Stanley Gibbons
Simplified Catalogue

Stamps of the World

Stanley Gibbons Simplified Catalogue

Stamps of the World

2013 Edition

1

Countries **Abu Dhabi – Charkhari**

Stanley Gibbons Ltd
London and Ringwood

By Appointment to
Her Majesty The Queen
Stanley Gibbons Limited
London
Philatelists

78th Edition
Published in Great Britain by
Stanley Gibbons Ltd
Publications Editorial, Sales Offices and Distribution Centre
7, Parkside, Christchurch Road,
Ringwood, Hampshire BH24 3SH
Telephone +44 (0) 1425 472363

British Library Cataloguing in
Publication Data.
A catalogue record for this book is available
from the British Library.

Volume 1
ISBN 10: 0-85259-853-X
ISBN 13: 978-0-85259-853-5

Boxed Set
ISBN 10: 0-85259-861-0
ISBN 13: 978-0-85259-861-0

Published as Stanley Gibbons Simplified Catalogue from 1934 to 1970, renamed Stamps of the World in 1971, and produced in two (1982-88), three (1989-2001), four (2002-2005) five (2006-2010) and six from 2011 volumes as Stanley Gibbons Simplified Catalogue of Stamps of the World.

Item No. 2881– Set13

Printed and bound in Wales by Stephens & George

Contents – Volume 1

Est 1856

STANLEY
GIBBONS

About Us

Our History

Edward Stanley Gibbons started trading postage stamps in his father's chemist shop in 1856. Since then we have been at the forefront of stamp collecting for over 150 years. We hold the Royal Warrant, offer unsurpassed expertise and quality and provide collectors with the peace of mind of a certificate of authenticity on all of our stamps. If you think of stamp collecting, you think of Stanley Gibbons and we are proud to uphold that tradition for you.

399 Strand

Our world famous stamp shop is a collector's paradise, with all of our latest catalogues, albums and accessories and, of course, our unrivalled stockholding of postage stamps.

www.stanleygibbons.com shop@stanleygibbons.com +44 (0)20 7836 8444

Specialist Stamp Sales

For the collector that appreciates the value of collecting the highest quality examples, Stanley Gibbons is the only choice. Our extensive range is unrivalled in terms of quality and quantity, with specialist stamps available from all over the world.

www.stanleygibbons.com/stamps shop@stanleygibbons.com +44 (0)20 7836 8444

Stanley Gibbons Auctions and Valuations

Sell your collection or individual rare items through our prestigious public auctions or our regular postal auctions and benefit from the excellent prices being realised at auction currently. We also provide an unparalleled valuation service.

www.stanleygibbons.com/auctions auctions@stanleygibbons.com +44 (0)20 7836 8444

Stanley Gibbons Publications

The world's first stamp catalogue was printed by Stanley Gibbons in 1865 and we haven't looked back since! Our catalogues are trusted worldwide as the industry standard and we print countless titles each year. We also publish consumer and trade magazines, Gibbons Stamp Monthly and Philatelic Exporter to bring you news, views and insights into all things philatelic. Never miss an issue by subscribing today and benefit from exclusive subscriber offers each month.

www.stanleygibbons.com orders@stanleygibbons.com +44 (0)1425 472 363

Stanley Gibbons Investments

The Stanley Gibbons Investment Department offers a unique range of investment propositions that have consistently outperformed more traditional forms of investment. You can own your very own piece of history. Whether it is the Penny Black, a Victoria Cross or an official royal document signed by the Queen of England in the 16th century, we have something to amaze you and potentially offer you excellent investment returns.

www.stanleygibbons.com/investment investment@stanleygibbons.com +44 (0)1481 708 270

Fraser's Autographs

Autographs, manuscripts and memorabilia from Henry VIII to current day. We have over 60,000 items in stock, including movie stars, musicians, sport stars, historical figures and royalty. Fraser's is the UK's market leading autograph dealer and has been dealing in high quality autographed material since 1978.

www.frasersautographs.com sales@frasersautographs.com +44 (0)20 7557 4404

stanleygibbons.com

Our website offers the complete philatelic service. Whether you are looking to buy stamps, invest, read news articles, browse our online stamp catalogue or find new issues, you are just one click away from anything you desire in the world of stamp collecting at stanleygibbons.com. Happy browsing!

www.stanleygibbons.com

Introduction

The ultimate reference work for all stamps issued around the world since the very first Penny Black of 1840, now with an improved layout.

Stamps of the World provides a comprehensive, illustrated, priced guide to postage stamps, and is the standard reference tool for every collector. It will help you to identify those elusive stamps, to value your collection, and to learn more about the background to issues. *Stamps of the World* was first published in 1934 and has been updated every year since 1950.

The helpful article 'Putting on a Good Show' provides expert advice on starting and developing a collection, then making the most of its presentation. Also included is a guide to stamp identification so that you can easily discover which country issued your stamp.

Re-designed to provide more colourful, clearer, and easy-to-navigate listings, these volumes continue to present you with a wealth of information to enhance your enjoyment of stamp collecting.

Features:

- Current values for every stamp in the world from the experts
- Easy-to-use simplified listings
- World-recognised Stanley Gibbons catalogue numbers
- A wealth of historical, geographical and currency information
- Indexing and cross-referencing throughout the volumes
- Worldwide miniature sheets listed and priced
- Thousands of new issues since the last edition

For this edition, prices have been thoroughly reviewed for Great Britain up to date, and all Commonwealth countries up to 1970, with further updates for Commonwealth countries which have appeared in our recently-published or forthcoming comprehensive catalogues under the titles *Channel Islands and Isle of Man, Southern and Central Africa, Indian Ocean, Leeward Islands, Cyprus, Gibraltar and Malta, Falkland Islands and Dependencies Australia*. Other countries with complete price updates from the following comprehensive catalogues are: *China, Czech Republic, Slovakia and Poland*. New issues received from all other countries have been listed and priced. The first *Gibbons Stamp Monthly* Catalogue Supplement to this edition is September 2012.

Information for users

Scope of the Catalogue

Stamps of the World contains listings of postage stamps only. Apart from the ordinary definitive, commemorative and air-mail stamps of each country there are sections for the following, where appropriate. Noted below are the Prefixes used for each section (see Guide to Entries for further information):

- postage due stamps – Prefix in listing D
- parcel post or postcard stamps – Prefix P
- official stamps – Prefix O
- express and special delivery stamps - Prefix E
- frank stamps – Prefix F
- charity tax stamps – Prefix J
- newspaper and journal stamps – Prefix N
- printed matter stamps – Prefix
- registration stamps - Prefix R
- acknowledgement of receipt stamps – Prefix AR
- late fee and too late stamps – Prefix L
- military post stamps- Prefix M
- recorded message stamps – Prefix RM
- personal delivery stamps – Prefix P
- concessional letter post – Prefix CL
- concessional parcel post – Prefix CP
- pneumatic post stamps – Prefix PE
- publicity envelope stamps – Prefix B
- bulk mail stamps – Prefix BP
- telegraph used for postage – Prefix PT
- telegraph (Commonwealth Countries) – Prefix T
- obligatory tax – Prefix T
- Frama Labels and Royal Mail Postage Labels No Prefix-

As this is a simplified listing, the following are NOT included:

Fiscal or revenue stamps: stamps used solely in collecting taxes or fees for non-postal purposes. For example, stamps which pay a tax on a receipt, represent the stamp duty on a contract, or frank a customs document. Common inscriptions found include: Documentary, Proprietary, Inter. Revenue and Contract Note.

Local stamps: postage stamps whose validity and use are limited in area to a prescribed district, town or country, or on certain routes where there is no government postal service. They may be issued by private carriers and freight companies, municipal authorities or private individuals.

Local carriage labels and Private local issues: many labels exist ostensibly to cover the cost of ferrying mail from one of Great Britain's offshore islands to the nearest mainland post office. They are not recognised as valid for national or international mail. Examples: Calf of Man, Davaar, Herm, Lundy, Pabay, Stroma.

Telegraph stamps: stamps intended solely for the prepayment of telegraphic communication.

Bogus or "phantom" stamps: labels from mythical places or non-existent administrations. Examples in the classical period were Sedang, Counani, Clipperton Island and in modern times Thomond and Monte Bello Islands. Numerous labels have also appeared since the War from dissident groups as propaganda for their claims and without authority from the home governments. Common examples are the numerous issues for Nagaland.

Railway letter fee stamps: special stamps issued by railway companies for the conveyance of letters by rail. Example: Talyllyn Railway. Similar services are now offered by some bus companies and the labels they issue likewise do not qualify for inclusion in the catalogue.

Perfins ("perforated initials"): stamps perforated with the initials or emblems of firms as a security measure to prevent pilferage by office staff.

Labels: Slips of paper with an adhesive backing. Collectors tend to make a distinction between stamps, which have postal validity and anything else, which has not.

However, Frama Labels and Royal Mail Postage Labels are both classified as postage stamps and are therefore listed in this catalogue.

Cut-outs: Embossed or impressed stamps found on postal stationery, which are cut out if the stationery has been ruined and re-used as adhesives.

Further information on a wealth of terms is in *Philatelic Terms Illustrated*, published by Stanley Gibbons, details are listed under Stanley Gibbons Publications. There is also a priced listing of the postal fiscals of Great Britain in our *Commonwealth & British Empire Stamps 1840-1970* Catalogue and in Volume 1 of the *Great Britain Specialised Catalogue* (5th and later editions). Again, further details are listed under the Stanley Gibbons Publications section (see p.xii).

Organisation of the Catalogue

The catalogue lists countries in alphabetical order with country headers on each page and extra introductory information such as philatelic historical background at the beginning of each section. The Contents list provides a detailed guide to each volume, and the Index has full cross-referencing to locate each country in each volume.

Each country lists postage stamps in order of date of issue, from earliest to most recent, followed by separate sections for categories such as postage due stamps, express stamps, official stamps, and so on (see above for a complete listing).

"Appendix" Countries

Since 1968 Stanley Gibbons has listed in an appendix stamps which are judged to be in excess of true postal needs. The appendix also contains stamps which have not fulfilled all the normal conditions for full catalogue listing. Full catalogue listing requires a stamp to be:

- issued by a legitimate postal authority
- recognised by the government concerned
- adhesive
- valid for proper postal use in the class of service for which they are inscribed
- available to the general public at face value with no artificial restrictions being imposed on their distribution (with the exception of categories as postage dues and officials)

Only stamps issued from component parts of otherwise united territories which represent a genuine political, historical or postal division within the country concerned have a full catalogue listing. Any such issues which do not fulfil this stipulation will be recorded in the Catalogue Appendix only.

Stamps listed in the Appendix are constantly under review in light of newly acquired information about them. If we are satisfied that a stamp qualifies for proper listing in the body of the catalogue it will be moved in the next edition.

"Undesirable Issues"

The rules governing many competitive exhibitions are set by the Federation Internationale de Philatelie and stipulate a downgrading of marks for stamps classed as "undesirable issues".

This catalogue can be taken as a guide to status. All stamps in the main listings are acceptable. Stamps in the Appendix are considered, "undesirable issues" and should not be entered for competition.

Correspondence

We welcome information and suggestions but we must ask correspondents to include the cost of postage for the return of any materials, plus registration where appropriate. Letters and emails should be addressed to Michelle Briggs, 7 Parkside, Christchurch Road, Ringwood, Hampshire BH24 3SH, UK. mrbriggs@stanleygibbons.co.uk. Where information is solicited purely for the benefit of the enquirer we regret we are seldom able to reply.

Identification of Stamps

We regret we do not give opinion on the authenticity of stamps, nor do we identify stamps or number them by our Catalogue.

Thematic Collectors

Stanley Gibbons publishes a range of thematic catalogues (see page xxxix for details) and *Stamps of the World* is ideal to use with these titles, as it supplements those listings with extra information.

Type numbers

Type numbers (in bold) refer to illustrations, and are not the Stanley Gibbons Catalogue numbers.

A brief description of the stamp design subject is given below or beside the illustrations, or close by in the entry, where needed. Where a design is not illustrated, it is usually the same shape and size as a related design, unless otherwise indicated.

Watermarks

Watermarks are not covered in this catalogue. Stamps of the same issue with differing watermarks are not listed separately.

Perforations

Perforations – all stamps are perforated unless otherwise stated. No distinction is made between the various gauges of perforation but early stamp issues which exist both imperforate and perforated are usually listed separately. Where a heading states, "Imperf or perf"or "Perf. or rouletted" this does not necessarily mean that all values of the issue are found in both conditions

Se-tenant Pairs

Se-tenant Pairs – Many modern issues are printed in sheets containing different designs or face values. Such pairs, blocks, strips or sheets are described as being "*se-tenant*" and they are outside the scope of this catalogue, although reference to them may occur in instances where they form a composite design.

Miniature Sheets are now fully listed.

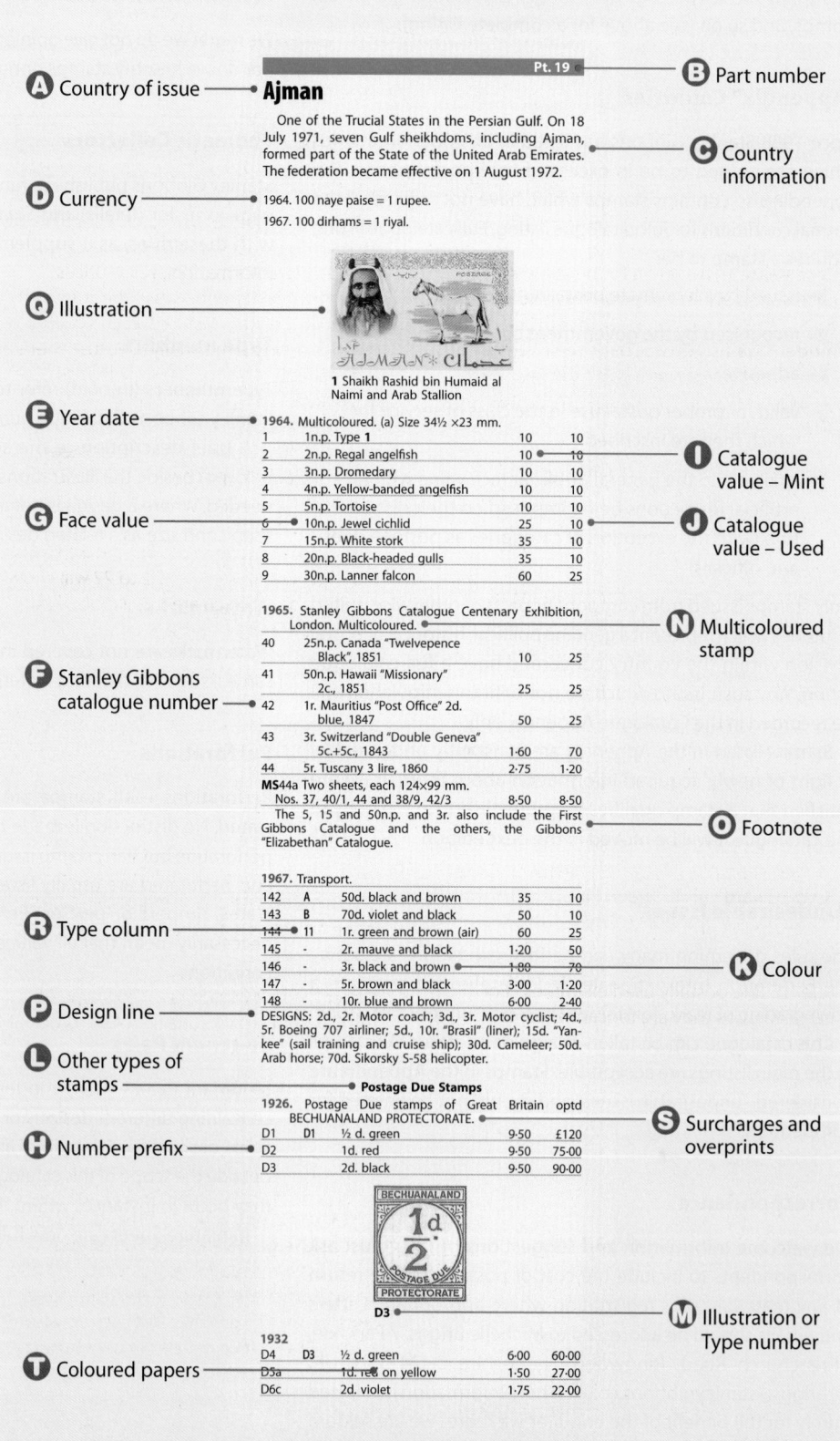

Guide to Entries

A Country of Issue

B Part Number – shows where to find more detailed listings in the Stanley Gibbons Comprehensive Catalogue. Part 6 refers to France and so on – see p. xli for further information on the breakdown of the Catalogue.

C Country Information – Brief geographical and historical details for the issuing country.

D Currency – Details of the currency, and dates of earliest use where applicable, on the face value of the stamps. Where a Colony has the same currency as the Mother Country, see the details given in that country.

E Year Date – When a set of definitive stamps has been issued over several years the Year Date given is for the earliest issue, commeorative sets are listed in chronological order. As stamps of the same design or issue are usually grouped together a list of King George VI stamps, for example, headed "1938" may include stamps issued from 1938 to the end of the reign.

F Stanley Gibbons Catalogue number – This is a unique number for each stamp to help the collector identify stamps in the listing. The Stanley Gibbons numbering system is universally recognized as definitive. The majority of listings are in chronological order, but where a definitive set of stamps has been re-issued with a new watermark, perforation change or imprint date, the cheapest example is given; in such cases catalogue numbers may not be in numerical order.

Where insufficient numbers have been left to provide for additional stamps to a listing, some stamps will have a suffix letter after the catalogue number. If numbers have been left for additions to a set and not used they will be left vacant.

The separate type numbers (in bold) refer to illustrations (see **M**).

B Part number — Pt. 19

A Country of issue — **Ajman**

C Country information — One of the Trucial States in the Persian Gulf. On 18 July 1971, seven Gulf sheikhdoms, including Ajman, formed part of the State of the United Arab Emirates. The federation became effective on 1 August 1972.

D Currency — 1964. 100 naye paise = 1 rupee.
1967. 100 dirhams = 1 riyal.

Q Illustration

1 Shaikh Rashid bin Humaid al Naimi and Arab Stallion

E Year date — **1964.** Multicoloured. (a) Size 34½ ×23 mm.

1	1n.p. Type **1**	10	10
2	2n.p. Regal angelfish	10	10
3	3n.p. Dromedary	10	10
4	4n.p. Yellow-banded angelfish	10	10
5	5n.p. Tortoise	10	10
6	10n.p. Jewel cichlid	25	10
7	15n.p. White stork	35	10
8	20n.p. Black-headed gulls	35	10
9	30n.p. Lanner falcon	60	25

G Face value — I Catalogue value – Mint — J Catalogue value – Used

1965. Stanley Gibbons Catalogue Centenary Exhibition, London. Multicoloured. — N Multicoloured stamp

40	25n.p. Canada "Twelvepence Black", 1851	10	25
41	50n.p. Hawaii "Missionary" 2c., 1851	25	25
42	1r. Mauritius "Post Office" 2d. blue, 1847	50	25
43	3r. Switzerland "Double Geneva" 5c.+5c., 1843	1·60	70
44	5r. Tuscany 3 lire, 1860	2·75	1·20
MS44a	Two sheets, each 124×99 mm. Nos. 37, 40/1, 44 and 38/9, 42/3	8·50	8·50

F Stanley Gibbons catalogue number

The 5, 15 and 50n.p. and 3r. also include the First Gibbons Catalogue and the others, the Gibbons "Elizabethan" Catalogue. — O Footnote

1967. Transport.

142	A	50d. black and brown	35	10
143	B	70d. violet and black	50	10
144	11	1r. green and brown (air)	60	25
145	-	2r. mauve and black	1·20	50
146	-	3r. black and brown	1·80	70
147	-	5r. brown and black	3·00	1·20
148	-	10r. blue and brown	6·00	2·40

R Type column — K Colour

P Design line — DESIGNS: 2d., 2r. Motor coach; 3d., 3r. Motor cyclist; 4d., 5r. Boeing 707 airliner; 5d., 10r. "Brasil" (liner); 15d. "Yankee" (sail training and cruise ship); 30d. Cameleer; 50d. Arab horse; 70d. Sikorsky S-58 helicopter.

L Other types of stamps — **Postage Due Stamps**

1926. Postage Due stamps of Great Britain optd BECHUANALAND PROTECTORATE. — S Surcharges and overprints

D1	D1	½ d. green	9·50	£120
D2		1d. red	9·50	75·00
D3		2d. black	9·50	90·00

H Number prefix

D3 — M Illustration or Type number

1932

D4	D3	½ d. green	6·00	60·00
D5a		1d. red on yellow	1·50	27·00
D6c		2d. violet	1·75	22·00

T Coloured papers

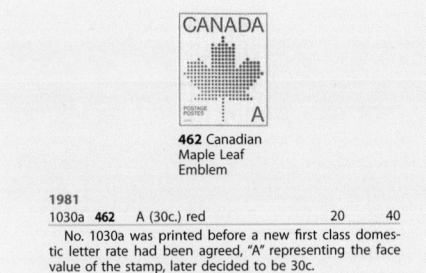

462 Canadian Maple Leaf Emblem

1981

1030a **462** A (30c.) red 20 40

No. 1030a was printed before a new first class domestic letter rate had been agreed, "A" representing the face value of the stamp, later decided to be 30c.

Ⓖ **Face value** – This refers to the value of each stamp and is the price it was sold for at the Post Office when issued. Some modern stamps do not have their values in figures but instead shown as a letter, see for example the entry above for Canada 1030a/Illustration 462.

Ⓗ **Number Prefix** – Stamps other than definitives and commemoratives have a prefix letter before the catalogue number. Such stamps may be found at the end of the normal listing for each country. (See Scope of the Catalogue p.viii for a list of other types of stamps covered, together with the list of the main abbreviations used in the Catalogue).

Other prefixes are also used in the Catalogue. Their use is explained in the text: some examples are A for airmail, E for East Germany or Express Delivery stamps.

Ⓘ **Catalogue Value** – Mint/Unused. Prices quoted for pre-1945 stamps are for lightly hinged examples. Prices quoted of unused King Edward VIII to Queen Elizabeth II issues are for unmounted mint.

Ⓙ **Catalogue Value** – Used. Prices generally refer to fine postally used examples. For certain issues they are for cancelled-to-order.

Prices

Prices are given in pence and pounds. Stamps worth £100 and over are shown in whole pounds:

Shown in Catalogue as	Explanation
10	10 pence
1.75	£1.75
15.00	£15
£150	£150
£2300	£2300

Prices assume stamps are in 'fine condition'; we may ask more for superb and less for those of lower quality. The minimum catalogue price quoted is 10p and is intended as a guide for catalogue users. The lowest price for individual stamps purchased from Stanley Gibbons is £1.

Prices quoted are for the cheapest variety of that particular stamp. Differences of watermark, perforation, or other details, outside the scope of this catalogue, often increase the value. Prices quoted for mint issues are for single examples. Those in *se-tenant* pairs, strips, blocks or sheets may be worth more. Where no prices are listed it is either because the stamps are not known to exist in that particular condition, or, more usually, because there is no reliable information on which to base their value.

All prices are subject to change without prior notice and we cannot guarantee to supply all stamps as priced. Prices quoted in advertisements are also subject to change without prior notice. Due to differing production schedules it is possible that new editions of Parts 2 to 22 will show revised prices which are not included in that year's Stamps of the World.

Ⓚ **Colour** – Colour of stamp (if fewer than four colours, otherwise noted as "multicoloured"– see N below). Colour descriptions are simple in this catalogue, and only expanded to aid identification – see other more comprehensive Stanley Gibbons catalogues for more detailed colour descriptions (see p.xxxix).

Where stamps are printed in two or more colours, the central portion of the design is the first colour given, unless otherwise stated.

Ⓛ **Other Types of Stamps** – See Scope of the Catalogue p.viii for a list of the types of stamps included.

Ⓜ **Illustration or Type Number** – These numbers are used to help identify stamps, either in the listing, type column, design line or footnote, usually the first value in a set. These type numbers are in a bold type face – **123**; when bracketed (**123**) an overprint or a surcharge is indicated. Some type numbers include a lower-case letter – **123a**, this indicates they have been added to an existing set. New cross references are also normally shown in bold, as in the example below.

1990. Small Craft of Canada (2nd series). Early Work Boats. As T **563**. Multicoloured.

Ⓝ **Multicoloured** – Nearly all modern stamps are multicoloured; this is indicated in the heading, with a description of the stamp given in the listing.

Ⓞ **Footnote** – further information on background or key facts on issues

Ⓟ **Design line** – Further details on design variations

Ⓠ **Illustration** – Generally, the first stamp in the set. Stamp illustrations are reduced to 75%, with overprints and surcharges shown actual size.

Ⓡ **Key Type** – indicates a design type (see p. xii for further details) on which the stamp is based. These are the bold figures found below each illustration. The type numbers are also given in bold in the second column of figures alongside the stamp description to indicate the design of each stamp. Where an issue comprises stamps of similar design, the corresponding type number should be taken as indicating the general design. Where there are blanks in the type number column it means that the type of the corresponding stamp is that shown by the number in the type column of the same issue. A dash (–) in the type column means that the stamp is not illustrated. Where type numbers refer to stamps of another country, e.g. where stamps of one country are overprinted for use in another, this is always made clear in the text.

Ⓢ **Surcharges and Overprints** – usually described in the headings. Any actual wordings are shown in bold type. Descriptions clarify words and figures used in the overprint. Stamps with the same overprints in different colours are not listed separately. Numbers in brackets after the descriptions are the catalogue numbers of the non-overprinted stamps. The words "inscribed" or "inscription" refer to the wording incorporated in the design of a stamp and not surcharges or overprints.

Ⓣ **Coloured Papers** – stamps printed on coloured paper are shown – e.g. "brn on yell" indicates brown printed on yellow paper. No information on the texture of paper, e.g. laid or wove, is provided in this catalogue.

Key-Types

Standard designs frequently occuring on the stamps of the French, German, Portuguese and Spanish colonies are illustrated below together with the descriptive names and letters by which they are referred to in the lists to avoid repetition. Please see the Guide to Entries for further information.

French Group

A "Blanc"

B "Mouchon"

C "Merson"

D "Tablet"

INTERNATIONAL COLONIAL EXHIBITION

E

F "

G

H

I "Faidherbe"

J "Palms"

K "Balay"

L "Natives"

M "Figure"

German Group

N "Yacht"

O "Yacht"

Spanish Group

X "Alfonso XII"

Y "Baby"

Z "Curly Head"

Portuguese Group

P "Crown"

Q "Embossed"

R "Figures"

S "Carlos"

T "Manoel"

U Ceres"

V "Newspaper"

W "Due"

Glossary of terms

English	French	German	Spanish	Italian
Agate	Agate	Achat	Agata	Agata
Air stamp	Timbre de la poste aérienne	Flugpostmarke	Sello de correo aéreo	Francobollo per posta aerea
Apple Green	Vert-pomme	Apfelgrün	Verde manzana	Verde mela
Barred	Annulé par barres	Balkenentwertung	Anulado con barras	Sbarrato
Bisected	Timbre coupé	Halbiert	Partido en dos	Frazionato
Bistre	Bistre	Bister	Bistre	Bistro
Bistre-brown	Brun-bistre	Bisterbraun	Castaño bistre	Bruno-bistro
Black	Noir	Schwarz	Negro	Nero
Blackish Brown	Brun-noir	Schwärzlichbraun	Castaño negruzco	Bruno nerastro
Blackish Green	Vert foncé	Schwärzlichgrün	Verde negruzco	Verde nerastro
Blackish Olive	Olive foncé	Schwärzlicholiv	Oliva negruzco	Oliva nerastro
Block of four	Bloc de quatre	Viererblock	Bloque de cuatro	Bloco di quattro
Blue	Bleu	Blau	Azul	Azzurro
Blue-green	Vert-bleu	Blaugrün	Verde azul	Verde azzuro
Bluish Violet	Violet bleuâtre	Bläulichviolett	Violeta azulado	Violtto azzurrastro
Booklet	Carnet	Heft	Cuadernillo	Libretto
Bright Blue	Bleu vif	Lebhaftblau	Azul vivo	Azzurro vivo
Bright Green	Vert vif	Lebhaftgrün	Verde vivo	Verde vivo
Bright Purple	Mauve vif	Lebhaftpurpur	Púrpura vivo	Porpora vivo
Bronze Green	Vert-bronze	Bronzegrün	Verde bronce	Verde bronzo
Brown	Brun	Braun	Castaño	Bruno
Brown-lake	Carmin-brun	Braunlack	Laca castaño	Lacca bruno
Brown-purple	Pourpre-brun	Braunpurpur	Púrpura castaño	Porpora bruno
Brown-red	Rouge-brun	Braunrot	Rojo castaño	Rosso bruno
Buff	Chamois	Sämisch	Anteado	Camoscio
Cancellation	Oblitération	Entwertung	Cancelación	Annullamento
Cancelled	Annulé	Gestempelt	Cancelado	Annullato
Carmine	Carmin	Karmin	Carmín	Carminio
Carmine-red	Rouge-carmin	Karminrot	Rojo carmín	Rosso carminio
Centred	Centré	Zentriert	Centrado	Centrato
Cerise	Rouge-cerise	Kirschrot	Color de ceresa	Color Ciliegia
Chalk-surfaced paper	Papier couché	Kreidepapier	Papel estucado	Carta gessata
Chalky Blue	Bleu terne	Kreideblau	Azul turbio	Azzurro smorto
Charity stamp	Timbre de bienfaisance	Wohltätigkeitsmarke	Sello de beneficenza	Francobollo di beneficenza
Chestnut	Marron	Kastanienbraun	Castaño rojo	Marrone
Chocolate	Chocolat	Schokolade	Chocolate	Cioccolato
Cinnamon	Cannelle	Zimtbraun	Canela	Cannella
Claret	Grenat	Weinrot	Rojo vinoso	Vinaccia
Cobalt	Cobalt	Kobalt	Cobalto	Cobalto
Colour	Couleur	Farbe	Color	Colore
Comb-perforation	Dentelure en peigne	Kammzähnung, Reihenzähnung	Dentado de peine	Dentellatura e pettine
Commemorative stamp	Timbre commémoratif	Gedenkmarke	Sello conmemorativo	Francobollo commemorativo
Crimson	Cramoisi	Karmesin	Carmesí	Cremisi

Arabic	English
عقيقي	Agate
طابع بريد جوي	Air stamp
أخضر تفاحي	Apple Green
	Barred
مقسوم الى شطرين	Bisected
الذهبي المطفي - بيج	Bistre
بيج غامق	Bistre-brown
أسود	Black
بني مسود	Blackish Brown
أخضر مسود	Blackish Green
زيتي مسود	Blackish Olive
أربعة قطعة واحدة	Block of four
أزرق	Blue
أخضر مزرق	Blue-green
بنفسجي مزرق	Bluish Violet
دفتر طوابع	Booklet
أزرق فاتح	Bright Blue
أخضر فاتح	Bright Green
بنفسجي فاتح	Bright Purple
أخضر برونزي	Bronze Green
بني	Brown
بني قرميدي	Brown-lake
البنفسجي الغامق	Brown-purple
أحمر غامق	Brown-red
أصفر داكن	Buff
الإلغاء	Cancellation
ملغى	Cancelled
قرمزي	Carmine
أحمر قرمزي	Carmine-red
متوسط	Centred
أحمر فاتح	Cerise
ورق سطحه طباشيري	Chalk-surfaced paper
أزرق طباشيري	Chalky Blue
طابع خيري	Charity stamp
بني فاتح - كستناوي	Chestnut
شوكولا	Chocolate
بني فاتح جدا - بيج	Cinnamon
أحمر داكن	Claret
أزرق سماوي	Cobalt
لون	Colour
تخريم مشطي	Comb-perforation
طابع تذكاري	Commemorative stamp
أحمر داكن - قرزي	Crimson

English	French	German	Spanish	Italian
Deep Blue	Blue foncé	Dunkelblau	Azul oscuro	Azzurro scuro
Deep bluish Green	Vert-bleu foncé	Dunkelbläulichgrün	Verde azulado oscuro	Verde azzurro scuro
Design	Dessin	Markenbild	Diseño	Disegno
Die	Matrice	Urstempel. Type Platte,	Cuño	Conio, Matrice
Double	Double	Doppelt	Doble	Doppio
Drab	Olive terne	Trüboliv	Oliva turbio	Oliva smorto
Dull Green	Vert terne	Trübgrün	Verde turbio	Verde smorto
Dull purple	Mauve terne	Trübpurpur	Púrpura turbio	Porpora smorto
Embossing	Impression en relief	Prägedruck	Impresión en relieve	Impressione a relievo
Emerald	Vert-eméraude	Smaragdgrün	Esmeralda	Smeraldo
Engraved	Gravé	Graviert	Grabado	Inciso
Error	Erreur	Fehler, Fehldruck	Error	Errore
Essay	Essai	Probedruck	Ensayo	Saggio
Express letter stamp	Timbre pour lettres par exprès	Eilmarke	Sello de urgencia	Francobollo per espresso
Fiscal stamp	Timbre fiscal	Stempelmarke	Sello fiscal	Francobollo fiscale
Flesh	Chair	Fleischfarben	Carne	Carnicino
Forgery	Faux, Falsification	Fälschung	Falsificación	Falso, Falsificazione
Frame	Cadre	Rahmen	Marco	Cornice
Granite paper	Papier avec fragments de fils de soie	Faserpapier	Papel con filamentos	Carto con fili di seta
Green	Vert	Grün	Verde	Verde
Greenish Blue	Bleu verdâtre	Grünlichblau	Azul verdoso	Azzurro verdastro
Greenish Yellow	Jaune-vert	Grünlichgelb	Amarillo verdoso	Giallo verdastro
Grey	Gris	Grau	Gris	Grigio
Grey-blue	Bleu-gris	Graublau	Azul gris	Azzurro grigio
Grey-green	Vert gris	Graugrün	Verde gris	Verde grigio
Gum	Gomme	Gummi	Goma	Gomma
Gutter	Interpanneau	Zwischensteg	Espacio blanco entre dos grupos	Ponte
Imperforate	Non-dentelé	Geschnitten	Sin dentar	Non dentellato
Indigo	Indigo	Indigo	Azul indigo	Indaco
Inscription	Inscription	Inschrift	Inscripción	Dicitura
Inverted	Renversé	Kopfstehend	Invertido	Capovolto
Issue	Émission	Ausgabe	Emisión	Emissione
Laid	Vergé	Gestreift	Listado	Vergato
Lake	Lie de vin	Lackfarbe	Laca	Lacca
Lake-brown	Brun-carmin	Lackbraun	Castaño laca	Bruno lacca
Lavender	Bleu-lavande	Lavendel	Color de alhucema	Lavanda
Lemon	Jaune-citron	Zitrongelb	Limón	Limone
Light Blue	Bleu clair	Hellblau	Azul claro	Azzurro chiaro
Lilac	Lilas	Lila	Lila	Lilla
Line perforation	Dentelure en lignes	Linienzähnung	Dentado en linea	Dentellatura lineare
Lithography	Lithographie	Steindruck	Litografía	Litografia
Local	Timbre de poste locale	Lokalpostmarke	Emisión local	Emissione locale
Lozenge roulette	Percé en losanges	Rautenförmiger Durchstich	Picadura en rombos	Perforazione a losanghe
Magenta	Magenta	Magentarot	Magenta	Magenta
Margin	Marge	Rand	Borde	Margine
Maroon	Marron pourpré	Dunkelrotpurpur	Púrpura rojo oscuro	Marrone rossastro
Mauve	Mauve	Malvenfarbe	Malva	Malva
Multicoloured	Polychrome	Mehrfarbig	Multicolores	Policromo
Myrtle Green	Vert myrte	Myrtengrün	Verde mirto	Verde mirto

Arabic	English
كحلي - أزرق غامق	Deep Blue
أخضر غامق	Deep bluish Green
التصميم	Design
قالب حديد يستخدم للصك	Die
ضعف الكمية	Double
لون كاكي	Drab
أخضر باهت	Dull Green
بنفسجي باهت	Dull purple
نافر - بارز	Embossing
الزمرد	Emerald
منقوش - طباعة بالحفر	Engraved
خطأ	Error
تجارب طباعية	Essay
طابع رسالة سريعه	Express letter stamp
طابع مالي	Fiscal stamp
زهري غامق	Flesh
تزييف	Forgery
إطار	Frame
ورق الجرانيت	Granite paper
أخضر	Green
أخضر مزرق	Greenish Blue
أخضر مصفر	Greenish Yellow
رمادي	Grey
رمادي مزرق	Grey-blue
رمادي مخضر	Grey-green
صمغ	Gum
فراغ أبيض يفصل بين طابعين	Gutter
غير مثقب - بدون تخريم	Imperforate
نيلي - أزرق غامق	Indigo
النقش	Inscription
معكوس - مقلوب	Inverted
اصدار	Issue
	Laid
أحمر غامق جداً - أحمر دموي	Lake
أحمر أجري	Lake-brown
لون الموف	Lavender
ليموني	Lemon
أزرق فاتح	Light Blue
لون نهدي	Lilac
ثقب الخط	Line perforation
طباعة حجرية	Lithography
محلي	Local
تخريم ناعم	Lozenge roulette
قرمزي	Magenta
هامش	Margin
بنفسجي غامق	Maroon
بنفسجي	Mauve
متعدد الألوان	Multicoloured
أخضر غامق	Myrtle Green

English	French	German	Spanish	Italian
New Blue	Bleu ciel vif	Neublau	Azul nuevo	Azzurro nuovo
Newspaper stamp	Timbre pour journaux	Zeitungsmarke	Sello para periódicos	Francobollo per giornali
Obliteration	Oblitération	Abstempelung	Matasello	Annullamento
Obsolete	Hors (de) cours	Ausser Kurs	Fuera de curso	Fuori corso
Ochre	Ocre	Ocker	Ocre	Ocra
Official stamp	Timbre de service	Dienstmarke	Sello de servicio	Francobollo di
Olive-brown	Brun-olive	Olivbraun	Castaño oliva	Bruno oliva
Olive-green	Vert-olive	Olivgrün	Verde oliva	Verde oliva
Olive-grey	Gris-olive	Olivgrau	Gris oliva	Grigio oliva
Olive-yellow	Jaune-olive	Olivgelb	Amarillo oliva	Giallo oliva
Orange	Orange	Orange	Naranja	Arancio
Orange-brown	Brun-orange	Orangebraun	Castaño naranja	Bruno arancio
Orange-red	Rouge-orange	Orangerot	Rojo naranja	Rosso arancio
Orange-yellow	Jaune-orange	Orangegelb	Amarillo naranja	Giallo arancio
Overprint	Surcharge	Aufdruck	Sobrecarga	Soprastampa
Pair	Paire	Paar	Pareja	Coppia
Pale	Pâle	Blass	Pálido	Pallido
Pane	Panneau	Gruppe	Grupo	Gruppo
Paper	Papier	Papier	Papel	Carta
Parcel post stamp	Timbre pour colis postaux	Paketmarke	Sello para paquete postal	Francobollo per pacchi postali
Pen-cancelled	Oblitéré à plume	Federzugentwertung	Cancelado a pluma	Annullato a penna
Percé en arc	Percé en arc	Bogenförmiger Durchstich	Picadura en forma de arco	Perforazione ad arco
Percé en scie	Percé en scie	Bogenförmiger Durchstich	Picado en sierra	Foratura a sega
Perforated	Dentelé	Gezähnt	Dentado	Dentellato
Perforation	Dentelure	Zähnung	Dentar	Dentellatura
Photogravure	Photogravure, Heliogravure	Rastertiefdruck	Fotograbado	Rotocalco
Pin perforation	Percé en points	In Punkten durchstochen	Horadado con alfileres	Perforato a punti
Plate	Planche	Platte	Plancha	Lastra, Tavola
Plum	Prune	Pflaumenfarbe	Color de ciruela	Prugna
Postage Due stamp	Timbre-taxe	Portomarke	Sello de tasa	Segnatasse
Postage stamp	Timbre-poste	Briefmarke, Freimarke, Postmarke	Sello de correos	Francobollo postale
Postal fiscal stamp	Timbre fiscal-postal	Stempelmarke als Postmarke verwendet	Sello fiscal-postal	Fiscale postale
Postmark	Oblitération postale	Poststempel	Matasello	Bollo
Printing	Impression, Tirage	Druck	Impresión	Stampa, Tiratura
Proof	Épreuve	Druckprobe	Prueba de impresión	Prova
Provisionals	Timbres provisoires	Provisorische Marken. Provisorien	Provisionales	Provvisori
Prussian Blue	Bleu de Prusse	Preussischblau	Azul de Prusia	Azzurro di Prussia
Purple	Pourpre	Purpur	Púrpura	Porpora
Purple-brown	Brun-pourpre	Purpurbraun	Castaño púrpura	Bruno porpora
Recess-printing	Impression en taille douce	Tiefdruck	Grabado	Incisione
Red	Rouge	Rot	Rojo	Rosso
Red-brown	Brun-rouge	Rotbraun	Castaño rojizo	Bruno rosso
Reddish Lilac	Lilas rougeâtre	Rötlichlila	Lila rojizo	Lilla rossastro
Reddish Purple	Poupre-rouge	Rötlichpurpur	Púrpura rojizo	Porpora rossastro
Reddish Violet	Violet rougeâtre	Rötlichviolett	Violeta rojizo	Violetto rossastro
Red-orange	Orange rougeâtre	Rotorange	Naranja rojizo	Arancio rosso
Registration stamp	Timbre pour lettre chargée (recommandée)	Einschreibemarke	Sello de certificado lettere	Francobollo per raccomandate
Reprint	Réimpression	Neudruck	Reimpresión	Ristampa

Arabic	English
أزرق جديد	New Blue
طابع جريدة	Newspaper stamp
طمس	Obliteration
لايستخدم	Obsolete
بيج	Ochre
طابع حكومي	Official stamp
بني زيتوني	Olive-brown
أخضر زيتوني	Olive-green
رمادي زيتوني	Olive-grey
أصفر زيتوني	Olive-yellow
برتقالي	Orange
بني برتقالي	Orange-brown
أحمر برتقالي	Orange-red
أصفر برتقالي	Orange-yellow
توشيح	Overprint
زوج	Pair
شطب على القيمة أو	Pale
لوح	Pane
ورقة	Paper
رزمة طوابع البريد	Parcel post stamp
ملغي بالقلم - مشطوب بالقلم	Pen-cancelled
ثقب	Percé en arc
تخريم	Percé en scie
صوة أبيض واسود	Perforated
ثقب دبوس	Perforation
صفحة لتحديد مكان الطبع	Photogravure
لون خوخي	Pin perforation
طابع أجرة بريد مستحق	Plate
لون خوخي	Plum
طابع مالي بريدي	Postage Due stamp
طابع بريدي	Postage stamp
طابع مالي بريدي	Postal fiscal stamp
ختم البريد	Postmark
طباعة	Printing
بروفا	Proof
مؤقت - طابع محلي	Provisionals
أزرق مسود	Prussian Blue
أرجواني	Purple
بني ارجواني	Purple-brown
طباعة زاحفة	Recess-printing
أحم	Red
بني محمر	Red-brown
أحمر زهري	Reddish Lilac
أرجواني محمر	Reddish Purple
بنفسجي محمر	Reddish Violet
برتقالي محمر	Red-orange
طابع تسجيل - مسجل	Registration stamp
إعادة طبع	Reprint

English	French	German	Spanish	Italian
Reversed	Retourné	Umgekehrt	Invertido	Rovesciato
Rose	Rose	Rosa	Rosa	Rosa
Rose-red	Rouge rosé	Rosarot	Rojo rosado	Rosso rosa
Rosine	Rose vif	Lebhaftrosa	Rosa vivo	Rosa vivo
Roulette	Percage	Durchstich	Picadura	Foratura
Rouletted	Percé	Durchstochen	Picado	Forato
Royal Blue	Bleu-roi	Königblau	Azul real	Azzurro reale
Sage green	Vert-sauge	Salbeigrün	Verde salvia	Verde salvia
Salmon	Saumon	Lachs	Salmón	Salmone
Scarlet	Écarlate	Scharlach	Escarlata	Scarlatto
Sepia	Sépia	Sepia	Sepia	Seppia
Serpentine roulette	Percé en serpentin	Schlangenliniger Durchstich	Picado a serpentina	Perforazione a serpentina
Shade	Nuance	Tönung	Tono	Gradazione de colore
Sheet	Feuille	Bogen	Hoja	Foglio
Slate	Ardoise	Schiefer	Pizarra	Ardesia
Slate-blue	Bleu-ardoise	Schieferblau	Azul pizarra	Azzurro ardesia
Slate-green	Vert-ardoise	Schiefergrün	Verde pizarra	Verde ardesia
Slate-lilac	Lilas-gris	Schierferlila	Lila pizarra	Lilla ardesia
Slate-purple	Mauve-gris	Schieferpurpur	Púrpura pizarra	Porpora ardesia
Slate-violet	Violet-gris	Schieferviolett	Violeta pizarra	Violetto ardesia
Special delivery stamp	Timbre pour exprès	Eilmarke	Sello de urgencia	Francobollo per espressi
Specimen	Spécimen	Muster	Muestra	Saggio
Steel Blue	Bleu acier	Stahlblau	Azul acero	Azzurro acciaio
Strip	Bande	Streifen	Tira	Striscia
Surcharge	Surcharge	Aufdruck	Sobrecarga	Soprastampa
Tête-bêche	Tête-bêche	Kehrdruck	Tête-bêche	Tête-bêche
Tinted paper	Papier teinté	Getöntes Papier	Papel coloreado	Carta tinta
Too-late stamp	Timbre pour lettres en retard	Verspätungsmarke	Sello para cartas retardadas	Francobollo per le lettere in ritardo
Turquoise-blue	Bleu-turquoise	Türkisblau	Azul turquesa	Azzurro turchese
Turquoise-green	Vert-turquoise	Türkisgrün	Verde turquesa	Verde turchese
Typography	Typographie	Buchdruck	Tipografia	Tipografia
Ultramarine	Outremer	Ultramarin	Ultramar	Oltremare
Unused	Neuf	Ungebraucht	Nuevo	Nuovo
Used	Oblitéré, Usé	Gebraucht	Usado	Usato
Venetian Red	Rouge-brun terne	Venezianischrot	Rojo veneciano	Rosso veneziano
Vermilion	Vermillon	Zinnober	Cinabrio	Vermiglione
Violet	Violet	Violett	Violeta	Violetto
Violet-blue	Bleu-violet	Violettblau	Azul violeta	Azzurro violetto
Watermark	Filigrane	Wasserzeichen	Filigrana	Filigrana
Watermark sideways	Filigrane couché liegend	Wasserzeichen	Filigrana acostado	Filigrana coricata
Wove paper	Papier ordinaire, Papier uni	Einfaches Papier	Papel avitelado	Carta unita
Yellow	Jaune	Gelb	Amarillo	Giallo
Yellow-brown	Brun-jaune	Gelbbraun	Castaño amarillo	Bruno giallo
Yellow-green	Vert-jaune	Gelbgrün	Verde amarillo	Verde giallo
Yellow-olive	Olive-jaunâtre	Gelboliv	Oliva amarillo	Oliva giallastro
Yellow-orange	Orange jaunâtre	Gelborange	Naranja amarillo	Arancio giallastro
Zig-zag roulette	Percé en zigzag	Sägezahnartiger Durchstich	Picado en zigzag	Perforazione a zigzag

Arabic	English
معكوس ـ مقلوب	Reversed
وردي	Rose
أحمر وردي	Rose-red
وردي غامق	Rosine
تخريم ناعم	Roulette
تخريم ناعم	Rouletted
أزرق ملكي	Royal Blue
أخضر معتدل	Sage green
برتقالي فاتح قريب للزهري	Salmon
قرمزي	Scarlet
بني داكن	Sepia
	Serpentine roulette
	Shade
صفحة	Sheet
لون رصاصي	Slate
أزرق رمادي	Slate-blue
أخضر مسود	Slate-green
نهدي مزرق	Slate-lilac
	Slate-purple
	Slate-violet
خدمة البريد السريعة	Special delivery stamp
نموذج ـ عينة	Specimen
أزرق فولاذي	Steel Blue
شريط	Strip
الضريبة الاضافية	Surcharge
	Tête-bêche
ورق لون خفيف	Tinted paper
طابع متأخر جداً	Too-late stamp
أزرق تركوازي	Turquoise-blue
أخضر تركوازي	Turquoise-green
نوع من الطباعة	Typography
أزرق لازوردي	Ultramarine
غير مستخدم	Unused
مستخدم	Used
لون بندقي ـ بني محمر	Venetian Red
لون برتقالي محمر (قمرديني)	Vermilion
بنفسج	Violet
أزرق بنفسجي	Violet-blue
علامة مائية	Watermark
	Watermark sideways
ورقة منسوجه	Wove paper
أصفر	Yellow
بني مصفر	Yellow-brown
أخضر مصفر	Yellow-green
زيتوني مصفر	Yellow-olive
برتقالي مصفر	Yellow-orange
تخريم ناعم متعرج	Zig-zag roulette

Abbreviations

Printers

A.B.N. Co.	American Bank Note Co, New York.
B.A.B.N.	British American Bank Note Co. Ottawa
B.W.	Bradbury Wilkinson & Co, Ltd.
C.B.N.	Canadian Bank Note Co, Ottawa.
Continental B.N. Co.	Continental Bank Note Co.
Courvoisier	Imprimerie Courvoisier S.A., La-Chaux-de-Fonds, Switzerland.
D.L.R.	De La Rue & Co, Ltd, London.
Enschedé	Joh. Enschedé en Zonen, Haarlem, Netherlands.
Harrison	Harrison & Sons, Ltd. London
P.B.	Perkins Bacon Ltd, London.
Waterlow	Waterlow & Sons, Ltd, London.

General Abbreviations

Alph	Alphabet
Anniv	Anniversary
Comp	Compound (perforation)
Des	Designer; designed
Diag	Diagonal; diagonally
Eng	Engraver; engraved
F.C.	Fiscal Cancellation
H/S	Handstamped
Horiz	Horizontal; horizontally
Imp, Imperf	Imperforate
Inscr	Inscribed
L	Left
Litho	Lithographed
mm	Millimetres
MS	Miniature sheet
N.Y.	New York
Opt(d)	Overprint(ed)
P or P-c	Pen-cancelled
P, Pf or Perf	Perforated
Photo	Photogravure
Pl	Plate
Pr	Pair
Ptd	Printed
Ptg	Printing
R	Right
R.	Row
Recess	Recess-printed
Roto	Rotogravure
Roul	Rouletted
S	Specimen (overprint)
Surch	Surcharge(d)
T.C.	Telegraph Cancellation
T	Type
Typo	Typographed
Un	Unused
Us	Used
Vert	Vertical; vertically
W or wmk	Watermark
Wmk s	Watermark sideways

(†) = Does not exist

(–) (or blank price column) = Exists, or may exist, but no market price is known.

/ between colours means "on" and the colour following is that of the paper on which the stamp is printed.

Colours of Stamps

Bl	(blue)
blk	(black)
brn	(brown)
car, carm	(carmine)
choc	(chocolate)
clar	(claret);
emer	(emerald)
grn	(green)
ind	(indigo)
mag	(magenta)
mar	(maroon)
mult	(multicoloured)
mve	(mauve)
ol	(olive)
orge	(orange)
pk	(pink)
pur	(purple)
scar	(scarlet)
sep	(sepia)
turq	(turquoise)
ultram	(ultramarine)
verm	(vermilion)
vio	(violet)
yell	(yellow).

Colour of Overprints and Surcharges

(B.)	= blue
(Blk.)	= black
(Br.)	= brown,
(C.)	= carmine
(G.)	= green
(Mag.)	= magenta
(Mve.)	= mauve
(Ol.)	= olive
(O.)	= orange,
(P.)	= purple
(Pk.)	= pink,
(R.)	= red,
(Sil.)	= silver
(V.)	= violet
(Vm.) or (Verm.)	= vermilion,
(W.)	= white
(Y.)	= yellow.

Arabic Numerals

As in the case of European figures, the details of the Arabic numerals vary in different stamp designs, but they should be readily recognised wit-h the aid of this illustration:

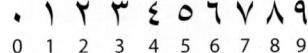

٠	١	٢	٣	٤	٥	٦	٧	٨	٩
0	1	2	3	4	5	6	7	8	9

How to Identify Stamps

From top to bottom: Stamps of Switzerland, Japan, Austria, Scandinavia (Denmark) and Latin America (Argentine Republic)

INTRODUCTION

Identification is the key to the catalogue as you must be able to recognise the country which has issued a stamp before you can look up a stamp in the catalogue. This guide will help you to do just that.

The main elements of a stamp design which provide clues to identity are:

- the country name,
- subordinate or secondary inscriptions,
- national emblems or symbols, such as a coat of arms or monarch's head
- currency or face value.

'Helvetia', for example, is the Latin name for Switzerland and it is used regularly on Swiss stamps. The chrysanthemum emblem appeared on Japanese stamps from 1872 to about 1947, while the modern issues are additionally inscribed 'Nippon', the Japanese name for Japan. Sometimes the actual design of a stamp indicates a particular country or at least the region of its location. The heraldic eagle relates to central Europe and as a design subject it will lead (supported by the inscriptions) to the identification of the early stamps of Austria ('KKPOST' or 'KREUZER'), Germany ('Deutsches Reich' or 'Reichpost'), Poland ('Poczta Polska') and possibly Albania, Finland and Russia. Centimes and Francs indicate a French-speaking country; Ore and Krone (or Krona) are Scandinavian; Centavos and Pesetas or Pesos appear on Spanish and Latin-American stamps.

Brazil

Finland

Spain

Some stamps without a country name

KEY INSCRIPTIONS

Inscriptions are all the words and figures appearing on the stamp in addition to the design. For purposes of identification the most important words are those representing the country of issue, which may appear in the Roman alphabet; in the Cyrillic or Greek alphabets; or in other alphabets and scripts such as Arabic, Chinese, Korean and Japanese, Hindi (the Devanagari script of India), and Urdu and Bengali (Pakistan). Urdu has many Arabic and Persian words, while Persian, with Pushtu, is also the written language of Afghanistan. Malay is the language of the natives of the Malay Archipelago and islands of South-east Asia (Malaysia) and has Arabic elements infused. The Siamese language (of the inhabitants of Thailand) is derived from a form of Sanskrit, and has affinities with Chinese. Hebrew is the official language of modern Israel, and Amharic is the official tongue of Ethiopia.

Fortunately many of these countries additionally inscribe their stamps in the Roman alphabet, while some use English versions, such as 'Israel' and 'Thailand'. Great Britain is the only country in the world which enjoys the privilege, granted by universal accord as the inventor of the postage stamp, of omitting the country name. Since the famous Penny Black of 1840, British stamps have borne a portrait of the reigning sovereign. New collectors will soon become familiar with the heads of Queen Victoria, King Edward VII, King George V, King Edward VIII, King George VI and Queen Elizabeth II, which also appear on many of the stamps of the Commonwealth territories. In recent times the head of the Queen has been shown in simplified form on GB special stamps, often just as a silhouette.

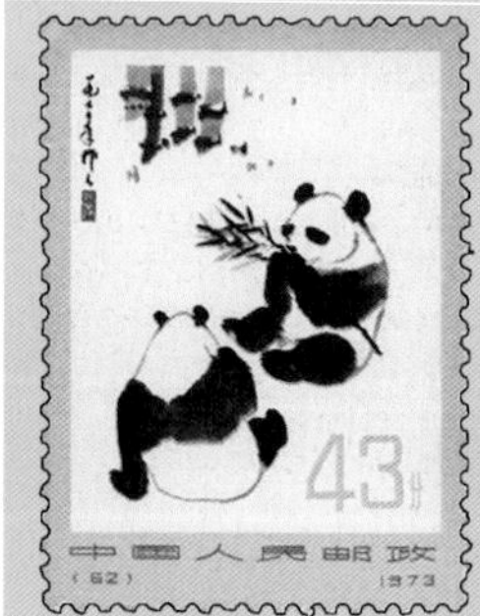

Chinese

Hebrew

Malay

Japanese

Thai

Korean

Hindi

Amharic

Arabic

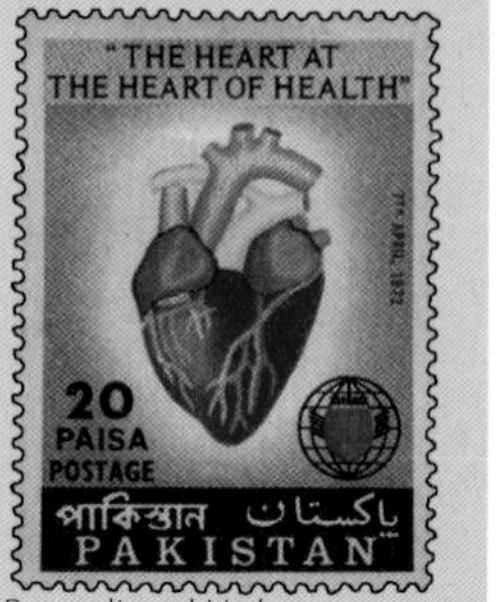

Bengali and Urdu

In early days, before the Universal Postal Union was founded, other countries sometimes omitted their names. These include Austria, Bosnia and Herzegovina, Brazil, Finland, Hungary, the Papal States, Portugal, Sardinia and Spain. The early postage dues of Switzerland comprised figures of value only. On the other stamps the principal clues are the figures of value and/or the portraits depicted on them. Examples are illustrated above and others will be found on pages 39 and 40. Modern stamps of Saudi Arabia use a palm tree emblem instead of a country name.

USING THE CATALOGUE

The *Stanley Gibbons Simplified Catalogue of Stamps of the World* is extremely simple to use. The countries are arranged in alphabetical order by the name of the stamp issuing country, so North Borneo, for example, will be found under 'N'. The index contains cross-referencing to help locate countries. Each country title is followed by a reference indicating the part of the comprehensive 22-part catalogue which contains the full detailed listing, and by summarised notes of the country's location, status and currency.

The Tristan da Cunha stamp below has a modern look and also depicts Queen Elizabeth II in silhouette in the top right-hand corner. Reference to the catalogue tells you that the stamp is the first or lowest value in a set of 'Bird' definitives issued in 1977. There are twelve stamps in the set and the style of listing is as follows:

83 Great-winged Petrel

1977. Birds. Multicoloured.

220	1p.	Type **83**
221	2p.	White-faced storm petrel
222	3p.	Hall's giant petrel
223	4p.	Soft-plumaged petrel
224	5p.	Wandering albatross
225	10p.	Kerguelen petrel
226	15p.	Swallow-tailed tern
227	20p.	Greater shearwater
228	25p.	Broad-billed prion
229	50p.	Great skua
230	£1	Common diving petrel
231	£2	Yellow-nosed albatross

The 3p. to £2 designs are vert.

As all the above stamps are multicoloured there was no need to repeat the colours against each stamp, those spaces being used for the design details. A little further on in your catalogue you will find a set of 'Fishes' with a slightly different arrangement:

31 Two-spined Thornfish

1978. Fishes

246	**31**	5p.	black, brown and green
247		10p.	black, brown and green
248		15p.	multicoloured
249		20p.	multicoloured

DESIGNS: 10p. Five-fingered morwong; 15p. Concha wrasse, 20p. Tristan jacopever.

Knowing the country obviously eases the task of locating a particular stamp in the catalogue – look for similarities of design, subject and style. And, of course, you will then know exactly which stamps you need to complete a set, while the detailed information about the stamps and their designs will assist you in writing-up your collection. Just browsing through the catalogue will help you enormously in getting to know the

This stamp was intended for use in the Channel Islands, but was also valid in the rest of the United Kingdom

'look' of a stamp and its various inscriptions. Most countries maintain a distinctive style of design which is easily recognizable and many of the stamps you want to identify will be illustrated. If the actual stamp is not shown you should be able to track down similar characteristics of design. Once you establish the country the rest should be straightforward.

Non Postage Stamps

Collectors will frequently find 'stamps' that are not listed in the Stamps of the World *catalogue. These are usually fiscal or revenue stamps, locals, telegraph stamps or souvenir labels of one kind or another. Some information about them can be found in the 'Information for Users' section of the catalogue. Such 'stamps' are normally referred to as 'cinderellas' and can form the basis of another collection.*

The Gibbons catalogue only lists stamps issued for postal purposes by official postal administrations.

French Equatorial Africa

THE ROMAN ALPHABET

A list of country names as they appear on stamps, subordinate inscriptions (including provisional overprints and surcharges, occupation issues and special-purpose inscriptions) and abbreviations.

The names in capital letters are those of the appropriate country in that catalogue. Where items are not listed in *Stamps of the World* the country name is followed by the appropriate part number of the main Stanley Gibbons catalogue.

Belgian Occupation of Germany

A. Overprint on stamps of Colombia for Avianca Air Company. COLOMBIA – Private Air Companies.

A & T. Overprint/surcharge on French Colonies 'Commerce' stamps for ANNAM AND TONGKING.

Açores. AZORES.

Admiralty Official. Overprint on British stamps 1903. GREAT BRITAIN – Official Stamps.

A.E.F. 'Afrique Equatoriale Française'. Inscription on 'Centenaire du Gabon' issue of 1938. FRENCH EQUATORIAL AFRICA.

Afghanes, Postes. AFGHANISTAN.

Africa. PORTUGUESE COLONIES, 1898. General issue.

Africa Occidental Española. SPANISH WEST AFRICA.

Africa Orientale Italiana. ITALIAN EAST AFRICA.

Afrique Equatoriale Française. FRENCH EQUATORIAL AFRICA.

Afrique Française Libre. Overprint on stamp of Middle Congo. FRENCH EQUATORIAL AFRICA.

Afrique Occidentale Française. FRENCH WEST AFRICA.

Albania. With surcharge in para currency. ITALIAN P.O.s IN THE LEVANT.

Alexandrie. ALEXANDRIA. French Post Office.

Algérie. ALGERIA.

Bavaria

Belgium – Railway Official

Belgium

Trieste

Bohemia and Moravia

Bosnia and Herzegovina

Allemagne Duitschland. Belgian stamps overprinted for Rhineland. BELGIAN OCCUPATION OF GERMANY.
A.M.G. F.T.T. 'Allied Military Government – Free Territory of Trieste'. Overprint on Italian stamps. TRIESTE.
A.M.G. V.G. 'Allied Military Goverment – Venezia Giulia'. Overprint on Italian stamps. VENEZIA GIULIA AND ISTRIA.
A.M. Post Deutschland. GERMANY (ALLIED OCCUPATION) – Anglo-American Zone, 1945.
Amtlicher Verkehr K. Württ. Post. WURTTEMBERG – Official Stamps.
Andorre. ANDORRA (French Post Offices).
Anna(s). Surcharged on British Stamps. BRITISH POSTAL AGENCIES IN EASTERN ARABIA. Also on French stamps for FRENCH P.O.s IN ZANZIBAR.
Antananarivo, British Consular Mail. MADACASGAR (*Part 1*).
A.O. 'Afrique Orientale'. Overprint on Belgian Congo Red Cross stamps for Belgian Occupation of RUANDA-URUNDI.
AOF. 'Afrique Occidentale Française'. Overprint on French stamp. FRENCH WEST AFRICA.
A.O.I. 'Africa Orientale Italiana'. Overprint on Italian Postage Due stamps. ITALIAN EAST AFRICA.
A payer te betalen. BELGIUM – Postage Dues.
A percevoir. 'To collect'. Postage Due stamps of BELGIUM, FRANCE, GUADELOUPE, CANADA, EGYPT, MONACO.

A percevoir timbre taxe. FRENCH COLONIES – Postage Dues.
Archipel des Comores. COMORO ISLANDS.
Army Official. Overprint on British stamps, 1896–1902. GREAT BRITAIN – Official Stamps. Also overprint on Sudan stamps. SUDAN – Army Service Stamps.
Army Service. Overprint on Sudan stamps, 1906. SUDAN – Army Service Stamps.
Arriba España as part of overprint on stamps of Spain. SPAIN – Civil War issues (*Part 9*).
Assistência D.L. no. 72. Educational Tax overprint. PORTUGUESE TIMOR, 1936–37.
Aunus. Overprint on Finnish stamps. FINNISH OCCUPATION OF AUNUS.

Autopaketti. For parcels carried by road. FINLAND, 1949 onwards.
Avila por España. Overprint on stamps of Spain. SPAIN – Civil War issues (*Part 9*).
Avion Nessre Tafari. Airmail stamps. ETHIOPIA, 1931.
Avisporto Maerke. DENMARK, 1907–15 – Newspaper Stamps.
Azarbaycan. AZERBAIJAN.
B. 'Bangkok'. Overprint on Straits Settlements stamps for BRITISH POST OFFICES IN SIAM.
B. Within oval. Overprint and inscription on Railway Official stamps of BELGIUM.
B. As part of overprint/surcharge on stamps of Nicaragua. NICARAGUA – Zelaya (*Part 15*).
B.A. Eritrea, B.A. Somalia or **B.A. Tripolitania**. Overprints/surcharges on British stamps. BRITISH OCCUPATION OF ITALIAN COLONIES.
Baden. German State until 1871, listed under BADEN. French zone of occupation 1947–9, listed under GERMANY (ALLIED OCCUPATION).
Baena por España. Overprint on stamps of Spain. SPAIN – Civil War issues (*Part 9*).
Bánát Bacska. Overprint on Hungarian stamps. ROMANIAN OCCUPATION OF HUNGARY.
Bani and lei. Surcharges for K.u.K.Feldpost. AUSTRO-HUNGARIAN MILITARY POST – Issues for Romania.
Baranya. Overprint/surcharge on Hungarian stamps. SERBIAN OCCUPATION OF HUNGARY.
Basel, Stadt Post. Basel Town Post. SWITZERLAND – Cantonal Administrations (*Part 8*).
Bayern. BAVARIA. Now part of Germany.
B.C.A. Overprint on Rhodesian stamps for British Central Africa Protectorate. NYASALAND PROTECTORATE, 1891–95.
B.C.M. British Consular Mail. MADAGASCAR, 1884–86 (*Part 1*).
B.C.O.F. Japan 1946. 'British Commonwealth Occupation Forces'. Overprint on Australian stamps. BRITISH OCCUPATION OF JAPAN.
België/Belgique. BELGIUM. Flemish/French inscriptions.
Belgien. Overprint/surcharge on German stamps. GERMAN OCCUPATION OF BELGIUM.
Belgisch Congo. BELGIAN CONGO.
Benadir. SOMALIA, 1903–05.
Bengasi. Overprint/surcharge on Italian stamps. ITALIAN P.O.s IN THE LEVANT.
Berlin. Overprint on Allied Occupation stamps (1947) for GERMANY (WEST BERLIN).
Berlin, Notopfer. GERMANY (ALLIED OCCUPATION) – Obligatory Tax Stamp.
Berlin, Stadt. Berlin – Brandenburg. ALLIED OCCUPATION OF GERMANY – Russian Zone (*Part 7*).
Beyrouth. Overprint on Russian stamps. RUSSIAN POST OFFICES IN THE TURKISH EMPIRE (*Part 10*).

B.I.E. 'Bureau International d'Education' (International Education Office). Overprint on Swiss stamp. SWITZERLAND – International Organizations.
B L C I (one letter in each corner). BHOPAL.
B.M.A. Malaya. Overprint on Straits Settlements stamps. MALAYA – British Military Administration.
B.M.A. Eritrea, B.M.A. Somalia or **B.M.A. Tripolitania**. Overprints/surcharges on British stamps. BRITISH OCCUPATION OF ITALIAN COLONIES.
B.N.F. Castellorizo. As overprint. See O.N.F. Castellorizo.
Board of Education. Overprint on British stamps 1902. GREAT BRITAIN – Official Stamps.
Böhmen und Mähren. BOHEMIA AND MORAVIA. German protectorate issues.
Boka Kotorska. Overprint/surcharge on stamps of Yugoslavia. GERMAN OCCUPATION OF DALMATIA.
Bollo Postale. 'Postage Stamp'. SAN MARINO, 1877–1935.
Bosna i Hercegovina. BOSNIA AND HERZEGOVINA – Sarajevo Government. Additionally inscribed 'Hrvatska Republika (or H.R.) Herceg Bosna' – Croatian Posts.
Bosnien Hercegovina (or Herzegowina). BOSNIA AND HERZEGOVINA. Military Post.
Brasil. BRAZIL.
Braunschweig. BRUNSWICK. Now part of Germany.
British Bechuanaland. Overprint and inscription. BECHUANALAND, 1885–91.
British Central Africa. NYASALAND PROTECTORATE, 1891–1903.
British New Guinea. Former name of PAPUA.
British Occupation. Overprint/ surcharge on Russian and Batum stamps. BATUM, 1919–20.
British Somaliland. Overprint on Indian stamps for the SOMALILAND PROTECTORATE.
British South Africa Company. Former name of RHODESIA.
Brunei Darussalam. BRUNEI since 1984.
Buchanan. Registration stamp of LIBERIA 1893.
Bureau International d'Education, also with Courrier du. 'International Education Office'. Overprint/ inscription on Swiss stamps. SWITZERLAND – International Organizations.
Bureau International du Travail, also with Courrier du. 'International Labour Office'. Overprint/inscription on Swiss stamps. SWITZERLAND – International Organizations.
C. As part of overprint on stamps of Nicaragua. NICARAGUA – Zelaya (*Part 15*).
Cabo. Overprint on stamps of Nicaragua. NICARAGUA – Zelaya (*Part 15*).
Cabo Jubi/Cabo Juby. Overprint on stamps of Rio de Oro, Spain or Spanish Morocco. CAPE JUBY.
Cabo Verde. CAPE VERDE ISLANDS.
Cache(s). (Unit of currency). Surcharge on Postage Due stamps of France. FRENCH INDIAN SETTLEMENTS.

Calchi/Karki. Overprint on Italian stamps for Khalki. DODECANESE ISLANDS.
Calimno/Calino. Overprint on Italian stamps for Kalimnos. DODECANESE ISLANDS.
Camb. Aust. Sigillum Nov. NEW SOUTH WALES.

Cambodge. CAMBODIA.
Cameroons U.K.T.T. 'United Kingdom Trust Territory'. Overprint on Nigerian stamps. CAMEROON.
Campione, Comune de. CAMPIONE (*Part 8*).
Canal Maritime de Suez. SUEZ CANAL COMPANY (*Part 19*).
Canarias. As part of surcharge on stamps of Spain. SPAIN – Civil War issues (*Part 9*).

Caso. Overprint on Italian stamps for Kasos. DODECANESE ISLANDS.
Castellorizo/Catelloriso. CASTELROSSO.
Cavalle. CAVALLA (KAVALLA). French Post Office.
C. CH. with figure '5' on French Colonies stamps. COCHIN-CHINA.
Čechy a Morava. BOHEMIA AND MORAVIA. German protectorate issues.
C.E.F. Overprint on Indian stamps for CHINA EXPEDITIONARY FORCE; also with surcharge on German 'Kamerun' stamps for Cameroons Expeditionary Force. CAMEROON.
Cefalonia e Itaca. Part of overprint on Greek stamps. ITALIAN OCCUPATION OF CEPHALONIA AND ITHACA.
Cent (s). Also **F** for franc. Surcharges for Belgium and Northern France. GERMAN COMMANDS. Surcharges on stamps of Russia. RUSSIAN P.O.s IN CHINA.
Centesimi and lire. Surcharges for K.u.K. Feldpost. AUSTRO-HUNGARIAN MILITARY POST – Issues for Italy.
Centesimo (or centesimi) di corona. Surcharge on Italian stamps for AUSTRIAN TERRITORIES ACQUIRED BY ITALY.
Centimes. Surcharge on German stamps for GERMAN P.O.s IN THE TURKISH EMPIRE. Also on stamps of Austria for AUSTRO-HUNGARIAN P.O.s IN THE TURKISH EMPIRE.
Centimos. Surcharge on French stamps for FRENCH P.O.s IN MOROCCO.
Centrafricaine, République. CENTRAL AFRICAN REPUBLIC.

Česká Republika. CZECH REPUBLIC. Former part of Czechoslovakia.
Československe Armady Siberske or Československe Vojsko Na Rusi. CZECHOSLOVAK ARMY IN SIBERIA.
Československo(a). CZECHOSLOVAKIA.
Česk'ych Skatu. CZECHOSLOVAKIA.
CFA 'Communaute Financielle Africaine'. Overprint/surcharge on French stamps for REUNION.

C.G.H.S. 'Commission de Gouvernement Haute Silésie'. Overprint on German Official stamps for plebiscite in UPPER SILESIA.
Chemins de Fer Spoorwegen. Railway Parcels stamps. BELGIUM.
Chiffre Tax. Postage Due stamps. FRANCE and FRENCH COLONIES. On stamps denominated in paras and piastres, TURKEY.
China. CHINA (PEOPLE'S REPUBLIC), from 1992.
China. Overprint on Hong Kong stamps for BRITISH POST OFFICES IN CHINA. Also on German stamps for GERMAN P.O.s IN CHINA.
China, Republic of. CHINA, 1913–29 and CHINA (TAIWAN), from 1953.
Chine. Overprint, surcharge and inscription for FRENCH P.O.s IN CHINA.
C.I.H.S. in circle. Overprint on German stamps for plebiscite in UPPER SILESIA.
Cilicie. CILICIA.
Cinquantenaire 24 Septembre 1853–1903 and eagle overprint on French stamps for 50th anniversary of French occupation. NEW CALEDONIA.
Cirenaica. CYRENAICA.
Città Del Vaticano. VATICAN CITY.

Vatican City

C.M.T. in box with value. 'Comandamentul Militar Territorial'. Surcharge on stamps of Austria. WEST UKRAINE – Romanian Occupation (*Part 10*).
Coamo. Type-set provisional. PUERTO RICO (*Part 22*).
Co. Ci. 'Commissariato Civile'. Overprint on Yugoslav stamps for the Italian Occupation of SLOVENIA.

Slovenia

Cocuk Esirgeme (or C.E.) Kurumu. Inscription on Child Welfare stamps of TURKEY.
Colombia. COLOMBIA. Also inscribed on stamps of PANAMA, 1887–92.
Coloniale Italiane, R.R. Poste. ITALIAN COLONIES. General issues, 1932–34.
Colonie Italiane. Overprint on Italian 'Dante' stamps of 1932 for ITALIAN COLONIES.
Colonies de l'Empire Français. FRENCH COLONIES. 'Eagle' issue, 1859.
Colonies Postes. FRENCH COLONIES. French 'Commerce' type, 1881. NOTE. French stamps without special distinction or inscription were also issued for the French Colonies up to 1877. For details see under FRANCE in the Catalogue.
Comité Français de la Liberation Nationale. With 'RF' or 'République Française'. FRENCH COLONIES.
Comité International Olympique. 'International Olympic Committee'. Inscription on Swiss stamps. SWITZERLAND – International Organizations.

Mozambique Company

Comores, Archipel des. or **Republique Federale Islamique des**. COMORO ISLANDS.
Communicaciones. SPAIN.
Companhia de Mozambique. MOZAMBIQUE COMPANY.
Companhia do Nyassa. NYASSA COMPANY.
Compañia Colombiana de Navegacíon Aérea. Private Air Company stamps. COLOMBIA (*Part 20*).
Confed. Granadina. COLOMBIA, 1859.
Confœderatio Helvetica. SWITZERLAND. 'National Fete' issues, etc. 1938–52.

Switzerland

Congo. CONGO (BRAZZAVILLE) 1991–. CONGO (KINSHASA) 1960. On key-types of Portuguese Group – PORTUGUESE CONGO.
Congo Belge. BELGIAN CONGO.
Congo Française Gabon. GABON.
Congo Française. FRENCH CONGO.
Congo, République Démocratique du. CONGO DEMOCRATIC REPUBLIC (EX ZAIRE). CONGO (KINSHASA), 1964–71.
Congo, République du. CONGO (BRAZZAVILLE), 1959–70, 1993; CONGO (KINSHASA), 1961–64.
Congo, République Populaire du. CONGO (BRAZZAVILLE), 1970–91.
Congreso de los Diputados. SPAIN – Official Stamps, 1895.
Congreso Internacional de Ferrocarriles. Inscription on stamps of SPAIN, 1930.
Constantinopol Posta Romana. Circular overprint on Romanian stamps. ROMANIAN P.O.s IN THE TURKISH EMPIRE.

Spain

Austrian Territories acquired by Italy

Constantinople. Overprint on stamps of Russia. RUSSIAN POST OFFICES IN THE TURKISH EMPIRE (*Part 10*).
Constantinopoli. Overprint and surcharge on Italian stamps. ITALIAN P.O.s IN THE TURKISH EMPIRE. For Constantinople.
Cordoba. ARGENTINE REPUBLIC – Cordoba (*Part 20*).
Corfu. Overprint on Italian stamps. ITALIAN OCCUPATION OF CORFU. Also overprint on Greek stamps. ITALIAN OCCUPATION OF CORFU AND PAXOS.
Corée, Postes de. KOREA, 1902–03.
Corona(e). Surcharge on Italian stamps for AUSTRIAN TERRITORIES ACQUIRED BY ITALY.
Corrientes. ARGENTINE REPUBLIC – Corrientes (*Part 20*).
Correspondencia Urgente. SPAIN – Express Letter Stamps.
Cos or Coo. Overprint on Italian stamps for Kos, DODECANESE ISLANDS.

Côte d'Ivoire. IVORY COAST.
Côte Française des Somalis. FRENCH SOMALI COAST.
Cour Internationale de Justice or Cour Permanente, etc. Overprint/ inscription on special stamps for the Court of International Justice, The Hague. NETHERLANDS – International Court of Justice.
Crete. Overprint and surcharge on French stamps. FRENCH P.O.s IN CRETE.
Crna Gora. MONTENEGRO.
C.S. or **C.S.A.** CONFEDERATE STATES OF AMERICA.
Dai Nippon. Overprint/surcharge on Malayan States stamps. MALAYA (JAPANESE OCCUPATION OF).
Danmark. DENMARK.
Dansk Vestindiske Öer/Dansk Vestindien. DANISH WEST INDIES.
Dardanelles. Overprint on stamps of Russia. RUSSIAN POST OFFICES IN THE TURKISH EMPIRE (*Part 10*).
Datia. DUTTIA. A state of central India.
DBP. 'Dalni-Vostochnaya Respublika' (Far Eastern Republic). Overprint in fancy letters on stamps of Russia or Siberia. SIBERIA.
D de A. 'Departmento de Antioquia'. Inscription on issue of 1890. ANTIOQUIA.

DDR. 'Deutsche Demokratische Republik' (German Democratic Republic). GERMANY (EAST GERMANY).
Dédéagh. DEDEAGATZ.
Deficit. Overprint/inscription on Postage Due stamps. PERU.
Demokratska Federativna Jugoslavija. Overprint/surcharge on Croatian stamps. YUGOSLAVIA (Democratic Federation). Regional issues.
Denda. Inscription on Postage Due stamps of MALAYSIA.
Deutsche Besetzung Zara. Overprint on stamps of Italy. GERMAN OCCUPATION OF DALMATIA.
Deutsche Bundespost. GERMANY (FEDERAL REPUBLIC).
Deutsche Bundespost Berlin. GERMANY (WEST BERLIN).
Deutsche Demokratische Republik. GERMANY (EAST GERMANY).
Deutsche Feldpost. GERMANY. Military Fieldpost stamps, 1944.
Deutsche Flugpost/Deutsche Luftpost. GERMANY. Airmail stamps, 1919–38.
Deutsche Militär-verwaltung Kotor. Overprint/surcharge on stamps of Italy. GERMAN OCCUPATION OF DALMATIA.
Deutsche Post. GERMANY (FEDERAL REPUBLIC) and (ALLIED OCCUPATION) – British and American Zone and Russian Zone.
Deutsche Post Osten. Overprint/ surcharge on German stamps for Nazi Occupation. POLAND, 1939.
Deutsche Reichspost/Deutsches Reich. GERMANY. 'Empire' issues, 1872–87 and 1902–43.
Deutschland. GERMANY (FEDERAL REPUBLIC) from 1995.

Deutsch-Neu-Guinea. GERMAN NEW GUINEA.
Deutsch-Ostafrika. GERMAN EAST AFRICA.

Deutschösterreich. AUSTRIA. Issues of 1918–20.
Deutsch-Sudwestafrika. GERMAN SOUTH WEST AFRICA.
Dienstmarke. GERMANY. Official stamps from 1920.
Diligencia. URUGUAY. 'Mailcoach' issue of 1856.
Dios Patria Libertad. DOMINICAN REPUBLIC. Inscription on early issues.
Dios, Patria, Rey. SPAIN – Carlist issues (*Part 9*). As overprint on stamps of Spain. SPAIN – Civil War issues (*Part 9*).
DJ. Overprint on Obock stamp for DJIBOUTI, 1893.

Dollar(s). Surcharge on stamps of Russia. RUSSIAN P.O.s IN CHINA.
Dominicana, República. DOMINICAN REPUBLIC.
Donau Dampfschiffahrt Gesellshaft, Erste k.k.pr. DANUBE STEAM NAVIGATION COMPANY (*Part 2*).

D.P.R.K. 'Democratic People's Republic of Korea'. KOREA (NORTH KOREA), 1977–80.
DPR Korea. KOREA (NORTH KOREA). Issues since 1980 (stamps inscribed DPR of Korea in 1976).
Drzava S.H.S. (also **with Bosna i Hercegovina**). YUGOSLAVIA – Issues for Bosnia and Herzegovina, or Slovenia.

Drzavna Posta Hrvatska. YUGOSLAVIA – Issues for Croatia, 1918–19.
Duc. di Parma Piac. Ecc. PARMA.
Durango. As part of overprint on stamps of Spain. SPAIN – Civil War issues (*Part 9*).
Durazzo. Overprint/surcharge on Italian stamps. ITALIAN P.O.s IN THE TURKISH EMPIRE.
EA. Overprint on stamps of France. ALGERIA.
E.A.F. 'East Africa Forces'. Overprint on British stamps. BRITISH OCCUPATION OF ITALIAN COLONIES – Somalia.
East Africa and Uganda Protectorates. Listed under KENYA, UGANDA AND TANGANYIKA.
East India Postage. INDIA. Stamps of 1860. Also, surcharged with a crown and value in cents – STRAITS SETTLEMENTS first issue of 1867.

EE. UU. De C., E.S. DEL T. 'Estados Unidos de Colombia, Estado Soberano del Tolima'. First issue of TOLIMA.
E.E.F. 'Egyptian Expeditionary Force'. Inscription on stamps of PALESTINE, 1918–22.

Eesti. ESTONIA.
Egeo. Overprint on Italian stamps. DODECANESE ISLANDS, 1912.
Egypte, **Royaume d'Egypte**, **Postes Egyptiennes** or **Poste Khedevie Egiziane**. EGYPT.

Eire. IRELAND (REPUBLIC).
Eireann, **Poblacht na h**. IRELAND (REPUBLIC).
Elsass. Overprint on German stamps. GERMAN OCCUPATION OF ALSACE.
Elua Keneta. 'Two Cents'. HAWAII.
E.R.I. 6d. Surcharge on 6d. stamp of ORANGE FREE STATE.
Escuelas. 'Schools'. Fiscals valid for postal use. VENEZUELA.
España or **Española**. SPAIN.
España Valencia. SPAIN – Carlist issues (*Part 9*).
Estado da India. PORTUGUESE INDIA.
Estados Unidos de Nueva Granada. COLOMBIA, 1861.
Est Africain Allemand Occupation Belge or **Duitsch Oost Afrika Belgische Bezetting** (Flemish). Overprint on Belgian Congo stamps for Belgian Occupation of RUANDA-URUNDI.
Estensi, Poste. MODENA, 1852.
Estero. 'Foreign'. Overprint on modified Italian stamps for ITALIAN P.O.s IN THE TURKISH EMPIRE.
Estland Eesti. GERMAN OCCUPATION OF ESTONIA.
Etablissements Française dans l'Inde. FRENCH INDIAN SETTLEMENTS.

Etablissements (or **Ets.**) **Française de l'Océanie**. OCEANIC SETTLEMENTS.
Etat Comorien. COMORO ISLANDS.
Etat Indépendant du Congo. BELGIAN CONGO – Independent State.
Ethiopie/Postes Ethiopiennes. ETHIOPIA.
Eupen & Malmédy. Overprint/ surcharge on Belgian stamps. BELGIAN OCCUPATION OF GERMANY.
Expossicion Gral. Sevilla Barcelona. SPAIN 1929.
Fanon(s). (Unit of currency). Surcharge on Postage Due stamps of France. FRENCH INDIAN SETTLEMENTS.
Fdo. Poo. Inscription on surcharged fiscal stamps. FERNANDO POO.
Filipinas (or **Filipas**). PHILIPPINES.
Fiume Rijeka. Overprint with date 3-V-1945 and surcharge on Italian stamps. VENEZIA GIULIA AND ISTRIA – Yugoslav Occupation.
Florida. With picture of heron. URUGUAY. Air stamp of 1925.
Forces Françaises Libres Levant with Lorraine Crosses. Overprint/ surcharge on Syrian and Lebanese stamps. FREE FRENCH FORCES IN THE LEVANT.

Føroyar. FAROE ISLANDS.
Franc. Surcharge on Austrian stamps. AUSTRO-HUNGARIAN P.O.s IN THE TURKISH EMPIRE.
Franc (with Empire or Repub.). FRANCE, FRENCH COLONIES.
France d'Outre-Mer. FRENCH COLONIES.
Franco. 'Helvetia' seated. SWITZERLAND, 1854.
Franco Bollo. 'Postage Stamp'. First issues of ITALY, NEAPOLITAN PROVINCES and SARDINIA. With 'Postale' added to crossed keys design, PAPAL STATES.
Francobollo di Stato. ITALY – Official Stamps.
Franco Marke. BREMEN, 1856.
Franco Scrisorei. ROMANIA, 1862.
Freimarke. 'Postage Stamp'. With portrait, PRUSSIA, 1850. With large numerals, THURN AND TAXIS.

Frimaerke (with 4 Skilling). First issue of NORWAY.
Frimaerke Kgl. Post or **Kgl. Post. Frm.** DENMARK/DANISH WEST INDIES. Kgl. or Kongeligt means 'Royal'.
G. Overprint on Cape of Good Hope stamps for GRIQUALAND WEST, 1877.
G. Overprint on stamps of CANADA for government use, 1950–63.
GAB. Overprint and surcharge on French Colonial stamp for GABON, 1886.
Gabonaise, République. GABON.
G.E.A. 'German East Africa'. Overprint on Kenya and Uganda stamps for British Occupation of TANGANYIKA.
Gen.-Gouv. Warschau. Overprint on German stamps. GERMAN OCCUPATION OF POLAND.

General Gouvernement. POLAND – German Occupation, 1940–44.
Genève, Post de. Geneva. SWITZERLAND – Cantonal Administrations (*Part 8*).
Georgie (La) or République Georgienne. GEORGIA, 1919–21.
Gerusalemme. Overprint/surcharge on Italian stamps for Jerusalem. ITALIAN P.O.s IN THE TURKISH EMPIRE.
G et D (or G & D). Overprint/surcharge on Guadeloupe stamps for Guadeloupe and Dependencies. GUADELOUPE.
G.F.B. 'Gaue Faka Buleaga' (On Government Service). Overprint on Tonga stamps, 1893. TONGA – Official Stamps.
G.K.C.A. Within dotted circle. Overprint on Yugoslav stamps for the Carinthian plebiscite, 1920. YUGOSLAVIA.
G.N.R. 'Guardia Nazionale Repubblicana'. Overprint on stamps of Italy. ITALY – Italian Social Republic.
Golfo de Guinea, Territorios (or Terrs.) del. Overprint on Spanish stamps for SPANISH GUINEA.
Govt. Parcels. Overprint on British stamps, 1883–1902. GREAT BRITAIN – Official Stamps.
G.P.E. Overprint/surcharge on French Colonies for GUADELOUPE.
Graham Land Dependency of. FALKAND ISLANDS DEPENDENCIES.

Italy – Italian Social Republic

Granadina, Confed. COLOMBIA, 1859.
Grande Comore. GREAT COMORO.
Grand Liban. 'Greater Lebanon'. LEBANON, 1924–26.
Grenada Carriacou & Petite Martinique. GRENADINES OF GRENADA.
Grenville. Registration stamp of LIBERIA, 1893.
G.R.I. 'Georgius Rex Imperator'. Overprint and surcharge in British currency on stamps and registration labels of German New Guinea and Marshall Islands during Australian Occupation of NEW GUINEA; also on German Cameroons stamps for New Zealand administration of SAMOA.
G.R. Post Mafia. Overprint on stamps of Indian Expeditionary Force. TANGANYIKA.
Grønland. GREENLAND.

Georgia

Grossdeutsches Reich. GERMANY. Issues of 1943–45.
Gruzija. GEORGIA.
Guiné. PORTUGUESE GUINEA.
Guinea Ecuatorial, Republica de. EQUATORIAL GUINEA.
Guinea Española. SPANISH GUINEA.
Guiné-Bissau. GUINEA-BISSAU.
Guinée, also Republique de. FRENCH GUINEA.
Guinée, République de. GUINEA.
Gultig 9. Armee. Overprint on stamps of Germany. GERMAN OCCUPATION OF ROMANIA.
Guyane Française. FRENCH GUIANA.
G.W. Overprint on Cape of Good Hope stamps for GRIQUALAND WEST. 1877.
Harper. Registration stamp of LIBERIA, 1893.
Haut (or Ht.) Sénégal-Niger. UPPER SENEGAL AND NIGER.
Haute-Silésie. UPPER SILESIA. Plebiscite issues, 1920–22.

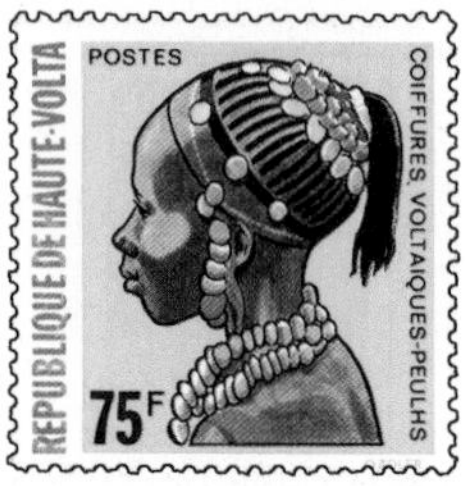

Haute-Volta. UPPER VOLTA.
H.E.H. The Nizam's Government/ Silver Jubilee. HYDERABAD.
Hellas. GREECE.
Helvetia. SWITZERLAND.
Herzogth. (or **Herzogthum**) **Holstein** or **Schleswig**. SCHLESWIG-HOLSTEIN.
H.H. Nawab Shah Jahan Begam. BHOPAL.
H.I. (**& U.S.**) **Postage.** 'Hawaiian Islands'. HAWAII.
Holkar State. INDORE.
Homenaje General Varela. As part of overprint on stamps of Spain. SPAIN – Civil War issues (*Part 9*).

Hrvatska (with ND, Nezavisna Drzava or Republika). CROATIA.
Hrvatska (with SHS, Drzavna Posta or DRZ SHS). YUGOSLAVIA – Issues for Croatia, 1918–19.
Hrvatska Republika (with Bosna i Hercegovina). BOSNIA AND HERZGOVINA – Croatian Posts.
Hrzgl. Frm(**rk**). SCHLESWIG-HOLSTEIN.
I.B. 'Irian Barat'. WEST IRIAN. Now part of Indonesia.
I.E.F. Overprint on Indian stamps for INDIAN EXPEDITIONARY FORCES.
I.E.F. 'D'. Overprint/surcharge in annas on Turkish fiscal stamps for Indian forces in Mesopotamia. MOSUL.
Ierusalem. Overprint on stamps of Russia. RUSSIAN POST OFFICES IN THE TURKISH EMPIRE (*Part 10*).
Ile de la Réunion. REUNION.
Ile Rouad. Overprint and surcharge on French stamps for ROUAD ISLAND (ARWAD).
Iles Wallis et Futuna. WALLIS AND FUTUNA ISLANDS.
Imperial British East Africa Company. BRITISH EAST AFRICA.
Imperio Colonial Portugues. Postage Due stamps. PORTUGUESE COLONIES.
Impuesto (or Impto.) de Guerra. SPAIN – War Tax Stamps.
India/India Portugueza (or Port. or **Portugesa**), **Estado da.** PORTUGUESE INDIA.
Inde Française (or Fçaise). FRENCH INDIAN SETTLEMENTS.
Independence 11th November 1965. Overprint on stamps of Southern Rhodesia. RHODESIA.
Indo-Chine/Indochine. INDO-CHINA.
Instruçao D.L. no. 7 de 3-2-1934. Educational Tax overprint. TIMOR, 1934.

Instruccion. 'Instruction' or 'Teaching'. Fiscals valid for postage. VENEZUELA.
Insufficiently Prepaid. Postage Due. No country name. ZANZIBAR, 1929–33.
Irian Barat. WEST IRIAN. Formerly Netherlands New Guinea and West New Guinea.
I.R. Official. Overprint on British stamps, 1882–1902. GREAT BRITAIN – Official Stamps (Inland Revenue).
Isla de Menorca. As part of overprint on stamps of Spain. SPAIN – Civil War issues (*Part 9*).

Island. ICELAND.
Islas Galapagos. GALAPAGOS ISLANDS.
Isole Italiani dell'Egeo. Overprint on Italian stamps. DODECANESE ISLANDS.
Isole Jonie. Overprint on Italian stamps. ITALIAN OCCUPATION OF IONIAN ISLANDS.

Istra. Overprint and surcharge on Italian stamps. VENEZIA GIULIA AND ISTRIA.

Itä-Karjala Sot. hallinto. Overprint on Finnish stamps. FINNISH OCCUPATION OF EASTERN KARELIA.
Italia/Poste Italiane. ITALY.
Jaffa. Overprint on stamps of Russia. RUSSIAN POST OFFICES IN THE TURKISH EMPIRE (*Part 10*).
Jam. Dim. Soomaaliya. SOMALIA, 1974–75.
Janina. Overprint and surcharge on Italian stamps. ITALIAN P.O.s IN THE TURKISH EMPIRE.
J.D. Soomaaliya. SOMALIA. 1976–77.
J.D. Soomaaliyeed. SOMALIA. 1977–.
Jeend (Jhind or Jind) State. Overprint on Indian stamps for JIND.
Jubilé de l'Union Postale Universelle. SWITZERLAND, 1900.
Jugoslavija. YUGOSLAVIA.

Julio 1936. Inscription on stamp of Spain. SPAIN – Civil War issues (*Part 9*).

K(ais). K(ön). Zeitungs-Stempel. 'Imperial/Royal Newspaper Stamp'. AUSTRIA or LOMBARDY AND VENETIA.

Kalayaan nang Pilipinas. JAPANESE OCCUPATION OF PHILIPPINES.

Kamerun. CAMEROUN. The former German colony.

Karabakh, Republic of Mountainous. NAGORNO-KARABAKH.

Karjala. KARELIA (*Part 10*).

Karki. Overprint on Italian stamps for Khalki. DODECANESE ISLANDS.

Karnten Abstimmung. Overprint on modified Austrian stamps for Carinthian plebiscite, 1920. AUSTRIA.

Karolinen. CAROLINE ISLANDS. The former German protectorate.

Kazahstan. KAZAKHSTAN.

Keneta. 'Cent' or 'cents'. HAWAII.

Kenttäpostia Fältpost. FINLAND – Military Field Post.

Kenya and Uganda. KENYA, UGANDA AND TANGANYIKA.

Kerassunde. Overprint on stamps of Russia. RUSSIAN POST OFFICES IN THE TURKISH EMPIRE (*Part 10*).

KGCA. Part of surcharge on Yugoslav Newspaper stamp for 1920 Carinthia Plebiscite. YUGOSLAVIA – Issues for Slovenia.

Kgl. Post. Frm. See 'Frimaerke Kgl'.

Kibris Türk Yonetimi/Kibris Türk Federe Devleti Postalari. CYPRUS (TURKISH CYPRIOT POSTS).

Kizilay Dernegi. (Red Crescent). Inscription on Obligatory Tax stamps of TURKEY.

K.K. Post-Stempel. 'Imperial/Royal Postage Stamp'. AUSTRIA (denominated in Kreuzer); LOMBARDY AND VENETIA (denominated in centes).

Klaipeda. Overprint, surcharge or inscription for MEMEL – Lithuanian Occupation.

Korea/Republic of Korea. KOREA (SOUTH KOREA).

Kosovo, United Nations Interim Administration in. UNITED NATIONS – Kosovo.

Kraljevstvo (or Kraljevina) Srba, Hrvata i Slovenaca. YUGOSLAVIA,1921–31.

K.S.A. Kingdom of SAUDI ARABIA. Stamps so inscribed 1975–82, since when inscription in Arabic only. Stamps identifiable by palm tree and crossed swords emblem.

K.u.K. Feldpost. 'Imperial and Royal Field Post'. AUSTRO-HUNGARIAN MILITARY POST.

K.u.K. Milit. Verwaltung Montenegro. Overprint on K.u.K. Feldpost stamps for the AUSTRO-HUNGARIAN MILITARY POST – Montenegro issues.

K.u.K. Militärpost. BOSNIA AND HERZEGOVINA. Austro-Hungarian Military Post.

Kurland. Overprint/surcharge on stamps of Germany. GERMAN OCCUPATION ISSUES, 1939–45 – Latvia (Courland) (*Part 7*).

Kuzey Kibris Türk Cumhuriyeti. CYPRUS (TURKISH CYPRIOT POSTS), since 1983.

K. Wurtt. Post. WURTTEMBERG.

La Canea. Overprint and surcharge on Italian stamps. ITALIAN P.O.s IN CRETE.

La Guaira. VENEZUELA – La Guaira (*Part 20*).

Läibäch, Provinz. Overprint/surcharge on stamps of Italy or inscription. SLOVENIA – German Occupation, 1943–45.

Land-Post Porto-Marke. BADEN – Rural Postage Due Samps.

LANSA (Lineas Aéreas Nacionales Sociedad Anonima). COLOMBIA – Private Air Companies.

Lao (Postes). LAOS since 1976.

L.A.R. 'Libyan Arab Republic'. LIBYA, 1969–77.

Lattaquie. Overprint on Syrian stamps for LATAKIA (formerly Alaouites).

Latvija (or Latwija). LATVIA.

Latvija 1941·I·VII. Overprint on Russian stamps for GERMAN OCCUPATION OF LATVIA.

Latvijas Aizsargi. 'Latvian Militia'. Overprint and surcharge. LATVIA.

Latvijas PSR. Issue inscribed for absorption of Latvia by Soviet Union, 1940. LATVIA.

Lero or Leros. Overprint on Italian stamps for Leros. DODECANESE ISLANDS.

Levant. Overprint on British stamps for Middle East post offices. BRITISH LEVANT. Also overprint on Polish stamps for POLISH P.O. IN TURKEY.

Levante. Overprint and surcharge on Italian Express Letter stamps. ITALIAN P.O.s IN THE TURKISH EMPIRE.

Liban/République Libanaise. LEBANON.

Libia or Libye. LYBIA.

Libra. (Unit of weight). SPAIN – Official Stamps.

Lietuva or Lietuvos. LITHUANIA.

Lignes Aeriennes F.A.F.L. Overprint and surcharge on Syrian Air stamps of 1931. FREE FRENCH FORCES IN THE LEVANT, 1942.

Lima. Inscription and overprint on early issues of PERU (Lima is the capital).

Limbagan 1593–1943. Overprint on stamp of Philippines. JAPANESE OCCUPATION OF PHILIPPINES.

Linja Autorahti Bussfrakt. FINLAND – Parcel Post Stamps.

Lipso or Lisso. Overprint on Italian stamps for Lipso. DODECANESE ISLANDS.

Litwa Srodkowa. CENTRAL LITHUANIA. Independence issues of 1920–22.

L. Marques. Overprint on Mozambique stamps for LOURENCO MARQUES.

Lebanon

Lithuania

North West Russia

Logroño. As part of overprint on stamps of Spain. SPAIN – Civil War issues (*Part 9*).
Lokalbref. Local issue for Stockholm. SWEDEN (*Part 11*).
Lösen. Inscription on postage due stamps for SWEDEN, 1874.
Lothringen. Overprint on German stamps for GERMAN OCCUPATION OF LORRAINE, 1940.
LP 'Latwija Pashparwalac' (Independent Latvia) and cross of Russia. NORTH WEST RUSSIA.
Lubiana, R. Commissariato Civile, etc. Overprint on Yugoslav stamps for the Italian Occupation of SLOVENIA.
Luftfeldpost. Inscription on Nazi Air stamp of 1942. GERMANY – Military Fieldpost.
Macau. MACAO.
Madagascar, British Inland Mail. MADAGASCAR (*Part 1*).
Mafia, G.R. Post. Overprint on Indian Expeditionary Force stamps for TANGANYIKA – British Occupation, 1915.

Magyar Kir. Posta/Magyar Posta/Magyarország. HUNGARY.
Makedonija. MACEDONIA.
Malgache, République/Malagasy, Repoblika. MALAGASY REPUBLIC.
Malmédy. See Eupen & Malmedy.
Marianen. Inscription and overprint on German stamps for the MARIANA ISLANDS.
Maroc. FRENCH MOROCCO.
Maroc, Royaume du.'Kingdom of Morocco'. MOROCCO.
Marocco or Marokko. Overprint and surcharge on German stamps for GERMAN P.O.s IN MOROCCO.
Marruecos, etc. SPANISH MOROCCO, SPANISH P.O.s IN TANGIER.
Marschall (or Marshall) Inseln. MARSHALL ISLANDS.
Mauritanie. MAURITANIA.
M.B.D. in oval. Overprint for Official stamps of NANDGAON.
Mecklenb. Schwerin. MECKLENBURG-SCHWERIN.
Mecklenb. Strelitz. MECKLENBURG-STRELITZ.
Mecklenburg-Vorpomm(ern). Mecklenburg-Vorpommern. ALLIED OCCUPATION OF GERMANY – Russian Zone (*Part 7*).

Spanish Morocco

Medellin. ANTIOQUIA (Colombia). Issue of 1888.
M.E.F. 'Middle East Forces'. Overprint on British stamps. BRITISH OCCUPATION OF ITALIAN COLONIES.
Mejico, Correos. MEXICO. Issues of 1856 and 1864.
Melaka Malaysia. MALACCA. Issues from 1965.
Memelgebiet. Overprint and surcharge on German stamps for MEMEL.
Memento Avdere Semper L1 Bvccari. Surcharge on Yugoslav stamp. FIUME AND KUPA ZONE.

British Postal Agencies in Eastern Arabia

Metelin. Overprint on stamps of Russia. RUSSIAN POST OFFICES IN THE TURKISH EMPIRE (*Part 10*).
Militärpost Eilmarke. BOSNIA AND HERZEGOVINA – Newspaper Stamps.
Militärpost Portomarke. BOSNIA AND HERZEGOVINA – Postage Due Stamps.
Milliemes/Mill. Surcharges on French Colonial stamps. ALEXANDRIA AND PORT SAID.

Norway

Moçambique. MOZAMBIQUE.
Moçambique, Companhia (or Comp.) de. MOZAMBIQUE COMPANY.
Modonensi, Provincie. MODENA.
Monrovia. Registration stamp of LIBERIA, 1893.
Mont-Athos. Overprint on stamps of Russia. RUSSIAN POST OFFICES IN THE TURKISH EMPIRE (*Part 10*).
Montevideo. URUGUAY. Issues of 1858–59 and Air stamp of 1925.

Moyen Congo. MIDDLE CONGO.
MQE. Surcharge on French Colonies 'Commerce' type for MARTINIQUE.
M.V.i.R. Within frame. 'Militärverwaltung in Rumänien' (Military Administration in Romania). Overprint/surcharge in 'bani' on German stamps for the GERMAN OCCUPATION OF ROMANIA.
Nandgan. NANDGAON.
Napoletana, Bollo della Posta. NAPLES.
Nationaler Verwaltungsausschus 10·XI·1943. Overprint on Italian occupation stamps for MONTENEGRO – German Occupation.

Nations Unies. UNITED NATIONS – Geneva Headquarters. Overprint/inscription on Swiss stamps (1950–63). SWITZERLAND – International Organizations.
Naxçivan Poçt. NAKHICHEVAN.
N.C.E. or **N.-C.E.** Overprint/surcharge on French Colonies stamps for NEW CALEDONIA.
Negeri Sembilan. NEGRI SEMBILAN. Malaysia.

Nederland. NETHERLANDS.
Nederlands (or Ned.) Nieuw-Guinea. NETHERLANDS NEW GUINEA.
Nederlandsch (Ned. or **Nederl) Indië**. NETHERLANDS INDIES.
Nederlandse (or Ned.) Antillen. NETHERLANDS ANTILLES.
Nepriklausoma Lietuva 1941·VI·23. Overprint on Russian stamps for GERMAN OCCUPATION OF LITHUANIA.
Nezavisna Drzava (or N.D.) Hrvatska. Inscription or overprint on Yugoslav stamps for CROATIA.
N.F. Overprint on Nyasaland stamps for Nyasa-Rhodesian Force during British Occupation of TANGANYIKA, 1916. Sometimes erroneously ascribed to '(Gen.) Northey's Force'.
Nieuwe Republiek. NEW REPUBLIC. South Africa.
Nippon. JAPAN.
Nisiro or Nisiros. Overprint on Italian stamps for Nisiros. DODECANESE ISLANDS.
Nlle. Caledonie. Inscription or overprint on French stamps. NEW CALEDONIA.
Norddeutscher Postbezirk. NORTH GERMAN CONFEDERATION.
Norge/Noreg. NORWAY.
Nouvelle (or Nlle.) Caledonie et Dependances. NEW CALEDONIA.
Nouvelles Hebrides, Condominium des. NEW HEBRIDES.
NP. 'Naye paise' (Indian currency). Surcharge on British stamps for BRITISH POSTAL AGENCIES IN EASTERN ARABIA.
NSB. Overprint/surcharge on French Colonies stamps for NOSSI-BE.
N. Sembilan. NEGRI SEMBILAN. Malaysia.
N.S.W. NEW SOUTH WALES.
Nueva Granada, etc. See Estados Unidos.
N.W. Pacific Islands. 'North-West Pacific Islands'. Overprint on Australian stamps. NEW GUINEA.

N.Z. Inscription on Postage Due stamps (1899), Express Delivery stamp (1903) and Life Insurance Department stamps of NEW ZEALAND.
O.B. Overprint for 'Official Business' mail. PHILIPPINES.
Occupation Française. Overprint and surcharge on Hungarian stamps for FRENCH OCCUPATION OF HUNGARY – Arad.
Océanie. OCEANIC SETTLEMENTS.
Oesterreich(ische)/Oesterr. Post. AUSTRIA.
O.F. Castellorisio. 'Occupation Française'. Overprint on French stamps for occupation of CASTELROSSO.

Offentlig Sak/Off. Sak./O.S. Official stamps of NORWAY.
Office des Postes et Telecommunications. FRENCH WEST AFRICA.
Official. Overprint or inscription on stamps for use by government departments, e.g. BRITISH GUIANA, NEW ZEALAND.
O.H.M.S. 'On His/Her Majesty's Service'. Overprint on stamps for government use, e.g. CANADA, COOK ISLANDS, MONTSERRAT, NIUE (**O.K.G.S.** KIRIBATI).
Oil Rivers, British Protectorate. Overprint/surcharge on British stamps for Oil Rivers Protectorate. NIGER COAST PROTECTORATE.
Olsztyn Allenstein. Overprint on stamps of Germany. ALLENSTEIN.

Oltre Giuba. JUBALAND.
O.M.F. Cilicie. 'Occupation Militaire Française'. Overprint/surcharge on French stamps for French Military Occupation of CILICIA. Also, in full, on Turkish fiscal stamps.

O.M.F. Syrie. 'Occupation Militaire Française'. Overprint/surcharge on French stamps for French Military Occupation of SYRIA.
O.N.F. (or **B.N.F.**) **Castellorizo**. 'Occupation (or Base) Navale Française'. Overprint/surcharge on French/French Levant stamps for French Occupation of CASTELROSSO.
Onza. (Unit of weight). SPAIN – Official Stamps.
O.P.S.O. 'On Public Service Only'. Overprint on NEW ZEALAND stamps, 1891–1906.
Orange River Colony. Overprint on Cape of Good Hope stamps, or inscription, for ORANGE FREE STATE.
Oranje Vrij Staat. ORANGE FREE STATE.
Organisation Internationale pour les Réfugiés. 'International Refugees Organisation'. Overprint on Swiss stamps. SWITZERLAND – International Organizations.
Organisation Météorologique Mondiale. 'World Meteorological Organization'. Inscription on Swiss stamps. SWITZERLAND – International Organizations.
Organisation Mondiale de la Propriete Intellectuelle. 'World Intellectual Property Organization'. Inscription on Swiss stamps. SWITZERLAND – International Organizations.

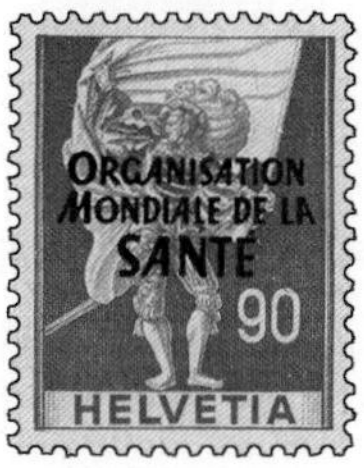

Organisation Modiale de la Santé. 'World Heath Organisation'. Overprint/inscription on Swiss stamps. SWITZERLAND – International Organizations.
Orts-Post. 'Local Post'. SWITZERLAND, 1850.
O.S. Overprint on Australian stamps. AUSTRALIA – Official Stamps. Also PAPUA, TRINIDAD. Also see 'Offentlig Sak', etc.
O.S.G.S. 'On Sudan Government Service'. Overprint on Sudanese stamps. SUDAN – Official Stamps.

Österreich(ische). AUSTRIA.
Ostland. Overprint on German stamps for GERMAN OCCUPATION OF RUSSIA, 1941.

German Occupation of Russia

Ottomanes, Postes. TURKEY, 1914.
Oubangui-Chari/Oubangui-Chari-Tchad. UBANGI-SHARI.
O.V.S. 'Oranje Vrij Staat'. Inscription on Military Frank and Police Frank stamps of ORANGE FREE STATE.
O.W. Official. Overprint on British stamps. GREAT BRITAIN – Official Stamps (Office of Works).
O'zbekiston. UZBEKISTAN,
P (in oval with crescent and star). Overprint on Straits Settlements stamp. PERAK.
Pacchi Postali. 'Parcel Post'. ITALY. Also, inscribed 'R.S. Marino', SAN MARINO.
Packhoi. Overprint and Chinese surcharge on Indo-Chinese stamps for PAKHOI.
Pakke-Porto. 'Parcel Post'. GREENLAND.
Palestine. Overprint on E.E.F. stamps of PALESTINE. Overprint on Egyptian stamps. GAZA – Egyptian Occupation.

Para(s). Currency inscription on first issues of EGYPT. Also surcharge on stamps for AUSTRIAN P.O.s IN TURKEY, BRITISH LEVANT, FRENCH LEVANT, GERMAN P.O.s IN TURKEY, ITALIAN P.O.s IN THE TURKISH EMPIRE, ROMANIAN P.O.s IN THE TURKISH EMPIRE, RUSSIAN P.O.s IN THE TURKISH EMPIRE.
Parm, Stati, Parma, Duc. di or **Parmensi, Stati**. PARMA.
Parlamento a Cervantes, El. Cervantes commemorative. Official stamps of SPAIN, 1916.
Patmo or Patmos. Overprint on Italian stamps for Patmos. DODECANESE ISLANDS.
P D and numeral. 'Payé à Destination'. Overprint on plain paper. ST PIERRE ET MIQUELON (*Part 6*).
Pechino. Overprint/surcharge on Italian stamps for Peking. ITALIAN P.O.s IN CHINA.

Pentru Cultura. Inscription on Postal Tax stamps of ROMANIA, 1932.
Persanes, Postes. IRAN. Formerly 'Persia'.

Persekutuan Tanah Melayu. MALAYAN FEDERATION.
Peruana, Republica. PERU.
Pesa. Surcharge on German stamps for GERMAN EAST AFRICA.
Peseta(s). Surcharge on French stamps for FRENCH P.O.s IN MOROCCO.
P.G.S. 'Perak Government Service'. Overprint on Straits Settlements stamps. PERAK – Official Stamps.
Piaster. Surcharge on Austrian stamps for AUSTRIAN P.O.s IN THE TURKISH EMPIRE. Also on German stamps for GERMAN P.O.s IN THE TURKISH EMPIRE.
Piastra. Surcharge on Italian stamp. ITALIAN P.O.s IN CRETE.

Piastre(s). Surcharge on stamps for BRITISH LEVANT, FRENCH LEVANT, ITALIAN P.O.s IN THE TURKISH EMPIRE, RUSSIAN P.O.s IN THE TURKISH EMPIRE.
Pilgrim Tercentenary. Inscription on UNITED STATES commemorative set of 1920.
Pilipinas. PHILIPPINES. Inscription since 1962.
Pilipinas, Republika ng. JAPANESE OCCUPATION OF THE PHILIPPINES.
Piscopi. Overprint on Italian stamps for Tilos (Piskopi). DODECANESE ISLANDS.
Plebiscite Olsztyn Allenstein. Overprint on German stamps for plebiscite in ALLENSTEIN, 1920.
Pohjois Inkeri. NORTH INGERMANLAND. Part of Russia.
Polska/Poczta Polska. POLAND.
Polynesie Française. FRENCH POLYNESIA.
Porteado Correio. PORTUGAL – Postage Due Stamps.
Porte de Mar. MEXICO (*Part 15*).
Porte Franco. PERU.

Great Britain – Postage Due

Ireland – Postage Due

Port Gdansk. Overprint on Polish stamps for POLISH POST IN DANZIG.
Porte Franco. Inscription on early issues of PERU.
Porto Gazetei (Moldavian 'Bulls') or Porto Scrisorei. Earliest issues of ROMANIA.
Porto Rico. Overprint on U.S. stamps. PUERTO RICO–US OCCUPATION.
Portuguesa, Republica. PORTUGAL.
Portzegel. Overprint and surcharge for Postage Dues. NETHERLANDS.
Postage Due. No country name. GREAT BRITAIN or AUSTRALIA.
Postal Charges. Overprint for Postage Due stamps. PAPUA NEW GUINEA.
Post & Receipt or Post Stamp. Inscriptions on 'annas' stamps of HYDERABAD.
Postas le híoc. IRELAND – Postage Dues.
Poste Khedivie e Giziane/Postes Egyptiennes. EGYPT, 1872–88.
Poste Locale. SWITZERLAND – Transitional Period (*Part 8*) or Federal Administration.
Postgebeit Ob. Ost. Overprint on stamps of Germany. GERMAN COMMANDS.
Postzegel. Inscription on first issues of NETHERLANDS.
P.P. in box. Overprint on French Postage Due stamps. FRENCH MOROCCO.
Preussen. PRUSSIA.
P.R.G. 'People's Revolutionary Government', overprint on stamps of GRENADA for official use, 1982. Also Grenadines.
Pro Juventute. 'For the Children'. Charity stamps of SWITZERLAND.
Pro Patria. 'For the Fatherland'. National culture fund stamps of SWITZERLAND.

Pro (Plebiscito) Tacna y Arica. Obligatory Tax stamps of PERU, 1927–28.
Protectorado Español en Marruecos. SPANISH MOROCCO.
Protectorat Français. Overprint on French 'Maroc' key-types for FRENCH MOROCCO.

Pro Tuberculosis Probres. Inscription on stamp of SPAIN, 1937.
Pro Union Iberoamericana. Inscription on stamps of SPAIN, 1930.

Provinz Laibach/Ljubljanska Pokrajina. Inscription/overprint on Italian stamps for German Occupation of SLOVENIA.
Pto. Rico. PUERTO RICO.
P S N C (one letter in each in corner). 'Pacific Steam Navigation Company'. Provisional issue of PERU (*Part 20*).

Pulau Pinang Malaysia. PENANG. Issues from 1965.
Puolustusvoimat Kenttäpostia. FINLAND – Military Field Post.
Puttialla State. Overprint on Indian stamps for first issues of PATIALA.
R. Overprint/surcharge on French Colonies stamps for REUNION, 1885.
Raj Shahpura. SHAHPURA.

Rarotonga. Overprint/surcharge on New Zealand stamps, also inscription. COOK ISLANDS.
Rayon. SWITZERLAND, 1850–54.
Recargo/Recargo Transitorio de Guerra. SPAIN – War Tax Stamps.
Recuerdo del 1 de Febrero 1916 and portrait of Francisco Bertrand. HONDURAS.
Regatul Romaniei. Overprint with values in bani, leu or lei on Hungarian stamps for ROMANIA – Transylvania, 1919.

Regno d'Italia Trentino 3 nov 1918/Venezia Giulia 3·XI·18. Overprint on Austrian stamps. AUSTRIAN TERRITORIES ACQUIRED BY ITALY.
Reichspost. GERMANY. Empire issues, 1889–1901.
R.E.P. (or **Republika**) **Shqiptare**. ALBANIA, 1925–30, 1939–43.
Repub. Franc. (Republique Française). Abbreviation on early stamps of FRANCE and FRENCH COLONIES.
Repubblica Sociale (or Rep. Soc.) Italiana. Overprint on stamps of Italy. ITALY – Italian Social Republic.
Républica Oriental. URUGUAY.
Republika Popullore e or R.P.S.E. Shqiperise. ALBANIA, 1946–91.
République Française. FRANCE, FRENCH COLONIES.
République Khmere. KHMER REPUBLIC. Cambodia, 1971–75.
Retymno. Rethymnon Province – RUSSIAN POST OFFICES IN CRETE.

R.F. 'République Française'. FRANCE, FRENCH COLONIES.
R.H. 'République d'Haiti'. Abbreviation on Postage Due stamps. HAITI, 1898.
R.H. Official. Overprint on British stamps. GREAT BRITAIN – Official Stamps (Royal Household).
Rheinland-Pfalz. GERMANY. Allied Occupation, 1947–49.
Rialtar Sealadac na Héireann 1922. 'Provisional Government of Ireland'. Overprint on British stamps for IRELAND (REPUBLIC).
Rizeh. Overprint on stamps of Russia. RUSSIAN POST OFFICES IN THE TURKISH EMPIRE (*Part 10*).
R.O. Overprint on stamps of Turkey. EASTERN ROUMELIA AND SOUTH BULGARIA.
Robertsport. Registration stamp of LIBERIA, 1893.

Rodi. Overprint on Italian stamps, or inscription, for Rhodes. DODECANESE ISLANDS.
Romagne, Franco Bollo Postale. ROMAGNA.
Romana/Romina. ROMANIA.
Rossija. RUSSIA – Russian Federation.
Roumelie Orientale. Overprint on stamps of Turkey, or inscription. EASTERN ROUMELIA AND SOUTH BULGARIA.
Royaume de l'Arabie Soudite (or Saoudite). SAUDI ARABIA.
R P SH. 'Republika Popullore e Shqiperise'. On stamp depicting dove with olive branch. ALBANIA.

RSA. 'Republic of South Africa'. SOUTH AFRICA.
R.S.M. 'Repubblica di San Marino'. SAN MARINO.
Ruanda. Overprint on stamps of Belgian Congo. RUANDA-URUNDI.
Rumänien. Overprint and value in 'bani' surcharged on German stamps. GERMAN OCCUPATION OF ROMANIA.
Rupee(s). Surcharge on British stamps for BRITISH POSTAL AGENCIES IN EASTERN ARABIA.
Russisch-Polen. Overprint on German stamps for GERMAN OCCUPATION OF POLAND.
Rwandaise, République. RWANDA, 1962–76.
Ryukus. RYUKU ISLANDS.
S. Overprint on Straits Settlements 2c. stamp for SELANGOR, 1882.
S.A. SAUDI ARABIA.

Saargebeit/Saarland. SAAR. Now part of Germany.
Sachsen. SAXONY.
Sachsen, Bundesland. East Saxony. ALLIED OCCUPATION OF GERMANY – Russian Zone (*Part 7*).

Sachsen, Provinz. Saxony. ALLIED OCCUPATION OF GERMANY – Russian Zone (*Part 7*).
Sahara Español. SPANISH SAHARA.
Sahara Occidental, Posesiones Españolas del. SPANISH SAHARA.
Salonicco. Overprint/surcharge on Italian stamps for Salonika (Thessaloniki). ITALIAN P.O.s IN THE TURKISH EMPIRE.
Salonique. Overprint on stamps of Russia. RUSSIAN POST OFFICES IN THE TURKISH EMPIRE (*Part 10*).
Salvador. EL SALVADOR.
Samoa i Sisifo. SAMOA.
Sandjak d'Alexandrette. Overprint/surcharge on Syrian stamps. ALEXANDRETTA.
Saorstát Eireann 1922. 'Irish Free State'. Overprint on British stamps for IRELAND (REPUBLIC).
S.A.R. 'Syrian Arab Republic'. SYRIA.
Sarkari. Overprint on Official stamps of SORUTH.
Sarre. Overprint on stamps of Germany and Bavaria. SAAR.
Saurashtra. SORUTH (Indian state).
Scarpanto. Overprint on Italian stamps for Karpathos. DODECANESE ISLANDS.
Scinde District Dawk. INDIA, 1852.
Scutari di Albania. Overprint/ surcharge on Italian stamps for ITALIAN P.O.s IN THE TURKISH EMPIRE.
Segnatasse. ITALY – Postage Due Stamps.
Sello 10Þ/25c. de Peso. Inscription on surcharged fiscal stamp. FERNANDO POO.
Senegambie et Niger. SENEGAMBIA AND NIGER.

Serbien. Overprint/surcharge on Yugoslav stamps for German Occupation of SERBIA; also overprint on Bosnian stamps for Serbian Issues of AUSTRO-HUNGARIAN MILITARY POST.
Sevilla. As part of overprint on stamps of Spain. SPAIN – Civil War issues (*Part 9*).
S H (one letter in each upper corner). SCHLESWIG-HOLSTEIN.
Shanghai China. Overprint/surcharge on U.S. stamps for UNITED STATES POSTAL AGENCY IN SHANGHAI.
Shqipenia. ALBANIA, 1913–20, 1995–.
Shqipenie. ALBANIA, 1920–22.
Shqiperia. ALBANIA, 1962–91.
Shqiperise. ALBANIA, 1948–62.
Shqipni. ALBANIA, 1937–38.

Albania

Slovakia

Shqipnija. ALBANIA, 1944, 1947.
Shqiptare. ALBANIA, 1991–95.
Shqyptare. ALBANIA, 1922–25, 1930.
Shri Lanka. SRI LANKA, issues of 1992–93.
S.H.S. 'Srba (Serbs), Hrvata (Croats), Slovena (Slovenes)'. Early issues of YUGOSLAVIA.
Siam. THAILAND, 1887–1939.
Sicilia, Bollo della Posta. SICILY.
Simi. Overprint on Italian stamps for Simi. DODECANESE ISLANDS.
Slesvig. SCHLESWIG. Plebiscite issues, 1920.
Slovenija. SLOVENIA.
Slovensko/Slovanska Posta. SLOVAKIA.
Slovenský Stat. Overprint on stamps of Czechoslovakia. SLOVAKIA.
Slova Posta. CZECHOSLOVAKIA – Postage Due stamps, 1919.
S. Marino, **Repubblica** (or **Rep.**) **di**. SAN MARINO.
Smirne. Overprint/surcharge on Italian stamps for Smyrna (Izmir). ITALIAN P.O.s IN THE TURKISH EMPIRE.
Smyrne. Overprint on stamps of Russia. RUSSIAN POST OFFICES IN THE TURKISH EMPIRE (*Part 10*).

S.O. 1920. 'Silesie Orientale'. Overprint on Czech and Polish stamps for EAST SILESIA.
Sobreporte. Special Fee stamp of COLOMBIA, 1865.
Socialist People's Libyan Arab Jamahiriya. LIBYA since 1977.
Sociedad Colombo-Alemana de Transportes Aéreos. Private Air Company stamps. SCADTA (*Part 20*), COLOMBIA (*Part 20*) and ECUADOR (*Part 20*).
Societé des Nations, also with Courrier de la or Service de la. Overprints on Swiss stamps for League of Nations. SWITZERLAND – International Organizations.
Soomaaliya (Soomaaliyeed or Somaliya). SOMALIA.
Soudan. Overprint on Egyptian stamps. SUDAN.
Soudan Français. FRENCH SUDAN.
South Georgia Dependency of. FALKAND ISLANDS DEPENDENCIES.
South Orkneys Dependency of. FALKAND ISLANDS DEPENDENCIES.
South Shetlands Dependency of. FALKAND ISLANDS DEPENDENCIES.
Sowjetische Besatszungs Zone. Overprint on German stamps for GERMANY (ALLIED OCCUPATION) – Russian Zone.

SPM or St-Pierre M-on. Overprint/surcharge on French Colonies stamps, or inscription. ST PIERRE ET MIQUELON.
Srbija. SERBIA.
Srbija i Crna Gora. SERBIA AND MONTENEGRO.
Srodkowa Litwa. CENTRAL LITHUANIA.
Stampalia. Overprint on Italian stamps for Astipalaia. DODECANESE ISLANDS.
S. Thomeé (or **Tomé**) **e Principe**. ST THOMAS AND PRINCE ISLANDS.
S.T. Trsta Vuja. TRIESTE – Zone B Yugoslav Military Government.
STT Vuja (or Vujna). Overprints on Yugoslav stamps. TRIESTE – Zone B Yugoslav Military Government.
Sud Kasai, Etat Autonome du. Overprint and inscription. SOUTH KASAI.
Sul Bolletino or Sulla Ricevuta. Inscriptions on left and right halves of Parcel Post stamps. ITALY. With star and crescent SOMALIA.
S.U./S. Ujong. SUNGEI UJONG.
Suidafrika (Suid-Afrika or Republiek van Suid-Afrika). SOUTH AFRICA.
Suidwes-Afrika. SOUTH WEST AFRICA.
Suomi. FINLAND.
Suriname. SURINAM.

Sverige. SWEDEN.

S.W.A. (or **SWA**). Overprints on South African stamps, also abbreviated inscription on stamps, for SOUTH WEST AFRICA.
Syrie/République Syrienne. SYRIA.
Syrie Grand Liban. Surcharge on French stamps. SYRIA – French Mandated Territory.
T with monetary unit in f(rancs). BELGIUM – Postage Due Stamps.
Tadzikistan. TAJIKISTAN.
Takse Pulu. Inscription on Postage Due stamps of TURKEY.
Tanganyika & Zanzibar, Republic of. TANZANIA.
Tanger. Overprint on French/French Morocco stamps for FRENCH P.O.s in TANGIER. Also overprint on Spanish stamps, or inscription, for SPANISH P.O.s IN TANGIER.
Tangier. Overprint on British stamps for MOROCCO AGENCIES – Tangier International Zone.
Tassa Gazette. MODENA – Newspaper Stamp.
Taxa de Guerra. War Tax surcharge. Distinguished by currencies. PORTUGUESE COLONIES ($), PORTUGUESE GUINEA (reis), PORTUGUESE INDIA (Rps), MACAO (avos).
Taxa Porto Pentru Cultura. Postal Tax Postage Due stamp of ROMANIA.
Te Betalen Port. Postage Due stamps of NETHERLANDS, CURAÇAO, SURINAM.
T.-C. Overprint on stamp of Cochin. TRAVANCORE-COCHIN.
T.C.E.K. 'Turkiye Cocuk Esirgeme Kurumu'. Inscription on Child Welfare stamps of TURKEY.
Tchad. CHAD.
T.C. Postalari. TURKEY.
T.E.O. 'Territoires Ennemis Occupés'. Overprint with surcharge in milliemes or piastres on French stamps for French Military Occupation of SYRIA. Also in paras on French Levant stamps for CILICIA.
T.E.O. Cilicie. Overprint on Turkish stamps for French Occupation of CILICIA.
Terres Australes et Antarctiques Françaises. FRENCH SOUTHERN AND ANTARCTIC TERRITORIES.
Territoire Français des Afars et des Issas. FRENCH TERRITORY OF THE AFARS AND THE ISSAS.
Territorios Espanoles del Golfo de Guinea. Inscription or overprint on Spanish stamps for SPANISH GUINEA.
Tetuan. Handstamp on Spanish stamps for SPANISH MOROCCO – Spanish P.O.s in Morocco.

Thailand, with value in cents. MALAYA (THAI OCCUPATION).
Thirty Two Cents. With sailing ship. LIBERIA, 1886.
Thuringen. Thuringia. ALLIED OCCUPATION OF GERMANY – Russian Zone (*Part 7*).
Tientsin. Overprint/surcharge on Italian stamps for ITALIAN P.O.s IN CHINA.
Timor-Leste. EAST TIMOR.
Timor Lorosae. UNITED NATIONS – East Timor (UN Transitional Administration).

Tjeneste Frimaerke. DENMARK – Official Stamps.
Tjenestefrimerke. NORWAY – Official Stamps, 1925.

To Pay. No country name. GREAT BRITAIN – Postage Due Stamps.

Toga. TONGA, 1897–1944.
Togolaise, République. TOGO.
Toscano, Francobollo Postale. TUSCANY.
Touva. TUVA.
Traité de Versailles. Overprint on stamps of Germany. ALLENSTEIN.
Transjordan. JORDAN.
Trebizonde. Overprint on stamps of Russia. RUSSIAN POST OFFICES IN THE TURKISH EMPIRE (*Part 10*).
Trieste Trst in surcharge with date 1.V.1945 on Italian stamps. VENEZIA GIULIA AND ISTRIA – Yugoslav Occupation.
Tripoli di Barberia. Overprint on Italian stamps for ITALIAN P.O.s IN THE TURKISH EMPIRE.
Tripoli, Fiera Campionaria. On stamps inscribed Poste Italiane, R.R. Poste Coloniali or Posta Aerea with date 1935. TRIPOLITANIA. On stamps with dates 1936, 1937, 1938. LIBYA.
T.Ta.C. Inscription on Aviation Fund stamp of TURKEY.
T T T T. In corners of stamps with large numerals. DOMINICAN REPUBLIC – Postage Due Stamps.
Tunis, Tunisie or République Tunisienne. TUNISIA.
Türkiye Cumhuriyeti (or T.C.) Postalari. TURKEY.
Türkiye (or Turk) Postalari. TURKEY.
Türkmenpoçta. TURKMENISTAN.
Two Pence. Denomination on stamps showing Queen Victoria on throne. VICTORIA, 1852.
U.A.E. UNITED ARAB EMIRATES.
U.A.R. 'United Arab Republic'. Inscription on issues of EGYPT (value in milliemes), 1958–71, and SYRIA (value in piastres), 1958–61.
U.G. Typewritten inscription on first 'Missionary' stamps for UGANDA, 1895.
Ukraina. UKRAINE.
Ukraine. Overprint on German stamps for GERMAN OCCUPATION OF RUSSIA, 1941.
Ultramar. 'Beyond the Seas'. Inscription with year dates on stamps of CUBA, also overprinted for PUERTO RICO. Appears also on postal-fiscals of MACAO (values in avos) and PORTUGUESE GUINEA (values in reis).
UNEF. Overprint on Indian stamp for INDIAN U.N. FORCE IN GAZA (PALESTINE).
UN Force (India) Congo. Overprint on stamps of India, 1962. INDIAN U.N. FORCE IN CONGO.
Union Internationale des Télécommunications. 'International Telecommunications Union'. Inscription on Swiss stamps. SWITZERLAND – International Organizations.
Union Postale Universelle. 'Universal Postal Union'. Inscription on Swiss stamps. SWITZERLAND – International Organizations.
Union Postale Universelle, Jubile de l'. SWITZERLAND, 1900.
UNTEA. 'United Nations Temporary Executive Authority'. Overprint on stamps of Netherlands New Guinea for WEST NEW GUINEA.
Urundi. Overprint on stamps of Belgian Congo. RUANDA-URUNDI.
U.S. or **U.S.A.** UNITED STATES OF AMERICA.
U.S.T.C. Overprint on stamp of Cochin. TRAVANCORE-COCHIN.
Vallées d'Andorre. ANDORRA (French Post Offices), 1932–37.
Valona. Overprint/surcharge on Italian stamps. ITALIAN P.O.s IN THE TURKISH EMPIRE.
Vancouver Island. BRITISH COLOMBIA AND VANCOUVER ISLAND.
Van Diemen's Land. First issues of TASMANIA.
Vaticane, Poste. VATICAN CITY, to 1993. (Posta Aerea Vaticana – Air stamps).
Venezia Giulia. Overprint/surcharge on Italian stamps. AUSTRIAN TERRITORIES ACQUIRED BY ITALY.
Venezia Tridentina. Overprint/ surcharge on Italian stamps. AUSTRIAN TERRITORIES ACQUIRED BY ITALY.

Vereinte Nationen. UNITED NATIONS – Vienna Centre.
VII Congreso U.P.U. Madrid 1920. Inscription on stamps of SPAIN.
VIII Världspost-Kongressen i Stockholm. SWEDEN, 1924.
Vilnius. Overprint on Russian stamps for GERMAN OCCUPATION OF LITHUANIA.
Virgin Islands. BRITISH VIRGIN ISLANDS.
Viva España as part of overprint on stamps of Spain. SPAIN – Civil War issues (*Part 9*).
Vojna Uprava Jugoslavenske Armije. Overprint/surcharge on Yugoslav stamps for VENEZIA GIULIA AND ISTRIA – Yugoslav Military Government.
Vojenska Posta. CZECHOSLOVAK ARMY IN SIBERIA.
Vom Empfänger Einzuziehen. DANZIG – Postage Due Stamps.
Vom Empfänger Zahlbar. BAVARIA – Postage Due Stamps.
V R in top corners. FIJI.
V.R.I. 'Victoria Regina Imperatrix'. Overprint with values in British currency on stamps of ORANGE FREE STATE.

Czechoslovak Army in Siberia

W or West Australia. WESTERN AUSTRALIA.
Wilayah Persekutuan. MALAYSIA – Federal Territory issues.
Wendenschen Kreises, Briefmarke des/Packenmarke des. WENDEN.
Western Samoa. SAMOA.
Württemberg. WURTTEMBERG. Independent Kingdom. Also GERMANY (ALLIED OCCUPATION).
Y.A.R. 'Yemen Arab Republic'. YEMEN.
Yemen PDR. YEMEN PEOPLE'S DEMOCRATIC REPUBLIC.
Yemen, Republic of. YEMEN REPUBLIC (Combined).
Yunnansen/Yunnanfou. Overprint/surcharge on Indo-Chinese stamps. YUNNANFU.
Z. Afr. Rep(ubliek). TRANSVAAL.
Zanzibar. Overprint/surcharge on French stamps for FRENCH P.O.s IN ZANZIBAR.

Yemeni Arab Republic

Zara. Overprint on Italian stamps. GERMANY OCCUPATION OF DALMATIA.
Zelaya, Dpto. NICARAGUA – Zelaya (*Part 15*).
Zeitungs Stempel. 'Newspaper Stamp'. AUSTRIA or LOMBARDY AND VENETIA.
Zil Eloigne Sesel Seychelles. 'Seychelles Outer Islands'. ZIL EL WANNYEN SESEL, 1980–82.
Zil Elwagne Sesel Seychelles. See above, 1982–84.
Zona de Ocupatie Romana in small oval. Overprint on Hungarian stamps for Debrecen. ROMANIAN OCCUPATION OF HUNGARY.
Zona Occupata Fiumano Kupa. Overprint on Yugoslav stamps. FIUME AND KUPA ZONE.
Zona (de) Protectorado Español/en Marruecos. SPANISH MOROCCO.

Turkey

Zone Française. GERMANY (ALLIED OCCUPATION) – French Zone, 1945–46.
Zuid Afrika. SOUTH AFRICA.
Zuid Afrikaansche (or Z. Afr.) Republiek. TRANSVAAL.
Zuidwest Afrika. SOUTH WEST AFRICA.
Zurich, Local Taxe. Zurich. SWITZERLAND – Cantonal Administrations (*Part 8*).

United Arab Emirates

The first Greek stamp showing Hermes

OTHER ALPHABETS AND SCRIPTS

The Greek Alphabet

Greek is one of the classic languages – its alphabet was 'borrowed' from the Phoenicians whose extinct Semitic language was allied to Carthaginian and akin to Hebrew, and was, perhaps, the first tongue written in an alphabet proper. The word 'alphabet' itself is derived from *alpha*, *beta*, the first two Greek letters. Greek stamps have the country name 'Hellas' expressed (in Greek), a word which can be spelled out from the table below as *Ellas*. In fact since 1966 the version 'Hellas' has been printed alongside the Greek characters on the stamps.

Aerospresso Co issue of 1926

Greek stamp marking the cession of the Ionian Islands

Modern Greek stamp inscribed 'ΕΛΛΑΣ ΔΗΜΟΚΡΑΤΙΑ'

Look out for the distinctive currency inscription – 100 lepta = 1 drachma. *Lepta* (singular, *lepton*) is expressed in a word which looks like 'AENTA' (although the first letter is an inverted 'V'), while *drachmai* (plural) appears at first glance as 'APAXMAI', though again the first letter is a triangle, the equivalent for 'D'. Sometimes these words are abbreviated. You may encounter overprints on Greek stamps and once you have decoded them it should be an easy matter to locate them in the catalogue. *Ellenike Dioikesis* ('Greek Administration') may be found on the Greek stamps of 1912 (provisionals for Balkan territories), or the Greek Occupation of Albania in 1940. The initials *S.D.D.* adjoining a surcharge within a scroll can be pinpointed to the Greek Occupation of the Dodecanese Islands. Thrace suffered various occupations in 1920, and a typical overprint reads, when decoded, *Diokesis Dutikes Frakes* or 'Administration of Western Thrace'. Stamps for the Greek island of Crete bear the inscription KPHTH which translates as *Krete*.

Anti Tuberculosis Fund

SIMPLIFIED GREEK TABLE *with English equivalents*

Greek	*English*	*Greek*	*English*
Α α	A	**Ξξ**	X
Β β	B	**Οο**	O
Γγ	G	**Ππ**	P
Δδ	D	**Ρρ**	R
Εε	E	**Σσ**	S
Ζζ	Z	**ς**	(final)
Ηη	E	**Ττ**	T
Θθ	TH	**Υυ**	U
Ιι	I	**Φφ**	F
Κκ	K	**Χχ**	KH
Λλ	L	**Ψψ**	PS
Μμ	M	**Ωω**	O
Νν	N		

Conventional English equivalents are given. The actual pronunciation of some letters differs in modern spoken Greek.

Greece – Administration of (Western) Thrace

A list of inscriptions in the Greek alphabet as they appear on stamps.

ΒΟΗΘΕΙΤΕ ΤΟΝ. Inscription on Charity Tax stamps. GREECE.
ΔΙΟΙΚΗΣΙΣ ΔΥΤΙΚΗΣ ΘΡΑΚΗΣ or Διοίκησις (Δυτικής) Θράκης. 'Administration of (Western) Thrace'. Overprint on stamps of Greece. THRACE.
Ε*Δ. Overprint on stamps of Greece for Khios. GREECE – Balkan War Issues (*Part 3*).
ΕΛΛΑΣ 2-Χ-43 in box. Handstamp on stamps for the Italian Occupation of Ionian Islands. GERMAN OCCUPATION OF ZANTE.
ΕΛΛΑΣ, ΕΛΛΑC or ΕΛΛ. GREECE.
ΕΛΛ. ΔΙΟΙΚ. ΓΚΙΟΥΜΟΥ ΛΤΖΙΝΑΣ. Overprint/surcharge on stamps of Turkey. THRACE – Greek Occupation, 1913, Issue for Gumultsina (*Part 3*).
ΕΛΛΗΝΙΚΗ ΧΕΙΜΑΡΡΑ. EPIRUS (*Part 3*).
ΕΛΛΗΝΙΚΗ ΔΗΜΟΚΡΑΤΙΑ. GREECE.
ΕΛΛΗΝΙΚΗ ΔΙΟΙΚΗCIC. Overprint on stamps of Greece. GREEK OCCUPATION OF ALBANIA.
ΕΛΛΗΝΙΚΗ ΔΙΟΙΚΗΣΙΣ. Overprint on stamps of Greece, 1912. GREECE. Also on stamps of Greece (Ikaria) and Bulgaria (Kavalla). GREECE – Balkan War Issues (*Part 3*).
ΕΛΛΗΝΙΚΗ ΔΙΟΙΚΗΣΙΣ ΔΕΔΕΑΓΑΤΣ. 'Greek Administration Dedeagtz'. THRACE – Greek Occupation, 1913. Issue for Dedeagatz (*Part 3*).
Ελληνική Κατοχή Μυτιλήνης. 'Greek Possession Mytilene'. Overprint on stamps of Turkey for Lesvos. GREECE – Balkan War Issues (*Part 3*).
ΕΝΑΡΙΘΜΟΝ ΓΡΑΜΜΑΤΟΣΗΜΟΝ. Postage Due. GREECE.
ΕΘΝΙΚΗ ΠΕΡΙΘΑΛΨΙΣ. Inscription on 1914 Charity Tax stamp. GREECE.
ΕΠΑΝΑΣΤΑΣΙΣ 1922. 'Revolution 1922'. Overprint on stamps of Crete (and Greece). GREECE.
ΗΠΕΙΡΟΣ. EPIRUS (*Part 3*).
ΙΚΑΡΙΑΣ. Ikaria. GREECE – Balkan War Issues (*Part 3*).
ΙΟΝΙΚΟΝ ΚΡΑΤΟΣ. IONIAN ISLANDS.
ΙΤΑΛΙΑΣ–ΕΛΛΑΔΟΣ–ΤΟΥΡΚΙΑΣ. Inscription on Aerospresso Co issue of 1926. GREECE.
ΚΟΙΝΟΝ ΝΗΣΙΩΤΩΝ. Island Committee for Union with Greece. DODECANESE ISLANDS (*Part 3*).
Κ. Π. Overprint on Fiscal stamps (inscribed ΧΑΡΤΟΣΗΜΟΝ) of GREECE.
ΚΡΗΤΗ. CRETE.
Λ(or Α)ΗΜΝΟΣ. Overprint on stamps of Greece for Limnos. GREECE – Balkan War Issues (*Part 3*).
ΟΛΥΜΠ. ΑΓΩΥΕΣ or **ΟΛΥΜΠΙΑΚΟΙ ΑΓΩΝΕΣ**. Olympic Games issue of 1906. GREECE.
Π.Ι.Π. (P.I.P. 'Patriotic Charity League'). Overprint on Red Cross stamp. GREECE.
ΠΡΟΣΤΑΣΙΑ ΦΥΜΑΤΙΚΩΝ. Anti-Tuberculosis Fund. GREECE.
ΠΡΟΣΩΡΙΝΗ ΚΥΒΕΡΝΗΣΙΣ. CRETE – Revolutionary Assembly.
ΠΡΟΣΩΡΙΝΟΝ ΤΑΧΥΔΡΟΜΕΙΟΝ ΗΡΑΚΛΕΙΟΥ. Candia Province – BRITISH P.O.s IN CRETE.
ΡΕΘΥΜΝΗΣ. Rethymnon Province – RUSSIAN POST OFFICES IN CRETE.
ΣΑΜΟΥ. Samos. GREECE – Balkan War Issues (*Part 3*).

Σ.Δ.Δ. Overprint on stamps of Greece. Greek Military Administration. DODECANESE ISLANDS (*Part 3*).
Υάτη Αρμοστεία Θράκης. 'High Commission of Thrace'. Overprint/surcharge on stamps of Turkey. THRACE.

Greek Occupation of Albania

Greek Administration

Greek Postage Due

Epirus

Ikaria

Stamps of Imperial China and the Chinese People's Republic and on the far right Taiwan (Republic of China)

From 1992 People's Republic stamps have included the name 'CHINA' in the Western alphabet.

The same rule applies to the stamps of Taiwan from 1949 – the birth of the Chinese Nationalist Republic. Modern Taiwan stamps are inscribed 'Republic of China'.

JAPAN

Japan. Design with Chrysanthemum emblem, stamp with name in Japanese characters only and issue including the name 'Nippon'

Japanese is written in ideographic (picture-symbol) characters, acquired from China. Indeed, through constant contact with the Chinese people down the centuries (in peace and war), the Japanese language has enriched itself with Chinese words and expressions. Japanese stamps up to 1947 often had an emblem representing a chrysanthemum included in the design. From 1966 the word 'Nippon' in the Roman alphabet has been added to Japanese stamp designs. Inscriptions in the native language include the country name which comprises a standard group of four characters. The first of these (which may be last depending in which direction the sentence has been written) is easily recognizable – it resembles a box with a horizontal line through the middle.

In 1930 Japan alleged that her interests in Manchuria were being jeopardized by the Chinese and began the military occupation of the area, setting up a new puppet state of Manchukuo, consisting of the former provinces of Fegtien, Kirin, Heilungchiang and Jehol. Pu Yi, who later became Emperor Kang-teh (of *The Last Emperor* film fame), was appointed Head of State. The stamps, identified by the orchid crest and by the currency – 100 fen = 1 yuan – are listed in the catalogue under Manchukuo.

RYUKYU ISLANDS

Ryukyu stamps, first issued in 1948, closely resembled those of Japan in style, inscriptions and currency – 100 sen = 1 yen. The main inscription, however, lacks the box-like character noted above for Japan. Under United States administration the stamps were issued in American cents and dollars from 1958 – note the distinctive '¢' for cents. From 1961 the word 'Ryukyus' appeared on the stamps, which ceased in 1972 when the islands were handed back to Japan.

KOREA

Korea. US military Government surcharge on Japanese stamp, issues of South and North Korea

The divided nation. Emblems and inscriptions help to distinguish the stamps of South and North Korea. Unlike Chinese, each sign in the Korean language is a separate letter of the alphabet – these are combined in groups to form complete characters. North Korean inscriptions have four such characters, those of South Korea have six, the first one resembling 'CH'. South Korean stamps additionally bear the *yin yang* symbol – a circle part light and part dark – and have been inscribed 'Republic of Korea' in English since 1966.

Japanese occupation of Malaya

OTHER SCRIPTS

Unfamiliar scripts and alphabets may present a problem if there is no other clue to a stamp's origins. Some are illustrated here as a general guide. Note the appearance and 'look' of an inscription, and observe particularly whether the script comprises separate characters (like the Amharic language from Ethiopia, or the Siamese language of Thailand

Turkey

Afganistan

which is derived from a form of Sanskrit and has affinities with Chinese), or in flowing style like Arabic or Persian, which is a version of Arabic. Most Arab countries inscribe their stamps additionally in English or French, but remember that Arabic is written from right to left and that there are six chief dialects – Algerian, Moroccan, Syrian, Egyptian,

Manchukuo

Ryukyu Islands

Iran

Saudi Arabia

Malaya (Perak)

Left to right: Different scripts on stamps of Georgia, Nepal, Burma and Tuva

Alsace and Lorraine

Austria

Austria – Postage Due

Austria – Newspaper stamps

Bosnia and Herzegovina

Belgium

Bahrain – War tax

Iraqi and Arabian. The Turkish language, formerly written in Arabic characters, was changed to Roman by the order of Ataturk in 1928. Note also that Israel stamps, following the first 'Coins' issue of 1948, have been inscribed not only in Hebrew and Arabic, but in English as well.

Some of the Malay States are easy to identify with the names shown in English – Johore, Kedah, Malacca (or Melaka), Penang (or Pulau Pinang) and Sungei Ujong. But some have the state's name only in Malay script – which contains 'dots and dashes' and has Arabic elements. These include Kelantan, Negri Sembilan (or Negeri Sembilan), Pahang, Perak, Perlis, Selangor and Trengganu. Look for a similar sultan's portrait or state arms in the catalogue. The Afghan languages are Persian or Pushtu (or Pashtu), but the stamps are usually inscribed in French – Postes Afghanes – as well as the native script. Nepali is the spoken language of the Gurkha peoples of Nepal, but all except the earliest stamps have been additionally inscribed 'Nepal' in English. Burmese, the language of the people of Burma (also known as Myanmar), is allied to Chinese and is written in an alphabet derived from India, the characters of which are more or less circular and thereby easily identifiable on Burmese stamps in addition to the 'Burma Postage' or 'Union of Burma' inscriptions. The stamps of Sri Lanka (Ceylon) are unusual in that they are inscribed trilingually – Sinhalese, Tamil and English.

United States of America

'No-name' Stamps

As mentioned in the beginning of this book, Great Britain is the only country in the world whose stamps do not bear the name of the issuing country, although all of them bear the likeness of the ruling monarch. In early days – before the foundation of the Universal Postal Union, other countries sometimes did not include their names either. Three stamps which apparently defied the U.P.U. convention were issued by the United States in 1920, marking the tercentenary of the Landing of the Pilgrim Fathers – they omitted the customary 'U.S. Postage'.

Some 'difficult' countries are listed below with a number of the stamps illustrated.

Austria. Check the currencies on early issues because, although the designs are similar, your stamps might be from Austrian Post Offices in Turkey, or from Lombardy and Venetia. The head of Mercury, messenger of the gods, appears on Austrian newspaper stamps.

Bahrain. Arabic inscription with 'key'-like word under circle – 1974 War Tax Stamp. (Also 1973 issue, without 'key'.)

Bosnia and Herzegovina. The Austrian coat-of-arms is prominent.

Brazil. The early 'numeral' stamps represented 'Bull's-eyes', 'Goat's-eyes' and 'Snake's-eyes' respectively. A 'Bull's-eye' is shown on page 5.

Finland. Circles in the designs distinguish the 1891 issue from the similar issues of Russia. Also issues between 1901 and 1911 bear the face value in Finnish *penni* and *markkaa*.

Hungary. 1871–88. Similar to Austria, but the designs are distinctive.

Papal States. The crossed keys are the main clue. Cf. First issue of Vatican City.

Portugal. 'Correio', the 'reis' currency and the Royal heads suggest Portugal.

Sardinia. Compare with very similar stamps of Italy, 1862.

Saudi Arabia. Palm tree emblem only on stamps from 1982.

Spain. Stamps with various portraits, often inscribed Communicaciones, sometimes dated, and with currencies in cuartos, centimos and pesetas, indicate 19th century Spain, but should be checked with contemporary issues of Cuba, Puerto Rico or the Philippines, particularly if the inscription includes Ultramar.

Switzerland. Early postage dues were unnamed, being regarded as of internal significance only.

Emblems on stamps can also aid identification. Shown below are Yin yang (South Korea), Chrysanthemum (Japan), Orchid (Manchukuo), Star and crescent (Turkey, Pakistan, Bahawalpur, Hyderabad), Toughra (Turkey, Saudi Arabia, Afghanistan), Palm tree and crossed scimitar (Saudi Arabia) and Trident (Ukraine)

Putting on a Good Show

Paul Brittain looks at the question of mounting and presentation

It's only natural—having acquired some stamps, you want to be able to enjoy them in the best possible way. And what better way than placing them on pages. Most collectors start by using a stamp album whose pages have been specifically designed, usually with large or small squares, making it easy to arrange the stamps neatly. Such albums normally have the names of countries printed at the tops of the pages, so that the correct stamps can be affixed to each page.

Mounting

It is the method of affixing that is key, however. Many try various ways—using glue; if the stamp is gummed, simply licking the back and using the stamp's own adhesive; using clear sticky tape; perhaps using the blank white paper that normally surrounds stamps in a sheet. None of these should be tried. In the initial stages, when putting stamps on a page, always use stamp hinges. These are small pieces of opaque paper, gummed on one side. You fold the piece of paper over about one third down its length (some are ready-folded), with the gummed side on the outside. The smaller portion is gently moistened, and affixed to the back of the stamp, at the top centrally, just below the perforations. A small portion of the part not affixed to the stamp is similarly moistened. By holding both stamp and hinge with a pair of stamp tweezers, it is now possible to position the stamp where required on the album page. With a little bit of pressure with a finger (some like to use a piece of paper between finger and stamp for this purpose), the stamp can be made secure on the page. If the hinge has been used correctly, it should be possible to lift the stamp up to examine the back. As long as the hinge has been gently moistened, no damage should occur to stamp or album page if the hinge is subsequently removed. However, do not be in a hurry to remove the hinge. If you find you have made a mistake, such as putting the stamp in the wrong place, leave the hinge to dry for a while before attempting to remove it.

Returning to the idea of pressing the stamp in place with a piece of paper, I recall seeing one collector, so keen to mount a new acquisition into his album, that he did not bother to wash his hands after coming in from gardening. When pressing the stamps in place with his finger, he left a lovely fingerprint on each.

Stamp mounts welded at top and bottom (left) and at bottom only

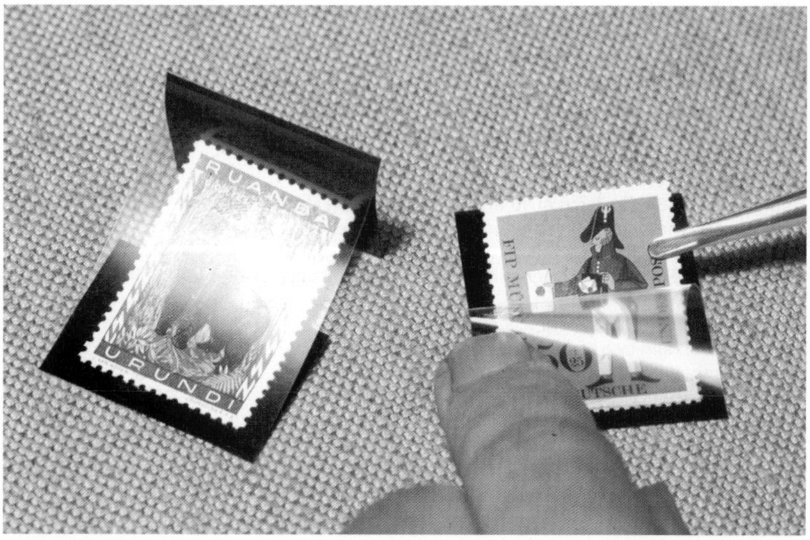

Mounted or unmounted?

Over the years there have been concerns about even affixing a hinge to a stamp. When you buy a stamp from a post office, it has all its gum on the back. Once you fix a hinge to the back, you damage part of that gum. For many stamps, especially the rarer ones, there can be a great difference in price between a stamp which has all its original gum intact (known as mint, unmounted, or unmounted mint) compared with one to which a hinge has been attached (known as mounted, or sometimes as mounted mint). Of course, generally speaking a stamp that still has its gum has not been on an item sent through the post, and therefore is regarded as unused. (Some countries deliberately postmark unused stamps for sale to collectors, and these may still have their gum, in addition to a post-mark.) If a stamp has been through the post, it will not normally still retain its gum: it is therefore known as used. It could be argued that it does not matter if you affix a hinge to a used stamp, as there is no gum to disturb. However, there are collectors who are concerned about leaving the marks where a stamp hinge has been, even on a used stamp.

The answer has been to use what are known as stamp mounts. These comprise two pieces of clear material, welded together, between which the stamp is placed. The front is always clear, so that the stamp is clearly visible. The back is sometimes clear, but can be dark coloured (virtually black) to highlight the stamp. Such mounts invariably come in strips of different heights, designed to accommodate various sizes of stamp. The strips can be cut into the required length for each stamp. Such strips are either welded just along the bottom edge, or along both the top and bottom edges. The latter tend to hold stamps more securely in place, but make it more difficult to remove stamps for closer inspection once mounted. Similar mounts are available for larger items, such as blocks of stamps or miniature sheets.

Such mounts are not cheap, especially when compared with the price of stamp hinges, while unmounted stamps will cost more to buy in the first place. Whether to use mounts must therefore be a personal choice. However, it must be added that over the years there has been growing concern that some mounts, especially those manufactured in the early years, inflict harm on material, and cannot be recommended for the long-term safety of your stamps. I have seen stamps which have been in such mounts for some years, and where the design of the stamp has migrated on to the mount itself. If you are going to use mounts, therefore, do ensure you buy the best conservation quality.

By the way, if you are mounting larger items, an alternative is to use photo corners, especially those with a clear face that enable the item to be fully viewed.

Some collectors adopt a variety of methods, putting their more precious stamps in mounts, using photo corners for larger items, and stamp hinges for the rest. The trouble is that this can look a mess, so might be best avoided, although the visual impact can be improved, as we shall see later.

Planning

Before any start is made designing your pages, it will first be necessary to plan your collection. If you are collecting the stamps of just one country, this can be fairly straightforward. Most choose a chronological approach, putting the stamps and sets in the date order they are issued. Since the stamp catalogues list the stamps for each country in this way, it becomes quite easy to arrange the stamps in order. The only decision that might need to be made is which stamps you are likely to acquire, and which, probably because of their cost, you might have to forget for a while. It is not ideal to see a collection with lots of gaps for stamps not yet obtained, especially if there is really no chance of being able to acquire the missing stamps in the foreseeable future. Much better therefore to arrange your collection as though those stamps do not

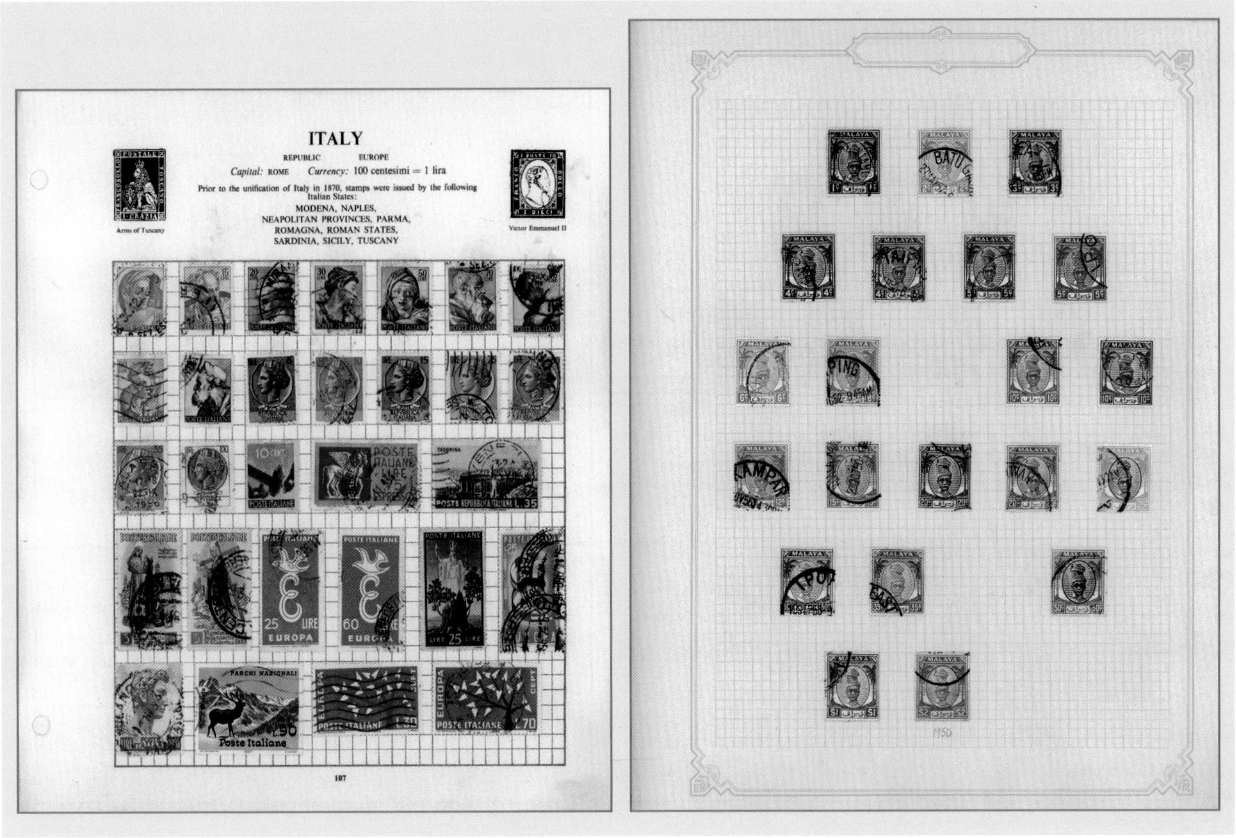

Album page with printed heading (left). Page with gaps left for stamps not yet obtained

exist: do not leave spaces for them. If, later on, some of these stamps come your way, you will be so pleased, you will not mind having to redesign a page or two of your collection.

With thematic collecting, life is a little more difficult. You will want to tell a `story' with your material, and therefore need to sort out that story before you start to plan your pages. In this case, it is often better to use a stockbook initially to arrange your stamps. You can easily move the material around until it is in the sequence in which you want it to appear finally on your album pages. Once again, there may be items you would still like to add for your theme: the joy of collecting is always finding new items. However, you cannot wait indefinitely before you start to put your collection on to pages: when more material comes along, you might need to redesign some pages.

Choosing your album pages

A question to be asked now is exactly what sort of paper you are going to use on which to mount your material. The obvious answer is to use the pages of a loose-leaf stamp album. However, the majority are not of a standard paper size. As will be discussed more fully later, many collectors are now designing their pages on a computer screen, often adding the written information at the same time. While printers attached to computers can accommodate various sizes of paper, many will only take a maximum paper size of A4. Increasingly therefore, collectors are turning to using blank A4 sheets of paper for their collections. As with the standard album pages, the paper used must be strong enough to take the material, and should also be of conservation quality. While pale shades can be attractive, white paper is still preferable. Also try to ensure that all the collection uses the same shade of paper (even white can vary), although this is not always easy to achieve. At one time black paper was popular, but is far less used these days.

Once you have decided what is going to be put on to each page, whether it be stamps, blocks, covers, miniature sheets, or whatever, the first thing is to arrange the items in the most attractive, yet still logical, way. While each page you prepare should look pleasing, it would lose its point if an item is simply out of place. Starting with a blank page, move the items around until the preferred layout is achieved. Some now indicate the positioning of each item with feint pencil marks, ready for mounting the material later. Those who have opted to use the help of a computer can design their pages on screen. By measuring each item to appear on a page, it is possible to create a 'box' of the correct size. The boxes can then be moved around until a pleasing layout is achieved. It is, in fact, a good idea to make such boxes slightly smaller than the item concerned: once the item is mounted, the actual box will then be obscured.

An alternative however is to make the boxes fractionally bigger than the items: that way the boxes become an effective border. It is also possible to scan each item, so that a better impression of the final layout can be gleaned. A border can still be added. (Another advantage of scanning is that it does provide a good record of the items in the collection—however, again for conservation reasons, it is best only to scan an item once.)

Writing up

Having 'designed' your page, it is invariably best to add any 'write up' before mounting your material. However, even before you start, you must decide what information is going to accompany your stamps. The advice usually given is to keep it to a minimum. Write out what you think should appear—then precis it, and precis it again. The point is, of course, that this is your collection, and you should include the information that you feel is interesting and relevant. If you want to show your collection to others then the extent of any writing up is important—you want to interest, even enthuse, the viewer, not bore them to tears. The key aspect is that whatever you include should be there to enhance the material you are showing, not detract from it.

Again, today many prefer to produce the writing up on computer. It allows you to position it in the best place in relation to the items you are showing, and to edit or correct as necessary. You can vary the type-face, type size, add italics or underlining as appropriate. The key is not to become carried away by all the computer can provide. Never forget that what should impress the viewer is your material, it should not be overwhelmed by the writing up. Clearly if designing and writing up your pages on computer, once you are satisfied on screen, then the page can be printed off on your chosen paper, and the items are ready to be mounted as previously described.

If you feel the computer does not provide the right 'personal' touch to the writing up, there are always the more traditional methods. For years collectors used their skills with a pen: some would demonstrate the fine art of calligraphy. The quality of pen, and thickness of nib are all important: ball-point pens don't produce the same effect. Some are quite content with pencil. You must be your own judge as to whether

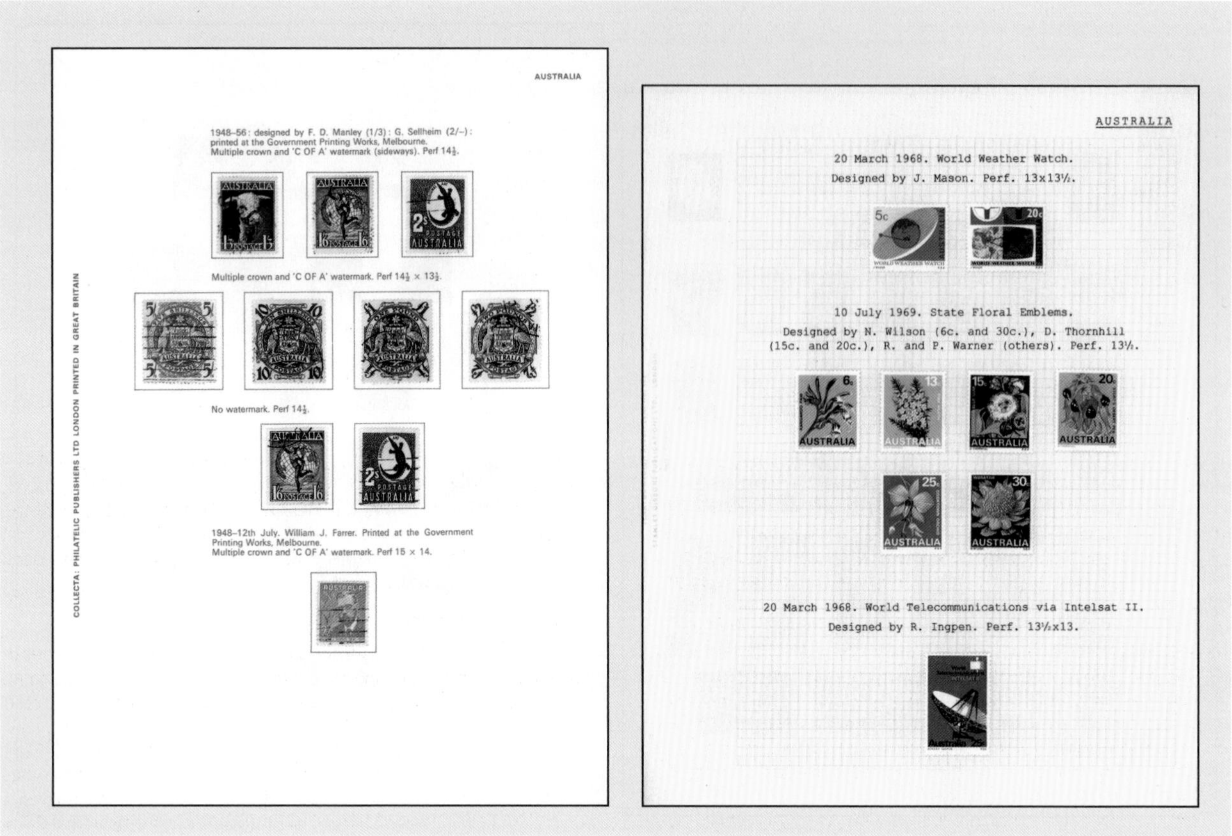

A printed page from a one-country album (left) and a type-written album page

your writing is sufficiently neat. Other methods that have been used include press-down dry lettering, such as the once famous Letraset brand, stencils, even cut-out labels. These have now been largely superseded. Some still use typewriters, perhaps typing directly on to the album page. Others prefer to type on to blank sheets of paper, which are then carefully cut out and positioned on the page. (The same principle can easily be used with a computer.) If using a more conventional method, it is better to complete the writing up before mounting: a mistake can occur, resulting in the page having to be rewritten, or in an item being damaged.

Having designed and written up each page, the material can be mounted. Even if various methods are used (hinges, mounts, photo corners), the final page should look uniform. For example, if your mounts have a black backing, ensure that covers, etc, even if mounted with photo corners, are on a similar, thin, black backing. Don't have some items with a backing, others without. If you prefer a black line to border each item, and do not wish to undertake this using a computer, ensure that these are drawn neatly, especially keeping the corners tidy.

There can be no doubt that a well presented collection, carefully arranged and neatly written up, is a joy to behold—for both its owner and others. It enhances not only the look but also the interest gained from the material. You are proud of your stamps, so you should do them proud.

Using a stamp hinge

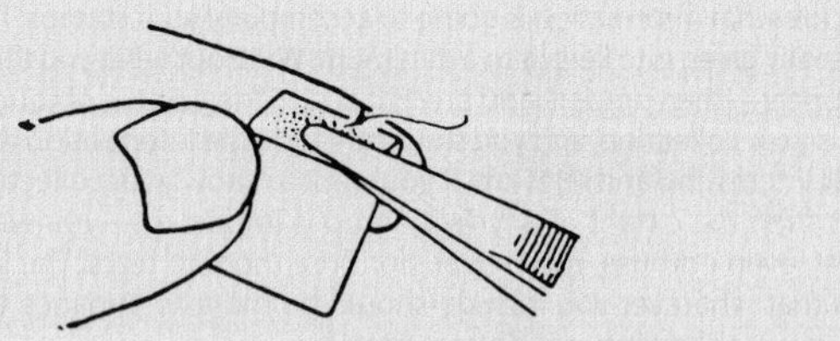

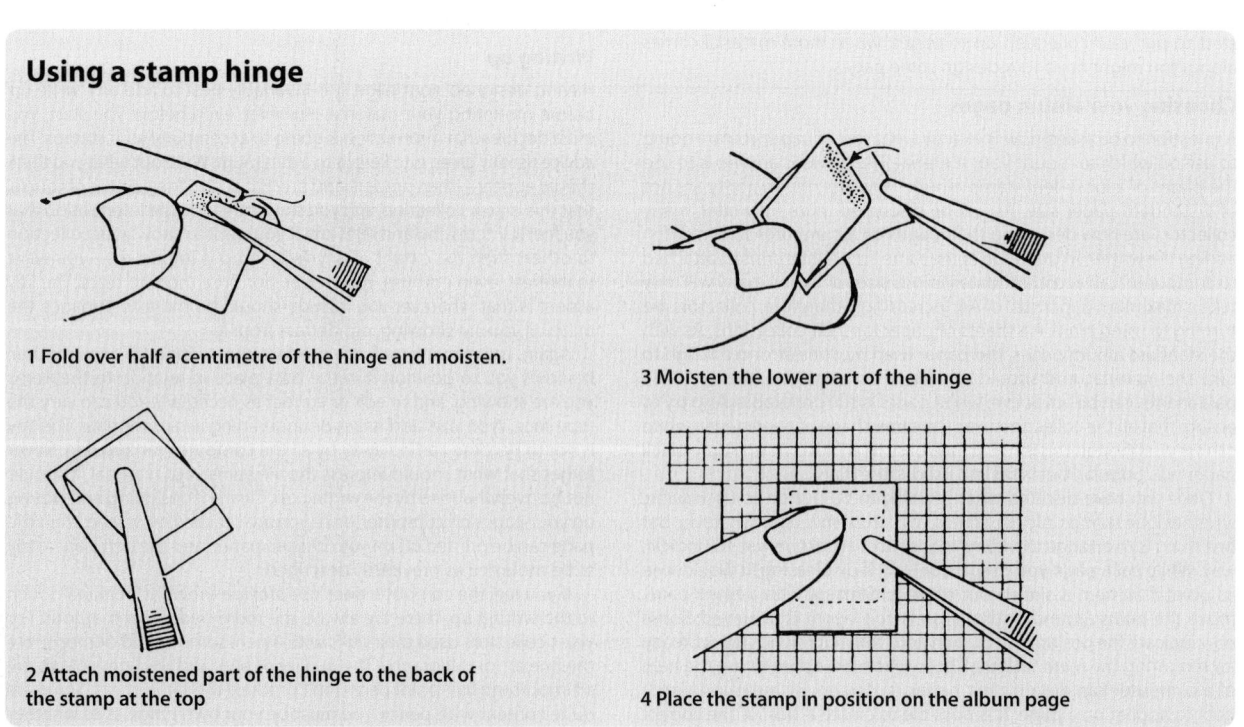

1 Fold over half a centimetre of the hinge and moisten.

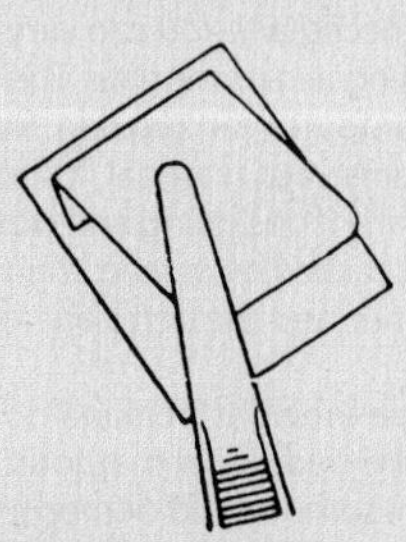

2 Attach moistened part of the hinge to the back of the stamp at the top

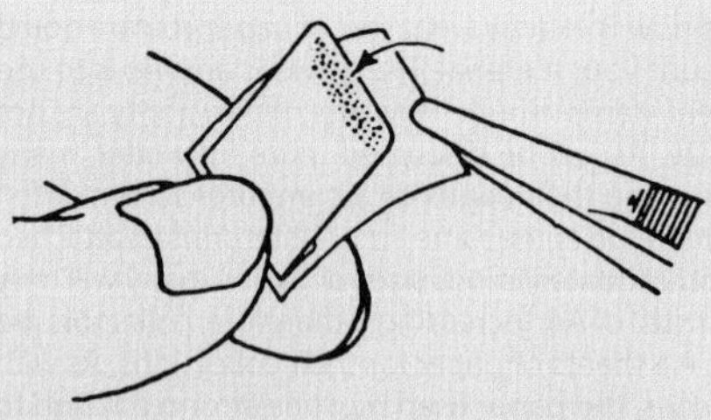

3 Moisten the lower part of the hinge

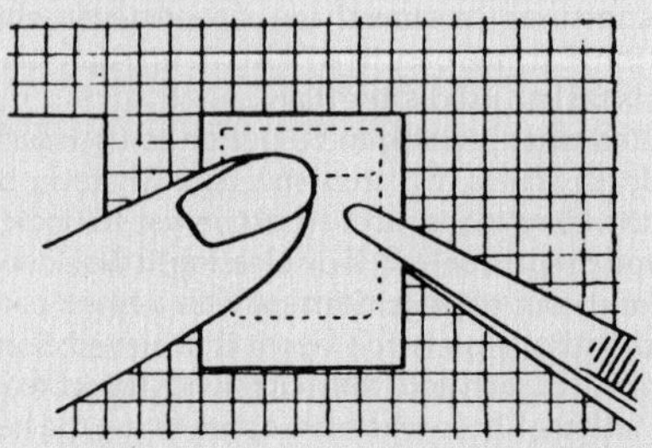

4 Place the stamp in position on the album page

To include, or not to include, that is the question

Paul Brittain explores the question of what is acceptable in a collection

What to include in a stamp collection is a matter that many ponder. The basic answer is that anything goes; for it is your personal collection, there to bring you pleasure. However, such an answer might be a little too simplistic. It really depends on how you intend to use the collection. Is it purely for personal enjoyment, or do you intend to share it with others? Are those others going to be stamp-collecting friends, perhaps fellow members of a stamp dub, or might they be non-collectors who you would like to see equally enthused by the hobby? Perhaps you intend to enter competitions, whether at local, regional, national or even international level. In each case a different approach might be needed.

There are many who develop several collections simultaneously, using each in different ways. In the days when thematic collecting was less established than today, there were several collectors I knew who would be very open about their more 'traditional' material, while secretly enjoying putting together a theme.

So let us consider from the outset what might be included in a collection that is for you to enjoy alone. In such cases, as stated, anything goes. If you want to include postcards, maps, newspaper cuttings, letters and so on, who is going to stop you, and who can say that you are wrong? Probably the only limit will be what can physically be mounted on an album page. If items are too large to fit on to a standard size page, they might prove more difficult to handle. That said, there are many collectors who put two album pages together in order to accommodate a larger piece. There needs to be a word of warning in such cases, however: odd-sized items are far more prone to damage, and therefore need special care at all times. Bulky or heavy items are also going to prove difficult, so do ensure that the quality of paper on which you mount items can stand their weight. At times thin card might be more appropriate.

The result could be that your collection looks more like a scrap book; at the other extreme it might appear more like a drawing exercise as you illustrate every nuance for your extensive study of a single stamp.

In addition to the material included comes the question of the amount of information you provide, the write-up. Again, for personal use what you include is up to you, and if it ends up looking like a book with a few illustrations, so be it.

Showing to others

Such points need to be addressed if you are going to show your collection to others, especially to those who may not be quite so absorbed by the subject as you are. If you are going to share your collection with those who do not collect, you must ensure you maintain their interest, hopefully creating such a fascination that they will want to know more and start exploring for themselves. It means that studies will not be appropriate, and a much lighter diet should be offered. I recall that when I started collecting, back in my primary school days, my next door neighbour was an avid collector. I was enthralled by his collection, and seeing it, and chatting with him, certainly encouraged me in my collecting. It was some years later when I came to see his collection again that I realised it was fairly straightforward.

Nothing wrong in that, of course, but the fact remains that had it been more specialised it might not have acted as such a catalyst for me.

The same can apply if showing part of the collection to members of a stamp club. If it is to members of a specialist society, then a fairly detailed study might be appropriate, but for a general audience, it is far better to keep it simple. We all have areas of collecting that we find particularly fascinating, but should never assume that others will derive the same satisfaction. It is equally true that some collectors are so blinkered they do not view displays, or read magazine articles, on anything other than their own particular interest. By adopting such a

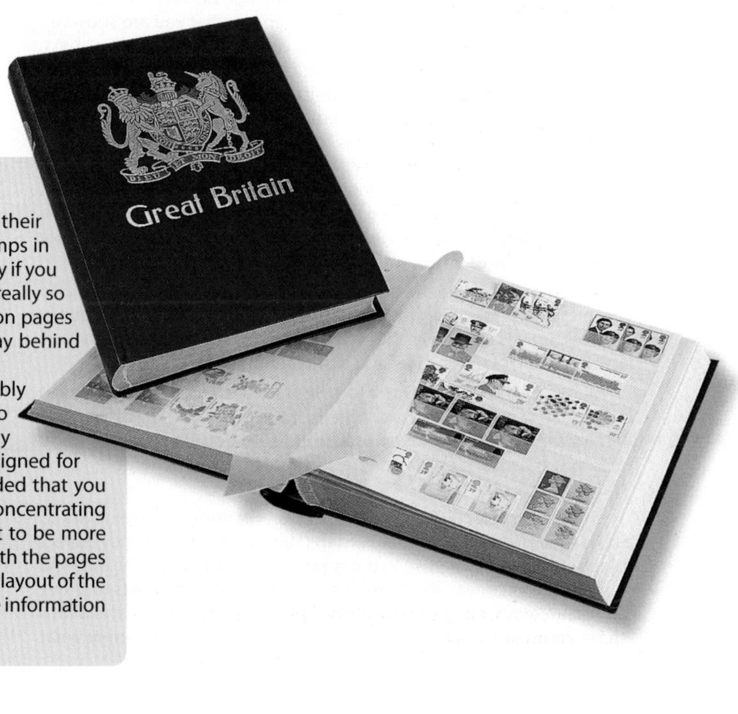

Stockbooks

There are collectors who never venture as far as mounting their material. They are quite content with arranging their stamps in stockbooks. This does have the advantage of making it easy if you want to rearrange the order, or add new items, but is not really so dynamic visually. The majority prefer to see the material on pages in albums, even though most will admit that they are way behind with the process.

As a youngster you begin with a printed album and probably place the stamps in rows on each page. (There are also albums produced, notably for a few countries particularly popular with collectors, which have the pages ready designed for the stamps to be added.) However, once you have decided that you want to be more specialised in your interest, perhaps concentrating on a particular country or a certain theme, you will want to be more adventurous. the next move will be to albums supplied with the pages blank. In such cases it is left to the individual to arrange the layout of the stamps on each page. In addition, most prefer to add some information about the stamps.

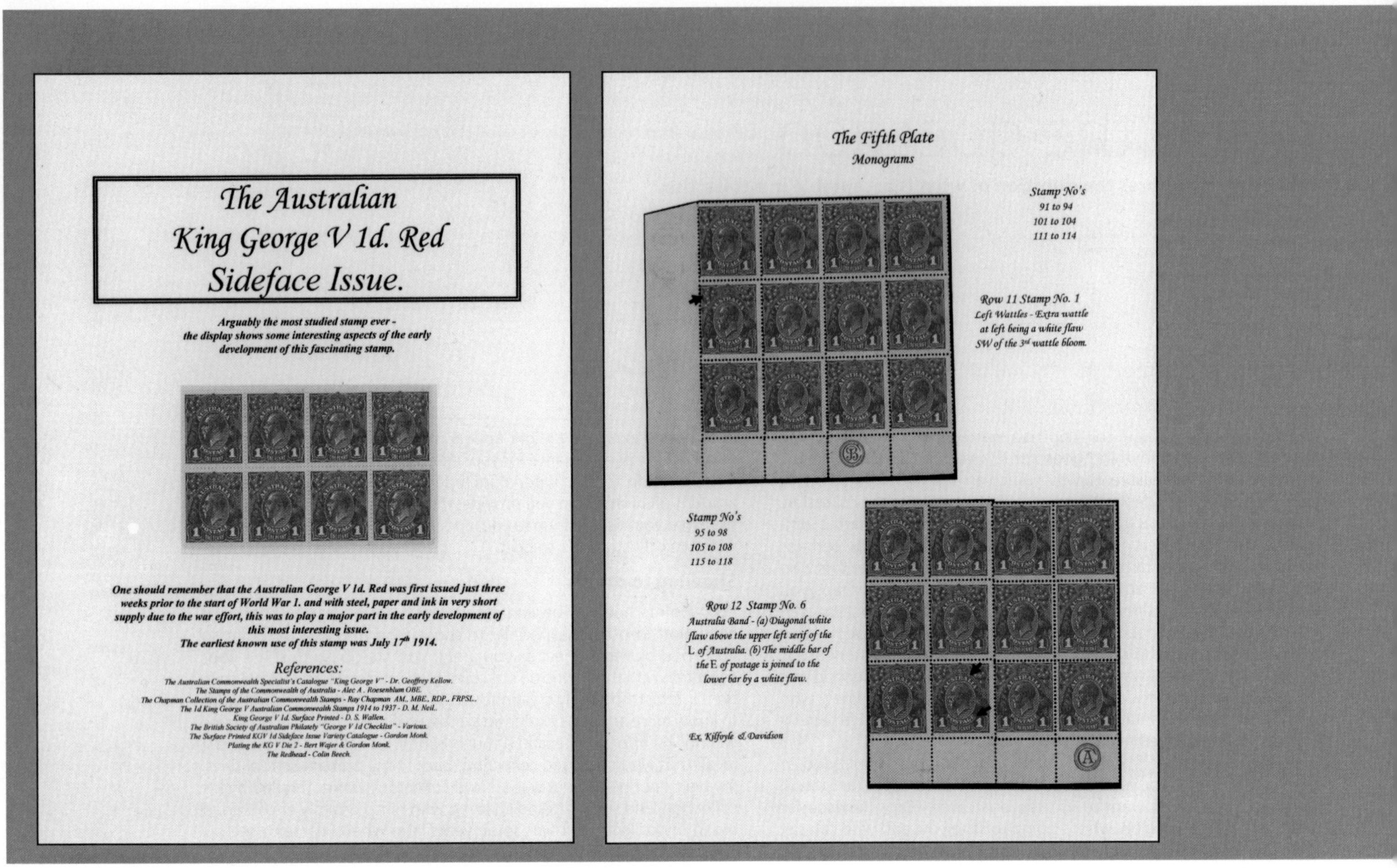

narrow-minded approach much useful information can be missed—it is surprising how the results of someone else's research can have a bearing on your own collecting..

The basic rule if showing to a more general audience, such as the members of a local stamp club, is to keep it interesting for all, irrespective of what they personally collect. Generally speaking such audiences will expect the material you show to be reasonably `conventional'. While you might include a great deal of ephemera or periphery material in your personal collection, those in your audience are stamp collectors, and expect primarily to see philatelic material. Equally, do not bore by including such minutiae that few can enjoy what you are showing. The point to re-member at any stamp club meeting is that, at best, the audience will only be able to glance at most of what you show, perhaps focusing on the one or two items that particularly catch the attention. There is simply not the time for a careful perusal of all you are showing, while the conditions may not make close inspection at all easy. By the same token, the writing up should be short and to the point. Long descriptions will simply not be read. One leading collector, sadly no longer with us, offered the advice that the write-up should be prepared, then edited to about half, then precised to half again: only then might it be of an acceptable length.

While not strictly on the theme of this article, remember if talking to any audience, not only should you not bore by your material, equally do not turn your audience off by your delivery. Speak to the audience, and keep what you say brief and stimulating.

Many collectors are invited to give talks and displays to societies other than of stamp collectors. With the right material and a fascinating tale to tell these can prove absorbing for the audience, but clearly the right balance is crucial in terms of material, the write up and the spoken word.

There are many collectors who, for whatever reason, are reluctant to show their material to others. Perhaps they feel that what they collect is not of sufficient interest, that it is poorly presented, or that they will not be able to convey their enthusiasm. Once someone starts to show, all such fears quickly prove unfounded. It becomes a great thrill to share your passion, and to discover that others really do enjoy what you have to say and show.

Competitions

The same reluctance is very evident when it comes to competitions. Some will use the argument that they do not approve of competitions, and the fact that to achieve the best result it is necessary to specially to prepare the required number of pages, usually from eight upwards. Would it not be fairer simply to take pages straight from the collection? There was a time when at competitions at events such as Stampex, the collection had to be submitted to support the pages that actually went on display, to demonstrate that what was shown was a true reflection of the entire collection. Today it is different, and there are many who exhibit who prepare the particular pages specifically for competition.

This is not the occasion to discuss the rights and wrongs of competitions: perhaps that can be the subject for a future article. However, I do not subscribe to the view that what goes into competition should necessarily be of the same standard as the rest of the collection, unless the entire collection is maintained to a high standard.

All competitions have their rules and regulations, which in the case of our hobby will include what material is acceptable and how it is presented. If you are entering any serious competition, whether a dog show, a flower or vegetable show, or a major sporting event, you know that you must abide by the rules. You would never dream of entering your pet dog into a major show without ensuring that all its features were exactly as looked for by the judges, and that it had been meticulously groomed. You would not expect to achieve the highest standards in a particular sport without years of practice and adopting all the correct techniques, gradually progressing from the lowest to the highest levels. So why should it be any different with a stamp competition?

You should expect to adhere to the rules, and to work up from local club level to as far as you personally aspire. So study the rules, particularly in relation to what can or should not be included. Most local/regional competitions are divided into the basic classes of traditional (often postal stationery is included within traditional), postal history, aerophilately, thematics, and Cinderellas and revenues.

Traditional philately is essentially the study of the stamps, and so would not include items that relate to postal history, although could well include covers to show the correct usage of the stamps

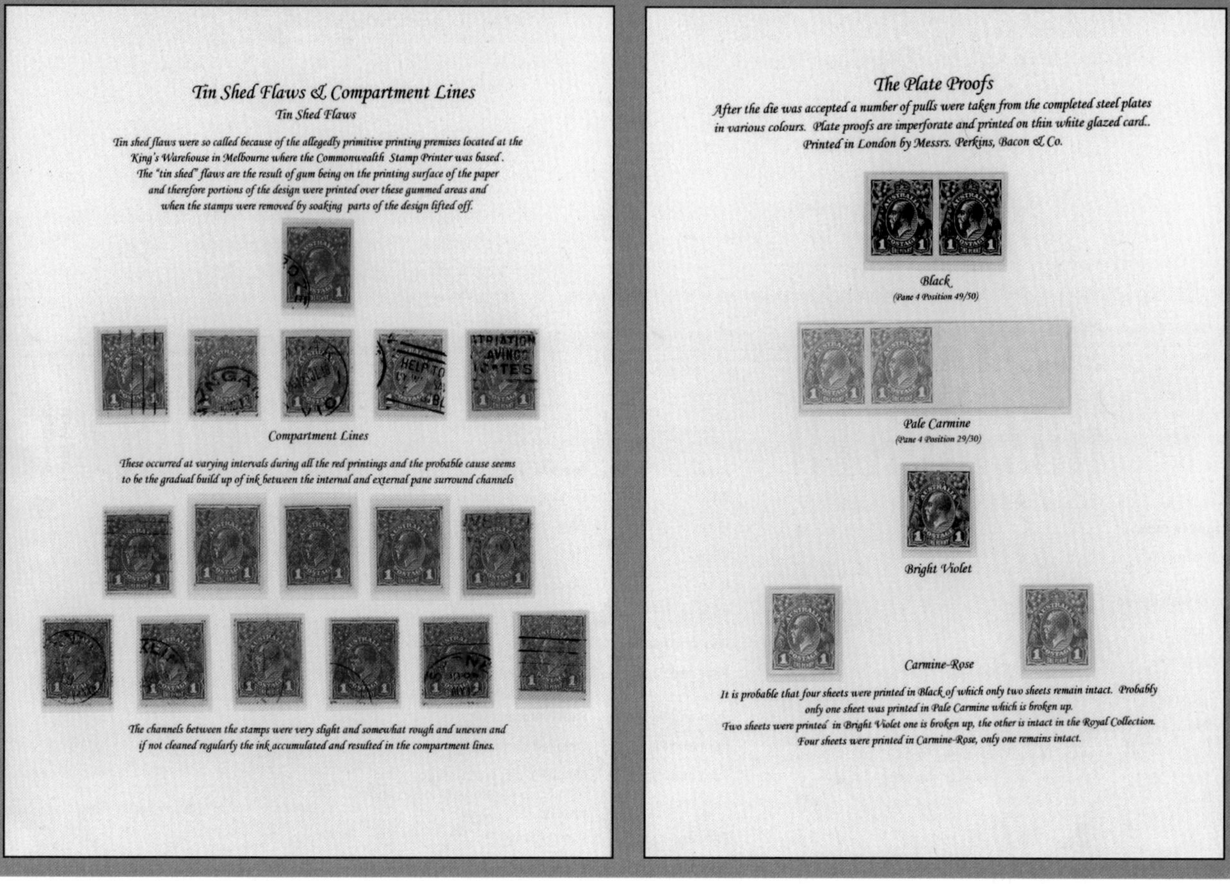

Pages from a traditional collection devoted to a specialised study of the King George V 1d. red stamp of Australia. Illustrations courtesy of Colin Mount.

in question. Covers are needed as they show not only the stamp and the service provided, but also that it was used during the valid period and to the right destination. A traditional exhibit will encompass the stamps, perhaps in plate blocks, with printings, shade, perforation or watermark variations, errors and varieties, 'Specimen' overprints, even proofs and essays. The stamps can be unused or used, although there is some debate as to whether mint and used should be mixed on the same page: in some cases this might be unavoidable if certain items are only known either unused or used. Postal history naturally relates to the development of the postal service, and thus will concentrate on the rates charged and the routes taken, although postal markings are usually also included in this class. Items will usually be covers, or perhaps fronts of covers, although stamps on piece are acceptable if sufficient to show the marking being demonstrated. Aerophilately of course relates to mail carried by air, and thus will normally involve covers, but can also include airmail stamps. Cinderellas and revenues are clearly less easy to define, but fascinating displays can be assembled which might involve local postage services, such as those on places such as Herm and Lundy islands, postal orders, railway letter stamps, the college stamps of Oxford and Cambridge, or stamps produced for fiscal purposes: these are, however, just a few examples. It is when it comes to thematics that the greatest confusion often arises. This is understandable, for what is regarded as acceptable has changed over the years. Again the whole question of thematics is a subject for another article, but suffice to say that these days it is expected that a far wider range of philatelic material will be included rather than just stamps. The material shown must however be relevant in some way to the chosen theme: there is often the temptation to stretch a point simply to include a prized item. It is also easy with thematics to become carried away by including interesting items that nevertheless should not have a place in a competitive exhibit: such items might include photographs, postcards and similar ephemera with no postal or philatelic relevance. Again these are fine in, and will often enhance, a personal collection, or even one used purely for showing to others, but not in competition.

It is because there is the realisation that many like to include additional items to add interest to the collection that in recent years new classes have been tested, such as the Open Class and Social Philately, which permit say up to 50 per cent of non-philatelic, yet still relevant, material to be included. A good example is the display of Supermarket Philately that has been developed by Dr Jean Alexander. Her focus is the many 'on-pack' offers where on offer are postally related items, such as first day covers, presentation packs or books of stamps. Her display includes the special packaging, such as cereal boxes, any promotional leaflets that were produced, perhaps the envelope in which the offered item arrived, plus of course the item itself. Such items would never have found a place within a conventional competitive entry a few years ago, although there is no doubt it would have delighted many a society audience. However, today Jean is able to include such material as part of a Social Philately exhibit.

I must repeat, however, that while non-philatelic material can be included, it must be relevant to the story being told, and certainly in the case of Social Philately should have a connection with the postal service in some way. This might take the form of letters, postal notices and documents, telegrams, packaging material used by Post Offices, and so on.

At an international exhibition in Amsterdam a few years ago special frames were created in which to display the Open Class entries. In the centre of the frame was a clear 'bubble' so that three-dimensional objects could be shown: I recall one exhibit on railway letter posts featured model locomotives. This, however, was unusual, and generally speaking the non-philatelic items will still be two-dimensional.

At the end of the day, what is important is that the collection becomes special to you, and brings you pleasure and pride. Without offending, hopefully, the many who are absorbed by the intricacies of a single issue, if you find it tedious to keep adding the new denominations, colour changes, booklets, and so on, to your collection, then why continue? If the collection has now become a bore, perhaps it is time to explore new ground.

Include what you find interesting, and in the early stages worry only about what pleases you. If later you decide to embark on the competition trail, then take a look at what others do, to see just what is acceptable for inclusion. Start at a modest level, and never be put off, even if you don't win straight away. Never forget: it is quite simply a hobby.

Features listing

Area	Feature	Collect British Stamps	Stamps of the World	Thematic Catalogues	Comprehensive Catalogue, Parts 1-22 (including Commonwealth and British Empire Stamps and one country catalogues)	Great Britain Concise	Specialised catalogues
General	SG number	√	√	√	√	√	√
General	Specialised Catalogue number						√
General	Year of issue of first stamp in design	√	√	√	√	√	√
General	Exact date of issue of each design				√	√	√
General	Face value information	√	√	√	√	√	√
General	Historical and geographical information	√	√	√	√	√	√
General	General currency information, including dates used	√	√	√	√	√	√
General	Country name	√	√	√	√	√	√
General	Booklet panes				√	√	√
General	Coil stamps				√		√
General	First Day Covers	√				√	√
General	Brief footnotes on key areas of note	√	√	√	√	√	√
General	Detailed footnotes on key areas of note				√	√	√
General	Extra background information				√	√	√
General	Miniature sheet information (including size in mm)	√	√	√	√	√	√
General	Sheetlets				√		
General	Stamp booklets				√	√	√
General	Perkins Bacon "Cancelled"				√		
General	PHQ Cards	√				√	√
General	Post Office Label Sheets					√	
General	Post Office Yearbooks	√				√	√
General	Presentation and Souvenir Packs	√				√	√
General	Se-tenant pairs	√			√	√	√
General	Watermark details - errors, varieties, positions				√	√	√
General	Watermark illustrations	√			√	√	√
General	Watermark types	√			√	√	√
General	Forgeries noted				√		√
General	Surcharges and overprint information	√	√	√	√	√	√
Design and Description	Colour description, simplified		√	√			
Design and Description	Colour description, extended	√			√	√	√
Design and Description	Set design summary information	√	√	√	√	√	√
Design and Description	Designer name				√	√	√
Design and Description	Short design description	√	√	√	√	√	√
Design and Description	Shade varieties				√	√	√
Design and Description	Type number	√	√		√	√	√
Illustrations	Multiple stamps from set illustrated	√			√	√	√
Illustrations	A Stamp from each set illustrated in full colour (where possible, otherwise mono)	√	√	√	√	√	√
Price	Catalogue used price	√	√	√	√	√	√
Price	Catalogue unused price	√	√	√	√	√	√
Price	Price - booklet panes				√	√	√
Price	Price - shade varieties				√	√	√
Price	On cover and on piece price				√	√	√
Price	Detailed GB pricing breakdown	√			√	√	√
Print and Paper	Basic printing process information	√	√	√	√	√	√
Print and Paper	Detailed printing process information, e.g. Mill sheets				√		√
Print and Paper	Paper information				√		√
Print and Paper	Detailed perforation information	√			√	√	√
Print and Paper	Details of research findings relating to printing processes and history						√
Print and Paper	Paper colour	√	√		√	√	√
Print and Paper	Paper description to aid identification				√	√	√
Print and Paper	Paper type				√	√	√
Print and Paper	Ordinary or chalk-surfaced paper				√	√	√
Print and Paper	Embossing omitted note						√
Print and Paper	Essays, Die Proofs, Plate Descriptions and Proofs, Colour Trials information						√
Print and Paper	Glazed paper				√	√	√
Print and Paper	Gum details				√		√
Print and Paper	Luminescence/Phosphor bands - general coverage	√			√	√	√
Print and Paper	Luminescence/Phosphor bands - specialised coverage						√
Print and Paper	Overprints and surcharges - including colour information	√	√	√	√	√	√
Print and Paper	Perforation/Imperforate information	√	√		√	√	√
Print and Paper	Perforation errors and varieties				√	√	√
Print and Paper	Print quantities				√		√
Print and Paper	Printing errors				√	√	√
Print and Paper	Printing flaws						√
Print and Paper	Printing varieties				√	√	√
Print and Paper	Punctured stamps - where official				√		
Print and Paper	Sheet positions				√	√	√
Print and Paper	Specialised plate number information						√
Print and Paper	Specimen overprints (only for Commonwealth & GB)				√	√	√
Print and Paper	Underprints				√	√	√
Print and Paper	Visible Plate numbers	√			√	√	√
Print and Paper	Yellow and Green paper listings				√	√	√
Index	Design index	√			√	√	

Stanley Gibbons Stamp Catalogue Complete list of parts

1 Commonwealth & British Empire Stamps 1840–1970
(115th edition, 2013)

Commonwealth Country Catalogues
Australia and Dependencies (7th edition, 2012)
Bangladesh, Pakistan & Sri Lanka (2nd edition, 2010)
Belize, Guyana, Trinidad & Tobago (1st edition, 2009)
Brunei, Malaysia & Singapore (2nd edition, 2009)
Canada (4th edition, 2011)
Central Africa (2nd edition, 2008)
Cyprus, Gibraltar & Malta (3rd edition, 2011)
East Africa with Egypt and Sudan (2nd edition, 2010)
Eastern Pacific (2nd edition, 2011)
Falkland Islands (5th edition, 2012)
Hong Kong (3rd edition, 2010)
India (including Convention and Feudatory States) (3rd edition, 2009)
Indian Ocean (2nd edition, 2012)
Ireland (4th edition, 2011)
Leeward Islands (2nd edition, 2012)
New Zealand (3rd edition, 2011)
Northern Caribbean, Bahamas & Bermuda (2nd edition, 2009)
St. Helena & Dependencies (4th edition, 2011)
Southern Africa (2nd edition, 2008)
Southern and Central Africa (1st edition, 2011)
West Africa (1st edition, 2009)
Western Pacific (2nd edition, 2009)
Windward Islands and Barbados (1st edition, 2007)

Stamps of the World 2011
Volume 1 ***Abu Dhabi – Charkhari***
Volume 2 ***Chile – Georgia***
Volume 3 ***German Commands – Jasdan***
Volume 4 ***Jersey – New Republic***
Volume 5 ***New South Wales – Singapore***
Volume 6 ***Sirmoor – Zululand***

Foreign Countries
2 ***Austria & Hungary*** (7th edition, 2009)
3 ***Balkans*** (5th edition, 2009)
4 ***Benelux*** (6th edition, 2010)
5 ***Czech Republic, Slovakia & Poland*** (7th edition, 2012)
6 ***France*** (7th edition, 2010)
7 ***Germany*** (9th edition, 2011)
8 ***Italy & Switzerland*** (7th edition, 2009)
9 ***Portugal & Spain*** (6th edition, 2011)
10 ***Russia*** (6th edition, 2008)
11 ***Scandinavia*** (6th edition, 2008)
12 ***Africa since Independence A-E*** (2nd edition, 1983)
13 ***Africa since Independence F-M*** (1st edition, 1981)
14 ***Africa since Independence N-Z*** (1st edition, 1981)
15 ***Central America*** (3rd edition, 2007)
16 ***Central Asia*** (4th edition, 2006)
17 ***China*** (9th edition, 2012)
18 ***Japan & Korea*** (5th edition, 2008)
19 ***Middle East*** (7th edition, 2009)
20 ***South America*** (4th edition, 2008)
21 ***South-East Asia*** (4th edition, 2004)
22 ***United States of America*** (7th edition, 2010)

Great Britain Catalogues
Collect British Stamps (62nd edition, 2011)
Great Britain Concise Stamp Catalogue (27th edition, 2012)
Volume 1 ***Queen Victoria*** (16th edition, 2012)
Volume 2 ***King Edward VII to King George VI*** (13th edition, 2009)
Volume 3 ***Queen Elizabeth II Pre-decimal issues*** (12th edition, 2011)
Volume 4 ***Queen Elizabeth II Decimal Definitive Issues – Part 1*** (10th edition, 2008)
Queen Elizabeth II Decimal Definitive Issues – Part 2 (10th edition, 2010)
Volume 5 ***Queen Elizabeth II Decimal Special Issues*** (3rd edition, 1998 with 1998-99 and 2000/1 Supplements)

Thematic Catalogues
Stanley Gibbons Catalogues for use with ***Stamps of the World.***
Collect Aircraft on Stamps (2nd edition, 2009)
Collect Chess on Stamps (2nd edition, 1999)
Collect Fish on Stamps (1st edition, 1999)
Collect Fungi on Stamps (2nd edition, 1994)
Collect Motor Vehicles on Stamps (1st edition 2004)
Collect Railways on Stamps (3rd edition, 1999)
Collect Shells on Stamps (1st edition, 1995)

Other publications
Africa Simplified (1st edition, 2011)
Asia Simplified (1st edition, 2010)
Antarctica (including Australian and British Antarctic Territories, French Southern and Antarctic Territories and Ross Dependency) (1st edition, 2010)
Collect Channel Islands and Isle of Man Stamps (27th edition, 2012)
Commonwealth Simplified (4th edition, 2010)
Enjoy Stamp Collecting (7th edition, 2006)
Great Britain Numbers Issued (3rd edition, 2008)
How to Identify Stamps (5th edition, 2011)
North America Combined (1st edition, 2010)
Philatelic Terms Illustrated (4th edition, 2003)
United Nations (also including International Organizations based in Switzerland and UNESCO) (1st edition, 2010)
Western Europe Simplified (2012)

For other titles, and further details on the above, please see *www.stanleygibbons.com*

The Stanley Gibbons Group plc - About us

Our History

Edward Stanley Gibbons started trading postage stamps in his father's chemist shop in Plymouth in 1856; we have been at the forefront of stamp collecting for more than 150 years, making us the world's oldest philatelic company.

As Royal Warrant holders since 1914 we offer unsurpassed expertise and provide collectors worldwide with peace of mind that all stamps purchased from us come with our certified lifetime guarantee of authenticity*.

If you think of stamp collecting, you think of Stanley Gibbons and we are proud to uphold that tradition for you.

399 Strand

Our world famous stamp shop is a collector's paradise, with all of our latest catalogues, albums and accessories and of course, our unrivalled stockholding of postage stamps.

www.stanleygibbons.com
shop@stanleygibbons.co.uk
+44 (0)20 7836 8444

Specialist Stamp Sales

For the collector that appreciates the value of collecting the highest quality examples, Stanley Gibbons is the only choice. Our extensive range is unrivalled in terms of quality and quantity, with specialist stamps available from all over the world.

www.stanleygibbons.com/stamps
shop@stanleygibbons.co.uk
+44 (0)20 7836 8444

Mail order

Stamp collecting made easy! Order anything you need to enhance your collection, from our world famous catalogues to brand new supplements, from our long-running range of albums to cutting edge accessories, all available via telephone, email or post.

orders@stanleygibbons.com
FREEPHONE (UK only) 0800 611 622
+44 (0) 1425 472363

Stanley Gibbons Auctions and Valuations

Sell your collection or individual rare items through our prestigious public auctions and regular postal auctions. You too can benefit from the excellent prices being realised at auction currently.

We also provide an unparalleled valuation service-drop your collection or rare items into us at 399 Strand, call us about our collection service or make an appointment at one of our valuation days held at venues across the UK.

www.stanleygibbons.com/auctions
auctions@stanleygibbons.co.uk
+44 (0)20 7836 8444

Stanley Gibbons Investments

The Stanley Gibbons Investment Department offers a unique range of investment propositions that have consistently outperformed more traditional forms of investment, from guaranteed minimum return products with unlimited upside to portfolios made up of the world's rarest stamps and autographs.

www.stanleygibbons.com/investment
investment@stanleygibbons.co.uk
+44 (0)1481 708 270

Stanley Gibbons Publications

The world's first stamp catalogue was printed by Stanley Gibbons in 1865 and we haven't looked back since! Our catalogues are trusted worldwide as the industry standard and we print countless titles each year. We also publish the consumer and trade magazines, Gibbons Stamp Monthly and Philatelic Exporter; bringing you news, views and insights into all things philatelic. For more information see 'Stanley Gibbons Publications Information.'

www.stanleygibbons.com/shop
orders@stanleygibbons.co.uk
+44 (0)1425 472 363

stanleygibbons.com

Our website offers the complete philatelic service. Whether you are looking to buy stamps, invest, read news articles, browse our online stamp catalogue or find new issues, you are just one click away from anything you desire in the world of stamp collecting at stanleygibbons.com. Happy browsing!

www.stanleygibbons.com

Fraser's Autographs

Autographs, manuscripts and memorabilia from Henry VIII to current day. We have over 60,000 items in stock, including movie stars, musicians, sport stars, historical figures and royalty. Fraser's is the UK's market leading autograph dealer and has been dealing in high quality autographed material since 1978.

www.frasersautographs.com
sales@frasersautographs.co.uk
+44 (0)20 7557 4404

The Stanley Gibbons Lifetime Guarantee of Authenticity

Stanley Gibbons sells stamps and philatelic items on the basis that they are genuine originals; if they are proved not to fit the description as represented by us, you may return them at any time and we will refund you the original purchase price.

All stamps supplied by Stanley Gibbons are guaranteed originals under the following terms:

If not as described, and returned by the purchaser, we undertake to refund the price paid in the original transaction.

If any stamp is certified as genuine by the Expert Committee of the Royal Philatelic Society, London, or by B.P.A. Expertising Ltd., the purchaser shall not be entitled to make any claim against us for any error, omission or mistake in such certificate.

Consumers' statutory rights are not affected by the above guarantee.

Stanley Gibbons Group plc- Contact us

The Stanley Gibbons Group plc

Stanley Gibbons Auctions

399 Strand, London WC2R OLX
Telephone + 44 (0)20 7836 8444
Fax + 44 (0) 20 7836 7342
enquires@stanleygibbons.co.uk
www.stanleygibbons.com for all departments

Auction and Specialist Stamp Departments

Open Monday–Friday 9.30am to 5pm
Shop open Monday–Friday 9am to 5.30pm and Saturday 9.30am to 5.30pm

Fraser's

(a division of Stanley Gibbons Group plc)
399 Strand, London WC2R OLX
Autographs, photographs, letters and documents
Telephone + 44 (0) 20 7836 8444
Fax +44 (0) 20 7836 7342,
info@frasersautographs.co.uk
www.frasersautographs.com
Monday–Friday 9 a.m. to 5.30 p.m. and Saturday 10 a.m. to 4 p.m.

Stanley Gibbons Publications

7 Parkside, Christchurch Road, Ringwood, Hampshire BH24 3SH.
Telephone + 44 (0)1425 472363 (24 hour answer phone service)
UK FREEPHONE 0800611 622
Fax +44 (0) 1425 470247
info@stanleygibbons.co.uk

Publications Mail Order

FREEPHONE 0800 611622
Monday–Friday 8.30 am to 5pm

Stanley Gibbons (Guernsey) Limited

Investments

18-20 Le Bordage, St Peter Port, Guernsey, Channel Islands, GY1 1DE
+44 (0) 1481 708 270
Toll free from USA +1 866 644 6146
investment@stanleygibbons.co.uk
www.stanleygibbons.com/investment

Gibbons Stamp Monthly and Philatelic Exporter

7 Parkside, Christchurch Road, Ringwood, Hampshire BH24 3SH.
Subscriptions. 01425 472363
Fax 01425 470247
gsm@stanleygibbons.co.uk

Pt. 1, Pt. 19

ABU DHABI

The largest of the Trucial States in the Persian Gulf. Treaty relations with Great Britain expired on 31 December 1966, when Abu Dhabi took over the postal services. On 18 July 1971, seven of the Gulf sheikhdoms, including Abu Dhabi, agreed to form the State of the United Arab Emirates. The federation came into being on 1 August 1972.

1964. 100 naye paise = 1 rupee.
1966. 1,000 fils = 1 dinar.

1 Shaikh Shakhbut bin Sultan

3 Ruler's Palace

1964

1	1	5n.p. green	4·25	4·50
2	1	15n.p. brown	4·00	2·25
3	1	20n.p. blue	4·25	2·00
4	1	30n.p. orange	4·25	1·75
5	-	40n.p. violet	6·00	1·50
6	-	50n.p. bistre	7·50	3·00
7	-	75n.p. black	9·50	6·00
8	3	1r. green	4·25	3·00
9	3	2r. black	8·50	4·50
10	-	5r. red	22·00	13·00
11	-	10r. blue	27·00	15·00

DESIGNS: As Type **1**: 40 to 75n.p. Mountain gazelle; As Type **3**: 5, 10r. Oil rig and camels.

5 Saker Falcon

1965. Falconry

12	5	20n.p. brown and blue	15·00	2·25
13	-	40n.p. brown and blue	18·00	3·00
14	-	2r. sepia and turquoise	32·00	15·00

DESIGNS: 40n.p., 2r. Other types of Saker falcon on gloved hand.

1966. Nos. 1/11 surch in new currency ("Fils" only on Nos. 5/7) and ruler's portrait obliterated with bars.

15	1	5f. on 5n.p. green	12·00	6·00
16	1	15f. on 15n.p. brown	18·00	10·00
17	1	20f. on 20n.p. blue	18·00	8·50
18	1	30f. on 30n.p. orange	16·00	20·00
19	-	40f. on 40n.p. violet	14·00	1·00
20	-	50f. on 50n.p. bistre	55·00	55·00
21	-	75f. on 75n.p. black	55·00	55·00
22	3	100f. on 1r. green	18·00	4·75
23	3	200f. on 2r. black	18·00	13·00
24	-	500f. on 5r. red	30·00	38·00
25	-	1d. on 10r. blue	55·00	65·00

9 Shaikh Zaid bin Sultan al Nahayyan

10

1967

26		5f. red and green	55	20
27		15f. red and brown	65	20
28		20f. red and blue	1·00	20
29		35f. red and violet	1·10	35
30	9	40f. green	1·60	35
38	10	40f. green	4·75	2·40
31	9	50f. brown	1·90	55
39	10	50f. brown	5·75	1·70
32	9	60f. blue	2·20	55
40	10	60f. blue	21·00	4·00
33	9	100f. red	3·25	80
41	10	100f. red	30·00	10·50
34	-	125f. brown and green	6·75	2·50
35	-	200f. brown and blue	36·00	11·00
36	-	500f. violet and orange	17·00	7·75
37	-	1d. blue and green	40·00	22·00

DESIGNS—As Types **9**&**10**—VERT: 5f. to 35f. National flag. HORIZ: (47×27 mm); 125f. Mountain gazelle; 200f. Lanner falcon; 500f., 1d. Palace. Each with portrait of Ruler.

11 Human Rights Emblem and Shaikh Zaid

1968. Human Rights Year.

42	11	35f. multicoloured	2·20	90
43	11	60f. multicoloured	3·50	1·30
44	11	150f. multicoloured	9·00	3·25

12 Arms and Shaikh Zaid

1968. Anniv of Shaikh Zaid's Accession.

45	12	5f. multicoloured	3·25	65
46	12	10f. multicoloured	3·25	90
47	12	100f. multicoloured	8·75	2·20
48	12	125f. multicoloured	13·00	4·00

13 New Construction

1968. Second Anniv of Shaikh's Accession. "Progress in Abu Dhabi". Multicoloured.

49	5f. Type **13**	2·75	55
50	10f. Airport buildings (46½×34 mm)	5·25	1·20
51	35f. Shaikh Zaid, bridge and Northern goshawk (59×34 mm)	24·00	9·50

14 Petroleum Installations

1969. Third Anniv of Shaikh's Accession. Petroleum Industry. Multicoloured.

52	35f. Type **14**	2·00	70
53	60f. Marine drilling platform	5·25	1·60
54	125f. Separator platform, Zakum field	8·75	3·25
55	200f. Tank farm	14·50	7·75

15 Shaikh Zaid

1970

56	-	5f. multicoloured	70	20
57	15	10f. multicoloured	1·00	20
58	-	25f. multicoloured	1·90	20
59	15	35f. multicoloured	2·50	35
60	15	50f. multicoloured	3·50	55
61	-	60f. multicoloured	4·00	65
62	15	70f. multicoloured	6·75	80
63	-	90f. multicoloured	8·50	1·50
64	-	125f. multicoloured	12·50	2·00
65	-	150f. multicoloured	12·50	2·50
66	-	500f. multicoloured	38·00	13·50
67	-	1d. multicoloured	65·00	22·00

DESIGNS: Nos. 56, 58, 61 and 63 as Type **15**, but frames changed, and smaller country name; 125f. Arab stallion; 150f. Mountain gazelle; 500f. Fort Jahili; 1d. Great Mosque.

No. 67 has face value in Arabic only.

17 Shaikh Zaid and "Mt. Fuji" (T. Hayashi)

1970. "Expo 70" World Fair, Osaka, Japan.

68	17	25f. multicoloured	3·25	1·20
69	17	35f. multicoloured	4·75	1·90
70	17	60f. multicoloured	8·75	2·75

18 Abu Dhabi Airport

1970. 40th Anniv of Shaikh's Accession. Completion of Abu Dhabi Airport. Mult.

71	25f. Type **18**	3·25	90
72	60f. Airport entrance	7·25	2·10
73	150f. Aerial view of Abu Dhabi (vert)	17·00	5·25

19 Pres. G. A. Nasser

1971. Gamal Nasser (President of Egypt) Commemoration.

74	19	25f. black on pink	6·00	3·75
75	19	35f. black on lilac	8·25	5·50

20 Military Land Rover Series II 88

1971. Fifth Anniv of Shaikh's Accession. Defence Force. Multicoloured.

76	35f. Type **20**	6·00	1·60
77	60f. Patrol-boat "Baniyas"	8·00	2·20
78	125f. Armoured car	17·00	3·50
79	150f. Hawker Hunter FGA.76 jet fighters	22·00	6·75

1971. No. 60 surch.

80	15	5f. on 50f. multicoloured	95·00	80·00

22 Dome of the Rock

1972. Dome of the Rock, Jerusalem. Multicoloured.

81	35f. Type **22**	25·00	5·00
82	60f. Mosque entrance	43·00	9·00
83	125f. Mosque dome	80·00	22·00

1972. Provisional Issue. Nos. 56/67 optd **UAE** and arabic inscr.

84	-	5f. multicoloured	2·50	2·50
85	15	10f. multicoloured	2·50	1·50
86	-	25f. multicoloured	3·25	3·25
87	15	35f. multicoloured	5·00	4·50
88	15	50f. multicoloured	7·75	7·75
89	-	60f. multicoloured	9·00	9·00
90	15	70f. multicoloured	11·00	11·00
91	-	90f. multicoloured	17·00	17·00
92	-	125f. multicoloured	55·00	55·00
93	-	150f. multicoloured	65·00	65·00
94	-	500f. multicoloured	£150	£150
95	-	1d. multicoloured	£300	£300

For later issues see **UNITED ARAB EMIRATES**.

Pt. 1

ADEN

Peninsula on southern coast of Arabia. Formerly part of the Indian Empire. A Crown Colony from 1 April 1937 to 18 January 1963, when Aden joined the South Arabian Federation, whose stamps it then used.

1937. 16 annas = 1 rupee.
1951. 100 cents = 1 shilling.

1 Dhow

1937

1	1	½a. green	3·75	2·75
2	1	9p. green	3·75	3·50
3	1	1a. brown	3·75	2·00
4	1	2a. red	5·00	3·00
5	1	2½a. blue	6·50	2·00
6	1	3a. red	10·00	8·50
7	1	3½a. blue	7·50	6·00
8	1	8a. purple	25·00	10·00
9	1	1r. brown	55·00	12·00
10	1	2r. yellow	£100	35·00
11	1	5r. purple	£225	£130
12	1	10r. olive	£600	£550

2 King George VI and Queen Elizabeth

1937. Coronation.

13	2	1a. brown	65	1·25
14	2	2½a. blue	75	1·40
15	2	3½a. blue	1·00	3·00

3 Aidrus Mosque, Crater

1939

16	3	½a. green	2·00	60
17	-	¾a. brown	3·00	1·25
18	-	1a. blue	75	40
19	-	1½a. red	3·00	60
20	3	2a. brown	1·25	25
21	-	2½a. blue	2·00	30
22	-	3a. brown and red	2·00	25
23	-	8a. orange	2·25	40
23a	-	14a. brown and blue	4·00	1·00
24	-	1r. green	5·00	2·50
25	-	2r. blue and mauve	9·50	3·00
26	-	5r. brown and olive	30·00	16·00
27	-	10r. brown and violet	45·00	17·00

DESIGNS: ¾a., 5r. Adenese Camel Corps; 1a., 2r. The Harbour; 1½a., 1r. Adenese dhow; 2½, 8a. Mukalla; 3, 14a., 10r. "Capture of Aden, 1839" (Capt. Rundle).

9 Houses of Parliament, London

1946. Victory.

28	9	1½a. red	20	1·75
29	9	2½a. blue	80	1·00

10

11 King George VI and Queen Elizabeth

1949. Royal Silver Wedding.

30	10	1½a. red	40	2·25
31	11	10r. purple	40·00	50·00

1949. 75th Anniv of U.P.U. As T **20/23** of Antigua surch with new values.

32	2½a. on 20c. blue	50	1·50
33	3a. on 30c. red	2·00	1·50
34	8a. on 50c. orange	1·40	2·00
35	1r. on 1s. blue	1·60	5·50

1951. Stamps of 1939 surch in cents or shillings.

36	5c. on 1a. blue	25	40
37	10c. on 2a. brown	15	45
38	15c. on 2½a. blue	30	1·25
39	20c. on 3a. brown and red	30	40
40	30c. on 8a. orange	50	65
41	50c. on 8a. orange	1·25	35
42	70c. on 14a. brown and blue	2·25	1·50
43	1s. on 1r. green	2·50	30
44	2s. on 2r. blue and mauve	16·00	3·75
45	5s. on 5r. brown and olive	27·00	15·00
46	10s. on 10r. brown and violet	40·00	16·00

13 Queen Elizabeth II

1953. Coronation.

47	**13**	15c. black and green	1·25	1·25

14 Minaret

15 Camel Transport

1953

48	**14**	5c. green	20	10
49a	**14**	5c. turquoise	10	1·25
50	**15**	10c. orange	40	10
51	**15**	10c. red	20	30
52	-	15c. turquoise	1·25	60
79	-	15c. grey	1·00	5·00
80	-	25c. red	2·75	40
56	-	35c. blue	2·50	1·50
58	-	50c. blue	20	10
60	-	70c. grey	20	10
61	-	70c. black	1·00	35
62	-	1s. brown and violet	30	10
63	-	1s. black and violet	1·50	10
64	-	1s.25 blue and black	9·00	60
65	-	2s. brown and red	1·50	50
66	-	2s. black and red	12·00	50
67	-	5s. brown and blue	1·50	1·00
68	-	5s. black and blue	13·00	1·25
69	-	10s. brown and green	1·75	8·00
70	-	10s. black and bronze	17·00	1·75
71	-	20s. brown and lilac	6·50	10·00
72	-	20s. black and lilac	65·00	19·00

DESIGNS—HORIZ: 15c. Crater; 25c. Mosque; 1s. Dhow building; 20s. (38×27 mm); Aden in 1572. VERT: 35c. Dhow; 50c. Map; 70c. Salt works; 1s.25, Colony's badge; 2s. Aden Protectorate Levy; 5s. Crater Pass; 10s. Tribesmen.

1954. Royal Visit. As No. 62 but inscr "ROYAL VISIT 1954".

73	1s. sepia and violet	75	75

1959. Revised Constitution. Optd **REVISED CONSTITUTION 1959** (in Arabic on No. 74).

74	15c. green (No. 53)	30	2·00
75	1s.25 blue and black (No. 64)	1·00	1·00

28 Protein Foods

1963. Freedom from Hunger.

76	**28**	1s.25 green	1·25	1·75

For later issues see **SOUTH ARABIAN FEDERATION**.

Pt. 16

AFGHANISTAN

An independent country in Asia, to N.W. of Pakistan. Now a republic, the country was formerly ruled by monarchs from 1747 to 1973.

1871. 60 paisa = 12 shahi = 6 sanar = 3 abasi = 2 kran = 1 rupee.
1920. 60 paisa = 2 kran = 1 rupee.
1926. 100 poul (pul) = 1 afghani (rupee).

The issues from 1860 to 1892 (Types **1** to **16**) are difficult to classify because the values of each set are expressed in native script and are generally all printed in the same colour. As it is not possible to list these in an intelligible simplified form we would refer users to the detailed list in the Stanley Gibbons Part 16 (Central Asia) Catalogue.

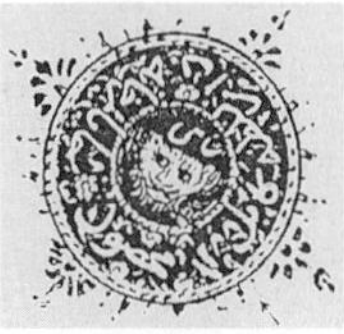
1

4

5

6

8

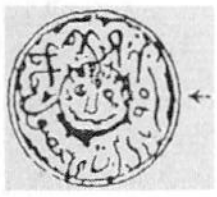
10

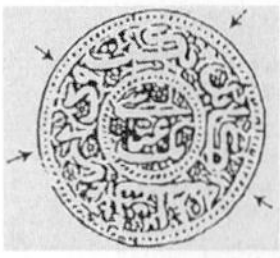
12

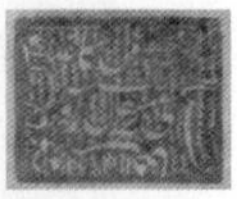
16

17 National Coat of Arms

1893. Dated "1310".

147	**17**	1a. black on green	3·25	3·25
148	**17**	1a. black on red	3·75	3·25
149a	**17**	1a. black on purple	3·75	3·50
150	**17**	1a. black on yellow	3·50	3·25
151	**17**	1a. black on orange	4·00	4·00
152	**17**	1a. black on blue	6·25	5·25

18 2 Abasi

1894. Undated

153	**18**	2a. black on green	12·50	8·25
154	**18**	1r. black on green	15·00	13·00

20 1 Abasi

1907. Imperf, roul or perf.

156a	**20**	1a. green	17·00	21·00
157	-	2a. blue	6·50	8·25
158	-	1r. green	45·00	23·00

The 2a. and 1r. are in similar designs.

23

24 1 Abasi

1909. Perf.

165	**23**	2 paisa brown	13·00	4·50
166	**24**	1a. blue	5·25	2·10
168	**24**	1a. red	1·20	1·00
169	-	2a. green	3·00	2·50
170a	-	2a. bistre	2·75	3·00
171	-	1r. brown	5·00	5·25
172	-	1r. olive	7·75	7·75

The frames of the 2a. and 1r. differ from Type **24**.

27 Royal Star of Order of Independence

1920. First Anniv of End of War of Independence. Size 39×47 mm.

173	**27**	10p. red	49·00	33·00
174	**27**	20p. purple	80·00	55·00
175	**27**	30p. green	£160	£160

1921. Size 23×29 mm.

177	10p. red	2·10	95
178	20p. purple	4·50	2·75
180b	30p. green	6·50	3·00

(28)

1923. Fifth Independence Day. Optd with T **28**.

181	10p. red	41·00	41·00
181a	20p. brown	49·00	49·00
182	30p. green	60·00	60·00

29 Crest of King Amanullah

1924. Sixth Independence Day.

183	**29**	10p. brown (24×32 mm)	37·00	37·00

29a

1924

183b	**29a**	5k. blue	41·00	41·00
183c	**29a**	5r. mauve	16·00	25·00

1925. Seventh Independence Day.

184	**29**	10p. brown (29×37 mm)	60·00	45·00

1926. Seventh Anniv of Independence.

185	10p. blue (26×33 mm)	6·50	8·25

30 Crest of King Amanullah

1927. Eighth Anniv of Independence.

186	**30**	10p. mauve	18·00	13·00

Types **31/3**, **36/37** and **41**, National Seal.

31

32

33

1927. Perf or imperf.

188A	**31**	15p. red	1·30	1·30
189A	**32**	30p. green	2·75	1·20
190B	**33**	60p. blue	3·00	2·10

See also Nos. 207A/13A.

34 Crest of King Amanullah

1928. Ninth Anniv of Independence.

191	**34**	15p. red	5·00	5·00

36

37

1928

193	**36**	10p. green	1·10	40
194	**37**	25p. red	1·20	80
195	-	40p. blue	1·20	80
196	-	50p. red	1·50	1·00

The frames of the 40 and 50p. differ from Type **37**.
See also Nos. 207A/13A.

41

1929

207A	**36**	10p. brown	1·50	1·30
208A	**31**	15p. blue	1·30	1·30
209A	**37**	25p. blue	1·30	1·20
210A	**41**	30p. green	1·30	1·20
211A	-	40p. red	1·60	1·50
212A	-	50p. blue	2·10	1·50
213A	**33**	60p. black	3·25	2·30

42 Independence Memorial

1931. 13th Independence Day.

214	**42**	20p. red	2·50	1·20

46 National Assembly Building

1932. Inauguration of National Council.

215	-	40p. brown (31×24 mm)	65	40
216	-	60p. violet (29×26 mm)	1·10	80
217	**46**	80p. red	1·50	1·20
218	-	1a. black (24×27 mm)	10·50	7·75
219	-	2a. blue (36×25 mm)	5·25	4·00
220	-	3a. green (36×24 mm)	5·50	3·75

DESIGNS: Nos. 215/16, 218/19, Council Chamber; 3a. National Assembly Building (different).

50 Mosque at Balkh

1932

221	**50**	10p. brown	60	25
222	-	15p. brown	40	35
223	-	20p. red	65	25
224	-	25p. green	80	25
225	-	30p. red	80	25
226	-	40p. orange	1·00	50
227	-	50p. blue	1·50	1·30
228	-	60p. blue	1·30	90
229	-	80p. violet	2·50	2·10
230	-	1a. blue	4·50	80
231	-	2a. purple	5·00	2·30
232	-	3a. red	5·75	3·00

DESIGNS—32×23 mm: 15p. Kabul Fortress; 20, 25p. Parliament House, Darul Funun, Kabul; 40p. Memorial Pillar of Knowledge and Ignorance, Kabul; 1a. Ruins at Balkh; 2a. Minarets at Herat. 32×16 mm: 30p. Arch of Paghman. 23×32 mm: 60p. Minaret at Herat. 23×25 mm: 30p. Arch at Qalai Bust, near Kandahar; 50p. Independence Memorial, Kabul. 16×32 mm: 3a. Great Buddha at Bamian.
See also Nos. 237/51.

62 Independence Memorial

1932. 14th Independence Day.

233	**62**	1a. red	5·00	3·25

63 National Liberation Monument, Kabul

1932. Commemorative Issue.

234	**63**	80p. red	2·10	1·50

64 Arch of Paghman

1933. 15th Independence Day.

235	**64**	50p. blue	2·10	1·50

65 Independence Memorial

1934. 16th Independence Day.

236	**65**	50p. green	3·25	2·75

1934. As Nos. 219/20 and 221/30, but colours changed and new values.

237	**50**	10p. violet	25	15
238	-	15p. green	40	15
239	-	20p. mauve	40	15
240	-	25p. red	50	25
241	-	30p. orange	60	35
242	-	40p. black	65	35
243	-	45p. blue	2·10	1·60
244	-	45p. red	40	15
245	-	50p. red	75	25
246	-	60p. violet	80	40
247	-	75p. red	3·00	2·10
248	-	75p. blue	80	65
248b	-	80p. brown	1·30	80
249	-	1a. mauve	2·10	1·60
250	-	2a. grey	4·00	2·50
251	-	3a. blue	4·50	3·00

DESIGNS (new values)—34×23 mm: 45p. Royal Palace, Kabul. 20×34 mm: 75p. Hunters Canyon Pass, Hindu Kush.

68 Independence Memorial

1935. 17th Independence Day.

252	**68**	50p. blue	3·00	2·50

69 Firework Display

1936. 18th Independence Day.

253	**69**	50p. mauve	3·25	2·75

70 Independence Memorial and Mohamed Nadir Shah

1937. 19th Independence Day. Perf or imperf.

254	**70**	50p. brown and violet	7·25	2·20

71 Mohamed Nadir Shah

1938. 20th Independence Day. Perf or imperf.

255	**71**	50p. brown and blue	2·50	2·50

72 Aliabad Hospital

1938. Obligatory Tax. International Anti-cancer Fund.

256	**72**	10p. green	3·25	5·00
257	-	15p. blue	3·25	5·00

DESIGN—44×28 mm: 15p. Pierre and Marie Curie.

74 Mohamed Nadir Shah

1939. 21st Independence Day.

258	**74**	50p. red	2·30	1·50

76 Darul Funun Parliament House, Kabul

79 Independence Memorial

82 Mohamed Zahir Shah

83 Sugar Mill, Baghlan

1939

259	**76**	10p. purple (36½×24 mm)	25	20
260	**76**	15p. green (34×21 mm)	35	20
261	**76**	20p. purple (34×22½ mm)	40	25
262	-	25p. red	50	35
263	-	25p. green	35	25
264	-	30p. orange	40	25
265	-	35p. orange	1·50	1·00
266	-	40p. grey	80	50
267	**79**	45p. red	80	40
268	**79**	50p. orange	65	25
269	**79**	60p. violet	80	25
270	-	70p. violet	2·10	1·00
271	-	70p. purple	2·10	1·00
272	-	75p. blue	2·30	80
273	-	75p. purple	1·80	1·60
274	-	75p. red	3·00	3·00
275	-	80p. brown	1·50	1·00
276	**82**	1a. purple	1·60	80
277	-	1a. purple	1·60	1·00
278d	**83**	1a.25 blue	2·10	70
279a	-	2a. red	2·50	1·20
280	-	3a. blue	3·75	2·50

DESIGNS—31×19 mm: 25, 30p. Royal Palace, Kabul. 30×18 mm: 40p. Royal Palace, Kabul. 30×21 mm: 70p. Ruins at Qalai Bust, near Kandahar. 35½×21½ mm: 75p. Independence Memorial and Mohamed Nadir Shah. 34½×21 mm: 80p. As 75p. 35×20 mm: 1a. (No. 277), 2a. Mohamed Zahir Shah; 3a. As Type **82** but head turned more to left. 19×31 mm: 35p. Minarets at Herat.

85 Potez 25A2 over Kabul

1939. Air.

280a	**85**	5a. orange	5·75	4·50
280b	**85**	10a. blue	5·75	4·50
280c	**85**	20a. green	11·50	7·75

See also Nos. 300/2.

86 Mohamed Nadir Shah

1940. 22nd Independence Day.

281	**86**	50p. green	2·10	1·50

87 Arch of Paghman

1941. 23rd Independence Day.

282	-	15p. green	9·00	5·75
283	**87**	50p. brown	2·50	2·10

DESIGN: (19×29½ mm): 15p. Independence Memorial.

87b Mohamed Nadir Shah and Arch of Paghman

1942. 24th Independence Day.

284	-	35p. green	3·75	3·75
285	**87b**	125p. blue	3·00	2·10

DESIGN—VERT: 35p. Independence Memorial in medallion.

88 Independence Memorial and Mohamed Nadir Shah

1943. 25th Independence Day.

286	-	35p. red	14·00	12·50
287	**88**	1a.25 blue	3·25	2·50

DESIGN—HORIZ: 35p. Independence Memorial seen through archway and Mohamed Nadir Shah in oval frame.

89 Arch of Paghman

90 Independence Memorial and Mohamed Nadir Shah

1944. 26th Independence Day.

288	**89**	35p. red	1·30	75
289	**90**	1a.25 blue	2·30	2·00

91 Mohamed Nadir Shah and Independence Memorial

92 Arch of Paghman and Mohamed Nadir Shah

1945. 27th Independence Day.

290	**91**	35p. red	2·30	80
291	**92**	1a.25 blue	3·75	2·10

93 Independence Memorial

1946. 28th Independence Day. Dated "1946".

292	-	15p. green	1·20	75
293	**93**	20p. mauve	2·10	90
294	-	125p. blue	3·25	2·10

DESIGNS—HORIZ: 15p. Mohamed Zahir Shah. VERT: 125p. Mohamed Nadir Shah.

94 Mohamed Nadir Shah and Independence Memorial

1947. 29th Independence Day. Dated "1947".

295		15p. green	1·20	60
296		35p. mauve	1·30	80
297	**94**	125p. blue	3·25	2·00

DESIGNS—HORIZ: 15p. Mohamed Zahir Shah and ruins of Kandahar Fort; 35p. Mohamed Zahir Shah and Arch of Paghman.

95 Hungry Boy

1948. Child Welfare Fund.

298	**95**	35p. green	5·00	4·00
299	-	125p. blue	5·00	4·00

DESIGN—26×33½ mm: 125p. Hungry boy in vert frame.
See also No. 307.

1948. Air. As T **85** but colours changed.

300	**85**	5a. green	23·00	23·00
301	**85**	10a. orange	23·00	23·00
302	**85**	20a. blue	23·00	23·00

96 Independence Memorial

1948. 30th Independence Day. Dated "1948".

303	-	15p. green	80	35
304	**96**	20p. mauve	1·00	40
305	-	125p. blue	2·20	1·10

DESIGNS—VERT: 15p. Arch of Paghman. HORIZ: 125p. Mohamed Nadir Shah.

97 U.N. Symbol

1948. Third Anniv of U.N.O.

306	**97**	1a.25 blue	11·00	9·00

98 Hungry Boy

1949. Obligatory Tax. Child Welfare Fund.

307	-	35p. orange	3·25	2·10
308	**98**	125p. blue	4·00	2·10

DESIGN—HORIZ: 35p. As Type **98** but 29×22½ mm.

99 Victory Monument

1949. 31st Independence Day. Dated "1949" (Nos. 310/11).

309	**99**	25p. green	1·00	50
310	-	35p. mauve	1·20	65
311	-	1a.25 blue	2·30	1·30

DESIGNS—HORIZ: 35p. Mohamed Zahir Shah and ruins of Kandahar Fort; 1a.25, Independence Memorial and Mohamed Nadir Shah.

100 Arch of Paghman

1949. Obligatory Tax. Fourth Anniv of U.N.O.

312	**100**	125p. green	15·00	9·00

101 King Mohamed Zahir Shah and Map of Afghanistan

1950. Obligatory Tax. Return of King Mohamed Zahir Shah from Visit to Europe.

313	**101**	125p. green	3·25	1·50

102 Hungry Boy

1950. Obligatory Tax. Child Welfare Fund.

314	**102**	125p. green	4·50	2·50

103 Mohamed Nadir Shah

1950. 32nd Independence Day.

315	**103**	35p. brown	65	40
316	**103**	125p. blue	1·80	60

104

1950. Obligatory Tax. Fifth Anniv of U.N.O.

317	**104**	1a.25 blue	9·00	3·00

106

1950. 19th Anniv of Faculty of Medicine, Kabul.

318	**106**	35p. green (postage)	1·20	75
319	-	1a.25 blue	4·25	2·30
320	**106**	35p. red (obligatory tax)	1·00	50
321	-	1a.25 black	7·00	2·30

DESIGN: Nos. 319 and 321, Sanatorium. Nos. 318 and 320 measure 38½×25½ mm and Nos. 319 and 321, 45×30 mm.

107 Minaret at Herat

109 Mohamed Zahir Shah

110 Mosque at Balkh

118

1951

322	**107**	10p. brown and yellow	50	15
323	**107**	15p. brown and blue	50	15
324	-	20p. black	9·75	5·25
325	**109**	25p. green	50	15
326	**110**	30p. red	60	15
327	**109**	35p. violet	65	15
328	-	40p. brown	65	15
329	-	45p. blue	65	15
330	-	50p. black	1·90	25
331	-	60p. black	1·50	25
332	-	70p. black, red and green	80	25
333	-	75p. red	1·20	50
334	-	80p. black and red	2·10	90
336	**118**	125p. black and purple	1·80	1·00
335	-	1a. violet and green	1·50	65
337	**118**	2a. blue	2·75	80
338	**118**	3a. blue and black	5·75	1·20

DESIGNS—19×29 mm: 20p. Buddha of Bamian; 45p. Maiwand Victory Monument; 60p. Victory Towers, Ghazni. 22×28 mm: 75, 80p., 1a. Mohamed Zahir Shah. 28×19 mm: 40p. Ruins at Qalai Bust; 70p. Flag. 30×19 mm: 50p. View of Kandahar.

See also Nos. 425/425k.

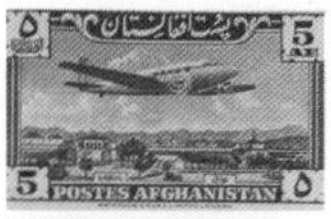

119 Douglas DC-3 over Kabul

1951. Air.

339	**119**	5a. red	3·25	65
339a	**119**	5a. green	1·80	40
340	**119**	10a. grey	7·50	1·80
341	**119**	20a. blue	10·50	3·00

See also Nos. 415a/b.

120 Shepherdess

1951. Obligatory Tax. Child Welfare Fund.

342	**120**	35p. green	1·50	90
343	-	125p. blue	1·50	90

DESIGN—34½×44 mm: 125p. Young shepherd.

121 Arch of Paghman

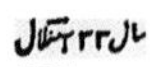

(122)

1951. 33rd Independence Day. Optd with T **122**.

344	**121**	35p. black and green	1·20	65
345	-	125p. blue	3·00	1·40

DESIGN (34×18½ mm): 125p. Mohamed Nadir Shah and Independence Memorial.

See also Nos. 360/1b and 418/19.

IMPERF STAMPS. From 1951 many issues were made available imperf from limited printings.

124 Flag of Pashtunistan

1951. Obligatory Tax. Pashtunistan Day.

346	**124**	35p. brown	1·50	80
347	-	125p. blue	3·00	2·10

DESIGN—42½×21½ mm: 125p. Afridi tribesman.

125 Dove and Globe

1951. Obligatory Tax. United Nations Day.

348	**125**	35p. mauve	80	40
349	-	125p. blue	2·10	1·60

DESIGN—VERT: 125p. Dove and globe.

126 Avicenna (physician)

1951. Obligatory Tax. 20th Anniv of Faculty of Medicine.

350	**126**	35p. mauve	7·75	1·50
351	**126**	125p. blue	3·00	4·00

127 Amir Sher Ali and First Stamp

1951. Obligatory Tax. 76th Anniv of U.P.U.

352	**127**	35p. brown	65	40
353	-	35p. mauve	65	40
354	**127**	125p. blue	1·20	80
355	-	125p. blue	1·20	80

DESIGN: Nos. 353 and 355, Mohamed Zahir Shah and first stamp.

128 Children and Postman

1952. Obligatory Tax. Child Welfare Fund.

356	**128**	35p. brown	80	65
357	-	125p. violet	1·60	1·00

DESIGN—HORIZ: 125p. Girl dancing (33×23 mm).

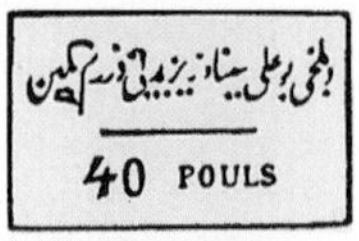

(129)

1952. Obligatory Tax. Birth Millenary of Avicenna (physician and philosopher). (a) Surch with T **129**.

358	**110** 40p. on 30p. red	5·25	3·00

(b) Surch **MILLIEME ANNIVERSAIRE DE BOALI SINAI BALKI 125 POULS** in frame.

359	125p. on 30p. red	7·50	3·50

(123)

1952. 34th Independence Day. As Nos. 344/5. (a) Optd with T **123**.

360	35p. black and green	3·25	2·30
361	125p. blue	3·25	2·30

(b) Without opt.

361a	35p. black and green	1·40	60
361b	125p. blue	3·00	1·20

131 Soldier and Flag of Pashtunistan

1952. Obligatory Tax. Pashtunistan Day.

362	**131**	35p. red	80	80
363	**131**	125p. blue	1·20	1·20

132 Orderly and Wounded Soldier

1952. Obligatory Tax. Red Crescent Day.

364	**132**	10p. green	80	65

133

1952. Obligatory Tax. United Nations Day.

365	**133**	35p. red	80	65
366	**133**	125p. turquoise	1·60	1·20

134 Staff of Aesculapius

1952. Obligatory Tax. 21st Anniv of Faculty of Medicine.

367	**134**	35p. brown	75	50
368	**134**	125p. blue	2·00	1·30

135 Stretcher Bearers and Wounded

1953. Obligatory Tax. Red Crescent Day.

369	**135**	10p. green and brown	80	80
370	-	10p. brown and orange	80	80

DESIGN: No. 370, Wounded soldier, orderly and eagle.

136 Prince Mohamed Nadir

1953. Obligatory Tax. Children's Day.

371	**136**	35p. orange	40	25
372	**136**	125p. blue	80	60

137 Mohamed Nadir Shah and Flag-bearer

1953. 35th Year of Independence. Inscr "1953".

373	**137**	35p. green	40	25
374	-	125p. violet	80	60

DESIGN—VERT: 125p. Independence Memorial and Mohamed Nadir Shah.

138 Flags of Afghanistan and Pashtunistan

1953. Obligatory Tax. Pashtunistan Day. Inscr "1953".

375	**138**	35p. red	40	15
376	-	125p. blue	80	65

DESIGN—HORIZ: 125p. Badge of Pashtunistan (26×20 mm).

139 U.N. Emblem

1953. Obligatory Tax. United Nations Day.

377	**139**	35p. mauve	1·00	80
378	**139**	125p. blue	2·10	1·50

140 Mohamed Nadir Shah

1953. Obligatory Tax. 22nd Anniv of Faculty of Medicine.

379	**140**	35p. orange	1·50	1·50
380	-	125p. blue	3·00	3·00

DESIGN: 125p. As Type **140** but inscribed "1953" and with French inscription.

No. 379 was wrongly inscribed "23rd" in Arabic (the extreme right-hand figure in the second row of the inscription) and No. 380 was wrongly inscr "XXIII" and had the words "ANNIVERSAIRE" and "MEDECINE" wrongly spelt "ANNIVERAIRE" and "MADECINE". These mistakes were subsequently corrected but the corrected stamps are much rarer than the original issue.

141 Children's Band and Map of Afghanistan

1954. Obligatory Tax. Child Welfare Fund.

381	**141**	35p. violet	65	40
382	**141**	125p. blue	1·80	80

142 Mohamed Nadir Shah and Cannon

1954. 36th Independence Day.

383	**142**	35p. red	65	40
384	**142**	125p. blue	1·80	80

143 Hoisting the Flag

1954. Obligatory Tax. Pashtunistan Day.

385	**143**	35p. orange	65	40
386	**143**	125p. blue	1·80	80

144

1954. Red Crescent Day.

387	**144**	20p. red and blue	60	35

145 U.N. Flag and Map

1954. United Nations Day and Ninth Anniv of U.N.O.

388	**145**	35p. red	1·20	1·20
389	**145**	125p. blue	3·25	2·20

146 Globe and Clasped Hands

1955. Tenth Anniv of Signing of U.N. Charter.

390	**146**	35p. green	1·00	60
391	-	125p. blue	1·80	1·10

DESIGN—28½×36 mm. 125p. U.N. emblem and flags.
See also Nos. 403/4.

147 Amir Sher Ali and Mohamed Zahir Shah

1955. 85th Anniv of Postal Service.

392	**147**	35p.+15p. red	1·00	60
393	**147**	125p.+25p. grey	1·90	1·10

148 Children on Swing

1955. Child Welfare Fund.

394	**148**	35p.+15p. green	1·20	75
395	**148**	125p.+25p. violet	2·50	1·20

149 Mohamed Nadir Shah (centre) and brothers

1955. 37th Year of Independence.

396	**149**	35p. blue	65	40
397	**149**	35p. mauve	65	40
398	-	125p. violet	1·40	90
399	-	125p. purple	1·40	90

DESIGN: 125p. Mohamed Zahir Shah and battle scene.

150

1955. Obligatory Tax. Pashtunistan Day.

400	**150**	35p. brown	60	25
401	**150**	125p. green	1·90	60

151 Red Crescent

1955. Obligatory Tax. Red Crescent Day.

402	**151**	20p. red and grey	60	35

152 U.N. Flag

1955. Obligatory Tax. Tenth Anniv of United Nations.

403	**152**	35p. brown	90	60
404	**152**	125p. blue	1·80	1·10

153 Child on Slide

1956. Children's Day.

405	**153**	35p.+15p. blue	90	40
406	**153**	140p.+15p. brown	2·30	80

154 Independence Memorial and Mohamed Nadir Shah

1956. 38th Year of Independence.

407	**154**	35p. green	60	35
408	**154**	140p. blue	2·30	90

155 Exhibition Building

1956. International Exhibition, Kabul.

409	**155**	50p. brown	80	40
410	**155**	50p. blue	80	40

156 Pashtun Square, Kabul

1956. Pashtunistan Day.

411	**156**	35p.+15p. violet	40	25
412	**156**	140p.+15p. brown	1·10	75

157 Mohamed Zahir Shah and Crescent

1956. Obligatory Tax. Red Crescent Day.

413	**157**	20p. green and red	40	25

158 Globe and Sun

1956. U.N. Day and Tenth Anniv of Admission of Afghanistan into U.N.O.

414	**158**	35p.+15p. blue	1·20	1·10
415	**158**	140p.+15p. brown	2·10	1·80

1957. Air. As Nos. 339/40, but colours changed.

415a	**119**	5a. blue	2·10	60
415b	**119**	10a. violet	3·00	1·10

159 Children on See-saw

1957. Child Welfare Fund.

416	**159**	35p.+15p. red	80	60
417	**159**	140p.+15p. blue	1·60	1·50

1957. 39th Independence Day. As Nos. 344/5 but 35p. has longer Arabic opt (19 mm) and 125p. optd **39 em Anv**.

418	**121**	35p. black and green	65	35
419	**121**	125p. blue	1·00	75

162 Pashtu Flag

1957. Pashtunistan Day.

420	**162**	50p. red	1·00	60
421	**162**	155p. violet	1·50	1·10

No. 421 is inscr "JOURNEE DU PASHTUNISTAN" beneath flag instead of Pushtu characters.

163 Red Crescent Headquarters, Kabul

1957. Obligatory Tax. Red Crescent Day.

422	**163**	20p. blue and red	90	60

164 U.N. Headquarters, New York

1957. U.N. Day.

423	**164**	35p.+15p. brown	60	40
424	**164**	140p.+15p. blue	1·10	1·10

165 Buzkashi Game

1957. As stamps of 1951, but colours changed and new value.

425	**110**	30p. brown	40	15
425a	-	40p. red	60	15
425b	-	50p. yellow	65	15
425c	-	60p. blue	80	15
425d	-	75p. violet	1·00	15
425e	-	80p. brown and violet	1·10	15
425g	**165**	140p. purple and green	2·75	65
425f	-	1a. blue and red	1·80	15
425k	**118**	2a. blue	5·75	80
425h	**118**	3a. black and orange	2·75	90

166 Children Bathing

1958. Child Welfare Fund.

426	**166**	35p.+15p. red	65	40
427	**166**	140p.+15p. brown	80	65

167 Mohamed Nadir Shah and Old Soldier

1958. 40th Independence Day.

428	**167**	35p. green	40	25
429	**167**	140p. brown	1·20	1·00

168 Exhibition Buildings

1958. International Exhibition, Kabul.

430	**168**	35p. green	50	25
431	**168**	140p. red	1·20	1·00

169

1958. Pashtunistan Day.

432	**169**	35p.+15p. turquoise	40	25
433	**169**	140p.+15p. brown	1·00	65

170 President Bayar

1958. Visit of Turkish President.

434	**170**	50p. blue	35	15
435	**170**	100p. brown	65	35

171 Red Crescent and Map of Afghanistan

1958. Obligatory Tax. Red Crescent Day.

436	**171**	25p. red and green	40	15

172

1958. 'Atoms for Peace'.

437	**172**	50p. blue	60	50
438	**172**	100p. purple	90	65

173 Flags of U.N. and Afghanistan

1958. U.N. Day.

439	**173**	50p. multicoloured	65	65
440	**173**	100p. multicoloured	1·40	1·20

174 UNESCO Headquarters, Paris

1958. Inauguration of UNESCO Headquarters Building, Paris.

441	**174**	50p. green	80	65
442	**174**	100p. brown	80	80

175 Globe and Torch

1958. Tenth Anniv of Declaration of Human Rights.

443	**175**	50p. mauve	50	50
444	**175**	100p. purple	1·00	1·20

176 Tug-of-War

1959. Child Welfare Fund.

445	**176**	35p.+15p. purple	60	35
446	**176**	165p.+15p. mauve	1·20	50

177 Mohamed Nadir Shah and Flags

1959. 41st Independence Day.

447	**177**	35p. red	60	50
448	**177**	165p. violet	1·50	65

178 Tribal Dance

1959. Pashtunistan Day.

449	**178**	35p.+15p. green	60	35
450	**178**	165p.+15p. orange	1·20	75

179 Badge-sellers

1959. Obligatory Tax. Red Crescent Day.

451	**179**	25p. red and violet	40	15

180 Horseman

1959. United Nations Day.

452	**180**	35p.+15p. orange	35	25
453	**180**	165p.+15p. green	65	40

181 "Uprooted Tree"

1960. World Refugee Year.

454	**181**	50p. orange	25	25
455	**181**	165p. blue	35	25
MS455a		108×80 mm. Nos. 454/5. Imperf	5·75	7·75
MS455b		As last, colours transposed	7·50	9·00

182 Buzkashi Game

183 Buzkashi Game

1960. Buzkashi Game

456	**182**	25p. pink	60	25
457	**182**	25p. violet	1·00	25
458	**182**	25p. olive	2·75	25
459	**182**	50p. turquoise	1·40	60
460	**182**	50p. blue	50	35
460a	**182**	50p. orange	50	35
461	**183**	100p. olive	80	25
462	**183**	150p. orange	65	35
463	**183**	175p. brown	2·50	50
464	**183**	2a. green	1·50	1·10

184 Children receiving Ball

1960. Child Welfare Fund.

465	**184**	75p.+25p. blue	90	35
466	**184**	175p.+25p. green	1·80	50

185 Douglas DC-6 over Mountains

1960. Air.

467	**185**	75p. violet	65	25
468	**185**	125p. blue	80	40
469	**185**	5a. olive	1·50	90

186 Independence Monument, Kabul

1960. 42nd Independence Day.

470	**186**	50p. blue	40	25
471	**186**	175p. mauve	1·10	40

187

1960. Pashtunistan Day.

472	**187**	50p.+50p. red	60	30
473	**187**	175p.+50p. blue	1·40	1·10

188 Insecticide Sprayer

1960. Anti-Malaria Campaign Day.

474	**188**	50p.+50p. orange	1·30	1·20
475	**188**	175p.+50p. brown	3·50	2·75

189 Mohamed Zahir Shah

1960. King's 46th Birthday.

476	**189**	50p. brown	65	25
477	**189**	150p. red	1·60	60

190 Ambulance

1960. Red Crescent Day.

478	**190**	50p.+50p. violet & red	65	50
479	**190**	175p.+50p. blue & red	1·60	1·00

191 Teacher with Globe and Children

1960. Literacy Campaign.

480	**191**	50p. mauve	40	35
481	**191**	100p. green	1·10	50

192 Globe and Flags

1960. U.N. Day.

482	**192**	50p. purple	25	15
483	**192**	175p. blue	1·00	65
MS483a		128×86 mm. Nos. 482/3. Imperf	6·25	4·50

1960. Olympic Games, Rome. Optd **1960** in figures and in Arabic and Olympic Rings.

484	**183**	175p. brown	1·80	2·10
MS484a		86×62 mm. No. 484. Imperf	6·25	8·25

1960. World Refugee Year. Nos. 454/5 surch **+25 Ps**.

485	**181**	50p.+25p. orange	1·80	1·80
486	**181**	165p.+25p. blue	1·80	1·80
MS486a		108×80 mm. Nos. 485/6. Imperf	6·25	6·50

195 Mir Wais Nika (patriot)

1960. Mir Wais Nika Commemoration.

487	**195**	50p. mauve	65	40
488	**195**	175p. blue	1·20	50
MS488a		108×78 mm. Nos. 487/8. Imperf	3·75	3·75

The very numerous issues of Afghanistan which we do not list appeared between 21 April 1961 and 15 March 1964 (both dates inclusive), and were made available to the philatelic trade by an agency acting under the authority of a contract granted by the Afghanistan Government.

It later became evident that token supplies were only placed on sale in Kabul for a few hours and some of these sets contained stamps of very low denominations for which there was no possible postal use.

When the contract for the production of these stamps expired in 1963 it was not renewed and the Afghanistan Government set up a Philatelic Advisory Board to formulate stamp policy. The issues from No. 489 onwards were made in usable denominations and placed on sale without restriction in Afghanistan and distributed to the trade by the Philatelic Department of the G.P.O. in Kabul.

Issues not listed here will be found recorded in the Appendix at the end of this country. It is believed that some of the higher values from the agency sets were utilised for postage in late 1979.

196 Band Amir Lake

1961. Band Amir Lake

489	**196**	3a. blue	50	25
490	**196**	10a. purple	1·30	1·20

197 Independence Memorial

1963. 45th Independence Day.

491	**197**	25p. green	15	15
492	**197**	50p. orange	35	25
493	**197**	150p. mauve	50	35

198 Tribesmen

1963. Pashtunistan Day.

494	**198**	25p. violet	15	15
495	**198**	50p. blue	25	25
496	**198**	150p. brown	65	40

199 Assembly Building

1963. National Assembly.

497	**199**	25p. brown	15	15
498	**199**	50p. red	15	15
499	**199**	75p. brown	25	15
500	**199**	100p. olive	25	15
501	**199**	125p. lilac	40	15

200 Balkh Gate

1963. Balkh Gate

502	**200**	3a. brown	1·00	25

201 Kemal Ataturk

1963. 25th Death Anniv of Kemal Ataturk.

503	**201**	1a. blue	15	15
504	**201**	3a. violet	65	50

202 Mohamed Zahir Shah

1963. King's 49th Birthday.

505	**202**	25p. green	15	15
506	**202**	50p. grey	25	15
507	**202**	75p. red	35	25
508	**202**	100p. brown	50	25

203 Afghan Stamp of 1878

1964. Stamp Day.

509	**203**	1a.25 black, green & gold	25	15
510	**203**	5a. black, red and gold	60	40

204 Kabul International Airport

1964. Air. Inauguration of Kabul Int Airport.

511	**204**	10a. green and purple	80	25
512	**204**	20a. purple and green	1·00	40
513	**204**	50a. turquoise and blue	2·75	1·20

205 Kandahar International Airport

1964. Air. Inauguration of Kandahar International Airport.

514	**205**	7a.75 brown	65	40
515	**205**	9a.25 blue	90	80
516	**205**	10a.50 green	1·20	1·00
517	**205**	13a.75 red	1·40	1·10

206 Unisphere and Flags

1964. New York World's Fair.

518	**206**	6a. black, red and green	25	15

207 "Flame of Freedom"

1964. First U.N. Human Rights Seminar, Kabul.

519	**207**	3a.75 multicoloured	25	15

208 Snow Leopard

1964. Afghan Wildlife.

520	**208**	25p. blue and yellow	1·80	25

521	-	50p. green and red	2·10	25
522	-	75p. purple and blue	2·50	25
523	-	5a. brown and green	2·75	90

ANIMALS—VERT: 50p. Ibex. HORIZ: 75p. Argali; 5a. Yak.

209 Herat

1964. Tourist Publicity. Inscr "1964".

524	**209**	25p. brown and blue	15	15
525	-	75p. blue and ochre	25	15
526	-	3a. black, red and green	50	25

DESIGNS—VERT: 75p. Tomb of Gowhar Shad, Herat. HORIZ: 3a. Map and flag.

210 Hurdling

1964. Olympic Games, Tokyo.

527	**210**	25p. sepia, red and bistre	15	10
528	-	1a. sepia, red and blue	15	15
529	-	3a.75 sepia, red and green	40	25
530	-	5a. sepia, red and brown	50	35
MS530a		95×95 mm. Nos. 527/30. Imperf. (sold at 15a.)	1·20	1·20

DESIGNS—VERT: 1a. Diving. HORIZ: 3a.75, Wrestling; 5a. Football.

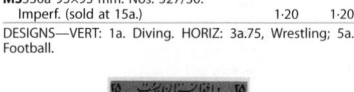

211 Afghan Flag

1964. 46th Independence Day.

531	**211**	25p. multicoloured	15	15
532	**211**	75p. multicoloured	35	15

On the above the Pushtu inscription "33rd Anniversary" is blocked out in gold.

212 Pashtu Flag

1964. Pashtunistan Day.

533	**212**	100p. multicoloured	25	15

213 Mohamed Zahir Shah

1964. King's 50th Birthday.

534	**213**	1a.25 green and gold	25	15
535	**213**	3a.75 red and gold	40	40
536	**213**	50a. black and gold	3·50	2·30

214 "Blood Transfusion"

1964. Red Crescent Day.

537	**214**	1a.+50p. red and black	35	25

215 Badges of Afghanistan and U.N.

1964. U.N. Day.

538	**215**	5a. blue, black and gold	25	15

216 Doves with Necklace

1964. Women's Day.

539	**216**	25p. blue, green and pink	60	35
540	**216**	75p. blue, green & lt blue	90	40
541	**216**	1a. blue, green and silver	1·20	60

217 M. Jami

1964. 550th Birth Anniv of Mowlana Jami (poet).

542	**217**	1a.50 cream, green & blk	1·00	80

218 Scaly-bellied Green Woodpecker

1965. Birds. Multicoloured.

543	1a.25 Type **218**	3·00	40
544	3a.75 Lanceolated jay (vert)	5·25	90
545	5a. Himalayan monal pheasant (vert)	6·25	2·00

219 I.T.U. Emblem and Symbols

1965. Centenary of I.T.U.

546	**219**	5a. black, red and blue	50	35

220 "The Red City"

1965. Tourist Publicity. Inscr "1965". Multicoloured

547	1a. Type **220**	25	10
548	3a.75 Bami Yan (valley and mountains)	40	15
549	5a. Band-E-Amir (lake and mountains)	60	25

221 I.C.Y. Emblem

1965. International Co-operation Year.

550	**221**	5a. multicoloured	50	35

222 Douglas DC-3 and Emblem

1965. Tenth Anniv of Afghan Airlines (ARIANA).

551	**222**	1a.25 multicoloured	35	10
552	-	5a. black, blue & purple	90	15
553	-	10a. multicoloured	1·60	60
MS553a		90×90 mm. Nos. 551/3. Imperf	3·00	3·00

DESIGNS: 5a. Convair CV 240; 10a. Douglas DC-6A.

223 Mohamed Nadir Shah

1965. 47th Independence Day.

554	**223**	1a. brown, black & green	40	15

224 Pashtu Flag

1965. Pashtunistan Day.

555	**224**	1a. multicoloured	40	15

225 Promulgation of New Constitution

1965. New Constitution.

556	**225**	1a.50 black and green	40	15

226 Mohamed Zahir Shah

1965. King's 51st Birthday.

557	**226**	1a.25 brown, blue & pink	25	15
558	**226**	6a. indigo, purple & blue	40	35

See also Nos. 579/80, 606/7 and 637/8.

227 First Aid Post

1965. Red Crescent Day.

559	**227**	1a.50+50 brn, grn & red	35	25

228 U.N. and Afghan Flags

1965. U.N. Day.

560	**228**	5a. multicoloured	25	15

229 Fat-tailed Gecko

1966. Reptiles. Multicoloured.

561	3a. Type **229**	1·00	25
562	4a. "Agama caucasica" (lizard)	1·20	35
563	8a. "Testudo horsfieldi" (tortoise)	2·00	65

230 Cotton

1966. Agriculture Day. Multicoloured.

564	1a. Type **230**	90	25
565	5a. Silkworm moth (caterpillar)	1·80	35
566	7a. Oxen	2·75	50

231 Footballer

1966. World Cup Football Championship, England.

567	**231**	2a. black and red	75	25
568	**231**	6a. black and blue	1·30	35
569	**231**	12a. black and brown	2·75	75

232 Independence Memorial

1966. Independence Day.

570	**232**	1a. multicoloured	35	25
571	**232**	3a. multicoloured	90	35

233 Pashtu Flag

1966. Pashtunistan Day.

572	**233**	1a. blue	60	25

234 Founding Members

1966. Red Crescent Day.

573	**234**	2a.+1a. green and red	35	25
574	**234**	5a.+1a. brown & mve	75	35

235 Map of Afghanistan

1966. Tourist Publicity. Multicoloured.

575	2a. Type **235**	25	25
576	4a. Bagh-i-Bala, former Palace of Abdur Rahman	50	35
577	8a. Tomb of Abdur Rahman, Kabul	75	75
MS578	111×80 mm. Nos. 575/7. Imperf	2·10	2·10

DESIGN: 6a. I.T.Y. emblem on map of Afghanistan.

1966. King's 52nd Birthday. Portrait similar to T **226** but with position of inscr changed. Dated "1966".

579	1a. green	25	25
580	5a. brown	60	35

236 Mohamed Zahir Shah and U.N. Emblem

1966. U.N. Day. Inscr "20TH ANNIVERSAIRE DES REFUGIES".

581	**236**	5a. green, brown & emer	40	15
582	**236**	10a. red, green & yellow	80	15

237 Children Dancing

1966. Child Welfare Day.

583	**237**	1a.+1a. red and green	15	10
584	**237**	3a.+2a. brown & yell	35	15
585	**237**	7a.+3a. green & purple	55	35

238 Construction of Power Station

1967. Afghan Industrial Development. Multicoloured

586	2a. Type **238**	25	25
587	5a. Handwoven carpet (vert)	25	25
588	8a. Cement works	50	35

239 UNESCO Emblem

1967. 20th Anniv (1966) of UNESCO.

589	**239**	2a. multicoloured	25	15
590	**239**	6a. multicoloured	40	15
591	**239**	12a. multicoloured	1·00	25

240 I.T.Y. Emblem

1967. International Tourist Year.

592	**240**	2a. black, blue and yellow	25	25
593	-	6a. black, blue and brown	50	25
MS594		110×70 mm. Nos. 592/3. Imperf. (sold at 10a.)	1·20	1·20

DESIGN: 6a. I.T.Y. emblem on map of Afghanistan.

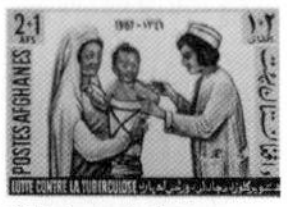

241 Inoculation

1967. Anti-Tuberculosis Campaign.

595	**241**	2a.+1a. black & yellow	25	25
596	**241**	5a.+2a. brown & pink	65	35

242 Hydroelectric Power Station, Dorunta

1967. Development of Electricity for Agriculture.

597	**242**	1a. lilac and green	15	15
598	-	6a. turquoise and brown	40	25
599	-	8a. blue and purple	60	40

DESIGNS—VERT: 6a. Dam. HORIZ: 8a. Reservoir, Jalalabad.

243 Rhesus Macaque

1967. Wildlife.

600	**243**	2a. blue and buff	75	25
601	-	6a. sepia and green	1·30	35
602	-	12a. brown and blue	2·10	80

ANIMALS—HORIZ: 6a. Striped hyena; 12a. Goitred gazelles.

244 *Saving the Guns at Maiwand* (after R. Caton Woodville)

1967. Independence Day.

603	**244**	1a. brown and red	35	25
604	**244**	2a. brown and mauve	60	25

245 Pashtu Dancers

1967. Pashtunistan Day.

605	**245**	2a. violet and purple	60	25

1967. King's 53rd Birthday. Portrait similar to T **226** but with position of inscr changed. Dated "1967".

606	2a. brown	15	15
607	8a. blue	65	35

246 Red Crescent

1967. Red Crescent Day.

608	**246**	3a.+1a. red, blk & ol	25	25
609	**246**	5a.+1a. red, blk & blue	40	25

247 U.N. Emblem and Fireworks

1967. U.N. Day.

610	**247**	10a. multicoloured	75	35

248 Wrestling

1967. Olympic Games, Mexico City.

611	**248**	4a. purple and green	50	25
612	-	6a. brown and red	1·00	25
MS613		100×65 mm. Nos. 611/12	2·10	2·10

DESIGN: 6a. Wrestling throw.

249 Said Jamal-ud-Din Afghan

1967. 70th Death Anniv of Said Afghan.

614	**249**	1a. purple	25	25
615	**249**	5a. brown	40	25

250 Bronze Vase

1967. Archaeological Treasures (11th–12th century Ghasnavide era).

616	**250**	3a. brown and green	35	15
617	-	7a. green and yellow	65	25
MS618		65×100 mm. Nos. 616/17. Imperf	3·00	3·00

DESIGN: 7a. Bronze jar.

251 W.H.O. Emblem

1968. 20th Anniv of W.H.O.

619	**251**	2a. blue and bistre	25	25
620	**251**	7a. blue and red	50	35

252 Karakul Sheep

1968. Agricultural Day.

621	**252**	1a. black and yellow	25	25
622	**252**	6a. brown, black and blue	1·00	35
623	**252**	12a. brown, sepia & blue	1·60	50

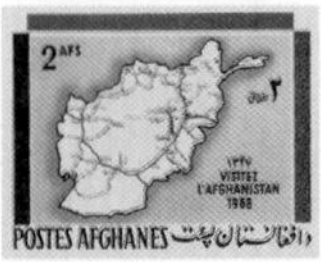

253 Road Map of Afghanistan

1968. Tourist Publicity. Multicoloured.

624	2a. Type **253**	25	25
625	3a. Victory Tower, Ghazni (21×31 mm)	35	25
626	16a. Mausoleum, Ghazni (21×31 mm)	1·20	60

254 Queen Humaira

1968. Mothers' Day.

627	**254**	2a.+2a. brown	35	25
628	**254**	7a.+2a. green	90	60

255 Cinereous Vulture

1968. Wild Birds. Multicoloured.

629	1a. Type **255**	1·80	65
630	6a. Eagle owl	4·25	2·00
631	7a. Greater flamingos	6·25	2·30

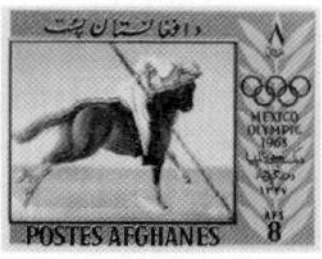

256 "Pig-sticking"

1968. Olympic Games, Mexico. Multicoloured.

632	2a. Olympic flame and rings (21×31 mm)	35	15
633	8a. Type **256**	65	40
634	12a. Buzkashi game	1·10	65

257 Flowers on Army Truck

1968. Independence Day.

635	**257**	6a. multicoloured	50	25

258 Pashtu Flag

1968. Pashtunistan Day.

636	**258**	3a. multicoloured	45	25

1968. King's 54th Birthday. Portrait similar to T **226** but differently arranged and in smaller size (21×31 mm).

637	2a. blue	25	25
638	8a. brown	60	35

259 Red Crescent

1968. Red Crescent Day.

639	**259**	4a.+1a. multicoloured	60	25

260 Human Rights Emblem

1968. U.N. Day and Human Rights Year.

640	**260**	1a. brown, bistre & green	25	25
641	**260**	2a. black, bistre & violet	25	25
642	**260**	6a. violet, bistre & purple	50	25
MS643		101×65 mm. **260** 10a. orange, bistre and purple. Imperf	1·80	1·80

261 Maolala Djalalodine Balkhi

1968. 695th Death Anniv of Maolala Djalalodine Balkhi (Rumi)

644	**261**	4a. mauve and green	35	25

262 Temple Painting

1969. Archaeological Treasures (Bagram era).

645	**262**	1a. red, yellow and green	35	25
646	-	3a. purple and violet	90	25
MS647		101×66 mm. Nos. 6545/6. Imperf. (sold at 10a.)	1·60	1·60

DESIGN: 3a. Carved vessel.

263 I.L.O. Emblem

1969. 50th Anniv of I.L.O.

648	**263**	5a. black and yellow	35	25
649	**263**	8a. black and blue	60	35

264 Red Cross Emblems

1969. 50th Anniv of League of Red Cross Societies.

650	**264**	3a.+1a. multicoloured	65	35
651	**264**	5a.+1a. multicoloured	80	35

On Nos. 650/1 the commemorative inscr in English and Pushtu for the 50th Anniv of the League of Red Cross Societies has been obliterated by gold bars.

266 Mother and Child

1969. Mothers' Day.

654	**266**	1a.+1a. brown & yell	25	25
655	**266**	4a.+1a. violet & mve	40	35
MS656		121×81 mm. Nos. 654/5. Imperf. (sold at 10a.)	2·10	2·10

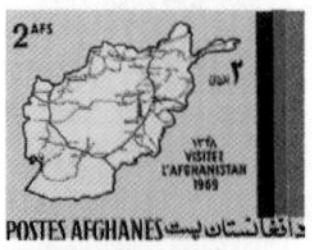

267 Road Map of Afghanistan

1969. Tourist Publicity. Badakshan and Pamir Region. Multicoloured.

657	**266**	2a. Type **267**	60	25
658	**266**	4a. Pamir landscape	65	35
659	**266**	7a. Mountain mule transport	1·10	65
MS660		136×90 mm. Nos. 657/9. Imperf (sold at 15a.)	2·50	2·50

268 Bust (Hadda era)

1969. Archaeological Discoveries. Multicoloured.

661	1a. Type **268**	15	10
662	5a. Vase and jug (Bagram period)	40	15
663	10a. Statuette (Bagram period)	65	35

269 Mohamed Zahir Shah and Queen Humaira

1969. Independence Day.

664	**269**	5a. red, blue and gold	40	25
665	**269**	10a. green, purple & gold	75	40

270 Map and Rising Sun

1969. Pashtunistan Day.

666	**270**	2a. red and blue	25	15

271 Mohamed Zahir Shah

1969. King's 55th Birthday.

667	**271**	2a. multicoloured	25	10
668	**271**	6a. multicoloured	60	25

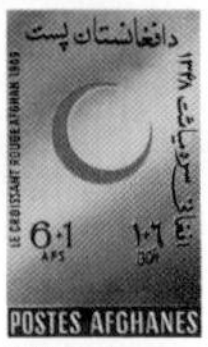

272 Red Crescent

1969. Red Crescent Day.

669	**272**	6a.+1a. multicoloured	80	25

273 U.N. Emblem, Afghan Arms and Flag

1969. United Nations Day.

670	**273**	5a. multicoloured	80	25

274 I.T.U. Emblem

1969. World Telecommunications Day.

671	**274**	6a. multicoloured	35	25
672	**274**	12a. multicoloured	75	40

275 Indian Crested Porcupine

1969. Wild Animals. Multicoloured.

673	**274**	1a. Type **275**	50	35
674	**274**	3a. Wild boar	1·20	40
675	**274**	8a. Bactrian red deer	1·60	50

276 Footprint on the Moon

1969. First Man on the Moon.

676	**276**	1a. multicoloured	25	25
677	**276**	3a. multicoloured	35	25
678	**276**	6a. multicoloured	50	25
679	**276**	10a. multicoloured	75	40

277 "Cancer the Crab"

1970. W.H.O. 'Fight Cancer' Day.

680	**277**	2a. red, dp green & green	25	25
681	**277**	6a. red, deep blue & blue	50	25

278 Mirza Bedel

1970. 250th Death Anniv of Mirza Abdul Quader Bedel (poet).

682	**278**	5a. multicoloured	40	15

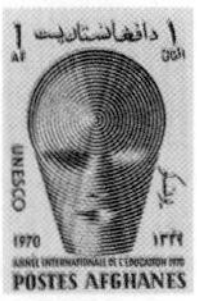

279 I.E.Y. Emblem

1970. International Education Year.

683	**279**	1a. black	25	25
684	**279**	6a. red	40	25
685	**279**	12a. green	90	40

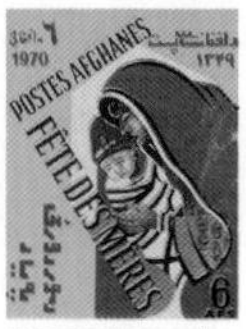

280 Mother and Child

1970. Mothers' Day.

686	**280**	6a. multicoloured	35	25

281 U.N. Emblem, Scales and Satellite

1970. 25th Anniv of United Nations.

687	**281**	4a. blue, dp blue & yellow	25	25
688	**281**	6a. blue, deep blue & red	40	25

282 Road Map of Afghanistan with Location of Sites

1970. Tourist Publicity. Inscr "1970". Multicoloured

689	**282**	2a. black, green and blue	15	15
690	-	3a. multicoloured	25	15
691	-	7a. multicoloured	60	25

DESIGNS: 36×26 mm: 3a. Lakeside mosque, Kabul; 7a. Arch of Paghman.

283 Common Quail

1970. Wild Birds. Multicoloured.

692	2a. Type **283**	2·10	65
693	4a. Golden eagle	4·00	1·00
694	6a. Common pheasant	5·25	1·60

284 Shah Reviewing Troops

1970. Independence Day.

695	**284**	8a. multicoloured	40	25

285 Group of Pashtus

1970. Pashtunistan Day.

696	**285**	2a. blue and red	40	25

286 Mohamed Zahir Shah

1970. King's 56th Birthday.

697	**286**	3a. violet and green	25	25
698	**286**	7a. purple and blue	75	35

287 Red Crescent Emblems

1970. Red Crescent Day.

699	**287**	2a. black, red and gold	25	15

288 U.N. Emblem and Plaque

1970. United Nations Day.

700	**288**	1a. multicoloured	25	25
701	**288**	5a. multicoloured	25	25

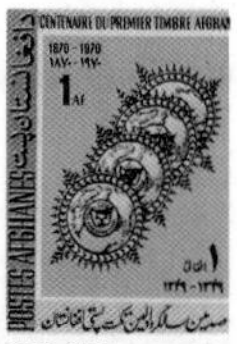

289 Afghan Stamps of 1871

1970. Centenary of First Afghan Stamps.

702	**289**	1a. black, blue & orange	35	25
703	**289**	4a. black, yellow & blue	60	25
704	**289**	12a. black, blue and lilac	1·00	40

290 Global Emblem

1971. World Telecommunications Day.

705	**290**	12a. multicoloured	65	40

291 *Callimorpha principalis*

1971. Butterflies and Moths. Multicoloured.

706	1a. Type **291**	1·30	60
707	3a. *Epizygaenella afghana*	2·75	1·20
708	5a. *Parnassius autocrator*	4·00	1·80

292 Lower half of old Kushan Statue

1971. UNESCO Kushan Seminar.

709	**292**	6a. violet and yellow	50	25
710	**292**	10a. purple and blue	80	35

293 Independence Memorial

1971. Independence Day.

711	**293**	7a. multicoloured	60	25
712	**293**	9a. multicoloured	90	35

294 Pashtunistan Square, Kabul

1971. Pashtunistan Day.

713	**294**	5a. purple	50	25

295 Mohamed Zahir Shah and Kabul Airport

1971. Air. Multicoloured.

714	50a. Type **295**	4·50	4·50
715	100a. King, airline emblem and Boeing 727 airplane	5·75	3·50

296 Mohamed Zahir Shah

1971. King's 57th Birthday.

716	**296**	9a. multicoloured	60	35
717	**296**	17a. multicoloured	1·20	65

297 Map, Nurse and Patients

1971. Red Crescent Day.

718	**297**	8a. multicoloured	50	35

298 Emblem of Racial Equality Year

1971. United Nations Day.

719	**298**	24a. blue	1·50	80

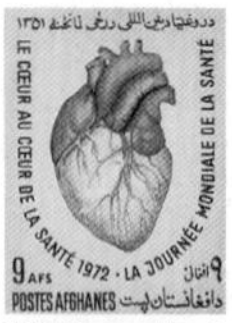

299 Human Heart

1972. World Health Day and World Heart Month.

720	**299**	9a. multicoloured	90	35
721	**299**	12a. multicoloured	1·80	40

300 *Tulipa lanata*

1972. Afghan Flora and Fauna. Multicoloured.

722	7a. Type **300**	1·30	75
723	10a. Chukar partridge (horiz)	7·75	1·60
724	12a. Lynx (horiz)	2·50	1·20
725	18a. *Allium stipitatum*	2·50	1·30

301 Buddha of Hadda

1972. Tourist Publicity.

726	**301**	3a. blue and brown	60	25
727	-	7a. green and red	90	35
728	-	9a. purple and green	1·30	40

DESIGNS: 7a. Greco-Bactrian seal, 250 B.C.; 9a. Greek temple, Ai-Khanum, 3rd–2nd century B.C.

302 King with Queen Humaira at Independence Parade

1972. Independence Day.

729	**302**	25a. multicoloured	4·50	1·20

303 Wrestling

1972. Olympic Games, Munich. Various Wrestling Holds as T **303**.

730	4a. multicoloured	35	15
731	8a. multicoloured	60	25
732	10a. multicoloured	65	35
733	19a. multicoloured	1·50	50
734	21a. multicoloured	1·60	60
MS735	160×110 mm. Nos. 730/4. Imperf (sold at 60a.)	3·25	3·25

304 Pathan and Mountain View

1972. Pashtunistan Day.

736	**304**	5a. multicoloured	60	25

305 Mohamed Zahir Shah

1972. King's 58th Birthday.

737	**305**	7a. blue, black and gold	75	25
738	**305**	14a. brown, black & gold	1·20	40

306 Ruined Town and Refugees

1972. Red Crescent Day.

739	**306**	7a. black, red and blue	65	25

307 E.C.A.F.E. Emblem

1972. U.N. Day. 25th Anniv of U.N. Economic Commission for Asia and the Far East.

740	**307**	12a. black and blue	60	35

308 Ceramics

1973. Afghan Handicrafts. Multicoloured.

741	7a. Type **308**	40	25
742	9a. Embroidered coat (vert)	50	35
743	12a. Coffee set (vert)	75	40
744	16a. Decorated boxes	1·10	50
MS745	110×110 mm. Nos. 741/4. Imperf (sold at 45a.)	3·75	3·75

309 W.M.O. and Afghan Emblems

1973. Cent of World Meteorological Organization.

746	**309**	7a. green and mauve	60	25
747	**309**	14a. red and blue	1·40	40

310 Emblems and Harvester

1973. Tenth Anniv of World Food Programme.

748	**310**	14a.+7a. purple & blue	1·40	90

311 Al-Biruni

1973. Birth Millenary of Abu-al Rayhan al-Biruni (mathematician and philosopher).

749	**311**	10a. multicoloured	65	40

312 Association Emblem

1973. Family Planning Week.

750	**312**	9a. purple and orange	65	25

313 Himalayan Monal Pheasant

1973. Birds. Multicoloured.

751	8a. Type **313**	3·00	2·10
752	9a. Great crested grebe	3·75	2·50
753	12a. Himalayan snowcock	4·50	3·25

314 Buzkashi Game

1973. Tourism.

754	**314**	8a. black	60	35

315 Firework Display

1973. Independence Day.

755	**315**	12a. multicoloured	65	35

316 Landscape and Flag

1973. Pashtunistan Day.

756	**316**	9a. multicoloured	65	15

317 Red Crescent

1973. Red Crescent.

757	**317**	10a. multicoloured	1·00	25

318 Kemal Ataturk

1973. 50th Anniv of Turkish Republic.

758	**318**	1a. blue	25	25
759	**318**	7a. brown	1·20	25

319 Human Rights Flame

1973. 25th Anniv of Declaration of Human Rights.

760	**319**	12a. blue, black and silver	60	40

320 Asiatic Black Bears

1974. Wild Animals. Multicoloured.

761	5a. Type **320**	65	15
762	7a. Afghan hound	1·10	40
763	10a. Goitred gazelle	1·40	50
764	12a. Leopard	1·80	60
MS765	120×100 mm. Nos. 761/4. Imperf	10·50	10·50

321 "Workers"

1974. Labour Day.

766	**321**	9a. multicoloured	50	35

322 Arch of Paghman and Independence Memorial

1974. Independence Day.

767	**322**	4a. multicoloured	40	10
768	**322**	11a. multicoloured	60	25

323 Arms of Afghanistan and Hands clasping Seedling

1974. First Anniv of Republic. Multicoloured.

769	4a. Type **323**	40	10
770	5a. Republican flag (36×26 mm)	60	15
771	7a. Gen. Mohammed Daoud (26×36 mm)	65	25
772	15a. Soldiers and arms	1·20	35
MS773	Two sheets. Imperf (a) 120×80 mm. Nos. 769 and 772. (b) 100×100 mm. Nos. 770/1	3·75	3·75

324 Lesser Spotted Eagle

1974. Afghan Birds. Multicoloured.

774	1a. Type **324**	2·10	50
775	6a. White-fronted goose, ruddy shelduck and greylag goose	4·50	80
776	11a. Black crane and common coots	7·50	1·30

325 Flags of Pashtunistan and Afghanistan

1974. Pashtunistan Day.

777	**325**	5a. multicoloured	35	25

326 Republic's Coat of Arms

1974. Coat of Arms

778	**326**	100p. green	80	25

327 Pres. Daoud

1974. Pres. Daoud

779	**327**	10a. multicoloured	65	25
780	**327**	16a. multicoloured	2·50	90
781	**327**	19a. multicoloured	90	50
782	**327**	21a. multicoloured	1·40	60
783	**327**	22a. multicoloured	3·75	2·00
784	**327**	30a. multicoloured	5·00	2·75

328 Arms and Centenary Years

1974. Centenary of U.P.U.

785	**328**	7a. green, black and gold	35	25

329 "UN" and U.N. Emblem

1974. United Nations Day.

786	**329**	5a. blue and ultramarine	40	15

330 Pres. Daoud

1975. Pres. Daoud

787	**330**	50a. multicoloured	2·75	1·40
788	**330**	100a. multicoloured	5·75	2·50

331 Minaret, Jam

1975. South Asia Tourist Year. Multicoloured.

789	7a. Type **331**	35	15
790	14a. "Griffon and Lady" (2nd century)	65	40
791	15a. Head of Buddha (4th–5th century)	80	40
MS792	130×90 mm. Nos. 789/91. Imperf	3·75	3·75

332 Afghan Flag

1975. Independence Day.

793	**332**	16a. multicoloured	80	25

333 Rejoicing Crowd

1975. Second Anniv of Revolution.

794	**333**	9a. multicoloured	50	15
795	**333**	12a. multicoloured	65	25

334 I.W.Y. Emblem

1975. International Women's Year.

796	**334**	9a. black, blue and purple	50	15

335 Rising Sun and Flag

1975. Pashtunistan Day.

797	**335**	10a. multicoloured	40	15

336 Wazir M. Akbar Khan

1976. 130th Death Anniv of Akbar Khan (resistance leader).

798	**336**	15a. multicoloured	60	40

337 Independence Monument and Arms

1976. Independence Day.

799	**337**	22a. multicoloured	75	50

338 Pres. Daoud raising Flag

1976. Third Anniv of Republic.

800	**338**	30a. multicoloured	80	60

339 Mountain

1976. Pashtunistan Day.

801	**339**	16a. multicoloured	65	50

340 Arms

340a

1976. Arms

802	-	25p. salmon	50	35
803	**340**	50p. green	60	25
803a	**340a**	50p. rosine	60	25
804	**340**	1a. blue	65	10

DESIGN: 25p. As Type **340** but with Arms on left and inscription differently arranged.

341 Flag and Monuments on Open Book

1977. Independence Day.

805	**341**	20a. multicoloured	75	65

342 Presidential Address

1977. Election of First President and New Constitution. Multicoloured.

806	7a. President Daoud and Election (45×27 mm)	80	60
807	8a. Type **342**	90	75
808	10a. Inaugural ceremony	1·20	90
809	18a. Promulgation of new constitution (45×27 mm)	2·00	1·60
MS810	136×106 mm. Nos. 806/9. Imperf	3·75	3·75

343 Medal

1977. 80th Death Anniv of Sayed Jamaluddin (Afghan reformer).

811	**343**	12a. black, blue & gold	40	15

344 Crowd with Afghan Flag

1977. Republic Day.

812	**344**	22a. multicoloured	75	40

345 Dancers around Fountain

1977. Pashtunistan Day.

813	**345**	30a. multicoloured	1·20	90

346 Dome of the Rock

1977. Palestinian Welfare.

814	**346**	12a.+3a. black, gold and pink	2·10	60

347 Arms and Carrier Pigeon

1977. Arms and Carrier Pigeon

815	**347**	1a. blue and black	40	15

348 President Daoud acknowledging Crowd

1978. First Anniv of Presidential Election.

816	**348**	20a. multicoloured	2·10	1·20

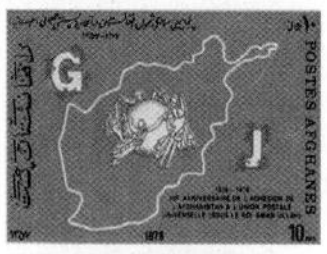

349 U.P.U. Emblem on Map of Afghanistan

1978. 50th Anniv of Admission to U.P.U.

817	**349**	10a. gold, green & black	40	15

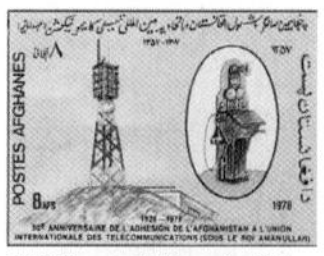

350 Transmitting Aerial and Early Telephone

1978. 50th Anniv of Admission to I.T.U.

818	**350**	8a. multicoloured	40	15

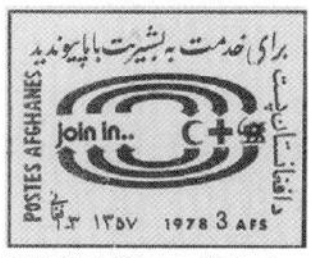

351 Red Crescent, Red Cross and Red Lion Emblems

1978. Red Crescent.

819	**351**	3a. black	1·20	65

352 Arms

1978. Arms

820	**352**	1a. red and gold	1·60	65
821	**352**	4a. red and gold	2·10	90

353 Ruin, Qalai Bust

1978. Independence Day. Multicoloured.

822	16a. Buddha, Bamian	1·20	50
823	22a. Type **353**	1·60	75
824	30a. Women in national costume	2·10	1·20

354 Afghans with Flag

1978. Pashtunistan Day.

825	**354**	7a. red and blue	50	15

355 Crest and Symbols of the Five Senses

1978. International Literacy Day.

826	**355**	20a. red	90	40

356 Flag

1978. 'The Mail is in the Service of the People'.

827	**356**	8a. red, gold and brown	65	15
828	**356**	9a. red, gold and brown	1·00	15

357 Martyr

1978. 'The People's Democratic Party Honours its Martyrs'.

829	**357**	18a. green	1·00	40

358 President Mohammed Taraki

1978. 14th Anniv of People's Democratic Party.

830	**358**	12a. multicoloured	75	25

359 Emancipated Woman

1979. Women's Day.

831	**359**	14a. blue and red	1·20	50

360 Farmers planting Tree

1979. Farmers' Day.

832	**360**	1a. multicoloured	65	35

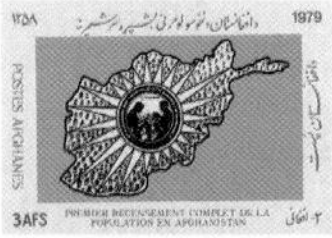

361 Map and Census Taking

1979. First Complete Population Census.

833	**361**	3a. black, blue and red	90	65

362 Pres. Taraki reading *Khalq*

1979. First Publication of *Khalq* (party newspaper).

834	**362**	2a. multicoloured	65	15

363 Pres. Taraki and Tank

1979. First Anniv of Sawr Revolution (1st issue).

835	**363**	50p. multicoloured	65	15

364 Pres. Taraki

1979. First Anniv of Sawr Revolution (2nd issue). Multicoloured.

836		4a. Type **364**	40	10
837		5a. Revolutionary H.Q. and Tank Monument, Kabul (47×32 mm)	60	15
838		6a. Command room, Revolutionary H.Q. (vert)	65	15
839		12a. House where first Khalq Party Congress was held (vert)	80	25

365 Carpenter and Blacksmith

1979. Workers' Solidarity.

840	**365**	10a. multicoloured	90	15

366 Children on Map of Afghanistan

1979. International Year of the Child.

841	**366**	16a. multicoloured	1·80	90

367 Revolutionaries and Kabul Monuments

1979. Independence Day.

842	**367**	30a. multicoloured	1·60	90

368 Afghans and Flag

1979. Pashtunistan Day.

843	**368**	9a. multicoloured	75	15

369 U.P.U. Emblem and Arms on Map

1979. Stamp Day.

844	**369**	15a. multicoloured	65	25

370 Headstone and Tomb

1979. Martyrs' Day.

845	**370**	22a. multicoloured	2·50	1·20

371 Doves around Globe

1979

845a	**371**	2a. blue and red	1·20	25

372 Woman with Baby, Dove and Rifle

1980. International Women's Day.

846	**372**	8a. multicoloured	1·60	50

373 Farmers receiving Land Grants

1980. Farmers' Day.

847	**373**	2a. multicoloured	2·10	65

374 Healthy Non-smoker and Prematurely Aged Smoker

1980. World Health Day. Anti-smoking Campaign.

848	**374**	5a. multicoloured	1·60	65

375 "Lenin speaking from Tribune"

1980. 110th Birth Anniv of Lenin.

849	**375**	12a. multicoloured	2·50	80

376 Crowd and Clenched Fist

1980. Second Anniv of Sawr Revolution.

850	**376**	1a. multicoloured	65	15

377 Quarry Worker and Blacksmith

1980. Workers' Solidarity.

851	**377**	9a. multicoloured	50	15

378 Football

1980. Olympic Games, Moscow. Multicoloured.

852		3a. Type **378**	60	15
853		6a. Wrestling	65	15
854		9a. Pigsticking	75	25
855		10a. Buzkashi	90	25

379 Soldiers attacking Fortress

1980. Independence Day.

856	**379**	3a. multicoloured	65	15

380 Pashtus with Flag

1980. Pashtunistan Day.

857	**380**	25a. multicoloured	1·00	40

381 Post Office

1980. World U.P.U. Day.

858	**381**	20a. multicoloured	1·00	40

382 Buzkashi

1980. Buzkashi

859	**382**	50a. multicoloured	2·10	1·50
860	**382**	100a. multicoloured	4·00	1·60

383 Arabic "H", Medina Mosque and Kaaba

1981. 1400th Anniv of Hegira.

861	**383**	13a.+2a. multicoloured	1·80	35

384 Mother and Child with Dove and Globe

1981. International Women's Day.

862	**384**	15a. multicoloured	1·20	35

385 Ox Plough, Tractor and Planting Trees

1981. Farmers' Day.

863	**385**	1a. multicoloured	1·00	25

386 Urial

1981. Protected Wildlife.

864	**386**	12a. multicoloured	2·30	65

387 Crowd and Afghan Arms

1981. Third Anniv of Sawr Revolution.

865	**387**	50p. brown	65	15

388 Road Workers in Ravine

1981. Workers' Day.

866	**388**	10a. multicoloured	90	35

389 Red Crescent enclosing Scenes of Disaster and Medical Aid

1981. Red Crescent Day.

867	**389**	1a.+4a. multicoloured	65	80

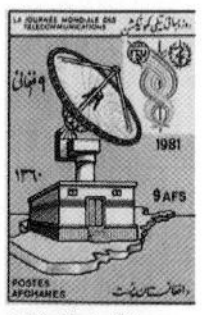
390 Satellite Receiving Station

1981. World Telecommunications Day.

868	**390**	9a. multicoloured	65	15

391 Map enclosing playing Children

1981. International Children's Day.

869	**391**	15a. multicoloured	90	40

392 Afghans and Monument

1981. Independence Day.

870	**392**	4a. multicoloured	90	15

393 Pashtus around Flag

1981. Pashtunistan Day.

871	**393**	2a. multicoloured	65	15

394 Terracotta Horseman

1981. World Tourism Day.

872	**394**	5a. multicoloured	65	15

395 Siamese Twins and I.Y.D.P. Emblem

1981. International Year of Disabled Persons.

873	**395**	6a.+1a. multicoloured	90	50

396 Harvesting

1981. World Food Day.

874	**396**	7a. multicoloured	80	15

397 Peace, Solidarity and Friendship Organization Emblem

1981. Afro-Asian Peoples' Solidarity Meeting.

875	**397**	8a. blue	75	15

398 Heads and Clenched Fist on Globe and Emblem

1981. International Anti-apartheid Year.

876	**398**	4a. multicoloured	1·00	25

399 Lion (bas-relief at Stara Zagora)

1981. 1300th Anniv of Bulgarian State.

877	**399**	20a. stone, purple and red	1·50	50

400 Mother rocking Cradle

1982. Women's Day.

878	**400**	6a. multicoloured	60	15

401 Farmers

1982. Farmers' Day.

879	**401**	4a. multicoloured	65	15

402 Judas Tree

1982. Plants. Multicoloured.

880	3a. Type **402**	35	15
881	4a. Hollyhock	60	15
882	16a. Rhubarb	1·20	35

403 Hands holding Flags and Tulip

1982. Fourth Anniv of Sawr Revolution.

883	**403**	1a. multicoloured	1·20	15

404 Dimitrov

1982. Birth Centenary of Georgi Dimitrov (Bulgarian statesman).

884	**404**	30a. multicoloured	2·30	80

405 Blacksmith, Factory Workers, Weaver and Labourer

1982. Workers' Day.

885	**405**	10a. multicoloured	75	25

406 White Storks

1982. Birds. Multicoloured.

886	6a. Type **406**	1·60	50
887	11a. Eurasian goldfinches	2·10	60

407 Brandt's Hedgehog

1982. Animals. Multicoloured.

888	3a. Type **407**	60	15
889	14a. Cobra	1·50	25

408 National Monuments

1982. Independence Day.

890	**408**	20a. multicoloured	1·20	50

409 Pashtus and Flag

1982. Pashtunistan Day.

891	**409**	32a. multicoloured	2·50	75

410 Tourists

1982. World Tourism Day.

892	**410**	9a. multicoloured	80	35

411 Postman delivering Letter, Post Office and U.P.U. Emblem

1982. World U.P.U. Day.

893	**411**	4a. multicoloured	90	25

412 Family eating Meal

1982. World Food Day.

894	**412**	9a. multicoloured	1·40	35

413 U.N. Emblem illuminating Globe

1982. 37th Anniv of United Nations.

895	**413**	15a. multicoloured	1·00	40

414 Earth Satellite Station

1982. I.T.U. Delegates' Conference, Nairobi.

896	**414**	8a. multicoloured	75	15

415 Dr. Robert Koch

1982. Centenary of Discovery of Tubercle Bacillus.

897	**415**	7a. black, brown & pink	50	25

416 Hand holding Torch, Globe and Scales

1982. 34th Anniv of Declaration of Human Rights.

898	**416**	5a. multicoloured	40	15

417 Lions

1982. Wild Animals. Multicoloured.

899	2a. Type **417**	40	15
900	7a. Asiatic wild asses	90	35
901	12a. Sable (vert)	2·00	50

418 Woman releasing Dove

1983. International Women's Day.

902	**418**	3a. multicoloured	25	15

419 Mir Alicher-e-Nawai (poet)

1983. 'Mir Alicher-e-Nawai and his Times' Study Decade.

903	**419**	22a. multicoloured	90	35

420 Distributing Land Ownership Documents

1983. Farmers' Day.

904	**420**	10a. multicoloured	65	25

421 Revolution Monument

1983. Fifth Anniv of Sawr Revolution.

905	**421**	15a. multicoloured	65	25

422 World Map and Hands holding Cogwheel

1983. Labour Day.

906	**422**	20a. multicoloured	65	25

423 Broadcasting Studio, Dish Aerial, Satellites and Television

1983. World Communications Year. Multicoloured.

907	4a. Type **423**	35	10
908	11a. Telecommunications headquarters	60	15

424 Hands holding Child

1983. International Children's Day.

909	**424**	25a. multicoloured	50	20

425 Arms and Map of Afghanistan

1983. Second Anniv of Nat Fatherland Front.

910	**425**	1a. multicoloured	35	15

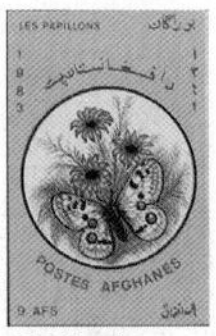

426 Apollo

1983. Butterflies. Multicoloured.

911	9a. Type **426**	1·00	75
912	13a. Swallowtail	2·30	1·30
913	21a. Small tortoiseshell (horiz)	3·00	1·60

427 Racial Segregation

1983. Anti-apartheid Campaign.

914	**427**	10a. multicoloured	50	15

428 National Monuments

1983. Independence Day.

915	**428**	6a. multicoloured	40	15

429 Pashtus with Flag

1983. Pashtunistan Day.

916	**429**	3a. multicoloured	40	15

430 Afghan riding Camel

1983. World Tourism Day.

917	**430**	5a. multicoloured	40	25
918	-	7a. brown and black	60	25
919	-	12a. multicoloured	90	25
920	-	16a. multicoloured	1·20	25

DESIGNS—VERT: 7a. Stone carving. 16a. Carved stele. HORIZ: 12a. Three statuettes.

431 Winter Landscape

1983. . Multicoloured.

921	50a. Type **431**	1·60	35
922	100a. Woman with camel	3·75	40

432 "Communications"

1983. World Communications Year. Multicoloured

923	14a. Type **432**	65	15
924	15a. Ministry of Communications, Kabul	65	15

433 Fish Breeding

1983. World Food Day.

925	**433**	14a. multicoloured	80	15

434 Football

1983. Sports. Multicoloured.

926	1a. Type **434**	25	25
927	18a. Boxing	1·00	35
928	21a. Wrestling	1·20	35

435 Jewellery

1983. Handicrafts. Multicoloured.

929	2a. Type **435**	15	10
930	8a. Polished stoneware	35	15
931	19a. Furniture	60	15
932	30a. Leather goods	1·40	15

436 Map, Sun, Scales and Torch

1983. 35th Anniv of Declaration of Human Rights.

933	**436**	20a. multicoloured	90	15

437 Polytechnic Buildings and Emblem

1983. 20th Anniv of Kabul Polytechnic.

934	**437**	30a. multicoloured	1·20	25

438 Ice Skating

1984. Winter Olympic Games, Sarajevo. Multicoloured.

935	5a. Type **438**	25	10
936	9a. Skiing	35	10
937	11a. Speed skating	50	10
938	15a. Ice hockey	60	10
939	18a. Biathlon	65	15
940	20a. Ski jumping	80	15
941	22a. Bobsleigh	1·00	15

439 Dove, Woman and Globe

1984. International Women's Day.

942	**439**	4a. multicoloured	50	30

440 Ploughing with Tractor

1984. Farmers' Day. Multicoloured.

943	2a. Type **440**	15	10
944	4a. Digging irrigation channel	15	10
945	7a. Saddling donkey by water-mill	15	10
946	9a. Harvesting wheat	25	10
947	15a. Building haystack	40	15
948	18a. Showing cattle	60	15
949	20a. Ploughing with oxen and sowing seed	75	15

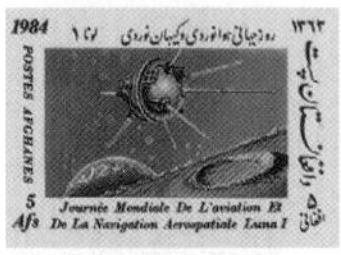

441 "Luna I"

1984. World Aviation and Space Navigation Day. Multicoloured.

950	5a. Type **441**	35	25
951	8a. "Luna II"	40	25
952	11a. "Luna III"	50	25
953	17a. "Apollo XI"	65	25
954	22a. "Soyuz VI"	80	35
955	28a. "Soyuz VII"	80	35
956	34a. "Soyuz VI", "VII" and "VIII"	1·00	40
MS957	66×87 mm. 25a. Sergei Korolev (rocket designer) and rocket (29×41 mm)	1·40	80

442 Flags, Soldier and Workers

1984. Sixth Anniv of Sawr Revolution.

958	**442**	3a. multicoloured	40	15

443 Hunting Dog

1984. Animals. Multicoloured.

959	1a. Type **443**	10	10
960	2a. Argali	25	15
961	6a. Przewalski's horse (horiz)	60	15
962	8a. Wild boar	80	25
963	17a. Snow leopard (horiz)	1·60	25
964	19a. Tiger (horiz)	2·75	25
965	22a. Indian elephant	3·00	35

444 Postal Messenger

1984. 19th U.P.U. Congress, Hamburg. Multicoloured

966	25a. Type **444**	90	15
967	35a. Post rider	1·40	35
968	40a. Bird with letter	1·80	35
MS969	97×66 mm. 50a. black	3·00	1·80

DESIGNS: As T **444**—35a. Post rider; 40a. Bird with letter; 25×37 mm—50a. Hamburg 1859 2s. stamp.

445 Antonov AN-2

1984. 40th Anniv of Ariana Airline. Multicoloured

970	1a. Type **445**	10	10
971	4a. Ilyushin Il-12	15	10
972	9a. Tupolev Tu-104A	60	15
973	10a. Ilyushin Il-18	80	15
974	13a. Yakovlev Yak-42	1·10	15
975	17a. Tupolev Tu-154	1·40	15
976	21a. Ilyushin Il-86	1·60	15

446 Ettore Bugatti (motor manufacturer) and Bugatti Type 43 Sports car, 1927

1984. Motor Cars. Multicoloured.

977	2a. Type **446**	15	10
978	5a. Henry Ford and Ford Model A two-seater, 1903	35	10
979	8a. Rene Panhard (engineer) and Panhard Limosine, 1899	60	10
980	11a. Gottlieb Daimler (engineer) and Daimler DB 18 saloon, 1935	75	10
981	12a. Karl Benz and Benz Viktoria two-seater (inscr "Victoris"), 1893	1·00	15
982	15a. Armand Peugeot (motor manufacturer) and Peugeot vis-a-vis, 1892	1·10	15
983	22a. Louis Chevrolet (car designer) and Chevrolet Superior sedan, 1925	1·50	15

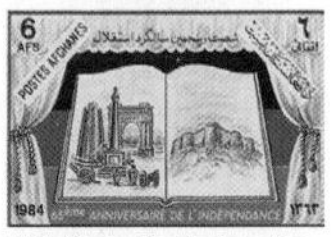

447 Open Book showing Monuments and Fortress

1984. Independence Day.

984	**447**	6a. multicoloured	40	15

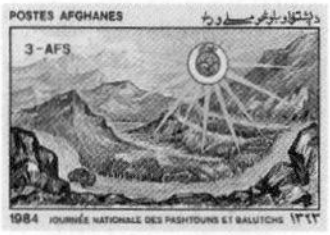

448 Truck on Mountain Road and Pashtunistan Badge

1984. Pashtunistan Day.

985	**448** 3a. multicoloured	40	15

449 Arch at Qalai Bust

1984. World Tourism Day. Multicoloured.

986	1a. Type **449**	10	10
987	2a. Ornamented belt	15	10
988	5a. Kabul monuments	15	15
989	9a. Statuette (vert)	25	15
990	15a. Buffalo riders in snow	40	25
991	19a. Camel in ornate caparison	80	25
992	21a. Buzkashi players	1·00	25

450 Pine Cone

1984. World Food Day. Multicoloured.

993	2a. Type **450**	15	10
994	4a. Walnuts	25	10
995	6a. Pomegranate	35	10
996	9a. Apples	50	10
997	13a. Cherries	60	15
998	15a. Grapes	75	15
999	26a. Pears	1·20	15

451 Globe and Emblem

1985. 20th Anniv (1984) of Peoples' Democratic Party.

1000	**451** 25a. multicoloured	1·20	40

452 Cattle

1985. Farmers' Day. Multicoloured.

1001	1a. Type **452**	35	15
1002	3a. Mare and foal	35	15
1003	7a. Galloping horse	35	15
1004	8a. Grey horse (vert)	60	25
1005	15a. Karakul sheep and sheepskins	90	25
1006	16a. Herder watching over cattle and sheep	1·10	35
1007	25a. Family with pack camels	1·50	40

453 Map and Geologist

1985. Geologists' Day.

1008	**453** 4a. multicoloured	35	15

454 Satellite

1985. 20th Anniv of 'Intelsat' Communications Satellite. Multicoloured.

1009	6a. Type **454**	50	15
1010	9a. "Intelsat III"	65	15
1011	10a. Rocket launch (vert)	90	15

455 *Visitors for Lenin* (V. Serov)

1985. 115th Birth Anniv of Lenin. Multicoloured.

1012	10a. Type **455**	65	25
1013	15a. "With Lenin" (detail, V. Serov)	80	25
1014	25a. Lenin and Red Army fighters	1·40	40
MS1015	90×21 mm. 50a. Lenin	2·30	1·40

456 Revolutionaries with Flags

1985. Seventh Anniv of Sawr Revolution.

1016	**456** 21a. multicoloured	1·00	15

457 Olympic Stadium and Moscow Skyline

1985. 12th World Youth and Students' Festival, Moscow. Multicoloured.

1017	7a. Type **457**	25	10
1018	12a. Festival emblem	40	25
1019	13a. Moscow Kremlin	50	35
1020	18a. Doll	65	60

458 Soviet Memorial, Berlin-Treptow, and Tank before Reichstag

1985. 40th Anniv of End of World War II. Multicoloured.

1021	6a. Type **458**	60	15
1022	9a. "Mother Homeland" war memorial, Volgograd, and fireworks over Moscow Kremlin	80	15
1023	10a. Cecilienhof Castle, Potsdam, and flags of United Kingdom, U.S.S.R. and U.S.A.	1·10	15

459 Weighing Baby

1985. UNICEF Child Survival Campaign. Multicoloured

1024	1a. Type **459**	10	15
1025	2a. Vaccinating child	15	15
1026	4a. Breast-feeding baby	35	15
1027	5a. Mother and child	40	15

460 Purple Blewit

1985. Fungi. Multicoloured.

1028	3a. Type **460**	15	10
1029	4a. Flaky-stemmed witches' mushroom	40	25
1030	7a. The blusher	60	35
1031	11a. Brown birch bolete	80	60
1032	12a. Common ink cap	1·10	60
1033	18a. *Hypholoma*	1·50	75
1034	20a. *Boletus aurantiacus*	1·60	75

461 Emblems

1985. United Nations Decade for Women.

1035	**461** 10a. multicoloured	65	25

462 Evening Primrose

1985. Argentina '85 International Stamp Exhibition, Buenos Aires. Flowers. Multicoloured.

1036	2a. Type **462**	15	10
1037	4a. Cockspur coral tree	35	15
1038	8a. *Tillandsia aeranthos*	60	15
1039	13a. Periwinkle	90	25
1040	18a. Marvel-of-Peru	1·30	35
1041	25a. *Cypella herbertii*	1·80	35
1042	30a. *Clytostoma callistegioides*	2·30	35
MS1043	80×100 mm. 75a. *Sesbania punicea* (51×36 mm)	5·75	80

463 Building

1985. Independence Day.

1044	**463** 33a. multicoloured	1·50	15

464 Dancers in Pashtunistan Square, Kabul

1985. Pashtunistan Day.

1045	**464** 25a. multicoloured	1·50	15

465 Guldara Stupa

1985. Tenth Anniv of World Tourism Organization. Multicoloured.

1046	1a. Type **465**	15	10
1047	2a. Mirwais tomb (vert)	15	10
1048	10a. Buddha of Bamian (vert)	60	10
1049	13a. No Gumbad mosque (vert)	80	10
1050	14a. Pule Kheshti mosque	90	15
1051	15a. Arch at Qalai Bust	1·00	15
1052	20a. Ghazni minaret (vert)	1·30	15

466 Boxing

1985. Sport. Multicoloured.

1053	1a. Type **466**	10	15
1054	2a. Volleyball	15	10
1055	3a. Football (vert)	50	10
1056	12a. Buzkashi	60	10
1057	14a. Weightlifting	65	15
1058	18a. Wrestling	75	15
1059	25a. Pigsticking	1·00	15

467 Fruit Stall

1985. World Food Day.

1060	**467** 25a. multicoloured	90	15

468 Flags and U.N. Building, New York

1985. 40th Anniv of United Nations Organization.

1061	**468** 22a. multicoloured	90	15

469 Black-billed Magpie

1985. Birds. Multicoloured.

1062	2a. Type **469**	25	10
1063	4a. Green woodpecker	1·00	50
1064	8a. Common pheasants	1·10	50
1065	13a. Bluethroat, Eurasian goldfinch and hoopoe	1·60	90
1066	18a. Peregrine falcons	2·00	1·00
1067	25a. Red-legged partridge	2·75	1·50
1068	30a. Eastern white pelicans (horiz)	3·50	1·70
MS1069	90×20 mm. 75a. Rose-ringed parakeets (29×41 mm)	7·50	80

470 Leopard and Cubs

1985. World Wildlife Fund. The Leopard. Multicoloured

1070	2a. Type **470**	40	25
1071	9a. Head of leopard	1·50	50
1072	11a. Leopard	2·50	80
1073	15a. Leopard cub	3·75	1·20

471 Triumph 650 and Big Ben Tower

1985. Motorcycles. Multicoloured.

1074	2a. Type **471**	15	10
1075	4a. Motobecane and Eiffel Tower, Paris	35	10
1076	8a. Bultaco motorcycles and Don Quixote monument, Madrid	60	15
1077	13a. Honda and Mt. Fuji, Japan	90	15
1078	18a. Jawa and Old Town Hall clock, Prague	1·10	25
1079	25a. MZ motorcycle and T.V. Tower, Berlin	1·60	25
1080	30a. Motorcycle and Colosseum, Rome	2·00	25
MS1081	100×80 mm. 75a. Moskva Dneipr motorcycle and Red Square, Moscow	6·50	80

472 Crowd with Flags

1986. 21st Anniv of Peoples' Democratic Party.

1082	**472** 2a. multicoloured	35	25

473 Lenin writing

1986. 27th Soviet Communist Party Congress, Moscow.

1083	**473**	25a. multicoloured	80	40

474 "Vostok 1"

1986. 25th Anniv of First Manned Space Flight. Multicoloured.

1084	3a. Type **474**	25	15
1085	7a. Russian Cosmonaut Medal (vert)	25	15
1086	9a. Launch of "Vostok 1" (vert)	40	15
1087	11a. Yuri Gagarin (first man in space) (vert)	50	15
1088	13a. Cosmonauts reading newspaper	60	25
1089	15a. Yuri Gagarin and Sergei Pavlovich Korolev (rocket designer)	60	25
1090	17a. Valentina Tereshkova (first woman in space) (vert)	75	25

475 Footballers

1986. World Cup Football Championship, Mexico.

1091	**475**	3a. multicoloured	25	15
1092	-	4a. multicoloured (horiz)	35	15
1093	-	7a. multicoloured (horiz)	40	15
1094	-	11a. multicoloured	65	15
1095	-	12a. mult (horiz)	80	25
1096	-	18a. multicoloured	1·20	25
1097	-	20a. multicoloured	1·40	25
MS1098		120×90 mm. 75a. multicoloured (39×26 mm)	4·50	80

DESIGNS: 4a. to 75a. Various footballing scenes.

476 Lenin

1986. 116th Birth Anniv of Lenin.

1099	**476**	16a. multicoloured	75	40

477 Delegates voting

1986. First Anniv of Supreme Council Meeting of Tribal Leaders.

1100	**477**	3a. brown, red and blue	25	15

478 Flags and Crowd

1986. Eighth Anniv of Sawr Revolution.

1101	**478**	8a. multicoloured	40	15

479 Worker with Cogwheel and Globe

1986. Labour Day.

1102	**479**	5a. multicoloured	25	15

480 Patient receiving Blood Transfusion

1986. International Red Cross and Red Crescent Day.

1103	**480**	7a. multicoloured	50	25

481 St. Bernard

1986. Pedigree Dogs. Multicoloured.

1104	5a. Type **481**	25	10
1105	7a. Rough collie	40	10
1106	8a. Spaniel	50	15
1107	9a. Long-haired dachshund	60	15
1108	11a. German shepherd	65	25
1109	15a. Bulldog	90	25
1110	20a. Afghan hound	1·20	25

482 Tiger Barb

1986. Fish. Multicoloured.

1111	5a. Type **482**	25	15
1112	7a. Mbuna	40	15
1113	8a. Clown loach	50	15
1114	9a. Lisa	60	25
1115	11a. Figure-eight pufferfish	80	25
1116	15a. Six-barred distichodus	1·10	35
1117	20a. Sail-finned molly	1·40	35

483 Mother and Children

1986. World Children's Day. Multicoloured.

1118	1a. Type **483**	15	15
1119	3a. Woman holding boy and emblem	15	15
1120	9a. Circle of children on map (horiz)	40	15

484 Italian Birkenhead Locomotive

1986. 19th-century Railway Locomotives. Multicoloured

1121	4a. Type **484**	25	10
1122	5a. Norris locomotive	35	10
1123	6a. Stephenson "Patentee" type locomotive	40	15
1124	7a. Bridges Adams locomotive	50	15
1125	8a. Ansoldo locomotive	65	25
1126	9a. Locomotive "St. David"	80	25
1127	11a. Jones & Potts locomotive	90	25

485 Cobra

1986. Animals. Multicoloured.

1128	3a. Type **485**	15	10
1129	4a. Lizards (vert)	25	15
1130	5a. Praying mantis	35	15
1131	8a. Beetle (vert)	50	25
1132	9a. Spider	60	35
1133	10a. Snake	65	35
1134	11a. Scorpions	80	35

Nos. 1130/2 and 1134 are wrongly inscr "Les Reptiles".

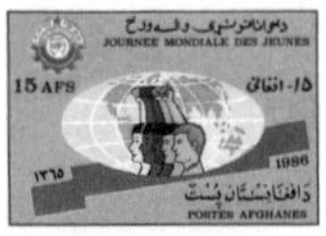

486 Profiles on Globe

1986. World Youth Day.

1135	**486**	15a. multicoloured	65	25

487 National Monuments

1986. Independence Day.

1136	**487**	10a. multicoloured	50	25

488 11th-century Ship

1986. Stockholmia 86 International Stamp Exhibition. Sailing Ships. Multicoloured.

1137	4a. Type **488**	40	15
1138	5a. Roman galley	50	25
1139	6a. English royal kogge	65	25
1140	7a. Early dhow	80	25
1141	8a. Nao	1·00	25
1142	9a. Ancient Egyptian ship	1·10	25
1143	11a. Medieval galeasse	1·30	25
MS1144	86×64 mm. 50a. Early dhow (as 7a.) (41×29 mm)	4·00	80

489 Tribesmen

1986. Pashtunistan Day.

1145	**489**	4a. multicoloured	25	15

490 State Arms

1986. Supreme Council Meeting of Tribal Leaders.

1146	**490**	3a. gold, blue and black	40	25

491 Labourer reading

1986. World Literacy Day.

1147	**491**	2a. multicoloured	25	15

492 Dove and U.N. Emblem

1986. International Peace Year.

1148	**492**	12a. black and blue	60	25

493 Tulips, Flame and Man with Rifle

1986. Afghanistan Youth Day.

1149	**493**	3a. red and black	40	25

494 Crowd and Flags

1987. Ninth Anniv of Sawr Revolution.

1150	**494**	3a. multicoloured	25	15

495 Map and Dove

1987. National Reconciliation.

1151	**495**	3a. multicoloured	25	15

496 Oral Rehydration

1987. International Children's Day. Multicoloured.

1152	1a. Type **496**	15	10
1153	5a. Weighing babies	15	10
1154	9a. Vaccinating babies	35	15

497 Conference Delegates

1987. First Anniv of Tribal Conference.

1155	**497**	5a. multicoloured	35	25

498 *Pieris* sp.

1987. Butterflies and Moths. Multicoloured.

1156	7a. Type **498**	60	35
1157	9a. Brimstone and unidentified butterfly	75	35
1158	10a. Garden tiger moth (horiz)	1·00	50
1159	12a. *Parnassius* sp.	1·40	50
1160	15a. Butterfly (unidentified) (horiz)	1·50	65
1161	22a. Butterfly (unidentified) (horiz)	2·10	90
1162	25a. Butterfly (unidentified)	2·50	90

499 People on Hand

1987. First Local Government Elections.

1163	**499**	1a. multicoloured	25	15

500 Khan Abdul Ghaffar Khan

1987. Pashtun and Baluch Day.

1164	**500**	4a. multicoloured	25	15

501 "Sputnik 1"

1987. 30th Anniv of Launch of *Sputnik* (first artificial satellite). Multicoloured.

1165	10a. Type **501**	40	15
1166	15a. Rocket launch	60	15
1167	25a. "Soyuz"–"Salyut" space complex	80	15

502 Old and Modern Post Offices

1987. World U.P.U. Day.

1168	**502**	22a. multicoloured	1·10	60

503 Monument and Arch of Paghman

1987. Independence Day.

1169	**503**	3a. multicoloured	25	15

504 "Communications"

1987. United Nations Day.

1170	**504**	42a. multicoloured	4·50	1·00

505 Lenin

1987. 70th Anniv of Russian Revolution.

1171	**505**	25a. multicoloured	1·20	65

506 Castor Oil Plant

1987. Plants. Multicoloured.

1172	3a. Type **506**	15	15
1173	6a. Liquorice	35	15
1174	9a. Camomile	60	15
1175	14a. Thorn apple	80	15
1176	18a. Chicory	1·00	15

507 Field Mice

1987. Mice. Multicoloured.

1177	2a. Type **507**	40	15
1178	4a. Brown and white mice (horiz)	50	15
1179	8a. Ginger mice (horiz)	60	15
1180	16a. Black mice (horiz)	1·00	15
1181	20a. Spotted and ginger mice (horiz)	1·20	15

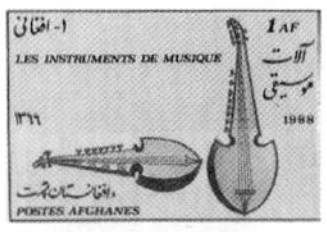

508 Four-stringed Instrument

1988. Musical Instruments. Multicoloured.

1182	1a. Type **508**	15	15
1183	3a. Drums	15	15
1184	5a. Two-stringed instruments with two pegs	25	15
1185	15a. Two-stringed instrument with ten pegs	60	15
1186	18a. Two-stringed instruments with fourteen or ten pegs	80	25
1187	25a. Four-stringed bowed instruments	1·20	25
1188	33a. Two-stringed bowed instruments	1·60	25

509 Mixed Arrangement

1988. Flowers. Multicoloured.

1189	3a. Type **509**	25	15
1190	5a. Tulips (horiz)	35	15
1191	7a. Mallows	50	25
1192	9a. Small mauve flowers	65	25
1193	12a. Marguerites	1·20	35
1194	15a. White flowers	1·50	35
1195	24a. Red and blue flowers (horiz)	2·10	35

510 Emblems and Means of Communication

1988. 60th Anniv of Membership of U.P.U. and I.T.U.

1196	**510**	20a. multicoloured	80	50

511 Tank Monument, Kabul, and Flags

1988. Tenth Anniv of Sawr Revolution.

1197	**511**	10a. multicoloured	80	50

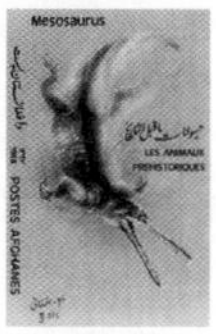

512 Mesosaurus

1988. Prehistoric Animals. Multicoloured.

1198	3a. Type **512**	15	10
1199	5a. Styracosaurus (horiz)	25	10
1200	10a. Uintatherium (horiz)	50	15
1201	15a. Protoceratops (horiz)	75	15
1202	20a. Stegosaurus (horiz)	1·00	25
1203	25a. Ceratosaurus	1·30	25
1204	30a. Moa ("Dinornis maximus")	1·80	25

513 Baskets and Bowl of Fruit

1988. Fruit. Multicoloured.

1205	2a. Type **513**	25	15
1206	4a. Baskets of fruit	35	15
1207	7a. Large basket of fruit	35	25
1208	8a. Bunch of grapes on branch (vert)	50	25
1209	16a. Buying fruit from market stall	80	35
1210	22a. Arranging fruit on market stall	1·20	35
1211	25a. Stallholder weighing fruit (vert)	1·80	35

514 Memorial Pillar of Knowledge and Ignorance, Kabul

1988. Independence Day.

1212	**514**	24a. multicoloured	1·20	65

515 Heads encircled with Rope

1988. Pashtunistan Day.

1213	**515**	23a. multicoloured	90	60

516 Flags and Globe

1988. Afghan–Soviet Space Flight.

1214	**516**	32a. multicoloured	1·20	50

517 Anniversary Emblem

1988. 125th Anniv of International Red Cross.

1215	**517**	10a. multicoloured	80	50

518 Rocket and V. Tereshkova

1988. 25th Anniv of First Woman Cosmonaut Valentina Tereshkova's Space Flight. Multicoloured

1216	10a. Type **518**	80	35
1217	15a. Bird, globe and rocket (vert)	65	15
1218	25a. "Vostok 6" and globe	1·00	15

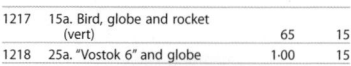

519 Decorated Metal Vessels

1988. Traditional Crafts. Multicoloured.

1219	2a. Type **519**	10	10
1220	4a. Pottery	15	10
1221	5a. Clothing (vert)	25	15
1222	9a. Carpets	35	15
1223	15a. Bags	35	25
1224	23a. Jewellery	90	25
1225	50a. Furniture	1·80	25

520 Indian Flag and Nehru

1988. Birth Centenary of Jawaharlal Nehru (Indian statesman).

1226	**520**	40a. multicoloured	2·10	80

521 Emeralds

1988. Gemstones. Multicoloured.

1227	13a. Type **521**	80	15
1228	37a. Lapis lazuli	1·80	35
1229	40a. Rubies	2·30	35

522 Ice Skating

1988. Winter Olympic Games, Calgary. Multicoloured

1230	2a. Type **522**	15	15
1231	5a. Slalom	25	15
1232	9a. Two-man bobsleigh	50	15
1233	22a. Biathlon	90	15
1234	37a. Speed skating	1·90	15
MS1235	80×60 mm. 75a. Ice hockey	4·00	80

523 Old City

1988. International Campaign for Preservation of Old Sana'a, Yemen.

1236	**523**	32a. multicoloured	1·50	1·10

524 Emblem

1989. Second Anniv of Move for National Reconciliation.

1237	**524**	4a. multicoloured	25	15

525 Bishop and Game from "The Three Ages of Man" (attr. Estienne Porchier)

1989. Chess. Multicoloured.

1238	2a. Type **525**	25	15
1239	3a. Faience queen and 14th century drawing of Margrave Otto IV of Brandenburg and his wife playing chess	35	15
1240	4a. French king and game	40	15
1241	7a. King and game	65	25
1242	16a. Knight and game	1·10	25
1243	24a. Arabian knight and "Great Chess"	1·50	35
1244	45a. Bishop and teaching of game	2·75	40

Nos. 1240/4 show illustrations from King Alfonso X's *Book of Chess, Dice and Tablings*.

526 *The Old Jew*

1989. Picasso Paintings. Multicoloured.

1245	4a. Type **526**	35	25
1246	6a. *The Two Harlequins*	40	25
1247	8a. *Portrait of Ambrouse Vollar*	50	25
1248	22a. *Majorcan Woman*	1·20	25
1249	35a. *Acrobat on Ball*	2·30	25
MS1250	70×90 mm. 75a. *Horta de Ebro Factory*. Imperf	4·00	80

527 Euphrates Jerboa

1989. Animals. Multicoloured.

1251	3a. Type **527**	35	25
1252	4a. Asiatic wild ass	35	25
1253	14a. Lynx	1·00	35
1254	35a. Lammergeier	3·50	1·50
1255	44a. Markhor	2·30	1·20
MS1256	70×90 mm. 100a. Oxus cobra	4·50	1·20

528 Bomb breaking, Dove and Woman holding Wheat

1989. International Women's Day (1988).

1257	**528**	8a. multicoloured	40	15

529 Cattle

1989. Farmers' Day. Multicoloured.

1258	1a. Type **529**	25	15
1259	2a. Ploughing with oxen and tractors	25	15
1260	3a. Picking cotton	25	15

530 Dish Aerial

1989. World Meteorology Day. Multicoloured.

1261	27a. Type **530**	1·20	25
1262	32a. World Meteorological Organization emblem and state arms	1·60	25
1263	40a. Data-collecting equipment (vert)	2·10	25

531 Rejoicing Crowd

1989. 11th Anniv of Sawr Revolution.

1264	**531**	20a. multicoloured	1·10	25

532 Outdoor Class

1989. Teachers' Day.

1265	**532**	42a. multicoloured	2·10	35

533 Eiffel Tower and Arc de Triomphe

1989. Bicentenary of French Revolution.

1266	**533**	25a. multicoloured	1·50	90

534 Transmission Mast

1989. Tenth Anniv of Asia-Pacific Telecommunity.

1267	3a. Type **534**	15	15
1268	27a. Dish aerial	1·10	25

535 National Monuments

1989. Independence Day.

1269	**535**	25a. multicoloured	1·20	35

536 Pashtu

1989. Pashtunistan Day.

1270	**536**	3a. multicoloured	35	25

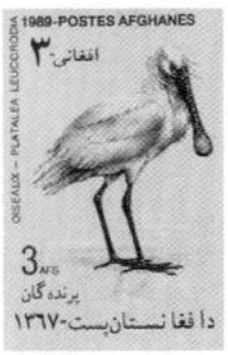

537 White Spoonbill

1989. Birds. Multicoloured.

1271	3a. Type **537**	25	15
1272	5a. Purple swamphen	50	25
1273	10a. Eurasian bittern (horiz)	90	40
1274	15a. Eastern white pelican	1·20	50
1275	20a. Red-crested pochard	1·50	60
1276	25a. Mute swan	2·10	65
1277	30a. Great cormorant (horiz)	2·30	90

538 Duchs Tourer, 1910

1989. Vintage Cars. Multicoloured.

1278	5a. Type **538**	40	25
1279	10a. Ford Model T touring car, 1911	75	25
1280	20a. Renault Type AX two-seater, 1911	1·20	25
1281	25a. Russo-Balte tourer, 1911	1·50	35
1282	30a. Fiat 509 tourer, 1926	1·80	35

It is reported no stamps were issued by the Post Office from 1990—2001 inclusive. Any in circulation for these years are considered spurious.

Nos. 1986/8 and Types **540/2** are left for the issues of 2002, not yet received.

543 Scales

2002. 55th (2003) Anniv of Universal Declaration of Human Rights

1989	4a. multicoloured	1·70	1·70

544 Tractor ploughing

2003. Farmers' Day. Multicoloured.

1990	3a. Type **544**	15·00	15·00
1991	6a. Ploughing with oxen	30·00	20·00

545 *Calanthe veitchii*

2003. Orchids. Multicoloured.

1992	9a. Type **545**	85	85
1993	13a. *Euanthe sanderiana* (inscr 'Eulanthe')	1·20	1·20
1994	17a. *Ordontoglossum vuyl-stekeae* (inscr 'Ordontioda')	1·40	1·40
1995	20a. *Dendrobium infundibulum*	1·50	1·50
1996	30a. *Miltoniopsis roezlii* (inscr 'Miltonsiopsis')	1·70	1·70
1997	40a. *Cattleya labiata*	2·40	2·40
1998	100a *Vanda coerulea*	5·25	5·25

546 Minaret, Mosque and Kaaba,

2003. Birthday of Prophet Mohammed.

1999	**546**	10a. multicoloured	70·00	30·00

547 Children and 'STOP TB'

2003. International Tuberculosis Awareness Day. Multicoloured.

2000	1a. Type **547**	10	10
2001	4a. Treatment (horiz)		
2002	9a. Infection (horiz)	60	25

548 Assembly

2003. First Anniv of Loya Jirga to elect President Hamid Karzai

2003	**548**	20a. multicoloured	1·90	1·90

549 Map enclosing Poppy Head overlaid with Ears of Corn

2003. Struggle Against Narcotics Day. Multicoloured.

2004	1a Type **549**	25	25
2005	2a Poppy head, resin and skulls (vert)	55	55
2006	5a Tractor ploughing in poppies	95	95
MS2006a	106×82 mmm. 10a. Poppy head, resin and skulls (different)	1·90	1·90

550 Rottweiler

2003. Dogs. Multicoloured.

2007	10a. Type **550**	95	95
2008	20a. Cocker spaniel	1·70	1·70
2009	30a. Doberman	1·90	1·90
2010	40a. Afghan hound	2·10	2·10
2011	50a. Giant schnauzer	2·50	2·50
2012	60a. Boxer	2·75	2·75
MS2013	106×82 mmm. 150a. Afghan hound (different)	9·00	9·00

551 Bird Island, South Africa

2003. Lighthouses. Multicoloured.

2014	10a. Type **551**	95	95
2015	20a Cordoun, France	1·90	1·90
2016	30a. Mahota Pagoda, China	2·30	2·30
2017	50a Bay Canh, Vietnam	2·75	2·75
2018	60a. Cap Roman Rock, South Africa	3·00	3·00
2019	100a Mikomoto Shima, Japan	4·75	4·75
MS2020	75×106 mmm. 150a. Bell Rock, UK (inscr 'British Islands')	9·00	9·00

552 Monument and Arch

2003. Independence Day.

2021	**552**	15a. multicoloured	80·00	35·00

553 Dove Outline enclosing Students

2003. International Literacy Day

2022	**553**	2a. multicoloured	15·00	15·00

554 Globe and Dove holding Envelope

2003. World Post Day

2023	**554**	8a. multicoloured	45·00	20·00

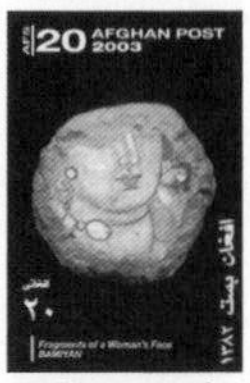

555 Fragment of Woman's Face (fresco), Bamiyan

2003. Cultural Heritage. Multicoloured.

MS2024		20a. Type **555**; 40a. Buddha's head, Gandhara; 60a. Buddha (statue), Takht-i-Bahi Monastery, Gandhara; 100a. Buddha's hand, Bamiyan	6·50	6·50

Nos. 2025/7 are vacant.

556 Quran

2003. Transmission of the Quran

2028	**556**	9a. multicoloured	3·25	3·25

557 Statue

2003. World Tourism Day. Historical Artefacts. Multicoloured.

2029	4a. Type **557**	25·00	10·00
2030	8a. Hill fort	45·00	20·00
2030a	12a. Pot, coins and inscribed tablets	70·00	30·00
MS2030b	108×82 mm. 25a. Hill fort (detail)	1·20	1·20

557a Leopard

2003. Animals. Multicoloured.

2030c	6c. Type **557a**	10·00	10·00
2030d	11a. Jackal	65·00	30·00
2030e	15a. Asiatic ibex	80·00	35·00
MS2030f	107×83 mm. 40s. Leopard (different)	6·25	6·25

558 Woman holding Book and Flame

2004. International Women's Day.

2031	**558**	6a. multicoloured	35·00	20·00

559 Woman, Pills and Blood-stained Hankerchief

2004. World TB Awareness Day. Multicoloured.

2032	1a. Type **559**	35	35
2033	4a. Woman wearing mask and child	50	50
2034	9a. Raising awareness	85	85
2035	12a. TB sufferer and pills (vert)	1·20	1·20
2036	15a. Doctor examining patient (vert)	1·40	1·40

560 President Karzai

2004. Inauguration of President Hamid Karzai. Multicoloured.

2037	12a. Type **560**	1·50	1·50
MS2038	150×82 mm. 100a. As Type **560** (50×50 mm)	9·25	9·25

561 Voters

2004. First Direct Presidential Elections.

2039	**561**	15a. multicoloured	85·00	40·00
2040	-	25a. multicoloured	1·20	55·00

No. 2041 and Type **562** are left for Inauguration of President, Issued on 7 December 2004, not yet received.

563 Clasped Hands and Symbols of Afghanistan and China

2005. 50th Anniv of Afghanistan–China Diplomatic Relations.

2042	**563**	25a. multicoloured	1·20	55·00
MS2042a		134×93 mm. Size 60×40 mm. 150a. As Type **563**	6·50	6·50

No. **MS**2042 was printed on silk coated paper.

565 Crowd

2006. 87th Anniv of Independence Day.

2046	**565**	45a. multicoloured	2·20	95·00

566 Classroom

2006. World Literacy Day.

2047	**566**	12a. multicoloured	70·00	30·00

567 Dove enclosing Globe

2006. World Post Day. Multicoloured.

2048	15a. Type **567**	85·00	40·00
2049	15a. As Type **567** but with inscription and colour of date changed	85·00	40·00

567a Flags of Members

2006. Third Meeting of ECO Postal Authorities.

2049a	**567a**	8a. multicoloured	45·00	20·00

569 Rumi, Dancers and Rûm (image scaled to 41% of original size)

2007. 800th Birth Anniv Mawlana Jalaluddin Mohammad al-Balkhi al-Rum (spiritual master and mystic poet). Sheet 116×78 mm

MS2053	**569**	150a. multicoloured		

570 Dancers

2007. Aten Milli, National Dance

2054	**570**	38a. multicoloured	3·00	3·00

No. 2054 carries the imprint date '2006'.

571 Ustad Awal Mir (master singer)

2007. National Day of Fine Arts. Multicoloured.

2055	20a. Type **571**	1·00	50·00
2056	22a. Mirmum Parwin (first female singer of Afghanistan)	1·10	50·00

NEWSPAPER STAMPS

N35

1928. Newspaper Stamps

N192	**N35**	2p. blue	4·00	4·50

1929. Newspaper Stamps

N205A	2p. red	30	50

N43

1932. Newspaper Stamps

N215	**N43**	2p. red	40	50
N216	**N43**	2p. black	35	80
N217	**N43**	2p. green	40	75
N219	**N43**	2p. red	50	75

N75 Coat-of-Arms

1939. Arms

N259	**N75**	2p. green	25	65
N260	**N75**	2p. mauve (no gum)	15	1·00

1969. As Type N **75**, but larger and with different Pushtu inscr.

N652	100p. green	25	25
N653	150p. brown	35	25

OFFICIAL STAMPS

O27

1909

O173	**O27**	(-) red	1·20	1·20

1939. Design 22¼×28 mm.

O281	**O86**	15p. green	1·10	80
O282	**O86**	30p. brown	1·50	1·50
O283	**O86**	45p. red	1·20	1·20
O284	**O86**	1a. mauve	2·00	1·80

O86

1954. Design 24½×31 mm.

O285b	50p. red	1·00	50

1965. Design 24×30½ mm.

O287	50p. pink	1·20	50

PARCEL POST STAMPS

P27

1909

P173	**P27**	3s. brown	1·20	2·10
P174	**P27**	3s. green	1·80	3·50
P175	**P27**	1k. green	2·10	3·50
P176	**P27**	1k. red	3·00	1·50
P177	**P27**	1r. orange	6·50	2·00
P178	**P27**	1r. grey	30·00	
P179	**P27**	1r. brown	3·50	3·50
P180	**P27**	2r. red	4·00	4·00
P181	**P27**	2r. blue	6·25	6·50

P28 Old Habibia College, Kabul

1921

P182	**P28**	10p. brown	4·00	5·75
P183	**P28**	15p. brown	5·75	6·50
P184	**P28**	30p. purple	10·50	6·50
P185	**P28**	1r. blue	12·50	12·50

1923. Fifth Independence Day. Optd with T **28**.

P186	10p. brown	90·00	
P187	15p. brown	£100	
P188	30p. purple	£200	

P35

P36

1928

P192	**P35**	2a. orange	6·50	5·00
P193	**P36**	3a. green	10·50	10·50

1930

P214	**P35**	2a. green	7·50	7·50
P215	**P36**	3a. brown	9·00	10·50

REGISTRATION STAMP

R19

1894. Undated.

R155	**R19**	2a. black on green	9·75	11·50

APPENDIX

The following stamps have either been issued in excess of postal needs or have not been available to the public in reasonable quantities at face value. Such stamps may later be given full listing if there is evidence of regular postal use. Sheets, imperforate stamps etc, are excluded from this section.

1961

Agriculture Day. Fauna and Flora. 2, 2, 5, 10, 15, 25, 50, 100, 150, 175p.
Child Welfare. Sports and Games. 2, 2, 5, 10, 15, 25, 50, 100, 150, 175p.
UNICEF Surch on 1961 Child Welfare issue. 2+25, 2+25, 5+25, 10+25, 15p.+25p.
Women's Day. 50, 175p.
Independence Day. Mohamed Nadir Shah. 50, 175p.
International Exhibition, Kabul. 50, 175p.
Pashtunistan Day. 50, 175p.
National Assembly. 50, 175p.
Anti-malaria Campaign. 50, 175p.

King's 47th Birthday. 50, 175p.
Red Crescent Day. Fruits. 2, 2, 5, 10, 15, 25, 50, 100, 150, 175p.
Afghan Red Crescent Fund. 1961 Red Crescent Day issue surch 2+25, 2+25, 5+25, 10+25, 15p.+25p.
United Nations Day. 1, 2, 3, 4, 50, 75, 175p.
Teachers' Day. Flowers and Educational Scenes. 2, 2, 5, 10, 15, 25, 50, 100, 150, 175p.
UNESCO 1961 Teachers' Day issue surch 2+25, 2+25, 5+25, 10+25, 15p.+25p.

1962

15th Anniv (1961) of UNESCO 2, 2, 5, 10, 15, 25, 50, 75, 100p.
Ahmed Shah Baba. 50, 75, 100p.
Agriculture Day. Animals and Products. 2, 2, 5, 10, 15, 25, 50, 75, 100, 125p.
Independence Day. Marching Athletes. 25, 50, 150p.
Women's Day. Postage 25, 50p.; Air 100, 175p.
Pashtunistan Day. 25, 50, 150p.
Malaria Eradication. 2, 2, 5, 10, 15, 25, 50, 75, 100, 150, 175p.
National Assembly. 25, 50, 75, 100, 125p.
4th Asian Games, Djakarta, Indonesia. Postage 1, 2, 3, 4, 5p.; Air 25, 50, 75, 100, 150, 175p.
Children's Day. Sports and Produce. Postage 1, 2, 3, 4, 5p.; Air 75, 150, 200p.
King's 48th Birthday. 25, 50, 75, 100p.
Red Crescent Day. Fruits and Flowers. Postage 1, 2, 3, 4, 5p.; Air 25, 50, 100p.
Boy Scouts' Day. Postage 1, 2, 3, 4p.; Air 25, 50, 75, 100p.
1st Anniv of Hammarskjold's Death. Surch on 1961 UNESCO issue. 2+20, 2+20, 5+20, 10+20, 15+20, 25+20, 50+20, 75+20, 100p.+20p.
United Nations Day. Postage 1, 2, 3, 4, 5p.; Air 75, 100, 125p.
Teachers' Day. Sport and Flowers. Postage 1, 2, 3, 4, 5p.; Air 100, 150p.
World Meteorological Day. 50, 100p.

1963

Famous Afghans Pantheon, Kabul. 50, 75, 100p.
Agriculture Day. Sheep and Silkworms. Postage 1, 2, 3, 4, 5p.; Air 100, 150, 200p.
Freedom from Hunger. Postage 2, 3, 300p.; Air 500p.
Malaria Eradication Fund. 1962 Malaria Eradication issue surch 2+15, 2+15, 5+15, 10+15, 15+15, 25+15, 50+15, 75+15, 100+15, 150+15, 175p.+15p.
World Meteorological Day. Postage 1, 2, 3, 4, 5p.; Air 200, 300, 400, 500p.
"GANEFO" Athletic Games, Djakarta, Indonesia. Postage 2, 3, 4, 5, 10p., 9a.; Air 300, 500p.
Red Cross Centenary Postage 2, 3, 4, 5, 10p.; Air 100, 200p., 4, 6a.
Nubian Monuments Preservation. Postage 100, 200, 500p.; Air 5a., 7a.50.

1964

Women's Day (1963). 2, 3, 4, 5, 10p.
Afghan Boy Scouts and Girl Guides. Postage 2, 3, 4, 5, 10p.; Air 2, 2, 2a.50, 3, 4, 5, 12a.
Child Welfare Day (1963). Sports and Games. Postage 2, 3, 4, 5, 10p.; Air 200, 300p.
Afghan Red Crescent Society. Postage 100, 200p.; Air 5a., 7a.50.
Teachers' Day (1963). Flowers. Postage 2, 3, 4, 5, 10p.; Air 3a., 3a.50.
United Nations Day (1963). Postage 2, 3, 4, 5, 10p.; Air 100p., 2, 3a.
15th Anniv of Human Rights Declaration. Surch on 1964 United Nations Day issue. Postage 2+50, 3+50, 4+50, 5+50, 10p.+50p.; Air 100p.+50p., 2a.+50p., 3a.+50p.
UNICEF (dated 1963). Postage 100, 200p.; Air 5a. 7a.50.
Malaria Eradication (dated 1963). Postage 2, 3, 4, 5p., 10p. on 4p.; Air 2, 10a.

2004

Deer. 80a.; 115a; 100a.

Pt. 1

AITUTAKI

Island in the South Pacific.

1903. 12 pence = 1 shilling; 20 shillings = 1 pound.
1967. 100 cents = 1 dollar.

A. NEW ZEALAND DEPENDENCY

The British Government, who had exercised a protectorate over the Cook Islands group since the 1880s, handed the islands, including Aitutaki, to New Zealand administration in 1901. Cook Islands stamps were used from 1932 to 1972.

1903. Pictorial stamps of New Zealand surch **AITUTAKI** and value in native language.

1	**23**	½d. green	4·75	6·50
2	**42**	1d. red	5·00	5·50
4	**26**	2½d. blue	15·00	12·00
5	**28**	3d. brown	18·00	15·00
6	**31**	6d. red	30·00	25·00
7	**34**	1s. orange	55·00	85·00

1911. King Edward VII stamps of New Zealand surch **AITUTAKI** and value in native language.

9	**51**	½d. green	1·00	7·00
10	**53**	1d. red	3·00	13·00
11	**51**	6d. red	50·00	£140
12	**51**	1s. orange	60·00	£150

1916. King George V stamps of New Zealand surch **AITUTAKI** and value in native language.

13a	**62**	6d. red	7·50	27·00
14	**62**	1s. orange	10·00	90·00

1917. King George V stamps of New Zealand optd **AITUTAKI**.

19		½d. green	1·00	6·00
20	**53**	1d. red	4·25	32·00
21	**62**	1½d. grey	3·75	30·00
22	**62**	1½d. brown	80	7·00
15a		2½d. blue	1·75	16·00
16a		3d. brown	1·50	28·00
17a		6d. red	4·75	21·00
18a		1s. orange	12·00	32·00

1920. As 1920 pictorial stamps of Cook Islands but inscr "AITUTAKI".

30	½d. black and green	2·00	21·00
31	1d. black and red	6·00	9·50
26	1½d. black and brown	6·00	12·00
32	2½d. black and blue	7·50	75·00
27	3d. black and blue	2·50	14·00
28	6d. brown and grey	5·50	14·00
29	1s. black and purple	9·50	16·00

B. PART OF COOK ISLANDS

On 9 August 1972 Aitutaki became a Port of Entry into the Cook Islands. Whilst remaining part of the Cook Islands, Aitutaki has a separate postal service.

1972. Nos. 227/8, 230, 233/4, 238, 240/1, 243 and 244 of Cook Islands optd **Aitutaki**.

33	**79**	½c. multicoloured	30	80
34	-	1c. multicoloured	70	1·40
35	-	2½c. multicoloured	2·25	7·00
36	-	4c. multicoloured	70	85
37	-	5c. multicoloured	2·50	7·50
38	-	10c. multicoloured	2·50	5·50
39	-	20c. multicoloured	3·75	1·00
40	-	25c. multicoloured	70	1·00
41	-	50c. multicoloured	2·75	2·75
42	-	$1 multicoloured	4·00	5·50

1972. Christmas. Nos. 406/8 of Cook Islands optd **Aitutaki**.

43	**130**	1c. multicoloured	10	10
44	-	5c. multicoloured	15	15
45	-	10c. multicoloured	15	25

1972. Royal Silver Wedding. As Nos. 413 and 415 of Cook Islands, but inscr "COOK ISLANDS Aitutaki".

46	**131**	5c. black and silver	2·75	2·25
47	-	15c. black and silver	1·25	1·25

1972. No. 245 of Cook Islands optd **AITUTAKI**.

48	$2 multicoloured	50	75

1972. Nos. 227/8, 230, 233, 234, 238, 240, 241, 243 and 244 of Cook Islands optd **AITUTAKI** within ornamental oval.

49	**79**	½c. multicoloured	15	10
50	-	1c. multicoloured	15	10
51	-	2½c. multicoloured	20	10
52	-	4c. multicoloured	25	15
53	-	5c. multicoloured	25	15
54	-	10c. multicoloured	35	25
55	-	20c. multicoloured	1·25	50
56	-	25c. multicoloured	50	55
57	-	50c. multicoloured	75	90
58	-	$1 multicoloured	1·25	1·75

13 *Christ Mocked* (Grunewald)

1973. Easter. Multicoloured.

59	1c. Type **13**	15	10
60	1c. *St. Veronica* (Van der Weyden)	15	10
61	1c. *The Crucified Christ with Virgin Mary, Saints and Angels* (Raphael)	15	10
62	1c. *Resurrection* (Piero della Francesca)	15	10
63	5c. *The Last Supper* (Master of Amiens)	20	15
64	5c. *Condemnation* (Holbein)	20	15
65	5c. *Christ on the Cross* (Rubens)	20	15
66	5c. *Resurrection* (El Greco)	20	15
67	10c. *Disrobing of Christ* (El Greco)	25	15
68	10c. *St. Veronica* (Van Oostsanen)	25	15
69	10c. *Christ on the Cross* (Rubens)	25	15
70	10c. *Resurrection* (Bouts)	25	15

1973. Silver Wedding Coinage. Nos. 417/23 of Cook Islands optd **AITUTAKI**.

71	**132**	1c. black, red and gold	10	10
72	-	2c. black, blue and gold	10	10
73	-	5c. black, green and silver	15	10
74	-	10c. black, blue and silver	20	10
75	-	20c. black, green and silver	30	15
76	-	50c. black, red and silver	50	30
77	-	$1 black, blue and silver	70	45

1973. Tenth Anniv of Treaty Banning Nuclear Testing. Nos. 236, 238, 240 and 243 of Cook Islands optd **AITUTAKI** within ornamental oval and **TENTH ANNIVERSARY CESSATION OF NUCLEAR TESTING TREATY**.

78	8c. multicoloured	15	15
79	10c. multicoloured	15	15
80	20c. multicoloured	30	20
81	50c. multicoloured	70	50

16 Red Hibiscus and Princess Anne

1973. Royal Wedding. Multicoloured.

82	25c. Type **16**	25	10
83	30c. Capt. Mark Phillips and blue hibiscus	25	10
MS84	114×65 mm. Nos. 82/3	50	40

17 "Virgin and Child" (Montagna)

1973. Christmas. "Virgin and Child" paintings by artists listed below. Multicoloured.

85	1c. Type **17**	10	10
86	1c. Crivelli	10	10
87	1c. Van Dyck	10	10
88	1c. Perugino	10	10
89	5c. Veronese (child at shoulder)	25	10
90	5c. Veronese (child on lap)	25	10
91	5c. Cima	25	10
92	5c. Memling	25	10
93	10c. Memling	25	10
94	10c. Del Colle	25	10
95	10c. Raphael	25	10
96	10c. Lotto	25	10

18 Rose-branch Murex

1974. Sea Shells. Multicoloured.

97	½c. Type **18**	90	1·00
98	1c. New Caledonia nautilus	90	1·00
99	2c. Common or major harp	90	1·00
100	3c. Striped bonnet	90	1·00
101	4c. Mole cowrie	90	1·00
102	5c. Pontifical mitre	90	1·00
103	8c. Trumpet triton	90	1·00
104	10c. Venus comb murex	90	80
105	20c. Red-mouth olive	1·25	80
106	25c. Ruddy frog shell	1·25	80
107	60c. Widest pacific conch	4·00	1·25
108	$1 Maple-leaf triton or winged frog shell	2·50	1·40
109	$2 Queen Elizabeth II and Marlin-spike auger	6·00	9·00
110	$5 Queen Elizabeth II and Tiger cowrie	32·00	10·00

The $2 and $5 are larger, 53×25 mm.

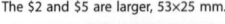

19 Bligh and H.M.S. *Bounty*

1974. William Bligh's Discovery of Aitutaki. Multicoloured.

114	1c. Type **19**	60	60
115	1c. H.M.S. *Bounty*	60	60
116	5c. Bligh, and H.M.S. *Bounty* at Aitutaki	1·00	1·00
117	5c. Aitutaki chart of 1856	1·00	1·00
118	8c. Captain Cook and H.M.S. *Resolution*	1·40	1·40
119	8c. Map of Aitutaki and inset location map	1·40	1·40

See also Nos. 123/8.

20 Aitutaki Stamps of 1903, Sand Map

1974. Centenary of U.P.U. Multicoloured.

120	25c. Type **20**	75	50
121	50c. Stamps of 1903 and 1920, and map	1·00	75
MS122	66×75 mm. Nos. 120/1	1·25	2·75

1974. Air. As Nos. 114/119 in larger size (46×26 mm), additionally inscr "AIR MAIL".

123	10c. Type **19**	70	65
124	10c. H.M.S. *Bounty*	70	65
125	25c. Bligh, and H.M.S. *Bounty* at Aitutaki	80	75
126	25c. Aitutaki chart of 1856	80	75
127	30c. Captain Cook and H.M.S. *Resolution*	90	85
128	30c. Map of Aitutaki and inset location map	90	85

21 *Virgin and Child* (Hugo van der Goes)

1974. Christmas. "Virgin and Child" paintings by artists named. Multicoloured.

129	1c. Type **21**	10	15
130	5c. Bellini	10	20
131	8c. Gerard David	10	20
132	10c. Antonello da Messina	10	15
133	25c. Joos van Cleve	20	30
134	30c. Master of the Life of St. Catherine	20	30
MS135	127×134 mm. Nos. 129/34	1·40	1·75

22 Churchill as Schoolboy

1974. Birth Centenary of Sir Winston Churchill. Multicoloured.

136	10c. Type **22**	20	25
137	25c. Churchill as young man	25	40
138	30c. Churchill with troops	25	45
139	50c. Churchill painting	30	60
140	$1 Giving "V" sign	40	75
MS141	115×108 mm. Nos. 136/40	1·25	1·50

1974. Children's Christmas Fund. Nos. 129/34 surch.

142	**21**	1c.+1c. multicoloured	10	10
143	-	5c.+1c. multicoloured	10	10
144	-	8c.+1c. multicoloured	10	10
145	-	10c.+1c. multicoloured	10	10
146	-	25c.+1c. multicoloured	20	20
147	-	30c.+1c. multicoloured	20	20

24 Soviet and U.S. Flags

1975. "Apollo–Soyuz" Space Project. Multicoloured.

148	25c. Type **24**	30	20
149	50c. Daedalus with space capsule	40	30
MS150	123×61 mm. Nos. 148/9	1·25	1·10

25 St. Francis

1975. Christmas. Multicoloured.

151	6c. Type **25**	10	10
152	6c. Madonna and Child	10	10
153	6c. St. John	10	10
154	7c. King and donkey	10	10
155	7c. Madonna, Child and King	10	10
156	7c. Kings with gifts	10	10
157	15c. Madonna and Child	15	15
158	15c. St. Onufrius	15	15
159	15c. John the Baptist	15	15
160	20c. Shepherd and cattle	20	15
161	20c. Madonna and Child	20	15
162	20c. Shepherds	20	15
MS163	104×201 mm. Nos. 151/62	2·25	2·50

Stamps of the same value were printed together, *se-tenant*, each strip forming a composite design of a complete painting as follows: Nos. 151/3, *Madonna and Child with Saints Francis and John* (Lorenzetti); 154/6, *Adoration of the Kings* (Van der Weyden); 157/9, *Madonna and Child Enthroneth with Saints Onufrius and John the Baptist* (Montagna); 160/2, *Adoration of the Shepherds* (Reni).

1975. Children's Christmas Fund. Nos. 151/62 surch.

164	**25**	6c.+1c. multicoloured	10	10
165	-	6c.+1c. multicoloured	10	10
166	-	6c.+1c. multicoloured	10	10
167	-	7c.+1c. multicoloured	10	10
168	-	7c.+1c. multicoloured	10	10
169	-	7c.+1c. multicoloured	10	10
170	-	15c.+1c. multicoloured	15	15
171	-	15c.+1c. multicoloured	15	15
172	-	15c.+1c. multicoloured	15	15
173	-	20c.+1c. multicoloured	20	20
174	-	20c.+1c. multicoloured	20	20
175	-	20c.+1c. multicoloured	20	20

26 *The Descent* (detail, 15th-century Flemish School)

1976. Easter. Multicoloured.

176	15c. Type **26**	15	10
177	30c. "The Descent" (detail)	20	15
178	35c. "The Descent" (detail)	25	20
MS179	87×67 mm. Nos. 176/8 forming a complete picture of "The Descent"	1·00	1·25

27 Left Detail

1976. Bicentenary of American Revolution. Paintings by John Turnbull.

180	**27**	30c. multicoloured	20	10
181	-	30c. multicoloured	20	10
182	-	30c. multicoloured	20	10
183	-	35c. multicoloured	20	15
184	-	35c. multicoloured	20	15
185	-	35c. multicoloured	20	15
186	-	50c. multicoloured	20	15
187	-	50c. multicoloured	20	15
188	-	50c. multicoloured	20	15
MS189		132×120 mm. Nos. 180/8	1·75	1·10

PAINTINGS: Nos. 180/2, *The Declaration of Independence*; 183/5, *The Surrender of Lord Cornwallis at Yorktown*; 186/8, *The Resignation of General Washington*.

Stamps of the same value were printed together, *se-tenant*, each strip forming a composite design of the whole painting.

28 Cycling

1976. Olympic Games, Montreal. Multicoloured.

190	15c. Type **28**	80	15
191	35c. Sailing	45	20
192	60c. Hockey	1·00	25
193	70c. Sprinting	70	30
MS194	107×97 mm. Nos. 190/3	2·50	1·25

1976. Royal Visit to the U.S.A. Nos. 190/3 optd **VISIT ROYAL JULY 1976**.

195	**28**	15c. multicoloured	50	15
196	-	35c. multicoloured	45	25
197	-	60c. multicoloured	80	40
198	-	70c. multicoloured	70	45
MS199		107×97 mm. Nos. 195/8	2·00	1·25

30 "The Visitation"

1976. Christmas.

200	**30**	6c. gold and green	10	10
201	-	6c. gold and green	10	10
202	-	7c. gold and purple	10	10
203	-	7c. gold and purple	10	10
204	-	15c. gold and blue	10	10
205	-	15c. gold and blue	10	10
206	-	20c. gold and violet	15	15
207	-	20c. gold and violet	15	15
MS208		128×96 mm. As Nos. 200/7 but with borders on three sides	1·00	1·40

DESIGNS: No. 201, Angel; 202, Angel; 203, Shepherds; 204, Joseph; 205, Mary and the Child; 206, Wise Man; 207, Two Wise Men.

Stamps of the same value were printed together, *se-tenant*, each pair forming a composite design.

1976. Children's Christmas Fund. Nos. 200/7 surch.

209	**30**	6c.+1c. gold and green	10	10
210	-	6c.+1c. gold and green	10	10
211	-	7c.+1c. gold and purple	10	10
212	-	7c.+1c. gold and purple	10	10
213	-	15c.+1c. gold and blue	15	15
214	-	15c.+1c. gold and blue	15	15
215	-	20c.+1c. gold and violet	15	15
216	-	20c.+1c. gold and violet	15	15
MS217		128×96 mm. As Nos. 209/16 but with a premium of "+2c." and borders on three sides	80	1·40

32 Alexander Graham Bell and First Telephone

1977. Centenary (1976) of Telephone.

218	**32**	25c. black, gold and red	20	15
219	-	70c. black, gold and lilac	40	40
MS220		116×59 mm. As Nos. 218/19 but with different colours	70	1·00

DESIGN: 70c. Satellite and Earth station.

33 *Christ on the Cross* (detail)

1977. Easter. 400th Birth Anniv of Rubens. Multicoloured.

221	15c. Type **33**	45	15
222	20c. *Lamentation for Christ*	60	20
223	35c. *Christ with Straw*	75	25
MS224	115×57 mm. Nos. 221/3	1·60	1·60

34 Captain Bligh, George III and H.M.S. "Bounty"

1977. Silver Jubilee. Multicoloured.

225	25c. Type **34**	35	35
226	35c. Rev. Williams, George IV and Aitutaki Church	40	40
227	50c. Union Jack, Queen Victoria and island map	45	45
228	$1 Balcony scene, 1953	50	50
MS229	130×87 mm. As Nos. 225/8 but with gold borders	1·25	1·25

35 The Shepherds

1977. Christmas. Multicoloured.

230	6c. Type **35**	10	10
231	6c. Angel	10	10
232	7c. Mary, Jesus and ox	10	10
233	7c. Joseph and donkey	10	10
234	15c. Three Kings	10	10
235	15c. Virgin and Child	10	10
236	20c. Joseph	10	10
237	20c. Mary and Jesus on donkey	10	10
MS238	130×95 mm. Nos. 230/7	70	1·25

Stamps of the same value were printed together, *se-tenant*, forming composite designs.

1977. Children's Christmas Fund. Nos. 230/7 surch **+1c**.

239	6c.+1c. Type **35**	10	10
240	6c.+1c. Angel	10	10
241	7c.+1c. Mary, Jesus and ox	10	10
242	7c.+1c. Joseph and donkey	10	10
243	15c.+1c. Three Kings	15	10
244	15c.+1c. Virgin and Child	15	10
245	20c.+1c. Joseph	15	10
246	20c.+1c. Mary and Jesus on donkey	15	10
MS247	130×95 mm. As Nos. 239/46 but each with premium of "+2c."	70	85

37 Hawaiian Goddess

1978. Bicentenary of Discovery of Hawaii. Multicoloured.

248	35c. Type **37**	35	25
249	50c. Figurehead of H.M.S. "Resolution" (horiz)	60	40
250	$1 Hawaiian temple figure	70	70
MS251	168×75 mm. Nos. 248/50	1·50	1·75

38 *Christ on the Way to Calvary* (Martini)

1978. Easter. Paintings from the Louvre, Paris. Multicoloured.

252	15c. Type **38**	15	10
253	20c. *Pieta of Avignon* (E. Quarton)	20	10
254	35c. *The Pilgrims at Emmaus* (Rembrandt)	25	10
MS255	108×83 mm. Nos. 252/4	75	75

1978. Easter. Children's Charity. Designs as Nos. 252/4, but smaller (34×26 mm) and without margins, in separate miniature sheets 75×58 mm, each with a face value of 50c. + 5c.

MS256	As Nos. 252/4 Set of 3 sheets	1·00	1·00

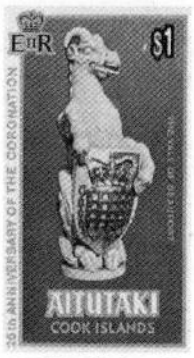

39 The Yale of Beaufort

1978. 25th Anniv of Coronation. Multicoloured.

257	$1 Type **39**	30	50
258	$1 Queen Elizabeth II	30	50
259	$1 Aitutaki ancestral statue	30	50
MS260	98×127 mm. Nos 257/9×2	75	75

Stamps from No. **MS**260 have coloured borders, the upper row in lavender and the lower in green.

40 *Adoration of the Infant Jesus*

1978. Christmas. 450th Death Anniv of Durer. Multicoloured.

261	15c. Type **40**	25	15
262	17c. *The Madonna with Child*	30	15
263	30c. *The Madonna with the Iris*	45	20
264	35c. *The Madonna of the Siskin*	60	45
MS265	101×109 mm. As Nos. 261/4 but each with premium of "+2c."	1·10	1·00

41 *Captain Cook* (Nathaniel Dance)

1979. Death Bicent of Captain Cook. Multicoloured.

266	50c. Type **41**	1·00	80
267	75c. *H.M.S. 'Resolution' and 'Adventure' at Matavai Bay, Tahiti* (W. Hodges)	1·75	95
MS268	94×58 mm. Nos. 266/7	2·00	2·25

42 Girl with Flowers

1979. International Year of the Child. Multicoloured.

269	30c. Type **42**	20	15
270	35c. Boy playing guitar	30	20
271	65c. Children in canoe	40	30
MS272	104×80 mm. As Nos. 269/71, but each with a premium of "+3c."	70	1·00

43 *Man writing a Letter* (painting by Gabriel Metsu)

1979. Death Centenary of Sir Rowland Hill. Multicoloured.

273	50c. Type **43**	45	45
274	50c. Sir Rowland Hill with Penny Black, 1903 ½d. and 1911 1d. stamps	45	45
275	50c. *Girl in Blue reading a Letter* (Jan Vermeer)	45	45
276	65c. *Woman writing a Letter* (Gerard Terborch)	50	50
277	65c. Sir Rowland Hill, with Penny Black, 1903 3d. and 1920 ½d. stamps	50	50
278	65c. *Lady reading a Letter* (Jan Vermeer)	50	50
MS279	151×85 mm. 30c.×6. As Nos. 273/8	1·75	1·75

44 *The Burial of Christ* (left detail) (Quentin Metsys)

1980. Easter. Multicoloured.

280	20c. Type **44**	40	25
281	30c. *The Burial of Christ* (centre detail)	50	35
282	35c. *The Burial of Christ* (right detail)	65	45
MS283	93×71 mm. As Nos. 280/2, but each with premium of "+2c."	75	75

45 Einstein as a Young Man

1980. 25th Death Anniv of Albert Einstein (physicist). Multicoloured.

284	12c. Type **45**	60	60

285	12c. Atom and "E=mc²" equation	60	60
286	15c. Einstein in middle-age	65	65
287	15c. Cross over nuclear explosion (Test Ban Treaty, 1963)	65	65
288	20c. Einstein as an old man	75	75
289	20c. Hand preventing atomic explosion	75	75
MS290	113×118 mm. Nos 284/9	3·00	3·00

46 Ancestor Figure, Aitutaki

1980. Third South Pacific Festival of Arts. Multicoloured.

291	6c. Type **46**	10	10
292	6c. Staff god image, Rarotonga	10	10
293	6c. Trade adze, Mangaia	10	10
294	6c. Carved image of Tangaroa, Rarotonga	10	10
295	12c. Wooden image Aitutaki	10	10
296	12c. Hand club, Rarotonga	10	10
297	12c. Carved mace "god", Mangaia	10	10
298	12c. Fisherman's god, Rarotonga	10	10
299	15c. Ti'i image, Aitutaki	15	15
300	15c. Fisherman's god, Rarotonga (different)	15	15
301	15c. Carved mace "god", Cook Islands	15	15
302	15c. Carved image of Tangaroa, Rarotonga (different)	15	15
303	20c. Chief's headdress, Aitutaki	15	15
304	20c. Carved mace "god", Cook Islands (different)	15	15
305	20c. Staff god image, Rarotonga (different)	15	15
306	20c. Carved image of Tangaroa, Rarotonga (different)	15	15
MS307	134×194 mm. Nos. 291/306	1·60	1·75

47 "Virgin and Child" (13th century)

1980. Christmas. Sculptures of "The Virgin and Child". Multicoloured.

308	15c. Type **47**	20	15
309	20c. 14th century	20	15
310	25c. 15th century	20	15
311	35c. 15th century (different)	30	20
MS312	82×120 mm. As Nos. 306/11 but each with premium of 2c.	70	80

48 "Mourning Virgin"

1981. Easter. Details of Sculpture "Burial of Christ" by Pedro Roldan.

313	**48**	30c. gold and green	25	25
314	-	40c. gold and lilac	30	30
315	-	50c. gold and blue	30	30
MS316		107×60 mm. As Nos. 313/15 but each with premium of 2c.	75	85

DESIGNS: 40c. "Christ"; 50c. "Saint John".

49 Goulдian Finch

1981. Birds (1st series). Multicoloured.

317	1c. Type **49**	45	30
318	1c. Common starling	45	30
319	2c. Golden whistler	50	30
320	2c. Scarlet robin	50	30
321	3c. Rufous fantail	60	30
322	3c. Peregrine falcon	60	30
323	4c. Java sparrow	70	30
324	4c. Barn owl	70	30
325	5c. Tahitian lory	70	30
326	5c. White-breasted wood swallow	70	30
327	6c. Purple swamphen	70	30
328	6c. Feral rock pigeon	70	30
329	10c. Chestnut-breasted mannikin	90	30
330	10c. Zebra dove	90	30
331	12c. Reef heron	1·00	40
332	12c. Common mynah	1·00	40
333	15c. Whimbrel (horiz)	1·25	40
334	15c. Black-browed albatross (horiz)	1·25	40
335	20c. Pacific golden plover (horiz)	1·50	55
336	20c. White tern (horiz)	1·50	55
337	25c. Pacific black duck (horiz)	1·75	70
338	25c. Brown booby (horiz)	1·75	70
339	30c. Great frigate bird (horiz)	2·00	85
340	30c. Pintail (horiz)	2·00	85
341	35c. Long-billed reed warbler	2·00	1·00
342	35c. Pomarine skua	2·00	1·00
343	40c. Buff-banded rail	2·25	1·25
344	40c. Spotted triller	2·25	1·25
345	50c. Royal albatross	3·00	1·50
346	50c. Stephen's lory	2·25	1·50
347	70c. Red-headed parrot-finch	5·50	3·00
348	70c. Orange dove	5·50	3·00
349	$1 Blue-headed flycatcher	4·50	3·75
350	$2 Red-bellied flycatcher	5·00	8·00
351	$4 Red munia	9·00	14·00
352	$5 Flat-billed kingfisher	12·00	16·00

See also Nos. 475/94.

50 Prince Charles

1981. Royal Wedding. Multicoloured.

391	60c. Type **50**	30	40
392	80c. Lady Diana Spencer	40	55
393	$1.40 Prince Charles and Lady Diana (87×70 mm)	60	80

1981. International Year for Disabled Persons. Nos. 391/3 surch **+5c.**

394	60c.+5c. Type **50**	50	90
395	80c.+5c. Lady Diana Spencer	60	1·10
396	$1.40+5c. Prince Charles and Lady Diana	70	1·40

52 Footballers

1981. World Cup Football Championship, Spain (1982). Football Scenes. Multicoloured.

397	12c. Ball to left of stamp	50	35
398	12c. Ball to right	50	35
399	15c. Ball to right	55	40
400	15c. Ball to left	55	40
401	20c. Ball to left	55	50
402	20c. Ball to right	55	50
403	25c. Type **52**	60	55
404	25c. "ESPANA 82" inscription	60	55
MS405	100×137 mm. 12c.+2c., 15c.+2c., 20c.+2c., 25c.+2c., each × 2. As Nos. 397/404	3·50	3·00

53 *The Holy Family*

1981. Christmas. Etchings by Rembrandt. Each brown and gold.

406	15c. Type **53**	45	45
407	30c. *Virgin with Child*	70	70
408	40c. *Adoration of the Shepherds* (horiz)	95	95
409	50c. *The Holy Family* (horiz)	1·25	1·25
MS410	Designs as Nos. 406/9 in separate miniature sheets, 65×82 mm or 82×65 mm, each with a face value of 80c.+5c. Set of 4 sheets	4·00	3·00

54 Princess of Wales

1982. 21st Birthday of Princess of Wales. Multicoloured.

411	70c. Type **54**	2·00	60
412	$1 Prince and Princess of Wales	2·00	75
413	$2 Princess Diana (different)	3·25	1·50
MS414	82×91 mm. Nos. 411/13	6·00	2·75

1982. Birth of Prince William of Wales (1st issue). Nos. 391/3 optd.

415	60c. Type **50**	90	70
416	60c. Type **50**	90	70
417	80c. Lady Diana Spencer	1·10	80
418	80c. Lady Diana Spencer	1·10	80
419	$1.40 Prince Charles and Lady Diana	1·25	1·00
420	$1.40 Prince Charles and Lady Diana	1·25	1·00

OPTS: Nos. 415, 417 and 419, **21 JUNE 1982. PRINCE WILLIAM OF WALES.** Nos. 416, 418 and 420, **COMMEMORATING THE ROYAL BIRTH.**

1982. Birth of Prince William of Wales (2nd issue). As Nos. 411/13 but inscr "ROYAL BIRTH 21 JUNE 1982 PRINCE WILLIAM OF WALES".

421	70c. Type **54**	70	60
422	$1 Prince and Princess of Wales	80	75
423	$2 Princess Diana (different)	1·60	1·50
MS424	81×91 mm. Nos. 421/3	5·50	3·00

56 "Virgin and Child" (12th-century sculpture)

1982. Christmas. Religious Sculptures. Multicoloured.

425	18c. Type **56**	70	70
426	36c. *Virgin and Child* (12th-century)	85	85
427	48c. *Virgin and Child* (13th-century)	1·00	1·00
428	60c. *Virgin and Child* (15th-century)	1·40	1·40
MS429	99×115 mm. As Nos. 425/8 but each with 2c. charity premium	2·50	2·75

57 Aitutaki Bananas

1983. Commonwealth Day. Multicoloured.

430	48c. Type **57**	75	50
431	48c. Ancient Ti'i image	75	50
432	48c. Tourist canoeing	75	50
433	48c. Captain William Bligh and chart	75	50

58 Scouts around Campfire

1983. 75th Anniv of Boy Scout Movement. Multicoloured.

434	36c. Type **58**	65	65
435	48c. Scout saluting	75	75
436	60c. Scouts hiking	80	80
MS437	78×107 mm. As Nos. 434/6 but each with premium of 3c.	1·50	1·75

1983. 15th World Scout Jamboree, Alberta, Canada. Nos. 434/6 optd **15TH WORLD SCOUT JAMBOREE.**

438	36c. Type **58**	80	45
439	48c. Scout saluting	1·00	55
440	60c. Scouts hiking	1·25	75
MS441	78×107 mm. As Nos. 438/40 but each with a premium of 3c.	1·50	2·00

60 Modern Sport Balloon

1983. Bicentenary of Manned Flight.

442	**60**	18c. multicoloured	55	30
443	-	36c. multicoloured	75	50
444	-	48c. multicoloured	90	60
445	-	60c. multicoloured	1·00	80
MS446	-	64×80 mm. $2.50, mult (48½×28½ mm)	1·50	2·00

DESIGNS: 36c. to $2.50, showing different modern sports balloons.

1983. Various stamps surch (a) Nos. 335/48 and 352.

447	18c. on 20c. Pacific golden plover	2·75	1·25
448	18c. on 20c. White tern	2·75	1·25
449	36c. on 25c. Pacific black duck	3·75	1·50
450	36c. on 25c. Brown booby	3·75	1·50
451	36c. on 30c. Great frigate bird	3·75	1·50
452	36c. on 30c. Pintail	3·75	1·50
453	36c. on 35c. Long-billed reed warbler	3·75	1·50
454	36c. on 35c. Pomarine skua	3·75	1·50
455	48c. on 40c. Buff-banded rail	4·25	1·50
456	48c. on 40c. Spotted triller	4·25	1·50
457	48c. on 50c. Royal albatross	4·25	1·50
458	48c. on 50c. Stephen's lory	4·25	1·50
459	72c. on 70c. Red-headed parrot finch	7·50	3·00
460	72c. on 70c. Orange dove	7·50	3·00
461	$5.60 on $5 Flat-billed kingfisher (vert)	21·00	10·00

63 International Mail

1983. World Communications Year. Multicoloured.

466	48c. Type **63**	65	50
467	60c. Telecommunications	95	70
468	96c. Space satellite	1·40	1·00
MS469	126×53 mm. Nos. 466/8	2·50	2·50

64 *Madonna of the Chair*

1983. Christmas. 500th Birth Anniv of Raphael. Multicoloured.

470	36c. Type **64**	75	40
471	48c. *The Alba Madonna*	90	50
472	60c. *Conestabile Madonna*	1·25	70
MS473	95×116 mm. Nos. 470/2, but each with a premium of 3c.	2·50	1·40

1983. Christmas. 500th Birth Anniv of Raphael. Children's Charity. Designs as Nos. 470/2 in separate miniature sheets 46×47 mm, but with different frames and a face value of 85c.+5c. Imperf.

MS474	As Nos. 470/2 Set of 3 sheets	3·75	2·75

65 Gouldian Finch

1984. Birds (2nd series). Multicoloured.

475	2c. Type **65**	1·75	1·25
476	3c. Common starling	1·75	1·25
477	5c. Scarlet robin	1·75	1·40
478	10c. Golden whistler	2·25	1·40
479	12c. Rufous fantail	2·25	1·40
480	18c. Peregrine falcon	2·25	1·75
481	24c. Barn owl	2·25	1·75
482	30c. Java sparrow	2·25	1·50
483	36c. White-breasted wood swallow	2·25	1·50

484	48c. Tahitian lory	2·25	1·50
485	50c. Feral rock pigeon	2·50	2·50
486	60c. Purple swamphen	2·50	2·00
487	72c. Zebra dove	3·00	2·50
488	96c. Chestnut-breasted mannikin	3·00	2·50
489	$1.20 Common mynah	3·50	2·75
490	$2.10 Reef heron	7·00	3·75
491	$3 Blue-headed flycatcher	7·50	6·00
492	$4.20 Red-bellied flycatcher	3·50	6·00
493	$5.60 Red munia	3·50	9·50
494	$9.60 Flat-billed kingfisher	7·50	12·00

66 Javelin throwing

1984. Olympic Games. Los Angeles. Multicoloured.

495	36c. Type **66**	35	35
496	48c. Shot-putting	40	45
497	60c. Hurdling	45	55
498	$2 Basketball	1·75	1·50
MS499	88×117 mm. As Nos. 495/8, but each with a charity premium of 5c.	3·00	3·50

DESIGNS: 48c. to $2, show Memorial Coliseum and various events.

1984. Olympic Gold Medal Winners. Nos. 495/8 optd.

500	36c. Type **66** (optd **Javelin Throw Tessa Sanderson Great Britain**)	35	35
501	48c. Shot-putting (optd **Shot Put Claudia Losch Germany**)	40	45
502	60c. Hurdling (optd **Heptathlon Glynis Nunn Australia**)	45	55
503	$2 Basketball (optd **Team Basketball United States**)	1·10	1·50

67 Captain William Bligh and Chart

1984. "Ausipex" International Stamp Exhibition, Melbourne. Multicoloured.

504	60c. Type **67**	4·00	3·75
505	96c. H.M.S. *Bounty* and map	4·00	4·00
506	$1.40 Aitutaki stamps of 1974, 1979 and 1981 with map	4·00	4·25
MS507	85×113 mm. As Nos. 504/6, but each with a premium of 5c.	7·50	4·00

1984. Birth of Prince Henry (1st issue). No. 391 optd **15-9-84 Birth Prince Henry** and surch also.

508	$3 on 60c. Type **50**	2·00	3·25

69 The Annunciation

1984. Christmas. Details from Altarpiece, St Paul's Church, Palencia, Spain. Multicoloured.

509	36c. Type **69**	30	35
510	48c. The Nativity	40	45
511	60c. The Epiphany	45	50
512	96c. The Flight into Egypt	75	80
MS513	Designs as Nos. 509/12 in separate miniature sheets, each 45×53 mm and with a face value of 90c.+7c. Imperf. Set of 4 sheets	2·50	3·25

70 Princess Diana with Prince Henry

1984. Birth of Prince Henry (2nd issue). Multicoloured.

514	48c. Type **70**	2·75	2·25
515	60c. Prince William with Prince Henry	2·75	2·25
516	$2.10 Prince and Princess of Wales with children	3·50	4·50
MS517	113×65 mm. As Nos. 514/16, but each with a face value of 96c.+7c.	7·00	4·50

71 Grey Kingbird ("Gray Kingbird")

1985. Birth Bicentenary of John J. Audubon (ornithologist). Designs showing original paintings. Multicoloured.

518	55c. Type **71**	1·10	1·10
519	65c. Bohemian waxwing	1·25	1·25
520	75c. Summer tanager	1·40	1·40
521	95c. Common cardinal ("Cardinal")	1·50	1·50
522	$1.15 White-winged crossbill	1·90	1·90

72 The Queen Mother, aged Seven

1985. Life and Times of Queen Elizabeth the Queen Mother. Multicoloured.

523	55c. Type **72**	45	50
524	65c. Engagement photograph, 1922	50	55
525	75c. With young Princess Elizabeth	60	65
526	$1.30 With baby Prince Charles	1·00	1·10
MS527	75×49 mm. $3 Queen Mother on her 63rd birthday	2·25	2·40

73 *The Calmady Children* (T. Lawrence)

1985. International Youth Year. Multicoloured.

528	75c. Type **73**	3·00	2·75
529	90c. *Madame Charpentier's Children* (Renoir)	3·00	3·00
530	$1.40 *Young Girls at Piano* (Renoir)	3·75	4·00
MS531	103×104 mm. As Nos. 528/30, but each with a premium of 10c.	4·75	3·75

74 *Adoration of the Magi* (Giotto) and "Giotto" Spacecraft

1985. Christmas. Appearance of Halley's Comet (1st issue). Multicoloured.

532	95c. Type **74**	2·00	1·75
533	95c. As Type **74** but showing "Planet A" spacecraft	2·00	1·75
534	$1.15 Type **74**	2·00	1·75
535	$1.15 As No. 533	2·00	1·75
MS536	52×55 mm. $6.40. As Type **74** but without spacecraft (30×31 mm). Imperf	14·00	8·50

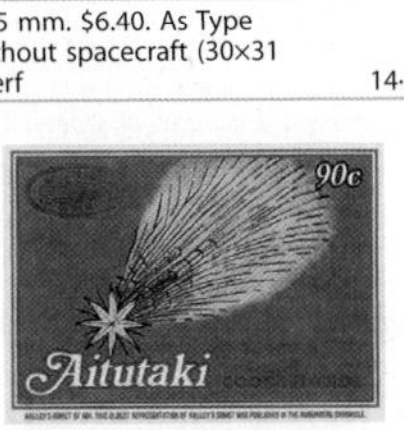

75 Halley's Comet A.D. 684 (from *Nuremberg Chronicle*)

1986. Appearance of Halley's Comet (2nd issue). Multicoloured.

537	90c. Type **75**	1·25	90
538	$1.25 Halley's Comet, 1066 (from Bayeux Tapestry)	1·60	1·10
539	$1.75 Halley's Comet, 1456 (from *Lucerne Chronicles*)	1·90	1·50
MS540	107×82 mm. As Nos. 537/9, but each with a face value of 95c.	5·50	2·50
MS541	65×80 mm. $4.20, *Melencolia I* (Albrecht Dürer woodcut) (61×76 mm). Imperf	6·50	3·50

76 Queen Elizabeth II on Coronation Day (from photo by Cecil Beaton)

1986. 60th Birthday of Queen Elizabeth II.

542	**76** 95c. multicoloured	2·00	2·25
MS543	58×68 mm. $4.20, As T **76**, but showing more of the portrait without oval frame	5·50	5·50

77 Head of Statue of Liberty

1986. Centenary of Statue of Liberty. Multicoloured.

544	$1 Type **77**	1·25	1·25
545	$2.75 Statue of Liberty at sunset	2·75	2·75
MS546	91×79 mm. As Nos. 544/5, but each with a face value of $1.25	3·25	2·50

78 Prince Andrew and Miss Sarah Ferguson

1986. Royal Wedding.

547	**78** $2 multicoloured	2·00	2·00
MS548	85×70 mm. Type **78** multicoloured	6·50	8·00

1986. "Stampex '86" Stamp Exhibition, Adelaide. No. **MS**507 with "Ausipex" emblems obliterated in gold.

MS549	As Nos. 504/6, but each with a premium of 5c.	13·00	14·00

The "Stampex '86" exhibition emblem is overprinted on the sheet margin.

1986. 86th Birthday of Queen Elizabeth the Queen Mother. Nos. 523/6 in miniature sheet, 132×82 mm.

MS550	Nos. 523/6	13·00	13·00

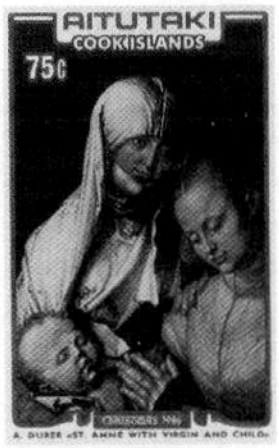

79 *St. Anne with Virgin and Child*

1986. Christmas. Paintings by Durer. Multicoloured.

551	75c. Type **79**	1·25	1·25
552	$1.35 *Virgin and Child*	1·75	1·75
553	$1.95 *The Adoration of the Magi*	2·25	2·25
554	$2.75 *Madonna of the Rosary*	3·00	3·00
MS555	88×125 mm. As Nos. 551/4, but each with a face value of $1.65	13·00	14·00

1986. Visit of Pope John Paul II to South Pacific. Nos. 551/4 optd **NOVEMBER 21-24 1986 FIRST VISIT TO SOUTH PACIFIC** and surch also.

556	75c.+10c. Type **79**	3·00	2·50
557	$1.35+10c. "Virgin and Child"	3·50	3·00
558	$1.95+10c. "The Adoration of the Magi"	4·25	3·50
559	$2.75+10c. "Madonna of the Rosary"	5·50	5·00
MS560	88×125 mm. As Nos. 556/9, but each with a face value of $1.65+10c.	17·00	15·00

1987. Hurricane Relief Fund. Nos. 544/5, 547, 551/4 and 556/9 surch **HURRICANE RELIEF +50c**.

561	75c.+50c. Type **79**	3·25	2·75
562	75c.+10c.+50c. Type **79**	4·00	3·50
563	$1+50c. Type **77**	3·50	3·00
564	$1.35+50c. *Virgin and Child* (Durer)	3·75	3·25
565	$1.35+10c.+50c. *Virgin and Child* (Durer)	4·50	4·00
566	$1.95+50c. *The Adoration of the Magi* (Durer)	4·50	4·00
567	$1.95+10c.+50c. *The Adoration of the Magi* (Durer)	5·00	4·00
568	$2+50c. Type **78**	4·50	4·00
569	$2.75+50c. Statue of Liberty at sunset	5·00	4·50
570	$2.75+50c. "Madonna of the Rosary" (Durer)	5·00	4·50
571	$2.75+10c.+50c. *Madonna of the Rosary* (Durer)	6·50	5·50

1987. Royal Ruby Wedding. Nos. 391/3 surch **2.50 Royal Wedding 40th Anniv**.

572	$2.50 on 60c. Type **50**	2·25	2·50
573	$2.50 on 80c. Lady Diana Spencer	2·25	2·50
574	$2.50 on $1.40 Prince Charles and Lady Diana (87×70 mm)	2·25	2·50

83 Angels

1987. Christmas. Details of angels from *Virgin with Garland* by Rubens.

575	**83** 70c. multicoloured	2·00	2·00
576	- 85c. multicoloured	2·25	2·25
577	- $1.50 multicoloured	2·50	2·50
578	- $1.85 multicoloured	3·25	3·25
MS579	92×120 mm. As Nos. 575/8, but each with a face value of 95c.	13·00	14·00
MS580	96×85 mm. $6 "Virgin with Garland" (diamond, 56×56 mm)	13·00	14·00

84 Chariot Racing and Athletics

1988. Olympic Games, Seoul. Ancient and modern Olympic sports. Multicoloured.

581	70c. Type **84**	2·25	2·00
582	85c. Greek runners and football	2·50	2·25
583	95c. Greek wrestling and handball	2·50	2·25
584	$1.40 Greek hoplites and tennis	3·25	3·00
MS585	103×101 mm. As Nos. 581 and 584, but each with face value of $2	8·00	8·50

1988. Olympic Medal Winners, Los Angeles. Nos. 581/4 optd.

586	70c. Type **84** (optd **FLORENCE GRIFFITH JOYNER UNITED STATES 100 M AND 200 M**)	2·50	2·40
587	85c. Greek runners and football (optd **GELINDO BORDIN ITALY MARATHON**)	2·50	2·40
588	95c. Greek wrestling and handball (optd **HITOSHI SAITO JAPAN JUDO**)	2·75	2·50
589	$1.40 Greek hoplites and tennis (optd **STEFFI GRAF WEST GERMANY WOMEN'S TENNIS**)	2·75	2·50

85 *Adoration of the Shepherds* (detail)

1988. Christmas. Paintings by Rembrandt. Multicoloured.

590	55c. Type **85**	2·00	1·75
591	70c. *The Holy Family*	2·25	2·00
592	85c. *Presentation in the Temple*	2·50	2·25
593	95c. *The Holy Family* (different)	2·50	2·25
594	$1.15 *Presentation in the Temple* (different)	2·75	2·50
MS595	85×101 mm. $4.50, As Type **85** but 52×34 mm.	5·50	6·50

86 H.M.S. *Bounty* leaving Spithead and King George III

1989. Bicentenary of Discovery of Aitutaki by Captain Bligh. Multicoloured.

596	55c. Type **86**	2·25	2·00
597	65c. Breadfruit plants	2·50	2·25
598	75c. Old chart showing Aitutaki and Captain Bligh	2·75	2·50
599	95c. Native outrigger and H.M.S. *Bounty* off Aitutaki	3·00	2·75
600	$1.65 Fletcher Christian confronting Bligh	4·00	3·50
MS601 94×72 mm. $4.20 *Mutineers casting Bligh adrift* (Robert Dodd) (60×45 mm)		8·50	10·00

87 "Apollo 11" Astronaut on Moon

1989. 20th Anniv of First Manned Landing on Moon. Multicoloured.

602	75c. Type **87**	2·75	2·00
603	$1.15 Conducting experiment on Moon	3·25	2·50
604	$1.80 Astronaut on Moon carrying equipment	4·00	3·50
MS605 105×86 mm. $6.40 Astronaut on Moon with U.S. flag (40×27 mm)		8·00	9·50

88 Virgin Mary

1989. Christmas. Details from *Virgin in the Glory* by Titian. Multicoloured.

606	70c. Type **88**	2·50	2·00
607	85c. Christ Child	3·00	2·50
608	95c. Angel	3·25	2·75
609	$1.25 Cherubs	3·75	3·25
MS610 80×100 mm. $6 *Virgin in the Glory* (45×60 mm)		8·50	10·00

89 Human Comet striking Earth

1990. Protection of the Environment. Multicoloured.

611	$1.75 Type **89**	1·90	2·25
612	$1.75 Comet's tail	1·90	2·25
MS613 108×43 mm. Nos. 611/12		3·50	4·50

Nos. 611/12 were printed together, *se-tenant*, forming a composite design.

1990. 90th Birthday of Queen Elizabeth the Queen Mother. No. **MS**550 optd **Ninetieth Birthday**.

MS614 132×82 mm. Nos. 523/6		13·00	12·00

91 *Madonna of the Basket* (Correggio)

1990. Christmas. Religious Paintings. Multicoloured.

615	70c. Type **91**	1·50	1·50
616	85c. *Virgin and Child* (Morando)	1·60	1·60
617	95c. *Adoration of the Child* (Tiepolo)	1·75	1·75
618	$1.75 *Mystic Marriage of St. Catherine* (Memling)	2·50	2·75
MS619 165×93 mm. $6 *Donne Triptych* (Memling) (horiz)		12·00	13·00

1990. "Birdpex '90" Stamp Exhibition, Christchurch, New Zealand. Nos. 349/50 optd **Birdpex '90** and bird's head.

620	$1 Blue-headed flycatcher	4·50	4·50
621	$2 Red-bellied flycatcher	6·00	6·00

1991. 65th Birthday of Queen Elizabeth II. No. 352 optd **COMMEMORATING 65th BIRTHDAY OF H.M. QUEEN ELIZABETH II**.

622	$5 Flat-billed kingfisher	12·00	12·00

93 "The Holy Family" (A. Mengs)

1991. Christmas. Religious Paintings. Multicoloured.

623	80c. Type **93**	1·75	1·75
624	90c. *Virgin and the Child* (Lippi)	1·75	1·75
625	$1.05 *Virgin and Child* (A. Durer)	2·00	2·00
626	$1.75 *Adoration of the Shepherds* (G. de la Tour)	2·75	3·25
MS627 79×103 mm. *The Holy Family* (Michelangelo)		13·00	14·00

94 Hurdling

1992. Olympic Games, Barcelona. Multicoloured.

628	95c. Type **94**	1·75	1·50
629	$1.25 Weightlifting	2·00	1·75
630	$1.50 Judo	2·50	2·25
631	$1.95 Football	2·75	2·75

95 Vaka Motu Canoe

1992. Sixth Festival of Pacific Arts, Rarotonga. Sailing Canoes. Multicoloured.

632	30c. Type **95**	65	65
633	50c. Hamatafua	80	80
634	95c. Alia Kalia Ndrua	1·50	1·50
635	$1.75 Hokule'a Hawaiian	2·25	2·75
636	$1.95 Tuamotu Pahi	2·50	3·00

1992. Royal Visit by Prince Edward. Nos. 632/6 optd **ROYAL VISIT**.

637	30c. Type **95**	1·50	1·25
638	50c. Hamatafua	2·00	1·75
639	95c. Alia Kalia Ndrua	3·00	2·50
640	$1.75 Hokule'a Hawaiian	4·50	4·25
641	$1.95 Tuamotu Pahi	4·50	4·25

96 *Virgin's Nativity* (detail) (Reni)

1992. Christmas. Different details from *Virgin's Nativity* by Guido Reni.

642	**96**	80c. multicoloured	1·40	1·40
643	-	90c. multicoloured	1·60	1·60
644	-	$1.05 multicoloured	1·75	1·75
645	-	$1.75 multicoloured	2·50	3·00
MS646 – 101×86 mm. $6 multicoloured (as $1.05, but larger (36×46 mm))			6·50	8·00

97 The Departure from Palos

1992. 500th Anniv of Discovery of America by Columbus. Multicoloured.

647	$1.25 Type **97**	2·25	2·50
648	$1.75 Map of voyages	2·75	3·00
649	$1.95 Columbus and crew in New World	3·25	3·50

98 Queen Victoria and King Edward VII

1993. 40th Anniv of Coronation. Multicoloured.

650	$1.75 Type **98**	3·50	3·00
651	$1.75 King George V and King George VI	3·50	3·00
652	$1.75 Queen Elizabeth II in 1953 and 1986	3·50	3·00

99 *Madonna and Child* (Nino Pisano)

1993. Christmas. Religious Sculptures. Multicoloured.

653	80c. Type **99**	90	90
654	90c. *Virgin on Rosebush* (Luca della Robbia)	1·00	1·00
655	$1.15 *Virgin with Child and St. John* (Juan Francisco Rustici)	1·40	1·40
656	$1.95 *Virgin with Child* (Miguel Angel)	2·25	2·25
657	$3 *Madonna and Child* (Jacopo della Quercia) (32×47 mm)	3·25	4·00

100 Ice Hockey

1994. Winter Olympic Games, Lillehammer. Multicoloured.

658	$1.15 Type **100**	4·00	3·25
659	$1.15 Ski-jumping	4·00	3·25
660	$1.15 Cross-country skiing	4·00	3·25

101 *Ipomoea pes–caprae*

1994. Flowers. Multicoloured.

661	5c. Type **101**	30	30
662	10c. *Plumeria alba*	35	35
663	15c. *Hibiscus rosa-sinensis*	45	45
664	20c. *Allamanda cathartica*	50	50
665	25c. *Delonix regia*	50	50
666	30c. *Gardenia taitensis*	50	50
667	50c. *Plumeria rubra*	70	70
668	80c. *Ipomoea littoralis*	1·00	1·00
669	85c. *Hibiscus tiliaceus*	1·00	1·00
670	90c. *Erythrina variegata*	1·00	1·00
671	$1 *Solandra nitida*	1·00	1·10
672	$2 *Cordia subcordata*	1·50	1·75
673	$3 *Hibiscus rosa-sinensis* (different) (34×47 mm)	4·50	4·50
674	$5 As $3 (34×47 mm)	6·00	6·50
675	$8 As $3 (34×47 mm)	5·00	6·50

Nos. 671/5 include a portrait of Queen Elizabeth II at top right.

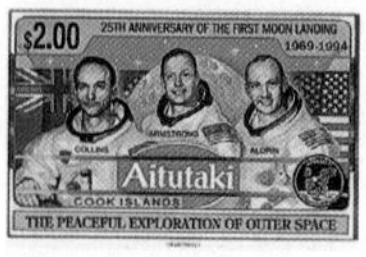

102 Cook Islands and U.S.A. Flags with Astronauts Collins, Armstrong and Aldrin

1994. 25th Anniv of First Manned Moon Landing. Multicoloured.

676	$2 Type **102**	7·50	7·50
677	$2 "Apollo 11" re-entering atmosphere and landing in sea	7·50	7·50

103 "The Madonna of the Basket" (Correggio)

1994. Christmas. Religious Paintings. Multicoloured.

678	85c. Type **103**	1·10	1·40
679	85c. *The Virgin and Child with Saints* (Memling)	1·10	1·40
680	85c. *The Virgin and Child with Flowers* (Dolci)	1·10	1·40
681	85c. *The Virgin and Child with Angels* (Bergognone)	1·10	1·40
682	90c. *Adoration of the Kings* (Dosso)	1·10	1·40
683	90c. *The Virgin and Child* (Bellini)	1·10	1·40
684	90c. *The Virgin and Child* (Schiavone)	1·10	1·40
685	90c. *Adoration of the Kings* (Dolci)	1·10	1·40

No. 678 is inscribed "Corregio" in error.

104 Battle of Britain

1995. 50th Anniv of End of Second World War. Multicoloured.

686	$4 Type **104**	9·50	8·50
687	$4 Battle of Midway	9·50	8·50

105 Queen Elizabeth the Queen Mother

1995. 95th Birthday of Queen Elizabeth the Queen Mother.

688	**105**	$4 multicoloured	7·50	8·00

106 Globe, Doves, United Nations Emblem and Headquarters

1995. 50th Anniv of United Nations.

689	**106**	$4.25 multicoloured	5·50	7·00

107 Green Turtle

1995. Year of the Sea Turtle. Multicoloured.

690	95c. Type **107**	1·75	1·75
691	$1.15 Leatherback turtle	2·00	2·00
692	$1.50 Olive Ridley turtle	2·25	2·25
693	$1.75 Loggerhead turtle	2·50	2·50

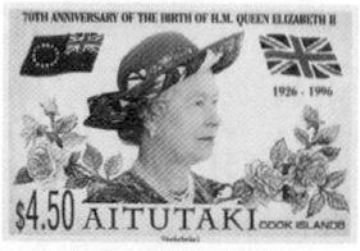

108 Queen Elizabeth II

1996. 70th Birthday of Queen Elizabeth II.

694	**108**	$4.50 multicoloured	8·50	8·00

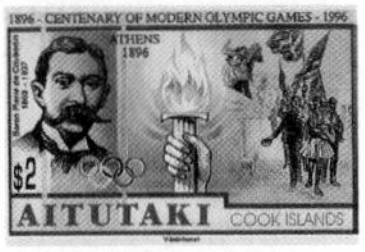

109 Baron Pierre de Coubertin, Torch and Opening of 1896 Olympic Games

1996. Centenary of Modern Olympic Games. Multicoloured.

695	$2 Type **109**	5·00	5·00
696	$2 Athletes and American flag, 1996	5·00	5·00

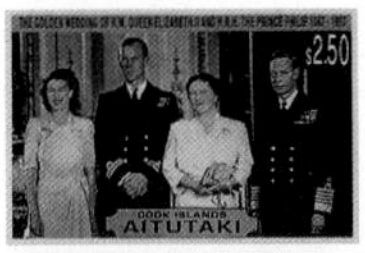

110 Princess Elizabeth and Lieut. Philip Mountbatten with King George VI and Queen Elizabeth, 1947

1997. Golden Wedding of Queen Elizabeth and Prince Philip.

697	**110** $2.50 multicoloured	4·50	3·50
MS698	78×102 mm. **110** $6 multicoloured	8·50	9·50

111 Diana, Princess of Wales

1998. Diana, Princess of Wales Commemoration.

699	**111** $1 multicoloured	1·00	1·00
MS700	70×100 mm. $4 Diana, Princess of Wales	2·50	3·75

1998. Children's Charities. No. **MS**1427 surch **+$1 CHILDREN'S CHARITIES**.

MS701	70×100 mm. $4 + $1 Diana, Princess of Wales	2·75	4·50

1999. New Millennium. Nos. 632/6 optd **KIA ORANA THIRD MILLENNIUM**.

702	30c. Type **95**	50	50
703	50c. Hamatafua	60	60
704	95c. Alia Kalia Ndrua	85	85
705	$1.75 Hokule'a Hawaiian	1·40	1·60
706	$1.95 Tuamotu Pahi	1·60	1·75

2000. Queen Elizabeth the Queen Mother's 100th Birthday. As T **277** of Cook Islands.

707	$3 blue and brown	3·50	3·50
708	$3 multicoloured	3·50	3·50
709	$3 multicoloured	3·50	3·50
710	$3 green and brown	3·50	3·50
MS711	73×100 mm. $7.50 multicoloured	7·00	8·00

DESIGNS: No. 707, Queen Mother in evening dress and tiara; 708, Queen Mother in evening dress standing by table; 709, Queen Mother in Garter robes; 710, King George VI and Queen Elizabeth; **MS**711 Queen Mother holding lilies.

2000. Olympic Games, Sydney. As T **278** of Cook Islands. Multicoloured.

712	$2 Ancient Greek wrestlers	2·00	2·25
713	$2 Modern wrestlers	2·00	2·25
714	$2 Ancient Greek boxer	2·00	2·25
715	$2 Modern boxers	2·00	2·25
MS716	99×90 mm. $2.75 Olympic torch and Cook Island canoes	2·25	2·75

113 Blue Lorikeets and Flowers

2002. Endangered Species. Blue Lorikeet. Multicoloured.

717	80c. Type **113**	1·10	1·25
718	90c. Lorikeets and bananas	1·10	1·25
719	$1.15 Lorikeets on palm leaf	1·40	1·60
720	$1.95 Lorikeets in tree trunk	1·90	2·10

2003. "United We Stand". Support for Victims of 11 September 2001 Terrorist Attacks. Design as T **282** of Cook Islands. Multicoloured.

MS721	75×109 mm. $1.15×4 Twin Towers and flags of U.S.A. and Cook Islands	4·75	5·50

2005. Pope John Paul II Commemoration. As T **285** of Cook Islands. Multicoloured.

722	$1.95 Pope praying	3·50	3·50

114 Caterpillar and Chrysalis

2008. Endangered Species. Blue Moon Butterfly (*Hypolimna bolinas*). Multicoloured.

723	80c. Type **114**	1·40	1·50
724	90c. Female butterfly	1·40	1·50
725	$1.15 Male butterfly (wings closed)	1·60	1·75
726	$1.95 Male butterfly (wings open)	2·10	2·25

115 Tomato Grouper swallowing Shrimp

2010. Endangered Species. Tomato Grouper (*Cephalopholis sonnerati*) and Peacock Grouper (*Cephalopholis argus*). Multicoloured.

727	80c. Type **115**	1·10	1·25
728	90c. Peacock grouper on reef	1·25	1·40
729	$1.10 Three tomato groupers on reef	1·50	1·60
730	$1.20 Peacock grouper (close up)	1·60	1·75

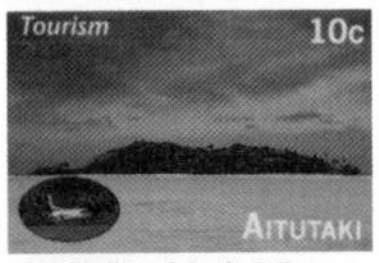

116 Atoll and Saab 340 Airplane

2010. Tourism. Island Views. Multicoloured.

731	10c. Type **116**	20	25
732	20c. Palm trees and sunset over ocean	35	40
733	30c. Turquoise sea and atoll with sandy beach	45	50
734	40c. Two small islands, ocean, cloudy sky and *Southern Express* (freighter)	50	55
735	50c. Tree lined road	55	60
736	60c. Two islands under dark stormy sky	85	80
737	70c. Islanders fishing from causeway	90	95
738	80c. Sandy beach with leaning palm tree and island	1·00	1·10
739	90c. Overwater bungalows, Aitutaki Lagoon Resort	1·10	1·25
740	$1 Two peninsulas with palm trees and sandy beaches	1·25	1·40
741	$1.10 Looking over fence to sandy beach with two deckchairs	1·25	1·40
742	$1.20 Sun and clouds reflecting in ocean	1·40	1·50
743	$1.50 Half moon over two islands, reflecting in water	1·60	1·75
744	$2 Dusk with waves lapping sandy beach, island in background	2·10	2·25
745	$3 Church	3·25	3·50
MS746	240×180 mm. Nos. 731/45	17·00	17·00

117 Miss Kate Middleton on Gold Cup Day, Cheltenham

2011. Royal Engagement. Multicoloured.

747	50c. Type **117**	55	60
748	$1 Prince William laying wreath at the Cenotaph, London, 2009 (horiz)	1·25	1·40
749	$1 Prince William competing in Chakravarty Cup, Beaufort Polo Club (horiz)	1·25	1·40
750	$1 Kate Middleton, Prince William in background (horiz)	1·25	1·40
751	$1 Prince William (horiz)	1·25	1·40
752	$1 Kate Middleton (horiz)	1·25	1·40
753	$1 Prince William and Kate Middleton (horiz)	1·25	1·40
754	$1 Kate Middleton wearing black hat (horiz)	1·25	1·40
755	$1 Prince William (head and shoulders) (horiz)	1·25	1·40
756	$1 Prince William and Kate Middleton (facing each other) (horiz)	1·25	1·40
757	$1 Engagement ring on Kate Middleton's hand (horiz)	1·25	1·40
758	$5 Prince William competing in Chakravarty Cup, Beaufort Polo Club	5·25	5·00
MS759	108×70 mm. Nos. 747 and 758. P 13½	1·90	1·90
MS760	144×93 mm. $8.10 Prince William and Kate Middleton (38×50 mm)	9·00	9·00
MS761	58×95 mm. $11 As No. 747 (38×50 mm)	13·75	13·75
MS762	58×95 mm. $11 As No. 758 (38×50 mm)		

118 Duke and Duchess of Cambridge

2011. Royal Wedding. Sheet 108×73 mm containing T **118** and similar vert designs. Multicoloured.

MS763	$1.10 Type **118**; $1.20 Duke and Duchess of Cambridge during wedding ceremony (back view, kneeling)	2·75	2·75

119 Suspended Cages

2011. Aitutaki Marine Research Center. Clams. Multicoloured.

764	10c. Type **119**	20	25
765	20c. Station Manager Richard Story	35	40
766	80c. *Tridacna maxima* (two clams and sea urchin)	1·00	1·10
767	90c. *Tridacna maxima* (clams and sea bed)	1·10	1·25
768	$1.10 *Tridacna derasa* (close-up of clam)	1·10	1·25
769	$1.20 *Tridacna derasa* (clam, fish and corals on sea bed)	1·25	1·40
MS770	127×76 mm. $2 Diver (30×38 mm); $3 Boat loaded with clam cages (30×38 mm)	5·50	5·50

OFFICIAL STAMPS

1978. Nos. 98/105, 107/10 and 227/8 optd **O.H.M.S.** or surch also.

O1	1c. multicoloured	90	10
O2	2c. multicoloured	1·00	10
O3	3c. multicoloured	1·00	10
O4	4c. multicoloured	1·00	10
O5	5c. multicoloured	1·00	10
O6	8c. multicoloured	1·25	10
O7	10c. multicoloured	1·50	15
O8	15c. on 60c. multicoloured	2·75	20
O9	18c. on 60c. multicoloured	2·75	20
O10	20c. multicoloured	2·75	20
O11	50c. multicoloured	1·00	55
O12	60c. multicoloured	10·00	70
O13	$1 multicoloured (No. 108)	10·00	80
O14	$2 multicoloured	9·00	75
O15	$4 on $1 mult (No. 228)	1·75	75
O16	$5 multicoloured	11·00	1·25

1985. Nos. 351/2, 430/3, 475 and 477/94 optd **O.H.M.S.** or surch also.

O17	2c. Type **65**	1·75	2·00
O18	5c. Scarlet robin	2·00	2·00
O19	10c. Golden whistler	2·25	2·25
O20	12c. Rufous fantail	2·50	2·50
O21	18c. Peregrine falcon	3·50	2·50
O22	20c. on 24 c Barn owl	3·25	2·50
O23	30c. Java sparrow	2·25	1·50
O24	40c. on 36c. White-breasted wood swallow	2·25	1·50
O25	50c. Feral rock pigeon	2·25	1·50
O26	55c. on 48c. Tahitian lory	3·50	1·75
O27	60c. Purple swamphen	2·50	1·75
O28	65c. on 72c. Zebra dove	2·50	1·75
O38	75c. on 48c. Type **57**	1·25	1·40
O39	75c. on 48c. Ancient Ti'i image	1·25	1·40
O40	75c. on 48c. Tourist canoeing	1·25	1·40
O41	75c. on 48c. Captain William Bligh and chart	1·25	1·40
O29	80c. on 96c. Chestnut-breasted mannikin	2·50	1·75
O30	$1.20 Common mynah	3·25	2·50
O31	$2.10 Reef heron	4·75	3·75
O32	$3 Blue-headed flycatcher	7·00	7·00
O33	$4.20 Red-bellied flycatcher	8·00	8·00
O34	$5.60 Red munia	9·00	9·00
O35	$9.60 Flat-billed kingfisher	14·00	14·00
O36	$14 on $4 Red munia (35×48 mm)	16·00	16·00
O37	$18 on $5 Flat-billed kingfisher (35×48 mm)	18·00	18·00

Pt. 19

AJMAN

One of the Trucial States in the Persian Gulf. On 18 July 1971, seven Gulf sheikhdoms, including Ajman, formed part of the State of the United Arab Emirates. The federation became effective on 1 August 1972.

1964. 100 naye paise = 1 rupee.
1967. 100 dirhams = 1 riyal.

1 Shaikh Rashid bin Humaid al Naimi and Arab Stallion

1964. Multicoloured. (a) Size 34½×23 mm.

1	1n.p. Type **1**	10	10
2	2n.p. Regal angelfish	10	10
3	3n.p. Dromedary	10	10
4	4n.p. Yellow-banded angelfish	10	10
5	5n.p. Tortoise	10	10
6	10n.p. Jewel cichlid	25	10
7	15n.p. White stork	35	10
8	20n.p. Black-headed gulls	35	10
9	30n.p. Lanner falcon	60	25

(b) Size 42½×27 mm.

10	40n.p. Type **1**	25	25
11	50n.p. Regal angelfish	25	25
12	70n.p. Dromedary	35	25
13	1r. Yellow-banded angelfish	35	35
14	1r.50 Tortoise	70	60
15	2r. Jewel cichlid	95	85

(c) Size 53×34 mm.

16	3r. White stork	1·60	1·20
17	5r. Black-headed gulls	4·25	3·00
18	10r. Lanner falcon	7·25	5·50

2 Kennedy in Football Kit

1964. Pres. Kennedy Commem. Perf or imperf.

19	**2**	10n.p. purple and green	10	10
20	-	15n.p. violet and turquoise	10	10
21	-	50n.p. blue and brown	25	10
22	-	1r. turquoise and sepia	60	35
23	-	2r. olive and purple	95	60
24	-	3r. brown and green	1·40	95
25	-	5r. brown and violet	2·40	2·10
26	-	10r. brown and blue	4·75	3·50
MS26a		105×140 mm. Nos. 23/6 in new colours	24·00	12·00

DESIGNS—Various pictures of Kennedy: 15n.p. Diving; 50n.p. As naval officer; 1r. Sailing with Mrs. Kennedy; 2r. With Mrs. Eleanor Roosevelt; 3r. With wife and child; 5r. With colleagues; 10r. Full-face portrait.

3 Start of Race

1965. Olympic Games, Tokyo. Perf or imperf.

27	**3**	5n.p. slate, brown & mauve	10	10
28	-	10n.p. red, bronze and blue	10	10
29	**3**	15n.p. brown, violet & green	10	10
30	-	25n.p. black, blue and red	25	10
31	-	50n.p. slate, purple and blue	35	25
32	-	1r. blue, green and purple	60	35
33	-	1r.50 purple, violet and green	95	60

34	-	2r. blue, purple and ochre	1·20	85
35	-	3r. violet, brown and blue	1·80	1·10
36	-	5r. purple, green and yellow	3·25	1·90
MS36a		120×100 mm. Nos. 33/6 in new colours	12·00	8·50

DESIGNS: 10n.p., 1r.50, Boxing; 25n.p., 2r. Judo; 50n.p., 5r. Gymnastics; 1, 3r. Sailing.

4 First Gibbons Catalogue and Alexandria (U.S.) 5c. Postmaster's Stamp

1965. Stanley Gibbons Catalogue Centenary Exhibition, London. Multicoloured.

37		5n.p. Type **4**	10	10
38		10n.p. Austria (6k.) scarlet "Mercury" newspaper stamp	10	10
39		15n.p. British Guiana "One Cent", 1856	10	10
40		25n.p. Canada "Twelvepence Black", 1851	10	25
41		50n.p. Hawaii "Missionary" 2c., 1851	25	25
42		1r. Mauritius "Post Office" 2d. blue, 1847	50	25
43		3r. Switzerland "Double Geneva" 5c.+5c., 1843	1·60	70
44		5r. Tuscany 3 lire, 1860	2·75	1·20
MS44a		Two sheets, each 124×99 mm. Nos. 37, 40/1, 44 and 38/9, 42/3	8·50	8·50

The 5, 15 and 50n.p. and 3r. also include the First Gibbons Catalogue and the others, the Gibbons "Elizabethan" Catalogue.

1965. Pan Arab Games, Cairo. Perf or imperf. Nos. 29, 31 and 33/5 optd. (a) Optd **PAN ARAB GAMES CAIRO 1965**.

45	3	15n.p. brown, violet & green	10	10
46	-	50n.p. slate, purple and blue	50	50
47	-	1r.50 purple, violet & green	1·40	1·40
48	-	2r. blue, red and ochre	2·10	2·10
49	-	3r. violet, brown and blue	3·25	3·25

(b) Optd as Nos. 45/9 but equivalent in Arabic.

50	3	15n.p. brown, violet & green	10	10
51	-	50n.p. slate, purple and blue	50	50
52	-	1r.50 purple, violet and green	1·40	1·40
53	-	2r. blue, red and ochre	2·10	2·10
54	-	3r. violet, brown and blue	3·25	3·25

1965. Air. Designs similar to Nos. 1/9, but inscr "AIR MAIL". Mult. (a) Size 42½×25½ mm.

55		15n.p. Type **1**	10	10
56		25n.p. Regal angelfish	25	25
57		35n.p. Dromedary	25	25
58		50n.p. Yellow-banded angelfish	35	35
59		75n.p. Tortoise	60	60
60		1r. Jewel cichlid	85	85

(b) Size 53×34 mm.

61		2r. White stork	1·80	1·80
62		3r. Black-headed gull	2·40	2·40
63		5r. Lanner falcon	4·25	4·25

1966. Stamp Cent Exn, Cairo. Nos. 38/9 and 41/3 optd **STAMP CENTENARY EXHIBITION CAIRO, JANUARY 1966** and pyramid motif.

73		10n.p. multicoloured	10	10
74		15n.p. multicoloured	25	25
75		50n.p. multicoloured	55	55
76		1r. multicoloured	1·00	1·00
77		3r. multicoloured	3·00	3·00
MS78		Two sheets, each 124×99 mm. as **MS**44a	7·75	4·25

8 Sir Winston Churchill and Tower Bridge

1966. Churchill Commemoration. Each design includes portrait of Churchill. Multicoloured.

79		25n.p. Type **8**	10	10
80		50n.p. Buckingham Palace	25	10
81		75n.p. Blenheim Palace	35	25
82		1r. British Museum	60	25
83		2r. St. Paul's Cathedral in wartime	1·10	60
84		3r. National Gallery and St. Martin in the Fields Church	1·70	85
85		5r. Westminster Abbey	2·75	1·40
86		7r.50 Houses of Parliament at night	4·00	2·10
MS87		101×120 mm. Nos. 85/6	16·00	8·50

9 Rocket

1966. Space Achievements. Multicoloured. (a) Postage. Size as T **9**.

88		1n.p. Type **9**	10	10
89		3n.p. Capsule	10	10
90		5n.p. Astronaut entering capsule in space	10	10
91		10n.p. Astronaut outside capsule in space	10	10
92		15n.p. Astronauts and globe	10	10
93		25n.p. Astronaut in space	10	10
MS94		98×88 mm. 1r. and 3r. in designs of 15n.p. and 10n.p.	3·50	3·00

(b) Air. Size 38×38 mm.

95		50n.p. As Type **9**	35	10
96		1r. Astronauts and globe	60	25
97		3r. Astronaut outside capsule in space	1·80	60
98		5r. Capsule	3·25	1·10

1967. Various issues with currency names changed by overprinting in **Dh.** or **Riyals**. (a) Postage. Nos. 1/18 (1964 Definitives).

99		1d. on 1n.p.	10	10
100		2d. on 2n.p.	10	10
101		3d. on 3n.p.	10	10
102		4d. on 4n.p.	10	10
103		5d. on 5n.p.	10	10
104		10d. on 10n.p.	25	25
105		15d. on 15n.p.	25	25
106		20d. on 20n.p.	35	35
107		30d. on 30n.p.	60	60
108		40d. on 40n.p.	85	85
109		50d. on 50n.p.	1·10	1·10
110		70d. on 70n.p.	1·40	1·40
111		1r. on 1r.	1·90	1·90
112		1r.50 on 1r.50	3·00	3·00
113		2r. on 2r.	4·00	4·00
114		3r. on 3r.	2·40	2·40
115		5r. on 5r.	4·00	4·00
116		10r. on 10r.	7·75	7·75

(b) Air. Nos. 55/63 (Airmails).

117		15d. on 15n.p.	10	10
118		25d. on 25n.p.	25	25
119		35d. on 35n.p.	35	35
120		50d. on 50n.p.	50	50
121		75d. on 75n.p.	70	70
122		1r. on 1r.	95	95
123		2r. on 2r.	1·80	1·80
124		3r. on 3r.	3·00	3·00
125		5r. on 5r.	4·50	4·50

NEW CURRENCY SURCHARGES. Nos. 19/44 and 79/98 are known surch in new currency (dirhams and riyals), in limited quantities, but there is some doubt as to whether they were in use locally.

11 Fiat 1500 Saloon, 1962

1967. Transport.

135	11	1d. brown & blk (postage)	10	10
136	-	2d. blue and brown	10	10
137	-	3d. mauve and black	10	10
138	-	4d. blue and brown	10	10
139	-	5d. green and black	10	10
140	-	15d. blue and brown	10	10
141	-	30d. brown and black	25	10
142	-	50d. black and brown	35	10
143	-	70d. violet and black	50	10
144	11	1r. green and brown (air)	60	25
145	-	2r. mauve and black	1·20	50
146	-	3r. black and brown	1·80	70
147	-	5r. brown and black	3·00	1·20
148	-	10r. blue and brown	6·00	2·40

DESIGNS: 2d., 2r. Motor coach; 3d., 3r. Motor cyclist; 4d., 5r. Boeing 707 airliner; 5d., 10r. "Brasil" (liner); 15d. "Yankee" (sail training and cruise ship); 30d. Cameleer; 50d. Arab horse; 70d. Sikorsky S-58 helicopter.

OFFICIAL STAMPS

1965. Designs similar to Nos. 1/9, additionally inscr "ON STATE'S SERVICE". Multicoloured. (i) Postage. Size 43×26 mm.

O64	25n.p. Type **1**	25	10
O65	40n.p. Regal angelfish	35	25
O66	50n.p. Dromedary	50	35
O67	75n.p. Yellow-banded angelfish	60	50
O68	1r. Tortoise	95	60

(ii) Air. (a) Size 43×26 mm.

O69	75n.p. Jewel cichlid	60	25

(b) Size 53×34 mm.

O70	2r. White stork	1·90	70
O71	3r. Black-headed gulls	3·00	1·10
O72	5r. Lanner falcon	4·75	1·80

1967. Nos. O64/72 with currency names changed by overprinting in **Dh.** or **Riyals**.

O126	25d. on 25n.p.	25	25
O127	40d. on 40n.p.	35	25
O128	50d. on 50n.p.	50	25
O129	75d. on 75n.p. (No. O67)	60	50
O130	75d. on 75n.p. (No. O69)	95	60
O131	1r. on 1r.	70	85
O132	2r. on 2r.	3·50	2·10
O133	3r. on 3r.	7·25	3·00
O134	5r. on 5r.	13·50	6·25

For later issues see **UNITED ARAB EMIRATES**.

APPENDIX

From June 1967 very many stamp issues were made by a succession of agencies which have been awarded contracts by the Ruler, sometimes two agencies operating at the same time. Several contradictory statements were made as to the validity of some of these issues which appeared 1967-72 and for this reason they are only listed in abbreviated form.

1967

50th Birth Anniv of President J. F. Kennedy. Air 10, 20, 40, 70d., 1r.50, 2, 3, 5r.
Paintings. Postage. Arab Paintings 1, 2, 3, 4, 5, 30, 70d.; Air. Asian Paintings 1, 2, 3, 5r.; Indian Painting 10r.
Tales from "The Arabian Nights". Postage 1, 2, 3, 10, 30, 50, 70d.; Air 90d., 1, 2, 3r.
World Scout Jamboree, Idaho. Postage 30, 70d., 1r.; Air 2, 3, 4r.
Olympic Games, Mexico (1968). Postage 35, 65, 75d., 1r.; Air 1r.25, 2, 3, 4r.
Winter Olympic Games, Grenoble (1968). Postage 5, 35, 60, 75d.; Air 1, 1r.25, 2, 3r.
Pres. J. F. Kennedy Memorial. Die-stamped on gold foil. Air 10r.
Paintings by Renoir and Terbrugghen. Air 35, 65d., 1, 2r.×3.

1968

Paintings by Velasquez. Air 1r.×2, 2r.×2.
Winter Olympic Games, Grenoble. Die-stamped on gold foil. Air 7r.
Paintings from Famous Galleries. Air 1r.×4, 2r.×6.
Costumes. Air 30d.×2, 70d.×2, 1r.×2, 2r.×2.
Olympic Games, Mexico. Postage 1r.×4; Air 2r.×4.
Satellites and Spacecraft. Air 30d.×2, 70d.×2, 1r.×2, 2r.×2, 3r.×2.
Paintings. Hunting Dogs. Air 2r.×6.
Paintings. Adam and Eve. Air 2r.×4.
Human Rights Year. Kennedy Brothers and Martin Luther King. Air 1r.×3, 2r.×3.
Kennedy Brothers Memorial. Postage 2r.; Air 5r.
Sports Champions. Inter-Milano Football Club. Postage 5, 10, 15, 20, 25d.; Air 10r.
Sports Champions. Famous Footballers. Postage 15, 20, 50, 75d., 1r.; Air 10r.
Cats. Postage 1, 2, 3d.; Air 2, 3r.
Olympic Games, Mexico. Die-stamped on gold foil. 5r.
5th Death Anniv of Pres. J. F. Kennedy. On gold foil. Air 10r.
Paintings of the Madonna. Air 30, 70d., 1, 2, 3r.
Space Exploration. Postage 5, 10, 15, 20, 25d.; Air 15r.
Olympic Games, Mexico. Gold Medals. Postage 2r.×4; Air 5r.×4.
Christmas. Air 5r.

1969

Sports Champions. Cyclists. Postage 1, 2, 5, 10, 15, 20d.; Air 12r.
Sports Champions. German Footballers. Postage 5, 10, 15, 20, 25d.; Air 10r.
Sports Champions. Motor-racing Drivers. Postage 1, 5, 10, 15, 25d.; Air 10r.
Motor-racing Cars. Postage 1, 5, 10, 15, 25d.; Air 10r.
Sports Champions. Boxers. Postage 5, 10, 15, 20d.; Air 10r.
Sports Champions. Baseball Players. Postage 1, 2, 5, 10, 15d.; Air 10r.
Birds. Air 1r.×11.
Roses. 1r.×6.
Wild Animals. Air 1r.×6.
Paintings. Italian Old Masters. 5, 10, 15, 20d., 10r.
Paintings. Famous Composers. Air 5, 10, 25d., 10r.
Paintings. French Artists. 1r.×4.
Paintings. Nudes. Air 2r.×4.
Three Kings Mosaic. Air 1r.×2, 3r.×2.
Kennedy Brothers. Air 2, 3, 10r.
Olympic Games, Mexico. Gold Medal Winners. Postage 1, 2d., 10r.; Air 10d., 5, 10r.
Paintings of the Madonna. Postage 10d.; Air 10r.
Space Flight of "Apollo 9". Optd on 1968 Space Exploration issue. Air 15r.
Space Flight of "Apollo 10". Optd on 1968 Space Exploration issue. Air 15r.
1st Death Anniv of Gagarin. Optd on 1968 Space Exploration issue. 5d.
2nd Death Anniv of Edward White. Optd on 1968 Space Exploration issue. 10d.
1st Death Anniv of Robert Kennedy. Optd on 1969 Kennedy Brothers issue. Air 2r.
European Football Championship. Optd on 1968 Famous Footballers issue. Air 10r.
Olympic Games, Munich (1972). Optd on 1969 Mexico Gold Medal Winners issue. Air 10d., 5, 10r.
Moon Landing of "Apollo 11". Air 1, 2, 5r.
Moon Landing of "Apollo 11". Circular designs on gold or silver foil. Air 3r.×3, 5r.×3, 10r.×14.
Paintings. Christmas. Postage 1, 2, 3, 4, 5, 15d.; Air 2, 3r.

1970

"Apollo" Space Flights. Postage 1, 2, 4, 5, 10d.; Air 3, 5r.
Birth Bicentenary of Napoleon Bonaparte. Die-stamped on gold foil. Air 20r.
Paintings. Easter. Postage 5, 10, 12, 30, 50, 70d.; Air 1, 2r.
Moon Landing. Die-stamped on gold foil. Air 20r.
Paintings by Michelangelo. Postage 1, 2, 4, 5, 8, 10d.; Air 3, 5r.
World Cup Football Championship, Mexico. Air 25, 50, 75d., 1, 2, 3r.
"Expo 70" World Fair, Osaka, Japan. Japanese Paintings. Postage 1, 2, 3, 4, 5, 10, 15d.; Air 1, 5r.
Birth Bicent Napoleon Bonaparte. Postage 1, 2, 4, 5, 10d.; Air 3, 5r.
Paintings. Old Masters. Postage 1, 2, 5, 6, 10d.; Air 1, 2, 3r.
Space Flight of "Apollo 13". Air 50, 75, 80d., 1, 2, 3r.
World Cup Football Championship, Mexico. Die-stamped on gold foil. Air 20r.
Olympic Games, 1960–1972. Postage 15, 30, 50, 70d.; Air 2, 5r.
"Expo 70" World Fair, Osaka, Japan. Pavilions. Postage 1, 2, 3, 4, 10, 15d.; Air 1, 3r.
Brazil's Victory in World Cup Football Championship. Optd on 1970 World Football Cup issue. Air 25, 50, 75d., 1, 2, 3r.
"Gemini" and "Apollo" Space Flights. Postage 1, 2, 3, 4, 5, 6, 8, 10, 12, 15, 20, 25, 30, 35, 40, 50d.; Air 1, 1r.50, 2, 3r.
Vintage and Veteran Cars. Postage 1, 2, 4, 5, 8, 10d.; Air 2, 3r.
Pres. D. Eisenhower Commem. Postage 30, 50, 70d.; Air 1, 2, 3r.
Paintings by Ingres. Air 25, 30, 35, 50, 70, 85d., 1, 2r.
500th Birth Anniv (1971) of Albrecht Durer. Air 25, 30, 35, 50, 70, 85d., 1, 2r.
Christmas Paintings. Air 25, 30, 35, 50, 70, 85d., 1, 2r.
Winter Olympic Games, Sapporo, Japan (1972). Die-stamped on gold foil. Air 20r.
Meeting of Eisenhower and De Gaulle, 1942. Die-stamped on gold foil. Air 20r.
General De Gaulle Commem. Air 25, 50, 75d., 1, 2, 3r.
Winter Olympic Games, Sapporo, Japan (1972). Sports. Postage 1, 2, 5, 10d.; Air 3, 5r.
J. Rindt, World Formula 1 Motor-racing Champion. Die-stamped on gold foil. Air 20r.

1971

"Philatokyo" Stamp Exhibition, Tokyo. Japanese Paintings. Air 25, 30, 35, 50, 70, 85d., 1, 2r.
Mars Space Project. Air 50, 75, 80d., 1, 2, 3r.
Napoleonic Military Uniforms. Postage 5, 10, 15, 20, 25, 30d.; Air 2, 3r.
Olympic Games, Munich (1972). Sports. Postage 10, 15, 25, 30, 40d.; Air 1, 2, 3r.
Paintings by Modern Artists. Air 25, 30, 35, 50, 70, 85d.; 1, 2r.
Paintings by Famous Artists. Air 25, 30, 35, 50, 70, 85d., 1, 2r.
25th Anniv of United Nations. Optd on 1971 Modern Artists issue. Air 25, 30, 35, 50, 70, 85d., 1, 2r.
Olympic Games, Munich (1972). Sports. Postage 1, 2, 3, 4, 5, 6, 8, 10, 12, 15, 20, 25, 30, 35, 40, 50d.; Air 1, 1r.50, 2, 3r.
Butterflies. Air 25, 30, 35, 50, 70, 85d., 1, 2r.
Space Flight of "Apollo 14". Postage 15, 25, 50, 60, 70d.; Air 5r.
Winter Olympic Games, 1924–1968. Postage 30, 40, 50, 75d., 1r.; Air 2r.
Signs of the Zodiac. 1, 2, 5, 10, 12, 15, 25, 30, 35, 45, 50, 60d.
Famous Men. Air 65, 70, 75, 80, 85, 90d., 1, 1r.25, 1r.50, 2, 2r.50, 3r.
Death Bicent of Beethoven. 20, 30, 40, 60d., 1r.50, 2r.
Dr. Albert Schweitzer Commem. 20, 30, 40, 60d., 1r.50, 2r.
Tropical Birds. Postage 1, 2, 3, 4, 5, 10d.; Air 2, 3r.
Paintings by French Artists. Postage 1, 2, 3, 4, 5, 10d.; Air 2, 3r.
Paintings by Modern Artists. Postage 1, 2, 3, 4, 5, 10d.; Air 2, 3r.
Paintings by Degas. Postage 1, 2, 3, 4, 5, 10d.; Air 2, 3r.
Paintings by Titian. Postage 1, 2, 3, 4, 5, 10d.; Air 2, 3r.
Paintings by Renoir. Postage 1, 2, 3, 4, 5, 10d.; Air 2, 3r.
Space Flight of "Apollo 15". Postage 25, 40, 50, 60d., 1r.; Air 6r.
"Philatokyo" Stamp Exhibition, Tokyo. Stamps. Postage 10, 15, 20, 30, 35, 50, 60, 80d.; Air 1, 2r.
Tropical Birds. Postage 1, 2, 3, 5, 7, 10, 12, 15, 20, 25, 30, 40d.; Air 50, 80d., 1, 3r.
Paintings depicting Venus. Postage 1, 2, 3, 4, 5, 10d.; Air 2, 3r.
13th World Scout Jamboree, Asagiri, Japan. Scouts. Postage 1, 2, 3, 5, 7, 10, 12, 15, 20, 25, 30, 35, 40, 50, 65, 80d.; Air 1, 1r.25, 1r.50, 2r.
Lions International Clubs. Optd on 1971 Famous Paintings issue. Air 25, 30, 35, 50, 70, 85d., 1, 2r.
13th World Scout Jamboree, Asagiri, Japan. Japanese Paintings. Postage 20, 30, 40, 60, 75d.; Air 3r.
25th Anniv of UNICEF Optd on 1971 Scout Jamboree (paintings) issue. Postage 20, 30, 40, 60, 75d.; Air 3r.
Christmas 1971. (1st series. Plain frames). Portraits of Popes. Postage 1, 2, 3, 4, 5, 10d.; Air 2, 3r.
Modern Cars. Postage 10, 15, 25, 40, 50d.; Air 3r.
Olympic Games, Munich (1972). Show-jumping. Embossed on gold foil. Air 20r.
Exploration of Outer Space. Postage 15, 25, 50, 60, 70d.; Air 5r.
Royal Visit of Queen Elizabeth II to Japan. Postage 1, 2, 3, 4, 5, 10d.; Air 2, 3r.
Meeting of Pres. Nixon and Emperor Hirohito of Japan in Alaska. Design as 3r. value of 1970 Eisenhower issue but value changed and optd with commemorative inscr. Air 5r. (silver opt), 5r. (gold opt).
"Apollo" Astronants. Postage 5, 20, 35, 40, 50d.; Air 1, 2, 3r.
Discoverers of the Universe. Astronomers and Space Scientists. Postage 5, 10, 15, 20, 25, 30d.; Air 2, 5r.
"ANPHILEX 71" Stamp Exn, New York. Air 2r.50.
Christmas 1971. Portraits of Popes (2nd series. Ornamental frames). Postage 1, 2, 3, 4, 5, 10d.; Air 2, 3r.

Royal Silver Wedding of Queen Elizabeth II and Prince Philip (1972). Air 1, 2, 3r.
Space Flight of "Apollo 16". Postage 20, 30, 40, 50, 60d.; Air 3, 4r.
Fairy Tales. "Baron Munchhausen" Stories. Postage 1, 2, 4, 5, 10d.; Air 3r.
World Fair, Philadelphia (1976). Paintings. Postage 25, 50, 75d.; Air 5r.
Fairy Tales. Stories of the Brothers Grimm. Postage 1, 2, 4, 5, 10d.; Air 3r.
European Tour of Emperor Hirohito of Japan. Postage 1, 2, 4, 5, 10d.; Air 6r.
13th World Scout Jamboree, Asagiri, Japan. Postage 5, 10, 15, 20, 25d.; Air 5r.
Winter Olympic Games, Sapporo, Japan (1972). Postage 5, 10, 15, 20, 25d.; Air 5r.
Olympic Games, Munich (1972). Postage 5, 10, 15, 20, 25d.; Air 5r.
"Japanese Life". Postage 10d.×4, 20d.×4, 30d.×4, 40d.×4, 50d.×4; Air 3r.×4.
Space Flight of "Apollo 15". Postage 5, 10, 15, 20, 25, 50d.; Air 1, 2, 3, 5r.
"Soyuz 11" Disaster. Air 50d., 1r., 1r.50.
"The Future in Space". Postage 5, 10, 15, 20, 25, 50d.
2500th Anniv of Persian Empire. Postage 10, 20, 30, 40, 50d., Air 3r.
Cats. Postage 10, 15, 20, 25d.; Air 50d., 1r.
50th Anniv of Tutankhamun Tomb Discovery. Postage 1, 2, 3, 4, 5, 6, 7, 8, 9, 10, 11, 12, 13, 14, 15, 16d.; Air 1r.×4.
400th Birth Anniv of Johannes Kepler (astronomer). Postage 50d.; Air 5r.
Famous Men. Air. 1r.×5.

1972

150th Death Anniv of Napoleon Bonaparte (1971). Postage 10, 20, 30, 40d.; Air 1, 2, 3, 4r.
1st Death Anniv of General de Gaulle. Postage 10, 20, 30, 40d.; Air 1, 2, 3, 4r.
Wild Animals (1st series). Postage 5, 10, 15, 20, 25, 30, 35, 40d.
Tropical Fishes. Postage 5, 10, 15, 20, 25d.; Air 50, 75d., 1r.
Famous Musicians. Postage 5d.×3, 10d.×3, 15d.×3, 20d.×3, 25d.×3, 30d.×3, 35d.×3, 40d.×3.
Easter. Postage 5, 10, 15, 20, 25d.; Air 5r.
Wild Animals (2nd series). Postage 5, 10, 15, 20, 25d.; Air 5r.
"Tour de France" Cycle Race. Postage 5, 10, 15, 20, 25, 30, 35, 40, 45, 50, 55d.; Air 60, 65, 70, 75, 80, 85, 90, 95d., 1r.

Many other issues were released between 1 September 1971 and 1 August 1972, but their authenticity has been denied by the Ajman Postmaster-General. Certain issues of 1967-69 exist overprinted to commemorate other events but the Postmaster General states that these are unofficial. Ajman joined the United Arab Emirates on 1 August 1972 and the Ministry of Communications assumed responsibility for the postal services. Further stamps inscribed "Ajman" issued after that date were released without authority and had no validity.

Pt. 11

ALAND ISLANDS

Aland is an autonomous province of Finland. From 1984 separate stamps were issued for the area although stamps of Finland could also still be used there. On 1 January 1993 Aland assumed control of its own postal service and Finnish stamps ceased to be valid there.

1984. 100 pennia = 1 markka.
2002. 100 cents = 1 euro.

1 Fishing Boat

1984

1	1	10p. mauve	15	20
2	1	20p. green	25	20
3	1	50p. green	25	20
4	-	1m. green	55	45
5	1	1m.10 blue	55	45
6	1	1m.20 black	55	55
7	1	1m.30 green	65	65
8	-	1m.40 multicoloured	1·20	80
9a	-	1m.50 multicoloured	1·00	55
10	-	1m.90 multicoloured	1·00	95
12	-	3m. blue, green and black	1·50	1·10
14	-	10m. black, chestnut & brn	4·25	2·75
15	-	13m. multicoloured	6·00	5·00

DESIGNS—20×29 mm: 1m.50, Midsummer pole, Storby village. 21×31 mm: 13m. Rug, 1793. 26×32 mm: 3m. Map of Aland Islands. 30×20 mm: 1m. Farjsund Bridge. 31×21 mm: 1m.40, Aland flag; 1m.90, Mariehamn Town Hall. 32×26 mm: 10m. Seal of Aland showing St. Olaf (patron saint).

2 *Pommern* (barque) and Car Ferries, Mariehamn West Harbour

1984. 50th Anniv of Society of Shipowners.

16	2	2m. multicoloured	4·75	2·30

3 Grove of Ashes and Hazels

1985. Aland Scenes. Multicoloured.

17	2m. Type **3**	1·90	1·00
18	5m. Kokar Church and shore (horiz)	1·90	1·70
19	8m. Windmill and farm (horiz)	3·25	2·75

4 Map, Compass and Measuring Instrument

1986. Nordic Orienteering Championships, Aland.

20	4	1m.60 multicoloured	3·00	1·70

5 Clay Hands and Burial Mounds, Skamkulla

1986. Archaeology. Multicoloured.

21	1m.60 Type **5**	1·90	80
22	2m.20 Bronze staff from Finby and Apostles	1·00	90
23	20m. Monument at ancient court site, Saltvik, and court in session (horiz)	7·75	7·50

6 "Onnigeby" (drawing, Victor Westerholm)

1986. Centenary of Onnigeby Artists' Colony.

24	6	3m.70 multicoloured	4·00	2·10

7 Eiders

1987. Birds. Multicoloured.

25	1m.70 Type **7**	7·75	7·25
26	2m.30 Tufted ducks	3·75	2·75
27	12m. Velvet scoters	5·00	4·75

8 Firemen in Horse-drawn Cart

1987. Centenary of Mariehamn Fire Brigade.

28	8	7m. multicoloured	7·00	7·75

9 Meeting and Item 3 of Report

1987. 70th Anniv of Aland Municipalities Meeting, Finstrom.

29	9	1m.70 multicoloured	1·70	1·20

10 Loading Mail Barrels at Eckero

1988. 350th Anniv of Postal Service in Aland.

30	10	1m.80 multicoloured	2·40	1·70

11 Ploughing with Horses

1988. Centenary of Agricultural Education in Aland.

31	11	2m.20 multicoloured	2·10	2·10

12 Baltic Galleass *Albanus*

1988. Sailing Ships. Multicoloured.

32	1m.80 Type **12**	2·50	1·50
33	2m.40 Schooner *Ingrid* (horiz)	3·75	3·25
34	11m. Barque *Pamir* (horiz)	10·00	8·50

13 St. Olaf's Church, Jomala

1988

35	13	1m.40 multicoloured	1·90	1·50

14 Elder-flowered Orchid

1989. Orchids. Multicoloured.

36	1m.50 Type **14**	2·50	1·60
37	2m.50 Narrow-leaved helleborine	3·25	2·20
38	14m. Lady's slipper	11·50	10·00

15 Teacher and Pupils

1989. 350th Anniv of First Aland School, Saltvik.

39	15	1m.90 multicoloured	1·50	1·30

16 St. Michael's Church, Finstrom

1989

40	16	1m.50 multicoloured	1·50	1·40

17 Baltic Herring

1990. Fish. Multicoloured.

41	1m.50 Type **17**	1·30	1·00
42	2m. Northern pike	1·30	1·00
43	2m.70 European flounder	1·30	1·40

18 St. Andrew's Church, Lumparland

1990

44	18	1m.70 multicoloured	1·50	1·30

19 *St. Catherine* (fresco, St. Anna's Church, Kumlinge)

1990

45	19	2m. multicoloured	90	85

20 West European Hedgehog

1991. Mammals. Multicoloured.

46	1m.60 Type **20**	1·30	85
47	2m.10 Eurasian red squirrel	1·30	1·00
48	2m.90 Roe deer	1·50	1·60

21 Volleyball

1991. Small Island Games, Mariehamn. Sheet 117×81 mm containing T **21** and similar vert designs. Multicoloured.

MS49 2m.10; Type **21**; 2m.10; Shooting; 2m.10; Football; 2m.10, Running 5·00 4·75

22 Canoeing

1991. Nordic Countries' Postal Co-operation. Tourism. Multicoloured.

50	2m.10 Type **22**	90	90
51	2m.90 Cycling	1·50	1·50

23 *League of Nations Meeting, Geneva, 1921* (print by F. Rackwitz)

1991. 70th Anniv of Aland Autonomy.

52	23	16m. multicoloured	9·00	7·00

24 St. Mathias's Church, Vardo

1991

53	24	1m.80 multicoloured	1·50	1·00

25 Von Knorring (after Karl Jansson)

1992. Birth Bicentenary of Rev. Frans Peter von Knorring (social reformer).

54	**25**	2 klass (1m.60) mult	1·30	90

26 Barque *Herzogen Cecilie* and Wheat Transport Route Map

1992. 48th International Association of Cape Horners Congress, Mariehamn.

55	**26**	1 klass (2m.10) mult	2·00	1·50

27 Ranno Lighthouse

1992. Lighthouses. Multicoloured.

56	2m.10 Type **27**	5·75	2·50
57	2m.10 Salskar	5·75	2·50
58	2m.10 Lagskar	5·75	2·50
59	2m.10 Market	5·75	2·50

28 *Lemland Landscape*

1992. Birth Cent of Joel Pettersson (painter). Multicoloured

60	2m.90 Type **28**	1·30	1·10
61	16m. *Self-portrait*	6·50	6·25

29 Delegates processing to Church Service

1992. 70th Anniv of First Aland Provincial Parliament.

62	**29**	3m.40 multicoloured	1·90	1·50

30 St. Catherine's Church, Hammarland

1992

63	**30**	1m.80 multicoloured	1·50	90

31 Arms

1993. Postal Autonomy. Multicoloured.

64	1m.60 Type **31**	1·20	85
MS65	129×80 mm. 1m.90 Cover with Kastelholm single-line postmark (26×35 mm); 1m.90 Mareinhamm Post Office; 1m.90 Post van leaving *Alfågeln* (ferry); 1m.90 Postal emblem (26×31 mm)	4·25	3·00

32 Fiddler

1993. Nordic Countries' Postal Co-operation. Tourism. Exhibits from Jan Karlsgarden Open-air Museum.

66	**32**	2m. red, pink and black	1·00	85
67	-	2m.30 blue, black and azure	1·00	1·00

DESIGN—HORIZ: 2m.30, Boat-house.

33 Saltvik Woman

1993. Costumes. Multicoloured.

68	1m.90 Type **33**	1·30	85
69	3m.50 Eckero and Brando women and Mariehamn couple	1·50	1·50
70	17m. Finstrom couple	8·25	7·25

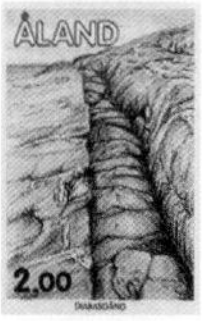

34 Diabase Dyke, Sottunga

1993. Aland Geology. Multicoloured.

71	10p. Boulder field, Dano Gamlan	25	20
72	1m.60 Drumlin (hillock), Markusbole	75	75
73	2m. Type **34**	90	70
74	2m.30 Pitcher of Kallskar	90	75
75	2m.70 Pillow lava, Kumlinge	1·20	90
76	2m.90 Red Cow (islet), Lumpurn	1·30	1·30
77	3m.40 Erratic boulder, Torsskar, Kokar Osterbygge (horiz)	1·40	1·40
78	6m. Folded gneiss	2·50	2·30
79	7m. Pothole, Bano Foglo (horiz)	2·75	2·50

35 Mary Magdalene Church, Sottunga

1993

80	**35**	1m.80 multicoloured	1·30	1·20

37 Glanville's Fritillary (*Melitaea cinxia*)

1994. Butterflies. Multicoloured.

81	2m.30 Type **37**	1·30	1·20
82	2m.30 *Quercusia querqus*	1·30	1·10
83	2m.30 Clouded apollo (*Parnassius mnemosyne*)	1·30	1·20
84	2m.30 *Hesperia comma*	1·30	1·10

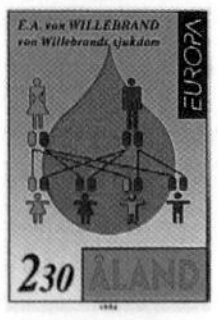

38 Genetic Diagram

1994. Europa. Medical Discoveries. Multicoloured.

85	2m.30 Type **38** (discovery of Von Willebrand's disease (hereditary blood disorder))	2·50	2·00
86	2m.90 Molecular diagram (purification of heparin by Erik Jorpes)	2·50	2·00

39 Comb Ceramic and Pitted Ware Pottery

1994. The Stone Age.

87	**39**	2m.40 brown	1·00	1·20
88	-	2m.80 blue	1·20	1·30
89	-	18m. green	7·75	7·75

DESIGNS—VERT: 2m.80, Stone tools. HORIZ: 18m. Canoe and tent by river (reconstruction of Stone-age village, Langbergsoda).

40 St. John the Baptist's Church, Sund

1994

90	**40**	2m. multicoloured	1·50	1·10

42 *Skuta* (Cargo Sailing Boat)

1995. Cargo Sailing Ships. Multicoloured.

91	2m.30 Type **42**	1·00	1·20
92	2m.30 *Sump* (well-boat)	1·00	1·20
93	2m.30 *Storbat* (farm boat)	1·00	1·20
94	2m.30 *Jakt*	1·00	1·20

43 National Colours and E.U. Emblem

1995. Admission of Aland Islands to European Union.

95	**43**	2m.90 multicoloured	1·70	1·30

44 Doves and Cliffs

1995. Europa. Peace and Freedom. Multicoloured.

96	2m.80 Type **44**	1·30	1·30
97	2m.90 Dove, night sky and island	1·30	1·40

45 Golf

1995. Nordic Countries' Postal Co-operation. Tourism. With service indicator. Multicoloured.

98	2 klass (2m.) Type **45**	1·30	1·20
99	1 klass (2m.30) Sport fishing	1·50	1·20

46 Racing Dinghies

1995. Optimist World Dinghy Championships, Mariehamn.

100	**46**	3m.40 multicoloured	2·00	1·40

47 St. George's Church, Geta

1995

101	**47**	2m. multicoloured	1·30	90

48 *St. Olaf* (Wooden Carving from Sund Church)

1995. Birth Millenary of St. Olaf.

102	**48**	4m.30 multicoloured	1·90	2·00

49 Fish holding Flag in Mouth ("Greetings from Aland")

1996. Greetings Stamps. With service indicator. Multicoloured.

103	1 klass Type **49**	1·50	1·20
104	1 klass Bird holding flower in beak ("Congratulations")	1·50	1·20

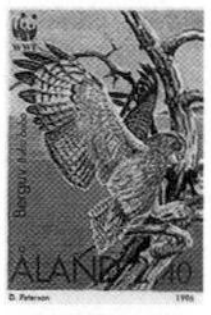

50 Landing on Branch

1996. Endangered Species. The Eagle Owl. Multicoloured.

105	2m.40 Type **50**	1·00	1·20
106	2m.40 Perched on branch	1·00	1·10
107	2m.40 Adult owl	1·00	1·20
108	2m.40 Juvenile owl	1·00	1·10

Nos. 105/6 form a composite design.

51 Sally Salminen (novelist)

1996. Europa. Famous Women. Multicoloured.

109	2m.80 Type **51**	1·20	1·10
110	2m.90 Fanny Sundstrom (politician)	1·20	1·40

52 Choir

1996. Aland '96 Song and Music Festival, Mariehamn.

111	**52**	2m.40 multicoloured	1·30	1·10

53 "Haircut"

1996. 150th Birth Anniv of Karl Jansson (painter).

112	**53**	18m. multicoloured	8·50	8·25

54 *Trilobita asaphus*

1996. Fossils. Multicoloured.

113	40p. Type **54**	25	35
114	9m. *Gastropoda euomophalus*	3·50	3·25

55 Brando Church

1996

115	**55**	2m. multicoloured	1·30	1·00

56 Giant Isopod (*Saduria entomon*) and Opossum Shrimp (*Mysis relicta*)

1997. Marine Survivors from the Ice Age. Multicoloured.

116	30p. Type **56**	25	25
117	2m.40 Four-horned sculpin (*Myotocephalus quadricornis*)	1·30	1·00
118	4m.30 Ringed seal (*Phoca hispida botrica*)	1·70	1·70

57 Coltsfoot (*Tussilago farfara*)

1997. Spring Flowers. Multicoloured.

119	2m.40 Type **57**	1·00	1·20
120	2m.40 Blue anemone (*Hepatica nobilis*)	1·00	1·20
121	2m.40 Wood anemone (*Anemone nemorosa*)	1·00	1·20
122	2m.40 Yellow anemone (*Anemone ranunculoides*)	1·00	1·20

58 Floorball

1997. First Women's Floorball World Championship, Mariehamn and Godby.

123	**58**	3m.40 multicoloured	2·00	1·30

59 The Devil's Dance

1997. Europa. Tales and Legends.

124	**59**	2m.90 multicoloured	2·50	2·30

60 Kastelholm Castle and Arms

1997. 600th Anniv of Kalmar Union between Sweden, Denmark and Norway.

125	**60**	2m.40 multicoloured	1·20	1·30

61 Hologram of Schooner *Linden* and "75 Years"

1997. 75th Anniv of Aland Autonomy. Sheet 128×80 mm.

MS126	**61** 20m. multicoloured	10·00	9·00

62 *Thornbury* (freighter)

1997. Steam Freighters. Multicoloured.

127	2m.80 Type **62**	1·20	1·20
128	3m.50 *Osmo* (freighter)	1·40	1·30

63 St George's Church, Mariehamn

1997. 70th Anniv of Mariehamn Church.

129	**63**	1m.90 multicoloured	1·30	1·00

64 Man harvesting Apples

1998. Horticulture. Multicoloured.

130	2m. Type **64**	75	85
131	2m.40 Woman harvesting cucumbers	1·30	85

65 Boy on Moped

1998. Youth Activities. Multicoloured.

132	2m.40 Type **65**	1·00	1·20
133	2m.40 Laptop computer	1·00	1·20
134	2m.40 CD disk and headphones	1·00	1·20
135	2m.40 Step aerobics	1·00	1·20

66 Midsummer Celebrations

1998. Europa. National Festivals.

136	**66**	4m.20 multicoloured	2·75	1·80

67 *Isabella* (car ferry)

1998. Nordic Countries' Postal Co-operation. Shipping.

137	**67**	2m.40 multicoloured	1·30	1·00

68 Waves breaking

1998. International Year of the Ocean.

138	**68**	6m.30 multicoloured	3·00	2·40

69 Players

1998. Association of Tennis Professionals Senior Tour, Mariehamn. Self-adhesive.

139	**69**	2m.40 multicoloured	1·30	1·00

70 Schooner, Compass Rose and Knots

1998. Ninth International Sea Scout Camp, Bomarsund Fortress, Aland.

140	**70**	2m.80 multicoloured	1·40	1·10

71 Seffers Homestead, Onningeby

1998. Traditional Porches. Multicoloured.

141	1m.60 Type **71**	65	65
142	2m. Labbas homestead, Storby	75	85
143	2m.90 Abras homestead, Bjorko	1·20	1·20

72 Eckero Church

1998

144	**72**	1m.90 multicoloured	1·30	85

73 Sword and Dagger

1999. Bronze Age Relics. Multicoloured.

145	2m. Type **73**	75	85
146	2m.20 "Ship" tumulus (vert)	90	1·00

74 Wardrobe

1999. Folk Art. Decorated Furniture. Multicoloured.

147	2m.40 Type **74**	1·00	1·00
148	2m.40 Distaff	1·00	1·00
149	2m.40 Chest	1·00	1·00
150	2m.40 Spinning wheel	1·00	1·00

75 'Pamir' and 'Passat' (barques) off Port Victoria (R. Castor)

1999. 50th Anniv of Rounding of Cape Horn by *Pamir* on Last Wheat-carrying Voyage.

151	**75**	3m.40 multicoloured	1·70	1·40

76 Cowslip

1999. Provincial Plant of Aland. Self-adhesive.

152	**76**	2m.40 multicoloured	1·20	1·00

77 Ido Island, Kokar

1999. Europa. Parks and Gardens.

153	**77**	2m.90 multicoloured	2·20	1·20

No. 153 is denominated both in markkas and in euros.

78 Racing Yachts

1999. Sailing.

154	**78**	2m.70 multicoloured	1·40	1·10

79 Puffed Shield Lichen (*Hypogymnia physodes*)

1999. Lichens. With service indicator. Multicoloured.

155	2 klass (2m.) Type **79**	1·30	90
156	1 klass (2m.40) Common orange lichen (*Xanthoria parietina*)	1·50	1·00

80 Loading Avions de Transport Regional ATR72

1999. 125th Anniv of Universal Postal Union.

157	**80**	2m.90 multicoloured	1·20	1·30

81 St. Bridget's Church, Lemland

1999

158	**81**	1m.90 multicoloured	1·20	1·00

82 Runners

1999. Finnish Cross-country Championships, Mariehamn.

159	**82**	3m.50 multicoloured	1·50	1·30

DENOMINATION. From No. 162 to 207 Aland Islands stamps are denominated both in markkas and in euros. As no cash for the latter is in circulation, the catalogue continues to use the markka value.

83 Arctic Tern (*Sterna paradisaea*)

2000. Sea Birds. Multicoloured.

162	1m.80 Type **83**	75	70
164	2m.20 Mew gull (*Larus canus*) (vert)	90	85
166	2m.60 Great black-backed gull (*Larus marinus*)	1·00	95

84 International Peace Symbol and State Flag

2000. New Millennium Sheet. 100×80 mm. Multicoloured.

MS171	**84** 3m.40, yellow; 3m.40, red; 3m.40, blue; 3m.40, white	8·00	5·25

85 Elk

2000. The Elk (*Alces alces*). Multicoloured.

172	2m.60 Type **85**	1·00	1·00
173	2m.60 With young	1·00	1·00
174	2m.60 Beside lake	1·00	1·00
175	2m.60 In snow	1·00	1·00

86 "Building Europe"

2000. Europa.

176	**86**	3m. multicoloured	2·20	1·60

87 Gymnast

2000. Finno-Swedish Gymnastics Association Exhibition, Mariehamn. Self-adhesive.

177	**87**	2m.60 multicoloured	1·30	1·00

88 Crew and *Linden* (schooner)

2000. Visit by *Cutty Sark* Tall Ships' Race Competitors to Mariehamn.

178	**88**	3m.40 multicoloured	1·60	1·20

89 Lange on prow of Longship

2000. Death Millenary of Hlodver Lange the Viking.

179	**89**	4m.50 multicoloured	2·40	1·90

90 Wooden Ornamented Swiss-style House, Mariehamn

2000. 48th Death Anniv of Hilda Hongell (architect). Multicoloured.

180	3m.80 Type **90**	1·50	1·30
181	10m. House with central front entrance, Mariehamn	3·75	3·50

91 The Nativity

2000. 2000 Years of Christianity.

182	**91**	3m. multicoloured	1·50	1·20

92 Kokar Church

2000

183	**92**	2m. multicoloured	1·20	95

93 Steller's Eider in Flight

2001. Endangered Species. The Steller's Eider (*Polysticta stelleri*). Multicoloured.

184	2m.70 Type **93**	1·00	1·20
185	2m.70 Duck and drake	1·00	1·20
186	2m.70 Duck and drake swimming	1·00	1·20
187	2m.70 Drake swimming	1·00	1·20

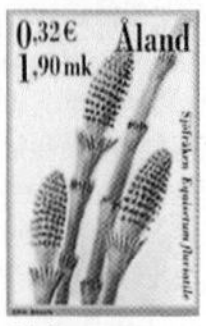

94 Swamp Horsetail (*Equisetum fluviatile*)

2001. Plants. Multicoloured.

188	1m.90 Type **94**	90	85
189	2m.80 Stiff clubmoss (*Lycopodium annotinum*)	1·20	1·20
190	3m.50 Polypody (*Polybodium vulgare*)	1·40	1·30

95 Heart and Graffiti on Brick Wall

2001. St. Valentine's Day.

200	**95**	3m.20 multicoloured	1·40	1·30

96 Fisherman and Fish

2001. Europa. Water Resources.

201	**96**	3m.20 multicoloured	2·10	1·90

97 Archipelago Windmill

2001. Windmills. Multicoloured.

202	3m. Type **97**	1·20	1·20
203	7m. Timbered windmill (horiz)	2·75	2·50
204	20m. Nest windmill (horiz)	8·00	7·50

98 Golden Retriever

2001. Puppies. Multicoloured.

205	2 klass (2m.30) Type **98**	1·20	90
206	1 klass (2m.70) Wire-haired dachshund	1·40	1·00

99 Foglo Church

2001

207	**99**	2m. multicoloured	90	75

100 Smooth Snake (*Coronella Austriaca*)

2002. Endangered Animals. Multicoloured.

208	5c. Type **100**	25	20
209	70c. Great crested newt (*Triturus cristatus*)	1·40	1·50

101 Woman pushing Shopping Trolley

2002. Euro Currency.

210	**101**	60c. multicoloured	1·50	1·30

102 Tidying up Christmas

2002. St. Canute's Day.

211	**102**	€2 multicoloured	4·75	4·50

103 Spiced Salmon and New Potatoes

2002. Traditional Dishes. Multicoloured.

212	1 klass (55c.) Type **103**	1·40	1·20
213	1 klass (55c.) Fried herring, mashed potatoes and beetroot	1·40	1·20
214	1 klass (55c.) Black bread and butter	1·40	1·20
215	1 klass (55c.) Aland pancake with stewed prune sauce and whipped cream	1·40	1·20

104 Building

2002. Inauguration of New Post Terminal, Sviby.

216	**104**	€1 multicoloured	2·50	2·20

105 Circus Elephant and Rider

2002. Europa. Circus.

217	**105**	40c. multicoloured	1·50	1·20

106 "Radar II" (sculpture, Stefan Lindfors)

2002. Nordic Countries' Postal Co-operation. Modern Art.

218	**106**	€3 multicoloured	7·00	6·25

107 Kayaking

2002

219	**107**	90c. multicoloured	2·30	2·50

108 8th-century Buckle, Persby, Sud

2002. Iron Age Jewellery found on Aland. Multicoloured.

220	2 klass. (45c.) Type **108**	1·20	1·00
221	1 klass. (55c.) 8th-century pin, Sylloda, Saltvik	1·40	1·20

109 Saltvik Church

2002

222	**109**	35c. multicoloured	1·00	85

110 Holmen

2002. Janne Holmen (Olympic gold medallist, men's marathon).

223	**110**	1 klass. (55c.) mult	1·40	1·20

111 *Cantharellus cibarius*

2003. Fungi. Multicoloured.

224	10c. Type **111**	25	30
225	50c. *Boletus edulis*	1·30	95
226	€2.50 *Macrolepiota procera*	6·50	5·75

112 Tovis (kitten)

2003. Cat Photograph Competition Winners. Multicoloured.

227	2 klass (45c.) Type **112**	1·20	1·10
228	1 klass (55c.) Randi (cat) (horiz)	1·40	1·30

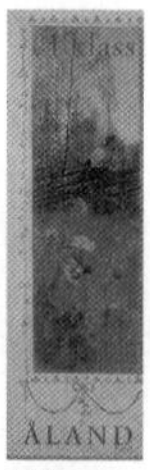

113 *Landscape in Summer* (detail) (Elin Danielson-Gambogi)

2003. Designs showing details of the painting. Multicoloured.

229	1 klass (55c.) Type **113**	1·40	1·30
230	1 klass (55c.) Trees and flowers	1·40	1·30
231	1 klass (55c.) Sunset over sea	1·40	1·30
232	1 klass (55c.) Shoreline and boats	1·40	1·30

114 *Freedom of Speech and Press* (Kurt Simons)

2003. Europa. Poster Art.

233	**114**	45c. multicoloured	1·70	1·30

115 *Pommern* (Arthur Victor Gregory)

2003. Centenary of *Pommern* (four mast steel barque, now museum). Self-adhesive.

234	**115**	55c. multicoloured	2·10	1·40

116 Two Boys

2003. 'My Aland'. Mark Levengood.

235	**116**	55c. multicoloured	1·40	1·30

117 Fiddle Player

2003. 50th Anniv of Aland Folk Music Association.

236	**117**	€1.10 multicoloured	2·50	2·10

118 Kumlinge Church

2003

237	**118**	40c. multicoloured	1·00	90

119 Children dressed as St. Lucia and her Attendants

2003. St. Lucia Celebrations.

238	**119**	60c. multicoloured	1·50	1·20

120 Ermine (*Mustela erminea*)

2004. Predators. Multicoloured.

239	20c. Type **120**	65	50
240	60c. Fox (*Vulpes vulpes*)	1·50	1·50
241	€3 Pine martin (*Martes martes*)	7·75	6·75

121 Fenja and Menja (giantesses)

2004. Nordic Mythology. Sheet 105×70 mm.

MS250 **121**	55c. multicoloured	1·40	1·30

Stamps of a similar theme were issued by Denmark, Faroe Islands, Finland, Greenland, Iceland, Norway and Sweden.

122 Flag

2004. 50th Anniv of Aland Flag. Self-adhesive.

251	**122**	1klass (60c.) multicoloured	1·40	1·30

123 *Cajsa* (longboat) and Passengers, 1986

2004. 'My Aland'. Mauno Koivisto (Finnish president 1982–94).

252	**123**	90c. multicoloured	2·20	2·00

124 Yacht moored in Inlet

2004. Europa. Holidays.

253	**124**	75c. multicoloured	1·80	1·60

125 Bomarsund Fortress

2004. 150th Anniv of Fall of Bomarsund Fortress. Sheet 170×95 mm containing T **125** and similar vert designs.

MS254	75c.×4, Type **125**; Bomarsund (different); Three soldiers; Six soldiers	7·25	6·75

The stamps and margin of No. **MS**254 form a composite design of painting by A. Lourde-Laplace.

126 Storklyndan, Brando

2004. Landscapes. Multicoloured.

255	2 klass (50c.) Type **126**	1·00	1·10
256	1 klass (60c.) Prästgardsnaset, Findstrom	1·70	1·30

127 Panathenaic Stadium, Athens

2004. Olympic Games, Athens.

257	**127**	80c. multicoloured	1·80	1·70

128 Father Christmas delivering Mail

2004. Christmas.

258	**128**	45c. multicoloured	1·20	1·10

129 Great Cormorant (*Phalacrocorax carbo sinensis*)

2005. Birds. Multicoloured.

259	15c. Type **129**	50	45
260	65c. Whooper swan (*Cygnus Cygnus*)	1·90	1·70
261	€4 Grey heron (*Ardea cinerea*)	9·50	8·25

130 Oakland Sport Chevrolet (1928) (⅔-size illustration)

2005. Vintage Cars. Multicoloured.

262	(60c.) Type **130**	1·70	1·30
263	(60c.) Ford V8 (1939)	1·70	1·30
264	(60c.) Buick Super 4D HT (1957)	1·70	1·30
265	(60c.) Volkswagen 1200 (1964)	1·70	1·30

131 Family and Bonfire

2005. Walpurgis Night. Self-adhesive.

266	**131**	(50c.) multicoloured	1·50	1·20

132 Fish

2005. Europa. Gastronomy.

267	**132**	90c. multicoloured	1·90	1·70

133 Bjorn Borg

2005. 'My Aland'. Bjorn Borg (tennis player).

268	**133**	55c. multicoloured	1·30	1·20

134 "A Visit to Bomarsund Fortress" (Fritz von Dardel)

2005. 150th Anniv of Fall of Bomarsund Fortress (2004) (2nd series).

269	**134**	€1.30 multicoloured	3·25	2·75

135 *Linden* (schooner)

2005

270	**135**	60c. multicoloured	1·70	1·40

136 Sando, Vardo

2005. Landscapes. Multicoloured.

271	70c. Type **136**	1·90	1·40
272	80c. Grondal, Geta	2·20	2·00

137 Boy and Girl Brownies

2005. Christmas.

273	**137**	45c. multicoloured	90	75

138 *Potosia cuprea*

2006. Beetles.

274	40c. Type **138**	75	35
275	65c. *Coccinella septempunctata*	1·30	85
276	€2 *Oryctes nasicornis*	4·50	3·00

139 Face

2006. Centenary of Women's Suffrage.

277	**139**	85c. multicoloured	2·40	2·00

140 Letesgubbe

2006. Nordic Mythology. Sheet 105×70 mm.

MS278 **140**	85c. multicoloured	2·40	2·40

Stamps of a similar theme were issued by Denmark, Greenland, Faroe Islands, Finland, Iceland, Norway and Sweden.

141 Bomarsund Fortress

2006. 150th Anniv of Demilitarization.

279	**141**	€1.50 multicoloured	4·25	4·00

142 Boy as King

2006. Europa. Integration.

280	**142**	€1.30 multicoloured	3·75	3·50

143 Girl posting Letter

2006. My Stamp. Self-adhesive.

281	**143**	1 klass multicoloured	1·75	1·50

144 Sail Boat

2006. 'My Aland'. Ake Lindman (actor and filmmaker).

282	**144**	75c. multicoloured	2·10	2·00

145 Soderby, Lemland

2006. Landscapes. Multicoloured.

283	55c. Type **145**	1·50	1·50
284	€1.20 Norra Essvik, Sottunga	3·50	3·25

146 Tribal-style Tattoo (Thomas Dahlgren)

2006. Tattoos. Multicoloured.

285	65c. Type **146**	2·10	2·00
286	65c. Seaman style (Mikael Sandholm)	2·10	2·00
287	65c. Floral (in memory of Tsunami disaster) (Linda Aberg)	2·10	2·00

147 Horse-drawn Sleigh

2006. Christmas. Inscribed 'JULPOST 06.

288	**147**	(50c.) multicoloured	1·40	1·40

148 *Tripolium vulgare*

2007. Waterside Plants. Multicoloured.

289	80c. Type **148**	2·20	2·00
290	90c. *Lythrum salicaria*	2·60	2·50
291	€5 *Angelica archangelica*	12·50	12·00

149 Junkers F13 flying boat

2007. Postal Transport. Multicoloured.

292	2klass Type **149**	1·60	1·50
293	1klass SAAB 340	2·00	1·80

150 Skaftö, Kumlinge

2007. Landscape.

294	**150**	2klass multicoloured	1·60	1·50

151 *Fillyjonks, Sea Monster and Cliffs* (painting by Tove Jansson)

2007. Art.

295	**151**	85c. multicoloured	2·50	2·40

152 Scout Emblem and Window

2007. Europa. Centenary of Scouting.

296	**152**	70c. multicoloured	2·20	2·10

153 Bridal Crown (Titti Sundblom)

2007. Arts and Crafts. Multicoloured.

297	1klass Type **153**	2·20	2·00
298	1klass Flower print (Maria Korpi-Gordon and Adam Gordon)	2·20	2·00
299	1klass Ceramics (Judy Kuitunen)	2·20	2·00

154 Two Players

2007. My Stamp. Girls' Football in Aland. Self-adhesive.

300	**154**	1klass multicoloured	2·00	1·90

155 *Windmills* (Ture Bengtz)

2007. Birth Centenary of Ture Bengtz (artist and emigrant to USA). Emigration.

301	**155**	75c. multicoloured	2·10	2·00

156 Landscape, Kjusan, Hammarland

2007. SEPAC (Ssmall European Postal Administration Co-operation).

302	**156**	1klass multicoloured	2·00	1·90

157 Santa Claus (poster by Haddon Sundblom)

2007. Christmas. Inscr 'Julpost 07'.

303	**157**	(50c.) multicoloured	1·40	1·30

158 *Perca fluviatilis*

2008. Fish. Paintings by Gosta Sundman. Multicoloured.

304	45c. Type **158**	1·30	1·30
305	€4.50 *Zander lucioperca*	11·50	11·50

159 Signhild at Drottningkleven

2008. Nordic Mythology. Mythical Places. Sheet 105×70 mm. Inscr 'VARLDEN'.

MS306	**159** multicoloured	2·75	2·75

Stamps of a similar theme were issued by Denmark, Faroe Islands, Finland, Greenland, Iceland, Norway and Sweden.

The stamp and margin of No. **MS**306 form a composite design.

MS306 was for use on international mail and was originally on sale for 85c.

160 Langvikshagen, Lumparland

2008. Landscapes. Inscr 'INRIKES'. Multicoloured.

307	(70c.) Type **160**	2·50	2·50
308	(70c.) Badhusberget, Mariehamn	2·50	2·50

Nos. 307/8 were for use on domestic mail and were originally on sale for 70c.

161 Emblem

2008. Olympic Games, Beijing. Inscr 'VARLDEN'.

309	**161**	(90c.) multicoloured	2·50	2·50

No. 309 was for use on international mail and was originally on sale for 90c.

162 Letter, Ship and Sailor's Wife

2008. Europa. The Letter.

310	**162**	€1 multicoloured	2·75	2·75

163 Marhallan

2008. Lighthouses. Inscr 'EUROPA'. Multicoloured.

311	(75c.) Type **163**	2·20	2·20
312	(75c.) Gustaf Dalen	2·20	2·20
313	(75c.) Bogskar	2·20	2·20
314	(75c.) Kokarsoren	2·20	2·20

Nos. 311/14 were for use on mail within Europe and were originally on sale for 75c.

164 Gravel Road and Profiles of Marcus Gronholm and Christoph Treier (trainer)

2008. My Aland. Marcus Gronholm (rally driver). Inscr 'VARLDEN'.

315	**164**	(90c.) multicoloured	2·75	2·75

No. 315 was for use on international mail and was originally on sale for 90c.

165 *Aland Peasant Bride* (Karl Emanuel Jansson)

2008. Art.

316	**165**	€1.50 multicoloured	4·50	4·50

166 Angel

2008. Christmas. Inscr 'JULPOST'.

317	**166**	(55c.) multicoloured	1·50	1·50

No. 317 was on sale for 55c.

167 Horse Rider

2008. My Stamp. Inscr 'EUROPA'. Self-adhesive.

318	**167**	(75c.) multicoloured	2·25	2·25

No. 318 was for use on mail within Europe and was originally on sale for 75c.

168 Boundary Post, Flojtan

2009. New Borders (bicentenary of Aland's integration into Russia). Inscr 'EUROPA'.

319	**168**	(80c.) multicoloured	3·00	3·00

No. 319 was for use on mail within Europe and was originally on sale for 80c.

169 Wind Turbine

2009. Preserve Polar Regions and Glaciers. Centenary of Electricity Supply. Sheet 120×80 mm.

MS320	**169** €2 multicoloured	7·25	7·25

170 Ulla-Lena Lundberg

2009. Authors. Inscr 'EUROPA'. Multicoloured.

321	(80c.) Type **170**	3·00	3·00
322	(80c.) Anni Blomqvist	3·00	3·00
323	(80c.) Valdemar Nyman	3·00	3·00

Nos. 321/3, were issued for use on mail within Europe and were originally on sale for 80c.

171 May Irwin and John Rice

2009. Centenary of Cinema in Aland.

324	**171**	€1.60 multicoloured	6·00	6·00

172 Divers and *Plus* (wreck)

2009. Diving. Inscr 'INRIKES'.

325	**172**	(75c.) multicoloured	2·75	2·75

No. 325 was for use on mail within Aland and Finland and was originally on sale for 75c.

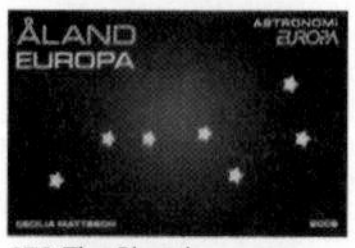

173 The Plough (constellation)

2009. Europa. Astronomy. Inscr 'EUROPA'.

326	**173**	(80c.) multicoloured	3·00	3·00

No. 326 was for use on mail within Europe and was originally on sale for 80c.

174 *Viking*

32

1925. Air.

186	**32**	5q. green	4·25	4·25
187	**32**	10q. red	4·25	4·25
188	**32**	25q. blue	4·25	4·25
189	**32**	50q. green	7·50	7·25
190	**32**	1f. black and violet	13·00	12·50
191	**32**	2f. violet and olive	22·00	21·00
192	**32**	3f. green and brown	27·00	21·00

33 Pres. Ahmed Zogu, later King Zog I

34

1925

193	**33**	1q. yellow	45	30
194	**33**	2q. brown	50	90
195	**33**	5q. green	35	30
196	**33**	10q. red	35	30
197	**33**	15q. brown	2·20	2·50
198	**33**	25q. blue	55	30
199	**33**	50q. green	2·20	1·90
200	**34**	1f. blue and red	4·25	2·50
201	**34**	2f. orange and green	5·50	2·50
202	**34**	3f. violet	11·00	6·25
203	**34**	5f. black and violet	13·00	9·00

1927. Air. Optd **Rep. Shqiptare**.

204	**32**	5q. green	13·00	12·50
205	**32**	10q. red	13·00	12·50
206	**32**	25q. blue	11·00	12·50
207	**32**	50q. green	8·25	7·75
208	**32**	1f. black and violet	16·00	12·50
209	**32**	2f. violet and olive	16·00	12·50
210	**32**	3f. green and brown	22·00	18·00

1927. Optd **A.Z.** and wreath.

211	**33**	1q. yellow	1·60	1·30
212	**33**	2q. brown	85	50
213	**33**	5q. green	3·50	75
214	**33**	10q. red	75	50
215	**33**	15q. brown	20·00	19·00
216	**33**	25q. blue	1·60	50
217	**33**	50q. green	1·60	50
218	**34**	1f. blue and red	3·75	75
219	**34**	2f. orange and green	3·75	1·00
220	**34**	3f. violet and brown	6·50	2·10
221	**34**	5f. black and violet	11·00	3·75

1928. Inauguration of Vlore (Valona)-Brindisi Air Service. Optd **REP. SHQYPTARE Fluturim' i I-ar Vlone-Brindisi 21.IV.1928**.

222	**32**	5q. green	13·00	12·50
223	**32**	10q. red	13·00	12·50
224	**32**	25q. blue	13·00	12·50
225	**32**	50q. green	27·00	26·00
226	**32**	1f. black and violet	£140	£140
227	**32**	2f. violet and olive	£140	£140
228	**32**	3f. green and brown	£140	£140

1928. Surch in figures and bars.

229	**33**	1 on 10q. red (No. 214)	1·60	75
230	**33**	5 on 25q. blue (No. 216)	1·60	75

39 Pres. Ahmed Zogu, later King Zog I

40

1928. National Assembly. Optd **Kujtim i Mbledhjes Kushtetuese 25.8.28.**

231	**39**	1q. brown	11·00	12·50
232	**39**	2q. grey	11·00	12·50
233	**39**	5q. green	11·00	16·00
234	**39**	10q. red	11·00	16·00
235	**39**	15q. brown	33·00	65·00
236	**39**	25q. blue	13·00	16·00
237	**39**	50q. lilac	22·00	21·00
238	**40**	1f. black and blue	13·00	16·00

1928. Accession of King Zog I. Optd **Mbretnia-Shqiptare Zog I 1.IX.1928.**

239	**39**	1q. brown	27·00	31·00
240	**39**	2q. grey	27·00	31·00
241	**39**	5q. green	22·00	26·00
242	**39**	10q. red	22·00	21·00
243	**39**	15q. brown	33·00	37·00
244	**39**	25q. blue	22·00	21·00
245	**39**	50q. lilac	22·00	21·00
246	**40**	1f. black and blue	27·00	26·00
247	**40**	2f. black and green	27·00	26·00

1928. Optd **Mbretnia-Shqiptare** only.

248	**39**	1q. brown	1·10	1·60
249	**39**	2q. grey	1·10	1·60
250	**39**	5q. green	7·50	4·75
251	**39**	10q. red	1·10	1·60
252	**39**	15q. brown	27·00	31·00
253	**39**	25q. blue	1·10	1·60
254	**39**	50q. lilac	2·20	2·50
255	**40**	1f. black and blue	4·25	3·25
256	**40**	2f. black and green	4·25	5·25
257	**40**	3f. olive and red	15·00	16·00
258	**40**	5f. black and violet	16·00	21·00

1929. Surch **Mbr. Shqiptare** and new value.

259	**33**	1 on 50q. green	75	1·00
260	**33**	5 on 25q. blue	75	1·00
261	**33**	15 on 10q. red	1·30	1·60

1929. King Zog's 35th Birthday. Optd **RROFT-MBRETI 8.X.1929.**

262		1q. yellow	16·00	26·00
263		2q. brown	16·00	26·00
264		5q. green	16·00	26·00
265		10q. red	16·00	26·00
266		25q. blue	16·00	26·00
267		50q. green	22·00	31·00
268	**34**	1f. blue and red	30·00	47·00
269	**34**	2f. orange and green	30·00	47·00

1929. Air. Optd **Mbr. Shqiptare**.

270	**32**	5q. green	11·00	16·00
271	**32**	10q. red	11·00	16·00
272	**32**	25q. blue	11·00	16·00
273	**32**	50q. green	£225	£300
274	**32**	1f. black and violet	£425	£500
275	**32**	2f. violet and olive	£500	£550
276	**32**	3f. green and brown	£600	£650

49 Lake Butrinto

50 King Zog I

1930. Second Anniv of Accession of King Zog I.

277	**49**	1q. grey	55	30
278	**49**	2q. red	55	30
279	**50**	5q. green	55	30
280	**50**	10q. red	55	50
281	**50**	15q. brown	55	50
282	**50**	25q. blue	55	50
283	**49**	50q. green	1·10	75
284	-	1f. violet	2·20	1·30
285	-	2f. blue	2·75	1·30
286	-	3f. green	8·25	2·10
287	-	5f. brown	11·00	5·25

DESIGNS—VERT: 1, 2f. Ahmed Zog Bridge, River Mati. HORIZ: 3, 5f. Ruins of Zogu Castle.

53 Junkers F-13 (over Tirana)

1930. Air. T **53** and similar view.

288	**53**	5q. green	2·20	2·50
289	**53**	15q. red	2·20	2·50
290	**53**	20q. blue	2·20	2·50
291	**53**	50q. olive	5·50	5·25
292	-	1f. blue	8·25	7·75
293	-	2f. brown	27·00	26·00
294	-	3f. violet	33·00	31·00

1931. Air. Optd **TIRANE-ROME 6 KORRIK 1931.**

295	**53**	5q. green	13·00	13·00
296	**53**	15q. red	13·00	13·00
297	**53**	20q. blue	13·00	13·00
298	**53**	50q. olive	13·00	13·00
299	-	1f. blue	75·00	75·00
300	-	2f. brown	75·00	75·00
301	-	3f. violet	75·00	75·00

1934. Tenth Anniv of Revolution. Optd **1924-24 Dhetuer-1934.**

302	**49**	1q. grey	13·00	16·00
303	**49**	2q. orange	13·00	16·00
304	**50**	5q. green	13·00	16·00
305	**50**	10q. red	13·00	16·00
306	**50**	15q. brown	13·00	16·00
307	**50**	25q. blue	16·00	17·00
308	**49**	50q. turquoise	22·00	21·00
309	-	1f. violet (No. 284)	22·00	26·00
310	-	2f. blue (No. 285)	33·00	40·00
311	-	3f. green (No. 286)	49·00	50·00

56 Horse and Flag of Skanderbeg

57 Albania in Chains

1937. 25th Anniv of Independence.

312	**56**	1q. violet	55	50
313	**57**	2q. brown	80	75
314	-	5q. green	1·10	75
315	**56**	10q. olive	1·10	1·00
316	**57**	15q. red	1·60	1·30
317	-	25q. blue	3·25	2·50
318	**56**	50q. green	8·25	4·50
319	**57**	1f. violet	22·00	7·75
320	-	2f. brown	27·00	12·50

MS320a 140×140 mm. 20q. purple (T **56**) 33·00 £190

DESIGN: 5, 25q., 2f. As Type **57**, but eagle with opened wings (Liberated Albania).

58 Countess Geraldine Apponyi and King Zog

1938. Royal Wedding.

321	**58**	1q. purple	55	50
322	**58**	2q. brown	55	50
323	**58**	5q. green	55	50
324	**58**	10q. olive	2·20	1·00
325	**58**	15q. red	2·20	1·00
326	**58**	25q. blue	5·50	2·50
327	**58**	50q. green	11·00	5·25
328	**58**	1f. violet	22·00	10·50

MS328a 110×140 mm. 2 each 20q. purple, 30q. brown 65·00 £200

59 National Emblems

60 King Zog

1938. Tenth Anniv of Accession.

329	-	1q. purple	45	75
330	**59**	2q. red	55	75
331	-	5q. green	1·10	80
332	**60**	10q. brown	1·10	1·30
333	-	15q. red	2·20	1·60
334	**60**	25q. blue	2·40	1·80
335	**59**	50q. black	20·00	7·75
336	**60**	1f. green	27·00	11·50

MS336a 110×65 mm. 15q. red (333), 20q. green (**59**), 30q. violet (**60**) 49·00 £140

DESIGN: 1, 5, 15q. As Type **60**, but Queen Geraldine's portrait.

ITALIAN OCCUPATION

1939. Optd **Mbledhja Kushtetuese 12-IV-1939 XVII**. (a) Postage.

337	**49**	1q. grey	1·60	1·60
338	**49**	2q. red	1·60	1·60
339	**50**	5q. green	1·10	1·00
340	**50**	10q. red	1·10	1·00
341	**50**	15q. brown	2·75	2·50
342	**50**	25q. blue	3·25	3·25
343	**49**	50q. turquoise	4·25	3·75
344	-	1f. violet (No. 284)	6·50	4·75
345	-	2f. blue (No. 285)	7·50	6·25
346	-	3f. green	16·00	14·50
347	-	5f. brown	22·00	25·00

(b) Air. Optd as Nos. 337/47 or surch also.

348	**53**	5q. green	7·50	6·75
349	**53**	15q. red	7·00	7·25
350	**53**	20q. on 50q. olive	12·00	11·50

62 Gheg

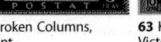

64 Broken Columns, Botrint

63 King Victor Emmanuel

65 King and Fiat G18V on Tirana–Rome Service

1939

351	**62**	1q. blue (postage)	1·10	50
352	-	2q. brown	1·10	50
353	-	3q. brown	1·10	50
354	-	5q. green	1·60	20
355	**63**	10q. brown	1·60	30
356	**63**	15q. red	1·70	30
357	**63**	25q. blue	1·70	1·30
358	**63**	30q. violet	2·75	2·10
359	-	50q. violet	4·25	1·80
360	-	65q. red	12·00	8·25
361	-	1f. green	12·00	5·75
362	-	2f. red	27·00	18·00
363	**64**	3f. black	46·00	33·00
364	-	5f. purple	55·00	46·00
365	**65**	20q. brown (air)	£110	18·00

DESIGNS—SMALL: 2q. Tosk man; 3q. Gheg woman; 5, 65q. Profile of King Victor Emmanuel; 50q. Tosk woman. LARGE: 1f. Kruje Fortress; 2f. Bridge over River Kiri at Mes; 5f. Amphitheatre ruins, Berat.

66 Sheep Farming

1940. Air.

366	**66**	5q. green	2·50	1·60
367	-	15q. red	2·75	2·10
368	-	20q. blue	5·50	3·25
369	-	50q. brown	7·75	7·75
370	-	1f. green	8·25	9·50
371	-	2f. black	18·00	18·00
372	-	3f. purple	35·00	31·00

DESIGNS: Savoia Marchetti S.M.75 airplane and—HORIZ: 20q. King of Italy and Durres harbour; 1f. Bridge over River Kiri at Mes. VERT: 15q. Aerial map; 50q. Girl and valley; 2f. Archway and wall, Durres; 3f. Women in North Eprius.

67 King Victor Emmanuel

1942. Third Anniv of Italian Occupation.

373	**67**	5q. green	2·40	2·50
374	**67**	10q. brown	2·40	2·50
375	**67**	15q. red	2·40	2·50
376	**67**	25q. blue	2·40	2·50
377	**67**	65q. brown	7·50	7·75
378	**67**	1f. green	7·50	7·75
379	**67**	2f. purple	7·50	7·75

1942. No. 352 surch **1 QIND**.

380		1q. on 2q. brown	4·25	5·25

69

1943. Anti-tuberculosis Fund.

381	**69**	5q.+5q. green	1·80	2·10
382	**69**	10q.+10q. brown	1·80	2·10
383	**69**	15q.+10q. red	1·80	2·10
384	**69**	25q.+15q. blue	2·20	3·25
385	**69**	30q.+20q. violet	2·20	3·25
386	**69**	50q.+25q. orange	2·20	3·25
387	**69**	65q.+30q. grey	3·25	4·50
388	**69**	1f.+40q. brown	5·50	6·25

GERMAN OCCUPATION

1943. Postage stamps of 1939 optd **14 Shtator 1943** or surch also.

389	-	1q. on 3q. brn (No. 353)	1·60	8·25
390	-	2q. brown (No. 352)	1·60	8·25
391	-	3q. brown (No. 353)	1·60	8·25
392	-	5q. green (No. 354)	1·60	8·25
393	**63**	10q. brown	1·60	8·25
394	-	15q. red (No. 356)	1·60	8·25
395	-	25q. blue (No. 357)	1·60	8·25
396	-	30q. violet (No. 358)	1·60	8·25
397	-	50q. on 65q. brn (No. 360)	2·20	12·00
398	-	65q. red (No. 360)	2·20	12·00
399	-	1f. green (No. 361)	11·00	24·00

400	-	2f. red (No. 362)	16·00	80·00
401	64	3f. black	65·00	£200

71 War Refugees

1944. War Refugees' Relief Fund.

402	71	5q.+5q. green	6·50	15·00
403	71	10q.+5q. brown	6·50	15·00
404	71	15q.+5q. red	6·50	15·00
405	71	25q.+10q. blue	6·50	15·00
406	71	1f.+50q. green	6·50	15·00
407	71	2f.+1f. violet	6·50	15·00
408	71	3f.+1f.50 orange	6·50	15·00

INDEPENDENT STATE

1945. Nos. 353/8 and 360/2 surch **QEVERIJA DEMOKRAT. E SHQIPERISE 22-X-1944** and value.

409	30q. on 3q. brown	8·25	16·00
410	40q. on 5q. green	8·25	16·00
411	50q. on 10q. brown	8·25	16·00
412	60q. on 15q. red	8·25	16·00
413	80q. on 25q. blue	8·25	16·00
414	1f. on 30q. violet	8·25	16·00
415	2f. on 65q. brown	8·25	16·00
416	3f. on 1f. green	8·25	16·00
417	5f. on 2f. red	8·25	16·00

73

1945. Second Anniv of Formation of People's Army. Surch as T **73**.

418	49	30q. on 1q. grey	5·50	7·75
419	49	60q. on 1q. grey	5·50	7·75
420	49	80q. on 1q. grey	5·50	7·75
421	49	1f. on 1q. grey	11·00	16·00
422	49	2f. on 2q. red	13·00	18·00
423	49	3f. on 50q. green	27·00	33·00
424	-	5f. on 2f. blue (No. 285)	33·00	50·00

1945. Red Cross Fund. Surch with Red Cross, **JAVA E K.K. SHQIPTAR 4-11 MAJ 1945** and value.

425	69	30q.+15q. on 5q.+5q. green	11·00	16·00
426	69	50q.+25q. on 10q.+10q. brown	11·00	16·00
427	69	1f.+50q. on 15q.+10q. red	27·00	33·00
428	69	2f.+1f. on 25q.+15q. blue	38·00	47·00

75 Permet Landscape

1945

429	-	20q. green	75	1·80
430	-	30q. orange	1·10	2·50
431	-	40q. brown	1·10	2·50
432	-	60q. red	1·60	3·75
433	-	1f. red	3·75	7·75
434	75	3f. blue	27·00	31·00

DESIGNS: 20q. Latinot; 40, 60q. Bridge at Berat; 1f. Permet landscape.

1946. Constitutional Assembly. Optd **ASAMBLEJA KUSHTETUESE 10 KALLNUER 1946.**

435		20q. green	1·60	2·10
436		30q. orange	2·20	2·50
437	-	40q. brown (No. 431)	2·75	3·25
438	-	60q. red (No. 432)	4·25	5·25
439	-	1f. red (No. 433)	16·00	19·00
440	-	3f. blue (No. 434)	27·00	31·00

PEOPLE'S REPUBLIC

77 Globe, Dove and Olive Branch

1946. International Women's Congress. Perf or imperf.

441A	77	20q. mauve and red	55	1·60
442A	77	40q. lilac and red	1·10	2·10
443A	77	50q. violet and red	2·20	3·25
444A	77	1f. blue and red	4·25	6·25
445A	77	2f. blue and red	5·50	10·50

1946. Proclamation of Albanian People's Republic. Optd **REPUBLIKA POPULLORE E SHQIPERISE.**

446	75	20q. green	1·50	1·60
447	75	30q. orange	1·70	2·10
448	-	40q. brown (No. 431)	3·00	4·25
449	-	60q. red (No. 432)	6·00	7·75
450	-	1f. red (No. 433)	16·00	21·00
451	-	3f. blue (No. 434)	27·00	31·00

1946. Albanian Red Cross Congress. Surch **KONGRESI K.K.SH. 24-25-11-46** and premium.

452	75	20q.+10q. green	24·00	37·00
453	75	30q.+15q. orange	24·00	37·00
454	-	40q.+20q. brown	24·00	37·00
455	-	60q.+30q. red	24·00	37·00
456	-	1f.+50q. red	24·00	37·00
457	-	3f.+1f.50 blue	24·00	37·00

79 Athletes

1946. Balkan Games.

458	79	1q. black	16·00	12·50
459	79	2q. green	16·00	12·50
460	79	5q. brown	16·00	12·50
461	79	10q. red	16·00	12·50
462	79	20q. blue	16·00	12·50
463	79	40q. lilac	16·00	12·50
464	79	1f. orange	38·00	37·00

80 Qemal Stafa

1947. Fifth Death Anniv of Qemal Stafa (Communist activist).

465	80	20q. dp brown & brown	13·00	16·00
466	80	28q. deep blue and blue	13·00	16·00
467	80	40q. dp brown & brown	13·00	16·00

81 Railway Construction

1947. Construction of Durres–Elbasan Railway.

468	81	1q. black and drab	5·50	1·80
469	81	4q. deep green and green	5·50	1·80
470	81	10q. dp brown & brown	5·75	2·10
471	81	15q. red and rose	5·75	2·10
472	81	20q. black and blue	13·00	2·50
473	81	28q. deep blue and blue	18·00	3·25
474	81	40q. red and purple	35·00	19·00
475	81	68q. dp brown & brown	43·00	31·00

82 Partisans

83 Enver Hoxha and Vasil Shanto

1947. Fourth Anniv of Formation of People's Army. Inscr "1943–1947".

476	82	16q. brown	9·75	10·50
477	83	20q. brown	9·75	10·50
478	-	28q. blue	9·75	10·50
479	-	40q. brown and mauve	9·75	10·50

DESIGNS—HORIZ: 28q. Infantry column. VERT: 40q. Portrait of Vojo Kushi.

84 Ruined Conference Building

1947. Fifth Anniv of Peza Conference.

480	84	2l. purple and mauve	7·00	7·75
481	84	2l.50 deep blue and blue	7·00	7·75

85 War Invalids

1947. First Congress of War Invalids.

482	85	1l. red	16·00	16·00

86 Peasants

1947. Agrarian Reform. Inscr "REFORMA AGRARE".

483	86	1l.50 purple	9·75	10·50
484	-	2l. brown	9·75	10·50
485	-	2l.50 blue	9·75	10·50
486	-	3l. red	9·75	10·50

DESIGNS—HORIZ: 2l. Banquet; 2l.50, Peasants rejoicing. VERT: 3l. Soldier being chaired.

87 Burning Village

1947. Third Anniv of Liberation. Inscr "29-XI-1944–1947".

487	87	1l.50 red	5·50	5·25
488	-	2l.50 purple	5·50	5·25
489	-	5l. blue	11·00	8·25
490	-	8l. mauve	16·00	12·50
491	-	12l. brown	27·00	21·00

DESIGNS: 2l.50, Riflemen; 5l. Machine-gunners; 8l. Mounted soldier; 12l. Infantry column.

1948. Nos. 429/34 surch **Lek** and value.

492	75	0l.50 on 30q. orange	55	75
493	75	1l. on 20q. green	1·10	1·30
494	-	2l.50 on 60q. red	2·75	3·75
495	-	3l. on 1f. red	3·75	4·75
496	-	5l. on 3f. blue	8·25	7·75
497	-	12l. on 40q. brown	22·00	21·00

88 Railway Construction

1948. Construction of Durres–Tirana Railway.

498	88	0l.50 red	2·75	1·60
499	88	1l. green	3·00	1·80
500	88	1l.50 red	4·50	2·50
501	88	2l.50 brown	6·50	3·25
502	88	5l. blue	11·00	6·25
503	88	8l. orange	18·00	10·50
504	88	12l. purple	22·00	12·50
505	88	20l. black	43·00	26·00

89 Parade of Infantrymen

1948. Fifth Anniv of People's Army.

506	89	2l.50 brown	5·50	5·25
507	89	5l. blue	7·50	7·25
508	-	8l. slate (Troops in action)	14·00	10·50

90 Labourer, Globe and Flag

1949. Labour Day.

509	90	2l.50 brown	1·60	2·50
510	90	5l. blue	3·25	4·25
511	90	8l. purple	6·00	6·75

91 Soldier and Map

1949. Sixth Anniv of People's Army.

512	91	2l.50 brown	1·60	2·50
513	91	5l. blue	3·25	4·25
514	91	8l. orange	6·00	7·75

92 Albanian and Kremlin Tower

1949. Albanian–Soviet Amity.

515	92	2l.50 brown	1·60	2·50
516	92	5l. blue	3·75	5·25

93 Gen. Enver Hoxha

1949

517	93	0l.50 purple	35	10
518	93	1l. green	40	10
519	93	1l.50 red	55	10
520	93	2l.50 brown	1·10	15
521	93	5l. blue	2·20	1·00
522	93	8l. purple	4·25	3·25
523	93	12l. purple	11·50	5·75
524	93	20l. slate	13·50	7·25

94 Soldier and Flag

1949. Fifth Anniv of Liberation.

525	94	2l.50 brown	1·10	1·60
526	-	3l. red	1·10	3·25
527	94	5l. violet	3·25	4·25
528	-	8l. black	6·50	7·75

DESIGN—HORIZ: 3, 8l. Street fighting.

96 Joseph Stalin

1949. Stalin's 70th Birthday.

529	96	2l.50 brown	1·10	2·10
530	96	5l. blue	2·75	3·75
531	96	8l. lake	7·00	9·00

97 Symbols of Transport and 'UPU'

1950. 75th Anniv of U.P.U.

532	97	5l. blue	3·00	6·75
533	97	8l. purple	5·50	9·50
534	97	12l. black	11·00	18·00

98 Sami Frasheri

1950. Literary Jubilee. Inscr "1950-JUBILEU I SHKRIMTAREVE TE RILINDJES".

535	98	2l. green	1·60	1·60

536	-	2l.50 brown	2·20	2·50
537	-	3l. red	4·25	5·25
538	-	5l. blue	5·50	6·25

PORTRAITS: 2l.50, A. Zako (Cajupi); 3l. Naim Frasheri; 5l. K. Kristoforidhi.

99 Vuno-Himare

1950. Air.

539	**99**	0l.50 black	1·00	1·00
540	-	1l. purple	1·00	1·00
541	-	2l. blue	1·70	2·10
542	**99**	5l. green	6·00	5·75
543	-	10l. blue	14·00	10·50
544	-	20l. violet	27·00	16·00

DESIGNS: Douglas DC-3 airplane over—1, 10l. Rozafat Shkodor; 2, 20l. Keshtjelle-Butrinto.

100 Stafa and Shanto

1950. Albanian Patriots.

545		2l. green	1·40	1·30
546		2l.50 violet	1·60	1·60
547		3l. red	3·25	3·25
548		5l. blue	5·50	5·25
549	**100**	8l. brown	11·00	10·50

PORTRAITS: 2l. Ahmet Haxhia, Hydajet Lezha, Naim Gjylbegu, Ndoc Mazi and Ndoc Deda; 2l.50, Asim Zeneli, Ali Demi, Kajo Karafili, Dervish Hakali and Asim Vokshi; 3l. Ataz Shehu, Baba Faja, Zoja Cure, Mustafa Matohiti and Gjok Doci; 5l. Perlat Rexhepi, Bako, Vojo Kushi, Reshit Collaku and Misto Mame.

101 Arms and Flags

1951. Fifth Anniv of Republic.

550	**101**	2l.50 red	2·20	3·25
551	**101**	5l. blue	4·25	6·25
552	**101**	8l. black	7·00	9·50

102 Skanderbeg

1951. 483rd Death Anniv of Skanderbeg (patriot).

553	**102**	2l.50 brown	2·20	2·50
554	**102**	5l. violet	4·25	5·25
555	**102**	8l. bistre	7·00	7·75

103 Gen. Enver Hoxha and Assembly

1951. Seventh Anniv of Permet Congress.

556	**103**	2l.50 brown	1·10	1·60
557	**103**	3l. red	1·20	2·10
558	**103**	5l. blue	2·75	3·75
559	**103**	8l. mauve	5·00	6·25

104 Child and Globe

1951. International Children's Day.

560	**104**	2l. green	2·75	2·10
561	-	2l.50 brown	3·75	2·50
562	-	3l. red	5·00	3·25
563	**104**	5l. blue	7·50	3·75

DESIGN—HORIZ: 2l.50, 3l. Nurse weighing baby.

105 Enver Hoxha and Meeting-house

1951. Tenth Anniv of Albanian Communists.

564	**105**	2l.50 brown	65	1·00
565	**105**	3l. red	75	1·40
566	**105**	5l. blue	1·70	2·10
567	**105**	8l. black	3·25	3·50

106 Young Partisans

1951. Tenth Anniv of Albanian Young Communists' Union. Inscr "1941–1951".

568	**106**	2l.50 brown	1·10	1·60
569	-	5l. blue	2·20	2·50
570	-	8l. red	5·00	5·25

DESIGNS: Schoolgirl, railway, tractor and factories; 8l. Miniature portraits of Stafa, Spiru, Mame and Kondi.

1952. Air. Surch in figures.

571		0.50l. on 2l. blue (No. 541)	£250	£190
572	**99**	0.50l. on 5l. green	49·00	36·00
573	**99**	2l.50 on 5l. green	£375	£200
574	-	2l.50 on 10l. blue (No. 543)	60·00	44·00

108 Factory

1953

575	**108**	0l.50 brown	80	10
576	-	1l. green	1·10	20
577	-	2l.50 sepia	1·50	50
578	-	3l. red	1·90	75
579	-	5l. blue	3·25	1·30
580	-	8l. olive	3·75	1·60
581	-	12l. purple	5·75	2·10
582	-	20l. blue	11·00	4·75

DESIGNS—HORIZ: 1l. Canal; 2l.50, Girl and cotton mill; 3l. Girl and sugar factory; 5l. Film studio; 8l. Girl and textile machinery; 20l. Dam. VERT: 12l. Pylon and hydroelectric station.

109 Soldiers and Flags

1954. Tenth Anniv of Liberation.

583	**109**	0l.50 lilac	20	15
584	**109**	1l. green	70	50
585	**109**	2l.50 brown	1·10	1·00
586	**109**	3l. red	2·20	2·10
587	**109**	5l. blue	3·25	3·25
588	**109**	8l. purple	6·50	6·25

110 First Albanian School

1956. 70th Anniv of Albanian Schools.

589	**110**	2l. purple	55	50
590	-	2l.50 green	90	1·00
591	-	5l. blue	2·00	2·10
592	**110**	10l. turquoise	6·50	3·75

DESIGN: 2l.50, 5l. Portraits of P. Sotiri, P. N. Luarasi and N. Naci.

111

1957. 15th Anniv of Albanian Workers' Party.

593	**111**	2l.50 brown	80	50
594	-	5l. blue	1·70	75
595	-	8l. purple	3·00	3·00

DESIGNS: 5l. Party headquarters, Tirana; 8l. Marx and Lenin.

112 Congress Emblem

1957. Fourth World Trade Unions Congress, Leipzig.

596	**112**	2l.50 purple	60	20
597	**112**	3l. red	65	50
598	**112**	5l. blue	75	75
599	**112**	8l. green	2·75	2·40

113 Lenin and Cruiser *Aurora*

1957. 40th Anniv of Russian Revolution.

600	**113**	2l.50 brown	85	50
601	**113**	5l. blue	1·60	1·60
602	**113**	8l. black	2·10	1·80

114 Raising the Flag

1957. 45th Anniv of Proclamation of Independence.

603	**114**	1l.50 purple	80	30
604	**114**	2l.50 brown	1·40	50
605	**114**	5l. blue	1·80	1·60
606	**114**	8l. green	4·25	2·10

115 N. Veqilharxhi

1958. 160th Birth Anniv of Veqilharxhi (patriot).

607	**115**	2l.50 brown	80	30
608	**115**	5l. blue	1·60	50
609	**115**	8l. purple	3·25	1·60

116 L. Gurakuqi

1958. Removal of Ashes of Gurakuqi (patriot).

610	**116**	1l.50 green	35	20
611	**116**	2l.50 brown	55	40
612	**116**	5l. blue	70	50
613	**116**	8l. sepia	3·25	1·40

117 Freedom Fighters

1958. 50th Anniv of Battle of Mashkullore.

614	**117**	2l.50 ochre	70	20
615	-	3l. green	70	20
616	**117**	5l. blue	1·60	80
617	-	8l. brown	2·75	1·60

DESIGN: 3, 8l. Tree and buildings.

118 Soldiers in Action

1958. 15th Anniv of Albanian People's Army.

618	**118**	1l.50 green	45	20
619	-	2l.50 brown	65	25
620	**118**	8l. red	1·60	1·40
621	-	11l. blue	2·50	2·30

DESIGN: 2l.50, 11l. Tank-driver, sailor, infantryman and tanks.

119 Bust of Apollo and Butrinto Amphitheatre

1959. Cultural Monuments Week.

622	**119**	2l.50 brown	80	30
623	**119**	6l.50 green	3·25	1·30
624	**119**	11l. blue	4·25	2·10

120 F. Joliot-Curie and Council Emblem

1959. Tenth Anniv of World Peace Council.

625	**120**	1l.50 red	2·20	50
626	**120**	2l.50 violet	5·00	1·60
627	**120**	11l. blue	11·50	5·25

121 Basketball

1959. First National Spartacist Games.

628	**121**	1l.50 violet	1·10	25
629	-	2l.50 green	1·20	30
630	-	5l. red	2·20	1·00
631	-	11l. blue	6·50	3·75

DESIGNS: 2l.50, Football; 5l. Running; 11l. Runners with torches.

122 Soldier

1959. 15th Anniv of Liberation.

632	**122**	1l.50 red	1·20	25
633	-	2l.50 brown	1·60	35
634	-	3l. green	2·20	45
635	-	6l.50 red	4·75	4·00
MS635a 141×96 mm. Nos. 632/5 but in red. Imperf			11·00	16·00

DESIGNS: 2l.50, Security guard. 3l. Harvester; 6l.50, Laboratory workers.

123 Mother and Child

1959. Tenth Anniv of Declaration of Human Rights.

636	**123**	5l. blue	6·25	3·25
MS636a 72×65 mm. No. 636. Imperf			7·50	11·50

124 Woman with Arm Raised

1960. 50th Anniv of International Women's Day.

637	**124**	2l.50 brown	1·10	50
638	**124**	11l. red	4·25	1·60

125 Congress Building

1960. 40th Anniv of Lushnje Congress.

639	**125**	2l.50 brown	55	30
640	**125**	7l.50 blue	1·60	1·00

126 A. Moisiu

1960. 80th Birth Anniv of Alexandre Moisiu (actor).

641	**126**	3l. brown	70	50
642	**126**	11l. green	2·40	1·00

127 Lenin

1960. 90th Birth Anniv of Lenin.

643	**127**	4l. turquoise	1·90	1·00
644	**127**	11l. red	6·00	5·25

128 Vaso Pasha

1960. 80th Anniv of Albanian Alphabet Study Association.

645	**128**	1l. olive	55	20
646	-	1l.50 brown	1·00	25
647	-	6l.50 blue	2·10	85
648	-	11l. red	5·50	2·10

DESIGNS: 1l.50, Jani Vreto; 6l.50, Sami Frasheri; 11l. Association statutes.

129 Frontier Guard

1960. 15th Anniv of Frontier Force.

649	**129**	1l.50 red	55	30
650	**129**	11l. blue	3·25	1·50

130 Family with Policeman

1960. 15th Anniv of People's Police.

651	**130**	1l.50 green	55	25
652	**130**	8l.50 brown	3·25	1·60

131 Normal School, Elbasan

1960. 50th Anniv of Normal School, Elbasan.

653	**131**	5l. green	2·75	1·60
654	**131**	6l.50 purple	2·75	1·60

132 Soldier and Cannon

1960. 40th Anniv of Battle of Vlore.

655	**132**	1l.50 brown	75	50
656	**132**	2l.50 purple	1·20	75
657	**132**	5l. blue	2·75	1·00

133 Tirana Clock Tower, Kremlin and Tupolev Tu-104A Jetliner

1960. Second Anniv of Tirana–Moscow Jet Air Service.

658	**133**	1l. brown	1·10	80
659	**133**	7l.50 blue	4·00	4·25
660	**133**	11l.50 grey	6·50	7·25

134 Federation Emblem

1960. 15th Anniv of World Democratic Youth Federation.

661	**134**	1l.50 blue	65	30
662	**134**	8l.50 red	2·20	1·00

135 Ali Kelmendi

1960. 60th Birth Anniv of Kelmendi (Communist).

663	**135**	1l.50 olive	55	30
664	**135**	11l. purple	2·20	1·00

136 Flags of Albania and Russia, and Clasped Hands

1961. 15th Anniv of Albanian-Soviet Friendship Society.

665	**136**	2l. violet	55	30
666	**136**	8l. purple	2·20	1·00

137 Marx and Lenin

1961. Fourth Albanian Workers' Party Congress.

667	**137**	2l. red	55	30
668	**137**	8l. blue	2·20	1·00

138 Malsi e Madhe (Shkoder) Costume

1961. Provincial Costumes.

669	**138**	1l. black	1·10	50
670	-	1l.50 purple	1·40	75
671	-	6l.50 blue	4·25	1·90
672	-	11l. red	6·50	4·75

COSTUMES: 1l.50, Malsi e Madhe (Shkoder) (female); 6l.50, Lume; 11l. Mirdite.

139 European Otter

1961. Albanian Fauna.

673	**139**	2l.50 blue	4·00	1·00
674	-	6l.50 green	8·00	2·40
675	-	11l. brown	16·00	8·25

DESIGNS: 6l.50, Eurasian badger; 11l. Brown bear.

140 Dalmatian Pelicans

1961. Albanian Birds.

676	**140**	1l.50 red on pink	5·75	1·00
677	-	7l.50 violet on blue	7·00	3·25
678	-	11l. brown on pink	9·75	3·75

BIRDS: 7l.50, Grey heron; 11l. Little egret.

141 Cyclamen

1961. Albanian Flowers.

679	**141**	1l.50 purple and blue	2·20	50
680	-	8l. orange and purple	6·00	2·50
681	-	11l. red and green	7·50	3·25

FLOWERS: 8l. Forsythia; 11l. Lily.

142 M. G. Nikolla

1961. 50th Birth Anniv of Nikolla (poet).

682	**142**	0l.50 brown	65	30
683	**142**	8l.50 green	2·20	1·60

143 Lenin and Marx on Flag

1961. 20th Anniv of Albanian Workers' Party.

684	**143**	2l.50 red	65	30
685	**143**	7l.50 purple	2·00	1·30

144 Anniversary Emblem

1961. 20th Anniv of Albanian Young Communists' Union.

686	**144**	2l.50 blue	65	30
687	**144**	7l.50 mauve	2·20	1·30

145 Yuri Gagarin and Vostok 1

1962. World's First Manned Space Flight. (a) Postage.

688	**145**	0l.50 blue	1·10	1·60
689	**145**	4l. purple	4·25	4·75
690	**145**	11l. green	11·00	11·50

(b) Air. Optd **POSTA AJRORE**.

691	0l.50 blue on cream	38·00	50·00
692	4l. purple on cream	38·00	50·00
693	11l. green on cream	38·00	50·00

147 P. N. Luarasi

1962. 50th Death Anniv of Petro N. Luarasi (patriot).

694	**147**	0l.50 blue	55	30
695	**147**	8l.50 brown	4·25	1·60

IMPERF STAMPS. Many Albanian stamps from No. 696 onwards exist imperf and/or in different colours from limited printings.

148 Campaign Emblem

1962. Malaria Eradication.

696	**148**	1l.50 green	35	15
697	**148**	2l.50 red	55	30
698	**148**	10l. purple	1·10	80
699	**148**	11l. blue	1·40	1·00
MS699a 90×106 mm. Nos. 696/9			38·00	38·00

149 Camomile

1962. Medicinal Plants.

700	**149**	0l.50 yellow, green & blue	55	30
701	-	8l. green, yellow and grey	2·20	1·20
702	-	11l.50 violet, grn & ochre	3·75	1·60

PLANTS: 8l. Silver linden; 11l.50, Sage.

150 Throwing the Javelin

1962. Olympic Games, Tokyo, 1964 (1st issue). Inscr as in T **102**.

703		0l.50 black and blue	20	10
704		2l.50 sepia and brown	40	15
705		3l. black and blue	55	20
706	**150**	9l. purple and red	2·20	1·00
707	-	10l. black and olive	2·40	1·60
MS707a 81×63 mm. 15l. (as 3l.)			38·00	50·00

DESIGNS—VERT: 0l.50, Diving; 2l.50, Pole-vaulting; 10l. Putting the shot. HORIZ: 3l. Olympic flame.

See also Nos. 754/**MS**758a, 818/**MS**821a and 842/**MS**851a.

151 Sputnil 1 in Orbit

1962. Cosmic Flights.

708	**151**	0l.50 yellow and violet	65	50
709	-	1l. sepia and green	1·10	85
710	-	1l.50 yellow and red	1·60	1·00
711	-	20l. blue and purple	11·00	4·25
MS711a 101×76 mm. 14l. (+ 6l.) brown and blue (rocket)			65·00	80·00

DESIGNS: 1l. Laika (dog) and Sputnik 2; 1l.50, Artificial satellite and Sun; 20l. Lunik 3 photographing Moon.

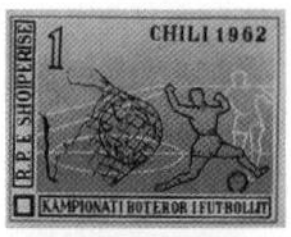

152 Footballer and Ball in Net

1962. World Cup Football Championship, Chile.

712	**152**	1l. violet and orange	55	30
713	-	2l.50 blue and green	1·60	85
714	**152**	6l.50 purple and brown	2·20	1·00
715	-	15l. purple and green	3·25	2·10
MS715a 82×66 mm. 20l. brown and green (as 713 but larger)			50·00	80·00

DESIGN: 2l.50, 15l. As Type **152** but globe in place of ball in net.

153 'Europa' and Albanian Maps

1962. Tourist Publicity.

716	**153**	0l.50 red, yellow & green	55	1·00
717	-	1l. red, purple and blue	1·10	2·50
718	-	2l.50 red, purple and blue	8·75	14·50
719	**153**	11l. red, yellow and grey	16·00	18·00
MS719a 82×63 mm. 7l. red, yellow and grey (**153**), 8l. red and grey (as 717)			50·00	80·00

DESIGN: 1, 2l.50, Statue and map.

154 Dardhe Woman

1962. Costumes of Albania's Southern Region.

720	**154**	0l.50 red, purple and blue	45	20
721	-	1l. brown and buff	55	40
722	-	2l.50 black, violet & grn	1·60	1·30
723	-	14l. red, brown and green	7·00	3·75

COSTUMES: 1l. Devoll man; 2l.50, Lunxheri woman; 14l. Gjirokaster man.

155 Chamois

1962. Albanian Animals.

724	**155**	0l.50 purple and green	55	40
725	-	1l. black and yellow	2·20	1·00
726	-	1l.50 black and brown	2·75	1·60
727	-	15l. brown and green	22·00	5·25

MS727a 72×89 mm. 20l. brown and green (as 727 but larger) £140 £180

ANIMALS—HORIZ. 1l. Lynx; 1l.50, Wild boar. VERT: 15l. Roe deer.

156 Golden Eagle

1962. 50th Anniv of Independence.

728	**156**	1l. brown and red	80	30
729	-	3l. black and brown	3·75	1·00
730	-	16l. black and mauve	7·50	3·75

DESIGNS: 3l. I. Qemali; 16l. "RPSH" and golden eagle.

157 Revolutionaries

1963. 45th Anniv of October Revolution.

731	**157**	5l. violet and yellow	1·30	75
732	-	10l. black and red	3·00	1·90

DESIGN: 10l. Statue of Lenin.

158 Henri Dunant and Globe

1963. Red Cross Centenary. Cross in red.

733	**158**	1l.50 black and red	70	30
734	**158**	2l.50 black, red and blue	1·10	50
735	**158**	6l. black, red and green	2·20	1·00
736	**158**	10l. black, red and yellow	3·75	2·50

159 Stalin and Battle

1963. 20th Anniv of Battle of Stalingrad.

737	**159**	8l. black & grn (postage)	11·00	4·25
738	-	7l. red and green (air)	11·00	4·25

DESIGN: 7l. 'Lenin' flag, map, tanks, etc.

160 Nikolaev and Vostok 3

1963. First 'Team' Manned Space Flights.

739	**160**	2l.50 brown and blue	65	40
740	-	7l.50 black and blue	1·60	1·00
741	-	20l. brown and violet	4·25	3·75

MS741a 88×73 mm. 25l. blue and brown (Popovich and Nikolaev) 45·00 45·00

DESIGNS—HORIZ: 7l.50, Globe, Vostok 3 snd Vostok 4. VERT: 20l. P. Popovic and Vostok 4.

161 Cockchafer Beetle

1963. Insects.

742	**161**	0l.50 brown and green	1·30	50
743	-	1l. brown and blue	2·20	1·00
744	-	8l. purple and red	9·25	2·50
745	-	10l. black and yellow	12·00	3·75

INSECTS: 1l.50, Stagbeetle; 8l. *Procerus gigas* (ground beetle); 10l. *Cicindela albanica* (tiger beetle).

162 Policeman and Allegorical Figure

1963. 20th Anniv of Albanian Security Police.

746	**162**	2l.50 black, purple & red	1·10	80
747	**162**	7l.50 black, lake and red	3·75	2·50

163 Great Crested Grebe

1963. Birds. Multicoloured.

748		0l.50 Type **163**	1·60	40
749		3l. Golden eagle	3·25	1·00
750		6l.50 Grey partridge	8·25	1·70
751		11l. Western capercaillie	11·00	2·50

164 Official Insignia and Postmark of 1913

1963. 50th Anniv of First Albanian Stamps.

752	**164**	5l. multicoloured	2·20	95
753	-	10l. green, black and red	3·75	2·10

DESIGN: 10l. Albanian stamps of 1913, 1937 and 1962.

165 Boxing

1963. Olympic Games, Tokyo (1964) (2nd issue).

754	**165**	2l. green, red and yellow	70	1·00
755	-	3l. brown, blue & orange	90	2·10
756	-	5l. purple, brown and blue	1·40	30
757	-	6l. black, grey and green	1·90	5·25
758	-	9l. blue and brown	3·75	8·25

MS758a 61×82 mm. 15l. mult (Torch, rings and map) 20·00 27·00

SPORTS: 3l. Basketball; 5l. Volleyball; 6l. Cycling; 9l. Gymnastics.

166 Gen. Enver Hoxha and Labinoti Council Building

1963. 20th Anniv of Albanian People's Army.

759	**166**	1l.50 yellow, black & red	55	30
760	-	2l.50 bistre, brown & blue	1·10	65
761	-	5l. black, drab & turq	1·60	1·00
762	-	6l. blue, buff and brown	2·20	1·50

DESIGNS: 2l.50, Soldier with weapons; 5l. Soldier attacking; 6l. Peacetime soldier.

167 Gagarin

1963. Soviet Cosmonauts. Portraits in yellow and brown.

763	**167**	3l. violet	1·10	40
764	-	5l. blue	1·30	50
765	-	7l. violet and grey	1·60	65
766	-	11l. blue and purple	3·25	1·00
767	-	14l. blue and turquoise	5·00	1·60
768	-	20l. blue	7·50	3·75

COSMONAUTS: 5l. Titov; 7l. Nikolaev; 11l. Popovich; 14l. Bykovsky; 20l. Valentina Tereshkova.

168 Volleyball (Rumania)

1963. European Sports Events, 1963.

769	**168**	2l. red, black and olive	55	30
770	-	3l. bistre, black and red	85	50
771	-	5l. orange, black & green	1·10	85
772	-	7l. green, black and pink	1·60	1·30
773	-	8l. red, black and blue	3·75	1·60

SPORTS: 3l. Weightlifting (Sweden); 5l. Football (European Cup); 7l. Boxing (Russia); 8l. Ladies' Rowing (Russia).

169 Celadon Swallowtail

1963. Butterflies and Moths.

774	**169**	1l. black, yellow and red	65	25
775	-	2l. black, red and blue	1·10	30
776	-	4l. black, yellow & purple	2·20	1·00
777	-	5l. multicoloured	3·25	95
778	-	8l. black, red and brown	5·50	2·10
779	-	10l. orange, brown & blue	7·00	3·25

DESIGNS: 2l. Jersey tiger moth; 4l. Brimstone; 5l. Death's-head hawk moth; 8l. Orange tip; 10l. Peacock.

170 Lunik 1

1963. Air. Cosmic Flights.

780	**170**	2l. olive, yellow & orange	55	30
781	-	3l. multicoloured	1·10	40
782	-	5l. olive, yellow & purple	1·60	65
783	-	8l. red, yellow and violet	2·75	1·20
784	-	12l. red, orange and blue	5·50	3·75

DESIGNS: 3l. Lunik 2; 5l. Lunik 3; 8l. Venus 1; 12l. Mars 1.

171 Food Processing Works

1963. Industrial Buildings.

785	**171**	2l.50 red on pink	1·10	50
786	-	20l. green on green	4·25	2·10
787	-	30l. purple on blue	9·75	4·25
788	-	50l. bistre on cream	11·00	5·25

DESIGNS—VERT: 20l. Naphtha refinery; 30l. Fruit-bottling plant. HORIZ: 50l. Copper-processing works.

172 Shield and Banner

1963. First Army and Defence Aid Assn Congress.

789	**172**	2l. multicoloured	75	30
790	**172**	8l. multicoloured	2·20	1·60

173 Young Men of Three Races

1963. 15th Anniv of Declaration of Human Rights.

791	**173**	3l. black and ochre	65	50
792	**173**	5l. blue and ochre	1·30	1·00
793	**173**	7l. violet and ochre	2·75	2·10

174 Bobsleighing

1963. Winter Olympic Games, Innsbruck. Inscr '1964'.

794	**174**	0l.50 black and blue	55	30
795	-	2l.50 black, red and grey	1·00	50
796	-	6l.50 black, yellow & grey	1·40	75
797	-	12l.50 red, black & green	2·75	2·10

MS797a 56×75 mm. 12l.50 black, green and blue (Ski jumper) (49×31 mm) 35·00 50·00

DESIGNS—VERT: 2l.50, Skiing; 12l.50, Figure-skating. HORIZ: 6l.50, Ice-hockey.

175 Lenin

1964. 40th Death Anniv of Lenin.

798	**175**	5l. olive and bistre	1·20	75
799	**175**	10l. olive and bistre	2·40	1·40

176 Hurdling

1964. GANEFO Games, Djakarta (1963).

800	**176**	2l.50 blue and lilac	55	30
801	-	3l. brown and green	1·10	50
802	-	6l.50 red and blue	1·60	1·30
803	-	8l. ochre and blue	2·75	2·10

SPORTS—HORIZ. 3l. Running; 6l.50, Rifle-shooting. VERT: 8l. Basketball.

177 Common Sturgeon

1964. Fish. Multicoloured.

804		0l.50 Type **177**	55	30
805		1l. Gilthead seabream	1·10	40
806		1l.50 Flat-headed grey mullet	1·60	50
807		2l.50 Common carp	2·20	1·00
808		6l.50 Atlantic mackerel	3·25	2·10
809		10l. Lake Ochrid salmon	5·50	3·25

178 Eurasian Red Squirrel

1964. Forest Animals. Multicoloured.

810		1l. Type **178**	55	25
811		1l.50 Beech marten	85	30
812		2l. Red fox	1·10	40
813		2l.50 East European hedgehog	1·60	50
814		3l. Brown hare	2·20	75

815		5l. Golden jackal	2·75	85
816		7l. Wild cat	4·25	95
817		8l. Wolf	5·50	1·30

179 Lighting Olympic Torch

1964. Olympic Games, Tokyo (3rd issue). Inscr "DREJT TOKIOS".

818	**179**	3l. yellow, buff and green	55	75
819	-	5l. blue, violet and red	75	1·00
820	-	7l. lt blue, blue & yellow	1·10	1·60
821	-	10l. multicoloured	1·60	2·50
MS821a		81×91 mm. 15l. buff, blue and violet (as 820) (49×62 mm)	30·00	40·00

DESIGNS: 5l. Torch and globes; 7l. Olympic flag and Mt. Fuji; 10l. Olympic Stadium, Tokyo.

180 Soldiers, Hand clutching Rifle, and Inscription

1964. 20th Anniv of Permet Congress.

822	**180**	2l. sepia, red and orange	1·60	1·00
823	-	5l. multicoloured	3·75	2·10
824	-	8l. sepia, red and brown	8·25	6·25

DESIGNS (each with different inscription at right): 5l. Albanian Arms; 8l. Gen. Enver Hoxha.

181 Revolutionaries with Flag

1964. 40th Anniv of Revolution.

825	**181**	2l.50 black and red	55	30
826	**181**	7l.50 black and mauve	1·60	1·00

1964. Verso Tokyo Stamp Exhibition, Rimini (Italy). Optd **Rimini 25-VI-64**.

827		10l. blue, violet, orange and black (No. 821)	8·75	8·75

183 Full Moon

1964. Moon's Phases.

828	**183**	1l. yellow and violet	55	20
829	-	5l. yellow and blue	1·10	85
830	-	8l. yellow and blue	1·60	1·00
831	-	11l. yellow and green	5·50	2·10
MS831a		67×78 mm. 15l. yellow and blue (New Moon) (34×39 mm). Imperf	27·00	35·00

PHASES: 5l. Waxing Moon; 8l. Half-Moon; 11l. Waning Moon.

184 Winter Wren

1964. Albanian Birds. Multicoloured.

832		0l.50 Type **184**	55	25
833		1l. Penduline tit	1·10	30
834		2l.50 Green woodpecker	1·60	40
835		3l. Common treecreeper	2·20	50
836		4l. Eurasian nuthatch	2·75	1·00
837		5l. Great tit	3·25	1·30
838		6l. Eurasian goldfinch	3·75	1·60
839		18l. Golden oriole	8·25	3·75

1964. Air. Riccione 'Space' Exhibition. Optd **Riccione 23-8-1964.**

840	**170**	2l. olive, yellow & orange	12·00	21·00
841	-	8l. red, yellow and violet (No. 783)	27·00	31·00

186 Running and Gymnastics

1964. Olympic Games, Tokyo.

842	**186**	1l. red, blue and green	20	15
843	-	2l. brown, blue and violet	25	20
844	-	3l. brown, violet and olive	35	20
845	-	4l. olive, turquoise & blue	55	30
846	-	5l. turquoise, purple & red	85	50
847	-	6l. ultram, lt blue & orge	1·10	80
848	-	7l. green, orange and blue	1·30	85
849	-	8l. grey, green and yellow	1·40	95
850	-	9l. lt blue, yellow & purple	1·50	1·00
851	-	10l. brown, green & turq	1·70	1·60
MS851a		70×96 mm. 20l. violet and bistre (Winners on Dais) (40×67 mm)	25·00	30·00

SPORTS: 2l. Weightlifting and judo; 3l. Horse-jumping and cycling; 4l. Football and water-polo; 5l. Wrestling and boxing; 6l. Various sports and hockey; 7l. Swimming and yachting; 8l. Basketball and volleyball; 9l. Rowing and canoeing; 10l. Fencing and pistol-shooting.

187 Chinese Republican Emblem

1964. 15th Anniv of Chinese People's Republic. Inscr 'I TETOR 1949 1964'.

852	**187**	7l. red, black and yellow	7·75	3·50
853	-	8l. black, red and yellow	7·75	4·75

DESIGN—HORIZ: 8l. Mao Tse-tung.

188 Karl Marx

1964. Centenary of 'First International'.

854	**188**	2l. black, red and lavender	1·10	50
855	-	5l. slate	2·75	1·60
856	-	8l. black, red and buff	5·50	2·10

DESIGNS: 5l. St. Martin's Hall, London; 8l. F. Engels.

189 J. de Rada

1964. 150th Birth Anniv of Jeronim de Rada (poet).

857	**189**	7l. green	1·60	1·00
858	**189**	8l. violet	2·75	1·60

190 Arms and Flag

1964. 20th Anniv of Liberation.

859	**190**	1l. multicoloured	55	40
860	-	2l. blue, red and yellow	1·10	85
861	-	3l. brown, red and yellow	1·60	1·30
862	-	4l. green, red and yellow	2·20	1·70
863	-	10l. black, red and blue	5·50	4·25

DESIGNS—HORIZ: 2l. Industrial scene; 3l. Agricultural scene. 4l. Laboratory worker. VERT: 10l. Hands holding Constitution, hammer and sickle.

191 Mercury

1964. Solar System Planets. Multicoloured.

864		1l. Type **191**	25	20
865		2l. Venus	55	30
866		3l. Earth	75	40
867		4l. Mars	80	45
868		5l. Jupiter	1·10	50
869		6l. Saturn	1·60	1·00
870		7l. Uranus	1·80	1·30
871		8l. Neptune	2·20	1·50
872		9l. Pluto	2·40	1·70
MS872a		88×72 mm. 15l. Solar system and rocket (61×51 mm). Imperf	35·00	47·00

192 Chestnut

1965. Winter Fruits. Multicoloured.

873		1l. Type **192**	35	20
874		2l. Medlars	55	30
875		3l. Persimmon	75	35
876		4l. Pomegranate	1·10	50
877		5l. Quince	2·20	75
878		10l. Orange	4·25	1·30

193 'Industry'

1965. 20th Anniv of Albanian Trade Unions. Inscr 'B.P.S.H. 1945–1965'.

879	**193**	2l. red, pink and black	7·50	7·25
880	-	5l. black, grey and ochre	11·50	11·00
881	-	8l. blue, lt blue & black	14·00	13·50

DESIGNS: 5l. Set square, book and dividers (Technocracy); 8l. Hotel, trees and sunshade (Tourism).

194 Buffalo Grazing

1965. Water Buffaloes.

882	**194**	1l. multicoloured	1·10	50
883	-	2l. multicoloured	2·20	1·00
884	-	3l. multicoloured	3·25	1·60
885	-	7l. multicoloured	7·50	2·10
886	-	12l. multicoloured	13·00	2·50

DESIGNS: 2l. to 12l. As Type **194**, showing different views of buffalo.

195 Coastal View

1965. Albanian Scenery. Multicoloured.

887		1l.50 Type **195**	1·60	50
888		2l.50 Mountain forest	3·50	1·00
889		3l. Lugina Peak (vert)	3·75	1·30
890		4l. White River, Thethi (vert)	5·00	1·60
891		5l. Dry Mountain	6·00	2·10
892		9l. Lake of Flowers, Lure	16·00	4·25

196 Frontier Guard

1965. 20th Anniv of Frontier Force.

893	**196**	2l.50 multicoloured	1·60	1·00
894	**196**	12l.50 multicoloured	9·25	4·25

197 Rifleman

1965. European Shooting Championships, Bucharest.

895	**197**	1l. purple, red and violet	35	20
896	-	2l. purple, ultram & blue	55	30
897	-	3l. red and pink	1·10	50
898	-	4l. multicoloured	2·20	50
899	-	15l. multicoloured	6·50	2·50

DESIGNS: 2, 15l. Rifle-shooting (different); 3l. Target map; 4l. Pistol-shooting.

198 I.T.U. Emblem and Symbols

1965. Centenary of I.T.U.

900	**198**	2l.50 mauve, black & grn	1·10	50
901	**198**	12l.50 blue, black & violet	6·50	1·80

199 Belyaev

1965. Space Flight of Vostod 2.

902	**199**	1l.50 brown and blue	20	10
903	-	2l. blue, ultram & lilac	35	20
904	-	6l.50 brown and mauve	1·10	50
905	-	20l. yellow, black & blue	4·25	2·10
MS906		71×86 mm. 20l. yellow, black and blue (as 905 but larger, 59×51 mm). Imperf	20·00	31·00

DESIGNS: 2l. Vostod 2; 6l.50, Leonov; 20l. Leonov in space.

200 Marx and Lenin

1965. Postal Ministers' Congress, Peking.

907	**200**	2l.50 sepia, red & yellow	85	50
908	**200**	7l.50 green, red & yellow	3·50	2·10

201 Mother and Child

1965. International Children's Day. Multicoloured.

909		1l. Type **201**	25	15
910		2l. Children planting tree	60	30
911		3l. Children and construction toy (horiz)	80	50
912		4l. Child on beach	1·10	85
913		15l. Child reading book	4·25	3·25

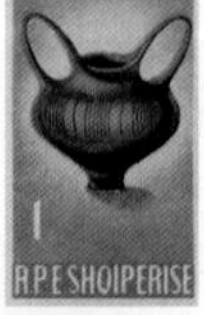
202 Wine Vessel

1965. Albanian Antiquities. Multicoloured.

914		1l. Type **202**	25	10
915		2l. Helmet and shield	55	30
916		3l. Mosaic of animal (horiz)	75	50
917		4l. Statuette of man	1·60	1·00
918		15l. Statuette of headless and limbless man	4·00	2·10

203 Fuchsia

1965. Albanian Flowers. Multicoloured.

919	1l. Type **203**	25	15
920	2l. Cyclamen	75	30
921	3l. Lilies	1·30	50
922	3l.50 Iris	1·60	75
923	4l. Dahlia	1·80	85
924	4l.50 Hydrangea	2·20	95
925	5l. Rose	2·40	1·00
926	7l. Tulips	3·25	1·30

1965. Surch.

927	5q. on 30l. (No. 787)	85	85
928	15q. on 30l. (No. 787)	1·10	1·00
929	25q. on 50l. (No. 788)	1·60	1·60
930	80q. on 50l. (No. 788)	3·75	3·75
931	1l.10 on 20l. (No. 786)	5·50	5·25
932	2l. on 20l. (No. 786)	8·75	8·25

205 White Stork

1965. Migratory Birds. Multicoloured.

933	10q. Type **205**	55	30
934	20q. European cuckoo	1·10	50
935	30q. Hoopoe	1·60	85
936	40q. European bee-eater	2·20	1·00
937	50q. European nightjar	2·75	1·30
938	1l.50 Common quail	8·25	3·75

206 *War Veterans* (after painting by B. Sejdini)

1965. War Veterans Conference.

939	**206**	25q. brown and black	3·25	85
940	**206**	65q. blue and black	8·25	2·10
941	**206**	1l.10 black	11·00	4·25

207 Hunter stalking Western Capercaillie

1965. Hunting.

942	**207**	10q. multicoloured	55	20
943	-	20q. brown, sepia & grn	1·10	20
944	-	30q. multicoloured	1·60	30
945	-	40q. purple and green	2·20	50
946	-	50q. brown, blue & black	2·75	1·00
947	-	1l. brown, bistre & green	5·50	1·60

DESIGNS: 20q. Shooting roe deer; 30q. Common pheasant; 40q. Shooting mallard; 50q. Dogs chasing wild boar; 1l. Hunter and brown hare.

208 *Nerium oleander*

1965. Mountain Flowers. Multicoloured.

948	10q. Type **208**	25	20
949	20q. *Myosotis alpestris*	55	25
950	30q. *Dianthus glacialis*	75	30
951	40q. *Nymphaea alba*	1·30	50
952	50q. *Lotus corniculatus*	1·60	75
953	1l. *Papaver rhoeas*	4·25	2·10

209 Tourist Hotel, Fier

1965. Public Buildings.

954	**209**	5q. black and blue	10	10
955	-	10q. black and buff	15	10
956	-	15q. black and green	20	10
957	-	25q. black and violet	75	20
958	-	65q. black and brown	1·60	40
959	-	80q. black and green	2·20	50
960	-	1l.10 black and purple	2·75	75
961	-	1l.60 black and blue	4·25	1·60
962	-	2l. black and pink	5·50	2·10
963	-	3l. black and grey	11·00	3·75

BUILDINGS: 10q. Peshkopi Hotel; 15q. Sanatorium, Tirana; 25q. 'House of Rest', Pogradec; 65q. Partisans Sports Palace, Tirana; 80q. 'House of Rest', Dajti Mountain; 1l.10. Palace of Culture, Tirana; 1l.60, Adriatic Hotel, Durres; 2l. Migjeni Theatre, Shkoder; 3l. 'A. Moisiu' Cultural Palace, Durres.

210 Freighter *Teuta*

1965. Evolution of Albanian Ships.

964	**210**	10q. green and light green	35	20
965	-	20q. bistre and green	45	20
966	-	30q. ultramarine and blue	55	30
967	-	40q. violet and light violet	75	50
968	-	50q. red and rose	1·60	75
969	-	1l. brown and ochre	3·75	1·30

DESIGNS: 20q. Punt; 30q. 19th-century sailing ship; 40q. 18th-century brig; 50q. Freighter *Vlora;* 1l. Illyrian galliots.

211 Head of Brown Bear

1965. Brown Bears. Different bear designs as T **211**.

970		10q. brown and buff	45	15
971		20q. brown and buff	55	20
972		30q. brown, red and buff	1·10	35
973		35q. brown and buff	1·30	40
974		40q. brown and buff	1·60	45
975	**211**	50q. brown and buff	2·75	50
976	-	55q. brown and buff	3·25	75
977	-	60q. brown, red and buff	6·00	2·75

The 10q. to 40q. are vert.

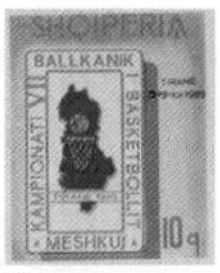

212 Championships Emblem

1965. Seventh Balkan Basketball Championships, Tirana. Multicoloured.

978	10q. Type **212**	35	10
979	20q. Competing players	45	15
980	30q. Clearing ball	75	20
981	50q. Attempted goal	1·60	50
982	1l.40 Medal and ribbon	3·25	1·30

213 Arms on Book

1966. 20th Anniv of Albanian People's Republic.

983	**213**	10q. gold, red and brown	20	10
984	-	20q. gold, blue & ultram	35	20
985	-	30q. gold, yellow and brown	75	50
986	-	60q. gold, lt grn & green	1·80	1·00
987	-	80q. gold, red and brown	2·30	1·60

DESIGNS (Arms and): 20q. Chimney stacks; 30q. Ear of corn; 60q. Hammer, sickle and open book; 80q. Industrial plant.

214 Cow

1966. Domestic Animals. Animals in natural colours; inscr in black: frame colours given.

988	**214**	10q. turquoise	20	20
989	-	20q. green	55	30
990	-	30q. blue	1·30	40
991	-	35q. lavender	1·60	50
992	-	40q. pink	2·20	50
993	-	50q. yellow	2·75	65
994	-	55q. blue	3·00	75
995	-	60q. yellow	5·50	1·00

ANIMALS—HORIZ. 20q. Pig; 30q. Sheep; 35q. Goat; 40q. Dog. VERT: 50q. Cat; 55q. Horse; 60q. Ass.

215 Football

1966. World Cup Football Championships (1st series).

996	**215**	5q. orange grey & buff	15	10
997	-	10q. multicoloured	20	10
998	-	15q. blue, yellow & buff	25	15
999	-	20q. multicoloured	35	20
1000	-	25q. sepia, red and buff	45	20
1001	-	30q. brown, green & buff	55	30
1002	-	35q. green, blue and buff	85	40
1003	-	40q. brown red and buff	90	50
1004	-	50q. multicoloured	1·10	75
1005	-	70q. multicoloured	1·60	1·00

DESIGNS—Footballer and map showing: 10q. Montevideo (1930); 15q. Rome (1934); 20q. Paris (1938); 25q. Rio de Janeiro (1950); 30q. Berne (1954); 35q. Stockholm (1958); 40q. Santiago (1962); 50q. London (1966); 70q. World Cup and football.

See also Nos. 1035/42.

216 A. Z. Cajupi

1966. Birth Centenary of Andon Cajupi (poet).

1006	**216**	40q. indigo and blue	1·10	60
1007	**216**	1l.10 bronze and green	3·25	2·10

217 Painted Lady

1966. Butterflies and Dragonflies. Multicoloured.

1008	10q. Type **217**	45	20
1009	20q. *Calopteryx virgo*	55	25
1010	30q. Pale clouded yellow	75	30
1011	35q. Banded agrion	1·10	35
1012	40q. Banded agrion (different)	1·60	40
1013	50q. Swallowtail	2·20	50
1014	55q. Danube clouded yellow	2·75	75
1015	60q. Hungarian glider	7·00	1·30

The 20, 35 and 40q. are dragonflies, remainder are butterflies.

218 W.H.O. Building

1966. Inauguration of W.H.O. Headquarters, Geneva.

1016	**218**	25q. black and blue	55	20
1017	-	35q. blue and orange	1·10	30
1018	-	60q. red, blue and green	1·60	75
1019	-	80q. blue, yellow & brn	2·20	1·30

DESIGNS—VERT: 35q. Ambulance and patient; 60q. Nurse and mother weighing baby. HORIZ: 80q. Medical equipment.

219 Leaf Star

1966. Starfish. Multicoloured.

1020	15q. Type **219**	45	30
1021	25q. Spiny Star	75	40
1022	35q. Brittle Star	1·30	50
1023	45q. Sea Star	1·60	65
1024	50q. Blood Star	1·80	75
1025	60q. Sea Cucumber	2·75	1·00
1026	70q. Sea Urchin	3·25	2·50

220 Luna 10

1966. Luna 10. Launching.

1027	**220**	20q. multicoloured	55	30
1028	-	30q. multicoloured	1·10	50
1029	**220**	70q. multicoloured	2·20	1·00
1030	-	80q. multicoloured	3·75	2·30

DESIGN: 30, 80q. Earth, Moon and trajectory of Luna 10.

221 Water-level Map of Albania

1966. International Hydrological Decade.

1031	**221**	20q. black, orge & red	55	30
1032	-	30q. multicoloured	85	50
1033	-	70q. black and violet	1·60	1·30
1034	-	80q. multicoloured	2·75	2·10

DESIGNS: 30q. Water scale and fields; 70q. Turbine and electricity pylon; 80q. Hydrological decade emblem.

222 Footballers (Uruguay, 1930)

1966. World Cup Football Championship (2nd series). Inscriptions and values in black.

1035	**222**	10q. purple and ochre	45	10
1036	-	20q. olive and blue	55	15
1037	-	30q. slate and red	75	20
1038	-	35q. red and blue	1·00	25
1039	-	40q. brown and green	1·10	30
1040	-	50q. green and brown	1·30	50
1041	-	55q. green and mauve	1·40	1·00
1042	-	60q. ochre and red	2·75	1·60

DESIGNS—Various footballers representing World Cup winners: 20q. Italy, 1934; 30q. Italy, 1938; 35q. Uruguay, 1950; 40q. West Germany, 1954; 50q. Brazil, 1958; 55q. Brazil, 1962; 60q. Football and names of 16 finalists in 1966 Championship.

223 Tortoise

1966. Reptiles. Multicoloured.

1043	10q. Type **223**	35	20
1044	15q. Grass snake	45	25
1045	25q. Swamp tortoise	55	30
1046	30q. Lizard	65	40
1047	35q. Salamander	1·10	50
1048	45q. Green lizard	1·30	60
1049	50q. Slow-worm	1·40	75
1050	90q. Sand viper	2·75	1·60

224 Siamese Cat

1966. Cats. Multicoloured.

1051	10q. Type **224**	45	20
1052	15q. Tabby	55	25
1053	25q. Kitten	1·10	30
1054	45q. Persian	1·70	75
1055	60q. Persian	2·75	1·00
1056	65q. Persian	3·00	1·20
1057	80q. Persian	3·75	1·40

Nos. 1053/7 are horiz.

225 P. Budi (writer)

1966. 400th Birth Anniv of P. Budi.

1058	**225**	25q. bronze and flesh	1·10	50
1059	**225**	1l.75 purple and green	3·25	2·50

226 UNESCO Emblem

1966. 20th Anniv of UNESCO. Multicoloured.

1060	5q. Type **226**	35	15
1061	15q. Tulip and open book	35	20
1062	25q. Albanian dancers	75	40
1063	1l.55 Jug and base of column	3·25	2·10

227 Borzoi

1966. Dogs. Multicoloured.

1064	10q. Type **227**	55	20
1065	15q. Kuvasz	75	25
1066	25q. Setter	1·30	50
1067	45q. Cocker spaniel	2·00	1·00
1068	60q. Bulldog	2·20	1·30
1069	65q. St. Bernard	3·00	1·60
1070	80q. Dachshund	4·25	2·10

228 Hand holding Book

1966. Fifth Workers Party Congress, Tirana. Multicoloured.

1071	15q. Type **228**	35	15
1072	25q. Emblems of agriculture and industry	60	15
1073	65q. Hammer and sickle, wheat and industrial skyline	1·60	85
1074	95q. Hands holding banner on bayonet and implements	2·20	1·30

229 Ndre Mjeda (poet)

1966. Birth Centenary of Ndre Mjeda.

1075	**229**	25q. brown and blue	65	50
1076	**229**	1l.75 brown and green	3·75	1·80

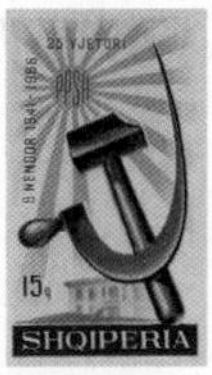

230 Hammer and Sickle

1966. 25th Anniv of Albanian Young Communists' Union. Multicoloured.

1077	15q. Type **230**	55	10
1078	25q. Soldier leading attack	75	20
1079	65q. Industrial worker	1·60	85
1080	95q. Agricultural and industrial vista	2·20	1·30

231 Young Communists and Banner

1966. 25th Anniv of Young Communists' Union. Multicoloured.

1081	5q. Manifesto (vert)	35	10
1082	10q. Type **231**	55	20
1083	1l.85 Partisans and banner (vert)	3·50	2·30

232 Golden Eagle

1966. Birds of Prey. Multicoloured.

1084	10q. Type **232**	55	20
1085	15q. White-tailed sea eagle	75	30
1086	25q. Griffon vulture	1·10	50
1087	40q. Northern sparrow hawk	1·30	65
1088	50q. Osprey	1·80	75
1089	70q. Egyptian vulture	2·75	1·30
1090	90q. Common kestrel	3·75	1·60

233 European Hake

1967. Fish. Multicoloured.

1091	10q. Type **233**	45	20
1092	15q. Striped red mullet	55	30
1093	25q. Opali	1·10	50
1094	40q. Atlantic wolffish	1·30	65
1095	65q. Lumpsucker	1·60	75
1096	80q. Swordfish	2·75	1·30
1097	1l.15 Short-spined sea- scorpion	3·25	1·60

234 Dalmatian Pelicans

1967. Dalmatian Pelicans. Multicoloured.

1098	10q. Type **234**	25	30
1099	15q. Three pelicans	55	40
1100	25q. Pelican and chicks at nest	1·60	50
1101	50q. Pelicans "taking off" and airborne	3·25	75
1102	2l. Pelican "yawning"	8·25	3·75

235 *Camellia williamsi*

1967. Flowers. Multicoloured.

1103	5q. Type **235**	20	10
1104	10q. *Chrysanthemum indicum*	25	15
1105	15q. *Althaea rosea*	35	20
1106	25q. *Abutilon striatum*	1·10	30
1107	35q. *Paeonia chinensis*	1·30	50
1108	65q. *Gladiolus gandavensis*	2·20	1·00
1109	80q. *Freesia hybrida*	2·75	1·60
1110	1l.15 *Dianthus caryophyllus*	3·25	1·80

236 Congress Emblem

1967. Sixth Trade Unions Congress, Tirana.

1111	**236**	25q. red, sepia and lilac	1·10	50
1112	**236**	1l.75 red, green and grey	3·25	2·10

237 Rose

1967. Roses.

1113	**237**	5q. multicoloured	45	20
1114	-	10q. multicoloured	55	30
1115	-	15q. multicoloured	65	40
1116	-	25q. multicoloured	75	50
1117	-	35q. multicoloured	1·10	65
1118	-	65q. multicoloured	1·40	75
1119	-	80q. multicoloured	1·60	1·00
1120	-	1l.65 multicoloured	3·25	1·60

DESIGNS: 10q. to 1l.65 Various roses as Type **237**.

238 Borsh Coast

1967. Albanian Riviera. Multicoloured.

1121	15q. Butrinti (vert)	45	20
1122	20q. Type **238**	55	25
1123	25q. Piqeras village	1·10	30
1124	45q. Coastal view	1·30	40
1125	50q. Himara coast	1·50	50
1126	65q. Fishing boat, Saranda	2·20	75
1127	80q. Dhermi	2·40	1·00
1128	1l. Sunset at sea (vert)	3·25	1·60

239 Fawn

1967. Roe Deer. Multicoloured.

1129	15q. Type **239**	55	20
1130	20q. Head of buck (vert)	55	30
1131	25q. Head of doe (vert)	1·10	50
1132	30q. Doe and fawn	1·10	50
1133	35q. Doe and new-born fawn	1·60	75
1134	40q. Young buck (vert)	1·60	75
1135	65q. Buck and doe (vert)	3·25	1·00
1136	70q. Running deer	4·25	1·60

240 Costumes of Malesia e Madhe Region

1967. National Costumes. Multicoloured.

1137	15q. Type **240**	45	15
1138	20q. Zadrima	50	20
1139	25q. Kukesi	55	30
1140	45q. Dardhe	85	50
1141	50q. Myzeqe	1·00	75
1142	65q. Tirana	1·30	85
1143	80q. Dropulli	2·20	1·00
1144	1l. Laberise	2·30	1·30

241 Battle Scene and Newspaper

1967. 25 Years of the Albanian Popular Press. Multicoloured.

1145	25q. Type **241**	65	30
1146	75q. Newspapers and printery	1·70	75
1147	2l. Workers with newspaper	4·25	2·10

242 University, Torch and Open Book

1967. Tenth Anniv of Tirana University.

1148	**242**	25q. multicoloured	55	40
1149	**242**	1l.75 multicoloured	3·50	1·80

243 Soldiers and Flag

1967. 25th Anniv of Albanian Democratic Front. Multicoloured.

1150	15q. Type **243**	35	20
1151	65q. Pick, rifle and flag	1·10	50
1152	1l.20 Torch and open book	2·40	1·30

244 Grey Rabbits

1967. Rabbit-breeding. Multicoloured.

1153	15q. Type **244**	35	15
1154	20q. Black and white rabbit (vert)	45	20
1155	25q. Brown hare	65	30
1156	35q. Brown rabbits	1·10	40
1157	40q. Common rabbits	1·30	50
1158	50q. Grey rabbit (vert)	2·20	75
1159	65q. Head of white rabbit (vert)	2·40	85
1160	1l. White rabbit	3·50	1·60

245 *Shkoder Wedding* (detail, Kole Idromeno)

1967. Albanian Paintings.

1161	**245**	15q. multicoloured	55	20
1162	-	20q. multicoloured	75	30
1163	-	25q. multicoloured	1·10	40
1164	-	45q. multicoloured	1·30	50
1165	-	50q. multicoloured	1·60	75
1166	-	65q. multicoloured	2·20	85
1167	-	80q. multicoloured	2·40	1·00
1168	-	1l. multicoloured	4·25	1·30

DESIGNS—VERT: 20q. *Head of the Prophet David* (detail, 16th-century fresco); 45q. Ancient mosaic head (from Durres); 50q. Detail, 16th-century icon (30×51 mm); 1l. *Our Sister* (K. Idromeno). HORIZ (51×30 mm): 25q. *Commandos of the Hakmarrja Battalion* (S. Shijaku); 65q. *Co-operative* (farm women, Z. Shoshi); 80q. *Street in Korce* (V. Mio).

246 Lenin and Stalin

1967. 50th Anniv of October Revolution. Multicoloured

1169	15q. Type **246**	35	20
1170	25q. Lenin with soldiers (vert)	75	50
1171	50q. Lenin addressing meeting (vert)	1·10	75
1172	1l.10 Revolutionaries	2·40	1·00

247 Common Turkey

1967. Domestic Fowl. Multicoloured.

1173	15q. Type **247**	20	10
1174	20q. Goose	35	20
1175	25q. Hen	55	30
1176	45q. Cockerel	1·10	50
1177	50q. Helmeted guineafowl	1·30	65
1178	65q. Greylag goose (horiz)	1·60	75
1179	80q. Mallard (horiz)	2·20	1·00
1180	1l. Chicks (horiz)	3·25	1·30

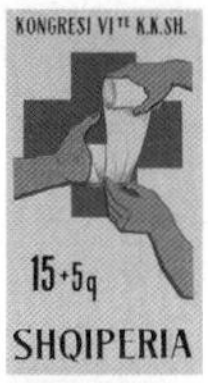

248 First Aid

1967. Sixth Red Cross Congress, Tirana. Multicoloured

1181	15q.+5q. Type **248**	1·10	65
1182	25q.+5q. Stretcher case	2·20	1·00
1183	65q.+25q. Heart patient	7·50	3·75
1184	80q.+40q. Nurse holding child	11·00	5·25

249 Arms of Skanderbeg

1967. 500th Death Anniv of Castriota Skanderbeg (patriot) (1st issue). Multicoloured.

1185	10q. Type **249**	20	10
1186	15q. Skanderbeg	35	15
1187	25q. Helmet and sword	55	20
1188	30q. Kruja Castle	65	30
1189	35q. Petrela Castle	75	40
1190	65q. Berati Castle	1·10	50
1191	80q. Meeting of chiefs	2·20	75
1192	90q. Battle of Albulena	2·30	1·00

See also Nos. 1200/7.

250 Winter Olympic Emblem

1967. Winter Olympic Games, Grenoble. Multicoloured

1193	15q. Type **250**	20	10
1194	25q. Ice hockey	25	15
1195	30q. Figure skating	35	20
1196	50q. Skiing (slalom)	55	30
1197	80q. Skiing (downhill)	1·10	50
1198	1l. Ski jumping	2·40	1·30
MS1199	58×67 mm. 2l. As Type **250** but larger. Imperf	9·25	10·50

251 Skanderbeg Memorial, Tirana

1968. 500th Death Anniv of Castriota Skanderbeg (2nd issue). Multicoloured.

1200	10q. Type **251**	35	20
1201	15q. Skanderbeg portrait	55	30
1202	25q. Skanderbeg portrait (different)	1·00	40
1203	30q. Equestrian statue, Kruja (vert)	1·10	45
1204	35q. Skanderbeg and mountains	1·30	50
1205	65q. Bust of Skanderbeg	2·20	75
1206	80q. Title page of biography	3·00	1·60
1207	90q. "Skanderbeg battling with the Turks" (painting) (vert)	3·50	2·10

252 Alpine Dianthus

1968. Flowers. Multicoloured.

1208	15q. Type **252**	20	10
1209	20q. Chinese dianthus	25	15
1210	25q. Pink carnation	35	20
1211	50q. Red carnation and bud	1·10	30
1212	80q. Two red carnations	1·60	50
1213	1l.10 Yellow carnations	2·20	1·00

253 Ear of Wheat and Electricity Pylon

1968. Fifth Agricultural Co-operative Congress. Multicoloured

1214	25q. Type **253**	55	30
1215	65q. Tractor (horiz)	1·60	85
1216	1l.10 Cow	2·20	1·30

254 Long-horned Goat

1968. Goats. Multicoloured.

1217	15q. Zane female	20	10
1218	20q. Kid	35	15
1219	25q. Long-haired capore	45	20
1220	30q. Black goat at rest	55	25
1221	40q. Kids dancing	65	30
1222	50q. Red and piebald goats	75	50
1223	80q. Long-haired ankara	1·60	65
1224	1l.40 Type **254**	3·25	1·60

The 15q., 20q. and 25q. are vert.

255 Zef Jubani

1968. 150th Birth Anniv of Zef Jubani (patriot).

1225	**255**	25q. brown and yellow	55	30
1226	**255**	1l.75 blue, black & vio	2·75	1·60

256 Doctor using Stethoscope

1968. 20th Anniv of W.H.O.

1227	**256**	25q. red and green	35	15
1228	-	65q. black, blue & yellow	1·30	85
1229	-	1l.10 brown and black	1·60	1·00

DESIGNS—HORIZ: 65q. Hospital and microscope. VERT: 1l.10, Mother feeding child.

257 Servicewoman

1968. 25th Anniv of Albanian Women's Union.

1230	**257**	15q. red and orange	45	20
1231	-	25q. turquoise and green	55	30
1232	-	60q. brown and ochre	1·60	75
1233	-	1l. violet and light violet	2·75	1·30

DESIGNS: 25q. Teacher; 60q. Farm-girl; 1l. Factory-worker.

258 Karl Marx

1968. 150th Birth Anniv of Karl Marx. Multicoloured.

1234	15q. Type **258**	1·10	50
1235	25q. Marx addressing students	1·60	75
1236	65q. "Das Kapital", "Communist Manifesto" and marchers	2·75	1·60
1237	95q. Karl Marx	4·25	3·75

259 Heliopsis

1968. Flowers. Multicoloured.

1238	15q. Type **259**	20	10
1239	20q. Red flax	35	15
1240	25q. Orchid	45	20
1241	30q. Gloxinia	50	30
1242	40q. Orange lily	55	40
1243	80q. Hippeastrum	1·60	1·00
1244	1l.40 Purple magnolia	2·75	1·60

260 A. Frasheri and Torch

1968. 90th Anniv of Prizren Defence League.

1245	**260**	25q. black and green	55	20
1246	-	40q. multicoloured	1·10	50
1247	-	85q. multicoloured	1·60	1·00

DESIGNS: 40q. League headquarters; 85q. Frasheri's manifesto and partisans.

261 *Shepherd* (A. Kushi)

1968. Paintings in Tirana Gallery. Multicoloured.

1248	15q. Type **261**	15	10
1249	20q. *Tirana* (V. Mio) (horiz)	20	10
1250	25q. *Highlander* (G. Madhi)	20	10
1251	40q. *Refugees* (A. Buza)	55	20
1252	80q. *Partisans at Shahin Matrakut* (S. Xega)	1·10	30
1253	1l.50 *Old Man* (S. Papadhimitri)	2·75	85
1254	1l.70 *Shkoder Gate* (S. Rrota)	3·25	1·00
MS1255	90×114 mm. 2l.50 *Shkoder Costume* (Z. Colombi) (51×71 mm)	4·00	2·50

262 Soldiers and Armoured Vehicles

1968. 25th Anniv of People's Army. Multicoloured.

1256	15q. Type **262**	55	20
1257	25q. Sailor and naval craft	65	25
1258	65q. Pilot and Ilyushin Il-28 and Mikoyan Gurevich MiG-17 aircraft (vert)	2·20	1·00
1259	95q. Soldier and patriots	3·25	1·60

263 Common Squid

1968. Marine Fauna. Multicoloured.

1260	15q. Type **263**	35	20
1261	20q. Common lobster	40	30
1262	25q. Common northern whelk	55	40
1263	50q. Edible crab	70	50
1264	70q. Spiny lobster	1·10	85
1265	80q. Common green crab	1·90	1·00
1266	90q. Norwegian lobster	2·20	1·60

264 Relay-racing

1968. Olympic Games, Mexico. Multicoloured.

1267	15q. Type **264**	15	10
1268	20q. Running	20	10
1269	25q. Throwing the discus	25	10
1270	30q. Horse-jumping	35	20
1271	40q. High-jumping	45	30
1272	50q. Hurdling	55	40
1273	80q. Football	1·10	50
1274	1l.40 High diving	2·20	1·30
MS1275	90×81 mm. 2l. Olympic Stadium (64×54 mm.)	4·00	2·50

265 Enver Hoxha (Party Secretary)

1968. Enver Hoxha's 60th Birthday.

1276	**265**	25q. blue	45	30
1277	**265**	35q. purple	65	50
1278	**265**	80q. violet	1·40	1·00
1279	**265**	1l.10 brown	1·70	1·30
MS1280	80½×91 mm. **265**	1l.50 violet, red and gold. Imperf	£160	£180

266 Alphabet Book

1968. 60th Anniv of Monastir Language Congress.

1281	**266**	15q. lake and green	65	40
1282	**266**	85q. brown and green	3·25	2·10

267 Bohemian Waxwing

1968. Birds. Multicoloured.

1283	15q. Type **267**	35	10
1284	20q. Rose-coloured starling	55	20
1285	25q. River kingfishers	75	30
1286	50q. Long-tailed tit	1·10	50
1287	80q. Wallcreeper	2·20	1·00
1288	1l.10 Bearded reedling	3·25	1·60

268 Mao Tse-tung

1968. Mao Tse-tung's 75th Birthday.

1289	**268**	25q. black, red and gold	1·10	50
1290	**268**	1l.75 black, red and gold	7·00	4·75

269 Adem Reka (dock foreman)

1969. Contemporary Heroes. Multicoloured.

1291	5q. Type **269**	45	30
1292	10q. Pjeter Lleshi (telegraph linesman)	55	40
1293	15q. M. Shehu and M. Kepi (fire victims)	1·10	85
1294	25q. Shkurte Vata (railway worker)	1·60	1·30
1295	65q. Agron Elezi (earthquake victim)	1·90	1·40
1296	80q. Ismet Bruca (school-teacher)	2·20	1·60
1297	1l.30 Fuat Cela (blind Co-op leader)	3·25	2·10

270 Meteorological Equipment

1969. 20th Anniv of Albanian Hydro-meteorology. Multicoloured.

1298	15q. Type **270**	55	30
1299	25q. "Arrow" indicator	85	50
1300	1l.60 Meteorological balloon and isobar map	4·25	2·30

271 *Student Revolutionaries* (P. Mele)

1969. Albanian Paintings since 1944. Multicoloured

1301	5q. Type **271**	20	10
1302	25q. *Partisans 1914* (F. Haxhiu) (horiz)	35	10
1303	65q. *Steel Mill* (C. Ceka) (horiz)	55	20
1304	80q. *Reconstruction* (V. Kilica) (horiz)	65	40
1305	1l.10 *Harvest* (N. Jonuzi) (horiz)	1·30	75
1306	1l.15 *Seaside Terraces* (S. Kaceli) (horiz)	1·60	1·30
MS1307	111×91 mm. 2l. *Partisans' Meeting* (N. Zajmi). Imperf	2·75	2·10

SIZES: The 25q., 80q., 1l.10 and 1l.15 are 50×30 mm.

272 *Self-portrait*

1969. 450th Death Anniv of Leonardo da Vinci.

1308	272	25q. agate, brown & gold	35	15
1309	-	35q. agate, brown & gold	65	20
1310	-	40q. agate, brown & gold	85	50
1311	-	1l. multicoloured	2·20	1·00
1312	-	2l. agate, brown & gold	4·25	1·80
MS1313		65×95 mm. 2l. multicoloured. Imperf	7·00	4·50

DESIGNS—VERT: 35q. *Lilies*; 1l. *Portrait of Beatrice*; 2l. *Portrait of a Lady*. HORIZ: 40q. Design for Helocopter.

273 Congress Building

1969. 25th Anniv of Permet Congress. Multicoloured.

1314	25q. Type **273**	55	30
1315	2l.25 Two partisans	4·25	3·25
MS1316	95×101 mm. 1l. Albanian arms. Imperf	50·00	65·00

274 *Viola albanica*

1969. Flowers. Viola Family. Multicoloured.

1317	5q. Type **274**	15	10
1318	10q. *Viola hortensis*	20	10
1319	15q. *Viola heterophylla*	35	15
1320	20q. *Viola hortensis*(different)	45	20
1321	25q. *Viola odorata*	55	20
1322	80q. *Viola hortensis* (different)	1·60	85
1323	1l.95 *Viola hortensis* (different)	2·75	2·10

275 Plum

1969. Fruit Trees. Blossom and Fruit. Multicoloured.

1324	10q. Type **275**	20	10
1325	15q. Lemon	35	15
1326	25q. Pomegranate	55	20
1327	50q. Cherry	1·10	50
1328	80q. Apricot	1·80	1·00
1329	1l.20 Apple	2·75	1·60

276 Throwing the Ball

1969. 16th European Basketball Championships, Naples. Multicoloured.

1330	10q. Type **276**	35	10
1331	15q. Trying for goal	45	15
1332	25q. Ball and net (horiz)	55	20
1333	80q. Scoring a goal	1·60	30
1334	2l.20 Intercepting a pass	3·25	1·60

277 Gymnastics

1969. National Spartakiad. Multicoloured.

1335	5q. Pickaxe, rifle, flag and stadium	15	10
1336	10q. Type **277**	20	10
1337	15q. Running	35	10
1338	20q. Pistol-shooting	45	15
1339	25q. Swimmer on starting block	55	20
1340	80q. Cycling	1·60	75
1341	95q. Football	2·20	1·30

278 Mao Tse-tung

1969. 20th Anniv of Chinese People's Republic. Multicoloured.

1342	25q. Type **278**	1·60	50
1343	85q. Steel ladle and control room (horiz)	5·50	2·10
1344	1l.40 Rejoicing crowd	9·25	3·75

279 Enver Hoxha

1969. 25th Anniv of Second National Liberation Council Meeting, Berat. Multicoloured.

1345	25q. Type **279**	35	20
1346	80q. Star and Constitution	85	50
1347	1l.45 Freedom-fighters	2·20	1·30

280 Entry of Provisional Government, Tirana

1969. 25th Anniv of Liberation. Multicoloured.

1348	25q. Type **280**	45	20
1349	30q. Oil refinery	55	25
1350	35q. Combine harvester	75	30
1351	45q. Hydroelectric power station	1·30	50
1352	55q. Soldier and partisans	1·80	75
1353	1l.10 People rejoicing	3·25	1·30

281 Stalin

1969. 90th Birth Anniv of Joseph Stalin.

1354	281	15q. lilac	20	10
1355	281	25q. blue	55	20
1356	281	1l. brown	1·80	75
1357	281	1l.10 blue	2·20	1·00

282 Head of Woman

1969. Mosaics. (1st series). Multicoloured.

1358	15q. Type **282**	20	10
1359	25q. Floor pattern	35	20
1360	80q. Bird and tree	1·10	50
1361	1l.10 Diamond floor pattern	1·60	65
1362	1l.20 Corn in oval pattern	2·20	75

Nos. 1359/61 are horiz.

See also Nos. 1391/6, 1564/70 and 1657/62.

283 Manifesto and Congress Building

1970. 50th Anniv of Lushnje Congress.

1363	283	25q. black, red and grey	55	30
1364	-	1l.25 black, yell & grn	3·25	2·10

DESIGN: 1l.25, Lushnje postmark of 1920.

284 '25' and Workers

1970. 25th Anniv of Albanian Trade Unions.

1365	284	25q. multicoloured	55	30
1366	284	1l.75 multicoloured	3·25	2·10

285 *Lilium cernum*

1970. Lilies. Multicoloured.

1367	5q. Type **285**	25	15
1368	15q. *Lilium candidum*	35	20
1369	25q. *Lilium regale*	55	30
1370	80q. *Lilium martagon*	1·60	1·00
1371	1l.10 *Lilium tigrinum*	2·20	1·40
1372	1l.15 *Lilium albanicum*	2·75	1·80

Nos. 1370/2 are horiz.

286 Lenin

1970. Birth Cent of Lenin. Each blk, silver & red.

1373	5q. Type **286**	20	10
1374	15q. Lenin making speech	45	20
1375	25q. As worker	55	30
1376	95q. As revolutionary	1·30	75
1377	1l.10 Saluting	2·40	1·00

Nos. 1374/6 are horiz.

287 Frontier Guard

1970. 25th Anniv of Frontier Force.

1378	287	25q. multicoloured	55	30
1379	287	1l.25 multicoloured	2·75	1·80

288 Jules Rimet Cup

1970. World Cup Football Championship, Mexico. Multicoloured.

1380	5q. Type **288**	10	10
1381	10q. Aztec Stadium	15	10
1382	15q. Three footballers	20	10
1383	25q. Heading goal	25	15
1384	65q. Two footballers	55	20
1385	80q. Two footballers	1·10	50
1386	2l. Two footballers	2·75	1·40
MS1387	81×74 mm. 2l. Mexican horseman and Mt. Popocatepetil	4·00	3·00

The design of **MS**1387 is larger, 56×45 mm.

289 New U.P.U. Headquarters Building

1970. New U.P.U. Headquarters Building, Berne.

1388	**289**	25q. blue, black and light blue	35	15
1389	**289**	1l.10 pink, black & orge	1·60	65
1390	**289**	1l.15 turq, blk & grn	1·80	1·00

290 Birds and Grapes

1970. Mosaics (2nd series). Multicoloured.

1391	5q. Type **290**	20	10
1392	10q. Waterfowl	35	10
1393	20q. Pheasant and tree stump	45	15
1394	25q. Bird and leaves	55	20
1395	65q. Fish	1·10	50
1396	2l.25 Peacock (vert)	3·75	2·10

291 Harvesters and Dancers

1970. 25th Anniv of Agrarian Reform.

1397	**291**	15q. lilac and black	45	20
1398	-	25q. blue and black	55	30
1399	-	80q. brown and black	1·60	50
1400	-	1l.30 brown and black	2·20	1·00

DESIGNS: 25q. Ploughed fields and open-air conference; 80q. Cattle and newspapers; 1l.30, Combine-harvester and official visit.

292 Partisans going into Battle

1970. 50th Anniv of Battle of Vlore.

1401	**292**	15q. brown, orge & black	35	20
1402	-	25q. brown, yell & black	75	30
1403	-	1l.60 myrtle, grn & blk	2·40	1·60

DESIGNS: 25q. Victory parade; 1l.60, Partisans.

293 *The Harvesters* (I. Sulovari)

1970. 25th Anniv of Liberation. Prize-winning Paintings. Multicoloured.

1404	5q. Type **293**	10	10
1405	15q. *Return of the Partisan* (D. Trebicka) (horiz)	20	10
1406	25q. *The Miners* (N. Zajmi) (horiz)	25	15
1407	65q. *Instructing the Partisans* (H. Nallbani) (horiz)	55	30
1408	95q. *Making Plans* (V. Kilica) (horiz)	1·10	75
1409	2l. *The Machinist* (Z. Shoshi)	3·25	2·10
MS1410	67×96 mm. 2l. *The Guerrilla* (S. Shijaku). (54×75 mm). Imperf	3·75	2·50

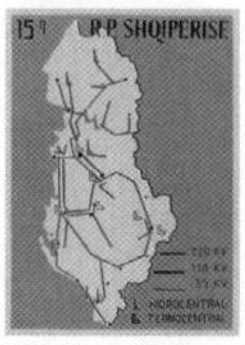

294 Electrification Map

1970. Rural Electrification Completion. Multicoloured

1411	15q. Type **294**	35	20
1412	25q. Lamp and graph	55	30
1413	80q. Erecting power lines	1·60	50
1414	1l.10 Uses of electricity	1·80	1·00

295 Engels

1970. 150th Birth Anniv of Friedrich Engels.

1415	**295**	25q. blue and bistre	55	20
1416	-	1l.10 purple and bistre	1·60	75
1417	-	1l.15 olive and bistre	1·80	85

DESIGNS: 1l.10, Engels as a young man; 1l.15, Engels making speech.

295a Tractor Factory, Tirana

1971. Industry. Multicoloured.

1417a	10q. Type **295a**	£275	£160
1417b	15q. Fertiliser factory, Fier	£275	£160
1417c	20q. Superphosphate factory, Lac (vert)	£275	£160
1417d	25q. Cement factory, Elbasan	£275	£160
1417e	80q. Factory, Oytreki Stalin	£275	£160

296 Beethoven's Birthplace

1970. Birth Bicentenary of Beethoven.

1418	**296**	5q. violet and gold	20	10
1419	-	15q. purple and silver	35	20
1420	-	25q. green and gold	55	30
1421	-	65q. purple and silver	1·30	85
1422	-	1l.10 blue and gold	2·40	1·00
1423	-	1l.80 black and silver	4·25	1·90

DESIGNS—VERT: Beethoven: 15q. In silhouette; 25q. As young man; 65q. Full-face; 1l.10, Profile. HORIZ: 1l.80, Stage performance of *Fidelio*.

297 Republican Emblem

1971. 25th Anniv of Republic.

1424	**297**	15q. multicoloured	35	20
1425	-	25q. multicoloured	45	30
1426	-	80q. black, gold & green	1·30	1·00
1427	-	1l.30 black, gold & brn	1·80	1·40

DESIGNS: 25q. Proclamation; 80q. Enver Hoxha; 1l.30, Patriots.

298 Storming the Barricades

1971. Centenary of Paris Commune.

1428		25q. blue and deep blue	55	20
1429		50q. green and grey	75	40
1430	**298**	65q. chestnut and brown	1·10	50
1431	-	1l.10 lilac and violet	2·20	1·00

DESIGNS—VERT: 25q. La Marseillaise; 50q. Women Communards. HORIZ: 1l.10, Firing squad.

299 Conflict of Race

1971. Racial Equality Year.

1432	**299**	25q. black and brown	35	20
1433	-	1l.10 black and red	1·10	50
1434	-	1l.15 black and red	1·30	65

DESIGNS—VERT: 1l.10, Heads of three races; 1l.15, Freedom fighters.

300 Tulip

1971. Hybrid Tulips.

1435	**300**	5q. multicoloured	15	10
1436	-	10q. multicoloured	20	10
1437	-	15q. multicoloured	35	10
1438	-	20q. multicoloured	45	15
1439	-	25q. multicoloured	55	20
1440	-	80q. multicoloured	1·60	50
1441	-	1l. multicoloured	2·75	1·00
1442	-	1l.45 multicoloured	4·25	2·10

DESIGNS: 10q. to 1l.45, Different varieties of tulips.

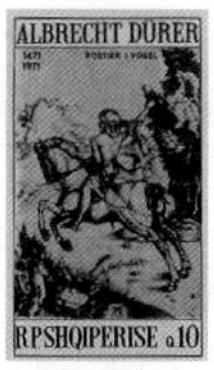

301 *Postrider*

1971. 500th Birth Anniv of Albrecht Durer (painter and engraver).

1443	**301**	10q. black and green	20	10
1444	-	15q. black and blue	45	15
1445	-	25q. black and blue	55	20
1446	-	45q. black and purple	1·10	50
1447	-	65q. multicoloured	2·20	1·00
1448	-	2l.40 multicoloured	6·50	2·10
MS1449		93×90 mm. 2l.50 multicoloured. Imperf	5·50	3·75

DESIGNS—VERT: 15q. *Three Peasants*; 25q. *Peasant Dancers*; 45q. *The Bagpiper*. HORIZ: 65q. *View of Kalchreut*; 2l.40, *View of Trient*. LARGER: 2l.50, Self-portrait.

302 Globe and Satellite (1970)

1971. Chinese Space Achievements. Multicoloured.

1450	60q. Type **302**	1·10	50
1451	1l.20 Public Building, Tirana	2·20	1·60
1452	2l.20 Globe and satellite (1971)	4·25	3·25
MS1453	65×112 mm. 2l.50 Globe and arrow. Imperf	6·50	3·75

The date on No. 1451 refers to the passage of Chinese satellite over Tirana.

303 Mao Tse-tung

1971. 50th Anniv of Chinese Communist Party. Multicoloured.

1454	25q. Type **303**	85	50
1455	1l.05 Party Birthplace (horiz)	2·20	1·60
1456	1l.20 Chinese celebrations (horiz)	3·25	2·50

304 Crested Tit

1971. Birds. Multicoloured.

1457	5q. Type **304**	35	10
1458	10q. European serin	45	15
1459	15q. Linnet	65	15
1460	25q. Firecrest	1·10	20
1461	45q. Rock thrush	1·60	40
1462	60q. Blue tit	2·40	1·00
1463	2l.40 Chaffinch	9·75	8·25

305 Running

1971. Olympic Games (1972). (1st issue). Multicoloured

1464	5q. Type **305**	10	10
1465	10q. Hurdling	15	10
1466	15q. Canoeing	20	15
1467	25q. Gymnastics	55	20
1468	80q. Fencing	1·10	40
1469	1l.05 Football	1·30	50
1470	3l.60 Diving	4·50	1·60
MS1471	70×83 mm. 2l. Runner breasting tape (47×54 mm). Imperf	4·00	3·00

See also Nos. 1522/**MS**1530.

306 Workers with Banner

1971. Sixth Workers' Party Congress. Multicoloured.

1472	25q. Type **306**	55	20
1473	1l.05 Congress hall	1·60	1·40
1474	1l.20 "VI", flag, star and rifle (vert)	2·20	1·60

307 'XXX' and Red Flag

1971. 30th Anniv of Albanian Workers' Party. Multicoloured.

1475	15q. Workers and industry (horiz)	20	10
1476	80q. Type **307**	1·40	1·00
1477	1l.55 Enver Hoxha and flags (horiz)	2·75	1·90

308 *Young Man* (R. Kuci)

1971. Albanian Paintings. Multicoloured.

1478	5q. Type **308**	10	10
1479	15q. *Building Construction* (M. Fushekati)	15	10
1480	25q. *Partisan* (D. Jukniu)	20	15
1481	80q. *Fighter Pilots* (S. Kristo) (horiz)	1·10	20
1482	1l.20 *Girl Messenger* (A. Sadikaj) (horiz)	1·40	85
1483	1l.55 *Medieval Warriors* (S. Kamberi) (horiz)	1·60	1·40
MS1484	89×70 mm. 2l. *Partisans in the Mountains* (I. Lulani). Imperf	4·00	3·00

309 Emblems and Flags

1971. 30th Anniv of Albanian Young Communists' Union.

1485	**309**	15q. multicoloured	20	10
1486	**309**	1l.35 multicoloured	2·00	1·00

310 Village Girls

1971. Albanian Ballet *Halili and Hajria*. Multicoloured

1487	5q. Type **310**	15	10
1488	10q. Parting of Halili and Hajria	20	10
1489	15q. Hajria before Sultan Suleiman	20	15
1490	50q. Hajria's marriage	75	50
1491	80q. Execution of Halili	1·30	75
1492	1l.40 Hajria killing her husband	2·20	1·30

311 Rifle-shooting (Biathlon)

1972. Winter Olympic Games, Sapporo, Japan. Multicoloured.

1493	5q. Type **311**	10	10
1494	10q. Tobogganing	15	10
1495	15q. Ice-hockey	15	10
1496	20q. Bobsleighing	20	10
1497	50q. Speed skating	85	50
1498	1l. Slalom skiing	1·30	85
1499	2l. Ski jumping	2·40	1·90
MS1500	71×91 mm. 2l.50 Figure skating. Imperf	4·00	3·00

312 Wild Strawberries

1972. Wild Fruits. Multicoloured.

1501	5q. Type **312**	15	10
1502	10q. Blackberries	15	10
1503	15q. Hazelnuts	20	10
1504	20q. Walnuts	45	15
1505	25q. Strawberry-tree fruit	55	20
1506	30q. Dogwood berries	75	50
1507	2l.40 Rowanberries	4·25	1·60

313 Human Heart

1972. World Health Day. Multicoloured.

1508	1l.10 Type **313**	1·80	1·30
1509	1l.20 Treatment of cardiac patient	2·00	1·40

314 Congress Delegates

1972. Seventh Albanian Trade Unions Congress. Multicoloured

1510	25q. Type **314**	75	50
1511	2l.05 Congress Hall	3·00	1·80

315 Memorial Flame

1972. 30th Anniv of Martyrs' Day, and Death of Qemal Stafa.

1512	**315** 15q. multicoloured	20	10
1513	- 25q. black, orge & grey	55	20
1514	- 1l.90 black and ochre	2·75	1·30

DESIGNS—VERT: 25q. *Spirit of Defiance* (statue). HORIZ: 1l.90, Qemal Stafa.

316 *Camellia japonica Kamelie*

1972. Camellias.

1515	**316** 5q. multicoloured	15	10
1516	- 10q. multicoloured	20	10
1517	- 15q. multicoloured	25	15
1518	- 25q. multicoloured	55	20
1519	- 45q. multicoloured	75	30
1520	- 50q. multicoloured	1·30	50
1521	- 2l.50 multicoloured	5·00	2·50

DESIGNS: Nos. 1516/21, Various camellias as Type **316**.

317 High Jumping

1972. Olympic Games, Munich (2nd issue). Multicoloured

1522	5q. Type **317**	10	10
1523	10q. Running	15	10
1524	15q. Putting the shot	20	10
1525	20q. Cycling	35	15
1526	25q. Pole-vaulting	45	20
1527	50q. Hurdling	55	30
1528	75q. Hockey	1·10	50
1529	2l. Swimming	3·25	1·00
MS1530	59×76 mm. 2l.50 High-diving (vert). Imperf	4·00	3·00

318 Articulated Bus

1972. Modern Transport. Multicoloured.

1531	15q. Type **318**	20	10
1532	25q. Czechoslovakian Class T699 diesel locomotive	55	15
1533	80q. Freighter *Tirana*	75	20
1534	1l.05 Motor-car	1·30	50
1535	1l.20 Container truck	2·20	1·00

319 Trial of Strength

1972. First Nat Festival of Traditional Games. Multicoloured

1536	5q. Type **319**	10	10
1537	10q. Pick-a-back ball game	15	10
1538	15q. Leaping game	20	10
1539	25q. Rope game	55	20
1540	90q. Leap-frog	1·60	75
1541	2l. Women's throwing game	2·75	2·10

320 Newspaper Mastheads

1972. 30th Anniv of Press Day.

1542	**320** 15q. black and blue	20	10
1543	- 25q. green, red & black	35	15
1544	- 1l.90 black and mauve	2·20	1·60

DESIGNS: 25q. Printing-press and partisan; 1l.90, Workers with newspaper.

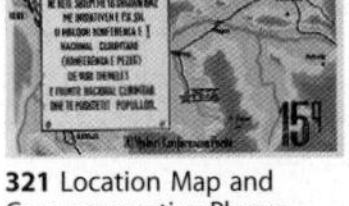

321 Location Map and Commemorative Plaque

1972. 30th Anniv of Peza Conference. Multicoloured

1545	15q. Type **321**	35	20
1546	25q. Partisans with flag	55	30
1547	1l.90 Conference Memorial	3·00	1·90

322 *Partisans Conference* (S. Capo)

1972. Albanian Paintings. Multicoloured.

1548	5q. Type **322**	10	10
1549	10q. *Head of Woman* (I. Lulani) (vert)	15	10
1550	15q. *Communists* (L. Shkreli) (vert)	20	10
1551	20q. *Nendorit*, 1941 (S. Shijaku) (vert)	35	15
1552	50q. *Farm Woman* (Z. Shoshi) (vert)	65	20
1553	1l. *Landscape* (D. Trebicka)	1·30	75
1554	2l. *Girls with Bicycles* (V. Kilica)	2·75	2·10
MS1555	55×83 mm. 2l.30 *Folk Dance* (A. Buza) (vert, 40×67 mm). Imperf	4·00	3·00

323 Congress Emblem

1972. Sixth Congress of Young Communists' Union.

1556	**323** 25q. gold, red and silver	75	50
1557	- 2l.05 multicoloured	3·00	1·80

DESIGN: 2l.05, Young worker and banner.

324 Lenin

1972. 55th Anniv of Russian October Revolution. Multicoloured.

1558	1l.10 multicoloured	1·60	1·00
1559	**324** 1l.20 red, blk & pink	3·25	1·30

DESIGN: 1l.10, Hammer and Sickle.

325 Albanian Soldiers

1972. 60th Anniv of Independence.

1560	**325** 15q. blue, red and black	15	15
1561	- 25q. black, red & yellow	35	20
1562	- 65q. multicoloured	85	50
1563	- 1l.25 black and red	2·75	1·30

DESIGNS—VERT: 25q. Ismail Qemali; 1l.25, Albanian double-eagle emblem. HORIZ: 65q. Proclamation of Independence, 1912.

326 Cockerel (mosaic)

1972. Ancient Mosaics from Apolloni and Butrint (3rd series). Multicoloured.

1564	5q. Type **326**	10	10
1565	10q. Bird (vert)	15	10
1566	15q. Partridges (vert)	20	10
1567	25q. Warrior's leg	45	30
1568	45q. Nude on dolphin (vert)	55	40
1569	50q. Fish (vert)	75	50
1570	2l.50 Warrior's head	3·75	2·50

327 Nicolas Copernicus

1973. 500th Birth Anniv of Copernicus. Multicoloured

1571	5q. Type **327**	10	10
1572	10q. Copernicus and signatures	15	10
1573	25q. Engraved portrait	20	15
1574	80q. Copernicus at desk	75	40
1575	1l.20 Copernicus and planets	2·20	1·00
1576	1l.60 Planetary diagram	3·25	1·60

328 Policeman and Industrial Scene

1973. 30th Anniv of State Security Police.

1577	**328** 25q. black, blue & lt blue	55	40
1578	- 1l.80 multicoloured	3·00	1·80

DESIGN: 1l.80, Prisoner under escort.

329/30 Cactus Flowers

1973. Cacti. As T **329/30**.

1579	**329** 10q. multicoloured	10	10
1580	**330** 15q. multicoloured	15	10
1581	- 20q. multicoloured	20	10
1582	- 25q. multicoloured	55	15
1583	- 30q. multicoloured	4·25	2·50
1584	- 65q. multicoloured	85	40
1585	- 80q. multicoloured	1·10	50
1586	- 2l. multicoloured	2·20	1·30

Nos. 1579/86 were issued together se-tenant within the sheet and in alternate formats as Types **329/30**.

331 Common Tern

1973. Sea Birds. Multicoloured.

1587	5q. Type **331**	25	15
1588	15q. White-winged black tern	45	20
1589	25q. Black-headed gull	55	30
1590	45q. Great black-headed gull	1·10	75
1591	80q. Slender-billed gull	2·20	1·60
1592	2l.40 Sandwich tern	4·25	3·25

332 Postmark of 1913, and Letters

1973. 60th Anniv of First Albanian Stamps. Multicoloured

1593	25q. Type **332**	1·10	50
1594	1l.80 Postman and postmarks	4·25	2·10

333 Albanian Woman

1973. Seventh Albanian Women's Congress.

1595	**333** 25q. red and pink	55	30
1596	- 1l.80 black, orge & yell	3·25	2·30

DESIGN: 1l.80, Albanian female workers.

334 *Creation of the General Staff* (G. Madhi)

1973. 30th Anniv of Albanian People's Army. Multicoloured

1597	25q. Type **334**	16·00	10·50
1598	40q. *August 1949* (sculpture by Sh. Haderi) (vert)	16·00	10·50
1599	60q. *Generation after Generation* (Statue by H. Dule) (vert)	16·00	10·50
1600	80q. *Defend Revolutionary Victories* (M. Fushekati)	16·00	10·50

335 *Electrification* (S. Hysa)

1973. Albanian Paintings. Multicoloured.

1601	5q. Type **335**	10	10
1602	10q. *Textile Worker* (E. Nallbani) (vert)	15	10
1603	15q. *Gymnastics Class* (M. Fushekati)	15	10
1604	50q. *Aviator* (F. Stamo) (vert)	65	40
1605	80q. *Downfall of Fascism* (A. Lakuriqi)	75	50
1606	1l.20 *Koci Bako* (demonstrators (P. Mele)) (vert)	1·10	85
1607	1l.30 *Peasant Girl* (Z. Shoshi) (vert)	2·20	1·60
MS1608	100×69 mm. 2l.05 *Battle of Tendes se Qypit* (F. Haxhiu) (88×47 mm). Imperf	4·00	3·00

336 *Mary Magdalene*

1973. 400th Birth Anniv of Caravaggio. Paintings. Multicoloured.

1609	5q. Type **336**	10	10
1610	10q. *The Guitar Player* (horiz)	15	10
1611	15q. Self-portrait	20	10
1612	50q. *Boy carrying Fruit*	65	40
1613	80q. *Basket of Fruit* (horiz)	85	65
1614	1l.20 *Narcissus*	1·30	1·00
1615	1l.30 *Boy peeling Apple*	2·20	1·60
MS1616	80×102 mm. 2l.05 *Man in Feathered Hat*. Imperf	6·00	5·25

337 Goalkeeper with Ball

1973. World Cup Football Championship, Munich (1974) (1st issue). Multicoloured.

1617	**337**	5q. multicoloured	10	10
1618	-	10q. multicoloured	15	10
1619	-	15q. multicoloured	15	10
1620	-	20q. multicoloured	20	15
1621	-	25q. multicoloured	25	15
1622	-	90q. multicoloured	1·30	40
1623	-	1l.20 multicoloured	1·50	75
1624	-	1l.25 multicoloured	2·20	1·00
MS1625		80×50 mm. 2l.05 multi-coloured (Ball in net, and list of Championships). Imperf	4·50	3·25

DESIGNS: Nos. 1618/24 are similar to Type **337**, showing goalkeepers saving goals.

See also Nos. 1663/70.

338 Weightlifting

1973. World Weightlifting Championships, Havana, Cuba.

1626	**338**	5q. multicoloured	10	10
1627	-	10q. multicoloured	15	10
1628	-	25q. multicoloured	20	10
1629	-	90q. multicoloured	75	40
1630	-	1l.20 mult (horiz)	1·10	75
1631	-	1l.60 mult (horiz)	2·20	1·20

DESIGNS: Nos. 1627/31 are similar to Type **338**, showing various lifts.

339 Ballet Scene

1973. Albanian Life and Work. Multicoloured.

1632	5q. Cement Works, Kavaje	10	10
1633	10q. Ali Kelmendi truck factory and trucks (horiz)	20	10
1634	15q. Type **339**	55	10
1635	20q. Combine-harvester (horiz)	25	10
1636	25q. "Telecommunications"	85	20
1637	35q. Skier and hotel, Dajt (horiz)	65	20
1638	60q. Llogora holiday village (horiz)	1·10	45
1639	80q. Lake scene	1·80	50
1640	1l. Textile mill (horiz)	45	20
1641	1l.20 Furnacemen (horiz)	1·30	50
1642	2l.40 Welder and pipeline (horiz)	2·75	1·60
1643	3l. Skanderbeg Statue, Tirana	4·25	2·50
1644	5l. Roman arches, Durres	5·00	3·25

340 Mao Tse-tung

1973. 80th Birth Anniv of Mao Tse-tung. Multicoloured

1645	85q. Type **340**	2·75	1·60
1646	1l.20 Mao Tse-tung at parade	3·75	2·50

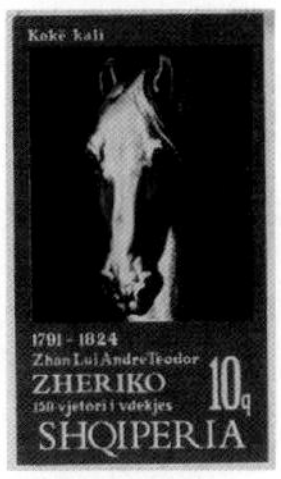

341 *Horse's Head* (Gericault)

1974. 150th Death Anniv of Jean-Louis Gericault (French painter).

1647	**341**	10q. multicoloured	15	10
1648	-	15q. multicoloured	15	10
1649	-	20q. black and gold	20	10
1650	-	25q. black, lilac and gold	55	30
1651	-	1l.20 multicoloured	2·20	75
1652	-	2l.20 multicoloured	3·75	2·10
MS1653		90×68 mm. 2l.05 multicol-oured. Imperf	4·00	3·00

DESIGNS—VERT: 15q. *Male Model* (Gericault); 20q. *Man and Dog*; 25q. *Head of a Negro*; 1l.20, Self-portrait. HORIZ: 2l.20, *Battle of the Giants*.

342 *Lenin with Crew of the Aurora* (D. Trebicka)

1974. 50th Death Anniv of Lenin. Multicoloured.

1654	25q. Type **342**	55	30
1655	60q. *Lenin* (P. Mele) (vert)	1·10	50
1656	1l.20 *Lenin* (seated) (V. Kilica) (vert)	3·25	2·10

343 Duck

1974. Ancient Mosaics from Butrint, Pogradec and Apolloni (4th series). Multicoloured.

1657	5q. Duck (different)	10	10
1658	10q. Bird and flower	15	10
1659	15q. Ornamental basket and grapes	20	15
1660	25q. Type **343**	35	20
1661	40q. Donkey and cockerel	45	30
1662	2l.50 Dragon	2·75	2·10

344 Shooting at Goal

1974. World Cup Football Championships, Munich (2nd issue).

1663	**344**	10q. multicoloured	15	10
1664	-	15q. multicoloured	15	10
1665	-	20q. multicoloured	20	10
1666	-	25q. multicoloured	35	15
1667	-	40q. multicoloured	55	20
1668	-	80q. multicoloured	1·10	50
1669	-	1l. multicoloured	1·30	75
1670	-	1l.20 multicoloured	1·80	1·40
MS1671		72×75 mm. 2l.05 multi-coloured (Trophy and names of competing countries). Imperf	4·00	3·00

DESIGNS: Nos. 1664/70, Players in action similar to Type **344**.

345 Memorial and Arms

1974. 30th Anniv of Permet Congress. Multicoloured.

1672	25q. Type **345**	55	30
1673	1l.80 Enver Hoxha and text	2·20	1·60

346 *Solanum dulcamara*

1974. Useful Plants. Multicoloured.

1674	10q. Type **346**	15	10
1675	15q. *Arbutus uva-ursi* (vert)	15	10
1676	20q. *Convallaria majalis* (vert)	20	10
1677	25q. *Colchicum autumnale* (vert)	55	10
1678	40q. *Borago officinalis*	75	20
1679	80q. *Saponaria officinalis*	1·30	50
1680	2l.20 *Gentiana lutea*	3·75	2·10

347 Revolutionaries

1974. 50th Anniv of 1924 Revolution.

1681	**347**	25q. mauve, black & red	55	30
1682	-	1l.80 multicoloured	2·20	1·60

DESIGN—VERT: 1l.80, Prominent revolutionaries.

348 Redwing

1974. Song Birds. Multicoloured.

1683	10q. Type **348**	20	10
1684	15q. European robin	25	15
1685	20q. Western greenfinch	35	15
1686	25q. Northern bullfinch (vert)	55	20
1687	40q. Hawfinch (vert)	85	25
1688	80q. Blackcap (vert)	2·40	75
1689	2l.20 Nightingale (vert)	4·25	2·10

349 Globe and Post Office Emblem

1974. Centenary of Universal Postal Union. Multicoloured.

1690	**349**	85q. multicoloured	1·80	85
1691	-	1l.20 green, lilac & violet	2·75	1·30
MS1692		78×78 mm. 2l.05 multicol-oured. Imperf	25·00	33·00

DESIGNS—Vert: 1l.20, U.P.U. emblem. Square: (70×70 mm.) 2l.50, Text on globe.

350 *Widows* (Sali Shijaku)

1974. Albanian Paintings. Multicoloured.

1693	10q. Type **350**	10	10
1694	15q. *Road Construction* (Danish Jukniu) (vert)	20	10
1695	20q. *Fulfilling the Plans* (Clirim Ceka)	25	10
1696	25q. *The Call to Action* (Spiro Kristo) (vert)	45	20
1697	40q. *The Winter Battle* (Sabaudin Xhaferi)	55	20
1698	80q. *Three Comrades* (Clirim Ceka) (vert)	1·10	50
1699	1l. *Step by Step, Aid the Partisans* (Guri Madhi)	1·60	1·00
1700	1l.20 *At the War Memorial* (Kleo Nini)	2·20	1·30
MS1701	87×78 mm. 2l.05 *Comrades* (Guri Madhi). Imperf	4·00	3·00

351 Chinese Festivities

1974. 25th Anniv of Chinese People's Republic. Multicoloured.

1702	**351**	85q. multicoloured	3·50	2·10
1703	-	1l.20 black, red and gold	5·50	3·25

DESIGN—VERT: 1l.20, Mao Tse-tung.

352 Volleyball

1974. National Spartakiad. Multicoloured.

1704	10q. Type **352**	10	10
1705	15q. Hurdling	10	10
1706	20q. Hoop exercises	15	10
1707	25q. Stadium parade	20	15
1708	40q. Weightlifting	55	20
1709	80q. Wrestling	75	40
1710	1l. Rifle shooting	1·10	45
1711	1l.20 Football	1·60	50

353 Berat

1974. 30th Anniv of Second Berat Liberal Council Meeting.

1712	**353**	25q. red and black	55	30
1713	-	80q. yellow, brown and black	1·60	75
1714	-	1l. purple and black	3·25	1·60

DESIGNS—HORIZ: 80q. "Liberation" frieze. VERT: 1l. Council members walking to meeting.

354 Security Guards patrolling Industrial Plant

1974. 30th Anniv of Liberation. Multicoloured.

1715	25q. Type **354**	15	10
1716	35q. Chemical industry	20	10
1717	50q. Agricultural produce	35	15
1718	80q. Cultural activities	45	25
1719	1l. Scientific technology	85	50
1720	1l.20 Railway construction	1·20	75
MS1721	81×70 mm. 2l.05 Albanians with book (60×40 mm). Imperf	4·00	3·25

355 Head of Artemis

1974. Archaeological Discoveries. Multicoloured.

1722	**355**	10q. black, mauve & sil	10	10
1723	-	15q. black, green and silver	20	10
1724	-	20q. black, buff & silver	35	20
1725	-	25q. black, mauve & sil	55	40
1726	-	40q. multicoloured	1·10	85
1727	-	80q. black, blue & silver	1·60	1·30
1728	-	1l. black, green & silver	2·20	1·60
1729	-	1l.20 black, sepia & sil	3·75	2·10
MS1730		96×96 mm. 2l.05 multicoloured. Imperf	4·00	3·25

DESIGNS: 15q. Statue of Zeus; 20q. Statue of Poseidon; 25q. Illyrian helmet; 40q. Greek amphora; 80q. Bust of Agrippa; 1l. Bust of Demosthenes; 1l.20, Bust of Bilia. Square: (84×84 mm.) 2l.50, Head of Artemis and Greek vase.

356 Clasped Hands

1975. 30th Anniv of Albanian Trade Unions. Multicoloured

1731	25q. Type **356**	55	20
1732	1l.80 Workers with arms raised (horiz)	2·20	1·40

357 *Cichorium intybus*

1975. Albanian Flowers. Multicoloured.

1733	5q. Type **357**	10	10
1734	10q. *Sempervivum montanum*	10	10
1735	15q. *Aquilegia alpina*	10	10
1736	20q. *Anemone hortensis*	15	10
1737	25q. *Hibiscus trionum*	15	10
1738	30q. *Gentiana kochiana*	20	10
1739	35q. *Lavatera arborea*	55	10
1740	2l.70 *Iris graminea*	3·00	1·90

358 Head of Jesus (detail, Doni Tondo)

1975. 500th Birth Anniv of Michelangelo. Multicoloured

1741	**358**	5q. multicoloured	10	10
1742	-	10q. brown, grey & gold	10	10
1743	-	15q. brown, grey & gold	15	10
1744	-	20q. sepia, grey and gold	20	10
1745	-	25q. multicoloured	20	10
1746	-	30q. brown, grey & gold	20	10
1747	-	1l.20 brn, grey & gold	1·10	65
1748	-	3l.90 multicoloured	2·75	1·90
MS1749		77×86 mm. 2l.05 multicoloured. Imperf	4·50	3·25

DESIGNS: 10q. *The Heroic Captive*; 15q. *Head of Dawn*; 20q. *Awakening Giant* (detail); 25q. *Cumaenian Sybil* (detail, Sistine chapel); 30q. *Lorenzo di Medici*; 1l.20, *Head and shoulders of David*; 3l.90, "Delphic Sybil" (detail, Sistine chapel). 70×77 mm. 2l.05, Head of Michelangelo.

359 Horseman

1975. Albanian Transport of the Past. Multicoloured.

1750	5q. Type **359**	10	10
1751	10q. Horse and cart	15	10
1752	15q. Ferry	25	10
1753	20q. Barque	25	15
1754	25q. Horse-drawn cab	35	15
1755	3l.35 Early car	3·75	1·60

360 Frontier Guard

1975. 30th Anniv of Frontier Force. Multicoloured

1756	25q. Type **360**	55	30
1757	1l.80 Guards patrolling industrial plant	2·20	1·60

361 Patriot affixing Anti-fascist Placard

1975. 30th Anniv of Victory over Fascism. Multicoloured.

1758	25q. Type **361**	35	20
1759	60q. Partisans in battle	75	50
1760	1l.20 Patriot defeating Nazi soldier	1·60	1·00

362 European Wigeon

1975. Albanian Wildfowl. Multicoloured.

1761	5q. Type **362**	10	10
1762	10q. Red-crested pochard	15	10
1763	15q. White-fronted goose	20	10
1764	20q. Pintail	20	10
1765	25q. Red-breasted merganser	35	15
1766	30q. Eider	65	15
1767	35q. Whooper swans	85	20
1768	2l.70 Common shoveler	5·00	2·50

363 *Shyqyri Kanapari* (Musa Qarri)

1975. Albanian Paintings. People's Art Exhibition, Tirana. Multicoloured.

1769	5q. Type **363**	10	10
1770	10q. *Sea Rescue* (Agim Faja)	10	10
1771	15q. *28 November 1912* (Petri Ceno) (horiz)	10	10
1772	20q. *Workers' Meeting* (Sali Shijaka)	15	10
1773	25q. *Shota Galica* (Ismail Lulani)	15	10
1774	30q. *Victorious Fighters* (Nestor Jonuzi)	20	15
1775	80q. *Partisan Comrades* (Vilson Halimi)	65	40
1776	2l.25 *Republic Day Celebration* (Fatmir Haxhiu) (horiz)	3·00	2·10
MS1777	68×98 mm. 2l.05 *Folk Dance* (Abdurahim Buza). Imperf	3·75	3·25

364 Farmer with Declaration of Reform

1975. 30th Anniv of Agrarian Reform. Multicoloured

1778	15q. Type **364**	55	30
1779	2l. Agricultural scene	2·75	1·80

365 Dead Man's Fingers

1975. Marine Corals. Multicoloured.

1780	5q. Type **365**	10	10
1781	10q. *Paramuricea chamaeleon*	15	10
1782	20q. Red Coral	20	10
1783	25q. Tube Coral or Sea Fan	35	15
1784	3l.70 *Cladocora cespitosa*	5·50	2·50

366 Cycling

1975. Olympic Games, Montreal (1976). Multicolured

1785	5q. Type **366**	10	10
1786	10q. Canoeing	10	10
1787	15q. Handball	20	10
1788	20q. Basketball	35	15
1789	25q. Water-polo	45	15
1790	30q. Hockey	55	20
1791	1l.20 Pole vaulting	1·60	85
1792	2l.05 Fencing	2·75	1·60
MS1793	73×77 mm. 2l.15 Games emblem and sportsmen. Imperf	6·50	6·50

367 Power Lines leading to Village

1975. Fifth Anniv of Electrification of Albanian Countryside. Multicoloured.

1794	**367**	15q. multicoloured	20	10
1795	-	25q. violet, red and lilac	35	20
1796	-	80q. black, turq & green	1·10	50
1797	-	85q. buff, brn & ochre	2·20	1·80

DESIGNS: 25q. High power insulators; 80q. Dam and power station; 85q. T.V. pylons and emblems of agriculture and industry.

368 Berat

1975. Air. Tourist Resorts. Multicoloured.

1798	20q. Type **368**	35	20
1799	40q. Gjirokaster	55	20
1800	60q. Sarande	85	30
1801	90q. Durres	1·60	50
1802	1l.20 Krujae	2·20	1·00
1803	2l.40 Boga	4·25	2·10
1804	4l.05 Tirana	6·50	3·75

369 Child, Rabbit and Bear planting Saplings

1975. Children's Tales. Multicoloured.

1805	5q. Type **369**	10	10
1806	10q. Mrs. Fox and cub	20	10
1807	15q. Ducks in school	25	10
1808	20q. Bears building	35	10
1809	25q. Animals watching television	45	10
1810	30q. Animals with log and electric light bulbs	50	10
1811	35q. Ants with spade and guitar	55	20
1812	2l.70 Boy and girl with sheep and dog	2·75	1·90

370 Arms and Rejoicing Crowd

1976. 30th Anniv of Albanian People's Republic. Multicoloured.

1813	25q. Type **370**	55	30
1814	1l.90 Folk-dancers	3·75	1·60

371 Ice Hockey

1976. Winter Olympic Games, Innsbruck. Multicoloured

1815	5q. Type **371**	10	10
1816	10q. Speed skating	15	10
1817	15q. Rifle shooting (biathlon)	20	10
1818	50q. Ski jumping	35	15
1819	1l.20 Skiing (slalom)	1·10	40
1820	2l.30 Bobsleighing	2·00	1·00
MS1821	66×80 mm. 2l.15 Figure skating (pairs)	3·25	2·10

372 *Colchicum autumnale*

1976. Medicinal Plants. Multicoloured.

1822	5q. Type **372**	10	10
1823	10q. *Atropa belladonna*	15	10
1824	15q. *Gentiana lutea*	20	10
1825	20q. *Aesculus hippocastanum*	20	10
1826	70q. *Polystichum filix*	75	20
1827	80q. *Althaea officinalis*	1·10	40
1828	2l.30 *Datura stamonium*	2·75	2·10

373 Wooden Bowl and Spoon

1976. Ethnographical Studies Conference, Tirana. Albanian Artifacts. Multicoloured.

1829	10q. Type **373**	10	10
1830	15q. Flask (vert)	15	10
1831	20q. Ornamental handles (vert)	20	10
1832	25q. Pistol and dagger	25	15
1833	80q. Hand-woven rug (vert)	75	30
1834	1l.20 Filigree buckle and earrings	1·10	50
1835	1l.40 Jugs with handles (vert)	2·20	1·40

374 *Founding the Co-operatives* (Zef Shoshi)

1976. Albanian Paintings. Multicoloured.

1836	5q. Type **374**	10	10
1837	10q. *Going to Work* (Agim Zajmi) (vert)	15	10
1838	25q. *Listening to Broadcast* (Vilson Kilica)	20	10
1839	40q. *Female Welder* (Sabaudin Xhaferi) (vert)	45	20
1840	50q. *Steel Workers* (Isuf Sulovari) (vert)	85	30
1841	1l.20 *1942 Revolt* (Lec Shkreli) (vert)	1·10	85
1842	1l.60 *Returning from Work* (Agron Dine)	1·60	1·00
MS1843	93×79 mm. 2l.05 *The Young Pioneer* (Andon Lakuriqi)	3·25	2·10

375 Demonstrators attacking Police

1976. 35th Anniv of Hoxha's Anti-fascist Demonstration. Multicoloured.

1844	25q. Type **375**	55	20
1845	1l.90 Crowd with flag	3·25	2·10

376 Party Flag, Industry and Agriculture

1976. Seventh Workers' Party Congress. Multicoloured.

1846	25q. Type **376**	55	20
1847	1l.20 Hand holding Party symbols, and flag	2·20	1·60

377 Communist Advance

1976. 35th Anniv of Workers' Party. Multicoloured.

1848	15q. Type **377**	20	10
1849	25q. Hands holding emblems and revolutionary army	55	30
1850	80q. "Reconstruction"	1·10	50
1851	1l.20 "Heavy Industry and Agriculture"	1·60	1·00
1852	1l.70 "The Arts" (ballet)	2·20	1·60

378 Young Communist

1976. 35th Anniv of Young Communists' Union. Multicoloured.

1853	80q. Type **378**	2·10	1·00
1854	1l.25 Young Communists in action	2·75	2·10

379 Ballet Dancers

1976. Albanian Ballet *Cuca e Malexe*.

1855	**379**	10q. multicoloured	10	30
1856	-	15q. multicoloured	20	50
1857	-	20q. multicoloured	35	1·00
1858	-	25q. multicoloured	55	2·10
1859	-	80q. multicoloured	1·30	3·25
1860	-	1l.20 multicoloured	1·80	3·75
1861	-	1l.40 multicoloured	2·20	4·25
MS1862		77×67 mm. 2l.05 multicoloured. Imperf	5·00	5·25

DESIGNS: 15q. to 2l.50, Various ballet scenes.

380 Bashtoves Castle

1976. Albanian Castles.

1863	**380**	10q. black and blue	10	10
1864	-	15q. black and green	15	10
1865	-	20q. black and grey	20	15
1866	-	25q. black and ochre	35	20
1867	-	80q. black, pink and red	1·10	50
1868	-	1l.20 black and blue	1·60	95
1869	-	1l.40 black, red & pink	1·70	1·00

DESIGNS: 15q. Gjirokaster; 20q. All Pash Tepelenes; 25q. Petreles; 80q. Berat; 1l.20, Durres; 1l.40, Krujes.

381 Skanderbeg's Shield and Spear

1977. Crest and Arms of Skanderbeg's Army. Multicoloured

1870	15q. Type **381**	2·20	50
1871	80q. Helmet, sword and scabbard	7·50	3·75
1872	1l. Halberd, spear, bow and arrows	12·00	9·50

382 Ilya Oiqi

1977. Albanian Heroes. Multicoloured.

1873	5q. Type **382**	10	10
1874	10q. Ilia Dashi	20	20
1875	25q. Fran Ndue Ivanaj	55	30
1876	80q. Zeliha Allmetaj	1·60	50
1877	1l. Ylli Zaimi	1·80	75
1878	1l.90 Isuf Plloci	3·75	1·30

383 Polyvinyl-chloride Plant, Vlore

1977. Sixth Five-year Plan. Multicoloured.

1879	15q. Type **383**	35	30
1880	25q. Naphtha plant, Ballsh	55	40
1881	65q. Hydroelectric station, Fjerzes	1·60	85
1882	1l. Metallurgical combinate, Elbasan	2·40	1·00

384 Shote Galica

1977. 50th Death Anniv of Shote Galica (Communist partisan).

1883	**384**	80q. red and pink	1·60	85
1884	-	1l.25 grey and blue	2·40	1·50

DESIGN: 1l.25, Shote Galica and father.

385 Crowd and Martyrs' Monument, Tirana

1977. 35th Anniv of Martyrs' Day. Multicoloured.

1885	25q. Type **385**	55	30
1886	80q. Clenched fist and Albanian flag	1·80	75
1887	1l.20 Bust of Qemal Stafa	3·25	1·60

386 Doctor calling at Village House

1977. Socialist Transformation of Villages. Multicoloured.

1888	5q. Type **386**	10	10
1889	10q. Cowherd with cattle	15	10
1890	20q. Harvesting	20	20
1891	80q. Modern village	1·60	75
1892	2l.95 Tractor and greenhouse	6·00	1·60

387 Workers outside Factory

1977. Eighth Trade Unions Congress. Multicoloured.

1893	25q. Type **387**	55	30
1894	1l.80 Three workers with flags	3·75	2·10

388 Advancing Soldiers

1977. All the People are Soldiers. Multicoloured.

1895	15q. Type **388**	40	20
1896	25q. Enver Hoxha and marching soldiers	55	30
1897	80q. Soldiers and workers	1·60	1·00
1898	1l. The Armed Forces	2·75	2·10
1899	1l.90 Marching soldiers and workers	4·25	3·75

389 Two Girls with Handkerchiefs

1977. National Costume Dances (1st series). Multicoloured

1900	5q. Type **389**	10	10
1901	10q. Two male dancers	15	10
1902	15q. Man and woman in kerchief dance	15	15
1903	25q. Two male dancers (different)	20	15
1904	80q. Two women dancers with kerchiefs	75	40
1905	1l.20 "Elbow dance"	1·10	50
1906	1l.55 Two women with kerchiefs (different)	1·60	1·00
MS1907	56×74 mm. 2l.05 Sabre dance	4·00	3·25

See also Nos. 1932/6 and 1991/5.

390 Armed Worker with Book

1977. New Constitution.

1908	**390**	25q. gold, red and black	55	30
1909	-	1l.20 gold, red and black	2·20	1·00

DESIGN: 1l.20, Industrial and agricultural symbols and hand with book.

391 *Beni Ecen Vet*

1977. Albanian Films.

1910	**391**	10q. green and grey	20	10
1911	-	15q. multicoloured	35	10
1912	-	25q. green, black & grey	55	30
1913	-	80q. multicoloured	2·20	1·60
1914	-	1l.20 brown and grey	3·25	2·50
1915	-	1l.60 multicoloured	3·75	3·25

DESIGNS: 15q. *Rruge te Bardha*; 25q. *Rrugicat qe Kerkonin Diell*; 80q. *Ne Fillim te Veres*; 1l.20, *Lulekuqet Mbi Mure*; 1l.60, *Zonja nga Qyteti*.

392 Rejoicing Crowd and Independence Memorial, Tirana

1977. 65th Anniv of Independence. Multicoloured.

1916	15q. Type **392**	15	15
1917	25q. Independence leaders marching in Tirana	55	30
1918	1l.65 Albanians dancing under national flag	3·75	2·10

393 *Farm Workers*

1977. Paintings by V. Mio. Multicoloured.

1919	5q. Type **393**	10	10
1920	10q. *Landscape in the Snow*	10	10
1921	15q. *Sheep under a Walnut Tree, Springtime*	15	10
1922	25q. *Street in Korce*	25	10
1923	80q. *Riders in the Mountains*	65	30
1924	1l. *Boats by the Seashore*	1·10	65
1925	1l.75 *Tractors Ploughing*	1·80	1·30
MS1926	67×102 mm. 2l.05 *Self-portrait*	4·00	3·25

394 Pan Flute

1978. Folk Music Instruments.

1927	**394**	15q. red, black and green	55	30
1928	-	25q. yellow, black & vio	1·10	50
1929	-	80q. red, black and blue	2·75	1·60
1930	-	1l.20 yellow, blk & blue	5·50	3·25
1931	-	1l.70 lilac, black & grn	12·00	7·25

DESIGNS: 25q. Single-string goat's head fiddle; 80q. Trumpet; 1l.20, Drum; 1l.70, Bagpipes.

1978. National Costume Dances (2nd series). As T **389**. Multicoloured.

1932	5q. Girl dancers with scarves	20	10
1933	25q. Male dancers	35	20
1934	80q. Kneeling dancers	85	50
1935	1l. Female dancers	1·10	85
1936	2l.30 Male dancers with linked arms	2·75	2·10

395 *Tractor Drivers* (D. Trebicka)

1978. Paintings of the Working Class. Multicoloured

1937	25q. Type **395**	20	10
1938	80q. *Steeplejack* (S. Kristo)	55	30
1939	85q. *A Point in the Discussion* (S. Milori)	65	40
1940	90q. *Oil Rig Crew* (A. Cini) (vert)	75	50
1941	1l.60 *Metal Workers* (R. Karanxha)	1·60	1·00
MS1942 73×99 mm. 2l.20 *The Political Discussion* (S. Sholla)		7·50	4·75

396 Boy and Girl

1978. International Children's Day. Multicoloured.

1943	5q. Type **396**	20	10
1944	10q. Boy and girl with pickaxe and rifle	35	20
1945	25q. Children dancing	75	50
1946	1l.80 Classroom scene	4·00	3·25

397 Woman with Pickaxe and Rifle

1978. Eighth Women's Union Congress.

1947	**397**	25q. red and gold	55	30
1948	-	1l.95 red and gold	8·25	5·25

DESIGN: 1l.95, Peasant, Militia Guard and industrial installation.

398 Battle of Mostar Bridge

1978. Centenary of the League of Prizren.

1949	**398**	10q. multicoloured	20	10
1950	-	25q. multicoloured	35	20
1951	-	80q. multicoloured	1·60	1·00
1952	-	1l.20 blue, black & vio	2·20	1·60
1953	-	1l.65 multicoloured	3·25	2·50
1954	-	2l.60 lt grn, blk & grn	5·50	4·75
MS1955 75×69 mm. 2l.20 multicoloured			5·50	4·25

DESIGNS: 25q. Spirit of Skanderbeg; 80q. Albanians marching under national flag; 1l.20, Riflemen; 1l.65, Abdyl Frasheri (founder); 2l.20, League building, crossed rifles, pens and paper; 2l.60, League Headquarters, Prizren.

399 Guerillas and Flag

1978. 35th Anniv of People's Army.

1956	5q. Type **399**	55	30
1957	25q. Men of armed forces (horiz)	1·10	50
1958	1l.90 Men of armed forces, civil guards and Young Pioneers	7·00	6·25

1978. International Fair, Riccione. No. 1832 surch **3.30L. RICCIONE 78 26.8.78.**

1959	3l.30 on 25q. multicoloured	17·00	15·00

401 Man with Target Rifle

1978. 32nd National Shooting Championships.

1960	**401**	25q. black and yellow	35	20
1961	-	80q. black and orange	75	65
1962	-	95q. black and red	1·10	85
1963	-	2l.40 black and red	2·75	2·50

DESIGNS—VERT: 80q. Woman with machine carbine; 2l.40, Pistol shooting. HORIZ: 95q. Shooting from prone position.

402 Kerchief Dance

1978. National Folklore Festival, Gjirokaster. Multicoloured

1964	10q. Type **402**	10	10
1965	15q. Musicians	15	10
1966	25q. Fiddle player	20	15
1967	80q. Singers	55	30
1968	1l.20 Sabre dance	1·20	75
1969	1l.90 Girl dancers	2·40	1·80

403 Enver Hoxha (after V. Kilica)

1978. Enver Hoxha's 70th Birthday.

1970	**403**	80q. multicoloured	55	30
1971	**403**	1l.20 multicoloured	1·10	50
1972	**403**	2l.40 multicoloured	2·20	1·60
MS1973 68×88 mm. **403** 2l.20 multicoloured			4·25	3·25

404 Woman with Wheatsheaf

1978. Agriculture and Stock Raising. Multicoloured.

1974	15q. Type **404**	55	30
1975	25q. Woman with boxes of fruit	75	50
1976	80q. Shepherd and flock	2·75	2·10
1977	2l.60 Dairymaid and cattle	9·75	7·25

405 Pupils entering School

1978

1978	**405**	5q. brown, lt brn & gold	15	10
1979	-	10q. blue, lt bl & gold	20	10
1980	-	15q. violet, lilac and gold	35	15
1981	-	20q. brown, drab & gold	45	20
1982	-	25q. red, pink and gold	55	30
1983	-	60q. green, lt grn & gold	1·60	50
1984	-	80q. blue, lt blue & gold	2·20	50
1985	-	1l.20 magenta, mauve and gold	3·25	1·00
1986	-	1l.60 blue, lt blue & gold	4·25	1·80
1987	-	2l.40 grn, lt grn & gold	6·50	3·25
1988	-	3l. blue, lt blue & gold	7·50	5·25

DESIGNS: 10q. Telephone, letters, telegraph wires and switchboard operators; 15q. Pouring molten iron; 20q. Dancers, musical instruments, book and artist's materials; 25q. Newspapers, radio, television and broadcasting tower; 60q. Assistant in clothes shop; 80q. Militiamen and women, tanks, ships, aircraft and radar equipment; 1l.20, Industrial complex and symbols of industry; 1l.60, Train and truck; 2l.40, Workers hoeing fields, cattle and girl holding wheat sheaf; 3l. Microscope and nurse holding up baby.

406 Dora D'Istria

1979. 150th Birth Anniv of Dora D'Istria (pioneer of women's rights).

1989	**406**	80q. green and black	1·60	1·00
1990	-	1l.10 grey and black	2·75	2·10

DESIGN: 1l.10, Full-face portrait.

1979. National Costume Dances (3rd series). As T **389**. Multicoloured.

1991	15q. Girl dancers with scarves	35	20
1992	25q. Male dancers	55	30
1993	80q. Girl dancers with scarves (different)	2·20	1·00
1994	1l.20 Male dancers with pistols	2·75	1·60
1995	1l.40 Female dancers with linked arms	3·25	2·10

407 Stone-built Galleried House

1979. Traditional Albanian Houses (1st series). Multicoloured.

1996	15q. Type **407**	20	10
1997	25q. Tower house (vert)	35	15
1998	80q. House with wooden galleries	1·10	50
1999	1l.20 Galleried tower house (vert)	1·60	75
2000	1l.40 Three-storied fortified house (vert)	2·20	1·30
MS2001 62×75 mm. 1l.90 Fortified tower house		8·75	5·25

See also Nos. 2116/19.

408 Aleksander Moissi

1979. Birth Centenary of Aleksander Moissi (actor).

2002	**408**	80q. green, black & gold	1·60	65
2003	-	1l.10 brown, blk & gold	2·20	1·60

DESIGN: 1l.10, Aleksander Moissi (different).

409 Vasil Shanto

1979. Anti-fascist Heroes (1st series). Multicoloured.

2004	15q. Type **409**	25	10
2005	25q. Qemal Stafa	55	30
2006	60q. Type **409**	2·20	1·00
2007	90q. As 25q.	3·25	2·10

See also Nos. 2052/5, 2090/3, 2126/9, 2167/70, 2221/4, 2274/7 and 2313/5.

410 Soldier, Crowd and Coat of Arms

1979. 35th Anniv of Permet Congress. Multicoloured.

2008	25q. Soldier, factories and wheat	1·10	50
2009	1l.65 Type **410**	5·00	2·50

411 Albanian Flag

1979. Fifth Albanian Democratic Front Congress.

2010	**411**	25q. multicoloured	1·10	50
2011	**411**	1l.65 multicoloured	5·00	3·25

412 *Ne Stervitje* (Arben Basha)

1979. Paintings. Multicoloured.

2012	15q. Type **412**	10	10
2013	25q. *Shtigje Lufte* (Ismail Lulani)	20	10
2014	80q. *Agim me Fitore* (Myrteza Fushekati)	1·10	50
2015	1l.20 *Gjithe Populli ushtare* (Muhamet Deliu)	1·80	75
2016	1l.40 *Zjarret Ndezur Mbajme* (Jorgji Gjikopulli)	2·20	1·00
MS2017 78×103 mm. 1l.90 *Cajime Rrethime* (Fatmir Haxhiu)		4·00	3·00

413 Athletes round Party Flag

1979. 35th Anniv of Liberation Spartakiad. Multicoloured.

2018	15q. Type **413**	10	10
2019	25q. Shooting	20	10
2020	80q. Girl gymnast	1·10	50
2021	1l.10 Football	1·60	1·00
2022	1l.40 High jump	1·80	1·30

414 Founder-president

1979. Centenary of Albanian Literary Society.

2023	-	25q. black, brown and gold	35	20
2024	**414**	80q. black, brown and gold	1·10	65
2025	-	1l.20 black, blue & gold	1·60	1·00
2026	-	1l.55 black, vio & gold	2·00	1·30
MS2027 78×66 mm. 1l.90 black, buff and gold			3·75	3·25

DESIGNS: 25q. Foundation document and seal of 1880; 1l.20, Headquarters building, 1979; 1l.55, Headquarters building, 1879; 1l.90, Four founder members, book and quill.

415 Congress Building

1979. 35th Anniv of Berat Congress. Multicoloured.

2028	25q. Arms and congress document	1·40	1·00
2029	1l.65 Type **415**	4·75	3·75

416 Workers and Industrial Complex

1979. 35th Anniv of Liberation. Multicoloured.

2030	25q. Type **416**	35	20
2031	80q. Wheat and hand grasping hammer and pickaxe	1·10	65
2032	1l.20 Open book, star and musical instrument	1·60	1·00
2033	1l.55 Open book, compasses and gear wheel	2·20	1·30

417 Joseph Stalin

1979. Birth Centenary of Joseph Stalin.

2034	**417**	80q. blue and red	1·60	1·00
2035	-	1l.10 blue and red	2·20	1·60

DESIGN: 1l.10, Stalin and Enver Hoxha.

418 Fireplace and Pottery, Korce

1980. Interiors (1st series). Multicoloured.

2036	25q. Type **418**	35	20
2037	80q. Carved bed alcove and weapons, Shkoder	75	50
2038	1l.20 Cooking hearth and carved chair, Mirdite	1·60	1·00
2039	1l.35 Turkish-style chimney, dagger and embroidered jacket, Gjirokaster	2·20	1·60

See also Nos. 2075/8.

419 Lacework

1980. Handicrafts. Multicoloured.

2040	25q. Pipe and flask	35	20
2041	80q. Leather handbags	75	50
2042	1l.20 Carved eagle and embroidered rug	1·60	1·00
2043	1l.35 Type **419**	2·20	1·60

420 Aleksander Xhuvani

1980. Birth Centenary of Dr. Aleksander Xhuvani.

2044	**420**	80q. blue, grey and black	2·20	1·60
2045	**420**	1l. brown, grey and black	2·75	2·10

421 Insurrectionists

1980. 70th Anniv of Kosovo Insurrection.

2046	**421**	80q. black and red	2·20	1·60
2047	-	1l. black and red	3·25	2·50

DESIGN: 1l. Battle scene.

422 *Soldiers and Workers helping Stricken Population* (D. Jukniu and L. Lulani)

1980. 1979 Earthquake Relief.

2048	**422**	80q. multicoloured	2·20	1·60
2049	**422**	1l. multicoloured	3·25	2·50

423 Lenin

1980. 110th Birth Anniv of Lenin.

2050	**423**	80q. grey, red and pink	2·20	1·60
2051	**423**	1l. multicoloured	3·25	2·50

424 Misto Mame and Ali Demi

1980. Anti-fascist Heroes (2nd series). Multicoloured,

2052	25q. Type **424**	35	20
2053	80q. Sadik Staveleci, Vojo Kushi and Xhoxhi Martini	1·10	75
2054	1l.20 Bule Naipi and Persefoni Kokedhima	1·80	1·00
2055	1l.35 Ndoc Deda, Hydajet Lezha, Naim Gjylbegu, Ndoc Mazi and Ahmet Haxhia	2·20	1·60

425 *Mirela*

1980. Children's Tales. Multicoloured.

2056	15q. Type **425**	10	10
2057	25q. *Shkarravina*	20	15
2058	80q. *Ariu Artist*	1·10	75
2059	2l.40 *Pika e Ujit*	4·00	3·25

426 *The Enver Hoxha Tractor Combine* (S. Shijaku and M. Fushekati)

1980. Paintings from Gallery of Figurative Arts, Tirana. Multicoloured.

2060	25q. Type **426**	35	20
2061	80q. *The Welder* (Harilla Dhima)	1·10	75
2062	1l.20 *Steel Erector* (Petro Kokushta)	1·80	1·60
2063	1l.35 *Harvest Festival* (Pandeli Lena)	2·20	1·80
MS2064	65×82 mm. 1l.80 *Communists* (Vilson Kilica) (48×71 mm)	5·00	5·00

427 Decorated Door (Pergamen miniature)

1980. Art of the Middle Ages. Each black and gold.

2065	25q. Type **427**	35	20
2066	80q. Bird (relief)	75	50
2067	1l.20 Crowned lion (relief)	1·40	1·00
2068	1l.35 Pheasant (relief)	1·60	1·30

428 Divjaka

1980. National Parks. Multicoloured.

2069	80q. Type **428**	1·10	85
2070	1l.20 Lura	1·60	1·30
2071	1l.60 Thethi	2·75	2·30
MS2072	89×90 mm. 1l.80 Llogara (77×80 mm)	5·50	5·50

429 Flag, Arms and rejoicing Albanians

1981. 35th Anniv of Albanian People's Republic. Multicoloured.

2073	80q. Type **429**	1·60	85
2074	1l. Crowd and flags outside People's Party headquarters	2·20	1·00

1981. Interiors (2nd series). Multicoloured.

2075	25q. As T **418**	20	15
2076	80q. Sleeping mats and spirit keg, Labara	65	50
2077	1l.20 Fireplace and covered dish mat	1·30	75
2078	1l.35 Interior and embroidered jacket, Dibres	1·80	1·40

430 Wooden Cot

1981. Folk Art. Multicoloured.

2079	25q. Type **430**	35	20
2080	80q. Bucket and flask	85	75
2081	1l.20 Embroidered slippers	1·20	1·00
2082	1l.35 Jugs	1·50	1·40

431 Footballers

1981. World Cup Football Championship Eliminating Rounds. Multicoloured.

2083	25q. Type **431**	1·30	60
2084	80q. Tackle	3·75	2·20
2085	1l.20 Player kicking ball	5·50	3·75
2086	1l.35 Goalkeeper saving goal	6·75	4·25

432 Rifleman

1981. Cent of Battle of Shtimje. Each purple & red.

2087	80q. Type **432**	1·20	85
2088	1l. Albanian with sabre	1·50	1·00
MS2089	84×68 mm. 1l.80 Albanian with pistol	5·00	5·00

1981. Anti-fascist Heroes (3rd series). As T **424**. Multicoloured.

2090	25q. Perlat Rexhepi and Branko Kadia	35	20
2091	80q. Xheladin Beqiri and Hajdah Dushi	1·10	50
2092	1l.20 Koci Bako, Vasil Laci and Mujo Ulqinaku	1·30	1·00
2093	1l.35 Mine Peza and Zoja Cure	2·20	1·30

433 Acrobats

1981. Children's Circus.

2094	-	15q. black, green & stone	15	10
2095	-	25q. black, blue and grey	20	15
2096	**433**	80q. black, mve & pink	65	50
2097	-	2l.40 black, orge & yell	2·20	2·00

DESIGNS: 15q. Monocyclists. 25q. Human pyramid; 2l.40, Acrobats spinning from marquee pole.

434 *Rallying to the Flag, December 1911* (A. Zajmi)

1981. Paintings. Multicoloured.

2098	25q. *Allies* (Sh. Hysa) (horiz)	55	20
2099	80q. *Azem Galica breaking the Ring of Turks* (A. Buza) (horiz)	85	50
2100	1l.20 Type **434**	1·30	1·00
2101	1l.35 *My Flag is my Heart* (L. Cefa)	1·60	1·40
MS2102	81×109 mm. 1l.80 *Unite under the Flag* (N. Vasia) (55×79 mm)	5·00	5·00

435 Weightlifting

1981. Albanian Participation in Inter Sports. Multicoloured

2103	25q. Rifle shooting	35	20
2104	80q. Type **435**	75	50
2105	1l.20 Volleyball	1·10	85
2106	1l.35 Football	1·30	1·00

436 Flag and Hands holding Pickaxe and Rifle

1981. Eighth Workers' Party Congress.

2107	**436**	80q. red, brown & black	85	65
2108	-	1l. red and black	1·30	1·20

DESIGN: 1l. Party flag, hammer and sickle.

437 Industrial and Agricultural Symbols

1981. 40th Anniv of Workers' Party. Multicoloured.

2109	80q. Type **437**	55	30
2110	2l.80 Albanian flag and hand holding pickaxe and rifle	2·75	2·10
MS2111	79×98 mm. 1l.80 Enver Hoxha and book (50×68 mm)	5·50	5·50

438 Pickaxe, Rifle and Young Communists Flag

1981. 40th Anniv of Young Communists' Union. Multicoloured.

2112	80q. Type **438**	1·30	1·00
2113	1l. Workers' Party flag and Young Communists emblem	2·20	1·90

439 F. S. Noli

1981. Birth Centenary of F. S. Noli (author).

2114	**439**	80q. green and gold	1·40	75
2115	**439**	1l.10 brown and gold	1·80	1·00

1982. Traditional Albanian Houses (2nd series). As T **407**, but vert. Multicoloured.

2116	25q. House in Bulqize	35	20
2117	80q. House in Kosovo	1·60	1·00
2118	1l.20 House in Bicaj	2·20	1·60
2119	1l.55 House in Mat	3·00	1·90

440 Map, Globe and Bacillus

1982. Centenary of Discovery of Tubercle Bacillus.

2120	**440**	80q. multicoloured	5·50	2·10
2121	-	1l.10 brown & dp brown	7·50	3·75

DESIGN: 1l.10, Robert Koch (discoverer), microscope and bacillus.

441 *Prizren Castle* (G. Madhi)

1982. Paintings of Kosovo. Multicoloured.

2122	25q. Type **441**	55	30
2123	80q. *House of the Albanian League, Prizren* (K. Buza) (horiz)	1·60	1·30
2124	1l.20 *Mountain Gorge, Rogove* (K. Buza)	2·75	1·60
2125	1l.55 *Street of the Hadhji, Zekes* (G. Madhi)	3·75	2·10

1982. Anti-fascist Heroes (4th series). As T **424.** Multicoloured.

2126	25q. Hibe Palikuqi and Liri Gero	55	30
2127	80q. Mihal Duri and Kojo Karafili	1·30	85
2128	1l.20 Fato Dudumi, Margarita Tutulani and Shejnaze Juka	2·00	1·40
2129	1l.55 Memo Meto and Gjok Doci	2·75	1·50

442 Factories and Workers

1982. Ninth Trade Unions Congress. Multicoloured.

2130	80q. Type **442**	3·75	2·20
2131	1l.10 Congress emblem	5·00	3·00

443 Ship in Harbour

1982. Children's Paintings. Multicoloured.

2132	15q. Type **443**	55	20
2133	80q. Forest camp	1·10	75
2134	1l.20 House	1·60	1·30
2135	1l.65 House and garden	3·25	2·00

444 *Village Festival* (Danish Jukniu)

1982. Paintings from Gallery of Figurative Arts, Tirana. Multicoloured.

2136	25q. Type **444**	35	20
2137	80q. *The Hydroelectric Station Builders* (Ali Miruku)	1·30	1·00
2138	1l.20 *Steel Workers* (Clirim Ceka)	1·60	1·30
2139	1l.55 *Oil Drillers* (Pandeli Lena)	2·75	1·60
MS2140	75×90 mm. 1l.90 *First Tapping of the Furnace* (Jorgji Gjikopulli)	5·50	3·75

445 *Voice of the People* (party newspaper)

1982. 40th Anniv of Popular Press. Multicoloured.

2141	80q. Type **445**	£120	£100
2142	1l.10 Hand duplicator producing first edition of *Voice of the People*	£120	£100

446 Heroes of Peza Monument

1982. 40th Anniv of Democratic Front. Multicoloured.

2143	80q. Type **446**	8·25	4·00
2144	1l.10 Peza Conference building and marchers with flag	12·00	5·50

447 Congress Emblem

1982. Eighth Young Communists' Union Congress.

2145	**447**	80q. multicoloured	7·25	4·25
2146	**447**	1l.10 multicoloured	11·50	6·25

448 Tapestry

1982. Handicrafts. Multicoloured.

2147	25q. Type **448**	55	30
2148	80q. Bags (vert)	1·30	75
2149	1l.20 Butter churns	1·80	1·00
2150	1l.55 Jug (vert)	2·75	1·60

449 Freedom Fighters

1982. 70th Anniv of Independence.

2151	**449**	20q. deep red, red & blk	45	30
2152	-	1l.20 black, grn & red	2·20	1·30
2153	-	2l.40 brown, buff and red	4·00	2·50
MS2154		90×89 mm. 1l.90 multicoloured	6·50	4·25

DESIGNS: 20q. Ismail Qemali (patriot) and crowd around building; 2l.40, Six freedom fighters. (58×55 mm) 1l.90, Independence Monument, Tirana.

450 Dhermi

1982. Coastal Views. Multicoloured.

2155	25q. Type **450**	35	20
2156	80q. Sarande	1·10	75
2157	1l.20 Ksamil	1·60	1·30
2158	1l.55 Lukove	2·40	1·60

451 Male Dancers

1983. Folk Dance Assemblies Abroad. Multicoloured

2159	25q. Type **451**	20	10
2160	80q. Male dancers and drummer	75	50
2161	1l.20 Musicians	1·30	1·00
2162	1l.55 Group of female dancers	1·60	1·50

452 Karl Marx

1983. Death Centenary of Karl Marx.

2163	**452**	80q. multicoloured	2·20	1·00
2164	**452**	1l.10 multicoloured	2·75	1·60

453 Electricity Generation

1983. Energy Development.

2165	**453**	80q. blue and orange	1·40	85
2166	-	1l.10 mauve and green	1·80	1·30

DESIGN: 1l.10, Gas and oil production.

1983. Anti-fascist Heroes (5th series). As T **424.** Multicoloured.

2167	25q. Asim Zeneli and Nazmi Rushiti	35	20
2168	80q. Shyqyri Ishmi, Shyqyri Alimerko and Myzafer Asqeriu	1·10	50
2169	1l.20 Qybra Sokoli, Qeriba Derri and Ylbere Bilibashi	1·80	1·00
2170	1l.55 Themo Vasi and Abaz Shehu	2·75	1·60

454 Congress Emblem

1983. Ninth Women's Union Congress.

2171	**454**	80q. multicoloured	1·50	1·00
2172	**454**	1l.10 multicoloured	2·00	1·60

455 Cycling

1983. Sport and Leisure. Multicoloured.

2173	25q. Type **455**	35	20
2174	80q. Chess	1·10	50
2175	1l.20 Gymnastics	1·80	1·00
2176	1l.55 Wrestling	2·20	1·40

456 Soldier and Militia

1983. 40th Anniv of People's Army.

2177	**456**	20q. gold and red	35	20
2178	-	1l.20 gold and red	1·80	1·00
2179	-	2l.40 gold and brown	3·25	1·90

DESIGNS: 1l.20, Soldier; 2l.40 Factory guard.

457 *Sunny Day* (Myrteza Fushekati)

1983. Paintings from Gallery of Figurative Arts, Tirana. Multicoloured.

2180	25q. Type **457**	35	20
2181	80q. *Morning Gossip* (Niko Progri)	1·30	75
2182	1l.20 *29th November, 1944* (Harilla Dhimo)	1·60	1·00
2183	1l.55 *Demolition* (Pandi Mele)	2·20	1·40
MS2184	111×74 mm. 1l.90 *Partisan Assault* (Sali Shijaku and Myrteza Fushekati) (99×59 mm)	11·00	7·50

1983. National Folklore Festival, Gjirokaster. As T **402.** Multicoloured.

2185	25q. Sword dance	25	15
2186	80q. Kerchief dance	1·80	1·00
2187	1l.20 Musicians	2·40	1·60
2188	1l.55 Women dancers with garlands	3·75	2·50

458 Enver Hoxha

1983. 75th Birthday of Enver Hoxha.

2189	**458**	80q. multicoloured	80	65
2190	**458**	1l.20 multicoloured	1·30	1·00
2191	**458**	1l.80 multicoloured	1·80	1·40
MS2192		77×98 mm. 1l.90 multicoloured (as T **458** but with inscriptions differently arranged)	4·25	4·25

459 W.C.Y. Emblem and Globe

1983. World Communications Year.

2193	**459**	60q. multicoloured	75	50
2194	**459**	1l.20 blue, orange & blk	2·00	1·60

460 *Combine to Triumph* (J. Keraj)

1983. Skanderbeg Epoch in Art. Multicoloured.

2195	25q. Type **460**	55	20
2196	80q. *The Heroic Resistance at Krujes* (N. Bakalli)	1·60	1·00
2197	1l.20 *United we are Unconquerable by our Enemies* (N. Progri)	2·20	1·30
2198	1l.55 *Assembly at Lezhe* (B. Ahmeti)	3·25	1·80
MS2199	77×90 mm. 1l.90 *Victory over the Turks* (G. Madhi)	8·25	7·75

461 Amphitheatre, Butrint (Buthrotum)

1983. Graeco-Roman Remains in Illyria. Multicoloured

2200	80q. Type **461**	2·20	1·60
2201	1l.20 Colonnade, Apoloni Cesma (Apollonium)	2·75	2·10
2202	1l.80 Vaulted gallery of amphitheatre, Dyrrah (Epidamnus)	3·25	2·50

462 Man's Head from Apoloni

1984. Archaeological Discoveries (1st series). Multicoloured

2203	15q. Type **462**	20	15
2204	25q. Tombstone from Korce	35	20
2205	80q. Woman's head from Apoloni	1·30	85
2206	1l.10 Child's head from Tren	1·60	1·00
2207	1l.20 Man's head from Dyrrah	2·00	1·30
2208	2l.20 Bronze statuette of Eros from Dyrrah	3·25	1·60

See also Nos. 2258/61.

463 Clock Tower, Gjirokaster

1984. Clock Towers.

2209	**463**	15q. purple	20	15
2210	-	25q. brown	35	20
2211	-	80q. violet	1·10	75
2212	-	1l.10 red	1·30	1·00
2213	-	1l.20 green	2·00	1·40
2214	-	2l.20 brown	3·25	2·30

DESIGNS: 25q. Kavaje; 80q. Elbasan; 1l.10, Tirana; 1l.20, Peqin; 2l.20, Kruje.

464 Student with Microscope

1984. 40th Anniv of Liberation (1st issue). Multicoloured

2215	15q. Type **464**	20	15
2216	25q. Soldier with flag	35	20
2217	80q. Schoolchildren	1·30	85
2218	1l.10 Soldier, ships, airplanes and weapons	1·60	1·00
2219	1l.20 Workers with flag	2·00	1·30
2220	2l.20 Armed guards on patrol	3·25	1·60

See also Nos. 2255/6.

1984. Anti-fascist Heroes (6th series). As T **424**. Multicoloured.

2221	15q. Manush Alimani, Mustafa Matohiti and Kastriot Muco	65	20
2222	25q. Zaho Koka, Reshit Collaku and Maliq Muco	1·30	55
2223	1l.20 Lefter Talo, Tom Kola and Fuat Babani	2·40	1·40
2224	2l.20 Myslysm Shyri, Dervish Hekali and Skender Caci	4·25	2·75

465 Enver Hoxha

1984. 40th Anniv of Permet Congress.

2225	**465**	80q. brown, orge & red	3·25	2·10
2226	-	1l.10 black, yell & lilac	4·00	2·50

DESIGN: 1l.10, Resistance fighter (detail of monument).

466 Children reading Comic

1984. Children. Multicoloured.

2227	15q. Type **466**	55	20
2228	25q. Children with toys	1·10	50
2229	60q. Children gardening and rainbow	2·20	1·00
2230	2l.80 Children flying kite bearing Albanian arms	5·00	2·50

467 Football in Goal

1984. European Football Championship Finals. Multicoloured.

2231	15q. Type **467**	1·10	30
2232	25q. Referee and football	1·60	50
2233	1l.20 Football and map of Europe	3·25	1·00
2234	2l.20 Football and pitch	3·75	2·10

468 *Freedom is Here* (Myrteza Fushekati)

1984. Paintings from Gallery of Figurative Arts, Tirana. Multicoloured.

2235	15q. Type **468**	55	20
2236	25q. *Morning* (Zamir Mati) (vert)	1·10	65
2237	80q. *My Darling* (Agim Zajmi) (vert)	2·75	1·60
2238	2l.60 *For the Partisans* (Arben Basha)	4·25	2·30
MS2239	80×93 mm. 1l.90 *Albania* (Zamir Mati)	11·00	9·00

469 Mulberry

1984. Flowers. Multicoloured.

2240	15q. Type **469**	3·25	85
2241	25q. Plantain	4·25	1·30
2242	1l.20 Hypericum	12·00	4·75
2243	2l.20 Edelweiss	24·00	9·00

470 Sabre Dance

1984. Ausipex 84 International Stamp Exhibition, Melbourne. Sheet 72×88 mm.

MS2244	**470**	1l.90 multicoloured	4·50	4·50

471 Truck driving through Forest

1984. Forestry. Multicoloured.

2245	15q. Type **471**	1·10	65
2246	25q. Transporting logs on overhead cable	1·60	1·00
2247	1l.20 Sawmill in forest	5·50	3·25
2248	2l.20 Lumberjack sawing down trees	8·25	4·50

472 Gjirokaster

1984. Eurphila '84 Int Stamp Exhibition, Rome.

2249	**472**	1l.20 multicoloured	2·75	2·50

473 Football

1984. Fifth National Spartakiad. Multicoloured.

2250	15q. Type **473**	20	15
2251	25q. Running	55	20
2252	80q. Weightlifting	1·10	65
2253	2l.20 Pistol shooting	3·00	2·10
MS2254	70×90 mm. 1l.90 Opening ceremony	4·25	3·50

474 Agriculture and Industry

1984. 40th Anniv of Liberation (2nd issue). Multicoloured

2255	80q. Type **474**	2·20	1·00
2256	1l.10 Soldiers and flag	2·75	1·60
MS2257	68×89 mm. 1l.90 Enver Hoxha making liberation speech	5·00	4·00

1985. Archaeological Discoveries (2nd series). As T **462**, showing Illyrian finds. Multicoloured.

2258	15q. Pot	55	20
2259	80q. Terracotta head of woman	2·20	1·00
2260	1l.20 Terracotta bust of Aphrodite	2·75	1·40
2261	1l.70 Bronze statuette of Nike	4·25	2·10

476 Kapo (bust)

1985. 70th Birthday of Hysni Kapo (politician).

2262	**476**	90q. black and red	2·20	1·60
2263	**476**	1l.10 black and blue	2·75	2·10

477 Running

1985. Olymphile '85 Olympic Stamps Exhibition, Lausanne. Multicoloured.

2264	25q. Type **477**	35	20
2265	60q. Weightlifting	85	65
2266	1l.20 Football	1·60	1·30
2267	1l.50 Pistol shooting	2·75	1·60

478 Bach

1985. 300th Birth Anniv of Johann Sebastian Bach (composer).

2268	**478**	80q. orange, brn & blk	22·00	13·00
2269	-	1l.20 blue, dp blue & blk	27·00	16·00

DESIGN—1l.20, Bach's birthplace, Eisenach.

479 Hoxha

1985. Enver Hoxha Commemoration.

2270	**479**	80q. multicoloured	2·75	2·10
MS2271		67×90 mm. **479** 1l.90 multicoloured	4·25	4·25

480 Frontier Guards

1985. 40th Anniv of Frontier Force. Multicoloured.

2272	25q. Type **480**	1·60	1·00
2273	80q. Frontier guard	3·75	3·25

1985. Anti-fascist Heroes (7th series). As T **424**. Multicoloured.

2274	25q. Mitro Xhani, Nimete Progonati and Kozma Nushi	85	50
2275	40q. Ajet Xhindoli, Mustafa Kacaci and Estref Caka	1·30	1·00
2276	60q. Celo Sinani, Llambro Andoni and Meleo Gosnishti	2·20	1·30
2277	1l.20 Thodhori Mastora, Fejzi Micoli and Hysen Cino	3·75	3·00

481 Scarf on Rifle Barrel

1985. 40th Anniv of V.E. (Victory in Europe) Day. Multicoloured.

2278	25q. Type **481**	33·00	50·00
2279	80q. Crumpled swastika and hand holding rifle butt	85·00	£130

482 *Primary School* (Thoma Malo)

1985. Paintings from Gallery of Figurative Arts, Tirana. Multicoloured.

2280	25q. Type **482**	35	20
2281	80q. *Heroes and Mother* (Hysen Devolli) (vert)	1·30	1·00
2282	90q. *Mother writing* (Angjelin Dodmasej) (vert)	1·60	1·30
2283	1l.20 *Women off to Work* (Ksenofen Dilo)	2·20	1·80
MS2284	74×88 mm. 1l.90 *Foundry Workers* (Mikel Gurashi)	5·00	3·75

483 Scoring a Goal

1985. Tenth World Basketball Championship, Spain.

2285	**483**	25q. blue and black	25	15
2286	-	80q. green and black	1·30	75
2287	-	1l.20 violet and black	1·80	1·30
2288	-	1l.60 red and black	2·75	2·10

DESIGNS: 80q. Player running with ball; 1l.20, Defending goal; 1l.60, Defender capturing ball.

484 Oranges

1985. Fruit Trees. Multicoloured.

2289	25q. Type **484**	55	30
2290	80q. Plums	2·75	1·60
2291	1l.20 Apples	4·25	2·10
2292	1l.60 Cherries	5·50	3·25

485 Kruja

1985. Architecture.

2293	**485**	25q. black and red	55	30
2294	-	80q. black, grey and brown	2·75	1·60
2295	-	1l.20 black, brown & bl	3·25	2·10
2296	-	1l.60 black, brown & red	4·25	2·50

DESIGNS: 80q. Gjirokastra; 1l.20, Berat; 1l.60, Shkoder.

486 War Horse Dance

1985. National Folklore Festival. Dances.

2297	**486**	25q. brown, red & black	55	30
2298	-	80q. brown, red & black	1·60	1·00
2299	-	1l.20 brown, red & blk	2·20	1·30
2300	-	1l.60 brown, red & blk	2·75	1·80
MS2301		56×82 mm. 1l.90 multicoloured. Imperf	4·25	3·75

DESIGNS: 80q. Pillow dance; 1l.20, Ladies' kerchief dance; 1l.60, Men's one-legged pair dance; 1l.90, Fortress dance.

487 State Arms

1986. 40th Anniv of Albanian People's Republic.

2302	**487**	25q. gold, red and black	1·60	1·00
2303	-	80q. multicoloured	3·25	2·10

DESIGN: 80q. *Comrade Hoxha announcing the News to the People* (Vilson Kilica) and arms.

488 Dam across River Drin

1986. Enver Hoxha Hydroelectric Power Station. Multicoloured.

2304	25q. Type **488**	5·50	2·10
2305	80q. Control building	12·00	7·25

489 *Gymnospermium shqipetarum*

1986. Flowers. Multicoloured.

2306	25q. Type **489**	2·20	1·00
2307	1l.20 *Leucojum valentinum*	8·75	4·25

490 Maksim Gorki (writer)

1986. Anniversaries.

2308	**490**	25q. brown	55	30
2309	-	80q. violet	2·20	1·30
2310	-	1l.20 green	3·75	2·10
2311	-	2l.40 purple	7·50	4·75

MS2312 88×72 mm. 1l.90 violet, blue and yellow 5·50 4·25

DESIGNS: 25q. Type **490** (50th death anniv); 80q. Andre Ampere (physicist and mathematician, 150th death anniv); 1l.20, James Watt (inventor, 250th birth); 2l.40, Franz Liszt (composer, death cent). 88×72 mm. 1l.90, Heads of Gorki, Ampere, Watt and Liszt.

1986. Anti-fascist Heroes (8th series). As T **424**. Multicoloured.

2313	25q. Ramiz Aranitasi, Inajete Dumi and Laze Nuro Ferraj	2·20	1·60
2314	80q. Dine Kalenja, Kozma Naska, Met Hasa and Fahri Raalbani	5·50	2·50
2315	1l.20 Hiqmet Buzi, Bajram Tusha, Mumin Selami and Hajredin Bylyshi	8·75	5·25

491 Trophy on Globe

1986. World Cup Football Championship, Mexico. Multicoloured.

2316	25q. Type **491**	55	30
2317	1l.20 Goalkeeper's hands and ball	2·75	2·10

MS2318 97×63 mm. 1l.90 Globe-football (40×32 mm) 4·25 3·25

492 Car Tyre within Ship's Wheel, Diesel Train and Traffic Lights

1986. 40th Anniv of Transport Workers' Day.

2319	**492**	1l.20 multicoloured	14·00	7·75

493 Naim Frasheri (poet)

1986. Anniversaries. Multicoloured.

2320	30q. Type **493** (140th birth anniv)	75	50
2321	60q. Ndre Mjeda (poet, 120th birth anniv)	1·30	1·00
2322	90q. Petro Nini Luarasi (jounalist, 75th death anniv)	2·20	1·60
2323	1l. Andon Zaka Cajupi (poet, 120th birth anniv)	2·75	1·90
2324	1l.20 Millosh Gjergj Nikolla (Migjeni) (revolutionary writer, 75th birth anniv)	3·25	2·30
2325	2l.60 Urani Rumbo (women's education pioneer, 50th death anniv)	8·75	4·25

494 Congress Emblem

1986. Ninth Workers' Party Congress, Tirana.

2326	**494**	30q. multicoloured	11·00	7·75

495 Party Stamp and Enver Hoxha's Signature

1986. 45th Anniv of Workers' Party.

2327	**495**	30q. red, grey and gold	3·25	1·60
2328	-	1l.20 red, orange & gold	8·75	3·75

DESIGNS: 1l.20, Profiles of Marx, Engels, Lenin and Stalin and Tirana house where Party was founded.

496 'Mother Albania'

1986

2329	**496**	10q. blue	10	10
2330	**496**	20q. red	10	10
2331	**496**	30q. red	10	10
2332	**496**	50q. brown	20	15
2333	**496**	60q. green	35	20
2334	**496**	80q. red	55	30
2335	**496**	90q. blue	75	50
2336	**496**	1l.20 green	1·10	75
2337	**496**	1l.60 purple	1·60	10
2338	**496**	2l.20 green	2·20	1·60
2339	**496**	3l. brown	2·75	2·10
2340	**496**	6l. yellow	5·50	3·75

497 Marble Head of Aesculapius

1987. Archaeological Discoveries (3rd series). Multicoloured.

2341	30q. Type **497**	1·10	65
2342	80q. Terracotta figure of Aphrodite	2·20	1·00
2343	1l. Bronze figure of Pan	3·25	1·50
2344	1l.20 Limestone head of Jupiter	4·25	2·75

498 Monument and Centenary Emblem

1987. Centenary of First Albanian School.

2345	**498**	30q. brown, lt brn & yell	55	30
2346	-	80q. multicoloured	1·60	75
2347	-	1l.20 multicoloured	2·20	1·60

DESIGNS: 80q. First school building; 1l.20, Woman soldier running, girl reading book and boy doing woodwork.

499 Victor Hugo (writer, 185th birth anniv)

1987. Anniversaries.

2348	**499**	30q. vio, lavender & blk	55	30
2349	-	80q. brown, lt brn & blk	1·30	75
2350	-	90q. dp blue, blue & blk	2·00	1·30
2351	-	1l.30 dp grn, grn & brn	2·75	2·10

DESIGNS: 80q. Galileo Galilei (astronomer, 345th death); 90q. Charles Darwin (naturalist, 105th death); 1l.30. Miguel de Cervantes Saavedra (writer, 440th birth).

500 *Forsythia europaea*

1987. Flowers. Multicoloured.

2352	30q. Type **500**	75	40
2353	90q. *Moltkia doerfleri*	1·40	1·00
2354	2l.10 *Wulfenia baldacii*	3·25	2·75

501 Congress Emblem

1987. Tenth Trade Unions Congress, Tirana.

2355	**501**	1l.20 dp red, red & gold	5·50	4·25

502 *The Bread of Industry* (Myrteza Fushekati)

1987. Paintings from Gallery of Figurative Arts, Tirana. Multicoloured.

2356	30q. Type **502**	55	30
2357	80q. *Partisan Gift* (Skender Kokobobo)	1·10	85
2358	1l. *Sowers* (Bujar Asllani) (horiz)	1·60	1·30
2359	1l.20 *At the Foundry* (Clirim Ceka) (horiz)	2·20	1·90

503 Throwing the Hammer

1987. World Light Athletics Championships, Rome. Multicoloured.

2360	30q. Type **503**	55	30
2361	90q. Running	1·50	1·00
2362	1l.10 Putting the shot	1·60	1·30

MS2363 85×59 mm. 1l.90 Runner, winners' podium and banner (64×24 mm) 4·25 4·25

504 Themistokli Germenji (revolutionary, 70th death)

1987. Anniversaries.

2364	**504**	30q. brown, red & black	35	25
2365	-	80q. red, scarlet & black	1·30	65
2366	-	90q. violet, red and black	1·60	1·00
2367	-	1l.30 green, red & black	2·75	1·90

DESIGNS: 80q. Bajram Curri (organizer of Albanian League, 125th birth); 90q. Aleks Stavre Drenova (poet, 40th death); 1l.30, Gjerasim Qiriazi (educational pioneer, 126th birth).

505 Emblem

1987. Ninth Young Communists' Union Congress, Tirana.

2368	**505**	1l.20 multicoloured	7·00	5·25

506 National Flag

1987. 75th Anniv of Independence.

2369	**506**	1l.20 multicoloured	7·00	5·25

507 Post Office Emblem

1987. 75th Anniv of Albanian Postal Administration. Multicoloured.

2370	90q. Type **507**	7·50	5·25
2371	1l.20 National emblem on bronze medallion	11·00	10·50

508 Lord Byron (writer, bicentenary)

1988. Birth Anniversaries.

2372	**508**	30q. black and orange	5·50	4·25
2373	-	1l.20 black and mauve	22·00	17·00

DESIGN: 1l.20, Eugene Delacroix (painter, 190th anniv).

509 Oil Derrick, Tap, Houses and Wheat Ears

1988. 40th Anniv of W.H.O.

2374	**509**	90q. multicoloured	30·00	25·00
2375	**509**	1l.20 multicoloured	41·00	33·00

510 *Sideritis raeseri*

1988. Flowers. Multicoloured.

2376	30q. Type **510**	11·00	6·25
2377	90q. *Lunaria telekiana*	22·00	14·50
2378	2l.10 *Sanguisorba albanica*	33·00	21·00

511 Flag and Woman with Book

1988. Tenth Women's Union Congress, Tirana.

2379	**511**	90q. black, red & orange	13·00	10·50

512 Footballers

1988. Eighth European Football Championship, West Germany. Multicoloured.

2380	30q. Type **512**	2·20	1·90
2381	80q. Players jumping for ball	3·25	3·00
2382	1l.20 Tackling	5·50	5·00
MS2383	78×67 mm. 1l.90 Goalkeeper saving ball. Imperf	13·00	13·00

513 Clasped Hands

1988. 110th Anniv of League of Prizren. Multicoloured

2384	30q. Type **513**	45·00	45·00
2385	1l.20 League Headquarters, Prizren	75·00	75·00

514 Flag, Woman with Rifle and Soldier

1988. 45th Anniv of People's Army. Multicoloured.

2386	60q. Type **514**	45·00	45·00
2387	90q. Army monument, partisans and Labinot house	75·00	75·00

515 Mihal Grameno (writer)

1988. Multicoloured.

2388	30q. Type **515**	16·00	16·00
2389	90q. Bajo Topulli (revolutionary)	27·00	27·00
2390	1l. Murat Toptani (sculptor and poet)	33·00	33·00
2391	1l.20 Jul Variboba (poet)	43·00	43·00

516 Migjeni

1988. 50th Death Anniv of Millosh Gjergj Nikolla (Migjeni) (writer).

2392	**516**	90q. silver and brown	13·00	12·50

517 *Dede Skurra*

1988. Ballads. Each black and grey.

2393	30q. Type **517**	11·00	8·25
2394	90q. *Young Omer*	27·00	23·00
2395	1l.20 *Gjergj Elez Alia*	33·00	26·00

518 Bride wearing Fezzes, Mirdita

1988. National Folklore Festival, Gjirokaster. Wedding Customs. Multicoloured.

2396	30q. Type **518**	33·00	31·00
2397	1l.20 Pan Dance, Gjirokaster	£120	95·00

519 Hoxha

1988. 80th Birth Anniv of Enver Hoxha. Multicoloured

2398	90q. Type **519**	5·50	5·25
2399	1l.20 Enver Hoxha Museum (horiz)	8·25	7·75

520 Detail of Congress Document

1988. 80th Anniv of Monastir Language Congress. Multicoloured.

2400	60q. Type **520**	27·00	23·00
2401	90q. Alphabet book and Congress building	43·00	37·00

521 Steam Locomotive and Map showing 1947 Railway Line

1989. Railway Locomotives. Multicoloured.

2402	30q. Type **521**	45	10
2403	90q. Polish steam locomotive and map of 1949 network	1·30	50
2404	1l.20 Diesel locomotive and 1978 network	1·70	85
2405	1l.80 Diesel locomotive and 1985 network	2·50	1·00
2406	2l.40 Czechoslovakian diesel-electric locomotive and 1988 network	5·00	2·10

522 Entrance to Two-storey Tomb

1989. Archaeological Discoveries in Illyria.

2407	**522**	30q. black, brown & grey	35	10
2408	-	90q. black and green	1·30	1·00
2409	-	2l.10 multicoloured	2·20	1·90

DESIGNS: 90q. Buckle showing battle scene; 2l.10, Earring depicting head.

523 Mother mourning Son

1989. *Kostandini and Doruntina* (folk tale). Multicoloured.

2410	30q. Type **523**	55	30
2411	80q. Mother weeping over tomb and son rising from dead	1·10	75
2412	1l. Son and his sister on horseback	1·30	1·00
2413	1l.20 Mother and daughter reunited	1·60	1·30

524 *Aster albanicus*

1989. Flowers. Multicoloured.

2414	30q. Type **524**	35	10
2415	90q. *Orchis paparisti*	1·30	1·00
2416	2l.10 *Orchis albanica*	2·20	1·90

525 Johann Strauss (composer, 90th death anniv)

1989. Anniversaries. Each brown and gold.

2417	30q. Type **525**	55	20
2418	80q. Marie Curie (physicist, 55th death anniv)	1·10	75
2419	1l. Federico Garcia Lorca (writer, 53rd death anniv)	1·60	1·30
2420	1l.20 Albert Einstein (physicist, 110th birth anniv)	2·20	1·80

526 State Arms, Workers' Party Flag and Crowd

1989. Sixth Albanian Democratic Front Congress, Tirana.

2421	**526**	1l.20 multicoloured	9·75	5·25

527 Storming of the Bastille

1989. Bicentenary of French Revolution. Multicoloured

2422	90q. Type **527**	75	50
2423	1l.20 Monument	1·40	85

528 Galley

1989. Ships.

2424	**528**	30q. green and black	55	20
2425	-	80q. blue and black	1·00	75
2426	-	90q. blue and black	1·10	95
2427	-	1l.30 lilac and black	1·60	1·40

DESIGNS: 80q. Kogge; 90q. Schooner; 1l.30, *Tirana* (freighter).

529 Pjeter Bogdani (writer, 300th anniv)

1989. Death Anniversaries. Multicoloured.

2428	30q. Type **529**	20	15
2429	80q. Gavril Dara (writer, centenary)	75	50
2430	90q. Thimi Mitko (writer, centenary (1990))	1·40	85
2431	1l.30 Kole Idromeno (painter, 50th anniv)	2·00	1·00

530 Engels, Marx and Marchers

1989. 125th Anniv of First International. Multicoloured.

2432	90q. Type **530**	1·10	50
2433	1l.20 Factories, marchers and worker with pickaxe and rifle	1·60	75

531 Gymnastics

1989. Sixth National Spartakiad.

2434	**531**	30q. black, orange & red	35	10
2435	-	80q. black, lt grn & grn	75	50
2436	-	1l. black, blue & dp blue	85	65
2437	-	1l.20 black, pur & red	1·30	1·00

DESIGNS: 80q. Football; 1l. Cycling; 1l.20, Running.

532 Soldier

1989. 45th Anniv of Liberation. Multicoloured.

2438	30q. Type **532**	55	20
2439	80q. Date	1·00	50
2440	1l. State arms	1·10	75
2441	1l.20 Young couple	1·60	1·30

533 Chamois

1990. Endangered Animals. The Chamois. Multicoloured.

2442	10q. Type **533**	35	10
2443	30q. Mother and young	75	30
2444	80q. Chamois keeping lookout	2·10	1·00
2445	90q. Head of chamois	2·20	1·30

534 Eagle Mask

1990. Masks. Multicoloured.

2446	30q. Type **534**	35	10
2447	90q. Sheep	75	50
2448	1l.20 Goat	1·10	75
2449	1l.80 Stork	1·60	1·00

535 Caesar's Mushroom

1990. Fungi. Multicoloured.

2450	30q. Type **535**	35	20
2451	90q. Parasol mushroom	85	50
2452	1l.20 Cep	1·40	1·20
2453	1l.80 *Clathrus cancelatus*	2·00	1·60

536 Engraving Die

1990. 150th Anniv of the Penny Black. Multicoloured.

2454	90q. Type **536**	75	50
2455	1l.20 Mounted postal messenger	1·10	85
2456	1l.80 Mail coach passengers reading letters	2·20	1·80

537 Mascot and Flags

1990. World Cup Football Championship, Italy. Multicoloured.

2457	30q. Type **537**	35	15
2458	90q. Mascot running	75	50
2459	1l.20 Mascot preparing to kick ball	1·30	1·00
MS2460	80×62 mm. 3l.30 Mascot as goalkeeper. Imperf	3·75	3·75

538 Young Van Gogh and Paintings

1990. Death Centenary of Vincent van Gogh (painter). Multicoloured.

2461	30q. Type **538**	45	20
2462	90q. Van Gogh and woman in field	85	50
2463	2l.10 Van Gogh in asylum	2·00	1·60
MS2464	88×73 mm. 2l.40 Van Gogh and *Wheatfield with Crows*. Imperf	3·25	3·25

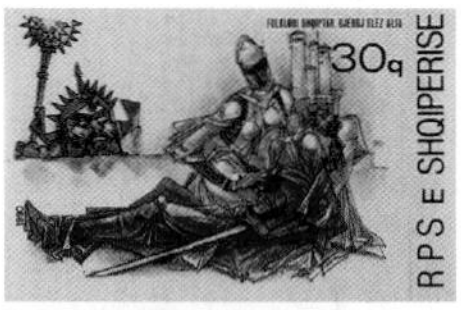

539 Gjergj Elez Alia lying Wounded

1990. Gjergj Elez Alia (folk hero). Multicoloured.

2465	30q. Type **539**	35	20
2466	90q. Alia being helped onto horse	75	50
2467	1l.20 Alia fighting Bajloz	1·10	85
2468	1l.80 Alia on horseback and severed head of Bajloz	1·60	1·00

540 Mosque

1990. 2400th Anniv of Berat. Multicoloured.

2469	30q. Type **540**	10	10
2470	90q. Triadha's Church	60	40
2471	1l.20 River	70	50
2472	1l.80 Onufri (artist)	1·20	95
2473	2l.40 Nikolla	1·40	1·20

541 Pirroja

1990. Illyrian Heroes. Each black.

2474	30q. Type **541**	20	10
2475	90q. Teuta	65	40
2476	1l.20 Bato	75	50
2477	1l.80 Bardhyli	1·10	85

542 School and Globe of Books

1990. International Literacy Year.

2478	**542** 90q. multicoloured	75	50
2479	**542** 1l.20 multicoloured	1·10	85

543 *Albanian Horsemen* (Eugene Delacroix)

1990. Albanians in Art. Multicoloured.

2480	30q. Type **543**	35	10
2481	1l.20 *Albanian Woman* (Camille Corot)	1·00	75
2482	1l.80 *Skanderbeg* (anon)	1·40	1·20

544 Boletini

1991. 75th Death Anniv of Isa Boletini (revolutionary). Multicoloured.

2483	90q. Type **544**	65	40
2484	1l.20 Boletini and flag	1·00	75

545 Armorial Eagle

1991. 800th Anniv (1990) of Founding of Arberi State.

2485	**545** 90q. multicoloured	65	50
2486	**545** 1l.20 multicoloured	1·00	75

546 *Woman reading*

1991. 150th Birth Anniv of Pierre Auguste Renoir (artist). Multicoloured.

2487	30q. Type **546**	55	10
2488	90q. *The Swing*	85	75
2489	1l.20 *The Boat Club* (horiz)	1·30	1·00
2490	1l.80 Still life (detail) (horiz)	2·20	1·80
MS2491	94×75 mm. 3l. *Portrait of Artist with Beard*. Imperf	4·25	4·25

547 *Cistus albanicus*

1991. Flowers. Multicoloured.

2492	30q. Type **547**	35	10
2493	90q. *Trifolium pilczii*	85	75
2494	1l.80 *Lilium albanicum*	1·60	1·30

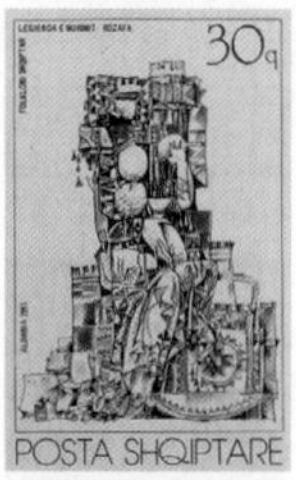

548 Rozafa breastfeeding Child

1991. Imprisonment of Rozafa (folk tale). Multicoloured

2495	30q. Type **548**	20	10
2496	90q. The three brothers talking to old man	65	50
2497	1l.20 Building of walls around Rozafa	1·10	75
2498	1l.80 Figures symbolizing water flowing between stones	1·50	1·20

549 Mozart conducting

1991. Death Bicentenary of Wolfgang Amadeus Mozart (composer). Multicoloured.

2499	90q. Type **549**	75	50
2500	1l.20 Mozart and score	1·20	85
2501	1l.80 Mozart composing	2·10	1·50
MS2502	88×69 mm. 3l. Mozart medallion and score. Imperf	6·50	6·50

550 Vitus Bering

1992. Explorers. Multicoloured.

2503	30q. Type **550**	35	20
2504	90q. Christopher Columbus and his flagship *Santa Maria*	75	40
2505	1l.80 Ferdinand Magellan and his flagship *Vitoria*	1·60	95

551 Otto Lilienthal's Biplane Glider, 1896

1992. Aircraft.

2506	**551** 30q. black, red and blue	35	20
2507	- 80q. multicoloured	55	40
2508	- 90q. multicoloured	75	65
2509	- 1l.20 multicoloured	1·00	85
2510	- 1l.80 multicoloured	1·30	1·20
2511	- 2l.40 black, grey & mve	1·60	1·50

DESIGNS: 80q. Clement Ader's *Avion III*, 1897; 90q. Wright Brothers' Type A, 1903; 1l.20, Concorde supersonic jetliner; 1l.80, Tupolev Tu-144 jetliner (wrongly inscr '114'); 2l.40, Dornier Do-31E (wrongly inscr 'Dernier').

552 Ski Jumping

1992. Winter Olympic Games, Albertville. Multicoloured.

2512	30q. Type **552**	35	20
2513	90q. Skiing	75	65
2514	1l.20 Ice skating (pairs)	1·10	85
2515	1l.80 Luge	1·60	1·40

553 'Europe' and Doves

1992. Admission of Albania to European Security and Co-operation Conference at Foreign Ministers' Meeting, Berlin. Multicoloured.

2516	90q. Type **553**	1·20	1·00
2517	1l.20 Members' flags and map of Europe	1·50	1·30

554 Envelopes and Emblem

1992. Admission of Albania to E.P.T. Conference. Multicoloured.

2518	90q. Type **554**	1·30	1·20
2519	1l.20 Emblem and tape reels	1·60	1·50

555 Everlasting Flame

1992. National Martyrs' Day. Multicoloured.

2520	90q. Type **555**	70	65
2521	4l.10 Poppies (horiz)	3·25	2·75

556 Pictograms

1992. European Football Championship, Sweden.

2522	**556** 30q. light green & green	60	30
2523	- 90q. red and blue	1·20	75
2524	- 10l.80 ochre and brown	7·00	5·25
MS2525	90×69 mm. 5l. pink, ochre and green. Imperf	4·00	4·00

DESIGNS: 90q. to 5l., Different pictograms.

557 Lawn Tennis

1992. Olympic Games, Barcelona. Multicoloured.

2526	30q. Type **557**	45	20
2527	90q. Baseball	1·40	85
2528	1l.80 Table tennis	2·75	1·90
MS2529	89×69 mm. 5l. Torch bearer and running tracks. Imperf	4·75	4·75

558 Map and Doves

1992. European Unity.

2530	**558** 1l.20 multicoloured	1·40	1·00

559 Native Pony

1992. Horses. Multicoloured.

2531	30q. Type **559**	35	20
2532	90q. Hungarian nonius	60	40
2533	1l.20 Arab (vert)	80	65
2534	10l.60 Haflinger (vert)	7·50	6·00

560 Map of Americas, Columbus and Ships

1992. Europa. 500th Anniv of Discovery of America by Columbus. Multicoloured.

2535		60q. Type **560**	60	40
2536		3l.20 Map of Americas and Columbus meeting Amerindians	4·00	3·75
MS2537		90×70 mm. 5l. Map of America and Columbus. Imperf	85·00	85·00

561 Mother Teresa and Child

1992. Mother Teresa (Agnes Gonxhe Bojaxhi) (founder of Missionaries of Charity).

2538	**561**	40q. red	10	10
2539	**561**	60q. brown	10	10
2540	**561**	1l. violet	10	10
2541	**561**	1l.80 grey	15	10
2542	**561**	2l. red	35	20
2543	**561**	2l.40 green	45	30
2544	**561**	3l.20 blue	60	50
2545	**561**	5l. violet	70	65
2546	**561**	5l.60 purple	95	85
2547	**561**	7l.20 green	1·20	1·00
2548	**561**	10l. orange	1·40	1·30
2549	**561**	18l. orange	1·50	1·40
2550	**561**	20l. purple	60	50
2551	**561**	25l. green	2·30	2·10
2552	**561**	60l. green	2·50	2·40

562 Pope John Paul II

1993. Papal Visit.

2555	**562**	16l. multicoloured	3·00	2·50

1993. Nos. 2329/32 and 2335 surch **POSTA SHQIPTARE** and new value.

2556	**496**	3l. on 10q. blue	25	20
2557	**496**	6l.50 on 20q. red	80	75
2558	**496**	13l. on 30q. red	2·30	2·10
2559	**496**	20l. on 90q. blue	3·50	3·25
2560	**496**	30l. on 50q. brown	5·25	4·75

564 Lef Nosi (first Postal Minister)

1993. 80th Anniv of First Albanian Stamps.

2561	**564**	6l.50 brown and green	1·20	1·00

565 *Life Weighs Heavily on Man* (A. Zajmi)

1993. Europa. Contemporary Art. Multicoloured.

2562		3l. Type **565**	1·20	1·00
2563		7l. *The Green Star* (E. Hila) (horiz)	4·75	4·25
MS2564		116×121 mm. 20l. *Gjirokaster* (B. Ahmeti). Imperf	8·25	8·25

566 Running

1993. Mediterranean Games, Agde and Roussillon (Languedoc), France. Multicoloured.

2565		3l. Type **566**	25	20
2566		16l. Canoeing	2·30	2·10
2567		21l. Cycling	3·25	3·00
MS2568		117×84 mm. 20l. Map of Mediterranean. Imperf	4·00	4·00

567 Bardhi

1993. 350th Death Anniv of Frang Bardhi (scholar).

2569	**567**	6l.50 brown and stone	1·40	1·30
MS2570		94×107 mm. 20l. brown and gold. Imperf	4·75	4·75

DESIGN: 20l. Bardhi writing at desk.

568 Mascot and Flags around Stadium

1994. World Cup Football Championship, U.S.A. Multicoloured.

2571		42l. Type **568**	1·40	1·30
2572		68l. Mascot kicking ball	2·10	1·90

569 Gjovalin Gjadri (construction engineer)

1994. Europa. Discoveries and Inventions.

2573	**569**	50l. dp brn, ches & brn	2·30	2·10
2574	-	100l. dp brn, ches & brn	3·50	3·25
MS2575		60×80 mm. 150l. drab and brown. Imperf	5·75	5·75

DESIGN: 100l. Karl Ritter von Ghega (railway engineer); 150l. Sketch of traffic project.

570 Emblem and Benz

1995. 150th Birth Anniv (1994) of Karl Benz (motor manufacturer). Multicoloured.

2576		5l. Type **570**	10	10
2577		10l. Mercedes-Benz C-class saloon, 1995 Daimler motor carriage, 1886	25	20
2578		60l. First four-wheel Benz motor-car, 1886	1·40	1·30
2579		125l. Mercedes-Benz 540 K cabriolet, 1936	4·00	3·75

571 Richard Wagner

1995. Composers. Each brown and gold.

2580		3l. Type **571**	10	10
2581		6l.50 Edvard Grieg	25	20
2582		11l. Charles Gounod	35	30
2583		20l. Pyotr Tchaikovsky	80	75

572 Intersections

1995. 50th Anniv (1994) of Liberation.

2584	**572**	50l. black and red	1·70	1·60

573 Ali Pasha

1995. 250th Birth Anniv (1994) of Ali Pasha of Tepelene (Pasha of Janina, 1788–1820).

2585	**573**	60l. black, yellow & brn	2·00	1·80
MS2586		80×60 mm. 100l. brown and orange (Administration building, Tepelene). Imperf	3·50	3·50

574 Veskopoja, 1744 (left half)

1995. 250th Anniv (1994) of Veskopoja Academy. Multicoloured.

2587		42l. Type **574**	1·20	1·00
2588		68l. Veskopoja, 1744 (right half)	1·70	1·60

Nos. 2587/8 were issued together, *se-tenant*, forming a composite design.

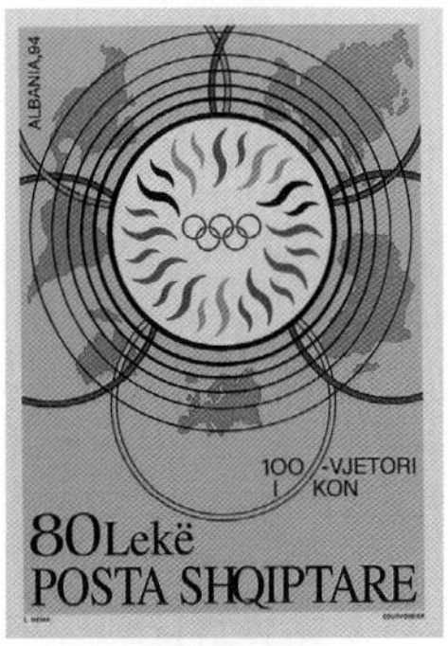

575 Olympic Rings and Map

1995. Centenary of International Olympic Committee. Sheet 60×80 mm. Imperf.

MS2589	**575**	80l. multicoloured	2·50	2·50

576 Palace of Europe, Strasbourg

1995. Admission of Albania to Council of Europe. Multicoloured.

2590		25l. Type **576**	95	85
2591		85l. State arms and map of Europe	3·75	3·25

577 Hands holding Olive Branch

1995. Europa. Peace and Freedom. Multicoloured.

2592		50l. Type **577**	2·30	2·10
2593		100l. Dove flying over hands	4·75	4·25
MS2594		80×60 mm. 150l. Figure stretching out hands. Imperf	7·00	7·00

578 Mice sitting around Table and Stork with Fox

1995. 300th Death Anniv of Jean de La Fontaine (writer). Multicoloured.

2595		2l. Type **578**	15	10
2596		3l. Stork with foxes around table	25	10
2597		25l. Frogs under tree	95	85
MS2598		80×60 mm. 60l. La Fontaine and animals. Imperf	2·30	2·30

579 Bee on Flower

1995. The Honey Bee. Multicoloured.

2599		5l. Type **579**	25	10
2600		10l. Bee and honeycomb	35	20
2601		25l. Bee on comb	1·60	1·30

580 Fridtjof Nansen

1995. Polar Explorers. Multicoloured.

2602		25l. Type **580**	80	70
2603		25l. James Cook	80	70
2604		25l. Roald Amundsen	80	70
2605		25l. Robert Scott	80	70

Nos. 2602/5 were issued together, *se-tenant*, forming a composite design.

581 Flags outside U.N. Building, New York

1995. 50th Anniv of U.N.O. Multicoloured.

2606		2l. Type **581**	25	10
2607		100l. Flags flying to right outside U.N. building, New York	3·25	3·00

582 Male Chorus

1995. National Folklore Festival, Berat. Multicoloured.

2608		5l. Type **582**	35	20
2609		50l. Female participant	1·70	1·60

583 *Poet*

1995. Jan Kukuzeli (11th-century poet, musician and teacher). Abstract representations of Kukuzeli. Multicoloured.

2610		18l. Type **583**	70	65
2611		20l. *Musician*	75	70
MS2612		80×80 mm. 100l. *Teacher*. Imperf	3·50	3·50

584 Church and Preacher, Berat Kruje

1995. 20th Anniv of World Tourism Organization. Multicoloured.

2613	18l. Type **584**	70	65
2614	20l. Street, Shkoder	80	75
2615	42l. Buildings, Gjirokaster	2·00	1·80

585 Paul Eluard

1995. Poets' Birth Centenaries. Multicoloured.

2616	25l. Type **585**	80	75
2617	50l. Sergei Yessenin	1·60	1·50

586 Louis, Film Reel and Projector

1995. Centenary of Motion Pictures. Lumiere Brothers (developers of cine camera). Multicoloured

2618	10l. Type **586**	25	20
2619	85l. Auguste, film reel and cinema audience	2·30	2·10

587 Presley

1995. 60th Birth Anniv of Elvis Presley (entertainer). Multicoloured.

2620	3l. Type **587**	25	20
2621	60l. Presley (different)	2·10	1·90

588 Banknotes of 1925

1995. 70th Anniv of Albanian National Bank. Multicoloured

2622	10l. Type **588**	35	20
2623	25l. Modern banknotes	95	85

589 '5', Crumbling Star, Open Book and Peace Dove

1995. Fifth Anniv of Democratic Movement. Multicoloured

2624	5l. Type **589**	25	10
2625	50l. Woman planting tree	1·90	1·70

590 Mother Teresa

1996. Europa. Famous Women. Mother Teresa (founder of Missionaries of Charity).

2626	**590**	25l. multicoloured	1·20	1·00
2627	**590**	100l. multicoloured	4·00	3·75
MS2628 60×80 mm. 150l. Mother Teresa (different). Imperf			8·25	8·25

591 Football, Union Flag, Map of Europe and Stadium

1996. European Football Championship, England. Multicoloured.

2629	25l. Type **591**	95	85
2630	100l. Map of Europe, ball and player	3·75	3·25

592 Satellite and Radio Mast

1996. Inauguration of Cellular Telephone Network. Multicoloured.

2631	10l. Type **592**	35	20
2632	60l. User, truck, container ship and mobile telephone (vert)	2·00	1·80

593 Running

1996. Olympic Games, Atlanta, U.S.A. Multicoloured.

2633	5l. Type **593**	25	10
2634	25l. Throwing the hammer	95	85
2635	60l. Long jumping	2·30	2·10
MS2636 60×80 mm. 100l. Games emblem. Imperf		3·00	3·00

594 Linked Hands

1996. 75th Anniv of Albanian Red Cross.

2637	**594**	50l.+10l. mult	2·10	1·90

595 Gottfried Wilhelm Leibniz (350th)

1996. Philosopher and Mathematicians' Birth Anniversaries. Multicoloured.

2638	10l. Type **595**	60	40
2639	85l. Rene Descartes (400th)	3·00	2·50

596 *The Naked Maja*

1996. 250th Birth Anniv of Francisco de Goya (artist). Multicoloured.

2640	10l. Type **596**	60	40
2641	60l. *Dona Isabel Cobos de Porcel*	2·10	1·90
MS2642 80×60 mm. 100l. *Self-portrait* (24×29 mm)		3·00	3·00

597 Book Binding

1996. Christian Art Exhibition. Multicoloured.

2643	5l. Type **597**	25	10
2644	25l. Book clasp showing crucifixion	95	85
2645	85l. Book binding (different)	3·00	2·50

598 Princess

1996. 50th Anniv of UNICEF Children's Paintings. Multicoloured.

2646	5l. Type **598**	25	10
2647	10l. Woman	35	20
2648	25l. Sea life	1·20	1·00
2649	50l. Harbour	1·70	1·60

599 State Arms, Book and Fishta

1996. 125th Birth Anniv of Gjergj Fishta (writer and politician). Multicoloured.

2650	10l. Type **599**	35	20
2651	60l. Battle scene and Fishta	2·00	1·80

600 Omar Khayyam and Writing Materials

1997. 950th Birth Anniv of Omar Khayyam (astronomer and poet). Multicoloured.

2652	20l. Type **600**	60	40
2653	50l. Omar Khayyam and symbols of astronomy	1·40	1·30

Nos. 2652/3 are inscribed '850' in error.

601 Gutenberg

1997. 600th Birth Anniv of Johannes Gutenberg (printer). Multicoloured.

2654	20l. Type **601**	60	40
2655	60l. Printing press	1·70	1·60

Nos. 2654/5 were issued together, *se-tenant*, forming a composite design.

602 Pelicans

1997. The Dalmatian Pelican. Multicoloured.

2656	10l. Type **602**	25	20
2657	80l. Pelicans on shore and in flight	2·30	2·10

Nos. 2656/7 were issued together, *se-tenant*, forming a composite design.

603 Dragon

1997. Europa. Tales and Legends. The Blue Pool. Multicoloured.

2658	30l. Type **603**	1·20	1·00
2659	100l. Dragon drinking from pool	4·00	3·75

604 Konica

1997. 55th Death Anniv of Faik Konica (writer and politician).

2660	**604**	10l. brown and black	35	20
2661	**604**	25l. blue and black	1·00	95
MS2662 60×80 mm. **604** 80l. brown			3·00	3·00

605 Male Athlete

1997. Mediterranean Games, Bari. Multicoloured.

2663	20l. Type **605**	60	40
2664	30l. Female athlete and rowers	1·20	1·00
MS2665 60×80 mm. 100l. Discus-thrower, javelin-thrower and runner. Imperf		3·00	3·00

606 Skanderbeg

1997

2666	**606**	5l. red and brown	25	10
2667	**606**	10l. green and olive	35	25
2668	**606**	20l. green and deep green	65	50
2669	**606**	25l. mauve and purple	75	65
2670	**606**	30l. violet and lilac	95	80
2671	**606**	50l. grey and black	1·50	1·30
2672	**606**	60l. lt brown & brown	1·80	1·60
2673	**606**	80l. lt brown & brown	2·40	2·20
2674	**606**	100l. red and lake	3·00	2·75
2675	**606**	110l. blue and deep blue	3·25	3·00

1997. Mother Teresa (founder of Missionaries of Charity) Commemoration. No. 2627 optd **HOMAZH 1910–1997.**

2676	**590**	100l. multicoloured	4·00	3·50

608 Codex Aureus (11th century)

1997. Codices (1st series). Multicoloured.

2677	10l. Type **608**	25	10
2678	25l. Codex Purpureus Beratinus (7th century) showing mountain and scribe	70	65
2679	60l. Codex Purpureus Beratinus showing church and scribe	1·60	1·50

See also Nos. 2712/14.

609 Twin-headed Eagle (postal emblem)

1997. 85th Anniv of Albanian Postal Service.

2680	**609**	10l. multicoloured	25	10
2681	**609**	30l. multicoloured	95	85

The 30l. differs from Type **609** in minor parts of the design.

610 Nikete of Ramesiana

1998. Nikete Dardani, Bishop of Ramesiana (philosopher and composer).

2682	**610**	30l. multicoloured	70	50
2683	**610**	100l. multicoloured	2·20	2·00

There are minor differences of design between the two values.

611 Man sitting at Table

1998. Legend of Pogradeci Lake. Multicoloured.

2684	30l. Type **611**	70	50
2685	50l. The Three Graces	1·00	85
2686	60l. Women drawing water	1·30	1·20
2687	80l. Man of ice	1·70	1·60

612 Stylized Dancers

1998. Europa. National Festivals. Multicoloured.

2688	60l. Type **612**	2·30	2·10
2689	100l. Female dancer	3·00	2·50
MS2690	60×80 mm. 150l. Two dancers. Imperf	5·25	5·25

613 Abdyl Frasheri (founder)

1998. 120th Anniv of League of Prizren. Multicoloured

2691	30l. Type **613**	70	50
2692	50l. Sulejman Vokshi and partisan	1·00	85
2693	60l. Iljaz Pashe Dibra and crossed rifles	1·30	1·20
2694	80l. Ymer Prizreni and partisans	1·70	1·60

614 Player with Ball

1998. World Cup Football Championship, France. Multicoloured.

2695	60l. Type **614**	1·30	1·20
2696	100l. Player with ball (different)	2·20	2·00
MS2697	60×80 mm. 120l. Championship mascot. Imperf	3·00	3·00

615 Wrestlers in National Costume

1998. European Junior Wrestling Championship. Multicoloured.

2698	30l. Type **615**	60	40
2699	60l. Ancient Greek wrestlers	1·30	1·20

616 Cacej

1998. 90th Birth Anniv of Eqerem Cabej (linguist).

2700	**616**	60l. black and yellow	80	65
2701	**616**	80l. yellow, black & red	1·20	1·00

617 Diana, Princess of Wales

1998. Diana, Princess of Wales Commemoration. Multicoloured.

2702	60l. Type **617**	1·70	1·60
2703	100l. With Mother Teresa	2·30	2·10

618 Mother Teresa holding Child

1998. Mother Teresa (founder of Missionaries of Charity) Commemoration. Multicoloured.

2704	60l. Type **618**	1·40	1·30
2705	100l. Mother Teresa (vert)	2·30	2·10

619 Detail of Painting

1998. 150th Birth Anniv of Paul Gauguin (artist). Multicoloured.

2706	60l. Type **619**	1·20	1·00
2707	80l. *Women of Tahiti*	1·60	1·50
MS2708	60×80 mm. 120l. Face. Imperf	3·00	3·00

620 Epitaph

1998. 625th Anniv of Epitaph of Gllavenica (embroidery of dead Christ). Multicoloured.

2709	30l. Type **620**	60	40
2710	80l. Close-up of upper body	1·60	1·50
MS2711	80×60 mm. 100l. Detail of epitaph (24×29 mm)	2·00	2·00

621 Page of Codex

1998. Codices (2nd series). 11th-century Manuscripts. Multicoloured.

2712	30l. Type **621**	60	40
2713	50l. Front cover of manuscript	95	75
2714	80l. Page showing mosque	1·60	1·50

1998. Italia '98 International Stamp Exhibition. No. **MS**2628 optd **Italia 98**.

MS2715	60×80 mm. 150l. mult	7·50	7·50

623 Koliqi

1998. First Death Anniv of Cardinal Mikel Koliqi (first Albanian Cardinal). Multicoloured.

2716	30l. Type **623**	60	40
2717	100l. Koliqi (different)	2·00	1·80

624 George Washington (first President, 1789–97)

1999. American Anniversaries. Multicoloured.

2718	150l. Type **624** (death bicentenary)	3·50	3·25
2719	150l. Abraham Lincoln (President 1861–65, 190th birth anniv)	3·50	3·25
2720	150l. Martin Luther King Jr. (civil rights campaigner, 70th birth anniv)	3·50	3·25

625 Monk Seals

1999. The Monk Seal. Multicoloured.

2721	110l. Type **625**	2·50	2·30
2722	110l. Two seals (both facing left)	2·50	2·30
2723	150l. As No. 2722 but both facing right	3·50	3·25
2724	150l. As Type **625** but seal at back facing left and seal at front facing right	3·50	3·25

Nos. 2721/4 were issued together, *se-tenant*, forming a composite design.

1999. 50th Anniv of Council of Europe. No. 2590 surch **150 LEKE** and emblem.

2725	**576**	150l. on 25l. mult	4·00	3·50

1999. iBRA '99 International Stamp Exhibition, Nuremberg, Germany. No. 2496 surch **150 LEKE** in black (new value) and multicoloured (emblem).

2726	150l. on 90q. multicoloured	3·75	3·25

628 Dove, Airplane and NATO Emblem

1999. 50th Anniv of North Atlantic Treaty Organization.

2727	**628**	10l. multicoloured	35	20
2728	**628**	100l. multicoloured	2·50	2·30
MS2729		69×85 mm. 250l. multicoloured	5·75	5·75

629 Mickey Mouse

1999. Mickey Mouse (cartoon film character). Multicoloured.

2730	60l. Type **629**	1·40	1·30
2731	80l. Mickey writing letter	2·10	1·90
2732	110l. Mickey thinking	2·30	2·10
2733	150l. Wearing black and red jumper	3·50	3·25

630 Thethi National Park, Shkoder

1999. Europa. Parks and Gardens. Multicoloured.

2734	90l. Type **630**	3·00	2·50
2735	310l. Lura National Park, Dibra	7·50	6·75
MS2736	80×60 mm. 350l. Divjaka National Park, Lushnje. Imperf	10·50	10·50

631 Coin

1999. Illyrian Coins. Multicoloured.

2737	10l. Type **631**	25	10
2738	20l. Coins from Labeateve, Bylisi and Scutari	45	30
2739	200l. Coins of King Monuni	5·00	4·50
MS2740	80×60 mm. 310l. Coin of King Gent (29×49 mm)	7·50	7·50

1999. Philexfrance 99 International Stamp Exhibition, Paris. No. 2512 surch with new value and Exhibition logo.

2741	**552**	150l. on 30q. mult	3·75	3·25

633 Chaplin

1999. 110th Birth Anniv of Charlie Chaplin (film actor and director). Multicoloured.

2742	30l. Type **633**	70	50
2743	50l. Raising hat	1·20	1·00
2744	250l. Dancing	6·50	6·50

634 Neil Armstrong on Moon

1999. 30th Anniv of First Manned Moon Landing. Multicoloured.

2745	30l. Type **634**	70	50
2746	150l. Lunar module	3·75	3·25
2747	300l. Astronaut and American flag	7·50	6·75
MS2748	60×80 mm. 280l. Launch of "Apollo 1" (25×29 mm)	7·00	7·00

Nos. 2745/7 were issued together, *se-tenant*, forming a composite design.

635 Prisoner behind Bars

1999. The Nazi Holocaust.

2749	**635**	30l. multicoloured	80	70
2750	**635**	150l. black and yellow	4·00	3·75

636 UPU Emblem

1999. 125th Anniv of Universal Postal Union.

2751	**636**	20l. multicoloured	45	30
2752	**636**	60l. multicoloured	1·50	1·40

1999. China 1999 International Stamp Exhibition, Peking. No. 2497 surch **150 LEKE.**

2753	150l. on 1l.20 multicoloured	3·75	3·25

638 Javelin

1999. 70th Anniv of National Athletic Championships. Multicoloured.

2754	10l. Type **638**	25	10
2755	20l. Discus	45	30
2756	200l. Running	5·00	4·50

639 Madonna and Child

1999. Icons by Onufri Shek (artist). Multicoloured.

2757	30l. Type **639**	90	80
2758	300l. The Resurrection	7·00	6·25

640 Bilal Golemi (veterinary surgeon)

1999. Birth Anniversaries. Multicoloured.

2759	10l. Type **640** (centenary)	25	10
2760	20l. Azem Galica (revolutionary) (centenary)	45	30
2761	50l. Viktor Eftimiu (writer) (centenary)	1·30	1·20
2762	300l. Lasgush Poradeci (poet) (centenary (2000))	7·50	6·75

641 Carnival Mask

1999. Carnivals. Multicoloured.

2763	30l. Type **641**	1·10	95
2764	300l. Turkey mask	7·50	6·75

642 Bell and Flowers

2000. New Millennium. The Peace Bell. Multicoloured

2765	40l. Type **642**	1·00	90
2766	90l. Bell and flowers (different)	2·30	2·00

643 Woman's Costume, Librazhdi

2000. Regional Costumes (1st series). Multicoloured

2767	5l. Type **643**	10	10
2768	10l. Woman's costume, Malesia E Madhe	25	15
2769	15l. Man's costume, Malesia E Madhe	35	20
2770	20l. Man's costume, Tropoje	45	30
2771	30l. Man's costume, Dumrea	70	50
2772	35l. Woman's costume, Tirana	80	65
2773	40l. Woman's costume, Tirana	95	75
2774	45l. Woman's costume, Arbereshe	1·00	85
2775	50l. Man's costume, Gjirokastra	1·20	1·00
2776	55l. Woman's costume, Lunxheri	1·30	1·20
2777	70l. Woman's costume, Cameria	1·60	1·50
2778	90l. Man's costume, Laberia	2·10	1·90

See also Nos. 2832/43, 2892/2903, 2943/54, 3053/64, 3080/91 and 3171/82.

644 Majer

2000. 150th Birth Anniv of Gustav Majer (etymologist).

2779	**644**	50l. green	1·20	1·00
2780	**644**	130l. red	3·00	2·75

645 Donald Duck

2000. Donald and Daisy Duck (cartoon film characters). Multicoloured.

2781	10l. Type **645**	25	10
2782	30l. Donald Duck	70	50
2783	90l. Daisy Duck	2·10	1·90
2784	250l. Donald Duck	5·75	5·25

646 Early Racing Car

2000. Motor Racing. Multicoloured.

2785	30l. Type **646**	1·00	90
2786	30l. Two-man racing car	1·00	90
2787	30l. Racing car with wire nose	1·00	90
2788	30l. Racing car with solid wheels	1·00	90
2789	30l. Car No. 1	1·00	90
2790	30l. Car No. 2	1·00	90
2791	30l. White Formula 1 racing car (facing left)	1·00	90
2792	30l. Blue Formula 1 racing car	1·00	90
2793	30l. Red Formula 1 racing car	1·00	90
2794	30l. White Formula 1 racing car (front view)	1·00	90

647 Ristoz of Mborja Church, Korca

2000. Birth Bimillenary of Jesus Christ. Multicoloured.

2795	15l. Type **647**	45	30
2796	40l. St. Kolli Church, Voskopoja	1·30	1·20
2797	90l. Church of Flori and Lauri, Kosovo	3·00	2·50
MS2798	80×60 mm. 250l. Fountain of Shengjin (mosaic), Tirana (37×37 mm)	5·25	5·25

648 'Building Europe'

2000. Europa. Multicoloured.

2799	130l. Type **648**	4·00	3·75
MS2800	60×80 mm. 300l. Detail of design showing boy holding star (24×29 mm)	10·50	10·50

649 Wolf

2000. Animals. Multicoloured.

2801	10l. Type **649**	25	10
2802	40l. Brown bear	95	75
2803	90l. Wild boar	2·10	1·90
2804	220l. Red fox	5·00	4·50

650 Gustav Mahler (composer) (40th death anniv)

2000. WIPA 2000 International Stamp Exhibition, Vienna.

2805	**650**	130l. multicoloured	3·00	2·75

651 Footballer saving Ball

2000. European Football Championship, Belgium and The Netherlands. Multicoloured.

2806	10l. Type **651**	25	10
2807	120l. Footballer heading ball	3·00	2·50
MS2808	80×60 mm. 260l. Footballer kicking ball. Imperf	6·25	6·25

652 Musicans

2000. Paintings by Picasso. Multicoloured.

2809	30l. Type **652**	70	50
2810	40l. Abstract face	1·00	85
2811	250l. Two women running along beach	5·75	5·25
MS2812	60×80 mm. 400l. Painting of man (24×29 mm)	9·25	9·25

653 Basketball

2000. Olympic Games, Sydney. Multicoloured.

2813	10l. Type **653**	25	10
2814	40l. Football	95	75
2815	90l. Athletics	2·10	1·90
2816	250l. Cycling	5·75	5·25

654 *LZ-1* (first Zeppelin airship) over Lake Constance, Friedrichshafen (first flight)

2000. Centenary of First Zeppelin Flight. Airship Development. Multicoloured.

2817	15l. Type **654**	35	20
2818	30l. Santos-Dumont airship *Ballon No. 5* and Eiffel Tower C attempted round trip from St. Cloud via Eiffel Tower, 1901	70	50
2819	300l. Beardmore airship *R-34* over New York (first double crossing of Atlantic)	6·50	5·75
MS2820	80×60 mm. 300l. Ferdinand von Zeppelin and airship (24×28 mm)	6·50	6·50

655 *Self-portrait* (Picasso)

2000. Espana 2000 World Stamp Exhibition, Madrid.

2821	**655**	130l. multicoloured	3·25	3·00

656 Yellow Gentian (*Gentiana lutea*)

2000. Medicinal Plants. Multicoloured.

2822	50l. Type **656**	1·30	1·20
2823	70l. Cross-leaved gentian (*Gentiana cruciata*)	1·60	1·50

657 Naim Frasheri (poet) and Landscape

2000. Personalities. Multicoloured.

2824	30l. Type **657**	70	50
2825	50l. Bajram Curri (revolutionary) and landscape	1·30	1·20

Nos. 2824/5 were issued together, *se-tenant*, forming a composite design.

658 Mother holding Child

2000. 50th Anniv of United Nations High Commission for Refugees. Multicoloured.

2826	50l. Type **658**	1·40	1·30
2827	90l. Mother breastfeeding child	2·10	1·90

659 Dede Ahmed Myftar Ahmataj

2001. Religious Leaders. Multicoloured.

2828	90l. Type **659**	2·30	2·10
2829	90l. Dede Sali Njazi	2·30	2·10

2001. For Kosovo. Nos. 2592/3 surch **PER KOSOVEN** and new value.

2830	80l.+10l. on 50l. multicoloured	5·25	4·75
2831	130l.+20l. on 100l. multicoloured	8·75	7·75

2001. Regional Costumes (2nd series). As T **643**. Multicoloured.

2832	20l. Man's costume, Tropoje	60	50
2833	20l. Woman's costume, Lume	60	50
2834	20l. Woman's costume, Mirdite	60	50
2835	20l. Man's costume, Lume	60	50
2836	20l. Woman's costume, Zadrime	60	50
2837	20l. Woman's costume, Shpati	60	50
2838	20l. Man's costume, Kruje	60	50
2839	20l. Woman's costume, Macukulli	60	50
2840	20l. Woman's costume, Dardhe	60	50
2841	20l. Man's costume, Lushnje	60	50
2842	20l. Woman's costume, Dropulli	60	50
2843	20l. Woman's costume, Shmili	60	50

661 Southern Magnolia (*Magnolia gandiflora*)

2001. Scented Flowers. Multicoloured.

2844	10l. Type **661**	35	20
2845	20l. Virginia rose (*Rosa virginiana*)	60	40
2846	90l. *Dianthus barbatus*	2·30	2·10
2847	140l. Lilac (*Syringa vulgaris*)	3·75	3·25

662 Goofy in Shorts

2001. Goofy (cartoon film character). Multicoloured.

2848	20l. Type **662**	45	30
2849	50l. Goofy in blue hat	1·20	1·00
2850	90l. Goofy in red trousers	2·10	1·90
2851	140l. Goofy in purple waistcoat	3·25	3·00

663 Vincenzo Bellini

2001. Composers' Anniversaries. Multicoloured.

2852	90l. Type **663** (birth centenary)	2·20	2·00
2853	90l. Guiseppe Verdi (death centenary)	2·20	2·00
MS2854	90×90 mm. 300l. Bellini and Verdi (75×38 mm)	7·00	7·00

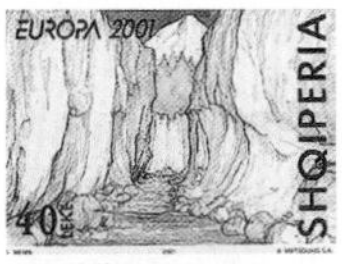

664 Cliffs and Stream

2001. Europa. Water Resources. Multicoloured.

2855	40l. Type **664**	1·20	1·00
2856	110l. Waterfall	2·30	2·10
2857	200l. Lake	4·75	4·25
MS2858	60×80 mm. 350l. Ripples (24×78 mm)	10·50	10·50

665 Horse

2001. Domestic Animals. Multicoloured.

2859	10l. Type **665**	25	10
2860	15l. Donkey	35	20
2861	80l. Siamese cat	1·90	1·70
2862	90l. Dog	2·20	2·00
MS2863	80×60 mm. 300l. Head of Siamese cat (49×29 mm)	7·00	7·00

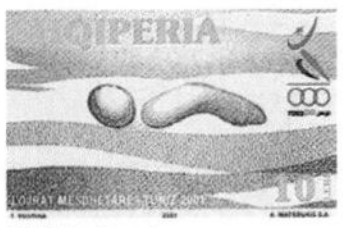

666 Swimming

2001. Mediterranean Games, Tunis. Multicoloured.

2864	10l. Type **666**	35	20
2865	90l. Athletics	2·30	2·10
2866	140l. Cycling	3·75	3·25
MS2867	60×80 mm. 260l. Discus (29×24 mm)	6·50	6·50

667 *Eole* (first powered take-off by Clement Ader, 1890)

2001. Aviation History. Multicoloured.

2868	40l. Type **667**	1·20	1·00
2869	40l. *Bleriot XI* (first powered crossing of English channel by Louis Bleriot, 1909)	1·20	1·00
2870	40l. *Spirit of St. Louis* (first solo non-stop crossing of North Atlantic from Paris to New York by Charles Lindbergh, 1927)	1·20	1·00
2871	40l. First flight to Tirana, 1925	1·20	1·00
2872	40l. Antonov AH-10 (first flight, 1956)	1·20	1·00
2873	40l. Concorde (first flight, 1969)	1·20	1·00
2874	40l. Concorde (first commercial flight, 1970)	1·20	1·00
2875	40l. Space shuttle *Colombia* (first flight, 1981)	1·20	1·00

668 Tabakeve

2001. Old Bridges.

2876	**668**	10l. multicoloured	25	10
2877	-	20l. multicoloured	35	20
2878	-	40l. multicoloured	1·00	85
2879	-	90l. black	2·10	1·90
MS2880		80×60 mm. 2l.50 multicoloured	6·50	6·50

DESIGNS: 20l. Kamares; 40l. Golikut; 90l. Mesit. 49×22 mm—2l.50, Tabakeve.

669 Dimitri of Arber

2001. Arms (1st series).

2881	20l. Type **669**	60	40
2882	45l. Balsha pricipality	1·20	1·00
2883	50l. Muzaka family	1·20	1·00
2884	90l. George Castriot (Skanderbeg)	2·30	2·10

See also Nos. 2921/4 and 2965/8.

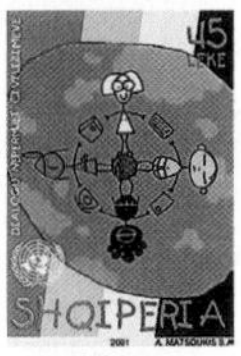

670 Children encircling Globe

2001. United Nations Year of Dialogue among Civilizations. Multicoloured, background colours given.

2885	**670**	45l. red, yellow and black	1·20	1·00
2886	**670**	50l. orange and green	1·20	1·00
2887	**670**	120l. black and red	3·00	2·50

There are minor differences in Nos. 2886/7, with each colour forming a solid block above and below the central motif.

671 Award Ceremony (Medicins sans Frontieres, 1999 Peace Prize) and Medal

2001. Centenary of Nobel Prizes. Showing winners and Nobel medal. Multicoloured.

2888	10l. Type **671**	25	10
2889	20l. Wilhelm Konrad Rontgen (1901 Physics prize)	45	30
2890	90l. Ferid Murad (1998 Medicine Prize)	2·30	2·10
2891	200l. Mother Teresa (1979 Peace Prize)	4·75	4·25

2002. Regional Costumes (3rd series). As T **643**. Multicoloured.

2892	30l. Woman's costume, Gjakova	70	65
2893	30l. Woman's costume, Prizreni	70	65
2894	30l. Man's costume, Shkodra	70	65
2895	30l. Woman's costume, Shkodra	70	65
2896	30l. Man's costume, Berati	70	65
2897	30l. Woman's costume, Berati	70	65
2898	30l. Woman's costume, Elbasani	70	65
2899	30l. Man's costume, Elbasani	70	65
2900	30l. Woman's costume, Vlora	70	65
2901	30l. Man's costume, Vlora	70	65
2902	30l. Woman's costume, Gjirokastra	70	65
2903	30l. Woman's costume, Delvina	70	65

672 Bambi and Thumper

2002. Bambi (cartoon film character). Multicoloured.

2904	20l. Type **672**	45	30
2905	50l. Bambi alone amongst flowers	1·20	1·00
2906	90l. Bambi and Thumper looking right	2·00	1·80
2907	140l. Bambi with open mouth	3·00	2·50

673 Fireplace

2002. Traditional Fireplaces. T **673** and similar vert designs showing fireplaces. Multicoloured.

MS2908	30l. Type **673**; 40l. With columns at each side; 50l. With foliage arch; 90l. With three medallions in arch	4·75	4·75

674 Acrobatic Jugglers

2002. Europa. Circus. Multicoloured.

2909	40l. Type **674**	95	75
2910	90l. Female acrobat	2·00	1·80
2911	220l. Tightrope performers	5·75	5·25
MS2912	60×80 mm. 350l. Equestrienne performer (38×38 mm)	11·50	11·50

675 Heading the Ball

2002. Football World Championship, Japan and South Korea. Multicoloured.

2913	20l. Type **675**	45	30
2914	30l. Catching the ball	70	50
2915	90l. Kicking the ball from horizontal position	2·10	1·90
2916	120l. Player and ball	2·50	2·30
MS2917	80×60 mm. 360l. Emblem (50×30)	8·25	8·25

2002. Arms (2nd series). As T **669**. Multicoloured.

2918	20l. Gropa family	45	30
2919	45l. Skurra family	1·00	85
2920	50l. Bua family	1·20	1·00
2921	90l. Topia family	2·30	2·10

676 *Opuntia catingiola*

2002. Cacti. T **676** and similar triangular designs. Multicoloured.

MS2922	50l. Type **676**; 50l. *Neoporteria pseudoreicheana*; 50l. *Lobivia shaferi* 50l. *Hylocereus undatus*; 50l. *Borzicactus madisoniorum*	5·25	5·25

677 Blood Group Symbols with Wings

2002. 50th Anniv of Blood Bank Service. Multicoloured.

2923	90l. Type **677**	2·30	2·10
2924	90l. Blood group symbols containing figures	2·30	2·10

678 Naim Kryeziu (footballer)

2002. Sports Personalities. Multicoloured.

2925	50l. Type **678**	1·20	1·00
2926	50l. Riza Lushta (footballer)	1·20	1·00
2927	50l. Ymer Pampuri (weight lifter)	1·20	1·00
MS2928	61× 81 mm. 300l. Loro Boriçi (footballer) (vert). Imperf	7·00	7·00

679 Stamp, Torso and Emblem

2002. 50th Anniv International Federation of Stamp Dealers'Associations (IFSDA). Multicoloured.

2929	50l. Type **679**	1·20	1·00
2930	100l. Part of stamp enlarged and emblem	2·40	2·20

680 Statue of Liberty

2002. First Anniv of Attacks on World Trade Centre, New York. Multicoloured.

2931	100l. Type **680**	2·40	2·20
2932	150l. Burning towers and skyline	3·50	3·25
MS2933	61×81 mm. 350l. Statue of Liberty and World Trade Centre tower (vert)	8·50	8·50

681 Loggerhead Turtle (*Caretta caretta*)

2002. Fauna of Mediterranean Sea. Sheet 100×107 mm containing T **681** and similar horiz designs. Multicoloured.

MS2934	50l. Type **681**; 50l. Common dolphin (*Delphinus delphis*); 50l. Blue shark (*Prionace glaucai*); 50l. Fin whale (*Balenoptera physalus*); 50l. Ray (*Torpedo torpedo*); 50l. Octopus (*Octopus vulgaris*)	7·25	7·25

682 Tefta Tashko Koço

2002. Personalities. The Stage. Multicoloured.

2935	50l. Type **682** (singer)	1·20	1·10
2936	50l. Naim Frasheri (actor)	1·20	1·10
2937	50l. Kristaq Antoniu (singer)	1·20	1·10
2938	50l. Panajot Kanaçi (choreographer)	1·20	1·10

683 Flags

2002. 90th Anniv of Independence. Multicoloured.

2939	20l. Type **683**	55	50
2940	90l. People and Albanian flag	2·20	2·00

684 Satellite Dish and Outline of Stamp

2002. 90th Anniv of Albanian Post and Telecommunications. Multicoloured.

2941	20l. Type **684**	55	50
2942	90l. Airmail envelope and telegraph machine	2·20	2·00

2003. Regional Costumes (4th series). As T **643**. Multicoloured.

2943	30l. Woman's costume, Kelmendi	90	85
2944	30l. Man's costume, Zadrime	90	85
2945	30l. Woman's costume, Zerqani	90	85
2946	30l. Man's costume, Peshkopi	90	85
2947	30l. Man's costume, Malesia Tiranes	90	85
2948	30l. Woman's costume, Malesia Tiranes	90	85
2949	30l. Woman's costume, Fushe Kruje	90	85
2950	30l. Man's costume, Shpati	90	85
2951	30l. Woman's costume, Myzeqe	90	85
2952	30l. Woman's costume, Labinoti	90	85
2953	30l. Man's costume, Korce	90	85
2954	30l. Woman's costume, Laberi	90	85

685 Popeye and Bluto

2003. Popeye (cartoon film character). Multicoloured.

2955	40l. Type **685**	1·20	1·10
2956	50l. Popeye running	1·50	1·30
2957	80l. Popeye and Olive Oyl	2·40	2·20
2958	150l. Popeye	4·25	3·75

686 Port Palemo Castle

2003. Castles. Sheet 118×98 mm. T **686** and similar horiz designs.

MS2959	10l. grey and black; 20l. green and black; 50l. grey and black; 20l. mauve and black	6·00	6·00

DESIGNS: 10l. Type **686**; 20l. Petrela; 50l. Kruja; 120l. Preza.

687 Bearded Man

2003. Europa. Poster Art. Multicoloured.

2960	150l. Type **687**	4·50	4·25
2961	200l. Eye, apple and piano	6·00	5·50
MS2962	80×61 mm. 350l. Detail of No. 2960	10·50	10·50

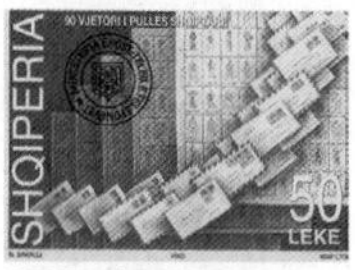

688 Envelopes

2003. 90th Anniv of Albanian Post and Telecommunications (2nd series). Multicoloured.

2963	50l. Type **688**	1·30	1·20
2964	1000l. Outline of stamps	29·00	26·00

2003. Arms (3rd series). As T **669**. Multicoloured.

2965	10l. Ariantet family	25	10
2966	20l. Jonimajt family	65	60
2967	70l. Dukagjini family	2·00	1·80
2968	120l. Kopili family	3·50	3·00

689 Pomegranate (*Punica granatum*)

2003. Fruit. Multicoloured. Self-adhesive.

MS2969	50l. Type **689**; 60l. Citron (*Citrus medica*); 70l. Cantaloupe (*Cucumis melo*); 80l. Fig (*Ficus*) (inscr "Fieus")	7·25	7·25

690 Diocletian

2003. Roman Emperors. Multicoloured.

2970	70l. Type **690**	2·00	1·80
2971	70l. Justinian	2·00	1·80
2972	70l. Claudius II	2·00	1·80
2973	70l. Constantine	2·00	1·80

691 White Stork (*Cicona cicona*)

2003. Birds. Sheet 100×119 mm containing T **691** and similar vert designs. Multicoloured.

MS2974	70l. Type **691**; 70l. Golden eagle (*Aquila chrysaetos*); 70l. Eagle owl (*Bubo bubo*); 70l. Capercaillie (*Tetrao urogallus*)	8·25	8·25

692 Players

2003. 90th Anniv of Albanian Football. Each grey, black and red.

2975	80l. Type **692**	2·20	2·00
2976	80l. Group of players	2·20	2·00

Nos. 2975/6 were issued together, *se-tenant*, forming a composite design.

693 *The Luncheon* (detail)

2003. 120th Death Anniv of Edouard Manet (artist). Multicoloured.

2977	40l. Type **693**	1·10	95
2978	100l. *The Fifer*	3·00	2·75
MS2979	80×60 mm. 250l. Edouard Manet (horiz)	7·00	7·00

694 Odhise Paskali

2003. Albanian Sculptors. Multicoloured.

2980	50l. Type **694**	1·30	1·20
2981	50l. Llazar Nikolla	1·30	1·20
2982	50l. Janaq Paco	1·30	1·20
2983	50l. Murat Toptani	1·30	1·20

695 Profile of Mother Teresa

2003. Mother Teresa (humanitarian) Commemoration. Multicoloured.

2984	40l. Type **695**	1·30	1·20
2985	250l. Mother Teresa facing front	6·50	6·00
MS2986	60×60 mm. 350l. Mother Teresa (statue) (40×40 mm)	9·25	9·25

696 Lake, Pelicans and Pine Trees (Divjaka)

2003. Natural Heritage. Multicoloured.

2987	20l. Type **696**	55	50
2988	30l. House and fir trees (Hotova forest)	85	75
2989	200l. Snow-covered fir trees (Drenova forest)	6·25	5·75

697 Stylized Cyclist and Map of France

2003. Centenary of Tour de France Cycle Race.

2990	**697**	50l. blue, red and black	1·40	1·30
2991	-	100l. multicoloured	2·75	2·50

DESIGN: 100l. Two cyclists.

698 Trees, Lake and Mountain, Pushimet

2004. Europa. Holidays. Multicoloured.

2992	200l. Type **698**	6·00	5·50
2993	200l. Grassland, hills and mountains, Pushimet	6·00	5·50
MS2994	61×81 mm. 350l. Island, Pushimet	11·00	11·00

699 Goalkeeper

2004. European Football Championship 2004, Portugal. Multicoloured.

2995	20l. Type **699**	75	70
2996	40l. Two players and goal-keeper catching ball	1·40	1·30
2997	50l. Two players	1·70	1·50
2998	200l. Players jumping for ball	7·00	6·50
MS2999	81×61 mm. 350l. Player with raised arms (38×38 mm) (circular)	11·00	11·00

700 Discus Thrower (statue)

2004. Olympic Games, Athens. Multicoloured.

3000	10l. Type **700**	30	25
3001	200l. Face (statue)	6·25	5·75
MS3002	61×81 mm. 350l. Athlete carrying Olympic torch (39×55 mm)	11·00	11·00

701 Wilhelm von Wied

2004. Wilhelm von Wied (ruler, February 6th—September 5th, 1914) Commemoration. Multicoloured.

3003	40l. Type **701**	1·30	1·20
3004	150l. Facing left	4·75	4·25

702 Bugs Bunny

2004. Bugs Bunny (cartoon character). Multicoloured.

3005	40l. Type **702**	1·30	1·20
3006	50l. With crossed arms	1·60	1·50
3007	80l. Wearing dinner jacket	2·75	2·40
3008	150l. Facing left	4·75	4·25

703 Damaged Painting

2004. Mural Paintings by Nikolla Onufri, Church of Saint Mary Vllherna. Multicoloured.

3009	10l. Type **703**	45	40
3010	20l. Mary	75	70
3011	1000l. Saint	34·00	31·00
MS3012	80×65 mm. 400l. Crowned Christ	12·50	12·50

704 Ladybird

2004. Ladybird (*Coccinella*). Sheet 120×95 mm containing T **704** and similar horiz designs showing ladybirds. Multicoloured.

MS3013	80l.×4, Type **704**; Six-spot; With open wings; 12-spot	10·00	10·00

705 Norek Luca

2004. Personalities. Multicoloured.

3014	50l. Type **705** (actor) (80th birth anniv)	1·50	1·40
3015	50l. Jorgjia Truja (singer) (10th death anniv)	1·50	1·40
3016	50l. Maria Kraja (singer) (5th death anniv)	1·50	1·40
3017	50l. Zina Andri (actor) (80th birth anniv)	1·50	1·40

706 Dushmani Principality

2004. Arms. Multicoloured.

3018	20l. Type **706**	80	75
3019	40l. Gjuraj family	1·40	1·30
3020	80l. Zahariaj family	2·75	2·50
3021	150l. Spani principality	5·00	4·75

707 Cactus-type Dahlia

2004. Dahlias. Sheet 164×77 mm containing T **707** and similar triangular designs showing dahlias. Multicoloured.

MS3022	80l.×4, Type **707**; Water lily type; Anemone type; Dahlia	10·00	10·00

708 *Madonna and Child* (Anonim Shen Meria)

2004. 50th Anniv of National Art Gallery. Multicoloured.

3023	20l. Type **708**	60	55
3024	20l. *Saint* (Mihal Anagnosti)	60	55
3025	20l. *Angel* (Onufer Qiprioti)	60	55
3026	20l. *Enthroned saint holding open book* (Cetiret)	60	55
3027	20l. *God and saints* (Onuferi)	60	55
3028	20l. *Woman wearing scarf* (Kel Kodheli)	60	55
3029	20l. *Crying woman* (Vangjush Mio)	60	55
3030	20l. *Woman wearing hat* (Abdurahim Buza)	60	55
3031	20l. *Semi-naked woman* (Mustapha Arapi)	60	55
3032	20l. *Man with moustache* (Guri Madhi)	60	55
3033	20l. *Soldier* (sculpture) (Janaq Paco)	60	55
3034	20l. *Still life with grapes* (Zef Kolombi)	60	55
3035	20l. *Flowers* (Hasan Reci)	60	55
3036	20l. *Still life with onions* (Vladimir Jani)	60	55
3037	20l. *Woman's head* (sculpture) (Halim Beqiri)	60	55
3038	20l. *Men seated* (Edison Gjergo)	60	55
3039	20l. *Men wearing traditional dress* (Naxhi Bakalli)	60	55
3040	20l. *Family* (Agron Bregu)	60	55
3041	20l. *Tree planting* (Edi Hila)	60	55
3042	20l. *Holding paintbrushes* (Artur Muharremi)	60	55
3043	20l. *Old man* (Rembrandt)	60	55
3044	20l. *Winged horseman* (Gazmend Leka)	60	55
3045	20l. *Multicoloured circle* (Damien Hirst)	60	55
3046	20l. *Corpse in cave* (Edvin Rama)	60	55
3047	20l. *Viking* (Ibrahim Kodra)	60	55

709 Bunting and NATO Emblem

2004. Fifth Anniv of NATO Peacekeeping in Kosovo. Multicoloured.

3048	100l. Type **709**	3·00	2·75
3049	200l. Doves and United Nations flag	6·00	5·50
MS3050	80×60 mm. 350l. Houses flying Kosovo flag	11·00	11·00

710 Two Doves

2004. 60th Anniv of Liberation. Multicoloured.

3051	50l. Type **710**	1·70	1·60
3052	200l. One dove	6·25	5·75

2004. Regional Costumes (5th series). As T **643**. Multicoloured.

3053	30l. Back view of woman's costume, Gramshi	90	85
3054	30l. Front view of woman's costume, Gramshi	90	85
3055	30l. Woman's costume, Korca	90	85
3056	30l. Man's costume, Kolonja	90	85
3057	30l. Woman's costume, Korca (different)	90	85
3058	30l. Woman's costume, Librazhdi	90	85
3059	30l. Woman's costume, Permeti	90	85
3060	30l. Woman's costume, Pogradeci	90	85
3061	30l. Man's costume, Skrapari	90	85
3062	30l. Woman's costume, Skrapari	90	85
3063	30l. Woman's costume, Tepelena	90	85
3064	30l. Woman's costume, Vlora	90	85

711 Emblem

2005. 50th Anniv of Europa Stamps. Multicoloured.

3065	200l. Type **711**	9·00	8·50
3066	250l. Stylized figure grasping '50'	10·50	10·00

712 Triangular Pies

2005. Europa. Gastronomy. Multicoloured.

3068	200l. Type **712**	7·00	6·50
3069	200l. Stew	7·00	6·50

713 Emblem

2005. 50th Anniv of United Nations Membership.

3071	**713**	40l. multicoloured	1·90	1·70

714 Tom and Jerry

2005. Tom and Jerry (cartoon characters). Multicoloured.

3072	40l. Type **714**	1·00	90
3073	50l. Heads of Tom and Jerry	1·30	1·20
3074	80l. Jerry	2·00	1·80
3075	150l. Tom	3·50	3·25

715 Mountain, City and Lake

2005. Art. Albanian Landscapes. Multicoloured.

3076	10l. Type **715**	30	30
3077	20l. Aqueduct and castle	65	60
3078	30l. Crowd and minaret	95	90
3079	1000l. Lake and mountain fortress	27·00	25·00

2005. Regional Costumes (6th series). As T **643**. Multicoloured.

3080	30l. Man's costume, Tirane	1·10	1·00
3081	30l. Woman's costume, Bende Tirane	1·10	1·00
3082	30l. Back of woman's costume, Zall Dajt	1·10	1·00
3083	30l. Man's costume, Kavaje-Durres	1·10	1·00
3084	30l. Woman's costume, Has	1·10	1·00
3085	30l. Man's costume, Mat	1·10	1·00
3086	30l. Woman's costume, Liqenas	1·10	1·00
3087	30l. Woman's costume, Klenje	1·10	1·00
3088	30l. Woman's costume, Maleshove	1·10	1·00
3089	30l. Woman's costume, German	1·10	1·00
3090	30l. Woman's costume, Kruje	1·10	1·00
3091	30l. Man's costume, Rec	1·10	1·00

716 Starting Blocks

2005. Mediterranean Games, Almera. Multicoloured.

3092	20l. Type **716**	85	70
3093	60l. Rings	2·10	1·80
3094	120l. Relay baton	4·25	3·50
MS3095	60×80 mm. 300l. Diver (30×50 mm)	14·50	14·50

717 Globe and Emblem

2005. Centenary of Rotary International. Multicoloured.

3096	30l. Type **717**	1·00	90
3097	150l. Emblem (vert)	5·25	4·50

2005. Arms (5th series). As T **706**. Multicoloured.

3098	10l. Bua	40	35
3099	20l. Karl Topia	1·00	90
3100	70l. Dukagjini II	3·50	3·00
3101	120l. Engjej	5·25	4·50

718 Yellow-flowered Portulaca

2005. Portulaca. Sheet 203×60 mm containing T **718** and similar triangular designs showing portulacas. Multicoloured.

MS3102	70l.×5, Type **718**; White flowers; Red and yellow flowers; Pale pink flowers; Double dark pink flower	12·50	12·50

719 Cyclists

2005. 80th Anniv of Cycle Race.

3103	**719**	50l. multicoloured	1·70	1·60
3104	**719**	60l. multicoloured	2·20	2·00
3105	**719**	120l. multicoloured	4·25	4·00

720 Battle Scene

2005. 600th Birth Anniv of Gjergj Kastrioti (Skanderbeg). Sheet 240×82 mm containing T **720** and similar multicoloured designs.

MS3106	40l. Type **720**; 50l. Chariot and fallen horse and rider; 60l. Archers, emblem and foot soldiers with spears; 70l. Shield bearer and archers; 80l. Soldier with raised sword and archers on rocks (30×30 mm) (circular); 90l. Archers firing from cliff ledge (30×30 mm) (circular)	14·00	14·00

The stamps and margins of **MS**3106 form a composite design of battle.

721 Roses growing through Helmet

2005. 60th Anniv of End of World War II. Multicoloured.

3107	50l. Type **721**	1·70	1·50
3108	200l. Allied flags and statues	7·25	6·50

722 Matia Kodheli-Marubi

2005. National Marubi Photograph Collection. Multicoloured.

3109	10l. Type **722**	30	25
3110	20l. Gege Marubi	70	65
3111	70l. Pjeter Marubi (Pietro Marubbi) (photographer, artist and architect)	2·50	2·30
3112	200l. Kel Marubi (Mikel Kodheli)	7·25	6·50

2006. Various stamps, numbers given in brackets, surch **40 lek**.

3113	40l. on 30q. multicoloured (2531)	1·40	1·30
3114	40l. on 18l. multicoloured (2549)	1·40	1·30
3115	40l. on 2l. multicoloured (2567)	1·40	1·30
3116	40l. on 2l. multicoloured (2595)	1·40	1·30
3117	40l. on 3l. multicoloured (2596)	1·40	1·30
3118	40l. on 25l. multicoloured (2597)	1·40	1·30
3119	40l. on 2l. multicoloured (2606)	1·40	1·30
3120	40l. on 18l. multicoloured (2610)	1·40	1·30
3121	40l. on 18l. multicoloured (2613)	1·40	1·30
3122	40l. on 25l. multicoloured (2620)	1·40	1·30
3123	40l. on 25l. multicoloured (2629)	1·40	1·30

724 Pres. George Bush

2007. President George Bush's visit to Albania. Multicoloured.

3124	20l. Type **724**	75	70
3125	40l. As Type **724** (suffused green)	1·50	1·40
3126	80l. As Type **724** (multicoloured)	3·00	2·75
MS3127	97×73 mm. 200l. Statue of Liberty	6·75	6·75

725 Arms of Italy and Albania

2007. Tenth Anniv of Italians in Albania.

3128	**725**	40l. multicoloured	1·80	1·60

Nos. 3129/41 and Type **726** have been left for 'Flags', issued 5 October 2007, not yet received.

Nos. 3142/52 have been left for 'Arms' (as Type **669**), issued on 15-23 October 2007, not yet received.

727 Flags and Scouts

2007. Centenary of Scouting. Multicoloured.

3153	100l. Type **727**	4·00	3·75
3154	150l. Flags and scouts (different)	6·00	5·75
MS3155	Sheet 80×60 mm. 250l. Knot (30×25 mm)	10·00	10·00

728 Pink Panther

2007. Pink Panther (cartoon character). Multicoloured.

3156	40l. Type **728**	1·60	1·40
3157	50l. With Inspector Clouseau	2·10	2·00
3158	80l. Leaning	3·00	2·75
3159	150l. Wearing tunic	6·50	6·00

729 Roads (Arkida)

2007. Children's Drawings. Multicoloured.

3160	10l. Type **729**	40	35
3161	40l. Boy and flowers (Amarilda Prifti)	1·70	1·60
3162	50l. Outline of houses and viaduct (Iliaz Kasa)	2·10	2·00
3163	80l. Buildings (K. Mezini) (horiz)	3·50	3·25

730 Galerio Maksimiliani

2007. Rulers. Multicoloured.

3164	30l. Type **730**	1·40	1·20
3165	120l. Flavio Anastasi	5·00	4·75

731 Sower (fresco by David Selenica)

2007. Art. Multicoloured.

3166	70l. Type **731**	3·00	2·75
3167	110l. Flowers and garlands (wall painting) (Et'hem Bey Mosque, Tirana)	4·75	4·25

732 Young People, Map and Stars

2007. Europa. Integration. Multicoloured.

3168	200l. Type **732**	6·75	6·25
3169	200l. Young people and double-headed eagle	6·75	6·25
MS3170	Sheet 80×60 mm. 350l. Young people and flag (30×25 mm)	12·00	12·00

2007. Regional Costumes (7th series). As T **643**. Multicoloured.

3171	40l. Woman's costume (inscr 'German')	1·30	1·20
3172	40l. Man's costume, Kubrin	1·30	1·20
3173	40l. Woman's costume, Golloborde	1·30	1·20
3174	40l. Man's costume, Kerrabe Malesi	1·30	1·20
3175	40l. Woman's costume, Gur I Bardhe	1·30	1·20
3176	40l. Woman's costume, Martanesh	1·30	1·20
3177	40l. Woman's costume, Puke	1·30	1·20
3178	40l. Woman's costume Serice Labinot	1·30	1·20
3179	40l. Woman's costume Shen Gjergj	1·30	1·20
3180	40l. Woman's costume, Tirane Qytet	1·30	1·20
3181	40l. Man's costume, Zalle Dajt	1·30	1·20
3182	40l. Woman's costume, Zaranike Godolesh	1·30	1·20

Nos. 3183/94 have been left for 'Regional Costumes (8th series)' (Vert designs as T **643**), issued on 2 November 2007, not yet received.

733 Thethi National Park (Inscr 'Parku Kombetar I Thethit')

2007. Tourism. Multicoloured.

3195	40l. Type **733**	1·60	1·40
3196	50l. Luras Lake (Inscr 'Liqenet e Lures')	2·00	1·80
3197	60l. Canine's Castle (Inscr 'Kalaja Kanines')	2·30	2·10
3198	70l. Laguna Karavastase	2·75	2·50

734 Plane Tree

2007. Natural Heritage. Elbasan Plane Trees. Multicoloured.

3199	70l. Type **734**	3·00	2·75
3200	90l. Hollow tree	3·50	3·25

735 Pope Clement II

2007. Pope Clement II

3201	**735**	30l. multicoloured	1·20	1·10
3202	**735**	90l. multicoloured	4·75	4·25

736 Leopold Senghor

2007. Birth Centenary (2006) of Leopold Sedar Senghor (poet and first President of Senegal 1960–80).

3203	**736**	40l. multicoloured	1·60	1·40
3204	**736**	80l. multicoloured	3·00	2·75

737 Team

2007. 60th Anniv of Albania as Balkan Football Champions.

3205	**737**	10l. multicoloured	80	70
3206	**737**	80l. multicoloured	7·00	6·25

738 Cannon

2007. World Heritage Site. Gjirokastra. Sheet 120×100 mm containing T **738** and similar vert designs. Multicoloured.

MS3207	10l. Type **738**; 20l. Flowers in a roundel; 30l. 'Kule' (building with tall basement, a first floor for use in the cold season, and a second floor for the warm season); 60l. Bridge ; 80l. Aerial view; 90l. Clock tower	12·00	12·00

739 Soldier wearing Gas Mask

2007. Tenth Anniv of Albania's Participation in International Military Missions. Multicoloured.

3208	10l. Type **739**	45	40
3209	100l. Soldiers in inflatable boat	4·25	3·75

740 Mother Teresa

2007. Tenth Death Anniv of Agnes Ganzhou Bojaxhiu (Mother Teresa). Multicoloured.

3210	**740**	60l. multicoloured	3·00	2·75
3211	**740**	130l. multicoloured No.	5·50	5·00

MS3212 has been left for miniature sheet, not yet received.

741 Gaia (statue)

2007. Archaeology. Durres City. Multicoloured.

3213	30l. Type **741**	1·20	1·10
3214	120l. Gaia (close up)	4·75	4·25

No. **MS**3215 has been left for miniature sheet, not yet received.

742 Drawings

2007. Cultural History. Tren Cave System (first occupied during Eneolithic period c. 2500–2000 BC). Multicoloured.

3216	20l. Type **742**	1·10	1·00
3217	100l. Drawings (different)	4·25	3·75
MS3218	81×61 mm. 300l. Cave (horiz)	12·50	12·50

743 Osman Kazazi

2007. Personalities (1st issue). Multicoloured.

3219	10l. Type **743** (politician)	40	35
3220	20l. Pjeter Arbnori (politician)	80	75
3221	60l. Llazar Sotir Gusho (Lagush Poradeci) (poet)	2·50	2·40
3222	100l. Cesk Zadeja (composer)	4·25	4·00

744 Abdurrahim Buza

2007. Personalities (2nd issue). Multicoloured.

3223	50l. Type **744** (artist)	2·00	1·90
3224	50l. Aleks Buda (historian)	2·00	1·90
3225	50l. Thimi Mitko (folklorist and nationalist)	2·00	1·90
3226	50l. Martin Camaj (writer)	2·00	1·90

745 Spheres as Player

2007. World Cup Football Championship, Germany. Multicoloured.

3227	30l. Type **745**	1·80	1·70
3228	60l. Triangles as player	3·00	2·75
3229	120l. Rectangles as player	5·25	4·75
MS3230	61×82 mm. 350l. Emblems	13·50	13·50

The stamp and margin of **MS**3230 form a composite design.

746 Ismail Kemal Bej Vlora (Ismail Qemali) (first head of state and government) and Arms

2007. 95th Anniv of Independence. Multicoloured.

3231	50l. Type **746**	2·00	1·90
3232	110l. Ismail Qemali	4·50	4·00

747 Garlic

2007. Domestic Plants. Multicoloured.

3233	80l. Type **747**	3·00	2·75
3234	80l. Onions	3·00	2·75
3235	80l. Peppers	3·00	2·75
3236	80l. Tomatoes	3·00	2·75

748 Blooms and Leaves

2007. *Wulfenia baldacci*. Multicoloured.

3237	70l. Type **748**	3·00	2·75
3238	100l. Flowers on single stem	4·25	4·00

749 Emblem

2007. 95th Anniv of National Post Office.

3239	**749**	80l. agate and vermilion	3·25	3·00
3240	**749**	90l. vermilion and black	3·75	3·25

750 New Road Surfacing

2007. Infrastructure Improvements. Sheet 133×107 mm containing T **750** and similar horiz designs. Multicoloured.

MS3241	10l. Type **750**; 20l. Durres port; 30l. New building, Tirana; 40l. Mother Teresa airport; 50l. Shkodra street, Hani i Hotit; 60l. Tepelene road, Gijirokastra; 70l. Fier road, Lushnje; 80l. Kalimash road, Morine	13·50	13·50

751 Emblem and Member Flags

2008. Albania in NATO. Multicoloured.

3242	40l. Type **751**	2·00	1·90
3243	60l. Arms and emblem	2·50	2·40

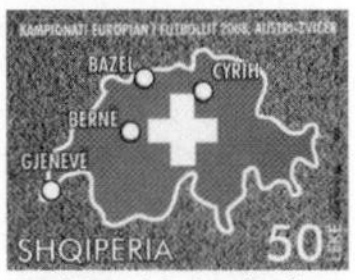

752 Map of Switzerland

2008. EURO 2008–European Football Championships, Austria and Switzerland. Multicoloured.

3244	50l. Type **752**	2·20	2·10
3245	250l. Map of Austria	10·50	10·00
MS3246	60×80 mm. 200l. Mascots (vert)	9·50	9·50

753 Script

2008. 130th Anniv of Albanian League of Prizren. Multicoloured.

3247	100l. Type **753**	4·25	4·00
3248	150l. Building	7·00	6·75

754 Postmark

2008. 95th Anniv of Postal Service.

3249	**754**	40l. multicoloured	2·00	1·90

755 John Belushi (actor)

2008. Personalities of Albanian Descent. Multicoloured.

3250	5l. Type **755**	20	15
3251	10l. Gjon Mili (photographer)	40	35
3252	20l. Koca Mi'mar Sinan Aga (Sinan) (Ottoman architect)	80	75
3253	200l. Ibrahim Kodra (artist)	8·75	8·50

756 Hand holding Quill

2008. Europa. The Letter. Multicoloured.

3254	100l. Type **756**	4·50	4·25
3255	150l. Hand holding quill writing Europa	7·00	6·75
MS3256	81×61 mm. 250l. 'Europa' (horiz)	11·50	11·50

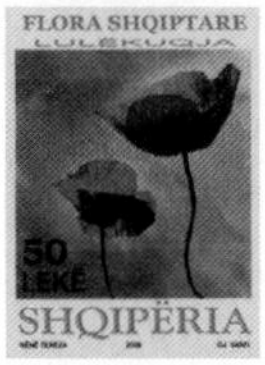

757 Two Poppies

2008. Poppy (*Papaver rhoeas*). Multicoloured.

3257	50l. Type **757**	2·20	2·10
3258	150l. Poppy	7·00	6·75

758 Swallows

2008. Universal Language of Art. Multicoloured.

3259	40l. Type **758**	2·00	1·90
3260	70l. Parachutists	3·00	2·75

759 Football

2008. Olympic Games, Beijing. Multicoloured.

3261	20l. Type **759**	80	75
3262	30l. Water polo	1·50	1·40
3263	40l. Athletics	2·00	1·90
3264	50l. Cycling	2·20	2·10

760 Osumi Canyons

2008. Tourism. Multicoloured.

3265	60l. Type **760**	2·50	2·40
3266	250l. Komani Lake	10·50	10·00

761 Ahmet Zogu

2008. 80th Anniv of Coronation of King Ahmet Zogu.

3267	**761**	40l. multicoloured	2·00	1·90
3268	**761**	100l. multicoloured	4·50	4·25

762 Azem Hajdari (politician)

2008. Personalities. Multicoloured.

3269	40l. Type **762**	2·00	1·90
3270	200l. Adem Jashari (Kosovo nationalist)	8·75	8·50

763 Ymer Prizreni

2008. Kosovo Nationalists. Multicoloured.

3271	20l. Type **763**	80	75
3272	30l. Isa Boletini	1·50	1·40
3273	40l. Ibrahim Rugova	2·00	1·90
3274	50l. Azem Galica	2·20	2·10
3275	70l. Adem Jashari	3·00	2·75

764 Decius

2008. Roman Emperors of Illyrian Ancestry. Multicoloured.

3276	30l. Type **764**	1·50	1·40

No. 3277 has been left for stamp not yet recieved.

765 Harry Potter (Daniel Radcliffe) and Professor Dumbledore (Michael Gambon)

2008. Youth Stamps. Harry Potter (character created by J. K. Rowling). Designs showing Harry Potter and other characters. Multicoloured.

3278	20l. Type **765**	80	75
3279	30l. With Dobby	1·50	1·40
3280	50l. With Hermione (Emma Watson) and friends	2·20	2·10
3281	100l. With Voldemort (Ralph Fiennes)	4·50	4·25

766 Congress Buildings, Monastir, Macedonia

2008. Centenary of Congress of Monastir (to decide on the use of Latin script for written Albanian). Multicoloured.

3282	40l. Type **766**	2·00	1·90
3283	100l. Albanian script using Latin alphabet	4·50	4·25

767 Sinagogue, Saranda

2008. Archaeological Excavations. Multicoloured.

3284	10l. Type **767**	80	75
3285	50l. Orikum	2·20	2·10
3286	80l. Antigonea	3·25	3·00

767a Emblem

2009. 135th Anniv of Universal Postal Union

3286a	**767a**	100l. multicoloured	9·50	9·50
3286aa		200l. As Type **767a** (vert)	4·50	4·50

767b Laurel and Hardy

2009. Laurel and Hardy (Arthur Stanley Jefferson and Norvell Hardy) (comedians). Multicoloured.

3286b	150l. Type **767b**	6·50	6·50
3286ba	200l. Wearing bowler hats	7·50	7·50
MS3286c	80×60 mm. 300l. Type **767b**	14·00	14·00

768 Completed Lift

2009. Weightlifting. Multicoloured.

3287	10l. Type **768**	80	75
3288	60l. Jerk and lunge	3·00	3·75
3289	120l. Squattin with barbell at shoulder hieght	4·75	4·25
3290	150l. Squatting and grasping barbell	7·00	6·75

769 Stylized Buildings

2009. 50th Anniv of Court of Human Rights.

3291	**769**	200l. multicoloured	9·00	8·50

770 Flags as Map of Europe

2009. 60th Anniv of Council of Europe.

3292	**770**	150l. multicoloured	7·00	6·75

771 Abidin Dino

2009. Painters of the Diaspora. Multicoloured.

3293	40l. Type **771**	2·00	1·90
3294	50l. Lin Delija	2·20	2·10
3295	60l. Lika Janko	3·00	2·75
3296	150l. Artur Tashko	7·00	6·75

772 Car and Traffic Controller

2009. Road Traffic Control. Multicoloured.

3297	5l. Type *772*	55	55
3298	1000l. Zebra crossing	30·00	30·00

773 Dove and Dragon

2009. Albania–China Diplomatic Relations.

3299	**773**	20l. multicoloured	1·50	1·40

774 Choir

2009. Albanian Folk Iso–Polyphony-UNESCO Oral and Intangible Cultural Heritage of Humanity (2005). Multicoloured.

3300	40l. Type **774**	2·00	2·00
3301	250l. Musicians	9·00	9·00

775 Soldier and Arms

2009. 65th Anniv of Liberation. Multicoloured.

3302	70l. Type **775**	3·00	2·75
3303	200l. Arms and aircraft	9·00	9·25

776 Mujit Dhe e Halilit

2009. Albanian Folklore. Mujo and Halili (epic poem). Multicoloured.

3304	30l. Type **776**	2·00	2·00
3305	200l. Couple on horseback	9·00	9·00

777 Mosque, Berat (1827)

2009. Religious Art. Multicoloured.

3306	90l. Type **777**	4·25	4·25
3307	100l. Fresco, Church of Mary and St. Ristozit, Mborje, Korce (1389)	4·75	4·75
3308	120l. Frescoes, Church of St. Venerandes, Pllane-Lezhe Shek, 18th-19th century	5·00	5·00

778 Satellite Receiver and Planets

2009. Europa. Multicoloured.

3309	200l. Type **778**	8·50	9·00
3310	200l. Landing craft and vehicles on the moon	9·00	8·50
MS3311	80×60 mm. Size 30×24 mm. 350l. Satellite.	10·50	10·00

779 Fortress of Tirana

2009. Archaeology. Multicoloured.

3312	30l. Type **779**	2·50	2·50
3313	250l. Artefacts, Tumulus of Kamenica	10·50	10·50

780 *Rainy Beach*

2009. National Theatre. Multicoloured.

3314	20l. Type **780**	2·25	2·25
3315	80l. *Pallati 176*	3·25	3·25
3316	200l. *True Apology of Socrates* (Apologjia e vertete e Sokratit)	8·50	8·50

781 Frontispiece

2009. 60th Anniv of State Archives. Multicoloured.

3317	40l. Type **781**	2·00	2·00
3318	60l. Roll of parchment	3·00	3·00

782 Emblems

2010. Albania–Italy Friendship

3319	**782**	40l. multicoloured	2·00	2·00

783 Mother Teresa

2010. Birth Centenary of Agnes Gonxha Bojaxhiu (Mother Teresa) (founder of Missionaries of Charity)

3320	**783**	100l. multicoloured	4·50	4·50

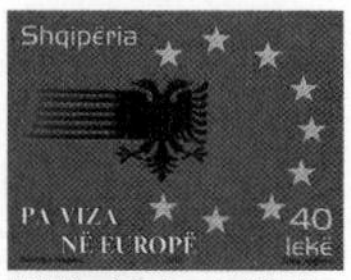

784 Double-headed Eagle and European Stars

2010. Introduction of Visa-free Travel for Albanians in the EU

3321	**784**	40l. multicoloured	2·20	2·20

785 Reading in Library

2011. 90th Anniv of State Library. Multicoloured.

3322	10l. Type **785**	5·00	5·00
3323	1000l. Using computer in library	45·00	45·00

Nos. 3322/3 were printed, *se-tenant*, forming a composite design

786 Students

2011. 20th Anniv of Student Unrest. Multicoloured.

3324	40l. Type **786**	2·50	2·50
3325	60l. Students protesting, rear view	3·00	3·00
MS3326	70×90 mm. 200l. Students making 'V' sign (vert)	9·75	9·75

787 Cockerel, Donkey and Sun

2011. Europa (2010). Children's Books. Multicoloured.

3327	100l. Type **787**	4·50	4·50
3328	150l. Girl, pigeon and cat	7·50	7·50
MS3329	80×60 mm. 250l. Girl with pile of books (horiz)	12·00	12·00

788 Bull's Head

2011. Underwater Archaeology. Multicoloured.

3330	50l. Type **788**	3·00	3·00
3331	250l. Amphorae	12·00	12·00

789 Player

2011. World Cup Football Championships, South Africa. Multicoloured.

3332	80l. Type **789**	4·50	4·50
3333	120l. Two players	5·25	5·25
MS3333a	60×80 mm. 200l. Two players (different)	9·75	9·75

790 Soldiers and Helicopter

2011. Albanian Peacekeepers. Multicoloured.

3334	50l. Type **790**	2·50	2·50
3335	200l. Soldier, wearing beret, and tank	10·00	10·00

791 Handstamp

2011. 90th (2010) Anniv of Congress of Lushnjë. Multicoloured.

3336	70l. Type **791**	3·50	3·50
3337	150l. Building	7·50	7·50

792 House of Zacat, Gjirokäster

2011. National Day of Cultural Heritage. Multicoloured.

3338	10l. Type **792**	85	85
3339	70l. Woven skirt from Dumre	3·25	3·25
3340	80l. Castle, Petrela	5·75	5·75
3341	120l. Lute, Shkodër	5·75	5·75
MS3341a	80×60 mm. 200l. Woman from Buzdrin, Zadrimë	9·75	9·75

793 Basket with Handle

2011. Silverwork. Multicoloured.

3342	20l. Type **793**	1·30	1·30
3343	30l. Evening bag	1·70	1·70
3344	50l. Butterfly	3·75	3·75
3345	100l. Closed cigarette case and holder	4·50	4·50
MS3346	80×60 mm. 200l. Open cigarette case and holder	9·75	9·75

794 Roadway and Plan of Junction

2011. Upgrade of Durres to Kukes Road. Multicoloured.

3347	40l. Type **794**	2·50	2·50
3348	60l. Roadworks and plan of roundabout	3·75	3·75
3349	90l. Tunnnel and plan of junction	5·50	5·50
3350	150l. Viaduct and plan	6·25	6·25

795 House with Balcony

2011. World Heritage Sites. Berat. Each black and scarlet-vermilion.

MS3351	10l. Type **795**; 20l. Hillside houses facing left; 30l. Bridge; 50l. Archway and gated courtyard; 60l. Hillside houses facing right; 80l. Church in castle grounds	12·00	12·00

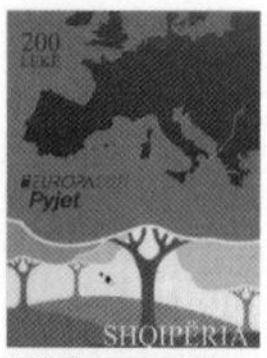

796 Tree containing Map of Europe

2011. Europa. Forests. Multicoloured.

3352	200l. Type **796**	11·50	11·50
MS3353	80×60 mm. 250l. As Type **796** but with colour change	9·50	9·50

797 Two Boxers

2011. Boxing. Multicoloured.

3354	50l. Type **797**	2·50	2·50
3355	100l. Two boxers (different)	4·50	4·50
MS3356	80×60 mm. 250l. Boxer wearing blue with raised fist	11·50	11·50

798 Ballot Box

2011. 20th Anniv of First Free Elections

3357	**798**	150l. multicoloured	7·00	7·00

799 Ismail Kadare

2011. 75th Birth Anniv of Ismail Kadare

3358	**799**	40l. multicoloured	2·10	2·10

800 Wooded Valley and River

2011. Tourism. Valbona River. Multicoloured.

3354	80l. Type **800**	3·00	3·00
3355	120l. Boulders in river	6·50	6·50

801 Worker holding Red Cross Parcel, Expectant Mother and Worker binding Injured Arm

2011. 90th Anniv of Albanian Red Cross. Each black and carmine-vermilion.

3361	70l. Type **801**	3·00	3·00
3362	120l. Giving and receiving aid	6·50	6·50

802 Pigeon wearing Helmet with Goggles and carrying Mail Bag and Globe

2011. Stamp Day. Carrier Pigeons. Multicoloured.

3363	10l. Type **802**	5·00	5·00
3364	1000l. Globe and pigeon (blue background)	42·00	42·00

EXPRESS LETTER STAMPS
ITALIAN OCCUPATION

E67 King Victor Emmanuel

1940

E373	**E67**	25q. violet	9·75	10·50
E374	**E67**	50q. red	18·00	19·00

No. E374 is inscr "POSTAT EXPRES".

1943. Optd **14 Shtator 1943**.

E402	25q. violet	27·00	33·00

POSTAGE DUE STAMPS

1914. Optd **TAKSE** through large letter **T**.

D33	**4**	2q. brown and yellow	13·00	5·25
D34	**4**	5q. green and yellow	13·00	5·25
D35	**4**	10q. red and pink	18·00	5·25
D36	**4**	25q. blue	22·00	5·25
D37	**4**	50q. mauve and red	33·00	17·00

1914. Nos. 40/4 optd **TAKSE**.

D46	10pa. on 5q. green & yell	6·50	5·25
D47	20pa. on 10q. red and pink	6·50	5·25
D48	1g. on 25q. blue	6·50	5·25
D49	2g. on 50q. mauve and red	6·50	5·25

1919. Fiscal stamps optd **TAXE**.

D89	**12**	4q. on 4h. pink	16·00	12·50
D90	**12**	10q. on 10k. red on grn	16·00	12·50
D91	**12**	20q. on 2k. orge on lilac	16·00	12·50
D92	**12**	50q. on 5k. brown on yell	16·00	12·50

D20 Fortress of Shkoder

1920. Optd with posthorn.

D129	**D20**	4q. olive	1·30	5·25
D130	**D20**	10q. red	2·50	7·75
D131	**D20**	20q. brown	2·50	7·75
D132	**D20**	50q. black	6·50	21·00

D22

1922

D141	**D22**	4q. black on red	1·80	5·25
D142	**D22**	10q. black on red	1·80	5·25
D143	**D22**	20q. black on red	1·80	5·25
D144	**D22**	50q. black on red	1·80	5·25

1922. Optd **Republika Shiqiptare**.

D186	4q. black on red	5·50	5·25
D187	10q. black on red	5·50	5·25
D188	20q. black on red	5·50	5·25
D189	50q. black on red	5·50	5·25

D35

1925

D204	**D35**	10q. blue	2·20	4·25
D205	**D35**	20q. green	2·20	4·25
D206	**D35**	30q. brown	4·25	8·25
D207	**D35**	50q. dark brown	7·50	16·00

D53 Arms of Albania

1930

D288	**D53**	10q. blue	18·00	26·00
D289	**D53**	20q. red	6·50	16·00
D290	**D53**	30q. violet	6·50	16·00
D291	**D53**	50q. green	6·50	16·00

1936. Optd **Takse**.

D312	**50**	10q. red	16·00	47·00

D67

1940

D373	**D67**	4q. red	43·00	65·00
D374	**D67**	10q. violet	43·00	65·00
D375	**D67**	20q. brown	43·00	65·00
D376	**D67**	30q. blue	43·00	65·00
D377	**D67**	50q. red	43·00	65·00

Pt. 6

ALEXANDRETTA

The territory of Alexandretta. Autonomous under French control from 1923 to September 1938.

1938. 100 centiemes = 1 piastre.

1938. Stamps of Syria of 1930/1 optd **Sandjak d'Alexandrette** (Nos. 1, 4, 7 and 11) or **SANDJAK D'ALEXANDRETTE** (others), Nos. 7 and 11 surch also.

1	0p.10 purple	1·40	5·50
2	0p.20 red	1·50	5·75
3	0p.50 violet	1·70	4·50
4	0p.75 red	2·40	5·50
5	1p. brown	2·00	4·25
6	2p. violet	2·00	4·75
7	2p.50 on 4p. orange	3·50	3·50
8	3p. green	3·00	8·25
9	4p. orange	4·00	2·75
10	6p. black	4·25	4·25
11	12p.50 on 15p. red (No. 267)	7·50	8·25
12	25p. purple	10·00	29·00

1938. Air. Stamps of Syria of 1937 (Nos. 322 etc.) optd **SANDJAK D'ALEXANDRETTE**.

13	½p. violet	1·70	3·00
14	1p. black	1·50	4·25
15	2p. green	3·25	5·50
16	3p. blue	3·75	9·75
17	5p. mauve	9·00	23·00
18	10p. brown	8·75	25·00
19	15p. brown	9·25	28·00
20	25p. blue	16·00	34·00

1938. 10Death of Kemal Ataturk. Nos. 4, 5, 7, 9 and 11 optd **10-11-1938** in frame.

27	0p.75 red	43·00	70·00
28	1p. brown	29·00	65·00
29	2p.50 on 4p. orange	16·00	13·00
30	4p. orange	10·00	17·00
31	12p.50 on 15p. red	65·00	80·00

POSTAGE DUE STAMPS

1938. Postage Due stamps of Syria of 1925 optd **SANDJAK D'ALEXANDRETTE**.

D21	**D20**	0p.50 brown on yellow	3·00	6·75
D22	**D20**	1p. purple on pink	2·30	7·25
D23	**D20**	2p. black on blue	3·00	8·00
D24	**D20**	3p. black on red	3·75	14·00
D25	**D20**	5p. black on green	5·75	11·00
D26	**D20**	8p. black on blue	8·25	11·50

Pt. 6

ALEXANDRIA

Issues of the French P.O. in this Egyptian port. The French Post Offices in Egypt closed on 31 March 1931.

1899. 100 centimes = 1 franc.
1921. 10 milliemes = 1 piastre.

1899. Stamps of France optd **ALEXANDRIE**.

1	**10**	1c. black on blue	1·50	1·80
2	**10**	2c. brown on yellow	2·50	2·50
3	**10**	3c. grey	1·80	2·30
4	**10**	4c. brown on grey	1·40	2·30
5	**10**	5c. green	3·75	2·10
7	**10**	10c. black on lilac	8·75	10·00
9	**10**	15c. blue	7·25	5·50
10	**10**	20c. red on green	9·25	8·50
11	**10**	25c. black on red	10·50	90
12	**10**	30c. brown	13·50	9·25
13	**10**	40c. red on yellow	13·00	11·00
15	**10**	50c. red	38·00	11·00
16	**10**	1f. olive	28·00	12·00
17	**10**	2f. brown on blue	90·00	£100
18	**10**	5f. mauve on lilac	£130	£100

1902. 'Blanc', 'Mouchon' and 'Merson' key-types, inscr 'ALEXANDRIE'.

19	**A**	1c. grey	1·80	1·20
20	**A**	2c. purple	60	1·90
21	**A**	3c. red	75	1·60
22	**A**	4c. brown	65	1·50
24	**A**	5c. green	75	60
25	**B**	10c. red	3·25	1·20
26	**B**	15c. red	7·00	2·50
27	**B**	15c. orange	2·50	2·50
28	**B**	20c. brown	3·50	1·80
29	**B**	25c. blue	2·00	20
30	**B**	30c. mauve	5·00	3·75
31	**C**	40c. red and blue	6·00	2·30
32	**C**	50c. brown and lilac	12·00	90
33	**C**	1f. red and green	22·00	2·30
34	**C**	2f. lilac and buff	18·00	7·25
35	**C**	5f. blue and buff	22·00	12·50

1915. Red Cross. Surch **5c** and Red Cross.

36	**B**	10c. + 5c. red	30	7·00

1921. Surch thus, **15 Mill.**, in one line (without bars).

37	**A**	2m. on 5c. green	4·00	9·25
38	**A**	3m. on 3c. red	10·50	16·00
39	**B**	4m. on 10c. red	3·75	6·50
40	**A**	5m. on 1c. grey	13·00	19·00
41	**A**	5m. on 4c. brown	10·50	19·00
42	**B**	6m. on 15c. orange	2·75	7·75
43	**B**	8m. on 20c. brown	5·00	14·00
44	**B**	10m. on 25c. blue	3·75	6·50
45	**B**	12m. on 30c. mauve	17·00	32·00
46	**A**	15m. on 2c. purple	7·75	14·00
47	**C**	15m. on 40c. red and blue	17·00	32·00
48	**C**	15m. on 50c. brown & lilac	9·50	25·00
49	**C**	30m. on 1f. red and green	£140	£140
50	**C**	60m. on 2f. lilac and buff	£160	£160
51	**C**	150m. on 5f. blue and buff	£250	£250

1921. Surch thus, **15 MILLIEMES**, in two lines (without bars).

53	**A**	1m. on 1c. grey	4·50	6·75
54	**A**	2m. on 5c. green	3·50	5·50
55	**B**	4m. on 10c. red	5·00	10·50
65	**B**	4m. on 10c. green	3·50	4·50
56	**A**	5m. on 3c. orange	6·50	10·00
57	**B**	6m. on 15c. orange	3·25	6·00
58	**B**	8m. on 20c. brown	3·75	3·75
59	**B**	10m. on 25c. blue	1·80	2·75
60	**B**	10m. on 30c. mauve	7·25	6·50
61	**C**	15m. on 50c. brown & lilac	7·75	6·50
66	**B**	15m. on 50c. blue	3·00	3·00
62	**C**	30m. on 1f. red and green	6·00	3·75
63	**C**	60m. on 2f. lilac and buff	£2000	£2000
67	**C**	60m. on 2f. red and green	20·00	23·00
64	**C**	150m. on 5f. blue and buff	21·00	25·00

1925. Surch in milliemes with bars over old value.

68	**A**	1m. on 1c. grey	20	4·00
69	**A**	2m. on 5c. orange	45	3·00
70	**A**	2m. on 5c. green	3·25	4·75
71	**B**	4m. on 10c. green	1·00	5·00
72	**A**	5m. on 3c. red	1·70	3·00
73	**B**	6m. on 15c. orange	1·50	4·50
74	**B**	8m. on 20c. brown	1·10	4·50
75	**B**	10m. on 25c. blue	65	1·60
76	**B**	15m. on 50c. blue	2·50	1·70
77	**C**	30m. on 1f. red and green	1·70	1·00
78	**C**	60m. on 2f. red and green	4·25	12·00
79	**C**	150m. on 5f. blue and buff	6·25	12·50

1927. Altered key-types, inscr 'Mm' below value.

80	**A**	3m. orange	2·75	6·25
81	**B**	15m. blue	2·50	1·40
82	**B**	20m. mauve	6·00	12·00
83	**C**	50m. red and green	13·00	24·00
84	**C**	100m. blue and yellow	16·00	27·00
85	**C**	250m. green and red	20·00	44·00

1927. Sinking Fund. As No. 81, colour changed, surch **+ 5 Mm Caisse d'Amortissement**.

86	**B**	15m.+5m. orange	3·75	12·00
87	**B**	15m.+5m. red	6·00	12·00
88	**B**	15m.+5m. brown	11·50	25·00
89	**B**	15m.+5m. lilac	15·00	40·00

POSTAGE DUE STAMPS

1922. Postage Due Stamps of France surch in milliemes.

D65	**D11**	2m. on 5c. blue	1·80	10·00
D66	**D11**	4m. on 10c. brown	3·75	10·00
D67	**D11**	10m. on 30c. red	3·00	11·00
D68	**D11**	15m. on 50c. purple	1·80	11·00
D69	**D11**	30m. on 1f. pur on yell	2·00	16·00

D10

1928

D90	**D10**	1m. grey	1·00	9·00
D91	**D10**	2m. blue	3·75	8·75
D92	**D10**	4m. pink	4·00	9·50
D93	**D10**	5m. olive	3·75	8·75
D94	**D10**	10m. red	4·25	9·50
D95	**D10**	20m. purple	5·50	8·75
D96	**D10**	30m. green	10·50	16·00
D97	**D10**	40m. lilac	7·25	16·00

This set was issued for use in both Alexandria and Port Said.

Pt. 6, Pt. 12

ALGERIA

French territory in N. Africa. Stamps of France were used in Algeria from July 1958 until 3 July 1962, when the country achieved independence following a referendum.

1924. 100 centimes = 1 franc.
1964. 100 centimes = 1 dinar.

1924. Stamps of France optd **ALGERIE**.

1	**11**	½c. on 1c. grey	55	80
2	**11**	1c. grey	60	2·50
3	**11**	2c. red	55	2·75
4	**11**	3c. red	70	2·50
5	**11**	4c. brown	70	1·90
6	**18**	5c. orange	1·40	70
7	**11**	5c. green	70	15
8	**30**	10c. green	1·60	1·40
9	**18**	10c. green	40	50
10	**15**	15c. green	1·60	1·40
11	**30**	15c. green	70	2·75
12	**18**	15c. brown	1·40	1·10
13	**18**	20c. brown	1·40	50
14	**18**	25c. blue	85	25
15	**30**	30c. red	85	90
16	**18**	30c. blue	70	15
17	**18**	30c. red*	85	1·50
18	**18**	35c. violet	1·50	1·70
19	**13**	40c. red and blue	2·50	2·10
20	**18**	40c. olive	1·80	1·90
21	**13**	45c. green and blue	1·40	2·30
22	**30**	45c. red	90	75
23	**30**	50c. blue	1·40	90
24	**15**	60c. violet	1·40	65
25	**15**	65c. red	55	65
26	**30**	75c. blue	70	40
27	**15**	80c. red	1·20	75
28	**15**	85c. red	1·00	40
29	**13**	1f. red and green	2·10	45
30	**18**	1f.05 red	1·10	1·50
31	**13**	2f. red and green	2·30	3·75
32	**13**	3f. violet and blue	2·50	3·00
33	**13**	5f. blue and yellow	11·00	16·00

*No. 17 was only issued pre-cancelled and the price in the unused column is for stamps with full gum.

3 Street in the Casbah

4 Mosque of Sidi Abderahman

5 Grand Mosque

6 Bay of Algiers

1926

34	**3**	1c. green	30	1·50
35	**3**	2c. purple	30	1·50
36	**3**	3c. orange	20	1·50
37	**3**	5c. green	45	15
38	**3**	10c. mauve	45	15
39	**4**	15c. brown	45	30
40	**4**	20c. green	40	15
41	**4**	20c. red	1·50	20
45	**4**	25c. blue	70	35
46	**4**	30c. blue	1·40	1·50
47	**4**	30c. green	1·70	60
48	**4**	35c. violet	1·70	5·25
49	**4**	40c. green	15	15
50	**5**	45c. purple	50	15
51	**5**	50c. blue	50	15
53	**5**	50c. red	1·60	15
54	**5**	60c. green	30	75
55	**5**	65c. brown	2·00	1·80
56	**3**	65c. blue	2·00	30
57	**5**	75c. red	75	15
58	**5**	75c. blue	3·25	30
59	**5**	80c. orange	1·20	2·50
60	**5**	90c. red	2·50	2·20
61	**6**	1f. purple and green	1·20	15
62	**5**	1f.05 brown	1·10	2·30
63	**5**	1f.10 mauve	4·50	7·25
64	**6**	1f.25 ultramarine and blue	1·90	6·75
65	**6**	1f.50 ultramarine and blue	3·75	1·50
66	**6**	2f. brown and green	2·75	45
67	**6**	3f. red and mauve	4·25	2·20
68	**6**	5f. mauve and red	5·25	3·00
69	**6**	10f. red and brown	75·00	50·00
70	**6**	20f. green and violet	11·50	13·00

1926. Surch **½ centime**.

71	**3**	½c. on 1c. olive	40	2·40

1927. Wounded Soldiers of Moroccan War Charity Issue. Surch with star and crescent and premium.

72		5c.+5c. green	1·00	6·00
73		10c.+10c. mauve	1·20	6·00
74	**4**	15c.+15c. brown	1·50	6·00
75	**4**	20c.+20c. red	1·50	6·00
76	**4**	25c.+25c. green	1·00	6·00
77	**4**	30c.+30c. blue	2·10	6·00
78	**4**	35c.+35c. violet	65	6·00
79	**4**	40c.+40c. olive	1·00	6·00
80	**5**	50c.+50c. blue	1·50	6·50
81	**5**	80c.+80c. orange	1·30	6·50
82	**6**	1f.+1f. purple and green	1·50	6·50
83	**6**	2f.+2f. brown and green	32·00	70·00
84	**6**	5f.+5f. mauve and red	70·00	90·00

1927. Surch in figures.

85	**4**	10 on 35c. violet	40	90
86	**4**	25 on 30c. blue	55	10
87	**4**	30 on 25c. green	40	10
88	**5**	65 on 60c. green	95	90
89	**5**	90 on 80c. orange	20	10
90	**5**	1f.10 on 1f.05 brown	15	10
91	**6**	1f.50 on 1f.25 ultramarine and blue	1·00	1·00

1927. Surch **5c.**

92	**11**	5c. on 4c. brown (No. 5)	90	1·60

11 Railway Terminus, Oran

1930. Centenary of French Occupation.

93		5c.+5c. orange	9·75	29·00
94	-	10c.+10c. olive	9·75	22·00
95	-	15c.+15c. brown	8·25	22·00
96	-	25c.+25c. grey	8·25	20·00
97	-	30c.+30c. red	7·00	28·00
98	-	40c.+40c. green	5·50	26·00
99	-	50c.+50c. blue	5·50	24·00
100	-	75c.+75c. purple	4·75	24·00
101	-	1f.+1f. orange	5·50	26·00
102	-	1f.50+1f.50 blue	6·25	24·00
103	-	2f.+2f. red	5·50	26·00
104	-	3f.+3f. green	7·00	26·00
105	-	5f.+5f. red and green	14·00	55·00

DESIGNS—HORIZ: 10c. Constantine; 15c. Admiralty, Algiers; 25c. Algiers; 30c. Ruins of Timgad; 40c. Ruins of Djemila. VERT: 50c. Ruins of Djemila; 75c. Tlemcen; 1f. Ghardaia; 1f.50, Tolga; 2f. Tuaregs; 3f. Native quarter, Algiers; 5f. Mosque, Algiers.

12 Bay of Algiers, after painting by Verecque

1930. N. African International Philatelic Exn.

106	**12**	10f.+10f. brown	34·00	65·00

15 Admiralty and Penon Lighthouse, Algiers

1936

107	**A**	1c. blue	35	1·50
108	**F**	2c. purple	30	75
109	**B**	3c. green	75	2·10
110	**C**	5c. mauve	45	15
111	**15**	10c. green	90	75
112	**D**	15c. red	45	15
113	**G**	20c. green	50	15
114	**E**	25c. purple	2·20	60
115	**C**	30c. green	60	20
116	**D**	40c. purple	90	20
117	**G**	45c. blue	1·30	3·75
118	**15**	50c. red	3·00	60
119	**A**	65c. brown	8·75	11·50
120	**A**	65c. red	1·90	60
121	**A**	70c. brown	75	90
122	**F**	75c. slate	75	20
124	**B**	90c. red	75	90
125	**E**	1f. brown	75	20
126	**15**	1f.25 violet	2·10	75
127	**15**	1f.25 red	75	1·50
128	**F**	1f.50 blue	2·75	90
129	**F**	1f.50 red	3·00	4·50
130	**C**	1f.75 orange	1·50	75
131	**B**	2f. purple	1·00	15
132	**A**	2f.25 green	19·00	26·00
133	**E**	2f.25 blue	1·90	2·00
134	**C**	2f.50 blue	2·20	3·25
135	**G**	3f. mauve	75	30
136	**E**	3f.50 blue	2·50	3·50
137	**15**	5f. slate	1·50	1·60
138	**F**	10f. orange	1·00	2·75
139	**D**	20f. blue	1·90	3·75

DESIGNS—HORIZ: A, In the Sahara; B, Arc de Triomphe, Lambese; C, Ghardaia, Mzab; D, Marabouts, Touggourt; E, El Kebir Mosque, Algiers. VERT: F, Colomb Bechar-Oued; G, Cemetery, Tlemcen.

17 Exhibition Pavilion

1937. Paris International Exhibition.

140	**17**	40c. green	1·00	65
141	**17**	50c. red	65	35
142	**17**	1f.50 blue	90	1·00
143	**17**	1f.75 black	1·90	1·70

18 Constantine in 1837

1937. Centenary of Capture of Constantine.

144	**18**	65c. red	1·00	50
145	**18**	1f. brown	3·00	65
146	**18**	1f.75 blue	30	75
147	**18**	2f.15 purple	45	50

19 Ruins of Roman Villa

1938. Centenary of Philippeville.

148	**19**	30c. green	1·50	2·50
149	**19**	65c. blue	45	50
150	**19**	75c. purple	1·80	2·75
151	**19**	3f. red	3·75	4·25
152	**19**	5f. brown	4·50	5·75

1938. 20th Anniv of Armistice Day. No. 132 surch **1918 - 11 Nov. - 1938 0.65 + 0.35.**

153		65c.+35c. on 2f.25 green	1·50	4·00

1938. Surch **0,25.**

154	**15**	25c. on 50c. red	45	15

22 Caillie, Lavigerie and Duveyrier

1939. Sahara Pioneers' Monument Fund.

155	**22**	30c.+20c. green	2·30	7·50
156	**22**	90c.+60c. red	2·20	5·75
157	**22**	2f.25+75c. blue	11·50	50·00
158	**22**	5f.+5f. black	29·00	75·00

23 "Extavia" (freighter) in Algiers Harbour

1939. New York World's Fair.

159	**23**	20c. green	1·50	3·75
160	**23**	40c. purple	1·90	4·25
161	**23**	90c. brown	2·10	65
162	**23**	1f.25 red	6·50	8·25
163	**23**	2f.25 blue	2·75	3·25

1939. Surch with new values and bars or cross.

173	**3**	50c. on 65c. blue	1·50	50
164	**3**	1f. on 90c. red	75	35
173c	**B**	90c.+60c. red (No. 124)	90	35

25 Algerian Soldiers

1940. Soldiers' Dependants' Relief Fund. Surch **+** and premium.

166	**25**	1f.+1f. blue	1·90	5·00
167	**25**	1f.+2f. red	1·90	5·75
168	**25**	1f.+4f. green	2·20	6·50
169	**25**	1f.+9f. brown	2·50	8·25

26 Algiers

1941

170	**26**	30c. blue	1·40	1·70
171	**26**	70c. brown	1·10	35
172	**26**	1f. red	1·10	35

28 Marshal Petain

1941

174	**28**	1f. blue	60	1·50

1941. National Relief Fund. As No. 174, but surch **+4 f** and colour changed.

175		1f.+4f. black	1·00	5·00

1942. National Relief Fund. Surch **SECOURS NATIONAL +4f**

176		1f.+4f. blue (No. 174)	1·20	6·50

1942. Various altered types. (a) As T **26**, but without 'RF'.

177	**26**	30c. blue	60	3·25

(b) As T **5**, but without 'REPUBLIQUE FRANCAISE'.

178	**5**	40c. grey	1·20	5·00
179	**5**	50c. red	75	1·30

(c) As No. 129 but without 'RF.

180	**F**	1f.50 red	1·80	1·10

32 Arms of Oran

1942. Coats-of-Arms.

190	**A**	10c. lilac	1·30	3·50
191	**32**	30c. green	1·00	3·75
181	**B**	40c. violet	75	4·25
192	**B**	40c. lilac	2·10	3·75
182	**32**	60c. red	1·30	2·50
194	**B**	70c. blue	90	2·30
195	**A**	80c. green	1·00	3·75
183	**B**	1f.20 green	1·30	3·00
184	**A**	1f.50 red	45	50
198	**32**	2f. blue	45	90
186	**B**	2f.40 red	1·80	3·00
187	**A**	3f. blue	45	65
188	**B**	4f. blue	1·20	1·50
201	**32**	4f.50 purple	90	15
189	**32**	5f. green	1·30	1·70

ARMS: A, Algiers; B, Constantine.

34 Marshal Petain

1943

202	**34**	1f.50 red	45	3·25

35 "La Marseillaise"

36 Allegory of Victory

1943

203	**35**	1f.50 red	1·00	3·00
204	**36**	1f.50 blue	30	65

1943. Surch **2f.**

205	**32**	2f. on 5f. orange	45	1·20

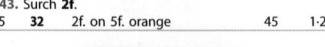

38 Summer Palace, Algiers

1943

206	**38**	15f. grey	1·50	2·10
207	**38**	20f. green	1·50	2·10
208	**38**	50f. red	1·20	1·30
209	**38**	100f. blue	3·00	3·25
210	**38**	200f. brown	4·50	5·00

39 Mother and Children

1943. Prisoners-of-war Relief Fund.

211	**39**	50c.+4f.50 pink	90	6·50
212	**39**	1f.50+8f.50 green	90	6·50
213	**39**	3f.+12f. blue	90	6·50
214	**39**	5f.+15f. brown	90	6·50

40 "Marianne"

1944

215	**40**	10c. grey	20	75
216	**40**	30c. lilac	20	50
217	**40**	50c. red	20	15
218	**40**	80c. green	45	90
219	**40**	1f.20 lilac	75	1·70
220	**40**	1f.50 blue	20	15
221	**40**	2f.40 red	30	50
222	**40**	3f. violet	45	25
223	**40**	4f.50 black	60	35

41 Gallic Cock

1944

224	**41**	40c. red	45	3·25
225	**41**	1f. green	50	15
226	**41**	2f. red	45	35
227	**41**	2f. brown	60	75
228	**41**	4f. blue	1·30	35
229	**41**	10f. black	1·50	2·50

1944. Surch **0f.30.**

230	**4**	0f.30 on 15c. brown	60	1·30

No. 230 was only issued pre-cancelled and the price in the unused column is for stamps with full gum.

1945. Types of France optd **ALGERIE**.

247	**239**	10c. black and blue	30	3·75
231	**217**	40c. mauve	15	50
232	**217**	50c. blue	30	35
248	-	50c. brown, yellow and red (No. 973)	90	50
233	**218**	60c. blue	60	85
236	**136**	80c. green	1·20	1·70
234	**218**	1f. red	60	50
237	**136**	1f. blue	90	50
238	**136**	1f.20 violet	90	4·25
235	**218**	1f.50 lilac	90	1·30
239	**136**	2f. brown	30	15
240	**136**	2f.40 red	1·00	2·10
242	**219**	2f. green	75	25
241	**136**	3f. orange	65	85
243	**219**	3f. red	45	15
244	**219**	4f.50 blue	2·10	50
245	**219**	5f. green	35	25
246	**219**	10f. blue	1·80	2·00

1945. Airmen and Dependants Fund. As No. 742 of France (bombers) optd **RF ALGERIE**.

249	**169**	1f.50+3f.50 blue	1·20	5·75

1945. Postal Employees War Victims' Fund. As No. 949 of France overprinted **ALGERIE**.

250	**223**	4f.+6f. brown	90	5·75

1945. Stamp Day. As No. 955 of France (Louis XI) optd **ALGERIE**.

251	**228**	2f.+3f. purple	1·20	5·00

1946. No. 184 surch **0f50 RF**.

252		50c. on 1f.50 red	30	50

1946. Type of France optd **ALGERIE** and surch **2F.**

253	**136**	2f. on 1f.50 brown	30	35

46 Potez 56 over Algiers

1946. Air.

254	**46**	5f. red	1·60	85
255	**46**	10f. blue	35	15
256	**46**	15f. green	1·50	75
257a	**46**	20f. brown	1·50	35
258	**46**	25f. violet	1·30	50
259	**46**	40f. black	1·90	1·70

1946. Stamp Day. As No. 975 of France (De la Varane), optd **ALGERIE**.

260	**241**	3f.+2f. red	90	6·50

47 Children at Spring

1946. Charity. Inscr as in T **47**.

261	**47**	3f.+17f. green	3·00	8·25
262	**47**	4f.+21f. red	3·25	7·50
263	**47**	8f.+27f. purple	4·00	18·00
264	**47**	10f.+35f. blue	3·75	8·25

DESIGNS—VERT: 4f. Boy gazing skywards; 8f. Laurel-crowned head. HORIZ: 10f. Soldier looking at Algerian coast.

1947. Air. Surch **-10%**.

265	**46**	"-10%" on 5f. red	45	60

1947. Stamp Day. As No. 1008 of France (Louvois), optd **ALGERIE**.

266	**253**	4f.50+5f.50 blue	1·20	7·00

49 Arms of Constantine

1947. Various Arms.

267	**49**	10c. green and red	15	2·50
268	**A**	50c. black and orange	15	35
269	**B**	1f. blue and yellow	15	15
270	**49**	1f.30 black and blue	1·50	4·25
271	**A**	1f.50 violet and yellow	30	15
272	**B**	2f. black and green	30	15
273	**49**	2f.50 black and red	1·20	1·30
274	**A**	3f. red and green	45	65
275	**B**	3f.50 green and purple	45	35
276	**49**	4f. brown and green	15	15
277	**A**	4f.50 blue and red	60	15
278	**A**	5f. black and blue	20	15
279	**B**	6f. brown and red	45	15
280	**B**	8f. brown and blue	30	15
281	**49**	10f. pink and brown	60	25
282	**A**	15f. black and red	1·80	15

ARMS: A, Algiers; B, Oran. See also Nos. 364/8 and 381/3.

1947. Air. Seventh Anniv of Gen. de Gaulle's Call to Arms. Surch with Lorraine Cross and **18 Juin 1940 + 10 Fr.**

283	**46**	10f.+10f. blue	3·25	8·25

1947. Resistance Movement. Type of France surch **ALGERIE+10f.**

284	**261**	5f.+10f. grey	1·80	8·25

1948. Stamp Day. Type of France (Arago) optd **ALGERIE**.

285	**267**	6f.+4f. green	1·50	8·25

1948. Air. Eighth Anniv of Gen. de Gaulle's Call to Arms. Surch with Lorraine Cross and **18 JUIN 1940 + 10 Fr.**

286	**46**	5f.+10f. red	3·00	6·50

1948. General Leclerc Memorial. Type of France surch **ALGERIE + 4f.**

287	**270**	6f.+4f. red	1·50	6·25

57 Battleship *Richelieu*

1949. Naval Welfare Fund.

288	**57**	10f.+15f. blue	5·75	25·00
289	-	18f.+22f. red	8·75	25·00

DESIGN: 18f. Aircraft-carrier *Arromanches*.

58 White Storks over Minaret

1949. Air.

290	**58**	50f. green	4·50	1·30
291	-	100f. brown	3·00	85
292	**58**	200f. red	8·75	4·25
293	-	500f. blue	31·00	46·00

DESIGN—HORIZ: 100, 500f. Dewoitine D-338 trimotor airplane over valley dwellings.

1949. Stamp Day. As No. 1054 of France (Choiseul) optd **ALGERIE**.

294	**278**	15f.+5f. mauve	95	6·50

60 French Colonials

1949. 75th Anniv of U.P.U.

295	**60**	5f. green	2·40	5·75
296	**60**	15f. red	3·00	5·75
297	**60**	25f. blue	4·75	15·00

61 Statue of Duke of Orleans

1949. Air. 25th Anniv of First Algerian Postage Stamp.

298	**61**	15f.+20f. brown	6·00	20·00

62 Grapes

1950

299	**62**	20f. purple, green & dp pur	1·20	65
300	-	25f. brown, green & black	2·40	1·00
301	-	40f. orange, green & brown	3·00	2·00

DESIGNS: 25f. Dates; 40f. Oranges and lemons.

1950. Stamp Day. As No. 1091 of France (Postman), optd **ALGERIE**.

302	**292**	12f.+3f. brown	2·40	9·00

63 Foreign Legionary

1950. Foreign Legion Welfare Fund.

303	**63**	15f.+5f. green	2·30	8·25

64 R. P. de Foucauld and Gen. Laperrine

1950. 50th Anniv of French in the Sahara (25f.) and Unveiling of Monument to Abd-el-Kader (40f.).

304	**64**	25f.+5f. black and green	6·00	20·00
305	-	40f.+10f. dp brown & brn	6·00	20·00

DESIGN: 40f. Emir Abd-el-Kader and Marshal Bugeaud.

65 Col. C. d'Ornano

1951. Col. d'Ornano Monument Fund.

306	**65**	15f.+5f. purple, brn blk	1·20	5·75

1951. Stamp Day. As No. 1107 of France (Travelling Post Office sorting van), optd **ALGERIE**.

307	**300**	12f.+3f. brown	4·25	8·25

66 Apollo of Cherchel

1952

308	**66**	10f. sepia	50	15
309	-	12f. brown	60	25
310	-	15f. blue	50	25
311	-	18f. red	70	50
312	-	20f. green	50	25
313	**66**	30f. blue	85	50

STATUES: 12, 18f. Isis of Cherchel; 15, 20f. Boy and eagle.

1952. Stamp Day. As No. 1140 of France (Mail Coach), optd **ALGERIE**.

314	**319**	12f.+3f. blue	2·40	11·50

67 Algerian War Memorial

1952. African Army Commemoration.

315	**67**	12f. green	95	2·50

68 Medaille Militaire

1952. Military Medal Centenary.

316	**68**	15f.+5f. brown, yell & grn	2·40	6·50

69 Fossil ("Berbericeras sekikensis")

1952. 19th Int Geological Convention, Algiers.

317	**69**	15f. red	3·50	5·75
318	-	30f. blue	2·40	4·25

DESIGN: 30f. Phonolite Dyke, Hoggar.

1952. Tenth Anniv of Battle of Bir-Hakeim. As No. 1146 of France surch **ALGERIE+5 F.**

319	**325**	30f.+5f. blue	2·30	6·50

72 Bou-Nara

1952. Red Cross Fund.

320	-	8f.+2f. red and blue	1·20	5·00
321	**72**	12f.+3f. red	1·80	8·25

DESIGN: 8f. El-Oued and map of Algeria.

73 Members of Corps and Camel

1952. 50th Anniv of Sahara Corps.

322	**73**	12f. brown	1·80	3·50

1953. Stamp Day. As No. 1161 of France (Count D'Argenson), optd **ALGERIE**.

323	**334**	12f.+3f. violet	1·20	8·25

74 "Victory" of Cirta

1954. Army Welfare Fund.

324	**74**	15f.+5f. brown and sepia	85	3·75

75 E. Millon

1954. Military Health Service.

325	**75**	25f. sepia and green	95	65
326	-	40f. red and brown	85	50
327	-	50f. indigo and blue	1·20	60

DOCTORS—VERT: 40f. F. Maillot. HORIZ: 50f. A. Laveran.

1954. Stamp Day. As No. 1202 of France (Lavalette), optd **ALGERIE**.

328	**346**	12f.+3f. red	95	5·25

76 French and Algerian Soldiers

1954. Old Soldiers' Welfare Fund.

329	**76**	15f.+5f. sepia	1·80	5·75

77 Foreign Legionary

1954. Foreign Legion Welfare Fund.

330	**77**	15f.+5f. green	2·50	8·25

78

1954. Third International Congress of Mediterranean Citrus Fruit Culture.

331	**78**	15f. blue and indigo	1·30	3·00

1954. Tenth Anniv of Liberation. As No. 1204 of France ("D-Day") optd **ALGERIE**.

332	**348**	15f. red	70	2·00

79 Darguinah Hydroelectric Station

1954. Inauguration of River Agrioun Hydroelectric Installations.

333	**79**	15f. purple	1·20	4·00

80 Courtyard of Bardo Museum

1954

334	**80**	10f. brown & light brown	70	15
335	**80**	12f. orange and brown (I)	95	20
336	**80**	12f. orange and brown (II)	60	50
337	**80**	15f. blue and light blue	70	20
338	**80**	18f. carmine and red	70	50
339	**80**	20f. green and light green	90	1·30
340	**80**	25f. lilac and mauve	95	30

12f. "POSTES" and "ALGERIE" in orange (I) or in white (II).

1954. 150th Anniv of Presentation of First Legion of Honour. As No. 1223 of France, optd **ALGERIE**.

341	**356**	12f. green	95	4·00

81 Red Cross Nurses

1954. Red Cross Fund. Cross in red.

342	**81**	12f.+3f. blue	3·50	9·00
343	-	15f.+5f. violet	4·75	12·00

DESIGN: 15f. J.H. Dunant and Djemila ruins.

82 St. Augustine

1954. 1600th Birth Anniv of St. Augustine.

344	**82**	15f. brown	1·20	2·20

83 Earthquake Victims and Ruins

1954. Orleansville Earthquake Relief Fund. Inscr as in T **83**.

345	**83**	12f.+4f. brown	1·40	6·25
346	**83**	15f.+5f. blue	1·50	6·50
347	-	18f.+6f. mauve	1·70	6·50
348	-	20f.+7f. violet	1·80	7·00
349	-	25f.+8f. lake	2·30	7·25
350	-	30f.+10f. turquoise	1·70	8·25

DESIGNS—HORIZ: 18, 20f. Red Cross workers. 25, 30f. Stretcher-bearers.

1955. Stamp Day. As No. 1245 of France (Balloon Post), optd **ALGERIE**.

351	**364**	12f.+3f. blue	65	5·00

84 Statue of Aesculapius and El Kettar Hospital

1955. 30th French Medical Congress.

352	**84**	15f. red	35	80

85 Ruins of Tipasa

1955. Bimillenary of Tipasa.

353	**85**	50f. brown	40	20

1955. 50th Anniv of Rotary International. As No. 1235 of France optd **ALGERIE**.

354	**361**	30f. blue	45	2·30

1955. As Nos. 1238 and 1238b of France ("France") inscr 'ALGERIE'.

355	**362**	15f. red	70	20
356	**362**	20f. blue	2·10	1·50

86 Widows and Children

1955. War Victims' Welfare Fund.

357	**86**	15f.+5f. indigo and blue	1·40	3·25

87 Grand Kabylie

1955

358	**87**	100f. indigo and blue	2·40	50

88

1956. Anti-cancer Fund.

359	**88**	15f.+5f. brown	1·60	5·50

1956. Stamp Day. As No. 1279 of France ("Francis of Taxis"), optd **ALGERIE**.

360	**383**	12f.+3f. red	95	4·50

89 Foreign Legion Retirement Home, Sidi Bel Abbes

1956. Foreign Legion Welfare Fund.

361	**89**	15f.+5f. green	1·70	6·00

90 Marshal Franchet d'Esperey (after J. Ebstein)

1956. Birth Cent of Marshal Franchet d'Esperey.

362	**90**	15f. indigo and blue	2·00	4·25

91 Marshal Leclerc and Memorial

1956. Marshal Leclerc Commemoration.

363	**91**	15f. brown and sepia	50	4·00

1956. Various arms as T **49**.

364	1f. green and red	85	70
365	3f. blue and green	80	2·75
366	5f. blue and yellow	1·10	50
367	6f. green and red	1·40	3·00
368	12f. blue and red	1·60	4·50

DESIGNS: 1f. Bone; 3f. Mostaganem; 5f. Tlemcen; 6f. Algiers; 12f. Orleansville.

92 Oran

1956

369	**92**	30f. purple	1·40	30
370	**92**	35f. red	1·90	5·25

1957. Stamp Day. As No. 1322 of France ("Felucca") optd **ALGERIE**.

371	**403**	12f.+3f. purple	1·80	5·00

93 Electric Train Crossing Viaduct

1957. Electrification of Bone-Tebessa Railway Line.

372	**93**	40f. turquoise and green	1·80	50

94 Fennec Fox

1957. Red Cross Fund. Cross in red.

373	**94**	12f.+3f. brown	3·50	15·00
374	-	15f.+5f. sepia (White storks)	3·50	15·00

1957. 17th Anniv of Gen. de Gaulle's Call to Arms. Surch **18 JUIN 1940 + 5F.**

375	**91**	15f.+5f. red and carmine	95	5·25

96 Beni Bahdel Barrage, Tlemcen

1957. Air.

376	**96**	200f. red	9·50	11·00

97 "Horseman Crossing Ford" (after Delacroix)

1957. Army Welfare Fund. Inscr 'OEUVRES SOCIALES DE L'ARMEE'.

377	**97**	15f.+5f. red	4·75	11·00
378	-	20f.+5f. green	4·25	11·50
379	-	35f.+10f. blue	4·25	12·00

DESIGNS—HORIZ: 20f. "Lakeside View" (after Fromentin). VERT: 35f. "Arab Dancer" (after Chasseriau).

1958. Stamp Day. As No. 1375 of France (Rural Postal Service), optd **ALGERIE**.

380	**421**	15f.+5f. brown	1·60	5·00

1958. Arms. As T **49** but inscr 'REPUBLIQUE FRANCAISE' instead of 'RF' at foot.

381	2f. red and blue	60	4·00
382	6f. green and red	36·00	60·00
383	10f. purple and green	1·20	4·50

ARMS: 2f. Tizi-Ouzou; 6f. Algiers; 10f. Setif.

99 "Strelitzia Reginae"

1958. Algerian Child Welfare Fund.

384	**99**	20f.+5f. orge, vio & grn	3·50	7·00

100

1958. Marshal de Lattre Foundation.

385	**100**	20f.+5f. red, grn & bl	3·50	7·00

INDEPENDENT STATE

1962. Stamps of France optd **EA** and with bars obliterating "REPUBLIQUE FRANCAISE".

386	**344**	10c. green	95	40
387	**463**	25c. grey and red	70	30
393	-	45c. violet, purple and sepia (No. 1463)	6·75	4·50
394	-	50c. pur & grn (No. 1464)	6·75	4·50
395	-	1f. brown, blue and myrtle (No. 1549)	4·50	1·80

103a Maps of Africa and Algeria

1962. War Orphans' Fund.

395a	**103a**	1f.+9f. green, black and red		£350

1962. As pictorial types of France but inscr 'REPUBLIQUE ALGERIENNE'.

396	-	5c. turquoise, grn & brn	25	10
397	**438**	10c. blue and sepia	25	10
398	-	25c. red, slate & brown	55	15
399	-	95c. blue, buff and sepia	3·50	1·10
400	-	1f. sepia and green	2·50	1·60

DESIGNS—VERT: 5c. Kerrata Gorges; 25c. Tlemcen Mosque; 95c. Oil derrick and pipeline at Hassi-Massaoud, Sahara. HORIZ: 1f. Medea.

104 Flag, Rifle and Olive Branch

1963. Return of Peace. Flag in green and red. Inscription and background colours given.

401	**104**	5c. bistre	25	10
402	**104**	10c. blue	25	10
403	**104**	25c. red	1·90	30
404	**104**	95c. violet	1·80	75
405	-	1f. green	2·20	15
406	-	2f. brown	3·75	80
407	-	5f. purple	7·00	3·00
408	-	10f. black	25·00	14·50

DESIGN: 1f. to 10f. As Type **104** but with dove and broken chain added.

105 Campaign Emblem and Globe

1963. Freedom from Hunger.

409	**105**	25c. yellow, green and red	70	25

106 Clasped Hands

1963. National Solidarity Fund.

410	**106**	50c.+20c. red, grn & blk	1·40	65

107 Map and Emblems

1963. First Anniv of Independence.

411	**107**	25c. multicoloured	70	25

108 "Arab Physicians" (13th-century MS.)

1963. Second Arab Physicians Union Congress.

412	**108**	25c. brown, green & bistre	2·10	55

109 Branch of Orange Tree

1963

413	**109**	8c. orange and bronze*	10	10
414	**109**	20c. orange and green*	25	15
415	**109**	40c. orange & turq*	75	35
416	**109**	55c. orange and green*	95	55

*These stamps were only issued pre-cancelled, the unused prices being for stamps with full gum.

110 "Constitution"

1963. Promulgation of Constitution.

417	**110**	25c. red, green and sepia	70	40

111 "Freedom Fighters"

1963. Ninth Anniv of Revolution.

418	**111**	25c. red, green and brown	70	25

112 Centenary Emblem

1963. Red Cross Centenary.

419	**112**	25c. blue, red and yellow	95	55

113 Globe and Scales of Justice

1963. 15th Anniv of Declaration of Human Rights.

420	**113**	25c. black and blue	70	25

114 Labourers

1964. Labour Day.

421	**114**	50c. multicoloured	1·40	45

115 Map of Africa and Flags

1964. First Anniv of Africa Day, and African Unity Charter.

422	**115**	45c. red, orange and blue	90	40

116 Tractors

1964

423	**116**	5c. purple	10	10
424	-	10c. brown	10	10
425	-	12c. green	50	25
426	-	15c. blue	45	25
427	-	20c. yellow	45	10
428	**116**	25c. red	55	10
429	-	30c. violet	55	15
430	-	45c. lake	70	25
431	-	50c. blue	70	10
432	-	65c. orange	90	25
433	**116**	85c. green	1·40	25
434	-	95c. red	1·80	25

DESIGNS: 10, 30, 65c. Apprentices; 12, 15, 45c. Research scientist; 20, 50, 95c. Draughtsman and bricklayer.

117 Rameses II in War Chariot, Abu Simbel

1964. Nubian Monuments Preservation.

435	**117**	20c. purple, red and blue	95	40
436	-	30c. ochre, turq & red	1·20	55

DESIGN: 30c. Heads of Rameses II.

118 Hertzian-wave Radio Transmitting Pylon

1964. Inauguration of Algiers–Annaba Radio-Telephone Service.

437	**118**	85c. black, blue & brown	2·10	65

119 Fair Emblems

1964. Algiers Fair.

438	**119**	30c. blue, yellow and red	55	25

120 Gas Plant

1964. Inauguration of Natural Gas Plant at Arzew.

439	**120**	25c. blue, yellow & violet	90	50

121 Planting Trees

1964. Reafforestation Campaign.

440	**121**	25c. green, red and yellow	55	25

122 Children

1964. Children's Charter.

441	**122**	15c. blue, green and red	50	25

123 Mehariste Saddle

1965. Saharan Handicrafts.

442	**123**	20c. multicoloured	55	25

124 Books Aflame

1965. Reconstitution of Algiers University Library.

443	**124**	20c.+5c. red, blk & grn	55	40

125 I.C.Y. Emblem

1965. International Co-operation Year.

444	**125**	30c. black, green and red	95	45
445	**125**	60c. black, green and blue	1·40	60

126 I.T.U. Emblem and Symbols

1965. Centenary of I.T.U.

446	**126**	60c. violet, ochre & green	95	50
447	**126**	95c. brown, ochre & lake	1·40	55

127 Musicians playing Rebbah and Lute

1965. Mohamed Racim's Miniatures (1st series). Multicoloured.

448	30c. Type **127**	1·80	65
449	60c. Musicians playing derbouka and tarr	2·75	1·50
450	5d. Algerian princess and sand gazelle	14·50	7·75

See also Nos. 471/3.

128 Cattle

1966. Rock-paintings of Tassili-N-Ajjer (1st series).

451	**128**	1d. brown, ochre & purple	5·25	2·75
452	-	1d. multicoloured	5·25	2·75
453	-	2d. dp brown, buff & brn	11·00	4·75
454	-	3d. multicoloured	12·00	6·25

DESIGNS—VERT: No. 452, Peuhl shepherd; 454, Peuhl girls. HORIZ: No. 453, Ostriches.

See also Nos. 474/7.

129 Pottery

1966. Grand Kahylie Handicrafts.

455	**129**	40c. brown, sepia and blue	55	40
456	-	50c. orange, green & bl	90	40
457	-	70c. black, red and blue	1·40	50

DESIGNS—HORIZ: 50c. Weaving. VERT: 70c. Jewellery.

130 Meteorological Instruments

1966. World Meteorological Day.

458	**130**	1d. purple, green and blue	1·40	50

131 Open Book, Cogwheel and Ear of Corn

1966. Literacy Campaign.

459	**131**	30c. black and ochre	50	25
460	-	60c. red, black and grey	75	40

DESIGN: 60c. Open primer, cogwheel and ear of corn.

132 W.H.O. Building

1966. Inauguration of W.H.O. Headquarters, Geneva.

461	**132**	30c. turq, grn & brn	45	40
462	**132**	60c. slate, blue and brown	90	40

133 Mohammedan Scout Emblem and Banner

1966. 30th Anniv of Algerian Mohammedan Scouts, and Seventh Arab Scout Jamboree, Jedaid (Tripoli). Multicoloured.

463	30c. Type **133**	70	40
464	1d. Jamboree emblem	1·80	65

134 Soldiers and Battle Casualty

1966. Freedom Fighters' Day.

465	**134**	30c.+10c. mult	95	65
466	**134**	95c.+10c. mult	1·80	1·30

135 Massacre Victims

1966. Deir Yassin Massacre (1948).

467	**135**	30c. black and red	55	25

136 Emir Abd-el-Kader

1966. Return of Emir Abd-el-Kader's Remains.

468	**136**	30c. multicoloured	25	10
469	**136**	95c. multicoloured	1·10	40

See also Nos. 498/502.

137 UNESCO Emblems

1966. 20th Anniv of UNESCO.

470	**137**	1d. multicoloured	1·10	40

1966. Mohamed Racim's Miniatures (2nd series). As T **127**. Multicoloured.

471	1d. Horseman	4·50	1·50
472	1d.50 Algerian bride	6·75	2·00
473	2d. Barbarossa	10·00	3·50

1967. Rock-paintings of Tassili-N-Ajjer (2nd series). As T **128**.

474	1d. violet, buff and purple	4·50	1·90
475	2d. brown, buff and purple	6·75	3·75
476	2d. brown, purple and buff	7·50	4·00
477	3d. brown, buff and black	10·50	5·50

DESIGNS: No. 474, Cow; No. 475, Antelope; No. 476, Archers; No. 477, Warrior.

138 Bardo Museum

1967. Musulman Art. Multicoloured.

478	35c. Type **138**	45	25
479	95c. La Kalaa minaret (vert)	95	45
480	1d.30 Sedrata ruins	1·70	65

139 Ghardaia

1967. Air.

481	**139**	1d. brown, green & purple	1·40	55
482	-	2d. brown, green and blue	3·25	1·40
483	-	5d. brown, green and blue	8·50	2·50

DESIGNS: 2d. Sud Aviation SE210 Caravelle over El Oued (Souf); 5d. Tipasa.

140 View of Moretti

1967. International Tourist Year. Multicoloured.

484	40c. Type **140**	70	40
485	70c. Tuareg, Tassili (vert)	1·40	55

141 Boy and Girl, and Red Crescent

1967. Algerian Red Crescent Organization.

486	**141**	30c.+10c. brn, red & grn	90	50

142 Ostrich

1967. Saharan Fauna. Multicoloured.

487	5c. Shiny-tailed Lizard (horiz)	50	40
488	20c. Type **142**	90	50
489	40c. Sand gazelle	1·40	65
490	70c. Fennec foxes (horiz)	1·90	1·00

143 Dancers with Tambourines

1967. National Youth Festival.

491	**143**	50c. black, yellow & blue	95	40

144 "Athletics"

1967. Fifth Mediterranean Games, Tunis.

492	**144**	30c. black, blue and red	70	40

145 Skiing

1967. Winter Olympic Games, Grenoble (1968).

493	**145**	30c. blue, green & ultram	95	40
494	-	95c. green, violet & brown	1·80	85

DESIGN—HORIZ (36×26 mm): 95c. Olympic rings and competitors.

1967

498	**136**	5c. purple	25	10
499	**136**	10c. green	10	10
500	**136**	25c. orange	35	10
501	**136**	30c. black	45	10
502	**136**	30c. violet	45	10
496	**136**	50c. red	70	25
497	**136**	70c. blue	90	25

The 10c. value exists in two versions, differing in the figures of value and inscription at bottom right.

146 Scouts supporting Jamboree Emblem

1967. World Scout Jamboree, Idaho.

503	**146**	1d. multicoloured	2·10	75

1967. No. 428 surch.

504	**116**	30c. on 25c. red	70	25

148 Kouitra

1968. Musical Instruments. Multicoloured.

505	30c. Type **148**	55	25
506	40c. Lute	90	40
507	1d.30 Rebbah	3·00	1·10

149 Nememcha Carpet

1968. Algerian Carpets. Multicoloured.

509	30c. Type **149**	95	55
510	70c. Guergour	1·80	85
511	95c. Djebel-Amour	3·00	1·20
512	1d.30 Kalaa	3·75	1·40

150 Human Rights Emblem and Globe

1968. Human Rights Year.

513	**150**	40c. red, yellow and blue	75	40

151 W.H.O. Emblem

1968. 20th Anniv of W.H.O.

514	**151**	70c. yellow, black & blue	90	40

152 Emigrant

1968. Emigration of Algerians to Europe.

515	**152**	30c. brown, slate & blue	55	25

153 Scouts holding Jamboree Emblem

1968. Eighth Arab Scouts Jamboree, Algiers.

516	**153**	30c. multicoloured	70	25

154 Torch and Athletes

1968. Olympic Games, Mexico. Multicoloured.

517	30c. Type **154**	60	45
518	50c. Football	1·10	65
519	1d. Allegory of Games (horiz)	1·80	95

155 Barbary Sheep

1968. Protected Animals. Multicoloured.

520	40c. Type **155**	90	40
521	1d. Red deer	2·10	65

156 "Neptune's Chariot", Timgad

1968. Roman Mosaics. Multicoloured.

522	40c. "Hunting Scene" (Djemila) (vert)	70	25
523	95c. Type **156**	1·50	55

157 Miner

1968. Industry, Energy and Mines.

524	**157**	30c. multicoloured	50	25
525	-	30c. silver and red	50	25
526	-	95c. red, black and silver	1·40	40

DESIGNS: No. 525, Coiled spring ("Industry"); No. 526, Symbol of radiation ("Energy").

158 Opuntia

1969. Algerian Flowers. Multicoloured.

527	25c. Type **158**	70	50
528	40c. Dianthus	1·10	65
529	70c. Rose	1·80	75
530	95c. Strelitzia	3·25	1·30

See also Nos. 621/4.

159 Djorf Torba Dam, Oued Guir

1969. Saharan Public Works. Multicoloured.

531	30c. Type **159**	70	25
532	1d.50 Route Nationale No. 51	2·10	80

160 Desert Mail-coach of 1870

1969. Stamp Day.

533	**160**	1d. sepia, brown and blue	2·75	85

161 The Capitol, Timgad

1969. Roman Ruins in Algeria. Multicoloured.

534	30c. Type **161**	55	25
535	1d. Septimius Temple, Djemila (horiz)	1·50	60

162 I.L.O. Emblem

1969. 50th Anniv of I.L.O.

536	**162**	95c. red, yellow and black	1·30	45

1969. No. 425 surch.

537	20c. on 12c. green	45	10

164 Carved Bookcase

1969. Handicrafts. Multicoloured.

538	30c. Type **164**	50	25
539	60c. Copper tray	90	40
540	1d. Arab saddle	1·60	60

165 "Africa" Head

1969. First Pan-African Cultural Festival, Algiers.

541	**165**	30c. multicoloured	55	25

166 Astronauts on Moon

1969. First Man on the Moon.

542	**166**	50c. multicoloured	1·10	45

167 Bank Emblem

1969. Fifth Anniv of African Development Bank.

543	**167**	30c. black, yellow blue	55	25

168 Flood Victims

1969. Aid for 1969 Flood Victims.

544	**168**	30c.+10c. black, flesh and blue	75	45
545	-	95c.+25c. brown, blue and purple	1·60	95

DESIGN: 95c. Helping hand for flood victims.

169 *Algerian Women* (Dinet)

1969. Dinet's Paintings. Multicoloured.

546	1d. Type **169**	2·10	85
547	1d.50 *The Look-outs* (Dinet)	2·75	1·20

170 "Mother and Child"

1969. Protection of Mother and Child

548	**170**	30c. multicoloured	70	40

171 "Agriculture"

1970. Four Year Plan.

549	**171**	25c. multicoloured	30	25
550	-	30c. multicoloured	55	25
551	-	50c. black and purple	55	25

DESIGNS: (LARGER, 49×23 mm): 30c. "Industry and Transport"; 50c. "Industry" (abstract).

172 Postal Deliveries by Donkey and Renault R4 Mail Van

1970. Stamp Day.

552	**172**	30c. multicoloured	70	25

173 Royal Prawn

1970. Marine Life. Multicoloured.

553	30c. Type **173**	70	25
554	40c. Noble pen (mollusc)	90	40
555	75c. Neptune's basket	1·40	50
556	1d. Red coral	2·10	75

174 Oranges

1970. Expo 70 World Fair, Osaka, Japan. Multicoloured.

557	30c. Type **174**	70	25
558	60c. Algerian Pavilion	70	40
559	70c. Bunches of grapes	1·40	60

175 Olives and Bottle of Olive-oil

1970. World Olive-oil Year.

560	**175**	1d. multicoloured	1·90	80

176 New U.P.U. H.Q. Building

1970. Inauguration of New U.P.U. Headquarters Building.

561	**176**	75c. multicoloured	1·10	40

177 Crossed Muskets

1970. Algerian 18th-century Weapons. Multicoloured.

562	40c. Type **177**	90	65
563	75c. Sabre (vert)	1·60	85
564	1d. Pistol	2·30	1·10

178 Arab League Flag, Arms and Map

1970. 25th Anniv of Arab League.

565	**178**	30c. multicoloured	55	25

179 Lenin

1970. Birth Centenary of Lenin.

566	**179**	30c. bistre and ochre	2·75	40

180 Exhibition Palace

1970. Seventh International Algiers Fair.

567	**180**	60c. green	70	40

181 I.E.Y. and Education Emblems

1970. International Education Year. Multicoloured.

568	30c. Type **181**	55	25
569	3d. Illuminated Koran (30×41 mm)	3·50	1·80

182 Great Mosque, Tlemcen

1970. Mosques.

570	**182**	30c. multicoloured	45	25
571	-	40c. brown and bistre	55	25
572	-	1d. multicoloured	1·00	40

DESIGNS—VERT: 40c. Ketchaoua Mosque, Algiers; 1d. Sidi-Okba Mosque.

183 *Fine Arts*

1970. Algerian Fine Arts.

573	**183**	1d. orange, grn & lt grn	1·10	45

184 G.P.O., Algiers

1971. Stamp Day.

574	**184**	30c. multicoloured	1·10	40

185 Hurdling

1971. Sixth Mediterranean Games, Izmir (Turkey).

575	**185**	20c. grey and blue	50	25
576	-	40c. grey and green	55	40
577	-	75c. grey and brown	1·10	65

DESIGNS—VERT: 40c. Gymnastics; 75c. Basket-ball.

186 "Racial Equality"

1971. Racial Equality Year.

578	**186**	60c. multicoloured	70	40

187 Symbols of Learning, and Students

1971. Inauguration of Technological Institutes.

579	**187**	70c. multicoloured	90	30

188 Red Crescent Banner

1971. Red Crescent Day.

580	**188**	30c.+10c. red and green	70	40

189 Casbah, Algiers

1971. Air.

581	**189**	2d. multicoloured	2·50	1·10
582	-	3d. violet and black	3·75	1·60
583	-	4d. multicoloured	4·25	2·00

DESIGNS: 3d. Port of Oran; 4d. Rhumel Gorges.

190 Aures Costume

1971. Regional Costumes (1st series). Multicoloured.

584		50c. Type **190**	1·30	60
585		70c. Oran	1·60	75
586		80c. Algiers	1·90	95
587		90c. Djebel-Amour	2·30	1·10

See also Nos. 610/13 and 659/62.

191 UNICEF Emblem, Tree and Animals

1971. 25th Anniv of UNICEF.

588	**191**	60c. multicoloured	90	45

192 Lion of St. Mark's

1971. UNESCO 'Save Venice' Campaign. Multicoloured.

589		80c. Type **192**	1·40	55
590		1d.15 Bridge of Sighs	2·30	95

193 Cycling

1972. Olympic Games, Munich. Multicoloured.

591		25c. Type **193**	45	25
592		40c. Throwing the javelin (vert)	60	25
593		60c. Wrestling (vert)	1·10	50
594		1d. Gymnastics (vert)	1·60	55

194 Book and Bookmark

1972. International Book Year.

595	**194**	1d.15 red, black and brown	90	45

195 Algerian Postmen

1972. Stamp Day.

596	**195**	40c. multicoloured	70	25

196 Jasmine

1972. Flowers. Multicoloured.

597		50c. Type **196**	70	40
598		60c. Violets	70	40
599		1d.15 Tuberose	2·10	65

197 Olympic Stadium

1972. Inauguration of Cheraga Olympic Stadium.

600	**197**	50c. green, brown & violet	70	40

198 Festival Emblem

1972. First Festival of Arab Youth.

601	**198**	40c. brown, yellow & grn	55	25

199 Rejoicing Algerians

1972. Tenth Anniv of Independence.

602	**199**	1d. multicoloured	1·30	60

1972. Regional Costumes (2nd series). As T **190**. Multicoloured.

610		50c. Hoggar	1·40	65
611		60c. Kabylie	1·80	65
612		70c. Mzab	1·90	85
613		90c. Tlemcen	2·40	1·10

201 Child posting Letter

1973. Stamp Day.

614	**201**	40c. multicoloured	55	25

202 Ho-Chi-Minh and Map

1973. Homage to the Vietnamese People

615	**202**	40c. multicoloured	90	40

203 Annaba Embroidery

1973. Algerian Embroidery. Multicoloured.

616		40c. Type **203**	55	25
617		60c. Algiers embroidery	90	50
618		80c. Constantine embroidery	1·30	70

204 "Food Cultivation"

1973. Tenth Anniv of World Food Programme.

619	**204**	1d.15 multicoloured	90	40

205 Serviceman and Flag

1973. National Service.

620	**205**	40c. multicoloured	55	25

1973. Algerian Flowers. As T **158**. Multicoloured.

621		30c. Type **158**	70	25
622		40c. As No. 529	90	40
623		1d. As No. 528	1·80	65
624		1d.15 As No. 530	2·75	1·10

206 O.A.U. Emblem

1973. Tenth Anniv of Organization of African Unity.

625	**206**	40c. multicoloured	55	25

207 Peasant Family

1973. Agrarian Revolution.

626	**207**	40c. multicoloured	70	25

208 Scout Badge on Map

1973. 24th World Scouting Congress, Nairobi, Kenya.

627	**208**	80c. mauve	75	40

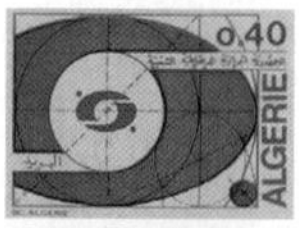

209 P.T.T. Symbol

1973. Inauguration of New P.T.T. Symbol.

628	**209**	40c. orange and blue	55	25

210 Conference Emblem

1973. Fourth Summit Conference of Non-Aligned Countries, Algiers.

629	**210**	40c. multicoloured	45	25
630	**210**	80c. multicoloured	90	40

211 "Skikda Harbour"

1973. Opening of Skikda Port.

631	**211**	80c. multicoloured	70	25

212 Young Workers

1973. Volontariat Students' Volunteer Service.

632	**212**	40c. multicoloured	55	25

213 Arms of Algiers

1973. Millenary of Algiers.

633	**213**	2d. multicoloured	3·00	1·40

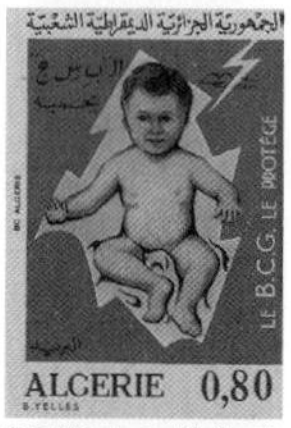

214 "Protected Infant"

1974. Anti-TB Campaign.

634	**214**	80c. multicoloured	90	45

215 Industrial Scene

1974. Four Year Plan.

635	**215**	80c. multicoloured	90	40

216 Arabesque Motif

1974. Birth Millenary of Abu-al Rayhan al-Biruni (mathematician and philosopher).

636	**216**	1d.50 multicoloured	2·50	1·40

217 Map and Arrows

1974. Meeting of Maghreb Committee for Co-ordination of Posts and Telecommunications, Tunis.

637	**217**	40c. multicoloured	55	25

218 Upraised Weapon and Fist

1974. Solidarity with South African People's Campaign.

638	**218**	80c. black and red	70	25

219 Algerian Family

1974. Homage to Algerian Mothers.

639	**219**	85c. multicoloured	70	25

220 Urban Scene

1974. Children's Drawings. Multicoloured.

640	70c. Type **220**	75	35
641	80c. Agricultural scene	90	40
642	90c. Tractor and sunrise	1·10	65

Nos. 641/2 are size 49×33 mm.

1974. Floralies 1974 Flower Show, Algiers. Nos. 623/4 optd **FLORALIES 1974**.

643	1d. multicoloured	1·80	85
644	1d.15 multicoloured	2·30	1·30

222 Automatic Stamp-vending Machine

1974. Stamp Day.

645	**222**	80c. multicoloured	80	35

223 U.P.U. Emblem on Globe

1974. Centenary of U.P.U.

646	**223**	80c. multicoloured	80	35

224 Revolutionaries

1974. 20th Anniv of Revolution. Multicoloured.

647	40c. Type **224**	55	25
648	70c. Armed soldiers (vert)	75	25
649	95c. Raising the flag (vert)	90	40
650	1d. Algerians looking to Independence	1·20	40

225 "Towards the Horizon"

1974. Horizon 1980.

651	**225**	95c. red, brown & black	75	40

226 Ewer

1974. Algerian 17th-century Brassware. Multicoloured.

652	50c. Type **226**	60	30
653	60c. Coffee pot	75	40
654	95c. Sugar basin	1·00	55
655	1d. Bath vessel	1·40	75

1975. No. 622 surch.

656	50c. on 40c. multicoloured	2·75	55

228 Games Emblem

1975. Seventh Mediterranean Games (1st issue).

657	**228**	50c. violet, green & yellow	50	25
658	**228**	1d. orange, violet & blue	90	40

See also Nos. 671/5.

1975. Regional Costumes (3rd series). As T **190**. Multicoloured.

659	1d. Algiers	1·60	85
660	1d. The Hogger	1·60	85
661	1d. Oran	1·60	85
662	1d. Tlemcen	1·60	85

229 Labour Emblems

1975. Tenth Anniv of Arab Labour Organization.

663	**229**	50c. brown	55	10

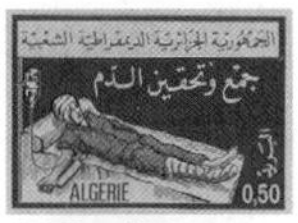

230 Transfusion

1975. Blood Collection and Transfusion Service.

664	**230**	50c. multicoloured	90	40

231 El Kantara Post Office

1975. Stamp Day.

665	**231**	50c. multicoloured	70	25

232 Policeman and Oil Rig on Map of Algeria

1975. Police Day.

666	**232**	50c. multicoloured	1·10	40

233 Ground Receiving Aerial

1975. Satellite Telecommunications. Multicoloured.

667	50c. Type **233**	55	15
668	1d. Map of receiving sites	90	25
669	1d.20 Main and subsidiary ground stations	1·20	50

234 Revolutionary with Flag

1975. 20th Anniv of 'Skikda' Revolution.

670	**234**	1d. multicoloured	75	40

235 Swimming

1975. Seventh Mediterranean Games, Algiers (2nd issue). Multicoloured.

671	25c. Type **235**	20	10
672	50c. Wrestling	45	25
673	70c. Football (vert)	70	30
674	1d. Athletics (vert)	90	40
675	1d.20 Handball (vert)	1·20	65
MS676	136×136 mm. Nos. 671/5	7·75	6·75

236 "Setif-Guelma-Kherrata"

1975. 30th Anniv of Setif, Guelma and Kherrata Massacres (1st issue).

677	**236**	5c. black and orange	10	10
678	**236**	10c. black and green	10	10
679	**236**	25c. black and blue	25	10
680	**236**	30c. black and brown	45	10
681	**236**	50c. black and green	45	10
682	**236**	70c. black and red	55	25
683	**236**	1d. black and red	90	40

See also No. 698.

237 Map of the Maghreb and A.P.U. Emblem

1975. Tenth Arab Postal Union Congress, Algiers.

684	**237**	1d. multicoloured	75	40

238 Mosaic, Palace of the Bey, Constantine

1975. Historic Buildings.

685	**238**	1d. multicoloured	1·10	40
686	-	2d. multicoloured	2·20	95
687	-	2d.50 black and brown	3·00	1·40

DESIGNS—VERT: 2d. Medersa Sidi-Boumedienne Oratory, Tlemcen. HORIZ: 2d.50, Palace of the Dey, Algiers.

239 University Building

1975. Millenary of Al-Azhar University, Cairo.

688	**239**	2d. multicoloured	2·10	80

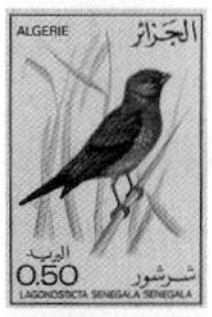

240 Red-billed Fire Finch

1976. Algerian Birds (1st series). Multicoloured.

689	50c. Type **240**	1·30	65
690	1d.40 Black-headed bush shrike (horiz)	2·50	1·30
691	2d. Blue-tit	3·25	1·40
692	2d.50 Black-bellied sand-grouse (horiz)	3·75	2·00

See also Nos. 722/5.

241 Early and Modern Telephones

1976. Telephone Centenary.

693	**241**	1d.40 multicoloured	1·10	55

242 Map and Angolan Flag

1976. Solidarity with Republic of Angola

694	**242**	50c. multicoloured	65	25

243 Child on Map

1976. Solidarity with People of Western Sahara.

695	**243**	50c. multicoloured	55	25

244 Postman

1976. Stamp Day.

696	**244**	1d.40 multicoloured	1·10	40

245 People, Microscope and Slide

1976. Campaign Against Tuberculosis.

697	**245**	50c. multicoloured	1·10	35

246 "Setif-Guelma-Kherrata"

1976. 30th Anniv of Setif, Guelma and Kherrata Massacres (2nd issue).

698	**246**	50c. yellow and blue	55	10

247 Ram's Head and Landscape

1976. Sheep Raising.

699	**247**	50c. multicoloured	65	25

248 Algerians holding Torch

1976. National Charter.

700	**248**	50c. multicoloured	55	25

249 Flag and Map

1976. Solidarity with the Palestinian People.

701	**249**	50c. multicoloured	70	25

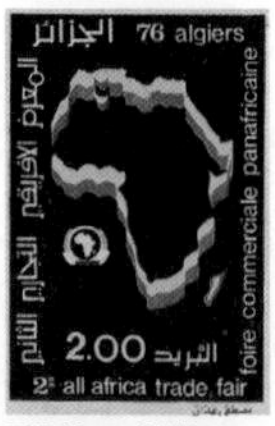
250 Map of Africa

1976. Second Pan-African Commercial Fair, Algiers.

702	**250**	2d. multicoloured	1·70	65

251 Blind Man making Brushes

1976. Rehabilitation of the Blind. Multicoloured.

703	1d.20 Type **251**	1·40	45
704	1d.40 *The Blind Man* (E. Dinet) (horiz)	2·10	65

252 Open Book

1976. The Constitution.

705	**252**	2d. multicoloured	1·70	65

253 Soldiers planting Seedlings

1976. Protection against Saharan Encroachment.

706	**253**	1d.40 multicoloured	1·40	55

254 Arabic Inscription

1976. Election of President Boumedienne.

707	**254**	2d. multicoloured	1·70	65

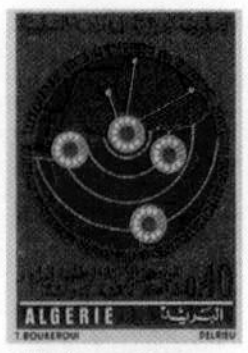
255 Map of Telephone Centres

1977. Inauguration of Automatic Telephone Dialling System.

708	**255**	40c. multicoloured	50	25

256 "Pyramid" of Heads

1977. Second General Population and Housing Census.

709	**256**	60c. on 50c. mult	60	25

257 Museum Building

1977. Sahara Museum, Ouargla.

710	**257**	60c. multicoloured	75	40

258 El Kantara Gorges

1977

711	**258**	20c. green and cream	10	10
712	**258**	60c. mauve and cream	25	10
713	**258**	1d. brown and cream	60	25

259 Assembly in Session

1977. National Assembly.

714	**259**	2d. multicoloured	1·40	55

260 Soldiers with Flag

1977. Solidarity with People of Zimbabwe.

715	**260**	2d. multicoloured	1·40	50

261 Soldier with Flag

1977. Solidarity with People of Namibia.

716	**261**	3d. multicoloured	2·30	75

262 *Winter*

1977. Roman Mosaics. The Seasons. Multicoloured.

717	1d.20 Type **262**	1·60	85
718	1d.40 *Autumn*	1·60	85
719	2d. *Summer*	2·50	1·30
720	3d. *Spring*	3·50	1·70
MS721	101×145 mm. Nos. 717/20	13·50	12·00

1977. Algerian Birds (2nd series). As T **240**. Multicoloured.

722	60c. Tristram's warbler	1·20	70
723	1d.40 Moussier's redstart (horiz)	2·10	1·10
724	2d. Temminck's horned lark (horiz)	3·25	1·50
725	3d. Hoopoe	4·00	2·00

263 Horseman

1977. The Cavaliers (performing horsemen). Multicoloured.

726	2d. Type **263**	2·10	85
727	5d. Three horsemen (horiz)	4·75	1·90

264 Ribbon and Games Emblem

1977. Third African Games, Algiers (1978) (1st issue). Multicoloured.

728	60c. Type **264**	55	25
729	1d.40 Symbolic design and emblem	1·50	50

See also Nos. 740/4.

265 Tessala el Merdja

1977. Socialist Agricultural Villages.

730	**265**	1d.40 multicoloured	1·00	40

266 12th-century Almohad Dirham

1977. Ancient Coins. Multicoloured.

731	60c. Type **266**	70	40
732	1d.40 12th-century Alomhad dinar	1·30	65
733	2d. 11th-century Almorarid dinar	1·90	95

267 Cherry (*Cerasus avium*)

1978. Fruit Tree Blossom. Multicoloured.

734	60c. Type **267**	70	25
735	1d.20 *Persica vulgaris* (peach)	1·10	75
736	1d.30 *Amygdalus communis* (almond)	1·10	75
737	1d.40 *Malus communis* (crab apple)	1·60	80

1978. Surch.

738	**236**	60c. on 50c. black & grn	70	25

269 Children with Traffic Signs opposing Car

1978. Road Safety for Children.

739	**269**	60c. multicoloured	60	25

270 Boxing and Map of Africa

1978. Third African Games, Algiers (2nd issue). Multicoloured.

740	40c. Sports emblems and volleyball (horiz)	25	10
741	60c. Olympic rings and table tennis symbol	40	25
742	1d.20 Basketball symbol (horiz)	1·00	40
743	1d.30 Hammerthrowing symbol	1·00	5·00
744	1d.40 Type **270**	1·30	60

271 Patient returning to Family

1978. Anti-tuberculosis Campaign.

745	**271**	60c. multicoloured	60	25

272 Ka'aba, Mecca

1978. Pilgrimage to Mecca.

746	**272**	60c. multicoloured	70	25

273 Road-building

1978. African Unity Road.

747	**273**	60c. multicoloured	70	25

274 Triangular Brooch

1978. Jewellery (1st series). Multicoloured.

748	1d.20 Type **274**	1·20	55
749	1d.35 Circular brooch	1·50	70
750	1d.40 Anklet	1·80	80

See also Nos. 780/2 and 833/5.

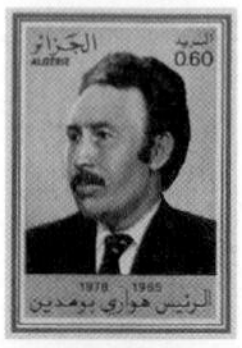
275 President Houari Boumedienne

1979. President Boumedienne Commem (1st issue).
751 **275** 60c. brown, red & turq 55 25
See also No. 753.

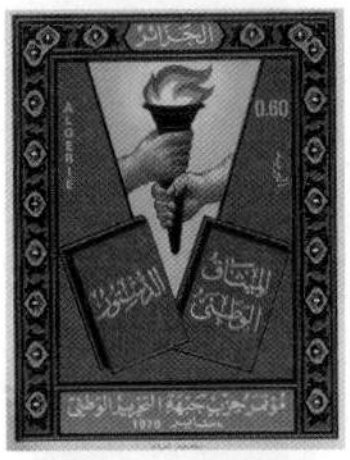
276 Books and Hands holding Torch

1979. National Liberation Front Party Congress.
752 **276** 60c. multicoloured 55 25

277 President Houari Boumedienne

1979. President Boumedienne Commem (2nd issue).
753 **277** 1d.40 multicoloured 1·40 50

278 Arabic Inscription

1979. Election of President Chadli Bendjedid.
754 **278** 2d. multicoloured 1·60 40

279 White Storks

1979. Air.
755 **279** 10d. blue, black and red 6·75 2·50

280 Ben Badis

1979. 90th Birth Anniv of Sheikh Abdelhamid Ben Badis (journalist and education pioneer).
756 **280** 60c. multicoloured 55 25

281 Globe within Telephone Dial

1979. Telecom 79 Exhibition. Multicoloured.
757 1d.20 Type **281** 90 35
758 1d.40 Sound waves 1·20 45

282 Children dancing on Globe

1979. International Year of the Child. Multicoloured.
759 60c. Picking Dates 55 10
760 1d.40 Type **282** (vert) 1·10 45

283 Kabylie Nuthatch

1979
761 **283** 1d.40 multicoloured 2·00 95

284 Fighting for the Revolution and Construction work

1979. 25th Anniv of Revolution. Multicoloured.
762 1d.40 Type **284** 1·00 30
763 3d. Algerians with flag 1·70 85

285 Arabic Inscription

1979. 1400th Anniv of Hegira.
764 **285** 3d. gold, turquoise & blue 2·10 80

286 Return of Dionysus (right detail)

1980. Dionysus Mosaic, Setif. Multicoloured.
765 1d.20 Type **286** 1·30 40
766 1d.35 Centre detail 1·30 55
767 1d.40 Left detail 1·60 80
Nos. 765/7 were issued together, *se-tenant*, forming a composite design.

287 Books

1980. Day of Knowledge.
768 **287** 60c. brown, yellow & grn 55 10

288 Five Year Plan

1980. Extraordinary Congress of National Liberation Front Party.
769 **288** 60c. multicoloured 55 25

289 Olympic Flame

1980. Olympic Games, Moscow. Multicoloured.
770 50c. Type **289** 50 10
771 1d.40 Olympic sports (horiz) 95 45

290 Figures supporting O.P.E.C. Emblem

1980. 20th Anniv of Organization of Petroleum Exporting Countries.
772 **290** 60c. green, blue and red 65 10
773 - 1d.40 green and blue 1·20 45
DESIGN: 1d.40, O.P.E.C. emblem on world map.

291 Aures

1980. World Tourism Conference, Manila. Multicoloured.
774 50c. Type **291** 50 25
775 1d. El Oued 90 25
776 1d.40 Tassili 1·10 40
777 2d. Algiers 1·90 65

292 Ibn Sina

1980. Birth Millenary of Ibn Sina (Avicenna) (philosopher).
778 **292** 3d. multicoloured 2·10 80

293 Earthquake Devastation

1980. El Asnam Earthquake Relief.
779 **293** 3d. multicoloured 2·10 55

1980. Jewellery (2nd series). As T **274**. Multicoloured.
780 60c. Necklace 60 25
781 1d.40 Earrings and bracelet 1·10 55
782 2d. Diadem (horiz) 1·60 70

294 Emblem

1981. Five Year Plan.
783 **294** 60c. multicoloured 40 10

295 Basket-worker

1981. Traditional Arts. Multicoloured.
784 40c. Type **295** 35 10
785 60c. Spinning 45 20
786 1d. Copper-smith 75 25
787 1d.40 Jeweller 1·20 40

296 Cedar *Cedrus atlantica*

1981. World Tree Day. Multicoloured.
788 60c. Type **296** 45 10
789 1d.40 Cypress *Cupressus dupreziana* 1·10 40

297 Mohamed Bachir el Ibrahimi

298 Children and Blackboard (Basic Schooling)

1981. Day of Knowledge.
790 **297** 60c. multicoloured 45 10
791 **298** 60c. multicoloured 45 10

299 Archer, Dog and Internal Organs

1981. 12th Int Hydatidological Congress, Algiers.
792 **299** 2d. multicoloured 1·80 55

300 Dish Aerial and Caduceus

1981. World Telecommunications Day.
793 **300** 1d.40 multicoloured 1·10 25

301 "Disabled"

1981. International Year of Disabled People.
794 **301** 1d.20 blue, red & orange 90 25
795 - 1d.40 multicoloured 1·00 30
DESIGN: 1d.40, Disabled people and hand holding flower.

302 "Papilio machaon"

1981. Butterflies. Multicoloured.

796	60c. Type **302**	70	35
797	1d.20 *Rhodocera rhamni gonepteryx rhamni*	1·20	50
798	1d.40 *Charaxes jasius*	1·60	85
799	2d. *Papilio podalirius*	2·10	90

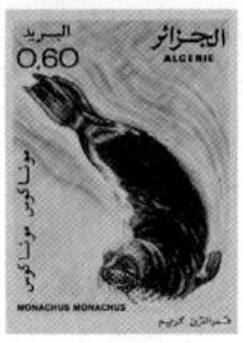
303 Mediterranean Monk Seal

1981. Nature Protection. Multicoloured.

800	60c. Type **303**	80	40
801	1d.40 Barbary ape	1·60	85

304 Man holding Ear of Wheat

1981. World Food Day.

802	**304** 2d. multicoloured	1·30	50

305 Cattle, Jabbaren

1981. Cave Paintings. Multicoloured.

803	60c. Mouflon, Tan Zoumaitek	55	25
804	1d. Type **305**	95	40
805	1d.60 Cattle, Iherir (horiz)	1·30	55
806	2d. One-horned bull, Jabbaren (horiz)	1·80	85

306 Galley

1981. Algerian Ships of 17th and 18th Centuries. Multicoloured.

807	60c. Type **306**	80	50
808	1d.60 Xebec	1·80	1·00

307 Footballers with Cup

1982. World Cup Football Championship, Spain. Multicoloured.

809	80c. Type **307**	60	25
810	2d.80 Footballers and ball (horiz)	1·90	75

308 Microscope

1982. Centenary of Discovery of Tubercle Bacillus.

811	**308** 80c. blue, lt blue & orge	55	25

309 Mirror

1982. Popular Traditional Arts. Multicoloured.

812	80c. Type **309**	60	25
813	2d. Whatnot	1·30	40
814	2d.40 Chest (48×32 mm)	1·70	75

310 New Mosque, Algiers

1982. Views of Algeria before 1830 (1st series). Size 32×22 mm.

815	**310** 80c. brown	45	15
816	- 2d.40 violet	1·20	50
817	- 3d. green	1·60	65

DESIGNS: 2d.40, Sidi Boumedienne Mosque, Tlemcen; 3d. Garden of Dey, Algiers.

See also Nos. 859/62, 873/5, 880/2, 999/1001, 1054/6 and 1075/86.

311 *Callitris articulata*

1982. Medicinal Plants. Multicoloured.

818	50c. Type **311**	45	10
819	80c. *Artemisia herba-alba*	55	25
820	1d. *Ricinus communis*	90	35
821	2d.40 *Thymus fontanesii*	1·90	75

312 Independence Fighter

1982. 20th Anniv of Independence. Multicoloured.

822	50c. Type **312**	40	15
823	80c. Modern soldiers	55	25
824	2d. Algerians and symbols of prosperity	1·40	55
MS825	74×82 mm. 5d. Sun rising over flames (31×39 mm)	4·25	4·00

313 Congress House

1982. Soumman Congress.

826	**313** 80c. multicoloured	55	15

314 Scout and Guide releasing Dove

1982. 75th Anniv of Boy Scout Movement.

827	**314** 2d.80 multicoloured	1·90	55

315 Child

1982. Palestinian Children.

828	**315** 1d.60 multicoloured	95	30

316 Waldrapp

1982. Nature Protection. Multicoloured.

829	50c. Type **316**	70	40
830	80c. Houbara bustard (vert)	95	65
831	2d. Tawny eagle	2·20	1·10
832	2d.40 Lammergeier (vert)	2·75	1·40

317 Mirror

1983. Silver Work.

833	**317** 50c. silver, black and red	35	10
834	- 1d. multicoloured	55	40
835	- 2d. silver, black, & purple	1·20	60

DESIGNS—VERT. 1d. Perfume flasks. HORIZ: 2d. Belt buckle.

318 *Abies numidica*

1983. World Tree Day. Multicoloured.

836	80c. Type **318**	70	25
837	2d.80 *Acacia raddiana*	2·10	75

319 Mineral

1983. Mineral Resources.

838	**319** 70c. multicoloured	90	35
839	**319** 80c. multicoloured	1·00	50
840	**319** 1d.20 mult (horiz)	1·20	65
841	**319** 2d.40 mult (horiz)	2·50	1·20

320 Customs Officer

1983. 30th Anniv of Customs Co-operation Council.

842	**320** 80c. multicoloured	70	25

321 Emir Abdelkader

1983. Death Centenary of Emir Abdelkader.

843	**321** 4d. multicoloured	2·30	95

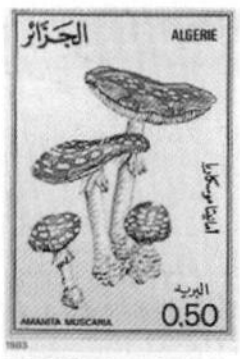
322 Fly Agaric

1983. Mushrooms. Multicoloured.

844	50c. Type **322**	80	25
845	80c. Death cap	1·10	65
846	1d.40 *Pleurotus eryngii*	2·40	1·00
847	2d.80 *Terfezia leonis*	3·75	1·70

323 Ibn Khaldoun

1983. Ibn Khaldoun Commemoration.

848	**323** 80c. multicoloured	70	25

324 W.C.Y. Emblem and Post Office

1983. World Communications Year. Multicoloured.

849	80c. Type **324**	55	25
850	2d.40 W.C.Y. emblem and telephone switch box	1·50	65

325 Goat and Tassili Mountains

1983. Tassili World Patrimony. Multicoloured.

851	50c. Type **325**	40	10
852	80c. Touaregs	55	25
853	2d.40 Rock paintings	1·40	55
854	2d.80 Rock formation	1·80	75

326 Sloughi

1983. Sloughi. Multicoloured.

855	80c. Type **326**	80	35
856	2d.40 Sloughi	2·10	1·00

327 Symbols of Economic Progress

1983. Fifth National Liberation Front Party Congress. Multicoloured.

857	80c. Type **327**	80	35
MS858	75×82 mm. 5d. Party emblem (31×38 mm)	4·25	4·00

1984. Views of Algeria before 1830 (2nd series). As T **310**.

859	10c. blue	10	10
860	1d. purple	45	10
861	2d. blue	95	45
862	4d. red	2·10	65

DESIGNS: 10c. Oran; 1d. Sidi Abderahmane Mosque, Et Taalibi; 2d. Bejaia; 4d. Constantine.

328 Jug

1984. Pottery. Multicoloured.

863	80c. Type **328**	55	25
864	1d. Dish (horiz)	75	40
865	2d. Lamp	1·40	60
866	2d.40 Jug (horiz)	1·60	75

329 Fountain

1984. Fountains of Old Algiers.

867	**329**	50c. multicoloured	20	10
868	-	80c. multicoloured	55	40
869	-	2d.40 multicoloured	1·30	65

DESIGNS: 80c., 2d.40, Different fountains.

330 Dove, Flames and Olympic Rings

1984. Olympic Games, Los Angeles.

870	**330**	1d. multicoloured	90	40

331 Stallion

1984. Horses. Multicoloured.

871	80c. Type **331**	70	40
872	2d.40 Mare	1·90	1·00

1984. Views of Algeria before 1830 (3rd series). As T **310**.

873	5c. purple	10	10
874	20c. blue	10	10
875	70c. violet	40	25

DESIGNS: 5c. Mustapha Pacha; 20c. Bab Azzoun; 70c. Mostaganem.

332 Lute

1984. Musical Instruments. Multicoloured.

876	80c. Type **332**	55	25
877	1d. Drum	90	40
878	2d.40 One-stringed instrument	1·80	75
879	2d.80 Bagpipes	2·00	1·00

1984. Views of Algeria before 1830 (4th series). As T **310**.

880	30c. red and black	25	10
881	40c. black	25	10
882	50c. brown	25	10

DESIGNS: 30c. Algiers from Admiralty; 40c. Kolea; 50c. Algiers from aqueduct.

333 Partisans in Mountains and Flag

1984. 30th Anniv of Revolution. Multicoloured.

883	80c. Type **333**	70	25
MS884	75×82 mm. 5d. Algerian flags (31×39 mm)	4·25	4·00

334 Map of M'Zab Valley

1984. M'Zab Valley. Multicoloured.

885	80c. Type **334**	65	10
886	2d.40 M'Zab town	1·70	60

335 Coffee Pot

1985. Ornamental Tableware.

887	**335**	80c. black, silver & yellow	55	25
888	-	2d. black, silver and green	1·20	60
889	-	2d.40 black, silver & pink	1·60	70

DESIGNS—HORIZ: 2d. Bowl. VERT: 2d.40, Lidded jar.

336 Blue-finned Tuna

1985. Fishes. Multicoloured.

890	50c. Type **336**	55	25
891	80c. Gilthead seabream	95	40
892	2d.40 Dusky grouper	2·20	1·10
893	2d.80 Smooth hound	2·75	1·20

337 Birds in Flight and Emblem

1985. National Games.

894	**337**	80c. multicoloured	65	25

338 Stylized Trees

1985. Environmental Protection. Multicoloured.

895	80c. Type **338**	80	25
896	1d.40 Stylized waves	90	40

339 Algiers Casbah

1985

897	**339**	20c. blue and cream	10	10
898	**339**	80c. green and cream	55	10
899	**339**	2d.40 brown and cream	1·70	10

340 Dove within "40"

1985. 40th Anniv of U.N.O.

900	**340**	1d. multicoloured	90	25

341 Figures linking arms and Emblem

1985. First National Youth Festival.

901	**341**	80c. multicoloured	70	25

342 Figures linking arms on Globe and Dove

1985. International Youth Year. Multicoloured.

902	80c. Type **342**	60	25
903	1d.40 Doves making globe with laurels	90	35

343 O.P.E.C. Emblem

1985. 25th Anniv of Organization of Petroleum Exporting Countries.

904	**343**	80c. multicoloured	70	25

344 Mother and Children

1985. Family Planning. Multicoloured.

905	80c. Type **344**	55	25
906	1d.40 Doctor weighing baby	90	40
907	1d.70 Mother breast-feeding baby	1·10	50

345 Chetaibi Bay

1985. Tourist Sites.

908	**345**	80c. blue, green & brown	45	25
909	-	2d. brown, green & blue	1·30	40
910	-	2d.40 brown, green & bl	1·60	65

DESIGNS—VERT: 2d. El Meniaa. HORIZ: 2d.40, Bou Noura.

346 *Palm Grove*

1985. Paintings by N. Dinet. Multicoloured.

911	2d. Type **346**	1·50	75
912	3d. *Palm Grove* (different)	2·10	1·20

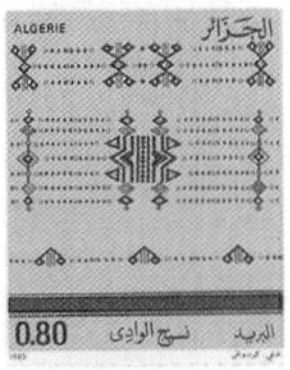

347 Line Pattern

1985. Weavings. Multicoloured.

913	80c. Type **347**	70	45
914	1d.40 Diamond pattern	1·40	65
915	2d.40 Patterned horizontal stripes	2·00	1·10
916	2d.80 Vertical and horizontal stripes	2·50	1·60

348 *Felis margarita*

1986. Wild Cats. Multicoloured.

917	80c. Type **348**	80	45
918	1d. Caracal	1·00	60
919	2d. Wild cat	1·90	1·10
920	2d.40 Serval (vert)	2·50	1·40

349 Oral Vaccination

1986. UNESCO Child Survival Campaign. Multicoloured.

921	80c. Type **349**	55	25
922	1d.40 Sun behind mother and baby	1·20	55
923	1d.70 Children playing	1·50	75

350 Industrial Skyline, Clasped Hands and Emblem

1986. 30th Anniv of Algerian General Workers' Union.

924	**350**	2d. multicoloured	1·50	55

351 Books and Crowd

1986. National Charter.

925	**351**	4d. multicoloured	2·75	1·20

352 Emblem on Book and Drawing Instruments

1986. Disabled Persons' Day.

926	**352**	80c. multicoloured	70	30

353 Children playing

1986. Anti-tuberculosis Campaign.

927	**353**	80c. multicoloured	70	35

354 Sombrero on Football

1986. World Cup Football Championship, Mexico. Multicoloured.

928	2d. Type **354**	1·40	55
929	2d.40 Players and ball	1·60	70

355 Courtyard with Fountain

1986. Traditional Dwellings. Multicoloured.

930	80c. Type **355**	70	30
931	2d.40 Courtyard with two beds of shrubs	1·80	1·00
932	3d. Courtyard with plants in tall pot	2·30	1·30

356 Heart forming Drop over Patient

1986. Blood Donors.

933	**356**	80c. multicoloured	1·40	40

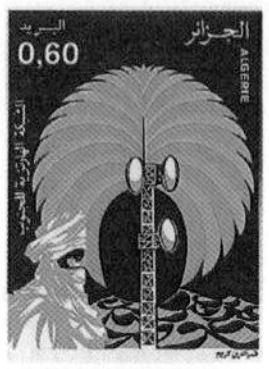

357 Transmission Mast as Palm Tree

1986. Opening of Hertzian Wave Communications (Southern District).

934	**357**	60c. multicoloured	45	25

358 Studded Gate

1986. Mosque Gateways. Multicoloured.

935	2d. Type **358**	1·30	55
936	2d.40 Ornate gateway	1·60	75

359 Dove

1986. International Peace Year.

937	**359**	2d.40 multicoloured	1·60	55

360 Girl dancing

1986. Folk Dances. Multicoloured.

938	80c. Type **360**	70	25
939	2d.40 Woman with purple dress dancing	1·70	65
940	2d.80 Veiled sword dancer	1·90	85

361 *Narcissus tazetta*

1986. Flowers. Multicoloured.

941	80c. Type **361**	70	30
942	1d.40 *Iris unguicularis*	1·20	55
943	2d.40 *Capparis spinosa*	1·70	90
944	2d.80 *Gladiolus segetum*	2·10	1·10

362 *Algerian Family*

1987. Paintings by Mohammed Issiakhem in National Museum. Multicoloured.

945	2d. Type **362**	1·50	75
946	5d. *Man and Books*	3·50	2·00

363 Earrings

1987. Jewellery from Aures. Multicoloured.

947	1d. Type **363**	75	40
948	1d.80 Bangles	1·20	60
949	2d.90 Brooches	1·70	1·10
950	3d.30 Necklace (horiz)	2·00	1·20

364 Boy and Girl

1987. Rock Carvings. Multicoloured.

951	1d. Type **364**	90	55
952	2d.90 Goat	2·00	1·30
953	3d.30 Animals	2·30	1·40

365 Baby holding Syringe "Umbrella"

1987. African Vaccination Year.

954	**365**	1d. multicoloured	55	25

366 Workers and Circles

1987. Voluntary Service.

955	**366**	1d. multicoloured	55	30

367 People and Buildings

1987. Third General Population Census.

956	**367**	1d. multicoloured	55	25

368 1962 War Orphans Fund Stamps and Magnifying Glass

1987. 25th Anniv of Independent Algeria Stamps.

957	**368**	1d.80 multicoloured	1·80	60

369 Hand holding Torch

1987. 25th Anniv of Independence. Multicoloured.

958	1d. Type **369**	55	25

MS959	75×82 mm. 5d. Sun, dove and "25" (32×39 mm)	3·50	3·25

370 Actors in Spotlight

1987. Amateur Theatre Festival, Mostaganem. Multicoloured.

960	1d. Type **370**	55	85
961	1d.80 Theatre	90	55

371 Discus Thrower

1987. Mediterranean Games, Lattaquie. Multicoloured.

962	1d. Type **371**	55	30
963	2d.90 Tennis player (vert)	1·50	70
964	3d.30 Footballer	1·80	95

372 Greater Flamingo

1987. Birds. Multicoloured.

965	1d. Type **372**	75	40
966	1d.80 Purple swamphen	1·30	80
967	2d.50 Black-shouldered kite	2·00	95
968	2d.90 Red kite	1·90	85

373 Reservoir

1987. Agriculture. Multicoloured.

969	1d. Type **373**	60	25
970	1d. Forestry (36×28 mm)	60	25
971	1d. Foodstuffs (25×37 mm)	60	25
972	1d. Erecting hedge against desert (25×37 mm)	55	25

374 Map, Transmitter and Radio Waves

1987. African Telecommunications Day.

973	**374**	1d. multicoloured	70	25

375 Motorway

1987. Transport. Multicoloured.

974	2d.90 Type **375**	1·50	60
975	3d.30 Diesel locomotive and passenger train	2·75	1·20

376 Houari Boumedienne University, Algiers

1987. Universities. Multicoloured.

976	1d. Type **376**	55	25
977	2d.50 Oran University	1·30	45
978	2d.90 Constantine University	1·50	60
979	3d.30 Emir Abdelkader University, Constantine (vert)	1·90	75

377 Wheat, Sun and Farmer ploughing with Oxen

1988. Tenth Anniv of International Agricultural Development Fund.

980	**377**	1d. multicoloured	70	25

378 Emblem as Sun above Factories

1988. Autonomy of State-owned Utilities.

981	**378**	1d. multicoloured	55	25

379 Woman's Face and Emblem

1988. International Women's Day.

982	**379**	1d. multicoloured	55	25

380 Globe, Flag, Wood Pigeon and Scout Salute

1988. 75th Anniv of Arab Scouting.

983	**380**	2d. multicoloured	1·10	45

381 Bau-Hanifia

1988. Spas. Multicoloured.

984	1d. Type **381**	55	25
985	2d.90 Chellala	1·50	55
986	3d.30 Righa-Ain Tolba	1·70	70

382 Running

1988. Olympic Games, Seoul.

987	**382**	2d.90 multicoloured	1·90	90

383 Pencil and Globe

1988. International Literacy Day.

988	**383**	2d.90 multicoloured	1·40	70

384 Barbary Ape

1988. Endangered Animals. Barbary Ape. Multicoloued.

989	50c. Type **384**	80	40
990	90c. Ape family	1·20	65
991	1d. Ape's head and shoulders (vert)	1·60	85
992	1d.80 Ape in tree (vert)	2·75	1·50

385 Family Group

1988. 40th Anniv of W.H.O.

993	**385**	2d.90 multicoloured	1·30	60

386 Different Races raising Fists

1988. Anti-apartheid Campaign.

994	**386**	2d.50 multicoloured	1·20	50

387 Emblem

1988. Sixth National Liberation Front Party Congress.

995	**387**	1d. multicoloured	55	25

388 Man irrigating Fields

1988. Agriculture. Multicoloured.

996	1d. Type **388**	55	25
997	1d. Fields, cattle and man picking fruit	55	25

389 Constantine

1989

998	**389**	1d. deep green and green	40	85

1989. Views of Algeria before 1830 (5th series). As T **310**.

999	2d.50 green	90	25
1000	2d.90 green	1·00	25
1001	5d. brown and black	2·10	40

DESIGNS: 2d.50, Bay; 2d.90, Harbour; 5d. View of harbour through archway.

390 Courtyard

1989. National Achievements. Multicoloured.

1002	1d. Type **390**	55	25
1003	1d. Flats (housing)	55	25
1004	1d. Gateway, Timimoun (tourism)	55	25
1005	1d. Dish aerial and telephones (communications)	55	25

391 Oran Es Senia Airport

1989. Airports. Multicoloured.

1006	2d.90 Type **391**	1·20	45
1007	3d.30 Tebessa airport	1·40	60
1008	5d. Tamanrasset airport (vert)	2·10	1·20

392 Irrigation

1989. Development of South. Multicoloured.

1009	1d. Type **392**	50	25
1010	1d.80 Ouargla secondary school	70	40
1011	2d.50 Gas complex, Hassi R'mel (vert)	1·10	50

393 Soldiers at Various Tasks

1989. 20th Anniv of National Service.

1012	**393**	2d. multicoloured	1·30	65

394 Locusts and Crop Spraying

1989. Anti-locusts Campaign.

1013	**394**	1d. multicoloured	55	25

395 Mother and Baby

1989. International Children's Day.

1014	**395**	1d.+30c. mult	65	40

396 Moon

1989. 20th Anniv of First Manned Landing on Moon. Multicoloured.

1015	2d.90 Type **396**	1·20	50
1016	4d. Astronaut on moon	1·50	80

397 Globe and Emblem

1989. Centenary of Interparliamentary Union.

1017	**397**	2d.90 mauve, brn & gold	1·20	40

398 Fruits and Vegetables

1989. National Production.

1018	**398**	2d. multicoloured	75	40
1019	-	3d. multicoloured	1·10	60
1020	-	5d. multicoloured	1·90	1·10

DESIGNS: 3, 5d. Various fruits and vegetables.

399 Atlantic Bonito

1989. Fish. Multicoloured.

1021	1d. Type **399**	60	30
1022	1d.80 John dory	1·10	45
1023	2d.90 Red seabream	1·60	60
1024	3d.30 Swordfish	1·80	75

400 "35" and Soldier with Rifle

1989. 35th Anniv of Revolution.

1025	**400**	1d. multicoloured	50	15

401 Bank Emblem, Cogwheel, Factory and Wheat

1989. 25th Anniv of African Development Bank.

1026	**401**	1d. multicoloured	45	25

402 Satan's Mushroom

1989. Fungi. Multicoloured.

1027	1d. Type **402**	70	30
1028	1d.80 Yellow stainer	1·20	45
1029	2d.90 Parasol mushroom	1·90	75
1030	3d.30 Saffron milk cap	2·20	95

403 Emblem

1990. Tenth Anniv of Pan-African Postal Union.

1031	**403**	1d. multicoloured	50	25

404 Sun, Arm and Face

1990. Rational Use of Energy.

1032	**404**	1d. multicoloured	60	25

405 Emblem

1990. African Nations Cup Football Championship.

1033	**405**	3d. multicoloured	1·30	50

406 Ceramics

1990. Industries. Multicoloured.

1034	2d. Type **406**	70	35
1035	2d.90 Car maintenance	1·10	45
1036	3d.30 Fishing	1·70	65

407 Pictogram and Olympic Rings

1990. World Cup Football Championship, Italy. Multicoloured.

1037	2d.90 Type **407**	1·10	50
1038	5d. Trophy, ball and flag	1·90	95

408 Pylons on Map

1990. Rural Electrification.

1039	**408**	2d. multicoloured	80	30

409 Young Workers

1990. Youth. Multicoloured.

1040	2d. Type **409**	80	30
1041	3d. Youth in crowd (vert)	1·20	45

410 Members' Flags

1990. Arab Maghreb Union Summit Conference.

1042	**410**	1d. multicoloured	50	25

411 Anniversary Emblem

1990. 30th Anniv of O.P.E.C.

1043	**411**	2d. multicoloured	80	30

412 House and Hand holding Coin

1990. Savings Day.

1044	**412**	1d. multicoloured	40	15

413 Flag, Rifle and Hands with Broken Manacles

1990. Namibian Independence.

1045	**413**	3d. multicoloured	1·00	30

414 Duck

1990. Domestic Animals. Multicoloured.

1046	1d. Type **414**	50	15
1047	2d. Hare (horiz)	95	35
1048	2d.90 Common turkey	1·30	55
1049	3d.30 Red junglefowl (horiz)	1·60	75

415 Dome of the Rock and Palestinians

1990. Palestinian "Intifada" Movement.

1050	**415**	1d.+30c. mult	60	40

416 Crowd with Banners

1990. 30th Anniv of 11 December 1960 Demonstration.

1051	**416**	1d. multicoloured	30	10

417 Families in Countryside

1990. Campaign against Respiratory Diseases.

1052	**417**	1d. multicoloured	30	10

418 Sunburst, Torch and Open Book

1991. Second Anniv of Constitution.

1053	**418**	1d. multicoloured	30	10

1991. Views of Algeria before 1830 (6th series). As T **310**.

1054	1d.50 red	50	10
1055	4d.20 green	1·40	55

DESIGNS: 1d.50, Kolea; 4d.20, Constantine.

419 Bejaia

1991. Air. Multicoloured.

1056	10d. Type **419**	2·75	1·20
1057	20d. Annaba	5·50	2·75

420 *Jasminum fruticans*

1991. Flowers. Multicoloured.

1058	2d. Type **420**	70	30
1059	4d. *Dianthus crinitus*	1·40	55
1060	5d. *Cyclamen africanum*	1·80	80

421 *Trip to the Country* (Mehdi Medrar)

1991. Children's Drawings. Multicoloured.

1061	3d. Type **421**	90	25
1062	4d. *Children playing* (Ouidad Bounab)	1·20	40

422 Emblem

1991. Third Anniv of Arab Maghreb Union Summit Conference, Zeralda.

1063	**422**	1d. multicoloured	30	10

423 Figures and Emblem

1991. 40th Anniv of Geneva Convention on Status of Refugees.

1064	**423**	3d. multicoloured	1·00	35

424 Coded Letter and Target

1991. World Post Day (1065) and "Telecom 91" International Telecommunications Exhibition, Geneva (1066). Multicoloured.

1065	1d.50 Type **424**	55	25
1066	4d.20 Exhibition and I.T.U. emblems (vert)	1·20	45

425 Spanish Festoon

1991. Butterflies. Multicoloured.

1067	2d. Type **425**	60	30
1068	4d. *Melitaea didyma*	1·00	45
1069	6d. Red admiral	1·40	65
1070	7d. Large tortoiseshell	1·70	95

426 Chest Ornament

1991. Silver Jewellery from South Algeria. Multicoloured.

1071	3d. Necklaces	60	30
1072	4d. Type **426**	80	45
1073	5d. Enamelled ornament	90	65
1074	7d. Bangles (horiz)	1·50	1·00

1992. Views of Algeria before 1830. As previous issues and new values. Size 30½×21 mm.

1075	5c. purple	60	30
1076	10c. blue	70	1·80
1077	20c. blue	90	50
1078	30c. red and black	1·30	35
1079	50c. brown	1·30	35
1080	70c. lilac	1·80	85
1081	80c. brown	2·00	75
1082	1d. brown	1·50	65
1083	2d. blue	2·75	1·30
1084	3d. green	3·75	95
1085	4d. red	5·25	1·30
1086	6d.20 blue	90	25
1087	7d.50 red	1·20	25

DESIGNS: 5c., 6d.20, As No. 873; 10c., 7d.50, As No. 859; 20c. As No. 1000; 30c. As No. 1001; 50c. As No. 882; 70c. As No. 875; 80c. Type **310**; 1d. As No. 860; 2d. As No. 861; 3d. As No. 817; 4d. As No. 1055.

427 Woman

1992. International Women's Day.

1095	**427**	1d.50 multicoloured	40	10

428 Dorcas Gazelle

1992. Gazelles. Multicoloured.

1096	1d.50 Type **428**	40	10
1097	6d.20 Edmi gazelle	1·10	60
1098	8d.60 Addra gazelle	1·50	75

429 Algiers

1992

1099	**429**	1d.50 brown & lt brown	25	10
1132	**429**	2d. blue	30	10
1147	**429**	3d. blue	50	10

430 Runners

1992. Olympic Games, Barcelona.

1100	**430**	6d.20 multicoloured	1·20	45

431 Doves and Flags

1992. 30th Anniv of Independence.

1101	**431**	5d. green, red and black	90	30

432 *Ajuga iva*

1992. Medicinal Plants. Multicoloured.

1102	1d.50 Type **432**	25	10
1103	5d.10 Buckthorn	90	40
1104	6d.20 Milk thistle	1·20	50
1105	8d.60 French lavender	1·60	70

433 Computerized Post Office Equipment

1992. World Post Day. Modernization of Postal Service.

1106	**433**	1d.50 multicoloured	40	10

434 Boudiaf

1992. Mohammed Boudiaf (chairman of Committee of State) Commemoration.

1107	**434**	2d. multicoloured	45	25
1108	**434**	8d.60 multicoloured	1·50	75

435 2nd-century B.C. Numidian Coin

1992. Coinage. Multicoloured.

1109	1d.50 Type **435**	20	10
1110	2d. 14th-century Zianide dinar	30	15
1111	5d.10 11th-century Almoravid dinar	85	40
1112	6d.20 19th-century Emir Abd-el-Kader coin	1·20	55

436 Short-snouted Seahorse

1992. Marine Animals. Multicoloured.

1113	1d.50 Type **436**	35	10
1114	2d.70 Loggerhead turtle	55	25
1115	6d.20 Mediterranean moray	1·20	55
1116	7d.50 Lobster	1·40	70

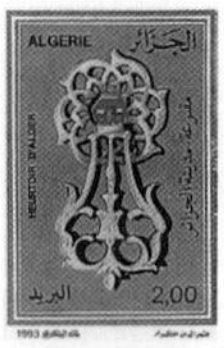

437 Algiers Door Knocker

1993. Door Knockers. Multicoloured.

1117	2d. Type **437**	30	10
1118	5d.60 Constantine	90	35
1119	8d.60 Tlemcen	1·40	70

438 Medlar Blossom

1993. Fruit-tree Blossom. Multicoloured.

1120	4d.50 Type **438**	80	40
1121	8d.60 Quince (vert)	1·40	70
1122	11d. Apricot (vert)	1·80	95

439 Patrol Boat, Emblem and Flag

1993. 20th Anniv of Coastguard Service.

1123	**439**	2d. multicoloured	95	35

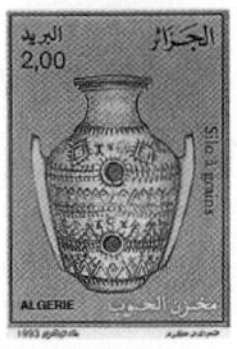

440 Grain Storage Jar

1993. Traditional Utensils. Multicoloured.

1124	2d. Type **440**	50	10
1125	5d.60 Grindstone	90	50
1126	8d.60 Oil-press	1·40	65

441 Mauretanian Royal Mausoleum, Tipaza

1993. Mausoleums. Multicoloured.

1127	8d.60 Type **441**	1·10	50
1128	12d. Royal Mausoleum, El Khroub	1·80	80

442 Jijelienne Coast

1993. Air.

1129	**442**	50d. green, brown & blue	5·75	2·00

443 Annaba

1993. Ports. Multicoloured.

1130	2d. Type **443**	40	10
1131	8d.60 Arzew	1·40	50

444 Chameleon

1993. Reptiles. Multicoloured.

1133	2d. Type **444**	50	10
1134	8d.60 Desert monitor (horiz)	1·60	85

445 Tipaza

1993. Tourism. Multicoloured.

1135	2d. Type **445**	40	10
1136	8d.60 Kerzaz	1·10	50

446 Map, Processing Plant and Uses of Hydrocarbons

1993. 30th Anniv of Sonatrach (National Society for Transformation and Commercialization of Hydrocarbons).

1137	**446**	2d. multicoloured	50	10

447 Dove, Flag and "18"

1994. National Chahid Day.

1138	**447**	2d. multicoloured	55	10

448 Crown of Statue of Liberty, Football, U.S. Flag and Trophy

1994. World Cup Football Championship, U.S.A.

1139	**448**	8d.60 multicoloured	2·75	85

449 Monkey Orchid

1994. Orchids. Multicoloured.

1140	5d.60 Type **449**	1·20	65
1141	8d.60 *Orphrys lutea*	1·50	85
1142	11d. Bee orchid	2·20	1·30

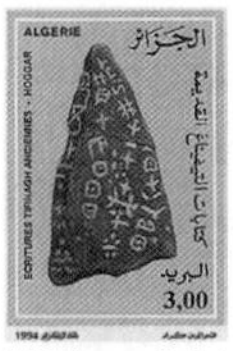

450 Hoggar Script on Stone

1994. Ancient Communication. Multicoloured.

1143	3d. Type **450**	80	25
1144	10d. Abizar stele	1·80	75

451 Flags and Olympic Rings

1994. Cent of International Olympic Committee.

1145	**451**	12d. multicoloured	1·90	65

452 Figures and City on Globe

1994. World Population Day.

1146	**452**	3d. multicoloured	50	10

453 Sandstone

1994. Minerals. Multicoloured.

1148	3d. Type **453**	55	25
1149	5d. Cipolin	90	45
1150	10d. Turitella shells in chalk	2·00	1·00

454 Brooches

1994. Saharan Silver Jewellery. Multicoloured.

1151	3d. Type **454**	65	15
1152	5d. Belt (horiz)	1·10	40
1153	12d. Bracelets (horiz)	2·75	1·00

455 Soldiers

1994. 40th Anniv of Revolution.

1154	**455**	3d. multicoloured	45	10

456 Ladybirds on Leaves

1994. Insects. Multicoloured.

1155	3d. Type **456**	50	15
1156	12d. Beetle (*Buprestidae*) on plant	1·90	75

457 Virus and Family

1994. World Anti-AIDS Campaign Day.

1157	**457**	3d. black, blue & mauve	50	10

458 Algiers

1994. Regional Dances. Multicoloured.

1158	3d. Type **458**	50	10
1159	10d. Constantine	1·30	65
1160	12d. Alaoui	1·40	75

459 Southern Algeria

1995. 20th Anniv of World Tourism Organization.

1161	**459**	3d. multicoloured	40	10

460 Honey Bee on Comb

1995. Bee-keeping. Multicoloured.

1162	3d. Type **460**	40	10
1163	13d. Bee on flower (horiz)	1·50	85

461 Dahlia

1995. Flowers. Multicoloured.

1164	3d. Type **461**	55	10
1165	10d. Zinnias	1·60	70
1166	13d. Lilac	1·80	85

462 Circular Design

1995. Stucco Work from Sedrata (4th century after Hegira).

1167	**462**	3d. brown	30	10
1168	-	4d. green	50	10
1169	-	5d. brown	55	25

DESIGNS—4d. Circular design within square; 5d. Stylized flowers.

463 Doves, Graves, Victims and Soldiers

1995. 50th Anniv of End of Second World War. Multicoloured.

1170	3d. Type **463**	40	10
MS1171	70×80 mm. 13d. National flag on dove (25×27 mm)	4·50	3·50

464 Water Pollution

1995. Environmental Protection. Multicoloured.

1172	3d. Type **464**	35	10
1173	13d. Air pollution	1·50	65

465 Players and Anniversary Emblem

1995. Centenary of Volleyball.

1174	**465**	3d. multicoloured	30	10

466 Map and Pylon

1995. Electrification.

1175	**466**	3d. multicoloured	35	10

467 Children and Schoolbag Contents

1995. National Solidarity.

1176	**467**	3d.+50c. mult	50	35

468 Doves and Anniversary Emblem

1995. 50th Anniv of U.N.O.

1177	**468**	13d. multicoloured	1·40	75

469 Pitcher from Lakhdaria

1995. Traditional Pottery.

1178	**469**	10d. brown	1·10	40
1179	-	20d. brown	2·10	65
1180	-	21d. brown	2·10	65
1181	-	30d. brown	3·00	90

DESIGNS: 20d. Water jug (Aokas); 21d. Jar (Larbaa nath Iraten); 30d. Jar (Ouadhia).

470 Common Shelduck

1995. Water Birds. Multicoloured.

1182	3d. Type **470**	55	25
1183	5d. Common snipe	90	35

471 Doves flying over Javelin Thrower and Olympic Rings

1996. Centenary of Modern Olympic Games and Olympic Games, Atlanta.

1184	**471**	20d. multicoloured	2·20	1·10

472 Fringed Bag

1996. Handicrafts. Leather Bags. Multicoloured.

1185	5d. Type **472**	1·20	50
1186	16d. Shoulder bag with handle (vert)	2·20	95

473 Pasteur Institute

1996. Centenary (1994) of Algerian Pasteur Institute.

1187	**473**	5d. multicoloured	55	20

474 Arabic Script and Computer

1996. Scientific and Technical Education Day. Multicoloured.

1188	5d. Type **474**	55	25
1189	16d. Dove, fountain pen and symbols (vert)	1·40	60
1190	23d. Pencil, pen, dividers and satellite over Earth on pages of open book (vert)	2·40	1·10

475 Iron Ore, Djebel Quenza

1996. Minerals. Multicoloured.

1191	10d. Type **475**	1·20	50
1192	20d. Gold, Tirek-Amesmessa	2·20	95

476 *Pandoriana pandora*

1996. Butterflies. Multicoloured.

1193	5d. Type **476**	65	25
1194	10d. *Coenonympha pamphilus*	1·10	50
1195	20d. Painted lady	2·30	1·10
1196	23d. Marbled white	2·50	1·30

477 Globe, Drug Addict and Drugs

1996. World Anti-drugs Day.

1197	**477**	5d. multicoloured	50	15

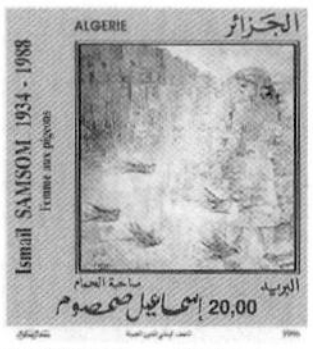

478 *Woman with Pigeons*

1996. Paintings by Ismail Samsom. Multicoloured.

1198	20d. Type **478**	1·50	80
1199	30d. *Interrogation*	2·30	1·30

479 Ambulance and Paramedic holding Child (Medical Aid)

1996. Civil Defence. Multicoloured.

1200	5d. Type **479**	50	25
1201	23d. Globe resting in cupped hands (natural disaster prevention) (vert)	1·80	85

480 Children, Syringe and Pens

1996. 50th Anniv of UNICEF Multicoloured.

1202	5d. Type **480**	40	10
1203	10d. Family holding pencil, key, syringe and flower	90	35

481 Dar Hassan Pacha

1996. Algiers Courtyards. Multicoloured.

1204	5d. Type **481**	40	15
1205	10d. Dar Kedaoudj el Amia	75	40
1206	20d. Palais des Rais	1·50	90
1207	30d. Villa Abdellatif	2·40	1·40

482 Minbar Inscription, Nedroma Mosque

1997. Mosque Carvings. Multicoloured.

1208	5d. Type **482**	40	15
1209	23d. Doors, Ketchaoua Mosque, Algiers	1·80	95

483 Outline Map, Graph and Roofs over People

1997. Fourth General Population and Housing Census.

1210	**483**	5d. multicoloured	40	10

484 Soldiers controlling Crowd with Flags

1997. 35th Anniv of Oargla Protest.

1211	**484**	5d. multicoloured	40	10

485 Doves above Crowd with Flags

1997. 35th Anniv of Victory Day.

1212	**485**	5d. multicoloured	40	10

486 *Ficaria verna*

1997. Flowers. Multicoloured.

1213	5d. Type **486**	50	20
1214	16d. Honeysuckle	1·20	70
1215	23d. Common poppy	1·80	1·00

487 "No Smoking" Sign on Map

1997. World No Smoking Day.

1216	**487**	5d. multicoloured	40	10

488 Crowd and Map

1997. Legislative Elections.

1217	**488**	5d. multicoloured	40	10

489 "Buthus occitanus"

1997. Scorpions. Multicoloured.

1218	5d. Type **489**	45	15
1219	10d. "Androctonus australis"	80	45

490 Crowd with Flags

1997. 35th Anniv of Independence. Multicoloured.

1220	5d. Type **490**	40	10
MS1221	70×80 mm. 10d. National flag behind doves and "35" between broken chain-link (25×36 mm)	1·10	85

491 Zakaria

1997. 20th Death Anniv of Moufdi Zakaria (poet).

1222	**491**	5d. multicoloured	40	10

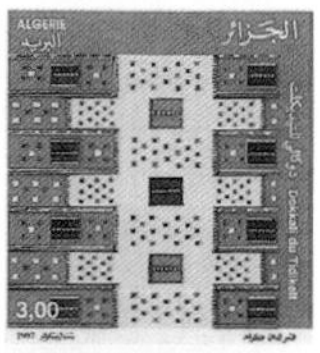

492 Dokkali Design, Tidikelt

1997. Textiles. Multicoloured.

1223	3d. Type **492**	30	10
1224	5d. Tellis design, Aures	45	25
1225	10d. Bou Taleb design, M'Sila	80	40
1226	20d. Ddil design, Ait-Hichem	1·50	85

493 Map, Emblem and Rainbow

1997. 25th Anniv of Pan-Arab Security Forces Organization.

1227	**493**	5d. multicoloured	40	15

494 Packages and Express Mail Service Emblem

1997. World Post Day.

1228	**494**	5d. multicoloured	40	15

495 Rising Sun on Map

1997. Local Elections.

1229	**495**	5d. multicoloured	40	15

496 Tenes Lighthouse

1997. Lighthouses. Multicoloured.

1230	5d. Type **496**	50	25
1231	10d. Cap Caxine, Algiers (vert)	1·00	50

497 Mail Plane and Mail Van

1997. First Anniv of Aeropostale.

1232	**497**	5d. multicoloured	50	15

498 Variable Scallop

1997. Sea Shells. Multicoloured.

1233	5d. Type **498**	55	15
1234	10d. *Bolinus brandaris*	1·00	40
1235	20d. *Hinia reticulata* (vert)	1·90	80

499 National Flag and Columned Facade

1997. Inauguration of Council of the Nation (upper parliamentary chamber).

1236	**499**	5d. multicoloured	40	15

500 Flag, Ballot Box, Constitution and People

1997. Completion of Government Reform. Multicoloured.

1237	5d. Type **500** (presidential election)	40	15
1238	5d. Constitution and torch (constitution referendum)	40	15
1239	5d. Ballot box and voting papers (elections to National Assembly (lower chamber of Parliament))	40	15
1240	5d. Flag, sun and rose (local elections)	40	15
1241	5d. Flag and Parliament (elections to National Council (upper chamber))	40	15

Nos. 1237/41 were issued together, *se-tenant*, forming a composite design.

501 Exhibition Emblem

1998. "Expo 98" World's Fair, Lisbon. Multicoloured.

1242	5d. Type **501**	40	15

MS1243	80×70 mm. 24d. Mosaic of fishes (40×31 mm) Imperf	2·00	1·80

502 Aerial Bombardment

1998. 40th Anniv of Bombing of Sakiet Sidi Youcef.

1244	**502**	5d. multicoloured	40	15

503 Archives Building

1998. National Archives.

1245	**503**	5d. multicoloured	40	15

504 Lalla Fadhma N'Soumeur

1998. International Women's Day.

1246	**504**	5d. multicoloured	35	15

505 Players and Eiffel Tower

1998. World Cup Football Championship, France.

1247	**505**	24d. multicoloured	1·90	55

506 View from Land

1998. Algiers Kasbah. Multicoloured.

1248	5d. Type **506**	40	30
1249	10d. Street	80	40
1250	24d. View from sea (horiz)	1·50	95

507 Crescent and Flag

1998. Red Crescent.

1251	**507**	5d.+1d. red, green and black	45	25

508 Battle Scene

1998. 150th Anniv of Insurrection of the Zaatcha.

1252	**508**	5d. multicoloured	40	15

509 Parent and Child and Hand holding Rose

1998. International Children's Day. National Solidarity. Multicoloured.

1253	5d.+1d. Type **509**	45	25
1254	5d.+1d. Children encircling emblem (horiz)	45	25

510 "Tourism and the Environment"

1998. Tourism. Multicoloured.

1255	5d. Type **510**	40	15
1256	10d. Young tourists and methods of transportation (horiz)	90	35
1257	24d. Taghit (horiz)	1·80	95

511 Map of North Africa and Arabia

1998. Arab Post Day.

1258	**511**	5d. multicoloured	90	10

512 Interpol and Algerian Police Force Emblems

1998. 75th Anniv of Interpol.

1259	**512**	5d. multicoloured	40	10

513 Provisional Government and State Flag

1998. 40th Anniv of Creation of Provisional Government of Algerian Republic.

1260	**513**	5d. multicoloured	40	15

514 Arrows leading from Algeria around the World

1998. National Diplomacy Day.

1261	**514**	5d. multicoloured	40	10

515 Dove and Olympic Rings

1998. 35th Anniv of Algerian Olympic Committee.

1262	**515**	5d. multicoloured	40	10

516 Osprey

1998. Birds. Multicoloured.

1263	5d. Type **516**	55	25
1264	10d. Audouin's gull	1·10	45
1265	24d. Shag (vert)	2·20	1·10
1266	30d. Common cormorant (vert)	2·75	1·40

517 Anniversary Emblem and Profiles

1998. 50th Anniv of Universal Declaration of Human Rights. Multicoloured.

1267	5d. Type **517**	55	10
1268	24d. Anniversary emblem, dove and people	2·00	90

518 Comb

1999. Spinning and Weaving Implements. Multicoloured.

1269	5d. Type **518**	50	25
1270	10d. Carding (horiz)	90	40
1271	20d. Spindle	1·90	90
1272	24d. Loom	2·20	1·00

519 Dove, Torch, Flag and Soldiers

1999. National Chahid Day.

1273	**519**	5d. multicoloured	40	15

520 Pear

1999. Fruit Trees. Multicoloured.

1274	5d. Type **520**	45	25
1275	10d. Plum	80	45
1276	24d. Orange (vert)	2·00	1·10

521 Calligraphy

1999. Presidential Election.

1277	**521**	5d. multicoloured	40	15

522 14th-century Ceramic Mosaic, Tlemcen

1999. Crafts. Multicoloured.

1278	5d. Type **522**	45	25
1279	10d. 11th-century ceramic mosaic, Kalaa des Beni Hammad	80	40
1280	20d. Cradle (horiz)	1·80	90
1281	24d. Table with raised rim (horiz)	2·00	1·00

523 Pictograms on Map of Africa and South African Flag

1999. Seventh African Games, Johannesburg. Multicoloured.

1282	5d. Type **523**	45	25
1283	10d. Pictograms of athletes and South African flag (horiz)	90	40

524 Gneiss

1999. Minerals. Multicoloured.

1284	5d. Type **524**	40	25
1285	20d. Granite	1·60	90
1286	24d. Sericite schist	2·00	1·10

525 Emblem

1999. Organization of African Unity Summit, Algiers.

1287	**525**	5d. multicoloured	40	15

526 Family and Map of Africa

1999. 40th Anniv of Organization of African Unity Convention on Refugees.

1288	**526**	5d. multicoloured	40	15

527 Emblem and Police Officers

1999. Police Day.

1289	**527**	5d. multicoloured	90	15

528 Linked Hands and "2000"

1999. International Year of Culture and Peace.

1290	**528**	5d. multicoloured	40	15

529 Dentex Seabream

1999. Fish. Multicoloured.

1291	5d. Type **529**	55	25
1292	10d. Striped red mullet	95	45
1293	20d. Pink dentex	2·00	1·00
1294	24d. White seabream	2·75	1·20

530 Rainbow

1999. Referendum.

1295	**530**	5d. multicoloured	40	15

531 Emblem and Rainbow

1999. 125th Anniv of Universal Postal Union. Multicoloured.

1296	5d. Type **531**	55	15
1297	5d. Globe, satellite and stamps	55	15

532 Woman's Face

1999. Rural Women's Day.

1298	**532**	5d. multicoloured	55	15

533 Partisans and Helicopters

1999. 45th Anniv of Revolution. Multicoloured.

1299	5d. Type **533**	55	20
1300	5d. Partisans and fires	55	20

Nos. 1299/300 were issued together, *se-tenant*, forming a composite design.

534 Chaoui

1999. Folk Dances. Multicoloured.

1301	5d. Type **534**	55	25
1302	10d. Targuie	1·00	45
1303	24d. M'zab	2·00	1·10

535 Doves

2000. New Millennium. Multicoloured. Self-adhesive.

1304	5d. Type **535** (peace)	55	40
1305	5d. Plants and tree (environment)	55	40
1306	5d. Umbrella over ears of grain (food security)	55	40
1307	5d. Wind farm (new energy sources)	55	40
1308	5d. Globe and ballot box (democracy)	55	40
1309	5d. Microscope (health)	55	40
1310	5d. Cargo ship at quayside (commerce)	55	40
1311	5d. Space satellite, dish aerial, jet plane and train (communications)	55	40
1312	5d. Astronaut and lunar buggy on Moon (space)	55	40
1313	5d. Film cave paintings, mandolin and music notes (culture)	55	40
1314	5d. Outline of dove (peace)	55	40
1315	5d. Hand above flora and fauna (environment)	55	40
1316	5d. Space satellites, computer and printed circuits forming maps of Europe and Africa (communications)	55	40
1317	5d. Sun, clouds, flame and water (new energy sources)	55	40
1318	5d. Hand holding seedling (food security)	55	40
1319	5d. Staff of Aesculapius and heart (health)	55	40
1320	5d. Arrows around globe (communication)	55	40
1321	5d. Cave paintings, book, painting and violin (culture)	55	40
1322	5d. Parthenon and envelopes (democracy)	55	40
1323	5d. Space satellite, solar system, space shuttle and astronaut (space)	55	40

536 Chaffinches

2000. Birds. Multicoloured.

1324	5d. Type **536**	50	35
1325	5d. Northern serin (horiz)	50	35
1326	10d. Northern bullfinch (horiz)	95	60
1327	24d. Eurasian goldfinch	2·50	1·40

537 Emblem

2000. "EXPO 2000" World's Fair, Hanover.

1328	**537**	5d. multicoloured	50	30

538 Sydney Opera House and Sports Pictograms

2000. Olympic Games, Sydney.

1329	**538**	24d. multicoloured	2·20	85

539 Emblem

2000. Telethon 2000 (fundraising event).

1330	**539**	5d. multicoloured	50	25

540 Crowd, Linked Hands and White Doves

2000. "Concorde Civile". Multicoloured.

1331	5d. Type **540**	50	15
1332	10d. Hands releasing doves (horiz)	95	40
1333	20d. Flag, doves and hands forming heart (horiz)	1·90	80
1334	24d. Doves and clasped hands above flowers	2·20	1·00

541 Building

2000. National Library.

1335	**541**	5d. multicoloured	50	20

542 Hand holding Blood Droplet

2000. Blood Donation Campaign.

1336	**542**	5d. multicoloured	50	25

543 Lock

2000. Touareg Cultural Heritage. Multicoloured.

1337	5d. Type **543**	50	40
1338	10d. Lock (vert)	95	40

544 Mohamed Racim (artist)

2000. Personalities. Multicoloured.

1339	10d. Type **544**	95	40
1340	10d. Mohammed Dib (writer)	95	40
1341	10d. Mustapha Kateb (theatre director)	95	40
1342	10d. Ali Maachi (musician)	95	40

545 Cock-chafer

2000. Insects. Multicoloured.

1343	5d. Type **545**	50	30
1344	5d. Carpet beetle	50	30
1345	10d. Drugstore beetle	95	55
1346	24d. Carabus	2·50	1·20

546 Jug

2000. Roman Artefacts, Tipasa. Multicoloured.

1347	5d. Type **546**	50	25
1348	10d. Vase	95	50
1349	24d. Jug	2·40	1·10

547 *Limodorum abortivum*

2000. Orchids. Multicoloured.

1350	5d. Type **547**	50	25
1351	10d. *Orchis papilionacea*	95	50
1352	24d. *Orchis provincialis*	2·40	1·10

548 Greylag Goose (*Anser anser*)

2001. Waterfowl. Multicoloured.

1353	5d. Type **548**	50	25
1354	5d. Avocet (*Recurvirostra avosetta*) (vert)	50	25
1355	10d. Eurasian bittern (*Botaurus stellaris*) (vert)	95	55

1356 24d. Western curlew (*Numenius arquata*) 2·50 1·10

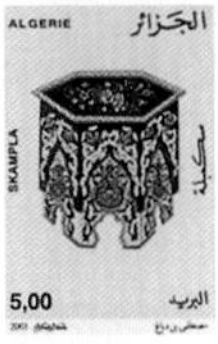
549 Painted Table

2001. Traditional Crafts. Multicoloured.
1357 5d. Type **549** 50 25
1358 10d. Decorated shelf (horiz) 95 60
1359 24d. Ornate mirror 2·40 95

550 Forest, Belezma National Park, Batna

2001. National Parks. Multicoloured.
1360 5d. Type **550** 50 25
1361 10d. Headland, Gouraya National Park, Bejaia (horiz) 95 45
1362 20d. Forest and mountains, Theneit el Had National Park, Tissemsilt (horiz) 1·90 80
1363 24d. El Tarf National Park 2·40 1·00

551 St. Augustine as Child (statue)

2001. St. Augustine of Hippo Conference, Algiers and Annaba. Multicoloured.
1364 5d. Type **551** 50 25
1365 24d. 4th-century Christian mosaic (43×31 mm) 2·40 1·10

552 Obverse and Reverse of Ryal Boudjou, 1830

2001. Coins. Multicoloured.
1366 5d. Type **552** 50 25
1367 10d. Obverse and reverse of Double Boudjou, 1826 95 45
1368 24d. Obverse and reverse of Ryal Drahem, 1771 2·40 1·00

553 Emblem and Scouts

2001. National Scouts' Day.
1369 **553** 5d. multicoloured 50 30

554 Child throwing Stones

2001. Intifida.
1370 **554** 5d. multicoloured 50 15

555 Asthma Sufferer

2001. National Asthma Day.
1371 **556** 5d. multicoloured 45 15

556 Hopscotch

2001. Children's Games. Multicoloured.
1372 5d. Type **556** 50 15
1373 5d. Jacks 50 15
1374 5d. Spinning top 50 15
1375 5d. Marbles 50 15

557 Runners

2001. 50th Anniv of Mediterranean Games. Multicoloured.
1376 5d. Type **557** 45 15
1377 5d. Race winners and tile decoration 45 15

558 Emblem

2001. 15th World Festival of Youth and Students, Algiers.
1378 **558** 5d. multicoloured 45 15

559 Burning Lorry

2001. Freedom Fighters' Day.
1379 **559** 5d. multicoloured 45 15

560 Tree of Pencils

2001. Teacher's Day.
1380 **560** 5d. multicoloured 45 15

561 Children encircling Globe

2001. United Nations Year of Dialogue among Civilisations.
1381 **561** 5d. multicoloured 45 15

562 Dove and Explosion

2001. National Immigration Day. 40th Anniv of Demonstrations in Paris.
1382 **562** 5d. multicoloured 45 20

563 El Mokrani

2001. Resistance Fighters. Multicoloured.
1383 5d. Type **563** 45 20
1384 5d. Cheikh Bouamama 45 20

564 Bab el Oued (flood damaged town)

2001. Flood Victims Relief Fund.
1385 **564** 5d.+5d. multicoloured 90 40

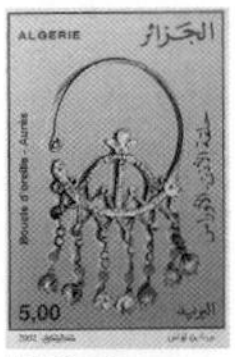
565 Earring

2002. Silver Jewellery from Aures Region. Multicoloured.
1386 5d. Type **565** 45 25
1387 5d. Fibula 45 25
1388 24d. Pendant 1·60 1·10

566 Ball, Net and Goalkeeper

2002. World Cup Football Championship, Japan and South Korea. Multicoloured.
1389 5d. Type **566** 45 25
1390 24d. Monk holding football (vert) 1·80 1·60

567 Flag, Doves and Soldiers

2002. 40th Anniv of Victory Day.
1391 **567** 5d. multicoloured 45 30

568 Ksar Sidi Ouali Tamentit, Touat

2002. Fortified Castles. Multicoloured.
1392 5d. Type **568** 45 30
1393 5d. Ksar Ighzar, Gourara 45 30

569 Basket, Ball and Players

2002. World Basketball Championship, Indianapolis, U.S.A.
1394 **569** 5d. multicoloured 45 10

570 Child and Table

2002. Children's Day. Multicoloured.
1395 5d. Type **570** 45 10
1396 5d. Two girls 45 10

571 Book Illustration

2002. 14th Death Anniv of Mohamed Temmam (artist and musician). Multicoloured.
1397 10d. Type **571** 90 40
1398 10d. Self-portrait 90 40

572 Anniversary Emblem

2002. 40th Anniv of Independence. Multicoloured.
1399 5d. Type **572** 45 10
1400 24d. Flags and crowd 1·30 1·00

573 Calcite

2002. Minerals. Multicoloured.
1401 5d. Type **573** 30 10
1402 5d. Feldspar 30 10
1403 5d. Galena (horiz) 30 10
1404 5d. Conglomerate (pudding stone) (horiz) 30 10

574 Cherchell

2002. Lighthouses. Multicoloured.
1405 5d. Type **574** 30 10
1406 10d. Cap de Fer 60 40
1407 24d. Rachgoun island 1·50 1·00

575 Postal Emblem

2002. Re-organization of Algerian Posts.
1408 **575** 5d. multicoloured 30 10

576 Small Jug

2002. Pots. Multicoloured.

1409	5d. Type **576**	30	10
1410	5d. Pot for cooking cous-cous	30	10
1411	5d. Two-handled jar	30	10
1412	5d. Oil lamp	30	10

577 Dove and Rainbow

2002. International Day of Tolerance.

1413	**577** 24d. multicoloured	1·50	1·00

578 *Venus verrucosa*

2002. Shells. Multicoloured.

1414	5d. Type **578**	30	10
1415	5d. *Acanthocardia aculeate*	30	10
1416	5d. *Xenophora crispa*	30	10
1417	5d. *Epitonium commune*	30	10

579 *Eucalyptus globules*

2002. Medicinal Plants. Multicoloured.

1418	5d. Type **579**	30	10
1419	10d. Mallow (*Malva sylvestris*)	60	40
1420	24d. Laurel (*Laurus nobilis*)	1·50	1·00

580 Eiffel Tower, Paris and Martyr's Monument, Algiers

2003. Djazair 2003, Year of Algeria in France. Multicoloured.

1421	5d. Type **580**	30	15
1422	24d. French and Algerian flags (horiz)	1·50	1·00

581 Emblem

2003. Tenth Arab Games.

1423	**581** 5d. multicoloured	30	10

582 El Maadjen, Relizane (oasis)

2003. International Year of Freshwater. Multicoloured.

1424	5d. Type **582**	30	10
1425	10d. Traditional well, M'zab valley	60	40
1426	24d. Kesria (irrigation), Timimoun	1·50	1·00

583 Slave Sale Contract (5 June 494)

2003. Vandal Carved Tablets. Multicoloured.

1427	10d. Type **583**	60	40
1428	24d. Mathematical chart (5 April 493) (vert)	1·50	1·00

584 Building Facade, Face and Books

2003. Student's Day.

1429	**584** 5d. multicoloured	30	10

585 *Rumina decollate*

2003. Snails. Multicoloured.

1430	5d. Type **585**	30	10
1431	24d. *Helix aspera*	1·50	1·00

586 Candle, Map of Africa and Members' Flags

2003. First Anniv of African Union.

1432	**586** 5d. multicoloured	30	10

587 *Ulva lactuca*

2003. Seaweeds. Multicoloured.

1433	5d. Type **587**	30	10
1434	24d. *Gymnogongrus crenulatus*	1·50	1·00

588 Ploughing with Oxen

2003. Roman Mosaics. Multicoloured.

1435	5d. Type **588**	30	10
1436	10d. Ulysses and the Sirens	60	40
1437	24d. Hunting scene	1·50	1·00

589 Maouche Mohand Amokrane (founder) and Emblem

2003. 40th Anniv of Algerian Olympic Committee.

1438	**589** 5d. multicoloured	30	10

590 Heart, Hand, Foot and Eye

2003. World Diabetes Awareness Day.

1439	**590** 5d. multicoloured	30	10

591 Ruins

2003. Support for Earthquake Victims (21 May 2003).

1440	**591** 5d.+5d. multicoloured	60	40

592 Doors

2003. Decorative Art. Multicoloured.

1441	5d. Type **592**	30	15
1442	10d. Window	60	40
1443	24d. Ceiling	1·50	1·00

593 Flags

2003. 45th Anniv of Algeria—China Diplomatic Relations.

1444	**593** 5d. multicoloured	30	10

594 Hurdler

2004. Olympic Games, Athens. Multicoloured.

1445	5d. Type **594**	30	10
1446	10d. Parthenon and hand holding Olympic torch	60	40

595 Woman with Raised Arms

2004. Women's Day.

1447	**595** 5d. multicoloured	30	10

596 Juba I

2004. Numidian Kings. Each brown, bronze and black.

1448	5d. Type **596**	30	10
1449	5d. Juba II	30	10
1450	5d. Micipsa	30	10
1451	5d. Massinassa	30	10
1452	5d. Jugurtha	30	10

597 Olive Tree

2004. Tree Day. Multicoloured.

1453	5d. Type **597**	30	10
1454	10d. Date palm (vert)	60	40

598 Entrance to Presidential Palace

2004. Presidential Elections.

1455	**598** 24d. multicoloured	1·50	1·00

599 Player catching Ball

2004. Centenary of FIFA (Federation Internationale de Football Association). Multicoloured.

1456	5d. Type **599**	30	10
1457	24d. Anniversary emblem	1·50	1·00

600 Dromedary

2004

1458	**600** 24d. multicoloured	1·50	1·00

601 Giving and Receiving Blood

2004. International Blood Donation Day.

1459	**601** 5d. vermilion and black	30	10

602 Tradesmen

2004. Acquiring a Trade.

1460	**602** 5d. multicoloured	30	10

603 Chess Pieces and Board

2004. 80th Anniv of World Chess Federation (FIDE).

1461	**603** 5d. multicoloured	30	10

604 Emblems and Currency

2004. 40th Anniv of CNEP Bank. Multicoloured.

1462	5d. Type **604**	30	10
1463	24d. Harbour	1·50	1·00

605 Yellow Rose

2004. Roses. Multicoloured.

1464	15d. Type **605**	1·30	65
1465	20d. Yellow rose (different)	1·40	85
1466	30d. Orange rose	1·80	1·30
1467	50d. Pink rose	2·75	2·10

606 Map and Flags

2004. Sixth Pan African Conference, Algiers.

1470	**606**	24d. multicoloured	1·50	1·00

607 In Tehaq Rock Formation

2004. Tourism. Sahara. Multicoloured.

1471	5d. Type **607**	30	15
1472	24d. Ekanassay (vert)	1·50	1·00

608 TeleFood Emblem, Houses and Flowers

2004. World Food Day. TeleFood (UN food agency). Multicoloured.

1473	5d.+1d. Type **608**	35	25
1474	5d.+1d. House and fruit trees	35	25

609 Group of Six

2004. 50th Anniv of Revolution. Multicoloured.

1475	15d. Type **609**	1·30	65
MS1476	70×80 mm. 30d. Emblem (30×40 mm)	1·80	1·80

610 Satellite and Earth

2004. Second Anniv of Launch of D'ALSAT 1 Satellite.

1477	**610**	30d. multicoloured	1·80	1·30

611 Rainbow and Plants

2004. Protection of the Environment.

1478	**611**	15d. multicoloured	1·10	60

612 Rabah Bitat

2004. Fourth Death Anniv of Rabah Bitat (politician).

1479	**612**	15d. multicoloured	1·10	60

613 Wood Pigeon (*Columba palumbus*)

2005. Pigeons. Multicoloured.

1480	10d. Type **613**	60	35
1481	15d. Rock dove (*Columba livia*)	1·10	60

614 *Echium australis*

2005. Flowers. Multicoloured.

1482	15d. Type **614**	1·30	65
1483	30d. *Borago officinalis*	1·80	1·30

615 Eye and Hands

2005. National Day for the Disabled.

1484	**615**	15d. multicoloured	1·10	60

616 Emblem

2005. Arab League Summit, Algeria (1485). 60th Anniv of Arab League (1486). Multicoloured.

1485	15d. Type **616**	1·10	60
1486	30d. Emblem and "2005–1945" (vert)	1·80	1·30

617 Medersa D'Alger

2005. Medersa (seats of learning). Multicoloured.

1487	10d. Type **617**	60	35
1488	15d. Medersa de Constantine	1·10	60
1489	30d. Medersa de Tlemcen	1·80	1·30

618 Emblem

2005. World Intellectual Property Day.

1490	**618**	15d. multicoloured	1·10	60

619 Workers and Hand holding Apple

2005. World Day for Safety and Health at Work.

1491	**619**	15d. multicoloured	1·10	60

620 "60" and Dove

2005. 60th Anniv of Massacre.

1492	**620**	15d. multicoloured	1·10	60

621 Medal and Stylized Sports

2005. 15th Mediterranean Games, Almeria. Multicoloured.

1493	15d. Type **621**	1·10	60
1494	30d. Emblem (horiz)	1·80	1·30

622 Lakhdar Ben Khlouf

2005. Poets. Multicoloured.

1495	10d. Type **622**	60	35
1496	15d. Ben M'sayeb	1·10	60
1497	20d. Si Mohand Ou M'Hand	1·40	85
1498	30d. Aissa El Djermouni	1·80	1·30

623 Children

2005. International Day against Drug Abuse.

1499	**623**	15d. multicoloured	1·10	60

624 Student and Soldiers

2005. 50th Anniv of UGEMA (General Union of the Algerian Moslem Students).

1500	**624**	15d. multicoloured	1·10	60

625 Cheetah

2005. Cheetah (inscr "Guepard"). Multicoloured.

1501	15d. Type **625**	1·10	60
1502	30d. Standing	1·80	1·30

626 Emblem

2005. World Information Society Summit, Tunis.

1503	**626**	15d. multicoloured	1·10	60

627 "50" and Soldiers

2005. 50th Anniv of Uprising.

1504	**627**	15d. multicoloured	1·10	60

628 Phare Fort

2005. Forts. Multicoloured.

1505	10d. Type **628**	60	35
1506	15d. Cap Matifou	1·10	60
1507	30d. Santa Cruz	1·80	1·30

629 Emblem and Runners

2005. International Year of Sports Education.

1508	**629**	30d. multicoloured	1·80	1·30

630 Clasped Hands

2005. National Reconciliation.

1509	**630**	15d. multicoloured	1·10	60

631 Flag

2005. Referendum.

1510	**631**	15d. multicoloured	1·10	60

632 Flag, Emblem and Buildings

2005. Recovery of National Sovereignty.

1511	**632**	30d. multicoloured	1·80	1·30

633 Saddle

2005. Emir Abdelkader's Possessions. Multicoloured.

1512	15d. Type **633**	1·10	60
1513	30d. Boots	1·80	1·30
1514	40d. Jacket (vert)	2·40	1·70
1515	50d. Seal (vert)	2·75	2·10

634 Miguel de Cervantes

2005. Miguel de Cervantes Saavedra (writer) Commemoration.

1516	**634**	30d. multicoloured	1·80	1·30

635 Amputee

2005. Anti-Personnel Mine Destruction Campaign.

1517	**635**	30d. multicoloured	1·80	1·30

636 Emblem

2005. International AIDS Awareness Day.

1518	**636**	30d. multicoloured	1·80	1·30

637 Ptolemy

2005. Kings. Multicoloured.

1519	15d. Type **637**	1·10	60
1520	30d. Syphax	1·80	1·30

638 Building Facade

2006. Posts.

1521	**638**	30d. multicoloured	1·80	1·30

639 *Ciconia ciconia*

2006. Waterside Birds. Multicoloured.

1522	10d. Type **639**	60	35
1523	15d. *Ciconia nigra*	1·10	60
1524	20d. *Platalea leucorodia*	1·40	85
1525	30d. *Grus grus*	1·80	1·30

640 Skier

2006. Winter Olympic Games, Turin.

1526	**640**	15d. multicoloured	1·10	60

641 Aissat Idir (founder)

2006. 50th Anniv of UGTA Trade Union.

1527	**641**	15d. multicoloured	1·10	60

642 Ball and Globe

2006. World Cup Football Championship, Germany.

1528	**642**	30d. multicoloured	1·80	1·30

643 Airport

2006. New Air Terminal, Algiers.

1529	**643**	30d. multicoloured	1·80	1·30

645 Students

2006. 50th Anniv of Student's Day.

1532	**645**	20d. multicoloured	1·40	85

646 Trees

2006. International Environment Day.

1533	**646**	30d. multicoloured	1·80	1·30

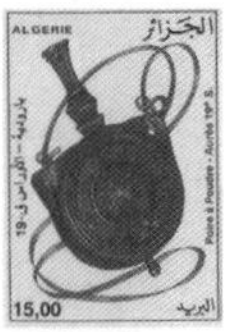
647 Powder Holder

2006. Poire a Poudre (powder holders). Multicoloured.

1534	15d. Type **647**	1·10	60
1535	20d. Powder holder (different)	1·40	85

648 Map

2006. 50th Anniv of La Soummam Congress.

1536	**648**	20d. multicoloured	1·40	85

649 Emblem

2006. 16th Arab School Games.

1537	**649**	30d. multicoloured	1·80	1·30

649a Hand holding Pencils

2006. Teacher's Day

1537a	**649a**	20d. multicoloured	1·40	85

649b Inscr "Pistachier de l'Atlas"

2006. Fruiting Trees. Multicoloured.

1537b	20d. Type **649b**	1·40	85
1537c	30d. Inscr "Grenadier"	1·80	1·30

649c Globe

2006. Sino-African Forum Summit, Beijing

1537d	**649c**	30d. multicoloured	1·80	1·30

650 Dunes and Oasis

2006. International Year of Deserts and Desertification.. Multicoloured.

1538	**650**	15d. multicoloured	1·10	60
1538a		15d. Ain Hammou-Tinerkouk-Adar	1·10	60

650a Map and building

2006. First Anniv of Arab Transient Parliament.

1538b	**650a**	15d. multicoloured	1·10	60

650b Early Edition

2006. 50th Anniv of El-Moudjohid (journal).

1538c	**650b**	30d. multicoloured	1·80	1·30

650c Desalination Plant

2006. Desalination Plant

1538d	**650c**	20d. multicoloured	1·40	85

651 Traditional Designs

2007. Algiers-Arab Cultural Capital-2007. Multicoloured.

1539	15d. Type **651**	1·10	60
1540	30d. "2007"	1·80	1·30

652 L'ilot d'Arzew

2007. Lighthouses. Multicoloured.

1541	15d. Type **652**	1·10	60
1542	20d. Cap Sigli	1·40	85
1543	38d. Ras-Afia	2·20	1·50

653 Women

2007. Development of Women's Employment.

1544	**653**	15d. multicoloured	1·10	60

653a Mohamed Ameziane Belhaddad

2007. Mohamed Ameziane Belhaddad Commemoration.

1545	**653a**	15d. multicoloured	1·10	60

654 Ksar de Kenadsa

2007. Cultural Heritage. Multicoloured.

1546	15d. Type **654**	1·10	60
1547	15d. Ksar de Temacine (vert)	1·10	60

655 Emblem, Map and 'JEUX AFRO-ASIATIQUES D'ALGER'

2007. Sport Events in Algiers. Multicoloured.

1548	15d. Type **655**	1·10	60
1549	15d. Emblem, map and 'ALL AFRICAN GAMES' (vert)	1·10	60

656 Count Landon's Garden, Biskra

2007. Gardens. Multicoloured.

1550	15d. Type **656**	1·10	60
1551	20d. Ibn Badis garden, Oran	1·40	85
1552	38d. Jardin d' Essai du Hamma, Algiers	2·20	1·50

657 Theatre de Setif

2007. Theatres. Multicoloured.

1553	15d. Type **657**	1·10	60
1554	15d. Theatre d'Oranen, Oran	1·10	60
1555	20d. Theatre de Annaba (*horiz*)	1·40	85
1555a	38d. Theatre d'Algers	2·20	1·50

658 Demonstrators

2007. 45th Anniv of Festival of Independence and Youth. Multicoloured.

1556	15d. Type **658**	1·10	60
MS1557	60×77 mm. 20d. Satellite, computer and inkwell. Imperf	1·40	1·40

659 Bottle

2007. Ceramics. Multicoloured.

1558	15d. Type **659**	1·10	60
1559	15d. Two handled jug	1·10	60
1560	20d. Censer	1·40	85
1561	38d. Oil lamp (horiz)	2·20	1·50

660 Emblem

2007. 45th Anniv of National Police. Multicoloured.

1562	15d. Type **660**	1·10	60
1563	38d. Policeman and patrol vehicle	2·20	1·50

661 Hyena

2007. Endangered Species. Multicoloured.

1564	15d. Type **661**	1·10	60
1565	38d. White-tailed red fox	2·20	1·50

662 Encyclopaedia of Algerian Postage Stamps

2007

1566	**662**	15d. multicoloured	1·10	60

663 Ahmed Bey

2007. Ahmed Bey (resistance fighter) Commemoration.

1567	**663**	15d. multicoloured	1·10	60

664 Emblem

2007. National Artisans' Day.

1568	**664**	15d. multicoloured	1·10	60

665 Nile Tilapia

2007. Nile Tilapia (Oreochromis niloticus).

1569	**665**	15d. multicoloured	1·10	60

666 Abd el-kader

2007. Birth Bicentenary of Abd al-Qadir al-Jaza'iri (Abd el-kader) (Islamic scholar, Sufi, political and military leader). Sheet 158×108 mm containing T **666** and similar vert designs.

MS1570 15d. Type **666**; 15d. Facing left; 38d. Wearing medals and belt 3·25 3·25

667 Emblem

2008. Census.

1571	**667**	15d. multicoloured	1·10	60

668 Doves and Emblem

2008. 50th Anniv of Bombing of Sakiet Sid Youcef, Tunisia.

1572	**668**	15d. multicoloured	1·10	60

A stamp of a similar design was issued by Tunisia.

669 Ain de la Grande Rue

2008. Fountains. Sheet 110×90 mm containing T **669** and similar vert designs. Multicoloured.

MS1573 10d. Type **669**; 15d. Ain Bir Djebbah; 20d. Ain Sidi Abdellah; 38d. Ain bir Chebana 5·00 5·00

670 Issakarassen Wetland, Tamanrasset

2008. Zaragoza 2008 International Water and Sustainable Development Exhibition. Sheet 110×90 mm containing T **670** and similar vert designs. Multicoloured.

MS1574 10d. Type **670**; 15d. Reghaia wetland; 20d. Guerbes wetland, Skikda; 38d. Emblem 2·75 2·75

671 '50'

2008. 50th Anniv of National Liberation Front Football Team. Sheet 158×108 mm.

MS1575 **671** 38d. multicoloured 2·30 2·30

672 Redha Houhou

2008. Writers. Multicoloured (background colour given).

1576	15d. Type **672** (green)	95	50
1577	15d. Abdelhamid Benhadouga (magenta)	95	50
1578	15d. Malek Bennabi (brown)	95	50
1579	15d. Kateb Yacine (blue)	95	50

It has been reported that No. 1577 (Abdelhamid Benhadouga) has been withdrawn by Algeria Posts due to a design error.

672a Fencing

2008. Olympic Games, Beijing. Multicoloured.

1580	15d. Type **672a**	95	50
1581	15d. Wrestling	95	50

673 Boy with Balloons

2008. Children and New Technologies.

1582	**673**	15d. multicoloured	95	50

674 *Self Portrait*

2008. Art from National Museums. 10th Death Anniv of Baya Mahieddine (artist). Sheet 88×80 mm containing T **674** and similar horiz design. Multicoloured.

MS1583 15d. Type **674**; 38d. *Femme et oiseau en cage* 3·25 3·25

675 Gare d'Alger

2008. Stations. Multicoloured.

1584	10d. Type **675**	60	35
1585	15d. Gare de Constantine	95	50
1586	20d. Gare d'Oran	1·25	65
1587	38d. Gare de Skikda	2·30	2·10

676 Ferhat Abbas

2008. Ferhat Abbas (political leader) Commemoration.

1588	**676**	15d. multicoloured	95	50

677 Script

2008. National Anthem.

1589	**677**	15d. multicoloured	95	50

678 Emblem

2008. Government Postage Stamp Printers' Association Conference.

1590	**678**	15d. multicoloured	95	50

679 Arms

2008. National Army.

1591	**679**	15d. multicoloured	95	50

680 Pont de Sidi M'Cid, Constantine

2008. Bridges. Sheet 110×88 mm containing T **680** and similar horiz designs. Multicoloured.

MS1592 10d. Type **680**; 15d. Pont de Sidi Rached; 20d. Pont d'El Knatara; 38d. Pont de la Medersa 5·00 5·00

681 Tebessa

2008. Towns. Multicoloured.

1593	10d. Type **681**	60	35
1594	15d. Saida	95	50
1595	20d. Miliana	1·25	65
1596	38d. Biskra	2·30	2·10

682 Globe and Flags

2008. 50th Anniv of Algeria–China Diplomatic Relations.

1597	**682**	15d. multicoloured	95	50

683 Emblem

2008. 60th Anniv of Anniv of Declaration of Human Rights.

1598	**683**	15d. multicoloured	95	50

684 Louis Braille and Alphabets

2009. Birth Bicentenary of Louis Braille (inventor of Braille writing for the blind).

1599	**684**	15d. multicoloured	95	50

685 Abderrahmene's Mausoleum, Algers

2009. Islamic Heritage. Mausoleums. Multicoloured.

1600	15d. Type **685**	95	50
1601	20d. Ibrahim El Atteuf, Mausoleum (horiz)	1·25	65

686 Figures

2009. National Day of Disabled Persons. Multicoloured.

1602	15d. Type **686**	95	50
1603	20d. Emblems	1·25	65

687 Polar Map and Hands enclosing Snowflake

2009. Preserve Polar Regions and Glaciers.

1604	**687**	38d. multicoloured	2·30	1·10

688 Emblem

2009. Presidential Elections.

1605	**688**	15d. multicoloured	95	50

689 Wooden Shoes

2009. Museum Exhibits. Multicoloured.

1606	15d. Type **689**	95	50
1607	20d. Silver brooch fragment	1·20	65
1608	30d. 19th-century waistcoat	1·90	1·00

690 Students and University Building

2009. Centenary of Universite d'Alger (university).

1609	**690**	15d. multicoloured	95	50

691 Silver Fibulae

2009. Jewellery.

1610	1d. dull green	10	10
1611	5d. pale brown-purple	30	20
1612	9d. bright reddish violet	50·00	30·00
1613	10d. olive-sepia	60	35

DESIGNS: 1d. Type **691**; 5d. Collar with amulets; 9d. Pectoral ornament; 10d. Circular brooch.

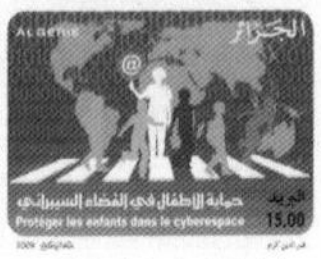

692 Digital Code, World Map and Children on Crossing

2009. Protection for Children using the Internet.

1614	**692**	15d. multicoloured	95	50

693 Windsurfing

2009. Mediterranean Games. Multicoloured.

1615	15d. Type **693**	95	50
1616	20d. Show jumping (horiz)	1·20	65

694 Madaure

2009. Roman Sites and Monuments. Multicoloured.

1617	15d. Type **694**	95	50
1618	20d. Khemissa	1·20	65
1619	30d. Theatre, Guelma	1·90	1·00

695 Symbols of Culture

2009. Pan African Cultural Festival, Algiers. Multicoloured.

1620	15d. Type **695**	95	50
1621	20d. Map of Africa as design	1·20	65

696 Symbols of Youth Development

2009. Algerian Youth. Multicoloured.

1622	15d. Type **696**	95	50
1623	20d. Heart, national flag and dove	1·20	65

697 '40'

2009. 40th Anniv of SONELGAZ.

1624	**697**	15d. multicoloured	95	50

698 Hand and Upturned Car

2009. Road Safety Campaign.

1625	**698**	15d. multicoloured	95	50

699 Bouharoun Fishing Port

2009. Fishing Ports. Multicoloured.

1626	15d. Type **699**	95	50
1627	20d. Beni Saf	1·20	65
1628	30d. Stora	1·90	1·00

700 Assistance

2009. Protection for the Elderly.

1629	**700**	15d. multicoloured	95	50

701 Symbols of Armed Forces

2009. National Army.

1630	**701**	15d. multicoloured	90	50

702 Women picking Olives

2009. Olive Cultivation. Multicoloured.

1631	15d. Type **702**	95	50
1632	20d. Pressing olives (vert)	1·20	65

703 *La fée colombe*

2009. Popular Tales. Multicoloured.

1633	15d. Type **703**	95	50
1634	15d. *La rose rouge*	95	50
1635	15d. *Loundja la fille de l'ogre*	95	50
1636	15d. *Badra*	95	50

704 *Aquila chrysaetos* (golden eagle)

2010. Raptors. Multicoloured.

1637	15d. Type **704**	95	50
1638	20d. *Falco biarmicus* (Lanner falcon) (vert)	1·20	65
1639	30d. *Falco peregrinus* (peregrine falcon) (vert)	1·90	1·00

705 Victim, Blast Fallout and Radiation

2010. Victims of Nuclear Testing.

1640	**705**	15d. multicoloured	95	50

706 Fort de l'Empereur (Bordj Moulay Hassan), Alger

2010. Forts. Multicoloured.

1641	15d. Type **706**	95	50
1642	20d. Fort Gouraya, Bejaia	1·20	65

707 Family and Emblem

2010. Expo 2010, Shanghai. Multicoloured.

1643	15d. Type **707**	95	50
1644	38d. China pavillion	2·30	1·10

708 Refinery and Conference Emblem

2010. International Conference on Natural Liquid Gas. Multicoloured.

1645	15d. Type **708**	95	50
1646	20d. Hill fort, coast line and conference emblem (horiz)	1·20	65

709 Jules Rimet Trophy and Flags

2010. World Cup Football Championships, South Africa. Multicoloured.

1647	15d. Type **709**	95	50
1648	15d. Algerian player and home crowd	95	50
MS1649	108×88 mm. 15d. ×2 Desert fox as footballer; Player and colours	1·90	1·90

710 Martyrs

2010. 65th Anniv of May 8th Massacre

1650	**710**	15d. multicoloured	95	50

711 Singers

2010. L'Ahellil du Gourara

1651	**711**	15d. multicoloured	95	50

712 Shrine

2010. Martyrs Shrine

1652	**712**	(-) multicoloured	95	50

713 Hands, Dove and Map

2010. Year of Peace and Security in Africa

1653	**713**	15d. multicoloured	95	50

714 Caves of Gor Beni-Add

2010. Caves and Grottoes. Multicoloured.

1654	15d. Type **714**	95	50
1655	15d. Ziama Mansouriah-Jijel Grotto	95	50

715 Anniversary Emblem

2010. 50th Anniv of Organization of Petroleum Exporting Countries. Multicoloured.

1656	15d. Type **715**	95	50
1657	38d. Emblem and oil tanker	2·30	1·10

716 El Hanafi-Blida Mosque

2010. Mosques. Multicoloured.

1658	15d. Type **716**	95	50
1659	20d. Ali Dib-Skida	1·20	65
1660	30d. Nedroma Gran Mosque	1·90	1·00

717 Dates (inscr 'Degla Beida')

2010. Dates. Multicoloured.

1661	15d. Type **717**	95	50
1662	15d. Inscr 'Akerbuch'	95	50
1663	15d. Inscr 'Deglet Noir' (vert)	95	50
1664	15d. Inscr 'Ghars' (vert)	95	50

718 Ceramic Candlestick

2010. Traditional Crafts. Multicoloured.

1665	15d. Type **718**	95	50
1666	20d. Quanoun (musical instrument)	1·20	65
1667	30d. Tuareg leather chest (horiz)	2·30	1·10

719 Ears of Corn

2010. Cereal

1668	**719**	1d. light green	20	15
1669	**719**	2d. blue	35	25

720 Cork Oak Tree

2011. International Year of Forests. Multicoloured.

1670	15d. Type **720**	95	50
1671	20d. Carob	1·20	65
1672	30d. Soapnut	2·30	1·10
1673	38d. Argan	2·30	1·10

721 Minaret of Mansourah Ruins, Tlemcen

2011. Tlemcen, Capital of Islamic Culture, 2011. Multicoloured.

1674	15d. Type **721**	1·10	60
1675	20d. Open work pendant	1·40	75

722 Horned Viper (inscr 'VIPERE A CORNES')

2011. Reptiles. Multicoloured.

1676	15d. Type **722**	1·10	60
1677	15d. Awl-headed snake (inscr 'COULEUVRE A DIADEME')	1·10	60

723 Symbols of Census

2011. First Algerian Economic Census

1678	**723**	15d. multicoloured	1·10	60

724 18th-century Couscous Dish

2011. Cultural Heritage. Culinary Utensils. Multicoloured.

1679	15d. Type **724**	1·10	60
1680	30d. 18th-century copper-plated butter dish	2·40	2·30

725 Computer Users and Satellite Dish

2011. Telecentres

1681	**725**	15d. multicoloured	1·10	60

726 AIDS Ribbon and Building

2011. 30th Anniv of Discovery of AIDS

1682	**726**	15d. multicoloured	1·10	60

727 Benyoucef Benkhadda

2011. Benyoucef Benkhadda (pharmacist, politician and Minister of Social Affairs and Chairman of the Provisional Government of the Algerian Republic (GPRA), August 1961-July 1962) Commemoration

1683	**727**	15d. multicoloured	1·10	60

728 Fez and Monument of Martyrs (Maquam E' chahid) in Algiers

2011. International Comics Festival of Algiers (Festival International de la Bande Dessinée d'Alger, FIBDA). Multicoloured.

1684	15d. Type **728**	1·10	60
1685	15d. M'Quidèch	1·10	60

729 Oran Post Office

2011. Stamp Day. Post Offices. Multicoloured.

1686	15d. Type **729**	1·10	60
1687	15d. Constantine	1·10	60

No. 1688 and Type **730** are left for Day of Immigration, issued on 17 October 2011, not yet received.

731 Anniversary Emblem

2011. 50th Anniv of Algeria Press Service Agency

1689	**731**	15d. multicoloured	1·10	60

732 Museum Façade

2011. Central Army Museum

1690	**732**	15d. multicoloured	1·10	60

733 Locomotive in Station

2011. Algiers Metro. Multicoloured.

MS1691	15d.×2, Type **733**; Locomotive facing right	2·25	1·25

734 Ouled-Djellal Sheep

2011. Algerian Sheep. Multicoloured.

1692	15d. Type **734**	1·10	60
1693	15d. Hamra sheep (brown with horns)		

POSTAGE DUE STAMPS

1926. As Postage Due stamps of France, but inscr "ALGERIE".

D34	**D11**	5c. blue	70	6·00
D35	**D11**	10c. brown	60	1·20
D36	**D11**	20c. olive	1·70	4·75
D37	**D11**	25c. red	1·40	7·25
D38	**D11**	30c. red	50	10
D39	**D11**	45c. green	2·50	7·75
D40	**D11**	50c. purple	25	35
D41	**D11**	60c. green	2·50	6·50
D42	**D11**	1f. red on yellow	55	95
D249	**D11**	1f.50 lilac	2·30	6·00
D250	**D11**	2f. blue	2·75	5·75
D43	**D11**	2f. mauve	1·10	3·00
D44	**D11**	3f. blue	85	1·80
D251	**D11**	5f. red	2·50	6·00
D252	**D11**	5f. green	4·00	8·25

1926. As Postage Due stamps of France, but inscr "ALGERIE".

D45	**D19**	1c. olive	25	4·75
D46	**D19**	10c. violet	1·20	2·75
D47	**D19**	30c. bistre	80	15
D48	**D19**	60c. red	1·30	15
D49	**D19**	1f. violet	9·00	1·90
D50	**D19**	2f. blue	13·00	2·75

1927. Nos. D36, D39 and D37 surch.

D92	**D11**	60 on 20c. olive	1·70	1·10
D93	**D11**	2f. on 45c. green	2·75	5·50
D94	**D11**	3f. on 25c. red	1·50	6·50

1927. Nos. D45/8 surch.

D95	**D19**	10c. on 30c. bistre	4·25	13·00
D96	**D19**	1f. on 1c. olive	2·75	4·50
D97	**D19**	1f. on 60c. red	14·00	75
D98	**D19**	2f. on 10c. violet	9·75	42·00

1942. As 1926 issue, but without "RF".

D181	**D11**	30c. red	2·20	8·25
D182	**D11**	2f. mauve	3·00	7·50

1944. No. 208 surch **TAXE P. C. V. DOUANE 20Fr**.

D230	**38**	20f. on 50f. red	3·00	5·25

1944. Surch **T 0.50**.

D231	**4**	50c. on 20c. green	1·50	5·25

1947. Postage Due Stamps of France optd ALGERIE.

D283	10c. brown (No. D985)	45	5·75
D284	30c. purple (No. D986)	45	5·75

D53

1947

D285	**D53**	20c. red	45	6·50
D286	**D53**	60c. blue	75	7·00
D287	**D53**	1f. brown	45	4·50
D288	**D53**	1f.50 olive	1·50	8·25
D289	**D53**	2f. red	35	3·75
D290	**D53**	3f. violet	60	4·25
D291	**D53**	5f. blue	60	1·70
D292	**D53**	6f. black	60	3·75
D293	**D53**	10f. purple	1·50	1·30
D294	**D53**	15f. myrtle	3·00	6·50
D295	**D53**	20f. green	1·50	1·30
D296	**D53**	30f. red	5·75	6·25
D297	**D53**	50f. black	6·50	10·00
D298	**D53**	100f. blue	28·00	28·00

1962. Postage Due stamps of France optd **EA** and with bar obliterating "REPUBLIQUE FRANCAISE".

D391	**D457**	5c. mauve	20·00	17·00
D392	**D457**	10c. red	20·00	17·00
D393	**D457**	20c. brown	20·00	17·00
D394	**D457**	50c. green	40·00	34·00
D395	**D457**	1f. green	60·00	55·00

The above also exist with larger overprint applied with handstamps.

D107 Scales of Justice

1963

D411	**D107**	5c. red and olive	10	10
D412	**D107**	10c. olive and red	10	10
D413	**D107**	20c. blue and black	50	30
D414	**D107**	50c. brown and green	1·10	75
D415	**D107**	1f. violet and orange	2·20	1·80

1968. No. D415 surch.

D508	60c. on 1f. violet and orange	80	60

D200 Ears of Corn

1972

D603	**D200**	10c. brown	10	10
D604	**D200**	20c. brown	10	10
D605	**D200**	40c. orange	25	10
D606	**D200**	50c. blue	30	10
D607	**D200**	80c. brown	65	30
D608	**D200**	1d. green	85	50
D609	**D200**	2d. blue	1·60	95
D610	**D200**	3d. violet	50	25
D611	**D200**	4d. purple	55	40

D644 Post Office

2006. Postage Due.

D1530	**D644**	5d. blue	15	10
D1531	**D644**	10d. green	20	10

Pt. 7

ALLENSTEIN

A district of E. Prussia retained by Germany as the result of a plebiscite in 1920. Stamps issued during the plebiscite period.

100 pfennig = 1 mark.

1920. Stamps of Germany inscr "DEUTSCHES REICH" optd **PLEBISCITE OLSZTYN ALLENSTEIN**.

1	**17**	5pf. green	55	1·10
2	**17**	10pf. red	55	1·10

3	**24**	15pf. violet	55	1·10
4	**24**	15pf. purple	7·50	12·50
5	**17**	20pf. blue	55	1·40
6	**17**	30pf. black & orge on buff	55	1·40
7	**17**	40pf. black and red	55	1·10
8	**17**	50pf. black & pur on buff	55	1·10
9	**17**	75pf. black and green	55	1·10
10	**18**	1m. red	2·10	4·25
11	**18**	1m.25 green	2·10	4·25
12	**18**	1m.50 brown	1·30	4·25
13b	**20**	2m.50 red	3·25	12·50
14	**21**	3m. black	3·25	4·75

1920. Stamps of Germany inscr "DEUTSCHES REICH" optd **TRAITE DE VERSAILLES** etc. in oval.

15	**17**	5pf. green	55	1·10
16	**17**	10pf. red	55	1·10
17	**24**	15pf. violet	55	1·10
18	**24**	15pf. purple	27·00	55·00
19	**17**	20pf. blue	85	1·70
20	**17**	30pf. black & orge on buff	55	1·10
21	**17**	40pf. black and red	55	1·10
22	**17**	50pf. black & pur on buff	55	1·10
23	**17**	75pf. black and green	85	1·70
24	**18**	1m. red	2·10	3·25
25	**18**	1m.25 green	2·10	3·25
26	**18**	1m.50 brown	1·60	3·25
27	**20**	2m.50 red	3·75	8·50
28	**21**	3m. black	2·30	3·25

Pt. 6

ALSACE AND LORRAINE

Stamps used in parts of France occupied by the German army in the war of 1870 -71, and afterwards temporarily in the annexed provinces of Alsace and Lorraine

100 pfennig = 1 mark

1

1870

1	**1**	1c. green	75·00	£130
3	**1**	2c. brown	95·00	£170
5	**1**	4c. grey	95·00	95·00
8	**1**	5c. green	65·00	12·50
10	**1**	10c. brown	85·00	18·00
14	**1**	20c. blue	85·00	15·00
16	**1**	25c. brown	£140	95·00

For 1940 issues see separate lists for Alsace and Lorraine under German Occupations.

Pt. 1

ALWAR

A state of Rajputana, N. India. Now uses Indian stamps.

12 pies = 1 anna; 16 annas = 1 rupee

1 Native Dagger

1877. Roul or perf.

1b		¼a. blue	6·00	1·10
5		¼a. green	7·50	2·50
2c		1a. brown	3·25	1·50

Pt. 6, Pt. 9

ANDORRA (FRENCH)

An independent state in the Pyrenees under the joint suzerainty of France and Spain.

French Post Office
1931. 100 centimes = 1 franc.
2002. 100 cents = 1 euro.

Spanish Post Office
1928. 100 centimos = 1 peseta.
2002. 100 cents = 1 euro.

FRENCH POST OFFICES

1931. Stamps of France optd **ANDORRE**.

F1	**11**	½c. on 1c. grey	1·10	6·50
F2	**11**	1c. grey	1·20	1·70
F3	**11**	2c. red	1·60	8·00
F4	**11**	3c. orange	2·10	4·25
F5	**11**	5c. green	3·25	8·25
F6	**11**	10c. lilac	5·25	10·00
F7	**18**	15c. brown	9·00	9·75
F8	**18**	20c. mauve	14·50	15·00
F9	**18**	25c. brown	12·50	17·00
F10	**18**	30c. green	12·50	15·00
F11	**18**	40c. blue	13·50	23·00
F12	**15**	45c. violet	26·00	31·00
F13	**15**	50c. red	18·00	20·00
F14	**15**	65c. green	37·00	41·00
F15	**15**	75c. mauve	42·00	46·00
F16	**18**	90c. red	55·00	70·00
F17	**15**	1f. blue	60·00	70·00
F18	**18**	1f.50 blue	65·00	80·00
F19	**13**	2f. red and green	60·00	90·00
F20	**13**	3f. mauve and red	£110	£150
F21	**13**	5f. blue and buff	£150	£250
F22	**13**	10f. green and red	£325	£450
F23	**13**	20f. mauve and green	£425	£500

F3 Our Lady's Chapel, Meritxell

F5 St. Michael's Church, Engolasters

1932

F24	**F3**	1c. slate	75	2·75
F25	**F3**	2c. violet	1·10	2·30
F26	**F3**	3c. brown	1·20	2·50
F27	**F3**	5c. green	95	2·75
F28	**A**	10c. lilac	1·80	3·25
F29	**F3**	15c. red	2·75	3·50
F30	**A**	20c. mauve	13·50	17·00
F31	**F5**	25c. brown	5·75	7·50
F32	**A**	25c. brown	13·50	34·00
F33	**A**	30c. green	3·75	4·50
F34	**A**	40c. blue	10·50	9·25
F35	**A**	40c. brown	1·60	4·00
F36	**A**	45c. red	15·00	29·00
F37	**A**	45c. green	7·50	22·00
F38	**F5**	50c. mauve	16·00	17·00
F39	**A**	50c. violet	7·50	20·00
F40	**A**	50c. green	2·10	10·50
F41	**A**	55c. violet	32·00	70·00
F42	**A**	60c. brown	2·10	7·50
F43	**F5**	65c. green	70·00	75·00
F44	**A**	65c. blue	19·00	33·00
F45	**A**	70c. red	2·40	5·75
F46	**F5**	75c. violet	11·50	12·50
F47	**A**	75c. blue	5·25	17·00
F48	**A**	80c. green	28·00	70·00
F49	**B**	80c. green	1·70	6·25
F50	**B**	90c. red	9·50	9·25
F51	**B**	90c. green	7·50	15·00
F52	**B**	1f. green	34·00	23·00
F53	**B**	1f. red	32·00	34·00
F54	**B**	1f. blue	1·40	3·50
F55	**B**	1f. 20 violet	1·30	6·50
F56	**F3**	1f. 25 mauve	65·00	80·00
F57	**F3**	1f.25 red	8·00	20·00
F58	**B**	1f.30 brown	1·70	6·50
F59	**C**	1f.50 blue	26·00	37·00
F60	**B**	1f.50 red	1·10	6·50
F61	**B**	1f.75 violet	£110	£140
F62	**B**	1f.75 blue	60·00	75·00
F63	**B**	2f. mauve	10·50	23·00
F64	**F 3**	2f. red	2·10	8·50
F65	**F 3**	2f. green	1·20	8·50
F66	**F 3**	2f.15 violet	60·00	90·00
F67	**F 3**	2f.25 blue	10·50	30·00
F68	**F 3**	2f.40 red	1·40	6·50
F69	**F 3**	2f.50 black	12·50	36·00
F70	**F 3**	2f.50 blue	2·75	10·50
F71	**B**	3f. brown	25·00	41·00
F72	**F 3**	3f. brown	2·20	7·00
F73	**F 3**	4f. blue	1·60	6·25
F74	**F 3**	4f.50 violet	2·10	8·25
F75	**C**	5f. brown	1·80	7·00
F76	**C**	10f. violet	2·40	7·00
F78	**C**	15f. blue	1·60	4·00
F79	**C**	20f. red	2·10	3·75
F81	**A**	50f. blue	3·00	9·25

DESIGNS—HORIZ: A, St. Anthony's Bridge; C, Andorra la Vella. VERT: B, Valley of Sant Julia.

1935. No. F38 surch **20c.**

F82	**F5**	20c. on 50c. purple	16·00	29·00

F9

1936

F83	**F9**	1c. black	55	3·25
F84	**F9**	2c. blue	55	3·25
F85	**F9**	3c. brown	55	3·25
F86	**F9**	5c. red	40	3·25
F87	**F9**	10c. blue	40	3·25
F88	**F9**	15c. mauve	3·25	5·25
F89	**F9**	20c. green	40	3·25
F90	**F9**	30c. red	75	7·00
F91	**F9**	30c. black	1·50	6·50
F92	**F9**	35c. green	60·00	90·00
F93	**F9**	40c. brown	1·10	6·25
F94	**F9**	50c. green	1·20	6·50
F95	**F9**	60c. blue	1·60	6·50
F96	**F9**	70c. violet	1·60	6·50

F13 Andorra la Vella

F10

F14 Councillor Jaume Bonell

1944

F97	**F10**	10c. violet	20	4·00
F98	**F10**	30c. red	20	4·00
F99	**F10**	40c. blue	40	4·00
F100	**F10**	50c. red	20	4·50
F101	**F10**	60c. black	40	4·00
F102	**F10**	70c. mauve	30	5·75
F103	**F10**	80c. green	20	5·75
F104	**F10**	1f. blue	1·10	2·40
F105	**D**	1f. purple	20	6·25
F106	**D**	1f.20 blue	20	6·25
F107	**D**	1f.50 red	20	6·25
F108	**D**	2f. green	20	4·00
F109	**E**	2f.40 red	20	4·00
F110	**E**	2f.50 red	4·25	7·00
F111	**E**	3f. brown	60	2·75
F112	**D**	3f. red	4·25	5·75
F113	**E**	4f. blue	55	6·25
F114	**E**	4f. green	1·10	7·50
F115	**D**	4f. brown	2·30	10·50
F116	**E**	4f.50 brown	60	5·75
F117	**F 13**	4f.50 blue	5·25	20·00
F118	**F 13**	5f. blue	55	6·25
F119	**F 13**	5f. green	1·40	6·50
F120	**E**	5f. green	3·25	11·50
F121	**E**	5f. violet	4·25	8·00
F122	**F 13**	6f. red	55	3·75
F123	**F 13**	6f. purple	55	5·75
F124	**E**	6f. green	3·25	7·50
F125	**F 13**	8f. blue	1·60	8·00
F126	**E**	8f. brown	1·10	3·50
F127	**F 13**	10f. green	40	5·75
F128	**F 13**	10f. blue	1·60	1·80
F129	**F 13**	12f. red	1·40	7·50
F130	**F 13**	12f. green	1·60	5·75
F131	**F 14**	15f. purple	65	6·50
F132	**F 13**	15f. red	85	3·50
F133	**F 13**	15f. brown	7·50	4·50
F134	**F 14**	18f. blue	3·25	12·00
F135	**F 13**	18f. red	12·50	26·00
F136	**F 14**	20f. blue	1·10	6·50
F137	**F 14**	20f. violet	3·25	10·00
F138	**F 14**	25f. red	3·75	10·50
F139	**F 14**	25f. blue	2·10	8·50
F140	**F 14**	30f. blue	21·00	29·00
F141	**F 14**	40f. green	3·25	9·25
F142	**F 14**	50f. brown	1·80	4·25

DESIGNS—HORIZ: D, Church of St. John of Caselles; E, House of the Valleys.

F15 Chamois and Pyrenees

1950. Air.

F143	**F15**	100f. blue	£110	£110

F16 Les Escaldes

1955

F144	**F16**	1f. blue (postage)	20	2·75
F145	**F16**	2f. green	55	2·10
F146	**F16**	3f. red	65	2·10
F147	**F16**	5f. brown	65	2·10
F148	-	6f. green	2·20	2·75
F149	-	8f. red	2·40	3·25
F150	-	10f. violet	4·25	2·75
F151	-	12f. blue	2·30	2·10
F152	-	15f. red	3·00	2·30
F153	-	18f. blue	2·75	3·75
F154	-	20f. violet	3·25	2·30
F155	-	25f. brown	3·50	4·00
F156	-	30f. blue	26·00	34·00
F157	-	35f. blue	13·50	14·50
F158	-	40f. green	35·00	55·00
F159	-	50f. red	4·25	4·50
F160	-	65f. violet	9·50	29·00
F161	-	70f. brown	9·25	22·00
F162	-	75f. blue	45·00	90·00
F163	-	100f. green (air)	10·50	15·00
F164	-	200f. red	21·00	23·00
F165	-	500f. blue	85·00	90·00

DESIGNS—VERT: 15f. to 25f. Gothic cross, Andorra la Vella; 100f. to 500f. East Valira River. HORIZ: 6f. to 12f. Santa Coloma Church; 30f. to 75f. Les Bons village.

F21

F22 Gothic Cross, Meritxell

1961

F166	**F21**	1c. grey, blue and slate (postage)	65	1·60
F167	**F21**	2c. lt orge, blk & orge	65	1·60
F168	**F21**	5c. lt grn, blk & grn	40	1·60
F169	**F21**	10c. pink, blk & red	45	45
F170a	**F21**	12c. yell, pur & grn	2·20	4·50
F171	**F21**	15c. lt bl, blk & bl	75	1·60
F172	**F21**	18c. pink, blk & mve	1·40	3·25
F173	**F21**	20c. lt yell, brn & yell	80	55
F174	**F22**	25c. blue, vio & grn	1·10	1·10
F175	**F22**	30c. pur, red & grn	1·10	80
F175a	**F22**	40c. green and brown	1·30	2·00
F176	**F22**	45c. blue, ind & grn	21·00	34·00
F176a	**F22**	45c. brown, bl & vio	1·30	2·75
F177	**F22**	50c. multicoloured	2·75	2·75
F177a	**F22**	60c. brown & chestnut	1·60	2·10
F178	**F22**	65c. olive, bl & brn	23·00	55·00
F179	**F22**	85c. multicoloured	23·00	40·00
F179a	**F22**	90c. green, bl & brn	1·60	3·50
F180	**F22**	1f. blue, brn & turq	2·75	2·75
F181	-	2f. green, red and purple (air)	2·20	2·30
F182	-	3f. purple, bl & grn	2·40	2·50
F183	-	5f. orange, pur & red	4·00	4·00
F184	-	10f. green and blue	6·00	5·50

DESIGNS—As Type F **22**: 60c. to 1f. Engolasters Lake; 2f. to 10f. Incles Valley.

F23 "Telstar" Satellite and part of Globe

1962. First Trans-Atlantic TV Satellite Link.

F185	**F23**	50c. violet and blue	1·60	2·75

F24 "La Sardane" (dance)

1963. Andorran History (1st issue).

F186	**F24**	20c. purple, mve & grn	3·75	6·50
F187	-	50c. red and green	6·75	12·50
F188	-	1f. green, blue & brn	9·50	21·00

DESIGNS—LARGER (48½×27 mm): 50c. Charlemagne crossing Andorra. (48×27 mm): 1f. Foundation of Andorra by Louis le Debonnaire.

See also Nos. F190/1.

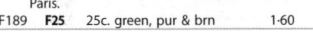

F25 Santa Coloma Church and Grand Palais, Paris

1964. "PHILATEC 1964" International Stamp Exhibition, Paris.

F189	**F25**	25c. green, pur & brn	1·60	3·25

1964. Andorran History (2nd issue). As Nos. F187/8, inscribed "1964".
F190 60c. green, chestnut and brown 11·50 32·00
F191 1f. blue, sepia and brown 16·00 32·00
DESIGNS (48½×27 mm): 60c. "Napoleon re-establishes the Andorran Statute, 1806"; 1f. "Confirmation of the Co-government, 1288".

F26 Virgin of Santa Coloma

1964. Red Cross Fund.
F192 **F26** 25c.+10c. red, green and blue 21·00 38·00

F27 "Syncom", Morse Key and Pleumeur-Bodou centre

1965. Centenary of I.T.U.
F193 **F27** 60c. violet, blue and red 4·75 8·00

F28 Andorra House, Paris

1965. Opening of Andorra House, Paris.
F194 **F28** 25c. brown, olive & bl 1·10 2·30

F29 Chair-lift

1966. Winter Sports.
F195 **F29** 25c. green, purple & bl 1·30 3·25
F196 - 40c. brown, blue & red 2·10 4·00
DESIGN—HORIZ: 40c. Ski-lift.

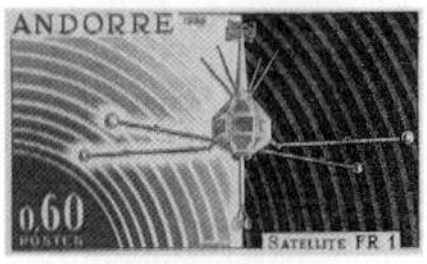
F30 Satellite "FR 1"

1966. Launching of Satellite "FR 1".
F197 **F30** 60c. blue, emer & grn 2·10 4·25

F31 Europa "Ship"

1966. Europa.
F198 **F31** 60c. brown 3·50 6·25

F32 Cogwheels

1967. Europa.
F199 **F32** 30c. indigo and blue 4·25 5·75
F200 **F32** 60c. red and purple 5·50 10·50

F33 "Folk Dancers" (statue)

1967. Centenary (1966) of New Reform.
F201 **F33** 30c. green, olive & slate 1·50 3·50

F34 Telephone and Dial

1967. Inaug of Automatic Telephone Service.
F202 **F34** 60c. black, violet & red 1·60 3·75

F35 Andorran Family

1967. Institution of Social Security.
F203 **F35** 2f.30 brown & purple 8·50 18·00

F36 "The Temptation"

1967. 16th-century Frescoes in House of the Valleys (1st series).
F204 **F36** 25c. red and black 1·10 2·75
F205 - 30c. purple and violet 1·20 3·50
F206 - 60c. blue and indigo 1·60 4·50
FRESCOES: 30c. *The Kiss of Judas*; 60c. *The Descent from the Cross*.
See also Nos. F210/12.

F37 Downhill Skiing

1968. Winter Olympic Games, Grenoble.
F207 **F37** 40c. purple, orge & red 1·40 3·75

F38 Europa "Key"

1968. Europa.
F208 **F38** 30c. blue and slate 5·25 8·50
F209 **F38** 60c. violet & brown 8·50 14·00

1968. 16th-century Frescoes in House of the Valleys (2nd series). Designs as Type **F36**.
F210 25c. deep green and green 95 3·25
F211 30c. purple and brown 1·20 4·75
F212 60c. brown and red 2·10 6·50
FRESCOES: 25c. "The Beating of Christ"; 30c. "Christ Helped by the Cyrenians"; 60c. "The Death of Christ".

F39 High Jumping

1968. Olympic Games, Mexico.
F213 **F39** 40c. brown and blue 2·10 3·75

F40 Colonnade

1969. Europa.
F214 **F40** 40c. grey, blue and red 9·50 11·50
F215 **F40** 70c. red, green and blue 13·00 22·00

F41 Canoeing

1969. World Kayak-Canoeing Championships, Bourg-St. Maurice.
F216 **F41** 70c. dp blue, bl & grn 2·10 5·25

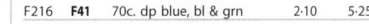

F41a "Diamond Crystal" in Rain Drop

1969. European Water Charter.
F217 **F41a** 70c. black, blue and ultramarine 5·25 9·75

F42 *The Apocalypse*

1969. Altar-screen, Church of St. John of Caselles (1st series). "The Revelation of St. John".
F218 **F42** 30c. red, violet & brn 1·10 2·10
F219 - 40c. bistre, brn & grey 1·60 2·75
F220 - 70c. purple, lake & red 2·10 3·50
DESIGNS: 40c. Angel "clothed with cloud with face as the sun, and feet as pillars of fire" (Rev. 10); 70c. Christ with sword and stars, and seven candlesticks.
See also Nos. F225/7, F233/5 and F240/2.

F43 Handball Player

1970. Seventh World Handball Championships, France.
F221 **F43** 80c. blue, brn & dp bl 2·75 5·25

F44 "Flaming Sun"

1970. Europa.
F222 **F44** 40c. orange 9·50 8·00
F223 **F44** 80c. violet 12·00 13·00

F45 Putting the Shot

1970. First European Junior Athletic Championships, Paris.
F224 **F45** 80c. purple and blue 2·75 5·50

1970. Altar-screen, Church of St. John of Caselles (2nd series). Designs as Type **F42**.
F225 30c. violet, brown and red 1·50 2·50
F226 40c. green and violet 1·60 2·75
F227 80c. red, blue and green 3·25 4·00
DESIGNS: 30c. Angel with keys and padlock; 40c. Angel with pillar; 80c. St. John being boiled in cauldron of oil.

F46 Ice Skaters

1971. World Ice Skating Championships, Lyon.
F228 **F46** 80c. violet, pur & red 3·00 4·75

F47 Western Capercaillie

1971. Nature Protection.
F229 **F47** 80c. multicoloured 4·75 6·25
F230 - 80c. brown, green & bl 4·75 6·25
DESIGN: No. F230, Brown bear.

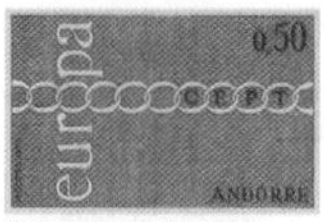
F48 Europa Chain

1971. Europa.
F231 **F48** 50c. red 10·50 12·50
F232 **F48** 80c. green 16·00 20·00

1971. Altar-screen, Church of St. John of Caselles (3rd series). As Type **F42**.
F233 30c. green, brown and myrtle 1·80 4·50
F234 50c. brown, orange and lake 2·40 5·25
F235 90c. blue, purple and brown 3·75 7·00
DESIGNS: 30c. St. John in temple at Ephesus; 50c. St. John with cup of poison; 90c. St. John disputing with pagan philosophers.

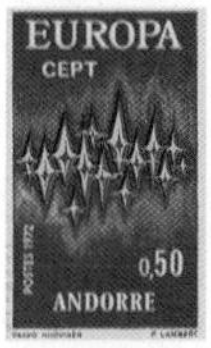
F49 "Communications"

1972. Europa.
F236 **F49** 50c. multicoloured 10·00 10·50
F237 **F49** 90c. multicoloured 15·00 18·00

F50 Golden Eagle

1972. Nature Protection.
F238 **F50** 60c. olive, green & pur 4·75 6·25

F51 Rifle-shooting

1972. Olympic Games, Munich.
F239 **F51** 1f. purple 3·25 4·50

1972. Altar-screen, Church of St. John of Caselles (4th series). As Type **F42**.
F240 30c. purple, grey and green 1·40 2·30
F241 50c. grey and blue 1·70 2·75
F242 90c. green and blue 2·75 4·00
DESIGNS: 30c. St. John in discussion with bishop; 50c. St. John healing a cripple; 90c. Angel with spear.

F52 General De Gaulle

1972. Fifth Anniv of Gen. De Gaulle's Visit to Andorra.
F243 **F52** 50c. blue 3·50 5·75
F244 - 90c. red 4·75 7·75

DESIGN: 90c. Gen. De Gaulle in Andorra la Vella, 1967.
See also Nos. F434/5.

F53 Europa "Posthorn"

1973. Europa.

F245	**F53**	50c. multicoloured	10·00	10·50
F246	**F53**	90c. multicoloured	10·50	21·00

F54 *Virgin of Canolich* (wood carving)

1973. Andorran Art.

F247	**F54**	1f. lilac, blue and drab	3·00	4·25

F55 Lily

1973. Pyrenean Flowers (1st series). Multicoloured.

F248	30c. Type F **55**	1·10	3·25
F249	50c. Columbine	2·10	4·50
F250	90c. Wild pinks	1·60	3·50

See also Nos. F253/5 and F264/6.

F56 Blue Tit ("Mesange Bleue")

1973. Nature Protection. Birds. Multicoloured.

F251	90c. Type **F56**	2·75	5·25
F252	1f. Lesser spotted woodpecker ("Pic Epeichette")	3·00	5·75

See also Nos. F259/60.

1974. Pyrenean Wild Flowers (2nd series). As Type F **55**. Multicoloured.

F253	45c. Iris	55	4·00
F254	65c. Tobacco Plant	65	4·50
F255	90c. Narcissus	1·40	4·75

F57 *The Virgin of Pal*

1974. Europa. Church Sculptures. Multicoloured.

F256	50c. Type F **57**	17·00	11·50
F257	90c. "The Virgin of Santa Coloma"	23·00	18·00

F58 Arms of Andorra

1974. Meeting of Co-Princes, Cahors.

F258	**F58**	1f. blue, violet & orge	1·40	5·75

1974. Nature Protection. Birds. As Type **F56**. Multicoloured.

F259	60c. Citril finch ("Venturon Montagnard")	4·25	7·00
F260	80c. Northern bullfinch ("Boureuil")	4·25	7·00

F59 Letters crossing Globe

1974. Centenary of U.P.U.

F261	**F59**	1f.20 red, grey & brn	2·30	4·25

F60 *Calvary*

1975. Europa. Paintings from La Cortinada Church. Multicoloured.

F262	80c. Type **F60**	8·50	15·00
F263	1f.20 *Coronation of St. Martin* (horiz)	10·50	23·00

1975. Pyrenean Flowers (3rd series). As Type F**55**.

F264	60c. multicoloured	65	3·25
F265	80c. multicoloured	1·80	4·00
F266	1f.20 yellow, red and green	1·30	3·50

DESIGNS: 60c. Gentian; 80c. Anemone; 1f.20, Colchicum.

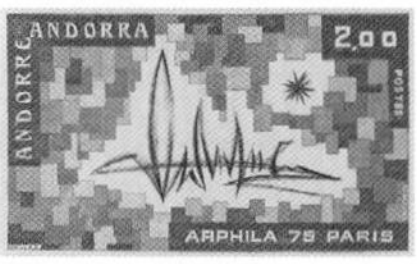

F61 "Arphila" Motif

1975. "Arphila 75" International Stamp Exhibition, Paris.

F267	**F61**	2f. red, green and blue	2·00	4·50

F62 Pres. Pompidou (Co-prince of Andorra)

1976. President Pompidou of France Commem.

F268	**F62**	80c. black and violet	1·10	3·25

F63 "La Pubilla" and Emblem

1976. International Women's Year.

F269	**F63**	1f.20 black, pur & bl	2·10	3·75

F64 Skier

1976. Winter Olympic Games, Innsbruck.

F270	**F64**	1f.20 black, green & bl	1·60	3·50

F65 Telephone and Satellite

1976. Telephone Centenary.

F271	**F65**	1f. green, black and red	1·60	3·75

F66 Catalan Forge

1976. Europa.

F272	**F66**	80c. brown, blue & grn	4·25	4·50
F273	-	1f.20 red, green & blk	5·25	5·75

DESIGN: 1f.20, Andorran folk-weaving.

F67 Thomas Jefferson

1976. Bicentenary of American Revolution.

F274	**F67**	1f.20 dp grn, brn & grn	1·40	3·50

F68 Ball-trap (clay pigeon) Shooting

1976. Olympic Games, Montreal.

F275	**F68**	2f. brown, violet & grn	2·10	4·00

F69 New Chapel

1976. New Chapel of Our Lady, Meritxell.

F276	**F69**	1f. green, purple & brn	1·20	3·25

F70 Apollo

1976. Nature Protection. Butterflies. Mult.

F277	80c. Type **F70**	3·25	6·50
F278	1f.40 Camberwell beauty	4·00	7·00

F71 Stoat

1977. Nature Protection.

F279	**F71**	1f. grey, black & blue	2·40	3·75

F72 Church of St. John of Caselles

1977. Europa.

F280	**F72**	1f. purple, green & bl	6·75	5·75
F281	-	1f.40 indigo, grn & bl	11·00	7·00

DESIGN: 1f.40, St. Vicens Chateau.

F73 Book and Flowers

1977. Frist Anniv of Institute of Andorran Studies.

F282	**F73**	80c. brown, green & bl	1·20	2·75

F74 St. Roma

1977. Reredos, St. Roma's Chapel, Les Bons.

F283	**F74**	2f. multicoloured	2·75	3·50

F75 General Council Assembly Hall

1977. Andorran Institutions.

F284	**F75**	1f.10 red, blue & brn	2·75	4·00
F285	-	2f. brown and red	2·75	4·00

DESIGN—VERT. 2f. Don Guillem d'Areny Plandolit.

F76 Eurasian Red Squirrel

1978. Nature Protection.

F286	**F76**	1f. brown, grn & olive	1·30	2·75

F77 Escalls Bridge

1978. 700th Anniv of Parity Treaties (1st issue).

F287	**F77**	80c. green, brown & bl	85	2·75

See also No. F292.

F78 Church at Pal

1978. Europa.

F288	**F78**	1f. brown, green & red	7·00	5·75
F289	-	1f.40 brown, bl & red	11·50	7·50

DESIGN: 1f.40, Charlemagne's House.

F79 *Virgin of Sispony*

1978. Andorran Art.
F290 **F79** 2f. multicoloured 2·10 3·50

F80 Tribunal Meeting

1978. Tribunal of Visura.
F291 **F80** 1f.20 multicoloured 1·80 2·75

F81 Treaty Text

1978. 700th Anniv of Parity Treaties (2nd issue).
F292 **F81** 1f.50 brown, grn & red 1·30 2·75

F82 Chamois

1978. Nature Protection.
F293 **F82** 1f. brown, lt brn & bl 85 2·40

F83 Rock Ptarmigans ("Perdiu Blanca")

1979. Nature Protection.
F294 **F83** 1f.20 multicoloured 1·70 3·25

F84 Early 20th Century Postman and Church of St. John of Caselles

1979. Europa.
F295 **F84** 1f.20 black, brn & grn 3·25 4·75
F296 - 1f.70 brown, grn & mve 5·25 5·75
DESIGN: 1f.70, Old French Post Office, Andorra.

F85 Wall painting, Church of St. Cerni, Nagol

1979. Pre-Romanesque Art.
F297 **F85** 2f. green, pink and brown 1·60 2·75
See also No. F309.

F86 Boy with Sheep

1979. International Year of the Child.
F298 **F86** 1f.70 multicoloured 1·30 2·75

F87 Co-princes Monument (Luigiteruggi)

1979. Co-princes Monument.
F299 **F87** 2f. dp green, grn & red 1·60 3·25

F88 Judo

1979. World Judo Championships, Paris.
F300 **F88** 1f.30 black, dp bl & bl 1·10 2·75

F89 Cal Pal, La Cortinada

1980
F301 **F89** 1f.10 brown, bl & grn 85 2·40

F90 Cross-country Skiing

1980. Winter Olympics, Lake Placid.
F302 **F90** 1f.80 ultram, bl & red 1·50 3·25

F91 Charlemagne

1980. Europa.
F303 **F91** 1f.30 brn, chest & red 2·10 3·50
F304 - 1f.80 green and brown 2·75 4·00
DESIGN: 1f.80, Napoleon I.

F93 Dog's-tooth Violet

1980. Nature Protection. Multicoloured.
F305 1f.30 Pyrenean lily 85 2·40
F306 1f.10 Type F **93** 95 2·50

F94 Cyclists

1980. World Cycling Championships.
F307 **F94** 1f.20 violet, mve & brn 1·20 2·50

F95 House of the Valleys

1980. 400th Anniv of Restoration of House of the Valleys (meeting place of Andorran General Council).
F308 **F95** 1f.40 brown, vio & grn 1·20 2·50

1980. Pre-Romanesque Art. As Type F**85**. Multicoloured.
F309 2f. Angel (wall painting, Church of St. Cerni, Nagol) (horiz) 1·70 3·25

F97 Shepherds' Huts, Mereig

1981. Architecture.
F310 **F97** 1f.40 brown and blue 1·10 1·70

F98 Bear Dance (Emcamp Carnival)

1981. Europa.
F311 **F98** 1f.40 black, green & bl 1·60 2·30
F312 - 2f. black, blue and red 2·10 3·50
DESIGN: 2f. El Contrapas (dance).

F99 Bonelli's Warbler

1981. Nature Protection. Birds. Multicoloured.
F313 1f.20 Type **F99** 1·10 2·75
F314 1f.40 Wallcreeper 1·30 2·75

F100 Fencing

1981. World Fencing Championships, Clermont-Ferrand.
F315 **F100** 2f. blue and black 1·30 2·75

F101 Chasuble of St. Martin (miniature)

1981. Art.
F316 **F101** 3f. multicoloured 1·80 2·75

F102 Fountain, Sant Julia de Loria

1981. International Decade of Drinking Water.
F317 **F102** 1f.60 blue and brown 1·10 2·50

F103 Symbolic Disabled

1981. International Year of Disabled Persons.
F318 **F103** 2f.30 blue, red & grn 1·50 2·75

F104 Scroll and Badge (creation of Andorran Executive Council, 1981)

1982. Europa.
F319 **F104** 1f.60 blue, brn & orge 2·10 2·75
F320 - 2f.30 blue, blk & orge 2·75 3·25
DESIGN: 2f.30, Hat and cloak (creation of Land Council, 1419).

F105 Footballer running to right

1982. World Cup Football Championship, Spain.
F321 **F105** 1f.60 brown and red 1·30 2·40
F322 - 2f.60 brown and red 1·90 2·75
DESIGN: 2f.60, Footballer running to left.

F 106 1933 1f.25 Stamp

1982. First Official Exhibition of Andorran Postage Stamps.
MSF323 **F106** 5f. black and red 2·75 4·00

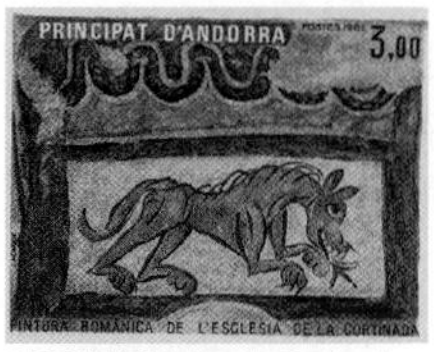

F107 Wall Painting, La Cortinada Church

1982. Romanesque Art.
F324 **F107** 3f. multicoloured 1·60 4·75

F108 Wild Cat

1982. Nature Protection.
F325 **F108** 1f.80 blk, grn & grey 1·60 3·75
F326 - 2f.60 brown & green 1·40 4·00
DESIGN: 2f.60, Scots Pine.

F109 Dr. Robert Koch

1982. Centenary of Discovery of Tubercle Bacillus.
F327 **F109** 2f.10 lilac 1·40 2·75

F110 St. Thomas Aquinas

1982. St. Thomas Aquinas Commemoration.
F328 **F110** 2f. deep brown, brown and grey 1·30 2·75

F111 Montgolfier and Charles Balloon over Tuileries, Paris

1983. Bicentenary of Manned Flight.

F329	**F111**	2f. green, red and brown	1·30	2·75

F112 Silver Birch

1983. Nature Protection.

F330	**F112**	1f. red, brown and green	1·50	3·75
F331	-	1f.50 green, bl & brn	1·60	4·00

DESIGN: 1f.50, Brown trout.

F113 Mountain Cheesery

1983. Europa.

F332	**F113**	1f. purple and violet	2·40	3·75
F333	-	2f.60 red, mve & pur	2·75	4·00

DESIGN: 2f.60, Catalan forge.

F114 Royal Edict of Louis XIII

1983. 30th Anniv of Customs Co-operation Council.

F334	**F114**	3f. black and slate	2·00	5·50

F115 Early Coat of Arms

1983. Inscr "POSTES".

F335	**F115**	5c. green and red	1·10	2·30
F336	**F115**	10c. dp green & green	1·10	2·30
F337	**F115**	20c. violet and mauve	1·10	2·30
F338	**F115**	30c. purple and violet	1·10	2·30
F339	**F115**	40c. blue & ultram	1·10	2·30
F340	**F115**	50c. black and red	1·10	2·30
F341	**F115**	1f. lake and red	1·10	2·30
F342	**F115**	1f.90 green	3·75	4·75
F343	**F115**	2f. red and brown	1·50	1·60
F344	**F115**	2f.10 green	1·50	2·75
F345	**F115**	2f.20 red	1·10	3·75
F346	**F115**	2f.30 red	1·40	3·75
F347	**F115**	3f. green and mauve	1·60	4·00
F348	**F115**	4f. orange and brown	3·25	6·25
F349	**F115**	5f. brown and red	2·10	5·75
F350	**F115**	10f. red and brown	4·25	6·25
F351	**F115**	15f. green & dp green	6·25	9·00
F352	**F115**	20f. blue and brown	8·00	9·25

For design as Type **F115** but inscribed "LA POSTE" see Nos. F446/9.

F116 Wall Painting, La Cortinada Church

1983. Romanesque Art.

F354	**F116**	4f. multicoloured	2·10	4·00

F117 Plandolit House

1983

F355	**F117**	1f.60 brown & green	1·10	1·70

F118 Snowflakes and Olympic Torch

1984. Winter Olympic Games, Sarajevo.

F356	**F118**	2f.80 red, blue & grn	1·70	2·75

F119 Pyrenees and Council of Europe Emblem

1984. Work Community of Pyrenees Region.

F357	**F119**	3f. blue and brown	1·80	3·25

F120 Bridge

1984. Europa.

F358	**F120**	2f. green	3·75	4·00
F359	**F120**	2f.80 red	4·75	5·25

F121 Sweet Chestnut

1984. Nature Protection.

F360	**F121**	1f.70 grn, brn & pur	1·30	3·75
F361	-	2f.10 green & brown	1·60	4·00

DESIGN: 2f.10, Walnut.

F122 Centre Members

1984. Pyrenean Cultures Centre, Andorra.

F362	**F122**	3f. blue, orange & red	1·80	3·50

F123 *St. George* (detail of fresco, Church of St. Cerni, Nagol)

1984. Pre-Romanesque Art.

F363	**F123**	5f. multicoloured	2·75	4·00

F124 Sant Julia Valley

1985

F364	**F124**	2f. green, olive & brn	1·50	2·75

F125 Title Page of "Le Val d'Andorre" (comic opera)

1985. Europa.

F365	**F125**	2f.10 green	3·75	4·00
F366	-	3f. brown & dp brown	4·75	5·25

DESIGN: 3f. Musical instruments within frame.

F126 Teenagers holding up ball

1985. International Youth Year.

F367	**F126**	3f. red and brown	1·60	3·25

F127 Mallard

1985. Nature Protection. Multicoloured.

F368	1f.80 Type **F127**	1·40	3·50
F369	2f.20 Eurasian goldfinch	1·70	4·00

F128 St. Cerni and Angel (fresco, Church of St. Cerni, Nagol)

1985. Pre-Romanesque Art.

F370	**F128**	5f. multicoloured	2·30	4·00

F130 1979 Europa Stamp

1986. Inauguration of Postal Museum.

F381	**F130**	2f.20 brown & green	1·40	3·25

F131 Ansalonga

1986. Europa.

F382	**F131**	2f.20 black and blue	4·25	4·50
F383	-	3f.20 black and green	5·25	5·50

DESIGN: 3f.20, Pyrenean chamois.

F132 Players

1986. World Cup Football Championship, Mexico.

F384	**F132**	3f. grn, blk & dp grn	2·10	3·50

F133 Angonella Lakes

1986

F385	**F133**	2f.20 multicoloured	1·40	2·75

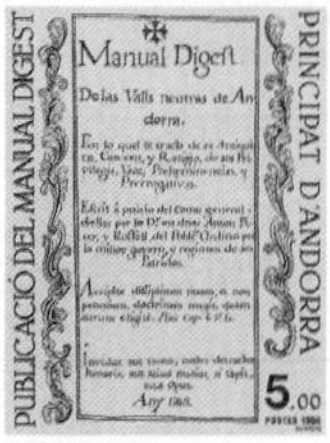

F134 Title Page of *Manual Digest*, 1748

1986. *Manual Digest*.

F386	**F134**	5f. black, grn & brn	2·75	4·00

F135 Dove with Twig

1986. International Peace Year.

F387	**F135**	1f.90 blue and indigo	1·30	2·75

F136 St. Vincent's Chapel, Enclar

1986

F388	**F136**	1f.90 brn, blk & grn	1·30	2·75

F137 Arms

1987. Visit of French Co-prince (French president).

F389	**F137**	2f.20 multicoloured	2·00	4·00

F138 Meritxell Chapel

1987. Europa.

F390	**F138**	2f.20 purple and red	5·25	4·50
F391	-	3f.40 violet and blue	7·50	6·25

DESIGN: 3f.40, Ordino.

F139 Ransol

1987

F392	**F139**	1f.90 multicoloured	1·50	3·50

F140 Horse

1987. Nature Protection. Multicoloured.

F393	1f.90 Type F **140**	1·70	4·25
F394	2f.20 Isabel (moth)	2·00	4·50

F141 Arualsu (fresco, La Cortinada Church)

1987. Romanesque Art.
F395 **F141** 5f. multicoloured 3·00 4·25

F142 Walker with Map by Signpost

1987. Walking.
F396 **F142** 2f. pur, grn & dp grn 1·40 2·75

F143 Key

1987. La Cortinada Church Key.
F397 **F143** 3f. multicoloured 1·70 3·50

F144 Arms

1988
F398 **F144** 2f.20 red 1·40 2·75
F399 **F144** 2f.30 red 1·60 4·50
F400 **F144** 2f.50 red 1·70 4·50
F401 **F144** 2f.80 red 1·80 4·25
Nos. F400/1 are inscribed "LA POSTE".

F145 Bronze Boot and Mountains

1988. Archaeology.
F407 **F145** 3f. multicoloured 1·70 3·75

F146 Players

1988. Rugby.
F408 **F146** 2f.20 blk, yell & grn 1·40 4·50

F147 Enclar Aerial

1988. Europa. Transport and Communications. Each green, brown and blue.
F409 2f.20 Type **F147** 3·75 4·00
F410 3f.60 Hand pointing to map on screen (tourist information) 4·75 5·75

F148 Les Escaldes Hot Spring

1988
F411 **F148** 2f.20 blue, brn & grn 1·40 2·75

F149 Ansalonga Pass

1988
F412 **F149** 2f. blue, green & olive 1·20 2·75

F150 Pyrenean Shepherd Dog

1988. Nature Protection. Multicoloured.
F413 2f. Type **F150** 1·90 4·50
F414 2f.20 Hare 2·00 4·50

F151 Fresco, Andorra La Vella Church

1988. Romanesque Art.
F415 **F151** 5f. multicoloured 3·00 4·00

F152 Birds

1989. Bicentenary of French Revolution.
F416 **F152** 2f.20 violet, blk & red 1·50 2·75

F153 Pal

1989
F417 **F153** 2f.20 violet and blue 1·50 2·75

F154 The Strong Horse

1989. Europa. Children's Games. Each brown and cream.
F418 2f.20 Type **F154** 3·25 3·50
F419 3f.60 The Handkerchief 4·25 4·75

F155 Wounded Soldiers

1989. 125th Anniv of International Red Cross.
F420 **F155** 3f.60 brn, blk & red 2·10 3·50

F156 Archaeological Find and St. Vincent's Chapel, Enclar

1989. Archaeology.
F421 **F156** 3f. multicoloured 1·60 3·50

F157 Wild Boar

1989. Nature Protection.
F422 **F157** 2f.20 blk, grn & brn 1·60 3·50
F423 - 3f.60 black, green and deep green 2·10 4·50
DESIGN: 3f.60, Palmate newt.

F158 Retable of St. Michael de la Mosquera, Encamp

1989
F424 **F158** 5f. multicoloured 3·25 5·50

F159 La Margineda Bridge

1990
F425 **F159** 2f.30 blue, brn & turq 1·60 2·75

F160 Llorts Iron Ore Mines

1990
F426 **F160** 3f.20 multicoloured 2·10 3·25

F161 Exterior of Old Post Office, Andorra La Vella

1990. Europa. Post Office Buildings.
F427 **F161** 2f.30 red and black 4·25 5·25
F428 - 3f.20 violet and red 6·25 7·00
DESIGN: 3f.20, Interior of modern post office.

F162 Censer, St. Roma's Chapel, Les Bons

1990
F429 **F162** 3f. multicoloured 2·10 3·25

F163 Wild Roses

1990. Nature Protection. Multicoloured.
F430 2f.30 Type **F163** 1·60 3·25
F431 3f.20 Otter (horiz) 2·10 3·50

F164 Tobacco-drying Sheds, Les Bons

1990
F432 **F164** 2f.30 yell, blk & red 1·60 2·75

F165 Part of Mural from Santa Coloma Church

1990
F433 **F165** 5f. multicoloured 2·75 3·75

1990. Birth Centenary of Charles de Gaulle (French statesman). As Nos. F243/4 but values and inscriptions changed.
F434 **F52** 2f.30 blue 2·10 3·25
F435 **F52** 3f.20 red 2·50 3·50

F166 Coin from St. Eulalia's Church, Encamp

1990
F436 **F166** 3f.20 multicoloured 2·10 3·25

F167 Chapel of Sant Roma Dels Vilars

1991
F437 **F167** 2f.50 blue, blk & grn 1·60 2·75

F168 Emblem and Track

1991. Fourth European Small States Games.
F438 **F168** 2f.50 multicoloured 1·50 2·75

F169 Television Satellite

1991. Europa. Europe in Space. Multicoloured.
F439 2f.50 Type **F169** 4·25 4·50
F440 3f.50 Globe, telescope and eye (horiz) 7·50 8·00

F170 Bottles

1991. Artefacts from Tomb of St. Vincent of Enclar.
F441 **F170** 3f.20 multicoloured 1·80 2·75

F171 Sheep

1991. Nature Protection.
F442 **F171** 2f.50 brown, bl & blk 2·10 4·50
F443 - 3f.50 brn, mve & blk 2·20 4·75
DESIGN: 3f.50, Pyrenean cow.

F172 Players

1991. World Petanque Championship, Engordany.
F444 **F172** 2f.50 blk, bistre & red 1·80 2·75

F173 Mozart, Quartet and Organ Pipes

1991. Death Bicentenary of Wolfgang Amadeus Mozart (composer).
F445 **F173** 3f.40 blue, blk & turq 2·20 3·25

1991. As Type **F115** but inscr "LA POSTE".
F446 **F115** 2f.20 green 1·40 4·00
F447 **F115** 2f.40 green 3·00 4·50
F448 **F115** 2f.50 red 1·60 4·00
F449 **F115** 2f.70 green 2·75 4·00
F450 **F115** 2f.80 red 2·75 4·00
F451 **F115** 3f. red 2·75 4·00

F174 *Virgin of the Remedy of Sant Julia and Sant Germa*

1991
F455 **F174** 5f. multicoloured 3·25 3·75

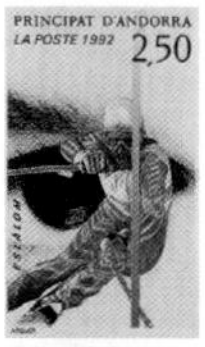

F175 Slalom

1992. Winter Olympic Games, Albertville. Multicoloured.
F456 2f.50 Type **F175** 2·40 2·75
F457 3f.40 Figure skating 2·75 3·25

F176 St. Andrew's Church, Arinsal

1992
F458 **F176** 2f.50 black and buff 1·80 2·20

F177 Navigation Instrument and Columbus's Fleet

1992. Europa. 500th Anniv of Discovery of America by Columbus. Multicoloured.
F459 2f.50 Type **F177** 4·75 4·50
F460 3f.40 Fleet, Columbus and Amerindians 7·50 5·75

F178 Canoeing

1992. Olympic Games, Barcelona. Multicoloured.
F461 2f.50 Type **F178** 1·90 2·30
F462 3f.40 Shooting 2·20 2·50

F179 Globe Flowers

1992. Nature Protection. Multicoloured.
F463 2f.50 Type **F179** 1·70 2·40
F464 3f.40 Griffon vulture ("El Voltor") (horiz) 2·30 2·75

F180 *Martyrdom of St. Eulalia* (altarpiece, St. Eulalia's Church, Encamp)

1992
F465 **F180** 4f. multicoloured 2·40 2·75

F181 *Ordino Arcalis 91* (Mauro Staccioli)

1992. Modern Sculpture. Multicoloured.
F466 5f. Type **F181** 3·25 3·50
F467 5f. *Storm in a Teacup* (Dennis Oppenheim) (horiz) 3·25 3·50

F182 Grau Roig

1993. Ski Resorts. Multicoloured.
F468 2f.50 Type **F182** 1·60 2·30
F469 2f.50 Ordino 1·60 2·30
F470 2f.50 Soldeu el Tarter 1·60 2·30
F471 3f.40 Pal 2·30 2·75
F472 3f.40 Arinsal 2·30 2·75

F183 *Estructures Autogeneradores* (Jorge du Bon)

1993. Europa. Contemporary Art.
F473 **F183** 2f.50 dp bl, bl & vio 2·20 3·25
F474 - 3f.40 multicoloured 2·40 3·50
DESIGN—HORIZ: 3f.40, *Fisicromia per Andorra* (Carlos Cruz-Diez).

F184 Common Blue

1993. Nature Protection. Butterflies. Multicoloured.
F475 2f.50 Type **F184** 2·10 3·25
F476 4f.20 *Nymphalidae* 3·00 4·00

F185 Cyclist

1993. Tour de France Cycling Road Race.
F477 **F185** 2f.50 multicoloured 2·20 3·50

F186 Smiling Hands

1993. Tenth Anniv of Andorran School.
F478 **F186** 2f.80 multicoloured 2·50 3·50

F187 *A Pagan Place* (Michael Warren)

1993. Modern Sculpture.
F479 **F187** 5f. black and blue 3·50 3·00
F480 - 5f. multicoloured 3·50 3·00
DESIGN: No. F480, *Pep, Lu, Canolic, Ton, Meritxell, Roma, Anna, Pau, Carles, Eugenia... and Others* (Erik Dietman).

F188 Cross-country Skiing

1994. Winter Olympic Games, Lillehammer, Norway.
F481 **F188** 3f.70 multicoloured 2·20 2·50

F189 Constitution Monument

1994. First Anniv of New Constitution.
F482 **F189** 2f.80 multicoloured 1·90 2·00
F483 - 3f.70 blk, yell & mve 2·40 3·50
DESIGN: 3f.70, Stone tablet.

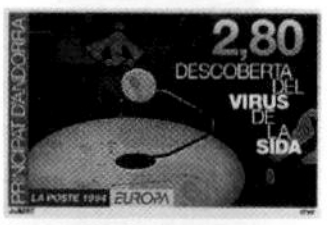

F190 AIDS Virus

1994. Europa. Discoveries and Inventions. Multicoloured.
F484 2f.80 Type F **190** 2·50 2·50
F485 3f.70 Radio mast 3·00 3·00

F191 Competitors' Flags and Football

1994. World Cup Football Championship, U.S.A.
F486 **F191** 3f.70 multicoloured 2·50 2·75

F192 Horse Riding

1994. Tourist Activities. Multicoloured.
F487 2f.80 Type **F192** 1·90 1·90
F488 2f.80 Mountain biking 1·90 1·90
F489 2f.80 Climbing 1·90 1·90
F490 2f.80 Fishing 1·90 1·90

F193 Scarce Swallowtail

1994. Nature Protection. Butterflies. Multicoloured.
F491 2f.80 Type **F193** 2·50 2·75
F492 4f.40 Small tortoiseshell 3·75 4·00

F194 "26 10 93"

1994. Meeting of Co-princes.
F493 **F194** 2f.80 multicoloured 1·70 2·00

F195 Emblem

1995. European Nature Conservation Year.
F494 **F195** 2f.80 multicoloured 1·90 2·10

F196 Globe, Goal and Player

1995. Third World Cup Rugby Championship, South Africa.
F495 **F196** 2f.80 multicoloured 1·90 2·10

F197 Dove and Olive Twig ("Peace")

1995. Europa. Peace and Freedom. Multicoloured.
F496 2f.80 Type **F197** 2·50 2·75
F497 3f.70 Flock of doves ("Freedom") 2·75 3·00

F198 Emblem

1995. 15th Anniv of Caritas Andorrana (welfare organization).
F498 **F198** 2f.80 multicoloured 1·90 2·30

F199 Caldea Thermal Baths, Les Escaldes-Engordany

1995
F499 **F199** 2f.80 multicoloured 1·90 2·30

F200 National Auditorium, Ordino

1995
F500 **F200** 3f.70 black and buff 2·50 2·75

F201 "Virgin of Meritxell"

1995
F501 **F201** 4f.40 multicoloured 2·75 3·00

F202 Brimstone

1995. Nature Protection. Butterflies. Multicoloured.
F502 2f.80 Type **F202** 2·50 2·75
F503 3f.70 Marbled white (horiz) 3·00 3·25

F203 National Flag over U.N. Emblem

1995. 50th Anniv of U.N.O. Multicoloured.
F504 2f.80 Type **F203** 2·50 2·75
F505 3f.70 Anniversary emblem over flag 2·75 3·00

F204 National Flag and Palace of Europe, Strasbourg

1995. Admission of Andorra to Council of Europe.

F506 **F204** 2f.80 multicoloured 1·90 2·00

F205 Emblem

1996. Fourth Borrufa Trophy Skiing Competition.

F507 **F205** 2f.80 multicoloured 1·90 2·00

F206 Basketball

1996

F508 **F206** 3f.70 red, blk & yell 3·00 3·75

F207 Children

1996. 25th Anniv of Our Lady of Meritxell Special School.

F509 **F207** 2f.80 multicoloured 1·90 2·10

F208 European Robin

1996. Nature Protection. Multicoloured.

F510 3f. Type **F208** 2·50 3·00

F511 3f.80 Great tit 3·00 3·25

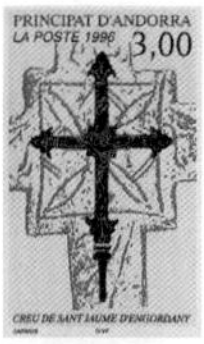

F209 Cross, St. James's Church, Engordany

1996. Religious Objects. Multicoloured.

F512 3f. Type **F209** 2·50 2·75

F513 3f.80 Censer, St. Eulalia's Church, Encamp (horiz) 2·75 3·00

F210 Ermessenda de Castellbo

1996. Europa. Famous Women.

F514 **F210** 3f. multicoloured 2·50 2·75

F211 Chessmen

1996. Chess.

F515 **F211** 4f.50 red, black & bl 2·50 2·75

F212 Canillo

1996. No value expressed. Self-adhesive.

F516 **F212** (3f.) multicoloured 3·00 3·25

F213 Cycling, Running and Throwing the Javelin

1996. Olympic Games, Atlanta.

F517 **F213** 3f. multicoloured 1·90 2·00

F214 Singers

1996. Fifth Anniv of National Youth Choir.

F518 **F214** 3f. multicoloured 1·90 2·00

F215 Man and Boy with Animals

1996. Livestock Fair.

F519 **F215** 3f. yellow, red and black 1·90 2·00

F216 St. Roma's Chapel, Les Bons

1996. Churches. Multicoloured.

F520 6f.70 Type F **216** 4·00 4·25

F521 6f.70 Santa Coloma 4·00 4·25

F217 Mitterrand

1997. Francois Mitterrand (President of France and Co-prince of Andorra, 1981–95) Commemoration.

F522 **F217** 3f. multicoloured 1·90 2·00

F218 Parish Emblem

1997. Parish of Encamp. No value expressed. Self-adhesive.

F523 **F218** (3f.) blue 1·90 2·00

F219 Volleyball

1997

F524 **F219** 3f. multicoloured 1·90 2·00

F220 The White Lady

1997. Europa. Tales and Legends.

F525 **F220** 3f. multicoloured 2·50 2·75

F221 House Martin approaching Nest

1997. Nature Protection.

F526 **F221** 3f.80 multicoloured 1·90 2·00

F222 Mill and Saw-mill, Cal Pal

1997. Tourism. Paintings by Francesc Galobardes. Multicoloured.

F527 3f. Type **F222** 2·50 2·75

F528 4f.50 Mill and farmhouse, Sole (horiz) 3·00 3·25

F223 Monstrance, St. Iscle and St. Victoria's Church

1997. Religious Silver Work. Multicoloured.

F529 3f. Type **F223** 2·50 2·75

F530 15f.50 Pax, St. Peter's Church, Aixirivall 7·50 8·00

F224 The Legend of Meritxell

1997. Legends. Multicoloured.

F531 3f. Type **F224** 1·90 2·10

F532 3f. The Seven-armed Cross 1·90 2·10

F533 3f.80 Wrestlers (The Fountain of Esmelicat) 3·00 3·25

F225 St. Michael's Chapel, Engolasters

1997. International Stamp Exn, Monaco.

F534 **F225** 3f. multicoloured 1·90 2·10

F226 Harlequin juggling Candles

1998. Birthday Greetings Stamp.

F535 **F226** 3f. multicoloured 1·90 2·10

F227 Super Giant Slalom

1997. Winter Olympic Games, Nagano, Japan.

F536 **F227** 4f.40 multicoloured 3·25 3·50

F228 Arms of Ordino

1998. No value expressed. Self-adhesive.

F537 **F228** (3f.) multicoloured 1·90 2·10

F229 Altarpiece and Vila Church

1998

F538 **F229** 4f.50 multicoloured 3·25 3·50

F230 Emblem and Cogwheels

1998. 20th Anniv of Rotary Int in Andorra.

F539 **F230** 3f. multicoloured 1·90 2·10

F231 Chaffinch and Berries

1998. Nature Protection.

F540 **F231** 3f.80 multicoloured 3·00 3·25

F232 Players

1998. World Cup Football Championship, France.

F541 **F232** 3f. multicoloured 1·90 2·10

F233 Treble Score and Stylized Orchestra

1998. Europa. National Festivals. Music Festival.

F542 **F233** 3f. multicoloured 1·90 2·10

F234 River

1998. "Expo '98" World's Fair, Lisbon, Portugal.

F543 **F234** 5f. multicoloured 3·75 4·25

F235 Chalice

1998. Chalice from the House of the Valleys.

F544	**F235**	4f.50 multicoloured	3·25	3·75

1998. French Victory in World Cup Football Championship. No. F541 optd **FINAL FRANCA/ BRASIL 3-0**.

F545	**F232**	3f. multicoloured	3·75	4·25

F237 Andorra, 1717

1998. Relief Maps. Multicoloured.

F546	3f. Type F **237**	1·90	2·10
F547	15f.50 Andorra, 1777 (horiz)	9·75	10·50

F238 Museum

1998. Inauguration of Postal Museum.

F548	**F238**	3f. multicoloured	1·90	2·10

F239 Front Page of First Edition

1998. 250th Anniv of *Manual Digest*.

F549	**F239**	3f.80 multicoloured	3·00	3·25

F240 Arms of La Massana

1999. No value expressed. Self-adhesive.

F550	**F240**	(3f.) multicoloured	1·90	2·10

F241 House and Recycling Bins

1999. "Green World". Recycling of Waste.

F551	**F241**	5f. multicoloured	3·75	4·25

F242 Vall de Sorteny

1999. Europa. Parks and Gardens.

F552	**F242**	3f. multicoloured	1·90	2·10

F243 Council Emblem and Seat, Strasbourg

1999. 50th Anniv of Council of Europe.

F553	**F243**	3f.80 multicoloured	3·00	3·25

F244 "The First Mail Coach"

1999

F554	**F244**	2f.70 multicoloured	1·70	1·90

F245 Footballer and Flags

1999. Andorra–France Qualifying Match for European Nations Football Championship.

F555	**F245**	4f.50 multicoloured	3·50	4·00

F246 St. Michael's Church, Engolasters, and Emblem

1999. "Philexfrance 99" International Stamp Exhibition, Paris, France.

F556	**F246**	3f. multicoloured	1·80	2·00

F247 Winter Scene

1999. Paintings of Pal by Francesc Galobardes. Multicoloured.

F557	3f. Type F **247**	1·80	2·00
F558	3f. Summer scene (horiz)	1·80	2·00

F248 Emblem and "50"

1999. 50th Anniv of International Photographic Art Federation.

F559	**F248**	4f.40 multicoloured	2·75	3·00

F249 Rull House, Sispony

1999

F560	**F249**	15f.50 multicoloured	7·25	8·00

F250 Chest with Six Locks

1999

F561	**F250**	6f.70 multicoloured	3·25	3·50

F251 Angels

1999. Christmas.

F562	**F251**	3f. multicoloured	1·80	2·00

F252 Revellers

2000. New Millennium.

F563	**F252**	3f. multicoloured	1·80	2·00

F253 Arms of La Vella

2000. No value expressed. Self-adhesive.

F564	**F253**	(3f.) multicoloured	1·80	2·00

F254 Snow Boarder

2000

F565	**F254**	4f.50 blue, brown and black	2·75	3·00

F255 Emblem

2000. Montserrat Caballe International Opera Competition, Saint Julia de Loria.

F566	**F255**	3f.80 yellow and blue	2·30	2·50

F256 *Campanula cochlearifolia*

2000

F567	**F256**	2f.70 multicoloured	1·80	2·00

F257 "Building Europe"

2000. Europa.

F568	**F257**	3f. multicoloured	2·50	2·75

F258 Church (Canolich Festival)

2000. Festivals. Multicoloured.

F569	3f. Type **F258**	1·80	2·00
F570	3f. People at Our Lady's Chapel, Meritxell (Meritxell Festival)	1·80	2·00

F259 Sparrow

2000

F571	**F259**	4f.40 multicoloured	2·75	3·00

F260 Hurdling

2000. Olympic Games, Sydney.

F572	**F260**	5f. multicoloured	3·00	3·50

F261 Goat, Skier and Walker

2000. Tourism Day.

F573	**F261**	3f. multicoloured	1·80	2·00

F262 Flower, Text, Circuit Board and Emblems

2000. "EXPO 2000" World's Fair, Hanover.

F574	**F262**	3f. multicoloured	1·80	2·00

F263 Stone Arch and Flag

2000. European Community.

F575	**F263**	3f.80 multicoloured	2·30	2·50

F264 Pottery

2000. Prehistoric Pottery.

F576	**F264**	6f.70 multicoloured	3·25	3·50

F265 Drawing

2000. 25th Anniv of National Archives.

F577	**F265**	15f.50 multicoloured	7·25	8·00

F266 Arms of Saint Julia de Loria

2001. No value expressed. Self-adhesive.

F578	**F266**	(3f.) multicoloured	1·80	2·00

F267 Ski Lift

2001. Canillo Aliga Club.

F579	**F267**	4f.50 multicoloured	2·75	3·00

F268 Decorative Metalwork

2001. Casa Cristo Museum.

F580	**F268**	6f.70 multicoloured	3·25	3·50

F269 Legend of Lake Engolasters

2001. Legends. Multicoloured.

F581	3f. Type F **269**	1·80	2·00
F582	3f. Lords before King (foundation of Andorra)	1·80	2·00

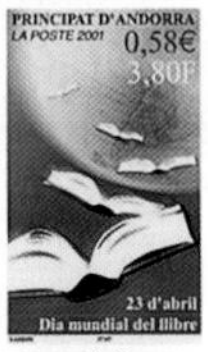
F270 Globe and Books

2001. World Book Day.

F583	**F270**	3f.80 multicoloured	2·30	2·50

F271 Water Splash

2001. Europa. Water Resources.

F584	**F271**	3f. multicoloured	2·50	2·75

F272 Raspberry

2001. Multicoloured.

F585	3f. Type **F272**	2·30	2·50
F586	4f.40 Jay (horiz)	3·00	3·50

F273 Profiles talking

2001. European Year of Languages.

F587	**F273**	3f.80 multicoloured	2·75	3·25

F274 Trumpeter

2001. Jazz Festival, Escaldes-Engordany.

F588	**F274**	3f. multicoloured	2·30	2·50

F275 Kitchen

2001

F589	**F275**	5f. multicoloured	3·00	3·50

F276 Chapel

2001. 25th Anniv of Chapel of Our Lady, Meritxell.

F590	**F276**	3f. multicoloured	2·30	2·50

F277 Hotel Pla

2001

F591	**F277**	15f.50 black, violet and green	7·75	8·75

F278 Cross

2001. Grossa Cross (boundary cross at the crossroads between Avinguda Meritxell and Carrer Bisbe Iglesias).

F592	**F278**	2f.70 multicoloured	1·60	1·70

F279 State Arms

2002. (a) With Face Value. Ordinary gum.

F593	**F279**	1c. multicoloured	30	35
F594	**F279**	2c. multicoloured	30	35
F595	**F279**	5c. multicoloured	30	35
F596	**F279**	60c. multicoloured	1·90	2·10

(b) No value expressed.

F598	(46c.) multicoloured	2·30	2·50
F599	(46c.) multicoloured	2·30	2·50

(ii) Size 17×23 mm. Self-adhesive gum.

F599a	(52c.) multicoloured	1·70	1·90

Nos. F598/9 were sold at the rate for inland letters up to 20 grammes.

F280 The Legend of Meritxell

2002. Legends. Designs as Nos. F525, F531/3 and F581/2 but with values in new currency as Type **F280**. Multicoloured.

F600	10c. Type **F280**	55	60
F601	20c. Wrestlers (The Fountain of Esmelicat)	55	60
F602	41c. The Piper (La joueurde cornemuse)	1·40	1·60
F603	45c. Legend of Saint Vincent Castle	1·40	1·60
F604	48c. Port Rat (horiz)	2·10	2·30
F604a	48c. The Cave of Ourses	1·40	1·60
F604b	49c. The Testament of llop	1·40	1·60
F604c	50c. El tresor de la font del Manego	1·40	1·60
F605	50c. The Seven-armed Cross	1·40	1·60
F606	51c. The Devils of Aiscirivall Ches Diables d'Aixirivall	2·10	2·30
F606a	75c. 'Le joueur de cornemuse'	2·75	3·00
F606b	90c. Legende du pin de la "Margin eda"	1·20	1·80
F610	€1 Lords before King (foundation of Andorra)	2·75	3·00
F611	€2 Legend of Lake Engolasters	5·50	6·25
F612	€5 The White Lady	12·50	14·00

F281 Pedestrians on Crossing

2002. Schools' Road Safety Campaign.

F615	**F281**	69c. multicoloured	2·50	2·75

F282 Skier

2002. Winter Olympic Games, Salt Lake City, U.S.A.

F616	**F282**	58c. multicoloured	1·90	2·10

F283 Hotel Rosaleda

2002

F617	**F283**	46c. multicoloured	1·70	1·80

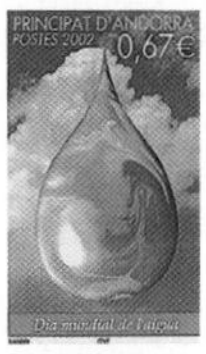
F284 Water Droplet and Clouds

2002. World Water Day.

F618	**F284**	67c. multicoloured	2·10	2·30

F285 Clown

2002. Europa. Circus.

F619	**F285**	46c. multicoloured	2·50	2·75

F286 Myrtle

2002

F620	**F286**	46c. multicoloured	1·70	1·80

F287 Seated Nude (Josep Viladomat)

2002

F621	**F287**	€2.26 multicoloured	6·50	7·00

F288 Mountains from Tunnel Entrance

2002. Completion of the Envalira Road Tunnel between Andorra and France.

F622	**F288**	46c. multicoloured	1·70	1·80

F289 Mural (detail) (Santa Coloma Church, Andorra la Vella)

2002

F623	**F289**	€1.02 multicoloured	3·25	3·50

F290 Arms of Escaldes – Engordany

2003. Arms. No value expressed. Self-adhesive.

F624	**F 290**	(46c.) multicoloured	1·90	2·10

No. F624 was sold at the rate for inland letters up to 20 grammes.

2003. Legends. 'Legende du pinde la Margineda'. As T **F280**.

F625	69c. multicoloured	1·90	2·10

F291 State Arms

2003. Tenth Anniv of Constitution.

F626	**F 291**	€2.36 multicoloured	6·50	7·00

F292 Les Bons

2003. Architecture.

F627	**F 292**	67c. multicoloured	2·50	2·10

F293 Hotel Mirador

2003

F628	**F 293**	€1.02 multicoloured	3·25	3·50

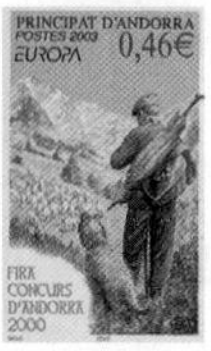
F294 Man, Dog and Sheep

2003. Europa. Poster Art.

F629	**F 294**	46c. multicoloured	2·50	2·75

F295 Dancers and Fire

2003. Fires of St. John the Baptist Festival.

F630	**F 295**	50c. multicoloured	1·90	2·10

F296 Cyclist and Map

2003. Centenary of Tour de France (cycle race).

F631	**F 296**	50c. multicoloured	1·90	2·10

F297 Pole Vault

2003. World Athletics Championship, Paris.

F632	**F 297**	90c. multicoloured	2·75	3·25

F298 *Greixa sparassis crispa*

2003
F633 **F298** 45c. multicoloured 1·30 1·40

F299 Red Currant

2003
F634 **F299** 75c. multicoloured 2·50 2·75

F300 Telephone, Satellite and Globe

2003. Centenary of First Telephone in Andorra.
F635 **F300** 50c. multicoloured 1·90 2·10

F301 *Maternity* (Paul Gauguin)

2003
F636 **F301** 75c. multicoloured 2·75 3·00

F302 St. Anthony's Market

2004
F637 **F302** 50c. multicoloured 1·90 2·10

F303 Children

2004
F638 **F303** 50c. multicoloured 1·90 2·10

F304 Hotel Valira

2004
F639 **F304** €1.11 multicoloured 3·50 3·75

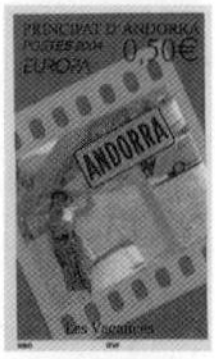

F305 Woman and Andorra Sign

2004. Europa. Holidays.
F640 **F305** 50c. orange, red and black 2·10 2·30

F306 Madriu-Perafita-Claror Valley

2004. UNESCO World Heritage Site.
F641 **F306** 75c. multicoloured 2·50 2·75

F307 Poblet de Fontaneda

2004
F642 **F307** 50c. multicoloured 1·90 2·10

F308 Runner and Swimmer

2004. Olympic Games, Athens 2004.
F643 **F308** 90c. multicoloured 3·00 3·25

F309 *Pont de la Margineda* (sketch)

2004. Arts. Margineda Bridge by Joaquim Mir (Spanish artist). Multicoloured.
F644 €1 Type F **309** 3·00 3·25
F645 €2 *Pont de la Margineda* (painting) 5·75 6·25

F310 Town Names and Post Codes

2004. Introduction of Postal Codes.
F646 **F310** 50c. vermilion, black and lemon 1·90 2·10

F311 Emblem

2004. Tenth Anniv of Entry into Council of Europe.
F647 **F311** €2.50 multicoloured 7·75 8·50

F312 Children's Nativity

2004. Christmas.
F648 **F312** 50c. black, brown and bistre 1·90 2·10

F313 Three Kings visiting Child

2005
F649 **F313** 50c. multicoloured 1·90 2·10

F314 Mountains and Lake

2005. World Heritage Site. Madriu-Claror-Perafita Valley.
F650 **F314** 50c. multicoloured 1·90 2·10

F315 Tengmalm's Owl (*Aegolius funereus*)

2005
F651 **F315** 90c. multicoloured 2·75 3·25

F316 Bottle, Glass, Jug and Fruit

2005. Europa. Gastronomy.
F652 **F316** 55c. multicoloured 2·00 2·20

F317 Marksman

2005. Small States of Europe Games. Sheet 151×70 mm containing Type **F317** and similar vert designs. Each black and magenta.
MSF653 53c. Type **F317**; 55c. Runner; 82c. Swimmer; €1 Diver 9·00 9·50

F318 Mountain Hut, Bordes d'Ensegur

2005
F654 **F318** €2.50 multicoloured 8·00 8·75

F319 Motorcycle

2005
F655 **F319** 53c. sepia, brown and black 1·60 1·70

F320 *Prats de Santa Coloma* (Joaquim Mir)

2005. Art.
F656 **F320** 82c. multicoloured 2·75 2·75

F321 Hostel Calones

2005
F657 **F321** €1.98 multicoloured 6·25 6·50

F322 Lorry in Snow (Josep Alsina)

2005. Photography.
F658 **F322** 53c. multicoloured 1·70 1·80

F323 Emblem

2005. Centenary of Rotary International.
F659 **F323** 55c. multicoloured 1·90 2·00

F324 *Adoration of the Shepherds* (A. Viladomat)

2005. Christmas.
F660 **F324** €1.22 multicoloured 4·00 4·25

F325 *Ursus arctos*

2006. Fauna. Multicoloured.
F661 53c. Type **F325** 1·70 1·80
F662 53c. *Rupicapra pyrenaica* (vert) 1·70 1·80

F326 Alpine Skier

2006. Winter Olympic Games, Turin. Multicoloured.
F663 55c. Type **F326** 1·70 1·80
F664 75c. Cross country skier 2·30 2·50

F326a Tobacco Leaves

2006. Tobacco Museum, Sant Julia de Loria.
F665 **F326a** 82c. multicoloured 2·75 2·75

F327 Napoleon

2006. Bicentenary of Napoleon's Decree restoring Statute of Co-Principality.
F666 **F327** 53c. blue, azure and black 1·70 1·80

F328 Coloured blocks

2006. Europa. Integration.
F667 **F328** 53c. multicoloured 2·00 2·10

F329 Sorteny Valley Nature Reserve

2006
F668 **F329** 55c. multicoloured 1·90 2·00

F330 Pablo Casals

2006. 130th Birth Anniv of Pablo Casals (cellist).
F669 **F330** 90c. multicoloured 3·00 3·25

F331 Model T Ford

2006
F670 **F331** 85c. multicoloured 2·75 3·00

F332 *Montserrat Procession* (Josep Borrell)

2006
F671 **F332** €1.30 multicoloured 4·25 4·50

F333 Reredos (retable), Sant Marti de la Cortinada, Ordino

2006
F672 **F333** 54c. multicoloured 1·90 2·00

F334 Marmot (*Marmota marmota*)

2007. Funa. Multicoloured.
F673 54c. Type **F334** 1·90 2·00
F674 60c. Eurasian red squirrel (*Sciurus vulgaris*) (horiz) 2·00 2·10

F335 *Predel-la de Prats* (Master of Canillo)

2007. *Pradel la des Prats...*
F675 **F335** €1.30 multicoloured 4·25 4·50

F336 Heart enclosing Rose

2007. Saint George.
F676 **F336** 86c. multicoloured 3·00 3·25

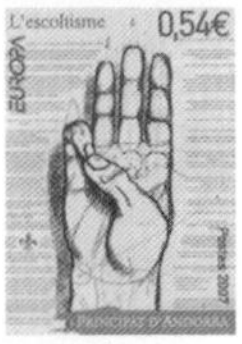

F337 Salute

2007. Europa. Centenary of Scouting.
F677 **F337** 54c. multicoloured 1·90 2·00

F338 Virgin, Meritxell

2007. Twinning of Meritxell and Sabart. Multicoloured.
F678 54c. Type F **338** 1·90 2·00
F679 54c. Virgin, Sabart 1·90 2·00

F339 'Pinette'

2007
F680 **F339** 60c. multicoloured 2·00 2·10

F340 Players

2007. Rugby World Cup, France.
F681 **F340** 85c. multicoloured 2·75 3·00

F341 Vall del Comapedrosa

2007
F682 **F341** €3.04 multicoloured 10·00 10·50

F341a Prehistoric Family

2007. Pre-Historic Sites. El Cedre.
F683 **F341a** 85c. multicoloured 3·00 3·25

F342 Cave Dwellers

2007. Pre-Historic Sites. La Barma de la Marginada.
F684 **F342** 60c. multicoloured 2·00 2·10

F343 Altarpiece, Sant Marti de la Cortinada

2007. Christmas.
F685 **F343** 54c. multicoloured 1·90 2·00

F344 *Vulpes vulpes* (red fox)

2008. Fauna. Multicoloured.
F686 54c. Type **F344** 2·00 2·10
F687 60c. *Sus scrofa* (wild boar) (vert) 2·20 2·30

F345 Predella's Altar of St. Michaels d'Pratts church

2008. Easter.
F688 **F345** €1.33 multicoloured 5·00 5·25

F346 Cartercar, 1906

2008
F689 **F346** 65c. multicoloured 2·75 2·75

F347 Symbols of Writing

2008. Europa. The Letter.
F690 **F347** 55c. multicoloured 2·30 2·40

F348 Rowing

2008. Olympic Games, Beijing. Sheet 210×60 mm containing Type **F348** and similar horiz designs. Multicoloured.
MSF691 55c.×4, Type **F348**; Running; Swimming; Judo 8·25 8·50
The stamps of **MS**F691 were not for sale separately.

F349 *Narcissus poeticus*

2008
F692 **F349** 55c. multicoloured 2·30 2·40

F350 Vall d'Incles (Incles valley)

2008
F693 **F350** €2.80 multicoloured 10·50 11·00

F351 Men

2008. 75th Anniv of Male Suffrage.
F694 **F351** 55c. multicoloured 2·30 2·40

F352 Valley

2008. Sustainable Development.
F695 **F352** 88c. multicoloured 3·75 4·00

F353 El roc d'Enclar

2008
F696 **F353** 85c. multicoloured 3·50 3·75

F354 St. Mark and St. Mary (alterpiece (reredos))

2008
F697 **F354** 55c. multicoloured 2·75 2·75

F355 Louis Braille

2009. Birth Bicentenary of Louis Braille (inventor of Braille writing for the blind).
F698 **F355** 88c. blue and brown 4·00 4·00

F356 *Equus mulus* (mule)

2009. Domestic Animals. Multicoloured.
F699 55c. Type **F356** 2·30 2·40
F700 65c. *Bos taurus* (cow) (horiz) 2·50 2·50

F357 Penguins

2009. Preserve Polar Regions and Glaciers. Sheet 143×120 mm containing Type **F357** and similar multicoloured design.
MSF701 56c. Type **F357**; 85c. Polar ice 6·25 6·50

F358 *Pradel la des Prats* (detail)

2009
F702 **F358** €1.35 multicoloured 6·00 6·25

F359 Nebula

2009. Europa. Astronomy.
F703 **F359** 56c. multicoloured 2·50 2·50

F360 Renault Voiturette, 1898

2009. First Car manufactured by Renault.
F704 **F360** 70c. multicoloured 3·00 3·25

F361 *Sant Joan de Caselles* (Maurice Utrillo)

2009. Art.
F705 **F361** 90c. multicoloured 4·00 4·00

F362 Cercle dels Pessons

2009
F706 **F362** €2.80 multicoloured 11·50 12·00

F363 Cyclist

2009. Tour de France (cycle race).
F707 **F363** 56c. multicoloured 2·50 2·50

F364 Allegory

2009. 40th Anniv of Circle of Arts and Letters.
F708 **F364** 51c. multicoloured 2·40 2·40

F365 Santa Coloma Church

2009. Romanesque Art in Andorra.
F709 **F365** 85c. multicoloured 3·75 3·75

F366 The Nativity

2009. Christmas.
F710 **F366** 56c. multicoloured 2·50 2·50

F366a Arms

2010. State Arms. Background colour given. (a) With face value.
F710a **F366a** 1c. multicoloured (pale lemon) 20 25
F711 5c. multicoloured (cobalt) 25 30
F712 10c. multicoloured (bright yellow-orange) 55 60
F713 20c. multicoloured (lavender) 55 60
F714 50c. multicoloured (olive-bistre) 1·40 1·60

(b) No value expressed.
F715 (60c.) multicoloured (aqua-marine) 2·40 2·50

Nos. F710a/F715 are as No. **F279** but with different inscriptions.

F367 Athlete

2010. Winter Olympic Games, Vancouver.
F716 **F367** 85c. multicoloured 3·75 3·75

F368 Casamanya Peak

2010. Mountains.
F717 **F368** €2.80 multicoloured 11·50 12·00

F369 Anniversary Emblem

2010. 20th Anniv of Convention on Rights of the Child. UNICEF
F718 **F369** 56c. multicoloured 2·50 2·50

F370 *Gyps fulvus* (griffon vulture)

2010. Vulture
F719 **F370** 56c. multicoloured 2·50 2·50

F371 Ovis aries (sheep)

2010. Sheep
F720 **F371** 90c. multicoloured 3·50 3·50

F372 Embassy of Andorra in Brussels

2010. Antverpia 2010–International Stamp Exhibition, Antwerp
F721 **F372** 70c. multicoloured 3·00 3·00

No. F722 and Type **F373** are left for Legends issued on 26 April 2010, not yet received.

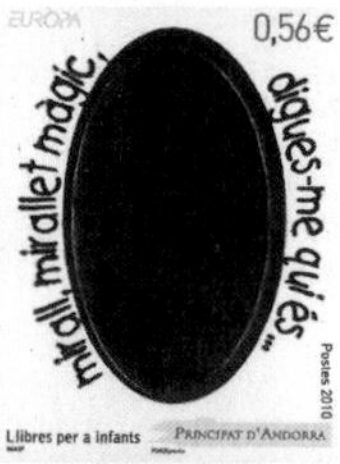

F374 Mirror and 'Mirror, Magic Mirror, tell me which is' (from Snow White)

2010. Europa. Children's Books
F723 **F374** 56c. silver and bright rose-red 2·50 2·50

F375 Radio Andorra

2010. Radio Andorra
F724 **F375** 56c. multicoloured 2·50 2·50

F377 Ferrari 328 GTS

2010. Classic Cars
F725 **F377** 70c. multicoloured 3·00 3·00

F378 Still Life (Carme Massana)

2010. Art
F726 **F378** 95c. multicoloured 3·75 3·75

F379 The Crucifixion of Christ, Predella of the Altar of Saint-Michel De Prats Church (detail)

2010. Religious Art
F727 **F379** €1.40 multicoloured 2·50 2·50
See also No. F702.

F380 Sant Joan de Caselles

2010. Romanesque Art in Andorra. Multicoloured.
MSF728 58c.×2, Type **F380;** Sant Romà de les Bons (horiz) 5·75 5·75

2010. State Arms. No value expressed.
F729 **F366a** (58c.) multicoloured (bright vermilion) 2·75 2·75
As Type **F366a**

F381 Signing of Paréage of Andorra on Escalls Bridge

2010. Feudal Andorra. Signing of Paréages of Andorra (Parity Treaties)
F730 **F381** 87c. multicoloured 3·75 3·75

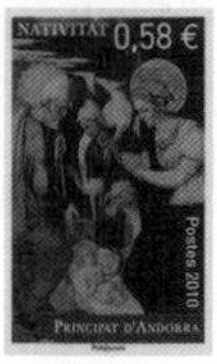

F382 The Epiphany

2010. Christmas
F731 **F382** 58c. multicoloured 2·50 2·50

F383 *Saint Joan de Caselle*

2011. Legends. 'Saint Joan de Caselle'
F732 **F383** €2.80 multicoloured 11·50 11·50

F384 Lighthouse Beam showing French Flag Colours

2011. Francophone
F733 **F384** 87c. multicoloured 4·00 4·00

F385 Taking of Christ, Predella of the Altar of Saint-Michel De Prats Church (detail)

2010. Religious Art
F734 **F385** €1.40 multicoloured 5·75 5·75
See also No. F702 and F727

F386 Tree Bark

2011. Europa. Forests. Self-adhesive

F735	**F386**	58c. multicoloured	2·75	2·75

F387 Francesc Borras

2011. Francesc Borras

F736	**F387**	95c. multicoloured	4·25	4·25

F388 Placeta de Sant Esteve

2011. Placeta de Sant Esteve

F737	**F388**	58c. multicoloured	2·75	2·75

F389 Soriano Pedroso Type P, 1922

2011. Soriano Pedroso Automobile Manufacturer

F738	**F389**	75c. m ulticoloured	3·50	3·50

F390 Games Emblem as Maori Shield

2011. Rugby World Cup Championship, New Zealand

F739	**F390**	89c. mutlicoloured	4·00	4·00

F391 Dansa de les 7 Parròquies, Placa Benlloch, Andorra la Vella

2011. Folk Dances. Sheet 105×71 mm.

MSF740 F**391** €1.45 multicoloured		6·50	6·50

F392 *Rhododendron ferrugineum*

2011. Flowers and Fruit. Multicoloured.

F741	60c. Type F**392**	2·75	2·75
F742	€1 Rose hips (*Rosa sempervirens*)	4·50	4·50

F393 Consell de la Terra

2011. Conseil de la Terra, 1866 (forerunner of Parliament)

F743	**F393**	89c. multicoloured	4·00	4·00

F394 Angel del Retaule de Santa Eulalia d'Encamp

2011. Angel from the Reredos of Santa Eulalia d'Encamp Church

F744	**F394**	60c. multicoloured	2·75	2·75

POSTAGE DUE STAMPS

1931. Postage Due stamps of France optd **ANDORRE**.

FD24	**D11**	5c. blue	2·10	5·75
FD25	**D11**	10c. brown	2·10	4·50
FD26	**D11**	30c. red	1·10	5·25
FD27	**D11**	50c. purple	2·10	5·75
FD28	**D11**	60c. green	26·00	55·00
FD29	**D11**	1f. brown on yellow	2·10	7·00
FD30	**D11**	2f. mauve	17·00	41·00
FD31	**D11**	3f. mauve	4·25	9·75

1931. Postage Due stamps of France optd **ANDORRE**.

FD32	**D43**	1c. green	3·25	5·75
FD33	**D43**	10c. red	6·25	14·00
FD34	**D43**	60c. red	31·00	48·00
FD35	**D43**	1f. green	95·00	£140
FD36	**D43**	1f.20 on 2f. blue	90·00	£160
FD37	**D43**	2f. brown	£180	£275
FD38	**D43**	5f. on 1f. purple	95·00	£130

FD7

1935

FD82	**FD7**	1c. green	4·25	9·25

FD10

1937

FD97	**FD10**	5c. blue	7·50	16·00
FD98	**FD10**	10c. brown	5·25	30·00
FD99	**FD10**	2f. mauve	11·50	16·00
FD100	**FD10**	5f. orange	25·00	40·00

FD11 Wheat Sheaves

1943

FD101a	**FD 11**	10c. brown	65	2·10
FD102	**FD 11**	30c. mauve	1·90	2·75
FD103	**FD 11**	50c. green	1·40	3·25
FD104	**FD 11**	1f. blue	2·10	4·75
FD105	**FD 11**	1f.50 red	5·75	14·50
FD106	**FD 11**	2f. blue	2·10	5·25
FD107	**FD 11**	3f. red	2·50	9·75
FD108	**FD 11**	4f. violet	5·25	15·00
FD109	**FD 11**	5f. mauve	4·25	14·50
FD110	**FD 11**	10f. orange	5·75	15·00
FD111	**FD 11**	20f. brown	8·00	22·00

1946. As Type **FD11**, but inscr "TIMBRE-TAXE".

FD143	10c. brown	1·10	7·25
FD144	1f. blue	1·30	4·00
FD145	2f. blue	1·40	4·00
FD146	3f. brown	2·75	6·00
FD147	4f. violet	3·75	7·25
FD148	5f. red	2·10	5·75
FD149	10f. orange	3·75	7·50
FD150	20f. brown	7·50	13·00
FD151	50f. green	60·00	55·00
FD152	100f. green	£110	£160

1961. As Nos. FD143/52 but new values and colours.

FD185	5c. red	4·25	8·25
FD186	10c. orange	9·50	17·00
FD187	20c. brown	13·50	29·00
FD188	50c. green	26·00	47·00

1964. Designs as Nos. D1650/6 of France, but inscr "ANDORRE".

FD192	5c. red, green and purple	55	4·25
FD193	10c. blue, grn & pur	85	4·25
FD194	15c. red, green and brown	95	4·25
FD195	20c. purple, green & turq	1·10	4·25
FD196	30c. blue, grn & brn	85	2·50
FD197	40c. yellow, red and green	2·10	2·75
FD198	50c. red, green and blue	1·70	1·70

FD129 Holly Berries

1985. Fruits.

FD371	**FD129**	10c. red and green	1·70	2·75
FD372	-	20c. brown & blue	1·70	2·75
FD373	-	30c. green and red	1·70	2·75
FD374	-	40c. brown & blk	1·70	2·75
FD375	-	50c. olive & violet	1·70	2·75
FD376	-	1f. green and blue	1·70	2·75
FD377	-	2f. red and brown	1·80	3·00
FD378	-	3f. purple & green	2·10	3·50
FD379	-	4f. olive and blue	2·75	3·75
FD380	-	5f. olive and red	3·25	4·25

DESIGNS: 20c. Wild plum; 30c. Raspberry; 40c. Dogberry; 50c. Blackberry; 1f. Juniper; 2f. Rose hip; 3f. Elder; 4f. Bilberry; 5f. Strawberry.

SPANISH POST OFFICES

1928. Stamps of Spain optd **CORREOS ANDORRA**.

1B	**68**	2c. green	1·70	2·30
2B	**68**	5c. red	2·30	2·75
3B	**68**	10c. green	3·50	4·00
5B	**68**	15c. blue	3·50	4·00
6B	**68**	20c. violet	3·75	4·25
7A	**68**	25c. red	8·50	8·50
8A	**68**	30c. brown	29·00	29·00
9A	**68**	40c. blue	34·00	34·00
10A	**68**	50c. orange	37·00	37·00
11B	**69**	1p. grey	34·00	36·00
12A	**69**	4p. red	£180	£180
13A	**69**	10p. brown	£250	£250

2 House of the Valleys

3 General Council of Andorra

1929

14A	**2**	2c. green	2·00	2·30
26	**2**	2c. brown	1·40	2·30
15A	-	5c. purple	3·75	4·00
27	-	5c. brown	2·10	2·75
16A	-	10c. green	3·75	4·00
17A	-	15c. blue	5·50	5·75
30	-	15c. green	5·75	7·00
18A	-	20c. violet	5·50	6·25
33	-	25c. red	2·75	3·50
20A	**2**	30c. brown	£150	£160
34	**2**	30c. red	2·75	4·00
21A	-	40c. blue	11·50	8·00
36	**2**	45c. red	2·30	2·75
22A	-	50c. orange	11·50	7·00
38	**2**	60c. blue	4·50	5·75
23A	**3**	1p. slate	23·00	29·00
39	**3**	4p. purple	46·00	50·00
40	**3**	10p. brown	70·00	75·00

DESIGNS: 5, 40c. Church of St. John of Caselles; 10, 20, 50c. Sant Julia de Loria; 15, 25c. Santa Coloma Church.

7 Councillor Manuel Areny Bons

11 Map

1948

41	**F**	2c. olive	1·10	1·70
42	**F**	5c. orange	1·10	1·70
43	**F**	10c. blue	1·10	1·70
44	**7**	20c. purple	10·50	7·00
45	**7**	25c. orange	7·00	3·50
46	**G**	30c. green	23·00	11·50
47	**H**	50c. green	34·00	15·00
48	**I**	75c. blue	33·00	16·00
49	**H**	90c. purple	17·00	11·50
50	**I**	1p. red	29·00	15·00
51	**G**	1p.35 violet	11·50	11·50
52	**11**	4p. blue	34·00	29·00
53	**11**	10p. brown	65·00	34·00

DESIGNS—VERT: F. Edelweiss; G. Arms; H. Market Place, Ordino; I. Shrine near Meritxell Chapel.

12 Andorra La Vella

1951. Air.

54	**12**	1p. brown	40·00	26·00

13 St. Anthony's Bridge

1963

55	**13**	25c. brown and black	25	30
56	-	70c. black and green	35	55
57	-	1p. lilac and grey	90	1·50
58	-	2p. violet and lilac	1·10	1·70
59	-	2p.50 deep red and purple	90	1·40
60	-	3p. slate and black	1·10	1·60
61	-	5p. purple and brown	3·50	3·75
62	-	6p. red and brown	4·50	4·00

DESIGNS—VERT: 70c. Anyos meadows (wrongly inscr "AYNOS"); 1p. Canillo; 2p. Santa Coloma Church; 2p.50, Arms; 6p. Virgin of Meritxell. HORIZ: 3p. Andorra la Vella; 5p. Ordino.

14 Daffodills

1966. Pyrenean Flowers.

63	**14**	50c. blue and slate	55	1·10
64	-	1p. purple and brown	1·10	1·30
65	-	5p. blue and green	3·25	3·50
66	-	10p. slate and violet	1·70	2·75

DESIGNS: 1p. Carnation; 5p. Narcissus; 10p. Anemone (wrongly inscr "HELEBORUS CONI").

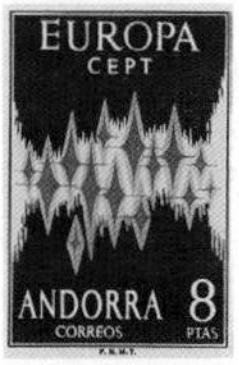

15 "Communications"

1972. Europa.

67	**15**	8p. multicoloured	£150	£140

16 Encamp Valley

1972. Tourist Views. Multicoloured.

68	1p. Type **16**	1·00	1·20
69	1p.50 La Massana	1·10	1·20
70	2p. Skis and snowscape, Pas de la Casa	2·10	2·40
71	5p. Lake Pessons (horiz)	2·30	2·40

17 Volleyball

1972. Olympic Games, Munich. Multicoloured.

72	2p. Type **17**	50	55
73	5p. Swimming (horiz)	70	75

18 St. Anthony's Auction

1972. Andorran Customs. Multicoloured.

74	1p. Type **18**	35	35
75	1p.50 "Les Caramelles" (choir)	35	35
76	2p. Nativity play (Christmas)	55	60
77	5p. Giant cigar (vert)	90	1·00
78	8p. Carved shrine, Meritxell (vert)	1·10	1·20
79	15p. "La Marratxa" (dance)	3·00	3·25

19 "Peoples of Europe"

1973. Europa.

80	**19**	2p. black, red and blue	55	60
81	-	8p. red, brown and black	1·70	1·90

DESIGN: 8p. Europa "Posthorn".

20 *The Nativity*

1973. Christmas. Frescoes from Meritxell Chapel. Multicoloured.

82	2p. Type **20**	55	60
83	5p. "Adoration of the Kings"	1·70	1·90

21 *Virgin of Ordino*

1974. Europa. Sculptures. Multicoloured.

84	2p. Type **21**	2·75	3·00
85	8p. Cross	4·00	4·25

22 Oak Cupboard and Shelves

1974. Arts and Crafts. Multicoloured.

86	10p. Type **22**	2·75	3·00
87	25p. Crown of the Virgin of the Roses	6·25	6·75

23 U.P.U. Monument, Berne

1974. Centenary of Universal Postal Union.

88	**23**	15p. multicoloured	3·50	3·75

24 *The Nativity*

1974. Christmas. Carvings from Meritxell Chapel. Multicoloured.

89	2p. Type **24**	1·10	1·20
90	5p. *Adoration of the Kings*	3·50	3·75

25 19th-century Postman and Church of St. John of Caselles

1975. "Espana 75" Int Stamp Exhibition, Madrid.

91	**25**	3p. multicoloured	55	60

26 *Peasant with Knife*

1975. Europa. 12th-century Romanesque Paintings from La Cortinada Church. Multicoloured.

92	3p. Type **26**	2·75	3·00
93	12p. *Christ*	5·75	6·25

27 Cathedral and Consecration Text

1975. 1100th Anniv of Consecration of Urgel Cathedral.

94	**27**	7p. multicoloured	3·50	3·75

28 *The Nativity*

1975. Christmas. Paintings from La Cortinada Church. Multicoloured.

95	3p. Type **28**	55	60
96	7p. *Adoration of The Kings*	1·10	1·20

29 Copper Cauldron

1976. Europa. Multicoloured.

97	3p. Type **29**	70	75
98	12p. Wooden marriage chest (horiz)	2·10	2·30

30 Slalom Skiing

1976. Olympic Games, Montreal. Multicoloured.

99	7p. Type **30**	70	75
100	15p. Canoeing (horiz)	2·10	2·30

31 *The Nativity*

1976. Christmas. Carvings from La Massana Church. Multicoloured.

101	3p. Type **31**	40	45
102	25p. *Adoration of the Kings*	2·50	2·75

32 Ansalonga

1977. Europa. Multicoloured.

103	3p. Type **32**	70	75
104	12p. Xuclar	2·10	2·30

33 Boundary Cross

1977. Christmas. Multicoloured.

105	5p. Type **33**	55	60
106	12p. St. Michael's Church, Engolasters	2·50	2·75

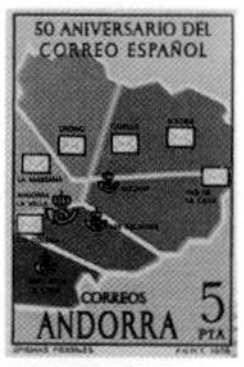

34 Map of Andorran Post Offices

1978. 50th Anniv of Spanish Post Offices. Sheet 105×149 mm containing T **34** and similar vert designs. Multicoloured.

MS107	5p. Type **34**; 10p. Postman delivering letter, 1923; 20p. Spanish Post Office, Andorra la Vella, 1928; 25p. Andorran arms	2·75	3·00

35 House of the Valleys

1978. Europa. Multicoloured.

108	5p. Type **35**	55	75
109	12p. Church of St. John of Caselles	1·40	2·30

36 Crown, Mitre and Crook

1978. 700th Anniv of Parity Treaties.

110	**36**	5p. multicoloured	85	1·50

37 *Holy Family*

1978. Christmas. Frescoes in St. Mary's Church, Encamp. Multicoloured.

111	5p. Type **37**	40	45
112	25p. *Adoration of the Kings*	95	1·10

38 Young Woman's Costume

1979. Local Costumes. Multicoloured.

113	3p. Type **38**	30	30
114	5p. Young man's costume	40	45
115	12p. Newly-weds	70	75

39 Old Mail Bus

1979. Europa.

116	**39**	5p. green & blue on yellow	70	75
117	-	12p. lilac and red on yellow	1·40	1·50

DESIGN: 12p. Pre-stamp letters.

40 Drawing of Boy and Girl

1979. International Year of the Child.

118	**40**	19p. blue, red and black	1·40	1·50

41 Agnus Dei, Santa Coloma Church

1979. Christmas. Multicoloured.

119	8p. Santa Coloma Church	40	45
120	25p. Type **41**	95	1·10

42 Pere d'Urg

1979. Bishops of Urgel, Co-princes of Andorra (1st series).

121	**42**	1p. blue and brown	30	30
122	-	5p. red and violet	40	45
123	-	13p. brown and green	85	90

DESIGNS: 5p. Joseph Caixal; 13p. Joan Benlloch.

See also Nos. 137/8, 171, 182 and 189.

43 Antoni Fiter i Rosell

1980. Europa.

124	**43**	8p. brown, ochre and green	40	45
125	-	19p. black, green & dp grn	1·70	1·80

DESIGN: 19p. Francesc Cairat i Freixes.

44 Skiing

1980. Olympic Games, Moscow.

126	**44**	5p. turquoise, red and blk	30	30
127	-	8p. multicoloured	40	45
128	-	50p. multicoloured	1·50	1·70

DESIGNS: 8p. Boxing; 50p. Shooting.

45 Nativity

1980. Christmas. Multicoloured.

129	10p. Type **45**	40	45
130	22p. Epiphany	95	1·10

46 Santa Anna Dance

1981. Europa. Multicoloured.

131	12p. Type **46**	70	75
132	30p. Festival of the Virgin of Canolich	1·40	1·50

47 Militia Members

1981. 50th Anniv of People's Militia.

133	**47**	30p. green, grey and black	1·40	1·50

48 Handicapped Child learning to Write

1981. International Year of Disabled Persons.

134	**48**	50p. multicoloured	2·10	2·30

49 *The Nativity*

1981. Christmas. Carvings from Encamp Church. Multicoloured.

135	12p. Type **49**	70	75
136	30p. *The Adoration*	1·40	1·50

1981. Bishops of Urgel, Co-princes of Andorra (2nd series). As T **42**.

137	7p. purple and blue	40	45
138	20p. brown and green	95	1·10

DESIGNS: 7p. Salvador Casanas; 20p. Josep de Boltas.

50 Arms of Andorra

1982. With "PTA" under figure of value.

139	**50**	1p. mauve	30	30
140	**50**	3p. brown	30	30
141	**50**	7p. red	30	30
142	**50**	12p. red	30	30
143	**50**	15p. blue	40	45
144	**50**	20p. green	70	75
145	**50**	30p. red	70	75
146	**50**	50p. green (25×31 mm)	1·70	1·90
147	**50**	100p. blue (25×31 mm)	3·00	3·50

See also Nos. 203/6.

51 The New Reforms, 1866

1982. Europa. Multicoloured.

154	14p. Type **51**	95	1·10
155	33p. Reform of the Institutions, 1981	1·80	2·00

52 Footballers

1982. World Cup Football Championship, Spain. Multicoloured.

156	14p. Type **52**	1·40	1·50
157	33p. Tackle	2·75	3·00

53 Arms and 1929 1p. stamp

1982. National Stamp Exhibition.

158	**53**	14p. black and green	1·40	1·50

54 Spanish and French Permanent Delegations Buildings

1982. Anniversaries.

159	**54**	9p. brown and blue	40	45
160	-	23p. blue and brown	70	75
161	-	33p. black and green	1·10	1·20

DESIGNS—VERT: 9p. Type **54** (centenary of Permanent Delegations); 23p. *St. Francis feeding the Birds* (after Ciambue) (800th birth anniv of St. Francis of Assisi); 33p. Title page of *Relacio sobre la Vall de Andorra* (birth centenary of Tomas Junoy (writer)).

55 *Virgin and Child* (statue from Andorra la Vella Parish Church)

1982. Christmas. Multicoloured.

162	14p. Type **55**	70	75
163	33p. Children beating log with sticks	2·10	2·30

56 Building Romanesque Church

1983. Europa.

164	**56**	16p. green, purple & black	70	75
165	-	38p. brown, blue and black	2·10	2·30

DESIGN: 38p. 16th-century water mill.

57 *Lactarius sanguifluus*

1983. Nature Protection.

166	**57**	16p. multicoloured	70	75

58 Ballot Box on Map and Government Building

1983. 50th Anniv of Universal Suffrage in Andorra.

167	**58**	10p. multicoloured	70	75

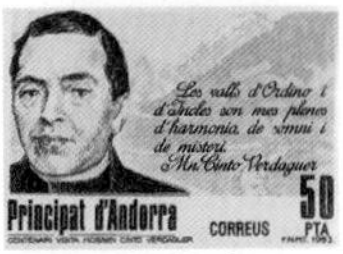

59 Mgr. Cinto Verdaguer

1983. Centenary of Mgr. Cinto Verdaguer's Visit.

168	**59**	50p. multicoloured	2·10	2·30

60 Jaume Sansa Nequi

1983. Air. Jaume Sansa Nequi (Verger-Episcopal) Commemoration.

169	**60**	20p. deep brown & brown	70	75

61 Wall Painting, Church of San Cerni, Nagol

1983. Christmas.

170	**61**	16p. multicoloured	70	75

1983. Bishops of Urgel, Co-princes of Andorra (3rd series). As T **42**.

171	26p. brown and red	1·40	1·50

DESIGN: 26p. Joan Laguarda.

62 Ski Jumping

1984. Winter Olympic Games, Sarajevo.

172	**62**	16p. multicoloured	95	1·10

63 Exhibition and F.I.P. Emblems

1984. "Espana 84" Int Stamp Exhibition, Madrid.

173	**63**	26p. multicoloured	1·40	1·50

64 Bridge

1984. Europa.

174	**64**	16p. brown	70	75
175	**64**	38p. blue	2·10	2·30

65 Hurdling

1984. Olympic Games, Los Angeles.

176	**65**	40p. multicoloured	2·10	2·30

66 Common Morel

1984. Nature Protection.

177	**66**	11p. multicoloured	4·25	7·50

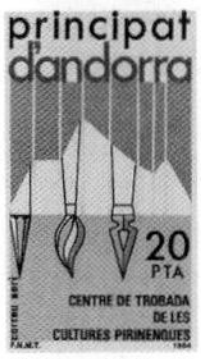

67 Pencil, Brush and Pen

1984. Pyrenean Cultures Centre, Andorra.

178	**67**	20p. multicoloured	85	90

68 The Holy Family (wood carvings)

1984. Christmas.

179	**68**	17p. multicoloured	70	75

69 Mossen Enric Marfany and Score

1985. Europa.

180	**69**	18p. green, purple & brown	95	1·10
181	-	45p. brown and green	1·80	2·00

DESIGN: 45p. Musician with viola (fresco detail, La Cortinada Church).

1985. Air. Bishops of Urgel, Co-princes of Andorra (4th series). As T **42**.

182	20p. brown and ochre	70	75

DESIGN: 20p. Ramon Iglesias.

70 Beefsteak Morel

1985. Nature Protection.

183	**70**	30p. multicoloured	1·40	1·50

71 Pal

1985

184	**71**	17p. deep blue and blue	70	75

72 Angels (St. Bartholomew's Chapel)

1985. Christmas.

185	**72**	17p. multicoloured	70	75

73 Scotch Bonnet

1986. Nature Protection.

186	**73**	30p. multicoloured	1·40	1·50

74 Sun, Rainbow, Lighthouse and Fish

1986. Europa. Each blue, red and green.

187	17p. Type **74**	1·40	1·50
188	45p. Sun and trees on rocks	2·10	2·30

1986. Bishops of Urgel, Co-princes of Andorra (5th series). As T **42**.

189	35p. blue and brown	1·40	1·50

DESIGN: 35p. Justi Guitart.

75 Bell of St. Roma's Chapel, Les Bons

1986. Christmas.

190	**75**	19p. multicoloured	70	75

76 Arms

1987. Meeting of Co-princes.

191	**76**	48p. multicoloured	1·40	1·50

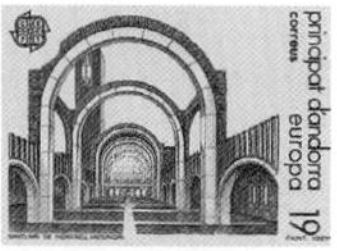

77 Interior of Chapel

1987. Europa. Meritxell Chapel.

192	**77**	19p. brown and blue	70	75
193	-	48p. blue and brown	1·40	1·50

DESIGN: 48p. Exterior of Chapel.

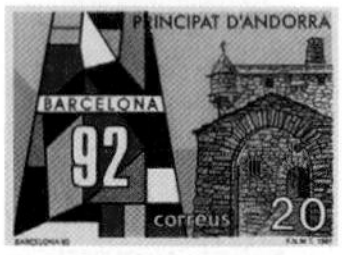

78 Emblem and House of Valleys

1987. Olympic Games, Barcelona (1992). Sheet 122×86 mm containing T **78** and similar horiz designs. Multicoloured.

MS194 20p. Type **78**; 50p. Torch carrier and St. Michael's Chapel, Fontaneda, bell tower		5·50	6·00

79 Cep

1987. Nature Protection.

195	**79**	100p. multicoloured	3·50	3·75

80 Extract from *Doctrina Pueril* by Ramon Llull

1987. Christmas.

196	**80**	20p. multicoloured	70	75

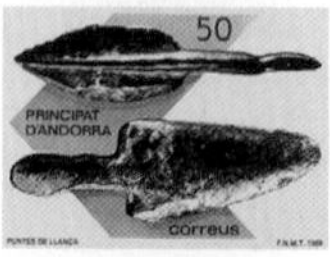

81 Copper Lance Heads

1988. Archaeology.

197	**81**	50p. multicoloured	1·70	1·80

82 Early 20th-century Trader and Pack Mules

1988. Europa. Communications. Each blue and red.

198	20p. Ancient road, Les Bons	70	75
199	45p. Type **82**	2·10	2·30

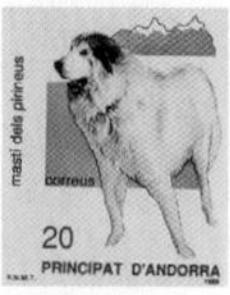

83 Pyrenean Mountain Dog

1988. Nature Protection.

200	**83**	20p. multicoloured	1·40	1·50

84 Commemorative Coin

1988. 700th Anniv of Second Parity Treaty.

201	**84**	20p. black, grey and brown	70	75

85 Church of St. John of Caselles

1988. Christmas.

202	**85**	20p. multicoloured	70	75

1988. As T **50** but without "PTA" under figure of value.

203	20p. green	70	75
204	50p. green (25×31 mm)	2·10	2·30
205	100p. blue (25×31 mm)	3·75	4·25
206	500p. brown (25×31 mm)	12·50	13·50

86 Leap-frog

1989. Europa. Children's Games. Multicoloured.

210	20p. Type **86**	1·40	1·50
211	45p. Girl trying to pull child from grip of other children (horiz)	2·10	2·30

87 St. Roma's Chapel, Les Bons

1989

212	**87**	50p. black, green and blue	2·10	2·30

88 Anniversary Emblem

1989. 125th Anniv of International Red Cross.

213	**88**	20p. multicoloured	70	75

89 "Virgin Mary" (detail of altarpiece, Les Escaldes Church)

1989. Christmas.

214	**89**	20p. multicoloured	70	75

90 Old French and Spanish Post Offices, Andorra La Vella

1990. Europa. Post Office Buildings. Multicoloured.

215	20p. Type **90**	70	75
216	50p. Modern Spanish post office, Andorra La Vella (vert)	2·10	2·30

91 *Gomphidius rutilus*

1990. Nature Protection.

217	**91**	45p. multicoloured	2·10	2·30

92 Plandolit House

1990

218	**92**	20p. brown and yellow	70	75

93 Angel, La Massana Church

1990. Christmas.

219	**93**	25p. brown, stone and red	85	90

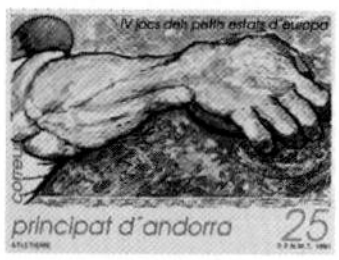

94 Throwing the Discus

1991. European Small States' Games. Multicoloured.

220	25p. Type **94**	95	1·10
221	45p. High jumping and running	1·80	2·00

95 "Olympus 1" Satellite

1991. Europa. Europe in Space. Multicoloured.

222	25p. Type **95**	2·10	2·30
223	55p. Close-up of "Olympus I" telecommunications satellite (horiz)	3·50	3·75

96 Parasol Mushroom

1991. Nature Protection.

224	**96**	45p. multicoloured	2·10	2·30

97 *Virgin of the Three Hands* (detail of triptych in Meritxell Chapel by Maria Assumpta Ortado i Maimo)

1991. Christmas.

225	**97**	25p. multicoloured	1·40	1·50

98 Woman fetching Water from Public Tap

1992

226	**98**	25p. multicoloured	1·40	1·50

99 *Santa Maria*

1992. Europa. 500th Anniv of Discovery of America by Columbus.

227	**99**	27p. multicoloured	2·10	2·30
228	-	45p. brown, red and orange	2·75	3·00

DESIGN—HORIZ: 45p. Engraving of King Ferdinand from map sent by Columbus to Ferdinand and Queen Isabella the Catholic.

100 White-water Canoeing

1992. Olympic Games, Barcelona.

229	**100**	27p. multicoloured	1·40	1·50

101 Benz Velo, 1894 and Sedanca de ville, 1920s

1992. National Motor Car Museum, Encamp.

230	**101**	27p. multicoloured	1·40	1·50

102 *Nativity* (Fra Angelico)

1992. Christmas.

231	**102**	27p. multicoloured	1·40	1·50

103 Chanterelle

1993. Nature Protection.

232	**103**	28p. multicoloured	1·40	1·50

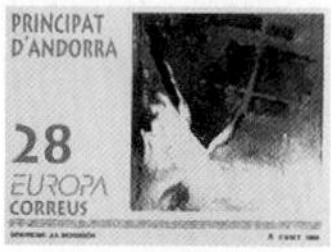

104 *Upstream* (J. A. Morrison)

1993. Europa. Contemporary Art. Multicoloured.
233 28p. Type **104** 1·40 1·50
234 45p. *Ritme* (Angel Calvente) (vert) 2·10 2·30

105 Society Emblem on National Colours

1993. 25th Anniv of Andorran Arts and Letters Circle.
235 **105** 28p. multicoloured 1·40 1·50

106 Illuminated "P" (Galceran de Vilanova Missal)

1993. Christmas.
236 **106** 28p. multicoloured 1·40 1·50

107 National Colours

1994. First Anniv of New Constitution. Sheet 105×78 mm.
MS237 **107** 29p. multicoloured 2·10 2·30

108 Sir Alexander Fleming and Penicillin

1994. Europa. Discoveries.
238 **108** 29p. multicoloured 1·40 1·50
239 - 55p. blue and black 2·75 3·00
DESIGN: 55p. Test tube and AIDS virus.

109 *Hygrophorus gliocyclus*

1994. Nature Protection.
240 **109** 29p. multicoloured 1·40 1·50

110 *Madonna and Child* (anon)

1994. Christmas.
241 **110** 29p. multicoloured 1·40 1·50

111 Madriu Valley (south)

1995. European Nature Conservation Year. Multicoloured.
242 30p. Type **111** 85 90
243 60p. Madriu Valley (north) 1·90 2·10

112 Sun, Dove and Barbed Wire

1995. Europa. Peace and Freedom.
244 **112** 60p. green, orange & blk 2·10 2·30

113 *Flight into Egypt* (altarpiece, St. Mark and St. Mary Church, Encamp)

1995. Christmas.
245 **113** 30p. multicoloured 1·40 1·50

114 Palace of Europe, Strasbourg

1995. Admission of Andorra to Council of Europe.
246 **114** 30p. multicoloured 1·40 1·50

115 *Ramaria aurea*

1996. Nature Protection. Multicoloured.
247 30p. Type **115** 1·40 1·50
248 60p. Black truffles 2·30 2·50

116 Isabelle Sandy (writer)

1996. Europa. Famous Women.
249 **116** 60p. multicoloured 2·75 3·00

117 Old Iron

1996. International Museums Day.
250 **117** 60p. multicoloured 2·10 2·30

118 *The Annunciation* (altarpiece, St. Eulalia's Church, Encamp)

1996. Christmas.
251 **118** 30p. multicoloured 1·40 1·50

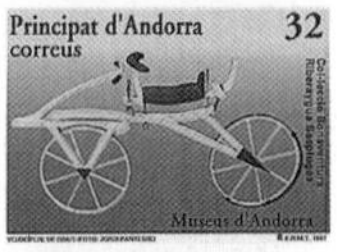

119 Drais Velocipede, 1818

1997. Bicycle Museum (1st series). Multicoloured.
252 32p. Type **119** 95 1·10
253 65p. Michaux velocipede, 1861 1·90 2·10
See also Nos. 258/9 and 264/5.

120 The Bear and The Smugglers

1997. Europa. Tales and Legends.
254 **120** 65p. multicoloured 2·75 3·00

121 Dove and Cultural Symbols

1997. National UNESCO Commission.
255 **121** 32p. multicoloured 70 75

122 Catalan Crib Figure

1997. Christmas.
256 **122** 32p. multicoloured 70 75

123 Giant Slalom

1998. Winter Olympic Games, Nagano, Japan.
257 **123** 35p. multicoloured 70 75

1998. Bicycle Museum (2nd series). As T **119**. Multicoloured.
258 35p. Kangaroo bicycle, Great Britain, 1878 95 1·10
259 70p. The Swallow, France, 1889 1·90 2·10

124 Harlequins of Canillo

1998. Europa. National Festivals.
260 **124** 70p. multicoloured 2·10 2·30

125 Front Page of First Edition and Landscape

1998. 250th Anniv of *Manual Digest*.
261 **125** 35p. multicoloured 70 75

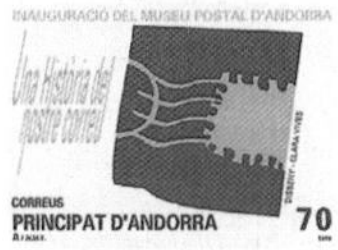

126 Emblem

1998. Inauguration of Postal Museum.
262 **126** 70p. violet and yellow 2·10 2·30

127 St. Lucia Fair

1998. Christmas.
263 **127** 35p. multicoloured 1·40 1·50

1999. Bicycle Museum (3rd series). As T **119**. Multicoloured.
264 35p. Salvo tricycle, 1878 (vert) 95 1·10
265 70p. Rudge tricycle, Coventry, England 1·90 2·10

128 Mules

1999. Postal History.
266 **128** 35p. black and brown 1·40 1·50

129 Palace of Human Rights, Strasbourg

1999. 50th Anniv of Council of Europe.
267 **129** 35p. multicoloured 1·40 1·50

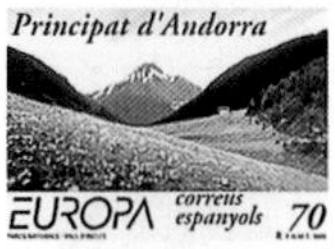

130 Vall d'Incles National Park, Canillo

1999. Europa. Parks and Gardens.
268 **130** 70p. multicoloured 2·10 2·30

131 Rull House, Sispony

1999
269 **131** 35p. multicoloured 1·40 1·50

132 Angel (detail of altarpiece, St. Serni's Church, Canillo)

1999. Christmas.
270 **132** 35p. brown and light brown 1·40 1·50

133 Santa Coloma Church

1999. European Heritage.
271 **133** 35p. multicoloured 1·40 1·50

134 "Building Europe"

2000. Europa.
272 **134** 70p. multicoloured 2·75 3·00

135 Angonella Lakes, Ordino

2000

273	**135**	35p. multicoloured	1·40	1·50

136 Casa Lacruz

2000. 131st Birth Anniv of Josep Cadafalch (architect).

274	**136**	35p. multicoloured	1·40	1·50

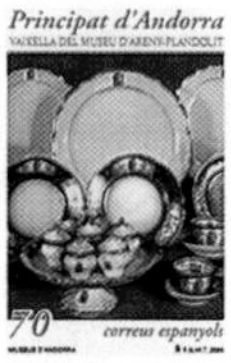
137 Dinner Service

2000. D'Areny-Plandolit Museum.

275	**137**	70p. multicoloured	2·10	2·30

138 Hurdling

2000. Olympic Games, Sydney.

276	**138**	70p. multicoloured	2·10	2·30

139 United Nations Headquarters, Strasbourg

2000. 50th Anniv of United Nations Declaration of Human Rights.

277	**139**	70p. multicoloured	2·10	2·30

140 Gradual, St. Roma, Les Bons

2000. 25th Anniv of the National Archives.

278	**140**	35p. multicoloured	70	75

141 *Quadre de les Animes* (Joan Casanovas)

2000. Christmas.

279	**141**	35p. multicoloured	70	75

142 Rec del Sola

2001. Natural Heritage.

280	**142**	40p. multicoloured	1·20	1·40

143 Roc del Metge (thermal spring), Escaldes-Engordany

2001. Europa. Water Resources.

281	**143**	75p. multicoloured	2·10	2·30

144 Casa Palau, Sant

2001

282	**144**	75p. multicoloured	2·10	2·30

145 Part of Sanctuary, Julia de Loria Meritxell

2001. 25th Anniv of Chapel of Our Lady, Meritxell.

283	**145**	40p. multicoloured	1·40	1·50

146 Building

2001. Tenth Anniv of National Auditorium, Ordino.

284	**146**	75p. multicoloured	2·10	2·30

147 Angel (detail of altarpiece, Church of St. John of Caselles)

2001. Christmas.

285	**147**	40p. multicoloured	1·40	1·50

148 State Arms

2002

286	**148**	25c. orange	70	75
286a	**148**	27c. blue	70	75
286b	**148**	28c. blue	85	90
286c	**148**	29c. sepia	85	90
286d	**148**	30c. carmine	85	90
287	**148**	50c. red	1·40	1·50
288	**148**	52c. yellow	1·50	1·70
289	**148**	53c. green	1·50	1·70
289a	**148**	57c. blue	1·70	1·80
289b	**148**	58c. black	1·70	1·80
290	**148**	77c. orange	2·20	2·40
291	**148**	78c. magenta	2·20	2·40

149 Alpine Accentor (*Prunella collaris*)

2002. Native Birds. Multicoloured.

300	25c. Type **149**	95	1·10
301	50c. Snow finch (*Montifringilla nivalis*)	1·90	2·10

150 Emblem

2002. International Year of the Mountain.

302	**150**	50c. multicoloured	2·10	2·30

151 Tightrope Walker

2002. Europa. Circus.

303	**151**	50c. multicoloured	14·00	15·00

152 Casa Fusile, Escaldes-Engordany

2002. Architectural Heritage. Multicoloured.

304	€1.80 Type **152**	5·50	6·00
305	€2.10 Farga Rossell Iron Museum, La Massana	6·25	6·75

153 Pinette Minim

2002. History of the Motor Car (1st series). Multicoloured.

306	25c. Type **153**	95	1·10
307	50c. Rolls Royce Silver Wraith	1·90	2·10

See also Nos. 317/18 and 324/5.

154 Placa Benlloch, Areny-Plandolit

2002. Christmas.

308	**154**	25c. multicoloured	1·40	1·50

155 Painted Medallion

2002. Cultural Heritage. Romanesque Murals from Santa Coloma Church, Andorra la Vella.. Multicoloured.

309	25c. Type **155**	70	75
310	50c. Part of damaged fresco showing seated figure	1·40	1·50
311	75c. Frieze	2·10	2·30

156 Sassanat Bridge

2003

312	**156**	26c. multicoloured	1·40	1·50

157 State Arms

2003. Tenth Anniv of Constitution.

313	**157**	76c. multicoloured	2·75	3·00

158 Man drinking, Donkey and Market Stalls

2003. Europa. Poster Art.

314	**158**	76c. multicoloured	2·75	3·00

159 Northern Wheatear (*Oenanthe oenanthe*)

2003. Native Birds.

315	**159**	50c. multicoloured	1·40	1·50

160 Multicoloured Stripes

2003. Tenth Anniv of Andorras' Membership of United Nations.

316	**160**	76c. multicoloured	2·75	3·00

161 Carter (1908)

2003. History of the Motor Car (2nd series). Multicoloured.

317	51c. Type **161**	1·70	1·80
318	76c. Peugeot (1928) (horiz)	2·50	2·75

162 Roadside Cross, Andorra la Vella

2003. Christmas.

319	**162**	26c. multicoloured	1·40	1·50

163 *Fira del Bestiar* (Joaquim Mir)

2004

320	**163**	27c. multicoloured	1·10	1·20

164 *L'Escorxador* (Joaquim Mir)

2004

321	**164**	52c. multicoloured	1·90	2·10

165 Coaches and Skiers in Snow

2004. Europa. Holidays.
322 **165** 77c. black 2·75 3·00

166 Chaffinch (*Fringilla coelebs*)

2004. Native Birds.
323 **166** 27c. multicoloured 1·10 1·20

167 Simca 508 C (1939)

2004. History of the Motor Car (3rd series).
324 €1.90 Type **167** 6·50 7·25
325 €2.19 Messerschmitt KR 1 (1955) 7·25 8·00

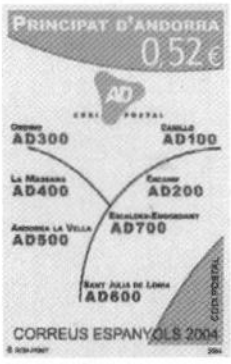

168 Map showing Postal Districts

2004. Introduction of Postal Codes.
326 **168** 52c. orange, magenta and black 2·10 2·30

169 Stars and Flag as Jigsaw Pieces

2004. Tenth Anniv of Entry into Council of Europe.
327 **169** 52c. multicoloured 2·10 2·30

170 Nativity

2004. Christmas.
328 **170** 27c. multicoloured 1·10 1·20

171 Madriu-Perafita-Claror Valley

2005. UNESCO World Heritage Site.
329 **171** 28c. multicoloured 1·10 1·20

172 *Endless* (Mark Brusse)

2005
330 **172** 53c. multicoloured 2·20 2·40

174 Cyclist

2005. Europa. Gastronomy.
331 **173** 78c. multicoloured 3·00 3·50

174 Cyclist

2005. Small States of Europe Games.
332 **174** €1.95 brown and black 5·50 6·00

175 Shrine

2005. 25th Anniv of Caritas Andorra (humanitarian organization).
333 **175** 28c. multicoloured 1·10 1·20

176 Dipper (*Cinclus cinclus*)

2005. Native Birds.
334 **176** €2.21 multicoloured 6·25 6·75

177 *The Nativity* (Sergei Mas)

2005. Christmas.
335 **177** 28c. multicoloured 1·10 1·20

178 Skiers

2006. Winter Olympic Games, Turin.
336 **178** 29c. multicoloured 1·40 1·50

179 *Ruta del Hierro* (sculpture) (Satora Sato)

2006. Cultural Heritage.
337 **179** 78c. multicoloured 2·50 2·75

180 Stylized People of Many Colours and Abilities

2006. Europa. Integration.
338 **180** 57c. multicoloured 2·20 2·40

181 Grey Partridge (*Perdix perdix*)

2006. Natural Heritage.
339 **181** €2.39 multicoloured 8·25 9·00

182 Scrabble Letters

2006. Fulbright Scholarships.
340 **182** 57c. multicoloured 2·20 2·40

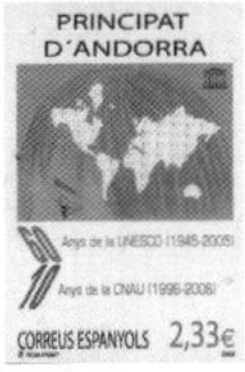

183 Head Containing World Map

2006. 60th Anniv of UNESCO and 10th Anniv of CNAU.
341 **183** €2.33 multicoloured 8·00 8·75

184 Nativity

2006. Christmas.
342 **184** 29c. multicoloured 1·20 1·20

185 *Encamp 1994* (F. Galobardes)

2007. Cultural Heritage.
343 **185** 30c. multicoloured 1·20 1·20

186 Doves and Emblem

2007. Europa. Centenary of Scouting.
344 **186** 58c. multicoloured 2·30 2·50

187 *La Familia Jordino* (sculpture by Rachid Khimoune)

2007. Cultural Heritage. The Iron Route (historical trail).
345 **187** €2.43 multicoloured 8·50 9·00

188 Capercaillie (*Tetrao urogallus*)

2007. Natural Heritage.
346 **188** €2.49 multicoloured 8·75 9·25

189 *Casa de la Vall* (Francesc Galobardes)

2007. Cultural Heritage.
347 **189** 78c. multicoloured 3·00 3·25

190 Stylized Figures

2007. 25th Anniv of Andorra Red Cross.
348 **190** 30c. carmine and black 1·20 1·20

191 *Lamb kneeling before Infant Jesus* (painting by Sergi Mas)

2007. Christmas.
349 **191** 30c. multicoloured 1·20 1·20

192 *Gypaetus barbatus* (Lammergeier or bearded vulture)

2008. Natural Heritage.
350 **192** 31c. multicoloured 1·40 1·50

193 *Carro Vortiu* (sculpture by Jordi Casamajor)

2008. Cultural Heritage.
351 **193** 60c. multicoloured 2·50 2·75

194 Flag and Ballot Box

2008. 15th Anniv of Constitution.
352 **194** 31c. multicoloured 1·80 2·10

195 Envelope

2008. Europa. The Letter.
353 **195** 60c. blue and black 2·75 3·00

196 Adam, Eve and Graph

2008. 25th Anniv of National Science Society.
354 **196** 78c. blue and black 3·75 4·00

197 Fluvi (exhibition mascot)

2008. Zaragoza 2008 International Water and Sustainable Development Exhibition. Sheet 105×79 mm.
MS355 **197** €2.60 multicoloured 10·50 11·50

198 Games Emblem

2008. Olympic Games, Beijing.
356 **198** 60c. multicoloured 2·75 3·00

199 Vall del Comapedrosa

2008. Natural Heritage.
357 **199** €2.44 multicoloured 9·25 10·00

200 *Sispony* (Carme Massana)

2008. Cultural Heritage.
358 **200** 31c. multicoloured 1·60 1·80

201 Midnight Mass

2008. Christmas.
359 **201** 31c. multicoloured 1·60 1·80

202 Narcissus

2009. Natural Heritage. Flora. Self adhesive.
360 **202** 32c. multicoloured 1·60 1·80

203 '25'

2009. 25th Anniv of Escola Andorrana.
361 **203** 62c. multicoloured 2·75 3·00

204 Merce Rodoreda

2009. Merce Rodoreda (Catalan writer) Commemoration.
362 **204** 78c. black 3·50 3·75

205 Emblem

2009. 60th Anniv of Council of Europe.
363 **205** 32c. multicoloured 1·60 1·80

206 Figures and Stars

2009. Europa. Astronomy.
364 **206** 62c. multicoloured 2·75 3·00

207 Bridge Strut

2009. Pont de Madrid (bridge designed by Carlos Fernandez Casado). Sheet 106×80 mm.
MS365 **207** €2.70 multicoloured 12·00 13·00

208 Eurasian Sparrowhawk

2009. Natural Heritage. Accipiter nisus.
366 **208** €2.47 multicoloured 9·25 10·00

209 *El Tarter* (Francesc Galobardes)

2009. Cultural Heritage. Multicoloured.
367 62c. Type **209** 2·75 3·00
368 78c. *Contrallum a Canillo* (Carme Massana) 3·50 3·75

210 Three Wise Men as Musicians (homage to National Classical Orchestra of Andorra by Sergei Mas)

2009. Christmas
369 **210** 32c. multicoloured 1·30 1·50

211 Iris

2010. Flora. Self-adhesive.
370 **211** 34c. multicoloured 1·70 1·90

212 Jacint Verdaguer

2010. 165th Birth Anniv of Jacint Verdaguer i Santaló (Catalan poet).
371 **212** 64c. black 2·75 3·00

213 Central Section

2010. Pont de Paris (bridge designed by Carlos Fernandez Casado).
372 **213** €2.75 multicoloured 12·00 13·00

214 Boy, Book and Fairy

2010. Europa
373 **214** 64c. multicoloured 2·75 3·00

215 Circle of Flame

2010. Cultural Heritage
374 **215** 64c. multicoloured 3·25 3·50

216 Emblem and Globe

2010. World Cup Football Championships, South Africa
375 **216** 78c. multicoloured 4·00 4·25

217 Multicoloured Ribbon

2010. Civic Values. Recycling
376 **217** €2.49 multicoloured 11·50 12·00

218 Mural (by Josep Oromí), Sant Joan de Sispony Church

2010. Christmas
377 **218** 34c. multicoloured 1·90 2·10

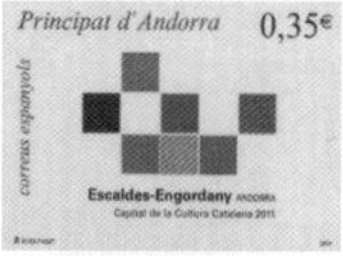

219 Capital of Culture Year Emblem

2011. Escaldes-Engordany, Capital of Catalan Culture
378 **219** 35c. multicoloured 2·00 2·20

220 Miquel Marti i Pol

2011. Personalities. Miquel Marti i Pol (poet) Commemoration
379 **220** 65c. black 3·25 3·50

221 Sorobilles Forest

2011. Europa. Forests
380 **221** 65c. multicoloured 4·00 4·25

222 Casa Farras

2011. Architecture. Casa Farras
381 **222** 80c. multicoloured 4·00 4·25

223 Decorated Stonework (Pedro Clau Sant Esteve)

2011. Cultural Heritage
382 **223** €2.55 multicoloured 12·00 13·00

224 Untitled (Helena Guàrdia)

2011. Venice Bienniale. Multicoloured.
383 80c. Type **224** 4·00 4·25
384 €2.55 Untitled (Francisco Sanchez) 11·00 12·00

225 Female and Masculine Figure

2011. Civic Values. Equality
385 **225** 80c. multicoloured 4·00 4·25

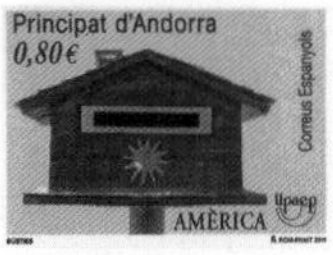

226 Mailbox

2011. America. Mailboxes
386 **226** 80c. multicoloured 4·00 4·25

227 Christmas Tree Baubles

2011. Christmas

387	**227**	35c. multicoloured	2·00	2·10

EXPRESS LETTER STAMPS

1928. Express Letter stamp of Spain optd **CORREOS ANDORRA**.

E15	**E53**	20c. red	70·00	90·00

E4 Lammergeier over Pyrenees

1929

E41	**E4**	20c. red	8·00	10·50

E12 Eurasian Red Squirrel (after Durer) and Arms

1949

E54	**E12**	25c. red	7·00	8·00

Pt. 9, Pt. 12

ANGOLA

Republic of Southern Africa. Independent of Portugal since 11 November 1975.

1870. 1000 reis = 1 milreis.
1913. 100 centavos = 1 escudo.
1932. 100 centavos = 1 angolar.
1954. 100 centavos = 1 escudo.
1977. 100 lweis = 1 kwanza.

1870. "Crown" key-type inscr "ANGOLA".

7	**P**	5r. black	3·50	2·10
17	**P**	10r. yellow	25·00	15·00
31	**P**	10r. green	9·75	5·50
9	**P**	20r. bistre	2·75	2·30
26	**P**	20r. red	23·00	16·00
10	**P**	25r. red	14·00	9·50
27	**P**	25r. purple	16·00	5·75
19b	**P**	40r. blue	£275	£190
33	**P**	40r. yellow	46·00	7·00
12	**P**	50r. green	65·00	17·00
30	**P**	50r. blue	50·00	10·50
21a	**P**	100r. lilac	6·25	3·75
22	**P**	200r. orange	5·25	2·30
23a	**P**	300r. brown	6·25	3·75

1886. "Embossed" key-type inscr "PROVINCIA DE ANGOLA".

35	**Q**	5r. black	20·00	8·00
36	**Q**	10r. green	20·00	8·00
37	**Q**	20r. red	29·00	16·00
39	**Q**	25r. mauve	20·00	5·25
40	**Q**	40r. brown	24·00	9·25
41	**Q**	50r. blue	30·00	5·75
42	**Q**	100r. brown	46·00	12·50
43	**Q**	200r. violet	55·00	17·00
44	**Q**	300r. orange	55·00	21·00

1894. "Figures" key-type inscr "ANGOLA".

49	**R**	5r. orange	4·00	1·60
62	**R**	10r. mauve	5·25	3·25
63	**R**	15r. brown	7·00	2·75
54	**R**	20r. lavender	8·00	3·50
74	**R**	25r. green	5·75	2·50
66	**R**	50r. blue	7·50	3·50
67	**R**	75r. red	14·00	11·50
68	**R**	80r. green	20·00	10·50
69	**R**	100r. brown on buff	20·00	10·50
70	**R**	150r. red on rose	25·00	18·00
77	**R**	200r. blue on blue	32·00	17·00
78	**R**	300r. blue on brown	32·00	17·00

1894. No. N51 with circular surch **CORREIOS DE ANGOLA 25 REIS**.

79b	**V**	25r. on 2½r. brown	80·00	70·00

1898. "King Carlos" key-type inscr "ANGOLA".

80	**S**	2½r. grey	70	55
81	**S**	5r. orange	70	55
82	**S**	10r. green	70	55
83	**S**	15r. brown	4·00	2·10
142	**S**	15r. green	2·00	1·80
84	**S**	20r. lilac	80	70
85	**S**	25r. green	2·10	80
143	**S**	25r. red	90	55
86	**S**	50r. blue	3·75	1·10
144	**S**	50r. brown	9·75	5·75
145	**S**	65r. blue	10·50	7·00
87	**S**	75r. red	12·50	8·00
146	**S**	75r. purple	4·00	2·50
88	**S**	80r. mauve	11·50	4·00
89	**S**	100r. blue on blue	2·50	1·60
147	**S**	115r. brown on pink	16·00	9·75
148	**S**	130r. brown on yellow	16·00	9·75
90	**S**	150r. brown on buff	12·50	7·50
91	**S**	200r. purple on pink	7·00	2·30
92	**S**	300r. blue on pink	8·00	7·00
149	**S**	400r. blue on yellow	7·00	4·50
93	**S**	500r. black on blue	8·00	7·00
94	**S**	700r. mauve on yellow	39·00	25·00

1902. "Embossed", "Figures" and "Newspaper" key-types of Angola surch.

98	**R**	65r. on 5r. orange	11·50	8·50
100	**R**	65r. on 10r. mauve	15·00	8·50
102	**R**	65r. on 20r. violet	13·50	8·50
104	**R**	65r. on 25r. green	14·00	10·50
95	**Q**	65r. on 40r. brown	14·00	8·50
96	**Q**	65r. on 300r. orange	14·00	8·50
106	**Q**	115r. on 10r. green	11·50	8·00
109	**R**	115r. on 80r. green	20·00	11·50
111	**R**	115r. on 100r. brn on buff	16·00	10·50
113	**R**	115r. on 150r. red on rose	21·00	12·50
108	**Q**	115r. on 200r. violet	11·50	8·00
120	**R**	130r. on 15r. brown	9·25	6·25
116	**Q**	130r. on 50r. blue	16·00	6·25
124	**R**	130r. on 75r. red	11·50	10·50
118	**Q**	130r. on 100r. brown	10·50	6·25
126	**R**	130r. on 300r. blue on brn	29·00	18·00
136	**V**	400r. on 2½r. brown	2·30	2·00
127	**Q**	400r. on 5r. black	23·00	17·00
128	**Q**	400r. on 20r. red	£110	70·00
130	**Q**	400r. on 25r. mauve	28·00	14·00
131	**R**	400r. on 50r. pale blue	10·50	7·00
133	**R**	400r. on 200r. blue on blue	11·50	9·75

1902. "King Carlos" key-type of Angola optd **PROVISORIO**.

138	**S**	15r. brown	2·75	1·80
139	**S**	25r. green	2·30	1·00
140	**S**	50r. blue	4·75	2·30
141	**S**	75r. red	8·00	6·25

1905. No. 145 surch **50 REIS** and bar.

150	50r. on 65r. blue	7·00	3·75

1911. "King Carlos" key-type optd **REPUBLICA**.

151	2½r. grey	55	45
152	5r. orange	55	45
153	10r. green	55	45
154	15r. green	80	70
155	20r. lilac	85	75
156	25r. red	85	75
157	50r. brown	3·25	2·00
232	50r. blue (No. 140)	2·50	2·10
224	75r. purple	2·50	1·30
234	75r. red (No. 141)	5·75	4·25
225	100r. blue on blue	4·00	3·75
160	115r. brown on pink	4·00	2·30
161	130r. brown on yellow	4·00	2·30
226	200r. purple on pink	2·75	1·80
163	400r. blue on yellow	4·50	2·00
164	500r. black on blue	4·50	2·30
165	700r. mauve on yellow	4·50	2·50

1912. "King Manoel" key-type inscr "ANGOLA" optd **REPUBLICA**.

166	**T**	2½r. lilac	70	45
167	**T**	5r. black	70	45
168	**T**	10r. green	70	45
169	**T**	20r. red	70	45
170	**T**	25r. brown	70	45
171	**T**	50r. blue	1·80	1·40
172	**T**	75r. brown	2·10	1·80
173	**T**	100r. brown on green	4·00	2·30
174	**T**	200r. green on pink	4·00	2·30
175	**T**	300r. black on blue	4·00	2·30

1912. "King Carlos" key-type of Angola optd **REPUBLICA** and surch.

176	**S**	2½ on 15r. green	5·75	3·25
177	**S**	5 on 15r. green	6·25	3·25
178	**S**	10 on 15r. green	4·75	3·25
179	**S**	25 on 75r. red (No. 141)	90·00	65·00
180	**S**	25 on 75r. purple	6·25	5·75

1913. Surch **REPUBLICA ANGOLA** and value in figures on "Vasco da Gama" issues of (a) Portuguese Colonies.

181	¼c. on 2½r. green	1·30	90
182	½c. on 5r. red	1·30	90
183	1c. on 10r. purple	1·30	90
184	2½c. on 25r. green	1·30	90
185	5c. on 50r. blue	1·30	90
186	7½c. on 75r. brown	7·50	6·25
187	10c. on 100r. brown	2·75	1·80
188	15c. on 150r. bistre	2·75	2·30

(b) Macao.

189	¼c. on ½a. green	2·75	2·20
190	½c. on 1a. red	2·75	2·20
191	1c. on 2a. purple	2·75	2·20
192	2½c. on 4a. green	2·30	1·60
193	5c. on 8a. blue	2·30	1·60
194	7½c. on 12a. brown	9·25	5·75
195	10c. on 16a. brown	3·50	2·50
196	15c. on 24a. bistre	4·25	2·50

(c) Timor.

197	¼c. on ½a. green	2·75	2·20
198	½c. on 1a. red	2·75	2·20
199	1c. on 2a. purple	2·75	2·20
200	2½c. on 4a. green	2·30	1·60
201	5c. on 8a. blue	2·30	1·60
202	7½c. on 12a. brown	9·25	5·75
203	10c. on 16a. brown	3·50	2·50
204	15c. on 24a. bistre	4·25	2·50

1914. "Ceres" key-type inscr "ANGOLA".

296	**U**	¼c. olive	40	35
297	**U**	½c. black	40	35
298	**U**	1c. green	40	35
299	**U**	1½c. brown	40	35
300	**U**	2c. red	40	35
301	**U**	2c. grey	70	55
281	**U**	2½c. violet	40	35
303	**U**	3c. orange	35	30
304	**U**	4c. red	35	30
305	**U**	4½c. grey	35	30
284a	**U**	5c. blue	40	35
307	**U**	6c. mauve	35	30
308	**U**	7c. blue	35	30
309	**U**	7½c. brown	45	40
288	**U**	8c. grey	45	40
311	**U**	10c. brown	40	35
312	**U**	12c. brown	70	55
313	**U**	12c. green	70	55
291	**U**	15c. purple	40	35
314	**U**	15c. pink	40	35
315	**U**	20c. green	2·00	1·70
316	**U**	24c. blue	1·70	1·40
317	**U**	25c. brown	1·70	1·40
217	**U**	30c. brown on green	2·75	2·50
318	**U**	30c. green	70	55
218	**U**	40c. brown on pink	2·75	2·50
319	**U**	40c. blue	1·40	70
219	**U**	50c. orange on pink	11·50	8·00
320	**U**	50c. purple	1·40	70
321	**U**	60c. blue	1·70	1·00
322	**U**	60c. red	£100	60·00
322a	**U**	80c. pink	2·10	1·00
220	**U**	1e. green on blue	8·50	5·25
323	**U**	1e. red	2·10	1·00
325	**U**	1e. blue	3·50	2·10
326	**U**	2e. purple	2·75	1·40
327	**U**	5e. brown	18·00	15·00
328	**U**	10e. pink	38·00	31·00
329	**U**	20e. green	£110	80·00

1914. Provisional stamps of 1902 optd **REPUBLICA**.

233	**S**	50r. on 65r. blue	5·50	3·75
256	**Q**	115r. on 10r. green	2·40	2·30
258	**R**	115r. on 80r. green	2·00	1·90
261	**R**	115r. on 100r. brn on buff	2·50	2·30
263	**R**	115r. on 150r. red on rose	1·90	1·90
266	**Q**	115r. on 200r. violet	2·75	2·30
267	**R**	130r. on 15r. brown	2·00	1·90
246	**Q**	130r. on 50r. blue	32·00	32·00
269	**R**	130r. on 75r. red	3·75	2·30
273	**Q**	130r. on 100r. brown	2·30	1·90
274	**R**	130r. on 300r. blue on brn	2·30	2·30
254	**V**	400r. on 2½r. brown	1·10	85

1919. Stamps of 1911, 1912 or 1914 surch.

331	**T**	½c. on 75r. brown	1·60	1·30
332	**S**	½c. on 75r. purple	1·80	1·60
336	**T**	1c. on 50r. blue	2·00	1·80
334	**S**	2½c. on 100r. brown on grn	3·00	2·30
335	**S**	2½c. on 100r. blue on blue	2·30	1·70
337	**S**	4c. on 130r. brown on yell	2·50	1·80
339	**U**	$04 on 15c. purple	2·50	1·80
340	**U**	$04 on 15c. pink	25·00	
341	**T**	$00.5 on 75r. brown	1·80	1·60
342	**U**	$00.5 on 7½c. brown	2·50	2·10

1925. Nos. 136 and 133 surch **Republica 40 C.**

343	**R**	40c. on 400r. on 200r. blue on blue	1·00	1·00
345	**V**	40c. on 400r. on 2½r. brn	1·50	1·10

1931. "Ceres" key-type of Angola surch.

347	**U**	50c. on 60c. red	2·30	2·00
348	**U**	70c. on 80c. pink	4·50	3·50
349	**U**	70c. on 1e. blue	4·25	3·50
350	**U**	1e.40 on 2e. purple	2·75	2·10

17 Ceres

1932

351	**17**	1c. brown	35	25
352	**17**	5c. sepia	35	35
353	**17**	10c. mauve	35	35
354	**17**	15c. black	35	35
355	**17**	20c. grey	35	35
356	**17**	30c. green	35	35
357	**17**	35c. green	9·25	4·25
358	**17**	40c. red	45	25
359	**17**	45c. blue	1·70	1·40
360	**17**	50c. brown	35	25
361	**17**	60c. olive	1·10	35
362	**17**	70c. brown	1·10	35
363	**17**	80c. green	70	25
364	**17**	85c. red	5·75	2·50
365	**17**	1a. red	1·10	35
366	**17**	1a.40 blue	11·50	3·50
367	**17**	1a.75 blue	20·00	5·25
368	**17**	2a. mauve	5·75	55
369	**17**	5a. green	11·50	1·80
370	**17**	10a. brown	23·00	5·75
371	**17**	20a. orange	55·00	5·75

1934. Surch.

380	5c. on 80c. green (A)	1·00	55
419	5c. on 80c. green (B)	1·00	55
413	10c. on 45c. blue	2·00	1·30
381	10c. on 80c. green	1·80	90
414	15c. on 45c. blue	2·00	1·30
382	15c. on 80c. green	2·50	90
415	20c. on 85c. red	2·00	1·30
374	30c. on 1a.40 blue	3·75	2·75
416	35c. on 85c. red	2·00	1·30
417	50c. on 1a.40 blue	2·00	1·30
418	60c. on 1a. red	11·00	8·50
375	70c. on 2a. mauve	6·25	2·75
376	80c. on 5a. green	9·75	2·75

(A) surch **0,05 Cent.** in one line; (B) surch **5 CENTAVOS** in two lines.

1935. "Due" key-type surch CORREIOS and new value.

377	**W**	5c. on 6c. brown	2·50	1·60
378	**W**	30c. on 50c. grey	2·50	1·60
379	**W**	40c. on 50c. grey	2·50	1·60

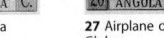

22 Vasco da Gama

27 Airplane over Globe

1938. Name and value in black.

383	**22**	1c. olive (postage)	25	25
384	**22**	5c. brown	35	35
385	**22**	10c. red	45	35
386	**22**	15c. purple	45	35
387	**22**	20c. grey	45	35
388	-	30c. purple	55	45
389	-	35c. green	1·10	80
390	-	40c. brown	35	25
391	-	50c. mauve	55	25
392	-	60c. black	1·10	35
393	-	70c. violet	1·10	35
394	-	80c. orange	1·10	35
395	-	1a. red	1·10	35
396	-	1a.75 blue	2·30	1·00
397	-	2a. red	3·50	1·10
398	-	5a. olive	16·00	1·10
399	-	10a. blue	32·00	1·30
400	-	20a. brown	44·00	4·00
401	**27**	10c. red (air)	45	40
402	**27**	20c. violet	45	40
403	**27**	50c. orange	45	40
404	**27**	1a. blue	45	40
405	**27**	2a. red	1·00	45
406	**27**	3a. green	1·80	70
407	**27**	5a. brown	7·00	1·00
408	**27**	9a. red	8·00	2·00
409	**27**	10a. mauve	11·00	2·75

DESIGNS: 30c. to 50c. Mousinho de Albuquerque; 60c. to 1a. "Fomento" (symbolizing Progress); 1a.75, 2, 5a. Prince Henry the Navigator; 10, 20a. Afonso de Albuquerque.

28 Portuguese Colonial Column

1938. President's Colonial Tour.

410	**28**	80c. green	3·50	2·20
411	**28**	1a.75 blue	23·00	6·25
412	**28**	20a. brown	70·00	40·00

1945. Nos. 394/6 surch.

420	5c. on 80c. orange	1·00	55
421	50c. on 1a. red	1·00	55
422	50c. on 1a.75 blue	1·00	55

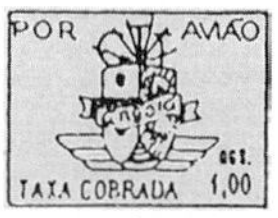

31 Arms of Angola

1947. Air.

423a	**31**	1a. brown	11·50	7·00
423b	**31**	2a. green	12·50	8·00
423c	**31**	3a. orange	12·50	8·00
423d	**31**	3a.50 orange	23·00	8·00
423e	**31**	5a. green	£110	29·00
423f	**31**	6a. pink	£110	23·00
423g	**31**	9a. red	£350	£225
423h	**31**	10a. green	£225	£100
423i	**31**	20a. blue	£375	£110
423j	**31**	50a. black	£500	£275
423k	**31**	100a. yellow	£800	£700

32 Sao Miguel Fortress, Luanda

1948. Tercentenary of Restoration of Angola. Inscr "Tricentenario da Restauracao de Angola 1648–1948".

424	**32**	5c. violet	35	25
425	-	10c. brown	90	35
426	-	30c. green	35	25
427	-	50c. purple	35	25
428	-	1a. red	90	25
429	-	1a.75 blue	1·60	25
430	-	2a. green	1·60	25
431	-	5a. black	3·75	70
432	-	10a. mauve	12·50	90
433	-	20a. blue	28·00	5·75
MS433a 162×225 mm. Nos. 424/33 (sold at 42a.50)			£140	£140

DESIGNS—HORIZ: 10c. Our Lady of Nazareth Hermitage, Luanda; 1a. Surrender of Luanda; 5a. Inscribed Rocks of Yelala; 20a. Massangano Fortress. VERT (portraits): 30c. Don John IV; 50c. Salvador Correia de Sa Benevides; 1a.75, Dioga Cao; 7a. Manuel Cerveira Pereira; 10a. Paulo Dias de Novais.

33 Our Lady of Fatima

1948. Honouring Our Lady of Fatima.

434	**33**	50c. red	2·75	1·70
435	**33**	3a. blue	11·00	3·50
436	**33**	6a. orange	34·00	8·50
437	**33**	9a. red	90·00	11·00

35 River Chiumbe

36 Pedras Negras

1949

438	**35**	20c. blue	80	25
439	**36**	40c. brown	80	25
440	-	50c. red	80	25
441	-	2a.50 blue	4·00	50
442	-	3a.50 grey	4·00	2·30
443	-	15a. green	29·00	2·30
444	-	50a. green	£160	9·25

DESIGNS—As T **35**: 50c. Luanda; 2a.50, Bandeira; 3a.50, Mocamedes; 50a. Braganza Falls. 31×26 mm: 15a. River Cubal.

37 Aircraft and Globe

1949. Air.

445	**37**	1a. orange	80	25
446	**37**	2a. brown	1·70	25
447	**37**	3a. mauve	2·30	25
448	**37**	6a. green	4·25	90
449	**37**	9a. purple	6·25	2·20

38 *Tentativa Feliz*

1949. Centenary of Founding of Mocamedes.

450	**38**	1a. purple	9·25	1·00
451	**38**	4a. green	28·00	2·75

39 Letter and Globe

1949. 75th Anniv of U.P.U.

452	**39**	4a. green	14·00	3·50

40 Reproduction of "Crown" key-type

1950. Philatelic Exhibition and 80th Anniv of First Angolan Stamp.

454	**40**	1a. red	1·70	90
455	**40**	4a. black	6·25	2·10
453	**40**	50a. green	1·70	55
MS455a 120×79 mm. Nos. 453/5 (sold at 6a.50)			34·00	29·00

41 Bells and Dove

42 Angels holding Candelabra

1950. Holy Year.

456	**41**	1a. violet	1·60	35
457	**42**	4a. black	6·25	1·10

43 Dark Chanting Goshawk

1951. Birds. Multicoloured.

458	5c. Type **43**	55	20
459	10c. Racquet-tailed roller	55	20
460	15c. Bateleur	90	20
461	20c. European bee eater	1·00	45
462	50c. Giant kingfisher	1·00	20
463	1a. Anchieta's barbet	1·00	20
464	1a.50 African open-bill stork	1·50	20
465	2a. Southern ground hornbill	4·00	20
466	2a.50 African skimmer	2·20	20
467	3a. Shikra	1·50	20
468	3a.50 Senham's bustard	2·20	20
469	4a. African golden oriole	2·50	20
470	4a.50 Magpie shrike	2·50	20
471	5a. Red-shouldered glossy starling	8·00	70
472	6a. Sharp-tailed glossy starling	10·50	1·70
473	7a. Fan-tailed whydah	11·50	2·30
474	10a. Half-collared kingfisher	46·00	2·75
475	12a.50 White-crowned shrike	14·50	4·00
476	15a. White-winged starling	13·00	4·00
477	20a. Southern yellow-billed hornbill	£100	9·75
478	25a. Violet starling	48·00	8·00
479	30a. Sulphur-breasted bush shrike	48·00	8·50
480	40a. Secretary bird	65·00	12·50
481	50a. Peach-faced lovebird	£140	30·00

The 10, 15 and 20c., 2a.50, 3a., 4a.50, 12a.50 and 30a. are horiz, the remainder vert.

44 Our Lady of Fatima

1951. Termination of Holy Year.

482	**44**	4a. orange	4·50	1·70

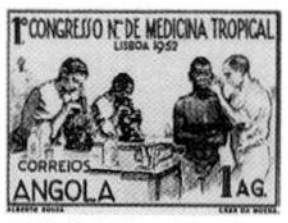

45 Laboratory

1952. First Tropical Medicine Congress, Lisbon.

483	**45**	1a. grey and blue	1·30	45

46 The Sacred Face

1952. Missionary Art Exhibition.

484	**46**	10c. blue and flesh	20	20
485	**46**	50c. green and stone	1·00	25
486	**46**	2a. purple and flesh	3·75	70

47 Leopard

1953. Angolan Fauna. Multicoloured.

487	5c. Type **47**	25	25
488	10c. Sable antelope (vert)	25	25
489	20c. African elephant (vert)	25	25
490	30c. Eland (vert)	25	25
491	40c. Crocodile	25	25
492	50c. Impala (vert)	25	25
493	1a. Mountain zebra (vert)	35	25
494	1a.50 Sitatunga (vert)	35	25
495	2a. Black rhinoceros	35	25
496	2a.30 Gemsbok (vert)	35	25
497	2a.50 Lion (vert)	45	25
498	3a. African buffalo	55	25
499	3a.50 Springbok (vert)	55	25
500	4a. Blue wildebeest (vert)	20·00	25
501	5a. Hartebeest (vert)	90	25
502	7a. Warthog (vert)	1·40	25
503	10a. Waterbuck (vert)	2·75	25
504	12a.50 Hippopotamus (vert)	7·50	1·50
505	15a. Greater kudu (vert)	9·25	1·50
506	20a. Giraffe (vert)	11·50	90

48 Stamp of 1853 and Colonial Arms

1953. Portuguese Stamp Centenary.

507	**48**	50c. multicoloured	1·30	55

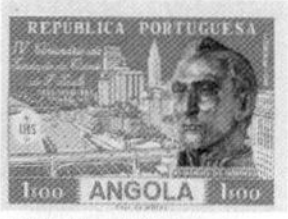

49 Father M. da Nobrega and Sao Paulo

1954. Fourth Centenary of Sao Paulo.

508	**49**	1e. black and buff	80	35

50 Route of President's Tour

1954. Presidential Visit.

509	**50**	35c. multicoloured	15	15
510	**50**	4e.50 multicoloured	1·70	80

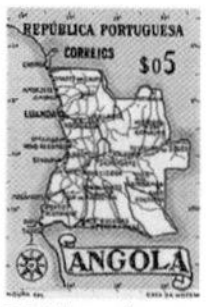

51 Map of Angola

1955. Map mult. Angola territory in colour given.

511	**51**	5c. white	20	20
512	**51**	20c. salmon	20	20
513	**51**	50c. blue	20	20
514	**51**	1e. orange	20	20
515	**51**	2e.30 yellow	1·30	45
516	**51**	4e. blue	2·50	25
517	**51**	10e. green	3·00	25
518	**51**	20e. white	4·25	1·80

52 Col. A. de Paiva

1956. Birth Centenary of De Paiva.

519	**52**	1e. black, blue and orange	45	35

53 Quela Chief

1957. Natives. Multicoloured.

520	5c. Type **53**	20	20
521	10c. Andulo flute player	20	20
522	15c. Dembos man and woman	20	20
523	20c. Quissama dancer (male)	20	20
524	30c. Quibala family	20	20
525	40c. Bocolo dancer (female)	20	20
526	50c. Quissama woman	20	20
527	80c. Cuanhama woman	45	45
528	1e.50 Luanda widow	2·75	45
529	2e.50 Bocolo dancer (male)	3·50	25
530	4e. Muquixe man	1·40	25
531	10e. Cabinda chief	3·00	55

54 Father J. M. Antunes

1957. Birth Centenary of Father Antunes.

532	**54**	1e. multicoloured	90	45

55 Exhibition Emblem, Globe and Arms

1958. Brussels International Exhibition.

533	**55**	1e.50 multicoloured	80	70

56 *Securidaca longipedunculata*

1958. Sixth Int Tropical Medicine Congress.

534	**56**	2e.50 multicoloured	3·50	1·00

57 Native Doctor and Patient

1958. 75th Anniv of Maria Pia Hospital, Luanda.

535	**57**	1e. brown, black and blue	55	35
536	-	1e.50 multicoloured	1·40	70
537	-	2e.50 multicoloured	2·50	1·30

DESIGNS: 1e.50, 17th-century doctor and patient; 2e.50, Present-day doctor, orderly and patients.

58 Welwitschia (plant)

1959. Centenary of Discovery of Welwitschia.

538	**58**	1e.50 multicoloured	1·10	55
539	-	2e.50 multicoloured	1·70	70
540	-	5e. multicoloured	2·75	70
541	-	10e. multicoloured	6·25	2·30

DESIGNS: 2e.50, 5, 10e. Various types of Welwitschia (*Welwitschia mirabilis*).

59 Old Map of West Africa

1960. 500th Death Anniv of Prince Henry the Navigator.

542	**59**	2e.50 multicoloured	70	35

60 "Agriculture" (distribution of seeds)

1960. Tenth Anniv of African Technical Co-operation Commission.

543	**60**	2e.50 multicoloured	80	35

61

1961. Angolan Women. As T **61**. Portraits multicoloured; background colours given.

544	10c. green	10	10
545	15c. blue	10	10
546	30c. yellow	10	10
547	40c. grey	10	10
548	60c. brown	10	10
549	1e.50 turquoise	15	10
550	2e. lilac	1·30	10
551	2e.50 lemon	1·30	10
552	3e. pink	4·50	35
553	4e. olive	2·30	35
554	5e. blue	1·50	35
555	7e.50 yellow	2·10	1·00
556	10e. buff	1·50	80
557	15e. brown	2·30	1·00
558	25e. red	3·25	1·50
559	50e. grey	5·75	3·25

62 Weightlifting

1962. Sports. Multicoloured.

560	50e. Flying	20	20
561	1e. Rowing	1·40	25
562	1e.50 Water polo	90	35
563	2e.50 Throwing the hammer	1·10	35
564	4e.50 High jumping	90	70
565	15e. Type **62**	2·30	1·70

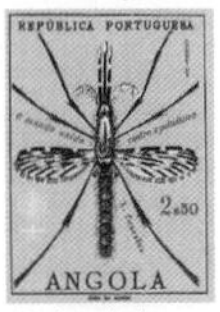

63 *Anopheles funestus* (mosquito)

1962. Malaria Eradication.

566	**63**	2e.50 multicoloured	2·10	90

64 Gen. Norton de Matos (statue)

1962. 50th Anniv of Nova Lisboa.

567	**64**	2e.50 multicoloured	70	35

65 Red Locusts

1963. 15th Anniv of Int Locust Eradication Service.

568	**65**	2e.50 multicoloured	2·10	55

66 Arms of St. Paul of the Assumption, Luanda

1963. Angolan Civic Arms (1st series). Multicoloured.

569	5c. Type **66**	20	20
570	10c. Massangano	20	20
571	30c. Muxima	20	20
572	50c. Carmona	20	20
573	1e. Salazar	80	20
574	1e.50 Malanje	1·50	20
575	2e. Henry of Carvalho	80	20
576	2e.50 Mocamedes	4·50	70
577	3e. Novo Redondo	1·10	20
578	3e.50 St. Salvador (Congo)	1·30	20
579	5e. Luso	1·10	35
580	7e.50 St. Philip (Benguela)	1·50	1·30
581	10e. Lobito	1·80	1·10
582	12e.50 Gabela	2·10	1·80
583	15e. Sa da Bandeira	2·10	1·80
584	17e.50 Silva Porto	3·50	3·00
585	20e. Nova Lisboa	3·50	2·50
586	22e.50 Cabinda	3·50	3·00
587	30e. Serpa Pinto	4·25	4·00

See also Nos. 589/610.

67 Rear-Admiral A. Tomas

1963. Presidential Visit.

588	**67**	2e.50 multicoloured	70	25

68 Arms of Sanza-Pombo

1963. Angolan Civic Arms (2nd series). Multicoloured.

589	15c. Type **68**	25	20
590	20c. St. Antonio do Zaire	25	20
591	25c. Ambriz	25	20
592	40c. Ambrizete	25	20
593	50c. Catete	25	20
594	70c. Quibaxe	25	20
595	1e. Maquela do Zombo	25	20
596	1e.20 Bembe	25	20
597	1e.50 Caxito	80	20
598	1e.80 Dondo	80	70
599	2e.50 Damba	3·00	25
600	4e. Cuimba	70	25
601	6e.50 Negage	70	45
602	7e. Quitexe	1·00	70
603	8e. Mucaba	1·00	80
604	9e. 31 de Janeiro	1·50	1·30
605	11e. Novo Caipemba	1·70	1·50
606	14e. Songo	2·00	1·70
607	17e. Quimbele	2·10	2·00
608	25e. Noqui	2·50	2·00
609	35e. Santa Cruz	3·75	3·00
610	50e. General Freire	4·75	2·50

69 Map of Africa, Boeing 707 and Lockheed Super Constellation Airliners

1963. Tenth Anniv of T.A.P. Airline.

611	**69**	1e. multicoloured	1·40	45

70 Bandeira Cathedral

1963. Angolan Churches. Multicoloured.

612	10c. Type **70**	10	10
613	20c. Landana	10	10
614	30c. Luanda (Cathedral)	10	10
615	40c. Gabela	10	10
616	50c. St. Martin, Bay of Tigers (Chapel)	10	10
617	1e. Melange (Cathedral) (horiz)	25	20
618	1e.50 St. Peter, Chibia	25	20
619	2e. Benguela (horiz)	35	20
620	2e.50 Jesus, Luanda	35	20
621	3e. Camabatela (horiz)	45	20
622	3e.50 Cabinda Mission	55	20
623	4e. Vila Folgares (horiz)	70	30
624	4e.50 Arrabida, Lobito (horiz)	90	35
625	5e. Cabinda	90	45
626	7e.50 Cacuso, Malange (horiz)	1·50	80
627	10e. Lubanga Mission	2·00	80
628	12e.50 Huila Mission (horiz)	2·30	1·30
629	15e. Island Cape, Luanda (horiz)	2·50	1·40

71 Dr. A. T. de Sousa

1964. Centenary of National Overseas Bank.

630	**71**	2e.50 multicoloured	90	45

72 Arms and Palace of Commerce, Luanda

1964. Cent of Luanda Commercial Association.

631	**72**	1e. multicoloured	45	25

73 I.T.U. Emblem and St. Gabriel

1965. Centenary of I.T.U.

632	**73**	2e.50 multicoloured	1·40	70

74 Boeing 707 over Petroleum Refinery

1965. Air. Multicoloured.

633	1e.50 Type **74**	1·40	20
634	2e.50 Cambabe Dam	1·40	20
635	3e. Salazar Dam	2·00	20
636	4e. Captain Trofilo Duarte Dam	2·00	25
637	4e.50 Creveiro Lopes Dam	1·40	25
638	5e. Cuango Dam	1·40	35
639	6e. Quanza Bridge	2·20	45
640	7e. Captain Trofilo Duarte Railway Bridge	3·25	45
641	8e.50 Dr. Oliveira Salazar Bridge	4·00	1·30
642	12e.50 Captain Silva Carvalho Railway Bridge	4·25	1·70

Nos. 634/42 are horiz and each design includes a Boeing 707 airliner overhead.

75 Fokker F.27 Friendship over Luanda Airport

1965. 25th Anniv of Direccao dos Transportes Aereos (Angolan airline).

643	**75**	2e.50 multicoloured	1·40	35

76 Arquebusier, 1539

1966. Portuguese Military Uniforms. Multicoloured.

644	50c. Type **76**	10	10
645	1e. Arquebusier, 1640	15	15
646	1e.50 Infantry officer, 1777	20	15
647	2e. Infantry standard-bearer, 1777	35	15
648	2e.50 Infantryman, 1777	40	15
649	3e. Cavalry officer, 1783	45	15
650	4e. Trooper, 1783	70	25
651	4e.50 Infantry officer, 1807	80	35
652	5e. Infantryman, 1807	90	35
653	6e. Cavalry officer, 1807	1·30	70
654	8e. Trooper, 1807	1·70	1·50
655	9e. Infantryman, 1873	2·10	1·70

77 St. Paul's Hospital, Luanda, and Sarmento Rodrigues Commercial and Industrial School

1966. 40th Anniv of National Revolution.

656	**77**	1e. multicoloured	45	25

78 Emblem of Brotherhood

1966. Centenary of Brotherhood of the Holy Spirit.

657	**78**	1e. multicoloured	45	25

79 Mendes Barata and Cruiser *Don Carlos I*

1967. Centenary of Military Naval Assn. Multicoloured.

658	1e. Type **79**	1·00	45
659	2e.50 Augusto de Castilho and sail/steam corvette *Mindelo*	1·40	80

80 Basilica of Fatima

1967. 50th Anniv of Fatima Apparitions.

660	**80**	50c. multicoloured	45	25

81 17th-century Map and M. C. Pereira (founder)

1967. 350th Anniv of Benguela.

661	**81**	50c. multicoloured	45	25

82 Town Hall, Uige-Carmona

1967. 50th Anniv of Uige-Carmona.

662	**82**	1e. multicoloured	25	20

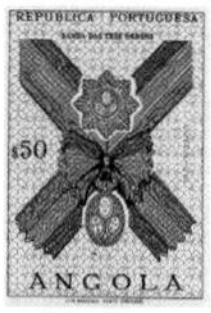

83 "The Three Orders"

1967. Portuguese Civil and Military Orders. Multicoloured.

663	50c. Type **83**	20	20
664	1e. "Tower and Sword"	20	20
665	1e.50 "Avis"	20	20
666	2e. "Christ"	20	20
667	2e.50 "St. James of the Sword"	20	20
668	3e. "Empire"	35	20
669	4e. "Prince Henry"	45	40
670	5e. "Benemerencia"	70	45
671	10e. "Public Instruction"	1·30	55
672	20e. "Agricultural and Industrial Merit"	2·75	1·50

84 Belmonte Castle

1968. 500th Birth Anniv of Pedro Cabral (explorer). Multicoloured.

673	50c. Our Lady of Hope (vert)	20	20
674	1e. Type **84**	55	20
675	1e.50 St. Jeronimo's hermitage (vert)	70	20
676	2e.50 Cabral's fleet (vert)	1·30	45

85 Francisco Inocencio de Souza Countinho

1969. Bicent of Novo Redondo (Angolan city).

677	**85**	2e. multicoloured	45	15

86 Gunboat *Loge* and Admiral Coutinho

1969. Birth Centenary of Admiral Gago Coutinho.

678	**86**	2e.50 multicoloured	1·00	35

87 Compass

1969. 500th Birth Anniv of Vasco da Gama (explorer).

679	**87**	1e. multicoloured	45	20

88 L. A. Rebello de Silva

1969. Cent of Overseas Administrative Reforms.

680	**88**	1e.50 multicoloured	25	20

89 Gate of Jeronimos

1969. 500th Birth Anniv of King Manoel I.

681	**89**	3e. multicoloured	45	20

90 *Angolasaurus bocagei*

1970. Fossils and Minerals. Multicoloured.

682	50c. Type **90**	55	25
683	1e. Ferro-meteorite	55	25
684	1e.50 Dioptase	90	55
685	2e. *Gondwanidium validium*	90	55
686	2e.50 Diamonds	90	55
687	3e. Estromatolitos	90	55
688	3e.50 Giant-toothed shark (*Pro-carcharodon megalodon*)	1·50	90
689	4e. Dwarf lungfish (*Micro-ceratodus angolensis*)	1·50	90
690	4e.50 Muscovite (mica)	1·50	90
691	5e. Barytes	1·50	90
692	6e. *Nostoceras helicinum*	2·75	1·30
693	10e. *Rotula orbiculus angolensis*	3·00	1·80

91 Marshal Carmona

1970. Birth Centenary of Marshal Carmona.

694	**91**	2e.50 multicoloured	45	20

92 Cotton-picking

1970. Centenary of Malanje Municipality.

695	**92**	2e.50 multicoloured	55	35

93 Mail Steamers *Infante Dom Henrique* and *Principe Perfeito* and 1870 5r. Stamp

1970. Stamp Centenary. Multicoloured.

696	1e.50 Type **93** (postage)	55	35
697	4e.50 Beyer-Garratt steam locomotive and 25r. stamp of 1870	3·00	3·00
698	2e.50 Fokker F.27 Friendship and Boeing 707 mail planes and 10r. stamp of 1870 (air)	2·10	90
MS699	150×105 mm. Nos. 696/8 (sold at 15e.)	14·00	14·00

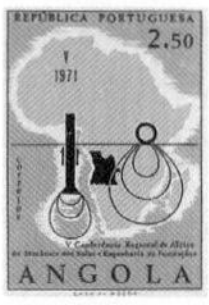

94 Map and Emblems

1971. Fifth Regional Soil and Foundation Engineering Conference, Luanda.

700	**94**	2e.50 multicoloured	45	20

96 16th-century Galleon at Mouth of Congo

1972. 400th Anniv of Camoens' *The Lusiads* (epic poem).

704	**96**	1e. multicoloured	70	25

97 Sailing Yachts

1972. Olympic Games, Munich.

705	**97**	50c. multicoloured	70	25

98 Fairey IIID Seaplane *Santa Cruz* near Fernando de Noronha

1972. 50th Anniv of First Flight Lisbon–Rio de Janeiro.

706	**98**	1e. multicoloured	35	20

99 W.M.O. Emblem

1974. Centenary of W.M.O.

707	**99**	1e. multicoloured	45	20

100 Dish Aerials

1974. Inauguration of Satellite Communications Station Network.

708	**100**	2e. multicoloured	45	20

101 Doris Harp

1974. Sea Shells. Multicoloured.

709	25c. Type **101**	10	10
710	30c. West African murex	10	10
711	50c. Scaly-ridged venus	10	10
712	70c. Filose latirus	20	10
713	1e. *Cymbium cisium*	20	10
714	1e.50 West African helmet	20	10
715	2e. Rat cowrie	20	10
716	2e.50 Butterfly cone	30	10
717	3e. Bubonian conch	40	20
718	3e.50 *Tympanotonus fuscatus*	45	20
719	4e. Great ribbed cockle	45	20
720	5e. Lightning moon	55	20
721	6e. Lion's-paw scallop	70	30
722	7e. Giant tun	85	30
723	10e. Rugose donax	1·10	45
724	25e. Smith's distorsio	3·50	1·30
725	30e. *Olivancilaria acuminata*	3·50	1·50
726	35e. Giant hairy melongena	3·75	2·00
727	40e. Wavy-leaved turrid	5·25	2·10
728	50e. American sundial	6·50	2·50

1974. Youth Philately. No. 511 optd **1974 FILATELIA JUVENIL**.

729	**51**	5c. multicoloured	25	80

103 Arm with Rifle and Star

1975. Independence.

730	**103**	1e.50 multicoloured	10	10

104 Diquiche-ua-Puheue Mask

1975. Angolan Masks. Multicoloured.

731	50c. Type **104**	10	10
732	3e. Bui ou Congolo mask	15	10

105 Workers

1976. Workers' Day.

733	**105**	1e. multicoloured	10	10

1976. Stamp Day. Optd **DIA DO SELO 15 Junho 1976 REP. POPULAR DE**.

734	**51**	10e. multicoloured	1·50	1·25

107 Pres. Agostinho Neto

1976. First Anniv of Independence.

735	**107**	50c. black and grey	10	10
736	**107**	2e. purple and grey	10	10
737	**107**	3e. blue and grey	10	10
738	**107**	5e. brown and buff	15	10
739	**107**	10e. brown and drab	25	10
MS740		59×75 mm. No. 739, but without President's name. Imperf	2·00	

1976. St. Silvestre Games. Optd **S Silvestre Rep. Popular de**.

741	**62**	15e. multicoloured	55	35

1977. Nos. 518, 724/5 and 728 optd **REPUBLICA POPULAR DE**.

742	20e. Type **51**	3·50	3·50
743	25e. "Cymatium trigonum"	60	15
744	30e. "Olivancilaria acuminata"	75	25
745	50e. "Solarium granulatum"	1·25	40

111 Child receiving Vaccine

1977. Polio Vaccination Campaign.

746	**111**	2k.50 blue and black	10	10

112 Map of Africa and Flag

1977. MPLA Congress.

747	**112**	6k. multicoloured	20	15

113 Human Rights Flame

1979. 30th Anniv of Declaration of Human Rights.

748	**113**	2k.50 yellow, red & black	15	10

114 Emblem

1979. International Anti-apartheid Year.

749	**114**	1k. multicoloured	10	10

115 Child raising Arms to Light

1980. International Year of the Child (1979).

750	**115**	3k.50 multicoloured	15	10

1980. Nos. 697/8 optd **REPUBLICA POPULAR DE.**

751	4e.50 multicoloured (postage)	2·75	1·75
752	2e.50 multicoloured (air)	15	10

117 Pres. Agostinho Neto

1980. National Heroes Day. Multicoloured.

753	4k.50 Type **117**	15	10
754	50k. Pres. Neto with machine-gun	1·25	70

118 Arms and Workers

1980. "Popular Power".

755	**118**	40k. blue and black	1·00	55

119 *The Liberated Angolan* (A. Vaz de Carvalho)

1980. Fifth Anniv of Independence.

756	**119**	5k.50 multicoloured	15	10

120 Running

1980. Olympic Games, Moscow.

757	**120**	9k. pink and red	20	10
758	-	12k. light blue and blue	30	10

DESIGN: 12k. Swimming.

121 Millet

1980. Angolan Produce. Multicoloured.

759	50l. Type **121**	10	10
760	5k. Coffee	15	10
761	7k.50 Sunflower	20	10
762	13k.50 Cotton	30	15
763	14k. Petroleum	30	15
764	16k. Diamonds	35	20

1981. Nos. 708, 713/16 and 718/27 with "REPUBLICA PORTUGUESA" inscr obliterated. (a) Dish aerials.

765	**100**	2e. multicoloured	10	10

(b) Sea Shells. Multicoloured.

766	1e. *Cymbium cisium*	10	10
767	1e.50 West African helmet	15	10
768	2e. Rat cowrie	20	10
769	2e.50 Butterfly cone	25	10
770	3e.50 *Tympanotonus fuscatus*	30	10
771	4e. Great ribbed cockle	35	15
772	5e. Lightning moon	40	15
773	6e. Lion's-paw scallop	45	20
774	7e. Giant tun	50	20
775	10e. Rugose donax	70	25
776	25e. Smith's distorsio	1·75	30
777	30e. *Olivancilaria acuminata*	1·90	65
778	35e. Giant hairy melongena	2·40	90
779	40e. Wavy-leaved turrid	3·00	1·00

122 Prisoner and Protesting Crowd

1981. Fifth Anniv of Soweto Riots in South Africa.

780	**122**	4k.50 black, red & silver	20	15

123 Basketball and Volleyball

1981. Second Central African Games. Multicoloured.

781	50l. Cycling and Tennis	10	10
782	5k. Judo and Boxing	20	15
783	6k. Type **123**	25	15
784	10k. Handball and football	40	20
MS784a	116×129 mm. 15k. Swimming and javelin. Imperf	80	85

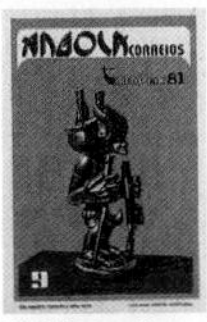

124 Statuette

1981. "Turipex 81".

785	**124**	9k. multicoloured	40	20

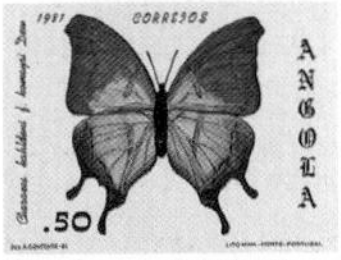

125 *Charaxes kahldeni f. homeyri*

1982. Butterflies. Multicoloured.

787	50l. Type **125**	10	10
788	1k. *Abantis gambesiaca*	10	10
789	5k. *Catacroptera cloanthe*	25	30
790	9k. *Myrina ficedula* (vert)	60	25
791	10k. *Colotis danae*	60	25
792	15k. *Acraea acrita bella*	80	30
793	100k. *Precis hierta cebrese*	5·25	2·40
MS793a	154×104 mm. Nos. 787/93. Imperf (sold at 30k.)	1·40	1·40

126 *Silence of Night*

1982. Fifth Anniv of Admission to United Nations. Multicoloured.

794	5k.50 Type **126**	25	15
795	7k.50 *Cotton Fields*	35	15

127 Worker and Building

1982. 20th Anniv of Angola Laboratory of Engineering. Multicoloured.

797	9k. Laboratory building (horiz)	40	20
798	13k. Type **127** (Research in construction materials)	45	25
799	100k. Geotechnical equipment	4·00	2·25

128 *Albizzia versicolor*

1983. Flowers (1st series). Multicoloured.

800	5k. *Dichrostachys glomerata*	25	10
801	12k. *Amblygonocarpus obtusangulus*	45	20
802	50k. Type **128**	2·00	1·10

129 Angolan Woman and Emblem

1983. First Angolan Women's Organization Congress.

803	**129**	20k. multicoloured	80	25

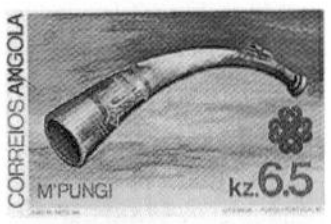

130 M'pungi (horn)

1983. World Communications Year. Multicoloured.

804	6k.50 Type **130**	25	20
805	12k. Mondu (drum)	50	45

131 Spear breaking Chain around South Africa

1983. 30th Anniv of Organization of African Unity.

806	**131**	6k.50 multicoloured	30	25

132 *Antestiopsis lineaticollis intricata*

1983. "Brasiliana 83" International Stamp Exn, Rio de Janeiro. Harmful Insects. Multicoloured.

807	4k.50 Type **132**	25	15
808	6k.50 *Stephanoderes hampei*	35	25
809	10k. *Zonocerus variegatus*	60	45

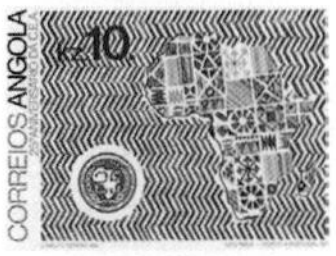

133 Map of Africa and E.C.A. Emblem

1983. 25th Anniv of Economic Commission for Africa.

810	**133**	10k. multicoloured	45	40

134 Collecting Mail

1983. 185th Anniv of Postal Service. Multicoloured.

811	50l. Type **134**	10	10
812	3k.50 Unloading mail from aircraft (horiz)	20	15
813	5k. Sorting mail (horiz)	35	25
814	15k. Posting letter	85	80
815	30k. Collecting mail from private box (horiz)	1·75	1·50
MS816	142×78 mm. Nos. 812, 813 and 815	2·20	1·90

135 *Parasa karschi*

1984. Moths. Multicoloured.

817	50l. Type **135**	10	10
818	1k. *Diaphone angolensis*	10	10
819	3k.50 *Choeropais jucunda*	30	15
820	6k.50 *Hespagarista rendalli*	50	35
821	15k. *Euchromia guineensis*	95	80
822	17k.50 *Mazuca roseistriga*	1·10	95
823	20k. *Utetheisa callima*	1·40	1·25

136 Dove

1984. First National Union of Angolan Workers Congress.

824	**136**	30k. multicoloured	1·75	1·50

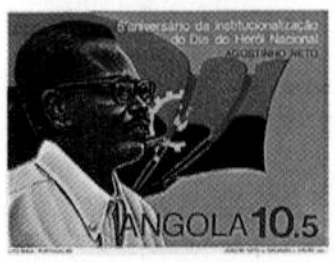

137 Flag and Agostinho Neto

1984. Fifth National Heroes Day. Multicoloured.

825	10k.50 Type **137**	50	45
826	36k.50 Flag and Agostinho Neto (different)	1·60	1·50

138 Southern Ground Hornbill

1984. Birds. Multicoloured.

827	10k.50 Type **138**	90	90

828	14k. Palm-nut vulture	1·25	1·25
829	16k. Goliath heron	1·50	1·50
830	19k.50 Eastern white pelican	1·75	1·75
831	22k. African spoonbill	2·00	2·00
832	26k. South African crowned crane	2·40	2·40

139 Greater Kudu

1984. Mammals. Multicoloured.

833	1k. Type **139**	10	10
834	4k. Springbok	25	15
835	5k. Chimpanzee	30	25
836	10k. African buffalo	55	50
837	15k. Sable antelope	80	65
838	20k. Aardvark	1·25	1·10
839	25k. Spotted hyena	1·50	1·25

140 Sao Pedro da Barra Fortress

1985. Monuments. Multicoloured.

840	5k. Type **140**	25	20
841	12k.50 Nova Oerias ruins	60	55
842	18k. Antiga cathedral ruins, M'Banza Kongo	80	75
843	26k. Massangano fortress	1·25	1·10
844	39k. Escravatura museum	1·75	1·60

141 Flags on World Map

1985. Fifth Anniv of Southern Africa Development Co-ordination Conference. Multicoloured.

845	1k. Type **141**	10	10
846	11k. Offshore drilling	1·25	50
847	57k. Conference session	2·50	2·40

142 Flags and "XXV"

1985. 25th Anniv of National Union of Angolan Workers.

848	**142** 77k. multicoloured	3·50	3·25

143 *Lonchocarpas sericeus*

1985. Medicinal Plants. Multicoloured.

849	1k. Type **143**	10	10
850	4k. *Gossypium* sp.	20	15
851	11k. Senna	50	45
852	25k.50 *Gloriosa superba*	1·10	1·00
853	55k. *Cochlospermum angolensis*	2·50	2·40

144 Map of Angola as Dove and Conference Emblem

1984. Ministerial Conference of Non-aligned Countries, Luanda.

854	**144** 35k. multicoloured	1·60	1·50

145 Dove and U.N. Emblem

1985. 40th Anniv of U.N.O.

855	**145** 12k.50 multicoloured	60	55

146 Cement Works

1985. Tenth Anniv of Independence. Multicoloured.

856	50l. Type **146**	10	10
857	5k. Timber yard	20	15
858	7k. Quartz	30	25
859	10k. Iron works	50	45
MS860	210×123 mm. Nos. 856/9	1·10	95

147 Emblem, Open Book, Soldier, Farmer and Factory

1985. Second MPLA Congress.

861	**147** 20k. multicoloured	90	85

148 Runner on Track

1985. 30th Anniv of Demostenes de Almeida Clington Races. Multicoloured.

862	50l. Type **148**	10	10
863	5k. Two runners on road	20	15
864	6k.50 Three runners on road	30	25
865	10k. Two runners on track	50	45

149 Map, Stadium and Players

1986. World Cup Football Championship, Mexico.

866	**149** 50l. multicoloured	10	10
867	- 3k.50 multicoloured	15	15
868	- 5k. multicoloured	30	25
869	- 7k. multicoloured	35	30
870	- 10k. multicoloured	50	45
871	- 18k. multicoloured	85	70

DESIGNS: 3k.50 to 18k. Different footballers.

150 Crowd

1986. 25th Anniv of Armed Independence Movement.

872	**150** 15k. multicoloured	75	70

151 Soviet Space Project

1985. 25th Anniv of First Man in Space. Multicoloured.

873	50l. Type **151**	10	10
874	1k. "Voskhod 1"	10	10
875	5k. Cosmonaut on space walk	20	15
876	10k. Moon vehicle	50	45
877	13k. "Soyuz"–"Apollo" link-up	60	55

152 National Flag and U.N. Emblem

1986. Tenth Anniv of Angolan Membership of U.N.O.

878	**152** 22k. multicoloured	1·00	90

153 People at Work

1986. 30th Anniv of Popular Movement for the Liberation of Angola. Multicoloured.

879	5k. Type **153**	20	15
880	5k. Emblem and people (29×36 mm)	20	15
881	5k. Soldiers fighting	20	15

Nos. 879/81 were printed together, *se-tenant*, forming a composite design.

154 Lecturer and Students (Faculty of Engineering)

1986. Tenth Anniv of Agostinho Neto University. Multicoloured.

882	50l. Type **154**	10	10
883	7k. Students and Judges (Faculty of Law)	30	25
884	10k. Students using micro-scopes and surgeons operating (Faculty of Medicine)	50	45

155 Ouioca

1987. Traditional Hairstyles. Multicoloured.

885	1k. Type **155**	10	10
886	1k.50 Luanda	10	10
887	5k. Humbe	20	15
888	7k. Muila	35	25
889	20k. Muila (different)	80	70
890	30k. Lunda, Dilolo	1·25	1·00

156 *Lenin in the Smolny Institute* (detail, Serov)

1987. 70th Anniv of Russian Revolution.

891	**156** 15k. multicoloured	60	25

157 Pambala Beach

1987. Scenic Spots. Multicoloured.

892	50l. Type **157**	10	10
893	1k.50 Quedas do Dala (waterfalls)	10	10
894	3k.50 Black Feet Rocks, Pungo Adongo (vert)	15	10
895	5k. Cuango River valley	20	15
896	10k. Luanda shore (vert)	40	35
897	20k. Serra da Leba road	80	75

158 Emblem

1988. Second Angolan Women's Organization Congress. Multicoloured.

898	2k. Type **158**	10	10
899	10k. Women engaged in various pursuits	40	35

159 Dancers

1988. Tenth Anniv of Vitoria Carnival. Multicoloured.

900	5k. Type **159**	15	10
901	10k. Revellers	40	35

160 Augusto N'Gangula (child revolutionary)

1989. Pioneers. Multicoloured.

902	12k. Type **160** (20th death anniv)	50	45
903	15k. Pioneers (25th anniv (1988) of Agostinho Neto Pioneers Organization)	60	55

161 Luanda 1st August Sports Club (1979–81)

1989. Tenth National Football League Championship. Championship Winners. Multicoloured.

904	5k. Type **161**	15	15
905	5k. Luanda Petro Atletico (1982, 1984, 1986–88)	15	15
906	5k. Benguela 1st May Sports Club (1983, 1985)	15	15

162 Watering Cabbages

1990. Tenth Anniv (1987) of International Fund for Agricultural Development.

907	**162** 10k. multicoloured	1·60	1·30

163 19th-century Middle-class Houses, Luanda

1990. Historical Buildings. Multicoloured.

908	1k. Type **163**	25	25
909	2k. Cidade Alta railway station, Luanda	50	30
910	5k. National Anthropology Museum	60	40
911	15k. Palace of Ana Joaquina dos Santos	1·20	1·20
912	23k. Iron Palace	1·60	2·00
913	36k. Meteorological observatory (vert)	2·75	2·50
914	50k. Governor's palace	3·75	3·50

164 *General Machado* and Route Map

1990. Benguela (915) and Luanda Railways. Multicoloured.

915	5k. Type **164**	1·00	1·00
916	12k. Beyer-Garratt steam locomotive (facing left)	2·00	2·00
917	12k. Beyer-Garratt steam locomotive (facing right)	2·00	2·00
918	14k. Mikado steam locomotive	2·50	2·50
MS919	88×69 mm. 25k. Diesel-electric locomotive (39×29 mm)	4·25	4·25

165 Hydroelectric Production

1990. Tenth Anniv of Southern Africa Development Co-ordinating Conference. Multicoloured.

920	5k. Type **165**	1·00	80
921	9k. Oil industry	2·00	1·75

166 Map in Envelope

1990. Tenth Anniv of Pan-African Postal Union. Multicoloured.

922	4k. Type **166**	90	70
923	10k. Map consisting of stamps and envelopes	2·60	1·80

167 *Muxima*

1990. "Stamp World London 90" International Stamp Exn. Paintings by Raul Indipwo. Multicoloured.

924	6k. *Three Graces* (horiz)	1·00	90
925	9k. Type **167**	1·80	1·25

168 Antelope

1990. Protected Animals. Sable Antelope. Multicoloured.

926	5k. Type **168**	2·60	1·90
927	5k. Male and female	2·60	1·90
928	5k. Female	2·60	1·90
929	5k. Female and young	2·60	1·90

169 Porcelain Rose

1990. "Belgica 90" International Stamp Exhibition, Brussels. Flowers. Multicoloured.

930	5k. Type **169**	55	60
931	8k. Indian carnation	90	80
932	10k. Allamanda	1·10	90
MS933	113×139 mm. 40k. Hibiscus and "Manneqin Pis", Brussels (49×39 mm)	4·50	4·00

170 Zebra Drinking

1990. International Literacy Year. Multicoloured.

934	5k. Type **170**	1·10	80
935	5k. Butterfly	1·10	80
936	5k. Horse's head	1·10	80
MS937	210×260 mm. 30×1k. Composite jungle-scene showing various animals and plants	7·50	7·00

171 Flag and People

1990. Tenth Anniv of People's Assembly.

938	**171**	10k. multicoloured	50	30

172 Dove, Flag and Workers

1990. Third Popular Movement for the Liberation of Angola-Labour Party Congress.

939	**172**	14k. multicoloured	80	50

173 Uniform, 1961

1991. 30th Anniv of Armed Independence Movement. Freedom Fighters' Uniforms. Multicoloured.

940	6k. Type **173**	1·40	1·00
941	6k. Pau N'Dulo, 1962–63	1·40	1·00
942	6k. Military uniform, 1968	1·40	1·00
943	6k. Military uniform from 1972	1·40	1·00

174 Marimba

1991. Musical Instruments. Multicoloured.

944	6k. Type **174**	1·20	85
945	6k. Ngoma ya Mucupela (double-ended drum)	1·20	85
946	6k. Ngoma la Txina (floor-standing drum)	1·20	85
947	6k. Kissange	1·20	85

175 Iona National Park

1991. African Tourism Year. Multicoloured.

948	3k. Type **175**	50	40
949	7k. Kalandula Falls	1·00	80
950	35k. Lobito Bay	3·00	2·40
951	60k. *Welwitschia mirabilis*	5·00	4·50

176 Kabir of the Dembos

1991. "Espamer '91" Spain–Latin America Stamp Exhibition, Buenos Aires. Dogs. Multicoloured.

953	5k. Type **176**	60	50
954	7k. Ombua	90	70
955	11k. Kabir massongo	1·50	1·10
956	12k. Kawa tchowe	1·60	1·20

177 Judo

1991. Olympic Games, Barcelona (1992) (1st issue). Multicoloured.

957	4k. Type **177**	30	20
958	6k. Yachting	40	30
959	10k. Marathon	70	50
960	100k. Swimming	6·50	5·25

178 Mother and Child

1991. 13th Anniv of Angolan Red Cross. Multicoloured.

961	20k.+5k. Type **178**	1·40	1·40
962	40k.+5k. Zebra and foal	2·40	2·40

179 Quadrant and Galleon

1991. "Iberex '91" Stamp Exhibition. Navigational Instruments. Multicoloured.

963	5k. Type **179**	50	35
964	15k. Astrolabe and caravel	1·40	1·00
965	20k. Cross-staff and caravel	1·80	1·30
966	50k. Navigation chart by Francisco Rodrigues and galleon	4·50	3·25

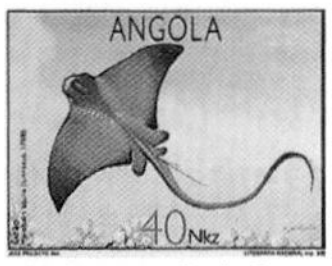

180 Common Eagle Ray

1992. Rays. Multicoloured.

967	40k. Type **180**	1·20	50
968	50k. Spotted eagle ray	1·50	80
969	66k. Manta ray	2·20	1·20
970	80k. Brown ray	2·75	1·60
MS971	112×140 mm. 25k. "Atlantic manta"	3·00	3·00

181 Mukixi wa Mbwesu Mask

1992. Quioca Painted Masks (1st series).

972	-	60k. orange and brown	50	35
973	-	100k. black, verm & red	70	60
974	**181**	150k. pink and orange	1·00	95
975	-	250k. red and brown	1·70	1·50

DESIGNS: 60k. Kalelwa mask; 100k. Mikixe wa Kino mask; 250k. Cikunza mask.

See also Nos. 1006/7 and 1021/4.

182 *Ptaeroxylon obliquum*

1992. "Lubrapex 92" Brazilian–Portuguese Stamp Exhibition, Lisbon. Medicinal Plants. Each brown, stone and deep brown.

976	200k. Type **182**	1·00	65
977	300k. *Spondias mombin*	1·50	1·00
978	500k. *Parinari curatellifolia*	2·50	1·60
979	600k. *Cochlospermum angolense*	3·00	1·90

183 King and Missionaries

1992. 500th Anniv (1991) of Baptism of First Angolans. Multicoloured.

980	150k. Type **183**	80	50
981	420k. Ruins of M'Banza Congo Church	2·20	1·40
982	470k. Muxima Church	2·40	1·50
983	500k. Cross superimposed on children's faces	2·60	1·60

184 Dimba House

1992. "Expo '92" World's Fair, Seville. Traditional Houses. Multicoloured.

984	150k. Type **184**	4·00	4·00
985	330k. Cokwe house	2·20	1·40
986	360k. Mbali house	2·40	1·60
987	420k. Ambwela house	2·60	1·80
988	500k. House of the Upper Zambezi	3·00	2·50

185 Lovebirds

1992. Nature Protection. Peach-faced Lovebirds. Multicoloured.

989	150k. Type **185**	1·20	80
990	200k. Birds feeding	1·50	1·00
991	250k. Bird in hand	1·90	1·30
992	300k. Bird on perch	2·30	1·50

186 *Crucifixion*

1992. Visit of Pope John Paul II. Sheet 151×90 mm containing T **186** and similar vert design plus two labels.

MS993	340k. Type **186** 370k. *The Lost Soul*	5·50	4·50

187 Hurdling

1992. Olympic Games, Barcelona (2nd issue). Multicoloured.

994	120k. Type **187**	70	60
995	180k. Cycling	1·30	1·10
996	240k. Roller hockey	1·50	1·30
997	360k. Basketball	2·20	1·80

188 Women with Nets

1992. Fishing. Multicoloured.

998	65k. Type **188**	60	50
999	90k. Fishermen pulling in nets	80	70
1000	100k. Fishermen checking traps	90	80
1001	120k. Fishing canoes	1·10	95

189 *Santa Maria*

1992. 500th Anniv of Discovery of America by Columbus and Genova 92 International Thematic Stamp Exhibition. Sheet 95×70 mm.

MS1002	**189** 500k. multicoloured	7·50	7·00

190 Crowd with Ballot Papers around Ballot Box

1992. First Free Elections. Multicoloured.

1003	120k. Type **190**	90	75
1004	150k. Doves, map, people and ballot box	1·10	1·10
1005	200k. Dove, crowd and ballot box	1·50	1·20

1992. Quioca Painted Masks (2nd series). As T **181**.

1006	72k. brown, black and yellow	60	50
1007	80k. red, black and brown	70	60
1008	120k. pink, black and red	1·00	90
1009	210k. black and yellow	1·70	1·50

DESIGNS: 72k. Cihongo mask; 80k. Mbwasu mask; 120k. Cinhanga mask; 210k. Kalewa mask.

191 Mail Van

1992. Introduction of Express Mail Service in Angola. Multicoloured.

1010	450k. Type **191**	4·75	4·50
1011	550k. Boeing 707 airplane	6·75	5·50

192 Weather Balloon

1993. World Meteorology Day. Meteorological Instruments. Multicoloured.

1012	250k. Type **192**	2·75	1·80
1013	470k. Actinometer	3·75	3·00
1014	500k. Rain-gauge	4·00	3·25

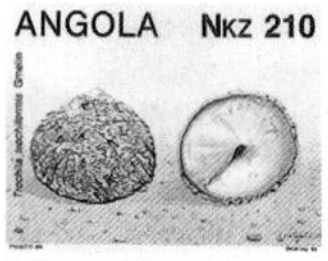

193 Rayed Hat

1993. Molluscs. Multicoloured.

1015	210k. Type **193**	75	60
1016	330k. Bubonian conch	1·20	90
1017	400k. African pelican's foot	1·50	1·20
1018	500k. White spindle	1·80	1·40
MS1019	70×90 mm. 1000k. "Pusionella nifat"	3·50	3·50

194 Leopard

1993. Africa Day. Sheet 95×70 mm.

MS1020 **194**	1500k. multicoloured	6·00	4·50

1993. Quioca Art (1st series). As T **181**.

1021	72k. grey, red and brown	25	20
1022	210k. pink and brown	60	55
1023	420k. black, brown & orge	1·80	1·50
1024	600k. black, red and brown	10	10

DESIGNS: 72k. Men with vehicles; 210k. Rider on antelope; 420k. Bird-plane; 600k. Carrying "soba".

See also Nos. 1038/41 and 1050/3.

195 *Sansevieria cylindrica*

1993. Cacti and Succulents. Multicoloured.

1025	360k. Type **195**	1·40	1·60
1026	400k. Milk-bush	1·80	1·60
1027	500k. Indian fig	2·00	2·30
1028	600k. *Dracaena aubryana*	2·75	2·40

196 Atlantic Hawksbill Turtle laying Eggs and Green Turtle

1993. Sea Turtles. Multicoloured.

1029	180k. Type **196**	80	70
1030	450k. Head of Atlantic hawksbill turtle and newly hatched turtles	2·00	1·70
1031	550k. Leather-back turtle	2·30	2·00
1032	630k. Loggerhead turtles	3·00	2·50

Nos. 1029/32 were issued together, *se-tenant*, forming a composite design.

197 People Dancing

1993. Union of Portuguese speaking Capital Cities. Sheet 95×71 mm.

MS1033 **197**	1500k. multicoloured	6·00	5·00

198 Vimbundi Pipe

1993. Tobacco Pipes. Multicoloured.

1034	72k. Type **198**	30	25
1035	200k. Vimbundi pipe (different)	9·00	70
1036	420k. Mutopa calabash water pipe	1·80	1·50
1037	600k. Pexi carved-head pipe	2·50	2·20

1993. Quioca Art (2nd series). As T **181**.

1038	300k. brown and orange	95	80
1039	600k. red and brown	2·00	1·60
1040	800k. black, orange and deep orange	2·50	2·20
1041	1000k. orange and brown	3·25	2·75

DESIGNS: 300k. Leopard and dog; 600k. Rabbits; 800k. Birds; 1000k. Birds and cockerel.

199 St. George's Mushroom

1993. Fungi. Multicoloured.

1042	300k. Type **199**	1·20	95
1043	500k. Death cap	2·00	1·50
1044	600k. *Amanita vaginata*	2·20	1·80
1045	1000k. Parasol mushroom	3·75	3·00

200 *Cinganji* (figurine of dancer, Bie province)

1994. National Culture Day. "Hong Kong '94" International Stamp Exhibition. Multicoloured.

1046	500k. Type **200**	80	75
1047	1000k. Chief's staff with carved woman's head (Bie province)	1·60	1·50
1048	1200k. Statuette of traveller riding ox (Huambo province)	2·00	1·80
1049	2200k. Corn pestle (Ovimbundu)	3·50	3·25

1994. Quioca Art (3rd series). As T **181**.

1050	500k. multicoloured	80	75
1051	2000k. red and brown	1·60	1·50
1052	2500k. red and brown	3·00	2·50
1053	3000k. carmine and red	3·50	3·25

DESIGNS: 500k. Bird on plant; 2000k. Plant with roots; 2500k. Plant; 3000k. Fern.

201 Orgy

1994. AIDS Awareness Campaign. Multicoloured.

1054	500k. Type **201**	1·00	80
1055	1000k. Masked figure using infected syringe passing box of condoms to young couple	2·00	1·70
1056	3000k. Victims	5·00	4·50

202 Flag, Arrows and Small Ball

1994. World Cup Football Championship, U.S.A. Multicoloured.

1057	500k. Type **202**	8·00	70
1058	700k. Flag, four arrows and large ball	1·10	1·00
1059	2200k. Flag, goal net and ball	3·50	3·00
1060	2500k. Flag, ball and boot	4·00	3·50

203 Brachiosaurus

1994. "Philakorea 1994" International and "Singpex '94" Stamp Exhibitions. Dinosaurs. Multicoloured.

1061	1000k. Type **203**	1·00	50
1062	3000k. Spinosaurus	1·50	1·00
1063	5000k. Ouranosaurus	2·00	1·50
1064	10000k. Lesothosaurus	3·50	3·00
MS1065	102×145 mm. 19000k. Lesothosaurus and map (43×34 mm)	4·50	4·50

204 Brown Snake Eagle, Ostrich, Yellow-billed Stork and Pink-backed Pelican

1994. Tourism. Multicoloured.

1066	2000k. Type **204**	1·00	80
1067	4000k. Animals	1·50	1·30
1068	8000k. Women	2·40	2·00
1069	10000k. Men	3·00	2·50

205 Dual-service Wall-mounted Post Box

1994. Post Boxes. Multicoloured.

1070	5000k. Type **205**	70	65
1071	7500k. Wall-mounted philatelic post box	1·30	1·20
1072	10000k. Free-standing post box	2·60	2·40
1073	21000k. Multiple service wall-mounted post box	3·50	3·00

206 *Heliothis armigera* (moth)

1994. Cotton Pests (Insects). Multicoloured.

1074	5000k. Type **206**	60	50
1075	6000k. *Bemisia tabasi*	75	60
1076	10000k. *Dysdercus* sp. (bug)	1·20	1·00
1077	27000k. *Spodoptera exigua* (moth)	3·25	2·50

207 "100"

1994. Cent of International Olympic Committee.

1078 **207**	27000k. red, yell & blk	2·40	2·00

208 Pot

1995. Traditional Ceramics. With service indicator. Multicoloured. (a) INLAND POSTAGE. Inscr "PORTE NACIONAL".

1079	(1°) Type **208**	8·00	70
1080	(2°) Pot with figure of woman on lid	80	70

(b) INTERNATIONAL POSTAGE. Inscr "PORTE INTERNACIONAL".

1081	(1°) Pot with man's head on lid	1·60	1·50
1082	(2°) Duck-shaped pot	1·80	1·70

209 Making Fire

1995. The !Kung (Khoisan tribe). Multicoloured.

1083	10000k. Type **209**	60	55
1084	15000k. Tipping darts with poison	95	80
1085	20000k. Smoking	1·30	1·00
1086	25000k. Hunting	1·50	1·40
1087	28000k. Women and children	1·75	1·50
1088	30000k. Painting animals on walls	1·90	1·60

210 Vaccinating Child against Polio

1995. 90th Anniv of Rotary International. Multicoloured. (a) Inscr in Portuguese.

1089	27000k. Type **210**	2·00	2·00
1090	27000k. Examining baby	2·00	2·00
1091	27000k. Giving child vaccination	2·00	2·00

(b) Inscr in English.

1092	27000k. Type **210**	2·00	2·00
1093	27000k. As No. 1090	2·00	2·00
1094	27000k. As No. 1091	2·00	2·00
MS1095	Two sheets, each 110×80 mm. 81000k. Dove flying over map. (a) Inscr in Portuguese; (b) Inscr in English Set of 2 sheets	15·00	15·00

Nos. 1089/91 and 1092/4 respectively were issued together, *se-tenant*, forming composite designs.

211 "Sputnik 1" (satellite)

1995. World Telecommunications Day. Multicoloured.

1096	27000k. Type **211**	1·70	1·70
1097	27000k. "Intelsat" satellite and space shuttle	1·70	1·70
MS1098	100×80 mm. Nos. 1096/7	3·50	3·50

212 Doves above Baby on Daisy-covered Map

1995. 20th Anniv of Independence.

1099 **212**	2900k. multicoloured	1·75	1·75

213 Child, Containers and Fork-lift Truck

1996. Goods Transportation. Multicoloured.

1100	200k. Type **213**	25	20
1101	1265k. Sailing boats and *Mount Cameroon* (ferry)	1·00	80
1102	2583k. Fork-lift trucks loading and unloading *Mount Cameroon* (ferry)	2·00	1·70
1103	2583k. Truck	3·00	1·70
MS1104	106×76 mm. 1265k. Ferry	1·50	1·20

214 Women in Agriculture

1996. Fourth World Conference on Women, Peking (1995). Multicoloured.

1105	375k. Type **214**	30	30
1106	1106k. Women in education	90	75
1107	1265k. Women in business	1·00	80
1108	2900k. Dimba servant girl (vert)	2·30	1·80
MS1109	106×76 mm. 1500k. Traditional education (vert)	1·30	1·30

215 Verdant Hawk Moth

1996. Flora and Fauna. Multicoloured.

1110	1500k. Type **215**	60	50
1111	1500k. Western honey buzzard	40	30
1112	1500k. Bateleur	40	30
1113	1500k. Common kestrel	40	30
1114	4400k. Water lily	90	60
1115	4400k. Red-crested turaco	45	35
1116	4400k. Giraffe	40	35
1117	4400k. African elephant	45	35
1118	5100k. Panther toad	1·10	70
1119	5100k. Hippopotamus	50	40
1120	5100k. Cattle egret	50	40
1121	5100k. Lion	50	40
1122	6000k. African hunting ("wild") dog	1·30	1·10
1123	6000k. Helmeted turtle	60	50
1124	6000k. African pygmy goose	60	50
1125	6000k. Egyptian plover	60	50
MS1126	100×70 mm. 12000k. Spotted hyena	2·00	1·60

Nos. 1111/13, 1115/17, 1119/21 and 1123/5 respectively were issued together, *se-tenant*, forming composite designs.

216 California Quail

1997. Birds. Multicoloured.

1127	5500k. Type **216**	50	35
1128	5500k. Prairie chicken ("Greater Prairie Chicken")	50	35
1129	5500k. Indian blue quail ("Painted Quail")	50	35
1130	5500k. Golden pheasant	50	35
1131	5500k. Crested wood partridge ("Roulroul Partridge")	50	35
1132	5500k. Ceylon spurfowl ("Ceylon Sourfowl")	50	35
1133	5500k. Himalayan snowcock	50	35
1134	5500k. Temminck's tragopan ("Temminicks Tragopan")	50	35
1135	5500k. Lady Amherst's pheasant	50	35
1136	5500k. Great curassow	50	35
1137	5500k. Red-legged partridge	50	35
1138	5500k. Himalayan monal pheasant ("Impeyan Pheasant")	50	35
1139	5500k. Anna's hummingbird	1·30	75
1140	5500k. Blue-throated hummingbird	1·30	75
1141	5500k. Broad-tailed hummingbird	1·30	75
1142	5500k. Costa's hummingbird	1·30	75
1143	5500k. White-eared hummingbird	1·30	75
1144	5500k. Calliope hummingbird	1·30	75
1145	5500k. Violet-crowned hummingbird	1·30	75
1146	5500k. Rufous hummingbird	1·30	75
1147	5500k. Crimson topaz ("Crimson Topaz Hummingbird")	1·30	75
1148	5500k. Broad-billed hummingbird	1·30	75
1149	5500k. Frilled coquette ("Frilled Coquette Hummingbird")	1·70	75
1150	5500k. Ruby-throated hummingbird	1·70	75
MS1151	Two sheets, each 100×70 mm. (a) 12000k. Ring-necked pheasant; (b) 12000k. Racquet-tailed hummingbird Set of 2 sheets	8·50	6·00

217 Lions attacking Zebra

1996. African Wildlife. Multicoloured.

1152	180k. Type **217**	80	55
1153	180k. Lions watching zebras	80	55
1154	180k. African hunting dogs attacking gnu	80	55
1155	180k. Pack of hunting dogs chasing herd of gnu	80	55
1156	450k. Lions stalking isolated zebra	80	55
1157	450k. Male lion	80	55
1158	450k. Hunting dogs surrounding gnu	80	55
1159	450k. Close-up of African hunting dog	80	55
1160	550k. Cheetah	80	55
1161	550k. Cheetah chasing springbok	80	55
1162	550k. Leopard	80	55
1163	550k. Leopard stalking oryx	80	55
1164	630k. Cheetah running beside herd of springbok	80	55
1165	630k. Cheetah overpowering springbok	80	55
1166	630k. Leopard approaching oryx	80	55
1167	630k. Leopard leaping at oryx	80	55

Nos. 1152/67 were issued together, *se-tenant*, in sheetlets with each horizontal strip forming a composite design of lions, cheetah, hunting dogs or leopard attacking prey.

218 Couple with Elderly Woman

1996. 50th Anniv of U.N.O. Multicoloured.

1168	3500k. Type **218**	2·30	1·70
1169	3500k. Children at water pump	2·30	1·70
MS1170	104×74 mm. 8000k. Unloading sacks from ship	5·50	4·50

219 *Styrbjorn* (Swedish sail warship), 1789

1996. Ships. Multicoloured.

1171	6000k. Type **219**	75	55
1172	6000k. U.S.S. *Constellation* (United States frigate), 1797	75	55
1173	6000k. *Taureau* (French torpedo-boat), 1865	75	55
1174	6000k. French bomb ketch	75	55
1175	6000k. *Sardegna* (Italian battleship), 1881	75	55
1176	6000k. H.M.S. *Glasgow* (frigate), 1867	75	55
1177	6000k. U.S.S. *Essex* (frigate), 1812	75	55
1178	6000k. H.M.S. *Inflexible* (battleship), 1881	75	55
1179	6000k. H.M.S. *Minotaur* (ironclad), 1863	75	55
1180	6000k. *Napoleon* (French steam ship of the line), 1854	75	55
1181	6000k. *Sophia Amalia* (Danish galleon), 1650	75	55
1182	6000k. *Massena* (French battleship), 1887	75	55
MS1183	Two sheets, each 105×74 mm. (a) 12000k. *Royal Prince* (English galleon), 1666 (vert); (b) 12000k. H.M.S. *Tremendous* (British ship of the line), 1806 (vert) Set of 2 sheets	5·00	4·00

220 Mask and Drilling Platform

1996. 20th Anniv of Sonangol. Multicoloured.

1184	1000k. Type **220**	60	40
1185	1000k. Storage tanks and mask of woman's face	50	40
1186	2500k. Mask with beard and gas bottles	1·10	90
1187	5000k. Refuelling airplane and mask of monkey's face	2·00	1·70

221 Slaves in Ship's Hold

1996. "Brapex 96" National Stamp Exhibition, Recife, Brazil. Multicoloured.

1188	20000k. Type **221**	3·00	2·50
1189	20000k. Ship capsizing	3·00	2·50
1190	30000k. Boats punting out to ship	4·75	3·50
1191	30000k. Inspection of slaves	4·75	3·50
MS1192	100×70 mm. 50000k. Boats (close-up of detail of No. 1190)	7·50	6·00

222 Mission Church, Huila

1996. Churches. Multicoloured.

1193	5000k. Type **222**	75	65
1194	10000k. Church of Our Lady, PoPulo	1·50	1·30
1195	10000k. Church of Our Lady, Nazare	1·50	1·30
1196	25000k. St. Adriao's Church	3·75	3·25

223 Handball

1996. Olympic Games, Atlanta, U.S.A. Multicoloured.

1197	5000k. Type **223**	10	10
1198	10000k. Swimming (horiz)	15	10
1199	25000k. Athletics	2·75	2·00
1200	35000k. Shooting (horiz)	3·75	3·00
MS1201	76×106 mm. 65000k. Basketball (horiz)	7·00	6·50

224 Dolphins, and Angola on Map of Africa

1996. 40th Anniv of Popular Movement for the Liberation of Angola (MPLA).

1202	**224**	30000k. multicoloured	4·50	4·00

The face value of No. 1202 is wrongly inscr as "300.00.00".

225 AVE, Spain

1997. Trains. Multicoloured.

1203	100000k. Type **225**	1·80	1·30
1204	100000k. "Hikari", Japan	1·80	1·30
1205	100000k. "Warbonnet" diesel locomotives, U.S.A.	1·80	1·30
1206	100000k. "Deltic" diesel locomotive, Great Britain	1·80	1·30
1207	100000k. "Eurostar", France and Great Britain	1·80	1·30
1208	100000k. ETR 450, Italy	1·80	1·30
1209	140000k. Class E1300 diesel locomotive, Morocco	2·30	1·70
1210	140000k. ICE, Germany	2·30	1·70
1211	140000k. Class X2000, Sweden	2·30	1·70
1212	140000k. TGV, France	2·30	1·70
1213	250000k. Steam locomotive	3·25	3·00
1214	250000k. Garratt steam locomotive	3·25	3·00
1215	250000k. General Electric electric locomotive	3·25	3·00
MS1216	Two sheets. (a) 106×76 mm. 11000k. Via Rail diesel locomotive, Canada (49×37 mm); (b) 76×106 mm. 11000k. Canadian Pacific steam locomotive, Canada (37×49 mm) Set of 2 sheets	12·50	11·00

Nos. 1203/8 were issued together, *se-tenant*, forming a composite design.

226 Thoroughbred

1997. Horses. Multicoloured.

1217	100000k. Type **226**	1·30	1·10
1218	100000k. Palomino and Appaloosa	1·30	1·10
1219	100000k. Grey and white Arabs	1·30	1·10
1220	100000k. Arab colt	1·30	1·10
1221	100000k. Thoroughbred colt	1·30	1·10
1222	100000k. Mustang (with hind quarters of another mustang)	1·30	1·10
1223	100000k. Head of mustang and hind quarters of Furioso	1·30	1·10
1224	100000k. Head and shoulders of Furioso	1·30	1·10
1225	120000k. Thoroughbred	1·70	1·30
1226	120000k. Arab and palomino	1·70	1·30
1227	120000k. Arab and Chincoteague	1·70	1·30
1228	120000k. Pintos	1·70	1·30
1229	120000k. Przewalski's Horse	1·70	1·30
1230	120000k. Thoroughbred colt	1·70	1·30
1231	120000k. Arabs	1·70	1·30
1232	120000k. New Forest pony	1·70	1·30
1233	140000k. Selle Francais	1·90	1·60
1234	140000k. Fjord	1·90	1·60
1235	140000k. Percheron	1·90	1·60
1236	140000k. Italian heavy draught horse	1·90	1·60
1237	140000k. Shagya Arab	1·90	1·60
1238	140000k. Avelignese	1·90	1·60
1239	140000k. Czechoslovakian warmblood	1·90	1·60
1240	140000k. New Forest pony	1·90	1·60
MS1241	Two sheets, each 100×70 mm. (a) 215000k. Thoroughbred mother and foal; (b) 220000k. Head and shoulders of thoroughbred Set of 2 sheets	8·00	6·00

Stamps of the same value were issued together, *se-tenant*, Nos. 1217/24 and 1225/32 respectively forming composite designs.

227 Jules Rimet Trophy (Uruguay, 1930)

1997. World Cup Football Championship, France.

1242	**227**	100000k. black	1·90	1·40
1243	-	100000k. black	1·90	1·40
1244	-	100000k. multicoloured	1·90	1·40
1245	-	100000k. multicoloured	1·90	1·40
1246	-	100000k. black	1·90	1·40
1247	-	100000k. multicoloured	1·90	1·40
1248	-	100000k. black	1·90	1·40
1249	-	100000k. black	1·90	1·40
1250	-	100000k. multicoloured	1·90	1·40
1251	-	100000k. multicoloured	1·90	1·40
1252	-	100000k. black	1·90	1·40
MS1253		Two sheets. (a) 127×102 mm. 220000k. multicoloured (Angola team); (b) 76×102 mm. 250000k. multicoloured (Angola team, 1997) Set of 2 sheets	10·00	8·50

DESIGNS—Victory celebrations: No. 1243, Germany (1954); 1244, Brazil (1970); 1245, Maradona holding trophy (Argentina, 1986); 1246, Brazil (1994). Official team photographs: 1247, Germany (1954); 1248, Uruguay (1958); 1249, Italy (1938); 1250, Brazil (1962); 1251, Brazil (1970); 1252, Uruguay (1930).

228 House Insurance

1998. 20th Anniv of ENSA Insurance. Multicoloured.

1254	240000k. Type **228**	2·10	1·80
1255	240000k. Forklift truck carrying egg (industrial risks)	2·10	1·80
1256	240000k. Egg on cross (personal accidents)	2·10	1·80
1257	240000k. Egg on waves (pleasure boating)	2·10	1·80
MS1258	99×155 mm. 350000k. Emblem (59×39 mm)	3·00	2·50

229 Coral

1998. "Expo '98" World's Fair, Lisbon, Portugal. Multicoloured.

1259	100000k. Type **229**	1·70	1·30
1260	100000k. Sea urchin	1·70	1·30
1261	100000k. Seahorses	1·70	1·30
1262	100000k. Sea anemone	1·70	1·30
1263	240000k. Sea slug	4·00	3·00
1264	240000k. Finger coral	4·00	3·00

230 Royal Assyrian (*Terinos terpander*)

1998. Butterflies. Multicoloured.

1265	120000k. Type **230**	1·60	1·30
1266	120000k. Wanderer (*Bematistes aganice*)	1·60	1·30
1267	120000k. Great orange-tip (*Hebomoia glaucippe*)	1·60	1·30
1268	120000k. Alfalfa butterfly (*Colias eurytheme*)	1·60	1·30
1269	120000k. Red-banded perelite (*Pereute leucodrosime*)	1·60	1·30
1270	120000k. Large copper (*Lycaena dispar*)	1·60	1·30
1271	120000k. Malachite (*Metamorpha stelenes*)	1·60	1·30
1272	120000k. Tiger swallowtail (*Papilio glaucus*)	1·60	1·30
1273	120000k. Monarch (*Danaus plexippus*)	1·60	1·30
1274	120000k. Grecian shoemaker (*Catonephele numili*)	1·60	1·30
1275	120000k. Silver-studded blue (*Plebejus argus*)	1·60	1·30
1276	120000k. Common eggfly (*Hypolimnas bolina*)	1·60	1·30
1277	120000k. Brazilian dynastor (*Dynastor napolean*) (horiz)	1·60	1·30
1278	120000k. Saturn butterfly (*Zeuxidia amethystus*) (horiz)	1·60	1·30
1279	120000k. Pipevine swallowtail (*Battus philenor*) (horiz)	1·60	1·30
1280	120000k. Orange-barred sulphur (*Phoebis philea*) (horiz)	1·60	1·30
1281	120000k. African monarch (*Danaus chrysippus*) (horiz)	1·60	1·30
1282	120000k. Green-underside blue (*Glaucopsyche alexis*) (horiz)	1·60	1·30
MS1283	Three sheets. (a) 68×98 mm. 250000k. Gold-banded forester (*Euphaedra neophron*); (b) 98×68 mm. 250000k. Hewitson's uraneis (*Uraneis ucubis*) on *Armillaria straminea* (fungus); (c) 98×68 mm. 250000k. Brown hairstreak (*Thecla betulae*) (horiz) Set of 3 sheets	23·00	19·00

Nos. 1265/70, 1271/6 and 1277/82 respectively were issued together, *se-tenant*, forming composite designs.

231 British Tortoiseshell

1998. Cats and Dogs. Multicoloured.

1284	140000k. Type **231**	1·10	95
1285	140000k. Chinchilla	1·10	95
1286	140000k. Russian blue	1·10	95
1287	140000k. Black persian (longhair) (wrongly inscribed "Longhiar")	1·10	95
1288	140000k. British red tabby	1·10	95
1289	140000k. Birman	1·10	95
1290	140000k. West Highland white terrier	1·10	95
1291	140000k. Red setter	1·10	95
1292	140000k. Dachshund	1·10	95
1293	140000k. St. John water-dog	1·10	95
1294	140000k. Shetland sheep-dog	1·10	95
1295	140000k. Dalmatian	1·10	95
MS1296	Two sheets, each 91×73 mm. (a) 500000k. Turkish van (swimming cat); (b) 500000k. Labrador retriever Set of 2 sheets	12·00	11·00

232 Dolphin, Yacht and Container Ship

1998. First Anniv of Government of Unity and National Reconciliation. Multicoloured.

1297	100000k. Type **232**	1·50	1·20
1298	100000k. Yacht, dolphin and container ship (different)	1·50	1·20
1299	100000k. Yacht, container ship and railway line	1·50	1·20
1300	100000k. Coastline and electricity pylons	1·50	1·20
1301	200000k. Grapes, goat and railway	3·00	2·40
1302	200000k. Village	3·00	2·40
1303	200000k. Tractor, grapes and railway	3·00	2·40
1304	200000k. Coal train	3·00	2·40
1305	200000k. Railway line with branch and pylons	3·00	2·40
1306	200000k. Elephant and tip of tree	3·00	2·40
1307	200000k. Edge of coastline with pylon	3·00	2·40
1308	200000k. Tree trunk and coastline	3·00	2·40

Nos. 1297/1308 were issued together, *se-tenant*, forming a composite design.

233 Ostrich, Children and Blackboard

1998. Decade of Education in Africa. Sheet 100×70 mm.

MS1309 **233** 400000k. mult — 5·00 4·00

234 Lion

1998. Animals of the Grande Porte. Multicoloured.

1310	100000k. Type **234**	1·50	1·20
1311	100000k. Hippopotamus (*Hippopotamus amphibius*)	1·50	1·20
1312	100000k. African elephant (*Loxodonta africana*)	1·50	1·20
1313	100000k. Giraffe (*Giraffa campelopardalis*)	1·50	1·20
1314	220000k. African buffalo (*Synceros caffer*)	3·00	2·40
1315	220000k. Gorilla (*Gorilla gorilla*)	3·00	2·40
1316	220000k. White rhinoceros (*Ceratotherium simum*)	3·00	2·40
1317	220000k. Gemsbok (*Oryx gazella*)	3·00	2·40

There are errors in the Latin inscriptions.

235 Man kicking Football

1998. Eradication of Polio in Angola. Sheet 100×70 mm.

MS1318 **235** 500000k. mult — 6·00 5·00

236 Diana, Princess of Wales

1998. Diana, Princess of Wales Commemoration. Multicoloured.

1319	100000k. Type **236**	1·40	1·20
1320	100000k. Wearing white balldress	1·40	1·20
1321	100000k. Holding handbag	1·40	1·20
1322	100000k. Wearing black evening dress	1·40	1·20
1323	100000k. Holding bouquet (white jacket)	1·40	1·20
1324	100000k. Wearing pearl necklace (looking down)	1·40	1·20
1325	100000k. Wearing pearl necklace (head raised)	1·40	1·20
1326	100000k. Speaking, wearing green velvet jacket	1·40	1·20
1327	100000k. Wearing sunglasses	1·40	1·20
1328	100000k. Wearing black jacket and white blouse	1·40	1·20
1329	100000k. Wearing green blouse	1·40	1·20
1330	100000k. Holding flowers (black jacket)	1·40	1·20
1331	150000k. With young girl amputee	2·20	1·80
1332	150000k. With two amputees	2·20	1·80
1333	150000k. Walking through minefield	2·20	1·80
MS1334	76×106 mm. 400000k. In mine protective clothing	6·50	5·50

237 *Pagurites* sp.

1998. International Year of the Ocean. Multicoloured.

1335	100000k. Type **237**	45	35
1336	100000k. *Callinectes marginatus* (crab)	90	80
1337	100000k. *Thais forbesi*	90	90
1338	100000k. *Ostrea tulipa*	90	80
1339	100000k. *Balanus amphitrite*	90	80
1340	100000k. *Uca tangeri*	90	80
1341	170000k. *Littorina angulifera*	1·60	1·40
1342	170000k. Great hairy melongena (*Semifusus morio*)	1·60	1·40
1343	170000k. *Thais coronata*	1·60	1·40
1344	170000k. *Cerithium atratum* on red branch	1·60	1·40
1345	170000k. *Ostrea tulipa* (different)	1·60	1·40
1346	170000k. *Cerithium atratum* on green branch	1·60	1·40
MS1347	Two sheets, each 85×110 mm. (a) 300000k. *Goniopsis* (crab) (horiz); (b) 300000k. Shell Set of 2 sheets	6·00	5·50

238 Mangos

1998. "Portugal 98" International Stamp Exhibition, Lisbon. Fruit and Vegetables. Multicoloured.

1348	100000k. Type **238**	1·40	1·10
1349	100000k. Guava	1·40	1·10
1350	120000k. Chillies	1·60	1·30
1351	120000k. Sweet corn	1·60	1·30
1352	140000k. Sliced bananas	1·90	1·50
1353	140000k. Avocadoes	1·90	1·50

239 Bimba Canoe

1998. Canoes. Multicoloured.

1354	250000k. Type **239**	2·75	2·50
1355	250000k. Sailing canoe, Ndongo	2·75	2·50
1356	250000k. Building canoes in Ndongo	2·75	2·50

240 *Titanic*

1998. The *Titanic* (liner that sank on maiden voyage, 1912). Sheet 200×160 mm containing T **240** and similar designs. Multicoloured.

MS1357 350000k. Type **240**; 350000k. Stern of *Titanic*; 350000k. *Titanic* under full steam (75×30 mm); 350000k. Bow of *Titanic* (37×60 mm) — 11·00 10·00

241 Ultralight Plane

1998. Aircraft. Multicoloured.

1358	150000k. Type **241**	1·00	80
1359	150000k. Gyroplane	1·00	80
1360	150000k. Business jet	1·00	80
1361	150000k. Convertible plane	1·00	80
1362	150000k. Chuterplane	1·00	80
1363	150000k. Twin-rotor craft	1·00	80
1364	150000k. Skycrane	1·00	80
1365	150000k. British Aerospace/Aerospatiale Concorde Supersonic airliner	1·00	80
1366	150000k. Flying boat	1·00	80
1367	200000k. Boeing 737-100	1·80	1·40
1368	200000k. Ilyushin Il-62M	1·80	1·40
1369	250000k. Pedal-powered plane	1·20	90
1370	250000k. Sail plane	1·20	90
1371	250000k. Aerobatic plane	1·20	90
1372	250000k. Hang-gliding	1·20	90
1373	250000k. Balloon	1·20	90
1374	250000k. Glidercraft	1·20	90
1375	250000k. Model airplane	1·20	90
1376	250000k. Air racing	1·20	90
1377	250000k. Solar-celled plane	1·20	90
MS1378	Four sheets. (a) 110×85 mm. 1000000k. Boeing 777 (84×28 mm); (b) 85×110 mm. 1000000k. Space shuttle Columbia (28×84 mm); (c) 100×70 mm. 1000000k. Boeing 737-200 (84×28 mm); (d) 100×70 mm. 1000000k. Boeing 747-300 (84×28 mm) Set of 4 sheets	18·00	15·00

Nos. 1358/66 and 1369/77 respectively were issued together, *se-tenant*, forming composite designs.

242 Parasaurolophus

1998. Prehistoric Animals. Multicoloured.

1379	120000k. Type **242**	90	80
1380	120000k. Elaphosaurus	90	80
1381	120000k. Iguanodon	90	80
1382	120000k. Maiasaura	90	80
1383	120000k. Brontosaurus	90	80
1384	120000k. Plateosaurus	90	80
1385	120000k. Brachiosaurus	90	80
1386	120000k. Anatosaurus	90	80
1387	120000k. Tyrannosaurus rex	90	80
1388	120000k. Carnotaurus	90	80
1389	120000k. Corythosaurus	90	80
1390	120000k. Stegosaurus	90	80
1391	120000k. Iguanodon (different)	90	80
1392	120000k. Hadrosaurus (horiz)	90	80
1393	120000k. Ouranosaurus (horiz)	90	80
1394	120000k. Hypsilophodon (horiz)	90	80
1395	120000k. Brachiosaurus (horiz)	90	80
1396	120000k. Shunosaurus (horiz)	90	80
1397	120000k. Amargasaurus (horiz)	90	80
1398	120000k. Tuojiangosaurus (horiz)	90	80
1399	120000k. Monoclonius	90	80
1400	120000k. Struthiosaurus (horiz)	90	80
MS1401	Two sheets, each 85×110 mm. (a) 550000k. Tyrannosaurus (different); (b) 550000k. Triceratops Set of 2 sheets	48·00	48·00

243 Head

1999. Endangered Species. The Lesser Flamingo (Phoenicopterus minor). Multicoloured.

1402	300000k. Type **243**	1·60	1·30
1403	300000k. Flamingo with wings outstretched	1·60	1·30
1404	300000k. Flamingo facing left	1·60	1·30
1405	300000k. Front view of flamingo	1·40	1·30

244 Hyacinth Macaw (*Anodorhynchus hyacinthinus*)

1999. Animals and Birds. Multicoloured.

1406	300000k. Type **244**	1·60	1·30
1407	300000k. Penguin (*Sphenisciformes*) (vert)	1·60	1·30
1408	300000k. Przewalski's horse (*Equus caballus przewalski*) (wrongly inscr "Equis")	1·60	1·30
1409	300000k. American bald eagle (*Haliaetus leucocephalus*) (vert)	1·60	1·30
1410	300000k. Spectacled bear (*Tremarctos ornatus*)	1·50	1·20
1411	300000k. Jay (*Aphelocoma*)	1·50	1·20
1412	300000k. Bare-legged scops owl (*Otus insularis*)	1·50	1·20
1413	300000k. Whale-headed stork (*Balaeniceps rex*)	1·50	1·20
1414	300000k. Atlantic ridley turtle (*Lepidochelys kempii*)	1·50	1·20
1415	300000k. Canadian river otter (*Lutra canadensis*)	1·50	1·20
1416	300000k. Swift fox (*Vulpes velox hebes*)	1·50	1·20
1417	300000k. Deer (*Odocoileus*)	1·50	1·20
1418	300000k. Orang-utan (*Pongo pygmaeus*)	1·50	1·20
1419	300000k. Golden lion tamarin (*Leontopithecus rosalia rosalia*) (inscr "Leontopitecus")	1·50	1·20
1420	300000k. Tiger (*Panthera tigris altaica*)	1·50	1·20
1421	300000k. Polecat (wrongly inscr "Tragelaphus eurycerus")	1·50	1·20
MS1422	Two sheets, each 110×85 mm. (a) 1000000k. Brown bear (*Ursus arctos horribilis*): (b) 1000000k. Giant panda (*Ailuropoda melanoleuca*)	10·00	9·00

245 Satellite circling Earth

1999. International Telecommunications Day.

1423	**245** 500000k. multicoloured	2·30	2·00

246 Waterfall, Andulo, Bie

1999. Waterfalls. Multicoloured.

1424	500000k. Type **246**	2·30	2·00
1425	500000k. Chiumbo, Lunda	2·30	2·00
1426	500000k. Ruacana, Cunene	2·30	2·00
1427	500000k. Coemba, Moxico	2·30	2·00

247 Emblem

1999. "Afrobasket '99" (Men's African Basketball Championship). Multicoloured.

1428	15000000k. Type **247**	1·30	1·30
1429	15000000k. Ball teetering on the edge of net, and players' hands	1·60	1·30
1430	15000000k. Hand scooping ball from edge of net	1·60	1·30
1431	15000000k. Flower holding ball	1·60	1·30
MS1432	95×83 mm. 25000000k. Enlarged detail from No. 1441 (39×29 mm)	7·25	2·20

248 African Continent

1999. South African Development Community (S.A.D.C.).

1433	**248** 1000000k. multicoloured	2·00	1·80

249 Duke and Duchess of York, 1923

1999. 100th Birthday of Queen Elizabeth, the Queen Mother. Multicoloured.

1434	**249** 200000k. black and gold	1·50	90
1435	- 200000k. mult	1·50	90
1436	- 200000k. mult	1·50	90
1437	- 200000k. mult	1·50	90
MS1438	154×157 mm. 500000k. Queen Mother in academic robes (37×50 mm)	3·00	2·50

DESIGNS: No. 1435, Portrait of Queen Mother wearing Star of the Garter; 1436, Queen Mother wearing fur stole; 1437, Queen Mother wearing blue hat.

250 Ekuikui II

1999. Rulers. Multicoloured.

1439	500000k. Type **250**	2·20	1·90
1440	500000k. Mvemba Nzinga	2·20	1·90
1441	500000k. Mwata Yamvu Nawej II	2·20	1·90
1442	500000k. Njinga Mbande	2·20	1·90
MS1443	104×76 mm. 1000000k. Mandume Ndemufayo	5·00	4·50

251 13th-century B.C. Pharaonic Barque

1999. Ships. Multicoloured.

1444	950000k. Type **251**	1·10	80
1445	950000k. Flemish carrack, 1480	1·10	80
1446	950000k. H.M.S. *Beagle* (Darwin), 1830	1·10	80
1447	950000k. *North Star* (paddle-steamer), 1852	1·10	80
1448	950000k. *Fram* (schooner, Amundsen and Nansen), 1892	1·10	80
1449	950000k. *Unyo Maru* (sail/steam freighter), 1909 (inscr "Unyon")	1·10	80
1450	950000k. *Juan Sebastian de Elcano* (cadet schooner), 1927	1·10	80
1451	950000k. *Tovarishch*, (three-masted cadet barque), 1933	1·10	80
1452	950000k. *Bucentaur* (Venetian state galley), 1728	1·10	80
1453	950000k. *Clermont* (first commercial paddle-steamer), 1807	1·10	80
1454	950000k. *Savannah* (paddle-steamer), 1819	1·10	80
1455	950000k. *Dromedary* (steam tug), 1844	1·10	80
1456	950000k. *Iberia* (steam freighter), 1881	1·10	80
1457	950000k. *Gluckauf* (tanker), 1886	1·10	80
1458	950000k. *Cidade de Paris* (ocean steamer), 1888	1·10	80
1459	950000k. *Mauretania* (liner), 1906	1·10	80
1460	950000k. *La Gloire* (first armoured-hull ship), 1859	1·10	80
1461	950000k. *L'Ocean*, (French battery ship), 1868	1·10	80
1462	950000k. *Dandolo* (Italian cruiser), 1876 (inscr "Dandalo") and stern of H.M.S. *Dreadnought*	1·10	80
1463	950000k. H.M.S. *Dreadnought* (battleship), 1906	1·10	80
1464	950000k. *Bismarck* (battleship), 1939 and stern of U.S.S. *Cleveland*	1·10	80
1465	950000k. U.S.S. *Cleveland* (cruiser), 1946	1·10	80
1466	950000k. U.S.S. *Boston* (first guided-missile cruiser), 1942 and stern of U.S.S. *Long Beach*	1·10	80
1467	950000k. U.S.S. *Long Beach* (first nuclear-powered cruiser), 1959	1·10	80
MS1468	Four sheets, each 75×70 mm. (a) 5000000k. 18th-century junk; (b) 5000000k. *Madre de Dios* (carrack) (wrongly inscr "Deus"), 1609; (c) 5000000k. Catamaran, 1861; (d) 5000000k. *Natchez* (Mississippi paddle-steamer), 1870	22·00	16·00

Nos. 1474/5, 1476/7 and 1478/9 respectively were issued together, *se-tenant*, forming a composite design.

252 Fly Agaric (*Amanita muscaria*)

1999. Fungi. Multicoloured.

1469	1000000k. Type **252** (wrongly inscr "Aminita")	1·00	75
1470	1000000k. Bronze boletus (*Boletus*)	1·00	75
1471	1000000k. Lawyer's wig (*Coprinus comatus*)	1·00	75
1472	1000000k. The blusher (*Amanita rubescens*) (inscr "Aminita")	1·00	75
1473	1000000k. Slimy-branded cort (*Cortinarius collinitus*)	1·00	75
1474	1000000k. Devil's boletus (*Boletus satanas*)	1·00	75
1475	1000000k. Parasol mushroom (*Lepiota procera*)	1·00	75
1476	1000000k. Trumpet agaric (*Clitocybe geotropa*)	1·00	75
1477	1000000k. *Morchella crassipes*	1·00	75
1478	1000000k. *Boletus rufescens*	1·00	75
1479	1000000k. Death cap (*Amanita phalloides*)	1·00	75
1480	1000000k. *Collybia iocephala*	1·00	75
1481	1000000k. *Tricholoma aurantium*	1·00	75
1482	1000000k. *Cortinarius violaceus*	1·00	75
1483	1000000k. *Mycena polygramma*	1·00	75
1484	1000000k. *Psalliota augusta*	1·00	75
1485	1000000k. *Russula nigricans*	1·00	75
1486	1000000k. Granulated boletus (*Boletus granulatus*)	1·00	75
1487	1000000k. *Mycena strobilinoides*	1·00	75
1488	1000000k. Caesar's mushroom (*Amanita caesarea*)	1·00	75
1489	1000000k. Fly agaric (*Amanita muscaria*) (different)	1·00	75
1490	1000000k. *Boletus crocipodius*	1·00	75
1491	1000000k. Cracked green russula (*Russula virescens*)	1·00	75
1492	1000000k. Saffron milk cap (*Lactarius deliciosus*)	1·00	75
1493	1250000k. Caesar's mushroom (*Amanita caesarea*) (different)	1·50	1·40
1495	1250000k. Red cracked boletus (*Boletus chrysenteron*) (wrongly inscr "chyrsenteron")	1·50	1·40
1496	1250000k. Butter mushroom (*Boletus luteus*)	1·50	1·40
1497	1250000k. Lawyer's wig (*Coprinus comatus*) (different)	1·50	1·40
1498	1250000k. Witch's hat (*Hygrocybe conica*)	1·50	1·40
1499	1250000k. *Psalliota xanthoderma*	1·50	1·40
MS1500	Two sheets, each 75×105 mm. (a) 5000000k. *Mycena lilacifolia*; (b) 5000000k. *Psalliota haemorrhoidaria*	11·00	8·00

253 Mercury and Venus

1999. 30th Anniv of First Manned Moon Landing. Multicoloured.

1501	3500000k. Type **253**	1·10	75
1502	3500000k. Jupiter	1·10	75
1503	3500000k. Neptune and Pluto	1·10	75
1504	3500000k. Earth and Mars	1·10	75
1505	3500000k. Saturn	1·10	75
1506	3500000k. Uranus	1·10	75
1507	3500000k. Explorer 17 satellite, 1963	1·10	75
1508	3500000k. Intelsat 4A satellite, 1975	1·10	75
1509	3500000k. GOES-D (Geostationary Operational Environmental Satellite), 1980	1·10	75
1510	3500000k. Intelsat 2 satellite, 1966	1·10	75
1511	3500000k. Navstar 2 (Navigation System with Timing And Ranging), 1978	1·10	75
1512	3500000k. S.M.S. (Solar Maximum Mission) satellite, 1980	1·10	75
1513	3500000k. Earth and astronaut walking in space	1·10	75
1514	3500000k. Mariner 8 spacecraft	1·10	75
1515	3500000k. Viking 10 spacecraft	1·10	75
1516	3500000k. Ginga satellite	1·10	75
1517	3500000k. Soyuz 19 spacecraft (inscr "satelite")	1·10	75
1518	3500000k. Voyager spacecraft	1·10	75
1519	3500000k. Hubble space telescope (vert)	1·10	75
1520	3500000k. Launch of space shuttle *Atlantis* (vert)	1·10	75
1521	3500000k. Uhuru satellite (vert)	1·10	75
1522	3500000k. Mir space station (vert)	1·10	75
1523	3500000k. Gemini 7 spacecraft (vert)	1·10	75
1524	3500000k. Venera 7 spacecraft (vert)	1·10	75
MS1525	Five sheets (a) 95×85 mm. 6000000k. Astronaut from Apollo 17 walking on moon (vert); (b) 95×85 mm. 6000000k. Astronaut driving moon buggy (vert); (c) 85×110 mm. 12000000k. Launch of commercial satellite SBS 4 (vert); (d) 85×110 mm. Neil Armstrong (astronaut) (vert); (e) 110×85 mm. 12000000k. Earth and *Columbia* spacecraft	18·00	15·00

No. 1523 is inscribed "GEMNI" in error.

254 *Night Attack by 47 Ronin*

1999. 150th Death Anniv of Katushika Hokusai (artist). Multicoloured.

1526	3500000k. Type **254**	1·10	75
1527	3500000k. *Usigafuchi no Kudan*	1·10	75
1528	3500000k. Sketch of seated man	1·10	75
1529	3500000k. Sketch of animals and birds	1·10	75
1530	3500000k. *Autumn Pheasant*	1·10	75
1531	3500000k. Rural landscape	1·10	75
1532	3500000k. *Survey of the region*	1·10	75
1533	3500000k. Kabuki theatre	1·10	75
1534	3500000k. Sketch of hen	1·10	75
1535	3500000k. Sketch of wheelwright	1·10	75
1536	3500000k. *Excursion to Enoshima*	1·10	75
1537	3500000k. Sumida River landscape	1·10	75
MS1538	Two sheets, each 100×70 mm. (a) 12000000k. Japanese calligraphy between woman and child (vert); (b) 12000000k. Woman dressing hair (vert)	8·00	6·50

255 SNCF Class 242 Steam Locomotive

2000. "PHILEX FRANCE 99" International Stamp Exhibition, Paris. Locomotives. Two sheets, each 111×80 mm containing T **255** and similar horiz design. Multicoloured.

MS1539	(a) 12k. Type **255** (b) 12k. Prototype Linear Propulsion Hover Train	13·50	12·00

257 Zebra

2000. Fauna. Multicoloured.

1540	1k.50 Type **256**	1·00	90
1541	2k. Short-tailed fruit bat	1·30	1·20
1542	3k. California condor	1·90	1·80
1543	5k.50 Lion	3·50	3·25

MS1544	Eight sheets:—140×179 mm. (a) 3k.50×6, Florida white-tailed deer; Turkey; Beaver; Bullfrog; Manatee; Greenback cutthroat trout; (b) 3k.50×6, White-faced sapajou; Toucan; Eyelash viper; Tree frog; Golden lion tamarin; Harpy eagle:—140×179 mm. (vert) (c) 3k.50×6, Mountain gorilla; Black rhino; Cape buffalo; Jackson chameleon; Cape cobra; Meerkats; (d) 3k.50×6, Kangaroo; Koala; Rainbow bee-eater; Red-eyed tree frog; Townsville blue-eye; Snake-necked tortoise:—107×77 mm. (vert) (e) 12k. Three-toed sloth; (f) 12k. Cheetah; (g) 12k. Orang-utan:—70×100 mm. (vert) 12k. Ring-tailed lemur	40·00	34·00

256 Harpy Eagle

2000. Birds. Multicoloured.

1545	1k.50 Type **257**	1·40	1·10
1546	2k. Andean condor	1·50	1·40
1547	3k. Lappet-faced vulture (vert)	2·30	2·00
1547a	5k.50 Vulture	4·25	4·00
MS1548	Eight sheets 128×127 mm. (a) 3k.50×6, American kestrel (*Falco sparverius*) (inscr "sperterius"); Spectacled owl (*Pulsatrix perspicillata*); White-tailed kite (*Eleanus leucurus*) (inscr "Elemus"); Boobook owl (*Ninox novaeseelandiae*) (inscr "novaseseeelandiar"); *Polemaetus bellicosus* (inscr "Polmactus"); Caracara (*Polyborus plancus*); (b) 3k.50×6, Northern goshawk (*Accipiter gentiles*) (inscr "Acolpiler genttlis"); Hawk owl (*Surnia ulula*) (wrongly inscr "Surnis"); Peregrine falcon (*Falco prregrinus*); Eastern screech owl (*Otus asio*); African fish eagle (*Haliaeetus vocifer*) (inscr "Haliaectus"); Laughing falcon (*Herpetotheres cachinnans*) (inscr "Herpetothers"):—85×127 mm. (c) 6k.50×3, Verreaux's eagle; Bonelli's eagle; African fish eagle:—127×85 mm. (d) 6k.50×3, Bald eagle (vert); Tawny eagle (vert); Eagle (vert); (e) 85×110 mm. 12k. Lanner falcon (vert); (f) 110×85 mm. 12k. King vultures; (g) 85×111 mm. 15k. Secretary bird (*Sagittarius serpentarius*); (h) 15k. Golden eagle (*Aquila chrysaetos*) (inscr "chrysectos")	40·00	40·00

258 Zebra (*Equs zebra*)

2000. Animals and Birds. Multicoloured.

1549	1k.50 Type **258**	1·00	80
1550	1k.50 Golden palm weaver (*Ploceus xanthops*)	1·00	80
1551	1k.50 Hunting dog (*Lycaon pictus*)	1·00	80
1552	1k.50 Cheetah (*Acinonyx jubatus*)	1·30	1·00
1553	1k.50 Gemsbok (*Oryx gazelle*)	1·00	80
1554	1k.50 Cape fox (*Vulpes chama*) (inscr "Otocyon megalotis")	1·00	80
1555	1k.50 Giraffe (*Giraffa camelopardalis*)	1·00	80
1556	1k.50 Golden jackal (*Canis aureus*) (inscr "adustus")	1·00	80
1557	1k.50 Potto (*Perodicticus potto*)	1·00	80
1558	1k.50 Lion (*Panthera leo*)	1·00	80
1559	1k.50 Lilac-breasted roller (*Coracias caudate*) (inscr "Coracus")	1·30	1·00
1560	1k.50 Bat-eared fox (*Otocyon megalotis*)	1·00	80
1561	2k. Ostrich (*Struthio camelus*)	1·50	1·20
1562	2k. African wild cat (*Felis lybica*)	1·50	1·20
1563	2k. Impala (*Aepyceros melampus*)	1·50	1·20
1564	2k. Savanna monkey (*Cercopithecus aethiops*)	1·50	1·20
1565	2k. Black rhino (*Diceros bicornis*)	1·50	1·20
1566	2k. Baboon (*Papio*)	1·50	1·20
1567	2k. Caracal (*Felis caracal*)	1·50	1·20
1568	2k. Secretary bird (*Sagittarius serpentarius*)	1·75	1·50
1569	2k. Warthog (*Phacochoerus aethiopicus*)	1·50	1·20
1570	2k. Afro-Australian fur seal (*Arctocephalus pusillus*)	1·50	1·20
1571	2k. Malachite kingfisher (*Alcedo cristata*)	2·00	1·75
1572	2k. Hippopotamus (*Hippopotamus amphibious*)	1·50	1·20
MS1573	Two sheets. (a) 85×110 mm.12k. Savanna monkey (vert); (b) 110×85 mm. 12k. Elephant (*Loxodonta Africana*) (vert)	13·00	13·00

259 Flowers and Birds (Lai-Ji)

2000. Millennium (1st issue). Cultural Events of the 16th-century. Multicoloured.

1574	2k.50 Type **259**	2·75	1·50
1575	2k.50 *Last Judgement*, Orvieto Cathedral (Luca Signorelli)	2·75	1·50
1576	2k.50 *Enchanted Garden* (Hieronymus Bosch)	2·75	1·50
1577	2k.50 Machiavelli (author of *O Principe* (beginning of modern politics))	2·75	1·50
1578	2k.50 Illustration from Utopia (Sir Thomas More)	2·75	1·50
1579	2k.50 Martin Luther (church reform)	2·75	1·50
1580	2k.50 Charles I of Spain (holy Roman Emperor (unification of Europe))	2·75	1·50
1581	2k.50 "School of Athens" (Rafael)	2·75	1·50
1582	2k.50 Juan Sebastion Elcano (first circumnavigation of the world)	3·25	1·50
1583	2k.50 Henry VIII (separation from Catholic church)	3·25	1·50
1584	2k.50 Spanish conquering Aztecs and Incas (exploration of Americas)	2·75	1·50
1585	2k.50 Plasencia Cathedral (beginning of Romanesque architecture)	2·75	1·50
1586	2k.50 Potatoes (first introduction into Europe)	3·25	1·50
1587	2k.50 Astrolabe (Copernicus' theory of the universe)	3·25	1·50
1588	2k.50 Priest and courtiers (Portuguese-Japanese trade)	2·75	1·50
1589	2k.50 *Self Portrait* (Albrecht Durer (death, 1528)) (60×40 mm)	2·75	1·50
1590	2k.50 Woman, hourglass, inkwell and cross (declaration of rights of indigenous Americans by Queen Isabel of Castille)	2·75	1·50

260 Henry II of Germany

2000. Millennium (2nd issue). Monarchs and Popes. Multicoloured.

MS1591	Twelve sheets:—165×198 mm. (a) 3k.×4, Type **260**; Marina Mniszech, Queen Consort of Tsar Lzhedmitry (false Dmitri); Tsar Ivan IV; Tsar Ivan III; (b) 3k.×4, Charles II of England; Lady Jane Grey; Leopold III of Belgium; Louis XV of France; (c) 3k.×6, James I of England; James II of England; James VI of Scotland; Brian Boru, King of Ireland; William I of Prussia (inscr "William I of Germany"); Edward VI of England; (d) 3k.×6, Pope Nicholas II; Pope Pascal II; Pope Sergius IV; Pope Victor II; Pope Victor III; Pope Urban III; Pope Innocent II; (e) 3k.×6, Pope John XIII; Pope Agapetus II; Pope John XVIII; Pope Lucius II; (f) 3k.×6, Pope Celestine II; Pope Clement II; Pope Clement III; Pope Gelasius II; Pope Benedict VII; Pope Gregory V:—109×129 mm. (g) 12k. William IV of England; (h) 12k. Tsar Fyodor I; (i) 12k. Tsar Lzhedmitry; (j) 12k. Pope Gregory VII; (k) 12k. Pope Leo XIII; (l) 12k. Pope Leo IX	60·00	60·00

261 Damaged Building, Kuito

2000. Buildings and People. Multicoloured.

1592	3k. Type **261**	1·90	1·90
1593	3k. People and Kunje–Kuito road	1·90	1·90
1594	4k. Post Office building	2·50	2·50
1595	4k. Police headquarters	2·50	2·50
1596	5k. Damaged apartments	3·25	3·25
1597	5k. Independence Plaza	3·25	3·25
1598	6k. Children	3·75	3·75
1599	6k. Man carrying sack	3·75	3·75

262 Trees

2000. Children's Paintings. Multicoloured.

1600	3k. Type **262**	1·50	1·50
1601	4k. Wall	1·90	1·90
1602	5k. Rural scene	2·40	2·40

263 Directorate of Communications, Telephones and Telegraphs, Luanda

2000. Postal Buildings. Multicoloured.

1603	5k. Type **263**	2·30	2·00
1604	5k. ETP building, Mbanza Congo	2·30	2·00
1605	5k. CTT building, Namibe	2·30	2·00
1606	8k. ECP building, Luanda	3·75	3·50
1607	8k. ETP building, Lobito	3·75	3·50
1608	8k. ECP building, Luanda (different)	3·75	3·50

264 Tank, Rifle and Dove

2001. 25th Anniv of Independence. Sheet 140×47 mm containing T **264** and similar horiz design. Multicoloured.

MS1609	12k. Type **264**; 12k. Dove, mattock and tractor	6·00	6·00

265 Radio Studio

2001. 25th Anniv of Public Radio (**MS**1613a, **MS**1613c) and Television (others). Four sheets containing T **265** and similar multicoloured designs.

MS1610	(a) 154×80 mm. 9k.50, Type **265**; 9k.50, Reporter in war zone; 9k.50 Carrying stretcher from burning aeroplane. (b) 154×80 mm. 9k.50, Television studio; 9k.50, Cameraman filming tank; 9k.50, Women and children crossing water. (c) 99×60 mm. 12k. Reporter in war zone (detail) (42×28 mm). (d) 99×60 mm. 12k. Cameraman filming tank (detail) (28×42 mm) (vert)	30·00	30·00

266 Hands holding Book

2001. Africa Day. Multicoloured.

1611	10k. Type **266**	2·75	2·30
1612	10k. Hands and xylophone	2·75	2·30
MS1613	130×90 mm. 30k. Map of Africa	8·00	8·00

267 *Nicolaia speciosa*

2001. Flowers. Belgica 2001 International Stamp Exhibition. Multicoloured.

1614	8k. Type **267**	2·75	2·50
1615	9k. *Allamanda cathartica* (inscr "cathartca")	3·00	2·75
1616	10k. *Welwitschia mirabilis*	3·50	3·00
1617	10k. *Tagetes patula*	3·50	3·00
MS1618	130×90 mm. 30k. No. 1616	10·50	10·00

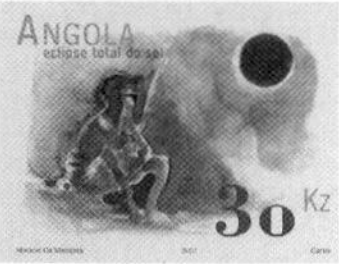

268 Man wearing Dark Glasses

2001. Total Eclipse of the Sun, 21 June 2001. Sheet 130×90 mm.

MS1619	30k. multicoloured	7·50	7·50

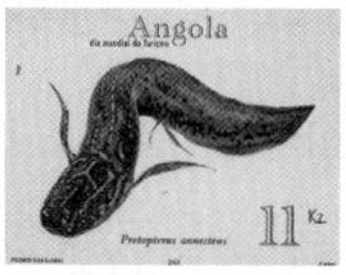

269 West African Lungfish (*Protopterus annectens*)

2001. Freshwater Fish. Multicoloured.

1620	11k. Type **269**	2·00	1·50
1621	17k. *Protopterus amphibious*	3·00	2·40
1622	18k. *Tilapia ruweti*	3·25	2·50
MS1623	130×90 mm. 36k. Red-breasted tilapia (*Tilapia rendalli*)	6·50	6·50

270 Ovambo Efundula, Cunene

2001. Traditional Dances. Multicoloured.

1624	11k. Type **270**	1·50	1·30
1625	11k. Massembo, Luanda	1·60	1·30
1626	17k. Macolo Batuque, Uige	2·50	2·00
1627	18k. Mukixi, Lunda Tchokwe	2·60	2·20
1628	18k. Humbi Puberdade, Namibe	2·60	2·20
MS1629	130×90 mm. 36k. Carnival Juvenil, Luanda	5·50	5·50

271 Hand-woven Hat, Banda

2001. Woven Crafts. Sheet 130×90 mm containing T **271** and similar horiz design. Multicoloured.

MS1630	17k. Type **271**; 18k. Hat with extensions, Kijinga	5·25	5·25

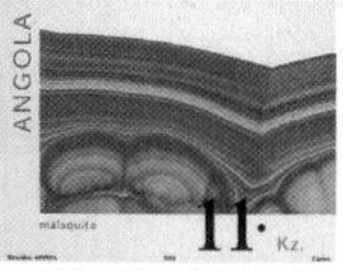

272 Malachite

2001. Minerals. Multicoloured.

1631	11k. Type **272**	2·00	1·80
1632	11k. Hematite	2·00	1·80
1633	18k. Diamond	3·25	2·75
1634	18k. Psilomelane	3·25	2·75

273 Mwana Mpwevo

2002. Masks. Multicoloured.

1635	10k. Type **273** (Ngangela animistic ritual)	1·40	1·30
1636	11k. Mukixi (Cokwe circumcision ritual)	1·80	1·40
1637	11k. Mbunda (comic)	1·80	1·40
1638	17k. Mwana Pwo (Cokwe circumcision ritual)	2·50	2·10
1639	18k. Likisi-Cinganji (supernatural incarnation)	2·75	2·20
MS1640	90×80 mm. 36k. Ndemba (Bakongo circumcision ritual)	6·00	5·00

274 Players and Football

2002. Football World Cup Championship, Japan and South Korea. Multicoloured.

1641	35k. Type **274**	4·50	3·00
1642	37k. Players and ball (different)	4·75	3·25
MS1643	55×120 mm. Nos. 1641/2	8·50	6·50

275 Figure with Target on Chest

2002. Socialist International Congress. Multicoloured.

1644	10k. Type **275** (abolition of the death penalty)	1·20	80
1645	10k. Woman (end to violence against women)	1·20	80
1646	10k. Faces (combating poverty)	1·20	80
1647	10k. Map and dollar sign (eliminate foreign debt)	1·20	80
1648	10k. Map ("Africa in Peril" combating poverty)	1·20	80
MS1649	40×30 mm. Nos. 1644/7	6·50	6·00

276 National Map, Rainbow and Dove

2002. Peace and Reconciliation Commission.

1650	**276**	35k. multicoloured	2·00	1·60

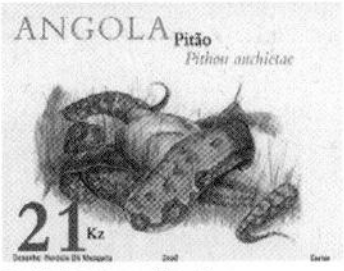

277 Python (*Python anchietae*) (inscr "pithon")

2002. Reptiles. Multicoloured.

1651	21k. Type **277**	1·50	1·10
1652	35k. *Lacerta* (lizard)	2·50	1·90
1653	37k. *Naja Nigricollis* (spitting cobra)	2·60	2·00
1654	40k. *Crocodylus niloticus*	2·75	2·20

278 Lighthouse, Barra do Dande

2002. Lighthouses and Buoys. Multicoloured.

1655	45k. Type **278**	3·50	2·50
1656	45k. Snake Head lighthouse, Soyo	3·50	2·50
1657	45k. Tafe lighthouse, Cabinda Bay	3·50	2·50
1658	45k. Moita Seca lighthouse, South Margin Bay	3·50	2·50
1659	45k. Red buoy no. 9, Luanda Bay	3·50	2·50
1660	45k. Green buoy no. 1, Luanda Bay	3·50	2·50

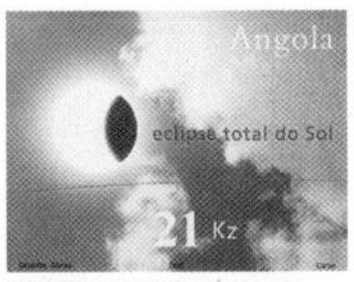

279 Partial Eclipse (one third)

2002. Total Eclipse of the Sun (21 June 2001). Sheet 155×80 mm containing T **279** and similar horiz designs showing stages of eclipse. Multicoloured.

MS1661	21k. Type **279**; 35k. Two thirds; 37k. Total eclipse	6·00	6·00

280 Antonio Manuel (17th-century Congolese ambassador to Pope Paul V) and Lion

2002. Angola—Italy Friendship. Multicoloured.

1662	35k. Type **280**	2·20	1·80
1663	45k. Antonio Manuel and papal plaque	3·00	2·20
MS1664	120×72 mm. Nos. 1662/3	4·00	4·00

281 Omolingui (Ovimbundo water pot)

2002. Pottery. Multicoloured.

1665	27k. Type **281**	2·00	1·20
1666	45k. Mulondo (Luvale drinking jar)	3·00	2·00
1667	47k. Ombya Yo Tuma (Ovimbundo food pot)	3·25	2·20
MS1668	120×72 mm. 51k. Sanga (Bakongo drinking vessel)	4·00	3·00

282 Trees, Satellite Dish and UN Emblem

2003. Third United Nations Science, Technology and Development Meeting.

1669	**282**	50k. multicoloured	2·75	2·20

283 Stylized Bi-plane

2003. Centenary of Powered Flight.

1670	**283**	25k. multicoloured	2·75	2·75

284 Antonio Jacinto

2003. Writers. Multicoloured.

1671	27k. Type **284**	1·50	1·20
1672	45k. Antonio Agostinho Neto	2·20	1·70
MS1673	121×90 mm. 27k. Antonio Jacinto wearing cap; 45k. Agostinho Neto as younger man	3·75	3·75

285 Two Antelope

2003. Sable Antelope (Hippotragus niger). Multicoloured.

1674	27k. Type **285**	1·50	1·20
1675	45k. Two antelope with straight horns	2·20	1·70
1676	47k. One antelope with curved horns	2·50	2·00

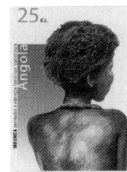

286 Mbunda Woman

2003. Traditional Women's Hairstyles. Sheet 130×120 mm containing T **286** and similar vert designs.

MS1677	25k.×6, Type **286**; Soyo; Huila; Humbi; Cabinda; Quipungu	8·00	8·00

287 Musicians (detail, *Ascensao*) (Jorge Afonso)

2003. Christmas. Multicoloured.

1678	27k. Type **287**	1·50	1·20
1679	27k. *Adoraçao dos Pastores* (Andre Reinoso)	1·50	1·20
1680	45k. Holy Family (detail, *Adoraçao dos Pastores*) (Josefa de Obidos)	2·20	1·70
1681	45k. Cherubs (detail, *Adoraçao dos Pastores*) (Josefa de Obidos)	2·20	1·70
MS1682	110×92 mm. Nos. 1678/81	7·50	7·50

288 Bryde's Whale (*Balaenoptera edeni*)

2003. Marine Mammals. Multicoloured.

1683	27k. Type **288**	2·50	2·20
1684	45k. Heaviside's dolphin (*Cephalorhynchus heavisidii*)	4·50	3·50
MS1685	120×84 mm. 27k. Type **288**; 47k. Pilot whale (*Globicephala melaena*) (inscr "Giobiocephaia")	7·00	6·00

289 Tawny Eagle (*Aquila rapax*)

2003. Eagles. Multicoloured.

1686	20k. Type **289**	2·00	1·70
1687	20k. Martial eagle (*Hieraaetus bellicosus*) (inscr "Polemaetus")	2·00	1·70
1688	25k. African fish eagle (*Haliaeetus vocifer*)	2·50	2·20
1689	25k. Bateleur (*Terathopius ecaudatus*)	2·50	2·20
MS1690	120×80 mm. 45k. Verreaux's eagle (*Aquila verreauxi*)	5·50	5·00

290 Chess Pieces

2003. Chess. Multicoloured.

1691	45k. Type **290**	3·50	3·00
1692	45k. Board and pieces	3·50	3·00

291 Pope John Paul II

2003. 25th Anniv of the Pontificate of Pope John Paul II. Multicoloured.

1693	27k. Type **291**	2·20	1·70
1694	27k. Pope John Paul II with raised hand	2·20	1·70

292 *Adansonia digitata*

2004. Southern African Development Community. Plants. Multicoloured.

1695	27k. Type **292**	1·80	1·30
1695a	27k. *Psidium guayava*	1·80	1·30
1696	45k. *Carica papaya*	3·00	2·20
1697	45k. *Cymbopogon citrates*	3·00	2·20
MS1698	129×105 mm. Nos. 1695/7	8·00	6·00

293 Basketball

2004. Olympic Games, Athens. Multicoloured.

1699	27k. Type **293**	1·50	1·10
1700	27k. Handball	1·50	1·10
1701	45k. Running	2·50	1·80
1702	45k. Volleyball	2·50	1·80

294 Humpback Whales (*Megaptera novaeangliae*)

2004. Sea Mammals. Multicoloured.

1703	27k. Type **294**	1·50	1·10
1704	27k. Heaviside's dolphin (*Cephalorhynchus heavisidii*)	1·50	1·10
1705	45k. Bottlenose dolphin (*Tursiops truncates*)	2·50	1·80
MS1706	135×80 mm. 99k. *Megaptera novaeangliae* (different)	5·50	5·00

Nos. 1703/5 were issued together, *se-tenant*, forming a composite design.

295 Saddle Tanker (Benguela)

2004. Trains. Multicoloured.

1707	27k. Type **295**	1·50	1·10
1708	27k. Diesel locomotive (Mocamedes)	1·50	1·10
1709	27k. Locomotive CFB 225 (Benguela)	1·50	1·10

296 Fireman and Campaign Emblem

2004. Fire Emergency Phone Number Publicity Campaign. Multicoloured.

1710	27k. Type **296**	1·50	1·10
1711	27k. Fire appliance	1·50	1·10
1712	45k. Fire appliance facing right	2·50	1·80
MS1713	130×80 mm. Nos. 1710/12	5·00	5·50

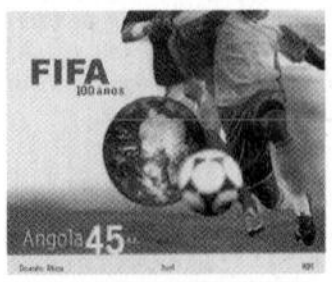

297 Globe and Footballers

2004. Centenary of FIFA (Federation Internationale de Football Association).

1714	**297**	45k. multicoloured	2·00	1·60

298 Three Kings

2004. Christmas. Multicoloured.

1715	27k. Type **298**	1·20	95
1716	45k. Nativity	2·00	1·60

Nos. 1715/16 were issued together, *se-tenant*, forming a composite design.

299 Family of Monkeys

2004. Colobus Monkey (*Colobus angolensis*). Multicoloured.

1717	27k. Type **299**	1·20	1·20
1718	27k. Mother and baby	1·20	1·20
1719	27k. Male	1·20	1·20
1720	27k. Facing left	1·20	1·20

300 Woman and City Skyline

2005. 50th Anniv of Rotary of Luanda. Multicoloured.

1721	45k. Type **300**	2·00	1·60
1722	51k. Woman and countryside	2·75	2·00
MS1723	120×80 mm. Nos. 1721/2	5·50	5·00

Nos. 1724/7 and Type **301** are left for Basketry, issued on 6 September 2005, not yet received.

Nos. 1728/9 and Type **302** are left for 30th Anniv of Independence, issued on 8 November 2005, not yet received.

Nos. 1730/1and Type **303** are left for World Summit on the Information Society (WSIS), issued on 8 November 2005, not yet received.

Nos. 1732/5 and Type **304** are left for Ministerial Conference of African Oil Producers , issued on 24 April 2006, not yet received.

Nos. 1736/7 and Type **305** are left for World Cup, issued on 30 August 2006, not yet received.

306 Dogs

2006. Tenth Anniv of Countries of Portuguese Language Community. Lubrapex International Stamp Exhibition, Rio de Janeiro, Brazil. Multicoloured.

1738	27k. Type **306**	35	15
1739	45k. Grey parrots	65	25
1740	45k. Helmeted guinea fowl	65	25

307 Currency

2006. 30th Anniv of National Bank. Multicoloured.

MS1745	200×136 mm. 90k. Type **307**	1·90	1·90

No. 1746 and Type **308** are left for Paralympic Committee, issued on 29 December 2006, not yet received.

No. 1747 and Type **309** are left for Five Years of Peace, issued on 20 April 2007, not yet received.

Nos. 1748/9 and Type **310** are left for Venice Biennial, issued on 20 April 2007, not yet received.

No. 1750 and Type **311** are left for Africa Day, issued on 25 May 2007, not yet received.

Nos. 1751/5 and Type **312** are left for Centenary of Scouting, issued on 1 June 2007, not yet received.

No. 1756 and Type **313** are left for 27th Anniv of SADC , issued on 17 August 2007, not yet received.

No. 1757 and Type **314** are left for Olympic Games, Beijing, issued on 20 September 2007, not yet received.

315 Malange

2007. World Post Day. Multicoloured.

MS1758	45k.×2, Type **315**; Huambo	1·10	1·10

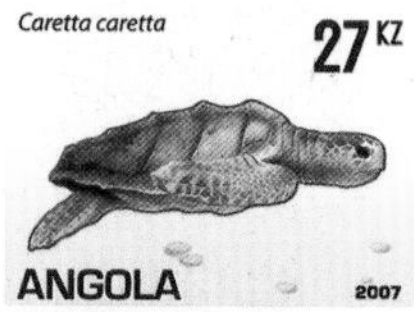

316 *Caretta caretta*

2007. Marine Turtles. Multicoloured.

MS1759	126×104 mm. 27k. Type **316**; 27k. *Chelonia mydas* ; 45k. *Eretmochelys imbricata* ; 45k. *Lepidochelys olivacea*	45	45
MS1760	142×108 mm. 130k. *Dermochelys coriacea* (37×39 mm)	1·30	1·30

317 Meat and Dumplings

2008. Angolan Gastronomy. Multicoloured.

1761	37k. Type **317**	40	14
1762	40k. Greens and dumplings	40	15
1763	59k. Stew with greens (Calulu)	1·10	35
MS1764	160×90 mm. 153k. Chicken stew (Muamba)	1·90	1·90

318 Rio Kuebe

2008. Rivers. Multicoloured.

1765	37k. Type **318**	40	15
1766	37k. Rapidos do Kuanza (Rapids of Kwanza)	40	15
1767	40k. Rio Kuanza	55	20
1768	40k. Foz do Rio Mbridge (Mbridge rivermouth)	55	20
MS1769	160×90 mm. 153k. Recursos Hidricos (waterfall (water resources))	1·90	1·10

319 Landmine Clearance

2008. Tenth Anniv of Lwini Social Solidarity Fund (to help landmine victims). Multicoloured.

MS1770	37k. Type **319**; 40k. Information literature (horiz); 40k. Princess Diana and Ana Paula dos Santos (foundation president) (horiz); 59k. Children in wheelchairs (horiz); 59k. Landmine victims making baskets (horiz)	2·75	2·75

320 Water Jug

2008. Water Jugs. Multicoloured.

1771	37k. Type **320**	40	15
1772	37k. Incised jug with several handles	40	15
1773	40k. Green jug with spout, handle and lid	55	20
1774	40k. White jug with figure as lid	55	20

321 Mangroves

2008. Mangroves on Rio Chiloango. Multicoloured.

1775	37k. Mangroves	60	25
1776	37k. River bordered by mangroves	60	25
1777	59k. Type **321**	85	35

322 Coffee Berries

2009. Angolan Coffee, Amboim. Multicoloured.

1778	37k. Type **322**	40	15
1779	45k. Branches of coffee plant	55	30
1780	45k. Woman picking coffee (horiz)	55	30

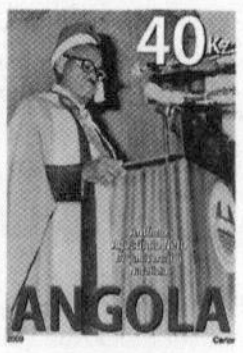

323 Antonio Agostinho Neto

2009. Antonio Agostinho Neto (first president of Angola) Commemoration.

1781	40k. black and scarlet-vermilion	45	30
1782	50k. multicoloured	45	35
MS1783	160×90 mm. 150k. multicoloured	1·20	1·20

DESIGNS: 40k. Type **323**; 50k. Wearing uniform; 150k. With school children.

324 Pope Benedict XVI

2009. Visit of Pope Benedict XVI to Angola

MS1784	**324** 150×60mm. 100k. multicoloured	2·75	2·75

325 Cabinda Stadium

2010. COCAN 2010, African Cup of Nations Football Competition. Multicoloured.

1785	40k. Type **325**	40	15
1786	40k. Benguela	40	15
1787	50k. Huila	45	20
1788	50k. Luanda	45	20

APPENDIX

1995

90th Anniv of Rotary International (on gold foil). 81000k.

CHARITY TAX STAMPS

Used on certain days of the year as an additional tax on internal letters. If one was not used in addition to normal postage, postage due stamps were used to collect the deficiency and the fine.

1925. Marquis de Pombal Commemorative stamps of Portugal but inscr "ANGOLA".

C343	**C73**	15c. violet	1·10	90
C344	-	15c. violet	1·10	90
C345	**C75**	15c. violet	1·10	90

C15

1929

C347	**C15**	50c. blue	7·00	2·00

C29

1939. No gum.

C413	**C29**	50c. green	4·00	35
C414	**C29**	1a. red	9·25	2·50

C52 Old Man

1955. Heads in brown.

C646	**C52**	50c. orange	35	25
C647	-	1e. red (Boy)	35	25
C648	-	1e.50 green (Girl)	55	35
C522	-	2e.50 blue (Old woman)	1·00	55

1957. Surch.

C535	**C52**	10c. on 50c. orange	35	35
C534	**C52**	30c. on 50c. orange	35	35

C58 Mother and Child

1959

C538	**C58**	10c. black and orange	35	35
C539	-	30c. black and slate	35	35

DESIGN: 30c. Boy and girl.

C65 Yellow, White and Black Men

1962. Provincial Settlement Committee.

C568	**C65**	50c. multicoloured	35	35
C569	**C65**	1e. multicoloured	55	25

C75 "Full Employment"

1965. Provincial Settlement Committee.

C644	**C75**	1e. multicoloured	55	35
C645	**C75**	2e. multicoloured	55	35
C643	**C75**	50e. multicoloured	55	35

C95 Planting Tree

1972. Provincial Settlement Committee.

C701	**C95**	50c. red and brown	35	35
C702	-	1e. black and green	35	35
C703	-	2e. black and brown	35	35

DESIGNS: 1e. Agricultural workers; 2e. Corncobs and flowers.

NEWSPAPER STAMP

1893. "Newspaper" key-type inscr "ANGOLA".

N51	**V**	2½r. brown	3·50	2·10

POSTAGE DUE STAMPS

1904. "Due" key-type inscr "ANGOLA".

D150	**W**	5r. green	45	45
D151	**W**	10r. grey	45	45
D152	**W**	20r. brown	1·00	70
D153	**W**	30r. orange	1·00	70
D154	**W**	50r. brown	1·30	1·00
D155	**W**	60r. brown	11·00	7·50
D156	**W**	100r. mauve	4·50	3·50
D157	**W**	130r. blue	4·50	3·50
D158	**W**	200r. red	14·00	9·25
D159	**W**	500r. lilac	11·50	7·50

See also Nos. D343/52.

1911. Nos. D150/9 optd **REPUBLICA**.

D166	5r. green	35	30
D167	10r. grey	35	30
D168	20r. brown	35	30
D169	30r. orange	55	45
D170	50r. brown	55	45
D171	60r. brown	1·50	1·10
D172	100r. mauve	1·50	1·10
D173	130r. blue	1·70	1·30
D174	200r. red	2·20	1·30
D175	500r. lilac	2·30	2·20

1921. Values in new currency.

D343	½c. green	40	35
D344	1c. grey	40	35
D345	2c. brown	40	35
D346	3c. orange	40	35
D347	5c. brown	40	35
D348	6c. brown	40	35
D349	10c. mauve	55	45
D350	13c. blue	1·00	90
D351	20c. red	1·00	90
D352	50c. grey	1·00	90

1925. Marquis de Pombal stamps of Angola, as Nos. C343/5, optd **MULTA**.

D353	**C73**	30c. violet	1·10	90
D354	-	30c. violet	1·10	90
D355	**C 75**	30c. violet	1·10	90

1949. Surch **PORTEADO** and value.

D438	**17**	10c. on 20c. grey	45	40
D439	**17**	20c. on 30c. green	55	50
D440	**17**	30c. on 50c. brown	1·00	90
D441	**17**	40c. on 1a. red	1·30	1·10
D442	**17**	50c. on 2a. mauve	2·00	1·80
D443	**17**	1a. on 5a. green	3·00	2·75

D45

1952. Numerals in red, name in black.

D483	**D45**	10c. brown and olive	35	30
D484	**D45**	30c. green and blue	35	30
D485	**D45**	50c. brown & lt brn	35	30
D486	**D45**	1a. blue, green & orge	65	55
D487	**D45**	2a. brown and red	80	75
D488	**D45**	5a. brown and blue	80	75

Pt. 9

ANGRA

A district of the Azores, which used the stamps of the Azores except from 1892 to 1905.

1000 reis = 1 milreis.

1892. As T **4** of Funchal, inscr "ANGRA".

16	5r. yellow	4·25	2·50
5	10r. mauve	4·75	2·50
6	15r. brown	5·50	3·75
7	20r. violet	5·50	3·75
8	25r. green	7·50	1·70
9	50r. blue	11·00	5·75
10	75r. red	13·00	7·50
11	80r. green	15·00	14·00
24	100r. brown on yellow	55·00	20·00
13	150r. red on rose	75·00	60·00
14	200r. blue on blue	75·00	60·00
15	300r. blue on brown	75·00	60·00

1897. "King Carlos" key-type inscr "ANGRA".

28	**S**	2½r. grey	1·00	65
29	**S**	5r. red	1·00	65
30	**S**	10r. green	1·00	65
31	**S**	15r. brown	13·00	8·50
43	**S**	15r. green	1·30	80
32	**S**	20r. lilac	2·50	1·90
33	**S**	25r. green	4·25	1·70
44	**S**	25r. red	90	80
34	**S**	50r. blue	7·75	2·40
46	**S**	65r. blue	1·80	80
35	**S**	75r. red	4·75	2·30
47	**S**	75r. brown on yellow	19·00	15·00
36	**S**	80r. mauve	2·10	1·70
37	**S**	100r. blue on blue	3·75	2·40
48	**S**	115r. red on pink	3·75	2·75
49	**S**	130r. brown on cream	3·75	2·75
38	**S**	150r. brown on yellow	3·75	2·40
50	**S**	180r. grey on pink	4·75	4·25
39	**S**	200r. purple on pink	7·75	6·75
40	**S**	300r. blue on pink	11·50	8·75
41	**S**	500r. black on blue	24·00	19·00

Pt. 1

ANGUILLA

St. Christopher, Nevis and Anguilla were granted Associated Statehood on 27 February 1967, but following a referendum Anguilla declared her independence and the St. Christopher authorities withdrew. On 7 July 1969, the Anguilla post office was officially recognised by the Government of St. Christopher, Nevis and Anguilla and normal postal communications via St. Christopher were resumed.

By the Anguilla Act of 27 July 1971, the island was restored to direct British control.

100 cents = 1 West Indian dollar.

1967. Nos. 129/44 of St. Kitts-Nevis optd **Independent Anguilla** and bar.

1	-	½c. sepia and blue	60·00	26·00
2	**33**	1c. multicoloured	75·00	11·00
3	-	2c. multicoloured	70·00	2·25
4	-	3c. multicoloured	70·00	6·00
5	-	4c. multicoloured	75·00	6·50
6	-	5c. multicoloured	£275	32·00
7	-	6c. multicoloured	£120	17·00
8	-	10c. multicoloured	70·00	9·50
9	-	15c. multicoloured	£140	15·00
10	-	20c. multicoloured	£300	22·00
11	-	25c. multicoloured	£225	38·00
12	-	50c. multicoloured	£4250	£750
13	-	60c. multicoloured	£5000	£1500
14	-	$1 yellow and blue	£3750	£650
15	-	$2.50 multicoloured	£2750	£425
16	-	$5 multicoloured	£3000	£450

Owing to the limited stocks available for overprinting, the sale of the stamps was personally controlled by the Postmaster and no orders from the trade were accepted.

2 Mahogany Tree, The Quarter

1967

17	**2**	1c. green, brown and orange	10	1·00
18	-	2c. turquoise and black	10	3·00
19	-	3c. black and green	10	10
20	-	4c. blue and black	10	10
21	-	5c. multicoloured	10	10
22	-	6c. red and black	10	10
23	-	10c. multicoloured	15	10
24	-	15c. multicoloured	2·50	20
25	-	20c. multicoloured	1·25	2·75
26	-	25c. multicoloured	60	20
27	-	40c. green, blue and black	1·00	25
28	-	60c. multicoloured	4·50	4·75
29	-	$1 multicoloured	1·75	3·25
30	-	$2.50 multicoloured	2·00	7·50
31	-	$5 multicoloured	3·00	4·25

DESIGNS: 2c. Sombrero Lighthouse; 3c. St. Mary's Church; 4c. Valley Police Station; 5c. Old Plantation House, Mt. Fortune; 6c. Valley Post Office; 10c. Methodist Church, West End; 15c. Wall Blake Airport; 20c. Beech A90 King Air aircraft over Sandy Ground; 25c. Island harbour; 40c. Map of Anguilla; 60c. Hermit crab and starfish; $1, Hibiscus; $2.50, Local scene; $5, Spiny lobster.

17 Yachts in Lagoon

1968. Anguillan Ships. Multicoloured.

32	10c. Type **17**	35	10
33	15c. Boat on beach	40	10
34	25c. Schooner *Warspite*	55	15
35	40c. Schooner *Atlantic Star*	65	20

18 Purple-throated Carib

1968. Anguillan Birds. Multicoloured.

36	10c. Type **18**	65	15
37	15c. Bananaquit	80	20
38	25c. Black-necked stilt (horiz)	85	20
39	40c. Royal tern (horiz)	90	30

19 Guides' Badge and Anniversary Years

1968. 35th Anniv of Anguillan Girl Guides. Multicoloured.

40	10c. Type **19**	10	10
41	15c. Badge and silhouettes of guides (vert)	15	10
42	25c. Guides' badge and Headquarters	20	15
43	40c. Association and proficiency badges (vert)	25	15

20 The Three Kings

1968. Christmas.

44	**20**	1c. black and red	10	10
45	-	10c. black and blue	10	10
46	-	15c. black and brown	15	10
47	-	40c. black and blue	15	10
48	-	50c. black and green	20	15

DESIGNS—VERT: 10c. The Wise Men; 15c. Holy Family and manger. HORIZ: 40c. The Shepherds; 50c. Holy Family and donkey.

21 Bagging Salt

1969. Anguillan Salt Industry. Multicoloured.

49	10c. Type **21**	25	10
50	15c. Packing salt	30	10
51	40c. Salt pond	35	10
52	50c. Loading salt	35	10

1969. Expiration of Interim Agreement on Status of Anguilla. Nos. 17/22, 23, 24 and 26/7 optd **INDEPENDENCE JANUARY 1969.**

52a	1c. green, brown and orange	10	40
52b	2c. green and black	10	40
52c	3c. black and green	10	40
52d	4c. blue and black	10	40
52e	5c. multicoloured	10	20
52f	6c. red and black	10	20
52g	10c. multicoloured	10	30
52h	15c. multicoloured	90	30
52i	25c. multicoloured	80	30
52j	40c. green, blue and black	1·00	40

The remaining values of the 1967 series, nos. 17/31, also come with this overprint but these are outside the scope of this catalogue.

22 *The Crucifixion* (Studio of Massys)

1969. Easter Commemoration. Multicoloured.

53	25c. Type **22**	25	15
54	40c. *The Last Supper* (ascribed to Roberti)	35	15

23 Amaryllis

1969. Flowers of the Caribbean. Multicoloured.

55	10c. Type **23**	15	20
56	15c. Bougainvillea	15	25
57	40c. Hibiscus	20	50
58	50c. *Cattleya* orchid	1·00	1·60

24 Superb Gaza, Channelled Turban, Chestnut Turban and Carved Star Shell

1969. Sea Shells. Multicoloured.

59	10c. Type **24**	20	20
60	15c. American thorny oysters	20	20
61	40c. Scotch, royal and smooth scotch bonnets	30	30
62	50c. Atlantic trumpet triton	40	30

1969. Christmas. Nos. 17 and 25/8 optd with different seasonal emblems.

63	1c. green, brown and orange	10	10
64	20c. multicoloured	20	10
65	25c. multicoloured	20	10
66	40c. green, blue and black	25	15
67	60c. multicoloured	40	20

30 Spotted Goatfish

1969. Fish. Multicoloured.

68	10c. Type **30**	45	15
69	15c. Blue-striped grunt	60	15
70	40c. Nassau grouper	75	20
71	50c. Banded butterflyfish	80	20

31 "Morning Glory"

1970. Flowers. Multicoloured.

72	10c. Type **31**	25	10
73	15c. Blue petrea	35	10
74	40c. Hibiscus	50	20
75	50c. "Flame Tree"	60	25

32 *The Crucifixion* (Masaccio)

1970. Easter. Multicoloured.

76	10c. *The Ascent to Calvary* (Tiepolo) (horiz)	15	10
77	20c. Type **32**	20	10
78	40c. *Deposition* (Rosso Fiorentino)	25	15
79	60c. *The Ascent to Calvary* (Murillo) (horiz)	25	15

33 Scout Badge and Map

1970. 40th Anniv of Scouting in Anguilla. Multicoloured.

80	10c. Type **33**	15	20
81	15c. Scout camp, and cubs practising first aid	20	20
82	40c. Monkey bridge	25	30
83	50c. Scout H.Q. building and Lord Baden-Powell	35	40

34 Boatbuilding

1970. Multicoloured.

84	1c. Type **34**	30	40
85	2c. Road construction	30	40
86	3c. Quay, Blowing Point	30	20
87	4c. Broadcaster, Radio Anguilla	30	50
88	5c. Cottage Hospital extension	40	50
89	6c. Valley Secondary School	30	50
90	10c. Hotel extension	30	30
91	15c. Sandy Ground	30	30
92	20c. Supermarket and cinema	70	30
93	25c. Bananas and mangoes	35	1·00
94	40c. Wall Blake Airport	4·00	3·25
95	60c. Sandy Ground jetty	65	3·50
96	$1 Administration buildings	1·25	1·40
97	$2.50 Livestock	1·50	4·00
98	$5 Sandy Hill Bay	3·25	3·75

35 *The Adoration of the Shepherds* (Reni)

1970. Christmas. Multicoloured.

99	1c. Type **35**	10	15
100	20c. *The Virgin and Child* (Gozzoli)	30	20
101	25c. *Mystic Nativity* (detail, Botticelli)	30	25
102	40c. *The Santa Margherita Madonna* (detail, Mazzola)	40	25
103	50c. *The Adoration of the Magi* (detail, Tiepolo)	40	25

36 *Ecce Homo* (detail, Correggio)

1971. Easter. Paintings. Multicoloured.

104	10c. Type **36**	25	10
105	15c. *Christ appearing to St Peter* (detail, Carracci)	25	10
106	40c. *Angels weeping over the Dead Christ* (detail, Guercino) (horiz)	30	10
107	50c. *The Supper at Emmaus* (detail, Caravaggio) (horiz)	30	15

37 *Hypolimnas misippus*

1971. Butterflies. Multicoloured.

108	10c. Type **37**	1·60	70
109	15c. *Junonia evarete*	1·60	80
110	40c. *Agraulis vanillae*	2·00	1·25
111	50c. *Danaus plexippus*	2·00	1·50

38 *Magnanime* and *Aimable* in Battle

1971. Sea-battles of the West Indies. Multicoloured.

112	10c. Type **38**	1·10	1·40
113	15c. H.M.S. *Duke*, *Glorieux* and H.M.S. *Agamemnon*	1·25	1·60
114	25c. H.M.S. *Formidabl* and H.M.S. *Namur* against *Ville de Paris*	1·50	1·75
115	40c. H.M.S. *Canada*	1·60	1·90
116	50c. H.M.S. *St. Albans* and wreck of *Hector*	1·75	2·00

Nos. 112/116 were issued together, se-tenant, forming a composite design.

39 *The Ansidei Madonna* (detail, Raphael)

1971. Christmas. Multicoloured.

117	20c. Type **39**	30	30
118	25c. *Mystic Nativity* (detail, Botticelli)	30	30
119	40c. *Adoration of the Shepherds* (detail, ascr to Murillo)	35	40
120	50c. *The Madonna of the Iris* (detail, ascr to Durer)	40	70

40 Map of Anguilla and St. Martin by Thomas Jefferys, 1775

1972. Caribbean Maps depicting Anguilla. Multicoloured.

121	10c. Type **40**	25	10
122	15c. Samuel Fahlberg's Map, 1814	35	15
123	40c. Thomas Jefferys' Map, 1775 (horiz)	50	25
124	50c. Captain E. Barnett's Map, 1847 (horiz)	60	25

41 "Jesus Buffeted"

1972. Easter. Multicoloured.

125	10c. Type **41**	25	25
126	15c. *The Way of Sorrows*	30	30
127	25c. *The Crucifixion*	30	30
128	40c. *Descent from the Cross*	35	35
129	50c. *The Burial*	40	40

42 Loblolly Tree

1972. Multicoloured.

130	1c. Spear fishing	10	40
131	2c. Type **42**	10	40
132	3c. Sandy Ground	10	40
133	4c. Ferry at Blowing Point	1·75	20
134	5c. Agriculture	15	1·00
135	6c. St. Mary's Church	25	20
136	10c. St. Gerard's Church	25	40
137	15c. Cottage hospital extension	25	30
138	20c. Public library	30	35
139	25c. Sunset at Blowing Point	40	2·00
140	40c. Boat building	5·00	1·50
141	60c. Hibiscus	4·00	4·00
142	$1 Magnificent frigate bird ("Man-o'-War")	10·00	8·00
143	$2.50 Frangipani	5·00	10·00
144	$5 Brown pelican	17·00	17·00
144a	$10 Green-back turtle	16·00	18·00

1972. Royal Silver Wedding. As T **52** of Ascension, but with Schooner and Common dolphin in background.

145	25c. green	50	75
146	40c. brown	50	75

44 Flight into Egypt

1972. Christmas. Multicoloured.

147	1c. Type **44**	10	10
148	20c. Star of Bethlehem	20	20
149	25c. Holy Family	20	20
150	40c. Arrival of the Magi	20	25
151	50c. Adoration of the Magi	25	25

45 *The Betrayal of Christ*

1973. Easter. Multicoloured.

152	1c. Type **45**	10	10
153	10c. *The Man of Sorrows*	10	10
154	20c. *Christ bearing the Cross*	10	15
155	25c. *The Crucifixion*	15	15
156	40c. *The Descent from the Cross*	15	15
157	50c. *The Resurrection*	15	20
MS158	140×141 mm. Nos. 152/7. Bottom panel in gold and mauve	70	80

46 *Santa Maria*

1973. Columbus Discovers the West Indies. Multicoloured.

159	1c. Type **46**	10	10
160	20c. Early map	1·50	1·25
161	40c. Map of voyages	1·60	1·40
162	70c. Sighting land	1·90	1·75
163	$1.20 Landing of Columbus	2·50	2·25
MS164	193×93 mm. Nos. 159/63	6·75	7·00

47 Princess Anne and Captain Mark Phillips

1973. Royal Wedding. Multicoloured. Background colours given.

165	47	60c. green	20	15
166	47	$1.20 mauve	30	15

48 *The Adoration of the Shepherds* (Reni)

1973. Christmas. Multicoloured.

167	1c. Type **48**	10	10
168	10c. *The Madonna and Child with Saints Jerome and Dominic* (Filippino Lippi)	10	10
169	20c. *The Nativity* (Master of Brunswick)	15	15
170	25c. *Madonna of the Meadow* (Bellini)	15	15
171	40c. *Virgin and Child* (Cima)	20	20
172	50c. *Adoration of the Kings* (Geertgen)	20	20
MS173	148×149 mm. Nos. 167/72	80	1·60

49 *The Crucifixion* (Raphael)

1974. Easter.

174	49	1c. multicoloured	10	10
175	-	15c. multicoloured	10	10
176	-	20c. multicoloured	15	15
177	-	25c. multicoloured	15	15
178	-	40c. multicoloured	15	15
179	-	$1 multicoloured	20	25
MS180		123×141 mm. Nos. 174/9	1·00	1·25

DESIGNS: 15c. to $1, Details of Raphael's *Crucifixion*.

50 Churchill Making "Victory" Sign

1974. Birth Centenary of Sir Winston Churchill. Multicoloured.

181	1c. Type **50**	10	10
182	20c. Churchill with Roosevelt	20	20
183	25c. Wartime broadcast	20	20
184	40c. Birthplace, Blenheim Palace	30	30
185	60c. Churchill's statue	30	35
186	$1.20 Country residence, Chartwell	45	55
MS187	195×96 mm. Nos. 181/6	1·40	2·50

51 U.P.U. Emblem

1974. Centenary of U.P.U.

188	51	1c. black and blue	10	10
189	51	20c. black and orange	15	15
190	51	25c. black and yellow	15	15
191	51	40c. black and mauve	20	25
192	51	60c. black and green	30	40
193	51	$1.20 black and blue	50	60
MS194		195×96 mm. Nos. 188/93	1·25	2·25

52 Anguillan pointing to Star

1974. Christmas. Multicoloured.

195	1c. Type **52**	10	10
196	20c. Child in Manger	10	20
197	25c. King's offering	10	20
198	40c. Star over map of Anguilla	15	20
199	60c. Family looking at star	15	20
200	$1.20 Angels of Peace	20	30
MS201	177×85 mm. Nos. 195/200	1·10	1·75

53 *Mary, John and Mary Magdalene* (Matthias Grunewald)

1975. Easter. Details from Isenheim Altarpiece, Colmar Museum. Multicoloured.

202	1c. Type **53**	10	10
203	10c. *The Crucifixion*	15	15
204	15c. *St. John the Baptist*	10	20
205	20c. *St. Sebastian and Angels*	15	20
206	$1 *The Entombment* (horiz)	15	20
207	$1.50 *St. Anthony the Hermit*	20	30
MS208	134×127 mm. Nos. 202/7 (imperf)	1·10	1·75

54 Statue of Liberty

1975. Bicentenary of American Revolution. Multicoloured.

209	1c. Type **54**	10	10
210	10c. The Capitol	15	15
211	15c. "Congress voting for Independence" (Pine and Savage)	30	15
212	20c. Washington and map	30	15
213	$1 Boston Tea Party	45	40
214	$1.50 Bicentenary logo	50	60
MS215	198×97 mm. Nos. 209/14	1·25	2·50

55 *Madonna, Child and the Infant John the Baptist* (Raphael)

1975. Christmas. "Madonna and Child" paintings by artists named. Multicoloured.

216	1c. Type **55**	10	10
217	10c. Cima	15	15
218	15c. Dolci	20	15
219	20c. Durer	20	20
220	$1 Bellini	35	25
221	$1.50 Botticelli	45	35
MS222	130×145 mm. Nos. 216/21	2·00	2·25

1976. New Constitution. Nos. 130 etc optd **NEW CONSTITUTION 1976** or surch also.

223	1c. Spear fishing	30	50
224	2c. on 1c. Spear fishing	30	50
225	2c. Type **42**	7·50	1·75
226	3c. on 40c. Boat building	75	70
227	4c. Ferry at Blowing Point	1·00	1·00
228	5c. on 40c. Boat building	30	60
229	6c. St. Mary's Church	30	60
230	10c. on 20c. Public library	30	50
231	10c. St. Gerard's Church	9·50	4·75
232	15c. Cottage Hospital extension	30	1·25
233	20c. Public library	30	50
234	25c. Sunset at Blowing Point	30	50
235	40c. Boat building	1·00	70
236	60c. Hibiscus	70	70
237	$1 Magnificent frigate bird	6·50	2·25
238	$2.50 Frangipani	2·25	2·25
239	$5 Brown pelican	8·00	10·00
240	$10 Green-back turtle	3·00	6·00

57 Almond

1976. Flowering Trees. Multicoloured.

241	1c. Type **57**	10	10
242	10c. Autograph	20	20
243	15c. Calabash	20	20
244	20c. Cordia	20	20
245	$1 Papaya	30	45
246	$1.50 Flamboyant	35	55
MS247	194×99 mm. Nos. 241/6	1·50	2·00

58 The Three Marys

1976. Easter. Showing portions of the Altar Frontal Tapestry, Rheinau. Multicoloured.

248	1c. Type **58**	10	10
249	10c. The Crucifixion	10	10
250	15c. Two Soldiers	15	15
251	20c. The Annunciation	15	15
252	$1 The complete tapestry (horiz)	65	65
253	$1.50 The Risen Christ	80	80
MS254	138×130 mm. Nos. 248/53 (imperf)	1·75	2·10

59 French Ships approaching Anguilla

1976. Bicentenary of Battle of Anguilla. Multicoloured.

255	1c. Type **59**	10	10
256	3c. *Margaret* (sloop) leaving Anguilla	1·25	35
257	15c. Capture of *Le Desius*	1·50	55
258	25c. *La Vaillante* forced aground	1·50	80
259	$1 H.M.S. *Lapwing*	2·00	1·25
260	$1.50 *Le Desius* burning	2·25	1·75
MS261	205×103 mm. Nos. 255/60	7·50	6·00

60 *Christmas Carnival* (A. Richardson)

1976. Christmas. Children's Paintings. Multicoloured.

262	1c. Type **60**	10	10
263	3c. *Dreams of Christmas Gifts* (J. Connor)	10	10
264	15c. *Carolling* (P. Richardson)	15	15
265	25c. *Candle-light Procession* (A. Mussington)	20	20
266	$1 *Going to Church* (B. Franklin)	30	30
267	$1.50 *Coming Home for Christmas* (E. Gumbs)	40	40
MS268	232×147 mm. Nos. 262/7	1·50	1·75

61 Prince Charles and H.M.S. *Minerva* (frigate)

1977. Silver Jubilee. Multicoloured.

269	25c. Type **61**	15	10
270	40c. Prince Philip landing by launch at Road Bay, 1964	15	10
271	$1.20 Coronation scene	20	20
272	$2.50 Coronation regalia and map of Anguilla	25	30
MS273	145×96 mm. Nos. 269/72	65	90

62 Yellow-crowned Night Heron

1977. Multicoloured.

274	1c. Type **62**	30	1·25
275	2c. Great barracuda	30	2·75
276	3c. Queen or pink conch	2·00	3·75
277	4c. Spanish bayonet (flower)	40	70
278	5c. Honeycomb trunkfish	1·50	30
279	6c. Cable and Wireless building	30	30
280	10c. American kestrel ("American Sparrow Hawk")	5·50	4·00
281	15c. Ground orchid	3·50	1·75
282	20c. Stop-light parrotfish	3·50	75
283	22c. Lobster fishing boat	50	60
284	35c. Boat race	1·40	70
285	50c. Sea bean	90	50
286	$1 Sandy Island	60	50
287	$2.50 Manchineel	1·00	1·00
288	$5 Ground lizard	2·00	2·00
289	$10 Red-billed tropic bird	9·00	4·50

No. 290 is vacant.

63 *The Crucifixion* (Massys)

1977. Easter. Paintings by Castagno ($1.50) or Ugolino (others). Multicoloured.

291	1c. Type **63**	10	10
292	3c. *The Betrayal*	10	10
293	22c. *The Way to Calvary*	20	20
294	30c. *The Deposition*	25	25
295	$1 *The Resurrection*	40	40
296	$1.50 *The Crucifixion*	45	45
MS297	192×126 mm. Nos. 291/6	1·60	1·75

1977. Royal Visit. Nos. 269/72 optd **ROYAL VISIT TO WEST INDIES.**

298	25c. Type **61**	10	10
299	40c. Prince Philip landing at Road Bay, 1964	10	15
300	$1.20 Coronation scene	20	25
301	$1.50 Coronation regalia and map of Anguilla	25	35
MS302	145×96 mm. Nos. 298/301	80	60

65 *Le Chapeau de Paille*

1977. 400th Birth Anniv of Rubens. Multicoloured.

303	25c. Type **65**	15	15
304	40c. *Helene Fourment and her Two Children*	20	25
305	$1.20 *Rubens and his Wife*	60	65
306	$2.50 *Marchesa Brigida Spinola-Doria*	75	95
MS307	90×145 mm. Nos. 303/6	2·00	2·10

1977. Christmas. Nos. 262/7 with old date blocked out and additionally inscr "1977", some also surch.

308	1c. Type **60**	10	10
309	5c. on 3c. *Dreams of Christmas Gifts*	10	10
310	12c. on 15c. *Carolling*	15	15
311	18c. on 25c. *Candle-light Procession*	20	20
312	$1 *Going to Church*	45	45
313	$2.50 on $1.50 *Coming Home for Christmas*	90	90
MS314	232×147 mm. Nos. 308/13	2·50	2·50

1978. Easter. Nos. 303/6 optd **EASTER 1978.**

315	25c. Type **65**	15	20
316	40c. *Helene Fourment with her Two Children*	15	20
317	$1.20 *Rubens and his Wife*	35	40
318	$2.50 *Marchesa Brigida Spinola-Doria*	45	60
MS319	93×145 mm. Nos. 315/18	1·25	1·50

68 Coronation Coach at Admiralty Arch

1978. 25th Anniv of Coronation. Multicoloured.

320	22c. Buckingham Palace	10	10
321	50c. Type **68**	10	10
322	$1.50 Balcony scene	15	15
323	$2.50 Royal coat of arms	25	25
MS324	138×92 mm. Nos. 320/3	60	60

1978. Anniversaries. Nos. 283/4 and 287 optd **VALLEY SECONDARY SCHOOL 1953–1978** and Nos. 285/6 and 288 optd **ROAD METHODIST CHURCH 1878–1978,** or surch also.

325	22c. Lobster fishing boat	25	15
326	35c. Boat race	35	20
327	50c. Sea bean	35	30
328	$1 Sandy Island	40	40
329	$1.20 on $5 Ground lizard	45	45
330	$1.50 on $2.50 Manchineel	50	55

71 Mother and Child

1978. Christmas. Children's Paintings. Multicoloured.

331	5c. Type **71**	10	10
332	12c. Christmas masquerade	15	10
333	18c. Christmas dinner	15	10
334	22c. Serenading	15	10
335	$1 Child in manger	35	20
336	$2.50 Family going to church	55	40
MS337	191×101 mm. Nos. 331/6	1·25	1·75

1979. International Year of the Child. As Nos. 331/6, but additionally inscr "1979 INTERNATIONAL YEAR OF THE CHILD" and emblem. Borders in different colours.

338	5c. Type **71**	10	10
339	12c. Christmas masquerade	10	10
340	18c. Christmas dinner	10	10
341	22c. Serenading	10	10
342	$1 Child in manger	30	30
343	$2.50 Family going to church	50	50
MS344	205×112 mm. Nos. 338/43	1·75	2·50

1979. Nos. 274/7 and 279/80 surch.

345	12c. on 2c. Great barracuda	50	50
346	14c. on 4c. Spanish bayonet	40	50
347	18c. on 3c. Queen conch	1·00	55
348	25c. on 6c. Cable and Wireless building	55	50
349	38c. on 10c. American kestrel	2·50	70
350	40c. on 1c. Type **62**	2·75	70

73 Valley Methodist Church

1979. Easter. Church Interiors. Multicoloured.

351	5c. Type **73**	10	10
352	12c. St. Mary's Anglican Church, The Valley	10	10
353	18c. St. Gerard's Roman Catholic Church, The Valley	15	15
354	22c. Road Methodist Church	15	15
355	$1.50 St. Augustine's Anglican Church, East End	40	40
356	$2.50 West End Methodist Church	50	50
MS357	190×105 mm. Nos. 351/6	1·50	2·25

74 Cape of Good Hope 1d. "Woodblock" of 1881

1979. Death Centenary of Sir Rowland Hill. Multicoloured.

358	1c. Type **74**	10	10
359	1c. U.S.A. "inverted Jenny" of 1918	10	10
360	22c. Penny Black ("V.R." Official)	15	15
361	35c. Germany 2m, *Graf Zeppelin* of 1928	20	20
362	$1.50 U.S.A. $5 *Columbus* of 1893	40	60
363	$2.50 Great Britain £5 orange of 1882	60	95
MS364	187×123 mm. Nos. 358/63	1·25	2·40

75 Wright *Flyer I* (1st powered Flight, 1903)

1979. History of Powered Flight. Multicoloured.

365	5c. Type **75**	20	10
366	12c. Louis Bleriot at Dover after Channel crossing, 1909	25	10
367	18c. Vickers FB-27 Vimy (1st non-stop crossing of Atlantic, 1919)	30	15
368	22c. Ryan NYP Special *Spirit of St Louis* (1st solo Atlantic flight by Charles Lindbergh, 1927)	30	20
369	$1.50 Airship LZ 127 *Graf Zeppelin*, 1928	65	60
370	$2.50 Concorde, 1979	3·50	90
MS371	200×113 mm. Nos. 365/70	4·25	3·25

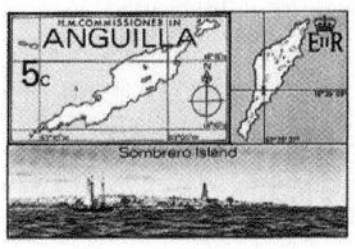

76 Sombrero Island

1979. Outer Islands. Multicoloured.

372	5c. Type **76**	15	10
373	12c. Anguillita Island	15	10
374	18c. Sandy Island	15	15
375	25c. Prickly Pear Cays	15	15
376	$1 Dog Island	40	40
377	$2.50 Scrub Island	60	70
MS378	180×91 mm. Nos. 372/7	2·75	2·25

77 Red Poinsettia

1979. Christmas. Multicoloured.

379	22c. Type **77**	15	20
380	35c. Kalanchoe	20	30
381	$1.50 Cream poinsettia	40	50
382	$2.50 White poinsettia	60	70
MS383	146×164 mm. Nos. 379/82	1·75	2·25

78 Exhibition Scene

1979. "London 1980" International Stamp Exhibition (1st issue). Multicoloured.

384	35c. Type **78**	15	20
385	50c. Earls Court Exhibition Centre	15	25
386	$1.50 Penny Black and Two-penny Blue stamps	25	60
387	$2.50 Exhibition Logo	45	95
MS388	150×94 mm. Nos. 384/7	1·40	2·00

See also Nos. 407/9.

79 Games Site

1980. Winter Olympic Games, Lake Placid, U.S.A. Multicoloured.

389	5c. Type **79**	10	10
390	18c. Ice hockey	20	10
391	35c. Ice skating	20	20
392	50c. Bobsleighing	20	20
393	$1 Skiing	20	35
394	$2.50 Luge-tobogganing	40	80
MS395	136×128 mm. Nos. 389/94	1·00	2·00

80 Salt ready for "Reaping"

1980. Salt Industry. Multicoloured.

396	5c. Type **80**	10	10
397	12c. Tallying salt	10	10
398	18c. Unloading salt flats	15	15
399	22c. Salt storage heap	15	15
400	$1 Salt for bagging and grinding	30	40
401	$2.50 Loading salt for export	50	70
MS402	180×92 mm. Nos. 396/401	1·10	1·75

1980. Anniversaries. Nos. 280, 282 and 287/8 optd **50th Anniversary Scouting 1980** (10c., $2.50) or **75th Anniversary Rotary 1980** (others).

403	10c. American kestrel	1·75	20
404	20c. Stop-light parrotfish	1·00	20
405	$2.50 Manchineel	1·75	1·50
406	$5 Ground lizard	2·50	2·50

83 Palace of Westminster and Great Britain 1970 9d. "Philympia" Commemoration

1980. "London 1980" International Stamp Exhibition (2nd issue). Multicoloured.

407	50c. Type **83**	55	75
408	$1.50 City Hall, Toronto and "Capex 1978" stamp of Canada	85	1·25
409	$2.50 Statue of Liberty and 1976 "Interphil" stamp of U.S.A.	1·10	1·60
MS410	157×130 mm. Nos. 407/9	2·25	3·00

84 Queen Elizabeth the Queen Mother

1980. 80th Birthday of The Queen Mother.

411	**84**	35c. multicoloured	70	40
412	**84**	50c. multicoloured	85	50
413	**84**	$1.50 multicoloured	1·25	1·50
414	**84**	$3 multicoloured	2·00	2·50
MS415		160×110 mm. Nos. 411/14	4·75	4·75

85 Brown Pelicans ("Pelican")

1980. Christmas. Birds. Multicoloured.

416	5c. Type **85**	45	10
417	22c. Great blue heron ("Great Grey Heron")	1·00	20
418	$1.50 Barn swallow ("Swallow")	2·00	60
419	$3 Ruby-throated hummingbird ("Hummingbird")	2·25	1·40
MS420	126×160 mm. Nos. 416/19	10·00	7·50

1980. Separation from St. Kitts. Nos. 274, 277, 280/9, 334 and 418/19 optd **SEPARATION 1980** or surch also.

421	1c. Type **62**	20	80
422	2c. on 4c. Spanish bayonet	20	80
423	5c. on 15c. Ground orchid	1·75	80
424	5c. on $1.50 Barn swallow	1·75	80
425	5c. on $3 Ruby-throated hummingbird	1·75	80
426	10c. American kestrel	2·25	80
427	12c. on $1 Sandy Island	30	80
428	14c. on $2.50 Manchineel	30	80
429	15c. Ground orchid	2·00	80
430	18c. on $5 Ground lizard	35	80
431	20c. Stop-light parrotfish	35	80
432	22c. Lobster fishing boat	35	80
433	25c. on 15c. Ground orchid	2·00	85
434	35c. Boat race	35	85
435	38c. on 22c. Serenading	35	85
436	40c. on 1c. Type **62**	1·00	85
437	50c. Sea bean	40	95
438	$1 Sandy Island	50	1·25
439	$2.50 Manchineel	1·25	3·00
440	$5 Ground lizard	2·25	4·00
441	$10 Red-billed tropic bird	5·00	6·00
442	$10 on 6c. Cable and Wireless Building	5·00	6·00

87 First Petition for Separation, 1825

1980. Separation from St. Kitts. Multicoloured.

443	18c. Type **87**	10	10
444	22c. Referendum ballot paper, 1967	15	10
445	35c. Airport blockade, 1967	40	15
446	50c. Anguillan flag	70	30
447	$1 Separation celebration, 1980	40	45
MS448	178×92 mm. Nos. 443/7	1·40	1·25

88 *Nelson's Dockyard* (R. Granger Barrett)

1981. 175th Death Anniv of Lord Nelson. Multicoloured.

449	22c. Type **88**	2·50	50
450	35c. *Ships in which Nelson Served* (Nicholas Pocock)	2·50	70
451	50c. *H.M.S. Victory* (Monamy Swaine)	3·00	1·50
452	$3 *Battle of Trafalgar* (Clarkson Stanfield)	3·75	6·50
MS453	82×63 mm. $5 *Horatio Nelson* (L. F. Abbott) and coat of arms	3·00	3·25

89 Minnie Mouse being chased by Bees

1981. Easter. Walt Disney Cartoon Characters. Multicoloured.

454	1c. Type **89**	10	10
455	2c. Pluto laughing at Mickey Mouse	10	10
456	3c. Minnie Mouse tying ribbon round Pluto's neck	10	10
457	5c. Minnie Mouse confronted by love-struck bird who fancies her bonnet	10	10
458	7c. Dewey and Huey admiring themselves in mirror	10	10
459	9c. Horace Horsecollar and Clarabelle Cow out for a stroll	10	10
460	10c. Daisy Duck with hat full of Easter eggs	10	10
461	$2 Goofy unwrapping Easter hat	1·40	1·40
462	$3 Donald Duck in his Easter finery	1·60	1·60
MS463	134×108 mm. $5 Chip and Dale making off with hat	3·50	3·50

90 Prince Charles, Lady Diana Spencer and St. Paul's Cathedral

1981. Royal Wedding. Multicoloured.

464	50c. Type **90**	15	20
465	$2.50 Althorp	30	50
466	$3 Windsor Castle	35	60
MS467	90×72 mm. Buckingham Palace	1·25	1·50

91 Children playing in Tree

1981. 35th Anniv of UNICEF Multicoloured.

470	5c. Type **91**	20	30
471	10c. Children playing by pool	20	30
472	15c. Children playing musical instruments	20	30
473	$3 Children playing with pets	2·50	3·00
MS474	78×106 mm. Children playing football (vert)	3·50	5·00

1981. Christmas. Designs as T **89** showing scenes from Walt Disney's cartoon film *The Night before Christmas*.

475	1c. multicoloured	10	10
476	2c. multicoloured	10	10
477	3c. multicoloured	10	10
478	5c. multicoloured	15	10
479	7c. multicoloured	15	10
480	10c. multicoloured	15	10
481	12c. multicoloured	15	10
482	$2 multicoloured	3·75	1·25
483	$3 multicoloured	3·75	1·60
MS484	130×105 mm. $5 multicoloured	5·50	3·50

92 Red Grouper

1982. Multicoloured.

485	1c. Type **92**	15	1·25
486	5c. Ferry service, Blowing Point	30	1·25
487	10c. Island dinghies	20	60
488	15c. Majorettes	20	60
489	20c. Launching boat, Sandy Hill	40	60
490	25c. Corals	1·50	60
491	30c. Little Bay cliffs	30	75
492	35c. Fountain Cave interior	1·50	80
493	40c. Sunset over Sandy Island	30	75
494	45c. Landing at Sombrero	50	80
495	60c. Seine fishing	3·25	3·25
496	75c. Boat race at sunset, Sandy Ground	1·00	2·00
497	$1 Bagging lobster at Island Harbour	2·25	2·00
498	$5 Brown pelicans	17·00	14·00
499	$7.50 Hibiscus	11·00	16·00
500	$10 Queen triggerfish	17·00	16·00

1982. No. 494 surch **50c.**

501	50c. on 45c. Landing at Sombrero	50	35

94 Anthurium and *Heliconius charithonia*

1982. Easter. Flowers and Butterflies. Multicoloured.

502	10c. Type **94**	1·10	15
503	35c. Bird of paradise and *Junonia evarete*	2·00	40
504	75c. Allamanda and *Danaus plexippus*	2·25	70
505	$3 Orchid tree and *Biblis hyperia*	3·50	2·25
MS506	65×79 mm. $5 Amaryllis and *Dryas julia*	2·75	3·50

95 Lady Diana Spencer in 1961

1982. 21st Birthday of Princess of Wales. Multicoloured.

507	10c. Type **95**	50	20
508	30c. Lady Diana Spencer in 1968	1·75	25
509	40c. Lady Diana in 1970	50	30
510	60c. Lady Diana in 1974	55	35
511	$2 Lady Diana in 1981	80	1·10
512	$3 Lady Diana in 1981 (different)	5·50	1·40
MS513	72×90 mm. $5 Princess of Wales	7·50	3·00
MS514	125×125 mm. As Nos. 507/12, but with buff borders	9·50	7·00

96 Pitching Tent

1982. 75th Anniv of Boy Scout Movement. Multicoloured.

515	10c. Type **96**	45	20
516	35c. Scout band	85	50
517	75c. Yachting	1·25	90
518	$3 On parade	3·00	2·75
MS519	90×72 mm. $5 Cooking	4·50	4·00

1982. World Cup Football Championship, Spain. Horiz designs as T **89** showing scenes from Walt Disney's cartoon film *Bedknobs and Broomsticks*.

520	1c. multicoloured	10	10
521	3c. multicoloured	10	10
522	4c. multicoloured	10	10
523	5c. multicoloured	10	10
524	7c. multicoloured	10	10
525	9c. multicoloured	10	10
526	10c. multicoloured	10	10
527	$2.50 multicoloured	2·50	1·75
528	$3 multicoloured	2·50	2·00
MS529	126×101 mm. $5 multicoloured	9·00	8·50

1982. Commonwealth Games, Brisbane. Nos. 487, 495/6 and 498 optd **COMMONWEALTH GAMES 1982.**

530	10c. Island dinghies	15	25
531	60c. Seine fishing	45	60
532	75c. Boat race at sunset, Sandy Ground	60	80
533	$5 Brown pelicans	3·25	3·75

1982. Birth Cent of A. A. Milne (author). As T **89.**

534	1c. multicoloured	25	20
535	2c. multicoloured	25	20
536	3c. multicoloured	25	20
537	5c. multicoloured	35	20
538	7c. multicoloured	35	25
539	10c. multicoloured	50	15
540	12c. multicoloured	60	20
541	20c. multicoloured	90	25
542	$5 multicoloured	9·00	9·50
MS543	120×93 mm. $5 multicoloured	7·50	9·00

DESIGNS—HORIZ: 1c. to $5 Scenes from various *Winnie the Pooh* stories.

98 Culture

1983. Commonwealth Day. Multicoloured.

544	10c. Type **98**	10	15
545	35c. Anguilla and British flags	30	30
546	75c. Economic co-operation	60	1·00
547	$2.50 Salt industry (salt pond)	3·75	5·25
MS548	76×61 mm. World map showing positions of Commonwealth countries	2·50	2·50

99 "I am the Lord Thy God"

1983. Easter. The Ten Commandments. Multicoloured.

549	1c. Type **99**	10	10
550	2c. "Thou shalt not make any graven image"	10	10
551	3c. "Thou shalt not take My Name in vain"	10	10
552	10c. "Remember the Sabbath Day"	25	10
553	35c. "Honour thy father and mother"	65	20
554	60c. "Thou shalt not kill"	1·00	40
555	75c. "Thou shalt not commit adultery"	1·25	50
556	$2 "Thou shalt not steal"	2·75	1·50
557	$2.50 "Thou shalt not bear false witness"	3·00	1·50
558	$5 "Thou shalt not covet"	4·25	2·75
MS559	126×102 mm. $5 "Moses receiving the Tablets" (16th-century woodcut)	2·75	3·00

100 Leatherback Turtle

1983. Endangered Species. Turtles. Multicoloured.

560	10c. Type **100**	4·00	80
561	35c. Hawksbill turtle	7·00	1·25
562	75c. Green turtle	8·00	3·50
563	$1 Loggerhead turtle	9·00	7·50
MS564	93×72 mm. $5 Leatherback turtle (different)	22·00	4·00

101 Montgolfier Hot Air Balloon, 1783

1983. Bicentenary of Manned Flight. Multicoloured.

565	10c. Type **101**	50	50
566	60c. Blanchard and Jefferies crossing English Channel by balloon, 1785	1·25	85
567	$1 Henri Giffard's steam-powered dirigible airship, 1852	1·75	1·50
568	$2.50 Otto Lillienthal and biplane glider, 1890–96	3·00	3·00
MS569	72×90 mm. $5 Wilbur Wright flying round Statue of Liberty, 1909	2·75	3·50

102 Boys' Brigade Band and Flag

1983. Centenary of Boys' Brigade. Multicoloured.

570	10c. Type **102**	50	15
571	$5 Brigade members marching	3·50	2·75
MS572	96×115 mm. Nos. 570/1	3·25	4·50

1983. 150th Anniv of Abolition of Slavery (1st issue). Nos. 487, 493 and 497/8 optd **150TH ANNIVERSARY ABOLITION OF SLAVERY ACT.**

573	10c. Island dinghies	20	10
574	40c. Sunset over Sandy Island	30	25
575	$1 Bagging lobster at Island Harbour	80	50
576	$5 Brown pelicans	10·00	2·75

See also Nos. 616/23.

104 Jiminy on Clock ("Cricket on the Hearth")

1983. Christmas. Walt Disney Cartoon Characters. Multicoloured.

577	1c. Type **104**	10	10
578	2c. Jiminy with fiddle (*Cricket on the Hearth*)	10	10
579	3c. Jiminy among toys (*Cricket on the Hearth*)	10	10
580	4c. Mickey as Bob Cratchit (*A Christmas Carol*)	10	10
581	5c. Donald Duck as Scrooge (*A Christmas Carol*)	10	10
582	6c. Mini and Goofy in *The Chimes*	10	10
583	10c. Goofy sees an imp appearing from bells (*The Chimes*)	10	10
584	$2 Donald Duck as Mr. Pickwick (*The Pickwick Papers*)	3·50	2·75
585	$3 Disney characters as Pickwickians (*The Pickwick Papers*)	4·00	2·25
MS586	130×104 mm. Donald Duck as Mr. Pickwick with gifts (*The Pickwick Papers*)	10·00	11·00

105 100 Metres Race

1984. Olympic Games, Los Angeles. Multicoloured. (A) Inscr "1984 Los Angeles".

587A	1c. Type **105**	10	10
588A	2c. Long jumping	10	10
589A	3c. Shot-putting	10	10
590A	4c. High jumping	10	10
591A	5c. 400 metres race	10	10
592A	6c. Hurdling	10	10
593A	10c. Discus-throwing	10	10
594A	$1 Pole-vaulting	3·25	1·25
595A	$4 Javelin-throwing	6·00	3·50
MS596A	117×93 mm. $5 1500 metres race	7·50	4·50

(B) Inscr "1984 Olympics Los Angeles" and Olympic emblem.

587B	1c. Type **105**	10	10
588B	2c. Long jumping	10	10
589B	3c. Shot-putting	10	10
590B	4c. High jumping	10	10
591B	5c. 400 metres race	10	10
592B	6c. Hurdling	10	10
593B	10c. Discus-throwing	10	10
594B	$1 Pole-vaulting	3·75	3·00
595B	$4 Javelin-throwing	7·50	8·50
MS596B	117×93 mm. $5 1500 metres race	8·00	4·50

106 *Justice*

1984. Easter. Multicoloured.

597	10c. Type **106**	15	10
598	25c. "Poetry"	20	20
599	35c. "Philosophy"	30	30
600	40c. "Theology"	30	30
601	$1 "Abraham and Paul"	85	95
602	$2 "Moses and Matthew"	1·60	2·25
603	$3 "John and David"	2·25	3·00
604	$4 "Peter and Adam"	2·50	3·00
MS605	83×110 mm. $5 "Astronomy"	3·00	3·00

Nos. 597/605 show details from "*La Stanza della Segnatura*" by Raphael.

1984. Nos. 485, 491, 498/500 surch.

606	25c. on $7.50 Hibiscus	65	35
607	35c. on 30c. Little Bay cliffs	50	40
608	60c. on 1c. Type **92**	55	45
609	$2.50 on $5 Brown pelicans	3·00	1·50
610	$2.50 on $10 Queen triggerfish	1·75	1·50

108 1913 1d. Kangaroo Stamp

1984. "Ausipex 84" International Stamp Exhibition. Multicoloured.

611	10c. Type **108**	40	30
612	75c. 1914 6d. Laughing Kookaburra	1·50	1·25
613	$1 1932 2d. Sydney Harbour Bridge	2·00	1·75
614	$2.50 1938 10s. King George VI	2·25	4·00
MS615	95×86 mm. $5 £1 Bass and £2 Admiral King	5·00	7·00

109 Thomas Fowell Buxton

1984. 150th Anniv of Abolition of Slavery (2nd issue). Multicoloured.

616	10c. Type **109**	15	10
617	25c. Abraham Lincoln	30	25
618	35c. Henri Christophe	40	35
619	60c. Thomas Clarkson	60	50
620	75c. William Wilberforce	70	60
621	$1 Olaudah Equiano	80	70
622	$2.50 General Charles Gordon	1·75	1·60
623	$5 Granville Sharp	3·00	3·00
MS624	150×121 mm. Nos. 616/23	7·50	10·00

1984. Universal Postal Union Congress, Hamburg. Nos. 486/7 and 498 optd **U.P.U. CONGRESS HAMBURG 1984** or surch also (No 626).

625	5c. Ferry service, Blowing Point	30	10
626	20c. on 10c. Island dinghies	30	15
627	$5 Brown pelicans	5·50	3·50

1984. Birth of Prince Henry. Nos. 507/12 optd **PRINCE HENRY BIRTH 15.9.84.**

628	10c. Type **95**	20	10
629	30c. Lady Diana Spencer in 1968	40	25
630	40c. Lady Diana in 1970	20	30
631	60c. Lady Diana in 1974	30	45
632	$2 Lady Diana in 1981	75	1·25
633	$3 Lady Diana in 1981 (different)	1·25	1·75
MS634	72×90 mm. $5 Princess of Wales	2·00	3·00
MS635	125×125 mm. As Nos. 628/33, but with buff borders	2·00	4·00

112 Christmas in Sweden

1984. Christmas. Walt Disney Cartoon Characters. National Scenes. Multicoloured.

636	1c. Type **112**	10	10
637	2c. Italy	10	10
638	3c. Holland	10	10
639	4c. Mexico	10	10
640	5c. Spain	10	10
641	10c. Disneyland, U.S.A.	10	10
642	$1 Japan	3·00	2·00
643	$2 Anguilla	4·00	4·50
644	$4 Germany	6·50	7·50
MS645	126×102 mm. $5 England	7·00	5·00

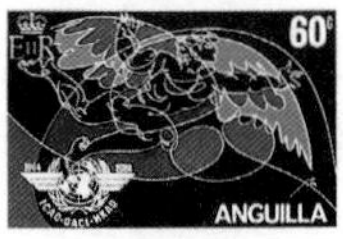

113 Icarus in Flight

1984. 40th Anniv of International Civil Aviation Authority. Multicoloured.

646	60c. Type **113**	60	75
647	75c. *Solar Princess* (abstract)	80	90
648	$2.50 I.C.A.O. emblem (vert)	2·25	3·00
MS649	65×49 mm. $5 Map of air routes serving Anguilla	3·00	4·50

114 Barn Swallow

1985. Birth Bicentenary of John J. Audubon (ornithologist). Multicoloured.

650	10c. Type **114**	1·25	75
651	60c. American wood stork ("Woodstork")	1·75	1·50
652	75c. Roseate tern	1·75	1·50
653	$5 Osprey	4·75	6·50
MS654	Two sheets, each 73×103 mm. $4 Western tanager (horiz); (b) $4 Solitary vireo (horiz) Set of 2 sheets	10·00	6·00

115 The Queen Mother visiting King's College Hospital, London

1985. Life and Times of Queen Elizabeth the Queen Mother. Multicoloured.

655	10c. Type **115**	10	10
656	$2 The Queen Mother inspecting Royal Marine Volunteer Cadets, Deal	80	1·25
657	$3 The Queen Mother outside Clarence House	1·10	1·50
MS658	56×85 mm. $5 At Ascot, 1979	1·75	2·50

116 White-tailed Tropic Bird

1985. Birds. Multicoloured.

659	5c. Brown pelican	1·75	1·75
660	10c. Mourning dove ("Turtle Dove")	1·75	1·75
661	15c. Magnificent frigate bird (inscr "Man-o-War")	1·75	1·75
662	20c. Antillean crested hummingbird	1·75	1·75
663	25c. Type **116**	1·75	1·75
664	30c. Caribbean elaenia	1·75	1·75
665	35c. Black-whiskered vireo	7·50	5·50
665a	35c. Lesser Antillean bullfinch	6·00	3·00
666	40c. Yellow-crowned night heron	2·00	1·75
667	45c. Pearly-eyed thrasher	1·75	1·75
668	50c. Laughing gull	1·75	1·75
669	65c. Brown booby	1·75	1·75
670	80c. Grey kingbird	2·25	3·00
671	$1 Audubon's shearwater	2·25	3·00
672	$1.35 Roseate tern	2·00	3·00
673	$2.50 Bananaquit	6·00	8·50
674	$5 Belted kingfisher	5·00	8·50
675	$10 Green-backed heron ("Green Heron")	7·00	11·00

1985. 75th Anniv of Girl Guide Movement. Nos. 486, 491, 496 and 498 optd **GIRL GUIDES 75TH ANNIVERSARY 1910–1985** and anniversary emblem.

676	5c. Ferry service, Blowing Point	30	30
677	30c. Little Bay cliffs	40	35
678	75c. Boat race at sunset, Sandy Ground	60	85
679	$5 Brown pelicans	10·00	10·00

118 Goofy as Huckleberry Finn Fishing

1985. 150th Birth Anniv of Mark Twain (author). Walt Disney cartoon characters in scenes from *Huckleberry Finn*. Multicoloured.

680	10c. Type **118**	70	20
681	60c. Pete as Pap surprising Huck	2·25	85
682	$1 "Multiplication tables"	2·75	1·25
683	$3 The Duke reciting Shakespeare	4·00	4·00
MS684	127×102 mm. $5 "In school but out"	8·50	8·00

119 Hansel and Gretel (Mickey and Minnie Mouse) awakening in Forest

1985. Birth Bicentenaries of Grimm Brothers (folklorists). Designs showing Walt Disney cartoon characters in scenes from *Hansel and Gretel*. Multicoloured.

685	5c. Type **119**	55	55
686	50c. Hansel and Gretel find the gingerbread house	1·50	60

687	90c. Hansel and Gretel meeting the Witch	2·00	1·00
688	$4 Hansel and Gretel captured by the Witch	3·50	5·00
MS689	128×101 mm. $5 Hansel and Gretel riding on swan	8·00	9·00

120 Statue of Liberty and *Danmark* (Denmark)

1985. Centenary of the Statue of Liberty (1986). The Statue of Liberty and Cadet ships.

690	10c. Type **120**	1·00	85
691	20c. *Eagle* (U.S.A.)	1·25	90
692	60c. *Amerigo Vespucci* (Italy)	1·60	1·50
693	75c. *Sir Winston Churchill* (Great Britain)	1·60	1·50
694	$2 *Nippon Maru* (Japan)	1·75	4·00
695	$2.50 *Gorch Fock* (West Germany)	1·75	4·00
MS696	96×69 mm. $5 Statue of Liberty (vert)	7·50	4·50

1985. 80th Anniv of Rotary (10, 35c.) and International Youth Year (others). Nos. 487, 491 and 497 optd or surch **80TH ANNIVERSARY ROTARY 1985** and emblem (10, 35c.) or **INTERNATIONAL YOUTH YEAR** and emblem ($1, $5).

697	10c. Island dinghies	30	25
698	35c. on 30c. Little Bay cliffs	60	45
699	$1 Bagging lobster at Island Harbour	1·50	1·25
700	$5 on 30c. Little Bay cliffs	4·25	5·25

123 Johannes Hevelius (astronomer) and Mayan Temple Observatory

1986. Appearance of Halley's Comet. Multicoloured.

701	5c. Type **123**	55	55
702	10c. "Viking Lander" space vehicle on Mars, 1976	55	55
703	60c. Comet in 1664 (from *Theatri Cosmicum*, 1668)	1·50	85
704	$4 Comet over Mississippi riverboat, 1835 (150th birth anniv of Mark Twain)	4·50	5·00
MS705	101×70 mm. $5 Halley's Comet over Anguilla	4·50	6·00

124 "The Crucifixion"

1986. Easter.

706	**124**	10c. multicoloured	20	20
707	-	25c. multicoloured	35	35
708	-	45c. multicoloured	65	65
709	-	$4 multicoloured	3·75	5·00
MS710	-	93×75 mm. $5 multicoloured (horiz)	6·00	8·50

DESIGNS: 25c. to $5 Different stained glass windows from Chartres Cathedral.

125 Princess Elizabeth inspecting Guards, 1946

1986. 60th Birthday of Queen Elizabeth II.

711	**125**	20c. black and yellow	40	20
712	-	$2 multicoloured	1·75	1·50
713	-	$3 multicoloured	1·75	1·75
MS714	-	120×85 mm. $5 black and brown	2·75	3·75

DESIGNS: $2 Queen at Garter Ceremony; $3 At Trooping the Colour; $5 Duke and Duchess of York with baby Princess Elizabeth, 1926.

1986. "Ameripex" International Stamp Exhibition, Chicago. Nos. 659, 667, 671, 673 and 675 optd **AMERIPEX 1986.**

715	5c. Brown pelican	60	1·00
716	45c. Pearly-eyed thrasher	1·25	50
717	$1 Audubon's shearwater	2·00	1·25
718	$2.50 Bananaquit	2·75	3·25
719	$10 Green-backed heron	6·50	9·50

127 Prince Andrew and Miss Sarah Ferguson

1986. Royal Wedding. Multicoloured.

720	10c. Type **127**	50	15
721	35c. Prince Andrew	85	35
722	$2 Miss Sarah Ferguson	2·25	1·50
723	$3 Prince Andrew and Miss Sarah Ferguson (diffferent)	2·50	2·00
MS724	119×90 mm. $6 Westminster Abbey	5·50	6·50

1986. International Peace Year. Nos. 616/23 optd **INTERNATIONAL YEAR OF PEACE.**

725	10c. Type **109**	90	60
726	25c. Abraham Lincoln	1·25	50
727	35c. Henri Christophe	1·40	55
728	60c. Thomas Clarkson	2·00	80
729	75c. William Wilberforce	2·00	1·00
730	$1 Olaudah Equiano	2·00	1·25
731	$2.50 General Gordon	3·75	4·75
732	$5 Granville Sharp	4·25	7·00
MS733	150×121 mm. Nos. 725/32	15·00	17·00

129 Trading Sloop

1986. Christmas. Ships. Multicoloured.

734	10c. Type **129**	1·75	60
735	45c. *Lady Rodney* (cargo liner)	3·25	1·10
736	80c. *West Derby* (19th-century sailing ship)	4·25	2·50
737	$3 *Warspite* (local sloop)	8·50	10·00
MS738	130×100 mm. $4 Boat-race day (vert)	18·00	20·00

130 Christopher Columbus with Astrolabe

1986. 500th Anniv (1992) of Discovery of America by Columbus (1st issue). Multicoloured.

739	5c. Type **130**	60	60
740	10c. Columbus on board ship	1·00	60
741	35c. *Santa Maria*	2·10	1·10
742	80c. King Ferdinand and Queen Isabella of Spain (horiz)	1·50	1·75
743	$4 Caribbean Indians smoking tobacco (horiz)	3·25	5·00
MS744	Two sheets, each 96×66 mm. (a) $5 Caribbean manatee (horiz). (b) $5 Dragon tree Set of 2 sheets	15·00	17·00

See also Nos. 902/6.

131 *Danaus plexippus*

1987. Easter. Butterflies. Multicoloured.

745	10c. Type **131**	1·50	70
746	80c. *Anartia jatrophae*	4·00	2·75
747	$1 *Heliconius charithonia*	4·25	2·75
748	$2 *Junonia evarete*	7·00	8·50
MS749	90×69 mm. $6 *Dryas julia*	11·00	13·00

132 Old Goose Iron and Modern Electric Iron

1987. 20th Anniv of Separation from St. Kitts-Nevis. Multicoloured.

750	10c. Type **132**	70	40
751	35c. Old East End School and Albena Lake-Hodge Comprehensive College	75	45
752	45c. Past and present markets	85	50
753	80c. Previous sailing ferry and new motor ferry, Blowing Point	2·50	1·25
754	$1 Original mobile post office and new telephone exchange	2·50	1·40
755	$2 Open-air meeting, Burrowes Park and House of Assembly in session	2·75	3·25
MS756	159×127 mm. Nos. 750/5	13·00	16·00

1987. "Capex '87" International Stamp Exhibition, Toronto. Nos. 665a, 667, 670 and 675 optd **CAPEX'87.**

757	35c. Lesser Antillean bullfinch	2·50	1·00
758	45c. Pearly-eyed thrasher	2·50	1·00
759	80c. Grey kingbird	3·75	1·50
760	$10 Green-backed heron	12·00	14·00

1987. 20th Anniv of Independence. Nos. 659, 661/4 and 665a/75 optd **20 YEARS OF PROGRESS 1967–1987,** No. 762 surch also.

761	5c. Brown pelican	3·25	3·25
762	10c. on 15c. Magnificent frigate bird	3·25	3·25
763	15c. Magnificent frigate bird	3·25	3·25
764	20c. Antillean crested hummingbird	3·25	3·25
765	25c. Type **116**	3·25	3·25
766	30c. Caribbean elaenia	3·25	3·25
767	35c. Lesser Antillean bullfinch	3·25	3·25
768	40c. Yellow-crowned night heron	3·25	3·25
769	45c. Pearly-eyed thrasher	3·25	3·25
770	50c. Laughing gull	3·25	3·25
771	65c. Brown booby	3·50	3·50
772	80c. Grey kingbird	3·50	3·50
773	$1 Audubon's shearwater	3·50	3·50
774	$1.35 Roseate tern	4·00	4·25
775	$2.50 Bananaquit	5·00	7·00
776	$5 Belted kingfisher	7·00	9·50
777	$10 Green-backed heron	9·00	12·00

135 Wicket Keeper and Game in Progress

1987. Cricket World Cup. Multicoloured.

778	10c. Type **135**	2·50	80
779	35c. Batsman and local Anguilla team	2·50	70
780	45c. Batsman and game in progress	3·00	75
781	$2.50 Bowler and game in progress	6·00	9·00
MS782	100×75 mm. $6 Batsman and game in progress (different)	16·00	17·00

136 West Indian Top Shell

1987. Christmas. Sea Shells and Crabs. Multicoloured.

783	10c. Type **136**	1·75	55
784	35c. Ghost crab	2·50	60
785	50c. Spiny Caribbean vase	3·25	1·40
786	$2 Great land crab	6·50	8·50
MS787	101×75 mm. $6 Queen or pink conch	14·00	15·00

1987. Royal Ruby Wedding. Nos. 665a, 671/2 and 675 optd **40TH WEDDING ANNIVERSARY H.M. QUEEN ELIZABETH II H.R.H. THE DUKE OF EDINBURGH.**

788	35c. Lesser Antillean bullfinch	1·50	55
789	$1 Audubon's shearwater	2·25	80
790	$1.35 Roseate tern	2·50	90
791	$10 Green-backed heron	6·50	10·00

138 *Crinum erubescens*

1988. Easter. Lilies. Multicoloured.

792	30c. Type **138**	70	25
793	45c. Spider lily	70	25
794	$1 *Crinum macowanii*	2·00	85
795	$2.50 Day lily	2·00	3·00
MS796	100×75 mm. $6 Easter lily	2·75	4·50

139 Relay Racing

1988. Olympic Games, Seoul. Multicoloured.

797	35c. Type **139**	45	30
798	45c. Windsurfing	55	45
799	50c. Tennis	1·50	1·10
800	80c. Basketball	6·50	2·75
MS801	104×78 mm. $6 Athletics	3·00	4·50

140 Common Sea Fan

1988. Christmas. Marine Life. Multicoloured.

802	35c. Type **140**	1·00	30
803	80c. Coral crab	1·75	70
804	$1 Grooved brain coral	2·00	1·00
805	$1.60 Queen triggerfish	2·75	3·25
MS806	103×78 mm. $6 West Indian spiny lobster	3·00	4·50

1988. Visit of Princess Alexandra. Nos. 665a, 670/1 and 673 optd **H.R.H. PRINCESS ALEXANDRA'S VISIT NOVEMBER 1988.**

807	35c. Lesser Antillean bullfinch	3·00	70
808	80c. Grey kingbird	4·00	1·40
809	$1 Audubon's shearwater	4·00	1·60
810	$2.50 Bananaquit	6·00	6·00

142 Wood Slave

1989. Lizards. Multicoloured.

811	45c. Type **142**	1·75	50
812	80c. Slippery back	2·50	85
813	$2.50 *Iguana delicatissima*	4·50	4·75
MS814	101×75 mm. $6 Tree lizard	14·00	4·75

143 *Christ Crowned with Thorns* (detail) (Bosch)

1989. Easter. Religious Paintings. Multicoloured.

815	35c. Type **143**	80	25
816	80c. *Christ bearing the Cross* (detail) (Gerard David)	1·25	75
817	$1 *The Deposition* (detail) (Gerard David)	1·40	80
818	$1.60 *Pieta* (detail) (Rogier van der Weyden)	2·00	2·75
MS819	103×77 mm. $6 *Crucified Christ with the Virgin Mary and Saints* (detail) (Raphael)	2·75	4·25

144 University Arms

1989. 40th Anniv of University of the West Indies.

820	**144** $5 multicoloured	4·50	5·00

1989. 20th Anniv of First Manned Landing on Moon. Nos. 670/2 and 674 optd **20TH ANNIVERSARY MOON LANDING.**

821	80c. Grey kingbird	3·25	90
822	$1 Audubon's shearwater	3·25	1·00
823	$1.35 Roseate tern	3·75	1·75
824	$5 Belted kingfisher	9·00	12·00

146 Lone Star (house), 1930

1989. Christmas. Historic Houses. Multicoloured.

825	5c. Type **146**	50	1·50
826	35c. Whitehouse, 1906	1·00	45
827	45c. Hodges House	1·10	50
828	80c. Warden's Place	1·75	1·75
MS829	102×77 mm. $6 Wallblake House, 1787	4·25	6·50

147 Bigeye ("Blear Eye")

1990. Fish. Multicoloured.

830B	5c. Type **147**	75	1·00
831B	10c. Long-spined squirrelfish ("Redman")	75	1·00
832A	15c. Stop-light parrotfish ("Speckletail")	80	60
833A	25c. Blue-striped grunt	1·00	80
834A	30c. Yellow jack	1·00	80
835B	35c. Red hind	1·00	75
836A	40c. Spotted goatfish	1·25	80
837A	45c. Queen triggerfish ("Old wife")	1·25	60
838A	50c. Coney ("Butter fish")	1·25	80
839A	65c. Smooth trunkfish ("Shell fish")	1·75	1·00
840A	80c. Yellow-tailed snapper	1·50	90
841A	$1 Banded butterflyfish ("Katy")	1·50	1·00
842A	$1.35 Nassau grouper	2·25	1·50
843A	$2.50 Blue tang ("Doctor fish")	2·50	3·75
844A	$5 Queen angelfish	3·00	6·00
845A	$10 Great barracuda	4·75	9·00

148 The Last Supper

1990. Easter. Multicoloured.

846	35c. Type **148**	1·25	40
847	45c. The Trial	1·25	40
848	$1.35 The Crucifixion	3·00	2·25
849	$2.50 The Empty Tomb	3·50	5·00
MS850	114×84 mm. $6 The Resurrection	12·00	14·00

149 G.B. 1840 Penny Black

1990. "Stamp World London 90" International Stamp Exhibition. Multicoloured.

851	25c. Type **149**	1·25	35
852	50c. G.B. 1840 Twopenny Blue	1·75	50
853	$1.50 Cape of Good Hope 1861 1d. "woodblock" (horiz)	3·00	3·25
854	$2.50 G.B. 1882 £5 (horiz)	3·50	4·25
MS855	86×71 mm. $6 Penny Black and Twopence Blue (horiz)	13·00	16·00

1990. Anniversaries and Events. Nos. 841/4 optd.

856	$1 Banded butterflyfish (optd **EXPO '90**)	1·75	1·25
857	$1.35 Nassau grouper (optd **1990 INTERNATIONAL LITERACY YEAR**)	1·75	1·25
858	$2.50 Blue tang (optd **WORLD CUP FOOTBALL CHAMPIONSHIPS 1990**)	7·00	7·00
859	$5 Queen angelfish (optd **90TH BIRTHDAY H.M. THE QUEEN MOTHER**)	12·00	12·00

151 Mermaid Flag

1990. Island Flags. Multicoloured.

860	50c. Type **151**	2·25	70
861	80c. New Anguilla official flag	2·75	1·00
862	$1 Three Dolphins flag	3·00	1·25
863	$5 Governor's official flag	7·50	10·00

152 Laughing Gulls

1990. Christmas. Sea Birds. Multicoloured.

864	10c. Type **152**	60	50
865	35c. Brown booby	1·00	50
866	$1.50 Bridled tern	2·00	2·00
867	$3.50 Brown pelican	3·25	5·50
MS868	101×76 mm. $6 Least tern	9·50	12·00

1991. Easter. Nos. 846/9 optd **1991**.

869	35c. Type **148**	1·50	60
870	45c. The Trial	1·60	60
871	$1.35 The Crucifixion	3·00	2·00
872	$2.50 The Empty Tomb	4·25	7·50
MS873	114×84 mm. $6 The Resurrection	13·00	16·00

154 Angel

1991. Christmas.

874	**154** 5c. violet, brown & black	1·00	1·00
875	- 35c. multicoloured	2·50	55
876	- 80c. multicoloured	2·50	2·25
877	- $1 multicoloured	3·50	2·25
MS878	- 131×97 mm. $5 multicoloured	13·00	15·00

DESIGNS—VERT: 35c. Father Christmas. HORIZ: 80c. Church and house; $1 Palm trees at night; $5 Anguilla village.

155 Angels with Palm Branches outside St. Gerard's Church

1992. Easter. Multicoloured.

879	30c. Type **155**	1·40	45
880	45c. Angels singing outside Methodist Church	1·60	45
881	80c. Village (horiz)	2·75	90
882	$1 Congregation going to St. Mary's Church	2·75	1·25
883	$5 Dinghy regatta (horiz)	7·00	11·00

1992. No. 834 surch **$1.60.**

884	$1.60 on 30c. Yellow jack	3·25	2·50

157 Anguillan Flags

1992. 25th Anniv of Separation from St. Kitts-Nevis. Multicoloured.

885	80c. Type **157**	3·25	1·50
886	$1 Present official seal	3·25	1·75
887	$1.60 Anguillan flags at airport	5·00	4·00
888	$2 Royal Commissioner's official seal	5·00	6·00
MS889	116×117 mm. $10 "Independent Anguilla" overprinted stamps of 1967 (85×85 mm)	16·00	18·00

158 Dinghy Race

1992. Sailing Dinghy Racing.

890	**158** 20c. multicoloured	2·00	1·00
891	- 35c. multicoloured	2·50	75
892	- 45c. multicoloured	2·75	75
893	- 80c. multicoloured	3·50	5·00
894	- 80c. black and blue	3·50	5·00
895	- $1 multicoloured	3·50	3·00
MS896	- 129×30 mm. $6 multicoloured	11·00	13·00

DESIGNS—VERT: 35c. Stylized poster; 80c. (No. 893) "Blue Bird" in race; 80c. (No. 894) Construction drawings of "Blue Bird" by Douglas Pyle; $1 Stylized poster (different). HORIZ: 45c. Dinghies on beach. (97×32 mm)—$6 Composite designs as 20 and 45c. values.

159 Mucka Jumbie on Stilts

1992. Christmas. Local Traditions. Multicoloured.

897	20c. Type **159**	1·25	40
898	70c. Masqueraders	2·50	60
899	$1.05 Baking in old style oven	2·75	1·25
900	$2.40 Collecting presents from Christmas tree	5·50	7·00
MS901	128×101 mm. $5 As No. 900	4·00	6·50

160 Columbus landing in New World

1992. 500th Anniv of Discovery of America by Columbus (2nd issue).

902	**160** 80c. multicoloured	3·25	1·25
903	- $1 black and brown	3·25	1·25
904	- $2 multicoloured	5·00	5·00
905	- $3 multicoloured	5·50	7·00
MS906	- 78×54 mm. $6 multicoloured	15·00	14·00

DESIGNS—VERT: $1 Christopher Columbus; $6 Columbus and map of West Indies. HORIZ: $2 Fleet of Columbus; $3 "*Pinta*.

161 *Kite Flying* (Kyle Brooks)

1993. Easter. Children's Paintings. Multicoloured.

907	20c. Type **161**	2·00	75
908	45c. *Clifftop Village Service* (Kara Connor)	2·50	70
909	80c. *Morning Devotion on Sombrero* (Junior Carty)	3·25	1·40
910	$1.50 *Hill Top Church Service* (Leana Harris)	4·50	7·00
MS911	90×110 mm. $5 *Good Friday Kites* (Marvin Hazel and Kyle Brooks) (39×53 mm)	5·50	7·50

162 Salt Picking

1993. Traditional Industries. Multicoloured.

912	20c. Type **162**	4·00	1·25
913	80c. Tobacco growing	2·75	1·25
914	$1 Cotton picking	2·75	1·25
915	$2 Harvesting sugar cane	5·00	7·00
MS916	111×85 mm. $6 Fishing	12·00	14·00

163 Lord Great Chamberlain presenting Spurs of Charity to Queen

1993. 40th Anniv of Coronation. Multicoloured.

917	80c. Type **163**	2·50	80
918	$1 The Benediction	2·75	90
919	$2 Queen Elizabeth II in Coronation robes	3·50	3·50
920	$3 St. Edward's Crown	4·00	4·50
MS921	114×95 mm. $6 The Queen and Prince Philip in Coronation coach	14·00	15·00

164 Carnival Pan Player

1993. Anguilla Carnival. Multicoloured.

922	20c. Type **164**	1·00	50
923	45c. Revellers dressed as pirates	1·50	40
924	80c. Revellers dressed as stars	2·50	80
925	$1 Mas dancing	2·75	3·25
926	$2 Masked couple	3·75	4·75
927	$3 Revellers dressed as commandos	4·25	6·00
MS928	123×94 mm. $5 Revellers in fantasy costumes	13·00	15·00

165 Mucka Jumbies Carnival Characters

1993. Christmas. Multicoloured.

929	20c. Type **165**	1·25	80
930	35c. Local carol singers	1·60	70
931	45c. Christmas home baking	1·75	70
932	$3 Decorating Christmas tree	5·50	7·50
MS933	123×118 mm. $4 Mucka Jumbies and carol singers (58½×47 mm)	3·50	5·00

166 Travelling Branch Post Van at Sandy Ground

1994. Delivering the Mail. Multicoloured.

934	20c. Type **166**	2·25	80
935	45c. *Betsy R* (mail schooner) at The Forest (vert)	2·75	80
936	80c. Mail van at old Post Office	3·25	1·60
937	$1 Jeep on beach, Island Harbour (vert)	3·25	1·60
938	$4 New Post Office	5·00	8·00

167 Princess Alexandra, 1988

1994. Royal Visitors. Multicoloured.

939	45c. Type **167**	2·00	1·00
940	50c. Princess Alice, 1960	2·00	1·00
941	80c. Prince Philip, 1993	3·00	1·50
942	$1 Prince Charles, 1973	3·00	1·75
943	$2 Queen Elizabeth II, 1994	4·50	5·50
MS944	162×90 mm. Nos. 939/43	14·00	15·00

168 *The Crucifixion*

1994. Easter. Stained-glass Windows. Multicoloured.

945	20c. Type **168**	1·25	60
946	45c. *The Empty Tomb*	1·60	45
947	80c. *The Resurrection*	2·25	90
948	$3 *Risen Christ with Disciples*	5·00	8·50

169 Cameroun Player and Pontiac Silverdome, Detroit

1994. World Cup Football Championship, U.S.A. Multicoloured.

949	20c. Type **169**	1·00	50
950	70c. Argentine player and Foxboro Stadium, Boston	1·75	70
951	$1.80 Italian player and RFK Memorial Stadium, Washington	2·75	3·25
952	$2.40 German player and Soldier Field, Chicago	3·75	4·75
MS953	112×85 mm. $6 American and Colombian players	13·00	14·00

170 *The Nativity* (Gustave Dore)

1994. Christmas. Religious Paintings. Multicoloured.

954	20c. Type **170**	1·00	80
955	30c. *The Wise Men guided by the Star* (Dore)	1·25	80
956	35c. *The Annunciation* (Dore)	1·25	80
957	45c. *Adoration of the Shepherds* (detail) (Poussin)	1·40	80
958	$2.40 *"The Flight into Egypt* (Dore)	5·00	7·25

171 Pair of Zenaida Doves

1995. Easter. Zenaida Doves. Multicoloured.

959	20c. Type **171**	65	40
960	45c. Dove on branch	85	50
961	50c. Guarding nest	90	55
962	$5 With chicks	5·50	7·00

172 Trygve Lie (first Secretary-General) and General Assembly

1995. 50th Anniv of United Nations. Multicoloured.

963	20c. Type **172**	30	30
964	80c. Flag and building showing "50"	60	65
965	$1 Dag Hammarskjold and U Thant (former Secretary-Generals) and U.N. Charter	70	75
966	$5 U.N. Building (vert)	4·00	7·00

173 Anniversary Emblem and Map of Anguilla

1995. 25th Anniv of Caribbean Development Bank. Multicoloured.

967	45c. Type **173**	1·75	2·00
968	$5 Bank building and launches	3·75	4·50

174 Blue Whale

1995. Endangered Species. Whales. Multicoloured.

969	20c. Type **174**	2·50	85
970	45c. Right whale (vert)	2·75	75
971	$1 Sperm whale	3·25	1·75
972	$5 Humpback whale	8·50	9·00

175 Palm Tree

1995. Christmas. Multicoloured.

973	10c. Type **175**	1·00	1·00
974	25c. Balloons and fishes	1·40	60
975	45c. Shells	1·75	60
976	$5 Fishes in shape of Christmas tree	10·00	11·00

176 Deep Water Gorgonia

1996. Corals. Multicoloured.

977	20c. Type **176**	1·75	80
978	80c. Common sea fan	2·75	1·00
979	$5 Venus sea fern	8·00	10·00

177 Running

1996. Olympic Games, Atlanta. Multicoloured.

980	20c. Type **177**	1·00	60
981	80c. Javelin throwing and wheelchair basketball	3·50	1·50
982	$1 High jumping and hurdles	1·50	1·50
983	$3.50 Olympic rings and torch with Greek and American flags	6·00	6·00

178 Siege of Sandy Hill Fort

1996. Bicentenary of the Battle for Anguilla. Multicoloured.

984	60c. Type **178**	1·50	1·25
985	75c. French troops destroying church (horiz)	1·50	1·25
986	$1.50 Naval battle (horiz)	3·25	3·00
987	$4 French troops landing at Rendezvous Bay	4·50	6·00

179 Gooseberry

1997. Fruit. Multicoloured.

988	10c. Type **179**	60	85
989	20c. West Indian cherry	70	40
990	40c. Tamarind	85	30
991	50c. Pomme-surette	90	40
992	60c. Sea almond	1·00	55
993	75c. Sea grape	1·25	85
994	80c. Banana	1·25	85
995	$1 Genip	1·50	1·00
996	$1.10 Coco plum	1·50	1·60
997	$1.25 Pope	2·00	2·25
998	$1.50 Pawpaw	2·00	2·25
999	$2 Sugar apple	2·75	3·25
1000	$3 Soursop	3·50	4·00
1001	$4 Pomegranate	4·50	4·75
1002	$5 Cashew	5·50	6·50
1003	$10 Mango	8·50	9·50

180 West Indian Iguanas hatching

1997. Endangered Species. West Indian Iguanas. Multicoloured.

1004	20c. Type **180**	1·75	1·50
1005	50c. On rock	2·00	1·60
1006	75c. On branch	2·25	2·00
1007	$3 Head of West Indian iguana	3·25	4·00

181 "Juluca, Rainbow Deity"

1997. Ancient Stone Carvings from Fountain Cavern. Multicoloured.

1008	30c. Type **181**	75	35
1009	$1.25 "Lizard with front legs extended"	1·50	1·00
1010	$2.25 "Chief"	2·50	2·75
1011	$2.75 "Jocahu, the Creator"	3·00	3·50

182 Diana, Princess of Wales

1998. Diana, Princess of Wales Commemoration. Multicoloured.

1012	15c. Type **182**	2·00	1·25
1013	$1 Wearing yellow blouse	2·75	1·60
1014	$1.90 Wearing tiara	3·00	3·00
1015	$2.25 Wearing blue short-sleeved Red Cross blouse	3·25	3·25

183 *Treasure Island* (Valarie Alix)

1998. International Arts Festival. Multicoloured.

1016	15c. Type **183**	60	60
1017	30c. *Posing in the Light* (Mel-sadis Fleming) (vert)	60	40
1018	$1 *Pescadores de Anguilla* (Juan Garcia) (vert)	90	80
1019	$1.50 *Fresh Catch* (Verna Hart)	1·25	1·75
1020	$1.90 *The Bell Tower of St. Mary's* (Ricky Racardo Edwards) (vert)	1·50	2·25

184 Roasting Corn-cobs on Fire

1998. Christmas. *Hidden Beauty of Anguilla.* Children's Paintings. Multicoloured.

1021	15c. Type **184**	35	30
1022	$1 Fresh fruit and market stallholder	80	50
1023	$1.50 Underwater scene	1·00	1·25
1024	$3 Cacti and view of sea	1·60	2·50

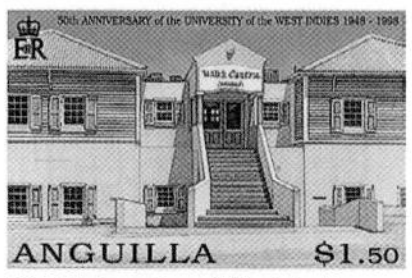

185 University of West Indies Centre, Anguilla

1998. 50th Anniv of University of West Indies. Multicoloured.

1025	$1.50 Type **185**	1·00	1·00
1026	$1.90 Man with torch and University arms	1·40	2·00

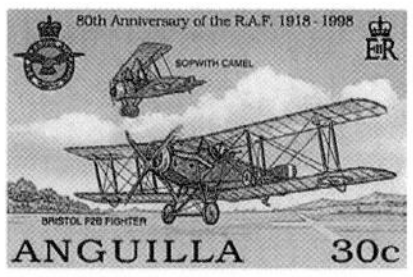

186 Sopwith Camel and Bristol F2B Fighters

1998. 80th Anniv of Royal Air Force. Multicoloured.

1027	30c. Type **186**	1·25	60
1028	$1 Supermarine Spitfire Mk II and Hawker Hurricane Mk I	2·25	90
1029	$1.50 Avro Lancaster	2·50	2·25
1030	$1.90 Panavia Tornado F3 and Harrier GR7	3·00	3·50

187 Saturn 5 Rocket and "Apollo 11" Command Module

1999. 30th Anniv of First Manned Landing on Moon. Multicoloured.

1031	30c. Type **187**	55	35
1032	$1 Astronaut Edwin Aldrin, Lunar Module Eagle and first footprint on Moon	1·00	70
1033	$1.50 Lunar Module leaving Moon's surface	1·00	1·00
1034	$1.90 Recovery of Command Module	1·40	2·00

188 Albena Lake Hodge

1999. Anguillan Heroes and Heroines (1st series). Each black, green and cream.

1035	30c. Type **188**	40	30
1036	$1 Collins O. Hodge	80	65
1037	$1.50 Edwin Wallace Rey	1·00	1·25
1038	$1.90 Walter G. Hodge	1·25	2·00

189 Library and Resource Centre

1999. Modern Architecture. Multicoloured.

1039	30c. Type **189**	45	35
1040	65c. Parliamentary building and Court House	75	70
1041	$1 Caribbean Commercial Bank	1·00	90
1042	$1.50 Police Headquarters	3·00	2·25
1043	$1.90 Post Office	2·00	3·00

190 Beach Barbeque and Fireworks

1999. Christmas and New Millennium. Multicoloured.

1044	30c. Type **190**	70	30
1045	$1 Musicians around globe	1·50	55
1046	$1.50 Family at Christmas dinner	2·25	1·75
1047	$1.90 Celebrations around decorated shrub	2·75	3·50

191 Shoal Bay (East)

2000. Beaches. Multicoloured.

1048	15c. Type **191**	40	60
1049	30c. Maundys Bay	45	30
1050	$1 Rendezvous Bay	90	60
1051	$1.50 Meads Bay	1·25	1·25
1052	$1.90 Little Bay	1·50	2·25
1053	$2 Sandy Ground	1·50	2·25
MS1054	144×144 mm. Nos. 1048/53	5·00	6·00

192 Toy Banjo (Casey Reid)

2000. Easter. Indigenous Toys. Multicoloured.

1055	25c. Type **192**	40	30
1056	30c. Spinning top (Johniela Harrigan)	40	30
1057	$1.50 Catapult (Akeem Rogers)	1·10	1·10
1058	$1.90 Roller (Melisa Mussington)	1·40	1·75
1059	$2.50 Killy Ban (trap) (Casey Reid)	1·75	2·25
MS1060	145×185 mm. 75c. Rag Doll (Jahia Esposito) (vert); $1 Kite (Javed Maynard) (vert); $1.25, Cricket ball (Jevon Lake) (vert); $4 Pond boat (Corvel Flemming) (vert)	4·75	5·50

193 Lanville Harrigan

2000. West Indies Cricket Tour and 100th Test Match at Lord's. Multicoloured.

1061	$2 Type **193**	2·25	2·25
1062	$4 Cardigan Connor	3·25	4·50
MS1063	119×102 mm. $6 Lord's Cricket Ground (horiz)	9·50	9·00

2000. "The Stamp Show 2000" International Stamp Exhibition, London. Beaches. As No. **MS**1054, but with exhibition logo on bottom margin. Multicoloured.

MS1064	144×144 mm. Nos. 1048/53	4·75	6·00

194 Prince William and Royal Family after Trooping the Colour

2000. 18th Birthday of Prince William. Multicoloured.

1065	30c. Type **194**	1·75	50
1066	$1 Prince and Princess of Wales with sons	2·50	85
1067	$1.90 With Prince Charles and Prince Harry	3·00	3·00
1068	$2.25 Skiing with father and brother	3·50	3·50
MS1069	125×95 mm. $8 Prince William as pupil at Eton	8·00	9·00

195 Queen Elizabeth the Queen Mother and Prince William

2000. 100th Birthday of Queen Elizabeth the Queen Mother. Showing different portraits. Multicoloured.

1070	30c. Type **195**	65	40
1071	$1.50 Island scene	1·50	1·00
1072	$1.90 Clarence House	1·75	1·60
1073	$5 Castle of Mey	3·25	4·00

196 *Anguilla Montage* (Weme Caster)

2000. International Arts Festival. Multicoloured.

1074	15c. Type **196**	30	40
1075	30c. *Serenity* (Damien Carty)	35	35
1076	65c. *Inter Island Cargo* (Paula Walden)	55	45
1077	$1.50 *Rainbow City where Spirits find Form* (Fiona Percy)	1·25	1·50
1078	$1.90 *Sailing Silver Seas* (Valerie Carpenter)	1·40	2·00
MS1079	75×100 mm. $7 *Historic Anguilla* (Melsadis Fleming) (42×28 mm)	4·75	6·00

197 Dried Flower Arrangement

2000. Christmas. Flower and Garden Show.

1080	**197**	15c. multicoloured	25	25
1081	-	25c. multicoloured	30	25
1082	-	30c. multicoloured	30	25
1083	-	$1 multicoloured	80	60
1084	-	$1.50 multicoloured	1·25	1·50
1085	-	$1.90 multicoloured	1·50	2·50

DESIGNS: 25c. to $1.90, Different floral arrangements.

198 Winning Primary School Football Team (Bank Sponsorship)

2000. 15th Anniv of National Bank of Anguilla. Multicoloured.

1086	30c. Type **198**	30	25
1087	$1 *De-Chan* (yacht) (Bank sponsorship) (vert)	70	60
1088	$1.50 Bank crest (vert)	1·25	1·50
1089	$1.90 New Bank Headquarters	1·50	2·25

199 Ebenezer Methodist Church in 19th Century

2000. 170th Anniv of Ebenezer Methodist Church.

1090	**199**	30c. brown and black	30	20
1091	-	$1.90 multicoloured	1·50	2·00

DESIGN: $1.90, Church in 2000.

200 Soroptomist Day Care Centre

2001. United Nations Women's Human Rights Campaign. Multicoloured.

1092	25c. Type **200**	30	30
1093	30c. Britannia Idalia Gumbs (Anguillan politician) (vert)	30	30
1094	$2.25 *Caribbean Woman II* (Leisel Renee Jobity) (vert)	1·60	2·25

201 John Paul Jones and U.S.S. *Ranger* (frigate)

2001. 225th Anniv of American War of Independence. Multicoloured.

1095	30c. Type **201**	1·75	80
1096	$1 George Washington and Battle of Yorktown	2·50	1·25
1097	$1.50 Thomas Jefferson and submission of Declaration of Independence to Congress	2·75	3·00
1098	$1.90 John Adams and the signing of the Treaty of Paris	3·00	4·00

202 Bahama Pintail

2001. Anguillian Birds. Multicoloured.

1099	30c. Type **202**	1·00	65
1100	$1 Black-faced grassquit (vert)	1·50	1·00
1101	$1.50 Common noddy	2·00	1·60
1102	$2 Black-necked stilt (vert)	2·50	2·50
1103	$3 Kentish plover ("Snowy Plover")	3·50	4·00
MS1104	124×88 mm. 25c. Snowy egret; 65c. Red-billed tropic bird; $1.35, Greater yellowlegs; $2.25, Sooty tern	6·50	6·50

203 "Children encircling Globe" (Urska Golob)

2001. U.N. Year of Dialogue among Civilisations.

1105	**203**	$1.90 multicoloured	1·60	2·25

204 Triangle

2001. Christmas. Indigenous Musical Instruments. Multicoloured.

1106	15c. Type **204**	25	30
1107	25c. Maracas	35	35
1108	30c. Guiro (vert)	35	35
1109	$1.50 Marimba	1·25	1·25
1110	$1.90 Tambu (hand drum) (vert)	1·50	1·75
1111	$2.50 Bass pan	2·00	2·50
MS1112	110×176 mm. 75c. Banjo (vert); $1 Quatro (vert); $1.25, Ukelele (vert); $3 Cello (vert)	5·00	6·00

205 Sombrero Lighthouse, 1962

2002. Commissioning of New Sombrero Lighthouse. Multicoloured.

1113	30c. Type **205**	1·00	65
1114	$1.50 Old and new lighthouses (horiz)	2·00	1·75
1115	$1.90 New, fully-automated lighthouse, 2001	2·50	3·00

206 Artist, Entertainer and Sportsmen

2002. 20th Anniv of Social Security Board. Multicoloured (except 30c.).

1116	30c. Type **206** (ultramarine and blue)	40	30
1117	75c. Anguillans of all ages	70	65
1118	$2.50 Anguillan workers (horiz)	2·25	3·50

207 H.M.S. *Antrim* (destroyer), 1967

2002. Ships of the Royal Navy. Multicoloured.

1119	30c. Type **207**	1·25	65
1120	50c. H.M.S. *Formidable* (aircraft carrier), 1939	1·75	85
1121	$1.50 H.M.S. *Dreadnought* (battleship), 1906	2·50	2·00
1122	$2 H.M.S. *Warrior* (ironclad), 1860	3·00	4·00
MS1123	102×77 mm. H.M.S. *Ark Royal* (aircraft carrier), 1981 (vert)	8·00	9·00

208 Princess Elizabeth with Prince Charles

2002. Golden Jubilee. Multicoloured.

1124	30c. Type **208**	75	45
1125	$1.50 Queen Elizabeth wearing white coat	1·40	1·10
1126	$1.90 Queen Elizabeth in evening dress	2·00	1·75
1127	$5 Wearing yellow hat and coat	4·75	6·00
MS1128	106×75 mm. $8 Queen Elizabeth sitting at desk	10·00	11·00

209 Valley Health Centre

2002. Centenary of Pan American Health Organization. Multicoloured.

1129	30c. Type **209**	45	40
1130	$1.50 Centenary of PAHO logo	1·25	1·60

210 *Finance* (sloop)

2003. Past Sailing Vessels of Anguilla. Multicoloured.

1131	15c. Type **210**	50	40
1132	30c. *Tiny Gull*	60	30
1133	65c. *Lady Laurel* (schooner)	80	40
1134	75c. *Spitfire* (gaff rigged sloop)	80	40
1135	$1 *Liberator* (schooner)	1·00	50
1136	$1.35 *Excelsior* (schooner)	1·25	70
1137	$1.50 *Rose Millicent*	1·50	1·00
1138	$1.90 *Betsy R.* (sloop)	1·75	1·10
1139	$2 *Sunbeam R.* (sloop)	2·00	1·60
1140	$2.25 *New London*	2·25	2·25
1141	$3 *Ismay* (schooner)	2·75	3·00
1142	$10 *Warspite* (schooner)	7·50	8·50

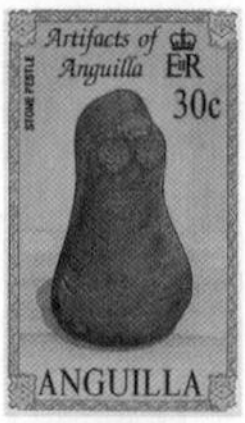

211 Stone Pestle

2003. Artifacts of Anguilla. Multicoloured.

1143	30c. Type **211**	50	25
1144	$1 Frog worked shell ornament	1·00	75
1145	$1.50 Pottery	1·25	1·25
1146	$1.90 Mask worked shell ornament	1·50	2·00

212 Frangipani Beach Club

2003. Hotels of Anguilla. Multicoloured.

1147	75c. Type **212**	70	45
1148	$1 Pimms, Cap Juluca	85	55
1149	$1.35 Cocoloba Beach Resort	1·00	1·00
1150	$1.50 Malliouhana Hotel	1·25	1·10
1151	$1.90 Carmiar Beach Club	1·40	1·40
1152	$3 Covecastles	2·00	3·00

213 *Eudice's Garden* (Eunice Summer)

2004. International Arts Festival. Multicoloured.

1153	15c. Type **213**	50	40
1154	30c. *Hammocks* (Lisa Davenport)	60	30
1155	$1 *Conched Out* (Richard Shaffett)	1·00	70
1156	$1.50 *Islands Rhythms*(Carol Garvin)	1·40	1·25
1157	$1.90 *Party at the Beach* (Jean–Pierre Ballagny)	1·75	1·75
1158	$3 *Shoal Bay before Luis*(Jacqueline Mariethoz)	2·50	3·25

214 Athlete (400 Metres)

2004. Olympic Games, Athens. Multicoloured.

1159	30c. Type **214**	60	30
1160	$1 Laser dinghies (sailing)	1·00	60
1161	$1.50 Gymnastics (rings)	1·40	1·25
1162	$1.90 The Acropolis, Athens, Pierre de Coubertin (founder of modern Olympics) and Dimetrios Vikelas (first IOC President) (horiz)	1·75	2·25

215 Goat

2004. Goats of Anguilla. Multicoloured.

1163	30c. Type **215**	60	30
1164	50c. Black and white goat	70	35
1165	$1 Black and tan goat (vert)	1·00	60
1166	$1.50 Chestnut goat	1·40	1·25
1167	$1.90 Chestnut and white goat (vert)	1·75	2·00
1168	$2.25 Two kids	2·00	2·50

216 Cordless Telephone

2004. Development of the Telephone. Multicoloured.

1169	30c. Type **216**	40	30
1170	$1 Touch tone telephone	1·00	70
1171	$1.50 Cellular phone	1·40	1·40
1172	$1.90 Circular dial telephone (horiz)	1·75	1·75
1173	$3.80 Magneto telephone	3·50	5·00

217 Santa baking in Traditional Rock Oven

2004. Christmas. Multicoloured.

1174	30c. Type **217**	45	25
1175	$1.50 Santa climbing coconut tree	1·40	1·40
1176	$1.90 Santa's string band	1·60	1·60
1177	$3.80 Santa delivering gifts by donkey	3·00	4·50
MS1178	107×76 mm. $8 Santa delivering gifts by boat	6·50	8·00

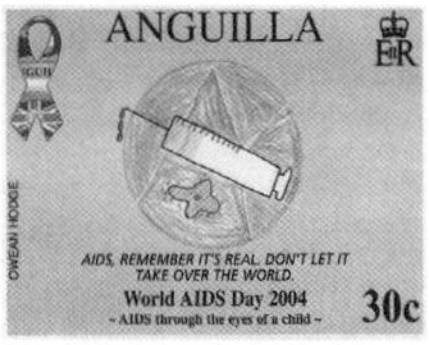

218 *AIDS, Remember it's Real. Don't let it take over the World* (Owean Hodge)

2005. World AIDS Day 2004—"AIDS through the Eyes of a Child". Children's paintings. Multicoloured.

1179	30c. Type **218**	45	30
1180	$1.50 *Arm Yourself against AIDS* (Lydia Fleming)	1·50	1·50
1181	$1.90 *AIDS is Your Concern* (Nina Rodriguez)	1·75	2·00
MS1182	144×144 mm. 15c. Classroom (Kenswick Richardson); 75c. Dancer, Schoolgirl, Teacher, Smoker (Toniquewah Ruan); $1 Girls and Tree (Elizabeth Anne Orchard); $2"*Even I can get AIDS* (Tricia Watty-Beard)	3·00	3·50

219 Arms of Anguilla and Rotary Emblem

2005. Centenary of Rotary International and 25th Anniv of Anguilla Rotary Club. Multicoloured.

1183	30c. Type **219**	40	30
1184	$1 Brown pelican and palm tree (District 7020)	1·25	85
1185	$1.50 Paul Harris (founder)	1·40	1·40
1186	$1.90 Children on slide (School Playground Project)	1·60	2·00

220 Grey Dog

2005. Dogs of Anguilla. Multicoloured.

1187	30c. Type **220**	65	40
1188	$1.50 Black and tan dog with puppy (vert)	1·75	1·40
1189	$1.90 Black and tan dog (vert)	2·00	2·00
1190	$2.25 Tan dog	2·50	2·75

221 Air Anguilla Cessna 402

2006. Early Airlines. Multicoloured.

1191	30c. Type **221**	65	40
1192	40c. LIAT DHC Dash 8	70	55
1193	60c. Winair Foxtrot DHC Twin Otter	1·00	80
1194	$1 Anguilla Airways Piper Aztec	1·50	1·00
1195	$1.50 St. Thomas Air Transport Piper Aztec	2·00	1·75
1196	$1.90 Carib Air Service Piper Aztec	2·25	2·50

222 *Appias drusillia*

2006. Butterflies. Multicoloured.

1197	30c. Type **222**	65	40
1198	$1.50 *Danaus plexippus megalippe*	1·75	1·40
1199	$1.90 *Phoebis sennae*	2·25	2·25
1200	$2.75 *Papilio demoleus*	3·50	4·00
MS1201	126×88 mm. 40c. *Aphrissa statira*; 60c. *Eurema elathea*; $1 *Danaus plexippusmegalippe*; $3 *Agraulis vanillae*	4·75	5·00

223 Soroptimist International Logo

2007. 25th Anniv (2006) of Anguilla Soroptimist Club. Multicoloured.

1202	$1.90 Type **223**	1·75	1·90
1203	$2.75 Alecia Ballin	2·75	3·25

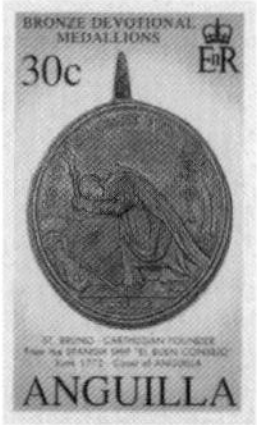

224 St. Bruno (Carthusian founder)

2007. Bronze Devotional Medallions. Designs showing medallions from Spanish ship El Buen Consejo, sunk in 1772 off Anguilla coast. Multicoloured.

1204	30c. Type **224**	40	30
1205	$1.50 Our Lady of Sorrows	1·40	1·40
1206	$1.90 Five Wounds of Jesus	1·60	1·75
1207	$2.75 Virgin and Child	2·50	3·25

225 Hyacinth Carty

2008. 40th Anniv of the Revolution (independence from St. Kitts-Nevis). Multicoloured.

1208	30c. Type **225**	40	30
1209	$1 Edward Duncan	1·00	80
1210	$1.50 Connell Harrigan	1·40	1·40
1211	$1.90 Reverend Leonard Carty	1·75	1·75
1212	$2.25 Jeremiah Gumbs	2·00	2·50
1213	$3.75 Atlin Harrigan	3·50	4·50

226 White-painted House with Gabled Roof and Lean-to

2008. Historical Architecture. Local Houses of the 1930s–1960s. Multicoloured.

1214	30c. Type **226**	40	30
1215	$1 House with gabled roof and lean-to at back	1·00	65
1216	$1.25 House with double hipped roof and flight of steps	1·25	1·00
1217	$1.50 House on seashore with hipped roof	1·50	1·10
1218	$1.90 House with double gabled roof	1·90	1·75
1219	$2.40 House with double hipped roof and verandah	2·50	2·75
1220	$2.75 House with hipped roof and verandah	3·00	3·50
1221	$3.75 House with gabled roof and flight of steps	4·50	5·00

227 Three Legged Pot

2009. Traditional Household Items. Multicoloured.

1222	30c Type **227**	40	30
1223	$1 Mortar and pestle	1·10	70
1224	$1.50 Gas and coal irons	1·60	1·25
1225	$1.90 Oil and gas lamps	2·00	1·75
1226	$2 Coal pots	2·25	2·50
1227	$2.25 Enamel and aluminium utensils (wrongly inscr 'USTENSILS')	3·25	3·50

228 *Tabebuia heterophylla*

2009. Wild Flowers. Multicoloured.

1228	30c Type **228**	55	50
1229	$1 *Argemone mexicana*	1·25	1·00
1230	$1.50 *Catharanthus roseus*	1·60	1·40
1231	$1.90 *Datura stramonium*	2·00	2·00
1232	$2 *Centrosema virginianum*	2·50	2·50
1233	$2.25 *Tetramicra canaliculata*	3·00	3·50

Pt. 6

ANJOUAN

One of the Comoro Is. between Madagascar and the East coast of Africa. Used stamps of Madagascar from 1914 and became part of the Comoro Islands in 1950.

100 centimes = 1 franc.

1892. "Tablet" key-type inscr "SULTANAT D'ANJOUAN".

1	**D**	1c. black on blue	1·40	2·00
2	**D**	2c. brown on buff	2·10	2·30
3	**D**	4c. brown on grey	3·25	3·75
4	**D**	5c. green on green	5·50	7·75
5	**D**	10c. black on lilac	7·75	7·25
14	**D**	10c. red	25·00	33·00
6	**D**	15c. blue	11·00	11·50
15	**D**	15c. grey	13·00	21·00
7	**D**	20c. red on green	12·00	15·00
8	**D**	25c. black on pink	12·00	15·00
16	**D**	25c. blue	16·00	28·00
9	**D**	30c. brown on grey	27·00	30·00
17	**D**	35c. black on yellow	8·25	9·25
10	**D**	40c. red on yellow	32·00	27·00
18	**D**	45c. black on green	£100	£120
11	**D**	50c. red on pink	36·00	48·00
19	**D**	50c. brown on blue	22·00	40·00
12	**D**	75c. brown on orange	33·00	55·00
13	**D**	1f. green	70·00	90·00

1912. Surch in figures.

20A	05 on 2c. brown on buff	2·75	5·50
21A	05 on 4c. brown on grey	1·40	3·00
22A	05 on 15c. blue	1·40	3·00
23A	05 on 20c. red on green	2·30	7·00
24A	05 on 25c. black on pink	1·60	3·50
25A	05 on 30c. brown on grey	2·50	3·00
26A	10 on 40c. red on yellow	1·50	1·80
27A	10 on 45c. black on green	1·40	1·70
28A	10 on 50c. red on pink	2·40	10·50
29A	10 on 75c. brown on orange	3·00	9·00
30A	10 on 1f. green	4·25	8·25

Pt. 6

ANNAM AND TONGKING

Later part of Indo-China and now included in Vietnam

100 centimes = 1 franc.

1888. Stamps of French Colonies, "Commerce" type, surch **A & T** and value in figures.

1	**J**	1 on 2c. brown on yellow	65·00	55·00
2	**J**	1 on 4c. lilac on grey	55·00	37·00
3	**J**	5 on 10c. black on lilac	50·00	50·00

Pt. 1

ANTIGUA

One of the Leeward Is., Br. W. Indies. Used general issues for Leeward Islands, concurrently with Antiguan stamps until 1 July 1956. Ministerial Government introduced on 1 January 1960. Achieved Associated Statehood on 3 March 1967 and Independence within the Commonwealth on 1 November 1981. Nos. 718/21 and 733 onwards are inscribed "Antigua and Barbuda".

1862. 12 pence = 1 shilling; 20 shillings = 1 pound.
1951. 100 cents = 1 West Indian dollar.

1

1862

5	1	1d. mauve	£130	70·00
25	1	1d. red	2·25	3·75
29	1	6d. green	60·00	£120

3

1879

21	3	½d. green	3·75	17·00
22	3	2½d. brown	£190	55·00
27	3	2½d. blue	7·00	14·00
23	3	4d. blue	£275	15·00
28	3	4d. brown	2·25	3·00
30	3	1s. mauve	£160	£140

4

1903

31	4	½d. black and green	3·75	6·50
41	4	½d. green	4·50	4·75
32	4	1d. black and red	10·00	1·25
44	4	1d. red	7·50	3·25
45	4	2d. purple and brown	4·75	32·00
34	4	2½d. black and blue	13·00	20·00
46	4	2½d. blue	21·00	16·00
47	4	3d. green and brown	6·50	19·00
48	4	6d. purple and black	7·50	40·00
49	4	1s. blue and purple	23·00	70·00
50	4	2s. green and violet	£110	£130
39	4	2s.6d. black and purple	27·00	65·00
40	5	5s. green and violet	£110	£150

5

1913. Head of King George V.

51	5	5s. green and violet	95·00	£150

1916. Optd **WAR STAMP**.

53	4	½d. green	1·50	2·50
54	4	1½d. orange	1·00	1·25

8

1921

62	8	½d. green	3·00	50
63	8	1d. red	4·25	50
64	8	1d. violet	6·50	1·50
67	8	1½d. orange	5·50	7·00
68	8	1½d. red	9·00	1·75
69	8	1½d. brown	3·00	60
70	8	2d. grey	4·00	75
72	8	2½d. yellow	2·50	17·00
73	8	2½d. blue	12·00	4·50
74	8	3d. purple on yellow	11·00	8·50
56	8	4d. black and red on yellow	2·25	5·50
75	8	6d. purple	7·00	4·75
57	8	1s. black on green	4·25	9·00
58	8	2s. purple and blue on blue	13·00	28·00
78	8	2s.6d. black and red on blue	48·00	35·00
79	8	3s. green and violet	50·00	£100
80	8	4s. black and red	50·00	75·00
60	8	5s. green and red on yellow	8·50	50·00
61	8	£1 purple and black on red	£250	£350

9 Old Dockyard, English Harbour

10 Government House, St. John's

1932. Tercentenary. Designs with medallion portrait of King George V.

81	9	½d. green	4·50	7·50
82	-	1d. red	6·00	7·50
83	-	1½d. brown	3·75	4·75
84	10	2d. grey	7·50	26·00
85	10	2½d. blue	7·50	8·50
86	10	3d. orange	7·50	12·00
87	-	6d. violet	15·00	12·00
88	-	1s. olive	20·00	32·00
89	-	2s.6d. purple	55·00	75·00
90	-	5s. black and brown	£110	£140

DESIGNS—HORIZ: 6d. to 2s.6d. Nelson's "Victory"; 5s. Sir Thomas Warner's "Conception".

13 Windsor Castle

1935. Silver Jubilee.

91	13	1d. blue and red	3·00	4·00
92	13	1½d. blue and grey	2·75	1·50
93	13	2½d. brown and blue	7·00	1·60
94	13	1s. grey and purple	8·50	17·00

1937. Coronation. As T **2** of Aden.

95	1d. red	70	2·75
96	1½d. brown	60	2·50
97	2½d. blue	2·25	3·00

15 English Harbour

16 Nelson's Dockyard

1938

98	15	½d. green	40	1·25
99	16	1d. red	3·50	2·50
100a	16	1½d. brown	2·75	4·00
101	15	2d. grey	1·00	1·00
102	16	2½d. blue	1·25	80
103	-	3d. orange	1·25	1·00
104	-	6d. violet	4·50	1·25
105	-	1s. black and brown	6·00	2·00
106a	-	2s.6d. purple	35·00	19·00
107	-	5s. olive	15·00	12·00
108	16	10s. mauve	21·00	35·00
109	-	£1 green	42·00	65·00

DESIGNS—HORIZ: 3d., 2s.6d., £1, Fort James. VERT: 6d., 1s., 5s. St. John's Harbour.

1946. Victory. As T **9** of Aden.

110	1½d. brown	30	10
111	3d. orange	30	50

1949. Silver Wedding. As T **10/11** of Aden.

112	2½d. blue	50	2·75
113	5s. green	15·00	12·00

20 Hermes, Globe and Forms of Transport

21 Hemispheres, Jet-powered Vickers Viking Airliner and Steamer

22 Hermes and Globe

23 U.P.U. Monument

1949. 75th Anniv of U.P.U.

114	20	2½d. blue	40	75
115	21	3d. orange	2·00	3·25
116	22	6d. purple	45	3·00
117	23	1s. brown	45	1·25

24 Arms of University

25 Princess Alice

1951. Inauguration of B.W.I. University College.

118	24	3c. black and brown	55	1·75
119	25	12c. black and violet	1·00	2·00

1953. Coronation. As T **13** of Aden.

120	2c. black and green	30	75

27 Martello Tower

1953. Designs as 1938 issues but with portrait of Queen Elizabeth II as in T **27**.

120a	-	½c. brown	40	40
121	15	1c. grey	30	1·75
122	16	2c. green	30	10
123	16	3c. black and yellow	40	20
153	15	4c. red	30	2·25
154	16	5c. black and lilac	20	10
155	-	6c. yellow	60	30
156	27	8c. blue	30	20
157	-	12c. violet	1·25	20
129	-	24c. black and brown	5·00	15
130	27	48c. purple and blue	10·00	2·75
131	-	60c. purple	7·50	80
132a	-	$1.20 olive	3·75	1·00
133	16	$2.40 purple	17·00	12·00
134	-	$4.80 slate	23·00	27·00

DESIGNS—HORIZ: ½, 6, 60c., $4.80, Fort James. VERT: 12, 24c., $1.20, St John's Harbour.

28 Federation Map

1958. Inaug of British Caribbean Federation.

135	28	3c. green	1·25	30
136	28	6c. blue	1·40	2·75
137	28	12c. red	1·60	75

1960. New Constitution. Nos. 123 and 157 optd **COMMEMORATION ANTIGUA CONSTITUTION**.

138	16	3c. black and yellow	15	15
139	-	12c. violet	15	15

30 Nelson's Dockyard and Admiral Nelson

1961. Restoration of Nelson's Dockyard.

140	30	20c. purple and brown	1·60	1·60
141	30	30c. green and blue	1·75	2·25

31 Stamp of 1862 and R.M.S.P. *Solent I* at English Harbour

1962. Stamp Centenary.

142	31	3c. purple and green	90	10
143	31	10c. blue and green	1·00	10
144	31	12c. sepia and green	1·10	10
145	31	50c. brown and green	1·50	2·25

1963. Freedom from Hunger. As T **28** of Aden.

146	12c. green	15	15

33 Red Cross Emblem

1963. Centenary of Red Cross.

147	33	3c. red and black	30	1·00
148	33	12c. red and blue	45	1·25

34 Shakespeare and Memorial Theatre, Stratford-upon-Avon

1964. 400th Birth Anniv of Shakespeare.

164	34	12c. brown	30	10

1965. No. 157 surch **15c.**

165	15c. on 12c. violet	10	10

36 I.T.U. Emblem

1965. Centenary of I.T.U.

166	36	2c. blue and red	25	15
167	36	50c. yellow and blue	75	1·25

37 I.C.Y. Emblem

1965. International Co-operation Year.

168	37	4c. purple and turquoise	20	10
169	37	15c. green and lavender	30	20

38 Sir Winston Churchill, and St. Paul's Cathedral in Wartime

1966. Churchill Commemoration. Designs in black, red and gold with background in colours given.

170	38	½c. blue	10	1·75
171	38	4c. green	65	10
172	38	25c. brown	1·50	45
173	38	35c. violet	1·50	55

39 Queen Elizabeth II and Duke of Edinburgh

1966. Royal Visit.

174	39	6c. black and blue	1·50	1·10
175	39	15c. black and mauve	1·50	1·40

40 Footballer's Legs, Ball and Jules Rimet Cup

1966. World Cup Football Championship.

176	**40**	6c. multicoloured	20	75
177	**40**	35c. multicoloured	60	25

41 W.H.O. Building

1966. Inaug of W.H.O. Headquarters, Geneva.

178	**41**	2c. black, green and blue	20	25
179	**41**	15c. black, purple & brn	1·25	25

42 Nelson's Dockyard

1966

180	**42**	½c. green and blue	10	1·25
181	-	1c. purple and mauve	10	30
182	-	2c. blue and orange	10	20
183a	-	3c. red and black	15	15
184a	-	4c. violet and brown	15	30
185	-	5c. blue and green	10	10
186a	-	6c. orange and purple	15	1·00
187	-	10c. green and red	15	10
188a	-	15c. brown and blue	55	10
189	-	25c. blue and brown	35	20
190a	-	35c. mauve and brown	60	1·00
191a	-	50c. green and black	70	2·25
192	-	75c. blue and ultramarine	4·25	2·50
193b	-	$1 mauve and green	1·25	5·00
194a	-	$2.50 black and mauve	1·50	8·00
195	-	$5 green and violet	12·00	6·50

DESIGNS: 1c. Old Post Office, St John's; 2c. Health Centre; 3c. Teachers' Training College; 4c. Martello Tower, Barbuda; 5c. Ruins of Officers' Quarters, Shirley Heights; 6c. Government House, Barbuda; 10c. Princess Margaret School; 15c. Air terminal building; 25c. General Post Office; 35c. Clarence House; 50c. Government House, St. John's; 75c. Administration building; $1 Court-house, St. John's; $2.50, Magistrates' Court; $5 St. John's Cathedral.

54 "Education"

55 "Science"

56 "Culture"

1966. 20th Anniv of UNESCO.

196	**54**	4c. violet, yellow & orange	20	10
197	**55**	25c. yellow, violet and olive	45	10
198	**56**	$1 black, purple and orange	90	2·25

57 State Flag and Maps

1967. Statehood. Multicoloured.

199	4c. Type **57**	10	10
200	15c. State Flag	10	20
201	25c. Premier's Office and State Flag	10	25
202	35c. As 15c.	15	25

60 Gilbert Memorial Church

1967. Attainment of Autonomy by the Methodist Church.

203	**60**	4c. black and red	10	10
204	-	25c. black and green	15	15
205	-	35c. black and blue	15	15

DESIGNS: 25c. Nathaniel Gilbert's House; 35c. Caribbean and Central American map.

63 Coat of Arms

1967. 300th Anniv of Treaty of Breda and Grant of New Arms.

206	**63**	15c. multicoloured	15	10
207	**63**	35c. multicoloured	15	10

64 *Susan Constant* (settlers' ship)

1967. 300th Anniv of Barbuda Settlement.

208	**64**	4c. blue	45	10
209	-	6c. purple	45	1·25
210	**64**	25c. green	50	20
211	-	35c. black	55	25

DESIGN: 6, 35c. Blaeu's Map of 1665.

66 Tracking Station

1968. N.A.S.A. Apollo Project. Inauguration of Dow Hill Tracking Station.

212	**66**	4c. blue, yellow and black	10	10
213	-	15c. blue, yellow and black	20	10
214	-	25c. blue, yellow and black	20	10
215	-	50c. blue, yellow and black	30	40

DESIGNS: 15c. Antenna and spacecraft taking off; 25c. Spacecraft approaching Moon; 50c. Re-entry of space capsule.

70 Limbo-dancing

1968. Tourism. Multicoloured.

216	½c. Type **70**	10	50
217	15c. Water-skier and bathers	30	10
218	25c. Yachts and beach	30	10
219	35c. Underwater swimming	30	10
220	50c. Type **70**	35	1·25

74 Old Harbour in 1768

1968. Opening of St. John's Deep Water Harbour.

221	**74**	2c. blue and red	10	40
222	-	15c. green and sepia	35	10
223	-	25c. yellow and blue	40	10
224	-	35c. salmon and emerald	50	10
225	**74**	$1 black	90	2·00

DESIGNS: 15c. Old harbour in 1829; 25c. Freighter and chart of new harbour; 35c. New harbour.

78 Parliament Buildings

1969. Tercentenary of Parliament. Multicoloured.

226	4c. Type **78**	10	10
227	15c. Antigua Mace and bearer	20	10
228	25c. House of Representative's Room	20	10
229	50c. Coat of arms and Seal of Antigua	30	1·60

82 Freight Transport

1969. First Anniv of Caribbean Free Trade Area.

230	**82**	4c. black and purple	10	10
231	**82**	15c. black and blue	20	30
232	-	25c. brown, black & ochre	25	30
233	-	35c. chocolate, blk & brn	25	30

DESIGN—VERT: 25, 35c. Crate of cargo.

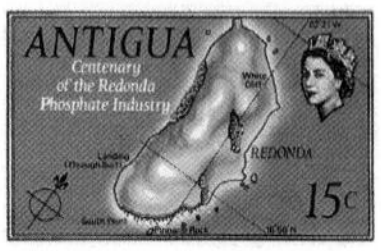

84 Island of Redonda (Chart)

1969. Centenary of Redonda Phosphate Industry. Multicoloured.

249	15c. Type **84**	20	10
250	25c. View of Redonda from the sea	20	10
251	50c. Type **84**	45	75

86 *The Adoration of the Magi* (Marcillat)

1969. Christmas. Stained Glass Windows. Multicoloured.

252	6c. Type **86**	10	10
253	10c. *The Nativity* (unknown German artist, 15th century)	10	10
254	35c. Type **86**	25	10
255	50c. As 10c.	50	40

1970. Surch **20c** and bars.

256	20c. on 25c. (No. 189)	10	10

89 Coat of Arms

1970. Coil Stamps.

257A	**89**	5c. blue	10	40
258A	**89**	10c. green	10	35
259A	**89**	25c. red	20	35

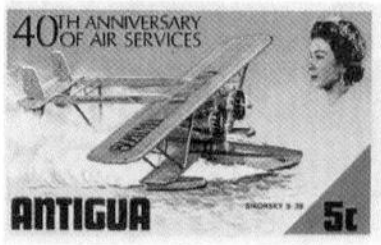

90 Sikorsky S-38 Flying Boat

1970. 40th Anniv of Antiguan Air Services. Multicoloured.

260	5c. Type **90**	50	10
261	20c. Dornier Do-X flying boat	80	10
262	35c. Hawker Siddeley H.S.748	1·00	10
263	50c. Douglas C-124C Globemaster II	1·00	1·50
264	75c. Vickers Super VC-10	1·25	2·00

91 Dickens and Scene from *Nicholas Nickleby*

1970. Death Centenary of Charles Dickens.

265	**91**	5c. bistre, sepia and black	10	10
266	-	20c. turq, sepia & blk	20	10
267	-	35c. blue, sepia and black	30	10
268	-	$1 red, sepia and black	75	80

DESIGNS: All stamps show Dickens and scene from: 20c. "Pickwick Papers"; 35c. "Oliver Twist"; $1 "David Copperfield".

92 Carib Indian and War Canoe

1970. Multicoloured.. Multicoloured..

323	½c. Type **92**	20	50
270	1c. Columbus and *Nina*	30	1·50
271	2c. Sir Thomas Warner's emblem and *Concepcion*	40	3·25
325	3c. Viscount Hood and H.M.S. *Barfleur*	1·00	1·25
273	4c. Sir George Rodney and H.M.S. *Formidable*	40	3·00
274	5c. Nelson and H.M.S. *Boreas*	50	40
275	6c. William IV and H.M.S. *Pegasus*	1·75	4·25
276	10c. *Blackbeard* and pirate ketch	80	20
277	15c. Collingwood and H.M.S. *Pelican*	11·00	1·00
278	20c. Nelson and H.M.S. *Victory*	1·25	40
279	25c. *Solent I* (paddle-steamer)	1·25	40
280	35c. George V (when Prince George) and H.M.S. *Canada* (screw corvette)	2·25	80
281	50c. H.M.S. *Renown* (battle cruiser)	4·00	6·00
331	75c. *Federal Maple* (freighter)	7·50	3·00
332	$1 *Sol Quest* (yacht) and class emblem	3·00	1·75
333	$2.50 H.M.S. *London* (destroyer)	2·75	6·50
285	$5 *Pathfinder* (tug)	2·50	6·00

93 *The Small Passion* (detail) (Durer)

1970. Christmas.

286	**93**	3c. black and blue	10	10
287	-	10c. purple and pink	10	10
288	**93**	35c. black and red	30	10
289	-	50c. black and lilac	45	50

DESIGN: 10, 50c. *Adoration of the Magi* (detail) (Durer).

94 4th King's Own Regiment, 1759

1970. Military Uniforms (1st series). Multicoloured.

290	½c. Type **94**	10	10
291	10c. 4th West India Regiment, 1804	65	10
292	20c. 60th Regiment, The Royal American, 1809	1·00	10
293	35c. 93rd Regiment, Sutherland Highlanders, 1826–34	1·25	10
294	75c. 3rd West India Regiment, 1851	1·75	2·00
MS295	128×164 mm. Nos. 290/4	5·50	11·00

See also Nos. 303/8, 313/18, 353/8 and 380/5.

95 Market Woman casting Vote

1971. 20th Anniv of Adult Suffrage.

296	**95**	5c. brown	10	10
297	-	20c. olive	10	10
298	-	35c. purple	10	10
299	-	50c. blue	15	30

DESIGNS: People voting: 20c. Executive; 35c. Housewife; 50c. Artisan.

96 *The Last Supper*

1971. Easter. Works by Durer.

300	**96**	5c. black grey and red	10	10
301	-	35c. black, grey and violet	10	10
302	-	75c. black, grey and gold	20	30

DESIGNS: 35c. *The Crucifixion*; 75c. *The Resurrection*.

1971. Military Uniforms (2nd series). As T **94**. Multicoloured.

303	½c. Private, 12th Regiment, The Suffolk (1704)	10	10
304	10c. Grenadier, 38th Regiment, South Staffordshire (1751)	35	10
305	20c. Light Company, 5th Regiment, Royal Northumberland Fusiliers (1778)	50	10
306	35c. Private, 48th Regiment, The Northamptonshire (1793)	60	10
307	75c. Private, 15th Regiment, East Yorks (1805)	1·00	3·00
MS308	127×144 mm. Nos. 303/7	4·50	6·50

97 *Madonna and Child* (detail, Veronese)

1971. Christmas. Multicoloured.

309	3c. Type **97**	10	10
310	5c. *Adoration of the Shepherds* (detail, Veronese)	10	10
311	35c. Type **97**	25	10
312	50c. As 5c.	40	30

1972. Military Uniforms (3rd series). As T **94**. Multicoloured.

313	½c. Battalion Company Officer, 25th Foot, 1815	10	10
314	10c. Sergeant, 14th Foot, 1837	70	10
315	20c. Private, 67th Foot, 1853	1·25	15
316	35c. Officer, Royal Artillery, 1854	1·40	20
317	75c. Private, 29th Foot, 1870	1·75	4·00
MS318	125×141 mm. Nos. 313/17	7·00	8·50

98 Reticulated Cowrie Helmet

1972. Shells. Multicoloured.

319	3c. Type **98**	50	10
320	5c. Measled cowrie	50	10
321	35c. West Indian fighting conch	1·40	15
322	50c. Hawk-wing conch	1·60	3·00

99 St. John's Cathedral, Side View

1972. Christmas and 125th Anniv of St. John's Cathedral. Multicoloured.

335	35c. Type **99**	20	10
336	50c. Cathedral interior	25	25
337	75c. St. John's Cathedral	30	60
MS338	165×102 mm. Nos. 335/7	65	1·00

1972. Royal Silver Wedding. As T **52** of Ascension, but with floral background.

339	20c. blue	15	15
340	35c. blue	15	15

101 Batsman and Map

1972. 50th Anniv of Rising Sun Cricket Club. Multicoloured.

341	5c. Type **101**	55	15
342	35c. Batsman and wicket-keeper	65	10
343	$1 Club badge	1·00	2·25
MS344	88×130 mm. Nos. 341/3	3·25	7·50

102 Yacht and Map

1972. Inauguration of Antigua and Barbuda Tourist Office in New York. Multicoloured.

345	35c. Type **102**	15	10
346	50c. Yachts	20	15
347	75c. St. John's G.P.O.	25	25
348	$1 Statue of Liberty	25	25
MS349	100×94 mm. Nos. 346, 348	75	1·25

103 "Episcopal Coat of Arms"

1973. Easter. Multicoloured.

350	**103**	5c. Type **103**	10	10
351	-	35c. "The Crucifixion"	15	10
352	-	75c. "Arms of 1st Bishop of Antigua"	25	30

Nos. 350/2 show different stained-glass windows from St. John's Cathedral.

1973. Military Uniforms (4th series). As T **94**. Multicoloured.

353	½c. Private, Zachariah Tiffin's Regiment of Foot, 1701	10	10
354	10c. Private, 63rd Regiment of Foot, 1759	40	10
355	20c. Light Company Officer, 35th Regiment of Foot, 1828	50	15
356	35c. Private, 2nd West India Regiment, 1853	65	15
357	75c. Sergeant, 49th Regiment, 1858	1·00	1·25
MS358	127×145 mm. Nos. 353/7	3·75	3·25

104 Butterfly Costumes

1973. Carnival. Multicoloured.

359	5c. Type **104**	10	10
360	20c. Carnival street scene	15	10
361	35c. Carnival troupe	20	10
362	75c. Carnival Queen	30	30
MS363	134×95 mm. Nos. 359/62	65	1·00

105 *Virgin of the Milk Porridge* (Gerard David)

1973. Christmas. Multicoloured.

364	3c. Type **105**	10	10
365	5c. *Adoration of the Magi* (Stomer)	10	10
366	20c. *The Granducal Madonna* (Raphael)	15	10
367	35c. *Nativity with God the Father and Holy Ghost* (Battista)	20	10
368	$1 *Madonna and Child* (Murillo)	40	60
MS369	130×128 mm. Nos. 364/8	1·10	1·75

106 Princess Anne and Captain Mark Phillips

1973. Royal Wedding.

370	**106**	35c. multicoloured	10	10
371	-	$2 multicoloured	25	25
MS372		78×100 mm. Nos. 370/1	50	40

The $2 is as Type **106** but has a different border.

1973. Nos. 370/1 optd **HONEYMOON VISIT DECEMBER 16TH 1973**.

373	**106**	35c. multicoloured	15	10
374	-	$2 multicoloured	30	30
MS375		78×100 mm. Nos. 373/4	55	55

108 Coat of Arms of Antigua and University

1974. 25th Anniv of University of West Indies. Multicoloured.

376	5c. Type **108**	15	10
377	20c. Extra-mural art	20	10
378	35c. Antigua campus	20	10
379	75c. Antigua chancellor	25	35

1974. Military Uniforms (5th series). As T **94**. Multicoloured.

380	½c. Officer, 59th Foot, 1797	10	10
381	10c. Gunner, Royal Artillery, 1800	35	10
382	20c. Private, 1st West India Regiment, 1830	50	10
383	35c. Officer, 92nd Foot, 1843	60	10
384	75c. Private, 23rd Foot, 1846	75	2·25
MS385	125×145 mm. Nos. 380/4	2·25	2·50

109 English Postman, Mailcoach and Westland Dragonfly Helicopter

1974. Centenary of U.P.U. Multicoloured.

386	½c. Type **109**	10	20
387	1c. Bellman, mail steamer *Orinoco* and satellite	10	20
388	2c. Train guard, post-bus and hydrofoil	10	20
389	5c. Swiss messenger, Wells Fargo coach and Concorde	60	50
390	20c. Postilion, Japanese post-men and carrier pigeon	35	10
391	35c. Antiguan postman, Sikorsky S-88 flying boat and tracking station	45	15
392	$1 Medieval courier, American express train and Boeing 747-100	1·75	2·00
MS393	141×161 mm. Nos. 386/92	3·00	2·50

On the ½c. English is spelt "Enlish" and on the 2c. Postal is spelt "Fostal".

110 Traditional Player

1974. Antiguan Steel Bands.

394	**110**	5c. dp red, red and black	10	10
395	-	20c. brown, lt brn & blk	10	10
396	-	35c. lt green, green & blk	10	10
397	-	75c. blue, dp blue & blk	20	1·10
MS398		115×108 mm. Nos. 394/7	35	1·25

DESIGNS—HORIZ: 20c. Traditional band; 35c. Modern band. VERT: 75c. Modern player.

111 Footballers

1974. World Cup Football Championships.

399	**111**	5c. multicoloured	10	10
400	-	35c. multicoloured	15	10
401	-	75c. multicoloured	30	30
402	-	$1 multicoloured	35	40
MS403		135×130 mm. Nos. 399/402	85	90

Nos. 400/2 show various footballing designs similar to Type **111**.

1974. Earthquake Relief Fund. Nos. 400/2 and 397 optd or surch **EARTHQUAKE RELIEF**.

404	35c. multicoloured	20	10
405	75c. multicoloured	30	30
406	$1 multicoloured	40	40
407	$5 on 75c. deep blue, blue and black	1·25	2·25

113 Churchill as Schoolboy and School College Building, Harrow

1974. Birth Centenary of Sir Winston Churchill. Multicoloured.

408	5c. Type **113**	15	10
409	35c. Churchill and St. Paul's Cathedral	20	10
410	75c. Coat of arms and catafalque	30	65
411	$1 Churchill, "reward" notice and South African escape route	45	1·00
MS412	107×82 mm. Nos. 408/11	1·00	1·50

114 *Madonna of the Trees* (Bellini)

1974. Christmas. *Madonna and Child* paintings by named artists. Multicoloured.

413	½c. Type **114**	10	10
414	1c. Raphael	10	10
415	2c. Van der Weyden	10	10
416	3c. Giorgione	10	10
417	5c. Mantegna	10	10
418	20c. Vivarini	20	10
419	35c. Montagna	30	10
420	75c. Lorenzo Costa	55	1·10
MS421	139×126 mm. Nos. 413/20	1·00	1·40

1975. Nos. 390/2 and 331 surch.

422	50c. on 20c. multicoloured	1·25	2·00
423	$2.50 on 35c. multicoloured	2·00	5·50
424	$5 on $1 multicoloured	6·50	7·00
425	$10 on 75c. multicoloured	2·00	7·50

116 Carib War Canoe, English Harbour, 1300

1975. Nelson's Dockyard. Multicoloured.

427	5c. Type **116**	20	10
428	15c. Ship of the line, English Harbour, 1770	80	15
429	35c. H.M.S. *Boreas* at anchor, and Lord Nelson, 1787	1·00	15
430	50c. Yachts during "Sailing Week", 1974	1·00	1·50
431	$1 Yacht Anchorage, Old Dockyard, 1970	1·00	2·25
MS432	130×134 mm. As Nos. 427/31, but in larger format, 43×28 mm	3·00	2·00

117 Lady of the Valley Church

1975. Antiguan Churches. Multicoloured.

433	5c. Type **117**	10	10
434	20c. Gilbert Memorial	10	10
435	35c. Grace Hill Moravian	15	10
436	50c. St. Phillips	20	20
437	$1 Ebenezer Methodist	35	50
MS438	91×101 mm. Nos. 435/7	65	1·25

118 Map of 1721 and Sextant of 1640

1975. Maps of Antigua. Multicoloured.

439	5c. Type **118**	30	15
440	20c. Map of 1775 and galleon	55	15
441	35c. Maps of 1775 and 1955	70	15
442	$1 1973 maps of Antigua and English Harbour	1·40	2·25
MS443	130×89 mm. Nos. 439/42	3·00	3·25

119 Scout Bugler

1975. World Scout Jamboree, Norway. Multicoloured.

444	15c. Type **119**	25	15
445	20c. Scouts in camp	30	15
446	35c. "Lord Baden-Powell" (D. Jagger)	50	20
447	$2 Scout dancers from Dahomey	1·50	2·25
MS448	145×107 mm. Nos. 444/7	2·75	3·50

120 *Eurema elathea*

1975. Butterflies. Multicoloured.

449	½c. Type **120**	10	30
450	1c. *Danaus plexippus*	10	30
451	2c. *Phoebis philea*	15	30
452	5c. *Hypolimnas misippus*	30	10
453	20c. *Eurema proterpia*	1·00	40
454	35c. *Battus polydamas*	1·50	50
455	$2 *Cynthia cardui*	4·25	9·00
MS456	147×94 mm. Nos. 452/5	6·00	11·00

No. 452 is incorrectly captioned "Marpesia petreus thetys".

121 *Madonna and Child* (Correggio)

1975. Christmas. *Madonna and Child* paintings by artists named. Multicoloured.

457	½c. Type **121**	10	10
458	1c. El Greco	10	10
459	2c. Durer	10	10
460	3c. Antonello	10	10
461	5c. Bellini	10	10
462	10c. Durer (different)	10	10
463	35c. Bellini (different)	40	10
464	$2 Durer (different again)	1·00	1·00
MS465	138×119 mm. Nos. 461/4	1·50	1·60

122 Vivian Richards

1975. World Cricket Cup Winners. Multicoloured.

466	5c. Type **122**	1·25	20
467	35c. Andy Roberts	2·25	60
468	$2 West Indies team (horiz)	4·25	8·00

123 Antillean Crested Hummingbird

1976. Multicoloured

469A	½c. Type **123**	40	50
470A	1c. Imperial amazon ("Imperial Parrot")	1·40	50
471A	2c. Zenaida dove	1·40	50
472A	3c. Loggerhead kingbird	1·40	60
473A	4c. Red-necked pigeon	1·40	2·25
474A	5c. Rufous-throated solitaire	2·00	10
475A	6c. Orchid tree	30	2·00
476A	10c. Bougainvillea	30	10
477A	15c. Geiger tree	35	10
478A	20c. Flamboyant	35	35
479A	25c. Hibiscus	40	15
480A	35c. Flame of the wood	40	40
481A	50c. Cannon at Fort James	55	60
482A	75c. Premier's Office	60	2·00
483A	$1 Potworks Dam	75	1·00
484A	$2.50 Diamond irrigation scheme (44×28 mm)	1·00	5·00
485B	$5 Government House (44×28 mm)	1·50	7·50
486A	$10 Coolidge International Airport (44×28 mm)	3·75	8·00

124 Privates, Clark's Illinois Regiment

1976. Bicentenary of American Revolution. Multicoloured.

487	½c. Type **124**	10	10
488	1c. Rifleman, Pennsylvania Militia	10	10
489	2c. Powder horn	10	10
490	5c. Water bottle	10	10
491	35c. American flags	40	10
492	$1 *Montgomery* (American brig)	75	30
493	$5 "Ranger" (privateer sloop)	1·50	1·75
MS494	71×84 mm. $2.50, Congress flag	1·00	1·40

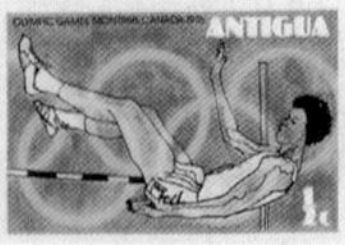

125 High Jump

1976. Olympic Games, Montreal.

495	125	½c. brown, yellow & black	10	10
496	-	1c. violet, blue and black	10	10
497	-	2c. green and black	10	10
498	-	15c. blue and black	15	10
499	-	30c. brown, yell & blk	20	15
500	-	$1 orange, red and black	40	40
501	-	$2 red and black	60	80
MS502		88×138 mm. Nos. 498/501	1·75	1·25

DESIGNS: 1c. Boxing; 2c. Pole vault; 15c. Swimming; 30c. Running; $1 Cycling; $2 Shot put.

126 Water Skiing

1976. Water Sports. Multicoloured.

503	½c. Type **126**	10	10
504	1c. Sailing	10	10
505	2c. Snorkeling	10	10
506	20c. Deep sea fishing	50	10
507	50c. Scuba diving	75	35
508	$2 Swimming	1·25	1·25
MS509	89×114 mm. Nos. 506/8	1·75	1·75

127 French Angelfish

1976. Fish. Multicoloured.

510	15c. Type **127**	40	15
511	30c. Yellow-finned grouper	55	30
512	50c. Yellow-tailed snapper	70	50
513	90c. Shy hamlet	90	1·50

128 The Annunciation

1976. Christmas. Multicoloured.

514	8c. Type **128**	10	10
515	10c. The Holy Family	10	10
516	15c. The Magi	10	10
517	50c. The Shepherds	20	25
518	$1 Epiphany scene	30	50

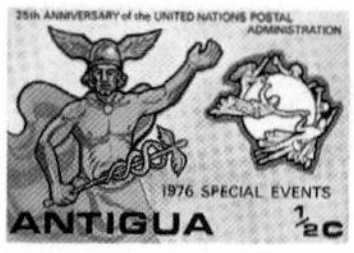

129 Mercury and U.P.U. Emblem

1976. Special Events, 1976. Multicoloured.

519	½c. Type **129**	10	10
520	1c. Alfred Nobel	10	10
521	10c. Space satellite	30	10
522	50c. Viv Richards and Andy Roberts	3·50	1·75
523	$1 Bell and telephones	1·00	2·00
524	$2 Yacht *Freelance*	2·25	4·50
MS525	127×101 mm. Nos. 521/4	7·50	13·00

130 Royal Family

1977. Silver Jubilee. Multicoloured. (a) Perf.

526	10c. Type **130**	10	10
527	30c. Royal Visit, 1966	10	10
528	50c. The Queen enthroned	15	15
529	90c. The Queen after Coronation	15	25
530	$2.50 Queen and Prince Charles	30	55
MS531	116×78 mm. $5 Queen and Prince Philip	65	85

(b) Roul×imperf. Self-adhesive.

532	50c. As 90c.	35	75
533	$5 The Queen and Prince Philip	2·00	3·75

Nos. 532/3 come from booklets.

131 Making Camp

1977. Caribbean Scout Jamboree, Jamaica. Multicoloured.

534	½c. Type **131**	10	10
535	1c. Hiking	10	10
536	2c. Rock-climbing	10	10
537	10c. Cutting logs	15	10
538	30c. Map and sign reading	40	10
539	50c. First aid	65	25
540	$2 Rafting	1·25	2·50
MS541	127×114 mm. Nos. 538/40	3·00	4·00

132 Carnival Costume

1977. 21st Anniv of Carnival. Multicoloured.

542	10c. Type **132**	10	10
543	30c. Carnival Queen	25	10
544	50c. Butterfly costume	30	15
545	90c. Queen of the band	40	25
546	$1 Calypso King and Queen	40	30
MS547	140×120 mm. Nos. 542/6	1·10	1·60

1977. Royal Visit. Nos. 526/30 optd **ROYAL VISIT 28TH OCTOBER 1977**.

548	10c. Type **130**	10	10
549	30c. Royal Visit, 1966	15	10
550	50c. The Queen enthroned	20	10
551	90c. The Queen after Coronation	30	20
552	$2.50 Queen and Prince Charles	50	35
MS553	116×178 mm. $5 Queen and Prince Philip	1·00	1·00

134 *Virgin and Child Enthroned* (Tura)

1977. Christmas. Paintings by artists listed. Multicoloured.

554	½c. Type **134**	10	20
555	1c. Crivelli	10	20
556	2c. Lotto	10	20
557	8c. Pontormo	15	10
558	10c. Tura (different)	15	10
559	25c. Lotto (different)	30	10
560	$2 Crivelli (different)	85	1·00
MS561	144×118 mm. Nos. 557/60	1·75	2·75

135 Pineapple

1977. Tenth Anniv of Statehood. Multicoloured.

562	10c. Type **135**	10	10
563	15c. State flag	60	20
564	50c. Police band	2·50	80
565	90c. Premier V. C. Bird	55	80
566	$2 State Coat of Arms	90	2·00
MS567	129×99 mm. Nos. 563/6	3·50	3·00

136 Wright Glider III, 1902

1978. 75th Anniv of Powered Flight. Multicoloured.

568	½c. Type **136**	10	10
569	1c. Wright Flyer I, 1903	10	10
570	2c. Launch system and engine	10	10
571	10c. Orville Wright (vert)	30	10
572	50c. Wright Flyer III, 1905	60	15
573	90c. Wilbur Wright (vert)	80	30
574	$2 Wright Type B, 1910	1·00	80
MS575	90×75 mm. $2.50, Wright Flyer I on launch system	1·25	2·75

137 Sunfish Regatta

1978. Sailing Week. Multicoloured.

576	10c. Type **137**	20	10
577	50c. Fishing and work boat race	35	20
578	90c. Curtain Bluff race	60	35

579	$2 Power boat rally	1·10	1·25
MS580	110×77 mm. $2.50, Guadeloupe–Antigua race	1·50	1·75

138 Queen Elizabeth and Prince Philip

1978. 25th Anniv of Coronation. Multicoloured. (a) Perf.

581	10c. Type **138**	10	10
582	30c. Crowning	10	10
583	50c. Coronation procession	15	10
584	90c. Queen seated in St. Edward's Chair	20	15
585	$2.50 Queen wearing Imperial State Crown	40	40
MS586	114×104 mm. $5 Queen and Prince Philip	80	80

(b) Roulximperf. Self-adhesive. Horiz designs as Type **138**.

587	25c. Glass Coach	15	30
588	50c. Irish State Coach	25	50
589	$5 Coronation Coach	1·75	3·00

Nos. 587/9 come from booklets.

140 Player running with Ball

1978. World Cup Football Championship, Argentina. Multicoloured.

590	10c. Type **140**	15	10
591	15c. Players in front of goal	15	10
592	$3 Referee and player	1·50	1·75
MS593	126×88 mm. 25c. Player crouching with ball; 30c. Players heading ball; 50c. Players running with ball; $2 Goalkeeper diving. All horiz	3·25	2·50

141 Petrea

1978. Flowers. Multicoloured.

594	25c. Type **141**	20	10
595	50c. Sunflower	30	20
596	90c. Frangipani	50	30
597	$2 Passion flower	90	2·00
MS598	118×85 mm. $2.50, Hibiscus	1·40	1·60

142 *St. Ildefonso receiving the Chasuble from the Virgin* (Rubens)

1978. Christmas. Multicoloured.

599	8c. Type **142**	10	10
600	25c. *The Flight of St. Barbara* (Rubens)	20	10
601	$2 *Madonna and Child, with St. Joseph, John the Baptist and Donor*	65	55
MS602	170×113 mm. $4 *The Annunciation* (Rubens)	1·25	1·50

The painting shown on No. 601 is incorrectly attributed to Rubens on the stamp. The artist was Sebastiano del Piombo.

143 1d. Stamp of 1863

1979. Death Centenary of Sir Rowland Hill. Multicoloured.

603	25c. Type **143**	10	10
604	50c. 1840 Penny Black	20	15
605	$1 Mail coach and woman posting letter, c. 1840	30	20
606	$2 Modern transport	1·10	60
MS607	108×82 mm. $2.50, Sir Rowland Hill	80	90

144 *The Deposition from the Cross* (painting)

1979. Easter. Works by Durer.

608	**144** 10c. multicoloured	10	10
609	- 50c. multicoloured	35	20
610	- $4 black, mauve and yellow	1·00	90
MS611	– 114×99 mm. $2.50, multicoloured	80	80

DESIGNS: 50c., $2.50, *Christ on the Cross–The Passion* (wood engravings) (both different); $4 *Man of Sorrows with Hands Raised* (wood engraving).

145 Toy Yacht and Child's Hand

1979. International Year of the Child. Multicoloured.

612	25c. Type **145**	10	10
613	50c. Rocket	25	15
614	90c. Car	40	25
615	$2 Toy train	1·00	90
MS616	80×112 mm. $5 Aeroplane	1·10	1·10

Nos. 612/16 also show the hands of children of different races.

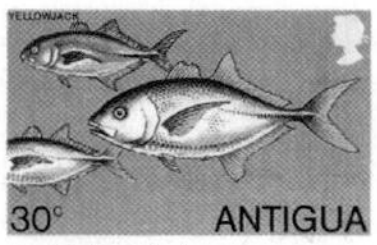

146 Yellow Jack

1979. Fish. Multicoloured.

617	30c. Type **146**	35	15
618	50c. Blue-finned tuna	40	25
619	90c. Sailfish	60	40
620	$3 Wahoo	1·50	1·75
MS621	122×75 mm. $2.50, Great barracuda	1·50	1·40

147 Cook's Birthplace, Marton

1979. Death Bicentenary of Captain Cook. Multicoloured.

622	25c. Type **147**	65	25
623	50c. H.M.S. *Endeavour*	1·25	60
624	90c. Marine chronometer	75	80
625	$3 Landing at Botany Bay	1·75	3·00
MS626	110×85 mm. $2.50, H.M.S. *Resolution*	2·25	1·50

148 The Holy Family

1979. Christmas. Multicoloured.

627	8c. Type **148**	10	10
628	25c. Virgin and Child on ass	15	10
629	50c. Shepherd and star	25	35
630	$4 Wise Men with gifts	85	2·50
MS631	113×94 mm. $3 Angel with trumpet	1·00	1·50

149 Javelin Throwing

1980. Olympic Games, Moscow. Multicoloured.

632	10c. Type **149**	20	10
633	25c. Running	20	10
634	$1 Pole vault	50	50
635	$2 Hurdles	70	1·75
MS636	127×96 mm. $3 Boxing (horiz)	80	90

150 Mickey Mouse and Airplane

1980. International Year of the Child. Walt Disney Cartoon Characters. Multicoloured.

637	½c. Type **150**	10	10
638	1c. Donald Duck driving car (vert)	10	10
639	2c. Goofy driving taxi	10	10
640	3c. Mickey and Minnie Mouse on motorcycle	10	10
641	4c. Huey, Dewey and Louie on a bicycle for three	10	10
642	5c. Grandma Duck and truck of roosters	10	10
643	10c. Mickey Mouse in jeep (vert)	10	10
644	$1 Chip and Dale in yacht	2·00	2·00
645	$4 Donald Duck riding toy train (vert)	4·00	6·50
MS646	101×127 mm. $2.50, Goofy flying biplane	4·50	3·25

1980. "London 1980" International Stamp Exhibition. Nos. 603/6 optd **LONDON 1980**.

647	25c. Type **143**	25	15
648	50c. Penny Black	35	35
649	$1 Stage-coach and woman posting letter, c. 1840	60	70
650	$2 Modern mail transport	3·25	3·00

152 *David* (statue, Donatello)

1980. Famous Works of Art. Multicoloured.

651	10c. Type **152**	10	10
652	30c. *The Birth of Venus* (painting, Botticelli) (horiz)	30	15
653	50c. *Reclining Couple* (sarcophagus), Cerveteri (horiz)	40	40
654	90c. *The Garden of Earthly Delights* (painting by Bosch) (horiz)	55	65
655	$1 *Portinari Altarpiece* (painting, van der Goes) (horiz)	65	75
656	$4 *Eleanora of Toledo and her Son, Giovanni de'Medici* (painting, Bronzino)	1·75	3·00
MS657	99×124 mm. $5 *The Holy Family* (painting, Rembrandt)	2·50	1·75

153 Anniversary Emblem and Headquarters, U.S.A.

1980. 75th Anniv of Rotary International. Multicoloured.

658	30c. Type **153**	30	30
659	50c. Rotary anniversary emblem and Antigua Rotary Club banner	40	50
660	90c. Map of Antigua and Rotary emblem	60	70
661	$3 Paul P. Harris (founder) and Rotary emblem	2·00	3·50
MS662	102×78 mm. $5 Antiguan flags and Rotary emblems	1·25	2·00

154 Queen Elizabeth the Queen Mother

1980. 80th Birthday of The Queen Mother.

663	**154** 10c. multicoloured	40	10
664	**154** $2.50 multicoloured	1·00	1·75
MS665	68×90 mm. As T **154**. $3 multicoloured	1·40	2·25

155 Ringed Kingfisher

1980. Birds. Multicoloured.

666	10c. Type **155**	70	30
667	30c. Plain pigeon	1·00	50
668	$1 Green-throated carib	1·50	2·00
669	$2 Black-necked stilt	2·00	4·00
MS670	73×73 mm. $2.50, Roseate tern	7·00	6·00

1980. Christmas. Walt Disney's "Sleeping Beauty". As T **150**. Multicoloured.

671	½c. The Bad Fairy with her raven	10	10
672	1c. The good fairies	10	10
673	2c. Aurora	10	10
674	4c. Aurora pricks her finger	10	10
675	8c. The prince	10	10
676	10c. The prince fights the dragon	15	10
677	25c. The prince awakens Aurora with a kiss	20	20
678	$2 The prince and Aurora's betrothal	2·25	2·25
679	$2.50 The prince and princess	2·50	2·50
MS680	126×101 mm. $4 multicoloured (vert)	5·00	3·25

156 Diesel Locomotive No. 15

1981. Sugar Cane Railway Locomotives. Multicoloured.

681	25c. Type **156**	15	15
682	50c. Narrow-gauge steam locomotive	30	30
683	90c. Diesel locomotives Nos. 1 and 10	55	60
684	$3 Steam locomotive hauling sugar cane	2·00	2·25
MS685	82×111 mm. $2.50, Antiguan sugar factory, railway yard and sheds	1·75	1·75

1981. Independence. Nos. 475/6 and 478/86 optd **"INDEPENDENCE 1981"**.

686B	6c. Orchid tree	10	50
687B	10c. Bougainvillea	10	10
688B	20c. Flamboyant	10	10
689B	25c. Hibiscus	15	15
690B	35c. Flame of the wood	20	20
691B	50c. Cannon at Fort James	35	45
692B	75c. Premier's Office	40	60
693B	$1 Potworks Dam	55	75

694B	$2.50 Irrigation scheme, Diamond Estate	75	2·00
695B	$5 Government House	1·40	3·50
696B	$10 Coolidge International Airport	3·25	6·00

158 *Pipes of Pan*

1981. Birth Centenary of Picasso. Multicoloured.

697	10c. Type **158**	10	10
698	50c. *Seated Harlequin*	30	30
699	90c. *Paulo as Harlequin*	55	55
700	$4 *Mother and Child*	2·00	2·00
MS701	115×140 mm. $5 *Three Musicians* (detail)	1·75	2·75

159 Prince Charles and Lady Diana Spencer

1981. Royal Wedding (1st issue). Multicoloured.

702	25c. Type **159**	10	10
703	50c. Glamis Castle	10	10
704	$4 Prince Charles skiing	80	80
MS705	96×82 mm. $5 Glass coach	80	80

160 Prince of Wales at Investiture, 1969

1981. Royal Wedding (2nd issue). Multicoloured. Roulximperf. Self-adhesive.

706	25c. Type **160**	15	25
707	25c. Prince Charles as baby, 1948	15	25
708	$1 Prince Charles at R.A.F. College, Cranwell, 1971	25	50
709	$1 Prince Charles attending Hill House School, 1956	25	50
710	$2 Prince Charles and Lady Diana Spencer	50	75
711	$2 Prince Charles at Trinity College, 1967	50	75
712	$5 Prince Charles and Lady Diana (different)	1·00	1·50

161 Irene Joshua (founder)

1981. 50th Anniv of Antigua Girl Guide Movement. Multicoloured.

713	10c. Type **161**	15	10
714	50c. Campfire sing-song	45	35
715	90c. Sailing	75	65
716	$2.50 Animal tending	1·50	2·00
MS717	110×85 mm. $5 Raising the flag	4·50	3·00

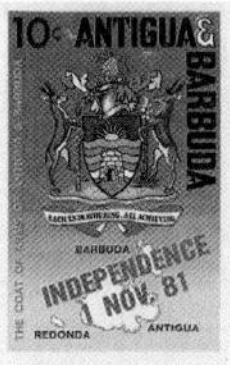

162 Antigua and Barbuda Coat of Arms

1981. Independence. Multicoloured.

718	10c. Type **162**	25	10
719	50c. Pineapple, with Antigua and Barbuda flag and map	2·00	60
720	90c. Prime Minister Vere Bird	55	55
721	$2.50 St. John's Cathedral (38×25 mm)	1·50	3·50
MS722	105×79 mm. $5 Map of Antigua and Barbuda (42×42 mm)	4·50	2·75

163 *Holy Night* (Jacques Stella)

1981. Christmas. Paintings. Multicoloured.

723	8c. Type **163**	15	10
724	30c. *Mary with Child* (Julius Schnorr von Carolfeld)	40	15
725	$1 *Virgin and Child* (Alonso Cano)	75	90
726	$3 *Virgin and Child* (Lorenzo di Credi)	1·10	3·75
MS727	77×111 mm. $5 *Holy Family* (Pieter von Avon)	2·50	4·50

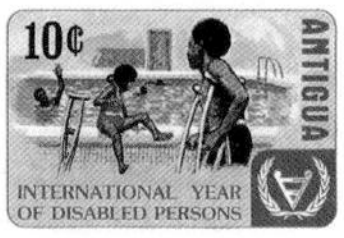

164 Swimming

1981. International Year of Disabled People. Sports for the Disabled. Multicoloured.

728	10c. Type **164**	10	10
729	50c. Discus-throwing	20	30
730	90c. Archery	40	55
731	$2 Baseball	1·00	1·40
MS732	108×84 mm. $4 Basketball	5·00	2·75

165 Scene from Football Match

1982. World Cup Football Championship, Spain.

733	**165**	10c. multicoloured	30	10
734	-	50c. multicoloured	60	35
735	-	90c. multicoloured	1·10	70
736	-	$4 multicoloured	3·00	3·50
MS737		75×92 mm. $5 multicoloured	6·00	10·00

DESIGNS: 50c. to $5, Scenes from various matches.

166 Airbus Industrie A300

1982. Coolidge International Airport. Multicoloured.

738	10c. Type **166**	10	10
739	50c. Hawker-Siddeley H.S.748	30	30
740	90c. de Havilland D.H.C.6 Twin Otter	60	60
741	$2.50 Britten Norman Islander	1·75	1·75
MS742	99×73 mm. $5 Boeing 747-100 (horiz)	2·75	4·00

167 Cordia

1982. Death Centenary of Charles Darwin. Fauna and Flora. Multicoloured.

743	10c. Type **167**	30	10
744	50c. Small Indian mongoose (horiz)	70	40
745	90c. Corallita	1·10	75
746	$2 Mexican bulldog bat (horiz)	2·50	3·25
MS747	107×85 mm. $5 Carribbean monk seal	7·50	8·00

168 Queen's House, Greenwich

1982. 21st Birthday of Princess of Wales. Multicoloured.

748	90c. Type **168**	45	45
749	$1 Prince and Princess of Wales	65	50
750	$4 Princess Diana	3·00	2·00
MS751	102×75 mm. $5 Type **169**	3·75	2·50

170 Boy Scouts decorating Streets for Independence Parade

1982. 75th Anniv of Boy Scout Movement. Multicoloured.

752	10c. Type **170**	25	10
753	50c. Boy Scout giving helping hand during street parade	50	40
754	90c. Boy Scouts attending H.R.H. Princess Margaret at Independence Ceremony	80	75
755	$2.20 Cub Scout giving directions to tourists	1·50	2·75
MS756	102×72 mm. $5 Lord Baden-Powell	4·50	5·50

1982. Birth of Prince William of Wales. Nos. 748/50 optd **ROYAL BABY 21.6.82.**

757	90c. Type **168**	45	45
758	$1 Prince and Princess of Wales	50	50
759	$4 Princess Diana	1·50	1·50
MS760	102×75 mm. $5 Type **169**	2·40	2·50

172 Roosevelt in 1940

1982. Birth Centenary of Franklin D. Roosevelt. (Nos. 761, 763 and 765/6) and 250th Birth Anniv of George Washington (others). Multicoloured.

761	10c. Type **172**	20	10
762	25c. Washington as blacksmith	45	15
763	45c. Churchill, Roosevelt and Stalin at Yalta Conference	1·75	40
764	60c. Washington crossing the Delaware (vert)	1·00	40
765	$1 "Roosevelt Special" train (vert)	1·75	90
766	$3 Portrait of Roosevelt (vert)	1·40	2·40
MS767	92×87 mm. $4 Roosevelt and Wife	2·00	1·75
MS768	92×87 mm. $4 Portrait of Washington (vert)	2·00	1·75

No. **MS**768 also exists imperf.

173 *Annunciation*

1982. Christmas. Religious Paintings by Raphael. Multicoloured.

769	10c. Type **173**	10	10
770	30c. *Adoration of the Magi*	15	15
771	$1 *Presentation at the Temple*	50	40
772	$4 *Coronation of the Virgin*	1·75	1·90
MS773	95×124 mm. $5 *Marriage of the Virgin*	2·75	2·50

174 Tritons and Dolphins

1983. 500th Birth Anniv of Raphael. Details from *Galatea* Fresco. Multicoloured.

774	45c. Type **174**	20	25
775	50c. Sea nymph carried off by Triton	25	30
776	60c. Winged angel steering dolphins (horiz)	30	35
777	$4 Cupids shooting arrows (horiz)	1·60	2·00
MS778	101×125 mm. $5 Galatea pulled along by dolphins	1·50	2·25

175 Pineapple Produce

1983. Commonwealth Day. Multicoloured.

779	25c. Type **175**	15	15
780	45c. Carnival	20	25
781	60c. Tourism	30	35
782	$3 Airport	1·00	1·50

176 T.V. Satellite Coverage of Royal Wedding

1983. World Communications Year. Multicoloured.

783	15c. Type **176**	40	20
784	50c. Police communications	2·25	1·50
785	60c. House-to-train telephone call	2·25	1·50
786	$3 Satellite earth station with planets Jupiter and Saturn	4·75	5·00
MS787	100×90 mm. $5 "Comsat" satellite over West Indies	2·00	3·75

177 Bottle-nosed Dolphin

1983. Whales. Multicoloured.

788	15c. Type **177**	85	20
789	50c. Fin whale	1·75	1·25
790	60c. Bowhead whale	2·00	1·25
791	$3 Spectacled porpoise	3·75	4·25
MS792	122×101 mm. $5 Narwhal	8·50	6·00

178 Cashew Nut

1983. Fruits and Flowers. Multicoloured.

793	1c. Type **178**	15	1·25
794	2c. Passion fruit	15	1·25
795	3c. Mango	15	1·25
796	5c. Grapefruit	20	1·25
797a	10c. Pawpaw	30	20
798	15c. Breadfruit	75	20
799	20c. Coconut	50	20
800a	25c. Oleander	75	20
801	30c. Banana	60	40
802a	40c. Pineapple	75	30
803a	45c. Cordia	85	40
804	50c. Cassia	90	60
805	60c. Poui	1·50	1·00
806a	$1 Frangipani	2·00	1·50
807a	$2 Flamboyant	3·50	4·50
808	$2.50 Lemon	3·75	6·50
809	$5 Linum vitae	5·00	13·00
810	$10 National flag and coat of arms	8·00	17·00

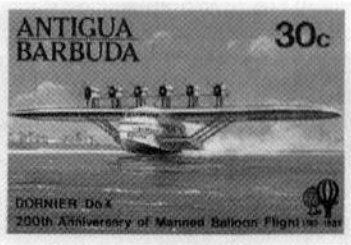

179 Dornier Do-X Flying Boat

1983. Bicentenary of Manned Flight. Multicoloured.

811	30c. Type **179**	1·00	30
812	50c. Supermarine S.6B seaplane	1·25	60
813	60c. Curtiss F-9C Sparrowhawk biplane and airship U.S.S. *Akron*	1·40	85
814	$4 Hot-air balloon *Pro Juventute*	3·25	6·00
MS815	80×105 mm. $5 Airship LZ-127 *Graf Zeppelin*	1·75	2·25

180 *Sibyls and Angels* (detail) (Raphael)

1983. Christmas. 500th Birth Anniv of Raphael.

816	**180** 10c. multicoloured	30	20
817	- 30c. multicoloured	65	35
818	- $1 multicoloured	1·50	1·25
819	- $4 multicoloured	2·50	5·00
MS820	– 101×103 mm. $5 multicoloured	1·50	2·25

DESIGNS—HORIZ: 10c. to $4, Different details from *Sibyls and Angels*. VERT: $5 *The Vision of Ezekiel*.

181 John Wesley (founder)

1983. Bicentenary of Methodist Church (1984). Multicoloured.

821	15c. Type **181**	25	15
822	50c. Nathaniel Gilbert (founder in Antigua)	70	50
823	60c. St. John Methodist Church steeple	75	65
824	$3 Ebenezer Methodist Church, St. John's	2·00	4·00

182 Discus

1984. Olympic Games, Los Angeles. Multicoloured.

825	25c. Type **182**	20	15
826	50c. Gymnastics	35	30
827	90c. Hurdling	65	70
828	$3 Cycling	2·50	4·25
MS829	82×67 mm. $5 Volleyball	2·75	3·00

183 *Booker Vanguard* (freighter)

1984. Ships. Multicoloured.

830	45c. Type **183**	1·00	55
831	50c. S.S. *Canberra* (liner)	1·25	80
832	60c. Yachts	1·50	1·00
833	$4 *Fairwind* (cargo liner)	3·00	7·00
MS834	107×80 mm. $5 18th-century British man-of-war (vert)	1·75	3·50

184 Chenille

1984. Universal Postal Union Congress, Hamburg. Multicoloured.

835	15c. Type **184**	40	15
836	50c. Shell flower	75	70
837	60c. Anthurium	75	1·10
838	$3 Angels trumpet	2·25	6·50
MS839	100×75 mm. $5 Crown of Thorns	1·50	3·25

1984. Various stamps surch. (a) Nos. 702/4.

840	$2 on 25c. Type **159**	2·50	2·50
841	$2 on 50c. Glamis Castle	2·50	2·50
842	$2 on $4 Prince Charles skiing	2·50	2·50
MS843	96×82 mm. $2 on $5 Glass coach	4·00	4·00

(b) Nos. 748/50.

844	$2 on 90c. Type **168**	2·50	2·50
845	$2 on $1 Prince and Princess of Wales	2·50	2·50
846	$2 on $4 Princess Diana	2·50	2·50
MS847	102×75 mm. Type **169**	4·00	4·00

(c) Nos. 757/9.

848	$2 on 90c. Type **168**	2·00	2·00
849	$2 on $1 Prince and Princess of Wales	2·00	2·00
850	$2 on $4 Princess Diana	2·00	2·00
MS851	102×75 mm. $2 on $5 Type **169**	4·00	4·00

(d) Nos. 779/82.

852	$2 on 25c. Type **175**	2·75	1·25
853	$2 on 45c. Carnival	2·75	1·25
854	$2 on 60c. Tourism	2·75	1·25
855	$2 on $3 Airport	2·75	1·25

187 Abraham Lincoln

1984. Presidents of the United States of America. Multicoloured.

856	10c. Type **187**	15	10
857	20c. Harry S. Truman	20	15
858	30c. Dwight D. Eisenhower	30	25
859	40c. Ronald W. Reagan	50	30
860	90c. Gettysburg Address, 1863	90	75
861	$1.10 Formation of N.A.T.O.,1949	2·00	1·25
862	$1.50 Eisenhower during the war	1·60	1·75
863	$2 Reagan and Caribbean Basin Initiative	1·75	2·00

188 View of Moravian Mission

1984. 150th Anniv of Abolition of Slavery. Multicoloured.

864	40c. Type **188**	90	50
865	50c. Antigua Courthouse, 1823	1·00	65
866	60c. Planting sugar-cane, Monks Hill	1·10	75
867	$3 Boiling house, Delaps' estate	4·25	6·00
MS868	95×70 mm. $5 Loading sugar, Willoughby Bay	6·50	4·75

189 Rufous-sided Towhee

1984. Songbirds. Multicoloured.

869	40c. Type **189**	1·25	85
870	50c. Parula warbler	1·40	1·10
871	60c. House wren	1·50	1·50
872	$2 Ruby-crowned kinglet	2·00	3·75
873	$3 Common flicker ("Yellow-shafted Flicker")	2·75	5·00
MS874	76×76 mm. $5 Yellow-breasted chat	2·50	6·00

190 Grass-skiing

1984. "Ausipex" International Stamp Exhibition, Melbourne, Australian Sports. Multicoloured.

875	$1 Type **190**	1·25	1·50
876	$5 Australian football	3·25	4·75
MS877	108×78 mm. $5 Boomerang-throwing	2·00	3·50

191 *The Virgin and Infant with Angels and Cherubs*

1984. 450th Death Anniv of Correggio (painter). Multicoloured.

878	25c. Type **191**	40	20
879	60c. *The Four Saints*	80	50
880	90c. *St. Catherine*	1·10	90
881	$3 *The Campori Madonna*	2·25	4·25
MS882	90×60 mm. $5 *St. John the Baptist*	1·75	2·75

192 *The Blue Dancers*

1984. 150th Birth Anniv of Edgar Degas (painter). Multicoloured.

883	15c. Type **192**	35	15
884	50c. *The Pink Dancers*	80	60
885	70c. *Two Dancers*	1·10	85
886	$4 *Dancers at the Bar*	2·50	4·75
MS887	90×60 mm. *The Folk dancers* (40×27 mm)	2·00	2·75

193 Sir Winston Churchill

1984. Famous People. Multicoloured.

888	60c. Type **193**	1·10	1·50
889	60c. Mahatma Gandhi	1·10	1·50
890	60c. John F. Kennedy	1·10	1·50
891	60c. Mao Tse-tung	1·10	1·50
892	$1 Churchill with General De Gaulle, Paris, 1944 (horiz)	1·25	1·75
893	$1 Gandhi leaving London by train, 1931 (horiz)	1·25	1·75
894	$1 Kennedy with Chancellor Adenauer and Mayor Brandt, Berlin, 1963 (horiz)	1·25	1·75
895	$1 Mao Tse-tung with Lin Piao, Peking, 1969 (horiz)	1·25	1·75
MS896	114×80 mm. $5 Flags of Great Britain, India, the United States and China	9·50	8·00

194 Donald Duck fishing

1984. Christmas. 50th Birthday of Donald Duck. Walt Disney Cartoon Characters. Multicoloured.

897	1c. Type **194**	10	10
898	2c. Donald Duck lying on beach	10	10
899	3c. Donald Duck and nephews with fishing rods and fishes	10	10
900	4c. Donald Duck and nephews in boat	10	10
901	5c. Wearing diving masks	10	10
902	10c. In deckchairs reading books	10	10
903	$1 With toy shark's fin	2·25	1·25
904	$2 In sailing boat	2·50	3·00
905	$5 Attempting to propel boat	4·00	6·00
MS906	Two sheets, each 125×100 mm. (a) $5 Nephews with crayon and paintbrushes (horiz). (b) $5 Donald Duck in deckchair Set of 2 sheets	7·50	13·00

195 Torch from Statue in Madison Square Park, 1885

1985. Centenary (1986) of Statue of Liberty (1st issue). Multicoloured.

907	25c. Type **195**	30	20
908	30c. Statue of Liberty and scaffolding ("Restoration and Renewal") (vert)	30	20
909	50c. Frederic Bartholdi (sculptor) supervising construction, 1876	40	40
910	90c. Close-up of statue	60	75
911	$1 Statue and cadet ship ("Operation Sail", 1976) (vert)	1·60	1·40
912	$3 Dedication ceremony, 1886	1·75	3·00
MS913	110×80 mm. $5 Port of New York	3·75	3·75

See also Nos. 1110/19.

196 Arawak Pot Sherd and Indians making Clay Utensils

1985. Native American Artefacts. Multicoloured.

914	15c. Type **196**	15	10
915	50c. Arawak body design and Arawak Indians tattooing	30	40
916	60c. Head of the god "Yocahu" and Indians harvesting manioc	40	50
917	$3 Carib war club and Carib Indians going into battle	1·25	2·50
MS918	97×68 mm. $5 Taino Indians worshipping stone idol	1·50	2·50

197 Triumph 2hp "Jap", 1903

1985. Centenary of the Motorcycle. Multicoloured.

919	10c. Type **197**	65	15
920	30c. "Indian Arrow", 1949	1·10	40
921	60c. BMW "R100RS", 1976	1·60	1·25
922	$4 Harley-Davidson "Model II", 1916	5·50	9·00
MS923	90×93 mm. $5 Laverda "Jota", 1975	5·50	7·00

198 Slavonian Grebe ("Horned Grebe")

1985. Birth Bicentenary of John J. Audubon (ornithologist) (1st issue). Multicoloured. Designs showing original paintings.

924	90c. Type **198**	1·75	1·25
925	$1 British storm petrel ("Least Petrel")	2·00	1·25
926	$1.50 Great blue heron	2·50	3·25
927	$3 Double-crested cormorant	3·75	6·00
MS928	103×72 mm. $5 White-tailed tropic bird (vert)	7·00	6·00

See also Nos. 990/4.

199 *Anaea cyanea*

1985. Butterflies. Multicoloured.

929	25c. Type **199**	1·00	30
930	60c. *Leodonta dysoni*	2·25	1·25
931	90c. *Junea doraete*	2·75	1·50
932	$4 *Prepona pylene*	7·50	10·50
MS933	132×105 mm. $5 *Caerois gerdtrudlus*	4·50	6·50

200 Cessna 172D Skyhawk

1985. 40th Anniv of International Civil Aviation Organization. Multicoloured.

934	30c. Type **200**	1·25	30
935	90c. Fokker D.VII	2·75	1·25
936	$1.50 SPAD VII	3·75	3·25
937	$3 Boeing 747-100	5·50	7·50
MS938	97×83 mm. $5 De Havilland D.H.C.6 twin otter	4·50	6·50

201 Maimonides

1985. 850th Birth Anniv of Maimonides (physician, philosopher and scholar).

939	**201**	$2 green	4·25	3·25
MS940		70×84 mm. Type **201** $5 brown	7·00	4·50

202 Young Farmers with Produce

1985. International Youth Year. Multicoloured.

941	25c. Type **202**	25	20
942	50c. Hotel management trainees	40	50
943	60c. Girls with goat and boys with football ("Environment")	1·00	70
944	$3 Windsurfing ("Leisure")	2·75	5·50
MS945	102×72 mm. $5 Young people with Antiguan flags	2·75	3·25

203 The Queen Mother attending Church

1985. Life and Times of Queen Elizabeth the Queen Mother. Multicoloured.

946	$1 Type **203**	45	60
947	$1.50 Watching children playing in London garden	60	85
948	$2.50 The Queen Mother in 1979	90	1·40
MS949	56×85 mm. $5 With Prince Edward at Royal Wedding, 1981	5·50	3·00

Stamps as Nos. 946/8, but with face values of 90c., $1 and $3 exist from additional sheetlets with changed background colours.

204 Magnificent Frigate Bird

1985. Marine Life. Multicoloured.

950	15c. Type **204**	1·00	30
951	45c. Brain coral	2·00	95
952	60c. Cushion star	2·25	1·75
953	$3 Spotted moray	7·00	9·00
MS954	110×80 mm. $5 Elkhorn coral	9·00	7·00

205 Girl Guides Nursing

1985. 75th Anniv of Girl Guide Movement. Multicoloured.

955	15c. Type **205**	75	20
956	45c. Open-air Girl Guide meeting	1·40	60
957	60c. Lord and Lady Baden-Powell	1·75	90
958	$3 Girl Guides gathering flowers	4·25	4·50
MS959	67×96 mm. $5 Barn swallow (Nature study)	6·50	8·50

206 Bass Trombone

1985. 300th Birth Anniv of Johann Sebastian Bach (composer).

960	**206**	25c. multicoloured	1·40	55
961	-	50c. multicoloured	1·75	1·10
962	-	$1 multicoloured	3·25	1·75
963	-	$3 multicoloured	6·00	7·00
MS964		– 104×73 mm. $5 black and grey	4·50	4·75

DESIGNS:50c. English horn; $1 Violino piccolo; $3 Bass rackett; $5 Johann Sebastian Bach.

207 Flags of Great Britain and Antigua

1985. Royal Visit. Multicoloured.

965	60c. Type **207**	1·00	65
966	$1 Queen Elizabeth II (vert)	1·50	1·25
967	$4 Royal Yacht "Britannia"	3·25	7·00
MS968	110×83 mm. $5 Map of Antigua	3·00	3·25

1985. 150th Birth Anniv of Mark Twain (author). As T **118** of Anguilla showing Walt Disney cartoon characters in scenes from *Roughing It*. Multicoloured.

969	25c. Donald Duck and Mickey Mouse meeting Indians	1·00	20
970	50c. Mickey Mouse, Donald Duck and Goofy canoeing	1·50	55
971	$1.10 Goofy as Pony Express rider	2·50	2·25
972	$1.50 Donald Duck and Goofy hunting buffalo	3·00	3·75
973	$2 Mickey Mouse and silver mine	3·50	4·50
MS974	127×101 mm. $5 Mickey Mouse driving stagecoach	8·00	7·50

1985. Birth Bicentenaries of Grimm Brothers (folklorists). As T **119** of Anguilla showing Walt Disney cartoon characters in scenes from "Spindle, Shuttle and Needle". Multicoloured.

975	30c. The Prince (Mickey Mouse) searches for a bride	1·25	40
976	60c. The Prince finds the Orphan Girl (Minnie Mouse)	1·75	80
977	70c. The Spindle finds the Prince	2·00	1·40
978	$1 The Needle tidies the Girl's house	2·50	1·75
979	$3 The Prince proposes	4·75	7·50
MS980	125×101 mm. $5 The Orphan Girl and spinning wheel on Prince's horse	8·00	7·50

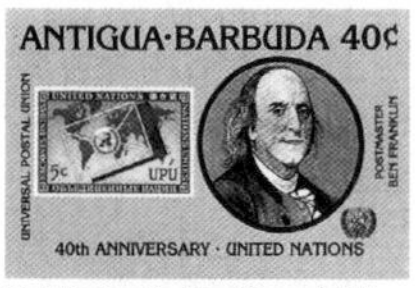

208 Benjamin Franklin and U.N. (New York) 1953 U.P.U. 5c. Stamp

1985. 40th Anniv of United Nations Organization. Multicoloured.

981	40c. Type **208**	1·00	70
982	$1 George Washington Carver (agricultural chemist) and 1982 Nature Conservation 28c. stamp	2·00	2·00
983	$3 Charles Lindbergh (aviator) and 1978 I.C.A.O. 25c. stamp	4·75	7·50
MS984	101×77 mm. $5 Marc Chagall (artist) (vert)	6·50	4·75

Nos. 981/4 each include a United Nations (New York) stamp design.

209 *Madonna and Child* (De Landi)

1985. Christmas. Religious Paintings. Multicoloured.

985	10c. Type **209**	30	15
986	25c. *Madonna and Child* (Berlinghiero)	55	25
987	60c. *The Nativity* (Fra Angelico)	70	60
988	$4 *Presentation in the Temple* (Giovanni di Paolo)	1·75	4·25
MS989	113×81 mm. $5 *The Nativity* (Antoniazzo Romano)	3·00	3·75

1986. Birth Bicentenary of John J. Audubon (ornithologist) (2nd issue). As T **198** showing original paintings. Multicoloured.

990	60c. Mallard	2·25	1·50
991	90c. North American black duck ("Dusky Duck")	2·75	2·00
992	$1.50 Pintail ("Common Pintail")	3·50	4·50
993	$3 American wigeon ("Wigeon")	4·75	6·50
MS994	102×73 mm. Eider ("Common Eider")	7·00	5·50

210 Football, Boots and Trophy

1986. World Cup Football Championship, Mexico. Multicoloured.

995	30c. Type **210**	1·50	40
996	60c. Goalkeeper (vert)	2·00	85
997	$1 Referee blowing whistle (vert)	2·50	1·75
998	$4 Ball in net	6·50	9·00
MS999	87×76 mm. $5 Two players competing for ball	8·50	7·50

1986. Appearance of Halley's Comet (1st issue). As T **123** of Anguilla. Multicoloured.

1000	5c. Edmond Halley and Old Greenwich Observatory	30	20
1001	10c. Messerschmitt Me 163B Komet (fighter aircraft), 1944	30	15
1002	60c. Montezuma (Aztec emperor) and Comet in 1517 (from *Historias de las Indias de Neuva Espana*)	1·50	70
1003	$4 Pocahontas saving Capt. John Smith and Comet in 1607	4·50	5·50
MS1004	101×70 mm. $5 Halley's Comet over English Harbour, Antigua	3·50	3·75

See also Nos. 1047/51.

1986. 60th Birthday of Queen Elizabeth II. As T **125** of Anguilla.

1005	60c. black and yellow	30	35
1006	$1 multicoloured	50	55
1007	$4 multicoloured	1·40	1·90
MS1008	120×85 mm. $5 black and brown	2·00	3·00

DESIGNS: 60c. Wedding photograph, 1947; $1 Queen at Trooping the Colour; $4 In Scotland; $5 Queen Mary and Princess Elizabeth, 1927.

211 Tug

1986. Local Boats. Multicoloured.

1009	30c. Type **211**	25	20
1010	60c. Game fishing boat	45	35
1011	$1 Yacht	75	60
1012	$4 Lugger with auxiliary sail	2·50	3·25
MS1013	108×78 mm. $5 Boats under construction	3·00	4·00

212 *Hiawatha* express

1986. "Ameripex '86" International Stamp Exhibition, Chicago. Famous American Trains. Multicoloured.

1014	25c. Type **212**	1·25	50
1015	50c. *Grand Canyon* express	1·50	80
1016	$1 *Powhattan Arrow* express	1·75	1·75
1017	$3 *Empire State* express	3·00	6·00
MS1018	116×87 mm. $5 Southern Pacific *Daylight* express	6·00	11·00

213 Prince Andrew and Miss Sarah Ferguson

1986. Royal Wedding. Multicoloured.

1019	45c. Type **213**	70	35
1020	60c. Prince Andrew	80	45
1021	$4 Prince Andrew with Prince Philip	2·75	3·50
MS1022	88×88 mm. $5 Prince Andrew and Miss Sarah Ferguson (different)	5·00	4·50

214 Fly-specked Cerith

1986. Sea Shells. Multicoloured.

1023	15c. Type **214**	75	50
1024	45c. Smooth Scotch bonnet	1·75	1·25
1025	60c. West Indian crown conch	2·00	2·00
1026	$3 Ciboney murex	5·50	10·00
MS1027	109×75 mm. $5 Colourful Atlantic moon (horiz)	7·50	8·50

215 Water Lily

1986. Flowers. Multicoloured.

1028	10c. Type **215**	20	15
1029	15c. Queen of the night	20	15
1030	50c. Cup of gold	55	55
1031	60c. Beach morning glory	70	70
1032	70c. Golden trumpet	80	80
1033	$1 Air plant	90	1·10
1034	$4 Purple wreath	1·75	3·00
1035	$4 Zephyr lily	2·00	3·75
MS1036	Two sheets, each 102×72 mm. (a) $4 Dozakie. (b) $5 Four o'clock flower Set of 2 sheets	5·00	7·50

1986. World Cup Football Championship Winners, Mexico. Nos. 995/8 optd **WINNERS Argentina 3 W.Germany 2**.

1037	30c. Type **210**	1·25	40
1038	60c. Goalkeeper (vert)	1·75	75
1039	$1 Referee blowing whistle (vert)	2·25	1·10
1040	$4 Ball in net	5·50	4·50
MS1041	87×76 mm. $5 Two players competing for ball	5·50	4·00

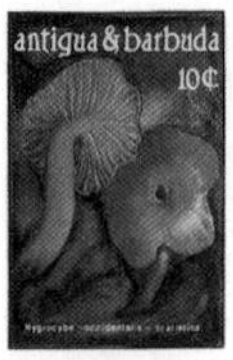

217 *Hygrocybe occidentalis var. scarletina*

1986. Mushrooms. Multicoloured.

1042	10c. Type **217**	30	25
1043	50c. *Trogia buccinalis*	70	55
1044	$1 *Collybia subpruinosa*	1·00	1·25
1045	$4 *Leucocoprinus brebissonii*	2·50	4·50
MS1046	102×82 mm. $5 *Pyrrhoglossum pyrrhum*	13·00	11·00

(218)

1986. Appearance of Halley's Comet (2nd issue). Nos. 1000/3 optd with T **218**.

1047	5c. Edmond Halley and Old Greenwich Observatory	20	10
1048	10c. Messerschmitt Me 163B Komet (fighter aircraft), 1944	50	10
1049	60c. Montezuma (Aztec emperor) and Comet in 1517 (from *Historias de las Indias de Neuva Espana*)	1·25	65

1050	$4 Pocahontas saving Capt. John Smith and Comet in 1607	4·50	4·00
MS1051	101×70 mm. $5 Halley's Comet over English Harbour, Antigua	6·00	6·50

219 Auburn "Speedster" (1933)

1986. Centenary of First Benz Motor Car. Multicoloured.

1052	10c. Type **219**	20	10
1053	15c. Mercury "Sable" (1986)	25	10
1054	50c. Cadillac (1959)	60	30
1055	60c. Studebaker (1950)	75	45
1056	70c. Lagonda "V-12" (1939)	85	55
1057	$1 Adler "Standard" (1930)	1·25	75
1058	$3 DKW (1956)	2·50	2·50
1059	$4 Mercedes "500K" (1936)	3·00	3·00
MS1060	Two sheets, each 99×70 mm. (a) $5 Daimler (1896). (b) $5 Mercedes "Knight" (1921) Set of 2 sheets	9·00	6·50

220 Young Mickey Mouse playing Santa Claus

1986. Christmas. Designs showing Walt Disney cartoon characters as babies. Multicoloured.

1061	25c. Type **220**	60	35
1062	30c. Mickey and Minnie Mouse building snowman	70	40
1063	40c. Aunt Matilda and Goofy baking	75	45
1064	60c. Goofy and Pluto	1·00	85
1065	70c. Pluto, Donald and Daisy Duck carol singing	1·10	1·00
1066	$1.50 Donald Duck, Mickey Mouse and Pluto stringing popcorn	1·75	2·50
1067	$3 Grandma Duck and Minnie Mouse	3·00	4·50
1068	$4 Donald Duck and Pete	3·25	4·50
MS1069	Two sheets, each 127×102 mm. (a) $5 Goofy, Donald Duck and Minnie Mouse playing with reindeer. (b) $5 Mickey Mouse, Donald and Daisy Duck playing with toys Set of 2 sheets	13·00	14·00

221 Arms of Antigua

1986

1070	**221**	10c. blue	1·00	1·00
1071	-	25c. red	1·00	1·00

DESIGN: 25c. Flag of Antigua.

222 *Canada I* (1981)

1987. America's Cup Yachting Championship. Multicoloured.

1072	30c. Type **222**	45	20
1073	60c. *Gretel II* (1970)	60	50
1074	$1 *Sceptre* (1958)	85	1·00
1075	$3 *Vigilant* (1893)	1·75	3·00
MS1076	113×84 mm. $5 *Australia II* defeating *Liberty* (1983) (horiz)	4·00	5·00

223 Bridled Burrfish

1987. Marine Life. Multicoloured.

1077	15c. Type **223**	2·50	50
1078	30c. Common noddy ("Brown Noddy")	5·00	60
1079	40c. Nassau grouper	3·00	70
1080	50c. Laughing gull	6·00	1·50
1081	60c. French angelfish	3·50	1·50
1082	$1 Porkfish	3·50	1·75
1083	$2 Royal tern	8·00	6·00
1084	$3 Sooty tern	8·00	8·00
MS1085	Two sheets, each 120×94 mm. (a) $5 Banded butterflyfish. (b) $5 Brown booby Set of 2 sheets	17·00	14·00

Nos. 1078, 1080 and 1083/5 are without the World Wildlife Fund logo shown on Type **223**.

224 Handball

1987. Olympic Games, Seoul (1988) (1st issue). Multicoloured.

1086	10c. Type **224**	60	10
1087	60c. Fencing	85	35
1088	$1 Gymnastics	1·00	80
1089	$3 Football	2·25	4·00
MS1090	100×72 mm. $5 Boxing gloves	3·00	4·25

See also Nos. 1222/6.

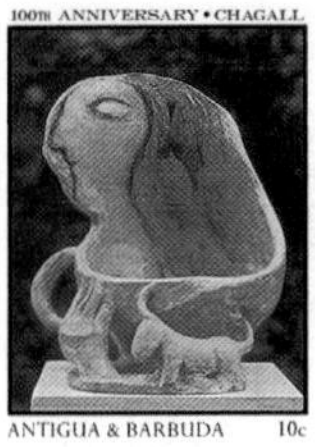

225 *The Profile*

1987. Birth Centenary of Marc Chagall (artist). Multicoloured.

1091	10c. Type **225**	30	15
1092	30c. *Portrait of the Artist's Sister*	45	30
1093	40c. *Bride with Fan*	50	40
1094	60c. *David in Profile*	55	45
1095	90c. *Fiancee with Bouquet*	75	60
1096	$1 *Self Portrait with Brushes*	75	65
1097	$3 *The Walk*	1·75	2·25
1098	$4 *Three Candles*	2·00	2·50
MS1099	Two sheets, each 110×95 mm. (a) $5 *Fall of Icarus* (104×89 mm). (b) $5 *Myth of Orpheus* (104×89 mm). Imperf Set of 2 sheets	6·50	6·00

226 *Spirit of Australia* (fastest powerboat), 1978

1987. Milestones of Transportation. Multicoloured.

1100	10c. Type **226**	80	40
1101	15c. Werner von Siemens's electric locomotive, 1879	1·50	50
1102	30c. U.S.S. *Triton* (first submerged circum-navigation), 1960	1·25	50
1103	50c. Trevithick's steam carriage (first passenger-carrying vehicle), 1801	1·75	60
1104	60c. U.S.S. *New Jersey* (battleship), 1942	1·75	85
1105	70c. Draisaine bicycle, 1818	2·00	1·00
1106	90c. *United States* (liner) (holder of Blue Riband), 1952	1·75	1·00
1107	$1.50 Cierva C.4 (first autogyro), 1923	1·75	2·75
1108	$2 Curtiss NC-4 flying boat (first transatlantic flight), 1919	2·00	3·00
1109	$3 *Queen Elizabeth 2* (liner), 1969	3·50	4·50

227 Lee Iacocca at Unveiling of Restored Statue

1987. Centenary of Statue of Liberty (1986) (2nd issue). Multicoloured.

1110	15c. Type **227**	15	15
1111	30c. Statue at sunset (side view)	20	20
1112	45c. Aerial view of head	30	30
1113	50c. Lee Iacocca and torch	35	35
1114	60c. Workmen inside head of Statue (horiz)	35	35
1115	90c. Restoration work (horiz)	50	50
1116	$1 Head of Statue	55	55
1117	$2 Statue at sunset (front view)	1·00	1·50
1118	$3 Inspecting restoration work (horiz)	1·00	2·00
1119	$5 Statue at night	1·75	3·50

228 Grace Kelly

1987. Entertainers. Multicoloured.

1120	15c. Type **228**	90	40
1121	30c. Marilyn Monroe	2·75	80
1122	45c. Orson Welles	90	60
1123	50c. Judy Garland	90	65
1124	60c. John Lennon	4·25	1·25
1125	$1 Rock Hudson	1·40	1·10
1126	$2 John Wayne	2·50	2·00
1127	$3 Elvis Presley	10·00	4·50

229 Scouts around Camp Fire and Red Kangaroo

1987. 16th World Scout Jamboree, Australia. Multicoloured.

1128	10c. Type **229**	65	20
1129	60c. Scouts canoeing and blue-winged kookaburra	1·25	80
1130	$1 Scouts on assault course and ring-tailed rock wallaby	1·00	85
1131	$3 Field kitchen and koala	1·50	4·25
MS1132	103×78 mm. $5 Flags of Antigua, Australia and Scout Movement	3·25	3·50

230 Whistling Frog

1987. "Capex '87" International Stamp Exhibition, Toronto. Reptiles and Amphibians. Mult.

1133	30c. Type **230**	55	20
1134	60c. Croaking lizard	75	40
1135	$1 Antiguan anole	1·00	70
1136	$3 Red-footed tortoise	2·00	3·00
MS1137	106×76 mm. $5 Ground lizard	2·25	2·75

1987. Tenth Death Anniv of Elvis Presley (entertainer). No. 1127 optd **10th ANNIVERSARY 16th AUGUST 1987**.

1138	$3 Elvis Presley	8·00	4·75

232 House of Burgesses, Virginia ("Freedom of Speech")

1987. Bicentenary of U.S. Constitution. Multicoloured.

1139	15c. Type **232**	10	10
1140	45c. State Seal, Connecticut	20	25
1141	60c. State Seal, Delaware	25	35
1142	$4 Governor Morris (Pennsylvania delegate) (vert)	1·75	2·25
MS1143	105×75 mm. $5 Roger Sherman (Connecticut delegate) (vert)	2·00	2·75

233 *Madonna and Child* (Bernardo Daddi)

1987. Christmas. Religious Paintings. Multicoloured.

1144	45c. Type **233**	50	15
1145	60c. St. Joseph (detail, *The Nativity* (Sano di Pietro))	65	30
1146	$1 Virgin Mary (detail, *The Nativity* (Sano di Pietro))	85	55
1147	$4 *Music-making Angel* (Melozzo da Forli)	2·25	3·50
MS1148	99×70 mm. $5 *The Flight into Egypt* (Sano di Pietro)	2·25	2·75

234 Wedding Photograph, 1947

1988. Royal Ruby Wedding.

1149	**234**	25c. brown, black and blue	30	15
1150	-	60c. multicoloured	60	40
1151	-	$2 brown, black and green	1·10	1·10
1152	-	$3 multicoloured	1·50	1·60
MS1153		107×77 mm. $5 multicoloured	2·50	2·75

DESIGNS: 60c. Queen Elizabeth II; $2 Princess Elizabeth and Prince Philip with Prince Charles at his christening, 1948; $3 Queen Elizabeth (from photo by Tim Graham), 1980; $5 Royal family, 1952.

235 Great Blue Heron

1988. Birds of Antigua. Multicoloured.

1154	10c. Type **235**	50	40
1155	15c. Ringed kingfisher (horiz)	55	40
1156	50c. Bananaquit (horiz)	1·00	50
1157	60c. American purple gallinule ("Purple Gallinule") (horiz)	1·00	50
1158	70c. Blue-hooded euphonia (horiz)	1·10	55
1159	$1 Brown-throated conure ("Caribbean Parakeet")	1·40	75
1160	$3 Troupial (horiz)	2·50	3·50
1161	$4 Purple-throated carib ("Hummingbird") (horiz)	2·50	3·50
MS1162	Two sheets, each 115×86 mm. (a) $5 Greater flamingo. (b) $5 Brown pelican Set of 2 sheets	4·50	5·50

236 First Aid at Daycare Centre, Antigua

1988. Salvation Army's Community Service. Multicoloured.

1163	25c. Type **236**	80	65
1164	30c. Giving penicillin injection, Indonesia	80	65
1165	40c. Children at daycare centre, Bolivia	90	75
1166	45c. Rehabilitation of the handicapped, India	90	75
1167	50c. Training blind man, Kenya	1·00	1·25
1168	60c. Weighing baby, Ghana	1·00	1·25
1169	$1 Training typist, Zambia	1·40	1·75
1170	$2 Emergency food kitchen, Sri Lanka	2·00	3·50
MS1171	152×83 mm. $5 General Eva Burrows	3·75	4·50

237 Columbus's Second Fleet, 1493

1988. 500th Anniv (1992) of Discovery of America by Columbus (1st issue). Multicoloured.

1172	10c. Type **237**	80	40
1173	30c. Painos. Indian village and fleet	80	45
1174	45c. *Santa Mariagalante* (flagship) and Painos. village	1·25	45
1175	60c. Painos Indians offering Columbus fruit and vegetables	80	50
1176	90c. Painos Indian and Columbus with scarlet macaw	2·50	1·00

1177	$1 Columbus landing on island	1·75	1·00
1178	$3 Spanish soldier and fleet	2·50	3·25
1179	$4 Fleet under sail	2·75	3·25

MS1180 Two sheets, each 110×80 mm. (a) $5 Queen Isabella's cross. (b) $5 Gold coin of Ferdinand and Isabella Set of 2 sheets 6·50 7·00

See also Nos. 1267/71, 1360/8, 1503/11, 1654/60 and 1670/1.

238 *Bust of Christ*

1988. Easter. 500th Birth Anniv of Titian (artist). Multicoloured.

1181	30c. Type **238**	40	20
1182	40c. *Scourging of Christ*	45	25
1183	45c. *Madonna in Glory with Saints*	45	25
1184	50c. *The Averoldi Polyptych (detail)*	45	35
1185	$1 *Christ Crowned with Thorns*	70	55
1186	$2 *Christ Mocked*	1·10	1·25
1187	$3 *Christ and Simon of Cyrene*	1·50	1·75
1188	$4 *Crucifixion with Virgin and Saints*	1·75	2·25

MS1189 Two sheets, each 110×95 mm. (a) $5 *Ecce Homo* (detail). (b) $5 *Noli me Tangere* (detail) Set of 2 sheets 5·50 7·50

239 Two Yachts rounding Buoy

1988. Sailing Week. Multicoloured.

1190	30c. Type **239**	35	20
1191	60c. Three yachts	50	40
1192	$1 British yacht under way	60	55
1193	$3 Three yachts (different)	1·10	2·50
MS1194	103×92 mm. $5 Two yachts	1·75	3·25

240 Mickey Mouse and Diver with Porpoise

1988. Disney EPCOT Centre, Orlando, Florida. Designs showing cartoon characters and exhibits. Multicoloured.

1195	1c. Type **240**	10	10
1196	2c. Goofy and Mickey Mouse with futuristic car (vert)	10	10
1197	3c. Mickey Mouse and Goofy as Atlas (vert)	10	10
1198	4c. Mickey Mouse and "Eda-phosaurus" (prehistoric reptile)	10	10
1199	5c. Mickey Mouse at Journey into Imagination exhibit	15	10
1200	10c. Mickey Mouse collecting vegetables (vert)	20	10
1201	25c. Type **240**	55	25
1202	30c. As 2c.	55	25
1203	40c. As 3c.	60	30
1204	60c. As 4c.	85	50
1205	70c. As 5c.	95	60
1206	$1.50 As 10c.	2·00	2·00
1207	$3 Goofy and Mickey Mouse with robot (vert)	2·50	2·75
1208	$4 Mickey Mouse and Clar-abelle at Horizons exhibit	2·50	2·75

MS1209 Two sheets, each 125×99 mm. (a) $5 Mickey Mouse and monorail (vert). (b) $5 Mickey Mouse flying over EPCOT Centre Set of 2 sheets 7·00 6·50

1988. Stamp Exhibitions. Nos. 1083/4 optd.

1210	$2 Royal tern (optd **Praga '88**, Prague)	7·00	3·50
1211	$3 Sooty tern (optd **INDE-PENDENCE 40**, Israel)	7·00	4·00

MS1212 Two sheets, each 120×94 mm. (a) $5 Banded butterflyfish (optd **"OLYM-PHILEX '88"**, Seoul). (b) $5 brown booby (optd **"FINLANDIA 88"**, Helsinki). Set of 2 sheets 23·00 14·00

242 Jacaranda

1988. Flowering Trees. Multicoloured.

1213	10c. Type **242**	30	20
1214	30c. Cordia	40	20
1215	50c. Orchid tree	60	40
1216	90c. Flamboyant	70	50
1217	$1 African tulip tree	75	55
1218	$2 Potato tree	1·40	1·60
1219	$3 Crepe myrtle	1·60	2·00
1220	$4 Pitch apple	1·75	2·75

MS1221 Two sheets, each 106×76 mm. (a) $5 Cassia. (b) $5 Chinaberry Set of 2 sheets 5·00 6·00

243 Gymnastics

1988. Olympic Games, Seoul (2nd issue). Multicoloured.

1222	40c. Type **243**	30	25
1223	60c. Weightlifting	40	30
1224	$1 Water polo (horiz)	80	50
1225	$3 Boxing (horiz)	1·50	2·25
MS1226	114×80 mm. $5 Runner with Olympic torch	2·00	3·00

244 *Danaus plexippus*

1988. Caribbean Butterflies. Multicoloured.

1227	1c. Type **244**	60	1·25
1228	2c. *Greta diaphanus*	70	1·25
1229	3c. *Calisto archebates*	70	1·25
1230	5c. *Hamadryas feronia*	85	1·25
1231	10c. *Mestra dorcas*	1·00	30
1232	15c. *Hypolimnas misippus*	1·50	30
1233	20c. *Dione juno*	1·60	30
1234	25c. *Heliconius charithonia*	1·60	30
1235	30c. *Eurema pyro*	1·60	30
1236	40c. *Papilio androgeus*	1·60	30
1237	45c. *Anteos maerula*	1·60	30
1238	50c. *Aphrissa orbis*	1·75	45
1239	60c. *Astraptes xagua*	2·00	60
1240	$1 *Heliopetes arsalte*	2·25	1·00
1241	$2 *Polites baracoa*	3·25	3·75
1242	$2.50 *Phocides pigmalion*	4·00	5·00
1243	$5 *Prepona amphitoe*	5·50	8·00
1244	$10 *Oarisma nanus*	7·50	12·00
1244a	$20 *Parides lycimenes*	17·00	22·00

245 President Kennedy and Family

1988. 25th Death Anniv of John F. Kennedy (American statesman). Multicoloured.

1245	1c. Type **245**	10	10
1246	2c. Kennedy commanding "PT109"	10	10
1247	3c. Funeral cortege	10	10
1248	4c. In motorcade, Mexico City	10	10
1249	30c. As 1c.	35	15
1250	60c. As 4c.	1·00	40
1251	$1 As 3c.	1·10	75
1252	$4 As 2c.	3·00	3·50
MS1253	105×75 mm. $5 Kennedy tak-ing presidential oath of office	2·50	3·25

246 Minnie Mouse carol singing

1988. Christmas. "Mickey's Christmas Chorale". Design showing Walt Disney cartoon characters. Multicoloured.

1254	10c. Type **246**	40	30
1255	25c. Pluto	55	45
1256	30c. Mickey Mouse playing ukelele	55	45
1257	70c. Donald Duck and nephew	90	80
1258	$1 Mordie and Ferdie carol singing	90	1·00
1259	$1 Goofy carol singing	90	1·00
1260	$1 Chip n'Dale sliding off roof	90	1·00
1261	$1 Two of Donald Duck's nephews at window	90	1·00
1262	$1 As 10c.	90	1·00
1263	$1 As 25c.	90	1·00
1264	$1 As 30c.	90	1·00
1265	$1 As 70c.	90	1·00

MS1266 Two sheets, each 127×102 mm. (a) $7 Donald Duck playing trumpet and Mickey and Minnie Mouse in carriage. (b) $7 Mickey Mouse and friends singing carols on roller skates (horiz) Set of 2 sheets 8·50 8·50

Nos. 1258/65 were printed together, *se-tenant*, forming a composite design.

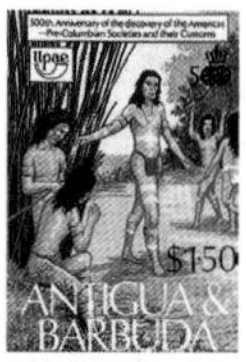

247 Arawak Warriors

1989. 500th Anniv of Discovery of America by Columbus (1992) (2nd issue). Pre-Columbian Arawak Society. Multicoloured.

1267	$1.50 Type **247**	1·10	1·40
1268	$1.50 Whip dancers	1·10	1·40
1269	$1.50 Whip dancers and chief with pineapple	1·10	1·40
1270	$1.50 Family and camp fire	1·10	1·40
MS1271	71×84 mm. $6 Arawak chief	2·75	3·00

Nos. 1267/70 were printed together, *se-tenant*, forming a composite design.

248 De Havilland Comet 4 Airliner

1989. 50th Anniv of First Jet Flight. Multicoloured.

1272	10c. Type **248**	90	45
1273	30c. Messerschmitt Me 262 fighter	1·50	45
1274	40c. Boeing 707 airliner	1·50	45
1275	60c. Canadair CL-13 Sabre (inscr "F-86") fighter	1·90	55
1276	$1 Lockheed F-104 Starfighters	2·25	1·10
1277	$2 McDonnell Douglas DC-10 airliner	3·00	3·00
1278	$3 Boeing 747-300/400 airliner	3·25	4·50
1279	$4 McDonnell Douglas F-4 Phantom II fighter	3·25	4·50

MS1280 Two sheets, each 114×83 mm. (a) $7 Grumman F-14A Tomcat fighter. (b) $7 Concorde airliner Set of 2 sheets 11·00 13·00

249 *Festivale*

1989. Caribbean Cruise Ships. Multicoloured.

1281	25c. Type **249**	2·00	50
1282	45c. *Southward*	2·25	50
1283	50c. *Sagafjord*	2·25	50
1284	60c. *Daphne*	2·25	60
1285	75c. *Cunard Countess*	2·50	1·00
1286	90c. *Song of America*	2·75	1·10
1287	$3 *Island Princess*	4·25	5·50
1288	$4 *Galileo*	4·25	6·00

MS1289 (a) 113×87 mm. $6 *Norway*. (b) 111×82 mm. $6 *Oceanic* Set of 2 sheets 7·50 11·00

250 *Fish swimming by Duck half-submerged in Stream*

1989. Japanese Art. Paintings by Hiroshige. Multicoloured.

1290	25c. Type **250**	1·00	50
1291	45c. *Crane and Wave*	1·25	50
1292	50c. *Sparrows and Morning Glories*	1·40	50
1293	60c. *Crested Blackbird and Flowering Cherry*	1·50	60
1294	$1 *Great Knot sitting among Water Grass*	1·75	80
1295	$2 *Goose on a Bank of Water*	2·50	2·50
1296	$3 *Black Paradise Flycatcher and Blossoms*	3·00	3·00
1297	$4 *Sleepy Owl perched on a Pine Branch*	3·00	3·00

MS1298 Two sheets, each 102×75 mm. (a) $5 *Bullfinch flying near a Clematis Branch*. (b) $5 *Titmouse on a Cherry Branch* Set of 2 sheets 9·00 9·50

251 Mickey and Minnie Mouse in Helicopter over River Seine

1989. "Philexfrance 89" International Stamp Exhibition, Paris. Walt Disney cartoon characters in Paris. Multicoloured.

1299	1c. Type **251**	10	10
1300	2c. Goofy and Mickey Mouse passing Arc de Triomphe	10	10
1301	3c. Mickey Mouse painting picture of Notre Dame	10	10
1302	4c. Mickey and Minnie Mouse with Pluto leaving Metro station	10	10
1303	5c. Minnie Mouse as model in fashion show	10	10
1304	10c. Daisy Duck, Minnie Mouse and Clarabelle as Folies Bergere dancers	10	10
1305	$5 Mickey and Minnie Mouse shopping in street market	7·00	7·00
1306	$6 Mickey and Minnie Mouse, Jose Carioca and Donald Duck at pavement cafe	7·00	7·00

MS1307 Two sheets, each 127×101 mm. (a) $5 Mickey and Minnie Mouse in hot air balloon. (b) $5 Mickey Mouse at Pompidou Centre cafe (vert) Set of 2 sheets 11·00 13·00

252 Goalkeeper

1989. World Cup Football Championship, Italy (1990). Multicoloured.

1308	15c. Type **252**	85	30
1309	25c. Goalkeeper moving towards ball	90	30
1310	$1 Goalkeeper reaching for ball	1·50	1·25
1311	$4 Goalkeeper saving goal	3·00	5·00

MS1312 Two sheets, each 75×105 mm. (a) $5 Three players competing for ball (horiz). (b) $5 Ball and player' legs (horiz) Set of 2 sheets 7·00 10·00

253 *Mycena pura*

1989. Fungi. Multicoloured.

1313	10c. Type **253**	75	50
1314	25c. *Psathyrella tuberculata* (vert)	1·10	40
1315	50c. *Psilocybe cubensis*	1·50	60

1316	60c. *Leptonia caeruleocapitata* (vert)	1·50	70
1317	75c. *Xeromphalina tenuipes* (vert)	1·75	1·10
1318	$1 *Chlorophyllum molybdites* (vert)	1·75	1·25
1319	$3 *Marasmius haematocephalus*	2·75	3·75
1320	$4 *Cantharellus cinnabarinus*	2·75	3·75
MS1321	Two sheets, each 88×62 mm. (a) $6 "*Leucopaxillus gracillimus* (vert). (b) $6 *Volvariella volvacea* Set of 2 sheets	13·00	15·00

254 Desmarest's Hutia

1989. Local Fauna. Multicoloured.

1322	25c. Type **254**	80	50
1323	45c. Caribbean monk seal	2·50	1·00
1324	80c. Mustache bat (vert)	1·50	1·00
1325	$4 American manatee (vert)	3·50	5·50
MS1326	113×87 mm. $5 West Indian giant rice rat	7·00	9·00

255 Goofy and Old Printing Press

1989. "American Philately". Walt Disney cartoon characters with stamps and the logo of the American Philatelic Society. Multicoloured.

1327	1c. Type **255**	10	10
1328	2c. Donald Duck cancelling first day cover for Mickey Mouse	10	10
1329	3c. Donald Duck's nephews reading recruiting poster for Pony Express riders	10	10
1330	4c. Morty and Ferdie as early radio broadcasters	10	10
1331	5c. Donald Duck and water buffalo watching television	10	10
1332	10c. Donald Duck with stamp album	10	10
1333	$4 Daisy Duck with computer system	4·75	6·00
1334	$6 Donald's nephews with stereo radio, trumpet and guitar	6·00	7·00
MS1335	Two sheets, each 127×102 mm. (a) $5 Donald's nephews donating stamps to charity. (b) $5 Minnie Mouse flying mailplane upside down (horiz) Set of 2 sheets	11·00	13·00

256 Mickey Mouse and Donald Duck with Camden and Amboy Locomotive *John Bull*, 1831

1989. "World Stamp Expo '89" International Stamp Exhibition, Washington. Walt Disney cartoon characters and locomotives. Mult.

1336	25c. Type **256**	90	50
1337	45c. Mickey Mouse and friends with *Atlantic*, 1832	1·10	50
1338	50c. Mickey Mouse and Goofy with *William Crooks*, 1861	1·10	50
1339	60c. Mickey Mouse and Goofy with *Minnetonka*, 1869	1·10	65
1340	$1 Chip n'Dale with *Thatcher Perkins*, 1863	1·40	75
1341	$2 Mickey and Minnie Mouse with *Pioneer*, 1848	2·25	2·25
1342	$3 Mickey Mouse and Donald Duck with cog railway locomotive *Peppersass*, 1869	3·00	4·00
1343	$4 Mickey Mouse with Huey, Dewey and Louie aboard N.Y. World's Fair *Gimbels Flyer*, 1939	3·25	4·00
MS1344	Two sheets, each 127×101 mm. (a) $6 Mickey Mouse and locomotive *Thomas Jefferson*, 1835 (vert). (b) $6 Mickey Mouse and friends at Central Pacific *Golden Spike* ceremony, 1869 Set of 2 sheets	8·50	10·00

258 Launch of "Apollo II"

1989. 20th Anniv of First Manned Landing on Moon. Multicoloured.

1346	10c. Type **258**	50	30
1347	45c. Aldrin on Moon	1·25	30
1348	$1 Module "Eagle" over Moon (horiz)	1·75	1·10
1349	$4 Recovery of "Apollo II" crew after splashdown (horiz)	2·75	5·00
MS1350	107×77 mm. $5 Astronaut Neil Armstrong	4·50	5·50

259 *The Small Cowper Madonna* (Raphael)

1989. Christmas. Paintings by Raphael and Giotto. Multicoloured.

1351	10c. Type **259**	30	15
1352	25c. *Madonna of the Goldfinch* (Raphael)	45	20
1353	30c. *The Alba Madonna* (Raphael)	45	20
1354	50c. Saint (detail, "Bologna Altarpiece") (Giotto)	65	30
1355	60c. Angel (detail, "Bologna Altarpiece") (Giotto)	70	35
1356	70c. Angel slaying serpent (detail, "Bologna Altarpiece") (Giotto)	80	40
1357	$4 Evangelist (detail, "Bologna Altarpiece") (Giotto)	3·00	4·50
1358	$5 *Madonna of Foligno* (detail) (Raphael)	3·00	4·50
MS1359	Two sheets, each 71×96 mm. (a) $5 "*The Marriage of the Virgin* (detail) (Raphael). (b) $5 Madonna and Child (detail, "Bologna Altarpiece") (Giotto) Set of 2 sheets	9·00	12·00

260 Star-eyed Hermit Crab

1990. 500th Anniv (1992) of Discovery of America by Columbus (3rd issue). New World Natural History–Marine Life. Multicoloured.

1360	10c. Type **260**	45	20
1361	20c. Spiny lobster	65	25
1362	25c. Magnificent banded fanworm	65	25
1363	45c. Cannonball jellyfish	80	40
1364	60c. Red-spiny sea star	1·00	60
1365	$2 Peppermint shrimp	2·00	2·50
1366	$3 Coral crab	2·25	3·75
1367	$4 Branching fire coral	2·25	3·75
MS1368	Two sheets, each 100×69 mm. (a) $5 Common sea fan. (b) $5 Portuguese man-of-war Set of 2 sheets	8·00	9·00

261 *Vanilla mexicana*

1990. "Expo '90" International Garden and Greenery Exhibition, Osaka. Orchids. Multicoloured.

1369	15c. Type **261**	75	50
1370	45c. *Epidendrum ibaguense*	1·10	50
1371	50c. *Epidendrum secundum*	1·25	55
1372	60c. *Maxillaria conferta*	1·40	55
1373	$1 *Oncidium altissimum*	1·50	1·00
1374	$2 *Spiranthes lanceolata*	2·00	2·50
1375	$3 *Tonopsis utricularioides*	2·25	3·50
1376	$5 *Epidendrum nocturnum*	3·25	4·50
MS1377	Two sheets, each 102×70 mm. (a) $6 *Octomeria graminifolia*. (b) $6 *Rodriguezia lanceolata* Set of 2 sheets	6·50	8·00

262 Queen Victoria and Queen Elizabeth II

1990. 150th Anniv of the Penny Black.

1378	**262** 45c. green	1·25	40
1379	- 60c. mauve	1·50	65
1380	- $5 blue	3·75	5·50
MS1381	102×80 mm. Type **262** $6 purple	5·00	6·50

DESIGNS: 60c., $5 As Type **262**, but with different backgrounds.

263 "*Britannia* (mail paddle-steamer), 1840

1990. "Stamp World London '90" International Stamp Exhibition.

1382	**263** 50c. green and red	1·25	35
1383	- 75c. brown and red	1·50	90
1384	- $4 blue and red	4·00	5·50
MS1385	– 104×81 mm. $6 brown and red	4·50	6·00

DESIGNS: 75c. Travelling Post Office sorting van, 1892; $4 Short S.23 Empire "C" Class flying boat *Centaurus*, 1938; $6 Post Office underground railway, London, 1927.

264 Flamefish

1990. Reef Fish. Multicoloured.

1386	10c. Type **264**	65	55
1387	15c. Coney	80	55
1388	50c. Long-spined squirrelfish	1·25	60
1389	60c. Sergeant major	1·25	60
1390	$1 Yellow-tailed snapper	1·50	85
1391	$2 Rock beauty	2·25	2·75
1392	$3 Spanish hogfish	2·75	3·75
1393	$4 Striped parrotfish	2·75	3·75
MS1394	Two sheets, each 90×70 mm. (a) $5 Black-barred soldierfish. (b) $4 Four-eyed butterflyfish Set of 2 sheets	10·00	11·00

265 "Voyager 2" passing Saturn

1990. Achievement in Space. Multicoloured.

1395	45c. Type **265**	1·10	85
1396	45c. "Pioneer 11" photographing Saturn	1·10	85
1397	45c. Astronaut in transporter	1·10	85
1398	45c. Space shuttle "Columbia"	1·10	85
1399	45c. "Apollo 10" command module on parachutes	1·10	85
1400	45c. "Skylab" space station	1·10	85
1401	45c. Astronaut Edward White in space	1·10	85
1402	45c. "Apollo" spacecraft on joint mission	1·10	85
1403	45c. "Soyuz" spacecraft on joint mission	1·10	85
1404	45c. "Mariner 1" passing Venus	1·10	85
1405	45c. "Gemini 4" capsule	1·10	85
1406	45c. "Sputnik 1"	1·10	85
1407	45c. Hubble space telescope	1·10	85
1408	45c. North American X-15 rocket plane	1·10	85
1409	45c. Bell XS-1 airplane	1·10	85
1410	45c. "Apollo 17" astronaut and lunar rock formation	1·10	85
1411	45c. Lunar Rover	1·10	85
1412	45c. "Apollo 14" lunar module	1·10	85
1413	45c. Astronaut Buzz Aldrin on Moon	1·10	85
1414	45c. Soviet "Lunokhod" lunar vehicle	1·10	85

266 Queen Mother in Evening Dress

1990. 90th Birthday of Queen Elizabeth the Queen Mother.

1415	**266** 15c. multicoloured	55	20
1416	- 35c. multicoloured	75	25
1417	- 75c. multicoloured	1·00	85
1418	- $3 multicoloured	2·50	3·50
MS1419	– 67×98 mm. mult	4·00	4·50

DESIGNS: Nos. 1416/19, Recent photographs of the Queen Mother.

267 Mickey Mouse as Animator

1990. Mickey Mouse in Hollywood. Walt Disney cartoon characters. Multicoloured.

1420	25c. Type **267**	60	25
1421	45c. Minnie Mouse learning lines while being dressed	80	25
1422	50c. Mickey Mouse with clapper board	90	30
1423	60c. Daisy Duck making-up Mickey Mouse	1·00	35
1424	$1 Clarabelle Cow as Cleopatra	1·25	70
1425	$2 Mickey Mouse directing Goofy and Donald Duck	1·75	2·25
1426	$3 Mickey Mouse directing Goofy as birdman	2·25	3·50
1427	$4 Donald Duck and Mickey Mouse editing film	2·25	3·50
MS1428	Two sheets, each 132×95 mm. (a) $5 Minnie Mouse, Daisy Duck and Clarabelle as musical stars. (b) $5 Mickey Mouse on set as director Set of 2 sheets.	7·00	9·00

268 Men's 20 Kilometres Walk

1990. Olympic Games, Barcelona (1992) (1st issue). Multicoloured.

1429	50c. Type **268**	75	40
1430	75c. Triple jump	1·00	75
1431	$1 Men's 10,000 metres	1·25	85
1432	$5 Javelin	3·50	6·00
MS1433	100×70 mm. $6 Athlete lighting Olympic flame at Los Angeles Olympics	5·50	7·00

See also Nos. 1553/61 and 1609/17.

269 Huey and Dewey asleep (*Christmas Stories*)

1990. International Literacy Year. Walt Disney cartoon characters illustrating works by Charles Dickens. Multicoloured.

1434	15c. Type **269**	65	35
1435	45c. Donald Duck as Poor Jo looking at grave (*Bleak House*)	1·00	45
1436	50c. Dewey as Oliver asking for more (*Oliver Twist*)	1·10	50
1437	60c. Daisy Duck as The Marchioness (*Old Curiosity Shop*)	1·25	55
1438	$1 Little Nell giving nosegay to her grandfather (*Little Nell*)	1·40	85
1439	$2 Scrooge McDuck as Mr. Pickwick (*Pickwick Papers*)	2·00	2·50
1440	$3 Minnie Mouse as Florence and Mickey Mouse as Paul (*Dombey and Son*)	2·25	3·50

1441 $5 Minnie Mouse as Jenny Wren (*Our Mutual Friend*) 2·75 4·50

MS1442 Two sheets, each 126×102 mm. (a) $6 Artful Dodger picking pocket (*Oliver Twist*). (b) $6 Unexpected arrivals at Mr. Peggoty's (*David Copperfield*) Set of 2 sheets 10·00 12·00

1990. World Cup Football Championship Winners, Italy. Nos. 1308/11 optd **Winners West Germany 1 Argentina 0**.

1443 15c. Type **252** 75 40
1444 25c. Goalkeeper moving towards ball 75 40
1445 $1 Goalkeeper reaching for ball 1·50 1·60
1446 $4 Goalkeeper saving goal 3·25 5·50

MS1447 Two sheets, each 75×105 mm. (a) $5 Three players competing for ball (horiz). (b) $5 Ball and players' legs (horiz) Set of 2 sheets 9·50 11·00

271 Pearly-eyed Thrasher

1990. Birds. Multicoloured.

1448 10c. Type **271** 55 30
1449 25c. Purple-throated carib 60 35
1450 50c. Common yellowthroat 75 40
1451 60c. American kestrel 1·00 70
1452 $1 Yellow-bellied sapsucker 1·25 80
1453 $2 American purple gallinule ("Purple Gallinule") 2·25 2·50
1454 $3 Yellow-crowned night heron 2·50 3·25
1455 $4 Blue-hooded euphonia 2·50 3·50

MS1456 Two sheets, each 76×60 mm. (a) $6 Brown pelican. (b) $6 Magnificent frigate bird Set of 2 sheets 14·00 16·00

272 *Madonna and Child with Saints* (detail, Sebastiano del Piombo)

1990. Christmas. Paintings by Renaissance Masters. Multicoloured.

1457 25c. Type **272** 80 30
1458 30c. *Virgin and Child with Angels* (detail, Grunewald) (vert) 90 30
1459 40c. *The Holy Family and a Shepherd* (detail, Titian) 1·00 30
1460 60c. *Virgin and Child* (detail, Lippi) (vert) 1·40 40
1461 $1 *Jesus, St. John and Two Angels* (Rubens) 2·00 70
1462 $2 *Adoration of the Shepherds* (detail, Vincenzo Catena) 2·50 2·75
1463 $4 *Adoration of the Magi* (detail, Giorgione) 4·00 5·50
1464 $5 *Virgin and Child adored by Warrior* (detail, Vincenzo Catena) 4·00 5·50

MS1465 Two sheets, each 71×101 mm. (a) $6 *Allegory of the Blessings of Jacob* (detail, Rubens) (vert). (b) $6 *Adoration of the Magi* (detail, Fra Angelico) (vert) Set of 2 sheets 7·00 8·50

273 *Rape of the Daughters of Leucippus* (detail)

1991. 350th Death Anniv of Rubens. Multicoloured.

1466 25c. Type **273** 1·00 40
1467 45c. *Bacchanal* (detail) 1·50 45
1468 50c. *Rape of the Sabine Women* (detail) 1·50 50
1469 60c. *Battle of the Amazons* (detail) 1·60 65
1470 $1 *Rape of the Sabine Women* (different detail) 2·00 1·00
1471 $2 *Bacchanal* (different detail) 2·50 2·50
1472 $3 *Rape of the Sabine Women* (different detail) 3·50 4·25
1473 $4 *Bacchanal* (different detail) 3·50 5·25

MS1474 Two sheets, each 101×71 mm. (a) $6 *Rape of Hippoda-meia* (detail). (b) $6 *Battle of the Amazons* (different detail) Set of 2 sheets 8·50 10·00

274 U.S. Troops cross into Germany, 1944

1991. 50th Anniv of Second World War. Multicoloured.

1475 10c. Type **274** 1·10 65
1476 15c. Axis surrender in North Africa, 1943 1·25 50
1477 25c. U.S. tanks invade Kwajalein, 1944 1·25 50
1478 45c. Roosevelt and Churchill meet at Casablanca, 1943 2·75 70
1479 50c. Marshal Badoglio, Prime Minister of Italian anti-fascist government, 1943 1·50 70
1480 $1 Lord Mountbatten, Supreme Allied Commander South-east Asia, 1943 3·25 1·50
1481 $2 Greek victory at Koritza, 1940 2·25 2·75
1482 $4 Anglo-Soviet mutual assistance pact, 1941 3·25 4·25
1483 $5 Operation Torch landings, 1942 3·50 4·25

MS1484 Two sheets, each 108×80 mm. (a) $6 Japanese attack on Pearl Harbor, 1941. (b) $6 U.S.A.A.F. daylight raid on Schweinfurt, 1943 Set of 2 sheets 11·00 12·00

275 Locomotive *Prince Regent*, Middleton Colliery, 1812

1991. Cog Railways. Multicoloured.

1485 25c. Type **275** 1·25 55
1486 30c. Snowdon Mountain Railway 1·25 55
1487 40c. First railcar at Hell Gate, Manitou Pike's Peak Railway, U.S.A 1·40 65
1488 60c. P.N.K.A. rack railway, Java 1·60 70
1489 $1 Green Mountain Railway, Maine, 1883 2·00 1·00
1490 $2 Rack locomotive *Pike's Peak*, 1891 3·00 3·00
1491 $4 Vitznau–Rigi Railway, Switzerland, and Mt. Rigi hotel local post stamp 3·75 4·75
1492 $5 Leopoldina Railway, Brazil 3·75 4·75

MS1493 Two sheets, each 100×70 mm. (a) $6 Electric towing locomotives, Panama Canal. (b) $6 Gornergracht Railway, Switzerland (vert) Set of 2 sheets 12·00 13·00

276 *Heliconius charithonia*

1991. Butterflies. Multicoloured.

1494 10c. Type **276** 65 50
1495 35c. *Marpesia petreus* 1·10 50
1496 50c. *Anartia amathea* 1·25 60
1497 75c. *Siproeta stelenes* 1·50 1·00
1498 $1 *Battus polydamas* 1·75 1·10
1499 $2 *Historis odius* 2·25 2·75
1500 $4 *Hypolimnas misippus* 3·25 4·25
1501 $5 *Hamadryas feronia* 3·25 4·25

MS1502 Two sheets. (a) 73×100 mm. $6 *Vanessa cardui* caterpillar (vert) (b) 100×73 mm. $6 *"Danaus plexippus* caterpillar (vert) Set of 2 sheets 14·00 16·00

277 Hanno the Phoenician, 450 B.C.

1991. 500th Anniv of Discovery of America by Columbus (1992) (4th issue). History of Exploration.

1503 **277** 10c. multicoloured 70 40
1504 - 15c. multicoloured 80 40
1505 - 45c. multicoloured 1·25 50
1506 - 60c. multicoloured 1·40 60
1507 - $1 multicoloured 1·75 85
1508 - $2 multicoloured 2·25 2·75
1509 - $4 multicoloured 3·00 4·00
1510 - $5 multicoloured 3·00 4·00

MS1511 – Two sheets, each 106×76 mm. (a) $6 black and red. (b) $6 black and red Set of 2 sheets 7·00 9·00

DESIGNS—HORIZ: 15c. Pytheas the Greek, 325 B.C.; 45c. Erik the Red discovering Greenland, 985 A.D.; 60c. Leif Eriksson reaching Vinland, 1000 A.D.; $1 Scylax the Greek in the Indian Ocean, 518 A.D.; $2 Marco Polo sailing to the Orient, 1259 A.D.; $4 Ship of Queen Hatshepsut of Egypt, 1493 B.C.; $5 St. Brendan's coracle, 500 A.D. VERT: $6 (No. **MS**1511a) Engraving of Columbus as Admiral; $6 (No. **MS**1511b) Engraving of Columbus bare-headed.

278 *Camille Roulin* (Van Gogh)

1991. Death Centenary (1990) of Vincent van Gogh (artist). Multicoloured.

1512 5c. Type **278** 70 85
1513 10c. *Armand Roulin* 70 60
1514 15c. *Young Peasant Woman with Straw Hat sitting in the Wheat* 85 50
1515 25c. *Adeline Ravoux* 1·00 50
1516 30c. *The Schoolboy* 1·00 50
1517 40c. *Doctor Gachet* 1·10 50
1518 50c. *Portrait of a Man* 1·25 50
1519 75c. *Two Children* 1·75 80
1520 $2 *The Postman Joseph Roulin* 2·75 2·75
1521 $3 *The Seated Zouave* 3·75 4·00
1522 $4 *L'Arlesienne* 4·00 4·50
1523 $5 *Self-Portrait, November/December 1888* 4·00 4·50

MS1524 Three sheets, each 102×76 mm. (a) $5 *Farmhouse in Provence* (horiz). (b) $5 *Flowering Garden* (horiz). (c) $6 *The Bridge at Trinquetaille* (horiz) Imperf Set of 3 sheets 16·00 18·00

279 Mickey Mouse as Champion Sumo Wrestler

1991. "Philanippon '91" International Stamp Exhibition, Tokyo. Walt Disney cartoon characters participating in martial arts. Multicoloured.

1525 10c. Type **279** 80 20
1526 15c. Goofy using the tonfa (horiz) 90 25
1527 45c. Donald Duck as a Ninja (horiz) 1·60 50
1528 60c. Mickey armed for Kung fu 2·00 65
1529 $1 Goofy with Kendo sword 2·50 1·25
1530 $2 Mickey and Donald demonstrating Aikido (horiz) 3·00 3·00
1531 $4 Mickey and Donald in Judo bout (horiz) 4·00 5·00
1532 $5 Mickey performing Yabusame (mounted archery) 4·00 5·00

MS1533 Two sheets, each 127×102 mm. (a) $6 Mickey delivering Karate kick (horiz). (b) $6 Mickey demonstrating Tamashiwara Set of 2 sheets 10·00 12·00

280 Queen Elizabeth and Prince Philip in 1976

1991. 65th Birthday of Queen Elizabeth II. Multicoloured.

1534 15c. Type **280** 40 10
1535 20c. The Queen and Prince Philip in Portugal, 1985 40 10
1536 $2 Queen Elizabeth II 1·75 1·50
1537 $4 The Queen and Prince Philip at Ascot, 1986 2·75 3·25

MS1538 68×90 mm. $4 The Queen at National Theatre, 1986, and Prince Philip 3·50 4·00

1991. Tenth Wedding Anniv of Prince and Princess of Wales. As T **280**. Multicoloured.

1539 10c. Prince and Princess of Wales at party, 1986 50 10
1540 40c. Separate portraits of Prince, Princess and sons 1·00 25
1541 $1 Prince Henry and Prince William 1·25 70
1542 $5 Princess Diana in Australia and Prince Charles in Hungary 4·50 4·50

MS1543 68×90 mm. $4 Prince Charles in Hackney and Princess and sons in Majorca, 1987 5·50 5·50

281 Daisy Duck teeing-off

1991. Golf. Walt Disney cartoon characters. Multicoloured.

1544 10c. Type **281** 70 50
1545 15c. Goofy playing ball from under trees 75 50
1546 45c. Mickey Mouse playing deflected shot 1·25 50
1547 60c. Mickey hacking divot out of fairway 1·50 65
1548 $1 Donald Duck playing ball out of pond 1·75 1·10
1549 $2 Minnie Mouse hitting ball over pond 2·50 2·75
1550 $4 Donald in a bunker 3·25 4·00
1551 $5 Goofy trying snooker shot into hole 3·25 4·00

MS1552 Two sheets, each 127×102 mm. (a) $6 Grandma Duck in senior tournament. (b) $6 Mickey and Minnie Mouse on course (horiz) Set of 2 sheets 10·00 12·00

282 Moose receiving Gold Medal

1991. 50th Anniv of Archie Comics, and Olympic Games, Barcelona (1992) (2nd issue). Multicoloured.

1553 10c. Type **282** 55 40
1554 25c. Archie playing polo on a motorcycle (horiz) 85 40
1555 40c. Archie and Betty at fencing class 1·10 45
1556 60c. Archie joining girls' volleyball team 1·40 65
1557 $1 Archie with tennis ball in his mouth 1·75 1·10
1558 $2 Archie running marathon 2·50 3·00
1559 $4 Archie judging women's gymnastics (horiz) 3·75 4·50
1560 $5 Archie watching the cheerleaders 3·75 4·50

MS1561 Two sheets, each 128×102 mm. (a) $6 Archie heading football. (b) $6 Archie catching baseball (horiz) Set of 2 sheets 11·00 13·00

283 Presidents De Gaulle and Kennedy, 1961

1991. Birth Centenary of Charles de Gaulle (French statesman). Multicoloured.

1562 10c. Type **283** 80 50
1563 15c. General De Gaulle with President Roosevelt, 1945 (vert) 80 50
1564 45c. President De Gaulle with Chancellor Adenauer, 1962 (vert) 1·25 50
1565 60c. De Gaulle at Arc de Triomphe, Liberation of Paris, 1944 (vert) 1·50 65
1566 $1 General De Gaulle crossing the Rhine, 1945 1·75 1·25
1567 $2 General De Gaulle in Algiers, 1944 2·50 3·00
1568 $4 Presidents De Gaulle and Eisenhower, 1960 3·25 4·50
1569 $5 De Gaulle returning from Germany, 1968 (vert) 3·25 4·50

MS1570 Two sheets. (a) 76×106 mm. $6 De Gaulle with crowd. (b) 106×76 mm. $6 De Gaulle and Churchill at Casablanca, 1943 Set of 2 sheets 15·00 13·00

284 Parliament Building and Map

1991. Tenth Anniv of Independence.

1571 **284**	10c. multicoloured	75	50
MS1572	87×97 mm. $6 Old Post Office, St. Johns, and stamps of 1862 and 1981 (50×37 mm)	6·00	7·50

285 Germans celebrating Reunification

1991. Anniversaries and Events. Multicoloured.

1573	25c. Type **285**	30	30
1574	75c. Cubs erecting tent	70	50
1575	$1.50 *Don Giovanni* and Mozart	5·50	3·00
1576	$2 Chariot driver and Gate at night	1·10	2·00
1577	$2 Lord Baden-Powell and members of 3rd Antigua Methodist cub pack (vert)	3·25	2·75
1578	$2 Lilienthal's signature and glider *Flugzeug Nr. 5*	3·50	2·75
1579	$2.50 Driver in Class P36 steam locomotive (vert)	6·50	4·00
1580	$3 Statues from podium	1·75	3·25
1581	$3.50 Cubs and camp fire	2·50	3·25
1582	$4 St. Peter's Cathedral, Salzburg	10·00	7·50
MS1583	Two sheets. (a) 100×72 mm. $4 Detail of chariot and helmet; (b) 89×117 mm. $5 Antiguan flag and Jamboree emblem (vert) Set of 2 sheets	9·00	11·00

ANNIVERSARIES AND EVENTS: Nos. 1573, 1576, 1580, **MS**1583a, Bicentenary of Brandenburg Gate, Germany; 1574, 1577, 1581, **MS**1583b, 17th World Scout Jamboree, Korea; 1575, 1582, Death bicentenary of Mozart (composer); 1578, Centenary of Otto Lilienthal's gliding experiments; 1579, Centenary of Trans-Siberian Railway.

286 "Nimitz" Class Carrier and "Ticonderoga" Class Cruiser

1991. 50th Anniv of Japanese Attack on Pearl Harbor. Multicoloured.

1585	$1 Type **286**	2·50	1·75
1586	$1 Tourist launch	2·50	1·75
1587	$1 U.S.S. *Arizona* memorial	2·50	1·75
1588	$1 Wreaths on water and aircraft	2·50	1·75
1589	$1 White tern	2·50	1·75
1590	$1 Mitsubishi A6M Zero-Sen fighters over Pearl City	2·50	1·75
1591	$1 Mitsubishi A6M Zero-Sen fighters attacking	2·50	1·75
1592	$1 Battleship Row in flames	2·50	1·75
1593	$1 U.S.S. *Nevada* (battleship) underway	2·50	1·75
1594	$1 Mitsubishi A6M Zero-Sen fighters returning to carriers	2·50	1·75

287 *The Annunciation*

1991. Christmas. Religious Paintings by Fra Angelico. Multicoloured.

1595	10c. Type **287**	40	30
1596	30c. *Nativity*	65	30
1597	40c. *Adoration of the Magi*	75	30
1598	60c. *Presentation in the Temple*	1·00	45
1599	$1 *Circumcision*	1·25	65
1600	$3 *Flight into Egypt*	2·50	3·50
1601	$4 *Massacre of the Innocents*	2·50	4·00
1602	$5 *Christ teaching in the Temple*	2·50	4·00
MS1603	Two sheets, each 102×127 mm. (a) $6 *Adoration of the Magi* (Cook Tondo). (b) $6 *Adoration of the Magi* (different) Set of 2 sheets	13·00	14·00

288 Queen Elizabeth II and Bird Sanctuary

1992. 40th Anniv of Queen Elizabeth II's Accession. Multicoloured.

1604	10c. Type **288**	1·25	40
1605	30c. Nelson's Dockyard	1·50	40
1606	$1 Ruins on Shirley Heights	1·50	70
1607	$5 Beach and palm trees	3·00	4·25
MS1608	Two sheets, each 75×98 mm. (a) $6 Beach. (b) $6 Hillside foliage Set of 2 sheets	8·50	9·00

289 Mickey Mouse awarding Swimming Gold Medal to Mermaid

1992. Olympic Games, Barcelona (3rd issue). Walt Disney cartoon characters. Multicoloured.

1609	10c. Type **289**	70	30
1610	15c. Huey, Dewey and Louie with kayak	80	30
1611	30c. Donald Duck and Uncle Scrooge in yacht	1·00	35
1612	50c. Donald and horse playing water polo	1·40	50
1613	$1 Big Pete weightlifting	2·00	85
1614	$2 Donald and Goofy fencing	3·00	3·00
1615	$4 Mickey and Donald playing volleyball	4·00	4·50
1616	$5 Goofy vaulting	4·00	4·50
MS1617	Four sheets, each 123×98 mm. (a) $6 Mickey playing football. (b) $6 Mickey playing basketball (horiz). (c) $6 Minnie Mouse on uneven parallel bars (horiz). (d) $6 Mickey, Goofy and Donald judging gymnastics (horiz) Set of 4 sheets	14·00	15·00

290 Pteranodon

1992. Prehistoric Animals. Multicoloured.

1618	10c. Type **290**	65	40
1619	15c. Brachiosaurus	65	40
1620	30c. Tyrannosaurus Rex	85	40
1621	50c. Parasaurolophus	1·00	50
1622	$1 Deinonychus (horiz)	1·50	1·00
1623	$2 Triceratops (horiz)	2·00	2·00
1624	$4 Protoceratops hatching (horiz)	2·25	3·25
1625	$5 Stegosaurus (horiz)	2·25	3·25
MS1626	Two sheets, each 100×70 mm. (a) $6 Apatosaurus (horiz). (b) $6 Allosaurus (horiz) Set of 2 sheets	8·50	9·50

291 *Supper at Emmaus* (Caravaggio)

1992. Easter. Religious Paintings. Multicoloured.

1627	10c. Type **291**	65	25
1628	15c. *The Vision of St. Peter* (Zurbaran)	80	25
1629	30c. *Christ driving the Money-changers from the Temple* (Tiepolo)	1·25	40
1630	40c. *Martyrdom of St. Bartholomew* (detail) (Ribera)	1·40	50
1631	$1 *Christ driving the Money-changers from the Temple* (detail) (Tiepolo)	2·25	1·00
1632	$2 *Crucifixion* (detail) (Altdorfer)	3·25	3·00
1633	$4 *The Deposition* (detail) (Fra Angelico)	4·25	5·00
1634	$5 *The Deposition* (different detail) (Fra Angelico)	4·25	5·00
MS1635	Two sheets. (a) 102×71 mm. $6 *The Last Supper* (detail, Masip). (b) 71×102 mm. $6 *Crucifixion* (detail, Altdorfer) (vert) Set of 2 sheets	9·50	12·00

292 *The Miracle at the Well* (Alonso Cano)

1992. "Granada '92" International Stamp Exhibition, Spain. Spanish Paintings. Multicoloured.

1636	10c. Type **292**	50	30
1637	15c. *The Poet Luis de Goingora y Argote* (Velazquez)	65	30
1638	30c. *The Painter Francisco Goya* (Vincente Lopez Portana)	85	40
1639	40c. *Maria de las Nieves Michaela Fourdinier* (Luis Paret y Alcazar)	95	50
1640	$1 *Carlos III eating before his Court* (Alcazar) (horiz)	1·75	1·25
1641	$2 *Rain Shower in Granada* (Antonio Munoz Degrain) (horiz)	2·50	2·75
1642	$4 *Sarah Bernhardt* (Santiago Rusinol i Prats)	3·50	4·00
1643	$5 *The Hermitage Garden* (Joaquim Mir Trinxet)	3·50	4·00
MS1644	Two sheets, each 120×95 mm. (a) $6 *The Ascent of Monsieur Boucle's Montgolfier Balloon in the Gardens of Aranjuez* (Antonio Carnicero) (112×87 mm). (b) $6 *Olympus: Battle with the Giants* (Francisco Bayeu y Subias) (112×87 mm). Imperf Set of 2 sheets	15·00	16·00

293 *Amanita caesarea*

1992. Fungi. Multicoloured.

1645	10c. Type **293**	70	40
1646	15c. *Collybia fusipes*	85	40
1647	30c. *Boletus aereus*	1·25	40
1648	40c. *Laccaria amethystina*	1·25	50
1649	$1 *Russula virescens*	2·00	1·25
1650	$2 *Tricholoma equestre* ("Tricholoma auratum")	2·75	2·75
1651	$4 *Calocybe gambosa*	3·50	4·00
1652	$5 *Lentinus tigrinus* ("Panus tigrinus")	3·50	4·00
MS1653	Two sheets, each 100×70 mm. (a) $6 *Clavariadelphus truncatus*. (b) $6 *Auricularia auricula-judae* Set of 2 sheets	12·00	13·00

294 Memorial Cross and Huts, San Salvador

1992. 500th Anniv of Discovery of America by Columbus (5th issue). World Columbian Stamp "Expo '92", Chicago. Multicoloured.

1654	15c. Type **294**	30	25
1655	30c. Martin Pinzon with telescope	55	25
1656	40c. Christopher Columbus	80	35
1657	$1 *Pinta*	2·75	1·50
1658	$2 *Nina*	3·00	3·00
1659	$4 *Santa Maria*	3·75	6·00
MS1660	Two sheets, each 108×76 mm. (a) $6 Ship and map of West Indies. (b) $6 Sea monster Set of 2 sheets	10·00	12·00

295 Antillean Crested Hummingbird and Wild Plantain

1992. "Genova '92" International Thematic Stamp Exhibition. Hummingbirds and Plants. Multicoloured.

1661	10c. Type **295**	45	50
1662	25c. Green mango and parrot's plantain	60	40
1663	45c. Purple-throated carib and lobster claws	80	45
1664	60c. Antillean mango and coral plant	90	55
1665	$1 Vervain hummingbird and cardinal's guard	1·40	85
1666	$2 Rufous-breasted hermit and heliconia	2·00	2·00
1667	$4 Blue-headed hummingbird and red ginger	3·00	3·75
1668	$5 Green-throated carib and ornamental banana	3·00	3·75
MS1669	Two sheets, each 100×70 mm. (a) $6 Bee hummingbird and jungle flame. (b) $6 Western streamertail and bignonia Set of 2 sheets	10·00	12·00

296 Columbus meeting Amerindians

1992. 500th Anniv of Discovery of America by Columbus (6th issue). Organization of East Caribbean States. Multicoloured.

1670	$1 Type **296**	85	65
1671	$2 Ships approaching island	1·40	1·60

297 Ts'ai Lun and Paper

1992. Inventors and Inventions. Multicoloured.

1672	10c. Type **297**	25	25
1673	25c. Igor Sikorsky and "Bolshoi Baltiskii" (first four-engined airplane)	1·75	40
1674	30c. Alexander Graham Bell and early telephone	55	45
1675	40c. Johannes Gutenberg and early printing press	55	45
1676	60c. James Watt and stationary steam engine	4·00	1·25
1677	$1 Anton van Leeuwenhoek and early microscope	2·00	1·60
1678	$4 Louis Braille and hands reading braille	5·00	5·50
1679	$5 Galileo and telescope	5·00	5·50
MS1680	Two sheets, each 100×73 mm. (a) $6 Edison and Latimer's phonograph. (b) $6 *Clermont* (first commercial paddle-steamer) Set of 2 sheets	9·50	12·00

298 Elvis looking Pensive

1992. 15th Death Anniv of Elvis Presley. Multicoloured.

1681	$1 Type **298**	1·90	1·25
1682	$1 Wearing black and yellow striped shirt	1·90	1·25
1683	$1 Singing into microphone	1·90	1·25
1684	$1 Wearing wide-brimmed hat	1·90	1·25
1685	$1 With microphone in right hand	1·90	1·25
1686	$1 In Army uniform	1·90	1·25
1687	$1 Wearing pink shirt	1·90	1·25
1688	$1 In yellow shirt	1·90	1·25
1689	$1 In jacket and bow tie	1·90	1·25

299 Madison Square Gardens

1992. Postage Stamp Mega Event, New York. Sheet 100×70 mm.

MS1690 **299**	$6 multicoloured	4·50	6·00

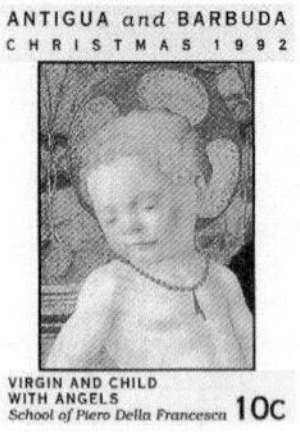

300 *Virgin and Child with Angels* (detail) (School of Piero della Francesca)

1992. Christmas. Details of the Holy Child from various paintings. Multicoloured.

1691	10c. Type **300**	60	30
1692	25c. *Madonna degli Alberelli* (Giovanni Bellini)	90	30
1693	30c. *Madonna and Child with St. Anthony Abbot and St. Sigismund* (Neroccio)	95	30
1694	40c. *Madonna and the Grand Duke* (Raphael)	1·00	30
1695	60c. *The Nativity* (Georges de la Tour)	1·50	60
1696	$1 *Holy Family* (Jacob Jordaens)	1·75	1·00
1697	$4 *Madonna and Child Enthroned* (Magaritone)	3·75	4·75
1698	$5 *Madonna and Child on a Curved Throne* (Byzantine school)	3·75	4·75
MS1699	Two sheets, each 76×102 mm. (a) $6 *Madonna and Child* (Domenco Ghirlando). (b) $6 *The Holy Family* (Pontormo) Set of 2 sheets	9·50	12·00

301 Russian Cosmonauts

1992. Anniversaries and Events. Multcoloured.

1700	10c. Type **301**	80	60
1701	40c. *Graf Zeppelin* (airship), 1929	1·75	65
1702	45c. Bishop Daniel Davis	50	40
1703	75c. Konrad Adenauer making speech	65	65
1704	$1 Bus Mosbacher and *Weatherly* (yacht)	1·25	1·25
1705	$1.50 Rain forest	1·75	1·75
1706	$2 Tiger	7·00	4·00
1707	$2 National flag, plant and emblem (horiz)	5·50	3·00
1708	$2 Members of Community Players company (horiz)	2·00	3·00
1709	$2.25 Women carrying pots	2·00	3·00
1710	$3 Lions Club emblem	2·25	3·25
1711	$4 Chinese rocket on launch tower	4·25	5·00
1712	$4 West German and N.A.T.O. flags	5·50	5·50
1713	$6 Hugo Eckener (airship pioneer)	5·00	6·00
MS1714	Four sheets, each 100×71 mm. (a) $6 Projected European space station. (b) $6 Airship LZ-129 *Hindenburg*, 1936. (c) $6 Brandenburg Gate on German flag. (d) $6 *Danaus plexippu*" (butterfly) Set of 4 sheets	23·00	25·00

ANNIVERSARIES AND EVENTS: Nos. 1700, 1711, **MS**1714a, International Space Year; 1701, 1713, **MS**1714b, 75th death anniv of Count Ferdinand von Zeppelin; 1702, 150th anniv of Anglican Diocese of North-eastern Caribbean and Aruba; 1703, 1712, **MS**1714c, 25th death anniv of Konrad Adenauer (German statesman); 1704, Americas Cup yachting championship; 1705/6, **MS**1714d, Earth Summit '92, Rio; 1707, 50th anniv of Inter-American Institute for Agricultural Co-operation; 1708, 40th anniv of Cultural Development; 1709, United Nations World Health Organization Projects; 1710, 75th anniv of International Association of Lions Clubs.

302 Boy Hiker resting

1993. Hummel Figurines. Multicoloured.

1715	15c. Type **302**	35	15
1716	30c. Girl sitting on fence	55	25
1717	40c. Boy hunter	65	35
1718	50c. Boy with umbrella	75	45
1719	$1 Hikers at signpost	1·25	75
1720	$2 Boy hiker with pack and stick	1·75	2·25
1721	$4 Girl with young child and goat	2·75	3·50
1722	$5 Boy whistling	2·75	3·50
MS1723	Two sheets, each 97×122 mm. (a) $1.50×4, As Nos. 1715/18. (b) $1.50×4, As Nos. 1719/22 Set of 2 sheets	13·00	14·00

303 Goofy playing Golf

1993. Opening of Euro-Disney Resort, Paris. Multicoloured.

1724	10c. Type **303**	80	30
1725	25c. Chip and Dale at Davy Crockett's campground	1·00	30
1726	30c. Donald Duck at the Cheyenne Hotel	1·00	35
1727	40c. Goofy at the Santa Fe Hotel	1·10	35
1728	$1 Mickey and Minnie Mouse at the New York Hotel	2·25	1·25
1729	$2 Mickey, Minnie and Goofy in car	2·75	2·75
1730	$4 Goofy at Pirates of the Caribbean	4·00	5·00
1731	$5 Donald at Adventureland	4·00	5·00
MS1732	Four sheets, each 127×102 mm. (a) $6 Mickey in bellboy outfit. (b) $6 Mickey on star (vert). (c) $6 Mickey on opening poster (vert). (d) $6 Mickey and balloons on opening poster (vert) Set of 2 sheets	16·00	18·00

304 Cardinal's Guard

1993. Flowers. Multicoloured.

1733	15c. Type **304**	1·00	40
1734	25c. Giant granadilla	1·10	40
1735	30c. Spider flower	1·10	40
1736	40c. Gold vine	1·25	40
1737	$1 Frangipani	2·00	1·25
1738	$2 Bougainvillea	2·75	2·75
1739	$4 Yellow oleander	3·75	4·50
1740	$5 Spicy jatropha	3·75	4·50
MS1741	Two sheets, each 100×70 mm. (a) $6 Birdlime tree. (b) Fairy lily Set of 2 sheets	9·00	12·00

305 *The Destiny of Marie de' Medici* (upper detail)

1993. Bicentenary of the Louvre, Paris. Paintings by Peter Paul Rubens. Multicoloured.

1742	$1 Type **305**	95	85
1743	$1 *The Birth of Marie de' Medici*	95	85
1744	$1 *The Education of Marie de' Medici*	95	85
1745	$1 *The Destiny of Marie de' Medici* (lower detail)	95	85
1746	$1 *Henry VI receiving the Portrait of Marie*	95	85
1747	$1 *The Meeting of the King and Marie at Lyons*	95	85
1748	$1 *The Marriage by Proxy*	95	85
1749	$1 *The Birth of Louis XIII*	95	85
1750	$1 *The Capture of Juliers*	95	85
1751	$1 *The Exchange of the Princesses*	95	85
1752	$1 *The Regency*	95	85
1753	$1 *The Majority of Louis XIII*	95	85
1754	$1 *The Flight from Blois*	95	85
1755	$1 *The Treaty of Angouleme*	95	85
1756	$1 *The Peace of Angers*	95	85
1757	$1 *The Reconciliation of Louis and Marie de' Medici*	95	85
MS1758	70×100 mm. $6 *Helene Faurment with a Coach* (52×85 mm)	5·50	7·00

Nos. 1742/57 depict details from *The Story of Marie de' Medici*.

306 St. Lucia Amazon ("St. Lucia Parrot")

1993. Endangered Species. Multicoloured.

1759	$1 Type **306**	90	90
1760	$1 Cahow	90	90
1761	$1 Swallow-tailed kite	90	90
1762	$1 Everglade kite ("Everglades Kite")	90	90
1763	$1 Imperial amazon ("Imperial Parrot")	90	90
1764	$1 Humpback whale	90	90
1765	$1 Plain pigeon ("Puerto Rican Plain Pigeon")	90	90
1766	$1 St. Vincent amazon ("St. Vincent Parrot")	90	90
1767	$1 Puerto Rican amazon ("Puerto Rican Parrot")	90	90
1768	$1 Leatherback turtle	90	90
1769	$1 American crocodile	90	90
1770	$1 Hawksbill turtle	90	90
MS1771	Two sheets, each 100×70 mm. (a) $6 As No. 1764. (b) West Indian manatee Set of 2 sheets	8·00	10·00

Nos. 1759/70 were printed together, *se-tenant*, with the background forming a composite design.

307 Queen Elizabeth II at Coronation (photograph by Cecil Beaton)

1993. 40th Anniv of Coronation (1st issue).

1772	**307**	30c. multicoloured	60	60
1773	-	40c. multicoloured	70	70
1774	-	$2 blue and black	1·75	2·00
1775	-	$4 multicoloured	2·25	2·50
MS1776		70×100 mm. $6 multicoloured	5·00	6·00

DESIGNS: 40c. Queen Elizabeth the Queen Mother's Crown, 1937; $2 Procession of heralds; $4 Queen Elizabeth II and Prince Edward. (28½×42½ mm)—$6 "Queen Elizabeth II" (detail) (Dennis Fildes).

308 Princess Margaret and Antony Armstrong-Jones

1993. 40th Anniv of Coronation (2nd issue).

1777-1808	$1×32 either grey and black or multicoloured	26·00	28·00

DESIGNS: Various views as Type **308** from each decade of the reign.

309 Edward Stanley Gibbons and Catalogue of 1865

1993. Famous Professional Philatelists (1st series).

1809	**309**	$1.50 brown, black & grn	1·75	1·50
1810	-	$1.50 multicoloured	1·75	1·50
1811	-	$1.50 multicoloured	1·75	1·50
1812	-	$1.50 multicoloured	1·75	1·50
1813	-	$1.50 multicoloured	1·75	1·50
1814	-	$1.50 multicoloured	1·75	1·50
MS1815		98×69 mm. $3 black; $3 black	5·50	6·50

DESIGNS: No. 1810, Theodore Champion and France 1849 1f. stamp; 1811, J. Walter Scott and U.S.A. 1918 24c. "Inverted Jenny" error; 1812, Hugo Michel and Bavaria 1849 1k. stamp; 1813, Alberto and Giulio Bolaffi with Sardinia 1851 5c. stamp; 1814, Richard Borek and Brunswick 1865 1gr. stamp; **MS**1815, Front pages of "*Mekeel's Weekly Stamp News* in 1891 (misdated 1890) and 1993.

See also No. 1957.

310 Paul Gascoigne

1993. World Cup Football Championship, U.S.A. (1st issue). English Players. Multicoloured.

1816	$2 Type **310**	1·50	1·40
1817	$2 David Platt	1·50	1·40
1818	$2 Martin Peters	1·50	1·40
1819	$2 John Barnes	1·50	1·40
1820	$2 Gary Lineker	1·50	1·40
1821	$2 Geoff Hurst	1·50	1·40
1822	$2 Bobby Charlton	1·50	1·40
1823	$2 Bryan Robson	1·50	1·40
1824	$2 Bobby Moore	1·50	1·40
1825	$2 Nobby Stiles	1·50	1·40
1826	$2 Gordon Banks	1·50	1·40
1827	$2 Peter Shilton	1·50	1·40
MS1828	Two sheets, each 135×109 mm. (a) $6 Bobby Moore holding World Cup. (b) $6 Gary Lineker and Bobby Robson Set of 2 sheets	9·00	11·00

See also Nos. 2039/45.

311 Grand Inspector W. Heath

1993. Anniversaries and Events. Multicoloured.

1829	10c. Type **311**	2·50	1·00
1830	15c. Rodnina and Oulanov (U.S.S.R.) (pairs figure skating) (horiz)	1·25	50
1831	30c. Present Masonic Hall, St. John's (horiz)	2·75	1·00
1832	30c. Willy Brandt with Helmut Schmidt and George Leber (horiz)	70	40
1833	30c. *Cat and Bird* (Picasso) (horiz)	70	40
1834	40c. Previous Masonic Hall, St. John's (horiz)	2·75	1·00
1835	40c. *Fish on a Newspaper* (Picasso) (horiz)	70	50
1836	40c. Early astronomical equipment	70	50
1837	40c. Prince Naruhito and engagement photographs (horiz)	70	50
1838	60c. Grand Inspector J. Jeffery	4·00	1·25
1839	$1 *Woman combing her Hair* (W. Slewinski) (horiz)	1·25	1·25
1840	$3 Masako Owada and engagement photographs (horiz)	2·50	3·00
1841	$3 *Artist's Wife with Cat* (Konrad Kryzanowski) (horiz)	2·50	3·00
1842	$4 Willy Brandt and protest march (horiz)	3·00	3·50
1843	$4 Galaxy	3·00	3·50
1844	$5 Alberto Tomba (Italy) (giant slalom) (horiz)	3·00	3·50
1845	$5 *Dying Bull* (Picasso) (horiz)	3·00	3·50
1846	$5 Pres. Clinton and family (horiz)	3·00	3·50
MS1847	Seven sheets. (a) 106×75 mm. $5 Copernicus. (b) 106×75 mm. $6 Womens' 1500 metre speed skating medallists (horiz). (c) 106×75 mm. $6 Willy Brandt at Warsaw Ghetto Memorial (horiz). (d) 106×75 mm. $6 *Woman with a Dog* (detail) (Picasso) (horiz). (e) 106×75 mm. $6 Masako Owada. (f) 70×100 mm. $6 *General Confusion* (S. I. Witkiewicz). (g) 106×75 mm. $6 Pres. Clinton taking the Oath (42½×57 mm) Set of 7 sheets	28·00	30·00

ANNIVERSARIES AND EVENTS: Nos. 1829, 1831, 1834, 1838, 150th anniv of St. John's Masonic Lodge No. 492; 1830, 1844, **MS**1847b, Winter Olympic Games '94, Lillehammer; 1832, 1842, **MS**1847c, 80th birth anniv of Willy Brandt (German politician); 1833, 1835, 1845, **MS**1847d, 20th death anniv of Picasso (artist); 1836, 1843, **MS**1847a, 450th death anniv of Copernicus (astronomer); 1837, 1840, **MS**1847e, Marriage of Crown Prince Naruhito of Japan; 1839, 1841, **MS**1847f, "Polska '93" International Stamp Exhibition, Poznan; 1846, **MS**1847g, Inauguration of U.S. President William Clinton.

312 Hugo Eckener and Dr. W. Beckers with Airship "Graf Zeppelin" over Lake George, New York

1993. Aviation Anniversaries. Multicoloured.

1848	30c. Type **312**	1·00	70
1849	40c. Chicago World's Fair from *Graf Zeppelin*	1·00	1·00
1850	40c. Gloster Whittle E.28/39, 1941	1·00	1·00
1851	40c. George Washington writing balloon mail letter (vert)	1·00	1·00
1852	$4 Pres. Wilson and Curtiss JN-4 Jenny	3·75	4·50
1853	$5 Airship *Hindenburg* over Ebbets Field baseball stadium, 1937	3·75	4·50
1854	$5 Gloster Meteor in dogfight	3·75	4·50
MS1855	Three sheets. (a) 86×105 mm. $6 Hugo Eckener (vert). (b) 105×86 mm. $6 Consolidated PBY-5 Catalina flying boat (57×42½ mm). (c) 105×86 mm. $6 Alexander Hamilton, Washington and John Jay watching Blanchard's balloon, 1793 (horiz) Set of 3 sheets	16·00	18·00

ANNIVERSARIES: Nos. 1848/9, 1853, **MS**1855a, 125th birth anniv of Hugo Eckener (airship commander); 1850, 1854, **MS**1855b, 75th anniv of Royal Air Force; 1851/2, **MS**1855c, Bicentenary of first airmail flight.

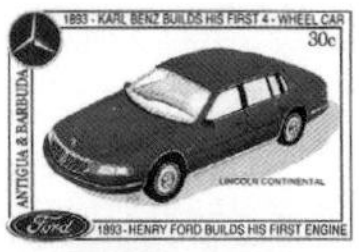

313 Lincoln Continental

1993. Centenaries of Henry Ford's First Petrol Engine (Nos. 1856, 1858), and Karl Benz's First Four-wheeled Car (others). Multicoloured.

1856	30c. Type **313**	1·00	75
1857	40c. Mercedes racing car, 1914	1·00	75
1858	$4 Ford "GT40", 1966	4·00	4·50
1859	$5 Mercedes Benz "gull-wing" coupe, 1954	4·00	4·50
MS1860	Two sheets. (a) 114×87 mm. $6 Ford's Mustang emblem. (b) 87×114 mm. $6 Germany 1936 12pf. Benz and U.S.A. 1968 12c. Ford stamps Set of 2 sheets	9·00	12·00

314 *The Musical Farmer*, 1932

1993. Mickey Mouse Film Posters. Multicoloured.

1861	10c. Type **314**	75	30
1862	15c. *Little Whirlwind*, 1941	85	35
1863	30c. *Pluto's Dream House*, 1940	1·00	40
1864	40c. *Gulliver Mickey*, 1934	1·00	40
1865	50c. *Alpine Climbers*, 1936	1·00	50
1866	$1 *Mr. Mouse Takes a Trip*, 1940	1·50	1·00
1867	$2 *The Nifty Nineties*, 1941	2·25	2·50
1868	$4 *Mickey Down Under*, 1948	3·25	4·50
1869	$5 *The Pointer*, 1939	3·25	4·50
MS1870	Two sheets, each 125×105 mm. (a) $6 *The Simple Things*, 1953. (b) $6 *The Prince and the Pauper*, 1990 Set of 2 sheets	11·00	14·00

315 Marie and Fritz with Christmas Tree

1993. Christmas. Mickey's Nutcracker. Walt Disney cartoon characters in scenes from *The Nutcracker*. Multicoloured.

1871	10c. Type **315**	75	40
1872	15c. Marie receives Nutcracker from Godfather Drosselmeir	80	40
1873	20c. Fritz breaks Nutcracker	80	40
1874	30c. Nutcracker with sword	90	40
1875	40c. Nutcracker and Marie in the snow	95	40
1876	50c. Marie and the Prince meet Sugar Plum Fairy	1·00	60
1877	60c. Marie and Prince in Crystal Hall	1·00	60
1878	$3 Huey, Dewey and Louie as Cossack dancers	3·25	4·00
1879	$6 Mother Ginger and her puppets	4·50	6·50
MS1880	Two sheets, each 127×102 mm. (a) $6 Marie and Prince in sleigh. (b) $6 The Prince in sword fight (vert) Set of 2 sheets	9·00	12·00

316 *Hannah and Samuel* (Rembrandt)

1993. Famous Paintings by Rembrandt and Matisse. Multicoloured.

1881	15c. Type **316**	40	30
1882	15c. *Guitarist* (Matisse)	40	30
1883	30c. *The Jewish Bride* (Rembrandt)	55	30
1884	40c. *Jacob wrestling with the Angel* (Rembrandt)	60	30
1885	60c. *Interior with a Goldfish Bowl* (Matisse)	80	50
1886	$1 *Mlle Yvonne Landsberg* (Matisse)	1·25	80
1887	$4 *The Toboggan* (Matisse)	3·00	4·25
1888	$5 *Moses with the Tablets of the Law* (Rembrandt)	3·00	4·25
MS1889	Two sheets. (a) 124×99 mm. $6 *The Blinding of Samson by the Philistines* (detail) (Rembrandt). (b) 99×124 mm. $6 *The Three Sisters* (detail) (Matisse) Set of 2 sheets	10·00	11·00

317 Hong Kong 1981 $1 Golden Threadfin Bream Stamp and Sampans, Shau Kei Wan

1994. "Hong Kong '94" International Stamp Exhibition (1st issue). Multicoloured.

1890	40c. Type **317**	80	80
1891	40c. Antigua 1990 $2 Rock beauty stamp and sampans, Shau Kei Wan	80	80

Nos. 1890/1 were printed together, *se-tenant*, forming a composite design.

See also Nos. 1892/7 and 1898/1905.

318 Terracotta Warriors

1994. "Hong Kong '94" International Stamp Exhibition (2nd issue). Qin Dynasty Terracotta Figures. Multicoloured.

1892	40c. Type **318**	60	60
1893	40c. Cavalryman and horse	60	60
1894	40c. Warriors in armour	60	60
1895	40c. Painted bronze chariot and team	60	60
1896	40c. Pekingese dog	60	60
1897	40c. Warriors with horses	60	60

319 Mickey Mouse in Junk

1994. "Hong Kong '94" International Stamp Exhibition (3rd issue). Walt Disney cartoon characters. Multicoloured.

1898	10c. Type **319**	70	30
1899	15c. Minnie Mouse as mandarin	75	35
1900	30c. Donald and Daisy Duck on houseboat	90	45
1901	50c. Mickey holding bird in cage	1·10	60
1902	$1 Pluto and ornamental dog	1·75	1·00
1903	$2 Minnie and Daisy celebrating Bun Festival	2·50	2·50
1904	$4 Goofy making noodles	3·50	4·50
1905	$5 Goofy pulling Mickey in rickshaw	3·50	4·50
MS1906	Two sheets, each 133×109 mm. (a) $5 Mickey and Donald on harbour ferry (horiz). (b) $5 Mickey in traditional dragon dance (horiz) Set of 2 sheets	7·00	9·00

320 Sumatran Rhinoceros lying down

1994. Centenary (1992) of Sierra Club (environmental protection society). Endangered Species. Multicoloured.

1907	$1.50 Type **320**	1·25	1·25
1908	$1.50 Sumatran rhinoceros feeding	1·25	1·25
1909	$1.50 Ring-tailed lemur on ground	1·25	1·25
1910	$1.50 Ring-tailed lemur on branch	1·25	1·25
1911	$1.50 Red-fronted brown lemur on branch	1·25	1·25
1912	$1.50 Head of red-fronted brown lemur	1·25	1·25
1913	$1.50 Head of red-fronted brown lemur in front of trunk	1·25	1·25
1914	$1.50 Sierra Club Centennial emblem	80	80
1915	$1.50 Head of Bactrian camel	1·25	1·25
1916	$1.50 Bactrian camel	1·25	1·25
1917	$1.50 African elephant drinking	1·25	1·25
1918	$1.50 Head of African elephant	1·25	1·25
1919	$1.50 Leopard sitting upright	1·25	1·25
1920	$1.50 Leopard in grass (emblem at right)	1·25	1·25
1921	$1.50 Leopard in grass (emblem at left)	1·25	1·25
MS1922	Four sheets. (a) 100×70 mm. $1.50, Sumatran rhinoceros (horiz). (b) 70×100 mm. $1.50, Ring-tailed lemur (horiz). (c) 70×100 mm. $1.50, Bactrian camel (horiz). (d) 100×70 mm. $1.50, African elephant (horiz) Set of 4 sheets	6·00	8·00

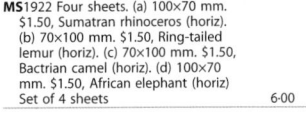

321 West Highland White Terrier

1994. Dogs of the World. Chinese New Year ("Year of the Dog"). Multicoloured.

1923	50c. Type **321**	75	65
1924	50c. Beagle	75	65
1925	50c. Scottish terrier	75	65
1926	50c. Pekingese	75	65
1927	50c. Dachshund	75	65
1928	50c. Yorkshire terrier	75	65
1929	50c. Pomeranian	75	65
1930	50c. Poodle	75	65
1931	50c. Shetland sheepdog	75	65
1932	50c. Pug	75	65
1933	50c. Shih Tzu	75	65
1934	50c. Chihuahua	75	65
1935	75c. Mastiff	75	65
1936	75c. Border collie	75	65
1937	75c. Samoyed	75	65
1938	75c. Airedale terrier	75	65
1939	75c. English setter	75	65
1940	75c. Rough collie	75	65
1941	75c. Newfoundland	75	65
1942	75c. Weimarana	75	65
1943	75c. English springer spaniel	75	65
1944	75c. Dalmatian	75	65
1945	75c. Boxer	75	65
1946	75c. Old English sheepdog	75	65
MS1947	Two sheets, each 93×58 mm. (a) $6 Welsh corgi. (b) $6 Labrador retriever Set of 2 sheets	9·00	12·00

322 *Spiranthes lanceolata*

1994. Orchids. Multicoloured.

1948	10c. Type **322**	70	60
1949	20c. *Ionopsis utricularioides*	1·00	50
1950	30c. *Tetramicra canaliculata*	1·25	50
1951	50c. *Oncidium picturatum*	2·00	1·25
1952	$1 *Epidendrum difforme*	3·00	2·75
1953	$2 *Epidendrum ciliare*	4·00	4·25
1954	$4 *Epidendrum ibaguense*	4·00	4·25
1955	$5 *Epidendrum nocturnum*	4·00	4·25
MS1956	Two sheets, each 100×73 mm. (a) $6 *Rodriguezia lanceolato*. (b) $6 *Encyclia cochleata* Set of 2 sheets	9·00	12·00

323 Hermann E. Sieger, Germany 1931 1m. Zeppelin Stamp and Airship LZ-127 *Graf Zeppelin*

1994. Famous Professional Philatelists (2nd series).

1957	**323**	$1.50 multicoloured	3·00	2·50

324 "Danaus plexippus"

1994. Butterflies. Multicoloured.

1958	10c. Type **324**	85	75
1959	15c. *Appias drusilla*	1·00	45
1960	30c. *Eurema lisa*	1·25	55
1961	40c. *Anaea troglodyta*	1·25	60
1962	$1 *Urbanus proteus*	2·00	1·25
1963	$2 *Junonia evarete*	2·75	2·75
1964	$4 *Battus polydamas*	3·50	4·50
1965	$5 *Heliconius charitonia*	3·50	4·50
MS1966	Two sheets, each 102×72 mm. (a) $6 *Phoebis sennae*. (b) $6 *Hemiargus hanno* Set of 2 sheets	9·00	12·00

No. 1959 is inscribed "Appisa drusilla" and No. 1965 "Heliconius charitonius", both in error.

325 Bottlenose Dolphin

1994. Marine Life. Multicoloured.

1967	50c. Type **325**	75	75
1968	50c. Killer whale	75	75
1969	50c. Spinner dolphin	75	75
1970	50c. Oceanic sunfish	75	75
1971	50c. Caribbean reef shark and short fin pilot whale	75	75
1972	50c. Copper-banded butterflyfish	75	75
1973	50c. Mosaic moray	75	75
1974	50c. Clown triggerfish	75	75
1975	50c. Red lobster	75	75
MS1976	Two sheets, each 106×76 mm. (a) $6 Seahorse. (b) $6 Swordfish ("Blue Marlin") (horiz) Set of 2 sheets	11·00	12·00

326 Edwin Aldrin (astronaut)

1994. 25th Anniv of First Manned Moon Landing. Multicoloured.

1977	$1.50 Type **326**	2·00	1·50
1978	$1.50 First lunar footprint	2·00	1·50

1979	$1.50 Neil Armstrong (astronaut)	2·00	1·50
1980	$1.50 Aldrin stepping onto Moon	2·00	1·50
1981	$1.50 Aldrin and equipment	2·00	1·50
1982	$1.50 Aldrin and U.S.A. flag	2·00	1·50
1983	$1.50 Aldrin at Tranquility Base	2·00	1·50
1984	$1.50 Moon plaque	2·00	1·50
1985	$1.50 "Eagle" leaving Moon	2·00	1·50
1986	$1.50 Command module in lunar orbit	2·00	1·50
1987	$1.50 First day cover of U.S.A. 1969 10c. First Man on Moon stamp	2·00	1·50
1988	$1.50 Pres. Nixon and astronauts	2·00	1·50
MS1989	72×102 mm. $6 Armstrong and Aldrin with postal official	5·00	4·00

327 Edwin Moses (U.S.A.) (400 m hurdles, 1984)

1994. Centenary of International Olympic Committee. Gold Medal Winners. Multicoloured.

1990	50c. Type **327**	40	30
1991	$1.50 Steffi Graf (Germany) (tennis, 1988)	2·00	1·75
MS1992	79×110 mm. $6 Johann Olav Koss (Norway) (500, 1500 and 10,000 metre speed skating), 1994	5·00	5·50

328 Antiguan Family

1994. International Year of the Family.

1993	**328**	90c. multicoloured	1·00	1·00

329 Mike Atherton (England) and Wisden Trophy

1994. Centenary (1995) of First English Cricket Tour to the West Indies. Multicoloured.

1994	35c. Type **329**	1·25	65
1995	75c. Viv Richards (West Indies) (vert)	2·00	1·25
1996	$1.20 Richie Richardson (West Indies) and Wisden Trophy	2·75	2·50
MS1997	80×100 mm. $3 English team, 1895 (black and brown)	2·50	3·00

330 Entrance Bridge, Songgwangsa Temple

1994. "Philakorea '94" International Stamp Exhibition, Seoul. Multicoloured.

1998	40c. Type **330**	50	40
1999	75c. Long-necked bottle	70	75
2000	75c. Punch'ong ware jar with floral decoration	70	75
2001	75c. Punch'ong ware jar with blue dragon pattern	70	75
2002	75c. Ewer in shape of bamboo shoot	70	75
2003	75c. Punch'ong ware green jar	70	75
2004	75c. Pear-shaped bottle	70	75
2005	75c. Porcelain jar with brown dragon pattern	70	75
2006	75c. Porcelain jar with floral pattern	70	75
2007	90c. Song-op Folk Village, Cheju	70	75
2008	$3 Port Sogwipo	1·75	2·25
MS2009	104×71 mm. $4 Ox herder playing flute (vert)	3·25	4·00

331 Short S.25 Sunderland (flying boat)

1994. 50th Anniv of D-Day. Multicoloured.

2010	40c. Type **331**	1·25	40
2011	$2 Lockheed P-38 Lightning fighters attacking train	3·00	2·75
2012	$3 Martin B-26 Marauder bombers	3·25	3·75
MS2013	108×78 mm. $6 Hawker Typhoon fighter bomber	6·75	6·25

332 Travis Tritt

1994. Stars of Country and Western Music. Multicoloured.

2014	75c. Type **332**	70	70
2015	75c. Dwight Yoakam	70	70
2016	75c. Billy Ray Cyrus	70	70
2017	75c. Alan Jackson	70	70
2018	75c. Garth Brooks	70	70
2019	75c. Vince Gill	70	70
2020	75c. Clint Black	70	70
2021	75c. Eddie Rabbit	70	70
2022	75c. Patsy Cline	70	70
2023	75c. Tanya Tucker	70	70
2024	75c. Dolly Parton	70	70
2025	75c. Anne Murray	70	70
2026	75c. Tammy Wynette	70	70
2027	75c. Loretta Lynn	70	70
2028	75c. Reba McEntire	70	70
2029	75c. Skeeter Davis	70	70
2030	75c. Hank Snow	70	70
2031	75c. Gene Autry	70	70
2032	75c. Jimmie Rodgers	70	70
2033	75c. Ernest Tubb	70	70
2034	75c. Eddy Arnold	70	70
2035	75c. Willie Nelson	70	70
2036	75c. Johnny Cash	70	70
2037	75c. George Jones	70	70
MS2038	Three sheets. (a) 100×70 mm. $6 Hank Williams Jr. (b) 100×70 mm. $6 Hank Williams Sr. (c) 70×100 mm. $6 Kitty Wells (horiz) Set of 3 sheets	15·00	15·00

333 Hugo Sanchez (Mexico)

1994. World Cup Football Championship, U.S.A. (2nd issue). Multicoloured.

2039	15c. Type **333**	75	30
2040	35c. Jurgen Klinsmann (Germany)	1·25	45
2041	65c. Antiguan player	1·50	55
2042	$1.20 Cobi Jones (U.S.A.)	2·00	1·75
2043	$4 Roberto Baggio (Italy)	3·25	4·00
2044	$5 Bwalya Kalusha (Zambia)	3·25	4·00
MS2045	Two sheets. (a) 72×105 mm. $6 Maldive Islands player (vert). (b) 107×78 mm. $6 World Cup trophy (vert) Set of 2 sheets	8·50	9·00

No. 2040 is inscribed "Klinsman" in error.

334 Sir Shridath Ramphal

1994. First Recipients of Order of the Caribbean Community. Multicoloured.

2046	65c. Type **334**	50	40
2047	90c. William Demas	65	60
2048	$1.20 Derek Walcott	2·50	1·75

335 Pair of Magnificent Frigate Birds

1994. Birds. Multicoloured.

2049	10c. Type **335**	60	45
2050	15c. Bridled quail dove	70	40
2051	30c. Magnificent frigate bird chick hatching	1·00	70
2052	40c. Purple-throated carib (vert)	1·00	70
2053	$1 Male magnificent frigate bird in courtship display (vert)	1·40	1·40
2054	$1 Broad-winged hawk (vert)	1·40	1·40
2055	$3 Young magnificent frigate bird	2·50	3·25
2056	$4 Yellow warbler	2·75	3·25
MS2057	Two sheets. (a) 70×100 mm. $6 Female magnificent frigate bird (vert). (b) 100×70 mm. $6 Black-billed whistling duck ducklings Set of 2 sheets	8·00	9·00

Nos. 2049, 2051, 2053 and 2055 also show the W.W.F. Panda emblem.

336 *The Virgin and Child by the Fireside* (Robert Campin)

1994. Christmas. Religious Paintings. Multicoloured.

2058	15c. Type **336**	80	30
2059	35c. *The Reading Madonna* (Giorgione)	1·10	30
2060	40c. *Madonna and Child* (Giovanni Bellini)	1·25	30
2061	45c. *The Litta Madonna* (Da Vinci)	1·25	30
2062	65c. *The Virgin and Child under the Apple Tree* (Lucas Cranach the Elder)	1·60	55
2063	75c. *Madonna and Child* (Master of the Female Half-lengths)	1·75	70
2064	$1.20 *An Allegory of the Church* (Alessandro Allori)	2·25	2·00
2065	$5 *Madonna and Child wreathed with Flowers* (Jacob Jordaens)	3·75	5·50
MS2066	Two sheets. (a) 123×88 mm. $6 *Madonna and Child with Commissioners* (detail) (Palma Vecchio) (b) 88×123 mm. $6 *The Virgin Enthroned with Child* (detail) (Bohemian master) Set of 2 sheets	13·00	9·00

337 Magnificent Frigate Bird

1995. Birds. Multicoloured.

2067	15c. Type **337**	45	20
2068	25c. Blue-hooded euphonia	60	20
2069	35c. Eastern meadowlark ("Meadowlark")	70	20
2070	40c. Red-billed tropic bird	75	20
2071	45c. Greater flamingo	75	25
2072	60c. Yellow-faced grassquit	1·00	30
2073	65c. Yellow-billed cuckoo	1·00	30
2074	70c. Purple-throated carib	1·00	35
2075	75c. Bananaquit	1·00	35
2076	90c. Painted bunting	1·10	40
2077	$1.20 Red-legged honeycreeper	1·50	65
2078	$2 Northern jacana ("Jacana")	2·50	1·75
2079	$5 Greater Antillean bullfinch	4·00	4·25
2080	$10 Caribbean elaenia	7·00	8·00
2081	$20 Brown trembler ("Trembler")	11·00	15·00

338 Head of Pachycephalosaurus

1995. Prehistoric Animals. Multicoloured.

2082	15c. Type **338**	60	60
2083	20c. Head of afrovenator	60	60
2084	65c. Centrosaurus	85	80
2085	75c. Kronosaurus (horiz)	85	85
2086	75c. Ichthyosaurus (horiz)	85	85
2087	75c. Plesiosaurus (horiz)	85	85
2088	75c. Archelon (horiz)	85	85
2089	75c. Pair of tyrannosaurus (horiz)	85	85
2090	75c. Tyrannosaurus (horiz)	85	85
2091	75c. Parasaurolophus (horiz)	85	85
2092	75c. Pair of parasaurolophus (horiz)	85	85
2093	75c. Oviraptor (horiz)	85	85
2094	75c. Protoceratops with eggs (horiz)	85	85
2095	75c. Pteranodon and protoceratops (horiz)	85	85
2096	75c. Pair of protoceratops (horiz)	85	85
2097	90c. Pentaceratops drinking	1·00	1·00
2098	$1.20 Head of tarbosaurus	1·25	1·25
2099	$5 Head of styracosaurus	3·50	4·50
MS2100	Two sheets, each 101×70 mm. (a) $6 Head of Corythosaurus (horiz). (b) $6 Head of Carnotaurus (horiz) Set of 2 sheets	11·00	13·00

339 Al Oerter (U.S.A.) (discus – 1956, 1960, 1964, 1968)

1995. Olympic Games, Atlanta (1996). Previous Gold Medal Winners (1st issue). Multicoloured.

2101	15c. Type **339**	60	30
2102	20c. Greg Louganis (U.S.A.) (diving – 1984, 1988)	60	30
2103	65c. Naim Suleymanoglu (Turkey) (weightlifting – 1988)	75	50
2104	90c. Louise Ritter (U.S.A.) (high jump – 1988)	1·00	70
2105	$1.20 Nadia Comaneci (Rumania) (gymnastics –1976)	2·00	1·40
2106	$5 Olga Bondarenko (Russia) (10,000 metres – 1988)	3·25	5·00
MS2107	Two sheets, each 106×76 mm. (a) $6 United States crew (eight-oared shell — 1964). (b) $6 Lutz Hessilch (Germany) (cycling — 1988) (vert) Set of 2 sheets	11·00	12·00

No. 2106 is inscribed "BOLDARENKO" in error.

See also Nos. 2302/23.

340 Map of Berlin showing Russian Advance

1995. 50th Anniv of End of Second World War in Europe. Multicoloured.

2108	$1.20 Type **340**	1·50	1·25
2109	$1.20 Russian tank and infantry	1·50	1·25
2110	$1.20 Street fighting in Berlin	1·50	1·25
2111	$1.20 German tank exploding	1·50	1·25
2112	$1.20 Russian air raid	1·50	1·25
2113	$1.20 German troops surrendering	1·50	1·25
2114	$1.20 Hoisting the Soviet flag on the Reichstag	1·50	1·25
2115	$1.20 Captured German standards	1·50	1·25
MS2116	104×74 mm. $6 Gen. Konev (vert)	4·50	5·50

See also Nos. 2132/8.

341 Signatures and Earl of Halifax

1995. 50th Anniv of United Nations. Multicoloured.

2117	75c. Type **341**	70	1·00
2118	90c. Virginia Gildersleeve	70	1·00
2119	$1.20 Harold Stassen	70	1·00
MS2120	100×70 mm. $6 Pres. Franklin D. Roosevelt	3·50	4·25

Nos. 2117/19 were printed together, *se-tenant*, forming a composite design.

342 Woman buying Produce from Market

1995. 50th Anniv of F.A.O. Multicoloured.

2121	75c. Type **342**	70	1·00
2122	90c. Women shopping	70	1·00
2123	$1.20 Women talking	70	1·00
MS2124	100×70 mm. $6 Tractor	3·00	3·75

Nos. 2121/3 were printed together, *se-tenant*, forming a composite design.

343 Beach and Rotary Emblem

1995. 90th Anniv of Rotary International.

2125 **343** $5 multicoloured 3·50 4·00
MS2126 74×104 mm. $6 National flag and emblem 3·50 4·00

344 Queen Elizabeth the Queen Mother

1995. 95th Birthday of Queen Elizabeth the Queen Mother.

2127 - $1.50 brown, light brown and black 1·50 1·50
2128 **344** $1.50 multicoloured 1·50 1·50
2129 - $1.50 multicoloured 1·50 1·50
2130 - $1.50 multicoloured 1·50 1·50
MS2131 100×127 mm. $6 multicoloured 5·50 5·50

DESIGNS: No. 2127, Queen Elizabeth the Queen Mother (pastel drawing); 2129, At desk (oil painting); 2130, Wearing green dress; **MS**2131, Wearing blue dress.

1995. 50th Anniv of End of Second World War in the Pacific. As T **340**. Multicoloured.

2132 $1.20 Gen. Chang Kai-Shek and Chinese guerrillas 1·10 1·25
2133 $1.20 Gen. Douglas MacArthur and beach landing 1·10 1·25
2134 $1.20 Gen. Claire Chennault and U.S. fighter aircraft 1·10 1·25
2135 $1.20 Brig. Orde Wingate and supply drop 1·10 1·25
2136 $1.20 Gen. Joseph Stilwell and U.S. supply plane 1·10 1·25
2137 $1.20 Field-Marshal Bill Slim and loading cow into plane 1·10 1·25
MS2138 108×76 mm. $3 Admiral Nimitz and aircraft carrier 2·75 3·50

345 Family ("Caring")

1995. Tourism. Sheet 95×72 mm, containing T **345** and similar horiz designs. Multicoloured.

MS2139 $2 Type **345**; $2 Market trader ("Marketing"); $2 Workers and housewife ("Working"); $2 Leisure pursuits ("Enjoying Life") 5·50 7·00

346 Purple-throated Carib

1995. Birds. Multicoloured.

2140 75c. Type **346** 1·10 1·00
2141 75c. Antillean crested hummingbird 1·10 1·00
2142 75c. Bananaquit 1·10 1·00
2143 75c. Mangrove cuckoo 1·10 1·00
2144 75c. Troupial 1·10 1·00
2145 75c. Green-throated carib 1·10 1·00
2146 75c. Yellow warbler 1·10 1·00
2147 75c. Antillean euphonia ("Blue-hooded Euphonia") 1·10 1·00
2148 75c. Scaly-breasted thrasher 1·10 1·00
2149 75c. Burrowing owl 1·10 1·00
2150 75c. Carib grackle 1·10 1·00
2151 75c. Adelaide's warbler 1·10 1·00
2152 75c. Ring-necked duck 1·10 1·00
2153 75c. Ruddy duck 1·10 1·00
2154 75c. Green-winged teal 1·10 1·00
2155 75c. Wood duck 1·10 1·00
2156 75c. Hooded merganser 1·10 1·00
2157 75c. Lesser scaup 1·10 1·00
2158 75c. Black-billed whistling duck ("West Indian Tree Duck") 1·10 1·00
2159 75c. Fulvous whistling duck 1·10 1·00
2160 75c. Bahama pintail 1·10 1·00
2161 75c. Northern shoveler 1·10 1·00
2162 75c. Masked duck 1·10 1·00
2163 75c. American wigeon 1·10 1·00
MS2164 Two sheets, each 104×74 mm. (a) $6 American purple gallinule. (b) $6 Heads of Blue-winged teal Set of 2 sheets 13·00 13·00

Nos. 2140/51 and 2152/63 respectively were printed together, *se-tenant*, forming composite designs.

347 Original Church, 1845

1995. 150th Anniv of Greenbay Moravian Church. Multicoloured.

2165 20c. Type **347** 70 30
2166 60c. Church in 1967 1·00 40
2167 75c. Present church 1·25 50
2168 90c. Revd. John Buckley (first minister of African descent) 1·40 60
2169 $1.20 Bishop John Ephraim Knight (longest-serving minister) 1·75 1·75
2170 $2 As 75c. 2·75 3·50
MS2171 110×81 mm. $6 Front of present church 4·50 6·00

348 Mining Bees

1995. Bees. Multicoloured.

2172 90c. Type **348** 1·00 70
2173 $1.20 Solitary bee 1·40 90
2174 $1.65 Leaf-cutter bee 2·00 2·00
2175 $1.75 Honey bees 2·00 2·00
MS2176 110×80 mm. $6 Solitary mining bee 4·00 5·00

349 Narcissus

1995. Flowers. Multicoloured.

2177 75c. Type **349** 80 80
2178 75c. Camellia 80 80
2179 75c. Iris 80 80
2180 75c. Tulip 80 80
2181 75c. Poppy 80 80
2182 75c. Peony 80 80
2183 75c. Magnolia 80 80
2184 75c. Oriental lily 80 80
2185 75c. Rose 80 80
2186 75c. Pansy 80 80
2187 75c. Hydrangea 80 80
2188 75c. Azaleas 80 80
MS2189 80×100 mm. $6 Calla lily 4·00 5·00

No. 2186 is inscribed "Pansie" in error.

350 Somali

1995. Cats. Multicoloured.

2190 45c. Type **350** 80 60
2191 45c. Persian and butterflies 80 60
2192 45c. Devon rex 80 60
2193 45c. Turkish angora 80 60
2194 45c. Himalayan 80 60
2195 45c. Maine coon 80 60
2196 45c. Ginger non-pedigree 80 60
2197 45c. American wirehair 80 60
2198 45c. British shorthair 80 60
2199 45c. American curl 80 60
2200 45c. Black non-pedigree and butterfly 80 60
2201 45c. Birman 80 60
MS2202 104×74 mm. $6 Siberian kitten (vert) 7·50 7·50

Nos. 2190/2201 were printed together, *se-tenant*, forming a composite design.

351 The Explorer Tent

1995. 18th World Scout Jamboree, Netherlands. Tents. Multicoloured.

2203 $1.20 Type **351** 1·60 1·60
2204 $1.20 Camper tent 1·60 1·60
2205 $1.20 Wall tent 1·60 1·60
2206 $1.20 Trail tarp 1·60 1·60
2207 $1.20 Miner's tent 1·60 1·60
2208 $1.20 Voyager tent 1·60 1·60
MS2209 Two sheets, each 76×106 mm. (a) $6 Scout and camp fire. (b) $6 Scout with back pack (vert) Set of 2 sheets 8·50 10·00

352 Trans-Gabon Diesel-electric Train

1995. Trains of the World. Multicoloured.

2210 35c. Type **352** 1·00 65
2211 65c. Canadian Pacific diesel-electric locomotive 1·50 90
2212 75c. Santa Fe Railway diesel-electric locomotive, U.S.A. 1·60 1·00
2213 90c. High Speed Train, Great Britain 1·60 1·00
2214 $1.20 TGV express train, France 1·60 1·60
2215 $1.20 Diesel-electric locomotive, Australia 1·60 1·60
2216 $1.20 Pendolino "ETR 450" electric train, Italy 1·60 1·60
2217 $1.20 Diesel-electric locomotive, Thailand 1·60 1·60
2218 $1.20 Pennsylvania Railroad Type K4 steam locomotive, U.S.A. 1·60 1·60
2219 $1.20 Beyer-Garratt steam locomotive, East African Railways 1·60 1·60
2220 $1.20 Natal Government steam locomotive 1·60 1·60
2221 $1.20 Rail gun, American Civil War 1·60 1·60
2222 $1.20 Locomotive *Lion* (red livery), Great Britain 1·60 1·60
2223 $1.20 William Hedley's *Puffing Billy* (green livery), Great Britain 1·60 1·60
2224 $6 Amtrak high speed diesel locomotive, U.S.A. 3·75 4·50
MS2225 Two sheets, each 110×80 mm. (a) $6 Locomotive *Iron Rooster*, China (vert). (b) $6 *Indian-Pacific* diesel-electric locomotive, Australia (vert) Set of 2 sheets 14·00 14·00

353 Dag Hammarskjold (1961 Peace)

1995. Centenary of Nobel Prize Trust Fund. Multicoloured.

2226 $1 Type **353** 1·10 1·10
2227 $1 Georg Wittig (1979 Chemistry) 1·10 1·10
2228 $1 Wilhelm Ostwald (1909 Chemistry) 1·10 1·10
2229 $1 Robert Koch (1905 Medicine) 1·10 1·10
2230 $1 Karl Ziegler (1963 Chemistry) 1·10 1·10
2231 $1 Alexander Fleming (1945 Medicine) 1·10 1·10
2232 $1 Hermann Staudinger (1953 Chemistry) 1·10 1·10
2233 $1 Manfred Eigen (1967 Chemistry) 1·10 1·10
2234 $1 Arno Penzias (1978 Physics) 1·10 1·10
2235 $1 Shmuel Agnon (1966 Literature) 1·10 1·10
2236 $1 Rudyard Kipling (1907 Literature) 1·10 1·10
2237 $1 Aleksandr Solzhenitsyn (1970 Literature) 1·10 1·10
2238 $1 Jack Steinberger (1988 Physics) 1·10 1·10
2239 $1 Andrei Sakharov (1975 Peace) 1·10 1·10
2240 $1 Otto Stern (1943 Physics) 1·10 1·10
2241 $1 John Steinbeck (1962 Literature) 1·10 1·10
2242 $1 Nadine Gordimer (1991 Literature) 1·10 1·10
2243 $1 William Faulkner (1949 Literature) 1·10 1·10
MS2244 Two sheets, each 100×70 mm. (a) $6 Elie Wiesel (1986 Peace) (vert). (b) $6 The Dalai Lama (1989 Peace) (vert) Set of 2 sheets 9·00 10·00

354 Elvis Presley

1995. 60th Birth Anniv of Elvis Presley. Multicoloured.

2245 $1 Type **354** 1·25 95
2246 $1 Holding microphone in right hand 1·25 95
2247 $1 In blue shirt and with neck of guitar 1·25 95
2248 $1 Wearing blue shirt and smiling 1·25 95
2249 $1 On wedding day 1·25 95
2250 $1 In army uniform 1·25 95
2251 $1 Wearing red shirt 1·25 95
2252 $1 Wearing white shirt 1·25 95
2253 $1 In white shirt with microphone 1·25 95
MS2254 101×71 mm. $6 "Ghost" image of Elvis amongst the stars 7·50 5·50

355 John Lennon and Signature

1995. 15th Death Anniv of John Lennon (entertainer). Multicoloured.

2255 45c. Type **355** 50 40
2256 50c. In beard and spectacles 50 50
2257 65c. Wearing sunglasses 55 55
2258 75c. In cap with heart badge 65 65
MS2259 103×73 mm. $6 As 75c. 5·50 6·50

1995. Hurricane Relief. Nos. 2203/8 optd **"Hurricane Relief"**.

2260 $1.20 Type **351** 1·25 1·25
2261 $1.20 Camper tent 1·25 1·25
2262 $1.20 Wall tent 1·25 1·25
2263 $1.20 Trail tarp 1·25 1·25
2264 $1.20 Miner's tent 1·25 1·25
2265 $1.20 Voyager tent 1·25 1·25
MS2266 Two sheets, each 76×106 mm. (a) $6 Scout and camp fire. (b) $6 Scout with back pack (vert) Set of 2 sheets 12·00 15·00

357 *Rest on the Flight into Egypt* (Paolo Veronese)

1995. Christmas. Religious Paintings. Multicoloured.

2267 15c. Type **357** 35 30
2268 35c. *Madonna and Child* (Van Dyck) 50 40
2269 65c. *Sacred Conversation Piece* (Veronese) 70 50
2270 75c. *Vision of St. Anthony* (Van Dyck) 80 60
2271 90c. *Virgin and Child* (Van Eyck) 90 65
2272 $6 *The Immaculate Conception* (Giovanni Tiepolo) 3·25 4·75
MS2273 Two sheets. (a) 101×127 mm. $5 *Christ appearing to his Mother* (detail) (Van der Weyden). (b) 127×101 mm. $6 *The Infant Jesus and Young St. John* (Murillo) Set of 2 sheets 8·00 9·00

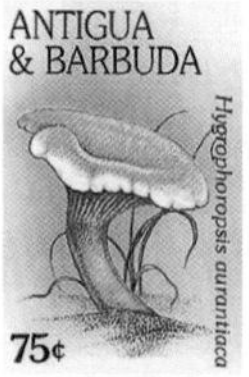

358 *Hygrophoropsis aurantiaca*

1996. Fungi. Multicoloured.

2274	75c. Type **358**	60	70
2275	75c. *Hygrophorus bakerensis*	60	70
2276	75c. *Hygrophorus conicus*	60	70
2277	75c. *Hygrophorus miniatus* ("Hygrocybe miniata")	60	70
2278	75c. *Suillus brevipes*	60	70
2279	75c. *Suillus luteus*	60	70
2280	75c. *Suillus granulatus*	60	70
2281	75c. *Suillus caerulescens*	60	70
MS2282	Two sheets, each 105×75 mm. (a) $6 *Conocybe filaris*. (b) $6 *Hygrocybe flavescens* Set of 2 sheets	7·00	8·00

359 H.M.S. *Resolution* (Cook)

1996. Sailing Ships. Multicoloured.

2283	15c. Type **359**	1·25	75
2284	25c. *Mayflower* (Pilgrim Fathers)	1·25	65
2285	45c. *Santa Maria* (Columbus)	1·50	65
2286	75c. *Aemilia* (Dutch galleon)	1·50	1·50
2287	75c. *Sovereign of the Seas* (English galleon)	1·50	1·50
2288	90c. H.M.S. *Victory* (Nelson)	1·75	1·25
2289	$1.20 As No. 2286	1·75	1·60
2290	$1.20 As No. 2287	1·75	1·60
2291	$1.20 *Royal Louis* (French galleon)	1·75	1·60
2292	$1.20 H.M.S. *Royal George* (ship of the line)	1·75	1·60
2293	$1.20 *Le Protecteur* (French frigate)	1·75	1·60
2294	$1.20 As No. 2288	1·75	1·60
2295	$1.50 As No. 2285	1·75	1·60
2296	$1.50 *Vitoria* (Magellan)	1·75	1·75
2297	$1.50 *Golden Hind* (Drake)	1·75	1·75
2298	$1.50 As No. 2284	1·75	1·75
2299	$1.50 *Griffin* (La Salle)	1·75	1·75
2300	$1.50 Type **359**	1·75	1·75
MS2301	Two sheets. (a) 102×72 mm. $6 U.S.S. *Constitution* (frigate). (b) 98×67 mm. $6 *Grande Hermine* (Cartier) Set of 2 sheets	10·00	11·00

360 Florence Griffith Joyner (U.S.A.) (Gold – track, 1988)

1996. Olympic Games, Atlanta. Previous Medal Winners (2nd issue). Multicoloured.

2302	65c. Type **360**	60	60
2303	75c. Olympic Stadium, Seoul (1988) (horiz)	65	65
2304	90c. Allison Jolly and Lynne Jewell (U.S.A.) (Gold – yachting, 1988) (horiz)	75	70
2305	90c. Wolfgang Nordwig (Germany) (Gold – pole vaulting, 1972)	75	75
2306	90c. Shirley Strong (Great Britain) (Silver – 100 metres hurdles, 1984)	75	75
2307	90c. Sergei Bubka (Russia) (Gold – pole vault, 1988)	75	75
2308	90c. Filbert Bayi (Tanzania) (Silver – 3000 metres steeplechase, 1980)	75	75
2309	90c. Victor Saneyev (Russia) (Gold – triple jump, 1968, 1972, 1976)	75	75
2310	90c. Silke Renk (Germany) (Gold – javelin, 1992)	75	75
2311	90c. Daley Thompson (Great Britain) (Gold – decathlon, 1980, 1984)	75	75
2312	90c. Robert Richards (U.S.A.) (Gold – pole vault, 1952, 1956)	75	75
2313	90c. Parry O'Brien (U.S.A.) (Gold – shot put, 1952, 1956)	75	75
2314	90c. Ingrid Kramer (Germany) (Gold – women's platform diving, 1960)	75	75
2315	90c. Kelly McCormick (U.S.A.) (Silver – women's springboard diving, 1984)	75	75
2316	90c. Gary Tobian (U.S.A.) (Gold – men's springboard diving, 1960)	75	75
2317	90c. Greg Louganis (U.S.A.) (Gold – men's diving, 1984 and 1988)	75	75
2318	90c. Michelle Mitchell (U.S.A.) (Silver – women's platform diving, 1984 and 1988)	75	75
2319	90c. Zhou Jihong (China) (Gold – women's platform diving, 1984)	75	75
2320	90c. Wendy Wyland (U.S.A.) (Bronze – women's platform diving, 1984)	75	75
2321	90c. Xu Yanmei (China) (Gold – women's platform diving, 1988)	75	75
2322	90c. Fu Mingxia (China) (Gold – women's platform diving, 1992)	75	75
2323	$1.20 2000 metre tandem cycle race (horiz)	1·00	1·00
MS2324	Two sheets, each 106×76 mm. (a) $5 Bill Toomey (U.S.A.) (Gold—Decathlon, 1968) (horiz). (b) $6 Mark Lenzi (U.S.A.) (Gold—Men's springboard diving, 1992) Set of 2 sheets	7·50	8·00

Nos. 2305/13 and 2314/22 respectively were printed together, *se-tenant*, with the background forming a composite design.

361 Black Skimmer

1996. Sea Birds. Multicoloured.

2325	75c. Type **361**	90	90
2326	75c. Black-capped petrel	90	90
2327	75c. Sooty tern	90	90
2328	75c. Royal tern	90	90
2329	75c. Pomarine skua ("Pomarine Jaegger")	90	90
2330	75c. White-tailed tropic bird	90	90
2331	75c. Northern gannet	90	90
2332	75c. Laughing gull	90	90
MS2333	Two sheets, each 105×75 mm. (a) $5 Magnificent frigate bird ("Great Frigate Bird"). (b) $6 Brown pelican Set of 2 sheets	8·00	9·00

362 Mickey and Goofy on Elephant (*Around the World in Eighty Days*)

1996. Novels of Jules Verne. Walt Disney cartoon characters in scenes from the books. Multicoloured.

2334	1c. Type **362**	15	25
2335	2c. Mickey, Donald and Goofy entering cave ("A Journey to the Centre of the Earth")	20	25
2336	5c. Mickey and Minnie driving postcart ("Michel Strogoff")	35	25
2337	10c. Mickey, Donald and Goofy in space rocket ("From the Earth to the Moon")	50	20
2338	15c. Mickey and Goofy in balloon ("Five Weeks in a Balloon")	50	20
2339	20c. Mickey and Goofy in China ("Around the World in Eighty Days")	50	20
2340	$1 Mickey, Goofy and Pluto on island ("The Mysterious Island")	2·25	85
2341	$2 Mickey, Pluto, Goofy and Donald on Moon ("From the Earth to the Moon")	2·75	2·75
2342	$3 Mickey being lifted by bird ("Captain Grant's Children")	3·25	3·50
2343	$5 Mickey with seal and squid ("Twenty Thousand Leagues Under the Sea")	4·25	5·00
MS2344	Two sheets, each 124×99 mm. (a) $6 Mickey on "Nautilus" ("Twenty Thousand Leagues Under the Sea"). (b) $6 Mickey and Donald on raft ("A Journey to the Centre of the Earth") Set of 2 sheets	12·50	12·50

363 Bruce Lee

1996. "CHINA '96" 9th Asian International Stamp Exhibition, Peking. Bruce Lee (actor). Multicoloured.

2345	75c. Type **363**	60	70
2346	75c. Bruce Lee in white shirt and red tie	60	70
2347	75c. In plaid jacket and tie	60	70
2348	75c. In mask and uniform	60	70
2349	75c. Bare-chested	60	70
2350	75c. In mandarin jacket	60	70
2351	75c. In brown jumper	60	70
2352	75c. In fawn shirt	60	70
2353	75c. Shouting	60	70
MS2354	76×106 mm. $5 Bruce Lee	3·75	4·00

364 Queen Elizabeth II

1996. 70th Birthday of Queen Elizabeth II. Multicoloured.

2355	$2 Type **364**	1·25	1·50
2356	$2 With bouquet	1·25	1·50
2357	$2 In Garter robes	1·25	1·50
MS2358	96×111 mm. $6 Wearing white dress	5·50	6·00

365 Ancient Egyptian Cavalryman

1996. Cavalry through the Ages. Multicoloured.

2359	60c. Type **365**	50	55
2360	60c. 13th-century English knight	50	55
2361	60c. 16th-century Spanish lancer	50	55
2362	60c. 18th-century Chinese cavalryman	50	55
MS2363	100×70 mm. $6 19th-century French cuirassier	3·25	3·75

366 Girl in Red Sari

1996. 50th Anniv of UNICEF Multicoloured.

2364	75c. Type **366**	60	60
2365	90c. South American mother and child	70	70
2366	$1.20 Nurse with child	90	1·00
MS2367	114×74 mm. $6 Chinese child	3·25	3·75

367 Tomb of Zachariah and "Verbascum sinuatum"

1996. 3000th Anniv of Jerusalem. Multicoloured.

2368	75c. Type **367**	75	65
2369	90c. Pool of Siloam and *Hyacinthus orientalis*	85	75
2370	$1.20 Hurva Synagogue and *Ranunculus asiaticus*	1·25	1·10
MS2371	66×80 mm. $6 Model of Herrod's Temple and *Cerics siliquastrum*	6·50	6·00

368 Kate Smith

1996. Cent of Radio. Entertainers. Multicoloured.

2372	65c. Type **368**	50	50
2373	75c. Dinah Shore	60	60
2374	90c. Rudy Vallee	75	70
2375	$1.20 Bing Crosby	1·10	1·00
MS2376	72×104 mm. $6 Jo Stafford (28×42 mm)	3·25	3·75

369 *Madonna Enthroned*

1996. Christmas. Religious Paintings by Filippo Lippi. Multicoloured.

2377	60c. Type **369**	80	40
2378	90c. *Adoration of the Child and Saints*	1·00	55
2379	$1 *The Annunciation*	1·10	90
2380	$1.20 *Birth of the Virgin*	1·25	1·25
2381	$1.60 *Adoration of the Child*	1·60	1·90
2382	$1.75 *Madonna and Child*	1·90	2·50
MS2383	Two sheets, each 76×106 mm. (a) $6 *Madonna and Child* (different). (b) $6 *The Circumcision* Set of 2 sheets	11·00	12·00

370 Robert Preston (*The Music Man*)

1997. Broadway Musical Stars. Multicoloured.

2384	$1 Type **370**	90	90
2385	$1 Michael Crawford (*Phantom of the Opera*)	90	90
2386	$1 Zero Mostel (*Fiddler on the Roof*)	90	90
2387	$1 Patti Lupone (*Evita*)	90	90
2388	$1 Raul Julia (*Threepenny Opera*)	90	90
2389	$1 Mary Martin (*South Pacific*)	90	90
2390	$1 Carol Channing (*Hello Dolly*)	90	90
2391	$1 Yul Brynner (*The King and I*)	90	90
2392	$1 Julie Andrews (*My Fair Lady*)	90	90
MS2393	106×76 mm. $6 Mickey Rooney (*Sugar Babies*)	4·00	5·00

371 Goofy and Wilbur

1997. Walt Disney Cartoon Characters. Multicoloured.

2394	1c. Type **371**	10	10
2395	2c. Donald and Goofy in boxing ring	10	10
2396	5c. Donald, Panchito and Jose Carioca	10	10
2397	10c. Mickey and Goofy playing chess	20	15
2398	15c. Chip and Dale with acorns	20	15
2399	20c. Pluto and Mickey	20	15
2400	$1 Daisy and Minnie eating ice-cream	90	75
2401	$2 Daisy and Minnie at dressing table	1·50	1·75
2402	$3 Gus Goose and Donald	2·00	2·50
MS2403	Two sheets. (a) 102×127 mm. $6 Goofy. (b) 127×102 mm. Donald Duck playing guitar (vert) Set of 2 sheets	8·50	9·00

372 Charlie Chaplin as Young Man

1997. 20th Death Anniv of Charlie Chaplin (film star). Multicoloured.

2404	$1 Type **372**	80	70
2405	$1 Pulling face	80	70
2406	$1 Looking over shoulder	80	70
2407	$1 In cap	80	70
2408	$1 In front of star	80	70
2409	$1 In *The Great Dictator*	80	70
2410	$1 With movie camera and megaphone	80	70
2411	$1 Standing in front of camera lens	80	70
2412	$1 Putting on make-up	80	70
MS2413	76×106 mm. $6 Charlie Chaplin	4·00	4·25

Nos. 2404/12 were printed together, *se-tenant*, with the backgrounds forming a composite design.

373 *Charaxes porthos*

1997. Butterflies. Multicoloured.

2414	90c. Type **373**	80	50
2415	$1.10 *Charaxes protoclea protoclea*	80	80
2416	$1.10 *Byblia ilithyia*	80	80
2417	$1.10 Black-headed tchagra (bird)	80	80
2418	$1.10 *Charaxes nobilis*	80	80
2419	$1.10 *Pseudacraea boisduvali trimeni*	80	80
2420	$1.10 *Charaxes smaragdalis*	80	80
2421	$1.10 *Charaxes lasti*	80	80
2422	$1.10 *Pseudacrea poggei*	80	80
2423	$1.10 *Graphium colonna*	80	80
2424	$1.10 Carmine bee eater (bird)	80	80
2425	$1.10 *Pseudacraea eurytus*	80	80
2426	$1.10 *Hypolimnas monteironis*	80	80
2427	$1.10 *Charaxes anticlea*	80	80
2428	$1.10 *Graphium leonidas*	80	80
2429	$1.10 *Graphium illyris*	80	80
2430	$1.10 *Nephronia argia*	80	80
2431	$1.10 *Graphium policenes*	80	80
2432	$1.10 *Papilio dardanus*	80	80
2433	$1.20 *Aethiopana honorius*	80	80
2434	$1.60 *Charaxes hadrianus*	1·25	1·10
2435	$1.75 *Precis westermanni*	1·25	1·40
MS2436	Three sheets, each 106×76 mm. (a) $6 *Charaxes lactitinctus* (horiz). (b) $6 *Eupheadra neophron*. (c) $6 *Euxanthe tiberius* (horiz) Set of 3 sheets	11·00	13·00

Nos. 2415/23 and 2424/32 respectively were printed together, *se-tenant*, with the backgrounds forming a composite design.

No. 2430 is inscribed "Nepheronia argia" in error.

374 Convent of The Companions of Jesus, Morelia, Mexico

1997. 50th Anniv of UNESCO Multicoloured.

2437	60c. Type **374**	70	35
2438	90c. Fortress at San Lorenzo, Panama (vert)	80	50
2439	$1 Canaima National Park, Venezuela (vert)	80	55
2440	$1.10 Aerial view of church with tower, Guanajuato, Mexico (vert)	80	90
2441	$1.10 Church facade, Guanajuato, Mexico (vert)	80	90
2442	$1.10 Aerial view of churches with domes, Guanajuato, Mexico (vert)	80	90
2443	$1.10 Jesuit Missions of the Chiquitos, Bolivia (vert)	80	90
2444	$1.10 Huascaran National Park, Peru (vert)	80	90
2445	$1.10 Jesuit Missions of La Santisima, Paraguay (vert)	80	90
2446	$1.10 Cartagena, Colombia (vert)	80	90
2447	$1.10 Fortification, Havana, Cuba (vert)	80	90
2448	$1.20 As No. 2444 (vert)	85	90
2449	$1.60 Church of San Fransisco, Guatemala (vert)	1·25	1·40
2450	$1.65 Tikal National Park, Guatemala	1·50	1·60
2451	$1.65 Rio Platano Reserve, Honduras	1·50	1·60
2452	$1.65 Ruins of Copan, Honduras	1·50	1·60
2453	$1.65 Antigua ruins, Guatemala	1·50	1·60
2454	$1.65 Teotihuacan, Mexico	1·50	1·60
2455	$1.75 Santo Domingo, Dominican Republic (vert)	1·75	1·90
MS2456	Two sheets, each 127×102 mm. (a) $6 Tikal National Park, Guatemala. (b) $6 Teotihuacan pyramid, Mexico Set of 2 sheets	9·00	9·50

No. 2446 is inscribed "Columbia" in error.

375 Red Bishop

1997. Endangered Species. Multicoloured.

2457	$1.20 Type **375**	1·40	1·40
2458	$1.20 Yellow baboon	1·40	1·40
2459	$1.20 Superb starling	1·40	1·40
2460	$1.20 Ratel	1·40	1·40
2461	$1.20 Hunting dog	1·40	1·40
2462	$1.20 Serval	1·40	1·40
2463	$1.65 Okapi	1·40	1·40
2464	$1.65 Giant forest squirrel	1·40	1·40
2465	$1.65 Lesser masked weaver	1·40	1·40
2466	$1.65 Small-spotted genet	1·40	1·40
2467	$1.65 Yellow-billed stork	1·40	1·40
2468	$1.65 Red-headed agama	1·40	1·40
MS2469	Three sheets, each 106×76 mm. (a) $6 South African crowned crane. (b) $6 Bat-eared fox. (c) $6 Malachite kingfisher Set of 3 sheets	15·00	16·00

Nos. 2457/62 and 2463/8 respectively were printed together, *se-tenant*, with the backgrounds forming composite designs.

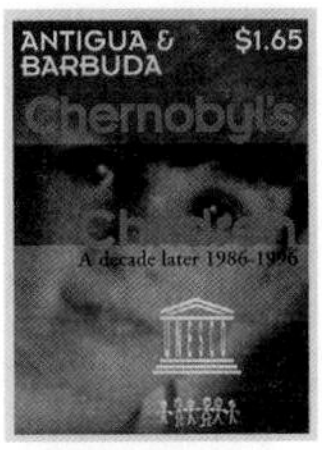

376 Child's Face and UNESCO Emblem

1997. Tenth Anniv of Chernobyl Nuclear Disaster. Multicoloured.

2470	$1.65 Type **376**	1·40	1·50
2471	$2 As Type **376**, but inscr "CHABAD'S CHILDREN OF CHERNOBYL" at foot	1·75	2·00

377 Paul Harris and James Grant

1997. 50th Death Anniv of Paul Harris (founder of Rotary International).. Multicoloured.

2472	$1.75 Type **377**	1·25	1·50
MS2473	78×107 mm. $6 Group study exchange, New Zealand	3·75	4·25

378 Queen Elizabeth II

1997. Golden Wedding of Queen Elizabeth and Prince Philip. Multicoloured.

2474	$1 Type **378**	1·10	1·10
2475	$1 Royal coat of arms	1·10	1·10
2476	$1 Queen Elizabeth and Prince Philip at reception	1·10	1·10
2477	$1 Queen Elizabeth and Prince Philip in landau	1·10	1·10
2478	$1 Balmoral	1·10	1·10
2479	$1 Prince Philip	1·10	1·10
MS2480	100×71 mm. $6 Queen Elizabeth with Prince Philip in naval uniform	4·25	4·50

379 Kaiser Wilhelm I and Heinrich von Stephan

1997. "Pacific '97" International Stamp Exhibition, San Francisco. Death Centenary of Heinrich von Stephan (founder of the U.P.U.).

2481	**379**	$1.75 blue	1·25	1·40
2482	-	$1.75 brown	1·25	1·40
2483	-	$1.75 mauve	1·25	1·40
MS2484		82×119 mm. $6 violet	3·75	4·50

DESIGNS: No. 2482, Von Stephan and Mercury; 2483, Carrier pigeon and loft; **MS**2484, Von Stephan and 15th-century Basle messenger.

No. 2483 is inscribed "PIDGEON" in error.

380 The Two Ugly Sisters and their Mother

1997. 175th Anniv of Brothers Grimm's Third Collection of Fairy Tales. *Cinderella*. Multicoloured.

2485	$1.75 Type **380**	1·60	1·60
2486	$1.75 Cinderella and her Fairy Godmother	1·60	1·60
2487	$1.75 Cinderella and the Prince	1·60	1·60
MS2488	124×96 mm. $6 Cinderella trying on slipper	4·25	4·50

381 *Marasmius rotula*

1997. Fungi. Multicoloured.

2489	45c. Type **381**	50	30
2490	65c. *Cantharellus cibarius*	60	40
2491	70c. *Lepiota cristata*	60	40
2492	90c. *Auricularia mesenteric*	70	50
2493	$1 *Pholiota alnicola*	75	55
2494	$1.65 *Leccinum aurantiacum*	1·10	1·25
2495	$1.75 *Entoloma serrulatum*	1·25	1·40
2496	$1.75 *Panaeolus sphinctrinus*	1·25	1·40
2497	$1.75 *Volvariella bombycina*	1·25	1·40
2498	$1.75 *Conocybe percincta*	1·25	1·40
2499	$1.75 *Pluteus cervinus*	1·25	1·40
2500	$1.75 *Russula foetens*	1·25	1·40
MS2501	Two sheets, each 106×76 mm. (a) $6 *Amanita cothurnata*. (b) $6 *Panellus serotinus* Set of 2 sheets	7·50	8·50

382 *Odontoglossum cervantesii*

1997. Orchids of the World. Multicoloured.

2502	45c. Type **382**	60	30
2503	65c. *Phalaenopsis* Medford Star	70	40
2504	75c. "Vanda Motes" Resplendent	75	45
2505	90c. *Odontonia* Debutante	80	50
2506	$1 *Iwanagaara* Apple Blossom	90	70
2507	$1.65 *Cattleya* Sophia Martin	1·25	1·25
2508	$1.65 Dogface Butterfly	1·25	1·25
2509	$1.65 *Laeliocattleya* Mini Purple	1·25	1·25
2510	$1.65 *Cymbidium* Showgirl	1·25	1·25
2511	$1.65 *Brassolaeliocattleya* Dorothy Bertsch	1·25	1·25
2512	$1.65 *Disa Blackii*	1·25	1·25
2513	$1.65 *Paphiopedilum leeanum*	1·25	1·25
2514	$1.65 *Paphiopedilum macranthum*	1·25	1·25
2515	$1.65 *Brassocattleya* Angel Lace	1·25	1·25
2516	$1.65 *Saphrolae liocattleya* Precious Stones	1·25	1·25
2517	$1.65 Orange Theope Butterfly	1·25	1·25
2518	$1.65 *Promenaea xanthina*	1·25	1·25
2519	$1.65 *Lycasle macrobulbon*	1·25	1·25
2520	$1.65 *Amestella philippinensis*	1·25	1·25
2521	$1.65 *Masdevallia* Machu Picchu	1·25	1·25
2522	$1.65 *Phalaenopsis* Zuma Urchin	1·25	1·25
2523	$2 *Dendrobium victoria-reginae*	1·60	1·60
MS2524	Two sheets, each 76×106 mm. (a)"*Mitonia* Seine. (b) *Pouphiopedilum gratrixanum* Set of 2 sheets	8·00	9·00

Nos. 2507/14 and 2515/22 respectively were printed together, *se-tenant*, with the backgrounds forming composite designs.

383 Maradona holding World Cup Trophy, 1986

1997. World Cup Football Championship, France (1998).

2525	**383**	60c. multicoloured	50	35
2526	-	75c. brown	60	45
2527	-	90c. multicoloured	70	50
2528	-	$1 brown	75	75
2529	-	$1 brown	75	75
2530	-	$1 brown	75	75
2531	-	$1 black	75	75
2532	-	$1 brown	75	75
2533	-	$1 brown	75	75
2534	-	$1 brown	75	75
2535	-	$1 brown	75	75
2536	-	$1.20 multicoloured	75	75
2537	-	$1.65 multicoloured	1·10	1·25
2538	-	$1.75 multicoloured	1·10	1·40
MS2539		Two sheets, each 102×127 mm. (a) $6 multicoloured. (b) $6 mult Set of 2 sheets	7·50	8·50

DESIGNS—HORIZ: No. 2526, Fritzwalter, West Germany, 1954; 2527, Zoff, Italy, 1982; 2536, Moore, England, 1966; 2537, Alberto, Brazil, 1970; 2538, Matthaus, West Germany, 1990; **MS**2539 (b) West German players celebrating, 1990. VERT: No. 2528, Ademir, Brazil, 1950; 2529, Eusebio, Portugal, 1966; 2530, Fontaine, France, 1958; 2531, Schillaci, Italy, 1990; 2532, Leonidas, Brazil, 1938; 2533, Stabile, Argentina, 1930; 2534, Nejedly, Czechoslovakia, 1934; 2535, Muller, West Germany, 1970; **MS**2539 (a) Bebeto, Brazil.

384 Scottish Fold Kitten

1997. Cats and Dogs. Multicoloured.

2540	$1.65 Type **384**	1·50	1·25
2541	$1.65 Japanese bobtail	1·50	1·25
2542	$1.65 Tabby manx	1·50	1·25
2543	$1.65 Bicolor American shorthair	1·50	1·25
2544	$1.65 Sorrel Abyssinian	1·50	1·25
2545	$1.65 Himalayan blue point	1·50	1·25
2546	$1.65 Dachshund	1·50	1·25
2547	$1.65 Staffordshire terrier	1·50	1·25
2548	$1.65 Shar-pei	1·50	1·25
2549	$1.65 Beagle	1·50	1·25
2550	$1.65 Norfolk terrier	1·50	1·25
2551	$1.65 Golden retriever	1·50	1·25
MS2552	Two sheets, each 107×77 mm. (a) $6 Red tabby (vert). (b) $6 Siberian husky (vert) Set of 2 sheets	8·50	9·00

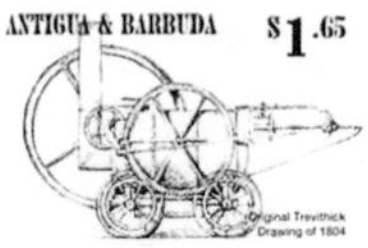

385 Original Drawing by Trevithick, 1803

1997. Railway Locomotives of the World. Multicoloured.

2553	$1.65 Type **385**	1·50	1·25
2554	$1.65 William Hedley's *Puffing Billy*, (1813–14)	1·50	1·25
2555	$1.65 Crampton locomotive of French Nord Railway, 1858	1·50	1·25
2556	$1.65 Lawrence Machine Shop locomotive, U.S.A., 1860	1·50	1·25
2557	$1.65 Natchez and Hamburg Railway steam locomotive *Mississippi*, U.S.A., 1834	1·50	1·25
2558	$1.65 Bury *Coppernob* locomotive, Furness Railway, 1846	1·50	1·25
2559	$1.65 David Joy's *Jenny Lind*, 1847	1·50	1·25

2560 $1.65 Schenectady Atlantic locomotive, U.S.A., 1899 1·50 1·25
2561 $1.65 Kitsons Class 1800 tank locomotive, Japan, 1881 1·50 1·25
2562 $1.65 Pennsylvania Railroad express frieght 1·50 1·25
2563 $1.65 Karl Golsdorf's 4 cylinder locomotive, Austria 1·50 1·25
2564 $1.65 Series "E" locomotive, Russia, 1930 1·50 1·25
MS2565 Two sheets, each 72×100 mm. (a) $6 George Stephenson "Patentee" type locomotive, 1843. (b) $6 Brunel's trestle bridge over River Lynher, Cornwall Set of 2 sheets 8·00 9·00

No. 2554 is dated "1860" in error.

386 *The Angel leaving Tobias and his Family* (Rembrandt)

1997. Christmas. Religious Paintings. Multicoloured.
2566 15c. Type **386** 30 15
2567 25c. *The Resurrection* (Martin Knoller) 40 20
2568 60c. *Astronomy* (Raphael) 60 40
2569 75c. *Music-making Angel* (Melozzo da Forli) 70 55
2570 90c. *Amor* (Parmigianino) 80 60
2571 $1.20 *Madonna and Child with Saints* (Rosso Fiorentino) 1·00 1·25
MS2572 Two sheets, each 105×96 mm. (a) $6 *The Wedding of Tobias* (Gianantonio and Francesco Guardi) (horiz). (b) $6 *The Portinari Altarpiece* (Hugo van der Goes) (horiz) Set of 2 sheets 7·50 8·50

387 Diana, Princess of Wales

1998. Diana, Princess of Wales Commemoration. Multicoloured (except Nos. 2574 and 2581/2).
2573 $1.65 Type **387** 1·10 1·10
2574 $1.65 Wearing hoop earrings (red and black) 1·10 1·10
2575 $1.65 Carrying bouquet 1·10 1·10
2576 $1.65 Wearing floral hat 1·10 1·10
2577 $1.65 With Prince Harry 1·10 1·10
2578 $1.65 Wearing white jacket 1·10 1·10
2579 $1.65 In kitchen 1·10 1·10
2580 $1.65 Wearing black and white dress 1·10 1·10
2581 $1.65 Wearing hat (brown and black) 1·10 1·10
2582 $1.65 Wearing floral print dress (brown and black) 1·10 1·10
2583 $1.65 Dancing with John Travolta 1·10 1·10
2584 $1.65 Wearing white hat and jacket 1·10 1·10
MS2585 Two sheets, each 70×100 mm. (a) $6 Wearing red jumper. (b) $6 Wearing black dress for papal audience (brown and black) Set of 2 sheets 7·50 8·00

388 Yellow Damselfish

1998. Fish. Multicoloured.
2586 75c. Type **388** 55 40
2587 90c. Barred hamlet 65 50
2588 $1 Yellow-tailed damselfish ("Jewelfish") 70 55
2589 $1.20 Blue-headed wrasse 75 60
2590 $1.50 Queen angelfish 85 85
2591 $1.65 Jackknife-fish 95 95
2592 $1.65 Spot-finned hogfish 95 95
2593 $1.65 Sergeant major 95 95
2594 $1.65 Neon goby 95 95
2595 $1.65 Jawfish 95 95
2596 $1.65 Flamefish 95 95
2597 $1.65 Rock beauty 95 95
2598 $1.65 Yellow-tailed snapper 95 95
2599 $1.65 Creole wrasse 95 95
2600 $1.65 Slender filefish 95 95
2601 $1.65 Long-spined squirrelfish 95 95
2602 $1.65 Royal gramma ("Fairy Basslet") 95 95
2603 $1.75 Queen triggerfish 1·00 1·10
MS2604 Two sheets, each 80×110 mm. (a) $6 Porkfish. (b) $6 Black-capped basslet Set of 2 sheets 8·00 9·00

Nos. 2591/6 and 2597/2602 respectively were printed together, *se-tenant*, with the backgrounds forming composite designs.

389 First Church and Manse, 1822–40

1998. 175th Anniv of Cedar Hall Moravian Church. Multicoloured.
2605 20c. Type **389** 20 20
2606 45c. Cedar Hall School, 1840 35 30
2607 75c. Hugh A. King, minister 1945–53 55 45
2608 90c. Present Church building 65 50
2609 $1.20 Water tank, 1822 75 75
2610 $2 Former Manse, demolished 1978 1·25 2·00
MS2611 100×70 mm. $6 Present church building (different) (50×37 mm.) 3·25 4·25

390 Europa Point Lighthouse, Gibraltar

1998. Lighthouses of the World. Multicoloured.
2612 45c. Type **390** 65 40
2613 65c. Tierra del Fuego, Argentina (horiz) 75 55
2614 75c. Point Loma, California, U.S.A. (horiz) 80 55
2615 90c. Groenpoint, Cape Town, South Africa 90 60
2616 $1 Youghal, Cork, Ireland 1·00 90
2617 $1.20 Launceston, Tasmania, Australia 1·10 1·10
2618 $1.65 Point Abino, Ontario, Canada (horiz) 1·40 1·75
2619 $1.75 Great Inagua, Bahamas 1·50 2·00
MS2620 99×70 mm. $6 Cap Hatteras, North Carolina, U.S.A. 5·50 6·00

No. 2613 is inscribed "Terra Del Fuego" in error.

391 Pooh and Tigger (January)

1998. Through the Year with Winnie the Pooh. Multicoloured.
2621 $1 Type **391** 1·00 1·00
2622 $1 Pooh and Piglet indoors (February) 1·00 1·00
2623 $1 Piglet hang-gliding with scarf (March) 1·00 1·00
2624 $1 Tigger, Pooh and Piglet on pond (April) 1·00 1·00
2625 $1 Kanga and Roo with posy of flowers (May) 1·00 1·00
2626 $1 Pooh on balloon and Owl (June) 1·00 1·00
2627 $1 Pooh, Eeyore, Tigger and Piglet gazing at stars (July) 1·00 1·00
2628 $1 Pooh and Piglet by stream (August) 1·00 1·00
2629 $1 Christopher Robin going to school (September) 1·00 1·00
2630 $1 Eeyore in fallen leaves (October) 1·00 1·00
2631 $1 Pooh and Rabbit gathering pumpkins (November) 1·00 1·00
2632 $1 Pooh and Piglet skiing (December) 1·00 1·00
MS2633 Four sheets, each 126×101 mm. (a) $6 Pooh, Rabbit and Piglet with blanket (Spring). (b) $6 Pooh by pond (Summer). (c) $6 Pooh sweeping fallen leaves (Autumn). (d) $6 Pooh and Eeyore on ice (Winter) Set of 4 sheets 16·00 16·00

392 Miss Nellie Robinson (founder)

1998. Centenary of Thomas Oliver Robinson Memorial School.
2634 **392** 20c. green and black 20 20
2635 - 45c. multicoloured 40 25
2636 - 65c. green and black 55 50
2637 - 75c. multicoloured 60 60
2638 - 90c. multicoloured 70 65
2639 - $1.20 brown, green and black 90 1·40
MS2640 106×76 mm. $6 brown 3·25 4·00

DESIGNS—HORIZ: 45c. School photo, 1985; 65c. Former school building, 1930–49; 75c. Children with Mrs. Natalie Hurst (present headmistress); $1.20, Present school building, 1950. VERT: 90c. Miss Ina Loving (former teacher); $6 Miss Nellie Robinson (different).

393 Spotted Eagle Ray

1998. International Year of the Ocean. Multicoloured.
2641-2665 40c.×25 Type **393**; Manta ray; Hawksbill turtle; Jellyfish; Queen angelfish; Octopus; Emperor angelfish; Regal angelfish; Porkfish; Racoon butterflyfish; Atlantic barracuda; Sea horse; Nautilus; Trumpetfish; White tip shark; Sunken Spanish galleon; Black-tip shark; Long-nosed butterflyfish; Green moray eel; Captain Nemo; Treasure chest; Hammerhead shark; Divers; Lionfish; Clownfish 7·00 8·00
2666-2677 75c.×12 Maroon-tailed conure; Cocoi heron; Common tern; Rainbow lory ("Rainbow Lorikeet"); Saddleback butterflyfish; Goatfish and cat shark; Blue shark and stingray; Majestic snapper; Nassau grouper; Black-cap gramma and blue tang; Stingrays; Stingrays and giant starfish 7·00 8·00
MS2678 Two sheets. (a) 68×98 mm. $6 Humpback whale. (b) 98×68 mm. $6 Fiddler ray Set of 2 sheets 9·00 9·50

Nos. 2641/65 and 2666/77 respectively were printed together, *se-tenant*, with the backgrounds forming composite designs.

394 *Savannah* (paddle-steamer)

1998. Ships of the World. Multicoloured.
2679 $1.75 Type **394** 1·50 1·50
2680 $1.75 Viking longship 1·50 1·50
2681 $1.75 Greek galley 1·50 1·50
2682 $1.75 Sailing clipper 1·50 1·50
2683 $1.75 Dhow 1·50 1·50
2684 $1.75 Fishing catboat 1·50 1·50
MS2685 Three sheets, each 100×70 mm. (a) $6 13th-century English warship (41×22 mm). (b) $6 Sailing dory (22×41 mm). (c) $6 Baltimore clipper (41×22 mm) Set of 3 sheets 13·00 14·00

395 Flags of Antigua and CARICOM

1998. 25th Anniv of Caribbean Community.
2686 **395** $1 multicoloured 1·25 1·25

396 Ford, 1896

1998. Classic Cars. Multicoloured.
2687 $1.65 Type **396** 1·10 1·10
2688 $1.65 Ford A, 1903 1·10 1·10
2689 $1.65 Ford T, 1928 1·10 1·10
2690 $1.65 Ford T, 1922 1·10 1·10
2691 $1.65 Ford Blackhawk, 1929 1·10 1·10
2692 $1.65 Ford Sedan, 1934 1·10 1·10
2693 $1.65 Torpedo, 1911 1·10 1·10
2694 $1.65 Mercedes 22, 1913 1·10 1·10
2695 $1.65 Rover, 1920 1·10 1·10
2696 $1.65 Mercedes-Benz, 1956 1·10 1·10
2697 $1.65 Packard V-12, 1934 1·10 1·10
2698 $1.65 Opel, 1924 1·10 1·10
MS2699 Two sheets, each 70×100 mm. (a) $6 Ford, 1908 (60×40 mm). (b) $6 Ford, 1929 (60×40 mm) Set of 2 sheets 7·50 8·00

397 Lockheed-Boeing General Dynamics Yf-22

1998. Modern Aircraft. Multicoloured.
2700 $1.65 Type **397** 1·25 1·25
2701 $1.65 Dassault-Breguet Rafale BO 1 1·25 1·25
2702 $1.65 MiG 29 1·25 1·25
2703 $1.65 Dassault-Breguet Mirage 2000D 1·25 1·25
2704 $1.65 Rockwell B-1B "Lancer" 1·25 1·25
2705 $1.65 McDonnell-Douglas C-17A 1·25 1·25
2706 $1.65 Space Shuttle 1·25 1·25
2707 $1.65 SAAB "Grippen" 1·25 1·25
2708 $1.65 Eurofighter EF-2000 1·25 1·25
2709 $1.65 Sukhoi SU 27 1·25 1·25
2710 $1.65 Northrop B-2 1·25 1·25
2711 $1.65 Lockheed F-117 "Nighthawk" 1·25 1·25
MS2712 Two sheets, each 110×85 mm. (a) $6 F18 Hornet. (b) $6 Sukhoi SU 35 Set of 2 sheets 8·50 9·00

No. **MS**2712b is inscribed "Sukhi" in error.

398 Karl Benz (internal-combustion engine)

1998. Millennium Series. Famous People of the Twentieth Century. Inventors. Multicoloured.
2713 $1 Type **398** 1·00 1·00
2714 $1 Early Benz car and Mercedes-Benz racing car (53×38 mm) 1·00 1·00
2715 $1 Atom bomb mushroom cloud (53×38 mm) 1·00 1·00
2716 $1 Albert Einstein (theory of relativity) 1·00 1·00
2717 $1 Leopold Godowsky Jr. and Leopold Damrosch Mannes (Kodachrome film) 1·00 1·00
2718 $1 Camera and transparencies (53×38 mm) 1·00 1·00
2719 $1 Heinkel He 178 (first turbo jet plane) (53×38 mm) 1·00 1·00
2720 $1 Dr. Hans Pabst von Ohain (jet turbine engine) 1·00 1·00
2721 $1 Rudolf Diesel (diesel engine) 1·00 1·00
2722 $1 Early Diesel engine and forms of transport (53×38 mm) 1·00 1·00
2723 $1 Zeppelin airship (53×38 mm) 1·00 1·00
2724 $1 Count Ferdinand von Zeppelin (airship pioneer) 1·00 1·00
2725 $1 Wilhelm Conrad Rontgen (X-rays) 1·00 1·00
2726 $1 X-ray of hand (53×38 mm) 1·00 1·00
2727 $1 Launch of Saturn rocket (53×38 mm) 1·00 1·00
2728 $1 Wernher von Braun (rocket research) 1·00 1·00

MS2729	Two sheets, each 106×76 mm. (a) $6 Hans Geiger (Geiger counter). (b) $6 William Shockley (research into semi-conductors) Set of 2 sheets	9·50	10·00

No. 2713 is inscribed "CARL BENZ" in error.

399 Stylized Americas

1998. 50th Anniv of Organization of American States.

2730	**399**	$1 multicoloured	80	90

400 *Figures on the Seashore*

1998. 25th Death Anniv of Pablo Picasso (painter). Multicoloured.

2731	$1.20 Type **400**	75	70
2732	$1.65 *Three Figures under a Tree* (vert)	85	1·00
2733	$1.75 *Two Women running on the Beach*	95	1·25
MS2734	126×102 mm. $6 *Bullfight*	3·25	3·75

401 Dino 246 GT-GTS

1998. Birth Centenary of Enzo Ferrari (car manufacturer). Multicoloured.

2735	$1.75 Type **401**	2·25	2·25
2736	$1.75 Front view of Dino 246 GT-GTS	2·25	2·25
2737	$1.75 365 GT4 BB	2·25	2·25
MS2738	104×72 mm. $6 Dino 246 GT-GTS (91×34 mm)	6·00	6·00

402 Scout Handshake

1998. 19th World Scout Jamboree, Chile. Multicoloured.

2739	90c. Type **402**	60	55
2740	$1 Scouts hiking	75	90
2741	$1.20 Scout salute	90	1·25
MS2742	68×98 mm. $6 Lord Baden-Powell	3·25	3·75

403 Mahatma Gandhi

1998. 50th Death Anniv of Mahatma Gandhi. Multicoloured.

2743	90c. Type **403**	1·00	60
2744	$1 Gandhi seated	1·25	85
2745	$1.20 As young man	1·60	1·25
2746	$1.65 At primary school in Rajkot, aged 7	2·25	2·25
MS2747	100×70 mm. $6 Gandhi with staff	4·00	4·25

404 McDonnell Douglas Phantom F-GR1

1998. 80th Anniv of Royal Air Force. Multicoloured.

2748	$1.75 Type **404**	1·60	1·60
2749	$1.75 Two Sepecat Jaguar GR1As	1·60	1·60
2750	$1.75 Panavia Tornado F3	1·60	1·60
2751	$1.75 McDonnell Douglas Phantom F-GR2	1·60	1·60
MS2752	Two sheets, each 90×68 mm. (a) $6 Golden eagle (bird) and Bristol F2B Fighter. (b) $6 Hawker Hurricane and EF-2000 Eurofighter Set of 2 sheets	10·00	10·00

405 Diana, Princess of Wales

1998. First Death Anniv of Diana, Princess of Wales.

2753	**405**	$1.20 multicoloured	1·00	1·00

406 Brown Pelican

1998. Sea Birds of the World. Multicoloured.

2754	15c. Type **406**	30	20
2755	25c. Dunlin	40	20
2756	45c. Atlantic puffin	50	25
2757	75c. King eider	65	70
2758	75c. Inca tern	65	70
2759	75c. Little auk ("Dovekie")	65	70
2760	75c. Ross's gull	65	70
2761	75c. Common noddy ("Brown Noddy")	65	70
2762	75c. Marbled murrelet	65	70
2763	75c. Northern gannet	65	70
2764	75c. Razorbill	65	70
2765	75c. Long-tailed skua ("Long-tailed Jaegar")	65	70
2766	75c. Black guillemot	65	70
2767	75c. Whimbrel	65	70
2768	75c. American oystercatcher ("Oystercatcher")	30	35
2769	90c. Pied cormorant	65	70
MS2770	Two sheets, each 100×70 mm. (a) $6 Black skimmer. (b) $6 Wandering albatross Set of 2 sheets	8·00	9·00

Nos. 2757/68 were printed together, *se-tenant*, with the backgrounds forming a composite design.

No. 2760 is inscribed "ROSS' BULL" in error.

407 Border Collie

1998. Christmas. Dogs. Multicoloured.

2771	15c. Type **407**	45	25
2772	25c. Dalmatian	55	25
2773	65c. Weimaraner	90	50
2774	75c. Scottish terrier	95	50
2775	90c. Long-haired dachshund	1·10	55
2776	$1.20 Golden retriever	1·40	1·25
2777	$2 Pekingese	2·00	2·50
MS2778	Two sheets, each 75×66 mm. (a) $6 Dalmatian. (b) $6 Jack Russell terrier Set of 2 sheets	8·50	9·00

408 Mickey Mouse Sailing

1999. 70th Birthday of Mickey Mouse. Walt Disney characters participating in water sports. Multicoloured.

2779	$1 Type **408**	95	95
2780	$1 Mickey and Goofy sailing	95	95
2781	$1 Goofy windsurfing	95	95
2782	$1 Mickey sailing and seagull	95	95
2783	$1 Goofy sailing	95	95
2784	$1 Mickey windsurfing	95	95
2785	$1 Goofy running with surfboard	95	95
2786	$1 Mickey surfing	95	95
2787	$1 Donald Duck holding surfboard	95	95
2788	$1 Donald on surfboard (face value at right)	95	95
2789	$1 Minnie Mouse surfing in green shorts	95	95
2790	$1 Goofy surfing	95	95
2791	$1 Goofy in purple shorts waterskiing	95	95
2792	$1 Mickey waterskiing	95	95
2793	$1 Goofy waterskiing with Mickey	95	95
2794	$1 Donald on surfboard (face value at left)	95	95
2795	$1 Goofy in yellow shorts waterskiing	95	95
2796	$1 Minnie in pink shorts surfing	95	95
MS2797	Four sheets, each 127×102 mm. (a) $6 Goofy (horiz). (b) $6 Donald Duck. (c) $6 Minnie Mouse. (d) $6 Mickey Mouse Set of 4 sheets	15·00	16·00

409 Hell's Gate Steel Orchestra, 1996

1999. 50th Anniv of Hell's Gate Steel Orchestra. Multicoloured.

2798	20c. Type **409**	25	20
2799	60c. Orchestra members, New York, 1992	50	40
2800	75c. Orchestra members with steel drums, 1950	60	50
2801	90c. Eustace Henry, 1964	70	55
2802	$1.20 Alston Henry playing double tenor	1·00	1·40
MS2803	Two sheets. (a) 100×70 mm. $4 Orchestra members, 1950 (vert). (b) 70×100 mm. $4 Eustace Henry, 1964 (vert) Set of 2 sheets	5·50	6·50

410 Tulips

1999. Flowers. Multicoloured.

2804	60c. Type **410**	40	30
2805	75c. Fuschia	50	35
2806	90c. Morning glory (horiz)	60	60
2807	90c. Geranium (horiz)	60	60
2808	90c. Blue hibiscus (horiz)	60	60
2809	90c. Marigolds (horiz)	60	60
2810	90c. Sunflower (horiz)	60	60
2811	90c. Impatiens (horiz)	60	60
2812	90c. Petunia (horiz)	60	60
2813	90c. Pansy (horiz)	60	60
2814	90c. Saucer magnolia (horiz)	60	60
2815	$1 Primrose (horiz)	70	70
2816	$1 Bleeding heart (horiz)	70	70
2817	$1 Pink dogwood (horiz)	70	70
2818	$1 Peony (horiz)	70	70
2819	$1 Rose (horiz)	70	70
2820	$1 Hellebores (horiz)	70	70
2821	$1 Lily (horiz)	70	70
2822	$1 Violet (horiz)	70	70
2823	$1 Cherry blossom (horiz)	70	70
2824	$1.20 Calla lily	75	75
2825	$1.65 Sweet pea	90	1·10
MS2826	Two sheets. (a) 76×100 mm. $6 Sangria lily. (b) 106×76 mm. $6 Zinnias Set of 2 sheets	7·50	8·00

Nos. 2806/14 and 2815/23 respectively were each printed together, *se-tenant*, forming composite designs.

411 Elle Macpherson

1999. "Australia '99" International Stamp Exhibition, Melbourne (1st issue). Elle Macpherson (model). Multicoloured.

2827	$1.20 Type **411**	1·00	1·00
2828	$1.20 Lying on couch	1·00	1·00
2829	$1.20 In swimsuit	1·00	1·00
2830	$1.20 Looking over shoulder	1·00	1·00
2831	$1.20 Wearing cream shirt	1·00	1·00
2832	$1.20 Wearing stetson	1·00	1·00
2833	$1.20 Wearing black T-shirt	1·00	1·00
2834	$1.20 Holding tree branch	1·00	1·00

See also Nos. 2875/92.

412 "Luna 2" Moon Probe

1999. Satellites and Spacecraft. Multicoloured.

2835	$1.65 Type **412**	1·10	1·10
2836	$1.65 "Mariner 2" space probe	1·10	1·10
2837	$1.65 "Giotto" space probe	1·10	1·10
2838	$1.65 Rosat satellite	1·10	1·10
2839	$1.65 International Ultraviolet Explorer	1·10	1·10
2840	$1.65 "Ulysses" space probe	1·10	1·10
2841	$1.65 "Mariner 10" space probe	1·10	1·10
2842	$1.65 "Luna 9" Moon probe	1·10	1·10
2843	$1.65 Advanced X-ray Astrophysics Facility	1·10	1·10
2844	$1.65 "Magellan" space probe	1·10	1·10
2845	$1.65 "Pioneer – Venus 2" space probe	1·10	1·10
2846	$1.65 Infra-red Astronomy Satellite	1·10	1·10
MS2847	Two sheets, each 106×76 mm. (a) $6 "Salyut 1" space station (horiz). (b) $6 "MIR" space station (horiz) Set of 2 sheets	7·50	8·00

Nos. 2835/40 and 2841/46 repectively were each printed together, *se-tenant*, with the backgrounds forming composite designs.

413 John Glenn entering "Mercury" Capsule, 1962

1999. John Glenn's Return to Space. Multicoloured.

2848	$1.75 Type **413**	1·25	1·25
2849	$1.75 Glenn in "Mercury" mission spacesuit	1·25	1·25
2850	$1.75 Fitting helmet for "Mercury" mission	1·25	1·25
2851	$1.75 Outside pressure chamber	1·25	1·25

414 Brachiosaurus

1999. Prehistoric Animals. Multicoloured.

2852	65c. Type **414**	65	40
2853	75c. Oviraptor (vert)	70	40
2854	$1 Homotherium	80	45
2855	$1.20 Macrauchenia (vert)	90	60
2856	$1.65 Struthiomimus	1·00	1·00
2857	$1.65 Corythosaurus	1·00	1·00
2858	$1.65 Dsungaripterus	1·00	1·00
2859	$1.65 Compsognathus	1·00	1·00
2860	$1.65 Prosaurolophus	1·00	1·00
2861	$1.65 Montanoceratops	1·00	1·00
2862	$1.65 Stegosaurus	1·00	1·00
2863	$1.65 Deinonychus	1·00	1·00
2864	$1.65 Ouranosaurus	1·00	1·00
2865	$1.65 Leptictidium	1·00	1·00
2866	$1.65 Ictitherium	1·00	1·00
2867	$1.65 Plesictis	1·00	1·00
2868	$1.65 Hemicyon	1·00	1·00
2869	$1.65 Diacodexis	1·00	1·00
2870	$1.65 Stylinodon	1·00	1·00
2871	$1.65 Kanuites	1·00	1·00
2872	$1.65 Chriacus	1·00	1·00
2873	$1.65 Argyrolagus	1·00	1·00
MS2874	Two sheets, each 110×85 mm. (a) $6 Eurhinodelphis. (b) $6 Pteranodon Set of 2 sheets	7·50	8·00

Nos. 2856/64 and 2865/73 respectively were each printed together, *se-tenant*, with the backgrounds forming composite designs.

415 Two White Kittens

1999. "Australia '99" International Stamp Exhibition, Melbourne (2nd issue). Cats. Multicoloured.

2875 35c. Type **415** 40 30
2876 45c. Kitten with string 50 35
2877 60c. Two kittens under blanket 60 50
2878 75c. Two kittens in basket 70 55
2879 90c. Kitten with ball 80 55
2880 $1 White kitten 90 80
2881 $1.65 Two kittens playing 1·10 1·10
2882 $1.65 Black and white kitten 1·10 1·10
2883 $1.65 Black kitten and sleeping cream kitten 1·10 1·10
2884 $1.65 White kitten with green string 1·10 1·10
2885 $1.65 Two sleeping kittens 1·10 1·10
2886 $1.65 White kitten with black tip to tail 1·10 1·10
2887 $1.65 Kitten with red string 1·10 1·10
2888 $1.65 Two long-haired kittens 1·10 1·10
2889 $1.65 Ginger kitten 1·10 1·10
2890 $1.65 Kitten playing with mouse 1·10 1·10
2891 $1.65 Kitten asleep on blue cushion 1·10 1·10
2892 $1.65 Tabby kitten 1·10 1·10
MS2893 Two sheets, each 70×100 mm. (a) $6 Cat carrying kitten in mouth. (b) $6 Kitten in tree Set of 2 sheets 8·50 9·00

416 Early Leipzig–Dresden Railway Carriage and Caroline Islands 1901 Yacht Type 5m. Stamp

1999. "iBRA '99" International Stamp Exhibition, Nuremberg. Multicoloured.

2894 $1 Type **416** 70 60
2895 $1.20 Golsdorf steam locomotive and Caroline Islands 1901 Yacht type 1m. 80 70
2896 $1.65 Early Leipzig–Dresden Railway carriage and Caroline Islands 1899 20pf. optd on Germany 1·00 1·10
2897 $1.90 Golsdorf steam locomotive and Caroline Islands 1901 Yacht type 5pf. and 20pf. 1·40 2·00
MS2898 165×110 mm. $6 Registration label for Ponape, Caroline Islands 3·25 3·75

417 *People on Balcony of Sazaido* (Hokusai)

1999. 150th Death Anniv of Katsushika Hokusai (Japanese artist). Multicoloured.

2899 $1.65 Type **417** 1·00 1·00
2900 $1.65 *Nakahara in Sagami Province* 1·00 1·00
2901 $1.65 *Defensive Positions* (two wrestlers) 1·00 1·00
2902 $1.65 *Defensive Positions* (three wrestlers) 1·00 1·00
2903 $1.65 *Mount Fuji in Clear Weather* 1·00 1·00
2904 $1.65 *Nihonbashi in Edo* 1·00 1·00
2905 $1.65 *Asakusa Honganji* 1·00 1·00
2906 $1.65 *Dawn at Isawa in Kai Province* 1·00 1·00
2907 $1.65 *Samurai with Bow and Arrow* (with arrows on ground) 1·00 1·00
2908 $1.65 *Samurai with Bow and Arrow* (trees in background) 1·00 1·00
2909 $1.65 *Kajikazawa in Kai Province* 1·00 1·00
2910 $1.65 *A Great Wave* 1·00 1·00
MS2911 Two sheets, each 100×71 mm. (a) $6 *A Netsuke Workshop* (vert). (b) $6 *Gotenyama at Shinagawa on Tokaido Highway* (vert) Set of 2 sheets 7·50 8·00

No. 2903 is inscribed "MOUNT FUGI" in error.

418 Sophie Rhys-Jones

1999. Royal Wedding. Multicoloured.

2912 $3 Type **418** 1·75 2·00
2913 $3 Sophie and Prince Edward 1·75 2·00
2914 $3 Prince Edward 1·75 2·00
MS2915 108×78 mm. $6 Prince Edward with Sophie Rhys-Jones and Windsor Castle (horiz) 3·50 4·00

419 Three Children

1999. Tenth Anniv of United Nations Rights of the Child Convention. Multicoloured.

2916 $3 Type **419** 1·75 2·00
2917 $3 Adult hand holding child's hand 1·75 2·00
2918 $3 Dove and U.N. Headquarters 1·75 2·00
MS2919 112×70 mm. $6 Dove 3·25 3·75

Nos. 2916/18 were printed together, *se-tenant*, forming a composite design.

420 Crampton Type Railway Locomotive, 1855–69

1999. "PhilexFrance '99" International Stamp Exhibition, Paris. Railway Locomotives. Two sheets, each 106×81 mm, containing T **420** and similar design. Multicoloured.

MS2920 (a) $6 Type **420**. (b) $6 Compound type No. 232-U1 steam locomotive, 1949 Set of 2 sheets 7·50 8·00

421 Three Archangels from *Faust*

1999. 250th Birth Anniv of Johann von Goethe (German writer).

2921 **421** $1.75 purple, mauve and black 1·10 1·25
2922 - $1.75 blue, violet and black 1·10 1·25
2923 - $1.75 green and black 1·10 1·25
MS2924 – 79×101 mm. $6 black and brown 3·25 3·75

DESIGNS: No. 2922, Von Goethe and Von Schiller; 2923, Faust reclining with spirits; **MS**2924 Wolfgang von Goethe.

422 *Missa Ferdie* (fishing launch)

1999. Local Ships and Boats. Multicoloured.

2925 25c. Type **422** 25 25
2926 45c. Yachts in 32nd Annual Antigua International Sailing Week 40 30
2927 60c. *Jolly Roger* (tourist ship) 50 40
2928 90c. *Freewinds* (cruise liner) (10th anniv of first visit) 70 60
2929 $1.20 *Monarch of the Seas* (cruise liner) 95 1·25
MS2930 98×62 mm. $4 *Freewinds* (11th anniv of maiden voyage) (50×37 mm) 2·75 3·25

423 Fiery Jewel

1999. Butterflies. Multicoloured.

2931 65c. Type **423** 70 45
2932 75c. Hewitson's blue hairstreak 80 55
2933 $1 California dog face (horiz) 90 90
2934 $1 Small copper (horiz) 90 90
2935 $1 Zebra swallowtail (horiz) 90 90
2936 $1 White "M" hairstreak (horiz) 90 90
2937 $1 Old world swallowtail (horiz) 90 90
2938 $1 Buckeye (horiz) 90 90
2939 $1 Apollo (horiz) 90 90
2940 $1 Sonoran blue (horiz) 90 90
2941 $1 Purple emperor (horiz) 90 90
2942 $1.20 Scarce bamboo page (horiz) 1·00 1·00
2943 $1.65 Paris peacock (horiz) 1·25 1·50
MS2944 Two sheets. (a) 85×110 mm. $6 Monarch. (b) 110×85 mm. $6 Cairns birdwing (horiz) Set of 2 sheets 9·00 9·50

Nos. 2933/41 were printed together, *se-tenant*, forming a composite design.

424 "Madonna and Child in Wreath of Flowers" (Rubens)

1999. Christmas. Religious Paintings.

2945 **424** 15c. multicoloured 25 15
2946 - 25c. black, stone & yellow 30 15
2947 - 45c. multicoloured 50 25
2948 - 60c. multicoloured 60 30
2949 - $2 multicoloured 1·75 1·75
2950 - $4 black, stone & yell 3·00 4·00
MS2951 – 76×106 mm. $6 multicoloured 4·00 4·25

DESIGNS: 25c. *Shroud of Christ held by Two Angels* (Durer); 45c. *Madonna and Child enthroned between Two Saints*"(Raphael); 60c. *Holy Family with Lamb* (Raphael); $2 *The Transfiguration* (Raphael); $4 "Three Putti holding Coat of Arms (Durer); $6 *Coronation of St. Catharine* (Rubens).

425 Katharine Hepburn (actress)

2000. Senior Celebrities of the 20th Century. Multicoloured.

2952 90c. Type **425** 85 85
2953 90c. Martha Graham (dancer) 85 85
2954 90c. Eubie Blake (jazz pianist) 85 85
2955 90c. Agatha Christie (novelist) 85 85
2956 90c. Eudora Welty (American novelist) 85 85
2957 90c. Helen Hayes (actress) 85 85
2958 90c. Vladimir Horowitz (concert pianist) 85 85
2959 90c. Katharine Graham (newspaper publisher) 85 85
2960 90c. Pablo Casals (cellist) 85 85
2961 90c. Pete Seeger (folk singer) 85 85
2962 90c. Andres Segovia (guitarist) 85 85
2963 90c. Frank Lloyd Wright (architect) 85 85

426 Sir Cliff Richard

2000. 60th Birthday of Sir Cliff Richard (entertainer).

2964 **426** $1.65 multicoloured 1·25 1·25

427 Charlie Chaplin

2000. Charlie Chaplin (actor and director) Commemoration. Showing film scenes. Multicoloured.

2965 $1.65 Standing in street (*Modern Times*) 95 95
2966 $1.65 Hugging man (*The Gold Rush*) 95 95
2967 $1.65 Type **427** 95 95
2968 $1.65 Wielding tools (*Modern Times*) 95 95
2969 $1.65 With hands on hips (*The Gold Rush*) 95 95
2970 $1.65 Wearing cape (*The Gold Rush*) 95 95

428 Streamertail

2000. "The Stamp Show 2000" International Stamp Exhibition, London. Birds of the Caribbean. Multicoloured.

2971 75c. Type **428** 50 35
2972 90c. Yellow-bellied sapsucker 60 40
2973 $1.20 Rufous-tailed jacamar 75 75
2974 $1.20 Scarlet macaw 75 75
2975 $1.20 Yellow-crowned amazon ("Yellow-fronted Amazon") 75 75
2976 $1.20 Golden conure ("Queen-of-Bavaria") 75 75
2977 $1.20 Nanday conure 75 75
2978 $1.20 Jamaican tody 75 75
2979 $1.20 Smooth-billed ani 75 75
2980 $1.20 Puerto Rican woodpecker 75 75
2981 $1.20 Ruby-throated hummingbird 75 75
2982 $1.20 Common ground dove 75 75
2983 $1.20 American wood ibis ("Wood Stork") 75 75
2984 $1.20 Saffron finch 75 75
2985 $1.20 Green-backed heron 75 75
2986 $1.20 Lovely cotinga 75 75
2987 $1.20 St. Vincent amazon ("St. Vincent Parrot") 75 75
2988 $1.20 Cuban grassquit 75 75
2989 $1.20 Red-winged blackbird 75 75
2990 $2 Spectacled owl 1·40 1·50
MS2991 Two sheets, each 80×106 mm. (a) $6 Vermillion flycatcher (50×37 mm). (b) $6 Red-capped manakin (37×50 mm) Set of 2 sheets 9·50 10·00

Nos. 2974/81 and 2982/9 were each printed together, *se-tenant*, with the backgrounds forming composite designs.

No. 2981 is inscribed "Arhilochus colubria" in error.

429 *Arthur Goodwin*

2000. 400th Birth Anniv of Sir Anthony Van Dyck (Flemish painter). Multicoloured.

2992 $1.20 Type **429** 75 75
2993 $1.20 *Sir Thomas Wharton* 75 75
2994 $1.20 *Mary Villiers, Daughter of Duke of Buckingham* 75 75
2995 $1.20 *Christina Bruce, Countess of Devonshire* 75 75
2996 $1.20 *James Hamilton, Duke of Hamilton* 75 75
2997 $1.20 *Henry Danvers, Earl of Danby* 75 75
2998 $1.20 *Marie de Raet, Wife of Philippe le Roy* 75 75
2999 $1.20 *Jacomo de Cachiopin* 75 75
3000 $1.20 *Princess Henrietta of Lorraine attended by a Page* 75 75
3001 $1.20 *Portrait of a Man* 75 75
3002 $1.20 *Portrait of a Woman* 75 75
3003 $1.20 *Philippe le Roy, Seigneur de Ravels* 75 75
3004 $1.20 *Charles I in State Robes* 75 75
3005 $1.20 *Queen Henrietta Maria* (in white dress) 75 75
3006 $1.20 *Queen Henrietta Maria with Sir Jeffrey Hudson* 75 75
3007 $1.20 *Charles I in Armour* 75 75
3008 $1.20 *Queen Henrietta Maria in Profile facing right* 75 75
3009 $1.20 *Queen Henrietta Maria* (in black dress) 75 75

MS3010	Six sheets. (a) 102×128 mm. $5 *Charles I on Horseback*. (b) 102×128 mm. $5 *Charles I Hunting*. (c) 128×102 mm. $5 *Charles I with Queen Henrietta Maria*. (d) 128×102 mm. $5 *Charles I* (from Three Aspects portrait). (e) 102×128 mm. $6 *William, Lord Russell*. (f) 102×128 mm. $6 *Two Sons of Duke of Lennox* Set of 6 sheets	20·00	22·00

No. 2994 is inscribed "Mary Villers", 3002 "Portrait of a Women", 3005 "Henrieta Maria" and **MS**3010f "Duke of Lenox", all in error.

430 *Eupolea miniszeki*

2000. Butterflies. Multicoloured.

3011	$1.65 Type **430**	90	90
3012	$1.65 *Heliconius doris*	90	90
3013	$1.65 *Evenus coronata*	90	90
3014	$1.65 *Papilio anchisiades*	90	90
3015	$1.65 *Syrmatia dorilas*	90	90
3016	$1.65 *Morpho patroclus*	90	90
3017	$1.65 *Mesosemia loruhama*	90	90
3018	$1.65 *Bia actorion*	90	90
3019	$1.65 *Anteos clorinde*	90	90
3020	$1.65 *Menander menande*	90	90
3021	$1.65 *Catasticta manco*	90	90
3022	$1.65 *Urania leilus*	90	90
3023	$1.65 *Theope eudocia* (vert)	90	90
3024	$1.65 *Uranus sloanus* (vert)	90	90
3025	$1.65 *Helicopis cupido* (vert)	90	90
3026	$1.65 *Papilio velovis* (vert)	90	90
3027	$1.65 *Graphium androcles* (vert)	90	90
3028	$1.65 *Mesene phareus* (vert)	90	90
MS3029	Three sheets. (a) 110×85 mm. $6 *Graphium encelades*. (b) 110×85 mm. $6 *Graphium milon*. (c) 85×110 mm. $6 *Hemlargus isola* (vert) Set of 3 sheets	13·00	14·00

Nos. 3011/16, 3017/22 and 3023/8 were each printed together, *se-tenant*, with the backgrounds forming composite designs.

431 Boxer

2000. Cats and Dogs. Multicoloured.

3030	90c. Type **431**	75	45
3031	$1 Alaskan malamute	85	70
3032	$1.65 Bearded collie	1·10	1·10
3033	$1.65 Cardigan Welsh corgi	1·10	1·10
3034	$1.65 Saluki (red)	1·10	1·10
3035	$1.65 Basset hound	1·10	1·10
3036	$1.65 White standard poodle	1·10	1·10
3037	$1.65 Boston terrier	1·10	1·10
3038	$1.65 Long-haired blue and white cat (horiz)	1·10	1·10
3039	$1.65 Snow shoe (horiz)	1·10	1·10
3040	$1.65 Persian (horiz)	1·10	1·10
3041	$1.65 Chocolate lynx point (horiz)	1·10	1·10
3042	$1.65 Brown and white sphynx (horiz)	1·10	1·10
3043	$1.65 White tortoiseshell (horiz)	1·10	1·10
3044	$2 Wirehaired pointer	1·40	1·40
3045	$4 Saluki (black)	2·50	3·00
MS3046	Two sheets. (a) 106×71 mm. $6 Cavalier King Charles spaniel. (b) 111×81 mm. $6 Lavender tortie Set of 2 sheets	12·00	12·00

432 *Epidendrum pseudepidendrum*

2000. Flowers of the Caribbean. Multicoloured.

3047	45c. Type **432**	85	35
3048	65c. *Odontoglossum cervantesii*	1·00	50
3049	75c. *Cattleya dowiana*	1·00	50
3050	90c. *Beloperone guttata*	1·00	50
3051	$1 *Colliandra haematocephala*	1·00	70
3052	$1.20 *Brassavola nodosa*	1·00	80
3053	$1.65 *Pseudocalymna alliaceum*	1·10	1·10
3054	$1.65 *Datura candida*	1·10	1·10
3055	$1.65 *Ipomoea tuberosa*	1·10	1·10
3056	$1.65 *Allamanda cathartica*	1·10	1·10
3057	$1.65 *Aspasia epidendroides*	1·10	1·10
3058	$1.65 *Maxillaria cucullata*	1·10	1·10
3059	$1.65 *Anthurium andreanum*	1·10	1·10
3060	$1.65 *Doxantha unguiscati*	1·10	1·10
3061	$1.65 *Hibiscus rosa-sinensis*	1·10	1·10
3062	$1.65 *Canna indica*	1·10	1·10
3063	$1.65 *Heliconius umilis*	1·10	1·10
3064	$1.65 *Strelitzia reginae*	1·10	1·10
3065	$1.65 *Masdevallia coccinea*	1·10	1·10
3066	$1.65 *Paphinia cristata*	1·10	1·10
3067	$1.65 *Vanilla planifolia*	1·10	1·10
3068	$1.65 *Cattleya forbesii*	1·10	1·10
3069	$1.65 *Lycaste skinneri*	1·10	1·10
3070	$1.65 *Cattleya percivaliana*	1·10	1·10
MS3071	Three sheets, each 74×103 mm. (a) $6 *Cattleya leopoldiie*. (b) $6 *Strelitzia reginae*. (c) $6 *Rossioglossum grande* Set of 3 sheets	13·00	14·00

No. 3061 is inscribed "rosa-senensis" and **MS**3071b "regenae", both in error.

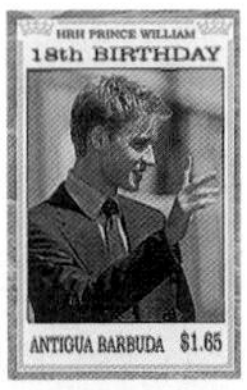

433 Prince William

2000. 18th Birthday of Prince William. Multicoloured.

3072	$1.65 Prince William waving	1·40	1·40
3073	$1.65 Wearing Eton school uniform	1·40	1·40
3074	$1.65 Wearing grey suit	1·40	1·40
3075	$1.65 Type **433**	1·40	1·40
MS3076	100×80 mm. $6 Princess Diana with Princes William and Harry (37×50 mm)	4·25	4·50

434 "Sputnik I"

2000. "EXPO 2000" World Stamp Exhibition, Anaheim, U.S.A. Space Satellites. Multicoloured.

3077	$1.65 Type **434**	1·10	1·10
3078	$1.65 "Explorer I"	1·10	1·10
3079	$1.65 "Mars Express"	1·10	1·10
3080	$1.65 "Lunik I Solnik"	1·10	1·10
3081	$1.65 "Ranger 7"	1·10	1·10
3082	$1.65 "Mariner 4"	1·10	1·10
3083	$1.65 "Mariner 10"	1·10	1·10
3084	$1.65 "Soho"	1·10	1·10
3085	$1.65 "Mariner 2"	1·10	1·10
3086	$1.65 "Giotto"	1·10	1·10
3087	$1.65 "Exosat"	1·10	1·10
3088	$1.65 "Pioneer Venus"	1·10	1·10
MS3089	Two sheets, each 106×76 mm. (a) $6 "Vostok I". (b) $6 Hubble Space Telescope Set of 2 sheets	8·50	9·50

Nos. 3077/82 and 3083/8 were each printed together, *se-tenant*, with the backgrounds forming composite designs.

435 Alexei Leonov (Commander of "Soyuz 19")

2000. 25th Anniv of "Apollo–Soyuz" Joint Project. Multicoloured.

3090	$3 Type **435**	1·75	2·00
3091	$3 "Soyuz 19"	1·75	2·00
3092	$3 Valeri Kubasov ("Soyuz 19" engineer)	1·75	2·00
MS3093	71×88 mm. $6 Alexei Leonov and Thomas Stafford (Commander of "Apollo 18")	3·25	3·75

436 Anna Karina in *Une Femme est Une Femme*, 1961

2000. 50th Anniv of Berlin Film Festival. Designs showing actors, directors and film scenes. Multicoloured.

3094	$1.65 Type **436**	1·00	1·00
3095	$1.65 *Carmen Jones*, 1955	1·00	1·00
3096	$1.65 *Die Ratten*, 1955	1·00	1·00
3097	$1.65 *Die Vier im Jeep*, 1951	1·00	1·00
3098	$1.65 Sidney Poitier in *Lilies of the Field*, 1963	1·00	1·00
3099	$1.65 *Invitation to the Dance*, 1956	1·00	1·00
MS3100	97×103 mm. $6 Kate Winslet in *Sense and Sensibility*, 1996	3·25	3·75

No. 3096 is inscribed "GOLDER BERLIN BEAR" and **MS**3100 shows the award date "1966" in error.

437 George Stephenson and *Locomotion No. 1*, 1825

2000. 175th Anniv of Stockton and Darlington Line (first public railway). Multicoloured.

3101	$3 Type **437**	2·50	2·50
3102	$3 Camden and Amboy Railroad locomotive *John Bull*, 1831	2·50	2·50

438 Statue of Johann Sebastian Bach

2000. 250th Death Anniv of Johann Sebastian Bach (German composer). Sheet 77×88 mm.

MS3103	$6 multicoloured	4·00	4·50

439 Albert Einstein

2000. Election of Albert Einstein (mathematical physicist) as Time Magazine "Man of the Century". Sheet 117×91 mm.

MS3104	$6 multicoloured	3·75	4·25

440 LZ-1 Airship, 1900

2000. Centenary of First Zeppelin Flight.

3105	**440**	$3 brown, black and blue	2·50	2·50
3106	-	$3 brown, black and blue	2·50	2·50
3107	-	$3 multicoloured	2·50	2·50
MS3108		93×66 mm. $6 multicoloured	3·75	4·00

DESIGNS: No. 3106, LZ-2, 1906; 3107, LZ-3, 1906. (50×37 mm)—No. **MS**3108, LZ-7 *Deutschland*, 1910.

Nos. 3105/7 were printed together, *se-tenant*, with the backgrounds forming a composite design.

441 Marcus Latimer Hurley (cycling), St. Louis (1904)

2000. Olympic Games, Sydney. Multicoloured.

3109	$2 Type **441**	2·25	2·25
3110	$2 Diving	2·25	2·25
3111	$2 Flaminio Stadium, Rome (1960) and Italian flag	2·25	2·25
3112	$2 Ancient Greek javelin thrower	2·25	2·25

442 Richie Richardson

2000. West Indies Cricket Tour and 100th Test Match at Lord's. Multicoloured.

3113	90c. Type **442**	1·50	70
3114	$5 Viv Richards	5·50	6·00
MS3115	121×104 mm. $6 Lord's Cricket Ground (horiz)	5·50	6·00

No. 3114 is inscribed "Viv Richard" in error.

443 Outreach Programme at Sunshine Home for Girls

2000. Girls Brigade. Multicoloured.

3116	20c. Type **443**	25	20
3117	60c. Ullida Rawlins Gill (International Vice President) (vert)	50	35
3118	75c. Officers and girls	60	45
3119	90c. Girl with flag (vert)	80	55
3120	$1.20 Members of 8th Antigua Company with flag (vert)	1·10	1·40
MS3121	102×124 mm. $5 Girl Brigade badge (vert)	3·25	3·75

444 Lady Elizabeth Bowes-Lyon as Young Girl

2000. "Queen Elizabeth the Queen Mother's Century".

3122	**444**	$2 multicoloured	1·75	1·75
3123	-	$2 black and gold	1·75	1·75
3124	-	$2 black and gold	1·75	1·75
3125	-	$2 multicoloured	1·75	1·75
MS3126		153×157 mm. $6 multicoloured	4·00	4·25

DESIGNS: No. 3123, Queen Elizabeth in 1940; 3124, Queen Mother with Princess Anne, 1951; 3125, Queen Mother in Canada, 1989; **MS**3126, Queen Mother inspecting guard of honour.

No. **MS**3126 also shows the Royal Arms embossed in gold.

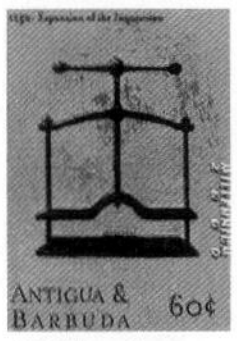

445 Thumbscrew (Expansion of Inquisition, 1250)

2000. New Millennium. People and Events of Thirteenth Century (1250–1300). Multicoloured (except No. 3127).

3127	60c. Type **445** (black and red)	90	90
3128	60c. Chartres Cathedral (completed, 1260)	90	90
3129	60c. Donor's sculpture, Naumberg (completed, 1260)	90	90
3130	60c. Delegates (Simon de Montfort's Parliament, 1261)	90	90
3131	60c. *Maesta* (Cimabue) (painted 1270)	90	90
3132	60c. Marco Polo (departure from Venice, 1271)	90	90
3133	60c. *Divine Wind* (Kamikaze wind saves Japan from invasion, 1274)	90	90
3134	60c. St. Thomas Aquinas (died 1274)	90	90
3135	60c. Arezzo Cathedral (completed 1277)	90	90

3136	60c. Margrethe ("The Maid of Norway") (crowned Queen of Scotland, 1286)	90	90
3137	60c. Jewish refugees (Expulsion of Jews from England, 1290)	90	90
3138	60c. Muslim horseman (capture of Acre, 1291)	90	90
3139	60c. Moshe de Leon (compiles *The Zohar*, 1291)	90	90
3140	60c. Knights in combat (German Civil War, 1292–98)	90	90
3141	60c. Kublai Khan (died 1294)	90	90
3142	60c. Dante (writes *La Vita Nuova*, 1295) (59×39 mm)	90	90
3143	60c. *Autumn Colours on Quiao and Hua Mountains* (Zhan Mengfu) (painted 1296)	90	90

446 *Admonishing the Court Ladies* (after Ku K'ai-Chih)

2000. New Millennium. Two Thousand Years of Chinese Paintings. Multicoloured.

3144	25c. Type **446**	40	40
3145	25c. Ink on silk drawing from Zhan Jadashan	40	40
3146	25c. Ink and colour on silk drawing from Mawangdui Tomb	40	40
3147	25c. *Scholars collating Texts* (attr Yang Zihua)	40	40
3148	25c. *Spring Outing* (attr Zhan Ziqian)	40	40
3149	25c. *Portrait of the Emperors* (attr Yen Liben)	40	40
3150	25c. *Sailing Boats and Riverside Mansion* (attr Li Sixun)	40	40
3151	25c. *Two Horses and Groom* (Han Kan)	40	40
3152	25c. *King's Portrait* (attr Wu Daozi)	40	40
3153	25c. *Court Ladies wearing Flowered Headdresses* (attr Zhou Fang)	40	40
3154	25c. *Distant Mountain Forest* (mountain) (Juran)	40	40
3155	25c. *Mount Kuanglu* (Jiang Hao)	40	40
3156	25c. *Pheasant and Small Birds* (Huang Jucai)	40	40
3157	25c. *Deer among Red Maples* (anon)	40	40
3158	25c. *Distant Mountain Forest* (river and fields) (Juran)	40	40
3159	25c. *Literary Gathering* (Han Huang) (57×39 mm)	40	40
3160	25c. *Birds and Insects* (Huang Quan)	40	40

No. 3148 is inscribed "SPRINTING", No. 3150 "MASION" and No. 3153 "HEADRESSES", all in error.

447 King Donald III of Scotland

2000. Monarchs of the Millennium.

3161	**447**	$1.65 black, stone and brown	1·50	1·50
3162	-	$1.65 black, stone and brown	1·50	1·50
3163	-	$1.65 black, stone and brown	1·50	1·50
3164	-	$1.65 black, stone and brown	1·50	1·50
3165	-	$1.65 black, stone and brown	1·50	1·50
3166	-	$1.65 black, stone and brown	1·50	1·50
3167	-	$1.65 multicoloured	1·50	1·50
3168	-	$1.65 multicoloured	1·50	1·50
3169	-	$1.65 multicoloured	1·50	1·50
3170	-	$1.65 multicoloured	1·50	1·50
3171	-	$1.65 multicoloured	1·50	1·50
3172	-	$1.65 multicoloured	1·50	1·50
MS3173		– Two sheets, each 115×135 mm. (a) $6 mult. (b) $6 mult Set of 2 sheets	8·50	9·50

DESIGNS: No. 3162, King Duncan I of Scotland; 3163, King Duncan II of Scotland; 3164, King Macbeth of Scotland; 3165, King Malcolm III of Scotland; 3166, King Edgar of Scotland; 3167, King Charles I of England and Scotland; 3168, King Charles II of England and Scotland; 3169, Prince Charles Edward Stuart ("The Young Pretender"); 3170, King James II of England and VII of Scotland; 3171, King James II of Scotland; 3172, King James III of Scotland; **MS**3173a, King Robert I of Scotland; **MS**3173b, Queen Anne of Great Britain.

No. 3169 is inscribed "George III 1760–1820 Great Britain" in error.

2000. Popes of the Millennium. As T **447**. Each black, yellow and green.

3174	$1.65 Alexander VI (bare-headed)	1·50	1·50
3175	$1.65 Benedict XIII	1·50	1·50
3176	$1.65 Boniface IX	1·50	1·50
3177	$1.65 Alexander VI (wearing cap)	1·50	1·50
3178	$1.65 Clement VIII	1·50	1·50
3179	$1.65 Clement VI	1·50	1·50
3180	$1.65 John Paul II	1·50	1·50
3181	$1.65 Benedict XV	1·50	1·50
3182	$1.65 John XXIII	1·50	1·50
3183	$1.65 Pius XI	1·50	1·50
3184	$1.65 Pius XII	1·50	1·50
3185	$1.65 Paul VI	1·50	1·50
MS3186	Two sheets, each 115×135 mm. (a) $6 Pius II (black, yellow and black). (b) $6 Pius VII (black, yellow and black) Set of 2 sheets	9·00	9·50

No. 3181 is inscribed "BENIDICT XV" in error.

448 Agouti

2000. Fauna of the Rain Forest. Multicoloured.

3187	75c. Type **448**	60	45
3188	90c. Capybara	70	50
3189	$1.20 Basilisk lizard	80	70
3190	$1.65 Green violetear ("Green Violet-Ear Hummingbird")	1·10	1·10
3191	$1.65 Harpy eagle	1·10	1·10
3192	$1.65 Three-toed sloth	1·10	1·10
3193	$1.65 White uakari monkey	1·10	1·10
3194	$1.65 Anteater	1·10	1·10
3195	$1.65 Coati	1·10	1·10
3196	$1.75 Red-eyed tree frog	1·10	1·10
3197	$1.75 Black spider monkey	1·10	1·10
3198	$1.75 Emerald toucanet	1·10	1·10
3199	$1.75 Kinkajou	1·10	1·10
3200	$1.75 Spectacled bear	1·10	1·10
3201	$1.75 Tapir	1·10	1·10
3202	$2 Heliconid butterfly	1·25	1·40
MS3203	Two sheets. (a) 90×65 mm. $6 Keel-billed toucan (horiz). (b) 65×90 mm. $6 Scarlet macaw Set of 2 sheets	10·00	11·00

Nos. 3190/5 and 3196/201 were printed together, *se-tenant*, forming composite designs.

449 "Sea Cliff" Submarine

2000. Submarines. Multicoloured.

3204	65c. Type **449**	85	45
3205	75c. "Beaver Mark IV"	1·00	50
3206	90c. "Reef Ranger"	1·10	50
3207	$1 "Cubmarine"	1·25	70
3208	$1.20 "Alvin"	1·40	80
3209	$2 H.M.S. *Revenge*	2·00	2·00
3210	$2 *Walrus*, Netherlands	2·00	2·00
3211	$2 U.S.S. *Los Angeles*	2·00	2·00
3212	$2 *Daphne*, France	2·00	2·00
3213	$2 U.S.S. *Ohio*	2·00	2·00
3214	$2 U.S.S. *Skipjack*	2·00	2·00
3215	$3 "Argus", Russia	2·50	2·75
MS3216	Two sheets, each 107×84 mm. (a) $6 "Trieste". (b) $6 Type 209 U-boat, Germany Set of 2 sheets	10·00	11·00

Nos. 3209/14 were printed together, *se-tenant*, with the backgrounds forming a composite design.

450 German Lookout

2000. 60th Anniv of Battle of Britain. Multicoloured (except No. 3222).

3217	$1.20 Type **450**	1·50	1·50
3218	$1.20 Children's evacuation train	1·50	1·50
3219	$1.20 Evacuating hospital patients	1·50	1·50
3220	$1.20 Hawker Hurricane (fighter)	1·50	1·50
3221	$1.20 Rescue team	1·50	1·50
3222	$1.20 Churchill cartoon (black)	1·50	1·50
3223	$1.20 King George VI and Queen Elizabeth inspecting bomb damage	1·50	1·50
3224	$1.20 Barrage balloon above Tower Bridge	1·50	1·50
3225	$1.20 Bristol Blenheim (bomber)	1·50	1·50
3226	$1.20 Prime Minister Winston Churchill	1·50	1·50
3227	$1.20 Bristol Blenheim and barrage balloons	1·50	1·50
3228	$1.20 Heinkel (fighter)	1·50	1·50
3229	$1.20 Supermarine Spitfire (fighter)	1·50	1·50
3230	$1.20 German rescue launch	1·50	1·50
3231	$1.20 Messerschmitt 109 (fighter)	1·50	1·50
3232	$1.20 R.A.F. rescue launch	1·50	1·50
MS3233	Two sheets, each 90×60 mm. (a) $6 Junkers 87B (dive bomber). (b) $6 Supermarine Spitfires at dusk Set of 2 sheets	12·00	13·00

No. **MS**3233a is inscribed "JUNKERS 878" in error.

451 *The Defence of Cadiz* (Zurbaran)

2000. "Espana 2000" International Stamp Exhibition, Madrid. Paintings from the Prado Museum. Multicoloured.

3234	$1.65 Type **451**	1·25	1·25
3235	$1.65 *The Defence of Cadiz* (General and galleys)	1·25	1·25
3236	$1.65 *The Defence of Cadiz* (officers)	1·25	1·25
3237	$1.65 *Vulcan's Forge* (Vulcan) (Velazquez)	1·25	1·25
3238	$1.65 *Vulcan's Forge* (working metal)	1·25	1·25
3239	$1.65 *Vulcan's Forge* (workers with hammers)	1·25	1·25
3240	$1.65 *Family Portrait* (three men) (Adriaen Key)	1·25	1·25
3241	$1.65 *Family Portrait* (one man)	1·25	1·25
3242	$1.65 *Family Portrait* (three women)	1·25	1·25
3243	$1.65 *The Devotion of Rudolf I* (horseman with lantern) (Rubens and Jan Wildens)	1·25	1·25
3244	$1.65 *The Devotion of Rudolf I* (priest on horseback)	1·25	1·25
3245	$1.65 *The Devotion of Rudolf I* (huntsman)	1·25	1·25
3246	$1.65 *The Concert* (lute player) (Vincente Gonzalez)	1·25	1·25
3247	$1.65 *The Concert* (lady with fan)	1·25	1·25
3248	$1.65 *The Concert* (two gentlemen)	1·25	1·25
3249	$1.65 *The Adoration of the Magi* (Wise Man) (Juan Maino)	1·25	1·25
3250	$1.65 *The Adoration of the Magi* (two Wise Men)	1·25	1·25
3251	$1.65 *The Adoration of the Magi* (Holy Family)	1·25	1·25
MS3252	Three sheets. (a) 115×90 mm. $6 *The Deliverance of St. Peter* (Jose de Ribera) (horiz). (b) 110×90 mm. $6 *The Fan Seller* (Jose del Castillo). (c) 110×90 mm. $6 *Family in a Garden* (Jan van Kessel the Younger) Set of 3 sheets	11·00	13·00

Nos. 3246/8 are inscribed "Gonzlez" with No. 3248 additionally inscribed "Francisco Rizi", all in error.

452 Two Angels

2000. Christmas and Holy Year. Multicoloured.

3253	25c. Type **452**	20	15
3254	45c. Heads of two angels looking down	35	25
3255	90c. Heads of two angels, one looking up	60	40
3256	$1.75 Type **452**	1·25	1·50
3257	$1.75 As 45c.	1·25	1·50
3258	$1.75 As 90c.	1·25	1·50
3259	$1.75 As $5	1·25	1·50
3260	$5 Two angels with drapery	3·00	3·50
MS3261	110×120 mm. $6 Holy Child	3·50	4·00

453 *Dr. Ephraim Bueno* (Rembrandt)

2000. Bicentenary of Rijksmuseum, Amsterdam. Dutch Paintings. Multicoloured.

3262	$1 Type **453**	85	85
3263	$1 *Woman writing a Letter* (Frans van Meris de Oude)	85	85
3264	$1 *Mary Magdalen* (Jan van Scorel)	85	85
3265	$1 *Anna Coddle* (Maerten van Heemskerck)	85	85
3266	$1 *Cleopatra's Banquet* (Gerard Lairesse)	85	85
3267	$1 *Titus in Friar's Habit* (Rembrandt)	85	85
3268	$1.20 *Saskia* (Rembrandt)	90	90
3269	$1.20 *In the Month of July* (Paul Joseph Constantin Gabriel)	90	90
3270	$1.20 *Maria Trip* (Rembrandt)	90	90
3271	$1.20 *Still Life with Flowers* (Jan van Huysum)	90	90
3272	$1.20 *Haesje van Cleyburgh* (Rembrandt)	90	90
3273	$1.20 *Girl in a White Kimono* (George Hendrick Breitner)	90	90
3274	$1.65 *Man and Woman at a Spinning Wheel* (Pieter Pietersz)	1·10	1·10
3275	$1.65 *Self-portrait* (Rembrandt)	1·10	1·10
3276	$1.65 *Jeremiah lamenting the Destruction of Jerusalem* (Rembrandt)	1·10	1·10
3277	$1.65 *The Jewish Bride* (Rembrandt)	1·10	1·10
3278	$1.65 *Anna accused by Tobit of stealing a Kid* (Rembrandt)	1·10	1·10
3279	$1.65 *The Prophetess Anna* (Rembrandt)	1·10	1·10
MS3280	Three sheets, each 118×88 mm. (a) $6 *Doubting Thomas* (Hendrick ter Brugghen). (b) $6 *Still Life with Cheeses* (Floris van Dijck); (c) $6 *Isaac Blessing Jacob* (Govert Flinck) Set of 3 sheets	11·00	13·00

454 "Starmie No. 121"

2001. Characters from "Pokemon" (children's cartoon series). Multicoloured.

3281	$1.75 Type **454**	1·10	1·10
3282	$1.75 "Misty"	1·10	1·10
3283	$1.75 "Brock"	1·10	1·10
3284	$1.75 "Geodude No. 74"	1·10	1·10
3285	$1.75 "Krabby No. 98"	1·10	1·10
3286	$1.75 "Ash"	1·10	1·10
MS3287	74×114 mm. $6 "Charizard No. 6"	3·25	3·50

455 Blue-toothed Entoloma

2001. "Hong Kong 2001" Stamp Exhibition. Tropical Fungi. Multicoloured.

3288	25c. Type **455**	45	30
3289	90c. Common morel	90	50
3290	$1 Red cage fungus	1·00	70
3291	$1.65 Copper trumpet	1·10	1·10

3292	$1.65 Field mushroom ("Meadow Mushroom")	1·10	1·10
3293	$1.65 Green gill ("Green-gilled Parasol")	1·10	1·10
3294	$1.65 The panther	1·10	1·10
3295	$1.65 Death cap	1·10	1·10
3296	$1.65 Royal boletus ("King Bolete")	1·10	1·10
3297	$1.65 Lilac fairy helmet ("Lilac Bonnet")	1·10	1·10
3298	$1.65 Silky volvar	1·10	1·10
3299	$1.65 Agrocybe mushroom ("Poplar Field Cap")	1·10	1·10
3300	$1.65 Saint George's mushroom	1·10	1·10
3301	$1.65 Red-stemmed tough shank	1·10	1·10
3302	$1.65 Fly agaric	1·10	1·10
3303	$1.75 Common fawn agaric ("Fawn Shield-Cap")	1·25	1·50
MS3304	Two sheets, each 70×90 mm. (a) $6 Yellow parasol. (b) $6 Mutagen milk cap Set of 2 sheets	8·50	9·50

Nos. 3291/6 and 3297/302 were each printed together, *se-tenant*, with the backgrounds forming composite designs.

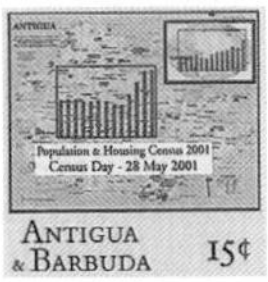

456 Map and Graphs

2001. Population and Housing Census.

3305	**456**	15c. multicoloured	15	15
3306	-	25c. multicoloured	20	20
3307	-	65c. multicoloured	55	55
3308	-	90c. multicoloured	70	70
MS3309		55×50 mm. $6 multicoloured (Map and census logo)	5·50	6·00

DESIGNS: 25c. to 90c. Map and different form of graph.

457 *Yuna (Bath-house Women)* (detail)

2001. "PHILANIPPON 2001" International Stamp Exhibition, Tokyo. Traditional Japanese Paintings. Multicoloured.

3310	45c. Type **457**	50	30
3311	60c. *Yuna (Bath-house Women)* (different detail)	60	50
3312	65c. *Yuna (Bath-house Women)* (different detail)	60	50
3313	75c. *The Hikone Screen* (detail)	70	50
3314	$1 *The Hikone Screen* (different detail)	75	60
3315	$1.20 *The Hikone Screen* (different detail)	80	70
3316	$1.65 Galleon and Dutch merchants with horse	95	95
3317	$1.65 Galleon and merchants with tiger	95	95
3318	$1.65 Merchants unpacking goods	95	95
3319	$1.65 Merchants with parasol and horse	95	95
3320	$1.65 Women packing food	95	95
3321	$1.65 Picnic under the cherry tree	95	95
3322	$1.65 Palanquins and resting bearers	95	95
3323	$1.65 Women dancing	95	95
3324	$1.65 Three samurai	95	95
3325	$1.65 One samurai	95	95
MS3326	Three sheets, each 80×110 mm. (a) $6 *Harunobu Suzuki* (Shiba Kokani) (38×50 mm). (b) $6 *Daruma* (Tsujo Kako) (38×50 mm). (c) $6 *Visiting a Shrine on a Rainy Night* (Harunobu Suziki) (38×50 mm) Set of 3 sheets	9·50	11·00

Nos. 3316/19 (*The Namban Screen* by Kano Nizen) and Nos. 3320/5 (*Merry-making under the Cherry Blossoms* by Kano Naganobu) were each printed together, *se-tenant*, with both sheetlets forming the entire painting.

458 Lucille Ball leaning on Mantelpiece

2001. Scenes from *I Love Lucy* (American T.V. comedy series). Eight sheets each containing multicoloured design as T **458**.

MS3327	(a) 118×92 mm. $6 Type **458**. (b) 98×120 mm. $6 Desi Arnaz laughing. (c) 93×130 mm. $6 William Frawley at table. (d) 114×145 mm. $6 Lucille Ball with William Frawley. (e) 114×145 mm. $6 Lucille Ball in blue dress. (f) 119×111 mm. $6 Lucille Ball sitting at table. (g) 128×100 mm. $6 Lucille Ball as scarecrow. (h) 93×125 mm. $6 William Frawley shouting at Desi Arnaz (horiz) Set of 8 sheets	22·00	24·00

459 *Hintleya burtii*

2001. Caribbean Orchids. Multicoloured.

3328	45c. Type **459**	50	25
3329	75c. *Neomoovea irrovata*	65	45
3330	90c. *Comparettia speciosa*	70	50
3331	$1 *Cypredepium crapeanum*	80	70
3332	$1.20 *Trichoceuos muralis* (vert)	90	90
3333	$1.20 *Dracula rampira* (vert)	90	90
3334	$1.20 *Psychopsis papilio* (vert)	90	90
3335	$1.20 *Lycaste clenningiana* (vert)	90	90
3336	$1.20 *Telipogon nevuosus* (vert)	90	90
3337	$1.20 *Masclecallia ayahbacana* (vert)	90	90
3338	$1.65 *Cattleya dowiana* (vert)	1·10	1·10
3339	$1.65 *Dendiobium cruentum* (vert)	1·10	1·10
3340	$1.65 *Bulbophyllum lobb* (vert)	1·10	1·10
3341	$1.65 *Chysis laevis* (vert)	1·10	1·10
3342	$1.65 *Ancistrochilus rothschildicanus* (vert)	1·10	1·10
3343	$1.65 *Angraecum sororium* (vert)	1·10	1·10
3344	$1.65 *Rhyncholaelia glanca* (vert)	1·10	1·10
3345	$1.65 *Oncidium barbatum* (vert)	1·10	1·10
3346	$1.65 *Phaius tankervillege* (vert)	1·10	1·10
3347	$1.65 *Ghies brechtiana* (vert)	1·10	1·10
3348	$1.65 *Angraecum leonis* (vert)	1·10	1·10
3349	$1.65 *Cycnoches loddigesti* (vert)	1·10	1·10
MS3350	Two sheets. (a) 68×104 mm. $6 *Symphalossum sanquinem* (vert). (b) 104×68 mm. $6 *Trichopilia fragrans* (vert) Set of 2 sheets	8·50	9·50

460 Yellowtail Damselfish

2001. Tropical Marine Life. Multicoloured.

3351	25c. Type **460**	35	25
3352	45c. Indigo hamlet	55	30
3353	65c. Great white shark	70	40
3354	90c. Bottle-nose dolphin	80	65
3355	90c. Palette surgeonfish	80	65
3356	$1 Octopus	80	65
3357	$1.20 Common dolphin	90	90
3358	$1.20 Franklin's gull	90	90
3359	$1.20 Rock beauty	90	90
3360	$1.20 Bicoloured angelfish	90	90
3361	$1.20 Beaugregory	90	90
3362	$1.20 Banded butterflyfish	90	90
3363	$1.20 Common tern	90	90
3364	$1.20 Flying fish	90	90
3365	$1.20 Queen angelfish	90	90
3366	$1.20 Blue-striped grunt	90	90
3367	$1.20 Porkfish	90	90
3368	$1.20 Blue tang	90	90
3369	$1.65 Red-footed booby	1·10	1·10
3370	$1.65 Bottle-nose dolphin	1·10	1·10
3371	$1.65 Hawksbill turtle	1·10	1·10
3372	$1.65 Monk seal	1·10	1·10
3373	$1.65 Great white shark (inscr "Bull Shark")	1·10	1·10
3374	$1.65 Lemon shark	1·10	1·10
3375	$1.65 Dugong	1·10	1·10
3376	$1.65 White-tailed tropicbird	1·10	1·10
3377	$1.65 Bull shark	1·10	1·10
3378	$1.65 Manta ray	1·10	1·10
3379	$1.65 Green turtle	1·10	1·10
3380	$1.65 Spanish grunt	1·10	1·10
MS3381	Four sheets. (a) 68×98 mm. $5 Sailfish. (b) 68×98 mm. $5 Brown pelican and beaugregory (vert). (c) 98×68 mm. $6 Queen triggerfish. (d) 96×68 mm. $6 Hawksbill turtle Set of 4 sheets	18·00	19·00

Nos. 3357/62, 3363/8, 3369/74 and 3375/80 were each printed together, *se-tenant*, the backgrounds forming composite designs.

461 *Freewinds* (liner) and Police Band, Antigua

2001. Work of Freewinds (Church of Scientology flagship) in Caribbean. Multicoloured.

3382	30c. Type **461**	40	30
3383	45c. At anchor off St. Barthelemy	45	30
3384	75c. At sunset	70	60
3385	90c. Off Bonaire	90	90
3386	$1.50 *Freewinds* anchored off Bequia	1·25	1·40
MS3387	Two sheets, each 85×60 mm. (a) $4 *Freewinds* alongside quay, Curacao. (b) $4 Decorated with lights Set of 2 sheets	5·50	6·00

462 Young Queen Victoria in Blue Dress

2001. Death Centenary of Queen Victoria. Multicoloured.

3388	$2 Type **462**	1·40	1·60
3389	$2 Queen Victoria wearing red head-dress	1·40	1·60
3390	$2 Queen Victoria with jewelled hair ornament	1·40	1·60
3391	$2 Queen Victoria, after Chalon, in brooch	1·40	1·60
MS3392	70×82 mm. $5 Queen Victoria in old age	3·00	3·75

463 *Water Lilies*

2001. 75th Death Anniv of Claude-Oscar Monet (French painter). Multicoloured.

3393	$2 Type **463**	1·50	1·50
3394	$2 *Rose Portals, Giverny*	1·50	1·50
3395	$2 *Water Lily Pond, Harmony in Green*	1·50	1·50
3396	$2 *Artist's Garden, Irises*	1·50	1·50
MS3397	136×111 mm. $5 *Jerusalem Artichoke Flowers* (vert)	3·25	3·75

No. 3396 is inscribed "Artists's" in error.

464 Duchess of York with Baby Princess Elizabeth (1926)

2001. 75th Birthday of Queen Elizabeth II. Multicoloured.

3398	$1 Type **464**	1·25	1·25
3399	$1 Queen in Coronation robes (1953)	1·25	1·25
3400	$1 Young Princess Elizabeth (1938)	1·25	1·25
3401	$1 Queen Elizabeth in Garter robes (1956)	1·25	1·25
3402	$1 Princess Elizabeth with pony (1939)	1·25	1·25
3403	$1 Queen Elizabeth in red dress and pearls (1985)	1·25	1·25
MS3404	90×72 mm. $6 Princess Elizabeth and Queen Elizabeth (1940)	4·50	5·00

465 Verdi in Top Hat

2001. Death Centenary of Giuseppe Verdi (Italian composer). Multicoloured.

3405	$2 Type **465**	2·75	2·75
3406	$2 Don Carlos and part of opera score	2·75	2·75
3407	$2 Conductor and score for *Aida*	2·75	2·75
3408	$2 Musicians and score for *Rigoletto*	2·75	2·75
MS3409	77×117 mm. $5 Verdi in evening dress	6·50	6·50

Nos. 3405/8 were printed together, *se-tenant*, the backgrounds forming a composite design.

466 *Georges-Henri Manuel*

2001. Death Centenary of Henri de Toulouse-Lautrec (French painter). Multicoloured.

3410	$2 Type **466**	1·75	1·75
3411	$2 *Louis Pascal*	1·75	1·75
3412	$2 *Romain Coolus*	1·75	1·75
3413	$2 *Monsieur Fourcade*	1·75	1·75
MS3414	67×84 mm. $5 *Dancing at the Moulin de la Galette*	5·00	5·00

No 3412 is inscribed "ROMAN" in error.

467 Marlene Dietrich smoking

2001. Birth Centenary of Marlene Dietrich (actress and singer).

3415	**467**	$2 black, purple and red	1·50	1·50
3416	-	$2 black, purple and red	1·50	1·50
3417	-	$2 multicoloured	1·50	1·50
3418	-	$2 black, purple and red	1·50	1·50

DESIGNS: No. 3416, Marlene Dietrich, in evening gown, sitting on settee; 3417, In black dress; 3418, Sitting on piano.

468 Collared Peccary

2001. Vanishing Fauna of the Caribbean. Multicoloured.

3419	25c. Type **468**	45	30
3420	30c. Baird's tapir	45	30
3421	45c. Agouti	60	30
3422	75c. Bananaquit	1·25	55
3423	90c. Six-banded armadillo	1·00	55
3424	$1 Roseate spoonbill	1·50	80
3425	$1.80 Mouse opossum	2·00	2·00
3426	$1.80 Magnificent black frigate bird	2·00	2·00
3427	$1.80 Northern jacana	2·00	2·00
3428	$1.80 Painted bunting	2·00	2·00
3429	$1.80 Haitian solenodon	2·00	2·00
3430	$1.80 St. Lucia iguana	2·00	2·00
3431	$2.50 West Indian iguana	2·75	2·75
3432	$2.50 Scarlet macaw	2·75	2·75
3433	$2.50 Cotton-topped tamarin	2·75	2·75
3434	$2.50 Kinkajou	2·75	2·75
MS3435	Two sheets. (a) 117×85 mm. $6 Ocelot (vert). (b) 162×116 mm. $6 King vulture (vert) Set of 2 sheets	14·00	15·00

469 Sara Crewe (*The Little Princess*) reading a Letter

2001. Shirley Temple Films. Multicoloured. Showing film scenes. (a) *The Little Princess*. Multicoloured.

3436	$1.50 Type **469**	95	95
3437	$1.50 Sara in pink dressing gown	95	95
3438	$1.50 Sara cuddling doll	95	95
3439	$1.50 Sara as Princess on throne	95	95
3440	$1.50 Sara talking to man in frock coat	95	95
3441	$1.50 Sara blowing out candles	95	95
3442	$1.80 Sara with Father (horiz)	1·10	1·10
3443	$1.80 Sara scrubbing floor (horiz)	1·10	1·10
3444	$1.80 Sara and friend with Headmistress (horiz)	1·10	1·10
3445	$1.80 Sara with Queen Victoria (horiz)	1·10	1·10
MS3446	106×76 mm. $6 Sara with wounded Father	3·25	3·75

(b) *Baby, Take a Bow*.

3447	$1.65 Shirley in dancing class (horiz)	95	95
3448	$1.65 Shirley cuddling Father (horiz)	95	95
3449	$1.65 Shirley at bedtime with parents (horiz)	95	95
3450	$1.65 Shirley in yellow dress with Father (horiz)	95	95
3451	$1.65 Shirley and Father at Christmas party (horiz)	95	95
3452	$1.65 Shirley and gangster looking in cradle (horiz)	95	95
3453	$1.65 Shirley in spotted dress	95	95
3454	$1.65 Shirley on steps with gangster	95	95
3455	$1.65 Shirley with gangster holding gun	95	95
3456	$1.65 Shirley with Mother	95	95
MS3457	106×76 mm. $6 Shirley in spotted dress	3·25	3·75

470 Rudolph Valentino in *Blood and Sand*, 1922

2001. 75th Death Anniv of Rudolph Valentino (Italian film actor).

3458	**470**	$1 brown and black	75	75
3459	-	$1 lilac and black	75	75
3460	-	$1 brown and black	75	75
3461	-	$1 brown and black	75	75
3462	-	$1 red and black	75	75
3463	-	$1 lilac and black	75	75
3464	-	$1 multicoloured	75	75
3465	-	$1 multicoloured	75	75
3466	-	$1 multicoloured	75	75
3467	-	$1 multicoloured	75	75
3468	-	$1 multicoloured	75	75
3469	-	$1 multicoloured	75	75
MS3470		Two sheets. (a) 90×125 mm. $6 multicoloured. (b) 68×95 mm. $6 multicoloured Set of 2 sheets	7·50	8·50

DESIGNS: No. 3459, In *Eyes of Youth* with Clara Kimbal Young, 1919; 3460, In *All Night Long* with Carmel Meyers, 1918; 3461, Valentino in 1926; 3462, In *Camille* with Alla Nazimova, 1921; 3463, In *Cobra* with Nita Naldi, 1925; 3464, In *The Son of the Sheik* with Vilma Banky, 1926; 3465, In *The Young Rajah*, 1922; 3466, In *The Eagle* with Vilma Banky, 1925; 3467, In *The Sheik* with Agnes Ayres, 1921; 3468, In *A Sainted Devil*, 1924; 3469, In *Monsieur Beaucaire*, 1924; **MS**3470, (a) Valentino with Natacha Rambova. (b) In *The Four Horseman of the Apocalypse*, 1921.

Nos. 3464 and 3466 are inscribed "BLANKY" and No. 3467 "AYERS", all in error.

471 Queen Elizabeth

2001. Golden Jubilee (1st issue).

3471	**471**	$1 multicoloured	1·50	1·50

No. 3471 was printed in sheetlets of 8, containing two vertical rows of four, separated by a large illustrated central gutter. Both the stamp and the illustration on the central gutter are made up of a collage of miniature flower photographs.

See also Nos. 3535/8.

472 Melvin Calvin, 1961

2001. Centenary of Nobel Prizes. Chemistry Winners. Multicoloured.

3472	$1.50 Type **472**	1·25	1·25
3473	$1.50 Linus Pauling, 1954	1·25	1·25
3474	$1.50 Vincent du Vigneaud, 1955	1·25	1·25
3475	$1.50 Richard Synge, 1952	1·25	1·25
3476	$1.50 Archer Martin, 1952	1·25	1·25
3477	$1.50 Alfred Werner, 1913	1·25	1·25
3478	$1.50 Robert Curl Jr., 1996	1·25	1·25
3479	$1.50 Alan Heeger, 2000	1·25	1·25
3480	$1.50 Michael Smith, 1993	1·25	1·25
3481	$1.50 Sidney Altman, 1989	1·25	1·25
3482	$1.50 Elias Corey, 1990	1·25	1·25
3483	$1.50 William Giauque, 1949	1·25	1·25
MS3484	Three sheets, each 107×75 mm. (a) $6 Ernest Rutherford, 1908. (b) $6 Ernst Fischer, 1973. (c) $6 American volunteers, International Red Cross (Peace Prize, 1944) Set of 3 sheets	12·50	13·00

473 *Madonna and Child with Angels* (Filippo Lippi)

2001. Christmas. Italian Religious Paintings. Multicoloured.

3485	25c. Type **473**	35	20
3486	45c. *Madonna of Corneto Tarquinia* (Lippi)	55	25
3487	50c. *Madonna and Child* (Domenico Ghirlandaio)	60	30
3488	75c. *Madonna and Child* (Lippi)	1·00	55
3489	$4 *Madonna Delceppo* (Lippi)	5·00	6·00
MS3490	106×136 mm. $6 *Madonna enthroned with Angels and Saints* (Lippi)	4·50	5·00

474 Final between Uruguay and Brazil, Brazil 1950

2001. World Cup Football Championship, Japan and Korea (2002). Multicoloured.

3491	$1.50 Type **474**	95	95
3492	$1.50 Ferenc Puskas (Hungary), Switzerland 1954	95	95
3493	$1.50 Raymond Kopa (France), Sweden 1958	95	95
3494	$1.50 Mauro (Brazil), Chile 1962	95	95
3495	$1.50 Gordon Banks (England), England 1966	95	95
3496	$1.50 Pele (Brazil), Mexico 1970	95	95
3497	$1.50 Daniel Passarella (Argentina), Argentina 1978	95	95
3498	$1.50 Karl-Heinz Rummenigge (Germany), Spain 1982	95	95
3499	$1.50 World Cup Trophy, Mexico 1986	95	95
3500	$1.50 Diego Maradona (Argentina), Italy 1990	95	95
3501	$1.50 Roger Milla (Cameroun), U.S.A. 1994	95	95
3502	$1.50 Zinedine Zidane (France), France 1998	95	95
MS3503	Two sheets, each 88×75 mm. (a) $6 Detail of Jules Rimet Trophy, Uruguay, 1930. (b) $6 Detail of World Cup Trophy, Japan/Korea, 2002 Set of 2 sheets	7·50	8·50

No. 3500 is inscribed "Deigo" in error.

475 Battle of Nashville, 1864

2002. American Civil War. Multicoloured.

3504	45c. Type **475**	85	85
3505	45c. Capture of Atlanta, 1864	85	85
3506	45c. Battle of Spotsylvania, 1864	85	85
3507	45c. Battle of The Wilderness, 1864	85	85
3508	45c. Battle of Chickamauga Creek, 1863	85	85
3509	45c. Battle of Gettysburg, 1863	85	85
3510	45c. Lee and Jackson at Chancellorsville, 1863	85	85
3511	45c. Battle of Fredericksburg, 1862	85	85
3512	45c. Battle of Antietam, 1862	85	85
3513	45c. Second Battle of Bull Run, 1862	85	85
3514	45c. Battle of Five Forks, 1865	85	85
3515	45c. Seven Days' Battles, 1862	85	85
3516	45c. First Battle of Bull Run, 1861	85	85
3517	45c. Battle of Shiloh, 1862	85	85
3518	45c. Battle of Seven Pines, 1862	85	85
3519	45c. Bombardment of Fort Sumter, 1861	85	85
3520	45c. Battle of Chattanooga, 1863	85	85
3521	45c. Grant and Lee at Appomattox, 1865	85	85
3522	50c. General Ulysses S. Grant (vert)	1·00	1·00
3523	50c. President Abraham Lincoln (vert)	1·00	1·00
3524	50c. President Jefferson Davis (vert)	1·00	1·00
3525	50c. General Robert E. Lee (vert)	1·00	1·00
3526	50c. General George Custer (vert)	1·00	1·00
3527	50c. Admiral Andrew Hull Foote (vert)	1·00	1·00
3528	50c. General "Stonewall" Jackson (vert)	1·00	1·00
3529	50c. General Jeb Stuart (vert)	1·00	1·00
3530	50c. General George Meade (vert)	1·00	1·00
3531	50c. General Philip Sheridan (vert)	1·00	1·00
3532	50c. General James Longstreet (vert)	1·00	1·00
3533	50c. General John Mosby (vert)	1·00	1·00
MS3534	Two sheets, each 105×76 mm. (a) $6 Confederate ironclad *Merrimack* attacking *Cumberland* (Federal sloop) (51×38 mm). (b) $6 *Monitor* (Federal ironclad) Set of 2 sheets	13·00	14·00

476 Queen Elizabeth presenting Rosettes

2002. Golden Jubilee (2nd issue). Multicoloured.

3535	$2 Type **476**	2·50	2·50
3536	$2 Queen Elizabeth at garden party	2·50	2·50
3537	$2 Queen Elizabeth in evening dress	2·50	2·50
3538	$2 Queen Elizabeth in cream coat	2·50	2·50
MS3539	76×108 mm. $6 Princesses Elizabeth and Margaret as bridesmaids	4·50	5·00

477 U.S. Flag as Statue of Liberty and Antigua & Barbuda Flag

2002. "United We Stand". Support for Victims of 11 September 2001 Terrorist Attacks.

3540	**477**	$2 multicoloured	1·25	1·40

478 Sir Vivian Richards waving Bat

2002. 50th Birthday of Sir Vivian Richards (West Indian cricketer). Multicoloured.

3541	25c. Type **478**	1·40	55
3542	30c. Sir Vivian Richards receiving presentation from Antigua Cricket Association	1·40	55
3543	50c. Sir Vivian Richards wearing sash	1·75	65
3544	75c. Sir Vivian Richards batting	2·00	90
3545	$1.50 Sir Vivian Richards and Lady Richards	3·25	3·50
3546	$1.80 Sir Vivian Richards with enlarged action photograph of himself	3·50	4·00
MS3547	Two sheets, each 68×95 mm. (a) $6 Sir Vivian Richards with guard of honour. (b) $6 Sir Vivian Richards in Indian traditional dress Set of 2 sheets	16·00	16·00

479 Thick-billed Parrot

2002. Flora and Fauna. Multicoloured.

3548	50c. Type **479**	1·00	55
3549	75c. Lesser long-nosed bat	1·00	60
3550	90c. Quetzal	1·25	1·25
3551	90c. Two-toed sloth	1·25	1·25
3552	90c. Lovely cotinga	1·25	1·25
3553	90c. *Pseudolycaena marsyas* (butterfly)	1·25	1·25
3554	90c. Magenta-throated woodstar	1·25	1·25
3555	90c. *Automeris rubrescens* (moth)	1·25	1·25
3556	90c. *Bufo periglenes* (toad)	1·25	1·25
3557	90c. Collared peccary	1·25	1·25
3558	90c. Tamandua anteater	1·25	1·25
3559	$1 St. Lucia parrot	1·25	1·25
3560	$1 Cuban kite	1·25	1·25
3561	$1 West Indian whistling-duck	1·25	1·25
3562	$1 *Eurema amelia* (butterfly)	1·25	1·25
3563	$1 Scarlet ibis	1·25	1·25
3564	$1 Black-capped petrel	1·25	1·25
3565	$1 *Cnemidophorus vanzoi* (lizard)	1·25	1·25
3566	$1 Cuban solenodon	1·25	1·25
3567	$1 *Papilio thersites* (butterfly)	1·25	1·25
3568	$1.50 Montserrat oriole	2·00	2·00
3569	$1.80 *Leptotes perkinsae* (butterfly)	2·50	2·50
MS3570	Two sheets, each 110×85 mm. (a) $6 Olive Ridley turtle. (b) $6 Margay Set of 2 sheets	11·00	12·00

Nos. 3550/8 and 3559/67 were each printed together, *se-tenant*, with the backgrounds forming composite designs.

480 Community Players wearing Straw Hats

2002. 50th Anniv of Community Players. Multicoloured. Showing scenes from various productions.

3571	20c. Type **480**	35	30
3572	25c. Men in suits with women in long dresses	35	30
3573	30c. In *Pirates of Penzance*	40	30

3574	75c. Female choir	75	50
3575	90c. In Mexican dress	90	55
3576	$1.50 Members at a reception	1·25	1·50
3577	$1.80 Production in the open air	1·50	2·00
MS3578	Two sheets, each 76×84 mm. (a) $4 Mrs. Edie Hill-Thibou (former President) (vert). (b) $4 Miss Yvonne Maginley (Acting President and Director of Music) (vert) Set of 2 sheets	7·00	8·00

481 Mount Fuji, Japan

2002. International Year of Mountains. Multicoloured.

3579	$2 Type **481**	1·50	1·50
3580	$2 Machu Picchu, Peru	1·50	1·50
3581	$2 The Matterhorn, Switzerland	1·50	1·50

482 Cross-country Skiing

2002. Winter Olympic Games, Salt Lake City. Multicoloured.

3582	$2 Type **482**	1·75	2·00
3583	$2 Pairs figure skating	1·75	2·00
MS3584	84×114 mm. Nos. 3582/3	3·50	4·00

483 Amerigo Vespucci wearing Skullcap

2002. 500th Anniv of Amerigo Vespucci's Third Voyage. Multicoloured.

3585	$2.50 Type **483**	2·50	2·50
3586	$2.50 Vespucci as an old man	2·50	2·50
3587	$2.50 16th-century map	2·50	2·50
MS3588	49×68 mm. $5 Vespucci holding dividers (vert)	4·50	5·00

484 *Spirit of St. Louis* and Charles Lindbergh (pilot)

2002. 75th Anniv of First Solo Transatlantic Flight. Multicoloured.

3589	$2.50 Type **484**	2·50	2·50
3590	$2.50 *Spirit of St. Louis* at Le Bourget, Paris, 1927	2·50	2·50
3591	$2.50 Charles Lindbergh in New York ticker-tape parade, 1927	2·50	2·50
MS3592	80×110 mm. $6 Charles Lindbergh wearing flying helmet	4·50	5·00

485 Princess Diana

2002. Fifth Death Anniv of Diana, Princess of Wales. Multicoloured.

3593	$1.80 Type **485**	1·40	1·40
3594	$1.80 Princess Diana in tiara (looking left)	1·40	1·40
3595	$1.80 Wearing hat	1·40	1·40
3596	$1.80 Princess Diana wearing pearl drop earrings and black dress	1·40	1·40
3597	$1.80 Wearing tiara (facing front)	1·40	1·40
3598	$1.80 Princess Diana wearing pearl drop earrings	1·40	1·40
MS3599	91×106 mm. $6 Princess Diana	4·50	5·00

486 Kennedy Brothers

2002. Presidents John F. Kennedy and Ronald Reagan Commemoration. Multicoloured.

3600	$1.50 Type **486**	1·60	1·60
3601	$1.50 John Kennedy with Danny Kaye (American entertainer)	1·60	1·60
3602	$1.50 Delivering Cuban Blockade speech, 1962	1·60	1·60
3603	$1.50 With Jacqueline Kennedy	1·60	1·60
3604	$1.50 Meeting Bill Clinton (future president)	1·60	1·60
3605	$1.50 Family at John Kennedy's funeral	1·60	1·60
3606	$1.50 President and Mrs. Reagan with Pope John Paul II, 1982	1·60	1·60
3607	$1.50 As George Gipp in *Knute Rockne - All American*, 1940	1·60	1·60
3608	$1.50 With General Matthew Ridgeway, Bitburg Military Cemetery, Germany, 1985	1·60	1·60
3609	$1.50 With George H. Bush and Secretary Mikhail Gorbachev of U.S.S.R., 1988	1·60	1·60
3610	$1.50 Presidents Reagan, Ford, Carter and Nixon at the White House, 1981	1·60	1·60
3611	$1.50 Horse riding with Queen Elizabeth, Windsor, 1982	1·60	1·60
MS3612	Two sheets, each 88×22 mm. (a) $6 President Kennedy at press conference (vert). (b) $6 President Reagan (vert) Set of 2 sheets	11·00	12·00

487 Red-billed Tropicbird

2002. Endangered Species of Antigua. Multicoloured.

3613	$1.50 Type **487**	2·00	2·00
3614	$1.50 Brown pelican	2·00	2·00
3615	$1.50 Magnificent frigate bird	2·00	2·00
3616	$1.50 Ground lizard	2·00	2·00
3617	$1.50 West Indian whistling duck	2·00	2·00
3618	$1.50 Antiguan racer snake	2·00	2·00
3619	$1.50 Spiny lobster	2·00	2·00
3620	$1.50 Hawksbill turtle	2·00	2·00
3621	$1.50 Queen conch	2·00	2·00

488 Elvis Presley

2002. 25th Death Anniv of Elvis Presley (American entertainer).

3622	**488**	$1 multicoloured	1·75	1·40

489 Cheerleader Teddy

2002. Centenary of the Teddy Bear. Girl Teddies. Multicoloured.

3623	$2 Type **489**	1·25	1·40
3624	$2 Figure skater	1·25	1·40
3625	$2 Ballet dancer	1·25	1·40
3626	$2 Aerobics instructor	1·25	1·40

490 "Croconaw No. 159"

2002. Pokemon (children's cartoon series). Multicoloured.

3627	$1.50 Type **490**	90	90
3628	$1.50 "Mantine No. 226"	90	90
3629	$1.50 "Feraligatr No. 160"	90	90
3630	$1.50 "Qwilfish No. 211"	90	90
3631	$1.50 "Remoraid No. 223"	90	90
3632	$1.50 "Quagsire No. 195"	90	90
MS3633	80×106 mm. $6 "Chinchou No. 170"	3·25	3·50

491 Charlie Chaplin

2002. 25th Death Anniv of Charlie Chaplin (British actor). Each black, grey and light grey.

3634	$1.80 Type **491**	1·75	1·75
3635	$1.80 Wearing waistcoat and spotted bow-tie	1·75	1·75
3636	$1.80 In top hat	1·75	1·75
3637	$1.80 Wearing coat and bowler hat	1·75	1·75
3638	$1.80 Charlie Chaplin in old age	1·75	1·75
3639	$1.80 With finger on chin	1·75	1·75
MS3640	90×105 mm. $6 Charlie Chaplin as The Tramp	4·50	4·75

492 Bob Hope

2002. Bob Hope (American entertainer) Commemoration. Designs showing him entertaining American troops. Multicoloured.

3641	$1.50 Type **492**	1·50	1·50
3642	$1.50 Wearing bush hat,Vietnam, 1972	1·50	1·50
3643	$1.50 On board U.S.S. *John F. Kennedy* (aircraft carrier)	1·50	1·50
3644	$1.50 With hawk badge on sleeve, Berlin, 1948	1·50	1·50
3645	$1.50 Wearing desert fatigues	1·50	1·50
3646	$1.50 In white cap and stars on collar	1·50	1·50

493 Lee Strasberg

2002. 20th Death Anniv of Lee Strasberg (pioneer of "Method Acting").

3647	**493**	$1 black and stone	1·00	1·00

494 Marlene Dietrich

2002. 10th Death Anniv of Marlene Dietrich (actress and singer). Each black and grey.

3648	$1.50 Type **494**	90	90
3649	$1.50 Wearing top hat	90	90
3650	$1.50 In chiffon dress	90	90
3651	$1.50 Resting chin on left hand	90	90
3652	$1.50 In cloche hat	90	90
3653	$1.50 Wearing black evening gloves	90	90
MS3654	83×108 mm. $6 Marlene Dietrich wearing chiffon scarf	3·25	3·75

495 Ferrari 801, 1957

2002. Ferrari Racing Cars. Multicoloured.

3655	20c. Type **495**	30	30
3656	25c. Ferrari 256, 1959	30	30
3657	30c. Ferrari 246 P, 1960	35	30
3658	90c. Ferrari 246, 1966	85	55
3659	$1 Ferrari 312 B2, 1971	95	70
3660	$1.50 Ferrari 312, 1969	1·40	1·40
3661	$2 Ferrari F310 B, 1997	1·75	2·00
3662	$4 Ferrari F2002, 2002	3·00	3·50

496 Antigua & Barbuda Flag

2002. 21st Anniv of Independence. Multicoloured.

3663	25c. Type **496**	50	35
3664	30c. Antigua & Barbuda coat of arms (vert)	50	35
3665	$1.50 Mount St. John's Hospital under construction	1·75	1·75
3666	$1.80 Parliament Building, St. John's	2·00	2·25
MS3667	Two sheets, each 77×81 mm. (a) $6 Sir Vere Bird (Prime Minister, 1967–94) (38×51 mm). (b) $6 Lester Bird (Prime Minister since 1994) (38×51 mm) Set of 2 sheets	10·00	11·00

497 Juan Valeron (Spain)

2002. World Cup Football Championship, Japan and Korea. Multicoloured.

3668	$1.65 Type **497**	1·00	1·00
3669	$1.65 Iker Casillas (Spain)	1·00	1·00
3670	$1.65 Fernando Hierro (Spain)	1·00	1·00
3671	$1.65 Gary Kelly (Ireland)	1·00	1·00
3672	$1.65 Damien Duff (Ireland)	1·00	1·00
3673	$1.65 Matt Holland (Ireland)	1·00	1·00
3674	$1.65 Pyo Lee (South Korea)	1·00	1·00
3675	$1.65 Ji Sung Park (South Korea)	1·00	1·00
3676	$1.65 Jung Hwan Ahn (South Korea)	1·00	1·00
3677	$1.65 Filippo Inzaghi (Italy)	1·00	1·00
3678	$1.65 Paolo Maldini (Italy)	1·00	1·00
3679	$1.65 Dammiano Tommasi (Italy)	1·00	1·00
MS3680	Four sheets, each 82×82 mm. (a) $3 Jose Camacho (Spanish coach); $3 Raul Gonzales Blanco (Spain). (b) $3 Robbie Keane (Ireland); $3 Mick McCarthy (Irish coach). (c) $3 Guus Hiddink (South Korean coach); $3 Chul Sang Yoo (South Korea). (d) $3 Francesco Totti (Italy); $3 Giovanni Trapattoni (Italian coach) Set of 4 sheets	13·00	14·00

No. **MS**3680a is inscribed "Carlos Gamarra" in error.

498 *Coronation of the Virgin* (Domenico Ghirlandaio)

2002. Christmas. Religious Paintings. Multicoloured.

3681	25c. Type **498**	40	20
3682	45c. *Adoration of the Magi* (detail) (D. Ghirlandaio)	60	25
3683	75c. *Annunciation* (Simone Martini) (vert)	1·00	45

3684 90c. *Adoration of the Magi* (different detail) (D. Ghirlandaio) 1·25 55

3685 $5 *Madonna and Child* (Giovanni Bellini) 5·00 6·00

MS3686 76×110 mm. $6 *"Madonnna and Child* (S. Martini) 5·00 6·00

499 Antiguan Racer Snake Head

2002. Endangered Species. Antiguan Racer Snake. Multicoloured.

3687 $1 Type **499** 1·25 1·25

3688 $1 Coiled Antiguan racer snake with tail at right 1·25 1·25

3689 $1 Antiguan racer snake with pebbles and leaves 1·25 1·25

3690 $1 Coiled Antiguan racer snake with tail at left 1·25 1·25

500 Magnificent Frigate Bird

2002. Fauna and Flora. Multicoloured.

3691 $1.50 Type **500** 1·75 1·75

3692 $1.50 Sooty tern 1·75 1·75

3693 $1.50 Bananaquit 1·75 1·75

3694 $1.50 Yellow-crowned night heron 1·75 1·75

3695 $1.50 Greater flamingo 1·75 1·75

3696 $1.50 Belted kingfisher 1·75 1·75

3697 $1.50 Killer whale 1·75 1·75

3698 $1.50 Sperm whale 1·75 1·75

3699 $1.50 Minke whale 1·75 1·75

3700 $1.50 Blainville's beaked whale 1·75 1·75

3701 $1.50 Blue whale 1·75 1·75

3702 $1.50 Cuvier's beaked whale 1·75 1·75

3703 $1.80 *Epidendrum fragans* 1·75 1·75

3704 $1.80 *Dombeya wallichii* 1·75 1·75

3705 $1.80 *Abebuia serratifolia* 1·75 1·75

3706 $1.80 *Cryptostegia grandiflora* 1·75 1·75

3707 $1.80 *Hylocereus undatus* 1·75 1·75

3708 $1.80 *Rodriguezia lanceolata* 1·75 1·75

3709 $1.80 *Diphthera festiva* 1·75 1·75

3710 $1.80 *Hypocrita dejanira* 1·75 1·75

3711 $1.80 *Eupseudosoma involutum* 1·75 1·75

3712 $1.80 *Composia credula* 1·75 1·75

3713 $1.80 *Citherania magnifica* 1·75 1·75

3714 $1.80 *Divana diva* 1·75 1·75

MS3715 Four sheets, each 75×45 mm. (a) $5 Snowy egret. (b) $5 *Rothschildia orizaba* (moth). (c) $6 Humpback whale. (d) $6 *Ionopsis utricularioides* (flower) Set of 4 sheets 22·00 23·00

Nos. 3691/6 (birds), 3697/702 (whales), 3703/8 (moths) and 3709/14 (flowers) were each printed together, *se-tenant*, with the backgrounds forming composite designs.

501 Dr. Margaret O'garro

2002. Centenary of Pan American Health Organization. Health Professionals. Multicoloured.

3716 $1.50 Type **501** 1·40 1·40

3717 $1.50 Ineta Wallace (nurse) 1·40 1·40

3718 $1.50 Vincent Edwards (public health official) 1·40 1·40

502 Antiguan Brownie

2002. 20th World Scout Jamboree, Thailand. Each lilac and brown (Nos. 3719/21) or multicoloured (others).

3719 $3 Type **502** 3·00 3·00

3720 $3 Brownie with badge on cap 3·00 3·00

3721 $3 Brownie without badge on cap 3·00 3·00

3722 $3 Robert Baden-Powell on horseback, 1896 (horiz) 3·00 3·00

3723 $3 Ernest Thompson Seton (founder, Boy Scouts of America), 1910, and American scout badge (horiz) 3·00 3·00

3724 $3 First black scout troop, Virginia, 1928 (horiz) 3·00 3·00

MS3725 Two sheets. (a) 80×113 mm. $6 Ernest Thompson Seton. (b) 110×83 mm. $6 Scout salute Set of 2 sheets 11·00 12·00

Nos. 3719/21 were printed together, *se-tenant*, forming a composite design.

503 Scene from *2001: A Space Odyssey* (Arthur C. Clarke)

2002. Famous Science Fiction Authors. Three sheets, each 150×108 mm, containg vert designs as T **503**. Multicoloured.

MS3726 Three sheets. (a) $6 Type **503**. (b) $6 Scene from *The Monuments of Mars* (Richard C. Hoagland). (c) $6 Nostradamus with globe Set of 3 sheets 13·00 14·00

504 "Goat and Kids" (Liu Jiyou)

2003. Chinese New Year ("Year of the Goat").

3727 **504** $1.80 multicoloured 1·60 1·60

505 *Lucretia*

2003. 450th Death Anniv of Lucas Cranach the Elder (artist). Multicoloured.

3728 75c. Type **505** 75 55

3729 90c. *Venus and Cupid* (detail) 90 65

3730 $1 *Judith with Head of Holofernes* (c. 1530) 1·00 1·00

3731 $1.50 *Portrait of a Young Lady* (detail) 1·25 1·75

MS3732 152×188 mm. $2 *Portrait of the Wife of a Jurist*; $2 *Portrait of a Jurist*; $2 *Johannes Cuspinian*; $2 *Portrait of Anna Cuspinian* 4·75 5·50

MS3733 120×100 mm. $6 *Judith with Head of Holofernes* (c. 1532) 4·75 5·50

506 *A High Class Maid training in a Samurai Household*

2003. Japanese Art of Taiso Yoshitoshi. Multicoloured.

3734 25c. Type **506** 35 20

3735 50c. *A Castle-Toppler known as a Keisei* 55 30

3736 $1 *Stylish Young Geisha battling a Snowstorm on her Way to Work* 90 65

3737 $5 *A Lady in Distress being treated with Moxa* 3·50 4·25

MS3738 178×140 mm. $2 *A Lady of the Imperial Court wearing Four Layers of Robes*; $2 *Young Mother adoring her Infant Son*; $2 *Lady-in-Waiting looking amused over a Veranda in the Household of a Great Lord*; $2 *A High Ranking Courtesan known as an "Oiran", waiting for a Private Assignation* 5·50 6·50

MS3739 135×67 mm. $6 *A Girl teasing her Cat* 4·50 5·00

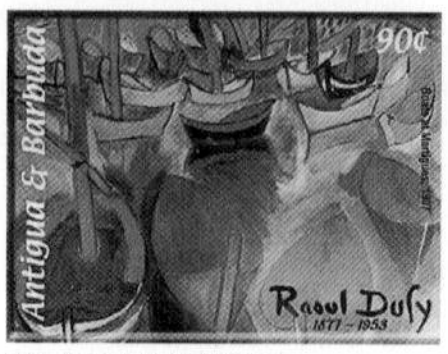

507 *Boats at Martigues*

2003. 50th Death Anniv of Raoul Dufy (artist). Multicoloured.

3740 90c. Type **507** 75 45

3741 $1 *Harvesting* 90 60

3742 $1.80 *Sailboats in the Port of Le Havre* 1·40 1·40

3743 $5 *The Big Bather* (vert) 4·00 4·50

MS3744 173×124 mm. $2 *The Beach and the Pier at Trouville*; $2 *Port with Sailing Ships*; $2 *Black Cargo*; $2 *Nice, The Bay of Anges* 5·50 6·00

MS3745 Two sheets, each 95×76 mm. (a) $6 *Vence*. (b) $6 *The Interior with an Open Window*. Both Imperf 8·50 9·50

508 Queen Elizabeth II at Trooping the Colour

2003. 50th Anniv of Coronation. Multicoloured.

MS3746 155×93 mm. $3 Type **508**; $3 Queen wearing fawn beret with single feather; $3 Queen wearing feathered hat 8·50 9·00

MS3747 105×75 mm. $6 Princess Elizabeth 5·00 5·50

509 Prince William

2003. 21st Birthday of Prince William of Wales. Multicoloured.

MS3748 147×77 mm. $3 Type **509**; $3 Prince william wearing polo helmet; $3 Wearing blue T-shirt 8·00 8·50

MS3749 67×97 mm. $6 As teenager holding bouquet 4·75 5·00

510 Tamarind Tree, Parham

2003. Centenary of Salvation Army in Antigua. Multicoloured.

3750 30c. Type **510** 60 30

3751 90c. Salvation Army pre-school 1·25 55

3752 $1 Meals on wheels (horiz) 1·40 80

3753 $1.50 St. John Citadel band (horiz) 1·75 1·75

3754 $1.80 Salvation Army Citadel (horiz) 2·00 2·50

MS3755 146×78 mm. $6 As Type **510** but without badge and centenary inscription 5·50 6·00

511 First Anglican Scout Troop, 1931

2003. 90th Anniv of Antigua and Barbuda Scouts Association. Multicoloured (except No. 3756).

3756 30c. Type **511** (black and brown) 50 30

3757 $1 National Scout Camp, 2002 1·25 80

3758 $1.50 Woodbadge Training course, 2000 (horiz) 1·60 1·60

3759 $1.80 Visitors to National Camp, 1986 (horiz) 1·90 2·25

MS3760 136×96 mm. 90c. Edris George; 90c. Theodore George; 90c. Edris James (all Deputy Commissioners) 3·00 3·25

MS3761 74×101 mm. $6 Scout leader demonstrating semaphore 5·00 5·50

512 Cesar Garin (1903)

2003. Centenary of Tour de France Cycle Race. Past winners. Multicoloured.

MS3762 160×100 mm. $2 Type **512**; $2 Caricature of Henri Cornet (1904); $2 Louis Trousselier (1905); $2 Rene Pottier (1906) 8·00 8·00

MS3763 160×100 mm. $2 Lucien Petit-Breton (1907); $2 Lucien Petit-Breton (1908); $2 Francois Faber (1909); $2 Octave Lapize (1910) 8·00 8·00

MS3764 160×100 mm. $2 Gustave Garrigou (1911); $2 Odile Defraye (1912); $2 Phillipe Thys (1913); $2 Phillipe Thys (1914) 8·00 8·00

MS3765 Three sheets, each 100×70 mm. (a) $6 Henri Desgranges (editor of *L'Auto*). (b) $6 Pierre Giffard (editor of *Le Velo*). (c) $6 Le Compte de Dion (sponsor) Set of 3 sheets 13·00 14·00

513 Frigate Bird and Emblem

2003. 30th Anniv of CARICOM.

3766 **513** $1 multicoloured 1·25 1·00

514 Cadillac Eldorado Convertible (1955)

2003. Centenary of General Motors Cadillac. Multicoloured.

MS3767 110×150 mm. $2 Type **514**; $2 Cadillac Series 60 (1937); $2 Cadillac Eldorado (1959); $2 Cadillac Eldorado (2002) 6·00 6·50

MS3768 102×76 mm. $6 Cadillac Eldorado (1953) 3·75 4·00

515 Chutes de Carbet Waterfall, Guadeloupe

2003. International Year of Freshwater. Multicoloured.

MS3769 94×180 mm. $2 Type **515**; $2 Foot of Chutes de Carbet waterfall; $2 Rapids at foot of Chutes de Carbet waterfall 4·50 4·75

MS3770 96×67 mm. $6 Waterfall, Ocho Rios, Jamaica (vert) 4·50 4·75

516 Corvette Convertible (1954)

2003. 50th Anniv of General Motors Chevrolet Corvette. Multicoloured.

MS3771 110×151 mm. $2 Type **516**; $2 Corvette Sting Ray (1964); $2 Corvette Sting Ray Convertible (1964); $2 Corvette Convertible (1998) 6·00 6·50

MS3772 102×74 mm. $6 Corvette Convertible (1956) 3·75 4·00

517 *Flyer I* (first manned powered flight), 1903

2003. Centenary of Powered Flight. Multicoloured.

MS3773 176×106 mm. $2 Type **517**; $2 Paul Cornu's helicopter on first helicopter flight, 1907; $2 E.B. Ely's biplane making first landing on ship, 1911; $2 Curtiss A-1 (first seaplane), 1911 8·00 8·00

MS3774 176×106 mm. $2 Bell X-5 research aircraft with variable wings, 1951; $2 Convair XFY-1 vertical take-off and landing; $2 North American X-15 rocket aircraft, 1959; $2 Alexei Leonov on first spacewalk, 1965 8·00 8·00

MS3775 176×106 mm. $2 Concorde, 1969; $2 Martin X-24 Lifting Body Vehicle Pre-Space Shuttle, 1969; $2 Apollo-Soyuz, 1975; $2 Viking Robot Mars Expedition, 1976 8·00 8·00

MS3776 Three sheets, each 106×76 mm. (a) $6 Boeing Model 200 Monomail with retractable landing gear, 1930. (b) $6 Bell XS-1 rocket plane breaking sound barrier, 1947. (c) $6 Grumman X-29 with forward swept wings, 1984 13·00 14·00

2003. As Nos. 2067/81, with country name overprint smaller and bird inscriptions in English only.

3777 $5 Greater Antillean bullfinch 4·50 5·00
3778 $10 Caribbean elaenia 8·50 9·50

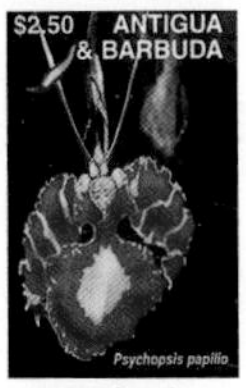

518 *Psychopsis papilio*

2003. Orchids. Multicoloured.

MS3779 96×138 mm. $2.50 Type **518**; $2.50 *Amesiella philippinensis*; $2.50 *Maclellanara* "Pagan Dove Song"; $2.50 *Phalaenopsis* "Little Hal" 8·00 8·00

MS3780 205×124 mm. $2.50 *Daeliocattleya* "Amber Glow"; $2.50 *Hygrochilus parishii*; $2.50 *Dendrobium crystallinum*; $2.50 *Disa* hybrid (all horiz) 8·00 8·00

MS3781 98×68 mm. $5 *Cattleya deckeri* (horiz) 5·00 5·00

519 Bull Shark

2003. Sharks. Multicoloured.

MS3782 128×128 mm. $2 Type **519**; $2 Grey reef shark; $2 Black tip shark; $2 Leopard shark 8·00 8·00

MS3783 88×88 mm. $5 Great white shark 5·00 5·00

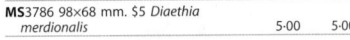

520 Esmeralda

2003. Butterflies. Multicoloured.

MS3784 105×86 mm. $2 Type **520**; $2 Tiger pierid; $2 Blue night butterfly; $2 *Charaxes nobilis* 8·00 8·00

MS3785 205×132 mm. $2.50 Orange-barred sulphur; $2.50 Scarce bamboo page; $2.50 *Charaxes latona*; $2.50 Hewitson's blue hairstreak 8·00 8·00

MS3786 98×68 mm. $5 *Diaethia merdionalis* 5·00 5·00

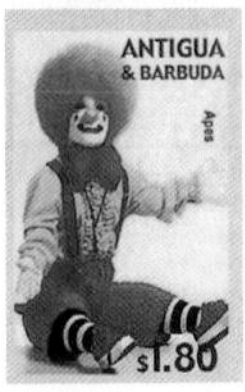

521 Apes

2003. Centenary of Circus Clowns. Multicoloured.

MS3787 119×195 mm. $1.80 Type **521**; $1.80 Mo Lite; $1.80 Gigi; $1.80 "Buttons" M. C. Bride 4·75 5·50

MS3788 145×218 mm. $1.80 Chun Group; $1.80 Casselly Sisters (acrobats); $1.80 Oliver Groszer; $1.80 Keith Nelson (sword swallower) 4·75 5·50

No. **MS**3787 is cut in the shape of a clown on a bicycle and No. **MS**3788 in the shape of a circus elephant.

522 *Madonna and Child* (detail) (Bartolommeo Vivarini)

2003. Christmas. Multicoloured.

3789 25c. Type **522** 35 20
3790 30c. *Holy Family* (detail) (Pompeo Girolano Batoni) 35 20
3791 45c. *Madonna and Child* (detail) (Benozzo Gozzoli) 50 25
3792 50c. *Madonna and Child* (detail) (Benozzo Gozzoli), Calci Parish Church 50 30
3793 75c. *Madonna and Child giving Blessings* (Benozzo Gozzoli) 75 50
3794 90c. *Madonna and Child* (detail) (Master of the Female Half-Figures) 90 55
3795 $2.50 *The Benois Madonna* (detail) (da Vinci) 2·50 3·25

MS3796 70×110 mm. $6 *The Virgin and Child with Angels* (Rosso Fiorentino) 5·50 6·00

523 Blue and Yellow Macaw ("Blue and Gold Macaw")

2003. Birds. Multicoloured.

MS3797 96×137 mm. $2.50 Type **523**; $2.50 Green-winged macaw; $2.50 Rainbow lory ("Green-naped Lorikeet"); $2.50 Lesser sulphur-crested cockatoo 8·50 8·50

MS3798 205×133 mm. $2.50 Chestnut-fronted macaw ("Severe Macaw"); $2.50 Blue-headed parrot; $2.50 Budgerigar; $2.50 Sun conure (all horiz) 8·50 8·50

MS3799 98×68 mm. $5 Waldrapp ("Bald Ibis") (horiz) 5·50 5·50

524 Diana Monkey

2004. Chinese New Year ("Year of the Monkey"). Multicoloured.

MS3800 152×95 mm. $1.50 Type **524**; $1.50 Mandrill; $1.50 Lar gibbon; $1.50 Red howler monkey 4·50 4·75

525 Mountain Landscape

2004. Hong Kong 2004 International Stamp Exhibition. Paintings by Ren Xiong. Multicoloured.

MS3801 131×138 mm. $1.50 Type **525**; $1.50 *Myriad Bamboo in Misty Rain*; $1.50 Winter landscape; $1.50 House and tree 4·50 4·75

MS3802 170×137 mm. $1.50 *Myriad Sceptres worshipping Heaven*; $1.50 Misty mountain landscape; $1.50 Myriad cherry trees; $1.50 Mountain landscape with two streams; $1.50 *Myriad Valleys with competing Streams*; $1.50 Myriad lights 5·50 6·00

MS3803 74×153 mm. $2.50 Bird singing from flowering cherry branch; $2.50 Bird in maple tree 3·75 4·00

Nos. **MS**3801/2 show paintings from *The Ten Myriads* album and No. **MS**3803 paintings from *Album after the Poems of Yao Xie*.

526 Binky skating

2004. Arthur the Aardvark by Marc Brown (children's books and TV programme). T **526** and similar vert designs. Multicoloured.

MS3804 150×183 mm. $1.50 Type **526**; $150 Buster skating; $1.50 Francine skating; $1.50 D.W.; $1.50 Sue Ellen; $1.50 Muffy skating 6·00 6·50

MS3805 150×183 mm. $1.80 Binky in baseball game; $1.80 Muffy with bat; $1.80 Francine running; $1.80 Buster catching ball 5·00 5·50

MS3806 150×183 mm. $2.50 Arthur hitting ball; $2.50 Sue Ellen with bat; $2.50 Binky holding bat; $2.50 Arthur with bat raised 5·00 5·50

No. **MS**3804 shows Arthur characters skating and **MS**3805/6 show them playing baseball.

527 *Freedom of Speech*

2004. 25th Death Anniv of Norman Rockwell (artist) (2003). T **527** and similar vert designs. Multicoloured.

MS3807 135×145 mm. $2 Type **527**; $2 *Freedom to Worship*; $2 "Freedom from Want"; $2 *Freedom from Fear* 6·00 6·50

MS3808 62×82 mm. $6 *Do Unto Others as you would have them Do Unto You*. Imperf 6·00 6·50

No. **MS**3807 shows a series of posters and **MS**3808 a painting for Saturday Evening Post cover, 1961.

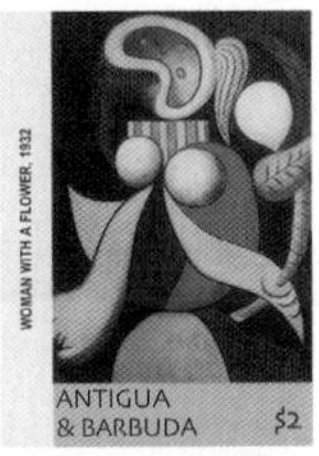

528 *Woman with a Flower*

2004. 30th Death Anniv of Pablo Picasso (artist). T **528** and similar vert designs. Multicoloured.

MS3809 177×127 mm. $2 Type **528**; $2"*Marie-Therese Seated*; $2 *The Red Armchair (Marie-Therese) Seated*; $2 *The Dream (Marie-Therese) Seated* 6·00 6·50

MS3810 58×69 mm. $5 *Bust of a Girl (Marie-Therese)*. Imperf 4·50 4·75

529 *The Smile of Flaming Wings, 1953*

2004. 20th Death Anniv of Joan Miro (artist). Multicoloured.

3811 75c. Type **529** 70 45
3812 90c. *The Bird's Song in the Dew of the Moon, 1955* 85 50
3813 $1 *Dancer II, 1957* (vert) 90 70
3814 $4 *Painting, 1954* (vert) 3·50 4·50

MS3815 Sheet 181×152 mm containing four different $2 designs, each entitled *Painting Based on a Collage, 1933* 6·50 7·00

MS3816 Two sheets. (a) 102×83 mm. $5 *Bather, 1932*. (b) 83×102 mm. $6 *Flame in Space and Nude Woman, 1932"* Both imperf. Set of 2 sheets 8·50 9·50

530 *Vaite Goupil*

2004. Death Centenary of Paul Gauguin (2003) (artist). Multicoloured.

3817 25c. Type **530** 40 25
3818 30c. *Autoportrait. Pres du Golgotha* 40 25
3819 75c. *Le Moulin David A Pont-Aven* (horiz) 85 60
3820 $2.50 *Moisson en Bretagne* 2·75 3·25

MS3821 77×62 mm. $4 *Cavaliers sur la Plage*. Imperf 4·25 4·50

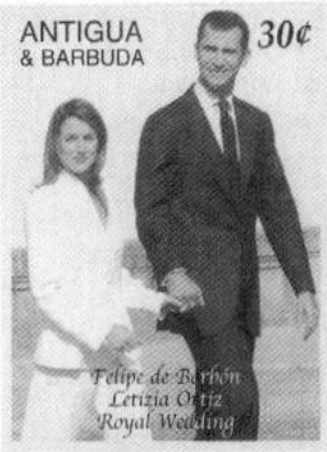

531 Felipe de Borbon and Letizia Ortiz

2004. Marriage of Crown Prince Felipe de Borbon and Letizia Ortiz. Multicoloured.

3822 30c. Type **531** 40 25
3823 50c. Felipe de Borbon and Letizia Ortiz in gardens 55 30
3824 75c. Letizia Ortiz 80 55
3825 90c. Felipe de Borbon 1·00 60
3826 $1 Felipe de Borbon and Letizia Ortiz wearing dark coats 1·10 85
3827 $5 Felipe de Borbon and Letizia Ortiz at social function 4·00 5·00

MS3828 190×174 mm. $1.80 Family photo; $1.80 Felipe de Borbon swearing allegiance to the Flag; $1.80 Felipe de Borbon with father and grandfather; $1.80 With King Juan Carlos I and Queen Sofia (horiz); $1.80 As No. 3824; $1.80 As No. 3825 9·00 10·00

MS3829 Six sheets, each 138×123 mm. (a) $5 Family photo. (b) $5 Felipe de Borbon with father and grandfather. (c) $5 Felipe de Borbon and Letizia Ortiz laughing. (d) $6 With King Juan Carlos I and Queen Sofia (horiz). (e) $6 Felipe de Borbon swearing allegiance to the Flag. (f) $6 Letizia Ortiz reading news Set of 6 sheets 26·00 29·00

532 Dove carrying Olive Branch

2004. United Nations International Year of Peace. Sheet 146×86 mm containing T **532** and similar horiz designs. Multicoloured.

MS3830 $3 Type **532**; $3 Dove with olive branch and globe; $3 Dove with olive branch and United Nations emblem 6·00 7·00

533 King Class 4-6-0

2004. Bicentenary of Steam Locomotives. Six sheets containing T **533** and similar multicoloured designs.

MS3831 Three sheets. (a) 147×175 mm. $1 Type **533**; $1 Argentinian 11B Class 2-8-0; $1 Baldwin Mikado; $1 Track signal; $1 Signal block instrument; $1 Forders Sidings signal box; $1 Signal on line; $1 Signal in snow; $1 Interior of signal box; $1 Two light signals. (b) 147×176 mm. $1 Class 2-4-0T, Douglas–Port Erin line; $1 Class 4-8-2S, South African; $1 Class 2-8-2, China; $1 St. Pancras Station; $1 Ulverston Station; $1 Bolton Station; $1 Liverpool Street Station; $1 Cannon Street Station; $1 Malvern Station. (c) 146×177 mm. $1 Evening Star (horiz); $1 Indian Railways XC Pacific (horiz); $1 German Kreigslokomotive (horiz); $1 Bullied Light Pacific and Corfe Castle (horiz); $1 Copper cap chimney (horiz); $1 Tallylyn Railway (horiz); $1 Preservation volunteers (horiz); $1 Class Y7 0-4-0T (horiz); $1 Asmara Locoshed and Breda 0-4-0, Eritrea (horiz) Set of 3 sheets	26·00	28·00
MS3832 Three sheets, each 97×67 mm. (a) $5 Settle–Carlisle line (horiz). (b) $6 Lake Egridir (horiz). (c) $6 Douro Valley railway (horiz) Set of 3 sheets	16·00	17·00

534 Pope John Paul II and Mother Teresa

2004. 25th Anniv of the Pontificate of Pope John Paul II. Sheet 162×152 mm containing T **534** and similar horiz designs. Multicoloured.

MS3833 $1.80 Type **534**; $1.80 At the Wailing Wall; $1.80 With Pres. George W. Bush; $1.80 Waving with left hand; $1.80 Waving with right hand	13·00	13·00

535 Poster of 1964 Olympic Games, Tokyo

2004. Olympic Games, Athens. Multicoloured.

3834	$1 Type **535**	1·00	60
3835	$1.65 Commemorative medal of 1964 Olympic Games, Tokyo	1·50	1·25
3836	$1.80 Fencing (horiz)	1·60	1·60
3837	$2 Pankration (wrestling, Greek art) (horiz)	1·75	2·25

536 Milan Galic (Yugoslav player)

2004. European Football Championship 2004, Portugal. Commemoration of First European Football Championship (1960). T **536** and similar multicoloured designs.

MS3838 147×86 mm. $2 Type **536**; $2 Slava Metreveli (USSR player); $2 Igor Netto (USSR player); $2 Parc des Princes stadium	6·50	7·00
MS3839 98×85 mm. $6 USSR football team, 1960 (50×37 *mm*)	4·50	4·75

537 Derrick Tysoe (Durham Light Infantry)

2004. 60th Anniv of D-Day Landings.

3840	**537**	30c. multicoloured	50	30
3841	-	45c. multicoloured	65	30
3842	-	$1.50 multicoloured	1·75	1·75
3843	-	$3 multicoloured	3·00	3·75

MS3844 Two sheets, each 177×107 mm. (a) $2 purple, mauve and black; $2 multicoloured; $2 purple; $2 lilac and black. (b) $2 deep blue and black; $2 blue and black; $2 slate and black; $2 slate violet and black Set of 2 sheets	17·00	17·00
MS3845 Two sheets, each 100×69 mm. (a) $6 purple and black. (b) $6 brown and black Set of 2 sheets	13·00	13·00

DESIGNS: No. 3840 Type **537**; No. 3841 Lt. Gen. Walter Bedell Smith; 3842 Les Perry, 1st Battalion, Suffolk Regiment; 3843 Major Gen. Percy Hobart; **MS**3844 (a) $2 Tiger II tank; $2 Kurt Meyer and tactics; $2 Canadian infantry; $2 British infantry; (b) $2 Hamilcar and Tetrarch tank; $2 Horsa Glider and soldiers; $2 Beachheads; $2 Soldiers and civilians; **MS**3845 (a) $6 Mulberry Harbour; (b) $6 Sherman tank.

538 Queen Juliana

2004. Queen Juliana of the Netherlands. Sheet, 170×180 mm, containing T **538** and similar horiz designs. Multicoloured.

MS3846 $2 Type **538**; $2 With Prince Bernhard; $2 With Princess Beatrix; $2 With Princess Irene; $2 With Princess Margriet; $2 With Princess Christina	12·00	12·00

539 Mike Bibby

2004. National Basketball Association, China. Sheet, 204×140 mm, containing T **539** and similar vert designs. Multicoloured.

MS3847 Type **539**; $1.50 Jim Jackson; $1.50 Tracy McGrady; $1.50 Chris Webber; $1.50 Peja Stojakovic; $1.50 Yao Ming	12·00	12·00

540 Zinedine Zidane (France)

2004. Centenary of FIFA (Federation Internationale de Football Association). T **540** and similar horiz designs. Multicoloured.

MS3848 193×97 mm. $2 Type **540**; $2 Roberto Baggio (Italy); $2 Franz Beckenbaur (Germany); $2 Ossie Ardiles (Argentina)	6·00	6·50
MS3849 108×87 mm. $6 Jimmy Greaves (England)	5·00	5·50

541 George Herman "Babe" Ruth

2004. Centenary of Baseball World Series. Sheet 127×118 mm containing T **541** and similar vert designs showing portraits of George Herman Ruth Jr ("Babe Ruth"). Multicoloured.

MS3850 $1.80 Type **541**; $1.80 Wearing crown; $1.80 Wearing striped cap; $1.80 Holding baseball bat over shoulder	4·50	5·00

542 John Denver

2004. John Denver Commemoration. Sheet 117×107 mm containing T **542** and similar vert designs. Multicoloured.

MS3851 $1.50 Type **542**; $1.50 John Denver (wearing pale waistcoat); $1.50 Wearing dark waistcoat; $1.50 Facing left	4·50	4·75

543 "If you had wider shoulders…"

2004. *The Family Circus* (cartoon). T **543** and similar vert designs. Multicoloured.

MS3852 115×176 mm. $2 Type **543**; $2 "Billy attacked me too hard!" (red border); $2 "Who tee-peed the mummies?"; $2 "Looking out there makes me realize its indeed the little things that count"	6·00	6·50
MS3853 115×176 mm. $2 "Billy attacked me too hard!" (purple border); $2 "His ears came from where his eyes are"; $2 "Tennessee!"; $2 "One candy, or one bowl?"	6·00	6·50
MS3854 176×115 mm. $2 "Someday I might travel to another planet, but I'm not sure why"; $2 "Adam and Eve were lucky. They didn't have any history to learn"; $2 "My backpack is too full. Will somebody help me to stand up?"; $2 "I tripped because one foot tried to hug the other foot"	6·00	6·50
MS3855 176×115 mm. $2 "If you don't put enough stamps on it the mailman will only take it part way"; $2 "Gee, Grandma, you have a lot of thoughts on your wall"; $2 "Shall I play for you, pa-rum-pa-rum-pummm…"; $2 "You have to do that when you're married"	6·00	6·50
MS3856 192×105 mm. $2 Billy; $2 Jeffy; $2 PJ; $2 Dolly	6·00	6·50

544 People holding Balloons forming AIDS Ribbon

2004. World AIDS Day.

3857	**544**	$2 multicoloured	2·00	2·00

545 *Madonna in Floral Wreath* (Bruegel the Elder with Rubens)

546 Santa on Skis

2004. Christmas. Multicoloured. (a) As T **545**.

3858	20c. Type **545**	30	25
3859	25c. *Madonna and Child* (detail) (Mabuse (Jan Gossaert))	30	25
3860	$1 *Floral Wreath with Virgin and Child* (detail) (Daniel Seghers)	1·00	75
3861	$1.80 *Madonna and Child* (detail) (Andrea Mantegna)	1·75	2·00
MS3862	70×100 mm. $6 *Madonna in a Floral Wreath* (Daniel Seghers)	5·50	6·00

(b) As T **546**.

3863	30c. Type **546**	30	25
3864	45c. Santa ornament with arms raised	50	25
3865	50c. Santa on chimney	55	35

547 American Pit (inscr "Pitt") Bull Terrier

2005. Cats and Dogs. Multicoloured.

3866	30c. Type **547**	50	30
3867	75c. Golden Persian	90	50
3868	90c. Maltese (dog)	1·10	55
3869	$1 Calico shorthair (cat)	1·25	80
3870	$1.50 Siamese	1·40	1·60
3871	$1.50 Rottweiler	1·40	1·60
3872	$3 Tabby Persian	2·75	3·50
3873	$3 Australian terrier	2·75	3·50
MS3874	Two sheets, each 100×70 mm. (a) $5 Turkish cat. (b) $5 German shepherd dog (horiz)	10·00	11·00

548 Yellowtail Damselfish

2005. Tropical Sea Life. Multicoloured.

MS3875 143×84 mm. $2 Type **548**; $2 French angelfish; $2 Horseshoe crab; $2 Emerald mithrax crab	8·00	8·00
MS3876 100×70 mm. $6 Spanish hogfish	5·50	6·00

The stamps within **MS**3875 form a composite design of a coral reef.

549 Figure-of-eight Butterfly

2005. Insects. Multicoloured.

MS3877 143×83 mm. $2 Type **549**; $2 Honey bee; $2 Migratory grasshopper; $2 Hercules beetle	8·00	8·00
MS3878 100×70 mm. $5 Cramer's mesene butterfly (vert)	5·00	5·50

550 Mammuthus imperator

2005. Prehistoric Animals. Multicoloured.

MS3879 Three sheets, each 140×110 mm. (a) $2 Type **550**; $2 Brontops; $2 Hyracotherium; $2 Propaleotherium. (b) $2.50 Ceratosaurs; $2.50 Coelurosaurs; $2.50 Ornitholestes; $2.50 Baryonyx. (c) $3 Plateosaurus; $3 Yangchuanosaurus; $3 Ceolophysis; $3 Lystrosaurus	25·00	27·00
MS3880 Three sheets, each 98×70 mm. (a) $4 Triceratops. (b) $5 Stegosaurus. (c) $6 Coelodonta	12·00	13·00

The stamps within Nos. **MS**3879a/c each form composite background designs.

551 Uruguay Team, 1930

2005. 75th Anniv of First World Cup Football Championship, Uruguay. Multicoloured.

3881	$2.50 Type **551**	2·00	2·00
3882	$2.50 Hector Castro scoring goal against Argentina, World Cup final, 1930	2·00	2·00
3883	$2.50 Estadio Centenario	2·00	2·00
3884	$2.50 Hector Castro	2·00	2·00
MS3885	111×86 mm. $6 Players after victory of Uruguay, 1930	5·00	6·00

552 Bust of Von Schiller (C. L. Richter), Central Park, New York

2005. Death Bicentenary of Friedrich von Schiller (poet and dramatist). Multicoloured.

3886	$3 Type **552**	2·50	2·50
3887	$3 Modern performance of *Kabale und Liebe*	2·50	2·50
3888	$3 Von Schiller's birthplace, Marbach, Germany	2·50	2·50
MS3889	66×95 mm. $6 Von Schiller and statue, Lincoln Park, Chicago	4·75	5·50

553 *Misterio en la Isla de los Monstruos*, 1961

2005. Death Centenary of Jules Verne (writer). Posters from films of Jules Verne's novels. Multicoloured.

3890	$2 Type **553**	2·25	2·25
3891	$2 *Journey to the Centre of the Earth*, 1961	2·25	2·25
3892	$2 *From the Earth to the Moon*, 1956	2·25	2·25
3893	$2 *Los Diablos del Mar*, 1961	2·25	2·25
MS3894	103×97 mm. $5 Michael Strogoff (56×41 mm)	5·00	5·00

554 British attempting to Board Spanish Ship *Santisima Trinidad*

2005. Bicentenary of the Battle of Trafalgar. Multicoloured.

3895	90c. Type **554**	1·75	1·00
3896	$1 Sailors clinging to wreckage and HMS *Royal Sovereign*, *Santa Ana*, HMS *Mars*, *Fougueux* and HMS *Temeraire*	2·00	1·25
3897	$1.50 HMS *Britannia* firing on crippled French *Bucentaure*	2·50	2·50
3898	$1.80 French *Redoubtable* and HMS *Victory*	3·00	3·50
MS3899	90×122 mm. $6 Crew of HMS *Victory* firing during battle	8·00	8·00

555 Ronald Reagan

2005. Ronald Reagan (US President 1981–9) Commemoration.

3900	**555**	$1.50 multicoloured	1·25	1·50

556 Defeated German Soldiers, Red Square, 9 May 1945

2005. 60th Anniv of Victory in Europe Day. Multicoloured.

3901	$1.50 Type **556**	2·00	2·00
3902	$1.50 General Montgomery	2·00	2·00
3903	$1.50 Marshal Zhukov	2·00	2·00
3904	$1.50 General Bradley	2·00	2·00

557 Churchill, Roosevelt and Stalin at Yalta Summit, 1945

2005. 60th Anniv of Victory in Japan Day. Multicoloured.

3905	$2 Type **557**	2·50	2·50
3906	$2 US troops raising flag on Mt. Suribachi	2·50	2·50
3907	$2 Gen. McArthur signing Japanese surrender documents	2·50	2·50
3908	$2 Surrendering Japanese officials, 2 September 1945	2·50	2·50

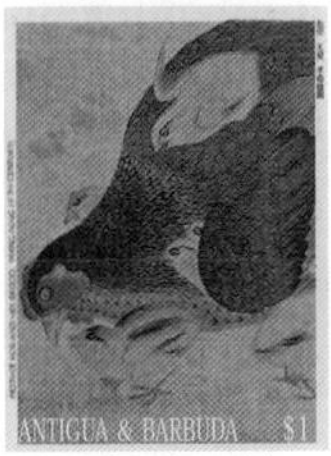

558 *Mother Hen and her Brood* (Wang Ning)

2005. Chinese New Year ("Year of the Rooster"). Multicoloured.

3909	$1 Type **558**	1·25	1·25
MS3910	75×105 mm. $4 *Mother Hen and her Brood* (Wang Ning)	3·50	4·00

559 Dwight Howard, Orlando Magic

2005. US National Basketball Association Players. Multicoloured.

3911	75c. Type **559**	1·25	90
3912	75c. Lucious Harris, Cleveland Cavaliers	1·25	90
3913	75c. Emeka Okafor, Charlotte Bobcats	1·25	90
3914	75c. Antonio McDyess, Detroit Pistons	1·25	90
3915	75c. Ray Allen, Seattle Supersonics	1·25	90

560 Pope John Paul II with Rabbi Meir Lau (Chief Rabbi of Israel, 1993–2003)

2005. Pope John Paul II Commemoration.

3916	**560**	$3 multicoloured	3·75	3·50

561 Italy 1979 World Rotary Congress Stamp

2005. Centenary of Rotary International. Multicoloured.

3917	$3 Type **561**	2·25	2·25
3918	$3 Paul Harris medallion and "Sow the Seeds of Love"	2·25	2·25
3919	$3 Paul Harris (founder), Tokyo, 1935	2·25	2·25
MS3920	100×70 mm. $6 Young African children (horiz)	4·75	5·00

562 Albert Einstein

2005. 50th Death Anniv of Albert Einstein (physicist). Multicoloured.

3921	$3 Type **562**	2·50	2·50
3922	$3 On bicycle	2·50	2·50
3923	$3 Albert Einstein (grey background)	2·50	2·50

563 Hans Christian Andersen

2005. Birth Bicentenary of Hans Christian Andersen (writer). Multicoloured.

3924	$3 Type **563**	2·25	2·25
3925	$3 Statue in Central Park, New York	2·25	2·25
3926	$3 Tombstone	2·25	2·25
MS3927	100×70 mm. $6 Hans Christian Andersen seated in chair	4·50	5·00

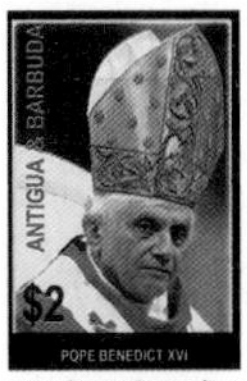

564 Pope Benedict XVI

2005. Election of Pope Benedict XVI.

3928	**564**	$2 multicoloured	2·50	2·50

565 Gilbert's Memorial Methodist Church

2005. Christmas. Churches. Multicoloured.

3929	25c. Type **565**	35	30
3930	30c. The People's Church, Barbuda	40	30
3931	30c. Tyrell's Roman Catholic Church	40	30
3932	45c. St. Barnabas Anglican Church	55	35
3933	50c. St. Peter's Anglican Church	60	35
3934	75c. Spring Gardens Moravian Church	75	75
3935	75c. St. Steven's Anglican Church	75	75
3936	90c. Pilgrim Holiness Church (vert)	90	90
3937	90c. Holy Family Catholic Cathedral	90	90
3938	$1 Ebenezer Methodist Church	1·00	1·00
MS3939	Two sheets, each 100×70 mm. (a) $5 St. John's Cathedral. (b) $5 Service at Spring Gardens Moravian Church (vert)	8·50	9·50

566 The Joiners Loft, Nelson's Dockyard

2005. National Parks of Antigua. Multicoloured.

3940	20c. Type **566**	30	30
3941	20c. Pay Office, Nelson's Dockyard (vert)	30	30
3942	30c. Bakery, Nelson's Dockyard	45	45
3943	30c. Admirals House Museum, Nelson's Dockyard	45	45
3944	75c. Devil's Bridge National Park	80	80
3945	75c. View from Shirley Heights Lookout, Nelson's Dockyard National Park	80	80
3946	90c. Green Castle Hill National Park	95	95
3947	90c. Fort Berkeley, Nelson's Dockyard National Park	95	95
3948	$1.50 Pigeon Point Beach, Nelson's Dockyard National Park	1·50	1·75
3949	$1.50 Half Moon Bay National Park	1·50	1·75
3950	$1.80 Cannon at Fort Berkeley	1·75	2·00
MS3951	Two sheets. (a) 96×67 mm. $5 Frigate birds nesting at Codrington Lagoon National Park, Barbuda. (b) 65×96 mm. $5 Cannon and Admirals House Museum, Nelson's Dockyard (vert)	10·00	11·00

567 Yellowstone National Park

2006. National Parks of the USA. Multicoloured.

3952	$1.50 Type **567**	1·40	1·40
3953	$1.50 Olympic National Park	1·40	1·40
3954	$1.50 Glacier National Park	1·40	1·40
3955	$1.50 Grand Canyon National Park	1·40	1·40
3956	$1.50 Yosemite National Park	1·40	1·40
3957	$1.50 Great Smoky Mountains National Park	1·40	1·40
MS3958	95×70 mm. $6 Mount Rainier National Park (42×28 mm)	4·75	5·50

568 Bishop John Ephraim Knight

2006. 250th Anniv of Moravian Church in Antigua. Moravian Church Antigua Conference. Multicoloured.

3959	30c. Type **568**	35	20
3960	$1 John Andrew Buckley (minister 1856–79)	1·00	85
3961	$1.50 Old Spring Gardens Moravian Church, 1854–1963 (horiz)	1·40	1·75
MS3962	Three sheets, each 95×60 mm. (a) $5 Westerby Memorial, St. John's. (b) $5 Sandbox Tree (site of beginnings of Antigua Moravian Church). (c) $5 Spring Gardens Teachers College, 1854–1958 (horiz)	12·00	13·00

569 Princess Elizabeth

2006. 80th Birthday of Queen Elizabeth II. Multicoloured.

3963	$2 Type **569**	2·25	2·25
3964	$2 Princess Elizabeth wearing cream dress and pearl necklace	2·25	2·25
3965	$2 Princess Elizabeth wearing white blouse	2·25	2·25
3966	$2 Queen Elizabeth II wearing diadem and red dress	2·25	2·25
MS3967	120×120 mm. $6 Queen Elizabeth II wearing diadem and drop earrings	6·00	6·00

570 Marilyn Monroe

2006. 80th Birth Anniv of Marilyn Monroe (actress).

3968	**570**	$3 multicoloured	2·50	2·50

571 Austria 2s.20 Ice Hockey Stamp

2006. Winter Olympic Games, Turin. Showing Austrian stamps issued for 1964 Olympic Games, Innsbruck (Nos. 3964/6) or poster (No. 3967). Multicoloured.

3969	75c. Type **571**	75	65
3970	75c. Poster for Winter Olympic Games, Sapporo, 1972 (vert)	75	65
3971	90c. Japan 1972 Winter Olympics 20y. skiing stamp (vert)	75	65
3972	90c. (1s.80) Figure skating stamp	75	65
3973	$2 4s. Bobsleighing stamp	1·75	2·00
3974	$3 Poster for Winter Olympic Games, Innsbruck, 1964 (vert)	2·75	3·25

572 Benjamin Franklin

2006. Washington 2006 International Stamp Exhibition. Showing Benjamin Franklin. Multicoloured.

MS3975	Two sheets, each 140×152 mm. (a) $3×4 Type **572**, Wearing red in oval portrait in gold frame (84×93 mm) (imperf); USA 1847 5c. stamp; Close-up portrait. (b) $3×3 Round portraits in gold frames: Wearing red; Sitting at desk; In close-up	17·00	19·00

573 Mozart's Viola

2006. 250th Birth Anniv of Wolfgang Amadeus Mozart (composer). Multicoloured.

3976	$3 Type **573**	3·50	3·00
3977	$3 Mozart aged eleven	3·50	3·00
3978	$3 Young Mozart	3·50	3·00
3979	$3 Mozart in Verona, 1770	3·50	3·00

574 Elvis Presley in *Charro!*

2006. 50th Anniv of Elvis Presley's Film Debut. Sheet 190×127 mm containing T **574** and similar vert designs showing film posters. Multicoloured.

3980	$3 Type **574**	2·50	2·50
3981	$3 *Follow That Dream*	2·50	2·50
3982	$3 *G I Blues*	2·50	2·50
3983	$3 *Blue Hawaii*	2·50	2·50

575 Leaders after Garbage Collection Race, 2002

2006. 75th Anniv of Antigua and Barbuda Girl Guides. Multicoloured.

3984	25c. Type **575**	35	20
3985	30c. Girl guides colour party (horiz)	35	20
3986	45c. Uniformed and non-uniformed members	55	25
3987	50c. Girl guides marching band (horiz)	60	30
3988	$1 Leeward Islands leaders training camp, 1946 (horiz)	1·00	1·25
MS3989	Three sheets, each 100×70 mm. (a) $5 Enrolment ceremony, 2006 (horiz). (b) $5 Girl guides gathering at Fort James, 1935 (horiz). (c) $5 Lisa Simon, Assistant Commissioner	12·00	13·00

576 HS-748 Hawker Siddely Avro

2006. 50th Anniv of LIAT (Leeward Islands Air Transport) Airline. Multicoloured.

3990	30c. Type **576**	50	25
3991	50c. BN2 Islanders on ground	70	70
3992	50c. BN2 Norman Islander	70	70
3993	50c. Beechcraft Twin Bonanza (vert)	70	70
3994	$1.50 BAC111-orange and HS748-pink/lilac on ground	2·00	2·00
3995	$2.50 Present brand DH8-300 50 seater De Havilland on ground	3·25	3·50
MS3996	70×100 mm. $5 Sir Frank Delisle (founder) and first Beechcraft Twin Bonanza N9614R (vert)	5·50	6·00

577 Magnificent Frigate Bird

2006. 25th Anniv of Independence. Multicoloured.

3997	25c. Type **577**	50	50
3998	25c. Fallow deer hinds	50	50
3999	25c. Fallow deer stag on beach	50	50
4000	25c. Magnificent frigate birds in flight and on nest	50	50
4001	30c. Pineapple	50	20
4002	$1 National flag	1·50	1·00
4003	$1.50 Coat of Arms	1·75	2·00
MS4004	100×70 mm. $5 New Parliament building (38×49 mm)	4·50	5·00

578 JSC Shuttle Mission Simulator (SMS)

2006. Space Anniversaries. Multicoloured. (a) 25th Anniv of First Flight of Space Shuttle "Columbia".

4005	$2 Type **578**	2·25	2·25
4006	$2 STS-1 prime crew during classroom session	2·25	2·25
4007	$2 STS-1 "Columbia" on launch pad	2·25	2·25
4008	$2 STS-1 "Columbia" blast-off	2·25	2·25
4009	$2 Pre-touchdown landing of "Columbia" at Edwards AFB, California	2·25	2·25
4010	$2 Space shuttle "Columbia" landing at Edwards Air Force Base	2·25	2·25

(b) 40th Anniv of "Luna 9" Moon Landing.

4011	$3 Molniya 8K78M rocket on launch vehicle	3·00	3·00
4012	$3 "Luna 9" flight apparatus	3·00	3·00
4013	$3 Image of Moon's surface transmitted by "Luna 9"	3·00	3·00
4014	$3 "Luna 9" capsule	3·00	3·00

(c) 30th Anniv (2005) of "Apollo-Soyuz" Test Project.

4015	$3 "Apollo" crew boarding transfer van	3·00	3·00
4016	$3 Handshake after "Apollo-Soyuz" linkup	3·00	3·00
4017	$3 Display of ASTP commemorative plaque	3·00	3·00
4018	$3 Recovery of ASTP Apollo command module	3·00	3·00
MS4019	Three sheets, each 100×70 mm. (a) $6 Calipso satellite. (b) $6 SS *Atlantis* docking on Space Station "MIR". (c) $6 Artist's concept of a NASA spaceship to orbit the Moon	16·00	16·00

579 Dalai Lama (Tibetan leader)

2006. Civil Rights. Multicoloured.

4020	$2 Type **579**	2·75	2·75
4021	$2 Abraham Lincoln (slavery abolitionist)	2·75	2·75
4022	$2 Susan Anthony (women's suffragist)	2·75	2·75
4023	$2 Harriet Tubman (slave liberator)	2·75	2·75
4024	$2 Mahatma Gandhi (Indian leader)	2·75	2·75
4025	$2 Nelson Mandela (anti-apartheid leader)	2·75	2·75
4026	$2 Rosa Parks (civil rights activist)	2·75	2·75
MS4027	70×100 mm. $5 Martin Luther King (civil rights leader)	4·50	5·00

580 *Landscape with the Baptism of the Eunuch* (detail)

2006. 400th Birth Anniv of Rembrandt Harmenszoon van Rijn (artist). Multicoloured.

4028	50c. Type **580**	60	30
4029	75c. *Landscape with a Coach* (detail)	1·00	55
4030	$1 *River Landscape with Ruins* (detail)	1·10	80
4031	$2 *Landscape with a Castle* (detail)	1·75	1·75
4032	$2 *Samson Posing the Riddle to the Wedding Guests* (detail, Samson's bride)	1·75	1·75
4033	$2 *Samson Posing the Riddle to the Wedding Guests* (detail, two men)	1·75	1·75
4034	$2 *Samson Posing the Riddle to the Wedding Guests* (detail, two guests listening)	1·75	1·75
4035	$2 *Samson Posing the Riddle to the Wedding Guests* (detail, woman)	1·75	1·75
4036	$2 *The Holy Family* (detail, man sitting at table)	1·75	1·75
4037	$2 *The Good Samaritan arriving at the Inn* (detail)	1·75	1·75
4038	$2 *Rebecca Taking Leave of her Family* (detail)	1·75	1·75
4039	$2 *The Holy Family* (detail, man sitting)	1·75	1·75
MS4040	Two sheets, each 70×100 mm. (a) $5 *Self-Portrait*. (b) $5 *Rembrandt's Mother*. Both imperf	8·00	9·00

581 Bauble

2006. Christmas. Multicoloured.

4041	30c. Type **581**	40	20
4042	90c. Gold star	1·10	55
4043	$1 Red bell	1·25	75
4044	$1.50 Miniature tree	1·75	2·00
MS4045	100×150 mm. $2×4 As Nos. 4041/4	8·00	9·00
MS4046	100×70 mm. $6 Santa on beach with wrapped presents	4·75	5·00

Nos. 4041/5 show Christmas tree decorations.

Stamps from **MS**4045 are in similar designs to Nos. 4041/4 but have the country inscription at top and no coloured panel at the foot of the stamp.

The background of **MS**4045 forms a composite design showing a decorated Christmas tree.

582 Betty Boop

2006. Betty Boop. Multicoloured.

4047	$1.50 Type **582**	1·00	1·00
4048	$1.50 Leaning forward	1·00	1·00
4049	$1.50 Holding mirror	1·00	1·00
4050	$1.50 Holding microphone	1·00	1·00
4051	$1.50 Seated, looking over shoulder	1·00	1·00
4052	$1.50 Wearing red heart garter	1·00	1·00
MS4053	70×100 mm. $3 "BETTY BOOP"; $3 With yellow fur stole	3·50	4·00

583 Columbus landing in New World

2007. 500th Death Anniv of Christopher Columbus. Multicoloured.

4054	75c. Type **583**	1·00	60
4055	90c. Christopher Columbus	1·10	65
4056	$2 Columbus (portrait in oval frame)	2·00	2·00
4057	$3 Columbus (in profile)	2·75	3·25
MS4058	100×70 mm. $6 *Nina*, *Pinta* and *Santa Maria*	5·50	6·00

584 National Flags forming Knot

2007. Centenary of World Scout Movement. Multicoloured.

4059	$4 Type **584**	4·00	4·25
MS4060	110×80 mm. $6 National flags forming knot	5·50	6·00

585 Ensign Kennedy

2007. 90th Birth Anniv of John F. Kennedy (American President 1960–3). Multicoloured.

4061	$3 Type **585**	2·50	2·50
4062	$3 Kennedy and crew members	2·50	2·50
4063	$3 Kennedy at the USS *PT-109*	2·50	2·50
4064	$3 Kennedy in the South Pacific	2·50	2·50
4065	$3 Campaigning on crutches	2·50	2·50
4066	$3 "The New Congressman"	2·50	2·50
4067	$3 John F. Fitzgerald, Joseph Kennedy and John F. Kennedy	2·50	2·50
4068	$3 "Celebrating Victory"	2·50	2·50

Nos. 4061/4 (showing John Kennedy in the Navy, 1941–5) and 4065/8 (showing his election to the House of Representatives, 1947–53).

586 *Alamanda*

587 *Callicore maimuna* (figure-of-eight butterfly)

2007. Flowers. Multicoloured.

4069	75c. Type **586**	90	50
4070	90c. *Bidens sulphurea*	1·00	50
4071	$1 *Alstroemeria caryophyllacea*	1·10	80
4072	$2 *Canna limbata* (horiz)	2·00	2·00
4073	$2 *Gazania rigens* (horiz)	2·00	2·00
4074	$2 *Gloriosa rothschildiana* (horiz)	2·00	2·00
4075	$2 *Hibiscus sinensis* (horiz)	2·00	2·00
4076	$4 *Bougainvillea*	3·50	4·00
MS4077	100×70 mm. $6 *Caesalpinia pulcherrima*	5·50	6·00

2007. Butterflies of the Caribbean. Multicoloured.

4078	75c. Type **587**	1·00	60
4079	90c. *Dismorphia amphione* (tiger pierid)	1·25	65
4080	$1 *Eryphanis polyxena* (purple mort bleu)	1·40	90
4081	$4 *Colobura dirce* (mosaic butterfly)	4·75	5·50
MS4082	130×108 mm. $2×4 *Actinote pellenea* (small lacewing); *Anteos clorinde* (clorinde); *Morpho peleides* (common morpho); *Anartia jatrophae* (white peacock)	8·00	8·00

MS4083	70×99 mm. $5 *Catonephele numilia* (Grecian shoemaker)	5·00	5·00

The stamps and margins of No. **MS**4082 form a composite design of palm tree foliage.

588 *Cantharellus cibarius*

590 Kenneth Benjamin

589 *Oncidium flexuosum*

2007. Mushrooms of the Caribbean. Multicoloured.

MS4084	131×108 mm. $2×4 Type **588**; *Auricularia auricula-judae*; *Mycena acicula*; *Peziza vesiculosa*	8·00	8·00
MS4085	100×70 mm. $6 *Pleurotus djamor*	6·00	6·00

The stamps and margins of No. **MS**4084 form a composite design.

2007. Orchids. Multicoloured.

4086	$3 Type **589**	3·00	3·00
4087	$3 *Paphiopedilum Pinocchio*	3·00	3·00
4088	$3 *Cattleyopsis lindenii*	3·00	3·00
4089	$3 *Cattleyopsis cubensis*	3·00	3·00
MS4090	100×70 mm. $6 *Osmoglossum pulchellum* (*vert*)	6·00	6·00

2007. World Cup Cricket, West Indies. Famous West Indian Cricketers. Multicoloured.

4091	25c. Type **590**	50	30
4092	30c. Anderson Roberts	50	30
4093	90c. Ridley Jacobs	1·25	60
4094	$1 Curtly Ambrose	1·40	1·00
4095	$1.50 Richard (Richie) Richardson	2·25	2·50
MS4096	117×90 mm. $5 Sir Vivian Richards	7·00	7·00

591 Princess Elizabeth and Duke of Edinburgh

2007. Diamond Wedding of Queen Elizabeth II and Duke of Edinburgh. Multicoloured.

4097	$1.50 Type **591**	1·50	1·50
4098	$1.50 Wedding shoes	1·50	1·50
MS4099	101×70 mm. $6 On wedding day with family (*vert*)	5·50	6·00

592 Camellias and Butterfly

2007. 50th Death Anniv of Qi Baishi (artist). Paintings on Fans. Multicoloured.

4100	$1.50 Type **592**	1·25	1·25
4101	$1.50 Two shrimps and arrow-head leaves	1·25	1·25
4102	$1.50 Gourd and ladybug	1·25	1·25
4103	$1.50 Bird	1·25	1·25
4104	$1.50 Landscape	1·25	1·25
4105	$1.50 Five shrimps	1·25	1·25
MS4106	(a) 102×72 mm. $3 Chrysanthemums; $3 Maple leaves (both vert). (b) 72×102 mm. $6 Wisteria (*vert*)	10·00	12·00

593 Ferrari 365 GTS4, 1969

2007. Ferrari Classic Cars. Multicoloured.

4107	$1.40 Type **593**	1·10	1·10
4108	$1.40 Superamerica, 2005	1·10	1·10
4109	$1.40 F1 90, 1990	1·10	1·10
4110	$1.40 400 Automatic, 1976	1·10	1·10
4111	$1.40 250 GT Coupe, 1954	1·10	1·10
4112	$1.40 156 F2, 1960	1·10	1·10
4113	$1.40 312 P, 1972	1·10	1·10
4114	$1.40 D 50, 1956	1·10	1·10

594 Concorde 01 rolled out, Filton, 20 Sept 1971

2007. Concorde. Multicoloured.

4115	$1.50 Type **594**	1·50	1·50
4116	$1.50 Concorde 01 (G-AXDN) in flight (green border)	1·50	1·50
4117	$1.50 As Type **594** (violet border)	1·50	1·50
4118	$1.50 As No. 4116 (magenta)	1·50	1·50
4119	$1.50 As Type **594** (green border)	1·50	1·50
4120	$1.50 As No. 4116 (violet border)	1·50	1·50
4121	$1.50 Concorde and London Eye (green inscr)	1·50	1·50
4122	$1.50 Concorde and Sydney Opera House (black inscr)	1·50	1·50
4123	$1.50 As No. 4121 (magenta inscr)	1·50	1·50
4124	$1.50 As No. 4122 (orange inscr)	1·50	1·50
4125	$1.50 As No. 4121 (black inscr)	1·50	1·50
4126	$1.50 As No. 4122 (blue inscr)	1·50	1·50

Nos. 4115/20 show Concorde 01, the first pre-production aircraft.

Nos. 4121/6 commemorate the London to Sydney flight record set on 13 February 1985. The colours given for Nos. 4121/6 are those of the country inscription 'ANTIGUA & BARBUDA'.

595 NH-90 Helicopter

2007. Centenary of the Helicopter. Multicoloured.

4127	$1.50 Type **595**	2·25	2·00
4128	$1.50 BO 105 helicopter carrying pipes	2·25	2·00
4129	$1.50 NH-90 helicopter on ground	2·25	2·00
4130	$1.50 AS-61 helicopter 6-15 over sea	2·25	2·00
4131	$1.50 BO 105 helicopter and lighthouse	2·25	2·00
4132	$1.50 AS-61 helicopter 6-26	2·25	2·00
MS4133	100×71 mm. $6 Bell UH-1 Iroquois 'Huey' troop carrier (*vert*)	7·50	7·00

596 Pope Benedict XVI

2007. 80th Birthday of Pope Benedict XVI.

4134	**596**	$1.40 multicoloured	2·00	2·00

597 Elvis Presley

2007. 30th Death Anniv of Elvis Presley. Multicoloured.

4135	$1.50 Type **597**	1·40	1·40
4136	$1.50 Wearing striped shirt, seen in profile	1·40	1·40
4137	$1.50 Holding guitar, wearing jacket and bow tie	1·40	1·40
4138	$1.50 Wearing striped shirt, smiling	1·40	1·40
4139	$1.50 Wearing red shirt	1·40	1·40
4140	$1.50 Holding guitar, seen in half-profile	1·40	1·40

598 Diana, Princess of Wales

2007. Tenth Death Anniv of Diana, Princess of Wales. Multicoloured.

4141	$2 Type **598**	1·75	1·75
4142	$2 Wearing pale mauve and drop earrings	1·75	1·75
4143	$2 Wearing purple jacket with black edging on collar	1·75	1·75
4144	$2 Wearing brownish grey and white dress and hat	1·75	1·75
MS4145	70×100 mm. $6 Wearing headscarf	4·50	4·75

599 *Strelitzia parvifolia* (bird of paradise)

2007. Plants and Trees. Multicoloured.

4146	15c. Type **599**	20	20
4147	20c. *Thespesia populnea* (sea-side mahoe)	25	20
4148	30c. *Hibiscus rosa sinensis*	30	20
4149	50c. *Agave karatto*	45	20
4150	70c. *Barringtonia asiatica*	65	35
4151	75c. *Cocos nucifera* (coconut)	70	40
4152	90c. *Prosopis chilensis* (mesquite) (*horiz*)	85	45
4153	$1 *Tamarindus indica*	1·00	55
4154	$1.50 *Capparis cynophallophora* (black willow) (*horiz*)	1·25	75
4155	$1.80 Baobab (*horiz*)	1·50	1·10
4156	$2 *Petrea volubilis*	1·75	1·50
4157	$2.50 *Opuntia cochenillifera* (cactus) (*horiz*)	2·00	2·00
4158	$5 *Hymenaea courbaril* (locust fruit) (*horiz*)	3·25	3·50
4159	$10 *Caesalpinia ciliata* (Barbuda black warri)	5·50	6·00
4160	$20 *Ricinus communis* (castor oil plant)	10·00	11·00

600 John W. Ashe, Antigua &; Barbuda

2007. Holocaust Remembrance. Multicoloured.

4161	$1.40 Type **600**	1·50	1·50
4162	$1.40 Alfred Capelle, Marshall Islands	1·50	1·50
4163	$1.40 Masao Nakayama, Micronesia	1·50	1·50
4164	$1.40 Gilles Noghes, Monaco	1·50	1·50
4165	$1.40 Baatar Choisuren, Mongolia	1·50	1·50
4166	$1.40 Filipe Chiduma, Mozambique	1·50	1·50
4167	$1.40 Marlene Moses, Nauru	1·50	1·50
4168	$1.40 Franciscus Majoor, Netherlands	1·50	1·50

601 Antigua and Barbuda on Bauble

2007. Christmas. Multicoloured.

4169	30c. Type **601**	40	20
4170	90c. Decorated palm tree and parade dancers on beach	90	50
4171	$1 Cake decorations	1·00	70
4172	$1.50 Parade costume	1·40	1·40

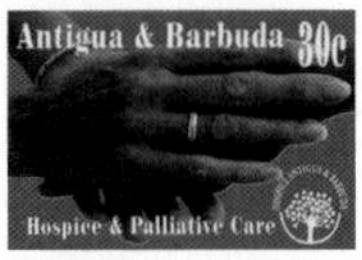

602 Hands

2007. World Hospice and Palliative Care Day. Multicoloured.

4173	30c. Type **602**	50	50
4174	30c. Clock	50	50

603 King Court (Prince Klaas), 1691–1736

2008. National Heroes. Multicoloured.

4175	90c. Type **603**	85	80
4176	90c. Dame Georgiana E. (Nellie) Robinson, 1880–1972	85	85
4177	$1 Sir Vivian Richards	1·50	1·00
4178	$1.50 Sir V. C. Bird Snr, 1909–99	1·50	1·75

603a Field Marshal William 'Bill' Slim

2008. Field Marshal William 'Bill' Slim Commemoration.

4178a	**603a**	$1.20 multicoloured	1·50	1·50

604 Americas Cup Yachts

2008. 32nd Americas Cup Yachting Championship, Valencia, Spain. Multicoloured.

4179	$1.20 Type **604**	1·25	1·50
4180	$1.80 Two yachts, yellow-hulled *Lladro* at right	1·60	1·75
4181	$3 Two yachts	2·25	2·50
4182	$5 Five yachts	3·75	4·00

605 Pierre de Coubertin (founder of modern Olympics), 1896

2008. Olympic Games, Beijing. Multicoloured.

4183	$1.40 Type **605**	1·50	1·50
4184	$1.40 Poster for first modern Olympic Games, Athens, 1896	1·50	1·50
4185	$1.40 Spiridon Louis of Greece, marathon gold medallist, 1896	1·50	1·50
4186	$1.40 Paul Masson of France, cycling gold medallist, 1896	1·50	1·50

606 King's Garden, Walls of Old City and Al-Aqsa Mosque, Jerusalem (image scaled to 44% of original size)

2008. Israel 2008 World Stamp Championship. Sheet 110×100 mm.

MS4187	**606**	$6 multicoloured	6·00	6·50

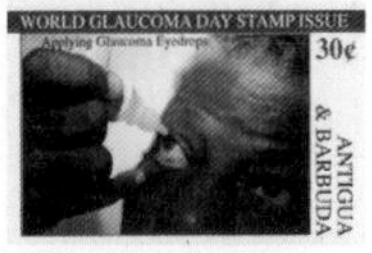

607 Applying Eye Drops

2008. World Glaucoma Day. Multicoloured.

4188	30c. Type **607**	45	30
4189	50c. Normal and glaucomatous optic nerves	70	35
4190	$1 Using braille typewriter	1·40	1·40

608 Pope Benedict XVI

2008. Frist Visit of Pope Benedict XVI to the United States

4191	**608**	$2 multicoloured	2·25	2·25

609 Elvis Presley

2008. 50th Anniv of Elvis Presley's Induction into the US Army. Sheet 160×130 mm containing T **609** and similar vert designs. Multicoloured.

MS4192	Type **609**; In light grey uniform; In dark grey uniform; In light grey uniform with cap	6·50	7·00

The stamps within **MS**4192 share a composite background design.

610 *Vanguard I*, 1958

2008. 50 Years of Space Exploration and Satellites. Multicoloured.

4193	$1.50 Type **610**	1·50	1·50
4194	$1.50 *Vanguard I* (green and white background)	1·50	1·50
4195	$1.50 *Vanguard I* (sphere and base)	1·50	1·50
4196	$1.50 *Explorer III*, 1958	1·50	1·50
4197	$1.50 *Explorer III* orbiting Earth	1·50	1·50
4198	$1.50 Van Allen radiation belt (discovered by Explorer programme)	1·50	1·50
4199	$2 *Vanguard I* and Moon	2·00	2·00
4200	$2 *Vanguard I* orbiting Earth at sunrise	2·00	2·00
4201	$2 *Explorer III* (deep brown-red and light green background)	2·00	2·00
4202	$2 *Explorer III*	2·00	2·00
MS4203	Two sheets, each 100×70 mm. (a) $6 *Vanguard I* above Earth (horiz). (b) $6 *Explorer III* and Earth (horiz)	12·00	12·00

611 Capt Kirk and Mr. Spock

2008. Star Trek. Multicoloured.

4204	$1.50 Type **611**	1·50	1·50
4205	$1.50 Mr. Spock, Capt. Kirk, Dr. Leonard McCoy and Lt. Cmdr Scott	1·50	1·50
4206	$1.50 Mr. Spock and Lt. Uhura	1·50	1·50
4207	$1.50 Enterprise crew in alien city	1·50	1·50
4208	$1.50 Lt. Uhura (Nichelle Nichols) on bridge of Enterprise	1·50	1·50
4209	$1.50 Lt. Cmdr Scott (James Doohan)	1·50	1·50
4210	$2 Dr. Leonard McCoy (DeForest Kelley) (50×37 mm)	2·00	2·00
4211	$2 Mr. Spock (Leonard Nimoy) (50×37 mm)	2·00	2·00
4212	$2 Captain Kirk (William Shatner) (50×37 mm)	2·00	2·00
4213	$2 Hikaru Sulu (George Takei) (50×37 mm)	2·00	2·00

612 Muhammad Ali

2008. Muhammad Ali (world heavyweight boxing champion, 1964, 1974–8). Multicoloured.

4214-4219	$1.50×6 Type **612** and similar designs showing Muhammad Ali speaking	7·00	6·75
4220-4223	$2×4 Hitting punchbag; Wearing white robe, speaking; With white robe over back of shoulders; Wearing helmet (all 37×50 mm)	6·00	6·75

613 John F. Kennedy (in profile)

2008. John F. Kennedy (US President 1960–3) Commemoration. Sheet 100×130 mm containing T **613** and similar vert designs showing President Kennedy. Multicoloured.

MS4224	Type **613**; Facing straight ahead; Head turned to left; With hand raised to chin	7·50	8·00

614 Marilyn Monroe

2008. Marilyn Monroe Commemoration. Sheet 100×140 mm containing T **614** and similar horiz designs. Multicoloured.

MS4225	Type **614**; Head turned to left; Wearing deep orange; Wearing mauve sweater	7·00	8·00

615 Holy Family

2009. Christmas. Designs showing stained glass windows. Multicoloured.

4226	30c. Type **615**	35	20
4227	90c. Baby Jesus in manger	90	55
4228	$1 Mary and infant Jesus with hands held together in prayer (vert)	1·10	80
4229	$1.50 Mary and infant Jesus standing on her lap (vert)	1·50	1·75

616 Baseball

2009. Olympic Games, Beijing (2008). Sports of the Summer Games. Sheet 130×94 mm containing T **616** and similar vert designs. Multicoloured.

MS4230	Type **616**; Beach volleyball; Gymnastics; Judo	4·50	5·00

617 First Inaugural Address of Pres. Lincoln, 4 March 1861

2009. Birth Bicentenary of Abraham Lincoln (US President 1861–5). Sheet 130×100 mm containing T **617** and similar horiz designs. Multicoloured.

MS4231	Type **617**; Abraham Lincoln; Crowd at his second inaugural address, 4 March 1865; Crowd and Abraham Lincoln	6·50	7·50

The stamps and margins of No. **MS**4231 form composite designs.

618 Pres. Barack Obama (in profile)

2009. Inauguration of President Barack Obama. Multicoloured.

MS4232	130×100 mm. $2.75 Type **618**×4	6·50	7·50
MS4232a	100×70 mm. $10 Pres. Obama (in front of US flag) (37×50 mm)	8·00	8·50

619 Ox

2009. Chinese New Year. Year of the Ox. Sheet 190×78 mm.

MS4233	$1 Type **619**×4 multicoloured	4·50	4·75

620 Xian

2009. China 2009 World Stamp Exhibition, Luoyang (1st issue). Sites and Scenes of China. Multicoloured.

MS4234	100×145 mm. $1.40×4 Type **620**; Harbinn; Chongqing; Tianjin	3·75	4·00

621 Emperor Quin Shi Huang

2009. China 2009 World Stamp Exhibition, Luoyang (2nd issue). First Emperor Quin Shi Huang (221–210BC) and his Terracotta Army. Multicoloured.

MS4235	120×150 mm. $1.40×4 Type **621**; Horses; Warriors; Excavation with army in columns	3·75	4·00

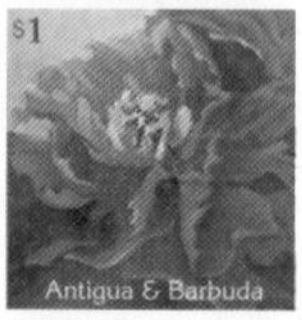

622 Peony

2009. China 2009 World Stamp Exhibition, Luoyang (3rd issue). Peonies. Multicoloured.

4236	$1 Type **622**	1·25	1·25
MS4237	100×70 mm. $5 Black and dull pink peony design (triangular 35×30 mm)	4·75	5·00

623 Elvis Presley

2009. Elvis Presley Commemoration. Multicoloured.

MS4238	185×125 mm. $1.50×6 Type **623**; Wearing jacket and tie (orange background); Standing with hands on hips; Wearing pale orange jacket with white stripe; Playing guitar, wearing lei; Wearing jacket and tie (sky background)	5·50	6·00

624

2009. National Stamp Day.

4239	**624**	$4 multicoloured	3·75	4·00

625 Labrador Retriever

2009. 125th Anniv of the American Kennel Club. Two sheets, each 100×120 mm, containing T **625** and similar horiz designs showing Labrador Retriever puppies (**MS**4240) or Dachshunds (**MS**4241). Multicoloured.

MS4240	Type **625**; Two golden labrador puppies; Black and golden labrador puppies carrying stick; Golden labrador puppy in tub	12·00	12·00
MS4241	Black and tan dachshund pawing case; Tan dachshund in green wooden crate; Two dachshund puppies in wooden trug; Wire-haired dachshund	12·00	12·00

626 Michael Jackson

2009. Michael Jackson Commemoration. Multicoloured.

MS4242	158×112 mm. $2.50×4 Type **626**; Wearing black with gold crossbelts and waistband; Wearing orange-red with black diagonal band; Wearing silver jacket with eagle design	9·75	9·75
MS4243	130×100 mm. $2.50×4 Wearing plain white shirt; Wearing white jacket with black armbands	9·75	9·75
MS4244	150×110 mm. $6 Wearing white T-shrit and white shirt (38×51 mm)	4·75	4·75

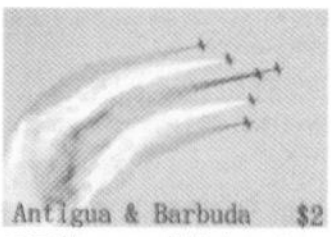

627 Flypast of Fighter Jets

2009. Centenary of Chinese Aviation and Aeropex 2009 Exhibition, Beijing. T **627** and similar horiz designs. Multicoloured.

MS4245	145×95 mm. $2×4 (All showing Chengdu J-7 fighters) Type **627**; Flying to right; Flying to left; Flying in fan formation	7·50	7·50
MS4246	120×80 mm. $6 Chengdu J-7GB fighter jet (50×38 mm)	6·00	6·00

628 Pres. Barack Obama

2009. Meeting of US President Barack Obama and Pope Benedict XVI, Vatican, 10 July 2009. Multicoloured.

MS4247	150×100 mm. $2.75×3 Type **628**; Pope Benedict XVI; Michelle Obama	7·50	7·50
MS4248	110×90 mm. $6 Pope Benedict XVI and Pres. Barack Obama (horiz)	6·50	6·50

629 Apollo 11 Emblem

2009. 40th Anniv of First Manned Moon Landing and International Year of Astronomy. Multicoloured.

MS4249	151×100 mm. $2.50×4 Type **629**; Lunar Module *Eagle*; Passive Seismic Experiment Package; Apollo 11	6·50	6·50
MS4250	101×71 mm. $6 Apollo 11 orbiting Moon	4·50	4·50

630 Poster for *King Creole*, 1958

2009. Elvis Presley in Film *King Creole*. Multicoloured.

MS4251	125×90 mm. $6 Type **630**	4·50	4·50
MS4252	90×125 mm. $6 Elvis Presley playing guitar	4·50	4·50
MS4253	90×125 mm. $6 Elvis Presley with arms raised (horiz)	4·50	4·50
MS4254	125×90 mm. $6 Elvis Presley playing guitar (horiz)	4·50	4·50

631 Candles and Wreath

2009. Christmas. Showing Christmas lights. Multicoloured.

4255	90c. Type **631**	1·00	85
4256	$1 Gold, red and green lights	1·10	90
4257	$1.80 Three bells and tree branches	2·00	1·75
4258	$3 Nativity	3·00	3·50

632 Pair of Caribbean Coot

2009. Endangered Species. Caribbean Coot (*Fulica caribaea*). Multicoloured.

4259	$2.65 Type **632**	3·00	3·00
4260	$2.65 Pair landing	3·00	3·00
4261	$2.65 Pair with chick	3·00	3·00
4262	$2.65 Adult feeding chick	3·00	3·00
MS4263	112×165 mm. Nos. 4259/62, each ×2	20·00	20·00

633 Sir Vere Cornwall Bird

2009. Birth Centenary of Rt. Honourable Dr. Sir Vere Cornwall Bird Sr. (first Chief Minister, Premier and Prime Minister of Antigua). Multicoloured.

4264	30c. Type **633**	40	25
4265	75c. Sir V. C. Bird (Antigua flag in background)	85	75
4266	90c. Wearing red jacket and hat	1·00	85
4267	$1.50 Sir V. C. Bird (black and white photo)	1·50	1·75
MS4268	160×110 mm. $2.50×4 As Nos. 4265/7	9·75	9·75
MS4269	100×70 mm. $6 Sir V. C. Bird (Antigua flag and outline map in background)	6·50	6·50

634 Glossy Ibis (*Plegadis falcinellus*)

2009. Birds of Antigua and Barbuda. Multicoloured.

4270	$1.20 Type **634**	1·75	1·25
4271	$1.80 Green-winged teal (*Anas carolinensis*)	2·25	1·75
4272	$3 California clapper rail (*Rallus longirostris obsoletus*)	3·50	3·50
4273	$5 Cattle egret (*Bubulcus ibis*) (vert)	5·50	6·50
MS4274	90×90 mm. $2.50×4 Green heron (*Butorides virescens*); Common ground dove (*Columbina passerina*); White-tailed hawk (*Buteo albicaudatus*); Black-faced grassquit (*Tiaris bicolor*)	10·00	10·00
MS4275	70×100 mm. $3×2 Bananaquit (*Coereba flaveola*); Osprey (*Pandion haliaetus*)	8·00	8·00

634a Nurse Shark (*Ginglymostoma cirratum*)

2010. Sharks of the Caribbean. Multicoloured.

4275*a*	$1.20 Type **634a**	1·75	1·25
4275*b*	$1.80 Caribbean reef shark (*Carcharhinus perezi*)	2·25	1·75
4275*c*	$3 Tiger Shark (*Galeocerdo cuvier*)	3·50	3·50
4275*d*	$5 Whale shark (*Rhincodon typus*)	5·50	6·50
MS4275*e*	170×100 mm. $2.75×4 Caribbean sharpnose shark (*Rhizoprionodon porosus*); Blacktip shark (*Carcharhinus limbatus*); Oceanic whitetip shark (*Carcharhinus longimanus*); Bull shark (*Carcharhinus leucas*	11·00	11·00

The stamps and margins of **MS**4275*e* form a composite design.

634b Rat

2010. Chinese Lunar Calendar.. Multicoloured.

MS4275*f*	60c.×12 Type **634b**; Ox; Tiger; Rabbit; Dragon; Snake; Horse; Ram; Monkey; Rooster; Dog; Pig	4·75	5·50

634c Bronze Tiger, Western Han Dynasty, China

2010. Chinese New Year. Year of the Tiger.. Multicoloured.

MS4275*g*	$5 Type **634c**; $5 Bronze tiger, Shang Dynasty, China	5·50	6·00

635 Risso's Dolphin (*Grampus griseus*)

2010. Whales and Dolphins of the Caribbean. Multicoloured.

4276	$1.20 Type **635**	1·75	1·25
4277	$1.80 Common dolphin (*Delphinus delphis*)	2·25	1·75
4278	$3 Humpback whale (*Megaptera novaeangliae*)	3·50	3·50
4279	$5 Sperm whale (*Physeter macrocephalus*)	5·50	6·50
MS4280	100×140 mm. $2×6 Short-snout dolphin (*Lagenodelphis hosei*); Spotted dolphin (*Stenella frontalis*); Cuvier's beaked whale (*Ziphius cavirostris*); Shortfin pilot whale (*Globicephala macrorhynchus*); Gulf Stream beaked whale (*Mesoplodon europaeus*); Rough-toothed dolphin (*Stenobredanensis*)	13·00	13·00

636 Diana, Princess of Wales

2010. Diana, Princess of Wales Commemoration. Sheet 130×90 mm containing T **636** and similar vert designs. Multicoloured.

MS4281	Type **636**; Wearing pink; Wearing pale mauve; Wearing pale green	7·00	7·50

637 Airfoil of Ferrari 312 F1-68, 1968

2010. Ferrari Cars. Multicoloured.

4282	$1.25 Type **637**	1·25	1·25
4283	$1.25 Ferrari 312 F1-68, 1968	1·25	1·25
4284	$1.25 Engine of Ferrari 246 P F1, 1960	1·25	1·25
4285	$1.25 Ferrari 246 P F1, 1960 (car no. 34)	1·25	1·25
4286	$1.25 Interior of Ferrari 365 P Speciale, 1966	1·25	1·25
4287	$1.25 Ferrari 365 P Speciale, 1966	1·25	1·25
4288	$1.25 Engine of Ferrari 158 F1, 1964	1·25	1·25
4289	$1.25 Ferrari 158 F1, 1964 (car no. 20)	1·25	1·25

638 Common Buckeye (Junonia coenia)

2010. Butterflies of the Caribbean. Multicoloured.

4290	$1.20 Type **638**	1·75	1·25
4291	$1.80 Red postman (*Heliconius erato*)	2·25	1·75
4292	$3 Red admiral (*Vanessa atalanta*)	3·50	3·50
4293	$5 Zebra longwing (*Heliconius charithonia*)	5·50	6·50
MS4294	140×100 mm. $2×6 Orange sulphur (inscr 'sulfur') (*Colias eurytheme*); Blue morpho (*Morpho peleides*); Queen butterfly (*Danaus gilippus*); Zebra swallowtail (*Eurytides marcellus*); Malachite (*Siproata stelenes*); Gatekeeper butterfly (*Pyronia tithonus*)	10·00	11·00

The stamps and margins of **MS**4294 form a composite background design of a flowering plant.

639 Dancers, Shanghai International Culture and Art Festival

2010. Expo 2010, Shanghai, China. Multicoloured.

MS4295	$1.50×4 Type **639**; China National Grand Theatre, Beijing; Green rice terrace, Guangxi Province, China; Dance performance, Beijing (yellow background)	4·25	4·50

640 Mother Teresa with Princess Diana, New York

2010. Birth Centenary of Mother Teresa. Multicoloured.

MS4296	$2.50×4 Type **640**; Receiving Order of Merit from Queen Elizabeth II, India; Receiving Medal of Freedom from Pres. Reagan; With Pope John Paul II, Calcutta, India	11·00	11·00

641 Scout giving Lecture ('Citizenship and Leadership')

2010. Centenary of Boy Scouts of America. Multicoloured.

MS4297	$2.50 Type **641**×2; $2.50 Two scouts in kayak ('Aquatic sport adventures')×2	7·50	8·50
MS4298	$2.50 Statue of Liberty giving Scout salute×2; $2.50 Two scouts ('Navigation with map and compass')×2	7·50	8·50

642 Elvis Presley

2010. 75th Birth Anniv of Elvis Presley. Multicoloured.

MS4299	$2.75×4 Type **642**; Facing forward, singing; Facing left, guitar strap over face; Three images of Elvis Presley	7·50	8·00
MS4300	$2.75×4 Wearing white with pattern; Wearing open neck shirt; Two images of Elvis Presley; Wearing white jacket with dark piping	7·50	8·00

The stamps and margins of **MS**4299 form a composite design spelling out 'ELV75'.

643 Pres. Obama holding Nobel Peace Prize

2010. Pres. Barack Obama's Nobel Peace Prize (2009). Multicoloured.

MS4301	$2.75×4 Type **643**; Speaking (side view) ; Speaking from podium; Holding Nobel Peace Prize, smiling	7·50	8·00

644 Princess Diana on Visit to Hindu Mission, UK

2010. Princess Diana Commemoration. Multicoloured.

MS4302	$2.75×4 Type **644**; Visit to Pakistan; Visit to Dubai; Visit to Japan	7·50	8·00
MS4303	$2.75×4 Wearing tiara with pearls and pearl drop earrings; Wearing tiara and sapphire and diamond earrings; Wearing tiara and pearl drop earrings; Wearing tiara and white jacket with stand-up collar	7·50	8·00

645 Rainbows

2010. Centenary of Girlguiding. Multicoloured.

MS4304	150×100 mm. $2.75×4 Type **645**; Brownies in kayaks; Three guides; Three Senior Section guides hiking	7·50	8·00
MS4305	70×100 mm. $6 Guides	4·75	5·50

646 Abraham Lincoln

2010. Birth Bicentenary (2009) of Abraham Lincoln (US President 1861–5). Multicoloured.

MS4306 $2.75×4 Type **646**; With beard, facing forward; With beard, looking to left; Profile, facing left	7·50	8·00
MS4307 $2.75×4 Type **646**; With beard, facing forward; With beard, looking to left; Profile, facing left	7·50	8·00

647 Pope John Paul II

2010. Pope John Paul II Commemoration. Multicoloured.

4308 $2.75 Type **647**	2·50	2·50

648 Pres. John F. Kennedy

2010. 50th Anniv of Election of Pres. John F. Kennedy. Multicoloured.

MS4309 $2.75×4 Type **648**; Pres. John F. Kennedy; Seated in chair (bookcase in background); Speaking	7·50	8·00

649 Three Stooges

2010. The Three Stooges. Multicoloured.

MS4310 $2.50×4 Type **649**; The Three Stooges as decorators, Curly holding cloth to Moe's neck; The Three Stooges as doctors and patient, Larry holding scissors to Curly's nose; Larry and Moe with Curly's head in guillotine	6·50	7·00

650 Maximiliano Pereira (Uruguay)

2010. World Cup Football Championship, South Africa. Multicoloured.

MS4311 130×150 mm. $1.50×6 Type **650**; John Heitinga (Netherlands); Edinson Cavani (Uruguay); Mark Van Bommel (Netherlands); Martin Caceres (Uruguay); Giovanni van Bronckhorst (Netherlands)	8·00	8·00
MS4312 85×90 mm. $3.50 Oscar Tabarez (Uruguay coach); $3.50 Uruguay flag on football	5·50	5·50
MS4313 85×90 mm. $3.50 Bert van Marwijk (Dutch coach); $3.50 Dutch flag on football	5·50	5·50

651 California Spangled Cat

2010. Cats of the World. Multicoloured.

MS4314 150×100 mm. $2.50×6 Type **651**; Siamese; British shorthair; Norwegian forest; Egyptian mau; American curl longhair	9·00	9·00
MS4315 100×70 mm. $6 Manx cat	5·00	5·00

652 Henri Dunant and Nurses with Wounded Soldiers

2010. Death Centenary of Henri Dunant (instigator of Red Cross). Multicoloured.

MS4316 150×100 mm. $2.50×4 Type **652**; Wounded laying on battlefield; Cavalry; Cavalry and soldiers	8·00	8·00
MS4317 70×100 mm. $6 Battle of Solferino	5·00	5·00

653 Pope Benedict XVI

2010. Fifth Anniv of Papacy of Pope Benedict XVI. Multicoloured.

MS4318 142×153 mm. $2.75 Type **653**×4	9·75	9·75
MS4319 171×113 mm. $2.75 Pope Benedict XVI (facing left)×4	9·75	9·75

654 Rabbit

2011. Chinese New Year. Year of the Rabbit

MS4320 $4 Type **654**; $4 Chinese rabbit symbol	6·00	6·00

655 Giant Panda

2011. Beijing 2010 International Stamp and Coin Exposition. Giant Panda. Multicoloured.

MS4321 170×95 mm. $2×4 Type **655**; Close-up of face; Panda with bamboo plant; Panda eating leaves (side view)	6·00	6·00
MS4322 62×90 mm. $5 Giant panda (facing right)	4·00	4·00

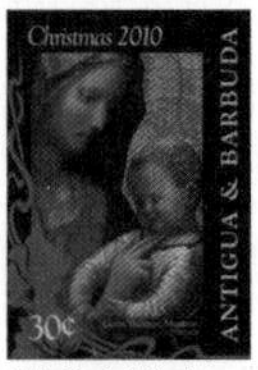

656 *Casini Madonna* (Masaccio)

2011. Christmas. Multicoloured.

4323 30c. Type **656**	30	25
4324 75c. *Madonna of the Stars* (Tintoretto)	70	70
4325 90c. Wall mosaic showing magi from Basilica of Sant Apollinare Nuovo, Ravenna, Italy	90	85
4326 $1.50 *The Annunciation* (Fra Angelico)	1·40	1·50

657 Prince William and Miss Catherine Middleton

2011. Royal Engagement. Multicoloured.

4327 $2.50 Type **657**	2·50	2·50
4328 $2.50 Prnce William	2·50	2·50
4329 $2.50 Miss Catherine Middleton	2·50	2·50

MS4330 120×70 mm. $6 Prince William (smiling)	5·00	5·00
MS4331 120×70 mm. $6 Prince William (speaking)	5·00	5·00

658 Mahatma Gandhi

2011. Indipex 2011 World Philatelic Exhibition, Delhi. Mahatma Gandhi. Multicoloured.

MS4332 $2.75×4 Type **658**; Gandhi and Asokan capital; Gandhi and towers and gateway; Gandhi and Taj Mahal, India	3·00	2·75
MS4333 $2.75×4 Gandhi (in profile, wearing white) and crowd; Gandhi (facing forward) and crowd; Gandhi (iin profile, lookinig down) and crowd; Gandhi (looking to right) and crowd	3·00	2·75

659 Pope John Paul II praying

2011. Beatification of Pope John Paul II. Multicoloured.

MS4334 176×91 mm. $2 Type **659**×3; $2 Pope John Paul II wearing red cape×3	10·00	10·00
MS4335 100×70 mm. $6 Pope John Paul II	10·00	10·00

660 Stephen Mallory, Lt-Commander Murray and Warships of Atlantic Blockading Squadron

2011. 150th Anniv of the American Civil War. Multicoloured.

MS4336 $2.50×4 Type **660**; Stephen Mallory (Confederate Secretary of Navy), Union Lt. Commander Alexander Murray and flotilla of Union warships; Mallory, Murray and Confederate privateers near Delaware Bay; Mallory, Murray and flagship USS *Minnesota*	10·00	10·00
MS4337 $2.50×4 Confederate General Henry Jackson, Union General Joseph Reynolds and map of battle of Greenbriar River by A. T. McRae of the Quitman Guards; Jackson, Reynolds and skirmish along the Greenbriar River; Jackson, Reynolds and Union forces assembling near Greenbriar River; Jackson, Reynolds and battle of Greenbriar River	10·00	10·00
MS4338 $2.50×4 Confederate Brigadier General Richard Anderson, Union Colonel Harvey Brown and Fort Pickens; Anderson, Brown and battle at Santa Rosa Island; Anderson, Brown and Union ships cutting off Confederate dispatch galley; Anderson, Brown and Colonel Brown in command of 3rd US Infantry	10·00	10·00

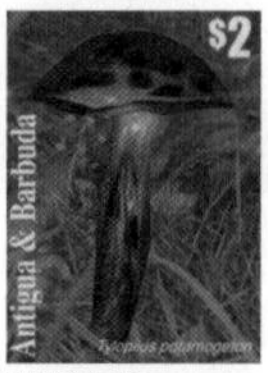

661 *Tylopilus potamogeton*

2011. Mushrooms of the Caribbean. Multicoloured.

MS4339 170×100 mm. $2×6 Type **661**; *Amanita campinaranae; Cantharellus atratus; Tylophilus orsonianus; Boletellus ananas; Amanita craseoderma*	10·00	10·00
MS4340 170×100 mm. $2.50×4 *Amanita cyanopus; Phyllobolites miniatus; Chroogomphus jamaicensis; Coltricia cf. montagnei*	9·00	9·00
MS4341 101×70 mm. $6 *Austroboletus festivus*	9·00	9·00
MS4342 101×70 mm. $6 *Austroboletus rostrupii*	6·00	6·00

662 Princess Diana in Barbuda, April 1997

2011. 50th Birth Anniv of Princess Diana. Multicoloured.

MS4343 150×100 mm. $10 Type **662**×5	10·00	10·00
MS4344 150×100 mm. $10 Princess Diana, Prince William and Prince Harry in Barbuda, April 1997×5	10·00	10·00
MS4345 101×70 mm. $50 Princess Diana wearing red dress and beach (horiz)	22·00	22·00

663 Pope Benedict XVI and Church

2011. Pope Benedict XVI visits Germany. Multicoloured.

MS4346 $3×3 Type **663**; Pope Benedict XVI and church with blue roof; Pope Benedict XVI and Brandenburg Gate, Berlin	10·50	10·50
MS4347 $3×3 Pope Benedict XVI and St. Mary's Cathedral and Church of St. Severus, Erfurt; Pope Benedict XVI and church with turquoise roof; Pope Benedict XVI and Bavarian houses and bell tower	10·50	10·50

664 Duke and Duchess of Cambridge

2011. Royal Wedding. Multicoloured.

MS4348 100×134 mm. $2.50 Type **664**×2; $2.50 Prince William (in profile); $2.50 Duchess of Cambridge (in profile)	9·00	9·00
MS4349 100×134 mm. $2.50 Prince William waving; $2.50 Duke and Duchess of Cambridge kissing×2; $2.50 Duchess of Cambridge	9·00	9·00
MS4350 100×106 mm. $6 Duke and Duchess of Cambridge	7·00	7·00

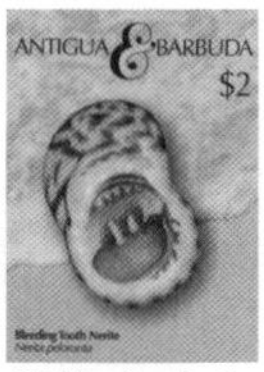

665 Bleeding Tooth Nerite (*Nerita peloronta*)

2011. Shells of the Caribbean. Multicoloured.

MS4351 100×150 mm. $2×6 Type **665**; Pen shell (*Atrina rigida*); Banded tulip shell (*Fasciolaria lillium*); Chank shell (*Turbinella pyrum*); Flame helmet (*Cassis flammea*); Atlantic partridge tun (*Tonna maculosa*)	10·00	10·00
MS4352 101×131 mm. $2.75×4 Pink conch (*Strombus gigas*); Sunrise tellin (*Tellina radiata*); Flamingo tongue (*Cyphoma gibbosum*); Queen's helmet (*Cassis madagascariensis*)	10·00	10·00
MS4353 101×101 mm. $6 King's helmet (*Cassis tuberosa*)	6·00	6·00
MS4354 101×101 mm. $6 Triton's trumpet (*Charonia tritonis*) (horiz)	6·00	6·00

666 Pres. Kennedy inspects Mercury Capsule, 23 February 1962

2011. 50th Anniv of Inauguration of Pres. John F. Kennedy. Multicoloured.

MS4355 150×110 mm. $2.75×4 Type **666**; Cape Canaveral tour, 16 November 1963; Saturn rocket briefing, 16 November 1963; Pres. Kennedy at Cape Canaveral, 16 November 1963 — 10·00 10·00

MS4356 100×100 mm. $6 Pres. John F. Kennedy (51×38 mm) — 6·00 6·00

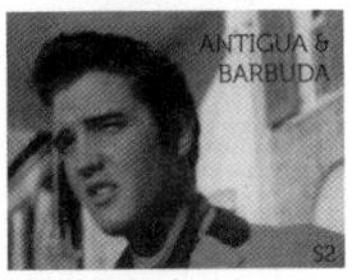

667 Elvis Presley

2011. Elvis Presley Commemoration. Multicoloured.

MS4357 90×140 mm. $2×3 Type **667**; Wearing white suit, boarding train; On motorbike — 10·00 10·00

MS4358 138×80 mm. $2.75×4 Elvis Presley in army uniform: Head and shoulders portrait; Leaning on railing; Wearing overalls; Reading letter (all vert) — 10·00 10·00

MS4359 176×124 mm. $2.75×4 In concert: Wearing red shirt; Wearing blue jacket and white shirt; Wearing white jacket with silver studs; Wearing white jacket with patterned collar (all vert) — 10·00 10·00

MS4360 140×90 mm. $3 On stage, wearing black; $3 Wearing sweater with two shoulder stripes (both vert) — 10·00 10·00

668 Pres. Barack Obama

2011. Pres. Barack Obama. Multicoloured.

MS4361 150×110 mm. $2.75×4 Type **668**; Pres. Obama facing forward, speaking; Facing forward; Facing left — 10·00 10·00

MS4362 100×70 mm. $6 Pres. Barack Obama — 10·00 10·00

669 Liftoff of Vostok 1, 1961

2011. 50th Anniv of the First Man in Space. Multicoloured.

MS4363 150×100 mm. $2.75×4 Type **669**; *Kosmonaut Yuri Gagarin* (tracking ship), 1970-91; Vostok 1 mission logo; Alan Shepard (first American astronaut) and Freedom 7, 1961 — 10·00 10·00

MS4364 150×100 mm. $2.75×4 Globe showing flightpath of Yuri Gagarin; Vostok 8K72K rocket; Yuri Gagarin in space; US astronaut Virgil Gus Grissom and rocket — 10·00 10·00

MS4365 100×71 mm. $6 Vostok 1 orbiting Earth — 6·00 6·00

MS4366 100×71 mm. $6 Yuri Gagarin — 6·00 6·00

670 Princess Diana

2011. 50th Birth Anniv of Princess Diana. Multicoloured.

MS4367 150×100 mm. $2.75×4 Type **670**; Princess Diana wearing beige top with white lapels and beige pleated skirt; Wearing white; On honeymoon with Prince Charles at Balmoral, 1981 — 10·00 10·00

MS4368 101×101 mm. $6 Princess Diana wearing pale mauve and white patterned dress (51×38 mm) — 10·00 10·00

671 Queen Angelfish (*Holacanthus ciliaris*)

2011. Tropical Fish. Multicoloured.

MS4369 161×100 mm. $3.50×4 Type **671**; Ocean surgeonfish (*Acanthurus bahianus*); Rock beauty (*Holacanthus tricolor*); Gray angelfish (*Pomacanthus arcuatus*) — 11·00 11·00

MS4370 161×100 mm. $3.50×4 Foureye butterflyfish (*Chaetodon capistratus*); French grunt (*Haemulon flavolineatum*); French angelfish (*Pomacanthus paru*); Spotfin butterflyfish (*Chaetodon ocellatus*) — 11·00 11·00

MS4371 121×81 mm. $9 Great barracuda (*Sphyraena barracuda*) (80×30 mm) — 14·00 14·00

MS4372 121×81 mm. $9 Banded butterflyfish (*Chaetodon striatus*) (40×40 mm) — 14·00 14·00

Pt. 20

ANTIOQUIA

One of the states of the Granadine Confederation. A department of Colombia from 1886, now uses Colombian stamps.

100 centavos = 1 peso.

1

1868. Various arms designs. Imperf.

1	**1**	2½c. blue	£1200	£700
2	-	5c. green	£900	£500
3	-	10c. lilac	£2750	£900
4	-	1p. red	£700	£450

5

6

1869. Various frames. Imperf.

5	**5**	2½c. blue	5·00	4·25
6	**5**	5c. green	7·75	7·00
8	**5**	10c. mauve	10·00	5·00
9	**5**	20c. brown	10·00	5·00
10	**6**	1p. red	20·00	17·00

7

1873. Arms designs inscr "E.S." (or "Eo. So." or "Estado Soberano") "de Antioquia". Imperf.

11	**7**	1c. green	7·25	5·25
12	-	5c. green	12·00	8·50
13	-	10c. mauve	35·00	28·00
14	-	20c. brown	12·00	10·00
15	-	50c. blue	2·75	2·10
16	-	1p. red	5·00	3·75
17	-	2p. black on yellow	12·00	10·50
18	-	5p. black on red	90·00	75·00

The 5p. is larger (25½×31½ mm).

15

1875. Imperf.

20	**15**	1c. black on green	2·40	3·25
21	**15**	1c. black	1·80	3·25
43	**15**	1c. mauve	3·50	5·25
52	**15**	1c. green	3·50	5·25
22	-	2½c. blue (Arms)	3·50	2·75
23	-	5c. green ("Liberty")	22·00	19·00
25	-	10c. mauve (J. Berrio)	35·00	28·00

20

21 Liberty

23 Liberty

1879. Imperf.

30	**20**	2½c. blue	3·75	3·50
38	**20**	2½c. green	3·50	2·75
45	**20**	2½c. black on buff	10·00	8·50
39	**21**	5c. green	6·00	5·00
40	**21**	5c. violet	13·00	10·00
32	-	10c. violet (Arms)	£1400	£900
36	**23**	10c. violet	£275	85·00
41	**23**	10c. red	3·50	2·75
42	**21**	20c. brown	6·00	5·00

25 Liberty

1883. Various frames. Head of Liberty to left. Imperf.

47	**25**	5c. yellow	7·75	5·75
48	**25**	5c. green	£225	£100
53	**25**	5c. brown	7·25	4·50
49	**25**	10c. green	7·75	7·00
50	**25**	10c. mauve	17·00	10·00
55	**25**	10c. blue	7·75	5·75
51	**25**	20c. blue	7·25	5·75

28

1886. Imperf.

57	**28**	1c. green on pink	90	75
65	**28**	1c. red on lilac	65	55
58	**28**	2½c. black on orange	90	75
66	**28**	2½c. mauve on pink	65	75
59	**28**	5c. blue on buff	5·00	4·25
67	**28**	5c. red on green	5·00	2·30
68	**28**	5c. lake on buff	90	85
60	**28**	10c. red on buff	1·00	1·20
69	**28**	10c. brown on green	1·00	1·20
61	**28**	20c. purple on buff	2·40	2·10
62	**28**	50c. yellow on buff	4·50	3·75
63	**28**	1p. yellow on green	7·25	5·75
64	**28**	2p. green on lilac	7·25	5·75

31

1888. Various sizes and frames. Inscr "MEDELLIN". Imperf.

70	**31**	2½c. black on yellow	22·00	19·00
71	**31**	2½c. red on white	11·00	9·00
72	**31**	5c. black on yellow	12·00	10·00
73	**31**	5c. red on orange	7·25	5·75

34

1889. Arms in various frames.

74	**34**	1c. black on red	35	30
75	**34**	2½c. black on blue	35	30
76	**34**	5c. black on yellow	45	45
77	**34**	10c. black on green	45	45
95	**34**	10c. brown	35	30
78	**34**	20c. blue	2·00	1·90
79	**34**	50c. brown	3·75	3·75
80	**34**	50c. green	2·75	2·75
81	**34**	1p. red	2·75	2·75
82	**34**	2p. black on mauve	20·00	19·00
83	**34**	5p. black on red	29·00	28·00

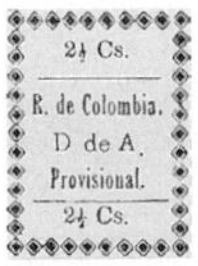

35

1890. Perf.

84	**35**	2½c. black on buff	2·75	2·75
85	**35**	5c. black on yellow	2·75	2·75
86	**35**	10c. black on buff	9·25	9·00
87	**35**	10c. black on red	12·00	11·50
88	**35**	20c. black on yellow	12·00	11·50

36

1892

89	**36**	1c. brown on buff	55	55
90	**36**	1c. blue	35	30
91	**36**	2½c. violet on lilac	55	55
92	**36**	2½c. green	55	55
93	**36**	5c. black	1·50	75
94	**36**	5c. red	35	30

37

1896

96	**37**	2c. grey	35	30
107	**37**	2c. red	35	55
97	**37**	2½c. brown	35	30
108	**37**	2½c. blue	35	30
98	**37**	3c. red	35	30
109	**37**	3c. olive	35	30
99	**37**	5c. green	35	30
110	**37**	5c. yellow	45	45
100	**37**	10c. lilac	75	75
111	**37**	10c. brown	75	75
101	**37**	20c. brown	2·00	1·90
112	**37**	20c. blue	2·00	1·90
102	**37**	50c. sepia	2·00	1·90
113	**37**	50c. red	1·80	1·70
103	**37**	1p. black and blue	24·00	23·00
114	**37**	1p. black and red	24·00	23·00
104	**37**	2p. black and orange	75·00	75·00
115	**37**	2p. black and green	75·00	75·00
105	**37**	5p. black and mauve	£130	£130

39 Gen. Cordoba

1899

118	**39**	½c. blue	20	20
119	**39**	1c. blue	20	20
120	**39**	2c. black	20	20
121	**39**	3c. red	20	20
122	**39**	4c. brown	20	20
123	**39**	5c. green	20	20
124	**39**	10c. red	20	20
125	**39**	20c. violet	20	20
126	**39**	50c. yellow	20	20
127	**39**	1p. green	20	20
128	**39**	2p. green	20	20

43

1901. Various frames.

132	**43**	1c. red	35	30
133	**43**	1c. brown	90	85
134	**43**	1c. blue	90	85

Nos. 132 and 134 also exist with "CENTAVO" inside the rectangle below figure "1".

46

47

48 Girardot

1902

138	**46**	1c. red	35	30
139	**46**	1c. blue	35	30
140	**46**	2c. blue	35	30
141	**46**	2c. violet	35	30
142	**46**	3c. green	35	30
143	**46**	4c. purple	35	30
144	**47**	5c. red	35	30
145	**47**	10c. mauve	35	30
147	**47**	20c. green	35	30
148	**47**	30c. red	35	30
149	**48**	40c. blue	35	30
150	**48**	50c. brown on yellow	35	30
152	-	1p. black and violet	1·10	1·10
153	-	2p. black and red	1·10	1·10
154	-	5p. black and blue	2·00	1·90

DESIGN: 1p. to 5p. Dr. J. Felix de Restrepo.

No. 145 also exists with smaller head.

54 55 56 Zea

1903

159	54	4c. brown	35	30
160	54	5c. blue	35	30
161	55	10c. yellow	35	30
162	55	20c. lilac	35	30
163	55	30c. brown	90	85
164	55	40c. green	90	85
165	55	50c. red	35	30
166	56	1p. green	90	85
167	56	2p. mauve (Rovira)	90	85
168	56	3p. blue (La Pola)	90	85
169	56	4p. red (Restrepo)	1·50	1·50
170	56	5p. brown (Madrid)	4·50	2·10
171	56	10p. red (Corral)	9·25	5·25

ACKNOWLEDGEMENT OF RECEIPT STAMPS

AR53

1902

AR157	AR53	5c. black on red	1·40	1·40
AR158	AR53	5c. green	45	45

REGISTRATION STAMPS

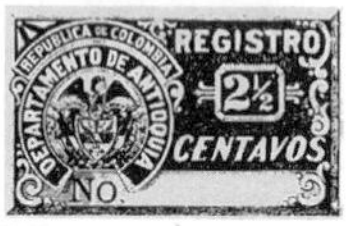

R38

1896

R106	R38	2½c. pink	1·80	1·80
R117	R38	2½c. blue	1·80	1·70

R41 Gen. Cordoba R42

1899

R130	R41	2½c. blue	35	30
R131	R42	10c. red	35	30

R52

1902

R156	R52	10c. violet on green	45	45

TOO LATE STAMPS

L40 Gen. Cordoba

1899

L129	L40	2½c. green	35	30

1901. As T **43**, but inscr "RETARDO" at sides.

L137a	2½c. purple	1·10	1·10

L51

1902

L155	L51	2½c. lilac	35	30

Pt. 8

ARBE

During the period of D'Annunzio's Italian Regency of Carnaro (Fiume), separate issues were made for Arbe (now Rab).

100 centesimi = 1lira

1920. No. 148, etc of Fiume optd **ARBE**.

1B	5c. green	10·50	10·50
2B	10c. red	21·00	21·00
3B	20c. brown	55·00	32·00
4B	25c. blue	32·00	32·00
5	50c. on 20c. brown	55·00	32·00
6	55c. on 5c. green	55·00	32·00

EXPRESS LETTER STAMPS

1920. Nos. E163/4 of Fiume optd **ARBE**.

E7	30c. on 20c. brown	£190	£110
E8	50c. on 5c. green	£130	£110

Pt. 20

ARGENTINE REPUBLIC

A republic in the S.E. of S. America formerly part of the Spanish Empire.

1858. 100 centavos = 1 peso.
1985. 100 centavos = 1 austral.
1992. 100 centavos = 1 peso.

1 Argentine Confederation

1858. Imperf.

1	1	5c. red	1·00	25·00
2	1	10c. green	1·50	55·00
3	1	15c. blue	14·00	£160

3 Argentine Confederation

1862. Imperf.

10	3	5c. red	16·00	18·00
8	3	10c. green	£150	60·00
9	3	15c. blue	£300	£190

5 Rivadavia 6 Rivadavia

1864. Imperf.

24	5	5c. red	£190	80·00
14	6	10c. green	£2250	£1300
15	5	15c. blue	£7500	£4500

1864. Perf.

16		5c. red	26·00	10·50
17	6	10c. green	70·00	24·00
18	5	15c. blue	£200	80·00

9 Rivadavia 10 Gen. Belgrano 11 Gen. San Martin

1867. Perf.

28	9	5c. red	12·50	1·00
29	10	10c. green	41·00	8·75
30a	11	15c. blue	85·00	16·00

12 Balcarce

1873. Portraits. Perf.

31	12	1c. violet	6·25	2·00
32	-	4c. brown (Moreno)	5·00	45
33	-	30c. orange (Alvear)	£100	19·00
34	-	60c. black (Posadas)	£100	4·50
35	-	90c. blue (Saavedra)	26·00	2·75

1877. Surch with large figure of value.

37	9	1 on 5c. red	55·00	20·00
38	9	2 on 5c. red	95·00	60·00
39	10	8 on 10c. green	£110	29·00

22 Sarsfield

1876. Roul.

36	9	5c. red	£180	75·00
40	9	8c. lake	21·00	35
41	10	16c. green	10·00	1·20
42	22	20c. blue	12·50	2·75
43	11	24c. blue	21·00	2·75

24 Lopez

1877. Perf.

46	24	2c. green	4·50	85
44	9	8c. lake	4·25	50
45	11	24c. blue	24·00	1·80
47	-	25c. lake (Alvear)	22·00	6·00

1882. Surch **1/2 (PROVISORIO)**.

51	9	½ on 5c. red	1·40	1·40

29

1882

52	29	½c. brown	1·60	1·00
55	29	1c. red	3·50	1·00
54	29	12c. blue	50·00	8·75

1884. Surch **1884** and value in figures or words.

90	9	½c. on 5c. red	2·75	2·20
92	11	½c. on 15c. blue	11·00	8·00
94	11	1c. on 15c. blue	11·00	8·75
100	9	4c. on 5c. red	7·00	4·50

33

1884

101	33	½c. brown	1·30	50
102	33	1c. red	6·25	50
103	33	12c. blue	30·00	1·20

34 Urquiza 45 Mitre

1888. Portrait types, inscr "CORREOS ARGENTINOS".

108	34	½c. blue	1·00	50
110	-	2c. green (Lopez)	12·00	7·25
111	-	3c. green (Celman)	2·10	75
113	-	5c. red (Rivadavia)	15·00	1·30
114	-	6c. red (Sarmiento)	31·00	18·00
115	-	10c. brown (Avellaneda)	18·00	1·00
116	-	15c. orange (San Martin)	21·00	1·60
117a	-	20c. green (Roca)	14·50	1·20
118	-	25c. violet (Belgrano)	21·00	2·50
119	-	30c. brown (Dorrego)	26·00	3·00
120a	-	40c. grey (Moreno)	31·00	3·50
121	45	50c. blue	£120	7·75

51 Rivadavia 60 Paz

1888. Portrait types, inscr "CORREOS Y TELEGRAFOS" except No. 126.

137	60	¼c. green	50	30
122	-	½c. blue (Urquiza)	50	30
123	-	1c. brown (Sarsfield)	1·00	50
125	-	2c. violet (Derqui)	1·00	50
126	-	3c. green (Celman)	3·00	80
127	51	5c. red	3·00	50
129	-	6c. blue (Sarmiento)	2·10	55
130	-	10c. brown (Avellaneda)	3·00	50
131	-	12c. blue (Alberti)	6·25	2·00
132	-	40c. grey (Moreno)	6·25	1·00
133	-	50c. orange (Mitre)	6·25	1·00
134	-	60c. black (Posadas)	15·00	3·00

1890. No. 131 surch **1/4** and bars.

135	¼ on 12c. blue	35	35

52 Rivadavia

1890

128a	52	5c. red	1·80	20

63 La Madrid

1891. Portraits.

139	-	1p. blue (San Martin)	55·00	9·75
140	63	5p. blue	£275	50·00
141	-	20p. green (G. Brown)	£425	£130

61 Rivadavia

1891

138	61	8c. red	1·30	50

65 Rivadavia 66 Belgrano 67 San Martin

1892

142	65	½c. blue	30	15
143	65	1c. brown	50	15
144	65	2c. green	60	20
145	65	3c. orange	1·20	20
146	65	5c. red	1·20	20
147	66	10c. red	9·50	35
148	66	12c. blue	7·25	35
149	66	16c. slate	12·00	45
150	66	24c. sepia	12·00	45
257	66	30c. orange	32·00	2·00
151	66	50c. green	18·00	45
188	66	80c. lilac	8·50	45
152a	67	1p. red	8·75	65
190	67	1p.20 black	8·50	1·70
153	67	2p. green	18·00	1·80
154	67	5p. blue	24·00	1·80

70 Fleet of Columbus

1892. Fourth Centenary of Discovery of America by Columbus.

219	70	2c. blue	7·75	3·25
220	70	5c. blue	8·25	4·00

71 "Liberty" and Shield

1899

221	71	½c. brown	30	20
222	71	1c. green	1·30	40
223	71	2c. grey	40	20
224	71	3c. orange	40	35
225	71	4c. yellow	65	40
226	71	5c. red	40	20
227	71	6c. black	40	40
228	71	10c. green	1·00	25
229a	71	12c. blue	65	40
230	71	12c. green	65	40
231	71	15c. blue	1·40	40
232	71	16c. orange	5·50	4·00
233	71	20c. red	1·10	20
234	71	24c. purple	2·75	70

235	71	30c. red	5·00	40
237	71	50c. blue	2·75	35
238	71	1p. black and blue	8·50	70
239	71	5p. black and orange	32·00	6·00
240	71	10p. black and green	42·00	10·00
241	71	20p. black and red	£110	20·00

The peso values are larger (19×32 mm).

73 Port Rosario

1902. Completion of Port Rosario Docks.

290	73	5c. blue	4·00	1·70

74 Gen. San Martin

1908

291B	74	½c. violet	35	20
292B	74	1c. brown	35	20
293B	74	2c. brown	40	20
294B	74	3c. green	40	25
295B	74	4c. mauve	85	25
296B	74	5c. red	40	20
297B	74	6c. green	60	40
298B	74	10c. green	1·30	20
299A	74	12c. brown	40	40
300B	74	12c. blue	1·30	20
301A	74	15c. green	4·25	1·20
302B	74	20c. blue	85	20
303B	74	24c. red	2·50	40
304B	74	30c. red	4·25	40
305B	74	50c. black	4·25	35
306A	74	1p. red and blue	12·50	1·70

The 1p. is larger (21½×27 mm) with portrait at upper left.

76 Pyramid of May

78 Azcuenaga and Alberti

80 Saavedra

1910. Cent of Deposition of the Spanish Viceroy.

366	76	½c. blue and grey	50	30
367	-	1c. black and green	50	30
368	-	2c. black and green	50	30
369	78	3c. green	1·00	40
370	-	4c. green and blue	1·00	40
371	80	5c. red	75	30
372	-	10c. black and brown	1·10	50
373	-	12c. blue	1·10	50
374	-	20c. black and brown	3·00	70
375	-	24c. blue and brown	2·75	1·20
376	-	30c. black and lilac	2·75	1·00
377	-	50c. black and red	6·25	1·20
378	-	1p. blue	9·50	3·00
379	-	5p. purple and orange	75·00	36·00
380	-	10p. black and orange	£100	60·00
381	-	20p. black and blue	£160	£100

DESIGNS—VERT: 50c. Crowds on 25 May 1810; 10p. Centenary Monument; 20p. San Martin. HORIZ: 1c. Pena and Vieytes; 2c. Meeting at Pena's house; 4c. Fort of the Viceroys, Buenos Aires; 10c. Distribution of cockades; 12c. Congress Building; 20c. Castelli and Matheu; 24c. First National Council; 30c. Belgrano and Larrea; 1p. Moreno and Paso; 5p. "Oath of the Junta".

90 Sarmiento

1911. Birth Centenary of Pres. Sarmiento.

382	90	5c. black and brown	85	40

91 Ploughman

1911

383	91	5c. red	40	15
384	91	12c. blue	5·25	45

92 Ploughman

94

1911

395	92	½c. violet	45	45
396	92	1c. brown	45	45
397	92	2c. brown	65	45
398	92	3c. green	65	65
399a	92	4c. purple	75	75
400	92	5c. red	55	45
401	92	10c. green	2·20	45
402	92	12c. blue	75	45
403	92	20c. blue	4·00	65
404	92	24c. brown	8·25	2·75
405	92	30c. red	9·25	1·40
406	92	50c. black	13·00	1·30
408	94	1p. red and blue	13·00	1·40
409	94	5p. green and grey	24·00	8·00
410	94	10p. blue and violet	£100	20·00
411	94	20p. red and blue	£225	£100

95 Dr. F. N. Laprida

96 Declaration of Independence

97 San Martin

1916. Centenary of Independence.

417	95	½c. violet	75	45
418	95	1c. brown	75	55
419	95	2c. brown	75	45
420	95	3c. green	75	75
421	95	4c. purple	75	75
422	96	5c. red	75	9·50
423	96	10c. green	2·10	45
424	97	12c. blue	75	45
425	97	20c. blue	75	75
426	97	24c. red	3·25	1·60
427	97	30c. red	3·25	95
428	97	50c. black	5·00	95
429	97	1p. red and blue	13·00	7·00
430	97	5p. green and grey	£130	80·00
431	97	10p. blue and violet	£200	£160
432	97	20p. red and grey	£170	£130

98 San Martin

1917

450A	98	½c. violet	45	20
451A	98	1c. buff	45	20
452A	98	2c. brown	45	20
453A	98	3c. green	65	20
454A	98	4c. purple	65	20
455B	98	5c. red	45	20
439A	98	10c. green	45	45
457B	-	12c. blue	1·70	20
458B	-	20c. blue	1·70	20
459B	-	24c. red	3·25	20
460B	-	30c. red	4·00	45
461B	-	50c. black	8·25	65
445B	-	1p. red and blue	8·25	75
446B	-	5p. green and grey	21·00	3·75
447B	-	10p. blue and violet	65·00	16·00
448B	-	20p. red and grey	£130	75·00

The 12c. to 20p. values are larger (21×27 mm).

100 Dr. Juan Pujol

1918. Birth Centenary of Juan Pujol, First P.M.G. of Argentina.

449	100	5c. grey and bistre	1·00	45

102 Mausoleum of Belgrano

103 Creation of Argentine Flag

1920. Death Centenary of Gen. Manuel Belgrano.

478	102	2c. red	70	15
479	103	5c. blue and red	70	15
480	-	12c. blue and green	1·40	60

DESIGN—VERT: 12c. Gen. Belgrano.

106 General Urquiza

1920. Gen. Urquiza's Victory at Cepada.

488	106	5c. blue	55	30

107 General Mitre

1921. Birth Centenary of Gen. Mitre.

490	107	2c. brown	55	30
491	107	5c. blue	55	30

108

1921. First Pan-American Postal Congress.

492	108	3c. lilac	75	45
493	108	5c. blue	1·90	10
494	108	10c. brown	2·20	45
495	108	12c. red	2·75	95

1921. As T **108**, but smaller. Inscr "BUENOS AIRES AGOSTO DE 1921".

496A		5c. red	40	25

1921. As No. 496, but inscr "REPUBLICA ARGENTINA" at foot.

511A		5c. red	3·00	25

112

1923. With or without stop below "c".

529	112	½c. purple	35	15
530	112	1c. brown	35	15
531	112	2c. brown	35	15
516A	112	3c. green	35	25
517A	112	4c. red	35	25
534	112	5c. red	35	15
535	112	10c. green	35	20
536	112	12c. blue	40	20
537	112	20c. blue	65	20
538	112	24c. brown	1·80	80
539	112	25c. violet	85	20
540	112	30c. red	1·80	20
541	112	50c. black	4·25	20
542	-	1p. red and blue	7·00	35
543	-	5p. green and lilac	21·00	4·00
544	-	10p. blue and red	65·00	10·00
545	-	20p. lake and slate	85·00	30·00

The peso values are larger (21×27 mm).

114 B. Rivadavia

1926. Rivadavia Centenary.

546	114	5c. red	55	30

115 Rivadavia

116 San Martin

117 G.P.O., 1926

118 G.P.O., 1826

1926. Postal Centenary.

547	115	3c. green	35	20
548	116	5c. red	35	20
549	117	12c. blue	1·10	30
550	118	25c. brown	2·75	85

120 Biplane and Globe

122

1928. Air.

558	120	5c. red	1·80	75
559	120	10c. blue	2·75	1·10
560	-	15c. brown	2·75	1·10
561	120	18c. violet	5·00	3·75
562	-	20c. blue	3·25	1·10
563	-	24c. blue	5·50	3·75
564	122	25c. violet	5·50	1·70
565	122	30c. red	6·50	1·30
566	-	35c. red	5·50	1·20
567a	120	36c. brown	3·00	1·50
568	-	50c. black	5·50	75
569	-	54c. brown	5·50	2·30
570	-	72c. green	6·50	2·30
571	122	90c. purple	12·00	2·30
572	122	1p. red and blue	14·50	1·10
573	122	1p.08 blue and red	22·00	5·75
574	-	1p.26 green and violet	29·00	10·50
575	-	1p.80 red and blue	29·00	10·50
576	-	3p.60 blue and grey	55·00	23·00

DESIGNS—VERT: 15, 20, 24, 54, 72c. Yellow-headed Caracara over sea. HORIZ: 35, 50c., 1p.26, 1p.80, 3p.60, Andean Condor on mountain top.

124 Arms of Argentina and Brazil

1928. Centenary of Peace with Brazil.

577	124	5c. red	1·90	65
578	124	12c. blue	3·25	85

125 Torch illuminating New World

1929. "Day of the Race" issue.

579	125	2c. brown	2·75	55
580	-	5c. red	2·75	45
581	-	12c. blue	8·25	1·30

DESIGNS: 5c. Symbolical figures, Spain and Argentina; 12c. American offering laurels to Columbus.

(128)

1930. Air. *Zeppelin* Europe–Pan-America Flight. Optd with T **128**.

587	-	20c. blue (No. 562)	14·50	8·50
588	-	50c. black (No. 568)	19·00	13·00
589	122	90c. purple	13·00	8·50
584	122	1p. red and blue	29·00	14·00
585	-	1p.80 (No. 575)	85·00	37·00
586	-	3p.60 (No. 576)	£225	£110

129 Soldier and Civilian Insurgents

130 The Victorious March, 6 September 30

1930. Revolution of 6 September 1930.

592	**129**	½c. violet	55	30
611	**130**	½c. mauve	45	30
593	**129**	1c. green	55	35
612	**130**	1c. black	1·30	1·10
594	**130**	2c. lilac	65	30
595	**129**	3c. green	55	45
613	**130**	3c. green	90	65
596	**129**	4c. violet	55	45
614	**130**	4c. lake	55	45
597	**129**	5c. red	45	30
615	**130**	5c. red	45	30
598	**129**	10c. black	1·10	55
616	**130**	10c. green	1·90	65
599	**130**	12c. blue	90	45
600	**130**	20c. buff	90	35
601	**130**	24c. brown	3·50	2·30
602	**130**	25c. green	4·25	2·30
603	**130**	30c. violet	6·50	3·50
604	**130**	50c. black	9·25	4·50
605	**130**	1p. red and blue	19·00	14·00
606	**130**	2p. orange and black	33·00	16·00
607	**130**	5p. black and green	£100	49·00
608	**130**	10p. blue and lake	£130	60·00
609	**130**	20p. blue and green	£350	£130
610	**130**	50p. violet and green	£1000	£750

1931. First Anniv of 1930 Revolution. Optd **6 Septembre 1930 - 1931**.

617	**112**	3c. green (postage)	45	45
618	**112**	10c. green	90	85
624	**129**	18c. violet (air)	2·75	1·60
619	**112**	30c. red	5·00	4·50
620	**112**	50c. black	5·00	4·50
625	-	72c. green (No. 570)	22·00	14·00
626	**122**	90c. purple	22·00	14·00
621	**112**	1p. red and blue	6·00	4·50
627	-	1p.80 red & bl (No. 575)	44·00	34·00
623	**130**	2p. orange and black	19·00	13·00
628	-	3p.60 bl & grey (No. 576)	85·00	60·00
622	**112**	5p. green and lilac	£100	28·00

1932. Zeppelin Air stamps. Optd **GRAF ZEPPELIN 1932**.

629	**120**	5c. red	3·25	2·10
630	**120**	18c. violet	14·00	9·50
631	**122**	90c. purple	50·00	28·00

134 Refrigerating Plant

1932. Sixth International Refrigerating Congress.

632	**134**	3c. green	1·30	65
633	**134**	10c. red	2·75	55
634	**134**	12c. blue	7·75	1·90

135 Port La Plata

1933. 50th Anniv of La Plata City.

635	**135**	3c. brown and green	55	35
636	-	10c. purple and orange	65	30
637	-	15c. blue	5·00	2·30
638	-	20c. brown and lilac	2·20	1·40
639	-	30c. red and green	21·00	8·00

DESIGNS: 10c. President J. A. Roca; 15c. Municipal buildings; 20c. La Plata Cathedral; 30c. Dr. D. Rocha.

139 Christ of the Andes

1934. 32nd Int Eucharistic Congress, Buenos Aires.

640	**139**	10c. red	1·10	30
641	-	15c. blue	2·20	65

DESIGN—HORIZ: 15c. Buenos Aires Cathedral.

141 "Liberty" with Arms of Brazil and Argentina

1935. Visit of President Vargas of Brazil. Inscr "MAYO DE 1935".

642	**141**	10c. red	1·10	30
643	-	15c. blue	2·20	65

DESIGN: 15c. Clasped hands and flags.

143 D. F. Sarmiento

1935. Portraits.

644	½c. purple (Belgrano)	30	20
645	1c. brown (Type **143**)	30	20
646	2c. brown (Urquiza)	35	20
647	3c. green (San Martin)	35	20
648	4c. grey (G. Brown)	35	20
653b	5c. brown (Moreno)	70	20
650	6c. green (Alberdi)	40	20
653d	10c. red (Rivadavia)	2·10	20
651	12c. purple (Mitre)	45	30
708	15c. grey (Martin Guemes)	55	35
652	20c. blue (Juan Martin Guemes)	90	20
653	20c. blue (Martin Guemes)	55	20

See also Nos. 671 etc.

1935. Philatelic Exhibition, Buenos Aires (Ex. Fl. B.A.). Sheet 83×100 mm.

MS654 **112** 10c. green ×4 (sold at 1p.) 95·00 45·00

146 Prize Bull

151 With Boundary Lines

1936. Production and Industry.

676	**146**	15c. blue	55	30
677a	**146**	20c. blue (19½×26 mm)	35	20
755	**146**	20c. blue (22×33 mm)	2·75	10
656	-	25c. red and pink	45	20
757	-	30c. brown and yellow	1·20	10
658	-	40c. purple and mauve	55	20
659	-	50c. red and salmon	45	20
660	**151**	1p. blue and brown	24·00	1·20
760	-	1p. blue and brown	5·00	10
661	-	2p. blue and purple	1·30	20
662	-	5p. green and blue	6·50	45
763	-	10p. black and purple	22·00	2·00
764	-	20p. brown and blue	19·00	2·00

DESIGNS—VERT: 25c. Ploughman; 50c. Oil well; 1p. (No. 760) as Type **151** but without country boundaries; 5p. Iguazu Falls; 10p. Grapes; 20p. Cotton plant. HORIZ: 30c. Patagonian ram; 40c. Sugar cane and factory; 2p. Fruit products.

157

1936. Pan-American Peace Conference.

665	**157**	10c. red	90	25

158 Pres. Sarmiento

1938. President's 50th Death Anniv.

666	**158**	3c. green	65	55
667	**158**	5c. red	65	55
668	**158**	15c. blue	1·30	65
669	**158**	50c. orange	4·25	1·40

159 *Presidente Sarmiento*

1939. Last Voyage of Cadet Ship *Presidente Sarmiento*.

670	**159**	5c. green	55	30

1939. Portraits as T **143**.

671	2½c. black	30	20
672	3c. grey (San Martin)	40	20
672a	3c. grey (Moreno)	40	20
673	4c. green	35	20
894	5c. brown (16½×22½ mm)	25	10
674	8c. orange	35	20
678	10c. purple	30	20
675	12c. red	30	20
895	20c. lilac (21×27 mm)	90	20
895b	20c. lilac (19½×25½ mm)	90	20

PORTRAITS: 2½c. L. Braille; 4c. G. Brown; 5c. Jose Hernandez; 8c. N. Avellaneda; 10c. B. Rivadavia; 12c. B. Mitre; 20c. G. Brown.

160 Allegory of the Post

1939. 11th U.P.U. Congress, Buenos Aires.

679	**160**	5c. red	90	20
680	-	15c. grey	90	45
681	-	20c. blue	90	20
682	-	25c. green	1·30	45
683	-	50c. brown	2·20	85
684	-	1p. purple	5·50	2·10
685	-	2p. mauve	24·00	13·00
686	-	5p. violet	55·00	27·00

DESIGNS—VERT: 20c. Seal of Argentina; 1p. Symbols of postal communications; 2p. Argentina, *Land of Promise* from a pioneer painting. HORIZ: 15c. G.P.O.; 25c. Iguazu Falls; 50c. Mt. Bonete; 5p. Lake Frias.

1939. International Philatelic Exhibition, Buenos Aires. Two sheets *se-tenant* horiz or vert, each comprising Nos. 679, 681/3 arranged differently.

MS686a Two sheets, 190×95 mm or 95×190 mm 17·00 16·00

165 Working-class Family and New Home

1939. First Pan-American Housing Congress.

687	**165**	5c. green	45	20

167 North and South America

1940. 50th Anniv of Pan-American Union.

688	**167**	15c. blue	55	20

168 Corrientes Type **5**

1940. Centenary of First Adhesive Postage Stamps and Philatelic Exhibition, Cordoba. Sheet 111×111 mm containing early Argentine issues as T **168**.

MS688a 5c. blue (Type **168**); 5c. blue (Cordoba T **3**); 5c. red (Type **1**); 5c. red (Type **3**); 10c. blue (Buenos Aires T **1**) 13·00 10·50

169 Airplane and Envelope

1940. Air.

689	**169**	30c. orange	8·75	45
690	-	50c. brown	13·00	45
691	**169**	1p. red	3·25	10
692	-	1p.25 green	90	10
693	**169**	2p.50 blue	2·75	50

DESIGNS—VERT: 50c. "Mercury"; 1p.25, Douglas DC-2 in clouds.

172 Gen. French, Col. Beruti and Rosette of the "Legion de Patricios"

1941. 131st Anniv of Rising against Spain.

694	**172**	5c. blue	45	20

173 Marco M. de Avellaneda

1941. Death Centenary of Avellaneda (patriot).

695	**173**	5c. blue	45	20

174 Statue of Gen. J. A. Roca

1941. Dedication of Statue of Gen. Roca.

696	**174**	5c. green	45	20

175 Pellegrini (founder) and National Bank

1941. 50th Anniv of National Bank.

697	**175**	5c. lake	45	20

176 Gen. Juan Lavalle

1941. Death Centenary of Gen. Lavalle.

698	**176**	5c. blue	45	20

177 New P.O. Savings Bank

1942. Inauguration of P.O. Savings Bank.

699	**177**	1c. green	35	20

178 Jose Manuel Estrada

1942. Birth Centenary of Estrada (patriot).

700	**178**	5c. purple	45	20

180 G.P.O., Buenos Aires

1942. Postage and Express Stamps.

717	**180**	35c. blue	4·75	20
746	**180**	35c. blue	1·90	30

No. 717 is inscr "PALACIO CENTRAL DE CORREOS Y TELEGRAFOS" and No. 746 "PALACIO CENTRAL DE CORREOS Y TELECOMUNICACIONES".

181 Proposed Columbus Lighthouse

1942. 450th Anniv of Discovery of America by Columbus.

721b	**181**	15c. blue	6·50	65

182 Dr. Paz (founder of "La Prensa")

1942. Birth Centenary of Dr. Jose C. Paz.

722	**182**	5c. blue	45	15

183 Flag of Argentina and Books

1943. First National Book Fair.

723	**183**	5c. blue	45	15

184 Arms of Argentina

1943. Revolution of 4 June 1943.

724	**184**	5c. red	35	15
725	**184**	15c. green	1·00	20
726	**184**	20c. blue (larger)	1·50	20

185 National Independence House

1943. Restoration of Tucuman Museum.

727b	**185**	5c. green	45	15

186 Head of Liberty, Money-box and Laurels

1943. First Savings Bank Conference.

728	**186**	5c. brown	35	10

187 Buenos Aires in 1800

1944. Export Day.

729	**187**	5c. black	35	10

188 Postal Union of the Americas and Spain

189 Alexander Graham Bell

1944. Postmen's Benefit Fund. Inscr "PRO-CARTERO".

730	-	3c.+2c. black and violet	80	65
731	**188**	5c.+5c. black and red	1·10	30
732	**189**	10c.+5c. black and orge	2·20	75
733	-	25c.+15c. black and brn	2·75	1·30
734	-	1p.+50c. black and green	13·00	10·50

DESIGNS: 3c. Samuel Morse; 25c. Rowland Hill; 1p. Columbus landing in America.

191 Liner, Warship and Yacht

1944. Naval Week.

735	**191**	5c. blue	35	10

192 Argentina

1944. San Juan Earthquake Relief Fund.

736	**192**	5c.+10c. black & olive	1·40	65
737	**192**	5c.+50c. black and red	5·50	2·30
738	**192**	5c.+1p. black & orange	17·00	10·50
739	**192**	5c.+20p. black & blue	40·00	21·00

193 Arms of Argentina

1944. First Anniv of Revolution of 4 June 1943.

740	**193**	5c. blue	45	15

193a National Flag

1944. National Anthem and Aid for La Rioja and Catamarca Provinces. Two sheets 75×110 mm each containing T **193a**.

MS740a	5c.+1p. blue and plum	22·00	7·00
MS740b	5c.+50p. blue and indigo	£650	£650

194 Archangel Gabriel

195 Cross of Palermo

1944. Fourth National Eucharistic Congress.

741	**194**	3c. green	50	20
742	**195**	5c. red	50	20

196 Allegory of Savings

1944. 20th Anniv of Universal Savings Day.

743	**196**	5c. black	35	15

197 Reservists

1944. Reservists' Day.

744	**197**	5c. blue	35	15

198 Bernardino Rivadavia

199 Rivadavia's Mausoleum

1945. Rivadavia's Death Centenary.

770	**198**	3c. green	45	15
771	-	5c. red	45	15
772	**199**	20c. blue	55	20

DESIGN—As Type **198**: 5c. Rivadavia and Scales of Justice.

200 San Martin

1945

773	**200**	5c. red	35	15

201 Monument to Andes Army, Mendoza

1946. "Homage to the Unknown Soldier of Independence".

776	**201**	5c. purple	45	15

202 Pres. Roosevelt

1946. First Death Anniv of Pres. Franklin Roosevelt.

777	**202**	5c. grey	35	15

203 "Affirmation"

1946. Installation of Pres. Juan Peron.

778	**203**	5c. blue	35	15

204 Airplane over Iguazu Falls

1946. Air.

779	**204**	15c. red	45	15
780	-	25c. green	45	15

DESIGN: 25c. Airplane over Andes.

205 "Flight"

1946. Aviation Week.

781	**205**	15c. green on green	90	30
782	-	60c. purple on buff	90	30

DESIGN: 60c. Hand upholding globe.

207 "Argentina and Populace"

1946. First Anniv of Peron's Defeat of Counter-revolution.

783	**207**	5c. mauve	65	45
784	**207**	10c. green	90	55
785	**207**	15c. blue	1·10	85
786	**207**	50c. brown	90	65
787	**207**	1p. red	2·10	1·70

208 Money-box and Map

1946. Annual Savings Day.

788	**208**	30c. red	90	30

209 Industry

1946. Industrial Exhibition.

789	**209**	5c. purple	55	15

210 Argentine–Brazil International Bridge

1947. Opening of Bridge between Argentina and Brazil.

790	**210**	5c. green	45	15

211 South Pole

1947. 43rd Anniv of 1st Argentine Antarctic Mail.

791	**211**	5c. violet	65	20
792	**211**	20c. red	1·40	20

212 "Justice"

1947. First Anniv of Col. Juan Peron's Presidency.

793	**212**	5c. purple and buff	45	15

213 Icarus Falling

1947. "Week of the Wing".

794	**213**	15c. purple	45	15

214 Presidente Sarmiento

1947. 50th Anniv of Launching of Cadet Ship *Presidente Sarmiento*.

795	**214**	5c. blue	45	15

215 Cervantes and "Don Quixote"

1947. 400th Birth Anniv of Cervantes.

796	**215**	5c. green	45	15

216 Gen. San Martin and Urn

1947. Arrival from Spain of Ashes of Gen. San Martin's Parents.

797	**216**	5c. green	45	15

217 Young Crusaders

1947. Educational Crusade for Universal Peace.

798	**217**	5c. green	45	15
799	**217**	20c. brown	55	15

218 Statue of Araucarian Indian

1948. American Indian Day.

801	**218**	25c. brown	45	15

219 Phrygian Cap and Sprig of Wheat

1948. Fifth Anniv of Anti-isolationist Revolution of 4 June 1943.

802	**219**	5c. blue	35	15

220 "Stop"

1948. Safety First Campaign.

803	**220**	5c. yellow and brown	40	15

221 Posthorn and Oak Leaves

1948. Bicent of Postal Service in Rio de la Plata.

804	**221**	5c. mauve	40	15

222 Argentine Farmers

1948. Agriculture Day.

805	**222**	10c. brown	35	15

223 "Liberty and Plenty"

1948. Re-election of President Peron.

806	**223**	25c. red	55	20

225 Statue of Atlas

226 Map, Globe and Compasses

1948. Air. Fourth Meeting of Pan-American Cartographers.

807	**225**	45c. brown	65	20
808	**226**	70c. green	1·30	55

226a Buenos Aires

1948. Bicentenary of Postal Service in Rio de la Plata (2nd issue). Two sheets containing designs as T **226a**.

MS808a 144×101 mm. (horiz designs). 15c. green (Mail coach, 1865); 45c. brown (Type **226a**); 55c. brown (First train, 1857); 85c. ultramarine (Sailing ship, 1767)		8·75	3·75
MS808b 102×144 mm (vert designs). 85c. brown (Domingo de Basavilibaso); 1p.50 green (Postrider, 1748); 1p.20 indigo (Sailing ship, 1798); 1p.90 purple (Courier in the Andes, 1772) Price for 2 sheets		60·00	13·00

227 Winged Railway Wheel

1949. First Anniv of Nationalization of Argentine Railways.

809	**227**	10c. blue	55	20

228 Head of Liberty

1949. Constitution Day.

810	**228**	1p. purple and red	70	30

229 Trophy and Target

1949. Air. International Shooting Championship.

811	**229**	75c. brown	1·20	30

230 "Intercommunication"

1949. 75th Anniv of U.P.U.

812	**230**	25c. green and olive	35	15

231 San Martin

232 San Martin at Boulogne

1950. San Martin's Death Cent. Dated "1850 1950".

813	-	10c. purple and blue	20	10
814	**231**	20c. brown and red	20	10
815	**232**	25c. brown	35	10
816	-	50c. blue and green	75	30
817	-	75c. green and brown	75	30
818	-	1p. green	2·00	30
819	-	2p. purple	1·10	55
MS819a 120×150 mm. Nos. 813/14 and 816/17. Imperf			3·75	2·75

DESIGNS—As Type **231**: 10, 50, 75c. Portraits of San Martin; 2p. San Martin Mausoleum. As Type **232**: 1p. House where San Martin died.

233 Stamp Designer

1950. Int Philatelic Exhibition, Buenos Aires.

820	**233**	10c.+10c. violet (postage)	20	15
821	-	45c.+45c. blue (air)	35	30
822	-	70c.+70c. brown	55	50
823	-	1p.+1p. red	2·20	1·60
824	-	2p.50+2p.50 olive	12·00	8·00
825	-	5p.+5p. green	19·00	13·00
MS825a 120×150 mm. Nos. 820/2. Imperf			8·75	8·00

DESIGNS: 45c. Engraver; 70c. Proofing; 1p. Printer; 2p.50, Woman reading letter; 5p. San Martin.

234 S. America and Antarctic

1951

826	**234**	1p. blue and brown	1·00	20

235 Douglas DC-3 and Andean Condor

1951. Air. Tenth Anniv of State Airlines.

827	**235**	20c. olive	70	20

236 Pegasus and Steam Locomotive

1951. Five-year Plan.

828	**236**	5c. brown (postage)	1·20	20
829	-	25c. green	2·40	35
830	-	40c. purple	3·25	35
831	-	20c. blue (air)	95	20

DESIGNS—HORIZ: 25c. *President Peron* (liner) and common dolphin. VERT: 20c. Douglas DC-4 and Andean condor; 40c. Head of Mercury and telephone.

237 Woman Voter and "Argentina"

1951. Women's Suffrage in Argentina.

832	**237**	10c. purple	55	15

238 "Piety"

1951. Air. Eva Peron Foundation Fund.

833	**238**	2p.45+7p.55 olive	34·00	20·00

239 Eva Peron

240 Eva Peron

1952. (a) Size 20×26 mm.

834	**239**	1c. brown	35	15
835	**239**	5c. grey	35	15
836	**239**	10c. red	35	15
837	**239**	20c. red	35	15
838	**239**	25c. green	35	15
839	**239**	40c. purple	35	15
841	**239**	45c. blue	70	20
840	**239**	50c. bistre	70	20

(b) Size 22×33 mm. Without inscr "EVA PERON".

842	**240**	1p. brown	70	20
843	**240**	1p.50 green	3·50	20
844	**240**	2p. red	70	20
845	**240**	3p. blue	2·10	20

(c) Size 22×33 mm. Inscr "EVA PERON".

846	1p. brown	55	20
847	1p.50 green	2·10	20
848	2p. red	2·10	20
849	3p. blue	5·25	75

(d) Size 30½×40 mm. Inscr "EVA PERON".

850		5p. brown	5·25	1·00
851	**239**	10p. red	12·50	2·20
852	**240**	20p. green	21·00	5·25
853	**239**	50p. blue	37·00	13·00

241 Indian Funeral Urn

1953. Fourth Centenary of Santiago del Estero.

854	**241**	50c. green	35	10

242 Rescue Ship *Uruguay*

1953. 50th Anniv of Rescue of the *Antarctic*.

855	**242**	50c. blue	1·90	65

243 Planting Flag in S. Orkneys

1954. 50th Anniv of Argentine P.O. in South Orkneys.

856	**243**	1p.45 blue	1·70	45

244 "Telegraphs"

1954. International Telecommunications Conference. Symbolical designs inscr as in T **244**.

857	**244**	1p.50 purple	70	20

858	-	3p. blue	2·10	35
859	-	5p. red	2·75	65

DESIGNS—VERT: 3p. "Radio". HORIZ: 5p. "Television".

245 Pediment, Buenos Aires Stock Exchange

1954. Centenary of Argentine Stock Exchange.

860	**245**	1p. green	70	10

246 Eva Peron

1954. Second Death Anniv of Eva Peron.

861	**246**	3p. red	3·00	55

247 San Martin

249 Wheat

250 Mt. Fitz Roy

1954

862	**247**	20c. red	25	10
863	**247**	40c. red	35	10
868	-	50c. blue (33×22 mm)	35	10
869	-	50c. blue (32×21 mm)	75	20
870	**249**	80c. brown	35	10
871	-	1p. brown	45	10
872	-	1p.50 blue	35	10
873	-	2p. red	55	20
874	-	3p. purple	55	20
875a	-	5p. green	10·50	25
876	-	10p. green and grey	11·00	25
877	**250**	20p. violet	16·00	70
1018	-	22p. blue	2·40	25
878	-	50p. indigo and blue (30½×40½ mm)	13·50	1·40
1023	-	50p. blue (29½×40 mm)	12·00	70
1287	-	50p. blue (22½×32½ mm)	1·80	25

DESIGNS—As Type **249**: HORIZ: 50c. Port of Buenos Aires; 1p. Cattle; 2p. Eva Peron Foundation; 3p. El Nihuil Dam. As Type **250**: VERT: 1p.50, 22p. Industrial Plant; 5p. Iguazu Falls; 50p. San Martin. HORIZ: 10p. Humahuaca Ravine.

For 43p. in the design of the 1p.50 and 22p. see No. 1021.

For 65c. in same design see No. 1313.

248 "Prosperity"

1954. Centenary of Argentine Corn Exchange.

867	**248**	1p.50 grey	1·00	25

251 Clasped Hands and Congress Emblem

1955. Productivity and Social Welfare Congress.

879	**251**	3p. brown	1·70	35

252 Father and Son with Model Airplane

1955. 25th Anniv of Commercial Air Services.

880	**252**	1p.50 grey	1·40	25

253 "Liberation"

1955. Anti-Peronist Revolution of 16 Sept. 1955.

881	**253**	1p.50 olive	1·00	25

254 Forces Emblem

1955. Armed Forces Commemoration.

882	**254**	3p. blue	70	20

255 Gen. Urquiza (after J. M. Blanes)

1956. 104th Anniv of Battle of Caseros.

883	**255**	1p.50 green	1·10	35

256 Detail from *Antiope* (Correggio)

1956. Infantile Paralysis Relief Fund.

884	**256**	20c.+30c. grey	45	30

257 Coin and Die

1956. 75th Anniv of National Mint.

885	**257**	2p. brown and sepia	45	25

258 Corrientes Stamp of 1856

259 Dr. J. G. Pujol

1956. Centenary of First Argentine Stamps.

886	**258**	40c. blue and green	35	10
887	**258**	2p.40 mauve and brown	45	20
888	**259**	4p.40 blue	1·00	35

The 40c. shows a 1r. stamp of 1856.

260 Cotton, Chaco

1956. New Provinces.

889	-	50c. blue	80	20
890	**260**	1p. lake	90	20
891	-	1p.50 green	1·00	20

DESIGNS—HORIZ: 50c. Lumbering, La Pampa. VERT: 1p.50, Mate tea plant, Misiones.

261 "Liberty"

1956. First Anniv of Revolution.

892	**261**	2p.40 mauve	1·10	35

262 Detail from *Virgin of the Rocks* (Leonardo)

1956. Air. Infantile Paralysis Victims, Gratitude for Help.

893	**262**	1p. purple	1·10	35

1956. Argentine Stamp Centenary (2nd issue) and Corrientes Stamp Centenary Exhibition. Nos. 886/7 but in litho and colours changed and No. 888 in sheet.

MS893a	147×169 mm. 40c. indigo and green; 2p.40 claret and purple; 4p.40 blue	7·50	7·25

264 Esteban Echeverria (writer)

265 F. Ameghino (anthropologist)

266 Roque Saenz Pena (statesman)

1956

896	**264**	2p. purple	35	20
897	**265**	2p.40 brown	45	20
898	**266**	4p.40 green	70	30

267 Franklin

1956. 250th Birth Anniv of Benjamin Franklin.

899	**267**	40c. blue	45	20

268 *Hercules* (sail frigate)

269 Admiral G. Brown

1957. Death Cent of Admiral Guillermo Brown.

900	**268**	40c. blue (postage)	25	10
902	-	60c. grey (air)	35	10
903	-	1p. mauve	25	10
904	**269**	2p. brown	35	10
901	-	2p.40 green	55	10

DESIGNS—HORIZ: 60c. *Zefiro* and *Nancy* (sail warships) at Battle of Montevideo; 1p. L. Rosales and T. Espora. VERT: 2p.40, Admiral Brown in later years.

270 Church of Santo Domingo

1957. 150th Anniv of Defence of Buenos Aires.

905	**270**	40c. green	35	10

271 Map of the Americas and Badge of Buenos Aires

1957. Air. Inter-American Economic Conference.

906	**271**	2p. purple	55	15

272 *La Portena*, 1857

1957. Centenary of Argentine Railways.

907	**272**	40c. sepia (postage)	1·40	35
908	-	60c. grey (air)	1·40	35

DESIGN: 60c. Diesel locomotive.

273 Globe, Flag and Compass Rose

1957. Air. Int Tourist Congress, Buenos Aires.

909	**273**	1p. brown	35	25
910	-	2p. turquoise	35	25

DESIGN: 2p. Symbolic key of tourism.

274 Head of Liberty

1957. Reform Convention.

911	**274**	40c. red	45	15

275

1957. Air. International Correspondence Week.

912	**275**	1p. blue	70	30

276 "Wealth in Oil"

1957. 50th Anniv of Argentine Oil Industry.

913	**276**	40c. blue	1·00	35

277 La Plata Museum

1958. 75th Anniv of Founding of La Plata.

914	**277**	40c. black	35	15

278 Health Emblem and Flower

1958. Air. Child Welfare.

915	**278**	1p.+50c. red	45	45

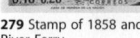

279 Stamp of 1858 and River Ferry

280 Stamp of 1858

1958. Centenary of Argentine Confederation Stamps and Philatelic Exhibition, Buenos Aires.

916	**279**	40c.+20c. purple and green (postage)	85	60
917	-	2p.40+1p.20 blue and black	90	65
918	-	4p.40+2p.20 pur & bl	95	70
919	**280**	1p.+50c. blue and olive (air)	90	85
920	**280**	2p.+1p. violet and red	1·10	95
921	**280**	3p.+1p.50 brown & grn	1·10	1·00
922	**280**	5p.+2p.50 red and olive	1·40	1·30
923	**280**	10p.+5p. sepia & olive	2·30	1·80

DESIGNS—HORIZ: 2p.40, Magnifier, stamp album and stamp of 1858; 4p.40, P.O. building of 1858.

281 Steam Locomotive and Arms of Argentina and Bolivia

1958. Argentine–Bolivian Friendship. (a) Inauguration of Yacuiba–Santa Cruz Railway.

924	**281**	40c. red and slate	90	30

282 Douglas DC-6 over Map of Argentine-Bolivian Frontier

(b) Exchange of Presidential Visits.

925	**282**	1p. brown	90	30

283 "Liberty and Flag"

1958. Transfer of Presidential Mandate. Head of "Liberty" in grey; inscr black; flag yellow and blue; background colours given.

926	**283**	40c. buff	15	10
927	**283**	1p. salmon	35	10
928	**283**	2p. green	70	35

284 Farman H.F.20 Biplane

1958. 50th Anniv of Argentine Aero Club.

929	**284**	2p. brown	35	20

285 National Flag Monument, Rosario

1958. First Anniv of Inauguration of National Flag Monument.

930	**285**	40c. grey and blue	35	20

286 Map of Antarctica

1958. International Geophysical Year.

931	**286**	40c. black and red	1·10	35

287 Confederation Stamp and *The Santa Fe Mail* (after J. L. Palliere)

1958. Cent of Argentine Confederation Stamps.

932	-	40c. grn & blue (postage)	35	25
933	-	80c. blue & yellow (air)	45	25
934	**287**	1p. blue and orange	40	25

DESIGNS: 40c. First local Cordoba 5c. stamp of 1858 and mail coach; 80c. Buenos Aires Type **1** of 1858 and *View of Buenos Aires* (after Deroy).

288 Aerial view of Flooded Town

1958. Flood Disaster Relief Fund. Inscr as in T **288**.

935	**288**	40c.+20c. brn (postage)	35	25
936	-	1p.+50c. plum (air)	35	25
937	-	5p.+2p.50 blue	1·20	1·10

DESIGNS—HORIZ: 1p. Different aerial view of flooded town; 5p. Truck in flood water and garage.

289 Child receiving Blood

1958. Leukaemia Relief Campaign.

938	**289**	1p.+50c. red and black	1·30	35

290 U.N. Emblem and *Dying Captive* (after Michelangelo)

1959. Tenth Anniv of Declaration of Human Rights.

939	**290**	40c. grey and brown	35	20

291 Hawker Siddeley Comet 4

1959. Air. Inauguration of Comet Jet Airliners by Argentine National Airlines.

940	**291**	5p. black and green	50	10

292 Orchids and Globe

1959. First Int Horticultural Exn, Buenos Aires.

941	**292**	1p. purple	35	20

293 Pope Pius XII

1959. Pope Pius XII Commemoration.

942	**293**	1p. black and yellow	50	20

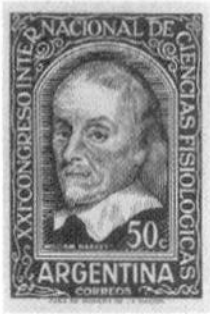

294 William Harvey

1959. 21st International Physiological Science Congress. Medical Scientists.

943	**294**	50c. green	25	10
944	-	1p. red	30	10
945	-	1p.50 brown	35	10

PORTRAITS: 1p. Claude Bernard; 1p.50, Ivan P. Pavlov.

295 Creole Horse

296 Tierra del Fuego

1959

946		10c. green	60	20
947		20c. purple	60	20
948		50c. ochre	60	20
950	**295**	1p. red	60	20
1016	-	1p. brown	25	10
1027	-	1p. brown	25	10
1035	-	2p. red	50	10
951	-	3p. blue	50	20
1036	-	4p. red	1·50	25
952	**296**	5p. brown	75	30
1037	-	8p. red	75	15
1038	-	10p. red	1·00	20
1286	-	10p. brown	75	25
1017	-	12p. purple	1·50	25
954	-	20p. green	4·25	25
1039	-	20p. red	50	10
1019	-	23p. green	7·25	25
1020	-	25p. lilac	2·20	25
1021	-	43p. lake	10·50	25
1022	-	45p. brown	6·00	25
1025	-	100p. blue	11·00	25
1026	-	300p. violet	5·50	25
1032	-	500p. green	2·20	25
1290	-	1000p. blue	5·25	85

DESIGNS—As Type **295**—HORIZ: 10c. Spectacled caiman; 20c. Llama; 50c. Puma. VERT: 2, 4, 8, 10p. (No 1038), 20p. (No. 1039) San Martin. As Type **296**—HORIZ: 3p. Zapata Hill, Catamarca; 300p. Mar del Plata (40×29½ mm). VERT: 1p. (No. 1016) Sunflowers; 1p. (No. 1027) Sunflower (22×32 mm); 10p. (No. 1286) Inca Bridge, Mendoza; 12, 23, 25p. Red quebracho tree; 20p. (No. 954) Lake Nahuel Huapi; 43, 45p. Industrial plant (30×39½ mm); 100p. Ski-jumper; 500p. Red deer (stag); 1,000p. Leaping salmon.

For these designs with face values in revalued currency, see Nos. 1300 etc.

298 Runner

1959. Third Pan-American Games, Chicago. Designs embody torch emblem. Centres and torch in black.

955	**298**	20c.+10c. green (postage)	25	10
956	-	50c.+20c. yellow	35	20
957	-	1p.+50c. purple	50	25
958	-	2p.+1p. blue (air)	60	25
959	-	3p.+1p.50 olive	85	70

DESIGNS—VERT: 50c. Basketball; 1p. Boxing. HORIZ: 2p. Rowing; 3p. High-diving.

299

1959. Red Cross Hygiene Campaign.

960	**299**	1p. red, blue and black	35	15

300 Child with Toys

1959. Mothers' Day.

961	**300**	1p. red and black	35	15

301 Buenos Aires 1p. stamp of 1859

1959. Stamp Day.

962	**301**	1p. blue and grey	35	15

302 B. Mitre and J. J. de Urquiza

1959. Centenary of Pact of San Jose de Flores.

963	**302**	1p. plum	35	15

303 Andean Condor

1960. Child Welfare. Birds.

964	**303**	20c.+10c. blue (postage)	1·50	25
965	-	50c.+20c. violet	1·80	25
966	-	1p.+50c. brown	1·50	25
967	-	2p.+1p. mauve (air)	1·50	35
968	-	3p.+1p.50 green	1·50	70

BIRDS: 50c. Fork-tailed flycatcher; 1p. Magellanic woodpecker; 2p. Red-winged tinamou; 3p. Greater rhea.

304 "Uprooted Tree"

1960. World Refugee Year.

969	**304**	1p. red and brown	50	25
970	**304**	4p.20 purple and green	50	25
MS971		113×85 mm. No. 969/70 with premium added for aid to refugees 1p.50c. and 4p.20+2p.10. Imperf	2·10	1·90

305 Abraham Lincoln

1960. 150th Birth Anniv of Abraham Lincoln.

972	**305**	5p. blue	60	25

306 Saavedra and Chapter Hall, Buenos Aires

1960. 150th Anniv of May Revolution.

973	**306**	1p. purple (postage)	25	10
974	-	2p. green	25	10
975	-	4p.20 green and grey	35	20
976	-	10p.70 blue and slate	60	25
977	-	1p.80 brown (air)	25	10
978	-	5p. purple and brown	50	20
MS979		Two sheets each 104×156 mm. Nos. 973/4, 977 in red-brown. Nos. 975/6, 978 in green	5·25	5·00

DESIGNS—Chapter Hall and: 1p.80, Moreno; 2p. Paso; 4p.20, Alberti and Azcuenaga; 5p. Belgrano and Castelli; 10p.70, Larrea and Matheu.

307 Dr. L. Drago

1960. Birth Centenary of Drago.

980	**307**	4p.20 brown	35	20

308 "Five Provinces"

1960. Air. New Argentine Provinces.

981	**308**	1p.80 blue and red	35	20

309 "Market Place 1810" (Buenos Aires)

1960. Air. Inter-American Philatelic Exhibition, Buenos Aires ("EFIMAYO") and 150th Anniv of Revolution. Inscr "EFIMAYO 1960".

982	**309**	2p.+1p. lake	25	10
983	-	6p.+3p. grey	50	20
984	-	10p.70+5p.30 blue	85	45
985	-	20p.+10p. turquoise	1·50	1·20

DESIGNS: 6p. "The Water Carrier"; 10p.70, "The Landing Place"; 20p. "The Fort".

310 J. B. Alberdi

1960. 150th Birth Anniv of J. B. Alberdi (statesman).

986	**310**	1p. green	35	20

311 Seibo (Argentine National Flower)

1960. Air. Chilean Earthquake Relief Fund. Inscr "AYUDA CHILE".

987	**311**	6p.+3p. red	50	25
988	-	10p.70+5p.30 red	75	45

DESIGN: 10p.70, Copihue (Chilean national flower).

312 Map of Argentina

1960. Census.

989	**312**	5p. lilac	1·20	35

313 Galleon

1960. Eighth Spanish-American P.U. Congress.

990	**313**	1p. green (postage)	35	10
991	**313**	5p. brown	85	25
992	**313**	1p.80 purple (air)	35	10
993	**313**	10p.70 turquoise	1·10	35

1960. Air. U.N. Day. Nos. 982/5 optd **DIA DE LAS NACIONES UNIDAS 24 DE OCTUBRE**.

994	**309**	2p.+1p. red	25	10
995	-	6p.+3p. black	50	35
996	-	10p.70+5p.30 blue	75	60
997	-	20p.+10p. turquoise	1·30	1·10

315 Blessed Virgin of Lujan

1960. First Inter-American Marian Congress.

998	**315**	1p. blue	1·00	25

316 Jacaranda

1960. International Thematic Stamp Exhibition ("TEMEX"). Inscr "TEMEX-61".

999	**316**	50c.+50c. blue	10	10
1000	-	1p.+1p. turquoise	20	10
1001	-	3p.+3p. brown	60	25
1002	-	5p.+5p. brown	85	60

FLOWERS: 1p. Passion flowers; 3p. Hibiscus; 5p. Black lapacho.

317 Argentine Scout Badge

1961. International Scout (Patrol) Camp.

1003	**317**	1p. red and black	50	20

318 *Shipment of Cereals* (after B. Q. Martin)

1961. Export Campaign.

1004	**318**	1p. brown	50	20

319 Emperor Penguin and Chick

1961. Child Welfare. Inscr "PRO-INFANCIA".

1005	-	4p.20+2p.10 brown (postage)	1·70	95
1006	**319**	1p.80+90c. black (air)	85	60

DESIGN: 4p.20, Blue-eyed cormorant.

320 *America*

1961. 150th Anniv of Battle of San Nicolas.

1007	**320**	2p. black	50	20

321 Dr. M. Moreno

1961. 150th Death Anniv of Dr. M. Moreno.

1008	**321**	2p. blue	35	15

322 Emperor Trajan

1961. Visit of President of Italy.

1009	**322**	2p. green	35	15

1961. Americas Day. Nos. 999/1002 optd **14 DE ABRIL DE LAS AMERICAS**.

1010	**316**	50c.+50c. blue	25	10
1011	-	1p.+1p. turquoise	25	10
1012	-	3p.+3p. brown	35	25
1013	-	5p.+5p. brown	75	45

324 Tagore

1961. Birth Centenary of Rabindranath Tagore (Indian poet).

1014	**324**	2p. violet on green	1·10	25

325 San Martin Monument, Madrid

1961. Inaug of Spanish San Martin Monument.

1015	**325**	1p. black	35	20

331a Gen. Belgrano (after monument by Rocha, Buenos Aires)

1961. Gen. Manuel Belgrano Commemoration.

1034	**331a**	2p. blue	1·00	25

333 Antarctic Scene

1961. Tenth Anniv of San Martin Antarctic Base.

1044	**333**	2p. black	1·00	25

334 Conquistador and Sword

1961. Fourth Centenary of Jujuy City.

1045	**334**	2p. red and black	35	20

335 Sarmiento Statue (Rodin)

1961. 150th Birth Anniv of Sarmiento.

1046	**335**	2p. violet	35	20

336 Cordoba Cathedral

1961. "Argentina 62" International Philatelic Exn.

1047	**336**	2p.+2p. purple (postage)	35	25
1048	-	3p.+3p. green	50	35
1049	-	10p.+10p. blue	1·10	95

MS1050 86×86 mm. Nos. 1047/9 each indigo. Imperf 3·75 2·50

DESIGNS-HORIZ: 10p. Buenos Aires Cathedral. VERT: 3p, As Type **336** but showing 10c. value and different inscr.

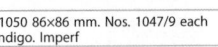

337

1961. World Town-planning Day.

1052	**337**	2p. blue and yellow	35	20

338 "The Flight into Egypt" (after Ana Maria Moncalvo)

1961. Child Welfare.

1053	**338**	2p.+1p. brown & lilac	25	10
1054	**338**	10p.+5p. purple & mve	75	20

339 Belgrano Statue (C. Belleuse)

1962. 150th Anniv of National Flag.

1055	**339**	2p. blue	35	20

340 Mounted Grenadier

1962. 150th Anniv of Gen. San Martin's Mounted Grenadiers.

1056	**340**	2p. red	1·00	25

341 Mosquito and Emblem

1962. Malaria Eradication.

1057	**341**	2p. black and red	60	20

342 Lujan Basilica

1962. 75th Anniv of Coronation of the Holy Virgin of Lujan.

1058	**342**	2p. black and brown	35	10

343 15c. Stamp of 1862

1962. Argentina 62 Philatelic Exhibition

1059	**343**	6p.50+6p.50 blue and turquoise (air)	1·00	85

344 Juan Jufre (founder)

1962. 400th Anniv of San Juan.

1060	**344**	2p. blue	35	20

345 UNESCO Emblem

1962. Air. 15th Anniv of UNESCO.

1061	**345**	13p. brown and ochre	60	35

346 "Flight"

1962. 50th Anniv of Argentine Air Force.

1062	**346**	2p. blue, black & purple	35	20

347 Juan Vucetich (fingerprints pioneer)

1962. Vucetich Commem.

1063	**347**	2p. green	35	15

348 19th-century Mail Coach

1962. Air. Postman's Day.

1064	**348**	5p.60 black and drab	1·00	25

1962. Air. Surch *AEREO* and value.

1065	**296**	5p.60 on 5p. brown	35	25
1066	**296**	18p. on 5p. brn on grn	1·50	35

350 U.P.A.E. Emblem

1962. Air. 50th Anniv of Postal Union of Latin America.

1067	**350**	5p.60 blue	50	15

351 Pres. Sarmiento

1962

1073	**351**	2p. green	1·00	25
1069	-	4p. red	75	25
1071	-	6p. brown	50	10
1075	-	6p. red	2·40	25
1072	-	90p. bistre	4·00	45

PORTRAITS: 4, 6p. Jose Hernandez; 90p. G. Brown.

352 Chalk-browed Mockingbird

1962. Child Welfare.

1076	**352**	4p.+2p. sepia, turquoise and brown	2·00	1·10
1077	-	12p.+6p. brown, yellow and slate	3·00	1·50

DESIGN—VERT: 12p. Rufous-collared sparrow.

See also Nos. 1101/2, 1124/5, 1165/6, 1191/2, 1214/15, 1264/5, 1293/4, 1394/5, 1415/16 and 1441/2.

353 Skylark 3 Glider

1963. Air. Ninth World Gliding Championships, Junin.

1078	**353**	5p.60 black and blue	25	10
1079	-	11p. black, red and blue	60	35

DESIGN: 11p. Super Albatross glider.

354 "20 de Febrero" Monument, Salta

1963. 150th Anniv of Battle of Salta.

1080	**354**	2p. green	1·00	25

355 Cogwheels

1963. 75th Anniv of Argentine Industrial Union.

1081	**355**	4p. red and grey	1·00	25

356 National College

1963. Centenary of National College, Buenos Aires.

1082	**356**	4p. black and buff	1·10	35

357 Child drinking Milk

1963. Freedom from Hunger.

1083	**357**	4p. ochre, black and red	35	20

358 "Flight"

1963. Air. (a) As T **358**.

1084	**358**	5p.60 green, mve & pur	35	20
1085	**358**	7p. black & yellow (I)	85	25
1086	**358**	7p. black & yellow (II)	7·25	1·40
1087	**358**	11p. purple, green & blk	35	20
1088	**358**	18p. blue, red and mauve	1·50	35
1089	**358**	21p. grey, red and brown	2·40	45

Two types of 7p. I, "ARGENTINA" reads down, and II, "ARGENTINA" reads up as in Type **358**.

(b) As T **358** but inscr "REPUBLICA ARGENTINA" reading down.

1147	12p. lake and brown	2·30	35
1148	15p. blue and red	1·60	35
1291	26p. ochre	25	10
1150	27p.50 green and black	2·50	60
1151	30p.50 brown and blue	3·25	95
1292	40p. lilac	4·00	25
1153	68p. green	5·75	70
1154	78p. blue	2·40	95

See also Nos. 1374/80 in revalued currency.

359 Football

1963. Fourth Pan-American Games, Sao Paulo.

1090	**359**	4p.+2p. green, black and pink (postage)	35	20
1091	-	12p.+6p. purple, black and salmon	75	60
1092	-	11p.+5p. red, black and green (air)	85	70

DESIGNS: 11p. Cycling; 12p. Show-jumping.

360 Frigate *La Argentina* (after Bouchard)

1963. Navy Day.

1093	**360**	4p. blue	1·10	35

361 Assembly House and Seal

1963. 150th Anniv of 1813 Assembly.

1094	**361**	4p. black and blue	1·00	25

362 Battle Scene

1963. 150th Anniv of Battle of San Lorenzo.

1095	**362**	4p. black & green on grn	1·00	25

363 Queen Nefertari (bas-relief)

1963. UNESCO Campaign for Preservation of Nubian Monuments.

1096	**363**	4p. black, green & buff	1·00	25

364 Government House

1963. Presidential Installation.

1097	**364**	5p. brown and pink	1·00	25

365 "Science"

1963. Tenth Latin-American Neurosurgery Congress.

1098	**365**	4p. blue, black & brown	1·10	35

366 Blackboards

1963. "Alliance for Progress".

1099	**366**	5p. red, black and blue	35	20

367 F. de las Carreras (President of Supreme Court)

1963. Centenary of Judicial Power.

1100	**367**	5p. green	35	20

1963. Child Welfare. As T **352**. Multicoloured.

1101	4p.+2p. Vermilion flycatcher (postage)	1·80	60
1102	11p.+5p. Great kiskadee (air)	2·40	95

368 Kemal Ataturk

1963. 25th Death Anniv of Kemal Ataturk.

1103	**368**	12p. grey	75	25

369 "Payador" (after Castagnino)

1964. Fourth National Folklore Festival.

1104	**369**	4p. black, blue & ultram	1·00	25

370 Map of Antarctic Islands

1964. Antarctic Claims Issue.

1105	**370**	2p. bl & ochre (postage)	2·50	35
1106	-	4p. bistre and blue	3·75	45
1107	-	18p. bl & bistre (air)	3·75	85

DESIGNS—VERT: (30×39½ mm): 4p. Map of Argentina and Antarctica. HORIZ: (as Type **291**): 18p. Map of "Islas Malvinas" (Falkland Islands).

371 Jorge Newbery in Airplane

1964. 50th Death Anniv of Jorge Newbery (aviator).

1108	**371**	4p. green	1·10	35

372 Pres. Kennedy

1964. President Kennedy Memorial Issue.

1109	**372**	4p. blue and mauve	75	25

373 Father Brochero

1964. 50th Death Anniv of Father J. G. Brochero.

1110	**373**	4p. brown	1·10	35

374 U.P.U. Monument, Berne

1964. Air. 15th U.P.U. Congress, Vienna.

1111	**374**	18p. purple and red	90	35

375 Soldier of the Patricios Regiment

1964. Army Day.

1112	**375**	4p. multicoloured	1·30	25

See also Nos. 1135, 1170, 1201, 1223, 1246, 1343, 1363, 1399, 1450, 1515, 1564, 1641 and 1678.

376 Pope John XXIII

1964. Pope John Commemoration.

1113	**376**	4p. black and orange	40	20

377 Olympic Stadium

1964. Olympic Games, Tokyo.

1114	**377**	4p.+2p. brown, yellow and red (postage)	40	20
1115	-	12p.+6p. black & green	75	35
1116	-	11p.+5p. blk & bl (air)	1·50	70

DESIGNS—VERT: 11p. Sailing; 12p. Fencing.

378 University Arms

1964. 350th Anniv of Cordoba University.

1117	**378**	4p. yellow, blue & black	40	10

379 Olympic Flame and Crutch

1964. Air. Invalids Olympic Games, Tokyo.

1118	**379**	18p.+9p. multicoloured	1·00	85

380 *The Discovery of America* (Florentine woodcut)

1964. Air. "Columbus Day" (or "Day of the Race").

1119	**380**	13p. black and drab	1·40	45

381 Pigeons and U.N. Headquarters

1964. United Nations Day.

1120	**381**	4p. ultramarine and blue	65	20

382 J. V. Gonzalez (medallion)

1964. Birth Centenary of J. V. Gonzalez.

1121	**382**	4p. red	1·00	25

383 Gen. J. Roca

1964. 50th Death Anniv of General Julio Roca.

1122	**383**	4p. blue	40	10

384 *Market-place, Montserrat Square* (after C. Morel)

1964. "Argentine Painters".

1123	**384**	4p. sepia	50	35

1964. Child Welfare. As T **352**. Multicoloured.

1124	4p.+2p. Red-crested cardinal (postage)	1·60	45
1125	18p.+9p. Chilean swallow (air)	3·25	1·20

385 Icebreaker *General San Martin* and Bearded Penguin

1965. "National Territory of Tierra del Fuego, Antarctic and South Atlantic Isles".

1126	-	2p. purple (postage)	75	20
1127	**385**	4p. blue	1·90	35
1128	-	11p. red (air)	90	25

DESIGNS: 2p. General Belgrano Base (inscr "BASE DE EJERCITO" etc); 11p. Teniente Matienzo Joint Antarctic Base (inscr "BASE CONJUNTA" etc).

1965. Air. First Rio Plata Philatelists' Day. Optd **PRIMERAS JORNADAS FILATELICAS RIOPLATENSES.**

1129	**358**	7p. black & yellow (II)	40	20

387 Young Saver

1965. 50th Anniv of National Postal Savings Bank.

1130	**387**	4p. black and red	35	10

388 I.T.U. Emblem

1965. Air. Centenary of I.T.U.

1131	**388**	18p. multicoloured	65	25

389 I.Q.S.Y. Emblem

1965. Int Quiet Sun Year and Space Research.

1132	**389**	4p. black, orange and blue (postage)	1·00	35
1133	-	18p. red (air)	1·10	45
1134	-	50p. blue	1·60	95

DESIGNS—VERT: 18p. Rocket launching. HORIZ: 50p. Earth, trajectories and space phenomena (both inscr "INVESTIGACIONES ESPACIALES").

391 Ricardo Guiraldes

1965. Army Day (29 May).

1135	**390**	8p. multicoloured	90	35

See also Nos. 1170, 1201, 1223, 1246, 1343, 1363, 1399, 1450, 1515, 1564 and 1641.

391 Ricardo Guiraldes

1965. Argentine Writers (1st series). Each brown.

1136	8p. Type **391**	65	25
1137	8p. E. Larreta	65	25
1138	8p. L. Lugones	65	25
1139	8p. R. J. Payro	65	25
1140	8p. R. Rojas	65	25

See also Nos 1174/8.

392 H. Yrigoyen (statesman)

1965. Hipolito Yrigoyen Commemoration.

1141	**392**	8p. black and red	40	20

393 "Children looking through a Window"

1965. International Mental Health Seminar.

1142	**393**	8p. black and brown	1·00	45

394 Ancient Map and Funeral Urn

1965. 400th Anniv of San Miguel de Tucuman.

1143	**394**	8p. multicoloured	50	25

395 Mgr. Dr. J. Cagliero

1965. Cagliero Commemoration.

1144	**395**	8p. violet	40	10

396 Dante (statue in Church of the Holy Cross, Florence)

1965. 700th Birth Anniv of Dante.

1145	**396**	8p. blue	1·00	25

397 Sail Merchantman *Mimosa*

1965. Centenary of Welsh Colonisation of Chubut and Foundation of Rawson.

1146	**397**	8p. black and red	50	20

398 Police Emblem on Map of Buenos Aires

1965. Federal Police Day.

1155	**398**	8p. red	50	35

399 Schoolchildren

1965. 81st Anniv of Law 1420 (Public Education).

1156	**399**	8p. black and green	50	20

400 St. Francis's Church, Catamarca

1965. Brother Mamerto Esquiu Commemoration.

1157	**400**	8p. brown and yellow	40	10

401 R. Dario (Nicaraguan poet)

1965. 50th Death Anniv of Ruben Dario.

1158	**401**	15p. violet on grey	40	20

402 *The Orange-seller* (detail)

1966. Prilidiano Pueyrredon's Paintings. Designs show details from the original works, each green.
1159 8p. Type **402** 1·10 60
1160 8p. *A Halt at the Village Grocer's Shop* 1·10 60
1161 8p. *San Fernando Landscape* 1·10 60
1162 8p. *Bathing Horses on the Banks of the River Plate* 1·10 60

403 Rocket "Centaur" and Antarctic Map

1966. Air. Rocket Launches in Antarctica.
1163 **403** 27p.50 red, black & blue 1·50 1·20

404 Dr. Sun Yat-sen

1966. Birth Centenary of Dr. Sun Yat-sen.
1164 **404** 8p. brown 1·10 25

1966. Child Welfare. As T **352**, inscr "R. ARGENTINA". Multicoloured.
1165 8p.+4p. Southern lapwing (postage) 2·00 85
1166 27p.50+12p.50 Rufous hornero (air) 1·60 1·20

405 "Rivadavia" 5c. stamp of 1864

1966. Second Rio Plata Philatelists Days and Exhibition. Miniature sheet containing designs as T **405**.
MS1167 141×100 mm. 4p. red and grey (T **405**); 5p. green and grey (10c. stamp); 8p. blue and grey (15c. stamp) 1·60 1·50

406 "Human Races"

1966. Inaug of W.H.O. Headquarters, Geneva.
1168 **406** 8p. black and brown 50 20

407 Magellan Gull

1966. Air. 50th Anniv of Naval Aviation School, Puerto Militar.
1169 **407** 12p. multicoloured 75 35

1966. Army Day (29 May). As T **390**.
1170 8p. multicoloured 1·00 25
DESIGN: 8p. Militiaman of Guemes's "Infernals".

408 Arms of Argentina

1966. Air. "Argentina '66" Philatelic Exhibition, Buenos Aires.
1171 **408** 10p.+10p. multicoloured 2·75 1·90

409

1966. 150th Anniv of Independence. Sheet of 25 (5×5) comprising different 10p. designs–national, federal and provincial arms and maps, as T **409**. Inscr "1816–1966". Multicoloured.
MS1172 Sheet of 25 stamps 65·00 60·00

410 "Charity" Emblem

1966. Argentine Charities.
1173 **410** 10p. blue, black & green 40 10

1966. Argentine Writers (2nd series). Portraits as T **391**. Each green.
1174 10p. H. Ascasubi 65 25
1175 10p. Estanislao del Campo 65 25
1176 10p. M. Cane 65 25
1177 10p. Lucio V. Lopez 65 25
1178 10p. R. Obligado 65 25

411 Anchor

1966. 25th Anniv of Argentine Mercantile Marine.
1179 **411** 4p. multicoloured 40 20

412 L. Agote

1966. Argentine Scientists. Each violet.
1180 10p. Type **412** 65 25
1181 10p. J. B. Ambrosetti 65 25
1182 10p. M. I. Lillo 65 25
1183 10p. F. P. Moreno 65 25
1184 10p. F. J. Muniz 65 25

413 Map and Flags of the American States

1966. Seventh American Armies Conf, Buenos Aires.
1185 **413** 10p. multicoloured 40 10

414 Bank Facade

1966. 75th Anniv of Argentine National Bank.
1186 **414** 10p. green 40 10

415 La Salle Statue and College

1966. 75th Anniv of La Salle College, Buenos Aires.
1187 **415** 10p. black and brown 40 10

416 Antarctic Map with Expedition Route

1966. Argentine South Pole Expedition, 1965–66.
1188 **416** 10p. multicoloured 1·30 25

417 Gen. J. M. de Pueyrredon

1966. Gen. J. M. de Pueyrredon Commemoration.
1189 **417** 10p. red 50 20

418 Gen. J. G. de Las Heras

1966. Gen. Juan G. de Las Heras Commemoration.
1190 **418** 10p. black 40 10

1967. Child Welfare. As T **352**, inscr "R. ARGENTINA". Multicoloured.
1191 10p.+5p. Scarlet-headed blackbird (horiz) (postage) 2·30 1·10
1192 15p.+7p. Blue and yellow tanager (air) 2·75 1·70

419 Ancient Pot

1967. 20th Anniv of UNESCO.
1193 **419** 10p. multicoloured 50 20

420 *The Meal* (after F. Fader)

1967. Fernando Fader (painter).
1194 **420** 10p. brown 50 20

421 Juana Azurduy de Padilla

1967. Famous Argentine Women. Each sepia.
1195 6p. Type **421** 65 25
1196 6p. J. M. Gorriti 65 25
1197 6p. C. Grierson 65 25
1198 6p. J. P. Manson 65 25
1199 6p. A. Storni 65 25

422 Schooner *Invencible*

1967. Navy Day.
1200 **422** 20p. multicoloured 1·80 45

1967. Army Day (29 May). As T **390**.
1201 20p. multicoloured 1·10 25
DESIGN: 20p. Soldier of the Arribenos Regiment.

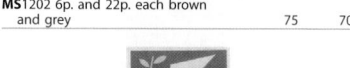

423 M. Belgrano (6p.) and J. G. de Artigas (22p.)

1967. Third Rio Plata Philatelists Days and Exhibition. Sheet 63×55 mm comprising designs as T **423**.
MS1202 6p. and 22p. each brown and grey 75 70

424 Suitcase and Dove

1967. International Tourist Year.
1203 **424** 20p. multicoloured 50 20

425 PADELAI Emblem and Sun

1967. 75th Anniv of PADELAI (Argentine Children's Welfare Association).
1204 **425** 20p. multicoloured 40 10

426 Teodoro Fels's Bleriot XI

1967. Air. 50th Anniv of First Argentine–Uruguay Airmail Flight.
1205 **426** 26p. brown, olive & blue 40 10

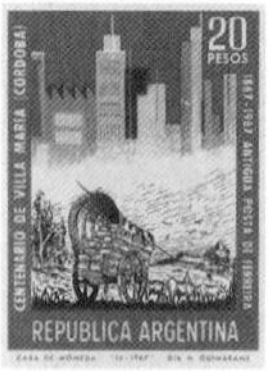

427 Ferreyra's Oxwagon and Skyscrapers

1967. Centenary of Villa Maria.
1206 **427** 20p. multicoloured 40 10

428 *General San Martin* (from statue by M. P. Nunez de Ibarra)

1967. 150th Anniv of Battle of Chacabuco.
1207 **428** 20p. brown and yellow 90 25
1208 - 40p. blue 1·40 45
DESIGN—(48×31 mm)—HORIZ: 40p. *Battle of Chacabuco* (from painting by P. Subercaseaux).

429 Interior of Museum

1967. Tenth Anniv of Government House Museum.
1209 **429** 20p. blue 40 20

430 Pedro Zanni and "Provincia de Buenos Aires"

1967. Aeronautics Week.
1210 **430** 20p. multicoloured 50 20

431 Cadet Ship *General Brown* (from painting by E. Biggeri)

1967. "Temex 67" Stamp Exhibition and 95th Anniv of Naval Military School.
1211 **431** 20p. multicoloured 1·90 60

432 Ovidio Lagos and Front Page of *La Capital* (newspaper)

1967. Centenary of *La Capital*.
1212 **432** 20p. brown 40 10

433 St. Barbara (from altar-painting, Segovia, Spain)

1967. Artillery Day (4 Dec).
1213 **433** 20p. red 50 15

1967. Child Welfare. Bird designs as T **352**. Multicoloured.
1214 20p.+10p. Amazon kingfisher (postage) 2·00 60
1215 26p.+13p. Toco toucan (air) 2·50 85

434 *Sivori's Wife*

1968. 50th Death Anniv of Eduardo Sivori (painter).
1216 **434** 20p. green 50 20

435 *Almirante Brown* Scientific Station

1968. "Antarctic Territories".
1217 - 6p. multicoloured 90 20
1218 **435** 20p. multicoloured 1·30 25
1219 - 40p. multicoloured 2·10 85
DESIGNS—VERT (22½×32 mm): 6p. Map of Antarctic radio-postal stations. HORIZ (as Type **435**): 40p. Aircraft over South Pole ("Trans-Polar Round Flight").

436 Man in Wheelchair

1968. Rehabilitation Day for the Handicapped.
1220 **436** 20p. black and green 40 25

437 "St. Gabriel" (detail from *The Annunciation* by Leonardo da Vinci)

1968. St. Gabriel (patron saint of army communications).
1221 **437** 20p. mauve 40 25

438 Children and W.H.O. Emblem

1968. 20th Anniv of W.H.O.
1222 **438** 20p. blue and red 40 25

1968. Army Day (29 May). As T **390**.
1223 20p. multicoloured 1·30 25
DESIGN: 20p. Iriarte's artilleryman.

439 Full-rigged Cadet Ship *Libertad* (E. Biggeri)

1968. Navy Day.
1224 **439** 20p. multicoloured 2·10 35

440 G. Rawson and Hospital

1968. Centenary of Guillermo Rawson Hospital.
1225 **440** 6p. bistre 50 25

441 Vito Dumas and *Legh II*

1968. Air. Vito Dumas' World Voyage in Yacht *Legh II*.
1226 **441** 68p. multicoloured 1·00 60

442 Children using Zebra crossing

1968. Road Safety.
1227 **442** 20p. multicoloured 1·00 35

443 *O'Higgins greeting San Martin* (P. Subercaseaux)

1968. 150th Anniv of Battle of the Maipu.
1228 **443** 40p. blue 1·10 45

444 Dr. O. Magnasco (lawyer)

1968. Magnasco Commemoration.
1229 **444** 20p. brown 65 30

445 *The Sea* (E. Gomez)

446 *Grandmother's Birthday* (P. Lynch)

1968. Children's Stamp Design Competition.
1230 **445** 20p. multicoloured 50 20
1231 **446** 20p. multicoloured 50 20

447 Mar del Plata at Night

1968. Fourth Plenary Assembly of Int Telegraph and Telephone Consultative Committee, Mar del Plata.
1232 **447** 20p. black, yellow and blue (postage) 40 20
1233 - 40p. black, mauve and blue (air) 75 20
1234 - 68p. multicoloured 1·10 45
DESIGNS (as Type **447**): 40p. South America in Assembly hemisphere. (Larger, 40×30 mm): 68p. Assembly emblem.

448 Mounted Gendarme

1968. National Gendarmerie.
1235 **448** 20p. multicoloured 50 20

449 Coastguard Cutter Lynch

1968. National Maritime Prefecture (Coastguard).
1236 **449** 20p. black, grey and blue 50 20

450 A. de Anchorena and *Pampero*

1968. Aeronautics Week.
1237 **450** 20p. multicoloured 50 20

451 St. Martin of Tours (A. Guido)

1968. St. Martin of Tours (patron saint of Buenos Aires).
1238 **451** 20p. brown and lilac 40 20

452 Bank Emblem

1968. Municipal Bank of Buenos Aires.
1239 **452** 20p. black, green & yell 40 20

453 Anniversary and A.L.P.I. Emblems

1968. 25th Anniv of "Fight Against Polio Association" (A.L.P.I.).
1240 **453** 20p. green and red 40 20

454 *My Grandmother's Birthday* (Patricia Lynch)

1968. First "Solidarity" Philatelic Exn, Buenos Aires.
1241 **454** 40p.+20p. multicoloured 90 60

455 *The Potter Woman* (Ramon Gomez Cornet)

1968. Cent of Whitcomb Gallery, Buenos Aires.
1242 **455** 20p. red 90 60

456 Emblem of State Coalfields

1968. Coal and Steel Industries. Multicoloured.
1243 20p. Type **456** 50 20
1244 20p. Ladle and emblem of Military Steel-manufacturing Agency ("FM") 50 20

457 Illustration from Schmidl's book *Journey to the River Plate and Paraguay*

1969. Ulrich Schmidl Commemoration.
1245 **457** 20p. yellow, red & black 90 60

1969. Army Day (29 May). As T **390**.
1246 20p. Sapper, Buenos Aires Army, 1856 1·50 25

459 Sail Frigate *Hercules*

1969. Navy Day.

1247	**459**	20p. multicoloured	2·75	45

460 *Freedom and Equality* (from poster by S. Zagorski)

1969. Human Rights Year.

1254	**460**	20p. black and yellow	40	20

461 I.L.O. Emblem within Honeycomb

1969. 50th Anniv of I.L.O.

1255	**461**	20p. multicoloured	40	20

462 P. N. Arata (biologist)

1969. Argentine Scientists.

1256	**462**	6p. brown on yellow	75	30
1257	-	6p. brown on yellow	75	30
1258	-	6p. brown on yellow	75	30
1259	-	6p. brown on yellow	75	30
1260	-	6p. brown on yellow	75	30

PORTRAITS: No. 1257, M. Fernandez (zoologist); 1258, A. P. Gallardo (biologist); 1259, C. M. Hicken (botanist); 1260, E. L. Holmberg (botanist).

463 Dish Aerial and Satellite

1969. Satellite Communications.

1261	**463**	20p. blk & yell (postage)	50	20
1262	-	40p. blue (air)	1·10	35

DESIGN—HORIZ: 40p. Earth station and dish aerial.

464 Nieuport 28 and Route Map

1969. 50th Anniv of First Argentine Airmail Service.

1263	**464**	20p. multicoloured	50	20

1969. Child Welfare. As T **352**, inscr "R. ARGENTINA". Multicoloured.

1264	20p.+10p. White-faced whistling duck (postage)	2·50	70
1265	26p.+13p. Lineated woodpecker (air)	2·75	85

465 College Entrance

1969. Centenary of Argentine Military College.

1266	**465**	20p. multicoloured	50	20

466 General Pacheco (from painting by R. Guidice)

1969. Death Centenary of General Angel Pacheco.

1267	**466**	20p. green	40	20

467 Bartolome Mitre and Logotypes of *La Nacion*

1969. Centenary of Newspapers *La Nacion* and *La Prensa*.

1268	**467**	20p. black, emer & grn	1·10	45
1269	-	20p. black orange & yell	1·10	45

DESIGN: No. 1269 "The Lantern" (masthead) and logotypes of "La Prensa".

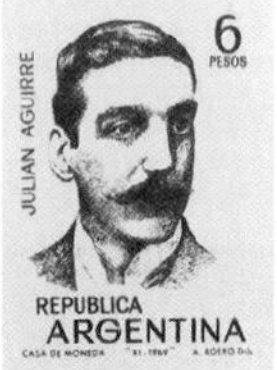

468 J. Aguirre

1969. Argentine Musicians.

1270	**468**	6p. green and blue	1·10	45
1271	-	6p. green and blue	1·10	45
1272	-	6p. green and blue	1·10	45
1273	-	6p. green and blue	1·10	45
1274	-	6p. green and blue	1·10	45

MUSICIANS: No. 1271, F. Boero; 1272, C. Gaito; 1273, C. L. Buchardo; 1274, A. Williams.

469 Hydro-electric Project on Rivers Limay and Neuquen

1969. National Development Projects. Multicoloured.

1275	6p. Type **469** (postage)	90	25
1276	20p. Parana–Santa Fe river tunnel	1·80	35
1277	26p. Atomic power plant, Atucha (air)	2·50	1·30

470 Lieut. B. Matienzo and Nieuport 28 Biplane

1969. Aeronautics Week.

1278	**470**	20p. multicoloured	90	20

471 Capital "L" and Lions Emblem

1969. 50th Anniv of Lions International.

1279	**471**	20p. olive, orge & green	1·10	25

472 *Madonna and Child* (after R. Soldi)

1969. Christmas.

1280	**472**	20p. multicoloured	1·10	35

1970. Child Welfare. As T **352**, but differently arranged and inscr "REPUBLICA ARGENTINA". Multicoloured.

1293	20c.+10c. Slender-tailed wood-star (postage)	2·00	70
1294	40c.+20c. Chilean flamingo (air)	2·50	85

See also Nos. 1394/5, 1415/16 and 1441/2.

474 *General Belgrano* (lithograph by Gericault)

1970. Birth Bicent of General Manuel Belgrano.

1295	**474**	20c. brown	65	20
1296	-	50c. black, flesh & blue	1·30	35

DESIGN—HORIZ (56×15 mm): 50c. *Monument to the Flag* (bas-relief by Jose Fioravanti).

475 Early Fire Engine

1970. Air. Centenary of Buenos Aires Fire Brigade.

1297	**475**	40c. multicoloured	2·30	45

476 Naval Schooner *Juliet*, 1814

1970. Navy Day.

1298	**476**	20c. multicoloured	2·00	60

477 San Jose Palace

1970. President Justo de Urquiza Commemoration.

1299	**477**	20c. multicoloured	40	20

478 General Belgrano

1970. Revalued currency. Previous designs with values in centavos and pesos as T **478**. Inscr "REPUBLICA ARGENTINA" or "ARGENTINA".

1300		1c. green (No. 1016)	25	10
1301	-	3c. red (No. 951)	25	10
1302	**296**	5c. blue	25	10
1303	**478**	6c. blue	40	15
1304	**478**	8c. green	25	10
1305	-	10c. brown (No. 1286)*	50	15
1306	-	10c. red (No. 1286)	2·40	45
1307	-	10c. brown (No. 1286)*	65	25
1308	**478**	10c. brown	25	10
1309	-	25c. brown	65	15
1310	**478**	30c. purple	50	20
1311	-	50c. red	1·50	30
1312	**478**	60c. yellow	50	25
1313	-	65c. brown (No. 878)	1·50	25
1314	-	70c. blue	25	15
1315	-	90c. green (No. 878)	4·50	30
1316a	-	1p. brown (as No. 1027, but 23×29 mm)	4·50	25
1317	-	1p.15 blue (No. 1072)	1·50	25
1318	-	1p.20 orange (No. 878)	1·60	30
1319	-	1p.20 red	50	20
1320	-	1p.80 brn (as No. 1072)	50	20
1321	**478**	1p.80 blue	50	25
1322	-	2p. brown	50	15
1323	-	2p.70 bl (as No. 878)	50	25
1323a	**478**	3p. grey	50	20
1392	-	4p.50 green (as No. 1288) (G. Brown)	1·10	20
1325	-	5p. green (as No. 1032)	1·90	35
1326	-	6p. red	50	20
1327	-	6p. green	50	20
1328	-	7p.50 grn (as No. 878)	1·60	30
1329	-	10p. blue (as No. 1033)	2·50	25
1329a	-	12p. green	65	20
1329b	-	12p. red	65	20
1330	-	13p.50 red (as No. 1072)	1·60	60
1331	-	13p.50 red (as No. 1072 but larger, 16×24 mm)	75	25
1332	-	15p. red	50	15
1333	-	15p. blue	50	15
1334	-	20p. red	50	20
1335	-	22p.50 blue (as No. 878) (22×32½ mm)	1·30	25
1393	-	22p.50 blue (as No. 878) (26×39 mm)	2·20	70
1336	-	30p. red	65	20
1337	**478**	40p. green	1·80	25
1338	-	40p. red	50	15
1339	**478**	60p. blue	2·50	30
1340	-	70p. blue	2·50	45
1340a	**478**	90p. green	1·30	30
1340b	-	100p. red	1·30	30
1340c	-	110p. red	65	25
1340d	-	120p. red	50	30
1340e	-	130p. red	90	35

DESIGNS—VERT (as Type **478**): 25, 50, 70c., 1p.20, 2, 6, 12, 15p. (No. 1332), 20, 30, 40p. (No. 1338), 100, 110, 120, 130p. General Jose de San Martin; 15p. (No. 1333), 70p. Guillermo Brown.

*No. 1307 differs from Nos. 1305/6 in being without imprint. It also has "CORREOS" at top right.

482 Wireless Set of 1920 and Radio "Waves"

1970. 50th Anniv of Argentine Radio Broadcasting.

1341	**482**	20c. multicoloured	75	45

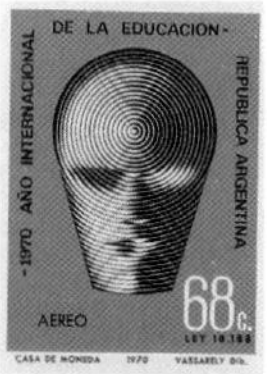

483 Emblem of Education Year

1970. Air. International Education Year.

1342	**483**	68c. black and blue	65	30

1970. Military Uniforms. As T **390**. Multicoloured.

1343	20c. Military courier, 1879	1·50	25

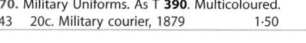

484 *Liberation Fleet leaving Valparaiso* (A. Abel)

1970. 150th Anniv of Peruvian Liberation.

1344	**484**	26c. multicoloured	1·90	60

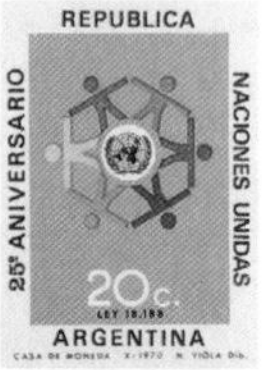

485 "United Nations"

1970. 25th Anniv of U.N.

1345	**485**	20c. multicoloured	40	20

486 Cordoba Cathedral

1970. 400th Anniv of Tucuman Diocese.

1346	**486**	50c. blk & grey (postage)	1·40	35
1347	-	40c. multicoloured (air)	1·50	60

DESIGN—HORIZ: 40c. Chapel, Sumampa.

487 Planetarium

1970. Air. Buenos Aires Planetarium.

1348	**487**	40c. multicoloured	1·10	35

488 "Liberty" and Mint Building

1970. 25th Anniv of State Mint Building, Buenos Aires.

1349	**488**	20c. black, green & gold	40	10

489 *The Manger* (H. G. Gutierrez)

1970. Christmas.

1350	**489**	20c. multicoloured	90	60

490 Jorge Newbery and Morane Saulnier Type L Airplane

1970. Air. Aeronautics Week.

1351	**490**	26c. multicoloured	65	25

491 St. John Bosco and College Building

1970. Salesian Mission in Patagonia.

1352	**491**	20c. black and green	40	20

492 "Planting the Flag"

1971. Fifth Anniv of Argentine Expedition to the South Pole.

1353	**492**	20c. multicoloured	2·30	35

493 Dorado

1971. Child Welfare. Fishes. Multicoloured.

1354	20c.+10c. Type **493** (postage)	2·00	70
1355	40c.+20c. River Plate pejerry (air)	1·80	60

494 Einstein and Scanners

1971. Electronics in Postal Development.

1356	**494**	25c. multicoloured	75	45

495 E. I. Alippi

1971. Argentine Actors and Actresses. Each black and brown.

1357	15c. Type **495**	50	15
1358	15c. J. A. Casaberta	50	15
1359	15c. R. Casaux	50	15
1360	15c. Angelina Pagano	50	15
1361	15c. F. Parravicini	50	15

496 Federation Emblem

1971. Inter-American Regional Meeting of International Roads Federation.

1362	**496**	25c. black and blue	50	20

1971. Army Day. As T **390**.

1363	25c. multicoloured	2·10	25

DESIGN: 25c. Artilleryman of 1826.

1971. Navy Day. As T **476**.

1364	25c. multicoloured	2·30	25

DESIGN: Sloop *Carmen*.

498 *General Guemes* (L. Gigli)

1971. 150th Death Anniv of General M. de Guemes. Multicoloured.

1365	25c. Type **498**	90	25
1366	25c. *Death of Guemes* (A. Alice) (84×29 mm)	90	25

499 Order of the Peruvian Sun

1971. 150th Anniv of Peruvian Independence.

1367	**499**	31c. yellow, black & red	1·10	25

500 Stylized Tulip

1971. Third Int and 8th Nat Horticultural Exhibition.

1368	**500**	25c. multicoloured	65	20

501 Dr. A. Saenz (founder) (after Jose Gut)

1971. 150th Anniv of Buenos Aires University.

1369	**501**	25c. multicoloured	50	20

502 Arsenal Emblem

1971. 30th Anniv of Fabricaciones Militares (Arsenals).

1370	**502**	25c. multicoloured	50	20

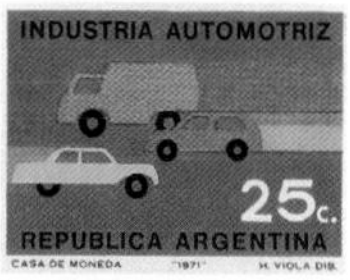

503 Road Transport

1971. Nationalized Industries.

1371	**503**	25c. mult (postage)	90	15
1372	-	65c. multicoloured	2·30	45
1373	-	31c. yell, blk & red (air)	1·00	35

DESIGNS: 31c. Refinery and formula ("Petrochemicals"); 65c. Tree and paper roll ("Paper and Cellulose").

1971. Air. Revalued currency. Face values in centavos.

1374	**358**	45c. brown	4·50	60
1375	**358**	68c. red	65	25
1376a	**358**	70c. blue	3·25	25
1377	**358**	90c. green	3·25	25
1378	**358**	1p.70 blue	1·00	25
1379	**358**	1p.95 green	1·00	25
1380	**358**	2p.65 purple	1·00	25

504 Constellation and Telescope

1971. Centenary of Cordoba Observatory.

1381	**504**	25c. multicoloured	1·10	25

505 Capt. D. L. Candelaria and Morane Saulnier Type P Airplane

1971. 25th Aeronautics and Space Week.

1382	**505**	25c. multicoloured	65	20

506 *Stamps* (Mariette Lydis)

1971. Second Charity Stamp Exhibition

1383	**506**	1p.+50c. multicoloured	75	45

507 *Christ in Majesty* (tapestry by Butler)

1971. Christmas.

1384	**507**	25c. multicoloured	40	20

1972. Child Welfare. As T **352**, but differently arranged and inscr "REPUBLICA ARGENTINA".

1394	25c.+10c. Saffron finch (vert)	1·90	45
1395	65c.+30c. Rufous-bellied thrush (horiz)	2·50	60

508 *Maternity* (J. Castagnino)

1972. 25th Anniv of UNICEF.

1396	**508**	25c. black and brown	40	15

509 Treaty Emblem, *Libertad* (liner) and Almirante Brown Base

1972. Tenth Anniv of Antarctic Treaty.

1397	**509**	25c. multicoloured	1·10	45

510 Postman's Mail Pouch

1972. Bicentenary of First Buenos Aires Postman.

1398	**510**	25c. multicoloured	35	10

1972. Army Day. As T **390**. Multicoloured.

1399	25c. Sergeant of Negro and Mulatto Battalion (1806–7)	1·10	45

1972. Navy Day. As T **476**. Multicoloured.

1400	25c. Brigantine "Santisima Trinidad"	1·60	50

512 Sonic Balloon

1972. National Meteorological Service.

1401	**512**	25c. multicoloured	50	15

513 Oil Pump

1972. 50th Anniv of State Oilfields (Y.P.F.).

1402	**513**	45c. black, blue & gold	1·40	25

514 Forest Centre

1972. Seventh World Forestry Congress, Buenos Aires.

1403	**514**	25c. black, blue & lt bl	1·10	35

515 Arms and Cadet Ship *Presidente Sarmiento*

1972. Centenary of Naval School.

1404	**515**	25c. multicoloured	1·30	25

516 Baron A. de Marchi, Balloon and Voisin *Boxkite*

1972. Aeronautics Week.
1405 **516** 25c. multicoloured 75 40

517 Bartolome Mitre

1972. 150th Birth Anniv of General Bartolome Mitre.
1406 **517** 25c. blue 70 40

518 Heart and Flower

1972. World Health Day.
1407 **518** 90c. blk, violet & blue 90 45

519 *Martin Fierro* (J. C. Castignino)

1972. Int Book Year and Cent of *Martin Fierro* (poem by Jose Hernandez). Multicoloured.
1408 50c. Type **519** 50 15
1409 90c. *Spirit of the Gaucho* (V. Forte) 1·00 45

520 Iguazu Falls

1972. American Tourist Year.
1410 **520** 45c. multicoloured 50 20

521 *Wise Man on Horseback* (18th-century wood-carving)

1972. Christmas.
1411 **521** 50c. multicoloured 75 25

522 Cockerel Emblem

1973. 150th Anniv of Federal Police Force.
1412 **522** 50c. multicoloured 50 20

523 Bank Emblem and First Coin

1973. 150th Anniv of Provincial Bank of Buenos Aires.
1413 **523** 50c. multicoloured 40 15

524 Douglas DC-3 Aircraft and Polar Map

1973. Tenth Anniv of Frist Argentine Flight to South Pole.
1414 **524** 50c. multicoloured 2·50 95

1973. Child Welfare. As T **473**, but differently arranged and inscr "R. ARGENTINA". Multicoloured.
1415 50c.+25c. Crested screamer (vert) 2·00 95
1416 90c.+45c. Saffron-cowled blackbird (horiz) 2·50 1·50

525 Presidential Chair

1973. Presidential Inauguration.
1417 **525** 50c. multicoloured 40 10

526 San Martin and Bolivar

1973. San Martin's Farewell to People of Peru. Multicoloured.
1418 50c. Type **526** 50 20
1419 50c. "San Martin" (after Gil de Castro) (vert) 50 20

527 "Eva Peron – Eternally with her People"

1973. Eva Peron Commemoration.
1420 **527** 70c. multicoloured 40 15

528 *House of Viceroy Sobremonte* (H. de Virgilio)

1973. Fourth Centenary of Cordoba.
1421 **528** 50c. multicoloured 45 15

529 *Woman* (L. Spilimbergo)

1973. Philatelists' Day. Argentine Paintings. Multicoloured.
1422 15c.+15c. *Nature Study* (A. Guttero) (horiz) 50 10
1423 70c. Type **529** 1·30 25
1424 90c.+90c. *Nude* (M. C. Victorica) (horiz) 1·60 1·10

See also Nos. 1434/6 and 1440.

530 *La Argentina* (sail frigate)

1973. Navy Day.
1425 **530** 70c. multicoloured 1·30 25

531 Early and Modern Telephones

1973. 25th Anniv of National Telecommunications Enterprise (E.N.T.E.L.).
1426 **531** 70c. multicoloured 65 15

532 Quill Pen of Flags

1973. 12th International Latin Notaries Congress.
1427 **532** 70c. multicoloured 40 15

533 Lujan Basilica

1973
1428 **533** 18c. brown and yellow 25 10
1429 **533** 50c. purple and black 25 10
1429a **533** 50c. blue and brown 25 10
1430 **533** 50c. purple 25 10

1973. Transfer of Presidency of General Juan Peron. No. 1318 optd **TRANSMISION DEL MANDO PRESIDENCIAL 12 OCTUBRE 1973**.
1431 1p.20 orange 1·40 25

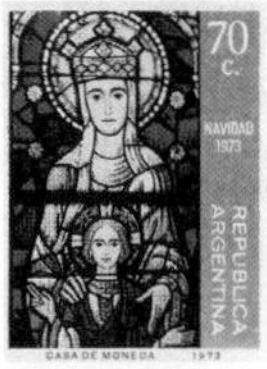

535 *Virgin and Child* (stained-glass window)

1973. Christmas. Multicoloured.
1432 70c. Type **535** 65 25
1433 1p.20 "The Manger" (B. Venier) 1·10 45

1974. Argentine Paintings. As T **529**. Multicoloured.
1434 50c. *Houses* (E. Daneri) (horiz) 65 20
1435 70c. *The Lama* (J. B. Planas) 70 25
1436 90c. *Homage to the Blue Grotto* (E. Pettoruti) (horiz) 75 35

536 View of Mar del Plata

1974. Centenary of Mar del Plata.
1437 **536** 70c. multicoloured 50 20

537 *Fray Justo Santa Maria de Oro* (anon.)

1974. Birth Bicentenary of Fray Justo Santa Maria de Oro.
1438 **537** 70c. multicoloured 40 10

538 Weather Contrasts

1974. Cent of World Meteorological Organization.
1439 **538** 1p.20 multicoloured 1·00 35

1974. "Prenfil 74" Philatelic Press Exhibition, Buenos Aires. As No. 1435.
1440 70c.+30c. multicoloured 75 30

1974. Child Welfare. As T **352** but differently arranged and inscr "REPUBLICA ARGENTINA". Multicoloured.
1441 70c.+30c. Double-collared seedeater 2·00 60
1442 1p.20+60c. Hooded siskin 2·50 85

539 B. Roldan

1974. Birth Centenary of Belisario Roldan (writer).
1443 **539** 70c. brown and blue 35 15

540 O.E.A. Member Countries

1974. 25th Anniv of Organization of American States' Charter.
1444 **540** 1p.38 multicoloured 40 15

541 Posthorn Emblem

1974. Creation of State Posts and Telecommunications Enterprise (E.N.C.O.T.E.L.).
1445 **541** 1p.20 blue, black & gold 75 15

542 Flags of Member Countries

1974. Sixth Meeting of River Plate Countries' Foreign Ministers.
1446 **542** 1p.38 multicoloured 40 20

543 El Chocon Hydro-electric Complex

1974. Nationalized Industries. Multicoloured.
1447 70c. Type **543** 65 15

1448 1p.20 Blast furnace, Somisa steel mills 1·00 45
1449 4p.50 General Belgrano Bridge (61×25 mm) 3·25 70

1974. Army Day. As T **390**. Multicoloured.
1450 1p.20 Mounted Grenadier 1·00 20

See also Nos. 1515 and 1564.

544 A. Mascias and Bleriot XI

1974. Air Force Day.
1451 **544** 1p.20 multicoloured 1·00 20

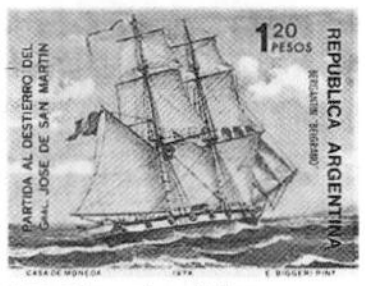

545 Brigantine *Belgrano*

1974. 150th Anniv of San Martin's Departure into Exile.
1452 **545** 1p.20 multicoloured 1·80 45

546 San Francisco Convent, Santa Fe

1974. 400th Anniv of Santa Fe.
1453 **546** 1p.20 multicoloured 65 15

547 Symbolic Posthorn

1974. Centenary of U.P.U.
1454 **547** 2p.65 multicoloured 1·40 35

548 Mariano Necochea

1974. 150th Anniv of Battles of Junin and Ayacucho. Sheet 143×134 mm comprising T **548** and similar vert designs. Multicoloured.
MS1455 (a) 1p. Type **548**; (b) 1p.20 San Martin; (c) 1p.70 Manuel Isidoro Suarez; (d) 1p.90 Juan Pascual Pringles; (e) 2p.70 Latin American flags; (f) 4p.50 Jose Felix Bogado 5·25 5·00

549 Congress Building, Buenos Aires

1974
1456 **549** 30p. purple and yellow 3·25 25

550 Boy examining Stamp

1974. International Year of Youth Philately.
1457 **550** 1p.70 black and yellow 65 15

551 *Christmas in Peace* (V. Campanella)

1974. Christmas. Multicoloured.
1458 1p.20 Type **551** 1·10 25
1459 2p.65 *St. Anne and the Virgin Mary* 1·30 45

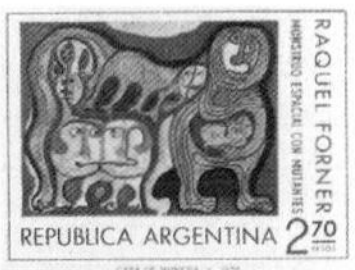

552 *Space Monsters* (R. Forner)

1975. Contemporary Argentine Paintings. Multicoloured.
1460 2p.70 Type **552** 1·50 35
1461 4p.50 *Sleep* (E. Centurion) 2·75 60

553 Cathedral and Weaver, Catamarca (image scaled to 58% of original size)

1975. Tourist Views (1st series). Multicoloured.
1462 1p.20 Type **553** 40 20
1463 1p.20 Street scene and carved pulpit, Jujuy 40 20
1464 1p.20 Monastery and tree- felling, Salta 40 20
1465 1p.20 Dam and vase, Santiago del Estero 40 20
1466 1p.20 Colombres Museum and farm cart, Tucuman 40 20

See also Nos. 1491/3.

554 *We're Vaccinated Now* (M. L. Alonso)

1975. Children's Vaccination Campaign.
1467 **554** 2p. multicoloured 75 20

555 *Don Quixote* (Zuloaga)

1975. Air. "Espana 75" International Stamp Exhibition, Madrid.
1468 **555** 2p.75 black, yell & red 1·00 40

556 Hugo S. Acuna and South Orkneys Base

1975. Antarctic Pioneers. Multicoloured.
1469 2p. Type **556** 50 15
1470 2p. Francisco P. Moreno and Quetrihue Peninsula 50 15
1471 2p. Capt. Carlos M. Moyano and Cerra Torre, Santa Cruz 50 15
1472 2p. Lt. Col. Luis PiedraBuena and naval cutter *Luisito* in the Antarctic 50 15
1473 2p. Ensign Jose M. Sobral and *Snow Hill* House 50 15

557 Valley of the Moon, San Juan Province

1975
1474 **557** 50p. multicoloured 4·00 45
1474a **557** 300p. multicoloured 4·50 45
1474b - 500p. multicoloured 8·75 1·20
1474c - 1000p. multicoloured 7·00 1·40

DESIGNS—HORIZ: 500p. Admiral Brown Antarctic Station; 1000p. San Francisco Church, Salta.

1975. Air. Surch.
1475 **358** 9p.20 on 5p.60 green, mauve and purple 1·50 35
1476 **358** 19p.70 on 5p.60 green, mauve and purple 2·10 70
1477 **358** 100p. on 5p.60 green, mauve and purple 9·50 3·75

559 Eduardo Bradley and Balloon

1975. Air Force Day.
1478 **559** 6p. multicoloured 75 25

560 Sail Frigate *25 de Mayo*

1975. Navy Day.
1479 **560** 6p. multicoloured 1·50 35

561 *Oath of the 33 Orientales on the Beach of La Agraciada* (J. Blanes)

1975. 150th Anniv of Uruguayan Independence.
1480 **561** 6p. multicoloured 1·30 35

1975. Air. Surch. **REVALORIZADO** and value.
1481 **358** 9p.20 on 5p.60 green, mauve and purple 1·10 45
1482 **358** 19p.70 on 5p.60 green, mauve and purple 2·00 95

563 Flame Emblem

1975. 30th Anniv of Pres. Peron's Seizure of Power.
1483 **563** 6p. multicoloured 65 25

1975. Surch **REVALORIZADO** and value.
1484 **533** 5p. on 18c. brown & yell 75 15

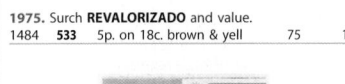

565 Bridge and Flags of Argentina and Uruguay

1975. "International Bridge" between Colon (Argentina) and Paysandu (Uruguay).
1485 **565** 6p. multicoloured 75 20

566 Posthorn Emblem

1975. Introduction of Postal Codes.
1486 **566** 10p. on 20c. yellow, black and green 90 20

1975. Nos. 951 and 1288 surch **REVALORIZADO** and value.
1487 6c. on 3p. blue 40 10
1488 30c. on 90p. bistre 40 10

568 *The Nativity* (stained-glass window)

1975. Christmas.
1489 **568** 6p. multicoloured 75 20

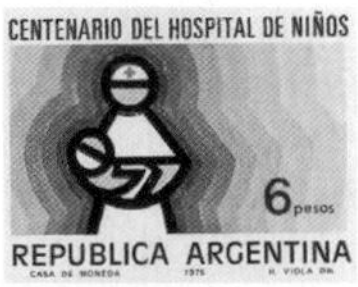

569 Stylized Nurse and Child

1975. Centenary of Children's Hospital.
1490 **569** 6p. multicoloured 1·30 35

1975. Tourist Views (2nd series). As T **553**. Multicoloured.
1491 6p. Mounted patrol and oil rig, Chubut 90 25
1492 6p. Glacier and sheep-shearing, Santa Cruz 90 25
1493 6p. Lake Lapataia, Tierra del Fuego, and Antarctic scene 90 25

570 "Numeral"

1976
1494 **570** 12c. grey and black 40 15
1495 **570** 50c. slate and green 40 15
1496 **570** 1p. red and black 40 15
1497 **570** 4p. blue and black 40 15
1498 **570** 5p. yellow and black 50 15
1499 **570** 6p. brown and black 50 15
1500 **570** 10p. grey and violet 90 20
1501 **570** 27p. green and black 65 20
1502 **570** 30p. blue and black 3·25 25
1503 **570** 45p. yellow and black 1·80 25
1504 **570** 50p. green and black 1·80 25
1505 **570** 100p. green and red 1·80 25

571 Airliner in Flight

1976. 25th Anniv of "Aerolineas Argentinas".
1513 **571** 30p. multicoloured 2·00 25

572 Sail Frigate *Heroina* and Map of Malvinas

1976. Argentine Claims to Falkland Islands (Malvinas).
1514 **572** 6p. multicoloured 5·75 60

1976. Army Day. As T **390**. Multicoloured.
1515 12p. Infantryman of Conde's 7th Regiment 75 20

573 Louis Braille

1976. Louis Braille (inventor of characters for the Blind) Commemoration.

1516	**573**	19p.70 blue	50	15

574 Plush-crested Jay

1976. Argentine Philately. Multicoloured.

1517	7p.+3p.50 Type **574**	1·40	80
1518	13p.+6p.50 Yellow-collared macaw	1·50	80
1519	20p.+10p. *Begonia micranthera*	1·70	85
1520	40p.+20p. *Echinopsis shaferi* (teasel)	2·10	1·00

575 Schooner *Rio de la Plata*

1976. Navy Day.

1521	**575**	12p. multicoloured	95	25

576 Dr. Bernardo Houssay (Medicine)

1976. Argentine Nobel Prize Winners.

1522	**576**	10p. black, orge & grey	50	15
1523	-	15p. black, yell & grey	50	15
1524	-	20p. black, brn & grey	65	25

DESIGNS: 15p. Dr. Luis Leloir (chemistry); 20p. Dr. Carlos Lamas (peace).

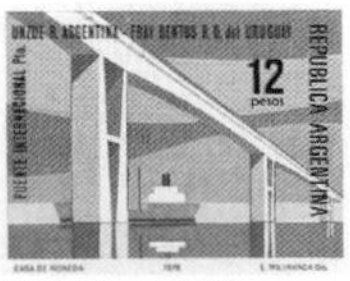

577 Bridge and Ship

1976. "International Bridge" between Unzue (Argentina) and Fray Bentos (Uruguay).

1525	**577**	12p. multicoloured	1·30	25

578 Cooling Tower and Pipelines

1976. General Mosconi Petrochemical Project.

1526	**578**	28p. multicoloured	75	20

579 Teodoro Fels and Bleriot XI

1976. Air Force Day.

1527	**579**	15p. multicoloured	65	15

580 *Nativity* (E. Chiapetto)

1976. Christmas.

1528	**580**	20p. multicoloured	1·10	45

581 Dr. D. Velez Sarsfield (statesman)

1977. Death Cent (1975) of Dr. D. V. Sarsfield.

1529	**581**	50p. brown and red	1·30	45

582 Conference Emblem

1977. United Nations Water Conference.

1530	**582**	70p. multicoloured	1·10	35

583 *The Visit* (Horacio Butler)

1977. Plastic Arts. Multicoloured.

1531	50p. Type **583**	1·00	25
1532	70p. *Consecration* (M. P. Caride) (vert)	1·40	45

584 World Cup Emblem

1977. World Cup Football Championship, Argentina. Multicoloured.

1533	30p. Type **584**	75	25
1534	70p. Stadium and flags (vert)	1·40	35

585 City of La Plata Museum

1977

1535	**585**	5p. black and brown	40	10
1536	-	10p. black and blue	25	10
1538	-	20p. black and yellow	40	10
1539	-	40p. black and blue	50	10
1540	-	50p. black and yellow	65	20
1541	-	50p. black and brown	65	15
1542	-	100p. black and pink	50	10
1543	-	100p. black and orange	65	15
1544	-	100p. black and green	50	10
1545	-	200p. black and blue	75	25
1546	-	280p. black and lilac	11·50	1·30
1547b	-	300p. black and yellow	1·20	25
1548	-	480p. black and yellow	1·80	35
1549b	-	500p. black and green	2·20	25
1550	-	520p. black and orange	2·40	35
1551	-	800p. black and purple	2·75	35
1552a	-	1000p. black and gold	3·75	35
1553	-	1000p. black and yellow	3·25	45
1554	-	2000p. multicoloured	2·75	45

DESIGNS—HORIZ: 10p. House of Independence, Tucuman; 20p. Type **585**; 50p. (No. 1541), Cabildo, Buenos Aires; 100p. (Nos. 1542/3), Columbus Theatre, Buenos Aires; 280p., 300p. Rio Grande Museum Chapel, Tierra del Fuego; 480p., 520p., 800p. San Ignacio Mission Church ruins; 500p. Candonga Chapel; 1000p. General Post Office, Buenos Aires (No. 1552 39×29 mm, No. 1553 32×21 mm); 2000p. Civic Centre, Bariloche. VERT: 40p. Cabildo, Salta; 50p. (No. 1540), Cabildo, Buenos Aires; 200p. Monument to the Flag, Rosario.

586 Morse Key and Satellite

1977. "Argentine Philately". Multicoloured.

1560	10p.+5p. Type **586**	55	30
1561	20p.+10p. Old and modern mail vans	65	65
1562	60p.+30p. Old and modern ships	1·30	1·00
1563	70p.+35p. SPAD XIII and Boeing 707 aircraft	1·60	1·00

1977. Army Day. As T **390**. Multicoloured.

1564	30p. Trooper of 16th Lancers	1·50	35

587 Schooner *Sarandi*

1977. Navy Day.

1565	**587**	30p. multicoloured	1·50	35

1977. 150th Anniv of Uruguay Post Office. As No. 1325 but colour changed. Surch **100 PESOS 150 ANIV. DEL CORREO NACIONAL DEL URUGUAY**.

1566	100p. on 5p. brown	2·50	1·10

1977. "Argentina '77" Exhibition. As No. 1474c, but inscr "EXPOSICION ARGENTINA '77".

1567	160p.+80p. multicoloured	4·50	3·00

589 Admiral Guillermo Brown

1977. Birth Bicent of Admiral Guillermo Brown.

1568	**589**	30p. multicoloured	65	20

590 Civic Centre, Santa Rosa (La Pampa)

1977. Provinces of the Argentine. Multicoloured.

1569	30p. Type **590**	65	25
1570	30p. Sierra de la Ventana (Buenos Aires)	65	25
1571	30p. Skiers at Chapelco, San Martin de los Andes (Neuquen)	65	25
1572	30p. Lake Fonck (Rio Negro)	65	25

591 Savoia S.16 ter Flying Boat over Rio de la Plata

1977. Air Force and 1926 Buenos Aires–New York Flight Commemoration.

1573	**591**	40p. multicoloured	50	20

592 Jet Fighter Outline

1977. 50th Anniv of Military Aviation Factory.

1574	**592**	30p. blue, pale blue and black	40	10

593 *The Adoration of the Kings* (stained-glass window, Holy Sacrament Basilica, Buenos Aires)

1977. Christmas.

1575	**593**	100p. multicoloured	1·60	25

1978. World Cup Football Championship, Argentina. Sheet 102×133 mm containing No. 1567×4 optd **Argentina 78** and logo.

MS1576	160p.+80p. multicoloured	33·00	31·00

595 World Cup Emblem

1978. World Cup Football Championship, Argentina.

1577	**595**	200p. green and blue	1·50	45

596 Rosario

1978. World Cup Football Championship (3rd issue). Match Sites. Multicoloured.

1578	50p. Type **596**	50	20
1579	100p. Cordoba	50	20
1580	150p. Mendoza	90	25
1581	200p. Mar del Plata	90	25
1582	300p. Buenos Aires	1·60	45

597 Children and Institute Emblem

1978. 50th Anniv of Inter-American Children's Institute.

1583	**597**	100p. multicoloured	65	30

598 *The Working Day* (B. Quinquela Martin)

1978. Argentine Art. Multicoloured.

1584	100p. Type **598**	90	25
1585	100p. *Bust of an Unknown Woman* (Orlando Pierri)	90	25

599 Players from Argentina, Hungary, France and Italy (Group One)

1978. World Cup Football Championship, Argentina. Multicoloured.

1586	100p. Type **599**	50	20
1587	200p. Group Two players	1·30	25
1588	300p. Group Three players	1·80	35
1589	400p. Group Four players	2·40	45
MS1590	89×60 mm. 700p. black and flesh	5·00	4·75

DESIGN: (39×26 mm) 700p. River Plate Stadium.

600 Hooded Siskin

1978. Inter-American Philatelic Exhibition. Multicoloured.

1591	50p.+50p. Type **600**	2·10	1·50
1592	100p.+100p. Double-collared seedeater	2·30	1·50
1593	150p.+150p. Saffron-cowled blackbird	3·25	2·20
1594	200p.+200p. Vermilion flycatcher	3·50	2·50
1595	500p.+500p. Great kiskadee	7·50	6·00

601 Young Tree with Support

1978. Technical Co-operation among Developing Countries Conference, Buenos Aires.

1596	**601**	100p. multicoloured	65	20

602 River Plate Stadium

1978. Argentina's Victory in World Cup Football Championship. Sheet 88×60 mm.

MS1597	**602**	1000p. black, stone and red	6·25	6·00

603 Bank Emblems of 1878 and 1978

1978. Centenary of Bank of Buenos Aires.

1598	**603**	100p. multicoloured	65	20

604 General Manuel Savio and Steel Production

1978. 30th Death Anniv of General Manuel Savio (director of military manufacturing).

1599	**604**	100p. multicoloured	65	20

605 San Martin

1978. Birth Bicentenary of Gen. San Martin.

1600	**605**	2000p. green	7·50	45
1600a	**605**	10000p. blue	11·50	60

606 Numeral

1978

1601	**606**	150p. blue and light blue	65	25
1602	**606**	180p. blue and light blue	65	25
1603	**606**	200p. blue and light blue	60	25

607 Chessboard, Pawn and Queen

1978. 23rd Chess Olympiad, Buenos Aires.

1604	**607**	200p. multicoloured	6·25	95

608 Argentine Flag supporting Globe

1978. 12th Int Cancer Congress, Buenos Aires.

1605	**608**	200p. multicoloured	1·40	25

609 "Correct Franking"

1978. Postal Publicity.

1606	**609**	20p. blue	25	10
1607	-	30p. green	40	15
1608	-	50p. red	65	15

DESIGN—VERT: 30p. "Collect postage stamps". HORIZ: 50p. "Indicate the correct post code".

610 Push-pull Tug

1978. 20th Anniv of Argentine River Fleet. Multicoloured.

1609	100p. Type **610**	50	20
1610	200p. Tug *Legador*	90	25
1611	300p. Tug *Rio Parana Mini*	1·30	35
1612	400p. River passenger ship *Ciudad de Parana*	1·80	35

611 Bahia Blanca and Arms

1978. 150th Anniv of Bahia Blanca.

1613	**611**	200p. multicoloured	90	35

612 *To Spain* (Arturo Dresco)

1978. Visit of King and Queen of Spain.

1614	**612**	300p. multicoloured	5·00	60

613 Stained-glass Window, San Isidro Cathedral, Buenos Aires

1978. Christmas.

1615	**613**	200p. multicoloured	1·10	25

614 *Chacabuco Slope* (Pedro Subercaseaux)

1978. Birth Bicent of General Jose de San Martin.

1616	500p. Type **614**	3·25	45
1617	1000p. *The Embrace of Maipo* (Pedro Subercaseaux) (vert)	6·25	60

615 San Martin Stamp of 1877 and U.P.U. Emblem

1979. Cent of Argentine Membership of U.P.U.

1618	**615**	200p. blue, black & brn	90	20

616 Mariano Moreno (revolutionary)

1979. Celebrities.

1619	**616**	200p. yellow, blk & red	90	20
1620	-	200p. blue, blk & dp bl	90	20

DESIGNS: No. 1620, Adolfo Alsina (statesman).

617 *Still Life* (Ernesto de la Carcova)

1979. Argentine Paintings. Multicoloured.

1621	200p. Type **617**	75	25
1622	300p. *The Washer-woman* (F. Brughetti)	1·50	45

618 Balcarce Antenna and Radio Waves

1979. Third Inter-American Telecommunications Conference.

1623	**618**	200p. multicoloured	1·00	35

619 Rosette

1979

1624	**619**	240p. blue and brown	65	25
1625	**619**	260p. blue and black	65	25
1626	**619**	290p. blue and brown	75	25
1627	**619**	310p. blue and purple	75	25
1628	**619**	350p. blue and red	1·00	25
1629	**619**	450p. blue and ultram	90	25
1630	**619**	600p. blue and green	90	25
1631	**619**	700p. blue and black	1·10	25
1632	**619**	800p. blue and orange	75	25
1632a	**619**	1100p. blue and grey	1·60	25
1632b	**619**	1500p. blue and black	90	2·40
1632c	**619**	1700p. blue and green	90	25

620 Olives

1979. Agricultural Products. Multicoloured.

1633	100p. Type **620**	75	45
1634	200p. Tea	1·00	60
1635	300p. Sorghum	1·90	70
1636	400p. Flax	2·10	95

621 "75" and Symbol

1979. 75th Anniv of Argentine Automobile Club.

1637	**621**	200p. multicoloured	65	30

622 Laurel Leaves and Army Emblem

1979. Naming of Village Subteniente Berdina, Tucuman.

1638	**622**	200p. multicoloured	70	30

623 Wheat Exchange and Emblem

1979. 125th Anniv of Wheat Exchange, Buenos Aires.

1639	**623**	200p. blue, gold & black	65	30

624 *Uruguay* (sail/steam gunboat)

1979. Navy Day.

1640	**624**	250p. multicoloured	1·50	60

1979. Army Day. As T **390**. Multicoloured.

1641	200p. Trooper of Mounted Chasseurs, 1817	1·80	45

625 *Comodoro Rivadavia* (hydrographic survey ship)

1979. Naval Hydrographic Service.

1642	**625**	250p. multicoloured	1·50	60

626 Tree and Man Symbol

1979. Ecology Day.

1643	**626**	250p. multicoloured	1·00	35

627 SPAD XIII and Vicente Almandos

1979. Air Force Day.

1644	**627**	250p. multicoloured	1·30	35

628 *Military Occupation of Rio Negro by Gen. Julio A. Roca's Expedition* (detail, J. M. Blanes)

1979. Centenary of Conquest of the Desert.

1645	**628**	250p. multicoloured	1·30	35

629 Caravel *Magdalena*

1979. "Buenos Aires '80" International Stamp Exhibition. Multicoloured.
1646 400p.+400p. Type **629** 6·25 3·75
1647 500p.+500p. Three-masted sailing ship 7·50 4·25
1648 600p.+600p. Corvette *Descubierta* 10·50 8·75
1649 1500p.+1500p. Yacht *Fortuna* 25·00 13·00

630 Rowland Hill

1979. Death Centenary of Sir Rowland Hill.
1650 **630** 300p. black, grey & red 1·00 35

631 Francisco de Viedma y Narvaez Monument (A. Funes and J. Agosta)

1979. Bicentenary of Founding of Viedma and Carmen de Patagones Towns.
1651 **631** 300p. multicoloured 1·50 35

632 Pope Paul VI

1979. Election of Pope John Paul I.
1652 **632** 500p. black 1·80 45
1653 - 500p. black 1·80 45
DESIGN: No. 1653, Pope John Paul I.

633 Molinas Church

1979. Churches. Multicoloured.
1654 100p.+50p. Purmamarca Church 50 20
1655 200p.+100p. Type **633** 75 25
1656 300p.+150p. Animana Church 1·10 45
1657 400p.+200p. San Jose de Lules Church 1·60 70

1979. 75th Anniv of Rosario Philatelic Society. No. 1545 optd **75 ANIV. SOCIEDAD FILATELICA DE ROSARIO**.
1658 200p. blue and black 1·10 35

635 Children's Faces, and Sun on Map of Argentina

1979. Resettlement Policy.
1659 **635** 300p. yellow, black & bl 1·30 45

636 Stained-glass Window, Salta Cathedral

1979. Christmas.
1660 **636** 300p. multicoloured 1·10 35

637 Institute Emblem

1979. Centenary of Military Geographical Institute.
1661 **637** 300p. multicoloured 1·30 45

638 General Mosconi and Oil Rig

1979. Birth Centenary of General Enrique Mosconi.
1662 **638** 1000p. blue and black 2·75 85

639 Buenos Aires 3p. Stamp of 1858

1979. Prenfil 80 International Exhibition of Philatelic Literature and Journalism, Buenos Aires. Four sheets 89×60 mm containing designs as T **639**.
MS1663 (a) 250p.+250p. stone and vermilion; (b) 750p.+750p. flesh and black; (c) 1000p.+1000p. multicoloured; (d) 2000p.+2000p. black, green and vermilion 32·00 30·00
DESIGNS—VERT: 750p. Rowland Hill; 2000p. International Year of the Child emblem. HORIZ: 1000p. Argentine 5c. Columbus stamp of 1892.

640 Rotary Emblem and Globe

1979. 75th Anniv of Rotary International.
1664 **640** 300p. multicoloured 3·25 60

641 Girl with Ruddy Ground Doves

1979. International Year of the Child.
1665 **641** 500p. brown, blue & blk 1·40 60
1666 - 1000p. multicoloured 2·75 70
DESIGN: 1000p. "Family".

642 Guillermo Brown

1980
1667 **642** 5000p. black 9·50 35
1668 **642** 30000p. black and blue 5·75 1·10

643 I.T.U. Emblem and Microphone

1980. Regional Administrative Conference on Broadcasting, Buenos Aires.
1669 **643** 500p. blue, gold & ultram 2·50 35

644 Organization of American States Emblem

1980. Day of the Americas.
1670 **644** 500p. multicoloured 1·00 30

645 Angel

1980. Centenary of Argentinian Red Cross.
1671 **645** 500p. multicoloured 1·00 30

646 Salto Grande Hydro-electric Complex

1980. National Development Projects. Multicoloured.
1672 300p. Type **646** 90 35
1673 300p. Zarate-Brazo Largo bridge 90 35
1674 300p. Dish aerials, Balcarce 90 35

647 Hipolito Bouchard and Sail Frigate *La Argentina*

1980. Navy Day.
1675 **647** 500p. multicoloured 1·30 45

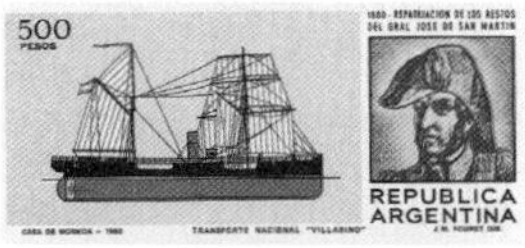

648 *Villarino* and Woodcut of San Martin Theodore by Gericault

1980. Centenary of Return of General Jose de San Martin's Remains.
1676 **648** 500p. multicoloured 1·30 45

649 *Gazeta de Buenos-Ayres* and Signature of Dr. Mariano Moreno (first editor)

1980. Journalists' Day.
1677 **649** 500p. multicoloured 1·00 25

650 Part of Mural

1980. 400th Anniv of Buenos Aires. Sheet 249×103 mm containing T **650** and similar vert designs forming a composite design depicting the ceramic mural by Rodolfo Franco in Cathedral Underground Station.
MS1678 500p.×14 multicoloured 23·00 21·00

651 Soldier feeding Dove

1980. Army Day.
1679 **651** 500p. green, blk & gold 1·50 45

652 Lt. Gen. Aramburu

1980. Tenth Death Anniv of Lt. Gen. Pedro Eugenio Aramburu.
1680 **652** 500p. yellow and black 1·00 35

653 Gen. Juan Gregorio de Las Heras

1980. National Heroes.
1681 **653** 500p. stone and black 1·00 35
1682 - 500p. yellow, blk & pur 1·00 35
1683 - 500p. mauve and black 1·00 35
DESIGNS: No. 1682, Bernardino Rivadavia; 1683, Brigadier-General Jose Matias Zapiola.

654 University of La Plata

1980. 75th Anniv of La Plata University.
1684 **654** 500p. multicoloured 1·00 30

655 Major Francisco de Arteaga and Avro 504K

1980. Air Force Day.
1685 **655** 500p. multicoloured 1·10 30

656 Flag and "Pencil" Figure

1980. National Census.
1686 **656** 500p. black and blue 2·00 30

657 King Penguin

1980. 75th Anniv of Argentine Presence in South Orkneys and 150th Anniv of Political and Military Command for the Malvinas. Two sheets each 151×174 mm containing T **657** and similar vert designs. Multicoloured.
MS1687 Two sheets (a) 150p.×12 Centre two stamps depict South Orkneys Naval Station; (b) 500p.×12 Centre two stamps depict "Puerto Soledad 1829" by Luisa Vernet 44·00 41·00

658 Congress Emblem

1980. National Marian Congress, Mendoza.
1688 **658** 700p. multicoloured 1·50 35

659 Heart pierced by Cigarette

1980. Anti-smoking Campaign.
1689 **659** 700p. multicoloured 1·60 35

660 Part of Mural

1980. Buenos Aires 80 International Stamp Exhibition. Sheet 251×105 mm containing T **660** and similar vert designs forming a composite design depicting the ceramic mural by Alfredo Guido in the 9th July Underground Station.
MS1690 500p.×14 multicoloured 20·00 19·00

661 Radio Antenna and Call Sign

1980. Radio Amateurs.
1691 **661** 700p. blue, black & green 1·40 35

662 Academy Emblem

1980. 50th Anniv of Technical Military Academy.
1692 **662** 700p. multicoloured 1·40 35

663 Commemorative Medallion

1980. Christmas. 150th Anniv of Appearance of Holy Virgin to St. Catherine Laboure.
1693 **663** 700p. multicoloured 1·40 35

664 Plan of Lujan Cathedral and Outline of Virgin

1980. Christmas. 350th Anniv of Appearance of Holy Virgin at Lujan.
1694 **664** 700p. green and brown 1·40 35

665 Simon Bolivar

1980. 150th Death Anniv of Simon Bolivar.
1695 **665** 700p. multicoloured 1·40 35

666 Football and Flags of Competing Nations

1981. Gold Cup Football Competition, Montevideo.
1696 **666** 1000p. multicoloured 2·00 35

667 *Lujan Landscape* (Marcos Tiglio)

1981. Paintings. Multicoloured.
1697 1000p. Type **667** 1·60 60
1698 1000p. *Effect of Light on Lines* (Miguel Angel Vidal) 1·60 60

668 Congress Emblem

1981. International Congress on Medicine and Sciences applied to Sport.
1699 **668** 1000p. blue, brown & blk 1·40 35

669 Esperanza Army Base, Antarctica

1981. 20th Anniv of Antarctic Treaty. Multicoloured.
1700 1000p. Type **669** 2·50 70
1701 2000p. Map of Vicecomodoro Marambio Island and De Havilland Twin Otter airplane (59½×25 mm) 4·50 95
1702 2000p. Icebreaker *Almirante Irizar* 4·50 95

670 Military Club

1981. Centenary of Military Club. Multicoloured.
1703 1000p. Type **670** 1·30 35
1704 2000p. Blunderbusses 1·50 45

671 *Minuet* (Carlos E. Pellegrini)

1981. "Espamer '81" International Stamp Exhibition, Buenos Aires (1st issue).
1705 **671** 500p.+250p. purple, gold and brown 1·40 70
1706 - 700p.+350p. green, gold and brown 2·00 1·20
1707 - 800p.+400p. brown, gold and deep brown 2·10 1·50
1708 - 1000p.+500p. mult 2·75 2·10

DESIGNS: 700p. *La Media Cana* (Carlos Morel); 800p. *Cielito* (Carlos E. Pellegrini); 1000p. *El Gato* (Juan Leon Palliere).
See also Nos. 1719 and 1720/1.

672 Juan A. Alvarez de Arenales

1981. Celebrities' Anniversaries.
1709 **672** 1000p. black, yell & brn 1·30 35
1710 - 1000p. blk, pink & lilac 1·30 35
1711 - 1000p. black, pale green and green 1·30 35

DESIGNS: No. 1709, Type **672** (patriot, 150th death anniv); 1710, Felix G. Frias (writer and politician, death centenary); 1711, Jose E. Uriburu (statesman, 150th birth centenary).

1981. 50th Anniv of Bahia Blanca Philatelic and Numismatic Society. No. 1553 optd **50 ANIV DE LA ASOCIACION FILATELICA Y NUMISMATICA DE BAHIA BLANCA**.
1712 1000p. black and yellow 3·25 60

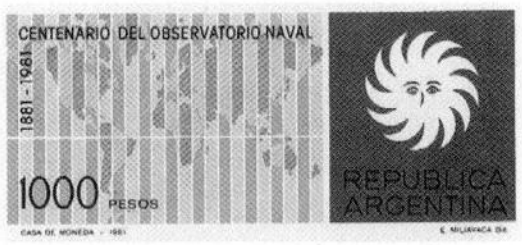

674 World Map divided into Time Zones and Sun

1981. Centenary of Naval Observatory.
1713 **674** 1000p. multicoloured 1·90 45

675 *St. Cayetano* (detail, stained-glass window, San Cayetano Basilica)

1981. 500th Death Anniv of St. Cayetano (founder of Teatino Order).
1714 **675** 1000p. multicoloured 1·30 35

676 Pablo Castaibert and Bleriot XI

1981. Air Force Day.
1715 **676** 1000p. multicoloured 2·10 45

677 First Argentine Blast Furnace, Sierra de Palpala

1981. 22nd Latin American Steel-makers Congress, Buenos Aires.
1716 **677** 1000p. multicoloured 1·10 30

678 Emblem of National Directorate for Special Education

1981. International Year of Disabled People.
1717 **678** 1000p. multicoloured 1·30 30

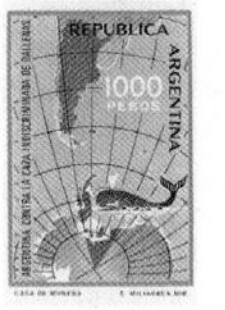

679 Sperm Whale and Map of Argentina and Antarctica

1981. Campaign against Indiscriminate Whaling.
1718 **679** 1000p. multicoloured 9·25 60

680 "Espamer 81" Emblem and 15th-century Caravel

1981. "Espamer 81" International Stamp Exhibition, Buenos Aires (2nd issue).
1719 **680** 1300p. pink, brn & blk 1·60 60

681 *San Martin at the Battle of Bailen* (equestrian statuette)

1981. "Espamer 81" International Stamp Exhibition, Buenos Aires (3rd issue).
1720 **681** 1000p. multicoloured 65 30
1721 **681** 1500p. multicoloured 90 35

682 Argentine Army Emblem

1981. Argentine Army. 175th Anniv of Infantry Regiment No. 1 "Patricios". Multicoloured.
1722 1500p. Type **682** 75 35
1723 1500p. "Patricios" badge 75 35

1981. Philatelic Services Course, Postal Union of the Americas and Spain Technical Training School, Buenos Aires. Optd **CURSO SUPERIOR DE ORGANIZACION DE SERVICIOS FILATELICOS-UPAE-BUENOS AIRES-1981**.
1724 **680** 1300p. pink, brn & blk 2·50 45

684 Football

1981. Espamer 81 International Stamp Exhibition, Buenos Aires (4th issue). Sheet 137×130 mm containing T **684** and similar vert designs. Multicoloured.
MS1725 2000p. Type **684**; 3000p. Tackle; 5000p. Dribbling; 15000p. Goalkeeper 12·50 12·00

685 "Patacon" (one peso piece)

1981. Centenary of First Argentine Coins.
1726 **685** 2000p. silver, blk & pur 90 25
1727 - 3000p. gold, black & bl 1·10 35
DESIGN: 3000p. Argentine oro (five pesos piece).

686 Stained-glass Window, Church of Our Lady of Mercy, Tucuman

1981. Christmas.
1728 **686** 1500p. multicoloured 3·75 85

687 "Drive Carefully"

1981. Road Safety. Multicoloured.

1729	1000p. "Observe traffic lights"	2·50	60
1730	2000p. Type **687**	1·30	70
1731	3000p. Zebra Crossing ("Cross at the white lines") (horiz)	1·90	75
1732	4000p. Headlights ("Don't dazzle") (horiz)	2·10	85

688 Francisco Luis Bernardez

1982. Authors. Multicoloured.

1733	1000p. Type **688**	2·50	60
1734	2000p. Lucio V. Mansilla	1·30	65
1735	3000p. Conrado Nale Roxlo	1·90	85
1736	4000p. Victoria Ocampo	2·50	95

689 Emblem

1982. 22nd American Air Force Commanders Conference, Buenos Aires.

1737	**689**	2000p. multicoloured	2·00	45

690 Dr. Robert Koch

1982. 25th World Tuberculosis Conf, Buenos Aires.

1738	**690**	2000p. brown, red & blk	1·90	45

691 Pre-Columbian Artwork and Signature of Hernando de Lerma (founder)

1982. 400th Anniv of Salta City.

1739	**691**	2000p. green, blk & gold	2·50	45
MS1740		89×60 mm. **691** 5000p. green, black and gold (39×26 mm)	5·00	4·75

1982. Argentine Invasion of the Falkland Islands. Optd **LAS MALVINAS SON ARGENTINAS**.

1741	**619**	1700p. blue and green	1·00	35

693 *Poseidon with Trophies of War* (sculpture) and Naval Centre Arms

1982. Centenary of Naval Centre.

1742	**693**	2000p. multicoloured	1·30	45

694 *Chorisia speciosa*

1982. Flowers. Multicoloured.

1743	200p. *Zinnia peruviana*	50	15
1744	300p. *Ipomoea purpurea*	50	15
1745	400p. *Tillandsia aeranthos*	50	15
1746	500p. Type **694**	50	15
1747	800p. *Oncidium bifolium*	50	15
1748	1000p. *Erythrina crista-galli*	50	15
1749	2000p. *Jacaranda mimosifolia*	55	15
1750	3000p. *Bauhinia candicans*	1·00	35
1751	5000p. *Tecoma stans*	1·00	35
1752	10000p. *Tabebuia ipe*	1·80	35
1753	20000p. *Passiflora coerulea*	1·90	35
1754	30000p. *Aristolochia littoralis*	2·75	60
1755	50000p. *Oxalis enneaphylla*	5·25	85

695 Juan C. Sanchez

1982. Tenth Death Anniv of Lt. Gen. Juan C. Sanchez.

1761	**695**	5000p. multicoloured	1·50	35

696 Don Luis Verne (first Commander)

1982. 153rd Anniv of Political and Military Command for the Malvinas.

1762	**696**	5000p. black and brown	2·50	85
1763	-	5000p. light bl, blk & bl	1·90	60

DESIGN (82×28 mm): No. 1763, Map of the South Atlantic Islands.

697 Pope John Paul II

1982. Papal Visit.

1764	**697**	5000p. multicoloured	3·25	85

698 San Martin

1982

1765	**698**	50000p. brown and red	12·00	1·40

699 *The Organ Player* (detail, Aldo Severi)

1982. Paintings. Multicoloured.

1766	2000p. Type **699**	1·30	40
1767	3000p. *Flowers* (Santiago Cogorno)	1·40	45

700 *Gen. de Sombras* (Sylvia Sieburger)

1982. "Argentine Philately". Tapestries. Multicoloured.

1768	1000p.+500p. Type **700**	75	60
1769	2000p.+1000p. *Inter-pretation of a Rectangle* (Silke Haupt)	90	70
1770	3000p.+1500p. *Canal* (detail, Beatriz Bongliani) (horiz)	1·00	85
1771	4000p.+2000p. *Pueblito de Tilcara* (Tana Sachs) (horiz)	1·10	95

701 Petrol Pump and Sugar Cane

1982. Alconafta (petrol-alcohol mixture) Campaign.

1772	**701**	2000p. multicoloured	1·40	35

1982. 50th Anniv of Tucuman Philatelic Society. No. 1751 optd **50 ANIVERSARIO SOCIEDAD FILATELICA DE TUCUMAN**.

1773	5000p. multicoloured	3·75	1·40

703 Belt Buckle with Argentine Scout Emblem

1982. 75th Anniv of Boy Scout Movement.

1774	**703**	5000p. multicoloured	3·50	60

704 Map of Africa showing Namibia

1982. Namibia Day.

1775	**704**	5000p. multicoloured	1·50	35

705 Rio Tercero Nuclear Power Station

1982. Atomic Energy. Multicoloured.

1776	2000p. Type **705**	65	15
1777	2000p. Control room of Rio Tercero power station	65	15

706 Our Lady of Itati, Corrientes

1982. Churches and Cathedrals of the North-east Provinces.

1778	**706**	2000p. green and black	90	55
1779	-	3000p. grey and purple	1·00	60
1780	-	5000p. blue and purple	1·60	65
1781	-	10000p. brown and black	2·50	85

DESIGNS—VERT: 3000p. Resistencia Cathedral, Chaco. HORIZ: 5000p. Formosa Cathedral; 10000p. Ruins of San Ignacio, Misiones.

707 *Sidereal Tension* (M. A. Agatiello)

1982. Art. Multicoloured.

1782	2000p. Type **707**	1·40	60
1783	3000p. *Sugerencia II* (E. MacEntyre)	1·50	65
1784	5000p. *Storm* (Carlos Silva)	2·10	70

708 Games Emblem and Santa Fe Bridge

1982. 2nd "Southern Cross" Games, Rosario and Santa Fe.

1785	**708**	2000p. blue and black	90	35

709 Volleyball

1982. Tenth Men's Volleyball World Championship.

1786	**709**	2000p. multicoloured	50	25
1787	**709**	5000p. multicoloured	1·00	35

710 Road Signs

1982. 50th Anniv of National Roads Administration.

1788	**710**	5000p. multicoloured	1·00	30

711 Monument to the Army of the Andes

1982. Centenary of *Los Andes* Newspaper.

1789	**711**	5000p. multicoloured	90	25

712 La Plata Cathedral

1982. Centenary of La Plata. Multicoloured.

1790	5000p. Type **712**	1·40	35
1791	5000p. Municipal Palace	1·40	35
MS1792	120×115 mm. 2500p.×6 (a) Cathedral; (b) Allegorical head (top); (c) Observatory; (d) Municipal Palace; (e) Allegorical head (bottom); (f) Natural Sciences Museum	4·00	3·75

713 First Oil Rig

1982. 75th Anniv of Discovery of Oil in Comodoro Rivadavia.

1793	**713**	5000p. multicoloured	1·90	35

714 Dr. Carlos Pellegrini (founder) (after J. Sorolla y Bastida)

1982. Cent of Buenos Aires Jockey Club. Multicoloured.

1794	5000p. Jockey Club emblem	1·50	35
1795	5000p. Type **714**	1·50	35

715 Cross of St. Damian, Assisi

1982. 800th Birth Anniv of St. Francis of Assisi.

1796	**715**	5000p. multicoloured	2·10	35

716 "St. Vincent de Paul" (stained-glass window, Our Lady of the Miraculous Medal, Buenos Aires)

1982. Christmas.

1797	**716**	3000p. multicoloured	3·25	60

717 Pedro B. Palacios

1982. Authors. Each red and green.

1798	1000p. Type **717**	40	10
1799	2000p. Leopoldo Marechal	50	15
1800	3000p. Delfina Bunge de Galvez	65	20
1801	4000p. Manuel Galvez	75	25
1802	5000p. Evaristo Carriego	90	30

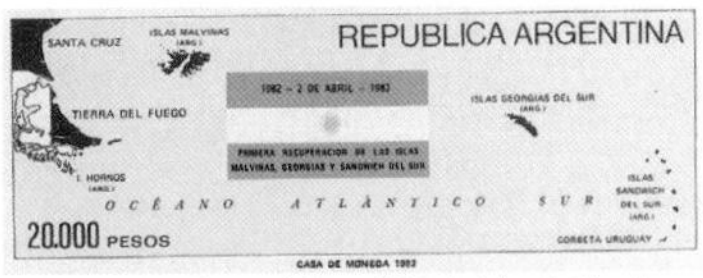

718 Argentine Flag and Map of South Atlantic Islands (image scaled to 58% of original size)

1983. First Anniv of Argentine Invasion of Falkland Islands.

1803	**718**	20000p. multicoloured	2·50	85

719 Sitram (automatic message transmission service) Emblem

1983. Information Technology. Multicoloured.

1804	5000p. Type **719**	2·00	95
1805	5000p. Red Arpac (data communications system) emblem	2·00	95

720 Naval League Emblem

1983. Navy Day. 50th Anniv of Naval League.

1806	**720**	5000p. multicoloured	1·00	35

721 Allegorical Figure (Victor Rebuffo)

1983. 25th Anniv of National Arts Fund.

1807	**721**	5000p. multicoloured	75	25

722 Golden Saloon

1983. 75th Anniv of Columbus Theatre, Buenos Aires. Multicoloured.

1808	5000p. Type **722**	1·10	60
1809	10000p. Stage curtain	1·60	70

723 Marbles

1983. Argentine Philately. Children's Games (1st series). Multicoloured.

1810	20c.+10c. Type **723**	50	30
1811	30c.+15c. Skipping	65	35
1812	50c.+25c. Hopscotch	1·40	45
1813	1p.+50c. Boy with kite	1·80	70
1814	2p.+1p. Boy with spinning top	2·50	95

See also Nos. 1870/4.

724 Maned Wolf

1983. Protected Animals (1st series). Multicoloured.

1815	1p. Type **724**	1·60	35
1816	1p.50 Pampas deer	2·40	45
1817	2p. Giant anteater	2·50	60
1818	2p.50 Jaguar	3·00	70

See also Nos 1883/87.

1983. Flowers. As T **694** but inscr in new currency. Multicoloured.

1819	5c. Type **694**	75	20
1820	10c. *Erythrina crista-galli*	25	10
1821	20c. *Jacaranda mimosifolia*	25	10
1822	30c. *Bauhinia candicans*	65	20
1823	40c. *Eichhornia crassipes*	40	10
1824	50c. *Tecoma stans*	25	10
1825	1p. *Tabebuia ipe*	50	10
1826	1p.80 *Mutisia retusa*	40	10
1827	2p. *Passiflora coerulea*	50	10
1828	3p. *Aristolochia littoralis*	65	10
1829	5p. *Oxalis enneaphylla*	90	15
1830	10p. *Alstroemeria aurantiaca*	1·50	25
1831	20p. *Ipomoea purpurea*	65	10
1832	30p. *Embothrium coccineum*	3·25	25
1833	50p. *Tillandsia aeranthos*	90	25
1834	100p. *Oncidium bifolium*	2·50	25
1835	300p. *Cassia carnaval*	2·75	70

725 *Founding of City of Catamarca* (detail, Luis Varela Lezana)

1983. 300th Anniv of San Fernando del Valle de Catamarca.

1836	**725**	1p. multicoloured	65	30

726 Brother Mamerto Esquiu

1983. Death Centenary of Brother Mamerto Esquiu, Bishop of Cordoba.

1837	**726**	1p. black, red and grey	65	30

727 Bolivar (painting by Herrera Toro after engraving by C. Turner)

1983. Birth Bicentenary of Simon Bolivar.

1838	**727**	1p. multicoloured	65	30
1839	-	2p. red and black	1·00	45

DESIGN: 2p. Bolivar (engraving by Kepper).

728 San Martin

1983

1840	**728**	10p. green and black	4·50	60
1841	-	20p. blue and black	4·00	2·40
1842	**728**	50p. brown and blue	3·50	2·50
1843	-	200p. black and blue	3·25	1·80
1844	-	500p. blue and brown	3·50	85

DESIGNS: 20, 500p. Guillermo Brown; 200p. Manuel Belgrano.

729 Gen. Toribio de Luzuriaga

1983. Birth Bicentenary (1982) of Gen. Toribio de Luzuriaga.

1845	**729**	1p. multicoloured	90	35

730 Grand Bourg House, Buenos Aires

1983. 50th Anniv of Sanmartinian National Institute.

1846	**730**	2p. brown and black	1·00	35

731 Dove and Rotary Emblem

1983. Rotary International South American Regional Conference, Buenos Aires.

1847	**731**	1p. multicoloured	1·00	35

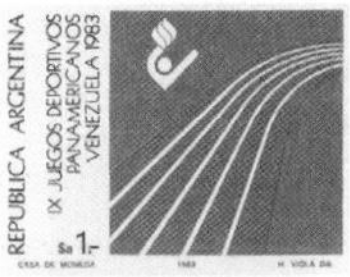

732 Running Track and Games Emblem

1983. 9th Pan-American Games, Venezuela.

1848	**732**	1p. red, green & black	75	25
1849	-	2p. multicoloured	1·00	35

DESIGN: 2p. Games emblem.

733 W.C.Y. Emblem

1983. World Communications Year (1st issue).

1850	**733**	2p. multicoloured	1·00	35

See also Nos. 1853/6 and 1857.

734 *The Squash Peddler* (Antonio Berni)

1983. Argentine Paintings. Multicoloured.

1851	1p. Type **734**	75	25
1852	2p. *Figure in Yellow* (Luis Seoane)	1·00	35

735 Ox-drawn Wagon

1983. World Communications Year (2nd issue). Mail Transport. Multicoloured.

1853	1p. Type **735**	90	45
1854	2p. Horse-drawn mail cart	1·00	60
1855	4p. Locomotive "La Portena"	1·50	65
1856	5p. Tram	1·60	70

736 *Central Post Office, Buenos Aires* (Lola Frexas)

1983. World Communications Year (3rd issue).

1857	**736**	2p. multicoloured	65	30

737 Rockhopper Penguin

1983. Fauna and Pioneers of Southern Argentina. Multicoloured.

1858a	2p. Type **737**	65	35
1858b	2p. Wandering albatross	65	35
1858c	2p. Black-browed albatross	65	35
1858d	2p. Macaroni penguin	65	35
1858e	2p. Luis Piedra Buena (after Juan R. Mezzadra)	65	35
1858f	2p. Carlos Maria Moyano (after Mezzadra)	65	35
1858g	2p. Luis Py (after Mezzadra)	65	35
1858h	2p. Augusto Lasserre (after Horacio Alvarez Boero)	65	35
1858i	2p. Light-mantled sooty albatross	65	35
1858j	2p. Leopard seal	65	35
1858k	2p. Crabeater seal	65	35
1858l	2p. Weddell seal	65	35

738 Coin of 1813

1983. Transfer of Presidency.

1859	**738**	2p. silver, black and blue	1·00	20

739 "Christmas Manger" (tapestry by Silke)

1983. Christmas. Multicoloured.

1860	2p. Type **739**	95	20
1861	3p. Stained-glass window, San Carlos de Bariloche Church	1·50	45

740 Printing Cylinder and Newspaper

1984. Centenary of *El Dia* Newspaper.

1862	**740**	4p. multicoloured	75	20

741 Compass Rose

1984. "Espana 84" (Madrid) and "Argentina 85" (Buenos Aires) International Stamp Exhibitions (1st issue). Multicoloured.

1863	5p.+2p.50 Type **741**	1·30	45
1864	5p.+2p.50 Arms of Spain and Argentine Republic	1·30	45
1865	5p.+2p.50 Arms of Christopher Columbus	1·30	45
1866	5p.+2p.50 *Nina*	1·30	45
1867	5p.+2p.50 *Pinta*	1·30	45
1868	5p.+2p.50 *Santa Maria*	1·30	45

See also Nos. 1906/10, 1917/18 and 1920/4.

742 College

1984. Centenary of Alejandro Carbo Teacher Training College, Cordoba.

1869	**742**	10p. multicoloured	75	30

1984. Argentine Philately. Children's Games (2nd series). As T **723**. Multicoloured.

1870	2p.+1p. Blind man's buff	65	35
1871	3p.+1p.50 Girls throwing hoop	70	40
1872	4p.+2p. Leap frog	75	55
1873	5p.+2p.50 Boy rolling hoop	90	60
1874	6p.+3p. Ball and stick	1·10	85

743 Rowing and Basketball

1984. Olympic Games, Los Angeles. Multicoloured.

1875	5p. Type **743**	50	35
1876	5p. Weightlifting and discus	50	35
1877	10p. Cycling and swimming	90	45
1878	10p. Pole vault and fencing	90	45

744 Wheat

1984. Food Supplies. Multicoloured.

1879	10p. Type **744** (18th F.A.O. Latin American Regional Conference, Buenos Aires)	1·00	45
1880	10p. Sunflowers (World Food Day)	1·00	45
1881	10p. Maize (3rd National Maize Congress, Pergamino)	1·00	45

745 Stock Exchange

1984. Centenary of Rosario Stock Exchange.

1882	**745**	10p. multicoloured	90	45

1984. Protected Animals (2nd series). As T **724**. Multicoloured.

1883	20p. Brazilian merganser	1·60	45
1884	20p. Black-fronted piping guan	1·60	45
1885	20p. Hooded grebes	1·60	45
1886	20p. Vicunas	1·60	45
1887	20p. Chilean guemal	1·60	45

746 Festival Emblem

1984. First Latin American Theatre Festival, Cordoba.

1888	**746**	20p. multicoloured	65	35

747 *Apostles' Communion* (detail, Fra Angelico)

1984. 50th Anniv of Buenos Aires International Eucharist Congress.

1889	**747**	20p. multicoloured	75	45

748 Antonio Oneto and Railway Station (Puerto Deseado)

1984. City Centenaries. Multicoloured.

1890	20p. Type **748**	1·30	45
1891	20p. 19th-century view and sail/steam corvette *Parana* (Ushuaia)	1·30	45

749 Glacier

1984. World Heritage Site. Los Glaciares National Park. Multicoloured.

1892	20p. Glacier (different)	1·10	35
1893	30p. Type **749**	1·90	45

1984. 50th Anniv of Buenos Aires Philatelic Centre. No. 1830 optd **1934–50°ANIVERSARIO-1984 CENTRO FILATELICO BUENOS-AIRES**.

1894	10p. multicoloured	75	55

751 *Jesus and the Star* (Diego Aguero)

1984. Christmas. Multicoloured.

1895	20p. Type **751**	1·00	40
1896	30p. *The Three Kings* (Leandro Ruiz)	1·30	45
1897	50p. *The Holy Family* (Maria Castillo) (vert)	1·40	55

752 *Sheds (La Boca)* (Marcos Borio)

1984. Argentine Paintings. Multicoloured.

1898	20p. Type **752**	90	40
1899	20p. *View of the Zoo* (Fermin Eguia) (horiz)	90	40
1900	20p. *Floodlit Congress Building* (Francisco Travieso)	90	40

753 Angel J. Carranza (historian, 150th)

1985. Birth Anniversaries.

1901	**753**	10p. deep blue & blue	75	35
1902	-	20p. deep brown & brn	90	45
1903	-	30p. deep blue & blue	1·00	60
1904	-	40p. black and green	1·60	65

DESIGNS: 20p. Estanislao del Campo (poet, 150th); 30p. Jose Hernandez (journalist, 150th); 40p. Vicente Lopez y Planes (President of Argentine Confederation 1827–28, birth bicent).

754 Guemes and "Infernal" (soldier)

1985. Birth Bicentenary of General Martin Miguel de Guemes (Independence hero).

1905	**754**	30p. multicoloured	50	30

755 Teodoro Fels's Bleriot XI Gnome

1985. "Argentina '85" International Stamp Exhibition, Buenos Aires (2nd issue). First Airmail Flights. Multicoloured.

1906	20p. Type **755** (Buenos Aires–Montevideo, 1917)	40	20
1907	40p. Junkers F-13L (Cordoba–Villa Dolores, 1925)	65	35
1908	60p. Saint-Exupery's Latecoere 25 (first Bahia Blanca-Comodoro Rivadavia, 1929)	1·00	40
1909	80p. *Graf Zeppelin* airship (Argentina-Germany, 1934)	1·30	60
1910	100p. Consolidated PBY-5A Catalina amphibian (to Argentine Antarctic, 1952)	1·80	70

756 Central Bank

1985. 50th Anniv of Central Bank, Buenos Aires.

1911	**756**	80p. multicoloured	1·10	35

757 Jose A. Ferreyra and "Munequitas Portenas"

1985. Argentine Film Directors. Multicoloured.

1912	100p. Type **757**	1·30	60
1913	100p. Leopoldo Torre Nilsson and "Martin Fierro"	1·30	60

758 *Carlos Gardel* (Hermenegildo Sabat)

1985. 50th Death Anniv of Carlos Gardel (entertainer). Multicoloured.

1914	200p. Type **758**	2·50	70
1915	200p. *Carlos Gardel* (Carlos Alonso)	2·50	70
1916	200p. *Carlos Gardel* (Aldo Severi and Martiniano Arce)	2·50	70

759 *The Arrival* (Pedro Figari)

1985. "Argentina '85" International Stamp Exhibition (3rd issue). Multicoloured.

1917	20c. Type **759**	1·50	60
1918	30c. *Mail Coach Square* (detail, Cesareo B. de Quiros)	1·80	65
MS1919	146×74 mm. 20c. (29×39 mm), 30c. (39×29 mm) Details of *Halt in the Country* (Prilidiano Pueyrredon)	6·25	6·00

760 Cover of 1917 Teodoro Fels Flight

1985. "Argentina '85" International Stamp Exhibition (4th issue). Multicoloured.

1920	10c. Type **760**	75	35
1921	10c. Cover of 1925 Cordoba–Villa Dolores flight	75	35
1922	10c. Cover of 1929 Saint-Exupery flight	75	35
1923	10c. Cover of 1934 *Graf Zeppelin* flight	75	35
1924	10c. Cover of 1952 Antarctic flight	75	35

1985. Flowers. As T **694** but with currency expressed as "A". Multicoloured.

1930	½c. *Oxalis enneaphylla*	90	15
1931	1c. *Alstroemeria aurantiaca*	50	10
1932	2c. *Ipomoea purpurea*	50	10
1933	3c. *Embothrium coccineum*	50	10
1934a	5c. *Tillandsia aeranthos*	50	10
1927	8½c. *Erythrina crista-galli*	50	10
1935a	10c. *Oncidium bifolium*	90	15
1936a	20c. *Chorisia speciosa*	65	35
1937	30c. *Cassia carnaval*	1·50	60
1938	50c. *Zinnnia peruviana*	1·90	45
1941	1a. *Begonia micranthera var. Hieronymi*	2·50	45
1941a	2a. *Bauhinia candicans*	1·00	30
1942	5a. *Gymnocalyciun bruchii*	6·25	4·25
1942a	10a. *Eichhornia crassipes*	50	30
1942b	20a. *Mutisia retusa*	15	10
1942c	50a. Passion flower	50	30
1943	100a. *Alstroemeria aurantiaca*	65	20
1943a	300a. *Ipomoea purpurea*	2·00	95
1943b	500a. *Embothrium coccineum*	3·25	1·50

1943c	1000a. *Aristolochia littoralis*	1·00	60
1943d	5000a. *Erythrina crista-galli*	4·75	65
1943e	10000a. *Jacaranda mimosifolia*	7·50	4·75

No. 1927 is 15×23 mm, the remainder 22×32 mm.

761 *Woman with Bird* (Juan del Prete)

1985. Argentine Paintings. Multicoloured.

1944	20c. Type **761**	1·50	60
1945	30c. *Illuminated Fruits* (Fortunato Lacamera)	1·80	70

762 Musical Bow

1985. Traditional Musical Instruments. Multicoloured.

1946	20c. Type **762**	1·00	40
1947	20c. Long flute with drum accompaniment	1·00	40
1948	20c. Frame drum	1·00	40
1949	20c. Pan's flute	1·00	40
1950	20c. Jew's harp	1·00	40

763 Juan Bautista Alberdi (writer)

1985. Anniversaries. Multicoloured.

1951	10c. Type **763** (death centenary (1984))	40	20
1952	20c. Nicolas Avellaneda (President 1874–80, death centenary)	75	35
1953	30c. Brother Luis Beltran (Independence hero, birth bicentenary (1984))	1·10	60
1954	40c. Ricardo Levene (historian) (birth centenary)	2·00	70

764 Roller Skaters

1985. International Youth Year.

1955	**764**	20c. black and blue	1·00	40
1956	-	30c. multicoloured	1·10	45

MS1957 146×74 mm. 1a. multicoloured. Imperf 6·25 6·00

DESIGNS: 30c. "Disappointment". 137×66 mm "Halt in the Country" (Prilidiano Pueyrredon).

765 *Rothschildia jacobaeae*

1985. Argentine Philately. Butterflies.

1958	5c.+2c. Type **765**	1·40	45
1959	10c.+5c. *Heliconius erato phyllis*	1·50	60
1960	20c.+10c. *Precis evarete hilaris*	2·10	1·10
1961	25c.+13c. *Cyanopepla pretiosa*	3·25	1·80
1962	40c.+20c. *Papilio androgeus*	4·25	2·50

766 Forclaz Windmill (Entre Rios)

1985. Tourism. Argentine Provinces. Multicoloured.

1963	10c. Type **766**	75	20
1964	10c. Sierra de la Ventana (Buenos Aires)	75	20
1965	10c. Potrero de los Funes artificial lake (San Luis)	75	20
1966	10c. Church belfry (North-west Argentina)	75	20
1967	10c. Magellanic penguins, Punta Tombo (Chubut)	75	20
1968	10c. Sea of Mirrors (Cordoba)	75	20

767 Hand holding White Stick

1985. National Campaign for the Prevention of Blindness.

1969	**767**	10c. multicoloured	65	20

768 *Birth of Our Lord* (Carlos Cortes)

1985. Christmas. Multicoloured.

1970	10c. Type **768**	65	25
1971	20c. *Christmas* (Hector Viola)	1·40	70

769 Rio Gallegos Cathedral

1985. Centenary of Rio Gallegos.

1972	**769**	10c. multicoloured	2·50	60

770 Grape Harvesting

1986. 50th Anniv of Grape Harvest Nat Festival.

1973	**770**	10c. multicoloured	75	15

771 House of Valentin Alsina (Italian Period)

1986. Buenos Aires Architecture, 1880–1930. Multicoloured.

1974	20c. Type **771**	1·00	45
1975	20c. 1441 Calle Cerrito (French period)	1·00	45
1976	20c. Customs House (Academic period) (horiz)	1·00	45
1977	20c. House, Avenido de Mayo (Art Nouveau)	1·00	45
1978	20c. Isaac Fernandez Blanco Museum (National Restoration period) (horiz)	1·00	45

772 Jubany Base

1986. Argentine Antarctic Research. Multicoloured.

1979	10c. Type **772**	1·50	1·00
1980	10c. Kerguelen fur seal	1·50	1·00
1981	10c. Southern sealion	1·50	1·00
1982	10c. General Belgrano Base	1·50	1·00
1983	10c. Pintado petrel	1·50	1·00
1984	10c. Black-browed albatross	1·50	1·00
1985	10c. King penguin	1·50	1·00
1986	10c. Giant petrel	1·50	1·00
1987	10c. Hugo Alberto Acuna (explorer)	1·50	1·00
1988	10c. Magellanic penguin	1·50	1·00
1989	10c. Magellan snipe	1·50	1·00
1990	10c. Capt. Augustin Servando del Castillo (explorer)	1·50	1·00

773 *Foundation of Nereid* (detail, Lola Mora)

1986. Sculpture. Multicoloured.

1991	20c. Type **773**	1·40	45
1992	30c. *Work Song* (detail, Rogelio Yrurtia)	1·50	55

774 Dr. Alicia Moreau de Justo (suffragist, d. 1986)

1986. Anniversaries.

1993	**774**	10c. black, yellow & brn	75	35
1994	-	10c. black, turq & blue	75	35
1995	-	30c. black, red & mauve	2·30	1·10

DESIGNS: No. 1994, Dr. Emilio Ravignani (historian, birth centenary); 1995, Indira Gandhi (Prime Minister of India, 1st death anniv).

775 Dr. Francisco Narciso Laprida

1986. Birth Bicentenaries of Independence Heroes. Each brown, yellow and black.

1996	20c. Type **775**	90	45
1997	20c. Brig. Gen. Estanislao Lopez	90	45
1998	20c. Gen. Francisco Ramirez	90	45

776 Namuncura

1986. Birth Centenary of Ceferino Namuncura (first Indian seminary student).

1999	**776**	20c. multicoloured	1·00	60

777 Drawing by Nazarena Pastor

1986. Argentine Philately. Children's Drawings. Multicoloured.

2000	5c.+2c. Type **777**	40	20
2001	10c.+5c. Girl and boy holding flowers and balloon (Tatiana Valleistein) (horiz)	65	30
2002	20c.+10c. Boy and girl (Juan Manel Flores)	1·00	95
2003	25c.+13c. Town and waterfront (Marcelo E. Pezzuto) (horiz)	1·40	1·20
2004	40c.+20c. Village (Esteban Diehl) (horiz)	2·00	1·80

1986. No. 1825 surch **A0,10.**

2005	10c. on 1p. *Tabebuia ipe*	1·90	85

779 Argentine Team (value top left)

1986. Argentina, World Cup Football Championship (Mexico) Winners. Multicoloured.

2006	75c. Type **779**	2·10	1·80
2007	75c. Argentine team (value top right)	2·10	1·80
2008	75c. Argentine team (value bottom left)	2·10	1·80
2009	75c. Argentine team (value bottom right)	2·10	1·80
2010	75c. Player shooting for goal	2·10	1·80
2011	75c. Player tackling and goal-keeper on ground	2·10	1·80
2012	75c. Player number 11	2·10	1·80
2013	75c. Player number 7	2·10	1·80
2014	75c. Crowd and Argentina player	2·10	1·80
2015	75c. West German player	2·10	1·80
2016	75c. Goalkeeper on ground	2·10	1·80
2017	75c. Footballers' legs	2·10	1·80
2018	75c. Hand holding World Cup trophy	2·10	1·80
2019	75c. Raised arm and crowded stadium	2·10	1·80
2020	75c. People with flags and cameras	2·10	1·80
2021	75c. Player's body and crowd	2·10	1·80

Nos. 2006/13 were printed together *se-tenant* in a sheetlet of eight stamps arranged in two blocks, each block forming a composite design. Nos. 2014/21 were similarly arranged in a second sheetlet.

780 Municipal Building

1986. Centenary of San Francisco City.

2022	**780**	20c. multicoloured	90	55

781 Old Railway Station

1986. Centenary of Trelew City.

2023	**781**	20c. multicoloured	90	55

782 Emblem and Colours

1986. Mutualism Day.

2024	**782**	20c. multicoloured	90	55

783 *Primitive Retable* (Aniko Szabo)

1986. Christmas. Multicoloured.
2025 20c. Type **783** 1·60 60
2026 30c. *Everybody's Tree* (Franca Delacqua) 1·90 70

784 St. Rosa of Lima

1986. 400th Birth Anniv of St. Rosa de Lima.
2027 **784** 50c. multicoloured 2·50 1·20

785 Municipal Building

1986. Anniversaries. Multicoloured.
2028 20c. Type **785** (bicentenary of Rio Cuarto city) 1·50 45
2029 20c. Palace of Justice, Cordoba (50th anniv) 1·50 45

786 Marine Biology

1987. 25th Anniv of Antarctic Treaty. Multicoloured.
2030 20c. Type **786** 1·50 60
2031 30c. Study of native birds 2·10 70
MS2032 159×89 mm. As Nos. 2030/1 but each 39×49 mm 9·50 8·75

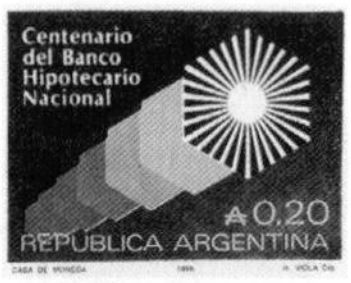

787 Emblem

1987. Centenary of National Mortgage Bank.
2033 **787** 20c. yellow, brown & blk 1·30 70

788 Stylized Pine Trees

1987. Argentine Co-operative Movement.
2034 **788** 20c. multicoloured 1·30 70

789 Pope

1987. Second Visit of Pope John Paul II.
2035 **789** 20c. blue and red 65 35
2036 - 80c. brown and green 2·50 1·20
MS2037 160×90 mm. 1a. multicoloured (34×45 mm) 4·50 4·25
DESIGNS: 80c. Pope in robes with Crucifix; 1a. Pope and children.

790 Flag forming "PAZ" (peace)

1987. International Peace Year.
2038 **790** 20c. blue, dp blue & blk 1·10 35
2039 - 30c. multicoloured 1·20 45
DESIGN: 30c. *Pigeon* (sculpture, Victor Kaniuka).

791 *Polo Players* (Alejandro Moy)

1987. World Polo Championships, Palermo.
2040 **791** 20c. multicoloured 1·50 35

792 *Supplicant* (Museum of Natural Sciences, La Plata)

1987. 14th International Museums Council General Conference, Buenos Aires. Multicoloured.
2041 25c. Conference emblem 75 35
2042 25c. Shield of Potosi (National History Museum, Buenos Aires) 75 35
2043 25c. Statue of St. Bartholomew (Enrique Larreta Spanish Art Museum, Buenos Aires) 75 35
2044 25c. Cudgel with animal design (Patagonia Museum, San Carlos de Bariloche) 75 35
2045 25c. Type **792** 75 35
2046 25c. Grate from Argentine Confederation House (Entre Rios Historical Museum, Parana) 75 35
2047 25c. Statue of St. Joseph (Northern Historical Museum, Salta) 75 35
2048 25c. Funeral urn (Provincial Archaeological Museum, Santiago del Estero) 75 35

793 Pillar Box

1987. No value expressed. (a) Inscr "C" and "TARIFA INTERNA/HASTA 10 GRAMOS".
2049 **793** (18c.) red, black & yell 1·60 45

(b) Inscr "C" and "TARIFA INTERNA/DE 11 A 20 GRAMOS".
2050 (33c.) black, yell & grn 1·90 60

794 Spotted Metynis (*Metynnis maculatus*)

1987. Argentine Philately. River Fish. Multicoloured.
2051 10c.+5c. Type **794** 45 15
2052 10c.+5c. Black-finned pearlfish (*Cynolebias nigripinnis*) 45 15
2053 10c.+5c. Solar's leporinus (*Leporinus solarii*) 45 15
2054 10c.+5c. Red-flanked bloodfin (*Aphyocharax rathbuni*) 45 15
2055 10c.+5c. Bronze catfish (*Corydoras aeneus*) 45 15
2056 10c.+5c. Giant hatchetfish (*Thoracocharax securis*) 45 15
2057 10c.+5c. Black-striped pearlfish (*Cynolebias melanotaenia*) 45 15
2058 10c.+5c. Chanchito cichlid (*Cichlasoma facetum*) 45 15
2059 20c.+10c. Silver tetra (*Tetragonopterus argente*) 80 30
2060 20c.+10c. Buenos Aires tetra (*Hemigrammus caudovittatus*) 80 30
2061 20c.+10c. Two-spotted astyanax (*Astyanax bimaculatus*) 80 30
2062 20c.+10c. Black widow tetra (*Gymnocorymbus ternetzi*) 80 30
2063 20c.+10c. Trahira (*Hoplias malabaricus*) 80 30
2064 20c.+10c. Blue-finned tetra (*Aphyocharax rubripinnis*) 80 30
2065 20c.+10c. Agassiz's dwarf cichlid (*Apistogramma agassizi*) 80 30
2066 20c.+10c. Fanning pyrrhulina (*Pyrrhulina rachoviana*) 80 30

795 College Facade and Arms

1987. 300th Anniv of Montserrat College, Cordoba and Montserrat/87 National Stamp Exhibition. Sheet 75×110 mm. Imperf.
MS2067 **795** 1a. multicoloured 2·50 2·40

796 Jorge Luis Borges (writer)

1987. Anniversaries. Multicoloured.
2068 20c. Type **796** (1st death anniv) 65 15
2069 30c. Armando Discepolo, (dramatist and theatre director, birth cent) 75 25
2070 50c. Dr Carlos Alberto Pueyrredon (historian, birth centenary) 90 40

797 Drawing by Leonardo da Vinci

1987. "The Post, a Medium for Communication and Prevention of Addictions".
2071 **797** 30c. multicoloured 1·90 45

798 *The Sower* (Julio Vanzo)

1987. 75th Anniv of Argentine Farmers' Union.
2072 **798** 30c. multicoloured 1·30 45

799 Basketball

1987. Tenth Pan-American Games, Indianapolis. Multicoloured.
2073 20c. Type **799** 75 35
2074 30c. Rowing 90 40
2075 50c. Dinghies 1·00 45

800 Col. Maj. Ignacio Alvarez Thomas

1987. Anniversaries. Multicoloured.
2076 25c. Type **800** (birth bicent) 90 35
2077 25c. Col. Manuel Dorrego (birth bicentenary) 90 35
2078 50c. 18th-century Spanish map of Falkland Islands (death bicentenary of Jacinto de Altolaguirre, governor of Islands) (horiz) 1·80 60
2079 50c. *Signing the Accord* (Rafael del Villar) (50th anniv of House of Accord Museum, San Nicolas) (horiz) 1·80 60

801 Children as Nurse and Mother

1987. UNICEF Child Vaccination Campaign.
2080 **801** 30c. multicoloured 90 30

802 Balloon

1987. Anniversaries. Multicoloured.
2081 50c. Type **802** (50th anniv of LRA National Radio) 1·30 70
2082 50c. Celendonio Galvan Moreno (first editor) (50th anniv of *Postas Argentinas* magazine) 1·30 70
2083 1a. Dr. Jose Marco del Pont (founder) (centenary of Argentine Philatelic Society) 2·50 95

803 *Nativity* (tapestry, Alisia Frega)

1987. Christmas. Multicoloured.
2084 50c. Type **803** 1·00 35
2085 1a. Doves and flowers (tapestry, Silvina Trigos) 2·10 95

804 Crested Oropendola, Baritu National Park

1987. National Parks (1st series). Multicoloured.
2086 50c. Type **804** 2·30 60
2087 50c. Otter, Nahuel Huapi National Park 2·30 60
2088 50c. Night monkey, Rio Pilcomayo National Park 2·30 60
2089 50c. Kelp goose, Tierra del Fuego National Park 2·30 60
2090 50c. Alligator, Iguazu National Park 2·30 60
See also Nos. 2150/4, 2222/6 and 2295/9.

805 *Caminito* (Jose Canella)

1988. Historical and Tourist Sites. Multicoloured.

2090a 3a. *Purmamarca* (Nestor Martin) (33×22 mm) 1·10 45
2091 5a. Type **805** 4·00 2·00
2092 10a. *Old Almacen* (Jose Canella) (A) 8·25 4·25
2092a 10a. *Old Almacen* (Jose Canella) (B) 2·10 95
2095 20a. *Ushuaia* (Nestor Martin) (vert) 7·50 3·00
2099 50a. Type **805** 2·10 95

10a. A. Inscr "Viejo Almacen". B. Inscr "El Viejo Almacen".

806 *Minstrel singing in a Grocer's Shop* (Carlos Morel)

1988. Argentine Paintings. Multicoloured.

2105 1a. Type **806** 1·50 60
2106 1a. *Curuzu* (detail, Candido Lopez) 1·50 60

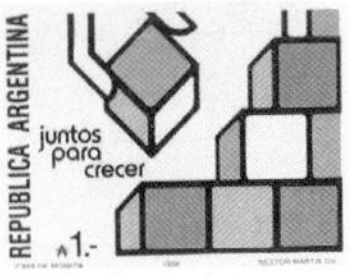

807 Hand arranging Coloured Cubes

1988. Argentine–Brazil Economic Co-operation.

2107 **807** 1a. multicoloured 1·00 45

808 St. Anne's Chapel, Corrientes

1988. 400th Annivs of Corrientes and Alta Gracia. Multicoloured.

2108 1a. Type **808** 1·50 60
2109 1a. Alta Gracia church 1·50 60

809 Men Stacking Sacks

1988. Labour Day. Details of mural *Cereals* (Nueve de Julio station, Buenos Aires underground railway). Multicoloured.

2110 50c. Type **809** 90 75
2111 50c. Sacks 90 75
2112 50c. Men unloading truck 90 75
2113 50c. Horse and cart 90 75

Nos. 2110/13 were printed together, *se-tenant*, forming a composite design.

810 Steam Locomotive *Yatay* and Tender, 1888 (image scaled to 54% of original size)

1988. "Prenfil '88" Philatelic Literature Exhibition, Buenos Aires (1st issue). Railways. Multicoloured.

2114 1a.+50c. Type **810** 1·30 85
2115 1a.+50c. Electric passenger coach, 1914 1·30 85
2116 1a.+50c. Type B-15 loco-motive and tender, 1942 1·30 85
2117 1a.+50c. Type GT-22 diesel loco-motive, 1988 1·30 85

See also Nos. 2134/7.

811 Running

1988. Olympic Games, Seoul. Multicoloured.

2118 1a. Type **811** 65 35
2119 2a. Football 1·60 45
2120 3a. Hockey 2·30 95
2121 4a. Tennis 2·75 1·20

812 Bank Facade

1988. Centenary of Bank of Mendoza.

2122 **812** 2a. multicoloured 1·30 55

813 Arms of Guemes and National Guard Emblem

1988. 50th Anniv of National Guard.

2123 **813** 2a. multicoloured 1·30 55

814 *St. Cayetano* (patron saint of workers)" (C. Quaglia)

1988. Philatelic Anniversaries and Events. Multicoloured.

2124 2a. Type **814** (50th anniv of Liniers (Buenos Aires) Philatelic Circle) 1·40 70
2125 3a. *Our Lady of Carmen (patron saint of Cuyo)* (window, Carlos Quaglia) (50th anniv of West Argentina Philatelic Society) 1·50 85
MS2126 145×73 mm. 5a. *Love* (mural, Antonio Berni) (Li-men 88 national stamp exhibition, Buenos Aires) (39×29 mm) 4·50 4·25

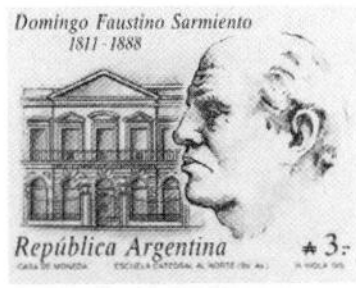

815 Sarmiento (after Mario Chierico) and Cathedral of the North School

1988. Death Centenary of Domingo Faustino Sarmiento (President, 1868–74).

2127 **815** 3a. multicoloured 2·10 85

816 *San Isidro* (Enrique Castro)

1988. Horse Paintings. Multicoloured.

2128 2a.+1a. Type **816** 1·90 95
2129 2a.+1a. *Waiting* (Gustavo Solari) 1·90 95
2130 2a.+1a. *Beside the Pond* (F. Romero Carranza) 1·90 95
2131 2a.+1a. *Mare and Colt* (Enrique Castro) 1·90 95
2132 2a.+1a. *Under the Tail* (Enrique Castro) 1·90 95

1988. 21st International Urological Society Congress. No. 2091 optd **XXI CONGRESO DE LA SOCIEDAD INTERNACIONAL DE UROLOGIA SIU 88**.

2133 **805** 5a. multicoloured 7·50 2·40

818 Cover of *References de la Poste*

1988. "Prenfil '88" Philatelic Literature Exhibition, Buenos Aires (2nd issue). Designs showing magazine covers. Multicoloured.

2134 1a.+1a. Type **818** 75 35
2135 1a.+1a. *Cronaca Filatelica* 75 35
2136 1a.+1a. *Co Fi* 75 35
2137 2a.+2a. *Postas Argentinas* 95 60

819 *Immaculate Conception*

1988. Arbrafax 88 Argentinian–Brazilian Stamp Exhibition, Buenos Aires. Sheet 156×80 mm containing T **819** and similar horiz design. Multicoloured.

MS2138 2a.+2a. *Candle Delivery at San Ignacio* (Leonie Matthis); 3a.+3a. Type **819** 5·00 4·75

820 Underground Train

1988. 75th Anniv of Buenos Aires Underground Railway.

2139 **820** 5a. multicoloured 2·10 95

821 *Virgin of Tenderness*

1988. Christmas. Virgins in Ucrania Cathedral, Buenos Aires. Multicoloured.

2140 5a. Type **821** 1·90 70
2141 5a. *Virgin of Protection* 1·90 70

822 Ushuaia and St. John

1989. Death Centenary (1988) of St. John Bosco (founder of Salesian Brothers).

2142 **822** 5a. multicoloured 1·30 35

823 *Rincon de los Areneros* (Justo Lynch)

1989. Paintings. Multicoloured.

2143 5a. Type **823** 2·75 45
2144 5a. *Blancos* (Fernando Fader) 2·75 45

824 *Crowning with Thorns* and Church of Our Lady of Carmen, Tandil

1989. Holy Week. Multicoloured.

2145 2a. Type **824** 50 25
2146 2a. *Jesus of Nazareth* and Buenos Aires Cathedral 50 25
2147 3a. *Our Lady of Sorrows* and Humahuaca Church, Jujuy 65 30
2148 3a. *Jesus Meets His Mother* (statue) and La Quebrada Church, San Luis 65 30

825 Shattering Drinking Glass

1989. Anti-alcoholism Campaign.

2149 **825** 5a. multicoloured 1·30 45

1989. National Parks (2nd series). As T **804**. Multicoloured.

2150 5a. Crested gallito (*Gallito Capeton*), Lihue Calel National Park 1·30 45
2151 5a. Lizard, El Palmar National Park 1·30 45
2152 5a. Tapirs, Calilegua National Park 1·30 45
2153 5a. Howler monkey, Chaco National Park 1·30 45
2154 5a. Magellanic wood-pecker (*Carpintero Negro Patagonico*), Los Glaciares National Park 1·30 45

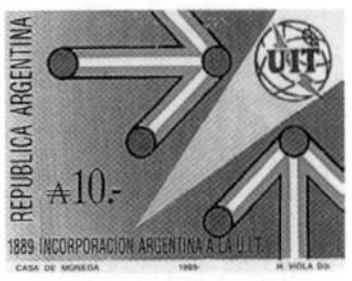

826 Emblem

1989. Cent of Argentine Membership of I.T.U.

2155 **826** 10a. multicoloured 2·75 60

827 Class 1A Glider Entries

1989. World Model Airplane Championships, La Cruz-Embals-Cordoba. Multicoloured.

2156 5a. Type **827** 1·00 35
2157 5a. Class 1B rubber-powered entries 1·00 35
2158 10a. Class 1C petrol-engined entries 1·80 50

828 Otuno (*Diplomystes viedmensis*)

1989. Argentine Philately. Fish. Multicoloured.

2159 10a.+5a. Type **828** 1·00 60
2160 10a.+5a. Striped galaxiid (*Haplochiton taeniatus*) 1·00 60
2161 10a.+5a. Creole perch (*Jenyns percichthys tucha*) 1·00 60
2162 10a.+5a. River Plate galaxiid (*Galaxias platei*) 1·00 60
2163 10a.+5a. Brown trout (*Salmo fario*) 1·00 60

829 "All Men are Born Free and Equal"

1989. Bicentenary of French Revolution.

2164 **829** 10a. red, blue and black 1·00 45
2165 - 15a. black, red and blue 1·10 50
MS2166 146×74 mm. 25a. multicoloured 2·10 2·00

DESIGNS: 15a. *Marianne* (Gandon) and French flag; 25a. *Liberty guiding the People* (detail, E. Delacroix).

830 *Weser* (steamer)

1989. Immigration. Multicoloured.
2167 150a. Type **830** 2·75 85
2168 200a. Immigrants' hostel 3·25 1·10
MS2169 155×80 mm. As Nos. 2167/8 but each 35×25 mm 5·00 4·75

831 "Republic" (bronze bust)

1989. Transference of Presidency. Unissued stamp surch as in T **831**.
2170 **831** 300a. on 50a. mult 2·75 85

832 Arms of Columbus and Title Page of *Book of Privileges*

1989. "Espamer '90" Spain–Latin America Stamp Exhibition. Chronicles of Discovery. Each yellow, black and red.
2171 100a.+50a. Type **832** 75 70
2172 150a.+50a. Illustration from *New Chronicle and Good Government* (Guaman Poma de Ayala) 1·00 95
2173 200a.+100a. Illustration from *Discovery and Conquest of Peru* (Pedro de Cieza de Leon) 1·50 1·40
2174 250a.+100a. Illustration from *A Journey to the River Plate* (Ulrico Schmidl) 1·80 1·70

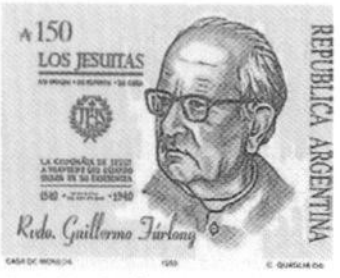

833 Fr. Guillermo Furlong and Title Page of *Los Jesuitas*

1989. Birth Anniversaries.
2175 **833** 150a. black, light green and green (centenary) 90 55
2176 - 150a. black, buff and brown (centenary) 90 55
2177 - 200a. black, light blue and blue (bicentenary) 1·00 60
DESIGNS: No. 2176, Dr. Gregorio Alvarez (physician) and title page of *Canto A Chos Mala*; 2177, Brigadier Gen. Enrique Martinez and *Battle of Maipu* (detail of lithograph, Theodore Gericault).

834 Wooden Mask from Atajo

1989. America. Pre-Columbian Artefacts. Multicoloured.
2178 200a. Type **834** 1·60 60
2179 300a. Urn from Punta de Balastro 2·10 65

835 *Policewoman with Children* (Diego Molinari)

1989. Federal Police Week. Winning entries in a schools' painting competition.
2180 100a. Type **835** 95 35
2181 100a. *Traffic policeman* (Carlos Alberto Sarago) 95 35
2182 150a. *Adults and child by traffic lights* (Roxana Andrea Osuna) 1·30 60
2183 150a. *Policeman and child stopping traffic at crossing* (Pablo Javier Quaglia) 1·30 60

836 *Dream of Christmas* (Maria Carballido)

1989. Christmas. Multicoloured.
2184 200a. Type **836** 1·10 35
2185 200a. *Cradle Song for Baby Jesus* (Gato Frias) 1·10 35
2186 300a. *Christ of the Hills* (statue, Chipo Cespedes) (vert) 1·30 45

837 *Battle of Vuelta de Obligado* (Ulde Todo)

1989
2187 **837** 300a. multicoloured 2·10 45

838 Port Building

1990. Cent of Buenos Aires Port. Multicoloured.
2188 200a. Type **838** 2·50 1·00
2189 200a. Crane and bows of container and sailing ships 2·50 1·00
2190 200a. Truck on quay and ships in dock 2·50 1·00
2191 200a. Van and building 2·50 1·00
Nos. 2188/91 were printed together, *se-tenant*, forming a composite design.

839 Aconcagua Peak and Los Horcones Lagoon

1990. Aconcagua International Fair. Multicoloured.
2192 500a. Type **839** 1·80 75
2193 500a. Aconcagua Peak and Los Horcones Lagoon (right-hand detail) 1·80 75
Nos. 2192/3 were printed together, *se-tenant*, forming a composite design.

840 "75" and Girl with Savings Box

1990. 75th Anniv of National Savings and Insurance Fund.
2194 **840** 1000a. multicoloured 1·00 45

841 Footballer in Striped Shirt

1990. World Cup Football Championship, Italy. Multicoloured.
2195 2500a. Type **841** 2·20 1·00
2196 2500a. Upper body of footballer in blue shirt 2·20 1·00
2197 2500a. Ball and footballers' legs 2·20 1·00
2198 2500a. Lower body of footballer 2·20 1·00
Nos. 2195/8 were printed together, *se-tenant*, forming a composite design.

842 Flowers

1990. Anti-drugs Campaign.
2199 **842** 2000a. multicoloured 1·90 85

843 School Emblem and Pellegrini

1990. Centenary of Carlos Pellegrini Commercial High School.
2200 **843** 2000a. multicoloured 1·90 85

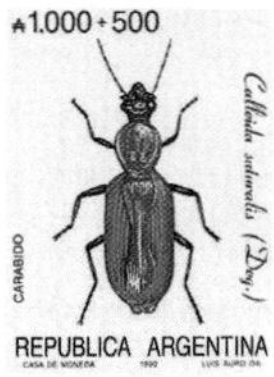

844 *Calleida suturalis*

1990. Argentine Philately. Insects. Multicoloured.
2201 1000a.+500a. Type **844** 1·80 1·20
2202 1000a.+500a. *Adalia bipunctata* 1·80 1·20
2203 1000a.+500a. *Hippodamia convergens* 1·80 1·20
2204 1000a.+500a. *Nabis punctipennis* 1·80 1·20
2205 1000a.+500a. *Podisus nigrispinus* 1·80 1·20

845 Letters and Globe

1990. International Literacy Year.
2206 **845** 2000a. multicoloured 1·50 85

846 Marcos Zar and Savoia S-16 Flying Boat

1990. Air. Aerofildae 90 National Air Mail Exhibition, Buenos Aires. Sheet 158×78 mm containing T **846** and similar horiz design. Multicoloured.
MS2207 2000a.+ 2000a. Type **846**; 3000a.+3000a. Capt. Antonio Parodi and biplane 12·50 12·00

847 Players

1990. World Basketball Championship. Multicoloured.
2208 2000a. Type **847** 3·25 2·10
MS2209 5000a. Detail of No. 2208 (29×39 mm) 8·25 7·00

848 Junkers Ju 52/3m

1990. Air. 50th Anniv of LADE (airline). Multicoloured.
2210 2500a. Type **848** 2·10 1·10
2211 2500a. Grumman SA-16 Albatross flying boat 2·10 1·10
2212 2500a. Fokker Friendship 2·10 1·10
2213 2500a. Fokker Fellowship 2·10 1·10

849 Arms of West Indies Maritime Post

1990. 14th Postal Union of the Americas and Spain Congress, Buenos Aires.
2214 **849** 3000a. brown & black 2·50 1·00
2215 - 3000a. multicoloured 2·50 1·00
2216 - 3000a. multicoloured 2·50 1·00
2217 - 3000a. multicoloured 2·50 1·00
DESIGNS: No. 2215, Sailing packet and despatch boat; 2216, "Rio Carcarana" (cargo liner); 2217, Boeing 707 airplane and mail van.

850 *Descubierta*

1990. Espamer 91 Spain–Latin America Stamp Exhibition, Buenos Aires. Sheet 109×114 mm containing T **850** and similar vert designs. Multicoloured.
MS2218 2000a.+1000a×4: Type **850**; Alejandro Malaspina (explorer) and *Atrevide*; Amerindians; Artist drawing Amerindians 12·50 12·00

851 *Hamelia erecta* and Iguazu Falls

1990. America. Natural World. Multicoloured.
2219 3000a. Type **851** 2·50 1·00
2220 3000a. Sea cow, Puerto Deseado 2·50 1·00

852 U.P.U. Emblem on "Stamp"

1990. World Post Day.
2221 **852** 3000a. multicoloured 2·30 85

1990. National Parks (3rd series). As T **804**. Multicoloured.
2222 3000a. Anteater, El Rey National Park 2·40 95
2223 3000a. Black-necked swans (*Cisne de Cuello Negro*), Laguna Blanca National Park 2·40 95
2224 3000a. Black-chested buzzard eagle (*Aguila Mora*), Lanin National Park 2·40 95
2225 3000a. Armadillo, Perito Moreno National Park 2·40 95
2226 3000a. Pudu, Puelo National Park 2·40 95

853 Hands (after Michelangelo) and Army Emblem

1990. Cent of Salvation Army in Argentina (2227) and Nat University of the Littoral (2228). Multicoloured.

2227	3000a. Type **853**	2·30	1·10
2228	3000a. University building and emblem	2·30	1·10

854 Archangel Gabriel

1990. Christmas. Stained-glass windows by Carlos Quaglia from Church of Immaculate Conception, Villaguay. Multicoloured.

2229	3000a. Dove's wing and hand	2·10	1·10
2230	3000a. Dove and Mary	2·10	1·10
2231	3000a. Type **854**	2·10	1·10
2232	3000a. Lower half of Mary and open book	2·10	1·10
2233	3000a. Joseph	2·10	1·10
2234	3000a. Star, shepherds and head of Mary	2·10	1·10
2235	3000a. Manger	2·10	1·10
2236	3000a. Baby Jesus in Mary's arms	2·10	1·10
2237	3000a. Joseph with two doves and Mary	2·10	1·10
2238	3000a. Simeon	2·10	1·10
2239	3000a. Lower halves of Joseph and Mary	2·10	1·10
2240	3000a. Lower half of Simeon and altar	2·10	1·10

Nos. 2229/32, 2233/6 and 2237/40 were printed together in se-tenant sheetlets of four stamps, each sheetlet forming a composite design of stained glass windows entitled *Incarnation of Son of God, The Birth of Christ* and *Presentation of Jesus in the Temple*.

855 Putting the Shot

1990. Espamer 91 Spain–Latin America Stamp Exhibition, Buenos Aires (2nd issue) and Olympic Games, Barcelona (1992). Sheet 103×125 mm containing T **855** and similar vert designs. Multicoloured.

MS2241	2000a.+2000a.×4: Type **855**; High jumping; Hurdling; Pole vaulting	19·00	18·00

856 *Landscape* (Pio Collivadino)

1991. Paintings. Multicoloured.

2242	4000a. Type **856**	1·80	1·00
2243	4000a. *Weeping Willows* (Atilio Malinverno) (horiz)	1·80	1·00

857 Juan Manuel Fangio

1991. Espamer 91 Spain–Latin America Stamp Exhibition, Buenos Aires (3rd issue). Racing Drivers. Sheet 104×125 mm containing T **857** and similar vert designs. Multicoloured.

MS2244	2500a.+2500a.×4: Type **857**; Juan Manuel Bordeau; Carlos Alberto Reutemann; Oscar and Juan Galvez	9·50	9·25

858 Rosas

1991. Return of Remains of Brig. Gen. Juan Manuel de Rosas.

2245	**858**	4000a. multicoloured	1·80	1·00

859 Freestyle Gymnastics

1991. Espamer 91 Spain–Latin America Stamp Exhibition, Buenos Aires (4th issue) and Olympic Games, Barcelona (1992) (2nd issue). Gymnastics. Sheet 103×125 mm containing T **859** and similar vert designs. Multicoloured.

MS2246	2500a.+2500a.×4: Type **859**; Asymmetric bars; Beam; Hoop exercise	9·50	9·25

860 *Hernan, the Pirate* (Jose Salinas)

1991. Comic Strips. Each black and blue.

2247	4000a. Type **860**	1·80	1·00
2248	4000a. *Don Fulgencio* (Lino Palacio)	1·80	1·00
2249	4000a. *Tablas Medicas de Salerno* (Oscar Conti)	1·80	1·00
2250	4000a. *Buenos Aires en Camiseta* (Alejandro del Prado)	1·80	1·00
2251	4000a. *Girls!* (Jose Divito)	1·80	1·00
2252	4000a. *Langostino* (Eduardo Ferro)	1·80	1·00
2253	4000a. *Mafalda* (Joaquin Lavado)	1·80	1·00
2254	4000a. *Mort Cinder* (Alberto Breccia)	1·80	1·00

861 "Flags" (Maria Augustina Ferreyra)

1991. 700th Anniv of Swiss Confederation.

2255	**861**	4000a. multicoloured	1·80	85

862 Divine Child Mayor

1991. 400th Anniv of La Rioja City.

2256	**862**	4000a. multicoloured	1·80	85

863 Eduardo Bradley, Angel Zuloaga and Balloon *Eduardo Newbery*

1991. 75th Anniv of Crossing of Andes by Balloon.

2257	**863**	4000a. multicoloured	1·80	85

864 *Vitoria* (Magellan's galleon)

1991. America. Voyages of Discovery. Multicoloured.

2258	4000a. Type **864**	2·50	1·00
2259	4000a. Juan Diaz de Solis's fleet	2·50	1·00

865 "Virgin of the Valley, Catamarca" (top half)

1991. Christmas. Stained-glass Windows from Church of Our Lady of Lourdes, Santos Lugares, Buenos Aires. Multicoloured.

2260	4000a. Type **865**	2·10	1·00
2261	4000a. "Virgin of the Valley" (bottom half)	2·10	1·00
2262	4000a. Church and "Virgin of the Rosary of the Miracle, Cordoba" (top half)	2·10	1·00
2263	4000a. "Virgin of the Rosary of the Miracle" (bottom half)	2·10	1·00

Nos. 2260/3 were issued together, *se-tenant*, Nos. 2260/1 and 2262/3 forming composite designs.

866 Enrique Pestalozzi (editor) and Masthead

1991. Centenaries. Multicoloured.

2264	4000a. Type **866** ("Argentinisches Tageblatt" (1989))	1·80	85
2265	4000a. Leandro Alem (founder) and flags (Radical Civic Union)	1·80	85
2266	4000a. Marksman (Argentine Shooting Federation)	1·80	85
2267	4000a. Dr. Nicasio Etchepareborda (first professor) and emblem (Buenos Aires Faculty of Odontology)	1·80	85
2268	4000a. Dalmiro Huergo and emblem (Graduate School of Economics)	1·80	85

867 Gen. Juan Lavalle and Medal

1991. Anniversaries. Multicoloured.

2269	4000a. Type **867** (150th death anniv)	1·80	85
2270	4000a. Gen. Jose Maria Paz and Battle of Ituzaingo medal (birth bicentenary)	1·80	85
2271	4000a. Dr. Marco Avellaneda and opening words of *Ode to the 25th May* (politician and writer, 150th death anniv)	1·80	85
2272	4000a. William Henry Hudson and title page of *Far Away and Long Ago* (writer, 150th birth anniv)	1·80	85

868 *Castor* (rocket)

1991. "Iberoprenfil '92" Iberia–Latin America Philatelic Literature Exhibition, Buenos Aires (1st issue). Multicoloured.

2273	4000a.+4000a. Type **868**	4·00	1·60
2274	4000a.+4000a. "Lusat-1" satellite	4·00	1·60

See also Nos. 2313/14 and 2325/8.

869 Guiana Crested Eagle (*Morphnu guianensis*)

1991. Birds. Multicoloured.

2275	4000a. Type **869**	2·50	1·10
2276	4000a. Green-winged macaw (*Ara chloroptera*)	2·50	1·10
2277	4000a. Lesser rhea (*Pterocnemia pennata*)	2·50	1·10

870 Gaucho with Woman

1992. Abrafex 92 Argentinian–Brazilian Stamp Exhibition, Porto Algere, Brazil. Sheet 103×126 mm containing T **870** and similar vert designs. Multicoloured.

MS2278	38c. Type **870**; 38c. Gaucho with horse; 38c. Gaucho in grocer's shop; 38c. Ranch owner	8·25	8·00

871 Golden Tops

1992. Fungi.

2279	10c. Type **871**	75	25
2280	25c. Common ink cap	1·30	35
2281	38c. Type **871**	1·30	45
2282	48c. As 25c.	1·50	55
2283	50c. Granulated boletus	2·50	70
2284	51c. Common morel	1·60	60
2285	61c. Fly agaric	2·00	65
2286	68c. Lawyer's wig	3·25	80
2289	1p. As 61c.	5·00	1·10
2290	1p.25 As 50c.	5·00	1·10
2293	2p. As 51c.	9·50	2·75

For redrawn, smaller, designs see Nos. 2365/77.

1992. National Parks (4th series). As T **804**. Multicoloured.

2295	38c. Chucao tapaculo (*Chucao*), Los Alerces National Park	1·50	85
2296	38c. Opossum, Los Arrayanes National Park	1·50	85
2297	38c. Giant armadillo, Formosa Nature Reserve	1·50	85
2298	38c. Cavy, Petrified Forests Natural Monument	1·50	85
2299	38c. James's flamingo (*Parina chica*), Laguna de los Pozuelos Natural Monument	1·50	85

872 Soldier and Truck

1992. National Heroes Commem. Multicoloured.

2300	38c. Type **872**	1·30	70
2301	38c. "General Belgrano" (cruiser)	1·30	70
2302	38c. FMA Pucara fighter	1·30	70

873 "Carnotaurus sastrei"

1992. Dinosaurs. Multicoloured.

2303	38c.+38c. Type **873**	2·75	1·80
2304	38c.+38c. "Amargasaurus cazaui"	2·75	1·80

874 *Tileforo Areco*

1992. Birth Centenary (1991) of Florencio Molina Campios (painter). Multicoloured.

2305	38c. Type **874**	1·50	85
2306	38c. *In the Shade* (horiz)	1·50	85

875 Deer

1992. Conference on Environment and Development, Rio de Janeiro. Sheet 85×82 mm containing T **875** and similar square designs. Multicoloured.

MS2307 38c. Type **875**; 38c. Birds; 38c. Butterflies; 38c. Whale — 12·00 12·00

876 General Lucio N. Mansilla and *San Martin* (frigate)

1992. Birth Anniversaries. Multicoloured.

2308	38c. Type **876** (bicentenary)	1·50	85
2309	38c. Jose Manuel Estrada (historian, 150th)	1·50	85
2310	38c. General Jose I. Garmendia (150th)	1·50	85

877 Hearts as Flowers

1992. Anti-drugs Campaign.

2311	**877**	38c. multicoloured	1·90	95

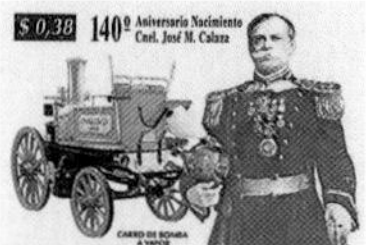

878 Steam Pump Fire Engine and Calaza

1992. 140th Birth Anniv of Col. Jose Calaza (founder of fire service).

2312	**878**	38c. multicoloured	1·60	90

879 *The Party*

1992. "Iberoprenfil '92" Iberia–Latin America Philatelic Literature Exhibition, Buenos Aires (2nd issue). Paintings by Raul Soldi. Multicoloured.

2313	76c.+76c. Type **879**	6·25	4·75
2314	76c.+76c. *Church of St. Anne of Glew*	6·25	4·75

880 Columbus, European Symbols and *Santa Maria*

1992. America. 500th Anniv of Discovery of America by Columbus. Multicoloured.

2315	38c. Type **880**	2·50	1·20
2316	38c. American symbols and Columbus	2·50	1·20

1992. 50th Anniv of Neuquen and Rio Negro Philatelic Centre. Unissued stamp as T **871** optd **50°ANIVERSARIO CENTRO FILATELICO DE NEUQUEN Y RIO NEGRO**. Multicoloured.

2317	1p.77 Verdigris agaric	7·50	4·75

882 *God Pays You*

1992. Argentine Films. Advertising posters. Multicoloured.

2318	38c. Type **882**	1·80	85
2319	38c. *The Turbid Waters*	1·80	85
2320	38c. *Un Guapo del 900*	1·80	85
2321	38c. *The Truce*	1·80	85
2322	38c. *The Official Version*	1·80	85

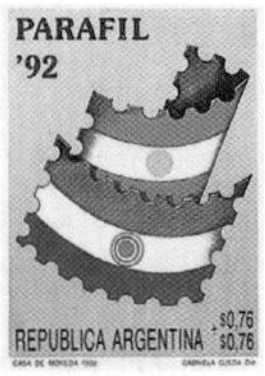

883 Flags of Paraguay and Argentina as Stamps

1992. "Parafil '92" Paraguay–Argentina Stamp Exhibition, Buenos Aires.

2323	**883**	76c.+76c. mult	6·00	4·50

884 Angel and Baby Jesus

1992. Christmas.

2324	**884**	38c. multicoloured	1·80	85

885 Punta Mogotes Lighthouse

1992. "Iberoprenfil '92" Iberia–Latin America Philatelic Literature Exhibition, Buenos Aires (3rd issue). Lighthouses. Multicoloured.

2325	38c. Type **885**	1·80	85
2326	38c. Rio Negro	1·80	85
2327	38c. San Antonio	1·80	85
2328	38c. Cabo Blanco	1·80	85

886 Campaign Emblem

1992. Anti-AIDS Campaign.

2329	**886**	10c. black, red and blue	3·25	60
2330	-	26c. multicoloured	5·75	1·00

DESIGN: 26c. AIDS cloud over house of life.

887 "Sac-B" Research Satellite

1992. International Space Year.

2331	**887**	38c. multicoloured	2·00	95

888 *The Lord of the Miracle* (Matriz Church, Salta)

1992. 400th Anniv of Arrival of the *Lord of the Miracle* in America. Sheet 72×112 mm.

MS2332 **888** 76c. multicoloured — 7·00 4·75

889 Footballers and Emblem

1993. Centenary of Argentine Football Assn.

2333	**889**	38c. multicoloured	1·80	85

890 Arquebusier and Arms of Francisco de Arganaras (founder)

1993. 400th Anniv of Jujuy.

2334	**890**	38c. multicoloured	1·80	85

891 Government Tower, Poznan

1993. International Stamp Exhibitions. Sheet 84×119 mm containing T **891** and similar square designs. Multicoloured.

MS2335 38c. Type **891** (Polska 93); 48c."Christ the Redeemer" (Statue), Rio de Janeiro (Brasiliana 93); 76c. Palace dome, Bangkok (Bangkok 1993) — 6·50 6·50

892 Order of San Martin

1993. Anniversaries. Multicoloured.

2336	38c. Type **892** (50th anniv)	1·80	85
2337	38c. Entrance to and emblem of National History Academy (centenary)	1·80	85

893 Flag-bearer and Arms of Gendarmerie

1993. National Heroes Commemoration. Multicoloured.

2338	38c. Type **893**	1·80	85
2339	38c. "Rio Iguazu" (coastguard corvette)	1·80	85

894 Luis Candelaria and Morane Saulnier Type P Monoplane

1993. 75th Anniv of First Flight over the Andes.

2340	**894**	38c. multicoloured	1·90	95

895 Snowy Egret (Egretta thula)

1993. Paintings of Birds by Axel Amuchastegui. Multicoloured.

2341	38c.+38c. Type **895**	2·75	2·10
2342	38c.+38c. Scarlet-headed blackbird (*Amblyramphus holosericeus*)	2·75	2·10
2343	38c.+38c. Red-crested cardinal (*Paroaria coronata*)	2·75	2·10
2344	38c.+38c. Amazon kingfisher (*Chloroceryle amazona*)	2·75	2·10

896 *Coming Home* (Adriana Zaefferer)

1993. Paintings. Multicoloured.

2345	38c. Type **896**	1·80	85
2346	38c. *The Old House* (Norberto Russo)	1·80	85

897 Pato

1993. 40th Anniv of Declaration of Pato as National Sport.

2347	**897**	1p. multicoloured	3·75	2·20

898 Segurola's Pacara (*Enterolobium contortisiliquum*)

1993. Old Trees in Buenos Aires. Multicoloured.

2348	75c. Type **898** (Puan and Baldomero Fernandez Moreno Streets)	2·50	1·40
2349	75c. Pueyrredon's carob tree (*Prosopis alba*) (Pueyrredon Square)	2·50	1·40
2350	1p.50 Alvear's coral tree (*Erythrina falcata*) (Lavalle Square)	5·25	2·50
2351	1p.50 Avellaneda's magnolia (*Magnolia grandiflora*) (Adolfo Berro Avenue)	5·25	2·50

899 Southern Right Whale

1993. America. Endangered Animals. Multicoloured.

2352	50c. Type **899**	2·00	1·10
2353	75c. Commerson's dolphin	3·00	1·80

900 Star, Leaf and Bell (Christmas)

1993. Christmas and New Year. Festive Symbols. Multicoloured.

2354	75c. Type **900**	3·00	1·80
2355	75c. Leaf, sun and moon (New Year)	3·00	1·80
2356	75c. Leaf and fir tree (Christmas)	3·00	1·80
2357	75c. Fish and moon (New Year)	3·00	1·80

Nos. 2354/7 were issued together, *se-tenant*, forming a composite design.

901 Cave Painting

1993. Cave of Hands, Santa Cruz.

2358	**901**	1p. multicoloured	3·75	2·20

902 Emblem

1994. New Argentine Post Emblem.

2359	**902**	75c. multicoloured	5·00	1·70

903 Brazil Player

1994. World Cup Football Championship, U.S.A. (1st issue). Multicoloured.

2360	25c. German player	1·00	60
2361	50c. Type **903**	1·90	1·20
2362	75c. Argentine player	2·50	1·80
2363	1p. Italian player	3·75	2·40
MS2364	151×99 mm. 1p.50 As No. 2362 but 39×49 mm	5·75	5·25

See also Nos. 2380/3.

904 Golden Tops

1994. Fungi. Multicoloured.

2365	10c. Type **904**	50	25
2366	25c. Common ink cap	75	45
2369	50c. Granulated boletus	1·50	95
2374	1p. Fly agaric	3·25	1·90
2377	2p. Common morel	6·25	3·75

905 Argentine Player with Ball (Matias Taylor)

1994. World Cup Football Championship, U.S.A. (2nd issue). Winning entries in children's competition. Multicoloured.

2380	75c. Type **905**	2·75	1·20
2381	75c. Tackle (Torcuato Santiago Gonzalez Agote)	2·75	1·20
2382	75c. Players (Julian Lisenberg) (horiz)	2·75	1·20
2383	75c. Match scene (Maria Paula Palma) (horiz)	2·75	1·20

906 Black-throated Finch

1994. Animals of the Falkland Islands (Islas Malvinas). Multicoloured.

2384	25c. Type **906**	1·00	60
2385	50c. Gentoo penguins	1·50	85
2386	75c. Falkland Islands flightless steamer ducks	2·50	1·20
2387	1p. Southern elephant-seal	3·25	2·10

907 Town Arms

1994. Anniversaries. Multicoloured.

2388	75c. Type **907** (400th anniv of San Luis)	2·75	1·20
2389	75c. Arms (3rd anniv of provincial status of Tierra del Fuego, Antarctica and South Atlantic Islands)	3·75	1·80

908 Ladislao Jose Biro

1994. Inventors. Multicoloured.

2390	75c. Type **908** (ball-point pen)	2·75	1·20
2391	75c. Raul Pateras de Pescara (helicopter)	2·75	1·20
2392	75c. Quirino Cristiani (animated films)	2·75	1·20
2393	75c. Enrique Finochietto (surgical instruments)	2·75	1·20

909 Star, Purple Bauble and Bell

1994. UNICEF Children's Fund in Argentina. Multicoloured.

2394	50c. Type **909**	1·90	85
2395	75c. Bell, red bauble and star	2·75	1·20

910 Children holding Globe (Ivana Mirna de Caro)

1994. *Care of the Planet*. Children's Painting Competition. Multicoloured.

2396	25c. Type **910**	90	40
2397	25c. Girl polishing sunbeam and boy tending tree (Elena Tsouprik)	90	40
2398	50c. Children of all races around globe (Estefania Navarro) (horiz)	1·90	85
2399	50c. Globe as house (Maria Belen Gidoni) (horiz)	1·90	85

911 Star and Angel (The Annunciation)

1994. Christmas. Multicoloured.

2400	50c. Type **911**	1·90	85
2401	75c. Madonna and Child (Nativity)	2·75	1·20

912 Running

1995. 12th Pan-American Games, Mar del Plata. Multicoloured.

2402	75c. Type **912**	2·75	1·20
2403	75c. Cycling	2·75	1·20
2404	75c. Diving	2·75	1·20
2405	1p.25 Football (vert)	3·75	1·80
2406	1p.25 Gymnastics (vert)	3·75	1·80

913 Postal Emblem

1995. Self-adhesive.

2407	**913**	25c. yellow, blue & black	10·00	95
2408	**913**	75c. yellow, blue & black	3·50	1·70

914 National Congress Building and "The Republic Triumphant" (statue, detail)

1995. New Constitution, August 1994.

2409	**914**	75c. multicoloured	2·75	1·80

915 Letters and Disk

1995. 21st International Book Fair.

2410	**915**	75c. multicoloured	2·75	1·80

916 Bay-winged Cowbird

1995. Birds. Multicoloured.

2412	5p. Hooded siskin	16·00	12·00
2413	9p.40 Type **916**	27·00	21·00
2414	10p. Rufous-collared sparrow	29·00	23·00

917 Clouds seen through Atrium

1995. Centenary of Argentine Engineers' Centre, Buenos Aires.

2420	**917**	75c. multicoloured	2·75	1·70

918 Antoine de Saint-Exupery (pilot and writer)

1995. Aerofila 96 Latin American Airmail Exhibition. Sheet 130×90 mm containing T **918** and similar multicoloured design.

MS2421	25c.+25c. Type **918**; 75c.+75c. Illustration from *The Little Prince*	12·50	12·00

919 *Bahia Aguirre* (supply ship)

1995. Argentine Antarctic. Sheet 171×91 mm containing T **919** and similar horiz design. Multicoloured.

MS2422	75c.+25c. Type **919**; 1p.25+75c. Lockheed C-130 Hercules transport plane	14·00	14·00

920 Jose Marti

1995. Revolutionaries' Anniversaries. Multicoloured.

2423	1p. Type **920** (death cent)	3·75	2·40
2424	1p. Antonio de Sucre (birth bicentenary)	3·75	2·40

921 Greater Rhea

1995. Birds. Multicoloured.

2425	5c. Type **921**	15	10
2425a	10c. Giant wood rail ("ipecae")	65	25
2426	25c. King penguin	90	40
2427	50c. Toco toucan	1·90	80
2428	75c. Andean condor	2·75	1·60
2429	1p. Barn owl	5·00	2·40
2430	2p. Olivaceous cormorant	8·75	4·75
2431	2p.75 Southern lapwing	10·50	6·25
2432	3p.25 Southern lapwing	15·00	7·75

1995. Animals. As T **921**. Multicoloured.

2436	25c. Alligator	90	55
2437	50c. Red fox	1·90	1·20
2438	75c. Anteater	2·75	1·70
2439	75c. Vicuna	2·75	1·70
2440	75c. Sperm whale	2·75	1·70

922 Cave Painting (Patagonia)

1995. Archaeology. Multicoloured.

2441	75c. Type **922**	2·75	1·70
2442	75c. Stone mask (Tafi culture, Tucuman)	2·75	1·70
2443	75c. Anthropomorphic vase (Catamarca)	2·75	1·70
2444	75c. Woven cloth (North Patagonia)	2·75	1·70

923 Peron

1995. Birth Centenary of Juan Peron (President, 1946–55 and 1973–74).

2445	**923**	75c. blue and bistre	2·75	1·70

924 Postal Emblem on Sunflower

1995

2446	**924**	75c. multicoloured	8·75	2·40

925 "50" Emblem

1995. Anniversaries. Sheet 110×80 mm containing T **925** and similar horiz designs. Multicoloured.

MS2447 75c. Type **925** (50th anniv of United Nations Organization); 75c. "50" and emblem (50th anniv of International Civil Aviation Organization); 75c. "50" and emblem (50th anniv of Food and Agriculture Organization); 75c. "75" and emblem (75th anniv of International Labour Organization) 12·00 12·00

926 Christmas Tree

1995. Christmas. Multicoloured.

2448	75c. Type **926**	2·75	1·70
2449	75c. "1996"	2·75	1·70
2450	75c. Glasses of champagne	2·75	1·70
2451	75c. Present	2·75	1·70
2452	75c. Type **926**	2·75	1·70

927 *Les 400 Coups* (dir. Francois Truffaut)

1995. Centenary of Motion Pictures. Each black, grey and orange.

2453	75c. *Battleship Potemkin* (dir. Sergei Eisenstein)	2·75	1·70
2454	75c. *Casablanca* (dir. Michael Curtiz)	2·75	1·70
2455	75c. *Bicycle Thieves* (dir. Vittorio de Sica)	2·75	1·70
2456	75c. Charlie Chaplin in *Limelight*	2·75	1·70
2457	75c. Type **927**	2·75	1·70
2458	75c. *Chronicle of an Only Child* (dir. Leonardo Favio)	2·75	1·70

928 Horse-drawn Mail Coach

1995. America (1994). Postal Transport. Multicoloured.

2459	75c. Type **928**	2·75	1·70
2460	75c. Early postal van	2·75	1·70

929 Dirigible Airship

1995. The Sky. Multicoloured.

2461	25c. Type **929**	1·00	65
2462	25c. Kite	1·00	65
2463	25c. Hot-air balloon	1·00	65
2464	50c. Balloons	2·00	1·30
2465	50c. Paper airplane	2·00	1·30
2466	75c. Airplane	2·75	1·70
2467	75c. Helicopter	2·75	1·70
2468	75c. Parachute	2·75	1·70

930 Ancient Greek and Modern Runners

1996. Multicoloured. (a) Centenary of Modern Olympic Games. Horiz designs.

2471	75c. Type **930**	2·75	1·70
2472	1p. *The Discus Thrower* (ancient Greek statue, Miron) and modern thrower	4·00	2·50

(b) Olympic Games. Vert designs.

2473	75c. Torch bearer (Buenos Aires, 2004)	2·75	1·70
2474	1p. Rowing (Atlanta, 1996)	4·00	2·50

931 Francisco Muniz (founder of Academy of Medicine and Public Hygiene Council)

1996. Physicians' Anniversaries. Multicoloured.

2475	50c. Type **931** (birth bicentenary (1995))	2·00	1·30
2476	50c. Ricardo Gutierrez (founder of Children's Hospital and co-founder of periodical *La Patria Argentina*, death centenary)	2·00	1·30
2477	50c. Ignacio Pirovano (death centenary (1995))	2·00	1·30
2478	50c. Esteban Maradona (birth centenary (1995) and first death anniv)	2·00	1·30

932 Mosaic Map of Jerusalem (left-hand detail)

1996. 3000th Anniv of Jerusalem. Multicoloured.

2479	75c. Type **932**	2·75	1·70
2480	75c. Map (right-hand detail)	2·75	1·70

Nos. 2479/80 were issued together, *se-tenant*, forming a composite design.

933 Capybaras

1996. America. Endangered Species. Multicoloured.

2481	75c. Type **933**	2·75	1·70
2482	75c. Guanacos	2·75	1·70

934 Ramon Franco's Seaplane *Plus Ultra*

1996. "Aerofila '96" Latin American Airmail Exhibition. Aircraft. Multicoloured.

2483	25c.+25c. Type **934**	2·00	1·30
2484	25c.+25c. Alberto Santos-Dumont's biplane *14 bis*	2·00	1·30
2485	50c.+50c. Charles Lindbergh's *Spirit of St. Louis*	4·00	2·50
2486	50c.+50c. Eduardo Olivero's biplane *Buenos Aires*	4·00	2·50

1996. As Nos. 2407/8. Self-adhesive. Imperf.

2486a	**913**	25c. yellow and blue	2·40	1·50
2486b	**913**	75c. yellow and blue	4·50	2·75

935 Dusky-legged Guan, Diamante National Park

1996. National Parks. Multicoloured.

2487	75c. Type **935**	2·75	1·70
2488	75c. Mountain viscacha, El Leoncito Nature Reserve	2·75	1·70
2489	75c. Marsh deer, Otamendi Nature Reserve	2·75	1·70
2490	75c. Red-spectacled amazon, San Antonio Nature Reserve	2·75	1·70

936 Dragon

1996. Murals from Buenos Aires Underground Railway. Multicoloured.

2491	1p.+50c. Type **936**	5·25	2·75
2492	1p.50+1p. Bird	8·75	4·75

937 *San Antonio* (tank landing ship)

1996. Cent of Port Belgrano Naval Base. Multicoloured.

2493	25c. Type **937**	1·30	80
2494	50c. *Rosales* (corvette)	2·00	1·30
2495	75c. *Hercules* (destroyer)	2·75	1·70
2496	1p. *25 de Mayo* (aircraft carrier)	3·75	2·40

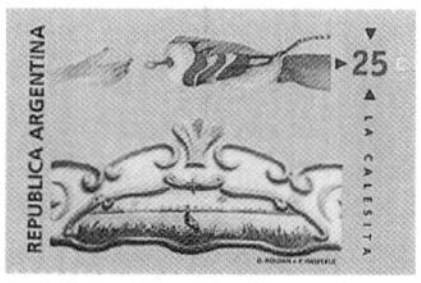

938 Decorative Panel

1996. Carousel. Multicoloured.

2497	25c. Type **938**	1·00	65
2498	25c. Child on horse	1·00	65
2499	25c. Carousel	1·00	65
2500	50c. Fairground horses	2·00	1·30
2501	50c. Child in airplane	2·00	1·30
2502	50c. Pig	2·00	1·30
2503	75c. Child in car	2·75	1·70

939 Head Post Office, Buenos Aires

1996. Size 24½×34½ mm. Self-adhesive. Imperf.

2504	**939**	75c. multicoloured	3·75	2·00

See also Nos. 2537/8.

940 *Adoration of the Wise Men* (Gladys Rinaldi)

1996. Christmas. Tapestries. Multicoloured.

2505	75c. Type **940**	2·75	1·70
2506	1p. *Abstract* (Norma Bonet de Maekawa) (horiz)	4·00	2·50

941 Melchior Base

1996. Argentinian Presence in Antarctic. Multicoloured.

2507	75c. Type **941**	2·75	1·70
2508	1p.25 "Irizar" (ice-breaker)	5·00	3·25

942 *Vahine no te Miti* (Gauguin)

1996. Cent of National Gallery of Fine Arts. Multicoloured.

2509	75c. Type **942**	2·50	1·60
2510	1p. *The Nymph surprised* (Edouard Manet)	3·25	2·00
2511	1p. *Figure of Woman* (Amedeo Modigliani)	3·25	2·00
2512	1p.25 *Woman lying down* (Pablo Picasso) (horiz)	3·75	2·40

943 Granite Mining, Cordoba

1997. Mining Industry. Multicoloured.

2513	75c. Type **943**	2·75	1·70
2514	1p.25 Borax mining, Salta	5·00	3·25

944 *They amuse Themselves in Dancing* (Raul Soldi)

1997. America (1996). National Costume.

2515	**944**	75c. multicoloured	2·75	1·70

945 Arms, Sabre and Shako

1997. Centenary of Repatriation of General San Martin's Sabre.

2516	**945**	75c. multicoloured	2·75	1·70

946 Match Scene

1997. 29th World Rugby Youth Championship, Argentina.

2517	**946**	75c. multicoloured	2·75	1·70

947 *Fortuna* (yacht)

1997. 50th Anniv of Buenos Aires to Rio de Janeiro Regatta.

2518	**947**	75c. multicoloured	2·75	1·70

948 Ceres Design, France (1849–52)

1997. "Mevifil '97" First Int Exn of Philatelic Audio-visual and Computer Systems. Multicoloured.

2519	50c.+50c. Type **948**	4·50	2·75
2520	50c.+50c. Queen Isabella II design, Spain (1851)	4·50	2·75
2521	50c.+50c. Rivadavia design, Argentine Republic (1864)	4·50	2·75
2522	50c.+50c. Paddle-steamer design, Buenos Aires (1858)	4·50	2·75

Nos. 2519/22 were issued together, *se-tenant*, with the centre of the block forming the composite design of an eye.

949 Museum

1997. Centenary of National History Museum, Buenos Aires.

2523	**949**	75c. multicoloured	2·75	1·70

950 Seal and Oak Leaf

1997. Centenary of La Plata National University.

2524	**950**	75c. multicoloured	2·75	1·70

951 Carcano (after Dolores Capdevila)

1997. 50th Death Anniv (1996) of Ramon Carcano (postal reformer).

2525	**951**	75c. multicoloured	2·75	1·70

952 Cabo Virgenes Lighthouse

1997. Lighthouses. Multicoloured.

2526	75c. Type **952**	2·75	1·70
2527	75c. Isla Pinguino	2·75	1·70
2528	75c. San Juan de Salvamento	2·75	1·70
2529	75c. Punta Delgada	2·75	1·70

953 Condor and Olympic Rings

1997. Inclusion of Buenos Aires in Final Selection Round for 2004 Olympic Games.

2530	**953**	75c. multicoloured	2·75	1·70

954 Lacroze Company Suburban Service, 1912

1997. Centenary of First Electric Tramway in Buenos Aires. Illustrations from *History of the Tram* by Marcelo Mayorga. Multicoloured.

2531	75c. Type **954**	2·75	1·70
2532	75c. Lacroze Company urban service, 1907	2·75	1·70
2533	75c. Anglo Argentina Company tramcar, 1930	2·75	1·70
2534	75c. City of Buenos Aires Transport Corporation tramcar, 1942	2·75	1·70
2535	75c. Fabricaciones Militares tramcar, 1956	2·75	1·70
2536	75c. Electricos de Sur Company tramcar, 1908	2·75	1·70

Nos. 2531/6 were issued together, *se-tenant*, showing a composite design of a tram in a city street.

1997. As No. 2504 but size 23×35 mm. Self-adhesive. Imperf.

2537	**939**	25c. multicoloured	1·00	65
2538	**939**	75c. multicoloured	2·75	1·70

955 Monument (by Mauricio Molina)

1997. Inauguration of Monument to Joaquin Gonzalez (politician) at La Rioja.

2539	**955**	75c. multicoloured	2·75	1·70

956 Alberto Ginastera (after Carlos Nine)

1997. Composers. Multicoloured.

2540	75c. Type **956**	2·75	1·70
2541	75c. Astor Piazzolla (after Carlos Alonso)	2·75	1·70
2542	75c. Anibal Troilo (after Hermenegildo Sabat)	2·75	1·70
2543	75c. Atahualpa Yupanqui (after Luis Scafati)	2·75	1·70

957 "Tren a las Nubes", Salta

1997. Trains. Multicoloured.

2544	50c.+50c. Type **957**	4·50	2·75
2545	50c.+50c. Preserved steam locomotive, Buenos Aires	4·50	2·75
2546	50c.+50c. Patagonian express *La Trochita* Rio Negro–Chubut	4·50	2·75
2547	50c.+50c. Austral Fueguino Railway locomotive No. 2, Tierra del Fuego	4·50	2·75

958 Eva Peron (after Raul Manteola)

1997. 50th Anniv of Women's Suffrage.

2548	**958**	75c. pink and grey	2·75	1·70

959 Jorge Luis Borges and Maze

1997. Writers. Multicoloured.

2549	1p. Type **959**	3·75	2·40
2550	1p. Julio Cortazar and hop-scotch grid	3·75	2·40

1997. 70th Anniv of Air Mail in Argentina. No. **MS**2421 optd **1927 1997 ANIVERSARIO AEROPOSTA ARGENTINA** in margin.

MS2551	25c.+25c. multicoloured; 75c.+75c. multicoloured	12·00	7·50

961 Members' Flags and Southern Cross

1997. Mercosur (South American Common Market).

2552	**961**	75c. multicoloured	3·25	2·00

962 *Presidente Sarmiento* (Hugo Leban)

1997. Centenary of Launch of *Presidente Sarmiento* (cadet ship). Multicoloured.

2553	75c. Type **962**	3·25	2·00
MS2554	150×100 mm. 75c. *Presidente Sarmiento* at sea; 75c. Figurehead (vert)	8·75	5·50

963 Guevara

1997. 30th Death Anniv of Ernesto "Che" Guevara (revolutionary).

2555	**963**	75c. brown, red & black	3·75	2·00

964 Vicuna (Julian Chiapparo)

1997. "Draw an Ecostamp" Children's Competition Winners. Multicoloured.

2556	50c. Type **964**	2·10	1·30
2557	50c. Vicuna (Leandro Lopez Portal)	2·10	1·30
2558	75c. Seal (Andres Lloren) (horiz)	3·00	1·90
2559	75c. Ashy-headed goose (Jose Saccone) (horiz)	3·00	1·90

965 *Nativity* (Mary Jose)

1997. Christmas. Tapestries of the Nativity. Designs by artists named. Multicoloured. (a) Size 45×34 mm.

2560	75c. Type **965**	3·00	2·00

(b) Size 44×27 mm. Self-adhesive. Imperf.

2561	25c. Elena Aguilar	95	65
2562	25c. Silvia Pettachi	95	65
2563	50c. Ana Escobar	2·00	1·30
2564	50c. Alejandra Martinez	2·00	1·30
2565	75c. As No. 2560 but with inscriptions differently arranged	3·00	2·00
2566	75c. Nidia Martinez	3·00	2·00

966 Mother Teresa

1997. Mother Teresa (founder of the Missionaries of Charity) Commemoration.

2567	**966**	75c. multicoloured	3·00	2·00

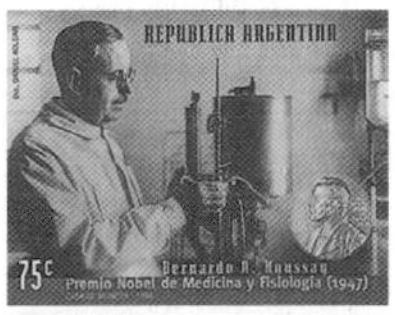

967 Houssay

1998. 50th Anniv (1997) of Award to Bernardo Houssay of Nobel Prize for Medicine and Physiology.

2568	**967**	75c. multicoloured	3·00	2·00

968 Mountaineers

1998. Cent of First Ascent of Mt. Aconcagua.

2569	**968**	1p.25 multicoloured	5·25	3·50

969 San Martin de los Andes and Lake Lacar

1998. Centenary of San Martin de los Andes.

2570	**969**	75c. multicoloured	3·00	2·00

970 Grenadier Monument (Juan Carlos Ferraro)

1998. Declaration as National Historical Monument of Palermo Barracks of General San Martin Horse Grenadiers. Multicoloured.

2571	75c. Type **970**	3·00	2·00
2572	75c. Sevres urn with portrait of San Martin	3·00	2·00
2573	75c. Regiment coat of arms	3·00	2·00
2574	75c. Main facade of barracks	3·00	2·00

971 Globe and Baby

1998. Protection of Ozone Layer.

2575	**971**	75c. multicoloured	3·00	2·00

972 Postman, 1920

1998. America. The Postman. Multicoloured.

2576	75c. Type **972**	3·00	2·00
2577	75c. Postman, 1998	3·00	2·00

973 *El Reino del Reves*

1998. Stories by Maria Elena Walsh. Illustrations by Eduardo and Ricardo Fuhrmann. Multicoloured. Self-adhesive.

2578	75c. Type **973**	3·00	2·00
2579	75c. *Zoo Loco*	3·00	2·00
2580	75c. *Dailan Kifki*	3·00	2·00
2581	75c. *Manuelita*	3·00	2·00

974 St Peter's, Fiambala, Catamarca

1998. Historic Chapels. Multicoloured.

2582	75c. Type **974**	3·00	2·00
2583	75c. Huacalera, Jujuy	3·00	2·00
2584	75c. St. Dominic's, La Rioja	3·00	2·00
2585	75c. Tumbaya, Jujuy	3·00	2·00

975 Raised Hands

1998. White Helmets (volunteer humanitarian workers).

2586	**975**	1p. multicoloured	4·25	2·75

976 Argentine Player

1998. World Cup Football Championship, France. Multicoloured.

2587	75c. Type **976**	3·00	2·00
2588	75c. Croatian player	3·00	2·00
2589	75c. Jamaican player	3·00	2·00
2590	75c. Japanese player	3·00	2·00

977 Typewriter, Camera, Pen, Computer and Satellite

1998. Journalism Day.

2591	**977**	75c. multicoloured	3·00	2·00

978 Corrientes 1860 3c. Stamps and Postal Emblem

1998. 250th Anniv of Establishment of Regular Postal Service in Rio de la Plata (Spanish dominion in South America). Multicoloured.

2592	75c. Type **978**	3·00	2·00
2593	75c. Buenos Aires Post Office and pillar box	3·00	2·00

979 Jesuit Ruins, San Ignacio Mini

1998. Mercosur Missions.

2594	**979**	75c. multicoloured	3·00	2·00

980 Aberdeen Angus

1998. Cattle. Multicoloured.

2595	25c. Type **980**	1·20	80
2596	25c. Brahman	1·20	80
2597	50c. Hereford	2·10	1·40
2598	50c. Criolla	2·10	1·40
2599	75c. Holando-Argentina	3·00	2·00
2600	75c. Shorthorn	3·00	2·00

981 Map and Base

1998. 50th Anniv of Decepcion Antarctic Base.

2601	**981**	75c. multicoloured	3·25	2·00

982 Anniversary Emblem

1998. 50th Anniv of State of Israel.

2602	**982**	75c. multicoloured	3·25	2·00

983 Bridge in Japanese Garden, Buenos Aires

1998. Cent of Argentina–Japan Friendship Treaty.

2603	**983**	75c. multicoloured	3·25	2·00

984 Facade and clock

1998. 70th Anniv of Head Post Office, Buenos Aires. Multicoloured.

2604	75c. Type **984**	3·25	2·00
2605	75c. Capital and bench	3·25	2·00

985 Patoruzu (Quinterno)

1998. Comic Strip Characters. Multicoloured.

2606	75c. Type **985**	3·25	2·00
2607	75c. Matias (Sendra)	3·25	2·00
2608	75c. Clemente (Caloi)	3·25	2·00
2609	75c. El Eternauta (Oesterheld Solano Lopez)	3·25	2·00
2610	75c. Loco Chavez (Trillo Altuna)	3·25	2·00
2611	75c. Inodoro Pereyra (Fontanarrosa)	3·25	2·00
2612	75c. Tia Vicenta (Landru)	3·25	2·00
2613	75c. Gaturro (Nik)	3·25	2·00

986 Heart with Arms holding Baby

1998. 220th Anniv of Dr. Pedro de Elizalde Children's Hospital.

2614	**986**	75c. multicoloured	3·25	2·00

987 Post Banner and Pennant, 1785, and Arms of Maritime Post

1998. "Espamer '98" Iberian–Latin American Stamp Exhibition, Buenos Aires. Multicoloured. Self-adhesive.

2615	25c. Type **987**	1·10	70
2616	75c. Mail brigantine	3·25	2·00
2617	75c.+75c. Mail brigantine (different)	6·50	4·25
2618	1p.25+1p.25 Mail brig	10·50	7·00

988 Passport and Wallenberg

1998. Raoul Wallenberg (Swedish diplomat in Hungary who helped Jews escape, 1944–45) Commemoration.

2619	**988**	75c. multicoloured	3·00	2·00

989 Aguada Culture Bird

1998. 50th Anniv of Organization of American States.

2620	**989**	75c. multicoloured	3·00	2·00

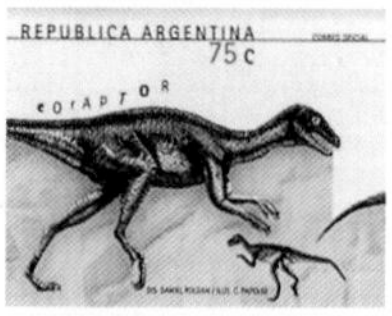
990 Eoraptor

1998. Prehistoric Animals. Multicoloured.

2621	75c. Type **990**	3·50	2·40
2622	75c. Gasparinisaura	3·50	2·40
2623	75c. Giganotosaurus	3·50	2·40
2624	75c. Patagosaurus	3·50	2·40

Nos. 2621/4 were issued together, *se-tenant*, forming a composite design.

991 Child as Angel, Stars and Score

1998. Christmas.

2625	**991**	75c. multicoloured	3·00	2·00

992 Juan Figueroa (founder) and First Issue

1998. Centenary of *El Liberal* (newspaper).

2626	**992**	75c. multicoloured	3·00	2·00

993 Postman

1998. Postmen. Size 25×35 mm. Multicoloured. Self-adhesive.

2627	25c. Type **993**	95	65
2628	75c. Modern postman	3·00	2·00

For 75c. in reduced size see No. 2640.

1998. Birds. As T **921**. Multicoloured. Self-adhesive.

2629	60c. Red-tailed comet	2·10	1·40

994 Child (painting, Francisco Ramirez)

1998. 50th Anniv of Universal Declaration of Human Rights.

2635	**994**	75c. multicoloured	3·00	2·00

995 Enrique Julio (founder) and Newspaper Offices

1998. Cent of *La Nueva Provincia* (newspaper).

2636	**995**	75c. multicoloured	3·00	2·00

996 *Haggadah* of Pessah (exhibit) and Carving on Cathedral

1998. Permanent Exhibition commemorating Holocaust Victims, Buenos Aires Cathedral.

2637	**996**	75c. multicoloured	3·00	2·00

1999. Postmen. Size 21×27 mm. Multicoloured. Self-adhesive.

2638	25c. Type **993**	85	55
2639	50c. Postman, 1950	1·50	1·00
2640	75c. As No. 2628	2·40	1·60

997 Oil-smeared Magellanic Penguin

1999. International Year of the Ocean. Multicoloured.

2641	50c. Type **997**	1·70	1·10
2642	75c. Dolphins (horiz)	2·50	1·70

998 Buildings and Draughtsman's Instruments

1999. National Arts Fund.

2643	**998**	75c. multicoloured	2·40	1·60

999 Computer and Book

1999. 25th Book Fair, Buenos Aires. Multicoloured.

2644	75c. Type **999**	2·75	1·80
2645	75c. Obelisk, compact disk case and readers	2·75	1·80

Nos. 2644/5 were issued together, *se-tenant*, forming a composite design.

1000 Rugby Balls and Player

1999. Centenary of Argentine Rugby Union. Multicoloured.

2646	75c. Type **1000**	2·75	1·80
MS2647	120×90 mm. 1p.50 19th-century and modern players	5·00	4·00

1001 Glass, La Giralda

1999. Cafes. Multicoloured. Self-adhesive.

2648	25c. Type **1001**	85	55
2649	75c. Two glasses, Cafe Homero Manzi	2·50	1·70
2650	75c. Hatstand, Confitenia Ideal	2·50	1·70
2651	1p.25 Cup and saucer, Cafe Tortoni	4·25	2·75

1002 Pierre de Coubertin, 1924 Olympic Gold Medal and Olympic Rings

1999. 75th Anniv of Argentine Olympic Committee.

2652	**1002**	75c. multicoloured	2·50	1·70

1003 Enrico Caruso (Italian tenor)

1999. Opera. Multicoloured.

2653	75c. Type **1003** (125th birth anniv and centenary of American debut)	2·50	1·60
2654	75c. Singer and musical instruments	2·50	1·60
2655	75c. Buenos Aires Opera House	2·50	1·60
2656	75c. Scene from *El Matrero* (Felipe Boero)	2·50	1·60

1004 Rosario Vera Penaloza (educationist)

1999. America (1998). Famous Women. Multicoloured.

2659	75c. Type **1004**	2·50	1·70
2660	75c. Julieta Lanteri (women's rights campaigner)	2·50	1·70

1005 *Portrait of L. E. S.* (Carlos Alonso)

1999. Paintings. Two sheets each 150×100 mm containing multicoloured designs as T **1005**.

MS2661 Two sheets. (a) 75c. *Anarchy of Year 20* (Luis Felipe Noe) (78×39 mm); 75c. Type **1005**. (b) 75c. *Typical Orchestra* (Antonio Berni) (69×49 mm); 75c. Unititled (Aida Carballo) (39×49 mm) 10·00 10·00

1006 Local Road Network

1999. Bulk Mailing Stamps. Multicoloured. Self-adhesive.

2662	35c. Type **1006**	1·20	80
2663	40c. Town plan	1·30	85
2664	50c. Regional map	1·70	1·10

1007 Carrier Pigeon

1999

2665	**1007**	75c. multicoloured	2·75	1·90

1008 Boxer

1999. Dogs. Multicoloured.

2666	25c. Type **1008**	70	45
2667	25c. Old English sheepdog	70	45
2668	50c. Welsh collie	1·30	85
2669	50c. St. Bernard	1·30	85
2670	75c. German shepherd	2·10	1·40
2671	75c. Siberian husky	2·10	1·40

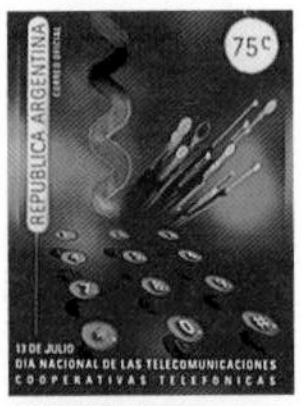

1009 Telephone Keypad

1999. National Telecommunications Day.

2672	**1009**	75c. multicoloured	2·50	1·70

1010 College Gates

1999. 150th Anniv of Justo Jose de Urquiza College, Concepcion del Uruguay.

2673	**1010**	75c. multicoloured	2·50	1·70

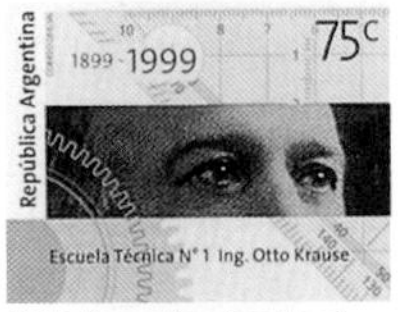

1011 Krause (engineer) and Industrial Instruments

1999. Centenary of Technical School No. 1 Otto Krause.

2674	**1011**	75c. multicoloured	2·50	1·70

1012 Nativity

1999. Bethlehem 2000.

2675	**1012**	75c. blue, gold and red	3·50	2·00

1013 Brotherhood among Men

1999. America. A New Millennium without Arms. Multicoloured.

2676	75c. Type **1013**	2·50	1·70
2677	75c. Liberty Tree (vert)	2·50	1·70

1014 Coypu (*Myocastor coypus*), Mburucuya National Park

1999. National Parks. Multicoloured.

2678	50c. Type **1014**	1·70	1·00
2679	50c. Andean condor, Quebrada de los Condoritos National Park	1·70	1·00
2680	50c. Vicuna, San Guillermo National Park	1·70	1·00
2681	75c. Puma, Sierra de las Quijadas National Park	2·50	1·70
2682	75c. Argentine grey fox (*Dusicyon griseus*), Talampaya National Park	2·50	1·70

1015 Map of the Americas, Road Network and Wickerwork

1999. 40th Anniv of Inter-American Development Bank.

2683	**1015**	75c. multicoloured	2·50	1·70

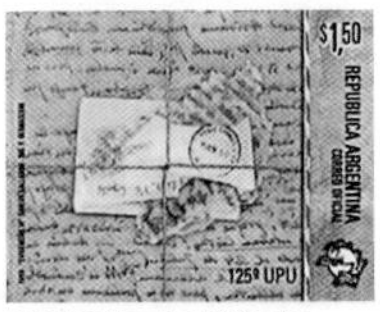

1016 *Evidencias VI* (Carlos Gallardo)

1999. 125th Anniv of Universal Postal Union.

2684	**1016**	1p.50 multicoloured	5·00	3·25

1017 *Fournier* and Map

1999. 50th Anniv of Sinking of the"*Fournier* (minesweeper) in Antarctica.

2685	**1017**	75c. multicoloured	2·50	1·70

1018 *Nothofagus pumillio*

1999. Trees (1st series). Multicoloured.

2686	75c. Type **1018**	2·50	1·70
2687	75c. *Prosopis caldenia*	2·50	1·70
2688	75c. *Schinopsis balansae*	2·50	1·70
2689	75c. *Cordia trichotoma*	2·50	1·70

Nos. 2686/9 were issued together, *se-tenant*, forming a composite design.

1019 Latecoere 25 Mailplane

1999. 50th Anniv of World Record for Consecutive Parachute Jumps. Multicoloured.

2690	75c. Type **1019**	2·50	1·70
2691	75c. Parachutists	2·50	1·70

1020 Accordionist *The Tango*

1999. The New Millennium. Three sheets each 150×100 mm containing multicoloured designs as T **1020**.

MS2692 Three sheets. (a) 50, 75c. *The Tango*; (b) 50, 75c. Jorge Luis Borges (writer); (c) 50, (horiz), 75c. Football 12·00 12·00

1021 Boca Juniors Club Supporters

1999. Football. Multicoloured. (a) Size 42×33 mm.

2693	75c. Type **1021**	2·50	1·70
2694	75c. River Plate Club supporters	2·50	1·70

(b) Size 37×34 mm (1p.50) or 37×27 mm (others) (i) Boca Juniors.

2695	25c. Two players and ball	85	55
2696	50c. Club badge	1·50	1·00
2697	50c. Players hugging	1·50	1·00
2698	75c. Supporters and balloons	2·40	1·60
2699	75c. Club banner	2·40	1·60
2700	75c. Players	2·40	1·60
2701	1p.50 Player making high kick	4·75	3·25

(ii) River Plate.

2702	25c. Stadium	85	55
2703	50c. Players arriving on pitch	1·50	1·00
2704	50c. Supporters waving flags	1·50	1·00
2705	75c. Club badge	2·40	1·60
2706	75c. Trophy	2·40	1·60
2707	75c. Supporters with banner	2·40	1·60
2708	1p.50 Player preparing to kick ball	4·75	3·25

Nos. 2695/708 are self-adhesive.

1022 Planisphere of Central South America (Pierre Descelliers, 1546)

1999. Maps. Multicoloured.

2709	25c.+25c. Type **1022**	1·50	1·00
2710	50c.+50c. 17th-century map of estuary of the River Plate (Claes Voogt)	3·00	2·00

2711	50c.+50c. Buenos Aires (Military Geographical Institute, 1910)	3·00	2·00
2712	75c.+75c. Mouth of Riachuelo river and Buenos Aires harbour (satellite picture, 1999)	4·75	3·25

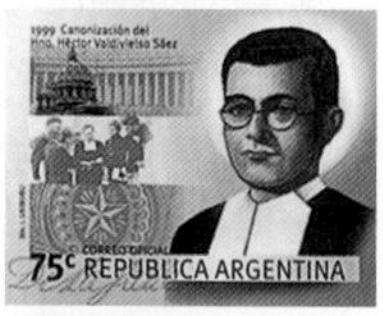

1023 Valdivielso and St. Peter's Cathedral, Rome

1999. Canonization of Hector Valdivielso Saez (Brother of the Christian Schools).

2713 **1023**	75c. multicoloured	2·50	1·70

1024 *San Francisco Xavier* (brig)

1999. Bicentenary of Manuel Belgrano Naval Academy.

2714 **1024**	75c. multicoloured	2·50	1·70

1025 *Uruguay*

1999. 125th Anniv of Launch of *Uruguay* (sail/steam corvette). Sheet 150×100 mm.

MS2715 **1025**	1p.50 multicoloured	4·75	4·75

1026 Holy Family

1999. Christmas. Multicoloured.

2716	25c. Wise Man (29×29 mm)	85	55
2717	25c. Bell (29×29 mm)	85	55
2718	50c. Two kings and camels (39×29 mm)	1·70	1·10
2719	50c. Holly leaf (39×29 mm)	1·70	1·10
2720	75c. Angel with star (39×30 mm)	2·50	1·70
2721	75c. Star (29×30 mm)	2·50	1·70
2722	75c. Nativity (39×29 mm)	2·50	1·70
2723	75c. Tree decorations (29×29 mm)	2·50	1·70
2724	75c. Type **1026**	2·50	1·70

1027 Grape on Vine

2000. Wine Making. Multicoloured.

2725	25c. Type **1027**	85	55
2726	25c. Glass and bottle of wine	85	55
2727	50c. Wine bottles	1·70	1·10
2728	50c. Cork screw and cork	1·70	1·10

1028 Mathematical Symbol and "2000"

2000. International Mathematics Year.

2729 **1028**	75c. multicoloured	2·50	1·70

1029 White-fronted Dove

2000. Doves and Pigeon. Mult. Self-adhesive.

2730	75c. Type **1029**	2·75	2·00
2731	75c. Picazuro pigeon (*Columba picazuro*)	2·75	2·00
2732	75c. Picui dove (*Columbina picni*)	2·75	2·00
2733	75c. Eared dove (*Fenaida auriculata*)	2·75	2·00

1030 *Venda coerulea*

2000. Bangkok 2000 International Stamp Exhibition. Plants. Sheet 100×76 mm containing T **1030** and similar horiz design. Multicoloured.

MS2734	25c. Type **1030**; 75c. Coral tree	3·50	3·50

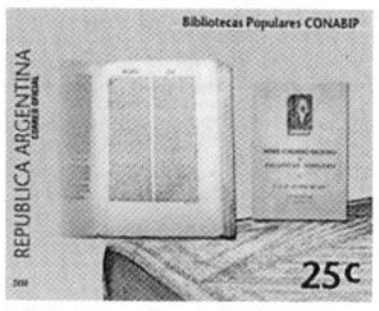

1031 Open Book (CONABIP Library)

2000. Libraries. Multicoloured.

2735	25c. Type **1031**	90	65
2736	50c. Building facade (Jujuy library)	1·80	1·30
2737	75c. Hands and braille book (Argentine Library for the Blind)	2·75	2·00
2738	$1 Open book and building (National Library)	3·50	2·75

No. 2737 has an inscription in braille across the stamp.

1032 Caravel, Compass Rose and Letter

2000. 500th Anniv of the Discovery of Brazil. Multicoloured.

2739	25c. Type **1032**	90	65
2740	75c. Pedro Alvares Cabral (discoverer) and map of South America	2·75	2·00

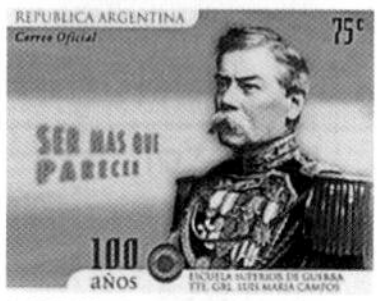

1033 Lieutenant General Luis Maria Campos (founder)

2000. Centenary of the Higher Military Academy.

2741 **1033**	75c. multicoloured	2·75	2·00

1034 Penny Black and *La Portena* (steam locomotive), 1857

2000. The Stamp Show 2000 International Stamp Exhibition, London. Sheet 99×76 mm containing T **1034** and similar horiz design. Multicoloured.

MS2742	25c. Type **1034**; 75c. Two 1862 15c. stamps and modern pillar box	3·50	3·50

1035 Convention Emblem

2000. 91st Rotary International Convention, Buenos Aires.

2743 **1035**	75c. multicoloured	2·75	2·10

1036 Futuristic Houses and Emblems (Rocio Casado)

2000. "Stampin' the Future". Winning Entries in Children's International Painting Competition. Multicoloured.

2744	25c. Type **1036**	1·00	75
2745	50c. Sea and clouds (Carolina Cacerez) (vert)	1·90	1·40
2746	75c. Flower (Valeria A. Pizarro)	3·00	2·30
2747	$1 Flying cars (Cristina Ayala Castro) (vert)	3·75	2·75

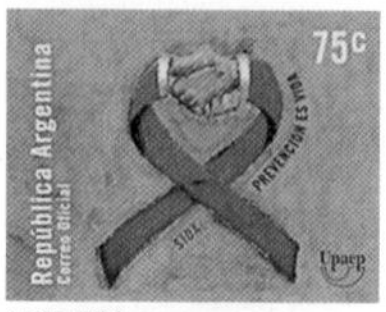

1037 Ribbon

2000. America. AIDS Awareness. Multicoloured.

2748	75c. Type **1037**	3·00	2·30
2749	75c. Arms circling faces	3·00	2·30

1038 Potez 25 Biplane

2000. Birth Centenary of Antoine de Saint-Exupery (novelist and pilot). Multicoloured.

2750	25c. Type **1038**	1·00	75
2751	50c. Late 28	2·00	1·50

1039 Potez 25 Biplane

2000. "Aerofila 2000" Mercosur Air Philately Exhibition, Buenos Aires. Multicoloured.

2752	25c. As Type **1039**	1·00	75
2753	25c. Antoine de Saint-Exupery (novelist and pilot) (29×29 mm)	1·00	75
2754	50c. Late 28	2·00	1·50
2755	50c. Henri Guillaumet, Almonacid and Jean Mermoz (aviation pioneers) (29×29 mm)	2·00	1·50
2756	50c. Map of South America and tail of Late 25 (39×39 mm)	2·00	1·50
2757	$1 Late 25 and cover (39×29 mm)	4·00	3·00

1040 Illia

2000. Birth Centenary of Arturo U. Illia (President, 1963–66).

2758 **1040**	75c. multicoloured	3·00	2·30

1041 San Martin

2000. 150th Death Anniv of General Jose de San Martin.

2759 **1041**	75c. multicoloured	3·00	2·30

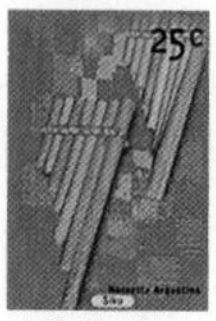

1042 Siku Pipes

2000. Argentine Culture. Multicoloured.

2760	10c. Ceremonial axe	30	25
2761	25c. Type **1042**	90	60
2762	50c. Andean loom	1·80	1·20
2763	60c. Pampeana poncho	2·30	1·50
2764	75c. Funeral mask	2·75	1·80
2765	$1 Basket	3·50	2·40
2766	$2 Kultun ritual drum	7·25	4·75
2767	$3.25 Ceremonial tiger mask	11·50	7·50
2768	$5 Funeral urn	18·00	12·00
2770	$9.40 Suri ceremonial costume	34·00	23·00

1043 Sarsfield, Signature and Cordoba Province Arms

2000. Birth Bicentenary of Dalmacio Velez Sarsfield (lawyer).

2775 **1043**	75c. multicoloured	3·25	2·40

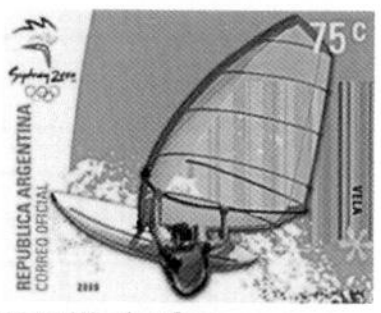

1044 Windsurfing

2000. Olympic Games, Sydney. Multicoloured.

2776	75c. Type **1044**	3·25	2·40
2777	75c. Hockey	3·25	2·40
2778	75c. Volleyball	3·25	2·40
2779	75c. High jump and pole vault	3·25	2·40

1045 Argentine Petiso

2000. "Espana 2000" International Stamp Exhibition, Madrid. Horses. Multicoloured.

2780	25c. Type **1045**	1·00	75
2781	25c. Carriage horse	1·00	75
2782	50c. Peruvian horse	2·00	1·50
2783	50c. Criolla	2·00	1·50
2784	75c. Saddle horse	3·25	2·40
2785	75c. Polo horse	3·25	2·40
MS2786	100×75 mm. 25c. Stagecoach (39×29 mm); 75c. Horse's head (39×29 mm)	4·25	4·25

1046 Man on Bicycle and Las Nereidas Fountain

2000. Transportation. Multicoloured.

2787	25c.+25c. Type **1046**	2·00	1·50
2788	50c.+50c. *Graf Zeppelin* over Buenos Aires	4·25	3·25
2789	50c.+50c. *Ganz* (diesel locomotive)	4·25	3·25
2790	75c.+75c. Tram	6·25	4·75

1047 Nuclear Reactor

2000. 50th Anniv of National Commission for Atomic Energy.

2791 **1047**	75c. multicoloured	3·25	2·40

1048 *Filete* (left-hand detail)

2000. Fileteado (painting genre) (Nos. 2792/3) and Tango (dance) (Nos. 2794/5). Multicoloured.

2792	75c. Type **1048**	3·25	2·40
2793	75c. *Filete* (right-hand detail) (Brunetti brothers)	3·25	2·40
2794	75c. Tango orchestra	3·25	2·40
2795	75c. Couple dancing	3·25	2·40

1049 Human Bodies on Jigsaw

2000. 40th Anniv of Organ Donation Publicity Campaign.

2796	**1049**	75c. multicoloured	3·25	2·40

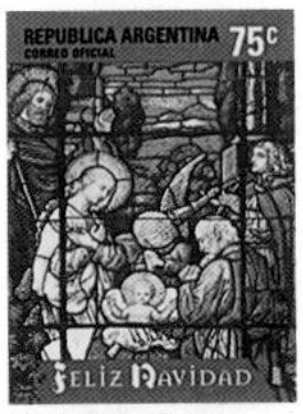

1050 *Birth of Jesus* (stained glass window, Sanctuary of Our Lady of the Rosary, New Pompeii)

2000. Christmas.

2797	**1050**	75c. multicoloured	3·25	2·40

1051 *Commelina erecta*

2000. Medicinal Plants. Multicoloured.

2798	75c. Type **1051**	3·25	2·40
2799	75c. *Senna corymbosa*	3·25	2·40
2800	75c. *Mirabilis jalapa*	3·25	2·40
2801	75c. *Eugenia uniflora*	3·25	2·40

1052 Human-shaped Vessel, Cienaga

2000. Traditional Crafts. Multicoloured.

2802	75c. Type **1052**	3·25	2·40
2803	75c. Painted human-shaped vase, Vaquerias	3·25	2·40
2804	75c. Animal-shaped vessel, Condorhuasi	3·25	2·40
2805	75c. Human-shaped vase, Candelaria	3·25	2·40

1053 "U. P." Unidad Postal

2001. Postal Agents' Stamps. Multicoloured, background colours given. Self-adhesive gum.

2806	**1053**	10c. turquoise	25	20
2807	**1053**	25c. green	70	55
2808	**1053**	60c. yellow	1·60	1·20
2809	**1053**	75c. red	2·20	1·70
2810	**1053**	$1 blue	3·00	2·20
2811	**1053**	$3 red	9·00	6·75
2812	**1053**	$3.25 yellow	9·75	7·25
2813	**1053**	$5.50 mauve	16·00	12·00

Nos. 2806/13 were issued for use by Postal Agents as opposed to branches of the Argentine Post Office.

1054 *Megatherium americanum* ("Megaterio")

2001. Cainozoic Mammals. Multicoloured.

2820	75c. Type **1054**	3·25	2·40
2821	75c. *Doedicurus clavcaudatus* ("Gliptodonte")	3·25	2·40
2822	75c. *Macrauchenia patachonica* ("Macrauqueria")	3·25	2·40
2823	75c. *Toxodon platensis* ("Toxodonte")	3·25	2·40

1055 Map, South Polar Skua and San Martin Base

2001. 50th Anniv of San Martín and Brown Antarctic Bases. Multicoloured.

2824	75c. Type **1055**	3·25	2·40
2825	75c. Blue-eyed cormorant, map and Brown Base	3·25	2·40

1056 Bees on Clover Flower

2001. Apiculture. Multicoloured.

2826	75c. Type **1056**	3·25	2·40
2827	75c. Bees on honeycomb	3·25	2·40
2828	75c. Bees and bee-keeper attending hives	3·25	2·40
2829	75c. Jar of honey and swizzle	3·25	2·40

Nos. 2826/9 were issued together, *se-tenant*, forming a composite design.

1057 Scientist with Fossilized Bones

2001. 50th Anniv of Argentine Antarctic Institute. Sheet 150×99 mm containing T **1057** and similar horiz design. Multicoloured.

MS2830	75c. Type **1057**; 75c. Scientist and surveying equipment	6·25	6·25

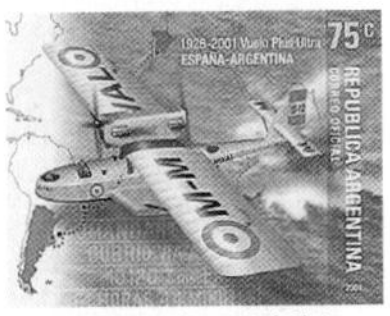

1058 Dornier Do-J Wal Flying Boat *Plus Ultra* and Route Map

2001. 75th Anniv of Major Ramon Franco's Flight from Spain to Argentina.

2831	**1058**	75c. multicoloured	3·25	2·40

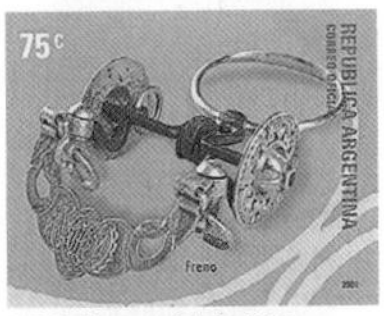

1059 Horse's Bridle Fittings

2001. Silver Work. Each blue, silver and black.

2832	75c. Type **1059**	3·25	2·40
2833	75c. Stirrups	3·25	2·40
2834	75c. Spurs	3·25	2·40
2835	75c. Rastra (gaucho belt decoration)	3·25	2·40

1060 *Washerwoman by the Banks of Belgrano* (detail, Prilidiano Pueyrredon)

2001. Belgica 2001 International Stamp Exhibition, Brussels. 500th Anniv of European Postal Service. Sheet 99×75 mm containing T **1060** and similar horiz design. Multicoloured.

MS2836	25c. Type **1060**; 75c. *Hay Harvest* (detail, Pieter Bruegel, the Elder)	4·50	4·50

1061 Goalkeeper catching Ball

2001. Under 20's World Youth Football Championship, Argentine Republic. Multicoloured.

2837	75c. Type **1061**	3·25	2·40
2838	75c. Player kicking ball	3·25	2·40

1062 People and Buildings

2001. National Census.

2839	**1062**	75c. multicoloured	3·25	2·40

1063 SAC-C Satellite, Seagulls and Sunflowers

2001. Environmental Protection. Satellite Tracking Project.

2840	**1063**	75c. multicoloured	3·25	2·40

1064 Puma

2001. Wild Cats. Multicoloured.

2841	25c. Type **1064**	1·00	75
2842	25c. Jaguar	1·00	75
2843	50c. Jaguarundi	2·00	1·50
2844	50c. Ocelot	2·00	1·50
2845	75c. Geoffroy's Cat	3·25	2·40
2846	75c. Kodkod	3·25	2·40

1065 *Bandoneon Recital* (painting, Aldo Severi)

2001

2847	**1065**	75c. multicoloured	3·25	2·40

1066 Couple dancing the Tango

2001. PHILA NIPPON 01 International Stamp Exhibition, Tokyo. Sheet 100×75 mm containing T **1066** and similar horiz design. Multicoloured.

MS2848	75c. Type **1066**; 75c. Kabuki performer	6·25	6·25

1067 Discepolo

2001. Birth Centenary of Enriques Santos Discepolo (actor and lyric writer).

2849	**1067**	75c. multicoloured	3·50	2·50

1068 Courtyard, Caroya Estancia, Angel and Chapel, Estancia Santa Catalina

2001. UNESCO World Heritage Sites. Multicoloured.

2850	75c. Type **1068**	3·50	2·50
2851	75c. Emblem and chapel, Estancia La Candelaria, dome of Estancia Alta Gracia and belfry, Estancia Jesus Maria	3·50	2·50

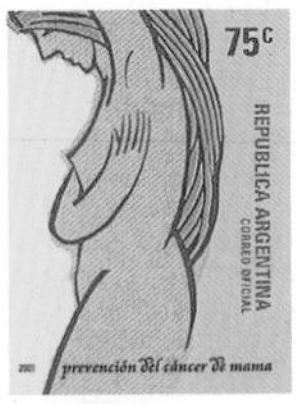

1069 Woman

2001. Breast Cancer Awareness.

2852	**1069**	75c. multicoloured	3·50	2·50

1070 Burmeister's Porpoise

2001. Marine Mammals. Multicoloured.

2853	25c.+25c. Type **1070**	2·30	2·10
2854	50c.+50c. La Plata River dolphin	4·75	4·25
2855	50c.+50c. Minke whale	4·75	4·25
2856	75c.+75c. Humpback whale	7·25	6·50

1071 Alfa Romeo 159 Alfetta, Spain, 1951

2001. Formula 1 Racing Cars driven by Juan Manuel Fangio. Multicoloured.

2857	75c. Type **1071**	3·25	2·40
2858	75c. Mercedes Benz W 196, France, 1954	3·25	2·40
2859	75c. Lancia-Ferrari D50, Monaco, 1956	3·25	2·40
2860	75c. Maserati 250 F, Germany, 1957	3·25	2·40

1072 Palo Santo Tree (*Bulnesia sarmientoi*)

2001. Mercosur (South American Common Market).

2861	**1072**	75c. multicoloured	3·25	2·40

1073 Justo Jose de Urquiza

2001. Birth Anniversaries. Multicoloured.

2862	75c. Type **1073** (politician) (bicentenary)	3·25	2·40
2863	75c. Roque Saenz Pena (President 1910—14) (150th anniv)	3·25	2·40

1074 18th-century Mail Courier

2001. HAFNIA 01 International Stamp Exhibition, Copenhagen. Sheet 100×75 mm containing T **1074** and similar horiz design. Multicoloured.

MS2864	25c. Type **1074**; 75c. 17th-century mail courier	5·00	5·00

1075 "La Pobladora" Carriage (Enrique Udaondo Graphic Museum Complex)

2001. Museums. Multicoloured.

2865	75c. Type **1075**	3·25	2·40
2866	75c. Ebony and silver crucifix (Brigadier General Juan Martin de Pueyrredon Museum) (vert)	3·25	2·40
2867	75c. Funerary urn (Emilio and Duncan Wagner Museum of Anthropological and Natural Sciences) (vert)	3·25	2·40
2868	75c. Skeleton of Carnotaurus sastrei (Argentine Natural Science Museum)	3·25	2·40

1076 *The Power of the Most High will Overshadow You* (Martin La Spina)

2001. Christmas.

2869	**1076** 75c. multicoloured	3·25	2·40

1077 Carola Lorenzini and Focke Wulf 44-J

2001. Aviation. Multicoloured.

2870	75c. Type **1077**	3·25	2·40
2871	75c. Jean Mermoz and Arc-en-Ciel	3·25	2·40

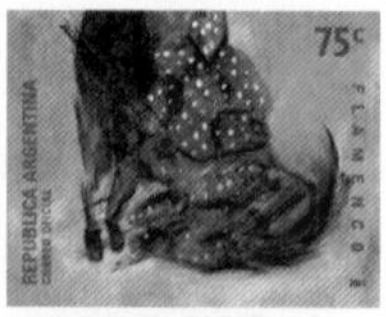

1078 Dancers (Flamenco)

2001. Dances. Multicoloured.

2872	75c. Type **1078**	3·25	2·40
2873	75c. Dancers (purple skirt) (Vals)	3·25	2·40
2874	75c. Dancers (orange skirt) (Zamba)	3·25	2·40
2875	75c. Dancers (Tango)	3·25	2·40

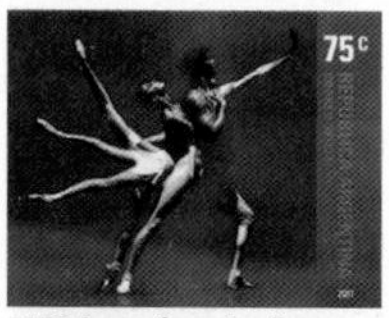

1079 Scene from *Apollon Musagete* (Igor Stravinsky)

2001. National Day of the Dancer.

2876	**1079** 75c. multicoloured	3·25	2·40

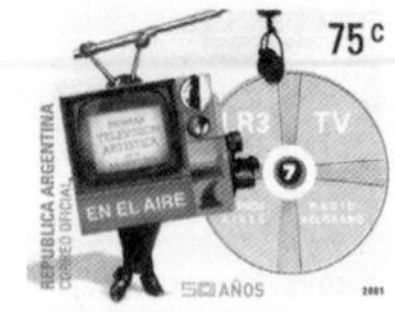

1080 Television Set, Camera and Microphone

2001. 50th Anniv of Television in Argentina. Multicoloured.

2877	75c. Type **1080**	3·25	2·40
2878	75c. Television set and video tapes	3·25	2·40
2879	75c. Satellite dish and astronaut	3·25	2·40
2880	75c. Colour television cables and remote control	3·25	2·40

1081 Consolidated PBY-5A Catalina (amphibian) and Cancellation

2002. 50th Anniv of Argentine Antarctic Programme. Multicoloured.

2881	75c. Type **1081** (first air and sea courier service)	3·25	2·40
2882	75c. *Chiriguano* (minesweeper) and buildings (foundation of Esparanza Base)	3·25	2·40

1082 House and Flag

2002. America. Education and Literacy Campaign. Multicoloured.

2883	75c. Type **1082**	3·25	2·40
2884	75c. Children playing hopscotch	3·25	2·40

1083 Two-banded Plover (*Charadrius falklandicus*)

2002. Birds. Multicoloured.

2885	50c. Type **1083**	1·80	1·30
2886	50c. Dolphin gull (*Larus scoresbii*)	1·80	1·30
2887	75c. Ruddy-headed goose (*Chloephaga rubidiceps*) (vert)	2·75	2·00
2888	75c. King penguin (*Aptenodytes patagonicus*) (vert)	2·75	2·00

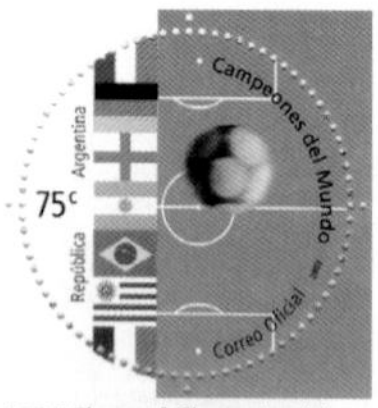

1084 Flags of Championship Winners and Football

2002. 20th-century World Cup Football Champions. Multicoloured.

2889	75c. Type **1084**	2·75	2·00
2890	75c. Argentine footballer	2·75	2·00

1085 Parana River and Emblem

2002. Anniversaries. Multicoloured.

2891	25c. Type **1085** (150th anniv of Rosario City)	90	65
2892	25c. National flag and monument	90	65
2893	50c. Mount Fitzroy (150th birth anniv of Francisco Pascasio Moreno (Perito) (explorer and founder of Argentine Scouts movement))	1·80	1·30
2894	50c. Dr. Moreno	1·80	1·30
2895	75c. Flower and view of city (centenary of foundation San Carlos de Bariloche)	2·75	2·00
2896	75c. Capilla San Eduardo (St. Edward's chapel) and city plan	2·75	2·00

1086 Fruit, Mother, Boy, Bread and Health Centre

2002. Centenary of Pan-American Health Organization.

2897	**1086** 75c. multicoloured	2·75	2·00

1087 Cosme Mariano Argerich, 1758–1820

2002. Doctors. Multicoloured.

2898	50c. Type **1087**	1·80	1·30
2899	50c. Jose Maria Ramos Mejia, 1849–1914	1·80	1·30
2900	50c. Salvador Mazza, 1886–1946	1·80	1·30
2901	50c. Carlos Arturo Giananonio, 1926–1995	1·80	1·30

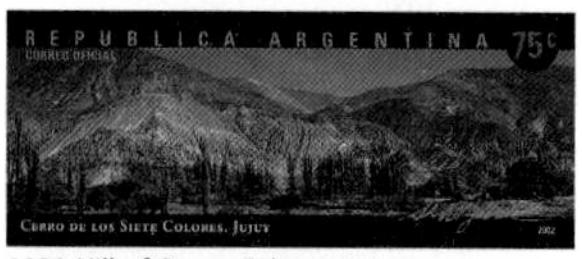

1088 Hill of Seven Colours, Jujuy

2002. Landscapes. Multicoloured.

2902	75c. Type **1088**	2·75	2·00
2903	75c. Iguazu waterfall, Misiones	2·75	2·00
2904	75c. Talampaya National Park	2·75	2·00
2905	75c. Agoncagua mountain, Mendoza	2·75	2·00
2906	75c. Rosedal Park, Buenos Aires	2·75	2·00
2907	75c. San Jorge lighthouse, Chubut	2·75	2·00
2908	75c. Perito Moreno glacier, Santa Cruz	2·75	2·00
2909	75c. Lapataia Bay, Tierra del Fuego	2·75	2·00

See also Nos. 2980/7 and 3022/9.

1089 Pampas Deer (*Ozotoceros bezoarticus*)

2002. Endangered Species. Multicoloured.

2910	$1 Type **1089**	3·25	2·20
2911	$1 Vicuna (*Vicugna vicugna*)	3·25	2·20
2912	$1 Southern pudu (*Pudu pudu*)	3·25	2·20
2913	$1 Chaco peccary (*Catgonus wagneri*)	3·25	2·20

1090 Eva Peron

2002. 50th Death Anniv of Eva Peron. Multicoloured.

2914	75c. Type **1090**	2·75	2·00
2915	75c. In cameo	2·75	2·00
2916	75c. At microphone	2·75	2·00
2917	75c. In profile wearing earrings	2·75	2·00

1091 Argentine Footballer

2002. Philakorea 2002 International Stamp Exhibition. Sheet 100×75 mm containing T **1091** and similar horiz design. Multicoloured.

MS2918	$1.50 Type **1091**; $1.50 Korean footballer	6·75	6·75

1092 Boa Constrictor (*Boa lampalagua*)

2002. Reptiles. Multicoloured.

2919	25c.+25c. Type **1092**	1·10	80
2920	50c.+50c. Caiman (*Caiman yacare*)	2·30	1·60
2921	50c.+50c. Argentine black and white tegu (*Tupinambis merianae*)	2·30	1·60
2922	75c.+75c. Red-footed tortoise (*Chelonoidis carbonaria*)	3·50	2·40

1093 Whale's Head

2002. Mercosur (South American Common Market). Multicoloured.

2923	75c. Type **1093**	1·30	85
2924	75c. Whale's tail	1·30	85

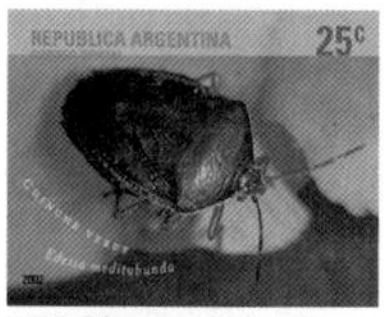

1094 *Edessa meditabunda*

2002. Insects. Multicoloured.

2925	25c. Type **1094**	65	45
2926	50c. *Elaeochlora viridis*	1·30	85
2927	75c. *Chrysodina aurata*	1·90	1·30
2928	75c. *Steirastoma breve*	2·50	1·70

1095 Players, Ball and Net

2002. World Men's Volleyball Championships. Multicoloured.

2929	75c. Type **1095**	1·90	1·30
2930	75c. Two players ball and net	1·90	1·30
2931	75c. Hands, net, ball and head	1·90	1·30
2932	75c. Players congratulating one another	1·90	1·30

1096 Roadway

2002. 50th Anniv of Argentine Highways Department.

2933	**1096** 75c. multicoloured	1·90	1·30

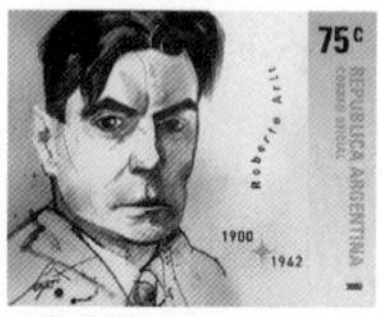

1097 Roberto Arlt

2002. Death Anniversaries. Multicoloured.

2934	75c. Type **1097** (writer, 60th)	1·90	1·30
2935	75c. Luis Sandrini (actor and director, 22nd)	1·90	1·30
2936	75c. Nini Marshall (actor, 6th)	1·90	1·30
2937	75c. Beatriz Guido (writer, 14th)	1·90	1·30

1101 Andres Chazarreta (composer)

2002. Folklorists. Multicoloured.

2945	75c. Type **1101**	1·90	1·30
2946	75c. Gustavo "Cuchi" Leguizamon (songwriter)	1·90	1·30
2947	75c. Carlos Vega (guitarist)	1·90	1·30
2948	75c. Armando Tejada Gomez (poet and songwriter)	1·90	1·30

1098 Immigrant Hotel, Mother and Child

2002. Immigration. Multicoloured.

2938	75c. Type **1098**	1·90	1·30
2939	75c. Two men and ship	1·90	1·30
2940	75c. Two men and immigrant hotel	1·90	1·30
2941	75c. Horse-drawn farm implement and family	1·90	1·30

Nos. 2938/41 were issued in horizontal *se-tenant* strips of four stamps within the sheet, each pair (2938/9 and 2940/1) forming a composite design.

1099 Envelope, Horse-drawn Coach and Head

2002. 50th Anniv of Argentine Federation of Philatelic Entities (FAEF). Multicoloured.

2942	75c. Type **1099**	1·90	1·30
2943	75c. Flag, figure, ship and arms	1·90	1·30

1100 Joseph leading Donkey carrying Mary and Jesus

2002. Christmas.

2944	**1100**	75c. multicoloured	1·90	1·30

1102 Girl (rod puppet)

2002. Puppets. Multicoloured.

2949	75c. Type **1102**	1·90	1·30
2950	75c. Fish and king (marionettes)	1·90	1·30
2951	75c. Man (marote puppet)	1·90	1·30
2952	75c. Figures (shadow puppets)	1·90	1·30

1103 Cabbage containing Hands

2003. "Pro Huerta" (communal gardens initiative). Multicoloured.

2953	75c. Type **1103**	1·90	1·30
2954	75c. Street map as corn cob (vert)	1·90	1·30

1104 Woven Bag and Band

2003. Mercosur (South American Common Market). Multicoloured.

2955	75c. Type **1104** (Pilaga and Toba people, Formosa province)	1·90	1·30
2956	75c. Basketwork sieve (Mbya people, Misiones province) and wooden servers (Wichi people, Salta province)	1·90	1·30

1105 Squirrel Cuckoo (*Piaya cayana*) (Colonia Benitez reserve)

2003. National Parks. Multicoloured.

2957	50c. Type **1105**	1·30	85
2958	50c. Grey brocket (*Mazama gouzoupira*) (Copo park)	1·30	85
2959	50c. Guanaco (*Lama guanicoe*) (Los Cardones)	1·30	85
2960	75c. Magellanic penguin (*Speniscus magellanicus*) (Monte Leon)	1·90	1·30
2961	75c. *Tinamotis pentlandii* (Campo de los Alisos)	1·90	1·30

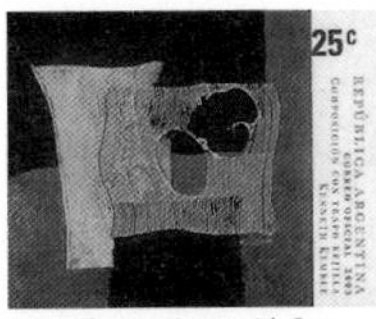

1106 *Composition with Rag Grid* (Kenneth Kemble)

2003. Art. Multicoloured.

2962	25c. Type **1106**	65	45
2963	25c. *Painting* (Roberto Aizenberg) (vert)	65	45
2964	50c. *Screen* (Romulo Maccio) (vert)	1·30	85
2965	75c. *La Gioconda* (Guillemo Roux)	1·90	1·30
2966	75c. *To Flee* (Antonio Segui)	1·90	1·30
2967	$1 *San P.* (Xul Solar) (vert)	2·50	1·70

1107 Hockey Player

2003. Sport. Multicoloured.

2968	75c. Type **1107** (Women's Hockey World Champions, 2002)	1·90	1·30
2969	75c. Footballer (World Blind Football Champions, 2002)	1·90	1·30

No. 2969 was embossed with the face value in Braille.

1108 Mago Fafa (Broccoli)

2003. Cartoons. Sheet 156×120 mm containing T **1108** and similar vert designs. Multicoloured.

MS2970	25c. Type **1108**; 25c. Astronauta (Crist); 50c. Hijitus (Garcia Ferre); 50c. Savarese (Mandrafina and Robin Wood); 75c. Sonoman (Oswal); 75c. El Tipito (Daniel Paz and Rudy); 75c. La Vaca Aurora (Mirco); 75c. Diogenes y el Linyera (Tabare)	7·50	7·50

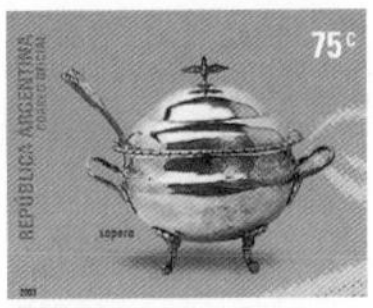

1109 19th-century Soup Tureen

2003. Silver Work. Multicoloured.

2971	75c. Type **1109**	1·90	1·30
2972	75c. Kettle, *mate de campana* and drinking tube	1·90	1·30
2973	75c. Chocolate pot and jug	1·90	1·30
2974	75c. 19th-century sugar bowl	1·90	1·30

Nos. 2971/4 were issued together, *se-tenant*, forming a composite design.

1110 Empanadas

2003. Traditional Foods. Multicoloured.

2975	75c. Type **1110** (turnovers)	1·90	1·30
2976	75c. Locro (corn and bean stew)	1·90	1·30
2977	75c. Parillada (mixed grill)	1·90	1·30
2978	75c. Pastilitos (miniature pastries)	1·90	1·30

1111 El Elastico (elastic)

2003. Children's Games. Sheet 108×88 mm containing T **1111** and similar horiz designs. Multicoloured.

MS2979	50c.×4 Type **1111**; La escondida (hide and seek); La mancha (tag); Martin pescador (Martin the fisherman)	4·50	4·50

2003. Landscapes. As T **1088**. Multicoloured.

2980	75c. Mbigua marsh, Formosa	1·90	1·30
2981	75c. Dead Man's salt flat, Catamarca	1·90	1·30
2982	75c. Quilmes ruins, Tucuman	1·90	1·30
2983	75c. Ibera marshland, Corrientes	1·90	1·30
2984	75c. Moon Valley, Ischigualasto park, San Juan	1·90	1·30
2985	75c. Mar del Plata city, Buenos Aires	1·90	1·30
2986	75c. Caleu Caleu, La Pampa	1·90	1·30
2987	75c. Lanin National Park, Neuqueen	1·90	1·30

1112 Velocipede (1855)

2003. Evolution of the Bicycle. Multicoloured.

2988	25c.+25c. Type **1112**	1·10	80
2989	50c.+50c. Penny farthing (1867)	2·30	1·60
2990	50c.+50c. Touring bicycle	2·30	1·60
2991	75c.+75c. Racing bicycle	3·50	2·40

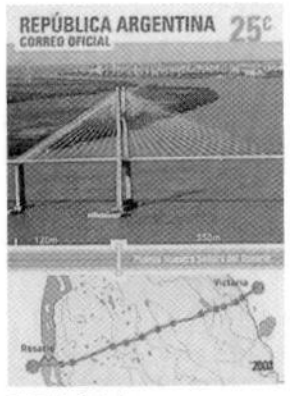

1113 Bridge

2003. Inauguration of Nuestra Senora de Rosario Bridge over Parana River. Multicoloured.

2992	25c. Type **1113**	65	45
2993	75c. Ship and bridge	1·90	1·30

Nos. 2992/3 were issued together, *se-tenant*, forming a composite design of the bridge.

1114 Provincial Emblem

2003. Rio Negro Province.

2994	**1114**	75c. multicoloured	1·90	1·30

1115 Dr. Vicente Fidel Lopez

2003. Anniversaries. Multicoloured.

2995	75c. Type **1115** (politician) (death centenary)	1·90	1·30
2996	75c. General San Martin Regiment (centenary of modern regiment)	1·90	1·30
2997	75c. Script and Bautista Alberdi (constitutional pioneer) (150th anniv of constitution)	1·90	1·30
2998	75c. Presidential palace and symbols of office	1·90	1·30

1116 Demon Mask

2003. Bangkok 2003 International Stamp Exhibition. Sheet 150×100 mm containing T **1116** and similar vert design. Multicoloured.

MS2999	75c.×2 Type **1116** (Quebrada de Humahuaca carnival, Argentine); Spirit mask (Phi Ta Khon festival, Thailand)	3·50	3·50

1117 Andean Condor (*Vultur gryphus*)

2003. America. Flora and Fauna. Multicoloured.

3000	75c. Type **1117**	1·90	1·30
3001	75c. *Nothofagus pumilio* (tree), forest and mountains	1·90	1·30

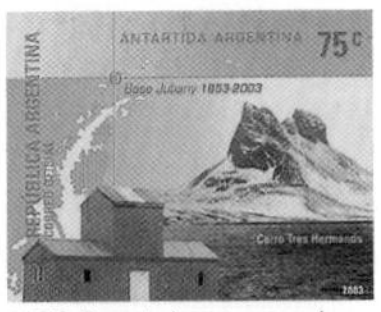

1118 Map, Laboratory and Tres Hermanos Mountain

2003. 50th Anniv of Jubany Antarctic Base.

3002	**1118**	75c. multicoloured	1·90	1·30

1119 Cattle

2003. National Products. Multicoloured.

3003	75c. Type **1119** (livestock)	1·90	1·30
3004	75c. Soya beans (agriculture)	1·90	1·30
3005	75c. Telecobalt therapy machines (nuclear medicine)	1·90	1·30
3006	75c. Drums and bars (aluminium production)	1·90	1·30

1120 Corvette *Uruguay*

2003. Centenary of Rescue of Swedish Scientists by Argentine Corvette Uruguay. Multicoloured.

3007	75c. Type **1120**	1·90	1·30
MS3008	150×99 mm. 75c.×2 Swedish ship (40×30 mm); Captain Julian Irizar and *Uruguay* (40×30 mm)	3·50	3·50

1121 The Nativity (clay figures)

2003. Christmas. Multicoloured.

3009	75c. Type **1121**	1·90	1·30
3010	75c. "Guacho Birth" (wooden carving) (Eloy Lopez)	1·90	1·30

1122 Savings Bank Building, Cordoba

2003. 20th-Century Architecture. Multicoloured.

3011	75c. Type **1122**	1·90	1·30
3012	75c. Bank, San Miguel de Tucuman	1·90	1·30
3013	75c. Minetti Palace, Rosario	1·90	1·30
3014	75c. Barolo Palace, Buenos Aires	1·90	1·30

1123 Helicopter over Orcados Base

2004. Centenary of Orcados Base and Orcados del Sud Post Office, Antarctica. Multicoloured.

3015	75c. Type **1123**	1·90	1·30
MS3016	150×100 mm. 75c.×2, 5 cent 1904 stamp and "Orcados del Sud" 1904 postmark; Orcados meteorological observatory, 1904	3·50	3·50

1124 Llama, Cave Painting, Painted Door and Rio Grande Valley

2004. UNESCO World Heritage Site. Quebrada de Humahuaca. Multicoloured.

3017	75c. Type **1124**	1·90	1·30
3018	75c. Church, festival procession and valley	1·90	1·30

Nos. 3017/18 were issued together, *se-tenant*, forming a composite design.

1125 Green Forest

2004. America. Endangered Species. Destruction of the Rainforest. Multicoloured.

3019	75c. Type **1125**	1·90	1·30
3020	75c. Dying forest	1·90	1·30

Nos. 3019/20 were issued together, *se-tenant*, forming a composite design.

The centre of No. 3020 has been removed to simulate burning.

1126 Masthead of First Edition and Modern Copy

2004. Centenary of *La Voz del Interior* Newspaper.

3021	**1126**	75c. multicoloured	1·90	1·30

2004. Landscapes. As T **1088**. Multicoloured.

3022	75c. Drying peppers, Molinas, Salta	1·90	1·30
3023	75c. Man leading donkey, Pampa del Indio Park, Chaco	1·90	1·30
3024	75c. Dam on Rio Dulce river, Rio Hondo, Santiago del Estero	1·90	1·30
3025	75c. Bridge over Setubal lagoon, Santa Fe de la Vera Cruz	1·90	1·30
3026	75c. San Roque lake, Cordoba	1·90	1·30
3027	75c. Palm Grove National Park, Entre Rios	1·90	1·30
3028	75c. Potero de los Funes, San Luis	1·90	1·30
3029	75c. Tronador mountain, Rio Negro	1·90	1·30

1127 Street Football

2004. Centenary of FIFA (Federation Internationale de Football Association). Paintings by Ruben Ramonda. Multicoloured.

3030	75c. Type **1127**	1·90	1·30
3031	75c. The Tunnel	1·90	1·30

1128 *Back from Fishing* (Joaquin Sorolla y Bastida)

2004. Espana 2004 International Stamp Exhibition, Valencia. Sheet 150×100 mm containing T **1128** and similar multicoloured design.

MS3032	75c. Type **1128**; 75c. "At Rest in the Pampa" (Angel Della Valle) (vert)	3·50	3·50

1129 Compass in Case

2004. 125th Anniv of Naval Hydro-Graphic Service. Multicoloured.

3033	75c. Type **1129**	1·90	1·30
3034	75c. Sextant	1·90	1·30
3035	75c. Cabo Virgenes lighthouse	1·90	1·30
3036	75c. *Puerto Deseado* (hydrographic ship)	1·90	1·30

1130 Performing Dogs

2004. Circus. Sheet 109×88 mm containing T **1130** and similar horiz designs. Multicoloured.

MS3037	50c. Type **1130**; 50c. Trapeze artiste; 50c. Clown riding unicycle; 50c. Equestrienne	4·00	4·00

The stamps of No. **MS**3037 form a composite design of a circus ring.

1131 Isidorito

2004. Patorutzito (character from graphic magazine by Dante Quinterno). Designs showing characters. Multicoloured.

3038	75c. Patoruzito (20×60 mm)	1·90	1·30
3039	75c. Pamperito (20×60 mm)	1·90	1·30
3040	75c. Isidorito (30×29 mm)	1·90	1·30
3041	75c. Malen	1·90	1·30
3042	75c. Upita	1·90	1·30
3043	75c. Chacha	1·90	1·30
MS3044	167×118 mm. 25c. Type **1131**; 25c. Upita (different); 50c. Patoruzito; 50c. Malen (different); 75c. Pamperito; 75c. Chacha plus 2 stamp size labels	7·00	7·00

The stamps and labels contained in **MS**3044 form a composite design.

1132 Woman and Guide Dog

2004. Working Dogs. Multicoloured.

3045	75c. Type **1132**	1·90	1·30
3046	75c. Rescue dog (horiz)	1·90	1·30

1133 *Patagonotothen ramsay*

2004. Endangered Species. Fish. Multicoloured.

3047	75c. Type **1133**	1·90	1·30
3048	75c. *Bathyraja griseocauda*	1·90	1·30
3049	75c. *Salilota australis*	1·90	1·30
3050	75c. *Dissostichus eleginoides*	1·90	1·30

1134 Cycling

2004. Olympic Games, Athens 2004. Multicoloured.

3051	75c. Type **1134**	1·90	1·30
3052	75c. Judo	1·90	1·30
3053	75c. Swimming	1·90	1·30
3054	75c. Tennis	1·90	1·30

1135 *Villarino*

2004. Naval Carriers. Multicoloured.

3055	25c.+25c. Type **1135**	90	70
3056	50c.+50c. *Pampa*	1·80	1·30
3057	50c.+50c. *Bahia Thetis*	1·80	1·30
3058	75c.+75c. *Cabo de Hornis*	2·50	2·20

Nos. 3055/8 were issued together, *se-tenant*, forming a composite design.

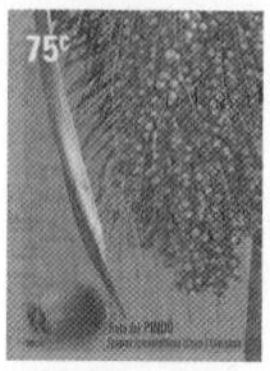

1136 Queen Palm Fruit (*Syagrus romanzoffiana*)

2004. Singapore 2004 International Stamp Exhibition. Fruit. Sheet 150×100 mm containing T **1136** and similar vert designs.

MS3059	75c.×2, Type **1136**; Mango	2·50	1·70

1137 El Pehuen

2004. Legends and Traditions. Multicoloured.

3060	75c. Type **1137** (legend of araucaria tree)	1·60	1·10
3061	75c. La Yacumama (Diaguita water goddess)	1·60	1·10
3062	75c. La Pachamama (earth goddess)	1·60	1·10
3063	75c. La Difunta Correa (legend of mother who died of thirst)	1·60	1·10

1138 Early Students and Microscope

2004. Centenaries. Multicoloured.

3064	75c. Type **1138** (Agronomy and Veterinary Science Institute)	1·60	1·10
3065	75c. Jose san Martin (statue) and road and rail bridges over Nequen river (Neuqin city)	1·60	1·10
3066	75c. Monument and cover of *La Coleccionista* (Rosario Philatelic Association)	1·60	1·10

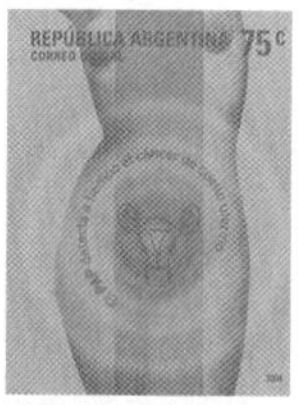

1139 Woman's Torso and Campaign Emblem

2004. Cervical Cancer Awareness Campaign.

3067	**1139**	75c. multicoloured	1·60	1·10

1140 Hourglass containing Clear Water

2004. Mercosur. Water Conservation Campaign. Multicoloured.

3068	75c. Type **1140**	1·60	1·10
3069	75c. Hourglass containing contaminated water	1·60	1·10

1141 Mary

2004. Christmas. Multicoloured.

3070	75c. Type **1141**	1·60	1·10
3071	75c. The Nativity	1·60	1·10

1142 Reverse

2004. 1813 One Ounce Gold Coin. Multicoloured.

3072	75c. Type **1142**	1·60	1·10
3073	75c. Obverse	1·60	1·10

Nos. 3072/3 were issued together, *se-tenant*, forming a composite design.

1143 "Spanish Grammar for Americans" and Andres Bello (author)

2004. Third International Spanish Language Congress.

3074	**1143**	75c. multicoloured	1·60	1·10

1144 Exchange Building

2004. 150th Anniv of Buenos Aires Commodities Exchange.

3075	**1144**	75c. multicoloured	1·60	1·10

1145 *Aloysia citriodora*

2004. Aromatic Plants. Multicoloured.

3076	75c. Type **1145**	1·60	1·10
3077	75c. *Minthostachys mollis*	1·60	1·10
3078	75c. *Tagetes minuta*	1·60	1·10
3079	75c. *Lippia turbinate*	1·60	1·10

1146 Emblem and Scout

2005. 12th Pan American Scout Jamboree, Mendoza.

3080	**1146**	75c. multicoloured	1·60	1·10

1147 Ram Klong Yao Dance (Thailand)

2005. 50th Anniv of Thailand—Argentina Diplomatic Relations. Multicoloured.

3081	75c. Type **1147**	1·60	1·10
3082	75c. Tango (Argentina)	1·60	1·10

1148 *Woman in Red Sweater*

2005. Birth Centenary of Alberto Berni (artist). Details from painting. Multicoloured.

3083	75c. Type **1148**	1·60	1·10
MS3084	150×99 mm. 75c.×2 Face (detail); Baby and men wearing hats (detail) (horiz)	3·25	3·25

The stamps and margin of No. **MS**3084 form a composite design of *Manifestation*.

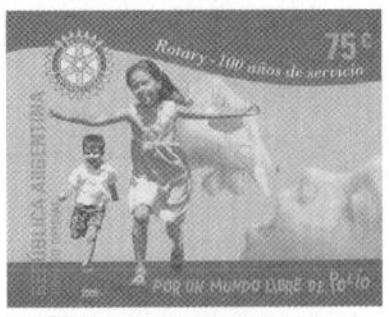

1149 Rotary International Emblem, Children and Vaccine

2005. Centenary of Rotary International (charitable organization). Eradication of Polio Campaign.

3085	**1149**	75c. multicoloured	1·60	1·10

1150 Silvina Ocampo

2005. Mercosaur. Writers. Multicoloured.

3086	75c. Type **1150** (1903–1993)	1·60	1·10
3087	75c. Ezequiel Martinez Estrada (1895–1964)	1·60	1·10

1151 Sedan Graciela

2005. National Motor Industry. Multicoloured.

3088	75c. Type **1151**	1·60	1·10
3089	75c. Justicalista sport	1·60	1·10
3090	75c. Rastrojero diesel	1·60	1·10
3091	75c. Siam di Tella 1500	1·60	1·10
3092	75c. Torino 380W	1·60	1·10

1152 Jose Antonio Balseiro (founder) and Nuclear Reactor

2005. 50th Anniv of Balseiro Institute. International Year of Physics. Multicoloured.

3093	75c. Type **1152**	1·60	1·10
3094	75c. Albert Einstein and frontispiece of *Theory of Special Relativity*	1·60	1·10

1153 Pope John Paul II

2005. Pope John Paul II Commemoration. Multicoloured.

3095	75c. Type **1153**	1·60	1·10
MS3096	150×99 mm. 75c.×2, (each 40×50 mm) Wearing mitre and carrying pastoral staff; Saying farewell	3·25	3·25

1154 Workers at Machines and Demonstrators

2005. Anniversaries. Multicoloured.

3097	75c. Type **1154** (75th anniv of Workers Confederation)	1·60	1·10
3098	75c. Mar del Plata and *La Capital* (centenary of *La Capital* newspaper)	1·60	1·10
3099	75c. Alfredo Palacios (centenary of Sunday blue law)	1·60	1·10

1155 Cesar Milstein

2005. Cesar Milstein (Nobel Prize for Medicine, 1984) Commemoration.

3100	**1155**	75c. multicoloured	1·60	1·10

1156 Orestes Liberti (1st Commander) and Horse-drawn Fire Engine

2005. Volunteer Fire Fighters. Multicoloured.

3101	75c. Type **1156**	1·60	1·10
3102	75c. Fighting fire and modern engine	1·60	1·10

1157 Early and Modern Red Cross Workers

2005. 125th Anniv of Argentine Red Cross Society.

3103	**1157**	75c. multicoloured	1·60	1·10

1158 Abyssinian

2005. Cats. Sheet 117×166 mm containing T **1158** and similar horiz designs. Multicoloured.

MS3104	25c. Birman; 25c. Siamese; 50c. Oriental shorthair; 50c. Persian; 75c. Type **1158**; 75c. European shorthair	5·00	5·00

1159 Juan Filloy

2005. Fifth Death Anniv of Juan Filloy (writer).

3105	**1159**	75c. multicoloured	1·60	1·10

1160 Malbec

2005. Tourism. Wine. Multicoloured.

3106	75c. Type **1160** (Mendoza, Tupungato Valley)	1·60	1·10
3107	75c. Merlot (Rio Negro, Alto Valle de Rio Negro)	1·60	1·10
3108	75c. Syrah (San Juan - Zonda Valley)	1·60	1·10
3109	75c. Torrontes (Salta - Cafayate, Calchaquies Valleys)	1·60	1·10

See also Nos. 3202/4.

1161 Our Lady of the Rosary Candonga Chapel, Sierras Chicas, Cordoba

2005. Places of Worship. Multicoloured.

3110	75c. Type **1161**	1·60	1·10
3111	75c. Al Ahmad Mosque, Buenos Aires	1·60	1·10
3112	75c. Israelite Congregation of Argentine Temple, Buenos Aires	1·60	1·10
3113	75c. Vision of the Middle Buddhist Temple, Buenos Aires	1·60	1·10

1162 Pulperia Perucho, Gral, Lavalle, Mendoza

2005. Stores (Pulperias). Multicoloured.

3114	75c. Type **1162**	1·60	1·10
3115	75c. El Torito, Baradero, Buenos Aires	1·60	1·10
3116	75c. Impini, Larroque, Entre Rios	1·60	1·10
3117	75c. Pulperia de Cacho di Catarina	1·60	1·10

1163 *Rio De la Plata* (merchant vessel)

2005. Ships. Multicoloured.

3118	25c.+25c. Type **1163**	95	60
3119	50c.+50c. *Libertad* (passenger ship)	1·80	1·00
3120	50c.+50c. *Camopo Duran* (tanker)	1·80	1·00
3121	75c.+75c. *Isla Soledad* (container ship)	2·50	2·20

Nos. 3118/21 were issued together, *se-tenant*, forming a composite design.

1164 Julio Bocca (dancer)

2005. Colon Theatre. Multicoloured.

3122	75c. Type **1164**	1·60	1·10
3123	75c. Theatre orchestra, opera singers and choir	1·60	1·10

1165 Ice Flow

2005. First Anniv of Antarctic Treaty Secretariat, Buenos Aires (3124). General Hernan Pujato's Expeditions to Antarctica (MS3125). Mult.

3124	75c. Type **1165**	1·60	1·10
MS3125	150×100 mm. 75c.×2, Divers and boat; General Pujato and team members	3·25	3·25

1166 Virgin and Child (detail)

2005. Christmas. Showing parts of the painting *Retablo* by Elena Stroni. Multicoloured.

3126	75c. Type **1166**	1·60	1·10
MS3127	150×100 mm. 75c.×4, The Annunciation (40×40 mm); The Nativity (40×40 mm); Three Wise Men (40×40 mm); Presenting Jesus in the temple (40×40 mm)	6·25	6·25

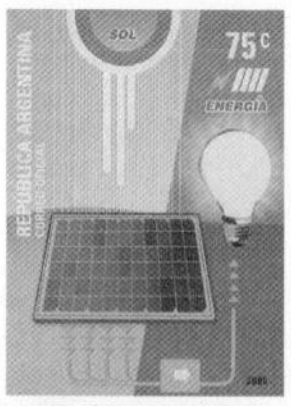

1167 Solar Panel and Light Bulb

2005. Alternative Energy. Multicoloured.

3128	75c. Type **1167**	1·60	1·10
3129	$4 Wind generators	6·25	4·75

1168 Mar de Plata Port and Summit Emblem

2005. Fourth Americas' Summit.

3130	**1168** 75c. multicoloured	1·60	1·10

1169 German Immigrants, Canada de Gomez, Santa Fe

2005. Immigration. Multicoloured.

3131	75c. Type **1169**	1·60	1·10
3132	75c. Slovakian women and children, Immigrant Hotel, Buenos Aires	1·60	1·10
3133	75c. Welsh immigrants, Chubut Central Railway, Trelew	1·60	1·10
3134	75c. Jewish colony, Moises Ville, Santa Fe	1·60	1·10

1170 Luis Angel Firpo

2005. Sport. Boxers. Multicoloured.

3135	75c. Type **1170**	1·60	1·10
3136	75c. Nicolino Locche	1·60	1·10

1171 Man (film, *Ivan & Eva*)

2005. Design. Multicoloured.

3137	75c. Type **1171**	1·60	1·10
3138	75c. Dress (Nadine Zlotogora) (clothes and textile) (vert)	1·60	1·10
3139	75c. Aluminium chair (Ricardo Blanco) (industrial design) (vert)	1·60	1·10
3140	75c. CD case (Claudia Smith) (graphic design)	1·60	1·10

1172 Bartolme Mitre

2006. Death Centenary of Bartolme Mitre (journalist and president 1862–8).

3141	**1172** 75c. multicoloured	1·60	1·10

1173 Snow-covered City

2006. Centenary of Esquel.

3142	**1173** 75c. multicoloured	1·60	1·10

2006. Tourism. Wine. As T **1160**. Multicoloured.

3143	50c. Vineyard, Alto Valle del Rio Negro (Merlot wine) (Rio Negro) (70×30 mm)	1·10	75
3144	75c. Wine barrels (Salta)	1·60	1·10
3145	1p. Grape harvest (San Juan)	2·20	1·50
3146	1p.25 Vineyard, Valle del Tupungato (Malbec wine) (Mendoza) (70×30 mm)	2·40	1·60
3147	2p.75 Wine tasting (Mendoza)	2·50	1·70
3148	3p. Vineyard, Valle del Zonda (Syrah wine) (San Juan) (70×30 mm)	2·75	1·90
3149	3p.25 Vineyard, Cafayate, Valles Calchaquies (Torrentes wine) (Salta) (70×30 mm)	3·00	2·00
3150	3p.50 Wine vats (Rio Negro)	3·25	2·20

1175 Ramon Carrillo

2006. Birth Centenary of Ramon Carrillo (health care specialist).

3151	**1175** 75c. multicoloured	1·60	95

1176 Guitar

2006. Mercosur. Musical Instruments. Multicoloured.

3152	75c. Type **1176**	1·60	95
3153	$3.50 Drum	5·00	3·50

1177 1 de Mayo Lighthouse

2006. Lighthouses. Multicoloured.

3154	75c. Type **1177**	1·60	90
3155	75c. Ano Nuevo	1·60	90
3156	75c. El Rincon	1·60	90
3157	75c. Recalada a Bahia Blanca	1·60	90

1178 Escuela de Mecanica de la Armada (concentration camp) (1976)

2006. *From Horror to Hope*. 30th Anniv of Military Dictatorship. Sheet 151×99 mm containing T 1178 and similar vert design. Multicoloured.

MS3158	75c.×2, Type **1178**; Escuela de Mecanica de la Armada (memorial museum) (2006)	3·25	3·25

1179 Crown

2006. 18th-century Religious Silverware. Multicoloured.

3159	75c. Type **1179**	1·60	95
3160	75c. Candelabra	1·60	95
3161	75c. Chalice	1·60	95
3162	75c. Viaticum	1·60	95

1180 Toyota Corolla WRC (Luis Perez Companc—Rally Nacional A8 category)

2006. National Motor Racing Champions. Multicoloured.

3163	75c. Type **1180**	1·60	95
3164	75c. Ford Falcon (Juan Manuel Silva—Turismo Carretera category)	1·60	95
3165	75c. Ford Focus (Gabriel Ponce de Leon—Turismo Competición 2000 category)	1·60	95
3166	75c. Ford Escort (Patricio di Palma—Class 3 Nacional category)	1·60	95

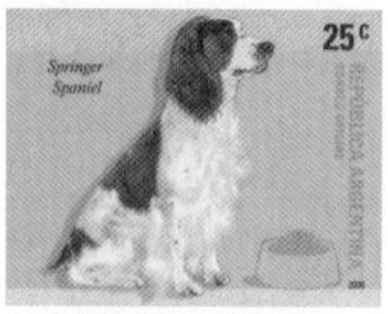

1181 Springer Spaniel

2006. Dogs. Sheet 117×166 mm containing T **1181** and similar horiz designs. Multicoloured.

MS3167	25c. Type **1181**; 25c. Yorkshire terrier; 50c. Argentine dogo (Argentinian mastiff); 50c. Miniature schnauzer; 75c. Poodle; 75c. Chow	6·50	2·75

No. **MS**3167 also contains two illustrated stamp size labels forming a composite design.

1182 Argentine Player

2006. World Cup Football Championship, Germany. Multicoloured.

	1p. Serbia and Montenegro	1·90	1·90
3168	1p. Type **1182**	1·90	1·90
3170	1p. Ivory Coast	1·90	1·90
3171	1p. Netherlands	1·90	1·90
3172	4p. Football in net	5·75	4·25
MS3173	149x100 mm. 1p.50 As No. 3168 (detail)	2·75	2·75

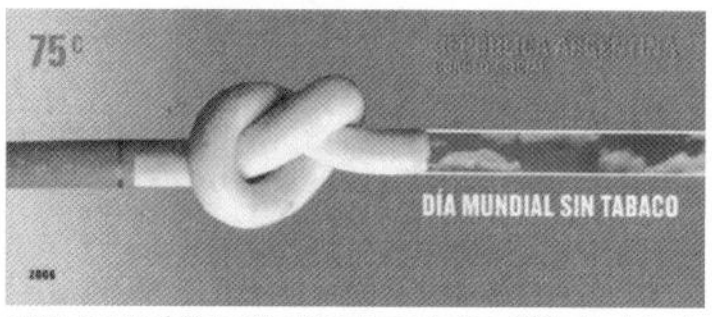

1183 Knotted Cigarette (image scaled to 49% of original size)

2006. World Health Organization No Tobacco Day.

3174	**1183** 75c. multicoloured	1·60	95

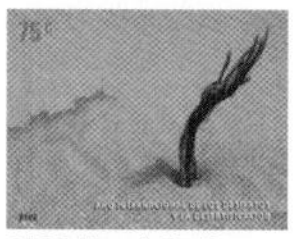

1184 Lizard Outline and Dead Tree

2006. International Year of Deserts and Desertification. Multicoloured.

3175	75c. Type **1184**	1·60	95
3176	75c. *Lilotaemus* (lizard) and *Calycera crassifolia*	1·60	95

1185 Mauricio Borensztein (Tato Bores) (actor)

2006. Personalities. Multicoloured.

3177	75c. Type **1185**	1·60	95
3178	75c. Rodolfo Walsh (journalist)	1·60	95

1186 Alpine Skiing

2006. Winter Sports. Multicoloured.

3179	75c. Type **1186**	1·60	95
3180	75c. Snowboarding	1·60	95
3181	75c. Cross-country skiing	1·60	95
3182	75c. Biathlon	1·60	95

1187 Musician

2006. Tango. Multicoloured.

3183	75c. Type **1187**	1·60	95
3184	$4 Dancers	1·60	95

Stamps of a similar design were issued by France.

1188 Patoruzito riding Pamperito

2006. Patoruzito (character from graphic magazine by Dante Quinterno). Opening of *Patoruzito—La Gran Adventura* (film).

3185	**1188** 75c. multicoloured	1·60	95

1189 Taruca (*Hippocamelus antisensis*)

2006. Natural Monuments. Multicoloured.

3186	75c. Type **1189**	1·60	95
3187	75c. Southern right whale (*Eubaluena australis*)	1·60	95
3188	75c. Huemul (*Hippocamelus bisculus*)	1·60	95
3189	75c. Jaguar (*Panthera onca*)	1·60	95

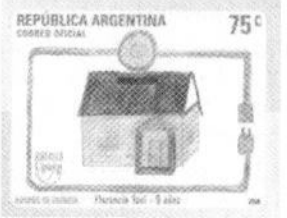

1190 House as Money Box and Plug connected to Sun (Florencia Tovi)

2006. America. Energy Conservation. Winning Designs in Children's Drawing Competition. Multicoloured.

3190	75c. Type **1190**	1·60	95
3191	75c. Window, table and standard lamp (Camila Suarez)	1·60	95

1191 *The Re-conquest of Buenos Aires* (Charles Fouqueray)

2006. Bicentenary of British Invasion and Defeat. Sheet 99×75 mm.

MS3192	**1191** 1p.50 multicoloured	2·75	2·75

1192 Flags as Ribbons

2006. 30th Council of the Common Market. Mercosur and Associate States' Presidents' Summit.

3193	**1192** 3p.50 multicoloured	1·60	95

1193 *Ciudad de Buenos Aires (image scaled to 49% of original size)*

2006. River Transport. Multicoloured.

3194	25c.+25c. Type **1193**	1·60	95
3195	50c.+50c. *Lambare*	1·60	95
3196	50c.+50c. *Madrid*	1·60	95
3197	75c.+75c. *Rawson*	1·60	95

1194 "150 Anos"

2006. 150th Anniv of First Argentine Stamp. Multicoloured.

3198	75c. Type **1194**	1·60	95
MS3199	151×99 mm. $1.50 As Type **3** (1856 1 real stamp) (40×40 mm)	2·75	2·75

1195 Colorado River Basin

2006. 30th Anniv of Comite Interjurisdiccional de Rio Colorado (COIRCO) (inter-jurisdictional committee on the Colorado river).

3200	**1195** 75c. multicoloured	1·60	95

1196 Legion de Patricios Rifleman (1806–9)

2006. Bicentenary of Infantry Corps "Patricios".

3201	**1196** 75c. multicoloured	1·60	95

2006. Tourism. Wine. As T **1160**. Multicoloured.

3202	75c. Syrah (Catamarcaungato Valley)	1·60	95
3203	75c. Torrontes Riojano (La Rioja)	1·60	95
3204	75c. Pinot noir (Neuquen)	1·60	95

1197 Cadets

2006. Centenary of Ramon L. Falcon Cadet School.

3205	**1197** 75c. multicoloured	1·60	95

1198 Puente San Roque Gonzalez de Santa Cruz, between Argentina and Paraguay

2006. International Bridges in Argentina. Multicoloured.

3206	75c. Type **1198**	1·60	95
3207	75c. Puente Presidente Tancredo Neves, between Argentina and Brazil	1·60	95

1199 *Madona y Paloma*

2006. Christmas. Paintings by Alfredo Guttero. Multicoloured.

3208	75c. Type **1199**	1·60	95
3209	75c. *Anunciacion* (horiz)	1·60	95

1200 Research Activities

2006. National Institute of Farming Technology.

3210	**1200** 75c. multicoloured	1·60	95

1201 Norberto Napolitano (Pappo)

2006. 40th Anniv of Argentinean Rock Music. Multicoloured.

3211	75c. Type **1201**	1·60	95
3212	75c. Luca George (Luca) Prodan	1·60	95
3213	75c. Miguel Angel Peralta (Miguel Abuelo)	1·60	95
3214	75c. Jose Alberto Iglesias (Tanguito)	1·60	95

1202 Valentin Sayhueque

2006. Caciques (tribal chiefs). Multicoloured.

3215	75c. Type **1202** (Huilliche people)	1·60	95
3216	75c. Casimiro Bigua (Tehuelche people)	1·60	95

1203 *Hercules* (detail from painting *Combate de Marin Garcia* by Emilio Biggeri)

2007. 150th Death Anniv of Admiral William Brown.

3217	**1203** 75c. multicoloured	1·60	95

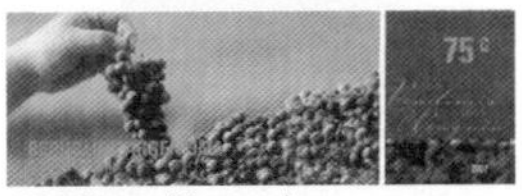

1204 Grapes (Neuquen)

2007. Tourism. Wine. Multicoloured.

3218	75c. Type **1204**	1·60	95
3219	75c. Grapes (Catamarca)	1·60	95
3220	75c. Grapes (La Rioja)	1·60	95
3221	3p.25 Bottle (Neuquen)	3·75	2·40
3222	3p.25 Bottle (Catamarca)	3·75	2·40
3223	3p.25 Bottle (La Rioja)	3·75	2·40

1205 1982 18 pesos Stamp and Ofincina Radiopostal Islas Malvinas Postmark

2007. 25th Anniv of South Atlantic Conflict. Multicoloured.

3224	75c. Type **1205**	1·60	95
3225	75c. IAI Dagger Fighter aircraft	1·60	95
3226	75c. Battle Cruiser *General Belgrano*	1·60	95
3227	75c. Decorated veteran	1·60	95
3228	75c. Decoration awarded to all veterans (*vert*)	1·60	95

1206 Postal Workers (detail from painting by Jose Murcia)

2007. 50th Anniv of Postal and Telecommunications Workers Federation (FOECYT).

3229	**1206** 75c. multicoloured	1·60	95

1207 *Phalacrocorax atriceps* (Imperial or blue-eyed cormorant)

2007. Argentina in Antarctica. Multicoloured.. Multicoloured.

3230	75c. Type **1207**	1·60	95
3231	75c. *Leptonychotes weddellii* (Weddell seal)	1·60	95
3232	75c. *Sterna vittata* (Antarctic tern)	1·60	95
3233	75c. *Sterna vittata* (Antarctic tern)	1·60	95
3234	75c. *Pysoscelis adeliae* (Adelie penguin)	1·60	95
3235	75c. *Chionis alba* (snowy or yellow-billed sheathbill)	1·60	95
3236	75c. *Pygoscelis papua* (gentoo penguins)	1·60	95
3237	75c. *Pygoscelis papua* (gentoo penguins)	1·60	95
3238	4p. *Almirante Irízar* (ice breaker)	5·00	3·50

Nos. 3232/3 and 3236/7 were issued together, *se-tenant*, forming a composite design.

1208 Latin American Art Museum, Buenos Aires

2007. Architecture. Multicoloured.

3239	75c. Type **1208**	1·60	95
3240	3p.25. High Mountain Archaeological Museum, Salta	4·50	3·00

1209 Rocking Horse

2007. Toys. Multicoloured.

3241	75c. Type **1209**	1·60	95
3242	75c. Tea set	1·60	95
3243	75c. Train set	1·60	95
3244	75c. Soldiers	1·60	95

1210 Emblem

2007. National Road Safety Campaign.

3245	**1210** 75c. red and silver	1·60	95

1211 Argentine Bases

2007. International Polar Year. Sheet 150×98 mm.

MS3246	**1211** 4p. multicoloured	5·00	3·50

1212 *Combate de Santo Domingo* (Eleodora Marenco)

2007. Bicentenary of Defence of Buenos Aires.

3247	**1212** 75c. multicoloured	1·60	95

1213 Radiation and Fluorescence Detectors

2007. Pierre Auger Observatory.

3248	**1213** 75c. multicoloured	1·60	95

1214 St. Jose de Calasanz and Pupils (stained glass window, San Jose de Calasanz Church, Buenos Aires)

2007. 450th Birth Anniv of Jose de Calasanz (founder of first free school in modern Europe).

3249	**1214** 1p. multicoloured	1·90	1·20

1215 Campfire

2007. Centenary of Scouting. Multicoloured.

3250	25c.+25c. Type **1215**	90	60
3251	50c.+50c. Tent and scout saluting	1·80	1·20
3252	75c.+75c. Scout wearing pack	2·20	1·50
3253	1p.+1p. Scouts pulling guy rope	2·50	1·70

Nos. 3250/3 were issued together, *se-tenant*, forming a composite design.

1216 *El Chaco* (meteorite)

2007. Meteorites of Campo Del Cielo. Sheet 148×99 mm.

MS3254	6p. multicoloured	6·25	6·00

1217 *Homero Manzi* (Hermenegildo Sabat)

2007. Birth Centenary of Homero Nicolas Manzione Prestera (Homero Manzi) (lyricist).

3255	**1217** 1p. multicoloured	1·60	95

1218 Road leading to S. C. de Bariloche (Rio Negro)

2007. Tourism. National Route 40. Sheet 496×99 mm containing T **1218** and similar horiz designs. Multicoloured.

MS3256 50c. Type **1218**; 50c. Abra El Acay (40×30 mm); 1p. Road to Perito Moreno (Santa Cruz) (70×30 mm); 1p. *La Trochita* locomotive (Chubut) (40×30 mm); 1p. Lanin volcano (Neuquen) (40×30 mm), 1p. Rio Grande (Mendoza) (50×30 mm); 1p. Goats, San Jose Jachal (San Juan) (40×30 mm); 1p. Cuesta de Miranda (La Rioja) (50×30 mm); 1p. Capel Nuestra Senora del Transito (Catamarca); 1p. Ruins of Quilmes (Tucuman); 1p. Road leading to Oratorio (Jujuy) (40×30 mm) 10·00 9·50

1219 Houses with Blocked and Free-flowing Chimneys (Julieta Saavedra Barrgan)

2007. Carbon Monoxide Inhalation Prevention Campaign. Winning Designs in Children's Drawing Competition. Multicoloured.

3257 1p. Type **1219** 1·80 1·20
3258 1p. Dirty and clean flames (Efrain Osvaldo Rost) (vert) 1·80 1·20
3259 1p. Engineer and gas cooker (Camila Micaela Alvarez Petrone) (vert) 1·80 1·20
3260 1p. Smoking fire (Leandro Ventancour) 1·80 1·20

1220 Accordion

2007. 150th Anniv of Argentine–Germany Bilateral Relations. Sheet 150×100 mm.

MS3261 4p. multicoloured 5·25 5·25

1221 Emblem

2007. Centenary of Club Atletico San Lorenzo de Almagro.

3262 **1221** 1p. multicoloured 1·80 1·20

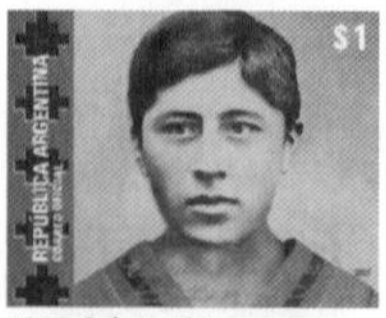

1222 Ceferino Namuncura

2007. Beatification of Ceferino Namuncura.

3263 **1222** 1p. multicoloured 1·80 1·20

1223 *Corrientes esquina Uruguay* (Horacio Cuppola)

2007. Contemporary Art. Multicoloured.

3264 1p. Type **1223** 1·80 1·20
3265 1p. *Dialogo* (Liliana Porter) (vert) 1·80 1·20
3266 1p. *0611* (detail) (Pablo Siqier) 1·80 1·20
3267 1p. *Imaginando el estupor* (detail) (Marta Minujin) (vert) 1·80 1·20

1224 Three Wise Men

2007. Christmas. Showing detail from The Birth (stained glass window)). Multicoloured.

3268 25c. Type **1224** 1·80 1·20
3269 1p. Holy Family 1·80 1·20

1225 Early Drilling Site

2007. Centenary of Oil and Gas Discovery in Argentina.

3270 **1225** 1p. multicoloured 1·80 1·20

1226 *Pampero* (balloon) and River Plate

2007. Centenary of Aaron de Anchorena and Jorge Newbery's Balloon Flight across the River Plate.

3271 **1226** 1p. multicoloured 1·80 1·20

1227 Ceremonial Staff

2007. Presidential Inauguration. 24th Anniv of Democracy.

3272 **1227** 1p. multicoloured 1·80 1·20

1228 Accordionist and Dancers

2007. Festivals. Multicoloured.

3273 1p. Type **1228** (National Chamame (dance) festival) 1·80 1·20
3274 1p. Ponchos and dancers (National and International Poncho festival) 1·80 1·20
3275 1p. Horseman, fireworks, guitar and dancers (National and International Dressage and Folklore festival) 1·80 1·20
3276 1p. Snow Queen and skier (National Snow festival) 1·80 1·20

1234 Piper Aircraft

2008. Centenary of Aero Club

3290 **1234** 1p. multicoloured 1·90 1·30

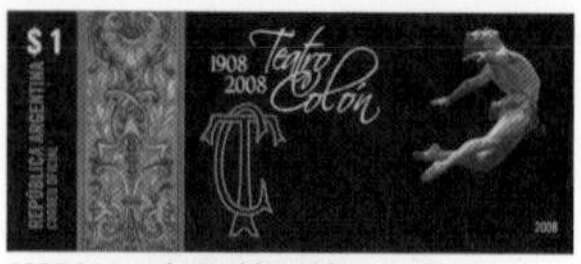

1235 Leonardo Realde performing 'pas de l'ange' from, Diane and Actaen (ballet)

2008. Centenary of Teatro Colon

3291 **1235** 1p. multicoloured 1·90 1·30

1236 Aimé Bonpland, Script, Yerba Mate Leaf and Flower

2008. 150th Death Anniv of Aimé Jacques Alexandre Bonpland (explorer and botanist)

3292 **1236** 1p. multicoloured 1·90 1·30

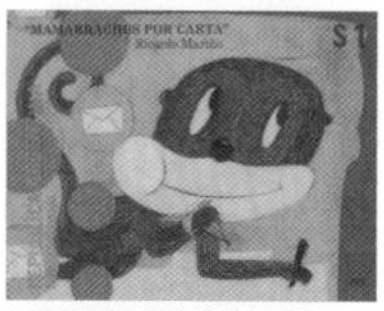

1239 'MAMRRACHOS POR CARTA' (Ricardo Mariño)

2008. Youth Philately

3296 1p. Type **1239** 1·90 1·30
3297 1p. 'CARTA A PAPÁ NOEL' (Luis Maria Pescetti) 1·90 1·30
3298 1p. 'CANCION DEL CORREO' (Maria Elena Walsh) (vert) 1·90 1·30
3299 1p. 'GRAN HERMANO' (Silvia Schujer) (vert) 1·90 1·30

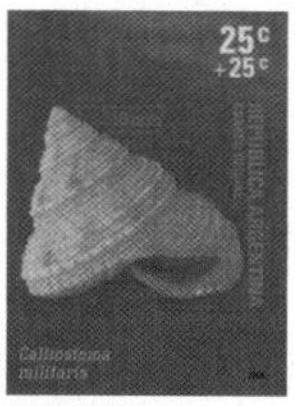

1240 *Callistoma militaris*

2008. Shells. Multicoloured.

3314 25c. Type **1240** 35 25
3315 50c. *Epitonium fabrizioi* 75 55
3316 75c. *Odontocymbiola magellanica* 1·40 95
3317 1p. *Trophon geverrrsianus* 1·90 1·30

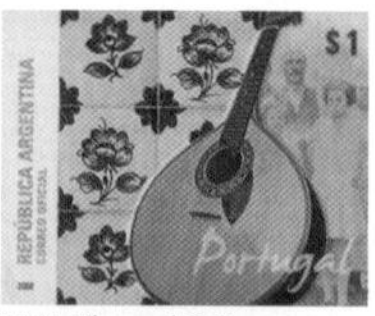

1241 Tiles and Guitar (Portugal)

2008. Immigration. Multicoloured.

3318 1p. Type **1241** (Portugal) 1·90 1·30
3319 1p. *Two Swimmers* (koi carp) (Kobayashi Katsushiro)and cherry blossom (Japan) 1·90 1·30
3320 1p. Virgin and child (plate) and Arabic script (Lebanon) 1·90 1·30
3321 1p. Wooden box, embroidered silk and Ugarithic alphabet tablet (Syria) 1·90 1·30

1242 Carnation, Lily and Delphinium

2008. National Flower Festival. Multicoloured.

MS3322 5p. Type **1242** 9·50 9·50
MS3323 5p. Gerbera, gardenia and rose 9·50 9·50

1243 Basket and Ball (Emanuel Ginóbili)

2008. Argentine Sporting Idols. Multicoloured.

MS3324 100×150 mm. 5p. Type **1243** 9·50 9·50
MS3325 100×150 mm. 5p. Golf ball and hole (Roberto de Vicenzo) 9·50 9·50
MS3326 100×150 mm. 5p. Rugby goal posts, ball and player silhouette (horiz) 9·50 9·50
MS3327 150×100 mm. 5p. Driver and race car (Juan Manuel Fangio) 9·50 9·50

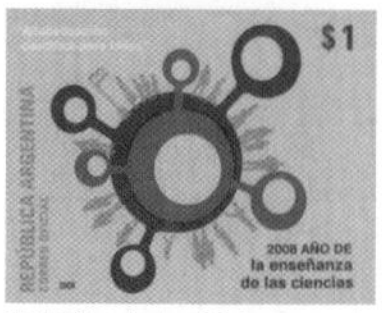

1244 Symbols of Science and Scientists

2008. 2008-Teaching of Sciences Year

3328 **1244** 1p. greenish blue, bright light green and silver 1·90 1·30

1245 *Nelumbo nucifera*

2008. 35th Anniv of Argentine-Vietnam Diplomatic Relations. Multicoloured.

3329 1p. Type **1245** 1·90 1·30
3330 1p. *Ceiba chodatii* 1·90 1·30

1246 First Stamp of Cordoba

2008. 150th Anniv of First Postage Stamps

MS3331 1p.×3, Type **1246**; Buenos Aires (40×30 mm); Argentine Federation (30×40 mm) 5·50 5·50

1247 Angel Gabriel (Renée T. Pietrantonio)

2008. Christmas

3332 **1247** 1p. multicoloured 1·90 1·30

1253 Sugar Cane, Soya Beans and Microscope

2009. Bishop Colombres Memorial Agribusiness Experimental Centre, Tucumán

3342 **1253** 1p. multicoloured 1·90 1·30

1254 Bull (Chinese New Year. Year of the Ox)

2009. China 2009 International Stamp Exhibition, Luoyang. Sheet 75×100 mm

MS3343 **1254** 5p. multicoloured 9·50 9·50

1255 Parish Church

2009. Centenary of Holy Cross Exaltation Parish Church, Puerto Santa Cruz

3344	**1255**	1p. multicoloured	1·90	1·30

1256 *Aguila coronada* (crowned eagle)

2009. Endangered Species. Multicoloured.

3345	1p. Type **1256**	1·90	1·30
3346	1p. *Chelonoidis chilensis* (Argentine tortoise) (horiz)	1·90	1·30

1257 Vintage Wine

2009. Mercosur. Exports. Multicoloured.

3347	1p. Type **1257**	1·90	1·30
3348	1p. Containers and tractor	1·90	1·30

No. 3349 and Type **1258** are left for R. R. Alfonsin, issued on 9 May 2009, not yet received.

No. 3350 and Type **1259** are left for R. S. Ortiz, issued on 23 May 2009, not yet received.

No. 3351 and Type **1260** are left for 150th Anniv of the Children of Holy Virgin at Orchard Congregation in Argentina , issued on 23 May 2009, not yet received.

Nos. 3352/3 and Type **1261** are left for 180th Anniv of Political and Military Command, issued on 13 June 2009, not yet received.

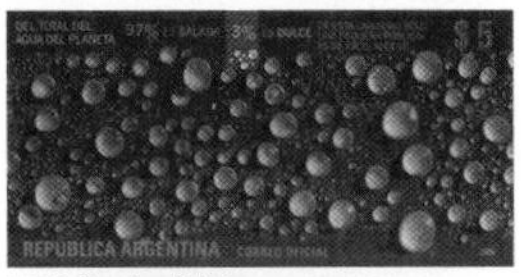

1262 Beads of Water

2009. Environmental Protection. Water

MS3354	5p.×2, Type **1262**; Hand and large water droplet (vert)	18·00	18·00

1263 *Polybetes pythagoricus*

2009. Native Flora and Fauna. Multicoloured .

3355	1p. Type **1263**	1·90	1·30
3356	1p. *Passiflora caerulea*	1·90	1·30

1264 Bumper Cars

2009. Youth Philately. Amusement Parks. Multicoloured.

3357	1p. Type **1264**	1·90	1·30
3358	1p. Roller coaster	1·90	1·30
3359	1p. Ferris wheel	1·90	1·30
3360	1p. Ghost train	1·90	1·30

Nos. 3357/60, plus stamp size label, were printed, *se-tenant*, in horizontal strips of four stamps plus label, the whole forming a composite design

1265 Merino Ram

2009. Sheep. Multicoloured.

MS3361	1p.×6, Type **1265**; Romney Marsh yearling; Corriedale ewe and lamb; Hampshire Down ewe and lamb; Lincoln ewe; Frisian ewe	11·00	11·00

Nos. 3362/5 and Type **1266** are left for Astronomy, issued on 22 August 2009, not yet received

Nos. 3366/7 and Type **1267** are left for Education, issued on 12 September 2009, not yet received

1268 Rainfall Damage, Erosion and Area under Conservation Management

2009. Natural Resources. The Soil. Multicoloured.

3368	1p. Type **1268**	1·90	1·30
3369	1p. Wind erosion of arid land and arid area under conservation management	1·90	1·30

Nos. 3368/9 were printed, *se-tenant*, in horizontal pairs within the sheet, each pair forming a composite design.

Nos. 3370/3 and Type **1269** are left for Sport, issued on 26 September 2009, not yet received.

Nos. 3374 and Type **1270** are left for 50th Anniv of UTN, issued on 17 October 2009, not yet received.

Nos. 3375/8 and Type **1271** are left for Italia 2009, issued on 24 October 2009, not yet received.

Nos. 3379/80 and Type **1272** are left for Astronomy, issued on 24 October 2009, not yet received.

Nos. 3381//4 and Type **1273** are left for TB Awareness, issued on 14 November 2009, not yet received.

Nos. 3385 and Type **1274** are left for Christmas, issued on 21 November 2009, not yet received.

Nos. 3386/93 and Type **1275** are left for Architecture, issued on 12 December 2009, not yet receivedNos. 3394/7 and Type **1276** are left for Festivals, issued on 20 February 2010, not yet received.

Nos. 3398/9 and Type **1277** are left for Ships, issued on 20 February 2010, not yet received.

No. 3400 and Type **1278** are left for Bicentenary, issued on 27 March 2010, not yet received.

Nos. 3401/2 and Type **1279** are left for America, issued on 27 March 2010, not yet received.

No. 3403 and Type **1280** are left for Centenary of Orchestra, issued on 24 April 2010, not yet received.

Nos. 3404/5 and Type **1281** are left for Mercosur, issued on 8 May 2010, not yet received.

No. 3406 and Type **1282** are left for Bicentenary, issued on 8 May 2010, not yet received.

Nos. 3407 and Type **1283** are left for Bicentenary, issued on 29 May 2010, not yet received.

1284 Buenos Aires Town Hall

2010. Bicentenary Mural (by Miguel Rep). Black, carmine and silver.

MS3408	1p.50×12, Type **1284**; General Manuel Belgrano creating National Flag; General San Martin crossing Andes (40×80 mm); National Constitution; Ships with immigrants; Confrontation (70×30 mm); National Congress; Symbols of literary expression (40×30 mm); People celebrating Loyalty Day (30×60 mm); 1976 Coup (30×40 mm); Mothers of May Square (40×60 mm); Symbols of Nineties economics (40×60 mm)	11·00	11·00

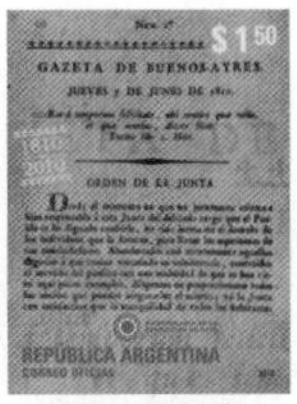

1285 First Issue of *Gazeta de Buenos Aires*

2010. Bicentenary of *Gazeta de Buenos Ayres* (newspaper)

3409	**1285**	1p.50 multicoloured	2·00	1·40

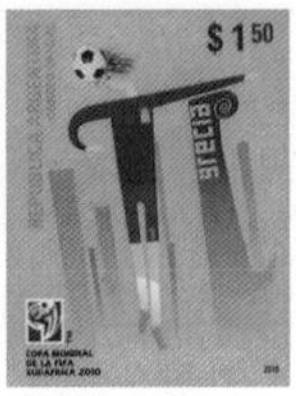

1286 Player, Greece

2010. World Cup Football Championships, South Africa. Multicoloured.

3410	1p.50 Type **1286**	1·90	1·30
3411	1p.50 Player, Nigeria (horiz)	1·90	1·30
3412	5p. Player, South Korea (horiz)	2·75	2·30
3413	7p. Player, Argentina	3·00	2·40
MS3414	100×75 mm. 5p. Goalkeeper making a save (40×60 mm)	9·50	9·50
MS3415	100×75 mm. 5p. Player diving for ball (70×40 mm)	9·50	9·50
MS3416	100×75 mm. 5p. Player heading ball towards goal (70×40 mm)	9·50	9·50
MS3417	100×75 mm. 5p. Player kicking ball into air with left leg raised (60×40 mm)	9·50	9·50

1287 Players

2010. Junior World Rugby Championships, Argentina

3418	**1287**	1p.50 multicoloured	1·90	1·30

1288 Dog and Hobby Horse

2010. Children's Games. Multicoloured.

3419	2p. Type **1288**	1·90	1·30
3420	2p. Boy with whip and ball (El balero)	1·90	1·30
3421	2p. Spinning top (El trompo)	1·90	1·30
3422	2p. Girls with hoops (El aro)	1·90	1·30
3423	2p. Girl with doll (La muñeca)	1·90	1·30

1289 *Members of Provisional Government Junta take the Oath on 25 May 1810* (Guillermo Da Ré)

2010. Bicentenary of the First Argentine Government Junta. Sheet 100×75 mm

MS3424	**1289**	5p. multicoloured	9·50	9·50

1290 Balea Lake, Romania

2010. 80th Anniv of Argentina–Romania Diplomatic Relations. Multicoloured.

3425	1p.50 Type **1290**	1·90	1·30
3426	7p. Nahuel Huapi Lake, Argentina	3·00	2·40

Stamps of a similar design were issued by Romania.

1291 Jorge Luis Borges

2010. Frankfurt Bookfair

3427	**1291**	7p. black, silver and scarlet-vermilion	3·00	2·40

1292 'Be Prepared' ('siempe LISTA')

2010. Centenary of Girl Guiding and Girl Scouting. Multicoloured.

3428	75c. Type **1292**	1·40	95
3429	75c. Clasped hands ('Always better' ('siempre MEJOR'))	1·40	95
3430	1p. Clasped hands and campfire ('Always forward' ('siempre ADELANTE'))	1·90	1·30
3431	1p. Hand on shoulder ('To serve' ('SERVIR'))	1·90	1·30

1293 Player's Silhouette and Pitch

2010. Women's World Hockey Championships, Argentina 2010

3432	**1293**	1p.50 multicoloured	2·00	1·40

1294 Bowls

2010. America. Traditional Games. Multicoloured.

3433	1p.50 Type **1294**	1·90	1·30
3434	1p.50 Cards ('truco')	1·90	1·30

1295 Symbols of Census

2010. Census-2010

3435	**1295**	1p.50 multicoloured	1·90	1·30

1296 *Juan Bautista Alberdi* (Liliana Ferrari)

2010. Birth Bicentenary of Juan Bautista Alberdi (writer and politician)

3436	**1296**	1p.50 multicoloured	1·90	1·30

1297 Library Building and Antique Books

2010. Bicentenary of National Library

3437	**1297**	1p.50 multicoloured	1·90	1·30

1298 Cherub (tiles, Carmo Church (Igreja do Carmo) (image scaled to 40% of original size)

2010. Portugal 2010, International Stamp Exhibition. Multicoloured.

MS3438 151×98 mm. 5p.×2,Querandi Lighthouse, Buenos Aires; Santa Marta lighthouse, Cascais, Lisbon 18·00 18·00

MS3439 120×120 mm. 10p.Type **1298**, Porto, Portugal) (50×50 mm) 18·00 18·00

1299 Postman (statue), World Map, FOECOP (postal workers' union) Emblem and Envelopes

2010. World Post Day. The Postman

3440 **1299** 1p.50 multicoloured 1·90 1·30

1300 Austria-Hungarian Community Meteorological Station, Botanical Garden, Buenos Aires

2010. Meteorological Architecture. Multicoloured.

MS3441 5p.×2, Type **1300**; Weather Station, City Park, Vienna 18·00 18·00

1301 *Canto al Trabajo* (statue) (Rogelio Yrurtia)

2010. Argentinian Workers

3442 **1301** 1p.50 multicoloured 1·90 1·30

1302 *The Child of Bethlehem* (Aldo Severi)

2010. Christmas

3443 **1302** 1p.50 multicoloured 1·90 1·30

1303 Map and Symbols of Electricity Generation and Distribution

2010. 50th Anniv of Electrical Power Federal Council

3444 **1303** 1p.50 multicoloured 1·90 1·30

1304 Race Start, Buenos Aires

2010. Dakar Rally, Argentina, 2009 and 2010. Multicoloured.

MS3445 480×100 mm (open), 140×100 mm. (closed). 1p.50 Type **1304**;1p.50 Philippe Peillon, Motor cycle No. 107 (Dakar 2009) (50×50 mm.);1p.50 Stephane Peterhansel, Car No. 303 (Dakar 2009) (60×40 mm.);1p.50 Ales Loprais, Lorry No. 502 (Dakar 2009) (50×50 mm.);1p.50 Caravan of vehicles (Dakar 2009) (50×50 mm.); 5p. Marcos Patronelli, Quad No. 251 (Dakar 2010) (40×80 mm.); 7p. Alejandro Patronelli Quad No. 277 (Dakar 2010) (40×80 mm.) 19·00 19·00

MS3446 492×100 mm (open) 170×100 mm. (closed). 1p.50 Jun Mitsuhashi, Car No. 375 (Dakar 2009) (60×50 mm.); 1p.50 Patronelli Brothers, Quads Nos. 252 and 277 (Dakar 2010) (60×40 mm.);1p.50 Roman Cabot, Car No. 377 (Dakar 2009) (40×50 mm.);1p.50 Marc Coma Motor cycle No. 1 (Dakar 2010) (60×40 mm.);1p.50 Laguna del Pescado, Entre Rios (40×50 mm.); 1p.50 Tafi del Valle, Tucuman (40×50 mm.);1p.50 Purmamarca, Jujuy (40×50 mm.); 10p. Firdaus Kabirov Lorry No. 500 (Dakar 2010) (70×50 mm.) 19·00 19·00

No. 3447 and Type **1305** are left for Year of Forests, issued on 19 March 2011, not yet received.

No. 3448 and Type **1306** are left for America, issued on 19 March 2011, not yet received.

Nos. 3449/50 and Type **1307** are left for Capital of Books, issued on 16 April 2011, not yet received.

1308 Ice Floe streaked with Colours

2011. 50th Anniv of Antarctic Treaty. 34th Antarctic Treaty Consultative Meeting. Multicoloured.

3451 2p. Type **1308** 1·90 1·30

MS3452 150×98 mm. Triangular Size 51×51mm. 8p.×2, *Pygocelis papua*; Researcher and equipment 7·50 7·50

1309 Mariano Moreno and Masthead of *Gazeta de Buenos Ayres*

2011. Death Bicentenary of Mariano Moreno (lawyer, journalist and politician.)

3453 **1309** 2p. multicoloured 1·90 1·30

1310 Blood Droplet

2011. Blood Donor Day

3453a **1310** 5p. multicoloured 9·50 6·00

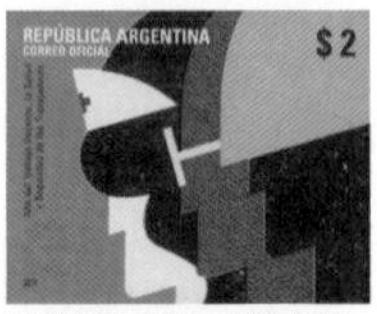

1311 Silhouettes of Workers' Heads

2011. 2011, Year of Decent Labour, Health and Safety for Workers

3454 **1311** 2p. multicoloured 1·90 1·30

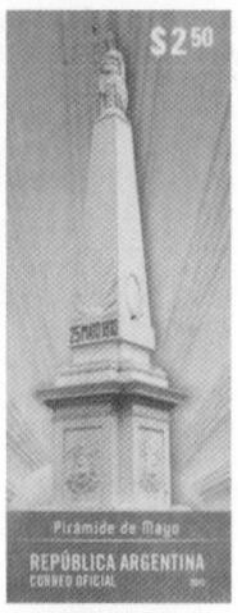

1312 Pirámide de Mayo

2011. Pirámide de Mayo, Buenos Aires (constructed to celebrate first anniversary of 1810 May Revolution)

3455 **1312** 2p.50 multicoloured 2·00 1·40

1313 Domingo Faustino Sarmiento

2011. Birth Bicentenary of Domingo Faustino Sarmiento (activist, intellectual, writer, statesman and seventh President of Argentina, 1868–74)

3456 **1313** 2p.50 multicoloured 2·00 1·40

1314 Argentina and Bolivia Players

2011. Copa America 2011, Argentina. Multicoloured.

MS3457 5p.×2, Group A, Type **1314**; Costa rica goalkeeper making save 18·00 18·00

MS3458 5p.×2, Group B, Venezuela and Brazil players tackling for ball (facing right); Paraguay and Ecuador players heading ball (facing left) 18·00 18·00

MS3459 5p.×2, Group C, Uruguay player wearing blue (facing right); Chile player preparing for goal kick (facing left) 18·00 18·00

1315 Satellite Sac-D/Aquarius

2011. Satellite Sac-D/Aquarius

3460 **1315** 2p.50 multicoloured 2·00 1·40

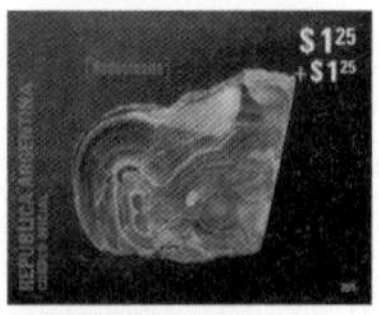

1316 Rhodochrosite

2011. Minerals. Multicoloured.

3461 1p.25 Type **1316** 2·00 1·40

3462 1p.25 Sulphur 2·00 1·40

3463 1p.25 Pyrite 2·00 1·40

3464 1p.25 Quartz 2·00 1·40

1317 Decorated Postbox

2011. America. Post Boxes

3465 2p.50 Type **1317** 2·00 1·40

3466 2p.50 Pillarbox (vert) 2·00 1·40

1318 National Beer Festival, Villa General Belgrano, Córdoba

2011. Festivals. Multicoloured.

3467 2p.50 Type **1318** 2·00 1·40

3468 2p.50 National Day of the Horse, San Cristobal, Santa Fe 2·00 1·40

3469 2p.50 Foreign Communities Fair, Comodoro Rivadavia, Chubut 2·00 1·40

3470 2p.50 National Tea Party, Campo Viera, Missiones. 2·00 1·40

1319 *Sacoila lanceolada*

2011. Orchids

3471 2p.50 Type **1319** 2·00 1·40

3472 2p.50 *Zygopetalum maxillare* (horiz) 2·00 1·40

1320 Carriages

2011. Tourism. Train to the Clouds. Multicoloured.

MS3473 5p.×4, Type **1320**; Locomotive; Rear of train crossing bridge; Crossing bridge viewed from below 18·00 18·00

1321 Physician and Hand holding Baby

2011. Centenary of Argentine Pediatric Society

3474 **1321** 2p.50 multicoloured 2·00 1·40

1322 Star of Bethlehem and Three Kings

2011. Christmas

3475 **1322** 2p.50 multicoloured 2·00 1·40

1323 Landrace

2011. Pigs. Multicoloured.

MS3476 2p.50×6, Type **1323**; Hampshire; Pietrain; Duroc Jersey; Spotted Poland; Yorkshire 12·00 12·00

1324 Nestor Carlos Kirchner and Casa Rosada (detail)

2011. Nestor Carlos Kirchner (president 2003-7) Commemoration. Sheet 100×150 mm

MS3477	**1324**	5p. multicoloured	9·50	9·50

1325 Polo Horse (Adolfo Cambiaso)

2011. Sports Personalities. Multicoloured.

MS3478	100×150 mm. 10p. Type **1325**	9·50	9·50
MS3479	100×150 mm. 10p. Skaters legs (Nora Vega) (60×40 mm)	9·50	9·50
MS3480	150×100 mm. 10p. Stylised windsurfer (Carlos Espinola) (50×60 mm)	9·50	9·50
MS3481	150×100 mm. 10p. Chessboard and Miguel Najdorf (50×60 mm)	9·50	9·50

1326 Family (Nicolas Agustin Bernachea)

2011. Rights of Children and Women. Centenary of Argentine Pediatrics Society . Multicoloured.

3482	2p.50 Type **1326**	2·00	1·40
3483	2p.50 Crying child and hand (Catalano Segesso)	2·00	1·40
3484	2p.50 Mother and child (Florencia Martinesi)	2·00	1·40
3485	2p.50 Girl jumping (Sofía Panagópulo)	2·00	1·40

1327 Douglas DC-3 making First Landing and Map showing Flight Route

2012. 50th Anniv of First Argentine Landing at South Pole

3486	**1327**	2p.50 multicoloured	2·00	1·40

No. 3487 and Type **1328** are left for Bicentenary of Argentina, issued on 3 March 2012, not yet received.

1329 Gen. Manuel Belgrano Monument, Buenos Aires

2012. General Manuel Belgrano Commemoration

3488	**1329**	2p.50 multicoloured	2·00	1·40

1330 'Islas Malvinas'

2012. Falkland Islands (Malvinas). Multicoloured.

3489	2p.50 Type **1330**	2·00	1·40
3490	2p.50 Inscr 'Islas Georgias del Sur'	2·00	1·40
3491	2p.50 Inscr 'Islas Sandwich del Sur' (28×67 mm)	2·00	1·40

1331 Presidential Staff and Flag

2012. Second Presidential Mandate of Cristina Elisabet Fernández de Kirchner

3492	**1331**	2p.50 multicoloured	2·00	1·40

1332 First Deed (detail) and Jose de San Martin Monument

2012. Centenary of Rio Gallegos Town Council

3493	**1332**	2p.50 multicoloured	2·00	1·40

BULK MAIL STAMPS

BP999 Post Office Building, Buenos Aires

1999. Bulk Mail. Self-adhesive. Imperf.

BP2644	**BP999**	$7 black and blue	21·00	14·00
BP2645	**BP999**	$11 black and red	33·00	22·00
BP2646	**BP999**	$16 black and yellow	50·00	35·00
BP2647	**BP999**	$23 black and green	70·00	47·00

BP1069

2001. Bulk Mail. Additionally overprinted UP. Imperf.

BP2853	**BP1069**	$7 black and blue	19·00	17·00
BP2854	**BP1069**	$11 black and red	29·00	26·00

EXPRESS SERVICE MAIL

E999 Express Service Emblem

1999. Self-adhesive.

E2644	**E999**	8p.75 blue and silver	30·00	20·00
E2645	-	17p.50 blue and gold	65·00	43·00

DESIGN: 24-hour service emblem.

No. E2644 was for express service mail and No. E2645 for use on 24-hour service mail.

OFFICIAL STAMPS

1884. Optd **OFICIAL**.

O66	**33**	½c. brown	15·00	12·00
O69	**33**	1c. red	60	40
O70	**24**	2c. green	60	40
O71	-	4c. brown (No. 32)	60	40
O72	**9**	8c. red	60	55
O73	**10**	10c. green	50·00	30·00
O76	**33**	12c. blue	1·00	80
O77	**10**	16c. green	2·00	1·20
O78	**22**	20c. blue	10·00	8·25
O79	**11**	24c. blue (roul)	12·50	8·50
O80	**11**	24c. blue (perf)	1·20	90
O81	-	25c. red (No. 47)	20·00	15·00
O82	-	30c. orange (No. 33)	42·00	24·00
O83	-	60c. black (No. 34)	25·00	15·00
O84	-	90c. blue (No. 35)	25·00	19·00

O73

1901

O275	**O73**	1c. grey	20	15
O276	**O73**	2c. brown	20	15
O277	**O73**	5c. red	20	15
O278	**O73**	10c. green	40	15
O279	**O73**	30c. blue	2·75	80
O280	**O73**	50c. orange	1·80	70

1938. (a) Optd **SERVICIO OFICIAL** in two lines.

O668	**143**	1c. brown (No. 645)	45	20
O669	-	2c. brown (No. 646)	45	20
O670	-	3c. green (No. 647)	1·20	20
O679	-	3c. grey (No. 672)	45	20
O771	-	3c. grey (No. 672a)	3·50	1·40
O671	-	5c. brown (No. 653b)	45	20
O782	**200**	5c. red (No. 773)	10	10
O667	-	10c. red (No. 653d)	55	20
O773	-	10c. purple (No. 678)	55	20
O681	**146**	15c. blue (No. 676)	55	20
O683	**146**	20c. blue (19½×26 mm)	1·40	45
O774	-	15c. grey (No. 708)	65	20
O872	**247**	20c. red	45	10
O813	-	25c. (No. 673)	65	20
O674	-	40c. (No. 658)	1·80	45
O675	-	50c. (No. 659)	45	20
O676	**152**	1p. (No. 760)	55	45
O827	**234**	1p. (No. 826)	90	20
O778	-	2p. (No. 661)	55	20
O779	-	5p. (No. 662)	55	20
O780	-	10p. (No. 763)	65	45
O781	-	20p. (No. 764)	1·80	1·40

(b) Optd **SERVICIO OFICIAL** in one line.

O897	20c. lilac (No. 895)	45	20

1953. Eva Peron stamps optd **SERVICIO OFICIAL**.

O854	**239**	5c. grey	45	15
O855	**239**	10c. red	45	15
O856	**239**	20c. red	45	15
O857	**239**	25c. green	45	15
O858	**239**	40c. purple	45	15
O859	**239**	45c. blue	55	45
O860	**239**	50c. bistre	45	15
O862	**240**	1p. brown (No. 846)	55	20
O863	**240**	1p.50 green (No. 847)	55	20
O864	**240**	2p. red (No. 848)	55	20
O865	**240**	3p. blue (No. 849)	70	45
O866	**240**	5p. brown	1·40	65
O867	**239**	10p. red	7·50	6·00
O868	**240**	20p. green	65·00	35·00

1955. Stamps of 1954 optd **SERVICIO OFICIAL** in one line.

O869	**247**	20c. red	45	10
O870	**247**	40c. red	45	10
O880	-	1p. brown (No. 871)	45	20
O882	-	3p. purple (No. 874)	55	20
O883	-	5p. green (No. 875)	55	20
O884	-	10p. green and grey (No. 876)	65	20
O886	**250**	20p. violet	1·50	70

1955. Various stamps optd. (a) Optd **S. OFICIAL**.

O896	-	5c. brown (No. 894)	45	20
O955	-	10c. green (No. 946)	50	20
O956	-	20c. purple (No. 947)	60	20
O879	-	50c. blue (No. 868)	45	20
O957	-	50c. ochre (No. 948)	50	20
O1034	-	1p. brn (No. 1016)	60	35
O899	**264**	2p. purple	45	20
O1050	-	2p. red (No. 1035)	50	10
O959	-	3p. blue (No. 951)	50	20
O1051	-	4p. red (No. 1036)	75	10
O961	**296**	5p. brown	60	20
O1052	-	8p. red (No. 1037)	50	10
O962	-	10p. brown (No. 1286)	60	20
O1036	-	12p. dull purple (No. 1028)	1·10	25
O1053	-	10p. red (No. 1038)	60	10
O964	-	20p. green (No. 954)	60	20
O1055	-	20p. red (No. 1039)	55	25
O1037	-	22p. blue (No. 1018)	1·30	45
O1038	-	23p. green (No. 1019)	1·60	60
O1039	-	25p. lilac (No. 1020)	1·30	60
O1040	-	43p. lake (No. 1021)	3·00	1·30
O1041	-	45p. brn (No. 1022)	3·00	1·30
O1042	-	50p. blue (No. 1023)	5·00	1·50
O1043	-	50p. blue (No. 1287)	6·75	1·50
O1045	-	100p. blue (No. 1289)	3·25	1·30
O1046	-	300p. violet (No. 1026)	9·75	4·75

(b) Optd **SERVICIO OFICIAL**.

O900	**265**	2p.40 brown	45	20
O958	-	3p. blue (No. 951)	50	20
O901	**266**	4p.40 green	45	20
O960	**296**	5p. brown	60	20
O887		50p. ind & bl (No. 878)	3·00	1·30
O1049	-	500p. grn (No. 1032)	16·00	7·75

For lists of stamps optd **M.A.**, **M.G.**, **M.H.**, **M.I.**, **M.J.I.**, **M.M.**, **M.O.P.** or **M.R.C.** for use in ministerial offices see the Stanley Gibbons Catalogue Part 20 (South America).

1963. Nos. 1068, etc., optd **S. OFICIAL**.

O1076	**351**	2p. green	60	10
O1080	-	4p. red (No. 1069)	75	15
O1081	-	6p. red (No. 1070)	85	45
O1078	-	90p. bistre (No. 1288)	8·00	3·75

RECORDED MESSAGE STAMPS

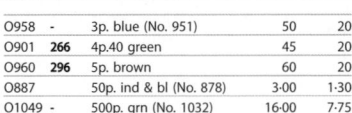

RM166 Winged Messenger

1939. Various symbolic designs inscr "CORREOS FONOPOSTAL".

RM688	**RM166**	1p.18 blue	19·00	10·50
RM689	-	1p.32 blue	19·00	10·50
RM690	-	1p.50 brown	65·00	45·00

DESIGNS—VERT: 1p.32, Head of Liberty and National Arms. HORIZ: 1p.50, Record and winged letter.

TELEGRAPH STAMPS USED FOR POSTAGE

PT34

PT35 (Sun closer to "NACIONAL")

1887

PT104	**PT34**	10c. red	1·10	15
PT105	**PT35**	10c. red	1·10	15
PT106	**PT34**	40c. blue	1·20	15
PT107	**PT35**	40c. blue	1·20	15

Pt. 10

ARMENIA

Formerly part of Transcaucasian Russia. Temporarily independent after the Russian revolution of 1917. From 12 March 1922, Armenia, Azerbaijan and Georgia formed the Transcaucasian Federation. Issues for the federation were superseded by those of the Soviet Union in 1924.

With the dissolution of the Soviet Union in 1991 Armenia once again became independent.

NOTE. Only one price is given for Nos. 3/245, which applies to unused or cancelled to order. Postally used copies are worth more.

All the overprints and surcharges were handstamped and consequently were applied upright or inverted indiscriminately, some occurring only inverted.

1919. 100 kopeks = 1 rouble.
1994. 100 luna = 1 dram.

NATIONAL REPUBLIC

28 May 1918 to 2 December 1920 and 18 February to 2 April 1921.

1919. Arms type of Russia and unissued Postal Savings Bank stamp (No. 6) surch. Imperf or perf. (a) Surch thus **k. 60 k** with or without stops.

3	**22**	60k. on 1k. orange	65
6	-	60k. on 1k. red on buff	12·00

(b) Surch in figures only.

7	**22**	60k. on 1k. orange	30·00
8	**22**	120k. on 1k. orange	30·00

(6)

1919. Stamps of Russia optd as T **6** in various sizes, with or without frame. Imperf or perf. (a) Arms types.

53B	**22**	1k. orange	12·50
54B	**22**	2k. green	3·00
55B	**22**	3k. red	2·40
11B	**23**	4k. red	80
12B	**22**	5k. red	1·30
13B	**23**	10k. blue	90
14B	**22**	10k. on 7k. blue	1·20
15B	**10**	15k. blue and purple	1·50
16B	**14**	20k. red and blue	1·60
17B	**10**	25k. mauve and green	2·00
45B	**10**	35k. green and purple	2·20

19B	14	50k. green and purple	1·00
30aB	22	60k. on 1k. orange (No. 3)	2·50
31B	10	70k. orange and brown	1·00
32B	15	1r. orange and brown	2·20
33B	11	3r.50 green and brown	3·50
23B	20	5r. green and blue	5·00
24B	11	7r. pink and green	9·00
62B	11	7r. yellow and black	40·00
52B	20	10r. grey, red and yellow	11·00

(b) Romanov type.

63B	20	4k. red (No. 129)	2·00

(c) Unissued Postal Savings Bank stamp.

64A	1k. red on buff	6·50

(8)

1920. Stamps of Russia surch as T **8** in various types and sizes. Imperf or perf. (a) Arms types.

65B	22	1r. on 1k. orange	3·25
94B	22	1r. on 60k. on 1k. orange (No. 3)	4·50
66B	22	3r. on 3k. red	2·10
67B	22	3r. on 4k. red	7·25
97B	22	5r. on 2k. green	2·50
69B	23	5r. on 4k. red	1·30
70B	22	5r. on 5k. red	1·80
71B	22	5r. on 7k. blue	1·20
72B	23	5r. on 10k. blue	1·60
73B	22	5r. on 10 on 7k. blue	2·10
74B	10	5r. on 14k. red and blue	2·30
75B	10	5r. on 15k. blue and purple	2·10
76aB	10	5r. on 20 on 14k. red and blue	8·50
76B	14	5r. on 20k. red and blue	2·10
77B	10	5r. on 25k. mauve and green	8·50
111B	22	5r. on 3r. on 5k. red	11·00
78B	10	10r. on 25k. mauve and green	2·00
79B	10	10r. on 35k. green and purple	1·50
80B	14	10r. on 50k. green and purple	4·00
80aB	9	25r. on 1k. orange	40·00
80bB	9	25r. on 3k. red	40·00
80cB	9	25r. on 5k. purple	40·00
80dB	22	25r. on 10 on 7k. blue	40·00
80eB	10	25r. on 15k. blue and purple	40·00
81B	14	25r. on 20k. red and blue	4·50
82B	10	25r. on 25k. mauve and green	3·75
83B	10	25r. on 35k. green and purple	2·75
84B	14	25r. on 50k. green and purple	3·50
85B	10	25r. on 70k. orange and brown	5·00
104aB	9	50r. on 1k. orange	45·00
104bB	9	50r. on 3k. red	48·00
85bB	10	50r. on 4k. red	45·00
104cB	14	50r. on 5k. purple	48·00
85cB	10	50r. on 15k. blue and purple	45·00
85dB	14	50r. on 20k. red and blue	45·00
85eB	10	50r. on 35k. green & purple	45·00
85fB	14	50r. on 50k. green & purple	25·00
105B	10	50r. on 70k. orange and brown	6·25
106B	15	50r. on 1r. orange and brown	6·50
107B	15	100r. on 1r. orange and brown	6·00
108B	11	100r. on 3r.50 green and brown	18·00
88B	20	100r. on 5r. green and blue	15·00
89B	11	100r. on 7r. yellow and black	19·00
90B	11	100r. on 7r. pink and green	10·00
93B	20	100r. on 10r. grey, red and yellow	15·00

(b) Romanov issue of 1913.

112	20	1r. on 1k. orange	10·50
113	20	3r. on 3k. red	13·00
114	20	5r. on 4k. red	5·50
115	20	5r. on 10 on 7k. brown	3·25
116	20	5r. on 14k. green	39·00
117	20	5r. on 20 on 14k. green	5·25
118	20	25r. on 4k. red	6·50
118a	20	100r. on 1k. orange	65·00
119	20	100r. on 2k. green	65·00
120	20	100r. on 3r. violet	65·00

(c) War Charity issues of 1914 and 1915.

121	15	25r. on 1k. green and red on yellow	39·00
122	15	25r. on 3k. green and red on rose	39·00
123	15	50r. on 7k. green and brown on buff	48·00
124	15	50r. on 10k. brown and blue	48·00
125	15	100r. on 1k. green and red on yellow	48·00
126	15	100r. on 1k. grey and brown	48·00
127	15	100r. on 3k. green and red on rose	48·00
128	15	100r. on 7k. green and brown on buff	48·00
129	15	100r. on 10k. brown and blue	48·00

1920. Arms types of Russia optd as T **6** in various sizes with or without frame, and surch as T **8** or with value only in various types and sizes. Imperf or perf.

155B	22	1r. on 60k. on 1k. orange (No. 3)	1·30
156A	22	3r. on 3k. red	2·50
157A	22	5r. on 2k. green	1·10
141A	23	5r. on 4k. red	4·50
158A	22	5r. on 5k. red	4·25
142A	23	5r. on 10k. blue	4·50
143A	22	5r. on 10 on 7k. blue	4·50
144A	10	5r. on 15k. blue & pur	2·40
145A	14	5r. on 20k. red and blue	2·40
132B	10	10r. on 15k. blue & pur	12·00
145aB	14	10r. on 20k. red & blue	1·20
146A	10	10r. on 25k. mauve and green	2·40
147B	10	10r. on 35k. green and purple	1·20
148A	14	10r. on 50k. green and purple	3·00
159A	10	10r. on 70k. orange and brown	14·00
163A	22	10r. on 5r. on 5k. red	30·00
164A	10	10r. on 5r. on 25k. mauve and green	32·00
165A	10	10r. on 5r. on 35k. green and purple	11·00
138A	10	25r. on 70k. orange and brown	8·00
161B	15	50r. on 1r. orange and brown	2·75
135B	11	100r. on 3r.50 green and brown	3·00
151A	20	100r. on 5r. green & bl	8·00
136A	11	100r. on 7r. pink and green	9·00
154aA	20	100r. on 10r. grey, red and yellow	12·00
166A	20	100r. on 25r. on 5r. green and blue	30·00

1920. Stamps of Russia optd as T **6** in various sizes, with or without frame and surch **10**. Perf. (a) Arms types.

168	14	10 on 20k. red and blue	30·00
169	10	10 on 25k. mauve and green	30·00
170	10	10 on 35k. green and purple	20·00
171	14	10 on 50k. green and purple	24·00

(b) Romanov type.

172	10 on 4k. red (No. 129)	48·00

1920. Stamps of Russia optd with monogram as in T **8** in various types and sizes and surch 10. Imperf or perf. (a) Arms types.

173	23	10 on 4k. red	48·00
174	22	10 on 5k. red	48·00
175	10	10 on 15k. blue & purple	48·00
176	14	10 on 20k. red and blue	45·00
176a	10	10 on 20 on 14k. red and blue	24·00
177	10	10 on 25k. mauve & green	24·00
178	10	10 on 35k. green & purple	24·00
179	14	10 on 50k. green & purple	24·00

(b) Romanov type.

181	10 on 4k. red (No. 129)	60·00

SOVIET REPUBLIC

Stamps in Types **11**, **12** and a similar horizontal type showing a woman spinning were printed in Paris to the order of the Armenian National Government, but were not issued in Armenia as the Bolshevists had assumed control. (Price 10p. each).

11

12 Mt. Ararat

(13)

1921. Arms types of Russia surch with T **13**. Perf.

182	15	5000r. on 1r. orange and brown	6·50
183	11	5000r. on 3r.50 grn & brn	6·50
184	20	5000r. on 5r. green & blue	6·50
185	11	5000r. on 7r. pink and green	6·50
186	20	5000r. on 10r. grey, red & yellow	6·50

TRANSCAUCASIAN FEDERATION ISSUES FOR ARMENIA

14 Common Crane

16 Village Scene

1922. Unissued stamps surch in gold kopeks. Imperf.

187	14	1 on 250r. red	9·75
188	14	1 on 250r. slate	13·00
189	16	2 on 500r. red	5·25
190	16	3 on 500r. slate	5·25
191	-	4 on 1000r. red	5·25
192	-	4 on 1000r. slate	9·75
193	-	5 on 2000r. slate	30·00
194	-	10 on 2000r. red	30·00
195	-	15 on 5000r. red	23·00
196	-	20 on 5000r. slate	5·25

DESIGNS (sizes in mm): 1000r. Woman at well (17×26); 2000r. Erivan railway station (35×24½); 5000r. Horseman and Mt. Ararat (39½×24½).

17 Soviet Emblems

18 Wall Sculpture at Ani

19 Mt. Aragatz

1922. Unissued stamps as T **17/19** surch in gold kopeks in figures. Imperf or perf.

210	17	1 on 1r. green	9·75
198	18	2 on 2r. slate	15·00
212	-	3 on 3r. red	18·00
213	-	4 on 25r. green	3·75
201	-	5 on 50r. red	5·00
215	-	10 on 100r. orange	13·00
203	-	15 on 250r. blue	2·20
204a	19	20 on 500r. purple	3·00
205	-	35 on 20,000r. red	24·00
206a	-	50 on 25,000r. green	48·00
209	-	50 on 25,000r. blue	6·50

DESIGNS (sizes in mm): 3r. (29×22) and 250r. (21×35) Soviet emblems; 25r. (30×22½); 100r. (34½×23) and 20,000r. (43×27) Mythological sculptures, Ani. 50r. (25½×37). Armenian soldier; 25,000r. (45½×27½) Mt. Ararat.

The above and other values were not officially issued without the surcharges.

1923. As T **19**, etc., surch in gold kopeks in figures. Imperf or perf.

219	-	1 on 250r. blue	6·50
217	19	2 on 500r. purple	6·50
218	-	3 on 20000r. lake	13·00

26 Mt. Ararat and Soviet Emblems

28 Ploughing

1923. Unissued stamps in various designs as T **26/28** surch in Transcaucasian roubles in figures. Perf.

227	26	10,000r. on 50r. green and red	1·80
228	-	15,000r. on 300r. blue and buff	1·80
229	-	25,000r. on 400r. blue and pink	1·80
240B	-	30,000r. on 500r. violet and lilac	2·00
231	-	50,000r. on 1000r. blue	1·80
232	-	75,000r. on 3000r. black and green	2·00
233	-	100,000r. on 2000r. black and grey	2·40
243	-	200,000r. on 4000r. black and brn	1·20
235	-	300,000r. on 5000r. black and red	3·25
245	28	500,000r. on 10,000r. black and red	1·50

DESIGNS (sizes in mm): 300r. (26×35) Star over Mt. Ararat; 400r. (26×34½) Soviet emblems; 500r. (26×34½) Crane (bird); 1000r. (19×25) Peasant in punt; 2000r. (26×31) Human-headed bird from old bas-relief; 3000r. (26½×36) Sower; 4000r. (26×31½) Star and dragon; 5000r. (26×32) Blacksmith.

INDEPENDENT REPUBLIC

31 Mount Ararat and National Colours

1992. Independence Day.

246	31	20k. multicoloured	15	15
247	31	2r. multicoloured	70	70
248	31	5r. multicoloured	1·70	1·70
MS249		80×80 mm. 7r. multicoloured (Mt. Ararat and eagle)	43·00	43·00

32 Dish Aerial and World Map

1992. Inauguration of International Direct-dial Telephone System.

250	32	50k. multicoloured	3·00	3·00

33 Ancient Greek Wrestling

1992. Olympic Games, Barcelona. Multicoloured.

251	40k. Type **33**	10	35
252	3r.60 Boxing	40	40
253	5r. Weightlifting	60	60
254	12r. Gymnastics (ring exercises)	1·40	1·40

34 National Flag

1992

255	34	20k. multicoloured (postage)	10	10
256	-	1r. black	15	15
257	-	3r. brown	45	45
258	-	3r. brown	30	30
259	-	5r. black	60	60
260	-	20r. grey	65	65
261	-	2r. blue (air)	30	30

DESIGNS: 1r. Goddess Waroubini statuette from Orgov radio-optical telescope; 2r. Zvartnots Airport, Yerevan; 3r. (No. 257) Goddess Anahit; 3r. (No. 258) Runic inscription Karmir-Blour; 5r. U.P.U. Monument, Berne, Switzerland; 20r. Silver cup from Karashamb.

See also Nos. 275/82.

35 *Noah's Descent from Mt. Ararat*

1993. 175th Birth Anniv of Hovhannes Aivazovsky (painter). Sheet 95×63 mm.

MS262	**35** 7r. multicoloured	2·10	2·10

36 Engraved 10th- century Tombstone, Makenis

1993. Armenian Cultural History. Multicoloured.

263		40k. Type **36**	10	10
264		80k. Illuminated page from Gospel of 1295	20	20
265		3r.60 13th-century bas-relief, Gandzasar	75	75
266		5r. *Glorious Mother of God* (18th-century painting, H. Hovnatanian)	1·30	1·30
MS267		93x73mm. 12r. *David of Sassoun*, 1922 (painting, H. Kojoian)	6·25	5·75

37 Garni Canyon

1993. Landscapes. Multicoloured.

268		40k. Type **37**	10	10
269		80k. Shaki Falls, Zangezur	10	10
270		3r.60 River Arpa gorge, Vike	35	35
271		5r. Lake Sevan (horiz)	50	50
272		12r. Mount Ararat (horiz)	1·20	1·20

38 Temple of Garni

1993. "YEREVAN '93" International Stamp Exn.

273	**38**	10r. red, black and brown	10	10
MS274		133×111 mm. No. 273×6 plus two labels	4·50	4·25

1994. As T **34** but new currency.

275		10l. agate and brown	10	10
277		50l. deep brown and brown	60	60
280		10d. brown and grey	60	60
282		25d. gold and red	1·50	1·50

DESIGNS: 10l. Shivini, Sun God (Karmir-Blour); 50l. Tayshaba, God of the Elements (Karmir-Blour); 10d. Khaldi, Supreme God (Karmir-Blour); 25d. National arms.

39 Reliquary for Arm of St. Thaddeus (17th century)

1994. Treasures of Etchmiadzin (seat of Armenian church). Multicoloured.

286		3d. Descent from the Cross (9th-century wooden panel)	10	10
287		5d. Gilded silver reliquary of Holy Cross of Khotakerats (1300)	10	10
288		12d. Cross with St. Karapet's right hand (14th century)	1·00	1·00
289		30d. Type **39**	50	50
290		50d. Gilded silver chrism vessel (1815)	1·40	1·40

40
(40)

40
(41)

1994. Stamp Exhibitions, Yerevan. (a) "Armenia '94" National Exn. No. 273 surch with T **40**.

291		40d. on 10r. red, blk & brn	3·75	3·75

(b) "Armenia–Argentina" Exhibition. No. 273 surch with T **41**.

292		40d. on 10r. red, blk & brn	3·75	3·75

42 Cancelled Stamps of 1919

1994. 75th Anniv of First Stamp Issue.

293	**42**	16d. multicoloured	30	30

43 Stadium and Arms of National Committee

1994. Olympic Committees. Multicoloured.

294		30d. Type **43**	45	45
295		40d. Olympic rings (centenary of Int Olympic Committee)	65	65

44 Haroutune Shmavonian

1994. Bicentenary of *Azdarar* (first Armenian periodical).

296	**44**	30d. brown and green	40	40

45 Ervand Otian

1994. 125th Birth Anniversaries.

297	**45**	50d. drab and brown	30	30
298	-	50d. brown	30	30

DESIGN—HORIZ: 50d. Levon Shant.

46 *Cross* (from Gospel)

1995. 1700th Anniv (2001) of Christianity in Armenia (1st issue). Works of art. Multicoloured.

299		60d. Type **46**	55	55
300		70d. *St. Bartholomew and St. Thaddeus the Apostles* (Hovnatan Hovnatanian) (45×39 mm)	55	55
301		70d. *Kings Abhar and Trdat* (Mkrtoum Hovnatanian) (45×39 mm)	55	55
302		80d. *St. Gregory the Illuminator*	70	70
303		90d. *The Baptism of Armenian People* (H. Aivazovsky)	85	85
MS304		97×71 mm. 400d. black and ochre (*Echmiadzin Monastery* (detail of engraving by Jacob Peeters))	2·75	2·75

See also Nos. **MS**331, 362/**MS**367, 382/**MS**387 and **MS**401.

47 Vazgen I

1995. First Death Anniv of Vazgen I (Patriarch of Armenian Orthodox Church).

305	**47**	150d. black and grey	70	70

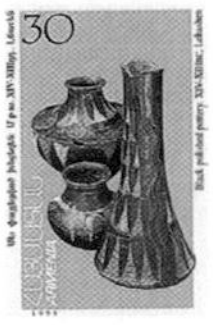

48 Black-polished Pottery

1995. Museum Artefacts (1st series). Multicoloured.

306		30d. Type **48**	25	25
307		60d. Silver horn	50	50
308		130d. Gohar carpet	1·20	1·20

See also Nos. 332/4.

49 Red Kite and Oak

1995. Birds and Trees. Multicoloured.

309		40d. Type **49**	40	55
310		60d. Golden eagle and juniper	50	60

50 Workers building "Honeycomb" Map

1995. Hyastan All-Armenian Fund.

311	**50**	90d. multicoloured	65	65

51 Rainbows around U.N. Emblem

1995. 50th Anniv of U.N.O.

312	**51**	90d. multicoloured	65	65

52 Commander P. Kitsook (408th Rifle Division)

1995. 50th Anniv of End of Second World War. (a) Size 40×23 mm. Each black, orange and blue.

313		60d. Type **52**	40	40
314		60d. Commanders S. Chernikov, N. Tavartkeladze and V. Penkovsky (76th Mountain Rifle Red-banner (51st Guard) Division)	40	40
315		60d. Commanders S. Zakian, H. Babayan and I. Lyudnikov (390th Rifle Division)	40	40
316		60d. Commanders A. Vasilian, M. Dobrovolsky, Y. Grechany and G. Sorokin (409th Rifle Division)	40	40
317		60d. Commanders A. Sargissian and N. Safarian (89th Taman Triple Order Bearer Rifle Division)	40	40

(b) Size 23×35 mm. Each blue, orange and brown.

318		60d. Marshal Hovhannes Baghramian	60	60
319		60d. Admiral Hovhannes Issakov	60	60
320		60d. General Marshal Hamazasp Babajanian	60	60
321		60d. Marshal Sergey Khoudyakov	60	60
MS322		120×90 mm. 300d. *Return of the Hero* (Mariam Aslamazian)	2·50	2·50

53 Ghevond Alishan (historian and geographer)

1995. Writers' Anniversaries.

323	**53**	90d. green and black	55	55
324	-	90d. sepia, brown & yellow	55	55
325	-	90d. blue and red	60	60

DESIGNS: No. 323, Type **53** (175th birth); 324, Grigor Artsruni (journalist, 150th birth); 325, Franz Werfel (50th death).

54 Sports and Concert Complex

1995. Yerevan.

326		60d. black and orange	30	30
327		80d. black and pink	40	40
328	**54**	90d. black and buff	45	45
329	-	100d. black and buff	60	60
330	-	120d. black and pink	80	80
MS331		90×65 mm. 400d. multicoloured	2·40	2·40

DESIGNS—As T **54**: 60d. Brandy distillery and wine cellars; 80d. Abovian Street; 400d. Panoramic view of Yerevan. 60×23 mm: 100d. Baghramian Avenue; 120d. Republic Square.

No. **MS**331 also commemorates the 1700th anniv (2001) of Christianity in Armenia.

1995. Museum Artefacts (2nd series). As T **48**. Multicoloured.

332		40d. Four-wheeled carriages (horiz)	25	25
333		60d. Bronze model of solar system	45	45
334		90d. Tombstone from Loriberd	65	65

55 Katsian and Spectators watching Flight

1995. Air. 86th Anniv of Artiom Katsian's 1909 World Record for Range and Altitude.

335	**55**	90d. ochre, brown and blue	60	60

(56)

1996. No. 275 surch as T **56**.

336		40d. on 10l. agate and brown	95	95
337		100d. on 10l. agate and brown	2·30	2·30
338		150d. on 10l. agate and brown	3·50	3·50
339		200d. on 10l. agate and brown	5·00	5·00

57 Griboedov

1996. Birth Bicentenary of Aleksandr Griboedov (historian).

340	**57**	90d. stone, brown and red	65	65

58 Hayrik Khrimian (patriarch of Armenian Orthodox Church, 175th birth anniv (1995))

1996. Anniversaries.

341	**58**	90d. blue & brn (postage)	55	55
342	-	90d. multicoloured	55	55
343	-	90d. grey, blue & red (air)	55	55

DESIGNS—HORIZ: No. 342, Lazar Serebryakov (Admiral of the Fleet, and 19th-century Russian warships, birth bicentenary (1995)). VERT: No. 343, Nelson Stepanian (Second World War pilot, 50th death anniv (1994)).

59 Opening Frame from First Armenian Film

1996. Centenary of Motion Pictures.

344	**59**	60d. black, grey and blue	40	40

60 Angel and Red Cross

1996. 75th Anniv of Armenian Red Cross Society.

345	**60**	60d. multicoloured	40	40

61 Wild Goats

1996. Mammals. Multicoloured.

346	40d. Type **61**	60	20
347	60d. Leopards	55	65

62 Nansen and *Fram*

1996. Centenary of Return of Fridtjof Nansen's Arctic Expedition.

348	**62**	90d. multicoloured	70	70

63 Cycling

1996. Olympic Games, Atlanta. Multicoloured.

349	40d. Type **63**	25	25
350	60d. Triple jumping	40	40
351	90d. Wrestling	70	70

Nos. 349/51 were issued together, *se-tenant*, the backgrounds forming a composite design showing ancient Greek athletes.

64 Torch Bearer

1996. Centenary of Modern Olympic Games.

352	**64**	60d. multicoloured	35	35

65 Genrikh Kasparian (first prize winner, "Chess in USSR" competition, 1939)

1996. 32nd Chess Olympiad, Yerevan. Designs showing positions from previous games. Multicoloured.

353	40d. Type **65**	35	35
354	40d. Tigran Petrosian v. Mikhail Botvinnik (World Championship, Moscow, 1963)	35	35
355	40d. Gary Kasparov v. Anatoly Karpov (World Championship, Leningrad, 1986)	35	35
356	40d. Olympiad emblem	35	35

66 Tigran Petrosian (World chess champion, 1963–69) and Tigran Petrosian Chess House, Yerevan

1996

357	**66**	90d. multicoloured	65	65

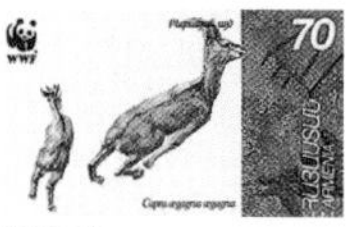

67 Goats

1996. The Wild Goat. Multicoloured.

358	70d. Type **67**	35	35
359	100d. Lone female	45	45
360	130d. Lone male	60	60
361	350d. Heads of male and female	1·70	1·70

68 Church of the Holy Mother, Samarkand, Uzbekistan

1997. 1700th Anniv (2001) of Christianity in Armenia (2nd issue). Armenian Apostolic Overseas Churches. Multicoloured.

362	100d. Type **68**	50	50
363	100d. Church of the Holy Mother, Kishinev, Moldova	50	50
364	100d. St. Hripsime's Church, Yalta, Ukraine	50	50
365	100d. St. Catherine's Church, St. Petersburg, Russia	50	50
366	100d. Church, Lvov, Ukraine	50	50
MS367	92×66 mm. 500d. St. George of Echmiadzin's Church, Tbilisi, Georgia	2·50	2·50

69 Man operating Printing Press

1997. 225th Anniv of First Printing Press in Armenia.

368	**69**	70d. multicoloured	85	85

70 Jivani and Mount Ararat

1997. 150th Birth Anniv of Jivani (folk singer).

369	**70**	90d. multicoloured	45	45

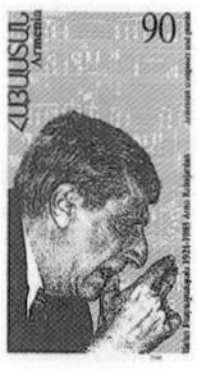

71 Babajanian and Score of *Heroic Ballad*

1997. 75th Birth Anniv (1996) of Arno Babajanian (composer and pianist).

370	**71**	90d. black, lilac & purple	45	45

72 *Countryside* (Gevorg Bashinjaghian)

1997. Exhibits in National Gallery of Armenia (1st series). Multicoloured.

371	150d. Type **72**	75	75
372	150d. *One of My Dreams* (Eghishe Tadevossian)	75	75
373	150d. *Portrait of Natalia Tehumian* (Hakob Hovnatanian) (vert)	75	75
374	150d. *Salome* (Vardges Sureniants) (vert)	75	75

See also Nos. 390/2 and 512/13.

73 Mamulian

1997. Birth Centenary of Rouben Mamulian (film director).

375	**73**	150d. multicoloured	80	80

74 St. Basil's Cathedral, Moscow

1997. "Moscow 97" Int Stamp Exhibition.

376	**74**	170d. multicoloured	85	85

75 Hayk and Bel

1997. Europa. Tales and Legends. Multicoloured.

377	170d. Type **75**	2·00	2·00
378	250d. The Song of Vahagn	2·50	2·50

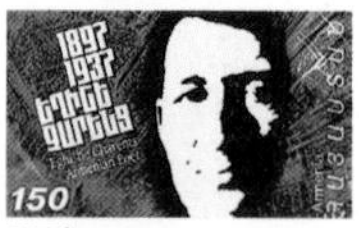

76 Charents

1997. Birth Centenary of Eghishe Charents (poet).

379	**76**	150d. brown and red	75	75

77 *Iris lycotis*

1997. Irises. Multicoloured.

380	40d. Type **77**	15	15
381	170d. "Iris elegantissima"	75	75

78 St. Gregory the Illuminator Cathedral, Anthelias, Libya

1997. 1700th Anniv (2001) of Christianity in Armenia (3rd issue). Armenian Overseas Educational Centres. Multicoloured.

382	100d. Type **78**	50	50
383	100d. St. Khach Armenian Church, Nakhijevan, Rostov-on-Don	50	50
384	100d. St. James's Monastery, Jerusalem (horiz)	50	50
385	100d. Nercissian School, Tbilisi, Georgia (60×21 mm)	50	50
386	100d. San Lazzaro Mekhitarian Congregation, Venice (horiz)	50	50
MS387	90×45 mm. 500d. Lazarian Seminary, Moscow (horiz)	2·40	2·40

79 Baby Jesus, Angel and Mary

1997. Christmas.

388	**79**	40d. multicoloured	30	30

80 Eagle and Demonstrator with Flag

1998. Tenth Anniv of Karabakh Movement.

389	**80**	250d. multicoloured	1·60	1·60

1998. Exhibits in National Gallery of Armenia (2nd series). As T **72**. Multicoloured.

390	150d. *Family. Generations* (Yervand Kochar) (vert)	75	75
391	150d. *Tartar Women's Dance* (Alexander Bazhbeouk-Melikian)	75	75
392	150d. *Spring in Our Yard* (Haroutiun Kalents) (vert)	75	75

81 Diana, Princess of Wales

1998. Diana, Princess of Wales Commemoration.

393	**81**	250d. multicoloured	90	90

82 Eiffel Tower, Ball and Pitch

1998. World Cup Football Championship, France.

394	**82**	250d. multicoloured	1·20	1·20

83 Couple leaping through Flames (Trndez)

1998. Europa. National Festivals. Multicoloured.

395	170d. Type **83**	1·30	1·30
396	250d. Girls in traditional costume (Ascension)	2·20	2·20

84 Southern Swallowtail

1998. Insects. Multicoloured.

397	170d. Type **84**	85	85
398	250d. *Rethera komarovi* (moth)	1·20	1·20

85 Ayrarat Couple

1998. Traditional Costumes (1st series). Multicoloured.

399	170d. Type **85**	85	85
400	250d. Vaspurakan family	1·20	1·20

See also Nos. 408/9, 492/3, 591/2 and 620/1.

86 St. Forty Children's Church, Milan

1998. 1700th Anniv (2001) of Christianity in Armenia (4th issue). Sheet 143×71 mm. Multicoloured.

MS401	100d. Type **86**; 100d. St. Sargis's Church, London; 100d. St. Vardan's Cathedral, New York; 100d. St. Hovhannes's Cathedral, Paris; 100d. St. Gregory the Illuminator's Cathedral, Buenos Aires	2·50	2·50

87 Fissure in Earth's Surface

1998. Tenth Anniv of Armenian Earthquake.

402	**87**	250d. black, red and lilac	1·20	1·20

88 Pyrite

1998. Minerals. Multicoloured.

403	170d. Type **88**	90	90
404	250d. Agate	1·30	1·30

89 Briusov

1998. 125th Birth Anniv of Valery Briusov (Russian translator of Armenian works).

405	**89**	90d. multicoloured	45	45

90 Parajanov

1999. 75th Birth Anniv of Sergei Parajanov (film director and artist). Sheet 74 ×65 mm.

MS406	**90** 500d. multicoloured	2·75	2·75
MS407	As No. **MS**406 but with emblem in margin of "iBRA" International Stamp Exhibition, Nuremberg, Germany	3·00	3·00

1999. Traditional Costumes (2nd series). As T **85**.

408	170d. Mother and child from Karin	90	90
409	250d. Zangezour couple	1·30	1·30

91 Khosrov Reserve

1999. Europa. Parks and Gardens. Multicoloured.

410	170d. Type **91**	85	85
411	250d. Dilijan Reserve	1·00	1·00

92 Anniversary Emblem on Flag

1999. 50th Anniv of Council of Europe.

412	**92**	170d. multicoloured	1·80	1·80

93 Medieval Kogge and Map

1999. Ships of the Armenian Kingdom of Cilicia (11–14th centuries). Multicoloured.

413	170d. Type **93**	85	85
414	250d. Medieval single-masted sailing ships	1·30	1·30
415	250d. As No. 414 but with emblem of "Philexfrance 99" International Stamp Exhibition, Paris, France, in lower right corner	1·30	1·30

94 Armenian Gampr

1999. Domestic Pets. Multicoloured.

416	170d. Type **94**	85	85
417	250d. Turkish van cat	1·30	1·30
418	250d. As No. 417 but with emblem of "China 1999" International Stamp Exhibition, Peking, China, in lower right corner	1·40	1·40

95 Obverse and Reverse of Medal

1999. First Pan-Armenian Games, Yerevan. Sheet 58×40 mm.

MS419	**95** 250d. multicoloured	2·20	2·20

96 St. Gregory the Illuminator's Church, Cairo

1999. 1700th Anniv (2001) of Christianity in Armenia (5th issue). Sheet 121×65 mm containing T **96** and similar horiz designs. Multicoloured.

MS420	70d. Type **96**; 70d. St. Gregory the Illuminator's Church, Singapore; 70d. St. Khach's Church, Suchava; 70d. St. Saviour's Church, Worcester; 70d. Church of the Holy Mother, Madras	1·90	1·90

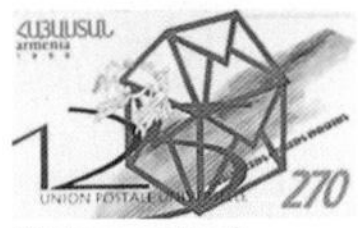

97 House made of Envelopes

1999. 125th Anniv of Universal Postal Union.

421	**97**	270d. multicoloured	1·60	1·60

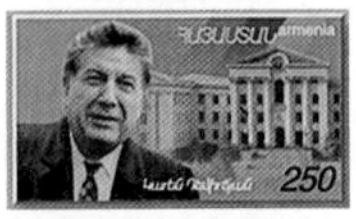

98 Karen Demirchyan (Speaker of the National Assembly)

2000. Commemoration of Victims of Attack on National Assembly. Multicoloured.

422	250d. Type **98**	1·40	1·40
423	250d. Vazgen Sargsyan (Prime Minister)	1·40	1·40
MS424	60×40 mm. 540d. Demirchyan Sargsyan, Yuri Bakshyan, Ruben Mirochyan, Henrik Abrahamyan, Armenak Armenakyan, Leonard Petrossyan and Mikael Kotanyan	3·00	3·00

99 Sevan Trout

2000. Fish. Multicoloured.

425	50d. Type **99**	35	35
426	270d. Sevan barbel	1·50	1·50

100 The Liar Hunter

2000. National Fairy Tales. Multicoloured.

427	70d. Type **100**	40	40
428	130d. The King and the Peddler	70	70

101 "Building Europe"

2000. Europa.

429	**101**	40d. multicoloured	35	35
430	**101**	500d. multicoloured	4·25	4·25

102 St. Gayane Church, Vagharshapat

2000. 1700th Anniv (2001) of Christianity in Armenia (6th issue). Sheet 121×65 mm containing T **102** and similar horiz designs. Multicoloured.

MS431	70d. Type **102**; 70d. Etchmiadzin Cathedral, Vagharshapat; 70d. Church of the Holy Mother, Khor Virap; 70d. St. Shoghakat Church, Vagharshapat; 70d. St. Hrip'sime Church, Vagharshapat	2·75	2·75

103 Basketball

2000. Olympic Games, Sydney. Multicoloured.

432	10d. Type **103**	10	10
433	30d. Tennis	25	25
434	500d. Weightlifting	4·25	4·25

104 Quartz

2000. Minerals. Multicoloured.

435	170d. Type **104**	1·30	1·30
436	250d. Molybdenite	1·90	1·90

105 Shnorhali

2000. 900th Birth Anniv of Nerses Shnorhali (writer and musician).

437	**105**	270d. multicoloured	1·60	1·60

106 Adoration of the Magi

2000. Christmas.

438	**106**	170d. multicoloured	1·00	1·00

107 Issahakian

2000. 125th Birth Anniv of Avetik Issahakian (poet).

439	**107**	130d. multicoloured	60	60

108 Dhol

2000. Musical Instruments. Multicoloured.

440	170d. Type **108**	95	95
441	250d. Duduk (wind instrument)	1·30	1·30

109 Viktor Hambartsoumian (astrophysicist)

2000. New Millennium. Famous Armenians. Multicoloured.

442	110d. Type **109**	65	65
443	110d. Abraham Alikhanov (physicist)	65	65
444	110d. Andranik Iossifan (electrical engineer)	65	65
445	110d. Sargis Saltikov (metallurgist)	65	65
446	110d. Samval Kocharients (electrical engineer)	65	65
447	110d. Artem Mikoyan (aircraft designer)	65	65
448	110d. Norayr Sisisakian (biochemist)	65	65
449	110d. Ivan Knunyants (chemist)	65	65
450	110d. Nikoghayos Yenikolopian (physical chemist)	65	65
451	110d. Nikoghayos Adonts (historian)	65	65
452	110d. Manouk Abeghian (folklore scholar)	65	65
453	110d. Hovhannes Toumanian (poet)	65	65
454	110d. Hrachya Ajarian (linguist)	65	65
455	110d. Gevorg Emin (poet)	65	65
456	110d. Yervand Lalayan (anthropologist)	65	65
457	110d. Daniel Varoujan (poet)	65	65
458	110d. Paruyr Sevak (poet)	65	65
459	110d. William Saroyan (dramatist and novelist)	65	65
460	110d. Hamo Beknazarian (film director)	65	65
461	110d. Alexandre Tamanian (architect)	65	65
462	110d. Vahram Papazian (actor)	65	65
463	110d. Vasil Tahirov (viticulturist)	65	65
464	110d. Leonid Yengibarian (mime artist)	65	65
465	110d. Haykanoush Danielian (singer)	65	65
466	110d. Sergo Hambartsoumian (weight lifter)	65	65
467	110d. Hrant Shahinian (gymnast)	65	65
468	110d. Toros Toramanian (architect)	65	65
469	110d. Komitas (composer)	65	65
470	110d. Aram Khachatourian (composer)	65	65
471	110d. Martiros Sarian (artist)	65	65
472	110d. Avet Terterian (composer)	65	65
473	110d. Alexandre Spendiarian (composer)	65	65
474	110d. Arshile Gorky (artist)	65	65
475	110d. Minas Avetissian (artist)	65	65
476	110d. (Levon Orbeli physiologist)	65	65
477	110d. Hripsimeh Simonian (ceramics artist)	65	65

110 Soldiers

2001. 1550th Anniv of Battle of Avarayr. Sheet 90×65 mm containing T **110** and similar vert design. Multicoloured.

MS478	170d. Type **110**; 270d. Vardan Mamikonian	3·00	3·00

111 Narekatsi and Text

2001. Millenary of A Record of Lamentations by Grigor Narekatsi.

479	**111**	25d. multicoloured	55	55

112 Lake Sevan

2001. Europa. Water Resources. Multicoloured.

480	50d. Type **112**	25	25
481	500d. Spandarian Reservoir	2·75	2·75

113 Emblem

2001. Armenian Membership of Council of Europe.

482	**113**	240d. multicoloured	1·10	1·10

114 Trophy

2001. Second Pan-Armenian Games. Sheet 58×40 mm.

MS483	**114** 300d. multicoloured	2·20	2·20

115 Persian Squirrel

2001. Endangered Species. Persian Squirrel (*Sciurus persicus*). Multicoloured.

484	**113**	40d. Type **115**	40	40
485	**113**	50d. Adult sitting on branch with young in tree hole	50	50
486	**113**	80d. Head of squirrel	85	85
487	**113**	120d. On ground	1·30	1·30

116 Cathedral Facade

2001. 1700th Anniv of Christianity in Armenia (7th issue). St. Gregory the Illuminator Cathedral, Yerevan. Multicoloured.

488	50d. Type **116**	35	35
489	205d. Interior elevation of Cathedral (44×30 mm)	1·40	1·40
490	240d. Exterior elevation of Cathedral (44×30 mm)	1·70	1·70

117 Lazarian and Institute

2001. Death Bicentenary of Hovhannes Lazarian (founder of Institute of Oriental Languages, Moscow).

491	**117**	300d. multicoloured	1·70	1·70

A stamp in a similar design was issued by Russia.

2001. Traditional Costumes (3rd series). As T **85**. Multicoloured.

492	50d. Javakhch couple	40	40
493	250d. Artzakh couple	1·70	1·70

118 Emblem

2001. Sixth World Wushu Championships, Yerevan.

494	**118**	180d. black	1·00	1·00

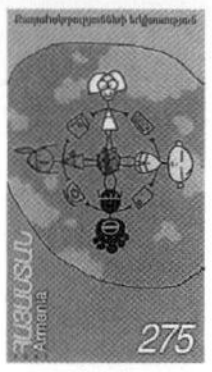

119 Children encircling Globe

2001. United Nations Year of Dialogue among Civilizations.

495	**119**	275d. multicoloured	1·60	1·60

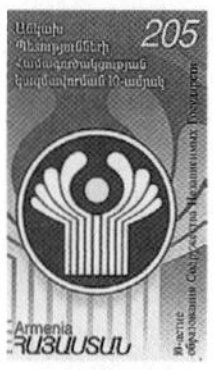

120 Emblem

2001. Tenth Anniv of Commonwealth of Independent States.

496	**120**	205d. multicoloured	1·20	1·20

121 Profiles

2001. European Year of Languages.

497	**121**	350d. multicoloured	2·30	2·30

122 Flag

2001. Tenth Anniv of Independence.

498	**122**	300d. multicoloured	1·70	1·70

123 Cart

2001. Transport. Multicoloured.

499	180d. Type **123**	1·30	1·30
500	205d. Phaeton	1·40	1·40

124 *Hypericum perforatum*

2001. Medicinal Plants. Multicoloured.

501	85d. Type **124**	60	60
502	205d. *Thymus serpyllum*	1·50	1·50

125 Eagle

2002

503	**125**	10d. brown	10	10
504	**125**	25d. green	20	20
506	**125**	50d. blue	35	35
507	**125**	70d. rose	20	20
508	**125**	300d. blue	1·50	1·50
509	**125**	500d. brown	1·90	1·90

126 Calendar Belt (2000 B.C.) and Copper Works

2002. Traditional Production. Multicoloured.

510	120d. Type **126**	75	75
511	350d. Beer vessels (7th century B.C.) and modern brewing equipment	2·10	2·10

2002. Exhibits in National Gallery of Armenia (3rd series). Vert designs as T **72**.

512	200d. black, grey and green	1·00	1·00
513	200d. black, grey and red	1·00	1·00

DESIGNS: No. 512, *Lily* (Edgar Chahine); 513, *Salome* (sculpture, Hakob Gurjian).

127 Football and Maps of Japan and South Korea

2002. World Cup Football Championships, Japan and South Korea.

514	**127**	350d. multicoloured	1·90	1·90

128 Pushman and *The Silent Order* (detail, painting)

2002. 125th Birth Anniv of Hovsep Pushman (artist). Sheet 75×65 mm.

MS515	**128** 650d. multicoloured	3·50	3·50

129 Technical Drawings, Tevossian and Factory

2002. Birth Centenary of Hovhannes Tevossian (metallurgical engineer).

516	**129**	350d. multicoloured	1·90	1·90

130 Birds, Playing Cards, Ribbons and Magician's Hat

2002. Europa. Circus. Multicoloured.

517	70d. Type **130**	40	40
518	500d. Clown juggling	2·10	2·10

131 Aivazian

2002. Birth Centenary of Artemy Aivazian (composer).

519	**131**	600d. multicoloured	3·25	3·25

132 Ani Cathedral

2002. Sheet 90×60 mm.

MS520	**132** 550d. multicoloured	2·75	2·75

133 Kaputjugh Mountain

2002. International Year of Mountains.

521	**133**	350d. multicoloured	2·10	2·10

134 Armenian Lizard (*Lacerta armeniaca*)

2002. Reptiles. Multicoloured.

522	170d. Type **134**	1·10	1·10
523	220d. Radde's viper (*Vipera raddei*)	1·40	1·40

135 Woman and Dove

2002. United Nations Development Fund for Women.

524	**135**	220d. multicoloured	1·60	1·60

136 Steam Locomotive

2002. Centenary of Alexandrapol–Yerevan Railway.

525	**136**	350d. multicoloured	2·50	2·50

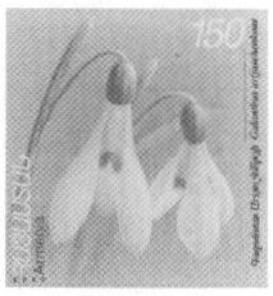

137 *Galanthus artjuschenkoae*

2002. Flowers. Multicoloured.

526	150d. Type **137**	1·00	1·00
527	200d. *Merendera mirzoevae*	1·50	1·50

138 Research Station, Yerevan Physics Institute

2002. Space Research. Multicoloured.

528	120d. Type **138**	85	85
529	220d. Orion 1 and Orion 2 space observatories	1·50	1·50

139 *Handle with Care* (Artak Baghdassaryan)

2003. Europa. Poster Art. Multicoloured.

530	170d. Type **139**	1·30	1·30
531	250d. *Armenia our Home* (Kearen Kojoyan)	1·70	1·70

140 Aram Khachatourian

2003. Birth Centenary of Aram Khachatourian (composer).

532	**140**	350d. multicoloured	1·90	1·90

141 Armenian Gull (*Larus Armenicus*)

2003. World Environment Day. Rehabilitation of Lake Gilli.

533	**141**	220d. multicoloured	1·30	1·30

142 Viaduct and Emblem

2003. Tenth Anniv of TRACEA (transport corridor Europe–Caucasus–Asia) Programme. Sheet 74×55 mm.

MS534 **142** 480d. multicoloured 2·75 2·75

143 Horse-drawn Cart, Map of Route and First Postal Seal

2003. 175th Anniv of First Armenian Postal Dispatch.

535 **143** 70d. multicoloured 40 40

144 Siamanto and Script

2003. 125th Birth Anniv of Siamanto (Atom Yarchanyan) (writer).

536 **144** 350d. multicoloured 1·90 1·90

145 Coins and Currency Notes

2003. Tenth Anniv of Armenian Currency.

537 **145** 170d. multicoloured 95 95

146 Vahan Tekeyan

2003. 125th Birth Anniv of Vahan Tekeyan (writer).

538 **146** 200d. multicoloured 1·10 1·10

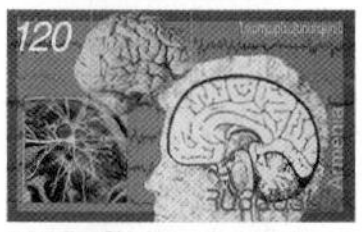

147 Profile showing Brain

2003. Neurophysiology.

539 **147** 120d. multicoloured 65 65

148 Sports and Culture Complex, Yerevan

2003. Third Armenian Games. Sheet 58×40 mm.

MS540 **148** 350d. multicoloured 2·00 2·00

149 *The Baptism* (6–7th century), Gospel of Ejmiatsin

2003. Armenian Miniatures (1st series). Sheet 65×74 mm.

MS541 **149** 550d. multicoloured 3·25 3·25

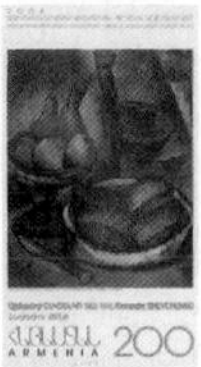

150 *Still Life* (Alexander Shevchenko)

2004. Art. Multicoloured.

542 200d. Type **150** 1·20 1·20

543 220d. *In a Restaurant* (Konstantin Roudakon) 1·30 1·30

151 "100" and Football

2004. Centenary of FIFA (Federation Internationale de Football Association).

544 **151** 350d. multicoloured 1·70 1·70

152 White Voskehat Grapes

2004. Grapes. Multicoloured.

545 170d. Type **152** 1·00 1·00

546 220d. Black Areni grapes 1·20 1·20

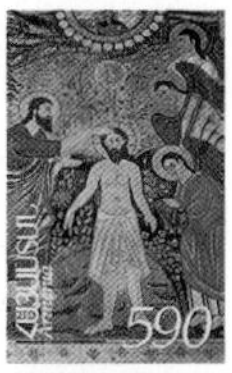

153 17th-century Frescos, Vifliem Church

2004. 400th Anniv of New Julfa (Armenian settlement in Iran). Sheet 55×56 mm.

MS547 **153** 590d. multicoloured 3·00 3·00

154 *The Cat and the Dog*, 1937

2004. Animated Films. Multicoloured.

548 70d. Type **154** 40 40

549 120d. *Foxbook*, 1975 70 70

155 Aramayis Yerznkian

2004. 125th Birth Anniv of Aramayis Yerznkian (politician).

550 **155** 220d. multicoloured 1·10 1·10

156 Karabakh Horse

2005

551 **156** 350d. multicoloured 1·80 1·80

157 Hand and Olympic Rings

2005. Olympic Games, Athens (2004). Multicoloured.

552 70d. Type **157** 40 40

553 170d. Hand as runner 1·00 1·00

554 350d. Hand as pistol 2·10 2·10

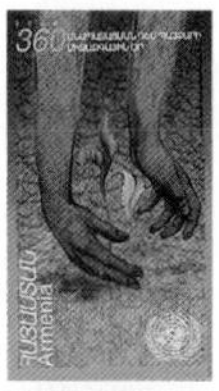

158 Hands enclosing Seedling

2005. International Day against Desertification.

555 **158** 360d. multicoloured 1·90 1·90

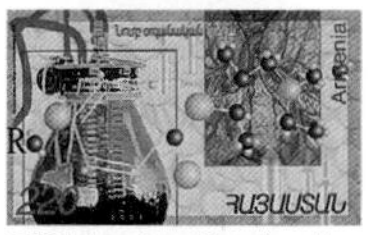

159 Laboratory Vessel and Chemical Formula

2005. Chemistry.

556 **159** 220d. multicoloured 1·10 1·10

160 Michael Nalbandian and Script

2005. 175th Birth Anniv of Michael Nalbandian (writer).

557 **160** 220d. multicoloured 1·10 1·10

161 Mouratsan and Forest

2005. 150th Birth Anniv of Grigor Ter-Hovhanissian (Mouratsan) (writer).

558 **161** 350d. multicoloured 1·80 1·80

162 Tigran petrossian

2005. 75th Birth Anniv of Tigran Petrossian (chess player).

559 **162** 220d. multicoloured 1·10 1·10

163 Man sitting on Flower

2005. Europa. Holidays (2004). Multicoloured.

560 70d. Type **163** 25 25

561 350d. Footprint in sand 1·70 1·70

164 Goshavank Church

2005. Goshavank Monastery (12th–13th century). Sheet 84×84 mm.

MS562 **164** 480d. multicoloured 2·40 2·40

165 Armen Tigranian, Musical Scores and Landscape

2005. 125th Birth Anniv of Armen Tigranian (composer and musician).

563 **165** 220d. multicoloured 1·10 1·10

166 Xachkar (cross)

2005. 90th Anniv of Armenian Genocide.

564 **166** 350d. multicoloured 1·90 1·90

167 Mother Armenia (statue)

2005. 60th Anniv of End of World War II.

565 **167** 350d. multicoloured 1·90 1·90

168 Anushavan Arzumanian

2005. Birth Centenary of Anushavan Arzumanian (economist).

566 **168** 220d. multicoloured 1·10 1·10

169 *Self Portrait*

2005. 125th Birth Anniv of Martiros Sarian (artist). Multicoloured.

567 170d. Type **169** 80 80

568 200d. *Mount Aragats* 90 90

170 Lavash Bread

2005. Europa. Gastronomy. Multicoloured.

569 70d. Type **170** 25 25

570 350d. Harisa porridge 1·90 1·90

171 Fragment of 16th-century Khachkar

2005. Mother's Day.

571 **171** 350d. multicoloured 1·90 1·90

172 Alphabet and Mesrob Mashots (inventor) (statue)

2005. 1600th Anniv of Armenian Alphabet.

572	**172**	70d. multicoloured	25	25

173 Vardan Ajemian (actor and theatre director)

2005. Anniversaries. Multicoloured.

573	70d. Type **173** (birth centenary)	25	25
574	170d. Anania Shirakatsi (scientist) (1400th birth anniv)	80	80

174 Carpet (Artzakh) (19th-century)

2005. Carpets. Multicoloured.

575	60d. Type **174**	15	15
576	350d. Carpet (Zangezour) (1904)	1·90	1·90
MS577	92×65 mm. 480d. Carpet (Artzakh) (18th-century) (28×42 mm)	2·50	2·50

175 Mher Mkrtchian (actor)

2005. Anniversaries. Multicoloured.

578	120d. Type **175** (75th birth anniv)	45	45
579	350d. Artem Mikoyan (aircraft designer) (birth centenary)	1·90	1·90

176 Armenian and Russian Flags and Arms

2006. Year of Armenia in Russia.

580	**176**	350d. multicoloured	1·90	1·90

A stamp of the same design was issued by Russia.

177 Alexandre Melik-Pashaev (conductor)

2006. Birth Centenaries. Multicoloured.

581	70d. Type **177**	25	25
582	170d. Vakhtang Ananian (writer)	80	80

178 Emblem

2006. Winter Olympic Games, Turin. Multicoloured.

583	120d. Type **178**	45	45
584	170d. Map of Italy on skis	80	80

179 Cathedral Facade

2006. St. Mary's Cathedral of Russian Orthodox.

585	**179**	170d. multicoloured	80	80

180 Raphael Patakanian

2006. 175th Birth Anniv of Raphael Patkanian (writer).

586	**180**	220d. multicoloured	1·10	1·10

181 "P" and Emblem

2006. 50th Anniv of Europa Stamps. Multicoloured.

587	70d. Type **181**	20	20
588	70d. "T" and emblem	20	20
589	70d. "C" and emblem	20	20
590	70d. "E" and emblem	20	20

2006. Traditional Costumes (4th series). As T **85**.

591	170d. Sassoun family	60	60
592	200d. Shatakhk couple	65	65

182 *Porphyrophora hamelii*

2006. Insects. Multicoloured.

593	170d. Type **182**	60	60
594	220d. *Procerus fallettianus*	70	70

183 Spiridon Melikian

2006. 125th (2005) Birth Anniv of Spiridon Melikian (composer).

595	**183**	350d. multicoloured	90	90

184 *Adoration of the Magi* (1391), Gospel of Vostan

2006. Armenian Miniatures (2nd series). Sheet 75×65 mm.

MS596	**184** 480d. multicoloured	1·40	1·40

185 "15"

2006. 15th Anniv of Republic of Armenia. Sheet 70×70 mm.

MS597	**185** 480d. multicoloured	1·80	1·80

186 Dove

2006. Peace.

598	**186**	50d. multicoloured	1·00	1·00

187 *To Jerusalem* (1211), Gospel of Haghpat

2006. Armenian Miniatures (3rd series). Sheet 65×76 mm.

MS599	**187** 220d. multicoloured	2·75	2·75

188 Watch Mechanism

2006. Europa. Integration. Multicoloured.

600	200d. Type **188**	2·75	2·75
601	350d. Golden key and rusty keys	4·50	4·50

189 Ball, Trophy, Flags and Emblem

2006. World Cup Football Championship, Germany.

602	**189**	350d. multicoloured	4·50	4·50

190 Boghos Nubar

2006. Centenary of General Benevolent Union. Sheet 110×77 mm containing T **190** and similar vert designs. Multicoloured.

MS603	120d.×3, Type **190** (benefactor); Minutes of first meeting; Alex Manoogian (benefactor)	4·50	4·50

191 Sergey Merkurov and "Naked" (sculpture)

2006. 125th Birth Anniv of Sergey Merkurov (artist and sculptor).

604	**191**	230d. multicoloured	2·75	2·75

192 *Testudo horsfieldii*

2007. Endangered Species. *Testudo horsfieldii*. Multicoloured.

605	70d. Type **192**	95	95
606	70d. Facing left	95	95
607	70d. Facing right	95	95
608	70d. Amongst leaves	95	95

193 Trophy

2007. Armenia—37th World Chess Olympiad Champions. Multicoloured.

609	170d. Type **193**	2·20	2·20
610	220d. Medal	2·75	2·75
611	280d. Chess pieces	2·75	2·75
612	350d. Queen	4·50	4·50

194 Decorated Tree

2007. Christmas and New Year.

613	**194**	70d. multicoloured	95	95

195 Clown and Circus Building

2007. 50th Anniv of National Circus Collective.

614	**195**	70d. multicoloured	95	95

196 Stepan Shahumian Monument

2007. Armenian Settlements. Stepanavan. Multicoloured.

615	110d. Type **196**	1·40	1·40
616	120d. Memorial fountain	1·50	1·50
617	170d. Rock of Lori Bridge	2·25	2·25
618	200d. Bear Rock	2·50	2·50

197 Sculpture

2007. 50th Anniv of Yerevan Mathematical Machines Scientific Research Institute.

619	**197**	120d. multicoloured	1·50	1·50

2007. Traditional Costumes (5th series). As T **85**.

620	170d. Taron couple	2·25	2·25
621	230d. Shirak couple	2·75	2·75

198 Voski

2007. Apricot (*Armeniaca vulgaris*). Multicoloured.

622	230d. Type **198**	2·25	2·25
623	230d. Yerevani	2·25	2·25
624	230d. Ghevondi	2·25	2·25
625	230d. Karmir Nakhijevanik	2·25	2·25
626	230d. Deghin Nakhijevanik	2·25	2·25
627	230d. Khosroveni karmir	2·25	2·25
628	230d. Deghnanush vaghahas	2·25	2·25
629	230d. Vaghahas vardaguyn	2·25	2·25
630	230d. Karmreni	2·25	2·25
631	230d. Sateni deghin	2·25	2·25

199 Earrings (8th–7th century BC)

2007. Jewellery. Multicoloured.

632	280d. Type **199**	2·75	2·75
633	280d. Pendant (3rd century BC)	2·75	2·75
634	280d. Earrings with pendants (10th–11th century)	2·75	2·75
635	280d. Gospel with encrusted cover (1484)	2·75	2·75
636	280d. Chalice (1623)	2·75	2·75
637	280d. Mitre (1765)	2·75	2·75
638	280d. Dove-shaped vessel (1797)	2·75	2·75
639	280d. Knar-diadem (19th century)	2·75	2·75
640	280d. Bracelet (early 20th century)	2·75	2·75
641	280d. Incensory (19th century)	2·75	2·75

200 *Pallas Athena or Armoured Figure*

2007. 400th Birth Anniv (2006) of Rembrandt Harmenszoon van Rijn (artist). Multicoloured.

642	70d. Type **200**	95	95
643	350d. *Portrait of an Old Man*	4·50	4·50
MS644	128×89 mm. 70d. *Self Portrait with Saskia*; 170d. *Juno*; 280d. *Woman with Fan*; 350d. *Portrait of Jan Six*	10·00	10·00

201 Mozart as a Young Man (detail)

2007. 250th Birth Anniv (2006) of Wolfgang Amadeus Mozart (composer and musician). Multicoloured.

645	70d. Type **201**	95	95
646	350d. Mozart facing left (vert)	4·50	4·50
MS647	128×89 mm. 70d. Mozart and score (42×28 mm); 170d. Mozart and script (42×28 mm); 280d. Mozart and stringed instrument (42×28 mm); 350d. Mozart as young man (28×42 mm)	10·00	10·00

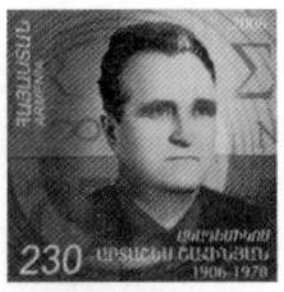

202 Artashes Shahinian

2007. Birth Centenary of Artashes Shahinian (scientist).

648	**202**	230d. multicoloured	1·90	1·90

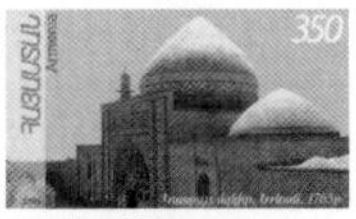

203 Blue Mosque

2007

649	**203**	350d. multicoloured	4·50	4·50

204 'L'Ange au Sourire' (the angel with a smile), Rheims Cathedral

2007. Year of Armenia in France. Multicoloured.

650	70d. Type **204**	1·00	1·00
651	350d. The Nativity (15th-century miniature)	4·50	4·50

205 Apricot

2007

652	**205**	350d. multicoloured	4·25	4·25

206 Tirgran the Great

2007

653	**206**	50d. multicoloured	80	80
654	**206**	60d. multicoloured	90	90
655	**206**	70d. multicoloured	1·00	1·00
656	**206**	120d. multicoloured	1·80	1·80

207 Hands

2007. Centenary of Scouting.

657	**207**	350d. multicoloured	4·50	4·50

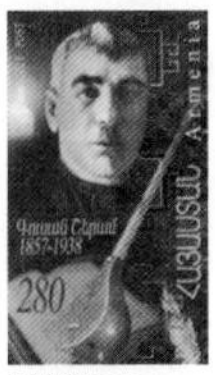

208 Gusan Sheram

2007. 150th Birth Anniv of Talyan Grigor Karapet (Gusan Sheram) (composer and singer).

658	**208**	280d. multicoloured	3·75	3·75

209 Margar Sedrakyan

2007. Birth Centenary of Margar Sedrakyan (Cognac maker).

659	**209**	170d. multicoloured	2·30	2·30

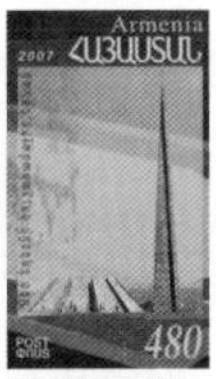

210 Memorial

2007. 40th Anniv of Genocide Museum. Sheet 74×65 mm.

MS660	480d. multicoloured	6·00	6·00

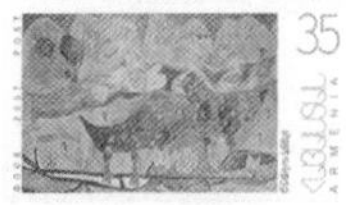

211 *Sparrows* (Yeva Karapetyan)

2007. Children's Drawings.

661	**211**	35d. multicoloured	1·00	1·00

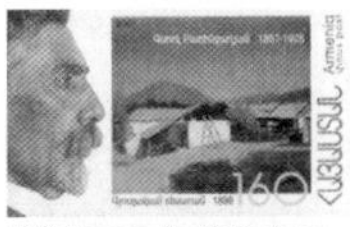

212 Gevorg Bashinjaghyan and *Gyughakan Tesaran*

2007. 150th Birth Anniv of Gevorg Bashinjaghyan (artist). Multicoloured.

662	160d. Type **212**	2·30	2·30
663	220d. *Aragats*	3·00	3·00

213 Jean Garzou in his Studio

2007. Birth Centenary of Garnik Zulumyan (Jean Garzou) (artist). Multicoloured.

664	180d. Type **213**	2·50	2·50
665	220d. *Portrait of Seda* (vert)	2·75	2·75

214 Hands holding Trophy

2007. Pan Armenian Games, Yerevan. Sheet 40×58 mm.

MS666	360d. multicoloured	4·75	4·75

215 Norayr Sisakyan

2007. Birth Centenary of Norayr Sisakyan (biochemist).

667	**215**	120d. multicoloured	1·60	1·60

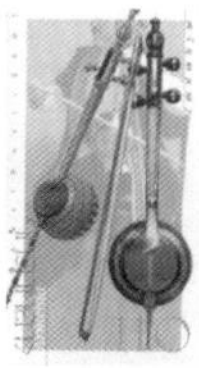

216 Kamancha

2007. Traditional Instruments.

668	**216**	110d. multicoloured	1·60	1·60

217 *Pelecanus crispus* (Dalmatian pelican)

2007. Endangered Species. Multicoloured.

669	120d. Type **217**	1·50	1·50
670	200d. *Aegypius monachus* (Eurasian black vulture)	2·75	2·75

218 Matenadaran

2007. Matenadaran Manuscript and Book Depository.

671	**218**	200d. multicoloured	2·50	2·50

219 Bagrat Nalbandyan

2007. Bagrat Nalbandyan (communications commissar) Commemoration.

672	**219**	230d. multicoloured	3·00	3·00

220 Nemrut Baghdasaryan

2007. Birth Centenary of Nemrut Baghdasaryan (photojournalist).

673	**220**	200d. multicoloured	2·50	2·50

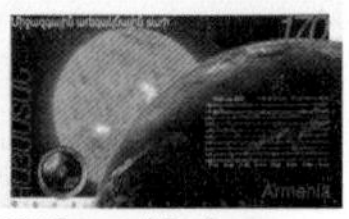

221 Sun and Earth

2007. International Year of Solar Physics. 50th Anniv of Geophysics.

674	**221**	170d. multicoloured	2·30	2·30

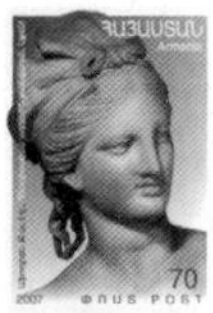

222 *Aphrodite* (Greek)

2007. Statues. Multicoloured.

675	70d. Type **222**	1·00	1·00
676	350d. *Anahit* (Armenian)	4·50	4·50

Stamps of the same design were issued by Greece.

223 Family (Eduard Ghazaryan)

2008. International Children's Day.

677	**223**	70d. multicoloured	1·50	1·50

No. 677 includes the *se-tenant* premium-carrying tab shown in Type **223**, the premium for the benefit of children's charities.

224 Chinese Dragon

2008. Olympic Games, Beijing.

678	**224**	350d. multicoloured	5·00	5·00

225 Carving

2008. Woodcraft.

679	**225**	120d. multicoloured	7·75	7·75

226 Envelopes and Map

2008. Europa. The Letter.

680	**226**	350d. multicoloured	5·00	5·00

227 Alexander Shirvanzade

2008. 150th Birth Anniv of Alexander Shirvanzade (writer).

681	**227**	280d. multicoloured	4·00	4·00

2008. Tirgran the Great.

682	**206**	10d. multicoloured	30	30
683	**206**	20d. multicoloured	55	55
684	**206**	50d. multicoloured	1·30	1·30
685	**206**	1100d. multicoloured	13·75	13·75

See also Nos. 653/6.

228 *Anemone fasciculata*

2008. Flowers. Multicoloured.

686		120d. Type **228**	2·75	2·75
687		280d. *Scabiosa caucasica*	4·00	4·00

229 Building Facade

2008. 75th Anniv of Polytechnic Institute.

688	**229**	220d. multicoloured	3·75	3·75

230 William Saroyan

2008. Birth Centenary of William Saroyan (dramatist and writer).

689	**230**	350d. multicoloured	5·75	5·75

231 Viktor Ambartsumyan

2008. Birth Centenary of Viktor Amazaspovich Ambartsumyan (scientist).

690	**231**	120d. multicoloured	2·00	2·00

232 Peyo Yavorov (Bulgarian poet and revolutionary)

2008. Nationalist Liberation Movements of Bulgaria and Armenia. Multicoloured.

691		70d. Type **232**	1·00	1·00
692		350d. Andranik Ozanyan (Armenian general in Balkan Wars of Independence)	4·75	4·75

2009. Tirgran the Great. Size 19×23 mm.

693	**206**	10d. multicoloured (dull yellow-green)	15	15
694	**206**	25d. multicoloured (orange-yellow)	25	25
695	**206**	50d. multicoloured (bright magenta)	55	55
696	**206**	70d. multicoloured (olive-sepia)	75	75
697	**206**	120d. multicoloured (reddish violet)	1·30	1·30
698	**206**	220d. multicoloured (deep blue)	2·75	2·75
699	**206**	280d. multicoloured (deep dull violet blue)	3·75	3·75
700	**206**	350d. multicoloured (bright crimson)	4·25	2·25

See also Nos. 653/6 and 682/5.

233 Dancer holding Sword

2009. Dances. Multicoloured.

701		70d. Type **233**	1·20	1·20
702		350d. Couple	3·75	3·75

234 Ruins

2009. Tushpa-Van–Ancient Capital of Armenia.

703	**234**	220d. multicoloured	2·50	2·50

235 Observatory

2009. Europa. Astronomy.

704	**235**	350d. multicoloured	4·75	4·75

236 Armenian Chess Team

2009. Armenia Gold Medalists at Chess Olympiad 2008, Dresden, Germany. Multicoloured.

705		70d. Type **236**	2·50	2·50
706		280d. Chess pieces	11·00	11·00

237 Stylized Buildings

2009. 50th Anniv of European Court of Human Rights.

707	**237**	70d. multicoloured	95	95

238 '60' and Emblem

2009. 60th Anniv of Council of Europe

708	**238**	280d. multicoloured	3·50	3·50

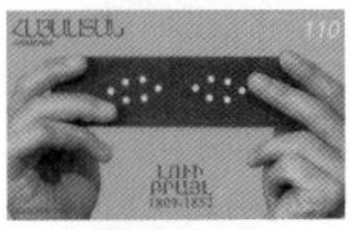

239 Braille Dots as Eyes

2009. Birth Bicentenary of Louis Braille (inventor of Braille writing for the blind).

709	**239**	110d. multicoloured	1·40	1·40

240 Daniel Varuzhan

2009. 125th Birth Anniv of Daniel Varuzhan (writer).

710	**240**	230d. multicoloured	2·75	2·75

241 Monument

2009. 50th Anniv of Monument to Davit of Sasun (epic hero). Sheet 69×90 mm.

MS711	**241**	multicoloured	4·50	4·50

242 Hrant Shahinyan, Helsinki–1952

2009. Olympic Champions. Sheet 119×59 mm containing T **242** and square designs. Multicoloured.

MS712	70d. Type **242**; 120d. Igor Novikov, Melbourne–1956, Tokyo–1964;160d. Albert Azaryan, Melbourne–1956, Rome–1960	4·50	4·50

243 Khachatur Abovyan

2009. Birth Bicentenary of Khachatur Abovyan (educator, poet and advocate of modernization).

713	**243**	170d. multicoloured	2·00	2·00

244 *Panna Paskevich* (Georgi Yakulov)

2009. Art from National Gallery. Multicoloured.

714		200d. Type **244**	2·50	2·50
715		200d. *Autumn. A Corner in Yerevan* (Sedrak Arakelyan)	2·50	2·50

245 *Lutra lutra meridionalis* (European otter)

2009. Fauna. Multicoloured.

716		120d. Type **245**	2·10	2·10
717		160d. *Ursus arctos syriacus* (Syrian brown bear)	2·75	2·75

246 Zvartnots Church, 642 AD,

2009. Churches in Vagharshapat. Sheet 145×69 mm containing T **246** and similar vert designs. Multicoloured.

MS718	70d.×4, Type **246**; St. Hripsime church, 618 AD; Mother See of Holy Etchmiadzin, 301–303 AD; St. Gayane church, 630 AD	3·50	3·50

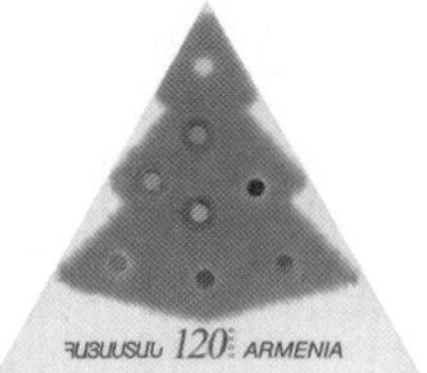

247 Decorated Tree

2009. New Year.

719	**247**	120d. multicoloured	1·60	1·60

The tree shown on No. 719 was printed with a flocked surface and simulated baubles.

248 Virgin and Child

2009. Christmas. Multicoloured.

720	280d. Type **248**	3·50	3·50
MS721	80×105 mm. Size 60×30 mm. 650d. As Type **248** but design enlarged	8·00	8·00

2010. Tirgran the Great

(a) Ordinary gum

722	**206**	10d. magenta	40	40
723		25d. ultramarine	60	60
724		50d. yellow-ochre	75	75
725		70d. bright vermilion	1·00	1·00
726		100d. purple-brown	1·50	1·50
727		120d. claret	1·80	1·80
728		200d. pale greenish grey	2·50	2·50
729		220d. bright reddish violet	2·75	2·75
730		280d. scarlet	3·75	3·75
731		650d. apple green	4·50	4·50

(b) Self-adhesive

732	**206**	10d. magenta	40	40
733		25d. ultramarine	60	60
734		50d. yellow-ochre	75	75
735		70d. bright vermilion	1·00	1·00
736		100d. purple-brown	1·50	1·50
737		120d. claret	1·80	1·80
738		200d. pale greenish grey	2·50	2·50
739		220d. bright reddish violet	2·75	2·75
740		280d. scarlet	3·75	3·75
741		650d. apple green	4·50	4·50

249 Henrik Kasparyan and Chessboard

2010. Birth Centenary of Henrik Kasparyan

742	**249**	870d. multicoloured	9·50	9·50

250 Victory Monument

2010. 65th Anniv of End of World War II

743	**250**	350d. multicoloured	4·75	4·75

251 Memorial Complex

2010. Russian Officer Cemetery. Multicoloured.

744	350d. Type **251**	5·00	5·00
MS745	102×77 mm. 650d. As Type **251**	5·00	8·00

252 Mount Ararat

2010. Independence Day

746	350d. Type **252**	4·50	4·50
747	650d. National flag (30×30 mm)	8·50	8·50

253 Armenian Pavillion

2010. Expo 2010, Shanghai. Multicoloured.

748	280d. Type **253**	3·75	3·75
749	280d. View of Yerevan and Mount Ararat (50×30 mm)	3·75	3·75

254 Medieval Women

2010. Europa

750	**254**	350d. multicoloured	4·50	4·50

255 Vladimir Yengibaryan (Melbourne, 1956)

2010. Olympic Champions. Multicoloured.

MS751	160d.×3, Type **255**; Faina Melnik (Munich, 1972); Yuri Vardanyan (Moscow, 1980)	6·50	6·50

256 Cross Country Skier

2010. Winter Olympic Games, Vancouver. Multicoloured.
MS752 350d. Type **256**; 500d. Alpine houses and cross country skier; 600d. Alpine skier 19·00 19·00

257 Games Emblem and Pictograms

2010. Olympic Youth Games, Singapore
753 **257** 870d. multicoloured 11·50 11·50

258 Ball and Globe

2010. Football World Cup Championships, South Africa
754 **258** 1100d. multicoloured 14·50 14·50

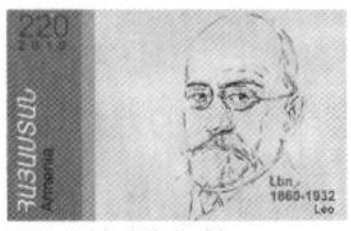
259 Arakel Babakhanyan

2010. 150th Birth Anniv of Araqel Babakhanyan (Leo) (historian and publicist)
755 **259** 220d. multicoloured 2·75 2·75

260 Raffi

2010. 175th Birth Anniv of Hakob Melik- Hakobyan (Raffi) (writer and publicist)
756 **260** 220d. multicoloured 2·75 2·75

261 Tigran the Great

2011. Tigran the Great. Background colour given in brackets.

757	**261**	10d. multicoloured (blue)	40	40
758	**261**	35d. multicoloured (deep brown)	60	60
759	**261**	50d. multicoloured (apple green)	75	75
760	**261**	70d. multicoloured pale (turquoise)	1·00	1·00
761	**261**	120d. multicoloured (orange-red)	1·80	1·80
762	**261**	160d. multicoloured (deep claret)	2·20	2·20
763	**261**	220d. multicoloured (deep rose-red)	3·75	3·75
764	**261**	280d. multicoloured (ultramarine)	3·75	3·75
765	**261**	350d. multicoloured (ochre)	4·00	4·00
766	**261**	1100d. multicoloured (brown)	14·00	14·00

262 Avet Avetisyan as Zimzimow and Davit Malyan as Kakuli

2011. First Armenian Sound Film - *Pepo* (1935). Each black and scarlet-vermilion.
MS767 170d. Type **262**; 200d. Hrachya Nercissyan as Pepo; 500d. Tatiana Makhmuryan as Kekel 11·00 11·00

263 Leonid Yengibarov

2011. Leonid Yengibarov (actor) Commemoration
768 **263** 220d. chrome yellow and black 3·00 3·00

264 Ruben Sevak

2011. 125th Birth Anniv of Ruben Chilinkiryan (Ruben Sevak) (writer, publicist and doctor)
769 **264** 280d. multicoloured 3·75 3·75

265 Vahan Teryan

2011. 125th Birth Anniv of Vahan Ter-Grigoryan (Vahan Teryan) (writer and politician)
770 **265** 280d. multicoloured 3·75 3·75

266 *Fritillaria armena*

2011. Flora and Fruit. Multicoloured.
771 280d. Type **266** 3·75 3·75
772 280d. *Sambucus tigranii* 3·75 3·75

267 Portrait of Actress Khmara (Haroutyun Kalents)

2011. Paintings from National Gallery. Multicoloured.
773 450d. Type **267** 5·75 5·75
774 450d. *Mkrtich Khriyan* (writer, newspaper editor, political and religious leader, Armenian Patriarch of Constantinople (1869–1873), Prelate of Van (1880–1885) and Catholicos of All Armenians (1892–1907)) (Vardghes Sourenyants) 5·75 5·75

268 Angel (detail from Resurrection (manuscript, c. 1319))

2011. Easter. Sheet 80×115 mm
MS775 **268** 1100d. multicoloured 14·00 14·00

269 Andranik Iosifyan

2011. Andranik Iosifyan (constructor of meteorological satellites) Commemoration
776 **269** 200d. multicoloured 2·50 2·50

270 Yuri Gagarin

2011. 50th Anniv of First Manned Space Flight
777 **270** 350d. multicoloured 4·00 4·00

271 Hovhannes Toumanyan

2011. Personalities. Writers. Multicoloured.
778 120d. Type **271** 1·80 1·80
779 230d. Valeri Bryusov 2·75 2·75

272 Minsk

2011. Capital Cities. Multicoloured.
780 200d. Type **272** 2·40 2·40
781 200d. Museum of Art and History, Yerevan 2·40 2·40

273 Globe and Commonwealth Emblem

2011. 20th Anniv of Regional Communication Community (RCC). Sheet 108×78 mm
MS782 **273** 200d. multicoloured 2·40 2·40

274 Athletes

2011. Pan Armenian Games. Sheet 120×104 mm
MS783 **274** 380d. multicoloured 4·25 4·25

275 *Luscinia scecica* (Bluethroat)

2011. Birds. Multicoloured.
784 230d. Type **275** 2·75 2·75
785 330d. *Parus major* (Great Tit) 2·75 2·75

276 Emblem and '20'

2011. 20th Anniv of Independence. Multicoloured.
786 330d. Type **276** 4·25 4·25
787 380d. National Arms and '2011' 4·25 4·25

Pt. 4

ARUBA

An island in the Caribbean, formerly part of Netherlands Antilles. In 1986 became an autonomous country within the Kingdom of the Netherlands.

100 cents = 1 gulden.

1 Map

1986. New Constitution.

1	1	25c. yellow, blue and black	1·70	55
2	-	45c. multicoloured	2·00	1·10
3	-	55c. black, grey and red	2·50	1·50
4	-	100c. multicoloured	3·25	2·50

DESIGNS—VERT: 45c. Aruban arms; 55c. National anthem. HORIZ: 100c. Aruban flag.

2 House

1986

5	**2**	5c. black and yellow	55	10
6	-	15c. black and blue	1·20	55
7	-	20c. black and grey	90	35
8	-	25c. black and violet	1·70	55
9	-	30c. black and red	1·70	90
10	-	35c. black and bistre	1·70	90
12	-	45c. black and blue	2·00	1·20
14	-	55c. black and grey	1·70	90
15	-	60c. black and blue	1·90	1·10
16	-	65c. black and blue	1·80	1·50
18	-	75c. black and brown	2·00	1·50
20	-	85c. black and orange	2·00	1·10
21	-	90c. black and green	2·20	1·50
22	-	100c. black and brown	2·20	1·50
23	-	150c. black and green	3·75	2·20
24	-	250c. black and green	5·25	4·50

DESIGNS: 15c. Clock tower; 20c. Container crane; 25c. Lighthouse; 30c. Snake; 35c. Burrowing owl; 45c. Carib-bean vase (shell); 55c. Frog; 60c. Water-skier; 65c. Fisherman casting net; 75c. Hurdy-gurdy; 85c. Pot; 90, 250c. Different cacti; 100c. Maize; 150c. Watapana Tree.

3 People and Two Ropes

1986. "Solidarity". Multicoloured.

25	30c.+10c. Type **3**	2·00	1·10
26	35c.+15c. People and three ropes	2·00	1·10
27	60c.+25c. People and one rope	2·75	1·70

4 Dove between Scenes of Peace and War

1986. International Peace Year. Multicoloured.
28 60c. Type **4** 5·00 1·70
29 100c. Doves flying over broken barbed wire 10·00 3·25

5 Boy and Caterpillar

1986. Child Welfare. Multicoloured.

30	45c.+20c. Type **5**	2·75	1·10
31	70c.+25c. Boy and shell	3·25	1·70
32	100c.+40c. Girl and butterfly	4·00	2·50

6 Engagement Picture

1987. Golden Wedding of Princess Juliana and Prince Bernhard.

33	**6**	135c. orange, black and gold	4·50	2·50

7 Queen Beatrix and Prince Claus

1987. Royal Visit. Multicoloured.

34	55c. Type **7**	2·20	1·10
35	60c. Prince Willem-Alexander	2·20	1·10

8 Woman looking at Beach

1987. Tourism. Multicoloured.

36	60c. Type **8**	2·20	1·50
37	100c. Woman looking at desert landscape	3·25	2·00

9 Child with Book on Beach

1987. Child Welfare. Multicoloured.

38	25c.+10c. Type **9**	1·70	90
39	45c.+20c. Children drawing Christmas tree	2·20	1·10
40	70c.+30c. Child gazing at Nativity crib	3·25	1·70

10 Plantation

1988. *Aloe vera.* Multicoloured.

41	45c. Type **10**	2·00	1·10
42	60c. Stem and leaves of plant	2·20	1·50
43	100c. Harvesting aloes	2·75	1·70

11 25c. Coin

1988. Coins. Multicoloured.

44	25c. Type **11**	1·50	55
45	55c. Square 50c. coin	2·00	1·10
46	65c. 5c. and 10c. coins	2·20	1·50
47	150c. 1 gulden coin	4·00	2·50

12 Bananaquits, Country Scene and "Love"

1988. Greetings Stamps. Multicoloured.

48	70c. Type **12**	2·00	1·10
49	135c. West Indian crown conch, West Indian chank (shells), seaside scene and "Love"	2·75	2·00

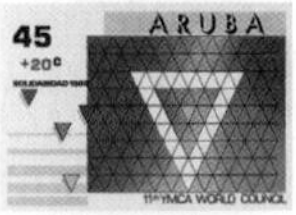

13 White Triangle on Shaded Background

1988. "Solidarity". 11th Y.M.C.A. World Council. Multicoloured.

50	45c.+20c. Type **13**	2·20	1·10
51	60c.+25c. Interlocking triangles	2·20	1·70
52	100c.+50c. Shaded triangle on white background	2·75	2·20

14 Torch

1988. Olympic Games, Seoul. Multicoloured.

53	35c. Type **14**	1·70	90
54	100c. Games and Olympic emblems	2·75	1·70

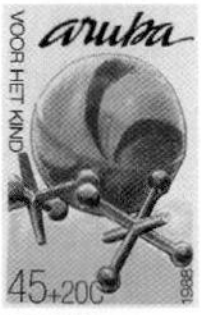

15 Jacks

1988. Child Welfare. Toys. Multicoloured.

55	45c.+20c. Type **15**	2·20	1·10
56	70c.+30c. Spinning top	2·20	1·70
57	100c.+50c. Kite	2·75	2·20

16 Children

1989. Carnival. Multicoloured.

58	45c. Type **16**	2·20	1·10
59	60c. Girl in costume	2·20	1·10
60	100c. Lights	2·75	1·70

17 Maripampun

1989. Maripampun. Multicoloured.

61	35c. Type **17**	1·70	85
62	55c. Seed pods	1·70	1·10
63	200c. Pod distributing seeds	4·50	3·25

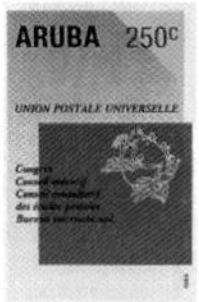

18 Emblem

1989. Universal Postal Union.

64	**18**	250c. multicoloured	6·75	4·25

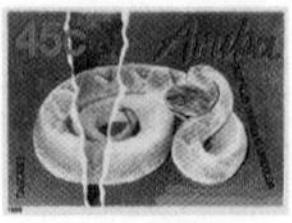
19 Snake

1989. South American Rattlesnake.

65	**19**	45c. multicoloured	1·70	90
66	-	55c. multicoloured	2·00	1·10
67	-	60c. multicoloured	2·00	1·10

DESIGNS: 55, 60c. Snake (different).

20 Spoon in Child's Hand

1989. Child Welfare. Multicoloured.

68	45c +20c. Type **20**	2·00	1·10
69	60c.+30c. Child playing football	2·20	1·20
70	100c.+50c. Child's hand in adult's hand (vert)	3·25	2·20

21 Violin, Tambour and Cuatro Players

1989. New Year. Dande Musicians. Multicoloured.

71	25c. Type **21**	1·10	55
72	70c. Guitar and cuatro players and singer with hat	1·60	1·10
73	150c. Cuatro, accordion and wiri players	3·00	2·20

22 Tractor and Natural Vegetation

1990. Environmental Protection. Multicoloured.

74	45c. Type **22**	1·50	1·10
75	55c. Face and wildlife (vert)	1·70	1·10
76	100c. Marine life	2·75	2·00

23 Giant Caribbean Anemone and Pederson's Cleaning Shrimp

1990. Marine Life. Multicoloured.

77	60c. Type **23**	1·70	1·10
78	70c. Queen angelfish and red coral	2·20	1·70
79	100c. Banded coral shrimp, fire sponge and yellow boring sponge	3·25	2·50

24 Ball

1990. World Cup Football Championship, Italy. Multicoloured.

80	35c. Type **24**	1·50	90
81	200c. Mascot	4·50	3·25

25 Emblem of Committee of Tanki Leendert Association Youth Centre

1990. "Solidarity". Multicoloured.

82	55c.+25c. Type **25**	2·20	1·80
83	100c.+50c. Emblem of Foundation for Promotion of Responsible Parenthood	4·00	3·00

26 Clay Painting Stamps

1990. Archaeology. Multicoloured.

84	45c. Type **26**	1·50	1·10
85	60c. Stone figure	1·70	1·10
86	100c. Dabajuroid-style jar	2·75	1·70

27 Sailboards and Fishes

1990. Child Welfare. Multicoloured.

87	45c.+20c. Type **27**	1·70	1·10
88	60c.+30c. Parakeets and coconut trees	2·20	1·70
89	100c.+50c. Kites and lizard	3·25	2·75

28 Mountain and Shoreline

1991. Landscapes. Multicoloured.

90	55c. Type **28**	1·40	1·10
91	65c. Cacti and Haystack mountain	1·70	1·50
92	100c. House, mountain and ocean, Jaburibari	2·50	2·20

29 Woman holding Herbs ("Carer")

1991. Women and Work. Multicoloured.

93	35c. Type **29**	1·10	55
94	70c. Women and kitchen ("Housewife")	1·70	1·50
95	100c. Women and telephone ("Woman in the World")	2·20	2·00

30 *Ocimum sanctum*

1991. Medicinal Plants. Multicoloured.

96	65c. Type **30**	1·70	1·10
97	75c. *Jatropha gossypifolia*	2·00	1·50
98	95c. *Croton flavens*	2·20	1·70

31 Fishing Net, Float and Needle

1991. Traditional Crafts.

99	**31**	35c. black, ultram & blue	1·10	90
100	-	250c. black, lilac & purple	5·00	4·25

DESIGNS: 250c. Hat, straw and hat-block.

32 Child's Hand taking Book from Shelf

1991. Child Welfare. Multicoloured.

101	45c.+25c. Type **32**	1·70	1·50
102	60c.+35c. Child's finger pointing to letter "B"	2·20	1·70
103	100c.+50c. Child reading	3·25	2·50

33 Toucan saying "Welcome"

1991. Tourism. Multicoloured.

104	35c. Type **33**	1·10	1·10
105	70c. Aruban youth welcoming tourist	1·70	1·10
106	100c. Windmill and Bubali swamp	2·75	2·20

34 Government Decree of 1892 establishing first Aruban Post Office

1992. Centenary of Postal Service (1st issue). Multicoloured.

107	60c. Type **34**	1·40	1·10
108	75c. Lt.-Governor's building (mail service office, 1892–1908) (horiz)	1·70	1·10
109	80c. Present Oranjestad P.O. (horiz)	2·20	1·70

See also Nos. 117/19.

35 Equality of Sexes

1992. Equality. Multicoloured.

110	100c. Type **35**	2·20	1·70
111	100c. People of different races (equality of nations)	2·20	1·70

36 Aruban Flag, Guide Emblem and Girl Guides

1992. "Solidarity". Multicoloured.

112	55c.+30c. Type **36**	2·20	1·70
113	100c.+50c. Open hand with Cancer Fund emblem	3·25	2·50

37 Columbus, Map and Clouds

1992. 500th Anniv of Discovery of America by Columbus. Multicoloured.

114	30c. Type **37**	1·70	55
115	40c. Caravel (from navigation chart, 1525)	1·70	90
116	50c. Indians, queen conch shell and 1540 map	1·70	1·10

38 *I Love Post* (Jelissa Boekhoudt)

1992. Child Welfare. Centenary of Postal Service (2nd issue). Children's Drawings. Multicoloured.

117	50c.+30c. Type **38**	2·00	1·50
118	70c.+35c. Airplane dropping letters (Marianne Fingal)	2·20	1·70
119	100c.+50c. Pigeon carrying letter in beak (Minorenti Jacobs) (vert)	3·25	2·50

39 Seroe Colorado Bridge

1992. Natural Bridges. Multicoloured.

120	70c. Type **39**	1·60	1·10
121	80c. Natural Bridge	2·00	1·70

41 Rocks at Ayo

1993. Rock Formations. Multicoloured.

123	50c. Type **41**	1·10	1·10
124	60c. Casibari	1·50	1·10
125	100c. Ayo (different)	2·20	2·00

42 Traditional Instruments

1993. Cock's Burial (part of St. John's Feast celebrations). Multicoloured.

126	40c. Type **42**	1·10	1·10
127	70c. *Cock's Burial* (painting, Leo Kuiperi)	1·50	1·10
128	80c. Verses of song, yellow flag, and calabashes	1·70	1·70

43 Sailfish dinghy

1993. Sports. Multicoloured.

129	50c. Type **43**	1·10	1·10
130	65c. Land sailing	1·50	1·10
131	75c. Sailboard	1·70	1·50

44 Young Iguana

1993. The Iguana. Multicoloured.

132	35c. Type **44**	1·50	90
133	60c. Young adult	1·70	1·50
134	100c. Adult (vert)	2·20	2·20

45 Aruban House, Landscape and Cacti

1993. Child Welfare. Multicoloured.

135	50c.+30c. Type **45**	1·60	1·50
136	75c.+40c. Face, bridge and sea (vert)	2·20	2·20
137	100c.+50c. Bridge, buildings and landscape	3·00	2·75

46 Owls

1994. The Burrowing Owl. Multicoloured.

138	5c. Type **46**	1·80	40
139	10c. Pair with young	1·80	90
140	35c. Owl with locust in claw (vert)	2·10	1·10
141	40c. Owl (vert)	2·10	1·70

47 Athlete

1994. Centenary of Int Olympic Committee. Multicoloured.

142	50c. Type **47**	1·30	1·10
143	90c. Baron Pierre de Coubertin (founder)	2·00	1·70

48 Family in House

1994. "Solidarity". Int Year of The Family. Multicoloured.

144	50c.+35c. Type **48**	1·70	1·60
145	100c.+50c. Family outside house	3·00	3·00

49 Flags of U.S.A. and Aruba, Ball and Players

1994. World Cup Football Championship, U.S.A. Multicoloured.

146	65c. Type **49**	1·70	1·50
147	150c. Mascot	3·25	2·75

50 West Indian Cherry

1994. Wild Fruits. Multicoloured.

148	40c. Type **50**	1·10	1·10
149	70c. Geiger tree	1·70	1·10
150	85c. *Pithecellobium unguis-cati*	2·00	1·70
151	150c. Sea grape	3·75	2·75

51 Children with Umbrella sitting on Anchor (shelter and security)

1994. Child Welfare. Influence of the Family. Multicoloured.

152	50c.+30c. Type **51**	2·00	1·70
153	80c.+35c. Children in smiling sun (warmth of nurturing home)	2·50	2·20
154	100c.+50c. Child flying on owl (wisdom guiding the child)	2·75	2·75

52 Government Building, 1888

1995. Historic Buildings. Multicoloured.

155	35c. Type **52**	90	75
156	60c. Ecury Residence, 1929 (vert)	1·50	1·10
157	100c. Protestant Church, 1846 (vert)	2·20	2·00

53 Dove, Emblem and Flags

1995. 50th Anniv of U.N.O. Multicoloured.

158	30c. Type **53**	1·50	90
159	200c. Emblem, flags, globe and doves	4·00	3·75

54 Casanova II and Rosettes

1995. Interpaso Horses. Multicoloured.

160	25c. Type **54**	90	50
161	75c. Horse performing Paso Fino	1·70	1·50
162	80c. Horse performing Figure 8 (vert)	1·70	1·70
163	90c. Girl on horseback (vert)	2·00	1·70

55 Cowpea

1995. Vegetables. Multicoloured.

164	25c. Type **55**	85	50
165	50c. Apple cucumber	1·40	1·10
166	70c. Okra	1·60	1·40
167	85c. Pumpkin	1·80	1·70

56 Hawksbill Turtle

1995. Turtles. Multicoloured.

168	15c. Type **56**	1·70	40
169	50c. Green turtle	2·10	90
170	95c. Loggerhead turtle	2·30	1·70
171	100c. Leatherback turtle	2·75	1·70

57 Children holding Balloons outside House (Christina Trejo)

1995. Child Welfare. Children's Drawings. Multicoloured.

172	50c.+25c. Type **57**	1·70	1·40
173	70c.+35c. Children at seaside (Julysses Tromp)	2·20	2·00
174	100c.+50c. Children and adults gardening (Ronald Tromp)	3·25	2·75

58 Henry Eman

1996. Tenth Anniv of Internal Autonomy. Politicians. Multicoloured.

175	100c. Type **58**	2·00	1·70
176	100c. Juancho Irausquin	2·00	1·70
177	100c. Shon Eman	2·00	1·70
178	100c. Betico Croes	2·00	1·70

59 Woman

1996. America. Traditional Costumes. Multicoloured.

179	65c. Type **59**	2·20	1·10
180	70c. Man	2·20	1·10
181	100c. Couple dancing (horiz)	2·75	1·70

60 Running

1996. Olympic Games, Atlanta. Multicoloured.

182	85c. Type **60**	2·20	1·50
183	130c. Cycling	2·75	2·50

61 Mathematical Instruments, "G" and Rising Sun

1996. "Solidarity". 75th Anniv of Freemasons' Lodge El Sol Naciente. Multicoloured.

184	60c.+30c. Type **61**	2·50	1·50

185	100c.+50c. Globes on top of columns and doorway	3·25	2·50

62 Livia Ecury (teacher and nurse)

1996. Anniversaries. Multicoloured.

186	60c. Type **62** (5th death)	1·50	1·50
187	60c. Laura Wernet-Paskel (teacher and politician, 85th birth)	1·50	1·50
188	60c. Lolita Euson (poet, 2nd death)	1·50	1·50

63 Rabbits at Bus-stop

1996. Child Welfare. Comic Strips. Multicoloured.

189	50c.+25c. Type **63**	1·90	1·50
190	70c.+35c. Mother accompanying young owl to school	2·30	2·00
191	100c.+50c. Boy flying kite with friend	2·75	2·50

64 Children at the Seaside and Words on Signpost

1997. "Year of Papiamento" (Creole language). Multicoloured.

192	50c. Type **64**	1·10	1·10
193	140c. Sunrise over ocean	2·75	2·75

65 Postman on Bicycle, 1936–57

1997. America. The Postman. Multicoloured.

194	60c. Type **65**	2·75	1·70
195	70c. Postman delivering package by jeep, 1957–88	2·75	1·70
196	80c. Postman delivering letter from motor scooter, 1995	2·75	1·70

66 Decorated Cunucu House

1997. Aruban Architecture. Multicoloured.

197	30c. Type **66**	90	60
198	65c. Bannistered steps	1·70	1·50
199	100c. Arends Building (vert)	2·20	2·00

67 Merlin and Lighthouse

1997. "Pacific 97" International Stamp Exhibition, San Francisco. Multicoloured.

200	90c. Type **67**	2·75	2·20
201	90c. Windswept trees and dolphin	2·75	2·20
202	90c. Iguana on rock and cacti	2·75	2·20
203	90c. Three types of fishes and one dolphin	2·75	2·20
204	90c. Two dolphins and fishes	2·75	2·20
205	90c. Burrowing owl on shore, turtle and lionfish	2·75	2·20
206	90c. Stingray, rock beauty, angelfishes, squirrelfish and coral reef	2·75	2·20
207	90c. Diver and stern of shipwreck	2·75	2·20
208	90c. Shipwreck, reef and fishes	2·75	2·20

Nos. 200/8 were issued together, *se-tenant*, forming a composite design.

68 Passengers approaching Cruise Liner

1997. Cruise Tourism. Multicoloured.

209	35c. Type **68**	1·10	90
210	50c. Passengers disembarking	1·50	1·10
211	150c. Cruise liner at sea and launch at shore	3·00	2·75

69 Coral Tree

1997. Trees. Multicoloured.

212	50c. Type **69**	1·50	1·10
213	60c. *Cordia dentata*	1·70	1·50
214	70c. *Tabebuia billbergii*	2·00	1·50
215	130c. *Lignum vitae*	2·75	2·20

70 Girl among Aloes

1997. Child Welfare. Child and Nature. Multicoloured.

216	50c.+25c. Type **70**	1·70	1·40
217	70c.+35c. Boy and butterfly (vert)	2·50	2·20
218	100c.+50c. Girl swimming underwater by coral reef	2·50	2·75

71 Fort Zoutman

1998. Bicentenary of Fort Zoutman.

219	**71** 30c. multicoloured	1·10	90
220	**71** 250c. multicoloured	4·75	4·25

Each design consists of alternating strips in brown tones or black and white. When the 250c. is laid on top of the 30c., the brown strips form a composite design of the fort in its early years and the black and white strips a composite design of the fort after 1929, when various alterations were made.

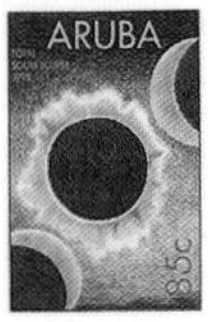

72 Stages of Eclipse

1998. Total Solar Eclipse. Multicoloured.

221	85c. Type **72**	2·20	1·50
222	100c. Globe showing path of eclipse and map of Aruba plotting duration of total darkness	2·50	1·70

73 Globe, Emblem and Wheelchair balanced on Map of Aruba

1998. "Solidarity" Anniversaries. Multicoloured.

223	60c.+30c. Type **73** (50th anniv of Lions Club of Aruba)	2·20	1·60
224	100c.+50c. Boy reading, emblem and grandmother in rocking chair (60th anniv of Rotary Club of Aruba)	3·25	2·50

74 Tropical Mockingbird

1998. Birds. Multicoloured.

225	50c. Type **74**	1·90	1·10
226	60c. American kestrel (vert)	2·20	1·50
227	70c. Troupial (vert)	2·20	1·50
228	150c. Bananaquit	3·75	3·25

75 Villagers processing Corn

1998. World Stamp Day.

229	**75** 225c. multicoloured	6·25	5·00

76 Ribbon Dance

1998. Child Welfare. Multicoloured.

230	50c.+25c. Type **76**	1·60	1·50
231	80c.+40c. Boy playing cuarta (four-string guitar)	2·50	2·50
232	100c. + 50c. Basketball	3·25	2·75

77 Two Donkeys

1999. The Donkey. Multicoloured.

233	40c. Type **77**	1·60	90
234	65c. Two adults and foal	1·80	1·50
235	100c. Adult and foal	2·75	2·20

78 *Opuntia wentiana*

1999. Cacti. Multicoloured.

236	50c. Type **78**	1·50	1·00
237	60c. *Lemaireocereus griseus*	1·70	1·20
238	70c. *Cephalocereus lanuginosus* ("Cadushi di carona")	1·70	1·50
239	75c. *Cephalocereus lanuginosus* ("Cadushi")	2·00	1·70

79 Creole Dog

1999. Creole Dogs (*Canis familiaris*). Multicoloured

240	40c. Type **79**	1·70	1·10
241	60c. White dog standing on rock	2·00	1·50
242	80c. Dog sitting by sea	2·20	1·70
243	165c. Black and tan dog sitting on rock	3·75	3·25

80 Indian Cave Drawings and Antique Map

1999. 500 Years of Cultural Diversity. Multicoloured.

244	150c. Type **80**	2·75	2·50
245	175c. Indian cave drawings and carnival headdress	3·25	3·00
MS246	90×60 mm. Nos. 244/5	6·75	5·50

81 Public Library and Children

1999. 50th Anniv of Public Library Service. Multicoloured.

247	70c. Type **81**	1·60	1·70
248	100c. Library, Santa Cruz	2·30	2·00

82 Boy with Fisherman

1999. Child Welfare. Multicoloured.

249	60c.+30c. Type **82**	1·70	1·50
250	80c.+40c. Man reading to children	2·50	2·20
251	100c.+50c. Woman with child (vert)	3·25	2·75

83 Three Wise Men

1999. Christmas. Multicoloured. Self-adhesive.

252	40c. Type **83**	1·80	1·10
253	70c. Shepherds	2·20	1·50
254	100c. Holy Family	2·75	2·00

84 *Norops lineatus*

2000. Reptiles. Multicoloured.

255	40c. Type **84**	7·75	80
256	60c. Green iguana (vert)	1·60	1·50
257	75c. Annulated snake (vert)	1·80	1·50
258	150c. Racerunner	3·75	2·50

85 Flags

2000. America. A.I.D.S. Awareness. Multicoloured.

259	75c. Type **85**	2·00	2·00
260	175c. Ribbon on globe (vert)	3·75	3·75

86 Bank Facade

2000. Anniversaries. Multicoloured.

261	150c. Type **86** (75th anniv of Aruba Bank)	3·25	2·50
262	165c. Chapel (250th anniv of Alto Vista Chapel)	3·25	2·75

87 West Indian Top Shell

2000. Aspects of Aruba. Multicoloured.

263	15c. Type **87**	50	40
264	25c. Guadirikiri cave	85	50
265	35c. Mud-house (vert)	1·00	80
267	55c. Cacti	1·50	1·10
269	85c. Hooiberg	2·00	1·70
271	100c. Gold smelter, Balashi (vert)	2·50	2·00
272	250c. Rock crystal	5·00	4·50
275	500c. Conchi	9·50	8·25

88 Children at Beach Playground

2000. "Solidarity". Multicoloured.

280	75c.+35c. Type **88**	2·10	1·80
281	100c.+50c. Children building sandcastles	3·50	2·75

89 *Solar Energy* (Nikki Johanna Teresia Willems)

2000. Child Welfare. "Stampin' the Future". Winning Entries in Children's International Painting Competition. Multicoloured.

282	60c.+30c. Type **89**	2·10	1·70
283	80c.+40c. *Environmental Protection* (Samantha Jeanne Tromp)	2·30	2·00
284	100c.+50c. *Future Vehicles* (Jennifer Huntington)	3·25	2·75

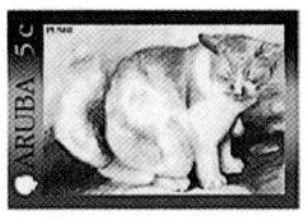

90 Cat

2001. Domestic Animals. Multicoloured.

285	5c. Type **90**	65	35
286	30c. Tortoise	1·70	1·10
287	50c. Rabbit	1·70	1·10
288	200c. Brown-throated conure	4·50	4·00

91 Shaman preparing for Sun Ceremony

2001. 40 Years of Mascaruba (amateur theatre group). Depicting scenes from *Macuarima, History or Legend?* (musical play). Multicoloured.

289	60c. Type **91**	1·60	1·10
290	150c. Love scene between Guadarikiri and Blanco	3·00	2·75

92 Ford Model A Roadster, 1930

2001. Motor Cars. Multicoloured.

291	25c. Type **92**	1·80	1·10
292	40c. Citroen Comerciale saloon, 1933	1·80	1·10
293	70c. Plymouth Pick-up, 1948	2·00	1·70
294	75c. Edsel corsair convertable, 1959	2·10	1·70

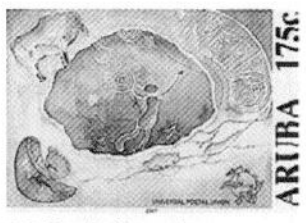

93 Rock Drawings

2001. Universal Postal Union. United Nations Year of Dialogue among Civilizations.

295	**93** 175c. multicoloured	4·00	3·25

94 Pedestrians using Crossing

2001. Child Welfare. International Year of Volunteers. Multicoloured.

296	40c. + 20c. Type **94**	1·60	1·10
297	60c. + 30c. Boys walking dogs	2·10	1·70
298	100c. + 50c. Children putting litter in bin	3·25	2·75

95 Dakota Airport, 1950

2002. Queen Beatrix Airport. Multicoloured.

299	30c. Type **95**	1·00	55
300	75c. Queen Beatrix Airport, 1972	1·90	1·50
301	175c. Queen Beatrix Airport, 2000	3·75	3·25

Dakota Airport was re-named Princess Beatrix Airport in 1955 and Queen Beatrix Airport in 1972.

96 Prince Willem-Alexander and Princess Maxima

2002. Wedding of Crown Prince Willem-Alexander to Maxima Zorreguieta. Multicoloured.

302	60c. Type **96**	1·50	1·10
303	300c. Prince Willem-Alexander and Princess Máxima facing right	5·50	5·50

97 Tap and Water Droplet

2002. 70th Anniv of Water Company (W. E. B.). Multicoloured.

304	60c. Type **97**	1·20	1·10
305	85c. Water pipes (horiz)	1·70	1·60
306	165c. Water meter and meter reader	3·25	3·25

98 Hand holding Quill Pen

2002. America. Literacy Campaign. Multicoloured.

307	25c. Type **98**	1·10	90
308	100c. Alphabet on wall and boy on step-ladder	2·20	1·90

99 *U-156* Submarine firing on Lago Oil Refinery

2002. Second World War. Multicoloured.

309	60c. Type **99**	2·20	1·10
310	75c. *Pedernales* (oil-tanker) in flames	2·20	1·40
311	150c. "Boy" Ecury (resistance fighter) (statue) (vert)	3·25	2·75

100 Boy, Iguana and Goat

2002. Child Welfare. Animals. Multicoloured.

312	40c.+20c. Type **100**	1·20	1·10
313	60c.+30c. Girl, turtle and crab (horiz)	2·50	1·70
314	100c.+50c. Pelicans, boy and parakeet	3·00	2·75

101 House at Fontein

2003. Mud Houses. Multicoloured.

315	40c. Type **101**	90	80
316	60c. House at Ari Kok	1·20	1·10
317	75c. House at Fontein	1·60	1·50

102 The Trupialen Boys Choir

2003. 50th Anniv of "De Trupialen" (boys' organization). Multicoloured.

318	30c. Type **102**	65	55
319	50c. Puppet theatre posters	1·10	1·00
320	100c. Organization emblems	2·20	1·90

103 *Schomburgkia humboldtii*

2003. Orchids. Multicoloured.

321	75c. Type **103**	1·80	1·70
322	500c. *Brassavola nodosa*	11·00	9·00

104 Orange-barred Sulphur Butterfly

2003. Butterflies. Multicoloured.

323	40c. Type **104**	1·30	1·10
324	75c. Monarch	1·90	1·60
325	85c. Hairstreak	2·20	1·80
326	175c. Gulf fritillary	3·75	3·25

105 Hawksbill Turtle (*Eretmochelys imbricate*)

2003. Endangered Species. Turtles. Multicoloured.

327	25c. Type **105**	1·20	1·00
328	60c. Leatherback turtle (*Dermochelys coricea*) (horiz)	1·40	1·20
329	75c. Green turtle (*Chelonia mydas*)	1·80	1·50
330	150c. Loggerhead turtle (*Caretta caretta*) (horiz)	3·50	3·00

106 Baseball

2003. Child Welfare. Children and Sport.. Multicoloured.

331	40c.+20c. Type **106**	1·20	1·00
332	60c.+30c. Volleyball	1·80	1·50
333	100c.+50c. Football	3·50	3·00

107 Masks and Headdresses

2004. 50th Anniv of Carnival. Multicoloured.

334	60c. Type **107**	95	80
335	75c. Woman's face (vert)	1·40	1·20
336	150c. Heads wearing carnival headdresses	3·00	2·50

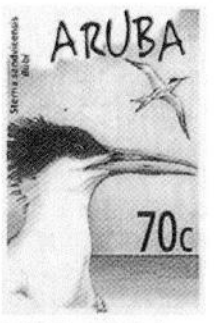

108 Sandwich Tern (*Sterna sandvicensis*)

2004. Birds. Multicoloured.

337	70c. Type **108**	1·40	1·20
338	75c. Brown pelican (*Pelecanus occidentalis*)	1·60	1·30
339	80c. Frigate bird (*Fregata magnificens*)	1·70	1·40
340	90c. Laughing gull (*Larus atricilla*)	1·80	1·50

109 Parrotfish

2004. Fish. Multicoloured.

341	40c. Type **109**	1·10	90
342	60c. Queen angelfish	1·30	1·10
343	75c. Squirrelfish	1·60	1·30
344	100c. Small-mouthed grunt	1·90	1·60

110 Children holding Maracas

2004. Child Welfare. Musical Instruments. Multicoloured.

345	60c.+30c. Type **110**	1·80	1·50
346	85c.+40c. Three children and steel drum	2·40	2·10
347	100c.+50c. Boy playing wiri and girl holding tambourine	3·00	2·50

111 Presents and Decorated Tree

2004. Christmas and New Year. Multicoloured.

348	50c. Type **111**	95	80
349	85c. Parcels, carol singers and candle	1·70	1·40
350	125c. Fireworks	2·40	2·10

112 Interconnecting Islands (Aruba, Curacao, Bonaire, Saba, St. Maarten and St. Eustatius)

2004. 50th Anniv of Charter of the Kingdom (statute establishing partial autonomy). Multicoloured.

351	160c. Type **112**	2·30	2·00
352	165c. Kingdom Statute monument	2·40	2·10

113 Sun and Flower

2004. Greetings Stamps. Multicoloured.

353	60c. Type **113** ("Thank you")	1·10	90
354	75c. Two rabbits ("Love")	1·20	1·00
355	135c. Fish ("Get well soon")	1·90	1·60
356	215c. Balloons ("Congratulations")	3·50	3·00

114 Race Car and Spectators

2005. Drag Racing. Multicoloured.

357	60c. Type **114**	1·20	1·00
358	85c. Parachute opening at race end	1·80	1·50
359	185c. Race start	3·00	2·50

115 Queen Beatrix and Prince Claus

2005. 25th Anniv of Coronation of Queen Beatrix. Sheet 144×75 mm containing T **115** and similar vert designs. Multicoloured.

MS360	30c. Type **115**; 60c. Seated; 75c. With Nelson Mandela; 105c.Wearing glasses; 215c. Wearing hat	7·75	7·75

116 Sunset

2005. Tourism. Sunsets. Multicoloured.

361	60c. Type **116**	95	80
362	100c. Palm tree	1·60	1·30
363	205c. Pelicans	3·25	2·75

117 American Kestrel (*Falco sparverius*)

2005. Birds. Multicoloured.

364	60c. Type **117**	1·20	1·00
365	75c. Burrowing owl (*Athene cunicularia*)	1·60	1·30
366	135c. Osprey (*Pandion haliaetus*)	2·30	2·00
367	200c. Common caracara (*Polyborus plancus*)	3·50	3·00
MS368	110×70 mm. Nos. 364/7	7·75	7·75

118 *Acropora cervicornis*

2005. Corals. Multicoloured.

369	60c. Type **118**	1·10	95
370	75c. *Millepora complanata*	1·40	1·20
371	100c. *Iciligorgia schrammi*	1·80	1·50
372	215c. *Diploria strigosa*	3·75	3·25

119 Girl and Stamps

2005. Child Welfare. Philately. Multicoloured.

373	75c. Type **119**	1·50	1·30
374	85c. Boy holding magnifier and album	1·60	1·40
375	125c. Boy putting stamps in album	2·30	2·00

120 "House of Savaneta" (Jean George Pandellis)

2006. Art. Multicoloured.

376	60c. Type **120**	1·20	1·00
377	75c. *Haf di Rei* (Mateo Hayde)	1·50	1·30
378	185c. *Landscape* (Julie Oduber)	3·50	3·00

121 Emblem

2006. 50th Anniv of YMCA. Multicoloured.

379	75c. Type **121**	1·50	1·30
380	205c. Children at play (horiz)	3·75	3·25

122 Tree and Log Bridge

2006. Washington 2006 International Stamp Exhibition. Sheet 98×88 mm containing T **122** and similar multicoloured design.

MS381	500c.×2, Type **122**; Cacti and boats (vert)	13·50	13·50

The stamps and margins of **MS**381 form a composite design.

123 Goalkeeper

2006. World Cup Football Championship, Germany. Multicoloured.

382	75c. Type **123**	1·40	1·20
383	215c. Hands holding globe as football	3·75	3·25

124 Surf Boards, Boats, Windsurfers and Kitesurfer

2006. 20th Anniv of Hi-Winds Windsurfing Competition. Multicoloured.

384	60c. Type **124**	1·00	85
385	100c. Leaping kitesurfer	1·60	1·30
386	125c. Windsurfers	2·00	1·70

125 Fire Hazards

2006. Fire Prevention. Multicoloured.

387	60c. Type **125**	1·00	85
388	100c. Firefighters	1·60	1·30
389	205c. Fire appliances	3·25	2·75

126 House and Goat

2006. Arikok National Park. Multicoloured.

390	75c. Type **126**	1·30	1·10
391	100c. Cacti, valley and eagle (vert)	1·60	1·30
392	200c. Cacti and owl	3·25	2·75

127 Dancers and Boar

2007. New Year. Year of the Pig. Sheet 78×62 mm containing T **127** and similar multicoloured design.

MS393	205c. Type **127**; 215c. Dragon (*vert*)	6·50	6·50

The stamp and margin of **MS**393 form a composite design.

128 Luciana Maria Koolman and Original Building

2007. 50th Anniv of Casa Cuna Children's Home Foundation. Multicoloured.

394	50c. Type **128**	85	70
395	125c. Children enclosed in hands	2·00	1·70
396	150c. New building	2·40	2·10

129 Museum of Antiquities

2007. Museums. Multicoloured.

397	70c. Type **129**	1·10	95
398	85c. Numismatic museum	1·30	1·10
399	100c. Archaeological museum	1·50	1·30
400	135c. Historical museum	2·10	1·80

130 Pipeline of *Pedernalis* (wrecked oil tanker)

2007. Wrecks and Reefs. Sheet 87×70 mm containing T **130** and similar horiz designs. Multicoloured.

MS401	200c. Type **130**; 300c. Convair 400 aircraft wreck; 500c. Sea turtle and *Jane* (wrecked freighter); 500c. *Antilla* (wrecked freighter) and fish	17·00	17·00

The stamps and margins of **MS**401 form a composite design.

131 Mother and Child

2007. Christmas. Multicoloured.

402	70c. Type **131**	1·20	1·10
403	100c. Girl with presents	1·70	1·50
404	150c. Child with balloon	2·50	2·30

132 Beached Catamarans

2007. Catamaran Regatta. Multicoloured.

405	40c. Type **132**	70	60
406	80c. Two catamarans and buoy	1·40	1·20
407	125c. Tacking	2·10	1·90
408	130c. Racing	2·20	2·00

133 As Small Child

2008. 70th Birth Anniv of Queen Beatrix. Multicoloured.

409	75c. Type **133**	1·30	1·10
410	125c. With Prince Claus and new born Prince Willem Alexander	2·10	1·90
411	250c. Wearing regalia on day of accession	4·25	3·75
412	300c. With Crown Prince Willem Alexander and his family	5·00	4·50

134 Carnival

2008. Cultural Heritage. Multicoloured.

413	80c. Type **134**	1·40	1·20
414	130c. Street entertainers	2·20	2·00
415	250c. Musicians, dancers, cockerel and campfire	3·50	3·00
416	300c. Musicians and householders	4·75	4·25

135 Athletics

2008. Olympic Games, Beijing. Multicoloured.

417	50c. Type **135**	85	75
418	75c. Synchronised swimming	1·30	1·10
419	100c. Gymnastics (vert)	1·70	1·50
420	175c. Judo	2·10	1·90

136 Burrowing Owl

2008. Aruban Cultural Year. Burrowing Owl Athene cunicularia arubensis . Multicoloured.

421	100c. Type **136**	1·80	1·60
422	150c. Two owls (horiz)	2·75	2·40
423	350c. Head	6·25	5·75

137 FRX Super Glide Big Boy

2008. Harley Davidson Motorcycles. Multicoloured.

424	175c. Type **137**	3·25	3·00
425	225c. Knucklehead	4·00	3·50
426	305c. Roadking	5·25	4·75

138 Script (poem by Frederico Oduber)

2008. Netherlands and Beyond. Sheet 145×75 mm containing T **138** and similar multicoloured designs.

MS427	240c. Type **138**; 240c. *Watapana* (first magazine in Papiamento (local language)) (vert); 240c. Henry Habibe and poem (vert)	14·50	14·50

No. **MS**427 also includes a Netherlands Antilles 5c. stamp (Houses (architecture)) and a Netherlands 92c. stamp (chillies and cheese (food)).

The 'foreign' stamps could only be used in their country of origin.

139 *Calatropis procea*

2008. Flowers. Multicoloured.

428	100c. Type **139**	1·80	1·60
429	185c. *Thespesia populnea*	3·50	3·00
430	200c. *Cryptostegia grandiflora*	3·50	3·25
431	215c. *Passiflora foetida*	3·75	3·50

140 *Self Portrait*

2008. International Culture. Drawings by Rembrandt. Multicoloured.

432	350c. Type **140**	7·00	6·25
433	425c. *Self Portrait*	8·25	7·50
434	500c. Beggars at the Door	9·75	9·00

141 Donkeys transporting Water

2008. Aruba in the Old Days. Each brown and ochre.

435	100c. Type **141**	2·00	1·80
436	200c. Two roomed clay house	4·00	3·50
437	215c. Harvesting *Aloe vera*	4·25	3·75

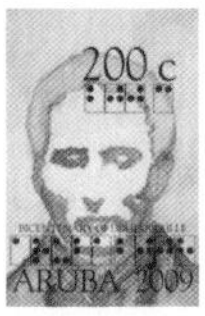

142 Louis Braille

2009. Birth Bicentenary of Louis Braille (inventor of Braille writing for the blind). Multicoloured.

438	200c. Type **142**	4·00	3·50
439	215c. Hand holding white stick	4·25	3·75

143 Carnival Queen

2009. 55th Anniv of Aruba Carnival. Sheet 115×95 mm containing T **143** and similar horiz designs. Multicoloured.

MS440	75c. Type **143**; 100c. Float with clown; 175c. Float with champagne bottle, large '55' bottom left; 225c. Dancers	11·00	11·50

143a Kapel Alto Vista

2009. Architecture

440a	**143a**	5c. multicoloured	10	10
440b		10c. multicoloured	15	10
440c		25c. multicoloured	40	25
440d		50c. multicoloured	85	65
440e		85c. multicoloured	1·20	1·00
440f		90c. multicoloured	1·50	1·30
440g		100c. multicoloured	1·70	1·50
440h		125c. multicoloured	2·40	1·90
440i		130c. multicoloured	2·50	1·90
440j		135c. multicoloured	2·60	2·20
440k		140c. multicoloured	2·60	2·20

440l	200c. multicoloured	3·50	2·75
440m	215c. multicoloured	3·75	3·25
440n	220c. multicoloured	4·00	3·50

144 Tunnel of Love (Baranca Suna) Cave

2009. Caves. Multicoloured.

441	175c. Type **144**	3·50	3·25
442	200c. Fountain (Fontein)	4·00	3·50
443	225c. Guardirikiri (Quadirikiri Grot)	4·25	4·00

145 Ozone Layer

2009. Global Warming Awareness Campaign. Sheet 82×64 mm containing T **145** and similar horiz designs. Multicoloured.

MS444	200c. Type **145**; 250c. Melting ice caps; 250c. Pollution; 300c. Alternative energy sources	17·00	17·00

146 California Lighthouse

2009. Architecture. Sheet 86×86 mm containing T **146** and similar multicoloured designs.

MS445	175c. Type **146**; 250c. Plaza Daniel Leo, Oranjestad (horiz); 275c. Henriquez Building (horiz); 325c. Main Building, Ecury Complex	18·00	18·00

147 Girl Reading

2009. 60th Anniv of National Library. Each black and new blue.

446	185c. Type **147**	3·50	3·25
447	300c. Woman reading	6·00	5·25

148 *Stenella frontalis* (Atlantic spotted dolphin)

2009. Dophins. Multicoloured.

448	125c. Type **148**	1·90	1·50
449	200c. *Steno bredanensis* (rough-toothed dolphin)	4·00	3·50
450	300c. Two Atlantic spotted dolphins facing right	6·00	5·25
451	325c. Several rough-toothed dolphins	6·50	5·75

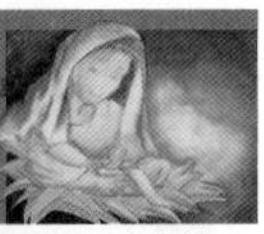

149 Virgin and Child

2009. Christmas. Multicoloured.

452	75c. Type **149**	1·30	1·10
453	120c. Angel	1·90	1·70
454	125c. Hands holding globe, '2009' and 'Peace'	2·10	1·90
455	210c. Shepherds and star	4·50	3·50

150 Palm Tree, Wall and Fish (paper)

2010. Recycle. Multicoloured.

456	90c. Type **150**	1·80	1·60
457	180c. House and cow (card-board and pasta)	3·50	3·25
458	325c. Fish and boat (paper, bottle tops and lolly sticks)	6·50	5·75

151 Seaplane

2010. Historic Aircraft. Multicoloured.

459	250c. Type **151**	4·50	4·25
460	500c. Curtiss NC-4	8·75	8·50

152 Two Junior Scouts

2010. Scouting. Multicoloured.

461	85c. Type **152**	60	55
462	95c. Two scouts and campfire	75	70
463	135c. Scout emerging from tent	1·50	1·40
464	180c. Four scouts map reading	2·00	1·90

153 Soldiers in Gun Placement

2010. 65th Anniv of End of World War II. Multicoloured.

465	140c. Type **153**	1·60	1·50
466	200c. Soldiers and missile	2·50	2·40
467	275c. Guns on foundering ship	3·00	2·75

154 Blue and Gold Macaw

2010. Parrots. Multicoloured.

468	85c. Type **154**	70	55
469	90c. Green Amazonian	90	65
470	180c. Scarlet macaw	2·00	1·70

155 Self-Portrait

2010. Art. Multicoloured.

471	200c. Type **155**	1·30	1·00
472	250c. *Vase with Fifteen Sunflowers*	1·90	1·50
473	305c. *The Starry Night*	3·00	2·50
474	500c. *Wheat Field Under Threatening Skies* (detail)	5·25	4·75

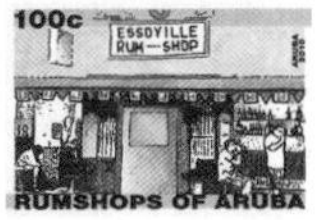

156 Essoville Rum Shop

2010. Rum Shops. Multicoloured.

475	100c. Type **156**	2·50	2·20
476	200c. Aruba Rum Shop	4·50	4·25
477	255c. Caribbean Store	5·50	5·25

157 *Caesalpinia pulcherrima*

2010. Flowers. Multicoloured.

478	200c. Type **157**	3·25	2·75
479	200c. *Dipladenia sanderi*	3·25	2·75
480	200c. *Dipladenia sanderi*	3·25	2·75
481	200c. *Adenium obesum*	3·25	2·75
482	200c. *Bougainvillea*	3·25	2·75
483	200c. *Ixora*	3·25	2·75
484	200c. *Eichhornia crassipes*	3·25	2·75
485	200c. *Passiflora caerulea*	3·25	2·75
486	200c. *Allamanda cathartica*	3·25	2·75
487	200c. *Nerium oleander*		

158 Beth Israel Synagogue

2010. Places of Worship. Multicoloured.

488	85c. Type **158**	1·50	1·20
489	90c. Protestant Church	1·90	1·50
490	135c. St. Fransiscus Catholic Church	3·00	2·50
491	240c. Interior, St. Fransiscus Church	5·50	2·00

159 *Falco sparverius* (American kestrel)

2010. Birds. Multicoloured.

492	200c. Type **159**	4·25	3·75
493	200c. *Icterus icterus* (troupial)	4·25	3·75
494	200c. *Mimus gilvus* (tropical mockingbird)	4·25	3·75
495	200c. *Egretta alba* (great white egret)	4·25	3·75
496	200c. *Aratinga pertinax* (brown-throated parakeet)	4·75	3·75
497	200c. *Pelicanus occidentalis* (eastern brown pelican)	4·25	3·75
498	200c. *Athena cunicularia* (burrowing owl)	4·25	3·75
499	200c. *Coereba flaveola* (bananaquit)	4·25	3·75
500	200c. *Polyborus plancus* (caracara)	4·25	3·75
501	200c. *Colibri thalassinus* (green violet-ear)	4·25	3·75

160 Caribbean Reef Octopus

2010. Caribbean Reef Octopus (*Octopus briareus*). Multicoloured.

502	100c. Type **160**	2·10	1·90
503	175c. With tenacles extended downwards	4·25	3·75
504	255c. With tenacles extended upwards	5·00	4·50
505	300c. Coiled on sea bed	6·00	5·50

161 *Heliconius hecale*

2010. Butterflies. Multicoloured.

506	200c. Type **161**	4·00	3·50
507	200c. *Morpho peleides* (inscr 'Morpho paleides')	4·00	3·50
508	200c. *Danaus plexippus*	4·00	3·50
509	200c. *Anartia jatrophae*	5·00	3·50
511	200c. *Phoebis sennae*	4·00	3·50
511	200c. *Heliconius charithorius* (inscr 'Heliconius charithorius')	4·00	3·50
512	200c. *Siproeta stelenes*	4·00	3·50
513	200c. *Caligo memmon*	4·00	3·50
514	200c. *Heliconius melpomene*	4·00	3·50
515	200c *Agraulis vanilla*	4·00	3·50

162 Flag

2011. 25th Anniv of Status Aparte (status of an autonomous state within Kingdom of the Netherlands). Multicoloured.

516	200c. Type **162**	4·50	4·50
517	300c. 'STATUS APARTE'	6·75	6·75
518	300c. Filipe Tromp and Henny Eman	6·75	6·75
519	400c. Fredis Refunjol and Betico Croes	6·75	6·75

163 *Delonix regia*

2011. Flowers. Multicoloured.

520	160c. Type **163**	3·50	3·50
521	160c. *Cassia fistula*	3·50	3·50
522	160c. *Ipomoea pes-caprae*	3·50	3·50
523	160c. *Allamanda cathartica*	3·50	3·50
524	160c. *Catharanthus roseus* (inscr 'Catharantnus roseus')	3·50	3·50
525	160c. *Nerium oleander*	3·50	3·50
526	160c. *Bougainvillea glabra*	3·50	3·50
527	160c. *Hibiscus rosa-sinensis*	3·50	3·50
528	160c. *Cordia sebestena*	3·50	3·50
529	160c. *Echinopsis lageniformis*	3·50	3·50

164 Hands as Flags of Portugal, Cuba, USA and Brazil

2011. Centenary of UPAEP (Unión Postal de las Américas, España y Portugal). Multicoloured.

530	200c. Type **164**	4·50	5·50
531	250c. Canada, Argentina and Colombia	6·75	6·75
532	350c. Brazil, USAand Panama	6·75	6·75
533	400c. Suriname, Portugal and Chile	8·75	8·75
MS534	108×78 mm. 300c.×4, As Nos. 530/3	28·00	28·00

165 Indonesia 1965 25sen Note

2011. 25th Anniv of Papermoney Fair, Maastricht. Multicoloured.

535	167c. Type **165**	3·50	3·50
536	167c. Bhutan 1986 - 2 Ngultrum	3·50	3·50
537	167c. Phippines 1949 - 50 centavos	3·50	3·50
538	167c. Sudan 1987 - 25 piastres	3·50	3·50
539	167c. Mozambique 1976 - 100 Escudos	3·50	3·50
540	167c. Haiti 1993 - 25 Gourdes	3·50	3·50
541	167c. Gottingen 1917 - 25 pt.	3·50	3·50
542	167c. Turkey 1997 - 250000 l.	3·50	3·50
543	167c. Solomon Islands1977 - 10 dollars	3·50	3·50
544	167c. Lille 1915 - 25 centimes	3·50	3·50
545	167c. Egypt 1985 - 25 piastres	3·50	3·50
546	167c. Albania 1976 - 100 leke	3·50	3·50

166 Peony Flower

2011. Peonies. Multicoloured.

547	110c. Type **166**	1·90	1·90
548	110c. Yellow flowered peony	1·90	1·90
549	110c. White flowered peony	1·90	1·90
550	110c. Large pale pink flowered peony with black centre	1·90	1·90
MS551	50×75 mm. 350c. Medium flowered pink peony	7·75	7·75

EXPRESS MAIL SERVICE

E40 Globe, Planets and Aruban Arms

1993

E122	**E40**	200c. multicoloured	4·50	3·25

Pt. 1

ASCENSION

An island in South Atlantic. A dependency of St. Helena.

1922. 12 pence = 1 shilling; 20 shillings = 1 pound.
1971. 100 pence = 1 pound.

1922. Stamps of St. Helena of 1912 optd **ASCENSION**.

1	½d. black and green	6·50	25·00
2	1d. green	6·50	24·00
3	1½d. red	17·00	48·00
4	2d. black and slate	17·00	13·00
4b	2d. black and slate	£425	£450
5	3d. blue	13·00	25·00
6	8d. black and purple	27·00	50·00
9	1s. black on green	28·00	48·00
7	2s. black and blue on blue	£110	£130
8	3s. black and violet	£140	£160

2 Badge of St. Helena

1924

10	2	½d. black	5·50	18·00
11	2	1d. black and green	6·00	13·00
12	2	1½d. red	10·00	40·00
13	2	2d. black and grey	19·00	12·00
14	2	3d. blue	8·00	18·00
15	2	4d. black on yellow	50·00	95·00
15d	2	5d. purple and green	17·00	26·00
16	2	6d. black and purple	60·00	£120
17	2	8d. black and violet	17·00	45·00
18	2	1s. black and brown	21·00	55·00
19	2	2s. black and blue on blue	75·00	£100
20	2	3s. black on blue	95·00	£100

3 Georgetown

4 Ascension Island

1934. Medallion portrait of King George V (except 1s.).

21	**3**	½d. black and violet	90	80
22	**4**	1d. black and green	1·75	1·50
23	-	1½d. black and red	1·75	2·25
24	**4**	2d. black and orange	1·75	2·50
25	-	3d. black and blue	2·25	1·50
26	-	5d. black and blue	2·25	3·25
27	**4**	8d. black and brown	4·25	5·00
28	-	1s. black and red	18·00	11·00
29	**4**	2s.6d. black and purple	45·00	48·00
30	-	5s. black and brown	50·00	60·00

DESIGNS—HORIZ: 1½d. The Pier; 3d. Long Beach; 5d. Three Sisters; 1s. Sooty tern ("Wideawake Fair"); 5s. Green mountain.

1935. Silver Jubilee. As T **13** of Antigua.

31	1½d. blue and red	3·50	13·00
32	2d. blue and grey	11·00	35·00
33	5d. green and blue	23·00	32·00
34	1s. grey and purple	23·00	40·00

1937. Coronation. As T **2** of Aden.

35	1d. green	50	1·40
36	2d. orange	1·00	60
37	3d. blue	1·00	50

10 Green Mountain

1938

38b	**A**	½d. black and violet	1·40	3·25
39	**10**	1d. black and green	45·00	13·00
39b	**10**	1d. black and orange	45	60
39d	**C**	1d. black and green	60	1·50
40b	**B**	1½d. black and red	1·00	80
40d	**B**	1½d. black and pink	1·50	1·00
41a	**10**	2d. black and orange	80	40
41c	**10**	2d. black and red	1·25	1·75
42	**D**	3d. black and blue	£100	29·00
42b	**D**	3d. black and grey	70	80
42d	**10**	4d. black and blue	5·00	3·00
43	**C**	6d. black and blue	10·00	2·25
44a	**A**	1s. black and brown	4·75	2·00
45	**B**	2s.6d. black and red	42·00	9·50
46a	**D**	5s. black and brown	38·00	38·00
47a	**C**	10s. black and purple	48·00	60·00

DESIGNS: A, Georgetown; B, The Pier; C, Three Sisters; D, Long Beach.

1946. Victory. As T **9** of Aden.

48	2d. orange	40	1·00
49	4d. blue	40	60

1948. Silver Wedding. As T **10/11** of Aden.

50	3d. black	50	30
51	10s. mauve	55·00	50·00

1949. U.P.U. As T **20/23** of Antigua.

52	3d. red	1·00	2·00
53	4d. blue	4·00	1·50
54	6d. olive	2·00	3·50
55	1s. black	2·00	1·50

1953. Coronation. As T **13** of Aden.

56	3d. black and grey	1·00	2·00

15 Water Catchment

1956

57	**15**	½d. black and brown	10	50
58	-	1d. black and mauve	4·00	2·25
59	-	1½d. black and orange	1·00	1·00
60	-	2d. black and red	5·50	3·00
61	-	2½d. black and brown	2·00	2·75
62	-	3d. black and blue	5·00	1·25
63	-	4d. black and turquoise	1·25	2·00
64	-	6d. black and blue	1·50	2·50
65	-	7d. black and olive	3·50	1·50
66	-	1s. black and red	1·00	1·25
67	-	2s.6d. black and purple	29·00	8·50
68	-	5s. black and green	40·00	18·00
69	-	10s. black and purple	50·00	40·00

DESIGNS: 1d. Map of Ascension; 1½d. Georgetown; 2d. Map showing Atlantic cables; 2½d. Mountain road; 3d. White-tailed tropic bird ("Boatswain Bird"); 4d. Yellow-finned tuna; 6d. Rollers on seashore; 7d. Turtles; 1s. Land crab; 2s.6d. Sooty tern ("Wideawake"); 5s. Perfect Crater; 10s. View of Ascension from north-west.

28 Brown Booby

1963. Birds. Multicoloured.

70	1d. Type **28**	1·50	30
71	1½d. White-capped noddy ("Black Noddy")	2·00	1·00
72	2d. White tern ("Fairy Tern")	1·25	30
73	3d. Red-billed tropic bird	1·75	30
74	4½d. Common noddy ("Brown Noddy")	1·75	30
75	6d. Sooty tern ("Wideawake Tern")	1·25	30
76	7d. Ascension frigate bird ("Frigate bird")	1·25	30
77	10d. Blue-faced booby ("White Booby")	1·25	50
78	1s. White-tailed tropic bird ("Yellow-billed Tropicbird")	1·25	30
79	1s.6d. Red-billed tropic bird	4·50	1·75
80	2s.6d. Madeiran storm petrel	8·50	11·00
81	5s. Red-footed booby (brown phase)	10·00	11·00
82	10s. Ascension frigate birds ("Frigate birds")	13·00	14·00
83	£1 Red-footed booby (white phase)	20·00	16·00

1963. Freedom from Hunger. As T **28** of Aden.

84	1s.6d. red	75	40

1963. Centenary of Red Cross. As T **33** of Antigua.

85	3d. red and black	1·25	1·25
86	1s.6d. red and blue	2·00	2·25

1965. Centenary of I.T.U. As T **36** of Antigua.

87	3d. mauve and violet	50	65
88	6d. turquoise and brown	75	65

1965. I.C.Y. As T **37** of Antigua.

89	1d. purple and turquoise	40	60
90	6d. green and lavender	60	90

1966. Churchill Commemoration. As T **38** of Antigua.

91	1d. blue	50	75
92	3d. green	1·75	1·00
93	6d. brown	2·00	1·25
94	1s.6d. violet	2·50	1·50

1966. World Cup Football Championship. As T **40** of Antigua.

95	3d. multicoloured	1·50	60
96	6d. multicoloured	1·50	80

1966. Inauguration of W.H.O. Headquarters, Geneva. As T **41** of Antigua.

97	3d. black, green and blue	1·75	1·00
98	1s.6d. black, purple and ochre	4·75	2·00

36 Satellite Station

1966. Opening of Apollo Communication Satellite Earth Station.

99	**36**	4d. black and violet	10	10
100	**36**	8d. black and green	15	15
101	**36**	1s.3d. black and brown	15	20
102	**36**	2s.6d. black and blue	15	20

37 B.B.C. Emblem

1966. Opening of B.B.C. Relay Station.

103	**37**	1d. gold and blue	10	10
104	**37**	3d. gold and green	15	15
105	**37**	6d. gold and violet	15	15
106	**37**	1s.6d. gold and red	15	15

1967. 20th Anniv of UNESCO As T **54/56** of Antigua.

107	3d. multicoloured	2·25	1·50
108	6d. yellow, violet and olive	3·00	2·00
109	1s.6d. black, purple and orange	4·75	2·50

44 Human Rights Emblem and Chain Links

1968. Human Rights Year.

110	**44**	6d. orange, red and black	20	15
111	**44**	1s.6d. blue, red and black	30	25
112	**44**	2s.6d. green, red and black	35	30

45 Black Durgon ("Ascension Black-Fish")

1968. Fish (1st series).

113	**45**	4d. black, grey and blue	30	35
114	-	8d. multicoloured	35	60
115	-	1s.9d. multicoloured	40	65
116	-	2s.3d. multicoloured	40	65

DESIGNS: 8d. Scribbled filefish ("Leather-jacket"); 1s.9d. Yellow-finned tuna; 2s.3d. Short-finned mako.

See also Nos. 117/20 and 126/9.

1969. Fish (2nd series). As T **45**. Multicoloured.

117	4d. Sailfish	75	90
118	6d. White seabream ("Old wife")	1·00	1·25
119	1s.6d. Yellowtail	1·25	2·50
120	2s.11d. Rock hind ("Jack")	1·50	3·00

46 H.M.S. *Rattlesnake*

1969. Royal Navy Crests (1st series).

121	**46**	4d. multicoloured	60	30
122	-	9d. multicoloured	75	35
123	-	1s.9d. blue and gold	1·10	45
124	-	2s.3d. multicoloured	1·25	55
MS125		165×105 mm. Nos. 121/4	6·50	13·00

DESIGNS: 9d. H.M.S. *Weston*; 1s.9d. H.M.S. *Undaunted*; 2s.3d. H.M.S. *Eagle*.

See also Nos. 130/3, 149/52, 154/7 and 166/9.

1970. Fish (3rd series). As T **45**. Multicoloured.

126	4d. Wahoo	4·50	2·75
127w	9d. Ascension jack ("Coalfish")	3·00	1·25
128	1s.9d. Pompouno dolphin	5·50	3·50
129w	2s.3d. Squirrelfish ("Soldier")	3·00	1·50

1970. Royal Navy Crests (2nd series). As T **46**. Multicoloured.

130	4d. H.M.S. *Penelope*	1·00	1·00
131	9d. H.M.S. *Carlisle*	1·25	1·50
132	1s.6d. H.M.S. *Amphion*	1·75	2·00
133	2s.6d. H.M.S. *Magpie*	1·75	2·00
MS134	159×96 mm. Nos. 130/3	11·00	15·00

50 Early Chinese Rocket

1971. Decimal Currency. Evolution of Space Travel. Multicoloured.

135	½p. Type **50**	15	20
136	1p. Medieval Arab astronomers	20	20
137	1½p. Tycho Brahe's observatory, quadrant and supernova (horiz)	30	30
138	2p. Galileo, Moon and telescope (horiz)	40	30
139	2½p. Isaac Newton, instruments and apple (horiz)	1·75	1·00
140	3½p. Harrison's chronometer and H.M.S. *Deptford* (frigate), 1735 (horiz)	2·50	1·50
141	4½p. Space rocket taking off	1·25	1·00
142	5p. World's largest telescope, Palomar (horiz)	1·00	1·00
143	7½p. World's largest radio telescope, Jodrell Bank (horiz)	4·00	1·75
144	10p. "Mariner VII" and Mars (horiz)	3·50	1·75
145	12½p. "Sputnik II" and Space dog, Laika (horiz)	5·00	2·00
146	25p. Walking in Space	6·00	2·25
147	50p. "Apollo XI" crew on Moon (horiz)	5·00	2·75
148	£1 Future Space Research station (horiz)	5·00	4·50

1971. Royal Navy Crests (3rd series). As T **46**. Multicoloured.

149	2p. H.M.S. "Phoenix"	1·00	30
150	4p. H.M.S. "Milford"	1·00	55
151	9p. H.M.S. "Pelican"	1·25	80
152	15p. H.M.S. "Oberon"	1·25	1·00
MS153	151×104 mm. Nos. 149/52	4·00	15·00

1972. Royal Navy Crests (4th series). As T **46**. Multicoloured.

154	1½p. H.M.S. *Lowestoft*	50	50
155	3p. H.M.S. *Auckland*	55	75
156	6p. H.M.S. *Nigeria*	60	1·25
157	17½p. H.M.S. *Bermuda*	90	2·50
MS158	157×93 mm. Nos. 154/7	2·25	7·50

51 Course of the *Quest*

1972. 50th Anniv of Shackleton's Death. Multicoloured.

159	2½p. Type **51**	30	60
160	4p. Shackleton and *Quest* (horiz)	35	60
161	7½p. Shackleton's cabin and *Quest* (horiz)	35	65
162	11p. Shackleton statue and memorial	40	80
MS163	139×114 mm. Nos. 159/62	1·25	6·00

52 Land Crab and Short-finned Mako

1972. Royal Silver Wedding. Multicoloured.

164	**52**	2p. violet	15	10
165	**52**	16p. red	35	30

1973. Royal Naval Crests (5th series). As T **46**. Multicoloured.

166	2p. H.M.S. *Birmingham*	2·00	1·50
167	4p. H.M.S. *Cardiff*	2·25	1·50
168	9p. H.M.S. *Penzance*	3·00	1·75
169	13p. H.M.S. *Rochester*	3·25	1·75
MS170	109×152 mm. Nos. 166/9	28·00	10·00

53 Green Turtle

1973. Turtles. Multicoloured.

171	4p. Type **53**	2·75	1·75
172	9p. Loggerhead turtle	3·00	2·00
173	12p. Hawksbill turtle	3·25	2·25

54 Sergeant, R.M. Light Infantry, 1900

1973. 50th Anniv of Departure of Royal Marines from Ascension. Multicoloured.

174	2p. Type **54**	1·50	1·50
175	6p. R.M. Private, 1816	2·25	1·50
176	12p. R.M. Light Infantry Officer, 1880	2·50	2·25
177	20p. R.M. Artillery Colour Sergeant, 1910	3·00	2·50

1973. Royal Wedding. As T **47** of Anguilla. Multicoloured. Background colours given.

178	2p. brown	15	10
179	18p. green	20	20

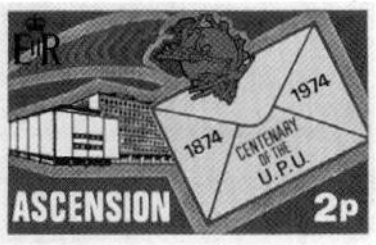

55 Letter and H.Q., Berne

1974. Centenary of Universal Postal Union. Multicoloured.

180	2p. Type **55**	20	30
181	9p. Hermes and U.P.U. monument	30	45

56 Churchill as a Boy, and Birthplace, Blenheim Palace

1974. Birth Centenary of Sir Winston Churchill. Multicoloured.

182	5p. Type **56**	20	35
183	25p. Churchill as statesman, and U.N. Building	30	75
MS184	93×87 mm. Nos. 182/3	1·00	2·50

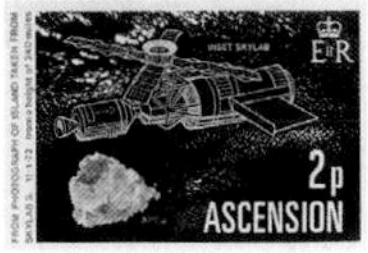

57 "Skylab 3" and Photograph of Ascension

1975. Space Satellites. Multicoloured.

185	2p. Type **57**	20	30
186	18p. "Skylab 4" Command module and photograph	30	40

58 U.S.A.F. Lockheed C-141A Starlifter

1975. Wideawake Airfield. Multicoloured.

187	2p. Type **58**	80	65
188	5p. R.A.F. Lockheed C-130 Hercules	80	85
189	9p. Vickers Super VC-10	80	1·40
190	24p. U.S.A.F. Lockheed C-5A Galaxy	1·25	2·50
MS191	144×99 mm. Nos. 187/90	14·00	22·00

1975. "Apollo-Soyuz" Space Link. Nos. 141 and 145/6 optd **APOLLO-SOYUZ LINK 1975**.

192	4½p. multicoloured	15	20
193	12½p. multicoloured	15	25
194	25p. multicoloured	25	40

60 Arrival of Royal Navy, 1815

1975. 160th Anniv of Occupation. Multicoloured.

195	2p. Type **60**	25	25
196	5p. Water supply, Dampiers Drip	25	40
197	9p. First landing, 1815	25	60
198	15p. The garden on Green Mountain	35	85

61 Yellow Canaries ("Canary")

1976. Multicoloured.. Multicoloured..

199	1p. Type **61**	40	1·50
200	2p. White tern ("Fairy Tern") (vert)	50	1·50
201	3p. Common waxbill ("Waxbill")	50	1·50
202	4p. White-capped noddy ("Black Noddy") (vert)	50	1·50
203	5p. Common noddy ("Brown Noddy")	70	1·50
204	6p. Common mynah	70	1·50
205	7p. Madeiran storm petrel (vert)	70	1·50
206	8p. Sooty tern	70	1·50
207	9p. Blue-faced booby ("White Booby") (vert)	70	1·50
208	10p. Red-footed booby	70	1·50
209	15p. Red-necked spurfowl ("Red-throated Francolin") (vert)	85	1·50
210	18p. Brown booby (vert)	85	1·50
211	25p. Red-billed tropic bird ("Red-billed Bo'sun Bird")	90	1·50
212	50p. White-tailed tropic bird ("Yellow-billed Tropic Bird")	1·00	1·75
213	£1 Ascension frigate-bird (vert)	1·00	2·25
214	£2 Boatswain Bird Island Sanctuary (50×38 mm)	2·00	5·00

63 G.B. Penny Red with Ascension Postmark

1976. Festival of Stamps, London.

215	**63**	5p. red, black and brown	15	15
216	-	9p. green, black and brown	15	20
217	-	25p. multicoloured	25	45

MS218 133×121 mm. No. 217 with St. Helena No. 318 and Tristan da Cunha No. 206 — 1·75 — 2·00

DESIGNS—VERT: 9p. ½d. stamp of 1922. HORIZ: 25p. *Southampton Castle* (liner).

64 U.S. Base, Ascension

1976. Bicentenary of American Revolution. Multicoloured.

219	8p. Type **64**	30	40
220	9p. NASA Station at Devils Ashpit	30	45
221	25p. "Viking" landing on Mars	50	80

65 Visit of Prince Philip, 1957

1977. Silver Jubilee. Multicoloured.

222	8p. Type **65**	15	15
223	12p. Coronation Coach leaving Buckingham Palace (horiz)	20	20
224	25p. Coronation Coach (horiz)	35	40

66 Tunnel carrying Water Pipe

1977. Water Supplies. Multicoloured.

225	3p. Type **66**	15	15
226	5p. Breakneck Valley wells	20	20
227	12p. Break tank (horiz)	30	35
228	25p. Water catchment (horiz)	45	65

67 Mars Bay Location, 1877

1977. Centenary of Visit of Professor Gill (astronomer). Multicoloured.

229	3p. Type **67**	15	20
230	8p. Instrument sites, Mars Bay	15	25
231	12p. Sir David and Lady Gill	20	40
232	25p. Maps of Ascension	60	70

68 Lion of England

1978. 25th Anniv of Coronation.

233	**68**	25p. yellow, brown and silver	35	50
234	-	25p. multicoloured	35	50
235	-	25p. yellow, brown and silver	35	50

DESIGNS: No 234, Queen Elizabeth II; No 235, Green turtle.

70 Flank of Sisters, Sisters' Red Hill and East Crater

1978. Ascension Island Volcanic Rock Formations. Multicoloured.

236	3p. Type **70**	15	20
237	5p. Holland's Crater (Hollow Tooth)	20	30
238	12p. Street Crater, Lower Valley Crater and Bear's Back	25	40
239	15p. Butt Crater, Weather Post and Green Mountain	30	45
240	25p. Flank of Sisters, Thistle Hill and Two Boats Village	35	50
MS241	185×100 mm. Nos. 236/40, each × 2	2·00	5·00

Nos. 236/40 were issued as a *se-tenant* strip within the sheet, forming a composite design.

71 *The Resolution* (H. Roberts)

1979. Bicentenary of Captain Cook's Voyages, 1768–79. Multicoloured.

242	3p. Type **71**	30	25
243	8p. Cook's chronometer	25	40
244	12p. Green turtle	30	50
245	25p. Flaxman/Wedgwood medallion of Cook	30	70

72 St. Mary's Church, Georgetown

1979. Ascension Day. Multicoloured.

246	8p. Type **72**	10	20
247	12p. Map of Ascension	15	30
248	50p. *The Ascension* (painting by Rembrandt)	30	90

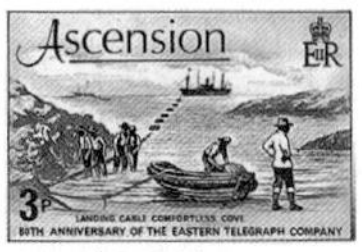

73 Landing Cable, Comfortless Cove

1979. 80th Anniv of Eastern Telegraph Company's Arrival on Ascension.

249	**73**	3p. black and red	10	10
250	-	8p. black and green	15	15
251	-	12p. black and yellow	20	20
252	-	15p. black and violet	20	25
253	-	25p. black and brown	25	35

DESIGNS—HORIZ: 8p. C.S. *Anglia*; 15p. C.S. *Seine*; 25p. Cable and Wireless earth station. VERT: 12p. Map of Atlantic cable network.

74 1938 6d. Stamp

1979. Death Centenary of Sir Rowland Hill.

254	**74**	3p. black and blue	10	10
255	-	8p. black, green and pale green	15	20
256	-	12p. black, blue and pale blue	15	25
257	-	50p. black and red	40	90

DESIGNS—HORIZ: 8p. 1956 5s. definitive. VERT: 12p. 1924 3s. stamp; 50p. Sir Rowland Hill.

75 *Anogramma ascensionis*

1980. Ferns and Grasses. Multicoloured.

258	3p. Type **75**	10	15
259	6p. *Xiphopteris ascensionense*	10	20
260	8p. *Sporobolus caespitosus*	10	20
261	12p. *Sporobolus durus* (vert)	15	30
262	18p. *Dryopteris ascensionis* (vert)	15	40
263	24p. *Marattia purpurascens* (vert)	20	55

76 17th-Century Bottle Post

1980. "London 1980" International Stamp Exhibition. Multicoloured.

264	8p. Type **76**	15	20

265	12p. 19th-century chance calling ship	20	25
266	15p. *Garth Castle* (regular mail service from 1863)	20	30
267	50p. *St. Helena* (mail services, 1980)	60	90
MS268	102×154 mm. Nos. 264/7	1·00	2·40

77 H.M. Queen Elizabeth the Queen Mother

1980. 80th Birthday of The Queen Mother.

269	**77**	15p. multicoloured	40	40

78 Lubbock's Yellowtail

1980. Fish. Multicoloured.

270	3p. Type **78**	20	25
271	10p. Resplendent angelfish	20	25
272	25p. Bicoloured butterflyfish	30	55
273	40p. Marmalade razorfish	40	75

79 H.M.S. *Tortoise*

1980. 150th Anniv of Royal Geographical Society. Multicoloured.

274	10p. Type **79**	20	40
275	15p. *Wideawake Fair*	25	45
276	60p. Mid-Atlantic Ridge (38×48 mm)	65	1·25

80 Green Mountain Farm, 1881

1981. Green Mountain Farm. Multicoloured.

277	12p. Type **80**	15	35
278	15p. Two Boats, 1881	15	40
279	20p. Green Mountain and Two Boats, 1981	20	50
280	30p. Green Mountain Farm, 1981	30	70

81 Cable and Wireless Earth Station

1981. "Space Shuttle" Mission and Opening of 2nd Earth Station.

281	**81**	15p. black, blue and pale blue	30	35

82 Poinsettia

83 Solanum

1981. Flowers. Multicoloured.

282A	1p. Type **82**	70	1·25
283B	2p. Clustered wax flower	50	1·25
284B	3p. Kolanchoe (vert)	50	1·25
285A	4p. Yellow pops	80	1·25
286A	5p. Camels foot creeper	80	1·25
287A	8p. White oleander	80	1·25
288B	10p. Ascension lily (vert)	45	75
289A	12p. Coral plant (vert)	1·50	1·10
290B	15p. Yellow allamanda	50	75
291B	20p. Ascension euphorbia	1·00	75
292A	30p. Flame of the forest (vert)	1·25	1·25
293A	40p. Bougainvillea "King Leopold"	1·25	3·00
294A	50p. Type **83**	1·75	3·25
295B	£1 Ladies petticoat	2·00	3·00
296A	£2 Red hibiscus	3·50	6·00

Nos. 294/6 are as Type **83**.

84 Map by Maxwell, 1793

1981. Early Maps of Ascension.

297	**84**	10p. black, gold and blue	20	35
298	-	12p. black, gold and green	20	35
299	-	15p. black, gold and stone	20	35
300	-	40p. black, gold and yellow	50	70
MS301		79×64 mm. 5p. × 4 multi-coloured	60	75

DESIGNS: 12p. Maxwell, 1793 (different); 15p. Ekeberg and Chapman, 1811; 40p. Campbell, 1819; miniature sheet, Linschoten, 1599.

Stamps from **MS**301 form a composite design.

85 Wedding Bouquet from Ascension

1981. Royal Wedding. Multicoloured.

302	10p. Type **85**	15	15
303	15p. Prince Charles in Fleet Air Arm flying kit	30	30
304	50p. Prince Charles and Lady Diana Spencer	65	90

87 "Interest"

1981. 25th Anniv of Duke of Edinburgh Award Scheme. Multicoloured.

305	5p. Type **87**	15	15
306	10p. "Physical activities"	15	15
307	15p. "Service"	20	20
308	40p. Duke of Edinburgh	45	45

88 Scout crossing Rope Bridge

1982. 75th Anniv of Boy Scout Movement.

309	**88**	10p. black, blue and light blue	15	35
310	-	15p. black, brown and yellow	15	50
311	-	25p. black, mve & lt mve	20	60
312	-	40p. black, red and orange	30	85
MS313		121×121 mm. 10, 15, 25, 40p. As Nos. 309/12 (each diamond 40×40 mm)	1·00	2·50

DESIGNS: 15p. 1st Ascension Scout Group flag; 25p. Scouts learning to use radio; 40p. Lord Baden-Powell.

89 Charles Darwin

1982. 150th Anniv of Charles Darwin's Voyage. Multicoloured.

314	10p. Type **89**	20	40
315	12p. Darwin's pistols	20	50
316	15p. Rock crab	25	55
317	40p. H.M.S. *Beagle*	60	95

90 Fairey Swordfish Torpedo Bomber

1982. 40th Anniv of Wideawake Airfield. Multicoloured.

318	5p. Type **90**	75	35
319	10p. North American B-25C Mitchell	1·00	40
320	15p. Boeing EC-135N Aria	1·25	55
321	50p. Lockheed C-130 Hercules	1·75	1·10

91 Ascension Coat of Arms

1982. 21st Birthday of Princess of Wales. Multicoloured.

322	12p. Type **91**	20	20
323	15p. Lady Diana Spencer in Music Room, Buckingham Palace	20	20
324	25p. Bride and Earl Spencer leaving Clarence House	30	30
325	50p. Formal portrait	65	65

1982. Commonwealth Games, Brisbane. Nos. 290/1 optd **1st PARTICIPATION COMMON-WEALTH GAMES 1982**.

326	15p. Yellow allamanda	30	40
327	20p. Ascension euphorbia	40	45

94 Bush House, London

1982. Christmas. 50th Anniv of B.B.C. External Broadcasting. Multicoloured.

328	5p. Type **94**	15	20
329	10p. Atlantic relay station	20	30
330	25p. Lord Reith, first Director-General	30	60
331	40p. King George V making his first Christmas broadcast, 1932	45	75

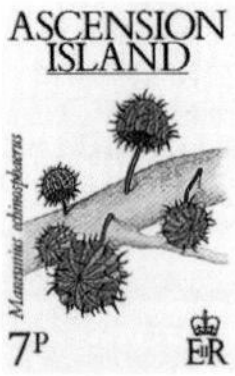

95 *Marasmius thwaitesii* (Marasmius echinosphaerus)

1983. Fungi. Multicoloured.

332	7p. Type **95**	25	30
333	12p. *Chlorophyllum molybdites*	35	45
334	15p. *Leucocoprinus cepaestripes*	40	50
335	20p. *Lycoperdon marginatum*	45	65
336	50p. *Marasmiellus distantifolius*	55	1·25

96 Aerial View of Georgetown

1983. Island Views (1st series). Multicoloured.

337	12p. Type **96**	15	25
338	15p. Green Mountain farm	15	25
339	20p. Boatswain Bird Island	20	40
340	60p. Telemetry Hill by night	40	80

See also Nos. 367/70.

97 Westland Wessex 5 Helicopter of No. 845 Naval Air Squadron

1983. Bicentenary of Manned Flight. British Military Aircraft. Multicoloured.

341	12p. Type **97**	40	65
342	15p. Avro Vulcan B.2 of No. 44 Squadron	40	75
343	20p. Hawker Siddeley Nimrod M.R.2P of No. 20 Squadron	40	85
344	60p. Handey Page Victor K2 of No. 55 Squadron	60	2·00

98 Iguanid

1983. Introduced Species. Multicoloured.

345	12p. Type **98**	25	30
346	15p. Common rabbit	30	35
347	20p. Cat	40	45
348	60p. Donkey	75	1·40

99 Speckled Tellin (*Tellina listeri*)

1983. Sea Shells. Multicoloured.

349	7p. Type **99**	15	20
350	12p. Lion's paw scallop	15	30
351	15p. Lurid cowrie	20	35
352	20p. Ascension nerite	20	45
353	50p. Miniature melo	40	1·10

100 1922 1½d. Stamp

1984. 150th Anniv of St. Helena as a British Colony. Multicoloured.

354	12p. Type **100**	20	45
355	15p. 1922 2d. stamp	20	50
356	20p. 1922 8d. stamp	20	55
357	60p. 1922 1s. stamp	50	1·40

101 Prince Andrew

1984. Visit of Prince Andrew. Sheet 124×90 mm.

MS358	12p. Type **101**; 70p. Prince Andrew in naval uniform	1·00	1·60

102 Naval Semaphore

1984. 250th Anniv of *Lloyd's List* (newspaper). Multicoloured.

359	12p. Type **102**	50	30
360	15p. *Southampton Castle* (liner)	50	35
361	20p. Pier head	55	45
362	70p. *Dane* (screw steamer)	1·25	1·50

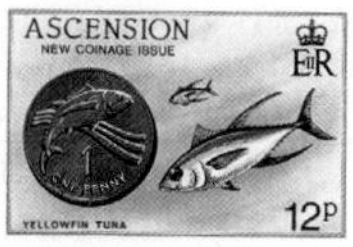

103 Penny Coin and Yellow-finned Tuna

1984. New Coinage. Multicoloured.

363	12p. Type **103**	35	35
364	15p. Twopenny coin and donkey	40	40
365	20p. Fifty pence coin and green turtle	45	50
366	70p. Pound coin and sooty tern	80	1·75

1984. Island Views (2nd series). As T **96**. Multicoloured.

367	12p. The Devil's Riding-school	20	30
368	15p. St. Mary's Church	25	35
369	20p. Two Boats Village	25	45
370	70p. Ascension from the sea	80	1·50

104 Bermuda Cypress

1985. Trees. Multicoloured.

371	7p. Type **104**	20	20
372	12p. Norfolk Island pine	25	30
373	15p. Screwpine	25	35
374	20p. Eucalyptus	25	45
375	65p. Spore tree	70	1·40

105 The Queen Mother with Prince Andrew at Silver Jubilee Service

1985. Life and Times of Queen Elizabeth the Queen Mother. Multicoloured.

376	12p. With the Duke of York at Balmoral, 1924	25	35
377	15p. Type **105**	25	40
378	20p. The Queen Mother at Ascot	30	55
379	70p. With Prince Henry at his christening (from photo by Lord Snowdon)	80	1·75

MS380 91×73 mm. 75p. Visiting the *Queen Elizabeth 2* at Southampton, 1968 — 1·10 — 1·60

106 32 Pdr. Smooth Bore Muzzle-loader, *c* 1820, and Royal Marine Artillery Hat Plate, *c* 1816

1985. Guns on Ascension Island. Multicoloured.

381	12p. Type **106**	40	90
382	15p. 7 inch rifled muzzle-loader, c. 1866, and Royal Cypher on barrel	40	1·00
383	20p. 7 pdr rifled muzzle-loader, c. 1877, and Royal Artillery Badge	40	1·25
384	70p. 5.5 inch gun, 1941, and crest from H.M.S. *Hood*	80	3·00

107 Guide Flag

1985. 75th Anniv of Girl Guide Movement and International Youth Year. Multicoloured.

385	12p. Type **107**	30	70
386	15p. Practising first aid	30	80
387	20p. Camping	30	90
388	70p. Lady Baden-Powell	80	2·50

108 *Clerodendrum fragrans*

1985. Wild Flowers. Multicoloured.

389	12p. Type **108**	30	75
390	15p. Shell ginger	30	90
391	20p. Cape daisy	35	90
392	70p. Ginger lily	70	2·50

109 Newton's Reflector Telescope

1986. Appearance of Halley's Comet. Multicoloured.

393	12p. Type **109**	40	1·10
394	15p. Edmond Halley and Old Greenwich Observatory	40	1·25
395	20p. Short's Gregorian telescope and comet, 1759	40	1·25
396	70p. Ascension satellite tracking station and ICE spacecraft	1·10	3·50

110 Princess Elizabeth in 1926

1986. 60th Birthday of Queen Elizabeth II. Multicoloured.

397	7p. Type **110**	15	25
398	15p. Queen making Christmas broadcast, 1952	15	40
399	20p. At Garter ceremony, Windsor Castle, 1983	20	50
400	35p. In Auckland, New Zealand, 1981	30	80
401	£1 At Crown Agents' Head Office, London, 1983	75	2·25

111 1975 Space Satellites 2p. Stamp

1986. "Ameripex '86" International Stamp Exhibition, Chicago. Designs showing previous Ascension stamps. Multicoloured.

402	12p. Type **111**	25	60
403	15p. 1980 "London 1980" International Stamp Exhibition 50p.	20	70
404	20p. 1976 Bicentenary of American Revolution 8p.	25	90
405	70p. 1982 40th anniv of Wideawake Airfield 10p.	70	2·00

MS406 60×75 mm. 75p. Statue of Liberty — 1·50 — 2·75

112 Prince Andrew and Miss Sarah Ferguson

1986. Royal Wedding. Multicoloured.

407	15p. Type **112**	25	50
408	35p. Prince Andrew aboard H.M.S. *Brazen*	50	1·00

113 H.M.S. *Ganymede* (*c* 1811)

1986. Ships of the Royal Navy. Multicoloured.

409	1p. Type **113**	55	1·50
410	2p. H.M.S. *Kangaroo* (c.1811)	60	1·50
411	4p. H.M.S. *Trinculo* (c.1811)	60	1·50
412	5p. H.M.S. *Daring* (c.1811)	60	1·50
413	9p. H.M.S. *Thais* (c.1811)	70	1·50
414	10p. H.M.S. *Pheasant* (1819)	70	1·50
415	15p. H.M.S. *Myrmidon* (1819)	80	1·75
416	18p. H.M.S. *Atholl* (1825)	90	1·75
417	20p. H.M.S. *Medina* (1830)	90	1·75
418	25p. H.M.S. *Saracen* (1840)	1·00	2·00
419	30p. H.M.S. *Hydra* (c.1845)	1·00	2·00
420	50p. H.M.S. *Sealark* (1849)	1·00	2·50
421	70p. H.M.S. *Rattlesnake* (1868)	1·00	3·00
422	£1 H.M.S. *Penelope* (1889)	1·25	3·75
423	£2 H.M.S. *Monarch* (1897)	2·50	6·50

114 Cape Gooseberry

1987. Edible Bush Fruits. Multicoloured.

424	12p. Type **114**	65	90
425	15p. Prickly pear	65	1·00
426	20p. Guava	70	1·10
427	70p. Loquat	1·10	2·75

115 Ignition of Rocket Motors

1987. 25th Anniv of First American Manned Earth Orbit. Multicoloured.

428	15p. Type **115**	55	75
429	18p. Lift-off	60	80
430	25p. Re-entry	75	95
431	£1 Splashdown	2·50	3·25

MS432 92×78 mm. 70p. "Friendship 7" capsule — 1·75 — 2·00

116 Captains in Full Dress raising Red Ensign

1987. 19th-century Uniforms (1st series). Royal Navy, 1815–20. Multicoloured.

433	25p. Type **116**	50	60
434	25p. Surgeon and seamen	50	60
435	25p. Seaman with water-carrying donkey	50	60
436	25p. Midshipman and gun	50	60
437	25p. Commander in undress uniform surveying	50	60

See also Nos. 478/82.

117 *Cynthia cardui*

1987. Insects (1st series). Multicoloured.

438	15p. Type **117**	55	65
439	18p. *Danaus chrysippus*	60	75
440	25p. *Hypolimnas misippus*	75	85
441	£1 *Lampides boeticus*	1·50	2·50

See also Nos. 452/5 and 483/6.

118 Male Ascension Frigate Birds

1987. Sea Birds (1st series). Multicoloured.

442	25p. Type **118**	1·60	2·00
443	25p. Juvenile Ascension frigate bird, brown booby and blue-faced boobies	1·60	2·00
444	25p. Male Ascension frigate bird and blue-faced boobies	1·60	2·00
445	25p. Female Ascension frigate bird	1·60	2·00
446	25p. Adult male feeding juvenile Ascension frigate bird	1·60	2·00

Nos. 442/6 were printed together, *se-tenant*, forming a composite design.

See also Nos. 469/73.

1987. Royal Ruby Wedding. Nos. 397/401 optd **40TH WEDDING ANNIVERSARY**.

447	7p. Type **110**	15	15
448	15p. Queen making Christmas broadcast, 1952	20	20
449	20p. At Garter ceremony, Windsor Castle, 1983	25	25
450	35p. In Auckland, New Zealand, 1981	40	45
451	£1 At Crown Agents' Head Office, London, 1983	1·00	1·10

1988. Insects (2nd series). As T **117**. Multicoloured.

452	15p. *Gryllus bimaculatus* (field cricket)	30	30
453	18p. *Ruspolia differeus* (bush cricket)	35	35
454	25p. *Chilomenus lunata* (ladybird)	40	40
455	£1 *Diachrysia orichalcea* (moth)	1·50	1·50

120 Bate's Memorial, St. Mary's Church

1988. 150th Death Anniv of Captain William Bate (garrison commander, 1828–38). Multicoloured.

456	9p. Type **120**	25	25
457	15p. Commodore's Cottage	30	30
458	18p. North East Cottage	35	35
459	25p. Map of Ascension	45	45
460	70p. Captain Bate and marines	1·00	1·00

121 H.M.S. *Resolution* (ship of the line), 1667

1988. Bicentenary of Australian Settlement. Ships of the Royal Navy. Multicoloured.

461	9p. Type **121**	1·25	45
462	18p. H.M.S. *Resolution* (Captain Cook), 1772	1·75	70
463	25p. H.M.S. *Resolution* (battleship), 1892	1·75	85
464	65p. H.M.S. *Resolution* (battleship), 1916	2·50	1·50

1988. "Sydpex '88" National Stamp Exhibition, Sydney. Nos. 461/4 optd **SYDPEX 88 30.7.88 - 7.8.88**.

465	9p. Type **121**	50	40
466	18p. H.M.S. *Resolution* (Captain Cook), 1772	75	60
467	25p. H.M.S. *Resolution* (battleship), 1892	85	70
468	65p. H.M.S. *Resolution* (battleship), 1916	1·60	1·40

1988. Sea Birds (2nd series). Sooty Tern. As T **118**. Multicoloured.

469	25p. Pair displaying	1·60	1·25
470	25p. Turning egg	1·60	1·25
471	25p. Incubating egg	1·60	1·25
472	25p. Feeding chick	1·60	1·25
473	25p. Immature sooty tern	1·60	1·25

Nos. 469/73 were printed together, *se-tenant*, forming a composite design of a nesting colony.

123 Lloyd's Coffee House, London, 1688

1988. 300th Anniv of Lloyd's of London. Multicoloured.

474	8p. Type **123**	25	25
475	18p. *Alert IV* (cable ship) (horiz)	65	65

476	25p. Satellite recovery in space (horiz)	80	80
477	65p. *Good Hope Castle* (cargo liner) on fire off Ascension, 1973	1·75	1·75

1988. 19th-century Uniforms (2nd series). Royal Marines 1821–34. As T **116**. Multicoloured.

478	25p. Marines landing on Ascension, 1821	1·10	1·60
479	25p. Officer and Marine at semaphore station, 1829	1·10	1·60
480	25p. Sergeant and Marine at Octagonal Tank, 1831	1·10	1·60
481	25p. Officers at water pipe tunnel, 1833	1·10	1·60
482	25p. Officer supervising construction of barracks, 1834	1·10	1·60

1989. Insects (3rd series). As T **117**. Multicoloured.

483	15p. *Trichoptilus wahlbergi* (moth)	75	50
484	18p. *Lucilia sericata* (fly)	80	55
485	25p. *Alceis ornatus* (weevil)	1·10	70
486	£1 *Polistes fuscatus* (wasp)	3·00	2·40

124 Two Land Crabs

1989. Ascension Land Crabs. Multicoloured.

487	15p. Type **124**	40	45
488	18p. Crab with claws raised	45	50
489	25p. Crab on rock	60	70
490	£1 Crab in surf	2·00	2·50
MS491	98×101 mm. Nos. 487/90	3·00	3·75

125 1949 75th Anniversary of U.P.U. 1s. Stamp

1989. "Philexfrance '89" International Stamp Exhibition, Paris, and "World Stamp Expo '89", Washington (1st issue). Sheet 104×86 mm.

MS492	**125** 75p. multicoloured	3·00	3·75

See also Nos. 498/503.

126 "Apollo 7" Tracking Station, Ascension

1989. 20th Anniv of First Manned Landing on Moon. Multicoloured.

493	15p. Type **126**	65	45
494	18p. Launch of "Apollo 7" (30×30 mm)	70	50
495	25p. "Apollo 7" emblem (30×30 mm)	90	70
496	70p. "Apollo 7" jettisoning expended Saturn rocket	1·75	1·75
MS497	101×83 mm. £1 Diagram of "Apollo 11" mission	2·00	2·10

127 *Queen Elizabeth 2* (liner) and U.S.S. *John F. Kennedy* (aircraft carrier) in New York Harbour

1989. "Philexfrance 89" International Stamp Exhibition, Paris, and "World Stamp Expo '89", Washington (1st issue). Designs showing Statue of Liberty and Centenary celebrations. Multicoloured.

498	15p. Type **127**	50	50
499	15p. Cleaning statue	50	50
500	15p. Statue of Liberty	50	50
501	15p. Crown of statue	50	50
502	15p. Warships and New York skyline	50	50
503	15p. *Jean de Vienne* (French destroyer) and skyscrapers	50	50

128 Devil's Ashpit Tracking Station

1989. Closure of Devil's Ashpit Tracking Station, Ascension. Multicoloured.

504	18p. Type **128**	80	50
505	25p. Launch of shuttle "Atlantis"	80	55

129 Bubonian Conch (*Strombus latus*)

1989. Sea Shells. Multicoloured.

506	8p. Type **129**	40	30
507	18p. Giant tun	70	50
508	25p. Doris loup	90	65
509	£1 Atlantic trumpet triton	2·75	2·50

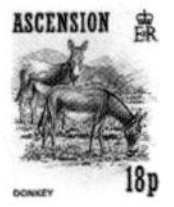

130 Donkeys

1989. Ascension Wildlife. Multicoloured.

510	18p. Type **130**	1·00	1·25
511	25p. Green turtle	1·00	1·25

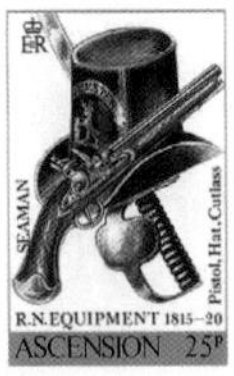

131 Seaman's Pistol, Hat and Cutlass

1990. Royal Navy Equipment, 1815–20. Multicoloured.

512	25p. Type **131**	70	70
513	25p. Midshipman's belt plate, button, sword and hat	70	70
514	25p. Surgeon's hat, sword and instrument chest	70	70
515	25p. Captain's hat, telescope and sword	70	70
516	25p. Admiral's epaulette, megaphone, hat and pocket	70	70

See also Nos. 541/5.

132 Pair of Ascension Frigate Birds with Young

1990. Endangered Species. Ascension Frigate Bird. Multicoloured.

517	9p. Type **132**	1·50	1·00
518	10p. Fledgeling	1·50	1·00
519	11p. Adult male in flight	1·50	1·00
520	15p. Female and immature birds in flight	1·75	1·25

133 Penny Black and Twopence Blue

1990. "Stamp World London 90" International Stamp Exhibition. Multicoloured.

521	9p. Type **133**	50	40
522	18p. Ascension postmarks used on G.B. stamps	70	60
523	25p. Unloading mail at Wideawake Airfield	95	85
524	£1 Mail van and Main Post Office	2·25	2·75

134 *Queen Elizabeth, 1940* (Sir Gerald Kelly)

1990. 90th Birthday of Queen Elizabeth the Queen Mother.

525	**134**	25p. multicoloured	75	75
526	-	£1 black and lilac	2·25	2·25

DESIGN—29×37 mm: £1 King George VI and Queen Elizabeth with Bren-gun carrier.

136 *Madonna and Child* (sculpture, Dino Felici)

1990. Christmas. Works of Art. Multicoloured.

527	8p. Type **136**	70	70
528	18p. *Madonna and Child* (anon)	1·25	1·25
529	25p. *Madonna and Child with St. John* (Johann Gebhard)	1·75	1·75
530	65p. *Madonna and Child* (Giacomo Gritti)	3·00	4·00

137 *Garth Castle* (mail steamer), 1910

1990. Maiden Voyage of *St. Helena II*. Multicoloured.

531	9p. Type **137**	90	90
532	18p. *St. Helena I* during Falkland Islands campaign, 1982	1·25	1·25
533	25p. Launch of *St. Helena II*	1·75	1·75
534	70p. Duke of York launching *St. Helena II*	3·00	4·25
MS535	100×100 mm. £1 *St. Helena II* and outline map of Ascension	3·50	5·00

1991. 175th Anniv of Occupation. Nos. 418, 420 and 422 optd **BRITISH FOR 175 YEARS**.

536	25p. H.M.S. *Saracen* (1840)	2·00	2·50
537	50p. H.M.S. *Sealark* (1849)	2·50	3·50
538	£1 H.M.S. *Penelope* (1889)	3·75	5·00

139 Queen Elizabeth II at Trooping the Colour

1991. 65th Birthday of Queen Elizabeth II and 70th Birthday of Prince Philip. Multicoloured.

539	25p. Type **139**	1·25	1·60
540	25p. Prince Philip in naval uniform	1·25	1·60

1991. Royal Marines Equipment, 1821–1844. As T **131**. Multicoloured.

541	25p. Officer's shako, epaulettes, belt plate and button	1·10	1·60
542	25p. Officer's cap, sword, epaulettes and belt plate	1·10	1·60
543	25p. Drum major's shako and staff	1·10	1·60
544	25p. Sergeant's shako, chevrons, belt plate and canteen	1·10	1·60
545	25p. Drummer's shako and side-drum	1·10	1·60

140 B.B.C. World Service Relay Station

1991. 25th Anniv of B.B.C. Atlantic Relay Station. Multicoloured.

546	15p. Type **140**	90	1·10
547	18p. Transmitters at English Bay	1·00	1·25
548	25p. Satellite receiving station (vert)	1·25	1·40
549	70p. Antenna support tower (vert)	2·50	4·00

141 St. Mary's Church

1991. Christmas. Ascension Churches. Multicoloured.

550	8p. Type **141**	55	55
551	18p. Interior of St. Mary's Church	1·00	1·00
552	25p. Our Lady of Ascension Grotto	1·25	1·25
553	65p. Interior of Our Lady of Ascension Grotto	2·75	5·00

142 Black Durgon ("Blackfish")

1991. Fish. Multicoloured.

554	1p. Type **142**	1·25	60
555	2p. Sergeant major ("Five finger")	1·25	60
556	4p. Resplendent angelfish	1·50	70
557	5p. Derbio ("Silver fish")	1·50	70
558	9p. Spotted scorpionfish ("Gurnard")	1·75	80
559	10p. St. Helena parrotfish ("Blue dad")	1·75	80
560	15p. St. Helena butterflyfish ("Cunning fish")	2·25	1·00
561	18p. Rock hind ("Grouper")	2·25	1·00
562	20p. Spotted moray	2·25	1·25
563	25p. Squirrelfish ("Hardback soldierfish")	2·25	1·25
564	30p. Blue marlin	2·25	1·40
565	50p. Wahoo	3·00	2·00
566	70p. Yellow-finned tuna	3·00	2·75
567	£1 Blue shark	3·25	3·50
568	£2.50 Bottlenose dolphin	7·00	7·00

143 Holland's Crater

1992. 40th Anniv of Queen Elizabeth II's Accession. Multicoloured.

569	9p. Type **143**	30	30
570	15p. Green Mountain	50	50
571	18p. Boatswain Bird Island	60	60
572	25p. Three portraits of Queen Elizabeth	80	80
573	70p. Queen Elizabeth II	2·00	2·00

The portraits shown on the 25p. are repeated from the three lower values of the set.

144 Compass Rose and *Eye of the Wind* (cadet brig)

1992. 500th Anniv of Discovery of America by Columbus and Re-enactment Voyages. Mult.

574	9p. Type **144**	1·25	80
575	18p. Map of re-enactment voyages and *Soren Larsen* (cadet brigantine)	1·75	1·25
576	25p. *Santa Maria*, *Pinta* and *Nina*	2·25	1·50
577	70p. Columbus and *Santa Maria*	3·75	3·50

145 Control Tower, Wideawake Airfield

1992. 50th Anniv of Wideawake Airfield. Multicoloured.

578	15p. Type **145**	65	65
579	18p. Nose hangar	70	70
580	25p. Site preparation by U.S. Army engineers	90	90
581	70p. Laying fuel pipeline	2·25	2·25

146 Hawker Siddeley Nimrod

1992. Tenth Anniv of Liberation of Falkland Islands. Aircraft. Multicoloured.

582	15p. Type **146**	1·50	1·75
583	18p. Vickers VC-10 landing at Ascension	1·50	1·75
584	25p. Westland Wessex HU Mk 5 helicopter lifting supplies	2·00	1·75
585	65p. Avro Vulcan B.2 over Ascension	3·25	4·75
MS586	116×116 mm. 15p.+3p. Type **146**; 18p.+4p. As No. 583; 25p.+5p. As No. 584; 65p.+13p. As No. 585	4·00	6·00

The premiums on No. **MS**586 were for the S.S.A.F.A.

147 *Christmas in Great Britain and Ascension*

1992. Christmas. Children's Paintings. Multicoloured.

587	8p. Type **147**	80	1·00
588	18p. *Santa Claus riding turtle*	1·25	1·50
589	25p. *Nativity*	1·50	1·75
590	65p. *Nativity with rabbit*	2·75	5·00

148 Male Canary Singing

1993. Yellow Canary. Multicoloured.

591	15p. Type **148**	75	80
592	18p. Adult male and female	85	90
593	25p. Young birds calling for food	95	1·10
594	70p. Adults and young birds on the wing	2·50	4·00

149 Sopwith Snipe

1993. 75th Anniv of Royal Air Force. Multicoloured.

595	20p. Type **149**	2·00	1·75
596	25p. Supermarine Southampton	2·00	1·75
597	30p. Avro Type 652 Anson	2·00	1·90
598	70p. Vickers-Armstrong Wellington	3·25	4·50
MS599	110×77 mm. 25p. Westland Lysander; 25p. Armstrong-Whitworth Meteor (*Gloster Meteor*); 25p. de Havilland D.H.106 Comet; 25p. Hawker Siddeley H.S.801 Nimrod	3·00	4·00

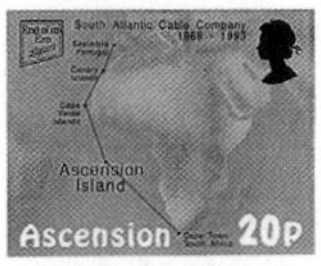

150 Map of South Atlantic Cable

1993. 25th Anniv of South Atlantic Cable Company. Multicoloured.

600	20p. Type **150**	80	90
601	25p. *Sir Eric Sharpe* laying cable	90	1·00
602	30p. Map of Ascension	1·00	1·25
603	70p. *Sir Eric Sharpe* (cable ship) off Ascension	2·25	2·75

151 Lanatana Camara

1993. Local Flowers. Multicoloured.

604	20p. Type **151**	1·50	1·00
605	25p. Moonflower	1·60	1·10
606	30p. Hibiscus	1·60	1·25
607	70p. Frangipani	3·00	3·25

152 Posting Christmas Card to Ascension

1993. Christmas. Multicoloured.

608	12p. Type **152**	45	45
609	20p. Loading mail onto R.A.F. Lockheed TriStar at Brize Norton	95	70
610	25p. TriStar over South Atlantic	1·25	90
611	30p. Unloading mail at Wideawake Airfield	1·40	1·10
612	65p. Receiving card and Georgetown Post Office	1·60	3·25
MS613	161×76 mm. Nos. 608/12	10·00	10·00

153 Ichthyosaurus

1994. Prehistoric Aquatic Reptiles. Multicoloured.

614	12p. Type **153**	70	1·10
615	20p. Metriorhynchus	85	1·25
616	25p. Mosasaurus	90	1·40
617	30p. Elasmosaurus	90	1·50
618	65p. Plesiosaurus	1·75	2·75

1994. "Hong Kong '94" International Stamp Exhibition. Nos. 614/18 optd **HONG KONG '94** and emblem.

619	12p. Type **153**	1·00	1·50
620	20p. Metriorhynchus	1·25	1·60
621	25p. Mosasaurus	1·25	1·90
622	30p. Elasmosaurus	1·40	2·00
623	65p. Plesiosaurus	2·50	4·00

155 Young Green Turtles heading towards Sea

1994. Green Turtles. Multicoloured.

624	20p. Type **155**	2·25	2·25
625	25p. Turtle digging nest	2·25	2·25
626	30p. Turtle leaving sea	2·25	2·25
627	65p. Turtle swimming	3·75	6·00
MS628	116×90 mm. 30p. Turtle leaving sea (different); 30p. Turtle digging nest (different); 30p. Young turtles heading towards sea (different); 30p. Young turtle leaving nest	12·00	12·00

156 *Yorkshireman* (tug)

1994. Civilian Ships used in Liberation of Falkland Islands, 1982. Multicoloured.

629	20p. Type **156**	2·75	2·25
630	25p. *St. Helena I* (minesweeper support ship)	2·75	2·25
631	30p. *British Esk* (tanker)	2·75	2·50
632	65p. *Uganda* (hospital ship)	5·00	6·00

157 Sooty Tern Chick

1994. Sooty Tern. Multicoloured.

633	20p. Type **157**	90	1·50
634	25p. Juvenile bird	95	1·50
635	30p. Brooding adult	1·10	1·60
636	65p. Adult male performing courting display	1·75	2·75
MS637	77×58 mm. £1 Flock of sooty terns	3·50	5·50

158 Donkey Mare with Foal

1994. Christmas. Donkeys. Multicoloured.

638	12p. Type **158**	1·60	1·40
639	20p. Juvenile	1·90	1·75
640	25p. Foal	1·90	1·75
641	30p. Adult and cattle egrets	1·90	1·90
642	65p. Adult	3·75	5·00

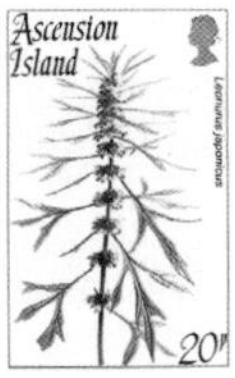

159 *Leonurus japonicus*

1995. Flowers. Multicoloured.

643	20p. Type **159**	2·75	2·25
644	25p. *Catharanthus roseus* (horiz)	2·75	2·25
645	30p. *Mirabilis jalapa*	3·00	2·50
646	65p. *Asclepias curassavica* (horiz)	3·75	5·50

160 Two Boats and Green Mountain

1995. Late 19th-century Scenes. Each in cinnamon and brown.

647	12p. Type **160**	50	80
648	20p. Island Stewards' Store	70	90
649	25p. Navy headquarters and barracks	90	1·10
650	30p. Police office	1·75	1·75
651	65p. Pierhead	2·00	3·50

161 5.5-inch Coastal Battery

1995. 50th Anniv of End of Second World War. Multicoloured.

652	20p. Type **161**	1·75	2·00
653	25p. Fairey Swordfish aircraft	2·00	2·00
654	30p. H.M.S. *Dorsetshire* (cruiser)	2·25	3·25
655	65p. H.M.S. *Devonshire* (cruiser)	3·75	4·50
MS656	75×85 mm. £1 Reverse of 1939–45 War Medal (vert)	2·50	3·25

162 Male and Female *Lampides boeticus*

1995. Butterflies. Multicoloured.

657	20p. Type **162**	1·50	1·50
658	25p. *Vanessa cardui*	1·75	1·75
659	30p. Male *Hypolimnas misippus*	1·75	1·75
660	65p. *Danaus chrysippus*	2·75	3·50
MS661	114×85 mm. £1 *Vanessa atalanta*	5·50	6·00

No. **MS**661 includes the "Singapore '95" International Stamp Exhibition logo on the sheet margin.

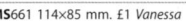

163 *Santa Claus on Boat* (Phillip Stephens)

1995. Christmas. Children's Drawings. Multicoloured.

662	12p. Type **163**	1·75	1·25
663	20p. *Santa sitting on Wall* (Kelly Lemon)	2·00	1·75
664	25p. *Santa in Chimney* (Mario Anthony)	2·00	1·75
665	30p. *Santa riding Dolphin* (Verena Benjamin)	2·00	1·75
666	65p. *Santa in Sleigh over Ascension* (Tom Butler)	3·50	5·00

164 *Cypraea lurida oceanica*

1996. Molluscs. Multicoloured.

667	12p. Type **164**	2·75	3·00
668	25p. *Cypraea spurca sanctaehelenae*	3·00	3·25
669	30p. *Harpa doris*	3·00	3·25
670	65p. *Umbraculum umbraculum*	3·75	4·00

Nos. 667/70 were printed together, *se-tenant*, forming a composite design.

165 Queen Elizabeth II and St. Mary's Church

1996. 70th Birthday of Queen Elizabeth II. Multicoloured.

671	20p. Type **165**	55	60
672	25p. The Residency	60	60
673	30p. The Roman Catholic Grotto	70	75
674	65p. The Exiles' Club	1·75	2·00

166 American Army Jeep

1996. "CAPEX '96" International Stamp Exhibition, Toronto. Island Transport. Multicoloured.

675	20p. Type **166**	1·50	1·50
676	25p. Citroen 7.5hp two-seater car, 1924	1·60	1·60
677	30p. Austin ten tourer car, 1930	1·60	1·60
678	65p. Series 1 Land Rover	2·75	3·25

167 Madeiran Storm Petrel

1996. Birds and their Young. Multicoloured.

679	1p. Type **167**	75	1·00
680	2p. Red-billed tropic bird	75	1·00
681	4p. Common mynah	75	1·00
682	5p. House sparrow	75	1·00
683	7p. Common waxbill	1·00	1·25
684	10p. White tern	1·25	1·25
685	12p. Red-necked spurfowl	1·50	1·25
686	15p. Common noddy ("Brown Noddy")	1·50	1·50
687	20p. Yellow canary	1·75	1·50
688	25p. White-capped noddy ("Black Noddy")	1·75	1·50
689	30p. Red-footed booby	1·75	1·50
690	40p. White-tailed tropic bird ("Yellow-billed Tropicbird")	2·00	2·00
691	65p. Brown booby	2·75	3·00

692	£1 Blue-faced booby ("Masked Booby")	3·25	3·50
693	£2 Sooty tern	5·00	6·00
694	£3 Ascension frigate bird	7·00	8·00

See also Nos. 726/7.

168 Pylons

1996. 30th Anniv of B.B.C. Atlantic Relay Station. Multicoloured.

695	20p. Type **168**	75	75
696	25p. Pylons (different)	80	80
697	30p. Pylons and station buildings	90	90
698	65p. Dish aerial, pylon and beach	1·90	1·90

169 Santa Claus on Dish Aerial

1996. Christmas. Santa Claus. Multicoloured.

699	12p. Type **169**	50	50
700	20p. Playing golf	75	75
701	25p. In deck chair	75	75
702	30p. On top of aircraft	85	85
703	65p. On funnel of *St. Helena II* (mail ship)	1·90	2·25

170 Date Palm

1997. "Hong Kong '97" International Stamp Exhibition. Trees. Multicoloured.

704	20p. Type **170**	75	75
705	25p. Mauritius hemp	85	85
706	30p. Norfolk Island pine	95	95
707	65p. Dwarf palm	2·00	2·50

1997. "HONG KONG '97" International Stamp Exhibition. Sheet 130×90 mm containing design as No. 691. Multicoloured.

MS708	65p. Brown booby	1·50	1·75

171 Red Ensign and *Maersk Ascension* (tanker)

1997. Flags. Multicoloured.

709	12p. Type **171**	1·00	80
710	25p. R.A.F. flag and Tristar airliner	1·40	1·10
711	30p. N.A.S.A. emblem and Space Shuttle "Atlantis" landing	1·40	1·25
712	65p. White Ensign and H.M.S. *Northumberland* (frigate)	2·75	2·75

172 *Solanum sodomaeum*

1997. Wild Herbs. Multicoloured.

713	30p. Type **172**	1·40	1·60
714	30p. *Ageratum conyzoides*	1·40	1·60
715	30p. *Leonurus sibiricus*	1·40	1·60
716	30p. *Cerastium vulgatum*	1·40	1·60
717	30p. *Commelina diffusa*	1·40	1·60

Nos. 713/17 were printed together, *se-tenant*, with the backgrounds forming a composite design.

1997. Return of Hong Kong to China. Sheet 130×90 mm containing design as No. 692, but with "1997" imprint date.

MS718	£1 Blue-faced booby	1·50	2·10

173 Queen Elizabeth II

1997. Golden Wedding of Queen Elizabeth and Prince Philip. Multicoloured.

719	20p. Type **173**	1·50	2·00
720	20p. Prince Philip on horseback	1·50	2·00
721	25p. Queen Elizabeth with polo pony	1·50	2·00
722	25p. Prince Philip in Montserrat	1·50	2·00
723	30p. Queen Elizabeth and Prince Philip	1·50	2·00
724	30p. Prince William and Prince Harry on horseback	1·50	2·00
MS725	110×70 mm. $1.50, Queen Elizabeth and Prince Philip in landau (horiz)	3·50	3·50

Nos. 719/20, 721/2 and 723/4 respectively were printed together, *se-tenant*, with the backgrounds forming composite designs.

1997. Birds and their Young. As Nos. 683 and 687, but smaller, size 20×24 mm. Multicoloured.

726	15p. Common waxbill	2·00	2·25
727	35p. Yellow canary	2·00	2·25

174 Black Marlin

1997. Gamefish. Multicoloured.

728	12p. Type **174**	75	75
729	20p. Atlantic sailfish	1·00	1·00
730	25p. Swordfish	1·10	1·10
731	30p. Wahoo	1·25	1·25
732	£1 Yellowfin tuna	3·00	4·00

175 Interior of St. Mary's Church

1997. Christmas. Multicoloured.

733	15p. Type **175**	1·00	1·00
734	35p. Falklands memorial window showing Virgin and child	1·60	1·60
735	40p. Falklands memorial window showing Archangel	1·75	1·90
736	50p. Pair of stained glass windows	2·00	2·25

176 *Cactoblastis cactorum* (caterpillar and moth)

1998. Biological Control using Insects. Multicoloured.

737	15p. Type **176**	2·00	1·75
738	35p. *Teleonemia scrupulosa* (lace-bug)	2·50	2·25
739	40p. *Neltumius arizonensis* (beetle)	2·50	2·75
740	50p. *Algarobius prosopis* (beetle)	2·75	3·25

177 Diana, Princess of Wales, 1985

1998. Diana, Princess of Wales Commemoration. Sheet 145×70 mm, containing T **177** and similar vert designs. Multicoloured.

MS741	35p. Type **177**; 35p. Wearing yellow blouse, 1992; 35p. Wearing grey jacket, 1984; 35p. Carrying bouquets (sold at £1.40+20p. charity premium)	2·25	3·75

178 Fairey Fawn

1998. 80th Anniv of Royal Air Force. Multicoloured.

742	15p. Type **178**	1·50	1·25
743	35p. Vickers Vernon	2·25	2·25
744	40p. Supermarine Spitfire F.22	2·25	2·50
745	50p. Bristol Britannia C.2	2·50	3·00
MS746	110×77 mm. 50p. Blackburn Kangaroo; 50p. S.E.5a; 50p. Curtiss Kittyhawk III; 50p. Boeing Fortress II	4·75	4·75

179 Barn Swallow

1998. Migratory Birds. Multicoloured.

747	15p. Type **179**	1·25	1·25
748	25p. House martin	1·50	1·50
749	35p. Cattle egret	1·75	1·75
750	40p. Eurasian swift ("Swift")	1·90	1·90
751	50p. Allen's gallinule	2·00	2·00

180 Cricket

1998. Sporting Activities. Multicoloured.

752	15p. Type **180**	2·75	1·75
753	35p. Golf	3·50	2·25
754	40p. Football	2·00	2·50
755	50p. Shooting	2·00	2·50

181 Children in Nativity Play

1998. Christmas. Multicoloured.

756	15p. Type **181**	1·25	1·25
757	35p. Santa Claus arriving on Ascension	1·75	1·75
758	40p. Santa Claus on carnival float	1·75	1·75
759	50p. Carol singers	1·75	1·75

182 Curtiss C-46 Commando

1999. Aircraft. Multicoloured.

760	15p. Type **182**	1·75	1·75
761	35p. Douglas C-47 Dakota	2·25	2·25
762	40p. Douglas C-54 Skymaster	2·25	2·25
763	50p. Consolidated Liberator Mk. V	2·25	2·50
MS764	120×85 mm. $1.50, Consolidated Liberator LB-30	11·00	11·00

No. **MS**764 also commemorates the 125th birth anniv of Sir Winston Churchill.

183 *Glengorm Castle* (mail ship), 1929

1999. "Australia '99" World Stamp Exhibition, Melbourne. Ships. Multicoloured.

765	15p. Type **183**	1·75	1·75
766	35p. *Gloucester Castle* (mail ship), 1930	2·25	2·25
767	40p. *Durham Castle* (mail ship), 1930	2·25	2·25
768	50p. *Garth Castle* (mail ship), 1930	2·25	2·50
MS769	121×82 mm. £1 H.M.S. *Endeavour* (Cook)	3·00	4·00

184 Pair of White Terns ("Fairy Terns")

1999. Endangered Species. White Tern ("Fairy Tern"). Multicoloured.

770	10p. Type **184**	45	55
771	10p. On branch	45	55
772	10p. Adult and fledgeling	45	55
773	10p. In flight	45	55

185 Prince Edward and Miss Sophie Rhys-Jones

1999. Royal Wedding. Multicoloured.

774	50p. Type **185**	1·25	1·50
775	£1 Engagement photograph	2·25	2·75

186 Command and Service Modules

1999. 30th Anniv of First Manned Landing on Moon. Multicoloured.

776	15p. Type **186**	75	1·10
777	35p. Moon from "Apollo 11"	1·25	1·60
778	40p. Devil's Ashpit Tracking Station and command module	1·25	1·60
779	50p. Lunar module leaving Moon	1·25	1·60
MS780	90×80 mm. $1.50, Earth as seen from Moon (circular, 40 mm diam)	3·75	5·00

187 King George VI, Queen Elizabeth and Prime Minister Winston Churchill, 1940

1999. "Queen Elizabeth the Queen Mother's Century". Multicoloured.

781	15p. Type **187**	1·25	1·25
782	35p. With Prince Charles at Coronation, 1953	1·75	1·75
783	40p. On her 88th Birthday, 1988	1·75	1·75
784	50p. With Guards' drummers, 1988	1·75	1·75
MS785	145×70 mm. £1.50, Lady Elizabeth Bowes-Lyon, and *Titanic* (liner) (black)	3·75	5·00

188 Babies with Toys

1999. Christmas. Multicoloured.

786	15p. Type **188**	1·50	1·50
787	35p. Children dressed as clowns	2·00	2·00
788	40p. Getting ready for bed	2·00	2·00
789	50p. Children dressed as pirates	2·00	2·00

189 *Anglia* (cable ship), 1900

1999. Centenary of Cable & Wireless Communications plc on Ascension.

790	**189**	15p. black, brown and bistre	1·75	1·75
791	-	35p. black, brown and bistre	2·25	2·25
792	-	40p. multicoloured	2·25	2·25
793	-	50p. black, brown and bistre	2·50	2·50
MS794		105×90 mm. £1.50, multicoloured	3·75	4·00

DESIGNS: 35p. *Cambria* (cable ship), 1910; 40p. Cable network map; 50p. *Colonia* (cable ship), 1910; £1.50, *Seine* (cable ship), 1899.

190 Baby Turtles

2000. Turtle Project on Ascension. Multicoloured.

795	15p. Type **190**	1·25	1·25
796	35p. Turtle on beach	1·75	1·75
797	40p. Turtle with tracking device	1·75	1·75
798	50p. Turtle heading for sea	1·75	1·75
MS799	197×132 mm. 25p. Head of turtle; 25p. Type **190**; 25p. Turtle on beach; 25p. Turtle entering sea (each 40×26 mm)	5·00	5·50

2000. "The Stamp Show 2000" International Stamp Exhibition, London. As No. **MS**799, but with "The Stamp Show 2000" added to the bottom right corner of the margin.

MS800	197×132 mm. 25p. Head of turtle; 25p. Type **190**; 25p. Turtle on beach; 25p. Turtle entering sea (each 40×26 mm)	2·75	3·25

191 Prince William as Toddler, 1983

2000. 18th Birthday of Prince William. Multicoloured.

801	15p. Type **191**	1·00	1·00
802	35p. Prince William in 1994	1·50	1·50
803	40p. Skiing at Klosters, Switzerland (horiz)	1·50	1·50
804	50p. Prince William in 1997 (horiz)	1·50	1·50
MS805	175×95 mm. 10p. As baby with toy mouse (horiz) and Nos. 801/4	7·00	7·00

192 Royal Marine and Early Fort, 1815

2000. Forts. Multicoloured.

806	15p. Type **192**	1·75	1·75
807	35p. Army officer and Fort Thornton, 1817	2·50	2·50
808	40p. Soldier and Fort Hayes, 1860	2·50	2·50
809	50p. Naval lieutenant and Fort Bedford, 1940	2·75	2·75

193 Ships and Dockside Crane (*I saw Three Ships*)

2000. Christmas. Carols. Multicoloured.

810	15p. Type **193**	1·50	1·20
811	25p. Choir and musicians on beach (*Silent Night*)	1·75	1·25
812	40p. Donkeys and church (*Away in a Manger*)	2·50	2·00
813	90p. Carol singers outside church (*Hark the Herald Angels Sing*)	4·50	7·00

194 Green Turtle

2001. "Hong Kong 2001" Stamp Exhibition. Sheet 150×90 mm, containing T **194**. Multicoloured.

MS814	25p. Type **194**; 40p. Loggerhead turtle	3·75	4·50

195 Captain William Dampier

2001. Centenary of Wreck of the Roebuck. Multicoloured.

815	15p. Type **195**	2·25	2·25
816	35p. Construction drawing (horiz)	2·75	2·75
817	40p. Cave dwelling at Dampier's Drip (horiz)	2·75	2·75
818	50p. Map of Ascension	3·50	3·50

196 Alfonso de Albuquerque

2001. 500th Anniv of the Discovery of Ascension Island. Multicoloured.

819	15p. Type **196**	2·25	2·25
820	35p. Portuguese caravel	3·25	3·25
821	40p. Cantino map	3·50	3·50
822	50p. Rear Admiral Sir George Cockburn	3·50	3·50

197 Great Britain 1d. Stamp used on Ascension, 1855

2001. Death Centenary of Queen Victoria. Multicoloured.

823	15p. Type **197**	1·25	1·25
824	25p. Navy church parade, 1901 (horiz)	1·50	1·50
825	35p. H.M.S. *Phoebe* (cruiser) (horiz)	2·00	2·00
826	40p. The Red Lion, 1863 (horiz)	2·00	2·00
827	50p. "Queen Victoria"	2·00	2·00
828	65p. Sir Joseph Hooker (botanist)	2·00	2·75
MS829	105×80 mm. £1.50, Queen Victoria's coffin on the steps of St. George's Chapel, Windsor (horiz)	5·50	6·50

198 Islander Hostel

2001. "BELGICA 2001" International Stamp Exhibition, Brussels. Tourism. Multicoloured.

830	35p. Type **198**	2·50	3·00
831	35p. The Residency	2·50	3·00
832	40p. The Red Lion	2·50	3·00
833	40p. Turtle Ponds	2·50	3·00

199 Female Ascension Frigate Bird

2001. Birdlife World Bird Festival (1st series). Ascension Frigate Birds. Multicoloured.

834	15p. Type **199**	1·25	1·25
835	35p. Fledgeling	1·75	1·75
836	40p. Male bird in flight (horiz)	1·75	1·75
837	50p. Male bird with pouch inflated (horiz)	1·75	1·75
MS838	175×80 mm. 10p. Male and female birds on rock (horiz) and Nos. 834/7	6·50	7·50

See also Nos. 889/94 and 921/**MS**926.

200 Princess Elizabeth and Dog

2002. Golden Jubilee.

839	**200**	15p. agate, mauve and gold	1·50	1·50
840	-	35p. multicoloured	2·00	2·00
841	-	40p. multicoloured	2·00	2·00
842	-	50p. multicoloured	2·00	2·00
MS843		162×95 mm. Nos. 839/42 and 60p. multicoloured	7·50	8·50

DESIGNS—HORIZ: 35p. Queen Elizabeth wearing tiara, 1978; 40p. Princess Elizabeth, 1946; 50p. Queen Elizabeth visiting Henley-on-Thames, 1998. VERT: (38×51 mm)—50p. Queen Elizabeth after Annigoni.

201 Royal Marines landing at English Bay

2002. 20th Anniv of Liberation of the Falkland Islands. Multicoloured.

844	15p. Type **201**	1·25	1·25
845	35p. Weapons testing	1·60	1·60
846	40p. H.M.S. *Hermes* (aircraft carrier)	1·60	1·60
847	50p. R.A.F. Vulcan at Wideawake Airfield	1·60	1·60

202 Duchess of York at Harrow Hospital, 1931

2002. Queen Elizabeth the Queen Mother Commemoration.

848	**202**	35p. black, gold and purple	1·40	1·40
849	-	40p. multicoloured	1·40	1·40
MS850		145×70 mm. 50p. brown and gold; £1 multicoloured	6·50	7·50

DESIGNS: 40p. Queen Mother on her birthday, 1997; 50p. Duchess of York, 1925; £1 Queen Mother, Scrabster, 1992.

203 Travellers Palm and Vinca

2002. Island Views. Multicoloured.

851	10p. Type **203**	75	1·00
852	15p. Broken Tooth (volcanic crater) and Mexican poppy	1·00	75
853	20p. St. Mary's Church and Ascension lily	1·00	75
854	25p. Boatswain Bird Island and goatweed	1·40	1·25
855	30p. Cannon and Mauritius hemp	1·40	1·40
856	35p. The Guest House and frangipani	1·50	1·25
857	40p. Wideawake tern and Ascension spurge	2·00	2·00
858	50p. The Pier Head and lovechaste	2·00	2·25
859	65p. Sisters' Peak and yellowboy	2·25	2·75
860	90p. Two Boats School and Persian lilac	3·00	3·25
861	£2 Green turtle and wild currant	6·00	7·00
862	£5 Wideawake Airfield and coral tree	13·00	14·00

204 *Ecce Ancilla Dominii* (Dante Rossetti)

2002. Christmas. Religious Paintings. Multicoloured.

863	15p. Type **204**	70	70
864	25p. *The Holy Family and Shepherd* (Titian) (horiz)	95	95
865	35p. *Christ carrying the Cross* (A. Bergognone)	1·25	1·25
866	75p. Sketch for *The Ascension* (Benjamin West)	2·50	2·50

205 Ariane 4 Rocket on Gantry

2003. Ariane Downrange Station. Multicoloured.

867	35p. Type **205**	1·40	1·40
868	40p. Map of Ariane Downrange stations (horiz)	1·50	1·50
869	65p. Automated Transfer Vehicle (ATV) in Space (horiz)	2·50	2·50
870	90p. Launch of Ariane 5	3·75	4·25
MS871	170×88 mm. Nos. 867/70	8·25	8·25

206 Coronation Coach in Procession

2003. 50th Anniv of Coronation. Multicoloured.

872	40p. Type **206**	1·50	1·00
873	£1 Newly crowned Queen with bishops and peers	3·25	3·75
MS874	95×115 mm. As Nos. 872/3	4·75	4·75

Nos. 872/3 have red frame; stamps from **MS**874 have no frame and country name in mauve panel.

207 Queen Elizabeth II

2003

875	**207**	£3 black, green and myrtle	6·50	7·00

208 Prince William at Tidworth Polo Club and on Skiing Holiday, 2002

2003. 21st Birthday of Prince William of Wales. Multicoloured.

876	75p. Type **208**	2·75	2·75
877	75p. On Raleigh International Expedition, 2000 and at Queen Mother's 101st Birthday, 2001	2·75	2·75

209 Bleriot XI

2003. Centenary of Powered Flight. Multicoloured.

878	15p. Type **209**	85	85
879	20p. Vickers VC-10	90	90
880	35p. BAe Harrier FRS Mk1	1·60	1·60

881	40p. Westland Sea King HAS Mk. 4 helicopter	1·75	1·75
882	50p. Rockwell Space Shuttle	1·75	1·75
883	90p. General Dynamics F-16 Fighting Falcon	3·25	3·50
MS884	115×65 mm. £1.50 Fairey Swordfish Mk II.	6·50	7·00

210 Casting Vote into Ballot Box

2003. Christmas. First Anniv of Democracy on Ascension. Multicoloured.

885	15p. Type **210**	75	55
886	25p. Island Council session	90	65
887	40p. Students ("HIGHER EDUCATION")	1·40	1·10
888	£1 Government Headquarters	2·75	3·50

211 Adult with Fledgling

2004. Birdlife International (2nd series). Masked Booby. Multicoloured.

889	15p. Type **211**	85	75
890	35p. Pair (vert)	1·40	1·00
891	40p. In flight (vert)	1·40	1·25
892	50p. Adult calling	1·50	1·50
893	90p. Masked booby	3·00	3·50
MS894	175×80 mm. Nos. 889/93	7·00	7·50

212 *Bougainvillea glabra* (orange)

2004. Bicentenary of the Royal Horticultural Society. Multicoloured.

895	15p. Type **212**	75	75
896	35p. *Bougainvillea glabra* (pink)	1·40	1·00
897	40p. *Bougainvillea glabra* (white)	1·50	1·10
898	90p. *Bougainvillea spectabilis* (red)	2·75	3·50
MS899	105×80 mm. £1.50 *Pteris adscensionis*	6·00	6·50

213 Blue Marlin

2004. Sport Fishing (1st series). Multicoloured.

900	15p. Type **213**	75	75
901	35p. Swordfish	1·40	1·00
902	40p. Sailfish	1·50	1·10
903	90p. White marlin	2·75	3·50
MS904	61×51 mm. £1.50 Blue marlin	5·00	6·00

See also Nos. 927/**MS**931.

214 Moon over Hummock Point

2004. Lunar Eclipse. Multicoloured.

905	15p. Type **214**	75	75
906	25p. Yellow moon over Sisters Peak (North side)	1·25	1·00
907	35p. Orange moon over Daly's Craggs	1·50	1·00
908	£1.25 Red moon and birds over Mars Bay	3·75	4·50
MS909	130×55 mm. £1.25 As No. 908	4·00	5·00

215 MV *Ascension*

2004. Merchant Ships. Multicoloured.

910	15p. Type **215**	1·25	1·00
911	35p. *St. Helena* (mail ship)	2·00	1·25
912	40p. *Caronia* (mail ship)	2·00	1·50
913	£1.25 MV *Maersk Gannet*	6·00	7·50

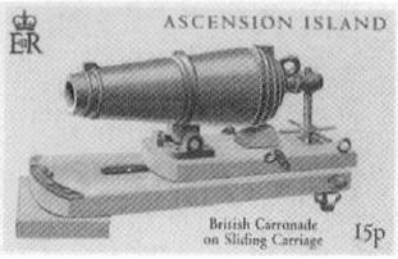

216 British Carronade on Sliding Carriage

2005. Bicentenary of Battle of Trafalgar (1st issue). Multicoloured.

914	15p. Type **216**	75	65
915	25p. Royal Marine drummer boy, 1805 (vert)	1·25	90
916	35p. HMS *Britannia* (vert)	1·40	1·25
917	40p. Admiral Nelson	1·50	1·50
918	50p. HMS *Neptune* and *Santissima Trinidad*	1·60	1·60
919	90p. HMS *Victory*	2·75	4·00
MS920	120×80 mm. £1 Lord Nelson (vert); £1 *Neptune* (vert)	6·50	7·50

No. 919 contains traces of powdered wood from HMS *Victory*.

See also Nos. 937/9.

217 White Tern ("Fairy Tern")

2005. Birdlife International (3rd series). "The Sea Birds Return". Multicoloured.

921	15p. Type **217**	55	55
922	35p. White-tailed tropic bird	1·10	1·10
923	40p. Brown booby	1·25	1·40
924	50p. Common noddy ("Brown Noddy")	1·40	1·40
925	£1.25 Red-billed tropic bird	3·25	4·25
MS926	170×80 mm. Nos. 921/5	8·00	8·50

218 Yellowfin Tuna

2005. Sport Fishing (2nd series). Tuna. Multicoloured.

927	35p. Type **218**	1·25	1·25
928	40p. Skipjack tuna	1·40	1·40
929	50p. Albacore tuna	1·50	1·50
930	£1.25 Bigeye tuna	3·50	4·00
MS931	61×51 mm. £1.50 Yellowfin tuna hunting herrings	4·50	5·50

219 Pope John Paul II

2005. Pope John Paul II Commemoration.

932	**219**	40p. multicoloured	1·75	1·75

220 *The Little Fir Tree*

2005. Christmas. Birth Bicentenary of Hans Christian Andersen (writer). Multicoloured.

933	15p. Type **220**	1·00	1·00
934	25p. *The Mail-Coach Passengers*	1·25	1·25
935	35p. *The Little Match Girl*	1·50	1·50
936	£1.25 *The Snow Man*	4·00	5·00

221 HMS *Victory*

2005. Bicentenary of the Battle of Trafalgar (2nd issue). Multicoloured.

937	40p. Type **221**	1·50	1·40
938	65p. Ships engaged in battle (horiz)	2·50	3·00
939	90p. *Admiral Lord Nelson*	3·50	4·00

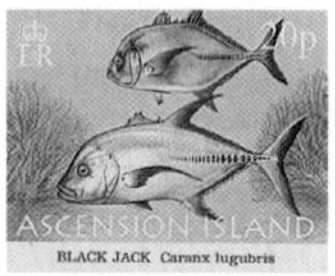

222 Black Jack

2006. Sport Fishing (3rd series). Jacks. Multicoloured.

940	20p. Type **222**	1·00	1·00
941	35p. Almaco jack	1·60	1·40
942	50p. Horse-eye jack	2·00	2·00
943	£1 Rainbow runner	3·50	4·25
MS944	61×50 mm. £1.50 Longfin crevalle jack	4·50	5·50

223 Princess Elizabeth

2006. 80th Birthday of Queen Elizabeth II. Multicoloured.

945	20p. Type **223**	80	80
946	40p. Queen Elizabeth II, c. 1952	1·00	1·25
947	50p. Queen Elizabeth II	1·75	1·90
948	£1.30 Wearing Garter robes	4·25	8·00
MS949	144×75 mm. £1 Queen, c. 1952; £1 Queen in 1960s	6·00	7·00

224 HMS *Beagle* (175th anniv of Darwin's voyage)

2006. Exploration and Innovation. Anniversaries. Multicoloured.

950	20p. Type **224**	1·25	1·25
951	20p. Charles Darwin (originator of theory of evolution)	1·25	1·25
952	35p. *Great Britain* (steam/sail)	2·00	2·00
953	35p. Isambard Kingdom Brunel (engineer, birth bicentenary)	2·00	2·00
954	40p. *Nina* (Columbus)	2·25	2·25
955	40p. Christopher Columbus (discoverer of New World, 500th death anniv)	2·25	2·25
956	50p. World map with lines of magnetic variation	2·25	2·25
957	50p. Edmund Halley (astronomer, 350th birth anniv) and Halley's comet	2·25	2·25

Nos. 950/1, 952/3, 954/5 and 956/7 were each printed together, *se-tenant*, forming a composite background design.

225 Long Beach ("Greetings from Ascension")

2006. Christmas. Views of Ascension Island. Multicoloured.

958	15p. Type **225**	85	85
959	25p. Coastal rocks at sunset ("Merry Christmas")	1·25	1·25
960	35p. Dewpond ("Seasons Greetings")	1·60	1·25
961	£1.25 Coast and Boatswain Bird Island ("Happy New Year")	4·25	5·00

226 Resplendent Angelfish

2007. Endangered Species. Resplendent Angelfish (Centropyge resplendens). Multicoloured.

962	35p. Type **226**	1·40	1·10
963	40p. Shoal of resplendent angelfish	1·60	1·60
964	50p. Three angelfish near red coral and rocks	1·60	1·60
965	£1.25 Large male angelfish and three smaller females	4·00	4·50

227 Handley Page Victor K Mk2 Tanker

2007. 25th Anniv of the Liberation of the Falkland Islands. Multicoloured.

966	35p. Type **227**	1·50	1·10
967	40p. HMS *Dumbarton Castle* (offshore patrol vessel) and Chinook helicopter	1·90	1·90
968	50p. HMS *Fearless* with helicopter and landing craft	1·90	1·90
969	£1.25 Vulcan XM607 taking off	4·50	5·00
MS970	Two sheets, each 183×89 mm. (a) As Type **227**; 40p. Vickers VC10 Transport; 50p. Nimrod MR2 Maritime Reconnaissance; As No. 969. (b) 35p. RFA *Tidespring* refuelling HMS *Antrim*; As No. 967; As No. 968; £1.25 *Atlantic Conveyor* and Harrier fighter	9·00	10·00

Stamps from the two miniature sheets **MS**970a/b do not have white borders.

The 50p. stamp from **MS**970(a) has an incorrect spelling "Reconaissance".

228 Ascension Scouts forming Fleur-de-Lis Emblem

2007. Centenary of Scouting. Multicoloured.

971	35p. Type **228**	1·40	1·10
972	40p. Scouts rescuing stranded turtle	1·60	1·60
973	50p. Ascension Scout Troop sitting on gun from HMS *Hood*	1·60	1·60
974	£1.25 Scouts on top of their Land Rover near Butt Crater	4·00	5·00

229 Mother Teresa and Princess Diana, Rome, 1992

2007. Tenth Death Anniv of Diana, Princess of Wales.

975	**229**	50p. multicoloured	1·60	1·60

230 Engagement Photograph, July 1947

2007. Diamond Wedding of Queen Elizabeth II and Duke of Edinburgh. Multicoloured.

976	35p. Type **230**	2·00	2·50
977	90p. Wedding programme	4·00	4·50
978	£1.25 Queen and Duke of Edinburgh at St. Paul's Cathedral for 80th birthday Thanksgiving Service	4·25	4·75

231 BOU Base Camp near Mars Bay

2007. 50th Anniv of the British Ornithologists' Union Centenary Expedition (1957–9). Multicoloured.

979	15p. Type **231**	1·00	1·25
980	15p. Peter Mundy's drawing of extinct flightless rail, 1656	1·00	1·25
981	25p. Team member recording sooty tern ('Wideawake')	1·25	1·50
982	25p. Sooty terns ('Wideawake')	1·25	1·50
983	40p. BOU outpost, Boatswain-bird Island	4·50	5·00
984	40p. Masked booby	2·25	2·50
985	50p. Team members with expedition dinghy *Overdraft*	2·25	2·50
986	50p. Red-footed booby	2·25	2·50

232 *Lampides boeticus* (long-tailed blue butterfly)

2008. Fauna and their Eggs. Multicoloured.

987	15p. Type **232**	45	50
988	20p. *Cheilomenes lunata* (ladybird)	60	65
989	25p. *Panulirus echinatus* (spiny lobster)	75	80
990	30p. *Schistocerca gregaria* (desert locust)	90	85
991	35p. *Chelonia mydas* (green turtle)	1·10	1·20
992	40p. *Gecarcinus lagostoma* (landcrab)	1·20	1·30
993	50p. *Sula sula* (red-footed booby)	1·50	1·60
994	65p. *Hemdactylus mercatorius* (coconut-palm gecko)	1·90	2·00
995	90p. *Estrilda astrild* (common waxbill)	2·75	3·00
996	£1 *Stegastes lubbocki* (yellowtail damselfish)	3·00	3·25
997	£2.50 *Oceanodroma castro* (Madeiran storm-petrel)	7·50	7·75
998	£5 *Francolinus afer* (red-necked francolin)	15·00	15·00

233 Bluntnose Sixgill Shark

2008. Sharks. Multicoloured.

999	35p. Type **233**	1·75	2·25
1000	40p. Scalloped hammerhead	1·75	2·25
1001	50p. Shortfin mako	1·75	2·25
1002	£1.25 Whale shark	3·75	2·25
MS1003	70×45 mm. £1.50 Bigeye thresher	5·00	5·50

234 Bell X-1E NACA X-Plane, 1958

2008. 50th Anniv of NASA. Multicoloured.

1004	35p. Type **234**	1·10	1·20
1005	35p. Apollo 11 Moon Walk, 1969	1·10	1·20
1006	40p. Apollo 17 Lunar Roving Vehicle, 1972	1·10	1·20
1007	50p. STS1 Space Shuttle *Columbia*, 1981	1·50	1·60
1008	65p. The Hubble Space Telescope, 1990	1·90	1·80
1009	90p. International Space Station, 2006	2·75	3·00

235 Sopwith 7F.1 Snipe

2008. 90th Anniv of the Royal Air Force. Multicoloured.

1010	15p. Type **235**	1·10	90
1011	35p. Vickers Wellington Mk 1C	1·90	1·75
1012	40p. Supermarine Spitfire Mk IX	2·00	2·00
1013	50p. Gloster Meteor F.IV	2·00	2·00
1014	65p. BAe Hawk	2·50	2·75
1015	90p. Typhoon F2 (Eurofighter)	3·25	3·50

236 Valerius Cordus (1515–44) and *Cordia sebestena*

2008. Botanists and Plants named after them. Multicoloured.

1016	35p. Type **236**	1·50	1·25
1017	40p. Nehemiah Grew (1641–1712) and *Grewia occidentalis*	1·75	1·75
1018	50p. Charles Plumier (1646–1704) and *Plumeria rubra*	1·75	1·75
1019	£2 Carl Peter Thunberg (1743–1828) and *Thunbergia grandiflora*	6·50	7·00

237 Father Christmas

2008. Christmas. Designs showing illustrations of Father Christmas from Father Christmas and Father Christmas Goes on Holiday by Raymond Briggs superimposed over Ascension Island scenes. Multicoloured.

1020	15p. Type **237**	70	70
1021	25p. Father Christmas in reindeer-drawn sleigh above surf of western coast	1·00	1·00
1022	50p. Father Christmas lying on inflatable	1·75	1·75
1023	£2 Father Christmas and his laden sleigh above Green Mountain and Two Boats Village	6·50	7·00

238 King Henry III (1216–72) and the Tower of London

2008. Britain's Longest Reigning Monarchs. Multicoloured.

1024	35p. Type **238**	1·90	1·60
1025	40p. King James VI (1567–1625) and Stirling Castle	2·00	2·00
1026	50p. King George III (1760–1820) and Windsor Castle	2·25	2·25
1027	65p. Queen Victoria (1837–1901) and Osborne House	2·50	2·75
1028	£1.25 Queen Elizabeth II (from 1952) and Buckingham Palace	4·75	5·50

239 Bottlenose Dolphin (*Tursiops truncatus*)

2009. Whales and Dolphins. Multicoloured.

1029	35p. Type **239**	1·10	1·20
1030	40p. Pantropical spotted dolphin (*Stenella attenuata*)	1·20	1·30
1031	50p. Sperm whale (*Physeter macrocephalus*) and squid (prey)	1·50	1·60
1032	£1.25 Gervais' beaked whale (*Mesoplodon europeus*)	3·75	4·00
MS1033	111×65 mm. £2 Humpback whale (*Megaptera novaeangliae*)	6·00	6·25

240 Flt. SLt. Rex Warneford

2009. Centenary of Naval Aviation. Victoria Cross of the Fleet Air Arm. Multicoloured.

1034	35p. Type **240**	1·75	1·75
1035	35p. Moraine-Saulnier L destroys Zeppelin LZ37, Belgium, 6/7 June 1915	1·75	1·75
1036	35p. Sqn. Cdr. Richard Bell Davies	1·75	1·75
1037	35p. Nieuport 10 takes off pursued by enemy soldiers, Bulgaria, 19 November 1915	1·75	1·75
1038	40p. Lt. Cdr. (A) Eugene Esmonde	1·75	1·75
1039	40p. Fairey Swordfish aircraft attacking German heavy cruisers, 12 February 1942	1·75	1·75
1040	50p. Lt. Robert Hampton Gray	1·75	1·75
1041	50p. Corsair bombing Japanese warship	1·75	1·75

241 Blue Water Lily (*Nymphaea capensis*)

2009. Introduced Plant Species. Multicoloured.

1042	35p. Type **241**	1·10	1·20
1043	35p. Raspberry (*Rubus rosifolius*)	1·10	1·20
1044	40p. Prickly pear (*Optunia vulgaris*)	1·20	1·30
1045	50p. Ascension lily (*Hippeastrum reginae*)	1·50	1·60
1046	65p. Yellowboy (*Tecoma stans*)	1·90	2·00
1047	90p. Portraits of young and old Joseph Dalton Hooker (botanist)	2·75	3·00

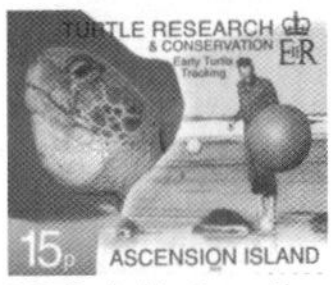

242 Dr. Archie Carr with Early Turtle Tracking Equipment

2009. Turtle Research and Conservation and Birth Centenary of Dr. Archie Carr (sea turtle biologist). T **242** and similar horiz designs, each showing either head of turtle at left (Nos. 1048, 1050, 1052, 1054) or outline map of Ascension Island at right (others). Multicoloured.

1048	15p. Type **242**	80	1·00
1049	15p. Dr. Archie Carr attaching tracking floats to turtle	80	2·00
1050	35p. Female laying eggs	1·40	1·60
1051	35p. Turtle hatchlings	1·40	1·60
1052	40p. Beach raking to remove turtle tracks after counting	1·40	1·75
1053	40p. Population monitoring	1·40	1·75
1054	65p. Rescuer with turtle	2·00	2·50
1055	65p. Two rescuers with turtle	2·00	2·50

Nos. 1048/9, 1050/1, 1052/3 and 1054/5 were each printed together, *se-tenant*, each pair forming a composite design.

243 Charles Darwin and Woodpecker Finch

2009. Birth Bicentenary of Charles Darwin (naturalist and evolutionary theorist). Each showing a different portrait. Multicoloured.

1056	35p. Type **243**	1·75	1·50
1057	40p. Charles Darwin (in profile) and marine iguanas	1·75	1·75
1058	50p. Charles Darwin and Galapagos tortoise	1·75	1·75
1059	£2 Charles Darwin as old man, Galapagos penguins and *Beagle*	6·50	7·00

244 Juvenile White-tailed Tropic Bird

2009. White-tailed Tropic Bird (Phaethon lepturus). Multicoloured.

1060	35p. Type **244**	1·75	2·00
1061	40p. Adult feeding juvenile	1·75	2·00
1062	50p. Juvenile in flight	1·75	2·00
1063	£1.25 Adult in flight	3·50	4·00

245 Hardback Soldier Fish (*Holocentrus adscensionis*)

2010. Reef Fish. Multicoloured.

1064	35p. Type **245**	1·60	1·60
1065	40p. Grouper (*Epinephelus adscensionis*)	1·75	1·75
1066	50p. Five fingers (*Abudefduf saxatilis*)	1·75	1·75
1067	£1.25 Rock bullseye (*Heteropriacanthus cruentatus*)	3·50	4·00
MS1068	84×59 mm. £2 Softback soldier fish (*Myripristis jacobus*)	6·50	7·00

246 Guides

2010. Centenary of Girl Guiding. Multicoloured.

1069	40p. Type **246**	1·60	1·60
1070	50p. Guides and large fish catch	1·75	1·75
1071	90p. Guide leaders and 'Celebrating 100 Years of Guiding' celebration cake	3·00	3·25
1072	£1.25 Guide abseiling	3·75	4·00
MS1073	160×80 mm. £1×3 Olave, Lady Baden-Powell (Chief Guide 1918–77); Agnes Baden-Powell (founder); Lord Baden-Powell (founder of Scout Movement) (all vert)	9·00	9·00

247 Supermarine Spitfire R6803, 65 Squadron

2010. London 2010 Festival of Stamps. 70th Anniv of the Battle of Britain. Multicoloured.

1074	50p. Type **247**	1·75	2·00
1075	50p. Hawker Hurricane V7383, 615 Squadron	1·75	2·00
1076	50p. Supermarine Spitfire X4036, 234 Squadron	1·75	2·00
1077	50p. Hawker Hurricane R4175, 303 Squadron	1·75	2·00
1078	50p. Supermarine Spitfire R6885, 41 Squadron	1·75	2·00
1079	50p. Hawker Hurricane V6684, 303 Squadron	1·75	2·00
1080	50p. Supermarine Spitfire K9998, 603 Squadron	1·75	2·00
1081	50p. Hawker Hurricane R4118, 605 Squadron	1·75	2·00

Nos. 1080/1 were printed together, *se-tenant*, forming composite background design.

248 Juvenile Yellow Canary

2010. Yellow Canary (*Serinus flaviventris*). Multicoloured.

1082	15p. Type **248**	70	70
1083	35p. Adult male (perched)	1·25	1·25
1084	60p. Adult female	2·00	2·00
1085	90p. Adult male (on ground)	2·75	2·75

249 Christmas Lunch

2010. Christmas on Ascension Island. Multicoloured.

1086	15p. Type **249**	45	50
1087	40p. Santa riding in decorated pick-up truck in Christmas parade	1·10	1·20
1088	50p. Three children at Christingle service	1·50	1·60
1089	£1.25 Children's nativity play	3·50	3·75

250 HMS Erebus and Terror approaching Ascension

2011. Parsley Fern (*Anogramma ascensionis*). Multicoloured.

1090	15p. Type **250**	15	15
1091	25p. Parsley fern	80	80
1092	35p. Parsley fern in situ	1·10	1·10
1093	40p. Parsley fern seedlings	1·25	1·25
1094	£1 Parsley fern cultivation, Kew Gardens	3·00	3·00

251 Queen Elizabeth II, Westminster Abbey, 12 April 2001

2011. Queen Elizabeth II and Prince Philip 'A Lifetime of Service'. Multicoloured.

1095	15p. Type **251**	45	45
1096	25p. Queen Elizabeth and Prince Philip, 1953	80	80
1097	35p. Queen Elizabeth and Prince Philip, Buckingham Palace, 1999	1·10	1·10
1098	40p. Queen Elizabeth and Prince Philip, The Mall, London, 24 February 2009	1·25	1·25
1099	60p. Queen Elizabeth and Prince Philip in Balmoral Castle grounds, September 1960	1·75	1·75
1100	£1.25 Duke of Edinburgh, Westminster Abbey, 12 April 2001	3·75	3·75
MS1101	174×163 mm. Nos. 1095/100 and three stamp-size labels	9·00	9·00
MS1102	110×70 mm. £2 Queen Elizabeth II and Prince Philip, Westminster Abbey, 1977	6·00	6·00

252 Unloading Sea King Helicopter from Hold of Short Belfast Aircraft, 8 May 1982

2011. 70th Anniv of RAF Search and Rescue. Multicoloured.

1103	35p. Type **252**	1·10	1·25
1104	40p. Westland Sea King HAR3 helicopter XZ593 over Ascension Island	1·25	1·40
1105	90p. Sea King helicopter XZ593 delivering stores to HMS *Dumbarton Castle* (Castle Class patrol ship), 1982	2·75	3·00
1106	£1 Sea King helicopter XZ593 airlifting casualty from nuclear submarine HMS *Spartan*, 1982	3·00	3·25
MS1107	64×94 mm. £2.50 Sea King helicopter XZ593	7·50	7·50

253 Red and Yellow Peonies

2011. The Peony. Multicoloured.

MS1108	50p.×4 Type **253**; White peony; Apricot peony; Pale yellow peony	5·25	5·25

254 Prince William and Miss Catherine Middleton at Friend's Wedding, 23 October 2010

2011. Royal Wedding. Multicoloured.

1109	35p. Type **254**	1·10	1·10
1110	90p. Prince William and Miss Catherine Middleton at St. James's Palace, November 2010	2·75	2·75
1111	£1.25 Duke and Duchess of Cambridge in carriage on their wedding day	3·75	3·75
MS1112	94×64 mm. £2 Duke and Duchess of Cambridge leaving Westminster Abbey after wedding (vert)	5·25	5·25

255 Red-billed Tropic Bird on Nest

2011. Endangered Species. Red-billed Tropicbird (*Phaethon aethereus*). Multicoloured.

1113	35p. Type **255**	90	90
1114	40p. Pair in flight	1·10	1·10
1115	50p. Adult and juvenile on nest	1·40	1·40
1116	£1.25 Red-billed tropic bird in flight over sea	3·50	3·50

256 Mother Goose

2011. Christmas. Pantomimes. Multicoloured.

1117	15p. Type **256**	45	45
1118	40p. Jack and the Beanstalk	1·25	1·25
1119	50p. Aladdin	1·50	1·50
1120	£1.25 Cinderella	3·75	3·75

257 Queen Elizabeth II, Windsor, 2011

2012. Diamond Jubilee. Multicoloured.

1121	15p. Type **257**	45	45
1122	25p. At reception on eve of Prince Charles' 50th birthday, Buckingham Palace, 13 November 1998	75	75
1123	35p. Attending Maundy Service, Lichfield, 1988	1·10	1·10
1124	40p. Official portrait by Peter Grugeon, Windsor Castle, October 1975	1·25	1·25
1125	60p. Formal photograph, Buckingham Palace, 1961	1·75	1·75
1126	£1.25 Wearing Coronation gown, 4 June 1953	3·75	3·75
MS1127	174×164 mm. Nos. 1121/6 and three stamp-size labels	9·00	9·00
MS1129	111×70 mm. £2 In Westminster Abbey, 1977	6·00	6·00

2012. Reef Fish (2nd series). Multicoloured.

1129	35p. Trumpetfish (*Aulostomus strigosus*)	1·10	1·10
1130	40p. Peacock flounder (*Bothus lunatus*)	1·25	1·25
1131	90p. Queen triggerfish (*Balistes vetula*)	2·50	2·50
1132	£1 Scrawled filefish (*Aluterus scriptus*)	2·75	2·75
MS1133	85×61 mm. £2 Yellow goatfish (*Mulloidichthys martinicus*)	6·00	6·00

POSTAGE DUE STAMPS

D1 Outline Map of Ascension

1986

D1	**D1**	1p. deep brown and brown	15	30
D2	**D1**	2p. brown and orange	15	30
D3	**D1**	5p. brown and orange	15	30
D4	**D1**	7p. black and violet	20	40
D5	**D1**	10p. black and blue	25	45
D6	**D1**	25p. black and green	65	1·10

Pt. 1

AUSTRALIA

An island continent to the S.E. of Asia. A Commonwealth consisting of the states of New S. Wales, Queensland, S. Australia, Tasmania, Victoria and W. Australia.

1913. 12 pence = 1 shilling; 20 shillings = 1 pound.
1966. 100 cents = 1 dollar.

1 Eastern Grey Kangaroo

1913

1	1	½d. green	8·50	4·75
2	1	1d. red	14·00	1·50
35	1	2d. grey	45·00	8·00
36	1	2½d. blue	24·00	10·00
37	1	3d. olive	38·00	4·75
6	1	4d. orange	85·00	25·00
8	1	5d. brown	70·00	38·00
38	1	6d. blue	75·00	7·50
73	1	6d. brown	26·00	1·75
133	1	9d. violet	35·00	2·25
40	1	1s. green	50·00	5·50
41	1	2s. brown	£225	13·00
134	1	2s. purple	8·00	1·00
135	1	5s. grey and yellow	£150	18·00
136	1	10s. grey and pink	£400	£140
15	1	£1 brown and blue	£2250	£2250
137	1	£1 grey	£600	£275
138	1	£2 black and pink	£3750	£550

3

1913

20	3	½d. green	3·75	1·00
94	3	½d. orange	2·25	1·40
17	3	1d. red	3·00	5·00
57	3	1d. violet	5·50	1·50
125	3	1d. green	1·75	20
59a	3	1½d. brown	6·50	60
61	3	1½d. green	4·00	80
77	3	1½d. red	2·25	40
62	3	2d. orange	12·00	1·00
98	3	2d. brown	12·00	9·50
127	3	2d. red	1·75	10
128	3	3d. blue	18·00	1·25
22	3	4d. orange	35·00	2·50
64	3	4d. violet	15·00	15·00
65	3	4d. blue	48·00	8·50
129	3	4d. olive	18·00	1·25
92	3	4½d. violet	18·00	3·75
130	3	5d. brown	15·00	20
131	3	1s.4d. blue	50·00	3·50

4 Laughing Kookaburra

1913

19	4	6d. purple	75·00	55·00

8 Parliament House, Canberra

1927. Opening of Parliament House.

105	8	1½d. lake	50	50

1928. National Stamp Exhibition, Melbourne.

106	4	3d. blue	4·25	6·50
MS106a		65×70 mm. No. 106×4	£110	£200

9 De Havilland Hercules and Pastoral Scene

1929. Air.

115	9	3d. green	8·00	4·25

10 Black Swan

1929. Centenary of Western Australia.

116	**10**	1½d. red	1·25	1·60

11 "Capt. Chas Sturt" (J. H. Crossland)

1930. Centenary of Sturt's Exploration of River Murray.

117	**11**	1½d. red	1·25	1·00
118	**11**	3d. blue	7·00	9·00

1930. Surch in words.

119	**3**	2d. on 1½d. red	1·50	1·00
120	**3**	5d. on 4½d. violet	11·00	14·00

13 The *Southern Cross* above Hemispheres

1931. Kingsford Smith's Flights.

121	**13**	2d. red (postage)	1·00	1·00
122	**13**	3d. blue	7·00	5·50
123	**13**	6d. violet (air)	5·50	16·00

1931. Air. As T **13** but inscr "AIR MAIL SERVICE".

139	6d. brown	18·00	17·00

1931. Air. No. 139 optd **O S**.

139a	6d. brown	30·00	55·00

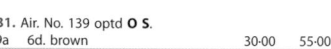

17 Superb Lyrebird

1932

140	**17**	1s. green	40·00	2·75

18 Sydney Harbour Bridge

1932. Opening of Sydney Harbour Bridge.

144	**18**	2d. red	5·00	1·40
142	**18**	3d. blue	8·00	9·00
143	**18**	5s. green	£425	£200

19 Laughing Kookaburra

1932

146	**19**	6d. brown	17·00	55

20 Melbourne and River Yarra

1934. Centenary of Victoria.

147	**20**	2d. red	3·00	1·75
148	**20**	3d. blue	4·00	5·50
149	**20**	1s. black	55·00	20·00

21 Merino Ram

1934. Death Centenary of Capt. John Macarthur (founder of Australian sheep-farming).

150	**21**	2d. red	8·00	1·50
151	**21**	3d. blue	15·00	18·00
152	**21**	9d. purple	32·00	50·00

22 Hermes

1934

153b	**22**	1s.6d. purple	2·00	1·40

23 Cenotaph, Whitehall

1935. 20th. Anniv of Gallipoli Landing.

154	**23**	2d. red	2·25	30
155	**23**	1s. black	50·00	45·00

24 King George V on "Anzac"

1935. Silver Jubilee.

156	**24**	2d. red	2·75	30
157	**24**	3d. blue	8·50	11·00
158	**24**	2s. violet	35·00	55·00

25 Amphitrite and Telephone Cable

1936. Opening of Submarine Telephone Cable to Tasmania.

159	**25**	2d. red	2·25	50
160	**25**	3d. blue	4·25	2·75

26 Site of Adelaide, 1836; Old Gum Tree, Glenelg; King William Street, Adelaide

1936. Centenary of South Australia.

161	**26**	2d. red	2·75	40
162	**26**	3d. blue	9·00	3·50
163	**26**	1s. green	16·00	10·00

27 Wallaroo **28** Queen Elizabeth **29** King George VI

30 King George VI **31** King George VI **33** Merino Ram

38 Queen Elizabeth

40 King George VI and Queen Elizabeth

1937

228	**27**	½d. orange	20	10
165	**28**	1d. green	1·00	50
180	-	1d. green	7·00	60
181	-	1d. purple	1·50	50
182	**29**	1½d. purple	4·75	14·00
183	**29**	1½d. green	1·25	1·75
167	**30**	2d. red	1·00	50
184	-	2d. red	5·50	20
185	**30**	2d. purple	50	2·00
186	**31**	3d. blue	45·00	3·75
187	**31**	3d. brown	40	10
188	-	4d. green	1·00	10
189	**33**	5d. purple	50	2·25
190a	-	6d. brown	1·75	10
191	-	9d. brown	1·00	30
192	-	1s. green	2·00	10
175	**31**	1s.4d. mauve	2·75	2·50
176a	**38**	5s. purple	4·50	2·75
177	-	10s. purple	50·00	17·00
178	**40**	£1 slate	70·00	35·00

DESIGNS—As Type **28**: 4d. Koala; 6d. Kookaburra; 1s. Lyrebird. As Type **33**: 9d. Platypus. As Type **38**: 10s. King George VI.

Nos. 180 and 184 are as Types **28** and **30** but with completely shaded background.

41 Governor Phillip at Sydney Cove (J. Alcott)

1937. 150th Anniv of New South Wales.

193	**41**	2d. red	3·25	30
194	**41**	3d. blue	7·00	2·25
195	**41**	9d. purple	24·00	14·00

42 A.I.F. and Nurse

1940. Australian Imperial Forces.

196	**42**	1d. green	2·50	2·75
197	**42**	2d. red	2·00	1·50
198	**42**	3d. blue	16·00	10·00
199	**42**	6d. purple	30·00	28·00

1941. Surch with figures and bars.

200	**30**	2½d. on 2d. red	1·00	70
201	**31**	3½d. on 3d. blue	2·50	2·25
202	**33**	5½d. on 5d. purple	4·00	6·00

46a Queen Elizabeth **47** King George VI **48** King George VI

49 King George VI **50** Emu

1942

203	**46a**	1d. purple	2·00	10
204	**46a**	1½d. green	2·50	10
205	**47**	2d. purple	1·75	2·00
206	**48**	2½d. red	50	10
207	**49**	3½d. blue	2·75	60
208	**50**	5½d. grey	1·00	20

52 Duke and Duchess of Gloucester

1945. Royal Visit.

209	**52**	2½d. red	20	10
210	**52**	3½d. blue	40	1·25
211	**52**	5½d. grey	50	1·25

53 Star and Wreath

1946. Victory. Inscr "PEACE 1945".

213	**53**	2½d. red	20	10
214	-	3½d. blue	55	1·75
215	-	5½d. green	60	1·00

DESIGNS—HORIZ: 3½d. Flag and dove. VERT: 5½d. Angel.

56 Sir Thomas Mitchell and Queensland

1946. Centenary of Mitchell's Central Queensland Exploration.

216	**56**	2½d. red	25	10
217	**56**	3½d. blue	75	1·50
218	**56**	1s. green	75	65

57 Lt. John Shortland, R.N. **58** Steel Foundry

1947. 150th Anniv of City of Newcastle.

219	**57**	2½d. lake	20	10
220	**58**	3½d. blue	60	1·50
221	-	5½d. green	60	75

DESIGNS—As Type **58**: HORIZ: 5½d. Coal carrier cranes.

60 Queen Elizabeth II when Princess

1947. Wedding of Princess Elizabeth.

222a	**60**	1d. purple	10	10

61 Hereford Bull **61a** Hermes and Globe **62** Aboriginal Art

62a Commonwealth Coat of Arms

1948

223	**61**	1s.3d. brown	2·25	1·10
223a	**61a**	1s.6d. brown	1·00	10
224	**62**	2s. brown	1·50	10
224a	**62a**	5s. red	3·75	20
224b	**62a**	10s. purple	19·00	85
224c	**62a**	£1 blue	40·00	4·25
224d	**62a**	£2 green	85·00	16·00

63 William J. Farrer

1948. W. J. Farrer (wheat research) Commem.

225	**63**	2½d. red	40	10

64 Ferdinand von Mueller

1948. Sir Ferdinand von Mueller (botanist) Commemoration.

226	**64**	2½d. red	30	10

65 Boy Scout

1948. Pan-Pacific Scout Jamboree, Wonga Park.

227	**65**	2½d. lake	30	10

For 3½d. value dates "1952–53", see No. 254.

66 "Henry Lawson" (Sir Lionel Lindsay)

1949. Henry Lawson (poet) Commemoration.

231	**66**	2½d. purple	40	10

67 Mounted Postman and Convair CV 240 Aircraft

1949. 75th Anniv of U.P.U.

232	**67**	3½d. blue	50	60

68 John, Lord Forrest of Bunbury

1949. John, Lord Forrest (explorer and politician) Commemoration.

233	**68**	2½d. red	55	10

69 Queen Elizabeth **70** King George VI **81** King George VI

80 King George VI **71** Aborigine **82** King George VI

1950

236	**69**	1½d. green	70	40
237	**69**	2d. green	15	10
234	**70**	2½d. red	10	10
237c	**70**	2½d. brown	15	35
235	**70**	3d. red	15	25
237d	**70**	3d. green	15	10
247	**80**	3½d. purple	10	10
248	**81**	4½d. red	15	1·25
249	**81**	6½d. brown	20	1·25
250	**81**	6½d. green	20	45
251	**80**	7½d. blue	15	80
238	**71**	8½d. brown	20	1·00
252	**82**	1s.0½d. blue	1·00	60
253	**71**	2s.6d. brown (21×25½ mm)	2·00	1·00

72 Reproduction of First Stamp of N.S.W. **73** Reproduction of First Stamp of Victoria

1950. Centenary of Australian States Stamps.

239	**72**	2½d. purple	50	10
240	**73**	2½d. purple	50	10

75 Sir Henry Parkes **77** Federal Parliament House, Canberra

1951. 50th Anniv of Commonwealth. Inscr as in T **75** and **77**.

241	**75**	3d. lake	1·50	10
242	-	3d. lake	1·50	10
243	-	5½d. blue	65	2·25
244	**77**	1s.6d. brown	1·25	50

DESIGNS—As Type **70**: No. 242, Sir Edmund Barton. As Type **77**: No. 243, Opening first Federal Parliament.

78 E. H. Hargraves **79** C. J. Latrobe

1951. Centenaries. Discovery of Gold in Australia and of Responsible Government in Victoria.

245	**78**	3d. purple	1·00	10
246	**79**	3d. purple	1·00	10

1952. Pan-Pacific Scout Jamboree, Greystanes. As T **65** but dated "1952–53".

254	**65**	3½d. lake	20	10

83 Butter

1953. Food Production. Inscr "PRODUCE FOOD!".

255	**83**	3d. green	30	10
256	-	3d. green (Wheat)	30	10
257	-	3d. green (Beef)	30	10
258	**83**	3½d. red	30	10
259	-	3½d. red (Wheat)	30	10
260	-	3½d. red (Beef)	30	10

86 Queen Elizabeth II

1953

261	**86**	1d. purple	15	15
261a	**86**	2½d. blue	20	15
262	**86**	3d. green	20	10
263	**86**	3½d. red	20	10
263a	**86**	6½d. orange	2·50	50

87 Queen Elizabeth II

1953. Coronation.

264	**87**	3½d. red	40	10
265	**87**	7½d. violet	75	1·40
266	**87**	2s. green	2·50	1·40

88 Young Farmers and Calf

1953. 25th Anniv of Australian Young Farmers' Clubs.

267	**88**	3½d. brown and green	10	10

89 Lt.-Gov. D. Collins

90 Lt.-Gov. W. Paterson

91 Sullivan Cove, Hobart, 1804

1953. 150th Anniv of Settlement in Tasmania.

268	**89**	3½d. purple	35	10
269	**90**	3½d. purple	35	10
270	**91**	2s. green	1·25	3·00

92 Stamp of 1853

1953. First Centenary of Tasmania Postage Stamps.

271	**92**	3d. red	10	40

93 Queen Elizabeth II and Duke of Edinburgh

94 Queen Elizabeth II

1954. Royal Visit.

272	**93**	3½d. red	20	10
273	**94**	7½d. purple	30	1·25
274	**93**	2s. green	60	65

95 "Telegraphic Communications"

1954. Centenary of Telegraph.

275	**95**	3½d. brown	10	10

96 Red Cross and Globe

1954. 40th Anniv of Australian Red Cross Society.

276	**96**	3½d. blue and red	10	10

97 Mute Swan

1954. Centenary of Western Australian Stamps.

277	**97**	3½d. black	20	10

98 Locomotives of 1854 and 1954

1954. Centenary of Australian Railways.

278	**98**	3½d. purple	30	10

99 Territory Badge

1954. Australian Antarctic Research.

279	**99**	3½d. black	15	10

100 Olympic Games Symbol

1954. Olympic Games Propaganda.

280	**100**	2s. blue	1·75	1·00
280a	**100**	2s. green	2·00	2·50

101 Rotary Symbol, Globe and Flags

1955. 50th Anniv of Rotary International.

281	**101**	3½d. red	10	10

101a Queen Elizabeth II

102 Queen Elizabeth II

1955

282a	**101a**	4d. lake	20	10
282b	**101a**	7½d. violet	1·00	1·50
282c	**101a**	10d. blue	60	1·25
282	**102**	1s.0½d. blue	1·25	1·25
282d	**102**	1s.7d. brown	1·25	45

103 American Memorial, Canberra

1955. Australian–American Friendship.

283	**103**	3½d. blue	10	10

104 Cobb & Co. Coach (from etching by Sir Lionel Lindsay)

1955. Mail-coach Pioneers Commemoration.

284	**104**	3½d. sepia	25	10
285	**104**	2s. brown	1·00	1·40

105 Y.M.C.A. Emblem and Map of the World

1955. World Centenary of Y.M.C.A.

286	**105**	3½d. green and red	10	10

106 Florence Nightingale and Young Nurse

1955. Nursing Profession Commemoration.

287	**106**	3½d. lilac	10	10

107 Queen Victoria

1955. Centenary of South Australian Postage Stamps.

288	**107**	3½d. green	10	10

108 Badges of N.S.W., Victoria and Tasmania

1956. Centenary of Responsible Government in N.S.W., Victoria and Tasmania.

289	**108**	3½d. lake	10	10

109 Arms of Melbourne

110 Olympic Torch and Symbol

111 Collins Street, Melbourne

1956. Olympic Games, Melbourne.

290	**109**	4d. red	30	10
291	**110**	7½d. blue	70	1·40
292	**111**	1s. multicoloured	80	30
293	-	2s. multicoloured	1·25	2·00

DESIGN—As Type **111**: 2s. Melbourne across River Yarra.

115 South Australia Coat of Arms

1957. Centenary of Responsible Government in South Australia.

296	**115**	4d. brown	10	10

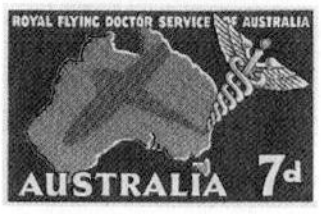

116 Map of Australia and Caduceus

1957. Royal Flying Doctor Service of Australia.

297	**116**	7d. blue	15	10

117 "The Spirit of Christmas" (after Sir Joshua Reynolds)

1957. Christmas.

298	**117**	3½d. red	10	20
299	**117**	4d. purple	10	10

118 Lockheed Super Constellation Airliner

1958. Inaug of Australian "Round-the-World" Air Service.

301	**118**	2s. blue	1·00	1·00

119 Hall of Memory, Sailor and Airman

1958

302	**119**	5½d. lake	40	30
303	-	5½d. lake	40	30

No. 303 shows a soldier and servicewoman instead of the sailor and airman.

120 Sir Charles Kingsford Smith and the *Southern Cross*

1958. 30th Anniv of First Air Crossing of the Tasman Sea.

304	**120**	8d. blue	60	1·00

121 Silver Mine, Broken Hill

1958. 75th Anniv of Founding of Broken Hill.

305	**121**	4d. brown	30	10

122 The Nativity

1958. Christmas Issue.

306	**122**	3½d. red	20	30
307	**122**	4d. violet	20	10

124 Queen Elizabeth II

126 Queen Elizabeth II

127 Queen Elizabeth II

128 Queen Elizabeth II

129 Queen Elizabeth II

1959

308	-	1d. purple	10	10
309	**124**	2d. brown	50	20
311	**126**	3d. turquoise	15	10
312	**127**	3½d. green	15	15
313	**128**	4d. red	1·75	10
314	**129**	5d. blue	1·25	10

No. 308 shows a head and shoulders portrait as in Type **128** and is vert.

131 Numbat

137 Christmas Bells

142 Aboriginal Stockman

1959

316	**131**	6d. brown	1·50	10
317	-	8d. brown	75	10
318	-	9d. sepia	2·00	55
319	-	11d. blue	1·00	15
320	-	1s. green	1·75	40
321	-	1s.2d. purple	1·00	15
322	**137**	1s.6d. red on yellow	1·75	1·00
323	-	2s. blue	70	10
324	-	2s.3d. green on yellow	1·00	10
324a	-	2s.3d. green	2·50	75
325	-	2s.5d. brown on yellow	3·50	75
326	-	3s. red	1·50	20
327	**142**	5s. brown	12·00	2·75

DESIGNS—As Type **131**: VERT: 8d. Tiger Cat; 9d. Eastern grey kangaroo; 11d. Common rabbit bandicoot; 1s. Platypus. HORIZ: 1s.2d. Thylacine. As Type **137**: 2s. Flannel flower; 2s.3d. Wattle; 2s.5d. Banksia (plant); 3s. Waratah.

143 Postmaster Isaac Nichols boarding the Brig *Experiment*

1959. 150th Anniv of Australian P.O.

331	**143**	4d. slate	15	10

144 Parliament House, Brisbane, and Arms of Queensland

1959. Centenary of Queensland Self-Government.

332	**144**	4d. lilac and green	10	10

145 "The Approach of the Magi"

1959. Christmas.

333	**145**	5d. violet	10	10

146 Girl Guide and Lord Baden-Powell

1960. 50th Anniv of Girl Guide Movement.

334	**146**	5d. blue	30	15

147 *The Overlanders* (after Sir Daryl Lindsay)

1960. Centenary of Northern Territory Exploration.

335	**147**	5d. mauve	50	15

148 *Archer* and Melbourne Cup

1960. 100th Melbourne Cup Race Commemoration.

336	**148**	5d. sepia	20	10

149 Queen Victoria

1960. Centenary of Queensland Stamps.

337	**149**	5d. green	25	10

150 Open Bible and Candle

1960. Christmas Issue.

338	**150**	5d. lake	10	10

151 Colombo Plan Bureau Emblem

1961. Colombo Plan.

339	**151**	1s. brown	10	10

152 Melba (after bust by Sir Bertram Mackennal)

1961. Birth Centenary of Dame Nellie Melba (singer).

340	**152**	5d. blue	30	15

153 Open Prayer Book and Text

1961. Christmas Issue.

341	**153**	5d. brown	10	10

154 J. M. Stuart

1962. Centenary of Stuart's South to North Crossing of Australia.

342	**154**	5d. red	40	10

155 Flynn's Grave and Nursing Sister

1962. 50th Anniv of Australian Inland Mission.

343	**155**	5d. multicoloured	30	15

156 "Woman"

1962. "Associated Country Women of the World" Conference, Melbourne.

344	**156**	5d. green	10	10

157 "Madonna and Child"

1962. Christmas.

345	**157**	5d. violet	15	10

158 Perth and Kangaroo Paw (plant)

1962. British Empire and Commonwealth Games, Perth. Multicoloured.

346	5d. Type **158**	50	10
347	2s.3d. Arms of Perth and running track	2·00	2·75

160 Queen Elizabeth II

1963. Royal Visit.

348	**160**	5d. green	35	10
349	-	2s.3d. lake	1·50	3·00

DESIGN: 2s.3d. Queen Elizabeth II and Duke of Edinburgh.

162 Arms of Canberra and W. B. Griffin (architect)

1963. 50th Anniv of Canberra.

350	**162**	5d. green	15	10

163 Centenary Emblem

1963. Centenary of Red Cross.

351	**163**	5d. red, grey and blue	60	10

164 Blaxland, Lawson and Wentworth on Mount York

1963. 150th Anniv of First Crossing of Blue Mountains.

352	**164**	5d. blue	15	10

165 "Export"

1963. Export Campaign.

353	**165**	5d. red	10	10

1963. As T **160** but smaller 17½×21½ mm "5D" at top right replacing "ROYAL VISIT 1963" and oak leaves omitted.

354	5d. green	1·00	10
354c	5d. red	55	10

167 Tasman and *Heemskerk*

1963. Navigators.

355	**167**	4s. blue	3·00	55
356	-	5s. brown	3·75	1·75
357	-	7s.6d. olive	19·00	19·00
358	-	10s. purple	25·00	5·00
359	-	£1 violet	35·00	16·00
360	-	£2 sepia	55·00	75·00

DESIGNS—As Type **167**: 7s.6d. Captain Cook; 10s. Flinders and *Investigator*. 20½×5½ mm: 5s. Dampier and *Roebuck* £1 Bass and *Tom Thumb* (whale boat); £2 Admiral King and *Mermaid* (survey cutter).

173 "Peace on Earth..."

1963. Christmas.

361	**173**	5d. blue	10	10

174 "Commonwealth Cable"

1963. Opening of COMPAC (Trans-Pacific Telephone Cable).

362	**174**	2s.3d. multicoloured	1·50	2·75

176 Black-backed Magpie

1964. Birds.

363	-	6d. multicoloured	1·00	25
364	**176**	9d. black, grey and green	1·00	2·75
365	-	1s.6d. multicoloured	75	1·40
366	-	2s. yellow, black and pink	1·40	50
367	-	2s.5d. multicoloured	1·75	3·50
368	-	2s.6d. multicoloured	2·50	3·75
369	-	3s. multicoloured	2·50	1·75

BIRDS—HORIZ: 6d. Yellow-tailed thornbill; 2s.6d. Scarlet robin. VERT: 1s.6d. Galah (cockatoo); 2s. Golden whistler (Thickhead); 2s.5d. Blue wren; 3s. Straw-necked ibis.

182 Bleriot XI Aircraft (type flown by M. Guillaux, 1914)

1964. 50th Anniv of 1st Australian Airmail Flight.

370	**182**	5d. green	30	10
371	**182**	2s.3d. red	1·50	2·75

183 Child looking at Nativity Scene

1964. Christmas.

372	**183**	5d. red, blue, buff and black	10	10

184 "Simpson and his Donkey"

1965. 50th Anniv of Gallipoli Landing.

373	**184**	5d. brown	50	10
374	**184**	8d. blue	75	2·50
375	**184**	2s.3d. purple	1·50	2·50

185 "Telecommunications"

1965. Centenary of I.T.U.

376	**185**	5d. black, brown and blue	60	10

186 Sir Winston Churchill

1965. Churchill Commemoration.

377	**186**	5d. multicoloured	30	10

187 General Monash

1965. Birth Centenary of General Sir John Monash (engineer and soldier).

378	**187**	5d. multicoloured	15	10

188 Hargrave and *Multiplane* Seaplane (1902)

1965. 50th Death Anniv of Lawrence Hargrave (aviation pioneer).

379	**188**	5d. multicoloured	25	10

189 I.C.Y. Emblem

1965. International Co-operation Year.

380	**189**	2s.3d. green and blue	65	1·50

190 "Nativity Scene"

1965. Christmas.

381	**190**	5d. multicoloured	15	10

191 Queen Elizabeth II

192 Blue-faced Honeyeater

1966. Decimal currency. As earlier issues but with values in cents and dollars as in T **191/2**. Also some new designs.

382	**191**	1c. brown	25	10
383	**191**	2c. green	70	10
384	**191**	3c. green	70	10
404	**191**	3c. black, pink and green	45	1·25
385	**191**	4c. red	20	10
405	**191**	4c. black, brown and red	35	60
386	-	5c. multicoloured (as 363)	25	10
386c	**191**	5c. blue	70	10
405a	**191**	5c. black, brown and blue	40	10
387	**192**	6c. multicoloured	1·25	1·00
387a	**191**	6c. orange	1·00	10
388	-	7c. multicoloured	60	10
388a	**191**	7c. purple	1·25	10
389	-	8c. multicoloured	60	1·00
390	-	9c. multicoloured	60	20
391	-	10c. multicoloured	60	10
392	-	13c. multicoloured	1·50	25
393	-	15c. multicoloured (as 365)	1·25	2·00
394	-	20c. yellow, black and pink (as 366)	1·50	15
395	-	24c. multicoloured	65	1·25
396	-	25c. multicoloured (as 368)	1·50	30
397	-	30c. multicoloured (as 369)	4·50	1·25
398	**167**	40c. blue	3·00	10
399	-	50c. brown (as 356)	3·00	10
400	-	75c. olive (as 357)	1·00	1·00
401	-	$1 purple (as 358)	1·50	20
402	-	$2 violet (as 359)	6·00	1·00
403	-	$4 brown (as 360)	6·00	6·50

DESIGNS—VERT: 7c. White-tailed Dascyllus ("Humbug fish"); 8c. Copper-banded butterflyfish ("Coral fish"); 9c. Hermit crab; 10c. Orange clownfish ("Anemone fish"); 13c. Red-necked avocet. HORIZ: 24c. Azure kingfisher.

200 "Saving Life"

1966. 75th Anniv of Royal Life Saving Society.

406	**200**	4c. black, lt bl & bl	15	10

201 "Adoration of the Shepherds"

1966. Christmas.

407	**201**	4c. black and olive	10	10

202 *Eendracht*

1966. 350th Anniv of Dirk Hartog's Landing in Australia.

408	**202**	4c. multicoloured	10	10

203 Open Bible

1967. 150th Anniv of British and Foreign Bible Society in Australia.

409	**203**	4c. multicoloured	10	10

204 Ancient Keys and Modern Lock

1967. 150th Anniv of Australian Banking.

410	**204**	4c. black, blue and green	10	10

205 Lions Badge and 50 Stars

1967. 50th Anniv of Lions International.

411	**205**	4c. black, gold and blue	10	10

206 Y.W.C.A. Emblem

1967. World Y.W.C.A. Council Meeting, Monash University, Melbourne.

412	**206**	4c. multicoloured	10	10

207 Anatomical Figures

1967. Fifth World Gynaecology and Obstetrics Congress, Sydney.

413	**207**	4c. black, blue and violet	10	10

1967. No. 385 surch.

414	**191**	5c. on 4c. red	25	10

209 Christmas Bells and Gothic Arches

1967. Christmas. Multicoloured.

415	5c. Type **209**	20	10
416	25c. Religious symbols (vert)	1·00	1·90

211 Satellite in Orbit

1968. World Weather Watch. Multicoloured.

417	5c. Type **211**	30	10
418	20c. World weather map	1·10	3·00

213 Radar Antenna

1968. World Telecommunications via Intelsat II.

419	**213**	25c. blue, black and green	1·00	2·00

214 Kangaroo Paw (Western Australia)

1968. State Floral Emblems. Multicoloured.

420	6c. Type **214**	45	1·25
421	13c. Pink Heath (Victoria)	50	70
422	15c. Tasmanian Blue Gum (Tasmania)	50	40
423	20c. Sturt's Desert Pea (South Australia)	1·00	75
424	25c. Cooktown Orchid (Queensland)	1·10	75
425	30c. Waratah (New South Wales)	50	10

220 Soil Sample Analysis

1968. International Soil Science Congress and World Medical Association Assembly. Multicoloured.

426	5c. Type **220**	10	10
427	5c. Rubber-gloved hands, syringe and head of Hippocrates	10	10

222 Athlete carrying Torch and Sunstone Symbol

1968. Olympic Games, Mexico City. Multicoloured.

428	5c. Type **222**	30	10
429	25c. Sunstone symbol and Mexican flag	40	1·50

224 Houses and Dollar Signs

1968. Building and Savings Societies Congress.

430	**224**	5c. multicoloured	10	40

225 Church Window and View of Bethlehem

1968. Christmas.

431	**225**	5c. multicoloured	10	10

226 Edgeworth David (geologist)

1968. Famous Australians (1st series).

432	**226**	5c. green on myrtle	25	20
433	-	5c. black on blue	25	20
434	-	5c. brown on buff	25	20
435	-	5c. violet on lilac	25	20

DESIGNS: No. 433, A. B. Paterson (poet); No. 434, Albert Namatjira (artist); No. 435, Caroline Chrisholm (social worker).

Nos. 432/5 were only issued in booklets and exist with one or two sides imperf.

See also Nos. 446/9, 479/82, 505/8, 537/40, 590/5, 602/7 and 637/40.

230 Macquarie Lighthouse

1968. 150th Anniv of Macquarie Lighthouse.

436	**230**	5c. black and yellow	50	70

231 Pioneers and Modern Building, Darwin

1969. Centenary of Northern Territory Settlement.

437	**231**	5c. brown, olive and ochre	10	10

232 Melbourne Harbour

1969. Sixth Biennial Conference of International Association of Ports and Harbours, Melbourne.

438	**232**	5c. multicoloured	20	10

233 Concentric Circles (symbolizing Management, Labour and Government)

1969. 50th Anniv of I.L.O.

439	**233**	5c. multicoloured	15	10

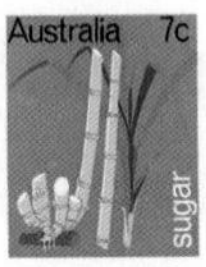

234 Sugar Cane

1969. Primary Industries. Multicoloured.

440	7c. Type **234**	50	1·50
441	15c. Timber	75	2·50
442	20c. Wheat	30	60
443	25c. Wool	50	1·50

238 *The Nativity* (stained glass window)

1969. Christmas. Multicoloured.

444	5c. Type **238**	20	10
445	25c. *Tree of Life*, Christ in crib and Christmas Star (abstract)	1·00	2·00

240 Edmund Barton

1969. Famous Australians (2nd series). Prime Ministers.

446	**240**	5c. black on green	40	20
447	-	5c. black on green	40	20
448	-	5c. black on green	40	20
449	-	5c. black on green	40	20

DESIGNS: No. 447, Alfred Deakin; 448, J. C. Watson; 449, G. H. Reid.

Nos. 446/9 were only issued in booklets and only exist with one or two adjacent sides imperf.

244 Capt. Ross Smith's Vickers Vimy, 1919

1969. 50th Anniv of 1st England–Australia Flight.

450	**244**	5c. multicoloured	15	10
451	-	5c. red, black and green	15	10
452	-	5c. multicoloured	15	10

DESIGNS: No. 451, Lt. H. Fysh and Lt. P. McGinness on 1919 survey with Ford Model T runabout; 452, Capt. Wrigley and Sgt. Murphy in Royal Aircraft Factory B.E.2E taking off to meet the Smiths.

247 Symbolic Track and Diesel Locomotive

1970. Sydney–Perth Standard Gauge Railway Link.

453	**247**	5c. multicoloured	15	10

248 Australian Pavilion, Osaka

1970. World Fair, Osaka.

454	**248**	5c. multicoloured	15	10
455	-	20c. red and black	35	65

DESIGN: 20c., *Southern Cross* and "from the Country of the south with warm feelings" (message).

251 Australian Flag

1970. Royal Visit.

456		5c. black and ochre	35	15
457	**251**	30c. multicoloured	1·10	2·50

DESIGN: 5c. Queen Elizabeth II and Duke of Edinburgh.

252 Lucerne Plant, Bull and Sun

1970. 11th International Grasslands Congress, Queensland.

458	**252**	5c. multicoloured	10	80

253 Captain Cook and H.M.S. *Endeavour*

1970. Bicentenary of Captain Cook's Discovery of Australia's East Coast. Multicoloured.

459	5c. Type **253**	35	10
460	5c. Sextant and H.M.S. *Endeavour*	35	10
461	5c. Landing at Botany Bay	35	10
462	5c. Charting and exploring	35	10
463	5c. Claiming possession	35	10
464	30c. Captain Cook, H.M.S. *Endeavour*, sextant, aborigines and kangaroo (63×30 mm)	1·25	2·50
MS465	157×129 mm. Nos. 459/64. Imperf	6·50	8·00

Nos. 459/63 were issued together, *se-tenant*, forming a composite design.

259 Sturt's Desert Rose

1970. Coil Stamps. Multicoloured.

465a	2c. Type **259**	40	20
466	4c. Type **259**	85	2·25
467	5c. Golden wattle	20	10
468	6c. Type **259**	1·25	1·00
468b	7c. Sturt's desert pea	40	70
468d	10c. As 7c.	60	1·50

264 Snowy Mountains Scheme

1970. National Development (1st series). Multicoloured.

469	7c. Type **264**	20	80
470	8c. Ord River scheme	10	15
471	9c. Bauxite to aluminium	15	15
472	10c. Oil and natural gas	30	10

See also Nos. 541/4.

265 Rising Flames

1970. 16th Commonwealth Parliamentary Association Conference, Canberra.

473	**265**	6c. multicoloured	10	10

266 Milk Analysis and Dairy Herd

1970. 18th International Dairy Congress, Sydney.

474	**266**	6c. multicoloured	10	10

267 "The Nativity"

1970. Christmas.

475	**267**	6c. multicoloured	10	10

268 U.N. "Plant" and Dove of Peace

1970. 25th Anniv of United Nations.

476	**268**	6c. multicoloured	15	10

269 Boeing 707 and Avro 504

1970. 50th Anniv of QANTAS Airline.

477	**269**	6c. multicoloured	30	10
478	-	30c. multicoloured	70	1·50

DESIGN: 30c. Avro 504 and Boeing 707.

1970. Famous Australians (3rd series). As T **226**.

479	6c. blue	35	20
480	6c. black on brown	35	20
481	6c. purple on pink	35	20
482	6c. red on pink	35	20

DESIGNS: No. 479, The Duigan brothers (pioneer aviators); 480, Lachlan Macquarie (Governor of New South Wales); 481, Adam Lindsay Gordon (poet); 482, E. J. Eyre (explorer).

271 "Theatre"

1971. "Australia–Asia". 28th International Congress of Orientalists, Canberra. Multicoloured.

483	7c. Type **271**	45	60
484	15c. "Music"	85	1·00
485	20c. "Sea Craft"	65	90

272 The Southern Cross

1971. Centenary of Australian Natives' Association.

486	**272**	6c. black, red and blue	10	10

273 Market "Graph"

1971. Centenary of Sydney Stock Exchange.

487	**273**	6c. multicoloured	10	10

274 Rotary Emblem

1971. 50th Anniv of Rotary International in Australia.

488	**274**	6c. multicoloured	15	10

275 Dassault Mirage Jets and de Havilland D.H.9A Biplane

1971. 50th Anniv of R.A.A.F.

489	**275**	6c. multicoloured	70	10

276 Draught-horse, Cat and Dog

1971. Animals. Multicoloured.

490	6c. Type **276**	20	10
491	12c. Vet and lamb ("Animal Science")	45	20
492	18c. Red Kangaroo ("Fauna Conservation")	1·25	35
493	24c. Guide-dog ("Animals Aid to Man")	1·00	1·50

The 6c. commemorates the Centenary of the Australian R.S.P.C.A.

277 Bark Painting

1971. Aboriginal Art. Multicoloured.

494	20c. Type **277**	20	20
495	25c. Body decoration	20	55
496	30c. Cave painting (vert)	65	20
497	35c. Grave posts (vert)	30	15

278 The Three Kings and the Star

1971. Christmas. Colours of star and colour of "AUSTRALIA" given.

498	**278**	7c. blue, mauve and brown	40	15
499	**278**	7c. mauve, brown and white	40	15
500	**278**	7c. mauve, white and black	2·50	80
501	**278**	7c. black, green and black	40	15
502	**278**	7c. lilac, green and mauve	40	15
503	**278**	7c. black, brown and white	40	15
504	**278**	7c. blue, mauve and green	11·00	2·25

1972. Famous Australians. (4th series). As T **240**. Prime Ministers.

505	7c. blue	30	20
506	7c. blue	30	20
507	7c. red	30	20
508	7c. red	30	20

DESIGNS: No. 505, Andrew Fisher; 506, W. M. Hughes; 507, Joseph Cook; 508, S. M. Bruce.

280 Cameo Brooch

1972. 50th Anniv of Country Women's Association.

509	**280**	7c. multicoloured	20	10

281 Fruit

1972. Primary Industries. Multicoloured.

510	20c. Type **281**	1·00	2·50
511	25c. Rice	1·00	4·00
512	30c. Fish	1·00	1·00
513	35c. Beef	2·25	75

282 Worker in Wheelchair

1972. Rehabilitation of the Disabled.

514	**282**	12c. brown and green	10	10
515	-	18c. green and orange	1·00	35
516	-	24c. blue and brown	15	10

DESIGNS—HORIZ: 18c. Patient and teacher. VERT: 24c. Boy playing with ball.

283 Telegraph Line

1972. Centenary of Overland Telegraph Line.

517	**283**	7c. multicoloured	15	15

284 Athletics

1972. Olympic Games, Munich. Multicoloured.

518	7c. Type **284**	25	25
519	7c. Rowing	25	25
520	7c. Swimming	25	25
521	35c. Equestrian	1·25	3·50

285 Numerals and Computer Circuit

1972. Tenth Int Congress of Accountants, Sydney.

522	**285**	7c. multicoloured	15	15

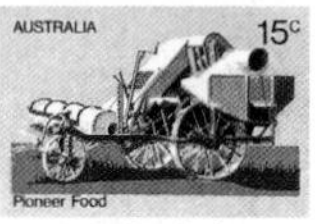

286 Australian-built Harvester

1972. Pioneer Life. Multicoloured.

523	5c. Pioneer family (vert)	10	10
524	10c. Water-pump (vert)	20	10
525	15c. Type **286**	15	10
526	40c. House	15	30
527	50c. Stage-coach	35	20
528	60c. Morse key (vert)	30	80
529	80c. *Gem* (paddle-steamer)	30	80

287 Jesus with Children

1972. Christmas. Multicoloured.

530	7c. Type **287**	30	10
531	35c. Dove and spectrum motif (vert)	2·75	5·00

288 "Length"

1973. Metric Conversion. Multicoloured.

532	7c. Type **288**	45	60
533	7c. "Volume"	45	60
534	7c. "Mass"	45	60
535	7c. "Temperature" (horiz)	45	60

289 Caduceus and Laurel Wreath

1973. 25th Anniv of World Health Organization.

536	**289**	7c. multicoloured	30	15

1973. Famous Australians (5th series). As T **226**.

537	7c. brown and black	35	45
538	7c. lilac and black	35	45
539	7c. brown and black	35	45
540	7c. lilac and black	35	45

PORTRAITS: No. 537, William Wentworth (statesman and explorer); 538, Isaac Issacs (1st Australian-born Governor-General); 539, Mary Gilmore (writer); 540, Marcus Clarke (author).

291 Shipping

1973. National Development (2nd series). Multicoloured.

541	20c. Type **291**	1·50	2·75
542	25c. Iron ore and steel	1·50	2·75
543	30c. Beef roads	1·50	2·75
544	35c. Mapping	2·25	2·75

292 Banded Coral Shrimp

1973. Marine Life and Gemstones. Multicoloured.

545	1c. Type **292**	10	10
546	2c. Fiddler crab	10	10
547	3c. Coral crab	10	10
548	4c. Mauve stinger	15	55
549	6c. Chrysoprase (vert)	65	80
550	7c. Agate (vert)	20	10
551	8c. Opal (vert)	35	10
552	9c. Rhodonite (vert)	50	15
552a	10c. Star sapphire (vert)	75	10

293 Children at Play

1973. 50th Anniv of Legacy (welfare organization).

553	**293**	7c. brown, red and green	30	10

294 John baptizing Jesus

1973. Christmas. Multicoloured.

554	7c. Type **294**	35	10
555	30c. The Good Shepherd	1·75	2·50

295 Sydney Opera House

1973. Architecture.

556	**295**	7c. blue and pale blue	30	15
557	-	10c. ochre and brown	80	70
558	-	40c. grey, brown and black	1·25	2·50
559	-	50c. multicoloured	1·25	3·00

DESIGNS—HORIZ: 10c. Buchanan's Hotel, Townsville; 40c. Como House, Melbourne. VERT: 50c. St. James's Church, Sydney.

296 Wireless Receiver and Speaker

1973. 50th Anniv of Regular Radio Broadcasting.

560	**296**	7c. blue, red and black	15	10

297 Common Wombat

1974. Animals. Multicoloured.

561	20c. Type **297**	25	10
562	25c. Short-nosed echidna (inscr "Spiny Anteater")	60	60
563	30c. Brush-tailed possum	75	15
564	75c. Pygmy (inscr "Feather-tailed") glider	80	1·00

298 *Sergeant of Light Horse* (G. Lambert)

1974. Australian Paintings. Multicoloured.

565	$1 Type **298**	1·00	10
566	$2 *Red Gums of the Far North* (H. Heysen) (horiz)	1·25	25
566b	$4 *Shearing the Rams* (Tom Roberts) (horiz)	2·00	2·25
567	$5 *McMahon's Point* (Sir Arthur Streeton)	3·25	2·25
567a	$10 *Coming South* (Tom Roberts)	4·50	3·50

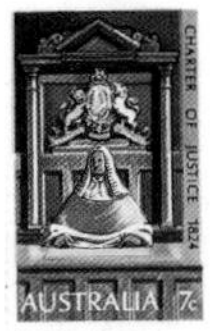

299 Supreme Court Judge

1974. 150th Anniv of Australia's Third Charter of Justice.

568	**299**	7c. multicoloured	20	10

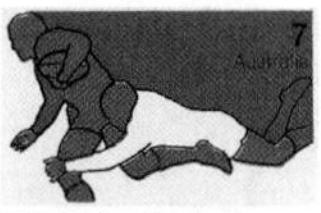

300 Rugby Football

1974. Non-Olympic Sports. Multicoloured.

569	7c. Type **300**	40	50
570	7c. Bowls	40	50
571	7c. Australian football (vert)	40	50
572	7c. Cricket (vert)	40	50
573	7c. Golf (vert)	40	50
574	7c. Surfing (vert)	40	50
575	7c. Tennis (vert)	40	50

301 "Transport of Mails"

1974. Centenary of U.P.U. Multicoloured.

576	7c. Type **301**	40	20
577	30c. Three-part version of T **301** (vert)	85	2·25

302 Letter "A" and W. C. Wentworth (co-founder)

1974. 150th Anniv of First Independent Newspaper,*The Australian*.

578	**302**	7c. black and brown	50	40

1974. No. 551 surch.

579	9c. on 8c. multicoloured	15	15

304 *The Adoration of the Magi*

1974. Christmas. Woodcuts by Durer.

580	**304**	10c. black on cream	25	10
581	-	35c. black on cream	80	1·00

DESIGN: 35c. *The Flight into Egypt*.

305 "Pre-school Education"

1974. Education in Australia. Multicoloured.

582	5c. Type **305**	25	40
583	11c. "Correspondence Schools"	25	60
584	15c. "Science Education"	40	40
585	60c. "Advanced Education" (vert)	50	2·00

306 "Road Safety"

1975. Environment Dangers. Multicoloured.

586	10c. Type **306**	50	50
587	10c. "Pollution" (horiz)	50	50
588	10c. "Bush Fires" (horiz)	50	50

307 Australian Women's Year Emblem

1975. International Women's Year.

589	**307**	10c. blue, green and violet	20	15

308 J. H. Scullin

1975. Famous Australians (6th series). Prime Ministers. Multicoloured.

590	10c. Type **308**	25	35
591	10c. J. A. Lyons	25	35
592	10c. Earle Page	25	35
593	10c. Arthur Fadden	25	35
594	10c. John Curtin	25	35
595	10c. J. B. Chifley	25	35

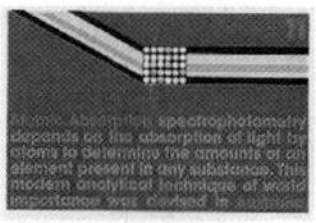

309 Atomic Absorption Spectrophotometry

1975. Scientfic Development. Multicoloured.

596	11c. Type **309**	70	75
597	24c. Radio astronomy	1·25	2·00
598	33c. Immunology	1·25	2·00
599	48c. Oceanography	1·50	2·75

310 Logo of Australian Postal Commission

1975. Inauguration of Australian Postal and Tele-communications Commissions.

600	**310**	10c. black, red and grey	25	10
601	-	10c. black, orange and grey	25	10

DESIGN: No. 601, Logo of Australian Tele-communications Commission.

311 Edith Cowan

1975. Famous Australians (7th series). Australian Women. Multicoloured.

602	10c. Type **311**	55	75
603	10c. Louisa Lawson	55	75
604	10c. "Henry Richardson" (pen name of Ethel Richardson)	55	75
605	10c. Catherine Spence	55	75
606a	10c. Constance Stone	65	75
607	10c. Truganini	55	75

312 *Helichrysum thomsonii*

1975. Wild Flowers. Multicoloured.

608	18c. Type **312**	25	10
609	45c. *Callistemon teretifolius* (horiz)	50	10

313 "Tambaran" House and Sydney Opera House

1975. Independence of Papua New Guinea. Multicoloured.

610	18c. Type **313**	20	10
611	25c. "Freedom" (bird in flight) (horiz)	50	1·50

314 Epiphany Scene

1975. Christmas.

612	**314**	15c. multicoloured	40	10
613	-	45c. violet, blue and silver	1·00	3·00

DESIGN—HORIZ: 45c. "Shining Star".

315 Australian Coat of Arms

1976. 75th Anniv of Nationhood.

614	**315**	18c. multicoloured	40	20

316 Telephone-user, c. 1878

1976. Centenary of Telephone.

615	**316**	18c. multicoloured	20	15

317 John Oxley

1976. 19th Century Explorers. Multicoloured.

616	18c. Type **317**	35	50
617	18c. Hume and Hovell	35	50
618	18c. John Forrest	35	50
619	18c. Ernest Giles	35	50
620	18c. William Gosse	35	50
621	18c. Peter Warburton	35	50

318 Measuring Stick, Graph and Computer Tape

1976. 50th Anniv of Commonwealth Scientific and Industrial Research Organization.

622	**318**	18c. multicoloured	20	15

319 Football

1976. Olympic Games, Montreal. Multicoloured.

623	18c. Type **319**	20	20
624	18c. Gymnastics (vert)	20	20
625	25c. Diving (vert)	35	80
626	40c. Cycling	1·25	1·25

320 Richmond Bridge, Tasmania

1976. Australian Scenes. Multicoloured.

627	5c. Type **320**	20	10
628	25c. Broken Bay, N.S.W	65	10
629	35c. Wittenoom Gorge, W.A	45	20
630	50c. Mt. Buffalo, Victoria (vert)	90	20
631	70c. Barrier Reef	1·25	1·25
632	85c. Ayers Rock, N.T	1·50	2·25

321 Blamire Young (designer of first Australian stamp)

1976. National Stamp Week.

633	**321**	18c. multicoloured	15	15
MS634		101×112 mm. Nos. 633×4	75	1·50

322 *Virgin and Child* (detail, Simone Contarini)

1976. Christmas.

635	**322**	15c. mauve and blue	20	10
636	-	45c. multicoloured	50	90

DESIGN: 45c. Toy koala bear and decorations.

323 John Gould

1976. Famous Australians. (8th series). Scientists. Multicoloured.

637	18c. Type **323**	35	50
638	18c. Thomas Laby	35	50
639	18c. Sir Baldwin Spencer	35	50
640	18c. Griffith Taylor	35	50

324 "Music"

1977. Performing Arts. Multicoloured.

641	20c. Type **324**	15	25
642	30c. Drama	20	35
643	40c. Dance	25	40
644	60c. Opera	1·50	1·75

325 Queen Elizabeth II

1977. Silver Jubilee. Multicoloured.

645	18c. Type **325**	30	10
646	45c. The Queen and Duke of Edinburgh	70	90

326 Fielder and Wicket Keeper

1977. Centenary of Australia–England Test Cricket.. Multicoloured.

647	18c. Type **326**	40	65
648	18c. Umpire and batsman	40	65
649	18c. Fielders	40	65
650	18c. Batsman and umpire	40	65
651	18c. Bowler and fielder	40	65
652	45c. Batsman facing bowler	50	1·25

327 Parliament House

1977. 50th Anniv of Opening of Parliament House, Canberra.

653	**327**	18c. multicoloured	15	10

328 Trade Union Workers

1977. 50th Anniv of Australian Council of Trade Unions.

654	**328**	18c. multicoloured	15	10

329 Surfing Santa

1977. Christmas. Multicoloured.

655	15c. Type **329**	25	10
656	45c. Madonna and Child	75	1·25

330 National Flag

1978. Australia Day.

657	**330**	18c. multicoloured	20	15

331 Harry Hawker and Sopwith Atlantic

1978. Early Australian Aviators. Multicoloured.

658	18c. Type **331**	40	50
659	18c. Bert Hinkler and Avro Type 581 Avian	40	50
660	18c. Sir Charles Kingsford Smith and *Southern Cross*	40	50
661	18c. Charles Ulm and *Southern Cross*	40	50
MS662	100×112 mm. Nos. 658/61×2. Imperf	75	1·75

332 Piper PA-31 Navajo landing at Station Airstrip

1978. 50th Anniv of Royal Flying Doctor Service.

663	**332**	18c. multicoloured	20	15

333 Illawarra Flame Tree

1978. Trees. Multicoloured.

664	18c. Type **333**	20	15
665	25c. Ghost gum	35	1·40
666	40c. Grass tree	45	2·00
667	45c. Cootamundra wattle	45	70

334 Sturt's Desert Rose and Map

1978. Establishment of State Government for the Northern Territory.

668	**334**	18c. multicoloured	20	15

335 Hooded Plover

1978. Birds (1st series). Multicoloured.

669	1c. Spotted-sided ("Zebra") finch	10	20
670	2c. Crimson finch	10	20
671	5c. Type **335**	50	10
672	15c. Forest kingfisher (vert)	20	20
673	20c. Australian dabchick ("Little Grebe")	70	10
674	20c. Yellow robin ("Eastern Yellow Robin")	75	10
675	22c. White-tailed kingfisher (22×29 mm)	30	10
676	25c. Masked ("Spur-wing") plover	1·00	1·25
677	30c. Pied oystercatcher	1·00	25
678	40c. Variegated ("Lovely") wren (vert)	30	45
679	50c. Flame robin (vert)	1·00	1·00
680	55c. Comb-crested jacana ("Lotus-Bird")	1·40	60

See also Nos. 734/40.

336 1928 3d. National Stamp Exhibition Commemorative

1978. 50th Anniv of National Stamp Week, and National Stamp Exhibition.

694	**336**	20c. multicoloured	15	15
MS695		78×113 mm. No. 694×4	75	1·50

337 *The Madonna and the Child* (after van Eyck)

1978. Christmas. Multicoloured.

696	15c. Type **337**	25	10
697	25c. *The Virgin and Child* (Marmion)	35	65
698	55c. *The Holy Family* (del Vaga)	50	1·00

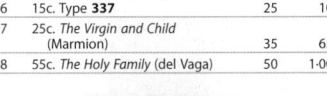

338 *Tulloch*

1978. Horse Racing. Multicoloured.

699	20c. Type **338**	30	10
700	35c. *Bernborough* (vert)	45	85
701	50c. *Phar Lap* (vert)	60	1·25
702	55c. *Peter Pan*	60	1·10

339 Raising the Flag, Sydney Cove, 26 January 1788

1979. Australia Day.

703	**339** 20c. multicoloured	15	15

340 *Canberra* (paddle-steamer)

1979. Ferries and Murray River Steamers. Multicoloured.

704	20c. Type **340**	20	10
705	35c. *Lady Denman*	40	70
706	50c. *Murray River Queen* (paddle-steamer)	50	1·40
707	55c. *Curl Curl* (hydrofoil)	55	1·25

341 Port Campbell, Victoria

1979. National Parks. Multicoloured.

708	20c. Type **341**	20	30
709	20c. Uluru, Northern Territory	20	30
710	20c. Royal, New South Wales	20	30
711	20c. Flinders Ranges, South Australia	20	30
712	20c. Nambung, Western Australia	20	30
713	20c. Girraween, Queensland (vert)	20	30
714	20c. Mount Field, Tasmania (vert)	20	30

342 *Double Fairlie* Type Locomotive, Western Australia

1979. Steam Railways. Multicoloured.

715	20c. Type **342**	30	10
716	35c. Locomotive, Puffing Billy Line, Victoria	60	70
717	50c. Locomotive, Pichi Richi Line, South Australia	70	1·50
718	55c. Locomotive, Zig Zag Railway, New South Wales	80	1·40

343 Symbolic Swan

1979. 150th Anniv of Western Australia.

719	**343** 20c. multicoloured	15	15

344 Children playing on Slide

1979. International Year of the Child.

720	**344** 20c. multicoloured	15	10

345 Letters and Parcels

1979. Christmas. Multicoloured.

721	15c. *Christ's Nativity* (Eastern European icon)	15	10
722	25c. Type **345**	15	65
723	55c. *Madonna and Child* (Buglioni)	25	80

346 Fly-fishing

1979. Fishing.

724	**346** 20c. multicoloured	15	10
725	- 35c. blue and violet	25	70
726	- 50c. multicoloured	35	90
727	- 55c. multicoloured	35	85

DESIGNS: 35c. Spinning; 50c. Deep sea game-fishing; 55c. Surf-fishing.

347 Matthew Flinders

1980. Australia Day.

728	**347** 20c. multicoloured	20	10

348 Dingo

1980. Dogs. Multicoloured.

729	20c. Type **348**	40	10
730	25c. Border collie	40	50
731	35c. Australian terrier	45	70
732	50c. Australian cattle dog	80	2·25
733	55c. Australian kelpie	80	1·40

1980. Birds (2nd series). As T **335**. Multicoloured.

734	10c. Golden-shouldered parrot (vert)	50	10
734b	18c. Spotted catbird (vert)	50	2·00
735	28c. Australian bee eater ("Rainbow Bird") (vert)	50	20
736	35c. Regent bower bird (vert)	50	10
737	45c. Masked wood swallow	50	10
738	60c. Australian king parrot ("King Parrot") (vert)	50	15
739	80c. Rainbow pitta	1·00	60
740	$1 Black-backed magpie ("Western Magpie") (vert)	1·00	10

349 Queen Elizabeth II

1980. Birthday of Queen Elizabeth II.

741	**349** 22c. multicoloured	30	20

350 Once a jolly Swagman camp'd by a Billabong

1980. Folklore. *Waltzing Matilda*. Multicoloured.

742	22c. Type **350**	25	40
743	22c. "And he sang as he shoved that jumbuck in his tuckerbag"	25	40
744	22c. "Up rode the squatter mounted on his thorough-bred"	25	40
745	22c. "Down came the troopers one, two, three"	25	40
746	22c. "And his ghost may be heard as you pass by that billabong"	25	40

351 High Court Building, Canberra

1980. Opening of High Court Building.

747	**351** 22c. multicoloured	20	20

352 Salvation Army

1980. Community Welfare. Multicoloured.

748	22c. Type **352**	30	30
749	22c. St. Vincent de Paul Society (vert)	30	30
750	22c. Meals on Wheels (vert)	30	30
751	22c. "Life. Be in it"	30	30

353 Postbox, c. 1900

1980. National Stamp Week. Multicoloured.

752	22c. Type **353**	25	40
753	22c. Postman, facing left	25	40
754	22c. Ford Model T mail van	25	40
755	22c. Postman, facing right	25	40
756	22c. Postman and postbox	25	40
MS757	95×100 mm. Nos. 752, 754 and 756	1·10	1·60

354 *Holy Family* (painting, Prospero Fontana)

1980. Christmas. Multicoloured.

758	15c. *The Virgin Enthroned* (Justin O'Brien) (detail)	15	10
759	28c. Type **354**	25	40
760	60c. *Madonna and Child* (sculpture by School of M. Zuern)	50	1·10

355 Commonwealth Aircraft Factory Wackett, 1941

1980. Australian Aircraft. Multicoloured.

761	22c. Type **355**	30	10
762	40c. Commonwealth Aircraft Factory Winjeel, 1955	50	75
763	45c. Commonwealth Aircraft Factory Boomerang, 1944	50	85
764	60c. Government Aircraft Factory Nomad, 1975	65	1·40

356 Flag in shape of Australia

1981. Australia Day.

765	**356** 22c. multicoloured	20	20

357 Caricature of Darby Munro (jockey)

1981. Sporting Personalities. Caricatures. Multicoloured.

766	22c. Type **357**	20	10
767	35c. Victor Trumper (cricket)	40	60
768	55c. Sir Norman Brookes (tennis)	40	1·00
769	60c. Walter Lindrum (billiards)	40	1·25

358 1931 Kingsford Smith's Flights 6d. Commemorative

1981. 50th Anniversary of Official Australia–U.K. Airmail Service.

770	**358** 22c. lilac, red and blue	15	10
771	- 60c. lilac, red and blue	40	90

DESIGN—HORIZ: 60c. As T **358**, but format changed.

359 Apex Emblem and Map of Australia

1981. 50th Anniv of Apex (young men's service club).

772	**359** 22c. multicoloured	20	20

360 Queen's Personal Standard for Australia

1981. Birthday of Queen Elizabeth II.

773	**360** 22c. multicoloured	20	20

361 *Licence Inspected*

1981. Gold Rush Era. Sketches by S. T. Gill. Multicoloured.

774	22c. Type **361**	20	25
775	22c. *Puddling*	20	25
776	22c. *Quality of washing stuff*	20	25
777	22c. *On route to deposit gold*	20	25

362 *On the Wallaby Track* (Fred McCubbin)

1981. Paintings. Multicoloured.

778	$2 Type **362**	1·00	30
779	$5 *A Holiday at Mentone, 1888* (Charles Conder)	3·00	70

363 Thylacine

363a Blue Mountain Tree Frog

363b *Papilio ulysses* (butterfly)

1981. Wildlife. Multicoloured.

781	1c. Lace monitor	10	20
782	3c. Corroboree frog	10	10
783	4c. Regent skipper (butterfly) (vert)	55	80
784	5c. Queensland hairy-nosed wombat (vert)	10	10
785	10c. Cairns birdwing (butterfly) (vert)	60	10
786	15c. Eastern snake-necked tortoise	1·00	1·00
787	20c. MacLeay's swallowtail (butterfly) (vert)	80	35
788	24c. Type **363**	45	10
789	25c. Greater Bilby (vert)	40	1·00
790a	27c. Type **363a**	1·00	1·00
791	27c. Type **363b**	1·00	30
792	30c. Bridle nail-tailed wallaby (vert)	90	20
792a	30c. Chlorinda hairstreak (butterfly) (vert)	1·00	20
793	35c. Blue tiger (butterfly) (vert)	1·00	30
794	40c. Smooth knob-tailed gecko	45	30
795	45c. Big greasy (butterfly) (vert)	1·00	30
796	50c. Leadbeater's possum	50	10
797	55c. Stick-nest rat (vert)	50	30
798	60c. Wood white (butterfly) (vert)	1·10	30
799	65c. Yellow-faced whip snake	1·75	1·50
800	70c. Crucifix toad	65	1·75
801	75c. Eastern water dragon	1·25	90
802	80c. Amaryllis azure (butterfly) (vert)	1·40	2·00
803	85c. Centralian blue-tongued lizard	1·10	1·25
804	90c. Freshwater crocodile	1·60	1·25
805	95c. Thorny devil	1·60	2·00
806	$1 Sword-grass brown (butterfly) (vert)	1·40	30

364 Prince Charles and Lady Diana Spencer

1981. Royal Wedding.

821	**364**	24c. multicoloured	20	10
822	**364**	60c. multicoloured	55	1·00

365 *Cortinarius cinnabarinus*

1981. Australian Fungi. Multicoloured.

823	24c. Type **365**	30	10
824	35c. *Coprinus comatus*	50	1·10
825	55c. *Armillaria luteobubalina*	65	1·25
826	60c. *Cortinarius austro-venetus*	75	1·40

366 Disabled People playing Basketball

1981. International Year for Disabled Persons.

827	**366**	24c. multicoloured	20	20

367 *Christmas Bush for His Adorning*

1981. Christmas. Scenes and Verses from Carols by W. James and J. Wheeler. Multicoloured.

828	18c. Type **367**	20	10
829	30c. *The Silver Stars are in the Sky*	25	25
830	60c. *Noeltime*	40	90

368 Globe depicting Australia

1981. Commonwealth Heads of Government Meeting, Melbourne.

831	**368**	24c. black, blue and gold	15	10
832	**368**	60c. black, blue and silver	45	75

369 *Ragamuffin* ocean racing yacht

1981. Yachts. Multicoloured.

833	24c. Type **369**	20	10
834	35c. *Sharpie*	30	55
835	55c. *12 Metre*	40	1·50
836	60c. *Sabot*	50	1·50

370 Aborigine, Governor Phillip (founder of N.S.W., 1788) and Post World War II Migrant

1982. Australia Day. "Three Great Waves of Migration".

837	**370**	24c. multicoloured	35	25

371 Humpback Whale

1982. Whales. Multicoloured.

838	24c. Sperm whale	30	10
839	35c. Black (inscr "Southern") right whale (vert)	40	60
840	55c. Blue whale (vert)	60	1·50
841	60c. Type **371**	70	1·50

372 Queen Elizabeth II

1982. Birthday of Queen Elizabeth II.

842	**372**	27c. multicoloured	35	15

373 "Marjorie Atherton"

1982. Roses. Multicoloured.

843	27c. Type **373**	25	15
844	40c. "Imp"	30	60
845	65c. "Minnie Watson"	50	2·00
846	75c. "Satellite"	50	1·25

374 Radio Announcer and 1930-style Microphone

1982. 50th Anniv of ABC (Australian Broadcasting Commission). Multicoloured.

847	27c. Type **374**	30	65
848	27c. ABC logo	30	65

375 Forbes Post Office

1982. Historic Australian Post Offices. Multicoloured.

849	27c. Type **375**	25	40
850	27c. Flemington Post Office	25	40
851	27c. Rockhampton Post Office	25	40
852	27c. Kingston S. E. Post Office (horiz)	25	40
853	27c. York Post Office (horiz)	25	40
854	27c. Launceston Post Office	25	40
855	27c. Old Post and Telegraph Station, Alice Springs (horiz)	25	40

376 Early Australian Christmas Card

1982. Christmas. Multicoloured.

856	21c. Bushman's Hotel with Cobb's coach arriving (horiz)	25	10
857	35c. Type **376**	40	60
858	75c. Little girl offering Christmas pudding to swagman	60	1·60

377 Boxing

1982. Commonwealth Games, Brisbane.

859	**377**	27c. stone, yellow and red	20	25
860	-	27c. yellow, stone and green	20	25
861	-	27c. stone, yellow and brown	20	25
862	-	75c. multicoloured	50	1·25
MS863		130×95 mm. Nos. 859/61	1·00	1·75

DESIGNS: No. 860, Archery; No. 861, Weight-lifting; No. 862, Pole-vaulting.

378 Sydney Harbour Bridge 5s. Stamp of 1932

1982. National Stamp Week.

864	**378**	27c. multicoloured	35	30

379 *Yirawala* Bark Painting

1982. Opening of Australian National Gallery.

865	**379**	27c. multicoloured	30	25

380 Mimi Spirits Dancing

1982. Aboriginal Culture. Music and Dance.

866	**380**	27c. multicoloured	20	10
867	-	40c. multicoloured	30	60
868	-	65c. multicoloured	45	1·00
869	-	75c. multicoloured	50	1·00

DESIGN: 40c. to 75c. Aboriginal bark paintings of Mimi Spirits.

381 *Eucalyptus calophylla* "Rosea"

1982. Eucalyptus Flowers. Multicoloured.

870	1c. Type **381**	10	30
871	2c. *Eucalyptus casia*	10	30
872	3c. *Eucalyptus ficifolia*	1·25	2·25
873	10c. *Eucalyptus globulus*	1·25	2·25
874	27c. *Eucalyptus forrestiana*	30	40

382 Shand Mason Steam Fire Engine, 1891

1983. Historic Fire Engines. Multicoloured.

875	27c. Type **382**	35	10
876	40c. Hotchkiss fire engine, 1914	45	75
877	65c. Ahrens-Fox fire engine, 1929	70	1·60
878	75c. Merryweather manual fire appliance, 1851	70	1·40

383 H.M.S. *Sirius*

1983. Australia Day. Multicoloured.

879	27c. Type **383**	40	75
880	27c. H.M.S.*Supply*	40	75

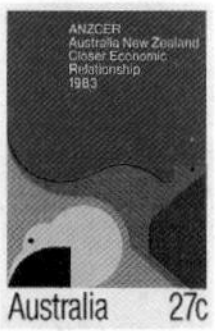

384 Stylized Kangaroo and Kiwi

1983. Closer Economic Relationship Agreement with New Zealand.

881	**384**	27c. multicoloured	30	30

385 Equality and Dignity

1983. Commonwealth Day. Multicoloured.

882	27c. Type **385**	20	25
883	27c. Liberty and Freedom	20	25
884	27c. Social Justice and Co-operation	20	25
885	75c. Peace and Harmony	50	1·50

386 R.Y. *Britannia* passing Sydney Opera House

1983. Birthday of Queen Elizabeth II.

886	**386**	27c. multicoloured	50	30

387 "Postal and Telecommunications Services"

1983. World Communications Year.

887	**387**	27c. multicoloured	30	30

388 Badge of the Order of St. John

1983. Centenary of St. John Ambulance in Australia.

888	**388**	27c. black and blue	35	30

389 Jaycee Members and Badge

1983. 50th Anniv of Australian Jaycees.

889	**389**	27c. multicoloured	30	30

390 "The Bloke"

1983. Folklore. *The Sentimental Bloke* (humorous poem by C. J. Dennis). Multicoloured.

890	27c. Type **390**	30	50
891	27c. "Doreen—The Intro"	30	50
892	27c. "The Stror' at Coot"	30	50
893	27c. "Hitched"	30	50
894	27c. "The Mooch o' Life"	30	50

391 Nativity Scene

1983. Christmas. Children's Paintings. Multicoloured.

895	24c. Type **391**	20	10
896	35c. Kookaburra	30	45
897	85c. Father Christmas in sleigh over beach	60	1·40

392 Sir Paul Edmund de Strzelecki

1983. Explorers of Australia. Multicoloured.

898	30c. Type **392**	25	40
899	30c. Ludwig Leichhardt	25	40
900	30c. William John Wills and Robert O'Hara Burke	25	40
901	30c. Alexander Forrest	25	40

393 Cook Family Cottage, Melbourne

1984. Australia Day.

902	**393**	30c. black and stone	30	35

394 Charles Ulm, *Faith in Australia* and Trans-Tasman Cover

1984. 50th Anniv of First Official Airmail Flights. New Zealand–Australia and Australia–Papua New Guinea. Multicoloured.

903	45c. Type **394**	75	1·25
904	45c. As Type **394** but showing flown cover to Papua New Guinea	75	1·25

395 Thomson "Steamer", 1898

1984. Veteran and Vintage Cars. Multicoloured.

905	30c. Type **395**	35	60
906	30c. Tarrant two seater, 1906	35	60
907	30c. Gordon & Co "Australian Six" two seater, 1919	35	60
908	30c. Summit tourer, 1923	35	60
909	30c. Chic two seater, 1924	35	60

396 Queen Elizabeth II

1984. Birthday of Queen Elizabeth II.

910	**396**	30c. multicoloured	30	35

397 *Cutty Sark*

1984. Clipper Ships. Multicoloured.

911	30c. Type **397**	35	25
912	45c. *Orient* (horiz)	50	80
913	75c. *Sobraon* (horiz)	70	1·75
914	85c. *Thermopylae*	70	1·50

398 Freestyle

1984. Skiing. Multicoloured.

915	30c. Type **398**	30	45
916	30c. Downhill racer	30	45
917	30c. Slalom (horiz)	30	45
918	30c. Nordic (horiz)	30	45

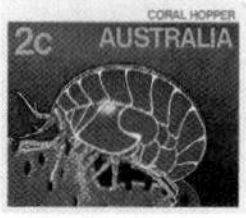

399 Coral Hopper

1984. Marine Life. Multicoloured.

919	2c. Type **399**	10	30
920	3c. Jimble	40	30
921	5c. Tasselled frogfish ("Anglerfish")	15	10
922	10c. Rough stonefish	1·00	50
923	20c. Red handfish	65	40
924	25c. Orange-lipped cowrie	45	40
925	30c. Choat's wrasse	45	40
926	33c. Leafy seadragon	65	10
927	40c. Red velvetfish	85	1·75
928	45c. Textile or cloth of gold cone	1·50	50
929	50c. Clown surgeonfish	80	50
930	55c. Bennet's nudibranch	80	50
931	60c. Zebra lionfish	1·50	70
932	65c. Banded stingray	1·50	2·25
933	70c. Southern blue-ringed octopus	1·50	1·75
934	80c. Pineconefish ("Pineapple fish")	1·25	1·75
935	85c. Royal angelfish	90	70
936	90c. Crab-eyed goby	1·60	75
937	$1 Crown of thorns starfish	1·50	80

400 Before the Event

1984. Olympic Games, Los Angeles. Multicoloured.

941	30c. Type **400**	25	40
942	30c. During the event	25	40
943	30c. After the event (vert)	25	40

401 Australian 1913 1d. Kangaroo Stamp

1984. "Ausipex '84" International Stamp Exhibition, Melbourne.

944	**401**	30c. multicoloured	35	30

MS945 126×175 mm. 30c. × 7, Victoria 1850 3d. "Half Length"; New South Wales 1850 1d. "Sydney View"; Tasmania 1853 1d.; South Australia 1855 1d.; Western Australia 1854 1d. "Black Swan"; Queensland 1860 6d.; Type **401** — 3·50 — 4·50

402 *Angel* (stained-glass window, St. Francis's Church, Melbourne)

1984. Christmas. Stained-glass Windows. Multicoloured.

946	24c. *Angel and Child* (Holy Trinity Church, Sydney)	15	10
947	30c. *Veiled Virgin and Child* (St. Mary's Catholic Church, Geelong)	20	10
948	40c. Type **402**	30	75
949	50c. *Three Kings* (St. Mary's Cathedral, Sydney)	40	90
950	85c. *Madonna and Child* (St. Bartholomew's Church, Norwood)	50	1·60

403 "Stick Figures" (Cobar Region)

1984. Bicentenary (1988) of Australian Settlement (1st issue). The First Australians. Multicoloured.

951	30c. Type **403**	20	45
952	30c. "Bunjil" (large figure), Grampians	20	45
953	30c. "Quikans" (tall figures), Cape York	20	45
954	30c. "Wandjina Spirit and Baby Snakes" (Gibb River)	20	45
955	30c. "Rock Python" (Gibb River)	20	45
956	30c. "Silver Barramundi" (fish) (Kakadu National Park)	20	45
957	30c. Bicentenary emblem	20	45
958	85c. "Rock Possum" (Kakadu National Park)	50	1·40

See also Nos. 972/5, 993/6, 1002/7, 1019/22, 1059/63, 1064/6, 1077/81, 1090/2, 1110, 1137/41, 1145/8 and 1149.

404 Yellow-tufted Honeyeater

1984. 150th Anniv of Victoria.. Multicoloured.

959	30c. Type **404**	40	65
960	30c. Leadbeater's possum	40	65

405 *Musgrave Ranges* (Sidney Nolan)

1985. Australia Day. Birth Bicentenary of Dorothea Mackellar (author of poem *My Country*). Multicoloured.

961	30c. Type **405**	50	80
962	30c. *The Walls of China* (Russell Drysdale)	50	80

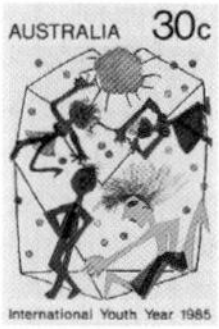

406 Young People of Different Races and Sun

1985. International Youth Year.

963	**406**	30c. multicoloured	40	30

407 Royal Victorian Volunteer Artillery

1985. 19th-Century Australian Military Uniforms. Multicoloured.

964	33c. Type **407**	40	65
965	33c. Western Australian Pinjarrah Cavalry	40	65
966	33c. New South Wales Lancers	40	65
967	33c. New South Wales Contingent to the Sudan	40	65
968	33c. Victorian Mounted Rifles	40	65

408 District Nurse of early 1900s

1985. Centenary of District Nursing Services.

969	**408**	33c. multicoloured	45	35

409 Sulphur-crested Cockatoos

1985. Multicoloured, background colour given.

970	**409**	1c. flesh	2·50	3·00
971	**409**	33c. turquoise	50	55

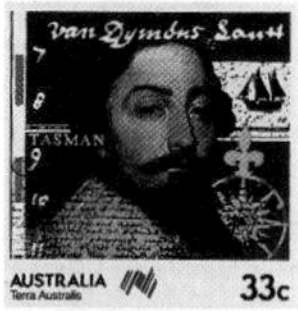

410 Abel Tasman and Journal Entry

1985. Bicentenary (1988) of Australian Settlement (2nd issue). Navigators. Multicoloured.

972	33c. Type **410**	40	35
973	33c. Dirk Hartog's *Eendracht* (detail, Aert Anthonisz)	40	35
974	33c. *William Dampier* (detail, T. Murray)	40	35
975	90c. Globe and hand with extract from Dampier's journal	75	2·50
MS976	150×115 mm. As Nos. 972/5, but with cream-coloured margins	2·25	4·50

411 Sovereign's Badge of Order of Australia

1985. Queen Elizabeth II's Birthday.

977	**411**	33c. multicoloured	40	30

412 Tree, and Soil running through Hourglass ("Soil")

1985. Conservation. Multicoloured.

978	33c. Type **412**	25	20
979	50c. Washing on line and smog ("air")	40	75
980	80c. Tap and flower ("water")	50	1·25
981	90c. Chain encircling flames ("energy")	60	1·75

413 *Elves and Fairies* (Annie Rentoul and Ida Rentoul Outhwaite)

1985. Classic Australian Children's Books. Multicoloured.

982	33c. Type **413**	40	75
983	33c. *The Magic Pudding* (Norman Lindsay)	40	75
984	33c. *Ginger Meggs* (James Charles Bancks)	40	75
985	33c. *Blinky Bill* (Dorothy Wall)	40	75
986	33c. *Snugglepot and Cuddlepie* (May Gibbs)	40	75

414 Dish Aerials

1985. Electronic Mail Service.

987	**414**	33c. multicoloured	35	30

415 Angel in Sailing Ship

1985. Christmas. Multicoloured.

988	27c. Angel with holly wings	20	10
989	33c. Angel with bells	25	10
990	45c. Type **415**	30	25
991	55c. Angel with star	40	60
992	90c. Angel with Christmas tree bauble	65	1·75

416 Astrolabe ("Batavia", 1629)

1985. Bicentenary (1988) of Australian Settlement (3rd issue). Relics from Early Shipwrecks. Multicoloured.

993	33c. Type **416**	35	15
994	50c. German beardman jug (*Vergulde Draeck*, 1656)	60	1·00
995	90c. Wooden bobbins (*Batavia*, 1629) and encrusted scissors (*Zeewijk*, 1727)	1·00	3·75
996	$1 Silver and brass buckle (*Zeewijk*, 1727)	1·00	2·25

417 Aboriginal Wandjina Spirit, Map of Australia and Egg

1986. Australia Day.

997	**417**	33c. multicoloured	40	30

418 AUSSAT Satellite, Moon and Earth's Surface

1986. AUSSAT National Communications Satellite System. Multicoloured.

998	33c. Type **418**	40	15
999	80c. AUSSAT satellite in orbit	1·00	2·25

419 H.M.S. *Buffalo*

1986. 150th Anniv of South Australia. Multicoloured.

1000	33c. Type **419**	70	1·25
1001	33c. *City Sign* sculpture (Otto Hajek), Adelaide	70	1·25

Nos. 1000/1 were printed together *se-tenant*, the background of each horiz pair showing an extract from the colony's Letters Patent of 1836.

420 *Banksia serrata*

1986. Bicentenary (1988) of Australian Settlement (4th issue). Cook's Voyage to New Holland. Multicoloured.

1002	33c. Type **420**	50	35
1003	33c. *Hibiscus meraukensis*	50	35
1004	50c. *Dillenia alata*	70	1·10
1005	80c. *Correa reflexa*	1·50	2·75
1006	90c. *Joseph Banks* (botanist) (Reynolds) and Banks with Dr. Solander	2·00	2·75
1007	90c. *Sydney Parkinson* (self-portrait) and Parkinson drawing	2·00	2·75

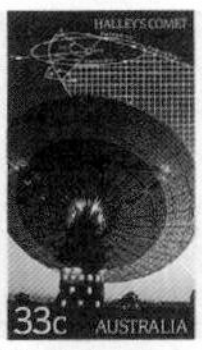

421 Radio Telescope, Parkes, and Diagram of Comet's Orbit

1986. Appearance of Halley's Comet.

1008	**421**	33c. multicoloured	50	35

422 Queen Elizabeth II

1986. 60th Birthday of Queen Elizabeth.

1009	**422**	33c. multicoloured	55	35

423 Brumbies (wild horses)

1986. Australian Horses. Multicoloured.

1010	33c. Type **423**	60	15
1011	80c. Mustering	1·50	2·25
1012	90c. Show-jumping	1·50	2·50
1013	$1 Child on pony	1·75	2·25

424 *The Old Shearer stands*

1986. Folklore. Scenes and Verses from the Folksong *Click go the Shears*. Multicoloured.

1014	33c. Type **424**	45	80
1015	33c. "The ringer looks around"	45	80
1016	33c. "The boss of the board"	45	80
1017	33c. "The tar-boy is there"	45	80
1018	33c. "Shearing is all over"	45	80

Nos. 1014/18 were printed together, *se-tenant*, forming a composite design.

425 *King George III* (A. Ramsay) and Convicts

1986. Bicentenary (1988) of Australian Settlement (5th issue). Convict Settlement in New South Wales. Multicoloured.

1019	33c. Type **425**	50	55
1020	33c. *Lord Sydney* (Gilbert Stuart) and convicts	50	55
1021	33c. *Captain Arthur Phillip* (F. Wheatley) and ship	50	55
1022	$1 *Captain John Hunter* (W. B. Bennett) and aborigines	1·50	5·00

426 Red Kangaroo

1986. Australian Wildlife (1st series). Multicoloured.

1023	36c. Type **426**	70	95
1024	36c. Emu	70	95
1025	36c. Koala	70	95
1026	36c. Laughing kookaburra ("Kookaburra")	70	95
1027	36c. Platypus	70	95

See also Nos. 1072/6.

427 Royal Bluebell

1986. Alpine Wildflowers. Multicoloured.

1028	3c. Type **427**	50	75
1029	5c. Alpine marsh marigold	2·00	3·25
1030	25c. Mount Buffalo sunray	2·00	3·25
1031	36c. Silver snow daisy	45	30

428 Pink Enamel Orchid

1986. Native Orchids. Multicoloured.

1032	36c. Type **428**	75	20
1033	55c. *Dendrobium nindii*	1·50	1·25
1034	90c. Duck orchid	2·25	4·00
1035	$1 Queen of Sheba orchid	2·25	2·75

429 *Australia II* crossing Finishing Line

1986. Australian Victory in America's Cup, 1983. Multicoloured.

1036	36c. Type **429**	75	75
1037	36c. Boxing kangaroo flag of winning syndicate	75	75
1038	36c. America's Cup trophy	75	75

430 Dove with Olive Branch and Sun

1986. International Peace Year.

1039	**430**	36c. multicoloured	65	40

431 Mary and Joseph

1986. Christmas. Scenes from children's nativity play. Multicoloured.

1040	30c. Type **431**	40	30
1041	36c. Three Wise Men leaving gifts	50	20
1042	60c. Angels (horiz)	90	2·00
MS1043	147×70 mm. 30c. Three angels and shepherd (horiz); 30c. Kneeling shepherds (horiz); 30c. Mary, Joseph and three angels; 30c. Innkeeper and two angels; 30c. Three Wise Men (horiz)	3·50	4·00

432 Australian Flag on Printed Circuit Board

1987. Australia Day. Multicoloured.

1044	36c. Type **432**	55	75
1045	36c. "Australian Made" Campaign logos	55	75

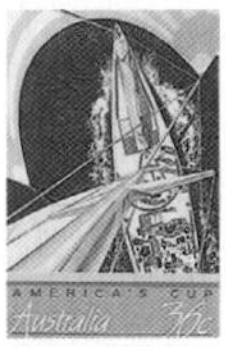

433 Aerial View of Yacht

1987. America's Cup Yachting Championship. Multicoloured.

1046	36c. Type **433**	30	20
1047	55c. Two yachts tacking	60	1·00
1048	90c. Two yachts beating	80	2·75
1049	$1 Two yachts under full sail	90	1·50

434 Grapes and Melons

1987. Australian Fruit. Multicoloured.

1050	36c. Type **434**	30	20
1051	65c. Tropical and sub-tropical fruits	80	1·50
1052	90c. Citrus fruit, apples and pears	1·25	2·75
1053	$1 Stone and berry fruits	1·25	1·60

435 Livestock

1987. Agricultural Shows. Multicoloured.

1054	36c. Type **435**	60	20
1055	65c. Produce	1·00	1·75
1056	90c. Sideshows	1·25	3·25
1057	$1 Competitions	1·50	2·50

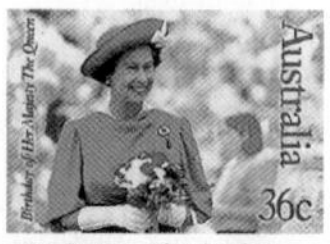

436 Queen Elizabeth in Australia, 1986

1987. Queen Elizabeth II's Birthday.

1058	**436**	36c. multicoloured	55	60

437 Convicts on Quay

1987. Bicentenary (1988) of Australian Settlement (6th issue). Departure of the First Fleet. Multicoloured.

1059	36c. Type **437**	65	1·10
1060	36c. Royal Marines officer and wife	65	1·10
1061	36c. Sailors loading supplies	65	1·10
1062	36c. Officers being ferried to ships	65	1·10
1063	36c. Fleet in English Channel	65	1·10

See also Nos. 1064/6, 1077/81 and 1090/2.

1987. Bicentenary (1988) of Australian Settlement (7th issue). First Fleet at Tenerife. As T **437**. Multicoloured.

1064	36c. Ferrying supplies, Santa Cruz	70	1·00
1065	36c. Canary Islands fishermen and departing fleet	70	1·00
1066	$1 Fleet arriving at Tenerife	1·75	2·25

Nos. 1064/5 were printed together, *se-tenant*, forming a composite design.

438 At the Station

1987. Folklore. Scenes and Verses from Poem *The Man from Snowy River*. Multicoloured.

1067	36c. Type **438**	80	1·10
1068	36c. "Mountain bred"	80	1·10
1069	36c. "That terrible descent"	80	1·10
1070	36c. "At their heels"	80	1·10
1071	36c. "Brought them back"	80	1·10

Nos. 1067/71 were printed together, *se-tenant*, forming a composite background design of mountain scenery.

1987. Australian Wildlife (2nd series). As T **426**. Multicoloured.

1072	37c. Common brushtail possum	55	85
1073	37c. Sulphur-crested cockatoo ("Cockatoo")	55	85
1074	37c. Common wombat	55	85
1075	37c. Crimson rosella ("Rosella")	55	85
1076	37c. Echidna	55	85

1987. Bicentenary (1988) of Australian Settlement (8th issue). First Fleet at Rio de Janeiro. As T **437**. Multicoloured.

1077	37c. Sperm whale and fleet	80	1·10
1078	37c. Brazilian coast	80	1·10
1079	37c. British officers in market	80	1·10
1080	37c. Religious procession	80	1·10
1081	37c. Fleet leaving Rio	80	1·10

Nos. 1077/81 were printed together, *se-tenant*, forming a composite design.

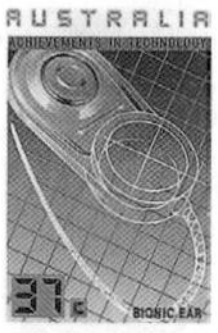

439 Bionic Ear

1987. Australian Achievements in Technology. Multicoloured.

1082	37c. Type **439**	25	15
1083	53c. Microchips	40	35
1084	63c. Robotics	50	60
1085	68c. Ceramics	55	65

440 Catching Crayfish

1987. "Aussie Kids". Multicoloured.

1086	37c. Type **440**	40	15
1087	55c. Playing cat's cradle	60	75
1088	90c. Young football supporters	1·00	2·50
1089	$1 Children with kangaroo	1·00	1·50

1987. Bicentenary (1988) of Australian Settlement (9th issue). First Fleet at Cape of Good Hope. As T **437**. Multicoloured.

1090	37c. Marine checking list of livestock	65	1·00
1091	37c. Loading livestock	65	1·00
1092	$1 First Fleet at Cape Town	1·50	2·50

Nos. 1090/1 were printed together, *se-tenant*, forming a composite design.

441 Detail of Spearthrower, Western Australia

1987. Aboriginal Crafts. Multicoloured.

1093	3c. Type **441**	1·10	1·50
1094	15c. Shield pattern, New South Wales	5·50	8·50
1095	37c. Basket weave, Queensland	1·10	1·50
1096	37c. Bowl design, Central Australia	90	1·25
1097	37c. Belt pattern, Northern Territory	1·10	1·50

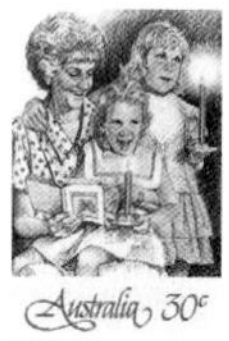

442 Grandmother and Granddaughters with Candles

1987. Christmas. Designs showing carol singing by candlelight. Multicoloured.

1098	30c. Type **442**	50	65
1099	30c. Father and daughters	50	65
1100	30c. Four children	50	65
1101	30c. Family	50	65
1102	30c. Six teenagers	50	65
1103	37c. Choir (horiz)	50	35
1104	63c. Father and two children (horiz)	85	1·60

1988. Bicentenary of Australian Settlement (10th issue). Arrival of First Fleet. As T **437**. Multicoloured.

1105	37c. Aborigines watching arrival of Fleet, Botany Bay	65	95
1106	37c. Aborigine family and anchored ships	65	95
1107	37c. Fleet arriving at Sydney Cove	65	95
1108	37c. Ship's boat	65	95
1109	37c. Raising the flag, Sydney Cove, 26 January 1788	65	95

Nos. 1105/9 were printed together, *se-tenant*, forming a composite design.

443 Koala with Stockman's Hat and Eagle dressed as Uncle Sam

1988. Bicentenary of Australian Settlement (11th issue). Joint issue with U.S.A.

1110	**443**	37c. multicoloured	60	35

444 *Religion* (A. Horner)

1988. "Living Together". Designs showing cartoons. Multicoloured (except 30c.).

1111	1c. Type **444**	50	70
1112	2c. *Industry* (P. Nicholson)	50	60
1113	3c. *Local Government* (A. Collette)	50	60
1114	4c. *Trade Unions* (Liz Honey)	10	20
1115	5c. *Parliament* (Bronwyn Halls)	30	50
1116	10c. *Transport* (Meg Williams)	30	50
1117	15c. *Sport* (G. Cook)	1·75	60
1118	20c. *Commerce* (M. Atcherson)	70	1·00
1119	25c. *Housing* (C. Smith)	45	40
1120	30c. *Welfare* (R. Tandberg) (black and lilac)	55	1·25
1121	37c. *Postal Services* (P. Viska)	50	50
1121b	39c. *Tourism* (J. Spooner)	60	50
1122	40c. *Recreation* (R. Harvey)	70	70
1123	45c. *Health* (Jenny Coopes)	70	1·25
1124	50c. *Mining* (G. Haddon)	70	50
1125	53c. *Primary Industry* (S. Leahy)	1·75	2·25
1126	55c. *Education* (Victoria Roberts)	1·50	2·25
1127	60c. *Armed Forces* (B. Green)	1·50	70
1128	63c. *Police* (J. Russell)	2·50	1·40
1129	65c. *Telecommunications* (B. Petty)	1·50	2·75
1130	68c. *The Media* (A. Langoulant)	2·25	3·50
1131	70c. *Science and Technology* (J. Hook)	1·75	1·75
1132	75c. *Visual Arts* (G. Dazeley)	1·00	1·00
1133	80c. *Performing Arts* (A. Stitt)	1·25	1·00
1134	90c. *Banking* (S. Billington)	1·50	1·50
1135	95c. *Law* (C. Aslanis)	1·00	2·25
1136	$1 *Rescue and Emergency* (M. Leunig)	1·10	1·00

445 *Government House, Sydney, 1790* (George Raper)

1988. Bicentenary of Australian Settlement (12th issue). *The Early Years, 1788–1809*. Multicoloured.

1137	37c. Type **445**	65	1·00
1138	37c. *Government Farm, Parramatta, 1791* ("The Port Jackson Painter")	65	1·00
1139	37c. *Parramatta Road, 1796* (attr Thomas Watling)	65	1·00
1140	37c. *View of Sydney Cove, c. 1800* (detail) (Edward Dayes)	65	1·00
1141	37c. *Sydney Hospital, 1803*, (detail) (George William Evans)	65	1·00

Nos. 1137/41 were printed together, *se-tenant*, forming a composite background design from the painting *View of Sydney from the East Side of the Cove, c. 1808* by John Eyre.

446 Queen Elizabeth II (from photo by Tim Graham)

1988. Queen Elizabeth II's Birthday.

1142	**446**	37c. multicoloured	50	40

447 Expo '88 Logo

1988. "Expo '88" World Fair, Brisbane.

1143	**447**	37c. multicoloured	50	40

448 New Parliament House

1988. Opening of New Parliament House, Canberra.

1144	**448**	37c. multicoloured	50	40

449 Early Settler and Sailing Clipper

1988. Bicentenary of Australian Settlement (13th issue). Multicoloured.

1145	37c. Type **449**	75	1·00
1146	37c. Queen Elizabeth II with British and Australian Parliament Buildings	75	1·00
1147	$1 W. G. Grace (cricketer) and tennis racquet	1·50	2·25
1148	$1 Shakespeare, John Lennon (entertainer) and Sydney Opera House	1·50	2·25

Stamps in similar designs were also issued by Great Britain.

450 Kiwi and Koala at Campfire

1988. Bicentenary of Australian Settlement (14th issue).

1149	**450**	37c. multicoloured	65	40

A stamp in a similar design was also issued by New Zealand.

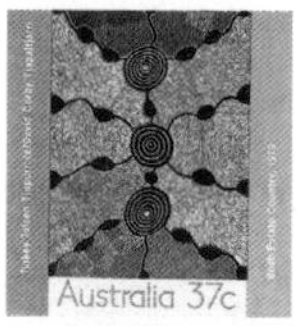

451 *Bush Potato Country* (Turkey Tolsen Tjupurrula and David Corby Tjapaltjarri)

1988. Art of the Desert. Aboriginal Paintings from Central Australia. Multicoloured.

1150	37c. Type **451**	25	30
1151	55c. *Courtship Rejected* (Limpi Puntungka Tjapangati)	45	70
1152	90c. *Medicine Story* (artist unknown)	65	2·40
1153	$1 *Ancestor Dreaming* (Tim Leura Tjapaltjarri)	65	1·50

452 Basketball

1988. Olympic Games, Seoul. Multicoloured.

1154	37c. Type **452**	40	25
1155	65c. Athlete crossing finish line	45	1·75
1156	$1 Gymnast with hoop	60	1·75

453 Rod and Mace

1988. 34th Commonwealth Parliamentary Conference, Canberra.

1157	**453**	37c. multicoloured	50	60

454 Necklace by Peter Tully

1988. Australian Crafts. Multicoloured.

1158	2c. Type **454**	4·00	6·50
1159	5c. Vase by Colin Levy	4·00	6·50
1160	39c. Teapot by Frank Bauer	50	35

455 Pinnacles Desert

1988. Panorama of Australia. Multicoloured.

1161	39c. Type **455**	55	30
1162	55c. Flooded landscape, Arnhem Land	75	75
1163	65c. Twelve Apostles, Victoria	1·25	2·25
1164	70c. Mountain Ash wood	1·25	2·25

456 *The Nativity* (Danielle Hush)

1988. Christmas. Multicoloured.

1165	32c. Type **456**	35	10
1166	39c. *Koala as Father Christmas* (Kylie Courtney)	35	10
1167	63c. *Christmas Cockatoo* (Benjamin Stevenson)	70	1·40

457 Sir Henry Parkes

1989. Australia Day. Centenary of Federation Speech by Sir Henry Parkes (N.S.W. Prime Minister).

1168	**457** 39c. multicoloured	45	40

458 Bowls

1989. Sports. Multicoloured.

1169	1c. Type **458**	10	50
1170	2c. Tenpin-bowling	10	20
1171	3c. Australian football	1·00	1·50
1172	5c. Kayaking and canoeing	15	10
1174	10c. Sailboarding	15	15
1176	20c. Tennis	20	25
1179	39c. Fishing	45	40
1180	41c. Cycling	40	35
1181	43c. Skateboarding	50	40
1184	55c. Kite-flying	50	45
1186	65c. Rock-climbing	80	70
1187	70c. Cricket	1·90	80
1188	75c. Netball	70	1·50
1189	80c. Squash	1·00	65
1190	85c. Diving	1·75	80
1191	90c. Soccer	1·75	2·00
1192	$1 Fun-run	1·00	50
1193	$1.10 Golf	4·25	1·00
1194	$1.20 Hang-gliding	5·00	1·10

459 Merino

1989. Sheep in Australia. Multicoloured.

1195	39c. Type **459**	70	50
1196	39c. Poll Dorset	70	50
1197	85c. Polwarth	1·75	3·50
1198	$1 Corriedale	1·75	2·00

460 Adelaide Botanic Garden

1989. Botanic Gardens. Multicoloured.

1199	$2 Noroo, New South Wales	1·50	30
1200	$5 Mawarra, Victoria	4·25	60
1201	$10 Type **460**	7·50	1·00
1201a	$20 *A View of the Artist's House and Garden in Mills Plains, Van Diemen's Land* (John Glover)	19·00	8·00

461 *Queen Elizabeth II* (sculpture, John Dowie)

1989. Queen Elizabeth II's Birthday.

1202	**461** 39c. multicoloured	55	50

462 Arrival of Immigrant Ship, 1830s

1989. Colonial Development (1st issue). Pastoral Era 1810–1850. Multicoloured.

1203	39c. Type **462**	45	60
1204	39c. Pioneer cottage and wool dray	45	60
1205	39c. Squatter's homestead	45	60
1206	39c. Shepherd with flock (from Joseph Lycett's *Views of Australia*)	45	60
1207	39c. Explorer in desert (after watercolour by Edward Frome)	45	60

See also Nos. 1254/8 and 1264/8.

463 Gladys Moncrieff and Roy Rene

1989. Australian Stage and Screen Personalities. Multicoloured.

1208	39c. Type **463**	30	25
1209	85c. Charles Chauvel and Chips Rafferty	70	2·00
1210	$1 Nellie Stewart and J. C. Williamson	70	1·00
1211	$1.10 Lottie Lyell and Raymond Longford	70	1·25

464 *Impression* (Tom Roberts)

1989. Australian Impressionist Paintings. Multicoloured.

1212	41c. Type **464**	45	50
1213	41c. *Impression for Golden Summer* (Sir Arthur Streeton)	45	50
1214	41c. *All on a Summer's Day* (Charles Conder) (vert)	45	50
1215	41c. *Petit Dejeuner* (Frederick McCubbin)	45	50

465 Freeways

1989. The Urban Environment.

1216	**465** 41c. black, purple and green	80	1·40
1217	- 41c. black, purple and mauve	80	1·25
1218	- 41c. black, purple and blue	80	1·40

DESIGNS: No. 1217, City buildings, Melbourne; No. 1218, Commuter train at platform.

466 Hikers outside Youth Hostel

1989. 50th Anniv of Australian Youth Hostels.

1219	**466** 41c. multicoloured	55	50

467 Horse Tram, Adelaide, 1878

1989. Historic Trams. Multicoloured.

1220	41c. Type **467**	60	75
1221	41c. Steam tram, Sydney, 1884	60	75
1222	41c. Cable tram, Melbourne, 1886	60	75
1223	41c. Double-deck electric tram, Hobart, 1893	60	75
1224	41c. Combination electric tram, Brisbane, 1901	60	75

468 *Annunciation* (15th-century Book of Hours)

1989. Christmas. Illuminated Manuscripts. Multicoloured.

1225	36c. Type **468**	30	10
1226	41c. *Annunciation to the Shepherds* (Wharncliffe Book of Hours, c. 1475)	35	10
1227	80c. *Adoration of the Magi* (15th-century Parisian Book of Hours)	1·00	1·75

469 Radio Waves and Globe

1989. 50th Anniv of Radio Australia.

1228	**469** 41c. multicoloured	55	50

470 Golden Wattle

1990. Australia Day.

1229	**470** 41c. multicoloured	55	50

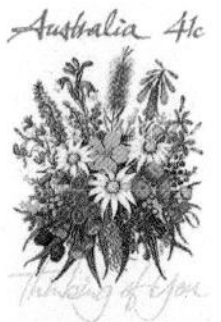

471 Australian Wildflowers

1990. Greetings Stamps.

1230	**471** 41c. multicoloured	65	65
1231	**471** 43c. multicoloured	50	50

472 Dr. Constance Stone (first Australian woman doctor), Modern Doctor and Nurses

1990. Centenary of Women in Medical Practice.

1232	**472** 41c. multicoloured	50	45

473 Greater Glider

1990. Animals of the High Country. Multicoloured.

1233	41c. Type **473**	60	45
1234	65c. Tiger cat ("Spotted-tailed Quoll")	90	1·90
1235	70c. Mountain pygmy-possum	95	1·90
1236	80c. Brush-tailed rock-wallaby	1·10	1·90

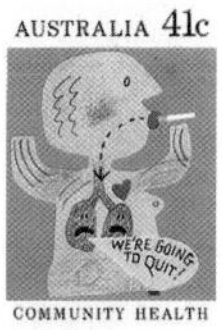

474 "Stop Smoking"

1990. Community Health. Multicoloured.

1237	41c. Type **474**	55	55
1238	41c. "Drinking and driving don't mix"	55	55
1239	41c. "No junk food, please"	55	55
1240	41c. "Guess who's just had a check up?"	55	55

475 Soldiers from Two World Wars

1990. "The Anzac Tradition". Multicoloured.

1241	41c. Type **475**	80	40
1242	41c. Fighter pilots and munitions worker	80	40
1243	65c. Veterans and Anzac Day parade	1·25	1·25
1244	$1 Casualty evacuation, Vietnam, and disabled veteran	1·75	1·40
1245	$1.10 Letters from home and returning troopships	1·75	1·50

476 Queen at Australian Ballet Gala Performance, London, 1988

1990. Queen Elizabeth II's Birthday.

1246	**476** 41c. multicoloured	1·00	50

477 New South Wales 1861 5s. Stamp

1990. 150th Anniv of the Penny Black. Designs showing stamps. Multicoloured.

1247	41c. Type **477**	75	1·00
1248	41c. South Australia 1855 unissued 1s.	75	1·00
1249	41c. Tasmania 1853 4d.	75	1·00
1250	41c. Victoria 1867 5s.	75	1·00
1251	41c. Queensland 1897 unissued 6d.	75	1·00
1252	41c. Western Australia 1855 4d. with inverted frame	75	1·00
MS1253	122×85 mm. Nos. 1247/52	4·00	5·50

478 Gold Miners on Way to Diggings

1990. Colonial Development (2nd issue). Gold Fever. Multicoloured.

1254	41c. Type **478**	85	1·00
1255	41c. Mining camp	85	1·00
1256	41c. Panning and washing for gold	85	1·00
1257	41c. Gold Commissioner's tent	85	1·00
1258	41c. Moving gold under escort	85	1·00

479 Glaciology Research

1990. Australian–Soviet Scientific Co-operation in Antarctica. Multicoloured.

1261	41c. Type **479**	65	40
1262	$1.10 Krill (marine biology research)	1·60	2·00
MS1263	85×65 mm. Nos. 1261/2	2·25	2·25

Stamps in similar designs were also issued by Russia.

480 Auctioning Building Plots

1990. Colonial Development (3rd issue). Boomtime. Multicoloured.

1264	41c. Type **480**	55	55
1265	41c. Colonial mansion	55	55
1266	41c. Stock exchange	55	55
1267	41c. Fashionable society	55	55
1268	41c. Factories	55	55

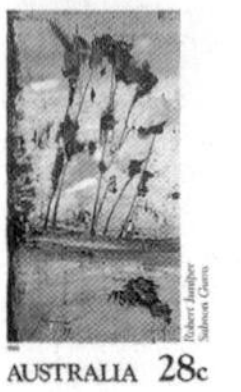

481 *Salmon Gums* (Robert Juniper)

1990. *Heidelberg and Heritage* Art Exhibition. Multicoloured.

1269	28c. Type **481**	2·50	4·00
1270	43c. *The Blue Dress* (Brian Dunlop)	40	45

482 *Adelaide Town Hall* (Edmund Gouldsmith)

1990. 150th Anniv of Local Government.

1271	**482**	43c. multicoloured	75	50

483 Laughing Kookaburras and Gifts

1990. Christmas. Multicoloured.

1272	38c. Type **483**	50	25
1273	43c. Baby Jesus with koalas and wallaby (vert)	50	25
1274	80c. Possum on Christmas tree	1·50	3·50

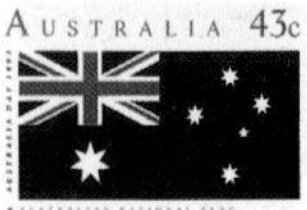

484 National Flag

1991. Australia Day. 90th Anniv of Australian Flag.

1275	**484**	43c. blue, red and grey	55	25
1276	-	90c. multicoloured	1·25	1·25
1277	-	$1 multicoloured	1·25	1·40
1278	-	$1.20 red, blue and grey	1·60	1·75

DESIGNS: 90c. Royal Australian Navy ensign; $1 Royal Australian Air Force standard; $1.20, Australian merchant marine ensign.

485 Black-necked Stork

1991. Waterbirds. Multicoloured.

1279	43c. Type **485**	80	60
1280	43c. Black swan (horiz)	80	60
1281	85c. Cereopsis goose ("Cape Barren")	2·25	3·50
1282	$1 Chestnut-breasted teal ("Chestnut Teal") (horiz)	2·25	2·50

486 Recruitment Poster (Women's Services)

1991. Anzac Day. 50th Anniversaries.

1283	**486**	43c. multicoloured	60	40
1284	-	43c. black, green & brn	60	40
1285	-	$1.20 multicoloured	2·25	2·00

DESIGNS: 43c. (No. 1284) Patrol (Defence of Tobruk); $1.20, "V-P Day Canberra" (Harold Abbot) (Australian War Memorial).

487 Queen Elizabeth at Royal Albert Hall, London

1991. Queen Elizabeth II's Birthday.

1286	**487**	multicoloured	1·00	50

488 *Tectocoris diophthalmus* (bug)

1991. Insects. Multicoloured.

1287	43c. Type **488**	75	45
1288	43c. *Cizara ardeniae* (hawk moth)	75	45
1289	80c. *Petasida ephippigera* (grasshopper)	2·25	2·00
1290	$1 *Castiarina producta* (beetle)	2·25	1·50

489 *Bondi* (Max Dupain)

1991. 150 Years of Photography in Australia.

1291	**489**	43c. black, brown and blue	80	65
1292	-	43c. black, green & brn	80	65
1293	-	70c. black, green & brn	1·50	1·10
1294	-	$1.20 black, brn & grn	2·00	1·50

DESIGNS: No. 1292, *Gears for the Mining Industry, Vickers Ruwolt, Melbourne* (Wolfgang Sievers): 1293, *The Wheel of Youth* (Harold Cazneaux): 1294, *Teacup Ballet* (Olive Cotton).

490 Singing Group

1991. Australian Radio Broadcasting. Designs showing listeners and scenes from radio programmes. Multicoloured.

1295	43c. Type **490**	70	45
1296	43c. "Blue Hills" serial	70	45
1297	85c. "The Quiz Kids"	1·40	2·25
1298	$1 "Argonauts' Club" children's programme	1·60	1·40

491 Puppy

1991. Domestic Pets. Multicoloured.

1299	43c. Type **491**	70	45
1300	43c. Kitten	70	45
1301	70c. Pony	1·40	2·50
1302	$1 Sulphur-crested cockatoo	1·90	1·50

492 George Vancouver (1791) and Edward Eyre (1841)

1991. Exploration of Western Australia.

1303	**492**	$1.05 multicoloured	1·25	1·10
MS1304		100×65 mm. No. 1303	1·25	1·40

493 *Seven Little Australians* (Ethel Turner)

1991. Australian Writers of the 1890s. Multicoloured.

1305	43c. Type **493**	50	45
1306	75c. *On Our Selection* (Steele Rudd)	80	1·00
1307	$1 *Clancy of the Overflow* (poem, A. B. Paterson) (vert)	1·10	1·00
1308	$1.20 *The Drover's Wife* (short story, Henry Lawson) (vert)	1·25	1·60

494 Shepherd

1991. Christmas. Multicoloured.

1309	38c. Type **494**	40	15
1310	43c. Infant Jesus	45	15
1311	90c. Wise Man	1·50	1·75

495 Parma Wallaby

1992. Threatened Species. Multicoloured. Ordinary or self-adhesive gum.

1312	45c. Type **495**	80	90
1313	45c. Ghost bat	80	90
1314	45c. Long-tailed dunnart	80	90
1315	45c. Little pygmy-possum	80	90
1316	45c. Dusky hopping-mouse	80	90
1317	45c. Squirrel glider	80	90

496 Basket of Wild Flowers

1992. Greetings Stamp.

1318	**496**	45c. multicoloured	50	50

497 Noosa River, Queensland

1992. Wetlands and Waterways. Multicoloured.

1319	20c. Type **497**	1·75	2·50
1320	45c. Lake Eildon, Victoria	40	45

498 "Young Endeavour" (brigantine)

1992. Australia Day and 500th Anniv of Discovery of America by Columbus (**MS**1337). Multicoloured. Sailing Ships.

1333	45c. Type **498**	80	50
1334	45c. *Britannia* (yacht) (vert)	80	50
1335	$1.05 *Akarana* (cutter) (vert)	1·75	2·75
1336	$1.20 *John Louis* (pearling lugger)	2·00	2·00
MS1337	147×64 mm. Nos. 1333/6	4·75	5·25

499 Bombing of Darwin

1992. 50th Anniv of Second World War Battles. Multicoloured.

1338	45c. Type **499**	90	45
1339	75c. Anti-aircraft gun and fighters, Milne Bay	1·75	1·90
1340	75c. Infantry on Kokoda Trail	1·75	1·90
1341	$1.05 H.M.A.S. *Australia* (cruiser) and U.S.S. *Yorktown* (aircraft carrier), Coral Sea	2·00	2·25
1342	$1.20 Australians advancing, El Alamein	2·25	2·00

500 *Helix Nebula*

1992. International Space Year. Multicoloured.

1343	45c. Type **500**	85	45
1344	$1.05 *The Pleiades*	2·00	1·25
1345	$1.20 *Spiral Galaxy, NGC 2997*	2·25	1·50
MS1346	133×70 mm. Nos. 1343/5	4·50	4·50

501 Hunter Valley, New South Wales

1992. Vineyard Regions. Multicoloured.

1347	45c. Type **501**	80	1·10
1348	45c. North-east Victoria	80	1·10
1349	45c. Barossa Valley, South Australia	80	1·10
1350	45c. Coonawarra, South Australia	80	1·10
1351	45c. Margaret River, Western Australia	80	1·10

502 3½d. Stamp of 1953

1992. Queen Elizabeth II's Birthday.

1352	**502**	45c. multicoloured	1·00	60

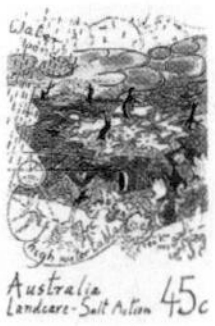

503 Salt Action

1992. Land Conservation. Multicoloured.

1353	45c. Type **503**	85	1·10
1354	45c. Farm planning	85	1·10
1355	45c. Erosion control	85	1·10
1356	45c. Tree planting	85	1·10
1357	45c. Dune care	85	1·10

504 Cycling

1992. Olympic Games and Paralympic Games (No. 1359), Barcelona. Multicoloured.

1358	45c. Type **504**	60	25

1359	$1.20 High jumping	1·50	1·75
1360	$1.20 Weightlifting	1·50	1·75

505 Echidna

1992. Australian Wildlife (1st series). Multicoloured.

1361	30c. Saltwater crocodile	35	20
1362	35c. Type **505**	65	30
1363	40c. Platypus	2·25	1·25
1364	50c. Koala	60	35
1365	60c. Common bushtail possum	1·50	1·50
1366	70c. Laughing kookaburra ("Kookaburra")	2·25	1·00
1367	85c. Australian pelican ("Pelican")	1·00	70
1368a	90c. Eastern grey kangaroo	2·50	2·75
1369	95c. Common wombat	1·00	2·50
1370a	$1.20 Major Mitchell's cockatoo ("Pink Cockatoo")	2·00	1·40
1371	$1.35 Emu	2·50	2·50

See also Nos. 1459/64.

506 Sydney Harbour Tunnel (value at left)

1992. Opening of Sydney Harbour Tunnel. Multicoloured.

1375b	45c. Type **506**	1·90	1·90
1376b	45c. Sydney Harbour Tunnel (value at right)	1·90	1·90

Nos. 1375/6 were printed together, *se-tenant*, forming a composite design.

507 Warden's Courthouse, Coolgardie

1992. Centenary of Discovery of Gold at Coolgardie and Kalgoorlie. Multicoloured.

1377	45c. Type **507**	80	50
1378	45c. Post Office, Kalgoorlie	80	50
1379	$1.05 York Hotel, Kalgoorlie	1·75	2·50
1380	$1.20 Town Hall, Kalgoorlie	2·25	2·50

508 Bowler of 1892

1992. Centenary of Sheffield Shield Cricket Tournament. Multicoloured.

1381	45c. Type **508**	1·00	50
1382	$1.20 Batsman and wicket-keeper	2·00	3·00

509 Children's Nativity Play

1992. Christmas. Multicoloured.

1383	40c. Type **509**	40	15
1384	45c. Child waking on Christmas Day	60	15
1385	$1 Children carol singing	2·00	1·75

510 *Ghost Gum, Central Australia* (Namatjira)

1993. Australia Day. Paintings by Albert Namatjira. Multicoloured.

1386	45c. Type **510**	90	1·40
1387	45c. *Across the Plain to Mount Giles*	90	1·40

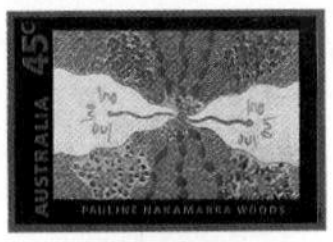
511 *Wild Onion Dreaming* (Pauline Nakamarra Woods)

1993. "Dreamings". Paintings by Aboriginal Artists. Multicoloured.

1388	45c. Type **511**	60	30
1389	75c. *Yam Plants* (Jack Wunuwun) (vert)	1·10	1·10
1390	85c. *Goose Egg Hunt* (George Milpurrurru) (vert)	1·25	1·60
1391	$1 *Kalumpiwarra-Ngulalintji* (Rover Thomas)	1·40	1·40

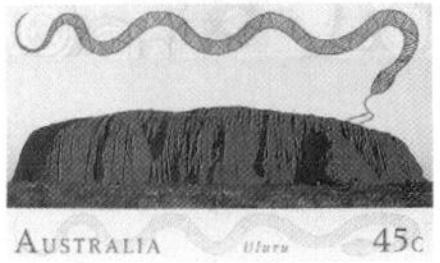
512 Uluru (Ayers Rock) National Park

1993. World Heritage Sites (1st series). Multicoloured.

1392	45c. Type **512**	60	30
1393	85c. Rain forest, Fraser Island	1·50	1·75
1394	95c. Beach, Shark Bay	1·50	1·75
1395	$2 Waterfall, Kakadu	2·75	3·50

See also Nos. 1582/5.

513 Queen Elizabeth II on Royal Visit, 1992

1993. Queen Elizabeth II's Birthday.

1396	**513**	45c. multicoloured	1·00	65

514 H.M.A.S. *Sydney* (cruiser, launched 1934) in Action

1993. Second World War Naval Vessels. Multicoloured.

1397	45c. Type **514**	1·00	45
1398	85c. H.M.A.S. *Bathurst* (mine-sweeper)	2·25	1·75
1399	$1.05 H.M.A.S. *Arunta* (de-stroyer)	2·50	2·75
1400	$1.20 *Centaur* (hospital ship) and tug	2·50	2·75

515 "Work in the Home"

1993. Working Life in the 1890s. Multicoloured.

1401	45c. Type **515**	45	45
1402	45c. "Work in the Cities"	45	45
1403	$1 "Work in the Country"	80	1·00
1404	$1.20 Trade Union banner	1·00	1·75

516 *Centenary Special*, Tasmania, 1971

1993. Australian Trains. Multicoloured.

1405	45c. Type **516**	65	95
1406	45c. *Spirit of Progress*, Victoria	65	95
1407	45c. *Western Endeavour*, West-ern Australia, 1970	65	95
1408	45c. *Silver City Comet*, New South Wales	65	95
1409	45c. Cairns–Kuranda tourist train, Queensland	65	95
1410	45c. *The Ghan*, Northern Territory	65	95

Nos. 1405/10 also come self-adhesive.

517 *Black Cockatoo Feather* (Fiona Foley)

1993. International Year of Indigenous Peoples. Aboriginal Art. Multicoloured.

1417	45c. Type **517**	30	20
1418	75c. *Ngarrgooroon Country* (Hector Jandany) (horiz)	50	1·25
1419	$1 *Ngak Ngak* (Ginger Riley Munduwalawala) (horiz)	65	1·25
1420	$1.05 *Untitled* (Robert Cole)	65	1·75

518 Conference Emblem

1993. Inter-Parliamentary Union Conference and 50th Anniv of Women in Federal Parliament. Multicoloured.

1421	45c. Type **518**	50	1·00
1422	45c. Dame Enid Lyons and Senator Dorothy Tangney	50	1·00

519 Ornithocheirus

1993. Prehistoric Animals. Multicoloured.

1423	45c. Type **519**	50	50
1424	45c. Leaellynasaura (25×30 mm)	50	50
1425	45c. Timimus (26×33 mm)	50	50
1426	45c. Allosaurus (26×33 mm)	50	50
1427	75c. Muttaburrasaurus (30×50 mm)	75	90
1428	$1.05 Minmi (50×30 mm)	1·00	1·50
MS1429	166×73 mm. Nos. 1423/8	3·50	6·50

Nos. 1423/4 also come self-adhesive.

520 "Goodwill"

1993. Christmas. Multicoloured.

1432	40c. Type **520**	40	10
1433	45c. "Joy"	55	10
1434	$1 "Peace"	1·50	1·60

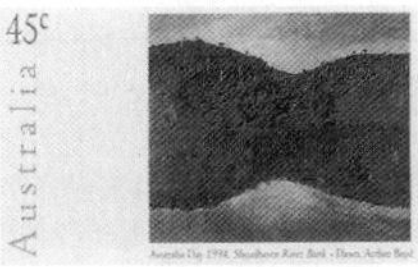
521 *Shoalhaven River Bank—Dawn* (Arthur Boyd)

1994. Australia Day. Landscape Paintings. Multicoloured.

1435	45c. Type **521**	40	20
1436	85c. *Wimmera* (Sir Sidney Nolan)	80	90
1437	$1.05 *Lagoon, Wimmera* (Nolan)	90	1·25
1438	$2 *White Cockatoos with Flame Trees* (Boyd) (vert)	1·60	2·10

522 Teaching Lifesaving Techniques

1994. Centenary of Organized Life Saving in Australia. Multicoloured.

1439	45c. Type **522**	35	25
1440	45c. Lifeguard on watch	35	25
1441	95c. Lifeguard team	70	1·00
1442	$1.20 Lifeguards on surf boards	1·00	1·25

Nos. 1439/40 also come self-adhesive.

523 Rose

1994. Greetings Stamps. Flower photographs by Lariane Fonseca. Multicoloured.

1445	45c. Type **523**	40	45
1446	45c. Tulips	40	45
1447	45c. Poppies	40	45

524 Bridge and National Flags

1994. Opening of Friendship Bridge between Thailand and Laos.

1448	**524**	95c. multicoloured	1·25	1·40

525 *Queen Elizabeth II* (Sir William Dargie)

1994. Queen Elizabeth II's Birthday.

1449	**525**	45c. multicoloured	1·00	70

526 *Family in Field* (Bobbie-Lea Blackmore)

1994. International Year of the Family. Children's Paintings. Multicoloured.

1450	45c. Type **526**	55	20
1451	75c. *Family on Beach* (Kathryn Teoh)	75	1·00
1452	$1 *Family around Fire* (Maree McCarthy)	1·00	1·25

1994. Australian Wildlife (2nd series). As T **505**. Multicoloured. Ordinary or self-adhesive gum.

1459	45c. Kangaroo	60	85
1460	45c. Female kangaroo with young	60	85
1461	45c. Two kangaroos	60	85
1462	45c. Family of koalas on branch	60	85
1463	45c. Koala on ground	60	85
1464	45c. Koala asleep in tree	60	85

527 Suffragettes

1994. Centenary of Women's Emancipation in South Australia.

1465	**527**	45c. multicoloured	60	60

528 Bunyip from Aboriginal Legend

1994. The Bunyip (mythological monster). Multicoloured.

1466	45c. Type **528**	45	70
1467	45c. Nature spirit bunyip	45	70
1468	90c. "The Bunyip of Berkeley's Creek" (book illustration)	70	1·75
1469	$1.35 Bunyip as natural history	1·00	2·00

529 *Robert Menzies* (Sir Ivor Hele)

1994. Wartime Prime Ministers. Multicoloured.

1470	45c. Type **529**	1·25	1·50
1471	45c. *Arthur Fadden* (William Dargie)	1·25	1·50
1472	45c. *John Curtin* (Anthony Dattilo-Rubbo)	1·25	1·50
1473	45c. *Francis Forde* (Joshua Smith)	1·25	1·50
1474	45c. *Joseph Chifley* (A. D. Colquhoun)	1·25	1·50

530 Lawrence Hargrave and Box Kites

1994. Aviation Pioneers.

1475	**530**	45c. brown, green and cinnamon	1·25	55
1476	-	45c. brown, red and lilac	1·25	55
1477	-	$1.35 brown, violet and blue	3·00	4·00
1478	-	$1.80 brown, deep green and green	3·25	4·00

DESIGNS: No. 1476, Ross and Keith Smith with Vickers Vimy (first England–Australia flight); 1477, Ivor McIntyre, Stanley Goble and Fairey IIID seaplane (first aerial circumnavigation of Australia); 1478, Freda Thompson and de Havilland Moth Major *Christopher Robin* (first Australian woman to fly solo from England to Australia).

531 Scarlet Macaw

1994. Australian Zoos. Endangered Species. Multicoloured.

1479	45c. Type **531**	90	55
1480	45c. Cheetah (25×30 mm)	90	55
1481	45c. Orang-utan (26×37 mm)	90	55
1482	45c. Fijian crested iguana (26×37 mm)	90	55
1483	$1 Asian elephants (49×28 mm)	2·75	1·60
MS1484	166×73 mm. Nos. 1479/83	4·50	4·50

Nos. 1479/80 also come self-adhesive.

532 *Madonna and Child* (detail)

1994. Christmas. *The Adoration of the Magi* by Giovanni Toscani. Multicoloured.

1487	40c. Type **532**	40	15
1488	45c. *Wise Man and Horse* (detail) (horiz)	45	15
1489	$1 *Wise Man and St. Joseph* (detail) (horiz)	1·00	1·00
1490	$1.80 Complete painting (49×29 mm)	1·75	2·75

533 Yachts outside Sydney Harbour

1994. 50th Sydney to Hobart Yacht Race. Mulicolouredt.

1491	45c. Type **533**	1·00	80
1492	45c. Yachts passing Tasmania coastline	1·00	80

Nos. 1491/92 also come self-adhesive.

534 Symbolic Kangaroo

1994. Self-adhesive. Automatic Cash Machine Stamps.

1495	**534**	45c. gold, emerald and green	55	90
1496	**534**	45c. gold, green and blue	55	90
1497	**534**	45c. gold, green and lilac	55	90
1498	**534**	45c. gold, emerald and green	55	90
1499	**534**	45c. gold, emerald and green	55	90
1500	**534**	45c. gold, green and pink	55	90
1501	**534**	45c. gold, green and red	55	90
1502	**534**	45c. gold, green and brown	55	90

535 *Back Verandah* (Russell Drysdale)

1995. Australia Day. Paintings. Multicoloured.

1503	45c. Type **535**	45	45
1504	45c. *Skull Springs Country* (Guy Grey-Smith)	45	45
1505	$1.05 *Outcamp* (Robert Juniper)	1·25	1·50
1506	$1.20 *Kite Flying* (Ian Fairweather)	1·40	1·50

536 Red Heart and Rose

1995. St. Valentine's Day. Multicoloured.

1507	45c. Type **536**	55	55
1508	45c. Gold and red heart with rose	55	55
1509	45c. Gold heart and roses	85	1·25

537 *Endeavour* Replica at Sea

1995. Completion of *Endeavour* Replica. Multicoloured.

1510	45c. Type **537**	1·50	1·75
1511	45c. *Captain Cook's Endeavour* (detail) (Oswald Brett)	1·50	1·75
1512	20c. Type **537** (44×26 mm)	1·00	2·75

538 Coalport Plate and Bracket Clock, Old Government House, Parramatta

1995. 50th Anniv of Australian National Trusts.

1514	**538**	45c. blue and brown	30	45
1515	-	45c. green and brown	30	45
1516	-	$1 red and blue	70	70
1517	-	$2 green and blue	1·40	1·90

DESIGNS: No. 1515, Steiner doll and Italian-style chair, Ayers House, Adelaide; 1516, "Advance Australia" teapot and parian-ware statuette, Victoria; 1517, Silver bowl and china urn, Old Observatory, Perth.

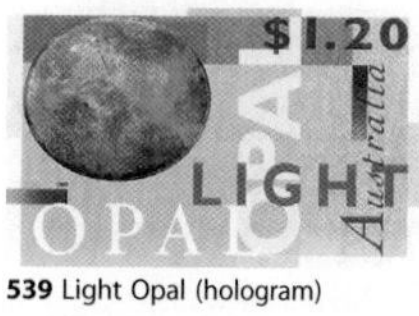

539 Light Opal (hologram)

1995. Opals. Multicoloured.

1518	$1.20 Type **539**	3·50	1·25
1519	$2.50 Black opal (hologram)	4·50	3·75

540 Queen Elizabeth II at Gala Concert, 1992

1995. Queen Elizabeth II's Birthday.

1520	**540**	45c. multicoloured	75	75

541 Sir Edward Dunlop and P.O.W. Association Badge

1995. Australian Second World War Heroes (1st series). Mult. Ordinary or self-adhesive gum.

1521	45c. Type **541**	60	60
1522	45c. Mrs. Jessie Vasey and War Widows' Guild badge	60	60
1523	45c. Sgt. Tom Derrick and Victoria Cross	60	60
1524	45c. Flt. Sgt. Rawdon Middleton and Victoria Cross	60	60

See also Nos. 1545/8.

542 Children and Globe of Flags

1995. 50th Anniv of United Nations.

1529	**542**	45c. multicoloured	75	75

543 *The Story of the Kelly Gang*

1995. Centenary of Cinema. Scenes from Films. Multicoloured. (a) Size 23×35 mm.

1530	45c. Type **543**	1·10	1·50
1531	45c. *On Our Selection*	1·10	1·50
1532	45c. *Jedda*	1·10	1·50
1533	45c. *Picnic at Hanging Rock*	1·10	1·50
1534	45c. *Strictly Ballroom*	1·10	1·50

(b) Self-adhesive. Size 19×30½ mm.

1535	45c. Type **543**	1·10	1·50
1536	45c. *On Our Selection*	1·10	1·50
1537	45c. *Jedda*	1·10	1·50
1538	45c. *Picnic at Hanging Rock*	1·10	1·50
1539	45c. *Strictly Ballroom*	1·10	1·50

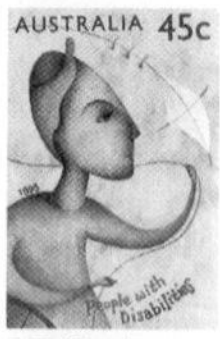

544 Man in Wheelchair flying Kite

1995. People with Disabilities. Multicoloured.

1540	45c. Type **544**	1·00	1·40
1541	45c. Blind woman playing violin	1·00	1·40

1995. 50th Anniv of Peace in the Pacific. Designs as 1946 Victory Commemoration (Nos. 213/15) redrawn with new face values.

1542	**53**	45c. red	1·00	70
1543	-	45c. green	1·00	70
1544	-	$1.50 blue	2·25	3·00

DESIGNS—VERT: No. 1543, Angel. HORIZ: No. 1544, Flag and dove.

1995. Australian Second World War Heroes (2nd series). As T **541**. Multicoloured.

1545	45c. Sister Ellen Savage and George Medal	1·50	1·75
1546	45c. Chief Petty Officer Percy Collins and Distinguished Service Medal and Bar	1·50	1·75
1547	45c. Lt-Comm. Leon Goldsworthy and George Cross	1·50	1·75
1548	45c. Warrant Officer Len Waters and R.A.A.F. wings	1·50	1·75

545 Koala with Cub

1995. Australia–China Joint Issue. Endangered Species. Multicoloured.

1549	45c. Type **545**	70	1·00
1550	45c. Giant panda with cubs	70	1·00
MS1551	Two sheets, each 106×70 mm. (a) No. 1549. (b) No. 1550 Set of 2 sheets	2·00	2·25

546 Father Joseph Slattery, Thomas Lyle and Walter Filmer (Radiology)

1995. Medical Scientists. Multicoloured.

1552	45c. Type **546**	1·50	1·50
1553	45c. Dame Jean Macnamara and Sir Macfarlane Burnet (viruses)	1·50	1·50
1554	45c. Fred Hollows (ophthalmology) (vert)	1·50	60
1555	$2.50 Sir Howard Florey (antibiotics) (vert)	6·00	7·00

547 Flatback Turtle

1995. Marine Life. Multicoloured. Ordinary or self-adhesive gum.

1556	45c. Type **547**	55	55
1557	45c. Flame angelfish and nudibranch	55	55
1558	45c. Potato grouper ("Potato cod") and hump-headed wrasse ("Maori wrasse")	55	55
1559	45c. Giant trevally	55	55
1560	45c. Black marlin	55	55
1561	45c. Mako and tiger sharks	55	55
MS1562	166×73 mm. Nos. 1556/61	3·50	3·00

548 *Madonna and Child*

1995. Christmas. Stained-glass Windows from Our Lady Help of Christians Church, Melbourne. Multicoloured.

1569	40c. Type **548**	80	15
1570	45c. *Angel carrying the Gloria banner*	80	15
1571	$1 *Rejoicing Angels*	3·00	3·25

No. 1569 also comes self-adhesive.

549 *West Australian Banksia* (Margaret Preston)

1996. Australia Day. Paintings. Multicoloured.

1573	45c. Type **549**	1·00	30
1574	85c. *The Babe is Wise* (Lina Bryans)	2·00	2·50
1575	$1 *The Bridge in Curve* (Grace Cossington Smith) (horiz)	2·25	2·00
1576	$1.20 *Beach Umbrellas* (Vida Lahey) (horiz)	2·50	3·50

550 Gold Heart and Rose

1996. St. Valentine's Day.

1577	**550**	45c. multicoloured	1·00	1·00

551 Bristol Type 156 Beaufighter and Curtiss P-40E Kittyhawk I

1996. Military Aviation. Multicoloured.

1578	45c. Type **551**	2·00	2·00
1579	45c. Hawker Sea Fury and Fairey Firefly	2·00	2·00
1580	45c. Bell Kiowa helicopters	2·00	2·00
1581	45c. Government Aircraft Factory Hornets	2·00	2·00

552 Tasmanian Wilderness

1996. World Heritage Sites (2nd series). Multicoloured.

1582	45c. Type **552**	90	7·25
1583	75c. Willandra Lakes	2·25	3·00
1584	95c. Naracoorte Fossil Cave	2·50	3·75
1585	$1 Lord Howe Island	2·50	2·25

553 Australian Spotted Cuscus

1996. Australia–Indonesia Joint Issue. Multicoloured.

1586	45c. Type **553**	90	1·50
1587	45c. Indonesian bear cuscus	90	1·50
MS1588	106×70 mm. Nos. 1586/7	2·00	3·50

554 Head of Queen Elizabeth II

1996. Queen Elizabeth II's Birthday.

1589	**554**	45c. multicoloured	1·25	1·00

555 North Melbourne Players

1996. Centenary of Australian Football League. Players from different teams. Multicoloured. Ordinary or self-adhesive gum.

1606	45c. Type **555**	50	90
1607	45c. Brisbane (red and yellow shirt)	50	90
1608	45c. Sydney (red and white shirt)	50	90
1609	45c. Carlton (black shirt with white emblem)	50	90
1610	45c. Adelaide (black, red and yellow shirt)	50	90
1611	45c. Fitzroy (yellow, red and blue shirt)	50	90
1612	45c. Richmond (black shirt with yellow diagonal stripe)	50	90
1613	45c. St. Kilda (red, white and black shirt)	50	90
1614	45c. Melbourne (black shirt with red top)	50	90
1615	45c. Collingwood (black and white vertical striped shirt)	50	90
1616	45c. Fremantle (green, red, white and blue shirt)	50	90
1617	45c. Footscray (blue, white and red shirt)	50	90
1618	45c. West Coast (deep blue shirt with yellow stripes)	50	90
1619	45c. Essendon (black shirt with red stripe)	50	90
1620	45c. Geelong (black and white horizontal striped shirt)	50	90
1621	45c. Hawthorn (black and yellow vertical striped shirt)	50	90

556 Leadbeater's Possum

1996. Fauna and Flora (1st series). Central Highlands Forest, Victoria. Multicoloured.

1622	5c. Type **556**	30	25
1623	10c. Powerful owl	1·75	45
1624	$2 Blackwood wattle	1·40	1·25
1625	$5 Soft tree fern and mountain ash (30×50 mm)	10·00	3·75

See also Nos. 1679/90, 1854/66, 2130/33, 2200/3, 2272/6 and 2377/80.

1996. "China '96" 9th Asian International Stamp Exhibition, Peking. Sheet 120×65 mm, containing Nos. 1453b, 1454b and 1455b. Multicoloured.

MS1626	45c. Kangaroo; 45c. Female kangaroo with young; 45c. Two kangaroos	2·00	2·25

557 Edwin Flack (800 and 1500 metres gold medal winner, 1896)

1996. Centennial Olympic Games and Tenth Paralympic Games, Atlanta. Multicoloured.

1627	45c. Type **557**	90	90
1628	45c. Fanny Durack (100 metres freestyle swimming gold medal winner, 1912)	90	90
1629	$1.05 Wheelchair athletes	2·25	2·25

558 *Animalia* (Graeme Base)

1996. 50th Anniv of Children's Book Council Awards. Designs taken from book covers. Ordinary or self-adhesive gum. Multicoloured.

1630	45c. Type **558**	60	60
1631	45c. *Greetings from Sandy Beach* (Bob Graham)	60	60
1632	45c. *Who Sank the Boat?* (Pamela Allen)	60	60
1633	45c. *John Brown, Rose and the Midnight Cat* (Jenny Wagner, illustrated by Ron Brooks)	60	60

559 American Bald Eagle, Kangaroo and Olympic Flame

1996. Passing of Olympic Flag to Sydney.

1638	**559**	45c. multicoloured	55	50

560 Margaret Windeyer

1996. Centenary of the National Council of Women.

1639	**560**	45c. purple and yellow	50	50
1640	-	$1 blue and yellow	1·25	2·00

DESIGN: $1 Rose Scott.

561 Pearl

1996. Pearls and Diamonds. Multicoloured.

1641	45c. Type **561**	60	50
1642	$1.20 Diamond	1·40	1·50

The pearl on the 45c. is shown as an exelgram (holographic printing on ultra thin plastic film) and the diamond on the $1.20 as a hologram, each embossed on to the stamp.

562 Silhouettes of Female Dancer and Musician on Rural Landscape

1996. 50th Anniv of Arts Councils. Multicoloured.

1643	20c. Type **562**	1·40	2·50
1644	45c. Silhouettes of musician and male dancer on landscape	35	45

563 Ginger Cats

1996. Australian Pets. Multicoloured.

1645	45c. Type **563**	75	75
1646	45c. Blue heeler dogs	75	75
1647	45c. Sulphur-crested cockatoo (30×25 mm)	75	75
1648	45c. Duck with ducklings (25×30 mm)	75	75
1649	45c. Dog and cat (25×30 mm)	75	75
1650	45c. Ponies (30×50 mm)	75	75
MS1651	166×73 mm. Nos. 1645/50	4·00	4·00

Nos. 1645/6 also come self-adhesive.

564 Ferdinand von Mueller

1996. Australia–Germany Joint Issue. Death Centenary of Ferdinand von Mueller (botanist).

1654	**564**	$1.20 multicoloured	1·25	2·00

565 Willem de Vlamingh

1996. 300th Anniv of the Visit of Willem de Vlamingh to Western Australia.

1655	**565**	45c. multicoloured	1·00	1·50

566 Madonna and Child

1996. Christmas. Multicoloured.

1656	40c. Type **566**	55	15
1657	45c. Wise man with gift	55	15
1658	$1 Shepherd boy with lamb	1·25	1·50

No. 1656 also comes self-adhesive.

567 *Landscape '74* (Fred Williams)

1997. Australia Day. Contemporary Paintings. Multicoloured.

1660	85c. Type **567**	1·10	1·10
1661	90c. *The Balcony 2* (Brett Whiteley)	1·10	1·10
1662	$1.20 *Fire Haze at Gerringong* (Lloyd Rees)	1·40	1·40

568 Sir Donald Bradman

1997. Australian Legends (1st series). Sir Donald Bradman (cricketer). Multicoloured.

1663	45c. Type **568**	55	55
1664	45c. Bradman playing stroke	55	55

See also Nos. 1731/42, 1838/9, 1947/50, 2069/70, 2165/9, 2264/7, 2348/9, 2473/8, 2577/81 and 2741/58.

569 Red Roses

1997. St. Valentine's Day. Ordinary or self-adhesive gum.

1665	**569**	45c. multicoloured	50	50

570 Ford Coupe Utility, 1934

1997. Classic Cars. Multicoloured. Ordinary or self-adhesive gum.

1667	45c. Type **570**	50	75
1668	45c. Holden 48-215 (FX) sedan, 1948	50	75
1669	45c. Austin Lancer sedan, 1958	50	75
1670	45c. Chrysler Valiant "R" Series sedan, 1962	50	75

571 May Wirth and Horse

1997. 150th Anniv of the Circus in Australia. Multicoloured.

1675	45c. Type **571**	55	75
1676	45c. Con Colleano on tightrope	55	75
1677	45c. Clowns	55	75
1678	45c. Acrobats	55	75

1997. Fauna and Flora (2nd series). Kakadu Wetlands, Northern Territory. As T **556**. Multicoloured.

1679	20c. Saltwater crocodile	15	20
1680	25c. Northern dwarf tree frog	20	25
1681	45c. Comb-crested jacana ("Jacana")	75	75
1682	45c. Mangrove kingfisher ("Little Kingfisher")	75	75
1683	45c. Brolga	75	75
1684	45c. Black-necked stork ("Jabiru")	75	75
1685	$1 "Cressida cressida" (butterfly)	70	75
1686	$10 Kakadu Wetlands (50×30 mm)	7·00	5·00
MS1686a	106×70 mm. No. 1686	9·00	11·00

Nos. 1681/84 also come self-adhesive.

572 Royal Wedding 1d. Stamp of 1947

1997. Queen Elizabeth II's Birthday.

1691	**572**	45c. purple	60	60

573 Hand holding Globe and Lion's Emblem

1997. 50th Anniv of First Australian Lions Club.

1692	**573**	45c. blue, brown and purple	50	50

574 Doll holding Teddy Bear (Kaye Wiggs)

1997. Dolls and Teddy Bears. Multicoloured.

1693	45c. Type **574**	40	50
1694	45c. Teddy bear standing (Jennifer Laing)	40	50
1695	45c. Doll wearing white dress with teddy bear (Susie McMahon)	40	50
1696	45c. Doll in brown dress and bonnet (Lynda Jacobson)	40	50
1697	45c. Teddy bear sitting (Helen Williams)	40	50

575 Police Rescue Helicopter

1997. Emergency Services. Multicoloured.

1698	45c. Type **575**	1·50	1·00
1699	45c. Emergency Service volunteers carrying victim	1·50	1·00
1700	$1.05 Fire service at fire	2·75	2·25
1701	$1.20 Loading casualty into ambulance	3·00	2·00

576 George Peppin Jnr (breeder) and Merino Sheep

1997. Bicentenary of Arrival of Merino Sheep in Australia. Multicoloured.

1702	45c. Type **576**	70	1·00
1703	45c. Pepe chair, cloth and wool logo	70	1·00

577 Dumbi the Owl

1997. *The Dreaming.* Cartoons from Aboriginal Stories. Multicoloured.

1704	45c. Type **577**	50	30
1705	$1 The Two Willy-Willies	80	70
1706	$1.20 How Brolga became a Bird	80	1·50
1707	$1.80 Tuggan-Tuggan	1·25	3·00

578 "Rhoetosaurus brownei"

1997. Prehistoric Animals. Multicoloured.

1708	45c. Type **578**	45	60
1709	45c. "Mcnamaraspis kaprios"	45	60
1710	45c. "Ninjemys oweni"	45	60
1711	45c. "Paracylotosaurus davidi"	45	60
1712	45c. "Woolungasaurus glendowerensis"	45	60

579 Spotted-tailed Quoll

1997. Nocturnal Animals. Multicoloured.

1713	45c. Type **579**	70	90
1714	45c. Barking owl	70	90
1715	45c. Platypus (30×25 mm)	70	90
1716	45c. Brown antechinus (30×25 mm)	70	90
1717	45c. Dingo (30×25 mm)	70	90
1718	45c. Yellow-bellied glider (50×30 mm)	70	90
MS1719	166×78 mm. Nos. 1713/18	4·75	4·75

Nos. 1713/14 also come self-adhesive.

580 Woman

1997. Breast Cancer Awareness Campaign.

1722	**580**	45c. multicoloured	1·25	60

581 Two Angels

1997. Christmas. Children's Nativity Play. Multicoloured.

1723	40c. Type **581**	50	15
1724	45c. Mary	55	15
1725	$1 Three Kings	1·25	1·50

No. 1723 also comes self-adhesive.

582 *Flying Cloud* (clipper) (J. Scott)

1998. Ship Paintings. Multicoloured.

1727	45c. Type **582**	60	30
1728	85c. *Marco Polo* (full-rigged ship) (T. Robertson)	1·00	1·00
1729	$1 *Chusan I* (steamship) (C. Gregory)	1·25	1·10
1730	$1.20 *Heather Belle* (clipper)	1·50	1·75

583 Betty Cuthbert (1956)

1998. Australian Legends (2nd series). Olympic Gold Medal Winners. Multicoloured. Ordinary or self-adhesive gum.

1731	45c. Type **583**	40	65
1732	45c. Betty Cuthbert running	40	65
1733	45c. Herb Elliott (1960)	40	65
1734	45c. Herb Elliott running	40	65
1735	45c. Dawn Fraser (1956, 1960 and 1964)	40	65
1736	45c. Dawn Fraser swimming	40	65
1737	45c. Marjorie Jackson (1952)	40	65
1738	45c. Marjorie Jackson running	40	65
1739	45c. Murray Rose (1956)	40	65
1740	45c. Murray Rose swimming	40	65
1741	45c. Shirley Strickland (1952 and 1956)	40	65
1742	45c. Shirley Strickland hurdling	40	65

584 "Champagne" Rose

1998. Greeting Stamp. Ordinary or self-adhesive gum.

1755	**584**	45c. multicoloured	55	50

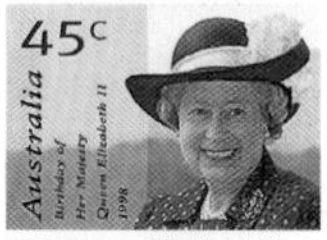

585 Queen Elizabeth II

1998. Queen Elizabeth II's Birthday.

1757	**585**	45c. multicoloured	70	50

586 Sea Hawk (helicopter) landing on Frigate

1998. 50th Anniv of Royal Australian Navy Fleet Air Arm.

1758	**586**	45c. multicoloured	1·00	50

587 Sheep Shearer and Sheep

1998. Farming. Multicoloured. Ordinary or self-adhesive gum.

1759	45c. Type **587**	45	50
1760	45c. Barley and silo	45	50
1761	45c. Farmers herding beef cattle	45	50
1762	45c. Sugar cane harvesting	45	50
1763	45c. Two dairy cows	45	50

588 Cardiograph Trace and Heart

1998. Heart Disease Awareness.

1769	**588**	45c. multicoloured	75	50

589 Johnny OKeefe (*The Wild One*, 1958)

1998. Australian Rock and Roll. Multicoloured. Ordinary or self-adhesive gum.

1770	45c. Type **589**	35	50
1771	45c. Col Joye (*Oh Yeah Uh Huh*, 1959)	35	50
1772	45c. Little Pattie (*He's My Blonde Headed Stompie Wompie Real Gone Surfer Boy*, 1963)	35	50
1773	45c. Normie Rowe (*Shakin all Over*, 1965)	35	50
1774	45c. Easybeats (*She's so Fine*, 1965)	35	50
1775	45c. Russell Morris (*The Real Thing*, 1969)	35	50
1776	45c. Masters Apprentices (*Turn Up Your Radio*, 1970)	35	50
1777	45c. Daddy Cool (*Eagle Rock*, 1971)	35	50
1778	45c. Billy Thorpe and the Aztecs (*Most People I know think I'm Crazy*, 1972)	35	50
1779	45c. Skyhooks (*Horror Movie*, 1974)	35	50
1780	45c. AC/DC (*It's a Long Way to the Top*, 1975)	35	50
1781	45c. Sherbet (*Howzat*, 1976)	35	50

590 Yellow-tufted Honeyeater ("Helmeted Honeyeater")

1998. Endangered Species. Multicoloured.

1794	5c. Type **590**	45	45
1795	5c. Orange-bellied parrot	45	45
1796	45c. Red-tailed cockatoo ("Red-tailed Black-Cockatoo")	80	80
1797	45c. Gouldian finch	80	80

591 French Horn and Cello Players

1998. Youth Arts, Australia. Multicoloured.

1798	45c. Type **591**	50	50
1799	45c. Dancers	50	50

592 *Phalaenopsis rosenstromii*

1998. Australia–Singapore Joint Issue. Orchids. Multicoloured.

1800	45c. Type **592**	55	40
1801	85c. *Arundina graminifolia*	1·00	1·00
1802	$1 *Grammatophyllum speciosum*	1·40	1·25
1803	$1.20 *Dendrobium phalaenopsis*	1·50	1·60
MS1804	138×72 mm. Nos. 1800/3	4·00	3·75

593 Flying Angel with Teapot (cartoon by Michael Leunig)

1998. *The Teapot of Truth* (cartoons by Michael Leunig). Multicoloured.

1805	45c. Type **593**	75	80
1806	45c. Two birds in heart-shaped tree	75	80
1807	45c. Pouring tea	75	80
1808	$1 Mother and child (29×24 mm)	1·40	1·75
1809	$1.20 Cat with smiling face (29×24 mm)	1·40	1·75

594 Red Lacewing

1998. Butterflies. Multicoloured. Ordinary or self-adhesive gum.

1815	45c. Type **594**	75	1·00
1816	45c. Dull oakblue	75	1·00
1817	45c. Meadow argus	75	1·00
1818	45c. Ulysses butterfly	75	1·00
1819	45c. Common red-eye	75	1·00

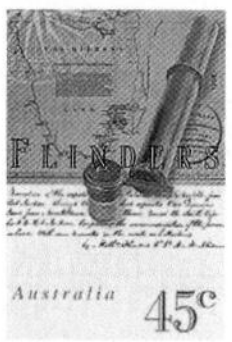

595 Flinders' Telescope and Map of Tasmania

1998. Bicentenary of the Circumnavigation of Tasmania by George Bass and Matthew Flinders. Multicoloured.

1820	45c. Type **595**	75	65
1821	45c. Sextant and letter from Bass	75	65

596 Weedy Seadragon

1998. International Year of the Ocean. Multicoloured.

1822	45c. Type **596**	65	65
1823	45c. Bottlenose dolphin	65	65
1824	45c. Fiery squid (24×29 mm)	65	65
1825	45c. Manta ray (29×24 mm)	65	65
1826	45c. White pointer shark (29×49 mm)	65	65
1827	45c. Southern right whale (49×29 mm)	65	65
MS1828	166×73 mm. Nos. 1822/7	2·75	2·75

Nos. 1822/3 also come self-adhesive.

597 Rose of Freedom

1998. 50th Anniv of Universal Declaration of Human Rights.

1831	**597**	45c. multicoloured	50	50

598 Three Kings

1998. Christmas. Multicoloured.

1832	40c. Type **598**	40	15
1833	45c. Nativity scene	40	15
1834	$1 Mary and Joseph	1·10	1·10

No. 1832 also comes self-adhesive.

599 Australian Coat of Arms

1999. 50th Anniv of Australian Citizenship. Ordinary or self-adhesive gum.

1837	**599**	45c. multicoloured	40	40

600 Arthur Boyd

1999. Australian Legends (3rd series). Arthur Boyd (painter). Multicoloured. Ordinary or self-adhesive gum.

1838	45c. Type **600**	50	50
1839	45c. *Nebuchadnezzer on fire falling over Waterfall* (Arthur Boyd)	50	50

601 Red Roses

1999. Greetings Stamp. Romance. Ordinary or self-adhesive gum.

1843	**601**	45c. multicoloured	40	40

602 Elderly Man and Grandmother with Boy

1999. International Year of Older Persons. Multicoloured.

1844	45c. Type **602**	50	50
1845	45c. Elderly woman and grandfather with boy	50	50

603 *Polly Woodside* (barque)

1999. Sailing Ships. Multicoloured.

1846	45c. Type **603**	60	35
1847	85c. *Alma Doepel* (topsail schooner)	1·00	1·10
1848	$1 *Enterprize* replica (topsail schooner)	1·25	1·10
1849	$1.05 *Lady Nelson* replica (topsail schooner)	1·40	1·90

1999. Australia—Ireland Joint Issue. *Polly Woodside* (barque). Sheet 137×72 mm. Multicoloured.

MS1850 45c. Type **603**; 30p. Type **374** of Ireland (No. **MS**1850 was sold at $1.25 in Australia) 1·25 1·40

1999. Australia—Canada. Joint Issue. *Marco Polo* (emigrant ship). Sheet 160×95 mm. Multicoloured.

MS1851 85c. As No. 1728; 46c. Type **701** of Canada (No. **MS**1851 was sold at $1.30 in Australia) 1·25 1·40

1999. "Australia '99" International Stamp Exhibition, Melbourne. Two sheets, each 142×76 mm, containing designs as Nos. 398/403 and all with face value of 45c.

MS1852 (a) 45c. ultramarine (Type **167**); 45c. grey (Captain Cook); 45c. brown (Flinders). (b) 45c. red (Type **168**); 45c. brown (Bass); 45c. purple (King) Set of 2 sheets 2·50 2·75

604 Olympic Torch and 1956 7½d. Stamp

1999. Olympic Torch Commemoration.

1853	**604**	$1.20 multicoloured	1·10	1·10

605 *Correa reflexa* (native fuchsia)

1999. Fauna and Flora (3rd series). Coastal Environment. Multicoloured.

1854	45c. Type **605**	50	60
1855	45c. *Hibbertia scandens* (guinea flower)	50	60
1856	45c. *Ipomoea pre-caprae* (beach morning glory)	50	50
1857	45c. *Wahlenbergia stricta* (Australian bluebells)	50	50
1858	70c. Humpback whales and zebra volute shell (29×24 mm)	1·00	70
1859	90c. Brahminy kite and checkerboard helmet shell (29×24 mm)	90	1·00
1860	90c. Fraser Island and chambered nautilus (29×24 mm)	90	1·00
1861	$1.05 Loggerhead turtle and melon shell (29×24 mm)	1·00	80
1862	$1.20 White-bellied sea eagle and Campbell's stromb shell (29×24 mm)	1·25	90

Nos. 1859/60 were printed together, *se-tenant*, forming a composite design.
Nos. 1854/7 also come self-adhesive.

606 Queen Elizabeth II with The Queen Mother

1999. Queen Elizabeth II's Birthday.

1870	**606**	45c. multicoloured	70	50

607 *Here's Humphrey*

1999. Children's Television Programmes. Multicoloured. Ordinary or self-adhesive gum.

1871	45c. Type **607**	45	45
1872	45c. *Bananas in Pyjamas*	45	45
1873	45c. *Mr. Squiggle*	45	45
1874	45c. *Play School* (teddy bears)	45	45
1875	45c. *Play School* (clock, toy dog and doll)	45	45

608 Obverse and Reverse of 1899 Sovereign

1999. Centenary of the Perth Mint.

1881	**608**	$2 gold, blue and green	2·00	1·75

609 Lineout against New Zealand

1999. Centenary of Australian Test Rugby. Multicoloured.

1882	45c. Type **609**	50	40
1883	45c. Kicking the ball against England	50	40
1884	$1 Try against South Africa (horiz)	1·00	85
1885	$1.20 Passing the ball against Wales (horiz)	1·10	1·25

Nos. 1882/3 also come self-adhesive.

610 Drilling at Burn's Creek and Rock Bolting in Tumut 2 Power Station Hall

1999. 50th Anniv of Snowy Mountain Scheme (hydro-electric project). Multicoloured. Ordinary or self-adhesive gum.

1888	45c. Type **610**	65	65
1889	45c. English class for migrant workers, Cooma	65	65
1890	45c. Tumut 2 Tailwater Tunnel and Eucumbene Dam	65	65
1891	45c. German carpenters and Island Bend Dam	65	65

611 Calligraphy Pen and Letter

1999. Greetings Stamps. Multicoloured.

1896	45c. Type **611**	65	65
1897	45c. Wedding rings	65	65
1898	45c. Birthday cake	65	65
1899	45c. Christmas decoration	65	65
1900	45c. Teddy bear	65	65
1901	$1 Koala	1·25	1·25

See also No. 1921.

612 Sydney Olympic Emblem

1999. Olympic Games, Sydney (2000) (1st issue).

1902	**612**	45c. multicoloured	1·50	60

See also Nos. 2015/24.

613 Australia Post Symbol, 1975

1999. "Sydney Design '99" International Congress and Exhibition. Multicoloured.

1903	45c. Type **613**	35	20
1904	90c. Embryo chair, 1988	65	70
1905	$1.35 Possum skin textile, c.1985	1·00	1·25
1906	$1.50 Storey Hall, R.M.I.T. University, 1995	1·00	1·25

614 Magnificent Tree Frog

1999. National Stamp Collecting Month, Small Pond Life. Multicoloured. Ordinary or self-adhesive gum.

1907	45c. Type **614**	55	55
1908	45c. Sacred kingfisher	55	55
1909	45c. Roth's tree frog (29×24 mm)	55	55
1910	45c. Dragonfly (29×24 mm)	55	55
1911	50c. Javelin frog (24×29 mm)	65	65
1912	50c. Northern dwarf tree frog (24×29 mm)	65	65
MS1913	166×73 mm. Nos. 1907/12	3·00	3·25

615 Madonna and Child

1999. Christmas. Multicoloured.

1918	40c. Type **615**	50	15
1919	$1 Tree of Life (horiz)	1·00	1·10

No. 1918 also comes self-adhesive.

616 Fireworks and Hologram

1999. Millennium Greetings stamp.

1921	**616**	45c. multicoloured	50	50

617 Rachel Thomson (college administrator)

2000. New Millennium. "Face of Australia". Multicoloured.

1922	45c. Nicholle and Meghan Triandis (twin babies)	35	60
1923	45c. David Willis (cattleman)	35	60
1924	45c. Natasha Bramley (scuba diver)	35	60
1925	45c. Cyril Watson (Aborigine boy)	35	60
1926	45c. Mollie Dowdall (wearing red hat) (vineyard worker)	35	60
1927	45c. Robin Dicks (flying instructor)	35	60
1928	45c. Mary Simons (retired nurse)	35	60
1929	45c. Peta and Samantha Nieuwerth (mother and baby)	35	60
1930	45c. John Matthews (doctor)	35	60
1931	45c. Edith Dizon-Fitzimmons (wearing drop earrings) (music teacher)	35	60
1932	45c. Philippa Weir (wearing brown hat) (teacher)	35	60
1933	45c. John Thurgar (in bush hat and jacket) (farmer)	35	60
1934	45c. Miguel Alzona (with face painted) (schoolboy)	35	60
1935	45c. Type **617**	35	60
1936	45c. Necip Akarsu (wearing blue shirt) (postmaster)	35	60
1937	45c. Justin Allan (R.A.N. sailor)	35	60
1938	45c. Wadad Dennaoui (wearing checked shirt) (student)	35	60
1939	45c. Jack Laity (market gardener)	35	60
1940	45c. Kelsey Stubbin (wearing cricket cap) (schoolboy)	35	60
1941	45c. Gianna Rossi (resting chin on hand) (church worker)	35	60
1942	45c. Paris Hansch (toddler)	35	60
1943	45c. Donald George Whatham (in blue shirt and tie) (retired teacher)	35	60
1944	45c. Stacey Coull (wearing pendant)	35	60
1945	45c. Alex Payne (wearing cycle helmet) (schoolgirl)	35	60
1946	45c. John Lodge (Salvation Army member)	35	60

618 Walter Parker

2000. Australian Legends (4th series). *The Last Anzacs.* Multicoloured. Ordinary of sels-adhesive gum.

1951	45c. Type **618**	35	40

1952	45c. Roy Longmore	35	40
1953	45c. Alec Campbell	35	40
1954	45c. 1914–15 Star (medal)	35	40

619 Scenes from *Cloudstreet* (play) (Perth Festival)

2000. Arts Festivals. Multicoloured.

1955	45c. Type **619**	45	50
1956	45c. Belgian dancers from Rosas Company (Adelaide Festival)	45	50
1957	45c. *Guardian Angel* (sculpture) and dancer (Sydney Festival)	45	50
1958	45c. Musician and Balinese dancer (Melbourne Festival)	45	50
1959	45c. Members of Vusa Dance Company of South Africa (Brisbane Festival)	45	50

620 Coast Banksia, False Sarsaparilla and Swamp Bloodwood (plants)

2000. Gardens. Multicoloured. Ordinary or self-adhesive gum.

1965	45c. Type **620**	40	55
1966	45c. Eastern spinebill on swamp bottlebrush in foreground	40	55
1967	45c. Border of cannas	40	55
1968	45c. Roses, lake and ornamental bridge	40	55
1969	45c. Hibiscus with bandstand in background	40	55

621 Queen Elizabeth II in 1996

2000. Queen Elizabeth II's Birthday.

1970	**621**	45c. multicoloured	80	50

622 Medals and Korean Landscape

2000. 50th Anniv of Korean War.

1971	**622**	45c. multicoloured	60	50

623 Daisy

2000. Nature and Nation. Greeting stamps. Multicoloured.

1972	45c. Type **623**	45	50
1973	45c. Australia on globe	45	50
1974	45c. Red kangaroo and flag	45	50
1975	45c. Sand, sea and sky	45	50
1976	45c. Rainforest	45	50

624 Taking the Vote, New South Wales

2000. Centenary of Commonwealth of Australia Constitution Act. Multicoloured.

1977	45c. Type **624**	45	40
1978	45c. Voters waiting for results, Geraldton, Western Australia	45	40
1979	$1.50 Queen Victoria (29×49 mm)	1·40	1·40
1980	$1.50 Women dancing ("The Fair New Nation") (29×49 mm)	1·40	1·40
MS1981	155×189 mm. Nos. 1977/80	3·25	3·25

625 Sydney Opera House, New South Wales

2000. International Stamps. Views of Australia (1st series). Multicoloured.

1982	50c. Type **625**	90	20
1983	$1 Nandroya Falls, Queensland	1·60	30
1984	$1.50 Sydney Harbour Bridge, New South Wales	2·00	75
1985	$2 Cradle Mountain, Tasmania	2·25	75
1986	$3 The Pinnacles, Western Australia	2·50	1·25
1987	$4.50 Flinders Ranges, South Australia (51×24 mm)	3·75	2·25
1988	$5 Twelve Apostles, Victoria (51×24 mm)	4·00	2·25
1989	$10 Devils Marbles, Northern Territory (51×24 mm)	8·25	4·50

Nos. 1982/9 were intended for international postage which, under changes in Australian tax laws from 1 July 2000, remained exempt from General Sales Tax.

From 1 February 2001 only international stamps were valid on overseas mail and from that date could not be used on items posted to Australian addresses.

See also Nos. 2121/4 and 2195/9.

626 Tennis Player in Wheelchair

2000. Paralympic Games, Sydney (1st issue). Multicoloured. Ordinary or self-adhesive gum.

1990	45c. Type **626**	50	50
1991	45c. Amputee sprinting	50	50
1992	49c. Basketball player in wheelchair	50	50
1993	49c. Blind cyclist	50	50
1994	49c. Amputee putting the shot	50	50

See also Nos. 2053/4.

627 Sir Neville Howse (first Australian recipient of Victoria Cross, 1900)

2000. Cent of Australia's First Victoria Cross Award.

2000	**627**	45c. multicoloured	70	50
2001	-	45c. brown, gold and black	70	50
2002	-	45c. multicoloured	70	50
2003	-	45c. multicoloured	70	50
2004	-	45c. brown, gold and black	70	50

DESIGNS: No. 2001, Sir Roden Cutler, 1941; 2002, Victoria Cross; 2003, Private Edward Kenna, 1945; 2004, Warrant Officer Keith Payne, 1969.

628 Water Polo

2000. Olympic Games, Sydney (2nd issue). Multicoloured. Ordinary or self-adhesive gum. Competitors highlighted in varnish.

2005	45c. Type **628**	40	50
2006	45c. Hockey	40	50
2007	45c. Swimming	40	50
2008	45c. Basketball	40	50
2009	45c. Cycling (triathlon)	40	50
2010	45c. Horse riding	40	50
2011	45c. Tennis	40	50
2012	45c. Gymnastics	40	50
2013	45c. Running	40	50
2014	45c. Rowing	40	50

Nos. 2005/14 were printed together, *se-tenant*, with the backgrounds forming a composite design.

629 Olympic Flag, Flame and Parthenon

2000. Transfer of Olympic Flag from Sydney to Athens. Joint issue with Greece. Multicoloured.

2025	45c. Type **629**	50	40
2026	$1.50 Olympic Flag, Flame and Sydney Opera House	1·50	1·50

Stamps in similar designs were issued by Greece.

630 Ian Thorpe (Men's 400m Freestyle Swimming)

2000. Australian Gold Medal Winners at Sydney Olympic Games. Multicoloured.

2027A	45c. Type **630**	40	45
2028A	45c. Australian team (Men's 4×100 m Freestyle Swimming Relay)	40	45
2029A	45c. Michael Diamond (Men's Trap Shooting)	40	45
2030A	45c. Australian team (Three Day Equestrian Event)	40	45
2031A	45c. Susie O'Neill (Women's 200 m Freestyle Swimming)	40	45
2032A	45c. Australian team (Men's 4×200 m Freestyle Swimming Relay)	40	45
2033A	45c. Simon Fairweather (Men's Individual Archery)	40	45
2034A	45c. Australian team (Men's Madison Cycling)	40	45
2035A	45c. Grant Hackett (Men's 1500 m Freestyle Swimming)	40	45
2036A	45c. Australian team (Women's Water Polo)	40	45
2037A	45c. Australian team (Women's Beach Volleyball)	40	45
2038A	45c. Cathy Freeman (Women's 400 m Athletics)	40	45
2039A	45c. Lauren Burns (Women's under 49 kg Taekwondo)	40	45
2040A	45c. Australian team (Women's Hockey)	40	45
2041A	45c. Australian crew (Women's 470 Dinghy Sailing)	40	45
2042A	45c. Australian crew (Men's 470 Dinghy Sailing)	40	45

631 Martian Terrain

2000. Stamp Collecting Month. Exploration of Mars. Multicoloured. (a) Ordinary gum.

2043	45c. Type **631**	45	45
2044	45c. Astronaut using thruster	45	45
2045	45c. Spacecraft (50×30 mm)	45	45
2046	45c. Flight crew (30×25 mm)	45	45
2047	45c. Launch site (30×50 mm)	45	45
2048	45c. Robots on kelp rod (25×30 mm)	45	45
MS2049	166×73 mm. Nos. 2043/8	2·50	2·50

(b) Self-adhesive. Designs 21×32 mm.

2050	45c. Type **631**	45	45
2051	45c. Astronaut using thruster	45	45

632 Cathy Freeman with Olympic Torch and Ring of Flames

2000. Opening Ceremony, Olympic Games, Sydney.

2052	**632**	45c. multicoloured	1·00	50

633 Blind Athlete carrying Olympic Torch

2000. Paralympic Games, Sydney (2nd issue). Multicoloured.

2053	45c. Type **633**	55	50
2054	45c. Paralympic Games logo	55	50

634 Siobhan Paton (swimmer)

2000. Siobhan Paton, Paralympian of the Year.

2055	**634**	45c. multicoloured	1·25	75

635 "Sleep in Heavenly Peace"

2000. Christmas. *Silent Night* (carol). Multicoloured. (a) Ordinary gum.

2056	40c. Type **635**	50	25
2057	45c. "All is Calm, All is Bright"	50	25
MS2058	165×75 mm. Nos. 2056/7	1·00	1·00

(b) Self-adhesive.

2059	40c. Type **635**	45	35

(c) International Mail. As T **625** inscr "Season's Greetings".

2060	80c. Byron Bay, New South Wales	70	85

2001. International Mail. No. 1901 optd International POST.

2061	$1 Koala	2·50	1·75

637 Parade passing Federation Arch, Sydney

2001. Centenary of Federation. Multicoloured. (a) Ordinary gum.

2062	49c. Type **637**	65	55
2063	49c. Edmund Barton (first Federal Prime Minister)	65	55
2064	$2 *Australia For Ever* (song sheet) and celebration picnic (50×30 mm)	2·40	2·10
2065	$2 State Banquet, Sydney (30×50 mm)	2·40	2·10
MS2066	166×73 mm. Nos. 2062/5	4·75	5·00

(b) Self-adhesive.

2067	49c. Type **637**	50	60
2068	49c. Edmund Barton (first Federal Prime Minister)	50	60

638 Slim Dusty with Guitar in 1940s

2001. Australian Legends (5th series). Slim Dusty (country music singer). Multicoloured. Ordinary or self-adhesive gum.

2069	45c. Type **638**	50	50
2070	45c. Slim Dusty wearing "Sundowner" hat	50	50

639 Light Horse Parade, 1940, and Command Post, New Guinea, 1943

2001. Centenary of Australian Army. Multicoloured.
2073 45c. Type **639** 1·00 65
2074 45c. Soldier carrying Rwandan child and officers on the Commando Selection Course 1·00 65

640 Entry Canopy, Skylights and Site Plan

2001. Opening of the National Museum, Canberra. Multicoloured.
2075 49c. Type **640** 50 50
2076 49c. Skylights and "Pangk" (wallaby sculpture) 50 50

2001. Sir Donald Bradman (cricketer) Commemoration. Nos. 1663/4 additionally inscribed "1908–2001" in red. Multicoloured.
2077 45c. Type **568** 50 50
2078 45c. Bradman playing stroke 50 50

641 *Khe Sanh* (Cold Chisel), 1978

2001. Australian Rock and Pop Music. Multicoloured. Ordinary or self-adhesive gum.
2089 45c. Type **641** 45 60
2090 45c. *Down Under* (Men at Work), 1981 45 60
2091 45c. *Power and the Passion* (Midnight Oil), 1983 45 60
2092 45c. *Original Sin* (INXS), 1984 45 60
2093 45c. *You're the Voice* (John Farnham), 1986 45 60
2094 45c. *Don't Dream it's Over* (Crowded House), 1986 45 60
2095 45c. *Treaty* (Yothu Yindi), 1991 45 60
2096 45c. *Tomorrow* (Silverchair), 1994 45 60
2097 45c. *Confide in Me* (Kylie Minogue), 1994 45 60
2098 45c. *Truly, Madly, Deeply* (Savage Garden), 1997 45 60

642 Queen Elizabeth II holding Bouquet

2001. Queen Elizabeth II's Birthday.
2099 **642** 45c. multicoloured 1·75 65

643 Party Balloons

2001. "Colour My Day". Greetings Stamps. (a) Domestic Mail.
2100 45c. Type **643** 30 35
2101 45c. Smiling Flower 30 35
2102 45c. Hologram and party streamers 30 35

(b) International Mail.
2103 $1 Kangaroo and joey 1·00 80
2104 $1.50 The Bayulu Banner 1·40 1·75

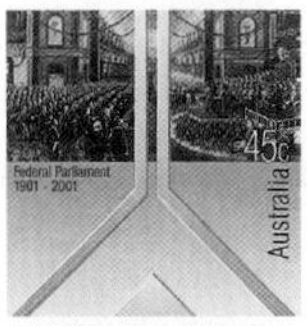

644 *Opening of the First Federal Parliament* (Charles Nuttall)

2001. Centenary of Federal Parliament. Paintings. Multicoloured.
2105 45c. Type **644** 50 25
2106 $2.45 *Prince George opening the First Parliament of the Commonwealth of Australia* (Tom Roberts) 1·75 2·25

MS2107 Two sheets, each 166×75 mm. (a) No. 2105. (b) No. 2106 Set of 2 sheets 2·75 3·00

645 Telecommunications Tower

2001. Outback Services. Multicoloured. Ordinary or self-adhesive gum.
2108 45c. Type **645** 1·00 75
2109 45c. Road train 1·00 75
2110 45c. School of the Air pupil 1·00 75
2111 45c. Outback family and mail box 1·00 75
2112 45c. Royal Flying Doctor Service aircraft and ambulance 1·00 75

646 Dragon Boat and Hong Kong Convention and Exhibition Centre

2001. Joint Issue with Hong Kong. Dragon Boat Racing. Multicoloured. (a) Domestic Mail.
2118 45c. Type **646** 50 45

(b) International Mail.
2119 $1 Dragon boat and Sydney Opera House 1·00 1·00
MS2120 115×70 mm. Nos. 2118/19 1·40 1·40

2001. International Stamps. Views of Australia (2nd series). As T **625**. Multicoloured.
2121 50c. The Three Sisters, Blue Mountains, New South Wales 1·25 40
2122 $1 The Murrumbidgee River, Australian Capital Territory 2·25 40
2123 $1.50 Four Mile Beach, Port Douglas, Queensland 3·25 1·00
2124 $20 Uluru Rock at dusk, Northern Territory (52×24 mm) 27·00 16·00

647 Variegated Wren ("Variegated Fairy-Wren")

2001. Fauna and Flora (4th series). Desert Birds. Multicoloured. Ordinary or self-adhesive gum.
2130 45c. Type **647** 50 50
2131 45c. Painted finch ("Painted Firetail") 50 50
2132 45c. Crimson chat 50 50
2133 45c. Budgerigar 50 50

648 Daniel Solander (Swedish botanist) and Mango Tree

2001. Australia–Sweden Joint Issue. Daniel Solander's Voyage with Captain Cook. Multicoloured. (a) Domestic Mail.
2134 45c. Type **648** 1·00 50

(b) International Mail.
2135 $1.50 H.M.S. *Endeavour* on reef and Kapok tree 3·50 3·50

649 Christmas Tree

2001. Christmas (1st issue). Multicoloured. (a) Domestic Mail.
2136 40c. Type **649** 50 20

(b) International Mail.
2137 80c. Star 1·50 1·10
See also Nos. 2157/8.

650 Australia on Globe

2001. Commonwealth Heads of Government Meeting (No. 2138) and Commonwealth Parliamentary Conference (No. 2139). Multicoloured.
2138 45c. Type **650** 50 50
2139 45c. Southern Cross 50 50

651 Wedge-tailed Eagle

2001. Centenary of Birds of Australia. Birds of Prey. Multicoloured.
2140 49c. Type **651** 1·00 75
2141 49c. Australian kestrel ("Nankeen Kestrel") 1·00 75
2142 98c. Red goshawk (vert) 2·00 2·00
2143 98c. Spotted harrier (vert) 2·00 2·00

652 Cockatoos dancing to Animal Band

2001. National Stamp Collecting Month. "Wild Babies" (cartoons). Multicoloured. Ordinary or self-adhesive gum.
2144 45c. Type **652** 55 45
2145 45c. Kevin Koala with birthday cake 55 45
2146 45c. Ring-tailed possums eating 55 45
2147 45c. Bilbies at foot of tree 55 45
2148 45c. James Wombat on rope ladder 55 45
2149 45c. Wallaby, echidna and platypus on rope ladder 55 45
MS2150 Two sheets, each 175×75 mm. (a) Nos. 2144/6. (b) 2147/9. Ordinary gum 2·50 2·50

653 *Adoration of the Magi*

2001. Christmas (2nd issue). Miniatures from *Wharncliffe Hours Manuscript*. Multicoloured.
2157 40c. Type **653** 1·10 30
2158 45c. *Flight into Egypt* 1·10 35
No. 2157 also comes self-adhesive.

654 Sir Gustav Nossal (immunologist)

2002. Australian Legends. (6th series). Medical Scientists. Ordinary or self-adhesive gum. Multicoloured.
2165 45c. Type **654** 45 55
2166 45c. Nancy Millis (microbiologist) 45 55
2167 45c. Peter Doherty (immunologist) 45 55
2168 45c. Fiona Stanley (epidemiologist) 45 55
2169 45c. Donald Metcalf (haematologist) 45 55

655 Queen Elizabeth in 1953

2002. Golden Jubilee. Multicoloured.
2170 45c. Type **655** 50 35
2171 $2.45 Queen Elizabeth in Italy, 2000 2·25 3·75
MS2172 160×77 mm. Nos. 2170/1 3·00 3·75

656 Steven Bradbury (Men's 1000m Short Track Speed Skating)

2002. Australian Gold Medal Winners at Salt Lake City Winter Olympic Games. Multicoloured.
2173 45c. Type **656** 95 60
2174 45c. Alisa Camplin (Women's Aerials Freestyle Skiing) 95 60

657 Austin 7 and Bugatti Type 40, Australian Grand Prix, Phillip Island, 1928

2002. Centenary of Motor Racing in Australia and New Zealand. Ordinary or self-adhesive gum. Multicoloured.
2175 45c. Type **657** 80 85
2176 45c. Jaguar Mark II, Australian Touring Car Championship, Mallala, 1963 80 85
2177 45c. Repco-Brabham, Tasman Series, Sandown, 1966 80 85
2178 45c. Holden Torana and Ford Falcon, Hardie-Ferodo 500, Bathurst, 1972 80 85
2179 45c. William's Ford, Australian Grand Prix, Calder, 1980 80 85
2180 45c. Benetton-Renault, Australian Grand Prix, Albert Park, 2001 80 85

658 Macquarie Lighthouse

2002. Lighthouses. Multicoloured.
2187 45c. Type **658** 75 35
2188 49c. Cape Naturaliste 90 80
2189 49c. Troubridge Island 90 80
2190 $1.50 Cape Bruny 2·25 2·25
Nos. 2188/9 also come self-adhesive.

659 Nicolas Baudin, Kangaroo, *Geographe* (ship) and Map

2002. Australia—France Joint Issue. Bicentenary of Flinders—Baudin Meeting at Encounter Bay. Multicoloured. (a) Domestic Mail.
2193 45c. Type **659** 60 40

(b) International Mail.
2194 $1.50 Matthew Flinders, Port Lincoln Parrot, *Investigator* (ship) and Map 2·00 1·75

2002. International Stamps. Views of Australia (3rd series). As T **625**. Multicoloured.
2195 50c. Walker Flat, River Murray, South Australia 65 40
2196 $1 Mt. Roland, Tasmania 1·25 60
2197 $1.50 Cape Leveque, Western Australia 1·60 1·25
Nos. 2195/6 also come self-adhesive.

660 Desert Star Flower

2002. Fauna and Flora (5th series). Great Sandy Desert. Multicoloured.
2200 50c. Type **660** 40 35
2201 $1 Bilby 80 65
2202 $1.50 Thorny Devil 1·20 1·60
2203 $2 Great Sandy Desert landscape (50×30 mm) 1·60 1·90
No. 2200 also comes self-adhesive.

661 *Ghost Gum, Mt Sonder* (Albert Namatjira)

2002. Birth Centenary of Albert Namatjira (artist). Multicoloured. Nos. 2204/7, ordinary or self-adhesive gum.

MS2208	133×70 mm. Nos. 2204/7	1·75	1·75
2209	45c. Type **661**	40	55
2210	45c. *Mt Hermannsburg*	40	55
2211	45c. *Glen Helen Country*	40	55
2212	45c. *Simpsons Gap*	40	55

662 *Nelumbo nucifera*

2002. Australia–Thailand Joint Issue. 50th Anniv of Diplomatic Relations. Water Lilies. Multicoloured. (a) Domestic Mail.

2213	45c. Type **662**	60	35

(b) International Mail.

2214	$1 *Nymphaea immutabilis*	1·40	75
MS2215	107×70 mm. Nos. 2214/15	1·75	1·75

663 Star, Presents and Baubles

2002. International Greetings. Multicoloured.

2216	90c. Type **663**	85	80
2217	$1.10 Koala	1·00	95
2218	$1.65 *Puja* (painting by Ngarralja Tommy May)	1·50	1·40

2002. International Stamps. Views of Australia (4th series). As T **625**. Multicoloured.

2219	$1.10 Coonawarra, South Australia	1·90	70
2220	$1.65 Gariwerd (Grampians), Victoria	2·75	1·40
2221	$2.20 National Library, Canberra	3·50	3·50
2222	$3.30 Cape York, Queensland	5·50	5·50

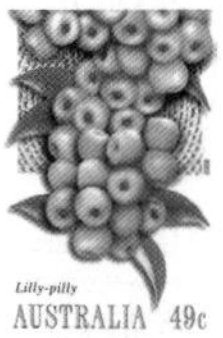

664 Lilly-pilly

2002. "Bush Tucker". Edible Plants from the Outback. Multicoloured. Ordinary or self-adhesive gum.

2228	49c. Type **664**	55	55
2229	49c. Honey Grevillea	55	55
2230	49c. Quandong	55	55
2231	49c. Acacia seeds	55	55
2232	49c. Murnong	55	55

665 Bunyip

2002. Stamp Collecting Month. *The Magic Rainforest*, (book by John Marsden). Multicoloured. Nos. 2233/8, ordinary or self-adhesive gum.

2233	45c. Type **665**	50	50
2234	45c. Fairy on branch	50	50
2235	45c. Gnome with sword	50	50
2236	45c. Goblin with stock whip	50	50
2237	45c. Wizard	50	50
2238	45c. Sprite	50	50
MS2239	170×90 mm. Nos. 2234/9	3·00	3·00

666 *Wakeful*

2002. Champion Racehorses. Multicoloured.

2246	45c. Type **666**	1·40	1·40
2247	45c. *Rising Fast*	1·40	1·40
2248	45c. *Manikato*	1·40	1·40
2249	45c. *Might and Power*	1·40	1·40
2250	45c. *Sunline*	1·40	1·40

667 Nativity

2002. Christmas. Multicoloured.

2251	40c. Type **667**	75	35
2252	45c. The Three Wise Men	75	35

No. 2251 also comes self-adhesive.

668 Two Daisies

2003. Greetings Stamps. Some adapted from previous issues. Multicoloured.

2254	50c. Type **668**	40	45
2255	50c. Wedding rings and yellow roses	40	45
2256	50c. Hearts and pink roses	40	45
2257	50c. Birthday cake and present	40	45
2258	50c. Seated teddy bear	40	45
2259	50c. Balloons	40	45
2260	50c. Red kangaroo and flag	40	45
2261	50c. Australia on globe	40	45
2262	50c. Sports car	40	45
2263	$1 Wedding rings and pink rose	80	85

669 Margaret Court with Wimbledon Trophy

2003. Australian Legends (7th series). Tennis Players. Ordinary or self-adhesive gum. Multicoloured.

2264	50c. Type **669**	65	50
2265	50c. Margaret Court in action	65	50
2266	50c. Rod Laver with Wimbledon Trophy	65	50
2267	50c. Rod Laver in action	65	50

670 Blue Orchid

2003. Fauna and Flora (6th series). Rainforest, Daintree National Park. Multicoloured. Ordinary or self-adhesive gum.

2272	50c. Orange-thighed tree frog	85	75
2273	50c. Green-spotted triangle (butterfly)	85	75
2274	50c. Striped possum	85	75
2275	50c. Yellow-bellied sunbird	85	75
2276	$1.45 Type **670**	2·00	1·25

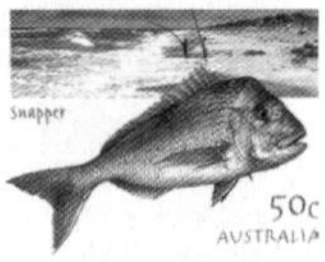

671 Snapper and Fishing from Beach

2003. Angling in Australia. Multicoloured.

2282	50c. Type **671**	60	60
2283	50c. Murray cod and flooded wood	60	60
2284	50c. Brown trout and fly-fishing	60	60
2285	50c. Yellow-finned tuna and sea-fishing from launch	60	60
2286	50c. Barramundi and anglers in mangrove swamp	60	60

672 "Hari Withers" Camellia

2003. Australian Horticulture. Multicoloured. (a) Size 25×36 mm. Ordinary gum.

2287	50c. Type **672**	55	50
2288	50c. "Victoria Gold" rose	55	50
2289	50c. "Superb" grevillea	55	50
2290	50c. "Bush Tango" kangaroo paw	55	50
2291	50c. "Midnight" rhododendron	55	50

(b) Size 21×33 mm. Self-adhesive.

2292	50c. Type **672**	50	60
2293	50c. "Victoria Gold" rose	50	60
2294	50c. "Superb" grevillea	50	60
2295	50c. "Bush Tango" kangaroo paw	50	60
2296	50c. "Midnight" rhododendron	50	60

673 *Ned Kelly* (Sir Sidney Nolan)

2003. Australian Paintings (1st series). Multicoloured.

2297	$1 Type **673**	1·50	1·75
2298	$1 *Family Home, Suburban Exterior* (Howard Arkley)	1·50	1·75
2299	$1.45 *Cord Long Drawn, Expectant* (Robert Jacks)	2·00	2·00
2300	$2.45 *Girl* (Joy Hester)	3·00	3·50

674 Queen Elizabeth II, 1953 (photograph by Cecil Beaton)

2003. 50th Anniv of Coronation. Multicoloured.

2301	50c. Type **674**	75	45
2302	$2.45 St. Edward's Crown	2·50	3·50
MS2303	105×70 mm. Nos. 2301/2	3·25	4·00

No. 2301 also comes self-adhesive.

675 Untitled Painting by Ningura Napurrula

2003. International Stamps. Art of Papunya Tula Movement. Showing untitled paintings by Aboriginal artists. Multicoloured.

2305	$1.10 Type **675**	1·60	70
2306	$1.65 Naata Nungurrayi	2·50	1·40
2307	$2.20 Graham Tjupurrula (55×24 mm)	3·00	2·00
2308	$3.30 Dini Campbell Tjampitjinpa (55×24 mm)	4·25	3·50

676 Kangaroo Chromosomes

2003. 50th Anniv of Discovery of DNA. Multicoloured.

2309	50c. Type **676**	1·00	1·00
2310	50c. DNA double helix	1·00	1·00

677 *Oscar W* (paddle-steamer)

2003. 150th Anniv of Murray River Shipping. Multicoloured. Ordinary or self-adhesive gum.

2311	50c. Type **677**	65	55
2312	50c. *Marion* (paddle-steamer)	65	55
2313	50c. *Ruby* (paddle-steamer)	65	55
2314	50c. *Pyap* (cruise vessel)	65	55
2315	50c. *Adelaide* (paddle-steamer)	65	55

678 Christmas Tree

2003. Greetings Stamps. Peace and Goodwill. Design, adapted from Christmas 2001 (1st issue) (Nos. 2136/7). Multicoloured. (a) Domestic Mail.

2321	50c. Type **678**	40	30

(b) International Mail.

2322	90c. Star	75	95

679 Sir Samuel Griffith (first Chief Justice)

2003. Centenary of High Court of Australia.

2323	**679**	50c. purple, black and red	55	45
2324	-	$1.45 vermilion, red and black	1·50	1·50
MS2325		105×70 mm. Nos. 2323/4	2·50	2·25

DESIGN: $1.45, "JUSTICE".

680 Ulysses Butterfly

2003. Stamp Collecting Month. Bugs and Butterflies. Multicoloured. Ordinary or self-adhesive gum.

2326	50c. Type **680**	50	45
2327	50c. Leichhardt's grasshopper	50	45
2328	50c. Vedalia ladybird	50	45
2329	50c. Green mantid and captured damselfly	50	45
2330	50c. Emperor gum moth caterpillar	50	45
2331	50c. Fiddler beetle	50	45
MS2332	170×85 mm. Nos. 2326/31	3·25	3·00

681 Hands passing Ball and Players

2003. Rugby World Cup Championship, Australia. Multicoloured. (a) Domestic Mail.

2339	50c. Type **681**	55	45

(b) International Mail.

2340	$1.10 Trophy (Webb Ellis Cup) and Telstra Stadium	1·10	1·00
2341	$1.65 Hand grasping ball and player taking shot at goal	1·50	2·00
MS2342	115×70 mm. Nos. 2339/41	2·75	3·00

682 "Active with ASTHMA" and Silhouettes of Sportspeople

2003. National Asthma Week Campaign.

2343	**682**	50c. multicoloured	1·00	45

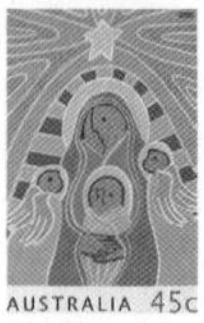

683 Mary, Baby Jesus and Angels

2003. Christmas. Multicoloured.

2344	45c. Type **683**	45	15
2345	50c. Three Wise Men	45	15
2346	90c. Angel appearing to shepherds	80	90

No. 2344 also comes self-adhesive.

684 Joan Sutherland as *Lucia di Lammermoor*, 1980

2004. Australian Legends (8th series). Dame Joan Sutherland (opera singer). Multicoloured. Ordinary or self-adhesive gum.

2350	50c. Type **684**	80	80
2351	50c. Joan Sutherland	80	80

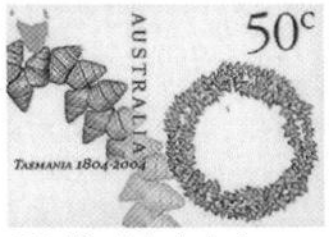

685 Aboriginal shell necklace and bracelet

2004. Bicentenary of Settlement of Hobart, Tasmania. Multicoloured.

2352	50c. Type **685**	85	70
2353	50c. Cheshunt House, Deloraine	85	70
2354	$1 *Mount Wellington and Hobart Town from Kangaroo Point* (John Glover)	1·75	1·75
2355	$1 Mountains, south west Tasmania	1·75	1·75
MS2356	135×72 mm. Nos. 2352/5	4·25	4·25

686 Ross Bridge, Tasmania, 1836

2004. Landmark Bridges. Multicoloured. Ordinary or self-adhesive gum.

2357	50c. Type **686**	90	70
2358	50c. Lockyer Creek Bridge, Queensland, 1911	90	70
2359	50c. Sydney Harbour Bridge, 1932	90	70
2360	50c. Birkenhead Bridge, Adelaide, 1940	90	70
2361	50c. Bolte Bridge, Melbourne, 1999	90	70

687 Stylized "Southern Cross"

2004. Greetings Stamp.

2367	**687**	50c. multicoloured	70	55

688 Solar Systems CS500 Dish ("solar")

2004. Renewable Energy. Multicoloured. Ordinary or self-adhesive gum.

2368	50c. Type **688**	85	85
2369	50c. Wind turbines ("wind")	85	85
2370	50c. Snowy Mountains Hydro-electric Scheme ("hydro")	85	85
2371	50c. Sugar cane field, bagasse (waste plant fibre) and sugar mill ("biomass")	85	85

689 Queen Elizabeth II (from photo by Dorothy Wilding)

2004. 50th Anniv of Royal Tour to Australia.

2376	**689**	50c. purple, black and grey	1·25	55

690 Red Lacewing

2004. Fauna and Flora (7th series). Rainforest Butterflies. Multicoloured.

2377	5c. Type **690**	15	15
2378	10c. Blue-banded eggfly	15	15
2379	75c. Cruiser	1·00	50
2380	$2 Ulysses and red lacewing butterflies and Daintree Rainforest (50×30 mm)	3·00	2·50

691 Cockatoos and Aircraft

2004. Australian Innovations. Multicoloured. Ordinary or self-adhesive gum.

2381	50c. Type **691** (black box flight recorder, 1961)	1·10	1·10
2382	50c. Pregnant woman (ultra-sound imaging equipment, 1976)	1·10	1·10
2383	50c. Driver's hands on wheel (Racecam TV sport coverage, 1979)	1·10	1·10
2384	50c. Kangaroo with joey and car (baby safety capsule, 1984)	1·10	1·10
2385	50c. Portion of banknote and tree (polymer banknotes, 1988)	1·10	1·10

692 Shaw Savill Lines *Dominion Monarch*

2004. "Bon Voyage". Ocean Liners. Advertising posters. Multicoloured.

2391	50c. Type **692**	90	45
2392	$1 Union Steam Ship Co. *Awatea*	1·50	85
2393	$1.45 Orient Line *Ormonde* & *Orsova*	2·00	2·00
2394	$2 Aberdeen & Commonwealth Line liner passing under bridge	2·75	2·75

No. 2395 also comes self-adhesive.

693 Eureka Flag (Southern Cross)

2004. 150th Anniv of Eureka Stockade. Multicoloured.

2396	50c. Type **693**	60	45
2397	$2.45 Peter Lalor (gold diggers leader) and detail from *Swearing allegiance to the Southern Cross 1854* (Alphonse Doudiet)	2·75	3·00
MS2398	106×69 mm. Nos. 2396/7	3·25	3·25

694 Koala

2004. "Impressions". Australian Wildlife and Heritage. Multicoloured.

2399	$1 Type **694**	1·50	1·75
2400	$1 Little penguin	1·50	1·75
2401	$1.45 Clown anemonefish (horiz)	1·75	1·75
2402	$2.45 Gold Coast (horiz)	2·75	3·50

695 Swimming

2004. Olympic Games, Athens, Greece. Multicoloured.

2403	50c. Type **695**	60	45
2404	$1.65 Sprinting	1·90	1·90
2405	$1.65 Cycling	2·75	1·90

696 Ian Thorpe (Men's 400m Freestyle Swimming)

2004. Australian Gold Medal Winners at Olympic Games, Athens. Multicoloured.

2406	50c. Type **696**	80	70
2407	50c. Women's 4×100m relay team	80	70
2408	50c. Sara Carrigan (Road Race Cycling)	80	70
2409	50c. Petria Thomas (Women's 100m Butterfly Swimming)	80	70
2410	50c. Suzanne Balogh (Women's Trap Shooting)	80	70
2411	50c. Ian Thorpe (Men's 200m Freestyle Swimming)	80	70
2412	50c. Jodie Henry (Women's 100m Freestyle Swimming)	80	70
2413	50c. Anna Meares (Women's 500m Time Trial Cycling)	80	70
2414	50c. James Tomkins and Drew Ginn (Men's Pair Rowing)	80	70
2415	50c. Grant Hacket (Men's 1500m Freestyle Swimming)	80	70
2416	50c. Women's 4×100m Medley Relay Swimming Team	80	70
2417	50c. Chantelle Newberry (Women's 10m Platform Diving)	80	70
2418	50c. Men's 4000m pursuit cycling team	80	70
2419	50c. Ryan Bayley (Men's Individual Sprint Cycling)	80	70
2420	50c. Graeme Brown and Stuart O'Grady (Men's Madison Cycling)	80	70
2421	50c. Ryan Bayley (Men's Keirin Cycling)	80	70
2422	50c. Men's hockey team	80	70

697 Entrance Beach, Broome, Western Australia

2004. International Stamps. Coastlines. Multicoloured.

2423	$1.20 Type **697**	2·00	50
2424	$1.80 Mt. William National Park, Tasmania	2·50	90
2425	$2.40 Potato Point, Bodalla, New South Wales	3·25	1·50
2426	$3.60 Point Gibbon, Eyre Peninsula, South Australia	4·50	2·75

698 Sheet of Early Australian Stamp (No. 16) (image scaled to 47% of original size)

2004. Treasures from the Archives (1st series). Ordinary or self-adhesive gum.

2427	**698**	$5 multicoloured	8·00	9·00

See also No. 2555.

699 Stephenson 2-4-0 (Melbourne–Sandridge, 1854)

2004. 150th Anniv of Australian Railways. Multicoloured. Ordinary or self-adhesive gum.

2429	50c. Type **699**	1·00	1·10
2430	50c. Locomotive No. 1 (Sydney–Parramatta, 1855)	1·00	1·10
2431	50c. B12 Class locomotive (Helidon–Toowoomba, 1867)	1·00	1·10
2432	50c. G Class train (Kalgoorlie–Port Augusta, 1917)	1·00	1·10
2433	50c. *The Ghan* (Alice Springs–Darwin, 2004)	1·00	1·10

700 "Ezzie" (black and white cat)

2004. Stamp Collecting Months. Cats and Dogs. Multicoloured. (a) Ordinary gum.

2439	50c. Type **700**	1·25	1·25
2440	50c. "Tinkerbell" (ginger and white kitten)	1·25	1·25
2441	50c. "Max" (Labrador puppy)	1·25	1·25
2442	50c. "Bridie" and "Lily" (West Highland terriers)	1·25	1·25
2443	$1 "Edward" (Jack Russell terrier)	2·25	1·50
MS2444	170×85 mm. Nos. 2439/43	6·50	6·00

(b) Self-adhesive.

2445	50c. "Max" (Labrador puppy)	70	80
2446	50c. Type **700**	70	80
2447	50c. "Bridie" and "Lily" (West Highland Terriers)	70	80
2448	50c. "Tinkerbell" (ginger and white kitten)	70	80
2449	$1 "Edward" (Jack Russell terrier)	1·50	1·60

701 Mick Doohan (Repsol)

2004. Formula 1 Motorcycle Racing. Multicoloured. Ordinary or self-adhesive gum.

2455	50c. Type **701**	80	90
2456	50c. Wayne Gardner (Racing Honda)	80	90
2457	50c. Troy Bayliss (Ducati)	80	90
2458	50c. Daryl Beattie (Team Suzuki)	80	90
2459	50c. Garry McCoy (Red Bull)	80	90

702 Mary and Jesus

2004. Christmas. Multicoloured. (a) Domestic mail.

2460	45c. Type **702**	40	15
2461	50c. The Angel and the shepherds	45	15

(b) International mail.

2462	$1 The Three Wise Men (horiz)	80	80

(c) Self-adhesive.

2464	$1 The Three Wise Men (horiz)	90	1·25

703 Tennis Player and Match, Warehousemen's Cricket Ground, Melbourne, c. 1905

2005. Centenary of Australian Open Tennis Championships. Multicoloured.

2465	50c. Type **703**	1·50	50
2466	$1.80 Woman player and match, Melbourne Park, c. 2005	3·00	2·75

704 Prue Acton

2005. Australian Legends (9th series). Fashion Designers. Multicoloured. Ordinary or self-adhesive gum.

2473	50c. Type **704**	90	1·10
2474	50c. Jenny Bannister	90	1·10
2475	50c. Collette Dinnigan	90	1·10
2476	50c. Akira Isogawa	90	1·10
2477	50c. Joe Saba	90	1·10
2478	50c. Carla Zampatti	90	1·10

705 Princess Parrot

2005. Australian Parrots. Multicoloured. Ordinary or self-adhesive gum.

2484	50c. Type **705**	1·10	1·10
2485	50c. Rainbow lorikeet	1·10	1·10
2486	50c. Green rosella	1·10	1·10
2487	50c. Red-capped parrot	1·10	1·10
2488	50c. Purple-crowned lorikeet	1·10	1·10

706 Sir Donald Bradman's Cap

2005. Sporting Treasures. Multicoloured.

2489	50c. Type **706**	1·00	85
2490	50c. Lionel Rose's boxing gloves	1·00	85
2491	$1 Marjorie Jackson's running spikes	1·50	1·50
2492	$1 Phar Lap's racing silks	1·50	1·50

707 Bumble Bee Toy

2005. Greetings Stamps (1st series). "Marking the Occasion". Multicoloured.

2493	50c. Type **707**	1·00	1·10
2494	50c. Red roses	1·00	1·10
2495	50c. Wrapped presents	1·00	1·10
2496	50c. Kangaroos at sunset	1·00	1·10
2497	50c. Bouquet of white flowers	1·00	1·10
2498	$1 Hand holding bouquet of cream roses	1·75	1·25
2499	$1.10 Koala	1·75	1·50
2500	$1.20 Shell on sandy beach	2·00	2·25
2501	$1.80 Sydney Opera House	3·50	3·50

Nos. 2493/8 are for domestic use and 2499/51 are for international use.

See also Nos. 2556/7.

708 Greater Blue Mountains Area, New South Wales

2005. World Heritage Sites. Multicoloured.

2502	50c. Type **708**	1·00	85
2503	50c. Blenheim Palace, England	1·00	85
2504	50c. Wet Tropics, Queensland	1·00	85
2505	50c. Stonehenge, England	1·00	85
2506	$1 Purnululu National Park, West Australia	1·75	1·50
2507	$1 Heart of Neolithic Orkney, Scotland	1·75	1·50
2508	$1.80 Uluru-Kata Tjuta National Park, Northern Territories	2·50	2·75
2509	$1.80 Hadrian's Wall, England	2·50	2·75

Nos. 2502/7 are for domestic use and 2508/9 are for international use.

Stamps in similar designs were also issued by Great Britain.

709 Tribrachidium

2005. Creatures of the Slime (Ediacaran fossils). Multicoloured.

2510	50c. Type **709**	1·25	1·00
2511	50c. Dickinsonia	1·25	1·00
2512	50c. Spriggina	1·25	1·00
2513	50c. Kimberella	1·25	1·00
2514	50c. Inaria	1·25	1·00
2515	$1 Charniodiscus 1.501	2·00	1·50
MS2516	170×210 mm. Nos. 2510/15	6·00	5·50

710 Rotary Emblem and Man supporting Globe

2005. Centenary of Rotary International. Ordinary or self-adhesive gum.

2517	**710** 50c. multicoloured	1·25	85

711 Obverse of Coin showing Head of Queen Victoria

2005. 150th Anniv of First Australian Coin. Design showing one sovereign coin and Sydney Mint building. Multicoloured.

2519	50c. Type **711**	1·50	85
2520	$2.45 Reverse of coin showing olive wreath	4·25	3·25
MS2521	105×69 mm. As Nos. 2519/20 but coins in gold foil	6·00	4·75

712 Queen at Opening Ceremony for Commonwealth Heads of Government Meeting, Queensland, 2002

2005. Queen's Birthday.

2522	**712** 50c. multicoloured	1·50	60

713 Superb Lyrebird

2005. International Stamps. Bush Wildlife. Multicoloured.

2523	$1 Type **713**	1·50	60
2524	$1.10 Laughing kookaburra	1·50	65
2525	$1.20 Koala	1·60	80
2526	$1.80 Red kangaroo	2·50	1·50

Nos. 2524/6 also come self-adhesive.

714 Sturt's Desert Pea

2005. Australian Wildflowers (1st series). Multicoloured. Ordinary or self-adhesive gum.

2530	50c. Type **714**	1·00	1·00
2531	50c. Coarse-leaved mallee	1·00	1·00
2532	50c. Common fringe lily	1·00	1·00
2533	50c. Swamp daisy	1·00	1·00

See also Nos. 2590/**MS**2594 and 2759/62.

715 Vineyard

2005. Australian Wine. Multicoloured.

2538	50c. Type **715**	1·00	1·00
2539	50c. Ripening grapes	1·00	1·00
2540	$1 Harvesting grapes	1·90	1·75
2541	$1 Casks of wine	1·90	1·75
2542	$1.45 Glasses of red and white wine and cheese	2·75	2·50

Nos. 2538/9 also come self-adhesive.

716 Snowgum

2005. Native Trees. Multicoloured. Ordinary or self-adhesive gum.

2550	50c. Type **716**	80	1·00
2551	50c. Wollemi pine	80	1·00
2552	50c. Boab	80	1·00
2553	50c. Karri	80	1·00
2554	50c. Moreton Bay fig	80	1·00

717 1888 20s. New South Wales Stamps (image scaled to 47% of original size)

2005. Treasures from the Archives (2nd issue).

2555	**717** $5 multicoloured	11·00	12·00

718 Christmas Tree with Lights

2005. Greetings Stamps. "Marking the Occasion" (2nd series). Multicoloured.

2556	45c. Type **718**	85	85
2557	50c. Map of Australia with stars	85	85

719 Chloe the Chicken

2005. Stamp Collecting Month. "Down on the Farm". Multicoloured.

MS2564	170×85 mm. Nos. 2558/63	5·00	5·50
2565	50c. Type **719**	1·00	1·25
2566	50c. Lucy the Lamb	1·00	1·25
2567	50c. Gilbert the Goat	1·00	1·25
2568	50c. Ralph the Piglet	1·00	1·25
2569	50c. Abigail the Cow	1·00	1·25
2570	$1 Harry the Horse	2·00	3·00

Nos. 2558/2563 also come self-adhesive.

720 Madonna and Child

2005. Christmas. Multicoloured. Ordinary or self-adhesive gum. (i) Domestic mail.

2571	45c. Type **720**	75	15

(ii) International Mail.

2572	$1 Adoring angel (horiz)	1·50	85

721 Emblem

2006. Commonwealth Games, Melbourne (1st issue). Ordinary or self-adhesive gum.

2575	**721** 50c. multicoloured	60	45

See also Nos. 2596/2600 and **MS**2607/**MS**2623.

722 Mrs. Norm Everage, 1969

2006. Australian Legends (10th series). Barry Humphries (satirist and actor). Multicoloured. Ordinary or self-adhesive gum.

2582	50c. Type **722**	1·00	1·50
2583	50c. As Mrs. Edna Everage, 1973	1·00	1·50
2584	50c. As Dame Edna Everage, 1982	1·00	1·50
2585	50c. As Dame Edna Everage, 2004	1·00	1·50
2586	50c. Barry Humphries	1·00	1·50

723 Red Rose

2006. Greetings Stamp. Roses. Ordinary or self-adhesive gum.

2587	**723** 50c. multicoloured	1·00	45

724 *Pincushion Hakea*

2006. Australian Wildflowers (2nd series). Multicoloured.

2590	$1 Type **724**	1·60	50
2591	$2 Donkey orchid	3·25	1·25
2592	$5 Mangles kangaroo paw (49×29 mm)	6·50	4·50
2593	$10 Waratah (49×29 mm)	12·00	9·00
MS2594	105×70 mm. $10 As No. 2593 (49×29 mm)	11·00	12·00

725 Dale Begg-Smith

2006. Dale-Begg Smith's Gold Medal for Men's Moguls Skiing at Winter Olympic Games, Turin.

2595	**725** 50c. multicoloured	1·00	75

726 Athlete at Start

2006. Commonwealth Games, Melbourne (2nd issue). Multicoloured. (a) Ordinary gum. (i) Domestic Mail.

2596	50c. Type **726**	50	45

(ii) International Post.

2597	$1.25 Cyclist	2·25	2·00
2598	$1.85 Netball	2·75	3·25
MS2599	142×75 mm. Nos. 2596/8	5·50	5·50

(b) Self-adhesive.

2600	50c. Type **726**	75	80

727 Platypus

2006. International Post. Native Wildlife. Multicoloured.

2601	5c. Type **727**	30	30
2602	25c. Short-beaked echidna	50	25
2603	$1.25 Common wombat	2·25	70
2604	$1.85 Tasmanian devil	3·25	1·40
2605	$2.50 Greater bilby	4·25	1·75
2606	$3.70 Dingo	6·00	3·25

728 Tram with Feathered "Wings" (Opening Ceremony)

2006. Commonwealth Games (3rd issue). Seventeen sheets each 180×200 mm containing horiz designs as T **728** showing opening/closing ceremonies (Nos. **MS**2607, **MS**2622) or Australian gold medal winners (others). Multicoloured.

MS2607	50c.×5 No. 1 Opening Ceremony	2·50	3·25
MS2608	50c.×5 No. 2	2·50	3·25
MS2609	50c.×10 No. 3	4·00	6·00
MS2610	50c.×5 No. 4	2·50	3·25
MS2611	50c.×10 No. 5	4·00	6·00
MS2612	50c.×5 No. 6	2·50	3·25

MS2613	50c.×5 No. 7	2·50	3·25
MS2614	50c.×10 No. 8	4·00	6·00
MS2615	50c.×5 No. 9	2·50	3·25
MS2616	50c.×10 No. 10	4·00	6·00
MS2617	50c.×5 No. 11	2·50	3·25
MS2618	50c.×10 No. 12	4·00	6·00
MS2619	50c.×10 No. 13	4·00	6·00
MS2620	50c.×10 No. 14	4·00	6·00
MS2621	50c.×5 No. 15	2·50	3·25
MS2622	50c.×5 No. 16 Closing Ceremony	2·50	3·25
MS2623	50c.×10 No. 17 Most memorable moment Kerryn McCann's Marathon victory	4·00	6·00

Nos. **MS**2607/23 are numbered from 1 to 17 at the foot of the sheet.

729 *Queen Elizabeth II in Garter Robes* (Pietro Annigoni)

2006. 80th Birthday of Queen Elizabeth II. Multicoloured. (a) Ordinary gum.

2624	50c. Type **729**	1·25	45
2625	$2.45 Queen Elizabeth II (photo by Cecil Beaton)	4·50	4·00
MS2626	105×70 mm. Nos. 2624/5	5·75	4·25

No. **MS**2626 also commemorates the 50th anniversary of the portrait by Annigoni.

(b) Self-adhesive.

2627	50c. Type **729**	75	1·00

730 Point Lonsdale, Victoria, 1902

2006. Lighthouses of the 20th Century. Ordinary or self-adhesive gum. Multicoloured.

2628	50c. Type **730**	1·10	1·00
2629	50c. Cape Don, Northern Territory, 1916	1·10	1·00
2630	50c. Wollongong Head, New South Wales, 1937	1·10	1·00
2631	50c. Casuarina Point, West Australia, 1971	1·10	1·00
2632	50c. Point Cartwright, Queensland, 1979	1·10	1·00

731 Koala with Cub

2006. International Stamps. "Greetings from Australia". Ordinary or self-adhesive gum. Multicoloured.

2638	$1.25 Type **731**	2·50	1·25
2639	$1.85 Royal Exhibition Building, Melbourne	3·50	2·75

732 Boy heading Ball ("PLAY")

2006. World Cup Football Championship, Germany. Soccer in Australia. Ordinary gum. Multicoloured. (i) Domestic Mail.

2642	50c. Type **732**	70	80
2643	50c. Player kicking ball ("GOAL")	70	80

(ii) International Post.

2644	$1.25 Goalkeeper ("SAVE")	1·75	1·50
2645	$1.85 Player with ball ("SHOT")	2·40	2·75
MS2646	Circular 170×170 mm. Nos. 2642/5	4·75	4·75

(b) Self-adhesive.

2647	50c. Type **732**	75	90
2648	50c. As No. 2643	75	90

733 Kate sorting Mail

2006. "Postie Kate". Ordinary or self-adhesive gum. Multicoloured.

2649	50c. Type **733**	80	80
2650	50c. On motorcycle, giving letter to woman	80	80
2651	50c. With van, delivering parcel	80	80
2652	50c. Riding motorcycle. passing mailbox	80	80
2653	50c. With mail satchel on shoulder	80	80

734 Blue Whale

2006. Endangered Species. Whales. Multicoloured. (a) Ordinary gum. (i) Domestic Mail.

2659	50c. Type **734**	75	60
2660	50c. Humpback whale	75	60

(ii) International Post.

2661	$1.25 Fin whale	1·75	1·25
2662	$1.85 Southern bottlenose whale	2·75	2·75
MS2663	69×66 mm. Nos. 2659/62	5·50	5·00

(b) Self-adhesive. (i) Domestic Mail.

2664	50c. Type **734**	75	90
2665	50c. As No. 2660	75	90

(ii) International Post.

2666	$1.25 As No. 2661	1·60	2·25
2667	$1.85 As No. 2662	2·40	3·75

2006. Le Salon du Timbre Stamp Exhibition, Paris. No. **MS**2646 inscr "LE SALON DU TIMBRE & DE L'ECRIT 17 AU 25 JUIN 2006 PARC FLORAL DE PARIS www. salondutimbre.fr" on sheet margin.

MS2668	Circular 170×170 mm. Nos. 2642/5	4·75	4·75

735 Surfing

2006. Extreme Sports. Multicoloured.

2669	50c. Type **735**	90	50
2670	$1 Snowboarding	1·75	1·25
2671	$1.45 Skateboarding	2·00	2·50
2672	$2 Freestyle motoX	3·50	4·00

736 Ford TT Truck, 1917

2006. Driving through the Years. Multicoloured. (a) Ordinary or self-adhesive gum.

2678	50c. Type **736**	70	1·00
2679	50c. Holden FE, 1956	70	1·00
2680	50c. Morris 850 (Mini Minor), 1961	70	1·00
2681	50c. Holden Sandman HX panel van, 1976	70	1·00
2682	50c. Toyota LandCruiser FJ60, 1985	70	1·00

737 "Sunbury Rock Festival" (1972)

2006. Rock Posters (1st series). Multicoloured. (a) Ordinary or self-adhesive gum.

2683	50c. Type **737**	95	1·00
2684	50c. "Magic Dirt" (2002)	95	1·00
2685	50c. "Masters Apprentices" (1969)	95	1·00
2686	50c. "Goanna's Spirit of Place" (1983)	95	1·00
2687	50c. "Angels/Sports/Paul Kelly" (c. 1979)	95	1·00
2688	50c. "Midnight Oil" (c. 1979)	95	1·00
2689	50c. "Big Day Out" (2003)	95	1·00
2690	50c. "Apollo Bay Music Festival" (1999)	95	1·00
2691	50c. "Rolling Stones Australian Tour" (1973)	95	1·00
2692	50c. "Mental as Anything" (1990)	95	1·00

See also Nos. 2808/11.

738 White Shark

2006. Stamp Collecting Month. Dangerous Australians. Multicoloured. (a) Ordinary gum.

2703	50c. Type **738**	1·25	1·25
2704	50c. Eastern brown snake	1·25	1·25
2705	50c. Box jellyfish	1·25	1·25
2706	50c. Saltwater crocodile	1·25	1·25
2707	50c. Blue-ringed octopus	1·25	1·25
2708	$1 Yellow-bellied sea snake	1·75	1·50
MS2709	130×90 mm. Nos. 2703/8	6·00	6·00

(b) Self-adhesive.

2710	50c. Type **738**	90	1·10
2711	50c. As No. 2704	90	1·10
2712	50c. As No. 2705	90	1·10
2713	50c. As No. 2706	90	1·10
2714	50c. As No. 2707	90	1·10
2715	$1 As No. 2708	1·40	1·75

739 *In Melbourne Tonight*

2006. 50th Anniv of Television in Australia. Multicoloured. (a) Ordinary or self-adhesive gum.

2716	50c. Type **739**	70	70
2717	50c. *Homicide*	70	70
2718	50c. *Dateline*	70	70
2719	50c. *Neighbours*	70	70
2720	50c. *Kath and Kim*	70	70

2006. China 2006 Stamp and Coin Expo. Two sheets, each 110×80 mm containing No. 2638, design on sheet margin given.

MS2726	**731** (a) $1.25 multicoloured (Great Wall of China). (b) $1.25 multicoloured (Sydney Opera House)	3·75	3·75

740 2s. Melbourne across River Yarra Stamp

2006. 50th Anniv of Olympic Games, Melbourne. Showing Australia 1956 Olympic Games stamps and contemporary photographs of Melbourne. Multicoloured.

2727	50c. Type **740**	1·25	1·25
2728	50c. River Yarra, Melbourne	1·25	1·25
2729	$1 1s. Collins Street stamp	1·75	2·00
2730	$1 Collins Street, Melbourne	1·75	2·00

741 Virgin Mary and Baby Jesus

2006. Christmas. Multicoloured. (a) Ordinary gum. (i) Domestic mail.

2731	45c. Type **741**	80	30
2732	50c. Magi with gift	80	35

(ii) International Mail.

2733	$1.05 Young shepherd with lamb	1·40	1·10

(b) Self-adhesive. Smaller design 22×33 mm. (i) Domestic mail.

2734	45c. Type **741**	70	60

(ii) International Mail.

2735	$1.05 As No. 2733	1·25	1·50

742 Victorious Australian Cricketers

2007. "Australia wins the Ashes". Multicoloured. (a) Ordinary gum. (i) Domestic Mail.

2736	50c. Type **742**	1·50	1·00

(ii) International Post.

2737	$1.85 Australian team with Ashes Urn	4·50	4·50
MS2738	160×80 mm. Nos. 2736/7	6·00	6·00

(b) Self-adhesive. (i) Domestic Mail.

2739	50c. As No. 2736	1·00	1·00

(ii) International Post.

2740	$1.85 As No. 2737	3·00	4·00

743 Scobie Breasley (jockey), 1936

2007. Australian Legends (11th series). Legends of Australian Horse Racing. Multicoloured. (a) Ordinary gum.

2741	50c. Type **743**	1·10	1·25
2742	50c. Scobie Breasley on *Santa Claus* after winning English Derby	1·10	1·25
2743	50c. Bart Cummings (trainer) holding binoculars, 1966	1·10	1·25
2744	50c. Bart Cummings holding Melbourne Cup	1·10	1·25
2745	50c. Roy Higgins (jockey), 1965	1·10	1·25
2746	50c. Roy Higgins riding *Light Fingers* to win Melbourne Cup, 1965	1·10	1·25
2747	50c. Bob Ingham (breeder), c. 1972	1·10	1·25
2748	50c. Bob Ingham leading *Lonhro*, 2004	1·10	1·25
2749	50c. George Moore (jockey), 1957	1·10	1·25
2750	50c. George Moore riding *Tulloch*, 1960	1·10	1·25
2751	50c. John Tapp (race commentator), 1972	1·10	1·25
2752	50c. John Tapp at microphone, 1998	1·10	1·25

(b) Self-adhesive.

2753	50c. Type **743**	85	1·25
2754	50c. As No. 2743	85	1·25
2755	50c. As No. 2746	85	1·25
2756	50c. As No. 2748	85	1·25
2757	50c. As No. 2749	85	1·25
2758	50c. As No. 2751	85	1·25

744 Tasmanian Christmas Bell

2007. Australian Wildflowers (3rd series). Multicoloured. Ordinary or self-adhesive gum.

2759	50c. Type **744**	1·25	1·40
2760	50c. Green spider flower	1·25	1·40
2761	50c. Sturt's desert rose	1·25	1·40
2762	50c. *Phebalium whitei*	1·25	1·40

745 Swimmer

2007. 12th FINA (Federation Internationale de Natation) World Championships, Melbourne. Ordinary or self-adhesive gum.

2767	**745** 50c. multicoloured	70	70

746 Maria Island, Tasmania

2007. International Post. Island Jewels. Multicoloured. (a) Ordinary gum.

2769	10c. Type **746**	15	10
2770	30c. Rottnest Island, West Australia	45	40
2771	$1.30 Green Island, Queensland	2·00	2·10
2772	$1.95 Fraser Island, Queensland	2·50	2·50
2773	$2.60 Kangaroo Island, South Australia	3·25	3·25
2774	$3.85 Lord Howe Island, New South Wales	3·75	4·00

(b) Self-adhesive gum.

2775	$1.30 As No. 2771	2·50	3·00
2776	$1.95 As No. 2772	3·00	4·25

747 Female Lifeguard with Reel

2007. Year of the Surf Lifesaver. Multicoloured. (a) Ordinary gum.

2777	50c. Type **747**	70	90
2778	50c. Male lifeguards	70	90
2779	$1 Surf boat	2·50	2·25
2780	$2 "Nippers" (life saving club's children's programme)	3·50	4·50

(b) Self-adhesive gum.

2781	50c. As No. 2778	70	1·00
2782	50c. Type **747**	70	1·00
MS2783	160×90 mm. $2.45 Inflatable rescue boat ×2	6·50	6·75

748 Aries

2007. Signs of the Zodiac. Multicoloured. Ordinary or self-adhesive gum.

2784	50c. Type **748**	70	80
2785	50c. Taurus	70	80
2786	50c. Gemini	70	80
2787	50c. Cancer	70	80
2788	50c. Leo	70	80
2789	50c. Virgo	70	80
2790	50c. Libra	70	80
2791	50c. Scorpio	70	80
2792	50c. Sagittarius	70	80
2793	50c. Capricorn	70	80
2794	50c. Aquarius	70	80
2795	50c. Pisces	70	80

749 *At the Beach* (Percy Trompf)

2007. Poster Art (2nd series). Nostalgic Tourism. Showing 1930s tourism posters. Multicoloured.

2808	50c. Type **749**	70	70
2809	$1 *Fishing* (John Vickery)	1·40	1·25
2810	$2 *Riding in the Country* (James Northfield)	3·00	3·75
2811	$2.45 *Winter Sport* (James Northfield)	3·75	5·50

750 Queen Elizabeth II in Australia, March 2006

2007. Queen's Birthday.

2812	**750**	50c. multicoloured	1·50	1·25

751 *Admella* (steamship), 1859

2007. Historic Shipwrecks. Multicoloured.

2813	50c. Type **751**	1·00	70
2814	$1 *Loch Ard* (clipper), 1878	1·75	1·25
2815	$2 *Dunbar* (clipper), 1857	3·00	4·50

752 Yellow-footed Rock-wallaby

2007. International Post. "Country to Coast". Multicoloured.

2816	$1.30 Type **752**	2·50	1·75
2817	$1.95 Sydney Harbour Bridge	4·50	2·75

753 "The Burning Bicycle"

2007. Circus: Under the Big Top. Multicoloured. Ordinary or self-adhesive gum.

2818	50c. Type **753**	80	1·00
2819	50c. "The Inside-out Man"	80	1·00
2820	50c. "The Dental Trapeze"	80	1·00
2821	50c. "The Banana Lady"	80	1·00
2822	50c. "The Human Cannonball"	80	1·00

754 Big Golden Guitar, Tamworth, New South Wales

2007. Big Things. Multicoloured..

2828	50c. Type **754**	80	85
2829	50c. Big lobster, Kingston SE, South Australia	80	85
2830	50c. Big banana, Coffs Harbour, New South Wales	80	85
2831	50c. Big Merino ram, Goulburn, New South Wales	80	85
2832	50c. Big pineapple, Nambour, Queensland	80	85

755 Sydney Harbour Bridge

2007. International Post. 75th Anniv of Sydney Harbour Bridge. Sheet 130×90 mm.

MS2838	(a) $1.95×2 multicoloured. (b) $1.95×2 multicoloured (emblem and '15 JUNE 2007 SYDNEY NSW 2000' inscr in gold on sheet margin) Set of 2 sheets	11·00	11·00

756 Grey-headed flying-fox

2007. Threatened Wildlife. Multicoloured. (i) Domestic mail.

2839	50c. Type **756**	90	1·25
2840	50c. Mountain Pygmy-possum	90	1·25

(ii) International Post.

2841	$1.25 Flatback turtle	2·25	2·50
2842	$1.30 Wandering albatross	2·25	2·50

757 Former ICI House, Melbourne, 1973

2007. Landmarks: Modernist Australian Architecture. Multicoloured.

2843	50c. Type **757**	90	90
2844	50c. Academy of Science, Canberra, 1958	90	90
2845	$1 Council House, Perth, 1962	1·60	1·25
2846	$2.45 Sydney Opera House, 1973	4·00	4·50
MS2847	90×90 mm. Nos. 2843/6	6·75	6·75

758 Delicatessen, Dairy Produce Hall, Queen Victoria Market, Melbourne

2007. Market Feast. Multicoloured. Ordinary or self-adhesive gum.

2848	50c. Type **758**	1·00	1·25
2849	50c. Banana seller, Rusty's Market, Cairns	1·00	1·25
2850	50c. Sydney Fish Market	1·00	1·25
2851	50c. Vegetable stall, Adelaide Central Market	1·00	1·25
2852	50c. Potato seller, Hume Murray Farmers Market, Albury Wodonga	1·00	1·25

2007. BANGKOK 2007

MS2857b	130×90 mm. **755** $1.95×2 multicoloured	7·50	6·00

759 APEC Logo and Half Globe

2007. Asia-Pacific Economic Cooperation Forum, Australia. Ordinary or self-adhesive gum.

2858	**759**	50c. multicoloured	70	70

760 SAS Soldiers, Helicopter and Parachutist

2007. 50th Anniv of the Special Air Service.

2860	**760**	50c. multicoloured	1·25	1·00

761 Brisbane Botanic Gardens, Mt. Coot-tha

2007. Australian Botanic Gardens. Multicoloured. Ordinary or self-adhesive gum.

2861	50c. Type **761**	1·10	1·10
2862	50c. Kings Park and Botanic Garden, Perth	1·10	1·10
2863	50c. Royal Botanic Gardens and Domain, Sydney	1·10	1·10
2864	50c. Royal Botanic Gardens, Melbourne	1·10	1·10
2865	50c. Botanic Gardens of Adelaide	1·10	1·10

2007. Collectors International Fair, Prague. No. MS2838 inscr 'SBERATEL SAMMLER COLLECTOR' and emblem on sheet margin.

MS2871	130×90 mm. **755** $1.95×2 multicoloured	5·75	5·75

762 Sputnik (first satellite), 1957

2007. Stamp Collecting Month. Blast Off! 50 Years in Space. Multicoloured.

2872	50c. Type **762**	70	70
2873	50c. Cosmonaut Alexei Leonov on first space walk, 1965	70	70
2874	50c. Neil Armstrong walking on Moon, 1969	70	70
2875	50c. *Voyager* space probe, 1977	70	70
2876	50c. International Space Station, 1998	70	70
2877	$1 Hubble Space Telescope and galaxy, 1990	1·25	1·25
MS2878	160×90 mm. Nos. 2872/7 and as No. 2877 but 51×37 mm	7·50	7·50

Nos. 2872/6 also come self-adhesive.

763 Family Picnic outside Caravan, 1950s

2007. Caravanning through the Years. Multicoloured. Ordinary or self-adhesive gum.

2884	50c. Type **763**	1·10	1·10
2885	50c. Family with kangaroos outside caravan, 1960s	1·10	1·10
2886	50c. Family outside caravan, 1970s	1·10	1·10
2887	50c. Woman and girl outside caravan, 1980s	1·10	1·10
2888	50c. Elderly couple sitting outside caravan, c. 2007	1·10	1·10

764 Surfing Santa Stamp Design by Roger Roberts, 1977

2007. Christmas. 50 Years of Christmas Stamps. Multicoloured designs showing Christmas stamp designs from previous years redrawn without the face values. (a) Ordinary gum. (i) Domestic Mail.

2894	45c. Type **764**	80	20
2895	45c. Bush Nativity (Baby Jesus with koalas and wallaby) by Marg Towt, 1990	80	1·00
2896	45c. Madonna and Child	80	1·00
2897	50c. The Spirit of Christmas	80	70

(ii) International Post.

2898	$1.10 Madonna and Child from stained-glass window, 1984	1·50	1·50

(b) Self-adhesive. (i) Domestic Mail.

2899	45c. As Type **764**	65	60
2900	45c. As No. 2895	90	90
2901	45c. As No. 2896	90	90
2902	50c. As No. 2897	90	1·25

(ii) International Post.

2903	$1.10 As No. 2898	1·75	2·00
MS2904	156×100 mm. As No. 2899 and Nos. 2900/3	4·75	4·75

765 Red Rose

2008. Greetings stamp. 'Love Blooms'. Ordinary or self-adhesive gum.

2905	**765**	50c. multicoloured	80	70

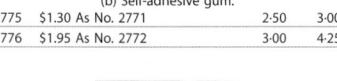

766 Dame Elisabeth Murdoch

2008. Australian Legends (12th series). Philanthropists. Multicoloured. Ordinary or self-dhesive gum.

2907	50c. Type **766**	1·40	1·40
2908	50c. Victor Smorgon and Loti Smorgon	1·40	1·40
2909	50c. Lady (Mary) Fairfax	1·40	1·40
2910	50c. Frank Lowy	1·40	1·40

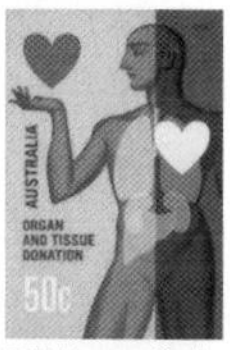

767 Human Body showing Organs

2008. Organ and Tissue Donation. Ordinary or self-adhesive gum.

2915	**767**	50c. multicoloured	75	75

768 Scout Camp

2008. Centenary of Scouting in Australia. T 768 and similar horiz designs. Multicoloured. (a) Ordinary gum. (i) Domestic Mail.

2917	50c. Type **768**	75	75

(ii) International Post.

2918	$1.35 Scouts in circle	1·90	2·00
2919	$2 Lord Baden-Powell (founder)	2·75	3·75

(b) Self-adhesive. (i) Domestic Mail.

2920	50c. As Type **768**	75	1·00

(ii) International Post.

2921	$1.35 As No. 2918	4·50	5·50
2922	$2 As No. 2919	6·50	8·50

769 Hanging Rock, Grose River Gorge, New South Wales

2008. International Post. 'Gorgeous Australia'. Multicoloured. (a) Ordinary gum.

2923	$1.35 Type **769**	1·90	1·90
2924	$2 Walpa Gorge, Northern Territory	3·00	2·75
2925	$2.70 Katherine Gorge, Northern Territory (horiz)	4·00	4·00
2926	$4 Geikie Gorge, West Australia (horiz)	6·50	6·50

(b) Self-adhesive

2927	$1.35 As Type 769	3·50	4·50
2928	$2 As No. 2924	4·75	7·00

770 Pope Benedict XVI

2008. World Youth Day, Sydney. Multicoloured. (a) Ordinary gum (i) Domestic Mail.

2929	50c. Type **770**	1·00	75

(ii) International Post

2930	$1.35 Pope holding crosier	2·50	2·50
2931	$2 Pope giving blessing	3·00	3·25

(b) Self-adhesive. (ii) International Post

2932	$1.35 As No. 2930	3·00	3·50
2933	$2 As No. 2931	4·50	6·00

2008. Canberra Stamp Show. Sheet 130×90 mm containing No. 2919×2. Multicoloured.

MS2934	$2×2 Lord Baden-Powell	7·50	6·50

771 Bulldogs

2008. Centenary of Rugby League. Multicoloured. (a) Ordinary gum.

2935	50c. Type **771**	80	90
2936	50c. Titans	80	90
2937	50c. Sharks	80	90
2938	50c. Knights	80	90
2939	50c. Cowboys	80	90
2940	50c. Broncos	80	90
2941	50c. Sea Eagles	80	90
2942	50c. Storm	80	90
2943	50c. Roosters	80	90
2944	50c. Raiders	80	90
2945	50c. Rabbitohs	80	90
2946	50c. Panthers	80	90
2947	50c. Dragons	80	90
2948	50c. Eels	80	90
2949	50c. Wests Tigers	80	90
2950	50c. Warriors	80	90

(b) Self-adhesive.

2951	50c. As No. 2942	75	1·00
2952	50c. As No. 2937	75	1·00
2953	50c. As No. 2943	75	1·00
2954	50c. As Type **771**	75	1·00
2955	50c. As No. 2938	75	1·00
2956	50c. As No. 2939	75	1·00
2957	50c. As No. 2945	75	1·00
2958	50c. As No. 2944	75	1·00
2959	50c. As No. 2948	75	1·00
2960	50c. As No. 2949	75	1·00
2961	50c. As No. 2947	75	1·00
2962	50c. As No. 2941	75	1·00
2963	50c. As No. 2940	75	1·00
2964	50c. As No. 2936	75	1·00
2965	50c. As No. 2946	75	1·00
2966	50c. As No. 2950	75	1·00

772 Face Shovel in Mine

2008. Heavy Haulers. Multicoloured. (a) Ordinary or self-adhesive gum.

2967	50c. Type **772**	1·50	1·50
2968	50c. 200 tonne mine haul truck	1·50	1·50
2969	50c. Road train	1·50	1·50
2970	50c. Ore train, West Australia	1·50	1·50
2971	50c. MS *Berge Stahl* (world?s largest bulk carrier)	1·50	1·50

773 Veterans marching

2008. 'Lest We Forget': ANZAC Day. Multicoloured. (a) Ordinary gum.

2977	50c. Type **773**	1·50	1·50
2978	50c. Laying wreaths at war memorial	1·50	1·50
2979	50c. Playing the *Last Post*	1·50	1·50
2980	50c. War veteran and young boy	1·50	1·50
2981	50c. Young Australians at Gallipoli	1·50	1·50
MS2982	160×90 mm. Nos. 2977/81	6·75	6·75

(b) Self-adhesive.

2983	50c. As Type **773**	1·10	1·25
2984	50c. As No. 2978	1·10	1·25
2985	50c. As No. 2979	1·10	1·25
2986	50c. As No. 2980	1·10	1·25
2987	50c. As No. 2981	1·10	1·25

774 Queen Elizabeth II at Official Dinner, Parliament House, Canberra, 2006

2008. Queen's Birthday. Multicoloured. (i) Domestic Mail.

2988	50c. Type**774**	1·50	75

(ii) International Post.

2989	$2 Sovereign's badge, Order of Australia	4·50	4·00
MS2990	106×70 mm. Nos. 2988/9	6·50	7·00

775 Balloons over Sydney, New South Wales

2008. 'Up Up and Away'. 150th Anniv of First Hot Air Balloon Flight in Australia. Multicoloured. Ordinary or self adhesive gum.

2991	50c. Type **775**	1·75	1·75
2992	50c. Orange and white balloons over Mt. Feathertop, Victoria	1·75	1·75
2993	50c. Multicoloured balloons over the Western MacDonnell Ranges, Northern Territories	1·75	1·75
2994	50c. Balloons over Canberra, Australian Central Territory	1·75	1·75

2008. WSC Israel 2008 World Stamp Championship, Tel-Aviv. Sheet 130×90 mm containing No. 2979×4. Multicoloured.

MS2999	50c.× 4 Playing *The Last Post*	7·00	6·00

776 German Shepherd Dog

2008. Working Dogs. Multicoloured. Ordinary or self-adhesive gum.

3005	50c. Type **776**	1·10	1·40
3006	50c. Australian cattle dog	1·10	1·40
3007	50c. Beagle	1·10	1·40
3008	50c. Border collie	1·10	1·40
3009	50c. Labrador	1·10	1·40

777 Chinese Dragon

2008. Olympic Games, Beijing. Ordinary or self-adhesive gum.

3010	**777**	50c. multicoloured	1·50	1·00

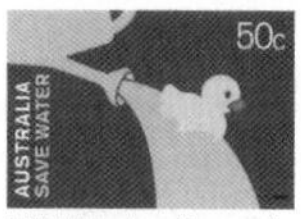

778 Watering Can and Rubber Duck ('SAVE WATER')

2008. Living Green. Ordinary or self-adhesive gum. Mulitcoloured.

3012	50c. Type **778**	80	80
3013	50c. Hand holding bin ('REDUCE WASTE')	80	80
3014	50c. Bus with legs ('TRAVEL SMART')	80	80
3015	50c. Crescent moon with light switch ('SAVE ENERGY')	80	80

779 Quarantine Detector Dog and Handler

2008. Centenary of the Quarantine Act. Ordinary or self-adhesive gum.

3020	**779**	50c. multicoloured	1·25	1·00

780 Pilgrims with Flags at Barangaroo for Opening Mass

2008. World Youth Day (2nd issue). Multicoloured.

3022	50c. Type **780**	2·00	2·00
3023	50c. Pope Benedict XVI at Barangaroo	2·00	2·00
3024	50c. Re-enactment of Stations of the Cross	2·00	2·00
3025	50c. Start of Pilgrimage Walk at Sydney Harbour Bridge	2·00	2·00
3026	50c. Pope Benedict XVI at Final Mass, Southern Cross Precinct	2·00	2·00

781 Football Game, Melbourne, 1866

2008. 150th Anniv of Australian Football.

3027	**781**	50c. multicoloured	1·00	1·00

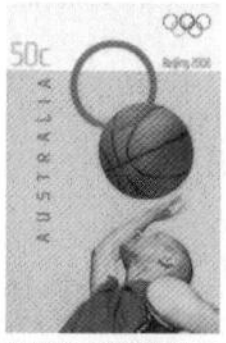

782 Basketball

2008. Olympic Games, Beijing. Multicoloured.

3028	50c. Type **782**	1·75	65
3029	$1.30 Cycling	3·50	2·75
3030	$1.35 Gymnastics	3·50	2·75

Nos. 3029/3030 also come self-adesive.

783 Bristol Tourer

2008. Aviation. Multicoloured. (a) Ordinary gum. (i) Domestic mail

3033	50c. Type **783**	1·40	1·40
3034	50c. Short S.30 Empire flying boat	1·40	1·40
3035	50c. Lockheed Super Constellation	1·40	1·40

(ii) International Post.

3036	$2 Airbus A320	4·50	4·50

(b) Self-adhesive.

3037	$2 As No. 3036	3·75	4·75

784 Stephanie Rice (swimming: women's 400m individual medley)

2008. Australian Gold Medal Winners at Olympic Games, Beijing. Multicoloured.

3038A	50c. Type **784**	1·25	1·25
3039A	50c. Lisbeth Trickett (swimming: women's 100m butterfly)	1·25	1·25
3040A	50c. Leisel Jones (swimming: women's 100m breaststroke)	1·25	1·25

3041A 50c. Stephanie Rice (swimming: women's 200m individual medley) 1·25 1·25
3042A 50c. Women's 4×200m freestyle relay swimming team 1·25 1·25
3043A 50c. Drew Ginn and Duncan Free (rowing: men's pair) 1·25 1·25
3044A 50c. David Crawshay and Scott Brennan (rowing: men's double sculls) 1·25 1·25
3045A 50c. Women's 4×100m medley relay swimming team 1·25 1·25
3046A 50c. Emma Snowsill (women's triathlon) 1·25 1·25
3047A 50c. Malcolm Page and Nathan Wilmott (sailing: men's 470) 1·25 1·25
3048A 50c. Tessa Parkinson and Elise Rechichi (sailing: women's 470) 1·25 1·25
3049A 50c. Ken Wallace (canoe/kayak: men's K-1 500m) 1·25 1·25
3050A 50c. Steven Hooker (athletics: men's pole vault) 1·25 1·25
3051A 50c. Matthew Mitcham (diving: men's 10m platform) 1·25 1·25

2008. SunStamp 2008 National Stamp Exhibition, Brisbane. Sheet 130×90 mm containing Nos. 2998 and 3036, each ×2. Multicoloured.
MS3052 50c.×2 Multicoloured balloons over the Western MacDonnell Ranges, Northern Territories; $2×2 Airbus A320 14·00 14·00

785 Luna Park, Melbourne

2008. Tourist Precincts. Multicoloured.
3053 55c. Type **785** 90 90
3054 55c. South Bank, Brisbane 90 90
3055 55c. The Rocks, Sydney 90 90
3056 55c. Fisherman's Wharf, Fremantle 90 90
3057 $1.10 Foreshore, Cairns 1·75 1·40
3058 $1.65 Salamanca Place, Hobart 2·75 2·25
3059 $2.75 Glenelg, Adelaide (50×30 mm) 4·25 4·75
Nos. 3053/3056 also come self-adhesive.

786 Russell Falls, Tasmania

2008. International Post. Waterfalls of Australia. Multicoloured.
3064 $1.40 Type **786** 2·00 1·25
3065 $2.05 Jim Jim Falls, Northern Territory 3·00 3·00
3066 $2.80 Spa Pool, Hamersley Gorge, Western Australia 4·00 4·00
3067 $4.10 Mackenzie Falls, Victoria 6·00 6·00
Nos. 3064/3065 also come self-adhesive.

787 Silver Rings

2008. Greetings Stamps. 'For Every Occasion'. Multicoloured.
3070 55c. Type **787** 1·10 1·10
3071 55c. Gold rings 1·10 1·10
3072 55c. Baby's feet 1·10 1·10
3073 55c. Gold heart and pink roses 1·10 1·10
3074 55c. Balloons 1·10 1·10
3075 55c. Bird flying over beach 1·10 1·10
3076 55c. Outline map of Australia as sun and stylised landscape 1·10 1·10
3077 55c. Sparklers 1·10 1·10
3078 55c. Australia and Antarctica on globe (30×30 mm) 1·10 1·10
3079 $1.10 Embroidery from wedding dress and pale pink roses 1·75 1·75

788 Genyornis

2008. Stamp Collecting Month. Megafauna of Australia. Multicoloured.
3080 55c. Type **788** 1·25 1·25
3081 55c. Diprotodon 1·25 1·25
3082 55c. Thylacoleo 1·25 1·25
3083 55c. Thylacine 1·25 1·25
3084 $1.10 Megalania (52×37 mm) 2·00 2·00
3085 $1.10 Procoptodon (52×37 mm) 2·00 2·00
MS3086 170×90 mm. Nos. 3080/5 8·00 8·00
Nos. 3080/3083 also come self-adhesive.

2008. Beijing Expo. No. **MS**3086 optd with emblem and **BEIJING 24-27 OCTOBER 2008**.
MS3091 170×90 mm. Nos. 3080/5 7·00 7·00

789 Matthew Cowdrey

2008. Paralympian of the Year.
3092 **789** 55c. multicoloured 1·50 1·00

790 Baubles

2008. Christmas. Multicoloured. (a) Ordinary gum. (i) Domestic Mail
3093 50c. Type **790** 75 75
3094 50c. Virgin Mary and baby Jesus 75 75
3095 55c. Angel 75 30

(ii) International Post.
3096 $1.20 Wise man carrying gift 1·75 2·50

(b) Self-adhesive. (i) Domestic Mail.
3097 50c. As Type **790** 85 85
3098 50c. As Type **790** but gold foil star on bottom left bauble 85 85
3099 50c. As No. 3094 85 85

(ii) International Post.
3100 $1.20 As No. 3096 1·75 2·00

791 *The Adventures of Priscilla, Queen of the Desert*

2008. Favourite Australian Films. Multicoloured. Self-adhesive.
3106 55c. Type **791** 85 95
3107 55c. *The Castle* 85 95
3108 55c. *Muriel's Wedding* 85 95
3109 55c. *Lantana* 85 95
3110 55c. *Gallipoli* 85 95
Nos. 3106/3110 also came with ordinary gum.

2008. Discovery of the HMAS Sydney. Sheet 130×90 mm containing Nos. 2977/8, each ×2. Multicoloured.
MS3111 50c.×2 Type **773**; 50c.×2 Laying wreaths at war memorial 3·00 3·00

2008. 90th Anniv of the End of World War I. Sheet 160×90 mm containing Nos. 2978/9, each ×2. Multicoloured.
MS3112 50c.×2 Laying wreaths at war memorial; 50c.×2 Playing the *Last Post* 3·00 3·00

792 Nicole Kidman

2009. Australian Legends (13th series). 'Legends of the Screen'. Multicoloured.
3113 55c. Type **792** 1·50 1·25
3114 55c. Russell Crowe 1·50 1·25
3115 55c. Geoffrey Rush 1·50 1·25
3116 55c. Cate Blanchett 1·50 1·25
3117 55c. Russell Crowe in *Gladiator*, 2000 1·50 1·25
3118 55c. Nicole Kidman in *Moulin Rouge!*, 2001 1·50 1·25
3119 55c. Cate Blanchett in *Elizabeth: The Golden Age*, 2007 1·50 1·25
3120 55c. Geoffrey Rush in *Shine*, 1996 1·50 1·25
Nos. 3113/3120 also come self-adhesive.

793 Red Roses

2009. Greetings Stamps. 'With Love'. Azure (3131, 3134, 3136) or multicoloured (others). (a) Ordinary gum.
3129 55c. Type **793** 95 70
3130 55c. Heart flowers 95 1·10
3131 55c. Fiigree heart 95 95

(b) Self-adhesive
3132 55c. Type **793** 95 95
3133 55c. As No. 3130 but with white border 95 95
3134 55c. As No. 3131 but with white border 95 95
3135 55c. As No. 3130 but with red foil applied to hearts and white border 95 95
3136 55c. As No. 3131 but with flocking applied to filigree heart and white border 95 95

794 Esky (coolbox) and Wine Cask

2009. Inventive Australia. Designs showing Australian inventions. Multicoloured. (a) Ordinary gum.
3137 55c. Type **794** 1·40 1·40
3138 55c. Girl swinging on Hills hoist (rotary clothes line) 1·40 1·40
3139 55c. Girl wearing Speedo swimsuit and boy and girl wearing zinc cream 1·40 1·40
3140 55c. Ute and B&D Roll-a-Door (garage door) 1·40 1·40
3141 55c. Victa rotary lawnmower 1·40 1·40
MS3142 170×84 mm. Nos. 3137/41 6·25 6·25

(b) Self-adhesive.
3143 55c. As Type **794** 95 1·40
3144 55c. As No. 3138 95 1·40
3145 55c. As No. 3139 95 1·40
3146 55c. As No. 3140 95 1·40
3147 55c. As No. 3141 95 1·40

2009. Greetings Stamps. 'For Every Occasion' (2nd series). As Nos. 3071/2, 3074, 3077 and 3079. Multicoloured. Self-adhesive.
3148 55c. Gold rings (3071) 95 95
3149 55c. Baby's feet (3072) 95 95
3150 55c. Balloons (3074) 95 95
3151 55c. Sparklers (3077) 95 95
3152 $1.10 Embroidery from wedding dress and pale pink roses (3079) 2·50 2·50
Nos. 3149/51 differ from Nos. 3072, 3074 and 3077 by having white borders.

795 Possum ('LIGHTS OUT')

2009. Earth Hour. Multicoloured. (a) Ordinary gum. (i) Domestic Mail
3153 55c. Type **795** 1·00 1·00
3154 55c. Owl ('SWITCH OFF') 1·00 1·00

(ii) International Post
3155 $2.05 Orang-utan ('SAVE ENERGY') 3·50 3·50

(b) Self-adhesive.
3156 55c. As Type **795** 90 90
3157 55c. As No. 3154 90 90

796 Isaac Nicholls, First Postmaster of New South Wales, boarding Ship to Collect Incoming Mail, 1809

2009. Bicentenary of Postal Services in Australia (1st issue). Multicoloured. Ordinary or self-adhesive gum.
3158 55c. Type **796** 1·50 1·25
3159 55c. Menzies Creek Post Office, Victoria, 1900s ('Early post office') 1·50 1·25
3160 55c. Early posting box 1·50 1·25
3161 55c. Australian soldiers reading letters, France, 1918 ('News from home') 1·50 1·25
3162 55c. First Quantas air mail service, Brisbane–Charleville, 1929 ('Early air mail') 1·50 1·25
3163 55c. Home delivery 1·50 1·25
3164 55c. Family reading letter ('Post-war immigration') 1·50 1·25
3165 55c. Retail PostShop 1·50 1·25
3166 55c. Express Post 1·50 1·25
3167 55c. Australia Post lorry ('Part of every day') 1·50 1·25

797 *Mamu* (Nura Rupert), 2002

2009. Indigenous Culture. Designs showing aboriginal paintings. Multicoloured. (a) Ordinary gum. (i) Domestic Mail
3178 55c. Type **797** 1·00 1·00
3179 55c. *All the Jila* (Jan Billycan), 2006 1·00 1·00
3180 55c. *Mina Mina* (Judy Napangardi Watson), 2004 1·00 1·00

(ii) International Post
3181 $1.40 Untitled (from the Mission series) (Elaine Russell), 2006 2·75 2·75
3182 $2.05 *Natjula* (Tjuruparu Watson), 2003 3·25 3·25

(b) Self-adhesive.
3183 $1.40 As No. 3181 2·25 2·50
3184 $2.05 As No. 3182 3·25 3·25

798 Queen Elizabeth II riding Side Saddle at Trooping the Colour

2009. Queen's Birthday. Multicoloured.
3185 55c. Type **798** 1·50 80
3186 $2.05 Queen Elizabeth and Prince Philip riding in carriage at Trooping the Colour 5·00 4·00
MS3187 106×70 mm. Nos. 3185/6 6·50 6·50

2009. 23rd Asian International Stamp Exhibition, Hong Kong. Sheet 130×90 mm containing Nos. 3053/6. Multicoloured.

MS3188	55c. Type **785**; 55c. South Bank, Brisbane; 55c. The Rocks, Sydney; 55c. Fisherman's Wharf, Fremantle	3·50	3·50

799 Anna Pavlova (ballerina) and Pavlova (meringue, whipped cream and fruit)

2009. 'Not Just Desserts'. Multicoloured.

3189	55c. Type **799**	1·75	1·75
3190	55c. Dame Nellie Melba (opera singer) and peach melba	1·75	1·75
3191	55c. Second Baron Lamington (Governor of Queensland, 1896–1901), Lady Lamington and lamingtons (sponge cake squares with chocolate and coconut)	1·75	1·75
3192	55c. ANZAC soldiers of 1915 and Anzac biscuits	1·75	1·75

Nos. 3189/3192 also come self-adhesive.

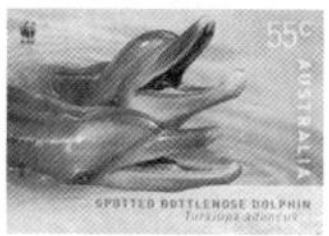

800 Indian Ocean ('Spotted') Bottlenose Dolphin

2009. Endangered Species. Dolphins of the Australian Coastline. Multicoloured. (a) Ordinary gum. (i) Domestic Mail.

3197	55c. Type **800**	1·50	90

(ii) International Post.

3198	$1.35 Hourglass dolphin	3·25	2·25
3199	$1.40 Southern right whale dolphin	3·25	2·25
3200	$2.05 Dusky dolphin	5·00	4·00
MS3201	136×70 mm. Nos. 3197/200	11·50	10·00

(b) Self-adhesive.

3202	$1.35 As No. 3198	2·25	2·25
3203	$1.40 As No. 3199	2·25	2·25
3204	$2.05 As No. 3200	3·75	3·75

801 Queensland Parliament House, Brisbane, Windmill and Outback Red Sands

2009. 150th Anniv of Queensland. Multicoloured.

3205	55c. Type **801**	1·00	90
3206	$2.75 Great Barrier Reef, red-eyed tree frog, rainforest and beach	4·50	5·00
MS3207	106×70 mm. Nos. 3205/6	5·25	5·25

802 1913 £2 Kangaroo and Map Stamp

2009. Bicentenary of Postal Services in Australia (2nd issue). Australia's Favourite Stamps. Multicoloured.

3208	55c. Type **802**	1·40	1·40
3209	55c. 1932 5s. Sydney Harbour Bridge stamp	1·40	1·40
3210	55c. 1946 Victory Commemoration 2½d. 'Peace' stamp	1·40	1·40
3211	55c. 1950 8½d. Aborigine stamp	1·40	1·40
3212	55c. 1914 6d. Kookaburra stamp	1·40	1·40

Nos. 3208/3212 also come self-adhesive.

803 Koala (*Phascolarctos cinereus*)

2009. International Post. Australian Bush Babies. Multicoloured.

3218	$1.45 Type **803**	3·00	1·75
3219	$2.10 Eastern grey kangaroo (*Macropus giganteus*)	5·00	3·00
3220	$2.90 Brushtail possum (*Trichosurus vulpecula*) (horiz)	7·00	5·50
3221	$4.20 Common wombat (*Vombatus ursinus*)	9·50	7·50

Nos. 3218/3219 also come self-adhesive.

804 Fitzroy Gardens, Melbourne

2009. Australian Parks and Gardens. Multicoloured.

3224	55c. Type **804**	1·40	1·40
3225	55c. Roma Street Parkland, Brisbane	1·40	1·40
3226	55c. St. David's Park, Hobart	1·40	1·40
3227	55c. Commonwealth Park, Canberra	1·40	1·40
3228	55c. Hyde Park, Sydney	1·40	1·40

Nos. 3224/3228 also come self-adhesive.

2009. Melbourne Stampshow 2009 National Stamp Exhibition. Sheet 140×95 mm. Sheet containing Nos. 3192, 3208, 3212 and 3224.

MS3234	55c.×4 ANZAC soldiers of 1915 and Anzac biscuits; Type **802**; 1914 6d. Kookaburra stamp; Type **804**	3·50	3·50

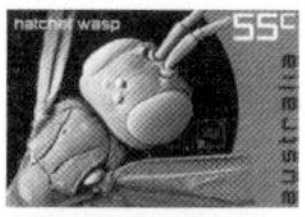

805 Hatchet Wasp

2009. Micro Monsters. Multicoloured.

3235	55c. Type **805**	1·10	1·10
3236	55c. Praying mantis	1·10	1·10
3237	55c. Ground beetle	1·10	1·10
3238	55c. Jumping spider	1·10	1·10
3239	55c. Ant	1·10	1·10
3240	$1.10 Weevil	2·10	2·10
MS3241	160×85 mm. As Nos. 3235/40	6·75	6·75

Nos. 3235/3239 also come self-adhesive.

806 Bridled Nailtail Wallaby (Australia)

2009. Species at Risk. Multicoloured.

3247	55c. Type **806**	1·75	1·75
3248	55c. Norfolk Island green parrot (Norfolk Island)	1·75	1·75
3249	55c. Subantarctic fur seal (Australian Antarctic Territory)	1·75	1·75
3250	55c. Christmas Island blue-tailed skink) (Christmas Island)	1·75	1·75
3251	55c. Green turtle (Cocos (Keeling) Islands)	1·75	1·75
MS3252	150×85 mm. As Nos. 3247/51	8·00	8·00

Nos. 3247/3251 also come self-adhesive.

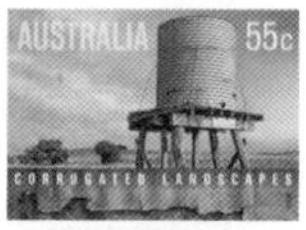

807 Water Tank, Fleurieu Peninsula, South Australia

2009. Corrugated Landscapes. Multicoloured.

3258	55c. Type **807**	1·10	1·10
3259	55c. Traditional home, Broken Hill, New South Wales	1·10	1·10
3260	55c. Nissen hut converted into shearing shed, Bushy Park Cattle Station, Queensland	1·10	1·10
3261	55c. Magney House, Bingie Bingie Point, New South Wales	1·10	1·10

Nos. 3258/3261 also come self-adhesive.

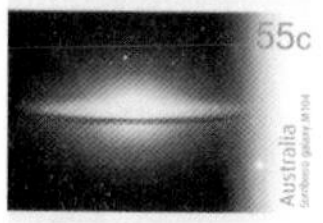

808 Sombrero Galaxy M104

2009. International Year of Astronomy. Stargazing: The Southern Skies. Multicoloured. (i) Domestic Mail.

3266	55c. Type **808**	1·25	1·00

(ii) International Post.

3267	$1.45 Reflection nebula M78	2·75	2·75
3268	$2.10 Spiral galaxy M83	3·75	4·00
MS3269	141×75 mm. Nos. 3266/8	7·00	7·00

809 Green Catbird (*Ailuroedus crassirostris*)

2009. Australian Songbirds. Multicoloured.

3270	55c. Type **809**	1·40	60
3271	$1.10 Noisy scrub-bird (*Atrichornis clamosus*)	2·50	1·90
3272	$1.65 Mangrove golden whistler (*Pachycephala melanura*) (male)	3·50	3·50
3273	$2.75 Pair of scarlet honeyeaters (*Myzomela sanguinolenta*)	5·50	7·00

No. 3270 also comes self-adhesive.

810 Cyclops Pedal Car

2009. Classic Toys. Multicoloured.

3275	55c. Type **810**	1·50	1·50
3276	55c. Test Match board game	1·50	1·50
3277	55c. Barbie doll	1·50	1·50
3278	55c. Malvern Star Dragstar bicycle	1·50	1·50
3279	55c. Cabbage Patch Kids doll	1·50	1·50

Nos. 3275/3279 also come self-adhesive.

811 Australian Rules Football

2009. Stamp Collecting Month. 'Let's Get active!'. Multicoloured.

3285	55c. Type **811**	1·10	1·10
3286	55c. Basketball	1·10	1·10
3287	55c. Soccer	1·10	1·10
3288	55c. Netball	1·10	1·10
3289	55c. Cricket	1·10	1·10
3290	55c. Tennis	1·10	1·10
MS3291	160×89 mm. Nos. 3285/90	6·00	6·00

Nos. 3285/3290 come self-adhesive.

812 Patrica Crabb

2009. Bicentenary of Postal Services in Australia (3rd issue). 'Our People Your Post'. Multicoloured.

3298	55c. Type **812**	1·25	1·25
3299	55c. Shirley Freeman (behind counter, wearing red blouse)	1·25	1·25
3300	55c. Vinko Romank (carrying box of Express Post)	1·25	1·25
3301	55c. Valda Knott (in front of shelving)	1·25	1·25
3302	55c. Gordon Morgan (in front of Australia Post motorcycles)	1·25	1·25
3303	55c. Vongpradith Phongsavan (wearing striped shirt and fluorescent tabard)	1·25	1·25
3304	55c. Norma Thomas and Australia Post contractor's van	1·25	1·25
3305	55c. John Marsh (wearing pale blue shirt)	1·25	1·25
3306	55c. Anne Brun (behind counter)	1·25	1·25
3307	55c. Russell Price (wearing blue jacket with Australia Post emblem)	1·25	1·25

813 Virgin Mary and Infant Jesus

2009. Christmas (1st issue). Multicoloured. (a) Ordinary gum. (i) Domestic mail.

3308	50c. Type **813**	95	50

(ii) International Post.

3309	$1.25 The Magi	2·40	2·75
MS3310	106×70 mm. Nos. 3308/9	3·25	3·25

(b) Self-adhesive. (i) Domestic mail.

3311	50c. As Type **813**	1·00	1·00

(ii) International Post.

3312	$1.25 As No. 3309	2·25	2·25

814 Candles enclosed in Star

2009. Christmas (2nd issue). Multicoloured. (a) Ordinary gum.

3313	50c. Type **814**	95	95
3314	50c. Decorated Christmas tree	95	95
3315	50c. Wrapped gifts enclosed in Santa hat	95	95
3316	50c. Baubles enclosed in bell	95	95
3317	50c. Candy canes enclosed in stocking	95	95

(b) Self-adhesive.

3318	50c. As Type **814**	95	95
3319	50c. As No. 3314	95	95
3320	50c. As No. 3315	95	95
3321	50c. As No. 3316	95	95
3322	50c. As No. 3317	95	95

(c) Self-adhesive.

3323	50c. As Type **814** but gold foil star outline	1·00	1·00
3324	50c. As No. 3314 but gold foil Christmas tree outline	1·00	1·00
3325	50c. As No. 3315 but gold foil Santa hat outline	1·00	1·00
3326	50c. As No. 3316 but gold foil bell outline	1·00	1·00
3327	50c. As No. 3317 but gold foil stocking outline	1·00	1·00

815 Peter Carey

2010. Australian Legends (14th series). 'Legends of the Written Word'. Multicoloured. (a) Ordinary gum.

3328	55c. Type **815**	1·10	1·10
3329	55c. Peter Carey (black/white photo)	1·10	1·10
3330	55c. David Malouf (black/white photo)	1·10	1·10
3331	55c. David Malouf	1·10	1·10
3332	55c. Colleen McCullough	1·10	1·10
3333	55c. Colleen McCullough (black/white photo)	1·10	1·10
3334	55c. Bryce Courtenay (black/white photo)	1·10	1·10
3335	55c. Bryce Courtenay	1·10	1·10
3336	55c. Thomas Keneally	1·10	1·10
3337	55c. Thomas Keneally (black/white photo)	1·10	1·10
3338	55c. Tim Winton (black/white photo)	1·10	1·10
3339	55c. Tim Winton	1·10	1·10

(b) Self-adhesive.

3340	55c. As Type **815**	1·00	1·10
3341	55c. As No. 3331	1·00	1·10
3342	55c. As No. 3332	1·00	1·10
3343	55c. As No. 3335	1·00	1·10
3344	55c. As No. 3336	1·00	1·10
3345	55c. As No. 3339	1·00	1·10

816 Governor Macquarie and North View of Sydney

2010. Bicentenary of Arrival of Governor Lachlan Macquarie in New South Wales. Multicoloured.

3346	55c. Type **816**	1·40	1·40
3347	55c. Port Jackson and Sydney Town	1·40	1·40
3348	55c. Parramatta Female Penitentiary, 1818	1·40	1·40
3349	55c. Government Stables, Sydney, 1817	1·40	1·40

817 Coat of Arms on Reverse of Florin

2010. Centenary of First Australian Commonwealth Coins. Multicoloured.

3350	55c. Type **817**	1·10	60
3351	$2.75 King Edward VII on Obverse of Florin	5·50	6·00
MS3352	106×70 mm. As Nos. 3350/1	6·50	6·50

818 Torah Bright (snowboard – halfpipe)

2010. Australian Gold Medallists at Olympic Winter Games, Vancouver. Multicoloured.

3353	55c. Type **818**	1·10	90
3354	55c. Lydia Lassila (freestyle skiing - aerials)	1·10	90

819 Colin Defries flying modified Wright Model A *The Stella*, Victoria Park Racecourse, Sydney, 9 December 1909

2010. Centenary of Powered Flight. Multicoloured. (a) Ordinary gum. (i) Domestic Mail.

3355	55c. Type **819** (first powered flight in Australia)	1·10	60

(ii) International Post.

3356	$1.45 John Duigan's flight, Mia Mia, Victoria, 7 October 1910 (first flight by Australian in Australian plane)	2·75	2·75
3357	$2.10 Harry Houdini flying Voisin aircraft, Diggers Rest, Victoria, 18 March 1910	3·75	4·25

(b) Self-adhesive.

3358	$1.45 As No. 3356	2·75	2·75
3359	$2.10 As No. 3357	3·75	4·25

2010. Canberra Stampshow 2010. Sheet 140×95 mm containing Nos. 3346, 3351, and 3355/6.

MS3360	55c. Type **816**; 55c. Type **819**; $1.45 John Duigan's flight, Mia Mia, Victoria, 7 October 1910 (first flight by Australian in Australian plane); $2.75 King Edward VII on obverse of florin coin	9·00	9·00

820 Prize Bull

2010. 'Come to the Show'. Multicoloured.

3361	55c. Type **820**	1·50	1·50
3362	55c. Cake decorating	1·50	1·50
3363	55c. Winning show horse	1·50	1·50
3364	55c. Wood chopping	1·50	1·50
3365	55c. Prizewinning dog	1·50	1·50
MS3366	170×85 mm. Nos. 3361/5	6·75	6·75

Nos. 3361/3365 also come self-adhesive.

821 Queen Elizabeth II leaving St. Andrew's Cathedral, Sydney, 2006

2010. Queen's Birthday. Ordinary or self-adhesive gum.

3372	**821**	55c. multicoloured	1·50	60

822 Australian Soldiers on Kokoda Trail, 1942

2010. Kokoda. Multicoloured. (a) Ordinary gum. (i) Domestic mail.

3374	55c. Type **822**	1·10	1·10
3375	55c. Papua New Guineans helping wounded soldiers along trail, 1942	1·10	1·10
3376	55c. Kokoda veterans	1·10	1·10
3377	55c. Trekker, guide and memorial	1·10	1·10

(ii) International Post.

3378	$1.45 Veterans at Kokoda Isurava Memorial	2·75	2·75
MS3379	160×90 mm. Nos. 3374/8	6·25	6·25

(b) Self-adhesive.

3380	55c. As Type **822**	1·25	1·40
3381	55c. As No. 3375	1·25	1·40
3382	55c. As No. 3376	1·25	1·40
3383	55c. As No. 3377	1·25	1·40

Stamps in similar designs were issued by Papua New Guinea.

823 The Ghan'

2010. Great Australian Railway Journeys. Multicoloured.

(a) Ordinary paper. (i) Domestic Mail.

3384	55c. Type **823**	1·10	1·10
3385	55c. West Coast Wilderness Railway, Tasmania	1·10	1·10
3386	55c. 'The Indian Pacific'	1·10	1·10

(ii) International Post. Size 50×30 mm.

3387	$2.10 Kuranda Scenic Railway, Queensland	3·75	3·75
MS3388	140×90 mm. No. 3387	7·00	7·00

(b) Self-adhesive. Phosphor over parts of design. (i) Domestic Mail.

3389	55c. As Type **823**	1·10	1·10
3390	55c. As No. 3385	1·10	1·10
3391	55c. As No. 3386	1·10	1·10

(ii) International Post. Size 50×30 mm.

3392	$2.10 As No. 3387	3·75	75

824 Queen Victoria

2010. Colonial Heritage: Empire (1st issue)

3393	**824**	$5 multicoloured	9·50	9·50
MS3394		140×90 mm. No. 3393	9·50	9·50

2010. London 2010 Festival of Stamps. Multicoloured.

MS3395	140×90 mm. Type **819**×2; No. 3356×2	4·00	4·00
MS3396	140×90 mm. Type **821**; Type **774**; Type **798**; Type **729**	9·50	9·50
MS3397	140×90 mm. No. 3387	7·50	7·50
MS3398	140×90 mm. No. 3393	4·00	4·00

825 Peng Peng (Australian kookaburra mascot)

2010. Expo 2010, Shanghai, China. Multicoloured.

3399	55c. Type **825**	1·10	1·10
3400	55c. Australian pavilion	1·10	1·00

826 Purnululu National Park, Western Australia

2010. Australian UNESCO World Heritage Sites. Multicoloured.

(a) Ordinary gum.

3401	55c. Type **826**	1·10	1·10
3402	55c. Kakadu National Park, Northern Territory	1·10	1·10
3403	$1.10 Mount Warning, Gondwana Rainforests	2·25	2·25
3404	$1.10 Tasmanian Wilderness	2·25	2·25

(b) Self-adhesive. Partial phosphor frame (at left and foot).

3405	55c. As No. 3402	1·10	1·10
3406	55c. As Type **826**	1·10	1·10

827 Coral Rabbitfish

2010. Fish of the Reef. Multicoloured.

(a) Ordinary gum

3407	5c. Type **827**	15	15
3408	60c. Clown triggerfish	1·10	1·10
3409	60c. Spotted sweetlips	1·10	1·10
3410	60c. Golden damselfish	1·10	1·10
3411	50c. Regal angelfish	1·10	1·10
3413	$1.80 Chevron butterflyfish	2·75	2·75
3414	$3 Orangefin anemonefish (50×30 mm)	5·50	5·50

(b) Self-adhesive

3415	5c. As Type **827**	15	15
3416	60c. As No. 3408	1·10	1·10
3417	60c. As No. 3409	1·10	1·10
3418	60c. As No. 3410	1·10	1·10
3419	60c. As No. 3411	1·10	1·10

Nos. 3420/5 are left vacant for possible additions to this series of definitive stamps.

828 Bay of Fires, Tasmania

2010. International Stamps. Australian Beaches. Multicoloured.

(a) Ordinary gum

3426	$1.50 Type **828**	3·25	3·25
3427	$2.20 Cape Tribulation, Queensland	4·25	4·25
3428	$4.30 Hellfire Bay, Western Australia (50×30 mm)	7·50	7·50

(b) Self-adhesive

3429	$1.50 As Type **828**	3·25	3·25
3430	$2.20 As No. 3427	4·25	4·25

829 'Piper'

2010. Adopted and Adored. Dogs. Multicoloured.

(a) Ordinary paper

3431	60c. Type **829**	1·20	1·20
3432	60c. Jessie	1·20	1·20
3433	60c. Buckley	1·20	1·20
3434	60c. Daisy	1·20	1·20
3435	60c. Tigger	1·20	1·20

(b) Self-adhesive

3436	60c. As Type **829**	1·20	1·20
3437	60c. As No. 3432	1·20	1·20
3438	60c. As No. 3433	1·20	1·20
3439	60c. As No. 3434	1·20	1·20
3440	60c. As No. 3435	1·20	1·20

830 'STAY FOCUSED STAY RELEVANT STAY ON LINE'

2010. Emergency Services. Multicoloured.

(a) Ordinary gum

3441	60c. Type **830**	1·20	1·20
3442	60c. Police helicopter	1·20	1·20
3443	60c. Fire emblem	1·20	1·20
3444	60c. Ambulance service emblem	1·20	1·20

(b) Self-adhesive

3445	60c. As Type **830**	1·20	1·20
3446	60c. As No. 3442	1·20	1·20
3447	60c. As No. 3443	1·20	1·20
3448	60c. As No. 3444	1·20	1·20

831 Gold and White Design

2010. Greetings Stamps. 'For Special Occasions'. Multicoloured.

(a) Ordinary gum

3449	60c. Type **831**	1·10	1·10
3450	60c. Pink tulips	1·10	1·10
3451	60c. Cream roses	1·10	1·10
3452	60c. Glasses of champagne	1·10	1·10
3453	60c. Three balloons	1·10	1·10
3454	60c. Teddy bear holding daisy	1·10	1·10
3455	60c. Wattle flowers	1·10	1·10
3456	60c. Southern Cross (deep blue background) (30×30 mm)	1·10	1·10
3457	60c. Southern Cross (orange and pink background) (30×30 mm)	1·10	1·10
3458	$1.20 Wedding and engagement rings	2·50	2·50

(b) Self-adhesive

3459	60c. As No. 3450	1·10	1·10
3460	60c. As No. 3451	1·10	1·10
3461	60c. As No. 3453	1·10	1·10
3462	60c. As No. 3454	1·10	1·10
3463	60c. As No. 3455	1·10	1·10
3464	$1.20 As No. 3458	2·50	2·50

832 Construction Worker, Doctor and Teacher

2010. Centenary of Australian Taxation Office

3465	**832**	60c. multicoloured	1·10	1·10

833

2010. 150th Anniv of Departure of Burke and Wills Expedition. Multicoloured.

(a) Ordinary gum

3466	60c. Type **833**	1·20	1·20
3467	60c. Expedition leaving Melbourne, August 1860	1·20	1·20
3468	$1.20 Return of Burke, Wills and John King from Gulf of Carpentaria to Cooper's Creek, April 1861	2·50	2·50
3469	$1.20 Burke, Wills and King on journey to Mount Hopeless	2·50	2·50

(b) Self-adhesive

3470	60c. As No. 3467	1·20	1·20
3471	60c. As Type **833**	1·20	1·20

2010. Bangkok 2010 25th Asian International Stamp Exhibition. Multicoloured.

MS3472	5c. Coral Rabbitfish×2; 60c. Oriental sweetlips; 60c. Clown triggerfish	2·40	2·40

2010. Stampex '10 National Stamp Exhibition, Adelaide. Multicoloured.

MS3473	60c. Type **833**; $2.05 Jade iceberg	5·25	5·25

834 Guide

2010. Centenary of Girl Guides Australia. Multicoloured.

(a) Ordinary gum. (i) Domestic Mail

3474	60c. Type **834**	1·50	1·50

(ii) International Mail

3475	$1.50 Two guides making guide sign	2·75	2·75
3476	$2.20 Olave Baden-Powell (founder)	4·50	4·50

(b) Self-adhesive. (i) Domestic Mail

3477	60c. As Type **834**	1·50	1·50

(ii) International Post

3478	$1.50 As No. 3475	2·75	4·50
3479	$2.20 As No. 3476	4·50	4·50

835

2010. National Service Memorial, Canberra

(a) Ordinary gum

3480	**835**	60c. multicoloured	1·30	1·30

(b) Self-adhesive. Irregular partial phosphor frame.

3481	**835**	60c. multicoloured	1·30	1·30

836 Children on Beach, 1950s

2010. 'Long Weekend'. Multicoloured.

(a) Ordinary gum

3482	60c. Type **836**	1·30	1·30
3483	60c. Family camping, 1960s	1·30	1·30
3484	60c. Surfers on beach, 1970s	1·30	1·30
3485	60c. Family on shore and houseboat on Lake Eildon, Victoria, 1980s	1·30	1·30
3486	60c. Children playing in snow, 1990s	1·30	1·30

(b) Self-adhesive. Phosphor over parts of design

3487	60c. As Type **836**	1·30	1·30
3488	60c. As No. 3483	1·30	1·30
3489	60c. As No. 3484	1·30	1·30
3490	60c. As No. 3485	1·30	1·30
3491	60c. As No. 3486	1·30	1·30

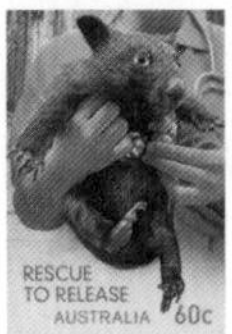

837 Common Wombat

2010. Wildlife Caring: Rescue to Release. Multicoloured.

(a) Ordinary gum

3492	60c. Type **837**	1·20	1·20
3493	60c. Eastern grey kangaroo	1·20	1·20
3494	60c. Koala	1·20	1·20
3495	60c. Grey-headed flying fox	1·20	1·20
3496	60c. Southern boobook owl	1·20	1·20
3497	$1.20 Ringtail possum	3·00	3·00
MS3498	170×85 mm. Nos. 3492/7	8·50	8·50

(b) Self-adhesive

3499	60c. As Type **837**	1·20	1·20
3500	60c. As No. 3493	1·20	1·20
3501	60c. As No. 3494	1·20	1·20
3502	60c. As No. 3495	1·20	1·20
3503	60c. As No. 3496	1·20	1·20

838 Mary MacKillop

2010. Canonisation of Mary MacKillop (Mother Mary of the Cross, founder of Sisters of St. Joseph of the Sacred Heart)

3504	**838**	60c. multicoloured	1·20	1·20

839 Red-backed Kingfisher (Todiramphus pyrrhopygius)

2010. Australian Kingfishers. Multicoloured.

(a) Ordinary gum

3505	60c. Type **839**	1·50	1·50
3506	$1.20 Sacred kingfisher (*Todiramphus sanctus*)	1·70	1·70
3507	$1.80 Blue-winged kookaburra (*Dacelo leachii*)	3·00	3·00
3508	$3 Yellow-billed kingfisher (*Syma torotoro*)	5·75	5·75

(b) Self-adhesive

3509	60c. As Type **839**	1·20	1·20

840 Melbourne Cup, 2010

2010. 150th Anniv of Melbourne Cup Horse Race. Multicoloured.

(a) Ordinary gum

3510	60c. Type **840**	1·20	1·20
3511	60c. Carbine, 1890 (horiz)	1·20	1·20
3512	60c. Phar Lap, 1930 (horiz)	1·20	1·20
3513	60c. Saintly, 1996 (horiz)	1·20	1·20
MS3514	160×85 mm. Nos. 3510/13	5·00	5·00

(b) Self-adhesive

3515	60c. As No. 3511	1·20	1·20
3516	60c. As No. 3512	1·20	1·20
3517	60c. As No. 3513	1·20	1·20

841 Young Girl writing Letter

2010. Christmas (1st issue). Dear Santa. Multicoloured.

(a) Ordinary gum

3518	55c. Type **841**	1·20	1·20
3519	55c. Santa reading letter	1·20	1·20

(b) Self-adhesive

3520	55c. As No. 3519	1·20	1·20
3521	55c. As Type **841**	1·20	1·20
3522	55c. As Type **841** but foil 'AUSTRALIA' and varnish on letter and stocking	1·20	1·20
3523	55c. As No. 3519 but foil 'AUSTRALIA' and varnish on Santa's beard, cuffs and boots	1·20	1·20

842 Madonna and Child

2010. Christmas (2nd issue). Multicoloured.

(a) Ordinary gum

(i) Domestic mail

3524	55c. Type **842**	1·20	1·20

(ii) International Post

3525	$1.30 Angel and shepherds	2·50	2·50

(b) Self-adhesive

(i) Domestic mail

3526	55c. As Type **842**	1·20	1·20

(ii) International Post

3527	$1.30 As No. 3525	2·50	2·50

843 'LOVE' and Red Roses

2011. Greetings Stamps. Special Occasions. 'LOVE'. Multicoloured.

(a) Ordinary gum

3528	60c. Type **843**	1·20	1·20
3529	60c. Pattern of hearts, flowers and vine leaves	1·20	1·20

(b) Self-adhesive

3530	60c. As Type **843**	1·20	1·20
3531	60c. As No. 3529	1·20	1·20
3532	60c. As No. 3452	1·20	1·20

844 Eva Cox (feminist)

2011. Australian Legends (15th series). Multicoloured.

(a) Ordinary gum

3533	60c. Type **844**	1·20	1·20
3534	60c. Germaine Greer (feminist author)	1·20	1·20
3535	60c. Elizabeth Evatt (former chief judge)	1·20	1·20
3536	60c. Anne Summers (writer and co-founder of first women's refuge)	1·20	1·20

(b) Self-adhesive

3537	60c. As Type **844**	1·20	1·20
3538	60c. As No. 3534	1·20	1·20
3539	60c. As No. 3535	1·20	1·20
3540	60c. As No. 3536	1·20	1·20

Nos. 3541/50, T **845** are left for Premier's Flood Relief Appeal sheetlet, issued 27 January 2011, not yet received.

845 Rescuer carrying Baby

2011. Premier's Flood Relief Appeal. Multicoloured.

3541	60c. Type **845**	1·30	1·30
3542	60c. House surrounded by floodwater	1·30	1·30
3543	60c. Rescuing cat from flooded house	1·30	1·30
3544	60c. Wallaby on debris in floodwater	1·30	1·30
3545	60c. Aerial view of flooded houses and street	1·30	1·30

Each sheetlet was sold at $8, a $2 premium over face value. This premium went to the Premier's Flood Relief Appeal.

Nos. 3546/50 are vacant.

846 Women's Eyes

2011. Centenary of International Women's Day

3551	**846**	60c. multicoloured	1·30	1·30

847 F-111 ('Pig')

2011. Royal Australian Air Force (RAAF) Aviation. Multicoloured.

(a) Ordinary gum

3552	60c. Type **847**	1·30	1·30
3553	60c. F/A -18F	1·30	1·30
3554	$1.20 Wedgetail	3·25	3·25
3555	$3 C-17 Globemaster III	5·75	5·75
MS3556	135×72 mm. Nos. 3552/5	11·50	11·50

(b) Self-adhesive

3557	60c. As Type **847**	1·30	1·30
3558	60c. As No. 3553	1·30	1·30

Nos. 3552/3 were printed together, *se-tenant*, as horizontal pairs, each pair forming a composite background design. The stamps and margins of **MS**3556 form a composite design.

848 Gerbera

2011. Floral Festivals Australia. Multicoloured.

(a) Ordinary paper

3559	60c. Type **848** (Melbourne International Flower and Garden Show)	1·30	1·30
3560	60c. Jacaranda (Jacaranda Festival, Grafton)	1·30	1·30
3561	60c. Australian everlasting (Kings Park Festival, Perth)	1·30	1·30
3562	60c. Violet (Toowoomba Carnival of Flowers)	1·30	1·30
3563	60c. Tulip (Floriade, Canberra)	1·30	1·30

(b) Self-adhesive

3564	60c. As Type **848**	1·30	1·30
3565	60c. As No. 3560	1·30	1·30
3566	60c. As No. 3561	1·30	1·30
3567	60c. As No. 3562	1·30	1·30
3568	60c. As No. 3563	1·30	1·30

849 *A Bunch of Flowers* (Nora Heysen), 1930

2011. The Gallery Series. National Gallery of Victoria: Flowers (1st series). Multicoloured.

(a) Ordinary gum

3569	60c. Type **849**	1·30	1·30
3570	60c. *Camellias* (Arnold Shore), 1937	1·30	1·30

3571	60c. *Fruit and Flowers* (Vida Lahey), c. 1924	1·30	1·30
3572	60c. *Still Life, Zinnias* (Roy de Maistre), 1925–30	1·30	1·30
3573	60c. *A Cottage Bunch* (Hans Heysen), 1930	1·30	1·30

(b) Self-adhesive

3574	60c. As Type **849**	1·30	1·30
3575	60c. As No. 3570	1·30	1·30
3576	60c. As No. 3571	1·30	1·30
3577	60c. As No. 3572	1·30	1·30
3578	60c. As No. 3573	1·30	1·30

2011. Sydney Stamp Expo 2011. Multicoloured.

MS3578a	60c. Type **847**; 60c. Type **833**; $1.20 Return of Burke, Wills and John King from Gulf of Carpentaria to Cooper's Creek, April 1861; $1.20 Wedgetail	7·75	7·75

850 Salt Pan ('The Dry')

2011. Lake Eyre. Multicoloured.

(a) Ordinary gum. (i) Domestic mail

3579	60c. Type **850**	1·30	1·30

(ii) Internatonal Post

3580	$1.55 Green land with pools of water ('New Growth')	3·00	3·00
3581	$2.25 Australian pelican flying over breeding colony on island ('Bird Life')	3·75	3·75
3582	$3.10 Lake Eyre ('In Flood')	6·75	6·75

(b) Self-adhesive

3583	$1.55 As No. 3580	2·10	2·10
3584	$2.25 As No. 3581	3·00	3·00

851 Queen Elizabeth II, 1984 (Brian Dunlop)

2011. 85th Birthday of Queen Elizabeth II. Multicoloured.

(i) Domestic Mail

3585	60c. Type **851**	1·30	1·30

(ii) International Post

3586	$2.25 Queen Elizabeth II, 2005 (Rolf Harris)	4·75	4·75
MS3587	106×70 mm. Nos. 3585/6	6·25	6·25

852 Prince William and Miss Catherine Middleton

2011. Royal Wedding (1st issue). Multicoloured.

(a) Ordinary gum. (i) Domestic mail

3588	60c. Type **852**	1·30	1·30

(ii) International Post

3589	$2.25 As Type **852** but white background	5·00	5·00
MS3590	106×70 mm. Nos. 3588/9	6·25	6·25

(b) Self-adhesive

3591	60c. As Type **852**	1·30	1·30

853 Wedding of Prince William and Miss Catherine Middleton

2011. Royal Wedding (2nd issue)

(a) Ordinary gum

3592	**853** 60c. multicoloured	1·50	1·50

(b) Self-adhesive

3593	**853** 60c. multicoloured	1·50	1·50

854 *Madame Melba* (Rupert Bunny)

2011. 150th Birth Anniv of Dame Nellie Melba (soprano)

(a) Ordinary paper

3594	**854** 60c. multicoloured	1·50	1·50

(b) Self-adhesive

3595	**854** 60c. multicoloured	1·50	1·50

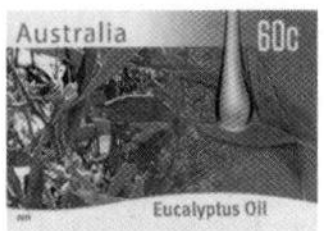

855 Eucalyptus Oil and Blue Mallee

2011. Farming Australia: Native Plants. Multicoloured.

(a) Ordinary gum

3596	60c. Type **855**	1·50	1·50
3597	60c. Eucalyptus flowers and honeycomb ('Australian Honey')	1·50	1·50
3598	60c. Macadamia nuts	1·50	1·50
3599	60c. Tea tree and tea tree oil	1·50	1·50

(b) Self-adhesive

3600	60c. As Type **855**	1·50	1·50
3601	60c. As No. 3597	1·50	1·50
3602	60c. As No. 3598	1·50	1·50
3603	60c. As No. 3599	1·50	1·50

856 HMAS *Australia* (I) (1913-22)

2011. Centenary of Royal Australian Navy. Multicoloured.

(a) Ordinary paper

3604	60c. Type **856**	1·50	1·50
3605	60c. HMAS *Sydney* (IV)	1·50	1·50

(b) Self-adhesive

3606	60c. As Type **856**	1·50	1·50
3607	60c. As No. 3605	1·50	1·50

857 Bilby

2011. Australian Bush Babies. Multicoloured.

(a) Ordinary paper. (i) Domestic mail

3608	60c. Type **857**	1·40	1·50

(ii) International Post

3609	$1.60 Dingo pup	3·75	4·00
3610	$1.65 Red kangaroo joey	3·75	4·00
3611	$2.35 Koala	5·50	5·75
3612	$4.70 Sugar glider	11·00	11·25

(b) Self-adhesive

3613	$1.65 As No. 3610	2·75	3·00
3614	$2.35 As No. 3611	5·25	5·50

858 Man and Dog ('Best Friends')

2011. 'Living Australian'. Winning Entries from Photography Competition. Multicoloured.

(a) Ordinary paper

3615	60c. Type **858**	1·75	1·75
3616	60c. Two girls ('Embrace Friendship')	1·75	1·75
3617	60c. Spectators reflected in sunglasses ('Cricket at the GABBA')	1·75	1·75
3618	60c. Aborigine boy performing Wedge Tail Eagle Dance ('Little Man's Business')	1·75	1·75
3619	60c. Red kangaroo lying on beach ('This is So Relaxing')	1·75	1·75

(b) Self-adhesive

3620	60c. As Type **858**	1·75	1·75
3621	60c. As No. 3616	1·75	1·75
3622	60c. As No. 3617	1·75	1·75
3623	60c. As No. 3618	1·75	1·75
3624	60c. As No. 3619	1·75	1·75

859 Hand enclosing Candle wrapped in Barbed Wire

2011. 50th Anniv of Amnesty International

3625	**859** 60c. black and greenish yellow	1·50	1·50

860 Child learning to Ski

2011. Skiing Australia. Multicoloured.

(a) Ordinary paper. (i) Domestic mail

3626	60c. Type **860**	1·50	1·50

(ii) International Post

3627	$1.60 Snowboarder (horiz)	3·50	3·50
3628	$1.65 Skiier (horiz)	3·75	3·75

(b) Self-adhesive. (i) Domestic mail

3629	60c. As Type **860**	1·50	1·50

(ii) International Post

3630	$1.60 As No. 3627	3·50	3·50
3631	$1.65 As No. 3628	3·75	3·75

2011. Colonial Heritage: Emerging Identity (2nd issue). Multicoloured.

3632	$2 Kangaroo	3·75	3·75
3633	$2 Black swan	3·75	3·75
MS3634	141×90 mm. Nos. 3632/3	7·50	7·50

2011. Phila Nippon '11 World Stamp Exhibition, Yokohama, Japan. Sheet 130×90 mm containing Nos. 3609/10. Multicoloured.

MS3635	$1.60 Dingo pup; $1.65 Red kangaroo joey	7·50	7·50

861 Quokka (*Setonix brachyurus*)

2011. 50th Anniv of Worldwide Fund for Nature (formerly World Wildlife Fund). Multicoloured.

3636	60c. Type **861**	1·60	1·75
3637	60c. Southern elephant seal (*Mirounga leonina*) (Australian Antarctic Territory)	1·60	1·75
3638	60c. Dugong (*Dugong dugon*) (Cocos (Keeling) Islands)	1·60	1·75
3639	60c. Christmas Island shrew (*Crocidura trichura*) (Christmas Island)	1·60	1·75
MS3640	135×72 mm. Nos. 3636/9	4·25	4·25

Nos. 3637/9 were all inscr 'AUSTRALIA' and also 'AUSTRALIAN ANTARCTIC TERRITORY' (3637), 'COCOS (KEELING) ISLANDS' (3638) or 'CHRISTMAS ISLAND' (3639).

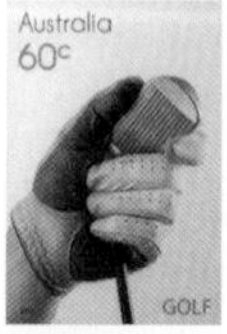

862 Hand holding Golf Club

2011. Golf. Multicoloured.

(a) Ordinary paper. (i) Domestic mail

3641	60c. Type **862**	1·40	1·50
3642	60c. The President's Cup	1·40	1·50
3643	60c. Golf shoes	1·40	1·50

(ii) International Post

3644	$1.65 Golf club and ball	3·00	3·25
3645	$2.35 Golf clubs	5·75	6·00
MS3646	170×85 mm. Nos. 3641/5	12·75	12·75

(b) Self-adhesive. (i) Domestic mail

3647	60c. As Type **862**	1·40	1·50
3648	60c. As No. 3642	1·40	1·50
3649	60c. As No. 3643	1·40	1·50

(ii) International Post

3650	$1.65 As No. 3644	3·00	3·25
3651	$2.35 As No. 3645	5·75	6·00

863 Fairy

2011. Stamp Collecting Month. Mythical Creatures. Multicoloured.

(a) Ordinary paper

3652	60c. Type **863**	1·50	1·60
3653	60c. Troll	1·50	1·60
3654	60c. Mermaid	1·50	1·60
3655	60c. Griffin	1·50	1·60
3656	60c. Unicorn	1·50	1·60
3657	$1.20 Dragon	3·00	3·25
MS3658	170×85 mm. Nos. 3652/7	9·25	9·25

(b) Self-adhesive

3659	60c. As Type **863**	1·25	1·40
3660	60c. As No. 3653	1·25	1·40
3661	60c. As No. 3654	1·25	1·40
3662	60c. As No. 3655	1·25	1·40
3663	60c. As No. 3656	1·25	1·40

864 Perth Skyline and Southern Cross

2011. Commonwealth Heads of Government Meeting, Perth

3664	**864** 60c. multicoloured	1·25	1·25

865 Haegeum Musician

2011. Australia - Korea Friendship. Multicoloured.

(a) Ordinary gum

(i) Domestic Mail

3665	60c. Type **865**	1·25	1·40

(ii) International Post

3666	$1.65 Didgeridoo musician	3·00	3·25

(b) Self-adhesive

3667	$1.65 As No. 3666	3·00	3·25

866 Virgin Mary and Baby Jesus

867 Christmas Tree

2011. Christmas. Multicoloured.

(a) Ordinary gum. (i) Domestic mail

3668	55c. Type **866**	1·25	1·25

(ii) International Post

3669	$1.50 Wise men following Star (horiz)	3·00	3·00

(b) Self-adhesive.

(i) Domestic mail

3670	55c. As Type **866**	1·25	1·25

(ii) International Post

3671	$1.50 As No. 3669	3·00	3·00

2011. Christmas (2nd issue). Multicoloured.

(a) Ordinary gum

3672	55c. Type **867**	1·25	1·25
3673	55c. Wrapped present	1·25	1·25
3674	60c. Star and berry decorations	1·25	1·25

(b) Self-adhesive

3675	55c. As Type **867**	1·25	1·25
3676	55c. As No. 3673	1·25	1·25
3677	55c. As Type **867** but gold and red foil tree decorations	1·25	1·25
3678	55c. As No. 3673 but gold foil on parcel, silver foil on bow and red foil on star and berry decorations	1·25	1·25

868 Poppy and Bugler

2011. Remembrance Day. Multicoloured.

(a) Ordinary gum

3679	60c. Type **868**	1·25	1·40
3680	$1.20 Two poppies and two soldiers	2·50	2·75
MS3681	Nos. 3679/80	3·75	3·75

(b) Self-adhesive

3682	60c. As Type **868**	1·25	1·40

2011. China 2011 27th Asian International Stamp Exhibition, Wuxi, China. Two sheets, each 130×90 mm. Multicoloured.

MS3683	No. 3609	3·50	3·50
MS3684	No. 3610	3·50	3·50

869 Lieut-Gen Rowell (Australia), Admiral Radford (US) and Maj-Gen Gentry (New Zealand), 1952

2011. 50th Anniv of ANZUS Treaty

3685	**869**	60c. multicoloured	1·25	1·40

870 Cupcake

2012. Greetings Stamps. 'Precious Moments'. Multicoloured.

(a) Ordinary gum

3686	60c. Type **870**	1·40	1·40
3687	60c. Teddy bear and stars within stars	1·40	1·40
3688	60c. Multicoloured balloons	1·40	1·40
3689	60c. 'LOVE' and hearts on strings	1·40	1·40
3690	60c. Love birds, 'with love' and branch of flowering tree	1·40	1·40
3691	$1.20 Pale gold rose	2·75	2·75

(b) Self-adhesive

3692	60c. As Type **870**	1·40	1·40
3693	60c. As No. 3687	1·40	1·40
3694	60c. As No. 3688	1·40	1·40
3695	60c. As No. 3689	1·40	1·40
3696	60c. As No. 3690	1·40	1·40

871 Ron Barassi (Australian rules football)

2012. Australian Legends (16th series). Legends of Football. Multicoloured.

(a) Ordinary gum

3697	60c. Type **871**	1·40	1·40
3698	60c. Gary Ablett (Australian rules football)	1·40	1·40
3699	60c. John Raper (Rugby League)	1·40	1·40
3700	60c. Billy Slater (Rugby League)	1·40	1·40
3701	60c. David Campese (Rugby Union)	1·40	1·40
3702	60c. David Pocock (Rugby Union)	1·40	1·40
3703	60c. Joe Marston (soccer)	1·40	1·40
3704	60c. Mark Schwarzer (soccer)	1·40	1·40

(b) Self-adhesive

3705	60c. As Type **871**	1·40	1·40
3706	60c. As No. 3698	1·40	1·40
3707	60c. As No. 3699	1·40	1·40
3708	60c. As No. 3700	1·40	1·40
3709	60c. As No. 3701	1·40	1·40
3710	60c. As No. 3702	1·40	1·40
3711	60c. As No. 3703	1·40	1·40
3712	60c. As No. 3704	1·40	1·40

872 Early Telephone and Modern 4G Phone

2012. Technology - Then and Now. Multicoloured.

(a) Ordinary gum

3713	60c. Type **872**	1·40	1·40
3714	60c. Ice chest and modern refrigerator	1·40	1·40
3715	60c. Early and modern television	1·40	1·40
3716	60c. Record player and digital media player	1·40	1·40
3717	60c. Road map and GPS (global positioning system)	1·40	1·40
MS3718	170×85 mm. Nos. 3713/17	7·50	7·50

(b) Self-adhesive

3719	60c. As Type **872**	1·40	1·40
3720	60c. As No. 3714	1·40	1·40
3721	60c. As No. 3715	1·40	1·40
3722	60c. As No. 3716	1·40	1·40
3723	60c. As No. 3717	1·40	1·40

873 O-Bahn Bus, Adelaide

2012. City Transport. Multicoloured.

(a) Ordinary gum

3724	60c. Type **873**	1·40	1·40
3725	60c. *Charlotte* (ferry) passing Luna Park, Sydney	1·40	1·40
3726	60c. Train running alongside roads, Perth	1·40	1·40
3727	60c. W-class tram, Melbourne	1·40	1·40
3728	60c. Double-decker train, Sydney	1·40	1·40

(b) Self-adhesive

3729	60c. As Type **873**	1·40	1·40
3730	60c. As No. 3725	1·40	1·40
3731	60c. As No. 3726	1·40	1·40
3732	60c. As No. 3727	1·40	1·40
3733	60c. As No. 3728	1·40	1·40

OFFICIAL STAMPS

1931. Optd **O.S.** (a) Kangaroo issue.

O133	**1**	6d. brown	30·00	20·00

(b) King George V issue.

O128	**3**	½d. orange	7·00	1·50
O129	**3**	1d. green	3·25	45
O130	**3**	2d. red	18·00	55
O131	**3**	3d. blue	7·50	4·50
O126	**3**	4d. olive	21·00	3·00
O132	**3**	5d. brown	42·00	27·00

(c) Various issues.

O123	**13**	2d. red	70·00	24·00
O134	**18**	2d. red	7·00	2·00
O124	**13**	3d. blue	£250	27·00
O135	**18**	3d. blue	15·00	5·00
O136	**17**	1s. green	48·00	27·00

POSTAGE DUE STAMPS

D1

1902. White space below value at foot.

D1	**D1**	½d. green	3·25	5·00
D2	**D1**	1d. green	55·00	10·00
D3	**D1**	2d. green	55·00	12·00
D4	**D1**	3d. green	45·00	27·00
D5	**D1**	4d. green	45·00	13·00
D6	**D1**	6d. green	60·00	9·50
D7	**D1**	8d. green	95·00	80·00
D8	**D1**	5s. green	£200	70·00

D3

1902. White space filled in.

D22	**D3**	½d. green	17·00	13·00
D23	**D3**	1d. green	17·00	4·50
D24	**D3**	2d. green	42·00	3·00
D25	**D3**	3d. green	70·00	16·00
D26	**D3**	4d. green	60·00	17·00
D17	**D3**	5d. green	60·00	14·00
D28	**D3**	6d. green	65·00	10·00
D29	**D3**	8d. green	£130	55·00
D18	**D3**	10d. green	85·00	18·00
D19	**D3**	1s. green	65·00	15·00
D20	**D3**	2s. green	£120	18·00
D33	**D3**	5s. green	£350	22·00
D43	**D3**	10s. green	£1900	£1800
D44	**D3**	20s. green	£4000	£2250

1908. As Type D **3**, but stroke after figure of value, thus "5/-".

D58	1s. green	£100	12·00
D60	2s. green	£1000	£15000
D59	5s. green	£250	48·00
D61	10s. green	£2500	£24000
D62	20s. green	£6500	£48000

D7

1909

D132	**D7**	½d. red and green	4·25	4·00
D133	**D7**	1d. red and green	2·50	3·00
D93	**D7**	1½d. red and green	1·50	9·00
D121	**D7**	2d. red and green	6·00	1·25
D134	**D7**	3d. red and green	1·75	3·00
D109	**D7**	4d. red and green	9·00	4·00
D124	**D7**	5d. red and green	17·00	8·00
D137	**D7**	6d. red and green	2·50	2·00
D126	**D7**	7d. red and green	2·25	1·50
D127	**D7**	8d. red and green	3·25	15·00
D139	**D7**	10d. red and green	3·25	1·75
D128	**D7**	1s. red and green	17·00	1·75
D70	**D7**	2s. red and green	70·00	8·50
D71	**D7**	5s. red and green	90·00	11·00
D72	**D7**	10s. red and green	£250	£150
D73	**D7**	£1 red and green	£500	£300

D10

1953

D140	**D10**	1s. red and green	5·50	1·75
D130	**D10**	2s. red and green	14·00	7·00
D131a	**D10**	5s. red and green	12·00	1·00

Pt. 1

AUSTRALIAN ANTARCTIC TERRITORY

By an Order in Council of 7 February 1933, the territory S. of latitude 60°S. between 160th and 145th meridians of East longitude (excepting Adelie Land) was placed under Australian administration. Until 1957 stamps of Australia were used from the base.

1957. 12 pence = 1 shilling; 20 shillings = 1 pound.
1966. 100 cents = 1 dollar.

1 1954 Expedition at Vestfold Hills and Map

1957

1	**1**	2s. blue	1·00	65

2 Members of Shackleton Expedition at S. Magnetic Pole, 1909

3 Weazel and Team

1959

2	**2**	5d. on 4d. black and sepia	60	15
3	**3**	8d. on 7d. black and blue	1·75	2·25
4	-	1s. myrtle	2·25	2·00
5	-	2s.3d. green	7·00	3·00

DESIGNS—VERT (as Type **3**): 1s. Dog-team and iceberg; 2s.3d. Map of Antarctica and emperor penguins.

6

1961

6	**6**	5d. blue	1·00	20

7 Sir Douglas Mawson (Expedition leader)

1961. 50th Anniv of 1911–14 Australian Antarctic Expedition.

7	**7**	5d. myrtle	35	20

8 Aurora and Camera Dome

1966. Multicoloured.. Multicoloured..

8	1c. Type **8**	70	30
9	2c. Emperor penguins	3·00	80
10	4c. Ship and iceberg	1·00	90
11	5c. Banding southern elephant-seals	2·25	1·75
12	7c. Measuring snow strata	80	80
13	10c. Wind gauges	1·00	1·10
14	15c. Weather balloon	5·00	2·00
15	20c. Bell Trooper helicopter (horiz)	9·00	2·50
16	25c. Radio operator (horiz)	1·75	2·25
17	50c. Ice-compression tests (horiz)	2·50	4·00
18	$1 Parahelion ("mock sun") (horiz)	19·00	12·00

11 Sastrugi (Snow Ridges)

1971. Tenth Anniv of Antarctic Treaty.

19	**11**	6c. blue and black	75	1·00
20	-	30c. multicoloured	2·25	5·50

DESIGN: 30c. Pancake ice.

12 Capt. Cook, Sextant and Compass

1972. Bicentenary of Cook's Circumnavigation of Antarctica. Multicoloured.

21	7c. Type **12**	1·00	75
22	35c. Chart and H.M.S. *Resolution*	3·00	1·25

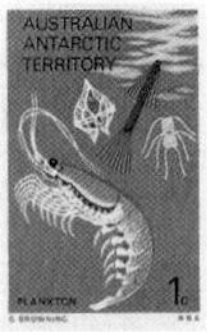

13 Plankton

1973. Multicoloured.. Multicoloured..

23	1c. Type **13**	30	20
24	5c. Mawson's de Havilland Gipsy Moth, 1931	55	1·00
25	7c. Adelie penguin	1·50	1·00
26	8c. de Havilland Fox Moth, 1934–37	60	1·25
27	9c. Leopard seal (horiz)	40	1·25
28	10c. Killer whale (horiz)	2·25	2·00
29	20c. Wandering albatross ("Albatross") (horiz)	1·50	1·00
30	25c. Wilkins's Lockheed Vega *San Francisco*, 1928 (horiz)	55	1·00
31	30c. Ellsworth's Northrop Gamma *Polar Star*, 1935	55	1·00
32	35c. Christensen's Avro Type 581 Avian, 1934 (horiz)	55	1·00
33	50c. Byrd's Ford Trimotor *Floyd Bennett*, 1929	55	1·25
34	$1 Sperm whale	75	1·40

14 Admiral Byrd (expedition leader), Ford Trimotor *Floyd Bennett* and Map of South Pole

1979. 50th Anniv of First Flight over South Pole. Multicoloured.

35	20c. Type **14**	25	60
36	55c. Admiral Byrd, aircraft and Antarctic terrain	50	1·25

15 *Thala Dan* (supply ship)

1979. Ships. Multicoloured.

37	1c. *Aurora* (horiz)	15	10
38	2c. *Penola* (Rymill's ship)	40	10
39	5c. Type **15**	30	40
40	10c. H.M.S. *Challenger* (survey ship) (horiz)	50	1·50
41	15c. *Morning* (bow view) (whaling ship) (horiz)	2·00	3·00
42	15c. *Nimrod* (stern view) (Shackleton's ship) (horiz)	1·40	2·50
43	20c. *Discovery II* (supply ship) (horiz)	1·50	1·50
44	22c. *Terra Nova* (Scott's ship)	1·00	1·25
45	25c. *Endurance* (Shackleton's ship)	60	1·00
46	30c. *Fram* (Amundsen's ship) (horiz)	60	1·75
47	35c. *Nella Dan* (supply ship) (horiz)	80	1·75
48	40c. *Kista Dan* (supply ship)	1·25	2·50
49	45c. *L'Astrolabe* (D'Urville's ship) (horiz)	70	1·50
50	50c. *Norvegia* (supply ship) (horiz)	70	70
51	55c. *Discovery* (Scott's ship)	1·00	2·00
52	$1 H.M.S. *Resolution* (Cook's ship)	1·75	2·50

No. 41 is incorrectly inscr "S.Y. Nimrod".

16 Sir Douglas Mawson in Antarctic Terrain

1982. Birth Centenary of Sir Douglas Mawson (Antarctic explorer). Multicoloured.

53	27c. Type **16**	25	25
54	75c. Sir Douglas Mawson and map of Australian Antarctic Territory	75	1·50

17 Light-mantled Sooty Albatross

1983. Regional Wildlife. Multicoloured.

55	27c. Type **17**	60	90
56	27c. King cormorant ("Macquarie Island shag")	60	90
57	27c. Southern elephant seal	60	90
58	27c. Royal penguin	60	90
59	27c. Dove prion ("Antarctic prion")	60	90

18 Antarctic Scientist

1983. 12th Antarctic Treaty Consultative Meeting. Canberra.

60	**18**	27c. multicoloured	55	1·00

19 Prismatic Compass and Lloyd-Creak Dip Circle

1984. 75th Anniv of Magnetic Pole Expedition. Multicoloured.

61	30c. Type **19**	30	30
62	85c. Aneroid barometer and theodolite	70	1·25

20 Dog Team pulling Sledge

1984. Antarctic Scenes. Multicoloured.

63	2c. Summer afternoon, Mawson Station	20	1·00
64	5c. Type **20**	20	30
65	10c. Late summer evening, MacRobertson Land	20	40
66	15c. Prince Charles Mountains	20	1·00
67	20c. Summer morning, Wilkesland	20	1·50
68	25c. Sea-ice and iceberg	60	1·50
69	30c. Mount Coates	25	50
70	33c. "Iceberg Alley", Mawson	25	1·00
71	36c. Early winter evening, Casey Station	1·00	50
72	45c. Brash ice (vert)	70	2·00
73	60c. Midwinter shadows, Casey Station	50	65
74	75c. Coastline	2·25	3·00
75	85c. Landing strip	2·50	3·00
76	90c. Pancake ice (vert)	75	80
77	$1 Emperor penguins	3·00	1·50

21 Prince Charles Mountains near Mawson Station

1986. 25th Anniv of Antarctic Treaty.

78	**21**	36c. multicoloured	1·25	1·10

22 Hourglass Dolphins and *Nella Dan*

1988. Environment, Conservation and Technology. Multicoloured.

79	37c. Type **22**	1·25	1·40
80	37c. Emperor penguins and Davis Station	1·25	1·40
81	37c. Crabeater seal and Hughes 500D helicopters	1·25	1·40
82	37c. Adelie penguins and tracked vehicle	1·25	1·40
83	37c. Grey-headed albatross and photographer	1·25	1·40

23 *Antarctica*

1989. Antarctic Landscape Paintings by Sir Sidney Nolan. Multicoloured.

84	39c. Type **23**	1·50	1·75
85	39c. *Iceberg Alley*	1·50	1·75
86	60c. *Glacial Flow*	2·50	2·75
87	80c. *Frozen Sea*	3·00	3·25

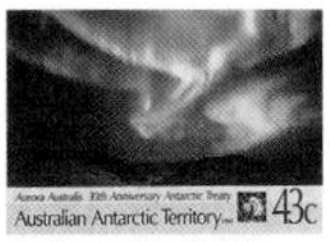

24 "Aurora Australis"

1991. 30th Anniv of Antarctic Treaty (43c.) and Maiden Voyage of *Aurora Australis* (research ship) ($1.20). Multicoloured.

88	43c. Type **24**	75	60
89	$1.20 *Aurora Australis* off Heard Island	2·75	4·25

25 Adelie Penguin and Chick

1992. Antarctic Wildlife. Multicoloured.

90	45c. Type **25**	1·00	50
91	75c. Elephant seal with pup	1·40	90
92	85c. Hall's giant petrel ("Northern giant petrel") on nest with fledgeling	2·00	1·00
93	95c. Weddell seal and pup	1·75	1·00
94	$1 Royal penguin	2·00	1·00
95	$1.20 Emperor penguins with chicks (vert)	2·50	1·40
96	$1.40 Fur seal	2·00	1·75
97	$1.50 King penguin (vert)	2·50	2·25

26 Head of Husky

1994. Departure of Huskies from Antarctica. Multicoloured.

104	45c. Type **26**	1·75	75
105	75c. Dogs pulling sledge (horiz)	2·00	2·25
106	85c. Husky in harness	2·25	2·50
107	$1.05 Dogs on leads (horiz)	2·50	3·00

27 Humpback Whale with Calf

1995. Whales and Dolphins. Multicoloured.

108	45c. Type **27**	1·75	80
109	45c. Pair of hourglass dolphins (vert)	1·75	2·00
110	45c. Pair of minke whales (vert)	1·75	2·00
111	$1 Killer whale	3·00	3·00
MS112	146×64 mm. Nos. 108/11	8·00	8·00

Nos. 109/10 were printed together, *se-tenant*, forming a composite design.

28 *Rafting Sea Ice* (Christian Clare Robertson)

1996. Paintings by Christian Clare Robertson. Multicoloured.

113	45c. Type **28**	90	1·40
114	45c. *Shadow on the Plateau*	90	1·40
115	$1 *Ice Cave*	1·90	2·00
116	$1.20 *Twelve Lake*	2·25	2·75

29 Apple Huts

1997. 50th Anniv of Australian National Antarctic Research Expeditions (A.N.A.R.E.). Multicoloured.

117	45c. Type **29**	1·00	1·25
118	45c. Tuning a radio receiver	1·00	1·25
119	95c. Summer surveying	1·60	2·25
120	$1.05 Scientists in cage above sea ice	1·75	2·25
121	$1.20 Scientists and tents	1·90	2·50

30 *Aurora Australis* (research ship)

1998. Antarctic Transport. Multicoloured.

122	45c. Type **30**	2·25	2·50
123	45c. Skidoo	2·25	2·50
124	$1 Helicopter lifting quad motorcycle (vert)	4·25	3·25
125	$2 Hagglunds tractor and trailer (vert)	4·75	6·50

31 Sir Douglas Mawson (expedition leader, 1911–14) and *Aurora* (research ship)

1999. Restoration of Mawson's Huts, Cape Denison. Each including a background drawing of a hut. Multicoloured.

126	45c. Type **31**	2·00	2·25
127	45c. Huts in blizzard	2·00	2·25
128	90c. Husky team	3·25	3·75
129	$1.35 Conservation in progress	3·25	3·75

32 Emperor Penguins

2000. Penguins. Multicoloured.

130	45c. Type **32**	3·50	3·50
131	45c. Adelie penguins	3·50	3·50

33 Adelie Penguins with Egg

2001. Centenary of Australian Antarctic Exploration. Multicoloured.

132	5c. Type **33**	90	1·00
133	5c. Louis Bernacchi (physicist)	90	1·00
134	5c. *Nimrod* (Shackleton)	90	1·00
135	5c. Mackay, Edgeworth David and Mawson at South Magnetic Pole, 1909	90	1·00
136	5c. Taylor and Debenham (geologists)	90	1·00
137	10c. Early radio set	90	1·00
138	10c. Lockheed-Vega aircraft and husky team	90	1·00
139	10c. Sir Douglas Mawson	90	1·00

140	10c. Members of BANZARE Expedition, 1929–31	90	1·00
141	10c. Hoisting Union Jack	90	1·00
142	25c. Hoisting Australian flag, 1948	1·10	1·25
143	25c. Hagglund vehicle and helicopter	1·10	1·25
144	25c. *Aurora australis* over Casey	1·10	1·25
145	25c. Scientist with weather balloon	1·10	1·25
146	25c. Modern Antarctic clothing and "apple" hut	1·10	1·25
147	45c. *Nella Dan* (supply ship) and emperor penguins	1·25	1·40
148	45c. Male and female scientists taking ice sample	1·25	1·40
149	45c. Scientist using satellite phone	1·25	1·40
150	45c. Weddell seal and tourists	1·25	1·40
151	45c. Satellite photograph of Antarctica	1·25	1·40

Nos. 132/51 were printed together, *se-tenant*, with the backgrounds forming a composite design.

Each stamp carries an inscription on the reverse, printed over the gum.

34 Female Leopard Seal and Pup

2001. Endangered Species. Leopard Seal. Multicoloured.

152	45c. Type **34**	2·00	2·25
153	45c. Male seal on ice floe chasing adelie penguins	2·00	2·25
154	45c. Female seal and pup swimming underwater	2·00	2·25
155	45c. Adult seal chasing adelie penguins underwater	2·00	2·25

35 Light Detection and Ranging Equipment, Davis Base

2002. Antarctic Research. Multicoloured.

156	45c. Type **35**	2·50	2·75
157	45c. Magnified diatom and coastline, Casey Base	2·50	2·75
158	45c. Wandering albatross, Macquarie Base	2·50	2·75
159	45c. Adelie penguin, Mawson Base	2·50	2·75

36 *Kista Dan* in Heavy Seas

2003. Antarctic Supply Ships. Multicoloured.

160	50c. Type **36**	3·00	3·25
161	50c. *Magga Dan* entering pack ice	3·00	3·25
162	$1 *Thala Dan* and iceberg (vert)	4·50	2·75
163	$1.45 *Nella Dan* unloading in Antarctic (vert)	5·50	6·50

37 Naming Ceremony, 1954

2004. 50th Anniv of Mawson Station. Multicoloured.

164	50c. Type **37**	2·75	3·25
165	50c. Mawson Station, 2004	2·75	3·25
166	$1 Accomodation "caravan", 1950s	3·50	2·75
167	$1.45 Emperor penguin rookery	4·50	5·50

38 Hughes 500 Helicopter

2005. Aviation in the Australian Antarctic Territory. Multicoloured.

168	50c. Type **38**	2·00	2·00
169	50c. de Haviland DHC-2 Beaver	2·00	2·00
170	$1 Pilatus PC06 Porter	3·00	2·25
171	$1.45 Douglas DC-3/Dakota C-47	3·75	3·75

39 Mackerel Icefish

2006. Fish of the Australian Antarctic Territory. Multicoloured.

172	50c. Type **39**	2·00	2·25
173	50c. Lanternfish	2·00	2·25
174	$1 Eaton's skate	2·50	2·75
175	$1 Patagonian toothfish	2·50	2·75

40 Royal Penguins

2007. Endangered Species. Royal Penguins (*Eudyptes schlegeli*). Multicoloured.

176	50c. Type **40**	2·50	2·50
177	50c. Penguin with egg	2·50	2·50
178	$1 Two penguins sparring	2·75	2·75
179	$1 Pair snuggling together	2·75	2·75

41 Telescope, AASTINO Observatory, Stars and Gas Cloud (Astronomy from the Polar Plateaus)

2008. International Polar Year 2007–08. Multicoloured.

180	55c. Type **41**	2·50	2·50
181	55c. Scientists drilling through sea ice (Sea Ice Physics and Ecosystem Experiment)	2·50	2·50
182	$1.10 Pteropod, pelagic snail *Limacina helicina* and emperor penguin (marine biology)	3·00	3·00
183	$1.10 CTD (conductivity-temperature-depth) probe and ocean (Climate of Antarctica and the Southern Ocean project)	3·00	3·00
MS184	160×90 mm. Nos. 180/3	10·00	10·00

42 Unloading *Nimrod*

2009. Centenary of the First Expedition to the South Magnetic Pole. Each black, grey and blue.

185	55c. Type **42**	2·00	2·00
186	55c. Arroll-Johnston car towing provisions on sledge	2·00	2·00
187	$1.10 Northern Party camp	2·75	2·75
188	$1.10 Alistair Mackay, Douglas Mawson and Edgeworth David raising Union Jack at South Magnetic Pole	2·75	2·75
MS189	170×85 mm. Nos. 185/8	8·50	8·50

43 Snow Petrel

2009. Preserve the Polar Regions and Glaciers. Multicoloured. (i) Domestic Mail

190	55c. Type **43**	2·00	1·25
191	$2.05 Jade iceberg	6·00	6·75
MS192	120x80mm. Nos. 190/1	8·00	8·00

44 Pleurophyllum hookeri

2010. Macquarie Island. Multicoloured.

193	60c. Type **44**	1·60	1·60
194	60c. Southern elephant seal	1·60	1·60
195	$1.20 Mawson Point Stacks	2·10	2·10
196	$1.20 Caroline Cove	2·10	2·10
MS197	159×85 mm. Nos. 193/6	7·25	7·25

45 Greenish Iceberg with Pinnacle

2011. Icebergs. Multicoloured.

(a) Ordinary paper

198	60c. Type **45**	1·40	1·40
199	60c. Flat-topped iceberg with overhang at left	1·40	1·40
200	60c. Dark iceberg with fluted sides	1·40	1·40
201	60c. Iceberg with low ridge in foreground and higher ridge with pinnacle at right	1·40	1·40
MS202	135×72 mm. Nos. 198/201	6·00	6·00

(b) Self-adhesive

203	60c. As Type **45**	1·40	1·40
204	60c. As No. 199	1·40	1·40
205	60c. As No. 200	1·40	1·40
206	60c. As No. 201	1·40	1·40

46 SY *Aurora* leaving Hobart, December 1911

2011. Centenary of the Australasian Antarctic Expedition, 1911-14 (1st issue). Multicoloured.

207	60c. Type **46**	1·00	1·25
208	60c. Captain John King Davis of the SY *Aurora*	1·00	1·25
209	60c. SY *Aurora* on Antarctic voyage	1·00	1·25
210	60c. Landing at Macquarie Island	1·00	1·25
211	60c. Birdlife on Macquarie Island	1·00	1·25
MS212	169x85 mm. Nos. 207/11	5·00	5·00

Nos. 207/11 were printed together in horizontal strips of five stamps throughout the sheets, each strip forming a composite background design of sea and coast.

47 (image scaled to 36% of original size)

2011. 50th Anniv of Worldwide Fund for Nature (formerly World Wildlife Fund). Sheet 135x72 mm containing Nos. 3637/9 and 3636 of Australia. Multicoloured.

MS213	**47** 60c.x4 Southern elephant seal (*Mirounga leonina*) (Australian Antarctic Territory); Dugong (*Dugong dugon*) (Cocos (Keeling) Islands); Christmas Island shrew (*Crocidura trichura*) (Christmas Island); Type **861** of Australia	5·00	5·00

Pt. 2

AUSTRIA

A state of central Europe, part of the Austro-Hungarian Monarchy and Empire until 1918. At the end of the First World War the Empire was dismembered and German-spealing Austria became a Republic.

Austria was absorbed into the German Reich in 1938 and remained part of Germany until 1945. Following occupation of the four Allied Powers the Austrian Republic was re-established on 14 May 1945.

1850. 60 kreuzer = 1 gulden.
1858. 100 kreuzer = 1 gulden.
1899. 100 heller = 1 krone.
1925. 100 groschen = 1 schilling.
1938. 100 pfennig = 1 German reichsmark.
1945. 100 groschen = 1 schilling.
2002. 100 cents = 1 euro.

1 Arms of Austria

1850. Imperf.

6a	1	1k. yellow	£1800	£110
7	1	2k. black	£2250	£100
8a	1	3k. red	£600	4·75
9	1	6k. brown	£1300	8·50
10	1	9k. blue	£1300	3·75

For stamps in Type **1** with values in "CENTES", see Lombardy and Venetia.

4 5

1858

22a	**5**	2k. yellow	£1500	70·00
23	**4**	3k. black	£2250	£375
24	**4**	3k. green	£1900	£225
25a	**5**	5k. red	£500	2·75
26a	**5**	10k. brown	£1200	4·25
27a	**5**	15k. blue	£1100	2·75

For stamps in Types **4** and **5** with values in "SOLDI", see Lombardy and Venetia.

The portraits on Austrian stamps to 1906 are of the Emperor Francis Joseph I.

10

1860

33	**10**	2k. yellow	£550	43·00
34	**10**	3k. green	£475	38·00
35	**10**	5k. red	£350	1·10
36	**10**	10k. brown	£450	2·75
37	**10**	15k. blue	£600	1·90

12 Arms of Austria

1863

45	**12**	2k. yellow	£250	17·00
46	**12**	3k. green	£250	17·00
47	**12**	5k. red	70·00	55
48	**12**	10k. blue	£300	4·25
49	**12**	15k. brown	£300	2·40

A H14 **A H16**

1867

59	**AH14**	2k. yellow	19·00	1·10
60	**AH14**	3k. green	95·00	1·10
62	**AH14**	5k. red	3·00	20
63	**AH14**	10k. blue	£225	1·10
64	**AH14**	15k. brown	21·00	17·00
AH56a	**AH14**	25k. grey	65·00	24·00
66	**AH16**	50k. brown	19·00	£250

20

1883

70c	**20**	2k. brown	8·25	45
71c	**20**	3k. green	8·25	30
72c	**20**	5k. red	£150	20
73c	**20**	10k. blue	21·00	45
74c	**20**	20k. grey	£200	4·25
75a	**20**	50k. mauve	£475	£160

23 **24**

1890

79	**23**	1k. grey	2·10	55
80	**23**	2k. brown	50	20
81	**23**	3k. green	60	20
82	**23**	5k. red	60	20
83	**23**	10k. blue	1·50	20
84	**23**	12k. purple	3·50	55
85	**23**	15k. purple	3·50	55

86	**23**	20k. green	55·00	3·25
87	**23**	24k. blue	3·00	1·90
88	**23**	30k. brown	3·00	1·30
89	**23**	50k. mauve	8·25	15·00
90	**24**	1g. blue	6·25	4·25
105	**24**	1g. lilac	£100	6·50
91	**24**	2g. red	10·50	38·00
106	**24**	2g. green	41·00	65·00

25

1891. Figures in black.

92	**25**	20k. green	5·25	20
93	**25**	24k. blue	7·25	1·30
94	**25**	30k. brown	5·25	20
95	**25**	50k. mauve	6·25	55

27

28

29

30

1899. Corner numerals in black on heller values.

107	**27**	1h. mauve	1·00	20
108	**27**	2h. grey	4·25	85
140	**27**	3h. brown	1·00	20
141b	**27**	5h. green	1·00	20
142b	**27**	6h. orange	1·00	20
143b	**28**	10h. red	1·00	20
144b	**28**	20h. brown	1·00	20
145b	**28**	25h. blue	1·00	20
146b	**28**	30h. mauve	2·10	1·10
147b	**29**	35h. green	1·50	30
148b	**29**	40h. green	2·10	5·25
149b	**29**	50h. blue	5·25	13·00
150b	**29**	60h. brown	2·10	1·10
119a	**30**	1k. red	11·50	20
120	**30**	2k. lilac	£150	65
121	**30**	4k. green	26·00	32·00

33

35

1904. Types as before, but with corners containing figures altered as T **33** and **35**. Figures in black on white on 10h. to 30h. only.

169	**33**	1h. purple	20	65
170	**33**	2h. black	20	45
171	**33**	3h. brown	40	10
173	**33**	6h. orange	60	10
160a	**28**	10h. red	2·30	10
a161	**28**	20h. brown	37·00	1·30
162a	**28**	25h. blue	37·00	1·10
a163	**28**	30h. mauve	55·00	2·10
178	**35**	35h. green	5·25	55
179	**35**	40h. purple	5·25	1·40
180	**35**	50h. blue	5·25	4·75
181	**35**	60h. brown	5·25	1·30
168	**35**	72h. red	6·25	2·10

1906. Figures on plain white ground and stamps printed in one colour.

183	**28**	5h. yellow-green	40	10
184	**28**	10h. red	50	20
185	**28**	12h. violet	1·50	1·10
186	**28**	20h. brown	5·00	30
187	**28**	25h. blue	5·00	75
188	**28**	30h. red	12·50	55

37 Francis Joseph I

38 Francis Joseph I

41 Schonbrunn

42 Francis Joseph I

1908. 60th Anniv of Emperor's Accession.

189A	-	1h. black	40	20
190A	-	2h. violet	40	20
191B	-	3h. purple	30	10
192B	**37**	5h. green	20	10
193A	-	6h. brown	95	1·10
194B	**37**	10h. red	20	10
195A	-	12h. red	2·10	1·60
196B	-	20h. brown	2·75	50
197B	**37**	25h. blue	2·50	45
198B	-	30h. green	6·25	65
199A	-	35h. grey	6·00	40
200	**38**	50h. green	2·00	55
201	-	60h. red	40	20
202	**38**	72h. brown	5·00	55
203	-	1k. violet	21·00	55
204	**41**	2k. green and red	36·00	1·10
205	-	5k. purple and brown	65·00	8·50
206	**42**	10k. brown, blue & ochre	£300	£110

DESIGNS—As Type **37**: 1h. Charles VI; 2h. Maria Theresa; 3h. Joseph II; 6h. Leopold II; 12h. Francis I; 20h. Ferdinand; 30h. Francis Joseph I in 1848; 35h. Same in 1878. As Type **38**: 60h. Francis Joseph I on horseback; 1k. Same in ceremonial robes. As Type **41**: 5k. Hofburg.

45

1910. 80th Birthday of Francis Joseph I. As issue of 1908 but with dates added as T **45**.

223	1h. black	6·25	10·50
224	2h. violet	8·25	21·00
225	3h. purple	7·25	18·00
226	5h. green	20	45
227	6h. brown	4·25	16·00
228	10h. red	20	45
229	12h. red	5·25	18·00
230	20h. brown	13·50	20·00
231	25h. blue	3·75	4·25
232	30h. green	5·25	16·00
233	35h. grey	5·25	17·00
234	50h. green	7·25	20·00
235	60h. red	7·25	20·00
236	1k. violet	5·75	9·50
237	2k. green and red	£200	£325
238	5k. purple and brown	£150	£300
239	10k. brown, blue and ochre	£275	£475

47

1914. War Charity Funds.

240	**47**	5h.+(2h.) green	30	45
241	**47**	10h.+(2h.) red	40	75

48 Cavalry

1915. War Charity Funds.

242	-	3h.+1h. brown	10	55
243	**48**	5h.+2h. green	10	10
244	-	10h.+2h. red	10	10
245	-	20h.+3h. green	60	3·25
246	-	35h.+3h. blue	3·00	7·50

DESIGNS: 3h. Infantry; 10h. Artillery; 20h. Battleship *Viribus Unitas* (Navy); 35h. Lohner Pfeilflieger B-1 biplane (Air Force).

49 Imperial Austrian Crown

50 Francis Joseph I

51 Arms of Austria

52

1916

247	**49**	3h. violet	10	10
248	**49**	5h. green	10	10
249	**49**	6h. orange	40	1·60
250	**49**	10h. red	10	10
251	**49**	12h. blue	40	2·75
252	**50**	15h. red	60	20
253	**50**	20h. brown	3·75	40
254	**50**	25h. blue	8·25	75
255	**50**	30h. slate	7·50	1·30
256	**51**	40h. olive	20	10
257	**51**	50h. green	20	10
258	**51**	60h. blue	20	10
259	**51**	80h. brown	20	10
260	**51**	90h. purple	20	10
261	**51**	1k. red on yellow	40	15
262aa	**52**	2k. blue	10	20
263aa	**52**	3k. red	30	1·10
264a	**52**	4k. green	4·25	1·60
265aa	**52**	10k. violet	10·50	43·00

On Nos. 254/5 the portrait is full face. The 1k. has floral sprays each side of the coat-of-arms.

60 Charles I

1917

290	**60**	15h. red	20	30
291a	**60**	20h. green	20	30
292	**60**	25h. blue	1·00	30
293	**60**	30h. violet	1·00	30

1918. Air. Optd **FLUGPOST** or surch also.

296A	**52**	1k.50 on 2k. mauve	2·10	9·75
297B	**52**	2k.50 on 3k. brown	10·50	32·00
298A	**52**	4k. grey	7·25	23·00

1918. Optd **Deutschosterreich**.

299	**49**	3h. violet	10	10
300	**49**	5h. green	10	10
301	**49**	6h. orange	30	2·75
302	**49**	10h. red	10	10
303	**49**	12h. blue	30	2·75
304	**60**	15h. red	30	1·60
305	**60**	20h. green	10	10
306	**60**	25h. blue	10	30
307	**60**	30h. violet	10	10
308	**51**	40h. olive	10	10
309	**51**	50h. green	60	2·10
310	**51**	60h. blue	55	2·00
311	**51**	80h. brown	20	20
312	**51**	90h. red	20	65
313	**51**	1k. red on yellow	20	30
314	**52**	2k. blue	10	10
315	**52**	3k. red	40	1·10
316	**52**	4k. green	2·10	4·25
317	**52**	10k. violet	10·50	27·00

64 Posthorn

65 Republican Arms

66 "New Republic"

1919. Imperf or perf.

336	**64**	3h. grey	10	10
337	**65**	5h. green	10	10
338	**65**	5h. grey	10	10
339	**64**	6h. orange	10	65
340	**65**	10h. red	10	10
342	**64**	12h. blue	10	1·30
343a	**64**	15h. brown	10	10
344	**66**	20h. green	10	10
346	**65**	25h. blue	10	10
347	**64**	25h. violet	10	10
348	**66**	30h. brown	10	10
349	**66**	40h. violet	10	10
350	**66**	40h. red	10	10
351	**65**	45h. green	20	1·10
352	**66**	50h. blue	10	10
353	**64**	60h. green	10	10
354	**65**	1k. red on yellow	10	10
355	**65**	1k. blue	40	1·10

67 Parliament Building

1919

356	**67**	2k. black and red	30	1·10
357	**67**	2½k. bistre	20	55
358	**67**	3k. brown and blue	10	10
359	**67**	4k. black and red	10	10
360	**67**	5k. black	10	30
361	**67**	7½k. purple	30	55
362	**67**	10k. brown and green	25	55
363	**67**	20k. brown and violet	10	55
364	**67**	50k. violet on yellow	70	1·60

71 Republican Arms

1920

402	**71**	80h. red	10	20
403	**71**	1k. brown	10	20
404	**71**	1½k. green	30	20
405	**71**	2k. blue	10	20
406	**71**	3k. black and green	10	30
407	**71**	4k. claret and red	10	20
408	**71**	5k. red and lilac	10	20
409	**71**	7½k. brown and orange	10	30
410	**71**	10k. blue and violet	10	20

The frames of the 3 to 10k. differ.

1920. Issues for Carinthian Plebiscite. Optd Karnten Abstimmung (T 65/7 in new colours). (a) Perf.

411	**65**	5h. (+10h.) grey on yell	70	2·10
412	**65**	10h. (+20h.) red on pink	70	1·60
413	**64**	15h. (+30h.) brn on yell	30	1·10
414	**66**	20h. (+40h.) green on bl	30	85
415	**64**	25h. (+50h.) pur on pink	30	90
416	**66**	30h. (+60h.) brn on buff	1·80	3·75
417	**66**	40h. (+80h.) red on yell	30	1·10
418	**66**	50h. (+100h.) indigo on blue	30	85
419	**64**	60h. (+120h.) green on bl	1·80	3·75
420	**71**	80h. (+160h.) red	45	95
421	**71**	1k. (+2k.) brown	45	1·10
422	**71**	2k. (+4k.) blue	45	1·10

(b) Imperf.

423	**67**	2½k. (+5k.) brown	50	1·40
424	**67**	3k. (+6k.) green & blue	60	1·70
425	**67**	4k. (+8k.) violet & red	85	2·00
426	**67**	5k. (+10k.) blue	75	1·70
427	**67**	7½k. (+15k.) green	75	1·70
428	**67**	10k. (+20k.) red & green	85	1·90
429	**67**	20k. (+40k.) brn & lilac	95	2·40

The plebiscite was to decide whether Carinthia should be part of Austria or Yugoslavia, and the premium was for a fund to promote a vote in favour of remaining in Austria. The result was a vote for Austria.

1921. Flood Relief Fund. Optd **Hochwasser 1920** (colours changed).

430	**65**	5h. (+10h.) grey on yell	30	1·10
431	**65**	10h. (+20h.) brown	30	1·10
432	**64**	15h. (+30h.) grey	30	1·10
433	**66**	20h. (+40h.) green on yell	30	1·10
434	**64**	25h. (+50h.) blue on yell	30	1·10
435	**66**	30h. (+60h.) purple on bl	65	2·10
436	**66**	40h. (+80h.) brn on red	75	2·75
437	**66**	50h. (+100h.) green on bl	1·70	4·75
438	**64**	60h. (+120h.) pur on yell	50	2·10
439	**71**	80h. (+160h.) blue	50	2·10
440	**71**	1k. (+2k.) orange on blue	45	2·10
441	**71**	1½k. (+3k.) green on yell	25	1·10
442	**71**	2k. (+4k.) brown	25	1·10
443	**67**	2½k. (+5k.) blue	30	1·10
444	**67**	3k. (+6k.) red & green	30	1·10
445	**67**	4k. (+8k.) brown & lilac	1·00	3·75
446	**67**	5k. (+10k.) green	30	2·10
447	**67**	7½k. (+15k.) red	30	2·10
448	**67**	10k. (+20k.) green & blue	30	2·10
449	**67**	20k. (+40k.) pur & red	60	3·25

80 Pincers and Hammer

81 Ear of Corn

1922

461	**81**	½k. brown	10	85
462	**80**	1k. brown	10	10
463	**80**	2k. blue	10	10
464	**81**	2½k. brown	10	10
465	**80**	4k. purple	10	1·40
466	**80**	5k. green	10	10
467	**81**	7½k. violet	10	10
468	**80**	10k. red	10	10
469	**81**	12½k. green	10	10
470	**81**	15k. turquoise	10	10
471	**81**	20k. blue	10	10
472	**81**	25k. red	10	10
473	**80**	30k. grey	10	10
474	**80**	45k. red	10	10
475	**80**	50k. brown	10	10
476	**80**	60k. green	10	10
477	**80**	75k. blue	10	10
478	**80**	80k. yellow	10	10
479	**81**	100k. grey	10	10
480	**81**	120k. brown	10	10
481	**81**	150k. orange	10	10
482	**81**	160k. green	10	10
483	**81**	180k. red	10	10
484	**81**	200k. pink	10	10
485	**81**	240k. violet	10	10
486	**81**	300k. blue	10	10
487	**81**	400k. green	1·50	55
488	**81**	500k. yellow	10	10
489	**81**	600k. slate	10	10
490	**81**	700k. brown	2·50	20
491	**81**	800k. violet	1·00	2·75
492	**80**	1000k. mauve	1·30	20
493	**80**	1200k. red	85	65
494	**80**	1500k. orange	85	20
495	**80**	1600k. slate	4·25	4·25
496	**80**	2000k. blue	5·25	3·75
497	**80**	3000k. blue	15·00	2·75
498	**80**	4000k. blue on blue	7·75	3·75

82

1922

499	**82**	20k. sepia	10	20
500	**82**	25k. blue	10	20
501	**82**	50k. red	10	20
502	**82**	100k. green	10	20
503	**82**	200k. purple	10	20
504	**82**	500k. orange	40	2·10
505	**82**	1000k. violet on yellow	10	20
506	**82**	2000k. green on yellow	10	20
507	**82**	3000k. red	13·00	1·10
508	**82**	5000k. black	2·40	2·10
509	**82**	10,000k. brown	5·75	7·50

85 Mozart

1922. Musicians' Fund.

519b	-	2½k. brown	9·25	13·00
520	**85**	5k. blue	1·50	2·75
521	-	7½k. black	2·50	4·25
522	-	10k. purple	3·00	5·25
523	-	25k. green	5·75	10·50
524	-	50k. red	3·00	5·25
525	-	100k. green	9·25	21·00

COMPOSERS: 2½k. Haydn; 7½k. Beethoven; 10k. Schubert; 25k. Bruckner; 50k. J. Strauss; 100k. Wolf.

87 Hawk

88 W. Kress

1922. Air.

546	**87**	300k. red	40	2·40
547	**87**	400k. green	6·25	21·00
548	**87**	600k. olive	40	2·10
549	**87**	900k. red	40	2·10
550	**88**	1200k. purple	40	2·10
551	**88**	2400k. slate	40	2·10
552	**88**	3000k. brown	4·25	13·00
553	**88**	4800k. blue	4·25	13·00

89 Bregenz

1923. Artists' Charity Fund.

554	**89**	100k. green	5·25	10·50
555	-	120k. blue	5·25	10·50
556	-	160k. purple	5·25	10·50
557	-	180k. purple	5·25	10·50
558	-	200k. red	5·25	10·50
559	-	240k. brown	5·25	10·50
560	-	400k. brown	5·25	10·50
561	-	600k. green	6·25	10·50
562	-	1000k. black	9·25	17·00

DESIGNS: 120k. Salzburg; 160k. Eisenstadt; 180k. Klagenfurt; 200k. Innsbruck; 240k. Linz; 400k. Graz; 600k. Melk; 1000k. Vienna.

90 "Art the Comforter"

1924. Artists' Charity Fund.

563	**90**	100k.+300k. green	5·25	13·00
564	-	300k.+900k. brown	5·25	13·00
565	-	500k.+1500k. purple	5·25	14·00
566	-	600k.+1800k. turquoise	10·50	25·00
567	-	1000k.+3000k. brown	15·00	31·00

DESIGNS: 300k. "Agriculture and Handicraft"; 500k. "Mother Love"; 600k. "Charity"; 1000k. "Fruitfulness".

91

92 Plains

93 Minorite Church, Vienna

1925

568	**91**	1g. grey	25	20
569	**91**	2g. red	50	20
570	**91**	3g. red	50	20
571	**91**	4g. blue	1·50	20
572	**91**	5g. brown	2·10	20
573	**91**	6g. blue	1·50	20
574	**91**	7g. brown	2·10	20
575	**91**	8g. green	5·25	20
576	**92**	10g. brown	1·00	20
577	**92**	15g. red	1·00	20
578	**92**	16g. blue	1·00	20
579	**92**	18g. green	1·50	1·10
580	-	20g. violet	1·00	20
581	-	24g. red	1·20	55
582	-	30g. brown	1·50	20
583	-	40g. blue	1·90	20
584	-	45g. brown	2·10	20
585	-	50g. grey	2·10	30
586	-	80g. blue	4·75	6·00
587	**93**	1s. green	23·00	2·10
588	-	2s. red	8·75	14·00

DESIGN—As T **92**—20g. to 80g. Golden eagle on mountains.

96 Pilot and Hansa Brandenburg C-1

97 de Havilland D.H.34 and Common Crane

1925. Air.

616	**96**	2g. brown	50	1·30
617	**96**	5g. red	30	45
618	**96**	6g. blue	1·00	2·10
619	**96**	8g. green	1·00	2·40
620	**97**	10g. red	1·30	3·75
621	**96**	10g. orange	1·30	2·75
622	**97**	15g. red	1·00	2·10
623	**96**	15g. mauve	50	1·10
624	**96**	20g. brown	14·00	16·00
625	**96**	25g. violet	6·25	12·00
626	**97**	30g. purple	1·20	3·75
627	**96**	30g. bistre	10·50	13·00
628	**97**	50g. grey	1·20	3·75
629	**96**	50g. blue	18·00	19·00
630	**96**	80g. green	3·00	5·25
631	**97**	1s. blue	10·50	14·00
632	**97**	2s. green	2·10	5·25
633	**97**	3s. brown	65·00	85·00
634	**97**	5s. blue	18·00	38·00
635	**97**	10s. brown on grey (25×32 mm)	10·50	32·00

98 Siegfried and Dragon

1926. Child Welfare. Scenes from the Nibelung Legend.

636	**98**	3g.+2g. brown	1·20	1·20
637	-	8g.+2g. blue	20	55
638	-	15g.+5g. red	40	55
639	-	20g.+5g. green	60	1·10
640	-	24g.+6g. violet	60	1·10
641	-	40g.+10g. brown	4·25	7·00

DESIGNS: 8g. Gunther's voyage; 15g. Kriemhild and Brunhild; 20g. Hagen and the Rhine maidens; 24g. Rudiger and the Nibelungs; 40g. Dietrich's fight with Hagen.

99 Dr. Michael Hainisch

1928. Tenth Anniv of Republic and War Orphans and Invalid Children's Fund.

642	**99**	10g. (+10g.) brown	6·25	16·00
643	**99**	15g. (+15g.) red	6·25	16·00
644	**99**	30g. (+30g.) black	6·25	16·00
645	**99**	40g. (+40g.) blue	6·25	16·00

100 Gussing

101 National Library, Vienna

1929. Views. Size 25½×21½ mm.

646	**100**	10g. orange	1·00	10
647	**100**	10g. brown	1·00	10
648	-	15g. purple	1·00	1·80
649	-	16g. black	20	10
650	-	18g. green	50	65
651	-	20g. black	50	10
653	-	24g. purple	7·25	75
654	-	30g. violet	8·25	10
655	-	40g. blue	10·50	30
656	-	50g. violet	39·00	30
657	-	60g. green	31·00	55
658	**101**	1s. brown	8·25	55
659	-	2s. green	19·00	17·00

VIEWS—As T **100**: 15g. Hochosterwitz; 16, 20g. Durnstein; 18g. Traunsee; 24g. Salzburg; 30g. Seewiesen; 40g. Innsbruck; 50g. Worthersee; 60g. Hohenems. As T **101**: 2s. St. Stephen's Cathedral, Vienna.

See also Nos. 678/91.

102 Pres. Wilhelm Miklas

1930. Anti-tuberculosis Fund.

660	**102**	10g. (+10g.) brown	10·50	30·00
661	**102**	20g. (+20g.) red	10·50	30·00
662	**102**	30g. (+30g.) purple	10·50	30·00
663	**102**	40g. (+40g.) blue	10·50	30·00
664	**102**	50g. (+50g.) green	10·50	30·00
665	**102**	1s. (+1s.) brown	10·50	30·00

1930. Rotarian Congress. Optd with Rotary Int emblem and **CONVENTION WIEN 1931**.

666	**100**	10g. (+10g.) brown	50·00	85·00
667	-	20g. (+20g.) grey (No. 651)	50·00	85·00
668	-	30g. (+30g.) vio (No. 654)	50·00	85·00
669	-	40g. (+40g.) bl (No. 655)	50·00	85·00
670	-	50g. (+50g.) vio (No. 656)	50·00	85·00
671	**101**	1s. (+1s.) brown	50·00	85·00

104 Johann Nestroy

1931. Austrian Writers and Youth Unemployment Fund.

672	-	10g. (+10g.) purple	21·00	45·00
673	-	20g. (+20g.) grey	21·00	45·00
674	**104**	30g. (+30g.) red	21·00	45·00
675	-	40g. (+40g.) blue	21·00	45·00
676	-	50g. (+50g.) green	21·00	45·00
677	-	1s. (+1s.) brown	21·00	45·00

DESIGNS: 10g. F. Raimund; 20g. E. Grillparzer; 40g. A Stifter; 50g. L. Anzengruber; 1s. P. Rosegger.

105

1932. Designs as No. 646 etc, but size reduced to 20½×16 mm as T 105.

678	**105**	10g. brown	1·00	20
679	-	12g. green	2·10	20
680	-	18g. green	2·10	3·50
681	-	20g. black	1·00	20
682	-	24g. red	6·75	20
683	-	24g. violet	4·25	20
684	-	30g. violet	23·00	20
685	-	30g. red	8·25	30
686	-	40g. blue	27·00	2·10
687	-	40g. violet	10·50	55
688	-	50g. violet	31·00	55
689	-	50g. blue	10·50	55
690	-	60g. green	70·00	5·25
691	-	64g. green	23·00	55

DESIGNS (new values): 12g. Traunsee; 64g. Hohenems.

106 Dr. Ignaz Seipel

1932. Death of Dr. Seipel (Chancellor), and Ex-servicemen's Fund.

692	**106**	50g. (+50g.) blue	19·00	38·00

107 Hans Makart

1932. Austrian Painters.

693	-	12g. (+12g.) green	31·00	65·00
694	-	24g. (+24g.) purple	31·00	65·00
695	-	30g. (+30g.) red	31·00	65·00
696	**107**	40g. (+40g.) grey	31·00	65·00
697	-	64g. (+64g.) brown	31·00	65·00
698	-	1s. (+1s.) red	31·00	65·00

DESIGNS: 12g. F. G. Waldmuller; 24g. Von Schwind; 30g. Alt; 64g. Klimt; 1s. A. Egger-Lienz.

108 The Climb

1933. International Ski Championship Fund.

699	**108**	12g. (+12g.) green	10·50	27·00
700	-	24g. (+24g.) violet	£140	£190
701	-	30g. (+30g.) red	21·00	38·00
702	-	50g. (+50g.) blue	£140	£190

DESIGNS: 24g. Start; 30g. Race; 50g. Ski jump.

109 *The Honeymoon* (M. von Schwind)

1933. International Philatelic Exn, Vienna (WIPA).

703	**109**	50g. (+50g.) blue	£200	£350
MS705		127×105 mm. As No. 703 (+1s.60 admission) in block of four	£3500	£5000

111 John Sobieski

1933. 250th Anniv of Relief of Vienna and Pan-German Catholic Congress.

706	-	12g. (+12g.) green	33·00	55·00
707	-	24g. (+24g.) violet	31·00	48·00
708	-	30g. (+30g.) red	31·00	48·00
709	**111**	40g. (+40g.) grey	44·00	85·00
710	-	50g. (+50g.) blue	31·00	48·00
711	-	64g. (+64g.) brown	36·00	75·00

DESIGNS—VERT: 12g. Vienna in 1683; 24g. Marco d'Aviano; 30g. Count von Starhemberg; 50g. Charles of Lorraine; 64g. Burgomaster Liebenberg.

1933. Winter Relief Fund. Surch with premium and **Winterhilfe** (5g.) or **WINTERHILFE** (others).

712	**91**	5g.+2g. green	20	75
713	-	12g.+3g. blue (as 679)	30	1·10
714	-	24g.+6g. brn (as 682)	20	75
715	**101**	1s.+50g. red	41·00	95·00

114

115

1934

716	**114**	1g. violet	10	10
717	**114**	3g. red	10	10
718	-	4g. green	10	10
719	-	5g. purple	10	10
721	-	6g. blue	20	10
722	-	8g. green	10	10
723	-	12g. brown	10	10
724	-	20g. brown	20	10
725	-	24g. turquoise	10	10
726	-	25g. violet	20	25
727	-	30g. red	20	10
728	-	35g. red	40	50
729	**115**	40g. grey	50	30
730	**115**	45g. brown	45	20
731	-	60g. blue	70	55
732	-	64g. brown	1·00	20
733	-	1s. purple	1·50	85
735	-	2s. green	4·75	8·50
736	-	3s. orange	18·00	32·00
737	-	5s. black	41·00	70·00

DESIGNS (Austrian costumes of the districts named)—As Type **114**: 1, 3g. Burgenland; 4, 5g. Carinthia; 6, 8g. Lower Austria; 12, 20g. Upper Austria; 24, 25g. Salzburg; 30, 35g. Styria (Steiermark). As Type **115**: 40, 45g. Tyrol; 60, 64g. Vorarlberg; 1s. Vienna; 2s. Army officer and soldiers. 30×31 mm: 3s. Harvesters; 5s. Builders.

117 Chancellor Dollfuss

1934. Dollfuss Mourning Stamp.

738	**117**	24g. black	60	1·10

See also No. 762.

118 Anton Pilgram

1934. Welfare Funds. Austrian Architects.

739	**118**	12g. (+12g.) black	14·50	32·00
740	-	24g. (+24g.) violet	14·50	32·00
741	-	30g. (+30g.) red	14·50	32·00
742	-	40g. (+40g.) brown	14·50	32·00
743	-	60g. (+60g.) blue	14·50	32·00
744	-	64g. (+64g.) green	14·50	32·00

DESIGNS: 24g. Fischer von Erlach; 30g. J. Prandtauer; 40g. A. von Siccardsburg and E. van der Null; 60g. H. von Ferstel; 64g. Otto Wagner.

119 *Mother and Child* (J. Danhauser)

1935. Mothers Day.

745	**119**	24g. blue	70	55

1935. First Anniv of Assassination of Dr. Dollfuss.

762	**117**	24g. blue	1·50	1·40

121 Maria Worth Castle, Carinthia

122 Zugspitze Aerial Railway

1935. Air. Designs showing Junkers airplane (except 10s.) and landscape.

763	-	5g. purple	30	85
764	**121**	10g. orange	10	55
765	-	15g. green	1·00	2·75
766	-	20g. blue	10	55
767	-	25g. purple	10	55
768	-	30g. red	10	55
769	-	40g. green	10	55
770	-	50g. blue	20	95
771	-	60g. sepia	40	1·40
772	-	80g. brown	50	1·80
773	-	1s. red	40	1·60
774	-	2s. green	3·00	8·50
775	-	3s. brown	9·25	32·00
776	**122**	5s. green	5·25	23·00
777	-	10s. blue	85·00	£170

DESIGNS—As T **121**: 5g. Gussing Castle; 15g. Durnstein; 20g. Hallstatt; 25g. Salzburg; 30g. Dachstein Mts.; 40g. Wettersee; 50g. Stuben am Arlberg; 60g. St. Stephen's Cathedral, Vienna; 80g. Minorite Church, Vienna. As T **122**: 1s. River Danube; 2s. Tauern railway viaduct; 3s. Grossglockner mountain roadway; 10s. Glider and yachts on the Attersee.

1935. Winter Relief Fund. As Nos. 719, 723, 725 and 733, but colours changed, surch **Winterhilfe** (778/80) or **WINTERHILFE** (781) and premium.

778	5g.+2g. green	70	1·60
779	12g.+3g. blue	1·20	2·10
780	24g.+6g. brown	70	1·60
781	1s.+50g. red	41·00	90·00

123 Prince Eugene of Savoy (born 1663, not 1667 as given)

1935. Welfare Funds. Austrian Heroes.

782	**123**	12g. (+12g.) brown	15·00	32·00
783	-	24g. (+24g.) green	15·00	32·00
784	-	30g. (+30g.) purple	15·00	32·00
785	-	40g. (+40g.) blue	15·00	32·00
786	-	60g. (+60g.) blue	15·00	32·00
787	-	64g. (+64g.) violet	15·00	32·00

PORTRAITS: 24g. Baron von Laudon; 30g. Archduke Charles; 40g. Field-Marshal Radetzky; 60g. Vice-Admiral von Tegetthoff; 64g. Field-Marshal Conrad von Hotzendorff.

124 Slalom Course Skier

1936. International Ski Championship Fund. Inscr "WETTKAMPFE 1936".

788	**124**	12g. (+12g.) green	3·00	6·50
789	-	24g. (+24g.) violet	5·25	8·50
790	-	35g. (+35g.) red	31·00	75·00
791	-	60g. (+60g.) blue	31·00	75·00

DESIGNS: 24g. Skier on mountain slope; 35g. Woman slalom course skier; 60g. View of Maria Theresienstrasse, Innsbruck.

125 Madonna and Child

1936. Mothers' Day.

792	**125**	24g. blue	40	1·30

126 Chancellor Dollfuss

1936. Second Anniv of Assassination of Dr. Dollfuss.

793	**126**	10s. blue	£950	£1500

127 *'St. Martin sharing Cloak*

1936. Winter Relief Fund. Inscr "WINTERHILFE 1936/37".

794	**127**	5g.+2g. green	35	1·10
795	-	12g.+3g. violet	35	1·10
796	-	24g.+6g. blue	35	1·10
797	-	1s.+1s. red	9·25	25·00

DESIGNS: 12g. "Healing the sick"; 24g. "St. Elizabeth feeding the hungry"; 1s. "Warming the poor".

128 J. Ressel

1936. Welfare Funds. Austrian Inventors.

798	**128**	12g. (+12g.) brown	3·50	10·00
799	-	24g. (+24g.) violet	3·50	10·00
800	-	30g. (+30g.) red	3·50	10·00
801	-	40g. (+40g.) black	3·50	10·00
802	-	60g. (+60g.) blue	3·50	10·00
803	-	64g. (+64g.) green	3·50	10·00

PORTRAITS: 24g. Karl Ritter von Ghega; 30g. J. Werndl; 40g. Carl Freih. Auer von Welsbach; 60g. R. von Lieben; 64g. V. Kaplan.

129 Mother and Child

1937. Mothers' Day.

804	**129**	24g. red	30	55

130 *Maria Anna*

1937. Centenary of Regular Danube Services of Danube Steam Navigation Co. Paddle-steamers.

805	**130**	12g. red	85	1·10
806	-	24g. blue	85	1·10
807	-	64g. green	85	2·10

DESIGNS: 24g. "Helios"; 64g. "Oesterreich".

131 "Child Welfare"

1937. Winter Relief Fund. Inscr "WINTERHILFE 1937 1938".

808	**131**	5g.+2g. green	20	65
809	-	12g.+3g. brown	20	65
810	-	24g.+6g. blue	20	65
811	-	1s.+1s. red	4·75	18·00

DESIGNS: 12g. "Feeding the Children"; 24g. "Protecting the Aged"; 1s. "Nursing the Sick".

132 Steam Locomotive *Austria*, 1837

1937. Railway Centenary.

812	**132**	12g. brown	20	40
813	-	25g. violet	85	1·60
814	-	35g. red	2·50	3·75

DESIGNS: 25g. Steam locomotive, 1936; 35g. Electric locomotive.

133 Dr. G. Van Swieten

1937. Welfare Funds. Austrian Doctors.

815	**133**	5g. (+5g.) brown	2·75	7·50
816	-	8g. (+8g.) red	2·75	7·50
817	-	12g. (+12g.) brown	2·75	7·50
818	-	20g. (+20g.) green	2·75	7·50
819	-	24g. (+24g.) violet	2·75	7·50
820	-	30g. (+30g.) red	2·75	7·50
821	-	40g. (+40g.) olive	2·75	7·50
822	-	60g. (+60g.) blue	2·75	7·50
823	-	64g. (+64g.) purple	2·75	7·50

DESIGNS: 8g. L. A. von Auenbrugg; 12g. K. von Rokitansky; 20g. J. Skoda; 25g. F. von Hebra; 30g. F. von Arlt; 40g. J. Hyrtl; 60g. T. Billroth; 64g. T. Meynert.

134 Nosegay and Signs of the Zodiac

1937. Christmas Greetings.

824		12g. green	10	30
825	**134**	24g. red	10	30

ALLIED OCCUPATION. Nos. 826/905 were issued in the Russian Zone of occupation and Nos. 906/22 were a joint issue for use in the British, French and American zones.

1945. Hitler portrait stamps of Germany optd. (a) Optd **Osterreich** only.

826	**173**	5pf. green	30	1·40
827	**173**	8pf. red	40	1·10

(b) Optd **Osterreich** and bar.

828	6pf. violet	60	1·60
829	12pf. red	60	1·60

(137)

1945. 1941 and 1944 Hitler stamps of Germany optd as T **137**.

830	**137**	1pf. grey	6·25	13·00
831	**137**	3pf. brown	3·25	11·00
832	**137**	4pf. grey	17·00	38·00
833	**137**	5pf. green	4·25	11·00
834	**137**	6pf. violet	1·60	2·20
835	**137**	8pf. red	1·30	3·25
836	**137**	10pf. brown	4·25	11·00
837	**137**	12pf. red	60	1·10
838	**137**	15pf. red	1·60	5·50
839	**137**	16pf. green	40·00	85·00
840	**137**	20pf. blue	4·25	8·50
841	**137**	24pf. brown	37·00	85·00
842	**173**	25pf. blue	5·25	11·00
843	**173**	30pf. green	5·25	11·00
844	**173**	40pf. mauve	5·75	11·50
845	**225**	42pf. green	8·25	19·00
846	**173**	50pf. green	6·75	13·00
847	**173**	60pf. brown	7·25	16·00
848	**173**	80pf. blue	6·25	15·00
853	**182**	1rm. green	34·00	70·00
850	**182**	2rm. violet	29·00	60·00
855	**182**	3rm. red	60·00	£130
856	**182**	5rm. blue	£425	£900

1945. Stamps of Germany surch **OSTERREICH** and new value.

857	**186**	5pf. on 12+88pf. green	85	2·75
858	-	6pf. on 6+14pf. brown and blue (No. 811)	10·50	24·00
859	**220**	8pf. on 42+108pf. brn	1·40	4·75
860	-	12pf. on 3+7pf. blue (No. 810)	85	2·75

(140)

1945. 1941 and 1944 Hitler stamps of Germany optd as T **140**.

862	**173**	5pf. green	1·60	5·50
863	**173**	6pf. violet	1·00	4·25
864	**173**	8pf. red	85	4·50
865	**173**	12pf. red	1·00	5·50
866	**173**	30pf. green	10·50	27·00
867a	**225**	42pf. green	23·00	44·00

141 New National Arms

142 New National Arms

1945

868	**141**	3pf. brown	20	20
869	**141**	4pf. blue	20	45
870	**141**	5pf. green	20	25
871	**141**	6pf. purple	20	25
872	**141**	8pf. orange	20	25
873	**141**	10pf. brown	20	25
874	**141**	12pf. red	20	25
875	**141**	15pf. orange	20	30
876	**141**	16pf. green	25	65
877	**141**	20pf. blue	20	30
878	**141**	24pf. orange	20	45
879	**141**	25pf. blue	20	35
880	**141**	30pf. green	20	25
881	**141**	38pf. blue	20	35
882	**141**	40pf. purple	20	40
883	**141**	42pf. grey	30	45
884	**141**	50pf. green	20	55
885	**141**	60pf. red	20	55
886	**141**	80pf. violet	20	45
887	**142**	1rm. green	40	1·10
888	**142**	2rm. violet	45	1·20
889	**142**	3rm. purple	50	1·70
890	**142**	5rm. brown	70	2·30

Nos. 877/86 are 24×28 mm.

144 Allegorical of the Home Land

1945. Austrian Welfare Charities.

905	**144**	1s.+10s. green	1·80	3·50

145 Posthorn

1945

906	**145**	1g. blue	20	85
907	**145**	3g. orange	20	30
908	**145**	4g. brown	20	30
909	**145**	5g. green	20	25
910	**145**	6g. purple	20	25
911	**145**	8g. red	20	25
912	**145**	10g. grey	20	25
913	**145**	12g. brown	20	25
914	**145**	15g. red	20	30
915	**145**	20g. brown	20	30
916	**145**	25g. blue	20	30
917	**145**	30g. mauve	20	30
918	**145**	40g. blue	20	30
919	**145**	60g. olive	20	45
920	**145**	1s. violet	40	85
921	**145**	2s. yellow	50	1·70
922	**145**	5s. blue	55	1·80

146 Salzburg

148 Durnstein

1945. Views as T **146/8**.

923	-	3g. blue	20	20
924	-	4g. red	20	20
925	-	5g. red	20	20
926	**146**	6g. green	20	20
927	-	8g. brown	20	20
928	-	8g. purple	20	20
929	-	8g. green	20	20
930	-	10g. green	20	20
931	-	10g. purple	20	20
932	-	12g. brown	20	20
933	-	15g. blue	20	20
934	-	16g. brown	20	20
935	-	20g. blue	20	20
936	-	24g. green	20	20
937	-	25g. grey	20	20
938	-	30g. red	20	20
939	-	30g. blue	50	55
940	-	35g. red	20	20
941	-	38g. green	20	20
942	-	40g. grey	20	20
943	-	42g. red	20	20
944	-	45g. blue	30	55
945	-	50g. blue	20	20
946	-	50g. purple	85	85
947	-	60g. blue	30	30
948	-	60g. violet	3·00	3·75
949	-	70g. blue	35	55
950	-	80g. brown	40	75
951	-	90g. green	1·70	3·25
952A	**148**	1s. brown	1·00	1·60
953A	-	2s. grey	3·50	5·50
954A	-	3s. green	1·20	2·75
955A	-	5s. red	2·10	3·75

DESIGNS—As Type **146**: 3g. Lermoos; 4g. Iron-ore mine, Erzberg; 5g. Leopoldsberg, Vienna; 8g. (927), Prater Woods, Vienna; 8g. (928/9), Town Hall Park, Vienna; 10g. (930/1), Hochosterwitz; 12g. Schafberg; 15g. Forchtenstein; 16g. Gesauseeingang. 23½×29 mm: 20g. Gebhartsberg; 24g. Holdrichsmuhle, near Modling; 25g. Vent im Otztal; 30g. (938/9), Neusiedler Lake; 35g. Belvedere Palace, Vienna; 38g. Langbath Lake; 40g. Mariazell; 42g. Traunstein; 45g. Burg Hartenstein; 50g. (945/6), Silvretta Peaks, Vorarlberg; 60g. (947/8), Semmering; 70g. Badgastein; 80g. Kaisergebirge; 90g. Wayside shrine near Tragoss. As T **148**: 2s. St. Christof; 3s. Heiligenblut; 5s. Schonbrunn Palace, Vienna.

See also Nos. 1072/86a.

1946. 1st Anniv of U.N.O. No. 938 surch **26. JUNI 1945+20 g 26. JUNI 1946** and globe.

971	30g.+20g. red	3·00	6·50

151 Dr. Karl Renner

1946. First Anniv of Establishment of Renner Government.

972	**151**	1s.+1s. green	6·25	11·00
973	**151**	2s.+2s. violet	6·25	11·00
974	**151**	3s.+3s. purple	6·25	11·00
975	**151**	5s.+5s. brown	6·25	11·00

MS976 Four sheets, each 180×155 mm, each with block of 8 of one value (972/5) and Arms in centre. Imperf Set 4 sheets £2500 £17000

152 Dagger and Map

1946. "Anti-Fascist" Exhibition.

977	**152**	5g.+3g. sepia	60	1·30
978	-	6g.+4g. green	40	95
979	-	8g.+6g. orange	40	95
980	-	12g.+12g. blue	40	95
981	-	30g.+30g. violet	40	1·10
982	-	42g.+42g. brown	60	1·10
983	-	1s.+1s. red	50	1·60
984	-	2s.+2s. red	1·20	2·75

DESIGNS: 6g. Broom sweeping Nazi and Fascist emblems; 8g. St. Stephen's Cathedral in flames; 12g. Hand and barbed wire; 30g. Hand strangling snake; 42g. Hammer and broken column; 1s. Hand and Austrian flag; 2s. Eagle and smoking Nazi emblem.

(153)

1946. Congress of Society for Promotion of Cultural and Economic Relations with the Soviet Union. No. 932 optd with T **153**.

985	12g. brown	20	55

154 Mare and Foal

1946. Austria Prize Race Fund.

986	**154**	16g.+16g. red	2·50	5·50
987	-	24g.+24g. violet	2·10	4·25
988	-	60g.+60g. green	2·10	4·25
989	-	1s.+1s. blue	2·10	4·25
990	-	2s.+2s. brown	7·25	11·00

DESIGNS: 24g. Two horses' heads; 60g. Racehorse clearing hurdle; 1s. Three racehorses; 2s. Three horses' heads.

155 Ruprecht's Church, Vienna

1946. 950th Anniv of First recorded use of name "Osterreich".

991	**155**	30g.+70g. red	50	1·10

156 Statue of Duke Rudolf

1946. St. Stephen's Cathedral Reconstruction Fund. Architectural and Sculptural designs.

992	**156**	3g.+12g. brown	20	1·10
993	-	5g.+20g. purple	20	1·10
994	-	6g.+24g. blue	20	1·10
995	-	8g.+32g. green	20	1·10
996	-	10g.+40g. blue	20	1·10
997	-	12g.+48g. violet	50	2·20
998	-	30g.+1s.20 red	1·80	2·20
999	-	50g.+1s.80 blue	2·30	6·50
1000	-	1s.+5s. purple	3·00	8·50
1001	-	2s.+10s. brown	6·25	11·00

DESIGNS: 5g. Tomb of Frederick III; 6g. Pulpit; 8g. Statue of St. Stephen; 10g. Statue of Madonna and Child; 12g. Altar; 30g. Organ; 50g. Anton Pilgram; 1s. N.E. Tower; 2s. S.W. Spire.

157 Franz Grillparzer (dramatic poet)

1947. Famous Austrians.

1002		12g. green	30	55
1003	**157**	18g. purple	30	30
1004	-	20g. green	50	30
1005	-	40g. brown	10·50	6·00
1006	-	40g. green	10·50	11·00
1007	-	60g. lake	50	45

PORTRAITS: 12g. Franz Schubert (composer); 20g. Carl Michael Ziehrer (composer); 40g. (No. 1005), Adalbert Stifter (poet); 40g. (No. 1006), Anton Bruckner (composer); 60g. Friedrich Amerling (painter).

158 Harvesting

1947. Vienna Fair Fund.

1009	**158**	3g.+2g. brown	50	1·10
1010	-	8g.+2g. green	50	1·10
1011	-	10g.+5g. slate	50	1·10
1012	-	12g.+8g. violet	50	1·10
1013	-	18g.+12g. olive	50	1·10
1014	-	30g.+10g. purple	50	1·10
1015	-	35g.+15g. red	50	1·60
1016	-	60g.+20g. blue	50	1·70

DESIGNS: 8g. Logging; 10g. Factory; 12g. Pithead; 18g. Oil wells; 30g. Textile machinery; 35g. Foundry; 60g. Electric cables.

159 Airplane over Hinterstoder

1947. Air.

1017		50g. brown	50	1·10
1018		1s. purple	50	1·10
1019		2s. green	50	2·20
1020	**159**	3s. brown	3·50	7·50
1021	-	4s. green	2·50	7·50
1022	-	5s. blue	2·50	7·50
1023	-	10s. blue	1·30	13·00

DESIGNS—Airplane over: 50g. Windmill at St. Andra; 1s. Heidentor; 2s. Gmund; 4s. Pragraten; 5s. Torsaule; 10s. St. Charles's Church, Vienna.

160 Beaker (15th century)

1947. National Art Exhibition Fund.

1024	**160**	3g.+2g. brown	50	85
1025	-	8g.+2g. green	50	85
1026	-	10g.+5g. red	50	85
1027	-	12g.+8g. violet	50	85
1028	-	18g.+12g. brown	50	85
1029	-	20g.+10g. violet	50	1·10
1030	-	30g.+10g. green	50	1·10
1031	-	35g.+15g. red	50	1·10
1032	-	48g.+12g. purple	1·60	1·40
1033	-	60g.+20g. blue	1·60	1·40

DESIGNS: 8g. Statue of "Providence" (Donner); 10g. Benedictine Monastery, Melk; 12g. "Wife of Dr. Brante of Vienna"; 18g. "Children in a Window" (Waldmuller); 20g. Belvedere Palace Gateway; 30g. Figure of "Egeria" on fountain at Schonbrunn; 35g. National Library, Vienna; 48g. "Copper Printer's (Ernst Rohm) Workshop" (Ferdinand Schmutzer); 60g. "Girl in Straw Hat" (Amerling).

161 Racehorse

1947. Vienna Prize Race Fund.

1034	**161**	60+20g. blue on pink	30	1·40

163 Prisoner-of-war

1947. Prisoners-of-war Relief Fund.

1063	**163**	8g.+2g. green	30	85
1064	-	12g.+8g. brown	30	85
1065	-	18g.+12g. black	30	85
1066	-	35g.+15g. purple	30	85
1067	-	60g.+20g. blue	30	85
1068	-	1s.+40g. brown	30	1·60

DESIGNS: 12g. Letter from home; 18g. Gruesome camp visitor; 35g. Soldier and family reunited; 60g. Industry beckons returned soldier; 1s. Soldier sowing.

1947. Nos. 934 and 941 surch.

1069	75g. on 38g. green	50	1·60
1070	1s.40 on 16g. brown	30	55

165 Globe and Tape Machine

1947. Telegraph Centenary.

1071	**165**	40g. violet	40	65

1947. Currency Revaluation. (a) As T **146**.

1072	3g. red (Lermoos)	40	20
1073	5g. red (Leopoldsberg)	40	20
1074	10g. red (Hochosterwitz)	40	20
1075	15g. red (Forchtenstein)	2·50	2·40

(b) As T **146** but larger (23½×29 mm).

1076	20g. red (Gebhartsberg)	50	20
1077	30g. red (Neusiedler Lake)	60	30
1078	40g. red (Mariazell)	1·00	20
1079	50g. red (Silvretta Peaks)	1·00	20
1080	60g. red (Semmering)	12·50	2·75
1081	70g. red (Badgastein)	5·25	20
1082	80g. red (Kaisergebirge)	5·25	55

1083		90g. red (Wayside shrine, Tragoss)	6·25	1·40

(c) As T **148**.

1084		1s. violet (Durnstein)	1·30	30
1085		2s. violet (St. Christof)	1·60	55
1086		3s. violet (Heiligenblut)	31·00	2·20
1086a		5s. violet (Schonbrunn)	31·00	2·75

Nos. 1072/86a in new currency replaced previous issue at rate of 3s. (old) = 1s. (new).

166 Sacred Olympic Flame

1948. Fund for Entries to 5th Winter Olympic Games, St. Moritz.

1087	**166**	1s.+50g. blue	50	85

167 Laabenbach Viaduct, Neulenbach

1948. Reconstruction Fund.

1088	**167**	10g.+5g. grey	20	30
1089	-	20g.+10g. violet	20	30
1090	-	30g.+10g. green	50	65
1091	-	40g.+20g. green	20	30
1092	-	45g.+20g. blue	20	30
1093	-	60g.+30g. red	20	30
1094	-	75g.+35g. purple	30	45
1095	-	80g.+40g. purple	30	45
1096	-	1s.+50g. blue	30	45
1097	-	1s.40+70g. lake	60	75

DESIGNS (showing reconstruction): 20g. Vermunt Lake Dam; 30g. Danube Port, Vienna; 40g. Erzberg open-cast mine; 45g. Southern Railway Station, Vienna; 60g. Flats; 75g. Vienna Gas Works; 80g. Oil refinery; 1s. Mountain roadway; 1s.40, Parliament Building.

169 Violets

1948. Anti-tuberculosis Fund.

1098	**169**	10g.+5g. violet, mauve and green	35	35
1099	-	20g.+10g. green, light green and yellow	35	35
1100	-	30g.+10g. brown, yellow and green	4·50	4·50
1101	-	40g.+20g. green, yellow and orange	85	85
1102	-	45g.+20g. purple, mauve and yellow	30	30
1103	-	60g.+30g. red, mauve and green	30	30
1104	-	75g.+35g. green, pink and yellow	30	30
1105	-	80g.+40g. blue, pink and green	40	40
1106	-	1s.+50g. blue, ultramarine and green	40	40
1107	-	1s.40+70g. green, blue and yellow	2·75	2·75

FLOWERS: 20g. Anemone; 30g. Crocus; 40g. Primrose; 45g. Pasque flower; 60g. Rhododendron; 75g. Wild rose; 80g. Cyclamen; 1s. Gentian; 1s.40, Edelweiss.

170 Vorarlberg Montafon

1948. Provincial Costumes.

1108		3g. grey	85	1·10
1109		5g. green	30	20
1110		10g. blue	30	20
1111		15g. brown	50	20
1112	**170**	20g. green	30	20
1113	-	25g. brown	30	20
1114	-	30g. red	3·50	20
1115	-	30g. violet	1·00	20
1116	-	40g. violet	4·25	20
1117	-	40g. green	85	20
1118	-	45g. blue	4·25	75
1119	-	50g. brown	1·20	20
1120	-	60g. red	85	20
1121	-	70g. green	85	20
1122	-	75g. blue	7·25	75
1123	-	80g. rose	1·00	20
1124	-	90g. purple	55·00	55
1125	-	1s. blue	16·00	20
1126	-	1s. red	£130	20
1127	-	1s. green	70	20
1128	-	1s.20 violet	1·00	20
1129	-	1s.40 brown	3·00	30
1130	-	1s.45 red	2·50	20
1131	-	1s.50 blue	2·10	20
1132	-	1s.60 red	85	20
1133	-	1s.70 blue	4·25	1·30
1134	-	2s. green	1·60	20
1135	-	2s.20 slate	8·25	30
1136	-	2s.40 blue	2·10	25
1137	-	2s.50 brown	5·75	2·20
1138	-	2s.70 brown	1·00	1·40
1139	-	3s. lake	4·25	20
1140	-	3s.50 green	34·00	30
1141	-	4s.50 purple	1·00	1·30
1142	-	5s. purple	1·60	20
1143	-	7s. olive	6·25	2·20
1144	-	10s. grey	50·00	7·50

DESIGNS—As T **170**: 3g. "Tirol Inntal"; 5g. "Salzburg Pinzgau"; 10, 75g. "Steiermark Salzkammergut" (different designs); 15g. "Burgenland Lutzmannsburg"; 25g., 1s.60, "Wien 1850" (two different designs); 30g. (2) "Salzburg Pongau"; 40g. (2) "Wien 1840"; 45g. "Karnten Lesachtal"; 50g. "Vorarlberg Bregenzerwald"; 60g. "Karnten Lavanttal"; 70g. "Niederosterreich Wachau"; 80g. "Steiermark Ennstal"; 90g. "Steiermark Mittelsteier"; 1s. (3) "Tirol Pustertal"; 1s.20, "Niederosterreich Wienerwald"; 1s.40, "Oberosterreich Innviertel"; 1s.45, "Wilter bei Innsbruck"; 1s.50, "Wien 1853"; 1s.70, "Ost Tirol Kals"; 2s. "Oberosterreich"; 2s.20, "Ischl 1820"; 2s.40, "Kitzbuhel"; 2s.50, "Obersteiermark 1850"; 2s.70, "Kleines Walsertal"; 3s. "Burgenland"; 3s.50, "Niederosterreich 1850"; 4s.50, "Gailtal"; 5s. "Zillertal"; 7s. "Steiermark Sulmtal". 25×35 mm: 10s. "Wien 1850".

172 Kunstlerhaus

173 Hans Makart

1948. 80th Anniv of Creative Artists' Association.

1145	**172**	20g.+10g. green	10·50	8·50
1146	**173**	30g.+15g. brown	3·50	4·25
1147	-	40g.+20g. blue	3·50	4·25
1148	-	50g.+25g. violet	6·25	7·50
1149	-	60g.+30g. red	7·25	6·50
1150	-	1s.+50g. blue	7·25	8·50
1151	-	1s.40+70g. brown	21·00	26·00

PORTRAITS: 40g. K. Kundmann; 50g. A. von Siccardsburg; 60g. H. Canon; 1s. W. Unger; 1s.40, Friedr. Schmidt.

174 St. Rupert

1948. Salzburg Cathedral Reconstruction Fund.

1152	**174**	20g.+10g. green	10·50	11·00
1153	-	30g.+15g. brown	3·00	4·25
1154	-	40g.+20g. green	3·50	4·25
1155	-	50g.+25g. brown	1·00	1·10
1156	-	60g.+30g. red	1·00	1·10
1157	-	80g.+40g. purple	1·00	1·10
1158	-	1s.+50g. blue	1·00	1·60
1159	-	1s.40+70g. green	3·00	4·25

DESIGNS: 30, 40, 50, 80g. Views of Salzburg Cathedral; 60g. St. Peter's; 1s. Cathedral and Fortress; 1s.40, Madonna.

175 Pres. Renner

1948. 30th Anniv of Republic.

1160	**175**	1s. blue	3·00	2·75

See also Nos. 1224 and 1333.

176 F. Gruber and J. Mohr

1948. 130th Anniv of Composition of Carol *Silent Night, Holy Night*.

1161	**176**	60g. brown	8·50	8·50

177 Boy and Hare

1949. Child Welfare Fund.

1162	**177**	40g.+10g. purple	22·00	24·00
1163	-	60g.+20g. red	22·00	24·00
1164	-	1s.+25g. blue	22·00	24·00
1165	-	1s.40+35g. green	25·00	27·00

DESIGNS: 60g. Two girls and apples in boot; 1s. Boy and birthday cake; 1s.40, Girl praying before candle.

178 Boy and Dove

1949. U.N. Int. Children's Emergency Fund.

1166	**178**	1s. blue	16·00	4·25

179 Johann Strauss

1949. 50th Death Anniv of Johann Strauss the Younger (composer).

1167	**179**	1s. blue	4·25	3·00

See also Nos. 1174, 1207 and 1229.

180 Esperanto Star

1949. Esperanto Congress, Vienna.

1168	**180**	20g. green	1·40	1·40

181 St. Gebhard

1949. Birth Millenary of St. Gebhard (Bishop of Vorarlberg).

1169	**181**	30g. violet	2·50	2·50

182 Seal of Duke Friedrich II, 1230

1949. Prisoners-of-war Relief Fund. Arms.

1170	**182**	40g.+10g. yell & brn	14·00	13·00
1171	-	60g.+15g. pink & pur	12·00	11·00
1172	-	1s.+25g. red & blue	12·00	11·00
1173	-	1s.60+40g. pink and green	16·00	16·00

ARMS: 60g. Princes of Austria, 1450; 1s. Austria, 1600; 1s.60, Austria, 1945.

1949. Death Centenary of Johann Strauss the Elder (composer). Portrait as T **179**.

1174		30g. purple	2·20	2·75

183 Allegory of U.P.U.

1949. 75th Anniv of U.P.U.

1175	**183**	40g. green	5·50	5·50
1176	-	60g. red	6·50	5·50
1177	-	1s. blue	11·00	9·75

DESIGNS: 60g. Children holding "75"; 1s. Woman's head.

185 Magnifying Glass and Covers

1949. Stamp Day.

1206	**185**	60g.+15g. brown	4·25	3·75

1949. 50th Death Anniv of Karl Millocker (composer). Portrait as T **179**.

1207		1s. blue	22·00	17·00

186 M. M. Daffinger

1950. 160th Birth Anniv of Moritz Michael Daffinger (painter).

1208	**186**	60g. brown	11·00	8·50

187 A. Hofer

1950. 140th Death Anniv of Andreas Hofer (patriot).

1209	**187**	60g. violet	17·00	13·00

See also Nos. 1211, 1223, 1232, 1234, 1243, 1253, 1288 and 1386.

188 Stamp of 1850

1950. Austrian Stamp Centenary.

1210	**188**	1s. black on yellow	2·75	2·20

1950. Death Centenary of Josef Madersperger (sewing machine inventor). Portrait as T **187**.

1211		60g. violet	9·75	5·50

189 Arms of Austria and Carinthia

1950. 30th Anniv of Carinthian Plebiscite.

1212	**189**	60g.+15g. grn & brn	43·00	38·00
1213	-	1s.+25g. red & orange	55·00	43·00
1214	-	1s.70+40g. blue and turquoise	55·00	49·00

DESIGNS: 1s. Carinthian waving Austrian flag; 1s.70, Hand and ballot box.

190 Rooks

1950. Air.

1215	**190**	60g. violet	6·50	5·50
1216	-	1s. violet (Barn swallows)	32·00	30·00
1217	-	2s. blue (Black-headed gulls)	22·00	11·00
1218	-	3s. turquoise (Great cormorants)	£190	£160
1219	-	5s. brown (Common buzzard)	£190	£160
1220	-	10s. purple (Grey heron)	85·00	75·00
1221	-	20s. sepia (Golden eagle)	16·00	4·25

191 Philatelist

1950. Stamp Day.

1222	**191**	60g.+15g. green	13·00	11·00

1950. Birth Centenary of Alexander Girardi (actor). Portrait as T **187**.

1223	30g. blue	2·40	1·90

192 Dr. Renner

1951. Death of Pres. Karl Renner.

1224	**192**	1s. black on lemon	1·90	85

193 Miner

1951. Reconstruction Fund.

1225	**193**	40g.+10g. purple	22·00	24·00
1226	-	60g.+15g. green	22·00	24·00
1227	-	1s.+25g. brown	22·00	24·00
1228	-	1s.70+40g. blue	22·00	24·00

DESIGNS: 60g. Bricklayer; 1s. Bridge-builder; 1s.70, Telegraph engineer.

1951. 150th Birth Anniv of Joseph Lanner (composer). Portrait as T **179**.

1229	60g. green	7·00	3·75

194 Martin Johann Schmidt

1951. 150th Death Anniv of Schmidt (painter).

1230	**194**	1s. red	10·00	4·75

195 Scout Badge

1951. Boy Scout Jamboree.

1231	**195**	1s. red, yellow & green	7·00	6·50

1951. Tenth Death Anniv of Wilhelm Kienzl (composer). Portrait as T **187**.

1232	1s.50 blue	4·75	3·25

196 Laurel Branch and Olympic Emblem

1952. Sixth Winter Olympic Games, Oslo.

1233	**196**	2s.40+60g. green	32·00	30·00

1952. 150th Birth Anniv of Karl Ritter von Ghega (railway engineer). Portrait as T 187.

1234	1s. green	11·00	3·25

197 Schrammel

1952. Birth Cent of Josef Schrammel (composer).

1235	**197**	1s.50 blue	11·00	3·25

See also No. 1239.

198 Cupid and Letter

1952. Stamp Day.

1236	**198**	1s.50+35g. purple	32·00	31·00

199 Breakfast Pavilion

1952. Bicentenary of Schonbrunn Menagerie.

1237	**199**	1s.50 green	9·75	3·25

200

1952. Int Union of Socialist Youth Camp, Vienna.

1238	**200**	1s.50 blue	11·00	2·20

1952. 150th Birth Anniv of Nikolaus Lenau (writer). Portrait as T 197.

1239	1s. green	11·00	3·25

202

1952. International Children's Correspondence.

1240	**202**	2s.40 blue	18·00	4·25

203 *Christus Pantocrator* (sculpture)

1952. Austrian Catholics' Day.

1241	**203**	1s.+25g. olive	16·00	15·00

204 Hugo Wolf

1953. 50th Death Anniv of Wolf (composer).

1242	**204**	1s.50 blue	12·00	3·25

1953. President Korner's 80th Birthday. As T **187** but portrait of Korner.

1243	1s.50 blue	12·00	3·25

For 1s.50 black, see No. 1288.

1953. 60th Anniv of Austrian Trade Union Movement. As No. 955 (colour changed) surch **GEWERKSCHAFTS BEWEGUNG 60 JAHRE 1s+25g**.

1244	1s.+25g. on 5s. blue	4·75	4·25

206 Linz National Theatre

1953. 150th Anniv of Linz National Theatre.

1245	**206**	1s.50 turquoise	27·00	4·25

207 Meeting-house, Steyr

1953. Vienna Evangelical School Rebuilding Fund.

1246	**207**	70g.+15g. purple	45	45
1247	-	1s.+25g. blue	45	45
1248	-	1s.50+40g. brown	1·10	1·10
1249	-	2s.40+60g. green	4·75	4·75
1250	-	3s.+75g. lilac	12·00	12·00

DESIGNS: 1s. J. Kepler (astronomer); 1s.50, Lutheran Bible, 1534; 2s.40, T. von Hansen (architect); 3s. School after reconstruction.

208 Child and Christmas Tree

1953. Christmas.

1251	**208**	1s. green	1·80	1·10

See also No. 1266.

209

1953. Stamp Day.

1252	**209**	1s.+25g. brown	12·00	11·00

1954. 150th Birth Anniv of M. Von Schwind (painter). As T **187** but portrait of Von Schwind.

1253	1s.50 lilac	23·00	4·25

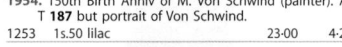

210 Baron K. von Rokitansky

1954. 150th Birth Anniv of Von Rokitansky (anatomist).

1254	**210**	1s.50 violet	26·00	4·25

See also No. 1264.

1954. Avalanche Fund. As No. 953 (colour changed) surch **LAWINENOPFER 1954 1s+20g**.

1255	1s.+20g. blue	55	55

212 Surgeon with Microscope

1954. Health Service Fund.

1256	-	30g.+10g. violet	1·60	1·60
1257	**212**	70g.+15g. brown	55	55
1258	-	1s.+25g. blue	55	55
1259	-	1s.45+35g. green	85	1·10
1260	-	1s.50+35g. red	7·75	11·00
1261	-	2s.40+60g. purple	9·25	12·00

DESIGNS: 30g. Boy patient and sun-ray lamp; 1s. Mother and children; 1s.45, Operating theatre; 1s.50, Baby on scales; 2s.40, Red Cross nurse and ambulance.

213 Esperanto Star

1954. 50th Anniv of Esperanto in Austria.

1262	**213**	1s. green and brown	7·50	75

214 J. M. Rottmayr von Rosenbrunn

1954. Birth Tercentenary of Rottmayr von Rosenbrunn (painter).

1263	**214**	1s. green	19·00	4·75

1954. 25th Death Anniv of Dr. Auer von Welsbach (inventor). Portrait as T **210**.

1264	1s.50 blue	55·00	4·25

216 Great Organ, Church of St. Florian

1954. Second International Congress of Catholic Church Music, Vienna.

1265	**216**	1s. brown	3·50	65

1954. Christmas. As No. 1251, but colour changed.

1266	**208**	1s. blue	6·00	1·10

217 18th-century River Boat

1954. Stamp Day.

1267	**217**	1s.+25g. green	11·00	9·75

218 Arms of Austria and Newspapers

1954. 150th Anniv of State Printing Works and 250th Anniv of *Wiener-Zeitung* (newspaper).

1268	**218**	1s. black and red	4·25	85

219 "Freedom"

1955. Tenth Anniv of Re-establishment of Austrian Republic.

1269	-	70g. purple	3·25	55
1270	-	1s. blue	8·50	55
1271	**219**	1s.45 red	14·00	7·00
1272	-	1s.50 brown	36·00	60
1273	-	2s.40 green	14·00	9·75

DESIGNS: 70g. Parliament Buildings; 1s. Western Railway terminus, Vienna; 1s.50, Modern houses; 2s.40, Limberg Dam.

1955. Austrian State Treaty. As No. 888, but colour changed, optd **STAATSVERTRAG 1955**.

1274	**142**	2s. grey	4·25	1·10

221 "Strength through Unity"

1955. Fourth World Trade Unions Congress, Vienna.

1275	**221**	1s. blue	4·25	3·75

222 "Return to Work"

1955. Returned Prisoners-of-war Relief Fund.

1276	**222**	1s.+25g. brown	3·75	3·25

223 Burgtheater, Vienna

1955. Re-opening of Burgtheater and State Opera House, Vienna.

1277	**223**	1s.50 brown	6·00	85
1278	-	2s.40 blue (Opera House)	8·00	4·50

224 Globe and Flags

1955. Tenth Anniv of U.N.O.

1279	**224**	2s.40 green	24·00	5·50

225 Stamp Collector

1955. Stamp Day.

1280	**225**	1s.+25g. brown	6·50	6·00

226 Mozart

1956. Birth Bicentenary of Mozart (composer).

1281	**226**	2s.40 blue	9·75	2·75

227

1956. Admission of Austria into U.N.

1282	**227**	2s.40 brown	19·00	3·75

228

1956. Fifth World Power Conference, Vienna.

1283	**228**	2s.40 blue	17·00	4·25

229 Vienna and Five New Towns

1956. 23rd International Town Planning Congress.

1284	**229**	1s.45 red, black & green	5·50	1·70

230 J. B. Fischer von Erlach

1956. Birth Tercentenary of Fischer von Erlach (architect).

1285	**230**	1s.50 brown	1·80	1·80

231 "Stamp Day"

1956. Stamp Day.

1286	**231**	1s.+25g. red	5·50	5·50

1956. Hungarian Relief Fund. As No. 1173, but colours changed, surch **1956 1.50 +50 UNGARNHILFE**.

1287	1s.50+50g. on 1s.60+40g. red and grey	1·10	1·10

1957. Death of Pres. Korner. As No. 1243, but colour changed.

1288	1s.50 black	3·25	2·75

233 J. Wagner von Jauregg

1957. Birth Centenary of Wagner von Jauregg (psychiatrist).

1289	**233**	2s.40 brown	6·50	4·25

234 Anton Wildgans

1957. 25th Death Anniv of Anton Wildgans (poet).

1290	**234**	1s. blue	85	75

235 Daimber (1907), Graf and Stift (1957) Post Buses

1957. 50th Anniv of Postal Coach Service.

1291	**235**	1s. black on yellow	85	75

237 Mt. Gasherbrum II

1957. Austrian Himalaya–Karakorum Expedition, 1956.

1293	**237**	1s.50 blue	75	75

236 Mariazell Basilica

1957. Buildings. (a) Size 20½×24½ mm.

1295	-	20g. purple	55	20
1296	-	30g. green	65	20
1297	-	40g. red	45	20
1298	-	50g. grey	45	20
1299	-	60g. brown	45	20
1300	-	70g. blue	90	20
1301	-	80g. brown	70	20
1302	**236**	1s. brown	1·90	30
1303	-	1s. brown	1·20	20
1304	-	1s.20 purple	1·30	45
1305	-	1s.30 green	30	20
1306	-	1s.40 blue	1·10	30
1307	-	1s.50 red	1·30	20
1308	-	1s.80 blue	1·40	20
1309	-	2s. blue	6·50	30
1310	-	2s. blue	2·20	60
1311	-	2s.20 green	1·40	20
1312	-	2s.50 violet	3·00	1·10
1313	-	3s. blue	1·60	20
1314	-	3s.40 green	2·30	1·10
1315	-	3s.50 mauve	2·40	65
1316	-	4s. violet	2·50	55
1317	-	4s.50 green	3·25	85
1318	-	5s.50 green	2·40	1·20
1319	-	6s. violet	2·50	50
1320	-	6s.40 blue	4·00	1·10
1321	-	8s. purple	5·50	1·10

(b) Larger.

1322	10s. green	5·50	55
1323	20s. purple	6·50	1·70

(c) Smaller, size 17½×21 mm.

1324	-	50g. grey	45	30
1325	**236**	1s. brown	45	30
1326	-	1s.50 purple	55	30

DESIGNS: 20g. Old Courtyard, Morbisch; 30g. Vienna Town Hall; 40g. Porcia Castle, Spittal; 50g. Heiligenstadt flats; 60g. Lederer Tower, Wels; 70g. Archbishop's Palace, Salzburg; 80g. Old farmhouse, Pinzgau; 1s. (1303) Millstatt; 1s.20, Corn Measurer's House, Bruck-on-the-Mur; 1s.30, Schattenburg Castle; 1s.40, Klagenfurt Town Hall; 1s.50, "Rabenhof" Flats, Erdberg, Vienna; 1s.80, Mint Tower, Hall-in-Tyrol; 2s. (1309) Christkindl Church; 2s. (1310) Dragon Fountain, Klagenfurt; 2s.20, Beethoven's House, Heiligenstadt, Vienna; 2s.50, Danube Bridge, Linz; 3s. "Swiss Portal", Imperial Palace, Vienna; 3s.40, Stein Gate, Krems-on-the-Danube; 3s.50, Esterhazy Palace, Eisenstadt; 4s. Vienna Gate, Hainburg; 4s.50, Schwechat Airport; 5s.50, Chur Gate, Feldkirch; 6s. Graz Town Hall; 6s.40, "Golden Roof", Innsbruck; 8s. Steyr Town Hall. 22×28½ mm: 10s. Heidenreichstein Castle. 28½×37½ mm: 20s. Melk Abbey.

238 Post Office, Linz

1957. Stamp Day.

1327	**238**	1s.+25g. green	4·75	4·25

239 Badgastein

1958. International Alpine Ski Championships, Badgastein.

1328	**239**	1s.50 blue	65	55

240 Vickers Viscount 800 OE-LAB

1958. Austrian Airlines Inaugural Flight, Vienna–London.

1329	**240**	4s. red	1·60	85

241 Mother and Child

1958. Mothers' Day.

1330	**241**	1s.50 blue	65	55

242 Walther von der Vogelweide (after 12th-century manuscript)

1958. Third Austrian Choir Festival, Vienna.

1331	**242**	1s.50 multicoloured	65	55

243 Dr. O. Redlich

1958. Birth Cent of Dr. Oswald Redlich (historian).

1332	**243**	2s.40 blue	95	65

1958. 40th Anniv of Republic. As T **175** but inscr "40 JAHRE".

1333	**175**	1s.50 green	1·10	95

244 Post Office, Kitzbuhel

1958. Stamp Day.

1334	**244**	2s.40+60g. blue	1·60	1·40

245 "E" building on Map of Europe

1959. Europa.

1335	**245**	2s.40 green	3·75	75

246 Monopoly Emblem and Cigars

1959. 175th Anniv of Austrian Tobacco Monopoly.

1336	**246**	2s.40 brown	95	55

247 Archduke Johann

1959. Death Cent of Archduke Johann of Austria.

1337	**247**	1s.50 green	65	45

248 Western Capercailie

1959. International Hunting Congress, Vienna.

1338	**248**	1s. purple	55	30
1339	-	1s.50 blue (Roebuck)	85	20
1340	-	2s.40 grn (Wild boar)	1·40	1·50
1341	-	3s.50 brown (Red deer family)	95	65

249 Haydn

1959. 150th Death Anniv of Haydn.

1342	**249**	1s.50 purple	85	55

250 Tyrolean Eagle

1959. 150th Anniv of Tyrolese Rising.

1343	**250**	1s.50 red	65	40

251 Microwave Transmitting Aerial, Zugspitze

1959. Inaug of Austrian Microwave Network.

1344	**251**	2s.40 blue	85	55

252 Handball Player

1959. Sports.

1345	-	1s. violet	65	30
1346	**252**	1s.50 green	95	65
1347	-	1s.80 red	65	55
1348	-	2s. purple	55	45
1349	-	2s.20 blue	65	55

DESIGNS: 1s. Runner; 1s.80, Gymnast; 2s. Hurdling; 2s.20, Hammer thrower.

253 Orchestral Instruments

1959. Vienna Philharmonic Orchestra's World Tour.

1350	**253**	2s.40 black and blue	85	60

254 Roman Coach

1959. Stamp Day.

1351	**254**	2s.40+60g. blk & mve	1·30	1·20

255 Refugees

1960. World Refugee Year.

1352	**255**	3s. turquoise	95	70

256 Pres. Adolf Scharf

1960. President's 70th Birthday.

1353	**256**	1s.50 green	95	50

257 Youth Hostellers

1960. Youth Hostels Movement.

1354	**257**	1s. red	55	50

258 Dr. Eiselsberg

1960. Birth Cent of Dr. Anton Eiselsberg (surgeon).

1355	**258**	1s.50 sepia and cream	1·10	50

259 Gustav Mahler

1960. Birth Centenary of Gustav Mahler (composer).

1356	**259**	1s.50 brown	1·10	50

260 Jakob Prandtauer

1960. 300th Birth Anniv of Jakob Prandtauer (architect).

1357	**260**	1s.50 brown	1·10	50

261 Grossglockner Highway

1960. 25th Anniv of Grossglockner Alpine Highway.

1358	**261**	1s.80 blue	2·20	90

262 Ionic Capital

1960. Europa.

1359	**262**	3s. black	2·75	2·30

263 Griffen, Carinthia

1960. 40th Anniv of Carinthian Plebiscite.

1360	**263**	1s.50 green	85	50

264 Examining Proof of Engraved Stamp

1960. Stamp Day.

1361	**264**	3s.+70g. brown	2·20	2·00

265 "Freedom"

1961. Austrian Freedom Martyrs' Commem.

1362	**265**	1s.50 red	95	60

266 Hansa Brandenburg C-1

1961. "LUPOSTA" Exhibition, Vienna, and First Austrian Airmail Service Commemoration.

1363	**266**	5s. blue	1·60	1·50

267 Transport and Multi-unit Electric Train

1961. European Transport Ministers' Meeting.

1364	**267**	3s. olive and red	1·10	1·00

268 *Mower in the Alps* (Detail, A. Egger-Lienz)

1961. Centenary of Kunstlerhaus, Vienna. Inscr as in T **268**.

1365	**268**	1s. purple and brown	55	30
1366	-	1s.50 lilac and brown	55	30
1367	-	3s. green and brown	1·60	1·20
1368	-	5s. violet and brown	1·60	1·20

PAINTINGS: 1s.50, *The Kiss* (after A. von Pettenkofen). 3s. *Portrait of a Girl* (after A. Romako). 5s. *The Triumph of Ariadne* (detail of Ariadne, after Hans Makart).

269 Observatory on Sonnblick Mountain

1961. 75th Anniv of Sonnblick Meteorological Observatory.

1369	**269**	1s.80 blue	85	60

270 Lavanttaler Colliery

1961. 15th Anniv of Nationalized Industries. Inscr "JAHRE VERSTAATLICHTE UNTERNEHMUNGEN".

1370	**270**	1s. black	30	25
1371	-	1s.50 green	30	25
1372	-	1s.80 red	95	90
1373	-	3s. mauve	1·30	1·20
1374	-	5s. blue	1·60	1·40

DESIGNS: 1s.50, Turbine; 1s.80, Industrial plant; 3s. Steelworks, Linz; 5s. Oil refinery, Schwechat.

271 Mercury

1961. World Bank Congress, Vienna.

1375	**271**	3s. black	95	90

272 Arms of Burgenland

1961. 40th Anniv of Burgenland.

1376	**272**	1s.50 red, yellow & sepia	65	60

273 Liszt

1961. 150th Birth Anniv of Franz Liszt (composer).

1377	**273**	3s. brown	85	60

274 Rust Post Office

1961. Stamp Day.

1378	**274**	3s.+70g. green	2·00	2·00

275 Court of Accounts

1961. Bicentenary of Court of Accounts.

1379	**275**	1s. sepia	55	50

276 Glockner-Kaprun Power Station

1962. 15th Anniv of Electric Power Nationalization. Inscr as in T **276**.

1380	**276**	1s. blue	20	25
1381	-	1s.50 purple	45	40
1382	-	1s.80 green	1·20	1·10
1383	-	3s. brown	85	80
1384	-	4s. red	95	90
1385	-	6s.40 black	2·75	2·50

DESIGNS: 1s.50, Ybbs-Persenbeug (Danube); 1s.80, Luner See; 3s. Grossraming (Enns River); 4s. Bisamberg Transformer Station; 6s.40, St. Andra Power Stations.

1962. Death Cent of Johann Nestroy (playwright). Portrait as T **187**.

1386		1s. violet	65	60

277 F. Gauermann

1962. Death Cent of Friedrich Gauermann (painter).

1387	**277**	1s.50 blue	65	60

278 Scout Badge and Handclasp

1962. 50th Anniv of Austrian Scout Movement.

1388	**278**	1s.50 green	85	80

279 Forest and Lake

1962. "The Austrian Forest".

1389	**279**	1s. grey	75	70
1390	-	1s.50 brown	85	80
1391	-	3s. myrtle	2·75	2·50

DESIGNS: 1s.50, Deciduous forest; 3s. Fir and larch forest.

280 Electric Locomotive and Steam Locomotive *Austria* (1837)

1962. 125th Anniv of Austrian Railways.

1392	**280**	3s. black and buff	2·20	1·50

281 Engraving Die

1962. Stamp Day.

1393	**281**	3s.+70g. violet	2·75	2·50

282 Postal Officials of 1863

1963. Centenary of Paris Postal Conference.

1394	**282**	3s. sepia and yellow	1·30	90

283 Hermann Bahr

1963. Birth Centenary of Hermann Bahr (writer).

1395	**283**	1s.50 sepia and blue	85	40

284 St. Florian (statue)

1963. Cent of Austrian Voluntary Fire Brigade.

1396	**284**	1s.50 black and pink	85	50

285 Flag and Emblem

1963. Fifth Austrian Trade Unions Federation Congress.

1397	**285**	1s.50 red, sepia & grey	65	40

286 Crests of Tyrol and Austria

1963. 600th Anniv of Tyrol as an Austrian Province.

1398	**286**	1s.50 multicoloured	65	40

287 Prince Eugene of Savoy

1963. Birth Tercent of Prince Eugene of Savoy.

1399	**287**	1s.50 violet	65	40

288 Centenary Emblem

1963. Centenary of Red Cross.

1400	**288**	3s. silver, red and black	95	80

289 Skiing (slalom)

1963. Winter Olympic Games, Innsbruck, 1964. Centres black; inscr gold; background colours given.

1401	**289**	1s. grey	30	20
1402	-	1s.20 blue	45	30
1403	-	1s.50 grey	55	40
1404	-	1s.80 purple	65	60
1405	-	2s.20 green	1·10	1·00
1406	-	3s. slate	75	60
1407	-	4s. blue	1·30	1·20

DESIGNS: 1s.20, Skiing (biathlon); 1s.50, Ski jumping; 1s.80, Figure skating; 2s.20, Ice hockey; 3s. Tobogganing; 4s. Bobsleighing.

290 Vienna "101" P.O. and Railway Shed

1963. Stamp Day.

1408	**290**	3s.+70g. black & drab	1·10	1·00

291 *The Holy Family* (Josef Stammel)

1963. Christmas.

1409	**291**	2s. green	65	40

292 Nasturtium

1964. Int Horticultural Exn, Vienna. Multicoloured.

1410		1s. Type **292**	30	20
1411		1s.50 Peony	40	25
1412		1s.80 Clematis	45	40
1413		2s.20 Dahlia	95	90
1414		3s. Convolvulus	1·10	1·00
1415		4s. Mallow	1·60	1·50

293 Gothic Statue and Stained-glass Window

1964. Romanesque Art Exhibition, Vienna.

1416	**293**	1s.50 blue and black	65	60

294 Pallas Athene and Interior of Assembly Hall, Parliament Building

1964. Second Parliamentary and Scientific Conference, Vienna.

1417	**294**	1s.80 black and green	55	50

295 *The Kiss* (Gustav Klimt)

1964. Re-opening of "Viennese Secession" Exn Hall.

1418	**295**	3s. multicoloured	95	90

296 "Comforting the Sick"

1964. 350th Anniv of Order of Brothers of Mercy in Austria.

1419	**296**	1s.50 blue	75	70

297 *Bringing News of the Victory at Kunersdorf* (Bellotto)

1964. 15th U.P.U. Congress, Vienna. Paintings.

1420	**297**	1s. purple	20	15
1421	-	1s.20 brown	45	30
1422	-	1s.50 blue	30	25
1423	-	1s.80 violet	65	60
1424	-	2s.20 black	85	80
1425	-	3s. purple	55	50
1426	-	4s. green	1·10	1·00
1427	-	6s.40 purple	3·50	3·25

PAINTINGS: 1s.20, *Changing Horses"* (Hormann); 1s.50, *The Wedding Trip* (Schwind); 1s.80, *Postboys returning Home* (Raffalt); 2s.20, *The Vienna Mail Coach* (Klein); 3s. *Changing Horses* (Gauermann); 4s. *Postal Tracked-vehicle in Mountain Village* (Pilch); 6s.40, *Saalbach Post Office and Post-bus* (Pilch).

298 Vienna, from the Hochhaus (N.)

1964. "WIPA" Stamp Exhibition, Vienna (1965) (1st issue). Multicoloured.

1428	1s.50+30g. Type **298**	65	65
1429	1s.50+30g. N.E.	65	65
1430	1s.50+30g. E.	65	65
1431	1s.50+30g. S.E.	65	65
1432	1s.50+30g. S.	65	65
1433	1s.50+30g. S.W.	65	65
1434	1s.50+30g. W.	65	65
1435	1s.50+30g. N.W.	65	65

The designs show a panoramic view of Vienna, looking to different points of compass (indicated on stamps). The inscription reads "Vienna welcomes you to WIPA 1965".

See also Nos. 1447/52.

299 "Workers"

1964. Centenary of Austrian Workers' Movement.

1436	**299**	1s. black	55	45

300 Europa "Flower"

1964. Europa.

1437	**300**	3s. blue	2·40	85

301 Radio Receiver Dial

1964. 40th Anniv of Austrian Broadcasting Service.

1438	**301**	1s. sepia and red	55	45

302 Old Printing Press

1964. Sixth International Graphical Federation Congress, Vienna.

1439	**302**	1s.50 black and drab	55	45

303 Post-bus Station, St. Gilgen

1964. Stamp Day.

1440	**303**	3s.+70g. multicoloured	1·60	1·30

304 Dr. Adolf Scharf

1965. Pres. Scharf Commemoration.

1441	**304**	1s.50 blue and black	85	45

305 "Reconstruction"

1965. "20 Years of Reconstruction".

1442	**305**	1s.80 lake	65	50

306 University Seal, 1365

1965. 600th Anniv of Vienna University.

1443	**306**	3s. red and gold	95	80

307 *St. George* (after engraving by Altdorfer)

1965. Danubian Art.

1444	**307**	1s.80 blue	65	50

308 I.T.U. Emblem, Morse Key and T.V. Aerial

1965. Centenary of I.T.U.

1445	**308**	3s. violet	95	50

309 F. Raimund

1965. 175th Birth Anniv of Ferdinand Raimund (actor and playwright).

1446	**309**	3s. purple	85	45

310 Egyptian Hieroglyphs on Papyrus

1965. "WIPA" Stamp Exhibition, Vienna (2nd issue). "Development of the Letter".

1447	**310**	1s.50+40g. black and pink	55	45
1448	-	1s.80+50g. black and yellow	65	50
1449	-	2s.20+60g. black and lilac	1·20	95
1450	-	3s.+80g. black & yell	95	80
1451	-	4s.+1s. black & blue	1·50	1·20
1452	-	5s.+1s.20 black & grn	2·20	1·70

DESIGNS: 1s.80, Cuneiform writing; 2s.20, Latin; 3c. Ancient letter and seal; 4s.19th-century letter; 5s. Typewriter.

311 Gymnasts with Wands

1965. Fourth Gymnaestrada, Vienna.

1453	**311**	1s.50 black and blue	55	25
1454	-	3s. black and brown	85	45

DESIGNS: 3s. Girls exercising with tambourines.

312 Dr. I. Semmelweis

1965. Death Cent of Ignaz Semmelweis (physician).

1455	**312**	1s.50 lilac	55	25

313 F. G. Waldmuller (self-portrait)

1965. Death Cent of F. G. Waldmuller (painter).

1456	**313**	3s. black	95	50

314 Red Cross and Gauze

1965. Red Cross Conference, Vienna.

1457	**314**	3s. red and black	95	45

315 Flag and Crowned Eagle

1965. 50th Anniv of Austrian Towns Union.

1458	**315**	1s.50 multicoloured	85	50

316 Austrian Flag, U. N. Emblem and Headquarters

1965. Tenth Anniv of Austria's Membership of U.N.O.

1459	**316**	3s. sepia, red and blue	95	50

317 University Building

1965. 150th Anniv of University of Technology, Vienna.

1460	**317**	1s.50 violet	65	35

318 Bertha von Suttner

1965. 60th Anniv of Nobel Peace Prize Award to Bertha von Suttner (writer).

1461	**318**	1s.50 black	65	35

319 Postman delivering Mail

1965. Stamp Day.

1462	**319**	3s.+70g. green	1·60	1·30

320 Postal Code Map

1966. Introduction of Postal Code System.

1463	**320**	1s.50 black, red & yell	65	35

321 P.T.T. Headquarters

1966. Centenary of Austrian Posts and Telegraphs Administration.

1464	**321**	1s.50 black on cream	65	35

322 M. Ebner-Eschenbach

1966. 50th Death Anniv of Maria Ebner-Eschenbach (writer).

1465	**322**	3s. purple	95	45

323 Big Wheel

1966. Bicentenary of Vienna Prater.

1466	**323**	1s.50 green	65	25

324 Josef Hoffmann

1966. Tenth Death Anniv of Josef Hoffmann (architect).

1467	**324**	3s. brown	95	50

325 Bank Emblem

1966. 150th Anniv of Austrian National Bank.

1468	**325**	3s. brown, grn & drab	95	50

326 Arms of Wiener Neustadt

1966. "Wiener Neustadt 1440–93" Art Exhibition.

1469	**326**	1s.50 multicoloured	65	35

327 Puppy

1966. 120th Anniv of Vienna Animal Protection Society.

1470	**327**	1s.80 black and yellow	65	50

328 Columbine

1966. Alpine Flora. Multicoloured.

1471	1s.50 Type **328**	50	25
1472	1s.80 Turk's cap	55	25
1473	2s.20 Wulfenia	65	40
1474	3s. Globe flower	75	45
1475	4s. Orange lily	85	60
1476	5s. Alpine anemone	1·90	85

329 Fair Building

1966. Wels International Fair.

1477	**329**	3s. blue	95	45

330 Peter Anich

1966. Death Bicent of Peter Anich (cartographer).

1478	**330**	1s.80 black	65	35

331 "Suffering"

1966. 15th International Occupational Health Congress, Vienna.

1479	**331**	3s. black and red	95	50

332 *Eunuchus* by Terence (engraving, Johann Gruninger)

1966. Austrian National Library, Vienna. Multicoloured.

1480	1s.50 Type **332** (Theatre collection)	45	20
1481	1s.80 Detail of title page of Willem Blaeu's atlas (Cartography collection)	50	25
1482	2s.20 *Herrengasse, Vienna* (Anton Stutzinger (Pictures and portraits collection))	55	35
1483	3s. Illustration from Rene of Anjou's *Livre du Cuer d'Amours Espris* (Manuscripts collection)	1·10	50

333 Young Girl

1966. Austrian "Save the Children" Fund.

1484	**333**	3s. black and blue	85	45

334 Strawberries

1966. Fruits. Multicoloured.

1485		50g. Type **334**	55	25
1486		1s. Grapes	55	20
1487		1s.50 Apple	55	25
1488		1s.80 Blackberries	85	70
1489		2s.20 Apricots	85	70
1490		3s. Cherries	95	80

335 16th-century Postman

1966. Stamp Day.

1491	**335**	3s.+70g. multicoloured	1·10	85

336 Arms of Linz University

1966. Inauguration of Linz University.

1492	**336**	3s. multicoloured	95	50

337 Skater of 1867

1967. Centenary of Vienna Skating Assn.

1493	**337**	3s. indigo and blue	95	50

338 Dancer with Violin

1967. Centenary of "Blue Danube" Waltz.

1494	**338**	3s. purple	95	45

339 Dr. Schonherr

1967. Birth Cent of Dr. Karl Schonherr (poet).

1495	**339**	3s. brown	95	50

340 Ice Hockey Goalkeeper

1967. World Ice Hockey Championships, Vienna.

1496	**340**	3s. blue and green	95	80

341 Violin and Organ

1967. 125th Anniv of Vienna Philharmonic Orchestra.

1497	**341**	3s.50 blue	95	45

342 *Mother and Children* (aquarelle, Peter Fendi)

1967. Mother's Day.

1498	**342**	2s. multicoloured	65	50

343 *Madonna* (Gothic wood-carving)

1967. "Gothic Art in Austria" Exhibition, Krems.

1499	**343**	3s. green	95	35

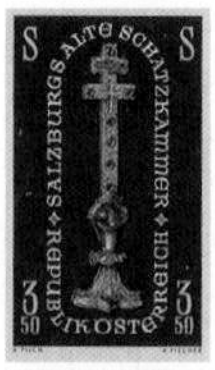

344 Jewelled Cross

1967. "Salzburg Treasures" Exhibition, Salzburg Cathedral.

1500	**344**	3s.50 multicoloured	95	50

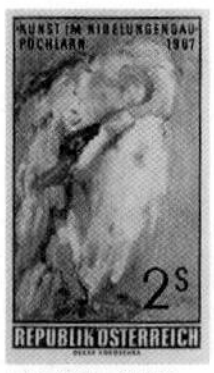

345 "The White Swan" (from Kokoschkas tapestry *Cupid and Psyche*)

1967. "Art of the Nibelungen District" Exhibition, Pochlarn.

1501	**345**	2s. multicoloured	65	35

346 Vienna

1967. Tenth European Talks, Vienna.

1502	**346**	3s. black and red	85	45

347 Champion Bull

1967. Centenary of Ried Fair.

1503	**347**	2s. purple	65	35

348 Colorado Potato Beetle

1967. Sixth Int Plant Protection Congress, Vienna.

1504	**348**	3s. multicoloured	95	50

349 Locomotive No. 671

1967. Centenary of Brenner Railway.

1505	**349**	3s.50 green and brown	95	50

350 *Christ* (fresco detail)

1967. Lambach Frescoes.

1506	**350**	2s. multicoloured	65	45

351 Prater Hall, Vienna

1967. International Trade Fairs Congress, Vienna.

1507	**351**	2s. purple and cream	85	45

352 Rector's Medallion and Chain

1967. 275th Anniv of Fine Arts Academy, Vienna.

1508	**352**	2s. brown, yellow & blue	85	45

353 Bible on Rock (from commemorative coin of 1717)

1967. 450th Anniv of the Reformation.

1509	**353**	3s.50 blue	85	45

354 Forest Trees

1967. 100 Years of Austrian University Forestry Studies.

1510	**354**	3s.50 green	1·30	70

355 Memorial, Vienna

1967. 150th Anniv of Land Registry.

1511	**355**	2s. green	55	25

356 *St. Leopold* (stained-glass window, Heiligenkreuz Monastery)

1967. Margrave Leopold the Holy.

1512	**356**	1s.80 multicoloured	55	25

357 "Music and Art"

1967. 150th Anniv of Academy of Music and Dramatic Art, Vienna.

1513	**357**	3s.50 black and violet	95	50

358 St. Mary's Altar, Nonnberg Convent, Salzburg

1967. Christmas.

1514	**358**	2s. green	65	35

359 "The Letter- carrier" (from playing-card)

1967. Stamp Day.

1515	**359**	3s.50+80g. mult	1·60	85

360 Ski Jump, Stadium and Mountains

1968. Winter University Games, Innsbruck.

1516	**360**	2s. blue	65	35

361 C. Sitte

1968. 125th Birth Anniv of Camillo Sitte (architect).

1517	**361**	2s. brown	55	45

362 Mother and Child

1968. Mothers' Day.

1518	**362**	2s. olive	55	45

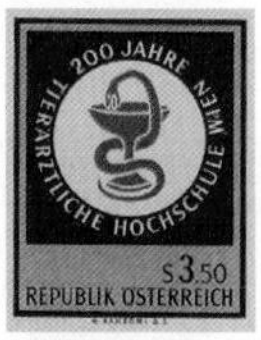

363 "Veterinary Medicine"

1968. Bicentenary of Vienna Veterinary College.
1519 **363** 3s.50 gold, pur & drab 85 70

364 Bride with Lace Veil

1968. Centenary of Vorarlberg Lace.
1520 **364** 3s.50 blue 85 70

365 Etrich Limousine

1968. "IFA Wien 1968" Airmail Stamp Exhibition, Vienna.
1521 **365** 2s. brown 55 45
1522 - 3s.50 green 95 80
1523 - 5s. blue 1·70 1·40
DESIGNS: 3s.50, Sud Aviation SE 210 Caravelle; 5s. Douglas DC-8 A-8021.

366 Horse-racing

1968. Centenary of Freudenau Gallop Races.
1524 **366** 3s.50 brown 95 50

367 Landsteiner

1968. Birth Centenary of Dr. Karl Landsteiner (physician and pathologist).
1525 **367** 3s.50 blue 95 50

368 P. Rosegger

1968. 50th Death Anniv of Peter Rosegger (writer).
1526 **368** 2s. green 65 35

369 *A. Kauffmann* (self-portrait)

1968. Exhibition of Angelica Kauffmann's Paintings, Bregenz.
1527 **369** 2s. violet 65 45

370 Statue of Young Man (Helenenberg site)

1968. Magdalensberg Excavations, Carinthia.
1528 **370** 2s. black and green 55 35

371 *The Bishop* (Romanesque carving)

1968. 750th Anniv of Graz-Seckau Diocese.
1529 **371** 2s. grey 55 35

372 K. Moser

1968. 50th Death Anniv of Koloman Moser (graphic artist).
1530 **372** 2s. brown and red 55 35

373 Human Rights Emblem

1968. Human Rights Year.
1531 **373** 1s.50 red, green & grey 95 50

374 Arms and Provincial Shields

1968. 50th Anniv of Republic. Multicoloured.
1532 2s. Type **374** 55 35
1533 2s. Karl Renner (first President of Second Republic) 55 35
1534 2s. First Article of Constitution 55 35

375 Crib, Oberndorf, Salzburg

1968. 150th Anniv of *Silent Night, Holy Night* (carol).
1535 **375** 2s. green 65 35

376 Mercury

1968. Stamp Day.
1536 **376** 3s.50+80g. green 1·10 1·10

377 Fresco (Troger), Melk Monastery

1968. Baroque Frescoes. Designs showing frescoes in locations given. Multicoloured.
1537 2s. Type **377** 65 60
1538 2s. Altenburg Monastery 65 60
1539 2s. Rohrenbach-Greillenstein 65 60
1540 2s. Ebenfurth Castle 65 60
1541 2s. Halbthurn Castle 65 60
1542 2s. Maria Treu Church, Vienna 65 60
Nos. 1537/9 are the work of Anton Troger and Nos. 1540/2 that of Franz Maulbertsch.

378 "Madonna and Child"

1969. 500th Anniv of Vienna Diocese. Statues in St. Stephen's Cathedral, Vienna.
1543 **378** 2s. blue 65 60
1544 - 2s. grey 65 60
1545 - 2s. green 65 60
1546 - 2s. purple 65 60
1547 - 2s. black 65 60
1548 - 2s. brown 65 60
DESIGNS: No. 1544, "St. Christopher"; No. 1545, "St. George"; No. 1546, "St. Paul"; No. 1547, "St. Sebastian"; No. 1548, "St. Stephen".

379 Parliament Building, Vienna

1969. Interparliamentary Union Meeting, Vienna.
1549 **379** 2s. green 55 35

380 Colonnade

1969. Europa.
1550 **380** 2s. multicoloured 1·60 45

381 "Council Members"

1969. 20th Anniv of Council of Europe.
1551 **381** 3s.50 multicoloured 95 60

382 Soldiers

1969. Austrian Armed Forces.
1552 **382** 2s. brown and red 65 35

383 *Don Giovanni*

1969. Centenary of State Opera, Vienna. Sheet 182×212 mm. T **383** and similar scenes.
MS1553 2s.×8 each brown, red and gold 6·50 6·50
DESIGNS—Scenes from Opera and Ballet: *Don Giovanni* (Mozart), *The Magic Flute* (Mozart), *Fidelio* (Beethoven), *Lohengrin* (Wagner), *Don Carlos* (Verdi), *Carmen* (Bizet), *Der Rosenkavlier* (R. Strauss) and *Swan Lake* (Tchaikovsky).

384 Maximilian's Armour

1969. "Maximilian I" Exhibition, Innsbruck.
1554 **384** 2s. black 65 35

385 Viennese "Privilege" Seal

1969. 19th International Union of Local Authorities Congress, Vienna.
1555 **385** 2s. red, brown & ochre 65 35

386 Young Girl

1969. 20th Anniv of "SOS" Children's Villages Movement.
1556 **386** 2s. brown and green 65 35

387 Hands clasping Spanner

1969. 50th Anniv of Int Labour Organization.
1557 **387** 2s. green 65 35

388 Austrian "Flag" encircling Globe

1969. "Austrians Living Abroad" Year.
1558 **388** 3s.50 red and green 95 50

389 *El Cid killing a Bull* (Goya)

1969. Bicentenary of Albertina Art Collection, Vienna. Multicoloured.
1559 2s. Type **389** 55 55
1560 2s. *Young Hare* (Durer) 55 55
1561 2s. *Madonna with Pomegranate* (Raphael) 55 55
1562 2s. *The Painter and the Amateur* (Bruegel) 55 55
1563 2s. *Rubens's Son, Nicholas* (Rubens) 55 55
1564 2s. *Self-portrait* (Rembrandt) 55 55
1565 2s. *Madame de Pompadour* (detail, Guerin) 55 55
1566 2s. *The Artist's Wife* (Schiele) 55 55

390 Pres. Jonas

1969. Pres. Franz Jonas's 70th Birthday.

1567	**390**	2s. blue and grey	55	45

391 Posthorn and Lightning over Globe

1969. 50th Anniv of Post and Telegraph Employees Union.

1568	**391**	2s. multicoloured	55	45

392 Savings Bank (c. 1450)

1969. 150th Anniv of Austrian Savings Bank.

1569	**392**	2s. green and silver	55	45

393 *The Madonna* (Egger-Lienz)

1969. Christmas.

1570	**393**	2s. purple and yellow	55	45

394 Unken, Salzburg, Post-house Sign (after F. Zeller)

1969. Stamp Day.

1571	**394**	3s.50+80g. black, red and stone	95	85

395 J. Schoffel

1970. 60th Death Anniv of Josef Schoffel ("Saviour of the Vienna Woods").

1572	**395**	2s. purple	45	35

396 St. Clement Hofbauer

1970. 150th Death Anniv of St. Clement Hofbauer (theologian).

1573	**396**	2s. brown and green	45	35

397 Chancellor Leopold Figl

1970. 25th Anniv of Austrian Republic.

1574	**397**	2s. olive	65	35
1575	-	2s. brown	65	35

DESIGN: No. 1575, Belvedere Castle.

398 Krimml Waterfalls

1970. Nature Conservation Year.

1576	**398**	2s. green	1·10	70

399 Oldest University Seal

1970. 300th Anniv of Leopold Franz University, Innsbruck.

1577	**399**	2s. black and red	55	45

400 "Musikverein" Organ

1970. Centenary of "Musikverein" Building.

1578	**400**	2s. purple and gold	55	45

401 Tower Clock, 1450–1550

1970. Antique Clocks.

1579	**401**	1s.50 brown and cream	55	45
1580	-	1s.50 green & lt green	55	45
1581	-	2s. blue and pale blue	65	50
1582	-	2s. red and purple	65	50
1583	-	3s.50 brown and buff	1·10	85
1584	-	3s.50 purple and lilac	1·10	85

DESIGNS: No. 1580, Empire "lyre" clock, 1790–1815; No. 1581, Pendant ball clock, 1600–50; No. 1582, Pocket-watch and signet, 1800–30; No. 1583, Bracket clock, 1720–60; No. 1584, "Biedermeier" pendulum clock and musical-box, 1820–50.

402 *The Beggar Student* (Millocker)

1970. Famous Operettas.

1585	**402**	1s.50 turquoise & green	55	45
1586	-	1s.50 blue and yellow	55	45
1587	-	2s. purple and pink	65	50
1588	-	2s. brown and green	65	50
1589	-	3s.50 blue and light blue	1·10	85
1590	-	3s.50 blue and buff	1·10	85

OPERETTAS: No. 1586, *Die Fledermaus* (Johann Strauss the younger); 1587, *A Waltz Dream* (O. Straus); 1588, *The Birdseller* (C. Zeller); 1589, *The Merry Widow* (F. Lehar); 1590,"*Two Hearts in Waltz-time* (R. Stoiz).

403 Scene from *The Gipsy Baron* (J. Strauss)

1970. 25th Anniv of Bregenz Festival.

1591	**403**	3s.50 blue, buff & ult	95	50

404 Festival Emblem

1970. 50th Anniv of Salzburg Festival.

1592	**404**	3s.50 multicoloured	95	50

405 T. Koschat

1970. 125th Birth Anniv of Thomas Koschat (composer and poet).

1593	**405**	2s. brown	55	45

406 "Head of St. John", from sculpture *Mount of Olive*, Ried Church (attribs, Ried Church (attributed to T. Schwanthaler)

1970. 13th World Veterans Federation General Assembly.

1594	**406**	3s.50 sepia	95	50

407 Climbers and Mountains

1970. "Walking and Mountaineering".

1595	**407**	2s. blue and mauve	55	35

408 A. Cossmann

1970. Birth Cent of Alfred Cossmann (engraver).

1596	**408**	2s. brown	55	35

409 Arms of Carinthia

1970. 50th Anniv of Carinthian Plebiscite.

1597	**409**	2s. multicoloured	55	35

410 U.N. Emblem

1970. 25th Anniv of United Nations.

1598	**410**	3s.50 blue and black	95	50

411 *Adoration of the Shepherds* (carving, Garsten Monastery)

1970. Christmas.

1599	**411**	2s. blue	45	35

412 Saddle, Harness and Posthorn

1970. Stamp Day.

1600	**412**	3s.50+80g. black, yellow and grey	1·10	1·10

413 Pres. K. Renner

1970. Birth Centenary of Pres. Renner.

1601	**413**	2s. purple	55	35

414 Beethoven (after painting by Waldmuller)

1970. Birth Bicentenary of Beethoven.

1602	**414**	3s.50 black and stone	95	60

415 E. Handel-Mazzetti

1971. Birth Centenary of Enrica Handel-Mazzetti (novelist).

1603	**415**	2s. brown	45	25

416 "Safety for Children"

1971. Road Safety.

1604	**416**	2s. multicoloured	65	35

417 Florentine Bowl, c. 1580

1971. Austrian Art Treasures (1st series). Sculpture and Applied Art.

1605	**417**	1s.50 green and grey	55	45
1606	-	2s. purple and grey	85	70
1607	-	3s.50 yellow, brn & grey	1·30	1·00

DESIGNS: 2s. Ivory equestrian statuette of Joseph I, 1693 (Matthias Steinle); 3s.50, Salt-cellar, c. 1570 (Cellini).

See also Nos. 1609/11, 1632/4 and 1651/3.

418 Shield of Trade Association

1971. 23rd International Chamber of Commerce Congress, Vienna.

1608	**418**	3s.50 multicoloured	85	50

419 *Jacopo de Strada* (Titian)

1971. Austrian Art Treasures (2nd series).

1609	**419**	1s.50 purple	55	45
1610	-	2s. black	85	70
1611	-	3s.50 brown	1·30	1·00

PAINTINGS: 2s. *The Village Feast* (Brueghel); 3s.50, *Young Venetian Woman* (Durer).

420 Notary's Seal

1971. Austrian Notarial Statute Cent Congress.

1612	**420**	3s.50 purple and brown	85	45

421 "St. Matthew" (altar sculpture)

1971. "Krems Millennium of Art" Exhibition.

1613	**421**	2s. brown and purple	45	25

422 Dr. A. Neilreich

1971. Death Cent of Dr. August Neilreich (botanist).

1614	**422**	2s. brown	45	25

423 Singer with Lyre

1971. International Choir Festival, Vienna.

1615	**423**	4s. blue, gold & lt blue	95	80

424 Arms of Kitzbuhel

1971. 700th Anniv of Kitzbuhel.

1616	**424**	2s.50 multicoloured	55	45

425 Stock Exchange Building

1971. Bicentenary of Vienna Stock Exchange.

1617	**425**	4s. brown	85	50

426 Old and New Fair Halls

1971. "50 Years of Vienna International Fairs".

1618	**426**	2s.50 purple	55	45

427 O.G.B. Emblem

1971. 25th Anniv of Austrian Trade Unions Federation.

1619	**427**	2s. multicoloured	45	35

428 Arms and Insignia

1971. 50th Anniv of Burgenland Province.

1620	**428**	4s. multicoloured	45	35

429 "Marcus" Veteran Car

1971. 75th Anniv of Austrian Automobile, Motor Cycle and Touring Club.

1621	**429**	4s. black and green	85	60

430 Europa Bridge, Brenner Highway

1971. Inauguration of Brenner Highway.

1622	**430**	4s. blue	85	60

431 Iron-ore Workings, Erzberg

1971. 25 Years of Nationalized Industries.

1623	**431**	1s.50 brown	55	45
1624	-	2s. blue	55	45
1625	-	4s. green	1·10	85

DESIGNS: 2s. Nitrogen Works, Linz; 4s. Iron and Steel works, Linz.

432 Electric Train on the Semmering Line

1971. Railway Anniversaries.

1626	**432**	2s. purple	55	45

433 E. Tschermak-Seysenegg

1971. Birth Centenary of Dr. E. Tshermak-Seysenegg (biologist).

1627	**433**	2s. purple and grey	45	35

434 Angling

1971. Sports.

1628	**434**	2s. brown	45	35

435 *The Infant Jesus as Saviour* (from miniature by Durer)

1971. Christmas.

1629	**435**	2s. multicoloured	55	45

436 "50 Years"

1971. 50th Anniv of Austrian Philatelic Clubs Association.

1630	**436**	4s.+1s.50 pur & gold	1·30	1·00

437 Franz Grillparzer (from miniature by Daffinger)

1972. Death Centenary of Grillparzer (dramatist).

1631	**437**	2s. black, brown & stone	65	35

438 Roman Fountain, Friesach

1972. Austrian Art Treasures (3rd series). Fountains.

1632	**438**	1s.50 purple	55	45
1633	-	2s. brown	85	70
1634	-	2s.50 green	1·30	1·00

DESIGNS: 2s. Lead Fountain, Heiligenkreuz Abbey; 2s.50. Leopold Fountain, Innsbruck.

439 Hofburg Palace

1972. Fourth European Postal Ministers' Conf, Vienna.

1635	**439**	4s. violet	95	80

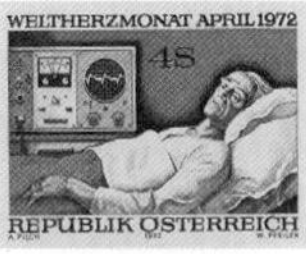

440 Heart Patient

1972. World Heart Month.

1636	**440**	4s. brown	95	80

441 *Woman's Head* (sculpture, Gurk Cathedral)

1972. 900th Anniv of Gurk Diocese.

1637	**441**	2s. purple and gold	65	50

442 Vienna Town Hall and Congress Emblem

1972. Ninth International Public and Co-operative Economy Congress, Vienna.

1638	**442**	4s. black, red and yellow	1·10	70

443 Lienz–Pelos Pylon Line

1972. 25th Anniv of Electric Power Nationalization.

1639	**443**	70g. violet and grey	45	35
1640	-	2s.50 brown and grey	65	50
1641	-	4s. blue and grey	1·10	85

DESIGNS: 2s.50, Vienna-Semmering Power Station; 4s. Zemm Dam and lake.

444 Runner with Torch

1972. Passage of the Olympic Torch through Austria.

1642	**444**	2s. brown and red	55	45

445 *Hermes* (C. Laib)

1972. "Late Gothic Art" Exhibition, Salzburg.

1643	**445**	2s. purple	55	45

446 Pears

1972. Amateur Gardeners' Congress, Vienna.

1644	**446**	2s.50 multicoloured	75	60

447 "Spanish Walk"

1972. 400th Anniv of the Spanish Riding School, Vienna. Sheet 136×181 mm containing T **447** and similar square designs each in purple, red and gold.

MS1645 2s. Type **447**; 2s. "Piaffe"; 2s.50 "Levade"; 2s.50 "On the long rein"; 4s. "Capriole"; 4s. "Courbette" 5·50 5·50

448 University Arms

1972. Cent of University of Agriculture, Vienna.

1646 **448** 2s. multicoloured 55 45

449 Old University Buildings (after F. Danreiter)

1972. 350th Anniv of Paris Lodron University, Salzburg.

1647 **449** 4s. brown 95 80

450 C. M. Ziehrer

1972. 50th Death Anniv of Carl M. Ziehrer (composer and conductor).

1648 **450** 2s. red 55 45

451 "Virgin and Child", Inzersdorf Church

1972. Christmas.

1649 **451** 2s. purple and green 65 50

452 18th-century Viennese Postman

1972. Stamp Day.

1650 **452** 4s.+1s. green 1·30 1·00

453 State Sledge of Maria Theresa

1972. Austrian Art Treasures (4th series). Carriages from the Imperial Coach House.

1651	**453**	1s.50 brown and bistre	55	45
1652	-	2s. green and bistre	85	70
1653	-	2s.50 purple and bistre	1·30	1·00

DESIGNS: 2s. Coronation landau; 2s.50, Hapsburg State Coach.

454 Telephone Network

1972. Completion of Austrian Telephone System Automation.

1654 **454** 2s. black and yellow 55 45

455 "Drug Addict"

1973. Campaign against Drug Abuse.

1655 **455** 2s. multicoloured 75 45

456 A. Petzold

1973. 50th Death Anniv of Alfons Petzold (writer).

1656 **456** 2s. purple 55 45

457 Korner

1973. Birth Centenary of Pres. Theodor Korner (President, 1951–57).

1657 **457** 2s. purple and grey 55 45

458 McDonell DC-9 OE-LDA

1973. Austrian Aviation Anniversaries.

1658 **458** 2s. blue and red 55 45

459 Otto Loewi

1973. Birth Cent of Otto Loewi (pharmacologist).

1659 **459** 4s. violet 95 70

460 "Succour"

1973. 25th Anniv of National Federation of Austrian Social Insurance Institutes.

1660 **460** 2s. blue 55 45

461 Telephone Dial within Posthorn

1973. Europa.

1661 **461** 2s.50 black, yell & orge 2·20 70

462 Fair Emblem

1973. 25th Dornbirn Fair.

1662 **462** 2s. multicoloured 65 35

463 Military Pentathlon

1973. 25th Anniv of International Military Sports Council and 23rd Military Pentathlon Championships, Wiener Neustadt.

1663 **463** 4s. green 1·00 55

464 Leo Slezak

1973. Birth Centenary of Leo Slezak (operatic tenor).

1664 **464** 4s. brown 1·00 55

465 Main Entrance, Hofburg Palace

1973. 39th International Statistical Institute's Congress, Vienna.

1665 **465** 2s. brown, red and grey 55 30

466 *Admiral Tegetthof Icebound* (J. Payer)

1973. Centenary of Discovery of Franz Josef Land.

1666 **466** 2s.50 green 80 45

467 I.U.L.C.S. Arms

1973. 13th International Union of Leather Chemists' Societies Congress, Vienna.

1667 **467** 4s. multicoloured 1·00 65

468 *Academy of Sciences, Vienna* (B. Bellotto)

1973. Cent of Int Meteorological Organization.

1668 **468** 2s.50 violet 80 45

469 Max Reinhardt

1973. Birth Centenary of Max Reinhardt (theatrical director).

1669 **469** 2s. purple 55 45

470 F. Hanusch

1973. 50th Death Anniv of Ferdinand Hanusch (politician).

1670 **470** 2s. purple 55 30

471 Light Harness Racing

1973. Centenary of Vienna Trotting Assn.

1671 **471** 2s. green 65 55

472 Radio Operator

1973. 50th Anniv of International Criminal Police Organization (Interpol).

1672 **472** 4s. violet 90 65

473 Petzval Camera Lens

1973. "Europhot" (professional photographers) Congress, Vienna.

1673 **473** 2s.50 multicoloured 90 55

474 Aqueduct, Hollen Valley

1973. Centenary of Vienna's 1st Mountain-spring Aqueduct.

1674 **474** 2s. brown, red & blue 55 30

475 Almsee

1973. Views. (a) Size 23×29 mm.

1674a	-	20g. blue and light blue	90	45
1675	-	50g. green & lt green	45	25
1676	-	1s. sepia and brown	45	25
1677	-	1s.50 purple and pink	65	30
1678	-	2s. indigo and blue	80	30
1679	-	2s.50 deep lilac & lilac	90	30
1680	-	3s. ultramarine & blue	1·10	30
1680a	-	3s.50 brown & orange	1·10	45
1681	**475**	4s. violet and lilac	1·10	30
1681a	-	4s.20 black and grey	1·70	95
1682	-	4s.50 dp green & green	1·50	45
1683	-	5s. violet and lilac	1·50	45
1683a	-	5s.50 blue and violet	2·50	1·90
1683b	-	5s.60 olive and green	3·25	2·75
1684	-	6s. lilac and pink	2·10	30
1684a	-	6s.50 blue & turquoise	2·00	45
1685	-	7s. deep green & green	2·75	45
1685a	-	7s.50 purple & mauve	3·25	45
1686	-	8s. brown and pink	2·75	65
1686a	-	9s. red and pink	3·25	65
1687	-	10s. myrtle and green	3·25	45
1688	-	11s. red and orange	4·00	45
1688a	-	12s. sepia and brown	4·00	95
1688b	-	14s. myrtle and green	5·00	95
1688c	-	16s. brown and orange	5·50	95
1688d	-	20s. green and bistre	6·75	95

(b) Size 28×37 mm.

1689 50s. violet and grey 20·00 2·40

(c) Size 17×20 mm.

1690 3s. ultramarine and blue 80 65

DESIGNS: 20g. Friedstadt Keep, Muhlviertel; 50g. Zillertal; 1s. Kahlenbergerdorf, Vienna; 1s.50, Bludenz; 2s. Old bridge, Finstermunz; 2s.50, Murau, Styria; 3s. Bischofsmutze and Alpine farm; 3s.50, Osterkirche, Oberwart; 4s.20, Hirschegg, Kleinwalsertal; 4s.50, Windmill, Retz; 5s. Ruins of Aggstein Castle; 5s.50, Peace Chapel, Stoderzinken; 5s.60, Riezlern, Kleinwalsertal; 6s. Lindauer Hut, Ratikon Massif; 6s.50, Villach, Carinthia; 7s. Falkenstein Castle; 7s.50, Hohensalzburg Fortress; 8s. Votive column, Reiteregg, Styria; 9s. Asten valley; 10s. Neusiedlersee; 11s. Enns; 12s. Kufstein Fortress; 14s. Weiszsee, Salzburg; 16s. Bad Tatzmannsdorf open-air museum; 20s. Myra Falls, Muggendorf; 50s. Hofburg, Vienna.

476 *The Nativity* (stained-glass window, St. Erhard Church, Bretenau)

1973. Christmas.

1691	**476**	2s. multicoloured	55	30

477 *Archangel Gabriel* (carving by Lorenz Luchsperger)

1973. Stamp Day.

1692	**477**	4s.+1s. purple	1·20	1·20

478 Dr. Fritz Pregl

1973. 50th Anniv of Award of Nobel Prize for Chemistry to Fritz Pregl.

1693	**478**	4s. blue	1·00	65

479 Telex Machine and Globe

1974. 50th Anniv of Radio Austria.

1694	**479**	2s.50 blue & ultramarine	80	45

480 Hugo Hofmannsthal

1974. Birth Cent of Hugo Hofmannsthal (writer).

1695	**480**	4s. blue	1·00	65

481 Anton Bruckner (composer)

1974. Inaug of Bruckner Memorial Centre, Linz.

1696	**481**	4s. brown	1·10	65

482 Vegetables

1974. Second Int Horticultural Show, Vienna. Multicoloured.

1697	2s. Type **482**	55	45
1698	2s.50 Fruit	90	75
1699	4s. Flowers	1·10	95

483 Head from Ancient Seal

1974. 750th Anniv of Judenburg.

1700	**483**	2s. multicoloured	65	40

484 Karl Kraus

1974. Birth Centenary of Karl Kraus (poet).

1701	**484**	4s. red	1·00	65

485 *St. Michael* (wood-carving, Thomas Schwanthaler)

1974. "Sculptures by the Schwanthaler Family" Exhibition, Reichersberg.

1702	**485**	2s.50 green	90	45

486 *King Arthur* (statue, Innsbruck)

1974. Europa.

1703	**486**	2s.50 blue and brown	2·20	95

487 Early De Dion-Bouton Motor-tricycle

1974. 75th Anniv of Austrian Association of Motoring, Motor Cycling and Cycling.

1704	**487**	2s. brown and grey	55	45

488 Mask of Satyr's Head

1974. "Renaissance in Austria" Exhibition, Schallaburg Castle.

1705	**488**	2s. black, brown & gold	55	45

489 I.R.U. Emblem

1974. 14th International Road Haulage Union Congress, Innsbruck.

1706	**489**	4s. black and orange	1·10	65

490 F. A. Maulbertsch

1974. 205th Birth Anniv of Franz Maulbertsch (painter).

1707	**490**	2s. brown	65	30

491 Gendarmes of 1849 and 1974

1974. 125th Anniv of Austrian Gendarmerie.

1708	**491**	2s. multicoloured	65	30

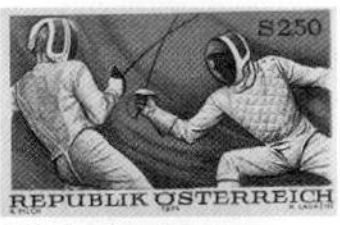

492 Fencing

1974. Sports.

1709	**492**	2s.50 black and orange	80	45

493 Transport Emblems

1974. European Transport Ministers' Conference, Vienna.

1710	**493**	4s. multicoloured	1·00	65

494 *St. Virgilius* (wood-carving)

1974. 1200 Years of Christianity in Salzburg.

1711	**494**	2s. blue	65	30

495 Pres. F. Jonas

1974. Pres. Franz Jonas Commemoration.

1712	**495**	2s. black	65	30

496 F. Stelzhamer

1974. Death Cent of Franz Stelzhamer (poet).

1713	**496**	2s. blue	65	30

497 Diving

1974. 13th European Swimming, Diving and Water-polo Championships.

1714	**497**	4s. brown and blue	1·10	65

498 F. R. von Hebra (founder of German scientific dermatology)

1974. 30th Meeting of German-speaking Dermatologists Association, Graz.

1715	**498**	4s. brown	1·00	65

499 A. Schonberg

1974. Birth Cent of Arnold Schonberg (composer).

1716	**499**	2s.50 purple	90	45

500 Broadcasting Studios, Salzburg

1974. 50th Anniv of Austrian Broadcasting.

1717	**500**	2s. multicoloured	65	30

501 E. Eysler

1974. 25th Death Anniv of Edmund Eysler (composer).

1718	**501**	2s. green	55	45

502 19th-century Postman and Mail Transport

1974. Centenary of U.P.U.

1719	**502**	2s. brown and mauve	65	55
1720	-	4s. blue and grey	1·00	85

DESIGN: 4s. Modern postman and mail transport.

503 Sports Emblem

1974. 25th Anniv of Football Pools in Austria.

1721	**503**	70g. red, black and green	55	30

504 Steel Gauntlet grasping Rose

1974. Nature Protection.

1722	**504**	2s. multicoloured	90	55

505 C. D. von Dittersdorf

1974. 175th Death Anniv of Carl Ditters von Dittersdorf (composer).

1723	**505**	2s. green	65	30

506 Mail Coach and P.O., 1905

1974. Stamp Day.
1724 **506** 4s.+2s. blue 1·50 95

507 *Virgin Mary and Child* (wood-carving)

1974. Christmas.
1725 **507** 2s. brown and gold 55 40

508 F. Schmidt

1974. Birth Centenary of Franz Schmidt (composer).
1726 **508** 4s. black and stone 1·00 65

509 *St. Christopher and Child* (altarpiece)

1975. European Architectural Heritage Year and 125th Anniv of Austrian Commission for Preservation of Monuments.
1727 **509** 2s.50 brown and grey 80 40

510 Slalom

1975. Winter Olympics, Innsbruck (1976) (1st issue). Multicoloured.
1728 1s.+50g. Type **510** 35 30
1729 1s.50+70g. Ice hockey 45 40
1730 2s.+90g. Ski-jumping 65 55
1731 4s.+1s.90 Bobsleighing 1·30 1·10
See also Nos. 1747/50.

511 Seat-belt around Skeletal Limbs

1975. Car Safety-belts Campaign.
1732 **511** 70g. multicoloured 45 40

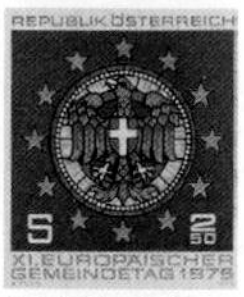

512 Stained-glass Window, Vienna Town Hall

1975. 11th European Communities' Day.
1733 **512** 2s.50 multicoloured 65 45

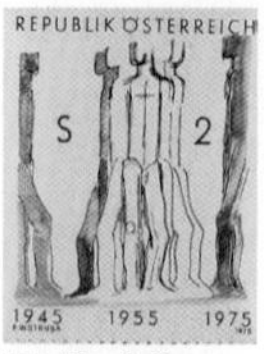

513 "The Buffer State"

1975. 30th Anniv of Foundation of Austrian Second Republic.
1734 **513** 2s. black and brown 55 30

514 Forest Scene

1975. 50th Anniv of Foundation of Austrian Forests Administration.
1735 **514** 2s. green 80 40

515 *The High Priest* (M. Pacher)

1975. Europa.
1736 **515** 2s.50 multicoloured 2·20 45

516 Gosaukamm Cable-way

1975. Fourth International Ropeways Congress, Vienna.
1737 **516** 2s. blue and red 65 30

517 J. Misson

1975. Death Centenary of Josef Misson (poet).
1738 **517** 2s. brown and red 55 30

518 "Setting Sun"

1975. Nat Pensioners' Assn Meeting, Vienna.
1739 **518** 1s.50 multicoloured 55 30

519 F. Porsche

1975. Birth Centenary of Prof. Ferdinand Porsche (motor engineer).
1740 **519** 1s.50 purple & green 55 30

520 L. Fall

1975. 50th Death Anniv of Leo Fall (composer).
1741 **520** 2s. violet 55 30

521 Judo "Shoulder Throw"

1975. World Judo Championships, Vienna.
1742 **521** 2s.50 multicoloured 80 45

522 Heinrich Angeli

1975. 50th Death Anniv of Heinrich Angeli (court painter).
1743 **522** 2s. purple 65 30

523 J. Strauss

1975. 150th Birth Anniv of Johann Strauss the Younger (composer).
1744 **523** 4s. brown and ochre 1·10 65

524 "The Cellist"

1975. 75th Anniv of Vienna Symphony Orchestra.
1745 **524** 2s.50 blue and silver 65 40

525 "One's Own House"

1975. 50th Anniv of Austrian Building Societies.
1746 **525** 2s. multicoloured 55 30

1975. Winter Olympic Games, Innsbruck (1976) (2nd issue). As T **510**. Multicoloured.
1747 70g.+30g. Figure-skating (pairs) 45 40
1748 2s.+1s. Cross-country skiing 55 45
1749 2s.50+1s. Tobogganing 90 75
1750 4s.+2s. Rifle-shooting (biathlon) 1·30 1·10

526 Scene on Folding Fan

1975. Bicentenary of Salzburg State Theatre.
1751 **526** 1s.50 multicoloured 55 30

527 Austrian Stamps of 1850, 1922 and 1945

1975. Stamp Day. 125th Anniv of Austrian Postage Stamps.
1752 **527** 4s.+2s. multicoloured 1·30 1·10

528 *Virgin and Child* (Schottenaltar, Vienna)

1975. Christmas.
1753 **528** 2s. lilac and gold 65 40

529 "Spiralbaum" (F. Hundertwasser)

1975. Modern Austrian Art.
1754 **529** 4s. multicoloured 1·70 1·20

530 Old Theatre Building

1976. Bicentenary of the Burgtheatre, Vienna. Sheet 130×60 mm containing T **530** and similar horiz design.
MS1755 3s. blue (Type **530**); 3s. brown (Interior of the modern theatre) 2·00 2·00

531 Dr. R. Barany

1976. Birth Centenary of Dr. Robert Barany (Nobel prizewinner for Medicine, 1915).
1756 **531** 3s. brown and blue 1·00 45

532 Ammonite Fossil

1976. Cent Exn, Vienna Natural History Museum.
1757 **532** 3s. multicoloured 1·00 45

533 9th-century Coronation Throne

1976. Millenary of Carinthia.
1758 **533** 3s. black and yellow 1·00 45

534 Stained-glass Window, Klosterneuburg

1976. Babenberg Exhibition, Lilienfeld.
1759 **534** 3s. multicoloured 1·00 45

535 *The Siege of Linz* (contemporary engraving)

1976. 350th Anniv of the Peasants' War in Upper Austria.
1760 **535** 4s. black and green 1·00 55

536 Bowler delivering Ball

1976. 11th World Skittles Championships, Vienna.
1761 **536** 4s. black and orange 1·00 55

537 *St. Wolfgang* (altar painting by Michael Pacher)

1976. International Art Exhibition, St. Wolfgang.
1762 **537** 6s. purple 1·70 95

538 Tassilo Cup, Kremsmunster

1976. Europa.
1763 **538** 4s. multicoloured 2·75 95

539 Fair Emblem

1976. 25th Austrian Timber Fair, Klagenfurt.
1764 **539** 3s. multicoloured 1·00 45

540 Constantin Economo

1976. Birth Centenary of Constantin Economo (brain specialist).
1765 **540** 3s. brown 1·00 45

541 Bohemian Court Chancellery, Vienna

1976. Centenary of Administrative Court.
1766 **541** 6s. brown 1·70 95

542 Arms of Lower Austria

1976. Millenary of Austria. Sheet 135×180 mm containing T **542** and similar vert designs showing provincial arms.
MS1767 2s.×9 multicoloured 5·00 5·00
DESIGNS: Arms of Lower Austria, Upper Austria, Styria, Carinthia, Vorarlberg, Salzberg, Burgenland and Vienna.

543 Cancer the Crab

1976. Fight against Cancer.
1768 **543** 2s.50 multicoloured 80 45

544 U.N. Emblem and Bridge

1976. Tenth Anniv of U.N. Industrial Development Organization.
1769 **544** 3s. blue and gold 1·00 55

545 Punched Tapes and Map of Europe

1976. 30th Anniv of Austrian Press Agency.
1770 **545** 1s.50 multicoloured 45 30

546 V. Kaplan

1976. Birth Centenary of Viktor Kaplan (inventor of turbine).
1771 **546** 2s.50 multicoloured 65 55

547 *The Birth of Christ* (Konrad von Friesach)

1976. Christmas.
1772 **547** 3s. multicoloured 90 45

548 Postilion's Hat and Posthorn

1976. Stamp Day.
1773 **548** 6s.+2s. black & lilac 1·80 1·50

549 R. M. Rilke

1976. 50th Death Anniv of Rainer Maria Rilke (poet).
1774 **549** 3s. violet 90 45

550 *Augustin the Piper* (Arik Brauer)

1976. Austrian Modern Art.
1775 **550** 6s. multicoloured 1·70 95

551 City Synagogue

1976. 150th Anniv of Vienna City Synagogue.
1776 **551** 1s.50 multicoloured 45 30

552 N. J. von Jacquin

1977. 250th Birth Anniv of Nikolaus Joseph Freiherrn von Jacquin (botanist).
1777 **552** 4s. brown 1·00 65

553 Oswald von Wolkenstein

1977. 600th Birth Anniv of Oswald von Wolkenstein (poet).
1778 **553** 3s. multicoloured 90 45

554 Handball

1977. World Indoor Handball Championships, Group B, Austria.
1779 **554** 1s.50 multicoloured 45 30

555 A. Kubin

1977. Birth Centenary of Alfred Kubin (writer and illustrator).
1780 **555** 6s. blue 1·70 95

556 Cathedral Spire

1977. 25th Anniv of Re-opening of St. Stephen's Cathedral, Vienna.
1781 **556** 2s.50 brown 90 75
1782 - 3s. blue 1·00 85
1783 - 4s. purple 1·50 1·20
DESIGNS: 3s. West front; 4s. Interior.

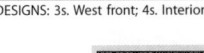

557 F. Herzmanovsky-Orlando

1977. Birth Centenary of Fritz Herzmanovsky-Orlando (writer).
1784 **557** 6s. green and gold 1·70 95

558 I.A.E.A. Emblem

1977. 20th Anniv of Int Atomic Energy Agency.
1785 **558** 3s. lt blue, gold & blue 90 45

559 Arms of Schwanenstadt

1977. 350th Anniv of Schwanenstadt.
1786 **559** 3s. multicoloured 90 45

560 Attersee

1977. Europa.
1787 **560** 6s. green 4·00 1·40

561 Globe (Vincenzo Coronelli)

1977. Fifth International Symposium and 25th Anniv of Coronelli World Federation of Globe Friends.
1788 **561** 3s. black and stone 90 45

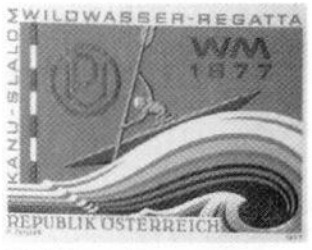

562 Canoeist

1977. World "White Water" Canoe Championships.
1789 **562** 4s. multicoloured 1·00 55

563 *The Samaritan* (Francesco Bassano)

1977. 50th Anniv of Austrian Workers' Samaritan Federation.
1790 **563** 1s.50 multicoloured 55 30

564 Papermakers' Arms

1977. 17th Conference of European Committee of Pulp and Paper Technology.
1791 **564** 3s. multicoloured 90 45

565 "Freedom"

1977. Martyrs for Austrian Freedom.
1792 **565** 2s.50 blue and red 80 45

566 Steam Locomotive, *Austria*, 1837

1977. 140th Anniv of Austrian Railways. Multicoloured.
1793 1s.50 Type **566** 65 55
1794 2s.50 Type 214 steam locomotive, 1928 1·00 85
1795 3s. Type 1044 electric locomotive, 1974 1·70 1·40

567 *Madonna and Child* (wood carving, Mariastein Pilgrimage Church)

1977. Christmas.
1796 **567** 3s. multicoloured 90 45

568 *Danube Maiden* (Wolfgang Hutter)

1977. Austrian Modern Art.
1797 **568** 6s. multicoloured 1·70 95

569 Emanuel Herrmann (inventor of postcard)

1977. Stamp Day.
1798 **569** 6s.+2s. brown and cinnamon 2·00 1·40

570 Egon Friedell

1978. Birth Centenary of Egon Friedell (writer).
1799 **570** 3s. black and blue 90 45

571 Underground Train

1978. Opening of Vienna Underground Railway.
1800 **571** 3s. multicoloured 1·10 55

572 Rifleman and Skier

1978. Biathlon World Championships, Hochfilzen.
1801 **572** 4s. multicoloured 1·10 65

573 Aztec Feather Shield

1978. 30th Anniv of Museum of Ethnology, Vienna.
1802 **573** 3s. multicoloured 1·00 45

574 Leopold Kunschak

1978. 25th Death Anniv of Leopold Kunschak (politician).
1803 **574** 3s. blue 1·00 45

575 "Mountain Peasants"

1978. Birth Centenary of Suitbert Lobisser (wood engraver).
1804 **575** 3s. brown and stone 1·00 45

576 Black Grouse, Hunting Satchel and Fowling Piece

1978. International Hunting Exn, Marchegg.
1805 **576** 6s. blue, brown & turq 1·70 95

577 Map of Europe and Austrian Parliament Building

1978. Third Interparliamentary European Security Conference, Vienna.
1806 **577** 4s. multicoloured 1·00 65

578 Riegersburg Castle, Styria

1978. Europa.
1807 **578** 6s. purple 4·00 95

579 *Admont Pieta* (Salzburg Circle Master)

1978. "Gothic Art in Styria" Exhibition.
1808 **579** 2s.50 black and ochre 65 55

580 Ort Castle

1978. 700th Anniv of Gmunden Town Charter.
1809 **580** 3s. multicoloured 1·10 45

581 Face surrounded by Fruit and Flowers

1978. 25th Anniv of Austrian Association for Social Tourism.
1810 **581** 6s. multicoloured 1·70 95

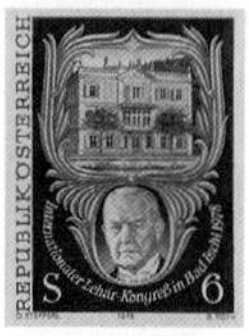

582 Franz Lehar and Villa at Bad Ischl

1978. International Lehar Congress.
1811 **582** 6s. blue 1·70 95

583 Tools and Globe

1978. 15th Congress of International Federation of Building and Wood Workers.
1812 **583** 1s.50 black, yellow & red 55 45

584 Knights Jousting

1978. 700th Anniv of Battle of Durnkrut and Jedenspeigen.
1813 **584** 3s. multicoloured 1·10 65

585 Bridge over River Drau

1978. 1100th Anniv of Villach.
1814 **585** 3s. multicoloured 1·10 65

586 City Seal, 1440

1978. 850th Anniv of Graz.
1815 **586** 4s. brown, green & grey 1·30 75

587 Angler

1978. 25th Sport Fishing Championships, Vienna.
1816 **587** 4s. multicoloured 1·30 75

588 Distorted Pattern

1978. Handicapped People.
1817 **588** 6s. black and brown 1·70 95

589 Concrete Chain

1978. Ninth International Concrete and Prefabrication Industry Congress, Vienna.
1818 **589** 2s.50 multicoloured 65 55

590 *Grace* (Albin Egger-Lienz)

1978. European Family Congress.
1819 **590** 6s. multicoloured 1·70 95

591 Lise Meitner

1978. Birth Centenary of Lise Meitner (physicist).
1820 **591** 6s. violet 1·70 95

592 Victor Adler (bust, Anton Hamek)

1978. 60th Death Anniv of Victor Adler (statesman).
1821 **592** 3s. black and red 1·10 45

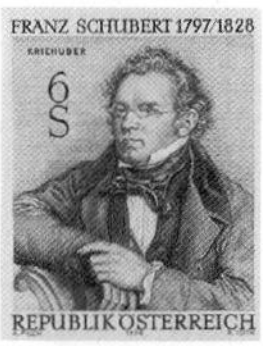

593 Franz Schubert (after Josef Kriehuber)

1978. 150th Death Anniv of Franz Schubert (composer).
1822 **593** 6s. brown 2·00 95

594 *Madonna and Child* (Martino Altomonte, Wilhering Collegiate Church)

1978. Christmas.
1823 **594** 3s. multicoloured 1·00 45

595 Postbus, 1913

1978. Stamp Day.
1824 **595** 10s.+5s. multicoloured 3·00 2·50

596 *Archduke Johann Hut, Grossglockner* (E. T. Compton)

1978. Centenary of Austrian Alpine Club.
1825 **596** 1s.50 violet and gold 55 45

597 *Adam* (Rudolf Hausner)

1978. Austrian Modern Art.
1826 **597** 6s. multicoloured 1·70 95

598 Bound Hands

1978. 30th Anniv of Declaration of Human Rights.
1827 **598** 6s. purple 1·70 95

599 "CCIR"

1979. 50th Anniv of International Radio Consultative Committee.
1828 **599** 6s. multicoloured 1·50 75

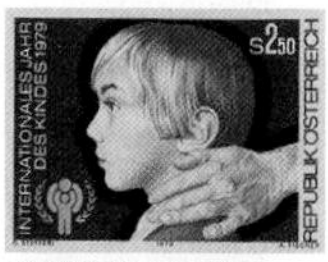

600 Adult protecting Child

1979. International Year of the Child.
1829 **600** 2s.50 multicoloured 65 55

601 Air Rifle, Pistol and Target

1979. Centenary of Austrian Shooting Club, and European Air Rifle and Air Pistol Shooting Championships.
1830 **601** 6s. multicoloured 1·70 75

602 *Franz I* (paddle-steamer)

1979. 150th Anniv of Danube Steam Navigation Company.
1831 **602** 1s.50 blue 55 45
1832 - 2s.50 brown 80 65
1833 - 3s. red 1·50 1·20
DESIGNS: 2s.50, Pusher tug "Linz"; 3s. "Theodor Korner" (passenger vessel).

603 Skater

1979. World Ice Skating and Dancing Championships. Vienna.
1834 **603** 4s. multicoloured 1·10 75

604 Fashion Drawing by Theo Zache, 1900

1979. 50th Viennese Int Ladies' Fashion Week.
1835 **604** 2s.50 multicoloured 65 55

605 Wiener Neustadt Cathedral

1979. 700th Anniv of Wiener Neustadt Cathedral.
1836 **605** 4s. blue and grey 1·10 65

606 Relief from Emperor Joseph II Monument, Vienna

1979. Bicentenary of Education for the Deaf.
1837 **606** 2s.50 green, black & gold 80 45

607 Population Graph

1979. 150th Anniv of Austrian Central Statistical Office.
1838 **607** 2s.50 multicoloured 90 45

608 Laurenz Koschier (postal reformer)

1979. Europa.
1839 **608** 6s. brown and ochre 3·75 95

609 Section through Diesel Engine

1979. 13th Congress of International Combustion Engine Council.
1840 **609** 4s. multicoloured 1·10 65

610 Town Arms of Ried, Braunau and Scharding

1979. Bicentenary of Innviertel District.
1841 **610** 3s. multicoloured 1·10 45

611 Water Pollution

1979. Prevention of Water Pollution.
1842 **611** 2s.50 green and grey 90 45

612 Arms of Rottenmann

1979. 700th Anniv of Rottenmann.
1843 **612** 3s. multicoloured 1·70 45

613 Jodok Fink

1979. 50th Death Anniv of Jodok Fink (politician).
1844 **613** 3s. brown 1·10 45

614 Arms of Wels and Returned Soldiers League Badge

1979. Fifth European Meeting of Returned Soldiers.
1845 **614** 4s. green and black 1·10 65

615 Flower

1979. U.N. Conference on Science and Technology for Development, Vienna.
1846 **615** 4s. blue 1·10 65

616 Vienna International Centre

1979. Opening of U.N.O. Vienna Int Centre.
1847 **616** 6s. slate 1·70 95

617 Eye and Blood Vessels of Diabetic

1979. Tenth World Congress of International Diabetes Federation, Vienna.
1848 **617** 2s.50 multicoloured 80 45

618 Stanzer Valley seen from Arlberg Road Tunnel

1979. 16th World Road Congress, Vienna.
1849 **618** 4s. multicoloured 1·10 65

619 Steam-driven Printing Press

1979. 175th Anniv of State Printing Works.
1850 **619** 3s. black and stone 90 55

620 Richard Zsigmondy

1979. 50th Death Anniv of Dr. Richard Zsigmondy (Nobel Prize winner for Chemistry).
1851 **620** 6s. brown 1·70 95

621 Bregenz Festival and Congress Hall

1979. Bregenz Festival and Congress Hall.
1852 **621** 2s.50 lilac 90 45

622 Burning Match

1979. "Save Energy".
1853 **622** 2s.50 multicoloured 90 45

623 Lions Emblem

1979. 25th European Lions Forum, Vienna.
1854 **623** 4s. yellow, gold and lilac 1·10 65

624 Wilhelm Exner (founder)

1979. Centenary of Industrial Museum and Technical School, Vienna.
1855 **624** 2s.50 dp purple & purple 80 45

625 *The Suffering Christ* (Hans Fronius)

1979. Austrian Modern Art.
1856 **625** 4s. black and stone 1·10 75

626 Series 52 Goods Locomotive

1979. Centenary of Raab (Gyor)–Odenburg (Sopron)-Ebenfurt Railway.
1857 **626** 2s.50 multicoloured 1·10 75

627 August Musger

1979. 50th Death Anniv of August Musger (pioneer of slow-motion photography).
1858 **627** 2s.50 black and grey 80 45

628 *Nativity* (detail of icon by Moses Subotic, St. Barbara Church, Vienna)

1979. Christmas.
1859 **628** 4s. multicoloured 1·10 65

629 Neue Hofburg, Vienna

1979. "WIPA 1981" International Stamp Exhibition, Vienna (1st issue). Inscr "1. Phase".
1860 **629** 16s.+8s. multicoloured 4·75 4·50

See also No. 1890.

630 Arms of Baden

1980. 500th Anniv of Baden.
1861 **630** 4s. multicoloured 1·10 65

631 Loading Exports

1980. Austrian Exports.
1862 **631** 4s. blue, red and black 1·10 65

632 Rheumatic Hand holding Stick

1980. Fight against Rheumatism.
1863 **632** 2s.50 red and blue 80 45

633 Emblems of 1880 and 1980

1980. Centenary of Austrian Red Cross.
1864 **633** 2s.50 multicoloured 80 45

634 Kirchschlager

1980. Pres. Rudolf Kirchschlager's 65th Birthday.
1865 **634** 4s. brown and red 1·10 65

635 Robert Hamerling

1980. 150th Birth Anniv of Robert Hamerling (writer).
1866 **635** 2s.50 green 80 45

636 Town Seal

1980. 750th Anniv of Hallein.
1867 **636** 4s. black and red 1·10 65

637 *Maria Theresa as a Young Woman* (Andreas Moller)

1980. Death Bicentenary of Empress Maria Theresa.
1868 **637** 2s.50 purple 1·10 95
1869 - 4s. blue 1·50 1·20
1870 - 6s. brown 2·50 2·10

DESIGNS: 4s. *Maria Theresa with St. Stephen's Crown* (Martin van Meytens); 6s. *Maria Theresa as Widow* (Joseph Ducreux).

638 Flags of Treaty Signatories

1980. 25th Anniv of Austrian State Treaty.
1871 **638** 4s. multicoloured 1·10 65

639 St. Benedict (statue, Meinrad Guggenbichler)

1980. Congress of Austrian Benedictine Orders, Mariazell.
1872 **639** 2s.50 green 80 45

640 *Hygieia* (Gustav Klimt)

1980. 175th Anniv of Hygiene Education.
1873 **640** 4s. multicoloured 1·10 65

641 Dish Aerial, Aflenz

1980. Inauguration of Aflenz Satellite Communications Earth Station.
1874 **641** 6s. multicoloured 1·70 95

642 Steyr (copperplate engraving, 1693)

1980. Millenary of Steyr.
1875 **642** 4s. brown, black & gold 1·10 65

643 Oil Driller

1980. 50th Anniv of Oil Production in Austria.
1876 **643** 2s.50 multicoloured 80 45

644 Town Seal of 1267

1980. 800th Anniv of Innsbruck.
1877 **644** 2s.50 yellow, blk & red 80 45

645 Ducal Crown

1980. 800th Anniv of Elevation of Styria to Dukedom.
1878 **645** 4s. multicoloured 1·10 65

646 Leo Ascher

1980. Birth Cent of Leo Ascher (composer).
1879 **646** 3s. violet 80 45

647 "Abraham" (illustration from *Viennese Genesis*)

1980. Tenth Congress of International Organization for Study of the Old Testament.
1880 **647** 4s. multicoloured 1·10 65

648 Robert Stolz

1980. Europa and Birth Centenary of Robert Stolz (composer).
1881 **648** 6s. red 3·25 95

649 Falkenstein Railway Bridge

1980. 11th International Association of Bridge and Structural Engineering Congress, Vienna.
1882 **649** 4s. multicoloured 1·10 65

650 *Moon Figure* (Karl Brandstatter)

1980. Austrian Modern Art.
1883 **650** 4s. multicoloured 1·10 65

651 Customs Officer

1980. 150th Anniv of Customs Service.
1884 **651** 2s.50 brown and red 80 45

652 Masthead of 1810

1980. 350th Anniv of *Linzer Zeitung* (Linz newspaper).
1885 **652** 2s.50 black, red & gold 80 45

653 Frontispiece of Waidhofen Municipal Book

1980. 750th Anniv of Waidhofen.
1886 **653** 2s.50 multicoloured 80 45

654 Heads

1980. 25th Anniv of Federal Army.
1887 **654** 2s.50 green and red 80 45

655 Alfred Wegener

1980. Birth Centenary of Alfred Wegener (explorer and geophysicist).
1888 **655** 4s. blue 1·10 65

656 Robert Musil

1980. Birth Centenary of Robert Musil (writer).
1889 **656** 4s. brown 1·10 65

1980. "WIPA 1981" International Stamp Exhibition, Vienna (2nd issue). Inscr "2. Phase".
1890 **629** 16s.+8s. mult 4·75 4·50

657 *Adoration of the Kings* (stained-glass window, Viktring Collegiate Church)

1980. Christmas.

1891	**657**	4s. multicoloured	1·10	65

658 Ribbon in National Colours

1981. 25th Anniv of General Social Insurance Act.

1892	**658**	2s.50 red, green & black	55	45

1981. WIPA. 1981 International Stamp Exhibtion, Vienna (3rd issue). Sheet 90×71 mm. containing horiz designs as T **629** but in finished state.

MS1893	16s. + 8s. multicoloured	5·50	5·50

659 Unissued Design for 1926 Child Welfare Stamps

1981. Birth Centenary of Wilhelm Dachauer (artist).

1894	**659**	3s. brown	80	45

660 Disabled Person operating Machine Tool

1981. Third European Regional Conference of Rehabilitation International.

1895	**660**	6s. brown, blue and red	1·30	85

661 Sigmund Freud

1981. 125th Birth Anniv of Sigmund Freud (psychoanalyst).

1896	**661**	3s. purple	80	45

662 Long-distance Heating System

1981. 20th International Union of Long-distance Heat Distributors Congress, Vienna.

1897	**662**	4s. multicoloured	1·10	65

663 *Azzo and his Vassals* (cover of Monastery's "bearskin" Manuscript)

1981. Kuenring Exhibition, Zwettl Monastery.

1898	**663**	3s. multicoloured	80	45

664 Maypole

1981. Europa.

1899	**664**	6s. multicoloured	4·50	1·40

665 Early Telephone

1981. Centenary of Austrian Telephone System.

1900	**665**	4s. multicoloured	1·10	65

666 "The Frog King"

1981. Art Education in Schools.

1901	**666**	3s. multicoloured	80	45

667 Research Centre

1981. 25th Anniv of Seibersdorf Research Centre.

1902	**667**	4s. blue, dp blue & orge	1·10	65

668 Town Hall and Seal

1981. 850th Anniv of St. Veit-on-Glan.

1903	**668**	4s. yellow, brown & red	1·10	65

669 Johann Florian Heller (chemist)

1981. 11th Int Clinical Chemistry Congress, Vienna.

1904	**669**	6s. brown	1·30	95

670 Boltzmann

1981. 75th Death Anniv of Ludwig Boltzmann (physicist).

1905	**670**	3s. green	80	45

671 Otto Bauer

1981. Birth Centenary of Otto Bauer (writer and politician).

1906	**671**	4s. multicoloured	1·10	65

672 Chemical Balance

1981. International Pharmaceutical Federation Congress, Vienna.

1907	**672**	6s. black, brown and red	1·20	75

673 Impossible Construction (M. C. Escher)

1981. Tenth International Austrian Mathematicians' Congress, Innsbruck.

1908	**673**	4s. lt blue, blue & dp blue	1·10	65

674 *Coronation of Virgin Mary* (detail)

1981. 500th Anniv of Michael Pacher's Altarpiece at St. Wolfgang, Abersee.

1909	**674**	3s. blue	80	45

675 Compass Rose

1981. 75th Anniv of Graz S.E. Exhibition.

1910	**675**	4s. multicoloured	1·10	65

676 *Holy Trinity* (illuminated MS, 12th century)

1981. 16th International Congress of Byzantine Scholars, Vienna.

1911	**676**	6s. multicoloured	1·20	75

677 Josef II

1981. Bicentenary of Toleration Act (giving freedom of worship to Protestants).

1912	**677**	4s. black, blue & bistre	1·10	65

678 Hans Kelsen

1981. Bicentenary of Hans Kelsen (law lecturer and contributor to shaping of Austrian Constitution).

1913	**678**	3s. red	80	45

679 Full and Empty Bowls and F.A.O. Emblem

1981. World Food Day.

1914	**679**	6s. multicoloured	1·20	75

680 *Between the Times* (Oscar Asboth)

1981. Austrian Modern Art.

1915	**680**	4s. multicoloured	1·10	65

681 Workers and Emblem

1981. Seventh International Catholic Employees' Meeting, Vienna-Lainz.

1916	**681**	3s. multicoloured	80	45

682 Hammer-Purgstall

1981. 125th Death Anniv of Josef Hammer-Purgstall (orientalist).

1917	**682**	3s. multicoloured	80	45

683 Julius Raab

1981. 90th Birth Anniv of Julius Raab (politician).

1918	**683**	6s. purple	1·10	95

684 Stefan Zweig

1981. Birth Centenary of Stefan Zweig (writer).

1919	**684**	4s. lilac	90	75

685 Christmas Crib, Burgenland

1981. Christmas.

1920	**685**	4s. multicoloured	90	75

686 Arms of St. Nikola

1981. 800th Anniv of St. Nikola-on-Danube.

1921	**686**	4s. multicoloured	90	75

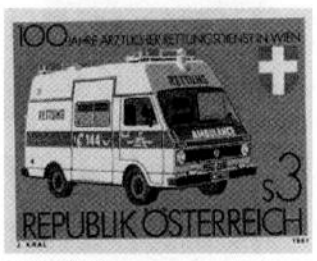

687 Volkswagen Transporter Ambulance

1981. Cent of Vienna's Emergency Medical Service.

1922	**687**	3s. multicoloured	80	45

688 Skier

1982. Alpine Skiing World Championship, Schladming-Haus.

1923	**688**	4s. multicoloured	80	45

689 Dorotheum Building

1982. 275th Anniv of Dorotheum Auction, Pawn and Banking Society.
1924 **689** 4s. multicoloured 80 45

690 Lifesaving

1982. 25th Anniv of Austrian Water Lifesaving Service.
1925 **690** 5s. blue, red & light blue 1·00 85

691 St. Severin

1982. "St. Severin and the End of the Roman Period" Exhibition, Enns.
1926 **691** 3s. multicoloured 80 45

692 Sebastian Kneipp (pioneer of holistic medicine)

1982. International Kneipp Congress, Vienna.
1927 **692** 4s. multicoloured 80 65

693 Printers' Coat-of-arms

1982. 500th Anniv of Printing in Austria.
1928 **693** 4s. multicoloured 80 65

694 Urine Analysis from *Canon Medicinae* by Avicenna

1982. Fifth European Union for Urology Congress, Vienna.
1929 **694** 6s. multicoloured 1·10 95

695 St. Francis preaching to Animals (miniature)

1982. "Franciscan Art and Culture in the Middle Ages" Exhibition, Krems-Stein.
1930 **695** 3s. multicoloured 80 45

696 Haydn and Birthplace, Rohrau

1982. "Joseph Haydn and His Time" Exhibition, Eisenstadt.
1931 **696** 3s. green 1·10 95

697 Globe within Milk Churn

1982. World Dairying Day.
1932 **697** 7s. multicoloured 1·70 95

698 Town Arms (1804 flag)

1982. 800th Anniv of Gfohl.
1933 **698** 4s. multicoloured 80 65

699 Tennis Player

1982. 80th Anniv of Austrian Lawn Tennis Assn.
1934 **699** 3s. multicoloured 80 45

700 Main Square, Langenlois

1982. 900th Anniv of Langenlois.
1935 **700** 4s. multicoloured 90 45

701 Town Arms

1982. 800th Anniv of Weiz.
1936 **701** 4s. multicoloured 1·70 75

702 Linz–Freistadt–Budweis Horse-drawn Railway

1982. Europa.
1937 **702** 6s. brown 5·00 1·00

703 Ignaz Seipel

1982. 50th Death Anniv of Ignaz Seipel (Federal Chancellor).
1938 **703** 3s. purple 80 50

704 Postbus

1982. 75th Anniv of Post-bus Service.
1939 **704** 4s. multicoloured 90 80

705 Rocket Launch

1982. Second U.N. Conference on the Exploration and Peaceful Uses of Outer Space, Vienna.
1940 **705** 4s. multicoloured 1·10 1·00

706 Globe (Federal Office for Standardization and Surveying, Vienna)

1982. Geodesists' Day.
1941 **706** 3s. multicoloured 80 50

707 Great Bustard ("Grosstrappe")

1982. Endangered Animals. Multicoloured.
1942 3s. Type **707** 80 70
1943 4s. Eurasian beaver 1·00 90
1944 6s. Western capercaillie ("Auerhahn") 1·60 1·40

708 Institute Building, Laxenburg

1982. Tenth Anniv of International Institute for Applied Systems Analysis.
1945 **708** 3s. black and brown 65 60

709 St. Apollonia (patron saint of dentists)

1982. 70th International Dentists Federation Congress, Vienna.
1946 **709** 4s. multicoloured 90 80

710 Emmerich Kalman

1982. Birth Cent of Emmerich Kalman (composer).
1947 **710** 3s. blue 80 50

711 Max Mell

1982. Birth Centenary of Max Mell (writer).
1948 **711** 3s. multicoloured 80 50

712 Christmas Crib, Damuls Church

1982. Christmas.
1949 **712** 4s. multicoloured 90 80

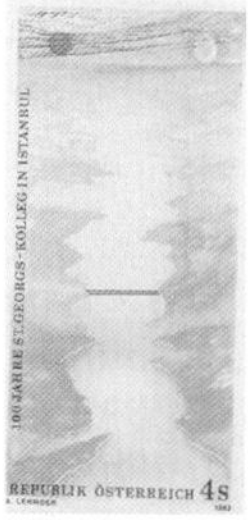

713 Aerial View of Bosphorus

1982. Centenary of St. George's Austrian College, Istanbul.
1950 **713** 4s. multicoloured 90 80

714 "Mainz-Weber" Mailbox, 1870

1982. Stamp Day.
1951 **714** 6s.+3s. multicoloured 2·20 2·00

715 *Muse of the Republic* (Ernst Fuchs)

1982. Austrian Modern Art.
1952 **715** 4s. red and violet 1·10 1·00

716 Bank, Vienna

1983. Centenary of Postal Savings Bank.
1953 **716** 4s. yellow, black and blue 90 80

717 Hildegard Burjan

1983. Birth Centenary of Hildegard Burjan (founder of Caritas Socialis (religious sisterhood)).
1954 **717** 4s. red 90 80

718 Linked Arms

1983. World Communications Year.
1955 **718** 7s. multicoloured 1·50 1·00

719 Young Girl

1983. 75th Anniv of Children's Friends Organization.
1956 **719** 4s. black, blue and red 90 80

720 Josef Matthias Hauer

1983. Birth Centenary of Josef Matthias Hauer (composer).
1957 **720** 3s. purple 65 60

721 Douglas DC-9-80 Super Eighty

1983. 25th Anniv of Austrian Airlines.
1958 **721** 6s. multicoloured 1·30 1·20

722 Hands protecting Workers

1983. Cent of Government Work Inspection Law.
1959 **722** 4s. grn, dp grn & brn 90 80

723 Wels (engraving, Matthaeus Merian)

1983. "Millenary of Upper Austria" Exn, Wels.
1960 **723** 3s. multicoloured 65 60

724 Human Figure, Heart and Electrocardiogram

1983. Seventh World Symposium on Pacemakers.
1961 **724** 4s. red, mauve and blue 90 80

725 Monastery Arms

1983. 900th Anniv of Gottweig Monastery.
1962 **725** 3s. multicoloured 65 60

726 Weitra

1983. 800th Anniv of Weitra.
1963 **726** 4s. black, red and gold 90 80

727 Cap, Stick, Ribbon and Emblems

1983. 50th Anniv of MKV and CCV Catholic Students' Organizations.
1964 **727** 4s. multicoloured 90 80

728 Glopper Castle and Town Arms

1983. 650th Anniv of Hohenems Town Charter.
1965 **728** 4s. multicoloured 90 80

729 Hess

1983. Europa. Birth Centenary of Viktor Franz Hess (physicist and Nobel Prize winner).
1966 **729** 6s. green 5·00 1·00

730 Vienna City Hall

1983. 25th Anniv of Vienna City Hall.
1967 **730** 4s. multicoloured 90 80

731 Kiwanis Emblem and View of Vienna

1983. Kiwanis International, World and European Conference, Vienna.
1968 **731** 5s. multicoloured 1·10 1·00

732 Congress Emblem

1983. Seventh World Psychiatry Congress, Vienna.
1969 **732** 4s. multicoloured 90 60

733 Hasenauer and Natural History Museum, Vienna

1983. 150th Birth Anniv of Carl Freiherr von Hasenauer (architect).
1970 **733** 3s. brown 90 50

734 Institute for Promotion of Trade and Industry, Linz

1983. 27th International Professional Competition for Young Skilled Workers, Linz.
1971 **734** 4s. multicoloured 1·10 70

735 Symbols of Penicillin V Efficacy and Cancer

1983. 13th Int Chemotherapy Congress, Vienna.
1972 **735** 5s. red and green 1·10 80

736 Pope John Paul II

1983. Papal Visit.
1973 **736** 6s. black, red and gold 1·70 1·00

737 *Relief of Vienna, 1683* (Franz Geffels)

1983. 300th Anniv of Relief of Vienna. Sheet 90×70 mm.
MS1974 **737** 6s. multicoloured 2·20 2·00

738 Spectrum around Cross

1983. Austrian Catholics' Day.
1975 **738** 3s. multicoloured 80 50

739 Vienna Town Hall

1983. Centenary of Vienna Town Hall.
1976 **739** 4s. multicoloured 1·10 60

740 Karl von Terzaghi

1983. Birth Centenary of Karl von Terzaghi (soil mechanics and foundations engineer).
1977 **740** 3s. blue 90 50

741 Initials of Federation

1983. Tenth Austrian Trade Unions Federation Congress.
1978 **741** 3s. red and black 80 50

742 *Evening Sun in Burgenland* (Gottfried Kumpf)

1983. Austrian Modern Art.
1979 **742** 4s. multicoloured 1·10 80

743 Tram No. 5, 1883

1983. Centenary of Modling–Hinterbruhl Electric Railway.
1980 **743** 3s. multicoloured 1·10 50

744 Boy looking at Stamped Envelope

1983. Stamp Day.
1981 **744** 6s.+3s. multicoloured 2·00 1·60

745 Francisco Carolinum Museum, Linz

1983. 150th Anniv of Upper Austrian Provincial Museum.
1982 **745** 4s. multicoloured 1·10 70

746 Crib by Johann Giner the Elder, Kitzbuhel Church

1983. Christmas.
1983 **746** 4s. multicoloured 90 80

747 Parliament Building

1983. Centenary of Parliament Building, Vienna.
1984 **747** 4s. blue 1·10 70

748 "St. Nicholas" (Maria Freund)

1983. Youth Stamp.
1985 **748** 3s. multicoloured 80 50

749 Wolfgang Pauli

1983. 25th Death Anniv of Wolfgang Pauli (Nobel Prize winner for Physics).
1986 **749** 6s. brown 1·30 1·00

750 Gregor Mendel

1984. Death Cent of Gregor Mendel (geneticist).
1987 **750** 4s. ochre and brown 90 80

751 Hanak at Work

1984. 50th Death Anniv of Anton Hanak (sculptor).

1988	**751**	3s. brown and black	80	50

752 Disabled Skier

1984. Third World Winter Games for the Disabled, Innsbruck.

1989	**752**	4s.+2s. multicoloured	1·30	1·20

753 Memorial, Wollersdorf

1984. 50th Anniv of 1934 Insurrections.

1990	**753**	4s.50 red and black	90	60

754 Founders' Stone

1984. 900th Anniv of Reichersberg Monastery.

1991	**754**	3s.50 stone, brown & bl	80	50

755 Geras Monastery

1984. Monasteries and Abbeys.

1992	-	50g. yellow, black & grey	20	20
1993	-	1s. yellow, black & mve	45	20
1994	-	1s.50 yellow, red & blue	45	25
1995	-	2s. yellow, green & black	80	30
1996	**755**	3s.50 yellow, sep & brn	1·30	40
1997	-	4s. yellow, purple & red	1·30	30
1998	-	4s.50 yellow, lilac & blue	1·50	50
1999	-	5s. yellow, purple & orge	1·50	50
2000	-	5s.50 yell, dp vio & vio	1·80	50
2001	-	6s. yellow, green & emer	1·80	30
2002	-	7s. yellow, green & blue	2·75	40
2003	-	7s.50 yell, dp brn & brn	2·50	50
2004	-	8s. yellow, blue and red	2·50	50
2005	-	10s. yellow, red & grey	3·00	50
2006	-	11s. yellow, black & brn	3·25	80
2007	-	12s. yellow, brn & orge	5·00	1·20
2008	-	17s. yellow, ultram & bl	5·50	1·30
2009	-	20s. yellow, brown & red	6·75	1·50

DESIGNS: 50g. Vorau Monastery; 1s. Wettingen Abbey, Mehrerau; 1s.50, Monastery of Teutonic Order, Vienna; 2s. Michaelbeuern Benedictine Monastery, Salzburg; 4s. Stams Monastery; 4s.50, Schlagl Monastery; 5s. St. Paul's Monastery, Lavanttal; 5s.50, St. Gerold's Priory, Vorarlberg; 6s. Rein Monastery; 7s. Loretto Monastery; 7s.50, Dominican Monastery, Vienna; 8s. Cistercian Monastery, Zwettl; 10s. Premonstratensian Monastery, Wilten; 11s. Trappist Monastery, Engelszell; 12s. Monastery of the Hospitallers, Eisenstadt; 17s. St. Peter's Abbey, Salzburg; 20s. Wernberg Convent, Carinthia.

756 Cigar Band showing Tobacco Plant

1984. Bicentenary of Tobacco Monopoly.

2012	**756**	4s.50 multicoloured	90	60

757 Kostendorf

1984. 1200th Anniv of Kostendorf.

2013	**757**	4s.50 multicoloured	90	60

758 Wheel Bearing

1984. 20th International Federation of Automobile Engineers' Associations World Congress, Vienna.

2014	**758**	5s. multicoloured	1·10	80

759 Bridge

1984. Europa. 25th Anniv of E.P.T. Conference.

2015	**759**	6s. blue and ultramarine	4·50	1·00

760 Archduke Johann (after Schnorr von Carolsfeld)

1984. 125th Death Anniv of Archduke Johann.

2016	**760**	4s.50 multicoloured	90	60

761 Aragonite

1984. "Ore and Iron in the Green Mark" Exhibition, Eisenerz.

2017	**761**	3s.50 multicoloured	65	50

762 Binding of *Das Buch vom Kaiser*, by Max Herzig

1984. Lower Austrian *Era of Emperor Franz Joseph: From Revolution to Grunderzeit* Exhibition, Grafenegg Castle.

2018	**762**	3s.50 red and gold	90	50

763 Upper City Tower and Arms

1984. 850th Anniv of Vocklabruch.

2019	**763**	4s.50 multicoloured	1·10	80

764 Dionysus (Virunum mosaic)

1984. Centenary of Carinthia Provincial Museum, Klagenfurt.

2020	**764**	3s.50 stone, brn & grey	80	50

765 *Meeting of Austrian Army with South Tyrolean Reserves* (detail, Schnorr von Carolsfeld)

1984. "Jubilee of Tyrol Province" Exhibition.

2021	**765**	3s.50 multicoloured	80	50

766 Ralph Benatzky

1984. Birth Cent of Ralph Benatzky (composer).

2022	**766**	4s. brown	90	60

767 Flood Control Barriers

1984. Centenary of Flood Control Systems.

2023	**767**	4s.50 green	1·10	70

768 Christian von Ehrenfels

1984. 125th Death Anniv of Christian von Ehrenfels (philosopher).

2024	**768**	3s.50 multicoloured	80	50

769 Models of European Monuments

1984. 25th Anniv of Minimundus (model world), Worthersee.

2025	**769**	4s. yellow and black	90	80

770 Blockheide Eibenstein National Park

1984. Natural Beauty Spots.

2026	**770**	4s. pink and olive	90	80

771 Electric Train on Schanatobel Bridge (Arlberg Railway Centenary)

1984. Railway Anniversaries.

2027	**771**	3s.50 brown, gold & red	1·10	1·00
2028	-	4s.50 blue, silver and red	1·30	1·20

DESIGN: 4s.50, Electric train on Falkenstein Bridge (75th anniv of Tauern Railway).

772 Johann Georg Stuwer's Flight in Montgolfier Balloon

1984. Bicentenary of First Manned Balloon Flight in Austria.

2029	**772**	6s. multicoloured	1·50	90

773 Lake Neusiedl

1984. Natural Beauty Spots.

2030	**773**	4s. purple and blue	90	80

774 Palace of Justice, Vienna

1984. 20th Int Bar Assn Congress, Vienna.

2031	**774**	7s. multicoloured	1·50	1·30

775 *Joseph Hyrtl* (window, Innsbruck Anatomy Institute)

1984. Seventh European Anatomists' Congress, Innsbruck.

2032	**775**	6s. multicoloured	1·30	80

776 *Window* (Karl Korab)

1984. Austrian Modern Art.

2033	**776**	4s. multicoloured	1·10	80

777 Clock of Imms (astrolabe)

1984. 600th Birth Anniv of Johannes von Gmunden (astronomer and mathematician).

2034	**777**	3s.50 multicoloured	80	50

778 Quill

1984. 125th Anniv of Concordia Press Club.

2035 **778** 4s.50 black, gold & red 90 60

779 Fanny Elssler

1984. Death Centenary of Fanny Elssler (dancer).

2036 **779** 4s. multicoloured 1·00 60

780 *Holy Family* (detail, Aggsbach Old High Altar)

1984. Christmas.

2037 **780** 4s.50 multicoloured 1·00 90

781 Detail from Burial Chamber Wall of Seschemnofer III

1984. Stamp Day.

2038 **781** 6s.+3s. multicoloured 2·00 1·60

782 Coat of Arms

1985. 400th Anniv of Graz University.

2039 **782** 3s.50 multicoloured 80 70

783 Dr. Lorenz Bohler

1985. Birth Centenary of Prof. Dr. Lorenz Bohler (surgeon).

2040 **783** 4s.50 purple 90 60

784 Ski Jumping, Skiing and Emblem

1985. World Nordic Skiing Championship, Seefeld.

2041 **784** 4s. multicoloured 1·00 90

785 Linz Cathedral

1985. Bicentenary of Linz Diocese.

2042 **785** 4s.50 multicoloured 90 60

786 Alban Berg

1985. Birth Centenary of Alban Berg (composer).

2043 **786** 6s. blue 1·30 1·00

787 Institute Emblem

1985. 25th Anniv of Institute for Vocational Advancement.

2044 **787** 4s.50 multicoloured 90 60

788 Stylized "B" and Clouds

1985. 2000th Anniv of Bregenz.

2045 **788** 4s. black, ultram & blue 80 50

789 1885 Registration Label

1985. Centenary of Registration Labels in Austria.

2046 **789** 4s.50 black, yell & grey 90 60

790 Josef Stefan

1985. 150th Birth Anniv of Josef Stefan (physicist).

2047 **790** 6s. brown, stone and red 1·30 90

791 St. Leopold (Margrave and patron saint)

1985. Lower Austrian Provincial Exhibition, Klosterneuburg Monastery.

2048 **791** 3s.50 multicoloured 80 50

792 *The Story-teller*

1985. 150th Birth Anniv of Franz Defregger (artist).

2049 **792** 3s.50 multicoloured 80 70

793 Barbed Wire, Broken Tree and New Shoot

1985. 40th Anniv of Liberation.

2050 **793** 4s.50 multicoloured 90 60

794 Johann Joseph Fux (composer)

1985. Europa. Music Year.

2051 **794** 6s. brown and grey 4·25 1·00

795 Flags and Caduceus

1985. 25th Anniv of European Free Trade Association.

2052 **795** 4s. multicoloured 1·00 70

796 Town and Arms

1985. Millenary of Boheimkirchen.

2053 **796** 4s.50 multicoloured 1·00 70

797 Bishop's Gate, St. Polten

1985. Bicentenary of St. Polten Diocese.

2054 **797** 4s.50 multicoloured 1·00 70

798 Johannes von Nepomuk Church, Innsbruck

1985. Gumpp Family (architects) Exn, Innsbruck.

2055 **798** 3s.50 multicoloured 80 60

799 Garsten (copperplate, George Matthaus Fischer)

1985. Millenary of Garsten.

2056 **799** 4s.50 multicoloured 1·10 80

800 U.N. Emblem and Austrian Arms

1985. 40th Anniv of U.N.O. and 30th Anniv of Austrian Membership.

2057 **800** 4s. multicoloured 1·00 70

801 Association Headquarters, Vienna

1985. 13th International Suicide Prevention Association Congress, Vienna.

2058 **801** 5s. brown, lt yell & yell 1·10 80

802 Woodland

1985. Forestry Year. Sheet 90×70 mm.

MS2059 **802** 6s. multicoloured 2·20 2·20

803 Operetta Emblem and Spa Building

1985. 25th Bad Ischl Operetta Week.

2060 **803** 3s.50 multicoloured 1·00 70

804 Fireman and Emblem

1985. Eighth International Fire Brigades Competition, Vocklabruck.

2061 **804** 4s.50 black, green & red 1·30 80

805 Grossglockner Mountain Road

1985. 50th Anniv of Grossglockner Mountain Road.

2062 **805** 4s. multicoloured 1·00 70

806 Chessboard as Globe

1985. World Chess Association Congress, Graz.

2063 **806** 4s. multicoloured 90 80

807 "Founding of Konigstetten" (August Stephan)

1985. Millenary of Konigstetten.

2064 **807** 4s.50 multicoloured 1·00 70

808 Webern Church and Arms of Hofkirchen and Taufkircher

1985. 1200th Anniversaries of Hofkirchen, Weibern and Taufkirchen.

2065 **808** 4s.50 multicoloured 1·00 70

809 Dr. Adam Politzer

1985. 150th Birth Anniv of Dr. Adam Politzer (otologist).
2066 **809** 3s.50 violet 90 60

810 Emblem and View of Vienna

1985. International Association of Forwarding Agents World Congress, Vienna.
2067 **810** 6s. multicoloured 1·30 90

811 "Clowns Riding High Bicycles" (Paul Flora)

1985. Austrian Modern Art.
2068 **811** 4s. multicoloured 1·10 1·00

812 St. Martin, Patron Saint of Burgenland

1985. 25th Anniv of Eisenstadt Diocese.
2069 **812** 4s.50 black, bistre & red 1·10 80

813 Roman Mounted Courier

1985. 50th Anniv of Stamp Day.
2070 **813** 6s.+3s. multicoloured 2·00 1·80

814 Hanns Horbiger

1985. 125th Birth Anniv of Hanns Horbiger (design engineer).
2071 **814** 3s.50 purple and gold 90 80

815 *Adoration of the Christ Child* (marble relief)

1985. Christmas.
2072 **815** 4s.50 multicoloured 80 50

816 Aqueduct

1985. 75th Anniv of Second Vienna Waterline.
2073 **816** 3s.50 black, red & blue 80 50

818 Chateau de la Muette (headquarters)

1985. 25th Anniv of Organization of Economic Co-operation and Development.
2080 **818** 4s. black, gold & mauve 95 85

819 Johann Bohm

1986. Birth Centenary of Johann Bohm (founder of Austrian Trade Unions Federation).
2081 **819** 4s.50 black and red 1·00 70

820 Dove and Globe

1986. International Peace Year.
2082 **820** 6s. multicoloured 1·30 85

821 Push-button Dialling

1986. Introduction of Digital Preselection Telephone System.
2083 **821** 5s. multicoloured 1·00 60

822 Albrechtsberger and Organ

1986. 250th Birth Anniv of Johann Georg Albrechtsberger (composer).
2084 **822** 3s.50 multicoloured 80 70

823 Main Square and Arms

1986. 850th Anniv of Korneuburg.
2085 **823** 5s. multicoloured 1·20 70

824 Kokoschka (self-portrait)

1986. Birth Centenary of Oskar Kokoschka (artist).
2086 **824** 4s. black and pink 1·00 60

825 Council Flag

1986. 30th Anniv of Membership of Council of Europe.
2087 **825** 6s. black, red and blue 1·30 85

826 Holzmeister and Salzburg Festival Hall

1986. Birth Centenary of Professor Clemens Holzmeister (architect).
2088 **826** 4s. grey, brown & lt brn 80 70

827 Road, Roll of Material, and Congress Emblem

1986. Third International Geotextile Congress, Vienna.
2089 **827** 5s. multicoloured 1·00 60

828 Schlosshof Palace (after Bernardo Bellotto) and Prince Eugene

1986. "Prince Eugene and the Baroque Era" Exhibition, Schlosshof and Niederweiden.
2090 **828** 4s. multicoloured 95 70

829 St. Florian Monastery

1986. Upper Austrian "World of Baroque" Exhibition, St. Florian Monastery.
2091 **829** 4s. multicoloured 1·00 70

830 Herberstein Castle and Styrian Arms

1986. "Styria – Bridge and Bulwark" Exhibition, Herberstein Castle, near Stubenberg.
2092 **830** 4s. multicoloured 1·00 70

831 Large Pasque Flower

1986. Europa.
2093 **831** 6s. multicoloured 3·50 1·00

832 Wagner and Scene from Opera *Lohengrin*

1986. International Richard Wagner (composer) Congress, Vienna.
2094 **832** 4s. multicoloured 95 85

833 Antimonite Crystal

1986. Burgenland "Mineral and Fossils" Exhibition, Oberpullendorf.
2095 **833** 4s. multicoloured 95 85

834 Martinswall, Zirl

1986. Natural Beauty Spots.
2096 **834** 5s. brown and blue 1·20 85

835 Waidhofen

1986. 800th Anniv of Waidhofen on Ybbs.
2097 **835** 4s. multicoloured 1·20 85

836 Tschauko Falls, Ferlach

1986. Natural Beauty Spots.
2098 **836** 5s. green and brown 1·20 85

837 19th-century Steam and Modern Articulated Trams

1986. Cent of Salzburg Local Transport System.
2099 **837** 4s. multicoloured 1·20 1·00

838 Enns and Seals of Signatories

1986. 800th Anniv of Georgenberg Treaty (between Duke Leopold V of Austria and Duke Otakar IV of Styria).
2100 **838** 5s. multicoloured 1·20 85

839 Tandler

1986. 50th Death Anniv of Julius Tandler (social reformer).
2101 **839** 4s. multicoloured 95 85

840 *Observatory, 1886* (A. Heilmann)

1986. Centenary of Sonnblick Observatory.
2102 **840** 4s. black, blue and gold 95 85

841 Man collecting Mandragora (from "Codex Tacuinum Sanitatis")

1986. 7th European Anaesthesia Congress, Vienna.
2103 **841** 5s. multicoloured 1·20 85

842 Fire Assistant

1986. 300th Anniv of Vienna Fire Brigade.
2104 **842** 4s. multicoloured 1·70 1·00

843 Stoessl

1986. 50th Death Anniv of Otto Stoessl (writer).
2105 **843** 4s. multicoloured 95 85

844 Viennese Hunting Tapestry (detail)

1986. Fifth International Oriental Carpets and Tapestry Conference, Vienna and Budapest.
2106 **844** 5s. multicoloured 1·20 85

845 Minister in Pulpit

1986. 125th Anniv of Protestants Act and 25th Anniv of Protestants Law.
2107 **845** 5s. black and violet 1·20 85

846 *Decomposition* (Walter Schmogner)

1986. Austrian Modern Art.
2108 **846** 4s. multicoloured 1·20 85

847 Liszt, Birthplace and Score

1986. 175th Birth Anniv of Franz Liszt (composer).
2109 **847** 5s. green and brown 1·20 85

848 Aerial View of Vienna

1986. European Security and Co-operation Conference Review Meeting, Vienna. Sheet 90×70 mm.
MS2110 **848** 6s. multicoloured 1·70 1·60

849 Strettweg Religious Carriage

1986. 175th Anniv of Styrian Joanneum Museum.
2111 **849** 4s. multicoloured 95 85

850 *Nuremberg Letter Messenger* (16th century woodcut)

1986. Stamp Day.
2112 **850** 6s.+3s. multicoloured 2·20 1·70

851 *Adoration of the Shepherds* (woodcut, Johann Georg Schwanthaler)

1986. Christmas.
2113 **851** 5s. brown and gold 1·20 85

852 Headquarters

1986. 40th Anniv of Federal Chamber of Trade and Industry.
2114 **852** 5s. multicoloured 1·20 85

853 Foundry Worker

1986. Austrian World of Work (1st series).
2115 **853** 4s. multicoloured 95 85

See also Nos. 2144, 2178, 2211, 2277, 2386, 2414, 2428, 2486, 2520, 2572 and 2605.

854 "The Educated Eye"

1987. Centenary of Adult Education in Vienna.
2116 **854** 5s. multicoloured 1·20 85

855 *Large Blue Madonna* (Anton Faistauer)

1987. Painters' Birth Centenaries. Multicoloured.
2117 4s. Type **855** 95 85
2118 6s. "Self-portrait" (Albert Paris Gutersloh) 1·40 1·20

856 Hundertwasser House, Vienna

1987. Europa and "Europalia 1987 Austria" Festival, Belgium.
2119 **856** 6s. multicoloured 6·50 2·10

857 Ice Hockey Players

1987. World Ice Hockey Championships, Vienna, and 75th Anniv of Austrian Ice Hockey Association.
2120 **857** 5s. multicoloured 1·50 1·00

858 Austria Centre

1987. Inaug of Austria Conference Centre, Vienna.
2121 **858** 5s. multicoloured 1·50 1·00

859 Salzburg

1987. 700th Anniv of Salzburg Town Charter.
2122 **859** 5s. multicoloured 1·50 1·00

860 Machine Shop, 1920

1987. Upper Austrian "Work–Men–Machines, the Route to Industrialized Society" Exhibition, Steyr.
2123 **860** 4s. black and red 1·20 70

861 Man and Woman

1987. Equal Rights for Men and Women.
2124 **861** 5s. multicoloured 1·20 85

862 *Adele Bloch-Bauer I* (detail, Gustav Klimt)

1987. Lower Austrian "Era of Emperor Franz Joseph: Splendour and Misery" Exhibition, Grafenegg Castle.
2125 **862** 4s. multicoloured 1·20 70

863 Archbishop and Salzburg

1987. 400th Anniv of Election of Prince Wolf Dietrich von Raitenau as Archbishop of Salzburg.
2126 **863** 4s. multicoloured 95 85

864 Schnitzler

1987. 125th Birth Anniv of Arthur Schnitzler (dramatist).
2127 **864** 6s. multicoloured 1·30 95

865 Lace and Arms

1987. 1100th Anniv of Lustenau.
2128 **865** 5s. multicoloured 1·20 85

866 Anniversary Emblem (William Slattery)

1987. 150th Anniv of Austrian Railways. Sheet 90×70 mm.
MS2129 **866** 6s. silver, red and black 2·30 2·10

867 Dachstein Giant Ice Cave

1987. Natural Beauty Spots.
2130 **867** 5s. green and black 1·20 85

868 Engraver at Work

1987. Eighth European Association of Engravers and Flexographers International Congress, Vienna.
2131 **868** 5s. brown, pink and grey 1·20 60

869 Dr. Karl Josef Bayer (chemist)

1987. Eighth International Light Metal Meeting, Leoben and Vienna.
2132 **869** 5s. multicoloured 1·20 60

870 Passenger Ferry

1987. Centenary of 1st Achensee Steam Service.
2133 **870** 4s. multicoloured 1·20 1·00

871 Office Building, Vienna

1987. Tenth Anniv of Office of Ombudsmen.
2134 **871** 5s. black, yellow and red 1·20 85

872 Schrodinger

1987. Birth Cent of Erwin Schrodinger (physicist).
2135 **872** 5s. brown, cream and bistre 1·20 85

873 Freistadt Town Square

1987. 125th Anniv of Freistadt Exhibitions.
2136 **873** 5s. multicoloured 1·20 60

874 Arbing Church

1987. 850th Anniv of Arbing.
2137 **874** 5s. multicoloured 1·20 60

875 Gauertal and Montafon Valleys, Voralberg

1987. Natural Beauty Spots.
2138 **875** 5s. brown and yellow 1·20 85

876 Cyclist

1987. World Cycling Championship, Vienna and Villach.
2139 **876** 5s. multicoloured 1·20 1·00

877 Emblem

1987. World Congress of International Institute of Savings Banks, Vienna.
2140 **877** 5s. multicoloured 1·20 85

878 Hofhaymer at Organ

1987. 450th Death Anniv of Paul Hofhaymer (composer and organist).
2141 **878** 4s. blue, black and gold 95 85

879 Haydn and Salzburg

1987. 250th Birth Anniv of Michael Haydn (composer).
2142 **879** 4s. lilac 95 85

880 Lammergeier ("Bartgeier")

1987. 25th Anniv of Alpine Zoo, Innsbruck.
2143 **880** 4s. multicoloured 95 85

881 Woman using Word Processor

1987. Austrian World of Work (2nd series).
2144 **881** 4s. multicoloured 1·00 70

882 *Tree Goddesses* (Arnulf Neuwirth)

1987. Austrian Modern Art.
2145 **882** 5s. multicoloured 1·20 85

883 Lottery Wheel

1987. Bicentenary of Gambling Monopoly.
2146 **883** 5s. multicoloured 1·20 85

884 Helmer

1987. Birth Centenary of Oskar Helmer (politician).
2147 **884** 4s. multicoloured 95 85

885 Gluck

1987. Death Bicentenary of Christoph Willibald Gluck (composer).
2148 **885** 5s. brown and ochre 1·20 85

886 Stagecoach and Passengers (lithograph, Carl Schuster)

1987. Stamp Day.
2149 **886** 6s.+3s. multicoloured 2·20 1·80

887 Josef Mohr and Franz Xaver Gruber (composers of *Silent Night*)

1987. Christmas.
2150 **887** 5s. multicoloured 1·70 1·00

888 Bosco and Boys

1988. International Educational Congress of St. John Bosco's Salesian Brothers, Vienna.
2151 **888** 5s. purple and orange 1·20 85

889 Cross-country Sledging

1988. Fourth World Winter Games for the Disabled, Innsbruck.
2152 **889** 5s.+2s.50 multicoloured 2·00 1·30

890 Mach

1988. 150th Birth Anniv of Ernst Mach (physicist and philosopher).
2153 **890** 6s. multicoloured 1·40 95

891 *Village with Bridge*

1988. 25th Death Anniv of Franz von Zulow (artist).
2154 **891** 4s. multicoloured 1·20 85

892 *The Confiscation* (Ferdinand Georg Waldmuller)

1988. "Patriotism and Protest: Viennese Biedermeier and Revolution" Exhibition, Vienna.
2155 **892** 4s. multicoloured 1·20 85

893 Barbed Wire, Flag and Crosses

1988. 50th Anniv of Annexation of Austria by Germany.
2156 **893** 5s. green, brown and red 1·40 90

894 Steam Locomotive *Aigen*, Muhlkreis Railway, 1887

1988. Railway Centenaries. Multicoloured.
2157 4s. Type **894** 1·20 1·00
2158 5s. Modern electric tram and Josefsplatz stop (Viennese Local Railways Stock Corporation) 1·50 1·30

895 European Bee Eater

1988. 25th Anniv of World Wildlife Fund, Austria.
2159 **895** 5s. multicoloured 1·40 1·00

896 Decanter and Beaker

1988. Styrian "Glass and Coal" Exn, Barnbach.
2160 **896** 4s. multicoloured 95 85

897 Late Gothic Silver Censer

1988. Lower Austrian "Art and Monastic Life at the Birth of Austria" Exhibition, Seitenstetten Benedictine Monastery.
2161 **897** 4s. multicoloured 95 85

898 Taking Casualty to Volkswagen Transporter Ambulance and Red Cross

1988. 125th Anniv of Red Cross.
2162 **898** 12s. black, red and green 2·50 1·90

899 Dish Aerials, Aflenz

1988. Europa. Telecommunications.
2163 **899** 6s. multicoloured 4·75 1·60

900 Mattsee Monastery

1988. Salzburg "Bajuvars from Severin to Tassilo" Exhibition, Mattsee Monastery.
2164 **900** 4s. multicoloured 95 85

901 Weinberg Castle

1988. Upper Austrian "Muhlviertel: Nature, Culture, Life" Exhibition, Weinberg Castle, near Kefermarkt.
2165 **901** 4s. multicoloured 95 85

902 Horvath

1988. 50th Death Anniv of Odon von Horvath (writer).
2166 **902** 6s. black and bistre 1·40 95

903 Stockerau Town Hall

1988. 25th Anniv of Stockerau Festival.
2167 **903** 5s. multicoloured 1·20 85

904 Motorway

1988. Completion of Tauern Motorway.
2168 **904** 4s. multicoloured 95 85

905 Brixlegg

1988. 1200th Anniv of Brixlegg.
2169 **905** 5s. multicoloured 1·20 85

906 Klagenfurt (after Matthaus Merian)

1988. 400th Anniv of Regular Postal Services in Carinthia.
2170 **906** 5s. multicoloured 1·20 85

907 Parish Church and Dean's House

1988. 1200th Anniv of Brixen im Thale, Tyrol.
2171 **907** 5s. multicoloured 1·20 85

908 Krimml Waterfalls, Upper Tauern National Park

1988. Natural Beauty Spots.
2172 **908** 5s. black and blue 1·20 85

909 Town Arms

1988. 1100th Anniv of Feldkirchen, Carinthia.
2173 **909** 5s. multicoloured 1·20 85

910 Feldbach

1988. 800th Anniv of Feldbach.
2174 **910** 5s. multicoloured 1·20 85

911 Ansfelden

1988. 1200th Anniv of Ansfelden.
2175 **911** 5s. multicoloured 1·20 85

912 Hologram of Export Emblem

1988. Federal Economic Chamber Export Congress.
2176 **912** 8s. multicoloured 3·00 2·30

913 Concert Hall

1988. 75th Anniv of Vienna Concert Hall.
2177 **913** 5s. multicoloured 1·20 85

914 Laboratory Assistant

1988. Austrian World of Work (3rd series).
2178 **914** 4s. multicoloured 1·00 70

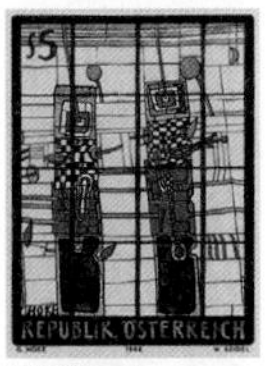
915 *Guards* (Giselbert Hoke)

1988. Austrian Modern Art.
2179 **915** 5s. multicoloured 1·20 85

916 Schonbauer

1988. Birth Centenary of Dr. Leopold Schonbauer (neurosurgeon and politician).
2180 **916** 4s. multicoloured 1·00 70

917 Carnation

1988. Cent of Austrian Social Democratic Party.
2181 **917** 4s. multicoloured 95 85

918 Loading Railway Mail Van at Pardubitz Station, 1914

1988. Stamp Day.
2182 **918** 6s.+3s. multicoloured 2·30 1·70

919 *Nativity* (St. Barbara's Church, Vienna)

1988. Christmas.
2183 **919** 5s. multicoloured 1·20 85

920 *Madonna* (Lucas Cranach)

1989. 25th Anniv of Diocese of Innsbruck.
2184 **920** 4s. multicoloured 95 60

921 Margrave Leopold II leading Abbot Sigibold and Monks to Melk (detail of fresco, Paul Troger)

1989. 900th Anniv of Melk Benedictine Monastery.
2185 **921** 5s. multicoloured 1·20 85

922 Marianne Hainisch

1989. 150th Birth Anniv of Marianne Hainisch (women's rights activist).
2186 **922** 6s. multicoloured 1·40 1·00

923 Glider and Paraskier

1989. World Gliding Championships, Wiener Neustadt, and World Paraskiing Championships, Damuls.
2187 **923** 6s. multicoloured 1·40 1·00

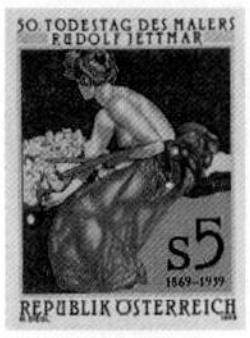
924 *The Painting*

1989. 50th Death Anniv of Rudolf Jettmar (painter).
2188 **924** 5s. multicoloured 1·20 85

925 *Bruck an der Leitha* (17th-century engraving, Georg Vischer)

1989. 750th Anniv of Bruck an der Leitha.
2189 **925** 5s. multicoloured 1·20 85

926 Wittgenstein

1989. Birth Centenary of Ludwig Wittgenstein (philosopher).
2190 **926** 5s. multicoloured 1·20 70

927 Holy Trinity Church, Stadl-Paura

1989. 250th Death Anniv of Johann Michael Prunner (architect).
2191 **927** 5s. multicoloured 1·20 70

928 Suess (after Josef Kriehuber) and Map

1989. 75th Death Anniv of Eduard Suess (geologist and politician).
2192 **928** 6s. multicoloured 1·30 85

929 *Judenburg* (17th-century engraving, Georg Vischer)

1989. Upper Styrian "People, Coins, Markets" Exhibition, Judenburg.
2193 **929** 4s. multicoloured 1·00 70

930 Steam Engine (Vinzenz Prick)

1989. Lower Austrian "Magic of Industry" Exhibition, Pottenstein.
2194 **930** 4s. blue and gold 1·00 70

931 Radstadt

1989. 700th Anniv of Radstadt.
2195 **931** 5s. multicoloured 1·20 85

932 Wooden Salt Barge from Viechtau

1989. Europa. Children's Toys.
2196 **932** 6s. multicoloured 4·00 1·00

933 *St. Adalbero and Family before Madonna and Child* (Monastery Itinerary Book)

1989. Upper Austrian "Graphic Art" Exhibition and 900th Anniv of Lambach Monastery Church.
2197 **933** 4s. multicoloured 1·00 70

934 *Gisela* (paddle-steamer)

1989. 150th Anniv of Passenger Shipping on Traunsee.
2198 **934** 5s. multicoloured 1·70 1·00

935 Hansa Brandenburg C-1 Mail Biplane at Vienna, 1918

1989. Stamp Day.
2199 **935** 6s.+3s. multicoloured 2·00 1·70

936 St. Andra (after Matthaus Merian)

1989. 650th Anniv of St. Andra.
2200 **936** 5s. multicoloured 1·20 85

937 Strauss

1989. 125th Birth Anniv of Richard Strauss (composer).
2201 **937** 6s. red, brown and gold 1·40 1·00

938 Locomotive

1989. Centenary of Achensee Steam Rack Railway.
2202 **938** 5s. multicoloured 1·50 85

939 Parliament Building, Vienna

1989. Centenary of Interparliamentary Union.
2203 **939** 6s. multicoloured 1·40 95

940 Anniversary Emblem

1989. Centenary of National Insurance in Austria.
2204 **940** 5s. multicoloured 1·20 70

941 U.N. Building, Vienna

1989. Tenth Anniv of U.N. Vienna Centre.
2205 **941** 8s. multicoloured 2·00 1·00

942 Lusthaus Water, Prater Woods, Vienna

1989. Natural Beauty Spots.
2206 **942** 5s. black and buff 1·20 1·00

943 Wildalpen and Hammerworks

1989. 850th Anniv of Wildalpen.
2207 **943** 5s. multicoloured 1·20 85

944 Emblem

1989. 33rd Congress of European Organization for Quality Control, Vienna.
2208 **944** 6s. multicoloured 1·40 95

945 Palace of Justice, Vienna

1989. 14th Congress of Int Assn of Criminal Law.
2209 **945** 6s. multicoloured 1·30 90

946 *Tree of Life* (Ernst Steiner)

1989. Austrian Modern Art.
2210 **946** 5s. multicoloured 1·40 95

947 Bricklayer

1989. Austrian World of Work (4th series).
2211 **947** 5s. multicoloured 1·40 95

948 Ludwig Anzengruber (150th birth anniv)

1989. Writers' Anniversaries. Multicoloured.
2212 4s. Type **948** 1·20 85
2213 4s. Georg Trakl (75th death anniv) 1·20 85

949 Fried

1989. 125th Birth Anniv of Alfred Fried (Peace Movement worker).
2214 **949** 6s. multicoloured 1·50 1·00

950 *Adoration of the Shepherds* (detail, Johann Carl von Reslfeld)

1989. Christmas.
2215 **950** 5s. multicoloured 1·20 85

951 "Courier" (Albrecht Durer)

1990. 500th Anniv of Regular European Postal Services.
2216 **951** 5s. chocolate, cinnamon and brown 1·30 85

952 Streif Downhill and Ganslern Slalom Runs

1990. 50th Hahnenkamm Ski Championships, Kitzbuhel.
2217 **952** 5s. multicoloured 1·20 85

953 Sulzer

1990. Death Centenary of Salomon Sulzer (creator of modern Synagogue songs).
2218 **953** 4s.50 multicoloured 1·00 60

954 Emich

1990. 50th Death Anniv of Friedrich Emich (microchemist).
2219 **954** 6s. purple and green 1·20 85

955 Emperor Friedrich III (miniature by Ulrich Schreier)

1990. 500th Anniv of Linz as Capital of Upper Austria.
2220 **955** 5s. multicoloured 1·20 85

956 University Seals

1990. 625th Anniv of Vienna University and 175th Anniv of Vienna University of Technology.
2221 **956** 5s. red, gold and lilac 1·20 85

957 South Styrian Vineyards

1990. Natural Beauty Spots.
2222 **957** 5s. black and yellow 1·20 85

958 Parish Church

1990. 1200th Anniv of Anthering.
2223 **958** 7s. multicoloured 1·90 95

959 1897 May Day Emblem

1990. Centenary of Labour Day.
2224 **959** 4s.50 multicoloured 1·00 95

960 "Our Dear Housewife of Seckau" (relief)

1990. 850th Anniv of Seckau Abbey.
2225 **960** 4s.50 blue 1·00 70

961 Ebene Reichenau Post Office

1990. Europa. Post Office Buildings.
2226 **961** 7s. multicoloured 5·25 1·20

962 Thematic Stamp Motifs

1990. Stamp Day.
2227 **962** 7s.+3s. multicoloured 2·30 1·90

963 Makart (self-portrait)

1990. 150th Birth Anniv of Hans Makart (painter).
2228 **963** 4s.50 multicoloured 1·20 1·00

964 Schiele (self-portrait)

1990. Birth Centenary of Egon Schiele (painter).

2229 **964** 5s. multicoloured 1·20 1·00

965 Raimund

1990. Birth Bicentenary of Ferdinand Raimund (actor and playwright).

2230 **965** 4s.50 multicoloured 1·20 1·00

966 *The Hundred Guilden Note* (Rembrandt)

1990. Second Int Christus Medicus Congress, Bad Ischl.

2231 **966** 7s. multicoloured 1·90 95

967 Hardegg

1990. 700th Anniv of Hardegg's Elevation to Status of Town.

2232 **967** 4s.50 multicoloured 1·20 85

968 Oberdrauburg (copperplate engraving, Freiherr von Valvasor)

1990. 750th Anniv of Oberdrauburg.

2233 **968** 5s. multicoloured 1·30 60

969 Church and Town Hall

1990. 850th Anniv of Gumpoldskirchen.

2234 **969** 5s. multicoloured 1·30 60

970 Zdarsky skiing

1990. 50th Death Anniv of Mathias Zdarsky (developer of alpine skiing).

2235 **970** 5s. multicoloured 1·30 60

971 *Telegraph*, 1880, and *Anton Chekhov*, 1978

1990. 150th Anniv of Modern (metal) Shipbuilding in Austria.

2236 **971** 9s. multicoloured 2·10 1·20

972 Perkonig

1990. Birth Centenary of Josef Friedrich Perkonig (writer).

2237 **972** 5s. sepia, brown & gold 1·20 85

973 "Man of Rainbows" (Robert Zeppel-Sperl)

1990. Austrian Modern Art.

2238 **973** 5s. multicoloured 1·20 85

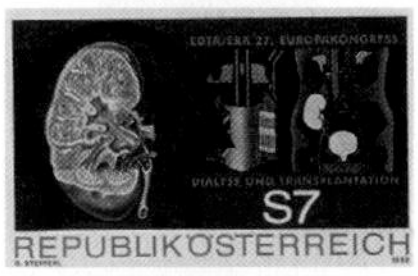

974 Kidney, Dialysis Machine and Anatomical Diagram

1990. 27th European Dialysis and Transplantation Federation Congress, Vienna.

2239 **974** 7s. multicoloured 1·90 95

975 Werfel

1990. Birth Centenary of Franz Werfel (writer).

2240 **975** 5s. multicoloured 1·20 85

976 U.N. and Austrian Flags

1990. 30th Anniv of Austrian Participation in U.N. Peace-keeping Forces.

2241 **976** 7s. multicoloured 1·90 95

977 Arms of Provinces

1990. 45th Anniv of First Provinces Conference (established Second Republic as Federal State).

2242 **977** 5s. multicoloured 1·20 60

978 University Seal

1990. 150th Anniv of Mining University, Leoben.

2243 **978** 4s.50 black, red & green 1·00 60

979 Vogelsang

1990. Death Centenary of Karl von Vogelsang (Christian social reformer).

2244 **979** 4s.50 multicoloured 1·00 60

980 Metal Workers

1990. Centenary of Metal, Mining and Energy Trade Union.

2245 **980** 5s. multicoloured 1·20 60

981 Player

1990. Third World Ice Curling Championships, Vienna.

2246 **981** 7s. multicoloured 1·90 95

982 Greenhouse

1990. Re-opening of Schonbrunn Greenhouse.

2247 **982** 5s. multicoloured 1·20 60

983 "Birth of Christ"

1990. Christmas. Detail of Altarpiece by Master Nikolaus of Verdun, Klosterneuburg Monastery.

2248 **983** 5s. multicoloured 1·20 60

984 Grillparzer

1991. Birth Bicent of Franz Grillparzer (dramatist).

2249 **984** 4s.50 multicoloured 1·20 60

985 Skier

1991. World Alpine Skiing Championships, Saalbach-Hinterglemm.

2250 **985** 5s. multicoloured 1·20 85

986 Kreisky

1991. 80th Birth Anniv of Bruno Kreisky (Chancellor, 1970–82).

2251 **986** 5s. multicoloured 1·20 85

987 Schmidt and Vienna Town Hall

1991. Death Centenary of Friedrich von Schmidt (architect).

2252 **987** 7s. multicoloured 1·90 1·20

988 Fountain, Vienna

1991. Anniversaries. Multicoloured.

2253 4s.50 Type **988** (250th death anniv of Georg Raphael Donner (sculptor)) 1·00 95

2254 5s. *Kitzbuhel in Winter* (birth centenary of Alfons Walde (artist and architect)) 1·20 1·00

2255 7s. Vienna Stock Exchange (death centenary of Theophil von Hansen (architect)) 1·70 1·60

See also No. 2269.

989 M. von Ebner-Eschenbach

1991. 75th Death Anniv of Marie von Ebner-Eschenbach (writer).

2256 **989** 4s.50 purple 1·20 85

990 Mozart

1991. Death Bicentenary of Wolfgang Amadeus Mozart (composer). Sheet 115×69 mm containing T **990** and similar vert design, each purple, mauve and gold.

MS2257 5s. Type **990**; 5s. *The Magic Flute* (statue, Vienna) 3·50 3·00

991 Obir Stalactite Caverns, Eisenkappel

1991. Natural Beauty Spots.

2258 **991** 5s. multicoloured 1·30 90

992 Spittal an der Drau (after Matthaus Merian)

1991. 800th Anniv of Spittal an der Drau.

2259 **992** 4s.50 multicoloured 1·30 90

993 "ERS-1" European Remote Sensing Satellite

1991. Europa. Europe in Space.

2260 **993** 7s. multicoloured 6·00 1·30

994 "Garden Party" (Anthoni Bays)

1991. Vorarlberg "Clothing and People" Exhibition, Hohenems.

2261 **994** 5s. multicoloured 1·30 90

995 Grein

1991. 500th Anniv of Grein Town Charter.
2262 **995** 4s.50 multicoloured 1·30 90

996 Bedding Plants forming Arms

1991. 1200th Anniv of Tulln.
2263 **996** 5s. multicoloured 1·30 90

997 Military History Museum

1991. Vienna Museum Centenaries. Multicoloured.
2264 5s. Type **997** 1·30 1·10
2265 7s. Museum of Art History 1·60 1·50

998 "B" and "P"

1991. Stamp Day.
2266 **998** 7s.+3s. brown, sepia and black 2·30 2·00

This is the first of a series of ten annual stamps, each of which will illustrate two letters. The complete series will spell out the words "Briefmarke" and "Philatelie".

999 Tunnel Entrance

1991. Opening of Karawanken Road Tunnel between Carinthia and Slovenia.
2267 **999** 7s. multicoloured 1·60 1·20

1000 Town Hall

1991. Fifth Anniv of St. Polten as Capital of Lower Austria.
2268 **1000** 5s. multicoloured 1·40 90

1991. 150th Birth Anniv of Otto Wagner (architect). As T **988**. Multicoloured.
2269 4s.50 Karlsplatz Station, Vienna City Railway 1·30 1·10

1001 Rowing

1991. Junior World Canoeing Championships and World Rowing Championships, Vienna.
2270 **1001** 5s. multicoloured 1·30 90

1002 X-ray Tube

1991. European Radiology Congress, Vienna.
2271 **1002** 7s. multicoloured 1·60 1·10

1003 Paracelsus

1991. 450th Death Anniv of Theophrastus Bombastus von Hohenheim (Paracelsus) (physician and scientist).
2272 **1003** 4s. black, red & brown 1·30 90

1004 "Mir" Space Station

1991. "Austro Mir 91" Soviet–Austrian Space Flight.
2273 **1004** 9s. multicoloured 2·10 1·50

1005 Almabtrieb (driving cattle from mountain pastures) (Zell, Tyrol)

1991. Folk Customs and Art (1st series). Multicoloured. . Multicoloured.
2274 4s.50 Type **1005** 1·00 90
2275 5s. Vintage Crown (Neustift, Vienna) 1·10 1·00
2276 7s. Harvest monstrance (Nestelbach, Styria) 1·60 1·50

See also Nos. 2305/7, 2349/51, 2363/5, 2393/5, 2418, 2432/3, 2450, 2482, 2491, 2500/1, 2508, 2524, 2546, 2547, 2550, 2552, 2569, 2581, 2587, 2595, 2718, 2776 and 2815.

1006 Weaver

1991. Austrian World of Work (5th series).
2277 **1006** 4s.50 multicoloured 1·10 80

1007 *The General* (Rudolf Pointner)

1991. Austrian Modern Art.
2278 **1007** 5s. multicoloured 1·30 90

1008 Raab

1991. Birth Centenary of Julius Raab (Chancellor, 1953–61).
2279 **1008** 4s.50 brown & chestnut 1·30 90

1009 "Birth of Christ" (detail of fresco, Baumgartenberg Church)

1991. Christmas.
2280 **1009** 5s. multicoloured 1·30 1·10

1010 Clerks

1992. Centenary of Trade Union of Clerks in Private Enterprise.
2281 **1010** 5s.50 multicoloured 1·40 1·00

1011 Emblems of Games and Olympic Rings

1992. Winter Olympic Games, Albertville, and Summer Games, Barcelona.
2282 **1011** 7s. multicoloured 2·00 1·10

1012 Competitor

1992. Eighth World Toboggan Championships on Natural Runs, Bad Goisern.
2283 **1012** 5s. multicoloured 1·30 90

1013 Hollow Stone, Klostertal

1992. Natural Beauty Spots.
2284 **1013** 5s. multicoloured 1·30 90

1014 Saiko

1992. Birth Centenary of George Saiko (writer).
2285 **1014** 5s.50 brown 1·40 1·00

1015 *Athlete with Ball* (Christian Attersee)

1992. Centenary of Workers' Sport Movement.
2286 **1015** 5s.50 multicoloured 1·40 1·00

1016 Franz Joseph Muller (chemist and mineralogist)

1992. Scientific Anniversaries. Multicoloured.
2287 5s. Type **1016** (250th birth anniv) 1·30 1·10
2288 5s.50 Paul Kitaibel (botanist, 175th death anniv) 1·40 1·20
2289 6s. Christian Doppler (physicist) (150th anniv of observation of Doppler Effect) 1·50 1·30
2290 7s. Richard Kuhn (chemist, 25th death anniv) 1·60 1·50

1017 Angels playing Instruments

1992. 150th Anniv of Vienna Philharmonic Orchestra. Sheet 90×70 mm.
MS2291 **1017** 5s.50 black, brown and gold 2·30 2·00

1018 First and Present Emblems

1992. Centenary of Railway Workers' Trade Union.
2292 **1018** 5s.50 red and black 1·30 80

1019 Hanrieder

1992. 150th Birth Anniv of Norbert Hanrieder (writer).
2293 **1019** 5s.50 lilac & brown 1·40 90

1020 Scenes from *"The Birdseller* (Zeller) and *The Beggar Student* (Millocker)

1992. 150th Birth Anniversaries of Carl Zeller and Karl Millocker (composers).
2294 **1020** 6s. multicoloured 1·50 1·10

1021 Foundry and Process

1992. Ironworks Day. 40th Anniv of First LD-Process Steel Works, Linz.
2295 **1021** 5s. multicoloured 1·30 90

1022 Woodcut of the Americas by Sebastian Munster (from *Geographia Universalis* by Claudius Ptolomaus)

1992. Europa. 500th Anniv of Discovery of America by Columbus.
2296 **1022** 7s. multicoloured 6·00 1·70

1023 Dredger

1992. Centenary of Treaty for International Regulation of the Rhine.
2297 **1023** 7s. multicoloured 2·00 1·30

1024 Rieger

1992. Centenary of Adoption of Pseudonym Reimmichl by Sebastian Rieger (writer).

2298	**1024**	5s. brown	1·30	90

1025 Flags and Alps

1992. Alpine Protection Convention.

2299	**1025**	5s.50 multicoloured	1·40	1·00

1026 Dr. Anna Dengel

1992. Birth Centenary of Dr. Anna Dengel (founder of Medical Missionary Sisters).

2300	**1026**	5s.50 multicoloured	1·50	90

1027 "R" and "H"

1992. Stamp Day.

2301	**1027**	7s.+3s. multicoloured	2·30	2·00

See note below No. 2266.

1028 Town Hall

1992. 750th Anniv of First Documentation of Lienz as a Town.

2302	**1028**	5s. multicoloured	1·30	90

1029 *"Billroth in Lecture Room* (A. F. Seligmann)

1992. Austrian Surgery Society International Congress, Eisenstadt.

2303	**1029**	6s. multicoloured	1·40	1·00

1030 Waldheim

1992. Presidency of Dr. Kurt Waldheim.

2304	**1030**	5s.50 black, red & grey	1·30	90

1992. Folk Customs and Art (2nd series). As T **1005**. Multicoloured.

2305	5s. Target with figure of Zieler, Lower Austria, 1732	1·30	1·10
2306	5s.50 Chest, Carinthia	1·50	1·30
2307	7s. Votive tablet from Venser Chapel, Vorarlberg	1·60	1·50

1031 Bridge over Canal

1992. Completion of Marchfeld Canal System.

2308	**1031**	5s. multicoloured	1·30	90

1032 "The Purification of Sea Water" (Peter Pongratz)

1992. Austrian Modern Art.

2309	**1032**	5s.50 multicoloured	1·50	1·10

1033 Gateway, Hofburg Palace (venue)

1992. Fifth Int Ombudsmen's Conference, Vienna.

2310	**1033**	5s.50 multicoloured	1·30	90

1034 Academy Seal

1992. 300th Anniv of Academy of Fine Arts, Vienna.

2311	**1034**	5s. blue and red	1·30	90

1035 *The Annunciation*

1992. Death Bicentenary of Veit Koniger (sculptor).

2312	**1035**	5s. multicoloured	1·30	1·10

1036 *Birth of Christ* (Johann Georg Schmidt)

1992. Christmas.

2313	**1036**	5s.50 multicoloured	1·40	90

1037 Earth and Satellite

1992. Birth Centenary of Hermann Potocnik (alias Noordung) (space travel pioneer).

2314	**1037**	10s. multicoloured	2·30	1·70

1038 Dome of Michael Wing, Hofburg Palace, Vienna

1993. Architects' Anniversaries. Multicoloured.

2315	5s. Type **1038** (Joseph Emanuel Fischer von Erlach, 300th birth)	1·10	1·00
2316	5s.50 Kinsky Palace, Vienna (Johann Lukas von Hildebrandt, 325th birth)	1·20	1·10
2317	7s. State Opera House, Vienna (Eduard van der Null and August Siccard von Siccardsburg, 125th death annivs)	1·80	1·70

1039 Emergency Vehicle's Flashing Lantern

1993. 25th Anniv of Radio-controlled Emergency Medical Service.

2318	**1039**	5s. multicoloured	1·20	90

1040 Wilder Kaiser Massif, Tyrol

1993. Natural Beauty Spots.

2319	**1040**	6s. multicoloured	1·40	1·00

1041 Mitterhofer Typewriter

1993. Death Centenary of Peter Mitterhofer (typewriter pioneer).

2320	**1041**	17s. multicoloured	4·25	2·75

1042 "Strada del Sole" (record sleeve)

1993. "Austro Pop" (1st series). Rainhard Fendrich (singer).

2321	**1042**	5s.50 multicoloured	1·40	1·10

See also Nos. 2356 and 2368.

1043 Games Emblem

1993. Winter Special Olympics, Salzburg and Schladming.

2322	**1043**	6s.+3s. multicoloured	3·50	2·00

1044 Sealsfield

1993. Birth Bicent of Charles Sealsfield (novelist).

2323	**1044**	10s. red, blue and gold	3·50	1·50

1045 Girl realizing her Rights

1993. Ratification of U.N. Convention on Children's Rights.

2324	**1045**	7s. multicoloured	1·80	1·10

1046 "Death" (detail of sculpture, Josef Stammel), Admont Monastery, Styria

1993. Monasteries and Abbeys.

2325	-	1s. brown, black & grn	35	35
2326	**1046**	5s.50 black, yell & grn	2·40	55
2327	-	6s. black, mauve & yell	1·40	35
2328	-	7s. brown, black & grey	2·40	1·50
2329	-	7s.50 brown, bl & blk	2·40	55
2330	-	8s. orange, black & bl	3·00	90
2331	-	10s. black, blue & orge	3·25	1·30
2332	-	20s. black, blue & yell	7·25	1·10
2333	-	26s. orange, black & bis	7·75	1·10
2334	-	30s. red, yellow & black	10·50	1·80

DESIGNS: 1s. The Annunciation (detail of crosier of Abbess), St. Gabriel Benedictine Abbey, Bertholdstein; 6s. St. Benedict of Nursia (glass painting), Mariastern Abbey, Gwiggen; 7s. Marble lion, Franciscan Monastery, Salzburg; 7s.50, Virgin Mary (detail of cupola painting by Paul Troger), Altenburg Monastery; 8s. Early Gothic doorway, Wilhering Monastery; 10s. *The Healing of St. Peregrinus* (altarpiece), Maria Luggau Monastery; 20s. Hartmann Crosier, St. Georgenberg Abbey, Fiecht; 26s. *Master Dolorosa* (sculpture), Franciscan Monastery, Schwaz; 30s. Madonna and Child, Monastery of the Scottish Order, Vienna.

1047 "Flying Harlequin" (Paul Flora)

1993. Europa. Contemporary Art.

2345	**1047**	7s. multicoloured	4·50	1·10

1048 Silhouette, Script and Signature

1993. 150th Birth Anniv of Peter Rosegger (writer and newspaper publisher).

2346	**1048**	5s.50 black and green	1·20	1·10

1049 *Hohentwiel* (lake steamer) and Flags

1993. Lake Constance European Region.

2347	**1049**	6s. multicoloured	1·80	1·10

1050 Knights in Battle and "I"s

1993. Stamp Day.

2348	**1050**	7s.+3s. gold, black and blue	2·20	2·00

See note below No. 2266.

1005 Almabtrieb (driving cattle from mountain pastures) (Zell, Tyrol)

1993. Folk Customs and Art (3rd series). As T **1005**. Multicoloured.

2349	5s. Corpus Christi Day procession, Hallstatt, Upper Austria	1·10	1·00

2350 5s.50 Drawing the block (log), Burgenland 1·20 1·10
2351 7s. Aperschnalzen (whipping the snow away), Salzburg 1·60 1·50

1051 Human Rights Emblem melting Bars

1993. U.N. World Conf on Human Rights, Vienna.
2352 **1051** 10s. multicoloured 2·20 1·50

1052 Jagerstatter

1993. 50th Death Anniv of Franz Jagerstatter (conscientious objector).
2353 **1052** 5s.50 multicoloured 1·20 1·10

1053 Train approaching Wolfgangsee

1993. Centenary of Schafberg Cog Railway.
2354 **1053** 6s. multicoloured 1·60 1·10

1054 *Self-portrait with Doll*

1993. Birth Centenary of Rudolf Wacker (artist).
2355 **1054** 6s. multicoloured 1·20 1·10

1993. "Austro Pop" (2nd series). Ludwig Hirsch (singer and actor). As T **1042**. Multicoloured.
2356 5s.50 "Die Omama" (record sleeve) 1·40 1·10

1055 *Concert in Dornbacher Park* (Balthasar Wigand)

1993. 150th Anniv of Vienna Male Choral Society.
2357 **1055** 5s. multicoloured 1·20 90

1056 *Easter* (Max Weiler)

1993. Austrian Modern Art.
2358 **1056** 5s.50 multicoloured 1·20 90

1057 "99 Heads" (detail, Friedensreich Hundertwasser)

1993. Council of Europe Heads of State Conference, Vienna.
2359 **1057** 7s. multicoloured 3·00 2·00

1058 Statue of Athene, Parliament Building

1993. 75th Anniv of Austrian Republic.
2360 **1058** 5s. multicoloured 1·20 90

1059 Workers

1993. Cent of First Austrian Trade Unions Congress.
2361 **1059** 5s.50 multicoloured 1·20 90

1060 "Birth of Christ" (Krainburg Altar, Styria)

1993. Christmas.
2362 **1060** 5s.50 multicoloured 1·20 90

1994. Folk Customs and Art (4th series). As T **1005**. Multicoloured.
2363 5s.50 Rocking cradle, Vorarlberg 1·20 1·10
2364 6s. Carved sleigh, Styria 1·40 1·30
2365 7s. Godparent's bowl and lid, Upper Austria 1·60 1·50

1061 Winter Sports

1994. Winter Olympic Games, Lillehammer, Norway.
2366 **1061** 7s. multicoloured 1·40 1·30

1062 Early Production of Coins

1994. 800th Anniv of Vienna Mint.
2367 **1062** 6s. multicoloured 1·20 1·10

1994. "Austro Pop" (3rd series). Falco (Johann Holzel) (singer). As T **1042**. Multicoloured.
2368 6s. "Rock Me Amadeus" (record sleeve) 1·40 1·10

1063 *Reclining Lady* (detail, Herbert Boeckl)

1994. Birth Centenary of Herbert Boeckl (painter).
2369 **1063** 5s.50 multicoloured 1·20 1·10

1064 N.W. Tower of City Wall

1994. 800th Anniv of Wiener Neustadt.
2370 **1064** 6s. multicoloured 1·20 1·10

1065 Lurgrotte (caves), Styria

1994. Natural Beauty Spots.
2371 **1065** 6s. multicoloured 1·20 1·10

1066 Lake Rudolf (Teleki–Hohnel expedition to Africa, 1887)

1994. Europa. Discoveries.
2372 **1066** 7s. multicoloured 3·75 1·80

1067 "E" and "L" as Ruins in Landscape

1994. Stamp Day.
2373 **1067** 7s.+3s. multicoloured 2·20 2·00
See note below No. 2266.

1068 "Allegory of Theology, Justice, Philosophy and Medicine" (detail of fresco, National Library)

1994. 300th Birth Anniv of Daniel Gran (artist).
2374 **1068** 20s. multicoloured 4·75 3·25

1069 Scene from *The Prodigal Son* (opera, Benjamin Britten)

1994. 25th Anniv of Carinthian Summer Festival, Ossiach and Villach.
2375 **1069** 5s.50 gold and red 1·20 1·10

1070 Steam Locomotive and Diesel Railcar (Gailtal)

1994. Railway Centenaries. Multicoloured.
2376 5s.50 Type **1070** 1·40 1·30
2377 6s. Steam locomotive and diesel railcar (Murtal) 1·60 1·50

1071 Gmeiner and Children

1994. 75th Birth Anniv of Hermann Gmeiner (founder of S.O.S. children's villages).
2378 **1071** 7s. multicoloured 1·40 1·30

1072 Seitz (bust, G. Ambrosi)

1994. 125th Birth Anniv of Karl Seitz (acting President, 1920).
2379 **1072** 5s.50 multicoloured 1·20 90

1073 Bohm

1994. Birth Centenary of Karl Bohm (conductor).
2380 **1073** 7s. blue and gold 1·40 1·30

1074 Ethnic Minorities on Map

1994. Legal and Cultural Protection of Ethnic Minorities.
2381 **1074** 5s.50 multicoloured 1·20 1·00

1075 Franz Theodor Csokor (dramatist and poet)

1994. Writers' Anniversaries. Multicoloured.
2382 6s. Type **1075** (25th death anniv) 1·20 1·10
2383 7s. Joseph Roth (novelist, birth cent) 1·40 1·30

1076 *Head* (Franz Ringel)

1994. Austrian Modern Art.
2384 **1076** 6s. multicoloured 1·40 1·10

1077 Money Box

1994. 175th Anniv of Savings Banks in Austria.
2385 **1077** 7s. multicoloured 1·40 1·00

1078 Air Hostess and Child

1994. Austrian World of Work (6th series).
2386 **1078** 6s. multicoloured 1·20 90

1079 Coudenhove-Kalergi and Map of Europe

1994. Birth Cent of Richard Coudenhove-Kalergi (founder of Paneuropa Union).

2387	**1079**	10s. multicoloured	2·10	1·20

1080 *Birth of Christ* (Anton Wollenek)

1994. Christmas.

2388	**1080**	6s. multicoloured	1·20	90

1081 Map and Austrian and E.U. Flags

1995. Austria's Entry into E.U.

2389	**1081**	7s. multicoloured	1·40	90

1082 Loos House, Michaelerplatz, Vienna

1995. 125th Birth Anniv of Adolf Loos (architect).

2390	**1082**	10s. multicoloured	1·90	1·50

1083 Sporting Activities

1995. 50th Anniv of Austrian Gymnastics and Sports Association.

2391	**1083**	6s. multicoloured	1·20	90

1084 Workers

1995. 75th Anniv of Workers' and Employees' Chambers (advisory body).

2392	**1084**	6s. multicoloured	1·20	80

1995. Folk Costumes and Art (5th series). As T **1005**. Multicoloured.

2393	5s.50 Belt, Carinthia	1·20	1·10
2394	6s. Costume of Hiata (vineyard guard), Vienna	1·40	1·30
2395	7s. Gold bonnet, Wachau	1·60	1·50

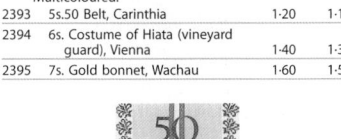

1085 State Seal

1995. 50th Anniv of Second Republic.

2396	**1085**	6s. multicoloured	1·20	90

1086 Heft Ironworks

1995. Carinthian "History of Mining and Industry" Exhibition, Heft, Huttenberg.

2397	**1086**	5s.50 multicoloured	1·20	90

1087 Hiker in Mountains

1995. Centenary of Friends of Nature.

2398	**1087**	5s.50 multicoloured	1·20	90

1088 Heidenreichstein National Park

1995. Natural Beauty Spots.

2399	**1088**	6s. multicoloured	1·30	1·00

1089 Woman and Barbed Wire around Skull

1995. Europa. Peace and Freedom.

2400	**1089**	7s. multicoloured	4·50	1·90

1090 Map, Woman and Child and Transport

1995. Meeting of European Ministers of Transport Conference, Vienna.

2401	**1090**	7s. multicoloured	1·40	90

1091 "F" and "A" on Vase of Flowers

1995. Stamp Day.

2402	**1091**	10s.+5s. multicoloured	3·00	2·75

See note below No. 2266.

1092 Set for *The Flying Dutchman*

1995. 50th Bregenz Festival.

2403	**1092**	6s. multicoloured	1·20	80

1093 St. Gebhard (stained-glass window, Martin Hausle)

1995. Death Millenary of St. Gebhard, Bishop of Konstanz (patron saint of Vorarlberg chuches).

2404	**1093**	7s.50 multicoloured	1·40	90

1094 Members' Flags

1995. 50th Anniv of U.N.O.

2405	**1094**	10s. multicoloured	2·10	1·20

1095 Loschmidt

1995. Death Centenary of Josef Loschmidt (physical chemist).

2406	**1095**	20s. black, stone & brn	5·75	3·00

1096 K. Leichter

1995. Birth Cent of Kathe Leichter (sociologist).

2407	**1096**	6s. cream, black & red	1·20	90

1097 Scene from *Jedermann* (Hugo von Hofmannsthal)

1995. 75th Anniv of Salzburg Festival.

2408	**1097**	6s. multicoloured	1·20	90

1098 *European Scene* (Adolf Frohner)

1995. Austrian Modern Art.

2409	**1098**	6s. multicoloured	1·20	90

1099 Franz von Suppe and *The Beautiful Galatea*

1995. Composers' Anniversaries. Scenes from operettas. Multicoloured.

2410	6s. Type **1099** (death cent)	1·20	1·10
2411	7s. Nico Dostal and *The Hungarian Wedding* (birth centenary)	1·40	1·30

1100 University Building

1995. 25th Anniv of Klagenfurt University.

2412	**1100**	5s.50 multicoloured	1·20	80

1101 Hollenburg Castle

1995. 75th Anniv of Carinthian Referendum.

2413	**1101**	6s. multicoloured	1·20	80

1102 Postman

1995. Austrian World of Work (7th series).

2414	**1102**	6s. multicoloured	1·20	80

1103 Anton von Webern (50th death)

1995. Composers' Anniversaries.

2415	**1103**	6s. blue and orange	1·20	1·10
2416	-	7s. red and orange	1·40	1·30

DESIGN: 7s. Ludwig van Beethoven (225th birth).

1104 Christ Child

1995. Christmas. 300th Anniv of Christkindl Church.

2417	**1104**	6s. multicoloured	1·20	80

1996. Folk Customs and Art (6th series). As T **1005**.

2418	6s. multicoloured	1·30	1·20

DESIGN: 6s. Masked figures Roller and Scheller (Imst masquerades, Tyrol).

1105 Empress Maria Theresia and Academy Building

1996. 250th Anniv of Theresian Academy, Vienna.

2419	**1105**	6s. multicoloured	1·30	1·20

1106 Ski Jumping

1996. World Ski Jumping Championships, Tauplitz and Bad Mitterndorf.

2420	**1106**	7s. multicoloured	1·60	90

1107 Terminal

1996. Completion of West Terminal, Vienna International Airport.

2421 **1107** 7s. multicoloured 1·60 90

1108 Hohe Tauern National Park

1996. Natural Beauty Spots.

2422 **1108** 6s. multicoloured 1·40 80

1109 "Mother and Child" (Peter Fendi)

1996. Artists' Birth Bicentenaries. Multicoloured.

2423 6s. Type **1109** 1·30 1·20

2424 7s. *Self-portrait* (Leopold Kupelwieser) 1·70 1·60

1110 Organ and Music

1996. Death Cent of Anton Bruckner (composer).

2425 **1110** 5s.50 multicoloured 1·30 80

1111 Kollmitz Castle (from copper engraving)

1996. 300th Death Anniv of Georg Vischer (cartographer and engraver).

2426 **1111** 10s. black and stone 2·20 1·30

1112 Old Market Square

1996. 800th Anniv of Klagenfurt.

2427 **1112** 6s. multicoloured 1·60 90

1113 Hotel Chef and Waitress

1996. Austrian World of Work (8th series).

2428 **1113** 6s. multicoloured 1·20 90

1114 Paula von Preradovic (writer)

1996. Europa. Famous Women.

2429 **1114** 7s. stone, brown & grey 1·60 1·10

1115 "M" and "T" and Bluebirds (mosaic)

1996. Stamp Day.

2430 **1115** 10s.+5s. mult 3·50 2·50

See note below No. 2266.

1116 Mascot with Olympic Flag

1996. Olympic Games, Atlanta.

2431 **1116** 10s. multicoloured 2·20 1·50

1996. Folk Customs and Art (7th series). As T **1005**.

2432 5s.50 Flower-bedecked poles, Salzburg 1·40 1·30

2433 7s. Tyrol militia 1·60 1·50

1117 Landscape

1996. 75th Anniv of Burgenland.

2434 **1117** 6s. multicoloured 1·20 80

1118 Mountaineers

1996. Cent of Austrian Mountain Rescue Service.

2435 **1118** 6s. multicoloured 1·20 80

1119 Deed of Otto III, 996

1996. Millenary of Austria. Multicoloured.

2436 6s. Type **1119** 1·20 90

2437 6s. Archduke Joseph II (after Georg Weikert) and Archduchess Maria Theresia (after Martin van Meytens) 1·20 90

2438 7s. *Duke Heinrich II* (stained-glass window, Monastery of the Holy Cross) 1·30 1·10

2439 7s. Arms in flames (1848 Revolution) 1·30 1·10

2440 7s. Rudolf IV, the Founder 1·30 1·10

2441 7s. Karl Renner (first Federal Republic president) 1·30 1·10

2442 10s. Archduke Maximilian I (Holy Roman Emperor) (miniature from Statute Book of Order of the Golden Fleece) 2·20 1·60

2443 10s. Seal and signature of Leopold Figl (State Treaty of 1955) 2·20 1·60

2444 20s. Imperial crown of Rudolf II 4·25 3·25

2445 20s. State arms, stars of Europe and *The Horsebreaker* (bronze by Josef Lax) (Austria and Europe) 4·25 3·25

1120 *Power Station* (Reinhard Artberg)

1996. Austrian Modern Art.

2446 **1120** 7s. multicoloured 1·60 1·10

1121 Children of Different Nations

1996. 50th Anniv of UNICEF.

2447 **1121** 10s. multicoloured 2·20 1·30

1122 Nativity and Vienna Town Hall

1996. Christmas.

2448 **1122** 6s. multicoloured 1·20 90

1123 Kramer

1997. Birth Centenary of Theodor Kramer (poet).

2449 **1123** 5s.50 blue 1·20 80

1997. Folk Customs and Art (8th series). As T **1005**. Multicoloured.

2450 7s. Epiphany carol singers, Eisenstadt Burgenland 1·60 1·50

1124 Vineyards on the Nussberg, Vienna

1997. Natural Beauty Spots.

2451 **1124** 6s. multicoloured 1·30 90

1125 Academy and Light

1997. 150th Anniv of Austrian Academy of Sciences, Vienna.

2452 **1125** 10s. multicoloured 2·30 1·30

1126 Emblem

1997. 50th Anniv of Verbund Electricity Company.

2453 **1126** 6s. multicoloured 1·20 90

1127 The Cruel Rosalia of Forchtenstein

1997. Myths and Legends.

2454 - 6s.50 grn, pink & blk 2·20 90

2455 **1127** 7s. black, stone & brn 2·40 65

2456 - 8s. orange, blk & lilac 2·20 1·10

2457 - 9s. black, stone & pur 3·00 1·70

2458 - 10s. black, grey & red 3·50 2·00

2459 - 13s. black, brn & pur 4·25 2·20

2460 - 14s. black, lt blue & bl 4·25 1·90

2461 - 20s. green, blk & stone 6·00 2·75

2462 - 22s. black, bl & stone 5·50 4·50

2463 - 23s. black, ochre and green 7·75 5·00

2464 - 25s. stone, black and yellow 7·25 3·25

2465 - 32s. black, brn & pink 11·00 5·50

DESIGNS: 6s.50, Lindworm of Klagenfurt; 8s. The Black Lady of Hardegg; 9s. Charming Augustin; 10s. Basilisk of Vienna; 13s. The Pied Piper of Korneuburg; 14s. The Strudengau Water-nymph; 20s. St. Notburga; 22s. Witches Whirl; 23s. Loaf Agony; 25s. St. Konrad and Altems Castle; 32s. The Discovery of Erzberg (Mountain of Ore).

1128 Stage Set for "Die tote Stadt"

1997. Birth Cent of Erich Korngold (composer).

2470 **1128** 20s. black, blue & gold 5·75 2·75

1129 Stadium, Badge and Players

1997. Rapid Vienna, National Football Champions, 1995–96.

2471 **1129** 7s. multicoloured 1·80 90

1130 Red Deer

1997. Hunting and the Environment. Deer Feeding in Winter.

2472 **1130** 7s. multicoloured 1·60 90

1131 Canisius and Children (altar by Josef Bachlechner in Innsbruck Seminary)

1997. 400th Death Anniv of St. Petrus Canisius (patron saint of Innsbruck).

2473 **1131** 7s.50 multicoloured 1·60 90

1132 Johannes Brahms (after L. Michalek)

1997. Composers' Anniversaries.

2474 **1132** 6s. violet and gold 1·30 1·20

2475 - 10s. purple and gold 2·30 2·10

DESIGNS: 6s. Type **1132** (death centenary); 10s. Franz Schubert (birth bicentenary).

1133 "A" and "E"

1997. Stamp Day.
2476 **1133** 7s. multicoloured 1·80 1·10
See note below No. 2266.

1134 The Four Friends

1997. Europa. Tales and Legends. *The Town Band of Bremen* by the Brothers Grimm.
2477 **1134** 7s. multicoloured 4·25 1·10

1135 1850 9k. Stamp and Postman

1997. "WIPA 2000" International Stamp Exhibition, Vienna (1st issue).
2478 **1135** 27s.+13s. mult 9·00 6·75
See also Nos. 2521, 2543, **MS**2551 and **MS**2564.

1136 Train on Hochschneeberg Line

1997. Railway Anniversaries. Multicoloured.
2479 6s. Type **1136** (centenary of Hochschneeberg rack-railway) 1·40 1·30
2480 7s.50 Steam locomotive *Licaon* and viaduct near Mattersburg (150th anniv of Odenburg–Wiener Neustadt line) 1·90 1·80

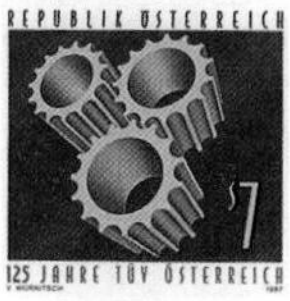

1137 Cogwheels

1997. 125th Anniv of Austrian Technical Supervisory Association.
2481 **1137** 7s. multicoloured 1·70 90

1997. Folk Customs and Art (9th series). As T **1005**. Multicoloured.
2482 6s.50 Tyrolean brass band 1·60 1·10

1138 Waggerl (self-portrait)

1997. Birth Centenary of Karl Waggerl (writer).
2483 **1138** 7s. green, yellow & blue 1·70 90

1139 Adolf Lorenz (founder of German Society of Orthopaedia)

1997. Orthopaedics Congress, Vienna.
2484 **1139** 8s. multicoloured 1·80 1·10

1140 Emblem

1997. 125th Anniv of College of Agricultural Sciences, Vienna.
2485 **1140** 9s. multicoloured 2·10 1·30

1141 Patient, Nurse and Doctor

1997. Austrian World of Work (9th series).
2486 **1141** 6s.50 multicoloured 1·40 90

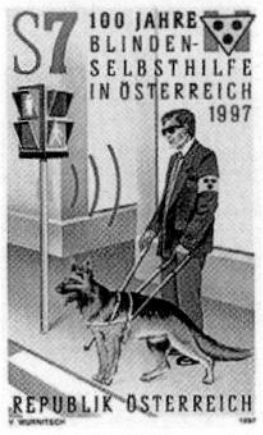

1142 Blind Man with Guide Dog

1997. Cent of Austrian Association for the Blind.
2487 **1142** 7s. multicoloured 1·60 90

1143 *House in Wind* (Helmut Schickhofer)

1997. Austrian Modern Art.
2488 **1143** 7s. multicoloured 1·80 1·10

1144 Klestil

1997. 65th Birthday of Pres. Thomas Klestil.
2489 **1144** 7s. multicoloured 1·80 90

1145 Werner

1997. 75th Birth Anniv of Oskar Werner (actor).
2490 **1145** 7s. black, orge & grey 1·80 90

1997. Folk Customs and Art (10th series). As T **1005**. Multicoloured.
2491 6s.50 Tower wind-band, Upper Austria 1·40 1·10

1146 Glowing Light

1997. 25th Anniv of Light in Darkness (umbrella organization of children's charities).
2492 **1146** 7s. blue 1·60 90

1147 "Mariazell Madonna"

1997. Christmas.
2493 **1147** 7s. multicoloured 1·60 90

1148 Kalkalpen National Park

1998. Natural Beauty Spots.
2494 **1148** 7s. multicoloured 1·40 90

1149 Courting Pair

1998. Hunting and the Environment. Preservation of Breeding Habitat of the Black Grouse.
2495 **1149** 9s. multicoloured 1·80 1·30

1150 Ice Skaters

1998. Winter Olympic Games, Nagano, Japan.
2496 **1150** 14s. multicoloured 2·75 2·00

1151 Austrian Poster Exposition Advertising Poster, 1928

1998. Birth Cent of Joseph Binder (designer).
2497 **1151** 7s. multicoloured 1·60 1·10

1152 Alois Senefelder (inventor) on Lithographic Stone

1998. Bicentenary of Invention of Lithography (printing process).
2498 **1152** 7s. blue, yellow & black 1·40 90

1153 Facade

1998. Centenary of Vienna Secession (exn hall).
2499 **1153** 8s. brown, gold & blue 1·80 1·10

1998. Folk Customs and Art (11th series). As T **1005**. Multicoloured.
2500 6s.50 Fiacre, Vienna 1·40 1·30

2501 7s. Palm Sunday procession, Thaur, Tyrol 1·60 1·50

1154 Player and Team Emblem

1998. Austria Memphis Football Club.
2502 **1154** 7s. multicoloured 1·80 1·00

1155 "St. Florian" (glass painting)

1998. St. Florian, Patron Saint of Firemen.
2503 **1155** 7s. multicoloured 1·80 1·00

1156 Rupertus Cross

1998. 1200th Anniv of Salzburg Archdiocese.
2504 **1156** 7s. multicoloured 1·80 1·00

1157 Series Yv Locomotive No. 2, 1895

1998. Centenary of Completion of Ybbs Valley Railway.
2505 **1157** 6s.50 multicoloured 1·80 1·10

1158 "Tyrolia" (Ferdinand Cosandier)

1998. 175th Anniv of Tyrol Ferdinandeum (state museum), Innsbruck.
2506 **1158** 7s. multicoloured 1·60 1·00

1159 Vienna Town Hall (Viennese festive weeks)

1998. Europa. National Festivals.
2507 **1159** 7s. multicoloured 4·00 1·10

1998. Folk Customs and Art (12th series). As T **1005**. Multicoloured.
2508 6s.50 Samson and the dwarves, Salzburg 1·80 1·10

1160 Christine Lavant

1998. 25th Death Anniv of Christine Lavant (poet).
2509 **1160** 7s. multicoloured 1·80 1·10

1161 Electric Railcar No. 1

1998. Centenary of Postlingberg Railway.

2510	**1161**	6s.50 multicoloured	1·80	1·10

1162 "R" and "L"

1998. Stamp Day.

2511	**1162**	7s. multicoloured	1·80	1·10

See note below No. 2266.

1163 Presidency Emblem

1998. Austrian Presidency of E.U.

2512	**1163**	7s. multicoloured	1·80	1·10

1164 Railcar No. 5090

1998. Centenary of Pinzgau Railway.

2513	**1164**	6s.50 multicoloured	1·80	1·10

1165 Volksoper, Vienna

1998. Centenary of Volksoper (theatre) and 50th Death Anniv of Franz Lehar (composer).

2514	**1165**	6s.50 multicoloured	1·60	1·10

1166 Empress Elisabeth (after Franz Winterhalter)

1998. Death Centenary of Empress Elisabeth.

2515	**1166**	7s. multicoloured	1·80	1·50

1167 School Building

1998. Centenary of Vienna Business School.

2516	**1167**	7s. multicoloured	1·80	1·50

1168 Kudlich and Farmers

1998. 175th Birth Anniv of Hans Kudlich (promoter of 1848 "Peasants' Liberation" Law).

2517	**1168**	6s.50 multicoloured	1·60	1·00

1169 *My Garden* (Hans Staudacher)

1998. Austrian Modern Art.

2518	**1169**	7s. multicoloured	1·80	1·10

1170 Town Hall and Arms

1998. 350th Anniv of Declaration of Eisenstadt as a Free Town.

2519	**1170**	7s. multicoloured	1·60	1·10

1171 Photographer and Reporter

1998. Austrian World of Work (10th series). Art, Media and Freelances.

2520	**1171**	6s.50 multicoloured	1·40	1·00

1172 1929 2s. Stamp and Post Van

1998. "WIPA 2000" International Stamp Exhibition, Vienna (2nd issue).

2521	**1172**	32s.+13s. mult	9·75	7·75

1173 "Nativity" (fresco, Tainach Church)

1998. Christmas.

2522	**1173**	7s. multicoloured	1·40	1·00

1174 Cross-country Skiing

1999. World Nordic Skiing Championships, Ramsau.

2523	**1174**	7s. multicoloured	1·80	1·20

1999. Folk Customs and Art (13th series). As T **1005**. Multicoloured.

2524	6s.50 Walking pilgrimage to Mariazell	1·40	1·10

1175 Stingl Rock, Bohemian Forest

1999. Natural Beauty Spots.

2525	**1175**	7s. multicoloured	1·40	1·10

1176 Books and Compact Disc

1999. Centenary of Austrian Patent Office.

2526	**1176**	7s. multicoloured	1·40	1·10

1177 Player and Club Emblem

1999. SK Puntigamer Sturm Graz Football Club.

2527	**1177**	7s. multicoloured	1·80	1·10

1178 Palace Facade

1999. World Heritage Site. Schonbrunn Palace, Vienna.

2528	**1178**	13s. multicoloured	2·75	2·20

1179 Partridges

1999. Hunting and the Environment. Living Space for Grey Partridges.

2529	**1179**	6s.50 multicoloured	1·40	1·10

1180 Snowboarder

1999. 50th Anniv of Austrian General Sport Federation.

2530	**1180**	7s. multicoloured	1·60	1·10

1181 Council Building, Strasbourg

1999. 50th Anniv of Council of Europe.

2531	**1181**	14s. multicoloured	3·00	2·20

No. 2531 is denominated both in Austrian schillings and in euros.

1182 Steyr Type 50 Baby Saloon

1999. Birth Centenary of Karl Jenschke (engineer and car manufacturer).

2532	**1182**	7s. multicoloured	1·60	1·20

1183 "St. Martin" (marble relief, Peuerbach Church)

1999. Ancient Arts and Crafts (1st series).

2533	**1183**	8s. brown, blue & orange	1·80	1·30

See also Nos. 2542, 2575, 2600 and 2602.

1184 Symbols of Aid and Emblem

1999. 125th Anniv of Diakonie (professional charitable services).

2534	**1184**	7s. multicoloured	1·40	1·10

1185 Johann Strauss, the Younger

1999. Composers' Death Anniversaries. Multicoloured.

2535	7s. Type **1185** (centenary)	1·70	1·60
2536	8s. Johann Strauss, the Elder (150th anniv)	1·80	1·70

1186 Rural Gendarmes

1999. 150th Anniv of National Gendarmerie.

2537	**1186**	7s. multicoloured	1·60	1·10

1187 Donau-auen National Park

1999. Europa. Parks and Gardens.

2538	**1187**	7s. multicoloured	1·80	1·10

1188 "K" and "I"

1999. Stamp Day.

2539	**1188**	7s. multicoloured	1·80	1·10

See note below No. 2266.

1189 Iron Stage Curtain

1999. Centenary of Graz Opera.

2540	**1189**	6s.50 multicoloured	1·80	1·10

1190 Couple on Bench

1999. International Year of the Elderly.

2541	**1190**	7s. multicoloured	1·40	1·10

1191 "St. Anne with Mary and Child Jesus" (wood-carving, St. George's Church, Purgg)

1999. Ancient Arts and Crafts (2nd series).
2542 **1191** 9s. multicoloured 2·20 2·00

1192 1949 25g. Stamp and Vienna Airport

1999. "WIPA 2000" International Stamp Exhibition, Vienna (3rd issue).
2543 **1192** 32s.+16s. mult 11·50 8·50

1193 "Security throughout Life"

1999. 14th Congress of Federation of Austrian Trade Unions.
2544 **1193** 6s.50 multicoloured 1·40 1·10

1194 "Cafe Girardi" (Wolfgang Herzig)

1999. Austrian Modern Art.
2545 **1194** 7s. multicoloured 1·80 1·10

1999. Folk Customs and Art (14th series). As T **1005**. Multicoloured.
2546 8s. Pumpkin Festival, Lower Austria 1·80 1·10

1999. Folk Customs and Art (15th series). As T **1005**. Multicoloured.
2547 7s. The Pummerin (great bell of St. Stephen's Cathedral) ringing in the New Year 1·80 1·10

1195 Institute and Fossils

1999. 150th Anniv of National Institute of Geology.
2548 **1195** 7s. multicoloured 1·80 1·10

1196 "Nativity" (altar painting, Pinkafeld Church)

1999. Christmas.
2549 **1196** 7s. multicoloured 1·40 1·10

2000. Folk Customs and Art (16th series). As T 1005. Multicoloured.
2550 7s. Chapel procession, Carinthia 1·40 1·30

2000. "WIPA 2000" International Stamp Exhibition, Vienna (4th issue). Sheet 150×95 mm.
MS2551 27s.+13s. No. 2478; 32s.+13s. No. 2521; 32s.+16s. No. 2543 36·00 39·00

2000. Folk Customs and Art (17th series). As T 1005. Multicoloured.
2552 6s.50 Three men wearing masks (Cavalcade of Beautiful Masks, Telfs) 1·40 1·10

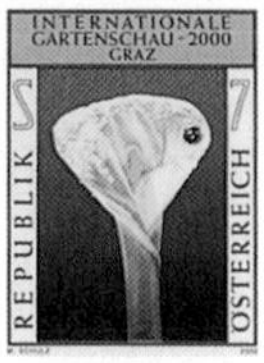

1197 *Zantadeschica aethiopica*

2000. International Garden Show, Graz.
2553 **1197** 7s. multicoloured 1·80 1·10

1198 Ibex

2000. Hunting and the Environment. Return of Ibex to Austrian Mountains.
2554 **1198** 7s. multicoloured 1·60 1·10

1199 Players

2000. F.C. Tirol Innsbruck, National Football Champion 2000.
2555 **1199** 7s. multicoloured 1·60 1·10

1200 Mt. Grossglockner and Viewing Point

2000. Bicentenary of First Ascent of Mt. Grossglockner.
2556 **1200** 7s. multicoloured 1·60 1·10

1201 Weisssee Lake

2000. Natural Beauty Spots.
2557 **1201** 7s. multicoloured 1·40 1·20

1202 "Building Europe"

2000. Europa.
2558 **1202** 7s. multicoloured 1·80 1·70

1203 Junkers F13 Airplane and Air Traffic Control Tower

2000. 75th Anniv of Civil Aviation at Klagenfurt Airport.
2559 **1203** 7s. multicoloured 1·40 1·30

1204 Madonna of Altenmarkt (statue) and Glass Roof, Palm House, Burggarten, Vienna

2000. 150th Anniv of Protection of Historic Monuments.
2560 **1204** 8s. multicoloured 1·80 1·50

1205 Illuminated Letter and Text

2000. Life of St. Malachy (treatise) by St. Bernard of Clairvaux.
2561 **1205** 9s. multicoloured 2·40 2·20

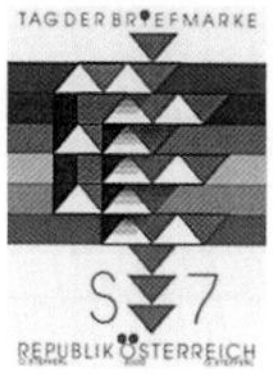

1206 "E" and "E"

2000. Stamp Day.
2562 **1206** 7s. multicoloured 1·80 1·30
See note below No. 2266.

1207 1850 9 Kreuzer and 2000 Stamp Day Stamps

2000. 150th Anniv of Austrian Stamps.
2563 **1207** 7s. multicoloured 1·80 1·30

2000. "WIPA 2000" International Stamp Exhibition, Vienna (5th series). Sheet 65×90 mm.
MS2564 10s. As No. 2458 36·00 34·00

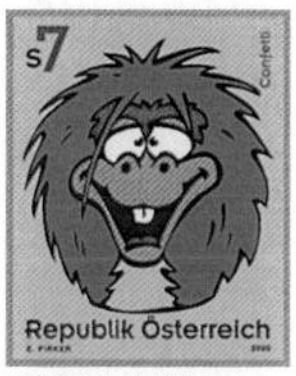

1208 "Confetti"

2000. Confetti (children's television programme).
2565 **1208** 7s. multicoloured 1·60 1·30

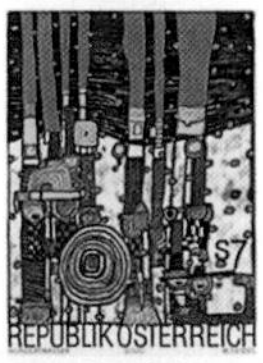

1209 *Blue Blues*

2000. Death Commemoration of Friedensreich Hundertwasser (artist). Sheet 129×126 mm, containing four versions of T **1209** identified by the colours of the vertical strips at the top of the design.
MS2566 7s. silver; 7s. red; 7s. mauve; 7s. black 9·75 9·00

1210 Blood Droplets

2000. Centenary of Discovery of Blood Groups by Karl Landsteiner (pathologist).
2567 **1210** 8s. pink, silver & black 1·60 1·50

1211 Daimler Cannstatter Bus

2000. Centenary of First Regular Bus Route between Purkersdorf and Gablitz.
2568 **1211** 9s. black, blue and light blue 2·40 2·00

2000. Folk Customs and Art (18th series). As T **1005**. Multicoloured.
2569 7s. Men on raft (International Rafting Meeting, Carinthia) 1·40 1·30

1212 Dachstein River and Hallstatt

2000. Natural Beauty Spots.
2570 **1212** 7s. multicoloured 1·40 1·30

1213 String Instrument and Emblem

2000. Centenary of Vienna Symphony Orchestra.
2571 **1213** 7s. multicoloured 1·40 1·30

1214 Dinghies

2000. Olympic Games, Sydney.
2572 **1214** 9s. multicoloured 2·20 1·80

1215 Old and Modern Paper Production Methods

2000. Austrian World of Work (11th series). Printing and Paper.
2573 **1215** 6s.50 multicoloured 1·40 1·30

1216 *Turf Turkey* (Ida Szigethy)

2000. Austrian Modern Art.
2574 **1216** 7s. multicoloured 1·40 1·30

1217 Codex 965 (National Library)

2000. Ancient Arts and Crafts (3rd series).
2575 **1217** 8s. multicoloured 1·80 1·70
See also Nos. 2600 and 2602.

1218 Child receiving Vaccination

2000. Bicentenary of Vaccination in Austria.
2576 **1218** 7s. black and cinnamon 1·40 1·30

1219 Urania Building, Vienna

2000. 50th Anniv of Adult Education Association.
2577 **1219** 7s. brown, grey & gold 1·40 1·30

1220 The Nativity (altar piece, Ludesch Church)

2000. Christmas.
2578 **1220** 7s. multicoloured 1·40 1·30

1221 Downhill Skier

2000. World Skiing Championship (2001), St. Anton am Arlberg.
2579 **1221** 7s. multicoloured 1·60 1·50

1222 Pair of Mallards

2001. Hunting and the Environment. Protection of Wetlands.
2580 **1222** 7s. multicoloured 1·60 1·50

2001. Folk Customs and Art (19th series). As T **1005**. Multicoloured.
2581 8s. Boat mill, Mureck, Styria 1·80 1·50

1223 Steam Locomotive No. 3

2001. Centenary of Zillertal Railway.
2582 **1223** 7s. multicoloured 1·60 1·50

1224 Players and Club Emblem

2001. SV Casino Salzburg, National Football Champion.
2583 **1224** 7s. multicoloured 1·80 1·30

1225 Rolf Rudiger

2001. Confetti (children's television programme).
2584 **1225** 7s. multicoloured 1·80 1·30

1226 Fieseler Fi-156 Storch and Airport

2001. 75th Anniv of Salzburg Airport.
2585 **1226** 14s. multicoloured 3·25 2·75

1227 Baerenschuetz Gorge

2001. Natural Beauty Spots.
2586 **1227** 7s. multicoloured 1·60 1·50

2001. Folk Customs and Art (20th series). As T 1005. Multicoloured.
2587 7s. Lent season cloth from Eastern Tyrol 1·60 1·50

1228 Water Droplet

2001. Europa. Water Resources.
2588 **1228** 15s. multicoloured 4·75 3·25

1229 Post Office Railway Car

2001. Stamp Day.
2589 **1229** 20s.+10s. mult 11·00 10·00

1230 Air Balloon

2001. Centenary of Austrian Flying Club.
2590 **1230** 7s. multicoloured 1·80 1·50

1231 Refugee

2001. 50th Anniv of United Nations High Commissioner for Refugees.
2591 **1231** 21s. multicoloured 4·75 4·50

1232 Kalte Rinne Viaduct

2001. UNESCO World Heritage Site. The Semmering Railway.
2592 **1232** 35s. multicoloured 11·00 10·00

1233 "Seppl" (mascot) (Michelle Schneeweiss)

2001. Seventh International Hiking Olympics, Seefeld.
2593 **1233** 7s. multicoloured 1·60 1·50

1234 Field Post Office at Famagusta

2001. Army Postal Services Abroad.
2594 **1234** 7s. multicoloured 1·60 1·50

2001. Folk Customs and Art (21st series). As T **1005**. Multicoloured.
2595 7s. Rifle and Clubhouse, Preberschiessen, Salzburg (Rifleman's gathering) 1·60 1·50

1235 *Taurus* (Railway Engine)

2001. Conversion of East–West Railway to Four-tracked Railway.
2596 **1235** 7s. multicoloured 1·80 1·70

1236 19th-century Theatrical Scene

2001. Birth Bicentenary of Johann Nestroy (playwright and actor).
2597 **1236** 7s. multicoloured 1·60 1·50

1237 *The Continents* (detail Helmut Leherb)

2001. Austrian Modern Art.
2598 **1237** 7s. multicoloured 1·60 1·50

1238 *False Friends* (Von Fuehrich)

2001. 125th Death Anniv of Joseph Ritter von Fuehrich (artist and engraver).
2599 **1238** 8s. deep green & green 1·70 1·60

1239 Pluviale (embroidered religious robe)

2001. Ancient Arts and Crafts (4th series).
2600 **1239** 10s. multicoloured 2·40 2·20

1240 Dobler

2001. Birth Bicentenary of Leopold Ludwig Dobler (magician and inventor).
2601 **1240** 7s. multicoloured 1·60 1·50

1241 Dalmatik (religious vestment) (Carmelite Monastery, Silbergrasse, Vienna)

2001. Ancient Arts and Crafts (5th series).
2602 **1241** 7s. multicoloured 1·60 1·50

1242 Building and Scientific Equipment

2001. 150th Anniv of the Central Institute for Meteorology and Geodynamics, Vienna.
2603 **1242** 12s. multicoloured 3·00 2·20

1243 Cat

2001
2604 **1243** 19s. multicoloured 6·00 5·50

1244 Civil Servants

2001. Austrian World of Work (12th series). Civil Service.
2605 **1244** 7s. multicoloured 1·60 1·50

1245 Figure of Infant Jesus

2001. Christmas. Glass Shrine, Fitzmoos Church.
2606 **1245** 7s. multicoloured 1·40 1·30

New Currency

1246 House of the Basilisk, Vienna

2002. Tourism.

2607	-	4c. multicoloured	25	10
2608	-	7c. blue and black	35	20
2609	-	13c. multicoloured	50	35
2610	-	17c. violet and black	60	45
2611	-	20c. multicoloured	70	65
2612	-	25c. multicoloured	85	80
2613	-	27c. blue and black	95	90
2614	-	45c. multicoloured	1·20	1·10

2615	**1246**	51c. multicoloured	1·40	1·30
2616	-	55c. multicoloured	1·40	1·20
2617	-	58c. multicoloured	1·60	1·50
2618	-	73c. multicoloured	1·80	1·70
2619	-	75c. multicoloured	2·10	1·80
2620	-	87c. multicoloured	2·40	2·20
2621	-	€1 multicoloured	2·75	2·20
2622	-	€1.25 multicoloured	3·25	2·50
2623	-	€2.03 multicoloured	6·00	5·50
2626	-	€3.75 multicoloured	9·25	8·50

DESIGNS: 4c. As No. 2615; 7c. As No. 2623; 13c. As No. 2620; 17c. As No. 2617; 20c. Yachts, Worthersee, Carintha; 25c. Crucifixes on rock, Mondsee, Upper Austria; 27c. As No. 2618; 45c. Snow covered chalet, Jungholz, Kleinwasler; 55c. Gothic houses, Steyr, Upper Austria; 58c. Wine cellars, Hadres, Lower Austria; 73c. Alpine chalet, Salzburg; 75c. Boat on Bodensee, Voralberg; 87c. Alpach Valley, Tyrol; €1 Farmhouse, Rossegg, Styria; €1.25 Wine press building, Eisenburg, Burgenland; €2.03 Heligenkreuz, Lower Austria; €3.75 Gothic shrine, Hochhosterwitz, Carinthia.

1247 Stars, Map of Europe and €1 Coin

2002. Euro Currency.

2630	**1247**	€3.27 multicoloured	9·75	9·00

No. 2630 is printed on the back under the gum with examples of Austrian schilling coins.

1248 Skiers and Olympic Rings

2002. Winter Olympic Games, Salt Lake City, U.S.A.

2631	**1248**	73c. multicoloured	2·20	2·00

1249 Bouquet of Flowers

2002

2632	**1249**	87c. multicoloured	2·30	2·10

1250 Woman and Skyline

2002. Women's Day.

2633	**1250**	51c. multicoloured	3·50	3·25

1251 Mel and Lucy

2002. "Philis" (children's stamp awareness programme) (1st issue).

2634	**1251**	58c. multicoloured	2·20	2·00

See also Nos. 2639 and 2662.

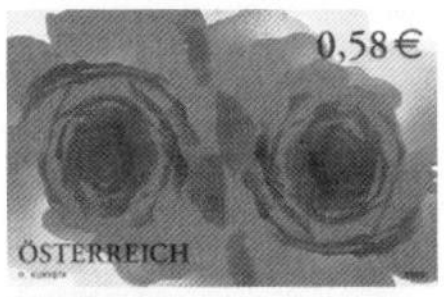

1252 Red Roses

2002. Greetings Stamp.

2635	**1252**	58c. multicoloured	1·80	1·70

1253 Kubin

2002. 125th Birth Anniv of Alfred Kubin (artist).

2636	**1253**	87c. black and buff	2·30	2·10

1254 St. Elizabeth of Thuringia and Sick Man

2002. Caritas (Catholic charity organization).

2637	**1254**	51c. multicoloured	1·90	1·80

1255 Tiger, Clown and Circus Tent

2002. Europa. The Circus.

2638	**1255**	87c. multicoloured	3·50	3·25

1256 Sisko and Mauritius

2002. "Philis" (children's stamp awareness programme) (2nd issue).

2639	**1256**	58c. multicoloured	1·90	1·80

1257 The Nativity

2002. 800th Anniv of Lilienfeld Abbey.

2640	**1257**	€2.03 multicoloured	5·75	5·50

1258 Mimi

2002. Confetti (children's television programme).

2641	**1258**	51c. multicoloured	1·80	1·70

1259 Railway Carriage, 1919

2002. Stamp Day.

2642	**1259**	€1.60+80c. multicoloured	8·50	7·75

1260 Cheetah, Zebra and Orang-utan

2002. 250th Anniv of Schonbrunn Zoo. Multicoloured.

2643	51c. Type **1260**	1·70	1·60
2644	58c. Gulls, flamingos and pelicans	1·80	1·70
2645	87c. Lion, turtle and crocodile	2·40	2·20
2646	€1.38 Elephant, birds and fish	3·50	3·25

Nos. 2643/6 were issued together, *se-tenant*, forming a composite design.

1261 Teddy Bears

2002. Centenary of the Teddy Bear.

2647	**1261**	51c. multicoloured	1·90	1·80

1262 Chair No. 14 (Michael Thonet)

2002. 75th Anniv of "Design Austria" (design group) (1st issue).

2648	**1262**	€1.38 multicoloured	3·50	3·25

See also Nos. 2661 and 2670.

1263 Crystal Cup

2002. Ancient Arts and Crafts.

2649	**1263**	€1.60 multicoloured	4·25	4·00

1264 Museum Buildings

2002. Museumsquartier (MQ), Messepalast, Vienna.

2650	**1264**	58c. multicoloured	2·20	2·00

1265 Figures supporting Emblem

2002. 50th Anniv of Union of Austrians Abroad.

2651	**1265**	€2.47 multicoloured	6·75	6·25

1266 Clown Doctor

2002. "Rote Nasen" (Red Noses (charity)).

2652	**1266**	51c. multicoloured	1·80	1·70

1267 Head

2002. Linzer Klangwolke (sound and light performance), Linz.

2653	**1267**	58c. multicoloured	1·90	1·80

1268 Graf & Stift Type 40/45

2002

2654	**1268**	51c. multicoloured	1·60	1·50

1269 Dog

2002

2655	**1269**	51c. multicoloured	1·60	1·50

1270 Steam Locomotive 109

2002

2656	**1270**	51c. multicoloured	1·80	1·70

1271 *Schutzenhaus* (Karl Goldammer)

2002. Austrian Modern Art.

2657	**1271**	51c. multicoloured	1·80	1·70

1272 Lottery Ball

2002. 250th Anniv of Austrian Lottery. Sheet 72×90 mm.

MS2658	**1272**	87c. multicoloured	3·00	2·75

1273 Thayatal National Park

2002

2659	**1273**	58c. multicoloured	1·80	1·70

1274 Puch 175 SV

2002

2660	**1274**	58c. multicoloured	1·90	1·80

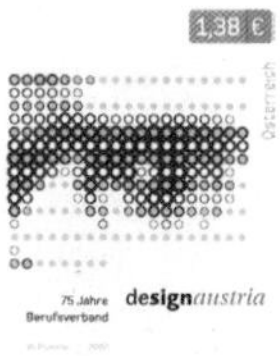

1275 "Eye"

2002. 75th Anniv of "Design Austria" (design group) (2nd issue). Winning Entry in Design Competition.

2661	**1275**	€1.38 multicoloured	4·25	4·00

1276 Edison and Gogo

2002. "Philis" (children's stamp awareness programme) (3rd issue).
2662 **1276** 58c. multicoloured 2·20 2·00

1277 Crib Aureola, Thaur, Tyrol

2002. Christmas.
2663 **1277** 51c. multicoloured 1·60 1·50

1278 Emblem

2003. Make-up Rate Stamp.
2664 **1278** 45c. yellow, silver and black 6·75 4·50

1279 Amphitheatre on River Mur

2003. Graz, Cultural Capital of Europe, 2003.
2665 **1279** 58c. multicoloured 1·80 1·70

1280 Billy Wilder

2003. First Death Anniv of Billy Wilder (film director).
2666 **1280** 58c. multicoloured 1·90 1·80

1281 Heart, Linked Rings and Doves

2003. Greetings Stamp. Wedding.
2667 **1281** 58c. multicoloured 1·90 1·80

1282 Kasperl

2003. Confetti (children's television programme). 45th Anniv of Kasperl (puppet).
2668 **1282** 51c. multicoloured 1·60 1·50

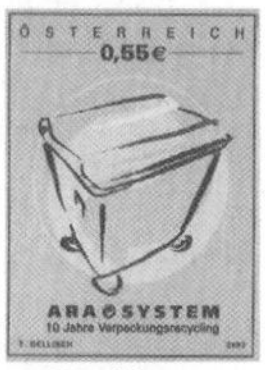

1283 Emblem

2003. Tenth Anniv of Recycling Enterprise.
2669 **1283** 55c. multicoloured 1·40 1·30

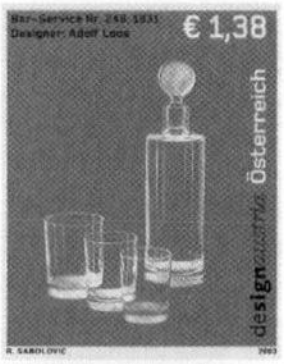

1284 Carafe and Glasses (Adolf Loos)

2003. 75th Anniv of "Design Austria" (design group) (3rd issue).
2670 **1284** €1.38 blue, black and orange 3·50 3·25

1285 Seated Pandas

2003. Schönbrunn Zoo's Acquisition of Pandas from People's Republic of China. Sheet 110×76 mm containing T **1285** and similar multicoloured design.
MS2671 75c. Pandas nuzzling (40×34 mm) (horiz); €1 Type **1285** 8·50 6·75

1286 St. George's Monastery

2003. Millenary of St. George's Monastery, Carintha.
2672 **1286** 87c. multicoloured 2·20 2·00

1287 Marcel Prawy

2003. Marcel Prawy Commemoration (musician). Sheet 100×100 mm.
MS2673 **1287** €1.75 multicoloured 6·75 6·75

1288 Face

2003. Europa. Poster Art.
2674 **1288** €1.02 multicoloured 3·00 2·75

1289 Siemmens M 320 Postal Wagon

2003. Stamp Day.
2675 **1289** €2.54+€1.26 multicoloured 11·00 10·00

1290 Series 5045 Locomotive *Blue Flash*

2003
2676 **1290** 75c. multicoloured 2·30 2·10

1291 Bridge over Salzach River

2003. Centenary of Oberndorf–Laufen Bridge.
2677 **1291** 55c. multicoloured 2·40 2·20

A stamp of the same design was issued by Germany.

1292 Ford Model T

2003. Centenary of Ford Motor Company. Sheet 150×81 mm containing T **1292** and similar horiz designs. Multicoloured.
MS2678 Type **1292**; 55c. Henry Ford; 55c. Ford Streetka 6·75 6·25

1293 Keith Richards

2003. Rolling Stones. Sheet 101×101 mm containing T **1293** and similar vert designs. Multicoloured.
MS2679 Type **1293**; 55c. Mick Jagger; 55c. Charlie Watts; 55c. Ronnie Woods 9·00 8·50

1294 Panther Airport Fire Appliance

2003
2688 **1294** 55c. multicoloured 1·80 1·70

1295 Apostle and Scribe

2003. Year of the Bible.
2689 **1295** 55c. multicoloured 1·40 1·30

1296 "Prenez le temps d'aimer" (Take time to enjoy) (Kiki Kogelnik)

2003
2690 **1296** 55c. multicoloured 1·80 1·70

1297 Lake

2003. UNESCO World Heritage Site. Lake Neusiedlersee.
2691 **1297** €1 multicoloured 3·00 2·75

1298 Geisha and Samurai

2003. Japan Exhibition, Leoben.
2692 **1298** 55c. multicoloured 1·80 1·70

1299 Princess Turandot

2003. Performance of Puccini's Opera *Turandot*, St. Margarethen Roman Quarry.
2693 **1299** 55c. multicoloured 1·80 1·70

1300 Family (Eva Wallner)

2003. Children's Stamp.
2694 **1300** 55c. multicoloured 1·80 1·70

1301 Water Tower

2003. 50th Anniv Local Government Conference, Wiener Neustadt.
2695 **1301** 55c. multicoloured 1·60 1·50

1302 TomTom (cartoon character) and Bouquet

2003. Greetings stamp.
2696 **1302** 55c. multicoloured 2·20 2·00

1303 TomTom throwing Parcel from Hot Air Balloon

2003
2697 **1303** 55c. multicoloured 2·20 2·00

1304 Werner Schlager

2003. Werner Schlager, World Table Tennis Champion, 2003.
2698 **1304** 55c. multicoloured 2·40 2·20

1305 Stylized Head (Cornelia Zell)

2003. Jugend-Phila '03 International Youth Stamp Exhibition, Graz.
2699 **1305** 55c. multicoloured 1·40 1·30

1306 Fan and *Elisabeth*

2003. Elisabeth, the Musical (musical based on life of Empress Elisabeth).
2700 **1306** 55c. multicoloured 1·90 1·80

1307 *Judith*

2003. 185th Death Anniv of Gustav Klimt (artist). Sheet 80×100 mm.
MS2701 **1307** €2.10 multicoloured 7·75 7·25

1308 Hands enclosing Light

2003. 30th Anniv of "Licht ins Dunkel" (Bringing light into darkness) (fund raising campaign).
2702 **1308** 55c. multicoloured 1·40 1·30

1309 Grand Piano

2003. 175th Anniv of Bosendorfer (piano manufacturer).
2703 **1309** 75c. multicoloured 2·20 2·00

1310 Oscar Peterson

2003. 78th Birth Anniv of Oscar Peterson (pianist).
2704 **1310** €1.25 multicoloured 3·50 3·25

1311 Stained Glass Window

2003. Christmas.
2705 **1311** 55c. multicoloured 1·90 1·80

1312 Postal Emblem

2003. Greeting Stamps. T **1312** and similar design. Each yellow, black and gold.
2706 55c. Type **1312** 1·40 1·30
2707 55c. Postal emblem (horiz) 1·40 1·30

Nos. 2706/7 could be personalised by the addition of photograph or logo, replacing the design shown on the stamp.

1313 Ricardo Muti

2004. Vienna Philharmonic Orchestra's New Year Concert conducted by Ricardo Muti (principal conductor, La Scala Milan).
2708 **1313** €1 multicoloured 3·50 3·25

1314 Seiji Ozawa

2004. Second Anniv of Seija Ozawa's Appointment as Musical Director of Vienna State Opera House.
2709 **1314** €1 multicoloured 3·50 3·25

1315 Jose Carreras

2004. 30th Anniv of Jose Carreras Association with Vienna State Opera House.
2710 **1315** €1 multicoloured 3·50 3·25

1316 Gerard Hanappi

2004. Centenary of Austrian Football. Sheet 196×113 mm containing T **1316** and similar vert designs. Multicoloured.
MS2711 55c.×10, Type **1316**; Mathias Sindelar; Football and anniversary emblem; Bruno Pezzey; Ernst Ocwirk; Walter Zeman; Herbert Prohaska; Hans Krankl; Andreas Herzog; Anton Polster 16·00 16·00

1317 Crucifixion (Werner Berg)

2004. Easter.
2712 **1317** 55c. multicoloured 1·40 1·30

1318 Dancers

2004. Life Ball (AIDS charity).
2713 **1318** 55c. multicoloured 1·60 1·30

1319 Cardinal Franz Konig

2004. Cardinal Franz Konig Commemoration.
2714 **1319** €1 multicoloured 3·00 2·75

1320 Emperor Franz Joseph and Empress Elisabeth

2004. 150th Anniv of the Marriage of Emperor Franz Joseph and Empress Elisabeth. Sheet 157×109 mm containing T **1320** and similar vert designs. Multicoloured.
MS2715 €1.25 Type **1320**; €1.50 Wedding procession; €1.75 Emperor Franz Joseph and Empress Elisabeth (35×42 mm) 13·50 13·50

1321 Catholics' Day Emblem

2004. Catholics' Day. Sheet 110×160 mm containing T **1321** and similar vert designs. Multicoloured.
MS2716 55c. Type **1321**; €1.25 Pope John Paul II; €1.25 Magna Mater Austriae (Romanesque statue) (Chapel of Grace, Basilica, Mariazell); €1.25 Mother of God on Column of the Blessed Virgin (Basilica, Mariazell); €1.25 Virgin Mary (Treasury Altar, Basilica, Mariazell); €1.25 Crucifix (High Altar, Basilica, Mariazell) 19·00 19·00

1322 Oeffag C.11 Mail Plane

2004. Stamp Day.
2717 **1322** €2.65+€1.30 multicoloured 11·50 10·50

2004. Folk Customs and Art (22nd series). As T **1005**. Multicoloured.
2718 55c. Barrel sliding, Kosterneuburgs 1·80 1·70

1323 Joe Zawinul (musician)

2004
2719 **1323** 55c. multicoloured 1·80 1·70

1324 Sun and Flowers

2004. Europa. Holidays.
2720 **1324** 75c. multicoloured 2·10 1·90

1325 Holy Sepulchre, Jerusalem

2004. Papal Order of the Holy Sepulchre.
2721 **1325** 125c. multicoloured 3·25 3·00

1326 Imperial and Royal Southern State Railway Locomotive *Engerth*

2004
2722 **1326** 55c. multicoloured 1·70 1·60

1327 Fireworks and Bubbles

2004. Danube Island Festival, Vienna.
2723 **1327** 55c. multicoloured 1·40 1·30

1328 Theodor Herzl

2004. Death Centenary of Theodor Herzl (writer and Zionist pioneer).
2724 **1328** 55c. multicoloured 2·30 2·10

A stamp of the same design was issued by Israel and Hungary.

1329 Arnold Schwarzenegger (governor of California)

2004
2725 **1329** 100c. multicoloured 5·50 5·00

1330 Ernst Happel

2004. 12th Death Anniv of Ernst Happel (football trainer).
2726 **1330** 100c. black and scarlet 5·50 5·00

1331 Tom Turbo (bicycle) (Andreas Wolkerstorfer)

2004. Tom Turbo (character from children's television series). Winning Entry in Children's Drawing Competition.
2727 **1331** 55c. multicoloured 1·70 1·60

1332 TomTom (cartoon character) greeting Snail

2004. Greetings Stamp.
2728 **1332** 55c. multicoloured 1·90 1·80

1333 Town Hall and Steam Tram

2004. Incorporation of Floridsdorf into Vienna.
2729 **1333** 55c. multicoloured 1·90 1·80

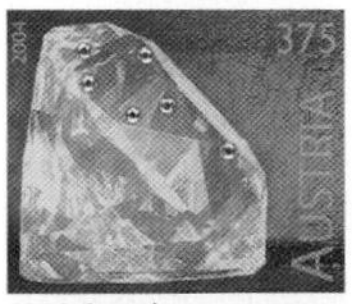

1334 Crystal

2004. Crystal Worlds (tourist attraction), Wattens. Sheet 147×85 mm containing T **1334** and similar horiz design. Multicoloured.
MS2730 375c.×2, Type **1334**; Swan 21·00 21·00

The stamps of **MS**2730 have crystals applied to the surface.

1335 Hermann Maier

2004. Hermann Maier—World Champion Giant Slalom Skier.
2731 **1335** 55c. multicoloured 2·40 2·20

1336 *Kaspar Winterbild* (Josef Bramer)

2004
2732 **1336** 55c. multicoloured 1·60 1·50

2004. No. 2607 surch **BASILISK**.
2733 55c. on 51c. multicoloured 1·80 1·70

1338 *Die Wartende* (Sylvia Gredenberg)

2004
2734 **1338** 55c. multicoloured 1·40 1·30

1339 *Junge Sonnenblume* (Max Weiler)

2004. Sheet 80×100 mm.
MS2735 **1339** €2.10 multicoloured 6·75 6·75

1340 Campaign Poster (Friednsreich Hundertwasser)

2004. 20th Anniv of Campaign to save Danube Meadows (now National Park).
2736 **1340** 55c. multicoloured 3·50 3·25

1341 Soldier and National Arms

2004. 50th Anniv of Federal Army.
2737 **1341** 55c. multicoloured 1·60 1·50

1342 Nikolaus Harnoncourt

2004. 75th Birthday of Nikolaus Harnoncourt (musician).
2738 **1342** €1 multicoloured 2·75 2·50

1343 Salzburg Christmas Market

2004. Christmas.
2739 **1343** 55c. multicoloured 1·40 1·30

1344 Lorin Maazel

2005. Vienna Philharmonic Orchestra's New Year Concert conducted by Lorin Maazel.
2740 **1344** €1 multicoloured 2·75 2·50

1345 Herbert von Karajan

2005. Tenth Anniv of Herbert von Karajan Centre.
2741 **1345** 55c. blue, black and deep blue 1·40 1·30

1346 Stephan Eberharter

2005. Stephan Eberharter—World Champion Skier.
2742 **1346** 55c. multicoloured 1·90 1·80

2005. Nos. 2607, 2609/10, 2613, 2617/18, 2620 and 2623 variously surch.

2743	55c. on 4c. multicoloured	1·40	1·30
2744	55c. on 13c. multicoloured	1·40	1·30
2745	55c. on 17c. multicoloured	1·40	1·30
2746	55c. on 27c. multicoloured	1·40	1·30
2747	55c. on 58c. multicoloured	1·40	1·30
2748	55c. on 73c. multicoloured	1·40	1·30
2749	55c. on 87c. multicoloured	1·40	1·30
2750	55c. on €2.03 multicoloured	1·40	1·30

1355 Globe and Rotary Emblem

2005. Centenary of Rotary International (charitable organization).
2751 **1355** 55c. multicoloured 1·60 1·50

1356 Max Schmeling

2005. Death Centenary of Max Schmeling (boxer).
2752 **1356** 100c. multicoloured 2·75 2·50

1357 *Venus in Front of the Mirror* (Peter Paul Rubens)

2005. Liechtenstein Museum, Garden Palace, Vienna.
2753 **1357** 125c. multicoloured 3·50 3·25

1358 Carl Djerassi

2005. 82nd Birth Anniv of Carl Djerassi (chemist and writer). Sheet 60×80 mm.
MS2754 **1358** 100c. multicoloured 3·50 3·50

1359 Pope John Paul II

2005. Pope John Paul II Commemoration.
2755 **1359** €1 multicoloured 2·75 2·50

1360 Taurus

2005. Astrology (1st issue). Multicoloured. Self-adhesive gum.

2756	55c. Type **1360**	1·60	1·50
2757	55c. Gemini	1·60	1·50
2758	55c. Cancer	1·60	1·50
2759	55c. Rooster (Year of the Rooster) (Chinese astrology) (red)	1·60	1·50

See also Nos. 2772/5, 2784/7 and 2799/2802.

1361 Post Office Building and Carriages

2005. Imperial Post Office in Jerusalem (1859–1914).
2760 **1361** 100c. multicoloured 2·75 2·50

1362 Saint Florian

2005. Saints (1st issue). Saint Florian (National Patron Saint).
2761 **1362** 55c. multicoloured 1·60 1·50

See also Nos. 2767, 2829, 2857, 2890, 2932 and 2959.

1363 Tracks

2005. 60th Anniv of Liberation of Mauthausen Concentration Camp.
2762 **1363** 55c. multicoloured 1·60 1·50

1364 State Arms

2005. 60th Anniv of Second Republic and 50th Anniv of State Treaty. Sheet 120×80 mm containing T **1364** and similar multicoloured design.
MS2763 55c.×2, Type **1364**; Seals and signatures on treaty (42×35 mm) 3·50 3·50

1365 Heidi Klum

2005. Life Ball (AIDS charity).
2764 **1365** 75c. multicoloured 2·20 2·00

1366 Junkers F13 Flying Boat

2005. Stamp Day.
2765 **1366** 265c.+130c. mult 11·00 11·00

1367 Waiter in Cup of Coffee

2005. Europa. Gastronomy.
2766 **1367** 75c. multicoloured 2·30 2·10

1368 Saint Joseph

2005. Saints (2nd issue).
2767 **1368** 55c. multicoloured 1·60 1·50

1369 Jochen Rindt

2005. 25th Death Anniv of Karl Jochen Rindt (1970—Formula 1 World Champion).
2768 **1369** 55c. multicoloured 1·80 1·70

1370 Melman, Marty, Alex and Gloria (characters)

2005. Madagascar (animated film).
2769 **1370** 55c. multicoloured 1·60 1·50

1371 Peacock Butterfly (*Inachis io*)

2005
2770 **1371** 55c. multicoloured 1·60 1·50

1372 Edelweiss

2005. Vorarlberg Embroidery.
2771 **1372** 375c. green 9·75 9·50

2005. Astrology (2nd issue). As T **1360**. Multicoloured. Self-adhesive.

2772	55c. Leo	1·60	1·50
2773	55c. Virgo	1·60	1·50
2774	55c. Libra	1·60	1·50
2775	55c. As No. 2759 (yellow)	1·60	1·50

2005. Customs and Art (23rd series). As T **1005**. Multicoloured.

2776	55c. Game of dice, Frankenburg	1·60	1·50

1373 Nikki Lauda

2005. Nikki Lauda (Formula 1 World Champion—1975, 1977 and 1984).

2777	**1373**	55c. multicoloured	1·70	1·60

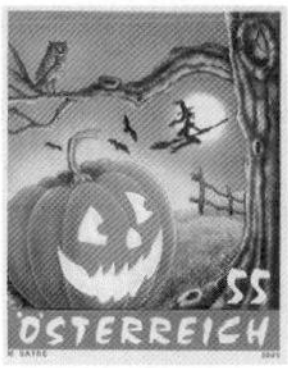

1374 Pumpkin

2005. Halloween.

2778	**1374**	55c. multicoloured	1·60	1·50

1375 "Houses" (Egon Schiele)

2005. Art. Sheet 100×80 mm.

MS2779	**1375** 210c. multicoloured	6·75	6·75

1376 ET 10.103 Railcar

2005. Centenary of Montafon Railway.

2780	**1376**	55c. multicoloured	1·60	1·50

1377 Presentation of Deed

2005. Landhaus (provincial government building), Klagenfurt.

2781	**1377**	75c. multicoloured	2·10	1·90

1378 *Master of the Woods* (Karl Hodina)

2005

2782	**1378**	55c. multicoloured	1·60	1·50

1379 Adalbert Stifter

2005. Birth Bicentenary of Adalbert Stifter (writer).

2783	**1379**	55c. multicoloured	2·40	2·20

2005. Astrology (3rd issue). As T **1360**. Multicoloured. Self-adhesive.

2784	55c. Scorpio	1·60	1·50
2785	55c. Sagittarius	1·60	1·50
2786	55c. Capricorn	1·60	1·50
2787	55c. As No. 2759 (orange)	1·60	1·50

1380 National Theatre

2005. 50th Anniv of Re-opening of National Theatre and Opera House. Sheet 130×60 mm containing T **1380** and similar horiz design.

MS2788	55c. sepia and agate; 55c. indigo and black	4·75	4·75

DESIGNS: 55c.×2, Type **1380**; State Opera House.

1381 Hills

2005. Restoration of Sattler's Cyclorama of Salzburg. Sheet 155×56 mm containing T **381** and similar horiz design. Multicoloured.

MS2789	125c.×2, Type **1381**; Townscape	7·75	7·75

1382 "Nude" (Veronika Zillner)

2005

2790	**1382**	55c. multicoloured	1·60	1·50

1383 Aslan (character)

2005. *The Chronicles of Narnia* (film of book by C. S. Lewis).

2791	**1383**	55c. multicoloured	1·60	1·50

1384 *Maria Heimsuchung* (Reinhold Stecher)

2005. Advent.

2792	**1384**	55c. multicoloured	1·40	1·30

1385 Shields

2005. 800th Anniv of Order of Teutonic Knights.

2793	**1385**	55c. multicoloured	1·40	1·30

1386 Snow-covered Houses

2005. Christmas.

2794	**1386**	55c. multicoloured	1·40	1·30

1387 Mariss Jansons

2006. Vienna Philharmonic Orchestra's New Year Concert conducted by Mariss Jansons.

2795	**1387**	75c. multicoloured	1·90	1·80

1388 Building Facade

2006. Austria's Presidency of European Union.

2796	**1388**	75c. multicoloured	1·90	1·80

1389 "Post" Philatelic Shop

2006. Greeting Stamp.

2797	**1389**	55c. multicoloured	1·40	1·30

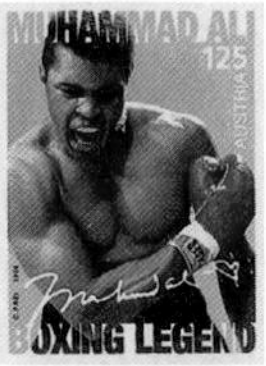

1390 Muhammad Ali

2006. Muhammad Ali (boxer).

2798	**1390**	€1.25 multicoloured	3·50	3·25

1391 Dog ("Year of the Dog")

2006. Astrology (4th issue). Multicoloured. Self-adhesive.

2799	55c. Type **1391**	1·60	1·50
2800	55c. Aquarius	1·60	1·50
2801	55c. Pisces	1·60	1·50
2802	55c. Aries	1·60	1·50

1392 Wolfgang Mozart

2006. 250th Birth Anniv of Wolfgang Amadeus Mozart (composer and musician).

2803	**1392**	55c. red and silver	1·60	1·50

1393 Europa (sculpture) (R. Chavanon)

2006. 50th Anniv of Europa Stamps.

2804	**1393**	125c. multicoloured	3·50	3·25

1394 *Lost in her Dreams* (Friedrich von Amerling)

2006. Liechtenstein Museum, Garden Palace, Vienna.

2805	**1394**	125c. multicoloured	3·50	3·25

A stamp of the same design was issued by Liechtenstein.

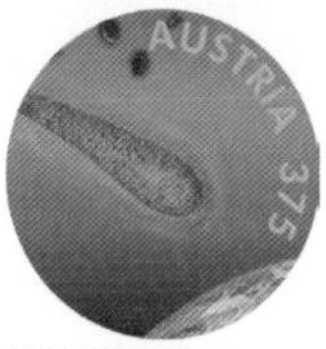

1395 Meteorite

2006. Post from another World. Meteorite H-chondrite on Stamps. Sheet 81×60 mm.

MS2806	**1395** 375c. multicoloured	11·00	11·00

No. **MS**2806 contains ground meteorite dust and is sold in a folder.

1396 Almaz and Karl Heinz Bohm (founders)

2006. 25th Anniv of Menschen fur Menschen (charity).

2807	**1396**	100c. multicoloured	2·50	2·40

1397 Initiation

2006. Freemasonry in Austria. Sheet 81×61 mm.

MS2808	**1397** 100c. multicoloured	3·50	3·50

1398 Couch

2006. 150th Birth Anniv of Sigmund Freud (psychoanalysis).

2809	**1398**	55c. multicoloured	1·30	1·20

1399 Franz Beckenbauer (Andy Warhol)

2006. Franz Beckenbauer (footballer).

2810	**1399**	75c. multicoloured	1·90	1·80

2006. Flood Relief. No. 2612 surch **75+425 HOCH WASSER HILFE 2006**.

2811	75c.+425c. on 25c. multicoloured	9·75	9·50

The surcharge was for the victims of the Marchfeld floods.

2006. No. 2608 surch **HEILIGENKREUZ NIEDEROSTERRICH** and tree.

2812	55c. on 7c. multicoloured	1·40	1·30

1402 Falco

2006. Hans Holzl (Falco) (rock musician) Commemoration.
2813 **1402** 55c. multicoloured 1·60 1·50

1403 Naomi Campbell

2006. Life Ball (AIDS charity).
2814 **1403** 75c. multicoloured 2·30 2·10

2006. Customs and Art (24th series). As T **1005**. Multicoloured.
2815 55c. Weitensfeld Kranzlreiten (race) 1·40 1·30

1404 Emblem

2006. Privatization of Post Office.
2816 **1404** 55c. multicoloured 1·40 1·30

1405 Jim Clark

2006. Formula I Motor Racing Legends. Sheet 140×185 mm containing T **1405** and similar horiz designs. Multicoloured.
MS2817 55c.×4, Type **1405**; Jacky Ickx; Jackie Stewart; Alain Prost; 75c.×2, Stirling Moss; Mario Andretti; 100c. Bruce McLaren; 125c. Jack Brabham 16·00 16·00

See also No. **MS**2868.

1406 Saint Hemma

2006
2818 **1406** 55c. multicoloured 1·40 1·30

1407 Emblem

2006. 60th Anniv of Federal Chamber of Industry and Commerce.
2819 **1407** 55c. silver, vermilion and black 1·80 1·70

1408 Mozart

2006. 250th Birth Anniv of Wolfgang Amadeus Mozart (composer and musician). Viva Mozart Exhibition, Salzburg.
2820 **1408** 55c. multicoloured 1·40 1·30

1409 Ottfried Fischer

2006. Ottfried Fischer (actor).
2821 **1409** 55c. multicoloured 1·40 1·30

1410 Figures

2006. Europa. Integration.
2822 **1410** 75c. multicoloured 1·90 1·80

1411 Airbus A310-300

2006. Stamp Day.
2823 **1411** 265c.+130c. multicoloured 10·50 10·50

1412 St. Anne's Column, Innsbruck

2006
2824 **1412** 55c. multicoloured 1·40 1·30

1413 K. K. STB Reihe 106 Locomotive

2006. Centenary of Pyhrn Railway.
2825 **1413** 55c. multicoloured 1·40 1·30

1414 Fireworks over Victoria Harbour, Hong Kong

2006. Fireworks. Sheet 146×85 mm containing T **1414** and similar horiz design. Multicoloured.
MS2826 €3.75×2, Type **1414**; Fireworks over Giant Ferris Wheel, Vienna, Austria 21·00 21·00

MS2826 has crystals applied to the surface of the stamps and was sold in a folder.

Stamps of a similar design were issued by Hong Kong.

1415 European Lynx (*Lynx lynx*)

2006. Fauna.
2827 **1415** 55c. multicoloured 1·40 1·30

1416 Emblem

2006. WIPA 2008 International Stamp Exhibition.
2828 **1416** 55c.+20c. multicoloured 2·20 2·00

1417 Saint Gebhard

2006. Saints (3rd issue).
2829 **1417** 55c. multicoloured 1·40 1·30

1418 Steyr 220 Motor Car

2006
2830 **1418** 55c. multicoloured 1·40 1·30

1419 KTM R 125 Tarzan Motorbike

2006
2831 **1419** 55c. multicoloured 1·40 1·30

1420 Benjamin Raich

2006. Benjamin Raich—World Champion Skier.
2832 **1420** 55c. multicoloured 1·40 1·30

1421 Piano

2006. Musical Instruments. Multicoloured.
2833 55c. Type **1421** 1·40 1·30
2834 55c. Guqin 1·40 1·30

Stamps of a similar design were issued by China.

1422 "Young Boy" (Cornelia Schlesinger)

2006
2835 **1422** 55c. multicoloured 1·40 1·30

1423 Alte Saline (salt refinery) and Saint Rupert

2006. German and Austrian Philatelic Exhibition, Bad Reichenhall.
2836 **1423** 55c.+20c. multicoloured 1·90 1·80

1424 *Homo sapiens* (detail) (Valentin Oman)

2006. Modern Art.
2837 **1424** 55c. multicoloured 1·40 1·30

1425 Pond Turtle

2006. Self-adhesive.
2838 **1425** 55c. multicoloured 1·40 1·30

1426 Bald Ibis

2006. Fauna. Multicoloured. Self-adhesive.
2839 55c. Type **1426** 1·40 1·30
2840 55c. Brown bear 1·40 1·30

1427 *The Holy Family at Rest* (Franz Weiss)

2006. Christmas (1st issue).
2841 **1427** 55c. multicoloured 1·40 1·30

1428 *Christkindl Pilgrimage Church* (Reinhold Stecher)

2006. Christmas (2nd issue).
2842 **1428** 55c. multicoloured 1·40 1·30

1429 *Ferdinand Square* (T. Chyshkovskii)

2006. 750th Anniv of Lvov.
2843 **1429** 55c. multicoloured 1·40 1·30

A stamp of a similar design was issued by Ukraine.

1430 Michael Schumacher

1430a Michael Schumacher

2006. Michael Schumacher (Formula 1 World Champion–1994/5 and 2000/4).
2844 **1430** 75c. multicoloured 2·20 2·00
2844a **1430a** 75c. multicoloured 3·25 3·00

No. 2844a has different (incorrect) championship year dates and includes designer and year of issue at lower margin.

1431 "Zinnoberroten Merkur" (No. N13 "Mercury")

2006. Centenary of National Stamp and Coin Dealers' Association.

2845 **1431** 55c. cerise and gold 1·40 1·30

1432 Zubin Mehta

2007. Vienna Philharmonic Orchestra's New Year Concert conducted by Zubin Mehta.

2846 **1432** 75c. multicoloured 1·90 1·80

1433 Alpine Flowers

2007. Flowers. Multicoloured.

2847 55c. Type **1433** 1·30 1·20

2848 75c. Hellebores 1·80 1·70

2849 €1.25 Spring flowers 3·00 2·75

1434 Symbols of Technology and Figure

2007. Mankind and Technology. Self-adhesive.

2850 **1434** 55c. multicoloured 1·40 1·30

1435 Fire and Earth

2007. Lower Austrian Provincial Exhibition.

2851 **1435** 55c. multicoloured 1·40 1·30

1436 Outline of Robert Baden-Powell

2007. Centenary of Scouting. Sheet 170×130 mm containing T **1436** and similar horiz designs. Multicoloured.

MS2852 55c.×4, Type **1436**; Campfire; Tent; Guitar 6·00 6·00

1437 Roe Deer

2007

2853 **1437** 75c. multicoloured 1·90 1·80

1438 *Portrait of a Lady* (Bernardino Zaganelli da Cottignola)

2007

2854 **1438** €1.25 multicoloured 3·25 3·00

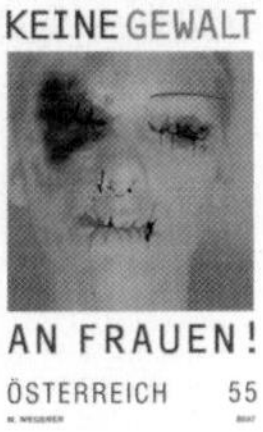

1439 Injured Woman

2007. Stop Violence against Women Campaign.

2855 **1439** 55c. multicoloured 1·40 1·30

1440 Easter Rattles

2007. Traditional Customs.

2856 **1440** 55c. multicoloured 1·40 1·30

1441 Saint Klemens Maria Holbauer

2007. Saints (4th issue).

2857 **1441** 55c. multicoloured 1·40 1·30

1442 Emblem

2007. WIPA 2008 International Stamp Exhibition.

2858 **1442** 55c.+20c. multicoloured 2·20 2·00

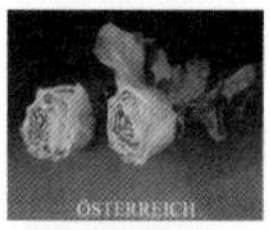

1443 Roses

2007. Mourning Stamp. No value expressed.

2859 **1443** (55c.) multicoloured 1·40 1·30

1444 Flowers

2007. Greetings Stamp. No value expressed.

2860 **1444** (55c.) multicoloured 1·40 1·30

1445 Salamander (*Salamandra salamandra*)

2007. Fauna. Multicoloured. Self-adhesive.

2861 55c. Type **1445** 1·40 1·30

2862 55c. Crayfish (*Astacus astacus*) 1·40 1·30

1446 Pope Benedict XVI

2007. 80th Birth Anniv of Pope Benedict XVI.

2863 **1446** 100c. multicoloured 2·75 2·50

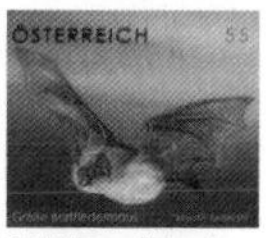

1447 Inscr "Myotis brandtii"

2007. Whiskered Bat. Self-adhesive.

2864 **1447** 55c. multicoloured 1·40 1·30

No. 2864 is described as "Whiskered Bat", that is Myotis mystacinus but is inscribed "Myotis brandtii", that is Brandt's Bat.

1448 Violet

2007

2865 **1448** 100c. multicoloured 2·40 2·20

1449 'The Good Samaritan' (fresco, Franciscan Monastery, Schwaz)

2007. 80th Anniv of Austrian Workers Samaritan Federation (medical assistance organization).

2866 **1449** 55c. multicoloured 1·40 1·30

1450 'Untitled' (painting by Hermann Nitsch)

2007. Modern Art. Sheet 61×80 mm. Imperf.

MS2867 **1450** scarlet and black 3·00 3·00

2007. Formula I Motor Racing Legends. Sheet 140×185 mm containing horiz designs (size 50×32 mm) as T **1405**. Multicoloured.

MS2868 55c.×8, Phil Hill; Clay Regazzoni; Gerhard Berger; Juan Manuel Fangio; John Surtees; Mika Hakkinen; Graham Hill; Emerson Fittipaldi 11·50 11·50

1451 Krause & Comp Electric Locomotive

2007. Centenary of Mariazell Narrow Gauge Railway.

2869 **1451** 55c. multicoloured 1·40 1·30

1452 Church Facade and Tower

2007. 850th Anniv of Mariazell Basilica.

2870 **1452** 55c. multicoloured 1·40 1·30

1453 Trix and Flix

2007. European Football Championships (Euro 2008), Austria and Switzerland. Sheet 100×80 mm containing T **1453** and similar horiz designs. Multicoloured.

MS2871 20c. Type **1453**; 25c. Holding trophy; 30c.Tackling for the ball; 35c. With arms around each other 3·00 3·00

1454 *Self-portrait* (painting by Angelika Kauffmann)

2007. Modern Art. Sheet 81×101 mm.

MS2872 **1454** 210c. scarlet and black 6·00 6·00

1455 *Wien* (steamer) (painting by Harry Heusser)

2007. Stamp Day.

2873 **1455** 265c.+130c. multicoloured 9·75 9·00

1456 Globe as Scout

2007. Europa. Centenary of Scouting.

2874 **1456** 55c. multicoloured 1·40 1·30

1457 Ignaz Pleyel

2007. 250th Birth Anniv of Ignaz Joseph Pleyel (composer).

2875 **1457** £1 multicoloured 2·40 2·20

1458 Shrek and Fiona

2007. *Shrek the Third* (animated film).

2876 **1458** 55c. multicoloured 1·40 1·30

1459 Museum Building

2007. Essel Museum. Self-adhesive.
2877 **1459** 55c. multicoloured 1·40 1·30

1460 Wilhelm Kienzl

2007. 150th Birth Anniv of Wilhelm Kienzl (composer).
2878 **1460** 75c. multicoloured 1·80 1·70

1461 U Series Steam Locomotive

2007. Bregenz Forest Railway.
2879 **1461** 75c. multicoloured 1·90 1·80

1462 *Man* (Astrid Bernhart)

2007
2880 **1462** 55c. multicoloured 1·40 1·30

1463 Dandelion

2007. Flora. Multicoloured.
2881 4c. Type **1463** 25 20
2882 10c. Scottish laburnum 35 35
2883 65c. Gelder rose 1·60 1·50
2884 115c. *Gentiana ciliate* 2·75 2·50
2885 140c. Clematis 3·50 3·25

1464 *Haliaeetus albicilla* (white-tailed eagle)

2007
2886 **1464** 55c. multicoloured 1·40 1·30

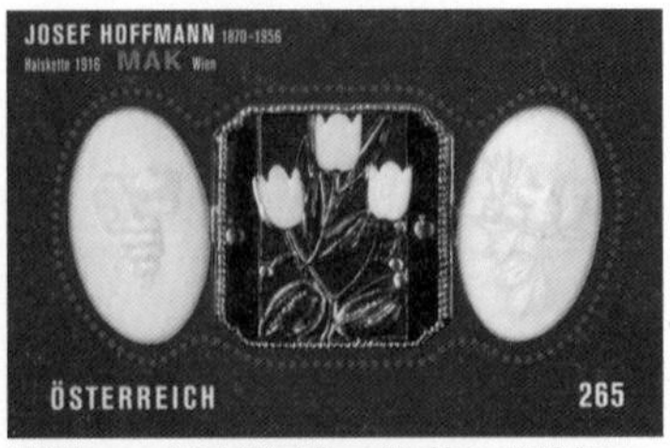

1465 Ivory and Gold Medallions (Necklace, 1916) (image scaled to 60% of original size)

2007. Josef Hoffman (designer and architect) Commemoration. Sheet 81×51 mm. Imperf.
MS2887 **1465** 265c. multicoloured 7·75 7·75

1466 Oil Derrick

2007. 75th Anniv of Austrian Oil Production.
2888 **1466** 75c. multicoloured 1·90 1·80
No. 2888 was impregnated with scent of oil which was released by rubbing part of the design.

1467 Stag and Hind

2007. Birth Bicentenary of Friedrich Gauermann (artist).
2889 **1467** 55c. multicoloured 1·40 1·30

1468 Saint Rupert

2007. Saints (5th issue).
2890 **1468** 55c. multicoloured 1·40 1·30

1469 Niki Hosp

2007. Niki Hosp–Women's World Cup Alpine Ski Champion, 2006–2007.
2891 **1469** 55c. multicoloured 1·40 1·30

1470 *Lucanus cervus* (stag beetle)

2007. Self-adhesive.
2892 **1470** 75c. multicoloured 2·10 1·90

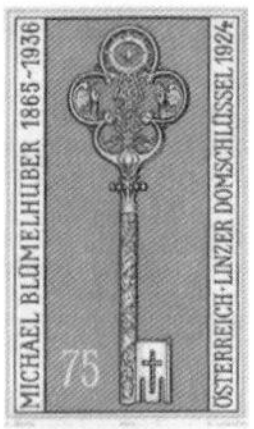

1471 Key

2007. Michel Blumelhuber (iron and steel carver) Commemoration.
2893 **1471** 75c. multicoloured 2·10 1·90

1472 Christiane Horbiger

2007. Christiane Horbiger (actress and recipient of Cross of Honour for Science and Art).
2894 **1472** 55c. multicoloured 1·40 1·30

1473 Scene from *Queen of Spades* (Peter Illyich Tchaikovsky)

2007. Vienna State Opera Opening Nights (1st issue).
2895 **1473** 55c. multicoloured 1·40 1·30
See also No. 2914.

1474 Nativity (altar painting, Oberwollan)

2007. Christmas. Multicoloured.
2896 55c. Type **1474** 1·40 1·30
2897 65c. Nativity (icon, Church of St. Barbara) 1·60 1·50

1475 Clownfish

2007. 50th Anniv of Haus des Meeres (Aqua Terra Zoo).
2898 **1475** 55c. multicoloured 1·40 1·30

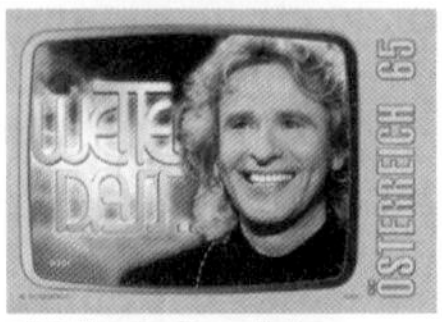

1476 Thomas Gottschalk

2007. Thomas Gottschalk and 'Wetten dass?' (TV presenter and game show).
2899 **1476** 65c. multicoloured 1·70 1·60

1477 *Cypripedium calceolus* (lady's slipper orchid)

2008
2900 **1477** 15c. multicoloured 35 35

1478 Vienna

2008. EURO 2008 Football Championships (1st issue). Venues. Sheet 150×90 mm containing T **1478** and similar square designs. Multicoloured.
MS2901 55c.×4, Type **1478**; Salzburg; Klagenfurt; Innsbruck, 65c.×4, Zurich; Basel; Bern; Geneva 12·00 12·00
The stamps of No. **MS**2901 share a common background design.
See also Nos. 2903/4, 2906/7, 2909, 2910, 2917, 2918, 2919, 2912, 2922, 2926, 2925, **MS**2929, 2930, **MS**2931 and 2951.

1479 Emblem and St Stephen's Cathedral

2008. WIPA 2008 International Stamp Exhibition.
2902 **1479** 55c.+20c. multicoloured 2·20 2·00
See also Nos. 2828 and 2858.

1480 Trix and Flix (mascots)

2008. EURO 2008 Football Championships (2nd issue). Multicoloured. Self-adhesive.
2903 55c. Type **1480** 1·40 1·30
2904 65c. Emblem 1·60 1·50

1481 *Portrait of Martina* (Hans Robert Pippal)

2008. Modern Art.
2905 **1481** 65c. multicoloured 1·60 1·50

1482 Trix and Flix (Alexandra Payer)

2008. EURO 2008 Football Championships (3rd issue). Children's Drawings. Multicoloured.
2906 55c. Type **1482** 1·40 1·30
2907 55c. Footballs as map of Europe (Corina Payr) 1·40 1·30

2008. WIPA 2008 International Stamp Exhibition. Gold. Sheet 126×73 mm containing triangular designs as T **1479**. Multicoloured.
MS2908 55c. As No. 2828; 55c. As No. 2858; 65c. As No. 2902 5·75 5·75

1483 Map of Europe, Football and Euro Stars (Saskia Puchegger)

2008. EURO 2008 Football Championships (4th issue). Children's Drawings.
2909 **1483** 65c. multicoloured 1·60 1·50

1484 *Defence* (Maria Lassnig)

2008. EURO 2008 Football Championships (5th issue).
2910 **1484** 55c. multicoloured 1·40 1·30

1485 *Hyla arborea* (tree frog)

2008. Fauna. Multicoloured. Self-adhesive.
2911 65c. Type **1485** 1·70 1·60
2912 65c. *Alcedo atthis* (kingfisher) 1·70 1·60

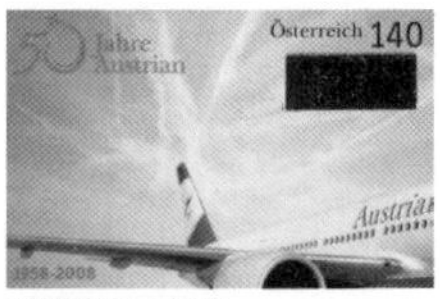

1486 Airbus A320

2008. 50th Anniv of Austrian Airlines.
2913 **1486** 140c. multicoloured 3·50 3·25
No. 2913 includes an area, which when scratched, could win a prize.

1487 Scene from *La Forza del Destino* (Giuseppe Verdi)

2008. Vienna State Opera Opening Nights (2nd issue).
2914 **1487** 55c. multicoloured 1·40 1·30

1488 *Princess Marie Franziska von Liechtenstein* (Friedrich von Amerling)

2008

2915 **1488** 125c. multicoloured 3·50 3·25

A stamp of a similar design was issued by Liechtenstein.

1489 Imaginary Landscape

2008. Modern Art. Sysanne Sculler (Soshana).

2916 **1489** 55c. multicoloured 1·40 1·30

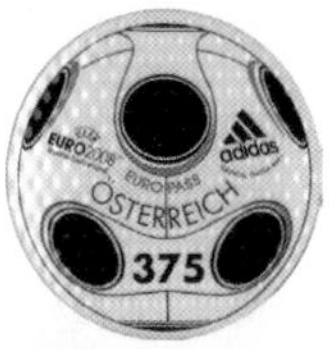

1490 Football

2008. EURO 2008 Football Championships (6th issue). Self-adhesive.

2917 **1490** 375c. multicoloured 9·75 9·25

No. 2917 is made from a synthetic mixture containing polyurethane, as the original ball used for the EURO 2008 (known as the 'Europass').

1491 Football Field, Ball and Player's Legs

2008. EURO 2008 Football Championships (7th issue).

2918 **1491** 55c. multicoloured 1·40 1·30

1492 Lindwurm (symbol of Klagenfurt) on Football and Karawanken Mountains (Bolona Jencic)

2008. EURO 2008 Football Championships (8th issue). Children's Drawings.

2919 **1492** 125c. multicoloured 3·00 2·75

1493 View from River

2008. World Heritage Site. Wachau.

2920 **1493** 100c. multicoloured 2·40 2·20

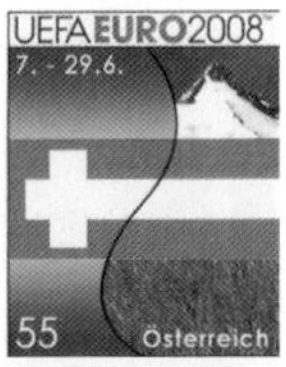

1494 Austrian and Swiss Flags, Alps and Turf (Stefan Gritsch)

2008. EURO 2008 Football Championships (9th issue). Children's Drawings.

2921 **1494** 55c. multicoloured 1·40 1·30

1495 Football wearing Lederhosen (Vanessa Schennach)

2008. EURO 2008 Football Championships (10th issue). Children's Drawings.

2922 **1495** 100c. multicoloured 2·40 2·20

1496 Traditional Clothes

2008. Centenary of Tyrolean Federation of Traditional Provincial Costumes.

2923 **1496** 75c. multicoloured 2·00 1·90

1497 *Erinaceus concolor* (southern white-breasted hedgehog)

2008. Fauna. Multicoloured. Self-adhesive.

2924 55c. Type **1497** 1·40 1·30

2925 55c. *Lepus europaeus* (hare) 1·40 1·30

1498 Preparation and Goal

2008. EURO 2008 Football Championships (11th issue). Andreas Herzog's Winning Goal—World Cup Qualifier, 1997. Self-adhesive.

2926 **1498** 545c. multicoloured 14·00 14·00

1499 Mare and Foal

2008. Federal Lipizzaner Stud, Piber.

2927 **1499** 55c. multicoloured 1·50 1·40

1500 Turf (Silvia Holemar, Denise Prossegger and Guso Aldijana)

2008. EURO 2008 Football Championships (12th issue). Children's Drawings.

2928 **1500** 75c. multicoloured 2·00 1·90

1501 Italy

2008. EURO 2008 Football Championships (13th issue). Participating Teams. Two sheets 150×90 mm containing T **1501** and similar square designs showing faces painted with team flag.

MS2929 (a) 10c. Type **1501**; 10c. Croatia; 15c. Sweden; 15c. Greece; 20c. Austria; 20c. Portugal; 65c. Spain; 65c. Czech Republic. (b) 25c. Switzerland; 25c. Germany; 30c. Romania; 30c. Turkey; 35c. Netherlands; 35c. Poland; 55c. Russia; 55c. France 12·50 12·50

1502 Ball and Chairs (Andrea Kastrun)

2008. EURO 2008 Football Championships (14th issue). Children's Drawings.

2930 **1502** 55c. multicoloured 1·50 1·40

1503 Henri Delaunay Cup (EURO 2008 trophy)

2008. EURO 2008 Football Championships (15th issue). Sheet 65×75 mm.

MS2931 **1503** 375c. multicoloured 10·00 10·00

No. **MS**2931 contains four crystals and was issued contained in a folder.

1504 Saint Notburga

2008. Saints (6th issue).

2932 **1504** 55c. multicoloured 1·50 1·40

1505 Script, Hand, Pen and Ink

2008. Europa. The Letter.

2933 **1505** 65c. multicoloured 1·80 1·60

1506 *Upupa epops* (hoopoe)

2008. Fauna. Multicoloured. Self-adhesive.

2934 75c. Type **1506** 1·90 1·70

2935 75c. *Hemaris fuciformis* (broad-bordered bee hawk-moth) 1·90 1·70

1507 Steam Locomotive

2008. 110th Anniv of Vienna Urban Railway.

2936 **1507** 75c. multicoloured 2·00 1·90

1508 Letterbox

2008. Death Centenary of Josef Maria Olbrich (artist and architect).

2937 **1508** 65c. multicoloured 1·80 1·60

1509 Statuette

2008. Centenary of Discovery of Willendorf Venus. Self-adhesive.

2938 **1509** 375c. multicoloured 10·00 9·75

1510 Columbine

2008. Flowers.

2939 **1510** 50c. multicoloured 1·40 1·30

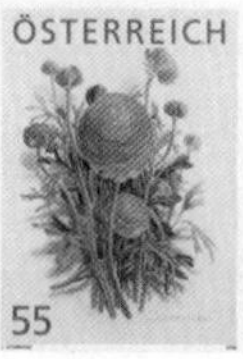

1511 Ranunculus

2008. Flowers.

2940 **1511** 55c. multicoloured 1·50 1·40

1512 Skyline

2008. WIPA 2008 International Stamp Exhibition. Self-adhesive.

2941 **1512** 55c. multicoloured 1·50 1·40

See also No. 2828, 2858 and 2902.

1513 Series 4130 Rail Car Set

2008. 150th Anniv of Empress Elizabeth Western Railway.

2942 **1513** 100c. multicoloured 2·75 2·50

1514 Express Mail (detail) (painting by K. Schorpfeil)

2008. Praga 2008 and WIPA 2008, International Stamp Exhibitions. Sheet 120×80 mm.

MS2943 **1514** 265c. multicoloured 7·25 7·00

Stamp of the same design was issued by Czech Republic.

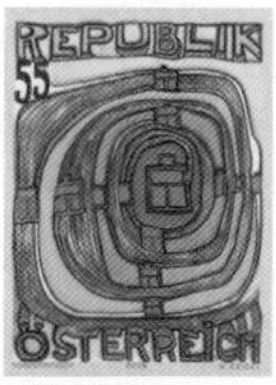

1515 Maze

2008. 80th Birth Anniv of Friedensreich Hundertwasser (artist). Sheet 97×127 mm containing T **1515** and similar vert designs. Multicoloured.

MS2944 55c. Type **1515**; 75c. House; 100c. Stylized lamps; 125c. Maze (different) 10·00 10·00

2008. WIPA 2008 International Stamp Exhibition. Silver. Sheet 126×73 mm containing triangular designs as T **1479**. Multicoloured.

MS2945 55c.+20c.×3, As No. 2828; As No. 2902; As No. 2858 6·25 6·25

1516 *Schonbrunn* (paddle steamer)

2008. Stamp Day.

2946 **1516** 265c.+130c. multicoloured 10·50 10·00

1517 Nude (Dina Larot)

2008

2947 **1517** 55c. multicoloured 1·50 1·40

1518 Gentian

2008. Vorarlberg Embroidery. Self-adhesive.

2948 **1518** 375c. blue 10·00 9·75

1519 *Maximilian Schell* ((Arnulf Rainer)

2008. Maximilian Schell (actor).

2949 **1519** 100c. multicoloured 2·75 2·50

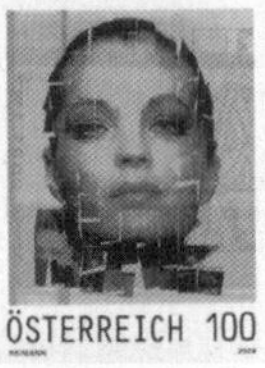

1520 Romy Schneider

2008. 70th Birth Anniv of Romy Schneider (actress).

2950 **1520** 100c. multicoloured 2·75 2·50

1521 Iker Casillas (winning Spanish team captain) holding Trophy

2008. Euro 2008 Football Championships (16th issue).

2951 **1521** 65c. multicoloured 1·80 1·60

1522 Thomas Morgenstern

2008. Thomas Morgenstern—World Champion Ski-jumper, 2007 and Olympic Gold Medallist.

2952 **1522** 100c. multicoloured 2·75 2·50

1523 Markus Rogan

2008. Markus Rogan—World Champion Backstroke Swimmer, 2008.

2953 **1523** 100c. multicoloured 2·75 2·50

1524 Heinz Fischer

2008. 70th Birth Anniv of Heinz Fischer (federal president 2004—present).

2954 **1524** 55c. multicoloured 1·50 1·40

1525 Manner Neapolitan Biscuits

2008. Classic Trademarks.

2955 **1525** 55c. multicoloured 1·50 1·40

1526 Koloman Moser

2008. Koloman Moser (artist and stamp designer) Commemoration.

2956 **1526** 130c. multicoloured 3·75 3·50

1527 Trieste Imperial and Royal Post Office Building

2008. Old Austria.

2957 **1527** 65c. multicoloured 2·00 1·90

1528 *First Christmas Tree in Ried* (Felix Ignaz Pollingger)

2008. Art History.

2958 **1528** 65c. multicoloured 2·00 1·90

1529 Saint Martin

2008. Saints (7th issue).

2959 **1529** 55c. multicoloured 1·50 1·40

1530 Karl Schranz

2008. 70th Birth Anniv of Karl Schranz (World Champion skier).

2960 **1530** 65c. multicoloured 2·00 1·90

1531 Adoration of the Magi (ceiling fresco, Collegiate Monastery and Parish Church of St Michael, Flachgau)

2008. Christmas.

2961 **1531** 55c. multicoloured 1·80 1·60

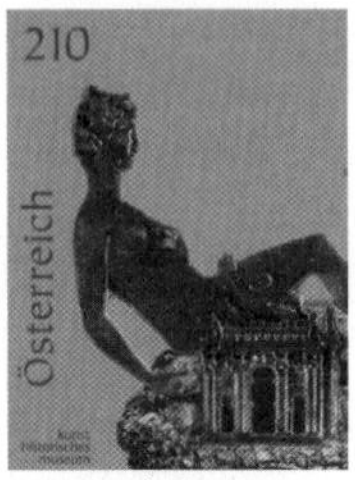

1532 Female Figure

2009. Saliera (salt cellar) by Benvento Cellini. Sheet 110×75 mm containing T **1532** and similar vert design. Multicoloured.

MS2962 210c.×2, Type **1532**; Male figure 14·00 14·00

The stamps of **MS**2962 form a composite design of the salt cellar.

1533 Landskron Castle

2009. Self-adhesive.

2963 **1533** 55c. multicoloured 1·90 1·70

1534 Pez Peppermint Sweets

2009. Classic Trademarks.

2964 **1534** 55c. multicoloured 1·90 1·70

1535 Post Building, Cracow

2009. Old Austria.

2965 **1535** 100c. multicoloured 3·00 2·75

1536 Raimondo Montecuccoli

2009. 400th Birth Anniv of Raimondo Montecuccoli (soldier and writer).

2966 **1536** 130c. multicoloured 4·00 3·75

1537 Girl

2009. 60th Anniv of SOS Children's Villages.

2967 **1537** 55c. multicoloured 1·90 1·70

1538 Lewis Hamilton and McLaren Race Car

2009. Lewis Hamilton (Formula I World Champion–2008).

2968 **1538** 100c. multicoloured 3·00 2·75

1539 Mercedes W 196 Silver Arrow

2009. Centenary of Technical Museum, Vienna. Self-adhesive.

2969 **1539** 265c. multicoloured 8·00 8·00

1540 Schonbrunn Imperial Palace

2009

2970 **1540** 65c. multicoloured 2·00 1·90

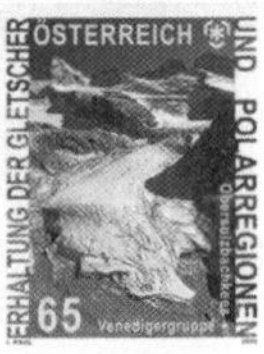

1541 Venediger Glacier

2009. Preserve Polar Regions and Glaciers.

2971 **1541** 65c. multicoloured 2·00 1·90

1542 Haflinger

2009. 50th Anniv of Steyr Daimler Puch Haflinger All Terrain Vehicle.

2972 **1542** 55c. murlticoloured 1·90 1·70

1543 Joseph Haydn

2009. Death Bicentenary of Franz Joseph Haydn (composer).

2973 **1543** 65c. multicoloured 2·00 1·90

1544 *Tyto alba* (barn owl)

2009. Self-adhesive.

2974 **1544** 55c. multicoloured 1·90 1·70

1545 Wrapped Flak Tower

2009. Art. Works by Christo Vladimirov Javashev (Christo, the packaging artist). Sheet 78×80 mm containing T **1545** and similar vert design. Multicoloured.
MS2975 55c.×2, Type **1545**; The 21st Century Collection 3·75 3·75

1546 Fred Zinnemann

2009. Fred Zinnemann (director) Commemoration
2976 **1546** 55c. multicoloured 1·60 1·40

1547 Old Town

2009. 850th Anniv of St Pölten
2977 **1547** 55c. multicoloured 1·60 1·40

1548 Burning Ring

2009. *The Ring of the Nibelungen* (opera) performed at Vienna State Opera House
2978 **1548** 100c. multicoloured 1·60 1·40

1549 *Thalia*

2009. Centenary of *Thalia* (pleasure steamer)
2979 **1549** 55c. multicoloured 1·60 1·60

1550 Baptismal Font, Old Cathedral, Linz

2009. Religious Art
2980 **1550** 55c. multicoloured 6·25 6·00

1551 State Opera House

2009. 140th Anniv of Vienna State Opera House
2981 **1551** 100c. multicoloured 3·00 2·75

1552 Wolfgang Graf Berghe von Trips

2009. Formula I Motor Racing Legends. Multicoloured.
MS2982 55c.×4, Type **1552**; Gilles Villeneuve; James Hunt; Bernie Ecclestone 6·25 6·25

1553 Napoleon

2009. Bicentenary of Battle of Aspern and Essling. Sheet 73×87 mm
MS2983 **1553** 110c. multicoloured 3·00 3·00

1554 TUGSAT-1 (nano-satellite)

2009
2984 **1554** 65c. multicoloured 2·10 1·90

1555 Graz

2009. Old Town, Graz–World Heritage Site
2985 **1555** 100c. multicoloured 3·00 2·75

1556 Early Aircraft

2009. Centenary of Wiener Neustadt Airfield
2986 **1556** 140c. multicoloured 4·00 3·75

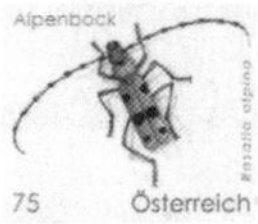

1557 *Rosalia alpina* (longhorn beetle)

2009. Longhorn Beetle
2987 **1557** 75c. multicoloured 2·10 1·90

1558 Steam Locomotive

2009. Centenary of Wachau Railway
2988 **1558** 75c. multicoloured 2·10 1·90

1559 *Apis mellifera* (honeybee)

2009. Fauna. Multicoloured.
2989 55c. Type **1559** 1·60 1·40
2990 55c. *Merops apiaster* (bee-eater) 1·60 1·40
Nos. 2989/90 were issued in *se-tenant* 'hang sell' sheetlets of ten stamps

1560 Anemones

2009. Flowers
2991 **1560** 55c. multicoloured 1·60 1·40

1561 Film Poster

2009. 60th Anniv of *The Third Man* (film by Carol Reed, based on book by Graham Greene)
2992 **1562** 65c. multicoloured 1·90 1·70

1562 '20'

2009. 20th Anniv of Opening of Border between Austria and Hungary
2993 **1562** 65c. multicoloured 1·90 1·70

1563 Gateway and Soldier, Carnuntum

2009. Archaeology. Multicoloured.
MS2994 55c. Type **1563**; 65c. Bas-relief and mounted soldier, Gerulata 5·00 5·00
Stamps of a similar design were issued by Slovakia.

1564 *MS Österreich* (oldest motor powered passenger ship on Lake Constance)

2009. Stamp Day
2995 **1564** 265c.+130c. multicoloured 11·50 10·00

1565 Berta von Suttner

2009. 120th Anniv of *Lay Down Your Arms!* (antiwar novel by Berta von Suttner)
2996 **1565** 55c. multicoloured 1·60 1·40

1566 *The Glorious Rosary*

2009. Tenth Anniv of the Return of Rosary Triptych (painted by Ernst Fuchs), Parish Church of Hetzendorf, Vienna. Multicoloured.
MS2997 55c. Type **1566**; 75c. *The Joyful Rosary*; 100c. *The Sorrowful Rosary* 6·75 6·75

1567 Wolfgang Loitzl (Four Hills Champion)

2009. Champion Ski Jumpers. Multicoloured.
2998 100c. Type **1567** 3·00 2·75
2999 100c. Gregor Schlierenzauer (World Cup winner 2008–9) 3·00 2·75

1568 5042 Series Rail Car in Zistersdorf Station

2009. 120th Anniv of Drösing–Zistersdorf Local Railway
3000 **1568** 100c. multicoloured 3·00 2·75

1569 *Woman rocking on a Chair* (Leander Kaiser)

2009. Modern Art
3001 **1569** 55c. multicoloured 1·90 1·70

1570 *Emilie Flöge* (Gustav Klimt)

2009. Austria–Japan Year. Multicoloured.
MS3002 140c.×2, Type **1570**; *Autumn Clothes* (Shoen Uemura) 8·50 8·50

1571 *Las Meninas (The Royal Family of Felipe IV)*

2009. Diego Rodríguez de Silva y Velázquez (artist) Commemoration. Multicoloured.
MS3003 55c. Type **1571**; 65c.*The Infanta Margarita Teresa in a Blue Dress* 4·25 4·25
Stamps of the same design were issued by Spain

1572 Ranui Church, Vilnös Valley, South Tyrol

2009. Christmas
3004 **1572** 65c. multicoloured 2·00 1·90

1573 Palmers Underwear

2009. Classic Trademarks
3005 **1573** 55c. multicoloured 1·90 1·70

1574 St. Leopold

2009. Patron Saints
3006 **1574** 55c. multicoloured 1·90 1·70

1575 Zum gnadenreichen Christkindl (Blessed Holy Child)

2009. Christmas
3007 **1575** 55c. multicoloured 1·90 1·70

1576 *Tribute to Vedova* (George Baselitz)

2009. Tenth Anniv of Essl Art Museum
3008 **1576** 55c. multicoloured 1·90 1·70

1577 Ape holding Book

2009. Birth Bicentenary of Charles Darwin (naturalist and evolutionary theorist). Multicoloured.
MS3009 55c.×3, Type **1577**; Cherub with head in hands and mirror; Ape holding mirror to cherub 5·75 5·75

The stamps and margins of **MS**3009 form a composite design

1578 *Lutra lutra* (otter)

2010. Fauna (1st issue). Multicoloured.
3010 75c. Type **1578** 2·10 2·00
3011 75c. *Salmo trutta fario* (brown trout) 2·10 2·00

1579 *Felis silvestris* (wild cat)

2010. Fauna (2nd issue)
3012 **1579** 65c. multicoloured 2·00 1·90

1580 View from Salzach River

2010. World Heritage Site
3013 **1580** 100c. multicoloured 3·00 2·75

1581 *Annual Rings of Scent and Bliss* (Helmut Kand)

2010. Modern Art
3014 **1581** 55c. multicoloured 1·90 1·70

1582 *Prince Eugene as Victor over the Turks* (Jacob van Schuppen)

2010. Prince Eugene of Savoy Exhibition, Belvedere, Vienna
3015 **1582** 65c. multicoloured 2·00 1·90

1583 Kleinbahn Model Railways

2010. Classic Trade Marks
3016 **1583** 55c. multicoloured 1·90 1·70

1584 *The Tyrolean Land Army Year Nine* (Joseph Anton Koch)

2010. Death Bicentenary of Andreas Hofer (revolutionary leader)
MS3017 **1584** 175c. multicoloured 5·75 5·75

1585 Stage Setting for *Medea* (by Marco Auturo Marelli)

2010. Vienna State Opera House
3018 **1585** 100c. multicoloured 3·00 2·75

1586 Otto Preminger

2010. Otto Ludwig Preminger (film director) Commemoration
3019 **1586** 55c. multicoloured 1·90 1·70

1587 Roger Federer

2010. Roger Federer (world champion tennis player)
3020 **1587** 65c. multicoloured 2·00 1·90

1588 *Soon the Sun will rise*

2010. Birth Centenary of Max Weiler (artist)
3021 **1588** 75c. multicoloured 2·10 2·00

1589 *Lady in Yellow* (Max Kurzwell)

2010. Wien Museum
3022 **1589** 65c. multicoloured 2·00 1·90

1590 Upper Belvedere

2010. Belvedere Palace, Vienna
3023 **1590** 65c. multicoloured 2·00 1·90

1591 671 Steam Locomotive (1860 (oldest operational steam locomotive in the world)

2010. 150th Anniv of Graz Köflach Railway
3024 **1591** 100c. multicoloured 3·00 2·75

1592 Prague Castle and St Vitus Cathedral.

2010. Old Austria
3025 **1592** 65c. multicoloured 2·00 1·90

1593 Empress Elisabeth (Sisi)

2010. Expo 2010, Shanghai
MS3026 **1593** 55c. multicoloured 1·50 1·50

1594 Railway

2010. Centenary (2003) of Mendel (Mendola) Railway (first electric funicular railway)
3027 **1594** 65c. multicoloured 1·90 1·80

1595 Post Box on Legs

2010. Post-Publicity Campaign 2010
3028 **1595** 55c. multicoloured 1·90 1·80

1596 Palace during Early 19th Century

2010. Imperial Festival Palace Hof
3029 **1596** 55c. multicoloured 1·50 1·40

1597 Baroque Church (painting by Franz Knapp

2010. 350th Anniv of Maria Taferl
3030 **1597** 55c. multicoloured 1·50 1·40

1598 Gustav Mahler

2010. 150th Birth Anniv of Gustav Mahler (composer and conductor)
3031 **1598** 100c. multicoloured 3·00 2·75

1599 Festival Poster, 1928 (by Leopoldine (Poldi) Wojtek)

2010. 90th Anniv of Salzburg Festival
3032 **1599** 55c. multicoloured 1·50 1·50

1600 Coracias garrulus (European roller)

2010. Fauna. Multicoloured.
3033 55c. Type **1600** 1·50 1·40
3034 75c. *Aquila chrysaetos* (golden eagle) 2·10 2·00

1601 Crozier

2010. Religious Art
3035 **1601** 75c. multicoloured 2·10 2·00

1602 Fridolin Fuchs (post fox) on Skateboard (illustration by Carola Holland)

2010. Europa
3036 **1602** 65c. multicoloured 1·90 1·80

1603 Self Portrait with Black Vase

2010. 120th Birth Anniv of Egon Schiele (artist)
3037 **1603** 140c. multicoloured 4·00 3·75

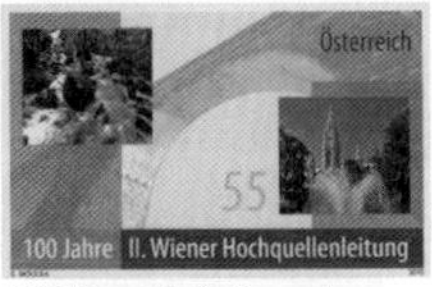

1604 Mountain Spring and Fountain in Front of Vienna City Hall

2010. Centenary of Second Pipeline carrying Mountain Spring Water to Vienna

3038 **1604** 55c. multicoloured 2·10 2·00

1605 Simon Wiesenthal in Star of David

2010. Simon Wiesenthal (holocaust survivor and pursuer of war criminals) Commemoration

3039 **1605** 75c. multicoloured 2·10 2·00

1606 Opera House Interior and Ioan Holender

2010. 75th Birth Anniv of Ioan Holender (director of Vienna State Opera)

3040 **1606** 100c. multicoloured 2·75 2·50

1607 Karnburg Church

2010. Churches

3041 **1607** 100c multicoloured 2·75 2·50

1608 Johann Flux

2010. 350th Birth Anniv of Johann Joseph Fux (composer and musical theorist)

3042 **0608** 100c. multicoloured 3·00 2·75

1609 Grete Rehor and Parliament Building, Vienna

2010. Birth Centenary of Grete Rehor (politician and first female Federal Minister)

3043 **1609** 55c. multicoloured 1·50 1·40

1610 'PARADE'

2010. 15th Anniv of Rainbow Parade

3044 **1610** 55c. multicoloured 3·00 2·75

1611 Steam Locomotive

2010. 125th Anniv of Spielfeld Strass-Bad Radkersburg Railway

3045 **1611** 65c. multicoloured 1·90 1·80

1612 Castle and Grounds

2010. Grafenegg Castle

3046 **1612** 55c. multicoloured 1·50 1·40

1613 Zodiac

2010. 150th Birth Anniv of Alfons Maria Mucha (artist)

3047 **1613** 115c. multicoloured 3·25 3·00

1614 Church

2010. 50th Anniv of Eisenstadt Diocese

3048 **1614** 55c. multicoloured 1·50 1·40

1615 Mother Teresa

2010. Birth Centenary of Agnes Gonxha Bojaxhiu (Mother Teresa) (founder of Missionaries of Charity)

3049 **1615** 130c. multicoloured 3·50 3·25

1616 Railjet Train and Gmunden

2010. Stamp Day

3050 **1616** 265c.+130c. multicoloured 11·00 10·50

1617 Rosa centifolia Bullata

2010. Flowers

3051 **1617** 55c. multicoloured 1·50 1·40

1618 Steam Locomotive, Salzburg, Austria

2010. *Orient Express*. Multicoloured.

MS3052 65c.×2, Type **1618**; Steam locomotive, Sinaia, Romania 3·50 3·50

1619 Crucifix (Jakob Adhart), ArchAbbey of St. Peter, Salzburg

2010. Sacred Art

3052a **1619** 100c. multicoloured 2·75 2·50

1620 Anniversary Emblem and Members Flags

2010. 50th Anniv of OPEC (Organization of Petroleum Exporting Countries)

3053 **1620** 140c. multicoloured 4·00 4·00

1621 Rose

2010. Petit Point

MS3054 multicoloured 7·25 7·25

1622 Imperial and Royal State Railways Series 199 Locomotive

2010. Centenary of Wechsel Railway

3055 **1622** 100c. multicoloured 2·75 2·50

1623 Andreas and Wolfgang Linger

2010. Andreas and Wolfgang Linger–Winners of Luge Olympic Gold Medal at Winter Olympic Games, Vancouver

3056 **1623** 100c. multicoloured 2·75 2·50

1624 Desk

2010. Austrian Design

3057 **1624** 65c. multicoloured 1·90 1·80

1625 Maria Theresa (Martin van Meytens)

2010. 230th Death Anniv of Archduchess Maria Theresia Walburga Amalia Christina von Österreich (Maria Theresa of Austria) (Archduchess of Austria and Queen of Hungary and Bohemia)

3058 65c. multicoloured 1·90 1·80

1626 Weather Station, City Park, Vienna

2010. Meteorological Architecture. Multicoloured.

MS3059 65c. Type **1626**; 140c. Austria-Hungarian community meteorological station, Botanical Garden, Buenos Aires 5·50 5·50

1627 Ornithopter (first controlled flight, November 1808)

2010. 250th Birth Anniv of Jakob Degen (inventor)

3060 **1627** 125c multicoloured 1·90 1·80

1628 Flag and Soldier

2010. 50th Anniv of Austrian Armed Forces International Assignments

3061 **1628** 65c. multicoloured 1·90 1·80

1629 St Stephen's Cathedral and St Peter's Church, Vienna

2010. Cultural Heritage

3062 **1629** 199c. multicoloured 3·00 2·75

1630 Goldenes Dachl, Innsbruck

2010. Advent

3063 **1630** 65c. multicoloured 2·00 1·90

1631 Three Wise Men (detail from 12th-century missal), St Florian's Monastery

2010. Christmas (1st issue)

3064 **1631** (55c.) multicoloured 1·50 1·40

1632 The Nativity (detail of antiphonal from Cistercian monastery, Rein, Styria)

2010. Christmas (2nd issue)

3065 **1632** 55c. multicoloured 1·50 1·40

1632a Emperor Franz Joseph and Dr. Anton Freiherr von Eiselsberg

2011. Centenary of Austrian Cancer Aid
3065a **1632a** 55c. multicoloured 1·50 1·40

1633 Post Office

2011. Old Austria
3066 **1633** 65c. multicoloured 1·90 1·80

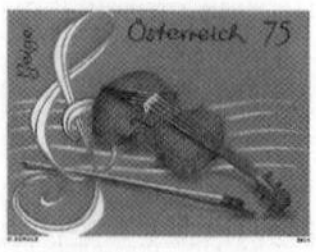

1634 Violin

2011. Musical Instruments
3067 **1634** 75c. multicoloured 2·20 2·10

1635 Bruno Kreisky

2011. Birth Centenary of Bruno Kreisky (politician)
3068 **1635** 55c. multicoloured 1·60 1·50

1636 Stylized Joanneum Graz and Kunsthaus Graz

2011. Bicentenary of Joanneum Graz Museum
3069 **1636** 100c. multicoloured 3·00 2·75

1637 Franz Liszt

2011. Birth Bicentenary of Franz Liszt
3070 **1637** 65c. multicoloured 1·90 1·90

1638 Hedy Lamarr

2011. Hedwig Eva Maria Kiesler (Hedy Lamarr) (film actor) Commemoration
3071 **1638** 55c. multicolured 1·60 1·50

1639 Niemetz Confectioners

2010. Classic Trade Marks
3072 **1639** 55c. multicoloured 1·90 1·80

1640 Luigi Hussak, Walter Nausch, Ernst Fiala and Herbert Prohaska (former captains) and Club Emblem

2011. Centenary of FC Austria Vienna
3073 **1640** 65c. multicoloured 2·00 1·90

1641 KTM 125 D.O.H.C. Apfelbeck

2011. Motorcycles
3074 **1641** 75c. multicoloured 2·25 2·10

1642 Puch 500

2011. Cars
3075 **1642** 65c. multicoloured 2·00 1·90

1643 Series 310 Locomotive and Karl Golsdorf

2011. 150th Birth Anniv of Karl Golsdorf (engineer and designer)
3076 **1643** 65c. multicoloured 2·00 1·90

1644 Museum Building

2011. 20th Anniv of Kunst Haus, Vienna
3077 **1644** 175c. multicoloured 5·25 5·00

1645 Cup of Coffee and Café Entrance

2011. Traditional Gastronomy
3078 **1645** 62c. multicoloured 2·00 1·90

1646 Space Walk

2011. 50th Anniv of Manned Space Flight
3079 **1646** 65c. multicoloured 2·00 1·90

1647 Roman Structures

2011. Lower Austrian Regional Exhibition 2011
3080 **1647** 62c. multicoloured 1·90 1·80

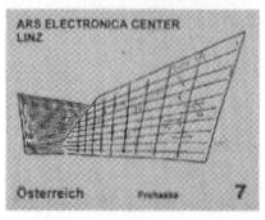

1648 Ars Electronica Centre, Linz

2011. Modern Architecture. All designs black, background colour given.

3081	7c. grey-brown	30	25
3082	62c. azure	1·90	1·80
3083	62c. azure	1·90	1·80
3084	62c. azure (vert)	1·90	1·80
3085	62c. azure (vert)	1·90	1·80
3086	70c. chrome yellow	2·20	2·10
3087	70c. pale yellow	2·20	2·10
3088	90c. pale lilac	2·50	2·40
3089	90c. pale lilac	2·50	2·40
3090	145c. pale turquoise-green	4·75	4·50
3091	170c. pale buff	5·75	5·50
3092	340c. pale greenish yellow (vert)	10·50	10·00

Designs: 7c. Type **1648**; 62c. Kunsthaus Graz Universal-museum, Joanneum; 62c. Museum of Modern Art Ludwig Foundation, Vienna (Museum Moderner Kunst Stiftung Ludwig, Wien); 62c. Kunsthaus Bregenz; 62c. Kunsthalle Krems; 70c. Museum der Moderne Monchsberg, Salzburg; 70c. Lentos Art Museum, Linz (Lentos Kunstmuseum, Linz); 90c. Forum Stadtpark, Graz; 90c. Essl Museum, Klosterneuburg; 145c. Kunsthalle Wien Project Space Karlsplatz, Vienna; 170c. MAK Centre Schindler Chase House, Los Angeles; 340c. Austrian Cultural Forum, New York.

1649 Horse pulling Railway Wagons

2011. 175 Years of Budweis (Budejowice)-Linz-Gmunden Horse-drawn Railway
3093 **1649** 62c. multicoloured 1·70 1·60

1650 Smiling Child

2011. 25th Anniv of CARE (humanitarian organization) Austria
3094 **1650** 70c. multicoloured 5·25 5·00

1651 Antique Bookcase from Mekhitarist's Library

2011. Bicentenary of Mekhitarists (congregation of Benedictine monks of Armenian Catholic Church founded in 1712 by Mechitar of Sebaste) in Vienna
3095 **1651** 90c. multicoloured 2·75 2·50

1652 Graz

2011. Stamp Day
3096 **1652** 272c. multicoloured 12·50 12·00

1653 Church

2011. Churches
3097 **1653** 62c. multicoloured 1·70 1·70

1654 *Tower of Babel* (Pieter Bruegel the Elder)

2011. Art
3098 **1654** 145c. multicoloured 4·50 4·25

1655 *Portrait of Dora Fournier-Gabillon*

2011. Art. Works by Hans Makart. Multicoloured.
MS3099 70c. Type **1655**; 170c. *The Triumph of Ariadne* 6·75 6·75

1656 Pheasant, Badger, Deer and Fungi

2011. Country of Forests. International Year of Forests
3100 **1656** 90c. multicoloured 2·50 2·25

2011. Modern Architecture. Horiz design as Type **1648**.
3101 5c. Liaunig Museum 1·00 90

1657 Etrich Taube Aircraft and Black Hawk Helicopter

2011. Centenary of Military Aviation
3102 **1657** 62c. multicoloured 2·00 1·90

1658 Chalice

2011. Religious Art
3103 **1658** 145c. multicoloured 4·50 4·25

1659 St Christoph Hospice

2011. 625th Anniv of St Christopher Brotherhood
3104 **1659** 62c. multicoloured 2·00 1·90

1660 Anniversary Emblem

2011. 50th Anniv of Organisation for Economic Co-operation and Development (OECD) (Organisation de coopération et de développement économiques, OCDE)
3105 **1660** 70c. multicoloured 2·25 2·10

1661 BBÖ 378 series Locomotive and Old Railway Station Building

2011. Centenary of Stammersdorf Railway
3106 **1661** 90c. multicoloured 2·50 2·25

1662 Curing a Woman (Ulrich Henn)

2011. Religious Art. Bronze Relief, Rankwil Basilica
3107 **1662** 90c. multicoloured 2·50 2·25

1663 Girl and Peddler

2011. 175th Death Anniv of Ferdinand Jakob Raimann (Ferdinand Raimund) (dramatist)
3108 **1663** 62c. multicoloured 2·00 1·90

1664 Football Boot

2011. Centenary of Austrian Football Championship
3109 **1664** 62c. multicoloured 2·00 1·90

1665 Vienna Künstlerhaus

2011. Centenary of Vienna Visual Artists Cooperative (Austrian Society of Artists, Künstlerhaus)
3110 **1665** 62c. multicoloured 2·00 1·90

1666 Lotto Ball

2011. 25th Anniv of Lottery. Sheet 70×90 mm
MS3111 **1666** 145c. multicoloured 4·50 4·25

1667 Coniferous Forest

2011. Europa. Forests. Sheet 112×73 mm
MS3112 **1667** 170c. multicoloured 4·25 2·25

1668 'C02 NEUTRAL ZUGESTELLT'

2011. CO_2 Neutral Post Delivery
3113 **1668** 62p. green 2·00 1·90

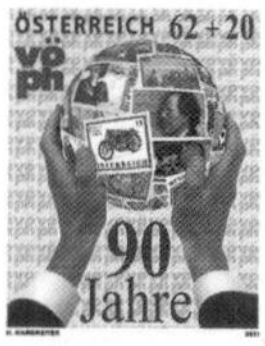

1669 Hand holding Globe of Stamps

2011. 90th Anniv of Federation of Austrian Philatelist Societies
3114 **1669** 62c. multicoloured 2·50 2·25

1670 Early Steam Locomotive

2011. 120th Anniv of Erzberg Railway
3115 **1670** 90c. multicoloured 2·50 2·25

1671 *Portrait of Walburga Neuzil* (Wally) (Egon Schiele)

2011. Tenth Anniv of Leopold Museum
3116 **1671** 62c. multicoloured 2·00 1·90

1672 Elisabeth Görgl

2011. Elisabeth Görgl (skiier) (gold medalist in Super-G and Downhill Race at World Skiing Championships, Garmisch-Partenkirchen)
3117 **1672** 62c. multicoloured 2·00 1·90

1673 Diana, the Huntress (As Type **2342** of USA)

2011. Breast Cancer Awareness Campaign
3118 **1673** 90c. multicoloured 3·00 2·75

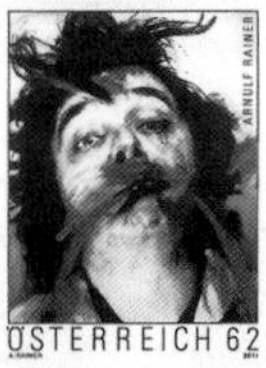

1674 *Angst* (Arnulf Rainer)

2011. Modern Art
3119 **1674** 62c multicoloured 2·00 1·90

1675 *o.T. 014, 2003*

2011. Photo Art Austria. Eva Schlegel
3120 **1675** 70c. multicoloured 2·25 1·10

1676 Looking down on Pasterze Glacier

2011. Trademark Austria. Winning Design in Austrian Identity Competition
3121 **1676** 62c. multicoloured 2·00 1·90

1677 Loisium Visitors' Centre, Langenlois (Steven Holl)

2011. Modern Architecture in Austria
3122 **1677** 62c. multicoloured 2·00 1·90

1678 *The Song of Songs* (Arik Brauer)

2011. Art
3123 **1678** 170c. multicoloured 5·00 4·75

1679 Nesting Storks

2011. 90th Anniv of Burgenland in Austria
3124 **1679** 90c. multicoloured 2·50 2·25

1680 St Quirinus Chapel

2011. Advent
3125 **1680** 70c. multicoloured 2·10 2·00

1681 Madonna of Plain

2011. Christmas (1st issue). Coil Stamp
3126 **1681** 62c. multicoloured 1·90 1·80

1682 Vienna BahnhofCity West Station

2011. Re-opening of Vienna BahnhofCity West
3127 **1682** 70c. multicoloured 2·10 2·00

1683 Birth of Christ (anon)

2011. Christmas (2nd issue)
3128 **1683** 62c. multicoloured 1·90 1·80

1684 Wolfgang Amadeus Mozart (detail)

2011. 220th Death Anniv of Wolfgang Amadeus Mozart
3129 **1684** 70c. multicoloured 2·10 2·00

1685 Interior of Great Hall and Caryatid

2012. Bicentenary of Gesellschaft der Musikfreunde (Friends of Music Society) in Vienna
3130 **1685** 90c. multicoloured 2·50 2·40

1686 Lohner L 125

2012. Motorcycles
3131 **1686** €1.45 multicoloured 4·00 3·75

1687 Carl Ritter von Ghega and Railway

2012. 210th Birth Anniv of Carl Ritter von Ghega (designer of Semmering Railway from Gloggnitz to Mürzzuschlag)
3132 **1687** 70c. multicoloured 2·00 1·90

1688 Early Mountaineer and Edelweiss

2012. 150th Anniv of Alpine Association
3133 **1688** 62c. multicoloured 1·75 1·60

1689 Locomotives

2012. 50th Anniv of Vienna Rapid Transit Railway

3134	**1689**	62c. multicoloured	1·75	1·60

IMPERIAL JOURNAL STAMPS

J18

1853. Imperf.

J67		1k. blue	15·00	2·10
J15	**J18**	2k. green	£4250	£120
J68		2k. brown	13·50	3·00
J32		4k. brown	£550	£1600

The 2k. green has different corner ornaments.

For similar values in black or red, see Lombardy and Venetia Imperial Journal stamps, Nos. J22/4.

J21 Arms of Austria

1890. Imperf.

J76	**J21**	1k. brown	15·00	2·10
J77	**J21**	2k. green	13·50	3·00

J22 Arms of Austria

1890. Perf.

J78	**J22**	25k. red	£140	£300

NEWSPAPER STAMPS

N2 Mercury

1851. Imperf.

N11b	**N2**	(0.6k.) blue	£225	£160
N12	**N2**	(6k.) yellow	£37000	£12000
N13	**N2**	(6k.) red	£62000	£108000
N14	**N2**	(30k.) red	£42000	£17000

N8 Francis Joseph I

1858. Imperf.

N28	**N8**	(1k.05) blue	£800	£900
N29	**N8**	(1k.05) lilac	£1100	£425

N11 Francis Joseph I

1861. Imperf.

N38	**N11**	(1k.05) grey	£250	£225

N13 Arms of Austria

1863. Imperf.

N44	**N13**	(1k.05) lilac	55·00	21·00

AHN17 Mercury

1867. Imperf.

AHN58b	**AHN17**	(1k.) lilac	50	30

N19 Mercury

1880. Imperf.

N69	**N19**	½k. green	11·50	1·60

N31 Mercury

1899. Imperf.

N122	**N31**	2h. blue	30	20
N123	**N31**	6h. orange	3·00	3·00
N124	**N31**	10h. brown	2·10	1·60
N125	**N31**	20h. pink	2·10	3·00

N43 Mercury

1908. Imperf.

N207C	**N43**	2h. blue	1·50	45
N208C	**N43**	6h. orange	6·75	1·10
N209C	**N43**	10h. red	6·75	85
N210C	**N43**	20h. brown	6·75	85

N53 Mercury

1916. Imperf.

N266	**N53**	2h. brown	10	20
N267	**N53**	4h. green	50	1·60
N268	**N53**	6h. blue	40	1·70
N269	**N53**	10h. orange	1·00	2·10
N270	**N53**	30h. red	50	1·90

N54 Mercury

1916. For Express. Perf.

N271	**N54**	2h. red on yellow	1·50	4·25
N272	**N54**	5h. green on yellow	1·50	4·25

N61 Mercury

1917. For Express. Perf.

N294	**N61**	2h. red on yellow	20	55
N295	**N61**	5h. green on yellow	20	55

1919. Optd **Deutschosterreich**. Imperf.

N318	**N53**	2h. brown	20	1·10
N319	**N53**	4h. green	50	8·50
N320	**N53**	6h. blue	30	10·50
N321	**N53**	10h. orange	1·20	16·00
N322	**N53**	30h. red	60	21·00

1919. For Express. Optd Deutschosterreich. Perf.

N334	**N61**	2h. red on yellow	10	30
N335	**N61**	5h. green on yellow	10	30

N68 Mercury

1920. Imperf.

N365A	**N68**	2h. violet	10	20
N366A	**N68**	4h. brown	10	30
N367A	**N68**	5h. slate	10	20
N368A	**N68**	6h. blue	15	20
N369A	**N68**	8h. green	10	55
N370A	**N68**	9h. bistre	10	20
N371A	**N68**	10h. red	10	20
N372A	**N68**	12h. blue	10	55
N373A	**N68**	15h. mauve	10	25
N374A	**N68**	18h. turquoise	10	30
N375A	**N68**	20h. orange	10	30
N376A	**N68**	30h. brown	10	20
N377A	**N68**	45h. green	10	55
N378A	**N68**	60h. red	10	30
N379A	**N68**	72h. brown	20	55
N380A	**N68**	90h. violet	30	85
N381A	**N68**	1k.20 red	30	1·10
N382A	**N68**	2k.40 green	30	1·10
N383A	**N68**	3k. grey	30	1·10

1921. For Express. No. N334 surch **50 50**.

N450	**N 61**	50 on 2h. red on yell	10	45

N78 Mercury

1921. Imperf.

N452	**N78**	45h. grey	20	20
N453	**N78**	75h. red	10	55
N454	**N78**	1k.50 green	10	75
N455	**N78**	1k.80 blue	10	95
N456	**N78**	2k.25 brown	10	1·30
N457	**N78**	3k. green	10	1·10
N458	**N78**	6k. purple	10	1·20
N459	**N78**	7k.50 brown	20	1·60

N79 Posthorn and Arrow

1921. For Express. Perf.

N460	**N79**	50h. lilac on yellow	20	2·10

POSTAGE DUE STAMPS

D26

1894. Perf.

D96	**D26**	1k. brown	6·25	2·10
D97	**D26**	2k. brown	8·25	4·25
D98	**D26**	3k. brown	10·50	2·10
D99	**D26**	5k. brown	10·50	75
D100	**D26**	6k. brown	8·25	9·25
D101	**D26**	7k. brown	4·25	9·25
D102	**D26**	10k. brown	8·25	85
D103	**D26**	20k. brown	4·25	9·25
D104	**D26**	50k. brown	90·00	£120

1899. As Type **D26**, but value in heller. Perf or imperf.

D126	1h. brown	75	30
D127	2h. brown	75	20
D128d	3h. brown	75	20
D129	4h. brown	95	20
D130	5h. brown	1·00	20
D131d	6h. brown	75	75
D132	10h. brown	1·20	10
D133	12h. brown	1·50	75
D134	15h. brown	1·20	1·40
D135	20h. brown	1·70	45
D136	40h. brown	3·00	75
D137d	100h. brown	8·25	4·25

D44

1908. Perf.

D210B	**D44**	1h. red	1·00	2·10
D211C	**D44**	2h. red	60	45
D212C	**D44**	4h. red	40	20
D213C	**D44**	6h. red	40	20
D214C	**D44**	10h. red	60	20
D215C	**D44**	14h. red	7·25	3·00
D216C	**D44**	20h. red	15·00	20
D217C	**D44**	25h. red	19·00	6·75
D218C	**D44**	30h. red	10·50	45
D219C	**D44**	50h. red	35·00	55
D220C	**D44**	100h. red	29·00	75
D221C	**D44**	5k. violet	85·00	20·00
D222C	**D44**	10k. violet	£300	5·25

D55

D56

1916

D273	**D55**	5h. red	10	20
D274	**D55**	10h. red	10	20
D275	**D55**	15h. red	10	20
D276	**D55**	20h. red	10	20
D277	**D55**	25h. red	25	1·30
D278	**D55**	30h. red	30	55
D279	**D55**	40h. red	20	85
D280	**D55**	50h. red	1·20	3·75
D281	**D 56**	1k. blue	1·00	55
D282	**D 56**	5k. blue	3·00	4·25
D283	**D 56**	10k. blue	4·25	2·30

1916. Nos. 189/90 optd **PORTO** or surch **15 15** also.

D284	1h. black	10	20
D285	15 on 2h. violet	35	75

1917. Unissued stamps as T **50** surch **PORTO** and value.

D286	**50**	10 on 24h. blue	2·10	75
D287	**50**	15 on 36h. violet	60	30
D288	**50**	20 on 54h. orange	35	55
D289	**50**	50 on 42h. brown	40	30

The above differ from Type **50** by showing a full-face portrait.

1919. Optd **Deutschosterreich**.

D323	**D55**	5h. red	10	20
D324	**D55**	10h. red	10	20
D325	**D55**	15h. red	30	55
D326	**D55**	20h. red	30	55
D327	**D55**	25h. red	10·50	32·00
D328	**D55**	30h. red	30	55
D329	**D55**	40h. red	30	1·10
D330	**D55**	50h. red	35	1·60
D331	**D 56**	1k. blue	5·75	19·00
D332	**D 56**	5k. blue	11·50	19·00
D333	**D 56**	10k. blue	13·50	5·25

D69

D70

1920. Imperf or perf (D 69), perf (D 70).

D384A	**D69**	5h. pink	20	45
D385A	**D69**	10h. pink	10	20
D386A	**D69**	15h. pink	10	1·60
D387A	**D69**	20h. pink	10	20
D388A	**D69**	25h. pink	20	1·60
D389A	**D69**	30h. pink	10	45
D390A	**D69**	40h. pink	10	45
D391A	**D69**	50h. pink	10	30
D392A	**D69**	80h. pink	10	55
D393A	**D 70**	1k. blue	10	40
D394A	**D 70**	1½k. blue	10	40
D395A	**D 70**	2k. blue	10	40
D396Aa	**D 70**	3k. blue	10	65
D397Aa	**D 70**	4k. blue	10	85
D398A	**D 70**	5k. blue	10	40
D399A	**D 70**	8k. blue	10	1·10
D400A	**D 70**	10k. blue	10	55
D401A	**D 70**	20k. blue	50	2·75

1921. No. 343a surch **Nachmarke 7½ K.** Perf.

D451	**64**	7½k. on 15h. brown	10	55

D83

1921

D510	**D83**	1k. brown	20	45
D511	**D83**	2k. brown	20	55
D512	**D83**	4k. brown	20	95
D513	**D83**	5k. brown	20	45
D514	**D83**	7½k. brown	20	1·30
D515	-	10k. blue	20	55
D516	-	15k. blue	20	75
D517	-	20k. blue	20	85
D518	-	50k. blue	20	75

The 10k. to 50k. are larger (22×30 mm).

D86

1922

D526	**D83**	10k. turquoise	10	65
D527	**D83**	15k. turquoise	10	95
D528	**D83**	20k. turquoise	10	75
D529	**D83**	25k. turquoise	10	1·60
D530	**D83**	40k. turquoise	10	55
D531	**D83**	50k. turquoise	10	1·90

D532	**D 86**	100k. purple	10	20
D533	**D 86**	150k. purple	10	20
D534	**D 86**	200k. purple	10	20
D535	**D 86**	400k. purple	10	20
D536	**D 86**	600k. purple	25	65
D537	**D 86**	800k. purple	10	20
D538	**D 86**	1000k. purple	10	20
D539	**D 86**	1200k. purple	1·50	9·25
D540	**D 86**	1500k. purple	10	55
D541	**D 86**	1800k. purple	4·25	18·00
D542	**D 86**	2000k. purple	50	1·30
D543	**D 86**	3000k. purple	9·25	37·00
D544	**D 86**	4000k. purple	6·25	30·00
D545	**D 86**	6000k. purple	10·50	47·00

D94

1925

D589	**D94**	1g. red	10	10
D590	**D94**	2g. red	10	10
D591	**D94**	3g. red	10	10
D592	**D94**	4g. red	10	10
D593	**D94**	5g. red	10	10
D594	**D94**	6g. red	30	45
D595	**D94**	8g. red	20	20
D596	**D94**	10g. blue	30	10
D597	**D94**	12g. blue	10	10
D598	**D94**	14g. blue	10	10
D599	**D94**	15g. blue	10	10
D600	**D94**	16g. blue	30	25
D601	**D94**	18g. blue	2·10	3·75
D602	**D94**	20g. blue	20	10
D603	**D94**	23g. blue	60	20
D604	**D94**	24g. blue	3·00	10
D605	**D94**	28g. blue	2·75	25
D606	**D94**	30g. blue	1·30	10
D607	**D94**	31g. blue	3·00	25
D608	**D94**	35g. blue	3·00	20
D609	**D94**	39g. blue	3·50	10
D610	**D94**	40g. blue	1·50	2·10
D611	**D94**	60g. blue	1·50	1·90
D612	-	1s. green	6·75	95
D613	-	2s. green	36·00	3·75
D614	-	5s. green	£140	60·00
D615	-	10s. green	55·00	5·25

DESIGN: 1 to 10s. Horiz bands of colour.

D120

1935

D746	**D120**	1g. red	10	20
D747	**D120**	2g. red	10	20
D748	**D120**	3g. red	10	20
D749	**D120**	5g. red	10	20
D750	-	10g. blue	10	10
D751	-	12g. blue	10	10
D752	-	15g. blue	30	65
D753	-	20g. blue	30	20
D754	-	24g. blue	35	20
D755	-	30g. blue	35	20
D756	-	39g. blue	40	20
D757	-	60g. blue	85	1·60
D758	-	1s. green	1·00	45
D759	-	2s. green	2·10	1·30
D760	-	5s. green	4·25	4·00
D761	-	10s. green	6·25	85

DESIGNS: 10 to 60g. As Type D **120** but with background of horizontal lines; 1 to 10s. As last, but with positions of figures, arms and inscriptions reversed.

D143

1945

D891	**D143**	1pf. red	20	20
D892	**D143**	2pf. red	20	20
D893	**D143**	3pf. red	20	20
D894	**D143**	5pf. red	20	20
D895	**D143**	10pf. red	20	20
D896	**D143**	12pf. red	20	25
D897	**D143**	20pf. red	20	25
D898	**D143**	24pf. red	20	45
D899	**D143**	30pf. red	20	50
D900	**D143**	60pf. red	20	55
D901	**D143**	1rm. violet	20	60
D902	**D143**	2rm. violet	20	95
D903	**D143**	5rm. violet	30	1·10
D904	**D143**	10rm. violet	30	1·30

1946. Optd **PORTO**.

D956	**145**	3g. orange	10	10
D957	**145**	5g. green	10	10
D958	**145**	6g. purple	10	10
D959	**145**	8g. red	10	10
D960	**145**	10g. grey	10	20
D961	**145**	12g. brown	10	10
D962	**145**	15g. red	10	20
D963	**145**	20g. brown	10	10
D964	**145**	25g. blue	20	20
D965	**145**	30g. mauve	10	10
D966	**145**	40g. blue	10	10
D967	**145**	60g. green	10	10
D968	**145**	1s. violet	20	20
D969	**145**	2s. yellow	70	1·20
D970	**145**	5s. blue	30	95

D162

1947

D1035	**D162**	1g. brown	10	10
D1036	**D162**	2g. brown	10	10
D1037	**D162**	3g. brown	10	20
D1038	**D162**	5g. brown	10	10
D1039	**D162**	8g. brown	10	10
D1040	**D162**	10g. brown	10	10
D1041	**D162**	12g. brown	10	10
D1042	**D162**	15g. brown	10	10
D1043	**D162**	16g. brown	50	95
D1044	**D162**	17g. brown	40	95
D1045	**D162**	18g. brown	40	95
D1046	**D162**	20g. brown	95	10
D1047	**D162**	24g. brown	40	1·10
D1048	**D162**	30g. brown	20	30
D1049	**D162**	36g. brown	95	1·60
D1050	**D162**	40g. brown	10	10
D1051	**D162**	42g. brown	1·10	1·60
D1052	**D162**	48g. brown	1·10	1·60
D1053	**D162**	50g. brown	95	30
D1054	**D162**	60g. brown	20	30
D1055	**D162**	70g. brown	20	25
D1056	**D162**	80g. brown	6·00	2·75
D1057	**D162**	1s. blue	20	10
D1058	**D162**	1s.15 blue	4·25	55
D1059	**D162**	1s.20 blue	4·50	2·20
D1060	**D162**	2s. blue	40	30
D1061	**D162**	5s. blue	50	40
D1062	**D162**	10s. blue	60	45

D184

1949

D1178	**D184**	1g. red	20	20
D1179	**D184**	2g. red	20	20
D1180	**D184**	4g. red	65	65
D1181	**D184**	5g. red	2·75	75
D1182	**D184**	8g. red	2·75	2·20
D1183	**D184**	10g. red	45	10
D1184	**D184**	20g. red	45	10
D1185	**D184**	30g. red	45	10
D1186	**D184**	40g. red	45	10
D1187	**D184**	50g. red	45	10
D1188	**D184**	60g. red	14·00	75
D1189	**D184**	63g. red	6·75	4·25
D1190	**D184**	70g. red	45	10
D1191	**D184**	80g. red	45	20
D1192	**D184**	90g. red	75	55
D1193	**D184**	1s. violet	75	10
D1194	**D184**	1s.20 violet	75	30
D1195	**D184**	1s.35 violet	45	20
D1196	**D184**	1s.40 violet	75	45
D1197	**D184**	1s.50 violet	75	25
D1198	**D184**	1s.65 violet	65	45
D1199	**D184**	1s.70 violet	65	45
D1200	**D184**	2s. violet	1·10	20
D1201	**D184**	2s.50 violet	75	20
D1202	**D184**	3s. violet	75	30
D1203	**D184**	4s. violet	1·20	1·10
D1204	**D184**	5s. violet	1·60	45
D1205	**D184**	10s. violet	1·80	60

D817

1985

D2074	**D817**	10g. yellow & black	10	10
D2075	**D817**	20g. red and black	10	10
D2076	**D817**	50g. orange & black	10	10
D2077	**D817**	1s. blue and black	20	20
D2078	**D817**	2s. brown & black	40	30
D2079	**D817**	3s. violet and black	50	40
D2080	**D817**	5s. yellow & black	90	60
D2081	**D817**	10s. green & black	1·80	90

Pt. 2

AUSTRIAN TERRITORIES ACQUIRED BY ITALY

Italian territory acquired from Austria at the close of the war of 1914-18, including Trentino and Trieste.

1918. 100 heller = 1 krone.
1918. 100 centesimi = 1 lira.
1919. 100 centesimi = 1 corona.

TRENTINO

1918. Stamps of Austria optd **Regno d'Italia Trentino 3 nov 1918.**

1	**49**	3h. purple	6·25	12·50
2	**49**	5h. green	4·25	6·25
3	**49**	6h. orange	70·00	£110
4	**49**	10h. red	4·25	9·25
5	**49**	12h. green	£200	£300
6	**60**	15h. brown	6·25	11·50
7	**60**	20h. green	3·00	10·50
8	**60**	25h. blue	55·00	70·00
9	**60**	30h. violet	17·00	26·00
10	**51**	40h. green	60·00	£100
11	**51**	50h. green	36·00	50·00
12	**51**	60h. blue	50·00	90·00
13	**51**	80h. brown	85·00	£130
14	**51**	90h. red	£1700	£3000
15	**51**	1k. red on yellow	85·00	£120
16	**52**	2k. blue	£500	£850
17	**52**	4k. green	£2000	£4000
18	**52**	10k. violet	£94000	

1918. Stamps of Italy optd **Venezia Tridentina**.

19	**30**	1c. brown	3·00	10·50
20	**31**	2c. brown	3·00	10·50
21	**37**	5c. green	3·00	10·50
22	**37**	10c. red	3·00	10·50
23	**41**	20c. orange	3·00	10·50
24	**39**	40c. brown	65·00	90·00
25	**33**	45c. olive	37·00	90·00
26	**39**	50c. mauve	37·00	90·00
27	**34**	1l. brown and green	37·00	90·00

1919. Stamps of Italy surch **Venezia Tridentina** and value.

28	**37**	5h. on 5c. green	3·00	5·25
29	**37**	10h. on 10c. red	3·00	5·25
30	**41**	20h. on 20c. orange	3·00	5·25

VENEZIA GIULIA

For use in Trieste and territory, Gorizia and province, and in Istria.

1918. Stamps of Austria optd **Regno d'Italia Venezia Giulia 3. XI. 18.**

31	**49**	3h. purple	1·60	3·00
32	**49**	5h. green	1·60	3·00
33	**49**	6h. orange	1·80	4·25
34	**49**	10h. red	5·25	5·25
35	**49**	12h. green	2·50	5·25
36	**60**	15h. brown	1·60	3·00
37	**60**	20h. green	1·60	3·00
38	**60**	25h. blue	8·25	13·50
39	**60**	30h. purple	3·00	6·25
40	**51**	40h. green	£100	£300
41	**51**	50h. green	8·25	12·50
42	**51**	60h. blue	29·00	36·00
43	**51**	80h. brown	18·00	23·00
44	**51**	1k. red on yellow	18·00	23·00
45	**52**	2k. blue	£275	£500
46	**52**	3k. red	£350	£600
47	**52**	4k. green	£550	£1200
48	**52**	10k. violet	£65000	£69000

1918. Stamps of Italy optd **Venezia Giulia**.

49	**30**	1c. brown	3·00	7·25
50	**31**	2c. brown	3·00	7·25
51	**37**	5c. green	2·10	3·00
52	**37**	10c. red	2·10	3·00
53	**41**	20c. orange	2·10	4·25
54	**39**	25c. blue	2·10	5·25
55	**39**	40c. brown	16·00	31·00
56	**33**	45c. green	5·25	11·50
57	**39**	50c. mauve	10·50	14·50
58	**39**	60c. red	90·00	£180
59	**34**	1l. brown and green	41·00	70·00

1919. Stamps of Italy surch **Venezia Giulia** and value.

60	**37**	5h. on 5c. green	2·10	4·25
61	**41**	20h. on 20c. orange	2·10	4·25

EXPRESS LETTER STAMPS

1919. Express Letter stamp of Italy optd **Venezia Giulia**.

E60	**E35**	25c. red	70·00	£120

POSTAGE DUE STAMPS

1918. Postage Due Stamps of Italy optd **Venezia Giulia**.

D60	**D 12**	5c. mauve and orange	1·00	2·10
D61	**D 12**	10c. mauve & orange	1·00	2·10
D62	**D 12**	20c. mauve & orange	1·60	4·25
D63	**D 12**	30c. mauve & orange	4·25	8·25
D64	**D 12**	40c. mauve & orange	36·00	55·00
D65	**D 12**	50c. mauve & orange	60·00	£160
D66	**D 12**	1l. mauve and blue	£200	£500

GENERAL ISSUE

For use throughout the liberated area of Trentino, Venezia Giulia and Dalmatia.

1919. Stamps of Italy surch in new currency.

62	**30**	1ce. di cor on 1c. brown	2·10	3·00
64	**31**	2ce. di cor on 2c. brown	2·10	3·00
65	**37**	5ce. di cor on 5c. green	2·10	2·10
67	**37**	10ce. di cor on 10c. red	2·10	2·10
68	**41**	20ce. di cor on 20c. orange	2·10	2·10
70	**39**	25ce. di cor on 25c. blue	2·10	5·25
71	**39**	40ce. di cor on 40c. brown	2·10	5·25
72	**33**	45ce. di cor on 45c. green	2·10	5·25
73	**39**	50ce. di cor on 50c. mauve	2·10	5·25
74	**39**	60ce. di cor on 60c. red	2·10	9·25
75	**34**	1cor. on 1l. brown & green	4·25	8·25
76	**34**	una corona on 1l. brn & grn	5·25	21·00
82	**34**	5cor. on 5l. blue and red	50·00	£120
83	**34**	10cor. on 10l. green & red	50·00	£120

EXPRESS LETTER STAMPS

1919. Express Letter stamps of Italy surch in new currency.

E76	**E35**	25ce. di cor on 25c. red	2·10	4·25
E77	**E41**	30ce. di cor on 30c. red and blue	3·00	8·25

POSTAGE DUE STAMPS

1919. Postage Due stamps of Italy surch in new currency.

D76	**D12**	5ce. di cor on 5c. mauve and orange	1·00	3·00
D77	**D12**	10ce. di cor. on 10c. mauve and orange	1·00	3·00
D78	**D12**	20ce. di cor on 20c. mauve and orange	2·10	3·00
D79	**D12**	30ce. di cor on 30c. mauve and orange	2·30	5·25
D80	**D12**	40ce. di cor on 40c. mauve and orange	2·30	5·25
D81	**D12**	50ce. di cor on 50c. mauve and orange	5·25	10·50
D82	**D12**	una corona on 1l. mauve and blue	5·25	12·50
D83	**D12**	due corona on 2l. mauve and blue	80·00	£180
D84	**D12**	cinque corona on 5l. mauve and blue	80·00	£180
D86	**D12**	1cor. on 1l. mve & blue	5·25	14·50
D87	**D12**	2cor. on 2l. mve & blue	50·00	£110
D88	**D12**	5cor. on 5l. mve & blue	50·00	£110

Pt. 2

AUSTRO-HUNGARIAN MILITARY POST

A. General Issues.
100 heller = 1 krone.

B. Issues for Italy.
100 centesimi = 1 lira.

C. Issues for Montenegro.
100 heller = 1 krone.

D. Issues for Romania.
100 bani = 1 leu.

E. Issues for Serbia.
100 heller = 1 krone.

A. GENERAL ISSUES

1915. Stamps of Bosnia and Herzegovina optd **K.U.K. FELDPOST.**

1	**25**	1h. olive	50	55
2	**25**	2h. blue	50	55
3	**25**	3h. lake	50	55
4	**25**	5h. green	40	30
5	**25**	6h. black	50	55
6	**25**	10h. red	30	30
7	**25**	12h. olive	50	75
8	**25**	20h. brown	60	1·10
9	**25**	25h. blue	50	75
10	**25**	30h. red	4·25	8·50
11	**26**	35h. green	3·00	7·50
12	**26**	40h. violet	3·00	7·50
13	**26**	45h. brown	3·00	7·50
14	**26**	50h. blue	3·00	7·50
15	**26**	60h. purple	60	1·40

16	**26**	72h. blue	3·00	6·25
17	**25**	1k. brown on cream	3·00	7·00
18	**25**	2k. indigo on blue	3·00	7·00
19	**26**	3k. red on green	31·00	70·00
20	**26**	5k. lilac on grey	28·00	47·00
21	**26**	10k. blue on grey	£200	£375

2

1915

22	**2**	1h. green	10	30
23	**2**	2h. blue	10	45
24	**2**	3h. red	10	30
25	**2**	5h. green	10	30
26	**2**	6h. black	10	45
27	**2**	10h. red	10	30
28	**2**	10h. blue	10	45
29	**2**	12h. green	10	55
30	**2**	15h. red	10	30
31	**2**	20h. brown	40	55
32	**2**	20h. green	40	65
33	**2**	25h. blue	20	45
34	**2**	30h. red	20	65
35	**2**	35h. green	40	95
36	**2**	40h. violet	40	95
37	**2**	45h. brown	40	95
38	**2**	50h. deep green	40	95
39	**2**	60h. purple	40	95
40	**2**	72h. blue	40	95
41	**2**	80h. brown	40	45
42	**2**	90h. red	1·10	1·80
43	-	1k. purple on cream	2·10	3·25
44	-	2k. green on blue	1·20	2·40
45	-	3k. red on green	1·10	7·50
46	-	4k. violet on grey	1·10	12·00
47	-	5k. violet on grey	27·00	49·00
48	-	10k. blue on grey	4·75	22·00

The kronen values are larger, with profile portrait.

1917. As 1917 issue of Bosnia, but inscr "K.u.K. FELDPOST".

49	1h. blue	10	20
50	2h. orange	10	20
51	3h. grey	10	20
52	5h. green	10	20
53	6h. violet	10	20
54	10h. brown	10	20
55	12h. blue	10	20
56	15h. red	10	20
57	20h. brown	10	20
58	25h. blue	40	65
59	30h. grey	10	20
60	40h. bistre	10	20
61	50h. green	10	20
62	60h. red	10	55
63	80h. blue	10	30
64	90h. purple	40	95
65	2k. red on buff	20	55
66	3k. green on blue	1·40	5·50
67	4k. red on green	22·00	38·00
68	10k. violet on grey	2·30	16·00

The kronen values are larger and the border is different.

1918. Imperial and Royal Welfare Fund. As 1918 issue of Bosnia, but inscr "K. UND K. FELDPOST".

69	**40**	10h. (+10h.) green	50	1·10
70	-	20h. (+10h.) red	50	1·10
71	**40**	45h. (+10h.) blue	50	1·10

NEWSPAPER STAMPS

N4
Mercury

1916

N49	**N4**	2h. blue	20	45
N50	**N4**	6h. orange	60	1·60
N51	**N4**	10h. red	60	1·60
N52	**N4**	20h. brown	60	1·60

B. ISSUES FOR ITALY

1918. General Issue stamps of 1917 surch in figs and words.

1	2c. on 1h. blue	10	55
2	3c. on 2h. orange	10	55
3	4c. on 3h. grey	10	55
4	6c. on 5h. green	10	55
5	7c. on 6h. violet	20	55
6	11c. on 10h. brown	10	55
7	13c. on 12h. blue	10	55
8	16c. on 15h. red	10	55
9	22c. on 20h. brown	10	55
10	27c. on 25h. blue	40	1·60
11	32c. on 30h. grey	20	1·50
12	43c. on 40h. bistre	30	1·20
13	53c. on 50h. green	20	1·10
14	64c. on 60h. red	30	1·60
15	85c. on 80h. blue	20	1·10
16	95c. on 90h. purple	20	1·10
17	2l.11 on 2k. red on buff	30	2·20
18	3l.16 on 3k. green on blue	70	3·25
19	4l.22 on 4k. red on green	85	4·25

NEWSPAPER STAMPS

1918. Newspaper stamps of General Issue surch in figs and words.

N20	3c. on 2h. blue	20	45
N21	7c. on 6h. orange	40	1·40
N22	11c. on 10h. red	40	1·40
N23	22c. on 20h. brown	50	1·40

1918. For Express. Newspaper stamps of Bosnia surch in figs and words.

N24	**N35**	3c. on 2h. red on yell	7·25	26·00
N25	**N35**	6c. on 5h. green on yell	7·25	26·00

POSTAGE DUE STAMPS

1918. Postage Due stamps of Bosnia surch in figs and words.

D20	**D 35**	6c. on 5h. red	4·25	11·00
D21	**D 35**	11c. on 10h. red	2·50	13·00
D22	**D 35**	16c. on 15h. red	1·00	5·50
D23	**D 35**	27c. on 25h. red	1·00	5·50
D24	**D 35**	32c. on 30h. red	1·00	5·50
D25	**D 35**	43c. on 40h. red	1·00	5·50
D26	**D 35**	53c. on 50h. red	1·00	5·50

C. ISSUES FOR MONTENEGRO

1917. Nos. 28 and 30 of General Issues optd **K.U.K. MILIT. VERWALTUNG MONTENEGRO.**

1	**2**	10h. blue	20·00	16·00
2	**2**	15h. red	20·00	16·00

D. ISSUES FOR ROMANIA

1917. General Issue stamps of 1917 optd **BANI** or **LEI**.

1	3b. grey	3·50	5·75
2	5b. green	3·50	4·00
3	6b. violet	3·50	4·00
4	10b. brown	60	1·20
5	12b. blue	2·30	4·00
6	15b. red	2·30	4·00
7	20b. brown	60	1·20
8	25b. blue	60	1·20
9	30b. grey	1·20	1·70
10	40b. bistre	1·20	1·70
11	50b. green	1·20	1·70
12	60b. red	1·20	1·70
13	80b. blue	60	1·20
14	90b. purple	1·20	2·30
15	2l. red on buff	1·70	3·00
16	3l. green on blue	1·70	3·50
17	4l. red on green	2·30	4·00

3 Charles I

1918

18	**3**	3b. grey	60	1·20
19	**3**	5b. green	60	1·20
20	**3**	6b. violet	60	1·70
21	**3**	10b. brown	60	1·70
22	**3**	12b. blue	60	1·70
23	**3**	15b. red	60	1·20
24	**3**	20b. brown	60	1·20
25	**3**	25b. blue	60	1·20
26	**3**	30b. grey	60	1·20
27	**3**	40b. bistre	60	1·20
28	**3**	50b. green	60	1·20
29	**3**	60b. red	60	1·70
30	**3**	80b. blue	60	1·70
31	**3**	90b. purple	60	1·20
32	**3**	2l. red on buff	60	1·70
33	**3**	3l. green on blue	1·20	4·00
34	**3**	4l. red on green	1·70	4·00

E. ISSUES FOR SERBIA

1916. Stamps of Bosnia optd **SERBIEN**.

22	**25**	1h. olive	2·75	6·50
23	**25**	2h. blue	2·75	6·50
24	**25**	3h. lake	2·75	6·50
25	**25**	5h. green	45	95
26	**25**	6h. black	1·90	4·75
27	**25**	10h. red	45	95
28	**25**	12h. olive	95	2·75
29	**25**	20h. brown	95	95
30	**25**	25h. blue	95	2·75
31	**25**	30h. red	95	1·90
32	**26**	35h. green	95	1·90
33	**26**	40h. violet	95	1·90
34	**26**	45h. brown	95	1·90
35	**26**	50h. blue	95	1·90
36	**26**	60h. brown	95	1·90
37	**26**	72h. blue	95	1·90
38	**25**	1k. brown on cream	1·90	2·75
39	**25**	2k. indigo on blue	1·90	2·75
40	**26**	3k. red on green	1·90	2·75
41	**26**	5k. lilac on grey	1·90	2·75
42	**26**	10k. blue on grey	19·00	37·00

Pt. 2

AUSTRO-HUNGARIAN POST OFFICES IN THE TURKISH EMPIRE

A. Lombardy and Venetia Currency.
100 soldi = 1 florin.

B. Turkish Currency.
40 paras = 1 piastre.

C. French Currency.
100 centimes = 1 franc.

A. LOMBARDY AND VENETIA CURRENCY

1

2

1867

1	**1**	2s. yellow	3·25	38·00
9	**1**	3s. green	1·60	38·00
10	**1**	5s. red	55	27·00
11	**1**	10s. blue	£140	1·70
5	**1**	15s. brown	36·00	11·00
6	**1**	25s. lilac	37·00	55·00
7a	**2**	50s. brown	1·60	85·00

3

1883

14	**3**	2s. black and brown	20	£225
15	**3**	3s. black and green	1·60	49·00
16	**3**	5s. black and red	30	28·00
17	**3**	10s. black and blue	1·10	85
18	**3**	20s. black and grey	8·00	13·00
19	**3**	50s. black and mauve	1·60	28·00

B. TURKISH CURRENCY

1886. Surch **10 PARA 10**.

21a	10p. on 3s. green	45	11·00

1888. Nos. 71/75a of Austria surch.

22	**20**	10pa. on 3k. green	5·50	17·00
23	**20**	20pa. on 5k. red	65	13·00
24	**20**	1pi. on 10k. blue	95·00	2·20
25	**20**	2pi. on 20k. grey	2·40	6·50
26	**20**	5pi. on 50k. purple	2·75	27·00

1890. Stamps of Austria of 1890, the kreuzer values with lower figures of value removed, surch at foot.

27	**23**	8pa. on 2k. brown	20	85
28	**23**	10pa. on 3k. green	75	85
29	**23**	20pa. on 5k. red	45	85
30	**23**	1pi. on 10k. blue	55	30
31	**23**	2pi. on 20k. olive	11·00	43·00
32	**23**	5pi. on 50k. mauve	16·00	95·00
33	**24**	10pi. on 1g. blue	14·00	60·00
37	**24**	10pi. on 1g. lilac	27·00	32·00
34	**24**	20pi. on 2g. red	22·00	90·00
38	**24**	20pi. on 2g. green	55·00	£110

1890. Stamps of Austria of 1891, with lower figures of value removed, surch at foot.

35	**25**	2pi. on 20k. green	8·50	2·20
36	**25**	5pi. on 50k. mauve	3·25	4·25

1900. Stamps of Austria of 1899, the heller values with lower figures of value removed, surch at foot.

46	**27**	10pa. on 5h. green	3·25	4·00
40	**28**	20pa. on 10h. red	7·50	1·20
48	**28**	1pi. on 25h. blue	2·20	1·10
49	**29**	2pi. on 50h. blue	5·50	8·50
43d	**30**	5pi. on 1k. red	75	55
44d	**30**	10pi. on 2k. lavender	3·25	4·75
45d	**30**	20pi. on 4k. green	3·25	13·00

1903. Stamps of Austria of 1899, with all figures of value removed, surch at top and at foot.

55	**27**	10pa. green	75	2·75
56	**28**	20pa. red	1·60	1·60
57	**28**	30pa. mauve	75	5·50
58	**28**	1pi. blue	1·10	55
59	**29**	2pi. blue	1·10	1·20

11 Francis Joseph I

12 Francis Joseph I

1908. 60th Anniv of Emperor's Accession.

60	**11**	10pa. green on yellow	20	55
61	**11**	20pa. red on pink	30	55
62	**11**	30pa. brown on buff	55	75
63	**11**	60pa. purple on blue	1·10	6·50
70	**11**	1pi. ultramarine on blue	45	75
65	**12**	2pi. red on yellow	1·10	20
66	**12**	5pi. brown on grey	1·10	1·30
67	**12**	10pi. green on yellow	1·60	2·75
68	**12**	20pi. blue on grey	3·75	5·50

POSTAGE DUE STAMPS

1902. Postage Due stamps as Type **D32** of Austria, but with value in heller, surch with new value.

D50	**D32**	10pa. on 5h. green	1·60	4·25
D51	**D32**	20pa. on 10h. green	1·60	5·50
D52	**D32**	1pi. on 20h. green	2·20	6·25
D53	**D32**	2pi. on 40h. green	2·20	6·25
D54	**D32**	5pi. on 100h. green	2·20	6·00

D13

1908

D71A	**D13**	¼pi. green	4·25	16·00
D72A	**D13**	½pi. green	2·75	13·00
D73A	**D13**	1pi. green	3·25	13·00
D74A	**D13**	1½pi. green	1·60	30·00
D75A	**D13**	2pi. green	2·20	27·00
D76A	**D13**	5pi. green	3·25	19·00
D77A	**D13**	10pi. green	23·00	£190
D78A	**D13**	20pi. green	15·00	£225
D79A	**D13**	30pi. green	23·00	19·00

C. FRENCH CURRENCY

1903. Stamps of Austria surch **CENTIMES** or **FRANC**.

F1A	**27**	5c. on 5h. green and black	1·60	6·50
F2A	**28**	10c. on 10h. red and black (No. 143)	1·20	6·50
F3A	**28**	25c. on 25h. blue and black (No. 145)	55·00	43·00
F4A	**29**	50c. on 50h. blue and black	14·00	£225
F5	**30**	1f. on 1k. red	1·60	£190
F6	**30**	2f. on 2k. lilac	14·00	£550
F7	**30**	4f. on 4k. green	16·00	£850

1904. Stamps of Austria surch **CENTIMES**.

F14	**33**	5c. on 5h. green	1·10	6·00
F13	**28**	10c. on 10h. red and black (No. 160)	75	22·00
F10B	**28**	25c. on 25h. blue and black (No. 176)	75	£170
F11A	**35**	50c. on 50h. blue	75	£750

1906. Type of Austria surch **CENTIMES**.

F15	**28**	10c. on 10h. red (No. 184)	1·60	55·00
F16	**28**	15c. on 15h. violet and black (as No. 185)	1·10	55·00

No. F16 was not issued without the surch.

1908. 60th Anniv of Emperor's Accession. As T **11/12** but in centimes or franc.

F17	**11**	5c. green on yellow	20	1·30
F18	**11**	10c. red on pink	45	1·60
F19	**11**	15c. brown on buff	65	9·75
F20	**11**	25c. blue on blue	19·00	8·50
F21	**12**	50c. red on yellow	5·50	49·00
F22	**12**	1f. brown on grey	7·50	75·00

Pt. 10

AZERBAIJAN

Formerly part of the Russian Empire. Became independent on 27 May 1918, following the Russian Revolution. Soviet troops invaded the country on 27 April 1920, and a Soviet Republic followed. From 1 October 1923 stamps of the Transcaucasian Federation were used but these were superseded by those of the Soviet Union in 1924.

With the dissolution of the Soviet Union in 1991, Azerbaijan once again became an independent state.

1919. 100 kopeks = 1 rouble.
1992. 100 qopik = 1 manat.
2006. 1 manat = 100 qepik.

1 Standard-bearer

1919. Imperf. Various designs.

1B	**1**	10k. multicoloured	20	20
2B	-	20k. multicoloured	20	20
3B	-	40k. olive, black and yellow	20	20
4B	-	60k. orange, black & yellow	20	25
5B	-	1r. blue, black and yellow	30	30
6B	-	2r. red, black and yellow	30	30
7B	-	5r. blue, black and yellow	40	55
8B	-	10r. olive, black & yellow	60	60
9B	-	25r. blue, black and red	1·00	1·00
10B	-	50r. olive, black and red	1·30	1·10

DESIGNS—HORIZ: 40k. to 1r. Reaper; 2r. to 10r. Citadel, Baku; 25r., 50r. Temple of Eternal Fires.

3 "Labour"

4 Petroleum Well

1921. Imperf.

11	**3**	1r. green	35	75
12	**4**	2r. brown	50	80
13	-	5r. brown	35	75
14	-	10r. grey	50	85
15	-	25r. orange	35	75
16	-	50r. violet	35	75
17	-	100r. orange	40	80
18	-	150r. blue	40	80
19	-	250r. violet and buff	40	80
20	-	400r. blue	40	80
21	-	500r. black and lilac	40	80
22	-	1000r. red and blue	40	80
23	-	2000r. black and blue	40	80
24	-	3000r. brown and blue	40	80
25	-	5000r. green on olive	55	50

DESIGNS—HORIZ: 5r., 3000r. Bibi Eibatt Oilfield; 100r., 5000r. Goukasoff House (State Museum of Arts); 400r., 1000r. Hall of Judgment, Khan's Palace. VERT: 10r., 2000r. Minaret of Friday Mosque, Khan's Palace, Baku; 25r., 250r. Globe and Workers; 50r. Malden's Tower, Baku; 150r., 500r. Blacksmiths.

6 Famine Supplies

1921. Famine Relief. Imperf.

26	**6**	500r. blue	50	1·50
27	-	1000r. brown	85	2·50

DESIGN—VERT: 1000r. Starving family.

For stamps of the above issues surch with new values, see Stanley Gibbons Part 10 (Russia) Catalogue.

13 Azerbaijan Map and Flag

1992. Independence.

83	**13**	35q. multicoloured	90	90

1992. Unissued stamp showing Caspian Sea surch **AZARBAYCAN** and new value.

84B	25q. on 15k. multicoloured	45	45
85B	35q. on 15k. multicoloured	65	65
86B	50q. on 15k. multicoloured	85	85
87B	1m.50 on 15k. multicoloured	2·75	2·75
88B	2m.50 on 15k. multicoloured	4·25	4·25

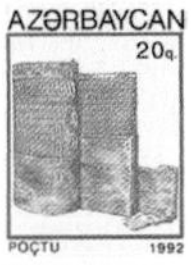

16 Maiden's Tower, Baku

1992. Dated "1992".

89	**16**	10q. green and black	15	15
90	**16**	20q. red and black	15	15
91	**16**	50q. yellow and black	20	20
92	**16**	1m.50 blue and black	85	85

See also Nos. 101/4.

17 Akhalteka Horse

1993. Horses. Multicoloured.

93	20q. Type **17**	10	10
94	30q. Kabarda horse	10	10
95	50q. Qarabair horse	10	10
96	1m. Don horse	10	10
97	2m.50 Yakut horse	45	45
98	5m. Orlov horse	85	85
99	10m. Diliboz horse	1·70	1·70
MS100	80×60 mm. 8m. Qarabag horse	1·70	1·70

1993. Dated "1993".

101	50q. blue and black	25	25
102	1m. mauve and black	15	15
103	2m.50 yellow and black	30	30
104	5m. green and black	55	55

18 *Tulipa eichleri*

1993. Flowers. Multicoloured.

105	25q. Type **18**	10	10
106	50q. *Puschkinia scilloides*	10	10
107	1m. *Iris elegantissima*	15	15
108	1m.50 *Iris acutiloba*	20	20
109	5m. *Tulipa florenskyii*	70	70
110	10m. *Iris reticulata*	1·30	1·30
MS111	78×58 mm. 10m. *Muscari elecostomum* (31×39 mm)	1·20	1·20

19 Russian Sturgeon

1993. Fish. Multicoloured.

112	25q. Type **19**	10	10
113	50q. Stellate sturgeon	10	10
114	1m. Iranian roach	15	10
115	1m.50 Caspian roach	25	25
116	5m. Caspian trout	90	90
117	10m. Black-backed shad	1·80	1·80
MS118	76×58 mm. 10m. Beluga (*Huso huso*) (39×31 mm)	1·60	1·20

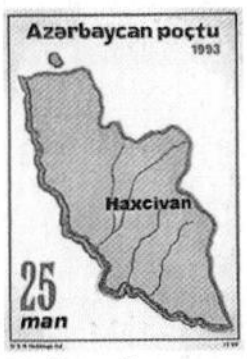

20 Map of Nakhichevan

1993. 70th Birthday of President Heydar Aliev.

119	-	25m. black and red	1·50	1·50
120	**20**	25m. multicoloured	1·50	1·50
MS121a		110×90 mm. Nos. 119/20 (map inscr "Naxcivan")	9·50	9·50

DESIGN: No. 119, President Aliev.

21 Government Building, Baku

1993

122	**21**	25q. black and yellow	15	15
123	**21**	30q. black and green	15	15
124	**21**	50q. black and blue	30	30
125	**21**	1m. black and red	60	60

22 Flags, and Dish Aerials on Maps

1993. Azerbaijan–Iran Telecommunications Co-operation.

126	**22**	15q. multicoloured	80	80

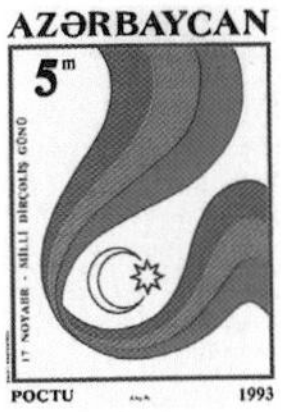

23 National Colours and Islamic Crescent

1994. National Day.

127	**23**	5m. multicoloured	35	35

24 State Arms

1994

128	**24**	8m. multicoloured	65	65

25 Sirvan Palace

1994. Baku Architecture.

129	**25**	2m. red, silver and black	15	15
130	-	4m. green, silver and black	25	25
131	-	8m. blue, silver and black	55	55

DESIGNS: 4m. 15th-century tomb; 8m. Divan-Khana.

26 Fuzuli

1994. 500th Birth Anniv (1992) of Mohammed ibn Suleiman Fuzuli (poet).

132	**26**	10m. multicoloured	45	45

1994. No. 126 surch **IRAN–AZERBAYGAN** and value.

133	**22**	2m. on 15q. multicoloured	30	30
134	**22**	20m. on 15q. multicoloured	85	85
135	**22**	25m. on 15q. multicoloured	1·00	1·00
136	**22**	50m. on 15q. multicoloured	2·40	2·40

1994. Nos. 122/5 surch.

137	**21**	5m. on 1m. black and red	30	30
138	**21**	10m. on 30q. black & grn	30	30
139	**21**	15m. on 30q. black & grn	30	30
140	**21**	20m. on 50q. black & blue	30	30
141	**21**	25m. on 1m. black & red	35	35
142	**21**	40m. on 50q. black & blue	65	65
143	**21**	50m. on 25q. black & yell	85	85
144	**21**	100m. on 25q. black & yell	1·70	1·70

29 Rasulzade

1994. 110th Birth Anniv of Mammed Amin Rasulzade (politician).

145	**29**	15m. brown, ochre & black	85	85

30 Mamedquluzade

1994. 125th Birth Anniv of Jalil Mamedquluzade (writer).

146	**30**	20m. black, gold and blue	85	85

31 Temple of the Fire Worshippers of Atashgah

1994. 115th Anniv of Nobel Partnership to Exploit Black Sea Oil. Multicoloured.

147	15m. Type **31**	25	25
148	20m. Oil wells	35	35
149	25m. *Zoroastr* (first oil tanker in Caspian Sea)	40	40
150	50m. Nobel brothers and Petr Bilderling (partners)	1·00	1·00
MS151	110×73 mm. No. 150	1·10	1·10

32 Laumontite

1994. Minerals. Multicoloured.

152	5m. Type **32**	25	25
153	10m. Epidot calcite	40	40
154	15m. Andradite	65	65
155	20m. Amethyst	85	85
MS156	120×110 mm. Nos. 152/5	2·10	2·10

33 Players

1994. World Cup Football Championship, U.S.A.

157	**33**	5m. multicoloured	10	10
158	-	10m. multicoloured	10	10
159	-	20m. multicoloured	25	25
160	-	25m. multicoloured	35	35
161	-	30m. multicoloured	40	40
162	-	50m. multicoloured	70	70
163	-	80m. multicoloured	1·10	1·10
MS164		90×65 mm. 100m. multicoloured (31×39 mm)	1·30	1·30

DESIGNS: 10m. to 100m. Match scenes.

34 Posthorn

1994

165	**34**	5m. red and black	10	10
166	**34**	10m. green and black	10	10
167	**34**	20m. blue and black	30	20
168	**34**	25m. yellow and black	30	30
169	**34**	40m. brown and black	55	55

35 Coelophysis and Segisaurus

1994. Prehistoric Animals. Multicoloured.

170	5m. Type **35**	10	15
171	10m. Pentaceratops and tyrannosaurids	10	15
172	20m. Segnosaurus and oviraptor	40	40
173	25m. Albertosaurus and corythosaurus	50	50
174	30m. Igaunodons	60	60
175	50m. Stegosaurus and allosaurus	1·10	1·10
176	80m. Tyrannosaurus and saurolophus	1·70	1·70
MS177	81×61 mm. 100m. Phobetor (39×31 mm)	1·80	1·80

36 Nesting Grouse

1994. The Caucasian Black Grouse. Multicoloured.

178	50m. Type **36**	60	60
179	80m. Grouse on mountain	95	95
180	100m. Pair of grouse	1·40	1·40
181	120m. Grouse in spring meadow	2·00	2·00

1994. No. 84 further surch **400 M.**

182	400m. on 25q. on 15k. multicoloured	1·60	1·60

38 *Kapitan Razhabov* (tug)

1994. Ships. Multicoloured.

183	50m. Type **38**	30	30
184	50m. *Azerbaijan* (ferry)	30	30
185	50m. *Merkuri 1* (ferry)	30	30
186	50m. *Tovuz* (container ship)	30	30
187	50m. *Ganzha* (tanker)	30	30

Nos. 183/7 were issued together, se-tenant, the backgrounds of which form a composite design of a map.

39 Pres. Aliev

1994. President Haidar Aliev. Sheet 102×72 mm.

MS188	**39** 150m. multicoloured	2·40	2·40

40 White-tailed Sea Eagle

1994. Birds of Prey. Multicoloured.

189	10m. Type **40**	60	60
190	15m. Imperial eagle	70	70
191	20m. Tawny eagle	85	85
192	25m. Lammergeier (vert)	1·00	1·00
193	50m. Saker falcon (vert)	2·40	2·40
MS194	83×64 mm. 100m. Golden eagle (*Aquila chrysaetos*) (39×31 mm)	1·60	1·60

Nos. 190/1 and **MS**194 are wrongly inscr "Aguila".

41 *Felis libica caudata*

1994. Wild Cats. Multicoloured.

195	10m. Type **41**	60	60
196	15m. Manul cat	70	70
197	20m. Lynx	85	85
198	25m. Leopard (horiz)	1·00	1·00
199	50m. Tiger (horiz)	2·40	2·40
MS200	64×56 mm. 100m. Tiger with cub (31×39 mm)	1·60	1·60

No. 197 is wrongly inscribed "Felis lyns lyns".

42 Ancient Greek and Modern Javelin Throwers

1994. Centenary of Int Olympic Committee. Multicoloured.

201	100m. Type **42**	60	60
202	100m. Ancient Greek and modern discus throwers	60	60
203	100m. Baron Pierre de Coubertin (founder of modern games) and flame	60	60

1995. Nos. 89/92 and 101/4 surch.

204	**15**	250m. on 10q. green & blk	50	50
205	**15**	250m. on 20q. red & black	50	50
206	**15**	250m. on 50q. yell & blk	50	50
207	**15**	250m. on 1m.50 bl & blk	50	50
208	**15**	500m. on 50q. blue & blk	1·10	1·10
209	**15**	500m. on 1m. mve & blk	1·10	1·10
210	**15**	500m. on 2m.50 yellow and black	1·10	1·10
211	**15**	500m. on 5m. green & blk	1·10	1·10

44 Apollo

1995. Butterflies. Multicoloured.

212	10m. Type **44**	30	30
213	25m. *Zegris menestho*	70	70
214	50m. *Manduca atropos*	1·40	1·40
215	60m. *Pararge adrastoides*	1·80	1·80
MS216	103×157 mm. Nos. 212/15	4·25	4·25

45 Aleksei Urmanov (Russia) (gold, men's figure skating)

1995. Winter Olympic Games, Lillehammer, Norway, Medal Winners. Multicoloured.

217	10m. Type **45**	10	10
218	25m. Nancy Kerrigan (U.S.A.) (silver, women's figure skating)	25	25
219	40m. Bonnie Blair (U.S.A.) (gold, women's 500m. speed skating) (horiz)	40	45
220	50m. Takanori Kano (Japan) (gold, men's ski jumping) (horiz)	40	40
221	80m. Philip Laros (Canada) (silver, men's freestyle skiing)	75	75
222	100m. German team (gold, three-man bobsleigh)	1·00	1·00
MS223	102×71 mm. 200m. Katya Seizinger (Germany) (gold, women's skiing)	2·20	2·20

46 Mary Cleave

1995. 25th Anniv (1994) of First Manned Moon Landing. Female Astronauts. Two sheets, each 137×78 mm, containing T **46** and similar vert designs. Multicoloured.

MS224	(a) 100m. Type **46**; 100m. Valentina Tereshkova; 100m. Tamara Jernigen; 100m. Wendy Lawrence. (b) 100m. Mae Jemison; 100m. Cathy Coleman; 100m. Ellen Shulman; 100m. Mary Weber	3·75	3·75

1995. Nos. 165/7 surch.

225	**34**	100m. on 5m. red & black	15	15
226	**34**	250m. on 10m. grn & blk	45	45
227	**34**	500m. on 20m. blue & blk	90	90

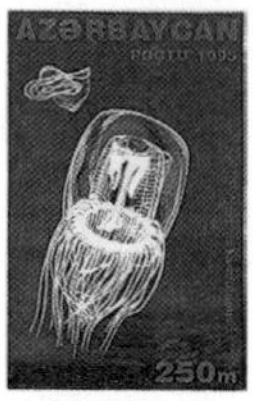

48 *Polyorchis karafutoensis*

1995. Marine Animals. Multicoloured.

228	50m. *Loligo vulgaris* (horiz)	15	15
229	100m. *Orchistoma pileus* (horiz)	40	40
230	150m. *Pegea confoederata* (horiz)	60	60
231	250m. Type **48**	1·00	1·00
232	300m. *Agalma okeni*	1·20	1·20
MS233	89×60 mm. 500m. *Corolla spectabilis* (39×31 mm)	3·00	2·00

49 Matamata Turtle

1995. Tortoises and Turtles. Multicoloured.

234	50m. Type **49**	15	15
235	100m. Loggerhead turtle	40	40
236	150m. Leopard tortoise	60	60
237	250m. Indian star tortoise	1·00	1·00
238	300m. Hermann's tortoise	1·20	1·20
MS239	79×65 mm. 500m. Alligator-snapping turtle (*Macroclemys temmincki*) (31×39 mm)	1·70	1·70

50 Uzeyir Hacibeyov (composer, 110th)

1995. Birth Anniversaries.

240	**50**	250m. silver and black	40	40
241	-	400m. gold and black	60	60

DESIGN: 400m. Vakhid (poet, centenary).

1995. Nos. 84/88 surch.

242	200m. on 2m.50 on 15k. mult	60	60
243	400m. on 25q. on 15k. mult	1·00	1·00
244	600m. on 35q. on 15k. mult	1·80	1·80
245	800m. on 50q. on 15k. mult	2·30	2·30
246	1000m. on 1m.50 on 15k. multicoloured	3·00	3·00

1995. Nos. 168/9 surch.

247	**34**	400m. on 25m. yell & blk	1·10	1·10
248	**34**	900m. on 40m. brn & blk	2·50	2·50

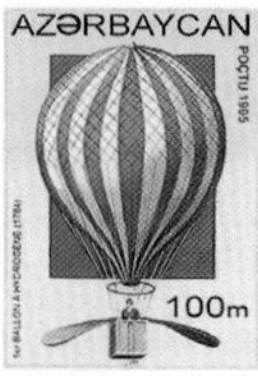

53 Charles's Hydrogen Balloon, 1783

1995. History of Airships. Multicoloured.

249	100m. Type **53**	15	15
250	150m. Tissandier Brothers' electrically-powered airship, 1883	30	30
251	250m. J.-B. Meusnier's elliptical balloon design, 1784 (horiz)	50	50
252	300m. Baldwin's dirigible airship, 1904 (horiz)	60	60
253	400m. U.S. Navy dirigible airship, 1917 (horiz)	85	85
254	500m. Pedal-powered airship, 1909 (horiz)	1·00	1·00
MS255	79×62 mm. 800m. First rigid dirigible airship by Hugo Eckener, 1924 (horiz)	1·70	1·70

No. 249 is wrongly dated.

54 *Gymnopilus spectabilis*

1995. Fungi. Multicoloured.

256	100m. Type **54**	35	35
257	250m. Fly agaric	95	95
258	300m. Parasol mushroom	1·10	1·10
259	400m. *Hygrophorus spectosus*	1·40	1·40
MS260	110×80 mm. 500m. Fly agaric (different)	2·40	2·40

The 250m. and 500m. are wrongly inscr "agaris".

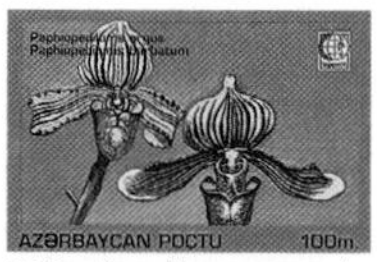

55 *Paphiopedilum argus* and *Paphiopedilum barbatum*

1995. "Singapore '95" International Stamp Exhibition. Orchids. Multicoloured.

261	100m. Type **55**	35	35
262	250m. *Maxillaria picta*	95	95
263	300m. *Laeliocattleya*	1·10	1·10
264	400m. *Dendrobium nobile*	1·40	1·40
MS265	110×80 mm. 500m. *Cattleya gloriette*	1·30	1·30

56 Pres. Aliev and U.N. Secretary-General Boutros Boutros Ghali

1995. 50th Anniv of U.N.O.

266	**56**	250m. multicoloured	2·10	2·10

57 Players

1995. World Cup Football Championship, France (1998). Multicoloured.

267	100m. Type **57**	35	35
268	150m. Dribbling	50	50
269	250m. Tackling	85	85
270	300m. Preparing to kick ball	1·00	1·00
271	400m. Contesting for ball	1·30	1·30
MS272	79×60 mm. 600m. Goalkeeper diving for ball	2·20	2·20

58 American Bald Eagle

1995. Air.

273	**58**	2200m. multicoloured	2·50	2·50

59 Persian

1995. Cats. Multicoloured.

274	100m. Type **59**	15	15
275	150m. Chartreux	30	30
276	250m. Somali	50	50
277	300m. Longhair Scottish fold	60	60
278	400m. Cymric	85	85
279	500m. Turkish angora	1·00	1·00
MS280	85×75 mm. 800m. Birman (31×39 mm)	1·70	1·70

60 Horse

1995. Flora and Fauna. Multicoloured.

281	100m. Type **60**	15	15
282	200m. Grape hyacinths (vert)	40	40
283	250m. Beluga	50	50
284	300m. Golden eagle	60	60
285	400m. Tiger	75	75
286	500m. Georgian black grouse nesting	1·00	1·00
287	1000m. Georgian black grouse in meadow	2·00	2·00

61 Lennon and Signature

1995. 15th Death Anniv of John Lennon (entertainer).

288	**61**	500m. multicoloured	1·10	1·10

62 Early Steam Locomotive, U.S.A.

1996. Railway Locomotives. Multicoloured.

289	100m. Type **62**	45	45
290	100m. New York Central Class J3 locomotive	45	45
291	100m. Steam locomotive on bridge	45	45
292	100m. Steam locomotive No. 1959, Germany	45	45
293	100m. Steam locomotive No. 4113, Germany	45	45
294	100m. Steam locomotive, Italy	45	45
295	100m. Class 59 steam locomotive, Japan	45	45
296	100m. Class QJ steam locomotive, China	45	45
297	100m. Class Sn 23 steam locomotive, China	45	45
MS298	110×80 mm. 500m. Electric train (vert)	2·75	2·75

63 Operating Theatre and Topcubasov

1996. Birth Centenary of M. Topcubasov (surgeon).

299	**63**	300m. multicoloured	1·00	1·00

64 Feast and Woman wearing Traditional Costume

1996. New Year.

300	**64**	250m. multicoloured	90	90

65 Carl Lewis (athletics, Los Angeles, 1984)

1996. Olympic Games, Atlanta. Previous Gold Medallists. Multicoloured.

301	50m. Type **65** (wrongly inscr "1994")	15	15
302	100m. Mohammed Ali (Cassius Clay) (boxing, Rome, 1960)	35	35
303	150m. Li Ning (gymnastics, Los Angeles, 1984)	55	55
304	200m. Said Aouita (5000m, Los Angeles, 1984)	70	70
305	250m. Olga Korbut (gymnastics, Munich, 1972)	90	90
306	300m. Nadia Comaneci (gymnastics, Montreal, 1976)	1·10	1·10
307	400m. Greg Louganis (diving, Los Angeles, 1984)	1·30	1·30
MS308	74×104 mm. 500m. Nazim Goussinev (bantamweight boxing, Barcelona, 1992) (vert)	1·80	1·80

66 *Maral-Gol*

1996. Fifth Death Anniv of G. Aliev (painter). Multicoloured.

309	100m. *Reka Cura*	55	55
310	200m. Type **66**	1·10	1·10

67 Behbudov and Globe

1996. Seventh Death Anniv of Resid Behbudov (singer).

311	**67**	100m. multicoloured	95	95

68 Mammadaliev and Flasks

1996. First Death Anniv of Yusif Mammadaliev (scientist).

312	**68**	100m. multicoloured	95	95

69 National Flag and Government Building

1996. Fifth Anniv of Republic.

313	**69**	250m. multicoloured	90	90

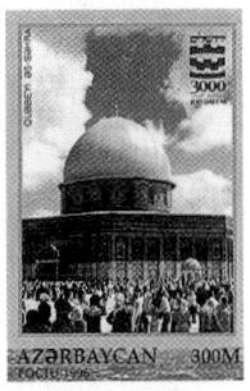

70 Dome of the Rock

1996. 3000th Anniv of Jerusalem. Multicoloured.

314	100m. Praying at the Wailing Wall	70	70
315	250m. Interior of church	1·70	1·70
316	300m. Type **70**	2·00	2·00
MS317	73×104 mm. 500m. Montefiore Windmill	3·50	3·50

71 German Shepherd

1996. Dogs. Multicoloured.

318	50m. Type **71**	10	10
319	100m. Basset hounds	40	40
320	150m. Collies	60	60
321	200m. Bull terriers	85	85
322	300m. Boxers	1·30	1·30
323	400m. Cocker spaniels	1·70	1·70
MS324	70×80 mm. 500m. Shar-pei (38×30 mm)	2·10	2·10

72 Shaft-tailed Whydah

1996. Birds. Multicoloured.

325	50m. Type **72**	10	10
326	100m. Blue-naped mousebird	40	40
327	150m. Asian black-headed oriole	60	60
328	200m. Golden oriole	85	85
329	300m. Common starling	1·30	1·30
330	400m. Yellow-fronted canary	1·70	1·70
MS331	60×80 mm. 500m. European bee eater (*Merops apaister*) (31×39 mm)	2·10	2·10

73 "Burgundy"

1996. Roses. Multicoloured.

332	50m. Type **73**	10	10
333	100m. "Virgo"	40	40
334	150m. "Rose Gaujard"	60	60
335	200m. "Luna"	85	85
336	300m. "Lady Rose"	1·30	1·30
337	400m. "Landora"	1·70	1·70
MS338	90×70 mm. 500m. "Luxor" (39×31 mm)	2·10	2·10

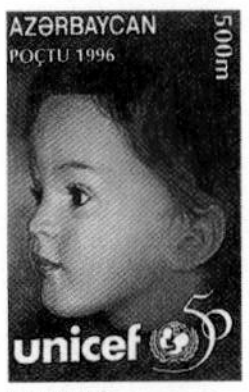

74 Child

1996. 50th Anniv of UNICEF.

339	**74**	500m. multicoloured	90	90

75 Spain v. Bulgaria

1996. European Football Championship, England. Multicoloured.

340	100m. Type **75**	25	25
341	150m. Rumania v. France	40	40
342	200m. Czech Republic v. Germany	50	50
343	250m. England v. Switzerland	70	70
344	300m. Croatia v. Turkey	75	75
345	400m. Italy v. Russia	1·10	1·10
MS346	110×80 mm. 500m. Detail of cup	1·40	1·40

76 Chinese Junk

1996. Ships. Multicoloured.

347	100m. Type **76**	25	25
348	150m. *Danmark* (Danish full-rigged cadet ship)	40	40
349	200m. *Nippon-Maru II* (Japanese cadet ship)	60	60
350	250m. *Mircea* (Rumanian barque)	75	75
351	300m. *Kruzenshtern* (Russian cadet barque)	95	95
352	400m. *Ariadne* (German cadet schooner)	1·30	1·30
MS353	107×77 mm. 500m. *Tovarishch* (Russian four-masted cadet barque) (vert)	2·75	2·75

77 Baxram Gur killing Dragon (fountain by A. Shulgin at Baku)

1997

354	**77**	100m. purple and black	35	35
356	**77**	250m. black and yellow	40	40
357	**77**	400m. black and red	55	55
358	**77**	500m. black and green	65	65
359	**77**	1000m. black and blue	1·30	1·30

78 Nariman Narimanov (politician and writer)

1997. Anniversaries. Multicoloured.

365	250m. Type **78** (125th birth anniv (1995))	80	80
366	250m. Fatali Xoyskin (politician, 120th birth anniv (1995))	80	80
367	250m. Aziz Mammed-Kerim ogli Aliyev (politician, birth centenary)	80	80
368	250m. Ilyas Afendiyev (writer, 1st death anniv)	80	80

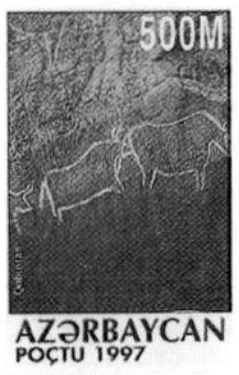

79 Bulls

1997. Qobustasn Rock Carvings. Sheet 127×84 mm containing T **79** and similar vert designs. Multicoloured.

MS369	500m. Type **79**; 500m. Goats; 500m. Dancers	4·50	4·50

1997. Red Cross. Various stamps optd **Red Cross** and cross. (a) Nos. 93/99.

370	20q. multicoloured	10	10
371	30q. multicoloured	10	10
372	50q. multicoloured	10	10

373		1m. multicoloured	35	35
374		2m.50 multicoloured	1·00	1·00
375		5m. multicoloured	2·00	2·00
376		10m. multicoloured	4·25	4·25
MS377		80×60 mm. 8m. multicoloured	4·25	4·25

(b) Nos. 195/9.

378		10m. multicoloured	40	40
379		15m. multicoloured	70	70
380		20m. multicoloured	95	95
381		25m. multicoloured	1·20	1·20
382		50m. multicoloured	2·40	2·40
MS383		64×56 mm. 100m. multicoloured	4·25	4·25

1997. 50th Anniv of Rotary Club International in Azerbaijan. Various stamps optd 50th Anniversary of the Rotary Club and emblem. (a) Nos. 314/16.

384		100m. multicoloured	95	95
385		250m. multicoloured	2·20	2·20
386		300m. multicoloured	2·75	2·75
MS387		74×103 mm. 500m. multicoloured	2·50	2·50

(b) Nos. 347/52.

388		100m. multicoloured	40	40
389		150m. multicoloured	70	70
390		200m. multicoloured	85	85
391		250m. multicoloured	1·10	1·10
392		300m. multicoloured	1·30	1·30
393		400m. multicoloured	1·70	1·70
MS394		106×76 mm. 500m. multicoloured	4·50	4·50

82 Dog

1997. *The Town Band of Bremen* by the Brothers Grimm. Multicoloured.

395		250m. Type **82**	1·50	1·50
396		250m. Donkey and cat	1·50	1·50
397		250m. Rooster	1·50	1·50
MS398		125×96 mm. 500m. Animals frightening robbers from hideaway	3·50	3·50

Nos. 395/7 were issued together, *se-tenant*, forming a composite design.

83 Seal Pup

1997. The Caspian Seal. Multicoloured.

399		250m. Type **83**	65	65
400		250m. Bull and mountain peak	65	65
401		250m. Bull and gull	65	65
402		250m. Cow (profile)	65	65
403		250m. Cow (full face)	65	65
404		250m. Young seal (three-quarter face)	65	65
MS405		106×77 mm. 500m. Cow (vert)	3·50	3·50

Nos. 399/404 were issued together, *se-tenant*, forming a composite design.

84 Tanbur

1997. Traditional Musical Instruments. Multicoloured.

406		250m. Type **84**	60	60
407		250m. Gaval (tambourine)	60	60
408		500m. Jang (harp)	1·20	1·20

85 19th-century Oil Derricks, Aspheron Peninsula

1997. 125th Anniv of First Industrial Oil Well in Azerbaijan. Sheet 115×91 mm containing T **85** and similar vert design. Multicoloured.

MS409		500m. Type **85**; 500m. Modern drilling platform, Caspian Sea	2·50	2·50

86 Sirvani

1997. 870th Birth Anniv (1996) of Xanqani Sirvani (poet).

410	**86**	250m. multicoloured	85	85

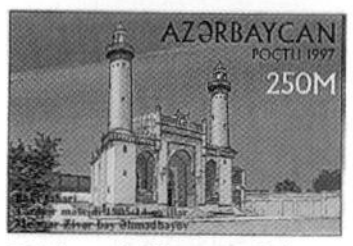

87 Taza-pir Mosque, Baku

1997. Mosques. Multicoloured.

411		250m. Type **87**	75	75
412		250m. Momuna-Xatun Mosque, Nakhichevan	75	75
413		250m. Govharaga Mosque, Shusha	75	75

88 Rasulbekov and Baku T.V. Tower

1997. 80th Birth Anniv of G. D. Rasulbekov (former Minister of Telecommunications).

414	**88**	250m. multicoloured	75	75

89 Italy, 1938

1997. World Cup Football Championship, France (1998).

415	**89**	250m. black	70	70
416	-	250m. multicoloured	70	70
417	-	250m. black	70	70
418	-	250m. multicoloured	70	70
419	-	250m. multicoloured	70	70
420	-	250m. multicoloured	70	70
MS421		85×90 mm. 1500m. black and blue (Tofiq Bahramov (referee))	3·25	3·25

DESIGNS—World Champion Teams: No. 416, Argentina, 1986; 417, Uruguay, 1930 (wrongly inscr "1980"); 418, Brazil, 1994; 419, England, 1966; 420, West Germany, 1990.

90 Katarina Wit, East Germany

1997. Winter Olympic Games, Nagano, Japan. Multicoloured.

422		250m. Type **90** (figure skating gold medal, 1984 and 1988)	3·75	50
423		250m. Elvis Stoyko, Canada (figure skating silver medal, 1994)	50	50
424		250m. Midori Ito, Japan (figure skating silver medal, 1992)	50	50
425		250m. Azerbaijan flag and silhouettes of sports	50	50
426		250m. Olympic torch and mountain	50	50
427		250m. Kristin Yamaguchi, U.S.A. (figure skating gold medal, 1992)	50	50
428		250m. John Curry, Great Britain (figure skating gold medal, 1976)	50	50
429		250m. Cen Lu, China (figure skating bronze medal, 1994)	50	50
MS430		76×106 mm. 500m. Yekaterina Gordeyeva and Sergi Grinkov, Russia (figure skating gold medal, 1984 and 1988)	3·00	3·00

91 Diana, Princess of Wales

1998. Diana, Princess of Wales Commem. Multicoloured.

431		400m. Type **91**	50	50
432		400m. Wearing black polo-neck jumper	50	50

92 Aliyev and Mountain Landscape

1998. 90th Birth Anniv of Hasan Aliyev (ecologist).

433	**92**	500m. multicoloured	85	85

93 Tourist Map, Flag and Pres. Aliev

1998. 75th Birthday of President Haidar Aliev. Sheet 114×89 mm.

MS434	**93**	500m. multicoloured	2·10	2·10

1998. "Israel 98" International Stamp Exhibition, Tel Aviv. No. **MS**369 optd **98** and emblem on each stamp and **Israel 98–WORLD STAMP EXHIBITION TEL-AVIV 13–21 MAY 1998** in margin.

MS435		500m. ×3 multicoloured	5·50	5·50

95 Ashug Alesker (singer)

1998. Birth Anniversaries. Multicoloured.

436		250m. Type **95** (175th anniv)	60	60
437		250m. Magomedhuseyn Shakhriyar (poet, 90th anniv)	60	60
438		250m. Qara Qarayev (composer, 80th anniv)	60	60

96 Bul-Bul

1998. Birth Centenary of Bul-Bul (Murtuz Meshadirza ogli Mamedov) (singer).

439	**96**	500m. multicoloured	85	85

97 Mickey and Minnie Mouse playing Chess

1998. World Rapid Chess Championship, Georgia. Multicoloured.

440		250m. Type **97**	2·10	2·10
441		500m. Mickey, Minnie, pawn and rook	2·40	2·40
442		500m. Goofy, bishop and knight	2·40	2·40
443		500m. Donald Duck, king and bishop	2·40	2·40
444		500m. Pluto, rook, pawn and clockwork pawn	2·40	2·40
445		500m. Minnie and queen	2·40	2·40
446		500m. Daisy Duck, bishop and king	2·40	2·40
447		500m. Goofy, Donald and pawn	2·40	2·40
448		500m. Mickey, queen and rook	2·40	2·40
MS449		Two sheets, each 127×101 mm. (a) 4000m. Mickey, Minnie, Pluto and queen; (b) 4000m. Donald, Mickey and pawn	19·00	19·00

98 Preparing Pastries

1998. Europa. National Festivals: New Year. Multicoloured.

450		1000m. Type **98**	1·20	1·20
451		3000m. Acrobat and wrestlers	3·00	3·00

1999. "iBRA" International Stamp Exhibition, Nuremberg, Germany. Nos. 450/1 optd with exhibition emblem.

452		1000m. multicoloured	75	75
453		3000m. multicoloured	2·30	2·30

100 Greater Flamingo, Gizilagach National Park

1999. Europa. Parks and Gardens. Multicoloured.

454		1000m. Type **100**	1·20	1·20
455		3000m. Stag, Girkan National Park	3·00	3·00

101 14th-century Square Tower

1999. Towers at Mardakyan.

456	**101**	1000m. black and blue	60	60
457	-	3000m. black and red	2·30	1·90

DESIGN: 3000m. 13th-century round tower.

See also Nos. 547 and 557.

102 President Aliev and Flag

1999. 75th Anniv of Nakhichevan Autonomous Region. Multicoloured.

460		1000m. Type **102**	1·00	1·00
461		1000m. Map of Nakhichevan	1·00	1·00
MS462		110×90 mm. Nos. 460/1	1·90	1·90

103 Cabbarli

1999. Birth Centenary of Cafar Cabbarli (dramatist).

463	**103**	250m. multicoloured	75	75

104 40k. Stamp

1999. 80th Anniv of First Azerbaijani Stamps. Sheet 131×106 mm containing T **104** and similar multicoloured designs showing stamps of 1919.

MS464		500m. 10k. stamp (Type **1**) (25×35 mm); 500m. Type **104**; 500m. 5r. stamp; 500m. 50r. stamp (Type **2**)	3·25	3·25

105 Flag, Pigeon and Emblem on Scroll

1999. 125th Anniv of Universal Postal Union. Multicoloured.

465	250m. Type **105**	10	10
466	300m. Satellite, computer and emblem	3·00	3·00

106 Caravanserai Inner Court and Maiden's Tower, Baku

1999. 19th-century Caravanserais. Multicoloured.

467	500m. Type **106**	1·30	1·30
468	500m. Camels outside caravan-serai, Sheki	1·30	1·30

107 Anniversary Emblem

1999. 50th Anniv of Council of Europe.

469	**107**	1000m. multicoloured	95	95

108 Beybur Khan's Son fighting Camel

1999. 1300th Anniv of Kitabi Dada Qorqud (folk epic). Sheet 90×125 mm containing T **108** and similar horiz designs. Multicoloured.

MS470	1000m. Type **108**; 1000m. Wounded Tural slumped on horse; 1000m. Gaza Khan asleep beside horse	2·75	2·75

109 "Building Europe"

2000. Europa.

471	**109**	1000m. multicoloured	90	90
472	**109**	3000m. multicoloured	3·25	3·25

110 Phaeton

2000. Baku City Transport. Sheet 111×88 mm containing T **110** and similar horiz designs. Multicoloured.

MS473	500m. Type **110**; 500m. Konka; 500m. Electric tram; 500m. Trolleybus	3·50	3·50

111 14th-century Square Tower, Ramana

2000. Towers of Mardakyan.

474	**111**	100m. black and orange	40	40
475	-	250m. black and green	1·00	1·00

DESIGN: 250m. 14th-century round tower, Nardaran.

See also Nos. 499/500.

112 Wrestling

2000. Olympic Games, Sydney. Multicoloured.

476	500m. Type **112**	95	95
477	500m. Weightlifting	95	95
478	500m. Boxing	95	95
479	500m. Relay	95	95

113 Duck flying

2000. The Ferruginous Duck. Multicoloured.

480	500m. Type **113**	70	70
481	500m. Ducks in water and standing on rocks	70	70
482	500m. Duck standing on rock and others swimming by grasses	70	70
483	500m. Ducks at sunset	70	70

114 Satellite Picture of Azerbaijan and Emblem

2000. 50th Anniv of World Meteorological Organization.

484	**114**	1000m. multicoloured	85	85

115 Quinces

2000. Fruits. Multicoloured.

485	500m. Type **115**	75	75
486	500m. Pomegranates (*Punica granatum*)	75	75
487	500m. Peaches (*Persica*)	75	75
488	500m. Figs (*Ficus carica*)	75	75

116 Ringed-necked Pheasant

2000. The Ringed-necked Pheasant (*Phasanus colchicus*). Sheet 102×72 mm.

MS489	**116** 2000m. multicoloured	2·50	2·50

117 Rasul-Rza

2000. 90th Birth Anniv of Rasul-Rza (poet).

490	**117**	250m. multicoloured	80	80

118 Levantine Viper

2000. Reptiles. Multicoloured.

491	500m. Type **118**	1·10	1·10
492	500m. Rock lizard (*Lacerta saxicola*) (wrongly inscr "Laserta saxcola")	1·10	1·10
493	500m. Ottoman viper (*Vipera xanthina*)	1·10	1·10
494	500m. Toad-headed agama (*Phrynocephalus mystaceus*)	1·10	1·10

MS495	90×63 mm. 500m. Watersnake (*Natrix tessellate*) and sunwatcher (*Phrynocephalus helioscopus*) (vert)	1·30	1·30

119 Rahman

2000. 90th Birth Anniv of Sabit Rahman (writer).

496	**119**	1000m. multicoloured	1·40	1·40

120 Emblem

2000. UNESCO International Year of Culture and Peace.

497	**120**	3000m. multicoloured	2·75	2·75

121 Namig Abullayev (gold, freestyle flyweight wrestling)

2001. Olympic Games, Sydney. Medal Winners. Sheet 99×127 mm containing T **121** and similar horiz designs. Multicoloured.

MS498	1000m. Type **121**; 1000m. Zemifira Meftahaddinova (gold, skeet shooting); 1000m. Vugar Alakbarov (bronze, middle-weight boxing)	3·00	3·00

122 Seal, Lesser White-fronted Goose and Oil Rig

2001. Europa. Water Resources. The Caspian Sea. Multicoloured.

499	1000m. Type **122**	1·00	1·00
500	3000m. Sturgeon, crab and oil rig	3·25	3·25

123 Building and Flags

2001. Admission of Azerbaijan to Council of Europe.

501	**123**	1000m. multicoloured	1·00	1·00

2001. Towers of Sheki. As T **111**.

502	100m. black and lilac	30	30
503	250m. black and yellow	80	80

DESIGNS: 100m. 18th-century round tower; 250m. Ruin of 12th-century tower.

124 Refugee Camp

2001. 50th Anniv of United Nations High Commissioner for Refugees. Sheet 100×73 mm.

MS504	**124** 3000m. black and blue	2·50	2·50

125 Tusi, Globe and Books

2001. 800th Birth Anniv of Nasraddin Tusi (mathematician and astronomer). Sheet 110×78 mm.

MS505	**125** 3000m. multicoloured	2·50	2·50

126 Handshake and Emblem

2001. Tenth Anniv of Union of Independent States.

506	**126**	1000m. multicoloured	1·00	1·00

127 Yuri Gagarin, "Vostok 1" and Globe

2001. 40th Anniv of First Manned Space Flight. Sheet 83×56 mm.

MS507	**127** 3000m. multicoloured	2·20	2·20

128 Short-eared Owl (*Asio flammeus*)

2001. Owls. Multicoloured.

508	1000m. Type **128**	75	75
509	1000m. Tawny owl (*Strix aluco*)	75	75
510	1000m. Scops owl (*Otus scops*)	75	75
511	1000m. Long-eared owl (*Asio otus*)	75	75
512	1000m. Eagle owl on branch (*Bubo bubo*)	75	75
513	1000m. Little owl (*Athene noctua*)	75	75
MS514	91×68 mm. 1000m. Eagle owl (*Bubo bubo*) in flight	1·90	1·90

129 Pres. Heydar Aliyev

2001. Tenth Anniv of Independence.

515	**129**	5000m. multicoloured	7·75	7·75

130 Pres. Vladimir Putin and Pres. Heydar Aliyev

2001. Visit of President Putin to Azerbaijan.

516	**130**	1000m. multicoloured	85	80

131 Emblem and Athletes

2002. Tenth Anniv of National Olympic Committee.

517	**131**	3000m. multicoloured	2·20	2·20

132 Circus Performers

2002. Europa. Circus. Multicoloured.

518	1000m. Type **132**	1·00	1·00
519	3000m. Equestrian juggler and trapeze artist	3·25	3·25

133 Presidents Heydar Aliyev and Jiang Zemin

2002. Tenth Anniv of Azerbaijan–China Diplomatic Relations.
520 **133** 1000m. multicoloured 90 90

134 Molla Panah Vagif's Mausoleum, Susa

2002. Towers of Karabakh.
521 **134** 100m. black and green 20 20
522 - 250m. black and cinnamon 50 50
DESIGNS: 250m. 19th-century mosque, Aghdam.

2002. Tenth Anniv of Azermarka Stamp Company. No. 83 surch **Azermarka 1992–2002 1000m.**
523 **13** 1000m. on 35q. multicoloured 85 85

136 Emblem

2002. Tenth Anniv of New Azerbaijan Party.
524 **136** 3000m. multicoloured 2·20 2·20

137 African Monarch (*Danaus chrysippus*)

2002. Butterflies and Moths. Multicoloured.
525 1000m. Type **137** (inscr "Danais") 95 95
526 1000m. Southern swallowtail (*Papilio alexanor*) 95 95
527 1000m. *Thaleropis jonia* 95 95
528 1000m. Red admiral (*Vanessa atalanta*) 95 95
529 1000m. *Argynnis alexandra* 95 95
530 1000m. *Brahmaea christoph* (moth) 95 95

138 Pres. Heydar Aliyev and Pope John Paul II

2002. Pope John Paul II's Visit to Azerbaijan. Sheet 80×65 mm.
MS531 **138** 1500m. multicoloured 2·00 2·00

139 Telegraph Machine, Building Facade and Emblem

2002. 70th Anniv of Baku Telegraph Office.
532 **139** 3000m. multicoloured 2·00 2·00

140 Gadjiyev and Piano

2002. 80th Birth Anniv of Ruaf Gadjiyev (composer).
533 **140** 5000m. multicoloured 2·50 2·50

141 Bearded Men with Swords, Black Pawns, White Pawn and White Rook

2002. European Junior Chess Championships, Baku. Showing chess board and views of Baku. Multicoloured.
534 1500m. Type **141** 1·20 1·20
535 1500m. Two knights on horseback 1·20 1·20
536 1500m. Two elephants 1·20 1·20
537 1500m. Black rook, black pawn, bearded men with swords and fallen knight 1·20 1·20
Nos. 534/7 were issued together, *se-tenant*, forming a composite design showing a chess game and views of ancient Baku.

142 World Trade Centre, New York, U.S.A. and Azerbaijan Flags and Globe

2002. First Anniv of Attack on World Trade Centre, New York. Sheet 130×65 mm containing vert design as T **142**. Multicoloured.
MS538 1500m. ×3 Type **142** 2·30 2·30

143 Turkish Football Team

2002. Football World Cup Championship, Japan and South Korea. Sheet 102×110 mm.
MS539 **143** 5000m. multicoloured 3·50 3·50

144 Dove, Woman, Flag and Emblems

2002. United Nations Development Fund for Women.
540 **144** 3000m. multicoloured 2·10 2·10

145 Siamese Fighting Fish (*Betta splendens*)

2002. Aquarium Fish. Multicoloured.
541 100m. Type **145** 75 75
542 100m. Blue discus (*Symphysodon aequifasciatus*) 75 75
543 100m. Freshwater angelfish (*Pterophyllum scalare*) 75 75
544 100m. Black moor (*Carassius auratus auratus*) 75 75
545 100m. Boeseman's rainbowfish (*Melanotaenia boesemani*) 75 75
546 1000m. Firemouth cichlid (*Cichlasoma meeki*) 75 75

2003. Towers of Karabakh. As T **101**.
547 250m. black and blue 45 45
DESIGN: No. 547, Askeran tower and fortress.

146 Bomb and Scissors ("Stop Terrorism")

2003. Europa. Poster Art. Multicoloured.
548 1000m. Type **146** 85 85
549 3000m. Wrestlers ("Sport is the Health of the Nation") 2·50 2·50

147 Flag and UPU Emblem

2003. Tenth Anniv of Azerbaijan Membership of Universal Postal Union.
550 **147** 3000m. multicoloured 2·10 2·10

148 H. Djavid Mausoleum and Hacha Mountain

2003. Nakhichevan.
551 **148** 3000m. multicoloured 2·10 2·10

149 Map and Pipeline

2003. Baku–Tbilisi–Jeychan Oil Pipeline.
552 **149** 3000m. multicoloured 2·10 2·10

150 Zarifa Aliyeva and Eye

2003. 80th Birth Anniv of Zarifa Aliyeva (ophthalmologist).
553 **150** 3000m. multicoloured 2·10 2·10

151 Heydar Aliyev

2003. 80th Birth Anniv of Pres. Heydar Aliyev. Sheet 130×160 mm.
MS554 **151** 10000m. multicoloured 6·00 6·00

2003. Nos. 131 and 168 surch.
555 500m. on 25m. yellow and black 50 50
556 1000m. on 8m. blue, silver and black 1·00 1·00

2003. Towers of Karabakh. As T **101**.
557 1000m. black 75 75
DESIGN: No. 557, Archway, walls and tower, Shusha Town.

153 QAZ-11-73 Saloon Car

2003. Cars. Sheet 100×77 mm containing T **153** and similar horiz designs. Multicoloured.
MS558 500m.×4 Type **153**; QAZ-M-20 Pobeda; QAZ 12 Zim; QAZ-21 Volga (inscr "Volqa") 2·40 2·00

154 Textile Seller

2003. 90th Anniv of U. Hajibekov's Musical Comedy *Arshin Mal Alan.*
559 **154** 10000m. multicoloured 5·00 5·00

2003. Nos. 91, 129, 130, 152/5, 165 and 169 surch.
560 500m. on 50q. yellow and black 40 40
561 500m. on 2m. red, silver and black 40 40
562 500m. on 4m. green, silver and black 40 40
563 500m. on 5m. multicoloured 40 40
567 500m. on 5m. red and black 40 40
564 500m. on 10m. multicoloured 40 40
565 500m. on 15m. multicoloured 40 40
566 500m. on 20m. multicoloured 40 40
568 500m. on 40m. brown and black 40 40

155 Bear (*Ursus arctos*) (inscr "arctors")

2003. Sheki National Park. Sheet 106×84 mm containing T **155** and similar horiz designs. Multicoloured.
MS569 3000m. Type **155**; Racoon (*Procyon lotor*); Wild boar (*Sus scrofa*); Fox (*Vulpes vulpes*) 6·75 6·75

156 Map and Monument

2004. 80th Anniversary of Nakhichevan Autonomous Republic.
570 **156** 3000m. multicoloured 1·70 1·70

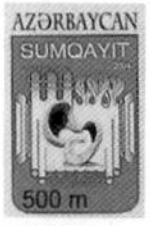

157 Dove of Peace (sculpture)

2004. Samgayit Town.
571 **157** 500m. blue and black 60 60

158 Geygel Lake

2004. Europa. Holidays. Multicoloured.
572 1000m. Type **158** 85 85
573 3000m. Baku at night 2·50 2·50

159 Molla Cuma

2004. 150th Birth Anniversary of Molla Cuma (singer).
574 **159** 500m. multicoloured 75 75

160 High Jump

2004. Olympic Games, 2004, Greece. Multicoloured.
575 500m. Type **160** 70 70
576 500m. Wrestlers 70 70
577 500m. Runner 70 70
578 500m. Greek vase 70 70
Nos. 575/8 were issued together, *se-tenant*, forming a composite design.

161 World Cup Trophy

2004. Centenary of FIFA (Federation Internationale de Football Association). Multicoloured.

579	500m. Type **161**	70	70
580	500m. Player facing left	70	70
581	500m. Player facing right	70	70
582	500m. Goalkeeper	70	70

Nos. 579/82 were issued together, *se-tenant*, forming a composite design.

162 Heydar Aliyev

2004. Heydar Aliyev Commemoration (president, 1993–2003) (1st issue).

583	**162**	500m. multicoloured	60	60

See also Nos. **MS**590, 607 and 632.

163 Mosques and Camels

2004. The Great Silk Route.

584	**163**	3000m. multicoloured	2·10	2·10

164 Carpet and Couple wearing 19th-century Costume, Baku

2004. Traditional Costumes. Carpets and 19th-century costumes.

585	500m. Type **164**	65	65
586	500m. Couple holding instruments, Karabakh	65	65
587	500m. Woman wearing long headdress, man with cane, Nakhichevan	65	65
588	500m. Man with dagger	65	65

165 Globe, Honeywell DDP 516 and Modern Computer

2004. 35th Anniv of the Internet.

589	**165**	3000m. multicoloured	1·80	1·80

166 Heydar Aliyev

2004. Heydar Aliyev Commemoration (president, 1993–2003) (2nd issue). Sheet 60×80 mm.

MS590	**166**	1000m. multicoloured	5·50	5·50

167 Leopard in Tree

2005. Endangered Species. Leopards. Multicoloured.

591	1000m. Type **167**	80	80
592	1000m. Two cubs	80	80
593	1000m. Adult	80	80
594	1000m. Mother and cubs	80	80

2005. Nos. 212/15 surch **1000 mm**.

595	1000m. on 10m. multicoloured	60	60
596	1000m. on 25m. multicoloured	60	60
597	1000m. on 50m. multicoloured	60	60
598	1000m. on 60m. multicoloured	60	60

169 Ministry Building and Emblem

2005. Fifth Anniv of Ministry of Taxes.

599	**169**	3000m. multicoloured	2·50	1·80

170 Observatory

2005. Shemakha Town.

600	**170**	500m. mauve and black	1·40	45

171 *Cephalanthera rubra*

2005. Orchids. Multicoloured.

601	500m. Type **171**	40	40
602	1000m. *Orchis papilionacea*	85	85
603	1500m. *Epipactis atrorubens*	1·30	1·30
604	3000m. *Orchis purpurea*	3·00	3·00
MS605	135×190 mm. Nos. 601/4	3·75	3·75

172 Aircraft, Tanks and Oil Tankers

2005. 60th Anniv of the End of World War II.

606	**172**	1000m. multicoloured	60	60

173 Heydar Aliyev

2005. Heydar Aliyev (president, 1993–2003) Commemoration (3rd issue).

607	**173**	1000m. multicoloured	60	60

174 Pilaf

2005. Europa. Gastronomy. Multicoloured.

608	1000m. Type **174**	70	70
609	3000m. Dolmasi	3·00	3·00

175 Rock Paintings and Academy Building

2005. 60th Anniv of Academy of Science.

610	**175**	1000m. multicoloured	45	45

176 Astronaut

2005. 40th Anniv of First Space Walk. Sheet 86×58 mm.

MS611	**176**	3000m. multicoloured	2·00	2·00

177 Computers and Emblem

2005. Tunis 2005 (World Summit on Information Society).

612	**177**	1000m. multicoloured	45	45

178 Pope John Paul II

2005. Pope John Paul II Commemoration.

613	**178**	3000m. multicoloured	2·00	2·00

179 *Paravespula germanica*

2005. Insects. Sheet 101×80 mm containing T **179** and similar horiz designs. Multicoloured.

MS614	500m. Type **179**; 1000m. *Bombus terrestris*; 1500m. *Vespa crabro*; 3000m. *Apis mellifera caucasica*	3·25	3·25

180 Emblem and Nos. 450/1

2005. 50th Anniv of Europa Stamps. Showing previous Europa stamps. Multicoloured.

615	3000m. Type **180**	1·40	1·40
616	3000m. Emblem and Nos. 471/2	1·40	1·40
617	3000m. Emblem and Nos. 548/9	1·40	1·40
618	3000m. Emblem and Nos. 1167/8 of West Germany	1·40	1·40
MS619	Four sheets, each 88×88 mm. (a) As No. 615; (b) As No. 616; (c) As No. 617; (d) As No. 618	5·00	5·00

Note: On 1 January 2006 the manat was re-valued at the rate 1 new manat = 5000 old manat.

2006. Nos. 131, 110, 114, 168, 521, 113, 457, 146 and 127/8 surch.

620	5q. on 8m. blue, silver and black (No. 131)	1·00	1·00
621	10q. on 1m. multicoloured (No. 110)	1·30	1·30
622	10q. on 1m. multicoloured (No. 114)	1·30	1·30
623	10q. on 25m. yellow and black (No. 168)	1·30	1·30
624	10q. on 100m. black and green (No. 521)	1·30	1·30
625	20q. on 50q. multicoloured (No. 113)	1·75	1·75
627	20q. on 20m. black, gold and blue (No. 146)	1·75	1·75
626	20q. on 3000m. black and scarlet (No. 457)	1·75	1·75
628	60q. on 5m. multicoloured (No. 127)	2·50	2·50
629	60q. on 8m. multicoloured (No. 128)	2·50	2·50

182 19th-century Mosque, Lankaran

2006. Towns.

630	**182**	10q. blue and black	1·00	1·00
631	-	20q. buff and brown	1·50	1·50

DESIGNS: Type **182**; 20q. 9th-century fortress, Lachin.

See also Nos. 652/3.

2006. Heydar Aliyev (president, 1993–2003) Commemoration (4th issue).

632	**162**	60q. multicoloured	4·25	4·25

183 Emblem

2006. 30th Anniv of OPEC Fund for International Development.

633	**183**	5q. multicoloured	1·00	1·00

184 Hands from Many Nations

2006. Europa. Integration. Multicoloured.

634	20q. Type **184**	2·50	2·50
635	60q. Globe enclosed in star	7·50	7·50

185 Emblem

2006. World Cup Football Championship, Germany. Multicoloured.

636	20q. Type **185**	1·50	1·50
637	60q. Player and map of Germany	1·40	1·40

186 Samad Vurgun

2006. Writers Birth Centenaries. Multicoloured.

638	10q. Type **186**	80	80
639	60q. Suleyman Rustam	2·40	2·40

187 Russian Flag and Arms and St. Basil's Cathedral, Moscow

2006. Year of Russia in Azerbaijan. Multicoloured.

640	10q. Type **187**	1·00	1·00
641	20q. Azerbaijan flag and arms and Taza Pir mosque, Baku	1·30	1·30
642	30q. Azerbaijan flag and arms and Maiden Tower, Baku	1·50	1·50
643	60q. Russian flag and arms and Kremlin, Moscow	2·50	2·50

188 Gulustan Mausoleum, Nakhichivan (13th-century)

2006

644	**188**	20q. multicoloured	1·40	1·40

189 Globe and Binary Code

2006. World Information Organization Day.

645	**189**	1m. multicoloured	6·00	6·00

190 Khan (1867)

2006. Karabakh Horses. Multicoloured.

646 20q. Type **190** 1·50 1·50
647 20q. Zaman (1952) 1·50 1·50
648 20q. Sarvan (1987) 1·50 1·50
649 20q. Gar-gar (2001) 1·50 1·50
MS650 122×94 mm. Size 52×37 mm. Nos. 646/9 9·00 9·00
MS651 82×65 mm. 60q. Rearing horse (vert) 6·50 6·50

2006. Towns. As T **182**. Multicoloured.

652 10q. lilac and black 1·00 1·00
653 20q. pink and black 1·50 1·50

DESIGNS: 10q. Sumuggala tower, Gakh; 20q. Nizami's mausoleum, Ganja.

2006. 50th Anniv of Europa Stamps. Nos. 608/609 surch. Multicoloured.

654 20q. on 1000m. multicoloured (Type **174**) 2·50 2·50
655 60q. on 3000m. multicoloured (Dolmasi) 8·00 8·00

192 Emblem

2006. 15th Anniv of Regional Concord of Communication.

656 **192** 20q. multicoloured 1·60 1·60

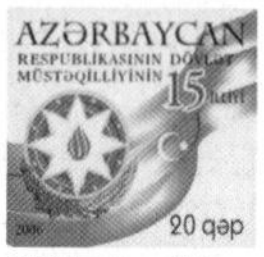

193 Arms and Flag

2006. 15th Anniv of Independence.

657 **193** 20q. multicoloured 1·60 1·60

194 Fire Appliance AMO-F15 (1926)

2006. Fire Engines. Sheet 101×76 mm containing T **194** and similar horiz designs showing fire engines. Multicoloured.

MS658 10q. Type **194**; 20q. PMQ-1 (1932); 60q. PMQ-9 (1950); 1m. ATS 2,5 (1998) 10·50 10·50

195 Pigeons and Tower

2007. Pigeons. Multicoloured.

659 20q. Type **195** 1·60 1·60
660 20q. Iridescent pigeons and domes 1·60 1·60
661 20q. Brown and white pigeons and oil derricks 1·60 1·60
662 20q. White pigeon, brown and white pigeon and buildings 1·60 1·60
663 20q. Dark pigeons and gateways 1·60 1·60
664 20q. Spotted pigeons and windmills 1·60 1·60
MS665 54×78 mm. 1m. White pigeon with feathered feet (vert) 5·00 5·00

The stamp and margins of **MS**665 form a composite design.

196 Baku Customs' Building

2007. Bicentenary of Baku Customs Services (20q.) or 15th Anniv of Azerbaijan Customs Services (60q.). Multicoloured.

666 20q. Type **196** 1·60 1·60
667 60q. Azerbaijan Customs' building 4·50 4·50

197 Monument to Victims

2007. 15th Anniv of Khojali Tragedy. Sheet 99×72 mm.

MS668 **197** multicoloured 6·25 6·25

198 Emblem

2007. Europa. Centenary of Scouting. Multicoloured.

669 20q. Type **198** 2·50 2·50
670 60q. Emblem on kite 7·00 7·00

199 Symbols of Azerbaijan and Japan

2007. Azerbaijan—Japan Friendly Relations.

671 **199** 1m. multicoloured 5·50 5·50

200 Mosque, Goycay

2007. Towns.

672 **200** 10q. yellow and black 1·00 1·00

2007 60qəp (201)

2007 60qəp (202)

60qəp (203)

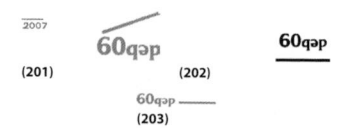

2007. Nos. 551 and 613 surch as T **201**, 615/18 surch as T **202** and 570 surch as T **203**.

673 60q. on 3000m. multicoloured (No. 551) 4·50 4·50
674 60q. on 3000m. multicoloured (No. 570) 4·50 4·50
675 60q. on 3000m. multicoloured (No. 613) 4·50 4·50
676 60q. on 3000m. multicoloured (No. 615) 3·75 3·75
677 60q. on 3000m. multicoloured (No. 616) 3·75 3·75
678 60q. on 3000m. multicoloured (No. 617) 3·75 3·75
679 60q. on 3000m. multicoloured (No. 618) 3·75 3·75

204 Dog Fight

2007. Azim Azimzade (artist) Commemoration. Paintings. Multicoloured.

680 20q. Type **204** 1·50 1·50
681 20q. Wedding 1·50 1·50

205 Emblem

2007. 15th Anniv of Azermarka (postal company).

682 **205** 50q. multicoloured 3·75 3·75

206 Polar Bear Cub

2007. Polar Bear (*Ursus maritimus*). Multicoloured.

683 60q. Type **206** 4·50 4·50
MS684 76×122 mm 1m. Cub with stick (*vert*) 8·50 8·50

No. **MS**684 was cut around in the shape of a bear cub.

207 *Gagea alexeenkoana*

2007. Local Flora. Two sheets containing T **207** and similar horiz designs. Multicoloured.

MS685 182×50 mm 10q. Type **207**; 20q. *Centaurea ficher*; 40q. *Galanthus caucasica*; 60q. *Ophrys caucasica* 7·00 7·00
MS686 50×54 mm 1m. *Ophrys caucasica* (different) 6·50 6·50

The stamp and margin of No. **MS**686 form a composite design.

208 Huseyn Cavid

2007. 160th Birth Anniv of Huseyn Cavid.

687 **208** 20q. multicoloured 1·60 1·60

209 Khudafarin Bridge, Jabrail

2007. Azim Azimzade (artist) Commemoration. Bridges. Multicoloured.

688 10q. Type **209** 80 80
689 20q. Gazanchi, Nakhchivan 1·60 1·60
690 30q. Gudyalchay, Guba 2·40 2·40
691 50q. Ganjachay, Ganja 3·00 3·00
MS692 74×58 mm 60q. 11th century bridge, Jabrail 4·00 4·00

The stamps and margin of No. **MS**692 form a composite design.

10 qəp 2007 (210)

2007. No. 145 surch as T **210**.

693 10q. on 15m. brown, ochre and black 1·20 1·20

211 11th-century Bridge, Jabrail

2007. Towns.

694 **211** 10q. pink and black 90 90
695 - 20q. emerald and black 1·00 1·00

DESIGNS: 10q. Type **211**; 20q. Fortress, Kalbajar.

212 Sputnik

2007. 50th Anniv of Space Exploration. Sheet 100×72 mm.

MS696 **212** multicoloured 6·75 6·75

213 Karim Karimov

2007. 90th Birth Anniv of Karim Karimov (Chairman of the Aeronautics Commission). Sheet 61×76 mm.

MS697 **213** multicoloured 6·25 6·25

214 Judo

2008. Olympic Games, Beijing. Showing stylized athletes. Multicoloured.

698 20q. Type **214** 1·60 1·60
699 30q. Weight lifting 2·20 2·20
700 40q. Wrestling 3·25 3·25
701 60q. Boxing 4·00 4·00

215 Stylized Envelope

2008. Europa. The Letter. Multicoloured.

702 20q. Type **215** 2·50 2·50
703 60q. Stylized computer screen 6·75 6·75
MS704 110×65 mm. 1m. Dove (20×27 mm) 10·00 10·00

216 17th-century Tower, Gazakh

2008. Towns.

705 **216** 10q. pink and black 1·50 1·50

217 Theatre Facade

2008. 125th Anniv of Musical Drama Theatre, Nakhchivan.

706 **217** 20q. multicoloured 2·50 2·50

218 Zafira Aliyeva

2008. 85th Birth Anniv of Zafira Aliyeva (ophthalmologist). Multicoloured.

707 1m. Type **218** 6·50 6·50
708 1m. Zafira Aliyeva (painting) 6·50 6·50

219 Heydar Aliyev

2008. 85th Birth Anniv of Heydar Aliyev (president, 1993–2003). Multicoloured.

709 1m. Type **219** 7·50 7·50
710 1m. Heydar Aliyev with national flag 7·50 7·50

220 Map as Flag and Meeting

2008. 90th Anniv of Independence.

711	**220**	20q. multicoloured	1·50	1·50

221 Mikayil Mushvig and Shirvan-Shakh Palace

2008. Birth Centenary of Mikayil Mushvig (writer).

712	**221**	20q. multicoloured	1·50	1·50

222 Lev Davidovich Landau

2008. Academicians. Multicoloured.

713	20q. Type **222** (physicist, winner of 1962 Nobel Prize for Physics) (birth centenary)	1·50	1·50
714	20q. Hasan Abdullayev (President of Academy of Science, 1970–1983) (90th birth anniv)	1·50	1·50

223 *Heydar Aliyev* (tanker)

2008. 150th Anniv of Caspian Shipping Company. Sheet 175×110 mm containing T **223** and similar horiz designs. Multicoloured.

MS715 20q. Type **223**; 30q. *Azerbaijan* (ferry); 50q. *Composer G. Garayev* (cargo boat); 60q. *Maestro Niyazi* (cargo); 1m. *Vandal* (tanker) 16·00 16·00

224 Earring (12th—13th century)

2008. Jewellery. Multicoloured.

716	60q. Type **224**	5·00	5·00
717	60q. Pendant (19th century)	5·00	5·00

Stamps of a similar design were issued by Ukraine.

225 Khanagah Mausoleum, Djulfa

2008. Towns.

718	10q. brown and black	1·25	1·25
719	20q. bgrey and black (vert)	2·00	2·00

DESIGNS: Type **225**; 20q. Garabaglar Mausoleum, Sharur.

226 *Galeodes araneoides*

2008. Arachnids. Two sheets containing T **226** and similar multicoloured designs.

MS720 100×106 mm. 5q. Type **226**; 10q. *Buthus occitanus*; 20q. *Pisaura mirabilis*; 30q. *Latrodectus tredecimguttatus*; 40q. *Araneus diadematus*; 60q. *Tegenaria domestica*

MS721 40×28 mm. 1m. *Argyroneta aquatica* (horiz) 6·50 6·50

227 Mir Jalal Pashayev

2008. Birth Centenary of Mir Jalal Pashayev (writer).

722	**227**	60q. multicoloured	15·00	15·00

228 Huseyn Javid Mausoleum

2009. 85th Anniv of Nakhchivan Autonomous Republic. Multicoloured.

723	20q. Type **228**	1·60	1·60
724	20q. Heydar Aliev School	1·60	1·60
725	20q. Ministry of Finance	1·60	1·60
726	20q. Nahchivan State University Library	1·60	1·60
727	20q. Nahchivan State University Conservatoire	1·60	1·60
728	20q. Physiotherapy Centre	1·60	1·60
729	20q. Tebriz Hotel	1·60	1·60
730	20q. Diagnostic Medical Centre	1·60	1·60

229 Emblem

2009. Baku–Islamic Cultural Centre–2009. Multicoloured.

731	10q. Type **229**	1·50	1·50
732	20q. Maiden Tower and emblem	2·50	2·50

230 Ice Cliffs, Emblem Antarctica Outline

2009. Preserve Polar Regions and Glaciers. Sheet 120×72 mm containing T **230** and similar vert design. Multicoloured.

MS733 1m.×2, Type **230**; Arctic outline 13·00 13·00

The stamps and margins of **MS**733 form a composite polar design.

231 Emblem and Map

2009. Tenth Economic Cooperation Organization Summit, Tehran.

734	**231**	1m. multicoloured	6·50	6·50

232 Nasiruddin Tusi (astronomer)

2009. Europa. Astronomy. Multicoloured.

735	20q. Type **232**	2·50	2·50
736	60q. Observatory, Shamakhi region	7·50	7·50

MS737 80×80 mm. 1m. First telescope invented by Galileo Galilei, 1609 10·00 10·00

233 Flags

2009. 15th Anniv of Azerbaijan–NATO Co-operation.

738	**233**	20q. multicoloured	1·90	1·90

234 '60', European Stars and Council Building

2009. 60th Anniv of Council of Europe.

739	**234**	60q. multicoloured	5·00	5·00

235 Court Building

2009. 50th Anniv of European Court of Human Rights.

740	**235**	60q. multicoloured	5·00	5·00

236 '60'

2009. 60th Anniv of Sumgait.

741	**236**	10q. multicoloured	1·00	1·00

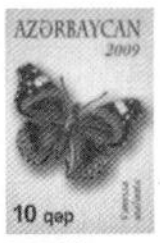

237 *Vanessa atalanta*

2009. Butterflies. Multicoloured.

742	10q. Type **237**	1·00	1·00
743	20q. *Papilio alexanor*	1·10	1·10

238 Anniversary Emblem

2009. 90th Anniv of Diplomatic Service.

744	**238**	60q. multicoloured	5·00	5·00

239 Jalil Mammadguluzadeh

2009. 140th Birth Anniv of Jalil Huseyngulu oglu Mammadguluzadeh (writer).

745	**239**	20q. multicoloured	1·60	1·60

240 Leyla Mammadbekova

2009. Birth Centenary of Leyla Mammadbekova (first Azerbaijani woman pilot).

746	**240**	20q. multicoloured	5·75	5·75

241 Anniversary Emblem

2009. Tenth Anniv of State Oil Fund

747	**241**	60q. multicoloured	5·00	5·00

242 Anniversary Emblem

2009. 135th Anniv of Universal Postal Union.

748	**242**	20q. multicoloured	2·50	2·50
749	**242**	60q. multicoloured	7·50	7·50

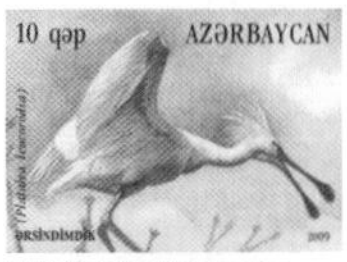

243 *Platalea leucorodia* (spoonbill)

2009. Marsh Waterfowl. Sheet 100×72 mm containing T **243** and similar horiz designs. Multicoloured.

MS750 10q. Type **243**; 20q. *Phalacrocorax pygmaeus* (pygmy cormorant); 60q. *Numenius tenuirostris* (slender-billed curlew); 1m. *Porphyrio porphyrio* (gallinule) 11·50 11·50

244 Chess Pieces on Map of Europe and Azerbaijan

2009. Azerbaijan–European Chess Champion 2009. Sheet 92×70 mm containing T **244** and similar square design. Multicoloured.

MS751 50q. Type **244**; 1m. Chess pieces on map of Azerbaijan 12·00 12·00

245 *Ancient Shamakha*

2009. Azerbaijan Art. Paintings by Sattar Bahlulzade. Sheet 135×100 mm containing T 245 and similar horiz designs. Multicoloured.

MS752 20q.×6, Type **245**; *Still-life with Pomegranates; Buzovna. Shore; Landscape; Poppies; Red View* 11·00 11·00

246 *Thaleropis jonia fisch*

2010. Butterflies. Multicoloured.

753	10q. Type **246**	70	70
754	20q. *Danais chrysippus*	1·40	1·40

247 Bodies

2010. 20th Anniv of 20 January 1990–National Day of Mourning Sheet 99×74 mm

MS755 **247** black and bright rose-red 1·90 1·90

248 Sunrise over Sea

2010. Tenth Anniv of Ministry of Taxes.

756	**248**	60q. multicoloured	5·00	5·00

249 Tiger

2010. Chinese New Year. Year of the Tiger.
757 **249** 60q. multicoloured 5·00 5·00

250 Hands

2010. 90th Anniv of Azerbaijan Red Crescent Society.
758 **250** 60q. multicoloured 5·00 5·00

251 *Bear's Dream*

2010. Europa. Children's Books. Multicoloured.
759 20q. Type **251** 1·40 1·40
760 60q. *Lion and Fox* 5·00 5·00
MS761 175×110 mm. Size 32×42 mm. 1m. *Jirtdan* 2·20 2·20

252 Yellow Peony

2010. Peonies. Two sheets containing T **252** and similar square designs. Multicoloured.
MS762 152×104 mm. 10q.×4, Type **252**; Pink peony; White peony; Magenta peony 4·75 4·75
MS763 104×72 mm. 20q. Vase of Peonies 5·00 5·00

253 Soldiers celebrating Victory in Berlin

2010. 65th Anniv of End of World War II. Multicoloured.
MS764 10q. Type **253**×2; 20q. Hoisting Soviet Flag over Reichstag×2; 60q. Oil container inscribed 'Baku - for front'×2 7·00 7·00

254 Player and Championship Emblem

2010. World Cup Football Championships, South Africa. Multicoloured.
765 Type **254** 1·50 1·50
766 60q. Horiz pair. Nos. 765/6 5·50 5·50

255 Shanghai Skyline

2010. Expo 2010, Shanghai
MS767 **255** 60q. multicoloured 4·75 4·75

256 Cinefilm and A. Alekperov

2010. Birth Centenary of Alesker Gadzhi Aga ogly Alekperov (actor)
768 **256** 20q. multicoloured 2·20 2·20

257 *Argynnis alexandra*

2010. Butterflies. Multicoloured.
769 10q. Type **257** 1·00 1·00
770 20q. *Brahmaea christophi* 1·00 1·10

258 Noah's Mausoleum, Nakhchivan

2010. Architectural Heritage
771 **258** 60q. multicoloured 4·75 4·75

259 Maiden Tower (6th century)

2010. Icheri Sheher Fortress, Baku Old City. Multicoloured.
MS772 10q. Type **259**; 20q. Mahammad mosque (11th century); 30q. Fortress walls (12th century); 40q. Palace Mosque (15th century); 50q. Shirvanshahlar tomb (15th century); 60q. Court-house (15th century) 9·25 9·25
MS773 Horiz. 10q. Palace building (12th-15th centuries); 20q. Bazar square (15th century); 30q. Two fortress archways (6th century); 40q. Jame mosque (14th century); 50q. Gasim Bay bathhouse (15th century); 60q. Multam and Bukhara Caravansaries (15th century) 9·25 9·25
MS774 Horiz. 1m. Shirvanshahlar Palace complex (12th–16th centuries) 6·50 6·50

260 Ateshgah (Zoroastrian fire temple), Baku

2010. Ancient Architecture. Multicoloured.
MS775 60q.×2, Type **260**; Pyramid of the Moon, Teotihuacan (Mexico) 7·50 7·50
Stamps of a similar design were issued by Mexico.

261 Shafaat Mehdiyev

2010. Birth Centenary of Shafaat Farhad Mehdiyev (academician)
776 **261** 60q. multicoloured 5·00 5·00

262 Scottish Fold Kitten

2010. Cats. Multicoloured.
MS777 104×104 mm. 10q. Type **262**; 20q. Persian kitten; 30q. Somali kitten; 40q. British Shorthair kitten; 50q. Birman kitten; 60q. Maine coon kitten 9·25 9·25
MS778 28x40 mm. 1m. Turkish Angora cat with kitten (28×40 mm) 6·50 6·50

263 *Phoenicopterus roseus* (greater flamingo)

2010. Ecology of Caspian Sea. Multicoloured.
779 60q. Type **263** 5·00 5·00
780 60q. *Ardeola ralloides* (Squacco heron) 5·00 5·00
Stamps of a similar design were issued by Kazakhstan.

264 *Parnassius apollo*

2010. Butterflies
781 **264** 10q. multicoloured 1·00 1·00

265 *Centaurea* (inscr 'Centaurea Ficher')

2011. Garabagh Flora. Multicoloured.
782 20q. Type **265** 1·60 1·60
783 50q. *Gagea* (inscr 'Gagea alekxeenkoana') 3·50 3·50

266 Samani and Fire (symbols of Novruz)

2011. Novruz Holiday
784 **266** 30q. multicoloured 2·20 2·20

267 Rabbit

2011. Chinese New Year. Year of the Rabbit
785 **267** 1m. multicoloured 6·25 6·25

268 '10'

2011. Tenth Anniversary of Azerbaijan Republic Joining to the Council of Europe
786 **268** 1m. multicoloured 6·25 6·25

269 *Ulmus densa*

2011. Europa. Multicoloured.
787 20q. Type **259** 2·25 2·25
788 60q. *Platanus orientalis* 7·50 7·50
MS789 109×170 mm. 1m. *Parrotia persica* 11·00 11·00

270 International Space Station

2011. 50th Anniv of First Manned Space Flight. Multicoloured.
MS790 20q. Type **270**; 50q. Spaceship *Vostok*-1 i(n which Yuri Gagarin made first space flight); 1m. *To you mankind* (painting by Tahir Salakhov) (80×28 mm) 6·25 6·25

271 Huseyn Aliyev

2011. Birth Centenary of Huseyn Aliyev (painter)
791 **271** 60q. multicoloured 4·50 4·50

272 Wheel Lyra

2011. Musical Instruments. Multicoloured.
792 50q. Type **272** 3·50 3·50
793 50q. Tar 3·50 3·50

273 *Ophrys Caucasica*

2011. Flowers of Garabagh. Multicoloured.
794 10q. Type **273** 85 85
795 30q. *Galanthus Caucasicus* 2·50 2·50

274 Ell and Nikki

2011. Azerbaijan, Winners of Eurovision 2011, Dusseldorf. Sheet 83×92 mm
MS796 **274** 1m. multicoloured 2·25 2·25

275 Heydar Aliyev Palace

2011. Heydar Aliyev Palace, Nakhchivan
797 **275** 60q. multicoloured 4·75 4·75

276 Behbud aga Shakhtakhtinsky

2011. Anniversaries. 130th Birth Anniv of Behbud aga Shakhtakhtinsky (politician) (No. 798) or 90th Anniv of International Treaty of Kars (No. 799). Multicoloured.
798 60q. Type **276** 4·75 4·75
799 60q. Map of Azerbaijan at time of treaty 4·75 4·75

277 Chrysanthemums

2011. Chrysanthemums. Multicoloured.
800 10q. Type **277** 85 85
801 20q. Chrysanthemums (different) 1·75 1·75

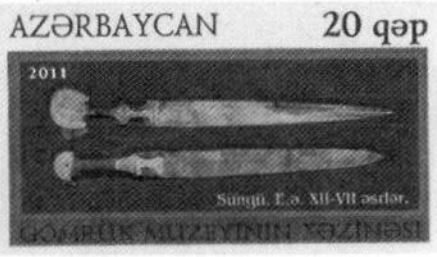

278 Two Bayonets

2011. Customs Museum Exhibits. Multicoloured.

802	20q. Type **278**	90	90
803	20q. Curved poniard and decorated sheath	90	90
804	20q. Poniard, metal sheath with chain and detail of poniard handle	90	90
805	20q. Wide decorated bladed knife with decorative sheath	90	90
806	20q. Dagger and sheath	90	90
807	20q. Decorated rifle and pistol with tassel	90	90
808	20q. Short barreled rifle	90	90
809	20q. Rifle with inlaid stock and powder flask	90	90
810	60q. Gold-coloured metal belt with solid rectangular links and large three piece buckle	2·50	2·50
811	60q. Bronze-coloured metal belt with solid vertical links and three piece buckle, all inlaid with black decorations	2·50	2·50
812	60q. Wide leather belt with coins and large buckle with raised decoration	2·50	2·50
813	60q. Cylindrical metal snuff box, with five suspended medallions and chain	2·50	2·50
814	60q. Bronze-coloured metal belt with solid interlocking links and raised circular buckle	2·50	2·50
815	60q. Two bronze animal statues, the left carrying two figures, the right, one figure	2·50	2·50
816	60q. Lute with tassels	2·50	2·50
817	60q. Five-headed metal dog and mounted horse-like statues	2·50	2·50

279 Order of Heydar Aliyev

2011. Orders of the Republic of Azerbaijan. Multicoloured.

818	60q. Type **279**	2·50	2·50
819	60q. Gold Star medal	2·50	2·50
820	60q. Order of Independence	2·50	2·50
821	60q. Order of Şah Ismayil	2·50	2·50
822	60q. Order of Azerbaijan Flag	2·50	2·50
823	60q. Order of Honour	2·50	2·50
824	60q. Order of Glory	2·50	2·50
825	60q. Order of Friendship	2·50	2·50
825	60q. Order of Service to Motherland	2·50	2·50

280 Nizami Ganjavi

2011. 870th Birth Anniv of Nizami Ganjavi (poet). Multicoloured.

827	30q. Type **280**	1·25	1·25
828	30q. Nizami Ganjavi, facing left	1·25	1·25

281 Clasped Hands and Emblem

2011. 20th Anniv of Regional Communication Community (RCC)

829	**281**	50q. multicoloured	2·25	2·25

282 Anniversary Emblem

2011. 20th Anniv of Community of Independent States (CIS)

830	**282**	60q. multicoloured	2·50	2·50

283 National Coat of Arms

2011. 20th Anniv of Independence. Multicoloured.

831	1m. Type **283**	1·90	1·90
832	1m. National flag	1·90	1·90
833	1m. National anthem	1·90	1·90
834	1m. Map of Azerbaijan	1·90	1·90
MS835	74×108 mm. 2m. National flag and map	3·75	3·75
MS836	74×108 mm. 2m. Heydar Aliyev (president 1993-2003)	3·75	

284 Emblem and UN Building, New York

2011. Azerbaijan Candidate for the United Nations Security Council

837	**284**	60q. multicoloured	2·50	2·50

285 *Circaetus gallicus* (short-toed snake eagle)

2011. Endangered Species. Short-toed Snake Eagle (*Circaetus gallicus*). Multicoloured.

838	20q. Type **285**	90	90
839	30q. Pair and chick on nest	1·25	1·25
840	50q. Pair and fledgling on nest	2·25	2·25
841	60q. Diving for snake	2·50	2·50
MS842	180×130mm. Nos. 838/41, each×2	13·00	13·00
MS843	105×140 mm. Nos. 838/41	6·50	6·50

286 National Flag Square

2011. Ninth November, National Flag Day

844	**286**	30q. multicoloured	1·25	1·25

287 Chestnut Garabagh Horse

2011. Garabagh Horses. Multicoloured.

845	10q. Type **287**	85	85
846	20q. Palomino	1·25	1·25
847	30q. Yellow dun	1·25	1·25
848	50q. Bay	2·25	2·25

288 Abbas Zamanov

2011. Birth Centenary of Abbas Zamanov (literary critic)

849	**288**	60q. multicoloured	2·50	2·50

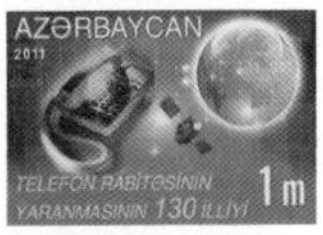

289 Telephone, Satellite and Globe

2011. 130th Anniv of Telephone Communication in Azerbaijan

850	**289**	1m. multicoloured	1·90	1·90

290 Shir Pai Puppy

2011. Dogs. Multicoloured.

MS851	105×105 mm. Puppies. 10q. Type **290**; 20q. Dalmatian; 30q. Labrador; 40q. Doberman; 50q. Chow Chow; 60q. German shepherd	3·75	3·75
MS852	70×75 mm. 1m. Caucasian Shepherd dogs (mother and two puppies)	1·90	1·90

291 Team Members

2011. Rabita Baku Volleyball Club - Fédération Internationale de Volleyball (FIVB) World Champions, 2011. Sheet 102×110 mm

MS853	**291** 1m. multicoloured	90	90

292 Dragon

2012. Chinese New Year. Year of the Dragon

854	**292**	20q. multicoloured	2·25	2·25

293 Anniversary Emblem

2012. 20th Anniv of Central Bank of Azerbaijan

855	**293**	50q. multicoloured	90	90

294 Bahruz Kengerli

2012. 120th Birth Anniv of Bahruz Kengerli (artist)

856	**294**	20q. multicoloured	90	90

295 Beach on Caspian Sea

2012. Europa. Visit Azerbaijan. Multicoloured.

857	20q. Type **295**	90	90
858	60q. Skiing	1·90	1·90
MS859	86×61 mm. 1m. Baku International Airport (vert)	2·50	2·50

Pt. 9

AZORES

A group of islands in the Atlantic Ocean.

1868. 1000 reis = 1 milreis.
1912. 100 centavos = 1 escudo.
2002. 100 cents = 1 euro.

NOTE. Except where otherwise stated, Nos. 1/393 are all stamps of Portugal optd **ACORES**.

1868. Curved value labels. Imperf.

1	**14**	5r. black	£4250	£2500
2	**14**	10r. yellow	£1800	£12000
3	**14**	20r. bistre	£250	£200
4	**14**	50r. green	£250	£200
5	**14**	80r. orange	£275	£225
6	**14**	100r. purple	£275	£225

1868. Curved value labels. Perf.

7	5r. black	85·00	85·00
9	10r. yellow	£110	85·00
10	20r. bistre	85·00	75·00
11	25r. pink	85·00	13·00
12	50r. green	£250	£225
13	80r. orange	£250	£225
14	100r. lilac	£250	£225
16	120r. blue	£225	£140
17	240r. lilac	£750	£475

1871. Straight value labels.

38	**15**	5r. black	16·00	10·50
39	**15**	10r. yellow	65·00	40·00
73	**15**	10r. green	£100	80·00
29	**15**	15r. brown	21·00	19·00
31	**15**	20r. bistre	36·00	21·00
109	**15**	20r. red	£170	£140
32	**15**	25r. pink	21·00	5·00
33	**15**	50r. green	£110	40·00
54	**15**	50r. blue	£190	£100
101b	**15**	80r. orange	90·00	70·00
103	**15**	100r. mauve	70·00	60·00
25	**15**	120r. blue	£200	£170
49	**15**	150r. blue	£225	£190
104	**15**	150r. yellow	70·00	60·00
26	**15**	240r. lilac	£1100	£800
50	**15**	300r. lilac	£110	70·00
94	**15**	1000r. black	£170	£140

1880

58	**16**	5r. black	29·00	12·50
60	**17**	25r. grey	£170	50·00
61	**16**	25r. grey	65·00	10·00
61b	**16**	25r. brown	65·00	10·00
67	**16**	50r. blue	£200	55·00

1882

136	**19**	5r. grey	17·00	6·25
125	**19**	10r. green	34·00	15·00
139	**19**	20r. red	38·00	20·00
126	**19**	25r. brown	34·00	5·00
141	**19**	25r. mauve	38·00	3·25
142	**19**	50r. blue	30·00	5·00
128	**19**	500r. black	£200	£180
129	**19**	500r. mauve	£170	£110

1894. Prince Henry the Navigator.

143	**32**	5r. orange	3·75	3·25
144	**32**	10r. red	3·75	3·25
145	**32**	15r. brown	4·75	4·25
146	**32**	20r. lilac	5·00	4·50
147	**32**	25r. green	5·50	4·75
148	**32**	50r. blue	13·50	7·25
149	**32**	75r. red	25·00	10·00
150	**32**	80r. green	29·00	11·00
151	**32**	100r. brown on buff	29·00	8·75
152	**32**	150r. red	39·00	29·00
153	**32**	300r. blue on buff	45·00	32·00
154	**32**	500r. purple	85·00	48·00
155	**32**	1000r. black on buff	£180	90·00

1895. St. Anthony of Padua.

156	**35**	2½r. black	3·25	1·30
157	-	5r. orange	10·50	3·25
158	-	10r. mauve	10·50	4·75
159	-	15r. brown	16·00	7·25
160	-	20r. grey	18·00	10·50
161	-	25r. purple and green	11·00	3·25
162	**37**	50r. brown and blue	37·00	16·00
163	**37**	75r. brown and red	55·00	45·00
164	**37**	80r. brown and green	60·00	50·00
165	**37**	100r. black and brown	60·00	46·00
166	-	150r. red and brown	£130	£110
167	-	200r. blue and brown	£130	£110
168	-	300r. black and brown	£160	£120
169	-	500r. brown & green	£225	£160
170	-	1000r. lilac and green	£375	£275

1898. Vasco da Gama stamps as Nos. 378/385 of Portugal but inscr "ACORES".

171	2½r. green	3·75	1·40
172	5r. red	3·75	1·70
173	10r. purple	7·50	3·25

174		25r. green	7·50	3·25
175		50r. blue	11·00	10·00
176		75r. brown	23·00	15·00
177		100r. brown	29·00	16·00
178		150r. bistre	46·00	32·00

1906. "King Carlos" key-type inscr "ACORES" and optd with letters **A**, **H** and **PD** in three of the corners.

179	**S**	2½r. grey	45	40
180	**S**	5r. orange	45	40
181	**S**	10r. green	45	40
182	**S**	20r. lilac	75	55
183	**S**	25r. red	75	40
184	**S**	50r. blue	6·75	5·00
185	**S**	75r. brown on yellow	2·30	1·40
186	**S**	100r. blue on blue	2·30	1·40
187	**S**	200r. purple on pink	2·40	1·40
188	**S**	300r. blue on pink	7·25	6·00
189	**S**	500r. black on blue	17·00	15·00

7 King Manoel

1910

190	**7**	2½r. lilac	50	40
191	**7**	5r. black	50	40
192	**7**	10r. green	50	40
193	**7**	15r. brown	1·00	70
194	**7**	20r. red	1·40	1·10
195	**7**	25r. brown	50	50
196	**7**	50r. blue	3·25	1·70
197	**7**	75r. brown	3·25	1·70
198	**7**	80r. grey	3·25	1·70
199	**7**	100r. brown on green	5·25	4·00
200	**7**	200r. green on pink	5·25	4·00
201	**7**	300r. black on blue	3·25	3·00
202	**7**	500r. brown and olive	10·50	11·00
203	**7**	1000r. black and blue	24·00	20·00

1910. Optd **REPUBLICA**.

204		2½r. lilac	40	35
205		5r. black	40	35
206		10r. green	45	35
207		15r. brown	2·00	1·40
208b		20r. red	2·00	1·40
209		25r. brown	40	30
210a		50r. blue	1·40	1·30
211		75r. brown	1·50	1·00
212		80r. grey	1·50	1·00
213		100r. brown on green	1·40	1·10
214		200r. green on orange	1·40	1·10
215		300r. black on blue	4·00	2·50
216		500r. brown and green	4·75	3·50
217		1000r. black and blue	12·00	7·00

1911. Vasco da Gama stamps of Azores optd **REPUBLICA**, some surch also.

218		2½r. green	70	50
219		15r. on 5r. red	70	50
220		25r. green	70	50
221		50r. blue	2·40	1·60
222		75r. brown	2·00	1·90
223		80r. on 150r. brown	2·10	2·00
224		100r. brown	2·40	2·10
225		1000r. on 10r. purple	22·00	16·00

1911. Postage Due stamps optd or surch **REPUBLICA ACORES**.

226	**D48**	5r. black	1·40	1·20
227	**D48**	10r. mauve	3·00	1·20
228	**D48**	20r. orange	5·75	4·00
229	**D48**	200r. brown on buff	25·00	22·00
230	**D48**	300r. on 50r. grey	24·00	21·00
231	**D48**	500r. on 100r. red on pink	24·00	20·00

1912. "Ceres" type.

250	**56**	¼c. brown	60	45
273	**56**	½c. black	60	60
252	**56**	1c. green	1·20	85
274	**56**	1c. brown	60	60
254	**56**	1½c. brown	1·20	85
255	**56**	1½c. green	60	60
256	**56**	2c. red	85	70
257	**56**	2c. orange	60	60
258	**56**	2½c. lilac	85	70
259	**56**	3c. red	60	60
278	**56**	3c. blue	45	35
260	**56**	3½c. green	60	60
261	**56**	4c. green	60	60
401	**56**	4c. orange	75	60
262	**56**	5c. blue	85	70
280	**56**	5c. brown	60	60
264	**56**	6c. purple	60	60
282	**56**	6c. brown	65	55
403	**56**	6c. red	50	35
265	**56**	7½c. brown	7·25	4·00
266	**56**	7½c. blue	2·00	1·80
267	**56**	8c. grey	85	70
283	**56**	8c. green	85	60
284	**56**	8c. orange	1·10	1·00
268	**56**	10c. brown	7·25	3·00
285	**56**	10c. red	60	60
286	**56**	12c. blue	3·00	1·90
287	**56**	12c. green	1·00	80
288	**56**	13½c. blue	3·00	1·90
249	**56**	14c. blue on yellow	2·50	2·50
269	**56**	15c. purple	90	70
289	**56**	15c. black	60	60
290	**56**	16c. blue	1·00	95
243	**56**	20c. brown on green	13·50	7·75
291	**56**	20c. brown	1·00	80
292	**56**	20c. green	1·30	1·00
293	**56**	20c. drab	85	70
294	**56**	24c. blue	1·00	65
295	**56**	25c. pink	75	60
244	**56**	30c. brown on pink	85·00	65·00
245	**56**	30c. brown on yellow	2·50	2·50
296	**56**	30c. brown	2·10	1·80
406	**56**	32c. green	3·50	2·40
298	**56**	36c. red	90	70
299	**56**	40c. blue	1·10	70
300	**56**	40c. brown	2·00	1·10
407	**56**	40c. green	1·90	95
408	**56**	48c. pink	4·50	3·75
246	**56**	50c. orange on orange	7·00	3·00
247	**56**	50c. orange on yellow	7·00	3·00
302	**56**	50c. yellow	2·00	1·60
410	**56**	50c. red	6·00	4·50
303	**56**	60c. blue	2·00	1·60
304	**56**	64c. blue	5·25	2·40
411	**56**	64c. red	6·00	4·50
305	**56**	75c. pink	5·50	4·25
412	**56**	75c. red	6·00	4·50
306	**56**	80c. purple	2·75	2·20
307	**56**	80c. lilac	3·00	2·10
413	**56**	80c. green	6·00	3·75
308	**56**	90c. blue	2·75	2·20
309	**56**	96c. red	8·25	3·75
248	**56**	1e. green on blue	7·75	6·50
310	**56**	1e. lilac	2·75	2·20
314	**56**	1e. purple	4·00	3·50
414	**56**	1e. red	55·00	36·00
311	**56**	1e.10 brown	3·00	2·20
312	**56**	1e.20 green	3·50	2·20
315	**56**	1e.20 buff	9·00	6·50
415	**56**	1e.25 blue	3·50	3·00
316	**56**	1e.50 purple	10·50	7·00
317	**56**	1e.50 lilac	9·25	7·25
400	**56**	1e.60 blue	5·25	2·20
313	**56**	2e. green	11·50	7·00
319	**56**	2e.40 green	80·00	50·00
320	**56**	3e. pink	90·00	55·00
321	**56**	3e.20 green	10·50	10·50
322	**56**	5e. green	20·00	11·00
323	**56**	10e. pink	55·00	30·00
324	**56**	20e. blue	£130	90·00

1925. C. C. Branco Centenary.

325	**65**	2c. orange	25	25
326	**65**	3c. green	25	25
327	**65**	4c. blue	25	25
328	**65**	5c. red	25	25
329	-	10c. blue	25	25
330	-	16c. orange	40	30
331	**67**	25c. red	40	30
332	-	32c. green	60	55
333	**67**	40c. black and green	60	55
334	**67**	48c. purple	1·30	1·30
335	-	50c. green	1·30	1·10
336	-	64c. brown	1·30	1·10
337	-	75c. grey	1·30	1·10
338	**67**	80c. brown	1·30	1·10
339	-	96c. red	1·50	1·30
340	-	1e.50 blue on blue	1·50	1·30
341	**67**	1e.60 blue	1·70	1·50
342	-	2e. green on green	2·75	2·40
343	-	2e.40 red on orange	3·75	2·50
344	-	3e.20 black on green	6·50	5·75

1926. First Independence Issue.

345	**76**	2c. black and orange	45	35
346	-	3c. black and blue	45	35
347	**76**	4c. black and green	45	35
348	-	5c. black and brown	45	35
349	**76**	6c. black and orange	45	35
350	-	15c. black and green	80	75
351	**77**	20c. black and violet	80	75
352	-	25c. black and red	80	75
353	**77**	32c. black and green	80	75
354	-	40c. black and brown	80	75
355	-	50c. black and olive	1·80	1·70
356	-	75c. black and red	1·90	1·80
357	-	1e. black and violet	2·40	2·30
358	-	4e.50 black and green	9·50	9·50

1927. Second Independence Issue.

359	**80**	2c. black and brown	35	35
360	-	3c. black and blue	35	35
361	**80**	4c. black and orange	35	35
362	-	5c. black and brown	35	35
363	-	6c. black and brown	35	35
364	-	15c. black and brown	45	35
365	**80**	25c. black and grey	1·70	1·70
366	-	32c. black and green	1·70	1·70
367	-	40c. black and green	95	95
368	-	96c. black and red	4·25	4·00
369	-	1e.60 black and blue	4·50	4·25
370	-	4e.50 black and yellow	11·50	11·50

1928. Third Independence Issue.

371		2c. black and blue	45	35
372	**84**	3c. black and green	45	35
373	-	4c. black and red	45	35
374	-	5c. black and olive	45	35
375	-	6c. black and brown	45	35
376	**84**	15c. black and grey	85	80
377	-	16c. black and purple	95	95
378	-	25c. black and blue	95	95
379	-	32c. black and green	1·00	1·00
380	-	40c. black and brown	1·00	1·00
381	-	50c. black and red	2·20	2·10
382	**84**	80c. black and grey	2·20	2·10
383	-	96c. black and red	4·25	4·00
384	-	1e. black and mauve	4·25	4·00
385	-	1e.60 black and blue	4·25	4·00
386	-	4e.50 black and yellow	11·00	10·50

1929. "Ceres" type surch **ACORES** and new value.

387	**56**	4c. on 25c. pink	95	95
388	**56**	4c. on 60c. blue	1·90	1·80
389	**56**	10c. on 25c. pink	1·90	1·80
390	**56**	12c. on 25c. pink	1·90	1·80
391	**56**	15c. on 25c. pink	1·90	1·80
392	**56**	20c. on 25c. pink	3·25	3·00
393	**56**	40c. on 1e.10 brown	6·25	6·00

14 10r. Stamp of 1868

1980. 112th Anniv of First Azores Stamps.

416	**14**	6e.50 black, yellow & red	45	25
417	-	19e.50 blk, purple & blue	1·50	1·00
MS418 140×115 mm. Nos. 416/17 (sold at 30e.)			6·75	6·75

DESIGN: 19e.50, 100r. stamp of 1868.

15 Map of the Azores

1980. World Tourism Conference, Manila, Philippines. Multicoloured.

419		50c. Type **15**	20	15
420		1e. Church	30	20
421		5e. Windmill	75	40
422		6e.50 Traditional costume	95	45
423		8e. Coastal scene	1·40	65
424		30e. Coastal village	2·75	1·10

16 St. Peter's Cavalcade, Sao Miguel Island

1981. Europa. Folklore.

425	**16**	22e. multicoloured	1·90	95
MS426 140×116 mm. No. 425×2			8·50	8·50

17 Bulls attacking Spanish Soldiers

1981. 400th Anniv of Battle of Salga. Multicoloured.

427		8e.50 Type **17**	80	10
428		33e.50 Friar Don Pedro leading attack	3·00	1·40

18 *Myosotis azorica*

1981. Regional Flowers. Multicoloured.

429		4e. Type **18**	20	10
430		7e. *Tolpis azorica*	45	30
431		8e.50 *Ranunculus azoricus*	60	30
432		10e. *Lactuca watsoniana*	85	30
433		12e.50 *Hypericum foliosum*	40	10
434		20e. *Platanthera micranta*	1·00	70
435		27e. *Vicia dennesiana*	1·90	1·20
436		30e. *Rubus hochstetterorum*	1·20	50
437		33e.50 *Azorina vidalii*	2·10	1·40
438		37e.50 *Vaccinium cylindraceum*	1·70	1·00
439		50e. *Laurus azorica*	2·75	1·50
440		100e. *Juniperus brevifolia*	3·50	1·60

19 Embarkation of the Heroes of Mindelo

1982. Europa. Multicoloured.

445	**19**	33e.50 multicoloured	2·75	1·40
MS446 140×113 mm. No. 445×3			21·00	21·00

20 Chapel of the Holy Ghost

1982. Regional Architecture. Multicoloured.

447		27e. Type **20**	2·00	1·20
448		33e.50 Chapel of the Holy Ghost (different)	2·75	1·60

21 Geothermal Power Station, Pico Vermeilho, São Miguel

1983. Europa.

449	**21**	37e.50 multicoloured	2·75	1·10
MS450 114×140 mm. No. 449×3			23·00	23·00

22 Flag of Azores

1983. Flag.

451	**22**	12e.50 multicoloured	1·10	20

23 Two "Holy Ghost" Jesters, São Miguel

1984. Traditional Costumes. Multicoloured.

452		16e. Type **23**	85	20
453		51e. Two women wearing Terceira cloak	3·00	2·10

23a Bridge

1984. Europa.

454	**23a**	51e. multicoloured	4·00	1·90
MS455 114×139 mm. No. 454×3			20·00	20·00

24 *Megabombus ruderatus*

1984. Insects (1st series). Multicoloured.

456 16e. Type **24** 50 10
457 35e. Large white (butterfly) 1·50 1·00
458 40e. *Chrysomela banksi* (leaf beetle) 2·20 1·00
459 51e. *Phlogophora interrupta* (moth) 2·50 1·60

1985. Insects (2nd series). As T **24**. Multicoloured.

460 20e. *Polyspilla polyspilla* (leaf beetle) 55 10
461 40e. *Sphaerophoria nigra* (hover fly) 1·60 85
462 46e. Clouded yellow (butterfly) 2·30 1·20
463 60e. Southern grayling (butterfly) 2·50 1·40

25 Drummer

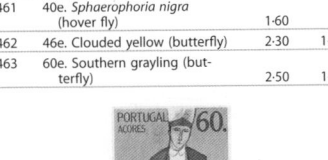

1985. Europa. Music Year.

464 **25** 60e. multicoloured 4·00 1·70
MS465 140×114 mm. No. 464×3 25·00 25·00

26 Jeque

1985. Traditional Boats. Multicoloured.

466 40e. Type **26** 2·10 1·20
467 60e. Bote 2·75 1·50

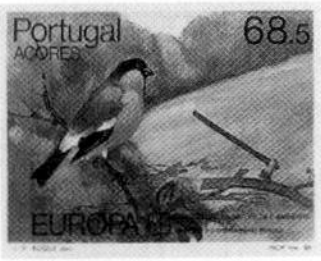

27 Northern Bullfinch

1986. Europa.

468 **27** 68e.50 multicoloured 4·75 1·90
MS469 140×114 mm. No. 468×3 21·00 21·00

28 Alto das Covas Fountain, Terceira

1986. Regional Architecture. Drinking Fountains. Multicoloured.

470 22e.50 Type **28** 90 20
471 52e.50 Faja de Baixo, Sao Miguel 2·75 1·40
472 68e.50 Portoes de S. Pedro, Terceira 4·00 1·80
473 100e. Agua d'Alto, Sao Miguel 5·50 1·60

29 Ox Cart, Santa Maria

1986. Traditional Carts. Multicoloured.

474 25e. Type **29** 90 10
475 75e. Ram cart, Sao Miguel 4·00 2·30

30 Regional Assembly Building (Correia Fernandes and Luis Miranda)

1987. Europa. Architecture.

476 **30** 74e.50 multicoloured 4·25 1·90
MS477 140×114 mm. No. 476×4 25·00 25·00

31 Santa Cruz, Graciosa

1987. Windows and Balconies. Multicoloured.

478 51e. Type **31** 2·50 1·40
479 74e.50 Ribeira Grande, São Miguel 3·00 1·40

32 A. C. Read's Curtiss NC-4 Flying Boat, 1919

1987. Historic Airplane Landings in the Azores. Multicoloured.

480 25e. Type **32** 75 10
481 57e. E. F. Christiansen's Dornier Do-X flying boat, 1932 2·75 1·90
482 74e.50 Italo Balbo's Savoia Marchetti S-55X flying boat, 1933 4·00 1·70
483 125e. Charles Lindbergh's Lockheed 8 Sirius seaplane *Tingmissartoq*, 1933 4·50 2·40

33 19th-century Mule-drawn Omnibus

1988. Europa. Transport and Communications.

484 **33** 80e. multicoloured 5·00 1·50
MS485 140×112 mm. As No. 484 ×4 but with cream background 25·00 25·00

34 Wood Pigeon

1988. Nature Protection. Birds (1st series). Multicoloured.

486 27e. Type **34** 90 30
487 60e. Eurasian woodcock 2·75 1·40
488 80e. Roseate tern 3·00 1·60
489 100e. Common buzzard 3·75 1·60

See also Nos. 492/5 and 500/3.

35 Azores Arms

1988. Coats-of-arms. Multicoloured.

490 55e. Type **35** 2·30 1·20
491 80e. Bettencourt family arms 3·00 1·60

1989. Nature Protection (2nd series). Goldcrest. As T **34**. Multicoloured.

492 30e. Goldcrest perched on branch 1·30 40
493 30e. Pair 1·30 40
494 30e. Goldcrest on nest 1·30 40
495 30e. Goldcrest with outspread wings 1·30 40

36 Boy in Boat

1989. Europa. Children's Games and Toys.

496 **36** 80e. multicoloured 3·75 1·60
MS497 139×112 mm. 80e. ×2, Type **36**; 80e. ×2, Boy with toy boat 25·00 25·00

37 Pioneers

1989. 550th Anniv of Portuguese Settlement in Azores. Multicoloured.

498 29e. Type **37** 85 30
499 87e. Settler breaking land 3·50 1·90

1990. Nature Protection (3rd series). Northern Bullfinch. As T **34**. Multicoloured.

500 32e. Two bullfinches 1·70 55
501 32e. Bullfinch on branch 1·70 55
502 32e. Bullfinch landing on twig 1·70 55
503 32e. Bullfinch on nest 1·70 55

38 Vasco da Gama P.O.

1990. Europa. P.O. Buildings.

504 **38** 80e. multicoloured 3·00 1·50
MS505 139×111 mm. 80e. ×2, Type **38**; 80e. ×2, Maia Post Office 23·00 23·00

39 Cart Maker

1990. Traditional Occupations. Multicoloured.

506 5e. Type **39** 20 15
507 10e. Viol maker 20 15
508 32e. Potter 80 40
509 35e. Making roof tiles 75 30
510 38e. Carpenter 75 35
511 60e. Tinsmith 2·30 1·20
512 65e. Laying pavement mosaics 1·80 1·10
513 70e. Quarrying 2·00 1·20
514 85e. Basket maker 1·90 1·00
515 100e. Cooper 3·25 1·80
516 110e. Shaping stones 3·00 1·40
517 120e. Boat builders 2·50 1·20

40 *Hermes* Spaceplane

1991. Europa. Europe in Space.

520 **40** 80e. multicoloured 5·25 4·00
MS521 140×112 mm. 80e. ×2, Type **40**; 80e. ×2, *Sanger* spaceplane 20·00 20·00

41 *Helena* (schooner)

1991. Inter-island Transport. Multicoloured.

522 35e. Type **41** 75 25
523 60e. Beech Model 18 airplane, 1947 1·50 85
524 80e. *Cruzeiro do Canal* (ferry), 1987 2·30 1·40
525 110e. British Aerospace ATP airliner, 1991 2·75 1·60

42 *Santa Maria* off Azores

1992. Europa. 500th Anniv of Discovery of America by Columbus.

526 **42** 85e. multicoloured 2·40 1·10

43 *Insulano* (steamer, 1868)

1992. The Empresa Insulana de Navegacao Shipping Fleet. Multicoloured.

527 38e. Type **43** 75 30
528 65e. *Carvalho Araujo* (ferry, 1930) 1·50 1·00
529 85e. *Funchal* (ferry, 1961) 1·90 1·20
530 120e. *Terceirense* (freighter, 1948) 2·50 1·40

44 Ox-mill

1993. Traditional Grinders. Multicoloured.

531 42e. Type **44** 75 35
532 130e. Hand-mill 3·00 1·80

45 *Two Sirens at the Entrance of a Grotto* (Antonio Dacosta)

1993. Europa. Contemporary Art.

533 **45** 90e. multicoloured 2·75 1·20
MS534 140×112 mm. 90e. ×2, Type **45**; 90e. ×2, *Acorinan III* 15·00 15·00

46 Main Entrance, Praia da Vitoria Church, Terceira

1993. Doorways. Multicoloured.

535 42e. Type **46** 75 35
536 70e. South door, Praia da Vitoria Church 1·40 85
537 90e. Main door, Ponta Delgada Church, Sao Miguel 1·80 1·10
538 130e. South door, Ponta Delgada Church 2·75 1·40

47 Floral Decoration, Our Lady of Sorrows, Caloura, Sao Miguel

1994. Tiles. Multicoloured.

539 40e. Type **47** 60 35
540 70e. Decoration of crosses, Our Lady of Sorrows, Caloura, Sao Miguel 1·40 80
541 100e. *Adoration of the Wise Men*, Our Lady of Hope Monastery, Ponta Delgada, Sao Miguel 1·80 1·10
542 150e. *St. Bras* (altar frontal), Our Lady of Anjos, Santa Maria 2·75 1·70

48 Monkey and Explorer with Model Caravel

1994. Europa. Discoveries. Multicoloured.

543 **48** 100e. multicoloured 2·20 1·10
MS544 140×112 mm. 100e. ×2, Type **48**; 100e. ×2, Armadilo and explorer with model caravel 12·50 12·50

49 Doorway, St. Barbaras Church, Cedros, Faial

1994. Manoeline Architecture. Multicoloured.

545	45e. Type **49**	65	35
546	140e. Window, Ribeira Grande, Sao Miguel	2·40	1·60

50 Aristides Moreira da Motta

1995. Centenary of Decree decentralizing Government of the Azores and Madeira Islands. Pro-autonomy activists. Multicoloured.

547	42e. Type **50**	65	35
548	130e. Gil Mont' Alverne de Sequeira	2·20	1·40

51 Santana Palace, Ponta Delgada

1995. Architecture of Sao Miguel. Multicoloured.

549	45e. Type **51**	65	35
550	80e. Chapel of Our Lady of the Victories, Furnas	1·30	75
551	95e. Hospital, Ponta Delgada	1·50	80
552	135e. Ernesto do Canto's villa, Furnas	1·80	1·10

52 Contendas Lighthouse, Terceira

1996. Lighthouses. Multicoloured.

553	47e. Type **52**	60	35
554	78e. Molhe Lighthouse, Sao Miguel	1·30	85
555	98e. Arnel Lighthouse, Sao Miguel	1·50	1·00
556	140e. Santa Clara Lighthouse, Sao Miguel	2·10	1·30
MS557	110×140 mm. 200e. Ponta da Barca Lighthouse, Graciosa	3·00	3·00

53 Natalia Correia (poet)

1996. Europa. Famous Women.

558	**53** 98e. multicoloured	1·70	85
MS559	140×112 mm. No. 558×3	5·75	5·75

54 Bird eating Grapes (St. Peter's Church, Ponta Delgada)

1997. Gilded Wooden Altarpieces. Multicoloured.

560	49e. Type **54**	65	35
561	80e. Cherub (St. Peter of Alcantara Convent, Sao Roque)	1·20	55
562	100e. Cherub with wings (All Saints Church, Jesuit College, Ponta Delgada)	1·40	1·00
563	140e. Caryatid (St. Joseph's Church, Ponta Delgada)	2·00	1·20

55 Island of the Seven Cities

1997. Europa. Tales and Legends.

564	**55** 100e. multicoloured	1·70	85
MS565	140×106 mm. No. 564×3	5·50	5·50

56 Emperor and Empress and young Bulls (Festival of the Holy Spirit)

1998. Europa. National Festivals.

566	**56** 100e. multicoloured	1·60	85
MS567	140×109 No. 566×3	4·75	4·75

57 Spotted Dolphin

1998. "Expo '98" World's Fair, Lisbon. Marine Life. Multicoloured.

568	50e. Type **57**	65	35
569	140e. Sperm whale (79×30 mm)	1·90	1·20

58 Mt. Pico Nature Reserve

1999. Europa. Parks and Gardens.

570	**58** 100e. multicoloured	1·40	85
MS571	154×109 mm. No. 570×3	4·75	4·75

59 *Emigrants* (Domingos Rebelo)

1999. Paintings. Multicoloured.

572	51e. Type **59**	65	35
573	95e. *Portrait of Vitorino Nemesio* (Antonio Dacosta) (vert)	1·30	85
574	100e. *Cattle loose on the Alto das Covas* (Ze van der Hagen Bretao)	1·30	85
575	140e. *Vila Franca Island* (Duarte Maia)	1·70	1·20

60 "Building Europe"

2000. Europa.

576	**60** 100e. multicoloured	1·70	95
MS577	154×108 mm. No. 576×3	5·25	5·25

61 Fishermen retrieving Mail Raft

2000. History of Mail Delivery in the Azores. Multicoloured.

578	85e. Type **61**	1·30	80
579	140e. Zeppelin airship dropping mail sacks	2·10	1·40

62 Coast Line

2001. Europa. Water Resources.

580	**62** 105e. multicoloured	1·70	95
MS581	140×110 mm. No. 580×3	5·25	5·25

63 Arch and Town

2001. UNESCO World Heritage Site, Angra do Heroismo. Multicoloured.

582	53e. Type **63**	70	35
583	85e. Monument and town	1·30	85
584	140e. Balcony and view over town	2·00	1·30
MS585	140×112 mm. 350e. Map of town	5·00	5·00

64 Clown

2002. Europa. Circus.

586	**64** 54c. multicoloured	1·70	1·90
MS587	140×110 mm. No. 586×3	5·00	5·00

65 Faial Island, Azores

2002. Windmills. Multicoloured.

588	43c. Type **65**	1·10	70
589	54c. Onze-Lieve-Vrouw-Lombeek, Roosdaal	1·50	85

Stamps of a similar design were issued by Belgium.

66 Birds (Sebastiao Rodrigues)

2003. Europa. Poster Art.

590	**66** 55c. multicoloured	1·80	95
MS591	140×113 mm. No. 591×2	3·25	3·25

67 Pineapple Groves

2003. Sao Miguel Island. Multicoloured.

592	30c. Type **67**	80	30
593	43c. Vineyards and grapes	1·10	70
594	55c. Date growing	1·40	90
595	70c. Coffee growing	1·80	1·20
MS596	140×112 mm. €1 Dancers and ceramic figure; €2 Fruit and ceramic bird (Espirito Santos festival)	8·00	8·00

68 Figures, Flowers and Island

2004. Europa. Holidays.

597	**68** 56c. multicoloured	1·60	90
MS598	141×112 mm. No. 597×2	3·25	3·25

69 Blue Marlin (*Makaira nigricans*)

2004. Endangered Species. Atlantic Marlin. Multicoloured.

599	30c. Type **69**	80	55
600	30c. Fin, body and tail	80	55
601	30c. White marlin (*Tetrapturus albidus*)	80	55
602	30c. Back and tail	80	55

Nos. 599/602 were issued together, *se-tenant*, forming a composite design.

70 Torresmos (marinated pork)

2005. Europa. Gastronomy. Multicoloured.

603	57c. Type **70**	1·60	90
MS604	125×95 mm. 57c.×2, *Polvo guisado* (octopus)×2	4·25	4·25

71 Cow

2005. Tourism. Multicoloured.

605	30c. Type **71**	70	50
606	30c. Arched window and lake	70	50
607	45c. Decorated house	1·10	75
608	45c. Windmill	1·10	75
609	57c. Whale's tail	1·40	90
610	74c. Pineapple and hot spring	1·80	1·30
MS611	125×95 mm. 30c. Santo Cristo dos Milagres (statue); €1.55 Bird	4·50	4·50

Nos. 605/10 were issued together, *se-tenant*, forming a composite design.

72 Figures standing on Head (Joao Dinis)

2006. Europa. Integration. Winning Entries in ANACED (association for art and creativity by and for people with disabilities) Painting Competition. Multicoloured.

612	60c. Type **72**	1·50	85
MS613	125×95 mm. 60c.×2, One legged figure; Figures with irregular outlines	3·00	3·00

73 Crabs, Lucky Strike

2006. Hydrothermal Springs. Multicoloured.

614	20c. Type **73**	45	30
615	30c. Fish, Lucky Strike	70	45
616	75c. Plumes, Rainbow	1·70	1·10
617	€2 Fish tower, Rainbow	4·50	3·00
MS618	125×95 mm. €2 No. 617	4·75	4·75

74 Mountain

2006. Wine from Pico Island. Multicoloured.

619	30c. Type **74**	70	45
620	60c. Terraces	1·30	85
621	75c. Wine barrel	1·70	1·10
622	€1 Harvesting	2·20	1·50
MS623	125×95 mm. 45c. Young vines; 60c. Harvesting; 75c. Winery; €1 Barrels	6·50	6·50

75 Scarf

2007. Europa. Centenary of Scouting. Multicoloured.

624	61c. Type **75**	1·40	85
MS625 125×95 mm. 61c.×2, Reef knot; Scouts in camp		3·00	3·00

The stamps of **MS**625 form a composite design.

76 Sao Miguel

2007. Windmills. Multicoloured.

626	30c. Type **76**	65	45
627	45c. Sao Jorge	95	65
628	61c. Corvo	1·30	85
629	75c. Blue windmill, Sao Jorge	1·70	1·10
MS630 125×95 mm. 45c. Sao Miguel (different); €2 Red windmill, Sao Jorge		5·50	5·50

77 Capelinhos Volcano

2007. 50th Anniv of Eruption of Capelinhos Volcano, Faial Island. Multicoloured.

631	30c. Type **77**	65	45
632	75c. Erupting volcano and lighthouse	1·70	1·10
MS633 125×95 mm. €2.45 Island showing lighthouse (80×30 mm)		5·75	5·75

The stamp and margin of **MS**633 form a composite design.

78 Envelope as Boat

2008. Europa. The Letter. Multicoloured.

634	61c. Type **78**	1·50	85
MS635 125×95 mm. 61c.×2, Windmill and envelopes; As Type **78**		3·00	3·00

The stamps of **MS**635 each form a composite design.

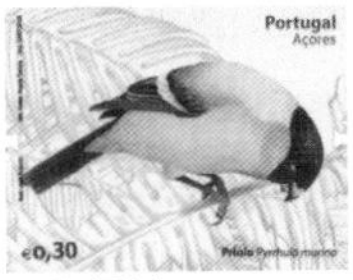

79 Cock Bird

2008. Azores Bullfinch (*Pyrrhula murina*). Multicoloured.

636	30c. Type **79**	75	45
637	61c. Female	1·50	85
638	75c. Male facing right	1·80	1·00
639	€1 Male facing left	2·50	1·40
MS640 Two sheets, each 125×95 mm. (a) €2.45 Head of male eating seed. (b) €2.95 Head of male with open beak		14·00	14·00

The stamps and margins of **MS**640a/b form a composite design.

80 Ponta do Arnel

2008. Lighthouse.

641	**80**	61c. multicoloured	1·50	85

81 Woodcock (Lagoa Comprida)

2009. Biodiversity. Lakes. Multicoloured.

642	32c. Type **81**	95	45
643	68c. Brown butterfly (Lagoa do Caldeirao)	2·10	1·00
644	80c. Dragonfly (Lagoa do Capitao)	2·40	1·20
645	€2 Azores juniper (Lagoinha)	6·00	3·00
MS646 125×95 mm. €2.50 Tessellate moray (80×30 mm)		7·50	7·50
MS647 125×95 mm. €2.50 Tufted duck, teal and capped heron (80×30 mm)		7·50	7·50

82 European Space Agency Satellite Tracking Station, Santa Maria Island, Azores

2009. Europa. Astronomy. Multicoloured.

648	68c. Type **82**	2·10	1·00
MS649 125×95 mm. 68c.×2, Ribeira Grande Astronomical Observatory, Sao Miguel Island, Azores; As Type **82**		4·25	4·25

The stamps and margins of **MS**649 form a composite design.

83 Milho (maize bread)

2009. Bread. Sheet 125×95 mm.

MS650 **83** €2 multicoloured	6·00	6·00

84 Girl

2010. Europa. Children's Books. Multicoloured.

651	68c. Type **84**	2·10	1·00
MS652 125×96 mm. 68c.× 2 King on horseback; As Type **84**		4·25	4·25

85 *Dardanus callidus*

2010. Invertebrates. Multicoloured.

653	32c. Type **85**	95	45
654	68c. *Alicia mirabilis*	2·10	1·00
655	80c. *Orphidiaster orphidianus*	2·40	1·20
MS656 125×95 mm. €2 *Grapsus adscencionis*		6·00	6·00
MS657 125×95 mm. €2 *Sphaerechinus granularis*		6·00	6·00

CHARITY TAX STAMPS

Used on certain days of the year as an additional postal tax on internal letters. The proceeds were devoted to public charities. If one was not affixed in addition to the ordinary postage, postage due stamps were used to collect the deficiency and the fine.

1911. No. 206 optd **ASSISTENCIA**.

C218a	**7**	10r. green	1·50	1·20

1913. No. 252 optd **ASSISTENCIA**.

C250	**56**	1c. green	5·25	4·00

1915. For the Poor. Charity stamp of Portugal optd **ACORES**.

C251	**C58**	1c. red	70	35

1925. No. C251 surch **15 ctvs**.

C325	15c. on 1c. red	1·20	95

1925. Portuguese Army in Flanders issue of Portugal optd **ACORES**.

C345	**C71**	10c. red	1·20	1·20
C346	**C71**	10c. green	1·20	1·20
C347	**C71**	10c. blue	1·20	1·20
C348	**C71**	10c. brown	1·20	1·20

1925. As Marquis de Pombal issue of Portugal, inscr "ACORES".

C349	**C73**	20c. green	1·20	1·20
C350	-	20c. green	1·20	1·20
C351	**C75**	20c. green	1·20	1·20

NEWSPAPER STAMPS

1876. Stamps of Portugal optd **ACORES**.

N146	**N16**	2r. black	7·00	3·25
N150a	**N17**	2½r. brown	6·50	1·90
N150b	**N17**	2½r. green	6·50	1·90

PARCEL POST STAMPS

1921. Stamps of Portugal optd **ACORES**.

P325	**P59**	1c. brown	60	50
P326	**P59**	2c. orange	60	50
P327	**P59**	5c. brown	60	50
P328	**P59**	10c. brown	80	50
P329	**P59**	20c. blue	80	50
P330	**P59**	40c. red	80	50
P331	**P59**	50c. black	1·60	1·10
P332	**P59**	60c. blue	1·60	1·10
P333	**P59**	70c. brown	3·00	2·50
P334	**P59**	80c. blue	3·00	2·50
P335	**P59**	90c. violet	3·00	2·50
P336	**P59**	1e. green	3·00	2·50
P337	**P59**	2e. lilac	4·75	3·75
P338	**P59**	3e. olive	8·50	4·00
P339	**P59**	4e. blue	10·00	4·00
P340	**P59**	5e. lilac	10·50	8·00
P341	**P59**	10e. brown	43·00	24·00

POSTAGE DUE STAMPS

Nos. D179/351 are stamps of Portugal overprinted **ACORES**.

1904

D179	**D49**	5r. brown	1·40	1·20
D180	**D49**	10r. orange	1·50	1·20
D181	**D49**	20r. mauve	2·50	1·40
D182	**D49**	30r. green	2·50	1·90
D183	**D49**	40r. lilac	4·25	2·50
D184	**D49**	50r. red	7·25	4·75
D185	**D49**	100r. blue	9·00	8·75

1911. As last, optd **REPUBLICA**.

D218	5r. brown	80	70
D219	10r. orange	80	70
D220	20r. mauve	1·00	90
D221	30r. green	1·00	90
D222	40r. lilac	1·60	1·20
D223	50r. red	8·50	8·00
D224	100r. blue	3·00	3·00

1918. Value in centavos.

D325	½c. brown	85	80
D326	1c. orange	85	80
D327	2c. purple	85	85
D328	3c. green	85	80
D329	4c. lilac	85	80
D330	5c. red	85	80
D331	10c. blue	85	80

1922

D332	½c. green	40	40
D333	1c. green	65	50
D334	2c. green	65	50
D335	3c. green	1·10	50
D336	8c. green	1·10	50
D337	10c. green	1·10	50
D338	12c. green	1·10	50
D339	16c. green	1·10	50
D340	20c. green	1·10	50
D341	24c. green	1·10	50
D342	32c. green	1·10	50
D343	36c. green	1·10	70
D344	40c. green	1·10	70
D345	48c. green	1·10	70
D346	50c. green	1·10	70
D347	60c. green	1·20	75
D348	72c. green	1·20	75
D349	80c. green	5·50	4·50
D350	1e.20 green	6·25	5·00

1925. Portuguese Army in Flanders.

D351	**D72**	20c. brown	1·20	1·20

1925. As Nos. C349/51, optd **MULTA**.

D352	**D73**	40c. green	1·20	1·20
D353	-	40c. green	1·20	1·20
D354	**D75**	40c. green	1·20	1·20

Pt. 7

BADEN

In S.W. Germany. Formerly a Grand Duchy, now part of the German Federal Republic.

60 kreuzer = 1 gulden.

1

1851. Imperf.

1	**1**	1k. black on buff	£650	£350
8	**1**	1k. black on white	£200	34·00
3	**1**	3k. black on yellow	£325	21·00
9	**1**	3k. black on green	£200	10·50
10	**1**	3k. black on blue	£900	42·00
5	**1**	6k. black on green	£1100	65·00
11	**1**	6k. black on orange	£350	34·00
6	**1**	9k. black on red	£275	32·00

2

1860. Shaded background behind Arms. Perf.

13	**2**	1k. black	£110	37·00
16	**2**	3k. blue	£120	26·00
17	**2**	6k. orange	£140	95·00
22	**2**	6k. blue	£200	£140
19	**2**	9k. red	£350	£250
25	**2**	9k. brown	£140	£170

1862. Uncoloured background behind Arms.

27	1k. black	65·00	19·00
28	3k. red	65·00	5·25
30	6k. blue	15·00	34·00
33	9k. brown	21·00	37·00
36	18k. green	£550	£750
38	30k. orange	42·00	£3000

1868. "K R." instead of "KREUZER".

39	1k. green	5·25	11·50
41	3k. red	3·25	5·25
44	7k. blue	27·00	48·00

RURAL POSTAGE DUE STAMPS

D4

1862

D39	**D4**	1k. black on yellow	6·25	£425
D40	**D4**	3k. black on yellow	3·75	£160
D41	**D4**	12k. black on yellow	48·00	£18000

For later issues of 1947 to 1964 see Germany: Allied Occupation (French Zone).

Pt. 1

BAGHDAD

A city in Iraq. Special stamps issued during British occupation in the War of 1914–18.

1917. 16 annas = 1 rupee.

1917. Various issues of Turkey surch **BAGHDAD IN BRITISH OCCUPATION** and new value in annas. A. Pictorial issues of 1913.

1	**32**	¼a. on 2pa. red	£300	£350
2	**34**	¼a. on 5pa. purple	£200	£225
3	-	½a. on 10pa. green (No. 516)	£1100	£1300
4	**31**	½a. on 10pa. green	£2250	£2500
5	-	1a. on 20pa. red (No. 504)	£750	£850
6	-	2a. on 1pi. blue (No. 518)	£350	£375

B. As last, but optd with small star.

7	1a. on 20pa. red	£500	£550
8	2a. on 1pi. blue	£6000	£6500

C. Postal Jubilee issue.

9	**60**	½a. on 10pa. red	£800	£900
10b	**60**	1a. on 20pa. blue	£1800	£2250
11b	**60**	2a. on 1pi. black & violet	£225	£250

D. Optd with Turkish letter "B".

12	**30**	2a. on 1pi. blue	£850	£1000

E. Optd with star and Arabic date within crescent.

13		½a. on 10pa. green	£200	£225
14		1a. on 20pa. red	£750	£800
15	**23**	1a. on 20pa. red	£800	£900
16	**21**	1a. on 20pa. red (No. N185)	£7000	£9000
17	**30**	2a. on 1pi. blue	£225	£250
18	**21**	2a. on 1pi. blue	£350	£400

F. Optd as last, but with date between star and crescent.

19	**23**	½a. on 10pa. green	£225	£275
20	**60**	½a. on 10pa. red	£350	£375
21	**30**	1a. on 20pa. red	£225	£275
22	**28**	1a. on 20pa. red	£800	£850
23	**15**	1a. on 10pa. on 20pa. red	£400	£425
24	**30**	2a. on 1pi. blue	£350	£400
25	**28**	2a. on 1pi. blue	£2750	£3000

Pt. 1

BAHAMAS

A group of islands in the Br. W. Indies, S.E. of Florida. Self-Government introduced on 7 January 1964. The islands became an independent member of the British Commonwealth on 10 July 1973.

1859. 12 pence = 1 shilling; 20 shillings = 1 pound.
1966. 100 cents = 1 dollar.

1

1859. Imperf.

2	**1**	1d. red	65·00	£1500

2

3

1860. Perf.

33	**1**	1d. red	70·00	15·00
26	**2**	4d. red	£300	60·00
31	**2**	6d. violet	£160	60·00
39ba	**3**	1s. green	8·00	9·50

1883. Surch **FOURPENCE**.

45	**2**	4d. on 6d. violet	£550	£400

5

1884

48	**5**	1d. red	7·50	2·00
52	**5**	2½d. blue	11·00	1·75
53	**5**	4d. yellow	9·50	4·00
54	**5**	6d. mauve	6·00	35·00
56	**5**	5s. green	80·00	90·00
57	**5**	£1 red	£275	£225

6 Queen's Staircase, Nassau

1901

111	**6**	1d. black and red	3·25	3·00
76a	**6**	3d. purple on buff	6·50	8·00
77	**6**	3d. black and brown	2·50	2·25
59	**6**	5d. black and orange	8·50	48·00
78	**6**	5d. black and mauve	3·25	5·50
113	**6**	2s. black and blue	22·00	22·00
61	**6**	3s. black and green	48·00	65·00

7

1902

71	**7**	½d. green	5·00	3·25
62	**7**	1d. red	1·50	1·50
63	**7**	2½d. blue	7·50	1·25
64	**7**	4d. yellow	15·00	60·00
66	**7**	6d. brown	5·00	27·00
67	**7**	1s. black and red	22·00	55·00
69	**7**	5s. purple and blue	70·00	90·00
70	**7**	£1 green and black	£300	£350

8

1912

115	**8**	½d. green	50	40
116	**8**	1d. red	1·00	15
117	**8**	1½d. brown	12·00	1·00
118	**8**	2d. grey	1·50	2·25
119	**8**	2½d. blue	1·00	2·25
120	**8**	3d. purple on yellow	6·50	16·00
121	**8**	4d. yellow	1·50	3·25
122	**8**	6d. brown	70	1·25
123	**8**	1s. black and red	5·00	5·50
124	**8**	5s. purple and blue	42·00	65·00
125	**8**	£1 green and black	£170	£325

1917. Optd **1.1.17.** and Red Cross.

90	**6**	1d. black and red	40	2·00

1918. Optd **WAR TAX** in one line.

96	**8**	½d. green	1·75	1·75
93		1d. black and red	3·50	8·00
97	**8**	1d. red	3·25	35
98	**6**	3d. purple on yellow	1·00	1·50
100	**6**	3d. black and brown	60	4·75
99	**8**	1s. black and red	10·00	4·75

1919. Optd **WAR CHARITY 3.6.18.**

101		1d. black and red	30	2·50

1919. Optd **WAR TAX** in two lines.

102	**8**	½d. green	30	1·25
103	**8**	1d. red	1·50	1·50
105	**6**	3d. black and brown	75	8·00
104	**8**	1s. black and red	27·00	55·00

16

1920. Peace Celebration.

106	**16**	½d. green	1·00	5·50
107	**16**	1d. red	2·75	1·00
108	**16**	2d. grey	2·75	7·50
109	**16**	3d. brown	2·75	9·00
110	**16**	1s. green	15·00	38·00

17 Seal of the Colony

1930. Tercentenary of the Colony.

126	**17**	1d. black and red	3·50	2·75
127	**17**	3d. black and brown	5·50	15·00
128	**17**	5d. black and violet	5·50	15·00
129	**17**	2s. black and blue	18·00	50·00
130	**17**	3s. black and green	48·00	85·00

1931. As T **17**, but without dates at top.

131b	2s. black and blue	14·00	8·50
132a	3s. black and green	12·00	4·50

1935. Silver Jubilee. As T **13** of Antigua.

141	1½d. blue and red	1·00	3·50
142	2½d. brown and blue	5·00	9·50
143	6d. blue and olive	7·00	15·00
144	1s. grey and purple	7·00	14·00

19 Greater Flamingo (in flight)

1935

145	**19**	8d. blue and red	8·00	3·25

1937. Coronation. As T **2** of Aden.

146	½d. green	15	15
147	1½d. brown	40	1·10
148	2½d. blue	55	1·10

20 King George VI

21 Sea Garden, Nassau

1938

149	**20**	½d. green	2·50	1·25
149e	**20**	½d. purple	1·00	3·50
150	**20**	1d. red	8·50	2·00
150ab	**20**	1d. grey	60	70
151	**20**	1½d. brown	1·50	1·25
152	**20**	2d. grey	19·00	3·50
152b	**20**	2d. red	1·00	65
152c	**20**	2d. green	2·00	80
153	**20**	2½d. blue	3·25	1·50
153a	**20**	2½d. violet	1·25	1·25
154	**20**	3d. violet	16·00	3·00
154a	**20**	3d. blue	2·25	1·25
154b	**20**	3d. red	2·00	3·25
158	**21**	4d. blue and orange	1·25	1·00
159	-	6d. green and blue	1·25	1·00
160	-	8d. blue and red	15·00	3·50
154c	**20**	10d. orange	2·50	20
155d	**20**	1s. black and red	17·00	1·50
156e	**20**	5s. purple and blue	24·00	24·00
157a	**20**	£1 green and black	60·00	55·00

DESIGNS—As Type **21**: 6d. Fort Charlotte; 8d. Greater flamingos.

1940. Surch **3d.**

161	**20**	3d. on 2½d. blue	1·50	2·75

1942. 450th Anniv of Landing of Columbus. Optd **1492 LANDFALL OF COLUMBUS 1942**.

162		½d. green	30	60
163		1d. grey	30	60
164		1½d. brown	40	60
165		2d. red	50	65
166		2½d. blue	50	65
167		3d. blue	30	65
168	**21**	4d. blue and orange	40	90
169	-	6d. green & blue (No. 159)	40	1·75
170	-	8d. blue and red (No. 160)	3·00	70
171	**20**	1s. black and red	12·00	5·00
172a	**17**	2s. black and blue	8·50	10·00
173	**17**	3s. black and green	9·00	6·50
174a	**20**	5s. purple and blue	23·00	14·00
175a	**20**	£1 green and black	30·00	25·00

1946. Victory. As T **9** of Aden.

176	1½d. brown	10	60
177	3d. blue	10	60

26 Infant Welfare Clinic

1948. Tercentenary of Settlement of Island of Eleuthera. Inscr as in T **26**.

178	**26**	½d. orange	40	1·75
179	-	1d. olive	40	35
180	-	1½d. yellow	40	80
181	-	2d. red	40	40
182	-	2½d. brown	70	75
183	-	3d. blue	2·50	85
184	-	4d. black	60	70
185	-	6d. green	2·50	80
186	-	8d. violet	1·25	70
187	-	10d. red	1·25	35
188	-	1s. brown	3·00	50
189	-	2s. purple	5·00	8·50
190	-	3s. blue	13·00	8·50
191	-	5s. mauve	20·00	5·50
192	-	10s. grey	17·00	13·00
193	-	£1 red	17·00	17·00

DESIGNS: 1d. Agriculture; 1½d. Sisal; 2d. Straw work; 2½d. Dairy; 3d. Fishing fleet; 4d. Island settlement; 6d. Tuna fishing; 8d. Paradise Beach; 10d. Modern hotels; 1s. Yacht racing; 2s. Water sports—skiing; 3s. Shipbuilding; 5s. Transportation; 10s. Salt production; £1 Parliament Buildings.

1948. Silver Wedding. As T **10/11** of Aden.

194	1½d. brown	20	25
195	£1 grey	45·00	32·00

1949. 75th Anniv of U.P.U. As T **20/23** of Antigua.

196	2½d. violet	35	75
197	3d. blue	2·25	3·50
198	6d. blue	55	3·25
199	1s. red	55	75

1953. Coronation. As T **13** of Aden.

200	6d. black and blue	1·50	60

42 Infant Welfare Clinic

1954. Designs as Nos. 178/93 but with portrait of Queen Elizabeth II and without commemorative inscr as in T **42**.

201	**42**	½d. black and red	10	1·50
202	-	1d. olive and brown	10	30
203	-	1½d. blue and black	15	80
204	-	2d. brown and green	15	30
205	-	3d. black and red	65	1·25
206	-	4d. turquoise and purple	30	30
207	-	5d. brown and blue	1·40	2·25
208	-	6d. blue and black	2·25	20
209	-	8d. black and lilac	70	40
210	-	10d. black and blue	30	10
211	-	1s. blue and brown	1·50	10
212	-	2s. orange and black	2·00	70
213	-	2s.6d. black and blue	3·50	2·00
214	-	5s. green and orange	22·00	75
215	-	10s. black and slate	32·00	2·50
216	-	£1 black and violet	29·00	7·00

DESIGNS: 1½d. Hatchet Bay, Eleuthera; 4d. Water sports—skiing; 5d. Dairy; 6d. Transportation; 2s. Sisal; 2s.6d. Shipbuilding; 5s. Tuna fishing. Other values the same as for the corresponding values in Nos. 178/93.

43 Queen Elizabeth II

1959. Centenary of 1st Bahamas Postage Stamp.

217	**43**	1d. black and red	50	20
218	**43**	2d. black and green	50	1·00
219	**43**	6d. black and blue	60	40
220	**43**	10d. black and brown	60	1·00

44 Christ Church Cathedral

1962. Centenary of Nassau.

221	**44**	8d. green	65	55
222	-	10d. violet	65	25

DESIGN: 10d. Nassau Public Library.

1963. Freedom from Hunger. As T **28** of Aden.

223	8d. sepia	40	40

1963. Bahamas Talks. Nos. 209/10 optd **BAHAMAS TALKS 1962.**

224	8d. black and lilac	50	75
225	10d. black and blue	50	75

1963. Centenary of Red Cross. As T **33** of Antigua.

226	1d. red and black	50	75
227	10d. red and blue	1·75	2·50

1964. New Constitution. Nos. 201/16 optd **NEW CONSTITUTION 1964.**

228	**42**	½d. black and red	15	1·50
229	-	1d. olive and brown	15	15
230	-	1½d. blue and black	70	1·50
231	-	2d. brown and green	15	20
232	-	3d. black and red	2·00	1·75
233	-	4d. turquoise and purple	70	55
234	-	5d. brown and blue	70	1·50
235	-	6d. blue and black	3·25	30
236	-	8d. black and lilac	70	30
237	-	10d. black and blue	30	15
238	-	1s. blue and brown	1·50	15
239	-	2s. brown and black	2·00	1·75
240	-	2s.6d. black and blue	3·00	2·75
241	-	5s. green and orange	7·00	3·25
242	-	10s. black and slate	7·00	5·50
243	-	£1 black and violet	7·50	25·00

1964. 400th Birth Anniv of Shakespeare. As T **34** of Antigua.

244	6d. turquoise	30	10

1964. Olympic Games, Tokyo. No. 211 surch **8d.** and Olympic rings.

245	8d. on 1s. blue and brown	45	15

49 Colony's Badge

1965

247	**49**	½d. multicoloured	15	2·25
248	-	1d. slate, blue and orange	30	1·00
249	-	1½d. red, green and brown	15	3·75
250	-	2d. slate, green and blue	15	10
251	-	3d. red, blue and purple	4·50	20
252	-	4d. green, blue and brown	5·00	3·50
253	-	6d. green, blue and red	1·25	10
254	-	8d. purple, blue & bronze	50	30
255	-	10d. brown, green and violet	25	10
256a	-	1s. multicoloured	40	10
257	-	2s. brown, blue and green	1·00	1·25
258	-	2s.6d. olive, blue and red	2·50	3·00
259	-	5s. brown, blue and green	2·75	1·00
260	-	10s. red, blue and brown	16·00	3·50
261	-	£1 brown, blue and red	21·00	11·00

DESIGNS: 1d. Out Island regatta; 1½d. Hospital; 2d. High School; 3d. Greater flamingo; 4d. R.M.S. *Queen Elizabeth*; 6d. "Development"; 8d. Yachting; 10d. Public square; 1s. Sea garden; 2s. Old cannons at Fort Charlotte; 2s.6d. Sikorsky S-38 flying boat, 1929, and Boeing 707 airliner; 5s. Williamson film project, 1914, and undersea post office, 1939; 10s. Queen or pink conch; £1 Columbus's flagship.

1965. Centenary of I.T.U. As T **36** of Antigua.

262	1d. green and orange	15	10
263	2s. purple and olive	65	45

1965. No. 254 surch **9d.**

264	9d. on 8d. purple, blue & bronze	30	15

1965. I.C.Y. As T **37** of Antigua.

265	½d. purple and turquoise	10	1·10
266	1s. green and lavender	30	40

1966. Churchill Commemoration. As T **38** of Antigua.

267	½d. blue	10	75
268	2d. green	50	30
269	10d. brown	85	85
270	1s. violet	85	1·40

1966. Royal Visit. As T **39** of Antigua but inscr "to the Caribbean" omitted.

271	6d. black and blue	1·00	50
272	1s. black and mauve	1·25	1·25

1966. Decimal currency. Nos. 247/61 surch.

273	**49**	1c. on ½d. multicoloured	10	30
274	-	2c. on 1d. slate, blue and orange	75	30
275	-	3c. on 2d. slate, green and blue	10	10
276	-	4c. on 3d. red, blue and purple	2·00	20
277	-	5c. on 4d. green, blue and brown	2·00	3·00
278	-	8c. on 6d. green, blue and red	20	20
279	-	10c. on 8d. purple, blue and bronze	30	75
280	-	11c. on 1½d. red, green and brown	15	30
281	-	12c. on 10d. brown, green and violet	15	10
282	-	15c. on 1s. multicoloured	25	10
283	-	22c. on 2s. brown, blue and green	60	1·25
284	-	50c. on 2s.6d. olive, blue and red	1·00	1·40
285	-	$1 on 5s. brown, blue and green	1·75	1·50
286	-	$2 on 10s. red, blue and brown	7·50	4·50
287	-	$3 on £1 brown, blue and red	7·50	4·50

1966. World Cup Football Championships. As T **40** of Antigua.

288	8c. multicoloured	35	15
289	15c. multicoloured	40	25

1966. Inauguration of W.H.O. Headquarters, Geneva. As T **41** of Antigua.

290	11c. black, green and blue	50	90
291	15c. black, purple and ochre	50	50

1966. 20th Anniv of UNESCO As T **54/6** of Antigua.

292	3c. multicoloured	10	10
293	15c. yellow, violet and olive	35	20
294	$1 black, purple and orange	1·10	2·00

1967. As Nos. 247/51, 253/9 and 261 but values in decimal currency, and new designs for 5c. and $2.

295	**49**	1c. multicoloured	10	3·25
296	-	2c. slate, blue and green	50	60
297	-	3c. slate, green and violet	10	10
298	-	4c. red, light blue and blue	4·75	50
299	-	5c. black, blue and purple	1·00	3·50
300	-	8c. green, blue and brown	2·00	10
301	-	10c. purple, blue and red	30	70
302	-	11c. red, green and blue	25	80
303	-	12c. brown, green and olive	25	10
304	-	15c. multicoloured	55	10
305	-	22c. brown, blue and red	70	65
306	-	50c. olive, blue and green	2·50	1·00
307	-	$1 maroon, blue and purple	2·00	60
308	-	$2 multicoloured	13·00	3·00
309	-	$3 brown, blue and purple	3·75	2·00

NEW DESIGNS: 5c. "Oceanic"; $2 Conch shell (different).

69 Bahamas Crest

1967. Diamond Jubilee of World Scouting. Multicoloured.

310	3c. Type **69**	35	15
311	15c. Scout badge	40	15

71 Globe and Emblem

1968. Human Rights Year. Multicoloured.

312	3c. Type **71**	10	10
313	12c. Scales of Justice and emblem	20	10
314	$1 Bahamas Crest and emblem	70	80

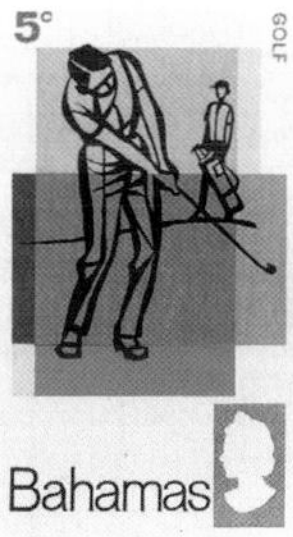

74 Golf

1968. Tourism. Multicoloured.

315	5c. Type **74**	1·75	1·75
316	11c. Yachting	1·25	50
317	15c. Horse-racing	1·75	55
318	50c. Water-skiing	2·50	7·00

78 Racing Yacht and Olympic Monument

1968. Olympic Games, Mexico City.

319	**78**	5c. brown, yellow and green	40	75
320	-	11c. multicoloured	40	25
321	-	50c. multicoloured	60	1·50
322	**78**	$1 grey, blue and violet	2·00	3·00

DESIGNS: 11c. Long jumping and Olympic Monument; 50c. Running and Olympic Monument.

81 Legislative Building

1968. 14th Commonwealth Parliamentary Conference. Multicoloured.

323	3c. Type **81**	10	30
324	10c. Bahamas Mace and Westminster Clock Tower (vert)	15	30
325	12c. Local straw market (vert)	15	25
326	15c. Horse-drawn surrey	20	35

85 Obverse and reverse of $100 Gold Coin

1968. Gold Coins commemorating the first General Election under the New Constitution.

327	**85**	3c. red on gold	40	40
328	-	12c. green on gold	45	50
329	-	15c. purple on gold	50	60
330	-	$1 black on gold	1·25	4·00

OBVERSE AND REVERSE OF: 12c. $50 gold coin; 15c. $20 gold coins; $1, $10 gold coin.

89 First Flight Postcard of 1919

1969. 50th Anniv of Bahamas Airmail Services.

331	**89**	12c. multicoloured	50	50
332	-	15c. multicoloured	60	1·75

DESIGN: 15c. Sikorsky S-38 flying boat of 1929.

91 Game-fishing Boats

1969. Tourism. One Millionth Visitor to Bahamas. Multicoloured.

333	3c. Type **91**	25	10
334	11c. Paradise Beach	35	15
335	12c. "Sunfish" sailing boats	35	15
336	15c. Rawson Square and parade	45	25
MS337	130×96 mm. Nos. 333/6	2·75	4·00

92 *The Adoration of the Shepherds* (Louis le Nain)

1969. Christmas. Multicoloured.

338	3c. Type **92**	15	20
339	11c. *The Adoration of the Shepherds* (Poussin)	20	30
340	12c. *The Adoration of the Kings* (Gerard David)	20	20
341	15c. *The Adoration of the Kings* (Vincenzo Foppa)	30	65

93 Badge of Girl Guides

1970. Diamond Jubilee of Girl Guides' Association. Multicoloured.

342	3c. Type **93**	30	30
343	12c. Badge of Brownies	45	40
344	15c. Badge of Rangers	50	50

94 New U.P.U. Headquarters and Emblem

1970. New U.P.U. Headquarters Building.

345	**94**	3c. multicoloured	10	40
346	**94**	15c. multicoloured	20	60

95 Coach and Globe

1970. "Goodwill Caravan". Multicoloured.

347	3c. Type **95**	85	20
348	11c. Diesel train and globe	1·60	60
349	12c. *Canberra* (liner), yacht and globe	1·60	60
350	15c. B.A.C. One Eleven airliner and globe	1·60	1·75
MS351	165×125 mm. Nos. 347/50	9·50	17·00

96 Nurse, Patients and Greater Flamingo

1970. Centenary of British Red Cross. Multicoloured.

352	3c. Type **96**	90	50
353	15c. Hospital and blue marlin	90	1·75

97 *The Nativity* (detail, Pittoni)

1970. Christmas. Multicoloured.

354	3c. Type **97**	15	15
355	11c. *The Holy Family* (detail, Anton Raphael Mengs)	20	25
356	12c. *The Adoration of the Shepherds* (detail, Giorgione)	20	20
357	15c. *The Adoration of the Shepherds* (detail, School of Seville)	30	75
MS358	114×140 mm. Nos. 354/7	1·40	4·25

98 International Airport

1971. Multicoloured

359	1c. Type **98**	10	30
360	2c. Breadfruit	15	35
361	3c. Straw market	15	30
362	4c. Hawksbill turtle	1·75	10·00
363	5c. Nassau grouper	60	60
364	6c. As 4c.	45	1·25
365	7c. Hibiscus	2·00	5·00
366	8c. Yellow elder	60	1·50
367	10c. Bahamian sponge boat	55	30
368	11c. Greater flamingos	2·50	3·25
369	12c. As 7c.	2·00	3·00
370	15c. Bonefish	55	55
466	16c. As 7c.	1·25	35
371	18c. Royal poinciana	65	65
467a	21c. As 2c.	80	1·25
372	22c. As 18c.	2·75	15·00
468	25c. As 4c.	90	40
469	40c. As 10c.	8·00	75
470	50c. Post Office, Nassau	1·50	1·75
471	$1 Pineapple (vert)	1·50	2·50
399	$2 Crawfish (vert)	1·50	6·00
473	$3 Junkanoo (vert)	1·50	9·00

99 Snowflake

1971. Christmas.

377	**99**	3c. purple, orange and gold	10	10
378	-	11c. blue and gold	20	15
379	-	15c. multicoloured	20	20
380	-	18c. blue, ultram & gold	25	25
MS381		126×95 mm. Nos. 377/80	1·25	1·50

DESIGNS: 11c. *Peace on Earth* (doves); 15c. Arms of Bahamas and holly; 18c. Starlit lagoon.

100 High Jumping

1972. Olympic Games, Munich. Multicoloured.

382	10c. Type **100**	35	60
383	11c. Cycling	1·75	75
384	15c. Running	60	75
385	18c. Sailing	95	1·25
MS386	127×95 mm. Nos. 382/5	3·25	3·00

101 Shepherd

1972. Christmas. Multicoloured.

387	3c. Type **101**	10	10
388	6c. Bells	10	10
389	15c. Holly and Cross	15	20

390	20c. Poinsettia	25	45
MS391	108×140 mm. Nos. 387/90	80	3·00

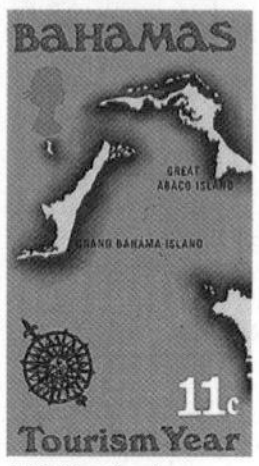

102 Northerly Bahama Islands

1972. Tourism Year of the Americas. Sheet 133×105 mm, containing T **102**.

MS392	11, 15, 18 and 50c. multicoloured	3·75	3·25

The four designs are printed, *se-tenant* in **MS**392, forming a composite map design of the Bahamas.

1972. Royal Silver Wedding. As T **52** of Ascension, but with mace and galleon in background.

393	11c. pink	15	15
394	18c. violet	15	20

104 Weather Satellite

1973. Centenary of I.M.O./W.M.O. Multicoloured.

410	15c. Type **104**	50	25
411	18c. Weather radar	60	35

105 C. A. Bain (national hero)

1973. Independence. Multicoloured.

412	3c. Type **105**	10	10
413	11c. Coat of arms	15	10
414	15c. Bahamas flag	20	15
415	$1 Governor-General, M. B. Butler	65	1·00
MS416	86×121 mm. Nos. 412/15	1·75	1·75

106 *The Virgin in Prayer* (Sassoferrato)

1973. Christmas. Multicoloured.

417	3c. Type **106**	10	10
418	11c. *Virgin and Child with St. John* (Filippino Lippi)	15	15
419	15c. *A Choir of Angels* (Simon Marmion)	15	15
420	18c. *The Two Trinities* (Murillo)	25	25
MS421	120×99 mm. Nos. 417/20	1·75	1·40

107 "Agriculture and Sciences"

1974. 25th Anniv of University of West Indies. Multicoloured.

422	15c. Type **107**	20	25
423	18c. "Arts, Engineering and General Studies"	25	30

108 U.P.U. Monument, Berne

1974. Centenary of U.P.U.

424	**108**	3c. multicoloured	10	15
425	-	13c. multicoloured (vert)	20	25
426	-	14c. multicoloured	20	30
427	-	18c. multicoloured (vert)	25	40
MS428		128×95 mm. Nos. 424/7	80	1·60

DESIGNS—As Type **108** but showing different arrangements of the U.P.U. Monument.

109 Roseate Spoonbills

1974. 15th Anniv of Bahamas National Trust. Multicoloured.

429	13c. Type **109**	1·60	1·10
430	14c. White-crowned pigeon	1·60	75
431	21c. White-tailed tropic birds	2·00	1·25
432	36c. Cuban amazon ("Bahamian parrot")	2·00	5·00
MS433	123×120 mm. Nos. 429/32	9·50	13·00

110 *The Holy Family* (Jacques de Stella)

1974. Christmas. Multicoloured.

434	8c. Type **110**	10	10
435	10c. *Madonna and Child* (16th-century Brescian School)	15	15
436	12c. *Virgin and Child with St. John the Baptist and St. Catherine* (Previtali)	15	15
437	21c. *Virgin and Child with Angels* (Previtali)	25	30
MS438	126×105 mm. Nos. 434/7	1·00	1·40

111 *Anteos maerula*

1975. Butterflies. Multicoloured.

439	3c. Type **111**	25	15
440	14c. *Eurema nicippe*	80	50
441	18c. *Papilio andraemon*	95	65
442	21c. *Euptoieta hegesia*	1·10	85
MS443	194×94 mm. Nos. 439/42	7·50	6·50

112 Sheep Husbandry

1975. Economic Diversification. Multicoloured.

444	3c. Type **112**	10	10
445	14c. Electric-reel fishing (vert)	20	15
446	18c. Farming	25	20
447	21c. Oil refinery (vert)	80	35
MS448	127×94 mm. Nos. 444/7	1·25	1·50

113 Rowena Rand (evangelist)

1975. International Women's Year.

449	**113**	14c. brown, lt blue & bl	20	50
450	-	18c. yellow, grn & brn	25	75

DESIGN: 18c. I.W.Y. symbol and harvest symbol.

114 *Adoration of the Shepherds* (Perugino)

1975. Christmas. Multicoloured.

451	3c. Type **114**	15	60
452	8c. *Adoration of the Magi* (Ghirlandaio)	20	10
453	18c. As 8c.	55	90
454	21c. Type **114**	60	95
MS455	142×107 mm. Nos. 451/4	2·25	4·50

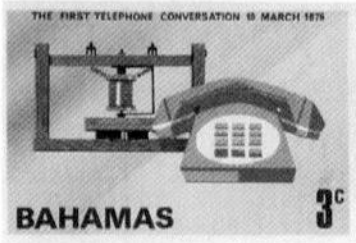

115 Telephones, 1876 and 1976

1976. Centenary of Telephone. Multicoloured.

456	3c. Type **115**	20	50
457	16c. Radio-telephone link, Deleporte	40	50
458	21c. Alexander Graham Bell	50	65
459	25c. Satellite	60	1·00

116 Map of North America

1976. Bicentenary of American Revolution. Multicoloured.

475	16c. Type **116**	30	30
476	$1 John Murray, Earl of Dunmore	1·50	1·75
MS477	127×100 mm. Nos. 476×4	6·00	7·50

117 Cycling

1976. Olympic Games, Montreal.

478	**117**	8c. mauve, blue and light blue	1·60	20
479	-	16c. orange, brown and light blue	35	30
480	-	25c. blue, mauve and light blue	45	50
481	-	40c. brown, orange and blue	55	1·60
MS482		100×126 mm. Nos. 478/81	3·00	3·25

DESIGNS: 16c. Jumping; 25c. Sailing; 40c. Boxing.

118 *Virgin and Child* (detail, Lippi)

1976. Christmas. Multicoloured.

483	3c. Type **118**	10	10
484	21c. *Adoration of the Shepherds* (School of Seville)	30	15
485	25c. *Adoration of the Kings* (detail, Foppa)	30	20
486	40c. *Virgin and Child* (detail, Vivarini)	40	40
MS487	107×127 mm. Nos. 483/6	1·00	2·00

119 Queen beneath Cloth of Gold Canopy

1977. Silver Jubilee. Multicoloured.

488	8c. Type **119**	10	10
489	16c. The Crowning	15	15
490	21c. Taking the Oath	15	15
491	40c. Queen with sceptre and orb	25	30
MS492	122×90 mm. Nos. 488/91	80	1·25

120 Featherduster

1977. Marine Life. Multicoloured.

493	3c. Type **120**	40	15
494	8c. Porkfish and cave	60	20
495	16c. Elkhorn coral	70	40
496	21c. Soft coral and sponge	80	55
MS497	119×93 mm. Nos. 493/6	2·75	4·50

121 Scouts around Campfire and Home-made Shower

1977. Sixth Caribbean Scout Jamboree. Multicoloured.

498	16c. Type **121**	75	30
499	21c. Boating scenes	85	35

1977. Royal Visit. Nos. 488/91 optd **Royal Visit October 1977**.

500	8c. Type **119**	15	10
501	16c. The Crowning	20	15
502	21c. Taking the Oath	25	25
503	40c. Queen with sceptre and orb	30	40
MS504	122×90 mm. Nos. 500/3	1·25	1·50

123 Virgin and Child

1977. Christmas. Multicoloured.

505	3c. Type **123**	10	10
506	16c. The Magi	30	25
507	21c. Nativity scene	30	40
508	25c. The Magi and star	40	45
MS509	136×74 mm. Nos. 505/8	1·00	1·75

124 Public Library, Nassau (Colonial)

1978. Architectural Heritage.

510	**124**	3c. black and green	10	10
511	-	8c. black and blue	15	10
512	-	16c. black and mauve	20	20
513	-	18c. black and pink	25	30
MS514		91×91 mm. Nos. 510/13	70	1·60

DESIGNS: 8c. St. Matthew's Church (Gothic); 16c. Government House (Colonial); 18c. Hermitage, Cat Island (Spanish).

125 Sceptre, St. Edward's Crown and Orb

1978. 25th Anniv of Coronation. Multicoloured.

515	16c. Type **125**	15	10
516	$1 Queen in Coronation regalia	50	65
MS517	147×96 mm. Nos. 515/16	1·25	1·00

126 Coat of Arms within Wreath and Three Ships

1978. Christmas.

532	**126**	5c. gold, lake and red	15	10
533	-	21c. gold, deep blue and blue	30	25
MS534		95×95 mm. Nos. 532/3	1·75	5·50

DESIGN: 21c. Three angels with trumpets.

127 Child reaching for Adult

1979. International Year of the Child. Multicoloured.

535	5c. Type **127**	20	15
536	16c. Boys playing leapfrog	40	45
537	21c. Girls skipping	50	60
538	25c. Bricks with I.Y.C. emblem	50	75
MS539	101×125 mm. Nos. 535/8	1·40	3·25

128 Sir Rowland Hill and Penny Black

1979. Death Centenary of Sir Rowland Hill. Multicoloured.

540	10c. Type **128**	30	10
541	21c. Printing press, 1840, and 6d. stamp of 1862	40	30
542	25c. Great Britain 1856 6d. with "A 05" (Nassau) cancellation, and 1840 2d. Blue	40	50
543	40c. Early mailboat and 1d. stamp of 1859	45	70
MS544	115×80 mm. Nos. 540/3	2·00	3·25

129 Commemorative Plaque and Map of Bahamas

1979. 250th Anniv of Parliament. Multicoloured.

545	16c. Type **129**	35	10
546	21c. Parliament buildings	40	15
547	25c. Legislative Chamber	40	15
548	$1 Senate Chamber	80	1·00
MS549	116×89 mm. Nos. 545/8	2·50	3·75

130 Goombay Carnival Headdress

1979. Christmas.

550	130	5c. multicoloured	10	10
551	-	10c. multicoloured	15	10
552	-	16c. multicoloured	20	10
553	-	21c. multicoloured	20	20
554	-	25c. multicoloured	25	20
555	-	40c. multicoloured	30	45
MS556		50×88 mm. Nos. 550/5	2·00	3·00

DESIGNS: 10c. to 40c. Various Carnival costumes.

131 Landfall of Columbus, 1492

1980. Multicoloured.

557	1c. Type **131**	1·25	2·50
558	3c. Blackbeard the pirate	30	2·50
559	5c. Eleutheran Adventurers (Articles and Orders, 1647)	30	1·25
560	10c. Ceremonial mace	20	40
561	12c. The Loyalists, 1783–88	30	2·25
562	15c. Slave trading, Vendue House	5·50	1·25
563	16c. Wrecking in the 1800s	1·75	1·25
564	18c. Blockade running (American Civil War)	2·50	2·50
565	21c. Bootlegging, 1919–29	60	2·50
566	25c. Pineapple cultivation	40	2·50
567	40c. Sponge clipping	70	1·50
568	50c. Tourist development	75	1·50
569	$1 Modern agriculture	75	4·25
570	$2 Boeing 737 and sea transport	4·25	5·50
571	$3 Banking (Central Bank)	1·25	4·00
572	$5 Independence, 10 July 1973	1·50	6·00

132 Virgin and Child

1980. Christmas. Straw-work. Multicoloured.

573	5c. Type **132**	10	10
574	21c. Three Kings	25	10
575	25c. Angel	25	15
576	$1 Christmas tree	75	85
MS577	168×105 mm. Nos. 573/6	1·25	2·25

133 Disabled Persons with Walking Stick

1981. International Year of Disabled People. Multicoloured.

578	5c. Type **133**	10	10
579	$1 Disabled person in wheelchair	1·25	1·25
MS580	120×60 mm. Nos. 578/9	1·40	2·50

134 Grand Bahama Tracking Site

1981. Space Exploration. Multicoloured.

581	10c. Type **134**	30	15
582	20c. Satellite view of Bahamas (vert)	60	50
583	25c. Satelite view of Eleuthera	65	60
584	50c. Satellite view of Andros and New Province (vert)	1·00	1·25
MS585	115×99 mm. Nos. 581/4	2·25	2·25

135 Prince Charles and Lady Diana Spencer

1981. Royal Wedding. Multicoloured.

586	30c. Type **135**	1·50	30
587	$2 Prince Charles and Prime Minister Pindling	1·50	1·25
MS588	142×120 mm. Nos. 586/7	5·00	1·25

136 Bahamas Pintail ("Bahama Duck")

1981. Wildlife (1st series). Birds. Multicoloured.

589	5c. Type **136**	1·50	60
590	20c. Reddish egret	2·00	60
591	25c. Brown booby	2·00	65
592	$1 Black-billed whistling duck ("West Indian Tree Duck")	4·00	7·50
MS593	100×74 mm. Nos. 589/92	8·50	8·50

See also Nos. 626/30, 653/7 and 690/4.

1981. Commonwealth Finance Ministers' Meeting. Nos. 559/60, 566 and 568 optd **COMMONWEALTH FINANCE MINISTERS' MEETING 21–23 SEPTEMBER 1981.**

594	5c. Eleutheran Adventurers (Articles and Orders, 1647)	15	15
595	10c. Ceremonial mace	20	20
596	25c. Pineapple cultivation	50	60
597	50c. Tourist development	85	1·50

138 Poultry

1981. World Food Day. Multicoloured.

598	5c. Type **138**	20	10
599	20c. Sheep	35	35
600	30c. Lobsters	45	50
601	50c. Pigs	75	1·50
MS602	115×63 mm. Nos. 598/601	1·50	3·25

139 Father Christmas

1981. Christmas. Multicoloured.

603	5c. Type **139**	55	85
604	5c. Mother and child	55	85
605	5c. St. Nicholas, Holland	55	85
606	25c. Lussibruden, Sweden	70	95
607	25c. Mother and child (different)	70	95
608	25c. King Wenceslas, Czechoslovakia	70	95
609	30c. Mother with child on knee	70	95
610	30c. Mother carrying child	70	95
611	$1 Christkindl Angel, Germany	1·00	1·50

140 Robert Koch

1982. Centenary of Discovery of Tubercle Bacillus by Robert Koch.

612	140	5c. black, brown and lilac	75	50
613	-	16c. black, brown & orge	1·40	50
614	-	21c. multicoloured	1·60	55
615	-	$1 multicoloured	3·00	7·50
MS616		94×97 mm. Nos. 612/15	6·00	7·50

DESIGNS: 16c. Stylised infected person; 21c. Early and modern microscopes; $1 Mantoux test.

141 Greater Flamingo (male)

1982. Greater Flamingos. Multicoloured.

617	25c. Type **141**	1·60	1·00
618	25c. Female	1·60	1·00
619	25c. Female with nestling	1·60	1·00
620	25c. Juvenile	1·60	1·00
621	25c. Immature bird	1·60	1·00

142 Lady Diana Spencer at Ascot, June, 1981

1982. 21st Birthday of Princess of Wales. Multicoloured.

622	16c. Bahamas coat of arms	20	10
623	25c. Type **142**	45	15
624	40c. Bride and Earl Spencer arriving at St. Paul's	60	20
625	$1 Formal portrait	1·00	1·25

1982. Wildlife (2nd series). Mammals. As T **136**. Multicoloured.

626	10c. Buffy flower bat	1·00	15
627	16c. Bahamian hutia	1·25	25
628	21c. Common racoon	1·50	55
629	$1 Common dolphin	3·00	1·90
MS630	115×76 mm. Nos. 626/9	6·00	3·50

143 House of Assembly Plaque

1982. 28th Commonwealth Parliamentary Association Conference. Multicoloured.

631	5c. Type **143**	15	10
632	25c. Association coat of arms	50	35
633	40c. Coat of arms	80	60
634	50c. House of Assembly	1·10	75

144 Wesley Methodist Church, Baillou Hill Road

1982. Christmas. Churches. Multicoloured.

635	5c. Type **144**	10	20
636	12c. Centreville Seventh Day Adventist Church	15	20
637	15c. The Church of God of Prophecy, East Street	15	30
638	21c. Bethel Baptist Church, Meeting Street	15	30
639	25c. St. Francis Xavier Catholic Church, Highbury Park	15	50
640	$1 Holy Cross Anglican Church, Highbury Park	60	3·00

145 Prime Minister Lyndon O. Pindling

1983. Commonwealth Day. Multicoloured.

641	5c. Type **145**	10	10
642	25c. Bahamian and Commonwealth flags	50	40
643	35c. Map showing position of Bahamas	50	50
644	$1 Ocean liner	1·10	1·40

1983. Nos. 562/5 surch.

645	20c. on 15c. Slave trading, Vendue House	50	35
646	31c. on 21c. Bootlegging, 1919–29	60	55
647	35c. on 16c. Wrecking in the 1800s	70	60
648	80c. on 18c. Blockade running (American Civil War)	80	1·40

147 Customs Officers and *Queen Elizabeth 2* (liner)

1983. 30th Anniv of Customs Co-operation Council. Multicoloured.

649	31c. Type **147**	1·50	45
650	$1 Customs officers and Lockheed L.1329 JetStar airliner	3·50	2·75

148 Raising the National Flag

1983. Tenth Anniv of Independence.

651	148	$1 multicoloured	1·00	1·40
MS652		105×65 mm. No. 651	1·00	1·40

1983. Wildlife (3rd series). Butterflies. As T **136**.

653	5c. multicoloured	1·50	20

654	25c. multicoloured	2·25	40
655	31c. black, yellow and red	2·25	55
656	50c. multicoloured	2·50	85
MS657	120×80 mm. Nos. 653/6	7·50	6·00

DESIGNS: 5c. *Atalopedes carteri*; 25c. *Ascia monuste*; 31c. *Phoebis agarithe*; 50c. *Dryas julia*.

149 *Loyalist Dreams*

1983. Bicentenary of Arrival of American Loyalists in the Bahamas. Multicoloured.

658	5c. Type **149**	10	10
659	31c. New Plymouth, Abaco (horiz)	30	50
660	35c. New Plymouth Hotel (horiz)	40	70
661	50c. *Island Hope*	45	90
MS662	111×76 mm. Nos. 658/61	1·25	2·50

150 Consolidated PBY-5 Catalina flying boatf

1983. Air. Bicentenary of Manned Flight. Multicoloured.

663	10c. Type **150**	55	15
664	25c. Avro Tudor IV "Star Lion"	75	30
665	31c. Avro Lancastrian	85	45
666	35c. Consolidated Commodore flying boat	1·00	50

For these stamps without the Manned Flight logo, see Nos. 699/702.

151 "Christmas Bells" (Monica Pinder)

1983. Christmas. Children's Paintings. Multicoloured.

667	5c. Type **151**	15	10
668	20c. *Flamingo* (Cory Bullard)	35	30
669	25c. *Yellow Hibiscus with Christmas Candle* (Monique Bailey)	45	40
670	31c. *Santa goes-a-sailing* (Sabrina Seiler) (horiz)	55	45
671	35c. *Silhouette scene with Palm Trees* (James Blake)	60	50
672	50c. *Silhouette scene with Pelicans* (Erik Russell) (horiz)	70	70

152 1861 4d. Stamp

1984. 125th Anniv of First Bahamas Postage Stamp. Multicoloured.

673	5c. Type **152**	25	10
674	$1 1859 1d. stamp	1·75	1·50

153 *Trent I* (paddle-steamer)

1984. 250th Anniv of *Lloyd's List* (newspaper). Multicoloured.

675	5c. Type **153**	50	10
676	31c. *Orinoco II* (mail ship), 1886	1·00	60
677	35c. Cruise liners in Nassau harbour	1·10	75
678	50c. *Oropesa* (container ship)	1·40	1·60

154 Running

1984. Olympic Games, Los Angeles.

679	**154** 5c. green, black and gold	15	20
680	- 25c. blue, black and gold	50	50
681	- 31c. red, black and gold	55	60
682	- $1 brown, black and gold	6·00	7·00
MS683	115×80 mm. Nos. 679/82	6·50	8·00

DESIGNS: 25c. Shot-putting; 31c. Boxing; $1 Basketball.

155 Bahamas and Caribbean Community Flags

1984. Fifth Conference of Caribbean Community Heads of Government.

684	**155** 50c. multicoloured	1·00	1·00

156 Bahama Woodstar

1984. 25th Anniv of National Trust. Multicoloured.

685	31c. Type **156**	3·75	3·75
686	31c. Belted kingfishers, greater flamingos and *Eleutherodactylus planirostris* (frog)	3·75	3·75
687	31c. Black-necked stilts, greater flamingos and *Phoebis sennae* (butterfly)	3·75	3·75
688	31c. *Urbanus proteus* (butterfly) and *Chelonia mydas* (turtle)	3·75	3·75
689	31c. Osprey and greater flamingos	3·75	3·75

Nos. 685/9 were printed together in horiz strips of 5 forming a composite design.

1984. Wildlife (4th series). Reptiles and Amphibians. As T **136**. Multicoloured.

690	5c. Allens' Cay iguana	85	20
691	25c. Curly-tailed lizard	1·75	60
692	35c. Greenhouse frog	2·00	85
693	50c. Atlantic green turtle	2·25	3·50
MS694	112×82 mm. Nos. 690/3	6·25	7·50

157 *The Holy Virgin with Jesus and Johannes* (19th-century porcelain plaque after Titian)

1984. Christmas. Religious Paintings. Multicoloured.

695	5c. Type **157**	30	10
696	31c. *Madonna with Child in Tropical Landscape* (aquarelle, Anais Colin)	1·00	60
697	35c. *The Holy Virgin with the Child* (miniature on ivory, Elena Caula)	1·25	65
MS698	116×76 mm. Nos. 695/7	2·50	4·25

1985. Air. As Nos. 663/6, but without Manned Flight logo.

699	10c. Type **150**	80	50
700	25c. Avro Tudor IV "Star Lion"	95	50
701	31c. Avro Lancastrian	95	60
702	35c. Consolidated Commodore flying boat	1·40	1·10

158 Brownie Emblem and Queen or Pink Conch

1985. International Youth Year. 75th Anniv of Girl Guide Movement. Multicoloured.

703	5c. Type **158**	60	50
704	25c. Tents and coconut palm	1·25	1·00
705	31c. Guide salute and greater flamingos	1·90	1·50
706	35c. Ranger emblem and marlin	1·90	1·50
MS707	95×74 mm. Nos. 703/6	5·50	7·50

159 Killdeer Plover

1985. Birth Bicent of John J. Audubon (ornithologist). Multicoloured.

708	5c. Type **159**	1·00	60
709	31c. Mourning dove (vert)	2·25	60
710	35c. *Mourning dove* (John J. Audubon) (vert)	2·25	65
711	$1 *Killdeer Plover* (John J. Audubon)	4·00	4·50

160 The Queen Mother at Christening of Peter Phillips, 1977

1985. Life and Times of Queen Elizabeth the Queen Mother. Multicoloured.

712	5c. Visiting Auckland, New Zealand, 1927	45	20
713	25c. Type **160**	70	40
714	35c. The Queen Mother attending church	75	55
715	50c. With Prince Henry at his christening (from photo by Lord Snowdon)	1·50	2·00
MS716	91×73 mm. $1.25, In horse-drawn carriage, Sark	2·75	1·90

161 Ears of Wheat and Emblems

1985. 40th Anniv of U.N.O. and F.A.O.

717	**161** 25c. multicoloured	1·25	70

162 Queen Elizabeth II

1985. Commonwealth Heads of Government Meeting, Nassau. Multicoloured.

718	31c. Type **162**	3·00	3·75
719	35c. Bahamas Prime Minister's flag and Commonwealth emblem	3·00	3·75

163 *Grandma's Christmas Bouquet* (Alton Roland Lowe)

1985. Christmas. Paintings by Alton Roland Lowe. Multicoloured.

736	5c. Type **163**	60	40
737	25c. *Junkanoo Romeo and Juliet* (vert)	1·50	1·00
738	31c. *Bunce Gal* (vert)	1·75	1·50
739	35c. *Home for Christmas*	1·75	2·75
MS740	110×68 mm. Nos. 736/9	2·75	3·25

1986. 60th Birthday of Queen Elizabeth II. As T **110** of Ascension. Multicoloured.

741	10c. Princess Elizabeth aged one, 1927	15	15
742	25c. The Coronation, 1953	30	30
743	35c. Queen making speech at Commonwealth Banquet, Bahamas, 1985	35	40
744	40c. In Djakova, Yugoslavia, 1972	35	45
745	$1 At Crown Agents Head Office, London, 1983	80	1·40

164 1980 1c. and 18c. Definitive Stamps

1986. "Ameripex '86" International Stamp Exn, Chicago.

746	**164** 5c. multicoloured	85	50
747	- 25c. multicoloured	2·00	50
748	- 31c. multicoloured	2·25	60
749	- 50c. multicoloured	3·00	5·00
750	- $1 black, green and blue	3·25	6·00
MS751	80×80 mm. No. 750	4·00	4·00

DESIGNS—HORIZ: (showing Bahamas stamps)—25c. 1969 50th Anniv of Bahamas Airmail Service pair; 31c. 1976 Bicentenary of American Revolution 16c., 50c. 1981 Space Exploration miniature sheet. VERT: $1 Statue of Liberty.

No. 750 also commemorates the Centenary of the Statue of Liberty.

1986. Royal Wedding. As T **112** of Ascension. Multicoloured.

756	10c. Prince Andrew and Miss Sarah Ferguson	20	20
757	$1 Prince Andrew	1·25	2·10

165 Rock Beauty (juvenile)

1986. Fish. Multicoloured.

758A	5c. Type **165**	75	75
759A	10c. Stoplight parrotfish	80	1·00
760A	15c. Jackknife-fish	1·50	1·50
761A	20c. Flamefish	1·25	1·25
762A	25c. Peppermint basslet ("Swiss-guard basslet")	1·50	1·50
763A	30c. Spot-finned butterflyfish	1·10	1·50
764A	35c. Queen triggerfish	1·10	2·75
765B	40c. Four-eyed butterflyfish	1·10	1·60
766A	45c. Royal gramma ("Fairy basslet")	1·50	1·25
767A	50c. Queen angelfish	2·00	3·75
797	60c. Blue chromis	2·25	5·50
769B	$1 Spanish hogfish	2·75	3·00
799	$2 Harlequin bass	3·00	8·50
771A	$3 Black-barred soldierfish	6·00	7·00
772A	$5 Cherub angelfish ("Pygmy angelfish")	6·50	8·00
773A	$10 Red hind	18·00	25·00

166 Christ Church Cathedral, Nassau, 1861

1986. 125th Anniv of City of Nassau. Diocese and Cathedral. Multicoloured.

774	10c. Type **166**	30	20
775	40c. Christ Church Cathedral, 1986	70	80
MS776	75×100 mm. Nos. 774/5	4·25	6·50

167 Man and Boy looking at Crib

1986. Christmas. International Peace Year. Multicoloured.

777	10c. Type **167**	35	20
778	40c. Mary and Joseph journeying to Bethlehem	85	75
779	45c. Children praying and Star of Bethlehem	95	1·00
780	50c. Children exchanging gifts	1·00	2·50
MS781	95×90 mm. Nos. 777/80	8·50	11·00

168 Great Isaac Lighthouse

1987. Lighthouses. Multicoloured.

782	10c. Type **168**	3·00	85
783	40c. Bird Rock lighthouse	6·00	1·75
784	45c. Castle Island lighthouse	6·00	2·00
785	$1 "Hole in the Wall" lighthouse	9·00	12·00

169 Anne Bonney

1987. Pirates and Privateers of the Caribbean. Multicoloured.

786	10c. Type **169**	3·50	1·25
787	40c. Edward Teach ("Blackbeard")	6·00	3·50
788	45c. Captain Edward England	6·00	3·50
789	50c. Captain Woodes Rogers	6·50	7·50
MS790	75×95 mm. $1.25, Map of Bahamas and colonial coat of arms	13·00	7·50

170 Boeing 737

1987. Air. Aircraft. Multicoloured.

800	15c. Type **170**	3·25	1·50
801	40c. Boeing 757-200	4·25	2·25
802	45c. Airbus Industrie A300 B4-200	4·25	2·25
803	50c. Boeing 747-200	4·75	4·50

171 *Norway* (liner) and Catamaran

1987. Tourist Transport. Multicoloured.

804	40c. Type **171**	2·00	2·00
805	40c. Liners and speedboat	2·00	2·00
806	40c. Game fishing boat and cruising yacht	2·00	2·00
807	40c. Game fishing boat and racing yachts	2·00	2·00
808	40c. Fishing boat and schooner	2·00	2·00
809	40c. Hawker Siddeley H.S.748 airliner	2·00	2·00
810	40c. Boeing 737 and Boeing 727-200 airliners	2·00	2·00
811	40c. Beech 200 Super King Air aircraft and radio beacon	2·00	2·00
812	40c. Aircraft and Nassau control tower	2·00	2·00
813	40c. Helicopter and parked aircraft	2·00	2·00

Nos. 804/8 and 809/13 were each printed together, *se-tenant*, forming composite design.

172 *Cattleyopsis lindenii*

1987. Christmas. Orchids. Multicoloured.

814	10c. Type **172**	1·75	60
815	40c. *Encyclia lucayana*	3·00	1·50
816	45c. *Encyclia hodgeana*	3·00	1·50
817	50c. *Encyclia lleidae*	3·00	3·00
MS818	120×92 mm. Nos. 814/17	11·00	12·00

173 King Ferdinand and Queen Isabella of Spain

1988. 500th Anniv (1992) of Discovery of America by Columbus (1st issue). Multicoloured.

819	10c. Type **173**	85	60
820	40c. Columbus before Talavera Committee	1·75	1·75
821	45c. Lucayan village	1·90	1·90
822	50c. Lucayan potters	2·00	3·50
MS823	65×50 mm. $1.50, Map of Antilles, c. 1500	6·00	3·75

See also Nos. 844/8, 870/4, 908/12 and 933/7.

174 Whistling Ducks in Flight

1988. Black-billed Whistling Duck. Multicoloured.

824	5c. Type **174**	2·25	1·75
825	10c. Whistling duck in reeds	2·25	1·75
826	20c. Pair with brood	4·00	2·75
827	45c. Pair wading	6·00	3·25

175 Grantstown Cabin, c.1820

1988. 150th Anniv of Abolition of Slavery. Multicoloured.

828	10c. Type **175**	50	30
829	40c. Basket-making, Grantstown	1·25	95

176 Olympic Flame, High Jumping, Hammer throwing, Basketball and Gymnastics

1988. Olympic Games, Seoul. Designs taken from painting by James Martin. Multicoloured.

830	10c. Type **176**	90	50
831	40c. Athletics, archery, swimming, long jumping, weightlifting and boxing	90	60
832	45c. Javelin throwing, gymnastics, hurdling and shot put	90	60
833	$1 Athletics, hurdling, gymnastics and cycling	3·50	5·00
MS834	113×85 mm. Nos. 830/3	6·00	3·25

1988. 300th Anniv of Lloyd's of London. As T **123** of Ascension. Multicoloured.

835	10c. *Lloyd's List* of 1740	30	15
836	40c. Freeport Harbour (horiz)	2·00	60
837	45c. Space shuttle over Bahamas (horiz)	2·00	60
838	$1 *Yarmouth Castle* (freighter) on fire	3·00	2·50

177 "Oh Little Town of Bethlehem"

1988. Christmas. Carols. Multicoloured.

839	10c. Type **177**	55	30
840	40c. *Little Donkey*	1·50	75
841	45c. *Silent Night*	1·50	90
842	50c. *Hark the Herald Angels Sing*	1·60	2·25
MS843	88×108 mm. Nos. 839/42	2·75	2·75

1989. 500th Anniv (1992) of Discovery of America by Columbus (2nd issue). As T **173**. Multicoloured.

844	10c. Columbus drawing chart	2·25	85
845	40c. Types of caravel	3·25	1·75
846	45c. Early navigational instruments	3·25	1·75
847	50c. Arawak artefacts	3·25	5·00
MS848	64×64 mm. $1.50, Caravel under construction (from 15th-cent *Nuremburg Chronicles*)	2·50	2·50

178 Cuban Emerald

1989. Hummingbirds. Multicoloured.

849	10c. Type **178**	1·75	1·25
850	40c. Ruby-throated hummingbird	3·00	2·00
851	45c. Bahama woodstar	3·00	2·00
852	50c. Rufous hummingbird	3·25	4·50

179 Teaching Water Safety

1989. 125th Anniv of Int Red Cross. Multicoloured.

853	10c. Type **179**	1·75	50
854	$1 Henri Dunant (founder) and Battle of Solferino	3·75	5·00

1989. 20th Anniv of First Manned Landing on Moon. As T **126** of Ascension. Multicoloured.

855	10c. "Apollo 8" Communications Station, Grand Bahama	1·25	50
856	40c. Crew of "Apollo 8" (30×30 mm)	2·00	90
857	45c. "Apollo 8" emblem (30×30 mm)	2·00	90
858	$1 The Earth seen from "Apollo 8"	2·75	5·00
MS859	100×83 mm. $2 "Apollo 11" astronauts in training, Manned Spacecraft Centre, Houston	5·00	6·00

180 Church of the Nativity, Bethlehem

1989. Christmas. Churches of the Holy Land. Multicoloured.

860	10c. Type **180**	1·50	30
861	40c. Basilica of the Annunciation, Nazareth	2·50	70
862	45c. Tabgha Church, Galilee	2·50	70
863	$1 Church of the Holy Sepulchre, Jerusalem	4·50	7·00
MS864	92×109 mm. Nos. 860/3	10·00	11·00

181 1974 U.P.U. Centenary 13c. Stamp and Globe

1989. "World Stamp Expo '89" International Stamp Exhibition, Washington. Multicoloured.

865	10c. Type **181**	70	40
866	40c. New U.P.U. Headquarters Building 3c. and building	1·40	85
867	45c. 1986 "Ameripex '86" $1 and Capitol, Washington	1·40	90
868	$1 1949 75th anniv of U.P.U. 2½d. and Boeing 737 airliner	5·50	7·00
MS869	107×80 mm. $2 Map showing route of Columbus, 1492 (30×38 mm)	10·00	14·00

1990. 500th Anniv (1992) of Discovery of America by Columbus (3rd issue). As T **173**. Multicoloured.

870	10c. Launching caravel	1·75	80
871	40c. Provisional ship	2·75	2·00
872	45c. Shortening sail	2·75	2·00
873	50c. Lucayan fisherman	2·75	4·00
MS874	70×61 mm. $1.50, Departure of Columbus, 1492	5·50	7·00

182 Bahamas Flag, O.A.S. Headquarters and Centenary Logo

1990. Centenary of Organization of American States.

875	**182** 40c. multicoloured	2·00	2·25

183 Supermarine Spitfire Mk I "Bahamas I"

1990. "Stamp World London 90" International Stamp Exhibition, London. Presentation Fighter Aircraft. Sheet 107×78 mm. containing T **183**. Multicoloured.

MS876	$1 Type **183**; $1 Hawker Hurricane Mk IIC "Bahamas V"	8·50	7·50

184 Teacher with Boy

1990. International Literacy Year. Multicoloured.

877	10c. Type **184**	1·00	50
878	40c. Three boys in class	1·75	1·25
879	50c. Teacher and children with books	1·75	5·00

1990. 90th Birthday of Queen Elizabeth the Queen Mother. As T **134** of Ascension.

880	40c. multicoloured	1·50	50
881	$1.50 black and ochre	2·75	6·00

DESIGNS—21×36 mm: 40c. *Queen Elizabeth 1938* (Sir Gerald Kelly); 29×37 mm: $1.50, Queen Elizabeth at garden party, France, 1938.

185 Cuban Amazon preening

1990. Cuban Amazon ("Bahamian Parrot"). Multicoloured.

882	10c. Type **185**	1·25	85
883	40c. Pair in flight	2·25	1·50
884	45c. Cuban amazon's head	2·25	1·50
885	50c. Perched on branch	2·50	3·75
MS886	73×63 mm. $1.50, Feeding on berries	8·00	10·00

186 The Annunciation

1990. Christmas. Multicoloured.

887	10c. Type **186**	65	50
888	40c. The Nativity	1·25	70
889	45c. Angel appearing to Shepherds	1·25	70
890	$1 The Three Kings	3·00	6·00
MS891	94×110 mm. Nos. 887/90	14·00	14·00

187 Green-backed Heron ("Green Heron")

1991. Birds. Multicoloured.

892	5c. Type **187**	80	1·25
893	10c. Turkey vulture	1·50	1·50
976	15c. Osprey	1·00	70
895	20c. Clapper rail	1·00	80
978	25c. Royal tern	1·00	70
979	30c. Key West quail dove	5·50	1·25
898	40c. Smooth-billed ani	1·75	55
899	45c. Burrowing owl	3·00	80
900	50c. Hairy woodpecker	2·50	80
983	55c. Mangrove cuckoo	2·00	80
902	60c. Bahama mockingbird	2·50	1·75
903	70c. Red-winged blackbird	2·50	1·75
904	$1 Thick-billed vireo	3·00	1·50

905	$2 Bahama yellowthroat	6·00	6·50
988	$5 Stripe-headed tanager	6·50	9·00
907	$10 Greater Antillean bullfinch	13·00	16·00

1991. 500th Anniv (1992) of Discovery of America by Columbus (4th issue). As T **173**. Multicoloured.

908	15c. Columbus navigating by stars	1·75	85
909	40c. Fleet in mid-Atlantic	2·50	2·25
910	55c. Lucayan family worshipping at night	2·50	2·50
911	60c. Map of First Voyage	3·25	5·00
MS912	56×61 mm. $1.50, *Pinta* look-out sighting land	6·00	7·00

1991. 65th Birthday of Queen Elizabeth II and 70th Birthday of Prince Philip. As T **139** of Ascension. Multicoloured.

913	15c. Prince Philip	1·00	1·50
914	$1 Queen Elizabeth II	1·75	2·00

188 Radar Plot of Hurricane Hugo

1991. International Decade for Natural Disaster Reduction. Multicoloured.

915	15c. Type **188**	1·25	65
916	40c. Diagram of hurricane	1·75	1·50
917	55c. Flooding caused by Hurricane David, 1979	2·00	2·25
918	60c. U.S. Dept of Commerce weather reconnaissance Lockhead WP-3D Orion	2·75	4·00

189 The Annunciation

1991. Christmas. Multicoloured.

919	15c. Type **189**	1·25	30
920	55c. Mary and Joseph travelling to Bethlehem	2·25	1·00
921	60c. Angel appearing to the shepherds	2·25	1·50
922	$1 Adoration of the kings	3·75	4·50
MS923	92×108 mm. Nos. 919/22	10·00	11·00

190 First Progressive Liberal Party Cabinet

1992. 25th Anniv of Majority Rule. Multicoloured.

924	15c. Type **190**	75	40
925	40c. Signing of Independence Constitution	1·60	1·10
926	55c. Prince of Wales handing over Constitutional Instrument (vert)	1·75	1·50
927	60c. First Bahamian Governor-General, Sir Milo Butler (vert)	2·00	3·50

1992. 40th Anniv of Queen Elizabeth II's Accession. As T **143** of Ascension. Multicoloured.

928	15c. Queen Elizabeth with bouquet	60	30
929	40c. Queen Elizabeth with flags	1·10	70
930	55c. Queen Elizabeth at display	1·10	90
931	60c. Three portraits of Queen Elizabeth	1·25	1·50
932	$1 Queen Elizabeth II	1·50	2·50

1992. 500th Anniv of Discovery of America by Columbus (5th issue). As T **173**. Multicoloured.

933	15c. Lucayans sighting fleet	2·00	1·00
934	40c. *Santa Maria* and dolphins	2·75	1·75
935	55c. Lucayan canoes approaching ships	2·75	2·25
936	60c. Columbus giving thanks for landfall	3·25	4·25
MS937	61×57 mm. $1.50, Children at Columbus Monument	3·50	6·00

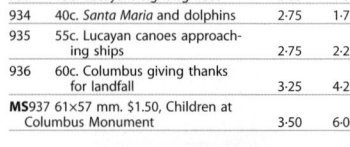

191 Templeton, Galbraith and Hansberger Ltd Building

1992. 20th Anniv of Templeton Prize for Religion.

938	**191** 55c. multicoloured	1·50	1·75

192 Pole Vaulting

1992. Olympic Games, Barcelona. Multicoloured.

939	15c. Type **192**	60	50
940	40c. Javelin	1·00	90
941	55c. Hurdling	1·10	1·25
942	60c. Basketball	7·00	5·00
MS943	70×50 mm. $2 Sailing	7·50	9·00

193 Arid Landscape and Starving Child

1992. International Conference on Nutrition, Rome. Multicoloured.

944	15c. Type **193**	1·25	75
945	55c. Seedling, cornfield and child	2·00	2·00

1992. 500th Anniv of Discovery of America by Columbus (6th issue). Sheet 65×65 mm, containing vert design as T **173**. Multicoloured.

MS946	$2 Columbus landing in Bahamas	7·50	8·00

194 Mary visiting Elizabeth

1992. Christmas. Multicoloured.

947	15c. Type **194**	40	20
948	55c. The Nativity	1·10	1·00
949	60c. Angel and shepherds	1·25	1·50
950	70c. Wise Men and star	1·40	2·50
MS951	95×110 mm. Nos. 947/50	6·50	7·50

1992. Hurricane Relief. No. **MS**876 showing each stamp surch **HURRICANE RELIEF+$1**.

MS952	$1+$1 Type **183**; $1+$1 Hawker Hurricane Mk IIc "Bahamas V"	12·00	15·00

196 Flags of Bahamas and U.S.A. with Agricultural Worker

1993. 50th Anniv of The Contract (U.S.A.–Bahamas farm labour programme). Each including national flags. Multicoloured.

953	15c. Type **196**	1·75	70
954	55c. Onions	2·25	1·50
955	60c. Citrus fruit	2·50	2·50
956	70c. Apples	2·75	3·25

1993. 75th Anniv of Royal Air Force. As T **149** of Ascension. Multicoloured.

957	15c. Westland Wapiti IIA	1·75	85
958	40c. Gloster Gladiator I	2·25	1·00
959	55c. de Havilland Vampire F.3	2·50	1·75
960	70c. English Electric Lightning F.3	3·00	5·00
MS961	110×77 mm. 60c. Avro Shackleton M.R.2; 60c. Fairey Battle; 60c. Douglas Boston III; 60c. de Havilland D.H.9a	8·75	7·75

197 1978 Coronation Anniversary Stamps

1993. 40th Anniv of Coronation. Multicoloured.

962	15c. Type **197**	70	50
963	55c. Two examples of 1953 Coronation stamp	1·75	1·75
964	60c. 1977 Silver Jubilee 8c. and 16c. stamps	1·75	2·00
965	70c. 1977 Silver Jubilee 21c. and 40c. stamps	2·00	2·75

198 *Lignum vitae* (national tree)

1993. 20th Anniv of Independence. Multicoloured.

966	15c. Type **198**	30	20
967	55c. Yellow elder (national flower)	90	90
968	60c. Blue marlin (national fish)	1·25	1·25
969	70c. Greater flamingo (national bird)	2·00	3·00

199 Cordia

1993. Environment Protection (1st series). Wild-flowers. Multicoloured.

970	15c. Type **199**	1·50	50
971	55c. Seaside morning glory	3·00	1·25
972	60c. Poinciana	3·25	2·25
973	70c. Spider lily	3·75	4·50

See also Nos. 1017/21, 1035/8, 1084/7, 1121/4, 1149/53 and 1193/6.

200 The Annunciation

1993. Christmas. Multicoloured.

990	15c. Type **200**	75	50
991	55c. Angel and shepherds	2·25	1·75
992	60c. Holy Family	2·25	2·00
993	70c. Three Kings	2·75	3·75
MS994	86×106 mm. $1 Virgin Mary and Child	5·50	7·50

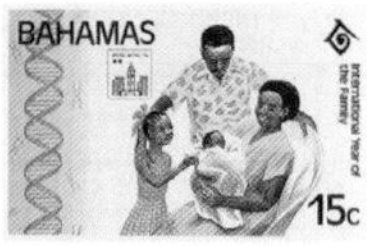

201 Family

1994. "Hong Kong '94" International Stamp Exhibition. International Year of the Family. Multicoloured.

995	15c. Type **201**	1·50	40
996	55c. Children doing homework	2·50	1·25
997	60c. Grandfather and grandson fishing	2·75	1·75
998	70c. Grandmother teaching grandchildren the Lord's Prayer	3·25	5·00

202 Flags of Bahamas and Great Britain

1994. Royal Visit. Multicoloured.

999	15c. Type **202**	1·25	50
1000	55c. Royal Yacht *Britannia*	2·50	1·75
1001	60c. Queen Elizabeth II	2·50	1·75
1002	70c. Queen Elizabeth and Prince Philip	2·50	4·50

203 Yachts

1994. 40th Anniv of National Family Island Regatta. Multicoloured.

1003	15c. Type **203**	80	40
1004	55c. Dinghies racing	1·75	1·25
1005	60c. Working boats	1·75	1·75
1006	70c. Sailing sloop	2·25	4·00
MS1007	76×54 mm. $2 Launching sloop (vert)	8·00	9·00

204 Logo and Bahamas 1968 Olympic Games Stamp

1994. Centenary of International Olympic Committee. Multicoloured.

1008	15c. Type **204**	1·75	50
1009	55c. 1976 Olympic Games stamps (vert)	2·75	1·25
1010	60c. 1984 Olympic Games stamps	2·75	2·25
1011	70c. 1992 Olympic Games stamps (vert)	3·00	4·50

205 Star of Order

1994. First Recipients of Order of the Caribbean Community. Sheet 90×69 mm.

MS1012	**205** $2 multicoloured	5·50	6·50

206 *Calpodes ethlius* and Canna

1994. Butterflies and Flowers. Multicoloured.

1013	15c. Type **206**	1·10	55
1014	55c. *Phoebis sennae* and cassia	2·00	1·50
1015	60c. *Anartia jatrophae* and passion flower	2·25	2·25
1016	70c. *Battus devilliersi* and calico flower	2·25	3·00

207 Spot-finned Hogfish and Spanish Hogfish

1994. Environment Protection (2nd series). Marine Life. Multicoloured.

1017	40c. Type **207**	1·00	1·25
1018	40c. Tomate and long-spined squirrelfish	1·00	1·25
1019	40c. French angelfish	1·00	1·25
1020	40c. Queen angelfish	1·00	1·25
1021	40c. Rock beauty	1·00	1·25
MS1022	57×55 mm. $2 Rock beauty, Queen angelfish and windsurfer	6·00	7·00

Nos. 1017/21 were printed together, *se-tenant*, with the backgrounds forming a composite design.

208 Angel

1994. Christmas. Multicoloured.

1023	15c. Type **208**	30	30
1024	55c. Holy Family	90	1·10
1025	60c. Shepherds	1·10	1·40
1026	70c. Wise Men	1·25	2·50
MS1027	73×85 mm. Jesus in manger	3·50	5·00

209 Lion and Emblem

1995. 20th Anniv of the College of the Bahamas. Multicoloured.

1028	15c. Type **209**	30	30
1029	70c. Queen Elizabeth II and College building	1·25	1·75

1995. 50th Anniv of End of Second World War. As T **161** of Ascension. Multicoloured.

1030	15c. Bahamian infantry drilling	75	50
1031	55c. Consolidated PBY-5A Catalina flying boat	2·00	1·25
1032	60c. Bahamian women in naval operations room	2·00	2·25
1033	70c. Consolidated B-24 Liberator bomber	2·50	3·75
MS1034	75×85 mm. $2 Reverse of 1939–45 War Medal (vert)	3·00	4·00

210 Kirtlands Warbler on Nest

1995. Environment Protection (3rd series). Endangered Species. Kirtland's Warbler. Mult.

1035	15c. Type **210**	55	75
1036	15c. Singing on branch	55	75
1037	25c. Feeding chicks	55	75
1038	25c. Catching insects	55	75
MS1039	73×67 mm. $2 On branch	7·50	8·50

No. **MS**1039 does not show the W.W.F. Panda emblem.

211 Eleuthera Cliffs

1995. Tourism. Multicoloured.

1040	15c. Type **211**	1·50	50
1041	55c. Clarence Town, Long Island	2·50	1·25
1042	60c. Albert Lowe Museum	2·75	2·50
1043	70c. Yachts	3·00	5·00

212 Pigs and Chick

1995. 50th Anniv of F.A.O. Multicoloured.

1044	15c. Type **212**	1·50	50
1045	55c. Seedling and hand holding seed	2·00	1·10
1046	60c. Family with fruit and vegetables	2·50	2·25
1047	70c. Fishes and crustaceans	3·50	4·50

213 Sikorsky S-55 Helicopter, Sinai, 1957

1995. 50th Anniv of United Nations. Multicoloured.

1048	15c. Type **213**	70	50
1049	55c. Ferret armoured car, Sinai, 1957	1·25	1·25
1050	60c. Fokker F.27 Friendship (airliner), Cambodia, 1991–93	1·50	2·00
1051	70c. Lockheed C-130 Hercules (transport)	1·60	2·75

214 St. Agnes Anglican Church

1995. Christmas. Churches. Multicoloured.

1052	15c. Type **214**	30	25
1053	55c. Church of God, East Street	90	90
1054	60c. Sacred Heart Roman Catholic Church	95	1·25
1055	70c. Salem Union Baptist Church	1·10	1·75

215 Microscopic View of AIDS Virus

1995. World AIDS Day. Multicoloured.

1056	25c. Type **215**	60	50
1057	70c. Research into AIDS	1·00	1·50

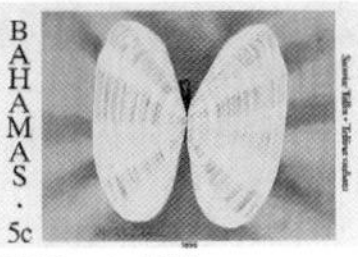

216 Sunrise Tellin

1996. Sea Shells. Multicoloured.

1058	5c. Type **216**	40	1·00
1059	10c. Queen conch	45	1·00
1060	15c. Angular triton	65	40
1061	20c. True tulip	80	60
1062	25c. Reticulated cowrie-helmet	80	60
1063	30c. Sand dollar	1·00	60
1063a	35c. As 30c.	1·50	55
1064	40c. Lace short-frond murex	1·25	60
1065	45c. Inflated sea biscuit	1·50	60
1066	50c. West Indian top shell	1·50	70
1067	55c. Spiny oyster	1·50	75
1068	60c. King helmet	1·50	80
1068a	65c. As 45c.	2·50	1·25
1069	70c. Lion's paw	1·60	1·00
1069a	80c. As 55c.	2·50	1·50
1070	$1 Crown cone	2·50	1·75
1071	$2 Atlantic partridge tun	3·75	4·00
1072	$5 Wide-mouthed purpura	8·00	9·50
1073	$10 Atlantic trumpet triton	22·00	22·00

217 East Goodwin Lightship with Marconi Apparatus on Mast

1996. Centenary of Radio. Multicoloured.

1074	15c. Type **217**	1·75	80
1075	55c. Newspaper headline concerning Dr. Crippen	2·50	1·25
1076	60c. *Philadelphia* (liner) and first readable transatlantic message	2·50	2·00
1077	70c. Guglielmo Marconi and *Elettra* (yacht)	2·75	3·50
MS1078	80×47 mm. $2 *Titanic* and *Carpathia* (liners)	8·50	8·50

218 Swimming

1996. Centenary of Modern Olympic Games. Multicoloured.

1079	15c. Type **218**	40	35
1080	55c. Running	90	90
1081	60c. Basketball	2·00	1·75
1082	70c. Long jumping	1·40	2·50
MS1083	73×86 mm. $2 Javelin throwing	3·00	4·00

219 Green Anole

1996. Environment Protection (4th series). Reptiles. Multicoloured.

1084	15c. Type **219**	55	50
1085	55c. Little Bahama bank boa	1·10	1·00
1086	60c. Inagua freshwater turtle	1·50	1·75
1087	70c. Acklins rock iguana	1·75	2·75
MS1088	85×105 mm. Nos. 1084/7	5·00	6·00

220 The Annunciation

1996. Christmas. Multicoloured.

1089	15c. Type **220**	1·25	40
1090	55c. Joseph and Mary travelling to Bethlehem	2·50	1·00
1091	60c. Shepherds and angel	2·50	1·50
1092	70c. Adoration of the Magi	2·75	4·00
MS1093	70×87 mm. $2 Presentation in the Temple	3·25	4·00

221 Department of Archives Building

1996. 25th Anniv of Archives Department.

1094	**221**	55c. multicoloured	1·50	1·00
MS1095		83×54 mm. $2 multicoloured	4·75	6·50

1997. "HONG KONG '97" International Stamp Exhibition. Sheet 130×90 mm, containing design as No. 1070, but with "1997" imprint date. Multicoloured.

MS1096	$1 Crown cone	3·00	3·50

1997. Return of Hong Kong to China. Sheet 130×90 mm, containing design as No. 1069, but with "1997" imprint date.

MS1097	70c. Lion's paw	2·00	2·50

1997. Golden Wedding of Queen Elizabeth and Prince Philip. As T **173** of Ascension. Multicoloured.

1114	50c. Queen Elizabeth II in Bonn, 1992	2·00	2·25
1115	50c. Prince Philip and Prince Charles at Trooping the Colour	2·00	2·25
1116	60c. Prince Philip	2·00	2·25
1117	60c. Queen at Trooping the Colour	2·00	2·25
1118	70c. Queen Elizabeth and Prince Philip at polo, 1970	2·00	2·25
1119	70c. Prince Charles playing polo	2·00	2·25
MS1120	110×70 mm. $2 Queen Elizabeth and Prince Philip in landau (horiz)	6·50	7·00

222 Underwater Scene

1997. Environment Protection (5th series). International Year of the Reefs.

1121	**222**	15c. multicoloured	1·25	60
1122	-	55c. multicoloured	2·25	1·00
1123	-	60c. multicoloured	2·25	1·75
1124	-	70c. multicoloured	2·50	3·00

DESIGNS: 55c. to 70c. Different children's paintings of underwater scenes.

223 Angel

1997. Christmas. Multicoloured.

1125	15c. Type **223**	1·50	40
1126	55c. Mary and Baby Jesus	2·25	80
1127	60c. Shepherd	2·25	1·25
1128	70c. King	2·75	3·75
MS1129	74×94 mm. $2 Baby Jesus wrapped in swaddling-bands.	8·00	8·50

223a Wearing Grey Jacket, 1988

1998. Diana, Princess of Wales Commemoration.

1130	**223a**	15c. multicoloured	50	50
MS1131		145×70 mm. 15c. As No. 1130; 55c. Wearing striped jacket, 1983; 60c. In evening dress, 1983; 70c. Meeting crowds, 1993	2·50	2·75

1998. 80th Anniv of the Royal Air Force. As T **178** of Ascension. Multicoloured.

1132	15c. Handley Page Hyderabad	55	40
1133	55c. Hawker Demon	1·00	85
1134	60c. Gloster Meteor F8	1·10	1·25
1135	70c. Lockheed P2 Neptune	1·40	2·25
MS1136	110×76 mm. 50c. Sopwith Camel; 50c. Short 184 (seaplane); 50c. Supermarine Spitfire PR.19; 50c. North American Mitchell III	4·00	4·25

224 Newsletters

1998. 50th Anniv of Organization of American States.

1137	15c. Type **224**	30	30
1138	55c. Headquarters building and flags, Washington	70	80

225 Start of Declaration and Birds

1998. 50th Anniv of Universal Declaration of Human Rights.

1139	**225**	55c. blue and black	1·75	1·00

226 University Arms and Graduates

1998. 50th Anniv of University of the West Indies.

1140	**226**	55c. multicoloured	1·50	1·00

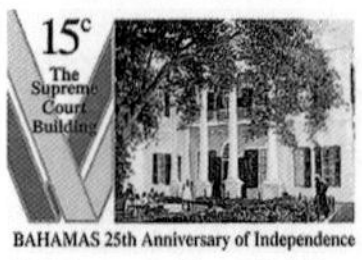

227 Supreme Court Building

1998. 25th Anniv of Independence. Multicoloured.

1141	15c. Type **227**	1·00	50
1142	55c. Nassau Library	1·75	1·00
1143	60c. Government House	1·90	1·50
1144	70c. Gregory Arch	2·00	3·00
MS1145	70×55 mm. $2 Island Regatta, George Town	3·50	5·00

228 *Disney Magic* (cruise liner) at Night

1998. Disney Cruise Line's Castaway Cay Holiday Development. Multicoloured.

1146	55c. Type **228**	2·00	2·00
1147	55c. *Disney Magic* by day	2·00	2·00

229 *Ryndam* (cruise liner)

1998. Holland America Line's Half Moon Cay Holiday Development.

1148	**229**	55c. multicoloured	2·75	1·25

230 Barrel Pink Rose

1998. Environment Protection (6th series). Roses. Multicoloured.

1149	55c. Type **230**	1·50	1·60
1150	55c. Yellow cream	1·50	1·60
1151	55c. Seven sisters	1·50	1·60
1152	55c. Big red	1·50	1·60
1153	55c. Island beauty	1·50	1·60
MS1154	100×70 mm. No. 1153	1·50	1·75

231 The Annunciation

1998. Christmas. Multicoloured.

1155	15c. Type **231**	50	30
1156	55c. Shepherds	1·00	70
1157	60c. Three Kings	1·25	1·10
1158	70c. The Flight into Egypt	1·50	2·75
MS1159	87×67 mm. The Nativity	3·00	4·00

232 Killer Whale and other Marine Life

1998. International Year of the Ocean. Multicoloured.

1160	15c. Type **232**	65	50
1161	55c. Tropical fish	85	90

233 Timothy Gibson (composer)

1998. 25th Anniv of *March on Bahamaland* (national anthem).

1162	**233**	60c. multicoloured	1·00	1·25

234 Head of Greater Flamingo and Chick

1999. 40th Anniv of National Trust (1st issue). Inagua National Park. Multicoloured.

1163	55c. Type **234**	1·50	1·60
1164	55c. Pair with two chicks	1·50	1·60
1165	55c. Greater flamingos asleep or stretching wings	1·50	1·60
1166	55c. Greater flamingos feeding	1·50	1·60
1167	55c. Greater flamingos in flight	1·50	1·60

Nos. 1163/7 were printed together, *se-tenant*, with the backgrounds forming a composite design.

See also Nos. 1173/7, 1198/1202 and 1207/11.

235 Arawak Indian Canoe

1999. "Australia '99" World Stamp Exhibition, Melbourne. Maritime History. Multicoloured.

1168	15c. Type **235**	55	30
1169	55c. *Santa Maria* (Columbus), 1492	1·75	1·10
1170	60c. *Queen Anne's Revenge* (Blackbeard), 1716	1·90	1·60
1171	70c. *The Banshee* (Confederate paddle-steamer) running blockade	2·00	3·25
MS1172	110×66 mm. $2 Firing on American ships, 1776	5·50	5·50

1999. 40th Anniv of National Trust (2nd issue). Exuma Cays Land and Sea Park. As T **234**. Multicoloured.

1173	55c. Dolphin	1·50	1·75
1174	55c. Angelfish and parrotfish	1·50	1·75
1175	55c. Queen triggerfish	1·50	1·75
1176	55c. Turtle	1·50	1·75
1177	55c. Lobster	1·50	1·75

Nos. 1173/7 were printed together, *se-tenant*, with the backgrounds forming a composite design.

236 Society Headquarters Building

1999. 40th Anniv of Bahamas Historical Society.

1178	**236**	$1 multicoloured	1·50	2·25

1999. 30th Anniv of First Manned Landing on Moon. As T **186** of Ascension. Multicoloured.

1179	15c. Constructing ascent module	45	40
1180	65c. Diagram of command and service module	1·25	1·25
1181	70c. Lunar module descending	1·25	1·75
1182	80c. Lunar module preparing to dock with service module	1·25	2·50
MS1183	90×80 mm. $2 Earth as seen from Moon (circular, 40 mm diam)	3·25	4·25

1999. "Queen Elizabeth the Queen Mother's Century". As T **187** of Ascension. Multicoloured.

1184	15c. Visiting Herts Hospital, 1940	60	35
1185	65c. With Princess Elizabeth, Hyde Park, 1944	1·50	1·00
1186	70c. With Prince Andrew, 1997	1·50	1·50
1187	80c. With Irish Guards' mascot, 1997	1·50	1·75
MS1188	145×70 mm. $2 Lady Elizabeth Bowes-Lyon with her brother David, 1904, and England World Cup team celebrating, 1966.	4·50	5·00

237 *Delaware* (American mail ship), 1880

1999. 125th Anniv of U.P.U. Ships. Multicoloured.

1189	15c. Type **237**	1·50	50
1190	65c. *Atlantis* (liner), 1923	2·50	1·25
1191	70c. *Queen of Bermuda 2* (liner), 1937	2·50	2·25
1192	80c. U.S.S. *Saufley* (destroyer), 1943	3·00	3·25

238 *Turtle Pond* (Green Turtle)

1999. Environment Protection (7th series). Marine Life Paintings by Ricardo Knowles. Multicoloured.

1193	15c. Type **238**	50	35
1194	65c. *Turtle Cliff* (Loggerhead turtle)	1·25	1·00
1195	70c. *Barracuda*	1·40	1·40
1196	80c. *Coral Reef*	1·50	2·25
MS1197	90×75 mm. $2 *Atlantic Bottle-nosed Dolphins*	3·25	4·50

The 65c. is inscribed "GREEN TURTLES" in error.

1999. 40th Anniv of National Trust (3rd issue). Birds. As T **234**. Multicoloured.

1198	65c. Bridled tern and white-tailed tropic bird	1·75	1·75
1199	65c. Louisiana heron	1·75	1·75
1200	65c. Bahama woodstar	1·75	1·75
1201	65c. Black-billed whistling duck	1·75	1·75
1202	65c. Cuban amazon	1·75	1·75

Nos. 1198/1202 were printed together, *se-tenant*, with the backgrounds forming a composite design.

239 Man on Elephant Float

1999. Christmas. Junkanoo Festival. Multicoloured.

1203	15c. Type **239**	50	30
1204	65c. Man in winged costume	1·00	1·00
1205	70c. Man in feathered mask	1·25	1·25
1206	80c. Man blowing conch shell	1·50	2·00

1999. 40th Anniv of National Trust (4th issue). Flora and Fauna. As T **234**. Multicoloured.

1207	65c. Foxglove	2·25	2·25
1208	65c. Vole	2·25	2·25
1209	65c. Cuban amazon	2·25	2·25
1210	65c. Lizard	2·25	2·25
1211	65c. Red hibiscus	2·25	2·25

Nos. 1207/11 were printed together, *se-tenant*, with the backgrounds forming a composite design.

240 New Plymouth

2000. Historic Fishing Villages. Multicoloured.

1212	15c. Type **240**	1·25	40
1213	65c. Cherokee Sound	2·25	1·00
1214	70c. Hope Town	2·50	2·00
1215	80c. Spanish Wells	2·75	3·25

241 Gold Medal Winning Bahamas Women's Relay Team

2000. "The Golden Girls" winners of 4×100 metre Relay at I.A.A.F. World Track and Field Championship '99, Spain. Sheet 100×55 mm.

MS1216	**241**	$2 multicoloured	3·00	3·50

242 Prickly Pear

2000. Medicinal Plants (1st series). Multicoloured.

1217	15c. Type **242**	35	30
1218	65c. Buttercup	1·25	1·25
1219	70c. Shepherd's needle	1·25	1·50
1220	80c. Five fingers	1·40	2·25

See also Nos. 1282/5 and 1324/7.

243 Re-arming and Re-fuelling Supermarine Spitfire

2000. "The Stamp Show 2000" International Stamp Exhibition, London. 60th Anniv of Battle of Britain. Multicoloured.

1221	15c. Type **243**	70	45
1222	65c. Sqdn. Ldr. Stanford-Tuck's Hurricane Mk I	1·40	1·40
1223	70c. Dogfight between Spitfires and Heinkel IIIs	1·60	1·75
1224	80c. Flight of Supermarine Spitfires attacking	1·60	2·25
MS1225	90×70 mm. $2 Presentation Spitfire Bahamas	3·50	4·00

244 Teachers' and Salaried Workers' Co-operative Credit Union Building

2000. Co-operatives Movement in Bahamas. Sheet 90×50 mm.

MS1226	**244**	$2 multicoloured	3·50	4·00

245 Swimming

2000. Olympic Games, Sydney. Each inscribed with details of previous Bahamian participation. Multicoloured.

1227	15c. Type **245**	50	30
1228	65c. Triple jump	1·40	1·25
1229	70c. Women's 4×100 m relay	1·40	1·40
1230	80c. Sailing	1·50	2·25

246 *Encyclia cochleata*

2000. Christmas. Orchids. Multicoloured.

1231	15c. Type **246**	70	30
1232	65c. *Encyclia plicata*	1·60	1·25
1233	70c. *Bletia purpurea*	1·75	1·60
1234	80c. *Encyclia gracilis*	1·90	2·25

247 Cuban Amazon and Primary School Class

2000. Bahamas Humane Society. Multicoloured.

1235	15c. Type **247**	1·50	50
1236	65c. Cat and Society stall	2·50	1·25
1237	70c. Dogs and veterinary surgery	3·00	2·50
1238	80c. Goat and animal rescue van	3·00	3·25

248 *Meadow Street, Inagua*

2001. Early Settlements. Paintings by Ricardo Knowles. Multicoloured.

1239	15c. Type **248**	40	30
1240	65c. *Bain Town*	1·25	1·00
1241	70c. *Hope Town, Abaco*	1·40	1·40
1242	80c. *Blue Hills*	1·50	2·25

249 Lynden Pindling presenting Independence Constitution, 1972

2001. Sir Lynden Pindling (former Prime Minister) Commemoration. Multicoloured.

1243	15c. Type **249**	50	40
1244	65c. Sir Lynden Pindling with Bahamas flag	1·40	1·50

250 *Cocoaplum*

2001. Edible Wild Fruits. Paintings by Alton Roland Lowe. Multicoloured.

1245	15c. Type **250**	35	25
1246	65c. *Guana Berry*	1·25	1·10
1247	70c. *Mastic*	1·25	1·25
1248	80c. *Seagrape*	1·50	2·25

251 Reddish Egret

2001. Birds and their Eggs. Multicoloured.

1249	5c. Type **251**	60	1·25
1250	10c. American purple gallinule	60	1·25
1251	15c. Antillean nighthawk	70	40
1252	20c. Wilson's plover	80	70
1253	25c. Killdeer plover	80	70
1254	30c. Bahama woodstar	85	70
1255	40c. Bahama swallow	90	80
1256	50c. Bahama mockingbird	1·25	80
1257	60c. Black-cowled oriole	1·50	1·25
1258	65c. Great lizard cuckoo	1·50	1·00
1259	70c. Audubon's shearwater	1·75	1·25
1260	80c. Grey kingbird	1·75	1·25
1261	$1 Bananaquit	2·50	2·50
1262	$2 Yellow warbler	4·50	4·75
1263	$5 Greater Antillean bullfinch	10·00	11·00
1264	$10 Roseate spoonbill	18·00	19·00

252 H.M.S. *Norfolk* (cruiser), 1933

2001. Royal Navy Ships connected to Bahamas. Multicoloured.

1265	15c. Type **252**	1·00	40
1266	25c. H.M.S. *Scarborough* (sloop), 1930s	1·25	65
1267	50c. H.M.S. *Bahamas* (frigate), 1944	1·75	1·50
1268	65c. H.M.S. *Battleaxe* (frigate), 1979	2·00	1·50
1269	70c. H.M.S. *Invincible* (aircraft carrier), 1997	2·00	2·00
1270	80c. H.M.S. *Norfolk* (frigate), 2000	2·00	2·75

253 *Adoration of the Shepherds*

2001. Christmas. Paintings by Rubens. Multicoloured.

1271	15c. Type **253**	55	25
1272	65c. "*Adoration of the Magi* (with Van Dyck)	1·40	1·10
1273	70c. *Holy Virgin in Wreath of Flowers* (with Breughel)	1·50	1·40
1274	80c. *Holy Virgin adored by Angels*	1·60	2·00

2002. Golden Jubilee. As T **200** of Ascension.

1275	15c. black, green and gold	45	25
1276	65c. multicoloured	1·25	1·00
1277	70c. multicoloured	1·40	1·50
1278	80c. multicoloured	1·40	2·00
MS1279	162×95 mm. Nos. 1275/8 and $2 multicoloured	6·50	6·50

DESIGNS—HORIZ: 15c. Princess Elizabeth; 65c. Queen Elizabeth in Bonn, 1992; 70c. Queen Elizabeth with Prince Edward, 1965; 80c. Queen Elizabeth at Sandringham, 1996. VERT (38×51 mm)—$2 Queen Elizabeth after Annigoni.

254 Avard Moncur (athlete)

2002. Award of BAAA Most Outstanding Male Athlete Title to Avard Moncur. Sheet 65×98 mm.

MS1280 **254**	$2 multicoloured	3·25	3·50

255 Statue of Liberty with U.S. and Bahamas Flags

2002. In Remembrance. Victims of Terrorist Attacks on U.S.A. (11 September 2001).

1281 **255**	$1 multicoloured	3·00	3·00

2002. Medicinal Plants (2nd series). As T **242**. Multicoloured.

1282	15c. Wild sage	50	35
1283	65c. Seaside maho	1·40	1·10
1284	70c. Sea ox-eye	1·50	1·60
1285	80c. Mexican poppy	1·50	2·00

2002. Queen Elizabeth the Queen Mother Commemoration. As T **202** of Ascension.

1286	15c. brown, gold and purple	75	40
1287	65c. multicoloured	1·75	1·50
MS1288	145×70 mm. 70c. black and gold; 80c. multicoloured	3·75	3·75

DESIGNS: 15c. Queen Elizabeth at American Red Cross Club, London, 1944; 65c. Queen Mother at Remembrance Service, 1989; 70c. Queen Elizabeth, 1944; 80c. Queen Mother at Cheltenham Races, 2000.

256 Rice Bird and Rice

2002. Illustrations from *The Natural History of Carolina, Florida and the Bahama Islands* by Mark Catesby (1747). Multicoloured.

1289	15c. Type **256**	85	45
1290	25c. Alligator and red mangrove	1·00	60
1291	50c. Parrot fish	1·40	1·10
1292	65c. Ilathera duck and sea ox-eye	1·75	1·50
1293	70c. Flamingo and gorgonian coral	1·90	2·00
1294	80c. Crested bittern and inkberry	2·00	2·25

257 *While Shepherds watched their Flocks*

2002. Christmas. Scenes from Carols. Multicoloured.

1295	15c. Type **257**	60	25
1296	65c. *We Three Kings*	1·40	1·10
1297	70c. *Once in Royal David's City*	1·50	1·50
1298	80c. *I saw Three Ships*	1·60	2·25

258 Flamingo on Nest

2003. Inagua National Park Wetlands. Flamingos. Multicoloured.

1299	15c. Type **258**	70	45
1300	25c. Flock of flamingos feeding	95	65
1301	50c. Group of flamingos	1·50	1·10
1302	65c. Group of flamingos walking	1·75	1·50
1303	70c. Flamingos taking-off	1·90	1·90
1304	80c. Flamingos in flight	2·00	2·25

259 Captain Edward Teach ("Blackbeard")

2003. Pirates. Multicoloured.

1305	15c. Type **259**	75	45
1306	25c. Captain "Calico Jack" Rackham	1·10	65
1307	50c. Anne Bonney	1·75	1·40
1308	65c. Captain Woodes Rogers	2·00	1·75
1309	70c. Sir John Hawkins	2·25	2·25
1310	80c. Captain Bartholomew Roberts ("Black Bart")	2·25	2·50

260 Dinghies

2003. 50th Anniv of Family Island Regatta. Multicoloured.

1311	15c. Type **260**	75	40
1312	65c. *New Courageous* (racing sloop)	2·00	1·50
1313	70c. *New Susan Chase* (racing sloop)	2·25	2·00
1314	80c. *Tida Wave* (racing sloop)	2·40	2·75

2003. 50th Anniv of Coronation. As T **206** of Ascension. Multicoloured.

1315	65c. Queen with crown, orb and sceptre	1·50	1·40
1316	80c. Royal family on Buckingham Palace balcony	2·00	2·25
MS1317	95×115 mm. 15c. As 65c.; 70c. As 80c.	2·25	2·50

Nos. 1315/16 have red frame; stamps from **MS**1317 have no frame and country name in mauve panel.

2003. Medicinal Plants (3rd series). As T **242**.

1318	15c. *Asystasia*	40	25
1319	65c. *Cassia*	1·40	1·25
1320	70c. *Lignum vitae*	1·50	1·60
1321	80c. Snowberry	1·60	2·00

2003. Centenary of Powered Flight. As T **209** of Ascension. Multicoloured.

1322	15c. Piper Cub	65	45
1323	25c. de Havilland Tiger Moth	85	70
1324	50c. Lockheed SR-71A Blackbird	1·60	1·50
1325	65c. Supermarine S6B	1·75	1·60
1326	70c. North American P-51D Mustang "Miss America"	1·90	1·90
1327	80c. Douglas DC-3 Dakota	2·25	2·50

261 Interior with Stained Glass Window

2003. Christmas. St. Matthew's Church, Nassau. Multicoloured.

1328	15c. Type **261**	60	25
1329	65c. Church interior (horiz)	1·50	1·10
1330	70c. St. Matthew's Church (horiz)	1·75	1·60
1331	80c. Church tower	2·00	2·00

262 *Crawfishin*

2003. "Waters of Life". Paintings by Alton Lowe. Multicoloured.

1332	15c. Type **262**	60	30
1333	65c. *Summer*	1·50	1·25
1334	70c. *The Whelkers*	1·75	1·75
1335	80c. *Annual Visit*	2·00	2·00

263 Egrets on Dead Tree

2004. Wetlands (2nd series). Harrold and Wilson Ponds, New Providence Island. Multicoloured.

1336	15c. Type **263**	60	40
1337	25c. Green-backed heron and duck	80	65
1338	50c. Birdwatchers in canoes	1·50	1·40
1339	65c. Egret and Bahama pintail ducks	1·75	1·60
1340	70c. Egret and Louisiana heron	2·00	2·00
1341	80c. Birdwatchers with binoculars and telescope	2·25	2·50

264 Methodist Church, Cupid's Cay, Governor's Harbour

2004. 300th Birth Anniv of John Wesley (founder of Methodist Church) (2003). Multicoloured.

1342	15c. Type **264**	60	30
1343	25c. Church, Grants Town, Nassau	80	45
1344	50c. Wooden Chapel, Marsh Harbour (vert)	1·50	1·40
1345	65c. Ebeneezer Methodist Church	1·75	1·75
1346	70c. Trinity Methodist Church	2·00	2·25
1346a	80c. Portrait by Antonius Roberts (vert)	2·25	2·50

265 Cattleya

2004. Bicentenary of the Royal Horticultural Society. Multicoloured.

1347	15c. Type **265**	75	30
1348	65c. Hibiscus	1·40	1·10
1349	70c. Canna	1·50	1·60
1350	80c. Thunbergia	1·60	2·00

266 Elbow Reef Lighthouse

2004. Lighthouses (1st series). Multicoloured.

1351	15c. Type **266**	1·00	50
1352	50c. Great Stirrup	1·75	1·25
1353	65c. Great Isaac	2·00	1·50
1354	70c. Hole in the Wall	2·25	2·00
1355	80c. Hog Island	2·50	2·50

See also Nos. 1396/1400.

267 Boxing

2004. Olympic Games, Athens. Multicoloured.

1356	15c. Type **267**	50	30
1357	50c. Swimming	1·25	1·10
1358	65c. Tennis	1·40	1·40
1359	70c. Relay racing	1·40	1·75

268 "Anticipation"

2004. Christmas. Junkanoo Festival. Multicoloured.

1360	15c. Type **268**	40	20
1361	25c. "First Time"	50	25
1362	50c. "On The Move" (vert)	1·00	60
1363	65c. "I'm Ready" (vert)	1·10	1·00
1364	70c. "Trumpet Player" (vert)	1·25	1·40
1365	80c. "Drummer Boy" (vert)	1·40	1·60

269 RMS *Mauretania*

2004. Merchant Ships. Multicoloured.

1366	15c. Type **269**	65	40
1367	25c. MV *Adonia*	85	55
1368	50c. MS *Royal Princess*	1·50	1·10
1369	65c. SS *Queen of Nassau*	1·60	1·40
1370	70c. RMS *Transvaal Castle*	1·75	1·75
1371	80c. SS *Norway*	1·90	2·25

2005. Medicinal Plants (4th series). As T **242**. Multicoloured.

1372	15c. Aloe vera	35	25
1373	25c. Red stopper	45	35
1374	50c. Blue flower	80	80
1375	65c. Bay lavender	1·10	1·25

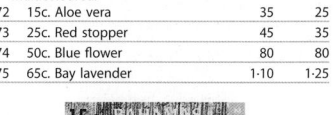

270 Commando Squadron

2005. 25th Anniv of the Royal Bahamas Defence Force. Multicoloured.

1376	15c. Type **270**	55	30
1377	25c. HMBS *Abaco*	75	45
1378	50c. HMBS *Bahamas*	1·40	1·10
1379	65c. Officers and marines in uniform	1·60	1·60

2005. Bicentenary of Battle of Trafalgar. Multicoloured (except **MS**1386) designs as T **216** of Ascension.

1380	15c. Tower Sea Service pistols, 1801 RN Pattern (vert)	50	30
1381	25c. Royal Marine, 1805 (vert)	70	45
1382	50c. HMS *Boreas* off Bahamas, 1787	1·25	1·10
1383	65c. "Death of Nelson" (A. W. Devis)	1·40	1·25
1384	70c. HMS *Victory*	1·60	1·60
1385	80c. *Achille* surrendering to HMS *Polyphemus*	1·75	2·00
MS1386	120×78 mm. $1 Admiral Collingwood (brown, black and grey) (vert); $1 HMS *Polyphemus* (vert)	6·00	6·50

No. 1384 contains traces of powdered wood from HMS *Victory*.

271 William Curry

2005. Abaco—Key West Connections. Multicoloured.

1387	15c. Type **271**	45	25
1388	25c. Captain John Bartlum's House (horiz)	60	40
1389	50c. Captain John Bartlum	1·25	1·10
1390	65c. Captain Tuggy Roberts' House (horiz)	1·50	1·60

272 Flags of EU and Bahamas and Map

2005. 50th Anniv of First Europa Stamp. Designs, all showing flags of EU and Bahamas, outline Map of Western Europe and different seascapes. Multicoloured.

1391	15c. Type **272**	45	45
1392	25c. Seascape with bands of thin high cloud	65	65
1393	50c. Seascape with small island	1·25	1·40
1394	$5 Seascape with clouds	9·00	11·00
MS1395	120×77 mm. Nos. 1391/4	10·00	12·00

2005. Lighthouses (2nd series). As T **266**. Multicoloured.

1396	15c. Bird Rock	80	40
1397	50c. Castle Island	1·75	1·10
1398	65c. San Salvador	2·00	1·40
1399	70c. Great Inagua	2·25	2·25
1400	80c. Cay Lobos	2·50	2·75

2005. Pope John Paul II Commemoration. As T **219** of Ascension.

1401	$1 multicoloured	2·25	2·50

273 College Entrance, Nassau

2005. 30th Anniv of the College of the Bahamas. Sheet 81×88 mm.

MS1402	**273** $2 multicoloured	3·25	3·75

2005. Christmas. Birth Bicentenary of Hans Christian Andersen (writer). As T **220** of Ascension. Multicoloured.

1403	15c. *The Little Fir Tree*	30	20
1404	25c. *The Princess and the Pea*	45	35
1405	50c. *The Tin Soldier*	90	90
1406	65c. *Thumbelina*	1·10	1·25

274 Bahama Nuthatch

2006. BirdLife International. Bahama Nuthatch (Sitta insularis). Multicoloured.

1407	15c. Type **274**	65	30
1408	25c. On thick branch (facing left)	80	45
1409	50c. On tree trunk (facing right)	1·40	1·10
1410	65c. On thin branch among pine needles	1·75	1·40
1411	70c. Nuthatch seen from underside	1·90	1·90
1412	80c. On tree trunk near hole (facing left)	2·00	2·25
MS1413	170×85 mm. Nos. 1407/12	7·75	7·75

The stamps within No. **MS**1413 form a composite design showing nuthatches in Caribbean pine trees.

2006. 80th Birthday of Queen Elizabeth II. As T **223** of Ascension. Multicoloured.

1414	15c. Princess Elizabeth	55	30
1415	25c. Queen Elizabeth II, c. 1952	75	40
1416	50c. Wearing blue feathered hat	1·25	1·10
1417	65c. Wearing hat with brim raised at one side	1·60	1·75
MS1418	144×75 mm. $1.50 As No. 1415; $1.50 As No. 1416	6·00	6·50

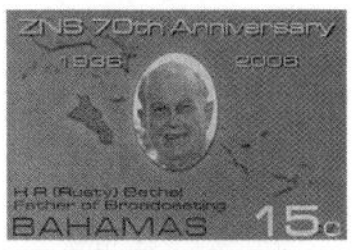

275 H. R. (Rusty) Bethel (Manager, ZNS Radio 1945–70)

2006. 70th Anniv of Broadcasting in the Bahamas. Multicoloured.

1419	15c. Type **275**	45	25
1420	25c. New Broadcasting Corporation of the Bahamas logo	65	30
1421	50c. National Headquarters of Broadcasting Corporation of the Bahamas	1·10	80
1422	65c. ZNS Nassau Radio stations building	1·40	1·25
1423	70c. Radio mast and map of Bahamas	1·50	1·50
1424	80c. "ZNS Radio" (70th anniv) and microphone	1·60	1·75

276 Amaryllis (*Hippeastrum puniceum*)

2006. Flowers of the Bahamas. Paintings by Alton Roland Lowe. Multicoloured.

1425	5c. Type **276**	20	30
1426	10c. *Barleria cristata*	25	30
1495a	15c. Yesterday, today, tomorrow (*Brunfelsia solanaceae*)	30	15
1427	25c. Desert rose (*Adenium obesum*)	40	20
1428	35c. Poor man's orchid (*Bauhinia* sp.)	55	25
1429	40c. Frangipani (*Plumeria* sp.)	85	50
1430	55c. Herald's trumpet (*Beaumontia grandiflora*)	1·25	1·00
1431	65c. Oleander (*Nerium oleander*)	1·40	1·00
1432	75c. Bird of Paradise (*Strelitzia reginae*)	1·60	1·25
1433	80c. *Plumbago capensis*	1·75	1·40
1434	90c. Rose (*Rosa* sp.)	1·90	1·50
1435	$1 Rubber vine (*Cryptostegia madagascariensis*)	2·25	2·00
1436	$2 Star of Bethlehem (*Jatropha integerrima*)	4·25	4·50
1437	$5 Angel's trumpet (*Brugmansia suaveolens*)	11·00	12·00
1438	$10 Wine lily (*Crinum* sp.)	22·00	24·00

277 *Centrosema virginianum* (blue pea)

2006. Wild Flowering Vines. Paintings by Alton Roland Lowe. Multicoloured.

1439	15c. Type **277**	40	25
1440	50c. *Urechites lutea* (allamanda)	90	60
1441	65c. *Ipomoea indica* (morning glory)	1·10	1·10
1442	70c. *Ipomoea microdactyla* (sky vine)	1·25	1·50

278 Christmas Sunday

2006. Christmas. Multicoloured.

1443	15c. Type **278**	40	25
1444	25c. Christmas dinner	60	30
1445	50c. Bay Street shopping	1·00	1·60
1446	65c. Boxing Day Junkanoo	1·25	85
1447	70c. Watch Night service	1·40	1·40
1448	80c. New Year's Day Junkanoo	1·50	1·75

279 Blainville's Beaked Whale

2007. Endangered Species. Blainville's Beaked Whale (*Mesoplodon densirostris*). Multicoloured.

1449	15c. Type **279**	40	40
1450	25c. Three whales	60	60
1451	50c. Whales just beneath surface	1·00	1·00
1452	60c. Two whales	1·10	1·10

280 Princess Elizabeth and Lt. Philip Mountbatten, 1949

2007. Diamond Wedding of Queen Elizabeth II and Prince Philip. Multicoloured.

1453	15c. Type **280**	30	15
1454	25c. Princess Elizabeth riding in carriage on her wedding day, 1949	50	35
1455	50c. Princess Elizabeth and Prince Philip waving from balcony on wedding day, 1949	1·00	1·00
1456	65c. Princess Elizabeth, Prince Philip and Queen Mary	1·40	1·50
MS1457	125×85 mm. $5 Wedding portrait (42×56 mm)	11·00	11·00

281 Bahamas Scouts at Church Service

2007. Centenary of Scouting. Multicoloured.

1458	15c. Type **281**	50	30
1459	25c. Scout in adventure playground	75	45
1460	50c. Scout barbecue	1·25	1·00
1461	65c. Bahamas girl scouts on parade	1·50	1·60
MS1462	90×65 mm. 70c. Scouts playing ball (*vert*); 80c. Lord Baden-Powell (*vert*)	2·40	2·40

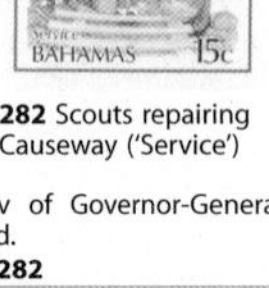

282 Scouts repairing Causeway ('Service')

2007. 20th Anniv of Governor-General's Youth Award. Multicoloured.

1463	15c. Type **282**	30	20
1464	25c. Painting ('Skills')	45	30
1465	50c. Kayaking ('Physical Recreation')	90	90
1466	65c. Hiking ('Adventurous Journey')	1·25	1·25
1467	70c. Conch shell emblem	1·50	1·75

283 Flower Decoration

2007. Christmas. Tree Decorations. Multicoloured.

1468	15c. Type **283**	25	15
1469	25c. Sea shells decoration	40	25
1470	50c. Sea shells decoration (different)	90	70
1471	65c. Bow and sea shells decoration	1·25	90
1472	70c. Gold woven decoration	1·40	1·40
1473	80c. 'Angel' made from sea shells	1·60	1·75

284 Choir

2007. 300th Birth Anniv of Charles Wesley. Multicoloured.

1474	15c. Type **284**	30	20
1475	50c. Charles and John Wesley (evangelists) (vert)	90	65
1476	65c. Revd. Charles Wesley and *Hymns and Sacred Poems* (vert)	1·10	90
1477	70c. Harbour Island Methodist Church (horiz)	1·50	1·60

285 *Heliconius charitonius* (zebra longwing)

2008. Bahamas Butterflies. Multicoloured.

1478	15c. Type **285**	30	20
1479	25c. *Dryas julia carteri* (Julia)	45	30
1480	50c. *Phoebis sennae* (cloudless sulphur)	1·10	85
1481	65c. *Danaus gilippus berenice* (The Queen)	1·40	1·10
1482	70c. *Urbanus proteus* (long-tailed skipper)	1·60	1·75
1483	80c. *Dione vanillae insularis* (Gulf fritillary)	1·75	2·00
MS1484	170×75 mm. Nos. 1478/83	5·50	6·00

286 His Majesty's Independant Company

2008. Military Uniforms. Multicoloured.

1485	15c. Type **286**	30	20
1486	25c. 47th Regiment of Foot	45	30
1487	50c. 99th Regiment of Foot	90	80
1488	65c. Royal Artillery	1·25	1·25
1489	70c. Black Garrison Companies	1·50	1·60

287 Athlete breaking Finish Tape

2008. Olympic Games, Beijing. Multicoloured.

1490	15c. Type **287**	25	15
1491	50c. High jump	90	80
1492	65c. Javelin thrower	1·25	1·25
1493	70c. Triple jump	1·40	1·60

288 Centenary Emblem

2008. Centenary of the Royal Bank of Canada in the Bahamas. Multicoloured.

1506	15c. Type **288**	40	25
1507	25c. Regional Head Office	55	40
1508	50c. Main Branch, Bay Street, Nassau, early 1900s	1·25	90
1509	65c. Artist's rendering of new Carmichael Road Branch, Nassau	1·50	1·60
1510	70c. Ross McDonald, Head of Caribbean Banking, and Nathaniel Beneby Jr., Vice President and Country Head	1·75	2·00

289 Launch of Space Shuttle *Discovery* in STS-26 'Return to Flight' Mission

2008. 50th Anniv of NASA. Multicoloured.

1511	15c. Type **289**	30	20
1512	25c. Apollo 16 Command and Service Module over the Moon, 1972	50	35
1513	50c. *Skylab 3*, 1973	1·10	80
1514	65c. Hubble Space Telescope	1·40	1·25
1515	70c. Gasses in the Swan Nebula	1·50	1·60
1516	80c. Star forming region in the Carina Nebula	1·75	1·90

290 The Three Kings worshipping Jesus

2008. Christmas. Book Illustrations by Leonhard Diefenbach from *The First Christmas for Our Dear Little Ones* by Rosa Mulholland. Multicoloured.

1517	15c. Type **290**	30	15
1518	50c. The Three Kings at the court of King Herod	1·10	70
1519	65c. Shepherds telling the news of the birth of Jesus	1·40	1·40
1520	70c. The shepherds visit the Baby Jesus	1·50	1·75

291 Students

2008. 60th Anniv of the University of the West Indies. Multicoloured.

1521	15c. Type **291**	50	30
1522	25c. Plaque marking Bahamas Clinical Training Programme becoming part of University of the West Indies, 2007	1·00	55
1523	65c. Scroll	3·00	2·00

292 Battle of Lexington, 1775

2008. 225th Anniv of the Treaty of Paris (recognising US Independence). Multicoloured.

1524	15c. Type **292**	40	30
1525	50c. Washington crossing the Delaware, 1776	1·25	90
1526	65c. American signatories of Treaty of Paris, 1783 (Benjamin West)	1·50	1·50
1527	70c. Detail of Treaty of Paris showing signatures	1·75	1·90

293 Bahamas Oriole (*Icterus northropi*)

2009. Endangered Species–Resident Breeders. Multicoloured.

1528	15c. Type **293**	65	25
1529	50c. Rose throated parrot (*Amazona leucocephala bahamensis*)	1·50	1·10
1530	65c. Great lizard cuckoo (*Saurothera merlini bahamensis*)	1·75	1·60
1531	70c. Audubon's shearwater (*Puffinus lherminieri*)	1·90	1·90

294 Peony

2009. China 2009 World Stamp Exhibition and Peony Festival, Luoyang. Sheet 180×110 mm. Multicoloured; colours of right-hand borders given.

MS1532	Type **294**×8 (colours of right-hand borders cream, white, pale pink, pale blue, pale flesh, pale green, pale yellow and pale azure)	8·25	8·25

295 'Tripod'

2009. Potcake Dogs. Multicoloured.

1533	15c. Type **295**	30	20
1534	50c. 'Amigo'	95	70
1535	65c. 'Turtle'	1·30	1·10
1536	70c. 'Oreo'	1·70	1·50

296 Bahamas 1859 1d Stamp

2009. 150th Anniv of the First Bahamas Stamp. Multicoloured, background colour given.

1537	**296** 15c. pink	35	25
1538	**296** 15c. azure	35	25
1539	**296** 15c. dull green	35	25
1540	**296** 15c. dull reddish lilac	35	25
MS1541	130×100 mm. Nos. 1537/40	1·40	1·40

2009. Centenary of Naval Aviation. As T **87** of British Antarctic Territory. Multicoloured.

1542	15c. Hawker Sea Hurricane	35	25
1543	65c. Hawker Sea Fury	1·20	1·00
1544	70c. Fairey Gannet	1·30	1·10
1545	80c. de Havilland Sea Vampire	1·60	1·40
MS1546	110×70 mm. $2 Aircraft on deck of merchant aircraft carrier MV *Empire MacKendrick*	4·25	4·25

297 East Street Tabernacle of Church of God of Prophecy

2009. Christmas. Churches. Multicoloured.

1547	15c. Type **297**	25	15
1548	25c. The Mission Baptist Church	40	30
1549	50c. Grant's Town Seventh-Day Adventist Church	85	65
1550	65c. Wesley Methodist Church, Harbour Island	1·40	1·20
1551	70c. St. Francis Xavier Cathedral	1·50	1·30
1552	80c. St. Ambrose Anglican Church	1·70	1·50

298 The House of Assembly

2009. 60th Anniv of the Commonwealth. Sheet 120×85 mm.

MS1553	**298** $2 multicoloured	4·00	4·00

299 Dolphin and Whale

2010. Friends of the Environment. Multicoloured.

1554	15c. Type **299**	25	15
1555	50c. Parrot and island map	85	65
1557	70c. Bird and tree	1·50	1·30

300 Winston Churchill

2010. 70th Anniv of the Battle of Britain. Multicoloured.

1558	15c. Type **300** ("...we shall never surrender...")	25	15
1559	25c. ..the Battle of Britain is about to begin...	45	25
1560	50c. "...never in the field of human conflict was so much owed by so many to so few..."	85	65
1561	65c. ...this was their finest hour...	1·40	1·20
1562	70c. ...upon this battle depends the survival of Christian civilization...	1·50	1·30
1563	80c. ...we shall fight on the beaches...	1·70	1·50
MS1563a	110×70 mm. $2 Sir Douglas Bader	4·00	4·00

301 Palm Trees in High Wind

2010. Hurricane Awareness. Multicoloured.

1564	15c. Type **301**	60	40
1565	50c. Map tracking hurricane across Bahamas	1·40	1·20
1566	65c. Reconnaissance aircraft flying through storm to measure intensity	2·00	1·80
1567	70c. Hurricane and NEMA (National Emergency Management Agency) logo	2·40	2·20

302 Cruise Ship and Fireworks

2010. Christmas. 'Tourist Winter Escapes'. Multicoloured.

1568	15c. Type **302**	60	40
1569	50c. Atlantis Hotel, Paradise Island and fireworks	1·40	1·20
1570	65c. Aircraft tailfin and fireworks	2·00	1·80
1571	70c. Fort Fincastle and Water Tower and fireworks	2·30	2·10

303 The Annual Heart Ball

2011. 50th Anniv of the Sir Victor Sassoon Heart Foundation. Multicoloured.

1572	15c. Type **303**	65	55
1573	50c. Doctor with young child	1·50	1·30
1574	65c. Doctor and young girl	2·10	1·90
1575	70c. Sir Victor Sassoon	2·50	2·30

2011. Queen Elizabeth II and Prince Philip. 'A Lifetime of Service'. Multicoloured.

1576	15c. Queen Elizabeth II, Balmoral, 6 February 1982	60	40
1577	50c. Queen Elizabeth II and Prince Philip, Windsor Castle, June 1959	1·60	1·40
1578	65c. Queen Elizabeth II and Prince Philip, Thames Valley University, London, 20 February 2009	2·00	1·80
1579	70c. Queen Elizabeth II and Prince Philip, Westminster Abbey, 8 March 2010	2·40	2·20
1580	$1 Queen Elizabeth II and Prince Philip, Buckingham Palace, 19 July 1957	3·50	3·25
1581	$2 Prince Philip, Balmoral, 6 February 1982	6·00	5·50
MS1582	175×164 mm. Nos. 1576/81 and three stamp-size labels	16·00	16·00
MS1583	110×70 mm. $2.50 Queen Elizabeth II and Prince Philip, Sandringham House, Norfolk, 1992	8·00	8·00

304 Prince William and Miss Catherine Middleton at Friend's Wedding, Austria, September 2008

2011. Royal Wedding. Multicoloured.

1584	15c. Type **304**	80	50
1585	50c. Engagement photograph, St. James's Palace, London, November 2010	1·40	1·20
1586	65c. Kissing on Buckingham Palace balcony after wedding	2·00	1·75
MS1587	94×64 mm. $5 Wedding in Westminster Abbey (vert)	16·00	16·00

305 Christ Church Cathedral

2011. 150th Anniv of the Anglican Diocese and City of Nassau. Multicoloured.

1588	15c. Type **305**	65	55
1589	50c. Rawson Square, 1861	1·50	1·30
1590	65c. Government House, 1861	2·10	1·90
1591	70c. Bay Street, 1861	2·50	2·30
1592	$1 Dr. Charles Caulfield (first Bishop of Nassau), 1862	3·00	3·25
1593	$2 Royal Governor Charles Bayley, 1857-64	6·00	5·50

306 Angel Gabriel appearing to Mary

2011. Christmas. Angels. Multicoloured.

1594	15c. Type **306**	65	55
1595	25c. Angel watching over Mary and Joseph on journey to Bethlehem	80	65
1596	50c. Angel guiding Wise Men	1·50	1·30
1597	65c. Angel watching over Infant Jesus in manger	2·10	1·90
1598	70c. Angel appearing to Shepherds	2·50	2·25
1599	80c. Angel watching over Mary and Infant Jesus	2·75	2·50

307 Common Sea Fan (*Gorgonia ventalina*)

2012. Marine Life. Multicoloured.

1600	5c. Type **307**	15	10
1601	10c. Christmas tree worm (*Spirobranchus giganteus*)	25	15
1602	15c. Elkhorn coral (*Acropora palmata*)	65	55
1603	20c. Cushion sea star (*Oreaster reticulatus*)	70	60

1604	25c. Queen conch (*Strombus gigas*)	75	65
1605	30c. Hawksbill turtle (*Eretmochelys imbricata*)	90	80
1606	40c. Green moray eel (*Gymnothorax funebris*)	1·20	1·00
1607	50c. Bonefish (*Albula vulpes*)	1·50	1·30
1608	60c. Spider crab (*Mithrax spinosissimus*)	1·90	1·70
1609	65c. Spiny lobster (*Panulirus argus*)	2·10	1·90
1610	70c. Nassau grouper (*Epinephelus striatus*)	2·50	2·30
1611	80c. Yellowtail snapper (*Ocyurus chrysurus*)	3·50	3·25
1612	$1 Great barracuda (*Sphyraena barracuda*)	4·00	3·75
1613	$2 Spotted eagle ray (*Aetobatus narinari*)	6·50	6·25
1614	$5 Caribbean reef shark (*Carcharhinus perezi*)	9·00	8·75
1615	$10 Bottlenose dolphin (*Tursiops truncatus*)	15·00	14·00

308 Caribbean Flamingo

2012. Endangered Species. Caribbean Flamingo (*Phoenicopterus ruber*). Multicoloured.

1616	15c. Type **308**	65	55
1617	50c. Chick and egg	1·50	1·30
1618	65c. Two flamingos feeding	2·10	1·90
1619	70c. Three flamingos in foreground	2·50	2·30
MS1620	90×70 mm. $5 Flamingos on beach	9·00	8·75

SPECIAL DELIVERY STAMPS

1916. Optd **SPECIAL DELIVERY**.

S2	6	5d. black and orange	50	9·50
S3	6	5d. black and mauve	30	3·75

Pt. 1

BAHAWALPUR

A former Indian Feudatory state which joined Pakistan in 1947 and continued to use its own stamps until 1953.

12 pies = 1 anna, 16 annas = 1 rupee.

(1)

1947. Nos. 265/8, 269a/77 and 259/62 of India optd with Type **1**.

1	**100a**	3p. slate	38·00
3	**100a**	9p. green	38·00
2	**100a**	½a. purple	38·00
4	**100a**	1a. red	38·00
5	**101**	1½a. violet	38·00
6	**101**	2a. red	38·00
7	**101**	3a. violet	38·00
8	**101**	3½a. blue	38·00
9	**102**	4a. brown	38·00
10	**102**	6a. green	38·00
11	**102**	8a. violet	38·00
12	**102**	12a. lake	38·00
13	-	14a. purple	85·00
14	**93**	1r. grey and brown	45·00
15	**93**	2r. purple and brown	£3500
16	**93**	5r. green and blue	£3500
17	**93**	10r. purple and red	£3500

2 Amir Muhammad Bahawal Khan I Abbasi

1948. Bicentenary Commemoration.

18	**2**	½a. black and red	3·75	7·00

4 H. H. the Amir of Bahawalpur

5 The Tombs of the Amirs

1948

19	**4**	3p. black and blue	2·75	20·00
21	**4**	9p. black and green	2·50	20·00
20	**4**	½a. black and red	2·50	20·00
22	**4**	1a. black and red	2·50	20·00
23	**4**	1½a. black and violet	3·50	16·00
24	**5**	2a. green and red	3·50	20·00
25	-	4a. orange and brown	3·50	20·00
26	-	6a. violet and blue	3·50	20·00
27	-	8a. red and violet	5·00	20·00
28	-	12a. green and red	5·50	30·00
29	-	1r. violet and brown	19·00	45·00
35	-	1r. green and orange	1·75	20·00
30	-	2r. green and red	55·00	80·00
36	-	2r. black and red	2·00	24·00
31	-	5r. black and violet	55·00	£100
37	-	5r. brown and blue	2·00	42·00
32	-	10r. red and black	32·00	£130
38	-	10r. brown and green	2·00	55·00

DESIGNS—HORIZ: 6a. Fort Derawar from the lake; 8a. Nur-Mahal Palace; 12a. Sadiq-Garh Palace. 46×32 mm: 10r. Three generations of Rulers. VERT (As Type **5**): 4a. Mosque in Sadiq-Garh; 1, 2, 5r. H.H. the Amir of Bahawalpur.

12 H.H. the Amir of Bahawalpur and Mohammed Ali Jinnah

1948. First Anniv of Union with Pakistan.

33	**12**	1½a. red and green	1·75	6·00

13 Soldiers of 1848 and 1948

1948. Centenary of Multan Campaign.

34	**13**	1½a. black and red	1·25	14·00

14 Irrigation

1949. Silver Jubilee of Accession of H.H. the Amir of Bahawalpur.

39	**14**	3p. black and blue	10	8·00
41	-	9p. black and green	10	8·00
40	-	½a. black and orange	10	8·00
42	-	1a. black and red	10	8·00

DESIGNS: ½a. Wheat; 9p. Cotton; 1a. Sahiwal bull.

18 UPU Monument, Berne

1949. 75th Anniv of U.P.U.

43	**17**	9p. black and green	20	2·25
44	**17**	1a. black and mauve	20	2·25
45	**17**	1½a. black and orange	20	2·25
46	**17**	2½a. black and blue	20	2·25

OFFICIAL STAMPS

O4 Eastern White Pelicans

1945. As Type O **4** with Arabic opt.

O1	-	½a. black and green	9·00	14·00
O2	-	1a. black and red	3·75	15·00
O7	-	1a. black and brown	90·00	80·00
O3	-	2a. black and violet	3·25	12·00
O4	**O 4**	4a. black and olive	13·00	26·00
O5	-	8a. black and brown	32·00	18·00
O6	-	1r. black and orange	32·00	18·00

DESIGNS: ½a. Panjnad Weir; 1a. (No. O2), Camel and calf; 1a. (No. O7), Baggage camels; 2a. Blackbuck antelopes; 8a. Friday Mosque, Fort Derawar; 1r. Temple at Pattan Munara.

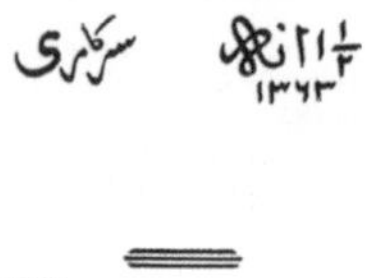

(O8)

1945. Types as Nos. O1, etc., in new colours and without Arabic opt. (a) Surch as Type O **8**.

O11	½a. on 8a. black and purple (as No. O5)	6·50	7·00
O12	1½a. on 5r. black and orange (as No. O6)	40·00	11·00
O13	1½a. on 2r. black and blue (as No. O1)	£140	8·50

(b) Optd **SERVICE** and Arabic inscription.

O14	½a. black and red (as No. O1)	1·25	11·00
O15	1a. black and red (as No. O2)	2·00	13·00
O16	2a. black and orange (as No. O3)	3·25	50·00

1945. As Type **4** but inscr "**SERVICE**" at left.

O17	3p. black and blue	7·00	15·00
O18	1½a. black and violet	24·00	8·00

O11 Allied Banners

1946. Victory.

O19	**O11**	1½a. green and grey	5·00	4·25

1948. Stamps of 1948 with Arabic opt as in Type O **4**.

O20	**4**	3p. black and blue	80	13·00
O21	**4**	1a. black and red	80	12·00
O22	**5**	2a. green and red	80	13·00
O23	-	4a. orange and brown	80	18·00
O24	-	1r. green and orange	80	20·00
O25	-	2r. black and red	80	26·00
O26	-	5r. chocolate and blue	80	42·00
O27	-	10r. brown and green	80	42·00

1949. 75th Anniv of U.P.U. optd as in Type O **4**.

O28	**17**	9p. black and green	15	4·50
O29	**17**	1a. black and mauve	15	4·50
O30	**17**	1½a. black and orange	15	4·50
O31	**17**	2½a. black and blue	15	4·50

Pt. 1, Pt. 19

BAHRAIN

An archipelago in the Persian Gulf on the Arabian coast. An independent shaikhdom with Indian and later British postal administration. The latter was closed on 1 January 1966, when the Bahrain Post Office took over.

1933. 12 pies = 1 anna; 16 annas = 1 rupee.
1957. 100 naya paise = 1 rupee.

Stamps of India optd **BAHRAIN**.

1933. King George V.

1	**55**	3p. grey	3·50	45
3	**80**	9p. green	3·75	4·25
2	**56**	½a. green	7·50	4·00
15	**79**	½a. green	7·50	2·00
4	**57**	1a. brown	8·00	2·50
16	**81**	1a. brown	11·00	40
5	**82**	1a.3p. mauve	15·00	3·75
6	**70**	2a. orange	10·00	19·00
17	**59**	2a. orange	45·00	7·50
7	**62**	3a. blue	19·00	65·00
18	**62**	3a. red	4·75	60
8	**83**	3a.6p. blue	3·75	40
9	**71**	4a. green	18·00	65·00
19	**63**	4a. olive	5·00	40
10	**65**	8a. mauve	6·00	30
11	**66**	12a. red	7·50	2·00
12	**67**	1r. brown and green	16·00	14·00
13	**67**	2r. red and orange	30·00	38·00
14w	**67**	5r. blue and violet	£140	£170

1938. King George VI.

20	**91**	3p. slate	19·00	7·50
22	**91**	9p. green	15·00	13·00
21	**91**	½a. brown	8·00	20
23	**91**	1a. red	14·00	20
24	**92**	2a. red	5·00	6·00
26	-	3a. green (No. 253)	12·00	12·00
27	-	3a.6p. blue (No. 254)	6·00	9·00
28	-	4a. brown (No. 255)	£170	70·00
30	-	8a. violet (No. 257)	£275	35·00
31	-	12a. red (No. 258)	£150	48·00
32	**93**	1r. slate and brown	7·50	1·75
33	**93**	2r. purple and brown	18·00	10·00
34	**93**	5r. green and blue	15·00	13·00
35	**93**	10r. purple and red	85·00	50·00
36w	**93**	15r. brown and green	90·00	90·00
37	**93**	25r. slate and purple	£130	£110

1942. King George VI.

38	**100a**	3p. slate	3·50	2·50
40	**100a**	9p. green	18·00	22·00
39	**100a**	½a. mauve	4·75	4·25
41	**100a**	1a. red	8·00	1·00
42	**101**	1a.3p. bistre	10·00	24·00
43	**101**	1½a. violet	7·00	8·00
44	**101**	2a. red	7·00	1·50
45	**101**	3a. violet	22·00	7·50
46	**101**	3½a. blue	6·50	22·00
47	**102**	4a. brown	6·50	2·00
48	**102**	6a. green	20·00	12·00
49	**102**	8a. violet	10·00	6·00
50	**102**	12a. purple	16·00	6·00

Stamps of Great Britain surch **BAHRAIN** and new value in Indian currency.

1948. King George VI.

71	**128**	½a. on ½d. orange	2·50	3·50
51	**128**	½a. on 1d. green	50	1·25
52	**128**	1a. on 1d. red	50	3·25
72	**128**	1a. on 1d. blue	3·00	20
53	**128**	1½a. on 1½d. brown	50	4·50
73	**128**	1½a. on 1½d. green	3·00	13·00
54	**128**	2a. on 2d. orange	50	20
74	**128**	2a. on 2d. brown	1·50	30
55	**128**	2½a. on 2½d. blue	50	5·00
75	**128**	2½a. on 2½d. red	3·00	16·00
56	**128**	3a. on 3d. violet	50	10
76	**129**	4a. on 4d. blue	5·00	1·50
57	**129**	6a. on 6d. purple	50	10
58	**130**	1r. on 1s. brown	1·25	10
59	**131**	2r. on 2s.6d. green	5·50	5·50
60	**131**	5r. on 5s. red	5·50	5·50
60a	-	10r. on 10s. blue (No. 478a)	90·00	80·00

1948. Silver Wedding.

61	**137**	2½a. on 2½d. blue	1·00	2·75
62	**138**	15r. on £1 blue	32·00	50·00

1948. Olympic Games.

63	**139**	2½a. on 2½d. blue	1·50	4·75
64	**140**	3a. on 3d. violet	1·00	4·25
65	-	6a. on 6d. purple	1·50	4·25
66	-	1r. on 1s. brown	2·75	4·25

1949. U.P.U.

67	**143**	2½a. on 2½d. blue	60	2·50
68	**144**	3a. on 3d. violet	70	4·50
69	-	6a. on 6d. purple	60	3·00
70	-	1r. on 1s. brown	1·25	3·50

1951. Pictorial stamps (Nos. 509/11).

77	**147**	2r. on 2s.6d. green	38·00	16·00
78	-	5r. on 5s. red	15·00	6·00
79	-	10r. on 10s. blue	35·00	9·50

1952. Queen Elizabeth II.

97	**154**	½a. on ½d. orange	10	15
81	**154**	1a. on 1d. blue	10	10
82	**154**	1½a. on 1½d. green	10	30
83	**154**	2a. on 2d. brown	30	10
84	**155**	2½a. on 2½d. red	20	1·75
85	**155**	3a. on 3d. lilac	3·00	10
86	**155**	4a. on 4d. blue	17·00	30
99	**157**	6a. on 6d. purple	50	75
88	**160**	12a. on 1s.3d. green	3·25	20
89	**160**	1r. on 1s.6d. blue	3·25	10

1953. Coronation.

90	**161**	2½a. on 2½d. red	1·25	75
91	-	4a. on 4d. blue	2·25	7·50
92	**163**	12a. on 1s.3d. green	6·00	6·00
93	-	1r. on 1s.6d. blue	7·50	50

1955. Pictorial stamps (Nos. 595a/598a).

94	**166**	2r. on 2s.6d. brown	5·50	2·00
95	-	5r. on 5s. red	16·00	2·75
96	-	10r. on 10s. blue	20·00	2·75

1957. Queen Elizabeth II.

102	**157**	1n.p. on 5d. brown	10	10
103	**154**	3n.p. on ½d. orange	50	3·00
104	**154**	6n.p. on 1d. blue	50	3·00
105	**154**	9n.p. on 1½d. green	50	3·25
106	**154**	12n.p. on 2d. pale brown	30	70
107	**155**	15n.p. on 2½d. red	30	15
108	**155**	20n.p. on 3d. lilac	30	10

109	**155**	25n.p. on 4d. blue	1·25	2·50
110	**157**	40n.p. on 6d. purple	40	10
111	**157**	50n.p. on 9d. olive	3·75	4·50
112	**157**	75n.p. on 1s.3d. green	2·50	50

1957. World Scout Jubilee Jamboree.

113	**170**	15n.p. on 2½d. red	35	35
114	**171**	25n.p. on 4d. blue	35	35
115	-	75n.p. on 1s.3d. green	40	45

16 Shaikh Sulman bin Hamed al-Khalifa

1960

117	**16**	5n.p. blue	20	10
118	**16**	15n.p. orange	20	10
119	**16**	20n.p. violet	20	10
120	**16**	30n.p. bistre	20	10
121	**16**	40n.p. grey	20	10
122	**16**	50n.p. green	20	10
123	**16**	75n.p. brown	30	15
124	-	1r. black	3·00	30
125	-	2r. red	3·00	2·50
126	-	5r. blue	5·00	3·25
127	-	10r. green	14·00	6·00

The rupee values are larger, 27×32½ mm.

18 Shaikh Isa bin Sulman al-Khalifa

19 Air Terminal, Muharraq

1964

128	**18**	5n.p. blue	10	10
129	**18**	15n.p. orange	15	1·00
130	**18**	20n.p. violet	15	10
131	**18**	30n.p. bistre	15	10
132	**18**	40n.p. slate	15	10
133	**18**	50n.p. green	15	1·50
134	**18**	75n.p. brown	25	10
135	**19**	1r. black	11·00	2·25
136	**19**	2r. red	11·00	4·50
137	-	5r. blue	15·00	18·00
138	-	10r. myrtle	15·00	18·00

DESIGN—As Type **19**: 5r., 10r. Deep water harbour.

21 Sheikh Isa bin Sulman al-Khalifa

22 Ruler and Bahrain Airport

1966

139	**21**	5f. green	20	20
140	**21**	10f. red	20	20
141	**21**	15f. blue	20	20
142	**21**	20f. purple	30	20
143	**22**	30f. black and green	45	20
144	**22**	40f. black and blue	55	20
145	-	50f. black and red	75	30
146	-	75f. black and violet	95	45
147	-	100f. blue and yellow	3·25	1·30
148	-	200f. green and orange	14·00	2·75
149	-	500f. brown and yellow	12·00	4·75
150	-	1d. multicoloured	21·00	10·50

DESIGNS—As Type **22**: 50f., 75f. Ruler and Mina Sulman deep-water harbour. VERT (26½×42½ mm): 100f. Pearl-diving; 200f. Lanner falcon and horse-racing; 500f. Serving coffee, and ruler's palace. LARGER (37×52½ mm): 1d. Ruler, crest, date palm, horse, dhow, pearl necklace, mosque, coffee-pot and Bab-al-Bahrain (gateway).

23 Produce

1966. Trade Fair and Agricultural Show.

151	**23**	10f. turquoise and red	55	10
152	**23**	20f. lilac and green	75	10
153	**23**	40f. blue and brown	2·10	55
154	**23**	200f. red and blue	10·00	4·75

24 W.H.O. Emblem and Map of Bahrain

1968. 20th Anniv of W.H.O.

155	**24**	20f. black and grey	95	65
156	**24**	40f. black and turquoise	3·25	1·70
157	**24**	150f. black and red	14·00	6·50

25 View of Isa Town

1968. Inauguration of Isa New Town. Multicoloured.

158	50f. Type **25**	4·75	1·40
159	80f. Shopping centre	7·00	2·75
160	120f. Stadium	10·50	5·00
161	150f. Mosque	13·00	6·50

26 Symbol of Learning

1969. 50th Anniv of School Education in Bahrain.

162	**26**	40f. multicoloured	1·90	1·20
163	**26**	60f. multicoloured	3·75	1·90
164	**26**	150f. multicoloured	10·00	5·00

27 Dish Aerial and Map of Persian Gulf

1969. Opening of Satellite Earth Station, Ras Abu Jarjour. Multicoloured.

165	20f. Type **27**	2·75	65
166	40f. Dish aerial and palms (vert)	6·00	1·10
167	100f. Type **27**	13·00	4·75
168	150f. As 40f.	21·00	7·00

28 Arms, Map and Manama Municipality Building

1970. Second Arab Cities Organization Conf, Manama.

169	**28**	30f. multicoloured	2·75	2·75
170	**28**	150f. multicoloured	15·00	15·00

29 Copper Bull's Head, Barbar

1970. Third International Asian Archaeology Conference, Bahrain. Multicoloured.

171	60f. Type **29**	4·75	2·50
172	80f. Palace of Dilmun excavations	7·50	3·25
173	120f. Desert gravemounds	9·00	4·25
174	150f. Dilmun seal	10·50	5·25

30 Vickers Super VC-10 Airliner, Big Ben, London, and Bahrain Minaret

1970. First Gulf Aviation Vickers Super VC-10 Flight, Doha–London.

175	**30**	30f. multicoloured	3·25	95
176	**30**	60f. multicoloured	6·50	2·10
177	**30**	120f. multicoloured	12·00	6·50

31 I.E.Y. Emblem and Open Book

1970. International Education Year. Multicoloured.

178	60f. Type **31**	5·25	5·25
179	120f. Emblem and Bahraini children	10·50	10·50

32 Allegory of Independence

1971. Independence Day and Tenth Anniv of Ruler's Accession. Multicoloured.

180	30f. Type **32**	2·40	1·30
181	60f. Government House	4·75	2·40
182	120f. Arms of Bahrain	12·00	6·00
183	150f. Arms of Bahrain (gold background)	16·00	8·00

33 Arab Dhow with Arab League and U.N. Emblems

1972. Bahrain's Membership of Arab League and U.N. Multicoloured.

184	30f. Type **33**	6·00	6·00
185	60f. Type **33**	9·75	9·75
186	120f. Dhow sails (vert)	13·00	13·00
187	150f. As 120f.	24·00	24·00

34 Human Heart

1972. World Health Day.

188	**34**	30f. multicoloured	6·00	6·00
189	**34**	60f. multicoloured	12·00	12·00

35 F.A.O. and U.N. Emblems

1973. Tenth Anniv of World Food Programme.

190	**35**	30f. brown, red and green	5·25	5·25
191	**35**	60f. brown, lt brown & grn	10·00	10·00

36 "Races of the World"

1973. 25th Anniv of Declaration of Human Rights.

192	**36**	30f. blue, brown and black	6·50	6·50
193	**36**	60f. red, brown and black	9·75	9·75

38 Flour Mill

1973. National Day. "Progress in Bahrain". Mult.

195	30f. Type **38**	2·40	65
196	60f. Muharraq Airport	3·25	1·20
197	120f. Sulmaniya Medical Centre	6·50	3·50
198	150f. Aluminium Smelter	6·50	3·75

39 U.P.U. Emblem within Letters

1974. Admission of Bahrain to U.P.U. Multicoloured.

199	30f. Type **39**	2·40	2·40
200	60f. U.P.U. emblem on letters	4·00	4·00
201	120f. Ruler and emblem on dove with letter in beak (37×28 mm)	4·00	4·00
202	150f. As 120f. (37×28 mm)	6·00	6·00

40 Traffic Lights and Directing Hands

1974. International Traffic Day.

203	**40**	30f. multicoloured	4·75	4·75
204	**40**	60f. multicoloured	8·50	8·50

41 U.P.U. "Stamp" and Mail Transport

1974. Centenary of U.P.U.

205	**41**	30f. multicoloured	1·30	1·30
206	**41**	60f. multicoloured	1·50	1·50
207	**41**	120f. multicoloured	4·00	4·00
208	**41**	150f. multicoloured	5·25	5·25

42 Emblem and Sitra Power Station

1974. National Day. Multicoloured.

209	30f. Type **42**	85	30
210	60f. Type **42**	2·75	1·40
211	120f. Emblem and Bahrain Dry Dock	4·50	2·75
212	150f. As 120f.	6·00	3·75

43 Costume and Headdress

1975. Bahrain Women's Costumes.

213	**43**	30f. multicoloured	85	85
214	-	60f. multicoloured	2·00	2·00
215	-	120f. multicoloured	4·00	4·00
216	-	150f. multicoloured	4·75	4·75

DESIGNS: Nos. 214/16, Costumes as Type **43**.

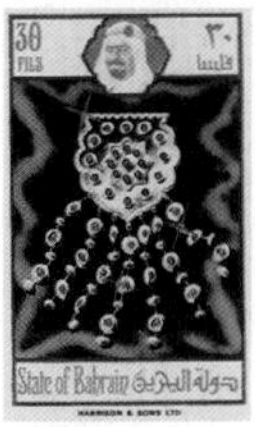
44 Jewelled Pendant

1975. Costume Jewellery. Multicoloured.

217	30f. Type **44**	1·10	1·10
218	60f. Gold crown	2·50	2·50
219	120f. Jewelled necklace	5·00	5·00
220	150f. Gold necklace	6·50	6·50

45 Women planting "Flower"

1975. International Women's Year. Multicoloured.

221	30f. Type **45**	2·40	1·10
222	60f. Woman holding I.W.Y. emblem	6·50	2·40

46 Head of Horse

1975. Horses. Multicoloured.

223a	60f. Type **46**	7·50	7·50
223b	60f. Grey	7·50	7·50
223c	60f. Grey with foal (horiz)	7·50	7·50
223d	60f. Close-up of Arab with grey	7·50	7·50
223e	60f. Grey and herd of browns (horiz)	7·50	7·50
223f	60f. Grey and brown (horiz)	7·50	7·50
223g	60f. Arabs riding horses (horiz)	7·50	7·50
223h	60f. Arab leading grey beside sea (horiz)	7·50	7·50

47 National Flag

48 Map of Bahrain within Cog and Laurel

1976

224	**47**	5f. red, pink and blue	30	30
225	**47**	10f. red, pink & green	30	30
226	**47**	15f. red, pink & black	30	30
227	**47**	20f. red, pink & brown	55	30
227b	**48**	25f. black and grey	65	30
228	**48**	40f. black and blue	65	45
228a	**48**	50f. green, black & olive	65	55
228b	**48**	60f. black and green	1·10	65
229	**48**	80f. black and mauve	1·70	75
229b	**48**	100f. black and red	1·70	95
230	**48**	150f. black and yellow	3·25	1·50
231	**48**	200f. black and yellow	3·75	1·80

49 Concorde Taking off

1976. First Commercial Flight of Concorde. Multicoloured.

232	80f. Type **49**	4·00	3·00
233	80f. Concorde landing	4·00	3·00
234	80f. Concorde en route	4·00	3·00
235	80f. Concorde on runway	4·00	3·00
MS236	154×115 mm. Nos. 232/5. Imperf	18·00	18·00

50 Soldier, Crest and Flag

1976. Defence Force Cadets' Day.

237	**50**	40f. multicoloured	3·00	3·00
238	**50**	80f. multicoloured	5·25	5·25

51 King Khalid of Saudi Arabia and Shaikh of Bahrain with National Flags

1976. Visit to Bahrain of King Khalid of Saudi Arabia.

239	**51**	40f. multicoloured	2·40	1·70
240	**51**	80f. multicoloured	4·75	3·75

52 Shaikh Isa bin Sulman al-Khalifa

1976

241	**52**	300f. green and pale green	5·25	2·75
242	**52**	400f. purple and pink	7·50	3·75
243	**52**	500f. blue and pale blue	9·00	4·75
244	**52**	1d. black and grey	16·00	8·50
244a	**52**	2d. violet and lilac	20·00	10·50
244b	**52**	3d. brown and pink	48·00	32·00

53 Ministry of Housing Emblem, Designs for Houses and Mosque

1976. National Day.

245	**53**	40f. multicoloured	2·10	95
246	**53**	80f. multicoloured	4·75	1·90

54 A.P.U. Emblem

1977. 25th Anniv of Arab Postal Union.

247	**54**	40f. multicoloured	2·10	1·60
248	**54**	80f. multicoloured	4·75	3·25

55 Dogs on Beach

1977. Saluki Dogs. Multicoloured.

249a	80f. Type **55**	3·75	3·75
249b	80f. Dog and dromedaries	3·75	3·75
249c	80f. Dog and antelope	3·75	3·75
249d	80f. Dog on lawn of building	3·75	3·75
249e	80f. Head of dog	3·75	3·75
249f	80f. Heads of two dogs	3·75	3·75
249g	80f. Dog in scrubland	3·75	3·75
249h	80f. Dogs fighting	3·75	3·75

56 Arab Students and Candle

1977. International Literacy Day.

250	**56**	40f. multicoloured	2·10	1·60
251	**56**	80f. multicoloured	4·75	3·25

57 Shipyard Installations and Arab Flags

1977. Inauguration of Arab Shipbuilding and Repair Yard Co.

252	**57**	40f. multicoloured	2·10	1·60
253	**57**	80f. multicoloured	4·75	3·25

58 Microwave Antenna

1978. Tenth World Telecommunications Day.

254	**58**	40f. multicoloured	2·10	1·60
255	**58**	80f. silver, dp blue & blue	4·75	3·25

59 Child being helped to Walk

1979. International Year of the Child. Multicoloured.

256	50f. Type **59**	2·10	1·50
257	100f. Hands protecting child	4·50	2·75

60 Boom Dhow

1979. Dhows. Multicoloured.

258	100f. Type **60**	6·50	6·50
259	100f. Baghla	6·50	6·50
260	100f. Shu'ai (horiz)	6·50	6·50
261	100f. Ghanja (horiz)	6·50	6·50
262	100f. Kotia	6·50	6·50
263	100f. Sambuk	6·50	6·50
264	100f. Jaliboot (horiz)	6·50	6·50
265	100f. Zarook (horiz)	6·50	6·50

61 Dome of Mosque, Mecca

1980. 1400th Anniv of Hejira.

266	**61**	50f. multicoloured	1·10	55
267	**61**	100f. multicoloured	2·40	1·80
268	**61**	150f. multicoloured	2·75	2·10
269	**61**	200f. multicoloured	3·75	3·00
MS270		84×91 mm. No. 267 (sold at 200f.)	10·00	10·00

62 Arab with Gyr Falcon

1980. Falconry. Multicoloured.

271	100f. Type **62**	4·25	2·40
272	100f. Arab looking at Lanner falcon on wrist	4·25	2·40
273	100f. Peregrine falcon resting with outstretched wings	4·25	2·40
274	100f. Peregrine falcon in flight	4·25	2·40
275	100f. Gyr falcon on pillar (with camels in background) (vert)	4·25	2·40
276	100f. Gyr falcon on pillar (closer view) (vert)	4·25	2·40
277	100f. Close-up of gyr falcon facing right (vert)	4·25	2·40
278	100f. Close-up of Lanner falcon full-face (vert)	4·25	2·40

63 Map and I.Y.D.P. Emblem

1981. International Year for Disabled Persons.

279	**63**	50f. multicoloured	2·75	75
280	**63**	100f. multicoloured	5·25	2·75

64 Jubilee Emblem

1981. 50th Anniv of Electrical Power in Bahrain.

281	**64**	50f. multicoloured	1·90	85
282	**64**	100f. multicoloured	4·50	2·40

65 Carving

1981. Handicrafts. Multicoloured.

283	50f. Type **65**	1·60	65
284	100f. Pottery	2·10	1·20
285	150f. Weaving	2·75	2·10
286	200f. Basket-making	4·25	2·75

66 Mosque

1981. Mosques.

287	**66**	50f. multicoloured	1·60	65
288	-	100f. multicoloured	2·10	1·20
289	-	150f. multicoloured	2·75	2·10
290	-	200f. multicoloured	4·25	2·75

DESIGNS: 100f. to 200f. As Type **66** but showing different mosques.

67 Shaikh Isa bin Sulman al-Khalifa

1981. 20th Anniv of Coronation of Shaikh Isa bin Sulman al-Khalifa.

291	**67**	15f. gold, grey and mauve	75	75
292	**67**	50f. gold, grey and red	1·50	1·50
293	**67**	100f. gold, grey and brown	2·50	2·50
294	**67**	150f. gold, grey and blue	4·00	4·00
295	**67**	200f. gold, grey and blue	4·75	4·75

68 Dorcas Gazelle

1982. Al-Areen Wildlife Park. Multicoloured.

296	100f. Goitred gazelle	2·75	2·75
297	100f. Type **68**	2·75	2·75
298	100f. Dhub lizard	2·75	2·75
299	100f. Brown hares	2·75	2·75
300	100f. Arabian oryx	2·75	2·75
301	100f. Addax	2·75	2·75

69 Flags and Clasped Hands encircling Emblem

1982. Third Supreme Council Session of Gulf Co-operation Council.

302	**69**	50f. multicoloured	1·20	1·20
303	-	100f. multicoloured	3·25	3·25

70 Madinat Hamad

1983. Opening of Madinat Hamad New Town. Multicoloured.

304	50f. Type **70**	2·10	65
305	100f. View of Madinat Hamad (different)	3·75	2·10

71 Shaikh Isa bin Sulman al-Khalifa

1983. Bicentenary of Al-Khalifa Dynasty. Multicoloured.

306	100f. Type **71**	1·30	1·30
307	100f. Cartouche of Ali bin Khalifa al-Khalifa	1·30	1·30
308	100f. Isa bin Ali al-Khalifa	1·30	1·30
309	100f. Hamad bin Isa al-Khalifa	1·30	1·30
310	100f. Salman bin Hamad al-Khalifa	1·30	1·30
311	100f. Cartouche of Ahmed bin Mohammed al-Khalifa	1·30	1·30
312	100f. Cartouche of Salman bin Ahmed al-Khalifa	1·30	1·30
313	100f. Cartouche of Abdullah bin Ahmed al-Khalifa	1·30	1·30
314	100f. Cartouche of Mohammed bin Khalifa al-Khalifa	1·30	1·30
MS315	109×83 mm. 500f. Type **71** (60×38 mm)	8·50	8·50

72 G.C.C. and Traffic and Licensing Directorate Emblems

1984. Gulf Co-operation Council Traffic Week.

316	**72**	15f. multicoloured	55	20
317	**72**	50f. multicoloured	1·60	55
318	**72**	100f. multicoloured	2·40	1·10

73 Hurdling

1984. Olympic Games, Los Angeles. Multicoloured.

319	15f. Type **73**	30	30
320	50f. Show-jumping	1·10	1·10
321	100f. Swimming	2·10	2·10
322	150f. Fencing	2·75	2·75
323	200f. Shooting	4·50	4·50

74 Manama and Emblem

1984. Centenary of Postal Services.

324	**74**	15f. multicoloured	55	20
325	**74**	50f. multicoloured	1·60	55
326	**74**	100f. multicoloured	2·75	1·40

75 Narrow-barred Spanish Mackerel

1985. Fish. Multicoloured.

327	100f. Type **75**	2·10	2·10
328	100f. Crocodile needlefish (three fishes)	2·10	2·10
329	100f. Sombre sweetlips (fish swimming to left, blue and lilac background)	2·10	2·10
330	100f. White-spotted rabbitfish (two fishes, blue and lilac background)	2·10	2·10
331	100f. Grey mullet (two fishes, green and pink background)	2·10	2·10
332	100f. Two-banded seabream (green and grey background)	2·10	2·10
333	100f. River seabream (blue background)	2·10	2·10
334	100f. Malabar grouper (green background)	2·10	2·10
335	100f. Small-toothed emperor (pink anemone background)	2·10	2·10
336	100f. Golden trevally (fish swimming to right, blue and lilac background)	2·10	2·10

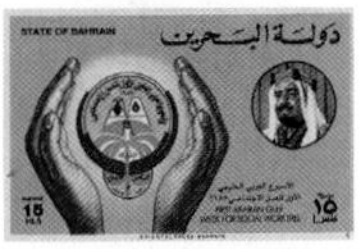

76 Hands cupping Emblem

1985. Arabian Gulf States Social Work Week.

337	**76**	15f. multicoloured	45	45
338	**76**	50f. multicoloured	1·30	1·30
339	**76**	100f. multicoloured	2·75	2·75

77 I.Y.Y. Emblem

1986. International Youth Year.

340	**77**	15f. multicoloured	45	45
341	**77**	50f. multicoloured	1·30	1·30
342	**77**	100f. multicoloured	2·75	2·75

78 Aerial View of Causeway

1986. Opening of Saudi–Bahrain Causeway. Multicoloured.

343	15f. Type **78**	45	45
344	50f. Aerial view of island	1·30	1·30
345	100f. Aerial view of road bridge	2·10	2·10

79 Shaikh Isa bin Sulman al-Khalifa

1986. 25th Anniv of Accession of Shaikh Isa bin Sulman al-Khalifa.

346	**79**	15f. multicoloured	45	45
347	**79**	50f. multicoloured	1·30	1·30
348	**79**	100f. multicoloured	2·10	2·10
MS349		148×110 mm. Nos. 346/8	8·50	8·50

80 Emblem

1988. 40th Anniv of W.H.O.

350	**80**	50f. multicoloured	75	75
351	**80**	150f. multicoloured	2·10	2·10

81 Centre

1988. Opening of Ahmed al-Fateh Islamic Centre.

352	**81**	50f. multicoloured	75	75
353	**81**	150f. multicoloured	2·10	2·10

82 Running

1988. Olympic Games, Seoul. Multicoloured.

354	50f. Type **82**	45	30
355	80f. Dressage	85	55
356	150f. Fencing	1·80	1·30
357	200f. Football	2·75	2·10

83 Emblem in "1988"

1988. Ninth Supreme Council Meeting of Gulf Co-operation Council.

358	**83**	50f. multicoloured	75	75
359	**83**	150f. multicoloured	2·10	2·10

84 Arab leading Camel

1989. Camels. Multicoloured.

360	150f. Type **84**	1·60	1·60
361	150f. Arab leading camel (different)	1·60	1·60
362	150f. Head of camel and pump-head	1·60	1·60
363	150f. Close-up of Arab on camel	1·60	1·60
364	150f. Arab riding camel	1·60	1·60
365	150f. Two Arab camel-riders	1·60	1·60
366	150f. Head of camel and camel-rider (horiz)	1·60	1·60
367	150f. Camels at rest in camp (horiz)	1·60	1·60
368	150f. Camels with calf (horiz)	1·60	1·60
369	150f. Heads of three camels (horiz)	1·60	1·60
370	150f. Camel in scrubland (horiz)	1·60	1·60
371	150f. Arab on camel (horiz)	1·60	1·60

85 Shaikh Isa bin Sulman al-Khalifa

1989. Multicoloured, colour of frame given.

372	**85**	25f. green	30	20
373	**85**	40f. grey	45	20
374	**85**	50f. pink	45	20
375	**85**	60f. brown	55	20
376	**85**	75f. mauve	75	20
377	**85**	80f. green	75	20
378	**85**	100f. orange	1·10	30
379	**85**	120f. violet	1·20	30
380	**85**	150f. grey	1·50	55
381	**85**	200f. blue	1·80	75
MS382		167×132 mm. Nos. 372/81	9·00	9·00

86 Houbara Bustards

1990. The Houbara Bustard. Multicoloured.

383	150f. Type **86**	1·50	1·50
384	150f. Two bustards (facing each other)	1·50	1·50
385	150f. Chicks and eggs	1·50	1·50
386	150f. Adult and chick	1·50	1·50
387	150f. Adult (vert)	1·50	1·50
388	150f. In flight	1·50	1·50
389	150f. Adult (facing right)	1·50	1·50
390	150f. Young bird (vert)	1·50	1·50
391	150f. Adult (facing left)	1·50	1·50
392	150f. Bird in display plumage	1·50	1·50
393	150f. Two bustards in display plumage	1·50	1·50
394	150f. Two bustards with bridge in background	1·50	1·50

87 Anniversary Emblem

1990. 40th Anniv of Gulf Air.

395	**87**	50f. multicoloured	55	30
396	**87**	80f. multicoloured	85	55
397	**87**	150f. multicoloured	1·60	1·10
398	**87**	200f. multicoloured	2·40	1·50

88 Anniversary Emblem

1990. 50th Anniv of Bahrain Chamber of Commerce and Industry.

399	**88**	50f. multicoloured	55	30
400	**88**	80f. multicoloured	75	55
401	**88**	150f. multicoloured	1·40	95
402	**88**	200f. multicoloured	1·80	1·30

89 I.L.Y. Emblem

1990. International Literacy Year.

403	**89**	50f. multicoloured	55	30
404	**89**	80f. multicoloured	75	55
405	**89**	150f. multicoloured	1·40	95
406	**89**	200f. multicoloured	1·90	1·30

90 Crested Lark

1991. Birds. Multicoloured.

407	150f. Type **90**	1·30	1·30
408	150f. Hoopoe (*Upupa epops*)	1·30	1·30
409	150f. White-cheeked bulbul (*Pycnonotus leucogenys*)	1·30	1·30
410	150f. Turtle dove (*Streptopelia turtur*)	1·30	1·30
411	150f. Collared dove (*Streptopelia decaocto*)	1·30	1·30
412	150f. Common kestrel (*Falco tinnunculus*)	1·30	1·30
413	150f. House sparrow (*Passer domesticus*) (horiz)	1·30	1·30
414	150f. Great grey shrike (*Lanius excubitor*) (horiz)	1·30	1·30
415	150f. Rose-ringed parakeet (*Psittacula krameri*)	1·30	1·30

91 Shaikh Isa bin Sulman al-Khalifa

1991. 30th Anniv of Amir's Coronation.

416	**91**	50f. multicoloured	45	30
417	**A**	50f. multicoloured	45	30
418	**91**	80f. multicoloured	65	45
419	**A**	80f. multicoloured	65	45
420	**91**	150f. multicoloured	1·40	85
421	**A**	150f. multicoloured	1·40	85
422	**91**	200f. multicoloured	1·80	1·10
423	**A**	200f. multicoloured	1·80	1·10

MS424 134×114 mm. **91** 500f. multicoloured; A 500f. multicoloured 10·50 10·50

DESIGN: A, The Amir and sunburst.

92 White Stork (*Ciconia ciconia*)

1992. Migratory Birds. Multicoloured.

425	150f. Type **92**	1·20	1·20
426	150f. European bee eater (*Merops apiaster*)	1·20	1·20
427	150f. Common starling (*Sturnus vulgaris*)	1·20	1·20
428	150f. Grey hypocolius (*Hypocolius ampelinus*)	1·20	1·20
429	150f. European cuckoo (*Cuculus canorus*)	1·20	1·20
430	150f. Mistle thrush (*Turdus viscivorus*)	1·20	1·20
431	150f. European roller (*Coracias garrulus*)	1·20	1·20
432	150f. Eurasian goldfinch (*Carduelis carduelis*)	1·20	1·20
433	150f. Red-backed shrike (*Lanius collurio*)	1·20	1·20
434	150f. Redwing (*Turdus iliacus*) (horiz)	1·20	1·20
435	150f. Pied wagtail (*Motacilla alba*) (horiz)	1·20	1·20
436	150f. Golden oriole (*Oriolus oriolus*) (horiz)	1·20	1·20
437	150f. European robin (*Erithacus rubecula*)	1·20	1·20
438	150f. Nightingale (*Luscinia luscinia*)	1·20	1·20
439	150f. Spotted flycatcher (*Muscicapa striata*)	1·20	1·20
440	150f. Barn swallow (*Hirundo rustica*)	1·20	1·20

93 Start of Race

1992. Horse-racing. Multicoloured.

441	150f. Type **93**	1·30	1·30
442	150f. Parading in paddock	1·30	1·30
443	150f. Galloping around bend	1·30	1·30
444	150f. Galloping past national flags	1·30	1·30
445	150f. Galloping past spectator stand	1·30	1·30
446	150f. Head-on view of horses	1·30	1·30
447	150f. Reaching winning post	1·30	1·30
448	150f. A black and a grey galloping	1·30	1·30

94 Show-jumping

1992. Olympic Games, Barcelona. Multicoloured.

449	50f. Type **94**	45	45
450	80f. Running	85	85
451	150f. Karate	1·60	1·60
452	200f. Cycling	2·10	2·10

95 Airport

1992. 60th Anniv of Bahrain International Airport.

453	**95**	50f. multicoloured	45	45
454	**95**	80f. multicoloured	85	85
455	**95**	150f. multicoloured	1·60	1·60
456	**95**	200f. multicoloured	2·10	2·10

96 Girl skipping

1992. Children's Paintings. Multicoloured.

457	50f. Type **96**	45	30
458	80f. Women	65	45
459	150f. Women preparing food (horiz)	1·30	85
460	200f. Pearl divers (horiz)	1·70	1·20

97 Cable-cars and Pylons

1992. Expansion of Aluminium Industry. Multicoloured.

461	50f. Type **97**	45	45
462	80f. Worker in aluminium plant	85	85
463	150f. Aerial view of aluminium plant	1·60	1·60
464	200f. Processed aluminium	2·10	2·10

98 Artillery Gun Crew

1993. 25th Anniv of Bahrain Defence Force. Multicoloured.

465	50f. Type **98**	45	45
466	80f. General Dynamics Fighting Falcon jet fighters, tanks and patrol boat	75	75
467	150f. "Ahmed al Fatah" (missile corvette) (horiz)	1·50	1·50
468	200f. Fighting Falcon over Bahrain (horiz)	1·90	1·90

99 Satellite View of Bahrain

1993. World Meteorological Day. Multicoloured.

469	50f. Type **99**	65	65
470	150f. Satellite picture of world (horiz)	1·60	1·60
471	200f. Earth seen from space	2·50	2·50

100 Purple Heron

1993. Water Birds. Multicoloured.

472	150f. Type **100**	1·60	1·60
473	150f. Moorhen (*Gallinula chloropus*)	1·60	1·60
474	150f. Socotra cormorant (*Phalacrocorax nigrogularis*)	1·60	1·60
475	150f. Crab plover (*Dromas ardeola*)	1·60	1·60
476	150f. River kingfisher (*Alcedo atthis*)	1·60	1·60
477	150f. Northern lapwing (*Vanellus vanellus*)	1·60	1·60
478	150f. Oystercatcher (*Haematopus ostralegus*) (horiz)	1·60	1·60
479	150f. Black-crowned night heron (*Nycticorax nycticorax*)	1·60	1·60
480	150f. Caspian tern (*Sterna caspia*) (horiz)	1·60	1·60
481	150f. Ruddy turnstone (*Arenaria interpres*) (horiz)	1·60	1·60
482	150f. Water rail (*Rallus aquaticus*) (horiz)	1·60	1·60
483	150f. Mallard (*Anas platyrhyncos*) (horiz)	1·60	1·60
484	150f. Lesser black-backed gull (*Larus fuscus*) (horiz)	1·60	1·60

101 Fawn

1993. The Goitered Gazelle. Multicoloured.

485	25f. Type **101**	1·20	1·20
486	50f. Doe walking	2·40	2·40
487	50f. Doe with ears pricked	2·40	2·40
488	150f. Male gazelle	7·00	7·00

102 *Lycium shawii*

1993. Wild Flowers. Multicoloured.

489	150f. Type **102**	1·10	1·10
490	150f. *Alhagi maurorum*	1·10	1·10
491	150f. Caper-bush (*Caparis spinosa*)	1·10	1·10
492	150f. *Cistanche phelypae*	1·10	1·10
493	150f. *Asphodelus tenuifolius*	1·10	1·10
494	150f. *Limonium axillare*	1·10	1·10
495	150f. *Cynomorium coccineum*	1·10	1·10
496	150f. *Calligonum polygonoides*	1·10	1·10

103 Children and Silhouettes of Parents' Heads

1994. International Year of the Family.

497	**103**	50f. multicoloured	45	45
498	**103**	80f. multicoloured	75	75
499	**103**	150f. multicoloured	1·50	1·50
500	**103**	200f. multicoloured	1·90	1·90

104 *Lepidochrysops arabicus*

1994. Butterflies. Multicoloured.

501	50f. Type **104**	30	30
502	50f. *Ypthima bolanica*	30	30
503	50f. Desert grass yellow (*Eurema brigitta*)	30	30
504	50f. *Precis limnoria*	30	30
505	50f. Small tortoiseshell (*Aglais urticae*)	30	30
506	50f. Protomedia (*Colotis protomedia*)	30	30
507	50f. Clouded mother-of-pearl (*Salamis anacardii*)	30	30
508	50f. *Byblia ilithyia*	30	30
509	150f. Swallowtail (*Papilio machaon*) (horiz)	95	95
510	150f. Blue (*Agrodiaetus loewii*) (horiz)	95	95
511	150f. Painted lady (*Vanessa cardui*) (horiz)	95	95
512	150f. Chequered swallowtail (*Papilio demoleus*) (horiz)	95	95
513	150f. Guineafowl (*Hamanumida daedalus*) (horiz)	95	95
514	150f. *Funonia orithya* (horiz)	95	95
515	150f. *Funonia chorimine* (horiz)	95	95
516	150f. *Colias croceus* (horiz)	95	95

105 Anniversary Emblem

1994. 75th Anniv of International Red Cross and Red Crescent.

517	**105**	50f. multicoloured	45	45
518	**105**	80f. multicoloured	75	75
519	**105**	150f. multicoloured	1·50	1·50
520	**105**	200f. multicoloured	1·90	1·90

106 Goalkeeper

1994. World Cup Football Championship, U.S.A. Multicoloured.

521	50f. Type **106**	55	55
522	80f. Players	85	85
523	150f. Players' legs	1·60	1·60
524	200f. Player on ground	2·10	2·10

107 Earth Station

1994. 25th Anniv of Ras Abu Jarjour Satellite Earth Station.

525	**107**	50f. multicoloured	45	45
526	**107**	80f. multicoloured	75	75
527	**107**	150f. multicoloured	1·50	1·50
528	**107**	200f. multicoloured	1·90	1·90

108 Children on Open Book, Pen as Torch and School

1994. 75th Anniv of Education in Bahrain.

529	**108**	50f. multicoloured	45	45
530	**108**	80f. multicoloured	75	75
531	**108**	150f. multicoloured	1·50	1·50
532	**108**	200f. multicoloured	1·90	1·90

109 Dove with "Olive Branch" of Members' Flags

1994. 15th Gulf Co-operation Council Supreme Council Session, Bahrain.

533	**109**	50f. multicoloured	45	45
534	**109**	80f. multicoloured	75	75
535	**109**	150f. multicoloured	1·40	1·40
536	**109**	200f. multicoloured	1·80	1·80

110 Date Palm in Bloom

1995. The Date Palm.

537	80f. Type **110**	75	75
538	100f. Date palm with unripened dates	85	85
539	200f. Dates ripening	1·80	1·80

540	250f. Date palm trees with ripened dates	2·10	2·10
MS541	134×126 mm. 500f. Dates, coffee pot, cups and date palms (65×47 mm)	4·25	4·25

111 Campaign Emblem

1995. World Health Day. Anti-poliomyelitis Campaign.

542	**111**	80f. multicoloured	55	55
543	**111**	200f. multicoloured	1·50	1·50
544	**111**	250f. multicoloured	2·00	2·00

112 Exhibition Emblem

1995. First National Industries Exhibition.

545	**112**	80f. multicoloured	55	55
546	**112**	200f. multicoloured	1·50	1·50
547	**112**	250f. multicoloured	2·00	2·00

113 Crops

1995. 50th Anniv of F.A.O. Multicoloured.

548	80f. Type **113**	55	55
549	200f. Field of crops	1·50	1·50
550	250f. Field of cabbages	2·00	2·00

114 Headquarters, Cairo

1995. 50th Anniv of Arab League.

551	**114**	80f. multicoloured	55	55
552	**114**	200f. multicoloured	1·50	1·50
553	**114**	250f. multicoloured	2·00	2·00

115 U.N. Headquarters and Map of Bahrain

1995. 50th Anniv of U.N.O.

554	**115**	80f. multicoloured	55	55
555	**115**	100f. multicoloured	75	75
556	**115**	200f. multicoloured	1·60	1·60
557	**115**	250f. multicoloured	2·00	2·00

116 Tower

1995. Traditional Architecture. Multicoloured.

558	200f. Type **116**	1·30	1·30
559	200f. Balcony	1·30	1·30
560	200f. Doorway	1·30	1·30
561	200f. Multi-storied facade	1·30	1·30
562	200f. Entrance flanked by two windows	1·30	1·30
563	200f. Three arched windows	1·30	1·30

117 National Flag and Shaikh Isa Bin Sulman al-Khalifa

1995. National Day.

564	**117**	80f. multicoloured	55	55
565	**117**	100f. multicoloured	75	75
566	**117**	200f. multicoloured	1·60	1·60
567	**117**	250f. multicoloured	2·00	2·00

118 Bookcase and Open Book

1996. 50th Anniv of Public Library.

568	**118**	80f. multicoloured	55	55
569	**118**	200f. multicoloured	1·60	1·60
570	**118**	250f. multicoloured	2·00	2·00

119 Divers on Dhow

1996. Pearl Diving. Multicoloured.

571	80f. Type **119**	55	55
572	100f. Divers	65	65
573	200f. Diver on sea-bed and dhow	1·30	1·30
574	250f. Diver with net	1·80	1·80
MS575	119×119 mm. 500f. Diving equipment (70×70 mm)	4·25	4·25

120 Globe, Ship and Olympic Rings

1996. Olympic Games, Atlanta.

576	**120**	80f. multicoloured	55	55
577	**120**	100f. multicoloured	65	65
578	**120**	200f. multicoloured	1·30	1·30
579	**120**	250f. multicoloured	1·80	1·80

121 Interpol Emblem and Map, Arms and Flag of Bahrain

1996. 24th Anniv of Membership of International Criminal Police (Interpol).

580	**121**	80f. multicoloured	55	55
581	**121**	100f. multicoloured	75	75
582	**121**	200f. multicoloured	1·60	1·60
583	**121**	250f. multicoloured	2·00	2·00

122 Anniversary Emblems in English and Arabic

1996. 25th Anniv of Aluminium Bahrain.

584	**122**	80f. multicoloured	45	45
585	**122**	100f. multicoloured	55	55
586	**122**	200f. multicoloured	1·30	1·30
587	**122**	250f. multicoloured	1·60	1·60

123 National Flag, Map and Shaikh Isa bin Sulman al-Khalifa

1996. 35th Anniv of Amir's Accession.

588	**123**	80f. multicoloured	55	55
589	**123**	100f. multicoloured	75	75
590	**123**	200f. multicoloured	1·60	1·60
591	**123**	250f. multicoloured	2·00	2·00

124 Tanker, Refinery and Storage Tanks

1997. 60th Anniv of Bahrain Refinery.

592	**124**	80f. multicoloured	55	55
593	**124**	200f. multicoloured	1·40	1·40
594	**124**	250f. multicoloured	1·90	1·90

125 Kuheilaan Weld umm Zorayr

1997. Arab Horses at Amiri Stud. Multicoloured.

595	200f. Musannaan (white horse), Al-Jellabieh and Rabdaan	1·40	1·40
596	200f. Type **125**	1·40	1·40
597	200f. Al-Jellaby	1·40	1·40
598	200f. Musannaan (brown horse)	1·40	1·40
599	200f. Kuheilaan Aladiyat	1·40	1·40
600	200f. Kuheilaan Aafas	1·40	1·40
601	200f. Al-Dhahma	1·40	1·40
602	200f. Mlolshaan	1·40	1·40
603	200f. Al-Kray	1·40	1·40
604	200f. Krush	1·40	1·40
605	200f. Al Hamdaany	1·40	1·40
606	200f. Hadhfaan	1·40	1·40
607	200f. Rabda	1·40	1·40
608	200f. Al-Suwaitieh	1·40	1·40
609	200f. Al-Obeyah	1·40	1·40
610	200f. Al-Shuwaimeh	1·40	1·40
611	200f. Al-Ma'anaghieh	1·40	1·40
612	200f. Al-Tuwaisah	1·40	1·40
613	200f. Wadhna	1·40	1·40
614	200f. Al-Saqlawieh	1·40	1·40
615	200f. Al-Shawafah	1·40	1·40

126 Championship Emblem

1997. Ninth World Men's Junior Volleyball Championship.

616	**126**	80f. multicoloured	55	55
617	**126**	100f. multicoloured	75	75
618	**126**	200f. multicoloured	1·40	1·40
619	**126**	250f. multicoloured	1·80	1·80

127 Emblem

1997. Tenth Anniv of Montreal Protocol (on reduction of use of chlorofluorocarbons).

620	**127**	80f. multicoloured	55	55
621	**127**	100f. multicoloured	75	75
622	**127**	200f. multicoloured	1·40	1·40
623	**127**	250f. multicoloured	1·80	1·80

128 Close-up of Support

1997. Inauguration of Shaikh Isa bin Salman Bridge between Manama and Muharraq. Multicoloured.

624	80f. Type **128**	55	55
625	200f. Distant view of middle section	1·50	1·50
626	250f. View of complete bridge (75×26 mm)	1·80	1·80
MS627	137×116 mm. 500f. As No. 626	3·75	3·75

129 Complex at Night

1998. Inauguration of Urea Plant at Gulf Petrochemical Industries Co Complex. Mult.

628	80f. Type **129**	55	55
629	200f. Refining towers	1·50	1·50
630	250f. Aerial view of complex	1·80	1·80

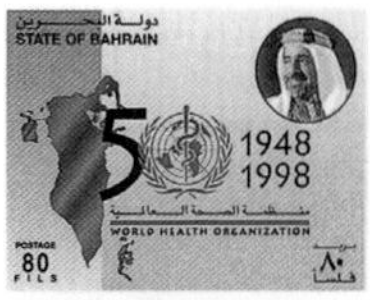

130 Map of Bahrain and Anniversary Emblem

1998. 50th Anniv of W.H.O.

631	**130**	80f. multicoloured	55	55
632	**130**	200f. multicoloured	1·50	1·50
633	**130**	250f. multicoloured	1·80	1·80

131 Emblem

1998. World Cup Football Championship, France. Multicoloured.

634	80f. Type **131**	55	55
635	200f. Globes and football forming "98" (vert)	1·50	1·50
636	250f. Footballers and globe (vert)	1·80	1·80

132 Football

1998. 14th Arabian Gulf Cup Football Championship, Bahrain. Multicoloured.

637	80f. Type **132**	55	55
638	200f. Close-up of football	1·50	1·50
639	250f. As No. 638	1·80	1·80

133 Emblem and Koran

1999. Holy Koran Reading Competition.

640	**133**	100f. multicoloured	75	75
641	**133**	200f. multicoloured	1·60	1·60
642	**133**	250f. multicoloured	1·80	1·80

134 Shaikh Isa bin Sulman al-Khalifa and State Flag

1999. Shaikh Isa bin Sulman al-Khalifa Commemoration. Multicoloured.

643	100f. Type **134**	75	75
644	200f. Shaikh and map of Bahrain (41×31 mm)	1·60	1·60
645	250f. Shaikh, map of Bahrain and state flag	1·80	1·80
MS646	125×170 mm. 500f. Type **134** (67×102 mm)	4·25	4·25

135 Emblem

1999. International Year of the Elderly. Multicoloured.

647	100f. Type **135**	75	75
648	200f. Emblem and flame	1·60	1·60
649	250f. Emblem (different)	1·80	1·80

136 Emblem

1999. Tenth Anniv of Bahrain Stock Exchange. Multicoloured.

650	100f. Type **136**	75	75
651	200f. Shaikh Isa bin Salman Bridge and emblem	1·60	1·60
652	250f. Globe and emblem	1·80	1·80

137 Shaikh Isa bin Salman and Shaikh Hamad bin Isa holding Flag

1999. National Day. Multicoloured.

653	100f. Type **137**	75	75
654	200f. Shaikh Hamad bin Isa and flag	1·60	1·60
655	250f. Shaikh Hamad bin Isa and globe	1·80	1·80
MS656	115×155 mm. 500f. As Type **137** (56×96 mm)	3·75	3·75

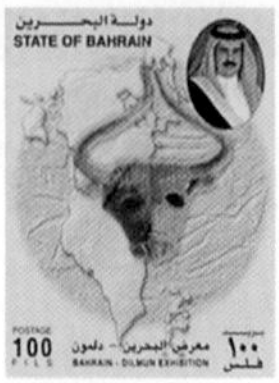

138 Map of Bahrain and Animal Skull

2000. Dilmun Exhibition. Multicoloured.

657	100f. Type **138**	75	75
658	200f. Map of Bahrain superimposed over animal skull	1·60	1·60
659	250f. Map of Bahrain and artefact	1·80	1·80

139 Map of Bahrain and Emblem

2000. 50th Anniv of Gulf Air. Multicoloured.

660	100f. Type **139**	1·20	1·20
661	200f. Map of Bahrain and emblem in circle	2·40	2·40
662	250f. Map of Bahrain, emblem and eagles	2·75	2·75

140 Emblem

2000. "Made in Bahrain 2000" Exhibition. Multicoloured.

663	100f. Type **140**	1·20	1·20
664	200f. Type **140**	2·40	2·40
665	250f. Oil refinery	2·75	2·75

141 Minarets and Fort

2000. Millennium. Multicoloured.

666	100f. Type **141**	1·30	1·30
667	100f. Dhows and factories	1·30	1·30
668	100f. Man harvesting dates	1·30	1·30
669	100f. Fort, globe and dish aerial	1·30	1·30
670	200f. Lake and bridge	1·80	1·80
671	200f. Modern building and woman	1·80	1·80
672	200f. Dhows, jug and wicker basket	1·80	1·80
673	200f. Horseman and falconer	1·80	1·80
674	250f. Pearl divers	2·20	2·20
675	250f. Opening clams	2·20	2·20
676	250f. Fishermen	2·20	2·20
677	250f. Man mending fishing nets	2·20	2·20

142 Emblem

2000. 21st Gulf Co-operation Council Supreme Council Session, Bahrain. Multicoloured.

678	100f. Type **142**	1·20	1·20
679	200f. Members' flags	2·40	2·40

143 Stained-glass Window

2001. Tenth Anniv of Beit Al Qur'an (Islamic institution). Multicoloured.

680	100f. Type **143**	75	75
681	200f. Beit Al Qur'an by night	1·50	1·50
682	250f. Facade	2·00	2·00
MS683	170×80 mm. 500f. Subjects as Nos. 680/2 but forming composite design. Imperf	3·75	3·75

144 Building

2001. 25th Anniv of Ministry of Housing and Agriculture. Multicoloured.

684	100f. Type **144**	75	75
685	150f. Sculpture and building	1·20	1·20
686	200f. Building viewed through arch	1·50	1·50
687	250f. Tall, arched building	2·00	2·00

145 Emblem and Stylized Figures

2001. International Year of Volunteers. Multicoloured.

688	100f. Type **145**	75	75
689	150f. Hands encircling emblem	1·20	1·20
690	200f. Star pattern and emblem	1·50	1·50
691	250f. Paper cut figures	2·00	2·00

146 Emblem

2002. Arab Women's Day. Multicoloured.

692	100f. Type **146**	75	75
693	200f. Elliptical shapes and emblem	1·60	1·60
694	250f. Women (horiz)	2·00	2·00

147 Football and Emblem

2002. World Cup Football Championship, Japan and South Korea. Sheet 124×64 mm containing T **147** and similar vert designs. Multicoloured.

MS695	100f. Type **147**; 200f. Earth, football and emblem; 250f. Football and white peaks	4·25	4·25

148 Shaikh Hamad Bin Isa Al Khalifa

2002. Multicoloured, background colour given. (a) Size 22×28 mm.

696	**148**	25f. brown	10	10
697	**148**	40f. purple	30	30
698	**148**	50f. grey	40	40
699	**148**	60f. blue	50	50
700	**148**	80f. blue	65	65
701	**148**	100f. orange	75	75
702	**148**	125f. mauve	95	95
703	**148**	150f. orange	1·10	1·10
704	**148**	200f. green	1·60	1·60
705	**148**	250f. pink	2·00	2·00
706	**148**	300f. brown	2·40	2·40
707	**148**	400f. green	3·25	3·25

(b) 26×36 mm.

708	500f. mauve	3·75	3·75
709	1d. orange	8·00	8·00
710	2d. blue	16·00	16·00
711	3d. brown	24·00	24·00
MS712	246×162 mm. Nos. 696/711	65·00	65·00

149 Stylized Teacher, Child and Symbols of Communication

2002. World Teacher's Day.

713	**149**	100f. multicoloured	65	65
714	**149**	200f. multicoloured	1·30	1·30

150 Emblem

2002. Parliamentary Election, 2002. Multicoloured.

715	100f. Type **150**	65	65
716	200f. Hand posting voting slip (vert)	1·30	1·30

151 Shaikh Hamad Bin Isa Al Khalifa and Flag

2002. National Day. Multicoloured.

717	100f. Type **151**	65	65
718	200f. Shaikh Hamad Bin Isa and flag (different) (vert)	1·30	1·30
719	250f. As No. 718 but with maroon background (vert)	1·60	1·60

152 Bahrain

2003. Arab Summit Conference, Sharm el-Sheikh, Egypt. Designs representing landmarks from each state.

720	100f. Type **152**	65	65
721	100f. Sudan	65	65
722	100f. Saudi Arabia	65	65
723	100f. Djibouti	65	65
724	100f. Algeria	65	65
725	100f. Tunisia	65	65
726	100f. UAE	65	65
727	100f. Jordan	65	65
728	200f. Comoros	1·30	1·30
729	200f. Qatar	1·30	1·30
730	200f. Palestine	1·30	1·30
731	200f. Oman	1·30	1·30
732	200f. Iraq	1·30	1·30
733	200f. Somalia	1·30	1·30
734	200f. Syria	1·30	1·30
735	250f. Yemen	1·60	1·60
736	250f. Mauritania	1·60	1·60
737	250f. Egypt	1·60	1·60
738	250f. Libya	1·60	1·60
739	250f. Lebanon	1·60	1·60
740	250f. Kuwait	1·60	1·60
MS741	120×103 mm. 500f. Buildings surrounding Holy Kabba. Imperf	3·25	3·25

153 Children, Emblem and Flowers

2003. World Health Day. Multicoloured.

742	100f. Type **153**	75	75
743	200f. Stylized figures and emblem	1·60	1·60

154 Swan

2003. World Environment Day. Flora and Fauna. Multicoloured.

744	100f. Type **154**	75	75
745	100f. Peacock	75	75
746	100f. Flamingos	75	75
747	100f. Ostrich	75	75
748	200f. *Rumex vesicarius*	1·50	1·50
749	200f. *Arnebia hispidissima*	1·50	1·50
750	200f. *Capparis spinosa*	1·50	1·50
751	200f. *Cassia italica*	1·50	1·50
752	250f. Crab	1·80	1·80
753	250f. Turtle	1·80	1·80
754	250f. Sting ray	1·80	1·80
755	250f. Shark	1·80	1·80

155 Girl Writing

2003. Children's Day. Multicoloured.

756	100f. Type **155**	60	60
757	150f. Girl painting	80	80
758	200f. Children playing (horiz)	1·20	1·20
759	250f. School class (horiz)	1·40	1·40

156 Shaikh Hamad Bin Isa Al Khalifa on Horseback

2003. National Day.

760	**156**	100f. multicoloured	60	60
761	**156**	200f. multicoloured	1·20	1·20
762	**156**	250f. multicoloured	1·40	1·40

MS763 125×167 mm. **156** 500f. multi-coloured (57×87 mm) 2·75 2·75

157 Mother and Baby

2004. Mothers' Day. Multicoloured.

764	100f. Type **157**	55	55
765	200f. Mother and child reading	1·10	1·10

158 Computer Model of Formula One Car (image scaled to 56% of original size)

2004. Bahrain Formula One Grand Prix. Sheet 180×180 mm containing T **158** and similar multicoloured designs.

MS766 100f. Type **158**; 150f. Model facing right; 200f. Side view; 250f. Rear view; 500f. Shakir tower, Bahrain International Circuit (40×40 mm) 6·50 6·50

159 Healthy Figures reaching for Drug Abuser

2004. International Day against Drug Abuse. Multicoloured.

767	100f. Type **159**	55	55
768	150f. Shrunken arm	70	70
769	200f. Needles and seated figure	1·10	1·10
770	250f. Healthy hands reaching to diseased hand	1·30	1·30

160 Running

2004. Olympic Games, Athens 2004. Sheet 211×65 mm containing T **160** and similar horiz designs. Multicoloured.

MS771 100f. Type **160**; 150f. Swimming; 200f. Windsurfing; 250f. Pistol Shooting 3·50 3·50

161 Hands holding Emblem

2004. 25th Session of Arabian Gulf States Co-operation Supreme Council. Multicoloured.

772	100f. Type **161**	55	55
773	200f. Emblem with flags as ribbons	1·10	1·10
774	250f. Emblem on background of flags	1·30	1·30

MS775 201×100 mm. 500f. Symbols of Gulf States (175×34 mm) 2·30 2·30

162 Amaryllis Flower and Fair Emblem

2005. Bahrain Garden Fair. Multicoloured.

776	100f. Type **162**	55	55
777	200f. Rose	1·10	1·10
778	250f. Jasmine	1·30	1·30

163 Scales and Court Building

2005. Inauguration of Constitutional Court.

779	**163**	100f. multicoloured	55	55
780	**163**	200f. multicoloured	1·10	1·10
791	**163**	250f. multicoloured	70	70

164 Statuette

2005. 50th Anniv of Discovery of Dilmon Civilization. Multicoloured.

782	100f. Type **164**	55	55
783	100f. Engraved seals	55	55
784	100f. Horseman (statue)	55	55
785	200f. pot spilling jewellery	1·10	1·10
786	200f. Two decorated pots	1·10	1·10
787	200f. Cylindrical vase and pot with lid	1·10	1·10
788	250f. Walls and gateway (horiz)	1·30	1·30
789	250f. Aerial view (horiz)	1·30	1·30
790	250f. Walls and steps (horiz)	1·30	1·30

MS791 Two sheets. (a) 195×155 mm. Nos. 782/90. (b) 140×105 mm. 500f. Sheikh Salman Bin Hamad Al Khalifa and archaeologists (88×58 mm) 10·50 10·50

165 King Hamad bin Isa Al Khalifa

2005. National Day. Multicoloured.

792	100f. Type **165**	55	55
793	200f. Flag and King Al Khalifa (vert)	1·10	1·10
794	250f. Towers and King Al Khalifa	1·30	1·30

166 Flag

2006. 25th Anniv of Gulf Co-operation Council. Multicoloured.

795	100f. Type **166**	1·00	1·00

MS796 165×105 mm. 500f. Flags of member states. Imperf 2·40 2·40

Stamps of similar designs were issued by Kuwait, Oman, Qatar, Saudi Arabia and United Arab Emirates.

167 Emblem

2006. World Cup Football Championship, Germany. Multicoloured.

797	100f. Type **167**	55	55
798	200f. Globe and balls	1·10	1·10
799	250f. Emblem (different)	1·30	1·30

168 King Hamad Bin Isa Al Khalifa

2006. National Day. Accession of King Hamad Bin Isa Al Khalifa. Multicoloured.

800	100f. Type **168**	55	55
801	200f. Facing front	1·10	1·10
802	250f. Facing left	1·30	1·30
803	500f. As Type **168** (40×54 mm)	2·40	2·40

169 Figures under Umbrella

2007. Consumer Protection Day. Multicoloured.

804	100f. Type **169**	50	50
805	200f. Flags as umbrella	1·00	1·00

170 King Hamad Bin Isa Al Khalifa

2007. National Day. Multicoloured.

806	100f. Type **170**	55	55
807	200f. Seated (horiz)	1·10	1·10
808	250f. King Hamad Bin Isa Al Khalifa and previous rulers (horiz)	1·30	1·30

MS809 125×201 mm. 100f.×2, No. 806×2; Horiz. 200f.×2, No. 807×2 2·75 2·75

171 Clay Carving and Basket Work

2008. Arab Productive Families Day. Multicoloured.

810	100f. Type **171**	50	50
811	200f. Stud work and embroiderey	1·00	1·00

172 Operating Theatre

2008. International Nurses Day. Multicoloured.

812	100f. Type **172**	50	50
813	200f. Neo-natal nurses	1·00	1·00

173 Symbols of Bahrain and China

2008. Arab–Chinese Cooperation Forum Ministerial Meeting, Manama. Multicoloured.

814	100f. Type **173**	50	50
815	200f. Great Wall and Bahrain World Trade Centre towers	1·00	1·00

174 'BUSINESS friendly'

2008. Economic Developement Board. Multicoloured.

816	100f. Type **174**	60	60
817	200f. BUSINESS FRIENDLY	1·20	1·20

175 Athletics

2008. Olympic Games, Beijing. Sheet 145×64 mm containing T 175 and similar square design. Multicoloured.

MS818 100f. Type **175**; 200f. Show jumping 1·80 1·80

176 Dancers

2008. National Day. Bahraini Ardha (dance). Two sheets containing T **176** and similar horiz designs. Multicoloured.

MS819 210×151 mm. 100f.×8, Type **176**; Dancer with lowered sword and two rows of dancers facing each other; Dancer with out-stretched sword and four dancers wearing blue and yellow costumes; Dancer with raised sword and large square of dancers; Unarmed dancer and men with raised swords; Dancer with rifle and three others; Dancer with sword to his left and three men; Dancer with sword to his right and drummers 4·50 4·50

MS820 210×151 mm. Size 54×40 mm. 200f.×3, Dancer holding flag and sword and dancers with flag; Dancer holding scabard and dancers wearing blue and yellow costumes; Dancer with raised sword and dancers 2·75 2·75

177 Dhow

2009. First GCC–ASEAN Ministerial Meeting, Manama. Multicoloured.

821	100f. Type **177**	60	60
822	200f. As Type **177**	1·00	1·00

178 Pigeon

2009. Arab Post Day. Sheet 170×60 mm containing T **178** and similar horiz design. Multicoloured.

MS823 500f.×2, Type **178**; Camels 5·25 5·25

179 Emblems

2009. Palm Tree–Life and Civilization Symposium.

824	**179**	100f. multicoloured	60	60

180 Emblem

2009. National Women's Day. Multicoloured.

825	100f. Type **180**	60	60
826	200f. Emblem and flag	1·00	1·00

181 Students

2009. 90th Anniv of Education in Bahrain. Sheet 160×99 mm containing T **181** and similar horiz designs. Multicoloured.

MS827	100f. Type **181**; 100f. Classroom, teacher at whiteboard; 200f. Students in laboratory; 200f. Graduating students; 250f. Students, teacher wearing blue lab coat; 250f. Classroom, female teacher with student	6·25	6·25

182 King Hamad Bin Isa Al Khalifa

2009. National Day. 10th Anniv of Accession of King Hamad Bin Isa Al Khalifa. Multicoloured.

828	100f. Type **182**	60	60
829	200f. As Type **182**	1·00	1·00
830	250f. King Hamad Bin Isa Al Khalifa, Isa bin Salman Al Khalifa, Salman Bin Hamad Al Khalifa, Hamad Bin Isa Al Khalifa and Isa bin Ali Al Khalifa	1·50	1·50
MS831	126×101 mm. 500f. As No. 830. Imperf	5·25	5·25

183 King Hamad Bin Isa Al Khalifa and Jet Fighter Aircraft

2010. International Airshow, Bahrain. Multicoloured.

832	100f. Type **183**	65	65
833	200f. Emblem	1·10	1·10

184 Championship Emblem

2010. World Cup Football Championship, South Africa

834	100f. Type **184**
835	200f. Championship mascot
836	250f. Football, emblem and globe (39×29 mm)

WAR TAX STAMPS

T36 "War Effort"

1973

T192	**T36**	5f. blue and cobalt	£130	85·00

T37 "War Effort"

1973

T194a	**T37**	5f. blue	5·25	45

Pt. 1

BAMRA

A state in India. Now uses Indian stamps.

12 pies = 1 anna; 16 annas = 1 rupee.

1

1888

1	**1**	¼a. black on yellow	£650	
2	**1**	½a. black on red	£110	
3	**1**	1a. black on blue	85·00	
4	**1**	2a. black on green	£120	£550
5	**1**	4a. black on yellow	£100	£550
6	**1**	8a. black on red	65·00	

8

1890. Imperf.

10	**8**	¼a. black on red	2·25	2·75
11	**8**	½a. black on green	5·50	5·50
30	**8**	1a. black on yellow	5·00	3·25
16	**8**	2a. black on red	5·50	5·50
19	**8**	4a. black on red	17·00	12·00
22	**8**	8a. black on red	14·00	22·00
25	**8**	1r. black on red	21·00	22·00

Pt. 1

BANGLADESH

Formerly the Eastern wing of Pakistan. Following a landslide victory at the Pakistan General Election in December 1970 by the Awami League party the National Assembly was suspended. Unrest spread throughout the eastern province culminating in the intervention of India on the side of the East Bengalis. The new state became effective after the surrender of the Pakistan army in December 1971.

1971. 100 paisa = 1 rupee.
1972. 100 paisa = 1 taka.

1 Map of Bangladesh

1971

1	**1**	10p. indigo, orange and blue	20	10
2	-	20p. multicoloured	20	10
3	-	50p. multicoloured	20	10
4	-	1r. multicoloured	30	10
5	-	2r. turquoise, blue and red	30	35
6	-	3r. light green, green and blue	30	65
7	-	5r. multicoloured	50	1·25
8	-	10r. gold, red and blue	1·00	2·25

DESIGNS: 20p. "Dacca University Massacre"; 50p. "75 Million People"; 1r. Flag of Independence; 2r. Ballot box; 3r. Broken chain; 5r. Shaikh Majibur Rahman; 10r. "Support Bangla Desh" and map.

1971. Liberation. Nos. 1 and 7/8 optd **BANGLADESH LIBERATED**.

9	10p. indigo, orange and blue	20	10
10	5r. multicoloured	2·00	2·25
11	10r. gold, red and blue	3·00	3·75

The remaining values of the original issue were also overprinted and placed on sale in Great Britian but were not issued in Bangladesh.

On 1 February 1972 the Agency placed on sale a further issue in the flag, map and Sheikh Mujib designs in new colours and new currency (100 paisa = 1 taka). This issue proved to be unacceptable to the Bangladesh authorities who declared them to be invalid for postal purposes, no supplies being sold within Bangladesh. The values comprise 1, 2, 3, 5, 7, 10, 15, 20, 25, 40, 50, 75p., 1, 2 and 5t.

3 "Martyrdom"

1972. In Memory of the Martyrs.

12	**3**	20p. green and red	30	50

4 Flames of Independence

1972. First Anniv of Independence.

13	**4**	20p. lake and red	25	10
14	**4**	60p. blue and red	40	45
15	**4**	75p. violet and red	45	55

5 Doves of Peace

1972. Victory Day.

16	**5**	20p. multicoloured	20	10
17	**5**	60p. multicoloured	30	55
18	**5**	75p. multicoloured	30	55

6 "Homage to Martyrs"

1973. In Memory of the Martyrs.

19	**6**	20p. multicoloured	15	10
20	**6**	60p. multicoloured	30	40
21	**6**	1t.35 multicoloured	65	1·75

7 Embroidered Quilt

8 Court of Justice

1973

22	**7**	2p. black	10	1·00
23	-	3p. green	30	1·00
24	-	5p. brown	30	10
25	-	10p. black	30	10
26	-	20p. green	50	10
27	-	25p. mauve	3·25	10
28	-	50p. purple	2·25	30
29	-	60p. grey	1·75	1·25
30	-	75p. orange	1·25	1·25
31	-	90p. brown	1·50	2·00
32	**8**	1t. violet	6·00	30
33	-	2t. green	6·00	1·00
34	-	5t. blue	7·50	2·50
35	-	10t. pink	10·00	5·00

DESIGNS—As Type **7**: 3p. Jute field; 5p. Jack fruit; 10p. Bullocks ploughing; 20p. Rakta jaba (flower); 25p. Tiger; 60p. Bamboo grove; 75p. Plucking tea; 90p. Handicrafts. (28×22 mm): 50p. Hilsa (fish). As Type **8**. VERT: 2t. Date tree. HORIZ: 5t. Fishing boat; 10t. Sixty-dome mosque, Bagerhat.

See also Nos. 49/51a, 64/75 and 711.

9 Flame Emblem

1973. 25th Anniv of Declaration of Human Rights.

36	**9**	10p. multicoloured	10	10
37	**9**	1t.25 multicoloured	20	20

10 Family, Map and Graph

1974. First Population Census.

38	**10**	20p. multicoloured	10	10
39	**10**	25p. multicoloured	10	10
40	**10**	75p. multicoloured	20	20

11 Copernicus and Heliocentric System

1974. 500th Birth Anniv of Copernicus.

41	**11**	25p. orange, violet and black	10	10
42	**11**	75p. orange, green and black	25	50

12 U.N. H.Q. and Bangladesh Flag

1974. Bangladesh's Admission to the U.N.

43	**12**	25p. multicoloured	10	10
44	**12**	1t. multicoloured	35	40

13 U.P.U. Emblem

1974. Centenary of Universal Postal Union. Multicoloured.

45	25p. Type **13**	10	10
46	1t.25 Mail runner	20	15
47	1t.75 Type **13**	20	25
48	5t. As 1t.25	80	1·60

14 Courts of Justice

1974. As Nos. 32/5 with revised inscriptions.

49	**14**	1t. violet	1·50	10
50	-	2t. olive	2·00	2·00
51	-	5t. blue	7·00	70
51a	-	10t. pink	23·00	15·00

For these designs redrawn to 32×20 mm or 20×32 mm, see Nos. 72/5 and, to 35×22 mm, see No. 711.

15 Tiger

1974. Wildlife Preservation. Multicoloured.

52	25p. Type **15**	70	10
53	50p. Tiger cub	1·00	70
54	2t. Tiger in stream	1·75	3·50

16 Symbolic Family

1974. World Population Year. "Family Planning for All". Multicoloured.

55	25p. Type **16**	15	10
56	70p. Village family	25	50
57	1t.25 Heads of family (horiz)	40	1·10

17 Radar Antenna

1975. Inauguration of Betbunia Satellite Earth Station.

58	**17**	25p. black, silver and red	10	10
59	**17**	1t. black, silver and blue	20	70

18 Woman's Head

1975. International Women's Year.

60	**18**	50p. multicoloured	10	10
61	**18**	2t. multicoloured	25	1·00

1976. As Nos. 24/31 and 49/51a but redrawn in smaller size.

64	-	5p. green	20	10
65	-	10p. black	20	10
66	-	20p. green	1·50	10
67	-	25p. mauve	5·00	10
68	-	50p. purple	3·75	10
69	-	60p. grey	40	40
70	-	75p. green	1·75	3·25
71	-	90p. brown	40	60
72	**14**	1t. violet	2·00	10
73	-	2t. green	9·00	10
74	-	5t. blue	3·25	3·00
75	-	10t. red	11·00	4·50

Nos. 64/71 are 23×18 mm (50p.) or 18×23 mm (others) and Nos. 72/75 are 20×32 mm (2t.) or 32×20 mm (others).

For the 10t. redrawn to 35×22 mm, see No. 711.

19 Telephones of 1876 and 1976

1976. Centenary of Telephone.

76	**19**	2t.25 multicoloured	25	20
77	-	5t. red, green and black	55	65

DESIGN: 5t. Alexander Graham Bell.

20 Eye and Nutriments

1976. Prevention of Blindness.

78	**20**	30p. multicoloured	50	10
79	**20**	2t.25 multicoloured	1·40	2·75

21 Liberty Bell

1976. Bicentenary of American Revolution. Multicoloured.

80	30p. Type **21**	10	10
81	2t.25 Statue of Liberty	20	25
82	5t. "Mayflower"	40	40
83	10t. Mount Rushmore	40	70
MS84 167×95 mm. No. 83		1·00	2·50

22 Industry, Science, Agriculture and Education

1976. 25th Anniv of Colombo Plan.

85	**22**	30p. multicoloured	15	10
86	**22**	2t.25 multicoloured	35	1·00

23 Hurdling

1976. Olympic Games, Montreal. Multicoloured.

87	25p. Type **23**	10	10
88	30p. Running (horiz)	10	10
89	1t. Pole vaulting	15	10
90	2t.25 Swimming (horiz)	30	45
91	3t.50 Gymnastics	55	1·25
92	5t. Football	1·00	2·00

24 The Blessing

1977. Silver Jubilee. Multicoloured.

93	30p. Type **24**	10	10
94	2t.25 Queen Elizabeth II	20	25
95	10t. Queen Elizabeth and Prince Philip	70	85
MS96 114×127 mm. Nos. 93/5		80	1·50

25 Qazi Nazrul Islam (poet)

1977. Qazi Nazrul Islam Commemoration.

97	**25**	40p. green and black	10	10
98	-	2t.25 brown, red & lt brn	50	30

DESIGN—HORIZ: 2t.25, Head and shoulders portrait.

26 Bird with Letter

1977. 15th Anniv of Asian–Oceanic Postal Union.

99	**26**	30p. red, blue and grey	10	10
100	**26**	2t.25 red, blue and grey	20	25

27 Sloth Bear

1977. Animals. Multicoloured.

101	40p. Type **27**	15	10
102	1t. Spotted deer	15	10
103	2t.25 Leopard (horiz)	30	20
104	3t.50 Gaur (horiz)	30	35
105	4t. Indian elephant (horiz)	80	50
106	5t. Tiger (horiz)	90	75

The Bengali numerals on the 40p. resemble "80", and that on the 4t. resembles "8".

28 Campfire and Tent

1978. First National Scout Jamboree.

107	**28**	40p. red, blue and pale blue	25	10
108	-	3t.50 lilac, green and blue	80	30
109	-	5t. green, blue and red	95	45

DESIGNS—HORIZ: 3t.50, Scout stretcher-team. VERT: 5t. Scout salute.

29 *Michelia champaca*

1978. Flowers. Multicoloured.

110	40p. Type **29**	20	10
111	1t. *Cassia fistula*	25	15
112	2t.25 *Delonix regia*	30	30
113	3t.50 *Nymphaea nouchali*	35	60
114	4t. *Butea monosperma*	35	80
115	5t. *Anthocephalus indicus*	35	85

30 St. Edward's Crown and Sceptres

1978. 25th Anniv of Coronation. Multicoloured.

116	40p. Type **30**	10	10
117	3t.50 Balcony scene	15	30
118	5t. Queen Elizabeth and Prince Philip	25	50
119	10t. Coronation portrait by Cecil Beaton	45	80
MS120 89×121 mm. Nos. 116/19		1·10	1·50

31 Sir Alan Cobham's de Havilland D.H.50

1978. 75th Anniv of Powered Flight.

121	**31**	40p. multicoloured	15	10
122	-	2t.25 brown and blue	25	45
123	-	3t.50 brown and yellow	25	65
124	-	5t. multicoloured	2·50	3·50

DESIGNS: 2t.25, Captain Hans Bertram's seaplane *Atlantis*; 3t.50, Wright brothers' Flyer III; 5t. Concorde.

32 Fenchuganj Fertiliser Factory

1978

125		5p. brown	10	10
126	**32**	10p. blue	10	10
127	-	15p. orange	10	10
128	-	20p. red	10	10
129	-	25p. blue	15	10
130	-	30p. green	3·00	10
131	-	40p. purple	30	10
132	-	50p. black	5·50	1·50
134	-	80p. brown	20	10
136	-	1t. violet	9·00	10
137	-	2t. blue	3·00	3·25

DESIGNS—HORIZ: 5p. Lalbag Fort; 25p. Jute on a boat; 40, 50p. Baitul Mukarram Mosque; 1t. Dotara (musical instrument); 2t. Karnaphuli Dam. VERT: 15p. Pineapple; 20p. Bangladesh gas; 30p. Banana tree; 80p. Mohastan Garh.

33 Tawaf-E-Ka'aba, Mecca

1978. Pilgrimage to Mecca. Multicoloured.

140	40p. Type **33**	20	10
141	3t. Pilgrims in Wuquf, Arafat (horiz)	60	45

34 Jasim Uddin

1979. Third Death Anniv of Jasim Uddin (poet).

142	**34**	40p. multicoloured	20	50

35 Moulana Abdul Hamid Khan Bhashani

1979. Third Death Anniv of Moulana Abdul Hamid Khan Bhashani (national leader).

143	**35**	40p. multicoloured	40	30

36 Sir Rowland Hill

1979. Death Centenary of Sir Rowland Hill.

144	**36**	40p. blue, red and light blue	10	10
145	-	3t.50 multicoloured	35	30
146	-	10t. multicoloured	80	1·00
MS147 176×96 mm. Nos. 144/6			2·25	2·75

DESIGNS: 3t.50, Sir Rowland Hill and first Bangladesh stamp; 10t. Sir Rowland Hill and Bangladesh U.P.U. stamp.

37 Children with Hoops

1979. International Year of the Child. Multicoloured.

148	40p. Type **37**	10	10
149	3t.50 Boy with kite	35	35
150	5t. Children jumping	50	50
MS151 170×120 mm. Nos. 148/50		1·50	2·75

38 Rotary International Emblem

1980. 75th Anniv of Rotary International.

152	**38**	40p. black, red and yellow	20	10
153	-	5t. gold and blue	65	1·00

DESIGN: 5t. Rotary emblem (different).

39 Canal Digging

1980. Mass Participation in Canal Digging.

154	**39**	40p. multicoloured	40	30

40 A. K. Fazlul Huq

1980. 18th Death Anniv of A. K. Fazlul Huq (national leader).

155	**40**	40p. multicoloured	30	30

41 Early Forms of Mail Transport

1980. "London 1980" International Stamp Exhibition. Multicoloured.

156	1t. Type **41**	15	10
157	10t. Modern forms of mail transport	1·25	1·40
MS158	140×95 mm. Nos. 156/7	1·40	2·00

42 Dome of the Rock

1980. Palestinian Welfare.

159	**42**	50p. lilac	1·00	30

43 Outdoor Class

1980. Education.

160	**43**	50p. multicoloured	40	30

44 Beach Scene

1980. World Tourism Conference, Manila. Multicoloured.

161	50p. Type **44**	35	50
162	5t. Beach scene (different)	65	1·10
MS163	140×88 mm. Nos. 161/2	1·00	1·60

45 Mecca

1980. Moslem Year 1400 A. H. Commemoration.

164	**45**	50p. multicoloured	50	20

46 Begum Roquiah

1980. Birth Centenary of Begum Roquiah (campaigner for women's rights).

165	**46**	50p. multicoloured	10	10
166	**46**	2t. multicoloured	35	20

47 Spotted Deer and Scout Emblem

1981. Fifth Asia–Pacific and Second Bangladesh Scout Jamboree.

167	**47**	50p. multicoloured	25	15
168	**47**	5t. multicoloured	1·00	2·00

1981. Second Population Census. Nos. 38/40 optd **2nd. CENSUS 1981**.

169	**10**	20p. multicoloured	10	10
170	**10**	25p. multicoloured	10	10
171	**10**	75p. multicoloured	20	30

49 Queen Elizabeth the Queen Mother

1981. 80th Birthday of the Queen Mother.

172	**49**	1t. multicoloured	15	15
173	**49**	15t. multicoloured	1·75	2·50
MS174		95×73 mm. Nos. 172/3	1·75	2·50

50 Revolutionary with Flag and Sub-machine-gun

1981. Tenth Anniv of Independence. Multicoloured.

175	50p. Type **50**	15	10
176	2t. Figures on map symbolizing Bangladesh life style	25	45

51 Bangladesh Village and Farm Scenes

1981. U.N. Conference on Least Developed Countries, Paris.

177	**51**	50p. multicoloured	45	15

52 Kemal Ataturk in Civilian Dress

1981. Birth Centenary of Kemal Ataturk (Turkish statesman).

178	50p. Type **52**	45	30
179	1t. Kemal Ataturk in uniform	80	1·25

53 Deaf People using Sign Language

1981. Int Year for Disabled Persons. Multicoloured.

180	50p. Type **53**	40	20
181	2t. Disabled person writing (horiz)	85	2·50

54 Farm Scene and Wheat Ear

1981. World Food Day.

182	**54**	50p. multicoloured	50	1·00

55 River Scene

1982. Tenth Anniv of Human Environment Conference.

183	**55**	50p. multicoloured	50	1·00

56 Dr. M. Hussain

1982. First Death Anniv of Dr. Motahar Hussain (educationist).

184	**56**	50p. multicoloured	50	1·00

57 Knotted Rope surrounding Bengali "75"

1982. 75th Anniv of Boy Scout Movement and 125th Birth Anniv of Lord Baden-Powell. Multicoloured.

185	50p. Type **57**	50	30
186	2t. Lord Baden-Powell (vert)	2·00	4·50

সম্মিলিত
সশস্ত্র বাহিনী দিবস
২১ নভেম্বর,৮২

(58)

1982. Armed Forces' Day. No. 175 optd with T **58**.

187	50p. Type **50**	3·50	3·00

59 Captain Mohiuddin Jahangir

1983. Heroes and Martyrs of the Liberation. Multicoloured, background colour of commemorative plaque given.

188	50p. Type **59** (orange)	30	50
189	50p. Sepoy Hamidur Rahman (green)	30	50
190	50p. Sepoy Mohammed Mustafa Kamal (red)	30	50
191	50p. Muhammed Ruhul Amin (yellow)	30	50
192	50p. Flt. Lt. M. Matiur Rahman (brown)	30	50
193	50p. Lance-Naik Munshi Abdur Rob (brown)	30	50
194	50p. Lance-Naik Nur Mouhammad (green)	30	50

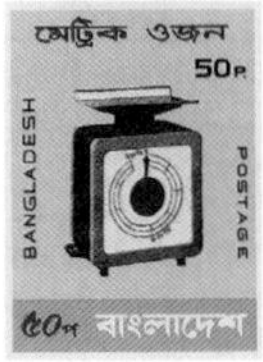

60 Metric Scales

1983. Introduction of Metric Weights and Measures. Multicoloured.

195	50p. Type **60**	40	30
196	2t. Weights, jug and tape measure (horiz)	1·40	2·75

61 Dr. Robert Koch

1983. Centenary (1982) of Robert Koch's Discovery of Tubercle Bacillus. Multicoloured.

197	50p. Type **61**	1·00	40
198	1t. Microscope, slide and X-ray	2·25	3·50

62 Open Stage Theatre

1983. Commonwealth Day. Multicoloured.

199	1t. Type **62**	10	15
200	3t. Boat race	20	30
201	10t. Snake dance	35	90
202	15t. Picking tea	50	1·50

63 Dr. Muhammed Shahidulla

1983. Dr. Muhammed Shahidulla (Bengali scholar) Commemoration.

203	**63**	50p. multicoloured	75	1·00

64 Magpie Robin

1983. Birds of Bangladesh. Multicoloured.

204	50p. Type **64**	75	40
205	2t. White-throated kingfisher (vert)	1·00	2·00
206	3t.75 Lesser flame-backed woodpecker (vert)	1·25	2·50
207	5t. White-winged wood duck	1·40	2·75
MS208	165×110 mm. Nos. 240/7 (sold at 13t.)	4·00	11·00

65 "Macrobrachium rosenbergii"

1983. Marine Life. Multicoloured.

209	50p. Type **65**	40	30
210	2t. White pomfret	60	1·50
211	3t.75 Rohu	75	1·75
212	5t. Climbing perch	90	2·50
MS213	119×98 mm. Nos. 209/12 (sold at 13t.)	2·50	6·00

1983. Visit of Queen Elizabeth II. No. 95 optd **Nov. '83 Visit of Queen**.

214	10t. Queen Elizabeth and Prince Philip	7·00	7·50

67 Conference Hall, Dhaka

1983. 14th Islamic Foreign Ministers' Conference, Dhaka. Multicoloured.

215	50p. Type **67**	35	30
216	5t. Old Fort, Dhaka	1·25	3·00

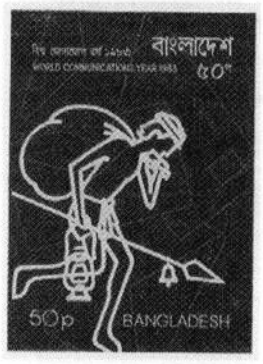

68 Early Mail Runner

1983. World Communications Year. Multicoloured.

217	50p. Type **68**	30	15
218	5t. Sailing ship, steam train and Boeing 707 airliner	2·00	1·50
219	10t. Mail runner and dish aerial (horiz)	2·75	4·50

69 Carrying Mail by Boat

1983. Postal Communications.

220	**69**	5p. blue	10	40
221	-	10p. purple	10	40
222	-	15p. blue	20	40
223	-	20p. black	1·25	40
224	-	25p. grey	30	40
225	-	30p. brown	30	40
226	-	50p. brown	1·00	10
227	-	1t. blue	1·25	10
228	-	2t. green	1·25	10
228a	-	3t. brown	4·00	70
229	-	5t. purple	2·00	1·00

DESIGNS—HORIZ (22×17 mm): 10p. Counter, Dhaka G.P.O.; 15p. I.W.T.A. Terminal, Dhaka; 20p. Inside railway travelling post office; 30p. Emptying pillar box; 50p. Mobile post office van. (30×19 mm): 1t. Kamalapur Railway Station, Dhaka; 2t. Zia International Airport; 3t. Sorting mail by machine; 5t. Khulna G.P.O. VERT (17×22 mm): 25p. Delivering a letter.

প্রথম বাংলাদেশ জাতীয় ডাকটিকিট প্রদর্শনী - ১৯৮৪

(70)

1984. First National Stamp Exhibition (1st issue). Nos. 161/2 optd with T **70** (5t.) or First Bangladesh National Philatelic Exhibition—1984 (50p.).

230	**44**	50p. multicoloured	1·50	2·00
231	-	5t. multicoloured	2·00	2·75

71 Girl with Stamp Album

1984. First National Stamp Exhibition (2nd issue). Multicoloured.

232	50p. Type **71**	65	1·25
233	7t.50 Boy with stamp album	1·10	2·25
MS234	98×117 mm. Nos. 232/3 (sold at 10t.)	3·00	4·25

72 Sarus Crane and Gavial

1984. Dhaka Zoo. Multicoloured.

235	1t. Type **72**	1·75	85
236	2t. Common peafowl and tiger	2·50	4·25

73 Eagle attacking Hen with Chicks

1984. Centenary of Postal Life Insurance. Multicoloured.

237	1t. Type **73**	50	25
238	5t. Bangladesh family and postman's hand with insurance cheque	1·50	2·25

74 Abbasuddin Ahmad

1984. Abbasuddin Ahmad (singer) Commemoration.

239	**74**	3t. multicoloured	1·00	1·25

খুলনাপেক্স—৮৪

(75)

1984. "Khulnapex-84" Stamp Exhibition. No. 86 optd with T **75**.

240	**22**	2t.25 multicoloured	1·00	1·75

76 Cycling

1984. Olympic Games, Los Angeles. Multicoloured.

241	1t. Type **76**	1·75	30
242	5t. Hockey	2·50	2·25
243	10t. Volleyball	2·75	4·25

77 Farmer with Rice and Sickle

1985. Ninth Annual Meeting of Islamic Development Bank, Dhaka. Multicoloured.

244	1t. Type **77**	35	15
245	5t. Citizens of four races	1·25	2·25

78 Mother and Baby

1985. Child Survival Campaign. Multicoloured.

246	1t. Type **78**	30	10
247	10t. Young child and growth graph	2·00	3·25

উপজেলা নির্বাচন ১৯৮৫

(79)

1985. Local Elections. Nos. 110/15 optd with T **79**.

248	40p. Type **29**	40	50
249	1t. *Cassia fistula*	50	30
250	2t.25 *Delonix regia*	70	75
251	3t.50 *Nymphaea nouchali*	80	1·25
252	4t. *Butea monosperma*	80	1·25
253	5t. *Anthocephalus indicus*	85	1·50

80 Women working at Traditional Crafts

1985. U.N. Decade for Women. Multicoloured.

254	1t. Type **80**	25	10
255	10t. Women with microscope, computer terminal and in classroom	1·25	2·25

81 U.N. Building, New York, Peace Doves and Flags

1985. 40th Anniv of United Nations Organization and 11th Anniv of Bangladesh Membership. Multicoloured.

256	1t. Type **81**	10	10
257	10t. Map of world and Bangladesh flag	1·40	1·75

82 Head of Youth, Flowers and Symbols of Commerce and Agriculture

1985. International Youth Year. Multicoloured.

258	1t. Type **82**	10	10
259	5t. Head of youth, flowers and symbols of industry	40	60

83 Emblem and Seven Doves

1985. First Summit Meeting of South Asian Association for Regional Co-operation, Dhaka. Multicoloured.

260	1t. Type **83**	10	10
261	5t. Flags of member nations and lotus blossom	1·75	1·25

84 Zainul Abedin

1985. Tenth Death Anniv of Zainul Abedin (artist).

262	**84**	3t. multicoloured	1·00	55

তৃতীয় বাংলাদেশ জাতীয় জাম্বুরী ১৯৮৬-৮৭

(85)

1985. Third National Scout Jamboree. No. 109 optd with T **85**.

263	5t. green, blue and red	2·50	3·50

86 "Fishing Net" (Safiuddin Ahmed)

1986. Bangladesh Paintings. Multicoloured.

264	1t. Type **86**	15	10
265	5t. *Happy Return* (Quamrul Hassan)	40	50
266	10t. *Levelling the Ploughed Field* (Zainul Abedin)	70	80

87 Two Players competing for Ball

1986. World Cup Football Championship, Mexico. Multicoloured.

267	1t. Type **87**	50	10
268	10t. Goalkeeper and ball in net	2·25	3·00
MS269	105×75 mm. 20t. Four players (60×44 mm) Imperf	5·50	6·50

88 General M. A. G. Osmani

1986. General M. A. G. Osmani (army commander-in-chief) Commemoration.

270	**88**	3t. multicoloured	1·75	1·00

1986. South Asian Association for Regional Co-operation Seminar. No. 183 optd **SAARC SEMINAR '86**.

271	**55**	50p. multicoloured	3·25	3·75

90 Butterflies and Nuclear Explosion

1986. International Peace Year. Multicoloured.

272	1t. Type **90**	50	25
273	10t. Flowers and ruined buildings	2·75	4·00
MS274	109×80 mm. 20t. Peace dove and soldier	1·50	2·00

1987. Conference for Development. Nos. 152/3 optd **CONFERENCE FOR DEVELOPMENT '87**, No. 275 also surch **TK. 1.00**.

275	**38**	1t. on 40p. black, red and yellow	10	20
276	-	5t. gold and blue	55	1·75

92 Demonstrators with Placards

1987. 35th Anniv of Bangla Language Movement. Multicoloured.

277	3t. Type **92**	1·40	2·50
278	3t. Martyrs' Memorial	1·40	2·50

Nos. 277/8 were printed together, se-tenant, forming a composite design.

93 Nurse giving Injection

1987. World Health Day.

279	**93**	1t. black and blue	1·75	2·00

See also No 295.

94 Pattern and Bengali Script

1987. Bengali New Year Day. Multicoloured.

280	1t. Type **94**	10	10
281	10t. Bengali woman	40	60

95 Jute Shika

1987. Export Products. Multicoloured.

282	1t. Type **95**	10	10
283	5t. Jute carpet (horiz)	30	35
284	10t. Cane table lamp	45	70

96 Ustad Ayet Ali Khan and Surbahar

1987. 20th Death Anniv of Ustad Ayet Ali Khan (musician and composer).

285	**96**	5t. multicoloured	1·50	1·00

97 Palanquin

1987. Transport. Multicoloured.

286	2t. Type **97**	20	15
287	3t. Bicycle rickshaw	1·00	35
288	5t. River steamer	1·25	65
289	7t. Express diesel train	3·25	1·25
290	10t. Bullock cart	60	1·50

98 H. S. Suhrawardy

1987. Hossain Shadid Suhrawardy (politician) Commemoration.

291	**98**	3t. multicoloured	20	30

99 Villagers fleeing from Typhoon

1987. International Year of Shelter for the Homeless. Multicoloured.

292	5t. Type **99**	50	70
293	5t. Villagers and modern houses	50	70

100 President Ershad addressing Parliament

1987. First Anniv of Return to Democracy.

294	**100**	10t. multicoloured	65	1·00

1988. World Health Day. As T **93**.

295	25p. brown	60	20

DESIGN: 25p. Oral rehydration.

101 Woman planting Palm Saplings

1988. I.F.A.D. Seminar on Agricultural Loans for Rural Women. Multicoloured.

296	3t. Type **101**	15	25
297	5t. Village woman milking cow	20	75

102 Basketball

1988. Olympic Games, Seoul. Multicoloured.

298	5t. Type **102**	1·25	80
299	5t. Weightlifting	1·25	80
300	5t. Tennis	1·25	80
301	5t. Rifle-shooting	1·25	80
302	5t. Boxing	1·25	80

103 Interior of Shait Gumbaz Mosque, Bagerhat

1988. Historical Buildings. Multicoloured.

303	1t. Type **103**	40	10
304	4t. Paharpur Monastery	80	30
305	5t. Kantanagar Temple, Dinajpur	80	30
306	10t. Lalbag Fort, Dhaka	1·25	1·00

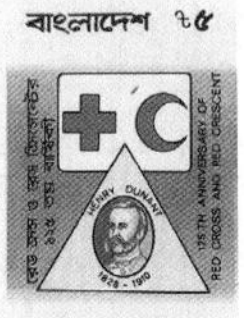

104 Henri Dunant (founder), Red Cross and Crescent

1988. 125th Anniv of International Red Cross and Red Crescent. Multicoloured.

307	5t. Type **104**	1·40	30
308	10t. Red Cross workers with patient	2·00	1·10

105 Dr. Qudrat-i-Khuda in Laboratory

1988. Dr. Qudrat-i-Khuda (scientist) Commem.

309	**105**	5t. multicoloured	50	40

106 Wicket-keeper

1988. Asia Cup Cricket. Multicoloured.

310	1t. Type **106**	80	90
311	5t. Batsman	1·00	1·25
312	10t. Bowler	1·75	2·25

107 Labourers, Factory and Technician

1988. 32nd Meeting of Colombo Plan Consultative Committee, Dhaka.

313	**107**	3t. multicoloured	10	10
314	**107**	10t. multicoloured	40	45

108 Dhaka G.P.O. Building

1988. 25th Anniv of Dhaka G.P.O. Building. Multicoloured.

315	1t. Type **108**	15	10
316	5t. Post Office counter	30	30

৫ম জাতীয় রোভার মুট
১৯৮৮-৮৯
(109)

1988. 5th National Rover Scout Moot. No. 168 optd with T **109**.

317	**47**	5t. multicoloured	3·50	3·00

110 Bangladesh Airport

1989. Bangladesh Landmarks.

318	**110**	3t. black and blue	40	10
318a	-	4t. blue	40	10
710	-	5t. black and brown	60	15
320	-	10t. red	4·00	35
321	-	20t. multicoloured	1·00	40

DESIGNS—VERT (22×33 mm): 5t. Curzon Hall. (19½×31½ mm): 10t. Fertiliser factory, Chittagong. HORIZ (33×23 mm): 4t. Chittagong port; 20t. Postal Academy, Rajshahi.

চতুর্থ দ্বিবার্ষিক এশীয়
চারুকলা প্রদর্শনী
বাংলাদেশ ১৯৮৯
(111)

1989. Fourth Biennial Asian Art Exhibition. No. 266 optd with T **111**.

322	10t. *Levelling the Ploughed Field* (Zainul Abedin)	75	1·00

112 Irrigation Methods and Student with Telescope

1989. 12th National Science and Technology Week.

323	**112**	10t. multicoloured	50	60

113 Academy Logo

1989. 75th Anniv of Police Academy, Sardah.

324	**113**	10t. multicoloured	75	60

114 Rejoicing Crowds, Paris, 1789

1989. Bicentenary of French Revolution. Multicoloured.

325	17t. Type **114**	70	75
326	17t. Storming the Bastille, 1789	70	75
MS327	125×125 mm 5t. Men with pickaxes; 10t. *Liberty guiding the People* (detail) (Delacroix); 10t. Crowd with cannon. P 14	2·00	3·00
MS328	152×88 mm. 25t. Storming the Bastille. Imperf	2·00	3·00

The design of No. **MS**328 incorporates the three scenes featured on No. **MS**327.

115 Sowing and Harvesting

1989. Tenth Anniv of Asia–Pacific Integrated Rural Development Centre. Multicoloured.

329	5t. Type **115**	65	65
330	10t. Rural activities	65	65

Nos. 329/30 were printed together, *se-tenant*, forming a composite design.

116 Helper and Child playing with Baby

1989. 40th Anniv of S.O.S. International Children's Village. Multicoloured.

331	1t. Type **116**	15	10
332	10t. Foster mother with children	85	90

117 U.N. Soldier on Watch

1989. First Anniv of Bangladesh Participation in U.N. Peace-keeping Force. Multicoloured.

333	4t. Type **117**	50	30
334	10t. Two soldiers checking positions	1·00	70

118 Festival Emblem

1989. Second Asian Poetry Festival, Dhaka.

335	**118**	2t. red, deep red and green	15	10
336	-	10t. multicoloured	85	90

DESIGN: 10t. Festival emblem and hall.

119 State Security Printing Press

1989. Inauguration of State Security Printing Press, Gazipur.

337	**119**	10t. multicoloured	65	65

120 Water Lilies and T.V. Emblem

1989. 25th Anniv of Bangladesh Television. Multicoloured.

338	5t. Type **120**	35	30
339	10t. Central emblem and water lilies	65	80

121 Gharial in Shallow Water

1990. Endangered Wildlife. Gharial. Multicoloured.

340	50p. Type **121**	80	45
341	2t. Gharial feeding	1·00	60
342	4t. Gharials basking on sand bank	1·40	70
343	10t. Two gharials resting	1·75	95

122 Symbolic Family

1990. Population Day.

344	**122**	6t. multicoloured	55	35

123 Justice S. M. Murshed

1990. Tenth Death Anniv of Justice Syed Mahbub Murshed.

345	**123**	5t. multicoloured	2·25	1·25

124 Boy learning Alphabet

1990. International Literacy Year. Multicoloured.

346	6t. Type **124**	1·00	50
347	10t. Boy teaching girl to write	1·50	1·25

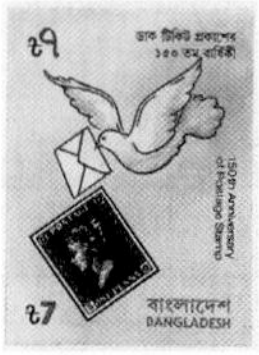

125 Penny Black with "Stamp World London 90" Exhibition Emblem

1990. 150th Anniv of the Penny Black. Multicoloured.

348	7t. Type **125**	1·50	2·00
349	10t. Penny Black, 1983 World Communications Year stamp and Bengali mail runner	1·75	2·50

126 Goalkeeper and Ball

1990. World Cup Football Championship, Italy. Multicoloured.

350	8t. Type **126**	1·75	1·75
351	10t. Footballer with ball	2·00	2·25
MS352	104×79 mm. 25t. Colosseum, Rome, with football. Imperf	12·00	12·00

127 Mango

1990. Fruit. Multicoloured.

353	1t. Type **127**	30	20
354	2t. Guava	30	20
355	3t. Water melon	35	25
356	4t. Papaya	40	30
357	5t. Bread fruit	65	65
358	10t. Carambola	1·25	1·50

128 Man gathering Wheat

1990. U.N. Conference on Least Developed Countries, Paris.

359	**128**	10t. multicoloured	1·25	1·25

129 Map of Asia with Stream of Letters

1990. 20th Anniv of Asia–Pacific Postal Training Centre. Multicoloured.

360	2t. Type **129**	1·75	1·75
361	6t. Map of Pacific with stream of letters	1·75	1·75

Nos. 360/1 were printed together, *se-tenant*, forming a composite map design.

130 Canoe Racing

1990. Asian Games, Beijing. Multicoloured.

362	2t. Type **130**	1·00	30
363	4t. Kabaddi	1·25	30
364	8t. Wrestling	1·75	1·50
365	10t. Badminton	3·00	2·00

131 Lalan Shah

1990. First Death Anniv of Lalan Shah (poet).

366	**131**	6t. multicoloured	1·50	1·00

132 U.N. Logo and "40"

1990. 40th Anniv of United Nations Development Programme.

367	**132**	6t. multicoloured	1·00	70

133 Baby

1990. Immunization.

368	**133**	1t. green	50	50
369	**133**	2t. brown	50	25

134 "Danaus chrysippus"

1990. Butterflies. Multicoloured.

370	6t. Type **134**	1·60	1·60
371	6t. *Precis almana*	1·60	1·60
372	10t. *Ixias pyrene*	1·75	1·75
373	10t. *Danaus plexippus*	1·75	1·75

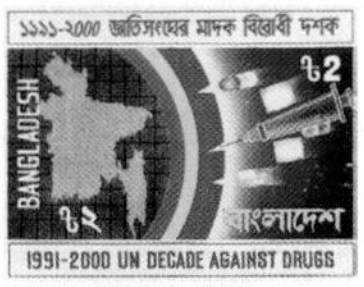

135 Drugs attacking Bangladesh

1991. U.N. Anti-drugs Decade. Multicoloured.

374	2t. Type **135**	1·25	50
375	4t. "Drug" snake around globe	1·75	1·25

136 Salimullah Hall

1991

376	**136**	6t. blue and yellow	20	15

137 Silhouetted People on Map

1991. Third National Census.

382	**137**	4t. multicoloured	1·50	1·50

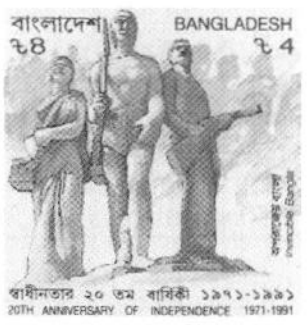

138 *Invincible Bangla* (statue)

1991. 20th Anniv of Independence. Multicoloured.

383	4t. Type **138**	85	1·00
384	4t. *Freedom Fighter* (statue)	85	1·00
385	4t. Mujibnagar Memorial	85	1·00
386	4t. Eternal flame	85	1·00
387	4t. National Martyrs' Memorial	85	1·00

Nos. 383/7 were issued together, *se-tenant*, forming a composite design.

139 President Rahman Seated

1991. Tenth Death Anniv of President Ziaur Rahman. Multicoloured.

388	50p. Type **139**	30	15
389	2t. President Rahman's head in circular decoration	1·00	1·10
MS390	146×75 mm. Nos. 388/9 (sold at 10t.)	1·90	2·75

140 Red Giant Flying Squirrel

1991. Endangered Species. Multicoloured.

391	2t. Type **140**	2·00	2·25
392	4t. Black-faced monkey (vert)	2·00	2·25
393	6t. Great Indian hornbill (vert)	2·00	2·25
394	10t. Armoured pangolin	2·00	2·25

141 Kaikobad

1991. 40th Death Anniv of Kaikobad (poet).

395	**141**	6t. multicoloured	1·60	1·25

142 Rabindranath Tagore and Temple

1991. 50th Death Anniv of Rabindranath Tagore (poet).

396	**142**	4t. multicoloured	1·00	65

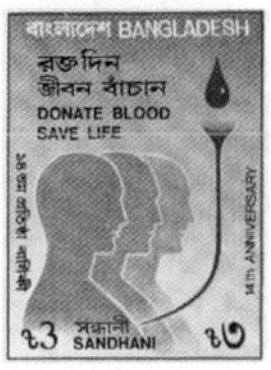

143 Voluntary Blood Programme

1991. 14th Anniv of "Sandhani" (medical students' association).

397	**143**	3t. black and red	1·00	50
398	-	5t. multicoloured	2·00	2·25

DESIGN: 5t. Blind man and eye.

144 Shahid Naziruddin and Crowd

1991. First Death Anniv of Shahid Naziruddin Jahad (democrat).

399	**144**	2t. black, green and brown	1·00	60

145 Shaheed Noor Hossain with Slogan on Chest

1991. Fourth Death Anniv of Shaheed Noor Hossain (democrat).

400	**145**	2t. multicoloured	1·00	55

146 Bronze Stupa

1991. Archaeological Relics from Mainamati. Multicoloured.

401	4t. Type **146**	1·50	1·60
402	4t. Earthenware and bronze pitchers	1·50	1·60
403	4t. Remains of Salban Vihara Monastery	1·50	1·60
404	4t. Gold coins	1·50	1·60
405	4t. Terracotta plaque	1·50	1·60

147 Demostrators

1991. First Anniv of Mass Uprising.

406	**147**	4t. multicoloured	1·25	80

148 Munier Chowdhury

1991. 20th Anniv of Independence. Martyred Intellectuals (1st series). Each black and brown.

407	2t. Type **148**	50	55
408	2t. Ghyasuddin Ahmad	50	55
409	2t. Rashidul Hasan	50	55
410	2t. Muhammad Anwar Pasha	50	55
411	2t. Dr. Muhammad Mortaza	50	55
412	2t. Shahid Saber	50	55
413	2t. Fazlur Rahman Khan	50	55
414	2t. Ranada Prasad Saha	50	55
415	2t. Adhyaksha Joges Chandra Ghose	50	55

416		2t. Santosh Chandra Bhattacharyya	50	55
417		2t. Dr. Gobinda Chandra Deb	50	55
418		2t. A. Muniruzzaman	50	55
419		2t. Mufazzal Haider Chaudhury	50	55
420		2t. Dr. Abdul Alim Choudhury	50	55
421		2t. Sirajuddin Hossain	50	55
422		2t. Shahidulla Kaiser	50	55
423		2t. Altaf Mahmud	50	55
424		2t. Dr. Jyotirmay Guha Thakurta	50	55
425		2t. Dr. Muhammad Abul Khair	50	55
426		2t. Dr. Serajul Haque Khan	50	55
427		2t. Dr. Mohammad Fazle Rabbi	50	55
428		2t. Mir Abdul Quyyum	50	55
429		2t. Golam Mostafa	50	55
430		2t. Dhirendranath Dutta	50	55
431		2t. S. Mannan	50	55
432		2t. Nizamuddin Ahmad	50	55
433		2t. Abul Bashar Chowdhury	50	55
434		2t. Selina Parveen	50	55
435		2t. Dr. Abul Kalam Azad	50	55
436		2t. Saidul Hassan	50	55

See also Nos. 483/92, 525/40, 568/83, 620/35, 656/71, 691/706, 731/46 and 779/94.

149 "Penaeus monodon"

1991. Shrimps. Multicoloured.

437		6t. Type **149**	2·00	2·25
438		6t. *Metapenaeus monoceros*	2·00	2·25

150 Death of Raihan Jaglu

1992. Fifth Death Anniv of Shaheed Mirze Abu Raihan Jaglu.

439	**150**	2t. multicoloured	1·50	60

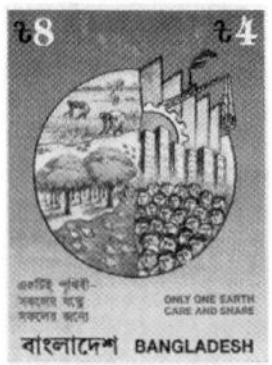

151 Rural and Urban Scenes

1992. World Environment Day. Multicoloured.

440		4t. Type **151**	75	25
441		10t. World Environment Day logo (horiz)	2·00	2·75

152 Nawab Sirajuddaulah

1992. 235th Death Anniv of Nawab Sirajuddaulah of Bengal.

442	**152**	10t. multicoloured	1·50	2·00

153 Syed Ismail Hossain Sirajee

1992. 61st Death Anniv of Syed Ismail Hossain Sirajee.

443	**153**	4t. multicoloured	1·25	60

154 Couple planting Seedling

1992. Plant Week. Multicoloured.

444		2t. Type **154**	1·00	80
445		4t. Birds on tree (vert)	2·00	1·25

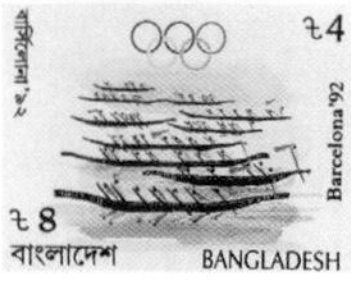

155 Canoe Racing

1992. Olympic Games, Barcelona. Multicoloured.

446		4t. Type **155**	1·40	1·75
447		6t. Hands holding torch with Olympic rings	1·40	1·75
448		10t. Olympic rings and doves	1·40	1·75
449		10t. Olympic rings and multiracial handshake	1·40	1·75

1992. "Banglapex '92", National Philatelic Exhibition (1st issue). No. 290 optd **Banglapex '92** in English and Bengali.

450		10t. Bullock cart	2·25	2·75

See also Nos. 452/3.

157 Masnad-e-Ala Isa Khan

1992. 393rd Death Anniv of Masnad-e-Ala Isa Khan.

451	**157**	4t. multicoloured	1·00	60

158 Ceremonial Elephant (19th-century ivory carving)

1992. "Banglapex '92" National Philatelic Exhibition (2nd issue). Multicoloured.

452		10t. Type **158**	1·60	2·25
453		10t. Victorian pillarbox between early and modern postmen	1·60	2·25
MS454		145×92 mm. Nos. 452/3. Imperf (sold at 25t.)	4·50	5·00

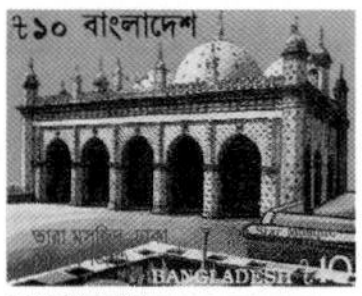

159 Star Mosque

1992. Star Mosque, Dhaka.

455	**159**	10t. multicoloured	2·00	2·00

160 Meer Nisar Ali Titumeer and Fort

1992. 161st Death Anniv of Meer Nisar Ali Titumeer.

456	**160**	10t. multicoloured	1·75	1·75

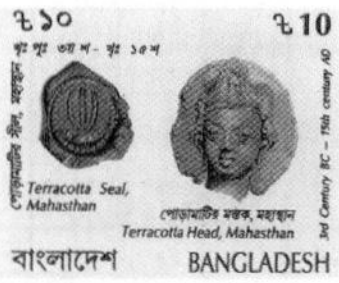

161 Terracotta Head and Seal

1992. Archaeological Relics from Mahasthangarh. Multicoloured.

457		10t. Type **161**	1·75	1·90
458		10t. Terracotta panel showing swan	1·75	1·90
459		10t. Terracotta statue of Surya	1·75	1·90
460		10t. Gupta stone column	1·75	1·90

162 Young Child and Food

1992. Int Conference on Nutrition, Rome.

461	**162**	4t. multicoloured	1·00	55

163 National Flags

1992. Seventh South Asian Association for Regional Co-operation Summit Conference, Dhaka. Mult.

462		6t. Type **163**	1·40	75
463		10t. S.A.A.R.C. emblem	1·60	2·00

164 Syed Abdus Samad

1993. Syed Abdus Samad (footballer) Commem.

464	**164**	2t. multicoloured	1·50	70

165 Haji Shariat Ullah

1993. Haji Shariat Ullah Commemoration.

465	**165**	2t. multicoloured	1·50	70

166 People digging Canal

1993. Irrigation Canals Construction Project. Multicoloured.

466		2t. Type **166**	80	80
467		2t. Completed canal and paddy-fields	80	80

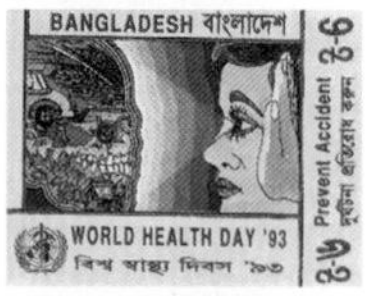

167 Accident Prevention

1993. World Health Day. Multicoloured.

468		6t. Type **167**	2·00	75
469		10t. Satellite photograph and symbols of trauma (vert)	2·25	2·75

168 National Images

1993. 1400th Year of Bengali Solar Calendar.

470	**168**	2t. multicoloured	1·00	50

169 Schoolchildren and Bengali Script

1993. Compulsory Primary Education. Multicoloured.

471		2t. Type **169**	80	80
472		2t. Books and slate (horiz)	80	80

170 Nawab Sir Salimullah and Palace

1993. 122nd Birth Anniv of Nawab Sir Salimullah.

473	**170**	4t. multicoloured	1·25	70

171 Fish Production

1993. Fish Fortnight.

474	**171**	2t. multicoloured	50	40

172 Sunderban

1993. Natural Beauty of Bangladesh. Multicoloured.

475		10t. Type **172**	1·00	1·40
476		10t. Kuakata beach	1·00	1·40
477		10t. Madhabkunda waterfall (vert)	1·00	1·40
478		10t. River Piyain, Jaflang (vert)	1·00	1·40
MS479		174×102 mm. Nos. 475/8. Imperf (sold at 50t.)	3·50	4·25

173 Exhibition Emblem

1993. Sixth Asian Art Biennale.

480	**173**	10t. multicoloured	80	1·00

174 Foy's Lake

1993. Tourism Month.

481	**174**	10t. multicoloured	1·00	1·25

175 Burdwan House

1993. Foundation Day, Bangla Academy.

482	**175**	2t. brown and green	1·25	40

1993. Martyred Intellectuals (2nd series). As T **148**. Each black and brown.

483		2t. Lt. Cdr. Moazzam Hussain	20	30
484		2t. Muhammad Habibur Rahman	20	30
485		2t. Khandoker Abu Taleb	20	30
486		2t. Moshiur Rahman	20	30
487		2t. Md. Abdul Muktadir	20	30
488		2t. Nutan Chandra Sinha	20	30
489		2t. Syed Nazmul Haque	20	30

490		2t. Dr. Mohammed Amin Uddin	20	30
491		2t. Dr. Faizul Mohee	20	30
492		2t. Sukha Ranjan Somaddar	20	30

176 Throwing the Discus

1993. Sixth South Asian Federation Games, Dhaka. Multicoloured.

493		2t. Type **176**	20	20
494		4t. Running (vert)	35	35

177 Tomb of Sultan Ghiyasuddin Azam Shah

1993. Muslim Monuments.

495	**177**	10t. multicoloured	75	1·00

178 Scouting Activities and Jamboree Emblem

1994. 14th Asian–Pacific and 5th Bangladesh National Scout Jamboree.

496	**178**	2t. multicoloured	40	30

179 Emblem and Mother giving Solution to Child

1994. 25th Anniv of Oral Rehydration.

497	**179**	2t. multicoloured	65	30

180 Interior of Chhota Sona Mosque, Nawabgonj

1994. Ancient Mosques. Multicoloured.

498		4t. Type **180**	40	20
499		6t. Exterior of Chhota Sona Mosque	50	65
500		6t. Exterior of Baba Adam's Mosque, Munshigonj	50	65

181 Agricultural Workers and Emblem

1994. 75th Anniv of I.L.O. Multicoloured.

501		4t. Type **181**	25	20
502		10t. Worker turning cog (vert)	1·00	1·00

182 Priest releasing Peace Doves

1994. 1500th Year of Bengali Solar Calendar.

503	**182**	2t. multicoloured	55	30

183 Scenes from Baishakhi Festival

1994. Folk Festivals. Multicoloured.

504		4t. Type **183**	35	35
505		4t. Scenes from Nabanna and Paush Parvana Festivals	35	35

184 Family, Globe and Logo

1994. International Year of the Family.

506	**184**	10t. multicoloured	1·00	1·50

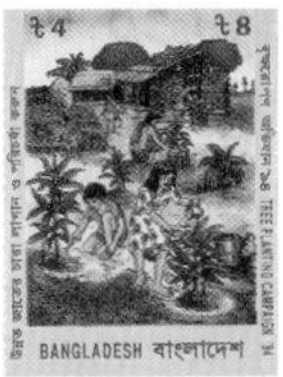

185 People planting Saplings

1994. Tree Planting Campaign. Multicoloured.

507		4t. Type **185**	50	25
508		6t. Hands holding saplings	75	60

186 Player kicking Ball

1994. World Cup Football Championship, U.S.A. Multicoloured.

509		20t. Type **186**	2·25	3·00
510		20t. Player heading ball	2·25	3·00

187 Traffic on Bridge

1994. Inauguration of Jamuna Multi-purpose Bridge Project.

511	**187**	4t. multicoloured	2·00	60

188 Asian Black-headed Oriole

1994. Birds. Multicoloured.

512		4t. Type **188**	40	40
513		6t. Greater racquet-tailed drongo	60	80
514		6t. Indian tree pie	60	80
515		6t. Red junglefowl	60	80
MS516		165×110 mm. Nos. 512/15 (sold at 25t.)	2·00	2·75

189 Dr. Mohammad Ibrahim and Hospital

1994. Fifth Death Anniv of Dr. Mohammad Ibrahim (diabetes treatment pioneer).

517	**189**	2t. multicoloured	40	20

190 Nawab Faizunnessa Chowdhurani

1994. 160th Birth Anniv of Nawab Faizunnessa Chowdhurani (social reformer).

518	**190**	2t. multicoloured	50	20

191 Boxing

1994. Asian Games, Hiroshima, Japan.

519	**191**	4t. multicoloured	1·50	60

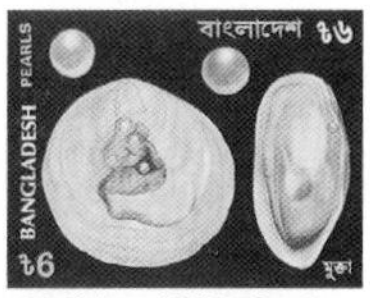

192 Pink and White Pearls with Windowpane Oysters

1994. Sea Shells. Multicoloured.

520		6t. Type **192**	1·40	1·60
521		6t. Tranquelous scallop and other shells	1·40	1·60
522		6t. Lister's conch, Asiatic Arabian cowrie, bladder moon and woodcock murex	1·40	1·60
523		6t. Spotted tun, spiny frog shell, spiral melongena and gibbous olive (vert)	1·40	1·60

193 Dr. Milon and Demonstrators

1994. Fourth Death Anniv of Dr. Shamsul Alam Khan Milon (medical reformer).

524	**193**	2t. multicoloured	25	20

1994. Martyred Intellectuals (3rd series). As T **148**. Each black and brown.

525		2t. Dr. Harinath Dey	25	30
526		2t. Dr. A. F. Ziaur Rahman	25	30
527		2t. Mamun Mahmud	25	30
528		2t. Mohsin Ali Dewan	25	30
529		2t. Dr. N. A. M. Jahangir	25	30
530		2t. Shah Abdul Majid	25	30
531		2t. Muhammad Akhter	25	30
532		2t. Meherunnesa	25	30
533		2t. Dr. Kasiruddin Talukder	25	30
534		2t. Fazlul Haque Choudhury	25	30
535		2t. Md. Shamsuzzaman	25	30
536		2t. A. K. M. Shamsuddin	25	30
537		2t. Lt. Mohammad Anwarul Azim	25	30
538		2t. Nurul Amin Khan	25	30
539		2t. Mohammad Sadeque	25	30
540		2t. Md. Araz Ali	25	30

194 *Diplazium esculentum*

1994. Vegetables. Multicoloured.

541		4t. Type **194**	70	50
542		4t. *Momordica charantia*	70	50
543		6t. *Lagenaria siceraria*	90	70
544		6t. *Trichosanthes dioica*	90	70
545		10t. *Solanum melongena*	1·40	2·00
546		10t. *Cucurbita maxima* (horiz)	1·40	2·00

195 Sonargaon

1995. 20th Anniv of World Tourism Organization.

547	**195**	10t. multicoloured	1·75	1·75

196 Exports

1995. Dhaka International Trade Fair '95. Multicoloured.

548		4t. Type **196**	20	20
549		6t. Symbols of industry	45	65

197 Soldiers of Ramgarh Battalion (1795) and of Bangladesh Rifles (1995)

1995. Bicentenary of Bangladesh Rifles. Multicoloured.

550		2t. Type **197**	1·25	50
551		4t. Riflemen on patrol	1·60	90

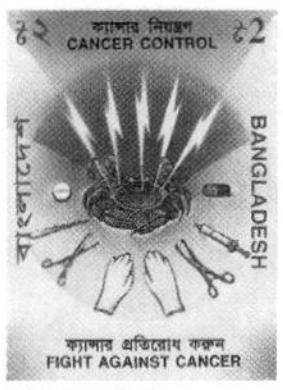

198 Surgical Equipment and Lightning attacking Crab (cancer)

1995. Campaign against Cancer.

552	**198**	2t. multicoloured	40	25

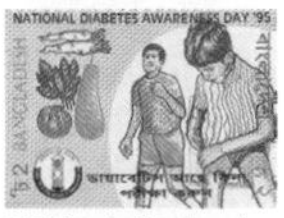

199 Fresh Food and Boy injecting Insulin

1995. National Diabetes Awareness Day.

553	**199**	2t. multicoloured	1·00	30

200 Munshi Mohammad Meherullah

1995. Munshi Mohammad Meherullah (Islamic educator) Commemoration.

554	**200**	2t. multicoloured	30	25

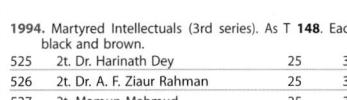

রাজশাহীপেক্স-৯৫

(201)

1995. "Rajshahipex '95" National Philatelic Exhibition. No. 499 optd with T **201**.

555	6t. Exterior of Chhota Sona Mosque	2·25	2·50

202 *Lagerstroemia speciosa*

1995. Flowers. Multicoloured.

556	6t. Type **202**	90	90
557	6t. *Bombax ceiba* (horiz)	90	90
558	10t. *Passiflora incarnata*	1·25	1·40
559	10t. *Bauhina purpurea*	1·25	1·40
560	10t. *Canna indica*	1·25	1·40
561	10t. *Gloriosa superba*	1·25	1·40

203 Aspects of Farming

1995. 50th Anniv of F.A.O.

562	**203** 10t. multicoloured	1·00	1·25

204 Anniversary Emblem, Peace Dove and U.N. Headquarters

1995. 50th Anniv of United Nations. Multicoloured.

563	2t. Type **204**	30	20
564	10t. Peace doves circling dates and Globe	90	1·40
565	10t. Clasped hands and U.N. Headquarters	90	1·40

205 Diseased Lungs, Microscope, Family and Map

1995. 18th Eastern Regional Conference on Tuberculosis, Dhaka.

566	**205** 6t. multicoloured	1·50	1·00

206 Peace Doves, Emblem and National Flags

1995. Tenth Anniv of South Asian Association for Regional Co-operation.

567	**206** 2t. multicoloured	1·40	55

1995. Martyred Intellectuals (4th series). As T **148**. Each black and brown.

568	2t. Abdul Ahad	25	30
569	2t. Lt. Col. Mohammad Qadir	25	30
570	2t. Mozammel Hoque Chowdhury	25	30
571	2t. Rafiqul Haider Chowdhury	25	30
572	2t. Dr. Azharul Haque	25	30
573	2t. A. K. Shamsuddin	25	30
574	2t. Anudwaipayan Bhattacharjee	25	30
575	2t. Lutfunnahar Helena	25	30
576	2t. Shaikh Habibur Rahman	25	30
577	2t. Major Naimul Islam	25	30
578	2t. Md. Shahidullah	25	30
579	2t. Ataur Rahman Khan Khadim	25	30
580	2t. A. B. M. Ashraful Islam Bhuiyan	25	30
581	2t. Dr. Md. Sadat Ali	25	30
582	2t. Sarafat Ali	25	30
583	2t. M. A. Sayeed	25	30

207 Aspects of COMDECA Projects

1995. Second Asia–Pacific Community Development Scout Camp.

584	**207** 2t. multicoloured	70	35

208 Volleyball Players

1995. Centenary of Volleyball.

585	**208** 6t. multicoloured	1·00	55

209 Man in Punjabi and Lungi

1995. Traditional Costumes. Multicoloured.

586	6t. Type **209**	1·00	1·00
587	6t. Woman in sari	1·00	1·00
588	10t. Christian bride and groom	1·40	1·50
589	10t. Muslim bride and groom	1·40	1·50
590	10t. Buddhist bride and groom (horiz)	1·40	1·50
591	10t. Hindu bride and groom (horiz)	1·40	1·50

210 Shaheed Amanullah Mohammad Asaduzzaman

1996. 27th Death Anniv of Shaheed Amanullah Mohammad Asaduzzaman (student leader).

592	**210** 2t. multicoloured	40	25

211 Bowler and Map

1996. World Cup Cricket Championship. Multicoloured.

593	4t. Type **211**	1·25	55
594	6t. Batsman and wicket keeper	1·50	80
595	10t. Match in progress (horiz)	2·00	2·25

212 Liberation Struggle, 1971

1996. 25th Anniv of Independence. Multicoloured.

596	4t. Type **212**	70	70
597	4t. National Martyrs Memorial	70	70
598	4t. Education	70	70
599	4t. Health	70	70
600	4t. Communications	70	70
601	4t. Industry	70	70

213 Michael Madhusudan Dutt

1996. Michael Madhusudan Dutt (poet) Commemoration.

602	**213** 4t. multicoloured	50	20

214 Gymnastics

1996. Olympic Games, Atlanta. Multicoloured.

603	4t. Type **214**	30	20
604	6t. Judo	40	35
605	10t. Athletics (horiz)	45	70
606	10t. High jumping (horiz)	45	70
MS607	165×110 mm. Nos. 603/6 (sold at 40t.)	1·50	2·00

1996. 25th Anniv of Bangladesh Stamps. No. **MS**234 optd **Silver Jubilee Bangladesh Postage Stamps 1971-96** on sheet margin.

MS608	98×117 mm. Nos. 232/3 (sold at 10t.)	1·40	1·75

215 Bangabandhu Sheikh Mujibur Rahman

1996. 21st Death Anniv of Bangabandhu Sheikh Mujibur Rahman.

609	**215** 4t. multicoloured	40	25

216 Maulana Mohammad Akrum Khan

1996. 28th Death Anniv of Maulana Mohammad Akrum Khan.

610	**216** 4t. multicoloured	40	20

217 Ustad Alauddin Khan

1996. 24th Death Anniv of Ustad Alauddin Khan (musician).

611	**217** 4t. multicoloured	70	30

218 *Kingfisher* (Mayeesha Robbani)

1996. Children's Paintings. Multicoloured.

612	2t. Type **218**	60	45
613	4t. *Fiver Crossing* (Iffat Panchlais) (horiz)	80	45

219 Syed Nazrul Islam

1996. 21st Death Anniv of Jail Martyrs. Multicoloured.

614	4t. Type **219**	30	40
615	4t. Tajuddin Ahmad	30	40
616	4t. M. Monsoor Ali	30	40
617	4t. A. H. M. Quamaruzzaman	30	40

220 Children receiving Medicine

1996. 50th Anniv of UNICEF Multicoloured.

618	4t. Type **220**	50	25
619	10t. Mother and child	1·10	1·40

1996. Martyred Intellectuals (5th series). As T **148**. Each black and brown.

620	2t. Dr. Jekrul Haque	45	45
621	2t. Munshi Kabiruddin Ahmed	45	45
622	2t. Md. Abdul Jabbar	45	45
623	2t. Mohammad Amir	45	45
624	2t. A. K. M. Shamsul Huq Khan	45	45
625	2t. Dr. Siddique Ahmed	45	45
626	2t. Dr. Soleman Khan	45	45
627	2t. S. B. M. Mizanur Rahman	45	45
628	2t. Aminuddin	45	45
629	2t. Md. Nazrul Islam	45	45
630	2t. Zahirul Islam	45	45
631	2t. A. K. Lutfor Rahman	45	45
632	2t. Afsar Hossain	45	45
633	2t. Abul Hashem Mian	45	45
634	2t. A. T. M. Alamgir	45	45
635	2t. Baser Ali	45	45

221 Celebrating Crowds

1996. 25th Anniv of Victory Day. Multicoloured.

636	4t. Type **221**	35	30
637	6t. Soldiers and statue (vert)	65	70

222 Paul P. Harris

1997. 50th Death Anniv of Paul Harris (founder of Rotary International).

638	**222** 4t. multicoloured	35	25

223 Shaikh Mujibur Rahman making Speech

1997. 25th Anniv of Shaikh Mujibur's Speech of 7 March (1996).

639	**223** 4t. multicoloured	35	25

224 Sheikh Mujibur Rahman

1997. 77th Birth Anniv of Sheikh Mujibur Rahman (first President).

640	**224**	4t. multicoloured	50	25

225 Sheikh Mujibur Rahman and Crowd with Banners

1997. 25th Anniv (1996) of Independence.

641	**225**	4t. multicoloured	35	25

226 Heinrich von Stephan

1997. Death Centenary of Heinrich von Stephan (founder of U.P.U.).

642	**226**	4t. multicoloured	35	25

227 Sheep

1997. Livestock. Multicoloured.

643	4t. Type **227**	75	75
644	4t. Goat	75	75
645	6t. Buffalo bull	90	90
646	6t. Cow	90	90

228 "Tilling the Field - 2" (S. Sultan)

1997. Bangladesh Paintings. Multicoloured.

647	6t. Type **228**	40	30
648	10t. *Three Women* (Quamrul Hassan)	60	1·25

229 Trophy, Flag and Cricket Ball

1997. Sixth International Cricket Council Trophy Championship, Malaysia.

649	**229**	10t. multicoloured	3·25	2·75

230 Kusumba Mosque, Naogaon

1997. Historic Mosques. Multicoloured.

650	4t. Type **230**	65	35
651	6t. Atiya Mosque, Tangail	85	45
652	10t. Bagha Mosque, Rajshahi	1·25	1·75

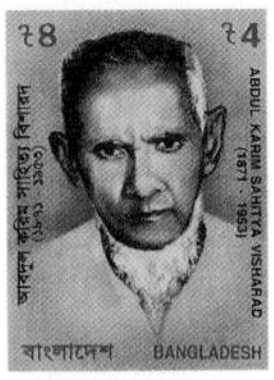

231 Adul Karim Sahitya Vishard

1997. 126th Birth Anniv of Abdul Karim Sahitya Vishard (scholar).

653	**231**	4t. multicoloured	40	25

232 River Moot Emblem and Scouts standing on top of World

1997. Ninth Asia-Pacific and Seventh Bangladesh Rover Moot, Lakkatura.

654	**232**	2t. multicoloured	50	25

233 Officers and Flag

1997. 25th Anniv of Armed Forces.

655	**233**	2t. multicoloured	1·50	60

1997. Martyred Intellectuals (6th series). As T **148**. Each black and brown.

656	2t. Dr. Shamsuddin Ahmed	65	65
657	2t. Mohammad Salimullah	65	65
658	2t. Mohiuddin Haider	65	65
659	2t. Abdur Rahin	65	65
660	2t. Nitya Nanda Paul	65	65
661	2t. Abdel Jabber	65	65
662	2t. Dr. Humayun Kabir	65	65
663	2t. Khaja Nizamuddin Bhuiyan	65	65
664	2t. Gulam Hossain	65	65
665	2t. Ali Karim	65	65
666	2t. Md. Moazzem Hossain	65	65
667	2t. Rafiqul Islam	65	65
668	2t. M. Nur Husain	65	65
669	2t. Captain Mahmood Hossain Akonda	65	65
670	2t. Abdul Wahab Talukder	65	65
671	2t. Dr. Hasimoy Hazra	65	65

234 Mohammad Mansooruddin

1998. Professor Mohammad Mansooruddin (folklorist) Commemoration.

672	**234**	4t. multicoloured	1·40	60

235 Standard-bearer and Soldiers

1998. 50th Anniv of East Bengal Regiment.

673	**235**	2t. multicoloured	1·00	55

236 Bulbul Chowdhury

1998. Bulbul Chowdhury (traditional dancer) Commemoration.

674	**236**	4t. multicoloured	40	25

237 World Cup Trophy

1998. World Cup Football Championship, France. Multicoloured.

675	6t. Type **237**	75	30
676	18t. Footballer and trophy	2·00	2·50

238 Eastern Approach Road, Bangabandhu Bridge

1998. Opening of Bangabandhu Bridge. Multicoloured.

677	4t. Type **238**	65	30
678	6t. Western approach road	75	40
679	8t. Embankment	95	1·40
680	10t. Main span, Bangabandhu Bridge	1·25	1·60

239 Diana, Princess of Wales

1998. Diana, Princess of Wales Commemoration. Multicoloured.

681	8t. Type **239**	1·40	1·40
682	18t. Wearing pearl choker	1·75	1·75
683	22t. Wearing pendant necklace	1·75	2·00

240 Means of collecting Solar Energy

1998. World Solar Energy Programme Summit.

684	**240**	10t. multicoloured	1·50	1·50

241 World Habitat Day Emblem and City Scene

1998. World Habitat Day.

685	**241**	4t. multicoloured	1·25	60

242 Farmworkers, Sunflower and "20"

1998. 20th Anniv of International Fund for Agricultural Development. Multicoloured.

686	6t. Type **242**	65	35
687	10t. Farmworker with baskets and harvested crops	1·10	1·40

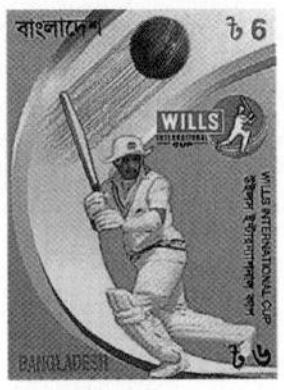

243 Batsman

1998. Wills International Cricket Cup, Dhaka.

688	**243**	6t. multicoloured	1·75	1·25

244 Begum Rokeya

1998. Begum Rokeya (campaigner for women's education) Commemoration.

689	**244**	4t. multicoloured	1·25	60

245 Anniversary Logo

1998. 50th Anniv of Universal Declaration of Human Rights.

690	**245**	10t. multicoloured	1·25	1·25

1998. Martyred Intellectuals (7th series). As T **148**. Each black and brown.

691	2t. Md. Khorshed Ali Sarker	50	50
692	2t. Abu Yakub Mahfuz Ali	50	50
693	2t. S. M. Nural Huda	50	50
694	2t. Nazmul Hoque Sarker	50	50
695	2t. Md. Taslim Uddin	50	50
696	2t. Gulam Mostafa	50	50
697	2t. A. H. Nural Alam	50	50
698	2t. Timir Kanti Dev	50	50
699	2t. Altaf Hossain	50	50
700	2t. Aminul Hoque	50	50
701	2t. S. M. Fazlul Hoque	50	50
702	2t. Mozammel Ali	50	50
703	2t. Syed Akbar Hossain	50	50
704	2t. Sk. Abdus Salam	50	50
705	2t. Abdur Rahman	50	50
706	2t. Dr. Shyamal Kanti Lala	50	50

246 Dove of Peace and U.N. Symbols

1998. 50th Anniv of U.N. Peace-keeping Operations.

707	**246**	10t. multicoloured	1·25	1·50

247 Kazi Nazrul Islam

1998. Birth Centenary (1999) of Kazi Nazrul Islam (poet).

708	**247**	6t. multicoloured	1·25	70

248 Jamboree Emblem and Scout Activities

1999. Sixth Bangladesh National Scout Jamboree.

709	**248**	2t. multicoloured	1·00	50

1999. As No. 75 but redrawn. Size 35×22 mm.

711	10t. red	1·10	30

No. 711 has been redrawn so that "SIXTY-DOME MOSQUE" appears above the face value at bottom right instead of below the main inscription at top left.

249 Surjya Sen and Demonstrators

1999. Surjya Sen (revolutionary) Commemoration.

715	**249**	4t. multicoloured	1·25	60

250 Dr. Fazlur Rahman Khan and Sears Tower

1999. 70th Birth Anniv of Dr. Fazlur Rahman Khan (architect).

716	**250**	4t. multicoloured	1·00	55

251 National Team Badges

1999. Cricket World Cup, England. Multicoloured.

717	8t. Type **251**	1·75	2·00
718	10t. Bangladesh cricket team badge and flag	2·50	2·50
MS719	139×89 mm. Nos. 717/18 (sold at 30t.)	4·50	4·75

252 Mother Teresa

1999. Mother Teresa Commemoration.

720	**252**	4t. multicoloured	1·50	65

253 Sheikh Mujibur Rahman, New York Skyline and Dove

1999. 25th Anniv of Bangladesh's Admission to U.N.

721	**253**	6t. multicoloured	1·00	65

254 Shaheed Mohammad Maizuddin

1999. 15th Death Anniv of Shaheed Mohammad Maizuddin (politician).

722	**254**	2t. multicoloured	60	30

255 Faces in Tree

1999. International Year of the Elderly.

723	**255**	6t. multicoloured	1·00	60

256 Shanty Town and Modern Buildings between Hands

1999. World Habitat Day.

724	**256**	4t. multicoloured	1·00	50

257 Mobile Post Office

1999. 125th Anniv of U.P.U. Multicoloured.

725	4t. Type **257**	80	65
726	4t. Postman on motorcycle	80	65
727	6t. Postal motor launch	1·00	90
728	6t. Douglas DC-10 and Boeing 737	1·00	90
MS729	141×90 mm. Nos. 725/8 (sold at 25t.)	3·25	3·25

258 Sir Jagadis Chandra Bose

1999. Sir Jagadis Chandra Bose (physicist and botanist) Commemoration.

730	**258**	4t. multicoloured	1·50	60

1999. Martyred Intellectuals (8th series). As T **148**. Each black and brown.

731	2t. Dr. Mohammad Shafi	50	50
732	2t. Maulana Kasimuddin Ahmed	50	50
733	2t. Quazi Ali Imam	50	50
734	2t. Sultanuddin Ahmed	50	50
735	2t. A. S. M. Ershadullah	50	50
736	2t. Mohammad Fazlur Rahman	50	50
737	2t. Captain A. K. M. Farooq	50	50
738	2t. Md. Latafot Hossain Joarder	50	50
739	2t. Ram Ranjan Bhattacharjya	50	50
740	2t. Abani Mohan Dutta	50	50
741	2t. Sunawar Ali	50	50
742	2t. Abdul Kader Miah	50	50
743	2t. Major Rezaur Rahman	50	50
744	2t. Md. Shafiqul Anowar	50	50
745	2t. A. A. M. Mozammel Hoque	50	50
746	2t. Khandkar Abul Kashem	50	50

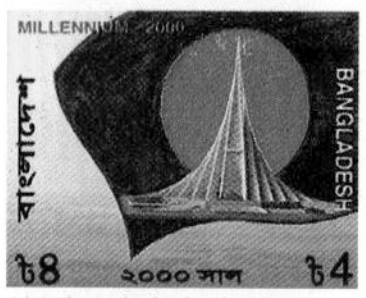

259 Bangladesh Flag and Monument

2000. New Millennium. Multicoloured.

747	4t. Type **259**	75	45
748	6t. Satellite, computer and dish aerial (vert)	1·00	1·10

260 Cub Scouts, Globe and Flag

2000. Fifth Bangladesh Cub Camporee.

749	**260**	2t. multicoloured	70	40

261 Jibananada Das

2000. Death Centenary (1999) of Jibananada Das (poet).

750	**261**	4t. multicoloured	70	40

262 Dr. Muhammad Shamsuzzoha

2000. 30th Death Anniv (1999) of Dr. Muhammad Shamsuzzoha.

751	**262**	4t. multicoloured	1·00	40

263 Shafiur Rahman

2000. International Mother Language Day. Multicoloured.

752	4t. Type **263**	65	75
753	4t. Abul Barkat	65	75
754	4t. Abdul Jabbar	65	75
755	4t. Rafiq Uddin Ahmad	65	75

264 Meteorological Equipment

2000. 50th Anniv of World Meteorological Organization.

756	**264**	10t. multicoloured	1·75	1·75

265 Cricket Week Logo and Web Site Address

2000. International Cricket Week.

757	**265**	6t. multicoloured	1·75	1·25

266 Wasp

2000. Insects. Multicoloured.

758	2t. Type **266**	50	30
759	4t. Grasshopper	70	35
760	6t. Bumble bee	90	65
761	10t. Silkworms	1·50	2·25

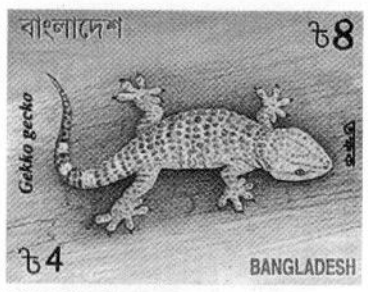

267 Gecko

2000. Native Fauna. Multicoloured.

762	4t. Type **267**	70	70
763	4t. Indian crested porcupine	70	70
764	6t. Indian black-tailed python	95	95
765	6t. Bengal monitor	95	95

268 Batsman

2000. Pepsi 7th Asia Cricket Cup.

766	**268**	6t. multicoloured	1·75	1·25

269 Water Cock

2000. Birds. Multicoloured.

767	4t. Type **269**	90	80
768	4t. White-breasted waterhen (*Amaurornis phoenicurus*)	90	80
769	6t. Javanese cormorant (*Phalacrocorax niger*) (vert)	1·25	1·10
770	6t. Indian pond heron (*Ardeola grayii*) (vert)	1·25	1·10

270 Women's Shotput

2000. Olympic Games, Sydney. Multicoloured.

771	6t. Type **270**	1·00	50
772	10t. Men's Shotput	1·50	1·75

271 Clasped Hands, Landmarks and Flags

2000. 25th Anniv of Diplomatic Relations with People's Republic of China.

773	**271**	6t. multicoloured	1·50	75

272 Idrakpur Fort, Munshigonj

2000. Archaeology. Multicoloured.

774	4t. Type **272**	75	40
775	6t. Statue of Buddha, Mainamati (vert)	1·25	1·00

273 Year Emblem

2000. International Volunteers' Year.

776	**273**	6t. multicoloured	1·25	65

274 Hason Raza

2000. 80th Death Anniv of Hason Raza (mystic poet).

777	**274**	6t. multicoloured	1·50	75

275 U.N.H.C.R. Logo

2000. 50th Anniv of United Nations High Commissioner for Refugees (U.N.H.C.R.).

778	**275**	10t. multicoloured	1·50	2·00

2000. Martyred Intellectuals (9th series). As T **148**. Each black and brown.

779	2t. M. A. Gofur	55	55
780	2t. Faizur Rahman Ahmed	55	55
781	2t. Muslimuddin Miah	55	55
782	2t. Sgt. Shamsul Karim Khan	55	55
783	2t. Bhikku Zinananda	55	55
784	2t. Abdul Jabber	55	55
785	2t. Sekander Hayat Chowdhury	55	55
786	2t. Chishty Shah Helalur Rahman	55	55
787	2t. Birendra Nath Sarker	55	55
788	2t. A. K. M. Nurul Haque	55	55
789	2t. Sibendra Nath Mukherjee	55	55
790	2t. Zahir Raihan	55	55
791	2t. Ferdous Dowla Bablu	55	55
792	2t. Capt A. K. M. Nurul Absur	55	55
793	2t. Mizanur Rahman Miju	55	55
794	2t. Dr. Shamshad Ali	55	55

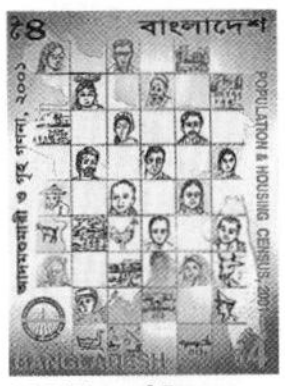

276 Map of Faces

2001. Population and Housing Census.

795	**276**	4t. multicoloured	1·25	55

277 Producing Food

2001. "Hunger-free Bangladesh" Campaign.

796	**277**	6t. multicoloured	1·25	65

278 "Peasant Women" (Rashid Chowdhury)

2001. Bangladesh Paintings.

797	**278**	10t. multicoloured	2·00	2·00

279 Lalbagh Kella Mosque

2001. Historic Buildings. Multicoloured.

798	6t. Type **279**	85	85
799	6t. Uttara Ganabhavan, Natore	85	85
800	6t. Armenian Church, Armanitola	85	85
801	6t. Panam Nagar, Sonargaon	85	85

280 Smoking Accessories, Globe and Paper People

2001. World No Tobacco Day.

802	**280**	10t. multicoloured	1·75	1·75

281 Ustad Gul Mohammad Khan

2001. Artists. Multicoloured.

803	6t. Type **281**	80	80
804	6t. Ustad Khadem Hossain Khan	80	80
805	6t. Gouhar Jamil	80	80
806	6t. Abdul Alim	80	80

282 Begum Sufia Kamal

2001. Begum Sufia Kamal (poet) Commemoration.

807	**282**	4t. multicoloured	75	40

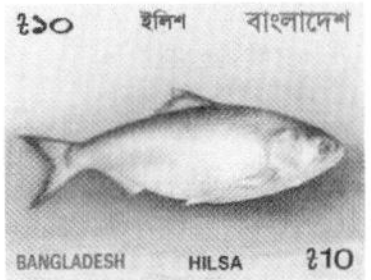

283 Hilsa

2001. Fish. Multicoloured.

808	10t. Type **283**	1·10	1·10
809	10t. Tengra	1·10	1·10
810	10t. Punti	1·10	1·10
811	10t. Khalisa	1·10	1·10

284 Parliament House, Dhaka

2001. Completion of First Full National Parliamentary Term.

812	**284**	10t. multicoloured	2·25	2·25

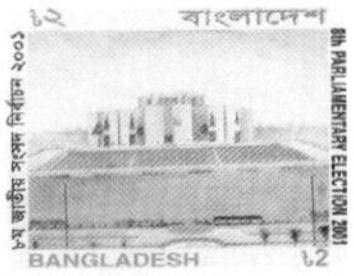

285 Parliament House, Dhaka

2001. Eighth Parliamentary Elections.

813	**285**	2t. multicoloured	70	45

286 "Children encircling Globe" (Urska Golob)

2001. U.N. Year of Dialogue among Civilizations.

814	**286**	10t. multicoloured	1·25	1·50
MS815 95×65 mm. **286** 10t. multicoloured (sold at 30t.)			1·75	3·00

287 Meer Mosharraf Hossain

2001. Meer Mosharraf Hossain (writer) Commemoration.

816	**287**	4t. black, red and crimson	65	40

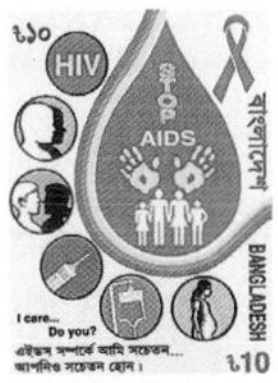

288 Drop of Blood surrounded by Images

2001. World AIDS Day.

817	**288**	10t. multicoloured	1·75	1·75

289 Sreshto Medal

2001. 30th Anniv of Independence. Gallantry Medals. Multicoloured.

818	10t. Type **289**	1·25	1·50
819	10t. Uttom medal	1·25	1·50
820	10t. Bikram medal	1·25	1·50
821	10t. Protik medal	1·25	1·50

290 Publicity Poster

2002. Tenth Asian Art Biennale, Dhaka.

822	**290**	10t. multicoloured	1·00	1·25

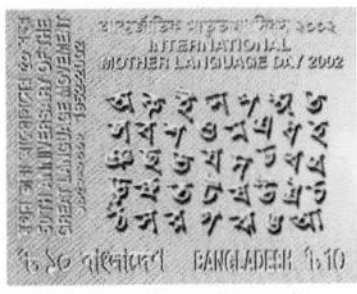

291 Letters from Bengali Alphabet

2002. 50th Anniv of Amar Ekushey (language movement). International Mother Language Day.

823	**291**	10t. black, gold and red	80	1·10
824	-	10t. black, gold and red	80	1·10
825	-	10t. black, gold and red	80	1·10
MS826 96×64 mm. 30t. multicoloured			2·00	2·25

DESIGNS—HORIZ: No. 824, Language Martyrs' Monument, Dhaka; 825, Letters from Bengali alphabet ("INTERNATIONAL MOTHER LANGUAGE DAY" inscr at right). VERT: No. **MS**826, Commemorative symbol of Martyrs' Monument.

292 Rokuon-Ji Temple, Japan

2002. 30th Anniv of Diplomatic Relations with Japan.

827	**292**	10t. multicoloured	1·00	1·25

293 Silhouetted Goats

2002. Goat Production.

828	**293**	2t. multicoloured	45	25

294 Children

2002. U.N. Special Session on Children.

829	**294**	10t. multicoloured	1·25	1·25

295 Mohammad Nasiruddin

2002. Mohammad Nasiruddin (journalist) Commemoration.

830	**295**	4t. black and brown	75	40

296 National Flags (trophy at top right)

2002. World Cup Football Championship, Japan and Korea. Multicoloured.

831	10t. Type **296**	1·00	1·25
832	10t. Pitch markings on world map	1·00	1·25
833	10t. National flags (trophy at top left)	1·00	1·25

297 Children tending Saplings

2002. National Tree Planting Campaign. Multicoloured.

834	10t. Type **297**	90	1·00
835	10t. Citrus fruit	90	1·00
836	10t. Trees within leaf symbol (vert)	90	1·00

298 Children inside Symbolic House

2002. 30th Anniv of S.O.S. Children's Village in Bangladesh.

837	**298**	6t. multicoloured	80	45

299 Rural Family

2002. World Population Day.

838	**299**	6t. multicoloured	80	45

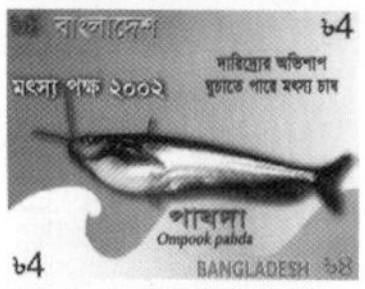

300 Ompook Pabda (fish)

2002. Fish. Multicoloured.
839 4t. Type **300** 50 50
840 4t. *Labeo gonius* 50 50

301 Bangladesh–U.K. Friendship Bridge, Bhairab

2002. Opening of Bangladesh–U.K. Friendship Bridge, Bhairab.
841 **301** 4t. multicoloured 1·00 45

302 Dhaka City Centre

2002. World Habitat Day.
842 **302** 4t. multicoloured 70 35

303 Dariabandha (Tag)

2002. Rural Games. Multicoloured.
843 4t. Type **303** 70 70
844 4t. Kanamachee (Blind-man's buff) 70 70

304 Jasimuddin

2003. Birth Centenary of Jasimuddin (poet).
845 **304** 5t. multicoloured 50 35

305 Books

2003. National Book Year.
846 **305** 6t. multicoloured 60 35

306 Footballers and Flags of Participating Countries

2003. Third SAFF Championship, Bangladesh.
847 **306** 10t. multicoloured 1·75 1·75

ইফাদ-এর ২৫ বছর
25 Years of IFAD
(307)

2003. 25th Anniv of International Fund for Agricultural Development. No. 687 optd with T **307**.
848 10t. Farmworker with baskets and harvested crops 1·75 1·75

308 Shefa-ul-Mulk Hakim Habib-ur-Rahman

2003. 56th Death Anniv of Shefa-ul-Mulk Hakim Habib-ur-Rahman.
849 **308** 4t. multicoloured 45 25

309 Ziaur Rahman

2003. 22nd Death Anniv of Ziaur Rahman (President 1977–1981).
850 **309** 4t. multicoloured 45 25

310 Sapling in Cupped Hands and Family

2003. National Tree Plantation Campaign. Multicoloured.
851 8t. Type **310** 1·00 60
852 12t. Trees, plant, fruit and adult with children inside "petals" 1·25 1·50

311 Fruit

2003. Fruit Tree Plantation Fortnight.
853 **311** 6t. multicoloured 1·25 60

312 *Labeo Calbasu* (Orange-fin labeo)

2003. Fish Fortnight.
854 **312** 2t. multicoloured 60 30

313 Train on Jamuna Bridge and Signals

2003. Inauguration of Direct Train Communication between Rajshahi and Dhaka.
855 **313** 10t. multicoloured 1·50 1·50

314 Jatiya Sangsad Bhaban (Parliament House)

2003. 49th Commonwealth Parliamentary Conference.
856 **314** 10t. multicoloured 1·25 1·40

315 Mosque

2003. Eid Mubarak.
857 **315** 4t. multicoloured 1·00 65

316 Emblem

2003. International Centre for Diarrhoeal Disease Research, Bangladesh.
858 **316** 10t. multicoloured 1·25 1·40

317 Rajshahi University

2003. 50th Anniv of Rajshahi University.
859 **317** 4t. multicoloured 1·00 55

318 Books

2004. National Library Year (2003).
860 **318** 6t. multicoloured 1·00 70

319 Tents inside Emblem and Member Flags

2004. Seventh Bangladesh and Fourth South Asian Association for Regional Co-operation Jamboree.
861 **319** 2t. multicoloured 1·00 45

320 Runner with Olympic Torch

2004. Sport and Environment.
862 **320** 10t. multicoloured 1·00 1·00

321 Emblems

2004. 11th Asian Art Biennale.
863 **321** 5t. multicoloured 45 25

322 Ziaur Rahman

2004. 33rd Anniv of Independence and National Day.
864 **322** 5t. multicoloured 45 25

323 Road and Emblems

2004. World Health Day.
865 **323** 6t. multicoloured 45 25

2004. 25th Anniv of Bangladesh National Philatelic Association. No. 843 optd **Silver Jubilee Bangladesh National Philatelic Association** and emblem.
866 4t. Type **303** 45 30

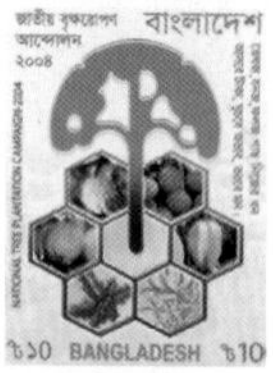

325 Stylized Tree, Fruits and Berries

2004. National Tree Plantation Campaign. Multicoloured.
867 10t. Type **325** 65 70
868 10t. Trees and saplings 65 70

326 Hafez Shirazi, Iranian Flag and Banay-e Azadi (Freedom Monument), Tehran

2004. Commemoration of Diplomatic Relations with Iran. Multicoloured.
869 10t. Type **326** 80 90
870 10t. Nazrul Islam, Bangladeshi flag and War memorial, Dhaka 80 90

327 Woman Planting Tree and Fruit

2004. Fruit Tree Plantation Campaign.
871 **327** 10t. multicoloured 75 75

328 Workers carrying Rice Harvest

2004. International Year of Rice.
872 **328** 5t. multicoloured 60 60

329 Man feeding Child and Two Women

2004. World Population Day.
873 **329** 6t. multicoloured 45 30

330 UN Headquarters and Flags

2004. 30th Anniv of United Nations Membership.
874 **330** 4t. multicoloured 30 20

331 Bhasani Novo Theatre, Dhaka

2004. Bhasani Novo Theatre, Dhaka.

875	**331**	4t. multicoloured	30	20

332 Centennial Bell

2004. Centenary of Rotary International.

876	**332**	4t. multicoloured	30	20

333 *Argemone mexicana*

2004. Wild Flowers. Multicoloured.

877	5t. Type **333**	70	70
878	5t. *Cyanotis axillaries*	70	70
879	5t. *Thevetia Peruvians*	70	70
880	5t. *Pentapetes phoenicea*	70	70
881	5t. *Aegle marmelos*	70	70
882	5t. *Datura stramonium*	70	70

2004. 13th SAARC (South Asian Association for Regional Co-operation) Summit, Dhaka (2005).

883	**334**	6t. multicoloured	40	25

335 *Sperata aor*

2004. Fish Fortnight. Multicoloured.

884	10t. Type **335**	80	95
885	10t. *Notopterus notepturus*	80	95

336 Cub in Sunflower

2004. Sixth National Cub Camporee.

886	**336**	6t. multicoloured	40	25

337 Woman Farmer and Microcredit Symbol

2005. United Nations International Year of Microcredit. Multicoloured.

887	4t. Type **337**	30	30
888	10t. Woman turning lever on coin and microcredit symbol pulley	70	80

338 Beach at Sunset

2005. South Asia Tourism Year.

889	**338**	4t. multicoloured	30	20

339 Major Ziaur Rahman and War Memorial, Dhaka

2005. Independence and National Day.

890	**339**	10t. multicoloured	75	75

340 Sewing Machinist, Fish in Net, Dairy Cattle, Hens and Goats

2005. Centenary of Co-operative Movement in Bangladesh.

891	**340**	5t. multicoloured	40	25

341 Family Planting Tree

2005. National Tree Plantation Campaign. Multicoloured.

892	6t. Type **341**	70	75
893	6t. Three types of different varieties	70	75

342 G. A. Mannan (choreographer)

2005. Talented Artists. Multicoloured.

894	6t. Type **342**	60	70
895	6t. Unstad Phuljhuri Khan (musician)	60	70
896	6t. Ustad Abed Hossian Khan (musician and composer)	60	70
897	6t. Ustad Munshi Raisuddin (musician)	60	70

343 *Nandus nandus*

2005. Fish Fortnight.

898	**343**	10t. multicoloured	1·00	75

344 Dr. Nawab Ali

2005. Dr. Nawab Ali (physician) Commemoration.

899	**344**	8t. multicoloured	60	60

345 Books, Compass and Dividers

2006. Science Book Year (2005).

900	**345**	10t. multicoloured	75	75

346 Emblems, Globe and Computer Screen

2006. World Summit on the Information Society, Tunis (2005).

901	**346**	10t. multicoloured	1·00	75

347 Verwaltungssitz, Vienna and Emblem

2006. 30th Anniv of OPEC Fund for International Development (2005).

902	**347**	10t. multicoloured	75	75

348 Palace of Heavenly Peace, Beijing

2006. 30th Anniv of Bangladesh–China Diplomatic Relations (2005). Multicoloured.

903	10t. Type **348**	70	70
904	10t. Parliament Building, Dhaka	70	70
905	10t. 5th Bangladesh–China Friendship Bridge over Gabkhan River	70	70
906	10t. Great Wall of China	70	70
MS907	140×90 mm. Nos. 903/6	2·50	2·50

349 Major Ziaur Rahman and War Memorial, Dhaka

2006. 35th Anniversary of Independence and National Day.

908	**349**	10t. multicoloured	1·00	75

350 Palm Tree

2006. National Tree Plantation Campaign and Tree Fair.

909	**350**	10t. multicoloured	1·00	75

351 Mother with Baby and Toddler

2006. World Health Day.

910	**351**	6t. multicoloured	1·25	1·00

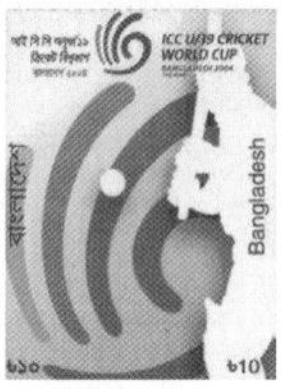

352 Silhouette of Batsman

2006. ICC Under 19 Cricket World Cup (2004), Bangladesh.

911	**352**	10t. multicoloured	1·50	1·25

353 Peace Dove and Modern Buildings and Roads

2006. Five Years of Peace and Development.

912	**353**	10t. multicoloured	1·00	1·00

354 AIDS Ribbon and Globe

2006. World AIDS Day.

913	**354**	10t. multicoloured	1·00	1·00

355 Profiles

2006. International Women's Day.

914	**355**	10t. multicoloured	1·00	1·00

356 Family and Jar of Coins ('Invest in health')

2007. World Health Day.

915	**356**	6t. multicoloured	1·00	1·00

357 Falling Wicket

2007. World Cup Cricket, West Indies. Multicoloured.

916	10t. Type **357**	1·00	1·00
917	10t. Tiger, bowler and trophy (horiz)	1·00	1·00
918	10t. Bangladesh team and Cricket World Cup trophy	1·00	1·00
919	10t. Batsman and trophy (horiz)	1·00	1·00

358 House and Girls in Plantation

2007. National Tree Plantation Campaign.

920	**358**	10t. multicoloured	1·00	1·00

359 Md. Habibullah Bahar Choudhury

2007. Birth Centenary (2006) of Md. Habibullah Bahar Choudhury (politician and writer).

921	**359**	10t. multicoloured	1·00	1·00

360 Boy and Girl Scouts

2007. Centenary of World Scouting. Multicoloured.

922	10t. Type **360**	1·00	1·00
923	10t. Lord Baden-Powell (founder)	1·00	1·00

(361)

2007. 20th Anniv of Philatelic Association of Bangladesh. No. 768 optd with T **361**.

924	4t. White-breasted waterhen (*Amaurornis phoenicurus*)	1·50	1·00

362 Dr. Muhammad Yunus and Peace Medal

2007. Dr. Muhammad Yunus and Grameen Bank–winner of Nobel Peace Prize (2006).

925	**362**	10t. multicoloured	1·50	1·50

363 Children standing in Flood Water

2008. In Charity of Flood Victims. Multicoloured.

926	2t. Type **363**	70	80
927	2t. Children and sheep in flood water	70	80
928	2t. People and goats taking refuge on corrugated iron roof	70	80
929	2t. Women queuing for food	70	80
930	2t. Woman and children with food bowls and flooded houses	70	80

364 Cricket Match

2007. ICC World Twenty20 2007 Cricket Cup, South Africa. Multicoloured.

931	4t. Type **364**	80	80
932	4t. Cricketer and map of South Africa	80	80

365 Emblem and Globe

2008. International Migrants Day.

933	**365**	10t. multicoloured	1·50	1·50

366 Soldiers with Flag

2008. Independence and National Day.

934	**366**	10t. multicoloured	1·50	1·50

367 Melting Glacier and Flooded Village

2008. World Health Day. 'Protecting Health From Climate Change'.

935	**367**	10t. multicoloured	1·50	1·50

368 Herd of Spotted Deer

2008. The Sundarbans World Heritage Site. Multicoloured.

936	10t. Type **368**	1·50	1·50
937	10t. Waterway and mangrove forest	1·50	1·50
938	10t. Collecting bee nests for honey	1·50	1·50
939	10t. Tiger	1·50	1·50
MS940	167×95 mm. Nos. 936/9	6·50	6·50

No. **MS**940 also exists imperforate.

369 'CELEBRATING 50 YEARS' and Pattern

2008. Golden Jubilee of the Aga Khan (2007).

941	**369**	3t. emerald and green	55	55
942	**369**	3t. red and rose	55	55
943	–	3t. gold pattern on white	55	55
944	–	3t. white pattern on gold	55	55

DESIGN: Nos. 943/4 'CELEBRATING 50 YEARS' in circle surrounded by pattern.

370 Athletes on Training Run

2008. Olympic Games, Beijing. Multicoloured.

945	10t. Type **370**	1·00	1·00
946	15t. Rifle shooting	1·25	1·25
947	20t. Olympic mascots Beibei, Jingjing, Huanhuan, Yingying and Nini	1·40	1·40
948	25t. Pierre de Coubertin (founder of modern Olympics) and Olympic stamps of Greece (1876) and Bangladesh (1976)	1·60	1·60

371 The First Stamps of Bangladesh, 1971

2008. Stamp Day. Sheet 140×90 mm.

MS949	**371**	50t. multicoloured	3·75	4·50

372 Khepupara Radar Station, Patuakhali

2008. Japanese International Cooperation Agency ('Friends from the Birth of Bangladesh'). Sheet 123×75 mm containing T **372** and similar horiz designs. Multicoloured.

MS950	3t. Type **372**; 7t. Vocational training programme; 10t. Jamuna Multi-purpose Bridge; 10t. Polio vaccination programme	2·50	2·75

373 Emblem

2008. 50th Anniv of Dhaka Chamber of Commerce and Industry.

951	**373**	10t. multicoloured	1·50	1·50

374 Farmer and Workers in Rice Field

2008. First National Agriculture Day.

952	**374**	4t. multicoloured	70	50

375 Nimtali Deuri (gateway of Nimtali Palace)

2008. 400th Anniv of Dhaka.

953	**375**	6t. multicoloured	80	60

376 Cox's Bazar

2008. Cox's Bazar (world's longest unbroken sea beach).

954	**376**	10t. multicoloured	1·00	1·00

377 Disabled Man

2008. International Day of Persons with Disabilities.

955	**377**	3t. multicoloured	70	45

378 Women and Child and Emblem

2008. International Year of Sanitation.

956	**378**	3t. multicoloured	70	45

379 1972 'In Memory of the Martyrs' 20p. Stamp

2009. International Mother Language Day. Sheet 180×119 mm.

MS957	**379**	50t. multicoloured	6·00	6·00

380 Sheikh Mujibur Rahman and Children

2009. Sheikh Mujibur Rahman Commemoration and National Children's Day.

958	**380**	10t. multicoloured	1·25	1·25

381 Ziaur Rahman, National Flag and Painting

2009. Independence and National Day.

959	**381**	3t. multicoloured	1·00	45

382 Doctors and Nurses with Patients and Hospital Building

2009. World Health Day.

960	**382**	3t. multicoloured	1·00	55

383 China 2009 Emblem

2009. China 2009 World Stamp Exhibition, Luoyang. Sheet 100×70 mm containing T **383** and similar horiz designs. Multicoloured.

MS961	10t. Type **383**; 10t. China 2009 'Tree Peony Messenger' mascot; 20t. Ox	4·75	4·75

No. **MS**5961 contains three stamps and a stamp size label.

384 Shamsun Nahar Mahmud

2009. Birth Centenary (2008) of Shamsun Nahar Mahmud (writer).

962	**384**	4t. multicoloured	70	50

385 Couple holding Tree Seedlings

2009. National Tree Plantation Campaign and Tree Fair.

963	**385**	3t. multicoloured	50	35

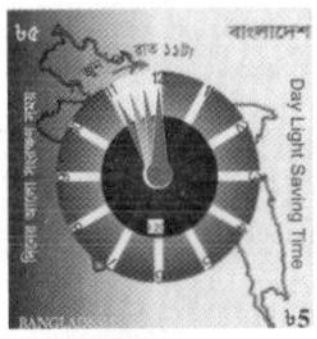

386 Clock

2009. Day Light Saving Time.

964	**386**	5t. multicoloured	65	65

387 Silhouette of Family

2009. World Population Day.

965	**387**	6t. multicoloured	70	70

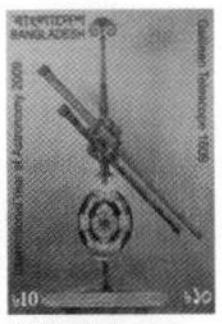

388 Galilean Telescope, 1609

2009. International Year of Astronomy. Multicoloured.

966	10t. Type **388**	1·50	1·50
967	10t. Andromeda Galaxy	1·50	1·50

389 Begum Fazilatunnessa Mujib

2009. National Mourning Day. Sheikh Mujibur Rahman and his Family. Multicoloured.

968	3t. Type **389**	35	35
969	3t. Sheikh Kamal	35	35
970	3t. Sheikh Jamal	35	35
971	3t. Sheikh Russel	35	35
972	3t. Sheikh Abu Naser	35	35
973	3t. Sultana Kamal Khuku	35	35
974	3t. Parveen Jamal Rosy	35	35
975	3t. Abdur Rab Serniabat	35	35
976	3t. Sheikh Fazlul Haque Moni	35	35
977	3t. Begum Arju Moni	35	35
978	3t. Colonel Jamiluddin Ahmed	35	35
979	3t. Baby Serniabat	35	35
980	3t. Arif Serniabat	35	35
981	3t. Sukanto Abdullah Babu	35	35
982	3t. Shahid Serniabat	35	35
983	3t. Abdul Nayeem Khan Rintu	35	35
984	15t. Sheikh Mujibur Rahman	35	35

390 Coin

2009. World Food Day. Multicoloured.

985	3t. Type **390**	45	45
986	3t. Bread and agricultural produce	45	45
987	3t. Boat loaded with produce	45	45
988	3t. Fishermen with catch	45	45

391 Valerie Taylor with Patient

2009. 30th Anniv of Centre for the Rehabilitation of the Paralysed, Dhaka.

989	7t. Type **391**	90	90
990	7t. Rehabilitation	90	90

392 Professor Abdul Moktader

2009. Birth Centenary of Professor Abdul Moktader.

991	**392**	4t. multicoloured	50	50

393 Scouts saluting

2010. Eighth National Scout Jamboree

992	**393**	10t. multicoloured	3·25	3·25

394 'Alec's Red'

2010. Roses: Cultivated Varieties in Bangladesh. Multicoloured.

993	10t. Type **394**	2·75	2·75
994	10t. Royal Highness	2·75	2·75
995	10t. Queen Elizabeth	2·75	2·75
996	10t. Ballerina	2·75	2·75
997	10t. Alexander	2·75	2·75
998	10t. Blue Moon	2·75	2·75
999	10t. Papa Meilland	2·75	2·75
1000	10t. Double Delight	2·75	2·75
1001	10t. Iceberg	2·75	2·75
1002	10t. Sonia	2·75	2·75
1003	10t. Sunblest	2·75	2·75
1004	10t. Piccadilly	2·75	2·75
1005	10t. Pascali	2·75	2·75

395 'Alec's Red'

2010. Inauguration of International Mother Language Institute, Dhaka

1006	**395**	15t. multicoloured	4·25	4·25

396 Women with Raised Fists

2010. Centenary of International Women's Day

1007	**396**	5t. multicoloured	2·00	2·00

397 1997 4t. Sheikh Mujibur Rahman Stamp

2010. National Children's Day. Sheet 140×100 mm.

MS1008	**397** 10t. multicoloured (sold at 25t.)	8·50	8·50

398 Liberation Monument, Public Library Campus, Brahman Baria

2010. Independence and National Day. Multicoloured.

MS1009	5t.×4, Type **398**; Liberation Monument, Shafipur, Gazipur; Liberation Monument, Jagannath Hall, Dhaka University; Liberation Monument, Vocational Training Institute, Rangpur	7·00	7·00

399 Cricket Badges

2010. ICC World Twenty20 2010 Cricket Cup

1010	**398**	15t. multicoloured	4·25	4·25

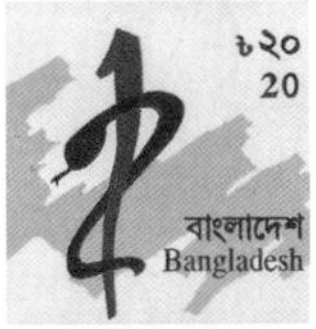

400 Emblem

2010. 12th Anniv of Bangabandhu Sheikh Mujib Medical University

MS1011	**400** 20t. multicoloured	7·25	7·25

401 City Park

2010. National Tree Plantation Campaign and Tree Fair

1012	**401**	6t. multicoloured	1·50	1·50

402 Bara Katra (Mughal Dhaka)

2010. 400th Anniv (2008) of Dhaka (2nd issue). Multicoloured.

1013	10t. Type **402**	3·00	3·00
1014	10t. Buriganga River and Buckland Bund (embankment) (British Dhaka)	3·00	3·00
1015	10t. Kamlapur Railway Station (Pakistan Period)	3·00	3·00
1016	10t. Dhaka City Corporation building and modern Dhaka	3·00	3·00

403 Anniversary Emblem

2010. 50th Anniv of ICDDR'B (International Centre for Diarrhoeal Disease Research, Bangladesh)

1017	**403**	5t. gold and black	1·75	1·75

404 Two Players

2010. World Cup Football Championships, South Africa. Multicoloured.

1018	10t. Type **404**	1·50	1·50
1019	10t. Three players pursuing headed ball	1·50	1·50
1020	20t. Zakumi mascot	3·00	3·00

405 Chakma Woman

2010. Indigenous Peoples in Bangladesh. Multicoloured.

1021	5t. Type **405**	60	60
1022	5t. Marma woman wearing flower in hair	60	60
1023	5r. Mru woman (head and shoulders, wearing red)	60	60
1024	5r. Tripura (head and shoulders, wearing red)	60	60
1025	5r. Pangkhua woman	60	60
1026	5r. Chakma woman (full length portrait, wearing sash)	60	60
1027	5r. Marma woman holding bouquet of flowers	60	60
1028	5r. Mru woman (threequarter length portrait, bracelets on arms)	60	60
1029	5r. Tripura woman (head and shoulders, wearing white)	60	60
1030	5r. Pangkhua man and woman	60	60
1031	5r. Chakma woman weaving	60	60
1032	5r. Two Marma women gathering crops	60	60
1033	5r. Two Mru women poundng grain	60	60
1034	5r. Two Tripura women carrying firewood	60	60
1035	5r. Pangkhua man making basket	60	60
1036	5r. Two Chakma women	60	60
1037	5r. Two Marma women dancing	60	60
1038	5r. Mru man spearing pig in pen	60	60
1039	5r. Tripura woman dancing	60	60
1040	5r. Pangkhua man with bull's skull	60	60

406 Rajban Bihar Pagoda, ('Raj Banbihar'), Rangamati

2010. Bangkok 2010 25th Asian International Stamp Exhibition, Bangkok, Thailand. Sheet 140×90 mm containing T **406** and similar horiz design. Multicoloured.

MS1041	20t. Type **406**; 20t. Buddha Dhatu Jadi, Bandarban	5·50	5·50

OFFICIAL STAMPS

1973. Nos. 22, etc. optd **SERVICE**.

O1	**7**	2p. black	10	1·50
O2	-	3p. green	10	1·50
O3	-	5p. brown	20	10
O4	-	10p. black	20	10
O5	-	20p. green	1·75	10
O6	-	25p. mauve	4·00	10
O7	-	60p. grey	4·00	2·25
O8	-	75p. orange	1·50	30
O9	**8**	1t. violet	17·00	6·50
O10	-	5t. blue	5·00	9·00

1974. Nos. 49/51 optd **SERVICE**.

O11	**14**	1t. violet	5·00	50
O12	-	2t. olive	7·00	2·25
O13	-	5t. blue	18·00	14·00

1976. Nos. 64/70 and 72/4 optd **SERVICE**.

O14		5p. green	1·50	1·00
O15		10p. black	3·00	1·00
O16		20p. green	3·25	1·25
O17		25p. mauve	3·50	1·00
O18		50p. purple	5·00	60
O19		60p. grey	30	3·00
O20		75p. olive	30	3·75
O21	**14**	1t. blue	3·25	70
O22	-	2t. green	35	2·50
O23	-	5t. blue	30	2·75

32 Fenchuganj Fertiliser Factory

1981. Nos. 125/37 optd **SERVICE**.

O24		5p. brown	2·75	2·50
O25	**32**	10p. blue	2·75	3·00
O26	-	15p. orange	2·75	2·75
O27	-	20p. red	1·50	2·75
O28	-	25p. blue	80	2·75
O29	-	30p. green	5·00	3·00
O30	-	40p. purple	2·75	2·75
O31	-	50p. black	30	10
O32	-	80p. brown	2·25	50
O33	-	1t. violet	30	10
O34	-	2t. blue	35	3·25

1983. Nos. 220/9, 318a and 710 (1989) optd **Service**.

O35	**69**	5p. blue	20	60
O36	-	10p. purple	20	30
O37	-	15p. blue	20	45
O38	-	20p. black	20	30
O39	-	25p. grey	20	40
O40	-	30p. brown	25	40
O41	-	50p. brown	25	20
O42	-	1t. blue	50	20
O43	-	2t. green	1·75	30
O44	-	3t. black and blue	50	50
O45	-	4t. blue	55	55
O46	-	5t. purple	2·25	1·00

সার্ভিস

(O5)

1989. Nos. 227 and 710 (1989) optd with Type **O5**.

O47		1t. blue	50	20
O48		5t. black and brown	1·00	1·00

(O6)

1990. Nos. 368/9 (Immunization) optd with Type **O6**.

O49	**133**	1t. green	25	50
O50	**133**	2t. brown	25	50

1992. No. 376 optd as Type **O6** but horiz.

O51	**136**	6t. blue and yellow	50	50

1995. No. 553 (National Diabetes Awareness Day) optd as Type **O6** but horiz.

O52	**199**	2t. multicoloured	1·00	1·00

সার্ভিস

(O7)

1996. Nos. 221 and 223 optd with Type **O7**.

O53		10p. purple	75	75
O54		20p. black	1·25	1·25

1999. No. 710 optd as Type **O5** but vert.

O56		5t. black and brown	1·00	1·00

Pt. 1

BARBADOS

An island in the Br. West Indies, E. of the Windward Islands, attained self-government on 16 October 1961 and achieved independence within the Commonwealth on 30 November 1966.

1852. 12 pence = 1 shilling; 20 shillings = 1 pound.
1950. 100 cents = 1 West Indian, later Barbados, dollar.

1 Britannia

2

1852. Imperf.

8	**1**	(½d.) green	£180	£200
10	**1**	(1d.) blue	75·00	60·00
4a	**1**	(2d.) slate	£300	£1200
5	**1**	(4d.) red	£120	£275
11	**2**	6d. red	£750	£120
12a	**2**	1s. black	£225	75·00

1860. Perf.

21	**1**	(½d.) green	27·00	29·00
24	**1**	(1d.) blue	65·00	3·75
25	**1**	(4d.) red	£140	65·00
31	**2**	6d. red	£140	30·00
33	**2**	6d. orange	£180	50·00
35	**2**	1s. black	65·00	9·50

1873. Perf.

72		½d. green	20·00	50
74		1d. blue	£120	1·50
63		3d. brown	£325	£110
75		3d. mauve	£160	13·00
76		4d. red	£150	14·00
79		6d. yellow	£150	2·25
81		1s. purple	£160	7·50

3

1873

64	**3**	5s. red	£950	£300

1878. Half of No. 64 surch **1D**.

86		1d. on half 5s. red	£5000	£650

4

1882

90	**4**	½d. green	26·00	2·00
92	**4**	1d. red	42·00	1·25
93	**4**	2½d. blue	£110	1·50
96	**4**	3d. purple	7·00	27·00
97	**4**	4d. grey	£350	4·50
99	**4**	4d. brown	12·00	2·00
100	**4**	6d. black	75·00	48·00
102	**4**	1s. brown	29·00	21·00
103	**4**	5s. bistre	£160	£200

1892. Surch **HALF-PENNY**.

104		½d. on 4d. brown	2·25	6·00

6 Seal of Colony

1892

105	**6**	¼d. grey and red	2·50	10
163	**6**	¼d. brown	10·00	30
106	**6**	½d. green	2·50	10
107	**6**	1d. red	4·75	10
108	**6**	2d. black and orange	9·00	75
166	**6**	2d. grey	9·00	20·00
139	**6**	2½d. blue	26·00	15
110	**6**	5d. olive	7·50	4·50
111	**6**	6d. mauve and red	16·00	2·00
168	**6**	6d. deep purple and purple	19·00	30·00
112	**6**	8d. orange and blue	4·25	29·00
113	**6**	10d. green and red	9·00	9·00
169	**6**	1s. black on green	14·00	16·00
114	**6**	2s.6d. black and orange	48·00	65·00
144	**6**	2s.6d. violet and green	65·00	£150

7

1897. Diamond Jubilee.

116	**7**	¼d. grey and red	8·50	60
117	**7**	½d. green	8·50	60
118	**7**	1d. red	9·00	60
119	**7**	2½d. blue	12·00	85
120	**7**	5d. brown	29·00	20·00
121	**7**	6d. mauve and red	40·00	25·00
122	**7**	8d. orange and blue	21·00	27·00
123	**7**	10d. green and red	60·00	55·00
124	**7**	2s.6d. black and orange	90·00	60·00

8 Nelson Monument

1906. Death Centenary of Nelson.

145	**8**	¼d. black and grey	15·00	1·75
146	**8**	½d. black and green	11·00	15
147	**8**	1d. black and red	12·00	15
148	**8**	2d. black and yellow	2·00	4·50
149	**8**	2½d. black and blue	3·75	1·25
150	**8**	6d. black and mauve	19·00	28·00
151	**8**	1s. black and red	23·00	50·00

9 *Olive Blossom*, 1650

1906. Tercentenary of Annexation of Barbados.

152	**9**	1d. black, blue and green	16·00	25

1907. Surch **Kingston Relief Fund. 1d.**

153	**6**	1d. on 2d. black and orange	6·00	12·00

11

1912

170	**11**	¼d. brown	1·75	1·50
171	**11**	½d. green	3·75	10
172	**11**	1d. red	11·00	10
173	**11**	2d. grey	6·00	19·00
174	**11**	2½d. blue	1·50	65
175	**11**	3d. purple on yellow	1·50	14·00
176	**11**	4d. black and red on yellow	4·00	23·00
177	**11**	6d. deep purple and purple	12·00	12·00

Larger type, with portrait at top centre.

178		1s. black on green	12·00	23·00
179		2s. purple and blue on blue	60·00	65·00
180		3s. green and violet	£110	£120

14

1916

181	**14**	¼d. brown	75	40
182	**14**	½d. green	3·00	15
183a	**14**	1d. red	2·50	15
184	**14**	2d. grey	11·00	32·00
185	**14**	2½d. blue	5·50	3·50
186	**14**	3d. purple on yellow	8·00	13·00
187	**14**	4d. red on yellow	1·00	14·00
199	**14**	4d. black and red	1·00	3·75
188	**14**	6d. purple	9·00	7·00
189	**14**	1s. black on green	10·00	12·00
190	**14**	2s. purple on blue	17·00	7·50
191	**14**	3s. violet	70·00	£170
200	**14**	3s. green and violet	25·00	£110

1917. Optd **WAR TAX**.

197	**11**	1d. red	50	15

16

1920. Victory. Inscr "VICTORY 1919".

201	**16**	¼d. black and brown	30	70
202	**16**	½d. black and green	1·50	15
203	**16**	1d. black and red	4·00	10
204	**16**	2d. black and grey	2·25	14·00
205	**16**	2½d. indigo and blue	2·75	26·00
206	**16**	3d. black and purple	3·25	6·50
207	**16**	4d. black and green	3·25	7·00
208	**16**	6d. black and orange	4·25	22·00
209	-	1s. black and green	18·00	48·00
210	-	2s. black and brown	48·00	70·00
211	-	3s. black and orange	50·00	90·00

The 1s. to 3s. show Victory full-face.

18

1921

217	**18**	¼d. brown	25	10
219	**18**	½d. green	1·50	10
220	**18**	1d. red	80	10
221	**18**	2d. grey	1·75	20
222	**18**	2½d. blue	1·50	9·00
213	**18**	3d. purple on yellow	2·00	8·50
214	**18**	4d. red on yellow	1·75	22·00
225	**18**	6d. purple	3·50	6·50
215	**18**	1s. black on green	5·50	22·00
227	**18**	2s. purple on blue	10·00	21·00
228	**18**	3s. violet	22·00	85·00

19

1925. Inscr "POSTAGE & REVENUE".

229	**19**	¼d. brown	25	10
230	**19**	½d. green	60	10
231	**19**	1d. red	60	10
231ca	**19**	1½d. orange	5·00	1·00
232	**19**	2d. grey	75	3·25
233	**19**	2½d. blue	50	80
234	**19**	3d. purple on yellow	1·00	45
235	**19**	4d. red on yellow	75	1·00
236	**19**	6d. purple	1·00	90
237	**19**	1s. black on green	2·00	8·00
238	**19**	2s. purple on blue	7·00	8·00
238a	**19**	2s.6d. red on blue	29·00	40·00
239	**19**	3s. violet	11·00	19·00

20 King Charles I and King George V

1927. Tercentenary of Settlement of Barbados.

240	**20**	1d. red	1·00	75

1935. Silver Jubilee. As T **13** of Antigua.

241		1d. blue and red	2·00	20
242		1½d. blue and grey	5·00	8·50
243		2½d. brown and blue	2·75	6·50
244		1s. grey and purple	24·00	32·00

1937. Coronation. As T **2** of Aden.

245		1d. red	30	15
246		1½d. brown	55	75
247		2½d. blue	1·25	75

21 Badge of the Colony

1938. "POSTAGE & REVENUE" omitted.

248	**21**	½d. green	6·00	15
248c	**21**	½d. bistre	15	30
249a	**21**	1d. red	16·00	10
249bc	**21**	1d. green	15	10
250	**21**	1½d. orange	15	40
250c	**21**	2d. purple	1·00	2·50
250d	**21**	2d. red	50	70
251	**21**	2½d. blue	50	60
252b	**21**	3d. brown	20	60
252c	**21**	3d. blue	60	1·75
253	**21**	4d. black	20	10
254	**21**	6d. violet	80	40
254a	**21**	8d. mauve	55	2·00
255a	**21**	1s. olive	1·50	10
256	**21**	2s.6d. purple	8·50	1·50
256a	**21**	5s. blue	8·50	12·00

22 Kings Charles I, George VI, Assembly Chamber and Mace

1939. Tercentenary of General Assembly.

257	**22**	½d. green	2·75	1·00
258	**22**	1d. red	2·75	1·25
259	**22**	1½d. orange	3·00	60
260	**22**	2½d. blue	4·50	8·50
261	**22**	3d. brown	4·50	5·50

1946. Victory. As T **9** of Aden.

262	1½d. orange	15	50
263	3d. brown	15	50

1947. Surch **ONE PENNY**.

264	**17**	1d. on 2d. red	2·25	4·50

1948. Silver Wedding. As T **10/11** of Aden.

265	1½d. orange	30	50
266	5s. blue	17·00	12·00

1949. U.P.U. As T **22/03** of Antigua.

267	1½d. orange	50	2·00
268	3d. blue	2·50	7·00
269	4d. grey	50	3·25
270	1s. olive	50	60

24 Dover Fort

35 Seal of Barbados

1950

271	**24**	1c. indigo	35	4·50
272	-	2c. green	15	3·00
273	-	3c. brown and green	1·25	4·00
274	-	4c. red	15	40
275	-	6c. blue	15	2·25
276	-	8c. blue and brown	1·50	3·75
277	-	12c. blue and olive	1·00	1·75
278	-	24c. red and black	1·00	50
279	-	48c. violet	9·00	7·00
280	-	60c. green and lake	10·00	12·00
281	-	$1.20 red and olive	12·00	4·50
282	**35**	$2.40 black	26·00	42·00

DESIGNS—As Type **24**: HORIZ: 2c. Sugar cane breeding; 3c. Public buildings; 6c. Casting net; 8c. "Frances W. Smith" (schooner); 12c. Four-winged flyingfish; 24c. Old Main Guard Garrison; 60c. Careenage. VERT: 4c. Statue of Nelson; 48c. St. Michael's Cathedral; $1.20, Map and wireless mast.

1951. Inauguration of B.W.I. University College. As T **24/25** of Antigua.

283	3c. brown and blue	30	40
284	12c. blue and olive	1·00	2·25

36 King George VI and Stamp of 1852

1952. Centenary of Barbados Stamps.

285	**36**	3c. green and slate	40	40
286	**36**	4c. blue and red	40	1·00
287	**36**	12c. slate and green	40	1·00
288	**36**	24c. brown and sepia	50	55

37 Harbour Police

1953. As 1950 issue but with portrait or cypher (No. 301) of Queen Elizabeth II as in T **37**.

289	**24**	1c. indigo	10	80
290	-	2c. orange and turquoise	15	1·50
291	-	3c. black and green	1·00	1·00
292	-	4c. black and orange	20	20
293	**37**	5c. blue and red	1·00	60
294	-	6c. brown	2·75	60
314	-	8c. black and blue	70	35
296	-	12c. blue and olive	1·00	10
297	-	24c. red and black	1·00	10
317	-	48c. violet	5·00	1·50
318	-	60c. green and purple	10·00	4·00
300	-	$1.20 red and olive	19·00	6·50
319	**35**	$2.40 black	1·25	1·75

1953. Coronation. As T **13** of Aden.

302	4c. black and orange	1·00	20

1958. British Caribbean Federation. As T **28** of Antigua.

303	3c. green	45	20
304	6c. blue	60	2·25
305	12c. red	60	30

38 Deep Water Harbour, Bridgetown

1961. Opening of Deep Water Harbour.

306	**38**	4c. black and orange	35	50
307	**38**	8c. black and blue	35	60
308	**38**	24c. red and black	40	60

39 Scout Badge and Map of Barbados

1962. Golden Jubilee of Barbados Boy Scout Association.

309	**39**	4c. black and orange	85	10
310	**39**	12c. blue and brown	1·25	15
311	**39**	$1.20 red and green	1·90	3·75

1965. Centenary of I.T.U. As T **36** of Antigua.

320	2c. lilac and red	20	40
321	48c. yellow and drab	45	1·00

40 Deep Sea Coral

1965

342	**40**	1c. black, pink and blue	10	20
323	-	2c. brown, yell & mve	20	15
324	-	3c. brown and orange	45	60
344	-	3c. brown and orange	30	2·75
325	-	4c. blue and green	15	10
326	-	5c. sepia, red and lilac	30	20
327	-	6c. multicoloured	45	20
328	-	8c. multicoloured	25	10
329	-	12c. multicoloured	35	10
330	-	15c. black, yellow and red	4·00	30
331	-	25c. blue and ochre	1·00	30
332	-	35c. red and green	1·50	15
333	-	50c. blue and green	2·00	40
334	-	$1 multicoloured	3·50	2·00
335	-	$2.50 multicoloured	2·75	6·50
355a	-	$5 multicoloured	21·00	15·00

DESIGNS—HORIZ: 2c. Lobster; 3c. (No. 324) Lined seahorse (wrongly inscribed "Hippocanpus"); 3c. (No. 344) (correctly inscribed "Hippocampus"); 4c. Sea urchin; 5c. Staghorn coral; 6c. Spot-finned butterflyfish; 8c. Rough file shell; 12c. Porcupinefish ("Balloon fish"); 15c Grey angel-fish; 25c. Brain coral; 35c. Brittle star; 50c. Four-winged flyingfish: $1 Queen or pink conch shell; $2.50, Fiddler crab. VERT: $5 Dolphin.

1966. Churchill Commemoration. As T **38** of Antigua.

336	1c. blue	10	3·25
337	4c. green	45	10
338	25c. brown	1·10	50
339	35c. violet	1·25	70

1966. Royal Visit. As T **39** of Antigua.

340	3c. black and blue	65	1·00
341	35c. black and mauve	1·60	1·00

54 Arms of Barbados

1966. Independence. Multicoloured.

356	4c. Type **54**	10	10
357	25c. Hilton Hotel (horiz)	15	10
358	35c. G. Sobers (Test cricketer)	1·50	65
359	50c. Pine Hill Dairy (horiz)	70	1·10

1967. 20th Anniv of U.N.E.S.C.O. As T **54/56** of Antigua.

360	4c. multicoloured	20	10
361	12c. yellow, violet and olive	45	50
362	25c. black, purple and orange	75	1·25

58 Policeman and Anchor

1967. Centenary of Harbour Police. Multicoloured.

363	4c. Type **58**	25	10
364	25c. Policeman and telescope	40	15
365	35c. "BPI" (police launch) (horiz)	45	15
366	50c. Policeman outside H.Q.	60	1·60

62 Governor-General Sir Winston Scott G.C.M.G

1967. Firstt Anniv of Independence. Multicoloured.

367	4c. Type **62**	15	10
368	25c. Independence Arch (horiz)	25	10
369	35c. Treasury Building (horiz)	30	10
370	50c. Parliament Building (horiz)	40	90

66 U.N. Building, Santiago, Chile

1968. 20th Anniv of Economic Commission for Latin America.

371	**66**	15c. multicoloured	10	10

67 Radar Antenna

1968. World Meteorological Day. Multicoloured.

372	3c. Type **67**	10	10
373	25c. Meteorological Institute (horiz)	25	10
374	50c. Harp Gun and Coat of Arms	30	90

70 Lady Baden-Powell and Guide at Campfire

1968. Golden Jubilee of Girl Guiding in Barbados.

375	**70**	3c. blue, black and gold	20	60
376	-	25c. blue, black and gold	30	60
377	-	35c. yellow, black and gold	35	60

DESIGNS: 25c. Lady Baden-Powell and Pax Hill; 35c. Lady Baden-Powell and Guides' Badge.

73 Hands breaking Chain, and Human Rights Emblem

1968. Human Rights Year.

378	**73**	4c. violet, brown and green	10	20
379	-	25c. black, blue and yellow	10	25
380	-	35c. multicoloured	15	25

DESIGNS: 25c. Human Rights emblem and family enchained; 35c. Shadows of refugees beyond opening fence.

76 Racehorses in the Paddock

1969. Horse Racing. Multicoloured.

381	4c. Type **76**	25	15
382	25c. Starting-gate	25	15
383	35c. On the flat	30	15
384	50c. The winning-post	35	2·40
MS385	117×85 mm. Nos. 381/4	2·00	2·75

80 Map showing "CARIFTA" Countries

1969. First Anniv of "CARIFTA". Multicoloured.

386	5c. Type **80**	10	10
387	12c. "Strength in Unity" (horiz)	10	10
388	25c. Type **80**	10	10
389	50c. As 12c.	15	20

82 I.L.O. Emblem and "1919–1969"

1969. 50th Anniv of I.L.O.

390	**82**	4c. black, green and blue	10	10
391	**82**	25c. black, mauve and red	20	10

1969. No. 363 surch **ONE CENT**.

392	**58**	1c. on 4c. multicoloured	10	10

84 National Scout Badge

1969. Independence of Barbados Boy Scouts Association and 50th Anniv of Barbados Sea Scouts. Multicoloured.

393	5c. Type **84**	15	10
394	25c. Sea Scouts rowing	45	10
395	35c. Scouts around campfire	55	10
396	50c. Scouts and National Scout H.Q.	80	1·25
MS397	155×115 mm. Nos. 393/6	15·00	13·00

1970. No. 326 surch **4**.

398	4c. on 5c. sepia, red and lilac	10	10

89 Lion at Gun Hill

1970. Multicoloured.. Multicoloured..

399	1c. Type **89**	10	2·00
400	2c. Trafalgar Fountain	30	1·25
401	3c. Montefiore Drinking Fountain	40	1·00
402a	4c. St. James' Monument	30	10
403	5c. St. Ann's Fort	10	10
404	6c. Old Sugar Mill, Morgan Lewis	35	3·00
405	8c. The Cenotaph	10	10
406a	10c. South Point Lighthouse	1·25	15
407	12c. Barbados Museum (horiz)	1·50	10
408	15c. Sharon Moravian Church (horiz)	30	15
409	25c. George Washington House (horiz)	25	15
410	35c. Nicholas Abbey (horiz)	30	85
411	50c. Bowmanston Pumping Station (horiz)	40	1·00
412	$1 Queen Elizabeth Hospital (horiz)	70	2·50
413	$2.50 Suger Factory (horiz)	1·50	4·00

467	$5 Seawell International Airport (horiz)	6·50	5·50

105 Primary Schoolgirl

1970. 25th Anniv of U.N. Multicoloured.

415	4c. Type **105**	10	10
416	5c. Secondary schoolboy	10	10
417	25c. Technical student	35	10
418	50c. University building	55	1·50

106 Minnie Root

1970. Flowers of Barbados. Multicoloured.

419	1c. Barbados Easter lily (vert)	10	2·00
420	5c. Type **106**	40	10
421	10c. Eyelash orchid	1·75	30
422	25c. Pride of Barbados (vert)	1·25	75
423	35c. Christmas hope	1·25	85
MS424	162×101 mm. Nos. 419/23. Imperf	2·00	6·50

107 "Via Dolorosa" Window, St. Margaret's Church, St. John

1971. Easter. Multicoloured.

425	4c. Type **107**	10	10
426	10c. *The Resurrection* (Benjamin West)	10	10
427	35c. Type **107**	15	10
428	50c. As 10c.	30	1·50

108 "Sailfish" Dinghy

1971. Tourism. Multicoloured.

429	1c. Type **108**	10	50
430	5c. Tennis	40	10
431	12c. Horse-riding	60	10
432	25c. Water-skiing	40	20
433	50c. Scuba-diving	50	90

109 S. J. Prescod (politician)

1971. Death Centenary of Samuel Jackman Prescod.

434	**109**	3c. multicoloured	10	15
435	**109**	35c. multicoloured	15	15

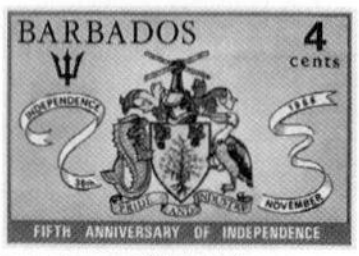
110 Arms of Barbados

1971. Fifth Anniv of Independence. Multicoloured.

436	4c. Type **110**	20	10
437	15c. National flag and map	45	10
438	25c. Type **110**	45	10
439	50c. As 15c.	90	1·60

111 Transmitting "Then and Now"

1972. Centenary of Cable Link. Multicoloured.

440	4c. Type **111**	10	10
441	10c. Cable Ship "Stanley Angwin"	20	10
442	35c. Barbados Earth Station and "Intelsat 4"	35	20
443	50c. Mt. Misery and Tropospheric Scatter Station	50	1·75

112 Map and Badge

1972. Diamond Jubilee of Scouts. Multicoloured.

444	5c. Type **112**	15	10
445	15c. Pioneers of scouting (horiz)	15	10
446	25c. Scouts (horiz)	30	15
447	50c. Flags (horiz)	60	1·00

113 Mobile Library

1972. International Book Year. Multicoloured.

448	4c. Type **113**	20	10
449	15c. Bedford mobile cinema truck	25	10
450	25c. Public library	25	10
451	$1 Codrington College	1·00	1·50

114 Potter's Wheel

1973. Pottery in Barbados. Multicoloured.

468	5c. Type **114**	10	10
469	15c. Kilns	20	10
470	25c. Finished products	25	10
471	$1 Market scene	90	1·10

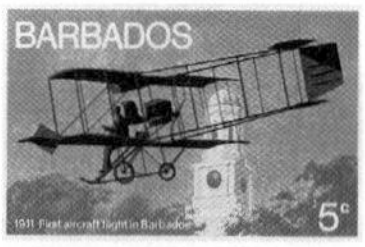
115 Wright Type B First Flight, 1911

1973. Aviation.

472	**115**	5c. multicoloured	30	10
473	-	15c. multicoloured	90	10
474	-	25c. blue, blk & cobalt	1·25	20
475	-	50c. multicoloured	2·00	1·90

DESIGNS: 15c. de Havilland Cirrus Moth on first flight to Barbados, 1928; 25c. Lockheed 14 Super Electra, 1939; 50c. Vickers Super VC-10 airliner, 1973.

116 University Chancellor

1973. 25th Anniv of University of West Indies. Multicoloured.

476	5c. Type **116**	10	10
477	25c. Sherlock Hall	25	15
478	35c. Cave Hill Campus	30	25

1974. No. 462 surch **4c.**

479	4c. on 25c. multicoloured	15	15

118 Old Sail Boat

1974. Fishing Boats of Barbados. Multicoloured.

480	15c. Type **118**	30	15
481	35c. Rowing-boat	55	25
482	50c. Motor fishing-boat	70	70
483	$1 *Calamar* (fishing boat)	1·10	1·40
MS484	140×140 mm. Nos. 480/3	3·50	3·00

119 *Cattleya gaskelliana alba*

1974. Orchids. Multicoloured.

510	1c. Type **119**	15	1·25
511	2c. *Renanthera storiei* (vert)	15	1·25
512	3c. *Dendrobium* "Rose Marie" (vert)	15	1·00
488	4c. *Epidendrum ibaguense* (vert)	1·75	90
514	5c. *Schomburgkia humboldtii* (vert)	35	15
490	8c. *Oncidium ampliatum* (vert)	1·75	90
515	10c. *Arachnis maggie oei* (vert)	35	10
492	12c. *Dendrobium aggregatum* (vert)	45	2·75
517	15c. *Paphiopedilum puddle* (vert)	70	15
493b	20c. *Spathoglottis* "The Gold"	5·00	4·75
518	25c. *Epidendrum ciliare* (Eyelash)	70	10
550	35c. *Bletia patula* (vert)	2·00	1·75
519	45c. *Phalaenopsis schilleriana* "Sunset Glow" (vert)	60	15
496	50c. As 45c. (vert)	7·00	4·50
497	$1 *Ascocenda* "Red Gem" (vert)	10·00	3·25
498	$2.50 *Brassolaeliocattleya* "Nugget"	2·50	7·00
499	$5 *Caularthron bicornutum*	2·50	6·00
500	$10 *Vanda* "Josephine Black" (vert)	2·75	13·00

120 4d. Stamp of 1882, and U.P.U. Emblem

1974. Centenary of Universal Postal Union.

501	**120**	8c. mauve, orange & grn	10	10
502	-	35c. red, orge & brown	20	10
503	-	50c. ultram, bl & silver	25	35
504	-	$1 blue, brown & black	55	1·00
MS505		126×101 mm. Nos. 501/4	1·75	2·50

DESIGNS: 35c. Letters encircling the globe; 50c. U.P.U. emblem and arms of Barbados; $1 Map of Barbados, sailing ship and Boeing 747 airliner.

121 Royal Yacht *Britannia*

1975. Royal Visit. Multicoloured.

506	8c. Type **121**	85	30
507	25c. Type **121**	1·40	30
508	35c. Sunset and palms	60	35
509	$1 As 35c.	1·75	5·00

122 St. Michael's Cathedral

1975. 150th Anniv of Anglican Diocese. Multicoloured.

526	5c. Type **122**	10	10
527	15c. Bishop Coleridge	15	10
528	50c. All Saints' Church	45	50
529	$1 "Archangel Michael and Satan" (stained glass window, St. Michael's Cathedral, Bridgetown)	70	80
MS530	95×96 mm. Nos. 526/9	1·40	2·00

123 Pony Float

1975. Crop-over Festival. Multicoloured.

531	8c. Type **123**	10	10
532	25c. Man on stilts	10	10
533	35c. Maypole dancing	15	10
534	50c. Cuban dancers	30	80
MS535	127×85 mm. Nos. 531/4	1·00	1·60

124 Barbados Coat of Arms

1975. Coil Definitives.

536	**124**	5c. blue	15	80
537	**124**	25c. violet	25	1·10

125 17th-Century Sailing Ship

1975. 350th Anniv of First Settlement. Multicoloured.

538	4c. Type **125**	50	20
539	10c. Bearded fig tree and fruit	30	15
540	25c. Ogilvy's 17th-century map	1·00	30
541	$1 Captain John Powell	1·00	5·00
MS542	105×115 mm. Nos. 538/41	2·50	7·00

126 Map of Caribbean

1976. West Indian Victory in World Cricket Cup.

559	**126**	25c. multicoloured	1·00	1·00
560	-	45c. black and purple	1·00	2·00

DESIGN—VERT: 45c. The Prudential Cup.

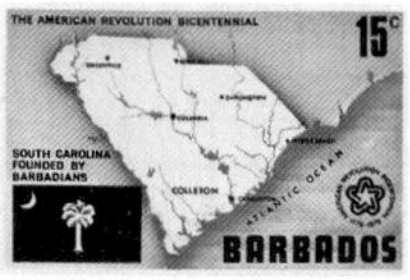
127 Flag and Map of South Carolina

1976. Bicentenary of American Revolution. Multicoloured.

561	15c. Type **127**	75	15
562	25c. George Washington and map of Bridgetown	75	15
563	50c. Independence Declaration	60	1·00
564	$1 Prince Hall	75	3·00

128 Early Postman

1976. 125th Anniv of Post Office Act. Multicoloured.

565	8c. Type **128**	10	10
566	35c. Modern postman	25	10
567	50c. Early letter	30	75
568	$1 Delivery van	50	1·75

129 Coast Guard *Commander Marshall* and *T. T. Lewis* launches

1976. Tenth Anniv of Independence. Multicoloured.

569	5c. Type **129**	30	20
570	15c. Reverse of currency note	30	10
571	25c. Barbados national anthem	30	20
572	$1 Independence Day parade	1·10	3·00

MS573 90×125 mm. Nos. 569/72 2·75 3·75

130 Arrival of Coronation Coach at Westminster Abbey

1977. Silver Jubilee. Multicoloured.

574	15c. Queen knighting Garfield Sobers, 1975	30	25
575	50c. Type **130**	30	40
576	$1 Queen entering Abbey	30	70

131 Underwater Park

1977. Natural Beauty of Barbados. Multicoloured.

577	5c. Type **131**	15	10
578	35c. Royal palms (vert)	30	10
579	50c. Underwater caves	40	50
580	$1 Stalagmite in Harrison's Cave (vert)	70	1·10
MS581	138×92 mm. Nos. 577/80	2·50	2·75

132 Maces of the House of Commons

1977. 13th Regional Conference of Commonwealth Parliamentary Association.

582	**132**	10c. orange, yellow & brn	10	10
583	-	25c. green, orge & dp grn	10	10
584	-	50c. multicoloured	20	20
585	-	$1 blue, orange and dp bl	55	75

DESIGNS—VERT: 25c. Speaker's Chair; 50c. Senate Chamber. HORIZ: $1 Sam Lord's Castle.

133 The Charter Scroll

1977. 350th Anniv of Granting of Charter to Earl of Carlisle. Multicoloured.

586	12c. Type **133**	15	10
587	25c. The earl receiving charter	15	10
588	45c. The earl and Charles I (horiz)	30	35
589	$1 Ligon's map, 1657 (horiz)	50	1·00

1977. Royal Visit. As Nos. 574/6 but inscr "SILVER JUBILEE ROYAL VISIT".

590	15c. Garfield Sobers being knighted, 1975	60	50
591	50c. Type **130**	20	75
592	$1 Queen entering Abbey	30	1·25

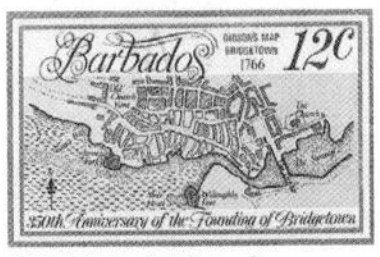

134 Gibson's Map of Bridgtown, 1766

1978. 350th Anniv of Founding of Bridgetown.

593	**134**	12c. multicoloured	15	10
594	-	25c. black, green & gold	15	10
595	-	45c. multicoloured	20	15
596	-	$1 multicoloured	30	60

DESIGNS: 25c. *A Prospect of Bridgetown in Barbados* (engraving by S. Copens, 1695); 45c. *Trafalgar Square, Bridgetown* (drawing by J. M. Carter, 1835); $1 The Bridges, 1978.

135 Brown Pelican

1978. 25th Anniv of Coronation.

597		50c. olive, black & blue	25	50
598		50c. multicoloured	25	50
599	**135**	50c. olive, black & blue	25	50

DESIGNS: No. 597, Griffin of Edward III. No. 598, Queen Elizabeth II.

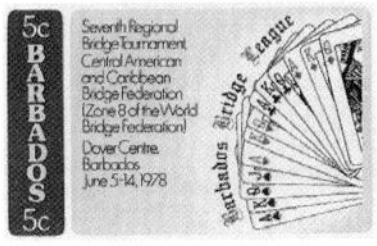

136 Barbados Bridge League Logo

1978. Seventh Regional Bridge Tournament, Barbados. Multicoloured.

600	5c. Type **136**	10	10
601	10c. Emblem of World Bridge Federation	15	10
602	45c. Central American and Caribbean Bridge Federation emblem	25	10
603	$1 Playing cards on map of Caribbean	40	60
MS604	134×83 mm. Nos. 600/3	2·00	2·75

137 Camp Scene

1978. Diamond Jubilee of Guiding. Multicoloured.

605	12c. Type **137**	25	15
606	28c. Community work	40	15
607	50c. Badge and "60" (vert)	55	30
608	$1 Guide badge (vert)	75	1·00

138 Garment Industry

1978. Industries of Barbados. Multicoloured.

609	12c. Type **138**	15	10
610	28c. Cooper (vert)	25	25
611	45c. Blacksmith (vert)	35	95
612	50c. Wrought iron working	40	1·50

139 *Forth* (early mail steamer)

1979. Ships. Multicoloured.

613	12c. Type **139**	35	10
614	25c. *Queen Elizabeth 2* in Deep Water Harbour	55	15
615	50c. *Ra II* nearing Barbados	75	1·00
616	$1 Early mail paddle-steamer	1·00	2·50

140 1953 1c. Definitive Stamp

1979. Death Cent of Sir Rowland Hill. Multicoloured.

617	12c. Type **140**	15	15
618	28c. 1975 350th anniv of first settlement 25c. commemorative (vert)	20	30
619	45c. Penny Black with Maltese Cross postmark (vert)	30	45
MS620	137×90 mm. 50c. Unissued "Brittannia" blue	55	50

1979. St. Vincent Relief Fund. No. 495 surch **28c+4c ST. VINCENT RELIEF FUND**.

621	28c.+4c. on 35c. "Bletia patula"	50	60

142 Grassland Yellow Finch ("Grass Canary")

1979. Birds. Multicoloured.

622	1c. Type **142**	10	1·25
623	2c. Grey kingbird ("Rainbird")	10	1·25
624	5c. Lesser Antillean bullfinch ("Sparrow")	10	70
625	8c. Magnificent frigate bird ("Frigate Bird")	75	2·25
626	10c. Cattle egret	10	40
627	12c. Green-backed heron ("Green Gaulin")	50	1·50
627a	15c. Carib grackle ("Blackbird")	4·50	5·00
628	20c. Antillean crested hummingbird ("Humming Bird")	20	55
629	25c. Scaly-breasted ground dove ("Ground Dove")	20	60
630	28c. As 15c.	2·00	2·00
631	35c. Green-throated carib	70	70
631b	40c. Red-necked pigeon ("Ramier")	4·50	5·50
632	45c. Zenaida dove ("Wood Dove")	1·50	1·50
633	50c. As 40c.	1·50	2·00
633a	55c. American golden plover ("Black breasted Plover")	4·00	3·50
633b	60c. Bananaquit ("Yellow Breasted")	4·50	6·00
634	70c. As 60c.	2·00	3·50
635	$1 Caribbean elaenia ("Peer whistler")	2·00	1·50
636	$2.50 American redstart ("Christmas Bird")	2·00	6·00
637	$5 Belted kingfisher ("Kingfisher")	3·25	9·00
638	$10 Moorhen ("Red-seal Coot")	4·50	14·00

143 Unloading H.A.R.P. Gun on Railway Wagon at Foul Bay

1979. Space Projects Commemorations. Multicoloured.

639	10c. Type **143**	30	10
640	12c. H.A.R.P. gun on railway wagon under tow (vert)	30	15
641	20c. Firing launcher (vert)	30	20
642	28c. Bath Earth Station and "Intelsat"	30	30
643	45c. "Intelsat" over Caribbean	35	50
644	50c. "Intelsat" over Atlantic (vert)	35	60
MS645	118×90 mm. $1 Lunar module descending on to Moon	1·50	1·00

144 Family

1979. International Year of the Child. Multicoloured.

646	12c. Type **144**	10	10
647	28c. Ring of children and map of Barbados	15	15
648	45c. Child with teacher	20	20
649	50c. Children playing	20	20
650	$1 Children and kite	35	45

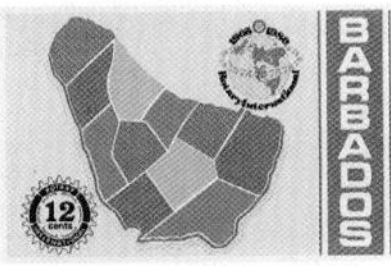

145 Map of Barbados

1980. 75th Anniv of Rotary International. Multicoloured.

651	12c. Type **145**	15	10
652	28c. Map of Caribbean	15	15
653	50c. Rotary anniversary emblem	20	35
654	$1 Paul P. Harris (founder)	30	95

146 Private, Artillery Company, Barbados Volunteer Force, c.1909

1980. Barbados Regiment. Multicoloured.

655	12c. Type **146**	25	10
656	35c. Drum Major, Zouave uniform	35	15
657	50c. Sovereign's and Regimental Colours	40	30
658	$1 Barbados Regiment Women's Corps	55	70

147 Early Postman

1980. "London 1980" International Stamp Exhibition. Two sheets each 122×125 mm containing T **147** or similar vert design. Multicoloured.

MS659 (a) 28c.×6, Type **147**. (b) 50c.×6, Modern postwoman and Inspector
Set of 2 sheets 1·00 1·25

148 Yellow-tailed Snapper

1980. Underwater Scenery. Multicoloured.

660	12c. Type **148**	20	10
661	28c. Banded butterflyfish	35	15
662	50c. Male and female blue-headed wrasse and princess parrotfish	45	25
663	$1 French grunt and French angelfish	70	70
MS664	136×110 mm. Nos. 660/3	2·50	3·75

149 Bathsheba Railway Station

1981. Early Transport. Multicoloured.

665	12c. Type **149**	30	10
666	28c. Cab stand at The Green	20	15
667	45c. Animal-drawn tram	30	30
668	70c. Horse-drawn bus	45	60
669	$1 Railway Station, Fairchild Street	70	95

150 The Blind at Work

1981. Int Year for Disabled Persons. Multicoloured.

670	10c. Type **150**	20	10
671	25c. Sign Language (vert)	25	15
672	45c. "Be alert to the white cane" (vert)	40	25
673	$2.50 Children at play	80	3·00

151 Prince Charles dressed for Polo

1981. Royal Wedding. Multicoloured.

674	28c. Wedding bouquet from Barbados	15	10
675	50c. Type **151**	20	15
676	$2.50 Prince Charles and Lady Diana Spencer	55	1·25

152 Landship Manoeuvre

1981. Carifesta (Caribbean Festival of Arts), Barbados. Multicoloured.

677	15c. Type **152**	15	15
678	20c. Yoruba dancers	15	15
679	40c. Tuk band	20	25
680	55c. Sculpture by Frank Collymore	25	35
681	$1 Harbour scene	50	75

1981. Nos. 630, 632 and 634 surch.

682	15c. on 28c. Carib grackle	30	15
683	40c. on 45c. Zenaida dove	30	35
684	60c. on 70c. Bananaquit	30	45

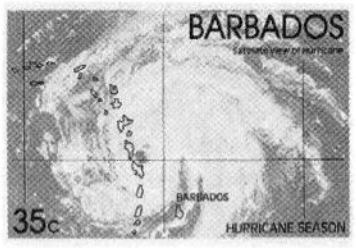

154 Satellite View of Hurricane

1981. Hurricane Season.

685	**154**	35c. black and blue	35	20
686	-	50c. multicoloured	45	35
687	-	60c. multicoloured	70	50
688	-	$1 multicoloured	85	90

DESIGNS: 50c. Hurricane *Gladys* from "Apollo 7"; 60c. Police Department on hurricane watch; $1 McDonnell Banshee "hurricane chaser" aircraft.

155 Twin Falls

1981. Harrison's Cave. Multicoloured.

689	10c. Type **155**	10	10
690	20c. Stream in Rotunda Room	20	15
691	55c. Formations in Rotunda Room	25	30
692	$2.50 Cascade Pool	60	2·25

156 Black Belly Ram

1982. Black Belly Sheep. Multicoloured.

693	40c. Type **156**	15	20
694	50c. Black belly ewe	15	20
695	60c. Ewe with lambs	20	45
696	$1 Ram and ewe, with map of Barbados	35	1·50

157 Barbados Coat of Arms and Flag

1982. President Reagan's Visit. Multicoloured.

697	20c. Type **157**	40	1·25
698	20c. U.S.A. coat of arms and flag	40	1·25
699	55c. Type **157**	50	1·50
700	55c. As No. 698	50	1·50

158 Lighter

1982. Early Marine Transport. Multicoloured.

701	20c. Type **158**	20	15
702	35c. Rowing boat	35	25
703	55c. Speightstown schooner	50	40
704	$2.50 Inter-colonial schooner	1·75	2·50

159 Bride and Earl Spencer Proceeding up the Aisle

1982. 21st Birthday of Princess of Wales. Mult.

705	20c. Barbados coat of arms	20	15
706	60c. Princess at Llanelwedd, October, 1981	45	50
707	$1.20 Type **159**	75	1·10
708	$2.50 Formal portrait	1·25	1·90

160 "To Help other People"

1982. 75th Anniv of Boy Scout Movement. Multicoloured.

709	15c. Type **160**	50	10
710	40c. "I Promise to do my Best" (horiz)	80	30
711	55c. "To do my Duty to God, the Queen and my Country" (horiz)	90	65
712	$1 National and Troop flags	1·40	1·75
MS713	119×93 mm. $1.50, The Scout Law	3·50	3·00

161 Arms of George Washington

1982. 250th Birth Anniv of George Washington. Multicoloured.

714	10c. Type **161**	10	10
715	55c. Washington House, Barbados	25	30
716	60c. Washington with troops	25	35
717	$2.50 Washington taking Oath	75	1·60

162 *Agraulis vanillae*

1983. Butterflies. Multicoloured.

718	20c. Type **162**	1·00	40
719	40c. *Danaus plexippus*	1·50	40
720	55c. *Hypolimnas misippus*	1·50	45
721	$2.50 *Hemiargus hanno*	3·25	3·75

163 Map of Barbados and Satellite View

1983. Commonwealth Day. Multicoloured.

722	15c. Type **163**	20	10
723	40c. Tourist beach	25	20
724	60c. Sugar cane harvesting	35	40
725	$1 Cricket match	1·25	1·10

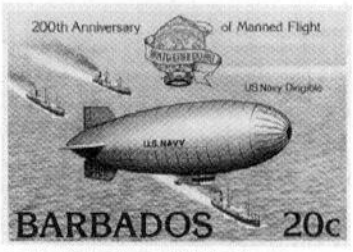

164 U.S. Navy "M" Class Airship M-20

1983. Bicentenary of Manned Flight.

726	20c. Type **164**	35	15
727	40c. Douglas DC-3	40	40
728	55c. Vickers Viscount 837	40	50
729	$1 Lockheed TriStar 500	65	2·50

165 Nash 600, 1934 (inscr "1941")

1983. Classic Cars. Multicoloured.

730	25c. Type **165**	35	20
731	45c. Dodge D-8 coupe, 1938	40	30
732	75c. Ford Model A tourer, 1930	60	1·50
733	$2.50 Dodge Four tourer, 1918	1·25	4·50

166 Game in Progress

1983. Table Tennis World Cup Competition. Multicoloured.

734	20c. Type **166**	25	20
735	65c. Map of Barbados	50	55
736	$1 World Table Tennis Cup	75	1·00

167 Angel playing Lute (detail *The Virgin and Child*) (Masaccio)

1983. Christmas. 50th Anniv of Barbados Museum.

737	**167**	10c. multicoloured	30	10
738	-	25c. multicoloured	60	20
739	-	45c. multicoloured	90	40
740	-	75c. black and gold	1·40	1·60
741	-	$2.50 multicoloured	4·50	6·00
MS742		59×98 mm. $2 multicoloured	1·75	2·00

DESIGNS—HORIZ: 45c. *The Barbados Museum* (Richard Day); 75c. *St. Ann's Garrison* (W. S. Hedges); $2.50, Needham's Point, Carlisle Bay. VERT: 25c., $2 Different details from *The Virgin and Child* (Masaccio).

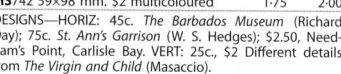

168 Track and Field Events

1984. Olympic Games, Los Angeles.

745	**168**	50c. green, black and brown	60	45
746	-	65c. orange, blk & brn	80	60
747	-	75c. blue, black & dp bl	1·00	85
748	-	$1 brown, black and yellow	2·50	2·00
MS749		115×97 mm. Nos. 745/8	8·00	9·00

DESIGNS: 65c. Shooting; 75c. Sailing; $1 Cycling.

169 Global Coverage

1984. 250th Anniv of *Lloyd's List* (newspaper). Multicoloured.

750	45c. Type **169**	80	40
751	50c. Bridgetown harbour	90	50
752	75c. "Philosopher" (full-rigged ship), 1857	1·40	1·25
753	$1 "Sea Princess" (liner), 1984	1·40	1·60

170 U.P.U. 1943 3d. Stamp and Logo

1984. Universal Postal Union Congress, Hamburg. Sheet 90×75 mm.

MS754	**170** $2 multicoloured	2·50	2·50

171 Local Junior Match

1984. 60th Anniv of International Chess Federation. Multicoloured.

755	25c. Type **171**	1·50	30
756	45c. Staunton and 19th-century knights	1·75	50
757	65c. Staunton queen and 18th-century queen from Macao	2·00	1·75
758	$2 Staunton and 17th-century rooks	3·75	6·50

172 Poinsettia

1984. Christmas. Flowers. Multicoloured.

759	50c. Type **172**	1·75	90
760	65c. Snow-on-the-Mountain	2·00	1·75
761	75c. Christmas Candle	2·25	3·25
762	$1 Christmas Hope	2·50	3·75

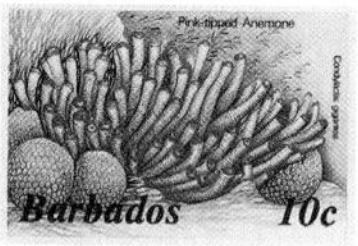

173 Pink-tipped Anemone

1985. Marine Life. Multicoloured.

794B	1c. Bristle worm	30	2·50
795B	2c. Spotted trunkfish	30	2·50
796A	5c. Coney	1·00	1·50
797B	10c. Type **173**	30	30
798B	20c. Christmas tree worm	30	40
799B	25c. Hermit crab	40	40
800A	35c. Animal flower	1·50	1·50
801B	40c. Vase sponge	50	50
802B	45c. Spotted moray	60	50
803B	50c. Ghost crab	60	60
804B	65c. Flamingo tongue snail	65	70
805B	75c. Sergeant major	70	75
806B	$1 Caribbean warty anemone	85	85
807B	$2.50 Green turtle	1·25	6·00
808B	$5 Rock beauty (fish)	1·50	8·00
809B	$10 Elkhorn coral	2·00	8·00

174 The Queen Mother at Docks

1985. Life and Times of Queen Elizabeth the Queen Mother. Multicoloured.

779	25c. In the White Drawing Room, Buckingham Palace, 1930s	50	20
780	65c. With Lady Diana Spencer at Trooping the Colour, 1981	2·50	1·00
781	75c. Type **174**	80	1·00
782	$1 With Prince Henry at his christening (from photo by Lord Snowdon)	85	1·25
MS783	91×73 mm. $2 In Land Rover Series I opening Syon House Garden Centre	2·50	1·50

175 Peregrine Falcon

1985. Birth Bicentenary of John J. Audubon (ornithologist). Designs showing original paintings. Multicoloured.

784	45c. Type **175**	2·25	80
785	65c. Prairie warbler (vert)	2·50	2·25
786	75c. Great blue heron (vert)	2·75	3·00
787	$1 Yellow warbler (vert)	3·00	4·00

176 Intelsat Satellite orbiting Earth

1985. 20th Anniv of Intelsat Satellite System.

788	**176**	75c. multicoloured	1·00	70

177 Traffic Policeman

1985. 150th Anniv of Royal Barbados Police. Multicoloured.

789	25c. Type **177**	80	20
790	50c. Police band on bandstand	1·40	80
791	65c. Dog handler	1·60	1·40
792	$1 Mounted policeman in ceremonial uniform	1·75	2·00
MS793	85×60 mm. $2 Police Band on parade (horiz).	1·50	2·75

1986. 60th Birthday of Queen Elizabeth II. As T **110** of Ascension. Multicoloured.

810	25c. Princess Elizabeth aged two, 1928	40	20
811	50c. At University College of West Indies, Jamaica, 1953	50	40
812	65c. With Duke of Edinburgh, Barbados, 1985	70	50
813	75c. At banquet in Sao Paulo, Brazil, 1968	70	60
814	$2 At Crown Agents Head Office, London, 1983	1·10	1·50

178 Canadair DC-4M2 North Star of Trans-Canada Airlines

1986. "Expo '86" World Fair, Vancouver. Multicoloured.

815	50c. Type **178**	75	50
816	$2.50 "Lady Nelson" (cargo liner)	2·00	2·50

1986. "Ameripex '86" International Stamp Exhibition, Chicago. As T **164** of Bahamas, showing Barbados stamps. Multicoloured.

817	45c. 1976 Bicentenary of American Revolution 25c.	70	35
818	50c. 1976 Bicentenary of American Revolution 50c.	80	55
819	65c. 1981 Hurricane Season $1	90	1·00
820	$1 1982 Visit of President Reagan 55c.	1·00	1·75
MS821	90×80 mm. $2 Statue of Liberty and liner "Queen Elizabeth 2"	10·00	12·00

No. **MS**821 also commemorates the Centenary of the Statue of Liberty.

1986. Royal Wedding. As T **112** of Ascension. Multicoloured.

822	45c. Prince Andrew and Miss Sarah Ferguson	75	35
823	$1 Prince Andrew in midshipman's uniform	1·25	75

179 Transporting Electricity Poles, 1923

1986. 75th Anniv of Electricity in Barbados. Multicoloured.

824	10c. Type **179**	15	10
825	25c. Heathman Ladder, 1935 (vert)	25	20
826	65c. Transport fleet, 1941	60	60
827	$2 Bucket truck, 1986 (vert)	1·60	2·00

180 *Alpinia purpurata* and Church Window

1986. Christmas. Multicoloured.

828	25c. Type **180**	20	20
829	50c. *Anthurium andraeanum*	45	45
830	75c. *Heliconia rostrata*	75	80
831	$2 *Heliconia* × *psittacorum*	1·50	4·25

181 Shot Putting

1987. Tenth Anniv of Special Olympics. Multicoloured.

832	15c. Type **181**	25	15
833	45c. Wheelchair racing	45	30
834	65c. Long jumping	60	65
835	$2 Logo and slogan	1·25	2·50

182 Barn Swallow

1987. "Capex '87" International Stamp Exhibition, Toronto. Birds. Multicoloured.

836	25c. Type **182**	2·00	50
837	50c. Yellow warbler	2·25	1·75
838	65c. Audubon's shearwater	2·25	1·75
839	75c. Black-whiskered vireo	2·50	3·25
840	$1 Scarlet tanager	2·75	4·00

183 Sea Scout saluting

1987. 75th Anniv of Scouting in Barbados. Multicoloured.

841	10c. Type **183**	20	10
842	25c. Scout jamboree	30	20
843	65c. Scout badges	65	45
844	$2 Scout band	1·60	1·75

184 Bridgetown Synagogue

1987. Restoration of Bridgetown Synagogue. Multicoloured.

845	50c. Type **184**	2·00	1·75
846	65c. Interior of Synagogue	2·25	2·25
847	75c. Ten Commandments (vert)	2·50	2·50
848	$1 Marble laver (vert)	2·75	3·75

185 Arms and Colonial Seal

1987. 21st Anniv of Independence. Multicoloured.

849	25c. Type **185**	50	20
850	45c. Flags of Barbados and Great Britain	1·25	35
851	65c. Silver dollar and one penny coins	1·25	55
852	$2 Colours of Barbados Regiment	2·50	2·75
MS853	94×56 mm. $1.50, Prime Minister E. W. Barrow (vert)	1·50	1·75

186 Herman C. Griffith

1988. West Indian Cricket. Each showing portrait, cricket equipment and early belt buckle. Multicoloured.

854	15c. E. A. (Manny) Martindale	2·50	75
855	45c. George Challenor	3·25	75
856	50c. Type **186**	3·50	2·25
857	75c. Harold Austin	3·75	3·50
858	$2 Frank Worrell	4·50	11·00

187 *Kentropyx borckianus*

1988. Lizards of Barbados. Multicoloured.

859	10c. Type **187**	1·75	50
860	50c. *Hemidactylus mabouia*	3·00	70
861	65c. *Anolis extremus*	3·00	1·25
862	$2 *Gymnophthalmus underwoodii*	6·00	10·00

188 Cycling

1988. Olympic Games, Seoul. Multicoloured.

863	25c. Type **188**	1·75	40
864	45c. Athletics	70	30
865	75c. Relay swimming	85	65
866	$2 Yachting	2·00	2·75
MS867	114×63 mm. Nos. 863/6	4·25	3·00

1988. 300th Anniv of Lloyd's of London. As T **123** of Ascension.

868	40c. multicoloured	55	30
869	50c. multicoloured	65	35
870	65c. multicoloured	1·50	45
871	$2 blue and red	6·50	3·00

DESIGNS—VERT: 40c. Royal Exchange, 1774; $2 Sinking of *Titanic*, 1912. HORIZ: 50c. Early sugar mill; 65c. *Author* (container ship).

189 Harry Bayley and Observatory

1988. 25th Anniv of Harry Bayley Observatory. Multicoloured.

872	25c. Type **189**	60	20
873	65c. Observatory with North Star and Southern Cross constellations	1·40	75
874	75c. Andromeda galaxy	1·60	90
875	$2 Orion constellation	3·00	6·00

190 L.I.A.T. Hawker Siddeley H.S.748

1989. 50th Anniv of Commercial Aviation in Barbados. Multicoloured.

876	25c. Type **190**	2·50	40
877	65c. Pan Am Douglas DC-8-62	3·25	1·25
878	75c. British Airways Concorde at Grantley Adams Airport	3·75	1·75
879	$2 Caribbean Air Cargo Boeing 707-351C	6·00	9·50

191 Assembly Chamber

1989. 350th Anniv of Parliament.

880	**191**	25c. multicoloured	40	20
881	-	50c. multicoloured	60	35
882	-	75c. blue and black	1·00	50
883	-	$2.50 multicoloured	2·50	2·25

DESIGNS: 50c. The Speaker; 75c. Parliament Buildings, c. 1882; $2.50, Queen Elizabeth II and Prince Philip in Parliament.

192 Brown Hare

1989. Wildlife Preservation. Multicoloured.

884	10c. Type **192**	80	30
885	50c. Red-footed tortoise (horiz)	2·00	70
886	65c. Savanna ("Green") monkey	2·25	1·25
887	$2 "Bufo marinus" (toad) (horiz)	4·00	8·00
MS888	87×97 mm. $1 Small Indian mongoose	1·25	1·50

1989. 35th Commonwealth Parliamentary Conference. Square design as T **191**. Multicoloured.

MS889	108×69 mm. $1 Barbados Mace	1·00	1·50

193 Bread 'n Cheese

1989. Wild Plants. Multicoloured.

921	2c. Type **193**	50	1·75
891	5c. Scarlet cordia	50	1·00
892	10c. Columnar cactus	50	30
893	20c. Spiderlily	50	30
925	25c. Rock balsam	65	20
895	30c. Hollyhock	70	25
895a	35c. Red sage	1·25	1·00
927	45c. Yellow shak-shak	75	35
928	50c. Whitewood	80	40
898	55c. Bluebell	1·00	55
930	65c. Prickly sage	90	55
900	70c. Seaside samphire	1·25	1·25
901	80c. Flat-hand dildo	1·75	1·40
901a	90c. Herringbone	1·75	2·25
902	$1.10 Lent tree	1·50	2·25
934	$2.50 Rodwood	1·90	4·00
935	$5 Cowitch	3·75	7·00
936	$10 Maypole	7·00	10·00

194 Water Skiing

1989. "World Stamp Expo '89" International Stamp Exhibition, Washington. Watersports. Multicoloured.

906	25c. Type **194**	1·50	40
907	50c. Yachting	2·50	1·00
908	65c. Scuba diving	2·50	1·75
909	$2.50 Surfing	6·50	11·00

195 Barbados 1852 1d. Stamp

1990. 150th Anniv of the Penny Black and "Stamp World London '90" International Stamp Exn.

910	195	25c. green, black and yellow	1·50	40
911	-	50c. multicoloured	2·00	1·00
912	-	65c. multicoloured	2·00	1·50
913	-	$2.50 multicoloured	5·00	9·00
MS914		90×86 mm. 50c. multicoloured; 50c. multicoloured	1·75	2·75

DESIGNS: 50c. 1882 1d. Queen Victoria stamp; 65c. 1899 2d. stamp; $2.50, 1912 3d. stamp; miniature sheet, 50c. Great Britain Penny Black, 50c. Barbados "1906" Nelson Centenary 1s.

196 Bugler and Jockeys

1990. Horse Racing. Multicoloured.

915	25c. Type **196**	60	30
916	45c. Horse and jockey in parade ring	85	50
917	75c. At the finish	1·25	85
918	$2 Leading in the winner (vert)	2·75	6·00

1990. 90th Birthday of Queen Elizabeth the Queen Mother. As T **134** of Ascension.

919	75c. multicoloured	75	60
920	$2.50 black and green	2·25	3·25

DESIGNS—21×36 mm: 75c. Lady Elizabeth Bowes-Lyon, April 1923 (from painting by John Lander). 29×37 mm: $2.50, Lady Elizabeth Bowes-Lyon on her engagement, January 1923.

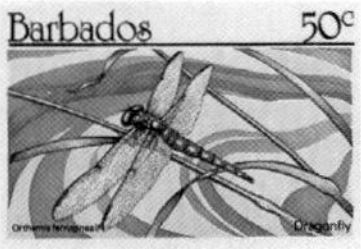

197 *Orthemis ferruginea* (dragonfly)

1990. Insects. Multicoloured.

937	50c. Type **197**	1·50	80
938	65c. *Ligyrus tumulosus* (beetle)	1·75	1·00
939	75c. *Neoconocephalus* sp. (grasshopper)	2·00	1·25
940	$2 *Bostra maxwelli* (stick-insect)	3·50	5·50

1990. Visit of the Princess Royal. Nos. 925, 901 and 903 optd **VISIT OF HRH THE PRINCESS ROYAL OCTOBER 1990.**

941	25c. Rock balsam	2·25	50
942	80c. Flat-hand dildo	3·50	2·00
943	$2.50 Rodwood	8·50	12·00

199 Star

1990. Christmas. Multicoloured.

944	20c. Type **199**	65	20
945	50c. Figures from crib	1·00	50
946	$1 Stained glass window	2·00	1·50
947	$2 Angel (statue)	3·00	5·50

200 Adult Male Yellow Warbler

1991. Endangered Species. Yellow Warbler. Multicoloured.

948	10c. Type **200**	1·40	80
949	20c. Pair feeding chicks in nest	2·00	80
950	45c. Female feeding chicks in nest	2·50	80
951	$1 Male with fledgeling	4·00	5·25

201 Sorting Daily Catch

1991. Fishing in Barbados. Multicoloured.

952	5c. Type **201**	50	50
953	50c. Line fishing (horiz)	1·75	90
954	75c. Fish cleaning (horiz)	2·25	1·25
955	$2.50 Game fishing	4·50	6·50

202 Masonic Building, Bridgetown

1991. 250th Anniv of Freemasonry in Barbados (1990).

956	202	25c. multicoloured	1·75	50
957	-	65c. multicoloured	2·50	1·25
958	-	75c. black, yellow & brn	2·50	1·25
959	-	$2.50 multicoloured	5·00	7·00

DESIGNS: 65c. Compass and square (masonic symbols); 75c. Royal Arch jewel; $2.50, Ceremonial apron, columns and badge.

203 *Battus polydamus*

1991. "Phila Nippon '91" International Stamp Exhibition, Tokyo. Butterflies. Multicoloured.

960	20c. Type **203**	1·00	40
961	50c. *Urbanus proteus* (vert)	1·50	65
962	65c. *Phoebis sennae*	1·60	95
963	$2.50 *Junonia evarete* (vert)	4·00	6·00
MS964	87×86 mm. $4 *Vanessa cardui*	9·00	10·00

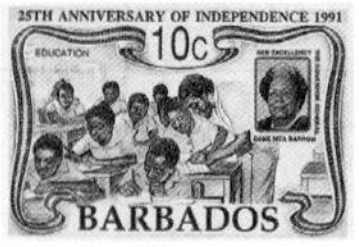

204 School Class

1991. 25th Anniv of Independence. Multicoloured.

965	10c. Type **204**	30	20
966	25c. Barbados Workers' Union Labour College	45	30
967	65c. Building a house	1·00	90
968	75c. Sugar cane harvesting	1·00	1·00
969	$1 Health clinic	1·25	2·00
MS970	123×97 mm. $2.50, Gordon Greenidge and Desmond Haynes (cricketers) (vert)	12·00	12·00

205 Jesus carrying Cross

1992. Easter. Multicoloured.

971	35c. Type **205**	80	30
972	70c. Crucifixion	1·40	90
973	90c. Descent from the Cross	1·50	1·25
974	$3 Risen Christ	4·00	6·50

206 Cannon Ball

1992. Conservation. Flowering Trees. Multicoloured.

975	10c. Type **206**	60	40
976	30c. Golden shower tree	1·00	50
977	80c. Frangipani	2·25	2·50
978	$1.10 Flamboyant	2·75	3·00

207 *Epidendrum* "Costa Rica"

1992. Orchids. Multicoloured.

979	55c. Type **207**	85	65
980	65c. *Cattleya guttaca*	1·00	1·00
981	70c. *Laeliacattleya* "Splashing Around"	1·00	1·00
982	$1.40 *Phalaenopsis* "Kathy Saegert"	1·60	3·00

208 Mini Moke and Gun Hill Signal Station, St. George

1992. Transport and Tourism. Multicoloured.

983	5c. Type **208**	65	60
984	35c. Tour bus and Bathsheba Beach, St. Joseph	1·25	30
985	90c. B.W.I.A. McDonnell Douglas MD-83 over Grantley Adams Airport	3·00	2·25
986	$2 *Festivale* (liner) and Bridgetown harbour	4·25	6·50

209 Barbados Gooseberry

1993. Cacti and Succulents. Multicoloured.

987	10c. Type **209**	55	30
988	35c. Night-blooming cereus	1·25	35
989	$1.40 Aloe	3·00	3·50
990	$2 Scrunchineel	3·50	5·50

1993. 75th Anniv of Royal Air Force. As T **149** of Ascension. Multicoloured.

991	10c. Hawker Hunter F.6	75	40
992	30c. Handley Page Victor K2	1·25	40
993	70c. Hawker Typhoon IB	1·75	1·50
994	$3 Hawker Hurricane Mk I	3·75	6·50
MS995	110×77 mm. 50c. Armstrong Whitworth Siskin IIIA; 50c. Supermarine S6B; 50c. Supermarine Walrus Mk I; 50c. Hawker Hart	2·50	2·75

1993. 14th World Orchid Conference, Glasgow. Nos. 979/82 optd **WORLD ORCHID CONFERENCE 1993.**

996	55c. Type **207**	1·25	1·25
997	65c. *Cattleya guttaca*	1·40	1·40
998	70c. *Laeliacattleya* "Splashing Around"	1·40	1·40
999	$1.40 *Phalaenopsis* "Kathy Saegert"	2·25	3·50

211 18 pdr Culverin of 1625, Denmark Fort

1993. 17th-century English Cannon. Multicoloured.

1000	5c. Type **211**	30	50
1001	45c. 6 pdr of 1649–60, St. Ann's Fort	85	50
1002	$1 9 pdr demi-culverin of 1691, The Main Guard	1·75	2·00
1003	$2.50 32 pdr demi–cannon of 1693–94, Charles Fort	2·75	4·50

212 Sailor's Shell-work Valentine and Carved Amerindian

1993. 60th Anniv of Barbados Museum. Multicoloured.

1004	10c. Type **212**	50	50
1005	75c. "Barbados Mulatto Girl" (Agostino Brunias)	1·50	1·50
1006	90c. Morris Cup and soldier of West India Regiment, 1858	2·25	2·50
1007	$1.10 Ogilby's map of Barbados, 1679, and Ashanti gold weights	2·75	3·25

213 Plesiosaurus

1993. Prehistoric Aquatic Animals. Multicoloured.

1008	90c. Type **213**	2·25	3·00
1009	90c. Ichthyosaurus	2·25	3·00
1010	90c. Elasmosaurus	2·25	3·00
1011	90c. Mosasaurus	2·25	3·00
1012	90c. Archelon	2·25	3·00

Nos. 1008/12 were printed together, *se-tenant*, with the background forming a composite design.

214 Cricket

1994. Sports and Tourism. Multicoloured.

1013	10c. Type **214**	1·25	75
1014	35c. Rally driving	1·40	50
1015	50c. Golf	2·25	1·75
1016	70c. Long distance running	1·75	2·50
1017	$1.40 Swimming	2·00	3·50

215 Whimbrel

1994. "Hong Kong '94" Int Stamp Exhibition. Migratory Birds. Multicoloured.

1018	10c. Type **215**	50	50
1019	35c. Pacific golden plover ("American Golden Plover")	1·00	50
1020	70c. Ruddy turnstone	1·50	1·50
1021	$3 Louisiana heron ("Tricoloured Heron")	3·50	5·50

216 Bathsheba Beach and Logo

1994. First United Nations Conference of Small Island Developing States. Multicoloured.

1022	10c. Type **216**	25	15
1023	65c. Pico Tenneriffe	1·00	70
1024	90c. Ragged Point Lighthouse	6·00	2·50
1025	$2.50 Consett Bay	3·00	5·50

217 William Demas

1994. First Recipients of Order of the Caribbean Community. Multicoloured.

1026	70c. Type **217**	70	1·00
1027	70c. Sir Shridath Ramphal	70	1·00
1028	70c. Derek Walcott	70	1·00

218 Dutch Flyut, 1695

1994. Ships. Multicoloured.

1075	5c. Type **218**	2·50	2·75
1076	10c. *Geestport* (freighter), 1994	75	50

1031B	25c. H.M.S. *Victory* (ship of the line), 1805	75	40
1078	30c. *Royal Viking Queen* (liner), 1994	50	30
1079	35c. H.M.S. *Barbados* (frigate), 1945	50	30
1080	45c. *Faraday* (cable ship), 1924	50	35
1081	50c. U.S.C.G. *Hamilton* (coast-guard cutter), 1974	6·50	75
1082	65c. H.M.C.S. *Saguenay* (destroyer), 1939	75	70
1083	70c. *Inanda* (cargo liner), 1928	75	70
1084	80c. H.M.S. *Rodney* (battleship), 1944	75	70
1085	90c. U.S.S. *John F. Kennedy* (aircraft carrier), 1982	75	70
1086	$1.10 *William and John* (immigrant ship), 1627	1·00	1·00
1087	$5 U.S.C.G. *Champlain* (coast-guard cutter), 1931	4·00	5·00
1042B	$10 *Artist* (full-rigged ship), 1877	7·00	9·00

219 Private, 2nd West India Regt, 1860

1995. Bicentenary of Formation of West India Regiment. Multicoloured.

1043	30c. Type **219**	75	35
1044	50c. Light Company private, 4th West India Regt, 1795	90	55
1045	70c. Drum Major, 3rd West India Regt, 1860	1·25	1·40
1046	$1 Privates in undress and working dress, 5th West India Regt, 1815	1·40	1·50
1047	$1.10 Troops from 1st and 2nd West India Regts in Review Order, 1874	1·60	1·90

1995. 50th Anniv of End of Second World War. As T **161** of Ascension. Multicoloured.

1048	10c. Barbadian Bren gun crew	60	50
1049	35c. Avro Type 683 Lancaster bomber	90	50
1050	55c. Supermarine Spitfire	1·25	75
1051	$2.50 *Davisian* (cargo liner)	3·00	4·75
MS1052	75×85 mm. $2 Reverse of 1939–45 War Medal (vert)	1·50	2·25

220 Member of 1st Barbados Combermere Scout Troop, 1912

1995. 300th Anniv of Combermere School. Multicoloured.

1053	5c. Type **220**	25	40
1054	20c. Violin and sheet of music	45	30
1055	35c. Sir Frank Worrell (cricketer) (vert)	1·50	55
1056	$3 Painting by pupil	2·25	4·50
MS1057	174×105 mm. Nos. 1053/6 and 90c. 1981 Carifesta 55c. stamp.	4·00	4·75

1995. 50th Anniv of United Nations. As T **213** of Bahamas. Multicoloured.

1058	30c. Douglas C-124 Globemaster (transport), Korea, 1950–53	70	40
1059	45c. Royal Navy Sea King helicopter	1·00	50
1060	$1.40 Westland Wessex helicopter, Cyprus, 1964	1·50	2·00
1061	$2 Sud Aviation SA 341 Gazelle helicopter, Cyprus, 1964	1·50	2·75

221 Blue Beauty

1995. Water Lilies. Multicoloured.

1062	10c. Type **221**	45	30
1063	65c. White water lily	1·25	60
1064	70c. Sacred lotus	1·25	60
1065	$3 Water hyacinth	3·00	5·00

222 Magnifying Glass, Tweezers and 1896 Colony Seal ¼d. Stamp

1996. Centenary of Barbados Philatelic Society. Each showing magnifying glass, tweezers and stamp. Multicoloured.

1066	10c. Type **222**	30	30
1067	55c. 1906 Tercentenary of Annexation 1d.	65	45
1068	$1.10 1920 Victory 1s.	1·25	1·40
1069	$1.40 1937 Coronation 2½d.	1·60	2·50

223 Football

1996. Cent of Modern Olympic Games. Multicoloured.

1070	20c. Type **223**	40	30
1071	30c. Relay running	45	30
1072	55c. Basketball	1·60	60
1073	$3 Rhythmic gymnastics	2·25	4·00
MS1074	68×89 mm. $2.50, "The Discus Thrower" (Myron)	2·00	3·25

224 Douglas DC-10 of Canadian Airlines

1996. "CAPEX '96" International Stamp Exhibition, Toronto. Aircraft. Multicoloured.

1089	10c. Type **224**	80	30
1090	90c. Boeing 767 of Air Canada	1·75	80
1091	$1 Airbus Industrie A320 of Air Canada	1·75	1·25
1092	$1.40 Boeing 767 of Canadian Airlines	2·25	3·50

225 Chattel House

1996. Chattel Houses.

1093	**225**	35c. multicoloured	40	25
1094	-	70c. multicoloured	70	60
1095	-	$1.10 multicoloured	90	1·10
1096	-	$2 multicoloured	1·60	3·25

DESIGNS: 70c. to $2, Different houses.

226 *Going to Church*

1996. Christmas. 50th Anniv of U.N.I.C.E.F. Children's Paintings. Multicoloured.

1097	10c. Type **226**	35	15
1098	30c. *The Tuk Band*	55	25
1099	55c. *Singing carols*	70	40
1100	$2.50 *Decorated house*	1·75	3·50

227 Doberman Pinscher

1997. "HONG KONG '97" International Stamp Exhibition. Dogs. Multicoloured.

1101	10c. Type **227**	1·00	50
1102	30c. German shepherd	1·75	40
1103	90c. Japanese akita	2·25	1·25
1104	$3 Irish red setter	4·75	7·00

228 Barbados Flag and State Arms

1997. Visit of President Clinton of U.S.A. Multicoloured.

1105	35c. Type **228**	1·00	75
1106	90c. American flag and arms	1·50	1·25

229 Measled Cowrie

1997. Shells. Multicoloured.

1107	5c. Type **229**	30	30
1108	35c. Trumpet triton	75	25
1109	90c. Scotch bonnet	1·40	90
1110	$2 West Indian murex	2·00	3·50
MS1111	71×76 mm. $2.50, Underwater scene	2·50	3·75

230 Lucas Manuscripts

1997. 150th Anniv of the Public Library Service. Multicoloured.

1112	10c. Type **230**	25	15
1113	30c. Librarian reading to children	50	25
1114	70c. Mobile library van	1·10	60
1115	$3 Man using computer	2·50	4·50

231 Barbados Cherry

1997. Local Fruits. Multicoloured.

1116	35c. Type **231**	45	30
1117	40c. Sugar apple	50	30
1118	$1.15 Soursop	1·10	1·25
1119	$1.70 Pawpaw	1·75	2·75

232 Arms of former British Caribbean Federation

1998. Birth Centenary of Sir Grantley Adams (statesman). Sheet 118×74 mm, containing T **232** and similar vert designs. Multicoloured.

MS1120	$1 Type **232**; $1 Sir Grantley Adams; $1 Flag of former British Caribbean Federation	6·50	7·00

1998. Diana, Princess of Wales Commemoration. Sheet 145×70 mm, containing vert designs as T **177** of Ascension. Multicoloured.

MS1121	$1.15, Wearing blue hat, 1985; $1.15, Wearing red jacket, 1981; $1.15, Wearing tiara, 1987; $1.15, Wearing black jacket	3·25	3·75

233 Environment Regeneration

1998. 50th Anniv of Organization of American States. Multicoloured.

1122	15c. Type **233**	20	15
1123	$1 Stilt dancing	70	80
1124	$2.50 Judge and figure of Justice	1·75	3·25

234 Frank Worrell Hall

1998. 50th Anniv of University of West Indies. Multicoloured.

1125	40c. Type **234**	50	30
1126	$1.15 Student graduating	1·25	1·25
1127	$1.40 50th anniversary plaque	1·50	2·00
1128	$1.75 Quadrangle	2·75	4·00

235 Catamaran

1998. Tourism. Multicoloured.

1129	10c. Type **235**	45	30
1130	45c. *Jolly Roger* (tourist schooner) (horiz)	1·00	35
1131	70c. *Atlantis* (tourist submarine) (horiz)	1·50	1·10
1132	$2 *Harbour Master* (ferry)	3·25	4·00

236 Racing Yacht

1999. "Australia '99" World Stamp Exhibition, Melbourne. Sheet 90×90 mm.

MS1133	**236** $4 multicoloured	3·50	5·00

237 Juvenile Piping Plover in Shallow Water

1999. Endangered Species. Piping Plover. Multicoloured.

1134	10c. Type **237**	20	20
1135	45c. Female with eggs	55	55
1136	50c. Male and female with fledglings	55	75
1137	70c. Male in shallow water	65	1·10

1999. 30th Anniv of First Manned Landing on Moon. As T **186** of Ascension. Multicoloured.

1138	40c. Astronaut in training	55	45
1139	45c. 1st stage separation	55	45
1140	$1.15 Lunar landing module	1·40	1·25
1141	$1.40 Docking with service module	1·50	2·25
MS1142	90×80 mm. $2.50, Earth as seen from Moon (circular, 40 mm diam)	2·25	3·25

238 Hare running

1999. "China '99" International Stamp Exhibition, Beijing. Hares. Multicoloured.

1143	70c. Type **238**	1·40	1·50
1144	70c. Head of hare	1·40	1·50
1145	70c. Baby hares suckling	1·40	1·50
1146	70c. Hares boxing	1·40	1·50
1147	70c. Two leverets	1·40	1·50

Nos. 1143/7 were printed together, *se-tenant*, forming a composite background design.

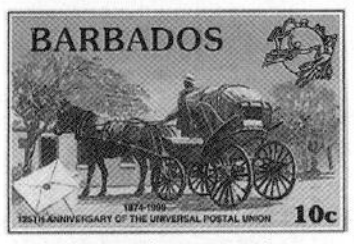

239 Horse-drawn Mail Cart

1999. 125th Anniv of U.P.U. Multicoloured.

1148	10c. Type **239**	1·25	35
1149	45c. Mail van	1·50	40
1150	$1.75 Sikorsky S42 flying boat	2·00	2·25
1151	$2 Computer and fax machine	2·00	2·50

240 Globe and Barbados Flag

2000. New Millennium. Sheet 90×80 mm.

MS1152	**240** $3 multicoloured	3·50	4·00

241 Drax Hall House

2000. Pride of Barbados. Multicoloured.

1153	5c. Type **241**	20	30
1154	10c. Reaping sugar cane (vert)	20	30
1155	40c. Needham's Point Lighthouse (vert)	1·50	60
1156	45c. Port St. Charles	60	30
1157	65c. Interior of Jewish synagogue	1·75	1·00
1158	70c. Bridgetown Port (I)	1·50	2·00
1158a	70c. Bridgetown Port (II)	1·50	1·50
1159	90c. Harrison's Cave	1·00	60
1160	$1.15 Villa Nova	1·10	85
1161	$1.40 Cricket at Kensington Oval	2·25	1·60
1162	$1.75 Sunbury House	1·50	1·75
1163	$2 Bethel Methodist Church	1·75	2·00
1164	$3 Peacock, Barbados Wildlife Reserve (vert)	2·75	3·00
1165	$5 Royal Westmoreland Golf Course (vert)	6·00	6·50
1166	$10 Grantley Adams International Airport	9·00	10·00

Two types of 70c.:

I. Central design reversed. The bows of three of the four liners shown point to the right.

II. Design corrected. The bows of three of the four liners point to the left.

242 Sir Conrad Hunte batting

2000. West Indies Cricket Tour and 100th Test Match at Lord's. Multicoloured.

1167	45c. Type **242**	75	35
1168	90c. Malcolm Marshall bowling	1·50	75
1169	$2 Sir Garfield Sobers batting	2·50	3·00
MS1170	121×104 mm. $2.50, Lord's Cricket Ground (horiz)	2·75	3·25

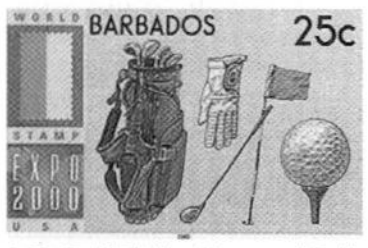

243 Golf Clubs, Flag and Ball on Tee Peg

2000. "EXPO 2000" World Stamp Exhibition, Anaheim, U.S.A. Golf. Multicoloured.

1171	25c. Type **243**	70	35
1172	40c. Golfer teeing off on top of giant ball	90	35
1173	$1.40 Golfer on green	1·75	1·90
1174	$2 Golfer putting	2·25	3·00

244 Bentley Mk VI Drophead Coupe, 1947

2000. Vintage Cars. Multicoloured.

1175	10c. Type **244**	25	15
1176	30c. Vanden Plas Princess Limousine, 1964	50	25
1177	90c. Austin Atlantic, 1952	1·00	70
1178	$3 Bentley Special, 1950	3·00	4·00

245 Thread Snake

2001. "HONG KONG 2001" Stamp Exhibition. Sheet 125×80 mm.

MS1179	**245** $3 multicoloured	3·50	4·00

246 Lizardfish

2001. Deep Sea Creatures. Multicoloured.

1180	45c. Type **246**	50	60
1181	45c. Golden-tailed moray	50	60
1182	45c. Black-barred soldierfish	50	60
1183	45c. Golden zoanthid	50	60
1184	45c. Sponge brittle star	50	60
1185	45c. Magnificent feather duster	50	60
1186	45c. Bearded fireworm	50	60
1187	45c. Lima shell	50	60
1188	45c. Yellow tube sponge	50	60

247 Octagonal, Fish and Butterfly Kites

2001. "Philanippon '01" International Stamp Exhibition, Tokyo. Kites. Multicoloured.

1189	10c. Type **247**	20	15
1190	65c. Hexagonal, bird and geometric kites	60	45
1191	$1.40 Policeman, Japanese and butterfly kites	1·40	1·50
1192	$1.75 Anti-drug, geisha and eagle kites	1·60	1·75

248 George Washington on the Quay, 1751

2001. 250th Anniv of George Washington's Visit to Barbados. Multicoloured.

1193	45c. Type **248**	65	40
1194	50c. George Washington in Barbados	65	40
1195	$1.15 George Washington superimposed on Declaration of Independence, 1776	1·50	1·00
1196	$2.50 Needham's Point Fort, 1750	2·50	3·25
MS1197	110×90 mm. $3 George Washington as President of U.S.A.	2·50	3·00

249 Shaggy Bear(Traditional Carnival Character)

2001. 35th Anniv of Independence. Multicoloured.

1198	25c. Type **249**	40	20
1199	45c. Tuk band	70	30
1200	$1 Landship Dancers	1·25	80
1201	$2 Guitar, saxophone and words of National Anthem	2·25	2·75

2002. Golden Jubilee. As T **200** of Ascension.

1202	10c. black, violet and gold	45	20
1203	70c. multicoloured	1·00	60
1204	$1 black, violet and gold	1·25	1·00
1205	$1.40 multicoloured	1·50	2·00
MS1206	162×95 mm. Nos. 1202/5 and $3 multicoloured	4·75	5·50

DESIGNS—HORIZ: 10c. Princess Elizabeth; 70c. Queen Elizabeth in cerise hat; $1 Queen Elizabeth wearing Imperial State Crown, Coronation, 1953; $1.40, Queen Elizabeth in purple feathered hat. VERT (38×51 mm)—$3 Queen Elizabeth after Annigoni.

Designs as Nos. 1202/5 in **MS**1206 omit the gold frame around each stamp and "Golden Jubilee 1952–2002" inscription.

250 1852 (½d.) Britannia Stamp and Map

2002. 150th Anniv of Inland Postal Service. Multicoloured.

1207	10c. Type **250**	30	15
1208	45c. Early twentieth-century postman delivering letter	60	35
1209	$1.15 *Esk* (mail steamer)	1·50	1·25
1210	$2 B.W.I.A. Tri-Star airliner	2·00	2·50

251 *Alpinia purpurata*

2002. Flowers. Multicoloured.

1211	10c. Type **251**	20	20
1212	40c. *Heliconia caribaea*	40	30
1213	$1.40 *Polianthes tuberosa* (horiz)	1·25	1·40
1214	$2.50 *Anthurium* (horiz)	2·00	2·75

252 Drax Hall Windmill, St. George

2002. 375th Anniv of First Settlement.

1215	**252**	10c. brown, agate and blue	35	15
1216	-	45c. brown, agate and blue	1·00	35
1217	-	$1.15 multicoloured	1·50	1·40
1218	-	$3 multicoloured	3·25	4·00

DESIGNS: 45c. Donkey cart; $1.15, Cattle Mill ruins, Gibbons; $3, Morgan Lewis windmill, St. Andrew.

253 Traditional Christmas Fare

2002. Christmas. Multicoloured.

1219	45c. Type **253**	60	35
1220	$1.15 Christmas morning in the park	1·25	1·25
1221	$1.40 Nativity scene from float parade	1·40	1·50

254 AIDS Ribbon

2002. Centenary of Pan American Health Organization. Multicoloured.

1222	10c. Type **254**	40	15
1223	70c. Amateur athletes	85	50
1224	$1.15 Sir George Alleyne (Director-General of P.A.H.O.)	1·25	1·10
1225	$2 Pregnant woman	1·75	2·00

255 H.M.S. *Tartar*, 1764

2003. Royal Navy Connections. Multicoloured.

1226	10c. Type **255**	55	20
1227	70c. H.M.S. *Barbadoes*, 1803	1·10	55
1228	$1.15 H.M.S. *Valerian*, 1926	1·40	1·25
1229	$2.50 H.M.S. *Victorious*, 1941	2·50	3·25

256 Broad Street, c. 1900

2003. 375th Anniv of the Settlement of Bridgetown. Multicoloured.

1230	10c. Type **256**	55	20
1231	$1.15 Swan Street, 1900	1·40	90
1232	$1.40 Roebuck Street, c. 1880	1·60	1·40
1233	$2 Chamberlain Bridge	2·25	3·00
MS1234	160×120 mm. Nos. 1230/3	5·50	6·00

2003. Centenary of Powered Flight. As T **209** of Ascension. Multicoloured.

1235	10c. McDonnell F2H-2P Banshee	40	20
1236	45c. Vickers Viscount 700	70	30
1237	50c. Douglas DC-9-30	80	30
1238	$1.15 Short Sunderland Mk II	1·10	70
1239	$1.40 North American P-51D Mustang	1·25	1·25
1240	$2.50 Concorde	2·75	3·50

257 Fishermen (Oistins Fish Festival)

2003. Barbados Festivals. Multicoloured.

MS1241	127×105 mm. 45c. Type **257**; 45c. Saxophone player (Barbados Jazz Festival); 45c. Man and woman in traditional costume (Crop Over Festival); 45c. Actresses (National Independence Festival of Creative Arts); 45c. School choir (National Independence Festival of Creative Arts); 45c. Carnival dancers (Crop Over Festival); 45c. Bass player (Barbados Jazz Festival); 45c. Competitor in fish boning competition (Oistins Fish Festival)	4·75	5·00

258 Cadet Corps Banner

2004. Centenary of the Cadet Corps. Multicoloured.

1242	10c. Type **258**	30	20
1243	25c. The Regular band marching	50	25
1244	50c. The Toy Soldier band	70	35
1245	$1 The Sea Cadets	1·00	80
1246	$3 Map reading	2·50	3·00

259 Swimming

2004. Olympic Games, Athens. Multicoloured.

1247	10c. Type **259**	35	20
1248	70c. Shooting	70	45
1249	$1.15 Running	1·10	1·10
1250	$2 Judo	2·00	2·50

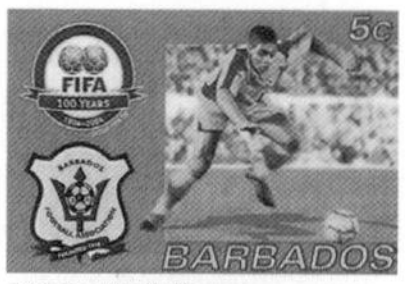

260 Football Player

2004. Centenary of FIFA (Federation Internationale de Football Association). Multicoloured.

1251	5c. Type **260**	15	30
1252	90c. Player in blue strip	1·00	70
1253	$1.40 Goal keeper	1·25	1·25
1254	$2.50 Player in yellow strip	2·00	2·50

261 Brain Coral

2004. Coral. Multicoloured.

1255	$1 Type **261**	1·40	1·50
1256	$1 Pillar coral	1·40	1·50
1257	$1 Pillar coral (different)	1·40	1·50
1258	$1 Fan coral	1·40	1·50
1259	$1 Yellow pencil coral	1·40	1·50
MS1260	85×85 mm. $3.50 Maze coral (36×36 mm)	3·50	3·75

262 White Peacock

2005. Pacific Explorer 2005 World Stamp Expo, Sydney, Australia. Butterflies. Multicoloured.

1261	50c. Type **262**	70	35
1262	$1 Great southern white	1·25	80
1263	$1.40 Orion	1·60	1·40
1264	$2.50 Mimic	2·25	3·00
MS1265	85×85 mm. $8 Monarch	7·00	8·00

263 Baobab

2005. Flowering Trees. Multicoloured.

1266	5c. Type **263**	15	15
1267	10c. African tulip tree	15	15
1268	25c. Rose of Sharon	25	25
1269	45c. Black willow	40	30
1270	50c. Black pearl tree	45	35
1271	75c. Seaside mahoe	70	50
1272	90c. Quickstick	80	55
1273	$1 Jerusalem Thorn	90	65
1274	$1.15 Pink cassia	1·00	70
1275	$1.40 Orchid tree	1·25	70
1276	$1.75 Yellow poui	1·50	1·50
1277	$2.10 Lignum vitae	1·90	2·10
1278	$3 Wild cinnamon	2·50	2·75
1279	$5 Pride of India	4·25	4·50
1280	$10 Immortelle	7·50	8·00

264 Firemen, c. 1955

2005. 50th Anniv of the Barbados Fire Service. Multicoloured.

1281	5c. Type **264**	40	40
1282	10c. Fire Officers marching, Fire Service Headquarters, Bridgetown, 2003	40	40
1283	90c. Rosenbauer-Panther FL 6x6 Airport Rescue and Fire Fighting tender	1·50	75
1284	$1.15 Fire Service parade with Dennis Pump Escape, Garrison Savannah, 1975	1·75	1·10
1285	$2.50 Scania 94G Water and Foam Tender	3·75	4·00

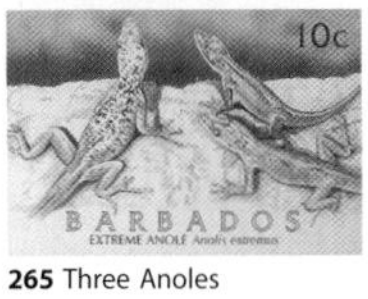

265 Three Anoles

2005. Extreme Anole (*Anolis extremus*). Multicoloured.

1286	10c. Type **265**	30	15
1287	50c. Two anoles	75	35
1288	$1.75 One anole	2·25	2·50
1289	$2 Young anole hatching	2·50	3·00

266 Queen Triggerfish and Diver

2006. Endangered Species. Queen Triggerfish (*Balistes vetula*). Multicoloured.

1290	10c. Type **266**	30	30
1291	$1.15 Pair at edge of coral reef	1·25	1·00
1292	$1.40 Queen Triggerfish above sandy sea floor	1·40	1·25
1293	$2.10 Queen Triggerfish on coral reef	2·00	2·25

267 Girls reading

2006. Washington 2006 International Stamp Exhibition. "Children – they are the future". Multicoloured.

1294	10c. Type **267**	30	20
1295	50c. Wheelchair basketball	75	40
1296	$2 Three children using computer	2·00	2·25
1297	$2.50 Two children playing violins	2·25	2·50

268 Cave Shepherd, c. 1911

2006. Centenary of Cave Shepherd Store, Bridgetown. Multicoloured.

1298	10c. Type **268**	30	20
1299	50c. Cave Shepherd, c. 2000	60	35
1300	$1.75 Cave Shepherd, c. 1975	1·75	2·00
1301	$2 Cave Shepherd, c. 1920	2·00	2·25

269 Old Town Hall, Bridgetown

2006. 175th Anniv of the Enfranchisement of Free Coloured and Black Barbadians. Multicoloured.

1302	10c. Type **269**	30	20
1303	50c. Samuel Jackman Prescod, 1806–71 (campaigner for enfranchisement)	60	35
1304	$1.40 Voting in ballot box (introduced 1885)	1·25	1·40
1305	$2.50 Sir James Lyon (Governor of Barbados, 1829–33)	2·00	2·50

270 Joel 'Big Bird' Garner

2007. World Cup Cricket, West Indies. Multicoloured.

1306	$1.75 Type **270**	1·75	2·00
1307	$2.10 Old Kensington Oval, Barbados (horiz)	2·00	2·25
1308	$3 New Kensington Oval, Barbados (horiz)	2·50	2·75
MS1309	161×121 mm. $10 World Cup Cricket trophy	8·25	8·50

271 Emancipation (Bussa) Statue

2007. Bicentenary of the Abolition of the Slave Trade Act. Multicoloured (except **MS**1314).

1310	10c. Type **271**	15	10
1311	$1 William Wilberforce (abolitionist)	95	1·00
1312	$1.75 Slave hut (horiz)	1·25	1·40
1313	$2 Freedom celebrations, 1838 (horiz)	1·60	1·75
MS1314	115×80 mm. $3 Slave ship (black and violet)	2·50	2·75

272 Interior of Nidhe Israel Synagogue, Bridgetown

2007. Opening of Nidhe Israel Museum, Bridgetown. Multicoloured.

1315	5c. Type **272**	10	10
1316	10c. Nidhe Israel Museum (adjacent to synagogue)	15	10
1317	$1.40 Hanukiah (candelabra)	1·00	1·10
1318	$2.50 Stained glass window in synagogue	2·00	2·25

273 Green Turtle

2007. Turtles. Multicoloured.

1319	10c. Type **273**	15	10
1320	50c. Loggerhead turtle	40	45
1321	$1 Hawksbill turtle	70	75
1322	$2.50 Leatherback turtle	2·00	2·25

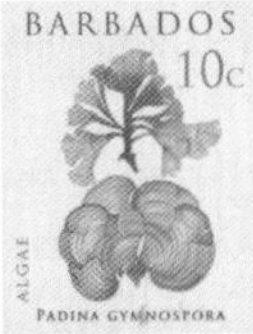

274 *Padina gymnospora*

2008. Algae. Multicoloured.

1323	10c. Type **274**	10	10
1324	50c. *Ulva lactuca*	40	45
1325	$1.75 *Sargassum platycarpum*	1·25	1·40
1326	$2 *Udotea conglutinata*	1·75	1·90

275 The Second Barbados Contingent of Volunteers for Armed Forces, 1940

2008. Airmen and Aircraft. Multicoloured.

1327	10c. Type **275**	10	10
1328	50c. Warren Alleyne (Telegraphist 1) and Supermarine Spitfire Mk IX, 1944	40	45
1329	$1.75 Wing Commander Aubrey Inniss and Bristol Beaufighter Mk VIC, 1943	1·25	1·40
1330	$2 Flying Officer Errol Barrow and Avro Lancaster B Mk 1, 1945	1·75	1·90
MS1331	100×73 mm. $6 Concorde over Barbados	4·75	4·75

Nos. 1327/30 commemorate the 90th anniversary of the Royal Air Force.

276 *Christmas Moon* (Alison Chapman-Andrews)

2008. Christmas. Designs showing paintings. Multicoloured.

1332	10c. Type **276**	15	10
1333	50c. *Preparing for Christmas* (Virgil Broodhagen)	60	45
1334	$1.40 *Christmas Candles* (Darla Trotman)	1·00	85
1335	$3 *Poinsettia and Snow on the Mountain* (Darla Trotman)	2·50	2·75

277 Mop making

2009. Birth Bicentenary of Louis Braille (inventor of Braille writing for the blind) and Barbados Association for the Blind and Deaf. Multicoloured.

1336	50c. Type **277**	60	45
1337	$1.40 Chair caning	1·00	85
1338	$1.75 Girl using Braille typewriter	1·25	1·40
1339	$2 Louis Braille	1·75	1·90

278 New Court House

2009. 300th Anniv of the Restructured Criminal Court. Multicoloured.

1340	10c. Type **278**	15	10
1341	50c. Handcuffs and seal of the Court	65	45
1342	$1.40 Judge's robe, wig and gavel	1·00	45
1343	$2.50 Old Court House	2·00	2·25

279 Queen's Park Fountain

2010. Centenary (2009) of Queen's Park, Bridgetown. Multicoloured.

1344	90c. Type **279**	85	90
1345	$1 The Boaba Tree (baobab *Adansonia digitata*)	90	95
1346	$1.40 Queen's Park House	1·50	1·60
1347	$2 The Band Stand	1·90	2·00
MS1348	140×91 mm. $4 Queen's Park in 1909	4·00	4·00

280 J 24 Keelboats flying Spinnakers

2010. Fireball International World Championships, Carlisle Bay. Multicoloured.

1349	10c. Type **280**	15	10
1350	50c. J24 keelboats	45	50
1351	90c. J24 keelboats	85	90
1352	$1.75 Laser dinghies	1·90	2·00
1353	$2 Racing keelboats	2·10	2·20

281 Guides camping

2010. Centenary of Girl Guiding. Multicoloured.

1354	10c. Type **281**	15	10
1355	50c. Guides saluting ('The Promise')	45	50
1356	$1 Brownies and guides ('Guiding Uniforms')	1·60	1·70
1357	$2.50 Parade of guides	2·10	2·00
MS1358	94×64 mm. $3.50 Emblem	3·50	3·50

282 Golden Apple (*Spondias cytherea*)

2011. Local Fruits. Multicoloured.

1359	5c. Type **282**	15	15
1360	10c. Coconut (*Cocos nucifera*)	20	25
1361	35c. Cashew (*Anacardium occidentale*)	40	45
1362	40c. Mammy apple (*Mammea americana*)	45	50
1363	60c. Barbados cherry (*Malpighia emarginata*)	70	75
1364	65c. Sugar apple (*Annona squamosa*)	75	80
1365	80c. Sea grape (*Coccoloba uvifera*)	90	95
1366	$1 Tamarind (*Tamarindus indica*)	1·10	1·20
1367	$1.25 Carambola (*Averrhoa carambola*)	1·20	1·30
1368	$1.50 Mango (*Mangifera indica*)	1·50	1·60
1369	$1.80 Banana (*Musa* X)	1·70	1·90

1370	$2.20 Guava (*Psidium guajava*)	2·10	2·20
1371	$2.75 Avocado (*Persea americana*)	2·40	2·50
1372	$3 Gooseberry (*Phyllanthus acidus*)	2·75	3·00
1373	$5 Soursop (*Annona muricata*)	5·25	5·50
1374	$10 Pomegranate (*Punica granatum*)	8·75	9·00

283 'Sailors' Valentine' from 1800s

2011. 'Sailors' Valentines' (collages of sea shells within octagonal wooden frames). Multicoloured.

1375	10c. Type **283**	20	25
1376	65c. Modern 'sailors' valentine' by Daphne Hunte	60	65
1377	$2.20 'Sailors' valentine' with 'Live Today Hope Tomorrow' inscription	2·20	2·30
1378	$2.75 Modern 'sailors' valentine' by Pamela Boynton	2·75	3·00

284 Miss Catherine Middleton and Maid of Honour Pippa Middleton arriving at Westminster Abbey

2011. Royal Wedding. Multicoloured.

1379	15c. Type **284**	35	40
1380	65c. Duke and Duchess of Cambridge in State Landau	75	80
1381	$1.80 Duke and Duchess of Cambridge at Westminster Abbey after wedding ceremony (vert)	1·75	1·90
1382	$2.20 Duke and Duchess of Cambridge waving from Buckingham Palace balcony (vert)	2·20	2·10

285 Queen Elizabeth II leaving 350th Anniversary Assembly of Parliament, Barbados, 1989

2012. Diamond Jubilee. Multicoloured.

1383	10c. Type **285**	30	35
1384	$1.40 Queen Elizabeth II wearing tiara on way to opening session of Parliament, London, 4 November 1952	1·50	1·75
1385	$2.10 Queen Elizabeth II inspecting Barbados Defence Force, 31 October 1977	2·20	2·10
1386	$2.50 Queen Elizabeth II at NASA's Goddard Space Flight Center, Maryland, USA, 8 May 2007	2·40	2·50

No. **MS**1387 is left for $4 miniature sheet not yet received.

POSTAGE DUE STAMPS

D1

1934

D1	**D1**	½d. green	1·25	8·50
D2	**D1**	1d. black	1·75	1·25
D3	**D1**	3d. red	20·00	23·00

1950. Values in cents.

D4a	1c. green	30	3·00
D8	2c. black	30	5·00
D9	6c. red	50	7·00

D2

1976

D14a	**D2**	1c. mauve and pink	10	10
D15a	-	2c. blue and light blue	10	10
D16a	-	5c. brown and yellow	10	15
D17a	-	10c. blue and lilac	15	20
D18a	-	25c. deep green and green	20	30
D19	-	$1 red and deep red	75	1·25

DESIGNS: Nos. D15/19 show different floral backgrounds.

Pt. 1

BARBUDA

One of the Leeward Is., Br. W. Indies. Dependency of Antigua. Used stamps of Antigua and Leeward Is. concurrently. The issues from 1968 are also valid for use in Antigua. From 1971 to 1973 the stamps of Antigua were again used.

1922. 12 pence = 1 shilling; 20 shillings = 1 pound.
1951. 100 cents = 1 West Indian dollar.

1922. Stamps of Leeward Islands optd **BARBUDA.**

1	**11**	½d. green	1·50	12·00
2	**11**	1d. red	1·50	12·00
3	**11**	2d. grey	1·50	7·00
4	**11**	2½d. blue	1·50	7·50
9	**11**	3d. purple on yellow	1·75	13·00
5	**11**	6d. purple	2·00	18·00
10	**11**	1s. black on green	1·50	8·00
6	**11**	2s. purple and blue on blue	14·00	50·00
7	**11**	3s. green and violet	35·00	80·00
8	**11**	4s. black and red	42·00	80·00
11	**11**	5s. green and red on yellow	65·00	£130

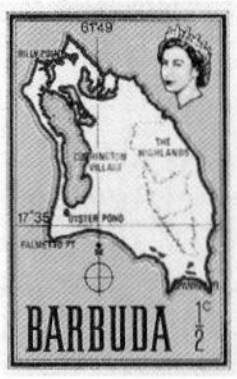

2 Map of Barbuda

3 Greater Amberjack

1968

12	**2**	½c. brown, black and pink	45	3·25
13	**2**	1c. orange, black and flesh	1·25	35
14	**2**	2c. brown, red and rose	2·25	1·25
15	**2**	3c. brown, yellow and lemon	1·25	55
16	**2**	4c. black, green & lt green	3·00	3·25
17	**2**	5c. turquoise and black	2·25	20
18	**2**	6c. black, purple and lilac	1·25	3·25
19	**2**	10c. black, blue and cobalt	1·75	1·25
20	**2**	15c. black, green & turq	2·00	3·75
20a	-	20c. multicoloured	1·50	2·00
21	**3**	25c. multicoloured	1·00	25
22	-	35c. multicoloured	3·00	25
23	-	50c. multicoloured	1·00	1·50
24	-	75c. multicoloured	1·00	80
25	-	$1 multicoloured	50	1·50
26	-	$2.50 multicoloured	55	2·00
27	-	$5 multicoloured	65	2·25

DESIGNS: As T **3**—20c. Great barracuda; 35c. French angelfish; 50c. Porkfish; 75c. Princess parrotfish; $1, Longspined squirrelfish; $2.50, Bigeye; $5, Blue chromis.

10 Sprinting and Aztec Sun-stone

1968. Olympic Games. Mexico. Multicoloured.

28	25c. Type **10**	50	30
29	35c. High-jumping and Aztec statue	55	30
30	75c. Dinghy-racing and Aztec lion mask	60	1·10
MS31	87×76 mm. $1 Football and engraved plate	2·00	3·25

14 "The Ascension" (Orcagna)"

1969. Easter Commemoration.

32	**14**	25c. black and blue	15	45
33	**14**	35c. black and red	15	50
34	**14**	75c. black and lilac	15	55

15 Scout Enrolment Ceremony

1969. Third Caribbean Scout Jamboree. Multicoloured.

35	25c. Type **15**	35	55
36	35c. Scouts around camp fire	45	65
37	75c. Sea Scouts rowing boat	55	1·40

18 *Sistine Madonna* (Raphael)

1969. Christmas.

38	**18**	½c. multicoloured	10	30
39	**18**	25c. multicoloured	10	15
40	**18**	35c. multicoloured	10	20
41	**18**	35c. multicoloured	20	35

19 William I (1066–87)

1970. English Monarchs. Multicoloured.

42	35c. Type **19**	30	15
43	35c. William II (1087–1100)	10	15
44	35c. Henry I (1100–35)	10	15
45	35c. Stephen (1135–54)	10	15
46	35c. Henry II (1154–89)	10	15
47	35c. Richard I (1189–99)	10	15
48	35c. John (1199–1216)	10	15
49	35c. Henry III (1216–72)	10	15
50	35c. Edward I (1272–1307)	10	15
51	35c. Edward II (1307–27)	10	15
52	35c. Edward III (1327–77)	10	15
53	35c. Richard II (1377–99)	10	15
54	35c. Henry IV (1399–1413)	10	15
55	35c. Henry V (1413–22)	10	15
56	35c. Henry VI (1422–61)	10	15
57	35c. Edward IV (1462–83)	10	15
58	35c. Edward V (April–June 1483)	10	15
59	35c. Richard III (1483–85)	10	15
60	35c. Henry VII (1485–1509)	35	15
61	35c. Henry VIII (1509–47)	35	15
62	35c. Edward VI (1547–53)	35	15
63	35c. Lady Jane Grey (1553)	35	15
64	35c. Mary I (1553–8)	35	15
65	35c. Elizabeth I (1558–1603)	35	15
66	35c. James I (1603–25)	35	15
67	35c. Charles I (1625–49)	35	15
68	35c. Charles II (1649–1685)	35	15
69	35c. James II (1685–1688)	35	15
70	35c. William III (1689–1702)	35	15
71	35c. Mary II (1689–1694)	35	15
72	35c. Anne (1702–1714)	35	15
73	35c. George I (1714–1727)	35	15
74	35c. George II (1727–1760)	35	15
75	35c. George III (1760–1820)	35	15
76	35c. George IV (1820–1830)	35	15
77	35c. William IV (1830–1837)	35	60
78	35c. Victoria (1837–1901)	35	60

See also Nos. 710/5.

1970. No. 12 surch **20c.**

79	**2**	20c. on ½c. brn, blk & pink	20	20

21 *The Way to Calvary* (Ugolino)

1970. Easter. Paintings. Multicoloured.

80	25c. Type **21**	15	30
81	35c. *The Deposition from the Cross* (Ugolino)	15	30
82	75c. Crucifix (The Master of St. Francis)	15	35

22 Oliver is introduced to Fagin (*Oliver Twist*)

1970. Death Centenary of Charles Dickens. Multicoloured.

83	20c. Type **22**	45	25
84	75c. Dickens and scene from *The Old Curiosity Shop*	80	75

23 *Madonna of the Meadows* (G. Bellini)

1970. Christmas. Multicoloured.

85	20c. Type **23**	10	25
86	50c. *Madonna, Child and Angels* (from Wilton diptych)	15	30
87	75c. *The Nativity* (della Francesca)	15	35

24 Nurse with Patient in Wheelchair

1970. Centenary of British Red Cross. Multicoloured.

88	20c. Type **24**	15	30
89	35c. Nurse giving patient magazines (horiz)	20	40
90	75c. Nurse and mother weighing baby (horiz)	25	70

25 *Angel with Vases*

1971. Easter. *Mond* Crucifixion by Raphael. Multicoloured.

91	35c. Type **25**	15	85
92	50c. *Christ crucified*	15	95
93	75c. *Angel with vase*	15	1·00

26 Martello Tower

1971. Tourism. Multicoloured.

94	20c. Type **26**	15	35
95	25c. "Sailfish" dinghy	25	40
96	50c. Hotel bungalows	25	45
97	75c. Government House and Mystery Stone	25	55

27 *The Granducal Madonna* (Raphael)

1971. Christmas. Multicoloured.

98	½c. Type **27**	10	10
99	35c. *The Ansidei Madonna* (Raphael)	10	20
100	50c. *The Madonna and Child* (Botticelli)	15	25
101	75c. *The Madonna of the Trees* (Bellini)	15	30

1973. Royal Wedding. Nos. 370/1 of Antigua optd **BARBUDA** twice.

102	**106**	25c. multicoloured	3·25	2·00
103	**106**	$2 multicoloured	1·25	1·25

Four stamps to commemorate the 500th Birth Anniv of Durer were prepared in late 1971, but their issue was not authorised by the Antigua Government.

1973. Ships. Nos. 269/85 of Antigua optd **BARBUDA**.

116	**92**	½c. multicoloured	15	20
104	-	1c. multicoloured	15	30
105	-	2c. multicoloured	25	30
117	-	3c. multicoloured	25	25
106	-	4c. multicoloured	30	30
107	-	5c. multicoloured	40	40
108	-	6c. multicoloured	40	40
109	-	10c. multicoloured	45	45
118	-	15c. multicoloured	45	50
110	-	20c. multicoloured	55	60
111	-	25c. multicoloured	55	60
112	-	35c. multicoloured	55	70
113	-	50c. multicoloured	55	70
114	-	75c. multicoloured	55	70
119	-	$1 multicoloured	55	70
115	-	$2.50 multicoloured	75	1·50
121	-	$5 multicoloured	1·10	2·50

1973. Military Uniforms. Nos. 353, 355 and 357 of Antigua optd **BARBUDA**.

122	½c. multicoloured	10	10
123	20c. multicoloured	15	10
124	75c. multicoloured	40	15
MS125	127×145 mm. Nos. 353/7 of Antigua	2·00	3·50

1973. Carnival. Nos. 360/3 of Antigua optd **BARBUDA**.

126	20c. multicoloured	10	10
127	35c. multicoloured	10	10
128	75c. multicoloured	20	25
MS129	134×95 mm. Nos. 359/62 of Antigua	1·00	2·25

1973. Christmas. Nos. 364/69 of Antigua optd **BARBUDA**.

130	**105**	3c. multicoloured	10	10
131	-	5c. multicoloured	10	10
132	-	20c. multicoloured	10	10
133	-	35c. multicoloured	15	15
134	-	$1 multicoloured	30	30
MS135		130×128 mm. Nos. 130/4	2·25	9·00

1973. Honeymoon Visit. Nos. 373/4 of Antigua additionally optd **BARBUDA**.

136	35c. multicoloured	30	20
137	$2 multicoloured	70	60
MS138	78×100 mm. Nos. 136/7	1·10	1·00

1974. University of West Indies. Nos. 376/9 of Antigua optd **BARBUDA**.

139	5c. multicoloured	10	10
140	20c. multicoloured	10	10
141	35c. multicoloured	15	15
142	75c. multicoloured	15	15

1974. Military Uniforms. Nos. 380/4 of Antigua optd **BARBUDA**.

143	½c. multicoloured	10	10
144	10c. multicoloured	20	10
145	20c. multicoloured	30	10
146	35c. multicoloured	35	10
147	75c. multicoloured	50	25

1974. Centenary of U.P.U. (1st issue). Nos. 386/92 of Antigua optd with either a or b. (a) **BARBUDA 13 JULY 1992**.

148	½c. multicoloured	10	10
150	1c. multicoloured	10	10
152	2c. multicoloured	20	15
154	5c. multicoloured	50	15
156	20c. multicoloured	40	70
158	35c. multicoloured	80	1·50
160	$1 multicoloured	1·75	4·00

(b) **BARBUDA 15 SEPT. 1874 G.P.U.** ("General Postal Union").

149	½c. multicoloured	10	10
151	1c. multicoloured	10	10
153	2c. multicoloured	20	15
155	5c. multicoloured	50	15
157	20c. multicoloured	40	70
159	35c. multicoloured	80	1·50
161	$1 multicoloured	1·75	4·00
MS162	141×164 mm. No. **MS**393 of Antigua optd **BARBUDA**	3·50	6·00

1974. Antiguan Steel Bands. Nos. 394/98 of Antigua optd **BARBUDA**.

163	5c. deep red, red and black	10	10
164	20c. brown, lt brown & blk	10	10
165	35c. light green, green and black	10	10
166	75c. deep blue, blue and black	20	20
MS167	115×108 mm. Nos. 163/6	65	80

39 Footballers

1974. World Cup Football Championships (1st issue).

168	**39**	35c. multicoloured	10	10
169	-	$1.20 multicoloured	25	35
170	-	$2.50 multicoloured	35	50
MS171		70×128 mm. Nos. 168/70	85	90

DESIGNS: $1.20, $2.50, Footballers in action similar to Type **39**.

1974. World Cup Football Championships (2nd issue). Nos. 399/403 of Antigua optd **BARBUDA**.

172	**111**	5c. multicoloured	10	10
173	-	35c. multicoloured	20	10
174	-	75c. multicoloured	25	15
175	-	$1 multicoloured	25	25
MS176		135×130 mm. Nos. 172/5	75	1·25

41 Ship Letter of 1833

1974. Cent of Universal Postal Union (2nd issue). Multicoloured.

177	35c. Type **41**	10	10
178	$1.20 Stamps and postmarks of 1922	25	50
179	$2.50 Britten Norman Islander mailplane over map of Barbuda	35	75
MS180	128×97 mm. Nos. 177/9	1·00	2·00

42 Greater Amberjack

1974. Multicoloured.

181	½c. Oleander, Rose Bay (vert)	10	40
182	1c. Blue petrea (vert)	15	40
183	2c. Poinsettia (vert)	15	40
184	3c. Cassia tree (vert)	15	40
185	4c. Type **42**	1·75	40
186	5c. Holy Trinity School	15	15
187	6c. Snorkeling	15	30
188	10c. Pilgrim Holiness Church	15	20
189	15c. New Cottage Hospital	15	20
190	20c. Post Office and Treasury	15	20
191	25c. Island jetty and boats (vert)	30	30
192	35c. Martello Tower	30	30
193	50c. Warden's House	30	30
194	75c. Britten Norman Islander aircraft	3·50	1·00
195	$1 Tortoise	70	80
196	$2.50 Spiny lobster	80	1·75
197	$5 Magnificent frigate bird	4·00	2·50
197b	$10 Hibiscus (vert)	1·50	4·50

The 50c. to $1 are 39×25 mm, $2.50 and $5 45×29 mm, $10 34×48 mm.

1974. Birth Centenary of Sir Winston Churchill (1st issue). Nos. 408/12 of Antigua optd **BARBUDA**.

198	**113**	5c. multicoloured	15	10
199	-	35c. multicoloured	25	15
200	-	75c. multicoloured	40	45
201	-	$1 multicoloured	75	70
MS202		107×82 mm. Nos. 198/201	7·00	14·00

43 Churchill making Broadcast

1974. Birth Centenary of Sir Winston Churchill (2nd issue). Multicoloured.

203	5c. Type **43**	10	10
204	35c. Churchill and Chartwell	10	10
205	75c. Churchill painting	20	20
206	$1 Churchill making "V" sign	25	30
MS207	146×95 mm. Nos. 203/6	75	2·50

1974. Christmas. Nos. 413/21 of Antigua optd **BARBUDA**.

208	**114**	½c. multicoloured	10	10
209	-	1c. multicoloured	10	10
210	-	2c. multicoloured	10	10
211	-	3c. multicoloured	10	10
212	-	5c. multicoloured	10	10
213	-	20c. multicoloured	10	10
214	-	35c. multicoloured	15	15
215	-	75c. multicoloured	30	30
MS216		139×126 mm. Nos. 208/15	80	1·40

1975. Nelson's Dockyard. Nos. 427/32 of Antigua optd **BARBUDA**.

217	**116**	5c. multicoloured	15	15
218	-	15c. multicoloured	35	25
219	-	35c. multicoloured	40	35
220	-	50c. multicoloured	45	50
221	-	$1 multicoloured	50	80
MS222		130×134 mm. As Nos. 217/21, but larger format; 43×28 mm	1·75	2·75

45 Ships of the Line

1975. Sea Battles. Battle of the Saints, 1782. Multicoloured.

223	35c. Type **45**	40	65
224	50c. H.M.S. *Ramillies*	40	75
225	75c. *Bonhomme Richard* (American frigate) firing broadside	50	90
226	95c. *L'Orient* (French ship of the line) burning	50	1·25

1975. "Apollo–Soyuz" Space Project. No. 197 optd **U.S.A.-U.S.S.R SPACE COOPERATION 1975** with **APOLLO** (No. 227) or **SOYUZ** (No. 228).

227	$5 multicoloured	3·25	6·00
228	$5 multicoloured	3·25	6·00

47 Officer, 65th Foot, 1763

1975. Military Uniforms. Multicoloured.

229	35c. Type **47**	60	60
230	50c. Grenadier, 27th Foot 1701–10	75	75
231	75c. Officer, 21st Foot, 1793–6	80	80
232	95c. Officer, Royal Regiment of Artillery, 1800	90	90

1975. 25th Anniv of United Nations. Nos. 203/6 optd **30TH ANNIVERSARY UNITED NATIONS 1945–1975**.

233	**43**	5c. multicoloured	10	10
234	-	35c. multicoloured	10	15
235	-	75c. multicoloured	15	20
236	-	$1 multicoloured	20	30

1975. Christmas. Nos. 457/65 of Antigua optd **BARBUDA**.

237	**121**	½c. multicoloured	10	15
238	-	1c. multicoloured	10	15
239	-	2c. multicoloured	10	15
240	-	3c. multicoloured	10	15
241	-	5c. multicoloured	10	15
242	-	10c. multicoloured	10	15
243	-	35c. multicoloured	15	20
244	-	$2 multicoloured	60	1·00
MS245		138×119 mm. Nos. 241/4	1·10	2·25

1975. World Cup Cricket Winners. Nos. 466/8 of Antigua optd **BARBUDA**.

246	**122**	5c. multicoloured	1·50	1·75
247	-	35c. multicoloured	2·75	2·00
248	-	$2 multicoloured	4·25	5·50

51 Surrender of Cornwallis at Yorktown (Trumbull)

1976. Bicentenary of American Revolution.

249	**51**	15c. multicoloured	10	15
250	-	15c. multicoloured	10	15
251	-	15c. multicoloured	10	15
252	-	35c. multicoloured	10	15
253	-	35c. multicoloured	10	15
254	-	35c. multicoloured	10	15
255	-	$1 multicoloured	15	25
256	-	$1 multicoloured	15	25
257	-	$1 multicoloured	15	25
258	-	$2 multicoloured	25	40
259	-	$2 multicoloured	25	40
260	-	$2 multicoloured	25	40
MS261		140×70 mm. Nos. 249/54 and 255/60 (two sheets)	1·40	9·00

DESIGNS—As Type **51**: Nos. 249/51; 252/4, The Battle of Princeton; 255/7, Surrender of General Burgoyne at Saratoga; 258/60, Jefferson presenting Declaration of Independence.

Type **51** shows the left-hand stamp of the 15c. design.

52 Bananaquits

1976. Birds. Multicoloured.

262	35c. Type **52**	20	25
263	50c. Blue-hooded euphonia	20	40
264	75c. Royal tern	20	50
265	95c. Killdeer plover ("Killdeer")	25	55
266	$1.25 Shiney-headed cowbird ("Glossy Cowbird")	25	70
267	$2 American purple gallinule ("Purple Gallinule")	30	85

1976. Royal Visit to the U.S.A. Nos. 249/60 additionally inscr "H.M. QUEEN ELIZABETH ROYAL *VISIT 6TH JULY 1976 H.R.H. DUKE OF EDINBURGH*.

268	15c. multicoloured	10	15
269	15c. multicoloured	10	15
270	15c. multicoloured	10	15
271	35c. multicoloured	10	20
272	35c. multicoloured	10	20
273	35c. multicoloured	10	20
274	$1 multicoloured	15	50
275	$1 multicoloured	15	50
276	$1 multicoloured	15	50
277	$2 multicoloured	25	70
278	$2 multicoloured	25	70
279	$2 multicoloured	25	70
MS280	143×81 mm. Nos. 268/73 and 274/9 (two sheets)	1·50	9·00

1976. Christmas. Nos. 514/18 of Antigua optd **BARBUDA**.

281	**128**	8c. multicoloured	10	10
282	-	10c. multicoloured	10	10
283	-	15c. multicoloured	10	10
284	-	50c. multicoloured	15	15
285	-	$1 multicoloured	25	30

1976. Olympic Games, Montreal. Nos. 495/502 of Antigua optd **BARBUDA**.

286	**125**	½c. brown, yellow and black	10	10
287	-	1c. violet and black	10	10
288	-	2c. green and black	10	10
289	-	15c. blue and black	10	10
290	-	30c. brown, yellow & blk	10	10
291	-	$1 orange, red and black	20	20
292	-	$2 red and black	35	35
MS293		88×138 mm. Nos. 289/92	1·75	2·40

55 P.O. Tower, Telephones and Alexander Graham Bell

1977. Cent of First Telephone Transmission. Multicoloured.

294	75c. Type **55**	15	35
295	$1.25 T.V. transmission by satellite	20	55
296	$2 Globe showing satellite transmission scheme	30	75
MS297	96×144 mm. Nos. 294/6	70	2·00

56 St. Margaret's Church, Westminster

1977. Silver Jubilee (1st issue). Multicoloured.

298	75c. Type **56**	10	15
299	75c. Street decorations	10	15
300	75c. Westminster Abbey	10	15
301	$1.25 Household Cavalry	15	20
302	$1.25 Coronation Coach	15	20
303	$1.25 Postillions	15	20
MS304	148×83 mm. As Nos. 298/303, but with silver borders.	75	1·50

Nos. 298/300 and 301/3 were printed together, se-tenant, forming composite designs.

See also Nos. 323/30 and 375/8.

1977. Nos. 469/86 of Antigua optd **BARBUDA**.

305	½c. Antillean crested hummingbird	1·00	75
306	1c. Imperial amazon ("Imperial Parrot")	1·00	75
307	2c. Zenaida dove	1·00	75
308	3c. Loggerhead kingbird	1·00	75
309	4c. Red-necked pigeon	1·00	75
310	5c. Rufous throated solitaire	1·00	75
311	6c. Orchid tree	50	50
312	10c. Bougainvillea	30	20
313	15c. Geiger tree	30	25
314	20c. Flamboyant	30	25
315	25c. Hibiscus	30	25
316	35c. Flame of the Wood	35	30
317	50c. Cannon at Fort James	40	40
318	75c. Premier's Office	40	40
319	$1 Potworks Dam	50	60
320	$2.50 Irrigation scheme	75	1·60
321	$5 Government House	1·25	3·25
322	$10 Coolidge Airport	3·50	7·50

1977. Silver Jubilee (2nd issue). Nos. 526/31 of Antigua optd **BARBUDA**. (a) Ordinary gum.

323	10c. Royal Family	10	15
324	30c. Royal visit, 1966	10	20
325	50c. The Queen enthroned	15	30
326	90c. The Queen after Coronation	15	40
327	$2.50 The Queen and Prince Charles	45	1·25
MS328	116×78 mm. $5 Queen Elizabeth and Prince Philip	80	1·25

(b) Self-adhesive.

329	50c. Queen after Coronation	40	70
330	$5 The Queen and Prince Philip	3·00	9·00

1977. Caribbean Scout Jamboree, Jamaica. Nos. 534/40 of Antigua optd **BARBUDA**.

331	½c. Type **131**	10	10
332	1c. Hiking	10	10
333	2c. Rock-climbing	10	10
334	10c. Cutting logs	10	10
335	30c. Map and sign reading	25	40
336	50c. First aid	25	65
337	$2 Rafting	55	2·25
MS338	127×114 mm. Nos. 335/7	1·75	4·00

1977. 21st Anniv of Carnival. Nos. 542/47 of Antigua optd **BARBUDA**.

339	10c. Type **312**	10	10
340	30c. Carnival Queen	10	10
341	50c. Butterfly costume	15	20
342	90c. Queen of the Band	20	35
343	$1 Calypso King and Queen	25	45
MS344	140×120 mm. Nos. 339/43	1·00	1·75

61 Royal Yacht *Britannia*

1977. Royal Visit (1st issue). Multicoloured.

345	50c. Type **61**	10	20
346	$1.50 Jubilee emblem	25	35
347	$2.50 Union Jack and flag of Antigua	35	55
MS348	77×124 mm. Nos. 345/7	85	2·25

1977. Royal Visit (2nd issue). Nos. 548/53 of Antigua optd **BARBUDA**.

349A	10c. Royal Family	10	10
350B	30c. Queen Elizabeth and Prince Philip in car	10	15
351B	50c. Queen enthroned	15	20
352B	90c. Queen after Coronation	20	30
353B	$2.50 The Queen and Prince Charles	45	80
MS354A	116×78 mm. $5 Queen and Prince Philip	1·50	4·00

1977. Christmas. Nos. 554/61 of Antigua optd **BARBUDA**.

355	½c. Type **134**	10	10
356	1c. Crivelli	10	10
357	2c. Lotto	10	10
358	8c. Pontormo	10	10
359	10c. Tura (different)	10	10
360	25c. Lotto (different)	15	10
361	$2 Crivelli (different)	45	45
MS362	144×118 mm. Nos. 358/61	1·00	1·75

64 Airship LZ-1

1977. Special Events, 1977. Multicoloured.

363	75c. Type **64**	30	30
364	75c. German battleship and German Navy airship L-31	30	30
365	75c. *Graf Zeppelin* in hangar	30	30
366	75c. Gondola of military airship	30	30
367	95c. Sputnik 1	35	35
368	95c. Vostok rocket	35	35
369	95c. Voskhod rocket	35	35
370	95c. Space walk	35	35
371	$1.25 Fuelling for flight	40	45
372	$1.25 Leaving New York	40	45
373	$1.25 *Spirit of St. Louis*	40	45
374	$1.25 Welcome to England	40	45
375	$2 Lion of England	50	70
376	$2 Unicorn of Scotland	50	70
377	$2 Yale of Beaufort	50	70
378	$2 Falcon of Plantagenets	50	70
379	$5 *Daniel in the Lion's Den* (Rubens)	50	1·25
380	$5 Different detail of painting	50	1·25
381	$5 Different detail of painting	50	1·25
382	$5 Different detail of painting	50	1·25
MS383	132×156 mm. Nos. 362/82	6·00	17·00

EVENTS: 75c. 75th anniv of navigable airships; 95c. 20th anniv of U.S.S.R. space programme; $1.25, 50th anniv of Lindbergh's transatlantic flight; $2 Silver Jubilee of Queen Elizabeth II; $5 400th birth anniv of Rubens.

Nos. 379/82 form a composite design.

1978. Tenth Anniv of Statehood. Nos. 562/7 of Antigua optd **BARBUDA**.

384	10c. Type **135**	10	10
385	15c. State flag	15	10
386	50c. Police band	1·25	80
387	90c. Premier V. C. Bird	20	40
388	$2 State Coat of Arms	40	1·00
MS389	122×99 mm. Nos. 385/88	7·00	4·00

66 *Pieta* (sculpture) (detail)

1978. Easter. Paintings and Sculptures by Michelangelo. Multicoloured.

390	75c. Type **66**	15	15
391	95c. *The Holy Family*	15	20
392	$1.25 *Libyan sibyl* (from the Sistine Chapel)	15	35
393	$2 *The Flood* (from the Sistine Chapel)	20	45
MS394	117×85 mm. Nos. 390/3	1·90	2·00

1978. 75th Anniv of Powered Flight. Nos. 568/75 of Antigua optd **BARBUDA**.

395	½c. Wright Glider No. III, 1902	10	10
396	1c. Wright Flyer I, 1903	10	10
397	2c. Launch system and engine	10	10
398	10c. Orville Wright (vert)	10	10
399	50c. Wright Flyer III, 1905	25	20
400	90c. Wilbur Wright (vert)	35	25
401	$2 Wright Type B, 1910	60	45
MS402	90×75 mm. $2.50, Wright Flyer I on launch system	1·50	2·50

1978. Sailing Week. Nos. 576/80 of Antigua optd **BARBUDA**.

403	10c. Sunfish regatta	20	10
404	50c. Fishing and work boat race	40	25
405	90c. Curtain Bluff race	55	35
406	$2 Power boat rally	85	75
MS407	110×77 mm. $2.50, Guadeloupe–Antigua race	1·25	1·60

68 St. Edward's Crown

1978. 25th Anniv of Coronation (1st issue). Multicoloured.

408	75c. Type **68**	15	20
409	75c. Imperial State Crown	15	20
410	$1.50 Queen Mary's Crown	20	30
411	$1.50 Queen Mother's Crown	20	30
412	$2.50 Queen Consort's Crown	35	50
413	$2.50 Queen Victoria's Crown	35	50
MS414	123×117 mm. Nos. 408/13	1·10	1·75

1978. 25th Anniv of Coronation (2nd issue). Nos. 581/5 of Antigua optd **BARBUDA**.

415	10c. Queen Elizabeth and Prince Philip	10	10
416	30c. The Crowning	10	10
417	50c. Coronation procession	10	15
418	90c. Queen seated in St. Edward's Chair	15	20
419	$2.50 Queen wearing Imperial State Crown	30	60
MS420	114×103 mm. $5 Queen Elizabeth and Prince Philip	1·00	1·50

1978. 25th Anniv of Coronation (3rd issue). As Nos. 587/9 of Antigua, additionally inscr "BARBUDA".

421	25c. Glass Coach	30	70
422	50c. Irish State Coach	30	70
423	$5 Coronation Coach	1·00	2·25

1978. World Cup Football Championship, Argentina. Nos. 590/3 of Antigua optd **BARBUDA**.

424	10c. Player running with ball	10	10
425	15c. Players in front of goal	10	10
426	$3 Referee and player	1·25	1·25
MS427	126×88 mm. 25c. Player crouching with ball; 30c. Players heading ball; 50c. Players running with ball; $2 Goalkeeper diving	80	90

1978. Flowers. As Nos. 594/7 of Antigua optd **BARBUDA**.

428	25c. Petrea	15	20
429	50c. Sunflower	25	40
430	90c. Frangipani	35	45
431	$2 Passion flower	60	90
MS432	118×85 mm. $2.50, Hibiscus	1·00	1·50

1978. Christmas. As Nos. 599/601 of Antigua optd **BARBUDA**.

433	8c. *St. Ildefonso receiving the Chasuble from the Virgin*	10	10
434	25c. *The Flight of St. Barbara*	15	15
435	$2 *Madonna and Child, with St. Joseph, John the Baptist and Donor*	60	1·25
MS436	170×113 mm. $4 *The Annuciation*	1·00	2·25

70 Black-barred Soldierfish

1978. Flora and Fauna. Multicoloured.

437	25c. Type **70**	75	1·50
438	50c. *Cynthia cardui* (butterfly)	1·50	2·25
439	75c. Dwarf poinciana	80	2·25
440	95c. *Heliconius charithonia* (butterfly)	1·50	2·50
441	$1.25 Bougainvillea	90	2·50

71 Footballers and World Cup

1978. Anniversaries and Events.

442	75c. Type **71**	30	30
443	95c. Wright Brothers and Flyer I (horiz)	30	40
444	$1.25 Balloon "Double Eagle II" and map of Atlantic (horiz)	55	45
445	$2 Prince Philip paying homage to the Queen	55	60
MS446	122×90 mm. Nos. 442/5. Imperf	5·00	6·00

EVENTS: 75c. Argentina—Winners of World Cup Football Championship; 95c. 75th anniv of powered flight; $1.25, First Atlantic crossing by balloon; $2 25th anniv of Coronation.

72 Sir Rowland Hill

1979. Death Centenary of Sir Rowland Hill (1st issue). Multicoloured.

447	75c. Type **72**	25	45
448	95c. Mail coach, 1840 (horiz)	25	50
449	$1.25 London's first pillar box, 1855 (horiz)	30	60
450	$2 Mail leaving St. Martin's Le Grand Post Office, London	45	85
MS451	129×104 mm. Nos. 447/50. Imperf	1·40	2·25

1979. Death Centenary of Sir Rowland Hill (2nd issue). Nos. 603/6 of Antigua optd **BARBUDA**.

452	25c. 1d. Stamp of 1863	15	15
453	50c. Penny Black	20	20
454	$1 Stage-coach and woman posting letter, c. 1840	35	30
455	$2 Modern mail transport	80	60
MS456	108×82 mm. $2.50, Sir Rowland Hill	75	80

1979. Easter. Works of Durer. Nos. 608/11 of Antigua optd **BARBUDA**.

457	10c. multicoloured	10	10
458	50c. multicoloured	20	20
459	$4 black, mauve and yellow	90	1·10
MS460	114×99 mm. $2.50, multicoloured	55	75

74 Passengers alighting from British Airways Boeing 747

1979. 30th Anniv of International Civil Aviation Organization. Multicoloured.

461	75c. Type **74**	25	50
462	95c. Air traffic control	25	50
463	$1.25 Ground crew-man directing Douglas DC-8 on runway	25	50

1979. International Year of the Child (1st issue). Nos. 612/15 of Antigua optd **BARBUDA**.

464	25c. Yacht	20	15
465	50c. Rocket	30	25
466	90c. Car	40	35
467	$2 Toy train	80	60
MS468	80×112 mm. $5 Airplane	1·10	1·10

1979. Fish. Nos. 617/21 of Antigua optd **BARBUDA**.

469	30c. Yellow jack	20	15
470	50c. Blue-finned tuna	25	20
471	90c. Sailfish	30	30
472	$3 Wahoo	65	1·10
MS473	122×75 mm. $2.50, Great barracuda	1·00	1·25

1979. Death Bicentenary of Captain Cook. Nos. 622/6 of Antigua optd **BARBUDA**.

474	25c. Cook's Birthplace, Marton	25	25
475	50c. H.M.S. *Endeavour*	70	35
476	90c. Marine chronometer	70	40
477	$3 Landing at Botany Bay	1·50	1·00
MS478	110×85 mm. $2.50, H.M.S. *Resolution*	1·25	1·50

77 *Virgin with the Pear*

1979. International Year of the Child (2nd issue). Paintings by Durer. Multicoloured.

479	25c. Type **77**	15	15
480	50c. *Virgin with the Pink* (detail)	20	25
481	75c. *Virgin with the Pear* (different detail)	25	30
482	$1.25 *Nativity* (detail)	25	40
MS483	86×118 mm. Nos. 479/82	1·00	1·75

1979. Christmas. Nos. 627/31 of Antigua optd **BARBUDA**.

484	8c. The Holy Family	10	10
485	25c. Mary and Jesus on donkey	15	10
486	50c. Shepherd looking at star	25	15
487	$4 The Three Kings	85	80
MS488	113×94 mm. $3 Angel with trumpet	80	1·10

1980. Olympic Games, Moscow. Nos. 632/6 of Antigua optd **BARBUDA**.

489	10c. Javelin	10	10
490	25c. Running	15	10
491	$1 Pole vault	35	20
492	$2 Hurdles	55	40
MS493	127×96 mm. $3 Boxing	70	1·10

1980. "London 1980" International Stamp Exhibition. Nos. 452/5 optd **LONDON 1980**.

494	25c. 1d. stamp of 1863	35	20
495	50c. Penny Black	45	40
496	$1 Stage-coach and woman posting letter, c. 1840	85	65
497	$2 Modern mail transport	2·75	1·50

80 "Apollo 11" Crew Badge

1980. Tenth Anniv of "Apollo 11" Moon Landing. Multicoloured.

498 75c. Type **80** 60 25
499 95c. Plaque left on Moon 60 30
500 $1.25 Rejoining the mother-ship 70 50
501 $2 Lunar module 90 75
MS502 118×84 mm. Nos. 498/501 1·60 2·50

81 American Wigeon ("American Widgeon")

1980. Birds. Multicoloured.

503 1c. Type **81** 70 1·50
504 2c. Snowy plover 70 80
505 4c. Rose-breasted grosbeak 75 80
506 6c. Mangrove cuckoo 75 80
507 10c. Adelaide's warbler 75 70
508 15c. Scaly-breasted thrasher 80 70
509 20c. Yellow-crowned night heron 80 70
510 25c. Bridled quail dove 80 70
511 35c. Carib grackle 85 1·50
512 50c. Northern pintail 90 55
513 75c. Black-whispered vireo 1·00 55
514 $1 Blue-winged teal 1·25 80
515 $1.50 Green-throated carib (vert) 1·50 80
516 $2 Red-necked pigeon (vert) 2·25 1·25
517 $2.50 Wied's crested flycatcher ("Stolid Flycatcher") (vert) 2·75 1·50
518 $5 Yellow-bellied sapsucker (vert) 3·50 3·75
519 $7.50 Caribbean elaenia (vert) 4·00 6·50
520 $10 Great egret (vert) 4·00 5·00

1980. Famous Works of Art. Nos. 651/8 of Antigua optd **BARBUDA**.

521 10c. *David* (statue, Donatello) 10 10
522 30c. *The Birth of Venus* (painting, Sandro Botticelli) 15 15
523 50c. *Reclining Couple* (sarcophagus), Cerveteri 15 20
524 90c. *The Garden of Earthly Delights* (painting, Hieronymus Bosch) 20 25
525 $1 *Portinari Altarpiece* (painting, Hugo van der Goes) 20 25
526 $4 *Eleanora of Toledo and her Son Giovanni de'Medici* (painting, Agnolo Bronzino) 60 80
MS527 99×124 mm. $5 *The Holy Family* (painting, Rembrandt) 1·50 1·75

1980. 75th Anniv of Rotary International. Nos. 658/62 of Antigua optd **BARBUDA**.

528 30c. Rotary Headquarters 15 15
529 50c. Antigua Rotary banner 20 20
530 90c. Map of Antigua 25 25
531 $3 Paul P. Harris (founder) 65 65
MS532 102×77 mm. $5 Antigua flags and Rotary emblems 1·50 2·25

1980. 80th Birthday of the Queen Mother. Nos. 663/5 of Antigua optd **BARBUDA**.

533 10c. multicoloured 50 15
534 $2.50 multicoloured 1·25 1·50
MS535 68×88 mm. $3 multicoloured 2·00 1·75

1980. Birds. Nos. 666/70 of Antigua optd **BARBUDA**.

536 10c. Ringed kingfisher 3·25 1·00
537 30c. Plain pigeon 3·75 1·10
538 $1 Green-throated carib 5·00 3·00
539 $2 Black necked stilt 6·00 6·00
MS540 73×73 mm. $2.50, Roseate tern 6·50 2·75

1981. Sugar Cane Railway Locomotives. Nos. 681/5 of Antigua optd **BARBUDA**.

541 25c. Diesel locomotive No. 15 1·00 25
542 50c. Narrow-gauge steam locomotive 1·25 35
543 90c. Diesel locomotive Nos. 1 and 10 1·75 45
544 $3 Steam locomotive hauling sugar cane 3·25 1·40
MS545 82×111 mm. $2.50, Antigua sugar factory, railway yard and sheds 1·50 1·75

84 Florence Nightingale

1981. Famous Women.

546 **84** 50c. multicoloured 15 30
547 - 90c. multicoloured 40 55
548 - $1 multicoloured 35 60
549 - $4 black, brown and lilac 50 1·75

DESIGNS: 90c. Marie Curie; $1 Amy Johnson; $4 Eleanor Roosevelt.

85 Goofy in Motor-boat

1981. Walt Disney Cartoon Characters. Multicoloured.

550 10c. Type **85** 90 15
551 20c. Donald Duck reversing car into sea 1·25 20
552 25c. Mickey Mouse asking tug-boat to take on more than it can handle 1·40 30
553 30c. Porpoise turning tables on Goofy 1·40 35
554 35c. Goofy in sailing boat 1·40 35
555 40c. Mickey Mouse and boat being lifted out of water by fish 1·40 40
556 75c. Donald Duck fishing for flying-fish with butterfly net 2·00 60
557 $1 Minnie Mouse in brightly decorated sailing boat 2·00 80
558 $2 Chip and Dale on floating ship-in-bottle 2·50 1·40
MS559 127×101 mm. $2.50, Donald Duck 4·50 3·00

1981. Birth Centenary of Picasso. Nos. 697/701 of Antigua optd with **BARBUDA**.

560 10c. "Pipes of Pan" 10 10
561 50c. *Seated Harlequin* 25 15
562 90c. *Paulo as Harlequin* 35 30
563 $4 *Mother and Child* 90 1·00
MS564 115×140 mm. $5 *Three Musicians* (detail) 1·40 1·40

87/8 Buckingham Palace

1981. Royal Wedding (1st issue). Buildings. Each printed in black on either pink, green or lilac backgrounds.

565 $1 Type **87** 25 40
566 $1 Type **88** 25 40
567 $1.50 Caernarvon Castle (right) 30 50
568 $1.50 Caernarvon Castle (left) 30 50
569 $4 Highgrove House (right) 55 90
570 $4 Highgrove House (left) 55 90
MS571 75×90 mm. $5 black and yellow (St. Paul's Cathedral—26×32 mm) 80 1·25

Same prices for any background colour. The two versions of each value form composite designs.

1981. Royal Wedding (2nd issue). Nos. 702/5 of Antigua optd **BARBUDA**.

572 25c. Prince Charles and Lady Diana Spencer 15 15
573 50c. Glamis Castle 25 25
574 $4 Prince Charles skiing 75 1·00
MS575 95×85 mm. $5 Glass coach 90 90

89 "Integration and Travel"

1981. International Year of Disabled Persons (1st issue).

576 **89** 50c. multicoloured 25 20
577 - 90c. black, orange and green 25 25
578 - $1 black, blue and green 30 30
579 - $4 black, yellow and brown 45 85

DESIGNS: 90c. Braille and sign language; $1 "Helping hands"; $4 "Mobility aids for disabled".

See also Nos. 603/6.

1981. Royal Wedding (3rd issue). Nos. 706/12 of Antigua optd **BARBUDA**.

580 25c. Prince of Wales at Investiture, 1969 40 70
581 25c. Prince Charles as baby, 1948 40 70
582 $1 Prince Charles at R.A.F. College, Cranwell, 1971 50 85
583 $1 Prince Charles attending Hill House School, 1956 50 85
584 $2 Prince Charles and Lady Diana Spencer 75 1·00
585 $2 Prince Charles at Trinity College, 1967 75 1·00
586 $5 Prince Charles and Lady Diana 4·25 6·50

1981. Independence. No. 686/96 of Antigua additionally optd **BARBUDA**.

587 6c. Orchid tree 50 15
588 10c. Bougainvillea 55 15
589 20c. Flamboyant 70 20
590 25c. Hibiscus 80 25
591 35c. Flame of the wood 90 30
592 50c. Cannon at Fort James 1·10 45
593 75c. Premier's Office 1·25 75
594 $1 Potworks Dam 1·50 80
595 $2.50 Irrigation scheme, Diamond Estate 2·50 2·75
596 $5 Government House and Gardens 2·75 3·75
597 $10 Coolidge International Airport 4·50 6·00

1981. 50th Anniv of Antigua Girl Guide Movement. Nos. 713/16 of Antigua optd **BARBUDA**.

598 10c. Irene Joshua (founder) 55 10
599 50c. Campfire sing-song 1·25 30
600 90c. Sailing 1·75 45
601 $2.50 Animal tending 3·00 1·40
MS602 170×113 mm. $4 "The Annunciation" (Rubens) 3·50 3·50

1981. International Year of Disabled Persons (2nd issue). Sport for the Disabled. Nos. 728/32 of Antigua optd **BARBUDA**.

603 10c. Swimming 15 15
604 50c. Discus throwing 20 25
605 90c. Archery 45 45
606 $2 Baseball 60 1·50
MS607 108×84 mm. $4 Basketball 2·00 1·75

1981. Christmas. Paintings. Nos. 723/7 of Antigua optd **BARBUDA**.

608 8c. *Holy Night* (Jacques Stella) 10 10
609 30c. *Mary with Child* (Julius Schnorr von Carolfeld) 20 20
610 $1 *Virgin and Child* (Alsono Cano) 40 40
611 $3 *Virgin and Child* (Lorenzo di Credi) 1·10 1·10
MS612 77×111 mm. $5 *Holy Family* (Pieter von Avon) 1·75 2·25

93 Princess of Wales

1982. Birth of Prince William of Wales (1st issue).

613 **93** $1 multicoloured 75 50
614 **93** $2.50 multicoloured 1·00 1·10
615 **93** $5 multicoloured 1·60 1·75
MS616 88×108 mm. $4 multicoloured 2·00 2·10

1982. South Atlantic Fund. Nos. 580/6 surch **S. Atlantic Fund + 50c.**

617 25c.+50c. Prince of Wales at Investiture, 1969 30 50
618 25c.+50c. Prince Charles as baby, 1948 30 50
619 $1+50c. Prince Charles at R.A.F. College, Cranwell, 1971 50 75
620 $1+50c. Prince Charles attending Hill House School, 1956 50 75
621 $2+50c. Prince Charles and Lady Diana Spencer 75 1·10
622 $2+50c. Prince Charles at Trinity College, 1967 75 1·10
623 $5+50c. Prince Charles and Lady Diana Spencer 3·00 4·25

1982. 21st Birthday of Princess of Wales (1st issue). As Nos. 613/16 but inscr "Twenty First Birthday Greetings to H.R.H. The Princess of Wales".

624 $1 multicoloured 1·50 45
625 $2.50 multicoloured 2·25 1·25
626 $5 multicoloured 3·00 2·40
MS627 88×108 mm. $4 multicoloured 2·75 2·25

1982. 21st Birthday of Princess of Wales (2nd issue). Nos. 748/51 of Antigua optd **BARBUDA MAIL**.

628 90c. Queen's House, Greenwich 80 45
629 $1 Prince and Princess of Wales 1·25 50
630 $4 Princess of Wales 3·00 1·50
MS631 114×94 mm. $3 Angel with trumpet 1·75 2·00

1982. Birth of Prince William of Wales (2nd issue). Nos. 757/60 of Antigua further optd **BARBUDA MAIL**.

632 90c. Queen's House, Greenwich 80 45
633 $1 Prince and Princess of Wales 1·50 50
634 $4 Princess of Wales 3·25 2·00
MS635 102×75 mm. $5 Princess of Wales (different) 4·50 2·50

1982. Birth Centenary of Franklin D. Roosevelt and 250th Birth Anniv of George Washington. Nos. 761/8 of Antigua optd **BARBUDA MAIL**.

636 10c. Roosevelt in 1940 10 10
637 25c. Washington as blacksmith 15 15
638 45c. Churchill, Roosevelt and Stalin at Yalta Conference 2·00 25
639 60c. Washington crossing Delaware 20 25
640 $1 *Roosevelt Special* train 2·00 40
641 $3 Portrait of Roosevelt 60 90
MS642 92×87 mm. $4 Roosevelt and wife 1·00 1·75
MS643 92×87 mm. $4 Portrait of Washington 1·00 1·75

1982. Christmas. Religious Paintings by Raphael. Nos. 769/73 of Antigua optd **BARBUDA MAIL**.

644 10c. *Annunciation* 10 10
645 30c. *Adoration of the Magi* 15 15
646 $1 *Presentation at the Temple* 40 40
647 $4 *Coronation of the Virgin* 1·00 1·00
MS648 95×142 mm. $5 *Marriage of the Virgin* 1·25 2·00

1983. 500th Birth Anniv of Raphael. Details from *Galatea* Fresco. Nos. 774/8 of Antigua optd **BARBUDA MAIL**.

649 45c. Tritons and dolphins 20 20
650 50c. Sea Nymph carried off by Triton 20 20
651 60c. Winged angel steering dolphins (horiz) 25 25
652 $4 Cupids shooting arrows 1·00 1·00
MS653 101×102 mm. $5 Galatea pulled along by dolphins 1·25 2·00

1983. Commonwealth Day. Nos. 779/82 of Antigua optd **BARBUDA MAIL**.

654 25c. Pineapple produce 45 55
655 45c. Carnival 55 70
656 60c. Tourism 70 1·25
657 $3 Airport 1·50 3·50

1983. World Communications Year. Nos. 783/6 of Antigua optd **BARBUDA MAIL**.

658 15c. T.V. satellite coverage of Royal Wedding 2·00 25
659 50c. Police communications 5·00 90
660 60c. House-to-diesel train telephone call 3·00 90
661 $3 Satellite earth station with planets Jupiter and Saturn 4·25 2·50
MS662 100×90 mm. $5 "Comsat" satellite over West Indies 1·50 2·25

97 Vincenzo Lunardi's Balloon Flight, London, 1785

1983. Bicent of Manned Flight (1st issue). Multicoloured.

663 $1 Type **97** 35 35
664 $1.50 Montgolfier brothers' balloon flight, Paris, 1783 50 55
665 $2.50 Blanchard and Jeffries' Cross-Channel balloon flight, 1785 70 90
MS666 111×111 mm. $5 Maiden flight of airship LZ-127 *Graf Zeppelin*, 1928 2·00 2·75

See also Nos. 672/6.

1983. Whales. Nos. 788/93 of Antigua optd **BARBUDA MAIL**.

667 15c. Bottlenose dolphin 1·25 40
668 50c. Finback whale 4·00 1·60
669 60c. Bowhead whale 4·50 1·75
670 $3 Spectacled porpoise 5·50 4·25
MS671 122×101 mm. $5 Narwhal 6·00 4·50

1983. Bicentenary of Manned Flight (2nd issue). Nos. 811/15 of Antigua optd **BARBUDA MAIL**.

672 30c. Dornier Do-X flying boat 1·50 35
673 50c. Supermarine S6B seaplane 1·75 60
674 60c. Curtiss Sparrowhawk biplane and airship U.S.S. *Akron* 2·25 70
675 $4 Hot-air balloon *Pro-Juventute* 5·50 4·00
MS676 0×105 mm. $5 Airship LZ-127 *Graf Zeppelin* 3·75 4·25

1983. Nos. 565/70 surch.

677 45c. on $1 Type **87** 25 45
678 45c. on $1 Type **88** 25 45
679 50c. on $1.45 Caernarvon Castle (right) 25 45
680 50c. on $1.45 Caernarvon Castle (left) 25 45
681 60c. on $4 Highgrove House (left) 25 45

682	60c. on $4 Highgrove House (right)	25	45

1983. Nos. 793/810 of Antigua optd **BARBUDA MAIL**.

683	1c. Cashew nut	10	40
684	2c. Passion fruit	15	40
685	3c. Mango	15	40
686	5c. Grapefruit	15	40
687	10c. Pawpaw	20	30
688	15c. Breadfruit	40	20
689	20c. Coconut	50	30
690	25c. Oleander	50	20
691	30c. Banana	55	20
692	40c. Pineapple	65	25
693	45c. Cordia	70	30
694	50c. Cassia	80	30
695	60c. Poui	80	30
696	$1 Frangipani	1·10	50
697	$2 Flamboyant	1·75	1·50
698	$2.50 Lemon	2·00	2·00
699	$5 Lignum vitae	3·00	3·25
700	$10 National flag and coat of arms	4·50	6·00

1983. Christmas. 500th Birth Anniv of Raphael. Nos. 816/20 of Antigua optd **BARBUDA MAIL**.

701	10c. multicoloured	10	10
702	30c. multicoloured	10	20
703	$1 multicoloured	30	50
704	$4 multicoloured	1·00	1·50
MS705	101×131 mm. $5 multicoloured	1·40	2·50

1983. Bicentenary (1984) of Methodist Church. Nos. 821/4 of Antigua optd **BARBUDA MAIL**.

706	15c. Type **181**	20	15
707	50c. Nathaniel Gilbert (founder in Antigua)	30	25
708	60c. St. John Methodist Church steeple	30	30
709	$3 Ebenezer Methodist Church, St John's	80	1·00

100 Edward VII

1984. Members of British Royal Family. Multicoloured.

710	$1 Type **100**	70	1·50
711	$1 George V	70	1·50
712	$1 George VI	70	1·50
713	$1 Elizabeth II	70	1·50
714	$1 Charles, Prince of Wales	70	1·50
715	$1 Prince William of Wales	70	1·50

1984. Olympic Games, Los Angeles (1st issue). Nos. 825/9 of Antigua optd **BARBUDA MAIL**.

716	25c. Discus	25	20
717	50c. Gymnastics	40	40
718	90c. Hurdling	50	60
719	$3 Cycling	2·75	1·50
MS720	82×67 mm. $5 Volleyball	2·00	3·25

1984. Ships. Nos. 830/4 of Antigua optd **BARBUDA MAIL**.

721	45c. *Booker Vanguard* (freighter)	1·50	45
722	50c. *Canberra* (liner)	1·50	50
723	60c. Yachts	1·75	60
724	$4 *Fairwind* (cargo liner)	4·25	2·75
MS725	101×80 mm. $5 18th-century British man-o-war (vert)	4·50	4·25

1984. Universal Postal Union Congress, Hamburg. Nos. 835/8 of Antigua optd **BARBUDA MAIL**.

726	15c. Chenille	25	15
727	50c. Shell flower	30	30
728	60c. Anthurium	40	40
729	$3 Angels trumpet	75	1·25
MS730	100×75 mm. $5 Crown of Thorns	2·00	2·50

101 Olympic Stadium, Athens, 1896

1984. Olympic Games, Los Angeles (2nd issue). Multicoloured.

731	$1.50 Type **101**	40	90
732	$2.50 Olympic stadium, Los Angeles, 1984	60	1·50
733	$5 Athlete carrying Olympic torch	95	2·25
MS734	121×95 mm. No. 733	1·50	2·50

1984. Presidents of the United States of America. Nos. 856/63 of Antigua optd **BARBUDA MAIL**.

735	10c. Abraham Lincoln	10	10
736	20c. Harry Truman	15	15
737	30c. Dwight Eisenhower	20	25
738	40c. Ronald Reagan	25	30
739	90c. Gettysburg Address, 1863	40	55
740	$1.10 Formation of N.A.T.O., 1949	40	65
741	$1.50 Eisenhower during Second World War	45	70
742	$2 Reagan and Caribbean Basin Initiative	50	1·00

1984. Abolition of Slavery. Nos. 864/8 of Antigua optd **BARBUDA MAIL**.

743	40c. View of Moravian Mission	30	30
744	50c. Antigua Courthouse, 1823	40	40
745	60c. Planting sugar-cane, Monks Hill	45	45
746	$3 Boiling house, Delaps' Estate	1·40	1·40
MS747	95×70 mm. $5 Loading sugar, Willoughby Bay	2·00	2·50

1984. Songbirds. Nos. 869/74 of Antigua optd **BARBUDA MAIL**.

748	40c. Rufous-sided towhee	2·25	55
749	50c. Parula warbler	2·25	70
750	60c. House wren	2·25	75
751	$2 Ruby-crowned kinglet	3·25	2·00
752	$3 Common flicker ("Yellow-shafted Flicker")	3·50	2·75
MS753	76×76 mm. $5 Yellow-breasted chat	4·00	4·50

1984. 450th Death Anniv of Correggio (painter). Nos. 878/82 of Antigua optd **BARBUDA MAIL**.

754	25c. *The Virgin and Infant with Angels and Cherubs*	15	20
755	60c. *The Four Saints*	40	45
756	90c. *St. Catherine*	50	55
757	$3 *The Campori Madonna*	1·25	1·75
MS758	90×60 mm. $5 *St. John the Baptist*	1·75	3·25

1984. "Ausipex" International Stamp Exibition Melbourne. Australian Sports. Nos. 875/7 of Antigua optd **BARBUDA MAIL**.

759	$1 Grass-skiing	50	40
760	$5 Australian Football	1·50	2·25
MS761	108×78 mm. Boomerang-throwing	1·50	2·75

1984. 150th Birth Anniv of Edgar Degas (painter). Nos. 883/7 of Antigua optd **BARBUDA MAIL**.

762	15c. *The Blue Dancers*	10	10
763	50c. *The Pink Dancers*	30	40
764	70c. *Two Dancers*	45	55
765	$4 *Dancers at the Bar*	1·25	3·50
MS766	90×60 mm. $5 *The Folk Dancers* (40×27 mm)	1·75	2·75

1985. Famous People. Nos. 888/96 of Antigua optd **BARBUDA MAIL**.

767	60c. Winston Churchill	7·00	3·00
768	60c. Mahatma Gandhi	7·00	3·00
769	60c. John F. Kennedy	7·00	3·00
770	60c. Mao Tse-tung	7·00	3·00
771	$1 Churchill with General De Gaulle, Paris, 1944 (horiz)	7·00	3·00
772	$1 Gandhi leaving London by train, 1931 (horiz)	7·00	3·00
773	$1 Kennedy with Chancellor Adenauer and Mayor Brandt, Berlin, 1963 (horiz)	7·00	3·00
774	$1 Mao Tse-tung with Lin Piao, Peking, 1969 (horiz)	7·00	3·00
MS775	114×80 mm. $5 Flags of Great Britain, India, the United States and China	12·00	8·50

103 Lady Elizabeth Bowes-Lyon, 1907, and Camellias

1985. Life and Times of Queen Elizabeth the Queen Mother. Multicoloured.

776	15c. Type **103**	35	20
777	45c. Duchess of York, 1926, and "Elizabeth of Glamis" roses	45	25
778	50c. The Queen Mother after the Coronation, 1937	45	25
779	60c. In Garter robes, 1971, and dog roses	45	30
780	90c. Attending Royal Variety Show, 1967, and red Hibiscus	60	45
781	$1 The Queen Mother in 1982, and blue plumbago	75	1·10
782	$3 Receiving 82nd birthday gifts from children, and morning glory	95	2·50

104 Roseate Tern

1985. Birth Bicentenary of John J. Audubon (ornithologist) (1st issue). Designs showing original paintings. Multicoloured.

783	45c. Type **104**	20	30
784	50c. Mangrove cuckoo	20	30
785	60c. Yellow-crowned night heron	20	40
786	$5 Brown pelican	80	3·50

See also Nos. 794/7 and 914/17.

1985. Centenary (1986) of Statue of Liberty (1st issue). Nos. 907/13 of Antigua optd **BARBUDA MAIL**.

787	25c. Torch from statue in Madison Square Park, 1885	20	20
788	30c. Statue of Liberty and scaffolding ("Restoration and Renewal") (vert)	20	20
789	50c. Frederic Bartholdi (sculpture) supervising construction, 1876	30	30
790	90c. Close-up of Statue	55	55
791	$1 Statue and sailing ship ("Operation Sail", 1976) (vert)	80	60
792	$3 Dedication ceremony, 1886 (vert)	1·75	1·75
MS793	110×80 mm. $5 Port of New York	5·75	4·75

See also Nos. 987/96.

1985. Birth Bicentenary of John J. Audubon (ornithologist) (2nd issue). Nos. 924/8 of Antigua optd **BARBUDA MAIL**.

794	90c. Slavonian grebe ("Horned Grebe")	10·00	4·25
795	$1 British storm petrel ("Least Petrel")	10·00	4·50
796	$1.50 Great blue heron	11·00	8·50
797	$3 Double-crested cormorant (white phase)	16·00	13·00
MS798	103×72 mm. $5 White-tailed tropic bird (vert)	28·00	11·00

1985. Butterflies. Nos. 929/33 of Antigua optd **BARBUDA MAIL**.

799	25c. *Anaea cyanea*	7·00	1·25
800	60c. *Leodonta dysoni*	9·00	2·00
801	90c. *Junea doraete*	10·00	2·50
802	$4 *Prepona pylene*	19·00	19·00
MS803	132×105 mm. $5 *Caervois gerdtrudtus*	17·00	9·00

1985. Centenary of Motorcycle. Nos. 919/23 of Antigua optd **BARBUDA MAIL**.

804	10c. Triumph 2hp "Jap", 1903	1·25	40
805	30c. Indian "Arrow", 1949	1·75	45
806	60c. BMW "R100RS", 1976	2·25	70
807	$4 Harley Davidson "Model II", 1916	5·75	5·00
MS808	90×93 mm. $5 Laverda "Jota", 1975	7·00	4·00

1985. 85th Birthday of Queen Elizabeth the Queen Mother. Nos. 776/82 optd **4TH AUG 1900–1985**.

809	15c. Type **103**	75	50
810	45c. Duchess of York, 1926 and "Elizabeth of Glamis" roses	1·10	60
811	50c. The Queen Mother after the Coronation, 1937	1·10	60
812	60c. In Garter robes, 1971, and dog roses	1·25	1·00
813	90c. Attending Royal Variey Show, 1967, and red hibiscus	1·25	1·25
814	$2 The Queen Mother in 1982, and blue plumbago	1·40	3·75
815	$3 Receiving 82nd birthday gifts from children, and morning glory	1·50	3·75

1985. Native American Artefacts. Nos. 914/18 of Antigua optd **BARBUDA MAIL**.

816	15c. Arawak pot sherd and Indians making clay utensils	15	10
817	50c. Arawak body design and Arawak Indians tattooing	25	25
818	60c. Head of the god "Yocahu" and Indians harvesting manioc	35	35
819	$3 Carib war club and Carib Indians going into battle	1·25	1·50
MS820	97×68 mm. $5 Taino Indians worshiping stone idol	2·00	3·00

1985. 40th Anniv of International Civil Aviation Organization. Nos. 934/8 of Antigua optd **BARBUDA MAIL**.

821	30c. Cessna Skyhawk	2·75	75
822	90c. Fokker D.VII	3·75	1·25
823	$1.50 SPAD VII	4·75	6·00
824	$3 Boeing 747	6·50	9·00
MS825	97×83 mm. De Havilland D.H.C.6 Twin Otter	3·25	3·50

1985. Life and Times of Queen Elizabeth the Queen Mother (2nd series). Nos. 946/9 of Antigua optd **BARBUDA MAIL**.

826	$1 The Queen Mother attending church	6·00	2·50
827	$1.50 Watching children playing in London garden	7·00	3·00
828	$2.50 The Queen Mother in 1979	8·00	3·50
MS829	56×85 mm. $5 With Prince Edward at Royal Wedding, 1981	17·00	11·00

1985. 850th Birth Anniv of Maimonides (physician philosopher and scholar). Nos. 939/40 of Antigua optd **BARBUDA MAIL**.

830	$2 green	4·50	4·50
MS831	70×84 mm. $5 brown	4·25	4·50

1985. Marine Life. Nos. 950/4 of Antigua optd **BARBUDA MAIL**.

832	15c. Magnificent frigate bird	7·00	1·25
833	45c. Brain coral	7·00	80
834	60c. Cushion star	7·00	1·25
835	$3 Spotted moray	15·00	5·50
MS836	110×80 mm. $5 Elkhorn coral	18·00	6·50

1986. International Youth Year. Nos. 941/5 of Antigua optd **BARBUDA MAIL**.

837	25c. Young farmers with produce	15	15
838	50c. Hotel management trainees	25	30
839	60c. Girls with goat and boys with football ("Environment")	30	35
840	$3 Windsurfing ("Leisure")	1·50	1·60
MS841	102×72 mm. $5 Young people with Antiguan flag	2·75	3·25

1986. Royal Visit. Nos. 965/8 of Antigua optd **BARBUDA MAIL**.

842	60c. Flags of Great Britain and Antigua	3·75	50
843	$1 Queen Elizabeth II (vert)	3·00	65
844	$4 Royal Yacht *Britannia*	8·50	2·50
MS845	110×83 mm. $5 Map of Antigua	12·00	4·00

1986. 75th Anniv of Girl Guide Movement. Nos. 955/9 of Antigua optd **BARBUDA MAIL**.

846	15c. Girl Guides nursing	1·50	80
847	45c. Open-air Girl Guide meeting	2·75	1·75
848	60c. Lord and Lady Baden-Powell	2·75	2·50
849	$3 Girl Guides gathering flowers	7·50	9·50
MS850	67×96 mm. $5 Barn swallow (Nature study)	35·00	23·00

1986. 300th Birth Anniv of Johann Sebastian Bach (composer). Nos. 960/4 of Antigua optd **BARBUDA MAIL**.

851	25c. multicoloured	3·50	70
852	50c. multicoloured	3·75	1·40
853	$1 multicoloured	5·00	2·00
854	$3 multicoloured	8·50	9·00
MS855	104×73 mm. $5 black and grey	27·00	12·00

1986. Christmas. Religious Paintings. Nos. 985/8 of Antigua optd **BARBUDA MAIL**.

856	10c. *Madonna and Child* (De Landi)	40	30
857	25c. *Madonna and Child* (Berlinghiero)	80	50
858	60c. *The Nativity* (Fra Angelico)	1·50	1·00
859	$4 *Presentation in the Temple* (Giovanni di Paolo)	4·00	7·00
MS860	113×81 mm. $5 *The Nativity* (Antoniazzo Romano)	4·25	5·50

108 Queen Elizabeth II meeting Members of Legislature

1986. 60th Birthday of Queen Elizabeth II (1st issue). Multicoloured.

861	$1 Type **108**	50	1·00
862	$2 Queen with Headmistress of Liberta School	60	1·10
863	$2.50 Queen greeted by Governor-General of Antigua	60	1·25
MS864	95×75 mm. $5 Queen Elizabeth in 1928 and 1986 (33×27 mm)	6·50	8·50

See also Nos. 872/5.

109 Halley's Comet over Barbuda Beach

1986. Appearance of Halley's Comet (1st issue). Multicoloured.

865	$1 Type **109**	60	1·25

866	$2.50 Early telescope and dish aerial (vert)	80	2·25
867	$5 Comet and world map	1·40	3·75

See also Nos. 886/9.

1986. 40th Anniv of United Nations Organization. Nos. 981/4 of Antigua optd **BARBUDA MAIL**.

868	40c. Benjamin Franklin and U.N. (New York) 1953 U.P.U. 5c. stamp	1·50	1·00
869	$1 George Washington Carver (agricultural chemist) and 1982 Nature Conservation 28c. stamp	2·25	2·25
870	$3 Charles Lindbergh (aviator) and 1978 I.C.A.O. 25c. stamp	4·00	5·00
MS871	101×77 mm. $5 Marc Chagell (artist) (vert)	13·00	14·00

1986. 60th Birthday of Queen Elizabeth II (2nd issue). Nos. 1005/8 of Antigua optd **BARBUDA MAIL**.

872	60c. black and yellow	2·50	1·25
873	$1 multicoloured	3·00	2·00
874	$4 multicoloured	4·75	4·50
MS875	120×85 mm. $5 black and brown	8·00	9·00

1986. World Cup Football Championship, Mexico. Nos. 995/9 of Antigua optd **BARBUDA MAIL**.

876	30c. Football, boots and trophy	4·00	1·00
877	60c. Goalkeeper (vert)	5·50	2·00
878	$1 Referee blowing whistle (vert)	6·00	2·25
879	$4 Ball in net	13·00	7·00
MS880	87×76 mm. $5 Two players competing for ball	24·00	15·00

1986. "Ameripex '86" International Stamp Exhibition, Chicago. Famous American Trains. Nos. 1014/18 of Antigua optd **BARBUDA MAIL**.

881	25c. *Hiawatha* express	2·00	1·50
882	50c. *Grand Canyon* express	2·75	2·25
883	$1 *Powhattan Arrow* express	3·50	3·00
884	$3 *Empire State* express	6·00	7·00
MS885	117×87 mm. $5 Southern Pacific *Daylight* express	9·00	9·50

1986. Appearance of Halley's Comet (2nd issue). Nos. 1000/4 of Antigua optd **BARBUDA MAIL**.

886	5c. Edmond Halley and Old Greenwich Observatory	2·75	1·00
887	10c. Messerschmitt Me 163B Komet (fighter aircraft), 1944	2·75	1·00
888	60c. Montezuma (Aztec Emperor) and Comet in 1517 (from "Historias de las Indias de Neuva Espana")	3·75	2·00
889	$4 Pocahontas saving Capt. John Smith and Comet in 1607	13·00	8·00
MS890	101×70 mm. $5 Halley's Comet over English Harbour, Antigua	7·00	5·00

1986. Royal Wedding. Nos. 1019/22 of Antigua optd **BARBUDA MAIL**.

891	45c. Prince Andrew and Miss Sarah Ferguson	75	50
892	60c. Prince Andrew	90	65
893	$4 Prince Andrew with Prince Philip	3·50	4·00
MS894	88×88 mm. $5 Prince Andrew and Miss Sarah Ferguson (different)	8·00	8·00

1986. Sea Shells. Nos. 1023/7 of Antigua optd **BARBUDA MAIL**.

895	15c. Fly-specked cerith	2·50	2·00
896	45c. Smooth Scotch bonnet	2·75	2·25
897	60c. West Indian crown conch	3·50	2·75
898	$3 Criboney murex	8·00	12·00
MS899	109×75 mm. $5 Colourful Atlantic moon (horiz)	20·00	18·00

1986. Flowers. Nos. 1028/36 of Antigua optd **BARBUDA MAIL**.

900	10c. *Nymphaea ampla* (water lily)	50	50
901	15c. Queen of the night	60	50
902	50c. Cup of gold	1·00	70
903	60c. Beach morning glory	1·10	70
904	70c. Golden trumpet	1·25	90
905	$1 Air plant	1·50	90
906	$3 Purple wreath	3·00	4·00
907	$4 Zephyr lily	3·50	4·25
MS908	Two sheets, each 102×72 mm. (a) $4 Dozakie. (b) $5 Four o'clock flower Set of 2 sheets	27·00	24·00

1986. Mushrooms. Nos. 1042/6 of Antigua optd **BARBUDA MAIL**.

909	10c. *Hygrocybe occidentalis var scarletina*	90	50
910	50c. *Trogia buccinalis*	3·25	1·75
911	$1 *Collybia subpruinosa*	4·75	2·75
912	$4 *Leucocoprinus brebissonii*	9·50	8·00
MS913	102×82 mm. $5 *Pyrrhoglossum pyrrhum*	27·00	18·00

1986. Birth Bicentenary of John J. Audubon (ornithologist) (3rd issue). Nos. 990/3 of Antigua optd **BARBUDA MAIL**.

914	60c. Mallard	7·50	2·50
915	90c. North American black duck ("Dusky Duck")	9·50	2·75
916	$1.50 American pintail ("Common Pintail")	13·00	8·50
917	$3 American wigeon ("Wigeon")	19·00	14·00

1987. Local Boats. Nos. 1009/13 of Antigua optd **BARBUDA MAIL**.

918	30c. Tugboat	1·50	1·50
919	60c. Game fishing boat	1·75	80
920	$1 Yacht	2·25	1·25
921	$4 Lugger with auxiliary sail	4·50	6·00
MS922	108×78 mm. $5 Boats under construction	24·00	17·00

1987. Centenary of First Benz Motor Car. Nos. 1052/60 of Antigua optd **BARBUDA MAIL**.

923	10c. Auburn "Speedster" (1933)	1·25	45
924	15c. Mercury "Sable" (1986)	1·50	50
925	50c. Cadillac (1959)	2·00	70
926	60c. Studebaker (1950)	2·00	70
927	70c. Lagonda "V-12" (1939)	2·00	1·00
928	$1 Adler "Standard" (1930)	2·50	1·00
929	$3 DKW (1956)	3·25	4·00
930	$4 Mercedes "500K" (1936)	3·25	4·00
MS931	Two sheets, each 99×70 mm. (a) $5 Daimler (1896). (b) $5 Mercedes "Knight" (1921) Set of 2 sheets	27·00	15·00

1987. World Cup Football Championship Winners, Mexico. Nos. 1037/40 of Antigua optd **BARBUDA MAIL**.

932	30c. Football, boots and trophy	4·50	1·00
933	60c. Goalkeeper (vert)	5·00	1·50
934	$1 Referee blowing whistle (vert)	6·00	2·25
935	$4 Ball in net	13·00	12·00

1987. America's Cup Yachting Championship. Nos. 1072/6 of Antigua optd **BARBUDA MAIL**.

936	30c. *Canada I* (1981)	90	40
937	60c. *Gretel II* (1970)	1·25	50
938	$1 *Sceptre* (1958)	1·60	80
939	$3 *Vigilant* (1893)	2·25	3·50
MS940	113×84 mm. $5 *Australia II* defeating *Liberty* (1983) (horiz)	4·75	5·00

1987. Marine Life. Nos. 1077/85 of Antigua optd **BARBUDA MAIL**.

941	15c. Bridled burrfish	7·00	1·50
942	30c. Common noddy ("Brown Noddy")	12·00	1·50
943	40c. Nassau grouper	9·00	1·50
944	50c. Laughing gull	14·00	2·25
945	60c. French angelfish	10·00	1·75
946	$1 Porkfish	10·00	2·50
947	$2 Royal tern	22·00	10·00
948	$3 Sooty tern	22·00	11·00
MS949	Two sheets, each 120×94 mm. (a) $5 Banded butterflyfish. (b) $5 Brown booby Set of 2 sheets	60·00	24·00

1987. Milestones of Transportation. Nos. 1100/9 of Antigua optd **BARBUDA MAIL**.

950	10c. *Spirit of Australia* (fastest powerboat), 1978	3·50	1·50
951	15c. Werner von Siemens's electric locomotive, 1879	4·50	1·25
952	30c. U.S.S. *Triton* (first submerged circumnavigation), 1960	4·50	1·25
953	50c. Trevithick's steam carriage (first passenger-carrying vehicle), 1801	5·00	2·00
954	60c. U.S.S. *New Jersey* (battleship), 1942	6·50	2·00
955	70c. Draisine bicycle, 1818	7·50	2·75
956	90c. *United States* (liner) (holder of the Blue Riband), 1952	7·50	2·25
957	$1.50 Cierva C.4 (first autogyro), 1923	7·50	7·00
958	$2 Curtiss NC-4 flying boat (first transatlantic flight), 1919	8·00	8·00
959	$3 *Queen Elizabeth 2* (liner), 1969	12·00	10·00

110 Shore Crab

1987. Marine Life. Multicoloured.

960	5c. Type **110**	10	20
961	10c. Sea cucumber	10	20
962	15c. Stop-light parrotfish	10	20
963	25c. Banded coral shrimp	15	20
964	35c. Spotted drum	15	20
965	60c. Thorny starfish	20	40
966	75c. Atlantic trumpet triton	20	60
967	90c. Feather star and yellow beaker sponge	20	65
968	$1 Blue gorgonian (vert)	20	65
969	$1.25 Slender filefish (vert)	20	85
970	$5 Barred hamlet (vert)	45	3·50
971	$7.50 Royal gramma ("Fairy basslet") (vert)	60	4·50
972	$10 Fire coral and banded butterflyfish (vert)	75	5·00

1987. Olympic Games, Seoul (1988). Nos. 1086/90 of Antigua optd **BARBUDA MAIL**.

973	10c. Handball	1·00	50
974	60c. Fencing	2·25	80
975	$1 Gymnastics	2·75	1·40
976	$3 Football	4·50	5·50
MS977	100×77 mm. $5 Boxing gloves	9·00	4·75

1987. Birth Centenary of Marc Chagall (artist). Nos. 1091/9 of Antigua optd **BARBUDA MAIL**.

978	10c. *The Profile*	25	40
979	30c. *Portrait of the Artist's Sister*	35	20
980	40c. *Bride with Fan*	40	30
981	60c. *David in Profile*	45	30
982	90c. *Fiancee with Bouquet*	60	50
983	$1 *Self Portrait with Brushes*	70	55
984	$3 *The Walk*	2·00	2·50
985	$4 *Three Candles*	2·25	2·75
MS986	Two sheets, each 110×95 mm. (a) $5 *Fall of Icarus* (104×89 mm). (b) $5 *Myth of Orpheus* (104×89 mm) Set of 2 sheets	7·00	8·00

1987. Centenary (1986) of Statue of Liberty (2nd issue). Nos. 1110/19 of Antigua optd **BARBUDA MAIL**.

987	15c. Lee Iacocoa at unveiling of restored statue	20	20
988	30c. Statue at sunset (side view)	30	20
989	45c. Aerial view of head	45	25
990	50c. Lee Iacocoa and torch	50	30
991	60c. Workmen inside head of statue (horiz)	55	30
992	90c. Restoration work (horiz)	70	50
993	$1 Head of statue	80	75
994	$2 Statue at sunset (front view)	1·25	1·75
995	$3 Inspecting restoration work (horiz)	1·60	2·50
996	$5 Statue at night	2·50	3·50

1987. Entertainers. Nos. 1120/7 of Antigua optd **BARBUDA MAIL**.

997	15c. Grace Kelly	2·00	70
998	30c. Marilyn Monroe	5·00	1·25
999	45c. Orson Welles	2·00	75
1000	50c. Judy Garland	2·00	1·00
1001	60c. John Lennon	15·00	2·50
1002	$1 Rock Hudson	2·75	1·75
1003	$1 John Wayne	4·50	3·50
1004	$3 Elvis Presley	26·00	11·00

1987. "Capex '87" International Stamp Exhibition, Toronto. Reptiles and Amphibians. Nos. 1133/7 of Antigua optd **BARBUDA MAIL**.

1005	30c. Whistling frog	7·00	2·00
1006	60c. Croaking lizard	8·00	2·00
1007	$1 Antiguan anole	9·00	3·00
1008	$3 Red-footed tortoise	18·00	17·00
MS1009	106×76 mm. $5 Ground lizard	30·00	12·00

1988. Christmas. Religious Paintings. Nos. 1144/8 of Antigua optd **BARBUDA MAIL**.

1010	45c. *Madonna and Child* (Bernardo Daddi)	2·00	30
1011	60c. St. Joseph (detail, *The Nativity* (Sano di Pietro))	2·00	55
1012	$1 Virgin Mary (detail, *The Nativity* (Sano di Pietro))	2·25	1·25
1013	$4 *Music-making Angel* (Melozzo da Forli)	6·50	8·50
MS1014	90×70 mm. $5 *The Flight into Egypt* (Sano di Pietro)	9·00	6·50

1988. Salvation Army's Community Service. Nos. 1163/71 of Antigua optd **BARBUDA MAIL**.

1015	25c. First aid at daycare centre, Antigua	2·25	1·00
1016	30c. Giving penicillin injection, Indonesia	2·25	1·00
1017	40c. Children at daycare centre, Bolivia	2·25	1·00
1018	45c. Rehabilitation of the handicapped, India	2·25	1·00
1019	50c. Training blind man, Kenya	2·75	1·50
1020	60c. Weighing baby, Ghana	2·75	1·50
1021	$1 Training typist, Zambia	3·25	2·50
1022	$2 Emergency food kitchen, Sri Lanka	3·75	4·00
MS1023	152×83 mm. $5 General Eva Burrows	28·00	25·00

1988. Bicentenary of U.S. Constitution. Nos. 1139/43 of Antigua optd **BARBUDA MAIL**.

1024	15c. House of Burgesses, Virginia ("Freedom of Speech")	10	15
1025	45c. State Seal, Connecticut	20	25
1026	60c. State Seal, Delaware	25	40
1027	$4 Gouverneur Morris (Pennsylvania delegate) (vert)	1·75	3·25
MS1028	105×75 mm. $5 Roger Sherman (Connecticut delegate) (vert)	2·75	3·25

1988. Royal Ruby Wedding. Nos. 1149/53 of Antigua optd **BARBUDA MAIL**.

1029	25c. brown, black and blue	2·75	40
1030	60c. multicoloured	3·25	65
1031	$2 brown, black and green	7·00	2·50
1032	$3 multicoloured	8·00	3·00
MS1033	102×77 mm. $5 multicoloured	17·00	6·50

1988. Birds of Antigua. Nos. 1154/62 of Antigua optd **BARBUDA MAIL**.

1034	10c. Great blue heron	4·00	1·75
1035	15c. Ringed kingfisher (horiz)	4·25	1·75
1036	50c. Bananaquit (horiz)	6·00	1·75
1037	60c. American purple gallinule ("Purple Gallinule") (horiz)	6·00	1·75
1038	70c. Blue-hooded euphonia (horiz)	6·50	2·75
1039	$1 Brown-throated concure ("Caribbean Parakeet")	7·50	2·75
1040	$3 Troupial (horiz)	13·00	8·50
1041	$4 Purple-throated carib (horiz)	13·00	8·50
MS1042	Two sheets, each 115×86 mm. (a) $5 Greater flamingo. (b) $5 Brown pelican Set of 2 sheets	40·00	19·00

1988. 500th Anniv (1992) of Discovery of America by Columbus (1st issue). Nos. 1172/80 of Antigua optd **BARBUDA MAIL**.

1043	10c. Columbus's second fleet, 1493	3·50	1·00
1044	30c. Painos Indian village and fleet	3·50	80
1045	45c. *Santa Mariagalante* (flag-ship) and Painos village	4·25	80
1046	60c. Painos Indians offering Columbus fruit and vegetables	3·00	85
1047	90c. Painos Indian and Columbus with scarlet macaw	7·50	1·75
1048	$1 Columbus landing on island	6·00	1·75
1049	$3 Spanish soldier and fleet	7·50	4·50
1050	$4 Fleet under sail	7·50	4·50
MS1051	Two sheets, each 110×80 mm. (a) $5 Queen Isabella's cross. (b) $5 Gold coin of Ferdinand and Isabella Set of 2 sheets	20·00	14·00

See also Nos. 1112/16, 1177/85, 1285/93, 1374/80 and 1381/2.

1988. 500th Birth Anniv of Titian. Nos. 1181/9 of Antigua optd **BARBUDA MAIL**.

1052	30c. *Bust of Christ*	1·00	20
1053	40c. *Scourging of Christ*	1·25	25
1054	45c. *Madonna in Glory with Saints*	1·25	25
1055	50c. *The Averoldi Polyptych* (detail)	1·40	30
1056	$1 *Christ Crowned with Thorns*	2·00	55
1057	$2 *Christ Mocked*	2·75	1·50
1058	$3 *Christ and Simon of Cyrene*	3·25	2·75
1059	$4 *Crucifixion with Virgin and Saints*	3·25	3·00
MS1060	Two sheets, each 110×95 mm. (a) $5 *Ecce Homo* (detail). (b) $5 *Noli me Tangere* (detail) Set of 2 sheets	11·00	8·00

1988. 16th World Scout Jamboree, Australia. Nos. 1128/32 of Antigua optd **BARBUDA MAIL**.

1061	10c. Scouts around campfire and red kangaroo	2·50	1·00
1062	60c. Scouts canoeing and blue-winged kookaburra	8·50	1·50
1063	$1 Scouts on assault course and ring-tailed rock wallaby	4·00	1·75
1064	$3 Field kitchen and koala	7·50	6·50
MS1065	103×78 mm. $5 Flags of Antigua, Australia and Scout Movement	10·00	6·50

1988. Sailing Week. Nos. 1190/4 of Antigua optd **BARBUDA MAIL**.

1066	30c. Two yachts rounding buoy	60	35
1067	60c. Three yachts	1·00	70
1068	$1 British yacht under way	1·25	1·10
1069	$3 Three yachts (different)	2·25	2·75
MS1070	103×92 mm. $5 Two yachts	7·50	4·50

1988. Flowering Trees. Nos. 1213/21 of Antigua optd **BARBUDA MAIL**.

1071	10c. Jacaranda	15	20
1072	30c. Cordia	30	20
1073	50c. Orchid tree	40	25
1074	90c. Flamboyant	60	45
1075	$1 African tulip tree	70	60
1076	$2 Potato tree	1·25	1·50
1077	$3 Crepe myrtle	1·50	2·00
1078	$4 Pitch apple	1·75	2·50
MS1079	Two sheets, each 106×76 mm. (a) $5 Cassia. (b) $5 Chinaberry Set of 2 sheets	6·00	6·50

1988. Olympic Games, Seoul. Nos. 1222/6 of Antigua optd **BARBUDA MAIL**.

1080	40c. Gymnastics	1·50	40
1081	60c. Weightlifting	1·75	55
1082	$1 Water polo (horiz)	2·00	1·00
1083	$3 Boxing (horiz)	2·75	3·00
MS1084	114×80 mm. $5 Runner with Olympic torch	3·00	2·40

1988. Caribbean Butterflies. Nos. 1227/44 of Antigua optd **BARBUDA MAIL**.

1085	1c. *Danaus plexippus*	50	1·00
1086	2c. *Greta diaphanus*	50	1·00
1087	3c. *Calisto archebates*	60	1·00
1088	5c. *Hamadryas feronia*	60	1·00
1089	10c. *Mestra dorcas*	75	1·00
1090	15c. *Hypolimnas misippus*	1·00	60
1091	20c. *Dione juno*	1·25	60
1092	25c. *Heliconius charithonia*	1·25	60

1093 30c. *Eurema pyro* 1·25 60
1094 40c. *Papilio androgeus* 1·50 60
1095 45c. *Anteos maerula* 1·50 60
1096 50c. *Aphrissa orbis* 1·75 85
1097 60c. *Astraptes xagua* 1·75 70
1098 $1 *Heliopetes arsalte* 2·50 1·00
1099 $2 *Polites baracoa* 4·25 4·25
1100 $2.50 *Phocides pigmalion* 4·50 4·75
1101 $5 *Prepona amphitoe* 6·00 7·00
1102 $10 *Oarisma nanus* 9·00 10·00
1102a $20 *Parides lycimenes* 16·00 17·00

1989. 25th Death Anniv of John F. Kennedy (American statesman). Nos. 1245/53 of Antigua optd **BARBUDA MAIL**.
1103 1c. President Kennedy and family 10 75
1104 2c. Kennedy commanding *PT109* 10 75
1105 3c. Funeral cortege 10 75
1106 4c. In motorcade, Mexico 10 75
1107 30c. As 1c. 1·50 50
1108 60c. As 4c. 3·50 60
1109 $1 As 3c. 3·50 1·50
1110 $4 As 2c. 9·00 11·00
MS1111 105×75 mm. $5 Kennedy taking presidential oath of office 4·50 6·00

1989. 500th Anniv (1992) of Discovery of America by Columbus (2nd issue). Pre-Columbian Arawak Society. Nos. 1267/71 of Antigua optd **BARBUDA MAIL**.
1112 $1.50 Arawak warriors 4·50 4·50
1113 $1.50 Whip dancers 4·50 4·50
1114 $1.50 Whip dancers and chief with pineapple 4·50 4·50
1115 $1.50 Family and camp fire 4·50 4·50
MS1116 71×84 mm. $6 Arawak chief 5·50 6·50

1989. 50th Anniv of First Jet Flight. Nos. 1272/80 of Antigua optd **BARBUDA MAIL**.
1117 10c. Hawker Siddeley Comet 4 airliner 3·50 2·00
1118 30c. Messerschmitt Me 262 fighter 4·50 1·50
1119 40c. Boeing 707 airliner 4·75 2·25
1120 60c. Canadair CL-13 Sabre fighter 6·00 1·25
1121 $1 Lockheed Starfighters 7·00 2·50
1122 $2 Douglas DC-10 airliner 9·00 8·00
1123 $3 Boeing 747-300/400 airliner 10·00 11·00
1124 $4 McDonnell Douglas Phantom II fighter 10·00 11·00
MS1125 Two sheets, each 114×83 mm. (a) $7 Grumman F-14 Tomcat fighter. (b) $7 Concorde airliner Set of 2 sheets 55·00 40·00

1989. Caribbean Cruise Ships. Nos. 1281/9 of Antigua optd **BARBUDA MAIL**.
1126 25c. *Festivale* 4·00 1·50
1127 45c. *Southward* 4·25 1·50
1128 50c. *Sagafjord* 4·25 1·75
1129 60c. *Daphne* 4·25 1·75
1130 75c. *Cunard Countess* 4·50 2·75
1131 90c. *Song of America* 4·50 2·75
1132 $3 *Island Princess* 12·00 10·00
1133 $4 *Galileo* 12·00 10·00
MS1134 (a) 113×87 mm. $6 *Norway*. (b) 111×82 mm. $6 *Oceanic* Set of 2 sheets 55·00 38·00

1989. Japanese Art. Paintings by Hiroshige. Nos. 1290/8 of Antigua optd **BARBUDA MAIL**.
1135 25c. *Fish swimming by Duck half-submerged in Stream* 4·50 1·00
1136 45c. *Crane and Wave* 5·50 1·00
1137 50c. *Sparrows and Morning Glories* 5·50 1·50
1138 60c. *Crested Blackbird and Flowering Cherry* 5·50 1·50
1139 $1 *Great Knot sitting among Water Grass* 6·50 1·75
1140 $2 *Goose on a Bank of Water* 8·50 4·25
1141 $3 *"Black Paradise Fly-catcher and Blossoms* 10·00 5·00
1142 $4 *Sleepy Owl perched on a Pine Branch* 11·00 5·50
MS1143 Two sheets, each 102×75 mm. (a) $5 *Bullfinch flying near a Clematis Branch*. (b) $5 *Titmouse on a Cherry Branch* Set of 2 sheets 50·00 23·00

1989. World Cup Football Championship, Italy (1990). Nos. 1308/12 of Antigua optd **BARBUDA MAIL**.
1144 15c. Goalkeeper 2·00 65
1145 25c. Goalkeeper moving towards ball 2·00 65
1146 $1 Goalkeeper reaching for ball 5·00 2·00
1147 $4 Goalkeeper saving goal 8·00 10·00
MS1148 Two sheets, each 75×105 mm. (a) $5 Three players competing for ball (horiz). (b) $5 Ball and players' legs (horiz) Set of 2 sheets 38·00 32·00

1989. Christmas. Paintings by Raphael and Giotto. Nos. 1351/9 of Antigua optd **BARBUDA MAIL**.
1149 10c. *The Small Cowper Madonna* (Raphael) 40 30
1150 25c. *Madonna of the Goldfinch* (Raphael) 50 20
1151 30c. *The Alba Madonna(* Raphael) 50 20
1152 50c. Saint (detail, *Bologna Altarpiece*) (Giotto) 80 30
1153 60c. Angel (detail, *Bologna Altarpiece*) (Giotto) 85 45
1154 70c. Angel slaying serpent (detail, *Bologna Altarpiece*) (Giotto) 90 60
1155 $4 Evangelist (detail, *Bologna Altarpiece*) (Giotto) 3·00 4·50
1156 $5 *Madonna of Foligno* (Raphael) 3·00 4·50
MS1157 wo sheets, each 71×96 mm. (a) $5 *"The Marriage of the Virgin* (detail) (Raphael). (b) $5 Madonna and Child (detail, *Bologna Altarpiece*) (Giotto) Set of 2 sheets 13·00 15·00

1990. Fungi. Nos. 1313/21 of Antigua optd **BARBUDA MAIL**.
1158 10c. *Mycena pura* 2·50 1·50
1159 25c. *Psathyrella turberculata* (vert) 2·75 65
1160 50c. *Psilocybe cubensis* 3·25 1·00
1161 60c. *Leptonia caeruleocapitata* (vert) 3·25 1·00
1162 75c. *Xeromphalina tenuipes* (vert) 3·25 1·40
1163 $1 *Chlorophyllum molybdites* (vert) 3·50 1·40
1164 $3 *Marasmius haematocephalus* 6·00 7·50
1165 $4 *Cantharellus cinnabarinus* 6·00 7·50
MS1166 Two sheets, each 88×62 mm. (a) $6 *Leucopaxillus gracillimus* (vert). (b) $6 *Volvariella volvacea* Set of 2 sheets 38·00 23·00

1990. Local Fauna. Nos. 1322/6 optd **BARBUDA MAIL**.
1167 25c. Desmarest's hutia 1·00 60
1168 45c. Caribbean monk seal 2·50 1·25
1169 60c. Mustache bat (vert) 1·75 1·25
1170 $4 American manatee (vert) 4·25 6·50
MS1171 113×87 mm. $5 West Indian giant rice rat 22·00 22·00

1990. 20th Anniv of First Manned Landing on Moon. Nos. 1346/50 optd **BARBUDA MAIL**.
1172 10c. Launch of "Apollo 11" 3·25 1·50
1173 45c. Aldrin on Moon 6·00 80
1174 $1 Module "Eagle" over Moon (horiz) 7·50 2·75
1175 $4 Recovery of "Apollo 11" crew after splashdown (horiz) 13·00 13·00
MS1176 107×77 mm. $5 Astronaut Neil Armstrong 24·00 23·00

1990. 500th Anniv (1992) of Discovery of America by Columbus (3rd issue). New World Natural History – Marine Life. Nos. 1360/8 of Antigua optd **BARBUDA MAIL**.
1177 10c. Star-eyed hermit crab 1·75 1·75
1178 20c. Spiny lobster 2·25 1·75
1179 25c. Magnificent banded fanworm 2·25 1·75
1180 45c. Cannonball jellyfish 3·25 1·00
1181 60c. Red-spiny sea star 3·50 1·00
1182 $2 Peppermint shrimp 4·75 5·00
1183 $3 Coral crab 5·00 6·00
1184 $4 Branching fire coral 5·00 6·00
MS1185 Two sheets, each 101×69 mm. (a) $5 Common sea fan. (b) Portuguese man-o-war Set of 2 sheets 28·00 27·00

1990. "EXPO 90" International Gardens and Greenery Exhibition, Osaka. Orchids. Nos. 1369/77 of Antigua optd **BARBUDA MAIL**.
1186 15c. *Vanilla mexicana* 2·00 80
1187 45c. *Epidendrum ibaguense* 2·50 80
1188 50c. *Epidendrum secundum* 2·50 90
1189 60c. *Maxillaria conferta* 2·75 1·10
1190 $1 *Onicidium altissimum* 3·00 1·75
1191 $2 *Spiranthes lanceolata* 5·00 5·00
1192 $3 *Tonopsis utricularioides* 5·50 6·50
1193 $5 *Epidendrum nocturnum* 7·00 8·50
MS1194 Two sheets, each 101×69 mm. (a) $6 *Octomeria graminifolia*. (b) $6 *"Rodriguezia lanceolata* Set of 2 sheets 38·00 23·00

1990. Reef Fishes. Nos. 1386/94 of Antigua optd **BARBUDA MAIL**.
1195 10c. Flamefish 2·50 1·75
1196 15c. Coney 2·50 1·75
1197 50c. Long-spined squirrelfish 3·50 1·50
1198 60c. Sergeant major 3·50 1·50
1199 $1 Yellow-tailed snapper 4·25 2·50
1200 $2 Rock beauty 7·00 7·00
1201 $3 Spanish hogfish 9·00 10·00
1202 $4 Striped parrotfish 9·00 10·00
MS1203 Two sheets, each 99×70 mm. (a) $5 Black-barred soldierfish. (b) $5 Four-eyed butterflyfish Set of 2 sheets 38·00 32·00

1990. First Anniv of Hurricane Hugo. Nos. 971/2 surch **1st Anniversary Hurricane Hugo 16th September, 1989-1990** and new value.
1204 $5 on $7.50 Fairy basslet (vert) 12·00 15·00
1205 $7.50 on $10 Fire coral and butterfly fish (vert) 13·00 17·00

1990. 90th Birthday of Queen Elizabeth the Queen Mother. Nos. 1415/19 of Antigua optd **BARBUDA MAIL**.
1206 15c. multicoloured 8·00 1·75
1207 35c. multicoloured 11·00 1·50
1208 75c. multicoloured 17·00 3·25
1209 $3 multicoloured 30·00 19·00
MS1210 67×98 mm. $6 multicoloured 55·00 26·00

1990. Achievements in Space. Nos. 1395/414 of Antigua optd **BARBUDA MAIL**.
1211 45c. "Voyager 2" passing Saturn 3·75 3·25
1212 45c. "Pioneer 11" photographing Saturn 3·75 3·25
1213 45c. Astronaut in transporter 3·75 3·25
1214 45c. Space shuttle *Columbia* 3·75 3·25
1215 45c. "Apollo 10" command module on parachutes 3·75 3·25
1216 45c. "Skylab" space station 3·75 3·25
1217 45c. Astronaut Edward White in space 3·75 3·25
1218 45c. "Apollo" spacecraft on joint mission 3·75 3·25
1219 45c. "Soyuz" spacecraft on joint mission 3·75 3·25
1220 45c. "Mariner 1" passing Venus 3·75 3·25
1221 45c. "Gemini 4" capsule 3·75 3·25
1222 45c. "Sputnik 1" 3·75 3·25
1223 45c. Hubble space telescope 3·75 3·25
1224 45c. North American X-15 rocket plane 3·75 3·25
1225 45c. Bell XS-1 airplane 3·75 3·25
1226 45c. "Apollo 17" astronaut and lunar rock formation 3·75 3·25
1227 45c. Lunar rover 3·75 3·25
1228 45c. "Apollo 14" lunar module 3·75 3·25
1229 45c. Astronaut Buzz Aldrin on Moon 3·75 3·25
1230 45c. Soviet "Lunokhod" lunar vehicle 3·75 3·25

1990. Christmas. Paintings by Renaissance Masters. Nos. 1457/65 of Antigua optd **BARBUDA MAIL**.
1231 25c. *Madonna and Child with Saints* (detail, Sebastiano del Piombo) 2·25 60
1232 30c. *Virgin and Child with Angels* (detail, Grunewald) (vert) 2·25 60
1233 40c. *The Holy Family and a Shepherd* (detail, Titian) 2·25 60
1234 60c. *Virgin and Child* (detail, Lippi) (vert) 3·00 1·10
1235 $1 *Jesus, St. John and Two Angels* (Rubens) 3·75 1·50
1236 $2 *Adoration of the Shepherds* (detail, Vincenzo Catena) 5·50 6·00
1237 $4 *Adoration of the Magi* (detail, Giorgione) 8·50 9·50
1238 $5 *Virgin and Child adored by Warriors* (detail, Vincenzo Catena) 8·50 9·50
MS1239 Two sheets, each 71×101 mm. (a) $6 *Allegory of the Blessings of Jacob* (detail, Rubens) (vert). (b) $6 *Adoration of the Magi* (detail, Fra Angelico) (vert) Set of 2 sheets 27·00 28·00

1991. 150th Anniv of the Penny Black. Nos. 1378/81 of Antigua optd **BARBUDA MAIL**.
1240 45c. green 5·00 1·00
1241 60c. mauve 5·00 1·10
1242 $5 blue 15·00 15·00
MS1243 102×80 mm. $6 purple 20·00 15·00

1991. "Stamp World London 90" International Stamp Exhibition. Nos. 1382/4 of Antigua optd **BARBUDA MAIL**.
1244 50c. green and red 5·00 1·00
1245 75c. brown and red 5·00 1·50
1246 $4 blue and red 15·00 15·00
MS1247 104×81 mm. $6 black and red 22·00 23·00

119 Troupial

1991. Wild Birds. Multicoloured.
1248 60c. Type **119** 2·25 65
1249 $2 Adelaide's warbler ("Christmas Bird") 3·75 3·00
1250 $4 Rose-breasted grosbeak 5·50 6·50
1251 $7 Wied's crested flycatcher ("Stolid Flycatcher") 7·50 11·00

1991. Olympic Games, Barcelona (1992). Nos. 1429/33 of Antigua optd **BARBUDA MAIL**.
1252 50c. Men's 20 kilometres walk 2·75 90
1253 75c. Triple jump 3·00 1·00
1254 $1 Men's 10,000 metres 3·25 1·75
1255 $5 Javelin 12·00 14·00
MS1256 100×70 mm. $6 Athlete lighting Olympic flame at Los Angeles Olympics 16·00 18·00

1991. Birds. Nos. 1448/56 of Antigua optd **BARBUDA MAIL**.
1257 10c. Pearly-eyed thrasher 3·00 1·75
1258 25c. Purple-throated carib 4·00 1·00
1259 50c. Common yellowthroat 5·00 1·25
1260 60c. American kestrel 5·00 1·25
1261 $1 Yellow-bellied sapsucker 5·50 2·00
1262 $2 American purple gallinule ("Purple Gallinule") 7·50 7·00
1263 $3 Yellow-crowned night heron 8·00 9·00
1264 $4 Blue-hooded euphonia 8·00 9·00
MS1265 Two sheets, each 76×60 mm. (a) $6 Brown pelican. (b) Magnificent frigate bird Set of 2 sheets 32·00 25·00

1991. 350th Death Anniv of Rubens. Nos. 1466/74 of Antigua optd **BARBUDA MAIL**.
1266 25c. *Rape of the Daughters of Leucippus* (detail) 2·50 80
1267 45c. *Bacchanal* (detail) 3·00 80
1268 50c. *Rape of the Sabine Women* (detail) 3·00 85
1269 60c. *Battle of the Amazons* (detail) 3·25 90
1270 $1 *Rape of the Sabine Women* (different detail) 3·75 1·75
1271 $2 *Bacchanal* (different detail) 6·00 6·50
1272 $3 *Rape of the Sabine Women* (different detail) 8·50 10·00
1273 $4 *Bacchanal* (different detail) 8·50 10·00
MS1274 Two sheets, each 111×71 mm. (a) $6 *Rape of Hippodameia* (detail). (b) *Battle of the Amazons* (different detail) Set of 2 sheets 30·00 32·00

1991. 50th Anniv of Second World War. Nos. 1475/88 of Antigua optd **BARBUDA MAIL**.
1275 10c. U.S. troops cross into Germany, 1944 3·25 2·25
1276 15c. Axis surrender in North Africa, 1943 3·75 2·00
1277 25c. U.S. tanks invade Kwajalein, 1944 4·00 1·50
1278 45c. Roosevelt and Churchill meet at Casablanca, 1943 12·00 2·50
1279 50c. Marshall Badoglio, Prime Minister of Italian anti-facist government, 1943 3·75 1·75
1280 $1 Lord Mountbatten, Supreme Allied Commander South-east Asia, 1943 15·00 4·75
1281 $2 Greek victory at Koritza, 1940 10·00 10·00
1282 $4 Anglo-Soviet mutual assistance pact, 1941 12·00 13·00
1283 $5 Operation Torch landings, 1942 13·00 13·00
MS1284 Two sheets, each 108×80 mm. (a) $6 Japanese attack on Pearl Harbor, 1941. (b) $6 U.S.A.A.F. daylight raid on Schweinfurt, 1943 Set of 2 sheets 60·00 40·00

1991. 500th Anniv (1992) of Discovery of America by Columbus (4th issue). History of Exploration. Nos. 1503/11 of Antigua optd **BARBUDA MAIL**.
1285 10c. multicoloured 2·25 2·00
1286 15c. multicoloured 2·50 2·00
1287 45c. multicoloured 3·50 1·00
1288 60c. multicoloured 3·75 1·25
1289 $1 multicoloured 4·00 2·00
1290 $2 multicoloured 6·50 6·00
1291 $4 multicoloured 10·00 11·00
1292 $5 multicoloured 10·00 11·00
MS1293 Two sheets, each 106×76 mm. (a) $6 black and red. (b) $6 black and red Set of 2 sheets 35·00 28·00

1991. Butterflies. Nos. 1494/502 of Antigua optd **BARBUDA MAIL**.
1294 10c. *Heliconius charithonia* 3·25 2·25
1295 35c. *Marpesia petreus* 4·50 1·25
1296 50c. *Anartia amathea* 5·00 1·40
1297 75c. *Siproeta stelenes* 6·00 2·25
1298 $1 *Battus polydamas* 6·00 2·50
1299 $2 *Historis odius* 9·00 8·50
1300 $4 *Hypolimnas misippus* 11·00 12·00
1301 $5 *Hamadryas feronia* 11·00 12·00
MS1302 Two sheets. (a) 73×100 mm. $6 *Vanessa cardui* (caterpillar) (vert). (b) 100×73 mm. $6 *Danaus plexippus* (caterpillar) (vert) Set of 2 sheets 40·00 35·00

1991. 65th Birthday of Queen Elizabeth II. Nos. 1534/8 of Antigua optd **BARBUDA MAIL**.
1303 15c. Queen Elizabeth and Prince Philip in 1976 6·00 1·50
1304 20c. The Queen and Prince Philip in Portugal, 1985 6·00 1·50
1305 $2 Queen Elizabeth II 17·00 8·00
1306 $4 The Queen and Prince Philip at Ascot, 1986 26·00 17·00
MS1307 68×90 mm. $4 The Queen at National Theatre, 1986 and Prince Philip 50·00 20·00

1991. Tenth Wedding Anniv of Prince and Princess of Wales. Nos. 1539/43 of Antigua optd **BARBUDA MAIL**.

1308 10c. Prince and Princess of Wales at party, 1986 5·50 2·50
1309 40c. Separate portraits of Prince, Princess and sons 11·00 1·75
1310 $1 Prince Henry and Prince William 13·00 4·50
1311 $5 Princess Diana in Australia and Prince Charles in Hungary 27·00 19·00
MS1312 68×90 mm. $4 Prince Charles in Hackney and Princess and sons in Majorca, 1987 50·00 20·00

1991. Christmas. Religious Paintings by Fra Angelico. Nos. 1595/1602 of Antigua optd **BARBUDA MAIL**.

1313 10c. *The Annunciation* 2·50 1·50
1314 30c. *Nativity* 3·00 70
1315 40c. *Adoration of the Magi* 3·00 70
1316 60c. *Presentation in the Temple* 3·75 70
1317 $1 *Circumcision* 5·00 1·75
1318 $3 *Flight into Egypt* 8·50 9·00
1319 $4 *Massacre of the Innocents* 8·50 10·00
1320 $5 *Christ teaching in the Temple* 8·50 10·00

1992. Death Centenary (1990) of Vincent van Gogh (artist). Nos. 1512/24 of Antigua optd **BARBUDA MAIL**.

1321 5c. *Camille Roulin* 2·00 2·00
1322 10c. *Armand Roulin* 2·25 2·00
1323 15c. *Young Peasant Woman with Straw Hat sitting in the Wheat* 2·50 2·00
1324 25c. *Adeline Ravoux* 2·50 2·00
1325 30c. *The Schoolboy* 2·50 1·25
1326 40c. *Doctor Gachet* 2·75 1·50
1327 50c. *Portrait of a Man* 2·75 1·75
1328 75c. *Two Children* 4·25 2·25
1329 $2 *The Postman Joseph Roulin* 8·00 7·50
1330 $3 *The Seated Zouave* 9·00 9·00
1331 $4 *L'Arlesienne* 9·50 10·00
1332 $5 *Self-Portrait, November/December 1888* 9·50 10·00
MS1333 Three sheets, each 102×76 mm. (a) $5 *Farmhouse in Provence* (horiz). (b) $5 *Flowering Garden* (horiz). (c) $6 *The Bridge at Trinquetaille* (horiz). Imperf Set of 3 sheets 45·00 42·00

1992. Birth Centenary of Charles de Gaulle (French statesman). Nos. 1562/70 of Antigua optd **BARBUDA MAIL**.

1334 10c. Pres. De Gaulle and Kennedy, 1961 3·00 2·00
1335 15c. General De Gaulle with Pres. Roosevelt, 1945 (vert) 3·00 2·00
1336 45c. President De Gaulle with Chancellor Adenauer, 1962 (vert) 3·75 80
1337 60c. De Gaulle at Arc de Triomphe, Liberation of Paris, 1944 (vert) 4·00 1·00
1338 $1 General De Gaulle crossing the Rhine, 1945 4·75 2·25
1339 $2 General De Gaulle in Algiers, 1944 8·00 8·00
1340 $4 Presidents De Gaulle and Eisenhower, 1960 10·00 13·00
1341 $5 De Gaulle returning from Germany, 1968 (vert) 10·00 13·00
MS1342 Two sheets. (a) 76×106 mm. $6 De Gaulle with crowd. (b) 106×76 mm. $6 De Gaulle and Churchill at Casablanca, 1943 Set of 2 sheets 42·00 35·00

1992. Easter. Religious Paintings. Nos. 1627/35 of Antigua optd **BARBUDA MAIL**.

1343 10c. *Supper at Emmaus* (Caravaggio) 1·75 1·50
1344 15c. *The Vision of St. Peter* (Zurbaran) 2·00 1·50
1345 30c. *Christ driving the Moneychangers from the Temple* (Tiepolo) 2·25 80
1346 40c. *Martyrdom of St. Bartholomew* (detail) (Ribera) 2·25 80
1347 $1 *Christ driving the Moneychangers from the Temple* (detail) (Tiepolo) 4·00 2·25
1348 $2 *Crucifixion* (detail) (Altdorfer) 6·00 6·50
1349 $4 *The Deposition* (detail) (Fra Angelico) 8·50 10·00
1350 $5 *The Deposition* (different detail) (Fra Angelico) 8·50 10·00
MS1351 Two sheets. (a) 102×71 mm. $6 *The Last Supper* (detail) (Masip). (b) 71×102 mm. $6 *Crucifixion* (detail) (vert) (Altdorfer) Set of 2 sheets 30·00 27·00

1992. Anniversaries and Events. Nos. 1573/83 of Antigua optd **BARBUDA MAIL**.

1352 25c. Germans celebrating Reunification 1·00 70
1353 75c. Cubs erecting tent 2·25 1·50
1354 $1.50 *Don Giovanni* and Mozart 12·00 4·25
1355 $2 Chariot driver and Gate at night 3·00 3·50
1356 $2 Lord Baden-Powell and members of the 3rd Antigua Methodist cub pack (vert) 3·00 3·50
1357 $2 Lilienthal's signature and glider *Flugzeug Nr. 5* 3·00 3·50
1358 $2.50 Driver in Class P36 steam locomotive (vert) 9·00 4·50
1359 $3 Statues from podium 3·00 4·50
1360 $3.50 Cubs and campfire 4·50 5·50
1361 $4 St. Peter's Cathedral, Salzburg 15·00 11·00
MS1362 Two sheets. (a) 100×72 mm. $4 Detail of chariot and helmet. (b) 89×117 mm. $5 Antiguan flag and Jamboree emblem (vert) Set of 2 sheets 45·00 35·00

1992. 50th Anniv of Japanese Attack on Pearl Harbor. Nos. 1585/94 of Antigua optd **BARBUDA MAIL**.

1364 $1 *Nimitz* class carrier and *Ticonderoga* class cruiser 7·00 4·00
1365 $1 Tourist launch 7·00 4·00
1366 $1 U.S.S. *Arizona* memorial 7·00 4·00
1367 $1 Wreaths on water and aircraft 7·00 4·00
1368 $1 White tern 7·00 4·00
1369 $1 Japanese torpedo bombers over Pearl City 7·00 4·00
1370 $1 Zeros attacking 7·00 4·00
1371 $1 Battleship Row in flames 7·00 4·00
1372 $1 U.S.S. *Nevada* (battleship) underway 7·00 4·00
1373 $1 Zeros returning to carriers 7·00 4·00

1992. 500th Anniv of Discovery of America by Columbus (5th issue). World Columbian Stamp "Expo '92", Chicago. Nos. 1654/60 of Antigua optd **BARBUDA MAIL**.

1374 15c. Memorial cross and huts, San Salvador 1·25 1·25
1375 30c. Martin Pinzon with telescope 1·50 90
1376 40c. Christopher Columbus 2·50 1·00
1377 $1 *Pinta* 7·00 3·00
1378 $2 *Nina* 9·00 8·00
1379 $4 *Santa Maria* 13·00 15·00
MS1380 Two sheets, each 108×76 mm. (a) $6 Ship and map of West Indies. (b) $6 Sea monster Set of 2 sheets 35·00 38·00

1992. 500th Anniv of Discovery of America by Columbus (6th issue). Organization of East Caribbean States. Nos. 1670/1 of Antigua optd **BARBUDA MAIL**.

1381 $1 Columbus meeting Amerindians 3·50 2·50
1382 $2 Ships approaching island 8·50 9·50

1992. Postage Stamp Mega Event, New York. No. MS1690 of Antigua optd **BARBUDA MAIL**.

MS1383 $6 multicoloured 15·00 17·00

1992. 40th Anniv of Queen Elizabeth II's Accession. Nos. 1604/8 of Antigua optd **BARBUDA MAIL**.

1384 10c. Queen Elizabeth II and bird sanctuary 8·00 2·25
1385 30c. Nelson's Dockyard 9·00 1·25
1386 $1 Ruins on Shirley Heights 13·00 2·75
1387 $5 Beach and palm trees 26·00 17·00
MS1388 Two sheets, each 75×98 mm. (a) $6 Beach. (b) $6 Hillside foliage Set of 2 sheets 55·00 29·00

1992. Prehistoric Animals. Nos. 1618/26 of Antigua optd **BARBUDA MAIL**.

1389 10c. Pteranodon 2·25 2·00
1390 15c. Brachiosaurus 2·75 2·00
1391 30c. Tyrannosaurus Rex 3·25 1·50
1392 50c. Parasaurolophus 3·25 2·50
1393 $1 Deinonychus (horiz) 4·00 2·50
1394 $2 Triceratops (horiz) 6·50 6·00
1395 $4 Protoceratops hatching (horiz) 7·50 9·50
1396 $5 Stegosaurus (horiz) 7·50 9·50
MS1397 Two sheets, each 100×70 mm. (a) $6 Apatosaurus (horiz). (b) $6 Allosaurus (horiz) Set of 2 sheets 45·00 38·00

1992. Christmas. Nos. 1691/9 of Antigua optd **BARBUDA MAIL**.

1398 10c. *Virgin and Child with Angels* (School of Piero della Francesca) 2·00 1·25
1399 25c. *Madonna degli Alberelli* (Giovanni Bellini) 2·00 1·00
1400 30c. *Madonna and Child with St. Anthony Abbot and St. Sigismund* (Neroccio) 2·00 85
1401 40c. *Madonna and the Grand Duke* (Raphael) 2·25 85
1402 60c. *The Nativity* (Georges de la Tour) 2·50 1·00
1403 $1 *Holy Family* (Jacob Jordaens) 3·25 1·50
1404 $4 *Madonna and Child Enthroned* (Magaritone) 7·50 9·50
1405 $5 *Madonna and Child on a Curved Throne* (Byzantine school) 7·50 9·50
MS1406 Two sheets, each 76×102 mm. (a) $6 *Madonna and Child* (Domenco Ghirlando). (b) $6 *The Holy Family* (Pontormo) Set of 2 sheets 27·00 30·00

1993. Fungi. Nos. 1645/53 of Antigua optd **BARBUDA MAIL**.

1407 10c. *Amanita caesarea* 1·75 1·75
1408 15c. *Collybia fusipes* 2·00 1·75
1409 30c. *Boletus aereus* 2·25 1·50
1410 40c. *Laccaria amethystina* 2·25 1·50
1411 $1 *Russula virescens* 3·25 2·00
1412 $2 *Tricholoma equestre* ("*Tricholoma auratum*") 4·50 4·00
1413 $4 *Calocybe gambosa* 5·50 7·00
1414 $5 *Lentinus tigrinus* ("*Panus tigrinus*") 5·50 7·00
MS1415 Two sheets, each 100×70 mm. (a) $6 *Clavariadelphus truncatus*. (b) $6 *Auricularia auricula-judae* Set of 2 sheets 28·00 26·00

1993. "Granada '92" International Stamp Exhibition, Spain. Spanish Paintings. Nos. 1636/44 of Antigua optd **BARBUDA MAIL**.

1416 10c. *The Miracle at the Well* (Alonzo Cano) 1·50 1·50
1417 15c. *The Poet Luis de Goingora y Argote* (Velazquez) 1·75 1·50
1418 30c. *The Painter Francisco Goya* (Vincente Lopez Portana) 2·00 1·00
1419 40c. *Maria de las Nieves Michaela Fourdinier* (Luis Paret y Alcazar) 2·00 1·00
1420 $1 *Carlos III eating before his Court* (Alcazar) (horiz) 3·50 2·25
1421 $2 *Rain Shower in Granada* (Antonio Munoz Degrain) (horiz) 5·50 5·50
1422 $4 *Sarah Bernhardt* (Santiago Ruisnol i Prats) 7·50 9·00
1423 $5 *The Hermitage Garden* (Joaquim Mir Trinxet) 7·50 9·00
MS1424 Two sheets, each 120×95 mm. (a) $6 *The Ascent of Monsieur Boucle's Montgolfier Balloon in the Gardens of Aranjuez* (Antonio Carnicero) (112×87 mm). (b) $6 *Olympus: Battle with the Giants* (Francisco Bayeu y Subias) (112×87 mm). Imperf Set of 2 sheets 22·00 25·00

1993. "Genova '92" International Thematic Stamp Exhibition. Hummingbirds and Plants. Nos. 1661/9 of Antigua optd **BARBUDA MAIL**.

1425 10c. Antillean crested hummingbird and wild plantain 2·75 2·00
1426 25c. Green mango and parrot's plantain 3·00 1·50
1427 45c. Purple-throated carib and lobster claws 3·50 1·25
1428 60c. Antillean mango and coral plant 3·50 1·50
1429 $1 Vervain hummingbird and cardinal's guard 4·50 2·25
1430 $2 Rufous-breasted hermit and heliconia 6·00 5·50
1431 $4 Blue-headed hummingbird and reed ginger 7·50 9·00
1432 $5 Green-throated carib and ornamental banana 7·50 9·00
MS1433 Two sheets, each 100×70 mm. (a) $6 Bee humming-bird and jungle flame. (b) $6 Western streamertail and bignonia Set of 2 sheets 35·00 25·00

1993. Inventors and Inventions. Nos. 1672/80 of Antigua optd **BARBUDA MAIL**.

1434 10c. Ts'ai Lun and paper 65 1·10
1435 25c. Igor Sikorsky and *Bolshoi Baltiskii* (first four-engined airplane) 4·00 1·00
1436 30c. Alexander Graham Bell and early telephone 1·50 80
1437 40c. Johannes Gutenberg and early printing press 1·50 80
1438 60c. James Watt and stationary steam engine 11·00 2·25
1439 $1 Anton van Leeuwenhoek and early microscope 3·50 2·75
1440 $4 Louis Braille and hands reading braille 10·00 11·00
1441 $5 Galileo and telescope 10·00 11·00
MS1442 Two sheets, each 100×71 mm. (a) $6 Edison and Latimer's phonograph. (b) $6 *Clermont* (first commercial paddle-steamer) Set of 2 sheets 32·00 35·00

1993. Anniversaries and Events. Nos. 900/14 of Antigua optd **BARBUDA MAIL**.

1443 10c. Russian cosmonauts 2·00 1·75
1444 40c. *Graf Zeppelin* (airship), 1929 3·50 1·00
1445 45c. Bishop Daniel Davis 1·00 70
1446 75c. Konrad Adenauer making speech 1·25 1·00
1447 $1 Bus Mosbacher and *Weatherly* (yacht) 2·50 1·75
1448 $1.50 Rain forest 3·50 3·25
1449 $2 Tiger 12·00 6·00
1450 $2 National flag, plant and emblem (horiz) 7·00 4·00
1451 $2 Members of Community Players company (horiz) 4·00 4·00
1452 $2.25 Women carrying pots 4·00 4·25
1453 $3 Lions Club emblem 4·25 4·75
1454 $4 Chinese rocket on launch tower 7·00 8·00
1455 $4 West German and N.A.T.O. flags 7·00 8·00
1456 $6 Hugo Eckener (airship pioneer) 7·50 8·50
MS1457 Four sheets, each 100×71 mm. (a) $6 Projected European space station. (b) $6 Airship LZ-129 *Hindenburg*, 1936. (c) $6 Brandenburg Gate on German flag. (d) $6 *Danaus plexippus* (butterfly) Set of 4 sheets 60·00 45·00

1993. Flowers. Nos. 1733/41 of Antigua optd **BARBUDA MAIL**.

1458 15c. Cardinal's guard 1·75 1·25
1459 25c. Giant granadilla 1·90 1·10
1460 30c. Spider flower 2·00 1·25
1461 40c. Gold vine 2·25 1·40
1462 $1 Frangipani 3·50 2·25
1463 $2 Bougainvillea 4·50 4·50
1464 $4 Yellow oleander 6·00 7·00
1465 $5 Spicy jatropha 6·00 7·00
MS1466 Two sheets, each 100×70 mm. (a) $6 Bird lime tree. (b) $6 Fairy lily Set of 2 sheets 32·00 32·00

1993. World Bird Watch. Nos. 1248/51 optd **WORLD BIRDWATCH 9-10 OCTOBER 1993**.

1467 60c. Type **119** 4·00 1·75
1468 $2 Adelaide's warbler 7·00 4·50
1469 $4 Rose-breasted grosbeak 9·50 10·00
1470 $7 Wied's crested flycatcher 12·00 13·00

1993. Endangered Species. Nos. 1759/71 of Antigua optd **BARBUDA MAIL**.

1471 $1 St. Lucia amazon ("St. Lucia Parrot") 5·50 4·00
1472 $1 Cahow 5·50 4·00
1473 $1 Swallow-tailed kite 5·50 4·00
1474 $1 Everglade kite ("Everglades Kite") 5·50 4·00
1475 $1 Imperial amazon ("Imperial Parrot") 5·50 4·00
1476 $1 Humpback whale 5·50 4·00
1477 $1 Plain pigeon ("Puerto Rican Plain Pigeon") 5·50 4·00
1478 $1 St. Vincent amazon ("St. Vincent Parrot") 5·50 4·00
1479 $1 Puerto Rican amazon ("Puerto Rican Parrot") 5·50 4·00
1480 $1 Leatherback turtle 5·50 4·00
1481 $1 American crocodile 5·50 4·00
1482 $1 Hawksbill turtle 5·50 4·00
MS1483 Two sheets, each 100×70 mm. (a) $6 As No. 1476. (b) $6 West Indian manatee Set of 2 sheets. 45·00 35·00

1994. Bicentenary of the Louvre, Paris. Paintings by Peter Paul Rubens. Nos. 1742/9 and MS1758 of Antigua optd **BARBUDA MAIL**.

1484 $1 *The Destiny of Marie de' Medici* (upper detail) 4·75 3·50
1485 $1 *The Birth of Marie de' Medici* 4·75 3·50
1486 $1 *The Education of Marie de' Medici* 4·75 3·50
1487 $1 *The Destiny of Marie de' Medici* (lower detail) 4·75 3·50
1488 $1 *Henry VI receiving the Portrait of Marie* 4·75 3·50
1489 $1 *The Meeting of the King and Marie at Lyons* 4·75 3·50
1490 $1 *The Marriage by Proxy* 4·75 3·50
1491 $1 *The Birth of Louis XIII* 4·75 3·50
MS1492 70×100 mm. $6 *Helene Fourment with a Coach* (52×85 mm) 22·00 23·00

1994. World Cup Football Championship, 1994, U.S.A. (1st Issue). Nos. 1816/28 of Antigua optd **BARBUDA MAIL**.

1493 $2 Paul Gascoigne 3·50 2·50
1494 $2 David Platt 3·50 2·50
1495 $2 Martin Peters 3·50 2·50
1496 $2 John Barnes 3·50 2·50
1497 $2 Gary Lineker 3·50 2·50
1498 $2 Geoff Hurst 3·50 2·50
1499 $2 Bobby Charlton 3·50 2·50
1500 $2 Bryan Robson 3·50 2·50
1501 $2 Bobby Moore 3·50 2·50
1502 $2 Nobby Stiles 3·50 2·50
1503 $2 Gordon Banks 3·50 2·50
1504 $2 Peter Shilton 3·50 2·50
MS1505 Two sheets, each 135×109 mm. (a) $6 Bobby Moore holding World Cup. (b) $6 Gary Lineker and Bobby Robson Set of 2 sheets 30·00 23·00

See also Nos. 1573/9.

1994. Anniversaries and Events. Nos. 1829/38, 1840 and 1842/7 of Antigua optd **BARBUDA MAIL**.

1506 10c. Grand Inspector W.Heath 5·00 2·50
1507 15c. Rodnina and Oulanov (U.S.S.R.) (pairs figure skating) (horiz) 2·00 2·00
1508 30c. Present Masonic Hall, St. John's (horiz) 6·50 2·50
1509 30c. Willy Brandt with Helmut Schmidt and George Leber (horiz) 1·50 1·50
1510 30c. *Cat and Bird* (Picasso) (horiz) 1·50 1·50
1511 40c. Previous Masonic Hall, St. John's (horiz) 6·50 2·50
1512 40c. *Fish on a Newspaper* (Picasso) (horiz) 1·50 1·50
1513 40c. Early astronomical equipment 1·50 1·50

1514 40c. Prince Naruhito and engagement photographs (horiz) 1·50 1·50
1515 60c. Grand Inspector J.Jeffery 7·50 2·50
1516 $3 Masako Owada and engagement photographs (horiz) 3·00 4·25
1517 $4 Willy Brandt and protest march (horiz) 4·50 5·50
1518 $4 Galaxy 4·50 5·50
1519 $5 Alberto Tomba (Italy) (giant slalom) (horiz) 4·50 5·50
1520 $5 *Dying Bull* (Picasso) (horiz) 4·50 5·50
1521 $5 Pres. Clinton and family (horiz) 4·50 5·50
MS1522 Six sheets. (a) 106×75 mm. $5 Copernicus. (b) 106×75 mm. $6 Womens' 1500 metre speed skating medallists (horiz). (c) 106×75 mm. $6 Willy Brandt at Warsaw Ghetto Memorial (horiz). (d) 106×75 mm. $6 *Woman with a Dog* (detail) (Picasso) (horiz). (e) 106×75 mm. $6 Masako Owada. (f) 106×75 mm. $6 Pres. Clinton taking the Oath (42½×57 mm) Set of 6 sheets 60·00 55·00

1994. Aviation Anniversaries. Nos. 1848/55 of Antigua optd **BARBUDA MAIL**.
1523 30c. Hugo Eckener and Dr. W. Beckers with airship *Graf Zeppelin* over Lake George, New York 3·25 1·75
1524 40c. Chicago World's Fair from *Graf Zeppelin* 3·25 1·75
1525 40c. Gloster Whittle E28/39, 1941 3·25 1·75
1526 40c. George Washington writing balloon mail letter (vert) 3·25 1·75
1527 $4 Pres. Wilson and Curtiss *Jenny* 10·00 11·00
1528 $5 Airship LZ-129 *Hindenburg* over Ebbets Field baseball stadium, 1937 10·00 11·00
1529 $5 Gloster Meteor in dogfight 10·00 11·00
MS1530 Three sheets. (a) 86×105 mm. $6 Hugo Eckener (vert). (b) 105×86 mm. $6 Consolidated Catalina PBY-5 flying boat (57×42½ mm). (c) 105×86 mm. $6 Alexander Hamilton, Washington and John Jay watching Blanchard's balloon, 1793 (horiz) Set of 3 sheets 42·00 35·00

1994. Centenaries of Henry Ford's First Petrol Engine (Nos. 1531, 1533, 1533a) and Karl Benz's First Four-wheeled Car (others). Nos. 1856/60 of Antigua optd **BARBUDA MAIL**.
1531 30c. Lincoln Continental 2·50 1·50
1532 40c. Mercedes racing car, 1914 2·50 1·50
1533 $4 Ford "GT40", 1966 7·50 8·50
1534 $5 Mercedes Benz "gull-wing" coupe, 1954 7·50 8·50
MS1535 Two sheets. (a) 114×87 mm. $6 Ford's Mustang emblem. (b) 87×114 mm. $6 Germany 1936 12pf. Benz and U.S.A. 1968 12c. Ford stamps Set of 2 sheets 24·00 21·00

1994. Famous Paintings by Rembrandt and Matisse. Nos. 1881/9 of Antigua optd **BARBUDA MAIL**.
1536 15c. *Hannah and Samuel* (Rembrandt) 2·50 2·00
1537 15c. *Guitarist* (Matisse) 2·50 2·00
1538 30c. *The Jewish Bride* (Rembrandt) 2·75 1·10
1539 40c. *Jacob wrestling with the Angel* (Rembrandt) 2·75 1·10
1540 60c. *Interior with a Goldfish Bowl* (Matisse) 3·25 1·25
1541 $1 *Mlle. Yvonne Landsberg* (Matisse) 4·00 1·75
1542 $4 *The Toboggan* (Matisse) 8·00 9·00
1543 $5 *Moses with the Tablets of the Law* (Rembrandt) 8·00 9·00
MS1544 Two sheets. (a) 124×99 mm. $6 *The Blinding of Samson by the Philistines* (detail) (Rembrandt). (b) 99×124 mm. $6 *The Three Sisters* (detail) (Matisse) Set of 2 sheets 23·00 23·00

1994. "Polska '93" International Stamp Exhibition, Poznan. Nos. 1839, 1841 and **MS**1847f of Antigua optd **BARBUDA MAIL**.
1545 $1 *Woman Combing her Hair* (W. Slewinski) (horiz) 5·00 2·50
1546 $3 *Artist's Wife with Cat* (Konrad Kryzanowski) (horiz) 9·00 10·00
MS1547 70×100 mm. $6 *General Confusion* (S. I. Witkiewicz) 10·00 12·00

1994. Orchids. Nos. 1949/56 of Antigua optd **BARBUDA MAIL**.
1548 10c. *Spiranthes lanceolata* 3·50 2·25
1549 20c. *Ionopsis utricularioides* 4·50 2·25
1550 30c. "*Tetramicra canaliculata* 5·00 1·50
1551 50c. *Oncidium picturatum* 5·50 1·50
1552 $1 *Epidendrum difforme* 6·50 2·50
1553 $2 *Epidendrum ciliare* 8·00 6·50
1554 $4 *Epidendrum ibaguense* 9·00 10·00
1555 $5 *Epidendrum nocturnum* 9·00 10·00
MS1556 Two sheets, each 100×73 mm. (a) $6 *Rodriguezia lanceolata*. (b) $6 Encyclia cochleata Set of 2 sheets 35·00 27·00

1994. Centenary of Sierra Club (environmental protection society) (1992). Endangered Species. Nos. 1907/22 of Antigua optd **BARBUDA MAIL**.
1557 $1.50 Sumatran rhinoceros lying down 3·00 2·50
1558 $1.50 Sumatran rhinoceros feeding 3·00 2·50
1559 $1.50 Ring-tailed lemur on ground 3·00 2·50
1560 $1.50 Ring-tailed lemur on branch 3·00 2·50
1561 $1.50 Red-fronted brown lemur on branch 3·00 2·50
1562 $1.50 Head of red-fronted brown lemur 3·00 2·50
1563 $1.50 Head of red-fronted brown lemur in front of trunk 3·00 2·50
1564 $1.50 Sierra Club Centennial emblem 1·75 1·60
1565 $1.50 Head of bactrian camel 3·00 2·50
1566 $1.50 Bactrian camel 3·00 2·50
1567 $1.50 African elephant drinking 3·00 2·50
1568 $1.50 Head of African elephant 3·00 2·50
1569 $1.50 Leopard sitting upright 3·00 2·50
1570 $1.50 Leopard in grass (emblem at right) 3·00 2·50
1571 $1.50 Leopard in grass (emblem at left) 3·00 2·50
MS1572 Four sheets. (a) 100×70 mm. $1.50, Sumatran rhinoceros (horiz). (b) 70×100 mm. $1.50, Ring-tailed lemur (horiz). (C) 70×100 mm. $1.50, Bactrian camel (horiz) (d) 100×70 mm. $1.50, African elephant (horiz) Set of 4 sheets 22·00 20·00

1995. World Cup Football Championship, U.S.A. (2nd issue). Nos. 2039/45 of Antigua optd **BARBUDA MAIL**.
1573 15c. Hugo Sanchez (Mexico) 2·25 1·25
1574 35c. Jurgen Klinsmann (Germany) 2·75 1·25
1575 65c. Antiguan player 3·00 1·25
1576 $1.20 Cobi Jones (U.S.A.) 4·00 2·75
1577 $4 Roberto Baggio (Italy) 8·00 8·50
1578 $5 Bwalya Kalusha (Zambia) 8·00 8·50
MS1579 Two sheets. (a) 72×105 mm. $6 Maldive Islands player (vert). (b) 107×78 mm. $6 World Cup trophy (vert) Set of 2 sheets 22·00 17·00

1995. Christmas. Religious Paintings. Nos. 2058/66 of Antigua optd **BARBUDA MAIL**.
1580 15c. *Virgin and Child by the Fireside* (Robert Campin) 1·75 1·00
1581 35c. *The Reading Madonna* (Giorgione) 2·25 70
1582 40c. *Madonna and Child* (Giovanni Bellini) 2·25 70
1583 45c. *The Little Madonna* (Da Vinci) 2·25 70
1584 65c. *The Virgin and Child under the Apple Tree* (Lucas Cranach the Elder) 2·75 1·00
1585 75c. *Madonna and Child* (Master of the Female Half-lengths) 2·75 1·25
1586 $1.20 *An Allegory of the Church* (Alessandro Allori) 4·25 4·00
1587 $5 *Madonna and Child wreathed with Flowers* (Jacob Jordaens) 8·50 13·00
MS1588 Two sheets. (a) 123×88 mm. $6 *Madonna and Child with Commissioners* (detail) (Palma Vecchio). (b) 88×123 mm. $6 *The Virgin Enthroned with Child* (detail) (Bohemian master) Set of 2 sheets 20·00 18·00

1995. "Hong Kong '94" International Stamp Exhibition (1st issue). Nos. 1890/1 of Antigua optd **BARBUDA MAIL**.
1589 40c. Hong Kong 1981 $1 Fish stamp and sampans, Shau Kei Wan 4·00 2·50
1590 40c. Antigua 1990 $2 Reef fish stamp and sampans, Shau Kei Wan 4·00 2·50
See also Nos. 1591/6.

1995. "Hong Kong '94" International Stamp Exhibition (2nd issue). Nos. 1892/7 of Antigua optd **BARBUDA MAIL**.
1591 40c. Terracotta warriors 1·25 1·00
1592 40c. Cavalryman and horse 1·25 1·00
1593 40c. Warriors in armour 1·25 1·00
1594 40c. Painted bronze chariot and team 1·25 1·00
1595 40c. Pekingese dog 1·25 1·00
1596 40c. Warriors with horses 1·25 1·00

1995. Centenary of International Olympic Committee. Nos. 1990/2 of Antigua optd **BARBUDA MAIL**.
1597 50c. Edwin Moses (U.S.A.) (400 metres hurdles), 1984 1·00 75
1598 $1.50 Steffi Graf (Germany) (tennis), 1988 8·50 4·25
MS1599 79×110 mm. $6 Johann Olav Koss (Norway) (500, 1500 and 10,000 metre speed skating), 1994 10·00 11·00

1995. Dogs of the World. Chinese New Year ("Year of the Dog"). Nos. 1923/47 of Antigua optd **BARBUDA MAIL**.
1600 50c. West Highland white terrier 1·60 1·10
1601 50c. Beagle 1·60 1·10
1602 50c. Scottish terrier 1·60 1·10
1603 50c. Pekingese 1·60 1·10
1604 50c. Dachshund 1·60 1·10
1605 50c. Yorkshire terrier 1·60 1·10
1606 50c. Pomeranian 1·60 1·10
1607 50c. Poodle 1·60 1·10
1608 50c. Shetland sheepdog 1·60 1·10
1609 50c. Pug 1·60 1·10
1610 50c. Shih tzu 1·60 1·10
1611 50c. Chihuahua 1·60 1·10
1612 50c. Mastiff 1·60 1·10
1613 50c. Border collie 1·60 1·10
1614 50c. Samoyed 1·60 1·10
1615 50c. Airedale terrier 1·60 1·10
1616 50c. English setter 1·60 1·10
1617 50c. Rough collie 1·60 1·10
1618 50c. Newfoundland 1·60 1·10
1619 50c. Weimarana 1·60 1·10
1620 50c. English springer spaniel 1·60 1·10
1621 50c. Dalmatian 1·60 1·10
1622 50c. Boxer 1·60 1·10
1623 50c. Old English sheepdog 1·60 1·10
MS1624 Two sheets, each 93×58 mm. (a) $6 Welsh corgi. (b) $6 Labrador retriever Set of 2 sheets 35·00 23·00

1995. Centenary of First English Cricket Tour to the West Indies (1995). Nos. 1994/7 of Antigua optd **BARBUDA MAIL**.
1625 35c. Mike Atherton (England) and Wisden Trophy 4·00 1·50
1626 75c. Viv Richards (West Indies) (vert) 6·00 2·75
1627 $1.20 Richie Richardson (West Indies) and Wisden Trophy 8·00 4·75
MS1628 80×100 mm. $3 English team, 1895 (black and brown) 13·00 11·00

1995. "Philakorea '94" International Stamp Exhibition (1st issue). Nos. 1998/2009 of Antigua optd **BARBUDA MAIL**.
1629 40c. Entrance bridge, Songgwangsa Temple 1·00 80
1630 75c. Long-necked bottle 1·25 1·50
1631 75c. Punch'ong ware jar with floral decoration 1·25 1·50
1632 75c. Punch'ong ware jar with blue dragon pattern 1·25 1·50
1633 75c. Ewer in shape of bamboo shoot 1·25 1·50
1634 75c. Punch'ong ware green jar 1·25 1·50
1635 75c. Pear-shaped bottle 1·25 1·50
1636 75c. Porcelain jar with brown dragon pattern 1·25 1·50
1637 75c. Porcelain jar with floral pattern 1·25 1·50
1638 90c. Song-op Folk Village, Cheju 1·25 1·25
1639 $3 Port Sogwipo 3·00 3·75
MS1640 104×71 mm. $4 Ox herder playing flute (vert) 4·75 6·50

1995. First Recipients of Order of the Caribbean Community. Nos. 2046/8 of Antigua optd **BARBUDA MAIL**.
1641 65c. Sir Shridath Ramphal 60 75
1642 90c. William Demas 90 1·00
1643 $1.20 Derek Walcott 4·50 4·25

1995. 25th Anniv of First Moon Landing. Nos. 1977/89 of Antigua optd **BARBUDA MAIL**.
1644 $1.50 Edwin Aldrin (astronaut) 4·25 2·75
1645 $1.50 First lunar footprint 4·25 2·75
1646 $1.50 Neil Armstrong (astronaut) 4·25 2·75
1647 $1.50 Aldrin stepping onto Moon 4·25 2·75
1648 $1.50 Aldrin and equipment 4·25 2·75
1649 $1.50 Aldrin and U.S.A. flag 4·25 2·75
1650 $1.50 Aldrin at Tranquility Base 4·25 2·75
1651 $1.50 Moon plaque 4·25 2·75
1652 $1.50 "Eagle" leaving Moon 4·25 2·75
1653 $1.50 Command module in lunar orbit 4·25 2·75
1654 $1.50 First day cover of U.S.A. 1969 10c. First Man on Moon stamp 4·25 2·75
1655 $1.50 Pres. Nixon and astronauts 4·25 2·75
MS1656 72×102 mm. $6 Armstrong and Aldrin with postal official 23·00 16·00

1995. International Year of the Family. No. 1993 of Antigua optd **BARBUDA MAIL**.
1657 90c. Antiguan family 1·75 1·50

1995. 50th Anniv of D-Day. Nos. 2010/13 of Antigua optd **BARBUDA MAIL**.
1658 40c. Short S.25 Sunderland flying boat 4·50 1·25
1659 $2 Lockheed P-38 Lightning fighters attacking train 13·00 6·50
1660 $3 Martin B-26 Marauder bombers 13·00 8·00
MS1661 108×78 mm. $6 Hawker Typhoon fighter bomber 21·00 19·00

122 Queen Elizabeth the Queen Mother (95th birthday)

1995. Anniversaries. Multicoloured.
1662 $7.50 Type **122** 12·00 13·00
1663 $8 German bombers over St. Paul's Cathedral, London (horiz) (50th anniv of end of Second World War) 27·00 18·00
1664 $8 New York skyline with U.N. and national flags (horiz) (50th anniv of United Nations) 16·00 18·00

1995. Hurricane Relief. Nos. 1662/4 surch **HURRICANE RELIEF** and premium.
1665 $7.50+$1 Type **122** (90th birthday) 8·00 11·00
1666 $8+$1 German bombers over St. Paul's Cathedral, London (horiz) (50th anniv of end of Second World War) 20·00 16·00
1667 $8+$1 New York skyline with U.N. and national flags (horiz) (50th anniv of United Nations) 8·00 11·00

1996. Marine Life. Nos. 1967/76 of Antigua optd **BARBUDA MAIL**.
1668 50c. Bottlenose dolphin 1·50 1·50
1669 50c. Killer whale 1·50 1·50
1670 50c. Spinner dolphin 1·50 1·50
1671 50c. Oceanic sunfish 1·50 1·50
1672 50c. Caribbean reef shark and short fin pilot whale 1·50 1·50
1673 50c. Copper-banded butterflyfish 1·50 1·50
1674 50c. Mosaic moray 1·50 1·50
1675 50c. Clown triggerfish 1·50 1·50
1676 50c. Red lobster 1·50 1·50
MS1677 Two sheets, each 106×76 mm. (a) $6 Seahorse. (b) $6 Swordfish ("Blue Marlin") (horiz) Set of 2 sheets 21·00 21·00

1996. Christmas. Religious Paintings. Nos. 2267/73 of Antigua optd **BARBUDA MAIL**.
1678 15c. *Rest on the Flight into Egypt* (Paolo Veronese) 65 60
1679 35c. *Madonna and Child* (Van Dyck) 75 50
1680 65c. *Sacred Conversation Piece* (Veronese) 1·00 70
1681 75c. *Vision of St. Anthony* (Van Dyck) 1·25 80
1682 90c. *Virgin and Child* (Van Eyck) 1·40 90
1683 $6 *The Immaculate Conception* (Giovanni Tiepolo) 4·75 9·00
MS1684 Two sheets. (a) 101×127 mm. $5 *Christ appearing to his Mother* (detail) (Van der Weyden). (b) 127×101 mm. $6 *The Infant Jesus and the Young St. John* (Murillo) Set of 2 sheets 18·00 20·00

1996. Stars of Country and Western Music. Nos. 2014/38 of Antigua optd **BRBAUDA MAIL**.
1685 75c. Travis Tritt 80 80
1686 75c. Dwight Yoakam 80 80
1687 75c. Billy Ray Cyrus 80 80
1688 75c. Alan Jackson 80 80
1689 75c. Garth Brooks 80 80
1690 75c. Vince Gill 80 80
1691 75c. Clint Black 80 80
1692 75c. Eddie Rabbit 80 80
1693 75c. Patsy Cline 80 80
1694 75c. Tanya Tucker 80 80
1695 75c. Dolly Parton 80 80
1696 75c. Anne Murray 80 80
1697 75c. Tammy Wynette 80 80
1698 75c. Loretta Lynn 80 80
1699 75c. Reba McEntire 80 80
1700 75c. Skeeter Davis 80 80
1701 75c. Hank Snow 80 80
1702 75c. Gene Autry 80 80
1703 75c. Jimmie Rodgers 80 80
1704 75c. Ernest Tubb 80 80
1705 75c. Eddy Arnold 80 80
1706 75c. Willie Nelson 80 80
1707 75c. Johnny Cash 80 80
1708 75c. George Jones 80 80
MS1709 Three sheets. (a) 100×70 mm. $6 Hank Williams Jr. (b) 100×70 mm. $6 Hank Williams Sr. (c) 70×100 mm. $6 Kitty Wells (horiz) Set of 3 sheets 17·00 17·00

1996. Birds. Nos. 2067/81 of Antigua optd **BARBUDA MAIL**.
1710 15c. Magnificent frigate bird 1·50 1·25

1711 25c. Antillean euphonia ("Blue-hooded Euphonia") 1·60 1·25
1712 35c. Eastern meadowlark ("Meadowlark") 1·75 1·00
1713 40c. Red-billed tropic bird 1·75 1·00
1714 45c. Greater flamingo 1·75 1·00
1715 60c. Yellow-faced grassquit 2·00 1·50
1716 65c. Yellow-billed cuckoo 2·00 1·50
1717 70c. Purple-throated carib 2·00 2·00
1718 75c. Bananaquit 2·00 1·25
1719 90c. Painted bunting 2·25 1·25
1720 $1.20 Red-legged honeycreeper 2·50 2·25
1721 $2 Northern jacana ("Jacana") 3·50 3·50
1722 $5 Greater Antillean bullfinch 5·50 7·50
1723 $10 Caribbean elaenia 8·50 13·00
1724 $20 Brown trembler ("Trembler") 13·00 19·00

1996. Birds. Nos. 2050, 2052 and 2054/7 of Antigua optd **BARBUDA MAIL.**
1725 15c. Bridled quail dove 2·00 1·50
1726 40c. Purple-throated carib (vert) 2·50 1·00
1727 $1 Broad-winged hawk ("Antigua Broad-winged Hawk") (vert) 3·75 2·50
1728 $4 Yellow warbler 6·00 8·00
MS1729 Two sheets. (a) 70×100 mm. $6 Female magnificent frigate bird (vert). (b) 100×70 mm. $6 Black-billed whistling duck ducklings Set of 2 sheets 17·00 18·00

1996. Prehistoric Animals. Nos. 2082/100 of Antigua optd **BARBUDA MAIL.**
1730 15c. Head of pachycephalosaurus 2·00 2·00
1731 20c. Head of afrovenator 2·00 2·00
1732 65c. Centrosaurus 2·00 2·00
1733 75c. Kronosaurus (horiz) 2·00 2·00
1734 75c. Ichthyosaurus (horiz) 2·00 2·00
1735 75c. Plesiosaurus (horiz) 2·00 2·00
1736 75c. Archelon (horiz) 2·00 2·00
1737 75c. Pair of tyrannosaurus (horiz) 2·00 2·00
1738 75c. Tyrannosaurus (horiz) 2·00 2·00
1739 75c. Parasaurolophus (horiz) 2·00 2·00
1740 75c. Pair of parasaurolophus (horiz) 2·00 2·00
1741 75c. Oviraptor (horiz) 2·00 2·00
1742 75c. Protoceratops with eggs (horiz) 2·00 2·00
1743 75c. Pteranodon and protoceratops (horiz) 2·00 2·00
1744 75c. Pair of protoceratops (horiz) 2·00 2·00
1745 90c. Pentaceratops drinking 2·25 1·50
1746 $1.20 Head of tarbosaurus 2·75 2·00
1747 $5 Head of styracosaurus 6·50 7·50
MS1748 Two sheets, each 101×70 mm. (a) $6 Head of Corythosaurus (horiz). (b) $6 Head of Carnotaurus (horiz) Set of 2 sheets 20·00 23·00

1996. Olympic Games, Atlanta (1st issue). Previous Gold Medal Winners. Nos. 2101/7 of Antigua optd **BARBUDA MAIL.**
1749 15c. Al Oerter (U.S.A.) (discus – 1956, 1960, 1964, 1968) 1·50 1·00
1750 20c. Greg Louganis (U.S.A.) (diving – 1984, 1988) 1·50 1·00
1751 65c. Naim Suleymanoglu (Turkey) (weightlifting – 1988) 2·00 1·00
1752 90c. Louise Ritter (U.S.A.) (high jump – 1988) 2·50 1·25
1753 $1.20 Nadia Comaneci (Rumania) (gymnastics – 1976) 4·00 2·75
1754 $5 Olga Bondarenko (Russia) (10,000 m – 1988) 6·00 8·50
MS1755 Two sheets, each 106×76 mm. (a) $6 United States crew (eight-oared shell – 1964). (b) $6 Lutz Hessilch (Germany) (cycling – 1988) (vert) Set of 2 sheets 18·00 16·00
See also Nos. 1922/44.

1996. 18th World Scout Jamboree, Netherlands. Tents. Nos. 2203/9 of Antigua optd **BARBUDA MAIL.**
1756 $1.20 The Explorer Tent 1·25 1·50
1757 $1.20 Camper tent 1·25 1·50
1758 $1.20 Wall tent 1·25 1·50
1759 $1.20 Trail tent 1·25 1·50
1760 $1.20 Miner's tent 1·25 1·50
1761 $1.20 Voyager tent 1·25 1·50
MS1762 Two sheets, each 76×106 mm. (a) $6 Scout and camp fire. (b) $6 Scout with back pack Set of 2 sheets 8·00 10·00

1996. Centenary of Nobel Prize Trust Fund. Nos. 2226/44 of Antigua optd **BARBUDA MAIL.**
1763 $1 Dag Hammarskjold (1961 Peace) 1·60 1·25
1764 $1 Georg Wittig (1979 Chemistry) 1·60 1·25
1765 $1 Wilhelm Ostwold (1909 Chemistry) 1·60 1·25
1766 $1 Robert Koch (1905 Medicine) 1·60 1·25
1767 $1 Karl Ziegler (1963 Chemistry) 1·60 1·25
1768 $1 Alexander Fleming (1945 Medicine) 1·60 1·25
1769 $1 Hermann Staudinger (1953 Chemistry) 1·60 1·25
1770 $1 Manfred Eigen (1967 Chemistry) 1·60 1·25
1771 $1 Arno Penzias (1978 Physics) 1·60 1·25
1772 $1 Shumal Agnon (1966 Literature) 1·60 1·25
1773 $1 Rudyard Kipling (1907 Literature) 1·60 1·25
1774 $1 Aleksandr Solzhenitsyn (1970 Literature) 1·60 1·25
1775 $1 Jack Steinburger (1988 Physics) 1·60 1·25
1776 $1 Andrei Sakharov (1975 Peace) 1·60 1·25
1777 $1 Otto Stern (1943 Physics) 1·60 1·25
1778 $1 John Steinbeck (1962 Literature) 1·60 1·25
1779 $1 Nadine Gordimer (1991 Literature) 1·60 1·25
1780 $1 William Faulkner (1949 Literature) 1·60 1·25
MS1781 Two sheets, each 100×70 mm. (a) $6 Elie Wiesel (1986 Peace) (vert). (b) $6 Dalai Lama (1989 Peace) (vert) Set of 2 sheets 14·00 17·00

1996. 70th Birthday of Queen Elizabeth II. Nos. 2355/8 of Antigua optd **BARBUDA MAIL.**
1782 $2 Queen Elizabeth II in blue dress 3·25 2·75
1783 $2 With bouquet 3·25 2·75
1784 $2 In Garter robes 3·25 2·75
MS1785 96×111 mm. $6 Wearing white dress 8·50 7·50

1997. Christmas. Religious Paintings by Filippo Lippi. Nos. 2377/83 of Antigua optd **BARBUDA MAIL.**
1786 60c. *Madonna Enthroned* 60 35
1787 90c. *Adoration of the Child and Saints* 85 55
1788 $1 *The Annunciation* 1·00 80
1789 $1.20 *Birth of the Virgin* 1·25 1·10
1790 $1.60 *Adoration of the Child* 1·60 2·00
1791 $1.75 *Madonna and Child* 1·75 2·25
MS1792 Two sheets, each 76×106 mm. (a) $6 *Madonna and Child* (different). (b) $6 *The Circumcision* Set of 2 sheets 12·00 15·00

1997. 50th Anniv of F.A.O. Nos. 2121/4 of Antigua optd **BARBUDA MAIL.**
1793 75c. Woman buying produce from market 1·00 1·00
1794 90c. Women shopping 1·10 1·10
1795 $1.20 Women talking 1·40 1·75
MS1796 100×70 mm. $6 Tractor 5·50 7·00

1997. 90th Anniv of Rotary International (1995). No. 2126 of Antigua optd **BARBUDA MAIL.**
1797 $5 Beach and rotary emblem 3·25 4·25
MS1798 74×104 mm. $6 National flag and emblem 4·50 5·50

1997. 50th Anniv of End of Second World War in Europe and the Pacific. Nos. 2108/16 and 2132/8 of Antigua optd **BARBUDA MAIL.**
1799 $1.20 Map of Berlin showing Russian advance 1·50 1·50
1800 $1.20 Russian tank and infantry 1·50 1·50
1801 $1.20 Street fighting in Berlin 1·50 1·50
1802 $1.20 German tank exploding 1·50 1·50
1803 $1.20 Russian air raid 1·50 1·50
1804 $1.20 German troops surrendering 1·50 1·50
1805 $1.20 Hoisting the Soviet flag on the Reichstag 1·50 1·50
1806 $1.20 Captured German standards 1·50 1·50
1807 $1.20 Gen. Chiang Kai-shek and Chinese guerrillas 1·50 1·50
1808 $1.20 Gen. Douglas MacArthur and beach landing 1·50 1·50
1809 $1.20 Gen. Claire Chennault and U.S. fighter aircraft 1·50 1·50
1810 $1.20 Brig. Orde Wingate and supply drop 1·50 1·50
1811 $1.20 Gen. Joseph Stilwell and U.S. supply plane 1·50 1·50
1812 $1.20 Field-Marshal Bill Slim and loading cow onto plane 1·50 1·50
MS1813 Two sheets, each 100×70 mm. (a) $3 Admiral Nimitz and aircraft carrier. (b) $6 Gen. Konev (vert) Set of 2 sheets 14·00 15·00

1997. Bees. Nos. 2172/6 of Antigua optd **BARBUDA MAIL.**
1814 90c. Mining bees 1·00 50
1815 $1.20 Solitary bee 1·25 80
1816 $1.65 Leaf-cutter bee 1·60 1·75
1817 $1.75 Honey bees 1·75 2·00
MS1818 110×80 mm. $6 Solitary mining bird 5·50 6·50

1997. Flowers. Nos. 2177/89 of Antigua optd **BARBUDA MAIL.**
1819 75c. Narcissus 75 85
1820 75c. Camellia 75 85
1821 75c. Iris 75 85
1822 75c. Tulip 75 85
1823 75c. Poppy 75 85
1824 75c. Peony 75 85
1825 75c. Magnolia 75 85
1826 75c. Oriental lily 75 85
1827 75c. Rose 75 85
1828 75c. Pansy 75 85
1829 75c. Hydrangea 75 85
1830 75c. Azaleas 75 85
MS1831 80×110 mm. $6 Calla lily 6·50 8·00

1997. Cats. Nos. 2190/202 of Antigua optd **BARBUDA MAIL.**
1832 45c. Somali 70 70
1833 45c. Persian and butterflies 70 70
1834 45c. Devon rex 70 70
1835 45c. Turkish angora 70 70
1836 45c. Himalayan 70 70
1837 45c. Maine coon 70 70
1838 45c. Ginger non-pedigree 70 70
1839 45c. American wirehair 70 70
1840 45c. British shorthair 70 70
1841 45c. American curl 70 70
1842 45c. Black non-pedigree and butterfly 70 70
1843 45c. Birman 70 70
MS1844 104×74 mm. $6 Siberian kitten (vert) 9·00 10·00

1997. 95th Birthday of Queen Elizabeth the Queen Mother. Nos. 2127/31 of Antigua optd **BARBUDA MAIL.**
1845 $1.50 brown, lt brown & black 5·00 3·50
1846 $1.50 multicoloured 5·00 3·50
1847 $1.50 multicoloured 5·00 3·50
1848 $1.50 multicoloured 5·00 3·50
MS1849 102×27 mm. $6 multicoloured 14·00 11·00

1997. 50th Anniv of United Nations. Nos. 2117/18 of Antigua optd **BARBUDA MAIL.**
1850 75c. Signatures and Earl of Halifax 80 80
1851 90c. Virginia Gildersleeve 90 90
1852 $1.20 Harold Stassen 1·25 1·50
MS1853 100×70 mm. $6 Pres. Franklin D. Roosevelt 4·50 6·00

1997. Trains of the World. Nos. 2210/25 of Antigua optd **BARBUDA MAIL.**
1854 35c. Trans-Gabon diesel-electric train 90 30
1855 65c. Canadian Pacific diesel-electric locomotive 1·00 40
1856 75c. Santa Fe Railway diesel-electric locomotive, U.S.A. 1·00 50
1857 90c. High Speed Train, Great Britain 1·00 60
1858 $1.20 TGV express train, France 1·00 1·25
1859 $1.20 Diesel-electric locomotive, Australia 1·00 1·25
1860 $1.20 Pendolino "ETR 450" electric train, Italy 1·00 1·25
1861 $1.20 Diesel-electric locomotive, Thailand 1·00 1·25
1862 $1.20 Pennsylvania Railroad Type 4 steam locomotive, U.S.A. 1·00 1·25
1863 $1.20 Beyer-Garratt steam locomotive, East African Railways 1·00 1·25
1864 $1.20 Natal Govt steam locomotive 1·00 1·25
1865 $1.20 Rail gun, American Civil War 1·00 1·25
1866 $1.20 Locomotive *Lion* (red livery), Great Britain 1·00 1·25
1867 $1.20 William Hedley's *Puffing Billy* (green livery), Great Britain 1·00 1·25
1868 $6 Amtrak high speed diesel locomotive, U.S.A. 3·50 4·50
MS1869 Two sheets, each 110×80 mm. (a) $6 Locomotive *Iron Rooster* China (vert). (b) $6 *Indian-Pacific* diesel-electric locomotive, Australia (vert) Set of 2 sheets 13·00 16·00

1997. Golden Wedding of Queen Elizabeth II and Prince Philip (1st issue). Nos. 1662/3 optd **Golden Wedding of H.M. Queen Elizabeth II and Prince Philip 1947-1997.**
1870 $7.50 Type **122** 7·50 8·00
1871 $8 German bombers over St. Paul's Cathedral, London (horiz) 9·50 10·00
See also Nos. 1925/30.

1997. Fungi. Nos. 2274/82 of Antigua optd **BARBUDA MAIL.**
1872 75c. *Hygrophoropsis aurantiaca* 1·50 1·50
1873 75c. *Hygrophorus bakerensis* 1·50 1·50
1874 75c. *Hygrophorus conicus* 1·50 1·50
1875 75c. *Hygrophorus miniatus* ("Hygrocybe miniata") 1·50 1·50
1876 75c. *Suillus brevipes* 1·50 1·50
1877 75c. *Suillus luteus* 1·50 1·50
1878 75c. *Suillus granulatus* 1·50 1·50
1879 75c. *Suillus caerulescens* 1·50 1·50
MS1880 Two sheets, each 106×76 mm. (a) $6 *Conocybe filaris*. (b) $6 *Hygrocybe flavescens* Set of 2 sheets 13·00 15·00

1997. Birds. Nos. 2140/64 of Antigua optd **BARBUDA MAIL.**
1881 75c. Purple-throated carib 90 90
1882 75c. Antillean crested hummingbird 90 90
1883 75c. Bananaquit 90 90
1884 75c. Mangrove cuckoo 90 90
1885 75c. Troupial 90 90
1886 75c. Green-throated carib 90 90
1887 75c. Yellow warbler 90 90
1888 75c. Antillean euphonia ("Blue-hooded Euphonia") 90 90
1889 75c. Scaly-breasted thrasher 90 90
1890 75c. Burrowing owl 90 90
1891 75c. Carib grackle 90 90
1892 75c. Adelaide's warbler 90 90
1893 75c. Ring-necked duck 90 90
1894 75c. Ruddy duck 90 90
1895 75c. Green-winged teal 90 90
1896 75c. Wood duck 90 90
1897 75c. Hooded merganser 90 90
1898 75c. Lesser scaup 90 90
1899 75c. Black-billed whistling duck ("West Indian Tree Duck") 90 90
1900 75c. Fulvous whistling duck 90 90
1901 75c. Bahama pintail 90 90
1902 75c. Northern shoveler ("Shoveler") 90 90
1903 75c. Masked duck 90 90
1904 75c. American wigeon 90 90
MS1905 Two sheets, each 104×74 mm. (a) $6 Head of purple gallinule. (b) $6 Heads of blue-winged teals Set of 2 sheets 14·00 13·00

1997. Sailing Ships. Nos. 2283/301 of Antigua optd **BARBUDA MAIL.**
1906 15c. H.M.S. "Resolution" (Cook) 1·25 1·00
1907 25c. "Mayflower" (Pilgrim Fathers) 1·00 50
1908 45c. "Santa Maria" (Columbus) 1·25 60
1909 75c. "Aemilia" (Dutch galleon) 1·00 60
1910 75c. "Sovereign of the Seas" (English galleon) 1·00 60
1911 90c. H.M.S. "Victory" (Nelson) 1·25 1·00
1912 $1.20 As No. 1909 1·25 1·25
1913 $1.20 As No. 1910 1·25 1·25
1914 $1.20 "Royal Louis" (French galleon) 1·25 1·25
1915 $1.20 H.M.S. "Royal George" (ship of the line) 1·25 1·25
1916 $1.20 "Le Protecteur" (French frigate) 1·25 1·25
1917 $1.20 As No. 1911 1·25 1·25
1918 $1.50 As No. 1908 1·25 1·40
1919 $1.50 "Victoria" (Magellan) 1·25 1·40
1920 $1.50 "Golden Hind" (Drake) 1·25 1·40
1921 $1.50 As No. 1907 1·25 1·40
1922 $1.50 "Griffin" (La Salle) 1·25 1·40
1923 $1.50 As No. 1906 1·25 1·40
MS1924 (a) 102×72 mm. $6 U.S.S. "Constitution" (frigate). (b) 98×67 mm. $6 "Grande Hermine" (Cartier) Set of 2 sheets 10·00 12·00

1997. Golden Wedding of Queen Elizabeth and Prince Philip (2nd issue). Nos. 2474/80 of Antigua optd **BARBUDA MAIL.**
1925 $1 Queen Elizabeth II 2·50 2·00
1926 $1 Royal coat of arms 2·50 2·00
1927 $1 Queen Elizabeth and Prince Philip at reception 2·50 2·00
1928 $1 Queen Elizabeth and Prince Philip in landau 2·50 2·00
1929 $1 Balmoral 2·50 2·00
1930 $1 Prince Philip 2·50 2·00
MS1931 100×71 mm. $6 Queen Elizabeth with Prince Philip in naval uniform 14·00 13·00

1997. Christmas. Religious Paintings. Nos. 2566/72 of Antigua optd **BARBUDA MAIL.**
1932 15c. "The Angel leaving Tobias and his Family" (Rembrandt) 80 60
1933 25c. "The Resurrection" (Martin Knoller) 90 60
1934 60c. "Astronomy" (Raphael) 1·25 75
1935 75c. "Music-making Angel" (Melozzo da Forli) 1·40 1·25
1936 90c. "Amor" (Parmigianino) 1·60 1·25
1937 $1.20 "Madonna and Child with Saints" (Rosso Fiorentino) 1·75 2·00
MS1938 Two sheets, each 105×96 mm. (a) $6 "The Wedding of Tobias" (Gianantonio and Francesco Guardi) (horiz). (b) $6 "The Portinari Altarpiece" (Hugo van der Goes) (horiz) Set of 2 sheets 9·00 11·00

1998. Sea Birds. Nos. 2325/33 of Antigua optd **BARBUDA MAIL.**
1939 75c. Black skimmer 1·50 1·50
1940 75c. Black-capped petrel 1·50 1·50
1941 75c. Sooty tern 1·50 1·50
1942 75c. Royal tern 1·50 1·50
1943 75c. Pomarine skua ("Pomarine Jaegger") 1·50 1·50
1944 75c. White-tailed tropic bird 5·50 5·50
1945 75c. Northern gannet 1·50 1·50

1946 75c. Laughing gull 1·50 1·50
MS1947 Two sheets, each 105×75 mm. (a) $5 Great frigate bird. (b) $6 Brown pelican Set of 2 sheets 9·00 11·00

1998. Centenary of Radio. Entertainers. Nos. 2372/6 of Antigua optd **BARBUDA MAIL**.
1948 65c. Kate Smith 90 65
1949 75c. Dinah Shore 1·00 85
1950 90c. Rudy Vallee 1·25 90
1951 $1.20 Bing Crosby 1·50 2·25
MS1952 72×104 mm. $6 Jo Stafford (28×42 mm) 5·50 7·50

1998. Olympic Games, Atlanta (2nd issue). Previous Medal Winners. Nos. 2302/23 of Antigua optd **BARBUDA MAIL**.
1953 65c. Florence Griffith Joyner (U.S.A.) (Gold – track, 1988) 85 75
1954 75c. Olympic Stadium, Seoul (1988) (horiz) 85 75
1955 90c. Allison Jolly and Lynne Jewell (U.S.A.) (Gold – yachting, 1988) (horiz) 1·00 1·00
1956 90c. Wolfgang Nordwig (Germany) (Gold – pole vaulting, 1972) 1·00 1·00
1957 90c. Shirley Strong (Great Britain) (Silver – 100 m hurdles, 1984) 1·00 1·00
1958 90c. Sergei Bubka (Russia) (Gold – pole vault, 1988) 1·00 1·00
1959 90c. Filbert Bayi (Tanzania) (Silver – 3000 m steeplechase, 1980) 1·00 1·00
1960 90c. Victor Saneyev (Russia) (Gold – triple jump, 1968, 1972, 1976) 1·00 1·00
1961 90c. Silke Renk (Germany) (Gold – javelin, 1992) 1·00 1·00
1962 90c. Daley Thompson (Great Britain) (Gold – decathlon, 1980, 1984) 1·00 1·00
1963 90c. Robert Richards (U.S.A.) (Gold – pole vault, 1952, 1956) 1·00 1·00
1964 90c. Parry O'Brien (U.S.A.) (Gold – shot put, 1952, 1956) 1·00 1·00
1965 90c. Ingrid Kramer (Germany) (Gold – Women's platform diving, 1960) 1·00 1·00
1966 90c. Kelly McCormick (U.S.A.) (Silver – Women's springboard diving, 1984) 1·00 1·00
1967 90c. Gary Tobian (U.S.A.) (Gold – Men's springboard diving, 1960) 1·00 1·00
1968 90c. Greg Louganis (U.S.A.) (Gold – Men's diving, 1984 and 1988) 1·00 1·00
1969 90c. Michelle Mitchell (U.S.A.) (Silver – Women's platform diving, 1984 and 1988) 1·00 1·00
1970 90c. Zhou Jihong (China) (Gold – Women's platform diving, 1984) 1·00 1·00
1971 90c. Wendy Wyland (U.S.A.) (Bronze – Women's platform diving, 1984) 1·00 1·00
1972 90c. Xu Yanmei (China) (Gold – Women's platform diving, 1988) 1·00 1·00
1973 90c. Fu Mingxia (China) (Gold – Women's platform diving, 1992) 1·00 1·00
1974 $1.20 2000 m tandem cycle race (horiz) 3·25 3·00
MS1975 Two sheets, each 106×76 mm. (a) $5 Bill Toomey (U.S.A.) (Gold – decathlon, 1968) (horiz). (b) $6 Mark Lenzi (U.S.A.) (Gold – Men's springboard diving, 1992) Set of 2 sheets 9·00 11·00

1998. World Cup Football Championship, France. Nos. 2525/39 of Antigua optd **BARBUDA MAIL**.
1976 60c. multicoloured 75 60
1977 75c. brown 75 60
1978 90c. multicoloured 80 65
1979 $1 brown 80 80
1980 $1 brown 80 80
1981 $1 brown 80 80
1982 $1 black 80 80
1983 $1 brown 80 80
1984 $1 brown 80 80
1985 $1 brown 80 80
1986 $1 brown 80 80
1987 $1.20 multicoloured 1·00 1·10
1988 $1.65 multicoloured 1·25 1·40
1989 $1.75 multicoloured 1·40 1·60
MS1990 Two sheets, each 102×127 mm. (a) $6 multicoloured. (b) $6 multicoloured Set of 2 sheets 9·00 11·00

1998. Cavalry through the Ages. Nos. 2359/63 of Antigua optd **BARBUDA MAIL**.
1991 60c. Ancient Egyptian cavalryman 1·50 1·25
1992 60c. 13th-century English knight 1·50 1·25
1993 60c. 16th-century Spanish lancer 1·50 1·25
1994 60c. 18th-century Chinese cavalryman 1·50 1·25
MS1995 100×70 mm. $6 19th-century French cuirassier (vert) 6·50 8·00

1998. 50th Anniv of UNICEF Nos. 2364/7 of Antigua optd **BARBUDA MAIL**.
1996 75c. Girl in red sari 90 90
1997 90c. South American mother and child 1·10 1·10
1998 $1.20 Nurse with child 1·40 2·00
MS1999 114×74 mm. $6 Chinese child 4·75 6·50

1998. 3000th Anniv of Jerusalem. Nos. 2368/71 of Antigua optd **BARBUDA MAIL**.
2000 75c. Tomb of Zachariah and "Verbascum sinuatum" 2·00 1·10
2001 90c. Pool of Siloam and "Hyacinthus orientalis" 2·25 1·10
2002 $1.20 Hurva Synagogue and "Ranunculus asiaticus" 2·50 2·75
MS2003 66×80 mm. $6 Model of Herod's Temple and "Cercis siliquastrum" 7·00 7·00

1998. Diana, Princess of Wales Commemoration. Nos. 2573/85 of Antigua optd **BARBUDA MAIL**.
2004 $1.65 Diana, Princess of Wales 1·25 1·10
2005 $1.65 Wearing hoop earrings (red and black) 1·25 1·10
2006 $1.65 Carrying bouquet 1·25 1·10
2007 $1.65 Wearing floral hat 1·25 1·10
2008 $1.65 With Prince Harry 1·25 1·10
2009 $1.65 Wearing white jacket 1·25 1·10
2010 $1.65 In kitchen 1·25 1·10
2011 $1.65 Wearing black and white dress 1·25 1·10
2012 $1.65 Wearing hat (brown and black) 1·25 1·10
2013 $1.65 Wearing floral print dress (brown and black) 1·25 1·10
2014 $1.65 Dancing with John Travolta 1·25 1·10
2015 $1.65 Wearing white hat and jacket 1·25 1·10
MS2016 Two sheets, each 70×100 mm. (a) $6 Wearing red jumper. (b) $6 Wearing black dress for Papal audience (brown and black) Set of 2 sheets 9·00 11·00

1998. Broadway Musical Stars. Nos. 2384/93 of Antigua optd **BARBUDA MAIL**.
2017 $1 Robert Preston (*The Music Man*) 1·50 1·50
2018 $1 Michael Crawford (*Phantom of the Opera*) 1·50 1·50
2019 $1 Zero Mostel (*Fiddler on the Roof*) 1·50 1·50
2020 $1 Patti Lupone (*Evita*) 1·50 1·50
2021 $1 Raul Julia (*Threepenny Opera*) 1·50 1·50
2022 $1 Mary Martin (*South Pacific*) 1·50 1·50
2023 $1 Carol Channing (*Hello Dolly*) 1·50 1·50
2024 $1 Yul Brynner (*The King and I*) 1·50 1·50
2025 $1 Julie Andrews (*My Fair Lady*) 1·50 1·50
MS2026 106×76 mm. $6 Mickey Rooney (*Sugar Babies*) 7·00 8·50

1998. 20th Death Anniv of Charlie Chaplin (film star). Nos. 2404/13 of Antigua optd **BARBUDA MAIL**.
2027 $1 Charlie Chaplin as young man 1·50 1·50
2028 $1 Pulling face 1·50 1·50
2029 $1 Looking over shoulder 1·50 1·50
2030 $1 In cap 1·50 1·50
2031 $1 In front of star 1·50 1·50
2032 $1 In *The Great Dictator* 1·50 1·50
2033 $1 With movie camera and megaphone 1·50 1·50
2034 $1 Standing in front of camera lens 1·50 1·50
2035 $1 Putting on make-up 1·50 1·50
MS2036 76×106 mm. $6 Charlie Chaplin 9·00 10·00

1998. Butterflies. Nos. 2414/36 of Antigua optd **BARBUDA MAIL**.
2037 90c. *Charaxes porthos* 1·00 70
2038 $1.10 *Charaxes protoclea protoclea* 1·00 1·00
2039 $1.10 *Byblia ilithyia* 1·00 1·00
2040 $1.10 Black-headed tchagra (bird) 1·00 1·00
2041 $1.10 *Charaxes nobilis* 1·00 1·00
2042 $1.10 *Pseudacraea boisduvali trimeni* 1·00 1·00
2043 $1.10 *Charaxes smaragdalis* 1·00 1·00
2044 $1.10 *Charaxes lasti* 1·00 1·00
2045 $1.10 *Pseudacraea poggei* 1·00 1·00
2046 $1.10 *Graphium colonna* 1·00 1·00
2047 $1.10 Carmine bee eater (bird) 1·00 1·00
2048 $1.10 *Pseudacraea eurytus* 1·00 1·00
2049 $1.10 *Hypolimnas monteironis* 1·00 1·00
2050 $1.10 *Charaxes anticlea* 1·00 1·00
2051 $1.10 *Graphium leonidas* 1·00 1·00
2052 $1.10 *Graphium illyris* 1·00 1·00
2053 $1.10 *Nephronia argia* 1·00 1·00
2054 $1.10 *Graphium policenes* 1·00 1·00
2055 $1.10 *Papilio dardanus* 1·00 1·00
2056 $1.20 *Aethiopana honorius* 1·00 1·10
2057 $1.60 *Charaxes hadrianus* 1·25 1·40
2058 $1.75 *Precis westermanni* 1·40 1·60
MS2059 Three sheets, each 107×76 mm. (a) $6 *Charaxes lactincus* (horiz). (b) $6 *Eupheadra reophron*. (c) *Euxantha tiberius* (horiz) Set of 3 sheets 19·00 22·00

1998. Christmas. Dogs. Nos. 2771/8 of Antigua optd **BARBUDA MAIL**.
2060 15c. Border collie 65 60
2061 25c. Dalmatian 75 60
2062 65c. Weimaraner 1·40 80
2063 75c. Scottish terrier 1·40 85
2064 90c. Long-haired dachshund 1·50 85
2065 $1.20 Golden retriever 1·75 1·75
2066 $2 Pekingese 2·25 2·75
MS2067 Two sheets, each 75×66 mm. (a) $6 Dalmatian. (b) $6 Jack Russell terrier Set of 2 sheets 13·00 12·00

1999. Lighthouses of the World. Nos. 2612/20 of Antigua optd **BARBUDA MAIL**.
2068 45c. Europa Point Lighthouse, Gibraltar 1·50 65
2069 65c. Tierra del Fuego, Argentina (horiz) 1·75 75
2070 75c. Point Loma, California, U.S.A. (horiz) 1·75 90
2071 90c. Groenpoint, Cape Town, South Africa 1·75 90
2072 $1 Youghal, Cork, Ireland 1·75 1·25
2073 $1.20 Launceston, Tasmania, Australia 1·90 1·50
2074 $1.65 Point Abino, Ontario, Canada (horiz) 2·25 2·75
2075 $1.75 Great Inagua, Bahamas (horiz) 2·25 2·75
MS2076 99×70 mm. $6 Cape Hatteras, North Carolina, U.S.A. 11·00 11·00

1999. Endangered Species. Nos. 2457/69 of Antigua optd **BARBUDA MAIL**.
2077 $1.20 Red bishop 2·00 2·00
2078 $1.20 Yellow baboon 2·00 2·00
2079 $1.20 Superb starling 2·00 2·00
2080 $1.20 Ratel 2·00 2·00
2081 $1.20 Hunting dog 2·00 2·00
2082 $1.20 Serval 2·00 2·00
2083 $1.65 Okapi 2·25 2·25
2084 $1.65 Giant forest squirrel 2·25 2·25
2085 $1.65 Lesser masked weaver 2·25 2·25
2086 $1.65 Small-spotted genet 2·25 2·25
2087 $1.65 Yellow-billed stork 2·25 2·25
2088 $1.65 Red-headed agama 2·25 2·25
MS2089 Three sheets, each 106×76 mm. (a) $6 South African crowned crane. (b) $6 Bat-eared fox. (c) $6 Malachite kingfisher Set of 3 sheets 19·00 22·00

1999. "Pacific 97" International Stamp Exhibition, San Francisco. Death Centenary of Heinrich von Stephan (founder of the U.P.U.). Nos. 2481/4 of Antigua optd **BARBUDA MAIL**.
2090 $1.75 blue 2·50 2·50
2091 $1.75 brown 2·50 2·50
2092 $1.75 mauve 2·50 2·50
MS2093 82×119 mm. $6 violet 4·75 6·00
DESIGNS: No. 2090, Kaiser Wilhelm I and Heinrich von Stephan; 2091, Von Stephan and Mercury; 2092, Carrier pigeon and loft; **MS**2093 Von Stephan and 15th-century Basel messenger.

1999. 175th Anniv of Brothers Grimm's Third Collection of Fairy Tales. Cinderella. Nos. 2485/8 of Antigua optd **BARBUDA MAIL**.
2094 $1.75 The Ugly Sisters and their Mother 2·75 2·75
2095 $1.75 Cinderella and her Fairy Godmother 2·75 2·75
2096 $1.75 Cinderella and the Prince 2·75 2·75
MS2097 124×96 mm. $6 Cinderella trying on slipper 6·00 7·50

1999. Orchids of the World. Nos. 2502/24 of Antigua optd **BARBUDA MAIL**.
2098 45c. *Odontoglossum cervantesii* 1·50 45
2099 65c. *Phalaenopsis* Medford Star 1·75 35
2100 75c. *Vanda* Motes Resplendent 1·75 85
2101 90c. *Odontonia* Debutante 2·00 1·00
2102 $1 *Iwanagaara* Apple Blossom 2·25 1·10
2103 $1.65 *Cattleya* Sophia Martin 2·25 2·00
2104 $1.65 Dogface Butterfly 2·25 2·00
2105 $1.65 *Laeliocattleya* Mini Purple 2·25 2·00
2106 $1.65 *Cymbidium* Showgirl 2·25 2·00
2107 $1.65 *Brassolaeliocattleya* Dorothy Bertsch 2·25 2·00
2108 $1.65 *Disa blackii* 2·25 2·00
2109 $1.65 *Paphiopedilum leeanum* 2·25 2·00
2110 $1.65 *Paphiopedilum macranthum* 2·25 2·00
2111 $1.65 *Brassocattleya* Angel Lace 2·25 2·00
2112 $1.65 *Saphrolae liocattleya* Precious Stones 2·25 2·00
2113 $1.65 Orange Theope Butterfly 2·25 2·00
2114 $1.65 *Promenaea xanthina* 2·25 2·00
2115 $1.65 *Lycasle macrobulbon* 2·25 2·00
2116 $1.65 *Amestella philippinensis* 2·25 2·00
2117 $1.65 *Masdevallia* Machu Picchu 2·25 2·00
2118 $1.65 *Phalaenopsis* Zuma Urchin 2·25 2·00
2119 $2 *Dendrobium victoria-reginae* 2·75 2·75
MS2120 Two sheets, each 76×106 mm. (a) $6 *Miltonia* Seine. (b) $6 *Paphiopedilum gratrixanum* Set of 2 sheets 15·00 15·00

1999. 50th Death Anniv of Paul Harris (founder of Rotary International). No. 2472/3 of Antigua optd **BARBUDA MAIL**.
2121 $1.65 Paul Harris and James Grant 2·50 3·25
MS2122 78×107 mm. $6 Group study exchange, New Zealand 5·00 7·00

1999. Royal Wedding. Nos. 2912/16 of Antigua optd **BARBUDA MAIL**.
2123 $3 Sophie Rhys-Jones 2·50 2·75
2124 $3 Sophie and Prince Edward 2·50 2·75
2125 $3 Prince Edward 2·50 2·75
MS2126 108×78 mm. $6 Prince Edward with Sophie Rhys-Jones and Windsor Castle 6·00 7·50
All examples of Nos. 2123/5 show the incorrect country overprint as above.

1999. Fungi. Nos. 2489/501 of Antigua optd **BARBUDA MAIL**.
2127 45c. *Marasmius rotula* 1·00 35
2128 65c. *Cantharellus cibarius* 1·25 55
2129 70c. *Lepiota cristata* 1·25 60
2130 90c. *Auricularia mesenterica* 1·40 70
2131 $1 *Pholiota alnicola* 1·40 1·00
2132 $1.65 *Leccinum aurantiacum* 1·40 1·75
2133 $1.75 *Entoloma serrulatum* 1·40 1·75
2134 $1.75 *Panaeolus sphinctrinus* 1·40 1·75
2135 $1.75 *Volvariella bombycina* 1·40 1·75
2136 $1.75 *Conocybe percincta* 1·40 1·75
2137 $1.75 *Pluteus cervinus* 1·40 1·75
2138 $1.75 *Russula foetens* 1·40 1·75
MS2139 Two sheets, each 106×76 mm. (a) $6 *Amanita cothurnata*. (b) $6 *Panellus serotinus* Set of 2 sheets 12·00 14·00

1999. First Death Anniv of Diana, Princess of Wales. No. 2753 of Antigua optd **BARBUDA MAIL**.
2140 $1.20 Diana, Princess of Wales 1·50 1·50

1999. Railway Locomotives of the World. Nos. 2553/65 of Antigua optd **BARBUDA MAIL**.
2141 $1.65 Original drawing by Richard Trevithick, 1803 1·75 1·75
2142 $1.65 William Hedley's *Puffing Billy*, (1813–14) 1·75 1·75
2143 $1.65 Crampton locomotive of French Nord Railway, 1858 1·75 1·75
2144 $1.65 Lawrence Machine Shop locomotive, U.S.A., 1860 1·75 1·75
2145 $1.65 Natchez and Hamburg Railway steam locomotive *Mississippi*, U.S.A., 1834 1·75 1·75
2146 $1.65 Bury "Coppernob" locomotive, Furness Railway, 1846 1·75 1·75
2147 $1.65 David Joy's *Jenny Lind*, 1847 1·75 1·75
2148 $1.65 Schenectady Atlantic locomotive, U.S.A., 1899 1·75 1·75
2149 $1.65 Kitson Class 1800 tank locomotive, Japan, 1881 1·75 1·75
2150 $1.65 Pennsylvania Railroad express freight 1·75 1·75
2151 $1.65 Karl Golsdorf's 4 cylinder locomotive, Austria 1·75 1·75
2152 $1.65 Series "E" locomotive, Russia, 1930 1·75 1·75
MS2153 Two sheets, each 72×100 mm. (a) $6 George Stephenson's "Patentee" Type locomotive, 1843. (b) $6 Brunel's trestle bridge over River Lynher, Cornwall 11·00 12·00

1999. 175th Anniv of Cedar Hall Moravian Church. Nos. 2605/11 of Antigua optd **BARBUDA MAIL**.
2154 20c. First Church and Manse, 1822–40 45 50
2155 45c. Cedar Hall School, 1840 55 40
2156 75c. Hugh A. King, minister, 1945–53 75 60
2157 90c. Present Church building 85 60
2158 $1.20 Water tank, 1822 1·25 1·25
2159 $2 Former Manse, demolished 1978 1·75 3·00
MS2160 100×70 mm. $6 Present church building (different) (50×37 mm) 4·75 6·50

1999. Christmas. Religious Paintings. Nos. 2945/51 of Antigua optd **BARBUDA MAIL**.
2161 15c. multicoloured 35 40
2162 25c. black, stone and yellow 40 40
2163 45c. multicoloured 55 30
2164 60c. multicoloured 80 35
2165 $2 multicoloured 1·75 2·50
2166 $4 black, stone and yellow 2·75 4·50
MS2167 76×106 mm. $6 multicoloured 4·50 6·00

1999. Centenary of Thomas Oliver Robinson Memorial School. Nos. 2634/40 of Antigua optd **BARBUDA MAIL**.
2168 20c. green and black 35 40
2169 45c. multicoloured 55 30

2170	65c. green and black	75	45
2171	75c. multicoloured	80	65
2172	90c. multicoloured	90	65
2173	$1.20 brown, green and black	1·10	1·50
MS2174	106×76 mm. $6 brown	4·50	6·00

2000. Cats and Dogs. Nos. 2540/52 of Antigua optd **BARBUDA MAIL**.

2175	$1.65 Scottish fold kitten	2·25	2·25
2176	$1.65 Japanese bobtail	2·25	2·25
2177	$1.65 Tabby manx	2·25	2·25
2178	$1.65 Bicolor American shorthair	2·25	2·25
2179	$1.65 Sorel Abyssinian	2·25	2·25
2180	$1.65 Himalayan blue point	2·25	2·25
2181	$1.65 Dachshund	2·25	2·25
2182	$1.65 Staffordshire terrier	2·25	2·25
2183	$1.65 Shar-pei	2·25	2·25
2184	$1.65 Beagle	2·25	2·25
2185	$1.65 Norfolk terrier	2·25	2·25
2186	$1.65 Golden retriever	2·25	2·25
MS2187	Two sheets, each 107×77 mm. (a) $6 Red tabby (vert). (b) $6 Siberian husky (vert)	15·00	17·00

2000. Fish. Nos. 2586/604 of Antigua optd **BARBUDA MAIL**.

2188	75c. Yellow damselfish	75	50
2189	90c. Barred hamlet	80	55
2190	$1 Yellow-tailed damselfish ("Jewelfish")	90	70
2191	$1.20 Blue-headed wrasse	1·10	1·00
2192	$1.50 Queen angelfish	1·25	1·25
2193	$1.65 Jackknife-fish	1·25	1·25
2194	$1.65 Spot-finned hogfish	1·25	1·25
2195	$1.65 Sergeant major	1·25	1·25
2196	$1.65 Neon goby	1·25	1·25
2197	$1.65 Jawfish	1·25	1·25
2198	$1.65 Flamefish	1·25	1·25
2199	$1.65 Rock beauty	1·25	1·25
2200	$1.65 Yellow-tailed snapper	1·25	1·25
2201	$1.65 Creole wrasse	1·25	1·25
2202	$1.65 Slender filefish	1·25	1·25
2203	$1.65 Long-spined squirrelfish	1·25	1·25
2204	$1.65 Royal gramma ("Fairy Basslet")	1·25	1·25
2205	$1.75 Queen triggerfish	1·40	1·40
MS2206	Two sheets, each 80×110 mm. (a) $6 Porkfish. (b) $6 Black-capped basslet	20·00	20·00

2000. Ships of the World. Nos. 2679/85 of Antigua optd **BARBUDA MAIL**.

2207	$1.75 *Savannah* (paddle-steamer)	1·75	1·75
2208	$1.75 Viking longship	1·75	1·75
2209	$1.75 Greek galley	1·75	1·75
2210	$1.75 Sailing clipper	1·75	1·75
2211	$1.75 Dhow	1·75	1·75
2212	$1.75 Fishing catboat	1·75	1·75
MS2213	Three sheets, each 100×70 mm. (a) $6 13th-century English warship (41×22 mm). (b) $6 Sailing dory (22×41 mm). (c) $6 Baltimore clipper (41×22 mm)	14·00	16·00

2000. Modern Aircraft. Nos. 2700/12 of Antigua optd **BARBUDA MAIL**.

2214	$1.65 Lockheed-Boeing General Dynamics Yf-22	1·75	1·75
2215	$1.65 Dassault-Breguet Rafale BO 1	1·75	1·75
2216	$1.65 MiG 29	1·75	1·75
2217	$1.65 Dassault-Breguet Mirage 2000D	1·75	1·75
2218	$1.65 Rockwell B-1B "Lancer"	1·75	1·75
2219	$1.65 McDonnell-Douglas C-17A	1·75	1·75
2220	$1.65 Space Shuttle	1·75	1·75
2221	$1.65 SAAB "Grippen"	1·75	1·75
2222	$1.65 Eurofighter EF-2000	1·75	1·75
2223	$1.65 Sukhoi SU 27	1·75	1·75
2224	$1.65 Northrop B-2	1·75	1·75
2225	$1.65 Lockheed F-117 "Night-hawk"	1·75	1·75
MS2226	Two sheets, each 110×85 mm. (a) $6 F18 Hornet. (b) $6 Sukhoi SU 35	13·00	15·00

2000. Classic Cars. Nos. 2687/MS2699 of Antigua optd **BARBUDA MAIL**.

2227	$1.65 Ford (1896)	1·75	1·75
2228	$1.65 Ford A (1903)	1·75	1·75
2229	$1.65 Ford T (1928)	1·75	1·75
2230	$1.65 Ford T (1922)	1·75	1·75
2231	$1.65 Ford Blackhawk (1929)	1·75	1·75
2232	$1.65 Ford Sedan (1934)	1·75	1·75
2233	$1.65 Torpedo (1911)	1·75	1·75
2234	$1.65 Mercedes 22 (1913)	1·75	1·75
2235	$1.65 Rover (1920)	1·75	1·75
2236	$1.65 Mercedes Benz (1956)	1·75	1·75
2237	$1.65 Packard V-12 (1934)	1·75	1·75
2238	$1.65 Opel (1924)	1·75	1·75
MS2239	Two sheets, each 70×100 mm. (a) $6 Ford (1908) (60×40 mm). (b) $6 Ford (1929) (60×40 mm) Set of 2 sheets	12·00	13·00

2000. 19th World Scout Jamboree, Chile. Nos. 2739/**MS**2742 of Antigua optd **BARBUDA MAIL**.

2240	90c. Scout handshake	1·50	1·00
2241	$1 Scouts hiking	1·75	1·25
2242	$1.20 Scout salute	2·25	2·50
MS2243	68×98 mm. $6 Lord Baden-Powell	7·50	8·50

2000. 50th Anniv of Organisation of American States (1998). No. 2730 of Antigua optd **BARBUDA MAIL**.

2244	$1 Stylized Americas	1·25	1·50

2000. International Year of the Ocean (1998). Nos. 2641/**MS**2678a/b of Antigua optd **BARBUDA MAIL**.

2245-2269	40c.×25 Spotted eagle ray; Manta ray; Hawksbill turtle; Jellyfish; Queen angelfish; Octopus; Emperor angelfish; Regal angelfish; Porkfish; Racoon butterflyfish; Atlantic barracuda; Sea horse; Nautilus; Trumpetfish; White tip shark; Sunken Spanish galleon; Black tip shark; Long-nosed butterflyfish; Green moray eel; Captain Nemo; Treasure chest; Hammerhead shark; Divers; Lionfish; Clownfish	14·00	15·00
2270-2281	75c.×12 Maroon-tailed conure; Cocoi heron; Common tern; Rainbow lorikeet; Saddleback butterflyfish; Goatfish and cat shark; Blue shark and stingray; Majestic snapper; Nassau grouper; Black-cap gramma and blue tang; Stingrays; Stingray and giant starfish	18·00	20·00
MS2282	Two sheets. (a) 68×98 mm. $6 Humpback whale. (b) 98×68 mm. $6 Fiddler ray Set of 2 sheets	15·00	16·00

Nos. 2245/69 and 2270/81 were each printed together, *se-tenant*, with the backgrounds forming composite designs.

2000. Olympic Games, Sydney. Nos. 3109/12 of Antigua optd **BARBUDA MAIL**.

2283	$2 Marcus Latimer Hurley (cycling), St Louis (1904)	4·50	3·75
2284	$2 Diving	4·50	3·75
2285	$2 Flaminio Stadium, Rome (1960) and Italian flag	4·50	3·75
2286	$2 Ancient Greek javelin thrower	4·50	3·75

2000. West Indies Cricket Tour and 100th Test Match at Lord's. Nos. 3113/MS3115 of Antigua optd **BARBUDA MAIL**.

2287	90c. Richie Richardson	2·25	1·60
2288	$5 Viv Richards	8·00	9·00
MS2289	121×104 mm. $6 Lord's Cricket Ground	9·00	10·00

2000. Satellites and Spacecraft. Nos. 2835/40 and **MS**2847b of Antigua optd **BARBUDA MAIL**.

2290	$1.65 "Luna 2" moon probe	2·50	2·50
2291	$1.65 "Mariner 2" space probe	2·50	2·50
2292	$1.65 Giotto space probe	2·50	2·50
2293	$1.65 Rosat satellite	2·50	2·50
2294	$1.65 International Ultraviolet Explorer	2·50	2·50
2295	$1.65 Ulysses space probe	2·50	2·50
MS2296	106×76 mm. $6 "MIR" space station	8·50	9·50

2000. No. **MS**3233 of Antigua optd **BARBUDA MAIL**.

MS2313	Two Sheets, each 90×60 mm. (a) $6 Junkers 87B (dive bomber). (b) $6 Supermarine Spitfires at dusk	17·00	18·00

Pt. 1

BARWANI

A State of Central India. Now uses Indian stamps.

12 pies = 1 anna; 16 annas = 1 rupee.

1 Rana Ranjit Singh

2

1921

5	**1**	¼a. green	24·00	£120
18	**1**	¼a. pink	3·50	18·00
19	**1**	¼a. blue	1·75	11·00
37B	**1**	¼a. black	5·50	48·00
4	**1**	½a. blue	22·00	£275
29	**1**	½a. green	2·75	20·00
10	**2**	1a. red	3·75	27·00
39B	**2**	1a. brown	15·00	38·00
11	**2**	2a. purple	2·50	32·00
41B	**2**	2a. red	40·00	£170
31	**2**	4a. orange	90·00	£325
42Ba	-	4a. green	17·00	60·00

DESIGN: 4a. Another portrait of Rana Ranjit Singh.

4 Rana Devi Singh

1932

32A	**4**	¼a. slate	4·00	28·00
33A	**4**	½a. green	5·00	28·00
34A	**4**	1a. brown	5·00	26·00
35A	**4**	2a. purple	4·00	55·00
36A	**4**	4a. olive	6·00	50·00

5

1938

43	**5**	1a. brown	50·00	85·00

Pt. 1

BASUTOLAND

An African territory under British protection, N.E. of Cape Province. Self-Government introduced on 1 April 1965. Attained independence on 4 October 1966, when the country was renamed Lesotho.

1933. 12 pence = 1 shilling; 20 shillings = 1 pound.
1961. 100 cents = 1 rand.

1 King George V, Nile Crocodile and Mountains

1933

1	**1**	½d. green	1·00	1·75
2	**1**	1d. red	75	1·25
3	**1**	2d. purple	1·00	80
4	**1**	3d. blue	75	1·25
5	**1**	4d. grey	2·00	7·00
6	**1**	6d. yellow	2·25	1·75
7	**1**	1s. orange	3·25	4·50
8	**1**	2s.6d. brown	35·00	55·00
9	**1**	5s. violet	65·00	85·00
10	**1**	10s. olive	£180	£190

1935. Silver Jubilee. As T **13** of Antigua.

11	1d. blue and red	65	3·25
12	2d. blue and grey	75	3·25
13	3d. brown and blue	4·00	7·50
14	6d. grey and purple	4·00	7·50

1937. Coronation. As T **2** of Aden.

15	1d. red	35	1·25
16	2d. purple	50	1·25
17	3d. blue	60	1·25

1938. As T **1**, but portrait of King George VI.

18	½d. green	30	1·25
19	1d. red	1·00	70
20	1½d. blue	60	50
21	2d. purple	40	60
22	3d. blue	40	1·25
23	4d. grey	2·00	3·75
24	6d. yellow	3·00	1·50
25	1s. orange	3·00	1·00
26	2s.6d. brown	18·00	8·50
27	5s. violet	42·00	9·50
28	10s. olive	42·00	22·00

1945. Victory. Stamps of South Africa optd **Basutoland**. Alternate stamps inscr in English or Afrikaans.

29	**55**	1d. brown and red	50	10
30	**55**	2d. blue and violet	50	10
31	**55**	3d. blue	50	15

Prices are for bi-lingual pairs.

5 King George VI and Queen Elizabeth

1947. Royal Visit.

32	-	1d. red	10	10
33	**5**	2d. green	10	10
34	-	3d. blue	10	10
35	-	1s. mauve	15	10

DESIGNS—VERT: 1d. King George VI. HORIZ: 3d. Queen Elizabeth II as Princess and Princess Margaret; 1s. The Royal Family.

1948. Silver Wedding. As T **10/11** of Aden.

36	1½d. blue	20	10
37	10s. green	48·00	50·00

1949. U.P.U. As T **20/23** of Antigua.

38	1½d. blue	20	1·50
39	3d. blue	2·00	2·00
40	6d. orange	1·00	5·00
41	1s. brown	50	1·40

1953. Coronation. As T **13** of Aden.

42	2d. black and purple	55	40

8 Qiloane

18 Mohair (Shearing Goats)

1954

43	**8**	½d. black and sepia	55	10
44	-	1d. black and green	40	10
45	-	2d. blue and orange	1·25	10
46	-	3d. sage and red	2·00	30
47	-	4½d. indigo and blue	1·50	15
48	-	6d. brown and green	2·00	15
49	-	1s. bronze and purple	2·00	30
50	-	1s.3d. brown and turquoise	27·00	9·00
51	-	2s.6d. blue and red	27·00	12·00
52	-	5s. black and red	11·00	12·00
53	**18**	10s. black and purple	35·00	27·00

DESIGNS—HORIZ: 1d. Orange River; 2d. Mosuto horseman; 3d. Basuto household; 4½d. Maletsunyane Falls; 6d. Herd-boy playing lesiba; 1s. Pastoral scene; 1s.3d. De Havilland Comet 1 airplane over Lancers' Gap; 2s.6d. Old Fort, Leribe; 5s. Mission cave house.

1959. No. 45 Surch **½d.** and bar.

54	½d. on 2d. blue and orange	20	20

20 "Chief Moshoeshoe I" (engraving by Delangle)

1959. Inauguration of National Council.

55	**20**	3d. black and olive	60	10
56	-	1s. red and green	60	20
57	-	1s.3d. blue and orange	80	45

DESIGNS: 1s. Council house; 1s.3d. Mosuto horseman.

1961. Nos. 43/53 surch.

58	**8**	½c. on ½d. black and sepia	10	30
59	-	1c. on 1d. black and green	10	10
60	-	2c. on 2d. blue and orange	1·25	1·25
61	-	2½c. on 3d. green and red	10	10
62	-	3½c. on 4½d. indigo and blue	35	10
63a	-	5c. on 6d. brown and green	40	10
64	-	10c. on 1s. green and purple	50	10
65a	-	12½c. on 1s.3d. brown and turquoise	6·00	2·50
66	-	25c. on 2s.6d. blue and red	1·50	60
67a	-	50c. on 5s. black and red	4·50	4·50
68b	**18**	1r. on 10s. black and purple	27·00	25·00

26 Basuto Household

1961. As 1954 but value in new currency as in T **26**.

69	**8**	½c. black and brown	20	20
70	-	1c. black and green (as 1d.)	20	40
71	-	2c. blue and orange (as 2d.)	3·00	1·40
86	**26**	2½c. green and red	25	25
73	-	3½c. indigo and blue (as 4½d.)	45	1·50
88	-	5c. brown and green (as 6d.)	40	50
75	-	10c. green and purple (as 1s.)	40	40
90	-	12½c. brown & grn (as 1s.3d.)	9·00	1·50
77	-	25c. blue and red (as 2s.6d.)	6·50	6·50

92	-	50c. black and red (as 5s.)	7·25	13·00
79	18	1r. black and purple	55·00	25·00

1963. Freedom from Hunger. As T **28** of Aden.

80	12½c. violet	40	15

1963. Centenary of Red Cross. As T **33** of Antigua.

81	2½c. red and black	20	10
82	12½c. red and blue	80	60

28 Mosotho Woman and Child

1965. New Constitution. Inscr "SELF GOVERNMENT 1965". Multicoloured.

94	2½c. Type **28**	20	10
95	3½c. Maseru border post	35	20
96	5c. Mountain scene	35	20
97	12½c. Legislative Buildings	60	70

1965. Centenary of I.T.U. As T **36** of Antigua.

98	1c. red and purple	15	10
99	20c. blue and brown	50	30

1965. I.C.Y. As T **37** of Antigua.

100	½c. purple and turquoise	10	90
101	12½c. green and lavender	45	35

1966. Churchill Commemoration. As T **38** of Antigua.

102	1c. blue	15	1·50
103	2½c. green	50	10
104	10c. brown	75	50
105	22½c. violet	1·25	1·50

OFFICIAL STAMPS

1934. Nos. 1/3 and 6 optd **OFFICIAL**.

O1	1	½d. green	£13000	£7000
O2	1	1d. red	£4500	£3500
O3	1	2d. purple	£5000	£1100
O4	1	6d. yellow	£13000	£4750

POSTAGE DUE STAMPS

1933. As Type D **1** of Barbados.

D1b	1d. red	2·00	8·00
D2a	2d. violet	30	25·00

D 2

1956

D3	**D2**	1d. red	30	3·00
D4	**D2**	2d. violet	30	6·00

1961. Surch.

D5		1c. on 1d. red	10	35
D6		1c. on 2d. violet	10	1·25
D7		5c. on 2d. violet	15	45
D8	-	5c. on 2d. violet (No. D2a)	1·00	7·00

1964. As Type D **2**, but value in decimal currency.

D9	1c. red	4·25	25·00
D10	5c. violet	4·25	25·00

For later issues see **LESOTHO**.

Pt. 1

BATUM

Batum, a Russian port on the Black Sea, had been taken by Turkish troops during the First World War. Following the Armistice, British Forces occupied the town on 1 December 1918. Batum was handed over to the National Republic of Georgia on 7 July 1920.

100 kopeks = 1 rouble.

1 Aloe Tree

1919. Imperf.

1	1	5k. green	7·00	24·00
2	1	10k. blue	7·50	24·00
3	1	50k. yellow	7·00	11·00
4	1	1r. brown	9·50	8·50
5	1	3r. violet	10·00	18·00
6	1	5r. brown	10·00	35·00

БАТУМ. ОБ.

Руб 10 Руб

(2)

1919. Arms types of Russia surch as T **2**. Imperf (Nos. 7/8), perf (Nos. 9/10).

7	10r. on 1k. orange	75·00	85·00
8	10r. on 3k. red	29·00	35·00
9	10r. on 5k. purple	£425	£475
10	10r. on 10 on 7k. blue	£500	£550

1919. T **1** optd **BRITISH OCCUPATION**.

11	5k. green	27·00	18·00
12	10k. blue	16·00	20·00
13	25k. yellow	26·00	20·00
14	1r. blue	7·50	20·00
15	2r. pink	1·00	8·00
16	3r. violet	1·00	8·00
17	5r. brown	1·25	8·00
18	7r. red	5·50	11·00

1919. Arms types of Russia surch with Russian inscr, **BRITISH OCCUPATION** and new value.

19	10r. on 3k. red	26·00	28·00
20a	15r. on 1k. orange	75·00	80·00
29	25r. on 5k. purple	50·00	70·00
30a	25r. on 10 on 7k. blue	85·00	95·00
31	25r. on 20 on 14k. red and blue	95·00	£120
32a	25r. on 25k. purple and green	£110	£140
33a	25r. on 50k. green and purple	90·00	£120
21	50r. on 1k. orange	£600	£700
34	50r. on 2k. green	£130	£160
35	50r. on 3k. red	£130	£160
36	50r. on 4k. red	£120	£140
37	50r. on 5k. purple	95·00	£120
27	50r. on 10k. blue	£2250	£2250
28	50r. on 15k. blue and brown	£750	£900

1920. Romanov type of Russia surch with Russian inscr, **BRITISH OCCUPATION** and new value.

41	50r. on 4k. red	£100	£120

1920. Nos. 11, 13 and 3 surch with new value (50r. with **BRITISH OCCUPATION** also).

42	25r. on 5k. green	48·00	50·00
43	25r. on 25k. yellow	38·00	40·00
44a	50r. on 50k. yellow	20·00	22·00

1920. T **1** optd **BRITISH OCCUPATION**.

45	1r. brown	2·25	14·00
46	2r. blue	2·25	14·00
47	3r. pink	2·25	14·00
48	5r. black	2·25	14·00
49	7r. yellow	2·25	14·00
50	10r. green	2·25	14·00
51	15r. violet	2·75	19·00
52	25r. red	2·50	18·00
53	50r. blue	2·75	22·00

Pt. 7

BAVARIA

In S. Germany. A kingdom till 1918, then a republic. Incorporated into Germany in 1920.

1849. 60 kreuzer = 1 gulden.
1874. 100 pfennig = 1 mark.

1

1849. Imperf.

1	1k. black	£1200	£1700

2 (Circle cut)

1849. Imperf. Circle cut by labels.

3	2	3k. blue	£300	4·75
23	2	3k. red	70·00	6·50
7	2	6k. brown	£8500	£300

1850. Imperf. As T **2**, but circle not cut.

8a	1k. red	£250	30·00
21	1k. yellow	95·00	25·00
11	6k. brown	60·00	12·00
25	6k. blue	95·00	50·00
16	9k. green	£275	20·00
28	9k. brown	£150	20·00
18	12k. red	£200	£170
31	12k. green	£130	80·00
19	18k. yellow	£180	£250
32	18k. red	£200	£600

3

6

1867. Imperf.

34	3	1k. green	85·00	15·00
37	3	3k. red	90·00	3·00
39	3	6k. blue	60·00	24·00
41	3	6k. brown	£110	60·00
43	3	7k. blue	£550	20·00
46	3	9k. brown	60·00	46·00
48	3	12k. mauve	£475	£120
50	3	18k. red	£180	£225
65	6	1m. mauve	£850	£100

1870. Perf.

51A	3	1k. green	15·00	2·00
69	3	3k. red	1·10	10·00
55A	3	6k. brown	42·00	41·00
56A	3	7k. blue	4·75	5·50
59A	3	9k. brown	5·75	5·00
60A	3	10k. yellow	7·50	17·00
61A	3	12k. mauve	£1600	£6000
63A	3	18k. red	16·00	18·00

8

1876. Perf.

120	8	2pf. grey	3·25	70
103	8	3pf. green	13·50	2·50
121	8	3pf. brown	40	80
107	8	5pf. mauve	27·00	10·00
122	8	5pf. green	40	80
123	8	10pf. red	55	1·00
124	8	20pf. blue	55	1·00
114	8	25pf. brown	42·00	8·75
125	8	25pf. orange	55	1·20
126	8	30pf. olive	1·10	1·00
127	8	40pf. yellow	1·10	1·40
86	8	50pf. red	75·00	9·25
117	8	50pf. brown	80·00	5·00
128	8	50pf. purple	65	2·00
129	8	80pf. mauve	4·25	5·00
100	6	1m. mauve	6·25	5·00
101a	6	2m. orange	7·50	10·00
136	6	3m. brown	11·50	46·00
137	6	5m. green	11·50	55·00

11

13 Prince Luitpold

1911. Prince Regent Luitpold's 90th Birthday.

138c	11	3pf. brown on drab	40	1·00
139c	11	5pf. green on green	40	1·00
140d	11	10pf. red on buff	40	1·00
141b	11	20pf. blue on blue	2·75	1·60
142a	11	25pf. deep brown on buff	4·25	3·00
143a	-	30pf. orange on buff	2·75	2·50
144a	-	40pf. olive on buff	4·25	2·50
145a	-	50pf. red on drab	4·25	13·00
146	-	60pf. green on buff	4·25	4·25
147a	-	80pf. violet on drab	12·50	13·00
148a	13	1m. brown on drab	4·25	5·00
149a	13	2m. green on green	6·25	15·00
150a	13	3m. red on buff	17·00	£100
151	13	5m. blue on buff	34·00	60·00
152	13	10m. orange on yellow	60·00	95·00
153	13	20m. brown on yellow	34·00	50·00

The 30 pf. to 80 pf. values are similar to Type **11**, but larger.

14

1911. 25th Anniv of Regency of Prince Luitpold.

154	14	5pf. yellow, green & black	1·10	1·80
155	14	10pf. yellow, red & black	1·60	3·00

15 King Ludwig III

16

1914. Imperf or perf.

171A	15	2pf. slate	35	2·75
172A	15	2½ on 2pf. slate	35	2·75
173A	15	3pf. brown	35	2·75
175A	15	5pf. green	35	2·75
176A	15	7½pf. green	35	2·75
178A	15	10pf. red	35	2·75
179A	15	15pf. red	35	2·75
182A	15	20pf. blue	35	2·75
183A	15	25pf. grey	35	2·75
184A	15	30pf. orange	1·60	2·75
185A	15	40pf. olive	35	2·75
186A	15	50pf. brown	35	2·75
187A	15	60pf. green	1·60	2·75
188A	15	80pf. violet	35	2·75
189A	16	1m. brown	35	2·75
190A	16	2m. violet	45	3·75
191A	16	3m. red	55	7·50
192A	-	5m. blue	75	27·00
193A	-	10m. green	2·40	75·00
194A	-	20m. brown	4·50	£110

The 5, 10 and 20m. are larger.

1919. Peoples' State Issue. Overprinted **Volksstaat Bayern**. Imperf or perf.

195A	15	3pf. brown	35	2·75
196A	15	5pf. green	35	2·75
197A	15	7½pf. green	35	2·75
198A	15	10pf. lake	35	2·75
199A	15	15pf. red	35	2·75
200A	15	20pf. blue	35	2·75
201A	15	25pf. grey	35	2·75
202A	15	30pf. orange	35	2·75
203A	15	35pf. orange	35	3·25
204A	15	40pf. olive	35	2·75
205A	15	50pf. brown	35	2·75
206A	15	60pf. turquoise	35	2·75
207A	15	75pf. brown	35	2·75
208A	15	80pf. violet	35	2·75
209A	16	1m. brown	35	2·75
210A	16	2m. violet	45	2·75
211A	16	3m. red	65	6·25
212A	-	5m. blue (No. 192)	1·30	16·00
213A	-	10m. green (No. 193)	2·00	75·00
214A	-	20m. brown (No. 194)	3·25	70·00

1919. First Free State Issue. Stamps of Germany (inscr "DEUTSCHES REICH") optd **Freistaat Bayern**.

215	24	2½pf. grey	35	2·75
216	10	3pf. brown	35	2·75
217	10	5pf. green	35	2·75
218	24	7½pf. orange	35	2·75
219	10	10pf. red	35	2·75
220	24	15pf. violet	35	2·75
221	10	20pf. blue	35	2·75
222	10	25pf. black & red on yell	35	2·75
223	24	35pf. brown	35	2·75
224	10	40pf. black and red	55	2·75
225	10	75pf. black and green	75	3·25
226	10	80pf. black & red on rose	75	4·25
227	12	1m. red	1·80	6·25
228	13	2m. blue	2·20	15·00
229	14	3m. black	2·20	17·00
230	15	5m. red and black	2·20	17·00

1919. Second Free State Issue. Stamps of Bavaria overprinted **Freistaat Bayern**. Imperf or perf.

231A		3pf. brown	35	2·75
232A		5pf. green	35	2·75
233A		7½pf. green	35	21·00
234A		10pf. lake	35	2·75
235A		15pf. red	35	2·75
236A		20pf. blue	35	2·75
237A		25pf. grey	35	2·75
238A		30pf. orange	35	2·75
239A		40pf. olive	35	19·00
240A		50pf. brown	35	2·75
241A		60pf. turquoise	35	19·00
242A		75pf. brown	55	19·00
243A		80pf. violet	35	4·75
244A	16	1m. brown	35	3·75
245A	16	2m. violet	35	7·50
246A	16	3m. red	90	9·50
247A	-	5m. blue (No. 192)	1·50	23·00
248A	-	10m. green (No. 193)	2·75	48·00
249A	-	20m. brown (No. 194)	3·25	80·00

1919. War Wounded. **Surch 5 Pf. fur Kriegs-beschadigte Freistaat Bayern.** Perf.

250	15	10pf.+5pf. lake	55	2·75
251	15	15pf.+5pf. red	55	2·75
252	15	20pf.+5pf. blue	55	3·25

1920. Surch **Freistaat Bayern** and value. Imperf or perf.

253A	16	1m.25pf. on 1m. green	35	3·25
254A	16	1m.50pf. on 1m. orange	35	4·25
255A	16	2m.50pf. on 1m. slate	65	8·50

1920. No. 121 surch **20** in four corners.

256	8	20 on 3pf. brown	35	2·75

26

27

28

29

30

1920

257	**26**	5pf. green	20	3·25
258	**26**	10pf. orange	20	3·25
259	**26**	15pf. red	20	3·25
260	**27**	20pf. violet	20	3·25
261	**27**	30pf. blue	20	4·25
262	**27**	40pf. brown	20	3·25
263	**28**	50pf. red	20	3·25
264	**28**	60pf. turquoise	20	3·25
265	**28**	75pf. red	20	3·25
266	**29**	1m. red and grey	45	3·25
267	**29**	1¼m. blue and brown	35	3·25
268	**29**	1½m. green and grey	35	4·25
269	**29**	2½m. black and grey	35	42·00
270	**30**	3m. blue	1·00	19·00
271	**30**	5m. orange	1·00	19·00
272	**30**	10m. green	1·60	32·00
273	**30**	20m. black	2·20	44·00

OFFICIAL STAMPS

O18

1916

O195	**O18**	3pf. brown	35	1·10
O196	**O18**	5pf. green	35	1·10
O197	**O18**	7½pf. green on green	35	65
O198	**O18**	7½pf. green	35	1·10
O199	**O18**	10pf. red	35	85
O200	**O18**	15pf. red on buff	90	95
O201	**O18**	15pf. red	35	1·10
O202	**O18**	20pf. blue on blue	2·75	2·75
O203	**O18**	20pf. blue	35	85
O204	**O18**	25pf. grey	35	85
O205	**O18**	30pf. orange	35	85
O206	**O18**	60pf. turquoise	35	1·60
O207	**O18**	1m. purple on buff	1·30	3·75
O208	**O18**	1m. purple	3·75	£650

1919. Optd **Volksstaat Bayern**.

O215	3pf. brown	35	18·00
O216	5pf. green	35	2·75
O217	7½pf. green	35	17·00
O218	10pf. red	35	3·00
O219	15pf. red	35	3·00
O220	20pf. blue	35	3·00
O221	25pf. grey	35	3·00
O222	30pf. orange	35	3·00
O223	35pf. orange	35	3·00
O224	50pf. olive	35	3·25
O225	60pf. turquoise	45	18·00
O226	75pf. brown	45	4·75
O227	1m. purple on buff	1·50	19·00
O228	1m. purple	5·50	£500

O31

O32

O33

1920

O274	**O31**	5pf. green	35	8·50
O275	**O31**	10pf. orange	35	8·50
O276	**O31**	15pf. red	35	8·50
O277	**O31**	20pf. violet	35	8·50
O278	**O31**	30pf. blue	35	9·50
O279	**O31**	40pf. brown	35	9·50
O280	**O32**	50pf. red	35	30·00
O281	**O32**	60pf. green	35	12·50
O282	**O32**	70pf. lilac	35	38·00
O283	**O32**	75pf. red	35	48·00
O284	**O32**	80pf. blue	35	48·00
O285	**O32**	90pf. olive	35	75·00
O286	**O33**	1m. brown	35	65·00
O287	**O33**	1¼m. green	35	85·00
O288	**O33**	1½m. red	35	85·00
O289	**O33**	2½m. blue	35	95·00
O290	**O33**	3m. lake	75	£140
O291	**O33**	5m. green	3·25	£160

POSTAGE DUE STAMPS

D6

1862. Inscr "Bayer. Posttaxe" at top. Imperf.

D34	**D6**	3k. black	£170	£400

1870. As Type D **6**, but inscr "Bayr. Posttaxe" at top. Perf.

D65B	1k. black	16·00	£1100
D66B	3k. black	16·00	£600

1876. Optd **Vom Empfanger zahlbar**.

D130a	**8**	2pf. grey	1·10	3·00
D131a	**8**	3pf. grey	1·10	5·00
D132a	**8**	5pf. grey	1·50	4·50
D133a	**8**	10pf. grey	1·10	2·50

1895. No. D131a surch **2** in each corner.

D134	2 on 3pf. grey	†	£61000

1908. Stamps of 1876 optd **E**.

R133	3pf. brown	1·10	4·00
R134	5pf. green	30	50
R135	10pf. red	30	50
R136	20pf. blue	65	1·00
R137	50pf. purple	5·75	9·25

Pt. 1

BECHUANALAND

A colony and protectorate in Central S. Africa. British Bechuanaland (colony) was annexed to Cape of Good Hope in 1895. Internal Self-Government in the protectorate was introduced on 1 March 1965. Attained independence on 30 September 1966, when the country was renamed Botswana.

1885. 12 pence = 1 shilling; 20 shillings = 1 pound.
1961. 100 cents = 1 rand.

A. BRITISH BECHUANALAND

1885. Stamps of Cape of Good Hope ("Hope" seated) optd **British Bechuanaland.**

4	**6**	½d. black	11·00	24·00
38	**6**	1d. red	3·00	2·25
32	**6**	2d. bistre	4·75	2·25
2	**6**	3d. red	45·00	60·00
3	**6**	4d. blue	85·00	80·00
7	**6**	6d. purple	£160	38·00
8	**6**	1s. green	£325	£170

1887. Stamp of Great Britain (Queen Victoria) optd **BRITISH BECHUANALAND.**

9	**71**	½d. red	1·25	1·25

3

4

1887

10	**3**	1d. lilac and black	22·00	3·25
11	**3**	2d. lilac and black	95·00	2·25
12	**3**	3d. lilac and black	7·00	6·00
13	**3**	4d. lilac and black	50·00	2·50
14	**3**	6d. lilac and black	65·00	2·50
15	**4**	1s. green and black	30·00	9·00
16	**4**	2s. green and black	60·00	50·00
17	**4**	2s.6d. green and black	70·00	75·00
18	**4**	5s. green and black	£110	£160
19	**4**	10s. green and black	£225	£375
20	-	£1 lilac and black	£850	£750
21	-	£5 lilac and black	£4000	£1700

Nos. 20/1 are as Type **4** but larger, 23×39½ mm.

1888. Surch.

22	**3**	"1d." on 1d. lilac and black	7·50	6·50
23	**3**	"2d." on 2d. lilac and black	48·00	3·75
25	**3**	"4d." on 4d. lilac and black	£425	£550
26	**3**	"6d." on 6d. lilac and black	£140	12·00
28	**4**	"1s." on 1s. green and black	£200	85·00

1888. Surch **ONE HALF PENNY** and bars.

29	**3**	½d. on 3d. lilac and black	£250	£300

1891. Stamps of Great Britain (Queen Victoria) optd **BRITISH BECHUANALAND.**

33	**57**	1d. lilac	7·00	1·50
34	**73**	2d. green and red	20·00	4·00
35	**76**	4d. green and brown	3·50	60
36	**79**	6d. purple on red	6·50	2·00
37	**82**	1s. green	13·00	16·00

B. BECHUANALAND PROTECTORATE

1888. No. 9 to 19 optd **Protectorate** or surch also.

40	**71**	½d. red	10·00	48·00
41	**3**	1d. on 1d. lilac and black	15·00	15·00
42	**3**	2d. on 2d. lilac and black	35·00	17·00
43	**3**	3d. on 3d. lilac and black	£180	£225
51	**3**	4d. on 4d. lilac and black	£110	50·00
45	**3**	6d. on 6d. lilac and black	£100	50·00
46	**4**	1s. green and black	£120	55·00
47	**4**	2s. green and black	£650	£1000
48	**4**	2s.6s. green and black	£600	£950
49	**4**	5s. green and black	£1300	£2250
50	**4**	10s. green and black	£4250	£6500

1889. Stamp of Cape of Good Hope ("Hope" seated) optd **Bechuanaland Protectorate.**

52	**6**	½d. black	5·50	55·00

1889. No. 9 surch **Protectorate Fourpence.**

53	**71**	4d. on ½d. red	38·00	5·50

1897. Stamp of Cape of Good Hope ("Hope" seated) optd **BRITISH BECHUANALAND.**

56	**6**	½d. green	2·50	18·00

1897. Queen Victoria stamps of Great Britain optd **BECHUANALAND PROTECTORATE.**

59	**71**	½d. red	1·50	2·25
60	**71**	½d. green	1·40	3·50
61	**57**	1d. lilac	4·00	75
62	**73**	2d. green and red	9·50	3·50
63	**75**	3d. purple on yellow	5·50	9·00
64	**76**	4d. green and brown	23·00	22·00
65	**79**	6d. purple on red	23·00	11·00

1904. King Edward VII stamps of Great Britain optd **BECHUANALAND PROTECTORATE.**

66	**83**	½d. turquoise	2·75	2·75
68	**83**	1d. red	9·50	30
69	**83**	2½d. blue	11·00	7·50
70	-	1s. green and red (No. 314)	55·00	£160

1912. King George V stamps of Great Britain optd **BECHUANALAND PROTECTORATE.**

73	**105**	½d. green	1·25	1·50
72	**102**	1d. red	3·00	60
92	**104**	1d. red	2·00	70
75	**105**	1½d. brown	7·00	2·50
93	**106**	2d. orange	2·00	1·00
78	**104**	2½d. blue	3·50	27·00
79	**106**	3d. violet	6·00	13·00
80	**106**	4d. grey	6·50	30·00
81	**107**	6d. purple	9·00	24·00
82	**108**	1s. brown	18·00	35·00
88	**109**	2s.6d. brown	90·00	£160
89	**109**	5s. red	£110	£275

22 King George V, Baobab Tree and Cattle drinking

1932

99	**22**	½d. green	2·75	30
100	**22**	1d. red	1·50	25
101	**22**	2d. brown	1·50	30
102	**22**	3d. blue	3·75	4·00
103	**22**	4d. orange	3·75	9·00
104	**22**	6d. purple	5·00	7·00
105	**22**	1s. black and olive	3·75	7·00
106	**22**	2s. black and orange	24·00	65·00
107	**22**	2s.6d. black and red	23·00	48·00
108	**22**	3s. black and purple	45·00	55·00
109	**22**	5s. black and blue	£100	£110
110	**22**	10s. black and brown	£225	£250

1935. Silver Jubilee. As T **13** of Antigua.

111	1d. blue and red	1·75	7·00
112	2d. blue and black	2·50	6·50
113	3d. brown and blue	4·00	8·00
114	6d. grey and purple	9·00	8·00

1937. Coronation. As T **2** of Aden.

115	1d. red	45	40
116	2d. brown	60	1·00
117	3d. blue	60	1·25

1938. As T **22**, but portrait of King George VI.

118	½d. green	4·00	3·75
119	1d. red	75	50
120a	1½d. blue	1·00	1·00
121	2d. brown	75	50
122	3d. blue	1·00	2·50
123	4d. orange	2·00	3·50
124a	6d. purple	4·75	2·50
125	1s. black and olive	5·50	9·00
126	2s.6d. black and red	14·00	19·00
127	5s. black and blue	45·00	30·00
128	10s. black and brown	28·00	35·00

1945. Victory. Stamps of South Africa optd **Bechuanaland**. Alternate stamps inscr in English or Afrikaans.

129	**55**	1d. brown and red	75	1·50
130	**55**	2d. blue and violet (No. 109)	50	1·50
131	**55**	3d. blue (No. 110)	50	1·75

Prices for bi-lingual pairs.

1947. Royal Visit. As Nos. 32/5 of Basutoland.

132	1d. red	10	10
133	2d. green	10	10
134	3d. blue	10	10
135	1s. mauve	10	10

1948. Silver Wedding. As T **10/11** of Aden.

136	1½d. blue	30	10
137	10s. grey	42·00	50·00

1949. U.P.U. As T **20/23** of Antigua.

138	1½d. blue	30	1·25
139	3d. blue	1·50	2·50
140	6d. mauve	60	4·75
141	1s. olive	60	1·50

1953. Coronation. As T **13** of Aden.

142	2d. black and brown	1·50	30

1955. As T **22** but portrait of Queen Elizabeth II, facing right.

143	½d. green	50	30
144	1d. red	80	10
145	2d. brown	1·25	30
146	3d. blue	3·00	2·50
146b	4d. orange	12·00	13·00
147	4½d. blue	1·50	35
148	6d. purple	1·25	60
149	1s. black and olive	1·25	1·00
150	1s.3d. black and lilac	14·00	9·50
151	2s.6d. black and red	12·00	10·00
152	5s. black and blue	17·00	18·00
153	10s. black and brown	40·00	19·00

26 Queen Victoria, Queen Elizabeth II and Landscape

1960. 75th Anniv of Protectorate.

154	**26**	1d. sepia and black	40	50
155	**26**	3d. mauve and black	40	30
156	**26**	6d. blue and black	40	50

1961. Stamps of 1955 surch.

157	1c. on 1d. red	30	10
158	2c. on 2d. brown	30	10
159	2½c. on 2d. brown	30	10
160	2½c. on 3d. blue	7·00	10·00
161d	3½c. on 4d. orange	20	60
162a	5c. on 6d. purple	20	10
163	10c. on 1s. black and olive	20	10
164	12½c. on 1s.3d. black and lilac	65	20
165	25c. on 2s.6d. black and red	1·50	50
166	50c. on 5s. black and blue	2·00	2·25
167b	1r. on 10s. black and brown	18·00	13·00

28 African Golden Oriole ("Golden Oriole")

1961

168	**28**	1c. multicoloured	1·50	50
169	-	2c. orange, black and olive	2·00	4·50
170	-	2½c. multicoloured	1·75	10
171	-	3½c. multicoloured	2·50	5·00
172	-	5c. multicoloured	3·25	1·00
173	-	7½c. multicoloured	2·25	2·25
174	-	10c. multicoloured	2·25	60
175	-	12½c. multicoloured	18·00	6·00
176	-	20c. brown and drab	4·00	4·25
177	-	25c. sepia and lemon	5·00	2·50
178	-	35c. blue and orange	4·50	4·75
179	-	50c. sepia and olive	3·25	2·50
180	-	1r. black and brown	10·00	2·50
181	-	2r. brown and turquoise	28·00	14·00

DESIGNS—VERT: 2c. Hoopoe ("African Hoopoe"); 2½c. Scarlet-chested sunbird; 3½c. Yellow-rumped bishop ("Cape Widow-bird"); 5c. Swallow-tailed bee eater; 7½c. African grey hornbill ("Grey Hornbill"); 10c. Red-headed weaver; 12½c. Brown-hooded kingfisher; 20c. Woman musician; 35c. Woman grinding maize; 1r. Lion; 2r. Police camel patrol. HORIZ: 25c. Baobab tree; 50c. Bechuana ox.

1963. Freedom from Hunger. As T **28** of Aden.

182	12½c. green	30	15

1963. Centenary of Red Cross. As T **33** of Antigua.

183	2½c. red and black	20	10
184	12½c. red and blue	40	50

1964. 400th Birth Anniv of Shakespeare. As T **34** of Antigua.

185	12½c. brown	15	15

C. BECHUANALAND

42 Map and Gaberones Dam

1965. New Constitution.

186	**42**	2½c. red and gold	30	10
187	**42**	5c. blue and gold	30	40
188	**42**	12½c. brown and gold	40	40
189	**42**	25c. green and gold	45	55

1965. Centenary of I.T.U. As T **36** of Antigua.

190	2½c. red and yellow	20	10
191	12½c. mauve and brown	45	30

1965. I.C.Y. As T **37** of Antigua.

192	1c. purple and turquoise	10	45
193	12½c. green and lavender	60	55

1966. Churchill Commemoration. As T **38** of Antigua.

194	1c. blue	20	2·50
195	2½c. green	35	10
196	12½c. brown	70	35
197	20c. violet	75	55

43 Haslar Smoke Generator

1966. Bechuanaland Royal Pioneer Corps.

198	**43**	2½c. blue, red and green	25	10
199	-	5c. brown and blue	30	20
200	-	15c. blue, red and green	1·25	25
201	-	35c. multicoloured	30	1·00

DESIGNS: 5c. Bugler; 15c. Gun-site; 35c. Regimental cap badge.

POSTAGE DUE STAMPS

1926. Postage Due stamps of Great Britain optd **BECHUANALAND PROTECTORATE**.

D1	**D1**	½d. green	12·00	£130
D2	**D1**	1d. red	12·00	80·00
D3	**D1**	2d. black	12·00	90·00

D 3

1932

D4	**D3**	½d. green	6·00	60·00
D5a	**D3**	1d. red	1·50	29·00
D6c	**D3**	2d. violet	1·75	22·00

1961. Surch.

D7	1c. on 1d. red	25	50
D8	2c. on 2d. violet	25	1·50
D9	5c. on ½d. green	20	60

1961. As Type D **3** but value in decimal currency.

D10	1c. red	30	2·00
D11	2c. violet	30	2·00
D12	5c. green	50	2·00

For later issues see **BOTSWANA**.

Pt. 10

BELARUS

Formerly a constituent republic of the Soviet Union, Belarus became independent in 1991.

100 kopeks = 1 rouble.
2000. Currency Revaluation.

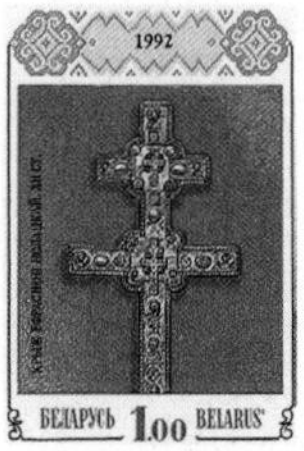

1 12th-century Cross

1992

1	**1**	1r. multicoloured	1·30	75

2 Shyrma

1992. Birth Cent of R. R. Shyrma (composer).

2	**2**	20k. lt blue, blue and black	50	30

3 Arms of Polotsk

1992

3	**3**	2r. multicoloured	80	55

See also Nos. 63 and 89/90.

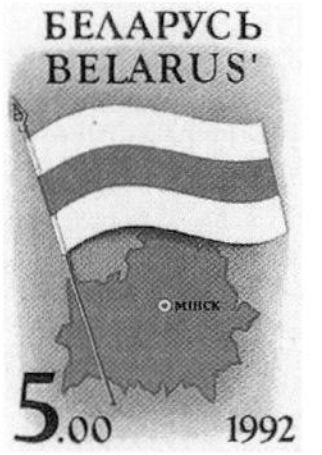

4 Flag and Map

1992

4	**4**	5r. multicoloured	1·30	95
5	-	5r. black, yellow and red	1·30	95

DESIGN: No. 5, State arms.

(5)

1992. Millenary of Orthodox Church in Belarus. (a) No. 1 optd with T **5**.

6	**1**	1r. multicoloured	1·00	75

(b) Sheet 91×66 mm.

MS7	5r. multicoloured	2·00	1·90

DESIGN: 24×36 mm—5r. Cross of Polotsk.

6 Kamen Tower

1992. Ancient Buildings and Monuments. Multicoloured.

8	2r. Type **6**	50	30
9	2r. Calvinist church, Zaslavl	50	30
10	2r. St. Euphrosyne's church, Polotsk	50	30
11	2r. St. Boris Gleb church, Grodno (horiz)	50	30
12	2r. Mir castle (horiz)	50	30
13	2r. Nesvizh castle (horiz)	50	30

7 State Arms

1992

14	**7**	30k. blue	20	15
15	**7**	45k. green	25	15
16	**7**	50k. green	25	15
17	**7**	1r. brown	25	15
18	**7**	2r. brown	25	15
19	**7**	3r. yellow	35	20
20	**7**	5r. blue	40	20
21	**7**	10r. red	95	55
22	**7**	15r. violet	55	35
23	**7**	25r. green	80	45
24	**7**	50r. mauve	25	20
25	**7**	100r. red	55	35
26	**7**	150r. purple	80	45
27	**7**	200r. green	20	20
28	**7**	300r. red	20	20
29	**7**	600r. mauve	25	20
30	**7**	1000r. red	45	20
31	**7**	3000r. blue	1·20	65

8 Jug and Bowl

1992. Pottery. Multicoloured.

40	1r. Type **8**	40	30
41	1r. Vases and jug on jug tree	40	30
42	1r. Flagon	40	30
43	1r. Jugs	40	30

9 Chickens

1993. Corn Dollies. Multicoloured.

44	5r. Type **9**	20	10
45	10r. Woman and gunman (vert)	30	20
46	15r. Woman (vert)	50	40
47	25r. Man and woman (vert)	1·00	75

10 Harezki

1993. Birth Centenary of M. I. Harezki (author).

48	**10**	50r. purple	60	35

11 Emblem

1993. World Belarussian Congress, Minsk.

49	**11**	50r. red, gold and black	2·00	1·60

12 *Man Over Vitebsk*

1993. Europa. Contemporary Art. Paintings by Marc Chagall. Multicoloured.

50	1500r. Type **12**	8·00	7·50
51	1500r. *Promenade* (vert)	8·00	7·50
MS52	142×103 mm. 2500r. *Allegory* (50×37 mm)	70·00	65·00

(13)

(14)

1993. Sports Events. Nos. 4/5 variously surch. (a) Winter Olympic Games, Lillehammer, Norway (1994). Surch **Winter Pre-Olympic Games Lillehammer, Norway 1500** (in capitals on No. 44) or in Cyrillic as T **13**.

53	**4**	1500r. on 5r. mult (in Cyrillic)	5·00	4·75
54	**4**	1500r. on 5r. mult (in English)	5·00	4·75
55	-	1500r. on 5r. black, yellow and red (in Cyrillic)	5·00	4·75
56	-	1500r. on 5r. black, yellow and red (in English)	5·00	4·75

MS57	Two sheets. (a) 1500r. on 5r. multicoloured (in Cyrillic); (b) 1500r. on 5r. (in English)	20·00	19·00

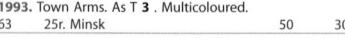

(b) World Cup Football Championship, U.S.A. (1994). Surch WORLD CUP USA 94 1500 or in Cyrillic as T **14**.

58	**4**	1500r. on 5r. mult (in Cyrillic)	5·00	4·75
59	**4**	1500r. on 5r. mult (in English)	5·00	4·75
60	-	1500r. on 5r. black, yellow and red (in Cyrillic)	5·00	4·75
61	-	1500r. on 5r. black, yellow and red (in English)	5·00	4·75

MS62	Two sheets. (a) 1500r. on 5r. multicoloured (in Cyrillic); (b) 1500r. on 5r. multicoloured (in English)	20·00	19·00

1993. Town Arms. As T **3** . Multicoloured.

63	25r. Minsk	50	30

15 St. Stanislav's Church, Mogilev

1993

64	**15**	150r. multicoloured	80	60

16 Kastus Kalinowski (leader)

1993. 130th Anniv of Peasants' Uprising.

65	**16**	50r. multicoloured	40	30

17 Princess Ragneda

1993. Tenth century Rulers of Polotsk. Multicoloured.

66	75r. Type **17**	50	30
67	75r. Prince Ragvalod and map	50	30

18 Statue of Budny

1993. 400th Death Anniv of Simon Budny (poet).

68	**18**	100r. multicoloured	70	65

19 Golden Eagle

1994. Birds in the Red Book. Multicoloured.

69	20r. Type **19**	20	20
70	40r. Mute swan (*Cygnus olor*)	30	30
71	40r. River kingfisher (*Alcedo atthis*)	30	30

1994. Nos. 14/16 surch.

72	**7**	15r. on 30k. blue	20	10
73	**7**	25r. on 45k. green	30	20
74	**7**	50r. on 50k. green	50	30

See also Nos. 86/8.

21 Map and Rocket Launchers (Liberation of Russia)

1994. 50th Anniv of Liberation. Multicoloured.

75	500r. Type **21**	60	45
76	500r. Map and Ilyushin 11-2 Shturmovick airplanes (Ukraine)	60	45
77	500r. Map, tank and soldiers (Byelorussia)	60	45

22 Yasev Drazdovich and "Persecution"

1994. Artists and Paintings. Multicoloured.

78	300r. Type **22**	30	20
79	300r. Pyotr Sergievich and *The Path through Life*	30	20
80	300r. Ferdinand Rushchyts and *The Land*	30	20

23 Figure Skating

1994. Winter Olympic Games, Lillehammer, Norway. Multicoloured.

81	1000r. Type **23**	40	30
82	1000r. Biathlon	40	30
83	1000r. Cross-country skiing	40	30
84	1000r. Speed skating	40	30
85	1000r. Ice hockey	40	30

1994. Birds in the Red Book. As Nos. 69/71 but values changed. Multicoloured.

86	300r. As Type **19**	50	30
87	400r. As No. 70	60	40
88	400r. As No. 71	60	40

1994. Town Arms. As T **3.** Multicoloured.

89	700r. Grodno	30	20
90	700r. Vitebsk	30	20

25 Church, Synkavichai (16th-century)

1994. Religious Buildings. Multicoloured.

91	700r. Type **25**	30	20
92	700r. Sts. Peter and Paul's Cathedral, Gomel (19th-century)	30	20

26 *Belarus*

1994. 150th Birth Anniv of Ilya Repin (painter). Multicoloured.

93	1000r. Type **26**	50	30
94	1000r. Repin Museum	50	30

Nos. 93/4 were issued together, *se-tenant*, forming a composite design.

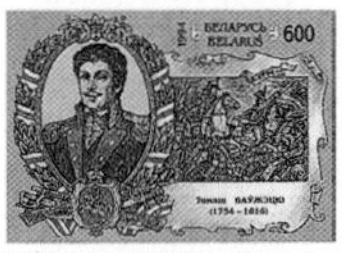

27 Tomasz Wojshezki and Battle Scene

1995. Bicentenary (1994) of Polish Insurrection. Multicoloured.

95	600r. Type **27**	45	35
96	600r. Jakub Jasinski	45	35
97	1000r. Mikhail Aginski	60	45
98	1000r. Tadeusz Kosciuszko	60	45

28 Memorial

1995. 50th Anniv of End of Second World War. Multicoloured.

99	180r. Type **28**	20	15
100	600r. Clouds and memorial	30	20

29 Aleksandr Stepanovich Popov (radio pioneer)

1995. Centenary of First Radio Transmission (by Guglielmo Marconi).

101	**29**	600r. multicoloured	50	40

30 Obelisk to the Fallen of the Red Army, Minsk

1995

102	**30**	180r. bistre and red	20	15
103	**30**	200r. green and bistre	30	20
104	**30**	280r. green and blue	40	30
107	**30**	600r. purple and bistre	50	40

31 Cherski

1995. 150th Birth Anniv of Ivan Cherski (explorer).

115	**31**	600r. multicoloured	50	40

32 Motal

1995. Traditional Costumes (1st series). Multicoloured.

116	180r. Type **32**	20	15
117	600r. Vaukavysk-Kamyanets	40	30
118	1200r. Pukhavits	70	55

See also Nos. 188/190, 256/8 and 460/1.

33 Head of Beaver

1995. The Eurasian Beaver. Multicoloured.

119	300r. Type **33**	30	20
120	450r. Beaver gnawing branch	40	30
121	450r. Beaver (horiz)	40	30
122	800r. Beaver swimming	75	45

34 Writer and Script

1995. Writers' Day.

123	**34**	600r. multicoloured	50	40

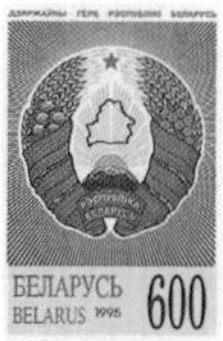

35 Arms

1995. National Symbols. Multicoloured.

124	600r. Type **35**	40	30
125	600r. Flag over map and arms	40	30

36 Anniversary Emblem

1995. 50th Anniv of U.N.O.

126	**36**	600r. blue, black and gold	50	40

37 Mstislavl Church

1995. Churches. Multicoloured.

127	600r. Type **37**	40	30
128	600r. Kamai Church	40	30

See also Nos. 227/8.

1995
125 год
з дня нараджэння

(38)

1995. 125th Birth Anniv of Ferdinand Rushchyts (artist). No. 80 optd with T **38.**

129	300r. multicoloured	1·00	95

39 Sukhoi and Aircraft

1995. Birth Centenary of P. V. Sukhoi (aircraft designer).

130	**39**	600r. multicoloured	40	30

40 Red Deer (*Cervus elaphus*)

1995. Nature. Sheet 100×64 mm. Imperf.

MS131	**40**	10000r. multicoloured	4·00	3·75

41 Leu Sapega (statesman)

1995. 17th-century Belarussians. Multicoloured.

132	600r. Type **41**	35	20
133	1200r. Kazimir Semyanovich (military scholar)	50	30
134	1800r. Simyaon Polatski (writer)	70	45

42 Lynx

1996. Mammals. Multicoloured.

135	1000r. Type **42**	45	30
136	2000r. Roe deer (vert)	75	45
137	2000r. Brown bear	75	45
138	3000r. Elk (vert)	95	75
139	5000r. European bison	1·50	1·30

1996. Nos. 17 and 23 optd with capital letter.

140	**7**	B (200r.) on 1r. brown	30	20
141	**7**	A (400r.) on 25r. green	30	20

44 Krapiva

1996. Birth Centenary of Kandrat Krapiva (writer).

142	**44**	1000r. multicoloured	50	30

45 Beaver

1996. The Eurasian Beaver (*Castor fiber*). Sheet 90×70 mm.

MS143	**45**	1200r. multicoloured	70	45

46 Purple Emperor (*Apatura iris*)

1996. Butterflies and Moths. Multicoloured.

144	300r. Type **46**	1·20	95
145	300r. *Lopinga achine*	1·20	95
146	300r. Scarlet tiger moth (*Callimorpha dominula*)	1·20	95
147	300r. Clifden's nonpareil (*Catocala fraxini*)	1·20	95
148	300r. Swallowtail (*Papilio machaon*)	1·20	95
149	300r. Apollo (*Parnassius apollo*)	1·20	95
150	300r. *Ammobiota hebe*	1·20	95
151	300r. Palaeno sulphur yellow (*Colias palaeno*)	1·20	95
MS152	Two sheets, each 100×70 mm. (a) 1000r. *Vacciniina optilete*; (b) 1000r. Willow-herb hawk moth (*Proserpinus proserpina*)	16·00	15·00

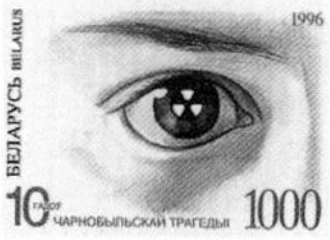

47 Radioactivity Symbol within Eye

1996. Tenth Anniv of Chernobyl Nuclear Disaster. Multicoloured.

153	1000r. Type **47**	30	20
154	1000r. Radioactivity symbol on diseased leaf	30	20
155	1000r. Radioactivity symbol on boarded-up window	30	20

48 State Arms

1996. Arms and value in black, background colours given.

159	**48**	100r. blue	15	10
160	**48**	200r. grey	30	25
161	**48**	400r. brown	20	15
162	**48**	500r. green	15	10
163	**48**	600r. red	15	10
164	**48**	800r. blue	20	15
165	**48**	1000r. orange	20	10
166	**48**	1500r. mauve	25	15
167	**48**	1500r. blue	25	25
168	**48**	1800r. violet	25	15
169	**48**	2000r. green	35	30
170	**48**	2200r. mauve	30	20
171	**48**	2500r. blue	35	30
172	**48**	3000r. brown	30	30
173	**48**	3300r. yellow	40	25
174	**48**	5000r. blue	50	40
175	**48**	10000r. green	1·00	75
176	**48**	30000r. brown	3·00	2·30
177	**48**	50000r. purple	5·25	3·75

49 Russian and Belarussian Flags

1996. Russian–Belarussian Treaty.

182	**49**	1500r. multicoloured	70	45

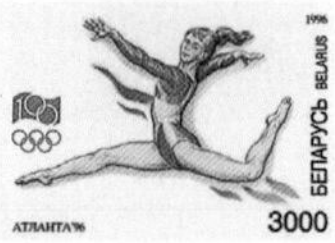

50 Gymnastics

1996. Olympic Games, Atlanta. Multicoloured.

183	3000r. Type **50**	90	65
184	3000r. Throwing the discus	90	65
185	3000r. Weightlifting	90	65
186	3000r. Wrestling	90	65
MS187	100×71 mm. 5000r. Rifle-shooting. Imperf	1·50	1·10

51 Kapyl-Kletski

1996. Traditional Costumes (2nd series). Multicoloured.

188	1800r. Type **51**	40	30
189	2200r. David-Garadots Turau	60	40
190	3300r. Kobryn	70	45
MS191	95×71 mm. 5000r. Naraulyanski. Imperf	1·50	1·10

See also Nos. 256/8 and 460/1.

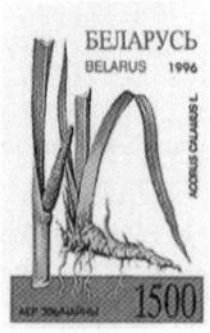

52 *Acorus calamus*

1996. Medicinal Plants. Multicoloured.

192	1500r. Type **52**	40	30
193	1500r. *Sanguisorba officinalis*	40	30
194	2200r. *Potentilla erecta*	60	40
195	3300r. *Frangula alnus*	70	45
MS196	96×71 mm. 5000r. *Menyanthes trifoliate*. Imperf	1·50	1·10

53 Grey Heron (*Ardea cinerea*)

1996. Birds. Multicoloured.

197	400r. Type **53**	60	40
198	400r. Black storks (*Ciconia nigra*)	60	40
199	400r. Great cormorant (*Phalacrocorax carbo*)	60	40
200	400r. White stork (*Ciconia ciconia*)	60	40
201	400r. Black-headed gulls (*Larus ridibundus*)	60	40
202	400r. Common snipe (*Gallinago gallinago*)	60	40
203	400r. White-winged black tern (*Chlidonias leucopterus*)	60	40
204	400r. Penduline tit (*Remiz pendulinus*)	60	40
205	400r. Eurasian bittern (*Botaurus stellaris*)	60	40
206	400r. Black coot (*Fulica atra*)	60	40
207	400r. Little bittern (*Ixobrychus minutus*)	60	40
208	400r. River kingfisher (*Alcedo atthis*)	60	40
209	400r. Green-winged teals (*Anas crecca*)	60	40
210	400r. Gadwalls (*Anas strepera*)	60	40
211	400r. Northern pintails (*Anas acuta*)	60	40
212	400r. Mallards (*Anas platyrhynchos*)	60	40
213	400r. Greater scaups (*Aythya marila*)	60	40
214	400r. Long-tailed duck (*Clangula hyemalis*)	60	40
215	400r. Northern shovelers (*Anas clypeata*)	60	40
216	400r. Garganeys (*Anas querquedula*)	60	40
217	400r. European wigeon (*Anas penelope*)	60	40
218	400r. Ferruginous ducks (*Aythya nyroca*)	60	40
219	400r. Common goldeneyes (*Bucephala clangula*)	60	40
220	400r. Goosander (*Mergus merganser*)	60	40
221	400r. Smew (*Mergus albellus*)	60	40
222	400r. Tufted duck (*Aythya fuligula*)	60	40
223	400r. Red-breasted merganser (*Mergus serrator*)	60	40
224	400r. Common pochard (*Aythya ferina*)	60	40
MS225	Two sheets, each 100×70 mm. (a) 1000r. Common snipe (*Gallinago gallinago*); (b) 1000r. European pochards (*Aythya farina*)	10·00	9·50

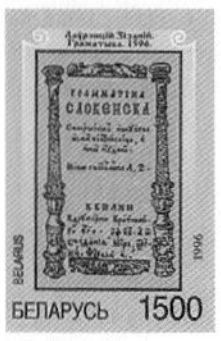

54 Title Page

1996. 400th Anniv of Publication of First Belarussian Grammar.

226	**54**	1500r. multicoloured	80	55

1996. Churches. As T **37**. Multicoloured.

227	3300r. St. Nicholas's Church, Mogilev	1·00	70
228	3300r. Franciscan church, Pinsk	1·00	70

55 Shchakatsikhin

1996. Birth Centenary of Mikola Shchakatsikhin (artist).

229	**55**	2000r. multicoloured	75	45

56 Old and New Telephones

1996. Cent of Telephone Service in Minsk.

230	**56**	2000r. multicoloured	75	45

57 Lukashenka

1996. President Alyaksandr Rygoravich Lukashenka.

231	**57**	2500r. multicoloured	60	45

58 Kiryla Turovski (12th-century Bishop of Turov)

1996. Multicoloured.

232	3000r. Type **58**	65	45
233	3000r. Mikolaj Radziwill (16th-century Chancellor of Lithuania)	65	45
234	3000r. Mikola Gusovski (15th-16th century writer)	65	45

59 Decorated Tree, Minsk

1996. New Year. Multicoloured.

235	1500r. Type **59**	30	20
236	2000r. Winter landscape (horiz)	50	40

60 *Paraskeva*

1996. Icons in National Museum, Minsk. Multicoloured.

237	3500r. Type **60**	60	45
238	3500r. *Illya* (17th-century)	60	45
239	3500r. *Three Holy Men* (Master of Sharashov)	60	45
240	3500r. *Madonna of Smolensk*	60	45
MS241	70×100 mm. 5000r. *Birth of the Madonna* (Patr Yavseevich)	1·50	1·10

61 Zhukov

1997. Birth Cent of Marshal G. K. Zhukov.

242	**61**	2000r. black, gold and red	50	40

62 Theatre

1997. Kupala National Theatre, Minsk.

243	**62**	3500r. black and gold	70	55

63 Byalnitsky-Birulya

1997. 125th Birth Anniv of W. K. Byalnitsky-Birulya (painter).

244	**63**	2000r. black and brown	50	40

(64)

1997. 105th Birth Anniv of R. R. Shyrma (composer). No. 2 surch with T **64**.

245	**2**	3500r. on 20k. light blue, blue and black	60	55

65 Salmon

1997. Fish. Multicoloured.

246	2000r. Type **65**	40	30
247	3000r. Vimba	60	45
248	4500r. Barbel (*Barbus barbus*)	80	65
249	4500r. European grayling (*Thymallus thymallus*)	80	65
MS250	90×60 mm. 5000r. Sterlet (*Acipenser ruthenus*)	1·50	1·10

66 "SOS" on Globe

1997. International Conference on Developing Countries, Minsk. Multicoloured.

251	3000r. Type **66**	50	40
252	4500r. Protective hand over ecosystem	70	55

Nos. 251/2 were issued together,*i se-tenant*, with intervening label showing the Conference emblem, the whole strip forming a composite design.

67 Emblem

1997. 50th Anniv of Belarussian Membership of Universal Postal Union.

253	**67**	3000r. multicoloured	60	45

1997. No. 18 surch **100 1997**.

254	**7**	100r. on 2r. brown	30	20

69 Map, National Flag and Monument to the Fallen of Second World War, Minsk

1997. Independence Day.

255	**69**	3000r. multicoloured	75	55

1997. Traditional Costumes (3rd series). As T **51**. Multicoloured.

256	2000r. Dzisensk	35	35
257	3000r. Navagrydsk	60	55
258	4500r. Bykhaisk	85	80

70 Page from Skorina Bible and Vilnius

1997. 480th Anniv of Printing in Belarus. Each red, black and grey.

259	3000r. Type **70**	60	55
260	3000r. Page from Skorina Bible and Prague	60	55
261	4000r. Franzisk Skorina and Polotsk	60	55
262	7500r. Skorina and Cracow	1·30	1·20

71 Jesuit College

1997. 900th Anniv of Pinsk.

263	**71**	3000r. multicoloured	60	55

72 Books and Entrance

1997. 75th Anniv of National Library.

264	**72**	3000r. multicoloured	60	55

73 Dark Glasses reflecting Hands reading Braille

1997. Centenary of Schools for the Blind in Belarus.

265	**73**	3000r. multicoloured	50	45

74 Child in Hand "Flower"

1997. World Children's Day.

266	**74**	3000r. multicoloured	60	55

75 Red Ribbon and Crowd

1997. Red Ribbon AIDS Solidarity Campaign.

267	**75**	4000r. multicoloured	70	65

76 Model 1221

1997. Belarussian Tractors. Multicoloured.

268	3300r. Type **76**	60	55
269	4400r. First Belarussian tractor, 1953	75	70
270	7500r. Model 680	1·20	1·10
271	7500r. Model 952	1·20	1·10

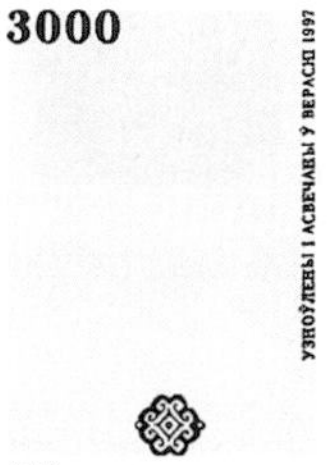

(77)

1997. Restoration of Cross of St. Ephrosina of Polotsk. No. 1 surch with T **77**.

272	**1**	3000r. on 1r. multicoloured	50	40

78 St. Nicholas hang-gliding over Houses (New Year)

1997. Greetings Stamps. Multicoloured.

273	1400r. Type **78**	30	20
274	4400r. Procession of musicians (Christmas)	60	45

79 Cross-country Skiing

1998. Winter Olympic Games, Nagano, Japan. Multicoloured.

275	2000r. Type **79**	40	30
276	3300r. Ice hockey	50	40
277	4400r. Biathlon	70	55
278	7500r. Freestyle skiing	90	75

80 Mashcherov

1998. 80th Birth Anniv of P. M. Mashcherov (writer).

279	**80**	2500r. multicoloured	50	40

81 MAZ-205 Lorry, 1947

1998. Tipper Trucks. Multicoloured.

280	1400r. Type **81**	30	20
281	2000r. MAZ-503, 1968	35	25
282	3000r. MAZ-5549, 1977	40	30
283	4400r. MAZ-5551, 1985	60	45
284	7500r. MAZ-5516, 1994	85	70

82 Entrance to Nyasvizh Castle

1998. Europa. National Festivals.

285	**82**	15000r. multicoloured	1·00	95

83 Mickiewicz

1998. Birth Bicentenary of Adam Mickiewicz (political writer).

286	**83**	8600r. multicoloured	65	65

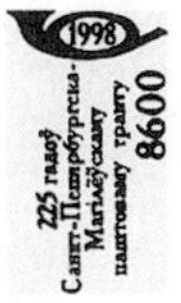

(84)

1998. 225th Anniv of Postal Service between Mogilov and St. Petersburg. No. 64 surch with T **84**.

287	**15**	8600r. on 150r. mult	65	65

85 Bluethroat

1998. Birds. Multicoloured.

288	1500r. Type **85**	20	10
289	3200r. Penduline tit	30	30
290	3800r. Aquatic warbler	40	35
291	5300r. Savi's warbler	50	45
292	8600r. Azure tit	85	80

86 Watermill

1998

293	**86**	100r. black and green	20	15
294	-	200r. black and brown	20	15
295	-	500r. black and blue	20	15
296	-	800r. black and violet	20	15
297	-	1000r. black and green	20	15
298	-	1500r. black and brown	30	30
299	-	2000r. black and blue	20	15
300	-	3000r. black and yellow	20	20
301	-	3200r. black and green	30	20
302	-	5000r. black and blue	25	30
303	-	5300r. black and yellow	30	30
304	-	10000r. black and orange	45	40
305	**86**	30000r. black and blue	50	45
306	-	50000r. black, orange and deep orange	60	55
308	-	100000r. black and mauve	80	75
309	-	500000r. black and brown	4·00	3·75

DESIGNS—VERT: 200, 50000r. Windmill; 500r. Stork; 800r. Cathedral of the Holy Trinity, Ishkold; 1000r. Bison; 1500, 3200r. Dulcimer; 2000r. Star; 3000, 5300r. Lute; 5000r. Church; 10000r. Flaming wheel; 500000r. Lyavoniha (folk dance). HORIZ: 100000r. Exhibition centre, Minsk.

87 Bulldozer Model 7821

1998. 50th Anniv of Belaz Truck Works. Multicoloured.

310	1500r. Type **87**	20	15
311	3200r. Tipper Model 75131	25	20
312	3800r. Tipper Model 75303	30	25
313	5300r. Tipper Model 75483	35	30
314	8600r. Tipper Model 7555	40	40

88 Common Morel

1998. Fungi. Multicoloured.

315	2500r. Type **88**	20	15
316	3800r. *Morchella conica*	25	20
317	4600r. Shaggy parasol	30	25
318	5800r. Parasol mushroom	35	30
319	9400r. Shaggy ink cap	65	50

89 Lion's Head

1998. Wood Sculptures. Multicoloured.

320	3400r. Type **89**	30	25
321	3800r. Archangel Michael	35	30
322	5800r. Prophet Zacharias	40	35
323	9400r. Madonna and Child	60	55

90 Emblem and Belarussian Stamps

1998. World Post Day.

324	**90**	5500r. multicoloured	60	45

91 *Kalozha* (V. K. Tsvirka)

1998. Paintings. Multicoloured.

325	3000r. Type **91**	20	20
326	3500r. *Hotel Lounge* (S. Yu. Zhukoiski)	20	20
327	5000r. *Winter Sleep* (V. K. Byalynitski-Birulya)	25	20
328	5500r. *Portrait of a Girl* (I. I. Alyashkevich) (vert)	25	20
329	10000r. *Portrait of an Unknown Woman* (I. F. Khrutski) (vert)	40	40

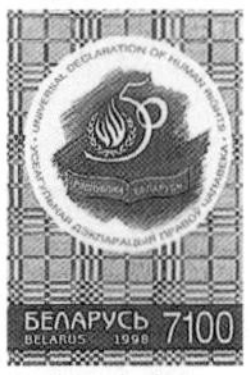

92 Anniversary Emblem

1998. 50th Anniv of Universal Declaration of Human Rights.

330	**92**	7100r. multicoloured	50	40

93 Girl, Rabbit and Fir Trees

1998. Christmas and New Year. Multicoloured.

331	5500r. Type **93**	25	25
332	5500r. Girl, rabbit and house	25	25

94 Pushkin and Adam Mickiewicz Monument, St. Petersburg (A. Anikeichyk)

1999. Birth Bicentenary of Aleksandr Pushkin (writer).

333	**94**	15300r. multicoloured	80	75

95 MAZ Model 8007 Truck and Excavator

1999. Minsk Truck and Military Works. Multicoloured.

334	10000r. Type **95**	25	20
335	15000r. MAZ model 543M and Smerch rocket system	30	25
336	30000r. MAZ model 7907 crane	45	40
337	30000r. MAZ model 543M Rubezh missile launcher	45	40
MS338	175×120 mm. Nos. 334/7; 5000r. Model 7917 and Topol missile; 150000r. Model 74135 low-loader	6·00	5·75

96 Dish, Jar and Vase

1999. Glasswork. Multicoloured.

339	30000r. Type **96**	50	45
340	30000r. Chalice	50	40
341	100000r. Oil lamp	1·00	95

(97)

1999. "iBRA '99" International Stamp Exhibition, Nuremberg. No. 69 surch with T **97**.

342	150000r. on 20r. multicoloured (Type **19**)	2·00	1·90

98 Belavezhskaya Pushcha Reserve

1999. Europa. Parks and Gardens. Multicoloured.

345	150000r. Type **98**	1·50	1·40
346	150000r. Beaver in Byarezinski Reserve	1·50	1·40

99 Well

1999. Wooden Buildings. Multicoloured.

347	50000r. Type **99**	70	45
348	50000r. Public house	70	45
349	100000r. Windmill	1·10	95

100 *Portrait of Yu. M. Pen* (A. M. Brazer)

1999. Vitebsk Art School. Paintings. Multicoloured.

350	30000r. Type **100**	30	20
351	60000r. *St. Anthony's Church, Vitebsk* (S. B.Yudovin)	70	45
352	100000r. *Street in Vitebsk* (Yu. M. Pen)	1·20	85
353	100000r. *Kryvaya Street, Vitebsk* (M. P. Mikhalap) (horiz)	1·20	85
MS354	104×82 mm. 200000r. *The World is a River without Banks* (Marc Chagall)	2·00	1·90

101 Karvat

1999. Third Death Anniv of Wing Commander Karvat.

355	**101**	25000r. multicoloured	1·20	95

102 Main Post Office, Minsk, 1954

1999. 125th Anniv of Universal Postal Union. Multicoloured.

356	150000r. Type **102**	1·80	1·60
357	150000r. First post office in Minsk, 1800	1·80	1·60

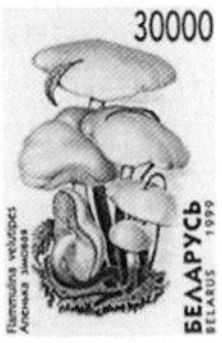
103 Golden Mushroom

1999. Fungi. Multicoloured.

358	30000r. Type **103**	30	20
359	50000r. Changeable agaric	55	40
360	75000r. *Lyophyllum connatum*	90	55
361	100000r. *Lyophyllum decastes*	1·20	85
MS362	97×79 mm. 150000r. Boot-lace fungus (*Armillariella mellea*)	1·80	1·60

104 East and West Belarussians Embracing

1999. 60th Anniv of Re-unification of Republic of Byelorussia.

363	**104**	29000r. multicoloured	40	30

105 MAZ MA3-6430, 1998

1999. Minsk Truck and Military Works. Lorries. Multicoloured.

364	51000r. Type **105**	50	30
365	86000r. Lorry Model MAZ MA3-4370	70	45

106 Landscape (Olya Smantser)

1999. Children's Painting Competition Winners. Multicoloured.

366	32000r. Type **106**	30	20
367	59000r. Girl (Masha Dudarenko) (vert)	50	30

107 Teddybear in Snow (Mitya Kutas)

1999. Christmas and New Year. Children's Paintings. Multicoloured.

368	30000r. Type **107**	40	30
369	30000r. Children building snow-man and ice-skating (Yulya Yakubovich)	40	30

108 Spasa-Praabrazhenskaya Church, Polatsk

2000. Birth Bimillenary of Jesus Christ (1st issue). Multicoloured.

370	50r. Type **108**	40	30
371	75r. St. Atsistratsiga Cathedral, Slutsk	70	45
372	100r. The Reverend Serafim Sarovskaga Church, Belaazersk	90	65

109 Our Lady Oranta (mosaic, Spohia Catherdral, Kiev, Ukraine)

2000. Birth Bimillenary of Jesus Christ (2nd issue). Sheet 150×100 mm containing T **109** and similar vert designs. Multicoloured.

MS373	100r. Type **109**; 100r. Jesus Christ (fresco, Spasa-Praabrazhenskaya Church, Polatsk); 100r. Our Lady Volodimirska (icon, National Tretyakov Gallery, Moscow, Russia)	3·00	2·75

110 Bison

2000

374	**110**	1r. black and green	20	10
375	-	2r. black and blue	20	10
376	-	3r. black and yellow	20	10
377	-	5r. black and blue	20	10
378	-	10r. black and orange	20	10
380	-	20r. black and mauve	30	15
382	-	30r. black and green	40	20
383	-	50r. black and yellow	60	40
387	-	100r. black and mauve	80	55

DESIGNS—VERT: 2r. Star; 3r. Lyre; 5r. Synkovichy Church; 10r. Flaming wheel; 20r. Type **111**; 30r. Watermill; 50r. Windmill. HORIZ: 100r. Exhibition Centre.

111 Kryzhachok (folk dance)

2000. Self-adhesive.

391	**111**	20r. black and red	30	15

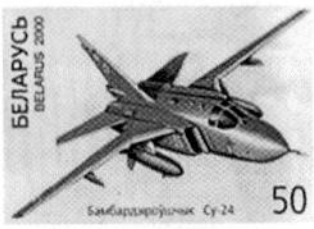
112 Su-24 Bomber

2000. 25th Death Anniv of Pavel Sukhoi (aircraft designer). Multicoloured.

392	50r. Type **112**	80	60
393	50r. Su-27 fighter	80	60
394	50r. Su-25 battle fighter	80	60
MS395	120×83 mm. 150r. Type **112**; 150r. As No. 394; 150r. As No. 393	2·50	2·30

113 Kupala Holiday

2000

396	**113**	A black and blue	40	30

No. 396 was for Inland Letter Post rate.

114 Stone-Curlew

2000. Birds in the Red Book. Multicoloured.

397	50r. Type **114**	60	40
398	50r. Smew (*Mergellus albellus*)	60	40
399	75r. Willow grouse	70	45
400	100r. Lesser spotted eagle (vert)	90	65

115 *The Partisan Madonna of Minsk* (M. Savitsky)

2000. 55th Anniv of End of Second World War.

401	**115**	100r. multicoloured	90	65

116 "Building Europe"

2000. Europa.

402	**116**	250r. multicoloured	3·00	2·75

117 Scene from *Creation of the World*

2000. National Ballet Company. Multicoloured.

403	100r. Type **117**	1·00	75
MS404	77×73 mm. 150r. Scene from *Passions*	1·80	1·60

118 Hands holding Lifebelt

2000. 50th Anniv of United Nations High Commission for Refugees.

405	**118**	50r. multicoloured	45	35

119 Head of Lynx

2000. Endangered Species. The Lynx. Multicoloured.

406	100r. Type **119**	80	65
407	100r. On branch	80	65
408	150r. Walking through woodland	1·20	95
409	150r. Adult and cub	1·20	95

120 People wearing National Costumes

2000. International Year of Culture.

410	**120**	100r. multicoloured	80	65

121 Rings

2000. Olympic Games, Sydney. Multicoloured.

411	100r. Type **121**	80	65
412	100r. Kayaking	80	65
413	100r. Rhythmic gymnastics	80	65
MS414	77×74 mm. 400r. Athletes	3·00	2·75

122 Amber

2000. Minerals. Multicoloured.

415	200r. Type **122**	1·30	1·10
416	200r. Galit	1·30	1·10
417	200r. Flint	1·30	1·10
418	200r. Silvin	1·30	1·10

123 People around decorated Tree

2000. New Year.

419	**123**	200r. multicoloured	1·50	1·30

124 Nativity Scene

2000. Christmas.

420	**124**	100r. multicoloured	1·20	95

125 *Connection of Times* (Roman Zabello)

2000. New Millennium. Children's Paintings. Multicoloured.

421	100r. Type **125**	80	65
422	100r. *Festival of Life* (Alena Emeliyanova)	80	65

126 Euphrosiniya Polotskaya and Church (image scaled to 52% of original size)

2001. 900th Birth Anniv of St. Euphrosiniya Polotskaya (Saint Euphrosyne). Imperf.

423	**126**	500r. multicoloured	2·30	2·10

127 Brest

2001. Town Arms. Multicoloured.

424	160r. Dubrovna	50	30
424a	200r. Type **127**	60	40
425	200r. Gomel	60	40
426	200r. Borisov	60	40
427	300r. Minsk	75	45
428	300r. David-Gorodok	75	45
429	350r. Kamjanets	80	55
430	460r. Slonim	90	65
431	500r. Novogrudok	95	75
432	500r. Turov	95	75
433	780r. Zaslavl	1·00	85
434	900r. Magilev	1·20	95

128 Runner

2001. Byelorussian Medal Winners, Olympic Games, Sydney. Sheet 78×75 mm.

MS435	**128**	1000r. multicoloured	4·00	3·75

No. **MS**435 is as No. **MS**414 but with face value changed and design altered to include list of winners.

129 Tupolev ANT-25 RD

2001. 25th Death Anniv of Pavel Sukhoy (aircraft designer). Multicoloured.

436	250r. Type **129**	1·20	95
437	250r. Tupolev ANT-37 Rodina	1·20	95

2001. As T **86**.

438	1r. black and green (inscr "2002")	20	10
439	2r. black and blue (inscr "2002")	20	10
440	3r. black and yellow (inscr "2002")	20	10
441	5r. black and blue (inscr "2002")	20	10
442	10r. black and brown (inscr "2002")	20	10
442a	20r. black and mauve (inscr "2002")	30	15
442b	30r. black and green (inscr "2002")	40	20
442c	50r. black and yellow (inscr "2002")	60	40
442d	100r. black and mauve (inscr "2002")	80	55
442e	100r. black and brown (inscr "2003")	80	55
443	200r. black and green	80	55
444	500r. black and brown	1·80	1·40

DESIGNS: 1r. Bison; 2r. Star; 3r. Lyre; 5r. Synkovichy Church; 10r. Flaming wheel; 20r. Dancers; 50r. Windmill; 100r. Exhibition centre; 100r. (442e), Layavoniha folk dance; 200r. 18th-century town house, Vitebsk; 500r. As No. 309.

130 Stag Beetle (*Lucanus cervus*)

2001. Beetles. Multicoloured.

445	300r. Type **130**	1·50	1·20
446	300r. European rhinoceros beetle (*Oryctes nasicornis*)	1·50	1·20

2001. As T **110**. Self-adhesive.

447	100r. black and mauve	60	40
448	200r. black and green (vert)	80	65

DESIGNS: 100r. As No. 387; 200r. As No. 438.

131 *Nymphaea alba*

2001. Endangered Species. Flowers. Multicoloured.

455	200r. Type **131**	80	65
456	400r. *Cypripedium calceolus*	1·70	1·40

132 Swans and Lake, Narochanskyi Nature Reserve

2001. Europa. Water Resources. Multicoloured.

457	400r. Geese and lake, Pripjatskyi Nature Reserve	2·00	1·40
458	1000r. Type **132**	5·00	4·25

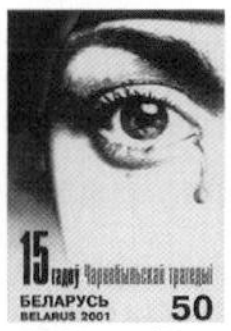

133 Eye and Tear

2001. 15th Anniv of Chernobyl Nuclear Disaster.

459	**133**	50r. black and rose	50	30

2001. Traditional Costumes (4th series). As T **51**. Multicoloured.

460	200r. 19th-century, Slutsk region	70	55
461	1000r. 19th-century, Pinsk region	3·50	3·25

134 National Arms

2001. Tenth Anniv of State Sovereignty.

462	**134**	500r. multicoloured	2·00	1·90

135 Union Emblem

2001. Tenth Anniv of Union of Independent States.

463	**135**	195r. multicoloured	80	55

2001. No. 166 surch **400**.

464	400r. on 1500r. mauve	1·20	95

137 King and Courtier (*The blue suit made inside out*)

2001. Folk Tales. Multicoloured.

465	100r. Type **137**	50	30
466	200r. Horse-drawn coach (*Okh and the golden snuff-box*)	90	65

138 Figures encircling Globe

2001. United Nations Year of Dialogue among Civilizations.

467	**138**	400r. multicoloured	1·20	95

139 Otto Schmidt

2001. 110th Birth Anniv of Otto Yulievich Schmidt (scientist and Arctic explorer). Sheet 78×74 mm.

MS468	**139**	3000r. multicoloured	8·00	7·50

2001. Surch.

469	400r. on 100r. blue (No. 159)	1·10	85
470	400r. on 600r. red (No. 163)	1·10	85
471	400r. on 1500r. blue (No. 167)	1·10	85
472	400r. on 3300r. yellow (No. 173)	1·10	85
473	1000r. on 100r. black and green (No. 293)	2·50	2·10
474	1000r. on 180r. brown and red (No. 102)	2·50	2·10
475	1000r. on 280r. green and blue (No. 104)	2·50	2·10

141 Wind-surfer

2001. Aquatic Sports. Multicoloured.

476	200r. Type **141**	70	45
MS477	102×66 mm. 1000r. Water-skier	3·00	2·75

142 Arms of Francisk Skorina

2001. Architecture and Arms. Multicoloured.

478	1000r. Type **142**	2·20	1·90
479	2000r. City Hall, Minsk	4·25	3·75
480	3000r. City Hall, Nesvizh	6·25	5·75
481	5000r. City Hall, Cherchersk	10·00	9·50

143 Building Facade

2001. House of Mercy (Orthodox Church humanitarian centre), Minsk.

495	**143**	200r. multicoloured	70	55

144 Calligraphy

2001. Christmas (496) and New Year (497). Multicoloured.

496	100r. Type **144**	50	30
497	100r. Snowy scene contained in bauble	50	30

145 E. V. Klumov

2001. 125th Birth Anniv of E. V. Klumov (surgeon and resistance worker).

498	**145**	100r. multicoloured	50	30

146 Ski Slalom

2002. Winter Olympics, Salt Lake City, USA (1st issue). Multicoloured.

499	300r. Type **146**	90	65
500	300r. Figure skating	90	65
501	500r. Biathlon	1·30	1·00
502	500r. Ski jumping	1·30	1·00

See also No. **MS**507.

147 *Formica rufa*

2002. Ants. Multicoloured.

503	200r. Type **147**	70	45
504	1000r. Grubs and worker ants (vert)	2·10	1·90
MS505	100×72 mm. 1000r. No. 504 plus label (vert) forming a composite design	2·50	1·90

148 Woman carrying Corn (Dozhinki Feast)

2002

506	**148**	B (55r.) black and yellow	30	20

149 Ice Hockey Player

2002. Winter Olympic Games, Salt Lake City, USA (2nd issue). Sheet 100×70 mm.

MS507	**149**	2000r. multicoloured	5·00	4·75

2002. As T **113** but inscr "2002".

508	**113**	A black and blue	40	30

No. 508 was for use on inland letters.

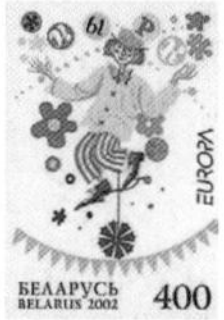

150 Clown riding Unicycle

2002. Europa. Circus. Multicoloured.

509	400r. Type **150**	1·50	1·40
510	500r. Horse	1·80	1·60

151 Yanka Kupala

2002. 120th Birth Annivs of Poets. Multicloured.

511	100r. Type **151**	30	20
512	100r. Yacub Kolas	30	20
MS513	100×70 mm. 500r.×2 Nos. 511/12	2·20	2·10

152 Church, Polotsk

2002. No value expressed. Multicoloured.

514	H (236r.) Type **152**	60	40
515	C (314r.) Railway Station, Brest	80	55

No. 514 was for use on letters up to 20 grams to Russia, Lithuania, Latvia, Uzbekistan, Tadjikistan and Turkmenistan.

No. 515 was for use on airmail letters up to 20 grams to the same countries.

153 Clover *Trifolium*

2002. Flowers. Multicoloured. Self-adhesive gum.

516	30r. Type **153**	30	15
517	50r. Matricaria	35	20
518	B (75r.) Flax (*Linium*)	20	10

519	A (90r.) Cornflower (*Centaurea cyanus*)	30	20
520	100r. Pasque flower (*Pulsatilla patens*)	40	25
521	200r. Yellow water lily (Nuphar lutea)	50	30
522	H (236r.) Campanula	70	45
523	C (314r.) Rhododendron	70	45
524	500r. Fireweed (*Chamaenerion angustifolium*)	90	65

No. 518 was for use on post cards within Belarus.

No. 519 was for use on letters up to 20 grams within Belarus.

No. 522 was for use on letters up to 20 grams to Russia, Lithuania, Latvia, Uzbekistan, Tadjikistan and Turkmenistan.

No. 523 was for use on airmail letters up to 20 grams to Russia, Lithuania, Latvia, Uzbekistan, Tadjikistan and Turkmenistan.

154 Go-Kart

2002. Children's Activities. Multicoloured.

525	90r. Type **154**	30	15
526	239r. Model aircraft	70	45

155 White Stork (*Ciconia ciconia*)

2002. Birds. Sheet 94×72 mm containing T **155** and similar horiz designs. Multicoloured.

MS527 200r. Type **155**; 200r. Golden oriole (*Oriolius oriolus)*; 200r. Pied wagtail (*Matacilla alba*) 1·50 1·40

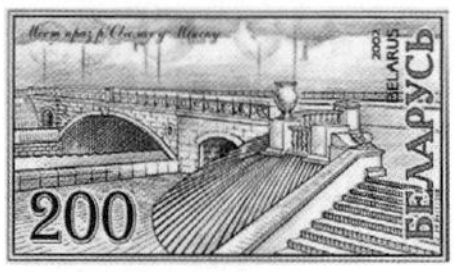

156 Bridge over River Svisloch, Minsk

2002. Bridges.

528	**156**	200r. black, mauve and blue	40	30
529	-	300r. multicoloured	70	55
530	-	500r. black, blue and green	1·00	85

DESIGNS: 200r. Type **156**; 300r. Bridge over River Sozh, Gomel; 500r. Bridge over River Zapadnaja Dvina, Vitebsk.

157 Lake, Braslav

2002. International Year of Eco-Tourism.

531	**157**	300r. multicoloured	1·00	95

158 *By the Church* (F. Rushchits)

2002. Art. Multicoloured.

532	300r. Type **158**	75	55
533	300r. *Battle at Nemiga* (M. Philippovich) (horiz)	75	55

159 V. V. Kovalyonok and P. I. Klimuk (cosmonauts)

2002. 45th Anniv of Space Exploration. Sheet 131×71 mm.

MS534 **159** 3000r. multicoloured 5·50 5·25

160 Father Christmas

2002. Christmas and New Year. Multicoloured.

535	300r. Type **160**	75	55
536	300r. Angel	75	55

161 Ksimir Malevich and *Black Square*

2003. 125th Birth Anniv of Kasimir Malevich (artist). Sheet 82×54 mm.

MS537 **161** 3000r. multicoloured 6·00 5·75

162 Smooth Snake (*Coronella austriaca*)

2003. Reptiles. Multicoloured.

538	300r. Type **162**	60	40
539	600r. European pond turtle (*Emys orbicularis*)	1·00	75

163 Glass containing Land and Water

2003. International Year of Freshwater.

540	**163**	370r. multicoloured	80	55

164 House Sparrow

2003

541	**164**	630r. multicoloured	1·20	95

165 In-line Skates

2003. Children's Sports. Multicoloured.

542	300r. Type **165**	60	40
543	300r. Scooter (vert)	60	40

166 "Europa"

2003. Europa. Poster Art. Multicoloured.

544	400r. Type **166**	80	55
545	700r. Painted wooden panels	1·30	1·00

167 Globeflower (*Trollius europaeus*)

2003. Endangered Flora. Multicoloured.

546	270r. Type **167**	60	40
547	740r. Siberian iris (*Iris sibirica*)	1·30	1·00

168 Women's Costumes, Polesye

2003. Traditional Costumes. Multicoloured.

548	380r. Type **168**	70	55
549	430r. Men and women's costumes, Mogilyov	80	65

See also Nos. 636/7.

169 470 Class Sailing Dinghy

2003. Dinghy Sailing. Sheet 128×78 mm, containing T 169 and similar multicoloured design.

MS550 1000r. Type **169**; 1000r. Laser dinghy (vert) 3·25 3·00

170 Bronze Age Axe Head

2003. National Museum of Natural History and Culture, Minsk. Three sheets, each 82×52 mm, containing T **170** and similar multicoloured designs.

MS551 (a) 1000r. Type **170**; (b) 1500r. Bronze age pot (28×30 mm); (c) 1500r. 14th-century bowl (28×30 mm) 7·00 6·50

171 Horse Stall, Povitie (19th-century)

2003. Architecture. Multicoloured.

552	270r. Type **171**	50	30
553	430r. Church, Sinkevichi (1724)	80	55
554	740r. Watermill, Volma (19th-century)	1·10	85
MS555	97×112 mm. Nos. 552/4	2·50	2·30

172 Golden Retriever

2003. Dogs. Multicoloured.

556	270r. Type **172**	60	40
557	380r. Great dane	70	50
558	430r. German shepherd	80	65

173 Young Player holding Ball

2003. Centenary of FIFA (Federation Internationale de Football Association). Multicoloured.

559	380r. Type **173**	70	50
560	380r. Five players (horiz)	70	50
561	460r. Three players (horiz)	80	65
562	780r. Player holding ball	1·30	1·00

174 Angel

2003. Christmas. Multicoloured.

563	380r. Type **174**	50	40
564	780r. Grandfather Frost	1·10	85

175 "Arrival of Spring" (Pavel Maslennikov)

2004

565	**175**	290r. multicoloured	60	40

176 Blackthorn (*Prunus spinosa*)

2004. Fruit. Multicoloured.

566	5r. Type **176**	30	15
567	10r. Lingonberry (*Vaccinium vitis idaea*)	30	15
568	20r. Bilberry (*Vaccinium myrtillus*)	30	15
569	30r. Cranberry (*Oxycoccus palustris*)	30	15
570	50r. Bog blueberry (*Vaccinium uliginosum*)	30	15
571	100r. Raspberry (*Rubus idaeus*)	30	15
572	B (100r.) Strawberry (*Fragaria ananassa*)	30	15
573	A (120r.) Red currant (*Ribes rubrum*)	30	15
574	200r. Dewberry (*Rubus caesius*)	30	15
575	H (290r.) Black currant (*Ribes nigrum*)	50	30
576	300r. Stone bramble (*Rubus saxatilis*)	50	30
577	C (420r.) Gooseberry (*Grossularia reclinata*)	60	40
578	500r. Wild strawberry (*Fragaria*)	70	50
579	P (780r.) Sea buckthorn (*Hippophae rhamnoides*)	1·00	75
580	1000r. Sour cherry (*Cerasus vulgaris*)	1·30	90

177 Queen and King of Hearts

2004. St. Valentine's Day.

581	**177**	H (290r.) black, scarlet and yellow	75	50

178 Alder (*Alnus incana*)

2004. Trees. Multicoloured. Self-adhesive gum.

582	100r. Type **178**	30	15
583	B (100r.) Birch (*Betula pendula*)	30	15
584	A (120r.) Scots pine (*Pinus sylvestris*)	30	15
585	200r. *Viburnum opulus*	30	15
586	H (290r.) Ash (*Fraxinus excelsior*)	50	30
587	300r. Lime (*Tillia cordata*)	50	30
588	400r. Hazel (*Corylus avellana*)	60	40
589	C (420r.) Rowan (*Sorbus aucuparia*)	60	40
590	500r. Oak (*Quercus robur*)	75	50
591	P (780r.) Hornbeam (*Carpinus betulus*)	1·00	85
592	1000r. Elm (*Ulmus laevis*)	1·30	1·00

179 Swallow

2004
593 **179** 870r. multicoloured 1·30 1·00

180 Player

2004. International Ice Hockey Federation World Under-18 Championships, Minsk.
594 **180** 320r. multicoloured 75 50

181 Forest and Walker

2004. Europa. Holidays. Multicoloured.
595 320r. Type **181** 60 40
596 870r. Fisherman 1·40 1·10

182 Mount of Glory Monument

2004. 60th Anniv of the Liberation of Minsk. Sheet 121×81 mm containing T **182** and similar multicoloured design.
MS597 500r. Type **182**; 1000r. *The Parade of Partisans* (Y. Zaitsev) (52×30 mm) 2·30 2·10

183 Class 130 Series D Locomotive and Early 20th-century Station, Mosty

2004. Railways. Multicoloured.
598 320r. Type **183** 70 45
599 870r. Class 230 series A locomotive and 19th-century station, Vitebsk 1·20 1·00

184 *Polistes gallicus*

2004. Insects. Multicoloured.
600 320r. Type **184** 60 40
601 505r. *Bombus lucorum* 80 65
MS602 75×102 mm. 2000r. *Apis mellifera* (40×30 mm) 3·00 2·75

185 *Self Portrait*

2004. 150th Birth Anniv of Yury Pan (artist). Sheet 115×75 mm containing T **185** Multicoloured.
MS603 1000m.×2, Type **185**; *Watchmaker* (horiz) 3·00 2·75

186 Cycling

2004. Olympic Games, Athens (1st issue). Multicoloured.
604 320r. Type **186** 60 40
605 505r. Hammer throwing 80 65
606 870r. Tennis 1·30 1·00
See also No. **MS**611.

187 *Euphydryas matuma*

2004. Butterflies. Multicoloured.
607 300r. Type **187** 50 30
608 500r. *Pericallia matronula* 70 50
609 800r. *Zerynthia polyxena* 1·00 75
610 1200r. *Eudia pavonia* 1·60 1·30

188 Yuiya Nesterenko

2004. Olympic Games, Athens (2nd issue). Gold Medal Winners. Sheet 103×73 mm containing T **188** and similar vert design. Multicoloured.
MS611 500r.×2, Type **188** (100 metres); Igor Makarov (judo) 2·00 1·90
The stamps and margin of No. **MS**611 form a composite design.

189 Byelorussian Harness Horse

2004. Horses. Sheet 120×100 mm containing T **189** and similar horiz designs. Multicoloured.
MS612 500r.×4, Type **89**; Andalusian horse; Head of Byelorussian horse; Head of Andalusian horse 3·00 2·75
The stamps and margin of No. **MS**612 form a composite design.

190 Black Persian

2004. Cats. Sheet 103×115 mm containing T **190** and similar horiz designs. Multicoloured.
MS613 300r. Type **190**; 500r. Siamese seal-point; 500r. Red Persian; 800r. Tortoiseshell Persian; 800r. British shorthair 4·50 4·25
The stamps and margin of No. **MS**613 form a composite design.

191 Father Christmas

2004. Christmas and New Year.
614 **191** 320r. multicoloured 75 50

192 Train in Station

2004. Minsk Underground Railway. Multicoloured.
615 560r. Type **192** 75 55
616 560r. Locomotive, decorated pillar and passengers 75 55

193 Gerasim Bogomolov

2005. Birth Centenary of Gerasim Vasilievich Bogomolov (hydrologist).
617 **193** 350r. black and vermilion 75 55

194 Madonna and Child (Protoierej Povnyji)

2005. 21st Century Icons. Sheet 151×101 mm containing T **194** and similar vert designs.
MS618 1500r.×3, Type **194**; Nativity (George Sutulin and Olga Belaja); Archangel Michael (Andrey Kosikov) 6·50 6·00

195 Great Grey Owl (*Strix nebulosa*)

2005
619 **195** 900r. multicoloured 1·00 85

196 Partisans

2005. 60th Anniv of the End of World War II. Multicoloured.
620 A (160r.) Type **196** 30 15
621 H (360r.) Liberation 50 30
622 H (360r.) Woman, bells and monument, Khatyn 50 30
623 P (930r.) Victory flag 1·00 80
MS624 150×74 mm. 1000r.×2, Signing treaty (40×30 mm); Victory parade (52×30 mm) 3·00 2·75

197 Greater Spotted Eagle (*Aquila clanga*)

2005. Fauna. Sheet 133×68 mm containing T **197** and similar horiz designs. Multicoloured.
MS625 500r. Type **197**; 500r. *Catocala sponsa*; 1000r. Beaver (*Castor fiber*); 1000r. Badger (*Meles meles*) 4·25 4·00
The stamps and margin of No. **MS**625 form a composite design. Stamps of the same design were issued by Russia.

198 Vegetables

2005. Europa. Gastronomy. Multicoloured.
626 500r. Type **198** 75 50
627 1000r. Bread and hat 1·30 95

199 Stefaniya Stanyuta

2005. Birth Centenary of Stanyuta Stefaniya Mikhailovna (Stefaniya Stanyuta) (actress).
628 **199** 160r. black and vermilion 40 20

200 Hans Christian Andersen

2005. Birth Bicentenary of Hans Christian Andersen (writer). Sheet 120×80 mm.
MS629 **200** 2000r. multicoloured 3·00 2·75

201 Black Stork

2005. Endangered Species. Black Stork (Ciconia nigra). Multicoloured.
630 500r. Type **201** 75 55
631 500r. In flight 75 55
632 1000r. Facing left 1·30 1·00
633 1000r. Nestlings 1·30 1·00

202 *Harvesting* (Mikhail Sevryuk)

2005. National Art Museum. Birth Centenary of Mikhail Sevryuk (artist).
634 **202** 360r. multicoloured 50 30

203 Emblem

2005. World Information Society Summit, Tunis.
635 **203** 360r. multicoloured 60 40

2005. Traditional Costumes. As T **168**. Multicoloured
636 380r. Women, Mosty 60 40
637 570r. Women, Lepel 80 65

204 Runner and Hockey Players

2005. International Year of Sports and Physical Education.
638 **204** 570r. multicoloured 80 65

205 Arms and Town

2005. Volkvoysk Millenary.
639 **205** 360r. multicoloured 70 45

206 Kiril Turovsky Monument

2005. Turov Diocese Millenary.
640 **206** 360r. gold and vermilion 60 40

207 Early Chess Players

2005. Chess. Background colour given.

641	**207**	500r. multicoloured (chestnut)	70	55
642	**207**	500r. multicoloured (red)	70	55

208 Vytautas Castle

2005. Architecture. Sheet 113×72 mm containing T **208** and similar horiz design. Multicoloured.

MS643	500r. Type **208**; 1000r. Lida Castle	1·80	1·60

209 Tree and Town

2005. Christmas and New Year.

644	**209**	360r. silver, ultramarine and emerald	60	40

210 Snowboarding

2005. Winter Olympic Games, Turin. Multicoloured.

645	500r. Type **210**	75	55
MS646	117×76 mm. 2000r. Freestyle skiing (30×40 mm)	2·30	2·10

211 Lapwing (*Vanellus vanellus*)

2006

647	**211**	930r. multicoloured	1·30	1·00

212 Atomic Symbol and Flowers

2006. 20th Anniv of Chernobyl Nuclear Disaster.

648	**212**	360r. multicoloured	60	40

213 Penguins (Lina Filippoch)

2006. Europa. Integration. Winning Designs in Children's Painting Competition. Multicoloured.

649	500r. Type **213**	75	55
650	1000r. Pegasus (Daria Buneeva) (horiz)	1·30	1·00

214 Ivan Shamyakin

2006. 85th Birth Anniv of Ivan Shamyakin (writer).

651	**214**	360r. multicoloured	60	40

215 Wheatear

2006. Birds. Multicoloured.

652	10r. Type **215**	20	10
653	20r. Blue tit	20	10
654	30r. Pied flycatcher	20	10
655	50r. Linnet	20	10
656	100r. Lesser whitethroat	25	15
657	B (160r.) Robin	30	20
658	A (190r.) Black redstart	35	20
659	200r. Chaffinch	40	25
660	300r. Tree sparrow	50	30
661	H (360r.) Great tit	55	35
662	500r. Greenfinch	70	50
663	1000r. Hawfinch	1·10	95

216 *Myotis dasycneme*

2006. Bats. Multicoloured.

664	500r. Type **216**	75	55
665	500r. *Vespertilio murinus*	75	55
666	500r. *Barbastella barbastellus*	75	55
MS667	97×115 mm. 1000r.×3, As Nos. 664/6	4·00	3·75

217 Silver Medals

2006. Free-style Ski Team and Dmitri Daschinski—Silver Medal Winners—Winter Olympic Games, Turin. Sheet 102×72 mm.

MS668 **217**	2000r. multicoloured	2·50	2·30

218 Canoeists

2006. Avgustovo Channel. Sheet 113×74 mm.

MS669 **218**	2000r. multicoloured	2·50	2·30

219 Series E Steam Locomotive, Railway Station, Molodechno

2006. Railways. Multicoloured.

670	1000r. Type **219**	1·40	1·30
671	1000r. Series O steam locomotive, railway station, Brest	1·40	1·30

220 *Cephalanthera rubra*

2006. Orchids. Multicoloured.

672	1000r. Type **220**	1·40	1·30
673	1000r. *Dactylorhiza majalis*	1·40	1·30
674	1000r. As Type **220** but with design reversed	1·40	1·30

221 Wind Turbines

2006. Renewable Energy. Multicoloured.

675	210r. Type **221**	30	30
676	970r. Hydro-electric dam	1·20	1·10

222 Emblem

2006. 15th Anniv of Regional Concord of Communication (RCC).

677	**222**	410r. multicoloured	70	65

2006. Fifth National Philatelic Exhibition (BelFILA 2006). No. MS131 surch. Sheet 100×70 mm. Imperf.

MS678	3500r. on 1000r. multicoloured	4·50	4·25

224 Red Discus

2006. Fish. Discus (*Symphysodon discus*). Multicoloured.

679	500r. Type **224**	75	70
680	500r. Violet	75	70
681	500r. Green striped	75	70
682	500r. Yellow, pink striped and green	75	70

225 Decorated Tree

2006. Happy New Year.

684	**225**	500r. ultramarine and blue	75	70
685	**225**	500r. blue	75	70

226 Napoleon Orda

2007. Birth Bicentenary of Napoleon Orda (artist).

686	**226**	2000r. multicoloured	5·25	5·00

2007. As T **152**. Multicoloured.

687	2000r. Minsk City Hall	2·50	2·30

227 Thrush Nightingale

2007

688	**227**	1000r. multicoloured	1·30	1·20

228 Reef Knot

2007. Europa. Centenary of Scouting. Multicoloured.

689	500r. Type **228**	65	40
690	1000r. Emblem	1·30	80

229 *Mustela putorius* (polecat)

2007. Fauna. Multicoloured.

691	B (190r.) Type **229**	20	15
692	B (190r.) *Vulpes vulpes* (red fox)	20	15
693	A (220r.) *Sciurus vulgaris* (red squirrel)	35	20
694	A (220r.) *Dryomys nitedula* (forest dormouse)	35	20

230 Map of Belarus

2007. World Heritage. Points of Struve Geodetic Arc (points where measurements were taken to determine the shape and size of Earth) in Belarus. Sheet 112×79 mm.

MS695 **230**	5000r. multicoloured	6·25	6·25

231 *Gallinago media* (snipe)

2007. Cepkeliai and Kotra Nature Reserves. Multicoloured.

696	1000r. Type **231**	1·20	70
697	1000r. *Crex crex* (corncrake)	1·20	70

Nos. 696/7 were issued together, *se-tenant*, forming a composite design. Stamps of a similar design were issued by Lithuania.

232 *Nyctea scandiaca* (snowy owl)

2007. Owls. Multicoloured.

698	500r. Type **232**	55	35
699	500r. *Surnia ulula* (northern hawk owl)	55	35
700	1000r. *Asio flammeus* (short eared owl)	1·20	70
701	1000r. *Athene noctua* (little owl)	1·20	70

233 *Alexandra Marianna Veselovskaya* (1640)

2007. Paintings from National Art Museum. Multicoloured.

702	1050r. Type **233**	2·40	1·40
703	1050r. *Griesel Sapega* (1632)	2·40	1·40
704	1050r. *Kshishtof Veselovsky* (1636)	2·40	1·40

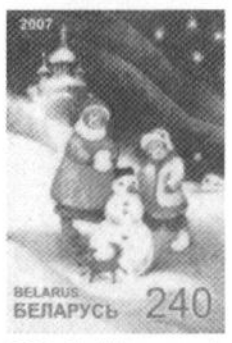

234 Children and Snowman

2007. Christmas and New Year. Multicoloured.

705	240r. Type **234**	40	25
706	240r. Children and parcel	40	25
707	1050r. Candle	2·10	1·30
708	1050r. Christmas tree	2·10	1·30
MS709	100×94 mm. 240r. As No. 705; 240r. As No. 706; 1500r. Child wearing Santa outfit; 1500r. Girl holding star	3·25	3·25

The stamps and margins of **MS**709 form a composite design.

235 Blagovest Bell (1937)

2007. Bells. Multicoloured.

710	600r. Type **235**	35	20
711	1000r. Blagovest bell (19th century)	1·40	85
712	1200r. Sub chime bell (1928)	1·75	1·00
MS713	106×79 mm. 2500r. Sub chime bell (18th century)	3·00	3·00

The stamps and margins of **MS**713 form a composite design.

236 Blacksmith and Armour

2007. Traditional Crafts. Multicoloured.

714	600r. Type **236**	75	45
715	600r. Weaver and cloth	75	45

237 Lamb, Sheep and Sheepdog

2007. Domestic Animals. Multicoloured.

716	240r. Type **237**	30	20
717	440r. Ram, sheep and sheepdog	60	35
718	500r. Piglets	70	40
719	1050r. Cattle	1·50	90
720	1500r. Goats	1·90	1·20

238 Medieval Falconers

2008. Hunting. Multicoloured.

721	440r. Type **238**	60	35
722	1050r. Deer hunting (horiz)	1·30	80

239 Vincent Dunin-Marcinkevich

2008. Birth Bicentenary of Vincent Dunin-Marcinkevich (writer and social activist).

723	**239**	440r. multicoloured	1·00	60

240 Konstantin Ostrozhsky

2008. 400th Death Anniv of Konstanty Wasyl Ostrogski (Konstantin Ostrozhsky) (Lithuanian prince). Sheet 93×78 mm.

MS724	**240** 2500r. multicoloured	1·70	1·70

241 *Egretta alba* (great white egret)

2008. Great White Egret.

725	**241**	1050r. multicoloured	1·30	80

242 Symbols of Information

2008. TIBO International Exhibition and Congress, Minsk.

726	**242**	H (440r.) multicoloured	60	35

243 Birch Parchment and Styli

2008. Europa. The Letter. Multicoloured.

727	1000r. Type **243**	1·20	75
728	1000r. Envelope, keyboard and '@'	1·20	75

244 *Nyctereutes procyonoides* (raccoon dog)

2008. Animals. Multicoloured.

729	10r. Type 244	10	10
730	200r. *Mustela lutreola* (European mink)	20	10
731	300r. *Lepus europaeus* (hare)	25	15
732	400r. *Canis lupus* (wolf)	40	25
733	1000r. *Martes martes* (pine martin)	1·30	80

245 *Paeonia lactiflora*

2008. Garden Flowers. Multicoloured.

734	20r. Type **245**	10	10
735	30r. *Petunia hybrida*	10	10
736	50r. *Narcissus hybridus*	15	10
737	100r. *Tulipa gesneriana*	20	15
738	B (200r.) *Dahlia cultorum*	30	20
739	A (240r.) *Rosa hybrida*	35	20
740	H (440r.) *Zinnia elegans*	45	30
741a	500r. *Lilium hybrida*	50	30

No. 739 was for use on domestic postcards and was originally on sale for 200r., No. 740 was for use on domestic mail and was originally on sale for 240r. and No. 741 was for use on mail to Russia, Lithuania and Turkmenistan, weighing up to 20 grams.

246 *Cantharellus cibarius*

2008. Fungi. Multicoloured.

741	1000r. Type **246**	1·50	90
742	1500r. *Boletus edulis*	2·00	1·20

247 Rowers

2008. Olympic Games, Beijing.

743	**247**	1000r. multicoloured	4·75	2·75

248 Order For Exceptional Courage

2008. State Medals. Multicoloured.

744	1000r. Type **248**	1·20	75
745	1000r. Order of Military Glory	1·20	75
746	1000r. Order of the Motherland classes I, II and III	1·20	75
747	1000r. Order For Service to Motherland classes I, II and III	1·20	75
748	1000r. Order of Friendship of Peoples	1·20	75
749	1000r. Order of Honour	1·20	75
750	1000r. Order of Francysk Skaryna	1·20	75
751	1000r. Order of Mothers	1·20	75
752	1000r. Military Service Medal	1·20	75
753	1000r. Hero of Belarus Medal	1·20	75
754	1000r. Medal For Bravery	1·20	75
755	1000r. Medal For Labor Achievements	1·20	75
756	1000r. Medal For Perfect Service classes I, II and III	1·20	75
757	1000r. Guarding Civil Order Medal	1·20	75
758	1000r. Guarding State Border Medal	1·20	75
759	1000r. Medal of Francysk Skaryna (different)	1·20	75

2008. Town Arms. As T **127**. Multicoloured.

760	600r. Vitsebsk	1·00	60

2008. Town Arms. As T **127**. Multicoloured.

761	500r Orsha	1·00	60
762	1000r. Nesvizh	1·00	60

249 Barbed Wire

2008. Holocaust Remembrance.

763	**249**	500r. multicoloured	1·20	75

250 Holy Virgin of Iljinsk and Chernigov

2008. 1020th Anniv of the Christianization of the Rus. Sheet 140×96 mm containing T **250** and similar vert designs showing icons. Multicoloured.

MS764	1500r.×3, Type **250**; Christ Pantocrator; Grand Prince Vladimir	5·75	5·75

251 Nesvizh

2008. 425th Anniv of Nesvizh Castle. Sheet 70×77 mm. Multicoloured.

MS765	**251** multicoloured	4·00	4·00

252 Angel

2008. Christmas.

766	**252**	500r. multicoloured	1·00	60

253 Signs of the Zodiac

2008. New Year.

767	**253**	1000r. multicoloured	1·25	75

254 *Bison bonasus* (European bison)

2008. Animals.

768	**254**	5000r. multicoloured	5·75	3·30

255 *Bubo bubo* (Eurasian eagle owl)

2008. Owls. Multicoloured.

769	500r. Type **255**	65	35
770	500r. *Athene noctua* (little owl)	65	35
771	1000r. *Otus scops* (common Scops owl)	1·25	75
772	1000r. *Strix uralensis* (Ural owl)	1·25	75

256 Hands reading and Louis Braille

2009. Birth Bicentenary of Louis Braille (inventor of Braille writing for the blind).

773	**256**	700r. multicoloured	1·00	60

257 Vladimir Muliavin

2009. Vladimir Muliavin (founder of Pesnyary folk-rock band) Commemoration.

774	**257**	1000r. multicoloured	1·25	75

258 Tanks

2009. 20th Anniv of Withdrawal of Troops.

775	**258**	400r. multicoloured	1·00	60

259 Executive Committee Building

2009

776	**259**	500r. multicoloured	1·00	60

260 Kaljady (winter holiday (7th–19th January))

2009. Holidays and Celebrations. Sheet 122×93 mm containing T **260** and similar vert designs. Multicoloured.

MS777	500r.×4, Type **260**; Invitation to Spring (pagan festival); Dozhinki (rye harvest); Kupalle (7th July)	2·40	2·40

261 *Anser anser* (grey goose)

2009. Grey Goose.

778	**261**	1000r. multicoloured	1·25	75

262 Symbols of Early Astronomy

2009. Europa. Astronomy. Multicoloured.

779	1000r. Type **262**	1·25	75

780 1000r. Symbols of modern astronomy 1·25 75

263 Globe and Butterflies

2009. Year of Native Land. Sheet 72×50 mm.
MS781 multicoloured 2·75 2·75

264 Ducks

2009. Poultry. Multicoloured.
782 1000r. Type **264** 1·50 90
783 1000r. Geese 1·50 90
MS784 69×91 mm. 3000r. Chickens (horiz) 4·00 4·00

265 *Scorzonera glabra*

2009. Endangered Flora. Multicoloured.
785 1500r. Type **265** 1·50 90
786 1500r. *Anemone sylvestris* 1·50 90

266 Monument and Fireworks

2009. 65th Anniv of Liberation. Sheet 81×66 mm. Multicoloured.
MS786 500r.×2 Type **266**; Women soldiers 1·00 1·00

267 Antonov An-2 and Parachutist

2009. Air Sports. Multicoloured.
787 1500r. Type **267** 1·50 90
788 1500r. Yakovlev Yak-52 1·50 90

268 Andrei Gromyko

2009. Birth Centenary of Andrei Andreyevich Gromyko (Soviet Union Minister for Foreign Affairs (1957–85) and Presidium of the Supreme Soviet Chairman (1985–88)).
789 **268** 800r. multicoloured 1·00 60

269 Holy Virgin of Borkolabovo

2009. 350th Anniv of Holy Virgin of Borkolabovo (icon).
790 **269** 1380r. multicoloured 1·50 90

2008. Arms. As T **127**. Multicoloured.
791 1000r. Smorgon 1·00 60

2008. Arms. As T **127**. Multicoloured.
792 1000r Kobrin 1·00 60

270 Red Deer

2009. 600th Anniv of the Nature Reserve—Belovezhskaya Puscha. Sheet 142×60 mm containing T 270 and similar horiz designs. Multicoloured.
MS793 1500r.×3, Type **270**; Bison; Wild boar 4·75 4·75

271 Telegraph Machine

2009. 150th Anniv of Minsk–Bobruisk Telegraph Line.
794 **271** 1380r. multicoloured 1·50 90

272 Galina Makarova

2009. 90th Birth Anniv of Galina Makarova (actress).
795 **272** 800r. multicoloured 75 45

273 *The Azure Day* (V.K. Tsvirko)

2009. 70th Anniv of National Museum. Multicoloured.
796 1000r. Type **273** 1·00 90
797 1000r. *Evening in Minsk Province* (A.G. Goravsky) 1·00 90

274 Decorated Tree

2009. Christmas and New Year. Bateleika–Christmas Puppet Show. Sheet 110×97 mm mm containing T **274** and similar vert design. Multicoloured.
MS798 1500r.×2, Type **274**; Angel 3·75 3·75

No. **MS**798 also contains a central stamp size label which, with the stamps and margins forms a composite design of a puppet theatre.

275 Kittens

2009. Russian Blue Cats. Sheet 131×101 mm containing T **275** and similar horiz designs. Multicoloured.
MS799 2500r.×3, Type **275**; Three kittens seated; Head of mother cat 3·25 3·25

276 Soccer Stadium, Minsk

2009. Sports Stadiums. Multicoloured.
800 1500r. Type **276** 1·90 90
801 1500r. MCSC, Minsk 1·90 90

277 Anniversary Emblem

2009. Tenth Anniv of Creation of Union State. Sheet 113×70 mm.
MS802 multicoloured 4·75 4·75

278 Games Emblem

2010. Winter Olympic Games, Vancouver. Sheet 132×71 mm.
MS803 multicoloured 3·00 3·00

No. 804 and Type **279** are left for Birth Bicentenary of I. Khrutski, issued on 8 February 2010, not yet received.

280 Ivan Naumenko

2010. 85th Birth Anniv of Ivan Naumenko (writer).
805 **280** 800r. multicoloured 1·00 60

281 *Falco tinnunculus* (kestrel)

2010. Birds.
806 **281** 1000r. multicoloured 1·00 90

282 *Iosif Zhagel*

2010. Slutsk Sashes. Sheet 138×67 mm containing T **282** and similar horiz designs. Multicoloured.
MS807 1000r.×3, Type **282**; Slutsk gate, Nesvizh; Slutsk sash (18th century) 2·50 2·50

The stamps and margin of **MS**807 form a composite design.

283 Boy reading

2010. Europa. Children's Books. Multicoloured.
808 1000r. Type **283** 1·00 90
809 1000r. Girl reading 1·00 90

284 Liberating Soldiers

2010. 65th Anniv of End of World War II. Multicoloured
810 500r. Type **284** 50 30
MS811 104×100 mm. 500r. Celebrating soldiers in Berlin; 1500r. Monument to Liberation, Berlin 3·00 3·00

285 Bears

2010. International Year of Biodiversity. Sheet 132×49 mm. Multicoloured
MS812 300r. Type **285**; 300r. Fish; 2400r. Emblem 4·00 4·00

286 Emblem

2010. Expo 2010, Shanghai
813 **286** 500r. multicoloured 2·20 1·30

287 Arms

2010. First Anniv of Belarus Sovereign Military Order of Malta Postal Agreement
814 **287** H (920r.) multicoloured 1·10 65

No. 814 was for international surface mail weighing 20g. or less.

288 Optimist

2010. Yachts. Multicoloured.
815 920r. Type **288** 1·10 65
816 1420r. *Luch* 1·70 1·00

289 Knights

2010. 600th Anniv of Battle of Grunwald
817 **289** 1500r. multicoloured 1·80 1·10

290 Darya Domracheva (Bronze medal winner (biathlon))

2010. Winter Olympic Games Medal Winners. Multicoloured.
818 A Type **290** 55 35
819 H Sergei Novikov (Silver medal winner (biathlon)) 95 60
820 P Aleksei Grishin (Olympic champion (freestyle skier)) 1·50 90
MS820a 100×135 mm. Nos. 818/20, each×2 2·10 1·60

291 Andrei Bahdanovich and Aliaksandr Bahdanovich (C2 1000m)

2010. Olympic Games Gold Medallists
MS821 1000r.×4, Type **291**; Aksana Miankova (women's hammer throw); Andrei Aramnau (weight lifter); Raman Piatrushenka, Aliaksei Abalmasau, Artur Litvinchuk and Vadzim Makhneu (K-4 1000m) 4·50 4·50

292 Locomotive S Class, Vilenski Station, Minsk

2010. Early 20th-century Locomotives and Stations. Multicoloured.

822	1000r. Type **292**	1·30	70
823	1000r. Locomotive Sch class, Mogilyov Station	1·30	70

293

2010. Endangered Species. Green Snaketail Dragonfly (*Ophiogomphus cecilia*). Multicoloured.

824	900r. Type **293**	95	60
825	1000r. Larva and adult	1·10	70
826	1400r. Adult facing left front	1·60	95
827	1500r. Facing left rear	1·80	1·10

294 *Clavariadelphus pistillaris*

2010. Endangered Species. Multicoloured.

828	Type **294**	45	30
829	500r. *Langermannia gigantea*	45	30
830	500r. *Hericium coralloides*	45	30
831	1000r. *Sparassis laminosa*	1·30	80
832	1000r. *Polyporus umbellatus*	1·30	80

2010. Arms. Multicoloured.

833	900r. Khoiniki	1·00	60

295 Trade Union Headquarters

2010. Sixth Trade Union Congress of Belarus

MS834	**295** 2000r. multicoloured	2·30	2·40

2010. Arms. Multicoloured.

835	1400r Lida	1·50	90

296 Dove, Globe, '65' and Emblem

2010. 65th Anniv of United Nations

836	**296** 1000r. multicoloured	1·30	80

297 Spaniel

2010. Hunting dogs. Multicoloured.

837	1000r. Type **297**	1·20	75
838	1000r Irish setter	1·20	75
839	1000r. Russian laika	1·20	75

298 Star, Angels and Snow-covered Bethlehem (Merry Christmas)

2010. Christmas and New Year. Multicoloured.

840	1000r. Type **298**	2·30	1·40
841	1000r. Children, snowman, Christmas tree and Santa Claus (Happy New Year)	2·30	1·40
MS841a	138×156 mm. Nos. 840/1, each×2	9·00	5·50

2010. Arms. Multicoloured.

842	900r Gantsevichi	1·00	60

299 Competition Emblem and Children

2010. Junior Eurovision Song Contest, Minsk

843	**299** H (1010r.) multicoloured	1·30	80

300 Castle Façade

2010. Mirsky Castle

844	**300** 5000r. multicoloured	5·75	5·75

301 *Primula elatior*

2011. Endangered Flora. Multicoloured.

845	H (1010r.) Type **301**	1·00	60
846	P (1560r.) *Orchis ustulata*	1·60	95
MS846a	107×103 mm. Nos. 845/6, each×2	5·25	2·10

302 Emperor Penguins and Ice Cap

2011. Preserve Polar Regions and Glaciers. Multicoloured.

847	1500r. Type **302**	1·10	65
848	2500r. Polar bear	2·50	1·50

303 Curlew

2011. Birds

849	**303** 1500r. multicoloured	1·60	95

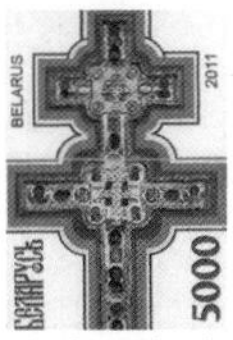

304 Cross (detail)

2011. 800th Anniv of Cross of St. Euphrosyne of Polotsk

MS850	5000r. Type **304**	1·00	60
MS851	10000r. As Type **304** (with colours reversed)	1·60	95

305 Yuri Gagarin

2011. 50th Anniv of the First Manned Space Flight

852	**305** H (1160r.) multicoloured	1·30	80

306 Deer in forest

2011. Europa. Forests. Multicoloured.

853	2000r. Type **306**	1·80	1·10
854	2500r. Bison	2·20	1·40

307 Tower and Flowers

2011. 25th Anniv of Chernobyl Nuclear Accident

855	**307** H (1330r.) multicoloured	1·20	75

308 Hands enclosing Ribbon

2011. 30th Anniv of AIDS Prevention Campaign

856	**308** H (1330r.) multicoloured	1·20	75

309 Tar

2011. Musical Instruments. Multicoloured.

857	H (1330r.) Type **309**	1·20	75
858	H (1330r.) Wheel Lyra	1·20	75

310 Minsk

2011. Capital Cities. Multicoloured.

859	H (1330r.) Type **310**	1·40	90
860	H (1330r.) Erevan	1·40	90

311 Anniversary Emblem

2011. 20th Anniv of Commonwealth of Independent States

861	**311** H (1330r.) multicoloured	1·40	90

312 Belarus and Venezuela Flags

2011. 15th Anniv of Friendship and Cooperation between Belarus and Venezuela. Sheet 93×62 mm

MS862	**312** 3000r. multicoloured	3·75	2·30

313 Summer Amphitheatre

2011. Slavianski Bazaar in Vitebsk, International Festival of Arts. Multicoloured.

863	A (360r.) Type **313**	45	30
864	H (1400r.) Vitebsk Town Hall	1·40	90

Nos. 863/4 were printed, *se-tenant*, forming a composite design.

314 Horse Racing

2011. Equestrian Sport

865	H (1400r.) Type **314**	1·40	90
866	H (1400r.) Jumping	1·40	90
867	H (1400r.) Dressage	1·40	90

MS868	6 90×60 mm. P (2160r.) Dressage, half-pass (vert)	2·75	1·90

315 Dove and Olive Branch

2011. 50th Anniv of Non-Aligned Movement

869	**315** H (1400r.) multicoloured	1·40	90

316 *Lota lota* (burbot)

2011. Fish. Multicoloured.

870	H (1400r.) Type **316**	1·40	90
871	P (2160r.) *Esox lucius* (northern pike)	2·75	1·90

317 Emblem

2011. 20th Anniv of Regional Communication Community (RCC)

872	**317** H (1540r.) multicoloured	1·30	80

318 Mir Castle (UNESCO World Heritage Site)

2011. Architecture. Multicoloured.

MS873	P (2380r.)×2, Type **318**; Karim-khani Citadel, Shiraz (prospective UNESCO World Heritage Site)	5·75	4·25

2011. Arms. Multicoloured.

874	H (1620r.) Molodechno	1·50	95

319 Malorita Region

2011. Traditional Costumes. Multicoloured.

875	H (1620r.) Type **319**	1·50	95
876	P (2500r.) Kalinkovichi region	3·00	2·20

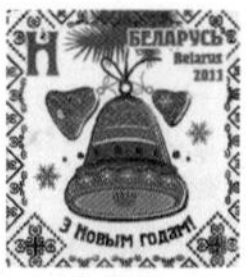

320 Christmas Bells

2011. Christmas and New Year. Multicoloured.

877	H (2450r.) Type **320**	2·30	1·50
878	P (3750r.) Angel	2·50	1·80

321 Pigeons

2011. Pigeons. Multicoloured.

879	5000r. Type **321**	4·50	3·25
880	5000r. Carrier pigeons	4·50	3·25
881	5000r. Fancy pigeons (white with pale brown ruff and base of tail)	4·50	3·25

322 Arms of Belarus and China

2012. 20th Anniv of Diplomatic Relations between Belarus and China. Sheet 100×55 mm

MS882	**322**	15000r. multicoloured	18·00	18·00

323 Textile

2012. Textile

883	**323**	N (1100r.) multicoloured (grey country name, vermilion value)	1·40	1·40
884	**323**	M (1650r.) multicoloured (vermilion name, vermilion value)	1·90	1·90

324 St. Sophia Cathedral, Polotsk

2012. Architecture. Orthodox Temples of Belarus. Multicoloured.

MS885	10000r.×2, Type **324**; All Saints' Monument Church, Minsk	1·70	1·70

325 Mogilev Town Hall

2012. Architecture. Architectural Monuments. Multicoloured.

(a) Ordinary gum

886		50r. Type **325**	10	10
887		100r. Tower, Kamenets	15	10
888		200r. Nesvizh Castle	20	10
889		500r. Church in Polatsk	50	30
890		1000r. Palace of Rumyantsev-Paskevich, Gomel	1·10	65
891		2000r. Mirski Castle	1·90	1·10
892		5000r. Main post office, Minsk	4·00	2·40
893		10000r. Lida Castle	4·50	4·75
894		20000r. Budslav Monastrey	7·00	4·25
895		A Kossov's Palace	50	30
896		H Red Castle, Minsk	2·00	1·20
897		P Church-fortress, Murovanka	2·50	1·50

(b) Self-adhesive

898		50r. Type **325** (As No. 886)	10	10
899	-	100r. Tower, Kamenets (As No. 887)	15	10
900	-	200r. Nesvizh Castle (As No. 888)	20	15
901	-	500r. Church in Polatsk (As No. 889)	50	30
902	-	1000r. Palace of Rumyantsev-Paskevich, Gomel (As No. 890)	1·10	65
903	-	2000r. Mirski Castle (As No. 891)	1·90	1·10
904	-	5000r. Main post office, Minsk (As No. 892)	4·00	2·40
905	-	10000r. Lida Castle (As No. 893)	4·50	2·75
906	-	20000r. Budslav Monastrey (As No. 894)	7·00	4·25
907	-	A Kossov's Palace (As No. 895)	50	30
908	-	H Red Castle, Minsk (As No. 896)	2·00	1·20
909	-	P Church-fortress, Murovanka (As No. 897)	2·50	1·50

326 Couple presenting Hen and Basket of Fruit

2012. Europa. Visit Belarus. Multicoloured.

910	5000r. Type **326**	1·00	60
911	5000r. Couple, facing left, presenting bread and jug of wine	1·00	60

Nos. 910/11 were printed, *se-tenant*, forming a composite design.

Pt. 4

BELGIAN CONGO

A Belgian colony in Central Africa. Became independent in July 1960. for later issues see Congo, Zaire, Democratic Republic of Congo, Katanga, and South Kasai.

100 centimes = 1 franc.

INDEPENDENT STATE OF THE CONGO

The Independent State of the Congo was established in 1885, with King Leopold II of the Belgians as ruler.

1 Leopold II

1886. Various frames.

1	1	5c. green	21·00	24·00
2	1	10c. red	7·50	9·50
3	1	25c. blue	50·00	26·00
4	1	50c. green	13·00	13·00
5	1	5f. lilac	£325	£180

1887. Surch **COLIS-POSTAUX Fr. 3.50**.

6	3f.50 on 5f. lilac	£900	£650

5 Leopold II

1887

7	**5**	5c. green	45	1·10
8	**5**	10c. red	1·70	85
9	**5**	25c. blue	2·30	1·40
10	**5**	50c. brown	65·00	15·00
11	**5**	50c. grey	5·00	12·00
12	**5**	5f. lilac	£900	£350
13	**5**	5f. grey	£110	90·00
14	**5**	10f. orange	£400	£225

1887. Surch **COLIS-POSTAUX Fr. 3.50**.

15	3f.50 on 5f. violet	£800	£450

1889. Surch **COLIS-POSTAUX Fr. 3.50** in frame.

16	3f.50 on 5f. violet	£600	£300
17	3f.50 on 5f. grey	£120	£120

7 Port of Matadi

8 Stanley Falls

13 Oil Palms

14 Native Canoe

1894. Inscr "ETAT INDEPENDANT DU "CONGO".

18	**7**	5c. black and blue	30·00	42·00
24	**7**	5c. black and brown	3·25	1·90
30	**7**	5c. black and green	1·30	60
19	**8**	10c. black and brown	36·00	50·00
25	**8**	10c. black and blue	1·70	1·00
31	**8**	10c. black and red	2·75	75
26	**13**	15c. black and brown	11·00	70
20	-	25c. black and orange	5·75	3·25
32	-	25c. black and blue	5·75	1·80
27	**14**	40c. black and green	18·00	3·50
21	-	50c. black and green	4·50	1·80
33	-	50c. black and brown	20·00	2·30
22	-	1f. black and violet	48·00	23·00
35	-	1f. black and red	£225	5·00
28	-	3f.50 black and red	£130	80·00
23	-	5f. black and red	75·00	20·00
29	-	10f. black and green	£120	18·00

DESIGNS—HORIZ: 25c. Inkissi Falls; 50c. Railway Bridge over the M'pozo; 1f. African elephant hunt; 3f.50 Congo village; 10f. *Deliverance* (stern wheel paddle-steamer). VERT: 5f. Bangala Chief Morangi and wife.

BELGIAN CONGO

The Congo was annexed to Belgium in 1908 and was renamed the Belgian Congo.

1909. Nos. 23, 26/29 and 30/33 optd **CONGO BELGE**.

36A	**7**	5c. black and green	4·50	3·50
37A	**8**	10c. black and red	7·50	2·75
38A	**13**	15c. black and brown	8·25	2·75
49	-	25c. black and blue	3·75	2·00
50	**14**	40c. black and green	10·00	6·75
51	-	50c. black and brown	16·00	3·75
52	-	1f. black and red	55·00	7·50
53	-	3f.50 black and red	60·00	18·00
54	-	5f. black and red	70·00	34·00
55b	-	10f. black and green	£120	40·00

1909. As 1894 issue but inscr "CONGO BELGE".

56	**7**	5c. black and green	2·75	3·75
57	**8**	10c. black and red	1·00	2·75
58	**13**	15c. black and brown	40·00	25·00
59	-	50c. black and bistre	4·50	5·75

1910. As 1894 issue but inscr "CONGO BELGE BELGISCH-CONGO" with values in French and Flemish.

60	**7**	5c. black and green	1·60	20
61	**8**	10c. black and red	1·30	20
62	**13**	15c. black and brown	40	10
63	-	25c. black and blue	3·50	90
64	**14**	40c. black and green	3·50	4·25
65	-	50c. black and bistre	5·75	3·25
66	-	1f. black and red	10·50	3·75
68	-	3f. black and red	28·00	34·00
67	-	5f. black and red	23·00	36·00
69	-	10f. black and green	50·00	46·00

32 Port of Matadi

33 Stanley Falls

34 Inkissi Falls

1915. New types as 32 to 34 (with value in words at top) and other types as 1910 all inscr "CONGO BELGE" and "BELGISCH-CONGO".

70	**32**	5c. black and green	90	1·00
71	**33**	10c. black and red	3·25	2·75
72b	**13**	15c. black and green	1·50	55
73	**34**	25c. black and blue	3·25	1·10
74	**14**	40c. black and red	9·50	4·50
75	-	50c. black and red	15·00	3·75
76	-	1f. black and olive	8·00	1·30
77	-	5f. black and orange	4·00	2·50

1918. Types as before, surch with red cross and premium.

78	**32**	5c.+10c. blue and green	30	5·50
79	**33**	10c.+15c. blue and red	70	5·50
80	**13**	15c.+20c. blue and green	50	4·50
81	**34**	25c.+25c. blue	1·50	6·00
82	**14**	40c.+40c. blue and red	1·30	7·75
83	-	50c.+50c. blue and red	60	7·50
84	-	1f.+1f. blue and olive	6·50	10·00
85	-	5f.+5f. blue and orange	17·00	40·00
86	-	10f.+10f. blue and green	£110	£120

38 Congo Wharf

1920. Air.

87	**38**	50c. black and orange	60	55
88	-	1f. black and violet	85	30
89	-	2f. black and blue	95	85
90	-	5f. black and green	1·50	1·00

DESIGNS—HORIZ: 1f. District stores; 2f. Native canoes on beach. VERT: 5f. Provinicial prison.

1921. Stamps of 1910 surch.

91	**14**	5c. on 40c. black and green	1·70	7·00
92	-	10c. on 5c. black and green	1·00	40
93	-	15c. on 50c. black and olive	40	2·75
94	**13**	25c. on 15c. black & yellow	4·25	1·10
95	**8**	30c. on 10c. black and red	85	1·10
96	-	50c. on 25c. black and blue	2·50	75

1921. Stamps of **1910 optd 1921**.

97	1f. black and red	1·40	1·40
98	3f. black and red	2·50	3·75
99	5f. black and lake	13·00	24·00
100	10f. black and green	14·00	11·50

1922. Stamps of previous issues variously surch without bars.

101	-	5c. on 50c. black and lake (No. 75)	45	1·90
102	**32**	10c. on 5c. black and green (No. 70)	55	25
103	**14**	25c. on 40c. black and lake (No. 74)	4·75	40
104	**33**	30c. on 10c. black and red (No. 71)	1·10	1·30
105	**34**	50c. on 25c. black and blue (No. 73)	45	35
114	**8**	0.25 on 30c. on 10c. black and red (No. 95)	23·00	50·00
115	**33**	0.25 on 30c. on 10c. black and red (No. 104)	10·00	48·00

1922. Stamps of 1915 surch with new value and two bars through old values.

108	**32**	10c. on 5c. black & green	6·75	7·75
110	-	10c. on 1f. black & olive	3·25	7·25
112	**14**	25c. on 40c. black & lake	1·40	60
113	-	25c. on 5f. blk & orange	5·25	11·00

46 Wood Carver

56 Native Cattle

1923

117	**A**	5c. yellow	35	85
118	**B**	10c. green	50	10
119	**C**	15c. brown	15	10
120	**D**	20c. olive	15	1·90
121	**E**	20c. green	85	1·40
122	**F**	25c. brown	15	10
123	**46**	30c. red	50	4·25
124	**46**	30c. olive	60	2·30
125	**46**	35c. green	8·00	6·00
126	**D**	40c. purple	50	10
142	**56**	45c. purple	70	1·20
127	**G**	50c. blue	55	1·00
128	**G**	50c. orange	70	10
143	**56**	60c. red	35	20
129	**E**	75c. orange	20	45
130	**E**	75c. blue	95	2·50
131	**46**	75c. red	1·00	15
132	**H**	1f. brown	60	95
133	**H**	1f. blue	30	10
134	**H**	1f. red	1·10	10
135	**D**	1f.25 blue	45	1·70
136	**D**	1f.50 blue	1·10	1·00
137	**D**	1f.75 blue	3·75	3·00
138	**I**	3f. brown	8·00	5·25
139	**J**	5f. grey	10·50	12·50
140	**K**	10f. black	22·00	21·00

DESIGNS: A, Ubangi woman; B, Baluba woman; C, Babuende woman; D, Ubangi man; E, Weaver; F, Basketmaker; G. Archer; H, Potter; I, Rubber worker; J, Palm oil; K, African elephant.

55 Native Canoe

1925. Great War Colonial Memorial Fund. Inscr in French or in Flemish.

141a	**55**	25c.+25c. black and red	1·30	12·00

1927. No. 136 surch **1.75**.

144	1.75 on 1f. 50 blue	45	35

58 H. M. Stanley

1928. 50th Anniv of Stanley's Exploration of the Congo.

145	**58**	5c. olive	10	35
146	**58**	10c. violet	10	10
147	**58**	20c. red	55	75

148	58	35c. green	2·30	3·25
149	58	40c. brown	1·60	1·90
150	58	60c. sepia	1·80	1·10
151	58	1f. red	45	10
152	58	1f.60 grey	6·75	6·00
153	58	1f.75 blue	1·40	1·00
154	58	2f. brown	90	45
155	58	2f.75 purple	4·50	1·80
156	58	3f.50 red	1·40	1·30
157	58	5f. turquoise	85	2·00
158	58	10f. blue	1·20	2·00
159	58	20f. red	7·50	5·25

59 Nurse weighing Children

60 Doctor and Tent Surgery

1930. Congo Natives Protection Fund.

160	59	10c.+5c. red	95	12·00
161	-	20c.+10c. brown	1·80	12·50
162	60	35c.+15c. green	3·50	19·00
163	-	60c.+30c. purple	3·25	18·00
164	-	1f.+50c. red	6·75	24·00
165	-	1f.75+75c. blue	6·00	36·00
166	-	3f.50+1f.50 red	9·50	60·00
167	-	5f.+2f.50 brown	10·00	65·00
168	-	10f.+5f. black	13·00	65·00

DESIGNS—VERT: 20c. Missionary and child; 1f. Dispenser attending patients. HORIZ: 60c. View of local hospital; 1f.75, Nurses and patients; 3f.50, Nurse bathing baby; 5f. Operating theatre in local hospital; 10f. Children in school.

61 Native Kraal

1930. Air.

169	61	15f. black and sepia	8·75	4·25
170	-	30f. black and purple	15·00	9·75

DESIGN: 30f. Native porters.

1931. Surch.

171	40c. on 35c. grn (No. 148)	1·80	2·75
177	40c. on 35c. green (125)	5·50	11·00
178	50c. on 45c. purple (142)	2·30	1·30
172	1f.25 on 1f. red (151)	2·00	10
173	2f. on 1f.60 grey (152)	75	15
174	2f. on 1f.75 blue (153)	90	20
179	2f. on 1f.75 blue (137)	10·00	9·75
175	3f.25 on 2f.75 purple (155)	2·50	1·60
180	3f.25 on 3f. brown (138)	11·00	20·00
176	3f.25 on 3f.50 red (156)	4·50	7·00

67 Sankuru River

68 Flute Players

1931

181	67	10c. brown	1·00	1·40
182	-	15c. grey	1·00	20
183	-	20c. mauve	1·20	1·10
184	-	25c. blue	70	35
185	68	40c. green	1·00	2·30
186	-	50c. violet	1·00	10
187	-	60c. purple	1·30	2·30
188	-	75c. red	50	35
189	-	1f. red	4·25	55
190	-	1f.25 brown	3·25	10
190b	-	1f.50 black	6·25	2·50
191	-	2f. blue	3·25	1·30
191a	-	2f.50 blue	5·00	5·00
192	-	3f.25 grey	3·75	6·75
193	-	4f. lilac	3·00	1·60
194	-	5f. purple	6·50	1·60
195	-	10f. orange	5·50	5·75
196	-	20f. sepia	6·25	5·75

DESIGNS—HORIZ: 15c., 25c. Native kraals (different views); 20c. Waterfall; 50c. Native musicians (seated); 1f.50, 2f., Riverside dwellings; 2f.50, 3f.25, Okapi; 4f. Canoes on river shore. VERT: 60c. Native musicians (standing); 75c. Mangbethu woman; 1f. Elephant transport; 1f.25., Native chief; 5f. Pressing out tapioca; 10f. Witch doctor; 20f. Woman carrying latex.

69 Fokker F.VIIb/3m over Congo

1934. Air.

197	69	50c. black	3·50	2·50
198	69	1f. red	2·30	1·30
199	69	1f.50 green	85	15
200	69	3f. brown	75	75
201	69	4f.50 blue	3·00	50
202	69	5f. red	1·70	95
203	69	15f. purple	5·50	5·50
204	69	30f. red	9·25	10·00
205	69	50f. violet	9·25	6·00

70 King Albert I

1934. Death of King Albert.

206	70	1f.50 black	95	55

71 The Kings of Belgium

1935. 50th Anniv of Independent State of the Congo.

207	71	50c. green	1·80	3·25
208	71	1f.25 red	1·10	60
209	71	1f.50 purple	1·10	20
210	71	2f.40 orange	6·50	6·50
211	71	2f.50 blue	3·50	2·75
212	71	4f. violet	5·25	3·50
213	71	5f. brown	5·75	6·00

1936. Air. Surch **3.50F**.

214	69	3f.50 on 3f. brown	70	10

1936. King Albert Memorial Fund. Surch **+ 50** c.

215	71	1f.50+50c. purple	4·50	12·50
216	71	2f.50+50c. blue	2·30	21·00

74 Queen Astrid and Congo Children

1936. Queen Astrid Fund for Congo Children.

217	74	1f.25+5c. brown	1·30	3·75
218	74	1f.50+10c. red	1·60	5·25
219	74	2f.50+25c. blue	1·80	11·50

75 Mitumba Forest

76 R. Molindi

1937. Promotion of National Parks. (a) Sheet (140×111 mm) comprising block of four.

MS219a	75 4f.50 black and red	11·00	27·00

(b) As T **76**.

220	76	5c. black and violet	10	10
221	-	90c. brown and red	2·00	2·75
222	-	1f.50 black and purple	45	1·30
223	-	2f.40 brown and grey	65	1·50
224	-	2f.50 black and blue	95	55
225	-	4f.50 brown and green	2·50	2·30

DESIGNS—VERT: 90c. Bamboo-canes; 1f.50, R. Suza; 2f.40, R. Rutshuru. HORIZ: 2f.50, Mt. Karisimbi; 4f.50, Mitumba Forest.

1938. Tourism Congress, Costermansville. Sheet 140×120 mm containing Nos. 220/5 but all printed in brown and blue.

MS225a	5c. to 4f.50	50·00	65·00

77 Marabou Stork and Ruppels Griffon

1939. Leopoldville Zoological Gardens.

226	77	1f.+1f. purple	13·50	21·00
227	-	1f.25+1f.25 red	10·00	20·00
228	-	1f.50+1f.50 violet	13·50	44·00
229	-	4f.50+4f.50 green	9·25	36·00
230	-	5f.+5f. brown	11·00	36·00

DESIGNS: 1f.25, Kob; 1f.50, Young chimpanzees; 4f.50, Crocodiles; 5f. Lioness.

78 King Albert Memorial, Leopoldville

1941

231	78	10c. grey	4·75	6·25
232	78	15c. brown	1·00	1·80
233	78	25c. blue	2·00	80
234	78	50c. lilac	2·75	1·30
235	78	75c. pink	4·00	2·00
236	78	1f.25 brown	3·00	2·30
237	78	1f.75 orange	8·00	11·00
238	78	2f.50 red	3·50	20
239	78	2f.75 blue	6·25	2·30
240	78	5f. olive	5·00	2·30
241	78	10f. red	9·50	7·00

1941. Surch.

242	-	5c. on 1f.50 black & purple (No. 222) (postage)	35	3·25
243	78	75c. on 1f.75 orange	10·50	14·00
244	-	2f.50 on 2f.40 brown and grey (No. 223)	2·00	2·50
245	69	50c. on 1f.50 green (air)	2·30	5·00

81 "Belgium Shall Rise Again"

1942. War Relief Fund.

246	81	10f.+40f. green	9·00	13·00
247	81	10f.+40f. blue	8·75	13·00

82 Oil Palms

84 Leopard

1942. (a) Inscr "BELGISCH CONGO BELGE".

248	82	5c. red	10	10
249	-	50f. black and blue	9·75	2·50
250	-	100f. black and red	19·00	1·80

(b) Inscr "CONGO BELGE BELGISCH CONGO", or vice versa.

251a	82	10c. olive	10	10
252a	82	15c. brown	10	50
253a	82	20c. blue	10	10
254a	82	25c. purple	10	10
255a	82	30c. blue	10	10
256	82	50c. green	1·50	10
257a	82	60c. brown	80	40
258	-	75c. black and violet	1·90	10
259a	-	1f. black and brown	1·70	10
260	-	1f.25 black and red	1·30	10
261	84	1f.75 brown	2·75	2·75
262a	84	2f. yellow	3·75	10
263a	84	2f.50 red	1·60	10
264a	-	3f.50 olive	1·60	10
265a	-	5f. orange	1·80	10
266a	-	6f. blue	2·00	10
267	-	7f. black	2·30	10
268	-	10f. brown	1·10	10
269a	-	20f. black and red	8·50	4·25

DESIGNS—As Type **82**: 75c. to 1f.25, Head of a native woman; 3f.50 to 10f. Askari sentry. As Type **84**: 20f. Okapi; 28×33 mm: 50 f. Head of woman; 100f. Askari sentry.

1944. Red Cross Fund. Surch **Au profit de la Croix Rouge Ten voordeele van het Roode Kruis** (or with French and Flemish reversed) and additional value.

269aa	82	50c.+50f. green	20·00	55·00
269b	-	1f.25+100f. black and red (No. 260)	19·00	55·00
269c	84	1f.75+100f. brown	20·00	55·00
269d	-	3f.50+100f. green (No. 264)	16·00	55·00

87 Driving Slaves to Market

88 Leopold II

1947. 50th Anniv of Abolition of Slavery in Belgian Congo.

270	87	1f.25 brown	60	15
270a	-	1f.50 violet	5·00	2·75
270b	-	3f. brown	2·75	45
271	-	3f.50 blue	35	10
272	88	10f. orange	80	1·30

PORTRAITS–As Type **88**: 1f.50, Lavigerie. 3f. Dhanis. 3f.50, Lambermont.

89 Seated Figure

1947. Native masks and carvings as T **89**.

273	89	10c. orange	35	10
274	A	15c. blue	10	10
275	B	20c. blue	35	35
276	C	25c. red	60	10
277	D	40c. purple	1·20	10
278	89	50c. brown	2·75	10
279	A	70c. green	35	50
280	B	75c. purple	85	10
281	C	1f. purple and orange	2·50	10
281a	A	1f.20 brown and grey	5·00	2·75
282	D	1f.25 purple and green	1·00	50
282a	E	1f.50 red and green	25·00	12·50
282b	B	1f.60 blue and grey	3·75	2·50
283	89	2f. red and orange	3·25	10
283a	C	2f.40 green and turquoise	2·00	60
284	A	2f.50 green and brown	60	10
284a	E	3f. indigo and blue	9·75	10
285	B	3f.50 green and blue	5·75	25
286	C	5f. purple and bistre	4·25	10
287	D	6f. green and orange	2·30	10
287a	F	6f.50 brown and red	5·50	10
287b	D	8f. green and blue	4·00	25
288	E	10f. brown and violet	20·00	15
289	F	20f. brown and red	3·50	10
290	E	50f. black and brown	5·25	80
291	F	100f. black and red	7·50	2·75

DESIGNS: A, Seated figure (different); B, Kneeling figure; C, Double mask; D, Mask; E, Mask with tassels; F, Mask with horns.

90 Railway Train and Map

1948. 50th Anniv of Matadi–Leopoldville Railway.

292	90	2f.50 green and blue	2·30	55

91 Globe and 19th-century Full-rigged Ship

1949. 75th Anniv of U.P.U.

293	91	4f. blue	80	1·40

92 Allegorical Figure and Map

1950. 50th Anniv of "Comite Special du Katanga" (Chartered Company).

294	**92**	3f. slate and blue	2·30	4·00
295	**92**	6f.50 sepia and red	2·30	1·90

93 "Littonia"

1952. Flowers. Multicoloured.

296	10c. "Dissotis"	35	10
297	15c. "Protea"	10	10
298	20c. "Vellozia"	10	10
299	25c. Type **93**	10	10
300	40c. "Ipomoea"	25	35
301	50c. "Angraecum"	80	10
302	60c. "Euphorbia"	60	60
303	75c. "Ochna"	1·10	20
304	1f. "Hibiscus"	1·20	10
305	1f.25 "Protea"	4·50	4·00
306	1f.50 "Schizoglossum"	1·20	85
307	2f. "Ansellia"	1·50	10
308	3f. "Costus"	1·00	10
309	4f. "Nymphaea"	2·30	10
310	5f. "Thunbergia"	1·90	10
311	6f.50 "Thonningia"	2·30	10
312	7f. "Gerbera"	2·20	10
313	8f. "Gloriosa"	5·75	60
314	10f. "Silene"	5·00	25
315	20f. "Aristolochia"	7·25	25
316	50f. "Eulophia"	18·00	1·40
317	100f. "Cryptosepalum"	22·00	7·50

SIZES: Nos. 296/315, 21×25½ mm. Nos. 316/17, 22½×32½ mm.

94 St. Francis Xavier

1953. 400th Death Anniv of St. Francis Xavier.

318	**94**	1f.50c. black and blue	4·00	1·40

95 Lake Kivu

1953. Kivu Festival.

319	**95**	3f. black and red	3·50	1·20
320	**95**	7f. brown and blue	4·75	30

96 Medallion

1954. 25th Anniv of Belgian Royal Colonial Institute. No. 322 has different frame.

321	**96**	4f.50 grey and blue	90	40
322	**96**	6f.50 brown and green	65	20

97 King Baudouin and Mountains

1955. Inscr "CONGO BELGE . BELGISCH CONGO" or vice versa.

323	**97**	1f.50 black and red	9·50	3·25
324	-	3f. black and green	6·50	90
325	-	4f.50 black and blue	7·25	1·00
326	-	6f.50 black & purple	9·50	3·00

DESIGNS: 3f. Forest; 4f.50, River; 6f.50, Grassland.

98 Badge and Map

1955. Fifth International Congress of African Tourism. Inscr in Flemish or French.

327	**98**	6f.50 blue	4·50	3·00

1956. Birth Bicentenary of Mozart. As T **316/17** of Belgium.

328	**316**	4f.50+1f.50 violet	9·75	14·50
329	**317**	6f.50+2f.50 blue	9·25	10·00

99 Nurse with Children

1957. Red Cross Fund. Cross in red.

330	**99**	3f.+50c. blue	5·00	10·50
331	-	4f.50+50c. green	8·00	11·50
332	-	6f.50+50c. brown	5·50	11·50

DESIGNS—HORIZ: 4f.50, Doctor inoculating patient; 6f.50, Nurse in tropical kit bandaging patient.

100 Belgian Monarchs

1958. 50th Anniv of Belgian Annexation of the Congo.

333	**100**	1f. red	60	10
334	**100**	1f.50 blue	70	10
335	**100**	3f. red	2·00	1·00
336	**100**	5f. green	3·00	85
337	**100**	6f.50 brown	2·30	25
338	**100**	10f. violet	2·00	1·20

101 Roan Antelope

1959. Wild Animals.

339	**101**	10c. brown, sepia & blue	20	95
340	-	20c. blue and red	10	3·25
341	-	40c. brown and blue	80	2·75
342	-	50c. multicoloured	1·30	95
343	-	1f. black, green & brown	1·90	1·30
344	-	1f.50 black and yellow	2·30	1·30
345	-	2f. black, brown and red	3·50	1·80
346	-	3f. black, purple & slate	2·75	2·00
347	-	5f. brown, green & sepia	3·25	2·30
348	-	6f.50 brn, yellow & blue	1·90	1·20
349	-	8f. bistre, violet & brown	3·75	2·50
350	-	10f. multicoloured	4·50	5·50

DESIGNS—HORIZ: 20c. White rhinoceros; 50c. Demidoff's galago; 1f.50, African buffaloes; 3f. African elephants; 6f.50, Impala; 10f. Eland and common zebras. VERT: 40c. Giraffe; 1f. Gorilla; 2f. Eastern Black and White Colobus monkey; 5f. Okapis; 8f. Giant ground pangolin.

102 Madonna and Child

1959. Christmas.

351	**102**	50c. brn, ochre & chestnut	15	15
352	**102**	1f. brown, violet & blue	15	15
353	**102**	2f. brown, blue and grey	25	55

103 "African Resources"

1960. Tenth Anniv of African Technical Co-operation Commission. Inscr in French or Flemish.

354	**103**	3f. orange and grey	1·20	3·00

104 High Jumping

1960. Child Welfare Fund.

355	**104**	50c.+25c. blue and red	1·50	7·50
356	-	1f.50+50c. red & green	1·30	7·50
357	-	2f.+1f. green and red	1·50	9·25
358	-	3f.+1f.25 purple & bl	3·25	12·50
359	-	6f.50+3f.50 brn & red	2·75	16·00

DESIGNS: 1f.50, Hurdling; 2f. Football; 3f. Throwing the javelin; 6f.60, Throwing the discus.

POSTAGE DUE STAMPS

D54

1923

D141	**D54**	5c. sepia	10	4·50
D142a	**D54**	10c. red	35	5·50
D143	**D54**	15c. violet	35	5·25
D144	**D54**	30c. green	50	1·60
D145	**D54**	50c. blue	35	2·00
D146	**D54**	1f. grey	40	65

D86

1943

D270a	**D86**	10c. olive	30	4·50
D271a	**D86**	20c. blue	15	2·75
D272a	**D86**	50c. green	20	4·75
D273a	**D86**	1f. brown	35	3·75
D274a	**D86**	2f. orange	15	3·50

D99

1957

D330	**D99**	10c. brown	90	3·00
D331	**D99**	20c. purple	1·00	3·00
D332	**D99**	50c. green	1·50	3·00
D333	**D99**	1f. blue	1·60	4·50
D334	**D99**	2f. red	2·00	4·50
D335	**D99**	4f. violet	2·30	5·00
D336	**D99**	6f. blue	3·00	5·50

For later issues see **CONGO (KINSHASA), ZAIRE REPUBLIC** and **DEMOCRATIC REPUBLIC OF CONGO**.

Pt. 7

BELGIAN OCCUPATION OF GERMANY

Stamps used in German territory occupied by Belgian Forces at the end of the War of 1914/18, and including the districts of Eupen and Malmedy, now incorporated in Belgium.

100 centimes = 1 Belgian franc.

1919. Stamps of Belgium optd **ALLEMAGNE DUITSCHLAND**.

1	**51**	1c. orange	40	85
2	**51**	2c. brown	40	85
3	**51**	3c. grey	40	3·25
4	**51**	5c. green	85	1·60
5	**51**	10c. red	1·60	3·25
6	**51**	15c. violet	85	1·60
7	**51**	20c. purple	1·30	1·60
8	**51**	25c. blue	1·60	2·75
9	**63**	25c. blue	5·25	16·00
10	**52**	35c. black and brown	1·60	1·60
11	-	40c. black and green	1·60	3·25
12	-	50c. black and red	8·00	15·00
13	-	65c. black and red	4·25	16·00
14	**55**	1f. violet	30·00	26·00
15	-	2f. grey	55·00	65·00
16	-	5f. blue (FRANK, No. 194)	11·50	16·00
17	-	10f. sepia	65·00	85·00

1920. Stamps of Belgium surch **EUPEN & MALMEDY** and value.

18	**51**	5pf. on 5c. green	40	55
19	**51**	10pf. on 10c. red	40	55
20	**51**	15pf. on 15c. violet	75	65
21	**51**	20pf. on 20c. purple	75	1·50
22	**51**	30pf. on 25c. blue	1·10	1·50
23	-	75pf. on 50c. black and red	21·00	26·00
24	**55**	1m.25 on 1f. violet	30·00	27·00

1920. Stamps of Belgium optd **Eupen**.

25	**51**	1c. orange	55	55
26	**51**	2c. brown	55	55
27	**51**	3c. grey	75	2·10
28	**51**	5c. green	75	1·30
29	**51**	10c. red	1·30	1·80
30	**51**	15c. violet	1·80	1·80
31	**51**	20c. purple	2·10	2·10
32	**51**	25c. blue	1·80	2·75
33	**63**	25c. blue	6·25	13·50
34	**52**	35c. black and brown	2·75	2·75
35	-	40c. black and green	3·25	3·25
36	-	50c. black and red	8·50	10·50
37	-	65c. black and red	4·75	16·00
38	**55**	1f. violet	34·00	26·00
39	-	2f. grey	60·00	42·00
40	-	5f. blue (FRANK, No. 194)	18·00	16·00
41	-	10f. sepia	75·00	70·00

1920. Stamps of Belgium optd **Malmedy**.

42	**51**	1c. orange	35	55
43	**51**	2c. brown	35	55
44	**51**	3c. grey	55	2·10
45	**51**	5c. green	85	1·30
46	**51**	10c. red	1·30	1·80
47	**51**	15c. violet	2·10	2·10
48	**51**	20c. purple	2·75	2·75
49	**51**	25c. blue	2·10	2·75
50	**63**	25c. blue	6·25	12·50
51	**52**	35c. black and brown	2·75	3·25
52	-	40c. black and green	2·75	3·25
53	-	50c. black and red	10·50	10·50
54	-	65c. black and red	4·75	16·00
55	**55**	1f. violet	34·00	23·00
56	-	2f. grey	60·00	42·00
57	-	5f. blue (FRANK, No. 194)	18·00	23·00
58	-	10f. sepia	75·00	80·00

POSTAGE DUE STAMPS

1920. Postage Due stamps of Belgium, 1919. (a) Optd **Eupen**.

D1	5c. green	1·30	1·60
D2	10c. red	2·75	2·75
D3	20c. green	5·25	6·25
D4	30c. blue	5·25	6·25
D5	50c. grey	26·00	21·00

(b) Optd **Malmedy**.

D6	5c. green	2·20	1·30
D7	10c. red	4·50	2·20
D8	20c. green	16·00	13·00
D9	30c. blue	8·75	9·75
D10	50c. grey	18·00	13·00

Pt. 4

BELGIUM

An independent Kingdom of N.W. Europe.

1849. 100 centimes = 1 franc.
2002. 100 cents = 1 euro.

1
"Epaulettes"

1849. Imperf.

1	**1**	10c. brown	£3500	£100
2a	**1**	20c. blue	£4000	70·00

3
"Medallions"

1861. Imperf.

12	**3**	1c. green	£300	£160
13	**3**	10c. brown	£650	11·50
14	**3**	20c. blue	£700	11·50
15	**3**	40c. red	£5500	£100

1863. Perf.

24	1c. green	85·00	35·00
25	10c. brown	£110	4·75
26	20c. blue	£110	4·75
27	40c. red	£600	32·00

5

8

1865. Various frames.

34	**5**	10c. grey	£250	3·00
35	**5**	20c. blue	£400	2·50
36	**5**	30c. brown	£850	13·50
37	**8**	40c. red	£1100	26·00
38	**5**	1f. lilac	£2750	£140

10 "Small Lion"

1866

43	**10**	1c. grey	£140	16·00
44	**10**	2c. blue	£500	£110
45	**10**	5c. brown	£600	£100

11

13

14

15

20

1869. Various frames.

46	**11**	1c. green	11·50	60
59a	**11**	2c. blue	27·00	4·00
60	**11**	5c. buff	75·00	1·70
49	**11**	8c. lilac	£100	70·00
50	**13**	10c. green	38·00	60
51b	**14**	20c. blue	£190	1·70
62	**15**	25c. bistre	£130	4·00
53a	**13**	30c. buff	£110	4·25
54b	**13**	40c. red	£190	8·75
55a	**15**	50c. grey	£375	14·50
56	**13**	1f. mauve	£550	21·00
57a	**20**	5f. brown	£2250	£1900

Types **13** to **20** and all later portraits to Type **38** are of Leopold II.

21

1883. Various frames.

63	**21**	10c. red	35·00	3·50
64	-	20c. grey	£250	14·00
65	-	25c. blue	£500	46·00
66	-	50c. violet	£475	46·00

25

1884. Various frames.

67	**11**	1c. olive	22·00	85
68	**11**	1c. grey	5·75	60
69	**11**	2c. brown	19·00	2·30
70	**11**	5c. green	50·00	60
71	**25**	10c. red	17·00	60
72	-	20c. olive	£275	2·30
73	-	25c. blue on red	21·00	3·50
74	-	35c. brown	26·00	3·50
75	-	50c. bistre	17·00	2·50
76	-	1f. brown on green	£1000	21·00
77	-	2f. lilac	80·00	44·00

32

33

1893

78a	**32**	1c. grey	95	35
79	**32**	2c. yellow	85	1·50
80	**32**	2c. brown	2·30	60
81	**32**	5c. green	13·00	60
82	**33**	10c. brown	3·75	25
83	**33**	10c. red	3·25	60
84	**33**	20c. olive	20·00	85
85	**33**	25c. blue	14·00	60
86a	**33**	35c. brown	29·00	1·70
87	**33**	50c. brown	75·00	25·00
88	**33**	50c. grey	85·00	3·75
89	**33**	1f. red on green	£110	29·00
90	**33**	1f. orange	£140	7·50
91	**33**	2f. mauve	95·00	75·00

The prices for the above and all following issues with the tablet are for stamps with the tablet attached. Without tablet, the prices will be about half those quoted.
See also Nos. 106/8.

34 Arms of Antwerp

1894. Antwerp Exhibition.

93	**34**	5c. green on red	7·00	4·75
94	**34**	10c. red on blue	3·50	3·00
95	**34**	25c. blue on red	1·20	1·20

35 St. Michael encountering Satan

36

1896. Brussels Exhibition of 1897.

96	**35**	5c. violet	85	85
97	**36**	10c. red	8·75	5·25
98	**36**	10c. brown	30	30

37

38

1905. Various frames.

99	**37**	10c. red	1·70	85
100	**37**	20c. olive	39·00	1·50
101	**37**	25c. blue	17·00	1·20
102	**37**	35c. purple	41·00	3·00
103	**38**	50c. grey	£140	3·00
104	**38**	1f. orange	£190	14·00
105	**38**	2f. mauve	£130	29·00

1907. As T **32** but no scroll pattern between stamps and labels.

106	1c. grey	2·00	30
107	2c. red	23·00	8·75
108	5c. green	20·00	85

40 St. Martin and the Beggar (from altarpiece by Van Dyck)

1910. Brussels Exhibition. A. Unshaded background. B. Shaded background. A.

109	**40**	1c. (+1c.) grey	1·20	1·20
110	**40**	2c. (+2c.) purple	13·00	13·00
111	**40**	5c. (+5c.) green	3·50	3·50
112	**40**	10c. (+5c.) red	3·50	3·50

B.

113	1c. (+1c.) green	3·50	3·50
114	2c. (+2c.) purple	9·25	9·25
115	5c. (+5c.) green	3·50	3·50
116	10c. (+5c.) red	3·50	3·50

1911. Nos. 109/16 optd **1911**. A.

117	1c. (+1c.) grey	42·00	29·00
118	2c. (+2c.) purple	£200	£100
119	5c. (+5c.) green	13·00	11·50
120	10c. (+5c.) red	13·00	11·50

B.

121	1c. (+1c.) green	65·00	41·00
122	2c. (+2c.) purple	£100	46·00
123	5c. (+5c.) green	13·00	11·50
124	10c. (+5c.) red	13·00	11·50

1911. Charleroi Exhibition. Nos. 109/16 optd **CHARLEROI–1911**. A.

125	1c. (+1c.) grey	8·25	4·25
126	2c. (+2c.) purple	21·00	17·00
127	5c. (+5c.) green	11·50	11·50
128	10c. (+5c.) red	11·50	11·50

B.

129	1c. (+1c.) green	8·25	4·25
130	2c. (+2c.) purple	21·00	17·00
131	5c. (+5c.) green	11·50	11·50
132	10c. (+5c.) red	11·50	11·50

42

43

44

45 Albert I

1912

133	**42**	1c. orange	25	25
134	**43**	2c. brown	35	35
135	**44**	5c. green	25	25
136	**45**	10c. red	70	60
137	**45**	20c. olive	22·00	5·75
138	**45**	35c. brown	1·20	85
139	**45**	40c. green	23·00	21·00
140	**45**	50c. grey	1·20	85
141	**45**	1f. orange	5·00	4·25
142	**45**	2f. violet	38·00	26·00
143	-	5f. purple	£120	38·00

The 5f. is as Type **45** but larger (23×35 mm).

46 (Larger head)

1912. Large head.

148	**46**	10c. red	25	25
145	**46**	20c. olive	35	45
150	**46**	25c. blue	35	35
147	**46**	40c. green	75	75

47 Merode Monument

1914. Red Cross.

151	**47**	5c. (+5c.) red & green	4·75	4·75
152	**47**	10c. (+10c.) red & pink	7·00	7·00
153	**47**	20c. (+20c.) red & vio	75·00	75·00

48 Albert I

1914. Red Cross.

154	**48**	5c. (+5c.) red and green	5·75	5·75
155	**48**	10c. (+10c.) red	60	60
156	**48**	20c. (+20c.) red & violet	18·00	18·00

49 Albert I

1915. Red Cross.

157	**49**	5c. (+5c.) red and green	13·00	3·00
158	**49**	10c. (+10c.) red and pink	37·00	14·50
159	**49**	20c. (+20c.) red & violet	65·00	23·00

51 Albert I

52 Cloth Hall, Ypres

55 Freeing of the Scheldt

1915

170	**51**	1c. orange	25	25
171	**51**	2c. brown	25	25
179	**51**	3c. grey	60	45
172	**51**	5c. green	1·50	25
173	**51**	10c. red	1·40	25
174	**51**	15c. violet	2·20	25
187	**51**	20c. purple	3·50	40
176	**51**	25c. blue	60	45
188	**52**	35c. black and brown	60	35
189	-	40c. black and green	60	35
190	-	50c. black and red	6·50	35
191	**55**	1f. violet	49·00	1·20
192	-	2f. grey	31·00	2·30
193	-	5f. blue (FRANKEN)	£500	£190
194	-	5f. blue (FRANK)	1·70	1·20
195	-	10f. brown	28·00	27·00

DESIGNS: As T **52**: 40c. Dinant; 50c. Louvain. As T **55**: 2f. Annexation of the Congo; 5f. King Albert at Furnes; 10f. The Kings of Belgium.

1918. Red Cross. Surch with new value and cross. Some colours changed.

222	**51**	1c.+1c. orange	30	30
223	**51**	2c.+2c. brown	30	30
224	**51**	5c.+5c. green	1·70	1·50
225	**51**	10c.+10c. red	3·50	3·25
226	**51**	15c.+15c. purple	7·00	7·00
227	**51**	20c.+20c. brown	14·50	13·00
228	**51**	25c.+25c. blue	29·00	29·00
229	**52**	35c.+35c. black & violet	14·00	13·50
230	-	40c.+40c. black & brown	14·00	13·50
231	-	50c.+50c. black and blue	14·50	13·50
232	**55**	1f.+1f. grey	46·00	45·00
233	-	2f.+2f. green	£100	£100
234	-	5f.+5f. brn (FRANKEN)	£250	£250
235	-	10f.+10f. blue	£850	£750

63 "Perron" at Liege

1919

236a	**63**	25c. blue	3·50	50

64 Albert I

1919

237	**64**	1c. brown	25	25
238	**64**	2c. olive	25	25
239	**64**	5c. green	25	25
240	**64**	10c. red	35	35
241	**64**	15c. violet	45	45
242	**64**	20c. sepia	1·70	1·70
243	**64**	25c. blue	2·30	2·30
244	**64**	35c. brown	2·50	2·50
245	**64**	40c. red	9·25	8·75
246	**64**	50c. brown	15·00	14·50
247	**64**	1f. orange	60·00	55·00
248	**64**	2f. purple	£550	£500
249	**64**	5f. red	£130	£130
250	**64**	10f. red	£170	£170

SIZES: 1c., 2c., 18½×21½ mm. 5c. to 2f., 22½×26½ mm. 5f., 10f., 27½×33 mm.

67 Discus thrower

68 Charioteer

1920. Olympic Games, Antwerp.

256	**67**	5c. (+5c.) green	2·50	2·30
257	**68**	10c. (+5c.) red	2·00	1·70
258	-	15c. (+5c.) brown	3·00	2·30

DESIGN—VERT: 15c. Runner.

73 Hotel de Ville, Termonde

1920

308b	**73**	65c. black and purple	85	45

1921. Nos. 256/8 surch **20c. 20c.**

309	**67**	20c. on 5c. green	85	30
310	**68**	20c. on 10c. red	60	30
311	-	20c. on 15c. brown	85	30

76 Albert I

1921

313	**76**	50c. blue	30	10
314	**76**	75c. red	40	35
315	**76**	75c. blue	50	10
316	**76**	1f. sepia	60	10
317	**76**	1f. blue	50	30
318	**76**	2f. green	1·20	30
319	**76**	5f. purple	19·00	18·00
320	**76**	5f. brown	11·50	11·50
321	**76**	10f. red	13·00	9·25

1921. Surch **55c 55c.**

322	**73**	55c. on 65c. black & pur	3·50	45

80

1922. War Invalids Fund.

348	**80**	20c.+20c. brown	1·70	1·70

81 Albert I

1922

349	**81**	1c. orange	10	10
350	**81**	2c. olive	30	30
351	**81**	3c. brown	10	10
352	**81**	5c. slate	10	10
353	**81**	10c. green	25	25
354	**81**	15c. plum	25	25
355	**81**	20c. brown	25	25
356	**81**	25c. purple	30	15
357	**81**	25c. violet	60	15
358	**81**	30c. red	45	25
359	**81**	30c. mauve	35	25
360	**81**	35c. brown	45	45
361	**81**	35c. green	60	30
362	**81**	40c. red	60	25
363	**81**	50c. bistre	65	30
364	**81**	60c. olive	4·25	15
365	**81**	75c. violet	1·30	85
366	**81**	1f. yellow	60	60
367	**81**	1f. red	1·50	30
368	**81**	1f.25 blue	1·70	1·50
369	**81**	1f.50 blue	3·00	60
370	**81**	1f.75 blue	2·00	25
371	**81**	2f. blue	4·25	60
372	**81**	5f. green	60·00	3·00
373	**81**	10f. brown	£100	13·00

83 Wounded Soldier

1923. War Invalids Fund.

374	**83**	20c.+20c. slate	1·70	1·70

87 Leopold I and Albert I

1925. 75th Anniv of 1st Belgian Stamps.

410	**87**	10c. green	11·00	11·00
411	**87**	15c. violet	4·25	4·25
412	**87**	20c. brown	4·25	4·25
413	**87**	25c. slate	4·25	4·25
414	**87**	30c. red	4·25	4·25
415	**87**	35c. blue	4·25	4·25
416	**87**	40c. sepia	4·25	4·25
417	**87**	50c. brown	4·25	4·25
418	**87**	75c. blue	4·25	4·25
419	**87**	1f. purple	9·25	9·25
420	**87**	2f. blue	5·75	5·75
421	**87**	5f. black	4·75	4·75
422	**87**	10f. red	9·75	9·75

88

1925. Anti-T.B. Fund.

423	**88**	15c.+5c. red and mauve	30	30
424	**88**	30c.+5c. red and grey	30	30
425	**88**	1f.+10c. red and blue	1·50	1·50

1926. Flood Relief. Type of 1922 surch **Inondations 30 c Watersnood.**

426	**81**	30c.+30c. green	1·20	1·20

90

1926. Flood Relief Fund. A. Shaded background. B. Solid background. A.

427	**90**	1f.+1f. blue	7·50	7·50

B.

428	1f.+1f. blue	1·70	1·70

91

92 Queen Elisabeth and King Albert

1926. War Tuberculosis Fund.

429	**91**	5c.+5c. brown	10	10
430	**91**	20c.+5c. brown	60	60
431	**91**	50c.+5c. violet	25	25
432	**92**	1f.50+25c. blue	80	80
433	**92**	5f.+1f. red	7·50	7·50

1927. Stamps of 1922 surch.

434	**81**	3c. on 2c. olive	25	25
435	**81**	10c. on 15c. plum	25	25
436	**81**	35c. on 40c. red	25	10
437	**81**	1f.75 on 1f.50 blue	1·60	1·20

94 Rowing Boat

1927. Anti-T.B. Fund.

438	**94**	25c.+10c. brown	1·20	1·20
439	**94**	35c.+10c. green	1·20	1·20
440	**94**	60c.+10c. violet	30	30
441	**94**	1f.75+25c. blue	1·50	1·50
442	**94**	5f.+1f. purple	5·25	5·25

96 Ogives

97 Ruins of Orval Abbey

1928. Orval Abbey Restoration Fund. Inscr "ORVAL 1928" or "ORVAL".

461	**96**	5c.+5c. red and gold	30	30
462	-	25c.+5c. violet and gold	45	45
463	-	35c.+10c. green	1·30	1·30
464	-	60c.+15c. brown	85	30
465	-	1f.75+25c. blue	3·50	2·30
466	-	2f.+40c. purple	29·00	24·00
467	-	3f.+1f. red	26·00	23·00
468	**97**	5f.+5f. lake	19·00	17·00
469	-	10f.+10f. sepia	19·00	17·00

DESIGNS—VERT: 35c., 2f. Cistercian monk stone-carving; 60c., 1f.75, 3f. Duchess Matilda retrieving her ring.

99 Mons Cathedral

101 Malines Cathedral

1928. Anti-T.B. Fund.

472	**99**	5c.+5c. red	30	30
473	-	25c.+15c. sepia	30	30
474	**101**	35c.+10c. green	1·50	1·50
475	-	60c.+15c. brown	60	60
476	-	1f.75+25c. violet	10·00	10·00
477	-	5f.+5f. purple	23·00	28·00

DESIGNS—As Type **99**: 25c. Tournai Cathedral. As Type **101**: 60c. Ghent Cathedral; 1f.75, St. Gudule Cathedral, Brussels; 5f. Louvain Library.

1929. Surch **BRUXELLES 1929 BRUSSEL 5 c** in frame.

478	**81**	5c. on 30c. mauve	15	15
479	**81**	5c. on 75c. violet	25	25
480	**81**	5c. on 1f.25c. blue	15	15

The above cancellation, whilst altering the original face value of the stamps, also constitutes a precancel, although stamps also come with additional ordinary postmark. The unused prices are for stamps with full gum and the used prices are for stamps without gum, with or without postmarks. We do not list precancels where there is no change in face value.

104 The Belgian Lion

105 Albert I

1929

487	**104**	1c. orange	25	25
488	**104**	2c. green	60	30
489	**104**	3c. brown	25	10
490	**104**	5c. green	25	10
491	**104**	10c. bistre	25	10
492	**104**	20c. mauve	1·40	40
493	**104**	25c. red	60	10
494	**104**	35c. green	60	10
495	**104**	40c. purple	45	15
496	**104**	50c. blue	45	10
497	**104**	60c. mauve	3·00	30
498	**104**	70c. brown	1·70	25
499	**104**	75c. blue	3·00	25
500	**104**	75c. brown	8·25	30
501	**105**	10f. brown	23·00	5·75
502	**105**	20f. green	£120	35·00
503a	**105**	50f. purple	29·00	29·00
504a	**105**	100f. red	35·00	35·00

1929. Laying of first Stone towards Restoration of Orval Abbey. Nos. 461/9 optd with crown over ornamental letter "L" and **19-8-29.**

543	5c.+5c. red and gold	£100	95·00
544	25c.+5c. violet and gold	£100	95·00
545	35c.+10c. green	£100	95·00
546	60c.+15c. brown	£100	95·00
547	1f.75c.+25c. blue	£100	95·00
548	2f.+40c. purple	£120	£100
549	3f.+1f. red	£100	95·00
550	5f.+5f. lake	£100	95·00
551	10f.+10f. sepia	£100	95·00

109 Canal and Belfry, Bruges

1929. Anti-T.B. Fund.

552	-	5c.+5c. brown	30	30
553	-	25c.+15c. grey	2·00	2·00
554	-	35c.+10c. green	1·70	1·70
555	-	60c.+15c. lake	60	60
556	-	1f.75+25c. blue	8·75	8·75
557	**109**	5f.+5f. purple	42·00	42·00

DESIGNS—HORIZ: 5c. Waterfall at Coo; 35c. Menin Gate, Ypres; 60c. Promenade d'Orleans, Spa; 1f.75, *Aquitania* and *Dinteldyk* (liners), Antwerp Harbour. VERT: 25c. Bayard Rock, Dinant.

110 Paul Rubens

111 Zenobe Gramme

1930. Antwerp and Liege Exns.

558	**110**	35c. green	60	30
559	**111**	35c. green	60	30

112 Fokker F. VIIa/m I-BOEO over Ostend

1930. Air.

560	**112**	50c. blue	60	30
561	-	1f.50 brown (St. Hubert)	3·50	3·50
562	-	2f. green (Namur)	2·30	1·20
563	-	5f. red (Brussels)	2·30	1·50
564	-	5f. violet (Brussels)	38·00	38·00

113 *Leopold II* by Jef Lempoels

1930. Centenary of Independence.

565		60c. purple	30	30
566	**113**	1f. red	1·20	85
567	-	1f.75 blue	3·00	1·70

PORTRAITS: 60c. *Leopold I* by Lievin de Winne. 1f.75, King Albert I.

114 Antwerp City Arms

1930. International Philatelic Exhibition, Antwerp. Sheet 138×136 mm.

MS568	**114** 4f. (+6f.) green	£350	£350

1930. I.L.O. Congress. Nos. 565/7 optd **B.I.T. OCT. 1930**.

569		60c. purple	3·00	3·00
570		1f. red	11·50	11·50
571		1f.75 blue	20·00	20·00

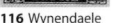

116 Wynendaele

117 Gaesbeek

1930. Anti-T.B. Fund.

572	-	10c.+5c. mauve	45	45
573	**116**	25c.+15c. sepia	1·30	1·30
574	-	40c.+10c. purple	1·20	1·20
575	-	70c.+15c. slate	1·20	1·20
576	-	1f.+25c. red	9·75	9·75
577	-	1f.75+25c. blue	6·50	6·50
578	**117**	5f.+5f. green	49·00	49·00

DESIGNS: 10c. Bornhem; 40c. Beloeil; 70c. Oydonck, 1f. Ghent; 1f.75, Bouillon.

1931. Surch **2c**.

579	**104**	2c. on 3c. brown	15	15

1931. Surch **BELGIQUE 1931 BELGIE 10c.**

580		10c. on 60c. mauve	70	30

See note below No. 480.

121 Albert I

123

1931

582	**121**	75c. brown (18×22 mm)	1·70	10
583	**121**	1f. lake (21×23½ mm)	35	30
584	**123**	1f.25 black	80	60
585	**123**	1f.50 purple	1·70	60
586	**123**	1f.75 blue	60	10
587	**123**	2f. brown	1·20	30
588	**123**	2f.45 violet	3·50	60
589	**123**	2f.50 sepia	13·50	60
590	**123**	5f. green	37·00	1·60
591	**123**	10f. red	70·00	19·00

See also No. 654.

124 Prince Leopold

1931. Disabled Soldiers' Relief Fund. Brussels National Philatelic Exhibition. Sheet 123×161 mm.

MS592	**124**	2f.45+55c. red (sold at 5f.)	£250	£225

125 Queen Elisabeth

1931. Anti-Tuberculosis Fund.

593	**125**	10c.+5c. brown	30	30
594	**125**	25c.+15c. violet	1·50	60
595	**125**	50c.+10c. green	85	60
596	**125**	75c.+15c. sepia	60	30
597	**125**	1f.+25c. lake	11·50	9·75
598	**125**	1f.75+25c. blue	8·50	5·75
599	**125**	5f.+5f. purple	75·00	75·00

1932. Surch **BELGIQUE 1932 BELGIE 10c.**

600	**104**	10c. on 40c. mauve	4·00	40
601	**104**	10c. on 70c. brown	4·00	15

See Note below No. 480.

126 Reaper

127 Mercury

1932

602	**126**	2c. green	50	50
603	**127**	5c. red	10	10
604	**126**	10c. green	15	10
605	**127**	20c. lilac	1·50	30
606	**126**	25c. red	85	25
607	**127**	35c. green	3·50	10

129 Cardinal Mercier

1932. Cardinal Mercier Memorial Fund.

609	**129**	10c.+10c. purple	60	60
610	**129**	50c.+30c. mauve	3·00	3·00
611	**129**	75c.+25c. brown	3·00	3·00
612	**129**	1f.+2f. red	11·00	11·00
613	-	1f.75+75c. blue	85·00	85·00
614	-	2f.50+2f.50 brown	85·00	85·00
615	-	3f.+4f.50 green	85·00	85·00
616	-	5f.+20f. purple	£120	£120
617	-	10f.+40f. red	£250	£225

DESIGNS: 1f.75, 3f. Mercier protecting refugees at Malines; 2f.50, 5f. Mercier with busts of Aristotle and Thomas Aquinas; 10f. Mercier when Professor at Louvain University.

132

1932. Infantry Memorial.

618	**132**	75c.+3f.25 red	95·00	95·00
619	**132**	1f.75+4f.25 blue	95·00	95·00

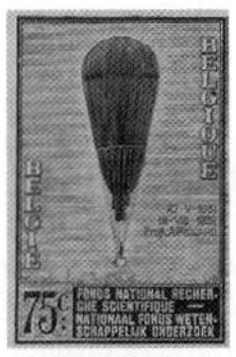

133 Prof Piccard's Stratosphere Balloon *F.N.R.S.*, 1931

1932. Scientific Research Fund.

621	**133**	75c. brown	3·50	30
622	**133**	1f.75 blue	20·00	3·25
623	**133**	2f.50 violet	23·00	17·00

134 Hulpe-Waterloo Sanatorium

1932. Anti-T.B. Fund.

624	**134**	10c.+5c. violet	30	30
625	**134**	25c.+15c. mauve	3·25	2·00
626	**134**	50c.+10c. red	3·00	85
627	**134**	75c.+15c. brown	1·70	30
628	**134**	1f.+25c. red	20·00	14·50
629	**134**	1f.75+25c. blue	13·00	11·00
630	**134**	5f.+5f. green	£110	£110

1933. Lion type surch **BELGIQUE 1933 BELGIE 10c.**

631	**104**	10c. on 40c. mauve	21·00	4·00
632	**104**	10c. on 70c. brown	19·00	1·70

See note below No. 480.

135 The Transept

1933. Orval Abbey Restoration Fund. Inscr "ORVAL".

633	-	5c.+5c. green	75·00	75·00
634	-	10c.+15c. green	75·00	75·00
635	-	25c.+15c. brown	55·00	50·00
636	**135**	50c.+25c. lake	55·00	50·00
637	-	75c.+50c. green	55·00	50·00
638	-	1f.+1f.25 lake	55·00	50·00
639	-	1f.25+1f.75 sepia	55·00	50·00
640	-	1f.75+2f.75 blue	85·00	85·00
641	-	2f.+3f. mauve	85·00	85·00
642	-	2f.50+5f. brown	85·00	85·00
643	-	5f.+20f. purple	85·00	85·00
644	-	10f.+40f. blue	£350	£350

DESIGNS—VERT: 10c. Abbey Ruins; 75c. Belfry, new abbey; 1f. Fountain, new abbey. HORIZ: 5c. The old abbey; 25c. Guests' Courtyard, new abbey; 1f.25, Cloister, new abbey; 1f.75, Foundation of Orval Abbey in 1131; 2f. Restoration of the abbey, XVI and XVII centuries; 2f.50, Orval Abbey, XVIII century; 5f. Prince Leopold laying foundation stone of new abbey; 10f. The Virgin Mary (30×45 mm).

138 Anti-T.B. Symbol

1933. Anti-tuberculosis Fund.

646	**138**	10c.+5c. grey	85	85
647	**138**	25c.+15c. mauve	3·75	3·75
648	**138**	50c.+10c. brown	3·00	3·00
649	**138**	75c.+15c. sepia	60·00	60·00
650	**138**	1f.+25c. red	23·00	21·00
651	**138**	1f.75+25c. blue	36·00	35·00
652	**138**	5f.+5f. purple	£160	£160

1934. Lion type surch **BELGIQUE 1934 BELGIE 10c.**

653	**104**	10c. on 40c. mauve	19·00	1·70

See note below No. 480.

1934. King Albert's Mourning Stamp.

654	**121**	75c. black	30	10

140 Peter Benoit

1934. Benoit Centenary Memorial Fund.

658	**140**	75c.+25c. brown	7·00	7·00

141 Brussels Palace

1934. International Exhibition, Brussels.

659	-	35c. green	85	45
660	**141**	1f. red	1·50	60
661	-	1f.50 brown	7·00	1·40
662	-	1f.75 blue	7·00	45

DESIGNS: 35c. Congo Palace; 1f.50, Old Brussels; 1f.75, Grand Palace of the Belgian section.

142 King Leopold III

1934. War Invalids' Fund. (a) Size 18×22 mm. (b) Size 21×24 mm. (i) Exhibition Issue.

663	**142**	75c.+25c. green (a)	20·00	20·00
664	**142**	1f.+25c. purple (b)	17·00	17·00

(ii) Ordinary postage stamps.

665		75c.+25c. purple (a)	5·25	5·25
666		1f.+25c. red (b)	8·75	8·75

143 King Leopold III

1934

667		70c. green	45	10
668		75c. brown	70	35
669	**143**	1f. red	3·50	40

144 Health Crusader

1934. Anti-tuberculosis Fund. Cross in red.

670	**144**	10c.+5c. black	25	25
671	**144**	25c.+15c. brown	4·50	4·50
672	**144**	50c.+10c. green	2·30	2·00
673	**144**	75c.+15c. purple	1·50	1·50
674	**144**	1f.+25c. red	14·50	14·50
675	**144**	1f.75+25c. blue	11·50	11·50
676	**144**	5f.+5f. purple	£150	£150

145 The Royal Children

1935. Queen Astrid's Appeal.

680	**145**	35c.+15c. green	1·20	1·20
681	**145**	70c.+30c. purple	1·20	1·20
682	**145**	1f.75+50c. blue	5·75	5·75

146 "Mail-diligence"

1935. Brussels Int Exn.

683	**146**	10c.+10c. olive	60	60
684	**146**	25c.+25c. brown	2·50	2·50
685	**146**	35c.+25c. green	3·75	3·75

1935. Air. Surch with new value twice.

686	**112**	1f. on 1f.50 brown	60	60
687	**112**	4f. on 5f. red	11·00	11·00

148 Francis of Taxis

1935. Brussels Philatelic Exhibition (SITEB). Sheet 93×118 mm.

MS688	**148**	5f.+5f. grey	£170	£170

151 Queen Astrid

1935. Death of Queen Astrid. Mourning Stamp.

713	**151**	70c.+5c. black	25	25

1935. Anti-tuberculosis Fund. Black borders.

714		10c.+5c. olive	25	25
715		25c.+15c. brown	45	45
716		35c.+5c. green	25	25
717		50c.+10c. mauve	60	60
718		1f. +25c. red	1·50	1·50
719		1f.75+25c. blue	2·00	2·00
720		2f.45+55c. violet	4·00	4·00

152 State arms

1936

727	**152**	2c. green	10	10
728	**152**	5c. orange	10	10
729	**152**	10c. olive	10	10
730	**152**	15c. blue	10	10
731	**152**	20c. violet	10	10
732	**152**	25c. red	10	10
733	**152**	25c. yellow	30	10
734	**152**	30c. brown	25	10
735	**152**	35c. green	10	10
736	**152**	40c. lilac	30	30
737	**152**	50c. blue	60	10
738	**152**	60c. grey	15	10
739	**152**	65c. mauve	4·25	45
740	**152**	70c. green	40	30
741	**152**	75c. mauve	1·00	10
742	**152**	80c. green	15·00	35
743	**152**	90c. violet	75	15
744	**152**	1f. brown	70	15

153

1936. Various frames. (a) Size 17½×22 mm.

745	**153**	70c. brown	30	10

746	153	75c. olive	30	30
747	153	1f. red	35	10

(b) Size 21×24 mm.

748		1f. red	35	10
749		1f.20 brown	2·50	15
750		1f.50 mauve	60	45
751		1f.75 blue	30	30
752		1f.75 red	30	10
753		2f. violet	1·70	1·70
754		2f.25 black	30	30
755		2f.50 red	10·50	40
756		3f.25 brown	30	30
757		5f. green	1·70	70

Nos. 746/7, 751/2, 754/5 and 757 are inscribed "BELGIE BELGIQUE".

155 King Leopold III

1936

760	155	1f.50 mauve	85	50
761	155	1f.75 blue	30	30
762	155	2f. violet	60	35
763	155	2f.25 violet	65	65
764	155	2f.45 black	60·00	85
765	155	2f.50 black	4·75	30
770	155	3f. brown	2·00	25
766	155	3f.25 brown	40	25
771	155	4f. blue	5·00	15
767	155	5f. green	3·50	60
772	155	6f. red	18·00	45
768	155	10f. purple	60	30
769	155	20f. red	1·20	60

See also No. 2775.

156 Borgerhout Town Hall

1936. Borgerhout Philatelic Exhibition. Sheet 95×119 mm.

MS775 **156** 70c.+30c. brown £100 95·00

157 Charleroi Town Hall

1936. Charleroi Philatelic Exhibition. Sheet 95×119 mm.

MS776 **157** 2f.45+55c. blue 75·00 75·00

158 Prince Baudouin

1936. Anti-tuberculosis Fund.

777	158	10c.+5c. brown	30	30
778	158	25c.+5c. violet	30	30
779	158	35c.+5c. green	35	35
780	158	50c.+5c. brown	60	60
781	158	70c.+5c. olive	25	25
782	158	1f.+25c. red	1·70	1·70
783	158	1f.75+25c. blue	2·30	2·30
784	158	2f.45+2f.55 purple	5·75	5·75

1937. Stamp of 1929 surch **BELGIQUE 1937 BELGIE 10c.**

785	104	10c. on 40c. purple	30	30

See note below No. 480.

1937. International Stamp Day.

786	158	2f.45c.+2f.55c. slate	3·00	3·00

159 Queen Astrid and Prince Baudouin

1937. Queen Astrid Public Utility Fund.

787	159	10c.+5c. purple	30	30
788	159	25c.+5c. olive	30	30
789	159	35c.+5c. green	30	30
790	159	50c.+5c. violet	60	60
791	159	70c.+5c. black	30	30
792	159	1f.+25c. red	1·70	1·70
793	159	1f.75c.+25c. blue	4·00	4·00
794	159	2f.45c.+1f.55c. brown	8·75	8·75

160 Queen Elisabeth

1937. Eugene Ysaye Memorial Fund.

795	160	70c.+5c. black	35	35
796	160	1f.75+25c. blue	80	80

MS797 113×146 mm. **160** 1f.50+2f.50 red (2); 2f.45+3f.55, violet (2) 44·00 20·00

See also **MS**1963.

161 Princess Josephine Charlotte

1937. Anti-tuberculosis Fund.

798	161	10c.+5c. green	35	35
799	161	25c.+5c. brown	40	40
800	161	35c.+5c. green	35	35
801	161	50c.+5c. olive	40	40
802	161	70c.+5c. purple	30	30
803	161	1f.+25c. red	2·00	2·00
804	161	1f.75+25c. blue	2·00	2·00
805	161	2f.45+2f.55 purple	5·75	5·75

163 King Albert Memorial, Nieuport

1938. King Albert Memorial Fund. Sheet 138×115 mm.

MS809 **163** 2f.45+7f.55 red 23·00 23·00

164 King Leopold

1938. Aeronautical Propaganda.

810	164	10c.+5c. purple	35	35
811	164	35c.+5c. green	50	50
812	164	70c.+5c. black	60	60
813	164	1f.75+25c. blue	3·75	3·75
814	164	2f.45+2f.55 violet	5·25	5·25

165 Basilica of the Sacred Heart, Koekelberg

1938. Building (Completion) Fund.

815	165	10c.+5c. brown	35	35
816	-	35c.+5c. green	35	35
817	165	70c.+5c. grey	35	35
818	-	1f.+25c. red	50	50
819	165	1f.75+25c. blue	50	50
820	-	2f.45+2f.55 red	5·50	5·50
821	-	5f.+5f. green	11·50	11·50

MS822 95×120 mm. 5f.+5f. violet (as 821) 19·00 17·00

DESIGNS—HORIZ: 35c., 1f., 2f.45, Front view of Basilica. VERT: 5f. Interior view.

1938. Surch **2F50.**

823	155	2f.50 on 2f.45 black	14·50	30

167 Exhibition Pavilion

1938. International Exhibition, Liege (1939). Inscr "LIEGE 1939 LUIK".

824	-	35c. green	25	25
825	167	1f. red	25	35
826	-	1f.50 brown	1·50	60
827	-	1f.75 blue	1·50	30

DESIGNS—VERT: 35c. View of Liege. HORIZ: 1f.50, R. Meuse at Liege; 1f.75, Albert Canal and King Albert.

1938. Koekelberg Basilica Completion Fund. Surch.

828		40c. on 35c.+5c. green (No. 816)	85	85
829	165	75c. on 70c.+5c. grey	60	60
830	-	2f.50+2f.50 on 2f.45+2f.55 red (No. 820)	7·75	7·75

170 Prince Albert of Liege

1938. Anti-tuberculosis Fund.

831	170	10c.+5c. brown	35	35
832	170	30c.+5c. purple	35	35
833	170	40c.+5c. olive	35	35
834	170	75c.+5c. grey	35	35
835	170	1f.+25c. red	1·60	1·60
836	170	1f.75+25c. blue	1·40	1·40
837	170	2f.50+2f.50 green	7·25	7·25
838	170	5f.+5f. purple	16·00	16·00

171 King Leopold and Royal Children

1939. Fifth Anniv of Int Red Cross Society.

839	-	10c.+5c. brown	30	30
840	-	30c.+5c. red	35	35
841	-	40c.+5c. olive	35	35
842	171	75c.+5c. black	35	35
843	-	1f.+25c. red	2·10	2·10
844	171	1f.75+25c. blue	1·50	1·50
845	-	2f.50+2f.50 violet	2·00	2·00
846	-	5f.+5f. green	9·25	9·25

DESIGNS—VERT: 10c. H. Dunant; 30c. Florence Nightingale; 40c. and 1f. Queen Elisabeth and Royal children; 2f.50, Queen Astrid. HORIZ: 5f. Queen Elisabeth and wounded soldier (larger).

173 Rubens's House (after engraving by Harrewijn)

1939. Rubens's House Restoration Fund.

847	173	10c.+5c. brown	35	35
848	-	40c.+5c. purple	35	35
849	-	75c.+5c. green	45	45
850	-	1f.+25c. red	2·30	2·30
851	-	1f.50+25c. brown	3·00	3·00
852	-	1f.75+25c. blue	4·75	4·75
853	-	2f.50+2f.50 purple	18·00	18·00
854	-	5f.+5f. grey	23·00	23·00

DESIGNS—As Type **173**: VERT: 40c. *Rubens's Sons, Albert and Nicholas*; 1f. *Helene Fourment (2nd wife) and Children*; 1f.50, *Rubens and Isabella Brant* (1st wife); 1f.75, Rubens (after engraving by Pontius); 2f.50, *Straw Hat* (Suzanne Fourment). HORIZ: 75c. Arcade of Rubens's house. 35 ×45 mm: 5f. *The Descent from the Cross.*

175 Portrait by Memling

1939. Exn of Memling's Paintings, Bruges.

855	175	75c.+75c. olive	2·30	2·30

177 Orval Abbey Cloisters and Belfry

1939. Orval Abbey Restoration Fund. Inscr "ORVAL".

861	-	75c.+75c. olive	5·25	5·25
862	177	1f.+1f. red	2·50	2·50
863	-	1f.50+1f.50 brown	2·50	2·50
864	-	1f.75+1f.75 blue	3·50	3·50
865	-	2f.50+2f.50 mauve	9·75	9·75
866	-	5f.+5f. purple	11·00	11·00

DESIGNS—As Type **177**: VERT: 75c. Monks in laboratory. HORIZ: 1f.50, Monks harvesting; 1f.75, Aerial view of Orval Abbey; 52½×35½ mm: 2f.50, Cardinal Van Roey, Statue of the Madonna and Abbot of Orval; 5f. Kings Albert and Leopold III and shrine.

180 Thuin

1939. Anti-tuberculosis Fund. Belfries.

868		10c.+5c. olive	35	35
869	180	30c.+5c. brown	35	35
870	-	40c.+5c. purple	35	35
871	-	75c.+5c. grey	35	35
872	-	1f.+25c. red	1·50	1·50
873	-	1f.75+25c. blue	1·20	1·20
874	-	2f.50+2f.50 brown	11·00	11·00
875	-	5f.+5f. violet	13·00	13·00

DESIGNS—As Type **180**: 10c. Bruges; 40c. Lier; 75c. Mons. LARGER (21½×34 mm): 1f. Furnes; 1f.75, Namur; 2f.50, Alost; 5f. Tournai.

182 Arms of Mons

1940. Winter Relief Fund.

901	182	10c.+5c. black, red and green	35	35
902	-	30c.+5c. multicoloured	35	35
903	-	40c.+10c. multicoloured	35	35
904	-	50c.+10c. multicoloured	35	35
905	-	75c.+15c. multicoloured	35	35
906	-	1f.+25c. multicoloured	45	45
907	-	1f.75c.+50c. mult	70	70
908	-	2f.50c.+2f.50c. olive, red and black	1·30	1·30
909	-	5f.+5f. multicoloured	1·60	1·60

MS910 103×145 mm. Nos. 901/9 each in first colour given, together with red 14·00 14·00

DESIGNS: 30c. to 5f. Arms of Ghent, Arlon, Bruges, Namur, Hasselt, Brussels, Antwerp and Liege, respectively.

183 Painting

184 Monks studying Plans of Orval Abbey

1941. Orval Abbey Restoration Fund.

935	183	10c.+15c. brown	50	50
936	-	30c.+30c. grey	50	50
937	-	40c.+60c. brown	50	50
938	-	50c.+65c. violet	50	50
939	-	75c.+1f. mauve	50	50
940	-	1f.+1f.50 red	50	50
941	183	1f.25+1f.75 green	50	50
942	-	1f.75+2f.50 blue	50	50
943	-	2f.+3f.50 mauve	50	50
944	-	2f.50+4f.50 brown	50	50

945	-	3f.+5f. green	50	50
946	**184**	5f.+10f. brown	1·80	1·80

MS947 183×165 mm. 5f.+15f. blue (as 946) 10·00 9·25

DESIGNS—As Type **183**. 30c., 1f., 2f.50, Sculpture; 40c., 2f. Goldsmiths (Monks carrying candlesticks and cross); 50c., 1f.75, Stained glass (Monk at prayer); 75c., 3f. Sacred music.

1941. Surch.

955	**152**	10c. on 30c. brown	10	10
956	**152**	10c. on 40c. lilac	10	10
957	**153**	10c. on 70c. brown	10	10
958	**153**	50c. on 75c. olive	30	30
959	**155**	2f.25 on 2f.50 black	65	65

189 Maria Theresa

1941. Soldiers' Families Relief Fund.

960	**189**	10c.+5c. black	25	25
961	-	35c.+5c. green	25	25
962	-	50c.+10c. brown	25	25
963	-	60c.+10c. violet	25	25
964	-	1f.+15c. red	25	25
965	-	1f.50+1f. mauve	25	25
966	-	1f.75+1f.75 blue	25	25
967	-	2f.25+2f.25 brown	30	30
968	-	3f.25+3f.25 brown	50	50
969	-	5f.+5f. green	1·00	1·00

PORTRAITS: 35c. to 5f. Charles of Lorraine, Margaret of Parma, Charles V, Johanna of Castile, Philip the Good, Margaret of Austria, Charles the Bold, Archduke Albert and Archduchess Isabella respectively.

190 St. Martin, Dinant

1941. Winter Relief Fund. Statues.

970	**190**	10c.+5c. brown	30	30
971	-	35c.+5c. green	30	30
972	-	50c.+10c. violet	30	30
973	-	60c.+10c. brown	30	30
974	-	1f.+15c. red	30	30
975	**190**	1f.50+25c. green	30	30
976	-	1f.75+50c. blue	35	35
977	-	2f.25+2f.25 mauve	35	35
978	-	3f.25+3f.25 brown	45	45
979	-	5f.+5f. green	85	85

MS980 105×139 mm. 5f.+20f. purple (as 979) 27·00 27·00

DESIGNS (Statues of St. Martin in churches)—As Type **190**: 35c., 1f. Lennick, St. Quentin; 50c., 3f. Beck, Limberg; 60c., 2f.25, Dave on the Meuse; 1f.75, Hal, Brabant. 35×50 mm: 5f. St. Trond.

192 Concert Hall, Argenteuil

1941. Fund for Queen Elisabeth's Concert Hall. Two sheets, each 103×133 mm.

MS981 **192** 10f.+15f. green 8·25 7·50

MS982 As last with perforated crown and monogram with violet control number on back 8·25 7·50

193 Mercator

1942. Anti-tuberculosis Fund. Portraits.

986	-	10c.+5c. brown	10	10
987	-	35c.+5c. green	10	10
988	-	50c.+10c. brown	10	10
989	-	60c.+10c. green	10	10
990	-	1f.+15c. red	10	10
991	**193**	1f.75+50c. blue	10	10
992	-	3f.25+3f.25 purple	10	10
993	-	5f.+5f. violet	25	25
994	-	10f.+30f. orange	1·70	1·70

MS995 77×59 mm. 3f.25+6f.75 green (as 968); 5f.+10f. red (as 969) 14·00 14·00

SCIENTISTS—As T **193**: 10c. Bolland. 35c. Versale. 50c. S. Stevin. 60c. Van Helmont. 1f. Dodoens. 3f.25, Oertell. 5f. Juste Lipse. 25½×28½ mm: 10f. Plantin.

198 Prisoner writing Letter

1942. Prisoners of War Fund.

1000	**198**	5f.+45f. grey	8·75	8·75

199 St. Martin

200 St. Martin sharing his cloak

1942. Winter Relief Fund.

1001	**199**	10c.+5c. orange	25	25
1002	-	35c.+5c. green	25	25
1003	-	50c.+10c. brown	25	25
1004	-	60c.+10c. black (horiz)	25	25
1005	-	1f.+15c. red	25	25
1006	-	1f.50+25c. green	30	30
1007	-	1f.75+50c. blue	30	35
1008	-	2f.25+2f.25 brn (horiz)	35	35
1009	-	3f.25+3f.25 purple (horiz)	60	60
1010	**200**	5f.+10f. brown	1·60	1·60
1011	**200**	10f.+20f. brown & vio	1·70	1·70
1012	**200**	10f.+20f. red & violet	1·50	1·50

201 Soldiers and Vision of Home

1943. Prisoners of War Relief Fund.

1013	**201**	1f.+30f. red	3·50	3·50
1014	-	1f.+30f. brown	2·30	2·30

DESIGN: No. 1014, Soldiers emptying parcel of books and vision of home.

202 Tiler

1943. Anti-tuberculosis Fund. Trades.

1015	**202**	10c.+5c. brown	25	25
1016	-	35c.+5c. green	25	25
1017	-	50c.+10c. brown	25	25
1018	-	60c.+10c. green	25	25
1019	-	1f.+15c. red	30	25
1020	-	1f.75+75c. blue	25	25
1021	-	3f.25+3f.25 purple	35	35
1022	-	5f.+25f. violet	1·20	1·20

DESIGNS: 35c. Blacksmith; 50c. Coppersmith; 60c. Gunsmith; 1f. Armourer; 1f.75, Goldsmith; 3f.25, Fishmonger; 5f. Clockmaker.

203 Ornamental Letter

204 Ornamental Letter

1943. Orval Abbey Restoration Fund. Designs showing single letters forming "ORVAL".

1023	**203**	50c.+1f. black	45	45
1024	-	60c.+1f.90 violet	35	35
1025	-	1f.+3f. red	35	35
1026	-	1f.75+5f.25 blue	35	35
1027	-	3f.25+16f.75 green	65	65
1028	**204**	5f.+30f. brown	1·10	1·10

205 St. Leonard's Church, Leon, and St. Martin

206 Church of Notre Dame, Hal, and St. Martin

207 St. Martin and River Scheldt

1943. Winter Relief Fund.

1029	**205**	10c.+5c. brown	30	30
1030	-	35c.+5c. green	30	30
1031	-	50c.+15c. green	30	30
1032	-	60c.+20c. purple	30	30
1033	-	1f.+1f. red	35	35
1034	-	1f.75+4f.25 blue	80	80
1035	-	3f.25+11f.75 mauve	1·60	1·60
1036	**206**	5f.+25f. blue	2·40	2·40
1037	**207**	10f.+30f. green	1·90	1·90
1038	-	10f.+30f. brown	1·90	1·90

DESIGNS: (Various churches and statues of St. Martin sharing his cloak). As Type **205**: HORIZ: 35c. Dion-le-Val; 50c. Alost; 60c. Liege; 3f.25, Loppem. VERT: 1f. Courtrai; 1f.75, Angre. As Type **207**: 10f. brown Meuse landscape.

208 "Daedalus and Icarus"

1944. Red Cross.

1039	**208**	35c.+1f.65 green	40	40
1040	-	50c.+2f.50 grey	40	40
1041	-	60c.+3f.40 brown	40	40
1042	-	1f.+5f. red	60	60
1043	-	1f.75+8f.25 blue	60	60
1044	-	5f.+30f. brown	95	95

DESIGNS: 50c. *The Good Samaritan* (Jacob Jordsen); 60c. *Christ healing the Paralytic* (detail); 1f. *Madonna and Child*; 1f.75, *Self-portrait*; 5f. *St. Sebastian*.

Nos. 1039 and 1041/4 depict paintings by Anthony van Dyck.

209 Jan van Eyck

1944. Prisoners of War Relief Fund.

1045	**209**	10c.+15c. violet	35	35
1046	-	35c.+15c. green	35	35
1047	-	50c.+25c. brown	35	35
1048	-	60c.+40c. olive	35	35
1049	-	1f.+50c. red	35	35
1050	-	1f.75+4f.25 blue	35	35
1051	-	2f.25+8f.25 slate	80	80
1052	-	3f.25+11f.25 brown	40	40
1053	-	5f.+35f. grey	85	85

PORTRAITS: 35c. "Godefroid de Bouillon". 50c. "Jacob van Maerlant". 60c. "Jean Joses de Dinant". 1f. "Jacob van Artevelde". 1f.75, "Charles Joseph de Ligne". 2f.25, "Andre Gretry". 3f.25, "Jan Moretus-Plantin". 5f. "Ruusbroeck".

210 "Bayard and Four Sons of Aymon", Namur

1944. Anti-tuberculosis Fund. Provincial legendary types.

1054	**210**	10c.+5c. brown	10	10
1055	-	35c.+5c. green	10	10
1056	-	50c.+10c. violet	10	10
1057	-	60c.+10c. brown	10	10
1058	-	1f.+15c. red	10	10
1059	-	1f.75+5f.25 blue	10	10
1060	-	3f.25+11f.75 green	35	35
1061	-	5f.+25f. blue	45	45

DESIGNS—VERT: 35c. "Brabo severing the giant's hand", Antwerp; 60c. "Thyl Ulenspiegel" and "Nele", Flanders; 1f. "St. George and the Dragon", Hainaut; 1f.75, "Genevieve of Brabant, with the Child and the Hind", Brabant. HORIZ: 50c. "St. Hubert encounters the Hind with the Cross", Luxemburg; 3f.25, "Tchantches wrestling with the Saracen", Liege; 5f. "St. Gertrude rescuing the Knight with the cards", Limburg.

211 Lion Rampant

1944. Inscr "BELGIQUE-BELGIE" or "BELGIE-BELGIQUE".

1062A	**211**	5c. brown	10	10
1063A	**211**	10c. green	10	10
1064A	**211**	25c. blue	10	10
1065A	**211**	35c. brown	10	10
1066A	**211**	50c. green	10	10
1067B	**211**	75c. violet	10	10
1068B	**211**	1f. red	10	10
1069B	**211**	1f.25 brown	25	25
1070B	**211**	1f.50 orange	40	40
1071A	**211**	1f.75 blue	10	10
1072B	**211**	2f. blue	1·70	1·70
1073A	**211**	2f.75 mauve	10	10
1074B	**211**	3f. red	25	25
1075B	**211**	3f.50 grey	15	10
1076B	**211**	5f. brown	3·50	3·50
1077B	**211**	10f. black	85	85

1944. Overprinted with large V.

1078	**152**	2c. green	10	10
1079	**152**	15c. blue	10	10
1080	**152**	20c. violet	10	10
1081	**152**	60c. grey	10	10

213 King Leopold III and "V"

1944

1082	**213**	1f. red	15	10
1083	**213**	1f.50 mauve	15	10
1084	**213**	1f.75 blue	45	45
1085	**213**	2f. violet	60	35
1086	**213**	2f.25 green	45	45
1087	**213**	3f.25 brown	30	15
1088	**213**	5f. green	1·20	35

214 War Victims

215 Rebuilding Homes

1945. War Victims' Relief Fund.

1114	**214**	1f.+30f. red	1·90	1·00
1115	**215**	1¾f.+30f. blue	1·90	1·00

Nos. 1114/15 measure 50×35 mm.

1945. Post Office Employers' Relief Fund.

1119	**214**	1f.+9f. red	40	25
1120	**215**	1f.+9f. red	45	25

217 Resister

218 Group of Resisters

1945. Prisoners of War Relief Fund.

1121	**217**	10c.+15c. orange	25	25
1122	-	20c.+20c. violet	25	25
1123	-	60c.+25c. brown	25	25
1124	-	70c.+30c. green	25	25
1125	**217**	75c.+50c. brown	25	25
1126	-	1f.+75c. green	30	25
1127	-	1f.50+1f. red	30	25
1128	-	3f.50+3f.50 blue	2·00	1·30
1129	**218**	5f.+40f. brown	2·50	1·50

DESIGNS—VERT: 20c., 1f. Father and child; 60c., 1f.50, Victim tied to stake. HORIZ: 70c., 3f.50, Rifleman.

219 West Flanders

1945. Anti-tuberculosis Fund.

1130	**219**	10c.+15c. green	60	30
1131	-	20c.+20c. red	35	30
1132	-	60c.+25c. brown	35	30
1133	-	70c.+30c. green	35	30
1134	-	75c.+50c. brown	35	30
1135	-	1f.+75c. violet	35	30
1136	-	1f.50+1f. red	35	30
1137	-	3f.50+1f.50 blue	75	75
1138	-	5f.+45f. mauve	4·25	2·40

ARMS DESIGNS—VERT: 20c. to 5f. Arms of Luxemburg, East Flanders, Namur, Limburg Hainaut, Antwerp, Liege and Brabant respectively.

222 Douglas DC-400-DAA

1946. Air.

1165	**222**	6f. blue	40	30
1166	**222**	8f.50 red	75	60
1167	**222**	50f. green	7·00	1·20
1168	**222**	100f. grey	11·50	2·50

1946. Surch *-10%*, reducing the original value by 10%.

1171	**213**	"-10%" on 1f.50 mauve	85	30
1172	**213**	"-10%" on 2f. violet	2·30	85
1173	**213**	"-10%" on 5f. green	2·00	30

224 *Marie Henriette* (paddle-steamer)

1946. Ostend–Dover Mail-boat Service Centenary.

1174a	-	1f.35 blue	45	25
1175	**224**	2f.25 green	60	40
1176	-	3f.15 grey	65	30

DESIGNS—21½×18½ or 21×17 mm: 1f.35, *Prince Baudouin* (mail steamer). As T **224**: 3f.15, *Diamant* (paddle-steamer), formerly *Le Chemin de Fer*.

225 Paratrooper

1946. Air. Bastogne Monument Fund.

1177	**225**	17f.50+62f.50 green	1·90	85
1178	**225**	17f.50+62f.50 purple	1·90	85

226 Father Damien

227 E. Vandervelde

228 Francois Bovesse

1946. Belgian Patriots. (a) Father Damien.

1179	**226**	65c.+75c. blue	2·30	1·50
1180	-	1f.35+2f. brown	2·30	1·50
1181	-	1f.75+18f. lake	2·30	1·50

DESIGNS—HORIZ: 1f.35, Molokai Leper Colony. VERT: 1f.75, Damien's statue.

(b) Emile Vandervelde.

1182	**227**	65c.+75c. green	2·30	1·50
1183	-	1f.35+2f. blue	2·30	1·50
1184	-	1f.75+18f. red	2·30	1·50

DESIGNS—HORIZ: 1f.35, Vandervelde, miner, mother and child. VERT: 1f.75, Sower.

(c) Francois Bovesse.

1185		65c.+75c. violet	2·30	1·50
1186	**228**	1f.35+2f. brown	2·30	1·50
1187	-	1f.75+18f. red	2·30	1·50

DESIGNS—VERT: 65c. Symbols of Patriotism and Learning; 1f.75, Draped memorial figures holding wreath and torch.

229 Pepin d'Herstal

1946. War Victims' Relief Fund.

1188	**229**	75c.+25c. green	60	25
1189	-	1f.+50c. violet	85	35
1190	-	1f.50+1f. purple	85	45
1191	-	3f.50+1f.50 blue	1·20	70
1192	-	5f.+45f. mauve	15·00	14·00
1194	-	5f.+45f. orange	13·00	13·00

DESIGNS: 1f. Charlemagne; 1f.50, Godfrey of Bouillon; 3f.50, Robert of Jerusalem; 5f. Baudouin of Constantinople.

See also Nos. 1207/11, 1258/9 and 1302/6.

230 Allegory of "Flight"

1946. Air.

1193	**230**	2f.+8f. violet	65	60

231 Malines

1946. Anti-tuberculosis Fund. No date.

1195	**231**	65c.+35c. red	70	25
1196	-	90c.+60c. olive	80	25
1197	-	1f.35+1f.15 green	80	25
1198	-	3f.15+1f.85 blue	1·20	45
1199	-	4f.50+45f.50 brown	19·00	16·00

DESIGNS—(Arms and Industries): 90c. Dinant; 1f.35, Ostend; 3f.15, Verviers; 4f.50, Louvain.

See also Nos. 1212/16.

1947. Air. "Cipex" International Stamp Exhibition, New York. Nos. 1179/87 surch **LUCHTPOST POSTE AERIENNE or POSTE AERIENNE LUCHTPOST** and new value. (a) Father Damien.

1199a		1f.+2f. on 65c. +75c. blue	95	60
1199b		1f.+50+2f.50 on 1f.35+2f. brown	95	60
1199c		2f.+45f. on 1f.75+18f. red	95	60

(b) Emile Vandervelde.

1199d		1f.+2f. on 65c.+75c. green	95	60
1199e		1f.50+2f.50 on 1f.35+2f. blue	95	60
1199f		2f.+45f. on 1f.75+18f. red	95	60

(c) Francois Bovesse.

1199g		1f.+2f. on 65c.+75c. vio	95	60
1199h		1f.50+2f.50 on 1f.35+2f. brown	95	60
1199i		2f.+45f. on 1f.75+18f. red	95	60

232 Joseph Plateau

1947. Int Film and Belgian Fine Arts Festival.

1200	**232**	3f.15 blue	1·50	30

233 Adrien de Gerlache

234 Explorers landing from *Belgica*

1947. 50th Anniv of Belgian Antarctic Expedition.

1201	**233**	1f.35 red	30	10
1202	**234**	2f.25 grey	4·75	70

1947. War Victims' Relief Fund. Mediaeval Princes as T **229**.

1207		65c.+35c. blue	1·30	60
1208		90c.+60c. green	1·90	85
1209		1f.35+1f.15 red	3·75	1·20
1210		3f.15+1f.85 blue	4·75	1·50
1211		20f.+20f. purple	60·00	48·00

DESIGNS: 65c. John II, Duke of Brabant; 90c. Philippe of Alsace; 1f.35, William the Good; 3f.15, Notger, Bishop of Liege; 20f. Philip the Noble.

1947. Anti-Tuberculosis Fund. Arms designs as T **231**, but dated "1947".

1212		65c.+35c. orange	70	60
1213		90c.+60c. purple	80	70
1214		1f.35+1f.15 brown	95	75
1215		3f.15+1f.85 blue	3·25	1·50
1216		20f.+20f. green	31·00	20·00

DESIGNS (Arms and Industries): 65c. Nivelles; 90c. St. Truiden; 1f.35, Charleroi; 3f.15, St. Nicholas; 20f. Bouillon.

237 Chemical Industry

240 Textile Machinery

239 Antwerp Docks

1948. National Industries.

1217	**237**	60c. blue	15	15
1218	**237**	1f.20 brown	3·00	30
1219	-	1f.35 brown	15	15
1220	-	1f.75 green	70	30
1221	-	1f.75 red	30	25
1222	**239**	2f.25 grey	85	60
1223	-	2f.50 mauve	9·50	65
1224	**239**	3f. purple	15·00	60
1225	**240**	3f.15 blue	1·40	70
1226	**240**	4f. blue	14·50	45
1227	-	6f. blue	36·00	65
1228	-	6f.30 purple	3·50	2·75

DESIGNS—As Type **237**: 1f.35, 1f.75 green, Woman making lace; 1f.75 red, 2f.50, Agricultural produce. As Type **239**: 6f., 6f.30, Steel works.

242 St. Benedict and King Totila

1948. Achel Abbey Fund. Inscr "ACHEL".

1232	**242**	65c.+65c. brown	1·20	85
1233	-	1f.35+1f.35 green	1·70	1·20
1234	-	3f.15+2f.85 blue	4·00	1·50
1235	-	10f.+10f. purple	14·00	11·50

DESIGNS—HORIZ: 1f.35, Achel Abbey. VERT: 3f.15, St. Benedict as Law-Giver; 10f. Death of St. Benedict.

243 St. Bega and Chevremont Castle

1948. Chevremont Abbey Fund. Inscr "CHEVREMONT".

1236	**243**	65c.+65c. blue	1·20	85
1237	-	1f.35+1f.35 red	1·70	1·20
1238	-	3f.15+2f.85 blue	3·50	1·50
1239	-	10f.+10f. brown	13·50	10·50

DESIGNS—HORIZ: 1f.35, Chevremont Basilica and Convent. VERT: 3f.15, Madonna of Chevremont and Chapel; 10f. Monk and Madonna of Mt. Carmel.

244 Statue of Anseele

245 Ghent and E. Anseele

1948. Inauguration of Edward Anseele (Socialist Leader) Statue.

1245	**244**	65c.+35c. red	3·00	1·70
1246	**245**	90c.+60c. grey	4·00	2·30
1247	-	1f.35+1f.15 brn	3·00	1·70
1248	-	3f.15+1f.85 blue	8·75	5·75
MS1249		82×145 mm. Nos. 1245/8	£250	£110

DESIGNS: 1f.35, Statue and Ed. Anseele; 3f.15, Reverse side of statue.

247 "Liberty"

248 "Resistance"

1948. Antwerp and Liege Monuments Funds.

1253	**247**	10f.+10f. green	60·00	29·00
1254	**248**	10f.+10f. brown	26·00	14·50

249 Cross of Lorraine

1948. Anti-tuberculosis Fund.

1255	**249**	20c.+5c. green	60	30
1256	**249**	1f.20+30c. purple	2·00	60
1257	**249**	1f.75+25c. red	2·30	85
1258	-	4f.+3f.25 blue	9·50	5·75
1259	-	20f.+20f. green	50·00	35·00

DESIGNS—As Type **229**: 4f. Isabel of Austria; 20f. Albert, Archduke of Austria.

250 *'Madonna and Child*

1949. Social and Cultural Funds. Sheets 140×90 mm sold at 50f. each incl premium (a) Paintings by R. van der Weyden.

MS1260	90c. brown (T **250** *Madonna and Child*); 1f.75 purple (*Crucifixion*); 4f. blue (*Mary Magdalene*)	£225	£200

(b) Paintings by J. Jordaens.

MS1261	90c. violet (*Woman Reading*); 1f.75 red (*Flute-player*); 4f. blue (*Old Woman and Letter*)	£225	£200

1949. Surch **1-1-49** at top, **31-XII-49** and value at bottom with posthorn in between. (a) Arms type.

1262	**152**	5c. on 15c. blue	10	10
1263	**152**	5c. on 30c. brown	10	10
1264	**152**	5c. on 40c. lilac	10	10
1265	**152**	20c. on 70c. green	10	10
1266	**152**	20c. on 75c. mauve	10	10

(b) Anseele Statue.

1267	**244**	10c. on 65c.+35c. red	3·00	3·00

1268	245	40c. on 90c.+60c. grey	1·70	1·70
1269	-	80c. on 1f.35+1f.15 brown	85	90
1270	-	1f.20 on 3f.15+1f.85 blue	1·50	1·50

251 King Leopold I

252 Forms of Postal Transport

1949. Belgian Stamp Centenary.

1271	251	90c. green (postage)	75	40
1272	251	1f.75 brown	40	30
1273	251	3f. red	11·00	3·50
1274	251	4f. blue	7·00	1·00
1275	252	50f. brown (air)	60·00	23·00

253 St. Madeleine from *The Baptism of Christ*

1949. Exhibition of Paintings by Gerard David, Bruges.

1276	253	1f.75 brown	85	30

255 Hemispheres and Allegorical Figure

1949. 75th Anniv of U.P.U.

1295	255	4f. blue	5·50	2·50

256 Guido Gezelle

1949. 50th Death Anniv of Gezelle (poet).

1297	256	1f.75+75c. green	2·00	1·50

257 Arnica

1949. Anti-tuberculosis and other Funds. (a) Flowers.

1298	257	20c.+5c. black, yellow and green	35	30
1299	-	65c.+10c. black, green and buff	1·40	45
1300	-	90c.+10c. black, blue and red	2·00	1·00
1301	-	1f.20+30c. mult	2·50	1·30

FLOWERS: 65c. Thistle. 90c. Periwinkle. 1f.20, Poppy.

(b) Portraits as T **229**.

1302	1f.75+25c. orange	1·20	40
1303	3f.+1f.50 red	13·00	8·25
1304	4f.+2f. blue	13·50	8·25
1305	6f.+3f. brown	23·00	11·50
1306	8f.+4f. green	27·00	15·00

PORTRAITS: 1f.75, Philip the Good. 3f. Charles V. 4f. Maria Christina. 6f. Charles of Lorraine. 8f. Maria Theresa.

260 Anglo-Belgian Monument, Hertain

1950. Anglo-Belgian Union and other Funds.

1307	-	80c.+20c. green	1·50	60
1308	-	2f.50+50c. red	6·75	4·00
1309	260	4f.+2f. blue	10·50	7·00

DESIGNS—HORIZ: 80c. Arms of Great Britain and Belgium; 2f.50, British tanks at Tournai.

261 Allegory of Saving

1950. National Savings Bank Centenary.

1310	261	1f.75 sepia	60	30

262 Hurdling

1950. European Athletic Championships. Inscr "HEYSEL 1950".

1311	262	20c.+5c. green	60	30
1312	-	90c.+10c. purple	4·75	2·30
1313	-	1f.75+25c. red	9·25	2·50
1314	-	4f.+2f. blue	44·00	23·00
1315	-	8f.+4f. green	46·00	30·00
MS1316		70×119 mm. 1f.75+25c. (+18f.) (No. 1313)	95·00	60·00

DESIGNS—HORIZ: 1f.75, Relay racing. VERT: 90c. Javelin throwing; 4f. Pole vaulting; 8f. Sprinting.

263 Sikorsky S-51 Helicopter and Douglas DC-4 leaving Melsbroeck Airport

1950. Air. Inauguration of Helicopter Airmail Services and Aeronautical Committee's Fund.

1317	263	7f.+3f. blue	9·75	5·75

265 Gentian

266 Sijsele Sanatorium

1950. Anti-tuberculosis and other Funds. Cross in red.

1326	265	20c.+5c. blue, green and purple	35	30
1327	-	65c.+10c. green and brown	1·40	45
1328	-	90c.+10c. light green and green	1·70	1·20
1329	-	1f.20+30c. blue, green and ultramarine	2·00	1·30
1330	266	1f.75+25c. red	2·50	1·70
1331	-	4f.+2f. blue	23·00	1·70
1332	-	8f.+4f. green	31·00	10·50

DESIGNS—Flowers as Type **265**: 65c. Rushes; 90c. Foxglove; 1f.20, Sea lavender. Sanatoria as Type **266**: HORIZ: 4f. Jauche. VERT: 8f. Tombeek.

267 The Belgian Lion

1951. (a) 17½×20½ mm.

1334	267	2c. brown	10	10
1335	267	3c. violet	10	10
1336	267	5c. lilac	10	10
1336a	267	5c. pink	10	10
1337	267	10c. orange	10	10
1338	267	15c. mauve	10	10
1333	267	20c. blue	30	10
1339	267	20c. red	10	10
1340	267	25c. green	1·70	15
1341	267	25c. blue	10	10
1342	267	30c. green	10	10
1343	267	40c. brown	10	10
1344a	267	50c. blue	15	25
1345	267	60c. mauve	10	10
1346	267	65c. purple	13·50	60
1347	267	75c. lilac	10	10
1348	267	80c. green	85	35
1349	267	90c. blue	1·30	35
1350	267	1f. red	10	10
1351	267	1f.50 grey	10	10
1353	267	2f. green	25	10
1354	267	2f.50 brown	25	10
1355	267	3f. mauve	25	10
1355a	267	4f. purple	35	10
1355b	267	4f.50 blue	25	10
1355c	267	5f. purple	15	10

(b) 20½×24½ mm.

1356	50c. blue	25	15
1357	60c. purple	80	65
1358a	1f. red	10	10

(c) Size 17½×22 mm.

1359	50c. blue	10	10
1360	1f. pink	1·30	75
1361	2f. green	50	25

268 "Science"

1951. UNESCO Fund. Inscr "UNESCO".

1365	268	80c.+20c. green	1·70	60
1366	-	2f.50+50c. brown	12·00	7·00
1367	-	4f.+2f. blue	15·00	8·75

DESIGNS—HORIZ: 2f.50, "Education". VERT: 4f. "Peace".

269 Fairey Tipsy Belfair Trainer I00-TIC

1951. Air. 50th Anniv of National Aero Club.

1368		6f. blue	38·00	20·00
1369	269	7f. red	38·00	20·00

DESIGN: 6f. Arsenal Air 100 glider.

1951. Air.

1370	-	6f. brown (glider)	7·25	30
1371	269	7f. green	7·25	85

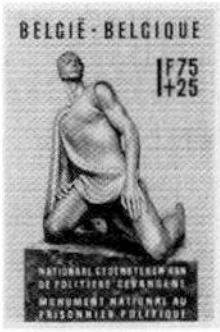

270 Monument

1951. Political Prisoners' National Monument Fund.

1372	270	1f.75+25c. brown	3·50	60
1373	-	4f.+2f. blue	37·00	20·00
1374	-	8f.+4f. green	38·00	23·00

DESIGNS—HORIZ: 4f. Breendonk Fort. VERT: 8f. Side view of monument.

272 Queen Elisabeth

1951. Queen Elisabeth Medical Foundation Fund.

1376	272	90c.+10c. grey	5·25	1·20
1377	272	1f.75+25c. red	11·50	2·50
1378	272	3f.+1f. green	38·00	17·00
1379	272	4f.+2f. blue	41·00	19·00
1380	272	8f.+4f. sepia	49·00	23·00

273 Lorraine Cross and Dragon

274 Beersel Castle

1951. Anti-tuberculosis and other Funds.

1381	273	20c.+5c. red	45	30
1382	273	65c.+10c. blue	70	35
1383	273	90c.+10c. brown	85	40
1384	273	1f.20+30c. violet	1·70	60
1385	274	1f.75+75c. brown	5·25	1·70
1386	-	3f.+1f. green	16·00	9·50
1387	-	4f.+2f. blue	20·00	11·50
1388	-	8f.+4f. black	30·00	16·00

CASTLES—As Type **274**: VERT: 3f. Horst Castle. 8f. Veves Castle. HORIZ: 4f. Lavaux St. Anne Castle.

For stamps as Type **273** but dated "1952" see Nos. 1416/19 and for those dated "1953" see Nos. 1507/10.

276 Consecration of the Basilica

1952. 25th Anniv of Cardinalate of Primate of Belgium and Koekelberg Basilica Fund.

1389		1f.75+25c. brown	1·70	60
1390		4f.+2f. blue	19·00	9·25
1391	276	8f.+4f. purple	28·00	13·50
MS1392		120×72 mm. Nos. 1389/91 (10f.)	£475	£200

DESIGNS—24×35 mm: 1f.75, Interior of Koekelberg Basilica; 4f. Exterior of Koekelberg Basilica.

277 King Baudouin

278 King Baudouin

1952

1393	277	1f.50 grey	1·70	25
1394	277	2f. red	60	25
1395	277	4f. blue	8·75	30
1396a	278	50f. purple	4·00	25
1397a	278	100f. red	20·00	70

279 Francis of Taxis

1952. 13th U.P.U. Congress, Brussels. Portraits of Members of the House of Thurn and Taxis.

1398	279	80c. green	35	30
1399	-	1f.75 orange	35	30
1400	-	2f. brown	70	45
1401	-	2f.50 red	1·40	45
1402	-	3f. olive	1·40	35
1403	-	4f. blue	1·50	30
1404	-	5f. brown	3·75	45
1405	-	5f.75 violet	5·25	1·50
1406	-	8f. black	23·00	4·00
1407	-	10f. purple	29·00	9·25
1408	-	20f. grey	£120	55·00
1409	-	40f.+10f. turquoise	£180	£150

DESIGNS—VERT: 1f.75, John Baptist; 2f. Leonard; 2f.50, Lamoral; 3f. Leonard Francis; 4f. Lamoral Claud; 5f. Eugene Alexander; 5f.75, Anselm Francis; 8f. Alexander Ferdinand; 10f. Charles Anselm; 20f. Charles Alexander; 40f. Beaulieu Chateau.

281 A. Vermeylen

1952. Culture Fund. Writers.

1410	281	65c.+30c. lilac	7·25	3·00
1411	-	80c.+40c. green	7·75	3·50
1412	-	90c.+45c. olive	8·25	4·00
1413	-	1f.75+75c. lake	17·00	5·75
1414	-	4f.+2f. blue	46·00	21·00
1415	-	8f.+4f. sepia	49·00	24·00

PORTRAITS: 80c. K. van de Woestijne. 90c. C. de Coster. 1f.75, M. Maeterlinck. 4f. E. Verhaeren. 8f. H. Conscience.

A 4f. blue as No. 1414 and an 8f. lake as No. 1415 each se-tenant with a label showing a laurel wreath and bearing a premium "+ 9 fr." were put on sale by subscription only.

282 Arms, Malmedy

1952. Anti-tuberculosis and other Funds. As T **273** but dated "1952" and designs as T **282**.

1416	**273**	20c.+5c. brown	35	30
1417	**273**	80c.+20c. green	80	40
1418	**273**	1f.20+30c. purple	2·00	1·20
1419	**273**	1f.50+50c. olive	2·30	1·30
1420	**282**	2f.+75c. red	3·25	1·50
1421	-	3f.+1f.50 brown	27·00	16·00
1422	-	4f.+2f. blue	25·00	15·00
1423	-	8f.+4f. purple	27·00	17·00

DESIGNS—HORIZ: 3f. Ruins, Burgreuland. VERT: 4f. Dam, Eupen; 8f. Saint and lion, St. Vith.

284 Dewe and Monument at Liege

1953. Walthere Dewe Memorial Fund.

1435	**284**	2f.+1f. lake	3·25	2·00

285 Princess Josephine Charlotte

1953. Red Cross National Disaster Fund. Cross in red.

1436	**285**	80c.+20c. green	4·00	1·70
1437	**285**	1f.20+30c. brown	3·75	1·50
1438	**285**	2f.+50c. lake	3·25	1·50
1439	**285**	2f.50+50c. red	20·00	11·50
1440	**285**	4f.+1f. blue	22·00	10·50
1441	**285**	5f.+2f. black	22·00	10·50

286 Fishing Boats *Marcel, De Meeuw* and *Jacqueline Denise*

1953. Tourist Propaganda and Cultural Funds.

1442	**286**	80c.+20c. green	2·30	1·20
1443	-	1f.20+30c. brown	7·00	3·25
1444	-	2f.+50c. sepia	8·25	3·25
1445	-	2f.50+50c. mauve	19·00	9·25
1446	-	4f.+2f. blue	30·00	15·00
1447	-	8f.+4f. green	38·00	18·00

DESIGNS—HORIZ: 1f.20, Bridge Bouillon; 2f. Antwerp. VERT: 2f.50, Namur; 4f. Ghent; 8f. Freyr Rocks and River Meuse.

289 King Baudouin

1953. (a) 21×24½ mm.

1453	**289**	1f.50 black	30	10
1454	**289**	2f. red	9·25	30
1455	**289**	2f. green	30	10
2188	**289**	2f.50 brown	25	10
1457	**289**	3f. purple	1·20	10
1458	**289**	3f.50 green	60	10
1459	**289**	4f. blue	4·00	25
2188A	**289**	4f.50 brown	80	50
1462	**289**	5f. violet	1·50	10
1463	**289**	6f. mauve	2·50	10
1464	**289**	6f.50 grey	£120	19·00
2189	**289**	7f. blue	50	25
1466	**289**	7f.50 brown	£110	21·00
1467	**289**	8f. blue	60	15
1468	**289**	8f.50 purple	26·00	60
1469	**289**	9f. olive	£120	2·30
1470	**289**	12f. turquoise	17·00	60
1471	**289**	30f. orange	14·50	35

(b) 17½×22 mm.

1472	1f.50 black	35	35
1473	2f.50 brown	7·50	6·50
1474	3f. mauve	25	10
1475	3f.50 green	35	10
1476	4f.50 brown	1·70	80

290

1953. European Child Welfare Fund.

1482	**290**	80c.+20c. green	5·75	3·50
1483	**290**	2f.50+1f. red	35·00	23·00
1484	**290**	4f.+1f.50 blue	37·00	26·00

293 Ernest Malvoz

1953. Anti-tuberculosis and other Funds. As T **273** but dated "1953" and portraits as T **293**.

1507	**273**	20c.+5c. blue	70	35
1508	**273**	80c.+20c. purple	1·90	80
1509	**273**	1f.20+30c. brown	3·00	1·20
1510	**273**	1f.50+50c. slate	3·50	1·50
1511	**293**	2f.+75c. green	4·25	2·00
1512	-	3f.+1f.50 red	20·00	10·50
1513	-	4f.+2f. blue	23·00	13·00
1514	-	8f.+4f. brown	29·00	16·00

PORTRAITS—VERT: 3f. Carlo Forlanini. 4f. Albert Calmette. HORIZ: 8f. Robert Koch.

1954. Surch **20c** and **I-I-54** at top, **31-XII-54** at bottom and bars in between.

1515	**267**	20c. on 65c. purple	1·70	15
1516	**267**	20c. on 90c. blue	1·70	15

See note below No. 480.

296 King Albert Statue

1954. King Albert Memorial Fund.

1520	**296**	2f.+50c. brown	11·50	4·75
1521	-	4f.+2f. blue	38·00	17·00
1522	-	9f.+4f.50 black	31·00	17·00

DESIGNS—HORIZ: 4f. King Albert Memorial. VERT: 9f. Marche-les-Dames Rocks and medallion portrait.

298 Monument

299 Breendonk Camp and Fort

1954. Political Prisoners' National Monument Fund.

1531	**298**	2f.+1f. red	27·00	24·00
1532	**299**	4f.+2f. brown	55·00	26·00
1533	-	9f.+4f.50 green	65·00	32·00

DESIGN—VERT: 9f. As Type **298** but viewed from different angle.

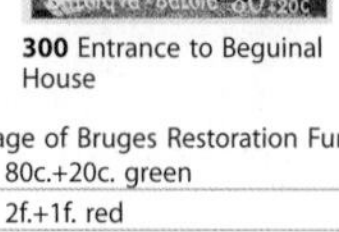

300 Entrance to Beguinal House

1954. Beguinage of Bruges Restoration Fund.

1534	**300**	80c.+20c. green	1·20	60
1535	-	2f.+1f. red	16·00	8·25
1536	-	4f.+2f. violet	21·00	11·50
1537	-	7f.+3f.50 purple	44·00	24·00
1538	-	8f.+4f. brown	44·00	24·00
1539	-	9f.+4f.50 blue	80·00	38·00

DESIGNS—HORIZ: 2f. River scene. VERT: 4f. Convent Buildings; 7f. Cloisters; 8f. Doorway; 9f. Statue of our Lady of the Vineyard (larger, 35×53 mm).

302 Map of Europe and Rotary Symbol

1954. 50th Anniv of Rotary International and Fifth Regional Conference, Ostend.

1540	**302**	20c. red	25	25
1541	-	80c. green	35	25
1542	-	4f. blue	1·70	35

DESIGNS: 80c. Mermaid, "Mercury" and Rotary symbol; 4f. Rotary symbol and hemispheres.

303 Child

304 "The Blind Man and the Paralytic" (after Anto-Carte)

1954. Anti-T.B. and other Funds.

1543	**303**	20c.+5c. green	30	30
1544	**303**	80c.+20c. black	85	35
1545	**303**	1f.20+30c. brown	2·30	1·40
1546	**303**	1f.50+50c. violet	4·75	2·50
1547	**304**	2f.+75c. red	9·25	4·75
1548	**304**	4f.+1f. blue	35·00	15·00

305 Begonia and the Rabot

1955. Ghent Flower Show.

1549	**305**	80c. red	60	60
1550	-	2f.50 sepia	10·50	3·00
1551	-	4f. lake	6·00	80

DESIGNS—VERT: 2f.50, Azaleas and Chateau des Comtes; 4f. Orchid and the "Three Towers".

306 *Homage to Charles V* (A. De Vriendt)

307 *Charles V* (Titian)

1955. Emperor Charles V Exhibition, Ghent.

1552	**306**	20c. red	25	25
1553	**307**	2f. green	95	25
1554	-	4f. blue	5·25	1·50

DESIGN—As Type **306**: 4f. *Abdication of Charles V* (L. Gallait).

308 Emile Verhaeren (after C. Montald)

1955. Birth Centenary of Verhaeren (poet).

1555	**308**	20c. black	25	25

309 "Textile Industry"

1955. Second Int Textile Exhibition, Brussels.

1556	**309**	2f. purple	1·30	30

310 *The Foolish Virgin* (R. Wouters)

1955. Third Biennial Sculpture Exn, Antwerp.

1557	**310**	1f.20 green	1·20	40
1558	**310**	2f. violet	2·00	30

311 "The Departure of the Liege Volunteers in 1830" (Soubre)

1955. Liege Exn. 125th Anniv of 1830 Revolution.

1559	**311**	20c. green	30	30
1560	**311**	2f. brown	85	30

312 Ernest Solvay

1955. Cultural Fund. Scientists.

1561	**312**	20c.+5c. brown	35	35
1562	-	80c.+20c. violet	1·40	50
1563	-	1f.20+30c. blue	7·50	4·00
1564	-	2f.+50c. red	7·00	3·75
1565	-	3f.+1f. green	16·00	9·75
1566	-	4f.+2f. brown	16·00	9·75

PORTRAITS—VERT: 80c. Jean-Jacques Dony. 2f. Leo H. Baekeland. 3f. Jean-Etienne Lenoir. HORIZ: 1f.20, Egide Walschaerts. 4f. Emile Fourcault and Emile Gobbe.

313 *The Joys of Spring* (E. Canneel)

314 E. Holboll (Danish postal official)

1955. Anti-T.B. and other Funds.

1567	**313**	20c.+5c. mauve	35	35
1568	**313**	80c.+20c. green	70	45
1569	**313**	1f.20+30c. brown	3·25	1·20
1570	**313**	1f.50+50c. violet	3·75	1·50
1571	**314**	2f.+50c. red	12·00	5·75
1572	-	4f.+2f. blue	30·00	14·50
1573	-	8f.+4f. sepia	31·00	18·00

PORTRAITS—As Type **314**: 4f. J. D. Rockefeller (philanthropist). 8f. Sir R. W. Philip (physician).

315 Blood Donors Emblem

1956. Blood Donors.

1574	**315**	2f. red	35	30

316 Mozart when a Child

317 Queen Elisabeth and Mozart Sonata

1956. Birth Bicentenary of Mozart. Inscr as in T **316**.

1575	-	80c.+20c. green	60	30
1576	**316**	2f.+1f. purple	4·75	3·00
1577	**317**	4f.+2f. lilac	10·50	5·50

DESIGN—As Type **316**: 80c. Palace of Charles de Lorraine, Brussels.

318

1956. "Scaldis" Exhibitions in Tournai, Ghent and Antwerp.

1578	**318**	2f. blue	30	30

319 Queen Elisabeth Medallion (Courtens)

1956. 80th Birthday of Queen Elisabeth and Foundation Fund.

1579	**319**	80c.+20c. green	60	40
1580	**319**	2f.+1f. lake	4·75	2·40
1581	**319**	4f.+2f. sepia	6·50	3·75

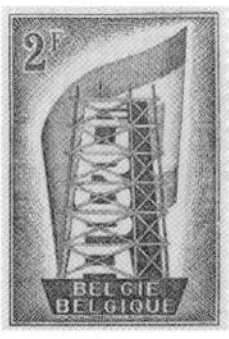

320

1956. Europa.

1582	**320**	2f. green	3·50	25
1583	**320**	4f. violet	13·00	35

321 Electric Train Type 122 and Railway Bridge

1956. Electrification of Brussels–Luxembourg Railway Line.

1584	**321**	2f. blue	30	25

322 E. Anseele

1956. Birth Centenary of Anseele (statesman).

1588	**322**	20c. purple	25	25

323 Medieval Ship

324 Weighing a Baby

1956. Anti-tuberculosis and other Funds.

1589	**323**	20c.+5c. brown	30	30
1590	**323**	80c.+20c. green	60	40
1591	**323**	1f.20+30c. purple	1·20	70
1592	**323**	1f.50+50c. slate	1·50	95
1593	**324**	2f.+50c. green	3·75	2·30
1594	-	4f.+2f. purple	15·00	9·25
1595	-	8f.+4f. red	17·00	11·50

DESIGNS—As Type **324**: HORIZ: 4f. X-ray examination. VERT: 8f. Convalescence and rehabilitation.

325 "Atomium" and Exhibition Emblem

1957. Brussels International Exhibition.

1596	**325**	2f. red	30	30
1597	**325**	2f.50 green	35	30
1598	**325**	4f. violet	70	25
1599	**325**	5f. purple	1·60	70

327 Emperor Maximilian I, with Messenger

1957. Stamp Day.

1603	**327**	2f. red	40	30

328 Charles Plisnier and Albrecht Rodenbach (writers)

1957. Cultural Fund. Belgian Celebrities.

1604	**328**	20c.+5c. violet	30	30
1605	-	80c.+20c. brown	40	30
1606	-	1f.20+30c. sepia	95	70
1607	-	2f.+50c. red	2·40	1·60
1608	-	3f.+1f. green	3·50	2·30
1609	-	4f.+2f. blue	4·00	3·00

DESIGNS: 80c. Professors Emiel Vliebergh and Maurice Wilmotte; 1f.20, Paul Pastur and Julius Hoste; 2f. Lodewijk de Raet and Jules Destree (politicians); 3f. Constantin Meunier and Constant Permeke (artists); 4f. Lieven Gevaert and Edouard Empain (industrialists).

329 Sikorsky S-58 Helicopter

1957. Conveyance of 100,000th Passenger by Belgian Helicopter Service.

1610	**329**	4f. blue, green and grey	95	45

330 Steamer entering Zeebrugge Harbour

1957. 50th Anniv of Completion of Zeebrugge Harbour.

1611	**330**	2f. blue	40	30

331 King Leopold I entering Brussels (after Simonau)

1957. 126th Anniv of Arrival of King Leopold I in Belgium.

1612	**331**	20c. green	30	30
1613	-	2f. mauve	70	30

DESIGN—HORIZ: 2f. King Leopold I at frontier (after Wappers).

332 Scout and Guide Badges

1957. 50th Anniv of Boy Scout Movement and Birth Centenary of Lord Baden-Powell.

1614	**332**	80c. brown	30	30
1615	-	4f. green	1·50	50

DESIGN—VERT: 4f. Lord Baden-Powell.

333 *Kneeling Woman* (after Lehmbruck)

1957. Fourth Biennial Sculpture Exn, Antwerp.

1616	**333**	2f.50 green	1·20	60

334 "Agriculture and Industry"

1957. Europa.

1617	**334**	2f. purple	1·20	30
1618	**334**	4f. blue	3·75	45

335 Sledge-dog Team

1957. Belgian Antarctic Expedition, 1957–58.

1619	**335**	5f.+2f.50 orange, brown and grey	4·00	3·00

MS1620 115×83 mm. Block of four of No. 1619 in new colours, brown, red and blue £200 £160

336 General Patton's Grave at Hamm

1957. General Patton Memorial Issue.

1621	**336**	1f.+50c. black	2·30	1·20
1622	-	2f.50+50c. green	3·50	1·70
1623	-	3f.+1f. brown	4·75	2·30
1624	-	5f.+2f.50 slate	10·50	6·50
1625	-	6f.+3f. red	14·00	9·25

DESIGNS—HORIZ: 2f.50, Patton Memorial project at Bastogne; 3f. Gen. Patton decorating Brig.-General A. MacAuliffe; 6f. (51×35½ mm) Tanks in action. VERT: 5f. General Patton.

337 Adolphe Max

1957. 18th Death Anniv of Burgomaster Adolphe Max (patriot).

1626	**337**	2f.50+1f. blue	1·50	65

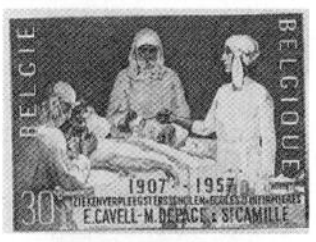

338 Queen Elisabeth with Doctors Depage and Debaisieux at a surgical operation

1957. 50th Anniv of "Edith Cavell-Marie Depage" and "St. Camille" Nursing Schools.

1627	**338**	30c. red	30	30

339 *Carnival Kings of Fosses* (Namur)

340 "Infanta Isabella with Crossbow" (Brussels)

1957. Anti-tuberculosis and other Funds. Provincial Legends.

1628	**339**	30c.+20c. pur & yell	30	30
1629	-	1f.+50c. sepia & blue	35	35
1630	-	1f.50+50c. grey & red	70	40
1631	-	2f.+1f. black & green	1·00	45
1632	**340**	2f.50+1f. grn & mve	2·30	1·70
1633	-	5f.+2f. black & blue	4·75	3·75
1634	-	6f.+2f.50 lake & red	5·75	4·75

DESIGNS: As Type **339**—HORIZ: 1f.50, "St. Remacle and the Wolf" (Liege). VERT: 1f. "Op Signoorken" (Antwerp); 2f. "The Long Man and the Pea Soup" (Limburg). As Type **340**—HORIZ: 6f. "Carnival Kings of Binche" (Hainaut). VERT: 5f. "The Virgin with the Inkwell" (West Flanders).

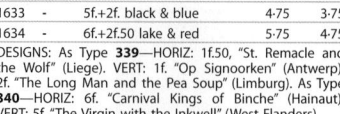

341 Posthorn and Postilion's Badges

1958. Postal Museum Day.

1635	**341**	2f.50 grey	30	30

342 Benelux Gate

1958. Inauguration of Brussels International Exhibition. Inscr as in T 342.

1636	**342**	30c.+20c. sepia, brown and violet	30	30
1637	-	1f.+50c. purple, slate and green	30	30
1638	-	1f.50+50c. violet, turquoise and green	35	30
1639	-	2f.50+1f. red, blue and vermilion	35	30
1640	-	3f.+1f.50 blue, black and red	85	60
1641	-	5f.+3f. mauve, black and blue	1·90	1·50

DESIGNS—HORIZ: 1f. Civil Engineering Pavilion; 1f.50, Belgian Congo and Ruanda-Urundi Pavilion; 2f.50, "Belgium, 1900"; 3f. Atomium; 5f. (49×33½ mm) Telexpo Pavilion.

343 "Food and Agriculture Organization"

1958. United Nations Commemoration.

1642		50c. grey (postage)	3·00	2·75
1643	**343**	1f. red	35	35
1644	-	1f.50 blue	40	35
1645	-	2f. purple	60	50
1646	-	2f.50 green	40	35
1647	-	3f. turquoise	65	60
1648	-	5f. mauve	40	35
1649	-	8f. brown	75	60
1650	-	11f. lilac	1·60	1·50
1651	-	20f. red	3·25	2·75
1652	-	5f. blue (air)	30	30
1653	-	6f. green	35	30
1654	-	7f.50 violet	45	35
1655	-	8f. sepia	50	40
1656	-	9f. red	60	45
1657	-	10f. brown	70	50

DESIGNS (Emblems and symbols)—HORIZ: 50c. I.L.O. 2f.50, UNESCO 3f. U.N. Pavilion, Brussels Int Exn; 6f. World Meteorological Organization; 8f. (No. 1649), Int Monetary Fund; 8f. (No. 1655), General Agreement on Tariffs and Trade; 10f. Atomic Energy Agency; 11f. W.H.O. 20f. U.P.U. VERT: 1f.50, U.N.O. 2f. World Bank; 5f. (No. 1648), I.T.U. 5f. (No. 1652), I.C.A.O. 7f.50, Protection of Refugees; 9f. UNICEF.

344 Eugene Ysaye

1958. Birth Centenary of Ysaye (violinist).

1658	**344**	30c. blue and red	30	25

345 "Europa"

1958. Europa.

1659	**345**	2f.50 blue and red	3·50	25
1660	**345**	5f. red and blue	7·75	35

346 *Marguerite Van Eyck* (after Jan Van Eyck)

1958. Cultural Relief Funds. Paintings as T **346**. Frames in brown and yellow.

1661	**346**	30c.+20c. myrtle	60	30
1662	-	1f.+50c. lake	85	60
1663	-	1f.+50+50c. blue	1·50	85
1664	-	2f.50+1f. sepia	3·00	2·00
1665	-	3f.+1f.50 red	4·00	2·50
1666	-	5f.+3f. blue	6·50	5·25

PAINTINGS—HORIZ: 1f. *Carrying the Cross* (Hieronymus Bosch). 3f. *The Rower* (James Ensor). VERT: 1f.50, *St. Donatien* (Jan Gossaert). 2f.50, Self-portrait (Lambert Lombard). 5f. *Henriette with the Large Hat* (Henri Evenepoel).

347 "Hoogstraten"

348 Pax—"Creche vivante"

1958. Anti-tuberculosis and other Funds. Provincial Legends.

1667	**347**	40c.+10c. blue & grn	30	30
1668	-	1f.+50c. sepia & yell	35	35
1669	-	1f.50+50c. pur & grn	65	35
1670	-	2f.+1f. brown & red	70	45
1671	**348**	2f.50+1f. red and green	2·10	1·20
1672	-	5f.+2f. purple & blue	4·75	3·25
1673	-	6f.+2f. blue & red	5·75	4·75

DESIGNS: As Type **347**—VERT: 1f. "Jean de Nivelles"; 1f.50, "Jeu de Saint Evermare a Russon". HORIZ: 2f. "Les penitents de Furnes". As Type **348**—HORIZ: "Marches de l'Entre Sambre et Meuse". VERT: 6f. "Pax—Vierge".

349 "Human Rights"

1958. Tenth Anniv of Human Rights Declaration.

1674	**349**	2f.50 slate	40	25

350 "Europe of the Heart"

1959. "Heart of Europe". Fund for Displaced Persons.

1675	**350**	1f.+50c. purple	45	35
1676	**350**	2f.50+1f. green	1·00	80
1677	**350**	5f.+2f.50 brown	1·70	1·20

351 J. B. de Taxis taking the oath at the hands of Charles V (after J.-E. Van den Bussche)

1959. Stamp Day.

1680	**351**	2f.50 green	50	30

352 N.A.T.O. Emblem

1959. Tenth Anniv of N.A.T.O.

1681	**352**	2f.50 blue and red	45	30
1682	**352**	5f. blue and green	1·30	60

On the 5f. value the French and Flemish inscriptions are transposed.

For similar design but inscr "1969", see No. 2112.

353 "Blood Transfusion"

354 J. H. Dunant and battle scene at Solferino, 1859

1959. Red Cross Commem. Inscr "1859 1959".

1683	**353**	40c.+10c. red & grey	35	35
1684	**353**	1f.+50c. red & sepia	1·30	50
1685	**353**	1f.50+50c. red and lilac	3·75	2·00
1686	-	2f.50+1f. red & grn	4·25	2·30
1687	-	3f.+1f.50 red and blue	7·75	4·75
1688	**354**	5f.+3f. red and sepia	14·50	7·00

DESIGN—As Type **353**—HORIZ: 2f.50, 3f. Red Cross and broken sword ("Aid for the wounded").

355 Philip the Good

356 Arms of Philip the Good

1959. Royal Library of Belgium Fund. Multicoloured.

1689	40c.+10c. Type **355**	30	30
1690	1f.+50c. Charles the Bold	45	45
1691	1f.50+50c. Maximillian of Austria	1·60	1·00
1692	2f.50+1f. Philip the Fair	2·75	2·30
1693	3f.+1f.50 Charles V	5·00	3·50
1694	5f.+3f. Type **356**	6·75	5·00

358 Town Hall, Oudenarde

1959. Oudenarde Town Hall Commem.

1699	**358**	2f.50 purple	40	30

359 Pope Adrian VI

1959. 500th Birth Anniv of Pope Adrian VI.

1700	**359**	2f.50 red	30	30
1701	**359**	5f. blue	40	30

360 "Europa"

1959. Europa.

1702	**360**	2f.50 red	85	30
1703	**360**	5f. turquoise	1·50	40

361 Boeing 707

1959. Inauguration of Boeing 707 Airliners by SABENA.

1704	**361**	6f. blue, grey and red	2·10	75

362 Antwerp fish (float)

363 Stavelot "Blancs Moussis" (carnival figures)

1959. Anti-tuberculosis and other Funds. Carnival scenes.

1705	**362**	40c.+10c. green, red and bistre	30	30
1706	-	1f.+50c. green, violet and olive	40	30
1707	-	2f.+50c. yellow, purple and brown	50	35
1708	**363**	2f.50+1f. blue, violet and grey	85	35
1709	-	3f.+1f. purple, yellow and grey	2·30	1·20
1710	-	6f.+2f. blue, red and olive	5·00	4·50
1711	-	7f.+3f. blk, yell, & bl	6·50	5·25

DESIGNS—As Type **362**—HORIZ: 1f. Mons dragon (float); 2f. Eupen and Malmedy clowns in chariot. As Type **363**—VERT: 3f. Ypres jester. HORIZ: 6f. Holy Family; 7f. Madonna and child.

364 Countess Alexandrine of Taxis (tapestry)

1960. Stamp Day.

1712	**364**	3f. blue	70	30

365 Indian Azalea

1960. Ghent Flower Show. Inscr as in T **365**.

1713	**365**	40c. red and purple	30	30
1714	-	3f. yellow, red and green	70	30
1715	-	6f. red, green and blue	1·70	60

FLOWERS: 3f. Begonia. 6f. Anthurium and bromelia.

366 Refugee

1960. World Refugee Year. Inscr as in T **366**.

1716		40c.+10c. purple	30	30
1717	**366**	3f.+1f.50 sepia	65	30
1718	-	6f.+3f. blue	1·40	1·20

MS1719 121×93 mm. Nos. 1716/18 in new colours, violet, brown and red respectively £100 85·00

DESIGNS: 40c. Child refugee; 6f. Woman refugee.

367 "Labour" (after Meunier)

1960. 75th Anniv of Belgian Socialist Party. Inscr as in T **367**.

1720	**367**	40c. purple and red	30	30
1721	-	3f. brown and red	60	30

DESIGN—HORIZ: 3f. "Workers" (after Meunier).

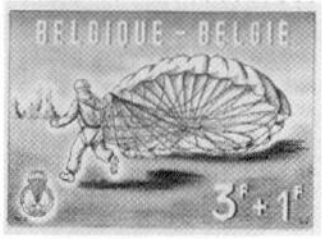

369 Parachutist on ground

1960. Parachuting. Designs bearing emblem of National Parachuting Club.

1726		40c.+10c. black & blue	35	30
1727		1f.+50c. black & blue	1·90	85
1728		2f.+50c. black, blue and green	4·00	2·30
1729		2f.50+1f. black, turquoise and green	7·00	3·75
1730	**369**	3f.+1f. black, blue and green	7·00	3·75
1731	**369**	6f.+2f. black, blue and green	7·75	4·75

DESIGNS—HORIZ: 40c., 1f., Parachutists dropping from Douglas DC-4 aircraft. VERT: 2f., 2f.50, Parachutists descending.

370 Ship's Officer and Helmsman

1960. Congo Independence.

1732	**370**	10c. red	30	30
1733	-	40c. red	30	30
1734	-	1f. purple	70	25
1735	-	2f. green	70	30
1736	-	2f.50 blue	1·30	30
1737	-	3f. blue	1·30	35
1738	-	6f. violet	3·25	80
1739	-	8f. brown	10·50	6·75

DESIGNS—As Type **370**: 40c. Doctor and nurses with patient; 1f. Tree-planting; 2f. Sculptors; 2f.50, Sport (putting the shot); 3f. Broadcasting from studio. (52×35½ mm): 6f. Children with doll; 8f. Child with globe.

371 Refugee Airlift

1960. Congo Refugees Relief Fund.

1740	**371**	40c.+10c. turquoise	30	30
1741	-	3f.+1f.50 red	3·00	1·70
1742	-	6f.+3f. violet	6·00	4·25

DESIGNS—As Type **371**: 3f. Mother and child. 35×51½ mm: 6f. Boeing 707 airplane spanning map of aircraft route.

1960. Surch.

1743	**267**	15c. on 30c. green	10	10
1744	**267**	15c. on 50c. blue	10	10
1745	**267**	20c. on 30c. green	10	10

373 Conference Emblem

1960. First Anniv of E.P.T. Conference.

1746	**373**	3f. lake	1·00	35
1747	**373**	6f. green	1·60	60

374 Young Stamp Collectors

1960. "Philately for the Young" Propaganda.

1748	**374**	40c. black and bistre	30	30

375 Pouring Milk for Child

1960. United Nations Children's Fund.

1749	**375**	40c.+10c. yellow, green and brown	30	30
1750	-	1f.+50c. red, blue and drab	85	60
1751	-	2f.+50c. bistre, green and violet	2·30	1·70
1752	-	2f.50+1f. sepia, blue and red	2·50	1·70
1753	-	3f.+1f. violet, orange and turquoise	3·25	2·00
1754	-	6f.+2f. brown, green and blue	5·25	3·00

DESIGNS: 1f. Nurse embracing children; 2f. Child carrying clothes, and ambulance; 2f.50, Nurse weighing baby; 3f. Children with linked arms; 6f. Refugee worker and child.

376 Frere Orban (founder)

1960. Centenary of Credit Communal (Co-operative Bank).

1755	**376**	10c. brown and yellow	30	30
1756	**376**	40c. brown and green	35	30
1757	**376**	1f.50 brown and violet	1·00	75
1758	**376**	3f. brown and red	1·00	30

377 Tapestry

1960. Anti-T.B. and other Funds. Arts and Crafts.

1759	**377**	40c.+10c. ochre, brown and blue	30	30
1760	-	1f.+50c. blue, brown and indigo	95	85
1761	-	2f.+50c. green, black and brown	1·70	1·20
1762	-	2f.50+1f. yellow and brown	3·75	2·50
1763	-	3f.+1f. black, brown and blue	4·25	3·00
1764	-	6f.+2f. lemon and black	6·25	3·75

DESIGNS—VERT: 1f. Crystalware; 2f. Lace. HORIZ: 2f.50, Brassware; 3f. Diamond-cutting; 6f. Ceramics.

378 King Baudouin and Queen Fabiola

1960. Royal Wedding.

1765	**378**	40c. sepia and green	35	30
1766	**378**	3f. sepia and purple	1·00	30
1767	**378**	6f. sepia and blue	2·75	35

1961. Surch in figs and **1961** at top, **1962** at bottom and bars in between.

1768	**267**	15c. on 30c. green	1·20	25
1769	**267**	20c. on 30c. green	2·40	1·20

See note below No. 480.

379 Nicolaus Rockox (after Van Dyck)

1961. 400th Birth Anniv of Nicolaus Rockox (Burgomaster of Antwerp).

1770	**379**	3f. black, bistre & brn	45	30

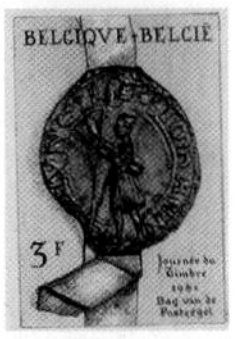

380 Seal of Jan Bode

1961. Stamp Day.

1771	**380**	3f. sepia and brown	45	30

381 K. Kats (playwright) and Father N. Pietkin (poet)

1961. Cultural Funds. Portrait in purple.

1772	40c.+10c. lake and pink	60	35
1773	1f.+50c. lake and brown	2·50	1·40
1774	2f.+50c. red and yellow	4·50	3·50
1775	2f.50+1f. myrtle and sage	4·75	3·50
1776	3f.+1f. blue and light blue	5·00	3·50
1777	6f.+2f. blue and lavender	7·00	4·75

PORTRAITS: 40c. Type **381**. 1f. A. Mockel and J. F. Willems (writers). 2f. J. van Rijswijck and X. Neujean (politicians). 2f.50, J. Demarteau (journalist) and A. van de Perre (politician). 3f. J. David (litterateur) and A. du Bois (writer). 6f. H. Vieuxtemps (violinist) and W. de Mol (composer).

382 White Rhinoceros

1961. Philanthropic Funds. Animals of Antwerp Zoo.

1778	40c.+10c. dp brown & brn	35	35
1779	1f.+50c. brown and green	1·30	80
1780	2f.+50c. sepia, red and black	2·00	1·60
1781	2f.50+1f. brown and red	2·20	1·70
1782	3f.+1f. brown and orange	2·50	1·90
1783	6f.+2f. ochre and blue	3·25	2·30

ANIMALS—VERT: 40c. Type **382**; 1f. Wild horse and foal; 2f. Okapi. HORIZ: 2f.50, Giraffe; 3f. Lesser panda; 6f. Elk.

383 Cardinal A.P. de Granville (first Archbishop)

1961. 400th Anniv of Archbishopric of Malines.

1784	**383**	40c.+10c. brown, red and purple	35	35
1785	-	3f.+1f.50 mult	95	80
1786	-	6f.+3f. bistre, violet and purple	1·60	1·50

DESIGNS: 3f. Cardinal's Arms; 6f. Symbols of Archbishopric and Malines.

385 "Interparliamentary Union"

1961. 50th Interparliamentary Union Conference, Brussels.

1791	**385**	3f. brown and turquoise	70	30
1792	**385**	6f. purple and red	1·00	60

386 Doves

1961. Europa.

1793	**386**	3f. black and olive	45	30
1794	**386**	6f. black and brown	95	45

387 Reactor BR 2, Mol

1961. Euratom Commemoration.

1795	**387**	40c. green	30	30
1796	-	3f. mauve	35	30
1797	-	6f. blue	50	45

DESIGNS—VERT: 3f. Heart of reactor BR 3, Mol. HORIZ: 6f. View of reactor BR 3, Mol.

388 *The Mother and Child* (after Paulus)

1961. Anti-T.B. and other Funds. Belgian paintings of mothers and children. Frames in gold.

1798	**388**	40c.+10c. sepia	30	30
1799	-	1f.+50c. blue	75	70
1800	-	2f.+50c. red	1·30	1·30
1801	-	2f.50+1f. lake	1·40	1·30
1802	-	3f.+1f. violet	1·30	1·20
1803	-	6f.+2f. myrtle	1·90	1·60

PAINTINGS: 1f. *Maternal Love* (Navez). 2f. *Maternity* (Permeke). 2f.50, *The Virgin and the Child* (Van der Weyden). 3f. *The Virgin with the Apple* (Memling), 6f. *The Myosotis Virgin* (Rubens).

389 Horta Museum

1962. Birth Cent of Victor Horta (architect).

1804	**389**	3f. brown	40	30

390 Male Castle

1962. Cultural and Patriotic Funds. Buildings.

1805	**390**	40c.+10c. green	30	30
1806	-	90c.+10c. mauve	35	35
1807	-	1f.+50c. lilac	50	50
1808	-	2f.+50c. violet	1·00	1·00
1809	-	2f.50+1f. brown	1·40	1·40
1810	-	3f.+1f. turquoise	1·50	1·50
1811	-	6f.+2f. red	2·40	2·40

BUILDINGS—HORIZ: 90c. Royal Library, Brussels. 1f. Collegiate Church, Soignies. 6f. Ypres Halls. VERT: 1f. Notre-Dame Basilica, Tongres. 2f.50, Notre-Dame Church, Hanswijk, Malines. 3f. St. Denis-en-Broqueroie Abbey.

391 16th-Century Postilion

1962. Stamp Day.

1812	**391**	3f. brown and green	40	30

See also No. 1997.

392 G. Mercator (after F. Hogenberg)

1962. 450th Birth Anniv of Mercator (geographer).

1813	**392**	3f. sepia	40	30

393 Brother A. M. Gochet (scholar)

1962. Gochet and Triest Commemoration.

1814	**393**	2f. blue	30	30
1815	-	3f. brown	35	30

PORTRAIT: 3f. Canon P.-J. Triest (benefactor of the aged).

394 Guianan Cock of the Rock ("Coq de Roch, Rotshann")

1962. Philanthropic Funds. Birds of Antwerp Zoo. Birds, etc., in natural colours; colours of name panel and inscription given.

1816	**394**	40c.+10c. blue	35	35
1817	-	1f.+50c. blue and red	60	60
1818	-	2f.+50c. mauve & blk	1·00	95
1819	-	2f.50+1f. turq & red	1·30	1·30
1820	-	3f.+1f. brown & grn	1·70	1·60
1821	-	6f.+2f. blue and red	2·00	1·90

BIRDS: 1f. Red lory ("Rode Lori, Lori Rouge"); 2f. Green turaco ("Touracou du Senegal, Senegal Toerakoe"); 2f.50, Keel-billed toucan ("Kortbek Toecan, Toucan a Bec Court"); 3f. Greater bird of paradise ("Grand Paradijsier, Grosse Paradisvogel"); 6f. Congo peafowl ("Kongo Pauw, Paon du Congo").

395 Europa "Tree"

1962. Europa.

1822	**395**	3f. black, yellow & red	75	30
1823	**395**	6f. black, yellow & olive	1·30	45

396 *Captive Hands* (after sculpture by Ianchelivici)

1962. Concentration Camp Victims.

1824	**396**	40c. blue and black	30	30

397 Reading Braille

1962. Handicapped Children Relief Funds.

1825	**397**	40c.+10c. brown	35	30
1826	-	1f.+50c. red	60	60
1827	-	2f.+50c. mauve	1·30	1·20
1828	-	2f.50+1f. green	1·30	1·20
1829	-	3f.+1f. blue	1·30	1·20
1830	-	6f.+2f. sepia	1·60	1·50

DESIGNS—VERT: 1f. Girl solving puzzle; 2f.50, Crippled child with ball; 3f. Girl walking with crutches. HORIZ: 2f. Child with earphones; 6f. Crippled boys with football.

398 *Adam* (after Michelangelo)

1962. *The Rights of Man.*

1831	**398**	3f. sepia and green	35	30
1832	**398**	6f. sepia and brown	60	40

399 Queen Louise-Marie

1962. Anti-tuberculosis and other Funds. Belgian Queens in green and gold.

1833	40c.+10c. Type **399**	30	30
1834	40c.+10c. As T **399** but inscr "ML"	30	30
1835	1f.+50c. Marie-Henriette	75	65

1836		2f.+1f. Elisabeth	1·50	1·40
1837		3f.+1f.50 Astrid	2·10	1·90
1838		8f.+2f.50 Fabiola	2·30	2·00

400 Menin Gate, Ypres

1962. Ypres Millenary.

1839	**400**	1f.+50c. multicoloured	45	45
MS1840		113×137 mm. Block of eight	7·00	7·00

401 H. Pirenne

1963. Birth Cent of Henri Pirenne (historian).

1841	**401**	3f. blue	40	30

402 "Peace Bell"

1963. Cultural Funds and Installation of "Peace Bell" in Koekelberg Basilica. Bell in yellow; "PAX" in black.

1842	**402**	3f.+1f.50 green & bl	1·90	1·90
1843	**402**	6f.+3f. chestnut & brn	1·00	1·00
MS1844		82×116 mm. No. 1842 (block of four)	9·25	9·25

403 *The Sower* (after Brueghel)

1963. Freedom from Hunger.

1845	**403**	2f.+1f. brown, black and green	35	35
1846	-	3f.+1f. brown, black and purple	40	40
1847	-	6f.+2f. yellow, black and brown	70	70

PAINTINGS—HORIZ: 3f. *The Harvest* (Brueghel). VERT: 6f. *The Loaf* (Anto Carte).

404 17th-century Duel

1963. 350th Anniv of Royal Guild and Knights of St. Michael.

1848	**404**	1f. red and blue	30	30
1849	-	3f. violet and green	35	30
1850	-	6f. multicoloured	80	45

DESIGNS—HORIZ: 3f. Modern fencing. VERT: 6f. Arms of the Guild.

405 19th-century Mail-coach

1963. Stamp Day.

1851	**405**	3f. black and ochre	35	30

See also No. 1998.

406 Hotel des Postes, Paris, and Belgian 1c. Stamp of 1863

1963. Centenary of Paris Postal Conference.

1852	**406**	6f. sepia, mauve & grn	70	40

407 Child in Wheatfield

1963. "8th May" Peace Movement.

1853	**407**	3f. multicoloured	40	30
1854	**407**	6f. multicoloured	1·00	40

408 "Transport"

1963. European Transport Ministers' Conference, Brussels.

1855	**408**	6f. black and blue	70	40

409 Town Seal

1963. Int Union of Towns Congress, Brussels.

1856	**409**	6f. multicoloured	70	40

410 Racing Cyclists

1963. Belgian Cycling Team's Participation in Olympic Games, Tokyo (1964).

1857	**410**	1f.+50c. multicoloured	30	30
1858	-	2f.+1f. multicoloured	35	35
1859	-	3f.+1f.50 mult	40	40
1860	-	6f.+3f. multicoloured	70	70

DESIGNS—HORIZ: 2f. Group of cyclists; 3f. Cyclists rounding bend. VERT: 6f. Cyclists being paced by motorcyclists.

411 Sud Aviation SE 210 Caravelle

1963. 40th Anniv of SABENA Airline.

1861	**411**	3f. black and turquoise	40	30

412 "Co-operation"

1963. Europa.

1862	**412**	3f. black, brown & red	1·30	30
1863	**412**	6f. black, brown & blue	2·40	45

No. 1863 is inscr with "6 F" on the left, "BELGIE" at foot and "BELGIQUE" on right.

413 Princess Paola with Princess Astrid

1963. Centenary of Red Cross and Belgian Red Cross Fund. Cross in red.

1864	-	40c.+10c. red & yell	25	25
1865	**413**	1f.+50c. grey & yellow	30	30
1866	-	2f.+50c. mauve & yell	40	40
1867	-	2f.50+1f. blue & yell	50	50
1868	-	3f.+1f. brown & yell	80	80
1869	-	3f.+1f. bronze & yell	2·50	2·50
1870	-	6f.+2f. green & yellow	2·10	2·10

DESIGNS—As T **413**: 40c. Prince Philippe; 2f. Princess Astrid; 2f.50, Princess Paola; 6f. Prince Albert; 46×35 mm: 3f. (2), Prince Albert and family.

414 J. Destree (writer)

1963. Jules Destree and H. Van de Velde Commems.

1871	**414**	1f. purple	25	25
1872	-	1f. green	25	25

DESIGN: No. 1872, H. Van de Velde (architect).

415 Bas-reliefs from Facade of Postal Cheques Office (after O. Jespars)

1963. 50th Anniv of Belgian Postal Cheques Office.

1873	**415**	50c. black, blue & red	25	25

416 *Balthasar Gerbier's Daughter*

1963. T.B. Relief and Other Funds. Rubens's Drawings. Background buff; inscr in black: designs colour given.

1874	**416**	50c.+10c. blue	30	30
1875	-	1f.+40c. red	35	35
1876	-	2f.+50c. violet	40	40
1877	-	2f.50+1f. green	80	80
1878	-	3f.+1f. brown	70	70
1879	-	6f.+2f. black	1·20	1·20

DRAWINGS—VERT: Rubens's children—1f. Nicolas (aged 2). 2f. Franz (aged 4). 2f.50, Nicolas (aged 6). 3f. Albert (aged 3). HORIZ: (46½×35½ mm): 6f. Infant Jesus, St. John and two angels.

417 Dr. G. Hansen and Laboratory

1964. Leprosy Relief Campaign.

1880	**417**	1f. black and brown	30	30
1881	-	2f. brown and black	30	30
1882	-	5f. black and brown	60	45
MS1883		135×98 mm. Nos. 1880/2 (+4f.)	3·50	3·50

DESIGNS: 2f. Leprosy hospital; 5f. Father Damien.

418 A. Vesale (anatomist) with Model of Human Arm

1964. Belgian Celebrities.

1884	**418**	50c. black and green	30	30
1885	-	1f. black and green	30	30
1886	-	2f. black and green	30	30

DESIGNS—HORIZ: 1f. J. Boulvin (engineer) and internal combustion engine; 2f. H. Jaspar (statesman) and medallion.

419 Postilion

1964. Stamp Day.

1887	**419**	3f. grey	35	30

420 Admiral Lord Gambier and U.S. Ambassador J. Q. Adams after signing treaty (from painting by Sir A. Forestier)

1964. 150th Anniv of Signing of Treaty of Ghent.

1888	**420**	6f.+3f. blue	70	70

421 Arms of Ostend

1964. Millenary of Ostend.

1889	**421**	3f. multicoloured	35	30

422 Ida of Bure (Calvin's wife)

1964. "Protestantism in Belgium".

1890	-	1f.+50c. blue	30	30
1891	**422**	3f.+1f.50 red	35	35
1892	-	6f.+3f. brown	65	65

PORTRAITS: 1f. P. Marnix of St. Aldegonde (Burgomaster of Antwerp). 6f. J. Jordaens (painter).

423 Globe, Hammer and Flame

1964. Centenary of Socialist International.

1893	**423**	50c. red and blue	30	30
1894	-	1f. red and blue	30	30
1895	-	2f. red and blue	30	30

DESIGNS: 1f. "SI" on Globe; 2f. Flames.

424 Infantryman of 1918

1964. 50th Anniv of German Invasion of Belgium. Multicoloured.

1896		1f.+50c. Type **424**	30	30
1897		2f.+1f. Colour sergeant of the Guides Regt, 1914	30	30
1898		3f.+1f.50 Trumpeter of the Grenadiers & Drummers of the Infantry and Carabiniers, 1914	45	45

425 Soldier at Bastogne

1964. "Liberation–Resistance". Multicoloured.

1899		3f.+1f. Type **425**	35	35
1900		6f.+3f. Soldier at estuary of the Scheldt	70	70

426 Europa "Flower"

1964. Europa.

1901	**426**	3f. grey, red and green	1·70	35
1902	**426**	6f. blue, green and red	4·00	45

427 "Philip the Good"

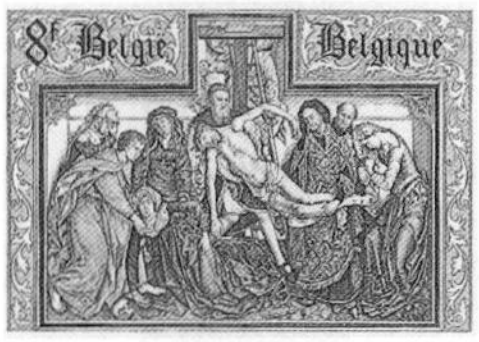

428 *Descent from the Cross*

1964. Cultural Funds. 500th Death Anniv of R. van der Weyden. Two sheets each 153×114 mm showing paintings by Van der Weyden.

MS1903 1f. Type **427**; 2f. *Portrait of a Lady*; 3f. *The Man with the Arrow* (+8f.)		5·00	5·00
MS1904 **428** 8f. (+8f.) brown		4·75	4·75

429 Pand Abbey, Ghent

1964. Pand Abbey Restoration Fund.

1905	**429**	2f.+1f. bl, turq & blk	35	30
1906	-	3f.+1f. brown, blue and purple	35	35

DESIGN: 3f. Waterside view of Abbey.

430 King Baudouin, Queen Juliana and Grand Duchess Charlotte

1964. 20th Anniv of "BENELUX".

1907	**430**	3f. purple, blue and olive	50	30

431 *One of Charles I's Children* (Van Dyck)

1964. T.B. Relief and Other Funds. Paintings of Royalty.

1908	**431**	50c.+10c. purple	30	30
1909	-	1f.+40c. red	30	30
1910	-	2f.+1f. purple	30	30
1911	-	3f.+1f. grey	35	35
1912	-	4f.+2f. violet	40	40
1913	-	6f.+3f. violet	50	50

DESIGNS—VERT: 1f. "William of Orange and his fiancee, Marie" (Van Dyck); 2f. "Portrait of a Little Boy" (E. Quellin and Jan Fyt); 3f. "Alexander Farnese at the age of 12 Years" (A. Moro); 4f. "William II, Prince of Orange" (Van Dyck). HORIZ—LARGER (46×35 mm): 6f. "Two Children of Cornelis De Vos" (C. de Vos).

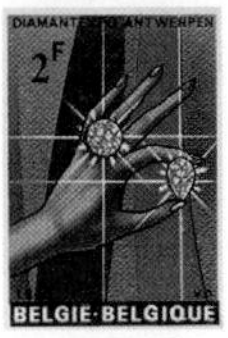

432 "Diamonds"

1965. "Diamantexpo" (Diamonds Exn) Antwerp.

1914	**432**	2f. multicoloured	30	25

433 "Textiles"

1965. "Textirama" (Textile Exn), Ghent.

1915	**433**	1f. black, red and blue	30	25

434 Vriesia

1965. Ghent Flower Show. Inscr "FLORALIES GANTOISES", etc. Multicoloured.

1916	1f. Type **434**	30	30
1917	2f. Echinocactus	30	30
1918	3f. Stapelia	30	30

435 Paul Hymans

1965. Birth Cent of Paul Hymans (statesman).

1919	**435**	1f. violet	30	30

436 Rubens

1965. Centenary of General Savings and Pensions Funds. Painters.

1920	**436**	1f. sepia and mauve	30	30
1921	-	2f. sepia and turquoise	30	30
1922	-	3f. sepia and purple	30	30
1923	-	6f. sepia and red	60	35
1924	-	8f. sepia and blue	75	60

PAINTERS: 2f. Franz Snyders. 3f. Adam van Noort. 6f. Anthony van Dyck. 8f. Jakob Jordaens.

437 *Sir Rowland Hill with Young Collectors* (detail from mural by J. Van den Bussche)

1965. "Philately for the Young".

1925	**437**	50c. green	30	30

438 19th-century Postmaster

1965. Stamp Day.

1926	**438**	3f. green	30	30

1965. U.N.W.R.A. Commemoration. Sheet 123×89 mm. Nos. 1916/18 in new colours.

MS1927 1f., 2f., 3f. (+14f.)	1·70	1·70

439 Globe and Telephone

1965. Centenary of I.T.U.

1928	**439**	2f. black and purple	30	30

440 Handclasp

1965. 20th Anniv of Liberation of Prison Camps.

1929	**440**	50c.+50c. purple, black and bistre	30	30
1930	-	1f.+50c. multicoloured	30	30
1931	-	3f.+1f.50 black, purple and green	40	35
1932	-	8f.+5f. multicoloured	95	95

DESIGNS—VERT: 1f. Hand reaching for barbed wire. HORIZ: 3f. Tank entering prison camp; 8f. Rose within broken wall.

441 Abbey Staircase

1965. Affligem Abbey.

1933	**441**	1f. blue	30	30

442 St. Jean Berchmans, Birthplace and Residence

1965. St. Jean Berchmans.

1934	**442**	2f. brown and purple	30	30

443 Toc H Lamp and Arms of Poperinge

1965. 50th Anniv of Founding of Toc H Movement at Talbot House, Poperinge.

1935	**443**	3f. multicoloured	35	30

444 Maison Stoclet, Brussels

1965. Josef Hoffman (architect) Commemoration.

1936	**444**	3f.+1f. grey and drab	45	45
1937	-	6f.+3f. brown	70	70
1938	-	8f.+4f. purple & drab	1·00	1·00

DESIGNS—Maison Stoclet: VERT: 6f. Entrance hall. HORIZ: 8f. Rear of building.

445 Tractor ploughing

1965. 75th Anniv of Boerenbond (Belgian Farmers' Association). Multicoloured.

1939	50c. Type **445**	30	30
1940	3f. Horse-drawn plough	35	30

446 Europa "Sprig"

1965. Europa.

1941	**446**	1f. black and pink	40	30
1942	**446**	3f. black and green	75	30

447 Jackson's Chameleon

1965. Philanthropic Funds. Reptiles of Antwerp Zoo. Multicoloured.

1943	1f.+50c. Type **447**	30	30
1944	2f.+1f. Iguana	30	30
1945	3f.+1f.50 Nile lizard	40	35
1946	6f.+3f. Komodo lizard	65	60
MS1947 118×98 mm. 8f.+4f. Soft-shelled turtle (larger)		1·20	1·20

448 J. Lebeau (after A. Schollaert)

1965. Death Cent of Joseph Lebeau (statesman).

1948	**448**	1f. multicoloured	30	30

449 Leopold I (after 30c. and 1f. Stamps of 1865)

1965. Death Centenary of King Leopold I.

1949	**449**	3f. sepia	35	30
1950	-	6f. violet	70	45

DESIGN: 6f. As 3f. but with different portrait frame.

450 Huy

1965. Tourist Publicity. Multicoloured.

1951	50c. Type **450**	10	10
1952	50c. Hoeilaart (vert)	10	10

See also Nos. 1995/6, 2025/6, 2083/4, 2102/3, 2123/4, 2159/60, 2240/1 and 2250/1.

451 Guildhouse

1965. T.B. Relief and Other Funds. Public Buildings, Brussels.

1953	**451**	50c.+10c. blue	30	30
1954	-	1f.+40c. turquoise	30	30
1955	-	2f.+1f. purple	30	30
1956	-	3f.+1f.50 violet	35	35
1957	-	10f.+4f.50 sepia and grey	95	95

BUILDINGS—HORIZ: 1f. Brewers' House; 2f. Builders' House; 3f. House of the Dukes of Brabant. VERT: (24½×44½ mm): 10f. Tower of Town Hall.

452 Queen Elisabeth (from medallion by A. Courtens)

1965. Queen Elisabeth Commem.

1958	**452**	3f. black	35	30

453 "Peace on Earth"

1966. 75th Anniv of *Rerum Novarum* (papal encyclical). Multicoloured.

1959	50c. Type **453**	30	30
1960	1f. "Building for Tomorrow" (family and new building)	30	30
1961	3f. Arms of Pope Paul VI (vert 24½×45 mm)	35	30

1966. Queen Elisabeth. Sheets 82×116 mm incorporating old designs, each with se-tenant label showing Crown over "E". (a) In brown, blue, gold and grey.

MS1962	3f. T **125** and 3f. T **317** (sold at 20f.)	1·60	1·60

(b) In brown, myrtle and green.

MS1963	3f. T **160** and 3f. T **172** (sold at 20f.)	1·60	1·60

454 Rural Postman

1966. Stamp Day.

1964	**454**	3f. black, lilac & buff	35	30

455 High Diving

1966. Swimming.

1965	**455**	60c.+40c. brown, green and blue	30	30
1966	-	10f.+4f. brown, purple and green	1·00	1·00

DESIGN: 10f. Diving from block.

456 Iguanodon Fossil (Royal Institute of Natural Sciences)

1966. National Scientific Institutions.

1967	**456**	1f. black and green	30	30
1968	-	2f. black, orge & cream	30	30
1969	-	2f. multicoloured	30	30
1970	-	3f. multicoloured	30	30
1971	-	3f. gold, black and red	30	30
1972	-	6f. multicoloured	40	30
1973	-	8f. multicoloured	65	60

DESIGNS—HORIZ: No. 1968, Kasai head (Royal Central African Museum); No. 1969, Snow crystals (Royal Meteorological Institute). VERT: No. 1970, *Scholar* (Royal Library); No. 1971, Seal (General Archives); No. 1972, Arend-Roland comet and telescope (Royal Observatory); No. 1973, Satellite and rocket (Space Aeronomy Inst.).

457 Eurochemic Symbol

1966. European Chemical Plant, Mol.

1974	**457**	6f. black, red and drab	45	35

458 A. Kekule

1966. Centenary of Professor August Kekule's Benzene Formula.

1975	**458**	3f. brown, black & blue	35	30

1966. 19th World I.P.T.T. Congress, Brussels. Optd XIXe CONGRES IPTT and emblem.

1976	**454**	3f. black, lilac and buff	35	30

460 *Rik Wouters* (self-portrait)

1966. 50th Death Anniv of Rik Wouters (painter).

1977	**460**	60c. multicoloured	10	10

461 Minorites Convent, Liege

1966. Cultural Series.

1978	**461**	60c.+40c. purple, blue and brown	30	30
1979	-	1f.+50c. blue, purple and turquoise	30	30
1980	-	2f.+1f. red, purple and brown	30	30
1981	-	10f.+4f.50 purple, turquoise and green	85	85

DESIGNS: 1f. Val-Dieu Abbey, Aubel; 2f. Huy and town seal; 10f. Statue of Ambiorix and castle, Tongres.

463 Europa "Ship"

1966. Europa.

1989	**463**	3f. green	45	25
1990	**463**	6f. purple	1·00	40

464 Surveying

1966. Antarctic Expeditions.

1991	**464**	1f.+50c. green	30	30
1992	-	3f.+1f.50 violet	30	30
1993	-	6f.+3f. red	60	60
MS1994		130×95 mm. 10f.+5f. multicoloured	1·20	1·20

DESIGNS: 3f. Commander A. de Gerlache and *Belgica* (polar barque); 6f. *Magga Dan* (Antarctic supply ship) and meteorological operations. 52×35½ mm.—10f. *Magga Dan* and emperor penguins.

1966. Tourist Publicity. As T **450**. Multicoloured.

1995	2f. Bouillon	10	10
1996	2f. Lier (vert)	10	10

1966. 75th Anniv of Royal Federation of Belgian Philatelic Circles. Stamps similar to Nos. 1812 and 1851 but incorporating "1890 1996" and F.I.P. emblem.

1997	**391**	60c. purple and green	30	30
1998	**405**	3f. purple and ochre	30	30

466 Children with Hoops

1966. "Solidarity" (Child Welfare).

1999	-	1f.+1f. black & pink	30	30
2000	-	2f.+1f. black & green	30	30
2001	-	3f.+1f.50 black & lav	30	30
2002	**466**	6f.+3f. brown & flesh	60	60
2003	-	8f.+3f.50 brown & grn	70	70

DESIGNS—VERT: 1f. Boy with ball and dog; 2f. Girl with skipping-rope; 3f. Boy and girl blowing bubbles. HORIZ: 8f. Children and cat playing "Follow My Leader".

467 Lions Emblem

1967. Lions International.

2004	**467**	3f. sepia, blue and olive	30	30
2005	**467**	6f. sepia, violet and green	45	40

468 Part of Cleuter Pistol

1967. Arms Museum, Liege.

2006	**468**	2f. black, yellow & red	30	30

469 I.T.Y. Emblem

1967. International Tourist Year.

2007	**469**	6f. blue, red and black	60	35

470 Young Refugee

1967. European Refugee Campaign Fund. Sheet 110×77 mm comprising T **470** and similar vert designs.

MS2008	1f. black and yellow (Type **470**); 2f. black and blue; 3f. black and orange (sold at 20f.)	1·20	1·20

471 Woodland and Trientalis (flowers), Hautes Fagnes

1967. Nature Conservation. Multicoloured.

2009	1f. Type **471**	30	30
2010	1f. Dunes and eryngium (flowers), Westhoek	30	30

472 Paul-Emile Janson (statesman)

1967. Janson Commemoration.

2011	**472**	10f. blue	85	60

473 19th-century Postman

1967. Stamp Day.

2012	**473**	3f. purple and red	30	30

474 Cogwheels

1967. Europa.

2013	**474**	3f. black, red and blue	60	30
2014	**474**	6f. black, yellow & green	1·20	45

475 Flax Plant and Shuttle

1967. Belgian Linen Industry.

2015	**475**	6f. multicoloured	45	35

476 Kursaal in 19th Century

1967. 700th Anniv of Ostend's Rank as Town.

2016	**476**	2f. sepia, buff and blue	30	30

478 With F.I.T.C.E. Emblem

1967. European Telecommunications Day. "Stamp Day" design of 1967 incorporating F.I.T.C.E. emblem as T **478** in green.

2021	**478**	10f. sepia and blue	30	30

"F.I.T.C.E." "Federation des Ingenieurs des Tele-communications de la Communaute Europeenne."

479 Robert Schuman (statesman)

1967. Charity.

2022	**479**	2f.+1f. green	30	30
2023	-	5f.+2f. brown, yellow and black	50	50
2024	-	10f.+5f. multicoloured	1·00	1·00

DESIGNS—HORIZ: 5f. Kongolo Memorial, Gentinnes (Congo Martyrs). VERT: 10f. "Colonial Brotherhood" emblem (Colonial Troops Memorial).

1967. Tourist Publicity. As T **450**. Multicoloured.

2025	1f. Ypres	10	10
2026	1f. Spontin	10	10

480 *Caesar Crossing the Rubicon* (Tournai Tapestry)

1967. Charles Plisnier and Lodewijk de Raet Foundations.

2028	**480**	1f. multicoloured	30	30
2029	-	1f. multicoloured	30	30

DESIGN No. 2029, "Maximilian hunting boar" (Brussels tapestry).

481 "Jester in Pulpit" (from Erasmus's *Praise of Folly*)

1967. Cultural Series. "Erasmus and His Time".

2030	1f.+50c. multicoloured	30	30
2031	2f.+1f. multicoloured	30	30
2032	3f.+1f.50 multicoloured	35	35
2033	5f.+2f. black, red & carmine	60	60
2034	6f.+3f. multicoloured	70	70

DESIGNS—VERT: 1f. Type **481**. 2f. "Jester declaiming" (from Erasmus' *Praise of Folly*); 3f. Erasmus; 6f. Pierre Gilles ("Aegidius" from painting by Metzijs). HORIZ: 5f. *Sir Thomas More's Family* (Holbein).

482 Princess Margaret of York (from miniature)

1967. "British Week".

2035	**482**	6f. multicoloured	55	40

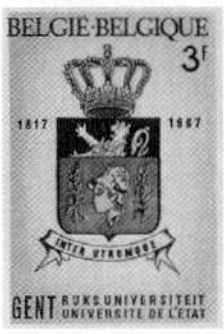

483 Arms of Ghent University

1967. Universities of Ghent and Liege. Multicoloured.

2036	3f. Type **483**	30	30
2037	3f. Liege	30	30

484 Emblem of "Pro-Post" Association

1967. "Postphila" Stamp Exhibition, Brussels. Sheet 110×77 mm.

MS2038 **484** 10f.+5f. black, green, red and brown 1·20 1·20

485 Our Lady of Virga Jesse, Hasselt

1967. Christmas.

2039	**485**	1f. blue	30	30

486 *Children's Games* (section of Brueghel's painting)

1967. "Solidarity".

2040	**486**	1f.+50c. multicoloured	30	30
2041	-	2f.+50c. multicoloured	30	30
2042	-	3f.+1f. multicoloured	40	30
2043	-	6f.+3f. multicoloured	65	60
2044	-	10f.+4f. multicoloured	1·00	90
2045	-	13f.+6f. multicoloured	1·25	1·25

Nos. 2040/5 together form the complete painting.

487 Worker in Protective Hand

1968. Industrial Safety Campaign.

2046	**487**	3f. multicoloured	30	30

489 Army Postman (1916)

1968. Stamp Day.

2068	**489**	3f. purple, brown & blue	30	30

490 Belgian 1c. "Small Lion" Stamp of 1866

1968. Cent of State Printing Works, Malines.

2069	**490**	1f. olive	30	30

491 Grammont and Seal of Baudouin VI

1968. "Historical Series". Multicoloured.

2070	2f. Type **491**	35	30
2071	3f. Theux-Franchimont Castle and battle emblems	35	30
2072	6f. Archaeological discoveries, Spiennes	55	35
2073	10f. Roman oil lamp and town crest, Wervik	85	60

492 Europa "Key"

1968. Europa.

2074	**492**	3f. gold, black & green	90	30
2075	**492**	6f. silver, black and red	1·80	50

493 Queen Elisabeth and Dr. Depage

1968. Belgian Red Cross Fund. Cross in red.

2076	**493**	6f.+3f. sepia, black and green	85	70
2077	-	10f.+5f. sepia, black and green	1·20	1·10

DESIGN: 10f. Queen Fabiola and baby.

494 Gymnastics

1968. Olympic Games, Mexico. Multicoloured.

2078	1f.+50c. Type **494**	30	30
2079	2f.+1f. Weightlifting	30	30
2080	3f.+1f.50 Hurdling	35	30
2081	6f.+2f. Cycling	70	60
2082	13f.+5f. Sailing (vert 24½×45 mm)	1·30	1·20

Each design includes the Olympic "rings" and a Mexican cultural motif.

1968. Tourist Publicity. As Type **450**.

2083	2f. multicoloured	10	10
2084	2f. black, blue and green	10	10

DESIGNS: No. 2083, Farm-house and windmill, Bokrijk; No. 2084, Bath-house and fountain, Spa.

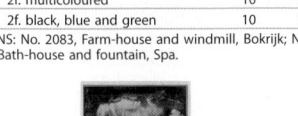

495 "Explosion"

1968. Belgian Disasters. Victims Fund. Multicoloured.

2085	10f.+5f. Type **495**	90	70
2086	12f.+5f. "Fire"	1·20	1·10
2087	13f.+5f. "Typhoon"	1·50	1·20

496 St. Laurent Abbey, Liege

1968. "National Interest".

2088	**496**	2f. black, bistre & blue	30	30
2089	-	3f. brown, grey & lt brn	35	30
2090	-	6f. black, blue & dp bl	70	35
2091	-	10f. multicoloured	95	40

DESIGNS: 3f. Church, Lissewege; 6f. *Mineral Seraing* and *Gand* (ore carriers), canal-lock, Zandvliet; 10f. Canal-lift, Ronquieres.

497 Undulate Triggerfish

1968. "Solidarity" and 125th Anniv of Antwerp Zoo. Designs showing fish. Multicoloured.

2092	1f.+50c. Type **497**	25	25
2093	3f.+1f.50 Ear-spotted angelfish	35	30
2094	6f.+3f. Lionfish	70	55
2095	10f.+5f. Diagonal butterflyfish	1·10	85

498 King Albert in Bruges (October, 1918)

1968. Patriotic Funds.

2096	**498**	1f.+50c. multicoloured	30	30
2097	-	3f.+1f.50 mult	35	30
2098	-	6f.+3f. multicoloured	60	55
2099	-	10f.+5f. multicoloured	90	85

DESIGNS—HORIZ: 3f. King Albert entering Brussels (November, 1918); 6f. King Albert in Liege (November, 1918). LARGER (46×35 mm): 10f. Tomb of the Unknown Soldier, Brussels.

499 Lighted Candle

1968. Christmas.

2100	**499**	1f. multicoloured	30	30

500 *Mineral Seraing* (ore carrier) in Ghent Canal

1968. Ghent Maritime Canal.

2101	**500**	6f. black brown, & blue	55	30

1969. Tourist Publicity. As Type **450**.

2102	1f. black, blue & pur (vert)	10	10
2103	1f. black, olive and blue	10	10

DESIGNS. No. 2102, Town Hall, Louvain; No. 2103, Valley of the Ourthe.

501 *Albert Magnis* (detail of wood carving by Quellin, Confessional, St. Paul's Church, Antwerp)

1969. St. Paul's Church, Antwerp, and Aulne Abbey Commemoration.

2104	**501**	2f. sepia	30	30
2105	-	3f. black and mauve	30	30

DESIGN: 3f. Aulne Abbey.

502 *The Travellers* (sculpture, Archaeological Museum, Arlon)

1969. 2,000th Anniv of Arlon.

2106	**502**	2f. purple	30	30

503 Broodjes Chapel, Antwerp

1969. "150 Years of Public Education in Antwerp".

2107	**503**	3f. black and grey	30	30

504 Mail Train

1969. Stamp Day.

2108	**504**	3f. multicoloured	30	30

505 Colonnade

1969. Europa.

2109	**505**	3f. multicoloured	50	30
2110	**505**	6f. multicoloured	85	35

506 *The painter and the Amateur* (detail, Brueghel)

1969. "Postphila 1969" Stamp Exhibition, Brussels. Sheet 91×124 mm.

MS2111 **506** 10f.+5f. brown 1·40 1·20

507 NATO Emblem

1969. 20th Anniv of N.A.T.O.

2112	**507**	6f. blue and brown	55	40

508 *The Builders* (F. Leger)

1969. 50th Anniv of I.L.O.

2113	**508**	3f. multicoloured	35	30

509 *Houses* (I. Dimitrova)

1969. UNICEF "Philanthropy" Funds. Multicoloured.

2114	1f.+50c. Type **509**	30	30
2115	3f.+1f.50 "My Art" (C. Patric)	35	30
2116	6f.+3f. "In the Sun" (H. Rejchlova)	70	60
2117	10f.+5f. "Out for a Walk" (P. Sporn) (horiz)	1·10	85

510 Racing Cyclist

1969. World Championship Cycle Races, Zolder.

2118	**510**	6f. multicoloured	60	30

511 Mgr. V. Scheppers

1969. Monseigneur Victor Scheppers (founder of "Brothers of Mechlin") Commemoration.

2119	**511**	6f.+3f. purple	85	60

512 National Colours

1969. 25th Anniv of BENELUX Customs Union.

2120	**512**	3f. multicoloured	35	30

513 Pascali Rose and Annevoie Gardens

1969. Flowers and Gardens. Multicoloured.

2121	2f. Type **513**	25	30
2122	2f. Begonia and Lochristi Gardens	30	30

1969. Tourist Publicity. As Type **450**.

2123	2f. brown, red and blue	25	10
2124	2f. black, green and blue	25	10

DESIGNS: No. 2123, Veurne Furnes; No. 2124, Vielsalm.

514 "Feats of Arms" from *History of Alexander the Great* (Tournai, 15th century)

1969. "Cultural Works" Tapestries. Multicoloured.

2125	1f.+50c. Type **514**	30	30
2126	3f.+1f.50 "The Violinist" from "Festival" (David Teniers II, Oudenarde, c.1700)	50	40
2127	10f.+4f. "The Paralytic", from "The Acts of the Apostles" (Brussels, c.1517)	1·20	1·10

515 Astronauts and Location of Moon Landing

1969. First Man on the Moon.

2128	**515**	6f. sepia	50	35
MS2129		95×130 mm. 20f.+10f. blue	3·50	3·00

DESIGN: **MS**2129 is as T **515**, but in vert format.

516 Wounded Soldier

1969. 50th Anniv of National War Invalids Works (O.N.I.G.).

2130	**516**	1f. green	30	30

517 "The Postman" (Daniella Sainteney)

1969. "Philately for the Young".

2131	**517**	1f. multicoloured	30	30

518 John F. Kennedy Motorway Tunnel, Antwerp

1969. Completion of Belgian Road-works. Multicoloured.

2132	3f. Type **518**	35	30
2133	6f. Loncin flyover, Wallonie motorway	55	50

519 Count H. Carton de Wiart (from painting by G. Geleyn)

1969. Birth Centenary of Count Henry Carton de Wiart (statesman).

2134	**519**	6f. sepia	65	50

520 *Barbu d'Anvers* (Cockerel)

1969. "The Poultry-yard" (poultry-breeding).

2135	**520**	10f.+5f. multicoloured	1·30	1·10

521 *Le Denombrement de Bethleem* (detail, Brueghel)

1969. Christmas.

2136	**521**	1f.50 multicoloured	30	30

522 Emblem, "Coin" and Machinery

1969. 50th Anniv of National Credit Society (S.N.C.I.).

2137	**522**	3f.50 brown and blue	35	30

523 Window, St. Waudru Church, Mons

1969. "Solidarity". Musicians in Stained-glass Windows. Multicoloured.

2138	1f.50+50c. Type **523**	30	30
2139	3f.50+1f.50 s-Herenelderen Church	35	30
2140	7f.+3f. St. Jacques Church, Liege	80	70
2141	9f.+4f. Royal Museum of Art and History, Brussels	1·20	1·10

No. 2141 is larger, 36×52 mm.

524 Camellias

1970. Ghent Flower Show. Multicoloured.

2142	1f.50 Type **524**	30	30
2143	2f.50 Water-lily	30	30
2144	3f.50 Azaleas	35	30
MS2145	122×92 mm. Nos. 2142/4 in slightly different shades	2·40	2·20

525 Beech Tree in National Botanical Gardens

1970. Nature Conservation Year. Multicoloured.

2146	3f.50 Type **525**	30	30
2147	7f. Birch	60	35

526 Young "Postman"

1970. "Philately for the Young".

2148	**526**	1f.50 multicoloured	30	30

527 New U.P.U. Headquarters Building

1970. New U.P.U. Headquarters Building.

2149	**527**	3f.50 green	35	30

528 "Flaming Sun"

1970. Europa.

2150	**528**	3f.50 cream, blk & lake	80	30
2151	**528**	7f. flesh, black and blue	1·20	4·75

529 Open-air Museum, Bokrijk

1970. Cultural Works. Multicoloured.

2152	1f.50+50c. Type **529**	30	30
2153	3f.50+1f.50 Relay Post-house, Courcelles	30	30
2154	7f.+3f. *The Reaper of Trevires* (bas-relief, Virton)	65	60
2155	9f.+4f. Open-air Museum, Middelheim, (Antwerp)	90	85

530 Clock-tower, Virton

1970. Historic Towns of Virton and Zelzate.

2156	**530**	2f.50 violet and ochre	30	30
2157	-	2f.50 black and blue	30	30

DESIGN—HORIZ: No. 2157, *Skaustand* (freighter), canal bridge, Zelzate.

531 Co-operative Alliance Emblem

1970. 75th Anniv of Int Co-operative Alliance.

2158	**531**	7f. black and orange	60	30

1970. Tourist Publicity, As Type **450**.

2159	1f.50 green, blue and black	20	20
2160	1f.50 buff, blue & deep blue	20	20

DESIGNS—HORIZ: No. 2159, Kasterlee. VERT: No. 2160, Nivelles.

532 Allegory of Resistance Movements

1970. 25th Anniv of Prisoner of War and Concentration Camps Liberation.

2161	**532**	3f.50+1f.50 black, red and green	40	30
2162	-	7f.+3f. black, red and mauve	80	60

DESIGN: 7f. Similar to Type **532**, but inscr "LIBERATION DES CAMPS", etc.

533 King Baudouin

1970. King Baudouin's 40th Birthday.

2163	**533**	3f.50 brown	30	10

See also Nos. 2207/23c and 2335/9b.

534 Fair Emblem

1970. 25th International Ghent Fair.

2164	**534**	1f.50 multicoloured	30	30

535 U.N. Headquarters, New York

1970. 25th Anniv of United Nations.
2165 **535** 7f. blue and black 60 35

536 Queen Fabiola

1970. Queen Fabiola Foundation.
2166 **536** 3f.50 black and blue 30 30

537 Angler's Rod and Reel

1970. Sports. Multicoloured.
2167 3f.50+1f.50 Type **537** 35 35
2168 9f.+4f. Hockey stick and ball (vert) 85 70

538 Belgian 8c. Stamp of 1870

1970. "Belgica 72" Stamp Exhibition, Brussels (1st issue).
MS2169 1f.50+50c. violet and black; 3f.50+1f.50 lilac and black; 9f.+4f. brown and black 4·25 3·50
DESIGNS: 3f.50, Belgian 1f. stamp of 1870; 9f. Belgian 5f. stamp of 1870.

539 "The Mason" (sculpture by G. Minne)

1970. 50th Anniv of National Housing Society.
2170 **539** 3f.50 brown & yell 30 30

540 Man, Woman and Hillside Town

1970. 25th Anniv of Belgian Social Security.
2171 **540** 2f.50 multicoloured 30 30

541 *Madonna and Child* (Jan Gossaert)

1970. Christmas.
2172 **541** 1f.50 brown 30 30

542 C. Huysmans (statesman)

1970. Cultural Works. Famous Belgians.
2173 **542** 1f.50+50c. brown and red 30 30
2174 - 3f.50+1f.50 brown and purple 30 30
2175 - 7f.+3f. brown & green 65 60
2176 - 9f.+4f. brown & blue 1·90 1·80
PORTRAITS: 3f.50, Cardinal J. Cardijn. 7f. Maria Baers (Catholic social worker). 9f. P. Pastur (social reformer).

543 Arms of Eupen, Malmedy and St. Vith

1970. 50th Anniv of Annexation of Eupen, Malmedy and St. Vith.
2177 **543** 7f. brown and sepia 50 35

544 *The Uneasy Town* (detail, Paul Delvaux)

1970. "Solidarity". Paintings. Multicoloured.
2178 3f.50+1f.50 Type **544** 35 35
2179 7f.+3f. *The Memory* (Rene Magritte) 35 60

545 Telephone

1971. Inaug of Automatic Telephone Service.
2183 **545** 1f.50 multicoloured 30 30

546 "Auto" Car

1971. 50th Brussels Motor Show.
2184 **546** 2f.50 black and red 30 30

547 Touring Club Badge

1971. 75th Anniv of Royal Touring Club of Belgium.
2185 **547** 3f.50 gold, red & blue 30 30

548 Tournai Cathedral

1971. 800th Anniv of Tournai Cathedral.
2186 **548** 7f. blue 50 40

549 *The Letter-box* (T. Lobrichon)

1971. "Philately for the Young".
2187 **549** 1f.50 brown 30 30

550 Notre-Dame Abbey, Marche-les-Dames

1971. Cultural Works.
2190 **550** 3f.50+1f.50 black, green and brown 35 30
2191 - 7f.+3f. black, red and yellow 70 65
DESIGN: 7f. Convent, Turnhout.

552 King Albert I, Jules Destree and Academy

1971. 50th Anniv of Royal Academy of French Language and Literature.
2201 **552** 7f. black and grey 30 10

553 Postman of 1855 (from lithograph, J. Thiriar)

1971. Stamp Day.
2202 **553** 3f.50 multicoloured 30 30

554 Europa Chain

1971. Europa.
2203 **554** 3f.50 brown and black 90 30
2204 **554** 7f. green and black 1·50 50

555 Satellite Earth Station

1971. World Telecommunications Day.
2205 **555** 7f. multicoloured 60 50

556 Red Cross

1971. Belgian Red Cross.
2206 **556** 10f.+5f. red & black 1·00 70

1971. As T **533**, but without dates.

2207	1f.75 green	70	60
2208	2f.25 green	30	10
2208a	2f.50 green	25	10
2209	3f. green	30	10
2209a	3f.25 plum	30	25
2210	3f.50 brown	50	10
2211	4f. blue	40	10
2212	4f.50 purple	95	10
2212a	4f.50 blue	40	10
2213	5f. violet	50	10
2214	6f. red	50	10
2214b	6f.50 violet	50	10
2215	7f. red	65	10
2215ba	7f.50 mauve	40	10
2216a	8f. black	70	10
2217	9f. sepia	95	10
2217a	9f. brown	90	10
2218a	10f. mauve	70	10
2218b	11f. sepia	1·00	10
2219	12f. blue	3·00	30
2219b	13f. blue	1·20	10
2219c	14f. green	1·40	10
2220	15f. violet	1·20	10
2220b	16f. green	2·10	10
2220c	17f. purple	1·40	10
2221	18f. blue	1·40	10
2221a	18f. turquoise	2·10	25
2222	20f. blue	1·60	10
2222b	22f. black	2·10	1·80
2222c	22f. turquoise	1·90	50
2222d	25f. purple	2·10	10
2223a	30f. orange	2·40	10
2223b	35f. turquoise	4·00	30
2223c	40f. blue	4·75	30
2223d	45f. brown	5·75	55

See also Nos. 2335/9.

557 Scientist, Adelie Penguins and "Erika Dan" (polar vessel)

1971. TEnth Anniv of Antarctic Treaty.
2230 **557** 10f. multicoloured 80 60

558 *The Discus thrower* and Munich Cathedral

1971. Olympic Games, Munich (1972) Publicity.
2231 **558** 7f.+3f. black & blue 80 70

559 G. Hubin (statesman)

1971. Georges Hubin Commemoration.
2232 **559** 1f.50 violet and black 30 30

560 Notre-Dame Abbey, Orval

1971. 900th Anniv of Notre-Dame Abbey, Orval.
2233 **560** 2f.50 brown 30 30

561 Processional Giants, Ath

1971. Historic Towns.
2234 **561** 2f.50 multicoloured 30 30
2235 - 2f.50 brown 30 30
DESIGN—HORIZ: (46×35 mm): No. 2235, View of Ghent.

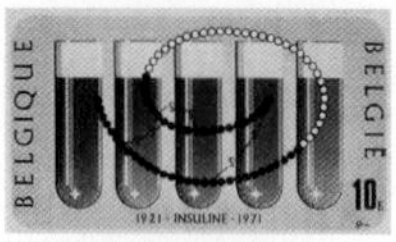

562 Test-tubes and Diagram

1971. 50th Anniv of Discovery of Insulin.

2236	**562**	10f. multicoloured	85	60

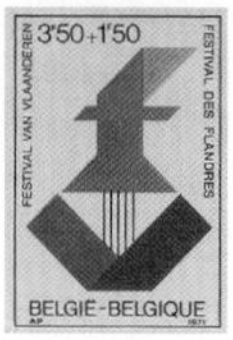

563 Flemish Festival Emblem

1971. Cultural Works. Festivals. Multicoloured.

2237	3f.50+1f.50 Type **563**	35	35
2238	7f.+3f. Walloon Festival emblem	85	70

564 Belgian Family and "50"

1971. 50th Anniv of "League of Large Families".

2239	**564**	1f.50 multicoloured	30	30

1971. Tourist Publicity. Designs similar to T **450**.

2240	2f.50 black, brown and blue	25	10
2241	2f.50 black, brown and blue	25	10

DESIGNS: No. 2240, St. Martin's Church, Alost; No. 2241, Town Hall and belfry, Mons.

565 Dr. Jules Bordet (medical scientist)

1971. Belgian Celebrities.

2242	**565**	3f.50 green	35	30
2243	-	3f.50 brown	35	30

DESIGN: No. 2242, Type **565** (10th death anniv); No. 2243, "Stijn Streuvels" (Frank Lateur, writer, birth cent.).

566 Achaemenid Tomb, Buzpar

1971. 2500th Anniv of Persian Empire.

2244	**566**	7f. multicoloured	60	50

567 Elewijt Chateau

1971. "Belgica 72" Stamp Exhibition, Brussels (2nd issue).

2245	-	3f.50+1f.50 green	35	35
2246	**567**	7f.+3f. brown	85	85
2247	-	10f.+5f. blue	1·20	1·20

DESIGNS—HORIZ: (52×35½ mm): 3f. Attre Chateau; 10f. Royal Palace, Brussels.

568 F.I.B./V.B.N. Emblem

1971. 25th Anniv of Federation of Belgian Industries.

2248	**568**	3f.50 gold, black & blue	35	30

569 *The Flight into Egypt* (15th-century Dutch School)

1971. Christmas.

2249	**569**	1f.50 multicoloured	30	30

1971. Tourist Publicity. Designs similar to T 450.

2250	1f.50 blue and buff	10	10
2251	2f.50 blue and buff	25	10

DESIGNS—HORIZ: 1f.50, Town Hall, Malines. VERT: 2f.50, Basilica, St. Hubert.

570 *Actias luna*

1971. "Solidarity". Insects in Antwerp Zoo. Multicoloured.

2252	1f.50+50c. Type **570**	30	30
2253	3f.50+1f.50 *Tabanus bromius* (horiz)	35	35
2254	7f.+3f. *Polistes gallicus* (horiz)	85	85
2255	9f.+4f. *Cicindela campestris*	95	95

572 Road Signs and Traffic Signals

1972. 20th Anniv of "Via Secura" Road Safety Organization.

2263	**572**	3f.50 multicoloured	30	30

573 Book Year Emblem

1972. International Book Year.

2264	**573**	7f. blue, brown & black	60	40

574 Coins of Belgium and Luxembourg

1972. 50th Anniv of Belgo–Luxembourgeoise Economic Union.

2265	**574**	1f.50 silver, black and orange	30	30

576 "Auguste Vermeylen" (I. Opsomer)

1972. Birth Centenary of Auguste Vemeylen (writer).

2267	**576**	2f.50 multicoloured	30	30

577 "Belgica 72" Emblem

1972. "Belgica 72" Stamp Exn., Brussels (3rd Issue).

2268	**577**	3f.50 purple, blue & brn	35	30

578 Heart Emblem

1972. World Heart Month.

2269	**578**	7f. multicoloured	60	40

579 Astronaut cancelling Letter on Moon

1972. Stamp Day.

2270	**579**	3f.50 multicoloured	35	30

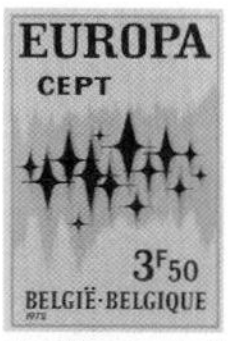

580 "Communications"

1972. Europa.

2271	**580**	3f.50 multicoloured	75	30
2272	**580**	7f. multicoloured	1·20	60

581 Quill Pen and Newspaper

1972. "Liberty of the Press". 50th Anniv of Belga News Agency and 25th Congress of International Federation of Newspaper Editors (F.I.E.J.).

2273	**581**	2f.50 multicoloured	30	30

582 "UIC" on Coupled Wagons

1972. 50th Anniv of Int Railways Union (U.I.C.).

2274	**582**	7f. multicoloured	60	40

See also No. P2266.

583 Couvin

1972. Tourist Publicity.

2275	**583**	2f.50 purple, blue & grn	25	25
2276	-	2f.50 brown and blue	25	25

DESIGN—VERT: No. 2276, Aldeneik Church, Maaseik.

584 Leopold I 10c. "Epaulettes" Stamp of 1849

1972. "Belgica 72" Stamp Exn, Brussels (4th issue).

2277	**584**	1f.50+50c. brown, black and gold	30	30
2278	-	2f.+1f. red, brown and gold	35	35
2279	-	2f.50+1f. red, brown and gold	40	40
2280	-	3f.50+1f.50 lilac, black and gold	45	45
2281	-	6f.+3f. violet, black and gold	60	60
2282	-	7f.+3f. red, black and gold	70	70
2283	-	10f.+5f. blue, black and gold	1·00	1·00
2284	-	15f.+7f.50 green, turquoise and gold	1·60	1·60
2285	-	20f.+10f. chestnut, brown and gold	2·10	2·10

DESIGNS: 2f. Leopold I 40c. "Medallion" of 1849; 2f.50, Leopold II 10c. of 1883. 3f.50, Leopold II 50c. of 1883; 6f. Albert I; 2f. "Tin Hat" of 1919; 7f. Albert I 50f. of 1929; 10f. Albert I 1f.75 of 1931; 15f. Leopold III 5f. of 1936; 20f. Baudouin 3f.50 of 1970.

585 *Beatrice* (G. de Smet)

1972. "Philately for the Young".

2287	**585**	3f. multicoloured	35	30

586 Emblem of Centre

1972. Inauguration of William Lennox Epileptic Centre, Ottignies.

2288	**586**	10f.+5f. multicoloured	1·20	1·20

587 Dish Aerial and "Intelstat 4" Satellite

1972. Inaug of Satellite Earth Station, Lessive.

2289	**587**	3f.50 black, silver & bl	35	30

588 Frans Masereel (wood-carver and painter)

1972. Masereel Commem.

2290	**588**	4f.50 black and green	40	30

589 "Adoration of the Magi" (F. Timmermans)

1972. Christmas.

2291	**589**	3f.50 multicoloured	35	30

590 *Empress Maria Theresa* (unknown artist)

1972. Bicentenary of Belgian Royal Academy of Sciences, Letters and Fine Arts.

2292	**590**	2f. multicoloured	30	30

591 Greylag Goose

1972. "Solidarity". Birds from Zwin Nature Reserve. Multicoloured.

2293	2f.+1f. Type **591**		35	35
2294	4f.50+2f. Northern lapwing		60	60
2295	8f.+4f. White stork		70	95
2296	9f.+4f.50 Common kestrel (horiz)		1·00	1·00

592 "Fire"

1973. Industrial Buildings Fire Protection Campaign.

2297	**592**	2f. multicoloured	30	30

593 W.M.O. Emblem and Meteorological Equipment

1973. Centenary of World Meteorological Organization.

2298	**593**	9f. multicoloured	80	45

594 Bijloke Abbey and Museum, Ghent

1973. Cultural Works. Religious Buildings.

2299	**594**	2f.+1f. green	40	40
2300	-	4f.50+2f. brown	50	50
2301	-	8f.+4f. red	95	95
2302	-	9f.+4f.50 blue	1·20	1·20

DESIGNS: 4f.50, Collegiate Church of St. Ursmer, Lobbes; 8f. Park Abbey, Heverlee; 9f. Floreffe Abbey.

595 W.H.O. Emblem as Man's "Heart"

1973. 25th Anniv of W.H.O.

2303	**595**	8f. black, yellow & red	60	45

596 Ball in Hands

1973. First World Basketball Championships for the Handicapped, Bruges.

2304	**596**	10f.+5f. multicoloured	1·20	1·20

597 Europa "Posthorn"

1973. Europa.

2305	**597**	4f.50 blue, yellow & brn	1·30	35
2306	**597**	8f. blue, yellow & green	2·50	35

598 Thurn and Taxis Courier (17th-cent)

1973. Stamp Day.

2307	**598**	4f.50 brown and red	40	30

599 Fair Emblem

1973. 25th International Fair, Liege.

2308	**599**	4f.50 multicoloured	40	30

600 Arrows encircling Globe

1973. Fifth World Telecommunications Day.

2309	**600**	3f.50 multicoloured	35	30

601 *Sport* (poster for Ghent Exhibition, 1913)

1973. 60th Anniv of Workers' International Sports Organization.

2310	**601**	4f.50 multicoloured	40	30

602 Douglas DC-10-30CF and De Havilland D.H.9

1973. 50th Anniv of SABENA.

2311	**602**	8f. black, blue and grey	70	45

603 Ernest Tips's Biplane, 1908

1973. 35th Anniv (1972) of "Les Vieilles Tiges de Belgique" (pioneer aviators' association).

2312	**603**	10f. black, blue & green	85	50

604 15th-Century Printing-press

1973. Historical Events and Anniversaries.

2313	**604**	2f.+1f. blk, brn & red	40	40
2314	-	3f.50+1f.50 mult	40	40
2315	-	4f.50+2f. mult	45	45
2316	-	8f.+4f. multicoloured	85	85
2317	-	9f.+4f.50 mult	1·00	1·00
2318	-	10f.+5f. multicoloured	1·30	1·30

DESIGNS—VERT (As Type **604**): 2f. (500th anniv of first Belgian printed book, produced by Dirk Martens); 3f.50, Head of Amon (Queen Elisabeth Egyptological Foundation. 50th anniv.); 4f.50, *Portrait of a Young Girl* (Petrus Christus, 500th death anniv). HORIZ (36×25 mm): 8f. Gold coins of Hadrian and Marcus Aurelius (Discovery of Roman treasure at Luttre-Liberchies); (52×35 mm); 9f. *Members of the Great Council* (Coessaert) (Great Council of Malines, 500th anniv.). 10f. *Jong Jacob* (East Indiaman) (Ostend Merchant Company, 250th anniv).

605 *Woman Bathing* (fresco by Lemaire)

1973. Thermal Treatment Year.

2319	**605**	4f.50 multicoloured	40	30

606 Adolphe Sax and Tenor Saxophone

1973. Belgian Musical Instrument Industry.

2320	**606**	9f. multicoloured	70	40

607 St. Nicholas Church, Eupen

1973. Tourist Publicity.

2321	**607**	2f. multicoloured	30	30

See also Nos. 2328/9, 2368/70, 2394/5, 2452/5, 2508/11, 2535/8, 2573/6, 2595/6 and 2614.

608 *Little Charles* (Evenepoel)

1973. "Philately for the Young".

2322	**608**	3f. multicoloured	35	30

609 J. B. Moens (philatelist) and Perforations

1973. 50th Anniv of Belgian Stamp Dealers Association.

2323	**609**	10f. multicoloured	80	60

610 *Adoration of the Shepards* (H. van der Goes)

1973. Christmas.

2324	**610**	4f. blue	40	30

611 Motorway and Emblem

1973. 50th Anniv of "Vlaamse Automobilistenbond" (VAB) (motoring organization).

2325	**611**	5f. multicoloured	45	30

612 L. Pierard (after sculpture by Ianchelevici)

1973. 21st Death Anniv of Louis Pierard (politician and writer).

2326	**612**	4f. red and cream	40	30

613 Early Microphone

1973. 50th Anniv of Belgium Radio.

2327	**613**	4f. black and blue	40	30

1973. Tourist Publicity. As T **607**.

2328		3f. grey, brown and blue	30	30
2329		4f. grey and green	40	35

DESIGNS—HORIZ: 3f. Town Hall, Leau; 4f. Chimay Castle.

614 F. Rops (self-portrait)

1973. 75th Death Anniv of Felicien Rops (artist and engraver).

2330	**614**	7f. black and brown	60	35

615 Jack of Diamonds

1973. "Solidarity". Old Playing Cards. Multicoloured.

2331	5f.+2f.50 Type **615**		60	60
2332	5f.+2f.50 Jack of Spades		60	60
2333	5f.+2f.50 Queen of Hearts		60	60
2334	5f.+2f.50 King of Clubs		60	60

1973. As Nos. 2207/23 but smaller, 22×17 mm.

2335	**583**	3f. green	30	10
2336	**583**	4f. blue	35	25
2337	**583**	4f.50 blue	40	10
2338	**583**	5f. mauve	40	25
2338c	**583**	6f. red	50	30
2339	**583**	6f.50 violet	50	30
2339b	**583**	8f. grey	65	30

616 King Albert (Baron Opsomer)

1974. 40th Death Anniv of King Albert I.

2340	**616**	4f. blue and black	35	30

617 "Blood Donation"

1974. Belgian Red Cross. Multicoloured.

2341	4f.+2f. Type **617**		45	45
2342	10f.+5f. "Traffic Lights" (Road Safety)		1·20	1·20

618 "Protection of the Environment"

1974. Robert Schuman Association for the Protection of the Environment.

2343 **618** 3f. multicoloured 35 30

619 *Armand Jamar* (Self-portrait)

1974. Belgian Cultural Celebrities. Multicoloured.

2344 4f.+2f. Type **619** 40 40

2345 5f.+2f.50 Tony Bergmann (author) and view of Lier 45 45

2346 7f.+3f.50 Henri Vieuxtemps (violinist) and view of Verviers 70 70

2347 10f.+5f. "James Ensor" (self-portrait with masks) (35×52 mm) 1·00 1·00

620 N.A.T.O. Emblem

1974. 25th Anniv of North Atlantic Treaty Organization.

2348 **620** 10f. blue and light blue 85 50

621 Hubert Krains (Belgian postal administrator)

1974. Stamp Day.

2349 **621** 5f. black and grey 40 30

622 "Destroyed Town" (O. Zadkine)

1974. Europa. Sculptures.

2350 **622** 5f. black and red 80 30

2351 - 10f. black and blue 1·60 50

DESIGN: 10f. *Solidarity* (G. Minne).

623 Heads of Boy and Girl

1974. Tenth Lay Youth Festival.

2352 **623** 4f. multicoloured 40 30

625 New Planetarium, Brussels

1974. Historical Buildings.

2354 **625** 3f. brown and blue 35 30

2355 - 4f. brown and red 45 30

2356 - 5f. brown and green 50 30

2357 - 7f. brown and yellow 65 35

2358 - 10f. brown, orange & bl 80 35

DESIGNS—As T **625**. HORIZ: 4f. Pillory, Braine-le-Chateau. VERT: 10f. Belfry, Bruges. 45×25 mm: 5f. Ruins of Soleilmont Abbey; 7f. *Procession* (fountain sculpture, Ghent).

626 "BENELUX"

1974. 30th Anniv of Benelux Customs Union.

2359 **626** 5f. blue, green & lt blue 40 30

627 *Jan Vekemans at the Age of Five* (Cornelis de Vos)

1974. "Philately for the Young".

2360 **627** 3f. multicoloured 35 30

628 Self-portrait and Van Gogh House, Cuesmes

1974. Opening of Vincent Van Gogh House, Cuesmes.

2361 **628** 10f.+5f. multicoloured 1·20 85

629 Corporal Tresignies and Brule Bridge

1974. 60th Death Anniv of Corporal Leon Tresignies (war hero).

2362 **629** 4f. green and brown 40 30

630 Montgomery Blair and U.P.U. Emblem

1974. Centenary of U.P.U.

2363 **630** 5f. black and green 45 30

2364 - 10f. black and red 80 50

DESIGN: 10f. H. von Stephan and U.P.U. Monument.

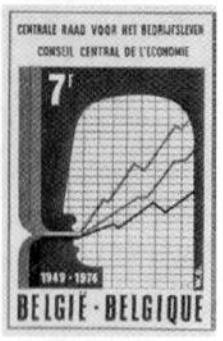

631 Graph within Head

1974. 25th Anniv of Central Economic Council.

2365 **631** 7f. multicoloured 65 40

632 Rotary Emblem on Belgian Flag

1974. 50th Anniv of Rotary Int in Belgium.

2366 **632** 10f. multicoloured 80 45

633 Wild Boar

1974. 40th Anniv of Granting of Colours to Ardennes Regiment of Chasseurs.

2367 **633** 3f. multicoloured 35 30

1974. Tourist Publicity. As T **607**.

2368 3f. brown and yellow 40 30

2369 4f. green and blue 40 35

2370 4f. green and blue 40 35

DESIGNS—VERT: No. 2368, Aarschot. HORIZ: No. 2369, Meeting of three frontiers, Gemmenich; 2370, Nassogne.

634 "Angel" (detail, "The Mystic Lamb", Brothers Van Eyck)

1974. Christmas.

2371 **634** 4f. purple 40 30

635 Gentian

1974. "Solidarity". Flora and Fauna. Multicoloured.

2372 4f.+2f. Type **635** 45 45

2373 5f.+2f.50 Eurasian badger (horiz) 65 65

2374 7f.+3f.50 *Carabus auratus* (beetle) (horiz) 75 75

2375 10f.+5f. Spotted cat's-ear 1·20 1·20

636 Adolphe Quetelet (after J. Odevaere)

1974. Death Centenary of Adolphe Quetelet. (scientist).

2376 **636** 10f. black and brown 80 50

637 Exhibition Emblem

1975. "Themabelga" Stamp Exhibition, Brussels (1st issue).

2377 **637** 6f.50 orange, blk & grn 45 30

See also Nos. 2411/16.

638 *Neoregelia carolinae*

1975. Ghent Flower Show. Multicoloured.

2378 4f.50 Type **638** 40 35

2379 5f. *Tussilago petasites* 45 30

2380 6f.50 *Azalea japonica* 50 30

639 Student and Young Boy

1975. Cent of Charles Buls Normal School.

2381 **639** 4f.50 multicoloured 40 30

640 Foundation Emblem

1975. Centenary of Davids Foundation (Flemish cultural organisation).

2382 **640** 5f. multicoloured 40 30

641 King Albert I

1975. Birth Centenary of King Albert I.

2383 **641** 10f. black and purple 80 45

642 Pesaro Palace, Venice

1975. Cultural Works.

2384 **642** 6f.50+2f.50 brown 65 65

2385 - 10f.+4f.50 purple 1·00 1·00

2386 - 15f.+6f.50 blue 1·50 1·50

DESIGNS—HORIZ: 10f. Sculpture Museum, St. Bavon Abbey, Ghent. VERT: 15f. *Virgin and Child* (Michelangelo, 500th Birth Anniv.).

643 *Postman of 1840* (J. Thiriar)

1975. Stamp Day.

2387 **643** 6f.50 purple 50 30

644 "An Apostle" (detail, *The Last Supper*, Dirk Bouts)

1975. Europa. Paintings.

2388 **644** 6f.50 black, blue & grn 80 30

2389 - 10f. black, red & orange 1·70 60

DESIGN: 10f. "The Suppliant's Widow" (detail, *The Justice of Otho*, Dirk Bouts).

645 Prisoners' Identification Emblems

1975. 30th Anniv of Concentration Camps' Liberation.

2390 **645** 4f.50 multicoloured 40 30

646 St John's Hospice, Bruges

1975. European Architectural Heritage Year.

2391 **646** 4f.50 purple 45 30

2392 - 5f. green 50 30

2393 - 10f. blue 1·00 45

DESIGNS—VERT: 5f. St. Loup's Church, Namur. HORIZ: 10f. Martyrs Square, Brussels.

1975. Tourist Publicity. As T **607**.

2394 4f.50 brown, buff and red 40 30

2395 5f. multicoloured 50 30

DESIGN—VERT: 4f.50, Church, Dottignies. HORIZ: 5f. Market Square, Saint Truiden.

647 G. Ryckmans and L. Cerfaux (founders), and Louvain University Library

1975. 25th Anniv of Louvain Colloquium Biblicum (Biblical Scholarship Association).

2396	**647**	10f. sepia and blue	85	45

648 *Metamorphosis* (P. Mara)

1975. Queen Fabiola Foundation for the Mentally Ill.

2397	**648**	7f. multicoloured	60	35

649 Marie Popelin (women's rights pioneer) and Palace of Justice

1975. International Women's Year.

2398	**649**	6f.50 purple and green	65	30

650 *Assia* (Charles Despiau)

1975. 25th Anniv of Middelheim Open-air Museum, Antwerp.

2399	**650**	5f. black and green	40	30

651 Dr. Hemerijckx and Leprosy Hospital, Zaire

1975. Dr. Frans Hemerijckx (treatment of leprosy pioneer) Commemoration.

2400	**651**	20f.+10f. mult	2·10	2·10

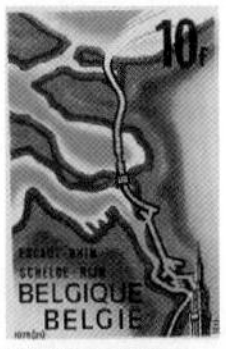

652 Canal Map

1975. Opening of Rhine–Scheldt Canal.

2401	**652**	10f. multicoloured	85	40

653 *Cornelia Vekemans at the Age of Seven* (Cornelis de Vos)

1975. "Philately for the Young".

2402	**653**	4f.50 multicoloured	45	30

654 National Bank and F. Orban (founder)

1975. 125th Anniv of Belgian National Bank.

2403	**654**	25f. multicoloured	2·20	60

655 Edmond Thieffry (pilot) and Hadley Page H.P.26 W.8e Hamilton OË-BAHO "Princess Marie-Jose"

1975. 50th Anniv of First Flight, Brussels–Kinshasa.

2404	**655**	7f. purple and black	60	40

656 University Seal

1975. 550th Anniv of Louvain University.

2405	**656**	6f.50 black, green & bl	60	30

657 "Angels", (detail, *The Nativity*, R. de le Pasture)

1975. Christmas.

2406	**657**	5f. multicoloured	40	25

658 Emile Moyson (Flemish Leader)

1975. "Solidarity".

2407	**658**	4f.50+2f. purple	45	45
2408	-	6f.50+3f. green	70	70
2409	-	10f.+5f. vio, blk & bl	1·00	1·00
2410	-	13f.+6f. multicoloured	1·30	1·30

DESIGNS—VERT: 6f.50, Dr. Augustin Snellaert (Flemish literature scholar); 13f. Detail of retable, St. Dymphne Church, Geel. HORIZ: 10f. Eye within hand, and Braille characters (150th anniv of introduction of Braille).

659 Cheese Seller

1975. "Themabelga" International Thematic Stamp Exhibition, Brussels (2nd issue). Traditional Belgian Trades. Multicoloured.

2411	4f.50+1f.50 Type **659**	45	45
2412	6f.50+3f. Potato seller	70	70
2413	6f.50+3f. Basket-carrier	70	70
2414	10f.+5f. Prawn fisherman and pony (horiz)	1·00	1·00
2415	10f.+5f. Knife-grinder and cart (horiz)	1·00	1·00
2416	30f.+15f. Milk-woman with dog-cart (horiz)	2·75	2·75

660 "African" Collector

1976. Centenary of "Conservatoire Africain" (Charity Organization).

2417	**660**	10f.+5f. multicoloured	1·20	1·20

661 Owl Emblem and Flemish Buildings

1976. 125th Anniv of Wilhems Foundation (Flemish cultural organization).

2418	**661**	5f. multicoloured	40	30

662 Bicentennial Symbol

1976. Bicentenary of American Revolution.

2419	**662**	14f. multicoloured	1·20	65

663 Cardinal Mercier

1976. 50th Death Anniv of Cardinal Mercier.

2420	**663**	4f.50 purple	40	30

664 "Vlaams Ekonomisch Verbond"

1976. 50th Anniv of Flemish Economic Federation.

2421	**664**	6f.50 multicoloured	50	30

665 Swimming

1976. Olympic Games, Montreal. Multicoloured.

2422	4f.50+1f.50 Type **665**	45	45
2423	5f.+2f. Running (vert)	45	45
2424	6f.50+2f.50 Horse jumping	70	70

666 Money Centre Building, Brussels

1976. Stamp Day.

2425	**666**	6f.50 brown	50	30

667 Queen Elisabeth playing Violin

1976. 25th Anniv of Queen Elisabeth International Music Competitions.

2426	**667**	14f.+6f. red & black	1·40	1·40

668 Basket-making

1976. Europa. Traditional Crafts. Multicoloured.

2427	6f.50 Type **668**	95	25
2428	14f. Pottery (horiz)	2·10	60

669 Truck on Motorway

1976. 14th Congress of International Road Haulage Union, Brussels.

2429	**669**	14f. black, red & yellow	1·30	50

670 Queen Elisabeth

1976. Birth Centenary of Queen Elisabeth.

2430	**670**	14f. green	1·20	50

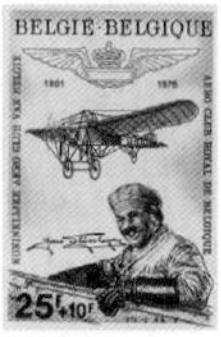

672 Jan Olieslagers (aviator), Bleriot XI Monoplane and club Badge

1976. 75th Anniv of Belgian Royal Aero Club. Sheet 82×116 mm.

MS2435	**672** 25f.+10f. black, yellow and blue	2·50	2·50

673 Ardennes Horses

1976. 50th Anniv of Ardennes Draught Horses Society.

2436	**673**	5f. multicoloured	45	35

674 King Baudouin

1976. 25th Anniv of King Baudouin's Accession. Two sheets each 110×62 mm containing stamps as T **674**.

MS2437	(a) 4f.50 grey; 6f.50 yellow; 10f. red (sold at 30f.). (b) 20f. green; 30f. blue (sold at 70f.)	7·50	7·50

675 *Madonna and Child* (detail)

1976. 400th Birth Anniv of Peter Paul Rubens (artist) (1st issue). Multicoloured.

2438	4f.50+1f.50 *Descent from the Cross* (detail)	60	60
2439	6f.50+3f. *Adoration of the Shepherds* (detail) (24½×35 mm)	70	60
2440	6f.50+3f. *Virgin of the Parrot* (detail) (24½×35 mm)	70	70

2441		10f.+5f. *Adoration of the Kings* (detail) (24½×35 mm)	1·20	1·20
2442		10f.+5f. *Last Communion of St. Francis* (detail) (24½×35 mm)	1·20	1·20
2443		30f.+15f. Type **675**	3·00	3·00

See also Nos. 2459 and 2497.

676 William the Silent, Prince of Orange

1976. 400th Anniv of Pacification of Ghent.

2444	**676**	10f. green	85	45

678 Underground Train

1976. Opening of Brussels Metro (Underground) Service.

2446	**678**	6f.50 multicoloured	65	30

679 *The Young Musician* (W. C. Duyster)

1976. "Philately for the Young" and Young Musicians' Movement.

2447	**679**	4f.50 multicoloured	40	30

680 Charles Bernard (writer, birth cent)

1976. Cultural Anniversaries.

2448	**680**	5f. purple	45	30
2449	-	5f. red	45	30
2450	-	6f.50 brown	65	30
2451	-	6f.50 green	65	30

DESIGNS—VERT: No. 2449, Fernand Toussaint van Boelaere (writer, birth cent 1975); No. 2450, *St. Jerome in Mountain Landscape* (J. le Patinier) (25th anniv of Charles Plisnier Foundation). HORIZ: No. 2451,*Story of the Blind* (P. Brueghel) (25th anniv of *Vereniging voor Beschaafde Omgangstaal* (Dutch language organisation)).

1976. Tourist Publicity. As T **607**.

2452		4f.50 multicoloured	45	35
2453		4f.50 multicoloured	45	35
2454		5f. brown and blue	45	35
2455		5f. brown and olive	45	35

DESIGNS—HORIZ: No. 2452, Hunnegem Priory, Grammont; No. 2454, River Lys, Sint-Martens-Latem; No. 2455, Chateau. Ham-sur-Heure. VERT: No. 2453, Remouchamps Caves.

681 *Child with Impediment* (Velasquez)

1976. National Association for Aid to the Mentally Handicapped.

2456	**681**	14f.+6f. multicoloured	1·60	1·60

682 *The Nativity* (detail, Master of Flemalle)

1976. Christmas.

2457	**682**	5f. violet	45	30

683 Monogram

1977. 400th Birth Anniv of Peter Paul Rubens (2nd issue).

2459	**683**	6f.50 black and lilac	60	30

684 Belgian Lion

1977. (a) Size 17×20 mm.

2460	**684**	50c. brown	10	10
2461	**684**	65c. red	10	10
2462	**684**	1f. mauve	10	10
2463	**684**	1f.50 grey	10	10
2464a	**684**	2f. orange	10	10
2465	**684**	2f.50 green	35	25
2466	**684**	2f.75 blue	35	35
2467a	**684**	3f. violet	25	10
2468	**684**	4f. brown	25	10
2469	**684**	4f.50 blue	45	25
2470	**684**	5f. green	35	10
2471	**684**	6f. red	45	10
2472	**684**	7f. red	60	10
2473	**684**	8f. blue	35	10
2474	**684**	9f. orange	1·20	10

(b) 17×22 mm.

2475	1f. mauve	25	25
2476	2f. orange	45	35
2477	3f. violet	50	40

685 Dr. Albert Hustin (pioneer of blood transfusion)

1977. Belgian Red Cross.

2478	**685**	6f.50+2f.50 red and black	75	75
2479	-	14f.+7f. red, blue and black	1·40	1·40

DESIGN: 14f.+7f. Knee joint and red cross (World Rheumatism Year).

686 "50 Years of F.A.B.I."

1977. 50th Anniv of Federation of Belgian Engineers.

2480	**686**	6f.50 multicoloured	60	30

687 Jules Bordet School, Brussels (bicent)

1977. Cultural Anniversaries.

2481	**687**	4f.50+1f. mult	40	40
2482	-	4f.50+1f. mult	40	40
2483	-	5f.+2f. multicoloured	50	45
2484	-	6f.50+2f. mult	60	60
2485	-	6f.50+2f. red & black	60	60
2486	-	10f.+5 slate	1·00	1·00

DESIGNS—VERT: 24×37 mm: No. 2482, Marie-Therese College, Herve (bicentenary); 2483, Detail from *La Grande Pyramide Musicale* (E. Tytgat) (50th anniv of Brussels Philharmonic Society). 35×45 mm: No. 2486, Camille Lemonnier (75th anniv of Society of Belgian Authors writing in French). HORIZ: 35×24 mm: No. 2484, Lucien van Obbergh and stage scene (50th anniv of Union of Artists). 37×24 mm: No. 2485, Emblem of Humanist Society (25th anniv).

688 Gulls in Flight

1977. 25th Anniv of District 112 of Lions International.

2487	**688**	14f. multicoloured	1·20	35

689 Footballers

1977. 30th International Youth Tournament of European Football Association.

2488	**689**	10f.+5f. multicoloured	1·20	1·20

690 Pillar Box, 1852

1977. Stamp Day.

2489	**690**	6f.50 olive	65	30

691 Gileppe Dam, Jalhay

1977. Europa. Multicoloured.

2490	6f.50 Type **691**	1·20	30
2491	14f. The Yser, Nieuport	2·00	60

692 "Mars and Mercury Association Emblem"

1977. 50th Anniv of Mars and Mercury Association of Reserve and Retired Officers.

2492	**692**	5f. green, black & brown	40	30

693 De Hornes Coat of Arms

1977. Historical Anniversaries.

2493	**693**	4f.50 lilac	40	30
2494	-	5f. red	45	30
2495	-	6f.50 brown	45	30
2496	-	14f. green	1·20	60

DESIGNS AND EVENTS—VERT: 4f.50, Type **693** (300th anniv of creation of principality of Overijse under Eugene-Maximilien de Hornes); 6f.50, Miniature (600th anniv of Froissart's *Chronicles*); 14f. *The Conversion of St. Hubert* (1250th death anniv). HORIZ: (45×24 mm): 5f. Detail from *Oxford Chest* (675th anniv of Battle of Golden Spurs).

694 *Self-Portrait*

1977. 400th Birth Anniv of Peter Paul Rubens (3rd issue).

2497	**694**	5f. multicoloured	45	30
MS2498		100×152 mm. As No. 2497 but larger (24×37 mm) ×3 (sold at 20f.)	1·40	1·40

695 *The Mystic Lamb* (detail, Brothers Van Eyck)

1977. 50th Anniv of International Federation of Library Associations and Congress, Brussels.

2499	**695**	10f. multicoloured	80	45

696 Gymnast and Footballer

1977. Sports Events and Anniversaries.

2500	**696**	4f.50 red, black & grn	45	30
2501	-	6f.50 black, violet and brown	50	30
2502	-	10f. turquoise, black and salmon	85	45
2503	-	14f. green, blk & ochre	1·30	60

DESIGNS—VERT: 4f.50, Type **696** (50th anniv of Workers' Central Sports Association); 10f. Basketball (20th European Championships); 14f. Hockey (International Hockey Cup competition). HORIZ: 6f.50, Disabled fencers (Rehabilitation through sport).

697 Festival Emblem

1977. "Europalia '77" Festival.

2504	**697**	5f. multicoloured	45	30

699 *The Egg-seller* (Gustave de Smet)

1977. Promoting Belgian Eggs.

2506	**699**	4f.50 black and ochre	40	30

700 *The Stamp Collectors* (detail, Constant Cap)

1977. "Philately for the Young".

2507	**700**	4f.50 sepia	40	30

1977. Tourist Publicity. As T **607**.

2508	4f.50 multicoloured	40	30
2509	4f.50 black, blue and green	40	30
2510	5f. multicoloured	40	30
2511	5f. multicoloured	40	30

DESIGNS—VERT: No. 2508, Bailiff's House, Gembloux; No. 2509, St. Aldegone's Church. HORIZ: No. 2510, View of Liege and statue of Mother and Child; No. 2511, View and statue of St. Nicholas.

701 *Nativity* (detail, R. de la Pasture)

1977. Christmas.

2512	**701**	5f. red	40	35

702 Albert-Edouard Janssen (financier)

1977. "Solidarity".

2513	**702**	5f.+2f.50 black	45	45
2514	-	5f.+2f.50 red	45	45
2515	-	10f.+5f. purple	1·00	1·00
2516	-	10f.+5f. grey	1·00	1·00

DESIGNS: No. 2514, Joseph Wauters (politician); No. 2516, Jean Capart (egyptologist); No. 2515, August de Boeck (composer).

703 Distressed Girl (Deserted Children)

1978. Philanthropic Works. Multicoloured.

2517	4f.50+1f.50 Type **703**	40	40
2518	6f.+3f. Blood pressure measurement (World Hypertension Month)	60	60
2519	10f.+5f. De Mick Sanatorium, Brasschaat (Anti-tuberculosis) (horiz)	1·00	1·00

704 Railway Signal as Arrows on Map of Europe

1978. "European Action". Multicoloured.

2520	10f. Type **704** (25th anniv of European Conference of Transport Ministers)	85	35
2521	10f. European Parliament Building, Strasbourg (first direct elections)	85	35
2522	14f. Campidoglio Palace, Rome and map of EEC countries (20th anniv of Treaties of Rome) (horiz)	1·20	50
2523	14f. Paul Henri Spaak (Belgian Prime Minister) (horiz)	1·20	50

705 Grimbergen Abbey

1978. 850th Anniv of Premonstratensian Abbey, Grimbergen.

2524	**705**	4f.50 brown	40	30

706 Emblem

1978. 175th Anniv of Ostend Chamber of Commerce and Industry.

2525	**706**	8f. multicoloured	60	30

707 5f. Stamp of 1878

1978. Stamp Day.

2526	**707**	8f. brown, blk & drab	60	30

708 Antwerp Cathedral

1978. Europa. Multicoloured.

2527	8f. Type **708**	1·20	35
2528	14f. Pont des Trous, Tournai (horiz)	2·30	60

709 Theatre and Characters from *The Brussels Street Singer*

1978. Cultural Anniversaries.

2529	**709**	6f.+3f. multicoloured	60	60
2530	-	6f.+3f. multicoloured	60	60
2531	-	8f.+4f. brown	75	75
2532	-	10f.+5f. brown	1·00	1·00

DESIGNS AND EVENTS: No. 2529, (Type **709**) (Royal Flemish Theatre Cent.); 2530, Arquebusier with standard, arms and Company Gallery, Vise (Royal Company of Crossbowmen of Vise 400th anniv); 2531, Karel van der Woestijne (poet) (birth cent); 2532, Don John of Austria (signing of Perpetual Edict, 400th anniv).

710 "Education"

1978. Teaching. Multicoloured.

2533	6f. Type **710** (Municipal education in Ghent, 150th anniv)	45	35
2534	8f. Paul Pastur Workers' University, Charleroi (75th anniv)	70	30

1978. Tourist Publicity. As T **607**.

2535	4f.50 sepia, buff and blue	40	35
2536	4f.50 multicoloured	40	35
2537	6f. multicoloured	50	35
2538	6f. multicoloured	50	35

DESIGNS—VERT: No. 2535, Jonathas House, Enghien. HORIZ: No. 2536, View of Wetteren and couple in local costume; 2537, Brussels tourist hostess; 2538, Carnival Prince and church tower.

711 "K.V.I."

1978. 50th Anniv of Royal Flemish Association of Engineers.

2539	**711**	8f. black and red	60	30

712 Young Stamp Collector

1978. "Philately for the Young".

2540	**712**	4f.50 violet	40	30

713 Mountain Scenery

1978. Olympic Games (1980) Preparation.

2541	**713**	6f.+2f.50 mult	65	65
2542	-	8f.+3f.50 green, brown and black	75	75

MS2543 150×100 mm. 7f. + 3f., 14f.+6f. multicoloured 2·30 2·30

DESIGNS: 7f. Ancient Greek athletes; 8f. Kremlin Towers, Moscow; 14f. Olympic flame.

714 *The Nativity* (detail, Bethlehem Door, Notre Dame, Huy)

1978. Christmas.

2544	**714**	6f. black	50	35

715 Tabernacle, Brussels Synagogue (centenary)

1978. "Solidarity". Anniversaries.

2545	**715**	6f.+2f. brown, grey and black	65	65
2546	-	8f.+3f. multicoloured	80	80
2547	-	14f.+7f. multicoloured	1·50	1·50

DESIGNS—HORIZ: (36×24 mm): 8f. Dancing figures (Catholic Students Action, 50th anniv); 14f. Father Dominique-Georges Pire and African Village (Award of Nobel Peace Prize, 20th anniv).

716 Relief Workers giving First Aid

1978. Belgian Red Cross. Multicoloured.

2548	8f.+3f. Type **716**	85	85
2549	16f.+8f. Skull smoking, bottle and syringe ("Excess kills")	1·70	1·70

717 "Till Eulenspiegel" (legendary character)

1979. Tenth Anniv of Lay Action Centres.

2550	**717**	4f.50 multicoloured	40	30

718 "European Dove"

1979. First Direct Elections to European Assembly.

2551	**718**	8f. multicoloured	70	30

719 Millenary Emblem

1979. Brussels Millenary (1st issue).

2552	**719**	4f.50 brown, blk & red	35	30
2553	**719**	8f. turquoise, blk & grn	80	30

See also Nos. 2559/62.

720 Sculpture at N.A.T.O. Headquarters and Emblem

1979. 30th Anniv of North Atlantic Treaty Organization.

2554	**720**	30f. blue, gold and light blue	2·30	60

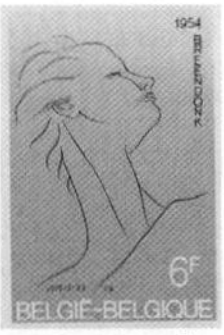

721 Drawing of Monument

1979. 25th Anniv of Breendonk Monument.

2555	**721**	6f. orange and black	45	35

722 Railway Parcels Stamp, 1879

1979. Stamp Day.

2556	**722**	8f. multicoloured	65	30

723 Mail Coach and Renault R4 Post Van

1979. Europa. Multicoloured.

2557	8f. Type **723**	1·70	30
2558	14f. Semaphore posts, satellite and dish aerial	3·00	60

724 *Legend of Our Lady of Sablon* (detail of tapestry, Town Museum of Brussels)

1979. Brussels Millenary (2nd issue). Multicoloured.

2559	6f.+2f. Type **724**	60	60
2560	8f.+3f. Different detail of tapestry	70	70
2561	14f.+7f. *Legend of Our Lady of Sablon* (tapestry)	1·50	1·50
2562	20f.+10f. Different detail of tapestry	2·20	2·20

MS2563 100×150 mm. 20f.+10f. Different detail of Town Museum tapestry (48×37 mm) 2·30 2·30

The tapestry shown on Nos. 2559/60 is from Brussels Town Museum and that on Nos. 2561/2 from the Royal Museum of Art and History.

725 Caduceus and Factory

1979. 175th Anniv of Verviers Chamber of Commerce.

2564 **725** 8f. multicoloured 60 30

726 "50" and Bank Emblem

1979. 50th Anniv of Professional Credit Bank.

2565 **726** 4f.50 blue and gold 40 30

727 Bas-relief

1979. 50th Anniv of Chambers of Trade and Commerce.

2566 **727** 10f. crimson, orange and red 75 40

728 Cambre Abbey

1979. Cultural Anniversaries.

2567 **728** 6f.+2f. multicoloured 60 60

2568 - 8f.+3f. multicoloured 70 75

2569 - 14f.+7f. black, orange and green 1·50 1·50

2570 - 20f.+10f. brown, red and grey 2·20 2·20

DESIGNS: 6f. Type **728** (50th anniv of restoration); 8f. Beauvoorde Chateau; 14f. Barthelemy Dumortier (founder) and newspaper "Courrier de L'Escaut" (150th anniv); 20f. Crypt, shrine and Collegiate Church of St. Hermes, Renaix (850th anniv of consecration).

729 "Tintin" with Dog, Stamps and Magnifier

1979. "Philately for the Young".

2571 **729** 8f. multicoloured 2·30 70

730 Le Grand-Hornu

1979. Le Grand-Hornu Industrial Archaeological Site.

2572 **730** 10f.+5f. black & grey 1·00 1·00

1979. Tourist Publicity. As T **607**.

2573 5f. multicoloured 45 35

2574 5f. multicoloured 45 35

2575 6f. black, turquoise & green 60 35

2576 6f. multicoloured 60 35

DESIGNS—HORIZ: No. 2573, Royal African Museum, Tervuren, and hunters with hounds; 2575, St. John's Church, Poperinge, and statue of Virgin Mary. VERT: No. 2574, Belfry, Thuin, and men carrying religious image; 2576, St. Nicholas's Church and cattle market, Ciney.

731 Francois Auguste Gevaert

1979. Music. Each brown and ochre.

2577 5f. Type **731** (150th birth anniv) 45 35

2578 6f. Emmanuel Durlet 65 35

2579 14f. Grand piano and string instruments (40th anniv of Queen Elisabeth Musical Chapel) 1·00 60

732 Madonna and Child, Foy-Notre-Dame Church

1979. Christmas.

2580 **732** 6f. black and blue 40 30

733 H. Heyman (politician, birth centenary)

1979. "Solidarity".

2581 **733** 8f.+3f. brown, green and black 60 60

2582 - 10f.+5f. multicoloured 95 95

2583 - 16f.+8f. black, green and yellow 1·60 1·60

DESIGNS—VERT: As Type **733**. 10f. War Invalids Organization medal (50th anniv). HORIZ: (44×24 mm): 16f. Child's head and International Year of the Child emblem.

734 "1830–1980"

1980. 150th Anniv of Independence (1st issue).

2584 **734** 9f. mauve & lt mauve 70 30

See also Nos. 2597/2601.

735 Frans Van Cauwelaert

1980. Birth Centenary of Frans Van Cauwelaert (politician).

2585 **735** 5f. black 45 30

736 Spring Flowers

1980. Ghent Flower Show. Multicoloured.

2586 5f. Type **736** 45 35

2587 6f.50 Summer flowers 60 35

2588 9f. Autumn flowers 70 35

737 Telephone and Diagram of Satellite Orbit

1980. 50th Anniv of Telegraph and Telephone Office.

2589 **737** 10f. multicoloured 80 35

738 5f. Airmail Stamp of 1930

1980. Stamp Day.

2590 **738** 9f. multicoloured 75 30

739 St. Benedict of Nursia

1980. Europa. Multicoloured.

2591 9f. Type **739** 1·40 30

2592 14f. Marguerite of Austria 2·10 70

740 Ivo van Damme

1980. Ivo van Damme (athlete) Commemoration.

2593 **740** 20f.+10f. mult 2·10 2·10

741 Palais de la Nation

1980. Fourth Interparliamentary Conference on European Co-operation and Security, Brussels.

2594 **741** 5f. blue, lilac and black 40 35

742 Golden Carriage, Mons

1980. Tourist Publicity. Multicoloured.

2595 6f.50 Type **742** 50 35

2596 6f.50 Damme 50 35

743 King Leopold I and Queen Louise-Marie

1980. 150th Anniv of Belgian Independence (2nd issue).

2597 **743** 6f.50+1f.50 pur & blk 65 65

2598 - 9f.+3f. blue & black 75 75

2599 - 14f.+6f. green & blk 1·40 1·40

2600 - 17f.+8f. orange. & blk 1·70 1·70

2601 - 25f.+10f. green & blk 2·40 2·40

MS2602 100×150 mm. 50f. black (sold at 75f.) 5·25 5·25

DESIGNS: 9f. King Leopold II and Queen Marie-Henriette; 14f. King Albert I and Queen Elisabeth; 17f. King Leopold III and Queen Astrid; 25f. King Baudouin and Queen Fabiola; 50f. Royal Mint Theatre, Brussels.

744 King Baudouin

1980. King Baudouin's 50th Birthday.

2603 **744** 9f. red 75 25

745 *Brewer* (detail, Reliquary of St. Lambert)

1980. Millenary of Liege. Multicoloured.

2604 9f.+3f. Type **745** 75 75

2605 17f.+6f. *The Miner* (sculpture by Constantin Meunier) (horiz) 1·70 1·70

2606 25f.+10f. *Seat of Wisdom* (Madonna, Collegiate Church of St. John, Liege) 2·40 2·40

MS2607 150×100 mm. 20f.+10f. Seal of Prince Bishop Notger (43×24 mm) 4·25 4·25

746 Chiny

1980. Tourist Publicity.

2608 **746** 5f. multicoloured 45 30

747 Emblem of Cardiological League of Belgium

1980. Heart Week.

2609 **747** 14f. light blue, red and blue 1·20 60

748 Rodenbach (statue at Roulers)

1980. Death Cent of Albrecht Rodenbach (poet).

2610 **748** 9f. brown, blue and deep blue 75 30

749 "Royal Procession" (children of Thyl Uylenspiegel Primary School)

1980. "Philately for the Young".

2611 **749** 5f. multicoloured 40 35

750 Emblem

1980. 50th Anniv of Belgian Broadcasting Corporation.

2612 **750** 10f. black and grey 80 45

751 "Garland of Flowers and Nativity" (attr. D. Seghers)

1980. Christmas.

2613 **751** 6f.50 multicoloured 50 35

752 Gateway, Diest

1980. Tourist Publicity.

2614	**752**	5f. multicoloured	45	35

See also Nos. 2648/51 and 2787/92.

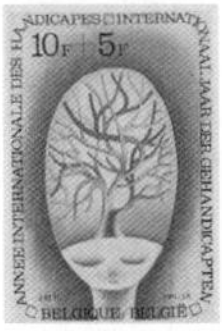

754 Brain

1981. International Year of Disabled Persons. Multicoloured.

2637	10f.+5f. Type **754**	1·20	1·20
2638	25f.+10f. Eye (horiz)	2·50	2·50

755 *Baron de Gerlache* (after F. J. Navez)

1981. Historical Anniversaries.

2639	**755**	6f. multicoloured	45	30
2640	-	9f. multicoloured	70	30
2641	-	50f. brown & yellow	3·75	70

DESIGNS—As T **755**: 6f. Type **755** (1st President of Chamber of Deputies) (150th anniv of Chamber); 9f. Baron de Stassart (1st President of Senate) (after F. J. Navez) (150th anniv of Senate). 35×51 mm: 50f. Statue of King Leopold I by Geefs (150th anniv of royal dynasty).

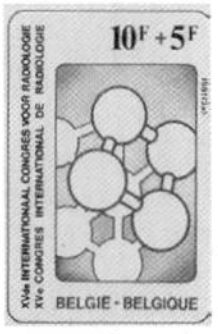

756 Emblem of 15th International Radiology Convention

1981. Belgian Red Cross.

2642	**756**	10f.+5f. bl, blk & red	1·00	1·00
2643	-	25f.+10f. blue, red and black	2·40	2·40

DESIGN: 25f. Dove and globe symbolizing international emergency assistance.

757 Tchantches and Op-Signoorke (puppets)

1981. Europa. Multicoloured.

2644	9f. Type **757**	1·50	30
2645	14f. D'Artagnan and Woltje (puppets)	2·50	85

758 Stamp Transfer-roller depicting A. de Cock (founder of Postal Museum)

1981. Stamp Day.

2646	**758**	9f. multicoloured	75	30

759 Ovide Decroly

1981. 110th Birth Anniv of Dr. Ovide Decroly (educational psychologist).

2647	**759**	35f.+15f. brown & bl	3·50	2·30

1981. Tourist Publicity. As T **752**. Multicoloured.

2648	6f. Statue of our Lady of Tongre	60	35
2649	6f. Egmont Castle, Zottegem	60	35
2650	6f.50 Dams on Eau d'Heure (horiz)	60	35
2651	6f.50 Tongerlo Abbey, Antwerp (horiz)	60	35

760 Footballer

1981. Cent of Royal Antwerp Football Club.

2652	**760**	6f. red, brown & black	60	30

761 Edouard Remouchamps (Walloon dramatist)

1981. 125th Anniv of Society of Walloon Language and Literature.

2653	**761**	6f.50 brown and stone	50	30

762 French Horn

1981. Centenary of De Vredekring Band, Antwerp.

2654	**762**	6f.50 blue, mve & blk	50	30

763 Audit Office

1981. 150th Anniv of Audit Office.

2655	**763**	10f. purple	80	30

764 Pietà

1981. 25th Anniv of Bois du Cazier Mining Disaster. Sheet 150×100 mm.

MS2656 **764**	20f. multicoloured (sold at 30f.)	2·30	2·30

765 Tombs of Marie of Burgundy and Charles the Bold

1981. Relocation of Tombs of Marie of Burgundy and Charles the Bold in Notre-Dame Church, Bruges.

2657	**765**	50f. multicoloured	3·75	85

766 Boy holding Globe in Tweezers

1981. "Philately for Youth".

2658	**766**	6f. multicoloured	45	30

767 King Baudouin

1981

2659	**767**	50f. light blue and blue	5·50	30
2660	**767**	65f. mauve and black	7·00	95
2661	**767**	100f. brown and blue	11·50	60

768 Max Waller (founder)

1981. Cultural Anniversaries.

2672	**768**	6f. multicoloured	45	30
2673	-	6f.50 multicoloured	50	30
2674	-	9f. multicoloured	70	30
2675	-	10f. multicoloured	80	45
2676	-	14f. lt brn & brn	1·30	60

DESIGNS: 6f. Type **768** (centenary of literary review *La Jeune Belgique*); 6f.50," Liqueur Drinkers" (detail, Gustave van de Woestijne (inscr "Woestyne") (birth centenary); 9f. Fernand Severin (poet, 50th death anniv); 10f. Jan van Ruusbroec (mystic, 600th death anniv); 14f. Owl (La Pensee et les Hommes organization, 25th anniv).

769 Nativity (miniature from *Missale ad usum d. Leodensis*)

1981. Christmas.

2677	**769**	6f.50 brown and black	45	30

770 Mounted Gendarme, 1832

1981. "Solidarity". Multicoloured.

2678	9f.+4f. Type **770**	1·00	1·00
2679	20f.+7f. Carabinier	2·00	2·00
2680	40f.+20f. Mounted Guide, 1843	4·00	4·00

771 Cellist and Royal Conservatory of Music, Brussels

1982. 150th Anniversaries. Multicoloured.

2681	6f.50 Type **771**	45	30
2682	9f. Front of former Law Court, Brussels (anniv of judiciary)	70	30

772 Sectional View of Cyclotron

1982. Science. Multicoloured.

2683	6f. Type **772** (Installation of cyclotron at National Radio-elements Institute, Fleurus)	45	35
2684	14f. Telescope and galaxy (Royal Observatory)	1·00	45
2685	50f. Dr. Robert Koch and tubercle bacillus (centenary of discovery)	3·50	80

773 Billiards

1982. Sports. Multicoloured.

2686	6f.+2f. Type **773**	95	95
2687	9f.+4f. Cycling	1·30	1·30
2688	10f.+5f. Football	1·40	1·40
2689	50f.+14f. *Treaty of Rome* (yacht)	4·00	4·00

MS2690	105×100 mm. 25f. multicoloured (Type **773**); 25f. brown, yellow and black (as No. 2687); 25f. red, yellow and black (as No. 2688); 25f. multicoloured (as No. 2689)	8·75	8·25

774 Joseph Lemaire (after Jean Maillard)

1982. Birth Centenary of Joseph Lemaire (Minister of State and social reformer).

2691	**774**	6f.50 multicoloured	50	30

775 Voting (Universal Suffrage)

1982. Europa.

2692	**775**	10f. multicoloured	2·30	35
2693	-	17f. green, black and grey	4·00	60

DESIGN: 17f. Portrait and signature of Emperor Joseph II (Edict of Toleration).

1982. Surch **1 F**.

2694	**684**	1f. on 5f. green	10	10

777 17th-century Postal Messenger

1982. Stamp Day.

2695	**777**	10f. multicoloured	75	30

778 *Tower of Babel* (Brueghel the Elder)

1982. World Esperanto Congress, Antwerp.

2696	**778**	12f. multicoloured	95	45

1982. Tourist Publicity. As T **752**.

2697	7f. blue and light blue	65	35
2698	7f. black and green	65	35
2699	7f.50 brown and light brown	65	35
2700	7f.50 violet and lilac	65	35
2701	7f.50 black and grey	65	35
2702	7f.50 black and pink	65	35

DESIGNS—VERT: No. 2697, Gosselies Tower; 2698, Zwijveke Abbey, Termonde; 2701, Entrance gate, Grammont Abbey; 2702, Beveren pillory. HORIZ: No. 2699, Stavelot Abbey; 2700, Abbey ruins, Villers-la-Ville.

780 Louis Paul Boon (writer)

1982. Cultural Anniversaries.

2707	**780**	7f. black, red and grey	45	30
2708	-	10f. multicoloured	70	30
2709	-	12f. multicoloured	95	45
2710	-	17f. multicoloured	1·70	45

DESIGNS: 7f. Type **780** (70th birth anniv); 10f. *Adoration of the Shepherds* (detail of Portinari retable) (Hugo van der Goes, 500th death anniv); 12f. Michel de Ghelderode (dramatist, 20th death anniv); 17f. *Motherhood* (Pierre Paulus, birth centenary (1981)).

781 Abraham Hans

1982. Birth Centenary of Abraham Hans (writer).

2711	**781**	17f. black, turquoise and blue	1·10	35

782 Children playing Football

1982. "Philately for the Young". Scout Year.

2712	**782**	7f. multicoloured	65	35

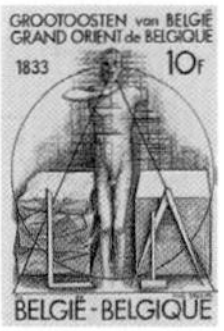

783 Masonic Emblems

1982. 150th Anniv of Belgium Grand Orient (Freemasonry Lodge).

2713	**783**	10f. yellow and black	75	30

784 Star over Village

1982. Christmas.

2714	**784**	10f.+1f. multicoloured	80	30

785 Cardinal Cardijn

1982. Birth Centenary of Cardinal Joseph Cardijn.

2715	**785**	10f. multicoloured	80	10

786 King Baudouin

787 King Baudouin

1982

2716	**786**	10f. blue	95	10
2717	**786**	11f. brown	1·20	10
2718	**786**	12f. green	3·00	60
2719	**786**	13f. red	1·30	10
2720	**786**	14f. black	1·20	10
2721	**786**	15f. red	2·00	35
2722	**786**	20f. blue	2·00	10
2723	**786**	22f. purple	3·00	1·20
2724	**786**	23f. green	3·00	60
2725	**786**	24f. grey	2·30	35
2726	**786**	25f. blue	2·50	30
2727	**786**	30f. brown	2·40	10
2728	**786**	40f. red	4·00	10
2729	**787**	50f. light brown, brown and black	5·75	10
2730	**787**	100f. blue, deep blue and black	16·00	25
2731	**787**	200f. light green, green and deep green	34·00	85

788 St. Francis preaching to the Birds

1982. 800th Birth Anniv of St. Francis of Assisi.

2736	**788**	20f. multicoloured	1·50	60

789 Messenger handing Letter to King in the Field

1982. "Belgica 82" Postal History Exhibition. Multicoloured.

2737		7f.+2f. Type **789**	60	60
2738		7f.50+2f.50 Messenger, Basel (vert)	70	70
2739		10f.+3f. Messenger, Nuremburg (vert)	85	85
2740		17f.+7f. Imperial courier, 1750 (vert)	1·60	1·60
2741		20f.+9f. Imperial courier, 1800	1·90	1·90
2742		25f.+10f. Belgian postman, 1886	2·20	2·20
MS2743		123×89 mm. 50f.+25f. Mail coach (48×37 mm)	5·25	5·25

790 Emblem

1983. 50th Anniv of Caritas Catholica Belgica.

2744	**790**	10f.+2f. red and grey	95	95

791 Horse Tram

1983. Trams. Multicoloured.

2745		7f.50 Type **791**	80	40
2746		10f. Electric tram	1·20	35
2747		50f. Tram with trolley (invented by K. van de Poele)	4·50	70

792 Mountaineer

1983. Belgian Red Cross. Multicoloured.

2748		12f.+3f. Type **792**	1·20	1·20
2749		20f.+5f. Walker	2·00	2·00

793 Brussels Buildings, Open Periodicals and Globe

1983. 24th International Periodical Press Federation World Congress, Brussels.

2750	**793**	20f. multicoloured	1·50	60

794 Woman at Work

1983. Women.

2751	**794**	8f. multicoloured	80	35
2752	-	11f. multicoloured	95	30
2753	-	20f. yellow, brown & bl	1·70	60

DESIGNS: 11f. Woman at home; 20f. Woman manager.

795 Graphic Representation of Midi Railway Station, Brussels

1983. Stamp Day. World Communications Year.

2754	**795**	11f. black, red and blue	95	30

796 Procession of the Holy Blood

1983. Procession of the Holy Blood, Bruges.

2755	**796**	8f. multicoloured	65	35

797 *The Man in the Street*

1983. Europa. Paintings by Paul Delvaux. Multicoloured.

2756		11f. Type **797**	1·70	35
2757		20f. *Night Trains* (horiz)	3·50	70

798 Hot-air Balloon over Town

1983. Bicentenary of Manned Flight. Multicoloured.

2758		11f. Type **798**	80	30
2759		22f. Hot-air balloon over countryside	1·70	70

799 Church of Our Lady, Hastiere

1983. Tourist Publicity. Multicoloured.

2760		8f. Type **799**	75	35
2761		8f. Tumulus, Landen	75	35
2762		8f. Park, Mouscron	75	35
2763		8f. Wijnendale Castle, Torhout	75	35

800 Milkmaid

1983. Tineke Festival, Heule.

2764	**800**	8f. multicoloured	65	35

801 Plaque on Wall

1983. European Small and Medium-sized Industries and Crafts Year.

2765	**801**	11f. yellow, black & red	85	30

802 Rainbow and Child

1983. "Philately for the Young". 20th Anniv of Queen Fabiola Village No. 1 (for handicapped people).

2766	**802**	8f. multicoloured	65	30

803 Textiles

1983. Belgian Exports (1st series). Multicoloured.

2767		10f. Type **803**	95	35
2768		10f. Steel beams (metallurgy)	95	35
2769		10f. Diamonds	95	35

See also Nos. 2777/80.

804 Conscience (after wood engraving by Nelly Degouy)

1983. Death Centenary of Hendrik Conscience (writer).

2770	**804**	20f. black and green	1·60	45

805 "Madonna" (Jef Wauters)

1983. Christmas.

2771	**805**	11f.+1f. multicoloured	95	95

806 2nd Foot Regiment

1983. "Solidarity". Military Uniforms. Multicoloured.

2772		8f.+2f. Type **806**	85	85
2773		11f.+2f. Lancer	1·50	1·50
2774		50f.+12f. Grenadier	4·25	4·25

1983. King Leopold III Commemoration.

2775	**155**	11f. black	85	30

807 Free University of Brussels

1984. 150th Anniv of Free University of Brussels.

2776	**807**	11f. multicoloured	95	25

1984. Belgian Exports (2nd series). As T **803**. Multicoloured.

2777		11f. Retort and test tubes (chemicals)	95	35
2778		11f. Combine harvester (agricultural produce)	95	35
2779		11f. Ship, coach and electric commuter train (transport)	95	35
2780		11f. Atomic emblem and computer terminal (new technology)	95	35

808 Albert I

1984. 50th Death Anniv of King Albert I.

2781	**808**	8f. black and stone	70	35

809 Judo

1984. Olympic Games, Los Angeles. Multicoloured.

2782		8f.+2f. Type **809**	70	70
2783		12f.+3f. Windsurfing (vert)	1·20	1·20
MS2784		125×90 mm. 10f. Archery; 24f. Dressage	2·50	2·50

810 Releasing Doves

1984. 25th Anniv of Movement without a Name.
2785 **810** 12f. multicoloured 95 30

811 Clasped Hands

1984. 50th Anniv of National Lottery.
2786 **811** 12f.+3f. multicoloured 1·20 1·20

812 St. John Bosco with Children

1984. 50th Anniv of Canonization of St. John Bosco (founder of Salesians).
2787 **812** 8f. multicoloured 70 30

813 Bridge

1984. Europa. 25th Anniv of European Posts and Telecommunications Conference.
2788 **813** 12f. red and black 1·50 30
2789 **813** 22f. blue and black 3·25 60

814 Leopold II 1884 10c. Stamp

1984. Stamp Day.
2790 **814** 12f. multicoloured 1·00 30

815 Dove and Pencils

1984. Second European Parliament Elections.
2791 **815** 12f. multicoloured 1·00 30

816 Shako

1984. 150th Anniv of Royal Military School.
2792 **816** 22f. multicoloured 1·70 50

817 Church of Our Lady of the Chapel, Brussels

1984. Tourist Publicity. Multicoloured.
2793 10f. Type **817** 85 40
2794 10f. St. Martin's Church and lime tree, Montigny-le-Tilleul 85 40
2795 10f. Belfry and Town Hall, Tielt (vert) 85 40

818 Curious Masks (detail, James Ensor)

1984. Inaug of Brussels Modern Art Museum.
2796 **818** 8f.+2f. multicoloured 85 85
2797 - 12f.+3f. multicoloured 1·50 1·50
2798 - 22f.+5f. multicoloured 2·00 2·00
2799 - 50f.+13f. grn, bl & blk 4·75 4·75
DESIGNS: 12f. *The Empire of Lights* (detail, Rene Magritte); 22f. *The End* (detail, Jan Cox); 50f. *Rhythm No. 6* (Jo Delahaut).

819 Symbolic Design

1984. 50th Anniv of Chirojeugd (Christian youth movement).
2800 **819** 10f. yellow, violet & bl 85 40

820 Averbode Abbey

1984. Abbeys.
2801 **820** 8f. green and brown 65 40
2802 - 22f. brown & dp brown 1·70 65
2803 - 24f. green & light green 1·70 65
2804 - 50f. lilac and brown 4·00 85
DESIGNS—VERT: 22f. Chimay; 24f. Rochefort. HORIZ: 50f. Affligem.

821 Smurf as Postman

1984. "Philately for the Young".
2805 **821** 8f. multicoloured 1·50 45

822 Child collecting Flowers

1984. Children.
2806 10f.+2f. Type **822** 95 95
2807 12f.+3f. Children with globe 1·20 1·20
2808 15f.+3f. Child on merry-go-round 1·40 1·40

823 Meulemans

1984. Birth Cent of Arthur Meulemans (composer).
2809 **823** 12f. black and orange 1·00 30

824 Three Kings

1984. Christmas.
2810 **824** 12f.+1f. multicoloured 1·20 1·20

825 St. Norbert

1985. 850th Death Anniv of St. Norbert.
2811 **825** 22f. brown & lt brown 1·80 60

826 *Virgin of Louvain* (attr. Jan Gossaert)

1985. "Europalia 85 Espana" Festival.
2812 **826** 12f. multicoloured 1·00 30

827 Press Card in Hatband

1985. Cent of Professional Journalists Association.
2814 **827** 9f. multicoloured 75 30

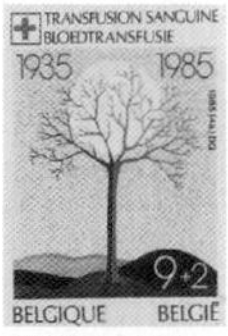

828 Blood System as Tree

1985. Belgian Red Cross. Blood Donations.
2815 **828** 9f.+2f. multicoloured 95 95
2816 - 23f.+5f. red, blue and black 2·20 2·20
DESIGN: 23f. Two hearts.

829 *Sophrolaelio cattleya* "Burlingama"

1985. Ghent Flower Festival. Orchids. Multicoloured.
2817 12f. Type **829** 95 30
2818 12f. Phalaenopsis "Malibu" 95 30
2819 12f. Tapeu orchid ("Vanda coerulea") 95 30

830 Pope John Paul II

1985. Visit of Pope John Paul II.
2820 **830** 12f. multicoloured 95 30

831 Rising Sun behind Chained Gates

1985. Centenary of Belgian Workers' Party.
2821 9f. Type **831** 70 40
2822 12f. Broken wall, flag and rising sun 95 30

832 Jean de Bast (engraver)

1985. Stamp Day.
2823 **832** 12f. blue 95 30

834 Class 18 Steam Locomotive, 1896

1985. Public Transport Year. Multicoloured.
2826 9f. Type **834** 80 35
2827 12f. Locomotive *Elephant*, 1835 95 30
2828 23f. Class 23 tank engine, 1904 1·90 70
2829 24f. Class I Pacific locomotive, 1935 1·90 70
MS2830 150×100 mm. 50f. Class 27 electric locomotive, 1979 4·75 4·75

835 Cesar Franck and Score

1985. Europa. Music Year. Multicoloured.
2831 12f. Type **835** 2·30 30
2832 23f. Queen and King with viola dressed in music score (Queen Elisabeth International Music Competition) 4·00 70

836 Planned Canal Lock, Strepy-Thieu

1985. Permanent International Navigation Congress Association Centenary Congress, Brussels. Multicoloured.
2833 23f. Type **836** 1·90 70
2834 23f. Aerial view of Zeebrugge harbour 1·90 70

837 Church of Our Lady's Assumption, Avernas-le-Bauduin

1985. Tourist Publicity. Multicoloured.
2835 12f. Type **837** 95 35
2836 12f. Saint Martin's Church, Marcinelle (horiz) 95 35
2837 12f. Roman tower and Church of old beguinage, Tongres 95 35
2838 12f. House, Wachtebeke (horiz) 95 35

838 Queen Astrid

1985. 50th Death Anniv of Queen Astrid.
2839 **838** 12f. lt brown & brown 1·00 30

839 Baking Matton Tart, Grammont

1985. Traditional Customs. Multicoloured.
2840 12f. Type **839** 1·00 30

2841	24f. Young people dancing on trumpet filled with flowers (cent of Red Youths, St. Lambert Cultural Circle, Hermalle-sous-Argenteau)	1·90	60

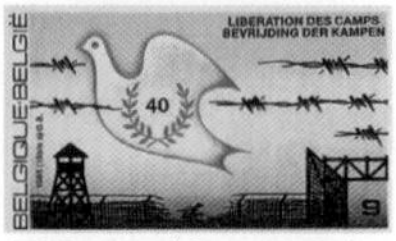

840 Dove and Concentration Camp

1985. 40th Anniv of Liberation. Multicoloured.

2842	9f. Type **840**	80	35
2843	23f. Battle of the Ardennes	1·90	70
2844	24f. Troops landing at Scheldt estuary	1·90	70

841 Hawfinch ("Appelvink – Gros Bec")

1985. Birds (1st series). Multicoloured.

2845	1f. Lesser spotted woodpecker ("Pic epeichette")	35	10
2846	2f. Eurasian tree sparrow ("Moineau friquet")	30	10
2847	3f. Type **841**	60	10
2847a	3f.50 European robin ("Rouge-gorge")	35	10
2848	4f. Bluethroat ("Gorge-bleue")	45	10
2848a	4f.50 Common stonechat ("Traquet patre")	50	25
2849	5f. Eurasian nuthatch ("Sittelle torche-pot")	45	10
2850	6f. Northern bullfinch ("Bouvreuil")	70	10
2851	7f. Blue tit ("Mesange bleue")	70	25
2852	8f. River kingfisher ("Martin-pecheur")	80	10
2853	9f. Eurasian goldfinch ("Chardonneret")	1·20	10
2854	10f. Chaffinch ("Pinson")	85	10

See also Nos. 3073/86 and 3306/23.

842 Claes and Fictional Character

1985. Birth Centenary of Ernest Claes (writer).

2855	**842**	9f. multicoloured	75	30

843 Youth

1985. "Philately for the Young". International Youth Year.

2856	**843**	9f. multicoloured	75	30

844 Trazegnies Castle

1985. "Solidarity". Castles. Multicoloured.

2857	9f.+2f. Type **844**	95	95
2858	12f.+3f. Laarne	1·20	1·20
2859	23f.+5f. Turnhout	2·00	2·00
2860	50f.+12f. Colonster	4·00	4·00

845 Miniature from *Book of Hours of Duc de Berry*

1985. Christmas.

2861	**845**	12f.+1f. multicoloured	1·00	1·00

846 King Baudouin and Queen Fabiola

1985. Royal Silver Wedding.

2862	**846**	12f. grey, blue and deep blue	1·20	30

847 Map and 1886 25c. Stamp

1986. Centenary of First Independent State of Congo Stamp.

2863	**847**	10f. blue, grey & dp blue	1·60	35

848 Giants and Belfry, Alost

1986. Carnivals. Multicoloured.

2864	9f. Type **848**	70	40
2865	12f. Clown, Binche	1·00	30

849 Dove as Hand holding Olive Twig

1986. International Peace Year.

2866	**849**	23f. multicoloured	2·00	60

850 Emblem

1986. Tenth Anniv of King Baudouin Foundation.

2867	**850**	12f.+3f. blue, light blue and grey	1·50	1·50

851 Virgin Mary

1986. *The Mystic Lamb* (altarpiece, Brothers Van Eyck). Multicoloured.

2868	9f.+2f. Type **851**	90	90
2869	13f.+3f. Christ in Majesty	1·30	1·30
2870	24f.+6f. St. John the Baptist	2·30	2·30
MS2871	92×150 mm. 50f.+12f. The Lamb (central panel) (48×37 mm)	9·00	9·00

852 Exhibits

1986. Stamp Day. 50th Anniv of Postal Museum, Brussels.

2872	**852**	13f. multicoloured	1·10	30

853 Living and Dead Fish and Graph

1986. Europa. Multicoloured.

2873	13f. Type **853**	1·90	30
2874	24f. Living and dead trees and graph	3·75	65

854 Malinois Shepherd Dog

1986. Belgian Dogs. Multicoloured.

2875	9f. Type **854**	85	40
2876	13f. Tervuren shepherd dog	1·30	30
2877	24f. Groenendael cattle dog	2·20	60
2878	26f. Flanders cattle dog	2·30	60

855 St. Ludger Church, Zele

1986. Tourist Publicity.

2879	**855**	9f. brown and flesh	70	35
2880	-	9f. red and pink	70	35
2881	-	13f. green & light green	1·10	35
2882	-	13f. black and green	1·10	35
2883	-	13f. blue and azure	1·10	35
2884	-	13f. brown & lt brown	1·10	35

DESIGNS—VERT: No. 2880, Town Hall, Wavre; 2882, Chapel of Our Lady of the Dunes, Bredene. HORIZ: 2881, Water-mills, Zwalm; 2883, Chateau Licot, Viroinval; 2884, Chateau d'Eynebourg, La Calamine.

856 Boy, Broken Skateboard and Red Triangle

1986. "Philately for the Young". 25th International Festival of Humour, Knokke.

2885	**856**	9f. black, green & red	70	40

857 Constant Permeke (artist)

1986. Celebrities. Multicoloured.

2886	9f. Type **857** (birth centenary)	70	35
2887	13f. Michael Edmond de Selys-Longchamps (naturalist)	1·20	35
2888	24f. Felix Timmermans (writer) (birth cent)	2·10	60
2889	26f. Maurice Careme (poet)	2·20	60

858 Academy Building, Ghent

1986. Centenary of Royal Academy for Dutch Language and Literature.

2890	**858**	9f. blue	70	35

859 Hops, Glass of Beer and Barley

1986. Belgian Beer.

2891	**859**	13f. multicoloured	1·20	30

860 Symbols of Provinces and National Colours

1986. 150th Anniv of Provincial Councils.

2892	**860**	13f. multicoloured	1·10	30

861 Lenoir Hydrocarbon Carriage, 1863

1986. "Solidarity". Cars. Multicoloured.

2893	9f.+2f. Type **861**	90	90
2894	13f.+3f. Pipe de Tourisme saloon, 1911	1·30	1·30
2895	24f.+6f. Minerva 22 h.p. coupe, 1930	2·40	2·40
2896	26f.+6f. FN 8 cylinder saloon, 1931	2·50	2·50

862 Snow Scene

1986. Christmas.

2897	**862**	13f.+1f. multicoloured	1·20	1·20

863 Tree and "100"

1986. Centenaries. Multicoloured.

2898	9f. Type **863** (Textile Workers Christian Union)	70	40
2899	13f. Tree and "100" (Christian Unions)	1·10	30

864 Corneel Heymans

1987. Belgian Red Cross. Nobel Physiology and Medicine Prize Winners. Each black, red and stone.

2900	13f.+3f. Type **864**	1·50	1·50
2901	24f.+6f. Albert Claude	2·75	2·75

865 Emblem

1987. "Flanders Technology International" Fair.

2902	**865**	13f. multicoloured	1·10	30

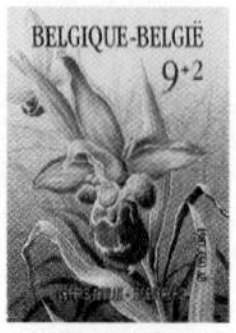

866 Bee Orchid

1987. European Environment Year. Multicoloured.

2903	9f.+2f. Type **866**	1·10	1·10
2904	24f.+6f. Small horse-shoe bat	2·40	2·40

2905		26f.+6f. Peregrine falcon (*Slechtvalk–Faucan Pelerin*)	2·75	2·75

867 *Waiting* (detail of mural, Gustav Klimt)

1987. "Europalia 87 Austria" Festival.

2906	**867**	13f. multicoloured	1·10	30

868 Jakob Wiener (engraver)

1987. Stamp Day.

2907	**868**	13f. deep green and green	1·10	30

869 Penitents' Procession, Furnes

1987. Folklore Festivals. Multicoloured.

2908		9f. Type **869**	70	40
2909		13f. "John and Alice" (play), Wavre	1·10	30

870 Louvain-la-Neuve Church (Jean Cosse)

1987. Europa. Architecture. Multicoloured.

2910		13f. Type **870**	2·40	30
2911		24f. St.-Maartensdal (Regional Housing Association tower block), Louvain (Braem, de Mol and Moerkerke)	4·25	90

871 Statue of Gretry and Stage Set

1987. 20th Anniv of Wallonia Royal Opera.

2912	**871**	24f. multicoloured	2·10	70

872 Virelles Lake

1987. Tourist Publicity. Multicoloured.

2913		13f. St. Christopher's Church, Racour	1·10	30
2914		13f. Type **872**	1·10	30
2915		13f. Heimolen windmill, Keerbergen	1·10	30
2916		13f. Boondael Chapel	1·10	30
2917		13f. Statue of Jan Breydel and Pieter de Coninck, Bruges	1·10	30

873 Rowing

1987. Centenary of Royal Belgian Rowing Association (2918) and European Volleyball Championships (2919). Multicoloured.

2918		9f. Type **873**	70	40
2919		13f. Volleyball (27×37 mm)	1·10	30

874 Emblem

1987. Foreign Trade Year.

2920	**874**	13f. multicoloured	1·10	30

875 *Leisure Time* (P. Paulus)

1987. Centenary of Belgian Social Law.

2921	**875**	26f. multicoloured	2·10	65

876 Willy and Wanda (comic strip characters)

1987. "Philately for the Young".

2922	**876**	9f. multicoloured	2·10	60

878 Rixensart Castle

1987. "Solidarity". Castles. Multicoloured.

2928		9f.+2f. Type **878**	90	90
2929		13f.+3f. Westerlo	1·20	1·20
2930		26f.+5f. Fallais	2·40	2·40
2931		50f.+12f. Gaasbeek	4·50	4·50

879 *Madonna and Child* (Remi Lens)

1987. Christmas.

2932	**879**	13f.+1f. multicoloured	1·20	1·20

880 Cross and Road

1987. 50th Anniv of Yellow and White Cross (home nursing organization).

2933	**880**	9f.+2f. multicoloured	1·20	1·20

881 Newsprint ("Le Soir")

1987. Newspaper Centenaries.

2934	**881**	9f. multicoloured	85	35
2935	-	9f. black and brown	85	35

DESIGN—VERT: No. 2935, Type characters (*Het Laatste Nieuws* (1988)).

882 Lighthouse, *Snipe* (trawler) and Horse Rider in Sea

1988. The Sea. Multicoloured.

2936		10f. Type **882**	85	70
2937		10f. *Asannot* (trawler) and people playing on beach	85	70
2938		10f. Cross-channel ferry, yacht and bathing huts	85	70
2939		10f. Container ship, spotted redshank and oystercatcher	85	70

Nos. 2936/9 were issued together, *se-tenant*, forming a composite design.

883 *Flanders Alive* (cultural activities campaign)

1988. Regional Innovations.

2940	**883**	13f. multicoloured	1·10	30
2941	-	13f. black, yellow & red	1·10	30

DESIGN: No. 2941, "Operation Athena" emblem (technological advancement in Wallonia).

884 19th-century Postman (after James Thiriar)

1988. Stamp Day.

2942	**884**	13f. brown and cream	1·10	30

885 *Bengale Triomphant*

1988. Philatelic Promotion Fund. Illustrations from *60 Roses for a Queen* by Pierre-Joseph Redoute (1st series). Multicoloured.

2943		13f.+3f. Type **885**	1·50	1·50
2944		24f.+6f. *Centfeuille cristata*	2·40	2·40
MS2945		150×100 mm. 50f.+12f. White tea rose	8·50	8·50

See also Nos. 2979/**MS**2981, 3009/**MS**3011 and **MS**3025.

886 Non-polluting Motor

1988. Europa. Transport and Communications. Multicoloured.

2946		13f. Dish aerial	2·40	30
2947		24f. Type **886**	4·75	90

887 Table Tennis

1988. Olympic Games, Seoul. Multicoloured.

2948		9f.+2f. Type **887**	1·30	1·30
2949		13f.+3f. Cycling	1·50	1·50
MS2950		125×85 mm. 50f.+12f. Running	8·50	8·50

888 Amay Tower

1988. Tourist Publicity.

2951	**888**	9f. black and brown	85	35
2952	-	9f. black and blue	85	35
2953	-	9f. black, green and pink	85	35
2954	-	13f. black and pink	1·10	30
2955	-	13f. black and grey	1·10	30

DESIGNS—VERT: No. 2952, Lady of Hanswijk Basilica, Malines; 2954, Old Town Hall and village pump, Peer. HORIZ: No. 2953, St. Sernin's Church, Waimes; 2955, Basilica of Our Lady of Bon Secours, Peruwelz.

889 Monnet

1988. Birth Centenary of Jean Monnet (statesman).

2956	**889**	13f. black and cream	1·10	30

890 Tapestry (detail) and Academy Building

1988. 50th Annivs of Royal Belgian Academy of Medicine (2957) and Royal Belgian Academy of Sciences, Literature and Fine Arts (2958). Multicoloured.

2957		9f. Type **890**	70	35
2958		9f. Symbols of Academy and building	70	35

891 Antwerp Ethnographical Museum Exhibits

1988. Cultural Heritage. Multicoloured.

2959		9f. Type **891**	85	35
2960		13f. Tomb of Lord Gilles Othon and Jacqueline de Lalaing, St. Martin's Church, Trazegnies	1·10	30
2961		24f. Organ, St. Bartholomew's Church, Geraardsbergen	2·10	70
2962		26f. St. Hadelin's reliquary, St. Martin's Church, Vise	2·30	70

892 Spirou (comic strip character) and Stamp

1988. "Philately for the Young". 50th Anniv of "Spirou" (comic).

2963	**892**	9f. multicoloured	1·80	60

893 Jacques Brel (songwriter)

1988. "Solidarity". Death Anniversaries. Multicoloured.

2964		9f.+2f. Type **893** (10th)	1·50	1·50
2965		13f.+3f. Jef Denyn (carilloner) (47th)	1·50	1·50
2966		26f.+6f. Fr. Ferdinand Verbiest (astronomer) (300th)	2·40	2·40

894 "75"

1988. 75th Anniv of Belgian Giro Bank.

2967	**894**	13f. multicoloured	1·20	30

895 Winter Scene

1988. Christmas.

2968	**895**	9f. multicoloured	80	35

896 Standard Bearer and Guards of Royal Mounted Escort

1988. 50th Anniv of Royal Mounted Escort.

2969	**896**	13f. multicoloured	1·10	30

897 Wooden Press, 1600

1988. Printing Presses.

2970	**897**	9f. black, pink and blue	85	30
2971	-	24f. brown, pink and deep brown	1·90	65
2972	-	26f. green, pink and light green	2·10	60

DESIGNS—VERT: 24f. 18th-cent Stanhope metal letter-press. HORIZ: 26f. 19th-cent Krause lithographic press.

898 *Crucifixion of Christ* (detail, Rogier van der Weyden)

1989. Belgian Red Cross. Paintings. Multicoloured.

2973	9f.+2f. Type **898**	1·20	1·20
2974	13f.+3f. "Virgin and Child" (Gerard David)	1·70	1·70
2975	24f.+6f. "The Good Samaritan" (detail, Denis van Alsloot)	2·50	2·50

899 Marche en Famenne

1989. Lace-making Towns.

2976	**899**	9f. green, black & brown	85	40
2977	-	13f. blue, black & grey	1·10	30
2978	-	13f. red, black & grey	1·10	30

DESIGNS: No. 2977, Bruges; 2978, Brussels.

1989. Philatelic Promotion Fund. *60 Roses for a Queen* by Pierre-Joseph Redoute (2nd series). As T **885**. Multicoloured.

2979	13f.+5f. *Centfeuille unique melee de rouge*	1·50	1·50
2980	24f.+6f. *Bengale a grandes feuilles*	2·40	2·40
MS2981	150×100 mm. 50f.+17f. *Aime vibere*	8·50	8·50

900 Post-chaise and Mail Coach

1989. Stamp Day.

2982	**900**	13f. yellow, black & brn	1·00	30

901 Marbles

1989. Europa. Children's Games and Toys. Multicoloured.

2983	13f. Type **901**	2·20	30
2984	24f. Jumping-jack	3·75	70

902 Palette on Column

1989. 325th Anniv of Royal Academy of Fine Arts, Antwerp.

2985	**902**	13f. multicoloured	1·00	30

903 Brussels

1989. Third Direct Elections to European Parliament.

2986	**903**	13f. multicoloured	1·00	30

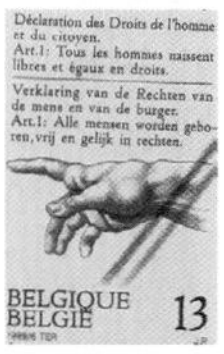

904 Hand (detail, "Creation of Adam", Michelangelo)

1989. Bicentenary of French Declaration of Rights of Man.

2987	**904**	13f. black, red and blue	1·00	30

905 St. Tillo's Church, Izegem

1989. Tourist Publicity. Multicoloured.

2988	9f. Type **905**	85	35
2989	9f. Logne Castle, Ferrieres (vert)	85	35
2990	13f. Antoing Castle (vert)	1·20	30
2991	13f. St. Laurentius's Church, Lokeren (vert)	1·20	30

906 Mallard

1989. Ducks. Multicoloured.

2992	13f. Type **906**	1·50	60
2993	13f. Green-winged teal ("Sarcelle d'Hiver")	1·50	60
2994	13f. Common shoveler ("Canard Souchet")	1·50	60
2995	13f. Pintail ("Canard Pilet")	1·50	60

907 *Shogun Uesugi Shigefusa* (Kamakura period wood figure)

1989. "Europalia 89 Japan" Festival.

2996	**907**	24f. multicoloured	1·90	70

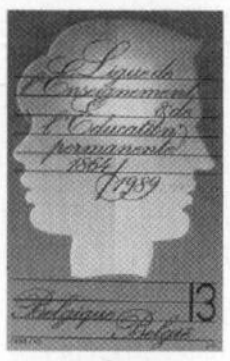

908 Profiles

1989. 125th Anniv of League of Teaching and Permanent Education.

2997	**908**	13f. multicoloured	1·00	30

909 Map

1989. 150th Anniv of Division of Limburg between Netherlands and Belgium.

2998	**909**	13f. multicoloured	1·00	30

910 Nibbs (comic strip character)

1989. "Philately for the Young".

2999	**910**	9f. multicoloured	1·50	50

911 Flower Beds in Greenhouse

1989. "Solidarity". Royal Greenhouses, Laeken. Multicoloured.

3000	9f.+3f. Statue and greenhouses (horiz)	1·20	1·20
3001	13f.+4f. Type **911**	1·60	1·60
3002	24f.+5f. External view of greenhouse	2·30	2·30
3003	26f.+6f. Trees in greenhouse	2·50	2·50

912 Treble Clef

1989. 50th Anniv of Queen Elisabeth Musical Chapel, Waterloo.

3004	**912**	24f.+6f. multicoloured	2·40	2·40

913 Army Musicians

1989. Christmas. Centenary of Salvation Army in Belgium.

3005	**913**	9f. multicoloured	80	30

914 Fr. Damien and Church

1989. Death Cent of Fr. Damien (missionary).

3006	**914**	24f. multicoloured	2·10	65

915 Fr. Daens

1989. 150th Birth Anniv of Fr. Adolf Daens (social reformer).

3007	**915**	9f. turquoise and green	70	30

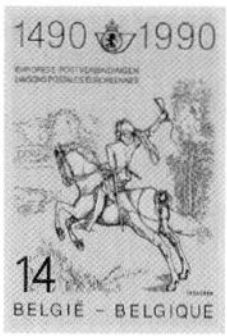

916 *Courier* (Albrecht Durer)

1990. 500th Anniv of Regular European Postal Services.

3008	**916**	14f. chocolate, buff and brown	1·10	30

1990. Philatelic Promotion Fund. *60 Roses for a Queen* by Pierre-Joseph Redoute (3rd series). As T **885**. Multicoloured.

3009	14f.+7f. *Bengale Desprez*	1·80	1·80
3010	25f.+12f. *Bengale Philippe*	3·00	3·00
MS3011	151×100 mm. 50f.+20f. *Maria Leonida*	8·50	8·50

917 *Iris florentina*

1990. Ghent Flower Show. Multicoloured.

3012	10f. Type **917**	85	50
3013	14f. *Cattleya harrisoniana*	1·20	35
3014	14f. *Lilium bulbiferum*	1·20	35

918 Emilienne Brunfaut (women's rights activist)

1990. International Women's Day.

3015	**918**	25f. red and black	2·10	85

919 Special Olympics

1990. Sporting Events. Multicoloured.

3016	10f. Type **919**	80	50
3017	14f. Football (World Cup football championship, Italy)	1·20	35
3018	25f. Disabled pictogram and ball (Gold Cup wheelchair basketball championship, Bruges)	1·90	70

920 Water, Tap and Heart

1990. 75th Anniv of Foundation of National Water Supply Society (predecessor of present water-supply companies).

3019	**920**	14f. multicoloured	1·10	30

921 *Postman Roulin* (Vincent van Gogh)

1990. Stamp Day.

3020	**921**	14f. multicoloured	1·10	30

922 Worker and Crowd

1990. Centenary of Labour Day.

3021	**922**	25f. brown, pink & black	2·10	85

923 Liege I Post Office

1990. Europa. Post Office Buildings.

3022	-	14f. black and blue	2·40	35
3023	**923**	25f. black and red	4·50	85

DESIGN—HORIZ: 14f. Ostend I Post Office.

924 Monument of the Lys, Courtrai

1990. 50th Anniv of the 18 Days Campaign (resistance to German invasion).

3024	**924**	14f. black, yellow & red	1·20	30

1990. "Belgica 90" International Stamp Exhibition, Brussels. *60 Roses for a Queen* by Pierre-Joseph Rerdoute (4th series). Sheet 189×120 mm containing vert designs as T **885**. Multicoloured.

MS3025	14f. Tricoloured rose; 14f. *Belle Rubanee*; 14f. *Mycrophylla*; 25f. *Amelie*; 25f. *Adelaide*; 25f. *Helene* (sold at 220f.)	36·00	36·00

925 Battle Scene

1990. 175th Anniv of Battle of Waterloo.

3026	**925**	25f. multicoloured	2·10	1·80

926 Berendrecht Lock, Antwerp

1990. Tourist Publicity. Multicoloured.

3027	10f. Type **926**	95	50
3028	10f. Procession of Bayard Steed, Termonde	95	50
3029	14f. St. Rolende's March, Gerpinnes (vert)	1·10	35
3030	14f. Lommel (1000th anniv)	1·10	35
3031	14f. St. Clement's Church, Watermael	1·10	35

927 King Baudouin

1990

3032	**927**	14f. multicoloured	1·30	25

928 Eurasian Perch

1990. Fishes. Multicoloured.

3033	14f. Type **928**	2·10	70
3034	14f. Eurasian minnow ("Vairon")	2·10	70
3035	14f. European bitterling ("Bouviere")	2·10	70
3036	14f. Three-spined stickle-back ("Epinoche")	2·10	70

929 Orchestra and Children

1990. "Solidarity". Multicoloured.

3037	10f.+2f. Type **929** (50th anniv of Jeunesses Musicales)	2·20	2·20
3038	14f.+3f. Count of Egmont (16th-century campaigner for religious tolerance) and Beethoven (composer of "Egmont" overture)	2·75	2·75
3039	25f.+6f. Jozef Cantre (sculptor) and sculptures (birth centenary)	3·75	3·75

930 Lucky Luke (comic strip character)

1990. "Philately for the Young".

3040	**930**	10f. multicoloured	1·80	60

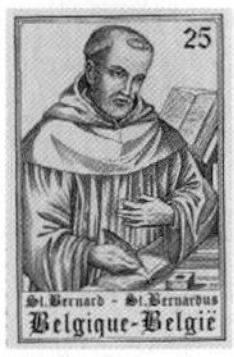

931 St. Bernard

1990. 900th Birth Anniv of St. Bernard (Abbot of Clairvaux and Church mediator).

3041	**931**	25f. black and flesh	2·10	70

932 *Pepingen, Winter 1977* (Jozef Lucas)

1990. Christmas.

3042	**932**	10f. multicoloured	85	30

933 *Self-portrait*

1990. 300th Death Anniv of David Teniers, the Younger (painter). Multicoloured.

3043	10f. Type **933**	85	35
3044	14f. *Dancers*	1·20	35
3045	25f. *Peasants playing Bowls outside Village Inn*	2·20	70

934 King Baudouin and Queen Fabiola (photograph by Valeer Vanbeckbergen)

1990. Royal 30th Wedding Anniversary.

3046	**934**	50f.+15f. mult	8·50	8·50

935 *Temptation of St. Anthony* (detail, Hieronymus Bosch)

1991. Belgian Red Cross. Paintings. Multicoloured.

3047	14f.+3f. Type **935**	2·75	2·75
3048	25f.+6f. *The Annunciation* (detail, Dirck Bouts)	4·00	4·00

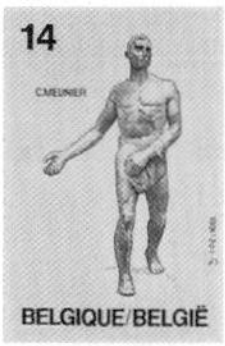

936 "The Sower" (detail of *Monument to Labour*, Brussels) (Constantin Meunier)

1991. 19th-Century Sculpture.

3049	**936**	14f. black & cinnamon	1·10	35
3050	-	25f. black and blue	1·80	70

DESIGN: 25f. Detail of Brabo Fountain, Antwerp (Jef Lambeaux).

937 Rhythmic Gymnastics (European Youth Olympic Days, Brussels)

1991. Sports Meetings.

3051	**937**	10f. grey, mauve & blk	80	30
3052	-	10f. grey, green & black	80	30

DESIGN: No. 3052, Korfball (Third World Championship, Belgium).

938 New Stamp Printing Office, Malines (Hugo van Hoecke)

1991. Stamp Day.

3053	**938**	14f. multicoloured	1·10	35

939 Cogwheels

1991. Centenary of Liberal Trade Union.

3054	**939**	25f. blue, light blue and deep blue	1·90	70

940 "Olympus 1" Communications Satellite

1991. Europa. Europe in Space. Multicoloured.

3055	14f. Type **940**	2·40	30
3056	25f. "Ariane 5" rocket carrying space shuttle *Hermes*	4·00	80

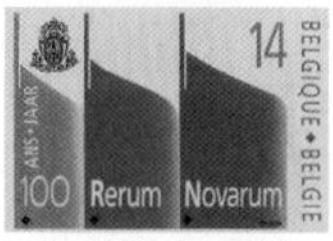

941 Leo XIII's Arms and Standard, and Christian Labour Movement Banners

1991. Centenary of "Rerum Novarum" (encyclical letter from Pope Leo XIII on workers' rights).

3057	**941**	14f. multicoloured	1·10	30

942 *Isabella of Portugal and Philip the Good* (anon)

1991. "Europalia 91 Portugal" Festival.

3058	**942**	14f. multicoloured	1·10	30

943 Neptune Grottoes, Couvin

1991. Tourist Publicity. Multicoloured.

3059	14f. Type **943**	1·10	35
3060	14f. Dieleghem Abbey, Jette	1·10	35
3061	14f. Niel Town Hall (vert)	1·10	35
3062	14f. Hautes Fagnes nature reserve	1·10	35
3063	14f. Giant Rolarius, Roeselare (vert)	1·10	35

944 King Baudouin (photograph by Dimitri Ardelean)

1991. 60th Birthday (1990) and 40th Anniv of Accession to Throne of King Baudouin.

3064	**944**	14f. multicoloured	2·20	30

945 Academy Building, Caduceus and Leopold I

1991. 150th Anniv of Royal Academy of Medicine.

3065	**945**	10f. multicoloured	80	35

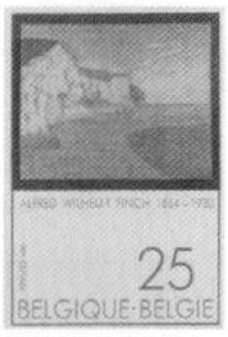

946 "The English Coast at Dover"

1991. 61st Death Anniv of Alfred Finch (painter and ceramic artist).

3066	**946**	25f. multicoloured	2·00	70

947 Death Cap

1991. Fungi. Multicoloured.

3067	14f. Type **947**	2·10	85
3068	14f. The Blusher (inscr "Golmotte")	2·10	85
3069	14f. Flaky-stemmed witches' mushroom (inscr "Bolet a pied rouge")	2·10	85
3070	14f. "Hygrocybe persistens" (inscr "Hygrophore jaune conique")	2·10	85

948 Hands reaching through Bars

1991. 30th Anniv of Amnesty International (3071) and 11th Anniv of Belgian Branch of Medecins sans Frontieres (3072). Multicoloured.

3071		25f. Type **948**	2·00	70
3072		25f. Doctor examining baby	2·00	70

1991. Birds (2nd series). As T **841**. Multicoloured.

3073		50c. Goldcrest ("Roitelet Huppe")	15	15
3074		1f. Redpoll ("Sizerin Flamme")	25	15
3075		2f. Blackbird ("Merle Noir")	25	15
3076		3f. Reed bunting ("Bruant des Roseaux")	50	15
3077		4f. Pied wagtail ("Bergeronette Grise")	45	15
3078		5f. Barn swallow ("Hirondelle de Cheminee")	45	15
3079		5f.50 Jay ("Geai des Chenes")	65	25
3080		6f. White-throated dipper ("Cincle Plongeur")	65	15
3081		6f.50 Sedge-warbler ("Phragmite des Jones")	65	25
3082		7f. Golden oriole ("Loriot")	75	15
3083		8f. Great tit ("Mesange Charbonniere")	75	15
3084		9f. Song thrush ("Grive Musicienne")	90	25
3085		10f. Western greenfinch ("Verdier")	95	25
3086		11f. Winter wren ("Troglodyte Mignon")	1·00	15
3087		13f. House sparrow ("Moineau Domestique")	1·30	15
3088		14f. Willow warbler ("Pouillot Fitis")	1·30	25
3088a		16f. Bohemian waxwing ("Jaseur Boreal")	1·60	15

949 Exhibition Emblem

1991. "Telecom 91" International Telecommuni- cations Exhibition, Geneva.

3089	**949**	14f. multicoloured	1·10	30

950 Blake and Mortimer in *The Yellow Mark* (Edgar P. Jacobs)

1991. "Philately for the Young". Comic Strips. Multicoloured.

3090		14f. Type **950**	2·00	1·30
3091		14f. Cori the ship boy in "The Ill-fated Voyage" (Bob de Moor)	2·00	1·30
3092		14f. *Cities of the Fantastic* (Francois Schuiten)	2·00	1·30
3093		14f. *Boule and Bill* (Jean Roba)	2·00	1·30

951 Charles Dekeukeleire

1991. "Solidarity". Film Makers.

3094	**951**	10f.+2f. black, brown and green	1·30	1·30
3095	-	14f.+3f. black, orange and brown	1·90	1·90
3096	-	25f.+6f. black, ochre and brown	3·50	3·50

DESIGNS: 14f. Jacques Ledoux; 25f. Jacques Feyder.

952 Printing Press forming "100" ("Gazet van Antwerpen")

1991. Newspaper Centenaries. Multicoloured.

3097	**952**	10f. black, lt grn & grn	80	30
3098	-	10f. yellow, blue & blk	80	30

DESIGN: No. 3098, Cancellation on "stamp" ("Het Volk").

953 *Our Lady rejoicing in the Child* (icon, Chevetogne Abbey)

1991. Christmas.

3099	**953**	10f. multicoloured	75	40

954 Mozart and Score

1991. Death Bicentenary of Wolfgang Amadeus Mozart (composer).

3100	**954**	25f. purple, bl & ultram	2·10	1·00

955 Speed Skating

1992. Olympic Games, Albertville and Barcelona. Multicoloured.

3101		10f.+2f. Type **955**	1·40	1·40
3102		10f.+2f. Baseball	1·40	1·40
3103		14f.+3f. Tennis (horiz)	1·90	1·90
3104		25f.+6f. Clay-pigeon shooting	3·50	3·50

956 Fire Hose and Service Emblem

1992. Fire Service.

3105	**956**	14f. multicoloured	1·10	30

957 Flames and Silhouette of Man

1992. The Resistance.

3106	**957**	14f. yellow, black & red	1·10	30

958 Tapestry and Carpet

1992. Prestige Occupations. Multicoloured.

3107		10f. Type **958**	75	45
3108		14f. Chef's hat and cutlery (10th anniv (1991) of Association of Belgian Master Chefs)	1·10	30
3109		27f. Diamond and "100" (centenary (1993) of Antwerp Diamond Club)	2·20	70

959 Belgian Pavilion and Exhibition Emblem

1992. "Expo '92" World's Fair, Seville.

3110	**959**	14f. multicoloured	1·10	30

960 King Baudouin

961

1992

3111	**960**	15f. red	1·10	15
3115	**960**	28f. green	2·50	70
3120	**961**	100f. green	9·50	65

962 Van Noten at Work

1992. Stamp Day. Tenth Death Anniv of Jean van Noten (stamp designer).

3124	**962**	15f. black and red	1·10	30

963 *White Magic No. VI*

1992. Original Art Designs for Stamps. Multicoloured.

3125		15f. Type **963**	1·10	40
3126		15f. *Colours* (horiz)	1·10	40

964 Compass Rose, Setting Sun and Harbour

1992. Europa. 500th Anniv of Discovery of America. Multicoloured.

3127		15f. Type **964**	2·50	45
3128		28f. Globe and astrolabe forming "500"	5·00	95

965 Faces of Different Colours

1992. Anti-racism.

3129	**965**	15f. grey, black & pink	1·10	30

966 *The Hamlet* (Jacob Smits)

1992. Belgian Paintings in Orsay Museum, Paris. Multicoloured.

3130		11f. Type **966**	80	40
3131		15f. *The Bath* (Alfred Stevens)	1·40	30
3132		30f. *Man at the Helm* (Theo van Rysselberghe)	2·50	90

967 Proud Margaret

1992. Folk Tales. Multicoloured.

3133		11f.+2f. Type **967**	1·60	1·60
3134		15f.+3f. Witches (*Les Macrales*)	2·20	2·20
3135		28f.+6f. Reynard the fox	3·75	3·75

968 Mannekin-Pis, Brussels

1992. Tourist Publicity. Multicoloured.

3136		15f. Type **968**	1·10	30
3137		15f. Former Landcommandery of Teutonic Order, Alden Biesen (now Flemish cultural centre) (horiz)	1·10	30
3138		15f. Andenne (1300th anniv)	1·10	30
3139		15f. Carnival revellers on Fools' Monday, Renaix (horiz)	1·10	30
3140		15f. Great Procession (religious festival), Tournai (horiz)	1·10	30

969 European Polecat

1992. Mammals. Multicoloured.

3141		15f. Type **969**	1·90	80
3142		15f. Eurasian red squirrel	1·90	80
3143		15f. Eurasian hedgehog	1·90	80
3144		15f. Common dormouse	1·90	80

970 Henri van der Noot, Jean van der Meersch and Jean Vonck

1992. 203rd Anniv of Brabant Revolution.

3145	**970**	15f. multicoloured	1·10	30

971 Arms of Thurn and Taxis

1992. 500th Anniv of Mention of Thurn and Taxis Postal Services in Lille Account Books.

3146	**971**	15f. multicoloured	1·10	30

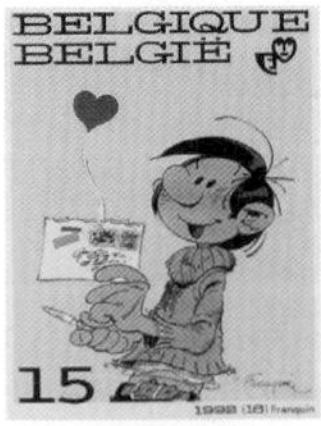

972 Gaston Lagaffe (cartoon character)

1992. "Philately for the Young".

3147	**972**	15f. multicoloured	1·50	45

973 Star, "B" and Map

1992. European Single Market.

3148	**973**	15f. multicoloured	1·10	40

974 Okapi

1992. 150th Anniv of Antwerp Zoo. Multicoloured.

3149	15f. Type **974**	1·10	40
3150	30f. Golden-headed tamarin	2·30	50

975 *Place Royale in Winter* (Luc de Decker)

1992. Christmas.

3151	**975**	11f. multicoloured	75	30

976 *Man with Pointed Hat* (Adriaen Brouwer)

1993. Belgian Red Cross. Paintings. Multicoloured.

3152	15f.+3f. Type **976**	2·40	2·40
3153	28f.+7f. *Nereid and Triton* (Peter Paul Rubens) (horiz)	4·75	4·75

977 Council of Leptines, 743

1993. Historical Events. Multicoloured.

3154	11f. Type **977**	75	40
3155	15f. Queen Beatrix and King Matthias I Corvinus of Hungary (detail of "Missale Romanum") (77×24 mm)	1·30	40
3156	30f. Battle scene (Battles of Neerwinden, 1673 and 1773)	2·50	75
MS3157	105×155 mm. 28f. Illustration from Matthias I Corvinus's *Missale Romanum*, 1485 (54×39 mm)	2·50	2·50

978 Town Hall

1993. Antwerp, European City of Culture. Multicoloured.

3158	15f. Panorama of Antwerp (76×24 mm)	1·30	30
3159	15f. Type **978**	1·30	30
3160	15f. "Study of Women's Heads and Male Torso" (Jacob Jordaens)	1·30	30
3161	15f. St. Job's altarpiece, Schoonbroek	1·30	30
3162	15f. "Angels" (stained glass window by Eugeen Yoors, Mother of God Chapel, Marie-Josee Institute, Elisabethville) (vert)	1·30	30

979 1893 2f. Stamp

1993. Stamp Day.

3163	**979**	15f. multicoloured	1·10	30

980 "Florence 1960" (Gaston Bertrand)

1993. Europa. Contemporary Art. Multicoloured.

3164	15f. Type **980**	1·30	30
3165	28f. *The Gig* (Constant Permeke)	2·50	75

981 Red Admiral (*Vanessa atalanta*)

1993. Butterflies. Multicoloured.

3166	15f. Type **981**	1·10	40
3167	15f. Purple emperor (*Apatura iris*)	1·10	40
3168	15f. Peacock (*Inachis io*)	1·10	40
3169	15f. Small tortoiseshell (*Aglais urticae*)	1·10	40

982 Knot

1993. 150th Anniv of Alumni of Free University of Brussels Association.

3170	**982**	15f. blue and black	1·10	30

983 Mayan Warrior (statuette)

1993. "Europalia 93 Mexico" Festival.

3171	**983**	15f. multicoloured	1·10	30

984 Ommegang, Brussels

1993. Folklore Festivals. Multicoloured.

3172	11f. Type **984**	95	45
3173	15f. Royale Moncrabeau, Namur	1·10	30
3174	28f. Stilt-walkers, Merchtem (vert)	1·90	75

985 La Hulpe Castle

1993. Tourist Publicity.

3175	**985**	15f. black and blue	1·10	30
3176	-	15f. black and lilac	1·10	30
3177	-	15f. black and grey	1·10	30
3178	-	15f. black and pink	1·10	30
3179	-	15f. black and green	1·10	30

DESIGNS—HORIZ: No. 3176, Cortewalle Castle, Beveren; 3177, Jehay Castle; 3179, Raeren Castle. VERT: No. 3178, Arenberg Castle, Heverlee.

986 Emblem

1993. Second International Triennial Textile Exhibition, Tournai.

3180	**986**	15f. blue, red and black	1·10	30

987 Presidency Emblem

1993. Belgian Presidency of European Community Council.

3181	**987**	15f. multicoloured	1·10	30

988 Magritte

1993. 25th Death Anniv (1992) of Rene Magritte (artist).

3182	**988**	30f. multicoloured	2·20	90

989 King Baudouin

1993. King Baudouin Commemoration.

3183	**989**	15f. black and blue	1·30	25

990 Red and White Cat

1993. Cats. Multicoloured.

3184	15f. Type **990**	1·40	75
3185	15f. Tabby and white cat standing on rock	1·40	75
3186	15f. Silver tabby lying on wall	1·40	75
3187	15f. Tortoiseshell and white cat sitting by gardening tools	1·40	75

991 Highlighted Cancer Cell

1993. Anti-cancer Campaign.

3188	**991**	15f.+3f. multicoloured	1·90	1·90

992 Frontispiece

1993. 450th Anniv of *De Humani Corporis Fabrica* (treatise on human anatomy) by Andreas Vesalius.

3189	**992**	15f. black, brown & red	1·10	30

993 Natacha (cartoon character)

1993. "Philately for the Young".

3190	**993**	15f. multicoloured	1·40	50

994 Sun's Rays

1993. 50th Anniv of Publication of *Le Faux Soir* (resistance newspaper).

3191	**994**	11f. multicoloured	80	50

995 *Madonna and Child* (statue, Our Lady of the Chapel, Brussels)

1993. Christmas.

3192	**995**	11f. multicoloured	75	30

996 Child looking at Globe

1993. Children's Town Councils.

3193	**996**	15f. multicoloured	1·10	30

997 King Albert II

998 King Albert II

1993

3194	**997**	16f. multicoloured	1·70	15
3195	**997**	16f. turquoise and blue	1·30	20
3196	**997**	20f. brown and stone	1·70	25
3197	**997**	30f. purple and mauve	1·90	25
3198	**997**	32f. orange and yellow	2·20	15
3199	**997**	40f. red and mauve	3·00	15
3200	**997**	50f. myrtle and green	5·25	25
3201	**998**	100f. multicoloured	7·50	45
3202	**998**	200f. multicoloured	16·00	65

999 *Ma Toute Belle* (Serge Vandercam)

1994. Painters' Designs. Multicoloured.

3210	16f. Type **999**	1·10	40
3211	16f. *The Malleable Darkness* (Octave Landuyt) (horiz)	1·10	40

1000 Olympic Flames and Rings

1994. Sports. Multicoloured.

3212	16f.+3f. Type **1000** (cent of International Olympic Committee)	2·20	2·20
3213	16f.+3f. Footballers (World Cup Football Championship, U.S.A.)	2·20	2·20
3214	16f.+3f. Skater (Winter Olympic Games, Lillehammer, Norway)	2·20	2·20

1001 Hanriot HD-1

1994. Biplanes. Multicoloured.

3215	13f. Type **1001**	1·10	45
3216	15f. Spad XIII	1·30	40
3217	30f. Schrenck FBA.H flying boat	2·20	75
3218	32f. Stampe SV-4B biplane	2·30	65

1002 Masthead of *Le Jour-Le Courrier* (centenary)

1994. Newspaper Anniversaries. Multicoloured.

3219	16f. Type **1002**	1·10	40
3220	16f. Masthead of *La Wallonie* (75th anniv) (horiz)	1·10	40

1003 *Fall of the Golden Calf* (detail, Fernand Allard l'Olivier)

1994. Centenary of Charter of Quaregnon (social charter).

3221	**1003**	16f. multicoloured	1·10	45

1004 1912 5f. Stamp

1994. Stamp Day. 60th Death Anniv of King Albert I.

3222	**1004**	16f. purple, mauve & bl	1·10	40

1005 Reconciliation of Duke John I and Arnold, Squire of Wezemaal

1994. 700th Death Anniv of John I, Duke of Brabant. Illustrations from 15th-century *Brabantse Yeesten*. Multicoloured.

3223	13f. Type **1005**	95	45
3224	16f. Tournament at wedding of his son John to Margaret of York, 1290	1·10	40
3225	30f. Battle of Woeringen (77×25 mm)	2·40	90

1006 Georges Lemaitre (formulator of expanding Universe and of "big bang" theory)

1994. Europa. Discoveries and Inventions. Multicoloured.

3226	16f. Type **1006**	1·30	40
3227	30f. Gerardus Mercator (inventor of Mercator projection in cartography)	2·50	90

1007 Father Damien (missionary and leprosy worker)

1994. Visit of Pope John Paul II. Multicoloured.

3228	16f. Type **1007** (beatification)	1·10	30
3229	16f. St. Mutien-Marie (5th anniv of canonization)	1·10	30

1008 St. Peter's Church, Bertem

1994. Tourist Publicity. Multicoloured.

3230	16f. Type **1008**	1·10	40
3231	16f. St. Bavo's Church, Kanegem (vert)	1·10	40
3232	16f. Royal St. Mary's Church, Schaarbeek	1·10	40
3233	16f. St. Gery's Church, Aubechies	1·10	40
3234	16f. Sts. Peter and Paul's Church, St.-Severin en Condroz (vert)	1·10	40

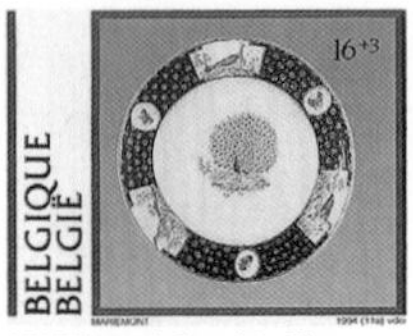

1009 Tournai Porcelain Plate from Duke of Orleans Service (Mariemont Museum)

1994. Museum Exhibits. Multicoloured.

3235	16f.+3f. Type **1009**	1·90	1·90
3236	16f.+3f. Etterbeek porcelain coffee cup and saucer (Louvain Municipal Museum)	1·90	1·90
MS3237	125×90 mm. 50f.+11f. Delft containers (Pharmacy Museum, Maaseik)	9·50	9·50

1010 Guillame Lekeu (composer)

1994. Anniversaries. Multicoloured.

3238	16f. Type **1010** (death cent)	1·10	40
3239	16f. Detail of painting by Hans Memling (500th death anniv)	1·10	40

1011 Generals Crerar, Montgomery and Bradley and Allied Troops

1994. 50th Anniv of Liberation.

3240	**1011**	16f. multicoloured	1·30	40

1012 Marsh Marigold (*Caltha palustris*)

1994. Flowers. Multicoloured.

3241	16f. Type **1012**	1·60	75
3242	16f. White helleborine ("Cephalanthera damasonium")	1·60	75
3243	16f. Sea bindweed ("Calystegia soldanella")	1·60	75
3244	16f. Broad-leaved helleborine ("Epipactis helleborine")	1·60	75

1013 Cubitus (cartoon character)

1994. "Philately for the Young".

3245	**1013**	16f. multicoloured	1·60	50

1014 Simenon and Bridge of Arches, Liege

1994. Fifth Death Anniv of Georges Simenon (novelist).

3246	**1014**	16f. multicoloured	1·60	40

The depiction of the bridge alludes to Simenon's first novel *Au Pont des Arches*.

1015 Deaf Man and Butterfly

1994. "Solidarity".

3247	**1015**	16f.+3f. mult	1·50	1·50

1016 Santa Claus on Rooftop

1994. Christmas.

3248	**1016**	13f. multicoloured	95	40

1017 Field and Flax Knife (Flax Museum, Courtrai)

1995. Museums. Multicoloured.

3249	16f.+3f. Type **1017**	1·40	1·40
3250	16f.+3f. River and pump (Water and Fountain Museum, Genval)	1·40	1·40
MS3251	125×90 mm. 34f.+6f. Mask (International Carnival and Mask Museum, Binche)	3·75	3·75

The premium was for the promotion of philately.

1018 Emblem

1995. Anniversaries. Anniversary emblems.

3252	**1018**	16f. red, blue & black	1·10	40
3253	-	16f. multicoloured	1·10	40
3254	-	16f. multicoloured	1·10	40
3255	-	16f. red, black & brown	1·10	40

ANNIVERSARIES: No. 3252, 50th anniv of August Vermeylen Fund; 3253, Centenary of Touring Club of Belgium; 3254, Centenary of Federation of Belgian Enterprises; 3255, 50th anniv of Social Security in Belgium.

1019 "*ibiscus rosa-sinensis*

1995. Ghent Flower Show. Multicoloured.

3256	13f. Type **1019**	95	50
3257	16f. Azalea	1·30	40
3258	30f. Fuchsia	2·20	75

1020 Crossword Puzzle

1995. Games and Pastimes. Multicoloured.

3259	13f. Type **1020**	95	45
3260	16f. King (chess piece)	1·10	40
3261	30f. Scrabble	2·20	75
3262	34f. Queen (playing cards)	2·30	95

1021 Frans de Troyer (promoter of thematic philately)

1995. Post Day.

3263	**1021**	16f. black, stone & orge	1·10	40

1022 Watch Tower and Barbed Wire Fence

1995. Europa. Peace and Freedom. Multicoloured.

3264	16f. Type **1022** (50th anniv of liberation of concentration camps)	2·50	90
3265	30f. Nuclear cloud (25th anniv of Non-Proliferation Treaty)	4·50	90

1023 Soldiers of the Irish Brigade and Memorial Cross

1995. 250th Anniv of Battle of Fontenoy.

3266	**1023**	16f. multicoloured	1·30	30

1024 U.N. Emblem

1995. 50th Anniv of U.N.O.

3267	**1024**	16f. multicoloured	1·10	40

1025 "Sauvagemont, Maransart" (Pierre Alechinsky)

1995. Artists' Philatelic Creations.

3268	**1025**	16f. red, black & yellow	1·10	40
3269	-	16f. multicoloured	1·10	40

DESIGN: No. 3269, "Telegram-style" (Pol Mara).

1026 Paul Cauchie (Brussels)

1995. Tourist Publicity. Art nouveau house facades by named architects. Multicoloured.

3270	16f. Type **1026**	1·10	40
3271	16f. Frans Smet-Verhas (Antwerp)	1·10	40
3272	16f. Paul Jaspar (Liege)	1·10	40

1027 Anniversary Emblem

1995. Cent of Royal Belgian Football Assn.

3273	**1027**	16f.+4f. mult	1·60	1·60

1028 *Mercator* (Belgian cadet barque)

1995. Sailing Ships. Multicoloured.

3274	16f. Type **1028**	1·40	75
3275	16f. *"ruzenshern* (Russian cadet barque) (inscr "Kruzenstern")	1·40	75
3276	16f. *Sagres II* (Portuguese cadet barque)	1·40	75

3277	16f. *Amerigo Vespucci* (Italian cadet ship)	1·40	75

1029 Princess Astrid and Globe

1995. Red Cross. Multicoloured.

3278	16f.+3f. Type **1029** (Chair-woman)	1·40	1·40
3279	16f.+3f. Wilhelm Rontgen (discoverer of X-rays) and X-ray of hand	1·40	1·40
3280	16f.+3f. Louis Pasteur (chemist) and microscope	1·40	1·40

1030 1908 Minerva

1995. Motorcycles. Multicoloured.

3281	13f. Type **1030**	95	50
3282	16f. 1913 FN (vert)	1·10	40
3283	30f. 1929 La Mondiale	2·00	75
3284	32f. 1937 Gillet (vert)	2·20	65

1031 Sammy (cartoon character)

1995. "Philately for the Young".

3285	**1031**	16f. multicoloured	1·40	45

1032 Couple and Condom in Wrapper

1995. "Solidarity". AIDS Awareness.

3286	**1032**	16f.+4f. mult	1·40	1·40

1033 King Albert II and Queen Paola (photograph by Christian Louis)

1995. King's Day.

3287	**1033**	16f. multicoloured	1·30	40

1034 *Nativity* (from 15th-century breviary)

1995. Christmas.

3288	**1034**	13f. multicoloured	95	40

1035 Puppets, Walloon Museum, Liege

1996. Museums. Multicoloured.

3289	16f.+4f. Type **1035**	1·40	1·40
3290	16f.+4f. National Gin Museum, Hasselt	1·40	1·40

MS3291 126×90 mm. 34f.+6f. *Fall of Saul* (detail of title panel), Butchers' Guild Hall Museum, Antwerp	3·75	3·75

The premium was used for the promotion of philately.

1036 *Emile Mayrisch*

1996. 70th Death Anniv of Theo van Rysselberghe (painter). No value expressed.

3292	**1036**	A (16f.) mult	1·30	40

1037 "LIBERALISME"

1996. 150th Anniv of Liberal Party.

3293	**1037**	16f. dp blue, violet & bl	1·30	40

1038 Oscar Bonnevalle (stamp designer) and *Gelatenheid*

1996. Stamp Day.

3294	**1038**	16f. multicoloured	1·30	40

1039 Dragonfly (*Sympetrum sanguineum*)

1996. 150th Anniv of Royal Institute of Natural Sciences of Belgium. Insects. Multicoloured.

3295	16f. Type **1039**	90	70
3296	16f. Buff-tailed bumble bee (*Bombus terrestris*)	90	70
3297	16f. Stag beetle (*Lucanus cervus*)	90	70
3298	16f. May beetle (*Melolontha melolontha*)	90	70
3299	16f. European field cricket (*Gryllus campestris*)	90	70
3300	16f. Seven-spotted ladybird (*Coccinella septempunctata*)	90	70

1040 Yvonne Nevejean (rescuer of Jewish children)

1996. Europa. Famous Women. Multicoloured.

3301	16f. Type **1040**	1·00	40
3302	30f. Marie Gevers (poet)	2·10	90

1996. Birds (3rd series). As T **841**. Multicoloured.

3303	1f. Crested tit ("Mesange Huppee")	25	15
3304	2f. Redwing ("Grive mauvis")	30	25
3305	3f. Eurasian skylark ("Alouette des champs")	30	25
3306	4f. Pied flycatcher ("Gore-mouche noir")	45	40
3307	5f. Common starling ("Etourneau sansonnet")	45	25
3308	6f. Spruce siskin ("Tarin des aulnes")	50	30
3309	7f. Yellow wagtail ("Bergeronnette printaniere")	45	15
3310	7f.50 Great grey shrike ("Pie-Grienche Grise")	50	40
3311	9f. Green woodpecker ("Pic Vert")	65	50
3312	10f. Turtle dove ("Tourterelle des Bois")	65	40
3313	15f. Willow tit ("Mesange boreale")	1·20	25
3314	16f. Coal tit ("Mesange noire")	1·00	30
3315	21f. Fieldfare ("Grive Litorne") (horiz)	1·40	80
3316	150f. Black-billed magpie ("Pie bavarde") (35×25 mm)	10·50	25

1042 King Albert II

1996. 62nd Birthday of King Albert II.

3327	**1042**	16f. multicoloured	1·40	25

1043 Han sur Lesse Grottoes

1996. Tourist Publicity. Multicoloured.

3328	16f. Type **1043**	1·20	40
3329	16f. Statue of beguine, Begijnendijk (vert)	1·20	40

1044 Royal Palace

1996. Brussels, Heart of Europe. Multicoloured.

3330	16f. Type **1044**	1·30	40
3331	16f. St. Hubert Royal Galleries	1·30	40
3332	16f. Le Petit Sablon, Egmont Palace (horiz)	1·30	40
3333	16f. Jubilee Park (horiz)	1·30	40

1045 1900 Germain 6CV Voiturette

1996. Cent of Motor Racing at Spa. Multicoloured.

3334	16f. Type **1045**	1·20	40
3335	16f. 1925 Alfa Romeo P2	1·20	40
3336	16f. 1939 Mercedes Benz W154	1·20	40
3337	16f. 1967 Ferrari 330P	1·20	40

1046 Table Tennis

1996. Olympic Games, Atlanta. Multicoloured.

3338	16f.+4f. Type **1046**	1·60	1·60
3339	16f.+4f. Swimming	1·60	1·60
MS3340	125×90 mm. 34f.+6f. High jumping (41×34 mm)	3·50	3·50

1996

3341	16f. blue	1·20	30
3342	17f. blue	1·40	15
3343	18f. green	1·30	50
3344	19f. lilac	1·60	40
3344a	20f. brown	1·40	20
3345	25f. brown	1·70	40
3346	28f. brown	2·40	50
3347	32f. violet	2·10	20
3348	34f. blue	1·90	40
3349	36f. blue	2·30	25
3350	50f. green	4·00	30

1047 *The Straw Hat* (Peter Paul Rubens)

1996. Paintings by Belgian Artists in the National Gallery, London. Multicoloured.

3351	14f. *St. Ivo* (Rogier van der Weyden)	1·20	40
3352	16f. Type **1047**	1·40	40
3353	30f. *Man in a Turban* (Jan van Eyck)	2·75	65

1048 Philip the Fair

1996. 500th Anniv of Marriage of Philip the Fair and Joanna of Castile and Procession into Brussels. Details of triptych by the Master of Affligem Abbey at Zierikzee Town Hall. Multicoloured.

3354	16f. Type **1048**	4·00	40
3355	16f. Joanna of Castile	1·30	40

1049 Cloro (cartoon character)

1996. "Philately for the Young".

3356	**1049**	16f. multicoloured	1·40	40

1050 Title of First Issue and Charles Letellier (founder)

1996. 150th Anniv of "Mons Almanac".

3357	**1050**	16f. black, yell & mve	1·30	40

1051 Arthur Grumiaux (violinist, 10th death anniv)

1996. Music and Literature Anniversaries.

3358	**1051**	16f. multicoloured	1·30	40
3359	-	16f. multicoloured	1·30	40
3360	-	16f. black and brown	1·30	40
3361	-	16f. multicoloured	1·30	40

DESIGNS: No. 3359, Flor Peeters (organist, 10th death anniv); 3360, Christian Dotremont (poet, 5th death anniv); 3361, Paul van Ostaijen (writer, birth centenary) and cover drawing by Oscar Jespers for "Bezette Stad".

1052 Globe and Children of Different Races

1996. "Solidarity". 50th Anniv of UNICEF.

3362	**1052**	16f.+4f. mult	1·40	1·40

1053 Christmas Trees

1996. Christmas. Sheet 185×145 mm containing T **1053** and similar horiz designs. Multicoloured.

MS3363 14f. Type **1053**; 14f. "Happy Christmas" in Flemish, German and French; 14f. Church; 14f. Cake stall; 14f. Stall with cribs; 14f. Meat stall; 14f. Father Christmas; 14f. Crowd including man smoking pipe; 14f. Crowd including man carrying holly	9·25	9·25

1054 Students

1997. Centenary of Catholic University, Mons.

3364	**1054**	17f. multicoloured	1·30	30

1055 Barbed Wire and Buildings

1997. Museums. Multicoloured.
3365 17f.+4f. Type **1055** (Deportation and Resistance Museum, Dossin Barracks, Malines) 1·60 1·60
3366 17f.+4f. Foundryman pouring molten metal (Fourneau Saint-Michel Iron Museum) 1·60 1·60
MS3367 90×125 mm. 41f.+9f. Horta Museum, Saint-Giles 5·75 5·75
The premium was used for the promotion of philately.

1056 Deer and Landscape

1997. "Cantons of the East" (German-speaking Belgium).
3368 **1056** 17f. black and brown 1·30 40

1057 Marie Sasse

1997. Opera Singers. Multicoloured.
3369 17f. Type **1057** 1·20 40
3370 17f. Ernest van Dijck 1·20 40
3371 17f. Hector Dufranne 1·20 40
3372 17f. Clara Clairbert 1·20 40

1058 Soldier on Duty

1997. Belgian Involvement in United Nations Peacekeeping Forces.
3373 **1058** 17f. multicoloured 1·20 40

1059 The Goat Riders

1997. Europa. Tales and Legends. Multicolourd.
3374 17f. Type **1059** 1·40 40
3375 30f. Jean de Berneau 2·50 90

1060 Spinoy working on Recess Plate

1997. Stamp Day. Fourth Death Anniv of Constant Spinoy (engraver).
3376 **1060** 17f. brown, yell & blk 1·20 40

1061 *The Man in the Street* (detail)

1997. Birth Centenary of Paul Delvaux (artist). Multicoloured.
3377 15f. Type **1061** 1·00 50
3378 17f. *The Public Voice* (horiz) 1·30 40
3379 32f. *The Messenger of the Night* 2·50 80

1062 Flower Arrangement

1997. Second International Flower Show, Liege.
3380 **1062** 17f. multicoloured 1·30 40

1063 Men's Judo

1997. Judo. Each black and red.
3381 17f.+4f. Type **1063** 1·40 1·30
3382 17f.+4f. Women's judo (showing female symbol) 1·40 1·30

1064 Queen Paola and Belvedere Villa

1997. 60th Birthday of Queen Paola.
3383 **1064** 17f. multicoloured 1·30 40

1065 Jommeke, Flip and Filiberke (comic strip characters)

1997. "Philately for the Young".
3384 **1065** 17f. multicoloured 1·60 45

1066 *Rosa damascena* "Coccinea"

1997. Roses. Illustrations by Pierre-Joseph Redoute. Multicoloured.
3385 17f. Type **1066** 1·30 40
3386 17f. *Rosa sulfurea* 1·30 40
3387 17f. *Rosa centifolia* 1·30 40

1067 St. Martin's Cathedral, Hal

1997. Tourist Publicity. Multicoloured.
3388 17f. Type **1067** 1·30 40
3389 17f. Notre-Dame Church, Laeken (horiz) 1·30 40
3390 17f. St. Martin's Cathedral, Liege 1·30 40

1068 Stonecutter

1997. Trades. Multicoloured.
3391 17f. Type **1068** 1·30 30
3392 17f. Bricklayer 1·30 30
3393 17f. Carpenter 1·30 30
3394 17f. Blacksmith 1·30 30

1069 Queen amidst Workers

1997. Centenary of Apimondia (International Apicultural Association) and 35th Congress, Antwerp. Bees. Multicoloured.
3395 17f. Type **1069** 1·30 90
3396 17f. Development of egg 1·30 90
3397 17f. Bees emerging from cells 1·30 90
3398 17f. Bee collecting nectar from flower 1·30 90
3399 17f. Bee fanning at hive entrance and worker arriving with nectar 1·30 90
3400 17f. Worker feeding drone 1·30 90

1070 *Belgica* (polar barque) ice-bound

1997. Cent of Belgian Antarctic Expedition.
3401 **1070** 17f. multicoloured 1·30 50

1071 Mask

1997. Centenary of Royal Central Africa Museum, Tervuren. Multicoloured.
3402 17f. Type **1071** 1·30 40
3403 17f. Museum (74×24 mm) 1·30 40
3404 34f. Statuette 2·50 1·00

1073 *Fairon* (Pierre Grahame)

1997. Christmas.
3408 **1073** 15f. multicoloured 1·20 40

1074 Disjointed Figure

1997. "Solidarity". Multiple Sclerosis.
3409 **1074** 17f.+4f. black & blue 1·60 1·60

1997. Willow Tit. As No. 3318 but horiz.
3410 15f. multicoloured 1·50 1·40

1075 Azalea "Mrs. Haerens A"

1997. Self-adhesive.
3411 **1075** (17f.) multicoloured 1·30 20

1076 Female Symbol

1998. 50th Anniv of Women's Suffrage in Belgium.
3412 **1076** 17f. red, brown & sepia 1·20 40

1077 Thalys High Speed Train on Antoing Viaduct

1998. Paris–Brussels–Cologne–Amsterdam High Speed Rail Network.
3413 **1077** 17f. multicoloured 1·30 40

1078 Gerard Walschap

1998. Writers' Birth Centenaries. Multicoloured.
3414 17f. Type **1078** 1·20 40
3415 17f. Norge (Georges Mogin) 1·20 40

1079 King Leopold III

1998. Kings of Belgium (1st series).
3416 **1079** 17f.+8f. green 1·70 1·70
3417 - 32f.+15f. brown 3·00 3·00
MS3418 125×90 mm. 50f.+25f. red 7·00 7·00
KINGS: 32f. Baudouin I; 50f. Albert II.
The premium was used for the promotion of philately.
See also Nos. 3466/8 and **MS**3508.

1080 *Black Magic*

1998. Birth Centenary of Rene-Ghislain Magritte (artist) (1st issue). Multicoloured.
3419 17f. Type **1080** 1·30 40
3420 17f. *The Sensitive Chord* (horiz) 1·30 40
3421 17f. *The Castle of the Pyrenees* 1·30 40
See also No. 3432.

1081 *La Foire aux Amours* (Felicien Rops)

1998. Art Anniversaries. Multicoloured.
3422 17f. Type **1081** (death cent) 1·20 1·00
3423 17f. *Hospitality for the Strangers* (Gustave van de Woestijne) (bicentenary of Museum of Fine Arts, Ghent) 1·20 1·00
3424 17f. *Man with Beard* (self-portrait of Felix de Boeck, birth centenary) 1·20 1·00
3425 17f. *black writing mixed with colours...* (Karel Appel and Christian Dotremont) (50th anniv of Cobra art movement) 1·20 1·00

1082 Anniversary Emblem

1998. 75th Anniv of Belgian Postage Stamp Dealers' Association.
3426 **1082** 17f. multicoloured 1·20 40

1083 Avro RJ85 Airplane

1998. 75th Anniv of Sabena Airlines.
3427 **1083** 17f. multicoloured 1·30 40

1084 Fox

1998. Wildlife of the Ardennes. Multicoloured.
3428 17f. Type **1084** 1·30 50
3429 17f. Red deer ("Cervus elaphus") 1·30 50
3430 17f. Wild boar ("Sus scrofa") 1·30 50
3431 17f. Roe deer ("Capreolus capreolus") 1·30 50

1085 *The Return* (Magritte)

1998. Birth Centenary of Rene-Ghislain Magritte (artist) (2nd issue).
3432 **1085** 17f. multicoloured 1·30 50

1086 Struyf

1998. Stamp Day. Second Death Anniv of Edmond Struyf (founder of Pro-Post (organization for promotion of philately)).
3433 **1086** 17f. black, red & yellow 1·20 40

1087 Guitarist (Torhout and Werchter Festival)

1998. Europa. National Festivals.
3434 **1087** 17f. violet and yellow 1·40 40
3435 - 17f. violet and mauve 1·40 40
DESIGN: No. 3435, Music conductor (Wallonie Festival).

1088 Pelote

1998. Sports. Multicoloured.
3436 17f.+4f. Type **1088** 1·50 1·50
3437 17f.+4f. Handball 1·50 1·50
MS3438 123×88 mm. 30f.+7f. Goalkeeper (World Cup Football Championship, France) 3·00 3·00

1089 Emblem

1998. European Heritage Days. Multicoloured.
3439 17f. Type **1089** 1·20 50
3440 17f. Bourla Theatre, Antwerp 1·20 50
3441 17f. La Halle, Durbuy 1·20 50
3442 17f. Halletoren, Kortrijk 1·20 50
3443 17f. Louvain Town Hall 1·20 50
3444 17f. Perron, Liege 1·20 50
3445 17f. Royal Theatre, Namur 1·20 50
3446 17f. Aspremont-Lynden Castle, Rekem 1·20 50
3447 17f. Neo-Gothic kiosk, Saint Nicolas 1·20 50
3448 17f. Saint-Vincent's Chapel, Tournai 1·20 50
3449 17f. Villers-la-Ville Abbey 1·20 50
3450 17f. Saint-Gilles Town Hall 1·20 50

1090 Marnix van Sint-Aldegonde

1998. 400th Death Anniv of Philips van Marnix van St. Aldegonde (writer).
3451 **1090** 17f. multicoloured 1·20 40

1091 Face

1998. Bicentenary of "Amis Philanthropes" (circle of free thinkers).
3452 **1091** 17f. black and blue 1·20 40

1092 Mniszech Palace

1998. Belgium Embassy, Warsaw, Poland.
3453 **1092** 17f. multicoloured 1·20 40

1093 King Albert II

1998
3454 **1093** 19f. lilac 1·70 1·60
No. 3454 was for use on direct mail by large companies.

1094 *The Eighth Day* (dir. Jaco van Dormael)

1998. 25th Anniv of Brussels and Ghent Film Festivals. Multicoloured.
3455 17f. Type **1094** 1·30 40
3456 17f. *Daens* (dir. Stijn Coninx) 1·30 40

1096 Chick Bill and Ric Hochet

1998. "Philately for the Young". Comic Strip Characters.
3460 **1096** 17f. multicoloured 1·30 50

1097 "Youth and Space"

1998. 14th World Congress of Association of Space Explorers.
3461 **1097** 17f. multicoloured 1·30 45

1098 Universal Postal Union Emblem

1998. World Post Day.
3462 **1098** 34f. blue & ultramarine 2·50 1·30

1099 "The Three Kings" (Michel Provost)

1998. Christmas. No value indicated.
3463 **1099** (17f.) multicoloured 1·20 40

1100 Detail of Triptych by Constant Dratz

1998. Cent of General Belgium Trade Union.
3464 **1100** 17f. multicoloured 1·20 40

1101 Blind Man with Guide Dog

1998. "Solidarity". Guide Dogs for the Blind.
3465 **1101** 17f.+4f. multicoloured 1·60 1·60
The face value is embossed in Braille.

1999. Kings of Belgium (2nd series). As T **1079**.
3466 17f.+8f. deep green & green 1·90 1·90
3467 32f.+15f. black 3·25 3·25
MS3468 125×90 mm. 50f.+25f. brown and purple 5·75 5·75
KINGS: 17f. Albert I; 32f. Leopold II; 50f. Leopold I.
The premium was used for the promotion of philately.

1102 Candle ("Happy Birthday")

1999. Greetings stamps. No value expressed. Multicoloured.
3469 (17f.) Type **1102** 1·20 50
3470 (17f.) Stork carrying heart ("Welcome" (new baby)) 1·20 50
3471 (17f.) Wristwatch ("Take your Time" (retirement)) 1·20 50
3472 (17f.) Four-leafed clover ("For your pleasure") 1·20 50
3473 (17f.) White doves ("Congratulations" (marriage)) 1·20 50
3474 (17f.) Arrow through heart ("I love you") 1·20 50
3475 (17f.) Woman with heart as head ("Happy Mother's Day") 1·20 50
3476 (17f.) Man with heart as head ("Happy Father's Day") 1·20 50

1103 Barn Owl

1999. Owls. Multicoloured.
3477 17f. Type **1103** 1·30 40
3478 17f. Little owl ("Athene noctua") 1·30 40
3479 17f. Tawny owl ("Strix aluco") 1·30 40
3480 17f. Long-eared owl ("Asio otus") 1·30 40

1104 Leopard Tank (Army)

1999. 50th Anniv of North Atlantic Treaty Organization. Multicoloured.
3481 17f. Type **1104** 1·20 40
3482 17f. Lockhead Martin F-16 Fighting Falcon (Air Force) 1·20 40
3483 17f. "De Wandelaar" (frigate) (Navy) 1·20 40
3484 17f. Field hospital (Medical Service) 1·20 40
3485 17f. Display chart of military operations (General Staff) 1·20 40

1105 Envelopes and World Map

1999. 125th Anniv of U.P.U.
3486 **1105** 34f. multicoloured 2·30 65

1106 De Bunt Nature Reserve, Hamme

1999. Europa. Parks and Gardens. Multicoloured.
3487 17f. Type **1106** 1·40 40
3488 17f. Harchies Marsh 1·40 40

1107 1849 10c. "Epaulettes" Stamp

1999. Stamp Day. 150th Anniv of First Belgian Postage Stamp. Multicoloured.
3489 17f. Type **1107** 1·10 30
3490 17f. 1849 20c. "Epaulettes" stamp 1·10 30

1108 Racing

1999. Sport. Belgian Motor Cycling. Multicoloured.
3491 17f.+4f. Type **1108** 1·60 1·60
3492 17f.+4f. Trial (vert) 1·60 1·60
MS3493 90×125 mm. 30f.+7f. Motocross (vert) 3·25 3·25

1109 *My Favourite Room*

1999. 50th Death Anniv of James Ensor (artist) (1st issue).
3494 **1109** 17f. multicoloured 1·10 40
See also Nos. 3501/3.

1110 Giant Family, Geraardsbergen

1999. Tourist Publicity. Multicoloured.

3495		17f. Type **1110**	1·10	40
3496		17f. Members of Confrerie de la Misericorde in Car d'Or procession, Mons (horiz)	1·10	40

1111 Harvesting of Cocoa Beans

1999. Belgian Chocolate. Multicoloured.

3497		17f. Type **1111**	1·10	40
3498		17f. Chocolate manufacture	1·10	40
3499		17f. Selling product	1·10	40

1112 Photographs of 1959 and 1999

1999. 40th Wedding Anniv of King Albert and Queen Paola.

3500	**1112**	17f. multicoloured	1·30	40

1113 *Woman eating Oysters*

1999. 50th Death Anniv of James Ensor (artist) (2nd issue).

3501	**1113**	17f. multicoloured	1·10	40
3502	-	30f. black, brown and grey	1·90	80
3503	-	32f. multicoloured	2·10	80

DESIGNS—30f. *Triumph of Death*; 32f. *Old Lady with Masks*.

1999. "Bruphila '99" National Stamp Exhibition, Brussels. Kings of Belgium (3rd series). Sheet 191×121 mm containing vert designs as T **1079**. Each deep blue and blue.

MS3508	17f. As No. 3466; 17f. Type **1079**; 32f. As No. 3467; 32f. As No. 3417; 50f. As No. **MS**3468; 50f. As No. **MS**3418	26·00	26·00

1115 Henri la Fontaine (President of International Peace Bureau), 1913

1999. Belgian Winners of Nobel Peace Prize.

3509	**1115**	17f. red and gold	1·10	40
3510	-	21f. blue and gold	1·30	80

DESIGNS: 3510, Auguste Beernaert (Prime Minister 1884–94), 1909.

DENOMINATION. From No. 3511 Belgian stamps are denominated both in Belgian francs and in euros.

1116 King Albert II

1116a King Albert II

1999

3511	**1116**	17f. multicoloured	1·20	15
3512	**1116**	17f. blue	1·20	15
3513	**1116**	19f. purple	1·30	40
3514	**1116**	20f. brown	1·30	30
3515	**1116**	25f. brown	2·50	2·30
3516	**1116**	30f. purple	2·10	25
3517	**1116**	32f. green	1·90	25
3518	**1116**	34f. blue	2·30	65
3519	**1116**	36f. brown	2·30	15
3520	**1116a**	50f. blue	3·25	65
3521	**1116a**	200f. lilac	13·00	1·60

1117 "Corentin" (Paul Cuvelier)

1999. "Philately for the Young". Comic Strips. Sheet 185×145 mm containing T **1117** and similar horiz designs. Multicoloured.

MS3525	17f. Type **1117**; 17f. "Jerry Spring" (Jije); 17f. "Gil Jourdan" (Maurice Tillieux); 17f. "Beaver Patrol" (Mitacq); 17f. Entrance Hall, Belgian Comic Strip Centre; 17f. "Hassan and Kadour" (Jacques Laudy); 17f. "Buck Danny" (Victor Hubinon); 17f. "Tif and Tondu" (Fernand Dineur); 17f. "Les Timour" (Sirius)	11·50	11·50

1118 Geranium "Matador"

1999. Flowers. No value expressed (geranium) or inscr "ZONE A PRIOR" (tulip). Multicoloured. Self-adhesive.

3528		(17f.) Type **1118**	1·60	45
3529		(21f.) Tulip (21×26 mm)	1·20	40

The geranium design was for use on inland letters up to 20g. and the tulip design for letters within the European Union up to 20g.

1119 Reindeer holding Glass of Champagne

1999. Christmas.

3530	**1119**	17f. multicoloured	1·20	40

1120 Child bandaging Teddy Bear

1999. "Solidarity". Red Cross. Multicoloured.

3531		17f.+4f. Type **1120**	1·50	1·50
3532		17f.+4f. Child and teddy bear cleaning teeth (vert)	1·50	1·50

1121 Prince Philippe and Mathilde d'Udekem d'Acoz

1999. Engagement of Prince Philippe and Mathilde d'Udekem d'Acoz.

3533		17f. Type **1121**	1·60	50
MS3534		120×89 mm. 21f. Prince Philippe and Mathilde d'Udekem d'Acoz (different)	1·80	1·80

1122 Pope John Paul XXIII

1999. The Twentieth Century (1st issue). Personalities, Sports and Leisure. Sheet 166×200 mm containing T **1122** and similar vert designs. Multicoloured.

MS3535	17f. Type **1122**; 17f. King Baudouin; 17f. Willy Brandt (German statesman); 17f. John F. Kennedy (U.S. President, 1961–3); 17f. Mahatma Gandhi (Indian leader); 17f. Martin Luther King (civil rights leader); 17f. Vladimir Lenin (Prime Minister of Russia, 1917–24; 17f. Che Guevara (revolutionary); 17f. Golda Meir (Prime Minister of Israel, 1969–74); 17f. Nelson Mandela (Prime Minister of South Africa, 1994–99); 17f. Jesse Owens (American athlete) (modern Olympics); 17f. Football; 17f. Eddy Merckx (racing cyclist) (Tour de France); 17f. Edith Piaf (French singer); 17f. The Beatles (English pop band); 17f. Charlie Chaplin (English film actor and director); 17f. Postcards (tourism); 17f. Children around campfire (youth movements); 17f. Tintin and Snowy (comic strip); 17f. Magnifying glass over stamp (hobbies)	23·00	23·00

See also Nos. **MS**3613 and **MS**3656.

1123 Fireworks and Streamer forming "2000"

2000. New Year.

3536	**1123**	17f. multicoloured	1·30	25

1124 Red-backed Shrike

2000. Birds. Multicoloured.

3537		50c. Goldcrest ("Roitelet Huppe")	15	25
3538		1f. Red crossbill ("Beccroisé des Sapins")	25	15
3539		2f. Short-toed treecreeper ("Grimpereau des Jardins")	25	15
3540		3f. Meadow pipit ("Pipit Farlouse")	25	15
3541		5f. Brambling ("Pinson du Nord")	30	15
3542		7f.50 Great grey shrike ("Pie-Grieche Grise")	50	50
3543		8f. Great tit ("Mesange Charbonniere")	65	30
3544		10f. Wood warbler ("Pouillot Siffleur")	65	40
3545		16f. Type **1124**	1·10	40
3546		16f. Common tern ("Sterne Pierregarin")	1·10	25
3547		21f. Fieldfare ("Grive Litorne") (horiz)	1·30	50
3548		150f. Black-billed magpie ("Pie Bavarde") (36×25 mm)	9·75	65

1125 Brussels Skyline and Group of People

2000. Brussels, European City of Culture. Multicoloured.

3555		17f. Type **1125**	1·10	50
3556		17f. Toots Tielmans (jazz musician), Anne Teresa de Keersmaeker (gymnast) and skyline	1·10	50
3557		17f. Lockhead L-1011 Tristar, train and skyline	1·10	50

Nos. 3555/7 were issued together, *se-tenant*, forming a composite design showing the Brussels skyline.

1126 Queen Astrid

2000. Queens of Belgium (1st series).

3558	**1126**	17f.+8f. green and deep green	1·90	1·90
3559	-	32f.+15f. brown and black	3·25	3·25
MS3560		125×89 mm. 50f.+25f. deep purple and purple	4·75	4·75

DESIGNS: 32f. Queen Fabiola; 50f. Queen Paola.

The premium was used for the promotion of philately.

See also Nos. 3615/**MS**3617 and **MS**3618.

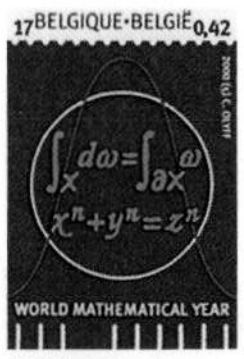

1127 Mathematical Formulae

2000. World Mathematics Year.

3561	**1127**	17f. multicoloured	1·10	40

1128 Globe and Technology (Joachim Beckers)

2000. "Stampin' the Future". Winning Entries in Children's International Painting Competition.

3562	**1128**	17f. multicoloured	1·10	40

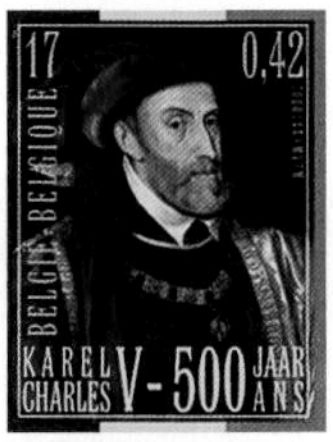

1129 *Charles V as Sovereign Master of the Order of the Golden Fleece* (anon)

2000. 500th Birth Anniv of Charles V, Holy Roman Emperor. Paintings of Charles V. Multicoloured.

3563		17f. Type **1129**	1·10	40
3564		21f. *Charles V* (Corneille de la Haye)	1·30	75
MS3565		125×88 mm. 34f. *Charles V on Horseback* (Titian)	2·50	2·50

1130 Common Adder

2000. Amphibians and Reptiles. Multicoloured.

3566		17f. Type **1130**	1·10	40
3567		17f. Sand lizard (*Lacerta agilis*) (vert)	1·10	40
3568		17f. Common tree frog (*Hyla arborea*) (vert)	1·10	40
3569		17f. Spotted salamander (*Salamander salamander*)	1·10	40

1131 Children flying Kites

2000. Red Cross and Red Crescent Movements.

3570	**1131**	17f.+4f. multicoloured	1·50	1·50

1132 Players Celebrating

2000. European Football Championship, Belgium and The Netherlands. Multicoloured. (a) With face value. Size 26×38 mm.

3571	17f. Type **1132**	1·30	25
3572	21f. Football	1·60	40

(b) Size 20×26 mm. Self-adhesive.

3573	(17f.) As Type **1132**	1·60	40

Nos. 3571/3 were printed together, *se-tenant*, with the backgrounds forming the composite design of a crowd of spectators and the Belgian flag.

1133 Cat and Rabbit reading Book

2000. Stamp Day. Winning Entry in Stamp Design Competition.

3574	**1133**	17f. black, blue and red	1·10	40

1134 Francois de Tassis (detail of tapestry)

2000. "Belgica 2001" Int Stamp Exhibition, Brussels, (1st issue).

3575	**1134**	17f. multicoloured	1·10	50

See also Nos. 3629/33.

1135 *Iris spuria*

2000. Ghent Flower Show. Multicoloured.

3576	16f. Type **1135**	1·30	50
3577	17f. Rhododendron (horiz)	1·50	40
3578	21f. Begonia (vert)	1·60	75

1136 Prince Philippe

2000. Second Anniv of Prince Philippe (cultural organization).

3579	**1136**	17f. brn, grey & sil	1·10	40

1137 Harpsichord

2000. 250th Death Anniv of Johann Sebastian Bach. No value expressed. Multicoloured.

3580	(17f.) Type **1137**	1·30	1·00
3581	(17f.) Violin	1·30	1·00
3582	(17f.) Two tenor lutes	1·30	1·00
3583	(17f.) Treble viol	1·30	1·00
3584	(17f.) Three trumpets	1·30	1·00
3585	(17f.) Bach	1·30	1·00

1138 Belgium Team Emblem and Olympic Rings

2000. Olympic Games, Sydney. Multicoloured.

3586	17f. Type **1138**	1·00	50
3587	17f.+4f. Tae-kwon-do	1·40	1·40
3588	17f.+4f. Paralympic athlete (horiz)	1·40	1·40
MS3589	125×90 mm. 30f.+7f. Swimmer (horiz)	2·50	2·50

1139 "Building Europe"

2000. Europa.

3590	**1139**	21f. multicoloured	1·50	75

1140 Flemish Beguinages

2000. UNESCO World Heritage Sites in Belgium. Multicoloured.

3591	17f. Type **1140**	1·10	30
3592	17f. Grand-Place, Brussels	1·10	30
3593	17f. Four lifts, Centre Canal, Wallonia	1·10	30

1141 Baroque Organ, Norbertine Abbey Church, Grimbergen

2000. Tourism. Churches and Church Organs. Multicoloured.

3594	17f. Type **1141**	1·10	40
3595	17f. St. Wandru Abbey, Mons	1·10	40
3596	17f. O.-L.-V. Hemelvaartkerk (former abbey church), Ninove	1·10	40
3597	17f. St. Peter's Church, Bastogne	1·10	40

1142 Red-backed Shrike ("Pie grieche ecorcheur")

2000

3598	**1142**	16f. multicoloured	2·20	1·60
3599	-	17f. mult (51×21 mm)	3·50	2·50
3600	-	23f. lilac	2·50	2·00

DESIGNS: 17f. Francois de Tassis (detail of tapestry) and Belgica 2001 emblem; 23f. King Albert II.

1143 Marcel, Charlotte, Fanny and Konstantinopel

2000. "Philately for the Young". Kiekeboe (cartoon series created by Robert Merhottein).

3601	**1143**	17f. multicoloured	1·10	50

1144 "Springtime"

2000. Hainaut Flower Show.

3602	**1144**	17f. multicoloured	1·10	40

1145 Pansies

2000. Flowers. No value expressed. Self-adhesive.

3603	**1145**	(17f.) multicoloured	1·30	25

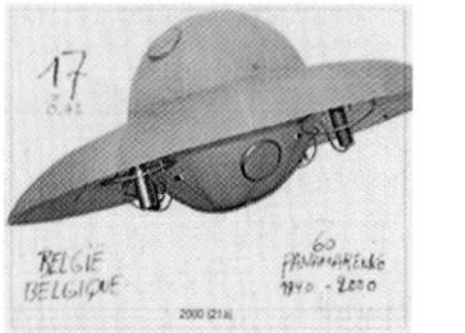

1147 "Bing of the Ferro Lusto X" (Panamarenko)

2000. Modern Art. Multicoloured.

3608	17f. Type **1147**	1·10	65
3609	17f. "Construction" (Anne-Mie van Kerckhoven) (vert)	1·10	65
3610	17f. "Belgique eternelle" (Jacques Charlier)	1·10	65
3611	17f. "Les Belles de Nuit" (Marie Jo Lafontaine)	1·10	65

1148 Postman

2000. Christmas.

3612	**1148**	17f. multicoloured	1·10	40

1149 Soldiers at Yser Front, West Flanders (First World War, 1914–18)

2000. The Twentieth Century (2nd issue). War, Peace and Art. Sheet 200×166 mm containing T **1149** and similar horiz designs. Multicoloured.

MS3613 17f. Type **1149**; 17f. German concentration camp and prisoners (black and scarlet); 17f. Atomic cloud and Hiroshima (atomic bomb, 1945); 17f. Winston Churchill, Franklin D. Roosevelt and Joseph Stalin (Yalta conference, 1945); 17f. Headquarters (United Nations established, 1945); 17f. Joseph Kasavubu (first President) and map of Africa (independence of Belgian Congo, 1960); 17f. American soldiers and Boeing CH-14 Chinook(Vietnam War); 17f. Collapse of Berlin Wall, 1989; 17f. Campaign for Nuclear Disarmament emblem and crowd; 17f. Dome of the Rock (Middle East conflict); 17f. Rene Magritte (artist); 17f. Le Corbusier (architect) and building; 17f. Bertolt Brecht (dramatist and poet) and actors; 17f. James Joyce (novelist); 17f. Anne Teresa de Keersmaeker (choreographer); 17f. Bila Bartok (composer); 17f. Andy Warhol (artist); 17f. Maria Callas (opera singer); 17f. Henry Moore (sculptor) and sculpture; 17f. Charlie Parker (alto saxophonist and composer) and Toots Thielemans (composer and jazz musician) 23·00 23·00

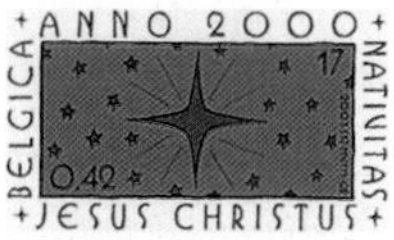

1150 Stars

2000. New Year.

3614	**1150**	17f. gold, blue & blk	1·30	50

2001. Queens of Belgium (2nd series). As T **1126**.

3615	17f.+8f. green & dp green	1·90	1·90
3616	32f.+15f. black and green	3·25	3·25
MS3617	126×91 mm. 50f.+25f. deep brown and brown	4·75	4·75

DESIGNS: 17f. Queen Elisabeth; 32f. Queen Marie-Henriette; 50f. Queen Louise-Marie.

The premium was used for the promotion of philately.

2001. Queens of Belgium (3rd series). Vert designs as T **1126**. Each blue, deep blue and ochre.

MS3618 190×121 mm. 17f. As No. 3615; 17f. As Type **1126**; 32f. As No. 3616; 32f. As No. 3559; 50f. As No. **MS**3617; 50f. As No. **MS**3560 23·00 23·00

1151 Movement of a Dynamo

2001. Death Centenary of Zenobe Gramme (physicist).

3619	**1151**	17f. black, red & black	1·10	40

1152 Virgin and Child (statue)

2001. 575th Anniv of Louvain Catholic University.

3620	**1152**	17f. multicoloured	1·10	40

2001. As T **998** but with face value expressed in francs and euros.

3621	100f. multicoloured	6·25	55

1153 Willem Elsschot (poet)

2001. Music and Literature.

3622	**1153**	17f. brown and black	1·10	40
3623	-	17f. grey and black	1·10	40
MS3624		125×90 mm. 21f. orange and brown	1·50	1·50

DESIGNS—VERT: No. 3623, Albert Ayguesparse (poet). HORIZ: **MS**3624 21f. Queen Elisabeth and emblem (50th anniv of Queen Elisabeth International Music Competition).

1154 Boy washing Hands

2001. Europa. Water Resources.

3625	**1154**	21f. multicoloured	1·40	75

1155 Type 12 Steam Locomotive

2001. 75th Anniv of National Railway Company. Multicoloured.

3626	17f. Type **1155**	1·10	65
3627	17f. Series 06 dual locomotive No. 671	1·10	65
3628	17f. Series 03 locomotive No. 328	1·10	65

Nos. 3626/8 were issued together, *se-tenant*, forming a composite design.

1156 16th-century Postman on horseback

2001. "Belgica 2001" International Stamp Exhibition, Brussels (2nd issue). 500th Anniv of European Post. Multicoloured.

3629	17f. Type **1156**	1·40	65

3630 17f. 17th-century postman with walking staff (vert) 1·40 65
3631 17f. 18th-century postman and hand using quill (vert) 1·40 65
3632 17f. Steam locomotive and 19th-century postman (vert) 1·40 65
3633 17f. 20th-century forms of communication (vert) 1·40 65
MS3634 190×120 mm. 150f. Female postal worker (35×46 mm) 20·00 20·00

1157 Hassan II Mosque, Casablanca

2001. Places of Worship. Multicoloured.
3635 17f. Type **1157** 1·10 40
3636 34f. Koekelberg Basilica 2·30 1·00

1158 *Winter Landscape with Skaters* (Pieter Bruegel the Elder)

2001. Art. Multicoloured.
3637 17f. Type **1158** 1·10 95
3638 17f. *Heads of Negros* (Peter Paul Rubens) 1·10 95
3639 17f. *Sunday* (Frits van den Berghe) 1·10 95
3640 17f. *Mussels* (Marcel Broodthaers) 1·10 95

1159 Pottery Vase

2001. Chinese Pottery. Multicoloured.
3641 17f. Type **1159** 1·10 30
3642 34f. Teapot 2·30 80

1160 Luc Orient

2001. "Philately for the Young". Cartoon Characters.
3643 **1160** 17f. multicoloured 1·10 50

1161 Cyclists (World Cycling Championship, Antwerp)

2001. Sports. Multicoloured.
3644 17f.+4f. Type **1161** 1·40 1·40
3645 17f.+4f. Gymnast (World Gymnastics Championships, Ghent) 1·40 1·40

1162 Emblem

2001. Belgian Presidency of European Union.
3646 **1162** 17f. multicoloured 1·10 50

1163 Binche

2001. Town Hall Belfries.
3647 **1163** 17f. mauve and black 1·10 40
3648 - 17f. blue, mauve & blk 1·10 40
DESIGN: No. 3648, Diksmuide.

1164 Damme

2001. Large Farmhouses. Multicoloured.
3649 17f. Type **1164** 1·10 40
3650 17f. Beauvechain 1·10 40
3651 17f. Louvain 1·10 40
3652 17f. Honnelles 1·10 40
3653 17f. Hasselt 1·10 40

1165 Red Cross and Doctor

2001. Red Cross.
3654 **1165** 17f.+4f. multicoloured 1·40 1·40

1166 Stam and Pilou

2001. Stamp Day. No value expressed. Self-adhesive.
3655 **1166** (17f.) multicoloured 1·40 50
No. 3655 was for use on inland standard letters up to 20g.

1167 Ovide Decroly (educational psychologist) and Road Sign

2001. The Twentieth Century. Science and Technology. Sheet 166×200 mm. Multicoloured.
MS3656 17f. Type **1167**; 17f. Dandelion and windmills (alternative energy sources); 17f. Globe, signature and map (first solo non-stop crossing of North Atlantic by Charles Lindbergh); 17f. Man with head on lap (Sigmund Freud, founder of psychoanalysis); 17f. Astronaut and foot print on moon surface (Neil Armstrong, first man on the moon, 1969); 17f. Claude Levi-Strauss (anthropologist); 17f. DNA double helix and athletes (human genetic code); 17f. Pierre Teilhard de Chardin (theologian palaeontologist and philosopher); 17f. Max Weber (sociologist) and crowd; 17f. Albert Einstein (physicist) (Theory of Relativity); 17f. Knight and jacket of pills (discovery of Penicillin, 1928); 17f. Ilya Prigogine (theoretical chemist and clock face; 17f. Text and Roland Barthes (writer and critic); 17f. Simone de Beauvoir (feminist writer); 17f. Globe and technology highway (computer science); 17f. John Maynard Keynes (economist) and folded paper; 17f. Marc Bloch (historian) and photographs; 17f. Tools and Julius Robert Oppenheimer (nuclear physicist); 17f. Marie and Pierre Curie, discoverers of radioactivity, 1896); 17f. Caricature of Ludwig Josef Wittgenstein (philosopher) 23·00 23·00

1168 Nativity

2001. Christmas.
3657 **1168** 15f. multicoloured 1·10 45

1169 Sunset

2001. Bereavement. No value expressed.
3658 **1169** (17f.) multicoloured 1·60 40
See also Nos. 3732 and 3856.

1170 Daffodil

2001. Flowers. No value expressed. Self-adhesive. (a) Without service indicator. Multicoloured.
3659 (17f.) Type **1170** 1·30 40

(b) Inscr "ZONE A PRIOR".
3660 (21f.) Tulip "Darwin" (vert) 1·40 50
No. 3659 was for use on inland letters up to 20g. and No. 3660 was for use on letters within the European Union up to 20g.

1171 Tintin

2001. 70th Anniv of Tintin in Congo (cartoon strip). Multicoloured.
3661 17f. Type **1171** 1·30 65
MS3662 123×88 mm. 34f. Tintin, Snowy and guide in car (48×37 mm) 3·25 3·25

1172 King Albert II

1173 King Albert II

2002

3663	**1173**	7c. blue and red (postage)	25	15
3666	**1172**	42c. red	1·10	40
3667	**1172**	47c. green	1·30	50
3668	**1173**	49c. red	1·30	50
3669	**1173**	52c. blue	1·40	50
3670	**1172**	59c. blue	1·80	55
3671	**1172**	60c. blue	1·20	90
3672	**1173**	79c. blue and red	2·50	65
3674	**1173**	€4.21 brown and red	10·00	2·50
3674a	**1172**	70c. blue (air)	1·50	65
3674b	**1172**	60c. blue	1·80	65
3674c	**1172**	80c. purple and red	2·00	65

Nos. 3663, 3668 and 3672 are inscribed "PRIOR" at left.

1174 Female Tennis Player

2002. Centenary of Royal Belgian Tennis Federation. Multicoloured.
3675 42c. Type **1174** 1·30 50
3676 42c. Male tennis player 1·30 50

1175 Cyclist

2002. International Cycling Events held at Circuit Zolder. Multicoloured.
3677 42c. Type **1175** (World Cyclo-Cross Championships) 1·30 50
3678 42c. Cyclist with hand raised (Road Cycling Championships) 1·30 50

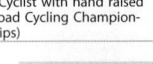

1176 Dinosaur

2002. Winning Entry in Children's Stamp Design Competition at "Belgica 2001".
3679 **1176** 42c.+10c. mult 1·50 1·50
The premium was used for the promotion of philately.

1177 Antwerp from River

2002. 150th Anniv of Antwerp University.
3680 **1177** 42c. blue and black 1·10 45

1178 Buildings and Architectural Drawing

2002. "Bruges 2002", European City of Culture. Multicoloured.
3681 42c. Type **1178** 1·30 45
3682 42c. Organ pipes and xylophone 1·30 45
3683 42c. Octopus 1·30 45

1179 16th-century Manuscript (poem, Anna Bijns)

2002. Women and Art. Multicoloured.
3684 42c. Type **1179** 1·30 45
3685 84c. *Woman writing* (painting, Anna Boch) (vert) 2·10 1·00

1180 Fountain Pen and Writing

2002. Stamp Day.
3686 **1180** 47c. multicoloured 1·40 55

1181 Papillon

2002. Centenary of Flanders Canine Society. Multicoloured.
3687 42c. Type **1181** 1·30 65
3688 42c. Brussels griffon 1·30 65
3689 42c. Bloodhounds 1·30 65
3690 42c. Bouvier des Ardennes 1·30 65
3691 42c. Schipperke 1·30 65

1182 Stock Dove ("Pigeon Colombin-Holenduif")

2002. Birds. Multicoloured.
3692 1c. Nightingale ("Rossignol philomele-Nachtegaal") (postage) 15 15
3693 2c. Snipe ("Becassine des Marais-Watersnip") 15 15
3693a 3c. Marsh tit ("Mesange Nonnette-Glanskopmees") 15 15
3693aa 5c. Little grebe ('Dodaars-Grebe castagneux') (23x27mm) 20 15

3693b	5c. Cirl bunting ("Bruant Zizi-Cirlors")	20	15
3693c	5c. Teal ("Wintertaling-Sarcelle D'Hiver")	20	15
3693d	6c. Little owl ('Steenuil-Chouette Cheveche')	25	15
3694	7c. Type **1182**	25	15
3694a	10c. Tengmalm's owl ("Chouette De Tengmalm-Ruigpootuil")	30	20
3694b	10c. Hedge sparrow (Heggemus-Accentor Maichet) (air/prior)	1·00	35
3694c	15c. Spotted nutcracker (Cassenoix Mouchete-Notenkracker) (air/prior)	1·00	35
3695	10c. Hedge Sparrow ('Heggemus-accenentor Mouchet') (AIRPRIOR)	30	20
3696	15c. Spotted nutcracker ('Cassenoix Mouchete-Noutenkotenkrake')(AIRPRIOR)	40	25
3697	20c. Mediterranean gull ("Zwarkopmeeuw-Mouette Melanocephale")	50	30
3697a	23c. Black-necked grebe ("Greb a Cou Noir - Geoorde Fuut")	55	30
3697b	23c. Jackdaw ("Kauw-Choucas des Tours")	55	30
3698	25c. Oystercatcher ("Scholekster-Huîtrier Pie")	65	40
3698a	27c. Eurasian woodcock ('Houtsnip-becasse des bois')	70	40
3699	30c. Corncrake ("Rale des Genets—Kwartelkoning")	95	40
3700	35c. Spotted woodpecker ("Pic Epeiche-Grote Bonte Specht")	1·00	45
3700a	40c. Spotted flycatcher ("Grauwe vliegenvanger-Gobemouche gris")	1·00	50
3700b	40c. Long-eared owl ("Hibou Moyen-Duc-Ransuil")	1·00	50
3701	41c. Collared dove ("Tourterelle Turque")	1·30	65
3701a	44c. House martin ("Hirondelle de fenetre-Huiszwaluw")	1·30	65
3701b	44c. Wood pigeon ("Hourduif-Pigeon Ramier")	1·30	65
3701c	46c. Avocet ("Kluut—Avocette")	1·30	70
3701d	52c. Hoopoe ("Hop-Huppe Fasciee")	1·40	75
3701e	55c. Plover ("Kleine plevier-Petit gravelot")	1·40	80
3702	57c. Black tern ("Guifette Noire")	1·40	90
3702a	60c. Partridge ("Perdrix Crise-Patrijs")	1·50	1·00
3703	65c. Black-headed gull ("Mouette rieuse-Kapmeeuw")	1·60	1·10
3704	70c. Redshank ("Chevalier Gambette")	2·10	1·10
3704a	70c. Swallow ('Aprus apus')	1·90	1·20
3704aa	75c. Golden plover ("Goudplevier-Pluvier dore")	1·90	1·20
3704b	75c. Firecrest ("Rottelet Triple-Bandeau Vuurgoudhaatje")	1·90	1·20
3704ba	75c. Kestrel ('Falco tinnunculus')	1·90	1·20
3704c	78c. Black-tailed godwit ("Gritto-Barge A Queue Noir")	2·30	1·30
3705	€1 Wheatear ("Traquet Motteux") (38×27 mm)	3·00	1·50
3706	€2 Ringed plover ("Grand Gravelot") (38×27 mm)	6·00	2·50
3707	€3.72 Moorhen ("Waterhoen-Poule d'eau") (38×27 mm)	11·50	3·25
3708	€4 Eagle owl ("Hibou grand-duc-Oehoe") (38×27 mm)	13·00	5·25
3708a	€4.30 Grebe ("Fuut-Grebe Huppe")	14·00	5·75
3708aa	€4.09 Pheasant ("Faisan de Colchide") (32×24 mm) (14.6.10)	13·50	5·25
3708b	€4.40 Peregrine falcon (Slechtwalk-Faucon Pelerin) (38×28 mm)	14·50	6·00
3708c	€ 4.60 Golden eagle	15·00	6·25
3708ca	€ 4.60 Barn owl ('Couette effraie-kerkuil')	15·00	6·25
3709	€5 Ruff ("Combattant Varie") (38×27 mm)	16·00	7·00

1183 Big Top, Ringmaster, Seal and Clown

2002. Europa. Circus. Winning Entry in Children's Drawing Competition.

3710	**1183**	52c. multicoloured	2·50	1·00

1184 Paramedic, Patient and Damaged Buildings

2002. Red Cross.

3711	**1184**	84c.+12c. multicoloured	2·50	2·50

1185 Abbey Buildings

2002. 850th Anniv of Leffe Abbey.

3712	**1185**	42c. multicoloured	1·50	50

1186 Loppem Castle

2002. Tourism. Castles. Sheet 161×141 mm containing T **1186** and similar horiz designs showing castles. Multicoloured.

MS3713	42c. Type **1186**; 42c. Horst; 42c. Wissekerke; 42c. Chimay; 42c. Ecaussinnes-Lalaing; 42c. Reinhardstein; 42c. Modave; 42c. Ooidonk; 42c. Corroy-le-Chateau; 42c. Alden Biesen	11·50	11·50

1187 Show Jumping

2002. Horses. Designs showing equestrian events. Multicoloured.

3714	40c. Type **1187**	1·00	45
3715	42c. Carriage driving (vert)	1·10	50
MS3716	126×91 mm. 52c. Two Brabant draught horses' heads (Centenary of St. Paul's horse procession, Opwijk) (37×48 mm)	1·60	1·60

1188 Golden Spur and Battle Scene

2002. 700th Anniv of Battle of the Golden Spurs (Flemish--French battle), Kortrijk. Multicoloured.

3717	42c. Type **1188**	1·10	40
3718	52c. Broel towers	1·30	75
MS3719	126×91 mm. 57c. Flemish and French soldiers, river and knight on horseback (48×38 mm)	1·60	1·60

1189 Onze-Lieve-Vrouw-Lombeek, Roosdaal

2002. Windmills. Multicoloured.

3720	42c. Type **1189**	1·10	40
3721	52c. Faial Island, Azores, Portugal	1·40	75

Stamps of a similar design were issued by Portugal.

1190 Liedekerke Lacework and Statue of Lace-maker

2002. Lace-making. Multicoloured.

3722	42c. Type **1190**	1·10	40
3723	74c. Pag lacework	2·00	90

Stamps of a similar design were issued by Croatia.

1191 Bakelandt, Red Zita and Stagecoach

2002. "Philately for the Young". Bakelandt (comic strip created by Hec Leemans).

3724	**1191**	42c. multicoloured	1·30	65

1192 Teddy Bear

2002. "The Rights of the Child".

3725	**1192**	42c. multicoloured	1·30	40

1193 Rey

2002. Birth Centenary of Jean Rey (politician).

3726	**1193**	52c. blue and cobalt	1·60	75

1194 Princess Elisabeth

2002. First Birthday of Princess Elisabeth. Multicoloured.

3727	49c. Type **1194**	1·60	50
3728	59c. Princess Elisabeth with parents (horiz)	1·90	75
MS3729	123×88 mm 84c. Princess Elisabeth (different) (59×38 mm)	2·75	2·75

No. 3727 was issued with a se-tenant label inscribed "PRIOR".

1195 Church, Ice Cream Van and Family

2002. Christmas. Sheet 166×40 mm containing T **1195** and similar vert designs. Multicoloured.

MS3730	41c. Type **1195**; 41c. Skier in snowy fir tree; 41c. Tobogganist and bird wearing hat; 41c. Skier wearing kilt; 41c. Skiers holding candles; 41c. Boy holding snowman-shaped ice cream; 41c. Children throwing snowballs; 41c. Children, snowman, and elderly man; 41c. Brazier, refreshment hut and people; 41c. Hut, robbers, cow and policeman	12·50	12·50

1196 Bricks

2002. The Twentieth Century. Society. Sheet 200×166 mm containing T **1196**.

MS3731	41c. purple, red and pink (Type **1196** (social housing)); 41c. deep purple, orange and purple ("MEI/MAI 68" and rubble (student protests)); 41c. slate, grey and green (telephone telecommunications)); 41c. red, orange and brown (slabs (gap between wealth and poverty)); 41c. brown, bistre and blue (broken crucifix (secularization of society)); 41c. multicoloured (towers of blocks (urbanization)); 41c. pink, violet and purple (combined female and male symbols (universal suffrage)); 41c. blue, orange and grey (enclosed circle (social security)); 41c. grey, green and bistre (schoolbag (equality in education)); 41c. grey, purple and deep purple (elderly man (ageing population)); 41c. blue, green and emerald ("E" (European Union)); 41c. chestnut, brown and yellow (stylized figure (declaration of Human Rights)); 41c. bistre, orange and light orange (pyramid of blocks (growth of consumer society)); 41c. blue, mauve and green (female symbol (feminism)); 41c. brown, sepia and light brown (mechanical arm (de-industrialization)); 41c. brown and green (dripping nozzle (oil crises)); 41c. multicoloured (vehicle (transportation)); 41c. lilac, brown and purple (sperm and egg (contraception)); 41c. green, red and grey (television (growth of television and radio)); 41c. pink, violet and blue (electric plug (increase in home appliances))	25·00	25·00

1197 Sunset

2002. Bereavement. No value expressed.

3732	**1197**	(49c.) multicoloured	1·50	65

1198 Crocus

2002. Flowers. No value expressed. Ordinary or self-adhesive gum.

3733	**1198**	(49c.) multicoloured	1·50	65

No. 3733 was for use on inland letters up to 50 g.

1199 Nero and Adhemar (cartoon characters)

2003. 80th (2002) Birth Anniv of Marc Sleen (cartoonist). Multicoloured.

3735	49c. Type **1199**	1·60	60
MS3736	121×91 mm 82c. Nero and Marc Sleen (49×38 mm)	2·75	2·75

1200 Firefighters, Engine and Ladders

2003. Public Services (Nos. 3737/41) and St. Valentine (3742). Multicoloured.

3737	49c. Type **1200**	1·60	60
3738	49c. Traffic police men and policewoman	1·60	60
3739	49c. Civil defence workers mending flood defences	1·60	60
3740	49c. Elderly woman wearing breathing mask, hand holding syringe and theatre nurse	1·60	60
3741	49c. Postman riding bicycle and obtaining signature for parcel	1·60	60
3742	49c. Hearts escaping from birdcage	1·60	60

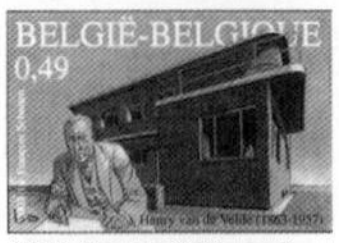

1201 Van de Velde and New House, Tervuren

2003. 140th Birth Anniv of Henry van de Velde (architect). Multicoloured.

3743	49c. Type **1201**	1·60	60
3744	59c. Van de Velde and Belgian pavilion, Paris International Exhibition, 1937 (vert)	1·90	70
3745	59c. Van de Velde and Book Tower, Central Library, Ghent University (vert)	1·90	70
MS3746	91×125 mm 84c. Woman and Art Nouveau newel post	2·75	2·75

1202 Bowls

2003. Traditional Sports. Multicoloured.

3747	49c. Type **1202**	1·80	65
3748	49c. Archery	1·80	65
MS3749	91×126 mm. 82c. Pigeon racing	3·00	3·00

1203 Berlioz

2003. Birth Bicentenary of Hector Berlioz (composer).

3750	**1203**	59c. multicoloured	2·10	75

1204 Statue of Men Conversing

2003. Anniversaries. Multicoloured.

3751	49c. Type **1204** (150th anniv of engineers' association)	1·80	65
3752	49c. Statue of seated man (centenary of Solvay Business School)	1·80	65

1205 Papy Ferdinand

2003. Red Cross. Cartoon characters in rescue attempt. Multicoloured.

3753	41c. + 9c. Type **1205**	2·10	1·30
3754	41c. + 9c. Pilou holding light	2·10	1·30
3755	41c. + 9c. Stam running for help	2·10	1·30

Nos. 3753/5 were issued together, se-tenant, forming a composite design.

1206 Bouquet

2003. Third International Flower Show, Liege.

3756	**1206**	49c. multicoloured	2·00	65

1207 "Maigret" (film poster)

2002. Birth Centenary of Georges Simenon (writer). Multicoloured.

3757	49c. Type **1207**	2·00	65
3758	59c. "Le chat" (film poster)	2·40	80
MS3759	91×126 mm. 84c. Simenon (38×49 mm)	3·25	3·25

1208 Bells of St. Rumbold's Cathedral, Maline

2003. 150th Anniv of Belgium–Russia Diplomatic Relations. Multicoloured.

3760	59c. Type **1208**	2·40	80
3761	59c. Bells of St. Peter and Paul's Cathedral, St. Petersburg	2·40	80

1209 Eternity Symbol and "Mail Art"

2003. Stamp Day. Mail Art.

3762	**1209**	49c. multicoloured	2·10	65

1210 Roland on Horseback

2003. "Philately for the Young". *The Valiant Knight* (comic strip created by Francois Craenhals).

3763	**1210**	49c. multicoloured	2·10	65

1211 Calcite

2003. Minerals. Multicoloured.

3764	49c. Type **1211**	2·10	65
3765	49c. Quartz	2·10	65
3766	49c. Barytes	2·10	65
3767	49c. Galena	2·10	65
3768	49c. Turquoise	2·10	65

1212 "Belgium, The Coast" (Leo Marfut)

2003. Europa. Poster Art.

3769	**1212**	59c. multicoloured	2·75	1·40

1213 *La Robe de Mariee* (Paul Delvaux, Koksijde)

2003. "This is Belgium" (1st series). Sheet 167×200 mm containing T **1213** and similar vert designs showing sites from smaller Belgian towns. Multicoloured.

MS3770	41c. Type **1213**; 41c. Mural, Town Hall, Oudenaarde; 41c. *De vius* (sculpture, Rik Poot) and Town Hall, Vilvoorde; 41c. Turnhout chateau; 41c. Ambiorix (sculpture), Gallo-Roman museum, Tongeren; 41c. Fountain (sculpture, Pol Bury), La Louviere; 41c. Town Hall, Braine; 52c. Mardasson Memorial, Bastogne; 52c. Tower and snow scene, Sankt Vith; 57c. Saxophone and Citadel, Dinant	20·00	11·00

See also Nos. **MS**3809, **MS**3943 and **MS**4033.

1214 *Monument to the Seasonal Worker, Rillaar* (Jan Peirelinck)

2003. Tourism. Statues. Multicoloured.

3771	49c. Type **1214**	2·20	70
3772	49c. *La Tionade, Treignes* (Yves and Claude Rahir)	2·20	70
3773	49c. *Textile Teut, Town Hall, Hamont-Achel* (Teo Groenen)	2·20	70
3774	49c. *The Canal Guy*, Brussels (Tom Frantzen)	2·20	70
3775	49c. *The Maca*, Wavre (Jean Godart)	2·20	70

1215 King Baudouin and Prince Albert

2003. Tenth Anniv of the Accession of King Albert. Multicoloured.

3776	49c. Type **1215**	2·20	70
MS3777	90×125 mm. 59c. King Baudouin (38×48 mm); 84c. King Albert (38×48 mm)	6·75	5·50

1216 *Argenteuil* (Edouard Manet)

2003. Art.

3778	**1216**	49c. + 11c. multicoloured	2·75	1·80

No. 3778 was issued with a se-tenant label inscribed "PRIOR".

1217 *Still Life* (Giorgio Morandi)

2003. "Europhalia 2003 Italy" Festival. Italian Presidency of European Union. Multicoloured.

3779	49c. Type **1217**	2·20	75
3780	59c. Cistalia 202 (1947)	2·75	90

No. 3779 was issued with a se-tenant label inscribed "PRIOR".

Stamps of the same design were issued by Italy.

1218 Elderly Couple, Family and Young People

2003. Social Cohesion.

3781	**1218**	49c. multicoloured	2·20	80

No. 3781 was issued with a se-tenant label inscribed "PRIOR".

1219 St. Nicholas

2003. Christmas.

3782	**1219**	49c. multicoloured	2·20	80

No. 3782 was issued with a se-tenant label inscribed "PRIOR".

1220 King Albert II

2003

3783	**1220**	49c. red	2·20	80
3784	**1220**	50c. red	2·20	80
3785	**1220**	79c. blue and red	3·50	1·30
3786	**1220**	80c. violet and red	3·50	1·30

Nos. 3783/6 are inscribed "PRIOR" at left.

1221 Woman holding Cat ("Jardin extraordinaire")

2003. 50th Anniv of Belgian Television. Sheet 166×140 mm containing T **1221** and similar vert designs. Multicoloured.

MS3795	41c.×5 Type **1221**; Cameraman and camera; Broadcasting tower; Brothers Cassiers and Jef Burm; Scene from "Schipper naast Mathide"	9·00	6·50

1222 Man leaning against Pile of Books

2003. The Book. Multicoloured.

3796	49c. Type **1222**	2·20	80
3797	49c. Man rolling through printing machine (horiz)	2·20	80
3798	49c. Books on shelves	2·20	80

Nos. 3796/8 were each issued with an attached label inscribed "Prior".

1223 Maurice Gilliams

2003. Writers.

3799	**1223**	49c. brown, sepia and light brown	2·20	80
3800	-	59c. brown and orange	2·75	95

DESIGN: 59c. Marguerite Yourcenar (Maugerite de Crayencour).

No. 3799 was issued with an attached label inscribed "Prior".

1224 Tulip

2003. Flowers. No value expressed. Self-adhesive.

3801	**1224**	(59c.) multicoloured	2·50	95

No. 3801 was for use on inland letters up to 50g.

1225 Herbeumont Church

2003. Christmas and New Year.

3802	**1225**	41c. multicoloured	1·70	65

1226 Justin Henin Hardenne

2003. Belgian Tennis Champions. Multicoloured.

3803	49c. Type **1226** (2003 Roland Garros and U.S. Open champion)	2·30	80
3804	49c. Kim Clijsters (2002 Masters Cup and 2003 WTA No. 1 champion) (horiz)	2·30	80

Nos. 3803/4 were each issued with an attached label inscribed "Prior", either at top or bottom (vert) or left or right (horiz).

1227 XIII and Lighthouse

2004. "Philately for the Young". XIII (comic strip created by Jean van Damme and William Vance).

3805	**1227**	41c. multicoloured	1·80	65

1228 *Portrait of Marguerite Khonopff*

2004. Fernand Khnopff (artist) Commemoration. Sheet 160×140 mm containing T **1228** and similar multicoloured designs.

MS3806	41c.×4, Type **1228**; *Caresses* (55×24 mm); *The Abandoned City*; *Brown Eyes and a Blue Flower* (55×24 mm)	5·25	4·75

1229 Carnation

2004. Flowers. No value expressed. Self-adhesive.

3807	**1229**	(49c.) multicoloured	1·80	80

No. 3807 was for use on inland letters up to 50g.

1230 Profile, Stamp and Kiss

2004. Stamp Day.

3808	**1230**	41c. multicoloured	1·40	65

1231 Peter Piot (AIDS agency director)

2004. "This is Belgium" (2nd series). Sheet 166×200 mm containing T **1231** and similar vert designs showing Belgian personalities. Multicoloured.

MS3809	57c.×10, Type **1231**; Nicole Van Goethem (film maker); Dirk Frimout and Frank de Winnie (astronaut and cosmonaut); Jaques Rogge (president, International Olympic Committee); Christian de Duve (winner, Nobel Prize for Medicine); Gabrielle Petit (war heroine); Catherine Verfaillie (director, Stem Cell Institute, Minnesota) and Christine Van Broeckhoven (director, Molecular Biology Laboratory, University of Antwerp); Jaques Stilbe (philatelist); Queen Fabiola; Adrien van der Burch (organizer, Brussels Exhibition, 1935)	18·00	14·50

1232 Herg and Models of Rocket and Tintin

2004. 75th Anniv of Tintin (cartoon character created by Georges Remi (Herge)). Sheet 163×126 mm containing T **1232** and similar vert designs. Multicoloured.

MS3810	41c.×5, Type **1232**; Technical sketch for Destination Moon; Tintin and Snowy (Bobbie); Tintin climbing up rocket (*Explorers on the Moon*); Tintin, Captain Haddock and Snowy on the moon (cover illustration, *Explorers on the Moon*)	7·25	6·50

1233 Sugar Beet

2004. Sugar Industry. Multicoloured.

3811	**49c.**	Type **1233**	1·60	70
3812	**49c.**	49c. Sugar refinery	1·60	70
3813	**49c.**	49c. Tienen city	1·60	70

Nos. 3811/13 were each issued with a *se-tenant* label inscribed "Prior".

1234 Stars

2004. European Elections.

3814	**1234**	22c. cobalt, ultramarine and yellow	80	35

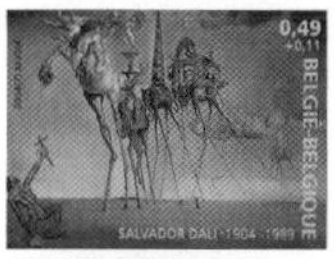

1235 *Temptation* (Salvador Dali)

2004. Birth Centenary of Salvador Dali (artist).

3815	**1235**	49c.+11c. multicoloured	2·10	1·90

No. 3815 was issued with a *se-tenant* label inscribed "Prior".

1236 Chapel, Buggenhout

2004. Tourism. Places of Pilgrimage.

3816	**1236**	49c. green	1·60	70
3817	-	49c. agate	1·60	70
3818	-	49c. purple	1·60	70
3819	-	49c. indigo	1·60	70

DESIGNS: No. 3817, Banneux; 3818, Scherpenheuvet; 3819, Beauraing (horiz).

Nos. 3816/19 were each issued with a *se-tenant* label inscribed "Prior".

1237 New Member's Flags and EU Emblem

2004. Enlargement of European Union (1st issue). Sheet 125×90 mm containing T **1237** and similar horiz designs. Multicoloured.

MS3820	50c.×2 Type **1237**×2; 60c.×2 Parliament building; As No. 3814	8·00	7·25

See also Nos. 3835/44.

1238 Le Faune Mordu (sculpture) (Jef Lambeaux), Boverie Park

2004. Liege ("Lidje todi"). Multicoloured.

3821	49c. Type **1238**	1·40	65
3822	49c. Bridge (Santiago Calatrava)	1·40	65
MS3823	90×125 mm. 75c. Blast furnace, Seraing (38×49 mm)	2·50	2·30

1239 Earth showing Clouds and Ozone Layer (climate and CO2)

2004. Climatology. Multicoloured.

3824	50c. Type **1239**	1·60	65
3825	65c. Sun and earth (earth–sun relationship)	2·00	85
3826	80c. Earth showing continent and viewed from space (earth)	2·50	1·00
3827	80c. Sun viewed through telescope and showing spots	2·50	1·00

Nos. 3824 and 3826 were issued with a *se-tenant* label inscribed "Prior".

1240 Edgar Jacobs

2004. Birth Centenary of Edgar Pierre Jacobs (creator of Blake and Mortimer (comic strip)). Black and yellow (60c.) or multicoloured (other).

3828	60c. Type **1240**	2·20	90
MS3829	125×90 mm. €1.20 Blake and Mortimer (45×36 mm)	3·75	3·00

Stamps of a similar design were issued by France.

1241 Django Reinhardt

2004. Jazz Musicians. Multicoloured.

3830	50c. Type **1241** (guitarist)	1·60	65
3831	50c. Fud Candrix (saxophonist)	1·60	65
3832	50c. Rene Thomas (guitarist)	1·60	65
3833	50c. Jack Sels (composer and saxophonist)	1·60	65
3834	50c. Bobby Jaspar (flautist and saxophonist)	1·60	65

Nos. 3830/4 were each issued with a *se-tenant* label inscribed "Prior".

1242 EU Emblem and Cyprus Flag

2004. Enlargement of European Union (2nd issue). Designs showing emblem and new member flag. Multicoloured. Self-adhesive.

3835	44c. Type **1242**	1·60	65
3836	44c. Estonia	1·60	65
3837	44c. Hungary	1·60	65
3838	44c. Latvia	1·60	65
3839	44c. Lithuania	1·60	65
3840	44c. Malta	1·60	65
3841	44c. Poland	1·60	65
3842	44c. Czech Republic	1·60	65
3843	44c. Slovakia	1·60	65
3844	44c. Slovenia	1·60	65

1243 King Albert II

2004. 70th Birthday of King Albert II. Each black and gold.

3845	50c. Type **1243**	1·60	65
MS3846	90×125 mm. 80c. As No. 3845 (38×48 mm)	2·50	2·10

No. 3845 was issued with a *se-tenant* label inscribed "Prior".

1244 Wind Break (Belgian Coast)

2004. Europa. Holidays. Winning Designs in Photographic Competition. Multicoloured.

3847	55c. Type **1244** (Muriel Vekemans)	1·70	1·40
3848	55c. Semois valley (Belgian Ardennes) (Freddy Deburghgraeve)	1·70	1·40

1245 Female Basketball Player

2004. Olympic Games, Athens 2004. Multicoloured.

3849	50c. Type **1245**	1·70	65
3850	55c. Cyclist (horiz)	1·80	75
3851	60c. Pole vaulter (horiz)	2·00	80
MS3852	136×90 mm. 80c. Olympic flame	2·75	2·10

No. 3849 was issued with a *se-tenant* label inscribed "Prior".

1246 Red Cross Workers

2004. Red Cross.

3853	**1246**	50c.+11c. multicoloured	2·00	1·60

No. 3853 was issued with a se-tenant label inscribed "Prior".

1247 *L'appel*

2004. Tenth Death Anniv of Idel Ianchelevici (sculptor). Multicoloured.

3854	50c. Type **1247**	1·70	65
3855	55c. "Perennis perdurat poeta"	1·80	75

No. 3854 was issued with a se-tenant label inscribed "Prior".

Stamps of the same design were issued by Romania.

2004. Mourning Stamp. As T **1197**.

3856	**1197**	50c. multicoloured	1·70	65

1248 Squirrel and Blackcap

2004. Forest Week. Sheet 90×125 mm containing T **1248** and similar vert designs. Multicoloured.
MS3857 44c.×4, Type **1248**; Nightingale, robin and red admiral butterfly; Bee, vole and weasel; Jay and peacock butterfly 6·50 5·25

The stamps and margin of **MS**3857 form a composite design of a forest scene.

1249 Volunteer Medal

2004. War Volunteers.
3858 **1249** 50c. multicoloured 1·70 65

1250 Impatiens

2004. Flowers. No value expressed. Self-adhesive.
3859 **1250** (50c.) multicoloured 1·70 65

No. 3859 was for use on inland letters up to 50g.

1251 Foal

2004. Belgica 2006 International Stamp Exhibition, Brussels (1st issue). Sheet 166×140 mm containing T **1251** and similar vert designs. Multicoloured.
MS3860 44c.×5, Type **1251**; Robin; Cat; Puppy; Fish 17·00 14·50

See also Nos. 3892/**MS**3897.

1252 Jack O' Lantern

2004. Halloween. Self-adhesive. Multicoloured.
3861 44c. Type **1252** 1·70 65
3862 44c. Witch, cat and bats 1·70 65

1253 Raymond Jean de Kramer

2004. Writers' Death Anniversaries. Multicoloured.
3863 50c. Type **1253** (writing as Jean Ray or John Flanders) (40th) 1·70 65
3864 75c. Johan Daisne (26th) 2·50 1·00
3865 80c. Thomas Owen (2nd) (vert) 2·75 1·10

Nos. 3863 and 3865 were issued with a *se-tenant* label inscribed "Prior".

1254 Soldiers, Mother and Child on Snow-covered Street

2004. 60th Anniv of Attack on Bastogne. Multicoloured.
3866 44c. Type **1254** 1·70 65
3867 55c. Soldiers assisting wounded (vert) 1·80 75
3868 65c. Soldiers amongst trees 2·10 85

1255 *Flight into Egypt*

2004. Christmas (1st issue). Paintings by Peter Paul Rubens. Multicoloured.
3869 44c. Type **1255** 1·70 65
3870 44c. *Adoration of the Magi* 1·70 65

Stamps of the same design were issued by Germany.
See also No. 3872.

1256 Rene Baeten

2004. Belgian International Motocross Champions. Sheet 151×166 mm containing T **1256** and similar horiz designs.
MS3871 50c.×12, (23bis a, d, e, f, g, i, j, k and l) multicoloured; (23bis b) green and brown; (23bis c) brown, lemon and deep brown; (23bis h) blue and brown 20·00 16·00

DESIGNS: Type **1256**; Jacky Martens; Georges Jobe; Joel Roberts; Eric Geboers; Roger de Coster; Stefan Everts; Gaston Rahier; Joel Smets; Harry Everts; Andre Malherbe and Steve Ramon.

The stamps of **MS**3871 were arranged around a central label, showing a motocross rider, each with a se-tenant label inscribed "Prior" attached at either left or right. The Belgium Post identification number is given in brackets to assist identification.

2004. Christmas (2nd issue). Paintings by Peter Rubens. Self-adhesive.
3872 44c. As No. 3870 (22×22 mm) 1·70 65

1257 Stylized Posthorn

2005
3873 **1257** 6c. scarlet 35 15
3874 **1257** 10c. blue 85 40
3877 **1257** 1 (52c.) scarlet 1·00 90

1258 Woman's Legs

2005. Centenary of Women's Council.
3882 **1258** 50c. multicoloured 1·70 65

No. 3882 was issued with a *se-tenant* label inscribed "Prior".

1259 Michel Vaillant

2005. "Philately for the Young". Michel Vaillant (comic strip created by Jean Graton).
3883 **1259** 50c. multicoloured 1·70 65

No. 3883 was issued with a *se-tenant* label inscribed "Prior".

1260 *The Violinist* (Kees van Dongen)

2005. "Promotion of Philately".
3884 **1260** 50c.+12c. multicoloured 2·10 1·70

1261 "www.175-25.be"

2005. 175th Anniv of Independence (1st issue). 25th Anniv of Federal State. No value expressed. Self-adhesive.
3885 **1261** (50c.) multicoloured 1·70 65

See also No. **MS**3889 and **MS**3891.

1262 Johan Hendrick van Dale and *van Dale* (Dutch dictionary)

2005. Language. Multicoloured.
3886 55c. Type **1262** 1·80 75
3887 55c. Maurice Grevisse and "le bon usage" (French grammar) 1·80 75

1263 Child receiving Polio Vaccine

2005. Centenary of Rotary International (charitable organization). Polio Eradication Campaign.
3888 **1263** 80c. multicoloured 2·75 1·30

1264 First Railway Journey from Brussels to Malines (1835)

2005. 175th Anniv of Independence (2nd issue). Sheet 166×200 mm containing T **1264** and similar horiz designs. Multicoloured.
MS3889 44c.×10, Type **1264** (transport); Bakuba dancers, Congo; Early school children (education); Factory workers (industrialization); Family (social development); Bombardment of Edingen, 1940; Brussels Expo, 1958 (trade); Rue de la Loi, Wetstraat (federalization); Berlaymont building, Brussels (Europe); "The Shadow and its Shadow" (Rene Mgritte) (art) 15·00 13·50

1265 "TSUNAMI" and Sea

2005. Red Cross. Support for Victims of Tsunami Disaster.
3890 **1265** 50c.+12c. multicoloured 2·10 1·70

No. 3890 was issued with a *se-tenant* label inscribed "Prior".

1266 King Albert II and Queen Paola

2005. 175th Anniv of Independence (3rd issue). Sheet 126×90 mm.
MS3891 **1266** 75c. multicoloured 2·50 2·00

1267 Go-Kart

2005. Belgica 2006 International Stamp Exhibition, Brussels (2nd issue). Multicoloured. (a) Self-adhesive.
3892 44c. Type **1267** 1·50 60
3893 44c. Motor boat 1·50 60
3894 44c. Train 1·50 60
3895 44c. Airplane 1·50 60
3896 44c. Spacecraft 1·50 60

(b) Size 27×39 mm. Miniature Sheet. Ordinary gum.
MS3897 166×131 mm. Nos. 3892/5 17·00 13·50

1268 Rose "Belinda"

2005. Ghent Flower Show. Multicoloured.
3898 44c. Type **1268** 1·50 60
3899 70c. Rose "Pink Iceberg" (vert) 2·30 95
3900 80c. Rose "Old Master" 2·75 1·10

Nos. 3898/3900 were impregnated with the scent of roses.
No. 3900 was issued with a *se-tenant* label inscribed "Prior".

1269 *The Children's Table* (Gustave van de Woestijne)

2005. Europa. Gastronomy. Multicoloured.
3901 60c. Type **1269** 2·00 1·60
3902 60c. *Still Life with Oysters, Fruit and Pastry* 2·00 1·60

1270 Black Stork

2005. Stamp Day.
3903 **1270** €4 multicoloured 13·00 5·25

1271 Soldiers

2005. 55th Anniv of Korean War.
3904 **1271** 44c. multicoloured 1·50 60

1272 Celebration

2005. 60th Anniv of End of World War II. Multicoloured.
3905 44c. Type **1272** 1·50 60
3906 44c. Camp prisoner 1·50 60
3907 44c. Returning service men and prisoners 1·50 60

1273 Zimmer Tower, Lier, Flanders

2005. Tourism. Clock Towers.
3908 **1273** 44c. black 1·50 60
3909 - 44c. agate 1·50 60
3910 - 44c. chocolate 1·50 60

DESIGNS: No. 3908 Type **1273**; 3909 Belfry, Mons, Wallonia; 3910 Mont des Arts Clock, Brussels.

1274 Hiker (Ardennes)

2005. Holidays. Multicoloured.
3911 50c. Type **1274** 1·70 65
3912 50c. Sunbather 1·70 65

Nos. 3911/12 were each issued with a se-tenant label inscribed "Prior".

1275 Hearts

2005. Greetings Stamps. Multicoloured. Self-adhesive.
3913 (50c.) Type **1275** 1·70 65

3914	80c. Doves (wedding)	2·75	1·10
3915	80c. Two rings (wedding)	2·75	1·10
3916	80c. Boy (birth)	2·75	1·10
3917	80c. Girl (birth)	2·75	1·10

No. 3913 was for use on inland letters up to 50g.

1276 Tulip

2005. Air. Flowers. No value expressed. Multicoloured. Self-adhesive.

3918	**1276**	(70c.) multicoloured	2·30	95

1277 *L'humanitie assaillie par les sept Peches capiteux* (Seven Deadly Sins) (16th-century tapestry, Brussels)

2005. Carpets and Tapestries. Multicoloured.

3919	44c. Type **1277**	1·50	60
3920	60c. Carpet, Hereke, Turkey	2·00	80

Stamps of a similar design were issued by Turkey.

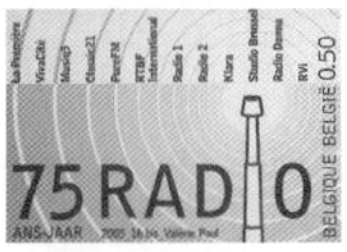

1278 Radio Waves

2005. 75th Anniv of Radio.

3921	**1278**	50c. magenta and black	1·70	65

No. 3921 was issued with a *se-tenant* label inscribed "Prior".

1279 Robert Van de Walle

2005. Belgian International Judo Champions. Sheet 100×167 mm containing T 1279 and similar horiz designs. Multicoloured.

MS3922 50c.×6, Type **1279**; Ingrid Berghmans; Ulla Werbrouck; Gella Vandecaveye; Christel Deliege; Johan Laats 10·00 8·00

The stamps of **MS**3922 were each issued with a *se-tenant* label inscribed "Prior" attached at either left or right.

1280 King Albert II

2005

3923	**1280**	50c. multicoloured (postage)	1·00	85
3923a	**1280**	52c. multicoloured	1·00	70
3928	**1280**	70c. blue and light (air)	2·30	95
3928a	**1280**	80c. blue, grey and black	95	65
3928b	**1280**	83c. multicoloured	1·00	70
3929	**1280**	90c. blue, grey and black	2·75	1·10

Nos. 3923 and 3928/9 were inscribed "Prior".

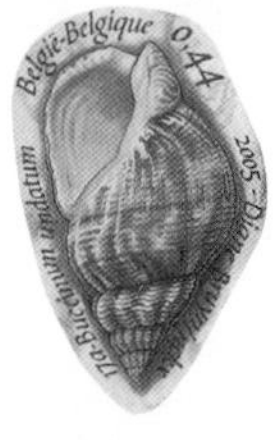

1281 *Buccinum undatum*

2005. Molluscs. Sheet 161×130 mm containing T **1281** and similar designs. Multicoloured. Self-adhesive.

MS3933 44c.×6, Type **1281**; *Epitonium clathrus*; *Cepea nemoralis and Arion rufus*; *Donax vittatus*; *Anodonta cygnea*; *Anodonta cygnea* (different) 9·00 7·25

1282 Centre for Comic Strip Art, Brussels

2005. Architecture. Multicoloured.

3934	44c. Type **1282**	1·50	60
3935	44c. Museum of Musical Instruments, Brussels	1·50	60
3936	65c. Bukit Pasoh Road, Singapore	2·10	85
3937	65c. Kandahar Street, Singapore	2·10	85

Stamps of the same design were issued by Singapore.

1283 Chrysanthemum

2005. Flowers. No value expressed. Self-adhesive.

3938	**1283**	(50c.) multicoloured	1·70	65

No. 3938 was for use on inland letters up to 50g.

1284 *The Reaper* (Kasimir Malevich)

2005. "Europhalia 2005—Russia" Festival. Multicoloured.

3939	50c. Type **1284**	1·70	65
3940	70c. "Allegory" (Sergei Sudeikin)	2·30	95

No. 3939 was issued with a *se-tenant* label inscribed "Prior".

1285 Shrine of Our Lady, Tournai

2005. 800th Anniv of Shrine of Our Lady by Nicolas of Verdun.

3941	**1285**	75c. bronze and gold	2·50	1·00

1286 Asterix

2005. Asterix (comic strip written by Rene Goscinny and illustrated by Albert Uderzo). Sheet 161×130 mm containing T **1286** and similar designs showing characters. Multicoloured.

MS3942 60c.×6, Type **1286**; Cacofonix (27×41 mm.); Getafix (41×27 mm.); Obelix (41×27 mm.); Abraracourcix (27×41 mm.); Asterix feasting (39×34 mm.) 11·50 10·50

1287 "Objet" (Joelle Tuerlinckx)

2005. "This is Belgium" (3rd series). Art. Sheet 166×201 mm containing T **1287** and similar designs.

MS3943 44c.×10, black and claret (Type **1287**); multicoloured (*ABC* (Jef Geys)); multicoloured (*La Traviata* (Lili Dujourie)); multicoloured (*Representation d'un corps rond* (Ann Veronica Janssens)); black (*Portrait of an Artist by Himself (XIII)* (Jan Vercuysse)); multicoloured (*Donderwolk* (Panamarenko)); multicoloured (*Tournus* (Marthe Wery)); multicoloured (*Figuur op de rug gezien (la nuque)* (I Luc Tuymans)); black and bright carmine (*Jeu de mains* (Michel Francois)); *Mur de la montee des Anges* (Jan Fabre)) 13·00 12·00

The stamps of No. **MS**3943 form a composite design.

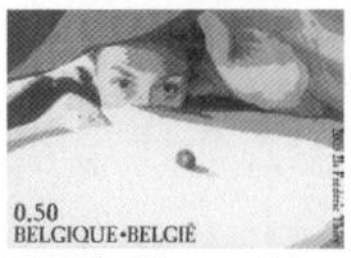

1288 *The Princess and the Pea*

2005. Birth Bicentenary of Hans Christian Andersen (writer). Multicoloured. (a) Ordinary gum.

3944	50c. Type **1288b**	1·70	65
3945	50c. *The Ugly Duckling*	1·70	65
3946	50c. *Thumbelina*	1·70	65
3947	50c. *The Little Mermaid*	1·70	65
3948	50c. *The Emperor's New Clothes*	1·70	65

(b) Size 28×22 mm. Self-adhesive.

3949	50c. As No. 3944	1·70	65
3950	50c. As No. 3945	1·70	65
3951	50c. As No. 3946	1·70	65
3952	50c. As No. 3947	1·70	65
3953	50c. As No. 3948	1·70	65

Nos. 3944/8 each have a label inscribed "Prior" attached at left.

1289 Father Christmas

2005. Christmas. (a) Ordinary gum.

3954	**1289**	44c. multicoloured	1·50	60

(b) Size 23×28 mm. Self-adhesive.

3955	44c. multicoloured	1·50	60

1290 Maurits Sabbe

2005. Popular Literature. Writers. Multicoloured.

3956	44c. Type **1290**	1·50	60
3957	44c. Arthur Masson	1·50	60

1291 Queen Astrid

2005. Birth Centenary of Queen Astrid. Each black and gold.

3958	44c. Type **1291**	1·50	60

MS3959 90×125 mm. 80c. Queen Astrid and Prince Albert (38×49 mm) 2·75 2·10

1292 Drum

2005. Music. Brass Bands. Multicoloured.

3960	50c. Type **1292**	1·70	70
3961	50c. Cornet	1·70	70
3962	50c. Sousaphone	1·70	70
3963	50c. Clarinet	1·70	70
3964	50c. Tuba	1·70	70

Nos. 3960/4 each have a label inscribed "Prior" attached at foot.

1293 Donkey

2006. Farm Animals. Multicoloured. Self-adhesive.

3965	46c. Type **1293**	1·40	65
3966	46c. Hens	1·40	65
3967	46c. Ducks	1·40	65
3968	46c. Pigs	1·40	65
3969	46c. Cow	1·40	65
3970	46c. Goat	1·40	65
3971	46c. Rabbits	1·40	65
3972	46c. Horses	1·40	65
3973	46c. Sheep	1·40	65
3974	46c. Geese	1·40	65

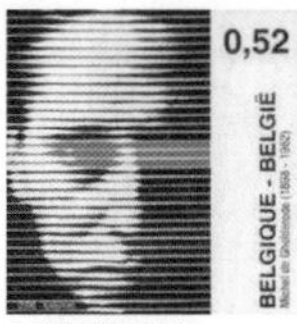

1294 Michel de Ghelderode

2006. Writers Commemorations.

3975	**1294**	52c. black and blue	1·60	70
3976	-	78c. black and magenta	1·90	85

DESIGN: 78c. Herman Terlinck.

No. 3975 has a label inscribed "Prior" attached at left.

1295 Guillaume Dufay and Gilles Binchois

2006. Renaissance Polyphonists (part song writers). Multicoloured.

3977	60c. Type **1295**	1·80	75
3978	60c. Johannes Ockeghem	1·80	75
3979	60c. Jacob Obrecht	1·80	75
3980	60c. Adriaan Willaert	1·80	75
3981	60c. Orlandus Lassus	1·80	75

1296 Musical Score and Mozart

2006. 250th Birth Anniv of Wolfgang Amadeus Mozart.

3982	**1296**	70c. multicoloured	2·30	1·00

1297 Cross Bowman

1298 Cross Bowman

2006. Cross Bowmen. (a) Ordinary gum.

3983	**1297**	46c. multicoloured	1·50	65

(b) Size 24×32 mm. Self-adhesive gum.

3984	**1298**	(52c.) multicoloured	1·70	70

1299 Senate

2006. 175th Anniv of Democracy. Sheet 200×83 mm containing T **1299** and similar multicoloured designs.

MS3985 46c.×3, Type **1299**; King Leopold (vert); Chamber of representatives 4·50 3·75

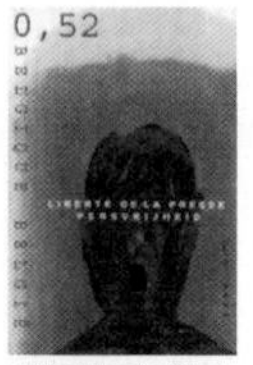

1300 Head with Open Mouth

2006. Freedom of the Press. Sheet 197×100 mm containing T **1300** and similar multicoloured designs.

MS3986 52c.×5, Type **1300** ×3; Blue sky ×2 (horiz) 8·25 7·25

The stamps of **MS**3986 each have a label inscribed "Prior" attached at foot. The stamp depicting a blue sky shows a woman's face when tilted.

1301 Mouth and Script

1302 Mouth and Script

2006. Stamp Festival. Winning Entry in Design a Stamp Competition. (a) Ordinary gum.

3987	**1301**	46c. multicoloured		1·50	65

(b) Size 29×25 mm. Self-adhesive gum.

3988	**1302**	(52c.) multicoloured	1·70	70
3988a	**1302**	(52c.) As Type **1302** but design reversed	1·70	70

Nos. 3988/a were each issued with a se-tenant label inscribed "Prior".

1303 Justus Lipsius

2006. 400th Death Anniv of Justus Lipsius (writer and scientist).

3989	**1303**	70c. brown and cinnamon	2·30	1·00

1304 Winner and Trophy

2006. First Four Stages—Giro Italia (cycle race), Wallonia.

3990	**1304**	52c. multicoloured	1·70	70

1305 John Walker

2006. 30th Anniv of Memorial Van Damme Track and Field Event. Sheet 167×100 mm containing T **1305** and similar vert designs. Multicoloured.

MS3991	52c.×5, Type **1305**; Alberto Juantorena; Ivo Van Damme; Sebastian Coe; Steve Ovett	8·25	7·25

The stamps of **MS**3991 were each issued with a label inscribed "Prior" at foot.

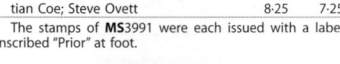

1306 Clement Van Hassel

2006. Belgian World Champions—Billiards. Sheet 153×167 mm containing T **1306** and similar horiz designs. Multicoloured.

MS3992	52c.×12, Type **1306**; Tony Schrauwen; Leo Corin; Emile Wafflard; Ludo Dielis; Jos Vervest; Frederic Caudron; Laurent Boulanger; Paul Stroobants, Eddy Leppens and Peter De Backer; Raymond Ceulemans; Raymond Steylaerts; Jozef Philipoom	18·00	16·00

The stamps of **MS**3992 were each issued with a label inscribed "Prior" at either left or right.

The stamps of **MS**3992 were not for sale separately.

1307 *L'offrande de Joachim Refusee* (Lambert Lombard)

2006. Art. 500th Birth Anniv of Lambert Lombard (3393/4) or 150th Birth Anniv of Leon Spilliaert (3395/6). Multicoloured.

3993	65c. Type **1307**	2·10	90
3994	65c. *August et la Sybille de Tibur* (Lambert Lombard)	2·10	90
3995	65c. *Duizeling* (Leon Spilliaert)	2·10	90
3996	65c. *De Dame met de Hoed* (Leon Spilliaert)	2·10	90

1308 Ostend Lighthouse

2006. Lighthouses. Multicoloured.

3997	46c. Type **1308**	1·50	65
3998	46c. Blankenberge	1·50	65
3999	46c. Nieuwport	1·50	65
4000	46c. Heist	1·50	65

1309 Dogfish

2006. North Sea Fish. Sheet 146×124 mm containing T **1309** and similar multicoloured designs.

MS4001	46c.×5, Type **1309**; Cod (47×26 mm); Thornback skate; Plaice (33×26 mm); Herring (33×26 mm)	7·50	6·50

The stamps and margins of **MS**4001 form a composite design.

1310 Emblem

1311 Emblem

2006. Belgica 2006 International Stamp Exhibition. (a) Ordinary Gum.

4002	**1310**	46c. multicoloured	1·50	65

(b) Size 24×28 mm. Self-adhesive gum.

4003	**1311**	(52c.) multicoloured	1·50	65

1312 Nurse, Patients and Bandages

1313 Nurse, Patients and Bandages

2006. Red Cross. Benjamin Secouriste (children's Red Cross certificate scheme). (a) Ordinary Gum.

4004	**1312**	52c.+12c. multicoloured	2·00	85

(b) Size 24×28 mm. Self-adhesive gum.

4005	**1313**	(52c.) multicoloured	1·70	70
4005a	**1313**	(52c.) As Type **1313** but design reversed	1·70	70

No. 4005/a were issued with a *se-tenant* label inscribed "Prior".

1314 Emblem

2006. Centenary of BOIC (Belgian Olympic and Interfederal Committee).

4006	**1314**	52c. multicoloured	1·70	70

No. 4006 was issued with a *se-tenant* label inscribed "Prior".

1315 Deigne

2006. Tourism. Wallonia. Showing village scenes. Multicoloured.

4007	52c. Type **1315**	1·70	70
4008	52c. Mein	1·70	70
4009	52c. Celles	1·70	70
4010	52c. Lompret	1·70	70
4011	52c. Ny	1·70	70

Nos. 4007/11 were each issued with a *se-tenant* label inscribed "Prior".

1316 Part of Football

2006. World Cup Football Championship, Germany. Sheet 126×90 mm.

MS4012	**1316**	€1.30 multicoloured	4·25	3·75

1317 *Centauria*

2006. Flowers. No value expressed. Self-adhesive.

4013	**1317**	(52c.) multicoloured	1·70	70

No. 4013 was for use on inland letters up to 50g.

1318 Miner

2006. 50th Anniv of Marcinelle Mine Disaster.

4014	**1318**	70c. multicoloured	2·30	1·00

1319 Tulip

2006. Air. Flowers. No value expressed. Self-adhesive. Multicoloured.

4015	**1319**	(70c.) multicoloured	2·30	1·00

No. 4015 was for use on letters of up to 50g. within Europe.

1320 *Oosterlinghuis* (beguinage (religious community), Bruges) (painting)

2006. 650th Anniv of Hanseatic League. Multicoloured.

4016	70c. Type **1320**	2·30	1·00
4017	80c. *Oosters Huis* (Bremen town hall) (painting)	2·50	1·10

1321 Institute Building

2006. Centenary of the Institute of Tropical Medicine.

4018	**1321**	80c. multicoloured	2·50	1·10

1322 "ABA"

2006. Academie de Philatelie de Belgique.

4019	**1322**	52c. multicoloured	1·60	70

No. 4019 was issued with a *se-tenant* label inscribed "Prior" attached at top.

1323 *Le Kleptomane* (Theodore Gericault)

2006. Foreign Masterpieces in Belgian Collections.

4020	**1323**	52c.+12c. multicoloured	2·10	95

No. 4020 was issued with a label inscribed "Prior" attached at left. The premium was for the promotion of philately.

1324 Ying Yang Symbol

2006. Belgica 2006 International Stamp Exhibition. Young Philatelist World Championship. Two sheets containing T **1324** and similar vert designs. Multicoloured.

MS4021	(a) 166×133 mm. 46c.×5, Type **1324**; Tulips as wine glasses; Butterflies as four leaf clover; Tent at night; Comic page containing all designs. (b) 190×120 mm. €1.95 Emblem (38×49 mm)	29·00	26·00

Nos. **MS**4021a/b were each sold for €5, the premium for the promotion of philately.

1325 Animals (Nassira Tadmiri)

2006. Europa. Integration. Multicoloured.

4022	52c. Type **1325**	1·60	70
4023	52c. Children of many nations and rainbow (Lize-Maria Verhaeghe)	1·60	70

1326 *New Skin* (Pierre Alechinsky)

1327 *New Skin* (Pierre Alechinsky)

2006. CoBrA (artistic movement). Multicoloured. (a) Miniature sheet. Ordinary gum.

MS4024	125×90 mm. 46c. Type **1326**; 70c. "Untitled" (Asger Jorn)	3·75	3·25

(b) Size 28×25 mm. No value expressed. Self-adhesive gum.

4025	(52c.) Type **1327**	1·60	70

Stamps of similar design were issued by Denmark.

1328 Rock and Roll

1329 Rock and Roll

2006. Dance. Multicoloured.

(a) Size 30×26 mm. No value expressed. Self-adhesive gum.

4026	(52c.) Type **1329**	1·60	70
4027	(52c.) Waltz	1·60	70
4028	(52c.) Tango	1·60	70
4029	(52c.) Cha-cha-cha	1·60	70
4030	(52c.) Samba	1·60	70

(b) Miniature sheet. Ordinary gum.

MS4031	166×125 mm. 60c.×5, Type **1328**; Waltz; Tango; Cha-cha-cha; Samba	8·75	8·75

1330 Kramikske

2006. Youth Philately. Kramikske Briochon, cartoon character created by Jean-Pol Vandenbroek.

4032	**1330** 46c. multicoloured	1·50	70

1331 Tomato and Shrimps

2006. "This is Belgium" (4th series). Food. Sheet 154×186 mm containing T **1331** and similar multicoloured designs.

MS4033	46c.×10, Type **1331**; Trappist beer (vert); Jenever (spirit) (vert); Chicory au gratin; Ham and sausages (vert); Waffles (vert); Stewed eels in chervil sauce; Chocolate; Mussels and fries (vert); Gueuze (beer) (vert)	13·50	13·00

1332 Angel playing Psaltery (detail)

1333 Angel playing Psaltery (detail)

2006. Christmas. Altarpiece by Hans Memling. Showing angel musicians. Multicoloured. (a) Ordinary gum.

4034	46c. Type **1332**	1·50	70
4035	46c. Tromba marina	1·50	70
4036	46c. Lute	1·50	70
4037	46c. Trumpet	1·50	70
4038	46c. Shawn	1·50	70

(b) Size 25×29 mm. Self-adhesive.

4039	46c. Type **1333**	1·50	70
4040	46c. Tromba marina	1·50	70
4041	46c. Lute	1·50	70
4042	46c. Trumpet	1·50	70
4043	46c. Shawn	1·50	70

Nos. 4034/8 were issued together, se-tenant, forming a composite design.

1334 "HAPPY BIRTHDAY TO YOU"

2006. Greetings Stamps. Self-adhesive. Multicoloured. No value expressed.

4044	(52c.) Type **1334**	1·50	70
4045	(52c.) Birthday cake (Prior at right)	1·50	70
4046	(52c.) As No. 4045 (Prior at left)	1·50	70
4047	(52c.) As No. 4044 (Prior at right)	1·50	70

1335 Cycle Wheel (cyclocross)

2007. Sport. Multicoloured. (a) Ordinary gum.

4048	46c. Type **1335**	1·40	65
4049	60c. Ball and skittles (bowling)	1·80	85
4050	65c. Club and ball (golf)	2·00	95

(b) Size 25×29 mm. Self-adhesive. No Value Expressed.

4051	(52c.) As Type **1335**	1·50	70
4052	(52c.) As No. 4049	1·50	70
4053	(52c.) As No. 4050	1·50	70

1336 *Nu Assis* (Amedo Modigliani)

2007. Sheet 90×125 mm.

MS4054	**1336** 60c.+30c. multicoloured	2·75	2·50

The premium was for the promotion of philately.

1337 Alix

2007. "Philately for the Young". Alix (comic strip created by Jacques Martin).

4055	**1337** 52c. multicoloured	1·70	80

1338 Piano Accordion

2007. Bellows-driven Aerophones. Sheet 166×100 mm containing T 1338 and similar vert designs. Multicoloured.

MS4056	52c.×5 Type **1338**; Concertina; Button accordion; Melodeon; Melodeon (different)	7·50	7·25

The stamps of **MS**4056 each have a se-tenant label inscribed "Prior" attached at foot.

The stamps of **MS**4056 were not for sale separately.

1339 Julia Tulkens

2007. Women in Literature. Sheet 166×100 mm containing T **1339** and similar vert designs. Multicoloured.

MS4057	52c.×5 Type **1339**; Madeleine Bourdhouxhe; Christine d'Haen; Jacqueline Harpman; Maria Rosseels	7·50	7·25

The stamps of **MS**4057 each have a se-tenant label inscribed "Prior" attached at foot and form a composite background design.

1340 Hospital Librarian and Patient

1341 Hospital Librarian and Patient

2007. Red Cross. Multicoloured. (a) Self-adhesive gum.

4058	(52c.) Type **1340**	1·50	70
4059	(52c.) As No. 4058 but with "Prior" at right	1·50	70

(b) Size 39×27 mm. Ordinary gum.

4060	52c.+25c. Type **1341**	2·40	1·10

No. 4060 has a label inscribed "Prior" attached at right.

1342 *Tati l'periki* (Tati the hairdresser) (Edouard Remouchamps)

2007. Belgian Popular Theatre. Sheet 198×83 mm containing T **1342** and similar multicoloured designs.

MS4061	46c.×3, Type **1342**; Romain DeConinck (vert); *Le Mariage de Melle Beulemans* (Jean-Francois Fonson and Fernand Wicheler)	4·50	4·25

The stamps of **MS**4061 form a composite background design.

1343 Stoclet Palace (interior) (Josef Hoffman)

2007. Architecture. Multicoloured.

4062	46c. Type **1343**	1·70	80
4063	80c. Stoclet Palace (exterior)	2·40	1·10

No. 4063 has a label inscribed "Prior" attached at top.

Stamps of a similar design were issued by Czech Republic.

1344 Robert Baden-Powell (founder)

2007. Europa. Centenary of Scouting. Multicoloured.

4064	52c. Type **1344**	1·60	80
MS4065	90×125 mm. 75c. Scouts (38×48 mm)	2·50	2·50

The stamp and margins of **MS**4065 form a composite background design.

1345 Country Identification Letters of Signatories

2007. 50th Anniv of Treaty of Rome.

4066	**1345** 80c. multicoloured	2·50	1·30

1346 'Tintin au pays de Soviets' (Tintin in the land of Soviets) (French)

2007. Birth Centenary of Georges Remi (Herge) (creator of Tintin). Designs showing Tintin book covers in different languages. Multicoloured.

4067	46c. Type **1346**	1·60	80
4068	46c. Tintin in the Congo (Danish)	1·60	80
4069	46c. Tintin in America	1·60	80
4070	46c. Cigars of the Pharaoh (Luxembourg)	1·60	80
4071	46c. The Blue Lotus (Chinese)	1·60	80
4072	46c. The Broken Ear (Portuguese)	1·60	80
4073	46c. The Black Island (Bengali)	1·60	80
4074	46c. King Ottokar's Sceptre (Slovakian)	1·60	80
4075	46c. The Crab with the Golden Claws (Russian)	1·60	80
4076	46c. The Shooting Star (Icelandic)	1·60	80
4077	46c. The Secret of the Unicorn (Polish)	1·60	80
4078	46c. Red Rackham's Treasure (Afrikaans)	1·60	80
4079	46c. Herge	1·60	80
4080	46c. The Seven Crystal Balls (Arabic)	1·60	80
4081	46c. Prisoners of the Sun (Spanish)	1·60	80
4082	46c. Land of Black Gold (German)	1·60	80
4083	46c. Destination Moon (Finnish)	1·60	80
4084	46c. Explorers of the Moon (Swedish)	1·60	80
4085	46c. The Calculus Affair (Japanese)	1·60	80
4086	46c. The Red Sea Sharks (Turkish)	1·60	80
4087	46c. Tintin in Tibet (Tibetan)	1·60	80
4088	46c. The Castifiore Emerald (Italian)	1·60	80
4089	46c. Flight 714 (Indonesian)	1·60	80
4090	46c. Tintin and the Picaros (Greek)	1·60	80
4091	46c. Tintin and the Alph-Art (Dutch)	1·60	80

1347 Dress (Museum of Fashion, Hasselt)

2007. Small Museums. Multicoloured.

4092	46c. Type **1347**	1·60	80
4093	75c. Skeleton and woman (Notre-Dame a la Rose Hospital Cultural Museum, Lessines)	2·40	1·20
4094	92c. Beaker (Jewish Museum, Brussels)	3·00	1·50

1348 Men carrying Canoe

1349 Men carrying Canoe

2007. Summer Stamps. No Value Expressed. Multicoloured. (a) Self-adhesive.

4095	(52c.) Type **1348**	1·60	80
4096	(52c.) As No. 4095 but with "Prior" at left	1·60	80
4097	(52c.) Couple with kite	1·60	80
4098	(52c.) As No. 4097 but with "Prior" at left	1·60	80

(b) Ordinary gum.

4099	52c. Type **1349**	1·60	80
4100	52c. As No. 4098	1·60	80

1350 Building

2007. 50th Anniv of King Baudouin Antarctic Base (1st Belgian Antarctic research station). Sheet 90×125 mm.

MS4101	75c. multicoloured	2·50	2·50

1351 Cyclists

2007. Tour de France Cycle Race.

4102	**1351** 52c. multicoloured	1·70	85

1352 Ship in Port

1353 Ship in Port

2007. Centenary of Zeebrugge. No Value Expressed. Multicoloured. (a) Self-adhesive.

4103	(52c.) Type **1352**	1·70	85
4104	(52c.) As No. 4103 but with 'Prior' at left	1·70	85

(b) Ordinary gum.

4105	€1.04 Type **1353** but with 'Prior' at left	3·50	1·80

1354 Athenee Royal Francois Bovesse, Namur

2007. Tourism. Multicoloured.

4106	52c. Type **1354**	1·90	1·10

4107	52c. Saint Michel College, Brussels	1·90	1·10
4108	52c. Heilig Hart College	1·90	1·10

1355 Scene from *Misere au Borinage* (film by Henri Storck)

2007. Belgium Cinema. Birth Centenary of Henri Storck (filmmaker). Sheet 98×167 mm containing T **1355** and similar horiz designs. Multicoloured.

MS4109	52c.×5, Type **1355**; Boy sleeping (*Les Fils* by Luc and Jean-Pierre Dardenne); Haircut (*L'homme au crane rase* (Man who had his hair cut short) by Andre Delvaux); Bedside scene (*Malpertius* by Harry Kumel); Seated woman (*Dust* by Marion Hansel)	8·50	8·50

1356 Tombeau du Geant, Botassart

2007. Luxembourg European Capital of Culture–2007. Multicoloured.

4110	52c. Type **1356**	1·90	1·10
4111	80c. Rotunda, Luxembourg Train Station	3·00	1·70

Stamp of a similar design was issued by Luxembourg.

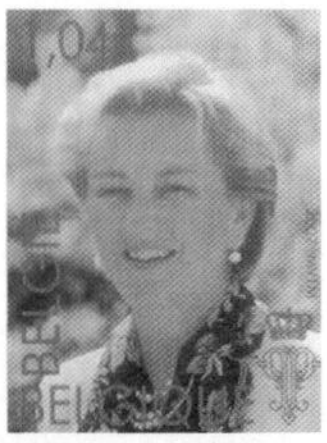

1357 Queen Paola

2007. 70th Birth Anniv of Queen Paola. Sheet 125×90 mm.

MS4112	**1357**	€1.04 multicoloured	3·75	3·75

1358 King Albert II

2007

4113	**1358**	1 (52c.) red and vermilion	1·80	1·10
4114	**1358**	2 (€1.04) olive, green and slate	3·50	2·10
4115	**1358**	3 (€1.56) blue, indigo and slate	5·25	3·25
4116	**1358**	5 (€2.60) violet, purple and slate	9·00	5·25
4117	**1358**	7 (€3.64) brown, deep brown and slate	12·50	7·50

This set is to introduce the new franking system which is in multiples of base price (currently 52c.). 1 (52c.) is for use on standard domestic mail from 0–50 grams, 2 (€1.04 (ie twice base rate of 52c.)) is for use on non-standard domestic mail from 0–100 grams, 3 (€1.56) is for use on non-standard domestic mail from 100–350 grams, 5 (€2.60) is for use on non-standard domestic mail from 350 grams–1 kilo, 7 (€3.64) is for use on non-standard domestic mail from 1–2 kilos.

1359 Pears

2007. Fruit. Multicoloured. Self-adhesive.

4118	1 (52c.) Type **1359**	1·80	1·10
4119	1 (52c.) Strawberries	1·80	1·10
4120	1 (52c.) Red currants	1·80	1·10
4121	1 (52c.) Apples	1·80	1·10
4122	1 (52c.) Grapes	1·80	1·10
4123	1 (52c.) Cherries	1·80	1·10
4124	1 (52c.) Raspberries	1·80	1·10
4125	1 (52c.) Peaches	1·80	1·10
4126	1 (52c.) Plums	1·80	1·10
4127	1 (52c.) Blackberries	1·80	1·10

1360 Remington (20th-century)

1361 Remington (20th-century)

2007. Stamp Festival. Typewriters. Multicoloured. (a) Self-adhesive.

4128	1 (52c.) Type **1360**	1·80	1·10
4129	1 (52c.) Royal (1925)	1·80	1·10
4130	1 (52c.) Olympia (1950)	1·80	1·10
4131	1 (52c.) Olivetti (1972)	1·80	1·10
4132	1 (52c.) Laptop word processor	1·80	1·10

(b) Ordinary gum.

MS4133	100×165 mm. 1 (52c.)×5, Type **1361**; As No. 4129; As No. 4130; As No. 4131; As No. 4132	9·00	9·00

1362 Dahlia

2007. Flowers. Multicoloured. Self-adhesive.

4134	1 (52c.) Type **1362**	1·80	1·10
4135	2 (€1.04) Petunia	3·50	2·10

1363 Marc Van Montagu (molecular genetics)

2007. This Belgium. Science. Sheet 166×193 mm containing T **1363** and similar circular designs. Multicoloured. Self-adhesive.

MS4136	70c.×9, Type **1363**; Paul Janssen (medicine); Lise Thirly (microbiology/virology); Chris Van den Wyngaert (international criminal law); Peter Carmeliet (molecular medicine); Philippe Van Parijs (social philosophy); Marie-Claire Foblets (anthropology); Andre Berger (climate studies); Pierre Rene Deligne (mathematics)	18·00	18·00

1364 Tulip 'Peach Blossom'

2007. Self-adhesive.

4137	**1364**	A (80c.) multicoloured	2·75	1·70

1365 Sunset

2007. Bereavement. No value expressed.

4138	**1365**	1 (52c.) multicoloured	1·80	1·10

1366 *Les chemins de la liberte* (*Le voyage*) (Thierry Merget)

2007. Postal Art.

4139	**1366**	1 (52c.) multicoloured	1·80	1·10

1367 Couple in Wedding Outfits

2007. Greetings Stamps. Multicoloured. Self-adhesive.

4140	1 (52c.) Type **1367**	1·80	1·10
4141	1 (52c.) Father holding boy baby	1·80	1·10
4142	1 (52c.) Mother holding girl baby	1·80	1·10

2007. Belgian Billiards World Champions. Sheet 80×140 mm containing horiz designs as T **1306**. Multicoloured.

MS4143	1 (52c.)×9, Piet J. Van Duppen; Albert Collette; Gustaaf Van Belle; Piet Sels; Gaston De Doncker; Theo Moons; Rene Gabriels; Victor Luypaerts; Rene Vingerhoerdt	14·50	14·50

See also **MS**3992.

1368 Christmas Tree

2007. Christmas and New Year. (a) Ordinary gum.

4144	**1368**	1 (52c.) multicoloured (postage)	1·80	1·10

1369 Christmas Tree

(b) Self-adhesive.

4145	**1369**	1 (52c.) multicoloured	1·80	1·10

1370 Christmas Tree

(c) Self-adhesive.

4146	**1370**	A (80c.) multicoloured (air)	2·75	1·70

1371 *The Man From the Sea*

2008. Rene Magritte (artist) Commemoration. Sheet 80×140 mm containing T **1371** and similar multicoloured designs.

MS4147	1 (52c.)×5, Type **1371**; *Scheherazade*; *The Midnight Marriage*; *Georgette* (32×41 mm); *The Ignorant Fairy* (49×37 mm)	9·00	9·00

1372 Give Blood

2008. Red Cross. Give Blood Campaign. (a) Self-adhesive.

4148	**1372**	1 (52c.) multicoloured	1·80	1·10

1373 Give Blood

(b) Ordinary gum.

4149	**1373**	1 (52c.)+25c. multicoloured	2·75	1·70

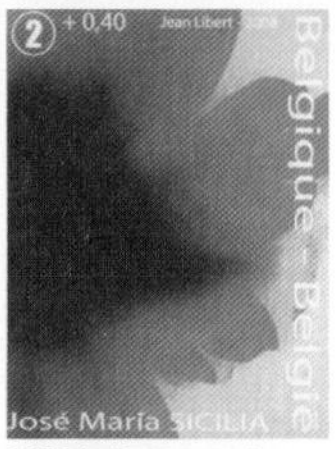

1374 *La Luz que se Apaga* (Jose Maria Sicilia)

2008. Art. Sheet 90×125 mm.

MS4150	**1374**	2 (€1.04)+40c. multicoloured	5·25	5·25

1375 Jeremiah and Kurdy Malloy

2008. 'Philately for the Young'. Jeremiah (comic strip created by Hermann Huppen (Hermann)).

4151	**1375**	1 (52c.) multicoloured	2·10	1·30

1376 Car

2008. Toys. Self-adhesive. Multicoloured.

4152	1 (52c.) Type **1376**	2·10	1·30
4153	1 (52c.) Pram	2·10	1·30
4154	1 (52c.) Doll	2·10	1·30
4155	1 (52c.) Airplane	2·10	1·30
4156	1 (52c.) Horse	2·10	1·30
4157	1 (52c.) Tram	2·10	1·30
4158	1 (52c.) Diablo	2·10	1·30
4159	1 (52c.) Teddy	2·10	1·30
4160	1 (52c.) Top	2·10	1·30
4161	1 (52c.) Wooden scooter	2·10	1·30

1377 Flowers

2008. Bicentenary of Ghent Flower Show. Sheet 90×125 mm.

MS4162	**1377**	80c. multicoloured	3·00	3·00

1378 Suzy Delair as Mila Malou and Pierre Fresnay as Wens (scene from film *L'assassin habite au 21*)

2008. Detective Novels. Multicoloured.

4163	1 (52c.) Type **1378** (novel by Stanislas–Andre Steeman)	2·10	1·30
4164	1 (52c.) Jan Decleir as Angelo Ledda (scene from film *De zaak Alzheimer*) (novel by Jef Geeraerts)	2·10	1·30

1379 Menorah

2008. Bicentenary of Belgian Jewish Community.

4165	**1379**	90c. blue and black	3·50	2·10

1380 Central Station

2008. Antverpia 2010 European Philatelic Championship, Antwerp. 120th Anniv of Royal National Association of Stamp Collectors. Sheet 161×141 mm containing T **1380** and similar vert designs. Multicoloured.

MS4166 1 (54c.)×5, Type **1380**; Cathedral of Our Lady and Pieter Paul Rubens memorial; Port; Fashion; Diamond necklace by Reena Ahluwalia 17·00 17·00

No. **MS**4166 was sold for €5.

1381 Comte de Champignac

2008. 70th Anniv of Spirou (cartoon character drawn by Andre Franquin). Sheet 166×100 mm containing T **1381** and similar vert designs. Multicoloured.

MS4167 1 (54c.)×5, Type **1381**; Fantasio; Spirou and Spip; Seccotine; Zorglub 10·50 10·50

1382 Coastal Route

2008. Trams. Trams enroute. Multicoloured.

4168	1 (54c.) Type **1382**	2·10	1·30
4169	80c. Charleroi	3·00	1·90
4170	90c. Brussels	3·50	2·10

1383 Mickey Mouse

2008. 80th Anniv of Mickey Mouse (cartoon character created by Walt Disney).

4171	**1383**	1 (54c.) multicoloured	2·10	1·30

1384 Letterbox and Envelope **1385** Letterbox and Envelope

2008. Europa. The Letter. (a) Self-adhesive gum.

4172	**1384**	1 (54c.) multicoloured	2·10	1·30

(b) Size 40×27 mm. Ordinary gum.

4173	**1385**	80c. multicoloured	3·00	1·90

1386 *Tagetes portula*

2008. Flowers. Multicoloured. Self-adhesive.

4174	1 (54c.) Type **1386**(postage)	2·10	1·30

No value expressed.

4175	(80c.) Tulip 'Orange Favourite' (air)	3·00	1·90

1387 Artificial Hand and Hands of Many Nations

2008. Diversity in the Workplace.

4176	**1387**	2 (€1.08) multicoloured	4·25	2·50

1388

2008. Freemasonry. Sheet 125×90 mm.

MS4177 **1388** 3 multicoloured 6·25 6·25

1389 Family hiking **1390** Family hiking

2008. Summer Stamps. Multicoloured. (a) Ordinary gum.

4178	1 (52c.) Type **1389**	2·10	1·30
4179	1 (52c.) Family cycling	2·10	1·30

(b) Size 30×25 mm. Self-adhesive.

4180	1 (52c.) Type **1390**	2·10	1·30
4181	1 (52c.) Family cycling	2·10	1·30

1391 Queen Fabiola and King Baudouin

2008. 80th Birth Anniv of Queen Fabiola. Sheet 170×120 mm containing T **1391** and similar vert designs. Multicoloured.

MS4182 1 (52c.)×3, Type **1391**; Portrait of Queen Fabiola; Queen Fabiola and King Baudouin, older, wearing casual dress 6·25 6·25

1392 Woman (George Grard), Musee George Grard, Gijverinkhove

2008. Tourism. Multicoloured.

4183	1 (52c.) Type **1392**	2·20	1·40
4184	80c. *Imago* (Emile Desmedt), Musee en Plein Air du Sart-Tilman, Liege	3·25	2·00
4185	90c. *Autoportrait* (Gerald Dederen), Jardin de sculptures de l'UCL, Brussels	3·50	2·30

1393 USSR Pavilion

2008. 50th Anniv of EXPO'58, Brussels. Multicoloured.

MS4186 1 (54c.)×5, Type **1393**; Thailand pavilion; Hostesses carrying flags; Expo logo as lighting; Atomium 10·50 10·50

The stamps of **MS**4186 were not for sale individually.

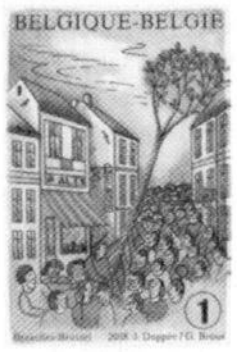

1394 Planting of May Tree (tree of joy), Brussels (700th anniv)

2008. Folklore and Traditions. Multicoloured.

4187	1 (54c.) Type **1394**	2·20	1·40
4188	1 (54c.) Hops, beer barrel, bonfire and hop devil, Asse (Hopduvelfeesten) (horiz)	2·20	1·40
4189	1 (54c.) Jugglers (Eupen carnival)	2·20	1·40
4190	1 (54c.) Men on stage (centenary (2007) of *La Royale Compagnie du Cabaret Wallon Tournaisien*) (philanthropic and literary company)	2·20	1·40

1395 BMX

2008. Olympic Games, Beijing. Multicoloured.

4191	1 (54c.) Type **1395**	2·30	1·50
4192	90c. Relay (horiz)	3·75	2·40

MS4193 125×90 mm. (2) €1.08 Tennis (49×38 mm) 4·50 4·50

1396 Angel Gabriel

2008. Stamp Day. 50th Anniv of Cercle St-Gabriel. 50th Anniv of Thematic Philately in Belgium.

4194	**1396**	1 (54c.) multicoloured	2·30	1·50

1397 Marten **1398** Marten

2008. Nature. Mustelidae. Multicoloured. (a) Self-adhesive gum.

4195	1 (54c.) Type **1397**	2·30	1·50
4196	1 (54c.) Stone marten	2·30	1·50
4197	1 (54c.) Polecat	2·30	1·50
4198	1 (54c.) Otter	2·30	1·50
4199	1 (54c.) Badger	2·30	1·50

(b) Ordinary gum. Sheet 178×146 mm.

MS4200 1 (54c.)×6, Type **1398** (48×38 mm); Ermine (38×42 mm); Stone marten (48×38 mm); Polecat (38×42 mm); Otter (38×48 mm); Badger (48×38 mm) 12·00 12·00

1399 Smurf **1400** Smurf and Smurfette

2008. The Smurfs (characters created by Peyo (Pierre Culliford)). Multicoloured. (a) Self-adhesive gum.

4201	1 (54c.) Type **1399**	2·30	1·50
4202	1 (54c.) Smurfette	2·30	1·50
4203	1 (54c.) Papa Smurf	2·30	1·50
4204	1 (54c.) Smurf and drum (horiz)	2·30	1·50
4205	1 (54c.) Poet Smurf	2·30	1·50
4206	1 (54c.) Jokey Smurf	2·30	1·50
4207	1 (54c.) Smurf carrying bag and envelope	2·30	1·50
4208	1 (54c.) Brainy Smurf	2·30	1·50
4209	1 (54c.) Gargamel	2·30	1·50
4210	1 (54c.) Harmony Smurf (horiz)	2·30	1·50

(b) Ordinary gum. Sheet 186×153 mm.

MS4211 1 (54c.)×5, Type **1400** (42×33 mm); Smurf in party hat (42×33 mm); Two smurfs (42×33 mm); Smurf carrying cake (42×33 mm); Smurf eating cake (38×42 mm) 12·00 12·00

1401 Mothers and Children (Tim Driven)

2008. Belgian Photographers. Sheet 100×166 mm containing **1401** and similar horiz designs. Multicoloured.

MS4212 80c.×5, Type **1401**; Jars (Paul Ausloos); Woman carrying pail (Leonard Misonne); Coloured lights in trees (Harry Gruyaert); Woman cycling (Stephan Vanfleteren) 16·00 16·00

1402 1909 Belgian Congo 1f. Stamp (As No. 40B)

2008. Centenary of Belgian Congo.

4213	**1402**	1 (54c.) multicoloured	2·30	1·50

1403 National Museum of Shoes, Izegem

2008. Museums. Multicoloured.

4214	1 (54c.) Type **1403**	2·30	1·50
4215	80c. Piconrue Museum (religious museum), Bastogne	3·25	2·10
4216	80c. David and Alice van Buuren Museum , Brussels	3·25	2·10

1404 Menin Gate, Ypres

2008. 90th Anniv of End of First World War. Sheet 201×85 mm containing T **1404** and similar vert designs. Multicoloured.

MS4217 90c.×3, Type **1404**; King Albert I (statue); Poppies 10·50 10·50

1405 The Nativity **1406** The Nativity

1407 Cardinal Mercier

2008. Christmas. Multicoloured. (a) Self-adhesive.

4218	1 (54c.) Type **1405**	2·40	1·70
4219	(80c.) Type **1406**	3·50	2·40

(b) Ordinary gum. Sheet 127×124 mm.

MS4220 1 (54c.)×5, Type **1407**; St. Francis; Mary and Joseph; Friar; Infant Jesus 12·00 12·00

No. 4219 was inscribed 'INTERNATIONAL' and was originally on sale for 80c.

No. **MS**4220 includes four labels which, with the stamps form a composite design of a stained glass window.

1408 Queen Elisabeth (Concours Reine Elisabeth (Queen Elisabeth International Music Competition))

2008. This Belgium. Music. Sheet 166×200 mm containing T **1408** and similar square designs. Multicoloured.

MS4221 80c.×10, Type **1408**; Jose van Dam (bass-baritone); Rock Werchter Festival; Philippe Herreweghe and Collegium Vocale Gent (music ensemble); dEus (rock band); Il Novecento (orchestra) and Robert Groslot (conductor); Philip Catherine (jazz guitarist); Dani Klein (singer with Vaya con Dios); Salvatore Adamo (composer and ballad singer); Jaques Brel (singer–songwriter) 32·00 32·00

The stamps of **MS**4136 were not for sale separately.

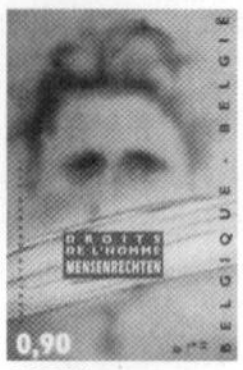

1409 Face

2008. Universal Declaration of Human Rights.

4222	**1409**	90c. multicoloured	4·25	3·00

1410 *Tulipa bakeri*

2009. Air. Flowers. Self-adhesive.

4223	**1410**	1 (90c.) multicoloured	4·25	3·00

1411 King Albert II

2009. Air.

4224	**1411**	1 (90c.) multicoloured	4·25	3·00
4225	**1411**	1 (€1.05) multicoloured	5·00	3·50
4226	**1411**	3 (€2.40) multicoloured	11·00	7·75
4227	**1411**	3 (€2.70) multicoloured	12·00	8·50

No. 4224 and 4225 were for use on airmail within Europe, Nos. 4226 and 4227 for use on international airmail. See also 4113/17.

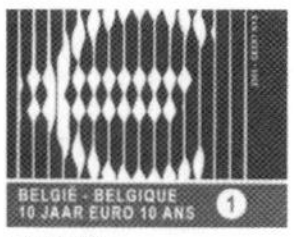

1412 '€'

2009. Tenth Anniv of European Union. Self-adhesive.

4228	**1412**	1 (59c.) multicoloured	2·75	2·00

1413 Monument

2009. Regions. German Community. Sheet 150×183 mm containing T **1413** and similar multicoloured designs.

MS4229 1 (90c.)×5, Type **1413**; Three handled pitcher; Lake Butgenbach; Eupen sanatorium (33×40 mm); Shooting (49×37 mm)	19·00	19·00

The stamps of **MS**4229 were not for sale separately.

1414 Hands 'reading' Braille

2009. Birth Bicentenary of Louis Braille (inventor of Braille writing for the blind).

4230	**1414**	1 (59c.) multicoloured	2·75	2·00

1415 Child and Tap

2009. Red Cross. Water.

4231	**1415**	1 (59c.) + 25c. black and vermillion	4·00	2·75

1416 Barge

2009. Transportation. Inland Waterways.

4232	**1416**	2 (€1.18) multicoloured	5·50	4·00

1417 Figure and Postbox (Emitis Mohsenin)

2009. Post Day.

4233	**1417**	1 (59c.) multicoloured	2·75	2·00

1418 Marthe Boel (promoter of women's issues)

2009. Women in Action. Multicoloured.

4234	1 (59c.) Type **1418**	2·75	2·00
4235	1 (59c.) Lily Boeykens (lawyer and journalist)	2·75	2·00

1419 Penguins

2009. Preserve Polar Regions and Glaciers. Sheet 120×80 mm containing T **1419** and similar multicoloured design.

MS4236 2 (€1.05)×2, Type **1419**; Polar bear	9·25	9·25

The stamps of **MS**4236 were for use on international priority mail and not for sale separately.

1420 Bob

2009. Bob and Bobette (comic series created by Willy Vandersteen) in *Les Diables du Texas* (animated film). Showing characters from the film. Multicoloured. Self-adhesive.

4237	1 (59c.) Type **1420**	2·75	2·00
4238	1 (59c.) Bobette	2·75	2·00
4239	1 (59c.) Jerome	2·75	2·00
4240	1 (59c.) Lambik	2·75	2·00
4241	1 (59c.) Aunt Sidonie	2·75	2·00

1421 Telescope and Globe

2009. Europa. Astronomy. Sheet 125×90mm.

MS4242 **1421** 1 (59c.) multicoloured	4·25	4·25

No. **MS**4242 was for use on mail within Europe.

1422 Neolithic Flint Mines, Spiennes

2009. World Heritage Sites. Sheet 166×100 mm containing T **1422** and similar vert designs. Multicoloured.

MS4243 1 (€1.05)×5, Type **1422**; Notre Dame Cathedral, Tournai; Plantin-Moretus Museum, Antwerp; Historic Centre, Bruges; Maison de Maitre (Victor Horta), Brussels	23·00	23·00

No. **MS**4243 was for use on International mail.

1423 Girl with Camera

2009. Summer Stamps. Holidays in Wallonia and Flanders. Multicoloured. Self-adhesive.

4244	1 (59c.) Type **1423**	2·75	2·00
4245	1 (59c.) Boy with camera	2·75	2·00

1424 Muhka and *Flemish Village* (Luc Tuymans)

2009. Antverpia 2010–International Stamp Exhibition, Antwerp. Artistic Antwerp (1st series). Sheet 180×64 mm containing T **1424** and similar vert designs. Multicoloured.

MS4246 1 (59c.)×5, Type **1424**; *Orbino* (Luc Deleu), Middelheim Sculpture Museum;Bourla Theater and Toneelhuis theatre company; *Hollywood on the Scheldt*, Robbe De Hert, Roma Cinema; *Willem Elschot* (writer) (sculpture by Wilfred Pas) and manuscript of *Kass*	23·00	23·00

See also Nos. **MS**4290.

1425 Henry Purcell (350th birth anniv)

2009. Composers Anniversaries. Sheet 180×64 mm containing T **1425** and similar vert designs. Multicoloured.

MS4247 1 (90c.)×5, Type **1425**; George Frideric Handel (250th death anniv); Franz Joseph Haydn (death bicentenary); Jakob Ludwig Felix Mendelssohn Bartholdy (birth bicentenary); Clara Schumann (nee Clara Josephine Wieck) (190th birth anniv)	21·00	21·00

The stamps and margins of **MS**4247 form a composite design.

The stamps of **MS**4247 were for use on mail within Europe

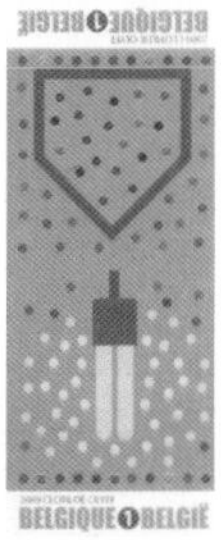

1426 Low Energy Lightbulb

2009. Green Stamps. Environmental Preservation. Multicoloured. Self-adhesive.

4248	1 (59c.) Type **1426**	2·75	2·00
4249	1 (59c.) Wind turbine	2·75	2·00
4250	1 (59c.) Shared transport	2·75	2·00
4251	1 (59c.) Solar panels	2·75	2·00
4252	1 (59c.) Insulated house	2·75	2·00

1427 International Space Station, 2009

2009. Aviation, From Bleriot to De Winne. Multicoloured.

4253	1 (59c.) Type **1427** (Frank de Winne, first European Space Agency astronaut to command mission)	2·75	2·00
4254	1 (59c.) Apollo 11, 1969 (first men on the moon)	2·75	2·00
4255	1 (59c.) Concorde, 1969 (first supersonic flight)	2·75	2·00
4256	1 (59c.) LZ 127 Graf Zeppelin, 1929 (flight around the world)	2·75	2·00
4257	1 (59c.) *Bleriot XI*, 1909 (first flight over English Channel)	2·75	2·00

1428 Yoko Tsuno

2009. Youth Philately. Yoko Tsuno (comic created by Roger Leloup).

4258	**1428**	1 (59c.) multicoloured	2·75	2·00

1429 King Albert and Queen Paola

2009. 50th Anniv of Wedding of King Albert and Queen Paola. Sheet 209×104 mm.

MS4259 **1429** 3 multicoloured	7·25	7·25

1430 Citroen 2CV Delivery Van, c. 1959

2009. Postal Vehicles. Multicoloured.

4260	1 (59c.) Type **1430**	2·75	2·00
4261	1 (59c.) Bedford van, c. 1960	2·75	2·00
4262	1 (59c.) Large Renault van, c. 1970	2·75	2·00
4263	1 (59c.) Renault 4 Fourgonnette van, c. 1980	2·75	2·00
4264	1 (59c.) Modern Citroen van	2·75	2·00

1431 Orchestra

2009. The Circus. Multicoloured. Self-adhesive.

4265	1 (59c.) Type **1431**	2·75	2·00
4266	1 (59c.) Highwire artistes	2·75	2·00
4267	1 (59c.) Illusionist	2·75	2·00
4268	1 (59c.) Acrobat pyramid	2·75	2·00
4269	1 (59c.) Trapeze artiste	2·75	2·00
4270	1 (59c.) Clowns	2·75	2·00
4271	1 (59c.) Acrobats balancing	2·75	2·00
4272	1 (59c.) Illusionist with tophat, rabbit and doves	2·75	2·00
4273	1 (59c.) Equestrian artiste	2·75	2·00
4274	1 (59c.) Clown juggling on uni-cycle	2·75	2·00

1432 Maurice Bejart

2009. Maurice Bejart (dancer) Commemoration.

4275	**1432**	1 (90c.) multicoloured	4·00	3·00

1433 Archives of Belgium

2009. Monts des Arts. Sheet 200×166 mm containing T **1433** and similar multicoloured designs.

MS4276 1 (59c.)×10, Type **1433**; Royal Museum of Fine Arts; Royal Library; Square Meeting Centre; Brussels Palace (38×49 mm); Saint Jaques sur Coudenberg Church and Protestant Chapel (49×38 mm); Palace of Fine Arts; Royal Belgian Filmarchive (Cinematheque Royale de Belgique); Belvue Museum; Musical Instruments Museum	25·00	25·00

1434 Seven Sacraments Altarpiece (detail)

2009. Master of Passions
4277 **1434** 2 (€1.18) multicoloured 5·00 4·00

1435 Lion Mask

2009. Europalia International Arts Festival, China. Self-adesive.
4278 **1435** 1 (59c.) multicoloured 2·75 2·00

1436 Mettoy Streamline Train, 1950

2009. Miniature Trains. Sheet 160×200 mm containing T **1436** and similar square designs. Multicoloured.
MS4279 1 (59c.)×10, Type **1436**; Bavarian locomotive *Aloisus*; Locomotive tender; Diesel locomotive; Locomotive tender *Storchenbein*; Locomotive Type 16; Tin toy train; ICE Deutsche Bahn; Wooden toy train with waggon; Blue and red wooden toy train 28·00 28·00

1437 Pine Tree

2009. La Foret de Soignes (Sonian Forest). Sheet 166×100 mm containing T **1437** and similar vert designs. Multicoloured.
MS4280 2 (€2.18)×5, Type **1437**; Beech; Birch; Larch; Oak 25·00 25·00

1438 Father Damien

2009. Canonization of Father Damien (Jozef De Veuster) (Roman Catholic missionary who ministered to lepers on the Hawaiian island of Molokai).
4281 **1438** 1 Europe (90c.) multicoloured 4·00 3·00

1439 Emblem

2009. 20th Anniv of Comic Strip Art Museum. Sheet 90×120 mm.
MS4282 **1439** 1 (59c.) multicoloured 4·50 3·25

1440 Tom Lanoye

2009. This is Belgium. Literature. Sheet 160×200 mm containing T **1440** and similar multicoloured designs.
MS4283 1 (59c.)×10, Type **1440**; Hugo Claus; Anne Provoost; Poeziezomers, Watou (summer poetry festival) (vert); Redu, Book Village (vert); Book Fair, Antwerp (vert); Book Fair, Brussels (vert); Pierre Mertens; Amelie Northomb; Henri Vernes 25·00 25·00

1441 Gold Baubles

2009. Christmas. Multicoloured. Self-adhesive.
4284 1 (59c.) Type **1441** 2·75 2·00
4285 1 (90c.) Blue baubles 2·75 2·00

No. 4284 were for use on domestic mail and were originally on sale for 59c.
No. 4285 were for use on international mail were originally on sale for 90c.

1442 1920 65c. Stamp (As No. 308b)

2009. Monacophil 2009. Promotion of Philately. Sheet 120×170 mm.
MS4286 **1442** 1 multicoloured 5·75 4·25

The premium was for the promotion of philately.

1443 Sunset

2010. Bereavement. Self-adhesive.
4288 **1443** (59c.) multicoloured 2·75 2·00

1444 Face as Jigsaw

2010. Organ Donation Awareness Campaign. Self-adhesive.
4289 **1444** (59c.) multicoloured 2·75 2·00

1445 Magnifying Glass

2010. Antverpia 2010–International Stamp Exhibition, Antwerp (2nd series). Sheet 160×140 mm containing T **1445** and similar vert designs. Multicoloured. Phosphorescent paper.
MS4290 (59c.)×6, Type **1445** (120th anniv of Royal Federation of Belgian Philatelic Circles); Commercial centre, Antwerp: Giraffes and Kai-Mook (elephant), Antwerp Zoo; painting by Eugeen van Mieghem and model, Museum aan de Stroom (MAS); *Self-portrait* and house of Peter Paul Rubens; City Hall and Cathedral, Old City Centre 15·00 15·00

No. **MS**4290 was on sale, above face value, at €6.50, the premium for the promotion of philately.

1446 Paul Otlet

2010. From Mundaneum (system for information storage, using Universal Decimal Classification, invented by Paul Otlet and Henri La Fontaine in 1910), the Internet. Sheet 90×125 mm.
MS4291 **1446** €4.60 multicoloured 12·00 12·00

1447 Largo Winch

2010. Youth Philately. Largo Winch (comic created by Philip Francq and writer Jean Van Hamme).
4292 **1447** 1 (59c.) multicoloured 2·75 2·00

1448 Paul Verlane and Arthur Rimbaud

2010. Literary Walk through Brussels. Sheet 180×64 mm containing T **1448** and similar vert designs. Multicoloured.
MS4293 2 (€1.18)×5, Type **1448**; Charles Baudelaire; Multatuli (Eduard Douwes Dekker); Charlotte and Emily Bronte; Victor Hugo 9·00 9·00

The stamps and margins of **MS**4293 form a composite design.
The stamps of **MS**4293 were for use on mail within Europe

1449 *Nicotiana alata*

2010. Ghent Flower Show. Multicoloured.
4294 1 (59c.) Type **1449** 2·75 2·00
4295 1 (59c.) *Lychnis coronaria* 2·75 2·00

1450 Chicks

2010. Young Animals. Multicoloured. Self-adhesive.
4296 1 (59c.) Type **1450** 2·75 2·00
4297 1 (59c.) Rabbits 2·75 2·00
4298 1 (59c.) Kitten 2·75 2·00
4299 1 (59c.) Ducklings 2·75 2·00
4300 1 (59c.) Foal cantering 2·75 2·00
4301 1 (59c.) Labrador puppy 2·75 2·00
4302 1 (59c.) Long-haired dachshund puppy 2·75 2·00
4303 1 (59c.) Two kittens 2·75 2·00
4304 1 (59c.) Foal, head and shoulders 2·75 2·00
4305 1 (59c.) Two lambs 2·75 2·00

1451 Dog reading to Boy

2010. Europa. Childrens' Books. Sheet 80×120 mm containing T **1451** and similar vert design. Multicoloured.
MS4306 3 Europe (€2.70)×2, Type **1451**; Cat reading to girl 12·00 12·00

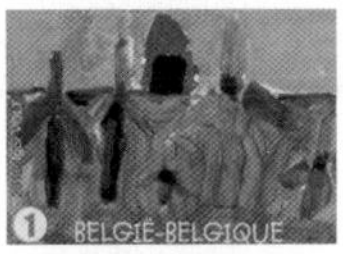

1452 Seas and Oceans (Igor Volt)

2010. Environmental Protection. Winning Designs in Childrens' Drawing Competition. Multicoloured.
4307 1 (59c.) Type **1452** 2·75 2·00
4308 1 (59c.) Forest (Lander Keyaerts) 2·75 2·00
4309 1 (59c.) Endangerd species (Eva Sterkens) 2·75 2·00
4310 1 (59c.) Climate (Lucie Octave) 2·75 2·00
4311 1 (59c.) Energy (Louise van Goylen) 2·75 2·00

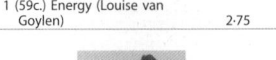

1453 Natan

2010. This is Belgium. Fashion. Sheet 200×160 mm containing T **1453** and similar multicoloured designs.
MS4312 1 (59c.)×10, Type **1453**; Walter Van Beirendonck; Veronique Branquinho (43×35 mm); A.F. Vandevorst (33×44 mm); Ann Demeulemeester (44×26 mm); Olivier Theyskens (32×48 mm); Dirk Bikkembergs (48×38 mm); Cathy Pill (38×48 mm); Veronique Leroy (29×33 mm); Martin Margiela (48×38 mm) 6·50 6·50

1454 Exhibition Emblem

2010. Antverpia 2010–International Stamp Exhibition, Antwerp (3rd issue). Sheet 190×120 mm.
MS4313 **1454** 3 (€1.77) multicoloured 7·75 7·75

1455 Gyrfalcon (inscr 'Buizerd–Buse Variable')

2010. 25th Anniv of Birds on Stamps drawn by André Buzin. Sheet 160×140 mm containing T **1455** and similar vert designs. Multicoloured.
MS4314 1 Europe (90c.)×5, Type **1455**; Hobby (Faucon hoberau–Boomvalk); Sparrow hawk (Sperwer–Epermer d'Europe); Red Kite (Milan Royal–Rode Wouw); Goshawk (Havik–Autour des Palombes) 25·00 25·00

See also No. 3692 etc.

1456 Prince Philippe

2010. 50th Birth Anniv of Prince Philippe, Duke of Brabant, Prince of Belgium.
4315 **1456** 2 (€1.18) multicoloured 5·00 4·00

1457 Early Steam and Modern High Speed Locomotives

2010. 175th Anniv of Belgian Railways
4316 **1457** 2 (€1.18) multicoloured 4·25 3·00

Nos. 4317/21 have wavy edges (simulating perforations) on two or three sides depending on position.

1458 Profiles and Party Favours

2010. Greetings Stamps. Multicoloured.
4317 1 (59c.) Type **1458** 2·75 2·00
4318 1 (59c.) Hands holding present and bouquet 2·75 2·00

4319	1 (59c.) Hand holding lantern and profile wearing mask	2·75	2·00
4320	1 (59c.) Hands holding tray of glasses and cake	2·75	2·00
4321	1 (59c.) Children	2·75	2·00

1459 Zebra-striped Ball and Player's Boot

2010. World Cup Football Championships, South Africa

4322	**1459**	1 (90c.) multicoloured	3·75	2·75

1460 Winners' Podiums and Athlete

2010. Youth Olympic Games, Singapore

4323	**1460**	1 (€1.05) multicoloured	4·25	3·00

1461 Child and Map as Flag

2010. 50th Anniv of Congo Independence

4324	**1461**	1 (€1.05) multicoloured	4·25	3·00

1462 Eddie Merckx

2010. 65th Birth Anniv of Edouard Louis Joseph Merckx (world champion cyclist)

4325	**1462**	2 (€1.08) multicoloured	5·00	3·50

1463 'eu'

2010. Belgium's Presidency of the European Union

4326	**1463**	1 (90c.) multicoloured	1·90	1·30

1464 Cyclist riding on Fietsknooppunten

2010. Tourism. Multicoloured.

4327	1 (59c.) Type **1464**	2·30	1·60
4328	1 (59c.) Tourist information board and cyclist, The Ravel	2·30	1·60

1465 Ford Bureau de Poste Vehicle (1953)

2010. Postal Transport. Multicoloured.

4329	1 (59c.) Type **1465**	2·30	1·60
4330	1 (59c.) Independent postal train (1931)	2·30	1·60
4331	1 (59c.) Bedford truck (1979)	2·30	1·60
4332	1 (59c.) Independent postal train (1968)	2·30	1·60
4333	1 (59c.) Volvo truck (2009)	2·30	1·60

1466 Le Tonneau, Brussels (S. Jasinsky)

2010. Pre-1960 Architecture. Multicoloured.

MS4334 1 (90c.)×5, Type **1466**; Saint-Maartensdal (Renaat Braem and A33 Architects), Louvain; Le fer à cheval (J. J. Eggericx and R.Verwilghen), Brussels; Boerentoren, Anvers (J. Vanhoenacker, J. Smolderen & E. Van Averbeke); Cité de Droixhe, Liège (EGAU architectural group) 18·00 18·00

1467 Fruit Trees, Saint-Trond

2010. Regions. Multicoloured.

MS4335 1 (90c.)×5, Type **1467**; Fruit blossom; Wine and glasses; Building façade, Hélécine (33×40 mm); Ploughed field and farm buildings, Perwez (49×37 mm) 18·00 18·00

1468 Leisure Centre, Rotselar (de Mena Brewery)

2010. Breweries, Change of Use. Multicoloured.

4336	1 (90c.) Type **1468**	3·25	2·25
4337	1 (€1.05) Telematics Support Centre, Marche-en-Famenne (Carmelite monastery and brewery)	4·00	2·75
4338	2 (€1.18) Weils Contemporary Art Centre, Brussels	5·25	3·50

1469 Shoe Making

2010. Craft Trades. Multicoloured.

4339	1 (59c.) Type **1469**	2·50	1·70
4340	1 (59c.) Clog making	2·50	1·70
4341	1 (59c.) Blacksmithing	2·50	1·70
4342	1 (59c.) Spinning	2·50	1·70
4343	1 (59c.) Laundry	2·50	1·70

1470 *Voyage dans la lune*

2010. Tenth Anniv of Folon Foundation. Multicoloured.

4344	1 (59c.) Type **1470**	2·50	1·70
4345	1 (59c.) *Pays de connaissance*	2·50	1·70
4346	1 (59c.) *Un cri* (horiz)	2·50	1·70
4347	1 (59c.) *La mer ce grand sculpteur* (Knokke) (horiz)	2·50	1·70
4348	1 (59c.) *L'étranger* (horiz)	2·50	1·70
4349	1 (59c.) *Oiseau* (horiz)	2·50	1·70
4350	1 (59c.) *Pluie* (La Hulpe)	2·50	1·70
4351	1 (59c.) Stained glass window, Eglise de Waha (Marche-en-Famenne)	2·50	1·70
4352	1 (59c.) *L'aube*	2·50	1·70
4353	1 (59c.) *Un monde*	2·50	1·70

1471 Virgin and Child (Caen)

2010. Flemish Primitive Art in French and Belgian Collections. Multicoloured.

MS4354 3 (€2.07)×2, Type **1471**; *Portrait of Laurent Froimont* (Brussels) 18·00 18·00

Stamps of a similar design were issued by France.

1472 Santa in his Sleigh

2010. Christmas. Multicoloured.

4355	1 (59c.) Type **1472**	2·75	2·00
4356	1 (90c.) Santa in his sleigh (different)	5·25	3·50

1473 '1-1-11'

2011. Liberalization of Postal Market from 1st January 2011

4357	**1473**	1 (59c.) multicoloured	2·75	2·00

EXPRESS LETTER STAMPS

E107 Ghent

1929

E530	-	1f.75 blue	70	35
E531	**E107**	2f.35 red	2·20	50
E581	-	2f.45 green	23·00	3·00
E532	-	3f.50 purple	14·00	14·00
E533	-	5f.25 olive	13·50	13·00

DESIGNS: 1f.75, Town Hall, Brussels; 2f.45, Eupen; 3f.50, Bishop's Palace, Liege; 5f.25, Antwerp Cathedral.

1932. No. E581 surch **2 Fr 50** and cross.

E608	2f.50 on 2f.45 green	16·00	2·30

MILITARY STAMPS

1967. As T **289** (Baudouin) but with letter "M" within oval at foot.

M2027	1f.50 green	25	20

1971. As No. 2207/8a and 2209a but with letter "M" within oval at foot.

M2224	1f.75 green	35	35
M2225	2f.25 green	30	40
M2226	2f.50 green	25	25
M2227	3f.25 plum	30	30

NEWSPAPER STAMPS

1928. Railway Parcels stamps of 1923 optd **JOURNAUX DAGBLADEN 1928.**

N443	**P 84**	10c. red	60	35
N444	**P 84**	20c. green	60	35
N445	**P 84**	40c. olive	60	35
N446	**P 84**	60c. orange	85	35
N447	**P 84**	70c. brown	85	35
N448	**P 84**	80c. violet	1·20	60
N449	**P 84**	90c. slate	10·50	3·50
N450	-	1f. blue	2·30	60
N451	-	2f. olive	4·75	85
N452	-	3f. red	4·75	85
N453	-	4f. red	4·75	85
N454	-	5f. violet	4·75	85
N455	-	6f. brown	7·25	2·00
N456	-	7f. orange	20·00	3·50
N457	-	8f. brown	14·50	2·30
N458	-	9f. purple	41·00	10·50
N459	-	10f. green	14·50	3·50
N460	-	20f. pink	41·00	14·50

1929. Railway Parcels stamps of 1923 optd **JOURNAUX DAGBLADEN** only.

N505	**P 84**	10c. red	1·20	60
N506	**P 84**	20c. green	60	60
N507	**P 84**	40c. olive	60	60
N508	**P 84**	60c. orange	85	60
N509	**P 84**	70c. brown	60	60
N510	**P 84**	80c. violet	1·20	1·20
N511	**P 84**	90c. slate	7·75	6·50
N512	-	1f. blue	1·70	60
N513	-	1f.10 brown	5·75	1·70
N514	-	1f.50 blue	5·75	1·70
N515	-	2f. olive	3·75	1·20
N516	-	2f.10 slate	17·00	12·00
N517	-	3f. red	3·75	1·20
N518	-	4f. red	3·75	1·20
N519	-	5f. violet	3·75	1·20
N520	-	6f. brown	8·75	1·70
N521	-	7f. orange	26·00	1·70
N522	-	8f. brown	17·00	1·70
N523	-	9f. purple	35·00	19·00
N524	-	10f. green	20·00	4·75
N525	-	20f. pink	49·00	17·00

PARCEL POST STAMPS

1928. **Optd COLIS POSTAL POSTCOLLO.**

B470	**81**	4f. brown	8·75	2·00
B471	**81**	5f. bistre	8·75	2·00

B106 G.P.O., Brussels

1929

B526	**B106**	3f. sepia	1·50	30
B527	**B106**	4f. slate	1·50	30
B528	**B106**	5f. red	1·50	30
B529	**B106**	6f. purple	36·00	36·00

1933. Surch **X4 4X.**

B645	4f. on 6f. purple	32·00	45

POSTAGE DUE STAMPS

D21

1870

D63	**D21**	10c. green	4·75	3·00
D64	**D21**	20c. blue	95·00	5·75

D35

1895

D96a	**D35**	5c. green	15	15
D97	**D35**	10c. brown	26·00	2·30
D101	**D35**	10c. red	15	10
D98a	**D35**	20c. green	15	15
D102	**D35**	30c. blue	20	15
D99	**D35**	50c. brown	26·00	7·00
D103	**D35**	50c. grey	45	45
D100	**D35**	1f. red	23·00	13·00
D104	**D35**	1f. yellow	5·75	5·75

1919. As Type **D35**, but value in colour on white background.

D251	5c. green	60	30
D323	5c. grey	10	10
D252b	10c. red	1·70	30
D324	10c. green	10	10
D253b	20c. green	8·75	1·50
D325	20c. brown	10	10
D254	30c. blue	4·75	60
D326	30c. red	80	60
D327	35c. green	25	15
D328	40c. brown	25	15
D329	50c. blue	1·50	25
D330	50c. grey	25	10
D331	60c. red	30	15
D1146	65c. green	7·50	3·50
D332	70c. brown	30	15
D333	80c. grey	30	15
D334	1f. violet	50	25
D335	1f. purple	60	30
D336	1f.20 olive	65	25
D337	1f.40 green	65	60
D338	1f.50 olive	65	60
D1147	1f.60 mauve	14·50	7·00
D1148	1f.80 red	16·00	5·75
D339	2f. mauve	65	30
D1149	2f.40 lavender	9·25	3·50
D1150	3f. red	1·70	60
D340	3f.50 blue	65	30
D1151	4f. blue	11·00	60
D1152	5f. brown	3·50	30
D1153	7f. violet	3·50	1·70

D1154		8f. purple	13·00	10·50
D1155		10f. violet	7·50	3·25

D218

1945. Inscr "A PAYER" at top and "TE BETALEN" at bottom, or vice versa.

D1130A	D218	10c. olive	10	10
D1131A	D218	20c. blue	10	10
D1132A	D218	30c. red	10	10
D1133A	D218	40c. blue	10	10
D1134A	D218	50c. green	10	10
D1135A	D218	1f. brown	10	10
D1136A	D218	2f. orange	10	10

D462

1966

D2812	D462	1f. mauve	10	10
D2813	D462	2f. green	10	10
D2814	D462	3f. blue	1·40	25
D2815	D462	4f. green	25	25
D1985ab	D462	5f. purple	30	30
D2816	D462	5f. lilac	30	30
D1986	D462	6f. brown	85	15
D1987	D462	7f. red	70	†
D2818	D462	7f. orange	45	45
D2819	D462	8f. grey	45	45
D2820	D462	9f. red	50	50
D2821	D462	10f. brown	60	60
D1988	D462	20f. green	1·30	50
D2822	D462	20f. green	1·20	1·20

On No. D1988 the "F" is outside the shield; on No. D2822 it is inside.

RAILWAY PARCELS STAMPS

P21

1879

P63	P21	10c. brown	£160	10·50
P64	P21	20c. blue	£400	29·00
P65	P21	25c. green	£550	17·00
P66	P21	50c. red	£2750	14·50
P67	P21	80c. yellow	£3000	85·00
P68	P21	1f. grey	£400	†

In Belgium the parcels service is largely operated by the Belgian Railways for which the following stamps were issued.

Certain stamps under this heading were also on sale at post offices in connection with a "small parcels" service. These show a posthorn in the design except for Nos. P1116/18.

P22

1882

P69	P22	10c. brown	35·00	3·00
P73	P22	15c. grey	14·50	10·50
P75	P22	20c. blue	£100	5·75
P77	P22	25c. green	£100	6·00
P78	P22	50c. red	£100	1·20
P81	P22	80c. yellow	£110	3·00
P84	P22	80c. brown	£110	3·00
P86	P22	1f. grey	£600	4·75
P87	P22	1f. purple	£650	5·75
P88	P22	2f. buff	£350	£100

P35

1895. Numerals in black except 1f. and 2f.

P96	P35	10c. brown	14·50	1·20
P97	P35	15c. slate	14·50	11·50
P98	P35	20c. blue	23·00	2·30
P99	P35	25c. green	23·00	3·50
P100	P35	30c. orange	28·00	2·50
P101	P35	40c. green	41·00	2·50
P102	P35	50c. red	41·00	1·20
P103	P35	60c. lilac	75·00	1·20
P104	P35	70c. blue	75·00	2·00
P105	P35	80c. yellow	75·00	2·00
P106	P35	90c. red	£110	3·00
P107	P35	1f. purple	£300	4·75
P108	P35	2f. buff	£350	23·00

P37 Winged Railway Wheel

1902

P109a		10c. slate and brown	30	30
P110		15c. purple and slate	30	30
P111		20c. brown and blue	30	30
P112		25c. red and green	30	30
P113		30c. green and orange	30	30
P114		35c. green and brown	30	30
P115		40c. mauve and green	30	30
P116		50c. mauve and pink	30	30
P117		55c. blue and purple	30	30
P118		60c. red and lilac	30	30
P119		70c. red and blue	30	30
P120		80c. purple and yellow	30	30
P121		90c. green and red	30	30
P122	P37	1f. orange and purple	30	30
P123	P37	1f.10 black and red	30	30
P124	P37	2f. green and bistre	30	30
P125	P37	3f. blue and black	30	30
P126	P37	4f. red and green	2·00	2·00
P127	P37	5f. green and orange	1·20	1·20
P128	P37	10f. purple and yellow	1·20	1·20

1915. Stamps of 1912–14 optd **CHEMINS DE FER SPOORWEGEN** and Winged Railway Wheel.

P160	44	5c. green	£225	
P161	46	10c. red	£250	
P162	46	20c. green	£300	
P163	46	25c. blue	£300	
P164	45	35c. brown	£400	
P165	46	40c. green	£350	
P166	45	50c. grey	£375	
P167	45	1f. orange	£350	
P168	45	2f. violet	£2000	
P169	-	5f. purple (No. 143)	£4000	

P59 Winged Railway Wheel

P60 Steam Locomotive

1915

P196	P59	10c. blue	1·20	60
P197	P59	15c. olive	2·00	2·00
P198	P59	20c. red	1·70	1·20
P199	P59	25c. brown	1·70	1·20
P200	P59	30c. mauve	1·70	1·20
P201	P59	35c. grey	2·00	1·20
P202	P59	40c. orange	3·25	3·00
P203	P59	50c. bistre	3·00	1·20
P204	P59	55c. brown	3·50	3·25
P205	P59	60c. lilac	3·00	1·20
P206	P59	70c. green	2·00	1·20
P207	P59	80c. brown	2·00	1·20
P208	P59	90c. blue	3·00	1·50
P209	P60	1f. grey	2·00	1·20
P210	P60	1f.10 bl (FRANKEN)	44·00	33·00
P211	P60	1f.10 blue (FRANK)	3·00	1·20
P212	P60	2f. red	65·00	1·70
P213	P60	3f. violet	65·00	1·70
P214	P60	4f. green	75·00	3·25
P215	P60	5f. brown	£150	4·25
P216	P60	10f. orange	£200	3·75

P69 Winged Railway Wheel

P70 Steam Train

1920

P259	P69	10c. green	2·30	1·20
P280	P69	10c. red	60	30
P281	P69	15c. green	60	30
P261	P69	20c. red	2·30	1·20
P282	P69	20c. green	2·00	30
P262	P69	25c. brown	3·50	1·20
P283	P69	25c. blue	85	30
P263	P69	30c. mauve	38·00	34·00
P284	P69	30c. brown	85	30
P285	P69	35c. brown	85	45
P286	P69	40c. orange	85	30
P265	P69	50c. bistre	11·50	2·00
P287	P69	50c. red	85	30
P266	P69	55c. brown	13·00	9·50
P288	P69	55c. yellow	7·00	5·75
P267	P69	60c. purple	15·00	1·70
P289	P69	60c. red	85	30
P290	P69	70c. green	4·00	60
P269	P69	80c. brown	65·00	2·00
P291	P69	80c. violet	3·00	45
P270	P69	90c. blue	17·00	1·70
P292	P69	90c. yellow	46·00	43·00
P293	P69	90c. purple	8·75	45
P271	P70	1f. grey	£120	2·00
P272	P70	1f.10 blue	38·00	2·00
P273	P70	1f.20 green	23·00	†
P274	P70	1f.40 brown	23·00	1·70
P275	P70	2f. red	£170	1·70
P276	P70	3f. mauve	£200	1·20
P277	P70	4f. green	£200	1·70
P278	P70	5f. brown	£200	1·20
P279	P70	10f. orange	£200	1·70

On Nos. P271/9 the engine has one head lamp.

1920. Three head lamps on engine.

P294	P70	1f. brown	8·75	30
P296	P70	1f.10 blue	3·00	30
P297	P70	1f.20 orange	3·75	30
P298	P70	1f.40 yellow	21·00	3·50
P299	P70	1f.60 green	38·00	70
P300	P70	2f. red	41·00	30
P301	P70	3f. red	41·00	30
P302	P70	4f. green	41·00	30
P303	P70	5f. violet	41·00	30
P304	P70	10f. yellow	£225	23·00
P305	P70	10f. brown	50·00	30
P306	P70	15f. red	50·00	30
P307	P70	20f. blue	£600	3·75

P75

1921

P312	P75	2f. black	11·50	95
P313	P75	3f. brown	£100	95
P314	P75	4f. green	26·00	95
P315	P75	5f. red	26·00	95
P316	P75	10f. brown	26·00	95
P317	P75	15f. red	26·00	1·50
P318	P75	20f. blue	£190	3·75

P84

1923

P375	P84	5c. brown	25	25
P376	P84	10c. red	10	10
P377	P84	15c. blue	30	30
P378	P84	20c. green	15	10
P379	P84	30c. purple	15	10
P380	P84	40c. olive	15	10
P381	P84	50c. red	15	10
P382	P84	60c. orange	15	10
P383	P84	70c. brown	15	10
P384	P84	80c. violet	15	10
P385	P84	90c. slate	1·00	10

Similar type, but horiz.

P386		1f. blue	30	15
P388		1f.10 orange	2·30	85
P389		1f.50 green	2·30	60
P390		1f.70 brown	60	60
P391		1f.80 red	3·50	85
P392		2f. olive	30	30
P393		2f.10 green	6·50	1·70
P394		2f.40 violet	3·00	1·70
P395		2f.70 grey	45·00	1·70
P396		3f. red	30	25
P397		3f.30 brown	70·00	1·70
P398		4f. red	30	25
P399		5f. violet	60	25
P400		6f. brown	30	25
P401		7f. orange	60	25
P402		8f. brown	60	25
P403		9f. purple	2·00	85
P404		10f. green	85	25
P405		20f. pink	1·20	25
P406		30f. green	4·00	60
P407		40f. slate	55·00	1·70
P408		50f. bistre	7·75	60

See Nos. P911/34.

1924. No. P394 surch **2F 30.**

P409		2f.30 on 2f.40 violet	5·75	85

P139 Type 5 Steam locomotive "Goliath", 1930

1934

P655	P139	3f. green	14·50	2·50
P656	P139	4f. mauve	5·75	30
P657	P139	5f. red	80·00	30

P149 Diesel Locomotive

1935. Centenary of Belgian Railway.

P689	P149	10c. red	35	30
P690	P149	20c. violet	35	30
P691	P149	30c. brown	60	30
P692	P149	40c. blue	60	30
P693	P149	50c. orange	60	30
P694	P149	60c. green	65	30
P695	P149	70c. blue	65	30
P696	P149	80c. black	65	30
P697	P149	90c. red	1·20	60

Horiz type. Locomotive *Le Belge*, 1835.

P698		1f. purple	85	30
P699		2f. black	2·30	30
P700		3f. orange	3·25	30
P701		4f. purple	3·25	30
P702		5f. purple	4·75	30
P703		6f. green	6·50	30
P704		7f. violet	26·00	30
P705		8f. black	26·00	35
P706		9f. blue	29·00	35
P707		10f. red	29·00	35
P708		20f. green	55·00	35
P709		30f. violet	£150	5·75
P710		40f. brown	£150	5·75
P711		50f. red	£200	5·25
P712		100f. blue	£375	85·00

P162 Winged Railway Wheel and Posthorn

1938

P806	P162	5f. on 3f.50 green	26·00	25
P807	P162	5f. on 4f.50 purple	30	10
P808	P162	6f. on 5f.50 red	60	10
P1162	P162	8f. on 5f.50 brown	60	15
P1163	P162	10f. on 5f.50 blue	85	15
P1164	P162	12f. on 5f.50 violet	1·50	25

P176 Seal of the International Railway Congress

1939. International Railway Congress, Brussels.

P856	P176	20c. brown	5·25	5·25
P857	P176	50c. blue	5·25	5·25
P858	P176	2f. red	5·25	5·25
P859	P176	9f. green	5·25	5·25
P860	P176	10f. purple	5·25	5·25

1939. Surch **M. 3Fr.**

P867	P162	3f. on 5f.50 red	30	25

1940. Optd **B** in oval and two vert bars.

P878	P84	10c. red	10	10
P879	P84	20c. green	10	10
P880	P84	30c. purple	10	10
P881	P84	40c. olive	10	10
P882	P84	50c. red	10	10
P883	P84	60c. orange	75	70
P884	P84	70c. brown	10	10
P885	P84	80c. violet	10	10
P886	P84	90c. slate	30	30
P887	P84	1f. blue	15	15
P888	P84	2f. olive	25	25
P889	P84	3f. red	25	25
P890	P84	4f. red	25	25
P891	P84	5f. violet	25	25

P892	**P84**	6f. brown	30	25
P893	**P84**	7f. orange	30	25
P894	**P84**	8f. brown	30	25
P895	**P84**	9f. purple	30	25
P896	**P84**	10f. green	30	25
P897	**P84**	20f. pink	75	45
P898	**P84**	30f. green	1·20	1·20
P899	**P84**	40f. slate	3·00	2·50
P900	**P84**	50f. bistre	1·70	1·70

1940. As Type **P84** but colours changed.

P911		10c. olive	10	10
P912		20c. violet	10	10
P913		30c. red	10	10
P914		40c. blue	10	10
P915		50c. green	10	10
P916		60c. grey	10	10
P917		70c. green	10	10
P918		80c. orange	30	10
P919		90c. lilac	3·00	10

Similar design, but horizontal.

P920		1f. green	30	10
P921		2f. brown	35	10
P922		3f. grey	35	10
P923		4f. olive	40	10
P924		5f. lilac	45	10
P925		5f. black	85	10
P926		6f. red	85	10
P927		7f. violet	85	10
P928		8f. green	85	10
P929		9f. blue	1·20	10
P930		10f. mauve	1·20	25
P931		20f. blue	3·50	50
P932		30f. yellow	5·75	1·00
P933		40f. red	7·25	1·00
P934		50f. red	11·50	85

No. P925 was for use as a railway parcels tax stamp.

P195 Engine Driver

1942. Various designs.

P1090	**P195**	10c. grey	30	25
P1091	**P195**	20c. violet	30	25
P1092	**P195**	30c. red	30	25
P1093	**P195**	40c. blue	30	25
P1094	**P195**	50c. blue	30	25
P1095	**P195**	60c. black	30	25
P1096	**P195**	70c. green	45	25
P1097	**P195**	80c. orange	45	25
P1098	**P195**	90c. brown	45	25
P1099	-	1f. green	30	25
P1100	-	2f. purple	30	25
P1101	-	3f. black	1·50	30
P1102	-	4f. blue	30	25
P1103	-	5f. brown	30	25
P1104	-	6f. green	1·50	60
P1105	-	7f. violet	30	25
P1106	-	8f. red	30	25
P1107	-	9f. blue	60	25
P996	-	9f.20 red	60	60
P1108	-	10f. red	3·25	35
P1109	-	10f. brown	2·30	45
P997	**P195**	12f.30 green	60	60
P998	-	14f.30 red	60	60
P1110	-	20f. green	1·20	25
P1111	-	30f. violet	1·20	25
P1112	-	40f. red	1·20	25
P1113	-	50f. blue	20·00	1·20
P999	-	100f. blue	24·00	24·00

DESIGNS—As Type P **195**: 1f. to 9f.20, Platelayer; 10f. and 14f.30 to 50f. Railway porter; 24½×34½ mm: 100f. Electric train.

No. P1109 was for use as a railway parcels tax stamp.

P216 Mercury

1945. Inscribed "BELGIQUE-BELGIE" or vice-versa.

P1116A	**P216**	3f. green	30	15
P1117A	**P216**	5f. blue	30	15
P1118A	**P216**	6f. red	30	15

P224 Level Crossing

1947

P1174	**P224**	100f. green	7·25	30

P230 Archer

1947

P1193	**P230**	8f. brown	1·20	40
P1194	**P230**	10f. blue and black	1·20	30
P1195	**P230**	12f. violet	1·70	30

1948. Surch.

P1229		9f. on 8f. brown	1·50	25
P1230		11f. on 10f. blue and black	1·50	40
P1231		13f.50 on 12f. violet	2·00	25

P246 "Parcel Post"

1948

P1250	**P246**	9f. brown	8·75	35
P1251	**P246**	11f. red	7·50	25
P1252	**P246**	13f.50 black	13·00	25

P254 Type 1 Locomotive, 1867 (dated 1862)

1949. Locomotives.

P1277	-	½f. brown	35	25
P1278	**P254**	1f. red	60	25
P1279	-	2f. blue	80	25
P1280	-	3f. red (1884)	2·50	25
P1281	-	4f. green (1901)	1·70	25
P1282	-	5f. red (1902)	1·70	25
P1283	-	6f. purple (1904)	2·50	25
P1284	-	7f. green (1905)	4·00	25
P1285	-	8f. blue (1906)	5·25	25
P1286	-	9f. brown (1909)	5·75	25
P1287	-	10f. olive (1910)	14·00	3·50
P1288	-	10f. black and red (1905)	7·00	25
P1289	-	20f. orange (1920)	13·00	25
P1290	-	30f. blue (1928)	23·00	25
P1291	-	40f. red (1930)	41·00	25
P1292	-	50f. mauve (1935)	70·00	25
P1293	-	100f. red (1939)	£120	30
P1294	-	300f. violet (1951)	£170	60

DESIGNS: 50c. Locomotive *Le Belge*, 1835; 2f. Type 29 locomotive, 1875; 3f. Type 25 locomotive, 1884; 4f. Type 18 locomotive, 1901; 5f. Type 22 locomotive, 1902; 6f. Type 53 locomotive, 1904; 7f. Type 8 locomotive, 1905; 8f. Type 16 locomotive, 1906; 9f. Type 10 locomotive, 1909; 10f. (P1287) Type 36 locomotive, 1910; 10f. (P 1288) Type 38 locomotive, 1905; 20f. Type 38 locomotive, 1920; 30f. Type 48 locomotive, 1928; 40f. Type 5 locomotive, 1935; 50f. Type 1 Pacific locomotive, 1935; 100f. Type 12 locomotive, 1939; 300f. Two-car electric train, 1951.

The 300f. is larger (37½×25 mm).

1949. Electrification of Charleroi–Brussels Line. As Type P254.

P1296		60f. brown	2·00	1·50

DESIGN: 60f. Type 101 electric locomotive, 1945.

P258 Loading Parcels

1950

P1307	-	11f. orange	5·75	25
P1308	-	12f. purple	22·00	2·00
P1309	-	13f. green	7·50	25
P1310	-	15f. blue	16·00	30
P1311	**P258**	16f. grey	5·75	25
P1312	-	17f. brown	7·50	25
P1313	**P258**	18f. red	16·00	25
P1314	**P258**	20f. orange	7·50	30

DESIGNS—HORIZ: 11, 12, 17f. Dispatch counter; 13, 15f. Sorting compartment.

P271 Mercury

1951. 25th Anniv of National Belgian Railway Society.

P1375	**P271**	25f. blue	15·00	13·00

1953. Nos. P1307, P1310 and P1313 surch.

P1442	-	13f. on 15f. blue	65·00	5·75
P1443	-	17f. on 11f. orange	32·00	1·20
P1444	**P258**	20f. on 18f. red	17·00	3·50

P288 Electric Train and Brussels Skyline

1953. Inauguration of Nord-Midi Junction.

P1451	**P288**	200f. green	£250	85
P1452	**P288**	200f. green & brown	£275	3·75

P291 Nord Station

P292 Central Station

1953. Brussels Railway Stations.

P1485	**P291**	1f. ochre	30	25
P1486	**P291**	2f. black	45	25
P1487	**P291**	3f. green	60	30
P1488	**P291**	4f. orange	85	40
P1489	**P291**	5f. brown	3·00	25
P1490	-	5f. brown	10·50	25
P1491	**P291**	6f. purple	1·20	25
P1492	**P291**	7f. green	1·20	25
P1493	**P291**	8f. red	1·50	25
P1494	**P291**	9f. blue	2·00	25
P1495	-	10f. green	2·40	25
P1496	-	10f. black	1·50	30
P1497	-	15f. red	14·50	45
P1498	-	20f. blue	4·00	25
P1498a	-	20f. green	2·30	45
P1499	-	30f. purple	6·50	25
P1500	-	40f. mauve	8·75	25
P1501	-	50f. mauve	10·50	25
P1501a	-	50f. blue	3·50	70
P1502	-	60f. violet	22·00	25
P1503	-	80f. purple	35·00	25
P1504	**P292**	100f. green	20·00	50
P1505	**P292**	200f. blue	£120	1·00
P1506	**P292**	300f. mauve	£200	1·70

DESIGNS—VERT: 5f. (P1490), 10f. (P1496), 15, 20f. (P1498a), 50f. (P1501a), Congress Station; 10f. (P1495), 20f. (P1498) to 50f. (P1501), Midi Station. HORIZ: 60, 80f. Chapelle Station.

Nos. P1490, P1496/7, P1498a and P1501a were for use as railway parcels tax stamps.

P295 Electric Train Type 121 and Nord Station, Brussels

1953

P1517	**P295**	13f. brown	23·00	30
P1518	**P295**	18f. blue	23·00	30
P1519	**P295**	21f. mauve	23·00	30

1956. Surch in figures.

P1585		14f. on 13f. brown	8·25	30
P1586		19f. on 18f. blue	8·25	30
P1587		22f. on 21f. mauve	8·25	30

P326 Mercury and Railway Winged Wheel

1957

P1600	**P326**	14f. green	8·25	25
P1601	**P326**	19f. sepia	8·25	25
P1602	**P326**	22f. red	8·25	40

1959. Surch **20 F.**

P1678		20f. on 19f. sepia	29·00	30
P1679		20f. on 22f. red	29·00	70

P357 Brussels Nord Station, 1861–1954

1959

P1695	**P357**	20f. olive	14·50	25
P1696	-	24f. red	5·75	30
P1697	-	26f. blue	5·75	3·50
P1698	-	28f. purple	5·75	3·50

DESIGNS—VERT: 24f. Brussels Midi station, 1869–1949. HORIZ: 26f. Antwerp Central station, 1905; 28f. Ghent St. Pieter's station.

P368 Congress Seal, Type 202 Diesel and Type 125 Electric Locomotives

1960. 75th Anniv of Int Railway Congress Assn.

P1722	**P368**	20f. red	50·00	35·00
P1723	**P368**	50f. blue	50·00	35·00
P1724	**P368**	60f. purple	50·00	35·00
P1725	**P368**	70f. green	50·00	35·00

1961. Nos. P1695/8 surch.

P1787	**P357**	24f. on 20f. olive	60·00	30
P1788	-	26f. on 24f. red	5·75	30
P1789	-	28f. on 26f. blue	5·75	30
P1790	-	35f. on 28f. purple	5·75	30

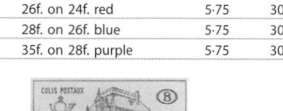

P477 Arlon Station

1967

P2017	**P477**	25f. ochre	9·25	45
P2018	**P477**	30f. green	2·30	45
P2019	**P477**	35f. blue	3·00	45
P2020	**P477**	40f. red	26·00	70

P488 Type 122 Electric Train

1968

P2047	**P488**	1f. bistre	30	30
P2048	**P488**	2f. green	30	30
P2049	**P488**	3f. green	60	30
P2050	**P488**	4f. orange	60	30
P2051	**P488**	5f. brown	60	30
P2052	**P488**	6f. plum	60	30
P2053	**P488**	7f. green	60	30
P2054	**P488**	8f. red	90	30
P2055	**P488**	9f. blue	1·50	30
P2056	-	10f. green	3·00	30
P2057	-	20f. blue	1·80	30
P2058	-	30f. lilac	5·50	30
P2059	-	40f. violet	6·00	30
P2060	-	50f. purple	7·50	30
P2061	-	60f. violet	11·00	30
P2062	-	70f. brown	48·00	30
P2063	-	80f. purple	7·50	30
P2063a	-	90f. green	7·25	50
P2064	-	100f. green	12·00	30
P2065	-	200f. violet	15·00	60
P2066	-	300f. mauve	27·00	1·50
P2067	-	500f. yellow	42·00	2·10

DESIGNS: 10f. to 40f. Type 126 electric train; 50, 60, 70, 80, 90f. Type 160 electric train; 100, 200, 300f. Type 205 diesel-electric train; 500f. Type 210 diesel-electric train.

1970. Surch.

P2180	**P477**	37f. on 25f. ochre	65·00	7·75
P2181	**P477**	48f. on 35f. blue	6·00	6·00
P2182	**P477**	53f. on 40f. red	6·00	6·00

P551 Ostend Station

1971. Figures of value in black.

P2192	**P551**	32f. ochre	1·80	1·50
P2193	**P551**	37f. grey	16·00	15·00
P2194	**P551**	42f. blue	2·40	1·80

P2195	**P551**	44f. mauve	2·40	1·80
P2196	**P551**	46f. violet	2·75	1·80
P2197	**P551**	50f. red	2·40	1·80
P2198	**P551**	52f. brown	17·00	16·00
P2199	**P551**	54f. green	6·75	6·00
P2200	**P551**	61f. blue	3·50	2·75

1972. Nos. P2192/5 and P2198/200 surch in figures.

P2256	34f. on 32f. ochre	2·75	1·20
P2257	40f. on 37f. grey	2·75	1·20
P2258	47f. on 44f. mauve	3·00	1·20
P2259	53f. on 42f. blue	4·00	1·20
P2260	56f. on 52f. brown	3·50	1·20
P2261	59f. on 54f. green	4·00	1·20
P2262	66f. on 61f. blue	4·25	1·20

P575 Emblems within Bogie Wheels

1972. 50th Anniv of Int Railways Union (U.I.C.).

P2266	**P575**	100f. black, red and green	9·00	2·40

See also No. 2274.

P624 Global Emblem

1974. Fourth International Symposium of Railway Cybernetics, Washington.

P2353	**P624**	100f. black, red and yellow	7·00	2·30

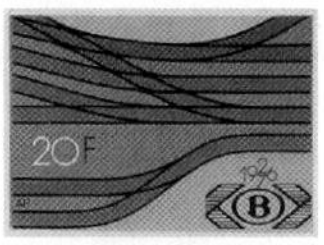

P671 Railway Junction

1976

P2431	**P671**	20f. black, bl & lilac	1·50	1·50
P2432	**P671**	50f. black, green and turquoise	2·50	1·50
P2433	**P671**	100f. black & orange	5·25	2·00
P2434	**P671**	150f. black, mauve and deep mauve	8·25	2·00

P677 Modern Electric Train

1976. 50th Anniv of National Belgian Railway Company.

P2445	**P677**	6f.50 multicoloured	50	15

P698 Railway Station at Night

1977

P2505	**P698**	1000f. mult	60·00	29·00

P753 Goods Wagon, Type 2216 A8

1980. Values in black.

P2615	**P753**	1f. ochre	30	30
P2616	**P753**	2f. red	30	30
P2617	**P753**	3f. blue	30	30
P2618	**P753**	4f. blue	30	30
P2619	**P753**	5f. brown	30	30
P2620	**P753**	6f. orange	45	45
P2621	**P753**	7f. violet	60	60
P2622	**P753**	8f. black	60	60
P2623	**P753**	9f. green	60	60
P2624	-	10f. brown	60	60
P2625	-	20f. blue	1·50	60
P2626	-	30f. ochre	2·30	60
P2627	-	40f. mauve	2·75	60
P2628	-	50f. purple	3·25	80
P2629	-	60f. olive	3·75	80
P2630	-	70f. blue	5·00	3·50
P2631	-	80f. purple	6·00	1·20
P2632	-	90f. mauve	6·50	4·00
P2633	-	100f. red	7·25	1·70
P2634	-	200f. brown	15·00	2·00
P2635	-	300f. olive	21·00	3·00
P2636	-	500f. purple	37·00	5·00

DESIGNS: 10f. to 40f. Packet wagon, Type 3614 A5; 50f. to 90f. Self-discharging wagon, Type 1000 D; 100f. to 500f. Tanker wagon, Type 2000 G.

P833 Electric Train entering Station

1985. 150th Anniv of Belgian Railways. Paintings by P. Delvaux. Multicoloured.

P2824	250f. Type P **833**	17·00	11·50
P2825	500f. Electric trains in station	41·00	20·00

RAILWAY PARCEL TAX STAMPS

1940. As Nos. P399 and P404 but colours changed.

P876	**P84**	5f. brown	60	60
P877	**P84**	10f. black	6·50	6·50

P779 Electric Locomotive at Station

1982

P2703	**P779**	10f. red & black	2·00	30
P2704	**P779**	20f. green & blk	2·30	1·50
P2705	**P779**	50f. brown & blk	4·25	85
P2706	**P779**	100f. blue & blk	7·50	1·20

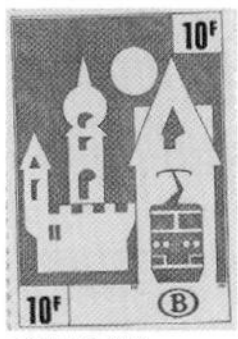

P877 Buildings and Electric Locomotive

1987

P2923	**P877**	10f. red	1·20	60
P2924	**P877**	20f. green	1·80	1·50
P2925	**P877**	50f. brown	5·50	2·10
P2926	**P877**	100f. purple	9·75	4·25
P2927	**P877**	150f. brown	15·00	5·50

RAILWAY OFFICIAL STAMPS

1929. Stamps of 1922 optd with winged wheel.

O481	**81**	5c. slate	35	30
O482	**81**	10c. green	35	30
O483	**81**	35c. green	45	30
O484	**81**	60c. olive	60	30
O485	**81**	1f.50 blue	19·00	9·25
O486	**81**	1f.75 blue	2·30	1·20

For use on the official mail of the Railway Company.

1929. Stamps of 1929 optd with winged wheel.

O534	**104**	5c. green	30	15
O535	**104**	10c. bistre	30	15
O536	**104**	25c. red	2·50	45
O537	**104**	35c. green	80	25
O538	**104**	40c. purple	80	25
O539	**104**	50c. blue	40	25
O540	**104**	60c. mauve	23·00	11·50
O541	**104**	70c. brown	4·00	1·40
O542	**104**	75c. blue	8·25	1·20

1932. Stamps of 1931–34 optd with winged wheel.

O620	**126**	10c. green	85	60
O677	**127**	35c. green	17·00	65
O678	**142**	70c. green	5·75	40
O679	**121**	75c. brown	2·50	50

1936. Stamps of 1936 optd with winged wheel.

O721	**152**	10c. olive	15	15
O722	**152**	35c. green	15	15
O723	**152**	40c. lilac	25	25
O724	**152**	50c. blue	60	60
O725	**153**	70c. brown	4·75	4·75
O726	**153**	75c. olive	60	60

1941. Optd B in oval frame.

O948	**152**	10c. green	15	15
O949	**152**	40c. lilac	15	15
O950	**152**	50c. blue	25	25
O951	**153**	1f. red (No. 747)	30	30
O952a	**153**	1f. red (No. 748)	60	60
O953	**153**	2f.25 black	70	70
O954	**155**	2f.25 violet	35	35

1942. Nos. O722, O725 and O726 surch.

O983	**152**	10c. on 35c. green	10	15
O984	**153**	50c. on 70c. brown	10	15
O985	**153**	50c. on 75c. olive	25	25

O221

1946. Designs incorporating letter "B".

O1156	**O 221**	10c. green	10	10
O1157	**O 221**	20c. violet	3·75	1·20
O1158	**O 221**	50c. blue	10	10
O1159	**O 221**	65c. purple	5·25	1·50
O1160	**O 221**	75c. mauve	25	15
O1161	**O 221**	90c. violet	6·00	35
O1240	-	1f.35 brn (as 1219)	3·00	60
O1241	-	1f.75 green (as 1220)	7·50	60
O1242	**239**	3f. purple	35·00	10·50
O1243	**240**	3f.15 blue	14·00	8·75
O1244	**240**	4f. blue	28·00	11·50

O283

1952

O1424	**O 283**	10c. orange	40	15
O1425	**O 283**	20c. red	4·25	85
O1426	**O 283**	30c. green	1·70	60
O1427	**O 283**	40c. brown	40	15
O1428	**O 283**	50c. blue	35	15
O1429	**O 283**	60c. mauve	85	30
O1430	**O 283**	65c. purple	35·00	29·00
O1431	**O 283**	80c. green	5·75	1·50
O1432	**O 283**	90c. blue	8·75	1·50
O1433	**O 283**	1f. red	60	15
O1433a	**O 283**	1f.50 grey	25	25
O1434	**O 283**	2f.50 brown	30	15

1954. As T **289** (King Baudouin) but with letter "B" incorporated in design.

O1523	1f.50 black	40	15
O1524	2f. red	46·00	40
O1525	2f. green	45	15
O1526	2f.50 brown	37·00	85
O1527	3f. mauve	2·00	15
O1528	3f.50 green	85	15
O1529	4f. blue	1·20	35
O1530	6f. red	2·00	60

1971. As Nos. 2209/20 but with letter "B" incorporated in design.

O2224	3f. green	1·30	90
O2225	3f.50 brown	50	30
O2226	4f. blue	1·50	60
O2227	4f.50 purple	40	30
O2228	4f.50 blue	30	30
O2229	5f. violet	30	30
O2230	6f. red	50	30
O2231	6f.50 violet	60	30
O2232a	7f. red	35	25
O2233	8f. black	60	30
O2233a	9f. brown	60	30
O2234	10f. red	60	30
O2235	15f. violet	60	30
O2236	25f. purple	1·80	60
O2237	30f. brown	1·90	90

1977. As T **684** but with letter "B" incorporated in design.

O2455	50c. brown	25	25
O2456	1f. mauve	25	25
O2457	2f. orange	25	25
O2458	4f. brown	30	30
O2459	5f. green	30	30

Pt. 1

BELIZE

British Honduras was renamed Belize on 1 June 1973 and the country became independent within the Commonwealth on 21 September 1981.

100 cents = 1 dollar.

1973. Nos. 256/66 and 277/8 of British Honduras optd **BELIZE** and two stars.

347	-	½c. multicoloured	10	20
348	**63**	1c. black, brown and yellow	10	20
349	-	2c. black, green and yellow	10	20
350	-	3c. black, brown and lilac	10	10
351	-	4c. multicoloured	10	20
352	-	5c. black and red	10	20
353	-	10c. multicoloured	15	15
354	-	15c. multicoloured	20	20
355	-	25c. multicoloured	35	35
356	-	50c. multicoloured	65	75
357	-	$1 multicoloured	75	1·50
358	-	$2 multicoloured	1·25	2·75
359	-	$5 multicoloured	1·40	4·75

1973. Royal Wedding. As T **47** of Anguilla. Background colours given. Multicoloured.

360	26c. blue	15	10
361	50c. brown	15	20

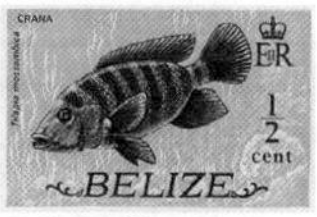

82 Mozambique Mouthbrooder

1974. As Nos. 256/66 and 276/78 of British Honduras. Multicoloured.

362	½c. Type **82**	10	50
363	1c. Spotted jewfish	10	30
364	2c. White-lipped peccary ("Waree")	10	30
365	3c. Misty grouper	10	30
366	4c. Collared anteater	10	30
367	5c. Bonefish	10	30
368	10c. Paca ("Gibnut")	15	15
369	15c. Dolphin	20	20
370	25c. Kinkajou ("Night Walker")	35	35
371	50c. Mutton snapper	60	70
372	$1 Tayra ("Bush Dog")	75	1·50
373	$2 Great barracuda	1·25	2·50
374	$5 Puma	1·50	5·50

83 Deer

1974. Mayan Artefacts (1st series). Pottery Motifs. Multicoloured.

375	3c. Type **83**	10	10
376	6c. Jaguar deity	10	10
377	16c. Sea monster	15	10
378	26c. Cormorant	25	10
379	50c. Scarlet macaw	40	40

See also Nos. 398/402.

84 "Parides arcas"

1974. Butterflies of Belize. Multicoloured.

380	½c. Type **84**	1·00	5·00
381	1c. *Evenus regalis*	1·00	1·75
405	2c. *Colobura dirce*	50	70
406	3c. *Catonephele numilia*	1·25	70
407	4c. *Battus belus*	3·00	30
408	5c. *Callicore patelina*	3·25	30
386	10c. *Diaethria astala*	1·50	70
410	15c. *Nessaea aglaura*	75	70
388	16c. *Prepona pseudojoiceyi*	5·00	9·00
412	25c. *Papilio thoas*	6·50	40
390	26c. *Hamadryas arethusa*	2·00	4·25
413	35c. Type **84**	13·00	4·50
391	50c. *Panthiades bathildis*	3·25	65
392	$1 *Caligo uranus*	6·50	7·00
393	$2 *Heliconius sapho*	4·00	1·25
394	$5 *Eurytides philolaus*	5·50	6·00
395	$10 *Philaethria dido*	10·00	4·00

85 Churchill when Prime Minister, and Coronation Scene

1974. Birth Centenary of Sir Winston Churchill. Multicoloured.

396	50c. Type **85**	20	20
397	$1 Churchill in stetson, and Williamsburg Liberty Bell	30	30

86 The Actun Balam Vase

1975. Mayan Artefacts (2nd series). Multicoloured.

398	3c. Type **86**	10	10
399	6c. Seated figure	10	10
400	16c. Costumed priest	25	15
401	26c. Head with headdress	35	20
402	50c. Layman and priest	45	1·75

87 Musicians

1975. Christmas. Multicoloured.

435	6c. Type **87**	10	10
436	26c. Children and "crib"	20	10
437	50c. Dancer and drummers (vert)	30	55
438	$1 Family and map (vert)	55	1·60

88 William Wrigley Jr. and Chicle Tapping

1976. Bicent of American Revolution. Multicoloured.

439	10c. Type **88**	10	10
440	35c. Charles Lindbergh	20	40
441	$1 J. L. Stephens (archaeologist)	50	1·50

89 Cycling

1976. Olympic Games, Montreal. Multicoloured.

442	35c. Type **89**	15	10
443	45c. Running	20	15
444	$1 Shooting	35	1·40

1976. No. 390 surch **20c**.

445	20c. on 26c. multicoloured	1·50	1·75

1976. West Indian Victory in World Cricket Cup. As Nos. 559/60 of Barbados.

446	35c. multicoloured	40	50
447	$1 black and purple	60	2·00

1976. No. 426 surch **5c**.

448	5c. on 15c. multicoloured	1·10	2·75

92 Queen and Bishops

1977. Silver Jubilee. Multicoloured.

449	10c. Royal Visit, 1975	10	10
450	35c. Queen and Rose Window	15	15
451	$2 Type **92**	45	90

93 Red-capped Manakin

1977. Birds (1st series). Multicoloured.

452	8c. Type **93**	75	55
453	10c. Hooded oriole	90	30
454	25c. Blue-crowned motmot	1·25	55
455	35c. Slaty-breasted tinamou	1·50	75
456	45c. Ocellated turkey	1·75	1·25
457	$1 White hawk	3·00	5·50
MS458	110×133 mm. Nos. 452/7	8·25	11·00

See also Nos. 467/78, 488/94 and 561/7.

94 Laboratory Workers

1977. 75th Anniv of Pan-American Health Organization. Multicoloured.

459	35c. Type **94**	20	20
460	$1 Mobile medical unit	40	65
MS461	126×95 mm. Nos. 459/60	85	1·40

1978. Nos. 386 and 413 optd **BELIZE DEFENCE FORCE 1ST JANUARY 1978**.

462	10c. "Diaethria astala"	75	1·50
463	35c. Type **84**	1·50	2·25

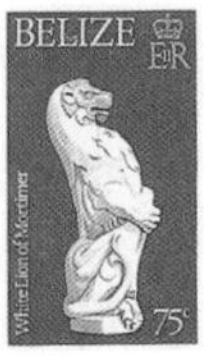

96 White Lion of Mortimer

1978. 25th Anniv of Coronation.

464	**96**	75c. brown, red and silver	20	30
465	-	75c. multicoloured	20	30
466	-	75c. brown, red and silver	20	30

DESIGNS: No. 465, Queen Elizabeth II; 466, Jaguar (Maya god of Day and Night).

1978. Birds (2nd series). As T **93**. Multicoloured.

467	10c. White-capped parrot("White-crowned Parrot")	55	30
468	25c. Crimson-collared tanager	80	45
469	35c. Black-headed trogon (*Citreoline Trogon*)	1·10	55
470	45c. American finfoot ("Sun-grebe")	1·25	1·75
471	50c. Muscovy duck	1·40	2·50
472	$1 King vulture	2·00	6·50
MS473	111×133 mm. Nos. 467/72	8·00	11·00

97 "Russelia sarmentosa"

1978. Christmas. Wild Flowers and Ferns. Multicoloured.

474	10c. Type **97**	15	10
475	15c. *Lygodium polymorphum*	20	15
476	35c. *Heliconia aurantiaca*	20	20
477	45c. *Adiantum tetraphyllum*	20	40
478	50c. *Angelonia ciliaris*	35	50
479	$1 *Thelypteris obliterata*	50	1·25

98 Fairchild Monoplane of Internal Airmail Service, 1937

1979. Centenary of U.P.U. Membership. Multicoloured.

480	5c. Type **98**	25	30
481	10c. *Heron H* (mail boat), 1949	25	10
482	35c. Internal mail service, 1920 (canoe)	25	20
483	45c. Steam Creek Railway mail, 1910	45	55
484	50c. Mounted mail courier, 1882	45	60
485	$2 *Eagle* (mail boat), 1856	80	2·50

1979. No. 413 surch **15c**.

487	**84**	15c. on 35c. multicoloured	2·25	1·75

1979. Birds (3rd series). As T **93**. Multicoloured.

488	10c. Boat-billed heron	50	30
489	25c. Grey-necked wood rail	75	30
490	35c. Lineated woodpecker	85	55
491	45c. Blue-grey tanager	90	70
492	50c. Laughing falcon	90	1·25
493	$1 Long-tailed hermit	1·40	4·50
MS494	113×136 mm. Nos. 488/93	4·75	7·00

101 Paslow Building, Belize G.P.O.

1979. 25th Anniv of Coronation. Multicoloured.

495	25c. Type **101**	1·50	10
496	50c. Houses of Parliament	2·00	10
497	75c. Coronation State Coach	2·50	15
498	$1 Queen on horseback (vert)	3·25	20
499	$2 Prince of Wales (vert)	3·25	35
500	$3 Queen and Duke of Edinburgh (vert)	3·25	35
501	$4 Portrait of Queen (vert)	3·25	40
502	$5 St. Edward's Crown (vert)	3·50	40
MS503	Two sheets, both 126×95 mm: (a) $5 Princess Anne on horseback at Montreal Olympics (vert); $10 Queen at Montreal Olympics (vert). (b) $15 As Type **101** Set of 2 sheets		25·00

102 Mortimer and Vaughan "Safety" Airplane, 1910

1979. Death Centenary of Sir Rowland Hill. 60th Anniv of I.C.A.O. (International Civil Aviation Organization), previously Int Commission for Air Navigation. Multicoloured.

504	4c. Type **102**	50	10
505	25c. Boeing 720	1·50	20
506	50c. Concorde	4·25	30
507	75c. Handley Page H.P.18 W.8b (1922)	2·00	30
508	$1 Avro Type F (1912)	2·00	30
509	$1.50 Samuel Cody's biplane (1910)	2·75	30
510	$2 A.V. Roe Triplane I (1909)	2·75	40
511	$3 Santos Dumont's biplane "14 bis" (1906)	2·75	45
512	$4 Wright Type A	3·00	65
MS513	Two sheets: (a) 115×95 mm. $5 Dunne D-5 (1910), $5 G.B. 1969 Concorde stamp; (b) 130×95 mm. $10 Boeing 720 (different) Set of 2 sheets		21·00

103 Handball

1979. Olympic Games, Moscow (1980). Multicoloured.

514	25c. Type **103**	45	10
515	50c. Weightlifting	65	10
516	75c. Athletics	90	15
517	$1 Football	1·25	20
518	$2 Yachting	1·75	25
519	$3 Swimming	2·00	30
520	$4 Boxing	2·50	30
521	$5 Cycling	11·00	1·25
MS522	Two sheets: (a) 126×92 mm. $5 Athletics (different), $10 Boxing (different); (b) 92×126 mm. $15 As $5 Set of 2 sheets		16·00

104 Olympic Torch

1979. Winter Olympic Games, Lake Placid (1980). Multicoloured.

523	25c. Type **104**	20	10
524	50c. Giant slalom	45	15
525	75c. Figure-skating	65	15
526	$1 Downhill skiing	80	15
527	$2 Speed-skating	1·60	20
528	$3 Cross-country skiing	2·50	30
529	$4 Shooting	3·00	40
530	$5 Gold, Silver and Bronze medals	3·50	45
MS531	Two sheets: (a) 127×90 mm. $5 Lighting the Olympic Flame, $10 Gold, Silver and Bronze medals (different); (b) 90×127 mm. $15 Olympic Torch (different) Set of 2 sheets		20·00

105 Measled Cowrie

1980. Shells. Multicoloured.

532	1c. Type **105**	65	10
533	2c. Callico clam	80	10
534	3c. Altantic turkey wing (vert)	90	10
535	4c. Leafy jewel box (vert)	90	10
536	5c. Trochlear latirus	90	10
537	10c. Alphabet cone (vert)	1·25	10
538	15c. Cabrits murex (vert)	1·75	10
539	20c. Stiff pen shell	1·75	10
540	25c. Little knobbed scallop (vert)	1·75	10
541	35c. Glory of the Atlantic cone (vert)	2·00	10
542	45c. Sunrise tellin (vert)	2·25	10
543	50c. *Leucozonia nassa leucozonalis*	2·25	10
544	85c. Triangular typhis	3·50	10
545	$1 Queen or pink conch (vert)	3·75	10
546	$2 Rooster-tail conch (vert)	6·00	30
547	$5 True tulip	8·50	50
548	$10 Star arene	10·00	90
MS549	Two sheets, each 125×90 mm. (a) Nos. 544 and 547. (b) Nos. 546 and 548	40·00	15·00

106 Girl and Flower Arrangement

1980. International Year of the Child (1st issue). Multicoloured.

550	25c. Type **106**	45	10
551	50c. Boy holding football	70	10
552	75c. Boy with butterfly	1·00	10
553	$1 Girl holding doll	1·00	10
554	$1.50 Boy carrying basket of fruit	1·50	15
555	$2 Boy holding reticulated cowrie-helmet shell	1·75	20
556	$3 Girl holding posy	2·25	25
557	$4 Boy and girl wrapped in blanket	2·50	30
MS558	130×95 mm. $5 Three children of different races. $5 "Madonna with Cat" (A. Dürer) (each 35×53 mm).		9·00
MS559	111×151 mm. $10 Children and Christmas tree (73×110 mm).		9·00

See also Nos. 583/91.

1980. No. 412 surch **10c**.

560	10c. on 25c. "Papilio thoas"	1·25	1·25

108 Jabiru

1980. Birds (4th series). Multicoloured.

561	10c. Type **108**	7·00	2·75
562	25c. Barred antshrike	8·00	2·75
563	35c. Northern royal flycatcher ("Royal Flycatcher")	8·00	2·75
564	45c. White-necked puffbird	8·00	3·00
565	50c. Ornate hawk-eagle	8·00	3·00
566	$1 Golden-masked tanager	8·50	3·75
MS567	85×90 mm. $2 Type **108**, $3 As $1	32·00	18·00

109 Speed Skating

1980. Winter Olympic Games, Lake Placid. Medal Winners. Multicoloured.

568	25c. Type **109**	45	20
569	50c. Ice-hockey	75	20
570	75c. Figure-skating	80	20
571	$1 Alpine-skiing	1·10	20
572	$1.50 Giant slalom (women)	1·50	30
573	$2 Speed-skating (women)	1·75	40
574	$3 Cross-country skiing	2·25	50
575	$5 Giant slalom	3·50	65
MS576	Two sheets: (a) 126×91 mm. $5 Type **109**; $10 Type **109**; (b) 91×126 mm. $10 As 75 c. Set of 2 sheets	16·00	

1980. "ESPAMER" International Stamp Exhibition, Madrid. Nos. 560/5 optd **BELIZE ESPAMER '80 MADRID 3-12 OCT 1980** and emblem (Nos. 577/9) or surch also.

577	10c. Type **107**	7·50	2·75
578	25c. Barred antshrike	8·00	3·00
579	35c. Northern royal flycatcher	8·00	3·00
580	40c. on 45c. White-necked puffbird	8·50	3·25
581	40c. on 50c. Ornate hawk eagle	8·50	3·25
582	40c. on $1 Golden-masked tanager	9·00	3·25

111 Witch in Sky

1980. International Year of the Child (2nd issue). "Sleeping Beauty".

583	**111**	25c. multicoloured	2·25	15
584	-	40c. multicoloured	2·50	15
585	-	50c. multicoloured	2·75	15
586	-	75c. multicoloured	3·00	20
587	-	$1 multicoloured	3·00	25
588	-	$1.50 multicoloured	3·50	40
589	-	$3 multicoloured	4·50	50
590	-	$4 multicoloured	4·50	55
MS591		Two sheets: (a) 82×110 mm. $8 "Paumgartner Altar-piece" (Dürer); (b) 110×82 mm. $5 Marriage ceremony, $5 Sleeping Beauty and Prince on horseback Set of 2 sheets	24·00	

DESIGNS: 40c. to $4, Illustrations from the story.

112 H.M. Queen Elizabeth the Queen Mother

1980. 80th Birthday of H.M. Queen Elizabeth the Queen Mother.

592	**112**	$1 multicoloured	3·00	65
MS593		82×110 mm, $5 As Type **112** (41×32 mm)	14·00	4·75

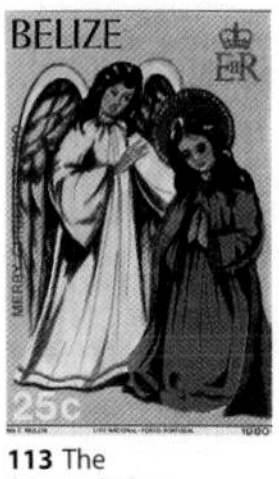

113 The Annunciation

1980. Christmas. Multicoloured.

594	25c. Type **113**	65	10
595	50c. Bethlehem	1·25	10
596	75c. The Holy Family	1·50	10
597	$1 The Nativity	1·60	15
598	$1.50 The Flight into Egypt	1·75	25
599	$2 Shepherds following the Star	2·00	35
600	$3 Virgin, Child and Angel	2·25	40
601	$4 Adoration of the Kings	2·25	45
MS602	Two sheets, each 82×111 mm: (a) $5 As $1: (b) $10 As $3 Set of 2 sheets	14·00	

1981. "WIPA" International Stamp Exhibition, Vienna. Nos. 598 and 601 surch.

603	$1 on $1.50 The Flight into Egypt	10·00	2·00
604	$2 on $4 Adoration of the Kings	11·00	3·00
MS605	82×111 mm. $2 on $10 Virgin, Child and Angel	18·00	6·00

115 Paul Harris (founder)

1981. 75th Anniv of Rotary International. Multicoloured.

606	25c. Type **115**	2·50	25
607	50c. Emblems of Rotary activities	3·00	35
608	$1 75th Anniversary emblem	3·50	65
609	$1.50 Educational scholarship programme (horiz)	4·25	1·00
610	$2 "Project Hippocrates"	4·75	1·40
611	$3 Emblems	6·50	2·00
612	$5 Emblems and handshake (horiz)	7·50	3·25
MS613	Two sheets: (a) 95×130 mm. $10 As 50c. (b) 130×95 mm, $5 As $1, $10 As $2 Set of 2 sheets	40·00	

116 Coat of Arms of Prince of Wales

1981. Royal Wedding. Multicoloured. (a) Size 22×38 mm.

614	50c. Type **116**	45	50
615	$1 Prince Charles in military uniform	80	90
616	$1.50 Royal couple	1·25	1·50

(b) Size 25×42 mm, with gold borders.

617	50c. Type **116**	45	30
618	$1 As No. 615	80	50
619	$1.50 As No. 616	1·25	70
MS620	145×85 mm. $3×3 As Nos 614/16, but 30×47 mm. P 14	2·50	4·25

1981. No. 538 surch **10c.**

621	10c. on 15c. "Murex cabritii"	3·50	3·75

118 Athletics

1981. History of the Olympics. Multicoloured.

622	85c. Type **118**	2·50	30
623	$1 Cycling	9·00	50
624	$1.50 Boxing	3·25	50
625	$2 1984 Games–Los Angeles and Sarajevo	4·25	50
626	$3 Baron de Coubertin	5·00	60
627	$5 Olympic Flame	6·00	70
MS628	Two sheets, each 175×123 mm: (a) $5 As $3, $10 As $5 (each 35×53 mm). P13½; (b) $15 As $2 (45×67 mm). P 14½. Set of 2 sheets	45·00	

1981. Independence Commemoration (1st issue). Optd **Independence 21 Sept., 1981**. (a) On Nos. 532/44 and 546/8.

629	1c. Type **105**	1·00	10
630	2c. Callico clam	1·00	10
631	3c. Atlantic turkey wing (vert)	1·00	10
632	4c. Leafy jewel box (vert)	1·00	10
633	5c. Trochlear latirus	1·25	10
634	10c. Alphabet cone (vert)	1·50	10
635	15c. Cabrits murex (vert)	2·25	10
636	20c. Stiff pen shell	2·25	15
637	25c. Little knobbed scallop (vert)	2·50	25
638	35c. Glory of the Atlantic cone	2·50	30
639	45c. Sunrise tellin (vert)	3·00	40
640	50c. *Leucozonia nassa leucozonalis*	3·00	40
641	85c. Triangular typhis	4·75	90
642	$2 Rooster-tail conch (vert)	9·00	2·50
643	$5 True tulip	11·00	5·50
644	$10 Star arene	13·00	9·50
MS645	Two sheets, each 126×91 mm; (a) Nos. 641 and 643; (b) Nos. 642 and 644 Set of 2 sheets	40·00	

(b) On Nos. 606/12.

646	25c. Type **115**	2·75	25
647	50c. Emblems of Rotary activities	3·00	35
648	$1 75th Anniversary emblem	3·50	65
649	$1.50 Educational scholarship programme	4·25	1·25
650	$2 *Project Hippocrates*	5·00	1·60
651	$3 Emblems	7·00	2·50
652	$5 Emblems and hand-shake	8·00	3·75
MS653	Two sheets: (a) 95×130 mm. $10 As 50c.; (b) 130×95 mm. $5 As $1, $10 As $2 Set of 2 sheets	40·00	

See also Nos. 657/63.

1981. "ESPAMER" International Stamp Exhibition, Buenos Aires. No. 609 surch **$1 ESPAMER 81 BUENOS AIRES 13-22 NOV** and emblem.

654	$1 on $1.50 Educational scholarship programme	13·00	3·50
MS655	95×130 mm. $1 on $5 75th anniversary emblem, $1 on $10 *Project Hippocrates*	18·00	9·00

(121)

1981. "Philatelia 81" International Stamp Exhibition, Frankfurt. No. **MS**549 surch with T **121**.

MS656	Two sheets, each 125×90 mm: (a) $1 on 85c. *Tripterotyphis triangularis*, $1 on $5 *Fasciolaria tulipa*; (b) $1 on $2 *Strombus gallus*, $1 on $10 *Arene cruentata* Set of 2 sheets	65·00	

122 Black Orchid

1981. Independence Commemoration (2nd issue). Multicoloured.

657	10c. Belize Coat of Arms (horiz)	2·25	20
658	35c. Map of Belize	5·00	40
659	50c. Type **122**	9·50	1·25
660	85c. Baird's tapir (horiz)	3·00	1·25
661	$1 Mahogany tree	2·50	1·25
662	$2 Keel-billed toucan (horiz)	14·00	4·00
MS663	130×98 mm. $5 As 10c.	18·00	6·50

123 Uruguayan Footballer

1981. World Cup Football Championship, Spain (1st issue). Multicoloured.

664	10c. Type **123**	2·25	20
665	25c. Italian footballer	3·25	20
666	50c. German footballer	4·00	45
667	$1 Brazilian footballer	5·00	70
668	$1.50 Argentinian footballer	6·50	1·50
669	$2 English footballer	7·00	1·75
MS670	Two sheets: (a) 145×115 mm. $2 "SPAIN '82" logo; (b) 155×115 mm. $3 Footballer (46×76 mm) Set of 2 sheets	30·00	7·50

See also Nos. 721/7.

124 H.M.S. *Centurion* (frigate)

1981. Sailing Ships. Multicoloured.

671	10c. Type **124**	3·25	40
672	25c. *Madagascar* (1837)	4·75	50
673	35c. Brig *Whitby* (1838)	5·50	55
674	55c. *China* (1838)	6·00	85
675	85c. *Swiftsure* (1850)	7·50	1·25
676	$2 *Windsor Castle* (1857)	11·00	3·00
MS677	110×87 mm. $5 Ships in battle	32·00	8·50

1982. "ESSEN '82" Int Stamp Exn, West Germany. Nos. 662 and 669 surch **$1 ESSEN 82.**

678	$1 on $2 Keel-billed toucan	11·00	2·75
679	$1 on $2 English footballer	11·00	2·75

126 Princess Diana

1982. 21st Birthday of Princess of Wales. (a) Size 22×38 mm.

680	**126**	50c. multicoloured	1·60	45
681	-	$1 multicoloured	2·00	75
682	-	$1.50 multicoloured	2·00	1·50

(b) Size 25×43 mm.

683	**126**	50c. multicoloured	1·60	30
684	-	$1 multicoloured	2·00	60
685	-	$1.50 multicoloured	2·00	1·10
MS686		145×85 mm. $3×3 As Nos. 680/2, but 30×47 mm.	2·75	3·00

DESIGNS: Portraits of Princess of Wales with different backgrounds.

127 Lighting Campfire

1982. 125th Birth Anniv of Lord Baden-Powell. Multicoloured.

687	10c. Type **127**	1·75	20
688	25c. Bird watching	5·00	30
689	35c. Three scouts, one playing guitar	2·75	30
690	50c. Hiking	3·25	55
691	85c. Scouts with flag	4·50	1·00
692	$2 Saluting	5·00	2·50
MS693	Two sheets: each 85×115 mm: (a) $2 Scout with flag; (b) $3 Portrait of Lord Baden-Powell Set of 2 sheets	35·00	13·00

128 *Gorgonia ventalina*

1982. First Anniv of Independence. Marine Life. Multicoloured.

694	10c. Type **128**	2·25	20
695	35c. *Carpiuis corallinus*	3·50	20
696	50c. *Plexaura flexuasa*	4·00	45
697	85c. *Condylactis gigantea*	4·25	60
698	$1 *Stenopus hispidus*	5·50	90
699	$2 Sergeant major	6·50	1·60
MS700	130×98 mm. $5 *Schyllarides aequinoclialis*	32·00	10·00

1982. "BELGICA 82" International Stamp Exhibition, Brussels. Nos. 687/92 optd **BELGICA 82 INT. YEAR OF THE CHILD SIR ROWLAND HILL 1795 1879 Picasso CENTENARY OF BIRTH** and emblems.

701	10c. Type **127**	2·75	40
702	25c. Bird watching	7·00	1·25
703	35c. Three scouts, one playing guitar	3·75	1·00
704	50c. Hiking	4·25	1·50
705	85c. Scouts with flag	10·00	2·75
706	$2 Saluting	11·00	7·50

1982. Birth of Prince William of Wales (1st issue). Nos. 680/5 optd **BIRTH OF H.R.H. PRINCE WILLIAM ARTHUR PHILIP LOUIS 21ST JUNE 1982**. (a) Size 22×38 mm.

707	50c. multicoloured	45	45
708	$1 multicoloured	55	60
709	$1.50 multicoloured	75	85

(b) Size 25×43 mm.

710	50c. multicoloured	45	45
711	$1 multicoloured	55	60
712	$1.50 multicoloured	75	85
MS713	145x85 mm. $3x3 as Nos. 707/9, but 30x477mm	3·25	3·50

1982. Birth of Prince William of Wales (2nd issue). Nos. 614/19 optd **BIRTH OF H.R.H. PRINCE WILLIAM ARTHUR PHILIP LOUIS 21ST JUNE 1982**. (a) Size 22×38 mm.

714	50c. Type **116**	3·25	1·00
715	$1 Prince Charles in military uniform	6·00	2·00
716	$1.50 Royal couple	8·50	3·00

(b) Size 25×42 mm.

717	50c. Type **116**	50	50
718	$1 As No. 715	70	70
719	$1.50 As No. 716	1·10	1·10
MS720	145×85 mm. $3×3 As Nos. 714/16 but 30×47 mm	7·50	7·00

131 Scotland v New Zealand

1982. World Cup Football Championship, Spain (2nd issue). Multicoloured.

721	20c.+10c. Type **131**	2·75	1·50
722	30c.+15c. Scotland v New Zealand (different)	2·75	1·50
723	40c.+20c. Kuwait v France	3·00	1·50
724	60c.+50c. Italy v Brazil	3·50	1·75
725	$1+50c. France v Northern Ireland	4·25	2·00
726	$1.50+75c. Austria v Chile	5·00	2·50
MS727	Two sheets: (a) 91×137 mm. $1+50c. Germany v Italy (50x70 mm); (b) 122×116 mm. $2+$1 England v France (50×70 mm) Set of 2 sheets	20·00	9·50

133 Belize Cathedral

1983. Visit of Pope John Paul II.

729	**133** 50c. multicoloured	2·75	1·50
MS730	135×110 mm. $2.50, Pope John Paul II (30×47 mm)	23·00	8·00

134 Map of Belize

1983. Commonwealth Day. Multicoloured.

731	35c. Type **134**	35	35
732	50c. *Maya Stella* from Lamanai Indian church (horiz)	40	50
733	85c. Supreme Court Building (horiz)	50	75
734	$2 University Centre, Belize (horiz)	85	2·50

1983. No. 658 surch **10c**.

735	10c. on 35c. Map of Belize	32·00	

136 De Lana-Terzis *Aerial Ship*, 1670

1983. Bicentenary of Manned Flight. Multicoloured.

736	10c. Type **136**	2·50	65
737	25c. De Gusmao's *La Passarole*, 1709	3·25	70
738	50c. Guyton de Morveau's balloon with oars, 1784	3·50	1·10
739	85c. Airship	4·25	1·25
740	$1 Airship "Clement Bayard"	4·50	1·60
741	$1.50 Beardmore airship R-34	5·00	3·25
MS742	Two sheets: (a) 125×84 mm. $3 Charles Green's balloon *Royal Vauxhall*; (b) 115×128 mm. $3 Montgolfier balloon, 1783 (vert) Set of 2 sheets	30·00	6·00

1983. Nos. 662 and 699 surch **$1.25**.

743	$1.25 on $2 Keel-billed toucan	18·00	12·00
744	$1.25 on $2 Sergeant major	6·00	8·50

1983. No. 541 surch **10c**.

746	10c. on 35c. Glory of the Atlantic cone	45·00	

141 Altun Ha

1983. Maya Monuments. Multicoloured.

747	10c. Type **141**	10	10
748	15c. Xunantunich	10	10
749	75c. Cerros	30	40
750	$3 Lamanal	70	1·75
MS751	102×72 mm. $3 Xunantunich (different)	1·00	1·75

142 Belmopan Earth Station

1983. World Communications Year. Multicoloured.

752	10c. Type **142**	30	10
753	15c. "Telstar 2"	40	25
754	75c. U.P.U. logo	70	1·75
755	$2 M.V. "Heron H" mail service	1·25	4·50

143 Jaguar Cub

1983. The Jaguar. Multicoloured.

756	5c. Type **143**	30	75
757	10c. Adult jaguar	35	45
758	85c. Jaguar in river	1·40	3·00
759	$1 Jaguar on rock	1·50	3·25
MS760	102×72 mm. $3 Jaguar in tree (44×28 mm). P 13½×14	1·50	2·50

144 Pope John Paul II

1983. Christmas.

761	**144** 10c. multicoloured	25	10
762	**144** 15c. multicoloured	25	10
763	**144** 75c. multicoloured	50	60
764	**144** $2 multicoloured	80	1·40
MS765	102×72 mm. $3 multicoloured	1·50	4·00

145 Four-eyed Butterflyfish

1984. Marine Life from the Belize Coral Reef. Multicoloured.

766	1c. Type **145**	25	1·25
767	2c. Cushion star	30	1·00
768	3c. Flower coral	35	1·00
769	4c. Royal gramma ("Fairy basslet")	40	1·00
770	5c. Spanish hogfish	45	1·00
771	6c. Star-eyed hermit crab	45	1·25
772a	10c. Sea fans and fire sponge	50	35
773a	15c. Blue-headed wrasse	70	60
774a	25c. Blue-striped grunt	80	80
775a	50c. Coral crab	1·00	1·75
776a	60c. Tube sponge	1·00	1·75
777	75c. Brain coral	1·00	1·50
778	$1 Yellow-tailed snapper	1·00	1·25
779	$2 Common lettuce slug	1·00	55
780	$5 Three-spotted damselfish	1·25	70
781	$10 Rock beauty	1·50	1·10

1984. Visit of the Archbishop of Canterbury. Nos. 772 and 775 optd **VISIT OF THE LORD ARCHBISHOP OF CANTERBURY 8th-11th MARCH 1984**.

782	10c. Sea fans and fire sponge	1·00	50
783	50c. Coral crab	1·75	2·00

147 Shooting

1984. Olympic Games, Los Angeles. Multicoloured. (a) As T **147**.

784	25c. Type **147**	30	25
785	75c. Boxing	50	70
786	$1 Marathon	60	90
787	$2 Cycling	2·75	2·75
MS788	101×72 mm. $3 Statue of discus thrower	1·60	3·00

(b) Similar designs to T **147** but Royal cypher replaced by Queen's Head.

789	5c. Marathon	20	90
790	20c. Sprinting	25	90
791	25c. Shot-putting	25	90
792	$2 Olympic torch	35	1·25

148 British Honduras 1866 1s. Stamp

1984. "Ausipex" International Stamp Exhibition, Melbourne. Multicoloured.

793	15c. Type **148**	25	15
794	30c. British mail coach, 1784	35	25
795	65c. Sir Rowland Hill and Penny Black	65	65
796	75c. British Honduras railway locomotive, 1910	70	75
797	$2 Royal Exhibition Buildings, Melbourne (46×28 mm)	1·00	2·25
MS798	103×73 mm. $3 Australia 1932 Sydney Harbour Bridge 5s. and British Honduras 1866 1s. stamps (44×28 mm). P 13½×14	1·10	2·00

149 Prince Albert

1984. 500th Anniv (1985) of British Royal House of Tudor. Multicoloured.

799	50c. Type **149**	25	45
800	50c. Queen Victoria	25	45
801	75c. King George VI	30	55
802	75c. Queen Elizabeth the Queen Mother	30	55
803	$1 Princess of Wales	40	75
804	$1 Prince of Wales	40	75
MS805	147×97 mm. $1.50, Prince Philip; $1.50, Queen Elizabeth II	1·25	2·00

150 White-fronted Amazon ("White-fronted Parrot")

1984. Parrots. Multicoloured.

806	$1 Type **150**	1·75	2·25
807	$1 White-capped parrot (horiz)	1·75	2·25
808	$1 Mealy amazon ("Mealy Parrot") (horiz)	1·75	2·25
809	$1 Red-lored amazon ("Red-lored Parrot")	1·75	2·25
MS810	102×73 mm. $3 Scarlet macaw	3·25	4·00

Nos. 806/9 were issued together, se-tenant, forming a composite design.

151 Effigy Censer, 1450 (Santa Rita Site)

1984. Maya Artefacts. Multicoloured.

811	25c. Type **151**	30	25
812	75c. Vase, 675 (Actun Chapat)	60	80
813	$1 Tripod vase, 500 (Santa Rita site)	65	1·00
814	$2 Sun god Kinich Ahau, 600 (Altun Ha site)	90	2·50

152 Governor-General inspecting Girl Guides

1985. International Youth Year and 75th Anniv of Girl Guides Movement. Multicoloured.

815	25c. Type **152**	30	15
816	50c. Girl Guides camping	45	30
817	90c. Checking map on hike	60	45
818	$1.25 Students in laboratory	70	60
819	$2 Lady Baden-Powell (founder)	90	75

153 White-tailed Kite

1985. Birth Bicentenary of John J. Audubon (ornithologist). Designs showing original paintings. Multicoloured.

820	10c. Type **153**	50	60
821	15c. Ruby-crowned kinglet ("Cuvier's Kinglet") (horiz)	50	60
822	25c. Painted bunting	60	60
822a	60c. As 25c.	24·00	9·00
823	75c. Belted kingfisher	60	1·40
824	$1 Common cardinal ("Northern Cardinal")	60	2·25
825	$3 Long-billed curlew (horiz)	1·00	3·00
MS826	139×99 mm. $5 "John James Audubon" (John Syme)	2·50	2·00

154 The Queen Mother with Princess Elizabeth, 1928

1985. Life and Times of Queen Elizabeth the Queen Mother. Multicoloured.

827	10c. Type **154**	10	10
828	15c. The Queen Mother, 1980	10	10
829	75c. Waving to the crowd, 1982	40	40
830	$5 Four generations of Royal Family at Prince William's Christening	1·50	2·75
MS831	Two sheets, each 138×98 mm. (a) $2 The Queen Mother with Prince Henry (from photo by Lord Snowdon) (38×50 mm); (b) $5 The Queen Mother, 1984 (38×50 mm) Set of 2 sheets	3·75	4·50

1985. Inauguration of New Government. Nos. 772/3 and 775 optd **INAUGURATION OF NEW GOVERNMENT – 21st. DECEMBER 1984.**

832	10c. Sea fans and fire sponge	1·50	60
833	15c. Blue-headed wrasse	1·50	60
834	50c. Coral crab	2·00	3·50

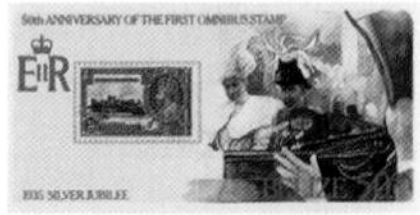

156 British Honduras 1935 Silver Jubilee 25c. stamp and King George V with Queen Mary in Carriage

1985. 50th Anniv of First Commonwealth Omnibus Issue. Designs showing British Honduras/Belize stamps. Multicoloured.

835	50c. Type **156**	55	85
836	50c. 1937 Coronation 3c., and King George VI and Queen Elizabeth in Coronation robes	55	85
837	50c. 1946 Victory 3c. and Victory celebrations	55	85
838	50c. 1948 Royal Silver Wedding 4c. and King George VI and Queen Elizabeth at Westminster Abbey service	55	85
839	50c. 1953 Coronation 4c. and Queen Elizabeth II in Coronation robes	55	85
840	50c. 1966 Churchill 25c., Sir Winston Churchill and fighter aircraft	55	85
841	50c. 1972 Royal Silver Wedding 50c. and 1948 Wedding photograph	55	85
842	50c. 1973 Royal Wedding 50c. and Princess Anne and Capt. Mark Phillips at their Wedding	55	85
843	50c. 1977 Silver Jubilee $2 and Queen Elizabeth II during tour	55	85
844	50c. 1978 25th anniversary of Coronation 75c. and Imperial Crown	55	85
MS845	138×98 mm. $5 Queen Elizabeth in Coronation robes (38×50 mm)	4·50	4·50

157 Mounted Postboy and Early Letter to Belize

1985. 350th Anniv of British Post Office. Multicoloured.

846	10c. Type **157**	50	25
847	15c. "Hinchinbrook II" (sailing packet) engaging "Grand Turk" (American privateer)	70	25
848	25c. "Duke of Marlborough II" (sailing packet)	85	30
849	75c. "Diana" (packet)	1·40	1·50
850	$1 Falmouth packet ship	1·40	2·00
851	$3 "Conway" (mail paddle-steamer)	2·25	5·50

1985. Commonwealth Heads of Government Meeting, Nassau, Bahamas. Nos. 827/30 optd **COMMONWEALTH SUMMIT CONFERENCE, BAHAMAS 16th-22nd OCTOBER 1985.**

852	10c. Type **154**	30	30
853	15c. The Queen Mother, 1980	40	35
854	75c. Waving to the crowd, 1982	80	80
855	$4 Four generations of Royal Family at Prince William's christening	2·00	3·75
MS856	Two sheets, each 138×98 mm. (a) $2 The Queen Mother with Prince Henry (from photo by Lord Snowdon) (38×50 mm): (b) $5 The Queen Mother, 1984 (38×50 mm) Set of 2 sheets	2·75	3·50

1985. 80th Anniv of Rotary International. Nos. 815/19 optd **80TH ANNIVERSARY OF ROTARY INTERNATIONAL.**

857	25c. Type **152**	70	40
858	50c. Girl Guides camping	1·25	75
859	90c. Checking map on hike	1·75	2·00
860	$1.25 Students in laboratory	2·25	2·75
861	$2 Lady Baden-Powell (founder)	2·75	3·50

160 Royal Standard and Belize Flag

1985. Royal Visit. Multicoloured.

862	25c. Type **160**	1·00	95
863	75c. Queen Elizabeth II	1·25	2·00
864	$4 Royal Yacht "Britannia" (81×39 mm)	4·50	4·00
MS865	138×98 mm. $5 Queen Elizabeth II (38×50 mm)	5·00	5·50

161 Mountie in Canoe (Canada)

1985. Christmas. 30th Anniv of Disneyland, U.S.A. Designs showing dolls from "It's a Small World" exhibition. Multicoloured.

866	1c. Type **161**	10	15
867	2c. Indian chief and squaw (U.S.A.)	10	15
868	3c. Incas climbing Andes (South America)	10	15
869	4c. Africans beating drums (Africa)	10	15
870	5c. Snake-charmer and dancer (India and Far East)	10	15
871	6c. Boy and girl with donkey (Belize)	10	15
872	50c. Musician and dancer (Balkans)	1·75	1·50
873	$1.50 Boys with camel (Egypt and Saudi Arabia)	2·75	3·50
874	$3 Woman and girls playing with kite (Japan)	3·75	5·00
MS875	127×102 mm. $4 Beefeater and castle (Great Britain). P 13½×14	5·50	8·00

1985. World Cup Football Championship, Mexico (1986) (1st issue). Nos. 835/44 optd **PRE "WORLD CUP FOOTBALL" MEXICO 1986** and trophy.

876	50c. Type **156**	75	90
877	50c. 1937 Coronation 3c., and King George VI and Queen Elizabeth in Coronation robes	75	90
878	50c. Victory 3c., and Victory celebrations	75	90
879	50c. 1948 Royal Silver Wedding 4c., and King George VI and Queen Elizabeth at Westminster Abbey service	75	90
880	50c. 1953 Coronation 4c., and Queen Elizabeth II in Coronation robes	75	90
881	50c. 1966 Churchill 25c., Sir Winston Churchill and fighter aircraft	75	90
882	50c. 1972 Royal Silver Wedding 50c. and 1948 wedding photograph	75	90
883	50c. 1973 Royal Wedding 5c., and Princess Anne and Capt. Mark Phillips at their Wedding	75	90
884	50c. 1977 Silver Jubilee $2 and Queen Elizabeth II during tour	75	90
885	50c. 1978 25th anniv of Coronation 75c. and Imperial Crown	75	90
MS886	138×98 mm. $5 Queen Elizabeth II in Coronation robes	4·25	4·25

See also Nos. 936/40.

163 Indian Costume

1986. Costumes of Belize. Multicoloured.

887	5c. Type **163**	75	30
888	10c. Maya	80	30
889	15c. Garifuna	1·00	35
890	25c. Creole	1·25	35
891	50c. Chinese	1·75	1·25
892	75c. Lebanese	2·00	2·00
893	$1 European c. 1900	2·00	2·50
894	$2 Latin	2·75	3·75
MS895	139×98 mm. Amerindian (38×50 mm)	6·00	7·00

164 Pope Pius X

1986. Easter. 20th-century Popes. Multicoloured.

896	50c. Type **164**	1·40	1·50
897	50c. Benedict XV	1·40	1·50
898	50c. Pius XI	1·40	1·50
899	50c. Pius XII	1·40	1·50
900	50c. John XXIII	1·40	1·50
901	50c. Paul VI	1·40	1·50
902	50c. John Paul I	1·40	1·50
903	50c. John Paul II	1·40	1·50
MS904	147×92 mm. $4 Pope John Paul II preaching (vert).	11·00	10·00

165 Princess Elizabeth aged Three

1986. 60th Birthday of Queen Elizabeth II. Multicoloured.

905	25c. Type **165**	40	55
906	50c. Queen wearing Imperial State Crown	60	75
907	75c. At Trooping the Colour	75	85
908	$3 Queen wearing diadem	1·40	2·25
MS909	147×93 mm. $4 Queen Elizabeth II (37×50 mm)	3·25	4·50

166 Halley's Comet and Japanese "Planet A" Spacecraft

1986. Appearance of Halley's Comet. Multicoloured.

910	10c. Type **166**	55	80
911	15c. Halley's Comet, 1910	65	90
912	50c. Comet and European "Giotto" spacecraft	70	1·00
913	75c. Belize Weather Bureau	90	1·00
914	$1 Comet and U.S.A. space telescope	1·25	1·40
915	$2 Edmond Halley	1·60	1·90
MS916	147×93 mm. $4 Computer enhanced photograph of Comet (37×50 mm)	6·50	8·50

167 George Washington

1986. United States Presidents. Multicoloured.

917	10c. Type **167**	35	60
918	20c. John Adams	35	65
919	30c. Thomas Jefferson	40	70
920	50c. James Madison	50	70
921	$1.50 James Monroe	80	1·25
922	$2 John Quincy Adams	1·00	1·50
MS923	147×93 mm. $4 George Washington (different)	3·75	5·50

168 Auguste Bartholdi (sculptor) and Statue's Head

1986. Centenary of Statue of Liberty. Multicoloured.

924	25c. Type **168**	40	65
925	50c. Statue's head at U.S. Centennial Celebration, Philadelphia, 1876	55	85
926	75c. Unveiling ceremony, 1886	55	90
927	$4 Statue of Liberty and flags of Belize and U.S.A.	1·50	2·50
MS928	147×92 mm. $4 Statue of Liberty and New York skyline (37×50 mm)	3·75	5·50

169 British Honduras 1866 1s. Stamp

1986. "Ameripex" International Stamp Exhibition, Chicago. Multicoloured.

929	10c. Type **169**	40	55
930	15c. 1981 Royal Wedding $1.50 stamps	55	75
931	50c. U.S.A. 1918 24c. airmail inverted centre error	75	80
932	75c. U.S.S. "Constitution" (frigate)	75	1·10
933	$1 Liberty Bell	80	1·40
934	$2 White House	90	1·60
MS935	147×93 mm. $4 Capitol, Washington (37×50 mm)	3·25	4·50

170 English and Brazilian Players

1986. World Cup Football Championship, Mexico (2nd issue). Multicoloured.

936	25c. Type **170**	1·50	1·75
937	50c. Mexican player and Maya statues	1·75	2·00
938	75c. Two Belizean players	2·00	2·25
939	$3 Aztec stone calendar	2·25	2·50
MS940	147×92 mm. $4 Flags of competing nations on two footballs (37×50 mm)	6·50	8·00

171 Miss Sarah Ferguson

1986. Royal Wedding. Multicoloured.

941	25c. Type **171**	65	40
942	75c. Prince Andrew	1·00	90
943	$3 Prince Andrew and Miss Sarah Ferguson (92×41 mm)	1·75	2·75
MS944	155×106 mm. $1 Miss Sarah Ferguson (different). $3 Prince Andrew (different)	4·25	6·00

1986. World Cup Football Championship Winners, Mexico. Nos. 936/9 optd **ARGENTINA – WINNERS 1986.**

945	25c. Type **170**	1·75	2·00
946	50c. Mexican player and Maya statues	2·00	2·25
947	75c. Two Belizean players	2·25	2·50
948	$3 Aztec stone calendar	3·25	3·50
MS949	147×92 mm. $4 Flags of competing nations on two footballs (37×50 mm)	8·00	10·00

1986. "Stockholmia '86" International Stamp Exhibition, Sweden. Nos. 929/34 optd **STOCKHOLMIA 86** and emblem.

950	10c. Type **169**	50	75
951	15c. 1981 Royal Wedding $1.50 stamp	65	90
952	50c. U.S.A. 1918 24c. airmail inverted centre error	80	1·10
953	75c. U.S.S. "Constitution"	1·00	1·50
954	$1 Liberty Bell	1·25	1·60
955	$2 White House	1·60	1·90
MS956	147×93 mm. $4 Capitol, Washington (37×50 mm)	5·00	7·00

174 Amerindian Girl

1986. International Peace Year. Multicoloured.

957	25c. Type **174**	65	80
958	50c. European boy and girl	80	1·10
959	75c. Japanese girl	1·00	1·60
960	$3 Indian boy and European girl	1·75	2·75
MS961	132×106 mm. $4 As 25c. but vert (35×47 mm)	5·50	7·00

175 *Amanita lilloi*

1986. Fungi and Toucans. Multicoloured.

962	5c. Type **175**	1·50	1·25
963	10c. Keel-billed toucan	1·75	1·60
964	20c. *Boletellus cubensis*	2·00	1·75
965	25c. Collared aracari	2·00	1·75
966	75c. *Psilocybe caerulescens*	2·25	2·00
967	$1 Emerald toucanet	2·25	2·00
968	$1.25 Crimson-rumped toucanet ("Crimson-rumped Toucan")	2·50	2·25
969	$2 *Russula puiggarii*	2·50	2·50

176 Jose Carioca

1986. Christmas. Designs showing Walt Disney cartoon characters in scenes from "Saludos Amigos". Multicoloured.

970	2c. Type **176**	20	20
971	3c. Jose Carioca, Panchito and Donald Duck	20	20
972	4c. Daisy Duck as Rio Carnival dancer	20	20
973	5c. Mickey and Minnie Mouse as musician and dancer	20	20
974	6c. Jose Carioca using umbrella as flute	20	20
975	50c. Donald Duck and Panchito	1·00	1·75
976	65c. Joe Carioca and Donald Duck playing hide and seek	1·25	2·00
977	$1.35 Donald Duck playing maracas	2·00	3·25
978	$2 Goofy as matador	2·75	3·75
MS979	131×111 mm. $4 Donald Duck	9·00	11·00

177 Princess Elizabeth in Wedding Dress, 1947

1987. Royal Ruby Wedding. Multicoloured.

980	25c. Type **177**	25	20
981	75c. Queen and Duke of Edinburgh, 1972	45	50
982	$1 Queen on her 60th birthday	50	60
983	$4 In Garter robes	1·00	2·00
MS984	171×112 mm. $6 Queen and Duke of Edinburgh (44×50 mm)	6·50	7·50

178 *America II*, 1983

1987. America's Cup Yachting Championship. Multicoloured.

985	25c. Type **178**	30	25
986	75c. *Stars and Stripes*, 1987	40	50
987	$1 *Australia II*, 1983	50	60
988	$4 *White Crusader*	1·00	2·00
MS989	171×112 mm. $6 Sails of *Australia II* (44×50 mm.)	5·00	7·50

179 "Mother and Child"

1987. Wood Carvings by George Gabb. Multicoloured.

990	25c. Type **179**	15	25
991	75c. *Standing Form*	35	50
992	$1 *Love-doves*	40	60
993	$4 *Depiction of Music*	1·10	2·00
MS994	173×114 mm. $6 *African Heritage* (44×50 mm.)	4·25	7·00

180 Black-handed Spider Monkey

1987. Primates. Multicoloured.

995	25c. Type **180**	25	20
996	75c. Black howler monkey	40	55
997	$1 Spider monkeys with baby	45	65
998	$4 Two black howler monkeys	1·10	2·25
MS999	171×112 mm. $6 Young spider monkey (44×50 mm.)	5·50	8·00

181 Guides on Parade

1987. 50th Anniv of Girl Guide Movement in Belize. Multicoloured.

1000	25c. Type **181**	45	20
1001	75c. Brownie camp	80	1·00
1002	$1 Guide camp	1·00	1·25
1003	$4 Olave, Lady Baden-Powell	3·00	5·00
MS1004	173×114 mm. $6 As $4 but vert (44×50 mm)	4·00	6·50

182 Indian Refugee Camp

1987. Int Year of Shelter for the Homeless. Multicoloured.

1005	25c. Type **182**	50	25
1006	75c. Filipino family and slum	90	90
1007	$1 Family in Middle East shanty town	1·10	1·25
1008	$4 Building modern house in Belize	2·00	4·50

183 "Laelia euspatha"

1987. Christmas. Orchids. Illustrations from Sander's *Reichenbachia*. Multicoloured.

1009	1c. Type **183**	95	95
1010	2c. *Cattleya citrina*	95	95
1011	3c. *Masdevallia backhousiana*	95	95
1012	4c. *Cypripedium tautzianum*	95	95
1013	5c. *Trichopilia suavis alba*	95	95
1014	6c. *Odontoglossum hebraicum*	95	95
1015	7c. *Cattleya trianaei schroederiana*	95	95
1016	10c. *Saccolabium giganteum*	95	95
1017	30c. *Cattleya warscewiczii*	1·25	1·25
1018	50c. *Chysis bractescens*	1·50	1·50
1019	70c. *Cattleya rochellensis*	1·75	1·75
1020	$1 *Laellia elegans schilleriana*	1·90	1·90
1021	$1.50 *Laelia anceps percivaliana*	2·00	2·00
1022	$3 *Laelia gouldiana*	2·50	2·50
MS1023	Two sheets, each 171×112 mm. (a) $3 *Odontoglossum roezlii* (40×47 mm). (b) $5 *Cattleya dowiana aurea* (40×47 mm) Set of 2 sheets	12·00	13·00

184 Christ condemned to Death

1988. Easter. The Stations of the Cross. Multicoloured.

1024	40c. Type **184**	35	60
1025	40c. Christ carrying the Cross	35	60
1026	40c. Falling for the first time	35	60
1027	40c. Christ meets Mary	35	60
1028	40c. Simon of Cyrene helping to carry the Cross	35	60
1029	40c. Veronica wiping the face of Christ	35	60
1030	40c. Christ falling a second time	35	60
1031	40c. Consoling the women of Jerusalem	35	60
1032	40c. Falling for the third time	35	60
1033	40c. Christ being stripped	35	60
1034	40c. Christ nailed to the Cross	35	60
1035	40c. Dying on the Cross	35	60
1036	40c. Christ taken down from the Cross	35	60
1037	40c. Christ being laid in the sepulchre	35	60

185 Basketball

1988. Olympic Games, Seoul. Multicoloured.

1038	10c. Type **185**	3·00	1·00
1039	25c. Volleyball	1·00	30
1040	60c. Table tennis	1·00	60
1041	75c. Diving	1·00	70
1042	$1 Judo	1·25	1·10
1043	$2 Hockey	7·00	5·00
MS1044	76×106 mm. $3 Gymnastics	6·00	6·50

186 Public Health Nurse, c. 1912

1988. 125th Anniv of Int Red Cross. Multicoloured.

1045	60c. Type **186**	3·25	1·25
1046	75c. "Aleda E. Lutz" (hospital ship) and ambulance launch, 1937	3·50	1·50
1047	$1 Ambulance at hospital tent, 1956	4·00	2·00
1048	$2 Auster ambulance plane, 1940	5·50	6·00

187 Collared Anteater ("Ants Bear")

1989. Small Animals of Belize. Multicoloured.

1049	10c. Paca ("Gibnut")	2·75	2·50
1050	25c. Four-eyed opossum (vert)	2·75	1·75
1051	50c. Type **187**	3·25	2·25
1052	60c. As 10c.	3·25	2·50
1053	75c. Red brocket	3·25	2·50
1054	$1 Collared peccary	4·50	6·50

1989. 20th Anniv of First Manned Landing on Moon. As T **126** of Ascension. Multicoloured.

1055	25c. Docking of "Apollo 9" modules	2·00	30
1056	50c. "Apollo 9" command service module in Space (30×30 mm)	2·50	75
1057	75c. "Apollo 9" emblem (30×30 mm)	2·75	1·25
1058	$1 "Apollo 9" lunar module in space	3·00	2·25
MS1059	83×100 mm. $5 "Apollo II" command service module undergoing test	11·00	10·00

1989. No. 771 surch **5c.**

1060	5c. on 6c. Star-eyed hermit crab	15·00	2·50

1989. "World Stamp Expo '89" International Stamp Exhibition, Washington. No. **MS**1059 optd **WORLD STAMP EXPO '89, United States Postal Service Nov 17—20 and Nov 24—Dec 3. 1989 Washington Convention Center Washington, DC** and emblem.

MS1061	83×100 mm. $5 "Apollo II" command service module undergoing tests	9·50	10·00

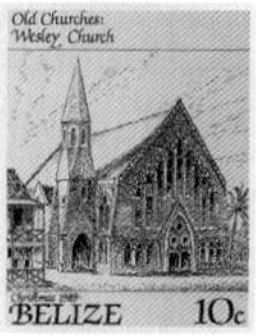

190 Wesley Church

1989. Christmas. Belize Churches.

1062	**190**	10c. black, pink and brown	20	10
1063	-	25c. black, lilac and mauve	25	20
1064	-	60c. black, turq & bl	50	70
1065	-	75c. black, grn & lt grn	65	90
1066	-	$1 black, lt yell & yell	80	1·25

DESIGNS: 25c. Baptist Church; 60c. St. John's Anglican Cathedral; 75c. St. Andrew's Presbyterian Church; $1 Holy Redeemer Roman Catholic Cathedral.

191 White-winged Tanager and *Catonephele numilia*

1990. Birds and Butterflies. Multicoloured.

1067A	5c. Type **191**	60	1·00
1068B	10c. Keel-billed toucan and *Nessaea aglaura*	80	80
1069A	15c. Magnificent frigate bird and *Eurytides philolaus*	80	40
1070A	25c. Jabiru and *Heliconius sapho*	80	40
1071A	30c. Great blue heron and *Colobura dirce*	80	50
1072A	50c. Northern oriole and *Hamadryas arethusia*	1·00	60
1073A	60c. Scarlet macaw and *Evenus regalis*	1·25	70
1074A	75c. Red-legged honey-creeper and *Callicore patelina*	1·25	75
1075A	$1 Spectacled owl and *Caligo uranus*	2·25	1·60
1076A	$2 Green jay and *Philaethria dido*	2·75	3·50
1077A	$5 Turkey vulture and *Battus belus*	4·50	6·50
1078A	$10 Osprey and *Papilio thoas*	8·50	11·00

1990. First Belize Dollar Coin. No. 1075 optd **FIRST DOLLAR COIN 1990.**

1079	$1 Spectacled owl and "Caligo uranus"	4·75	2·75

193 Green Turtle

1990. Turtles. Multicoloured.

1080	10c. Type **193**	65	40
1081	25c. Hawksbill turtle	1·00	40
1082	60c. Saltwater loggerhead turtle	1·50	1·50
1083	75c. Freshwater loggerhead turtle	1·60	1·60
1084	$1 Bocatora turtle	2·00	2·00
1085	$2 Hicatee turtle	2·75	5·50

194 Fairey Battle

1990. 50th Anniv of the Battle of Britain. Multicoloured.

1086	10c. Type **194**	1·00	50
1087	25c. Bristol Type 152 Beaufort	1·60	50

1088	60c. Bristol Type 142 Blenheim Mk IV	2·00	2·00
1089	75c. Armstrong-Whitworth Whitley	2·00	2·00
1090	$1 Vickers-Armstrong Wellington Mk 1c	2·00	2·00
1091	$1 Handley Page Hampden	2·50	4·00

195 *Cattleya bowringiana*

1990. Christmas. Orchids. Multicoloured.

1092	25c. Type **195**	85	20
1093	50c. *Rhyncholaelia digbyana*	1·25	50
1094	60c. *Sobralia macrantha*	1·50	1·00
1095	75c. *Chysis bractescens*	1·50	1·00
1096	$1 *Vanilla planifolia*	1·75	1·75
1097	$2 *Epidendrum polyanthum*	2·50	4·00

196 Common Iguana

1991. Reptiles and Mammals. Multicoloured.

1098	25c. Type **196**	80	35
1099	50c. Morelet's crocodile	1·25	90
1100	60c. American manatee	1·50	1·50
1101	75c. Boa constrictor	1·75	1·75
1102	$1 Baird's tapir	2·00	2·00
1103	$2 Jaguar	2·75	3·75

1991. 65th Birthday of Queen Elizabeth II and 70th Birthday of Prince Philip. As T **139** of Ascension. Multicoloured.

1104	$1 Queen Elizabeth II wearing tiara	1·00	1·50
1105	$1 Prince Philip wearing panama	1·00	1·50

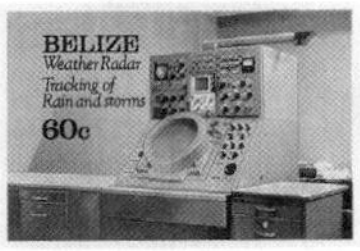

197 Weather Radar

1991. International Decade for Natural Disaster Reduction.

1106	**197**	60c. multicoloured	1·50	1·25
1107	-	75c. multicoloured	1·60	1·40
1108	-	$1 blue and black	1·75	1·75
1109	-	$2 multicoloured	2·50	3·25

DESIGNS: 75c. Weather station; $1 Floods in Belize after Hurricane Hattie, 1961; $2 Satellite image of Hurricane Gilbert.

198 Thomas Ramos and Demonstration

1991. Tenth Anniv of Independence. Famous Belizeans (1st series). Multicoloured.

1110	25c. Type **198**	60	30
1111	60c. Sir Isaiah Morter and palm trees	1·25	1·50
1112	75c. Antonio Soberanis and political meeting	1·25	1·75
1113	$1 Santiago Ricalde and cutting sugar-cane	1·50	2·00

See also Nos. 1126/9 and 1148/51.

199 "Anansi the Spider"

1991. Christmas. Folklore. Multicoloured.

1114	25c. Type **199**	1·75	20
1115	50c. "Jack-o-Lantern"	2·25	55
1116	60c. "Tata Duende" (vert)	2·50	1·25
1117	75c. "Xtabai"	2·50	1·25
1118	$1 "Warrie Massa" (vert)	2·75	2·25
1119	$2 "Old Heg"	4·00	7·00

200 *Gongora quinquenervis*

1992. Easter. Orchids. Multicoloured.

1120	25c. Type **200**	1·25	20
1121	50c. *Oncidium sphacelatum*	1·75	75
1122	60c. *Encyclia bratescens*	2·00	1·75
1123	75c. *Epidendrum ciliare*	2·00	1·75
1124	$1 *Psygmorchis pusilla*	2·25	2·25
1125	$2 *Galeandra batemanii*	3·75	4·50

1992. Famous Belizeans (2nd series). As T **198**, but inscr "EMINENT BELIZEANS" at top. Multicoloured.

1126	25c. Gwendolyn Lizarraga (politician) and High School	75	30
1127	60c. Rafael Fonseca (civil servant) and Government Offices, Belize	1·50	1·50
1128	75c. Vivian Seay (health worker) and nurses	1·75	1·75
1129	$1 Samuel Haynes (U.N.I.A. worker) and words of National Anthem	2·00	2·50

201 Xunantunich and National Assembly

1992. 500th Anniv of Discovery of America by Columbus. Mayan sites and modern buildings. Multicoloured.

1130	25c. Type **201**	1·00	25
1131	60c. Altun Ha and Supreme Court	1·50	1·00
1132	75c. Santa Rita and Tower Hill Sugar Factory	1·60	1·25
1133	$5 Lamanai and Citrus Company works	8·00	11·00

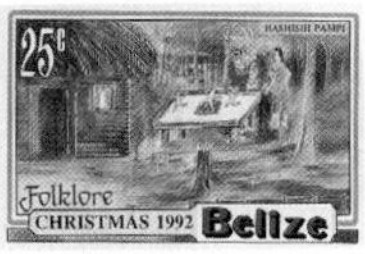

202 Hashishi Pampi

1992. Christmas. Folklore. Multicoloured.

1134	25c. Type **202**	30	20
1135	60c. Cadejo	60	60
1136	$1 La Sucia (vert)	90	1·00
1137	$5 Sisimito	4·00	7·00

1993. 75th Anniv of Royal Air Force. As T **149** of Ascension. Multicoloured.

1138	25c. Sud Aviation SA 330L Puma helicopter	1·25	60
1139	50c. Hawker Siddeley Harrier GR3	1·50	80
1140	60c. de Havilland DH98 Mosquito Mk XVIII	1·60	1·10
1141	75c. Avro Type 683 Lancaster	1·60	1·10
1142	$1 Consolidated Liberator I	1·75	1·40
1143	$3 Short Stirling Mk I	3·50	6·00

203 *Lycaste aromatica*

1993. 14th World Orchid Conference, Glasgow. Multicoloured.

1144	25c. Type **203**	40	25
1145	60c. *Sobralia decora*	75	80
1146	$1 *Maxillaria alba*	1·00	1·25
1147	$2 *Brassavola nodosa*	1·75	3·00

1993. Famous Belizeans (3rd series). As T **198**, but inscr "EMINENT BELIZEANS" at top. Multicoloured.

1148	25c. Herbert Watkin Beaumont, Post Office and postmark	40	25
1149	60c. Dr. Selvyn Walford Young and score of National Anthem	75	85
1150	75c. Cleopatra White and health centre	90	1·25
1151	$1 Dr. Karl Heusner and early car	1·10	1·40

204 Boom and Chime Band

1993. Christmas. Local Customs. Multicoloured.

1152	25c. Type **204**	1·00	20
1153	60c. John Canoe dance	2·00	75
1154	75c. Cortez dance	2·00	80
1155	$2 Maya musical group	4·50	7·00

1994. "Hong Kong '94" International Stamp Exhibition. No. 1075 optd **HONG KONG '94** and emblem.

1156	$1 Spectacled owl and "Caligo uranus"	2·75	2·50

1994. Royal Visit. As T **202** of Bahamas. Multicoloured.

1157	25c. Flags of Belize and Great Britain	1·75	55
1158	60c. Queen Elizabeth II in yellow coat and hat	2·25	1·25
1159	75c. Queen Elizabeth in evening dress	2·50	1·50
1160	$1 Queen Elizabeth, Prince Philip and Yeomen of the Guard	2·75	2·50

205 *Lonchorhina aurita* (bat)

1994. Bats. Multicoloured.

1161	25c. Type **205**	45	20
1162	60c. *Vampyrodes caraccioli*	75	65
1163	75c. *Noctilio leporinus*	90	80
1164	$2 *Desmodus rotundus*	2·00	3·50

1994. 75th Anniv of I.L.O. No. 1074 surch **10c** and anniversary emblem.

1165	10c. on 75c. multicoloured	2·00	1·75

207 "Cycnoches chlorochilon"

1994. Christmas. Orchids. Multicoloured.

1166	25c. Type **207**	45	20
1167	60c. *Brassavola cucullata*	75	70
1168	75c. *Sobralia mucronata*	90	90
1169	$1 *Nidema boothii*	1·10	1·50

208 Ground Beetle

1995. Insects. Multicoloured.

1170A	5c. Type **208**	45	70
1171A	10c. Harlequin beetle	50	70
1172A	15c. Giant water bug	60	80
1173A	25c. Peanut-head bug	70	20
1174A	30c. Coconut weevil	70	25
1175A	50c. Mantis	85	40
1176B	60c. Tarantula wasp	1·10	50
1177B	75c. Rhinoceros beetle	1·40	60
1178B	$1 Metallic wood borer	1·75	1·50
1179B	$2 Dobson fly	4·00	4·50
1180B	$5 Click beetle	7·00	8·50
1181B	$10 Long-horned beetle	10·00	12·00

1995. 50th Anniv of End of Second World War. As T **161** of Ascension. Multicoloured.

1182	25c. War memorial	35	25
1183	60c. Remembrance Day parade	1·00	1·00
1184	75c. British Honduras forestry unit	1·10	1·10
1185	$1 Vickers Type **271** Wellington bomber	1·40	1·75

(209)

1995. "Singapore '95" International Stamp Exhibition. Nos. 1166/9 optd with T **209**.

1186	25c. Type **207**	1·00	30
1187	60c. *Brassavola cucullata*	1·50	90
1188	75c. *Sobralia mucronata*	1·75	1·25
1189	$1 *Nidema boothii*	2·00	2·25

1995. 50th Anniv of United Nations. As T **213** of Bahamas. Multicoloured.

1190	25c. M113-light reconnaisance vehicle	25	20
1191	60c. Sultan armoured command vehicle	60	65
1192	75c. Leyland-Daf 8×4 drop truck	75	80
1193	$2 Warrior infantry combat vehicle	1·50	2·50

210 Male and Female Blue Ground Dove

1995. Christmas. Doves. Multicoloured.

1194	25c. Type **210**	35	20
1195	60c. White-fronted doves	70	70
1196	75c. Pair of ruddy ground doves	85	90
1197	$1 White-winged doves	1·25	1·50

1996. "CHINA '96" 9th Asian International Stamp Exhibition, Peking. Nos. 1172, 1174/5 and 1179 optd **'96 CHINA** and emblem.

1198	15c. Giant water bug	20	15
1199	30c. Coconut weevil	40	30
1200	50c. Mantis	55	50
1201	$2 Dobson fly	1·75	2·50

212 Unloading Banana Train, Commerce Bight Pier

1996. "CAPEX '96" International Stamp Exhibition, Toronto. Railways. Multicoloured.

1202	25c. Type **212**	1·50	55
1203	60c. Locomotive No. 1 Stann Creek station	2·00	1·25
1204	75c. Locomotive No. 4 pulling mahogany log train	2·00	1·40
1205	$3 L.M.S. No. 5602 *British Honduras* locomotive	3·75	6·00

213 *Epidendrum stamfordianum*

1996. Christmas. Orchids. Multicoloured.

1206	25c. Type **213**	50	20
1207	60c. *Oncidium cartha- genense*	80	70
1208	75c. *Oerstedella verrucosa*	90	90
1209	$1 *Coryanthes speciosa*	1·25	1·50

214 Red Poll

1997. "HONG KONG '97" International Stamp Exhibition. Chinese New Year ("Year of the Ox"). Cattle Breeds. Multicoloured.

1210	25c. Type **214**	60	25
1211	60c. Brahman	95	1·00
1212	75c. Longhorn	1·25	1·40
1213	$1 Charbray	1·40	1·90

215 Coral Snake

1997. Snakes. Multicoloured.

1214	25c. Type **215**	45	20
1215	60c. Green vine snake	70	70
1216	75c. Yellow-jawed tommygoff	80	80
1217	$1 Speckled racer	95	1·25

216 Adult Male Howler Monkey

1997. Endangered Species. Howler Monkey. Multicoloured.

1218	10c. Type **216**	25	25
1219	25c. Female feeding	40	25
1220	60c. Female with young	70	80
1221	75c. Juvenile monkey feeding	90	1·10

217 *Maxillaria elatior*

1997. Christmas. Orchids. Multicoloured.

1222	25c. Type **217**	65	25
1223	60c. *Dimmerandra emarginata*	1·00	75
1224	75c. *Macradenia brassavolae*	1·25	1·00
1225	$1 *Ornithocephalus gladiatus*	1·60	1·50

1998. Diana, Princess of Wales Commemoration. Sheet, 145×70 mm, containing vert designs as T **177** of Ascension. Multicoloured.

MS1226	$1 Wearing floral dress, 1988; $1 In evening dress, 1981; $1 Wearing pearl drop earrings, 1988; $1 Carrying bouquet, 1983	3·00	3·50

218 School Children using the Internet

1998. 50th Anniv of Organization of American States. Multicoloured.

1227	25c. Type **218**	25	20
1228	$1 Map of Central America	1·50	1·50

219 University Arms

1998. 50th Anniv of University of West Indies.

1229 **219**	$1 multicoloured	1·00	1·00

220 Baymen Gun Flats

1998. Bicentenary of Battle of St. George's Cay. Multicoloured.

1230	10c. Boat moored at quayside (vert)	30	50
1231	10c. Three sentries and cannon (vert)	30	50
1232	10c. Cannon and rowing boats (vert)	30	50
1233	25c. Type **220**	60	25
1234	60c. Baymen sloops	80	80
1235	75c. British schooners	85	85
1236	$1 H.M.S. *Merlin* (sloop)	1·00	1·00
1237	$2 Spanish flagship	1·75	2·25

221 *Brassia maculata*

1998. Christmas. Orchids. Multicoloured.

1238	25c. Type **221**	35	20
1239	60c. *Encyclia radiata*	50	40
1240	75c. *Stanhopea ecornuta*	50	55
1241	$1 *Isochilus carnosiflorus*	60	80

222 *Eucharis grandiflora*

1999. Easter. Flowers. Multicoloured.

1242	10c. Type **222**	20	10
1243	25c. *Hippeastrum puniceum*	30	20
1244	60c. *Zephyranthes citrina*	50	50
1245	$1 *Hymenocallis littoralis*	60	80

223 Postman on Bicycle

1999. 125th Anniv of UPU. Multicoloured.

1246	25c. Type **223**	50	30
1247	60c. Postal truck	65	55
1248	75c. "Dee" (mail ship)	85	80
1249	$1 Modern airliner	1·00	1·25

224 *Holy Family with Jesus and St. John* (School of Rubens)

1999. Christmas. Religious Paintings. Multicoloured.

1250	25c. Type **224**	30	20
1251	60c. *Holy Family with St. John* (unknown artist)	60	55
1252	75c. *Madonna and Child with St. John and Angel* (unknown artist)	65	70
1253	$1 *Madonna with Child and St. John* (Andrea del Salerno)	90	1·10

225 Iguana

2000. Wildlife. Multicoloured.

1254	5c. Type **225**	15	40
1255	10c. Gibnut	15	35
1256	15c. Howler monkey	20	35
1257	25c. Collared anteater	30	25
1258	30c. Hawksbill turtle	30	25
1259	50c. Red brocket antelope	50	40
1260	60c. Jaguar	60	45
1261	75c. American manatee	70	60
1262	$1 Crocodile	1·00	85
1263	$2 Baird's tapir	1·75	2·00
1264	$5 Collared peccary	4·50	6·00
1265	$10 Boa constrictor	8·50	11·00

226 Mango

2000. Fruits. Multicoloured.

1266	25c. Type **226**	35	25
1267	60c. Cashew	65	60
1268	75c. Papaya	80	75
1269	$1 Banana	1·10	1·40

227 Meeting in Battlefield Park and Supreme Court, 1950

2000. 50th Anniv of People's United Party. Multicoloured.

1270	10c. Type **227**	20	15
1271	25c. Voters queuing, 1954	30	25
1272	60c. Legislative Council and Mace, 1964	55	50
1273	75c. National Assembly Building (under construction and completed), Belmopan, 1967–70	70	80
1274	$1 Belizean flag in searchlights, Independence, 1981	2·25	1·75

228 *Bletia purpurea*

2000. Christmas. Orchids. Multicoloured.

1275	25c. Type **228**	55	25
1276	60c. *Cyrtopodium punctatum*	85	50
1277	75c. *Cycnoches egertonianum*	1·00	85
1278	$1 *Catasetum integerrimum*	1·40	1·60

229 Children at Computers

2001. 20th Anniv of Independence. Multicoloured.

1279	25c. Type **229**	35	25
1280	60c. Shrimp farm	60	50
1281	75c. Privassion Cascade (vert)	75	60
1282	$2 Map of Belize (vert)	3·00	3·50

230 *Sobralia fragrans*

2001. Christmas. Orchids. Multicoloured.

1283	25c. Type **230**	65	25
1284	60c. *Encyclia cordigera*	1·00	60
1285	75c. *Maxillaria fulgens*	1·25	1·00
1286	$1 *Epidendrum nocturnum*	1·60	1·75

2002. Golden Jubilee. As T **200** of Ascension.

1287	25c. black, violet and gold	45	25
1288	60c. multicoloured	75	60
1289	75c. black, violet and gold	90	80
1290	$1 multicoloured	1·10	1·25
MS1291	162×95 mm. Nos. 1287/90 and $5 multicoloured	6·50	7·50

DESIGNS—Horiz: 25c. Princess Elizabeth in pantomime, Windsor, 1943; 60c. Queen Elizabeth in floral hat; 75c. Queen Elizabeth in garden with Prince Charles and Princess Anne, 1952; $1 Queen Elizabeth in South Africa, 1995. VERT (38×51 mm)—$5 Queen Elizabeth after Annigoni.

231 *Dichaea neglecta*

2002. Christmas. Orchids. Multicoloured.

1292	25c. Type **231**	65	25
1293	50c. *Epinendrum hawkesii*	80	55
1294	60c. *Encyclia belizensis*	90	60
1295	75c. *Eriopsis biloba*	1·00	70
1296	$1 *Harbenaria monorrhiza*	1·25	1·50
1297	$2 *Mormodes buccinator*	1·75	2·75

232 B.D.F. Emblem

2003. 25th Anniv of Belize Defence Force.

1298 **232**	25c. multicoloured	50	35

233 Avro Shackleton MK 3

2003. Centenary of Powered Flight. Multicoloured.

1299	25c. Type **233**	75	45
1300	60c. Lockheed L-749 Constellation	1·00	70
1301	75c. Sepecat Jaguar GR. 1	1·25	80
1302	$3 British Aerospace Harrier GR. 3	3·00	4·00
MS1303	116×66 mm. $5 Ryan NYP *Spirit of St. Louis*, Belize, 1927	4·50	5·00

234 Head of Scarlet Macaw

2003. Christmas. Scarlet Macaw. Multicoloured.

1304	25c. Type **234**	80	45
1305	60c. Pair on tree	1·25	65
1306	75c. Three macaws feeding on clay	1·40	75
1307	$5 Pair in flight	4·75	6·50

235 Whale Shark

2004. Whale Shark. Multicoloured.

1308	25c. Type **235**	50	30
1309	60c. Near surface of water	80	50
1310	75c. Whale shark and diver	90	55
1311	$5 Near coral reef	4·50	5·50

2004. Wildlife. Nos. 1259/1261 surch.

1312	10c. on 50c. Red brocket antelope	30	40
1313	10c. on 60c. Jaguar	30	40
1314	15c. on 75c. American manatee	40	40

237 Woolly Opossum

2005. Endangered Species. Woolly Opossum. Showing the Woolly Opossum with the country name in different colours. Multicoloured.

1315	25c. Type **237**	50	30
1316	60c. Bright new blue	80	50
1317	75c. Dull orange (horiz)	90	55
1318	$5 Magenta (horiz)	4·50	5·50

2005. No. 1300 surch.

1318a	10c. on 60c. Lockheed L-749 Constellation	80	80

2005. No. 1305 surch.

1318b	10c. on 60c. Pair (of scarlet macaws) on tree	10·00	10·00

2005. Pope John Paul II Commemoration. As T **219** of Ascension.

1319	$1 multicoloured	2·00	2·00

239 Blue-crowned Motmot and Flower, Guanacaste National Park, Cayo District

2005. Ecological and Cultural Heritage. Multicoloured.

1320	5c. Type **239**	15	15
1321	10c. Government House of Culture, Belize City	15	15
1322	15c. Lubaantun Archaeological Reserve and ball court warriors, Toledo District	20	20
1323	25c. Altun Ha Archaeological Reserve and jade head, Belize District	30	30
1324	30c. Nohoch Che'n Archaeological Reserve and jar, Cayo District	30	30
1325	50c. Goff's Caye, Belize District	50	50
1326	60c. Blue Hole Natural Monument and diver, Belize District	60	60
1327	75c. Lamanai Archaeological Reserve and crocodile effigy, Orange Walk District	75	75

1328	$1 Half Moon Caye, lighthouse and red footed booby (bird), Belize District	1·25	1·25
1329	$2 Beach and starfish, Placencia Peninsula, Stann Creek District	2·25	2·50
1330	$5 Museum of Belize, Belize City	5·50	6·00
1331	$10 Cerros Archaeological Reserve and Olmec jade pendant, Corozal District	9·00	9·50

240 25c. Postman on Bicycle Stamp

2006. 50th Anniv of First Europa Stamp. Designs showing Belize 1999 125th Anniv of Universal Postal Union stamps. Multicoloured.

1332	25c. Type **240**	75	40
1333	75c. 60c. Postal truck stamp	1·50	75
1334	$3 75c. Mail ship *Dee* stamp	4·00	4·50
1335	$5 $1 Airliner stamp	7·00	8·00
MS1336	Nos. 1332/5	12·00	13·00

241 George Price (Independence negotiator and first Prime Minister)

2006. 25th Anniv of Independence. Multicoloured.

1337	25c. Type **241**	40	30
1338	30c. Black orchid, Baird's tapir, keel-billed toucan and mahogany tree (national symbols) (horiz)	1·00	45
1339	60c. Map of Belize	1·50	70
1340	$1 1981 Independence logo	1·50	1·40
1341	$5 The Constitution of Belize (horiz)	6·50	7·50

242 Roman Goddess Diana reaching for Arrow

2006. Breast Cancer Research.

1342	**242**	$1 multicoloured	1·75	1·75

A similar stamp was issued by the USA on 29 July 1998.

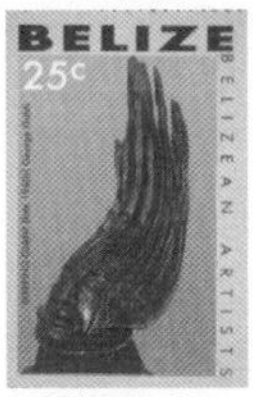

243 *Sleeping Giant* sculpture (George Gabb)

2007. Belizean Artists. Multicoloured.

1343	25c. Type **243**	15	10
1344	30c. *Market Scene* (Louis Belisle) (horiz)	25	20
1345	60c. *The Original Turtle Shell Band* (Pen Cayetano) (horiz)	50	45
1346	75c. *Have Some Coconut Water* (Benjamin Nicholas)	65	65
1347	$2 Woodcarving by Reuben Miguel	1·75	1·75
1348	$3 Mural of Corozal Town (Manuel Villamor)	2·40	2·50

244 Slave

2007. Bicentenary of the Abolition of the Slave Trade Act.

1349	**244**	$2 multicoloured	2·40	3·00

245 Scroll

2008. 60th Anniv of the University of the West Indies.

1350	**245**	$1 multicoloured	1·25	1·25

2009. As No. 1323

1351	25c. Altun Ha Archaeological Reserve and jade head, Belize District	40	30

Nos. 1352/62 are left for possible additions.

246 Yellow-headed Parrot (*Amazona oratrix*)

2009. Endangered Birds. Multicoloured.

1363	25c. Type **246**	40	30
1364	60c. Harpy eagle (*Harpia harpyja*)	50	45
1365	$1 Slate-colored seedeater (*Sporophila schistacea*)	1·25	1·25
1366	$2 Green honeycreeper (*Chlorophanes spiza*)	2·40	3·00
1367	$5 Great curassow (*Crax rubra*)	6·50	5·50

247 Encyclia polybulbon

2010. Christmas. Orchids. Multicoloured.

1368	25c. Type **247**	15	20
1369	60c. *Oncidium ensatum*	45	35
1370	$2 *Encyclia livida*	2·40	2·50
1371	$5 *Epidendrum difforme*	5·75	6·00

248 Queen Elizabeth II

2012. Diamond Jubilee. Multicoloured.

1372	25c. Type **248**	20	25
1373	60c. Queen Elizabeth II wearing pale grey hat, c. 2005	50	55
1374	75c. Queen Elizabeth II, c. 1970	1·00	1·10
1375	$1 Queen Elizabeth II wearing blue, c. 1990	1·25	1·50
1376	$2 Queen Elizabeth II wearing tiara, c. 1952	2·50	2·75
1377	$5 Queen Elizabeth II, c. 1980	6·00	6·25
MS1378	174×163 mm. Nos. 1372/7 and three stamp-size labels	11·50	12·00
MS1379	110×70 mm. $10 Queen Elizabeth II, c. 2005	11·00	11·00

POSTAGE DUE STAMPS

D2

1976

D6	**D2**	1c. red and green	10	1·00
D7	-	2c. purple and violet	15	1·00
D8	-	5c. green and brown	20	1·25
D9	-	15c. green and red	30	1·50
D10	-	25c. orange and green	40	1·75

DESIGNS: Nos. D7/10 as Type D **2** but with different frames.

Pt. 6, Pt. 12

BENIN

A French possession on the west coast of Africa incorporated, in 1899, into the colony of Dahomey.

100 centimes = 1 franc.

A. FRENCH COLONY

1892. Stamps of French Colonies. "Commerce" type, optd **BENIN**.

1	**J**	1c. black on blue	£140	£140
2	**J**	2c. brown on yellow	£130	£130
3	**J**	4c. brown on grey	75·00	75·00
4	**J**	5c. green on light green	18·00	16·00
5	**J**	10c. black on lilac	£100	80·00
6	**J**	15c. blue on light blue	60·00	26·00
7	**J**	20c. red on green	£225	£200
8	**J**	25c. black on red	£120	70·00
9	**J**	30c. brown on drab	£180	£160
10	**J**	35c. black on orange	£180	£160
11	**J**	40c. red on yellow	£160	£150
12	**J**	75c. red on pink	£300	£275
13	**J**	1f. green	£325	£275

A. FRENCH COLONY

1892. Stamps of French Colonies. "Commerce" type, optd **BENIN**.

1	**J**	1c. black on blue	£140	£140
2	**J**	2c. brown on yellow	£130	£130
3	**J**	4c. brown on grey	75·00	75·00
4	**J**	5c. green on light green	18·00	16·00
5	**J**	10c. black on lilac	£100	80·00
6	**J**	15c. blue on light blue	60·00	26·00
7	**J**	20c. red on green	£225	£200
8	**J**	25c. black on red	£120	70·00
9	**J**	30c. brown on drab	£180	£160
10	**J**	35c. brown on orange	£180	£160
11	**J**	40c. red on yellow	£160	£150
12	**J**	75c. red on pink	£300	£275
13	**J**	1f. green	£325	£275

1892. Nos. 4 and 6 surch.

14	01 on 5c. green on lt green	£275	£225
15	40 on 15c. blue on lt blue	£170	£120
16	75 on 15c. blue on lt blue	£750	£450

1893. "Tablet" key-type inscr "GOLFE DE BENIN" in red (1, 5, 15, 25, 75c., 1f.) or blue (others).

17	**D**	1c. black on blue	3·00	8·75
18	**D**	2c. brown on buff	3·75	4·50
19	**D**	4c. brown on grey	3·25	8·50
20	**D**	5c. green on light green	10·00	12·50
21	**D**	10c. black on lilac	10·50	15·00
22	**D**	15c. blue	40·00	50·00
23	**D**	20c. red on green	7·25	11·00
24	**D**	25c. black on pink	40·00	19·00
25	**D**	30c. brown on drab	14·50	15·00
26	**D**	40c. red on yellow	2·75	7·00
27	**D**	50c. red on pink	3·75	5·50
28	**D**	75c. brown on orange	11·50	22·00
29	**D**	1f. green	75·00	80·00

1894. "Tablet" key-type inscr "BENIN" in red (1, 5, 15, 25, 75c., 1f.) or blue (others).

33	1c. black on blue	2·75	3·25
34	2c. brown on buff	3·75	4·50
35	4c. brown on grey	2·75	4·25
36	5c. green on light green	7·25	8·75
37	10c. black on lilac	6·00	8·25
38	15c. blue	18·00	3·25
39	20c. red on green	14·00	17·00
40	25c. black on pink	11·00	4·50
41	30c. brown on drab	7·25	12·00
42	40c. red on yellow	17·00	18·00
43	50c. red on pink	25·00	29·00
44	75c. brown on orange	18·00	8·75
45	1f. green	7·00	12·50

POSTAGE DUE STAMPS

1894. Postage Due stamps of French Colonies optd **BENIN**. Imperf.

D46	**U**	5c. black	£150	85·00
D47	**U**	10c. black	£150	85·00
D48	**U**	20c. black	£150	85·00
D49	**U**	30c. black	£150	85·00

B. PEOPLE'S REPUBLIC

The Republic of Dahomey was renamed the People's Republic of Benin on 30 November 1975.

185 Celebrations

1976. Republic of Benin Proclamation. Multicoloured.

603	50f. Type **185**	75	30
604	60f. President Kerekou making Proclamation	1·10	40
605	100f. Benin arms and flag	1·80	70

186 Skiing

1976. Air. Winter Olympic Games, Innsbruck. Multicoloured.

606	60f. Type **186**	1·30	70
607	150f. Bobsleighing (vert)	2·30	1·20
608	300f. Figure-skating	4·75	2·30

1976. Various Dahomey stamps surch **POPULAIRE DU BENIN** and new value (609/11) or surch only (617/18).NIN

609	-	135f. brown, purple and blue (No. 590) (air)	2·00	90
610	-	210f. on 300f. brown, red and blue (No. 591)	2·75	1·30
611	-	380f. on 500f. brown, red and green (No. 592)	4·75	2·20
617	**108**	50f. on 1f. multicoloured (postage)	70	30
618	-	60f. on 2f. multicoloured (No. 415)	95	45

188 Alexander Graham Bell, Early Telephone and Satellite

1976. Telephone Centenary.

612	**188**	200f. red, violet & brown	3·25	1·70

189 Basketball

1976. Air. Olympic Games, Montreal. Multicoloured.

613	60f. Long jump (horiz)	1·00	45
614	150f. Type **189**	2·00	95
615	200f. Hurdling (horiz)	2·50	1·70
MS616	150×120 mm. Nos. 613/15	7·50	6·75

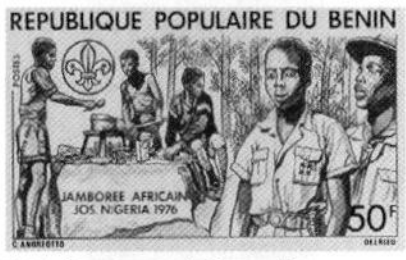

191 Scouts and Camp-fire

1976. African Scout Jamboree, Jos, Nigeria.

619	**191**	50f. purple, brown & blk	75	35
620	-	70f. brown, green & blk	1·00	55

DESIGN: 70f. "Comradeship".

192 Konrad Adenauer

1976. Air. Birth Centenary of Konrad Adenauer (German statesman).

621	**192**	90f. slate, blue and red	1·50	65
622	-	250f. blue, red & lt blue	4·00	1·50

DESIGN—HORIZ: 250f. Adenauer and Cologne Cathedral.

193 Benin 1c. Stamp, 1893, and Lion Cub

1976. Air. "Juvarouen 76" Youth Stamp Exhibition, Rouen.

623		60f. blue and turquoise	1·00	50
624	**193**	210f. red, brown & olive	3·25	1·50

DESIGN—HORIZ: 60f. Dahomey 60f. Stamp of 1965, and children's silhouettes.

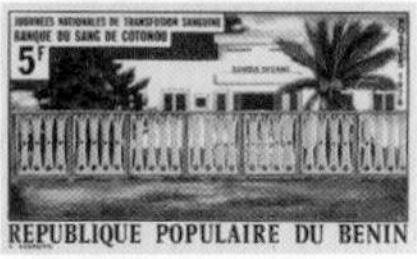

194 Blood Bank, Cotonou

1976. National Days of Blood Transfusion Service. Multicoloured.

625	5f. Type **194**	20	10
626	50f. Casualty and blood clinic	70	40
627	60f. Donor, patient and ambulance	1·10	55

195 Manioc

1976. National Products Campaign Year. Multicoloured.

628	20f. Type **195**	50	15
629	50f. Maize cultivation	75	25
630	60f. Cocoa trees	1·00	40
631	150f. Cotton plantation	2·30	80

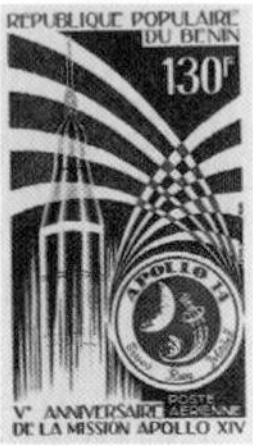

196 "Apollo" Emblem and Rocket

1976. Air. Fifth Anniv of "Apollo 14" Space Mission.

632	**196**	130f. lake, brown & blue	1·50	70
633	-	270f. blue, turquoise & red	3·00	1·50

DESIGN: 270f. Landing on Moon.

197 Classroom

1976. Third Anniv of Bariba Periodical "Kparo".

634	**197**	50f. multicoloured	1·00	55

198 Roan Antelope

1976. Mammals in Pendjari National Park. Multicoloured.

635	10f. Type **198**	45	25
636	30f. African buffalo	80	50
637	50f. Hippopotamus (horiz)	1·60	85
638	70f. Lion	1·80	1·00

199 "Freedom"

1976. First Anniv of Proclamation of Republic. Multicoloured.

639	40f. Type **199**	60	25
640	150f. Maize cultivation	1·80	85

200 *The Annunciation* (Master of Jativa)

1976. Air. Christmas. Multicoloured.

641	50f. Type **200**	80	40
642	60f. *The Nativity* (David)	90	50
643	270f. *Adoration of the Magi* (Dutch school)	3·75	1·80
644	300f. *The Flight into Egypt* (Fabriano) (horiz)	4·00	2·30

201 Table Tennis and Games Emblem

1976. West African University Games, Cotonou. Multicoloured.

645	10f. Type **201**	55	10
646	50f. Sports Hall, Cotonou	80	25

202 Loser with Ticket and Winner with Money

1977. Air. Tenth Anniv of National Lottery.

647	**202**	50f. multicoloured	75	45

203 Douglas DC-10 crossing Globe

1977. Europafrique.

648	**203**	200f. multicoloured	3·00	2·10

204 Chateau Sassenage, Grenoble

1977. Air. Tenth Anniv of International French Language Council.

649	**204**	200f. multicoloured	2·50	1·10

205 Adder

1977. Reptiles and Domestic Animals. Mult.

650	2f. Type **205**	45	10
651	3f. Tortoise	45	10
652	5f. Zebus	45	10
653	10f. Cats	85	25

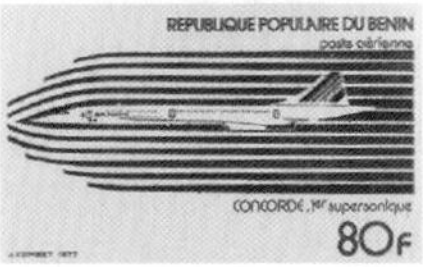

206 Concorde

1977. Air. Aviation.

654	**206**	80f. red and blue	95	40
655	-	150f. red, violet & green	2·10	90
656	-	300f. violet, red & mauve	3·00	1·60
657	-	500f. red, blue & green	6·25	3·25

DESIGNS: 150f. *Graf Zeppelin*; 300f. Charles Lindbergh and *Spirit of St. Louis*; 500f. Charles Nungesser and Francois Coli with *L'Oiseau Blanc*.

207 Footballer heading Ball

1977. Air. World Football Cup Eliminators. Multicoloured.

658	60f. Type **207**	80	35
659	200f. Goalkeeper and players	2·30	1·30

208 Rheumatic Patients

1977. World Rheumatism Year.

660	**208**	100f. multicoloured	1·50	75

209 Karate

1977. Second African Games, Lagos.

661	**209**	90f. multicoloured	1·40	70
662	-	100f. multicoloured	1·40	90
663	-	150f. multicoloured	2·30	1·10
MS664		144×92 mm. Nos. 661/3	6·75	6·50

DESIGNS—HORIZ: 100f. Javelin. VERT: 150f. Hurdles.

210 Mao Tse-tung

1977. First Death Anniv of Mao Tse-tung.

665	**210**	100f. multicoloured	2·75	1·40

211 Sterilising Scalpels

1977. 150th Birth Anniv of Joseph Lister.

666	**211**	150f. grey, red & carmine	2·00	90
667	-	210f. olive, green & red	2·50	1·30

DESIGN: 210f. Lister and antiseptic spray.

212 *Miss Haverfield* (Gainsborough)

1977. Air. Paintings.

668	**212**	100f. green and brown	2·40	60
669	-	150f. brown, bistre & red	3·50	1·30
670	-	200f. red and bistre	4·75	1·80

DESIGNS: 150f. *Self-Portrait* (Rubens); 200f. *Study of an Old Man* (da Vinci).

213 *Jarre Trouee* Emblem of King Ghezo (D'Abomey Museum)

1977. Historic Museums of Benin. Multicoloured.

671	50f. Type **213**	75	40
672	60f. Mask (Porto-Novo Museum) (horiz)	1·30	55
673	210f. D'Abomey Museum	2·75	1·20

214 Atacora Waterfall

1977. Tourism. Multicoloured.

674	50f. Type **214**	70	40
675	60f. Stilt houses, Ganvie (horiz)	95	55
676	150f. Hut village, Savalou	2·30	1·10
MS677	144×92 mm. Nos. 674/6	5·25	5·25

1977. Air. First Commercial Concorde Flight. Paris–New York. No. 654 optd **1er VOL COMMERCIAL 22.11.77 PARIS NEW-YORK**.

678	**206**	80f. red and blue	1·70	85

216 "Viking" on Mars ("Operation Viking", 1977)

1977. Air. Space Conquest Anniversaries.

679	**216**	100f. brown, olive & red	1·00	60
680	-	150f. blue, turq & mve	1·80	85
681	-	200f. brown, blue & red	2·75	1·10
682	-	500f. blue, brn & olive	6·50	3·00

DESIGNS AND EVENTS: 150f. Sir Isaac Newton, apple and stars (250th death anniv); 200f. Komarov and "Soyuz 2" over Moon (10th death anniv); 500f. Space dog "Laika" and rocket (20th anniv of ascent into Space).

217 Monument, Red Flag Square, Cotonou

1977. Air. First Anniv of Inauguration of Red Flag Square Monument.

683	**217**	500f. multicoloured	6·25	2·75

218 Mother and Child with Owl of Wisdom

1977. Fight against Witchcraft. Multicoloured.

684	60f. Type **218**	1·30	55
685	150f. Felling the tree of sorcery	2·50	1·10

219 *Suzanne Fourment*

1977. Air. 400th Birth Anniv of Rubens.

686	**219**	200f. brown, red & green	3·25	1·30
687	-	380f. orange and brown	5·50	2·20

DESIGN: 380f. *Albert Rubens*.

220 Battle Scene

1978. "Victory over Imperialism".

688	**220**	50f. multicoloured	1·20	45

221 Benin Houses and Map of Heads

1978. General Population Census.

689	**221**	50f. multicoloured	80	35

222 Sir Alexander Fleming, Microscope and Drugs

1978. 50th Anniv of Discovery of Antibiotics.

690	**222**	300f. multicoloured	4·50	2·10

223 Abdoulaye Issa

1978. First Death Anniv of Abdoulaye Issa.

691	**223**	100f. multicoloured	1·00	50

224 El Hadj Omar

1978. Heroes of Anti-colonial Resistance.

692	-	90f. multicoloured	1·30	45
693	**224**	100f. green, grey & blue	1·30	65

DESIGN: 90f. Samory Toure.

225 "Communications"

1978. Tenth World Telecommunications Day.

694	**225**	100f. multicoloured	1·50	75

226 Footballer and Stadium

1978. World Cup Football Championship, Argentina. Multicoloured.

695	200f. Type **226**	2·30	1·00
696	300f. Tackling (vert)	3·00	1·60
697	500f. Footballer and world map	5·50	2·50
MS698	190×121 mm. Nos. 695/7 in different colours	12·00	9·00

1978. Argentina's Victory in World Cup Football Championship. Nos. 695/7 optd.

699	**226**	200f. multicoloured	2·00	1·10
700	-	300f. multicoloured	3·00	1·90
701	-	500f. multicoloured	5·50	3·25
MS702		190×121 mm. Nos. 699/701 multicoloured	13·50	12·50

OPTS: 200f. **FINALE ARGENTINE: 3 HOLLANDE: 1**; 300f. **CHAMPION 1978 ARGENTINE**; 500f. **3e BRESIL 4e ITALIE**.

228 Map, Olympic Flag and Basketball Players

1978. Third African Games, Algiers. Multicoloured.

703	50f. Type **228**	55	25
704	60f. African map and Volleyball	95	45
705	80f. Cyclists and map of Algeria	1·00	55
MS706	208×80 mm. Nos. 703/5 in different colours	4·00	3·75

229 Martin Luther King

1978. Tenth Anniv of Martin Luther King's Assassination.

707	**229**	300f. multicoloured	3·50	1·70

230 Bicycle Taxi (Oueme)

1978. Benin Provinces. Multicoloured.

708	50f. Type **230**	1·20	40
709	60f. Leather work (Borgou)	1·10	40
710	70f. Drums (Oueme)	1·20	45
711	100f. Calabash with burnt-work ornamentation (Zou)	1·50	55

231 "Stamps" and Magnifying Glass

1978. Philatelic Exhibition, Riccione, Italy.

712	**231**	200f. multicoloured	2·30	1·10

232 Parthenon and Frieze showing Horsemen

1978. Air. UNESCO Campaign for the Preservation of the Acropolis. Multicoloured.

713	70f. Acropolis and Frieze showing Procession	80	25
714	250f. Type **232**	2·50	1·20
715	500f. The Parthenon (horiz)	5·00	2·20

235 Turkeys

1978. Domestic Poultry. Multicoloured.

722	10f. Type **235**	35	10
723	20f. Ducks	60	25
724	50f. Chickens	1·70	50
725	60f. Helmeted guineafowl	1·90	70

236 Post Runner and Boeing 747

1978. Centenary of UPU. Paris Congress. Multicoloured.

726	50f. Messenger of the Dahomey Kings (horiz)	1·00	40
727	60f. Pirogue oarsman, boat and post car	1·10	40
728	90f. Type **236**	1·30	55

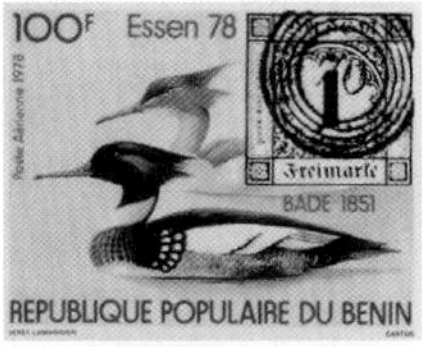

237 Red-breasted Merganser and Baden 1851 1k. Stamp

1978. Air. "Philexafrique" Exhibition, Libreville (Gabon) (1st issue) and International Stamp Fair, Essen, West Germany. Multicoloured.

729	100f. Type **237**	4·00	1·50
730	100f. African Buffalo and Dahomey 1966 50f. African Pygmy Goose stamp	4·00	1·50

See also Nos. 747/8.

238 Raoul Follereau

1978. First Death Anniv of Raoul Follereau (leprosy pioneer).

731	**238**	200f. multicoloured	2·00	95

239 Wilbur and Orville Wright and Wright Flyer 1

1978. Air. 75th Anniv of First Powered Flight.

732	**239**	500f. blue, yellow & brn	6·00	3·00

240 I.Y.C. Emblem

1979. International Year of the Child. Multicoloured.

733	10f. Type **240**	15	10
734	20f. Children in balloon	30	10
735	50f. Children dancing around globe	45	30

241 Hydrangea

1979. Flowers. Multicoloured.

736	20f. Type **241**	20	25
737	25f. Assangokan	45	25
738	30f. Geranium	70	35
739	40f. Water Lily (horiz)	90	40

242 Flags around Map of Africa

1979. OCAM Summit Meeting, Cotonou (1st series). Multicoloured.

740	50f. Type **242**	55	40
741	60f. Flags and map of Benin	85	45
742	80f. OCAM flag and map of member countries	1·20	60

See also Nos. 754/6.

1979. Various stamps surch.

743	**205**	50f. on 2f. multicoloured (postage)	£190	2·75
743a	-	50f. on 3f. multicoloured (651)	95·00	2·75
743b	-	50f. on 70f. brown, green and black (620)	95·00	2·75
744	**207**	50f. on 60f. mult (air)	95·00	2·75
745	**192**	50f. on 90f. blue, deep blue and red	95·00	2·75
746	-	50f. on 150f. mult (607)	95·00	2·75
747	**189**	50f. on 150f. mult	95·00	2·75

244 Antenna, Satellite and Wave Pattern

1979. World Telecommunications Day.

748	**244**	50f. multicoloured	80	45

245 Headquarters Building

1979. West African Savings Bank Building Opening.

749	**245**	50f. multicoloured	75	40

246 *Resolution* and *Discovery* in Karakakoa Bay, Hawaii

1979. Air. Death Bicentenary of Capt. James Cook.

750	**246**	20f. blue, green & brown	1·30	40
751	-	50f. brown, green & blue	1·00	45

DESIGN: 50f. Cook's death at Kowrowa.

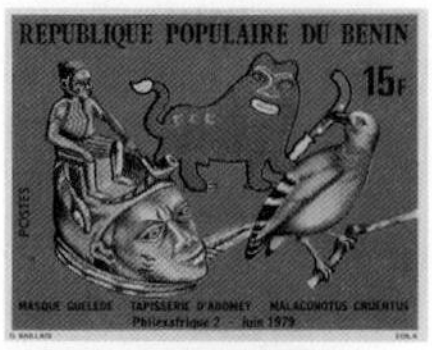

247 Guelede Mask, Abomey Tapestry and Fiery-breasted Bush Shrike

1979. "Philexafrique" Stamp Exhibition, Gabon (2nd issue).

752	**247**	15f. multicoloured	1·50	55
753	-	50f. orange, yellow & turq	2·00	95

DESIGN: 50f. Lockheed L-1011 Tristar 500, satellite, U.P.U. emblem and canoe post.

1979. Common African and Mauritian Organization Summit Conference, Cotonou (2nd issue). Nos. 740/2 optd **26 Au 28 Juin 1979**.

754	50f. Type **242**	80	40
755	60f. Map of Benin and flags of members	95	50
756	80f. OCAM flag and map showing member countries	1·10	55

249 Olympic Flame, Benin Flags and Pictograms

1979. Pre-Olympic Year. Multicoloured.

757	10f. Type **249**	30	10
758	50f. High jump	1·00	45

250 Roan Antelope

1979. Endangered Animals. Multicoloured.

759	5f. Type **250**	40	20
760	10f. Giraffes (vert)	55	35
761	20f. Chimpanzee	85	50
762	50f. African elephants (vert)	1·80	75

251 Emblem, Concorde and Map of Africa

1979. 20th Anniv of ASECNA (African Air Safety Organization). Multicoloured.

763	50f. Type **251**	50	25
764	60f. As No. 763 but emblem at bottom right and without dates	55	25

252 Post Offices, Antenna, Telephone and Savings Book

1979. 20th Anniv of Posts and Telecommunications Office. Multicoloured.

765	50f. Type **252**	50	25
766	60f. Collecting, sorting and delivering mail	55	25

253 Rotary Emblem, Symbols of Services and Globe

1980. 75th Anniv of Rotary International. Multicoloured.

767	90f. Cotonou Rotary Club banner (vert)	95	45
768	200f. Type **253**	1·80	95

254 Copernicus and Planetary System

1980. 50th Anniv of Discovery of Planet Pluto. Multicoloured.

769	70f. Kepler and astrolabe	80	45
770	100f. Type **254**	1·20	55

255 Pharaonic Capital

1980. 20th Anniv of Nubian Monuments Preservation Campaign. Multicoloured.

771	50f. Type **255**	55	30
772	60f. Rameses II, Abu Simbel	95	45
773	150f. Temple, Abu Simbel (horiz)	1·50	85

256 Lenin in Library

1980. 110th Birth Anniv of Lenin. Multicoloured.

774	50f. Lenin and globe	75	25
775	150f. Type **256**	2·00	85

257 Monument

1980. Martyrs Square, Cotonou.

776	**257**	50f. multicoloured	45	10
777	-	60f. multicoloured	55	25
778	-	70f. multicoloured	75	25
779	-	100f. multicoloured	1·20	40

DESIGNS—HORIZ: 60f. to 100f. Different views of the monument.

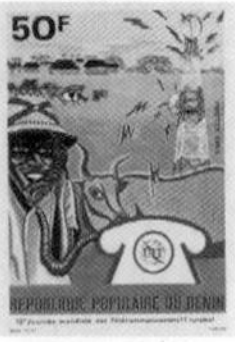

258 Farmer using Telephone

1980. World Telecommunications Day. Multicoloured.

780	50f. Type **258**	45	25
781	60f. Telephone	55	30

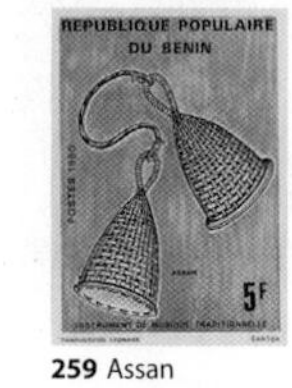

259 Assan

1980. Traditional Musical Instruments. Multicoloured.

782	5f. Type **259**	25	10
783	10f. Tinbo (horiz)	25	10
784	15f. Tam-tam sato	55	25
785	20f. Kora (horiz)	55	25
786	30f. Gangan (horiz)	85	40
787	50f. Sinhoun (horiz)	1·60	55

260 Monument

1980. King Gbehanzin Monument.

788	**260**	1000f. multicoloured	13·00	8·50

261 Dieudonne Costes, Maurice Bellonte and *Point d'Interrogation*

1980. 50th Anniv of First Paris–New York Non-stop Flight.

789	-	90f. red, lt blue & blue	1·00	45
790	**261**	100f. red, blue and flesh	1·20	55

DESIGN: 90f. Airplane *Point d'Interrogation* and scenes of New York and Paris.

262 "Lunokhod I"

1980. Tenth Anniv of "Lunokhod I".

791	-	90f. brown, blue and violet (postage)	95	55
792	**262**	210f. purple, blue and yellow (air)	2·75	1·30

DESIGN (48×36 mm): 90f. Rocket and "Lunokhod I".

263 Show-jumping

1980. Olympic Games, Moscow. Multicoloured.

793	50f. Olympic Flame, running track, emblem and mascot Mischa the bear (horiz)	50	25
794	60f. Type **263**	55	40
795	70f. Judo (horiz)	95	45
796	200f. Olympic flag and globe surrounded by sports pictogram	2·00	90
797	300f. Weightlifting	3·00	1·50

264 OCAM Building

1980. Common African and Mauritian Organization Village, Cotonou. Multicoloured.

798	50f. Entrance to OCAM village	60	25
799	60f. View of village	75	25
800	70f. Type **264**	95	55

265 Dancers

1980. Agbadja Dance. Multicoloured.

801	30f. Type **265**	55	25
802	50f. Singer and musicians	95	45
803	60f. Dancers and musicians	95	55

266 Casting a Net

1980. Fishing. Multicoloured.

804	5f. Type **266**	10	10
805	10f. Fisherman with catch (vert)	30	10
806	15f. Line fishing	30	25
807	20f. Fisherman emptying eel-pot	35	25
808	50f. Hauling in a net	95	45
809	60f. Fish farm	95	45

267 Philippines under Magnifying Glass

1980. World Tourism Conference, Manila. Multicoloured.

810	50f. Type **267**	55	25
811	60f. Conference flag on globe	95	30

268 "Othreis materna"

1980. Insects. Multicoloured.

812	40f. Type **268**	80	35
813	50f. *Othreis fullonia* (butterfly)	1·20	45
814	200f. *Oryctes* sp. (beetle)	3·75	1·60

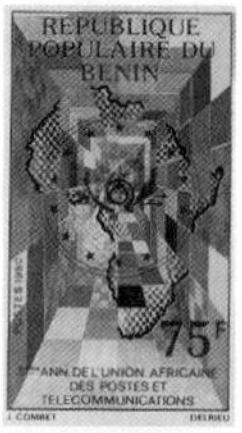

269 Map of Africa and Posthorn

1980. Fifth Anniv of African Posts and Telecommunications.

815	**269**	75f. multicoloured	75	25

270 Hands freed from Chains

1980. 30th Anniv of Signing of Human Rights Convention. Multicoloured.

816	30f. Type **270**	30	10
817	50f. African pushing through bars	50	25
818	60f. Figure holding Human Rights flame	75	25

271 *Self-portrait*

1980. 90th Death Anniv of Van Gogh (artist). Multicoloured.

819	100f. Type **271**	2·00	70
820	300f. *The Postman Roulin*	5·00	2·20

272 Offenbach and Scene from *Orpheus in the Underworld*

1980. Death Centenary of Jacques Offenbach (composer).

821	**272**	50f. black, red and green	1·30	50
822	-	60f. blue, brown & dp brn	1·90	75

DESIGN: 60f. Offenbach and scene from *La Vie Parisienne*.

273 Kepler and Astronomical Diagram

1980. 30th Death Anniv of Johannes Kepler (astronomer).

823	**273**	50f. red, blue and grey	75	25
824	-	60f. blue, black and green	95	45

DESIGN: 60f. Kepler, satellite and dish aerials.

274 Footballers

1981. Air. World Cup Football Championship. Multicoloured.

825	200f. Football and globe	1·80	70
826	500f. Type **274**	5·00	1·90

275 Disabled Person holding Flower

1981. International Year of Disabled People.

827	**275**	115f. multicoloured	1·20	50

276 Yuri Gagarin

1981. 20th Anniv of First Man in Space.

828	**276**	500f. multicoloured	5·50	2·75

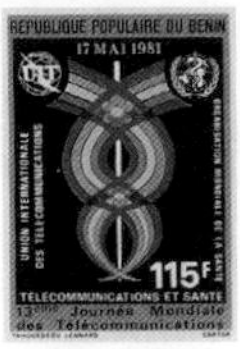

277 ITU and WHO Emblems and Ribbons forming Caduceus

1981. World Telecommunications Day.

829	**277**	115f. multicoloured	1·20	45

278 Amaryllis

1981. Flowers. Multicoloured.

830	10f. Type **278**	20	15
831	20f. *Eischornia crassipes*	45	30
832	80f. *Parkia biglobosa*	1·50	50

279 Hotel and Map

1981. Opening of Benin Sheraton Hotel.

833	**279**	100f. multicoloured	1·00	45

1981. Surch **50F**.

834	**216**	50f. on 100f. brown, green and red	85	25
835	**193**	50f. on 210f. red, brown and green	85	25

281 Prince Charles, Lady Diana Spencer and Tower Bridge

1981. Air. British Royal Wedding.

836	**281**	500f. multicoloured	4·50	2·00

282 Guinea Pig

1981. Domestic Animals. Multicoloured.

837	5f. Type **282**	35	25
838	60f. Cat	1·00	45
839	80f. Dogs	1·40	70

283 Heinrich von Stephan (founder of UPU)

1981. World Universal Postal Union Day.

840	**283**	100f. slate and red	95	45

284 Heads, Quill, Paper Darts and U.P.U. Emblem

1981. International Letter Writing Week.

841	**284**	100f. blue and purple	95	45

285 *The Dance*

1981. Air. Birth Centenary of Pablo Picasso. Multicoloured.

842	300f. Type **285**	3·00	1·20
843	500f. *The Three Musicians*	5·50	2·00

286 Globe, Map of Member Countries and Communication Symbols

1981. Fifth Anniv of ECOWAS (Economic Community of West African States).

844	**286**	60f. multicoloured	75	25

287 *St. Theodore Stratilates* (tile painting)

1981. Air. 1300th Anniv of Bulgarian State.

845	**287**	100f. multicoloured	95	45

288 Tractor and Map

1981. Tenth Anniv of West African Rice Development Association.

846	**288**	60f. multicoloured	75	25

289 Pope John Paul II

1982. Air. Papal Visit.

847	**289**	80f. multicoloured	2·00	90

290 John Glenn

1982. Air. 20th Anniv of First United States Manned Space Flight.

848	**290**	500f. multicoloured	5·50	2·20

291 Dr. Robert Koch

1982. Centenary of Discovery of Tubercle Bacillus.

849	**291**	115f. multicoloured	1·80	70

292 Washington, U.S. Flag and Map

1982. 250th Birth Anniv of George Washington.

850	**292**	200f. multicoloured	2·30	85

1982. Red Cross. Surch **Croix Rouge 8 Mai 1982 60f.**

851	**266**	60f. on 5f. multicoloured	75	25

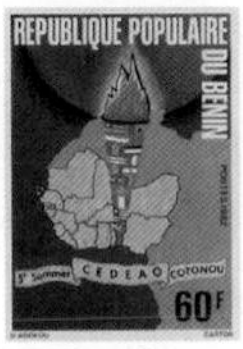

294 Map of Member Countries and Torch

1982. Fifth Economic Community of West African States Summit, Cotonou.

852	**294**	60f. multicoloured	60	25

295 Scouts round Campfire

1982. Air. 75th Anniv of Boy Scout Movement.

853	**295**	105f. multicoloured	1·20	60

296 Footballers

1982. World Cup Football Championship, Spain. Multicoloured.

854	90f. Type **296**	95	40
855	300f. Leg with sock formed from flags of participating countries and globe/football	3·00	1·20

1982. African Posts and Telegraph Union. Surch **UAPT 1982 60f.**

856	**282**	60f. on 5f. multicoloured	75	25

298 Stamp of Map of France and Magnifying Glass

1982. "Philexfrance 82" International Stamp Exhibition, Paris.

857	**298**	90f. multicoloured	95	45

1982. World Cup Football Championship Results. Nos. 854/5 optd.

858	90f. Type **296**	1·20	45
859	300f. Leg with flags of participating countries and football "globe"	3·75	1·30

OVERPRINTS: 90f. **COUPE 82 ITALIE bat RFA 3-1**; 300f. **COUPE 82 1 ITALIE 2 RFA 3 POLOGNE**.

1982. Riccione Stamp Exhibition. Optd **RICCIONE 1982**.

860	**231**	200f. multicoloured	1·80	80

301 Laughing Kookaburra (*Dacelo Gigas*)

1982. Birds. Multicoloured.

861	5f. Type **301**	65	30
862	10f. Bluethroat ("La Gorge Bleue") (horiz)	1·00	30
863	15f. Barn swallow ("L'Hirondelle")	1·00	35
864	20f. Woodland kingfisher ("Martin-Pecheur") and Village weaver ("Tisserin")	1·60	40
865	30f. Reed warbler ("La Rousserolle") (horiz)	2·20	50
866	60f. Warbler sp. ("Faurette Commoune") (horiz)	3·00	75
867	80f. Eagle owl ("Hibou Grand Doc")	5·50	1·40
868	100f. Sulphur-crested cockatoo ("Cacatoes")	6·50	1·80

302 World Map and Satellite

1982. I.T.U. Delegates' Conference, Nairobi.

869	**302**	200f. turq, blue & blk	2·00	80

303 UPU Emblem and Heads

1982. UPU Day.

870	**303**	100f. green, blue & brown	1·00	45

305 *Claude Monet in his Studio*

1982. Air. 150th Birth Anniv of Edouard Manet (artist).

876	**305**	300f. multicoloured	6·75	2·40

306 *"irgin and Child* (Grunewald)

1982. Air. Christmas. Multicoloured.

877		200f. Type **306**	2·20	1·10
878		300f. *Virgin and Child with Angels and Cherubins* (Correggio)	3·25	1·40

307 Pres. Mitterrand and Pres. Kerekou

1983. Visit of President Mitterrand.

879	**307**	90f. multicoloured	1·50	70

1983. Various stamps surch.

880	-	60f. on 50f. multicoloured (No. 798) (postage)	1·20	45
881	-	60f. on 70f. multicoloured (No. 778)	1·20	45
882	**279**	60f. on 100f. mult	47·00	2·75
883	-	75f. on 80f. multicoloured (No. 832)	1·40	55
884	-	75f. on 80f. multicoloured (No. 839)	1·50	85
885	**262**	75f. on 210f. red, blue and yellow (air)	1·50	85

309 *Tender Benin* (tug) and *Amazone* (oil rig)

1983. Seme Oilfield.

886	**309**	125f. multicoloured	1·50	60

1983. Various stamps surch.

887	**267**	5f. on 50f. multicoloured	3·00	50
888	**284**	10f. on 100f. blue & pur	3·00	50
889	-	10f. on 200f. mult (No. 659)	3·00	50
890	-	15f. on 200f. red and bistre (No. 670)	3·00	50
891	-	15f. on 200f. mult (No. 796)	3·00	50
892	-	15f. on 210f. green, deep green and red (No. 667)	3·00	50
893	-	15f. on 270f. mult (No. 643)	3·00	50
894	**219**	20f. on 200f. brown, red and olive	3·00	50
895	-	25f. on 70f. mult (No. 795)	3·00	60
896	-	25f. on 210f. mult (No. 673)	3·00	60
897	-	25f. on 270f. blue, turq & red (No. 633)	3·00	50
898	-	25f. on 380f. brown and red (No. 687)	3·00	50
899	-	30f. on 200f. brown, blue and red (No. 681)	3·00	60
900	**290**	40f. on 500f. mult	3·00	60
901	**282**	75f. on 5f. multicoloured	3·25	65
902	-	75f. on 100f. red, blue and pink (No. 790)	3·25	65
903	-	75f. on 150f. mult (No. 631)	3·25	65
904	-	75f. on 150f. violet, red and green (No. 655)	3·25	65
905	**211**	75f. on 150f. grey, orange and red	3·25	65
906	-	75f. on 150f. dp brown, brown & red (No. 669)	3·25	65

311 WCY Emblem

1983. World Communications Year.

907	**311**	185f. multicoloured	1·80	80

312 Stamps of Benin and Thailand and World Map

1983. Air. "Bangkok 1983" International Stamp Exhibition.

908	**312**	300f. multicoloured	3·00	1·40

313 Hand with Tweezers and Stamp

1983. "Riccione 83" Stamp Fair, San Marino.

909	**313**	500f. multicoloured	4·50	2·00

314 First Aid

1983. 20th Anniv of Benin Red Cross.

910	**314**	105f. multicoloured	1·20	60

315 Carved Table and Chairs

1983. Benin Woodwork. Multicoloured.

911		75f. Type **315**	1·00	25
912		90f. Rustic table and chairs	1·10	40
913		200f. Monkeys holding box	2·00	75

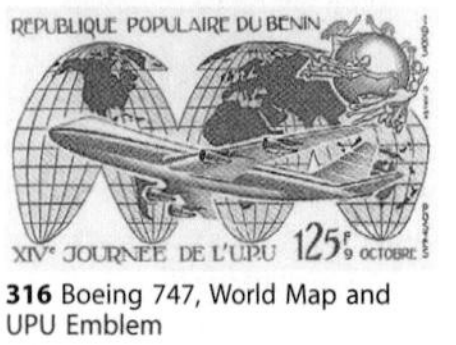

316 Boeing 747, World Map and UPU Emblem

1983. UPU Day.

914	**316**	125f. green, blue & brown	1·20	60

317 Egoun

1983. Religious Cults. Multicoloured.

915		75f. Type **317**	1·00	45
916		75f. Zangbeto	1·00	45

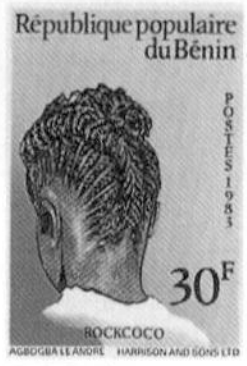

318 Rockcoco

1983. Hair-styles. Multicoloured.

917		30f. Type **318**	30	15
918		75f. Serpent	75	45
919		90f. Songas	1·30	55

319 Alfred Nobel

1983. 150th Birth Anniv of Alfred Nobel.

920	**319**	300f. multicoloured	3·00	1·50

320 *Madonna of Lorette* (Raphael)

1983. Air. Christmas.

921	**320**	200f. multicoloured	2·75	1·20

1984. Various stamps surch.

922	-	5f. on 150f. mult (No. 685) (postage)	3·25	75
923	**316**	5f. on 125f. green, blue and brown	3·25	75
924	**292**	10f. on 200f. mult	3·25	75
925	-	10f. on 200f. mult (No. 913)	3·25	75
926	-	15f. on 300f. mult (No. 820)	3·25	80
927	-	25f. on 300f. mult (No. 644)	3·25	80
928	**276**	40f. on 500f. mult	3·25	80
929	**314**	75f. on 105f. mult	3·50	1·00
930	**275**	75f. on 115f. mult	3·50	90
931	**277**	75f. on 115f. mult	3·50	90
932	**291**	75f. on 115f. mult	3·50	90
933	**311**	75f. on 185f. mult	3·50	1·00
934	**302**	75f. on 200f. turquoise, blue and black	3·50	1·00
935	**320**	15f. on 200f. mult (air)	3·25	75
936	**285**	15f. on 300f. mult	3·25	75
937	**312**	25f. on 300f. mult	3·25	80
938	**281**	40f. on 500f. mult	3·50	90
939	**295**	75f. on 105f. mult	3·50	90
940	**306**	90f. on 200f. mult	3·75	95
941	**305**	90f. on 300f. mult	3·75	95

322 Flags, Agriculture and Symbol of Unity and Growth

1984. 25th Anniv of Council of Unity.

942	**322**	75f. multicoloured	75	25
943	**322**	90f. multicoloured	95	40

323 UPU Emblem and Magnifying Glass

1984. 19th Universal Postal Union Congress, Hamburg.

944	**323**	90f. multicoloured	95	45

324 Abomey-Calavi Ground Station

1984. Inauguration of Abomy-Calavi Ground Station.

945	**324**	75f. multicoloured	75	45

325 Koumboro (Borgou)

1984. Traditional Costumes. Multicoloured.

946		5f. Type **325**	15	10
947		10f. Taka (Borgou)	30	25
948		20f. Toko (Atacora Province)	30	25

326 Olympic Mascot

1984. Air. Olympic Games, Los Angeles.

949	**326**	300f. multicoloured	3·00	1·40

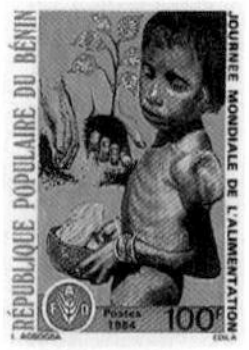

327 Plant and Starving Child

1984. World Food Day.

950	**327**	100f. multicoloured	95	45

328 Anatosaurus

1984. Prehistoric Animals. Multicoloured.

951		75f. Type **328**	3·75	65
952		90f. Brontosaurus	4·00	90

329 *Virgin and Child* (detail, Murillo)

1984. Air. Christmas.

953	**329**	500f. multicoloured	5·50	2·20

1984. Various stamps surch.

954	**203**	75f. on 200f. mult (post)	6·00	1·30
955	**226**	75f. on 200f. mult	6·00	1·30

956	-	75f. on 300f. mult (No. 696)	6·00	1·30
957	229	75f. on 300f. mult	6·00	1·30
958	-	90f. on 300f. mult (No. 855)	6·25	1·40
959	-	90f. on 500f. mult (No. 697)	6·25	1·40
960	-	90f. on 500f. mult (No. 701)	6·75	1·40
961	204	75f. on 200f. mult (air)	4·50	1·30
962	-	75f. on 200f. mult (No. 825)	4·50	1·30
963	-	75f. on 300f. violet, red and mauve (No. 656)	4·50	1·30
964	-	75f. on 300f. mult (No. 878)	4·50	1·30
965	239	90f. on 500f. blue, yellow and brown	4·50	1·40
966	-	90f. on 500f. mult (No. 715)	4·50	1·40
967	-	90f. on 500f. mult (No. 843)	4·50	1·40

331 Sidon Merchant Ship (2nd century)

1984. Air. Ships.

968	331	90f. black, green & blue	1·30	60
969	-	125f. multicoloured	2·00	85

DESIGN—VERT: 125f. Sail merchantman *Wavertree*, 1895.

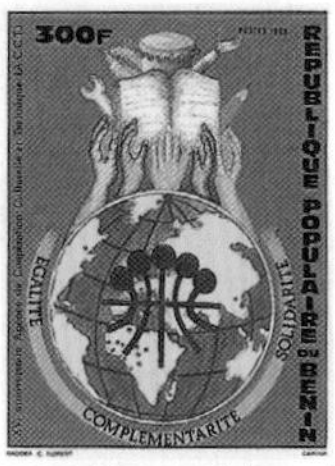

332 Emblem on Globe and Hands reaching for Cultural Symbols

1985. 15th Anniv of Cultural and Technical Co-operation Agency.

970	332	300f. multicoloured	3·25	1·20

333 Benin Arms

1985. Air. Postal Convention between Benin and Sovereign Military Order of Malta. Multicoloured.

971	75f. Type **333**	75	25
972	75f. Arms of Sovereign Military Order	75	25

334 Soviet Flag, Soldier and Tank

1985. 40th Anniv of End of Second World War.

973	334	100f. multicoloured		

335 Teke Dance, Borgou

1985. Traditional Dances. Multicoloured.

974	75f. Type **335**	1·00	40
975	100f. Tipen ti dance, Atacora	1·30	60

1985. Various Dahomey Stamps optd **POPULAIRE DU BENIN** (985/6) or **REPUBLIQUE POPULAIRE DU BENIN** (others), Nos. 976/7 and 979/85 surch also.

976	174	15f. on 40f. mult (post)	2·75	60
977	182	25f. on 40f. brown, blue and violet (air)	1·20	60
978	115	40f. black, purple & bl	1·30	70
978a	-	75f. on 85f. brown, blue and green (No. 468)	48·00	1·60
979	-	75f. on 85f. brown, blue and green (No. 482)	3·00	75
980	135	75f. on 100f. purple, violet and green	3·00	75
981	-	75f. on 125f. green, blue and purple (No. 509)	3·00	75
982	127	90f. on 20f. brown, blue and green	3·00	80
983	-	90f. on 150f. purple, blue & brown (No. 456)	3·00	80
984	-	90f. on 200f. green, red and blue (No. 438)	3·00	80
985	-	90f. on 200f. mult (No. 563)	3·00	80
986	-	150f. mult (No. 562)	3·50	1·00

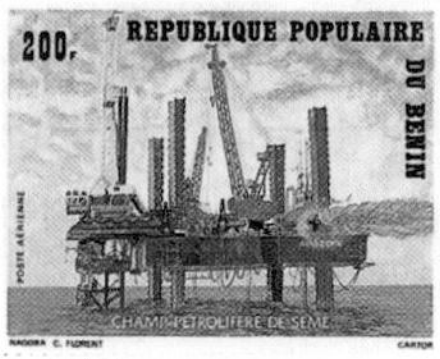

338 Oil Rig

1985. Air. "Philexafrique" International Stamp Exhibition, Lome, Togo (1st issue). Multicoloured.

987	200f. Type **338**	2·30	1·50
988	200f. Footballers	2·30	1·50

See also Nos. 999/1000.

339 Emblem

1985. International Youth Year.

989	339	150f. multicoloured	1·40	75

340 Football between Globes

1985. World Cup Football Championship, Mexico (1986) (1st issue).

990	340	200f. multicoloured	1·80	95

See also No. 1015.

341 Boeing 727, Map and Emblem

1985. 25th Anniv of Aerial Navigation Security Agency for Africa and Malagasy.

991	341	150f. multicoloured	1·80	75

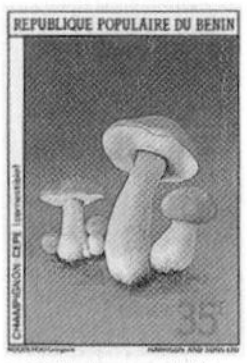

342 *Boletus edulis*

1985. Fungi. Multicoloured.

992	35f. Type **342**	1·50	45
993	40f. *Amanita phalloides*	1·80	75
994	100f. *Paxillus involutus*	4·50	1·70

343 Audubon and Arctic Skua ("Labbe Parasite")

1985. Birth Bicentenary of John J. Audubon (ornithologist). Multicoloured.

995	150f. Type **343**	3·00	1·50
996	300f. Audubon and oyster-catcher ("Huitrier Pie")	7·00	2·20

344 Emblem, Hands and Dove

1985. 40th Anniv of United Nations Organization and 25th Anniv of Benin's Membership.

997	344	250f. multicoloured	2·30	1·10

345 Stamps and Globe

1985. "Italia '85" International Stamp Exhibition, Rome.

998	345	200f. multicoloured	1·80	95

1985. "Philexafrique" International Stamp Exhibition, Lome, Togo (2nd issue). As Type **338**. Multicoloured.

999	250f. Forest and hand holding tools	4·25	1·80
1000	250f. Magnifying glass over judo stamp	3·00	1·50

1985. Various Dahomey stamps optd **Republique Populaire du Benin**. Nos. 1001/9 and 1011 surch also.

1001	-	75f. on 35f. mult (No. 596) (postage)	2·50	60
1002	-	90f. on 70f. multicoloured (No. 419)	2·50	65
1003	-	90f. on 140f. multicoloured (No. 446)	2·50	65
1004	113	100f. on 40f. red, brown and green	1·90	65
1005	-	150f. on 45f. multicoloured (No. 597)	2·10	80
1006	-	75f. on 70f. multicoloured (No. 342) (air)	4·25	90
1007	-	75f. on 100f. multicoloured (No. 251)	4·25	90
1008	59	75f. on 200f. mult	4·25	90
1009	-	90f. on 250f. multicoloured (No. 272)	4·25	90
1010	110	100f. multicoloured	2·75	90
1011	-	150f. on 500f. multicoloured (No. 252)	2·75	90

No. 1010 is surcharged on the unoverprinted unissued stamp subsequently issued as No. 422.

349 Church, Children playing and Nativity Scene

1985. Air. Christmas.

1012	349	500f. multicoloured	5·25	2·30

350 Emblem

1986. Tenth Anniv of African Parliamentary Union and Ninth Conference, Cotonou.

1013	350	100f. multicoloured	95	50

351 Halley, Comet and "Giotto" Space Probe

1986. Appearance of Halley's Comet.

1014	351	205f. multicoloured	3·00	1·50

352 Footballers

1986. World Cup Football Championship, Mexico (2nd issue). Multicoloured.

1015	352	500f. Footballers	4·50	2·30

353 Dead and Healthy Trees

1986. Anti-desertification Campaign.

1016	353	150f. multicoloured	1·50	70

354 Amazone

1986

1017	354	100f. blue	75	30
1018	354	150f. purple	1·30	50

355 *Haemanthus*

1986. Flowers. Multicoloured.

1019	100f. Type **355**	1·10	70
1020	205f. *Hemerocallis*	2·75	1·20

356 "*Inachis io*, *Aglais urticae* and *Nymphalis antiopa*

1986. Butterflies. Multicoloured.

1021	150f. Type **356**	3·00	1·30
1022	150f. *Anthocharis cardamines*, *Papilio machaon* and *Cynthia cardui*	3·00	1·30

1986. Various stamps of Dahomey surch **Republique Populaire du** Benin and new value.

1024	-	150f. on 100f. mult (444) (postage)	55·00	2·75
1025	-	15f. on 85f. mult (600) (air)	33·00	2·75
1026	-	25f. on 200f. mult (432)	55·00	2·75
1027	150	25f. on 200f. deep green, violet and green	55·00	2·75
1030	175	100f. purple, indigo & bl	55·00	2·75
1031	128	150f. on 100f. blue, violet and red		

358 Statue and Buildings

1986. Centenary of Statue of Liberty.

1032	358	250f. multicoloured	3·00	1·20

359 Bust of King Behanzin

1986. King Behanzin.

1033	359	440f. multicoloured	5·00	2·20

For design in smaller size, see Nos. 1101/4.

360 Family with Crib, Church and Nativity Scene

1986. Air. Christmas.

1034	**360**	300f. multicoloured	5·25	1·80

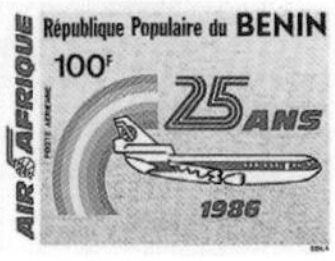

361 Rainbow and Douglas DC-10

1986. Air. 25th Anniv of Air Afrique.

1035	**361**	100f. multicoloured	1·00	50

362 Emblem around Map in Cog

1987. Brazil Culture Week, Cotonou.

1036	**362**	150f. multicoloured	1·40	65

363 Cotonou Centre for the Blind and Partially Sighted

1987. Rotary International 910 District Conference, Cotonou.

1037	**363**	300f. multicoloured	3·25	1·40

1987. Various stamps of Dahomey optd **Republique Populaire du Benin**. Nos. 1038/9 and 1042/53 surch also.

1038	**129**	10f. on 65f. black, violet and red (postage)		
1039	-	15f. on 100f. red, blue and green (434)	43·00	1·80
1040	**98**	40f. green, blue and brown	55·00	2·75
1042	-	150f. on 200f. mult (560)		
1043	**144**	10f. on 65f. black, yellow & purple (air)		
1046	-	25f. on 150f. mult (487)	55·00	2·75
1047	-	30f. on 300f. mult (602)		
1048	**140**	40f. on 15f. purple, green and blue	47·00	2·75
1049	-	40f. on 100f. mult (453)	43·00	2·75
1051	-	50f. on 140f. mult (601)	55·00	2·75
1052	-	50f. on 500f. mult (252)	55·00	2·75
1053	-	70f. on 250f. mult (462)		
1054	-	80f. mult (286)	55·00	2·75
1055	-	100f. mult (429)	55·00	2·75
1055a	-	100f. mult (447)	55·00	2·75

365 De Dion-Bouton and Trepardoux Steam Tricycle and Ford Coupe

1987. Centenary of Motor Car. Multicoloured.

1058	150f. Type **365**	1·50	70
1059	300f. Daimler motor carriage, 1886 and Mercedes Benz W124 series saloon	3·25	1·40

366 Baptism in the Python Temple

1987. Ritual Ceremonies.

1060	**366**	100f. multicoloured	1·50	70

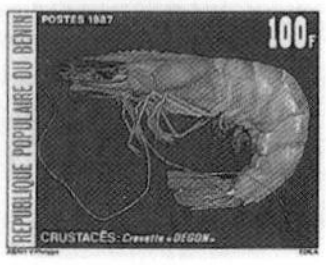

367 Shrimp

1987. Shellfish. Multicoloured.

1061	100f. Type **367**	1·30	75
1062	150f. Crab	2·00	1·00

368 G. Hansen and R. Follereau (leprosy pioneers) and Patients

1987. Anti-leprosy Campaign.

1063	**368**	200f. multicoloured	2·50	1·20

369 Crop-spraying and Locusts

1987. Anti-locust Campaign.

1064	**369**	100f. multicoloured	1·20	65

370 Fisherman and Farmer

1987. Air. Tenth Anniv of International Agricultural Development Fund.

1065	**370**	500f. multicoloured	4·50	2·40

371 Nativity Scene in Moon and Father Christmas giving Sweets to Crowd

1987. Christmas.

1066	**371**	150f. multicoloured	1·50	85

372 Rally

1988. 15th Anniv (1987) of Start of Benin Revolution.

1067	**372**	100f. multicoloured	£100	2·75

1988. Various stamps surch. (a) Stamps of Dahomey surch **Populaire du Benin** (1081c) or **Republique Populaire du Benin** (others).

1068	-	5f. on 3f. black and blue (173) (postage)	55·00	2·75
1069	-	20f. on 100f. mult (506)	55·00	2·75
1071	-	25f. on 100f. mult (576)	55·00	2·75
1073	-	50f. on 45f. mult (320)	65·00	2·75
1074	**178**	55f. on 200f. olive, brown and green	95·00	2·75
1075a	**178**	125f. on 100f. mult (557)		
1076	**116**	10f. on 50f. black, orange and blue (air)	55·00	2·75
1077	**161**	15f. on 150f. red and black	55·00	2·75
1078	-	25f. on 100f. mult (526)	75·00	2·75
1079	**156**	25f. on 100f. blue, brown and violet	75·00	2·75
1079a	**153**	40f. on 35f. mult	55·00	2·75
1080	-	40f. on 100f. mult (495)	55·00	
1081	**162**	40f. on 150f. red, brown and blue	55·00	2·75
1081a	**148**	100f. brown and green	55·00	2·75
1081b	**181**	125f. on 75f. lilac, red and green	45·00	2·75
1081c	-	125f. on 150f. blue and purple (541)		2·75
1082	-	125f. on 250f. mult (491)	55·00	2·75
1082a	-	125f. red and brown (540)	55·00	2·75
1083	-	190f. on 250f. brown, green and red (594)	90·00	
1084	-	1000f. on 150f. multicoloured (545)	55·00	2·75

(b) No. 618 of Benin surch **Republique Populaire du Benin**.

1085	10f. on 60f. on 2f. mult	55·00	2·75

(c) Stamps of Benin surch only.

1086	**359**	125f. on 440f. mult (postage)		
1087	**338**	125f. on 200f. mult (air)		
1088	-	190f. on 250f. mult (999)		90·00
1089	-	190f. on 250f. mult (1000)		

375 Hands holding Pot Aloft

1988. 25th Anniv of Organization of African Unity.

1094	**375**	125f. multicoloured	1·20	50

376 Resuscitation of Man pulled from River

1988. 125th Anniv of Red Cross Movement.

1095	**376**	200f. multicoloured	3·25	1·60

377 King

1988. 20th Death Anniv of Martin Luther King (Civil Rights leader).

1096	**377**	200f. multicoloured	2·00	95

378 Scout and Camp

1988. First Benin Scout Jamboree, Savalou.

1097	**378**	125f. multicoloured	1·20	55

379 Healthy Family and Health Care

1988. 40th Anniv of W.H.O. and 10th Anniv of "Health for All by 2000" Declaration.

1098	**379**	175f. multicoloured	1·50	80

380 Dugout Canoes and Houses

1988. Ganvie (lake village). Multicoloured.

1099	125f. Type **380**	1·20	55
1100	190f. Boatman and houses	1·80	85

1988. As T **359** but smaller (17×24 mm).

1101	**359**	40f. black	30	15
1102	**359**	125f. red	1·00	45
1103	**359**	190f. blue	1·50	65
1104	**359**	220f. green	1·80	80

381 Adoration of the Magi

1988. Air. Christmas.

1105	**381**	500f. multicoloured	4·50	2·20

382 Offering to Hebiesso, God of Thunder

1988. Ritual Ceremony.

1106	**382**	125f. multicoloured	1·20	55

383 Roseate Tern

1989. Endangered Animals. Roseate Tern. Multicoloured.

1107	10f. Type **383**	1·10	70
1108	15f. Tern with fish	1·10	70
1109	50f. Tern on rocks	2·50	1·40
1110	125f. Tern flying	5·00	2·75

384 Eiffel Tower

1989. Centenary of Eiffel Tower.

1111	**384**	190f. multicoloured	2·50	1·10

386 Tractor, Map and Pump

1989. 30th Anniv of Agriculture Development Council.
1113 **386** 75f. multicoloured 95·00

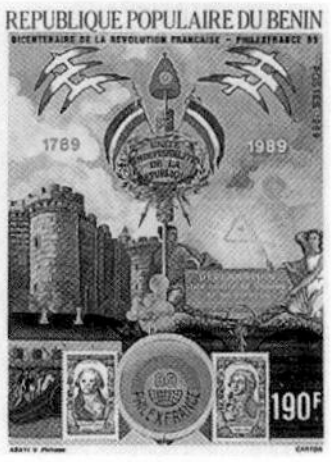

387 Symbols of Revolution and France 1950 National Relief Fund Stamps

1989. Bicentenary of French Revolution and "Philexfrance 89" International Stamp Exhibition, Paris.
1114 **387** 190f. multicoloured 2·50 1·50

388 Burbot

1989. Fish. Multicoloured.
1115 125f. Type **388** 1·30 60
1116 190f. Northern pike and Atlantic salmon 2·00 95

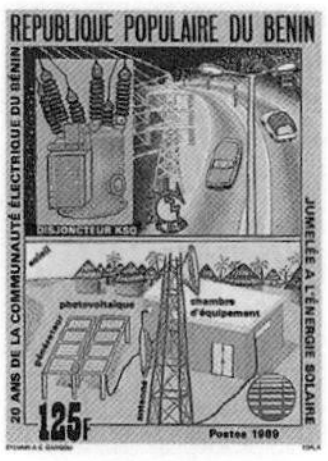

389 Circuit Breaker, Illuminated Road and Solar Energy Complex

1989. 20th Anniv of Benin Electricity Community.
1117 **389** 125f. multicoloured 1·30 60

390 Lion within Wreath

1989. Death Centenary of King Glele.
1118 **390** 190f. multicoloured 1·70 90

391 Nativity

1989. Christmas.
1119 **391** 200f. multicoloured 1·80 95

392 Anniversary Emblem and Means of Communications

1990. Centenary of Postal and Telecommunications Ministry (1st issue).
1120 **392** 125f. multicoloured 1·30 60
See also No. 1127.

393 Oranges

1990. Fruit and Flowers. Multicoloured.
1121 60f. Type **393** 75 40
1122 190f. Kaufmannia tulips (vert) 2·00 95
1123 250f. Cashew nuts (vert) 2·50 1·30

394 Launch of "Apollo 11" and Footprint on Moon

1990. 21st Anniv of First Manned Moon Landing.
1124 **394** 190f. multicoloured 1·70 85

395 Footballers

1990. World Cup Football Championship, Italy. Multicoloured.
1125 125f. Type **395** 1·20 60
1126 190f. Mascot holding torch and pennant (vert) 1·90 85

396 Balloons, Emblem and Means of Communication

1990. Centenary of Postal and Telecommunications Ministry (2nd issue).
1127 **396** 150f. multicoloured 1·40 65

1990. World Cup Finalists. No. 1125 optd **FINALE R.F.A.-ARGENTINE 1-0**.
1128 **395** 125f. multicoloured 1·20 60

398 De Gaulle

1990. Birth Centenary of Charles de Gaulle (French statesman) (1st issue).
1129 **398** 190f. multicoloured 2·00 1·20
See also No. 1160.

399 "Galileo" Space Probe orbiting Jupiter

1990. Space Exploration.
1130 **399** 100f. multicoloured 1·00 60

400 Nativity

1990. Christmas.
1131 **400** 200f. multicoloured 1·90 1·20

401 Hands pointing to Scales of Justice

1990. National Conference of Active Forces.
1132 **401** 125f. multicoloured

406 Different Cultures and Emblem

1991. African Tourism Year.
1150 **406** 190f. multicoloured 1·90 1·20

407 Tennis Player

1991. Cent of French Open Tennis Championships.
1151 **407** 125f. multicoloured 1·50 95

408 Flag and Arms

1991. 31st Anniv of Independence.
1152 **408** 125f. multicoloured 1·30 50

1991. "Riccione 91" Stamp Fair. No. 1130 optd "**Riccione 91**".
1153 **399** 100f. multicoloured 95 70

410 Adoration of the Magi

1991. Christmas.
1154 **410** 125f. multicoloured 1·30 60

411 Guelede Dancer

1991
1155 **411** 190f. multicoloured 2·00 80

412 Mozart

1991. Death Bicentenary of Wolfgang Amadeus Mozart (composer).
1156 **412** 1000f. multicoloured 10·00 5·75

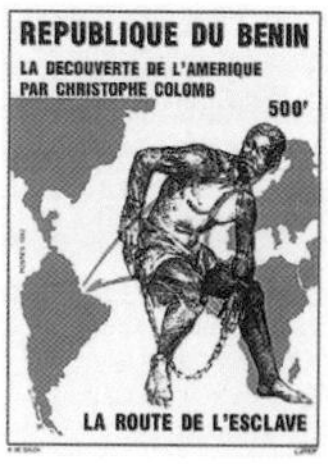

413 Slave in Chains and Route Map

1992. 500th Anniv of Discovery of America by Columbus.
1157 **413** 500f. black, brown & bl 4·50 3·00
1158 - 1000f. multicoloured 9·00 5·75
MS1159 133×93 mm. Nos. 1157/8 15·00 14·00
DESIGN—HORIZ: 1000f. Columbus landing at Guanahami, Bahamas.

1992. Birth Centenary (1990) of Charles de Gaulle (French statesman) (2nd issue). As No. 1129 but value changed.
1160 **398** 300f. multicoloured 3·00 1·60

414 Child, Produce and Emblems

1992. International Nutrition Conference, Rome.
1161 **414** 190f. multicoloured 1·80 1·20

415 Pope John Paul II

1993. Papal Visit.
1162 **415** 190f. multicoloured 2·00 1·10

416 Emblem and Voodoo Culture

1993. "Ouidah 92" Voodoo Culture Festival.
1163 **416** 125f. multicoloured 1·20 60

417 Well and Blue-throated Roller

1993. Possotome Artesian Well.
1164 **417** 125f. multicoloured 2·20 1·40

418 Map, Clasped Hands and Flags of Member Countries

1993. 30th Anniv of Organization of African Unity.

1165	**418**	125f. multicoloured	1·20	70

419 John F. Kennedy (President of United States, 1961–63)

1993. Death Anniversaries. Multicoloured.

1166	190f. Type **419** (30th anniv)	1·90	1·10
1167	190f. Dr. Martin Luther King (American civil rights campaigner, 25th anniv) (vert)	2·00	1·10

1993. Stamps of Dahomey variously optd or surch. (a) **REPUBLIQUE DU BENIN**.

1167a	**139**	5f. multicoloured (postage)	80·00	2·75
1170	**108**	50f. on 1f. multicoloured (617)	55·00	2·75
1171	**113**	80f. on 40f. red, brown and green	43·00	2·75
1173	**113**	135f. on 20f. black, green and red (190)	95·00	
1175	**113**	135f. on 30f. black, brown and violet (472)	55·00	
1177	**107**	135f. on 40f. mult	38·00	
1179	-	135f. on 60f. olive, red and purple (181)	55·00	2·75
1181	-	200f. on 100f. mult (322)	65·00	2·75
1186	-	15f. on 40f. mult (458) (air)	47·00	2·75
1190	**126**	100f. multicoloured	55·00	2·75
1190a	**119**	125f. on 40f. mult	23·00	2·75
1191	-	125f. on 65f. red and blue (552)	55·00	2·75
1201	-	200f. on 250f. mult (569)	47·00	

(b) **DU BENIN**.

1207	**60**	5f. on 1f. multicoloured (postage)	65·00	2·75
1208	-	10f. on 3f. black and blue (173)	55·00	
1211	-	25f. multicoloured (441)	47·00	2·75
1220	-	135f. on 3f. mult (274)	80·00	
1223	-	20f. on 200f. mult (451) (air)	55·00	
1225	-	25f. on 85f. mult (600)	47·00	2·75
1227	**140**	30f. on 15f. purple, green and blue	38·00	
1231	-	125f. on 70f. mult (383)	65·00	2·75
1235	-	150f. purple, blue and brown (456)	80·00	
1236	-	150f. multicoloured (527)	55·00	2·75
1239	**150**	200f. green, violet and emerald	65·00	2·75
1242	-	200f. on 150f. mult (562)	95·00	
1243	**179**	300f. multicoloured	55·00	2·75

(c) **BENIN**.

1257	-	25f. on 500f. brown, red and green (592) (air)	47·00	2·75
1258	-	30f. on 200f. mult (528)	24·00	2·75
1260a	-	100f. brown, green and blue (522)	55·00	2·75
1261	**116**	125f. on 50f. black, orange and blue	43·00	2·75
1263a	-	190f. on 200f. mult (478)	£190	2·75
1266	-	300f. brn, red & bl (591)	70·00	2·75

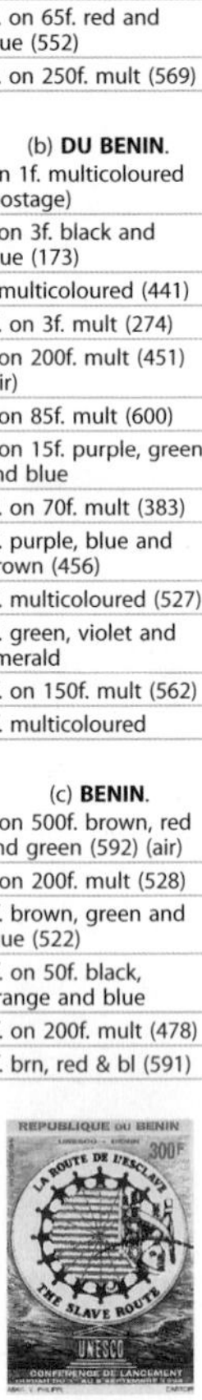

422 Conference Emblem

1994. UNESCO Conference on the Slave Route, Ouidah.

1275	**422**	300f. multicoloured	47·00	2·75

423 World Map

1994. International Year of the Family.

1276	**423**	200f. multicoloured	75·00	2·75

425 Water Polo

1995. Olympic Games, Atlanta (1996) (1st issue). Multicoloured.

1278	45f. Type **425**	20	20
1279	50f. Throwing the javelin (vert)	30	25
1280	75f. Weightlifting (vert)	45	35
1281	100f. Tennis (vert)	60	50
1282	135f. Baseball (vert)	75	55
1283	200f. Synchronised swimming (vert)	1·30	1·00
MS1284	60×79 mm. 300f. Diving (31×39 mm)	2·40	2·20

See also Nos. 1347/**MS**1353.

426 Paddle-steamer

1995. Ships. Multicoloured.

1285	40f. Type **426**	25	15
1286	50f. *Charlotte* (paddle steamer)	30	15
1287	75f. *Citta di Catania* (Italian liner)	45	20
1288	100f. *Mountbatten* SR-N4 (hovercraft)	45	25
1289	135f. *Queen Elizabeth 2* (liner)	85	30
1290	200f. *Matsu-Nef* (Japanese nuclear-powered freighter)	1·30	60
MS1291	72×58 mm. 300f. *Savannah* (sail/paddle-steamer) (39×31 mm)	2·40	2·40

427 Chimpanzee

1995. Primates. Multicoloured.

1292	50f. Type **427**	30	15
1293	75f. Mandrill	45	20
1294	100f. Colobus	60	25
1295	135f. Barbary ape	85	30
1296	200f. Hamadryas baboon	1·30	70
MS1297	93×72 mm. 300f. Yellow baboons (31×39 mm)	2·50	2·10

428 Tabby Shorthair

1995. Cats. Multicoloured.

1298	40f. Type **428**	25	15
1299	50f. Sorrel Abyssinian ("Ruddy red")	30	15
1300	75f. White Persian long-hair	45	20
1301	100f. Seal colourpoint	60	25
1302	135f. Tabby point	85	30
1303	200f. Black shorthair	1·30	60
MS1304	82×86 mm. 300f. Kitten climbing out of basket (38×31 mm)	2·50	2·50

429 German Shepherd

1995. Dogs. Multicoloured.

1305	40f. Type **429**	25	15
1306	50f. Beagle	30	15
1307	75f. Great dane	45	20
1308	100f. Boxer	60	25
1309	135f. Pointer	85	30
1310	200f. Long-haired fox terrier	1·30	60
MS1311	80×70 mm. 300f. Schnauzer	2·50	2·50

430 Arms

1995

1312	**430**	135f. multicoloured	85	25
1313	**430**	150f. multicoloured	95	55
1314	**430**	200f. multicoloured	1·30	55

See also Nos. 1458 and 1480/2.

431 Lion

1995. Mammals. Multicoloured.

1315	50f. Type **431**	30	15
1316	75f. African buffalo	45	20
1317	100f. Chimpanzee	65	25
1318	135f. Impala	85	30
1319	200f. Cape ground squirrel (horiz)	1·30	70
MS1320	80×60 mm. 300f. African elephant (31×39 mm)	2·50	2·50

432 Hawfinches

1995. Birds and their Young. Multicoloured.

1321	40f. Type **432**	25	15
1322	50f. Spotted-necked doves	30	15
1323	75f. Peregrine falcons	45	20
1324	100f. Blackburnian warblers	60	25
1325	135f. Black-headed gulls	80	30
1326	200f. Eastern white pelican	1·20	60

433 *Dracunculus vulgaris*

1995. Flowers. Multicoloured.

1327	40f. Type **433**	25	15
1328	50f. Daffodil	30	15
1329	75f. Amaryllis	45	20
1330	100f. Water-lily	60	25
1331	135f. *Chrysanthemum carinatum*	80	30
1332	200f. Iris	1·20	60

434 Lynx

1995. Big Cats and their Young. Multicoloured.

1333	40f. Type **434**	25	15
1334	50f. Pumas	30	15
1335	75f. Cheetahs	45	20
1336	100f. Leopards	60	25
1337	135f. Tigers	80	30
1338	200f. Lions	1·30	60

435 *Angraecum sesquipedale*

1995. Orchids. Multicoloured.

1339	40f. Type **435**	25	15
1340	50f. *Polystachya virginea*	30	15
1341	75f. *Disa uniflora*	45	20
1342	100f. *Ansellia africana*	60	25
1343	135f. *Angraecum eichlerianum*	95	30
1344	200f. *Jumellea confusa*	1·30	60

436 Emblem

1995. Sixth Francophone Summit, Cotonou.

1345	**436**	150f. multicoloured	85	55
1346	**436**	200f. multicoloured	1·10	80

437 Diving

1996. Olympic Games, Atlanta (2nd issue). Multicoloured.

1347	40f. Type **437**	30	25
1348	50f. Tennis	35	30
1349	75f. Running	45	35
1350	100f. Gymnastics	60	50
1351	135f. Weightlifting	90	65
1352	200f. Shooting	1·30	1·00
MS1353	65×65 mm. 1000f. Water polo (31×39 mm)	5·25	4·00

438 Player with Ball

1996. World Cup Football Championship, France (1998) (1st issue).

1354	**438**	40f. multicoloured	25	20
1355	-	50f. multicoloured	25	20
1356	-	75f. multicoloured	50	40
1357	-	100f. multicoloured	60	50
1358	-	135f. multicoloured	1·00	65
1359	-	200f. multicoloured	1·30	1·10
MS1360		88×63 mm. 1000f. Tackle (31×39 mm)	4·75	4·00

DESIGNS: 50f. to 1000f. Different players.

See also Nos. 1614/**MS**1620.

439 Small Striped Swallowtail

1996. Butterflies. Multicoloured.

1361	40f. Type **439**	25	20
1362	50f. Red admiral	25	20
1363	75f. Common blue	45	35
1364	100f. African monarch	55	45
1365	135f. Painted lady	95	60
1366	200f. *Argus celbulina ortbitulus*	1·30	1·00
MS1367	60×70 mm. 1000f. Foxy charaxes (*Charaxes jasius*) (31×39 mm)	4·50	4·00

440 Dancer

1996. "China '96" International Stamp Exhibition, Peking. Multicoloured.

1368	40f. Type **440**	35	30
1369	50f. Exhibition emblem	40	35

1370	75f. Water-lily	60	50
1371	100f. Temple of Heaven, Peking	85	75

Nos. 1368/71 were issued together, *se-tenant*, forming a composite design.

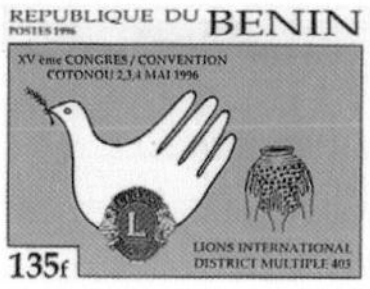

441 Emblem

1996. 15th Convention of Lions Club International, Cotonou.

1372	**441**	135f. multicoloured	1·10	75
1373	**441**	150f. multicoloured	1·10	80
1374	**441**	200f. multicoloured	1·50	1·10
1457	**441**	100f. multicoloured	55	25

442 *Holy Family of Rouvre* (Raphael)

1996. Christmas. Multicoloured.

1375	40f. Type **442**	25	20
1376	50f. *The Holy Family* (Raphael)	25	20
1377	75f. *St. John the Baptist* (Bartolome Murillo)	50	40
1378	100f. *The Virgin of the Scales* (Leonardo da Vinci)	65	50
1379	135f. *The Virgin and Child* (Gerhard David)	90	65
1380	200f. *Adoration of the Magi* (Juan Mayno)	1·30	1·10
MS1381	99×74 mm. 1000f. *Rest during the Flight into Egypt* (Murillo) (39×31 mm)	5·25	3·75

443 *Thermopylae* (clipper) (inscr "Thermopyles")

1996. Ships. Multicoloured.

1382	40f. Type **443**	20	15
1383	50f. Barque	25	20
1384	75f. *Nightingale* (full-rigged ship)	45	30
1385	100f. Opium clipper	50	40
1386	135f. *Torrens* (full-rigged ship)	80	60
1387	200f. English tea clipper	1·20	1·00
MS1388	78×58 mm. 1000f. Opium clipper (31×39 mm)	5·25	4·00

444 Serval

1996. Big Cats. Multicoloured.

1389	40f. Type **444**	25	20
1390	50f. Golden cat	25	20
1391	75f. Ocelot	45	35
1392	100f. Bobcat	55	45
1393	135f. Leopard cat	95	60
1394	200f. "Felis euptilura"	1·30	1·00
MS1395	80×64 mm. 1000f. Clouded leopard (*Neofelis nebulosa*) (31×39 mm)	5·25	4·00

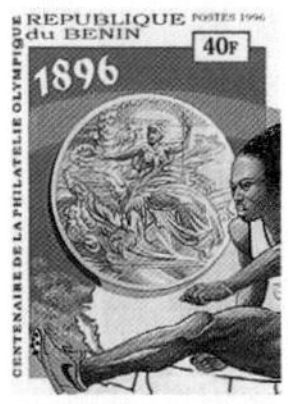

445 Hurdler and Gold Medal

1996. Centenary of Issue by Greece of First Olympic Stamps. Multicoloured.

1396	40f. Type **445**	35	30
1397	50f. Hurdler and Olympic flames	40	35
1398	75f. Pierre de Coubertin (founder of modern Olympics) and map showing south-west U.S.A.	60	50
1399	100f. Map showing south-east U.S.A.	85	75

Nos. 1396/9 were issued together, *se-tenant*, forming a composite design.

446 Running

1996. "Olymphilex '96" Olympics and Sports Stamp Exhibition, Atlanta. Multicoloured.

1400	40f. Type **446**	25	20
1401	50f. Canoeing	25	20
1402	75f. Gymnastics	50	40
1403	100f. Football	60	50
1404	135f. Tennis	1·00	65
1405	200f. Baseball	1·40	1·10
MS1406	65×95 mm. 1000f. Basketball (31×39 mm)	5·25	4·00

447 *Parodia subterranea*

1996. Flowering Cacti. Multicoloured.

1407	40f. Type **447**	25	20
1408	50f. *Astrophytum senile*	25	20
1409	75f. *Echinocereus melanocentrus*	50	40
1410	100f. *Turbinicarpus klinkerianus*	60	50
1411	135f. *Astrophytum capricorne*	1·00	65
1412	200f. *Nelloydia grandiflora*	1·40	1·10

448 Chestnut Horse

1996. Horses. Multicoloured.

1413	40f. Type **448**	25	20
1414	50f. Horse on hillside	25	20
1415	75f. Foal by fence	45	35
1416	100f. Mother and foal	55	45
1417	135f. Pair of horses	95	60
1418	200f. Grey horse (horiz)	1·30	1·00

449 Longisquama

1996. Prehistoric Animals. Multicoloured.

1419	40f. Type **449**	25	20
1420	50f. Dimorphodon	25	20
1421	75f. Dunkleosteus (horiz)	45	35
1422	100f. Eryops (horiz)	55	45
1423	135f. Peloneustes (horiz)	85	60
1424	200f. Deinonychus (horiz)	1·30	1·00

450 Ivory-billed Woodpecker

1996. Birds. Multicoloured.

1425	40f. Type **450**	25	20
1426	50f. Grey-necked bald crow	25	20
1427	75f. Kakapo	45	35
1428	100f. Puerto Rican amazon	55	45
1429	135f. Japanese crested ibis	95	60
1430	200f. California condor	1·30	1·00
MS1431	65×91 mm. 1000f. Blue bird of paradise (*Paradisaea rudolphi*) (31×39 mm)	5·25	4·00

451 Golden Tops

1996. Fungi. Multicoloured.

1432	40f. Type **451**	25	20
1433	50f. *Psilocybe zapotecorum*	25	20
1434	75f. *Psilocybe mexicana*	55	40
1435	100f. *Conocybe siligineoides*	65	50
1436	135f. *Psilocybe caerulescens mazatecorum*	1·00	65
1437	200f. *Psilocybe caerulescens nigripes*	1·40	1·10
MS1438	93×71 mm. 1000f. *Psilocybe aztecorum* (39×31 mm)	5·25	4·00

452 Impala

1996. Mammals. Multicoloured.

1439	40f. Type **452**	25	20
1440	50f. Waterbuck	25	20
1441	75f. African buffalo	45	35
1442	100f. Blue wildebeest	55	45
1443	135f. Okapi	85	60
1444	200f. Greater kudu	1·30	1·00

453 White Whale

1996. Marine Mammals. Multicoloured.

1445	40f. Type **453**	25	20
1446	50f. Bottle-nosed dolphin	25	20
1447	75f. Blue whale	45	35
1448	100f. "Eubalaena australis"	55	45
1449	135f. "Gramphidelphis griseus"	95	60
1450	200f. Killer whale	1·30	1·00

454 Grey Angelfish

1996. Fish. Multicoloured.

1451	50f. Type **454**	30	25
1452	75f. Sail-finned tang (horiz)	40	35
1453	100f. Golden trevally (horiz)	60	45
1454	135f. Pyramid butterflyfish (horiz)	85	60
1455	200f. Racoon butterflyfish (horiz)	1·30	1·00
MS1456	80×61 mm. 1000f. Parrotfish (horiz)	5·25	4·00

1996. Arms. Dated "1996".

1458	**430**	100f. multicoloured	65	25

1996. Stamps of Benin variously surch.

1469	**311**	15f. on 185f. mult (postage)	65·00	2·75
1470	**379**	25f. on 175f. mult		
1473	**359**	50f. on 220f. green (1104)	65·00	2·75
1479	**414**	150f. on 190f. mult		
1480	**415**	150f. on 190f. mult		
1484	**412**	250f. on 1000f. mult	65·00	2·75
1494	**193**	40f. on 210f. red, brown and green (air)	65·00	2·75
1495	-	40f. on 210f. purple, blue and yellow (792)		
1499	-	150f. on 500f. red, ultramarine and green (657)		

1996. Stamps of Dahomey variously optd or surch. (a) **Republique de Benin** (1510, 1516, 1519, 1522, 1526/9, 1535, 1544, 1556, 1558 and 1568) or **REPUBLIQUE DU BENIN** (others).

1510		35f. on 85f. brown, orange and green (493) (postage)		
1511		125f. on 100f. violet, red and black (510)		
1516	**85**	150f. on 30f. mult		
1519	**113**	150f. on 40f. red, brown and green		
1522	-	150f. on 45f. mult (597)		
1526	-	35f. on 100f. deep blue and blue (326) (air)		
1527	-	35f. on 100f. on 200f. multicoloured (409)		
1528	-	35f. on 125f. green, blue and light blue (553)		
1529	-	35f. on 300f. brown, red and blue (591)		
1535	-	150f. multicoloured (527)		
1544	**112**	150f. on 40f. multicoloured		
1556	-	150f. on 110f. mult (386)		
1558	-	150f. on 120f. mult (404)		
1568	-	200f. on 500f. mult (252)		

(b) **DU BENIN**.

1578		35f. on 125f. brown and green (540) (air)		
1579		125f. on 65f. mult (465)		
1580	**168**	135f. on 35f. mult		

(c) **BENIN**.

1587	**68**	150f. on 30f. mult (post)	75·00	2·75
1591	**68**	25f. on 85f. mult (600) (air)		

455 Grenadier, Glassenapps Regiment

1997. Military Uniforms. Multicoloured.

1600	135f. Type **455**	60	30
1601	150f. Officer, Von Groben's Regiment	80	35
1602	200f. Private, Dohna's Regiment	1·00	60
1603	270f. Artilleryman	1·30	70
1604	300f. Cavalry trooper	1·60	90
1605	400f. Trooper, Mollendorf's Dragoons	2·10	1·30
MS1606	90×108 mm. 1000f. Standard bearer (31×39 mm)	5·25	4·00

456 Reid Macleod Gas-turbine Locomotive, 1920

1997. Railway Locomotives. Multicoloured.

1607	135f. Type **456**	60	30
1608	150f. Class O5 steam locomotive, 1935, Germany	80	40
1609	200f. Locomotive "Silver Fox", Great Britain	1·00	55
1610	270f. Class "Merchant Navy" locomotive, 1941, Great Britain	1·30	75
1611	300f. Diesel locomotive, 1960, Denmark	1·60	80
1612	400f. GM Type diesel locomotive, 1960	2·10	1·10
MS1613	94×64 mm. 1000f. "Coronation", 1937 (39×31 mm)	5·25	4·00

No. 1607 is wrongly inscr "Reid Maclead 1920".

457 Footballer and Map

1997. World Cup Football Championship, France (1998) (2nd issue).

1614	**457**	135f. multicoloured	60	30
1615	-	150f. multicoloured	80	35
1616	-	200f. multicoloured	1·00	60
1617	-	270f. multicoloured	1·30	70
1618	-	300f. mult (horiz)	1·60	90
1619	-	400f. mult (horiz)	2·10	1·30
MS1620		107×83 mm. 1000f. multicoloured (39×31 mm)	5·25	4·00

DESIGNS: 135f. to 1000f. Each showing map of France and player.

458 Arms

1997. T **430** redrawn as T **458**. Dated "1997".

1621	**458**	135f. multicoloured	70	25
1622	**458**	150f. multicoloured	1·00	60
1623	**458**	200f. multicoloured	1·20	60

459 Horse's Head

1997. Horses. Multicoloured.

1624	135f. Type **459**	70	30
1625	150f. Bay horse	80	45
1626	200f. Chestnut horse looking forward	1·00	55
1627	270f. Chestnut horse looking backwards	1·30	70
1628	300f. Black horse	1·70	80
1629	400f. Profile of horse	2·10	1·00
MS1630	84×109 mm. 1000f. Bay horse with white nose	5·25	4·00

460 Irish Setter

1997. Dogs. Multicoloured.

1631	135f. Type **460**	60	30
1632	150f. Saluki	80	45
1633	200f. Dobermann pinscher	1·00	55
1634	270f. Siberian husky	1·60	70
1635	300f. Basenji	1·60	80
1636	400f. Boxer	2·30	1·00
MS1637	110×90 mm. 1000f. Rhodesian ridgeback (31×39 mm)	5·25	4·00

461 *Phalaenopsis penetrate*

1997. Orchids. Multicoloured.

1638	135f. Type **461**	70	35
1639	150f. *Phalaenopsis* "Golden Sands"	80	45
1640	200f. *Phalaenopsis* "Sun Spots"	1·00	60
1641	270f. *Phalaenopsis fuscata*	1·70	70
1642	300f. *Phalaenopsis christi floyd*	1·70	85
1643	400f. *Phalaenopsis cayanne*	2·50	1·10
MS1644	99×99 mm. 1000f. *Phalaenopsis* "Janet Kuhn" (31×39 mm)	5·25	4·00

462 Buick Model C Tourer, 1905

1997. Motor Cars. Multicoloured.

1645	135f. Type **462**	70	30
1646	150f. Ford model A tonneau, 1903	80	45
1647	200f. Stanley steamer tourer, 1913	1·00	60
1648	270f. Stoddar-Dayton tourer, 1911	1·30	70
1649	300f. Cadillac convertible sedan, 1934	1·70	85
1650	400f. Cadillac convertible sedan, 1931	2·10	1·10
MS1651	112×85 mm. 1000f. Ford, 1928 (39×31 mm)	5·25	4·00

463 Northern Bullfinch

1997. Birds. Multicoloured.

1652	135f. Type **463**	60	30
1653	150f. Spruce siskin	80	40
1654	200f. Ring ousel	1·00	55
1655	270f. Crested tit	1·30	70
1656	300f. Spotted nutcracker	1·60	80
1657	400f. Nightingale	2·10	1·10
MS1658	107×87 mm. 1000f. Yellow wagtail (31×39 mm)	5·25	4·00

464 *Faucaria lupina*

1997. Cacti. Multicoloured.

1659	135f. Type **464**	60	30
1660	150f. *Conophytum bilobun*	80	45
1661	200f. *Lithops aucampiae*	1·00	60
1662	270f. *Lithops helmutii*	1·30	75
1663	300f. *Stapelia grandiflora*	1·60	80
1664	400f. *Lithops fulviceps*	2·10	1·20
MS1665	109×90 mm. 1000f. *Pleiospilos willowmorensis* (31×38 mm)	5·25	4·00

465 Egyptian Merchant Ship

1997. Ancient Sailing Ships. Multicoloured.

1666	135f. Type **465**	60	30
1667	150f. Greek merchant ship	80	40
1668	200f. Phoenician galley	1·00	55
1669	270f. Roman merchant ship	1·30	70
1670	300f. Norman knarr	1·60	80
1671	400f. Mediterranean sailing ship	2·10	1·00
MS1672	109×89 mm. 1000f. English kogge of Richard II's reign (28×36 mm)	5·25	4·00

466 Black-tipped Grouper

1997. Fish. Multicoloured.

1673	135f. Type **466**	60	30
1674	150f. Cardinal fish	75	40
1675	200f. Indo-Pacific humpheaded parrotfish	1·00	55
1676	270f. Regal angelfish	1·30	70
1677	300f. Wrasse	1·60	80
1678	400f. Hawkfish	2·10	1·00
MS1679	109×90 mm. 1000f. Hogfish (39×31 mm)	5·25	4·00

467 Emblem

1997. Tenth Anniv of African Petroleum Producers' Association.

1680	**467**	135f. multicoloured	60	30
1681	**467**	200f. multicoloured	1·00	55
1682	**467**	300f. multicoloured	1·50	80
1683	**467**	500f. multicoloured	2·75	1·40

468 Caesar's Mushroom

1997. Fungi. Multicoloured.

1684	135f. Type **468**	60	30
1685	150f. Slimy-banded cort	80	40
1686	200f. *Amanita bisporigera*	1·00	55
1687	270f. The blusher	1·30	70
1688	300f. Cracked green russula	1·60	80
1689	400f. Strangulated amanita	2·10	1·00
MS1690	90×110 mm. 1000f. Fly agaric (31×37 mm)	5·25	4·00

469 *Puffing Billy*, 1813

1997. Steam Railway Locomotives. Multicoloured.

1691	135f. Type **469**	60	30
1692	150f. *Rocket*, 1829	80	40
1693	200f. *Royal George*, 1827	1·00	55
1694	270f. *Novelty*, 1829	1·30	70
1695	300f. *Locomotion*, 1825 (vert)	1·60	80
1696	400f. *Sans Pareil*, 1829 (vert)	2·10	1·00
MS1697	110×89 mm. 1000f. Richard Trevithick's locomotive, 1803 (39×31 mm)	5·25	4·00

470 *Tephrocybe carbonaria*

1998. Fungi. Multicoloured.

1698	135f. Type **470**	55	30
1699	150f. Butter mushroom	75	40
1700	200f. Oyster fungus	95	55
1701	270f. *Hohenbuehelia geogenia*	1·20	70
1702	300f. Bitter bolete	1·50	80
1703	400f. *Lepiota leucothites*	2·00	1·00
MS1704	108×90 mm. 1000f. *Gymnopilius junonius*	4·75	3·75

471 Philadelphia or "Double Deck", 1885

1998. Fire Engines. Multicoloured.

1705	135f. Type **471**	55	30
1706	150f. *Veteran*, 1850	75	40
1707	200f. Merryweather, 1894	95	55
1708	270f. 19 19th-century Hippomobile	1·20	70
1709	300f. Jeep *Willy*, 1948	1·50	80
1710	400f. Chevrolet 6400	2·00	1·00
MS1711	110×89 mm. 1000f. Foamite, 1952 (38×30 mm)	4·75	3·75

472 Uranite

1998. Minerals. Multicoloured.

1712	135f. Type **472**	55	30
1713	150f. Quartz	75	40
1714	200f. Aragonite	95	55
1715	270f. Malachite	1·20	70
1716	300f. Turquoise	1·50	80
1717	400f. Corundum	2·00	1·00
MS1718	89×109 mm. 1000f. Marble (short side as base)	4·75	3·75

473 Locomotive

1998. Steam Railway Locomotives. Multicoloured.

1719	135f. Type **473**	55	30
1720	150f. Green locomotive	75	40
1721	200f. Brown locomotive	95	55
1722	270f. Lilac locomotive	1·20	70
1723	300f. Toledo Furnace Co No. 1	1·50	80
1724	400f. No. 1 *Helvetia*	2·00	1·00
MS1725	109×86 mm. Shelby Steel Tube Co. Locomotive (39×31 mm)	4·75	3·75

474 Diana, Princess of Wales

1998. First Death Anniv of Diana, Princess of Wales. Multicoloured.

1726	135f. Type **474**	55	35
1727	150f. Wearing pink dress	75	40
1728	200f. Wearing beige jacket	95	55
1729	270f. Wearing white jacket with revers	1·20	75
1730	300f. Making speech	1·50	80
1731	400f. Wearing collarless single-breasted white jacket	2·00	1·10
1732	500f. Wearing red jacket	2·40	1·40
1733	600f. Wearing black jacket	2·75	1·70
1734	700f. Wearing double-breasted white jacket	3·25	2·00

475 Sordes

1998. Prehistoric Animals. Multicoloured.

1735	135f. Type **475**	55	35
1736	150f. Scaphognatus	70	40
1737	200f. Dsungaripterus	95	55
1738	270f. Brontosaurus	1·20	75
1739	300f. Diplodocus	1·50	80
1740	400f. Coelurus and baryonyx	2·00	1·10
1741	500f. Kronosaurus and ichthyosaurus	2·40	1·40
1742	600f. Ceratosaurus	2·75	1·70
1743	700f. Yangchuansaurus	3·25	2·00

Nos. 1735/43 were issued together, *se-tenant*, forming a composite design.

476 Beagle

1998. Dogs. Multicoloured.

1744	135f. Type **476**	55	30
1745	150f. Dalmatians	70	40
1746	200f. Dachshund	95	55
1747	270f. Cairn terrier	1·20	70
1748	300f. Shih-tzus	1·50	80

1749	400f. Pug	2·00	1·00
MS1750	110×90 mm. 1000f. Springer spaniels (39×31 mm)	4·75	3·75

477 Abyssinian

1998. Cats. Multicoloured.

1751	135f. Type **477**	55	30
1752	150f. Striped silver tabby	70	40
1753	200f. Siamese	95	55
1754	270f. Red tabby (horiz)	1·20	70
1755	300f. Wild cat (horiz)	1·50	80
1756	400f. Manx (horiz)	2·00	1·00
MS1757	110×89 mm. 1000f. Tortoise-shell and white (39×31 mm)	4·75	3·75

478 Bugatti 13 Torpedo, 1910

1998. Motor Cars. Multicoloured.

1758	135f. Type **478**	55	30
1759	150f. Clement voiturette, 1903	70	40
1760	200f. Stutz Bearcat speedster, 1914	95	55
1761	270f. Darracq phaeton, 1907	1·20	70
1762	300f. Napier delivery car, 1913	1·50	80
1763	400f. Pierce Arrow roadster, 1911	2·00	1·00
MS1764	109×91 mm. 1000f. Piccolo, 1904 (31×39 mm)	4·75	3·75

479 Apollo

1998. Butterflies. Multicoloured.

1765	135f. Type **479**	55	30
1766	150f. Orange-tip	70	40
1767	200f. Camberwell beauty	95	55
1768	250f. Speckled wood	1·20	70
1769	300f. Purple-edged copper	1·50	80
1770	400f. Chequered skipper	2·00	1·10
MS1771	106×76 mm. 1000f. Small tortoiseshell (39×31 mm)	4·75	3·75

480 Gouldian Finch

1999. Birds. Multicoloured.

1772	135f. Type **480**	55	30
1773	150f. Saffron finch	70	40
1774	200f. Red-billed quelea	95	55
1775	270f. Golden bishop	1·20	70
1776	300f. Red-crested cardinal	1·50	80
1777	400f. Golden-breasted bunting	2·00	1·10
MS1778	110×89 mm. 1000f. Green-backed twin-spot (31×39 mm)	4·75	3·75

481 Boat, Ceylon

1999. Sailing Boats. Multicoloured.

1779	135f. Type **481**	55	30
1780	150f. Tanka-Tim, Canton, Macao	70	40
1781	200f. Sampan, Hong Kong	95	55
1782	270f. Outrigger sailing canoe, Polynesia	1·20	70
1783	300f. Junk, Japan	1·50	80
1784	400f. Dacca-Pulwar, Bengal	2·00	1·10
MS1785	84×109 mm. 1000f. Junk, China (39×31 mm)	4·75	3·75

482 White Rhinoceros

1999. Mammals.

1786	**482**	50f. grey	15	10
1787	-	100f. violet	45	25
1788	-	135f. green	50	25
1789	-	135f. black	50	25
1790	-	150f. blue	65	30
1791	-	150f. green	65	30
1792	-	200f. blue	85	45
1793	-	200f. brown	85	45
1794	-	300f. brown	1·40	70
1795	-	300f. red	1·40	70
1796	-	400f. brown	1·80	90
1797	-	500f. brown	2·20	1·10

DESIGNS: No. 1787, Sable antelope; 1788, Warthog (*Phacochoerus aethiopicus*); 1789, Brown hyena (*Hyaena brunnea*); 1790, Eastern black-and-white colobus (*Colobus guereza*); 1791, Hippopotamus (*Hippopotamus amphibius*); 1792, Mountain zebra (*Equus zebra*); 1793, African buffalo (*Synceros caffer*) (wrongly inscr "Cyncerus"); 1794, Lion (*Panthera leo*); 1795, Cheetah (*Acinonyx jubatus*); 1796, Hunting dog; 1797, Potto.

483 Mikhail Tal

1999. Chess Players. Multicoloured.

1798	135f. Type **483**	55	30
1799	150f. Emanuel Lasker	70	40
1800	200f. Jose Raul Capablanca	95	55
1801	270f. Aleksandr Alekhine	1·20	70
1802	300f. Max Euwe	1·50	80
1803	400f. Mikhail Botvinnik	2·00	1·10
MS1804	85×109 mm. 1000f. Wilhelm Steinitz (29×36 mm)	4·75	3·75

484 *Brassocattleya cliftonii*

1999. Orchids. Multicoloured.

1805	50f. Type **484**	25	10
1806	100f. Wilsonara	45	25
1807	150f. *Cypripedium paeony*	70	40
1808	300f. *Cymbidium babylon*	1·50	80
1809	400f. Cattleya	2·00	1·10
1810	500f. *Miltonia minx*	2·40	1·50
MS1811	87×110 mm. 1000f. "Isis miltonia" (28×36 mm)	4·75	3·75

485 Royal Python

1999. Snakes. Multicoloured.

1812	135f. Type **485**	55	35
1813	150f. Royal python (different)	70	40
1814	200f. African rock python	95	55
1815	2000f. Head of African rock python	9·50	6·75

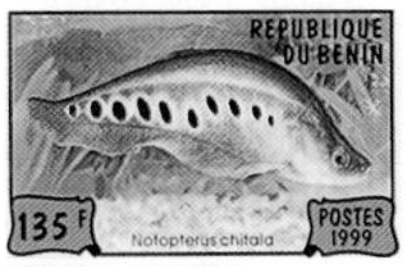

486 Clown Knifefish

1999. Fish. Multicoloured.

1816	135f. Type **486**	55	30
1817	150f. Puntius filamentosus	70	40
1818	200f. *Epalzeorhynchos bicolor*	95	55
1819	270f. Spotted rasbora	1·20	70
1820	300f. Tigernander	1·50	80
1821	400f. Siamese fighting fish	2·00	1·10
MS1822	96×86 mm. 1000f. Three-spotted gourami (39×31 mm)	4·75	3·75

487 A. Murdock's Steam Tricycle, 1786

1999. Steam-powered Vehicles. Multicoloured.

1823	135f. Type **487**	55	30
1824	150f. Richard Trevithick's locomotive, 1800	70	40
1825	200f. Trevithick's locomotive, 1803	95	55
1826	270f. John Blenkinsop's locomotive, 1811	1·20	70
1827	300f. Foster and Rastik's *Stourbridge Lion*, 1829	1·50	80
1828	400f. Peter Cooper's *Tom Thumb*, 1829	2·00	1·10
MS1829	110×85 mm. 1000f. Isaac Newton's locomotive, 1760 (36×28 mm)	4·75	3·75

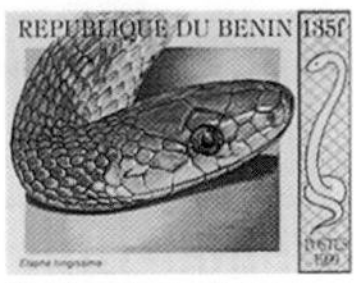

488 Aesculapian Snake

1999. Snakes. Multicoloured.

1830	135f. Type **488**	55	30
1831	150f. Common pine snake	70	40
1832	200f. Grass snake	95	55
1833	270f. Green whip snake	1·20	70
1834	300f. Jamaica boa	1·50	80
1835	400f. Diamond-back rattlesnake	2·00	1·10
MS1836	109×86 mm. 1000f. Common European adder (39×29 mm)	4·75	3·75

489 Testing Chinese Lantern (14th-century)

1999. "China 1999" International Stamp Exhibition, Peking. Multicoloured.

1837	50f. Type **489**	15	10
1838	100f. Satellite launching centre, Jiuquan	45	25
1839	135f. DFH-3 communications satellite	55	40
1840	150f. Satellite launch	70	45
1841	200f. Launch of *Long March* (rocket)	95	60
1842	300f. *Yuan Wang* (passenger ferry) at sea	1·50	90
1843	400f. Dish aerial	2·00	1·20
1844	500f. Items of space post	2·40	1·80

Nos. 1837/44 were issued together, *se-tenant*, with the backgrounds forming a composite design of the Earth.

490 Cheetah

1999. Big Cats. Multicoloured.

1845	135f. Type **490**	55	30
1846	150f. Jaguar	70	40
1847	200f. Snow leopard	95	55
1848	270f. Leopard	1·20	55
1849	300f. Puma	1·50	65
1850	400f. Tiger	2·00	90
MS1851	110×85 mm. 2000f. Lion	4·75	3·75

490a *Mammillaria lenta*

1999. Cacti. Multicoloured.

1856	135f. Type **490a**		
1857	150f. *Oehmea nelsonii*		
1858	200f. *Neobesseya rosiflora*		
1859	270f. *Opuntia gosseliniana*		
1860	300f. *Parodia nivosa*		
1861	400f. *Rebutia senilis*		
MS1862	90×110 mm. 1000f. *Opuntia retrorsa*		

492 Team Members

1999. Manchester United—Triple Cup Winners. Sheet 180×132 mm containing T **492** and similar horiz designs. Multicoloured.

MS1867 135f. Type **492**; 200f. Winning goal; 300f. Celebrating; 400f. Old Trafford football ground; 500f. Champions League, FA Cup and European Cup trophies; 1000f. Alex Ferguson (manager) and Champions League trophy

493 Inscr 'Estrilda locustella'

1999. Birds. Multicoloured.

1868	135f. Type **493**		
1869	150f. *Estrilda melanotis*		
1870	200f. Inscr 'Pyrelia melba'		
1871	270f. *Uraeginthus bengalensis*		
1872	300f. *Pyromelana orix*		
1873	400f. *Ploceus cucullatus*		
MS1874	90×110 mm. 1000f. *Steganura paradisea*		

PARCEL POST STAMPS

1982. Optd or surch **Colis Postaux**.

P871	-	100f. multicoloured (No. 779) (postage)	95	50
P872	**256**	100f. on 150f. mult	95	50
P873	-	300f. mult (No. 797)	2·75	1·40
P874	**260**	1000f. multicoloured	8·25	4·00
P875	**274**	5000f. on 500f. mult (air)	41·00	19·00

1988. No. 543 of Dahomey surch **Republique Populaire du Benin** colis postaux.

P1089	**174**	5f. on 40f. multicoloured (postage)		
P1092	-	300f. on 200f. blue, yellow & brown (air)		
P1093	-	500f. on 200f. mult	5·25	2·30

POSTAGE DUE STAMPS

D 233 Pineapples

1978. Fruits. Multicoloured.

D716	10f. Type D **233**	30	25
D717	20f. Cashew nuts (vert)	45	25
D718	40f. Oranges	95	55
D719	50f. Breadfruit	1·10	75

D234 Village Postman on Bicycle

1978. Rural Post.

D720	**D234**	60f. brown, grn & red	95	45
D721	-	80f. blue, brn & red	95	55

DESIGN: 80f. River village and postman in canoe.

APPENDIX

The following stamps have either been issued in excess of postal needs, or have not been available to the public in reasonable quantities at face value. Such stamps may later be given full listings if there is evidence of regular postal use. Miniature sheets and imperforate stamps are excluded from this listing.

2000

Year of the Dragon. 135, 150, 200, 270, 300, 400f.
Dogs. 135, 150, 200, 270, 300, 400f.
Insects. 135, 150, 200, 270, 300, 400f.
Birds. 135×2, 150×2, 200×2, 270×2, 300×2, 400f.×2

Pt. 7

BERGEDORF

A German city on the Elbe, governed by Hamburg and Lubeck until 1867 when it was purchased by the former. In 1868 became part of North German Confederation.

16 schilling = 1 Hamburg mark.

1

1861. Various sizes. Imperf.

1	1	½s. black on lilac	£600	
2	1	½s. black on blue	60·00	£950
4	1	1s. black on white	60·00	£500
5	1	1½s. black on yellow	26·00	£1800
6	1	3s. black on red	£900	
7	1	3s. blue on red	32·00	£2750
8	1	4s. black on brown	32·00	£3000

Pt. 1

BERMUDA

A group of islands in the W. Atlantic, E. of N. Carolina. Usually regarded by collectors as part of the Br. W. Indies group, though this is not strictly correct.

1865. 12 pence = 1 shilling; 20 shillings = 1 pound.
1970. 100 cents = 1 dollar (U.S.).

9 Queen Victoria

1865. Portrait. Various frames.

19	9	½d. stone	7·00	4·75
21a	9	½d. green	4·25	80
24a	9	1d. red	15·00	20
25	9	2d. blue	65·00	6·50
26a	9	2d. purple	4·25	1·75
27b	9	2½d. blue	14·00	40
10	9	3d. yellow	£180	60·00
28	9	3d. grey	23·00	9·00
20	9	4d. red	18·00	1·75
28a	9	4d. brown	35·00	60·00
7	9	6d. mauve	23·00	12·00
11	9	1s. green	15·00	£120
29b	9	1s. brown	14·00	20·00

1874. Surch in words.

15	1d. on 2d. blue	£700	£375
16	1d. on 3d. yellow	£450	£350
17	1d. on 1s. green	£500	£250
12	3d. on 1d. red	£18000	
14	3d. on 1s. green	£1500	£650

1901. Surch **ONE FARTHING** and bar.

30	¼d. on 1s. grey	4·50	75

13 Dry Dock

1902

34	13	¼d. brown and violet	1·75	1·50
31	13	½d. black and green	12·00	3·50
36	13	½d. green	19·00	4·25
32	13	1d. brown and red	8·00	10
38	13	1d. red	20·00	10
39	13	2d. grey and orange	7·50	10·00
40	13	2½d. brown and blue	27·00	7·00
41	13	2½d. blue	20·00	9·00
33	13	3d. mauve and green	4·50	2·00
42	13	4d. blue and brown	3·00	16·00

14 Badge of the Colony

15

1910

44a	14	¼d. brown	1·75	1·50
77	14	½d. green	1·50	3·00
78	14	1d. red	17·00	60
79b	14	1½d. brown	9·00	35
80	14	2d. grey	1·50	1·50
81a	14	2½d. green	3·00	1·50
82b	14	2½d. blue	1·75	70
83	14	3d. blue	18·00	26·00
84	14	3d. purple on yellow	4·00	1·00
85	14	4d. red on yellow	2·00	1·00
86	14	6d. purple	1·25	80
51	14	1s. black on green	5·00	4·50
51b	15	2s. purple and blue on blue	20·00	55·00
52	15	2s.6d. black and red on blue	32·00	80·00
52b	15	4s. black and red	60·00	£160
53d	15	5s. green and red on yellow	60·00	£120
92	15	10s. green and red on green	£140	£250
93	15	12s.6d. black and orange	£250	£375
55	15	£1 purple and black on red	£325	£550

1918. Optd **WAR TAX**.

56	14	1d. red	50	1·25

18

19

1920. Tercentenary of Representative Institutions. (a) 1st Issue.

59	18	¼d. brown	3·50	26·00
60	18	½d. green	9·00	18·00
65	18	1d. red	4·50	30
61	18	2d. grey	16·00	50·00
66	18	2½d. blue	19·00	20·00
62	18	3d. purple on yellow	12·00	50·00
63	18	4d. black and red on yellow	12·00	40·00
67	18	6d. purple	28·00	90·00
64	18	1s. black on green	16·00	48·00

(b) 2nd Issue.

74	19	¼d. brown	4·25	3·75
75	19	½d. green	3·50	8·50
76	19	1d. red	8·00	35
68	19	2d. grey	11·00	48·00
69	19	2½d. blue	14·00	5·50
70	19	3d. purple on yellow	5·50	17·00
71	19	4d. red on yellow	19·00	30·00
72	19	6d. purple	19·00	60·00
73	19	1s. black on green	25·00	60·00

1935. Silver Jubilee. As T **13** of Antigua.

94	1d. blue and red	1·00	2·25
95	1½d. blue and grey	1·00	3·50
96	2½d. brown and blue	1·50	2·50
97	1s. grey and purple	22·00	50·00

20 Hamilton Harbour

22 "Lucie" (yacht)

1936

98	20	½d. green	10	10
99	-	1d. black and red	65	30
100	-	1½d. black and brown	1·00	50
101	22	2d. black and blue	5·00	1·50
102	-	2½d. blue	1·00	25
103	-	3d. black and red	4·00	2·75
104	-	6d. red and violet	80	10
105	-	1s. green	14·00	18·00
106	20	1s.6d. brown	50	10

DESIGNS—HORIZ: 1d., 1½d. South Shore, near Spanish Rock; 3d. Point House, Warwick Parish. VERT: 2½d., 1s. Grape Bay, Paget Parish; 6d. House at Par-la-Ville, Hamilton.

The 1d., 1½d., 2½d. and 1s. values include a portrait of King George V.

1937. Coronation. As T **2** of Aden.

107	1d. red	90	1·50
108	1½d. brown	60	1·75
109	2½d. blue	70	1·75

26 Ships in Hamilton Harbour

28 White-tailed Tropic Bird, Arms of Bermuda and Native Flower

1938

110	26	1d. black and red	2·50	20
111b	26	1½d. blue and brown	2·25	1·75
112	22	2d. blue and brown	50·00	10·00
112a	22	2d. blue and red	3·00	2·25
113	-	2½d. blue and deep blue	11·00	1·25
113b	-	2½d. blue and black	3·75	3·50
114	-	3d. black and red	40·00	5·50
114a	-	3d. black and blue	1·75	40
114bc	28	7½d. black, blue and green	7·50	2·75
115	-	1s. green	2·00	50

DESIGNS—VERT: 3d. St. David's Lighthouse. The 2½d. and 1s. are as 1935, but with King George VI portrait.

1938. As T **15**, but King George VI portrait.

116c	2s. purple and blue on blue	10·00	1·50
117d	2s.6d. black and red on blue	16·00	21·00
118f	5s. green and red on yellow	35·00	30·00
119e	10s. green and red on green	48·00	50·00
120b	12s.6d. grey and orange	£110	55·00
121d	£1 purple and black on red	55·00	85·00

1940. Surch **HALF PENNY**.

122	26	½d. on 1d. black and red	1·25	3·25

1946. Victory. As T **9** of Aden.

123	1½d. brown	15	15
124	3d. blue	40	65

1948. Silver Wedding. As T **10/11** of Aden.

125	1½d. brown	30	50
126	£1 red	45·00	55·00

31 Postmaster Perot's Stamp

1949. Centenary of Postmaster Perot's Stamp.

127	31	2½d. blue and brown	35	35
128	31	3d. black and blue	35	15
129	31	6d. violet and green	40	15

1949. U.P.U. As T **20/23** of Antigua.

130	2½d. black	30	2·00
131	3d. blue	1·75	1·25
132	6d. purple	40	75
133	1s. green	40	1·50

1953. Coronation. As T **13** of Aden.

134	1½d. black and blue	1·00	40

34 Easter Lily

43 Hog Coin

1953

135a	-	½d. olive	40	2·00
136	-	1d. black and red	2·00	50
137	34	1½d. green	30	10
138	-	2d. blue and red	50	40
139	-	2½d. red	2·00	50
140	-	3d. purple	30	10
141	-	4d. black and blue	55	1·75
142	-	4½d. green	1·50	1·00
143	-	6d. black and turquoise	6·50	60
156	-	6d. black and mauve	1·50	15
143a	-	8d. black and red	3·25	30
143b	-	9d. violet	11·00	2·50
144	-	1s. orange	50	15
145	-	1s.3d. blue	3·75	30
146	-	2s. brown	4·00	85
147	-	2s.6d. red	9·00	45
148	43	5s. red	20·00	85
149	-	10s. blue	17·00	8·00
150	-	£1 multicoloured	42·00	21·00

DESIGNS—HORIZ: ½d. Easter lilies; 1d., 4d. Postmaster Perot's stamp; 2d. *Victory II* (racing dinghy); 2½d. Sir George Somers and *Sea Venture*; 3d., 1s.3d. Map of Bermuda; 4½d. 9d. *Sea Venture* (galleon), coin and Perot stamp; 6d. (No. 143), 8d. White-tailed tropic bird; 6d. (No. 156), Perot's Post Office; 1s. Early Bermuda coins; 2s. Arms of St. George's 10s. Obverse and reverse of hog coin; £1 Arms of Bermuda. VERT: 2s.6d. Warwick Fort.

No. 156 commemorates the restoration and reopening of Perot's Post Office.

1953. Royal Visit. As No. 143a but inscr "ROYAL VISIT 1953".

151	6d. black and turquoise	75	20

1953. Three Power Talks. Nos. 140 and 145 optd **Three Power Talks December, 1953**.

152	3d. purple	10	10
153	1s.3d. blue	15	10

1956. 50th Anniv of United States-Bermuda Yacht Race. Nos. 143a and 145 optd **50TH ANNIVERSARY US – BERMUDA OCEAN RACE 1956**.

154	8d. black and red	25	45
155	1s.3d. blue	25	55

49 Arms of King James I and Queen Elizabeth II

1959. 350th Anniv of Settlement. Arms in red, yellow and blue. Frame colours given.

157	49	1½d. blue	30	10
158	49	3d. grey	35	50
159	49	4d. purple	40	55
160	49	8d. violet	40	15
161	49	9d. olive	40	1·25
162	49	1s.3d. brown	40	30

50 The Old Rectory, St George's, c.1730

1962

163	50	1d. purple, black and orange	10	75
164	-	2d. multicoloured	1·00	35
165	-	3d. brown and blue	10	10
166	-	4d. brown and mauve	20	40
167	-	5d. blue and red	75	3·00
168	-	6d. blue, green & lt blue	30	30
169	-	8d. blue, green and orange	30	35
170	-	9d. blue and brown	30	60
197	-	10d. violet and ochre	75	60
171	-	1s. multicoloured	30	10
172	-	1s.3d. lake, grey and bistre	75	15
173	-	1s.6d. violet and ochre	75	1·00
199	-	1s.6d. blue and red	1·00	50
200	-	2s. brown and orange	1·00	75
175	-	2s.3d. sepia and green	1·00	7·00
176	-	2s.6d. sepia, green & yell	55	50
177	-	5s. purple and green	1·25	1·50
178	-	10s. mauve, green and buff	4·50	7·00
179	-	£1 black, olive and orange	14·00	14·00

DESIGNS: 2d. Church of St. Peter, St. George's; 3d. Government House, 1892; 4d. The Cathedral. Hamilton, 1894; 5d., 1s.6d. (No. 199) H.M. Dockyard, 1811; 6d. Perot's Post Office, 1848; 8d. G.P.O., Hamilton, 1869; 9d. Library, Par-la-Ville; 10d., 1s.6d. (No. 173) Bermuda cottage, c. 1705; 1s. Christ Church, Warwick, 1719; 1s.3d. City Hall, Hamilton, 1960; 2s. Town of St. George; 2s.3d. Bermuda house, c. 1710; 2s.6d. Bermuda house, early 18th century; 5s. Colonial Secretariat, 1833; 10s. Old Post Office, Somerset, 1890; £1 The House of Assembly, 1815.

1963. Freedom from Hunger. As T **28** of Aden.

180	1s.3d. sepia	60	40

1963. Centenary of Red Cross. As T **33** of Antigua.

181	3d. red and black	50	25
182	1s.3d. red and blue	1·00	2·50

67 *Tsotsi in the Bundu* (Finn class yacht)

1964. Olympic Games, Tokyo.

183	67	3d. red, violet and blue	10	10

1965. Centenary of ITU. As T **36** of Antigua.

184	3d. blue and green	35	25
185	2s. yellow and blue	65	1·50

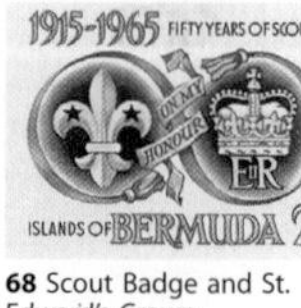

68 Scout Badge and St. Edward's Crown

1965. 50th Anniv of Bermuda Boy Scouts Association.

186	68	2s. multicoloured	50	50

1965. ICY. As T **37** of Antigua.

187	4d. purple and turquoise	40	20
188	2s.6d. green and lavender	60	80

1966. Churchill Commemoration. As T **38** of Antigua.

189	3d. blue	30	20

190	6d. green	70	1·00
191	10d. brown	1·00	75
192	1s.3d. violet	1·25	2·50

1966. World Cup Football Championship. As T **40** of Antigua.

193	10d. multicoloured	1·00	15
194	2s.6d. multicoloured	1·25	1·25

1966. 20th Anniv of UNESCO. As T **54/56** of Antigua.

201	4d. multicoloured	45	15
202	1s.3d. yellow, violet and olive	75	50
203	2s. black, purple and orange	1·00	1·10

69 GPO Building

1967. Opening of New General Post Office.

204	**69**	3d. multicoloured	10	10
205	**69**	1s. multicoloured	10	10
206	**69**	1s.6d. multicoloured	20	25
207	**69**	2s.6d. multicoloured	20	70

70 *Mercury* (cable ship) and Chain Links

1967. Inauguration of Bermuda–Tortola Telephone Service. Multicoloured.

208	3d. Type **70**	15	10
209	1s. Map, telephone and microphone	25	10
210	1s.6d. Telecommunications media	25	25
211	2s.6d. "Mercury" (cable ship) and marine fauna	40	70

74 Human Rights Emblem and Doves

1968. Human Rights Year.

212	**74**	3d. indigo, blue and green	10	10
213	**74**	1s. brown, blue and light blue	10	10
214	**74**	1s.6d. black, blue and red	10	15
215	**74**	2s.6d. green, blue and yellow	15	25

75 Mace and Queen's Profile

1968. New Constitution.

216	**75**	3d. multicoloured	10	10
217	**75**	1s. multicoloured	10	10
218	-	1s.6d. yellow, black and blue	10	20
219	-	2s.6d. lilac, black and yellow	15	75

DESIGNS: 1s.6d., 2s.6d., Houses of Parliament, and House of Assembly, Bermuda.

77 Football, Athletics and Yachting

1968. Olympic Games, Mexico.

220	**77**	3d. multicoloured	15	10
221	**77**	1s. multicoloured	25	10
222	**77**	1s.6d. multicoloured	50	30
223	**77**	2s.6d. multicoloured	50	1·40

78 Brownie and Guide

1969. 50th Anniv of Girl Guides. Multicoloured.

224	3d. Type **78**	10	10
225	1s. Type **78**	20	10
226	1s.6d. Guides and Badge	25	40
227	2s.6d. As 1s.6d.	35	1·40

80 Emerald-studded Gold Cross and Seaweed

1969. Underwater Treasure. Multicoloured.

228	4d. Type **80**	20	10
229	1s.3d. Emerald-studded gold cross and sea-bed	35	15
230	2s. As Type **80**	45	90
231	2s.6d. As 1s.3d.	45	1·75

1970. Decimal Currency. Nos. 163/79 surch.

232	1c. on 1d. purple, black & orge	10	1·75
233	2c. on 2d. multicoloured	10	10
234	3c. on 3d. brown and blue	10	30
235	4c. on 4d. brown and mauve	10	10
236	5c. on 8d. blue, green & orge	15	2·25
237	6c. on 6d. blue, green & lt blue	15	1·75
238	9c. on 9d. blue and brown	30	2·75
239	10c. on 10d. violet and ochre	30	25
240	12c. on 1s. multicoloured	30	1·25
241	15c. on 1s.3d. lake, grey & bis	2·00	1·75
242	18c. on 1s.6d. blue and red	80	65
243	24c. on 2s. brown and orange	85	4·00
244	30c. on 2s.6d. sepia, grn & yell	1·00	3·00
245	36c. on 2s.3d. sepia and green	1·75	8·00
246	60c. on 5s. purple and green	2·25	4·00
247	$1.20 on 10s. mve, grn & buff	5·00	12·00
248	$2.40 on £1 black, ol & orge	6·00	15·00

83 Spathiphyllum

1970. Flowers. Multicoloured.

249	1c. Type **83**	10	20
250	2c. Bottlebrush	20	25
251	3c. Oleander (vert)	15	10
252	4c. Bermudiana	15	10
253	5c. Poinsettia	2·50	20
254	6c. Hibiscus	30	30
255	9c. Cereus	20	45
256	10c. Bougainvillea (vert)	20	15
257	12c. Jacaranda	60	60
258	15c. Passion flower	90	1·40
258a	17c. As 15c.	2·75	4·75
259	18c. Coralita	2·25	1·00
259a	20c. As 18c.	2·75	4·00
260	24c. Morning glory	1·50	5·00
260a	25c. As 24c.	2·75	4·50
261	30c. Tecoma	1·00	1·25
262	36c. Angel's trumpet	1·25	1·25
262a	40c. As 36c.	2·75	5·50
263	60c. Plumbago	1·75	1·25
263a	$1 As 60c.	3·25	6·50
264	$1.20 Bird of paradise flower	2·25	1·25
264a	$2 As $1.20	9·00	10·00
265	$2.40 Chalice cup	4·50	2·00
265a	$3 As $2.40	11·00	11·00

84 The State House, St. George's

1970. 350th Anniv of Bermuda Parliament. Multicoloured.

266	4c. Type **84**	10	10
267	15c. The Sessions House, Hamilton	25	20
268	18c. St. Peter's Church, St. George's	25	25
269	24c. Town Hall, Hamilton	35	1·00
MS270	131×95 mm. Nos. 266/9	1·10	1·50

85 Street Scene, St. George's

1971. "Keep Bermuda Beautiful". Multicoloured.

271	4c. Type **85**	20	10
272	15c. Horseshoe Bay	65	65
273	18c. Gibbs Hill Lighthouse	1·50	2·25
274	24c. Hamilton Harbour	1·25	2·50

86 Building of the *Deliverance*

1971. Voyage of the "Deliverance". Multicoloured.

275	4c. Type **86**	60	20
276	15c. *Deliverance* and *Patience* at Jamestown (vert)	1·50	1·75
277	18c. Wreck of the *Sea Venture* (vert)	1·50	2·25
278	24c. *Deliverance* and *Patience* on high seas	1·75	2·50

87 Green overlooking Ocean View

1971. Golfing in Bermuda. Multicoloured.

279	4c. Type **87**	70	10
280	15c. Golfers at Port Royal	1·25	65
281	18c. Castle Harbour	1·25	1·00
282	24c. Belmont	1·50	2·00

1971. Anglo-American Talks. Nos. 252, 258, 259 and 260 optd **HEATH-NIXON DECEMBER 1971**.

283	4c. Bermudiana	10	10
284	15c. Passion flower	10	20
285	18c. Coralita	15	65
286	24c. Morning glory	20	1·00

89 Bonefish

1972. World Fishing Records. Multicoloured.

287	4c. Type **89**	30	10
288	15c. Wahoo	30	50
289	18c. Yellow-finned tuna	35	75
290	24c. Greater amberjack	40	1·25

1972. Silver Wedding. As T **52** of Ascension, but with "Admiralty Oar" and Mace in background.

291	4c. violet	15	10
292	15c. red	15	50

91 Palmetto

1973. Tree Planting Year. Multicoloured.

293	4c. Type **91**	25	10
294	15c. Olivewood bark	65	75
295	18c. Bermuda cedar	70	1·25
296	24c. Mahogany	75	1·60

1973. Royal Wedding. As T **47** of Anguilla, background colour given. Multicoloured.

297	15c. mauve	15	15
298	18c. blue	15	15

92 Bernard Park, Pembroke, 1973

1973. Centenary of Lawn Tennis. Multicoloured.

299	4c. Type **92**	30	10
300	15c. Clermont Court, 1873	40	65
301	18c. Leamington Spa Court, 1872	45	1·75
302	24c. Staten Island Courts, 1874	50	2·00

93 Weather Vane, City Hall

1974. 50th Anniv of Rotary in Bermuda. Multicoloured.

320	5c. Type **93**	15	10
321	17c. St. Peter's Church, St. George's	45	35
322	20c. Somerset Bridge	50	1·50
323	25c. Map of Bermuda, 1626	60	2·25

94 Jack of Clubs and "good bridge hand"

1975. World Bridge Championships, Bermuda. Multicoloured.

324	5c. Type **94**	20	10
325	17c. Queen of Diamonds and Bermuda Bowl	35	50
326	20c. King of Hearts and Bermuda Bowl	40	1·75
327	25c. Ace of Spades and Bermuda Bowl	40	2·50

95 Queen Elizabeth II and the Duke of Edinburgh

1975. Royal Visit.

328	**95**	17c. multicoloured	60	65
329	**95**	20c. multicoloured	65	2·10

96 Short S.23 Flying Boat *Cavalier*, 1937

1975. 50th Anniv of Air-mail Service to Bermuda. Multicoloured.

330	5c. Type **96**	40	10
331	17c. U.S. Navy airship *Los Angeles*, 1925	1·25	85
332	20c. Lockheed Constellation, 1946	1·40	2·75
333	25c. Boeing 747-100, 1970	1·50	3·50
MS334	128×85 mm. Nos. 330/3	11·00	15·00

97 Supporters of American Army raiding Royal Magazine

1975. Bicentenary of Gunpowder Plot, St. George's. Multicoloured.

335	5c. Type **97**	15	10
336	17c. Setting off for raid	30	40
337	20c. Loading gunpowder aboard American ship	35	1·40
338	25c. Gunpowder on beach	35	1·50
MS339	165×138 mm. Nos. 335/8	2·75	7·00

98 Launching *Ready* (bathysphere)

1976. 50th Anniv of Bermuda Biological Station. Multicoloured.

357	5c. Type **98**	30	10
358	17c. View from the sea (horiz)	60	60
359	20c. H.M.S. *Challenger*, 1873 (horiz)	65	2·25
360	25c. Beebe's Bathysphere descent, 1934	70	3·00

99 *Christian Radich* (cadet ship)

1976. Tall Ships Race. Multicoloured.

361	5c. Type **99**	75	20
362	12c. *Juan Sebastian de Elcano* (Spanish cadet schooner)	80	2·25
363	17c. *Eagle* (U.S. coastguard cadet ship)	80	1·50
364	20c. *Sir Winston Churchill* (cadet schooner)	80	1·75
365	40c. *Kruzenshtern* (Russian cadet barque)	1·00	2·75
366	$1 *Cutty Sark* trophy	1·25	7·00

100 Silver Trophy and Club Flags

1976. 75th Anniv of St. George's v. Somerset Cricket Cup Match. Multicoloured.

367	5c. Type **100**	30	10
368	17c. Badge and pavilion, St. George's Club	50	65
369	20c. Badge and pavilion, Somerset Club	65	2·75
370	25c. Somerset playing field	1·00	3·75

101 Royal Visit, 1975

1977. Silver Jubilee. Multicoloured.

371	5c. Type **101**	10	10
372	20c. St. Edward's Crown	15	20
373	$1 The Queen in Chair of Estate	40	1·25

102 Stockdale House, St. George's, 1784–1812

1977. Centenary of U.P.U. Membership. Multicoloured.

374	5c. Type **102**	15	10
375	15c. Perot Post Office and stamp	25	50
376	17c. St. George's P.O. c. 1860	25	50
377	20c. Old G.P.O., Hamilton, c. 1935	30	60
378	40c. New G.P.O., Hamilton, 1967	45	1·10

103 17th-Century Ship approaching Castle Island

1977. Piloting. Multicoloured.

379	5c. Type **103**	50	10
380	15c. Pilot leaving ship, 1795	70	60
381	17c. Pilots rowing out to paddle-steamer	80	60
382	20c. Pilot gig and brig *Harvest Queen*	85	2·25
383	40c. Modern pilot cutter and R.M.S. *Queen Elizabeth 2*	1·60	3·75

104 Great Seal of Queen Elizabeth I

1978. 25th Anniv of Coronation. Multicoloured.

384	8c. Type **104**	10	10
385	50c. Great Seal of Queen Elizabeth II	30	30
386	$1 Queen Elizabeth II	60	75

105 White-tailed Tropic Bird

1978. Wildlife. Multicoloured.

387	3c. Type **105**	2·50	2·50
388	4c. White-eyed vireo	3·00	3·00
389	5c. Eastern bluebird	1·25	1·75
390	7c. Whistling frog	50	1·50
391	8c. Common cardinal ("Cardinal Redbird")	1·25	55
392	10c. Spiny lobster	20	10
393	12c. Land crab	30	70
394	15c. Lizard (Skink)	30	15
395	20c. Four-eyed butterflyfish	30	30
396	25c. Red hind	30	20
397	30c. *Danaus plexippus* (butterfly)	2·25	2·50
398	40c. Rock beauty	50	1·75
399	50c. Banded butterflyfish	55	1·50
400	$1 Blue angelfish	2·50	1·75
401	$2 Humpback whale	2·00	2·25
402	$3 Green turtle	2·50	2·50
403	$5 Cahow	5·50	5·00

106 Map by Sir George Somers, 1609

1979. Antique Maps. Multicoloured.

404	8c. Type **106**	15	10
405	15c. Map by John Seller, 1685	20	15
406	20c. Map by H. Moll, 1729–40 (vert)	25	25
407	25c. Map by Desbruslins, 1740	30	30
408	50c. Map by Speed, 1626	45	80

107 Policeman and Policewoman

1979. Centenary of Police Force. Multicoloured.

409	8c. Type **107**	30	10
410	20c. Policeman directing traffic (horiz)	50	55
411	25c. *Blue Heron* (police launch) (horiz)	60	65
412	50c. Police Morris Marina and motorcycle	80	1·50

108 1d. "Perot" Stamp of 1848 and 1840 Penny Black

1980. Death Cent of Sir Rowland Hill. Multicoloured.

413	8c. Type **108**	20	10
414	20c. "Perot" and Sir Rowland Hill	30	25
415	25c. "Perot" and early letter	30	30
416	50c. "Perot" and "Paid 1" cancellation	35	1·00

109 Lockheed L-1011 TriStar 500 approaching Bermuda

1980. "London 1980" International Stamp Exhibition. Multicoloured.

417	25c. Type **109**	30	15
418	50c. "Orduna I" (liner) at Grassy Bay, 1926	45	35
419	$1 "Delta" (screw steamer) at St. George's Harbour, 1856	85	1·10
420	$2 "Lord Sidmouth" (sailing packet) in Old Ship Channel, St. George's	1·40	2·25

110 Gina Swainson ("Miss World 1979–80")

1980. "Miss World 1979–80" Commem. Multicoloured.

421	8c. Type **110**	15	10
422	20c. Miss Swainson after crowning ceremony	20	20
423	50c. Miss Swainson on Peacock Throne	35	35
424	$1 Miss Swainson in Bermuda carriage	70	90

111 Queen Elizabeth the Queen Mother

1980. 80th Birthday of The Queen Mother.

425	**111** 25c. multicoloured	30	1·00

112 Bermuda from Satellite

1980. Commonwealth Finance Ministers Meeting. Multicoloured.

426	8c. Type **112**	10	10
427	20c. *Camden*	20	40
428	25c. Princess Hotel, Hamilton	20	50
429	50c. Government House	35	1·50

113 Kitchen, 18th-century

1981. Heritage Week. Multicoloured.

430	8c. Type **113**	15	10
431	25c. Gathering Easter lilies, 20th-century	20	35
432	30c. Fishing, 20th-century	30	50
433	40c. Stone cutting, 19th-century	30	80
434	50c. Onion shipping, 19th-century	50	90
435	$1 Privateering, 17th-century	1·10	2·50

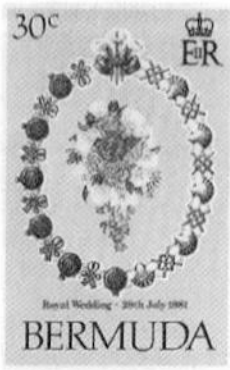

114 Wedding Bouquet from Bermuda

1981. Royal Wedding. Multicoloured.

436	30c. Type **114**	20	20
437	50c. Prince Charles as Royal Navy Commander	35	40
438	$1 Prince Charles and Lady Diana Spencer	55	80

115 "Service", Hamilton

1981. 25th Anniv of Duke of Edinburgh Award Scheme. Multicoloured.

439	10c. Type **115**	15	10
440	25c. "Outward Bound", Paget Island	20	20
441	30c. "Expedition", St. David's Island	20	30
442	$1 Duke of Edinburgh	55	1·25

116 Lightbourne's Cone

1982. Sea Shells. Multicoloured.

443	10c. Type **116**	30	10
444	25c. Finlay's frog shell	55	55
445	30c. Royal bonnet	60	60
446	$1 Lightbourne's murex	1·75	3·25

117 Regimental Colours and Colour Party

1982. Bermuda Regiment. Multicoloured.

447	10c. Type **117**	60	10
448	25c. Queen's Birthday Parade	80	80
449	30c. Governor inspecting Guard of Honour	1·10	1·40
450	40c. Beating the Retreat	1·25	1·75
451	50c. Ceremonial gunners	1·25	2·00
452	$1 Guard of Honour, Royal visit, 1975	1·75	3·50

118 Charles Fort

1982. Historic Bermuda Forts. Multicoloured.

453	10c. Type **118**	20	20
454	25c. Pembroks Fort	50	85
455	30c. Southampton Fort (horiz)	60	1·25
456	$1 Smiths Fort and Pagets Fort (horiz)	1·75	4·50

119 Arms of Sir Edwin Sandys

1983. Coat of Arms (1st series). Multicoloured.

457	10c. Type **119**	45	15
458	25c. Arms of the Bermuda Company	1·10	1·00
459	50c. Arms of William Herbert, Earl of Pembroke	1·90	3·75
460	$1 Arms of Sir George Somers	2·50	6·50

See also Nos. 482/5 and 499/502.

120 Early Fitted Dinghy

1983. Fitted Dinghies. Multicoloured.

461	12c. Type **120**	45	15
462	30c. Modern dinghy inshore	60	75
463	40c. Early dinghy (different)	70	90
464	$1 Modern dinghy with red and white spinnaker	1·40	3·25

121 Curtiss N-9 Seaplane

1983. Bicentenary of Manned Flight. Multicoloured.

465	12c. Type **121** (First flight over Bermuda)	60	20
466	30c. Stinson Pilot Radio seaplane (First completed flight between U.S. and Bermuda)	1·25	1·25
467	40c. S.23 Flying boat *Cavalier* (First scheduled passenger flight)	1·50	1·75
468	$1 U.S.N. *Los Angeles* (airship) moored to U.S.S. *Patoka*	2·75	5·00

122 Joseph Stockdale

1984. Bicentenary of Bermuda's First Newspaper and Postal Service. Multicoloured.

469	12c. Type **122**	25	15
470	30c. *The Bermuda Gazette*	45	80
471	40c. Stockdale's postal service (horiz)	60	1·10
472	$1 *Lady Hammond* (mail boat) (horiz)	2·00	3·25

123 Sir Thomas Gates and Sir George Somers

1984. 375th Anniv of First Settlement. Multicoloured.

473	12c. Type **123**	20	15
474	30c. Jamestown, Virginia	50	1·25
475	40c. Wreck of *Sea Venture*	90	1·25
476	$1 Fleet leaving Plymouth, Devon	2·00	6·00
MS477	130×73 mm. Nos. 474 and 476	3·75	10·00

124 Swimming

1984. Olympic Games, Los Angeles. Multicoloured.

478	12c. Type **124**	40	15
479	30c. Track and field events (horiz)	70	75
480	40c. Equestrian	1·10	1·25
481	$1 Sailing (horiz)	2·00	5·50

1984. Coat of Arms (2nd series). As T **119**. Multicoloured.

482	12c. Arms of Henry Wrothesley, Earl of Southampton	50	15
483	30c. Arms of Sir Thomas Smith	1·00	85
484	40c. Arms of William Cavendish, Earl of Devonshire	1·25	1·50
485	$1 Town arms of St. George	2·75	4·50

125 Buttery

1985. Bermuda Architecture. Multicoloured.

486	12c. Type **125**	35	15
487	30c. Limestone rooftops (horiz)	80	70
488	40c. Chimneys (horiz)	95	1·00
489	$1.50 Entrance archway	3·00	3·75

126 Osprey

1985. Birth Bicentenary of John J. Audubon (ornithologist). Designs showing original drawings. Multicoloured.

490	12c. Type **126**	2·00	65
491	30c. Yellow-crowned night heron	2·00	95
492	40c. Great egret (horiz)	2·25	1·25
493	$1.50 Eastern bluebird ("Bluebird")	3·75	6·50

127 The Queen Mother with Grandchildren, 1980

1985. Life and Times of Queen Elizabeth the Queen Mother. Multicoloured.

494	12c. Queen Consort, 1937	35	15
495	30c. Type **127**	60	50
496	40c. At Clarence House on 83rd birthday	70	60
497	$1.50 With Prince Henry at his christening (from photo by Lord Snowdon)	2·00	2·75
MS498	91×73 mm. $1 With Prince Charles at 80th birthday celebrations	3·75	3·50

1985. Coats of Arms (3rd series). As T **119**. Multicoloured.

499	12c. Hamilton	75	15
500	30c. Paget	1·40	80
501	40c. Warwick	1·60	1·40
502	$1.50 City of Hamilton	3·75	4·25

128 Halley's Comet and Bermuda Archipelago

1985. Appearance of Halley's Comet. Multicoloured.

503	15c. Type **128**	85	25
504	40c. Halley's Comet, A.D. 684 (from Nuremberg Chronicles, 1493)	1·60	1·75
505	50c. *Halley's Comet, 1531* (from Peter Apian woodcut, 1532)	1·90	2·50
506	$1.50 *Halley's Comet, 1759* (Samuel Scott)	3·50	6·50

129 *Constellation* (schooner) (1943)

1986. Ships Wrecked on Bermuda. Multicoloured.

507A	3c. Type **129**	70	2·00
508A	5c. *Early Riser* (pilot boat), 1876	20	20
509A	7c. *Madiana* (screw steamer), 1903	65	2·75
510A	10c. *Curlew* (sail/steamer), 1856	30	30
511A	12c. *Warwick* (galleon), 1619	60	80
512A	15c. H.M.S. *Vixen* (gun-boat), 1890	40	60
512cA	18c. As 7c.	6·00	4·25
513A	20c. *San Pedro* (Spanish galleon), 1594	1·10	80
514A	25c. *Alert* (fishing sloop), 1877	60	3·00
515A	40c. *North Carolina* (barque), 1880	65	1·25
516A	50c. *Mark Antonie* (Spanish privateer), 1777	1·50	3·25
517A	60c. *Mary Celestia* (Confederate paddle-steamer), 1864	1·50	1·75
517cA	70c. *Caesar* (brig), 1818	6·50	6·50
518B	$1 *L'Herminie* (French frigate), 1839	1·50	1·60
519A	$1.50 As 70c.	4·50	6·00
520B	$2 *Lord Amherst* (transport), 1778	2·50	6·50
521B	$3 *Minerva* (sailing ship), 1849	4·25	9·00
522A	$5 *Caraquet* (cargo liner), 1923	4·50	11·00
523A	$8 H.M.S. *Pallas* (frigate), 1783	6·00	13·00

1986. 60th Birthday of Queen Elizabeth II. As T **110** of Ascension. Multicoloured.

524	15c. Princess Elizabeth aged three, 1929	45	30
525	40c. With Earl of Rosebery at Oaks May Meeting, Epsom, 1954	80	60
526	50c. With Duke of Edinburgh, Bermuda, 1975	80	75
527	60c. At British Embassy, Paris, 1972	90	90
528	$1.50 At Crown Agents Head Office, London, 1983	2·00	2·50

1986. "Ameripex '86" International Stamp Exhibition, Chicago. As T **164** of Bahamas, showing Bermuda stamps. Multicoloured.

529	15c. 1984 375th Anniv of Settlement miniature sheet	1·50	30
530	40c. 1973 Lawn Tennis Centenary, 24c.	2·25	70
531	50c. 1983 Bicentenary of Manned Flight 12c.	2·25	1·00
532	$1 1976 Tall Ships Race 17c.	3·75	3·00
MS533	80×80 mm. $1.50, Statue of Liberty and *Monarch of Bermuda*	8·75	7·00

No. **MS**533 also commemorates the Centenary of the Statue of Liberty.

1986. 25th Anniv of World Wildlife Fund. No. 402 surch **90c.**

534	90c. on $3 Green turtle	3·00	4·25

131 Train in Front Street, Hamilton, 1940

1987. Transport (1st series). Bermuda Railway. Multicoloured.

535	15c. Type **131**	2·00	25
536	40c. Train crossing Springfield Trestle	2·50	90
537	50c. *St. George Special* at Bailey's Bay Station	2·50	1·50
538	$1.50 Boat train at St. George	4·00	6·25

See also Nos. 557/60, 574/7 and 624/9.

132 "Bermuda Settlers", 1901

1987. Bermuda Paintings (1st series). Works by Winslow Homer. Multicoloured.

539	15c. Type **132**	60	25
540	30c. *Bermuda*, 1900	85	45
541	40c. *Bermuda Landscape*, 1901 (buff frame)	95	55
544	40c. Type **132**	1·00	1·75
545	40c. As No. 540	1·00	1·75
546	40c. As No. 541 (grey frame)	1·00	1·75
547	40c. As No. 542	1·00	1·75
548	40c. As No. 543	1·00	1·75
542	50c. *Inland Water*, 1901	1·10	70
543	$1.50 *Salt Kettle*, 1899	2·50	2·50

See also Nos. 607/10 and 630/3.

133 Sikorsky S-42B Flying Boat "Bermuda Clipper"

1987. 50th Anniv of Inauguration of Bermuda–U.S.A. Air Service. Multicoloured.

549	15c. Type **133**	2·00	15
550	40c. Short S.23 flying boat *Cavalier*	3·00	70
551	50c. *Bermuda Clipper* in flight over signpost	3·25	80
552	$1.50 *Cavalier* on apron and *Bermuda Clipper* in flight	6·00	3·50

134 19th-century Wagon carrying Telephone Poles

1987. Centenary of Bermuda Telephone Company. Multicoloured.

553	15c. Type **134**	75	15
554	40c. Early telephone exchange	1·40	60
555	50c. Early and modern telephones	1·75	70
556	$1.50 Communications satellite orbiting Earth	2·75	5·75

135 Mail Wagon, c. 1869

1988. Transport (2nd series). Horse-drawn Carts and Wagons. Multicoloured.

557	15c. Type **135**	25	15
558	40c. Open cart, c. 1823	55	55
559	50c. Closed cart, c. 1823	65	70
560	$1.50 Two-wheeled wagon, c. 1930	2·00	3·25

136 "Old Blush"

1988. Old Garden Roses (1st series). Multicoloured.

561	15c. Type **136**	85	25
562	30c. "Anna Olivier"	1·25	45
563	40c. *Rosa chinensis semperflorens* (vert)	1·40	85
564	50c. "Archduke Charles"	1·50	1·25
565	$1.50 *Rosa chinensis viridiflora* (vert)	3·00	6·50

See also Nos. 584/8 and, for designs with the royal cypher instead of the Queen's head, Nos. 589/98 and 683/6.

1988. 300th Anniv of Lloyd's of London. As T **123** of Ascension. Multicoloured.

566	18c. Loss of H.M.S. *Lutine* (frigate), 1799	85	25
567	50c. *Sentinel* (cable ship) (horiz)	1·60	65
568	60c. *Bermuda* (liner), Hamilton, 1931 (horiz)	1·75	75
569	$2 Loss of H.M.S. *Valerian* (sloop) in hurricane, 1926	3·00	4·00

137 Devonshire Parish Militia, 1812

1988. Military Uniforms. Multicoloured.

570	18c. Type **137**	1·50	25
571	50c. 71 st (Highland) Regiment, 1831–34	2·00	1·10
572	60c. Cameron Highlanders, 1942	2·25	1·25
573	$2 Troop of horse, 1774	4·75	8·00

138 *Corona* (ferry)

1989. Transport (3rd series). Ferry Services. Multicoloured.

574	18c. Type **138**	35	25
575	50c. Rowing boat ferry	75	65
576	60c. St. George's barge ferry	85	75
577	$2 *Laconia*	2·50	4·50

139 Morgan's Island

1989. 150 Years of Photography. Multicoloured.

578	18c. Type **139**	85	25
579	30c. Front Street, Hamilton	1·10	45
580	50c. Waterfront, Front Street, Hamilton	1·60	1·25
581	60c. Crow Lane from Hamilton Harbour	1·75	1·40
582	70c. Shipbuilding, Hamilton Harbour	1·90	2·50
583	$1 Dockyard	2·25	3·50

1989. Old Garden Roses (2nd series). As T **136**. Multicoloured.

584	18c. "Agrippina" (vert)	90	25
585	30c. "Smith's Parish" (vert)	1·25	60
586	50c. "Champney's Pink Cluster"	1·75	1·40
587	60c. "Rosette Delizy"	1·75	1·60
588	$1.50 *Rosa bracteata*	2·75	6·00

1989. Old Garden Roses (3rd series). Designs as Nos. 561/5 and 584/8, but with royal cypher at top left instead of Queen's head. Multicoloured.

589	50c. As No. 565 (vert)	1·75	2·25
590	50c. As No. 563 (vert)	1·75	2·25
591	50c. Type **136**	1·75	2·25
592	50c. As No. 562	1·75	2·25
593	50c. As No. 564	1·75	2·25
594	50c. As No. 585 (vert)	1·75	2·25
595	50c. As No. 584 (vert)	1·75	2·25
596	50c. As No. 586	1·75	2·25
597	50c. As No. 587	1·75	2·25
598	50c. As No. 588	1·75	2·25

140 Main Library, Hamilton

1989. 150th Anniv of Bermuda Library. Multicoloured.

599	18c. Type **140**	60	25
600	50c. The Old Rectory, St. George's	1·25	65
601	60c. Somerset Library, Springfield	1·25	85
602	$2 Cabinet Building, Hamilton	3·25	4·50

141 1865 1d. Rose

1989. Commonwealth Postal Conference. Multicoloured.

603	**141**	18c. grey, pink and red	1·50	25
604	-	50c. grey, blue & lt blue	2·00	75
605	-	60c. grey, purple and mauve	2·25	1·25
606	-	$2 grey, green and emerald	3·75	5·00

DESIGNS: 50c. 1866 2d. blue; 60c. 1865 6d. purple; $2 1865 1s. green.

142 *Fairylands, c. 1890* (Ross Turner)

1990. Bermuda Paintings (2nd series). Multicoloured.

607	18c. Type **142**	75	25
608	50c. *Shinebone Alley, c. 1953* (Ogden Pleissner)	1·25	1·25
609	60c. *Salt Kettle, 1916* (Prosper Senat)	1·25	1·50
610	$2 *St. George's, 1934* (Jack Bush)	3·25	7·00

1990. "Stamp World London 90" International Stamp Exhibition. Nos. 603/6 optd **Stamp World London 90** and logo.

611	18c. grey, pink and red	1·25	25
612	50c. grey, blue and light blue	1·75	1·50
613	60c. grey, purple and mauve	2·00	1·75
614	$2 grey, green and emerald	3·50	6·00

1990. Nos. 511, 516 and 519 surch.

615	30c. on 12c. "Warwick" (galleon), (1619)	1·75	1·25
616	55c. on 50c. "Mark Antonie" (Spanish privateer), 1777	2·25	2·25
617	80c. on $1.50 "Caesar" (brig), 1818	2·50	4·75

145 The Halifax and Bermudas Cable Company Office, Hamilton

1990. Centenary of Cable and Wireless in Bermuda.

618	**145**	20c. brown and black	70	25
619	-	55c. brown and black	2·00	1·25
620	-	70c. multicoloured	2·00	2·75
621	-	$2 multicoloured	4·75	7·50

DESIGNS: 55c. "Westmeath" (cable ship), 1890; 70c. Wireless transmitter station, St. George's, 1928; $2 "Sir Eric Sharp" (cable ship).

1991. President Bush–Prime Minister Major Talks, Bermuda. Nos. 618/19 optd **BUSH-MAJOR 16 MARCH 1991**.

622	**145**	20c. brown and black	2·00	1·50
623	-	55c. brown and black	3·00	3·50

147 Two-seater Pony Cart, 1805

1991. Transport (4th series). Horse-drawn Carriages. Multicoloured.

624	20c. Type **147**	80	30
625	30c. Varnished rockaway, 1830	90	60
626	55c. Vis-a-Vis victoria, 1895	1·60	1·10
627	70c. Semi-formal phaeton, 1900	2·25	2·50
628	80c. Pony runabout, 1905	2·50	3·75
629	$1 Ladies phaeton, 1910	2·75	4·50

148 *Bermuda, 1916* (Prosper Senat)

1991. Bermuda Paintings (3rd series). Multicoloured.

630	20c. Type **148**	1·00	30
631	55c. *Bermuda Cottage* 1930 (Frank Allison) (horiz)	2·00	1·40
632	70c. *Old Maid's Lane*, 1934 (Jack Bush)	2·50	3·25
633	$2 *St. George's*, 1953 (Ogden Pleissner) (horiz)	5·00	8·50

1991. 65th Birthday of Queen Elizabeth II and 70th Birthday of Prince Philip. As T **139** of Ascension. Multicoloured.

634	55c. Prince Philip in tropical naval uniform	1·25	1·75
635	70c. Queen Elizabeth II in Bermuda	1·25	1·75

149 H.M.S. *Argonaut* (cruiser) in Floating Dock

1991. 50th Anniv of Second World War. Multicoloured.

636	20c. Type **149**	1·50	40
637	55c. Kindley Airfield	2·25	1·40
638	70c. Boeing 314A flying boat and map of Atlantic route	2·75	3·25
639	$2 Censored trans-Atlantic mail	4·50	7·50

1992. 40th Anniv of Queen Elizabeth II's Accession. As T **143** of Ascension. Multicoloured.

640	20c. Old fort on beach	60	30
641	30c. Public gardens	75	55
642	55c. Cottage garden	1·25	90
643	70c. Beach and hotels	1·60	2·25
644	$1 Queen Elizabeth II	1·90	2·75

150 Rings and Medallion

1992. 500th Anniv of Discovery of America by Columbus. Spanish Artifacts. Multicoloured.

645	25c. Type **150**	1·25	35
646	35c. Ink wells	1·40	75
647	60c. Gold ornaments	2·25	2·00
648	75c. Bishop buttons and crucifix	2·50	3·25
649	85c. Earrings and pearl buttons	2·75	3·75
650	$1 Jug and bowls	3·00	4·25

151 "Wreck of 'Sea Venture' "

1992. Stained Glass Windows. Multicoloured.

651	25c. Type **151**	1·50	40
652	60c. "Birds in tree"	2·75	2·00
653	75c. "St. Francis feeding bird"	3·25	3·00
654	$2 "Shells"	7·00	10·00

152 German Shepherd

1992. Seven World Congress of Kennel Clubs. Multicoloured.

655	25c. Type **152**	1·25	40
656	35c. Irish setter	1·50	70
657	60c. Whippet (vert)	2·25	2·25
658	75c. Border terrier (vert)	2·25	3·25
659	85c. Pomeranian (vert)	2·50	3·75
660	$1 Schipperke (vert)	2·50	4·25

153 Policeman, Cyclist and Cruise Liner

1993. Tourism Posters by Adolph Treidler. Multicoloured.

679	25c. Type **153**	2·25	80
680	60c. Seaside golf course	3·00	2·75
681	75c. Deserted beach	2·50	2·75
682	$2 Dancers in evening dress and cruise liner	4·50	7·00

154 "Duchesse de Brabant" and Bee

1993. Garden Roses (4th series).

683	**154**	10c. multicoloured	75	1·40
684	**154**	25c. multicoloured	75	60
685	**154**	50c. multicoloured	2·75	4·00
686	**154**	60c. multicoloured	1·25	1·75

1993. 75th Anniv of Royal Air Force. As T **149** of Ascension. Multicoloured.

687	25c. Consolidated PBY-5 Catalina	85	35
688	60c. Supermarine Spitfire Mk IX	2·00	2·00
689	75c. Bristol Type 156 Beaufighter Mk X	2·25	2·25
690	$2 Handley Page Halifax Mk III	3·75	6·00

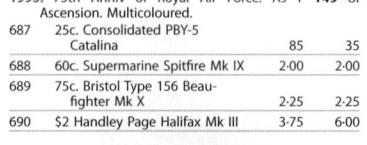

155 Hamilton from the Sea

1993. Bicentenary of Hamilton. Multicoloured.

691	25c. Type **155**	1·00	35
692	60c. Waterfront	2·00	2·00
693	75c. Barrel warehouse	2·00	2·50
694	$2 Sailing ships off Hamilton	5·00	7·00

156 *Queen of Bermuda* (liner) at Hamilton

1994. 75th Anniv of Furness Line's Bermuda Cruises. Adolphe Treidler Posters. Multicoloured.

695	25c. Type **156**	65	35
696	60c. *Queen of Bermuda* entering port (horiz)	1·50	1·60
697	75c. *Queen of Bermuda* and *Ocean Monarch* (liners) (horiz)	1·60	1·75
698	$2 Passengers on promenade deck at night	3·50	6·00

157 Queen Elizabeth II in Bermuda

1994. Royal Visit. Multicoloured.

699	25c. Type **157**	1·00	35
700	60c. Queen Elizabeth and Prince Philip in open carriage	2·50	1·75
701	75c. Royal Yacht "Britannia"	5·00	3·50

158 Peach

1994. Flowering Fruits. Multicoloured.

792	5c. Type **158**	40	1·00
703A	7c. Fig	40	1·25
704A	10c. Calabash (vert)	35	35
795	15c. Natal plum	65	35
796	18c. Locust and wild honey	70	30
797	20c. Pomegranate	70	35
798	25c. Mulberry (vert)	70	40
709A	35c. Grape (vert)	70	55
710A	55c. Orange (vert)	1·00	80
711A	60c. Surinam cherry	1·25	1·40
802	75c. Loquat	2·00	1·75
803	90c. Sugar apple	2·25	2·00
804	$1 Prickly pear (vert)	2·50	3·50
715A	$2 Paw paw	4·50	5·50
716A	$3 Bay grape	5·00	6·00
717A	$5 Banana (vert)	7·50	8·00
718A	$8 Lemon	11·00	12·00

159 Nurse with Mother and Baby

1994. Centenary of Hospital Care. Multicoloured.

719	25c. Type **159**	1·00	35
720	60c. Patient on dialysis machine	2·00	1·90
721	75c. Casualty on emergency trolley	2·25	2·25
722	$2 Elderly patient in wheelchair with physiotherapists	4·75	7·00

160 Gombey Dancers

1994. Cultural Heritage (1st series). Multicoloured.

723	25c. Type **160**	75	35
724	60c. Christmas carol singers	1·40	1·50
725	75c. Marching band	2·50	2·00
726	$2 National Dance Group performers	4·75	7·50

See also Nos. 731/4.

161 Bermuda 1970 Flower 1c. Stamps and 1c. Coin

1995. 25th Anniv of Decimal Currency. Multicoloured.

727	25c. Type **161**	75	35
728	60c. 1970 5c. stamps and coin	1·40	1·50
729	75c. 1970 10c. stamps and coin	1·75	2·00
730	$2 1970 25c. stamps and coin	4·50	6·50

1995. Cultural Heritage (2nd series). As T **160**. Multicoloured.

731	25c. Kite flying	75	35
732	60c. Majorettes	1·50	1·50
733	75c. Portuguese dancers	1·75	2·00
734	$2 Floral float	4·00	6·00

162 Bermuda Coat of Arms

1995. 375th Anniv of Bermuda Parliament.

735	**162**	25c. multicoloured	1·25	35
736	**162**	$1 multicoloured	2·50	3·25

For design as No. 736 but inscr "Commonwealth Finance Ministers Meeting", see No. 765.

163 U.S. Navy Ordnance Island Submarine Base

1995. Military Bases. Multicoloured.

737	20c. Type **163**	70	60
738	25c. Royal Naval Dockyard	75	35
739	60c. U.S.A.F. Fort Bell and Kindley Field	1·60	1·25
740	75c. R.A.F. Darrell's Island flying boat base	1·75	2·00
741	90c. U.S. Navy operating base	1·90	2·75
742	$1 Canadian Forces Communications Station, Daniel's Head	1·90	2·75

164 Triple Jump

1996. Olympic Games, Atlanta. Multicoloured.

743	25c. Type **164**	70	35
744	30c. Cycling	3·00	1·00
745	65c. Yachting	2·00	2·00
746	80c. Show jumping	2·00	3·00

165 Jetty and Islets, Hamilton

1996. Panoramic Paintings of Hamilton (Nos. 747/51) and St. George's (Nos. 752/6) by E. J. Holland. Multicoloured.

747	60c. Type **165**	1·75	2·25
748	60c. End of island and buildings	1·75	2·25
749	60c. Yachts and hotel	1·75	2·25
750	60c. Islet, hotel and cathedral	1·75	2·25
751	60c. Cliff and houses by shore	1·75	2·25
752	60c. Islet and end of main island	1·75	2·25
753	60c. Yacht and houses on hillside	1·75	2·25
754	60c. Yacht and St. George's Hotel on hilltop	1·75	2·25
755	60c. Shoreline and fishing boats	1·75	2·25
756	60c. Entrance to harbour channel	1·75	2·25

166 Somerset Express Mail Cart, c. 1900

1996. "CAPEX '96" International Stamp Exhibition, Toronto. Local Transport. Multicoloured.

757	25c. Type **166**	1·25	35
758	60c. Victoria carriage and railcar, 1930s	2·75	1·75
759	75c. First bus, 1946	2·75	2·00
760	$2 Sightseeing bus, c. 1947	5·00	7·50

167 Hog Fish Beacon

1996. Lighthouses. Multicoloured.

761	30c. Type **167**	1·50	50
762	65c. Gibbs Hill Lighthouse	2·00	1·25
763	80c. St. David's Lighthouse	2·50	2·00
764	$2 North Rock Beacon	4·50	7·00

See also Nos. 770/3.

1996. Commonwealth Finance Ministers' Meeting. As No. 736, but inscr "Commonwealth Finance Ministers Meeting" at top and with wider gold frame.

765	$1 multicoloured	2·50	3·00

168 Waterville

1996. Architectural Heritage. Multicoloured.

766	30c. Type **168**	1·00	45
767	65c. Bridge House	1·40	1·50
768	80c. Fannie Fox's Cottage	1·75	2·00
769	$2.50 Palmetto House	4·00	7·00

1997. "HONG KONG '97" International Stamp Exhibition. Designs as Nos. 761/4, but incorporating "HONG KONG '97" logo and with some values changed.

770	30c. As Type **167**	2·00	65
771	65c. Gibbs Hill Lighthouse	2·75	1·50
772	80c. St David's Lighthouse	3·00	2·25
773	$2.50 North Rock Beacon	6·00	9·50

169 White-tailed Tropic Bird

1997. Bird Conservation. Multicoloured.

774	30c. Type **169**	60	50
775	60c. White-tailed tropic bird and chick (vert)	1·25	1·25
776	80c. Cahow and chick (vert)	1·75	2·00
777	$2.50 Cahow	4·00	6·50

170 Queen Elizabeth II with Crowd

1997. Golden Wedding of Queen Elizabeth and Prince Philip. Multicoloured.

778	30c. Type **170**	50	40
779	$2 Queen Elizabeth and Prince Philip	3·25	4·50
MS780	90×56 mm. Nos. 778/9	3·75	4·50

171 Father playing with Children

1997. Education. Multicoloured.

781	30c. Type **171**	50	40
782	40c. Teacher and children with map	60	55
783	60c. Boys holding sports trophy	85	1·25
784	65c. Pupils outside Berkeley Institute	90	1·25
785	80c. Scientific experiments	1·25	2·00
786	90c. New graduates	1·40	2·50

1998. Diana, Princess of Wales Commemoration. Sheet, 145×170 mm, containing vert designs as T **177** of Ascension. Multicoloured.

MS787	30c. Wearing black hat, 1983; 40c. Wearing floral dress; 65c. Wearing blue evening dress, 1996; 80c. Carrying bouquets, 1993 (sold at $2.15 + 25c. charity premium)	3·00	4·00

172 *Fox's Cottage, St. Davids* (Ethel Tucker)

1998. Paintings by Catherine and Ethel Tucker. Multicoloured.

788	30c. Type **172**	1·25	40
789	40c. *East Side, Somerset*	1·40	70
790	65c. *Long Bay Road, Somerset*	2·25	1·25
791	$2 *Flatts Village*	5·00	7·50

173 Horse and Carriage

1998. Hospitality in Bermuda. Multicoloured.

809	25c. Type **173**	1·25	40
810	30c. Golf club desk	1·75	75
811	65c. Chambermaid preparing room	1·50	1·25
812	75c. Kitchen staff under training	1·50	2·00
813	80c. Waiter at beach hotel	1·75	2·25
814	90c. Nightclub bar	2·00	3·00

174 *Agave attenuata*

1998. Centenary of Botanical Gardens. Multicoloured.

815	30c. Type **174**	1·25	40
816	65c. Bermuda palmetto tree	2·25	90
817	$1 Banyan tree	2·75	2·75
818	$2 Cedar tree	4·00	7·00

175 Lizard with Fairy Lights (Claire Critchley)

1998. Christmas. Children's Paintings. Multicoloured.

819	25c. Type **175**	1·25	35
820	40c. *Christmas stairway* (Cameron Rowling) (horiz)	1·50	1·25

176 Shelly Bay

1999. Bermuda Beaches. Multicoloured.

821	30c. Type **176**	80	40
822	60c. Catherine's Bay	1·10	1·00
823	65c. Jobson's Cove	1·25	1·10
824	$2 Warwick Long Bay	3·50	5·50

177 Tracking Station

1999. 30th Anniv of First Manned Landing on Moon. Multicoloured.

825	30c. Type **177**	1·00	40
826	60c. Mission launch (vert)	1·50	90
827	75c. Aerial view of tracking station, Bermuda	1·75	1·25
828	$2 Astronaut on Moon (vert)	3·75	6·00
MS829	90×80 mm. 65c. Earth as seen from Moon (circular, 40 mm diam)	3·25	4·00

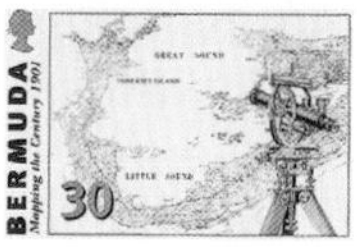

178 Theodolite and Map, 1901

1999. Centenary of First Digital Map of Bermuda.

830	**178**	30c. multicoloured	1·50	40
831	-	65c. black, stone & silver	2·25	1·50
832	-	80c. multicoloured	2·75	2·50
833	-	$1 multicoloured	2·75	4·00

DESIGNS: 65c. Street map, 1901; 80c. Street plan and aerial photograph, 1999; $1 Satellite and Bermuda from Space, 1999.

179 Victorian Pillar Box and Bermuda 1865 1s. Stamp

1999. Bermuda Postal History. Multicoloured.

834	30c. Type **179**	1·00	40
835	75c. King George V pillar box and 1920 2s. stamp	2·00	1·50
836	95c. King George VI wall box and 1938 3d. stamp	2·25	2·75
837	$1 Queen Elizabeth II pillar box and 1953 Coronation 1½d. stamp	2·25	2·75

180 Sir Henry Tucker and Meeting of House of Assembly

2000. Pioneers of Progress (1st series). Each brown, black and gold.

838	30c. Type **180**	85	1·00
839	30c. Gladys Morrell and suffragettes	85	1·00
840	30c. Dr. E. F. Gordon and workers	85	1·00

See also Nos. 988/92 and 1018/1019.

181 *Amerigo Vespucci* (full-rigged ship)

2000. Tall Ships Race. Multicoloured.

841	30c. Type **181**	1·25	50
842	60c. *Europa* (barque)	1·75	1·50
843	80c. *Juan Sebastian de Elcano* (schooner)	2·00	2·50

182 Prince William

2000. Royal Birthdays. Multicoloured.

844	35c. Type **182**	1·25	45
845	40c. Duke of York	1·25	50
846	50c. Princess Royal	1·40	90
847	70c. Princess Margaret	1·75	2·50
848	$1 Queen Elizabeth the Queen Mother	2·00	3·25
MS849	169×90 mm. Nos. 844/8	8·00	8·50

183 Santa Claus with Smiling Vegetable (Meghan Jones)

2000. Christmas. Children's Paintings. Multicoloured.

850	30c. Type **183**	1·00	45
851	45c. *Christmas tree and presents (Carlita Lodge)*	1·25	80

2001. Endangered Species. Bird Conservation. Designs as Nos. 774/7, but with different face values, inscriptions redrawn and WWF panda emblem added. Multicoloured.

852	15c. As Type **169**	90	1·00
853	15c. Cahow	90	1·00
854	20c. White-tailed tropic bird with chick (vert)	90	1·00
855	20c. Cahow with chick (vert)	90	1·00
MS856	200×190 mm. Nos. 852/5 each × 4	12·00	13·00

No. **MS**856 includes the "HONG KONG 2001" logo on the margin.

184 King's Castle

2001. Historic Buildings, St. George's. Multicoloured.

857	35c. Type **184**	1·10	55
858	50c. Bridge House	1·50	75
859	55c. Whitehall	1·60	1·00
860	70c. Fort Cunningham	1·90	2·25
861	85c. St. Peter's Church	2·50	3·25
862	95c. Water Street	2·50	3·25

185 Boer Prisoners on Boat and Plough

2001. Centenary of Anglo-Boer War. Multicoloured.

863	35c. Type **185**	85	55
864	50c. Prisoners in shelter and boot	1·10	75
865	70c. Elderly Boer with children and jewellery	1·60	1·75
866	95c. Bermuda residents and illustrated envelope of 1902	2·00	3·00

186 Girl touching Underwater Environment

2001. 75th Anniv of Bermuda Aquarium. Multicoloured.

867	35c. Type **186**	90	55
868	50c. Museum exhibits (horiz)	1·25	75
869	55c. Feeding giant tortoise (horiz)	1·25	95
870	70c. Aquarium building (horiz)	1·75	1·75
871	80c. Lesson from inside tank	1·75	2·25
872	95c. Turtle	2·25	3·00

187 *Fishing Boats* (Charles Lloyd Tucker)

2001. Paintings of Charles Lloyd Tucker. Multicoloured.

873	35c. Type **187**	1·40	55
874	70c. *Bandstand and City Hall, Hamilton*	2·00	1·50
875	85c. *Hamilton Harbour*	2·25	2·50
876	$1 *Train in Front Street, Hamilton*	3·00	4·25

2002. Golden Jubilee. As T **200** of Ascension.

877	10c. black, violet and gold	60	60
878	35c. multicoloured	1·50	1·10
879	70c. black, violet and gold	2·00	1·60
880	85c. multicoloured	2·25	2·25
MS881	162×95 mm. Nos. 887/80 and $1 multicoloured	7·00	7·50

DESIGNS—HORIZ: 10c. Princess Elizabeth with corgi; 35c. Queen Elizabeth in evening dress, 1965; 70c. Queen Elizabeth in car, 1952; 85c. Queen Elizabeth on Merseyside, 1991. VERT (38×51 mm)—$2 Queen Elizabeth after Annigoni.

Designs as Nos. 877/80 in No. **MS**881 omit the gold frame around each stamp and the "Golden Jubilee 1952–2002" inscription.

188 Fantasy Cave

2002. Caves. Multicoloured.

882	35c. Type **188**	1·40	55
883	70c. Crystal Cave	2·00	1·50
884	80c. Prospero's Cave	2·25	2·50
885	$1 Cathedral Cave	2·75	4·00

189 Fielder and Somerset Club Colours

2002. Centenary of Bermuda Cup Cricket Match. Multicoloured.

886	35c. Type **189**	1·25	1·00
887	35c. Batsman and wicket-keeper with St. George's Club colours	1·25	1·00
MS888	110×85 mm. $1 Batsman (48×31 mm)	3·25	3·50

2002. Queen Elizabeth the Queen Mother Commemoration. As T **202** of Ascension.

889	30c. brown, gold and purple	1·00	45
890	$1.25 multicoloured	2·50	3·00
MS891	145×70 mm. Nos. 889/90	4·50	4·75

DESIGNS: 30c. Duchess of York, 1923; $1.25, Queen Mother on her birthday, 1995.

Designs as Nos. 889/90 in No. **MS**891 omit the "1900–2002" inscription and the coloured frame.

190 Slit Worm-shell

2002. Shells. Multicoloured.

892	5c. Type **190**	10	10
893	10c. Netted olive	15	15
894	20c. Angular triton (horiz)	35	30
895	25c. Frog shell (horiz)	40	35
896	30c. Colourful atlantic moon (horiz)	45	40
897	35c. Noble wentletrap	50	45
898	40c. Atlantic trumpet triton (horiz)	60	50
899	45c. Zigzag scallop	70	55
900	50c. Bermuda cone	80	65
901	75c. Very distorted distorsio (horiz)	1·25	90
902	80c. Purple sea snail (horiz)	1·40	95
903	90c. Flame helmet (horiz)	1·40	1·10
904	$1 Scotch bonnet (horiz)	1·50	1·40
905	$2 Gold mouth triton (horiz)	2·75	2·50
906	$3 Bermuda's slit shell (horiz)	4·25	4·00
907	$4 Reticulated cowrie-helmet (horiz)	5·50	6·00
908	$5 Dennison's morum (horiz)	6·50	7·00
909	$8 Sunrise tellin	10·00	11·00

191 Dove of Peace

2002. World Peace Day.

910	**191** 35c. multicoloured	1·25	50
911	- 70c. multicoloured	2·00	2·25

DESIGN: 70c. Dove.

192 Research Station and *Weatherbird II* (research ship)

2003. Centenary of Bermuda Biological Research Station. Multicoloured.

912	35c. Type **192**	1·00	50
913	70c. Spotfin butterflyfish (horiz)	1·75	1·50
914	85c. Collecting coral (horiz)	1·90	2·25
915	$1 Krill	2·00	3·00

193 Costume Dolls

2003. Heritage "Made in Bermuda". (1st Series). Multicoloured.

916	35c. Type **193**	75	40
917	70c. Model sailing ship	1·25	1·10
918	80c. Abstract sculpture in wood	1·40	1·60
919	$1 Silverware	1·75	2·25

See also Nos. 934/7, 952/5 and 980/3.

2003. 50th Anniv of Coronation. As T **206** of Ascension. Multicoloured.

920	35c. Queen in Coronation Coach	75	40
921	70c. Queen in Coronation chair, flanked by bishops of Durham and Bath & Wells	1·25	1·50
MS922	95×115 mm. $1.25 As 35c.; $2 As 70c.	5·00	6·00

Nos. 920/1 have red frame; stamps from **MS**922 have no frame and country name in mauve panel.

194 Red Poinsettias

2003. Christmas Greetings. Poinsettias. Multicoloured.

925	30c. Type **194**	75	35
926	45c. White poinsettias	1·10	55
927	80c. Pink poinsettias	2·00	2·50

195 Gateway

2004. Royal Naval Dockyard, Bermuda. Multicoloured.

928	25c. Type **195**	65	50
929	35c. Fountain and Clock Tower	90	80
930	70c. Waterside seat and Clock Tower	1·75	1·50
931	85c. Marina	1·90	2·00
932	95c. Window in ramparts	2·25	2·50
933	$1 Boats moored at pontoon and Clocktower Centre	2·40	3·00

2004. Heritage "Made in Bermuda" (2nd series). As T **193**. Multicoloured.

934	35c. Carver chair	65	45
935	70c. Ceramic jug and plate	1·10	90
936	80c. Glass fish and glass plate with shell design	1·25	1·40
937	$1.25 Quilt	1·75	2·50

196 Bluefin Tuna

2004. Endangered Species. Bluefin Tuna. Multicoloured.

938	10c. Type **196**	30	50
939	35c. Five bluefin tuna	85	50
940	85c. Bluefin tuna near surface of water	1·90	1·90
941	$1.10 Bluefin tuna swimming left	2·25	2·50

197 Yellow Oncydium Orchids

2004. 50th Anniv of the Orchid Society. Multicoloured.

942	35c. Type **197**	90	45
943	45c. *Encyclia radiate*	1·10	55
944	85c. Purple and white orchids	2·00	2·00
945	$1.10 *Paphiopedilum spicerianum*	2·50	2·75

198 1940 Map of Bermuda and Compass

2005. 500th Anniv of Discovery of Bermuda by Juan de Bermudez (Spanish navigator). Multicoloured.

946	25c. Type **198**	1·00	50
947	35c. 1846 map and sextant	1·10	55
948	70c. 1764 map and box compass	1·90	1·40
949	$1.10 1692 map and telescope	2·75	3·00
950	$1.25 1548 map and calipers	2·75	3·25
MS951	115×95 mm. $5 Aerial view of Bermuda	11·00	12·00

2005. Heritage "Made in Bermuda" (3rd series). As T **193**. Multicoloured.

952	35c. Picture of Bermuda Gombey dancers	70	45
953	70c. Papier-mache sculpture of parrotfish on tube coral	1·25	1·25
954	85c. Stained glass picture of lion and lamb	1·60	1·75
955	$1 Earrings and pendant of silver, pearls and garnets	1·90	2·50

2005. Bicentenary of Battle of Trafalgar. As T **216** of Ascension but horiz. Multicoloured.

956	10c. HMS *Victory*	60	60
957	35c. HMS *Pickle* under construction in Bermuda	1·00	50
958	70c. HMS *Pickle* picking up survivors from burning *Achille*	1·60	1·50
959	85c. HMS *Pickle* racing back to England with news of victory	1·90	2·25

No. 956 contains traces of powdered wood from HMS *Victory*.

199 Ruddy Turnstone and Semipalmated Sandpiper

2005. Bermuda Habitats. Scenes from dioramas in Bermuda Natural History Museum. Multicoloured.

960	10c. Type **199**	45	50
961	25c. Least bittern in reeds	65	40
962	35c. White-tailed tropic bird	85	45
963	70c. Eastern bluebird	1·50	1·25
964	85c. Saw-whet owl	2·00	2·00
965	$1 Yellow-crowned night heron	2·25	2·50

200 Christmas Tree with Lights

2005. Christmas Greetings. Festival of Lights. Multicoloured.

966	30c. Type **200**	50	50
967	45c. Dolphin	65	60
968	80c. Snowman	1·25	1·25

201 Man working on Overhead Power Cables

2006. Centenary of the Bermuda Electric Light Company Ltd. Multicoloured.

969	35c. Type **201**	70	45
970	70c. Engineer, power lines and vehicle	1·40	1·10
971	85c. Power plant	1·75	1·90
972	$1 Office block	1·90	2·50

2006. 80th Birthday of Queen Elizabeth II. As T **223** of Ascension. Multicoloured.

973	35p. Princess Elizabeth with corgi	90	45
974	70p. Queen wearing tiara (black/white photo)	1·40	1·10
975	85p. Wearing tiara and drop earrings (colour photo)	1·75	1·75
976	$1.25 Wearing blue hat	2·75	3·25
MS977	144×75 mm. $1.25 As No. 974; $2 As No. 975	6·00	7·00

202 Map of Bermuda, 1747

2006. Washington 2006 International Stamp Exhibition.

978	**202** $1.10 multicoloured	1·90	2·00
MS979	82×65 mm. No. 978	1·90	2·00

2006. Heritage "Made in Bermuda" (4th series). As T **193**. Multicoloured.

980	35c. Bees, honeycomb and honey	90	45
981	70c. *Stonecutters* (detail) (Sharon Wilson)	1·60	1·25
982	85c. *I've Caught Some Whoppers* (sculpture) by Desmond Fountain	2·00	2·00
983	$1.25 Flower and perfume (Bermuda Perfumery)	2·75	3·25

203 Advent Wreath

2006. Christmas. Greetings. Advent Wreaths.

984	**203** 30c. multicoloured	80	45
985	- 35c. multicoloured	90	30
986	- 45c. multicoloured	1·10	40
987	- 80c. multicoloured	2·00	2·25

DESIGNS: 35c. to 80c. Showing different advent wreaths.

204 Francis L. Patton

2007. Pioneers of Progress (2nd series). Educators. Multicoloured.

988	35c. Type **204**	65	70
989	35c. Adele Tucker	65	70
990	35c. Edith and Matilda Crawford	65	70
991	35c. Millie Neversen	65	70
992	35c. May Francis	65	70

205 Hull under Construction at Rockport, Maine, USA

2007. *Spirit of Bermuda*. Sail training schooner. Multicoloured.

993	10c. Type **205**	50	40
994	35c. Close-up view	85	40
995	70c. *Spirit of Bermuda* at sea	1·50	1·10
996	85c. Off coast of Bermuda	1·75	1·40
997	$1.10 At Hamilton, Bermuda	2·00	2·00
998	$1.25 *Spirit of Bermuda* seen from stern	2·25	2·50

206 *Deliverance* off Building Bay

2007. 400th Anniv of Jamestown, Virginia, USA. Voyage of the Deliverance from Bermuda to Jamestown, 1610. Multicoloured.

999	35c. Type **206**	1·00	50
1000	$1.10 *Deliverance* sailing from Building Bay, St. George's, Bermuda	2·50	2·75

2007. Centenary of World Scouting. As T **281** of Bahamas. Multicoloured.

1001	35c. Bishop's Own Cubs, Government House, 22 February 1930	75	35
1002	70c. Lord Baden-Powell inspecting the Cubs, Hamilton, February 1930	1·25	85
1003	85c. Scout parade, Front Street, Hamilton, 25 February 1930	1·60	1·25
1004	$1.10 Dance of Kaa, Government House, 25 February 1930	1·75	2·00
MS1005	90×65 mm. $1.25 Bermuda Scouts emblem; $2 Lord Baden-Powell inspecting the Cubs, Hamilton, February 1930 (both vert)	5·25	5·75

207 *Celeste & Al Harris*

2008. Bermuda Calypso Music. Designs showing album covers. Multicoloured.

1006	35c. Type **207**	75	35
1007	70c. *Bermuda Calypsos*	1·25	90
1008	85c. *Calypso Varieties from Bermuda*	1·50	1·25
1009	$1.10 *The Talbot Brothers of Bermuda*	1·75	2·00

208 Perot Stamp, 1848

2008. 160th Anniv of the Perot Stamp (stamps prepared and issued by W. B. Perot, postmaster at Hamilton).

1010	**208** 35c. brown and black	80	35
1011	**208** 70c. blue and black	1·50	1·10
1012	**208** 85c. sepia and black	1·75	1·60
1013	**208** $1.25 silver and black	2·50	2·75

209 Deep Bay, West Pembroke

2008. Bermuda Scenes. Multicoloured. Self-adhesive.

1014	(35c.) Type **209**	75	75
1015	(70c.) Spanish Point Park	1·40	1·40
1016	(85c.) Flatts Inlet	1·60	1·75
1017	(95c.) Tucker's Town Bay	1·75	2·00

No. 1014 is inscribed 'Postage Paid Local', No. 1015 'Postage Paid Zone 1', No. 1016 'Postage Paid Zone 2' and No. 1017 'Postage Paid Zone 3'.

210 Dame Lois Browne-Evans

2008. Pioneers of Progress (3rd series). Multicoloured.

1018	35c. Type **210** (barrister and PLP leader 1968–72, 1976–85)	90	65
1019	35c. Dr. Pauulu Roosevelt Brown Kamarakafego (civil rights campaigner and rural technologist)	90	65

211 Sprinter at Start

2008. Olympic Games, Beijing. Multicoloured.

1020	10c. Type **211**	40	40
1021	35c. Swimmer diving from start	90	40
1022	70c. Horse and rider jumping	1·75	1·50
1023	85c. Yachting	1·90	2·00

212 Reindeer Lights outside Houses

2008. Christmas. Greetings. Designs showing Christmas lights. Multicoloured.

1024	30c. Type **212**	60	30
1025	35c. Lights on balcony and across street	65	35
1026	45c. Horse and carriage and street lamp lights on roof	85	40
1027	80c. Single storey house with lights around roof and verandah and in garden	1·40	1·25

213 Hamilton in 1930s and Modern Photographs

2009. 400th Anniv of Settlement of Bermuda. Each showing scene from past and modern photograph. Multicoloured.

1028	35c. Type **213**	80	35
1029	70c. St. George's in 1830s painting by Thomas Driver and modern photograph	1·60	1·10
1030	85c. Flatts Village in 1797 watercolour by Capt. George Tobin and modern photograph	2·00	1·90
1031	$1.25 17th-century map and aerial photograph of Bermuda	3·00	2·75

214 Aerial View of Cooper's Island

2009. International Year of Astronomy. 40th Anniv of First Moon Landing. Multicoloured.

1032	35c. Type **214**	85	50
1033	70c. Tracking Station, Cooper's Island	1·50	90
1034	85c. Apollo 11 Lunar Landing Module, 1969	1·90	1·10
1035	95c. STS 126, 2008	2·10	1·25
1036	$1.25 International Space Station	2·50	1·50
MS1037	100×80 mm. $1.10 Lunar Landing Module on Moon (39×59 mm)	2·25	2·25

215 Winner and Trophy

2009. Centenary of Bermuda Marathon Derby.

1038	**215** 35c. black, brown-red and brown	75	45
1039	- 70c. black, orange-yellow and brown	1·25	75
1040	- 85c. black, orange-yellow and brown	1·60	95
1041	- $1.10 black, brown-red and brown	2·40	1·50

DESIGNS: 70c. Winner with trophy (different); 85c. Runners and motorcycle; $1.10 Runners.

216 *Concordia*

2009. Tall Ships Atlantic Challenge 2009. Multicoloured.

1042	35c. Type **216**	75	45
1043	70c. *Picton Castle*	1·25	75
1044	85c. *Jolie Brise* (horiz)	1·50	90
1045	95c. *Tecla*	1·90	1·10
1046	$1.10 *Europa*	2·10	1·25
1047	$1.25 *Etoile* (horiz)	2·40	1·50

217 *Theatre Boycott, Upstairs Right, 1959* (Robert Barritt)

2009. 50th Anniv of Theatre Boycott (ended segregation in public buildings). Multicoloured.

1048	35c. Type **217**	75	45
1049	70c. *Storm in a Teacup* (Charles Lloyd Tucker) (vert)	1·25	75
1050	85c. Bronze statue of boycott leaders by Chesley Trott (vert)	1·60	95
1051	$1.25 Scene from documentary *When Voices Rise*	2·40	1·50

218 Basket with Berries and Red Bow

2009. Christmas Greetings. Tree Decorations. Multicoloured.

1052	30c. Type **218**	50	35
1053	35c. Angel	60	45
1054	70c. Circular basket with red bow	1·40	85
1055	85c. Gold bow and tassels	1·60	95

219 Guides and Leaders

2010. Centenary of Girlguiding. Multicoloured.

1056	35c. Type **219**	75	45
1057	70c. Guide camp	1·20	75
1058	85c. Parade of guides and brownies	1·60	95
1059	$1.10 Guides with carnival float carrying model galleon	75	75
MS1060	127×89 mm. $1.25 1st and 2nd Excelsior Gudies (Bermuda's first Black Unit)	2·50	2·50

220 Cobbs Hill Methodist Church

2010. African Diaspora Heritage Trail. Multicoloured.

1061	35c. Type **220**	85	55
1062	70c. The Bermudian Heritage Museum	1·40	85
1063	85c. St. Peter's Church	1·80	1·10
1064	$1.10 Barr's Bay Park	2·75	1·90

221 Lined Seahorse

2010. Endangered Species. Multicoloured.

1065	35c. Type **221**	85	55
1066	70c. Pair of seahorses	1·40	85
1067	85c. Pair hiding in seaweed	1·80	1·10
1068	$1.25 Adults and young	3·00	2·10

222 HMS *Urgent* in Floating Dock, c.1880

2010. Pioneers of Progress (4th series). Dockyard Apprentices. Multicoloured.

1069	35c. Type **222**	75	45
1070	70c. Dockyard Gate and part of dockyard clock	2·00	75
1071	85c. George Dixon (senior shipfitter) in front of power saw	1·60	95
1072	$1.10 Workmen outside chief constructor's shipfitting shop and tools	2·40	1·50

2011. Queen Elizabeth II and Prince Philip 'A Lifetime of Service'. Multicoloured.

1073	10c. Queen Elizabeth II, c. 1952	15	20
1074	35c. Queen Elizabeth II and Prince Philip (black and white photo)	80	55
1075	70c. Queen Elizabeth II (wearing red) and Prince Philip (in white uniform)	1·40	95
1076	85c. Queen Elizabeth II (wearing blue) and Prince Philip	1·50	1·10
1077	$1.10 Princess Elizabeth and Prince Philip (in uniform)	2·40	1·50
1078	$1.25 Prince Philip, c. 1952	2·75	2·00
MS1079	174×164 mm. Nos. 1073/8 and three stamp-size labels	9·00	9·00
MS1080	110×70 mm. $2.50 Queen Elizabeth II (wearing pale blue) and Prince Philip	5·25	5·25

223 Piloting Crew bringing Gig ashore and the Heathers Chart

2011. Pioneers of Progress (5th series). Piloting. Multicoloured.

1081	35c. Type **223**	85	60
1082	70c. Painting of pilot sloop *Gibbs Hill*	1·40	95
1083	85c. Pilot sloop and portrait of pilot Jacob Miners	1·50	1·10
1084	$1.10 Photographs of gig in rough seas and pilot crew at leisure	2·50	1·75

224 Bermuda Dockyard and Casemates Barracks, 1857

2011. Casemates Barracks, Bermuda Dockyard. Multicoloured.

1085	35c. Type **224**	85	60
1086	70c. Watercolour of western warehouse of Victualling Yard and construction of main Dockyard buildings, 1857	1·40	95
1087	85c. Casemates Barracks and Great Eastern Storehouse, late 1850s	1·50	1·10
1088	$1.25 Casemates Barracks complex, late 1800s	2·75	1·90

2011. Royal Wedding. Multicoloured.

MS1089	35c. Duke and Duchess of Cambridge at Westminister Abbey after Wedding ceremony (vert); 70c. Waving from State Landau; 85c. Leaving Buckingham Palace in car with 'JUST WED' numberplate; $1.25 Kissing on Buckingham Palace balcony (vert)	6·50	6·50

225 Queen Elizabeth II, c. 1955

2012. Diamond Jubilee. Multicoloured.

1090	10c. Type **225**	15	20
1091	35c. At State Opening of Parliament, c. 2005	85	55
1092	70c. Queen Elizabeth II wearing headscarf, c. 1970	1·40	95
1093	85c. Queen Elizabeth II wearing bright pink, c. 2005	1·50	1·10
1094	$1.10 Queen Elizabeth II wearing blue dress, jacket and hat, c. 1955	2·40	1·50
1095	$1.25 Queen Elizabeth II wearing pearl and diamond earrings and necklace, c. 1970	2·75	2·00
MS1096	174×164 mm. Nos. 1090/5 and three stamp-size labels	9·00	6·25
MS1097	110×70 mm. $2.50 Coronation photograph, 1953	5·50	3·75

EXPRESS LETTER STAMP

E1 Queen Elizabeth II

1996

E1	**E1**	$22 orange and blue	25·00	26·00

2003. As T **207** of Ascension.

E2	$25 black, blue and violet	29·00	30·00

Pt. 1

BHOPAL

A state of C. India. Now uses Indian stamps.

12 pies = 1 anna; 16 annas = 1 rupee.

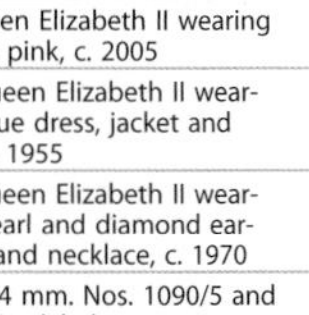

3

1876. Imperf.

5	**3**	¼a. black	8·00	21·00
2	**3**	½a. red	20·00	65·00

4

1878. Imperf or perf.

7	**4**	¼a. green	12·00	23·00
15	**4**	¼a. red	7·00	5·00
8	**4**	½a. red	7·00	22·00
9	**4**	½a. brown	38·00	60·00

1881. As T **3**, but larger. Imperf or perf.

29	¼a. black	2·25	2·75
37	½a. red	2·00	3·75
46	½a. black	2·00	1·75
30	1a. brown	2·50	4·75
31	2a. blue	2·00	3·00
32	4a. yellow	2·50	3·75

13

1884. Perf.

49	**13**	¼a. green	6·00	24·00
76	**13**	¼a. black	2·00	1·50

15

1884. Imperf or perf.

64	**15**	¼a. green	80	70
65	**15**	¼a. black	50	50
53	**15**	½a. black	1·00	3·50
56	**15**	½a. red	65	1·75

17

1890. Imperf or perf.

71	**17**	8a. greenish black	23·00	23·00

19

1902. Imperf.

90	**19**	¼a. red	1·25	6·50
91	**19**	½a. black	1·25	5·00
92	**19**	1a. brown	4·50	10·00
94	**19**	2a. blue	9·50	30·00
96	**19**	4a. yellow	20·00	65·00
97	**19**	8a. lilac	70·00	£160
98	**19**	1r. red	£110	£275

20 State Arms

1908. Perf.

100	**20**	1a. green	3·75	6·00

OFFICIAL STAMPS

1908. As T **20** but inscr "H.H. BEGUM'S SERVICE" optd **SERVICE**.

O301	½a. green	2·25	10
O302	1a. red	4·25	40
O307	2a. blue	4·00	60
O304	4a. brown	15·00	55

O4

1930. Type **O4** optd **SERVICE**.

O309	**O4**	½a. green	14·00	1·75
O310	**O4**	1a. red	15·00	15
O311	**O4**	2a. blue	9·50	45
O312	**O4**	4a. brown	14·00	90

1932. As T **20**, but inscr "POSTAGE" at left and "BHOPAL STATE" at right, optd **SERVICE**.

O313	¼a. orange	2·50	1·00

1932. As T **20**, but inscr "POSTAGE" at left and "BHOPAL GOVT" at right, optd **SERVICE**.

O314	½a. green	9·00	10
O315	1a. red	11·00	15
O316	2a. blue	15·00	45
O317	4a. brown	13·00	1·00

1935. Nos. O314, etc, surch.

O319	3p. on ½a. green	4·00	4·00
O321	3p. on 2a. blue	4·50	5·50
O325	3p. on 4a. brown	2·50	3·50
O318	¼a. on ½a. green	42·00	17·00
O320	¼a. on 2a. blue	42·00	25·00
O323	¼a. on 4a. brown	£110	35·00
O326	1a. on ½a. green	5·00	1·50
O328	1a. on 2a. blue	70	2·50
O329	1a. on 4a. brown	7·50	5·00

O8

1935

O330	**O8**	1a.3p. blue and red	3·50	1·75
O331	**O8**	1a.6p. blue and red	2·50	1·50
O332	**O8**	1a.6p. red	6·00	2·75

Nos. O331/2 are similar to Type O **8**, but inscr "BHOPAL STATE POSTAGE".

O9

1936. Type **O9** optd **SERVICE**.

O333	**O9**	¼a. yellow	90	60
O335	**O9**	1a. red	1·50	10

O10 The Moti Mahal

1936. As Type **O4** optd **SERVICE**.

O336d	**O10**	½a. purple and green	70	50
O337	-	2a. brown and blue	2·00	1·00
O338	-	2a. green and violet	16·00	30
O339	-	4a. blue and brown	3·75	50
O340	-	8a. purple and blue	5·50	2·50
O341b	-	1r. blue and purple	20·00	4·50

DESIGNS: 2a. The Moti Masjid; 4a. Taj Mahal and Be-Nazir Palaces; 8a. Ahmadabad Palace; 1r. Rait Ghat.

Nos. O336 is inscr "BHOPAL GOVT" below the arms, other values have "BHOPAL STATE".

1940. Animal designs, as Type **O10** but inscr "SERVICE" in bottom panel.

O344	¼a. blue (Tiger)	6·00	1·75
O345	1a. purple (Spotted deer)	40·00	4·00

1941. As Type **O8** but "SERVICE" inscr instead of optd.

O346	**O8**	1a.3p. green	3·00	3·00

1944. Palaces as Type **O10** but smaller.

O347	½a. green (Moti Mahal)	1·00	1·00
O348	2a. violet (Moti Masjid)	17·00	4·00
O348c	2a. purple (Moti Masjid)	4·25	3·75
O349	4a. brown (Be-Nazir)	10·00	2·25

The 2a. and 4a. are inscr "BHOPAL STATE", and the other "BHOPAL GOVT".

O14 Arms of Bhopal

1944

O350	**O14**	3p. blue	1·00	1·00
O351b	**O14**	9p. brown	2·25	5·00
O352	**O14**	1a. purple	8·00	1·75
O352b	**O14**	1a. violet	12·00	3·25
O353	**O14**	1½a. red	2·50	1·25
O354	**O14**	3a. yellow	21·00	22·00
O354d	**O14**	3a. brown	£120	£140
O355	**O14**	6a. red	26·00	65·00

1949. Surch 2 As. and bars.

O356	2a. on 1½a. red	2·50	9·50

1949. Surch 2 As. and ornaments.

O357	2a. on 1½a. red	£1700	£1700

Pt. 1

BHOR

A state of W. India, Bombay district. Now uses Indian stamps.

12 pies = 1 anna; 16 annas = 1 rupee.

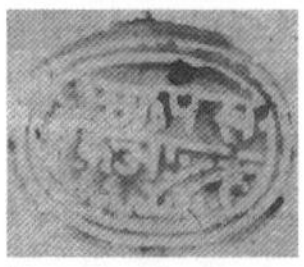

1

1879. Imperf.

1	1	½a. red	4·75	7·00

Similar to T 1, but rectangular.

2	1a. red	6·50	9·50

3 Pandit Shankar Rao

1901. Imperf.

3	3	½a. red	18·00	45·00

Pt. 21

BHUTAN

An independent territory in treaty relations with India and bounded by India, Sikkim and Tibet.

100 chetrum = 1 ngultrum.

1 Postal Runner

1962

1	1	2ch. red and grey	15	15
2	-	3ch. red and blue	25	25
3	-	5ch. brown and green	80	80
4	-	15ch. yellow, black and red	15	30
5	1	33ch. green and violet	25	25
6	-	70ch. ultramarine and blue	50	35
7	-	1n.30 black and blue	1·40	1·40

DESIGNS—HORIZ: 3, 70ch. Archer. 5ch., 1n.30, Yak. 15ch. Map of Bhutan, Maharaja Druk Gyalpo and Paro Dzong (fortress and monastery).

2 "Uprooted Tree" Emblem and Crest of Bhutan

1962. World Refugee Year.

8	2	1n. red and blue	2·75	2·75
9	2	2n. violet and green	2·50	2·50

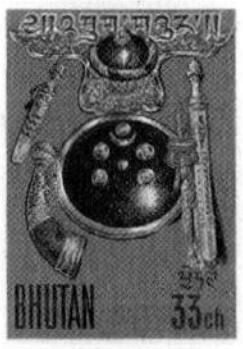

3 Accoutrements of Ancient Warrior

1962. Membership of Colombo Plan.

10	3	33ch. multicoloured	25	25
11	3	70ch. multicoloured	50	50
12	3	1n.30 red, brown & yellow	75	75

4 "Boy filling box" (with grain)

1963. Freedom from Hunger.

13	4	20ch. brown, blue & yellow	25	25
14	4	1n.50 purple, brown & blue	65	65

1964. Winter Olympic Games, Innsbruck, and Bhutanese Winter Sports Committee Fund. Nos. 10/12 surch **INNSBRUCK 1964 +50 ch**, Olympic rings and emblem.

15	3	33ch.+50ch. multicoloured	2·40	2·40
16	3	70ch.+50ch. multicoloured	2·40	2·40
17	3	1n.30+50ch. multicoloured	2·40	2·40

6 Dancer with upraised hands

1964. Bhutanese Dancers. Multicoloured.

18	2ch. Standing on one leg (vert)	10	10
19	3ch. Type **6**	10	10
20	5ch. With tambourine (vert)	10	10
21	20ch. As 2ch.	10	10
22	33ch. Type **6**	10	10
23	70ch. With sword	15	15
24	1n. With tasselled hat (vert)	35	35
25	1n.30 As 5ch.	65	65
26	2n. As 70ch.	1·10	1·10

7 Bhutanese Athlete

1964. Olympic Games, Tokyo. Multicoloured.

27	2ch. Type **7**	15	10
28	5ch. Boxing	10	10
29	15ch. Type **7**	10	10
30	33ch. As 5ch.	15	15
31	1n. Archery	35	35
32	2n. Football	70	70
33	3n. As 1n.	1·30	1·30
MS33a	85×118 mm. Nos. 31/2	10·00	10·00

8 Flags at Half-mast

1964. Pres. Kennedy Commemoration.

34	8	33ch. multicoloured	25	25
35	8	1n. multicoloured	60	60
36	8	3n. multicoloured	90	90
MS36a		82×119 mm. Nos. 35/6	3·75	3·75

9 Primula

1965. Flowers. Multicoloured.

37	2ch. Type **9**	10	10
38	5ch. Gentian	10	10
39	15ch. Type **9**	10	10
40	33ch. As 5ch.	15	15
41	50ch. Rhododendron	25	25
42	75ch. Peony	35	35
43	1n. As 50ch.	35	35
44	2n. As 75ch.	85	85

1965. Churchill Commemoration. Optd **WINSTON CHURCHILL 1874 1965**.

45	1	33ch. green and violet	35	35
46	8	1n. multicoloured	55	55
47	-	1n. multicoloured (No. 43)	50	50
48	-	2n. multicoloured (No. 44)	85	85
49	8	3n. multicoloured	1·30	1·30

11 Pavilion and Skyscrapers

1965. New York World's Fair. Multicoloured.

50	1ch. Type **11**	10	10
51	10ch. Buddha and Michelangelo's "Pieta"	10	10
52	20ch. Bhutan houses and New York skyline	10	10
53	33ch. Bhutan and New York bridges	10	10
54	1n.50 Type **11**	50	50
55	2n. As 10ch.	80	80
MS55a	120×86 mm. Nos. 54/5	3·50	5·50

1965. Surch.

56	2	5ch. on 1n. (No. 8)	28·00	28·00
57	2	5ch. on 2n. (No. 9)	28·00	28·00
58	-	10ch. on 70ch. (No. 23)	7·75	7·75
59	-	10ch. on 2n. (No. 26)	7·75	7·75
60	-	15ch. on 70ch. (No. 6)	6·50	6·50
61	-	15ch. on 1n.30 (No. 7)	6·50	6·50
62	-	20ch. on 1n. (No. 24)	9·25	9·25
63	-	20ch. on 1n.30 (No. 25)	9·25	9·25

13 "Telstar" and Portable Transmitter

1966. Centenary of I.T.U. Multicoloured.

64	35ch. Type **13**	15	15
65	2n. "Telstar" & morse key	40	40
66	3n. "Relay" and headphones	75	75
MS67	118×78 mm. Nos. 65/6	4·25	4·25

14 Asiatic Black Bear

1966. Animals. Multicoloured.

68	1ch. Type **14**	10	10
69	2ch. Snow leopard	10	10
70	4ch. Pygmy hog	10	10
71	8ch. Tiger	10	10
72	10ch. Dhole	10	10
73	75ch. As 8ch.	25	25
74	1n. Takin	40	40
75	1n.50 As 10ch.	55	55
76	2n. As 4ch.	70	70
77	3n. As 2ch.	1·00	1·00
78	4n. Type **14**	1·40	1·40
79	5n. As 1n.	2·00	2·00

15 Simtoke Dzong (fortress)

1966

80	-	5c. brown	15	10
81	15	15ch. brown	15	15
82	15	20ch. green	25	25

DESIGN: 5ch. Rinpung Dzong (fortress).

16 King Jigme Dorji Wangchuck (obverse of 50n.p. coin)

1966. 40th Anniv of King Jigme Wangchuck's Accession (father of King Jigme Dorji Wangchuck). Circular designs, embossed on gold foil, backed with multicoloured patterned paper. Imperf. Sizes: (a) Diameter 38 mm; (b) Diameter 50 mm; (c) Diameter 63 mm. (i) 50n.p. Coin.

83	16	10ch. green (a)	15	15
		(ii) 1r. Coin.		
84		25ch. green (b)	25	25
		(iii) 3r. Coin.		
85		50ch. green (c)	45	45
		(iv) 1 sertum Coin.		
86		1n. red (a)	80	80
87	-	1n.30 red (a)	1·20	1·20
		(v) 2 sertum Coin.		
88	16	2n. red (b)	1·80	1·80
89	-	3n. red (b)	2·50	2·50
		(vi) 5 sertum Coin.		
90	16	4n. red (c)	3·25	3·25
91	-	5n. red (c)	3·75	3·75

Nos. 87, 89 and 91 show the reverse side of the coins (Symbol).

17 "Abominable Snowman"

1966. "Abominable Snowman". Various triangular designs.

92	17	1ch. multicoloured	10	10
93	-	2ch. multicoloured	10	10
94	-	3ch. multicoloured	10	10
95	-	4ch. multicoloured	10	10
96	-	5ch. multicoloured	10	10
97	-	15ch. multicoloured	10	10
98	-	30ch. multicoloured	10	10
99	-	40ch. multicoloured	15	15
100	-	50ch. multicoloured	15	15
101	-	1n.25 multicoloured	30	30
102	-	2n.50 multicoloured	50	50
103	-	3n. multicoloured	60	60
104	-	5n. multicoloured	85	85
105	-	6n. multicoloured	85	85
106	-	7n. multicoloured	95	95

1967. Air. Optd **AIR MAIL** and Sikorsky S-55 helicopter.

107	6	33ch. multicoloured	10	15
108	-	50ch. mult (No. 41)	25	25
109	-	70ch. mult (No. 23)	30	30
110	-	75ch. mult (No. 42)	25	25
111	-	1n. mult (No. 24)	35	35
112	-	1n.50 mult (No. 75)	55	55
113	-	2n. mult (No. 76)	80	80
114	-	3n. mult (No. 77)	1·20	1·20
115	14	4n. multicoloured	1·80	1·80
116	-	5n. mult (No. 79)	2·30	2·30

20 "Lilium sherriffiae"

1967. Flowers. Multicoloured.

117	3ch. Type **20**	10	10
118	5ch. "Meconopsis"	10	10
119	7ch. "Rhododendron dhwoju"	10	10
120	10ch. "Pleione hookeriana"	10	10
121	50ch. Type **20**	15	15
122	1n. As 5ch.	30	30
123	2n.50 As 7ch.	75	75
124	4n. As 10ch.	1·00	1·00
125	5n. "Rhododendron giganteum"	1·30	1·30

21 Scouts planting Sapling

1967. Bhutanese Boy Scouts. Multicoloured.

126	5ch. Type **21**	10	10
127	10ch. Scouts preparing meal	10	10
128	15ch. Scout mountaineering	15	15
129	50ch. Type **21**	25	25
130	1n.25. As 10ch.	70	70
131	4n. As 15ch.	1·70	1·70
MS132	93×93 mm. Nos. 130/1	6·25	6·25

1967. World Fair, Montreal. Nos. 53/5 optd expo67 and emblem.

133	-	33ch. multicoloured	30	30

134	11	1n.50 multicoloured	40	40
135	-	2n. multicoloured	45	45
MS136		120×86 mm. Nos. 134/5	2·00	2·00

23 Avro Type **683** Lancaster

1967. Churchill and Battle of Britain Commemoration. Multicoloured.

137	45ch. Type **23**	20	20
138	2n. Supermarine Spitfire Mk IIB	45	45
139	4n. Hawker Hurricane Mk IIC	90	90
MS140	118×75 mm. Nos. 138/9	2·40	2·40

1967. World Scout Jamboree, Idaho. Nos. 126/31 optd **WORLD JAMBOREE IDAHO, U.S.A. AUG. 1-9/67.**

141	21	5ch. multicoloured	15	15
142	-	10ch. multicoloured	20	20
143	-	15ch. multicoloured	25	25
144	-	50ch. multicoloured	35	35
145	-	1n.25 multicoloured	70	75
146	-	4n. multicoloured	1·80	1·80
MS147		93×93 mm. Nos. 145/6	3·75	3·75

25 Painting

1967. Bhutan Girl Scouts. Multicoloured.

148	5ch. Type **25**	10	10
149	10ch. Playing musical instrument	10	10
150	15ch. Picking fruit	10	10
151	1n.50 Type **25**	45	45
152	2n.50 As 10ch.	1·10	1·10
153	5n. As 15ch.	2·50	2·50
MS154	93×93 mm. Nos. 152/3	5·50	5·50

26 Astronaut in Space

1967. Space Achievements. With laminated prismatic-ribbed plastic surface. Multicoloured.

155	3ch. Type **26** (postage)	25	25
156	5ch. Space vehicle and astronaut	25	25
157	7ch. Astronaut and landing vehicle	45	45
158	10ch. Three astronauts in space	50	50
159	15ch. Type **26**	75	75
160	30ch. As 5ch.	90	90
161	50ch. As 7ch.	1·30	1·30
162	1n.25 As 10ch.	2·75	2·75
163	2n.50 Type **26** (air)	1·90	1·90
164	4n. As 5ch.	2·75	2·75
165	5n. As 7ch.	3·75	3·75
166	9n. As 10ch.	6·50	6·50
MS167	Three sheets, each 130×111 mm. Nos. 155/8, 159/62 and 163/6. Imperf	29·00	29·00

The laminated plastic surface gives the stamps a three-dimensional effect.

27 Tashichho Dzong

1968

168	**27**	10ch. purple and green	20	10

28 Elephant

1968. Mythological Creatures.

169	**28**	2ch. red, blue and brown (postage)	10	10
170	-	3ch. pink, blue & green	10	10
171	-	4ch. orange, green & blue	10	10
172	-	5ch. blue, yellow & pink	10	10
173	-	15ch. green, purple & blue	10	10
174	**28**	20ch. brown, blk & orge	10	10
175	-	30ch. yellow, black & blue	15	15
176	-	50ch. bistre, green & black	15	15
177	-	1n.25 black, green & red	15	15
178	-	2n. yellow, violet & black	30	30
179	**28**	1n.50 green, purple and yellow (air)	25	25
180	-	2n.50 red, black & blue	35	35
181	-	4n. orange, green & black	60	60
182	-	5n. brown, grey & orange	80	80
183	-	10n. violet, grey & black	1·50	1·50

DESIGNS: 3, 30ch., 2n.50, Garuda; 4, 50ch., 4n. Tiger; 5ch., 1n.25, 5n. Wind horse; 15ch., 2, 10n. Snow lion.

29 Tongsa Dzong

1968

184	**29**	50ch. green	30	15
185	-	75ch. brown and blue	35	20
186	-	1n. blue and violet	40	25

DESIGNS: 75ch. Daga Dzong; 1n. Lhuntsi Dzong.

30 Ward's Trogon

1968. Rare Birds.

187	2ch. Red-faced liocichla ("Crimson-winged Laughing Thrush") (horiz) (postage)	10	10
188	3ch. Type **30**	10	10
189	4ch. Burmese ("Grey") Peacock-pheasant (horiz)	10	10
190	5ch. Rufous-necked hornbill	10	10
191	15ch. Fire-tailed 'myzornis' ("Myzornis") (horiz)	15	15
192	20ch. As No. 187	20	20
193	30ch. Type **30**	20	20
194	50ch. As No. 189	25	25
195	1n.25 As No. 190	35	35
196	2n. As No. 191	45	45
197	1n.50 As No. 187 (air)	50	50
198	2n.50 Type **30**	60	55
199	4n. As No. 189	90	90
200	5n. As No. 190	1·20	1·20
201	10n. As No. 191	1·80	1·80

31 Mahatma Gandhi

1969. Birth Centenary of Mahatma Gandhi.

202	**31**	20ch. brown and blue	15	15
203	**31**	2n. brown and yellow	75	75

1970. Various stamps surch **5 CH** or **20 CH.** (a) Freedom from Hunger (No. 14).

223	20ch. on 1n.50 purple, brown and blue	2·75	2·75

(b) Animals (Nos. 75/9).

224	20ch. on 1n.50 multicoloured	2·75	2·75
225	20ch. on 2n. multicoloured	2·75	2·75
204	20ch. on 3n. multicoloured	2·10	2·10
205	20ch. on 4n. multicoloured	2·10	2·10
206	20ch. on 5n. multicoloured	2·10	2·10

(c) Abominable Snowmen (Nos. 101/6).

226	20ch. on 1n.25 multicoloured	2·75	2·75
227	20ch. on 2n.50 multicoloured	2·75	2·75
207	20ch. on 3n. multicoloured	1·90	1·90
208	20ch. on 5n. multicoloured	2·10	2·10
209	20ch. on 6n. multicoloured	2·75	2·75
210	20ch. on 7n. multicoloured	2·75	2·75

(d) Flowers (Nos. 124/5).

211	20ch. on 4n. multicoloured	2·10	2·10
212	20ch. on 5n. multicoloured	2·50	2·50

(e) Boy Scouts (Nos. 130/1).

228	20ch. on 1n.25 multicoloured	2·75	2·75
213	20ch. on 4n. multicoloured	17·00	17·00

(f) Churchill (Nos. 138/9).

229	20ch. on 2n. multicoloured	2·75	2·75
230	20ch. on 4n. multicoloured	2·75	2·75

(g) 1968 Pheasants (Appendix).

231	20ch. on 2n. multicoloured	3·75	3·75
214	20ch. on 4n. multicoloured	2·10	2·10
232	20ch. on 7n. multicoloured	3·75	3·75

(h) Mythological Creatures (Nos. 175/80 and 182/3).

215	20ch. on 2n. yellow, violet and black	3·75	3·75
216	20ch. on 5n. brown, grey and orange	2·40	2·40
217	20ch. on 10n. violet, grey and black	2·10	2·10
233	5ch. on 30ch. yellow, black and blue (postage)	85	85
234	5ch. on 50ch. bistre, green and black	85	85
235	5ch. on 1n.25 black, green and red	85	85
236	5ch. on 2n. yellow, vio & blk	85	85
237	5ch. on 1n.50 green, purple and brown (air)	85	85
238	5ch. on 2n.50 red, black and blue	85	85

(i) Rare Birds (Nos. 193/201).

218	20ch. on 2n. multicoloured	2·75	2·75
219	20ch. on 2n.50. multicoloured	2·75	2·75
220	20ch. on 4n. multicoloured	2·10	2·10
221	20ch. on 5n. multicoloured	2·50	2·50
222	20ch. on 10n. multicoloured	3·50	3·50
239	20ch. on 30ch. mult (postage)	3·75	3·75
240	20ch. on 50ch. multicoloured	3·75	3·75
241	20ch. on 1n. 25. multicoloured	3·75	3·75
242	20ch. on 1n.50. mult (air)	3·75	3·75

(j) 1969 U.P.U. (Appendix).

243	20ch. on 1n.05. multicoloured	2·75	2·75
244	20ch. on 1n.40. multicoloured	2·75	2·75
245	20ch. on 4n. multicoloured	2·75	2·75

For stamps surcharged with 55 or 90ch. values, see Nos. 253/65 and for 25ch. surcharges see Nos. 385/410.

33 Wangdiphodrang Dzong and Bridge

1971

246	**33**	2ch. grey	25	10
247	**33**	3ch. mauve	35	15
248	**33**	4ch. violet	35	25
249	**33**	5ch. green	10	10
250	**33**	10ch. brown	15	10
251	**33**	15ch. blue	20	15
252	**33**	20ch. purple	30	15

1971. Various stamps surch **55 CH** or **90 CH.** I. Dancers (Nos. 25/6).

253	55ch. on 1n.30 multicoloured	85	85
254	90ch. on 2n. multicoloured	85	85

II. Animals (Nos. 77/8).

255	55ch. on 3n. multicoloured	85	85
256	90ch. on 4n. multicoloured	85	85

III. Boy Scouts (No. 131).

257	90ch. on 4n. multicoloured	1·60	1·60

IV. 1968 Pheasants (Appendix).

258	55ch. on 5n. multicoloured	3·00	3·00
259	90ch. on 9n. multicoloured	3·00	3·00

V. Air. Mythological Creatures (No. 181).

260	55ch. on 4n. orange, green and black	55	55

VI. 1968 Mexico Olympics (Appendix).

261	90ch. on 1n.05 multicoloured	1·40	1·40

VII. Rare Birds (No. 196).

262	90ch. on 2n. multicoloured	3·00	3·00

VIII. 1969 UPU (Appendix).

263	55ch. on 60ch. multicoloured	85	85

IX. 1970 New UPU Headquarters (Appendix).

264	90ch. on 2n.50 gold and red	2·75	2·75

X. 1971 Moon Vehicles (plastic-surfaced) (Appendix).

265	90ch. on 1n.70 multicoloured	4·00	4·00

34 Book Year Emblem

1972. International Book Year.

266	**34**	2ch. green and blue	10	10
267	**34**	3ch. brown and yellow	10	10
268	**34**	5ch. brown, orange & red	10	10
269	**34**	20ch. brown and blue	10	10

35 Dochi

1972. Dogs. Multicoloured.

270	5ch. Apsoo standing on hind legs (vert)	10	10
271	10ch. Type **35**	10	10
272	15ch. Brown and white damci	10	10
273	25ch. Black and white damci	10	10
274	55ch. Apsoo lying down	10	10
275	8n. Two damci	1·40	1·40
MS276	100×119 mm. Nos. 274/5	1·40	1·40

36 King and Royal Crest

1974. Coronation of King Jigme Singye Wangchuck. Multicoloured.

277	10ch. Type **36**	10	10
278	25ch. Bhutan Flag	15	15
279	1n.25 Good Luck signs	30	30
280	2n. Punakha Dzong	45	45
281	3n. Royal Crown	60	60
MS282	Two sheets, each 177×127 mm. (a) 5ch. As 10ch.; 5ch. As 3n.; (b) 90ch. As 1n.25; 4n. As 2n. Perf or imperf	4·75	4·75

37 Mail Delivery by Horse

1974. Centenary of UPU. Multicoloured.

283	1ch. Type **37** (postage)	10	10
284	2ch. Early and modern locomotives	10	10
285	3ch. "Hindoostan" (paddle-steamer) and "Iberia" (liner)	10	10
286	4ch. Vickers FB-27 Vimy and Concorde aircraft	10	10
287	25ch. Mail runner and four-wheel drive post car	10	10
288	1n. As 25ch. (air)	20	20
289	1n.40 As 2ch.	45	45
290	2n. As 4ch.	80	80
MS291	91×78 mm. 10n. As 4 ch	3·75	3·75

38 Family and WPY Emblem

1974. World Population Year.

292	**38**	25ch. multicoloured	10	10
293	**38**	50ch. multicoloured	10	10
294	**38**	90ch. multicoloured	25	25
295	**38**	2n.50 multicoloured	55	55
MS296		116×79 mm. **38** 10n. multi-coloured	2·10	2·10

39 Eastern Courtier

1975. Butterflies. Multicoloured.

297	1ch. Type **39**	10	10
298	2ch. Bamboo forester	10	10
299	3ch. Tailed labyrinth	10	10
300	4ch. Blue duchess	10	10
301	5ch. Cruiser	10	10
302	10ch. Bhutan glory	10	10
303	3n. Bi-coloured commodore	65	65
304	5n. Red-breasted jezebel	1·40	1·40
MS305	116×91 mm. 10n. Brown gorgon (*Dabasa gyas*)	2·75	2·75

40 King Jigme Singye Wangchuck

1976. King Jigme's 20th Birthday. Imperf. (a) Diameter 39 mm.

306	**40**	15ch. green on gold	10	10
307	**40**	1n. red on gold	25	25
308	-	1n.30 red on gold	25	25

(b) Diameter 50 mm.

309	**40**	25ch. green on gold	10	10
310	**40**	2n. red on gold	45	45
311	-	3n. red on gold	70	70

(c) Diameter 63 mm.

312	**40**	90ch. green on gold	75	75
313	**40**	4n. red on gold	1·40	1·40
314	-	5n. red on gold	1·70	1·70

DESIGN: 1n.30, 3, 5n. Decorative motif.

41 "Apollo"

1976. "Apollo"–"Soyuz" Space Link. Multicoloured.

315	10n. Type **41**	2·40	2·40
316	10n. "Soyuz"	2·40	2·40
MS317	130×89 mm. 15n. Type **41**; 15n. As No. 316	6·75	6·75

42 Jewellery

1976. Handicrafts and Craftsmen. Multicoloured.

318	1ch. Type **42**	10	10
319	2ch. Coffee-pot, hand bell and sugar dish	10	10
320	3ch. Powder horns	10	10
321	4ch. Pendants and inlaid box	10	10
322	5ch. Painter	10	10
323	15ch. Silversmith	10	10
324	20ch. Wood carver with tools	10	10
325	1n.50 Textile printer	40	40
326	10n. Printer	1·90	1·90
MS327	105×79 mm. 5n. As No. 326	1·70	1·70

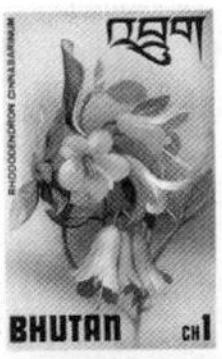

43 *Rhododendron cinnabarinum*

1976. Rhododendrons. Multicoloured.

328	1ch. Type **43**	10	10
329	2ch. *R. campanulatum*	10	10
330	3ch. *R. fortunei*	10	10
331	4ch. *R. arboreum*	10	10
332	5ch. *R. arboreum* (different)	25	10
333	1n. *R. falconeri*	20	40
334	3n. *R. hodgsonii*	55	55
335	5n. *R. keysii*	1·10	1·10
MS336	105×79 mm. 10n. *R. cinnabarinum* (different)	2·75	2·75

44 Skiing

1976. Winter Olympic Games, Innsbruck. Multicoloured.

337	1ch. Type **44**	10	10
338	2ch. Bobsleighing	10	10
339	3ch. Ice hockey	10	10
340	4ch. Cross-country skiing	10	10
341	5ch. Women's figure skating	10	10
342	2n. Downhill skiing	25	25
343	4n. Speed skating	60	55
344	10n. Pairs figure skating	1·90	1·70
MS345	78×104 mm. 6n. Ski jumping	1·60	1·60

45 Dragon Mask

1976. Ceremonial Masks. Laminated prismatic-ribbed plastic surface.

346	**45**	5ch. mult (postage)	10	10
347	-	10ch. multicoloured	10	10
348	-	15ch. multicoloured	10	10
349	-	20ch. multicoloured	10	10
350	-	25ch. multicoloured	10	10
351	-	30ch. multicoloured	10	10
352	-	35ch. multicoloured	10	10
353	-	1n. multicoloured (air)	25	25
354	-	2n. multicoloured	45	45
355	-	2n.50 multicoloured	75	75
356	-	3n. multicoloured	90	90
MS357		Two sheets, each 119×160 mm. (a) 5n. As No. 348; (b) 10n. As No. 351	4·00	4·00

DESIGNS:10ch. to 10n. Similar Bhutanese masks.

46 Orchid

1976. Flowers. Multicoloured.

358	1ch. Type **46**	10	10
359	2ch. Orchid (different)	10	10
360	3ch. Orchid (different)	10	10
361	4ch. *Primula denticulata*	10	10
362	5ch. Arum	10	10
363	2n. Orchid (different)	35	35
364	4n. *Leguminosa*	80	80
365	6n. Rhododendron	1·20	1·20
MS366	106×80 mm. 10n. Arum (*different*)	3·75	3·75

47 Double Carp Emblem

1976. 25th Anniv of Colombo Plan.

367	3ch. Type **47**	10	10
368	4ch. Vase emblem	10	10
369	5ch. Geometric design	10	10
370	25ch. Design incorporating animal's face	10	10
371	1n.25 Ornamental design	25	25
372	2n. Floral design	40	35
373	2n.50 Carousel design	50	45
374	3n. Wheel design	70	65

48 Bandaranaike Conference Hall

1976. Fifth Non-aligned Countries Summit Conference, Colombo.

375	**48**	1n.25 multicoloured	35	35
376	**48**	2n.50 multicoloured	75	65

49 Liberty Bell

1978. Anniversaries and Events. Multicoloured.

377	20n. Type **49** (bicentenary of U.S. independence)	4·00	4·00
378	20n. Alexander Graham Bell early telephone (telephone centenary)	4·00	4·00
379	20n. Archer (Olympic Games, Montreal)	4·00	4·00
380	20n. Alfred Nobel (75th anniv of Nobel Prizes)	4·00	4·00
381	20n. "Spirit of St. Louis" (50th anniv of Lindbergh's transatlantic flight)	4·00	4·00
382	20n. Airship LZ3 (75th anniv of Zeppelin)	4·50	4·50
383	20n. Queen Elizabeth II (25th anniv of Coronation)	4·00	4·00
MS384	Seven sheets, each 103×79 mm. (a) 25n. Flags of Bhutan and United States; (b) 25n. "Syncom II" communications satellite; (c) 25n. Shot putter; (d) 25n. Nobel medal; (e) 25n. "Spirit of St. Louis" landing at Le Bourget; (f) 25n. Airship "Viktoria Luise"; (g) 25n. Westminster Abbey	42·00	42·00

1978. Provisionals. Various stamps surch **25 Ch** (385, 394) or **25 CH** (others). I. Girl Scouts (No. 153).

385	25ch. on 5n. mult (postage)	12·50	10·00

II. Air. 1968 Mythological Creatures (Nos. 181 and 183).

386	25ch. on 4n. orange, green and black	2·50	2·10
387	25ch. on 10n. violet, grey and black	2·50	2·10

III. 1971 Admission to U.N. (Appendix).

388	25ch. on 3n. mult (postage)	2·10	1·70
389	25ch. on 5n. mult (air)	2·10	1·70
390	25ch. on 6n. multicoloured	2·10	1·70

IV. Boy Scouts Anniv (Appendix).

391	25ch. on 6n. multicoloured	13·00	11·00

V. 1972 Dogs (No. 275).

392	25ch. on 8n. multicoloured	3·75	3·25

VI. 1973 Dogs (Appendix).

393	25ch. on 4n. multicoloured	3·75	3·25

VII. 1973 "Indipex 73" (Appendix).

394	25ch. on 3n. mult (postage)	3·25	3·00
395	25ch. on 5n. mult (air)	3·25	3·00
396	25ch. on 6n. multicoloured	3·25	3·00

VIII. U.P.U. (Nos. 289/90).

397	25ch. on 1n. 40 multicoloured	3·00	2·50
398	25ch. on 2n. multicoloured	3·00	2·50

IX. World Population Year (No. 295).

399	25ch. on 2n.50 multicoloured	5·00	4·25

X. Butterflies (Nos. 303/4).

400	25ch. on 3n. multicoloured	5·00	4·25
401	25ch. on 5n. multicoloured	5·00	4·25

XI. "Apollo"–"Soyuz" (Nos. 315/16).

402	25ch. on 10n. mult (315)	12·50	10·00
403	25ch. on 10n. mult (316)	12·50	10·00

XII. Handicrafts (No. 326).

404	25ch. on 10n. multicoloured	2·50	2·10

XIII. Rhododendrons (No. 335).

405	25ch. on 5n. multicoloured	4·25	3·50

XIV. Winter Olympics (Nos. 343/4).

406	25ch. on 4n. multicoloured	5·75	5·00
407	25ch. on 10n. multicoloured	5·75	5·00

XV. Flowers (Nos. 364/5).

408	25ch. on 4n. multicoloured	2·10	1·80
409	25ch. on 6n. multicoloured	2·10	1·80

XVI. Colombo Plan (No. 373).

410	25ch. on 2n.50 multicoloured	2·50	2·10

50 Mother and Child

1979. International Year of the Child. Multicoloured.

411	2n. Type **50**	50	50
412	5n. Mother carrying two children	1·10	95
413	10n. Children at school	1·60	1·50
MS414	131×103 mm. Nos. 411/13	3·25	2·75

51 Conference Emblem and Dove

1979. Sixth Non-Aligned Countries Summit Conference, Havana. Multicoloured.

415	25ch. Type **51**	15	15
416	10n. Emblem and Bhutanese symbols	2·50	2·20

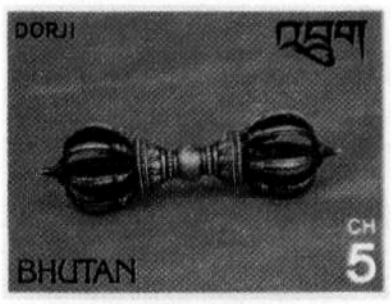

52 Dorji (rattle)

1979. Antiquities. Multicoloured.

417	5ch. Type **52**	10	10
418	10ch. Dilbu (hand bell) (vert)	10	10
419	15ch. Jadum (cylindrical pot) (vert)	10	10
420	25ch. Jamjee (teapot)	10	10
421	1n. Kem (cylindrical container) (vert)	35	30
422	1n.25 Jamjee (different)	40	40
423	1n.70 Sangphor (ornamental vessel) (vert)	60	60
424	2n. Jamjee (different) (vert)	75	70
425	3n. Yangtho (pot with lid) (vert)	95	90
426	4n. Battha (circular case)	1·20	1·20
427	5n. Chhap (ornamental flask) (vert)	1·70	1·60

53 Rinpiang Dzong, Bhutan Stamp and Rowland Hill Statue

1980. Death Cent of Sir Rowland Hill. Multicoloured.

428	1n. Type **53**	45	40
429	2n. Dzong, Bhutan stamp and statue	80	75
430	5n. Ounsti Dzong, Bhutan stamp and statue	1·30	1·20
431	10n. Lingzi Dzong and British 1912 1d. stamp	2·75	2·50
MS432	102×103 mm. 20n. Rope bridge, British 1d. black stamp and statue	9·50	9·50

54 Dungtse Lhakhang, Paro

1981. Monasteries. Multicoloured.

433	1n. Type **54**	20	15
434	2n. Kich Lhakhang, Paro (horiz)	40	35
435	2n.25 Kurjey Lhakhang (horiz)	55	50
436	3n. Tangu, Thimphu (horiz)	70	65
437	4n. Cheri, Thimphu (horiz)	95	85
438	5n. Chorten, Kora (horiz)	1·50	1·30
439	7n. Tak-Tsang, Paro	2·10	1·90

55 St. Paul's Cathedral

1981. Wedding of Prince of Wales. Multicoloured.

440	1n. Type **55**	10	10
441	5n. Type **55**	90	75
442	20n. Prince Charles and Lady Diana Spencer	3·25	2·75
443	25n. As No. 442	4·00	3·75
MS444	69×90 mm. 20n. Wedding procession	4·00	3·50

56 Orange-bellied Leafbird ("Orange-billed Chiropsis")

1982. Birds. Multicoloured.

445	2n. Type **56**	70	65
446	3n. Himalayan monal pheasant ("Monal Pheasant")	1·00	95
447	5n. Ward's trogon	2·00	1·80
448	10n. Mrs. Gould's sunbird	3·25	3·00
MS449	95×101 mm. 25n. Maroon oriole (*Oriolus trailii*)	6·75	6·00

57 Footballers

1982. World Cup Football Championship, Spain.

450	**57**	1n. multicoloured	20	15
451	-	2n. multicoloured	45	40
452	-	3n. multicoloured	65	60
453	-	20n. multicoloured	3·75	3·25
MS454		79×108 mm. 25n. multicoloured (horiz)	6·75	5·25

DESIGNS: 2n. to 25n. Various football scenes.

No. **MS**454 exists in two versions, differing in the list of qualifying countries in the border.

58 St. James's Palace

1982. 21st Birthday of Princess of Wales. Multicoloured.

455	1n. Type **58**	40	35
456	10n. Prince and Princess of Wales	2·20	2·00
457	15n. Windsor Castle	3·75	4·00
458	25n. Princess in wedding dress	5·75	5·25
MS459	102×76 mm. 20n. Princess of Wales	5·00	4·50

59 Lord Baden-Powell (founder)

1982. 75th Anniv of Boy Scout Movement. Multicoloured.

460	3n. Type **59**	55	50
461	5n. Scouts around campfire	1·10	95
462	15n. Map reading	2·75	2·50
463	20n. Pitching tents	4·00	3·75
MS464	91×70 mm. 25n. Scout	5·25	4·75

60 Rama finds Mowgli

1982. *The Jungle Book* (cartoon film). Multicoloured.

465	1ch. Type **60**	10	10
466	2ch. Bagheera leading Mowgli to Man-village	10	10
467	3ch. Kaa planning attack on Bagheera and Mowgli	10	10
468	4ch. Mowgli and elephants	10	10
469	5ch. Mowgli and Baloo	10	10
470	10ch. Mowgli and King Louie	10	10
471	30ch. Kaa and Shere Khan	10	10
472	2n. Mowgli, Baloo and Bagheera	45	35
473	20n. Mowgli carrying jug for girl	4·00	3·50
MS474	Two sheets, each 127×102 mm. (a) 20n. Mowgli and Baloo; (b) 20n. Mowgli and Baloo floating down river	8·75	7·75

1982. Birth of Prince William of Wales. Nos. 455/MS459 optd **ROYAL BABY 21.6.82.**

475	1n. multicoloured	40	40
476	10n. multicoloured	1·40	1·20
477	15n. multicoloured	2·75	2·50
478	25n. multicoloured	4·50	4·00
MS479	102×76 mm. 20n. multicoloured	5·00	4·75

62 Washington surveying

1982. 250th Birth Anniv of George Washington and Birth Centenary of Franklin D. Roosevelt. Multicoloured.

480	50ch. Type **62**	10	10
481	1n. Roosevelt and Harvard University	10	10
482	2n. Washington at Valley Forge	30	30
483	3n. Roosevelt's mother and family	45	40
484	4n. Washington at Battle of Monmouth	55	50
485	5n. Roosevelt and the White House	80	75
486	15n. Washington and Mount Vernon	2·40	2·20
487	20n. Churchill, Roosevelt and Stalin at Yalta	3·25	3·00
MS488	Two sheets, each 102×73 mm. (a) 25n. Washington (vert); (b) 25n. Roosevelt (vert)	8·00	7·25

1983. "Druk Air" Bhutan Air Service. Various stamps optd **DRUK AIR** (491) or **Druk Air** (others), No. 489 surch also.

489	**42**	30ch. on 1n. multicoloured (postage)	1·30	1·30
490	-	5n. multicoloured (Scouts, Appendix)	2·40	2·10
491	-	8n. mult (No. 275)	2·50	2·20
492	-	5n. mult ("Indipex 73", Appendix) (air)	3·75	3·50
493	-	7n. mult (Munich Olympics, Appendix)	3·75	3·50

64 *Angelo Doni*

1983. 500th Birth Anniv of Raphael (artist). Multicoloured.

494	1n. Type **64**	15	10
495	4n. *Maddalena Doni*	70	60
496	5n. *Baldassare Castiglione*	1·00	85
497	20n. *Woman with Veil*	4·00	3·50
MS498	Two sheets, each 127×101 mm. (a) 25n. Self-portrait (detail from *Mass of Bolsena*); (b) 25n. Self-portrait (detail from *Expulsion of Heliodorus*)	10·50	9·75

65 Ta-Gyad-Boom-Zu (the eight luck-bringing symbols)

1983. Religious Offerings. Multicoloured.

499	25ch. Type **65**	10	10
500	50ch. Doeyun Nga (the five sensory symbols)	15	15
501	2n. Norbu Chadun (the seven treasures) (47×41 mm)	35	35
502	3n. Wangpo Nga (the five sensory organs)	60	55
503	8n. Sha Nga (the five kinds of flesh)	1·30	1·10
504	9n. Men-Ra-Tor Sum (the sacrificial cake) (47×41 mm)	1·60	1·60
MS505	180×135 mm. Nos. 499/504	4·50	4·25

66 Dornier Wal Flying Boat *Boreas*

1983. Bicentenary of Manned Flight. Multicoloured.

506	50ch. Type **66**	10	10
507	3n. Savoia-Marchetti S.66 flying boat	60	55
508	10n. Hawker Osprey biplane	2·00	1·90
509	20n. Astra airship *Ville de Paris*	4·00	3·75
MS510	106×80 mm. 25n. Henri Giffard's balloon *Le Grand Ballon Captif*	5·00	4·50

67 Mickey Mouse as Caveman

1984. World Communications Year. Multicoloured.

511	4ch. Type **67**	10	10
512	5ch. Goofy as printer	10	10
513	10ch. Chip 'n' Dale with morse key	10	10
514	20ch. Pluto talks to girlfriend on telephone	10	10
515	25ch. Minnie Mouse pulling record from bulldog	10	10
516	50ch. Morty and Ferdie with microphone and loudhailers	10	10
517	1n. Huey, Dewey, and Louie listening to radio	30	30
518	5n. Donald Duck watching television on buffalo	1·10	1·10
519	20n. Daisy Duck with computers and abacus	4·25	4·00
MS520	Two sheets, each 127×102 mm. (a) 20n. Mickey Mouse on television (horiz); (b) 20n. Donald Duck and satellite (horiz)	8·75	8·25

68 Golden Langur

1984. Endangered Species. Multicoloured.

521	50ch. Type **68**	20	20
522	1n. Golden langur family in tree (horiz)	30	30
523	2n. Male and female Golden langurs with young (horiz)	70	70
524	4n. Group of langurs	1·40	1·30
MS525	Three sheets. (a) 88×121 mm. 20n. Snow leopard (horiz); (b) 121×88 mm. 25n. Yak; (c) 121×88 mm. 25n. Bharal (horiz)	14·50	12·00

69 Downhill Skiing

1984. Winter Olympic Games, Sarajevo. Multicoloured.

526	50ch. Type **69**	10	10
527	1n. Cross-country skiing	20	15
528	3n. Speed skating	70	65
529	20n. Four-man bobsleigh	3·50	3·25
MS530	108×76 mm. 25n. Ice hockey	4·75	4·00

70 *Sans Pareil*, 1829

1984. Railway Locomotives. Multicoloured.

531	50ch. Type **70**	10	10
532	1n. *Planet*, 1830	15	15
533	3n. *Experiment* 1832	65	60
534	4n. *Black Hawk*, 1835	85	80
535	5n.50 *Jenny Lind*, 1847 (horiz)	1·10	1·10
536	8n. *Bavaria*, 1851 (horiz)	1·60	1·50
537	10n. Great Northern locomotive No. 1, 1870 (horiz)	2·10	1·90
538	25n. Steam locomotive Type 110, Prussia, 1880 (horiz)	5·00	4·50
MS539	Four sheets, each 92×65 mm. (a) 20n. Crampton's locomotive, 1846 (horiz); (b) 20n. *Erzsebet*, 1870 (horiz); (c) 20n. Sondermann freight, 1896 (horiz); (d) 20n. Darjeeling–Himalaya railway (horiz)	16·00	14·50

71 Riley Sprite Sports Car, 1936

1984. Cars. Multicoloured.

540	50ch. Type **71**	10	10
541	1n. Lanchester Forty saloon, 1919	15	15
542	3n. Itala 35/45 racer, 1907	55	50
543	4n. Morris Oxford (Bullnose) tourer, 1913	80	70
544	5n.50 Lagonda LG6 drophead coupe, 1939	1·10	95
545	6n. Wolseley four seat tonneau, 1903	1·30	1·10
546	8n. Buick Super convertible, 1952	1·50	1·40
547	20n. Maybach Zeppelin limousine, 1933	4·00	3·50
MS548	Two sheets, each 126×99 mm. (a) 25n. Renault (1901); (b) 25n. Simplex (1912)	8·00	7·25

72 Women's Archery

1984. Olympic Games, Los Angeles. Multicoloured.

549	15ch. Type **72**	10	10
550	25ch. Men's archery	15	10
551	2n. Table tennis	40	35
552	2n.25 Basketball	50	45
553	5n.50 Boxing	1·00	95
554	6n. Running	1·20	1·10
555	8n. Tennis	1·70	1·60
MS556	115×82 mm. 25n. Couple practising archery (72×43 mm)	4·50	4·00

73 Domkhar Dzong

1984. Monasteries.

557	**73**	10ch. blue	10	10
558	-	25ch. red	10	10
559	-	50ch. violet	10	10
560	-	1n. brown	20	20
561	-	2n. red	35	35
562	-	5n. green	85	85

DESIGNS: 25ch. Shemgang Dzong; 50ch. Chapcha Dzong; 1n. Tashigang Dzong; 2n. Pungthang Dzong; 5n. Dechhenphoda Dzong.

74 "Magician Mickey"

1984. 50th Anniv of Donald Duck. Scenes from films. Multicoloured.

563	4ch. Type **74**	10	10
564	5ch. "Slide, Donald, Slide"	10	10
565	10ch. "Donald's Golf Game"	10	10
566	20ch. "Mr. Duck Steps Out"	10	10
567	25ch. "Lion Around"	10	10
568	50ch. "Alpine Climbers"	10	10
569	1n. "Flying Jalopy"	10	10
570	5n. "Frank Duck brings 'Em Back Alive"	55	45
571	20n. "Good Scouts"	2·20	1·80
MS572	Two sheets, each 128×101 mm. (a) 20n. "Sea Scouts"; (b) 20n. "The Three Caballeros"	9·00	8·25

1984. Various stamps surch. (a) World Cup Football Championship, Spain (Nos. 450/3).

573	5n. on 1n. multicoloured	1·60	1·40
574	5n. on 2n. multicoloured	1·60	1·40
575	5n. on 3n. multicoloured	1·60	1·40
576	5n. on 20n. multicoloured	1·60	1·40
MS577	79×108 mm. 20n. on 25n. multicoloured	6·25	6·25

No. **MS**577 exists in two versions, differing in the list of qualifying countries in the border.

(b) 21st Birthday of Princess of Wales (Nos. 455/8).

578	5n. on 1n. multicoloured	1·40	1·30
579	5n. on 10n. multicoloured	1·40	1·30
580	5n. on 15n. multicoloured	1·40	1·30
581	40n. on 25n. multicoloured	11·00	10·00
MS582	102×76 mm. 25n. on 20n. multicoloured	7·50	7·50

(c) Birth of Prince William of Wales (Nos. 475/8).

583	5n. on 1n. multicoloured	1·30	1·30
584	5n. on 10n. multicoloured	1·30	1·30
585	5n. on 15n. multicoloured	1·30	1·30
586	40n. on 25n. multicoloured	11·00	10·50
MS587	102×76 mm. 25n. on 20n. multicoloured	10·00	10·00

(d) Wedding of Prince of Wales (Nos. 440/3).

588	10n. on 1n. multicoloured	2·40	2·20
589	10n. on 5n. multicoloured	2·40	2·20
590	10n. on 20n. multicoloured	2·40	2·20
591	10n. on 25n. multicoloured	2·40	2·20
MS592	69×90 mm. 30n. on 20n. multicoloured	10·00	10·00

On Nos. 588/**MS**592 the new value is surcharged twice.

(e) 75th Anniv of Boy Scout Movement (Nos. 460/3).

593	10n. on 3n. multicoloured	2·40	2·20
594	10n. on 5n. multicoloured	2·40	2·20
595	10n. on 15n. multicoloured	2·40	2·20
596	10n. on 20n. multicoloured	2·40	2·20
MS597	91×70 mm. 20n. on 25n. multicoloured	10·00	10·00

76 Shinje Choegyel

1985. The Judgement of Death Mask Dance. Multicoloured.

598	5ch. Type **76**	10	10
599	35ch. Raksh Lango	10	10
600	50ch. Druelgo	10	10
601	2n.50 Pago	40	35
602	3n. Telgo	55	50
603	4n. Due Nakcung	75	70
604	5n. Lha Karpo	90	85
605	5n.50 Nyalbum	1·00	95
606	6n. Khimda Pelkyi	1·10	1·10

MS607	90×135 mm. Nos. 598/9 and 603/4	2·30	2·20

77 Bhutan and UN Flags

1985. 40th Anniv of UNO.

608	**77**	50ch. multicoloured	20	20
609	-	15n. multicoloured	2·00	1·70
610	-	20n. black and blue	3·00	2·50
MS611		65×80 mm. 25n. black, yellow and scarlet	3·75	3·25

DESIGNS—VERT: 15n. UN building, New York; 25n. 1945 charter; HORIZ: 20n. Veterans' War Memorial Building San Francisco (venue of signing charter, 1945).

78 Mickey Mouse tramping through Black Forest

1985. 150th Birth Anniv of Mark Twain (writer) and International Youth Year. Multicoloured.

612	50ch. Type **78**	10	10
613	2n. Mickey Mouse, Donald Duck and Goofy on steam-boat trip on Lake Lucerne	35	30
614	5n. Mickey Mouse, Donald Duck and Goofy climbing Rigi-Kulm	85	75
615	9n. Mickey Mouse and Goofy rafting to Heidelberg on River Neckar	1·60	1·40
616	20n. Mickey Mouse leading Donald Duck on horse back up the Riffelberg	3·50	3·25
MS617	126×101 mm. 25n. Mickey Mouse and Goofy	4·75	4·25

Nos. 612/**MS**617 show scenes from "A Tramp Abroad" (cartoon film of Twain novel).

79 Prince sees Rapunzel

1985. Birth Bicentenaries (1985 and 1986) of Grimm Brothers (folklorists). Multicoloured.

618	1n. Type **79**	10	10
619	4n. Rapunzel (Minnie Mouse) in tower	50	45
620	7n. Mother Gothel calling to Rapunzel to let down her hair	1·10	95
621	8n. Prince climbing tower using Rapunzel's hair	1·40	1·30
622	15n. Prince proposing to Rapunzel	2·40	2·10
MS623	126×101 mm. 25n. Prince riding away with Rapunzel	5·00	4·75

80 *Brewers Duck* (mallard)

1985. Birth Bicentenary of John J. Audubon (ornithologist). Audubon illustrations. Multicoloured.

624	50ch. Type **80**	10	10
625	1n. "Willow Ptarmigan" (Willow/red Grouse)	15	15
626	2n. "Mountain Plover"	35	30
627	3n. "Red-throated Loon" (Red-throated Diver)	50	50
628	4n. "Spruce Grouse"	80	70
629	5n. "Hooded Merganser"	95	90
630	15n. "Trumpeter Swan" (Whooper Swan)	2·75	2·50
631	20n. Common goldeneye	3·75	3·25
MS632	75×105 mm. 25n. "Sharp-shinned Hawk"	4·50	4·00
MS633	75×105 mm. 25n."Tufted Titmouse"	4·50	4·00

81 Members' Flags around Buddhist Design

1985. South Asian Regional Co-operation Summit, Dhaka, Bangladesh.

634	**81**	50ch. multicoloured	15	15
635	**81**	5n. multicoloured	95	85

82 Precious Wheel

1986. The Precious Symbols. Multicoloured.

636	30ch. Type **82**	10	10
637	50ch. Precious Gem	10	10
638	1n.25 Precious Queen	15	15
639	2n. Precious Minister	30	30
640	4n. Precious Elephant	55	55
641	6n. Precious Horse	80	80
642	8n. Precious General	1·10	1·10

1986. Olympic Games Gold Medal Winners. Nos. 549/50 and 552/5 optd.

643	**72**	15ch. **GOLD HYANG SOON SEO SOUTH KOREA**	10	10
644	-	25ch. **GOLD DARRELL PACE USA**	10	10
645	-	2n.25 **GOLD MEDAL USA**	35	35
646	-	5n.50 **GOLD MARK BRELAND USA**	70	70
647	-	6n. **GOLD DALEY THOMPSON ENGLAND**	80	80
648	-	8n. **GOLD STEFAN EDBERG SWEDEN**	1·10	1·10
MS649		Two sheets, each 115×82 mm. (a) 25n. **HYANG SOON SEO, SOUTH KOREA**; (b) 25n. **DARRELL PACE, U.S.A.**	7·50	6·25

1986. "Ameripex 86" International Stamp Exhibition, Chicago. Various stamps optd **AMERIPEX 86.** (a) Nos. 615/**MS**617.

650	8n. multicoloured	2·20	1·80
651	20n. multicoloured	3·25	3·00
MS652	126×101 mm. 25n. multicoloured	4·00	3·50

(b) Nos. 621/**MS**623.

653	8n. multicoloured	1·40	1·20
654	15n. multicoloured	1·90	1·70
MS655	126×101 mm. 25n. multicoloured	4·00	3·50

85 Mandala of Phurpa (Ritual Dagger)

1986. Kilkhor Mandalas of Mahayana Buddhism. Multicoloured.

656	10ch. Type **85**	10	10
657	25ch. Mandala of Amitayus in Wrathful Form	10	10
658	50ch. Mandala of Overpowering Deities	10	10
659	75ch. Mandala of the Great Wrathful One	10	10
660	1n. Type **85**	15	15
661	3n. As 25ch.	45	45
662	5n. As 50ch.	65	65
663	7n. As 75ch.	85	85

1986. 75th Anniv of Girl Guides. Nos. 460/3 optd **75th ANNIVERSARY GIRL GUIDES.**

664	3n. multicoloured	40	40
665	5n. multicoloured	1·00	1·00
666	15n. multicoloured	3·00	3·00
667	20n. multicoloured	4·00	4·00
MS668	91×70 mm. 25n. multicoloured	5·50	5·50

87 Babylonian Tablet and Comet over Noah's Ark

1986. Appearance of Halley's Comet. Multicoloured.

669	50ch. Type **87**	10	10
670	1n. 17th-century print	10	10
671	2n. 1835 French silhouette	25	25
672	3n. Bayeux tapestry	40	35
673	4n. Woodblock from *Nuremburg Chronicle*	60	50
674	5n. Illustration of Revelation 6, 12–13 from 1650 Bible	80	75
675	15n. Comet in constellation of Cancer	2·30	2·10
676	20n. Decoration on Delft plate	3·25	2·75
MS677	Two sheets, each 109×79 mm. (a) 25n. Comet over dzong in Himalayas; (b) 25n. Comet over shrine	8·00	7·25

88 Statue and *Libertad* (Argentine full-rigged cadet ship)

1986. Centenary of Statue of Liberty. Multicoloured.

678	50ch. Type **88**	10	10
679	1n. "Shalom" (Israeli liner)	10	10
680	2n. "Leonardo da Vinci" (Italian liner)	25	25
681	3n. "Mircea" (Rumanian cadet barque)	40	35
682	4n. "France" (French liner)	55	50
683	5n. S.S. *United States* (American liner)	80	75
684	15n. "Queen Elizabeth 2" (British liner)	2·30	2·10
685	20n. "Europa" (West German liner)	3·25	2·75
MS686	Two sheets, each 114×83 mm. (a) Statue (27×41 mm); (b) Statue and tower blocks (27×41 mm)	7·50	6·75

The descriptions of the ships on Nos. 678 and 681 were transposed in error.

89 "Santa Maria"

1987. 500th Anniv (1992) of Discovery of America by Columbus. Multicoloured.

687	20ch. Type **89**	25	30
688	25ch. Queen Isabella of Spain	25	25
689	50ch. Flying fish	25	25
690	1n. Columbus's coat of arms	50	40
691	2n. Christopher Columbus	85	70
692	3n. Columbus landing with Spanish soldiers	1·10	1·10
MS693	Seven sheets, each 97×65 mm. (a) 20ch. Pineapple; (b) 25ch. Indian hammock (horiz); (c) 50ch. Tobacco plant; (d) 1n. Greater flamingo; (e) 2n. Astrolabe; (f) 3n. Lizard (horiz); (g) 5n. Iguana (horiz)	11·50	11·50
MS694	170×144 mm. As Nos. 687/92 but with white backgrounds	23·00	23·00

90 Canadian National Class "U1-f" Steam Locomotive No. 6060

1987. "Capex '87" International Stamp Exhibition, Toronto. Canadian Railways. Multicoloured.

695	50ch. Type **90**	10	10
696	1n. Via Rail "L.R.C." electric locomotive No. 6903	10	10
697	2n. Canadian National GM "GF30t" diesel locomotive No. 5341	35	30
698	3n. Canadian National steam locomotive No. 6157	45	40
699	8n. Canadian Pacific steam locomotive No. 2727	1·30	1·20
700	10n. Via Express diesel locomotive No. 6524	1·60	1·40

701	15n. Canadian National "Turbotrain"	2·40	2·10
702	20n. Canadian Pacific diesel-electric locomotive No. 1414	3·00	2·75
MS703	Two sheets, each 102×75 mm. (a) 25n. Cab and tender of Royal Hudson steam locomotive (27×41 mm); (b) 25n. Canadian National steam locomotive (27×41 mm)	7·50	6·75

91 *Two Faces* (sculpture)

1987. Birth Centenary of Marc Chagall (artist). Multicoloured.

704	50ch. Type **91**	15	15
705	1n. *At the Barber's*	25	25
706	2n. Old Jew with Torai	40	40
707	3n. *Red Maternity*	65	65
708	4n. *Eve of Yom Kippur*	1·00	1·00
709	5n. *The Old Musician*	1·20	1·20
710	6n. *The Rabbi of Vitebsk*	1·30	1·30
711	7n. *Couple at Dusk*	1·50	1·50
712	9n. *The Artistes*	1·80	1·80
713	10n. *Moses breaking the Tablets*	2·00	2·00
714	12n. *Bouquet with Flying Lovers*	2·30	2·30
715	20n. *In the Sky of the Opera*	4·00	4·00
MS716	12 sheets, each 95×110 mm (e) or 110×95 mm (others). Imperf. (a) 25n. *The Red Gateway*. (b) 25n. *Romeo and Juliet*. (c) 25n. *Maternity*. (d) 25n. *The Carnival for Aleko, Scene II*. (e) 25n. *Magician of Paris*. (f) 25n. *Visit to the Grandparents*. (g) 25n. *Cow with Parasol*. (h) 25n. *Russian Village*. (i) 25n. *Still Life*. (j) 25n. *Composition with Goat*. (k) 25n. *The Smolensk Newspaper*. (l) 25n. *The Concert*	47·00	47·00

92 Goofy (slalom)

1988. Winter Olympic Games, Calgary. Multicoloured.

717	50ch. Type **92**	10	10
718	1n. Donald Duck pushing Goofy at start (downhill skiing)	15	15
719	2n. Goofy in goal (ice hockey)	25	25
720	4n. Goofy (biathlon)	55	50
721	7n. Goofy and Donald Duck (speed skating)	1·10	95
722	8n. Minnie Mouse (figure skating)	1·30	1·20
723	9n. Minnie Mouse (free-style skating)	1·50	1·30
724	20n. Goofy and Mickey Mouse (two-man bobsleigh)	3·00	2·75
MS725	Two sheets, each 127×101 mm. (a) 25n. Goofy (ski jumping); (b) 25n. Donald and Daisy Duck (ice skating)	7·00	7·00

93 Stephenson's Railway Locomotive *Rocket*, 1829

1988. Transport. Multicoloured.

726	50ch. Pullman "Pioneer" sleeper, 1985	10	10
727	1n. Type **93**	15	15
728	2n. Pierre Lallement's *Velocipede*, 1866	25	25
729	3n. Benz *Patent Motor Wagon*, 1866	45	35
730	4n. Volkswagen Beetle	55	50
731	5n. Mississippi paddle-steamers *Natchez* and *Robert E. Lee*, 1870	65	60
732	6n. American La France motor fire engine, 1910	80	75
733	7n. Frigate U.S.S. *Constitution*, 1797 (vert)	95	85
734	9n. Bell rocket belt, 1961 (vert)	1·20	1·10
735	10n. Trevithick's railway locomotive, 1804	1·30	1·20
MS736	Four sheets, each 118×89 mm. (a) 25n. Steam locomotive *Mallar"* (27×41 mm); (b) 25n. French "TGV" express train (41×27 mm); (c) 25n. Japanese Shinkansen *Tokaido* bullet train (41×27 mm); (d) 25n. Concorde supersonic airplane (41×27 mm)	17·00	17·00

No. 731 is wrongly inscribed "Natches" and No. 733 is wrongly dated "1787".

94 Dam and Pylon

1988. Chhukha Hydro-electric Project.

737	**94** 50ch. multicoloured	30	30

1988. World Aids Day. Nos. 411/13 optd **WORLD AIDS DAY**.

738	**50** 2n. multicoloured	40	35
739	- 5n. multicoloured	1·00	90
740	- 10n. multicoloured	2·10	1·90

96 *Diana and Actaeon* (detail)

1989. 500th Birth Anniv of Titian (painter). Multicoloured.

741	50ch. *Gentleman with a Book*	10	10
742	1n. *Venus and Cupid, with a Lute Player* (detail)	15	15
743	2n. Type **96**	30	30
744	3n. *Cardinal Ippolito dei Medici*	50	45
745	4n. *Sleeping Venus* (detail)	75	70
746	5n. *Venus risen from the Waves* (detail)	90	85
747	6n. *Worship of Venus* (detail)	1·20	1·10
748	7n. *Fete Champetre* (detail)	1·40	1·30
749	10n. *Perseus and Andromeda* (detail)	1·80	1·70
750	15n. *Danae* (detail)	2·75	2·50
751	20n. *Venus at the Mirror*	3·75	3·50
752	25n. *Venus and the Organ Player* (detail)	4·50	4·25
MS753	12 sheets, each 109×94 (a/d) or 94×109 mm (others). (a) 25n. *Bacchus and Ariadne*; (b) 25n. *Danae with the Shower of Gold* (horiz); (c) 25n. *The Pardo Venus* (horiz); (d) 25n. *Venus and Cupid with an Organist*; (e) 25n. *Diana and Callisto*; (f) 25n. *Mater Dolorosa with Raised Hands*; (g) 25n. *Miracle of the Irascible Son*; (h) 25n. *Portrait of Johann Friedrich*; (i) 25n. *Portrait of Laura Dianti*; (j) 25n. *St. John the Almsgiver*; (k) 25n. *Venus blindfolding Cupid*; (l) 25n. *Venus of Urbino*	47·00	47·00

97 Volleyball

1989. Olympic Games, Seoul (1988). Multicoloured.

754	50ch. Gymnastics	10	10
755	1n. Judo	10	10
756	2n. Putting the shot	25	25
757	4n. Type **97**	55	50
758	7n. Basketball (vert)	95	85
759	8n. Football (vert)	1·10	95
760	9n. High jumping (vert)	1·30	1·10
761	20n. Running (vert)	2·75	2·50
MS762	Two sheets. (a) 109×79 mm. 25n. Fencing. (b) 79×109 mm. 25n. Archery (vert)	7·00	7·00

1989. "Fukuoka '89" Asia-Pacific Exhibition. Nos. 598/606 optd **ASIA-PACIFIC EXPOSITION FUKUOKA '89**.

763	5ch. multicoloured	10	10
764	35ch. multicoloured	10	10
765	50ch. multicoloured	10	10
766	2n.50 multicoloured	25	25
767	3n. multicoloured	40	35
768	4n. multicoloured	50	45
769	5n. multicoloured	60	55
770	5n.50 multicoloured	75	65
771	6n. multicoloured	85	80

99 Mickey Mouse

1989. 60th Anniv of Mickey Mouse. Film Posters. Multicoloured.

772	1ch. Type **99**	15	15
773	2ch. "Barnyard Olympics"	15	15
774	3ch. "Society Dog Show"	15	15
775	4ch. "Fantasia"	15	15
776	5ch. "The Mad Dog"	15	15
777	10ch. "A Gentleman's Gentleman"	15	15
778	50ch. "Symphony hour"	15	15
779	10n. "The Moose Hunt"	1·50	1·50
780	15n. "Wild Waves"	2·30	2·30
781	20n. "Mickey in Arabia"	3·25	3·25
782	25n. "Tugboat Mickey"	3·75	3·75
783	30n. "Building a Building"	4·75	4·75
MS784	12 sheets, each 127×101 mm. (a) 25n. *The Klondike Kid*; (b) 25n. "The Mad Doctoe" (c) 25n. "The Meller Drammer"; (d) 25n. "Mickey's Good Deed"; (e) 25n. "Mickey's Nightmare"; (f) 25n. "Mickey's Pal Pluto"; (g) 25n. "Steamboat Willie"; (h) 25n. "Touchdown Mickey"; (i) 25n. "Trader Mickey"; (j) 25n. "The Wayward Canary"; (k) 25n. "The Whoopee Party"; (l) 25n. "Ye Olden Days"	42·00	42·00

100 *Tricholoma pardalotum*

1989. Fungi. Multicoloured.

785	50ch. Type **100**	10	10
786	1n. *Suillus placidus*	10	10
787	2n. Royal boletus	25	25
788	3n. *Gomphidius glutinosus*	45	35
789	4n. Scarlet-stemmed boletus	55	50
790	5n. Elegant boletus	70	65
791	6n. *Boletus appendiculatus*	85	80
792	7n. Griping toadstool	1·10	95
793	10n. *Macrolepiota rhacodes*	1·40	1·30
794	15n. The blusher	2·10	1·90
795	20n. Death cap	2·75	2·50
796	25n. False death cap	3·50	3·25
MS797	12 sheets, each 97×68 mm. (a) 25n. *Boletus rhodoxanthus*; (b) 25n. Chanterelle *Chanterelle repdandum*; (c) 25n. *Dentinum repandum*; (d) 25n. Chestnut boletus (*Gyroporus castaneus*); (e) 25n. Indigo boletus (*Gyroporus cyanescens*); (f) 25n. *Hydnum imbricatum*; (g) 25n. Blue leg (*Lepista nuda*); (h) 25n. *Lepista saeva*; (i) 25n. Brown roll-rim (*Paxillus involutus*); (j) 25n. Golden russula (*Russula aurata*); (k) 25n. *Russula olivacea*; (l) 25n. Downy boletus (*Xerocomus subtomentosus*)	42·00	42·00

101 *La Reale* (Spanish galley), 1680

1989. 30th Anniv of International Maritime Organization. Multicoloured.

798	50ch. Type **101**	10	10
799	1n. *Turtle* (submarine), 1776	15	15
800	2n. *Charlotte Dundas* (steamship), 1802	30	30
801	3n. *Great Eastern* (paddle-steamer), 1858	50	45
802	4n. H.M.S. *Warrior* (armoured ship), 1862	65	60
803	5n. Mississippi river steamer, 1884	85	75
804	6n. *Preussen* (full-rigged ship), 1902	1·00	90
805	7n. U.S.S. *Arizona* (battleship), 1915	1·20	1·10
806	10n. *Bluenose* (fishing schooner), 1921	1·60	1·50
807	15n. Steam trawler, 1925	2·50	2·20
808	20n. *Liberty* freighter, 1943	3·25	3·00
809	25n. *United States* (liner), 1952	4·00	3·50
MS810	12 sheets, each 100×70 mm. (a) 25n. Chinese junk, 1988; (b) 25n. *U.S.S. Constitution* (frigate); (c) 25n. VIIC type U-boat, 1942; (d) 25n. *Cutty Sark* (clipper), 1869; (e) 25n. H.M.S. *Dreadnought* (battleship), 1906; (f) 25n. U.S.S. *Monitor* (ironclad), 1862; (g) 25n. Moran Company tug, 1950; (h) 25n. *Normandie* (French liner), 1933; (i) 25n. H.M.S. *Resolution* (Capt. Cook); (j) 25n. *Titanic* (liner), 1912; (k) 25n. H.M.S. *Victory* (ship of the line), 1805; (l) 25n. *Yamato* (Japanese battleship), 1944	42·00	42·00

102 Nehru

1989. Birth Centenary of Jawaharlal Nehru (Indian statesman).

811	**102** 1n. brown	30	30

No. 811 is erroneously inscribed "ch".

103 Greater Flamed-backed Woodpecker

1989. Birds. Multicoloured.

812	50ch. Type **103**	10	10
813	1n. Black-naped blue monarch ("Black–naped Monarch")	15	15
814	2n. White-crested laughing thrush	30	30
815	3n. Blood pheasant	50	45
816	4n. Plum-headed ("Blossom-headed") parakeet	65	60
817	5n. Rosy minivet	85	75
818	6n. Chestnut-headed fulvetta ("Tit-Babbler") (horiz)	1·00	90
819	7n. Blue pitta (horiz)	1·20	1·10
820	10n. Black-naped oriole (horiz)	1·60	1·50
821	15n. Green magpie (horiz)	2·50	2·20
822	20n. Three-toed kingfisher ("Indian Three-toed Kingfisher") (horiz)	3·25	3·00
823	25n. Ibis bill (horiz)	4·00	3·50
MS824	12 sheets, each 76×104 mm (vert designs) or 104×76 mm (horiz). (a) 25n. Fire-tailed sunbird; (b) 25n. Crested tree swift (inscr "Indian Crested Swift"); (c) 25n. Greater (inscr "Large") racket-tailed drongo; (d) 25n. Little spider hunter; (e) 25n. Blue-backed fairy bluebird (horiz); (f) 25n. Great Indian (inscr "Pied") hornbill (horiz); (g) 25n. Red-legged (inscr "Himalayan Redbreasted") falconet (horiz); (h) 25n. Lammergeier (horiz); (i) 25n. Satyr tragopan (horiz); (j) 25n. Spotted forktail (horiz); (k) 25n. Wallcreeper (horiz); (l) 25n. White eared-pheasant (wrongly inscr "White-eared") (horiz)	42·00	42·00

104 *Best Friend of Charleston*, 1830, U.S.A.

1990. Steam Railway Locomotives. Multicoloured.

825	50ch. Type **104**	10	10
826	1n. Class U locomotive, 1948, France	10	10
827	2n. Consolidation locomotive, 1866, U.S.A.	25	25
828	3n. Luggage engine, 1843, Great Britain	45	35
829	4n. Class 60-3 Shay locomotive No. 18, 1913, U.S.A.	55	50
830	5n. "John Bull", 1831, U.S.A.	70	65
831	6n. "Hercules", 1837, U.S.A.	85	80
832	7n. Locomotive No. 947, 1874, Great Britain	1·10	95
833	10n. "Illinois", 1852, U.S.A.	1·40	1·30
834	15n. Class O5 locomotive, 1935, Germany	2·10	1·90
835	20n. Standard locomotive, 1865, U.S.A.	2·75	2·50
836	25n. Class Ps-4 locomotive, 1936, U.S.A.	3·50	3·25

MS837 12 sheets, each 74×100 mm (horiz designs) or 100×74 mm (vert). (a) 25n. "The Cumberland" (U.S.A., 1845); (b) 25n. "Ariel" (U.S.A., 1877); (c) 25n. No. 22 Baldwin locomotive (U.S.A., 1873); (d) 25n. Class "A" (U.S.A., 1935) (vert); (e) 25n. Class "K-36" (U.S.A., 1923); (f) 25n. No. 999 "Empire State Express" (U.S.A., 1893); (g) 25n. "John Stevens" (U.S.A., 1849) (vert); (h) 25n. Class "A4" (Great Britain, 1935) (vert); (i) 25n. "Puffing Billy" (Great Britain, 1814) (vert); (j) 25n. "The Rocket" (Great Britain, 1829) (vert); (k) 25n. Class "P-1" (U.S.A., 1943) (vert); (l) 25n. No. 1301 Webb compound engine (Great Britain, 1889) 42·00 42·00

105 *Charaxes harmodius*

1990. Butterflies. Multicoloured.

838	50ch. Type **105**	10	10
839	1n. *Prioneris thestylis*	10	10
840	2n. Eastern courtier	25	25
841	3n. *Penthema lisarda* (horiz)	45	35
842	4n. Golden birdwing	55	50
843	5n. Great nawab	70	65
844	6n. *Polyura dolon* (horiz)	85	80
845	7n. Tailed labyrinth (horiz)	1·10	95
846	10n. *Delias descombesi*	1·40	1·30
847	15n. *Childreni childrena* (horiz)	2·10	1·90
848	20n. Leaf butterfly (horiz)	2·75	2·50
849	25n. *Elymnias malelas* (horiz)	3·50	3·25

MS850 12 sheets, each 110×80 mm. (a) 25n. Bhutan glory; (b) 25n. Blue (inscr "Blue Banded") peacock; (c) 25n. Camberwell beauty; (d) 25n. Chequered swallowtail; (e) 25n. Chestnut tiger; (f) 25n. Common birdwing; (g) 25n. Common map butterfly; (h) 25n. Common (inscr "Great") eggfly; (i) 25n. Jungle glory; (j) 25n. Kaiser-i-hind; (k) 25n. Red lacewing; (l) 25n. Swallowtail 42·00 42·00

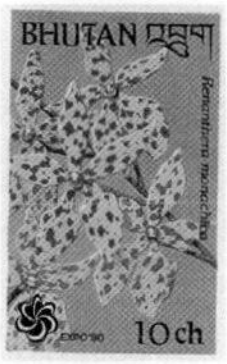
106 *Renanthera monachica*

1990. "Expo '90" International Garden and Greenery Exposition, Osaka. Orchids. Multicoloured.

851	10ch. Type **106**	10	10
852	50ch. *Vanda coerulea*	10	10
853	1n. *Phalaenopsis violacea*	15	15
854	2n. *Dendrobium nobile*	30	25
855	5n. *Vandopsis lissochiloides*	60	55
856	6n. *Paphiopedilum rothschildianum*	85	75
857	7n. *Phalaenopsis schilleriana*	1·00	90
858	9n. *Paphiopedilum insigne*	1·30	1·10
859	10n. *Paphiopedilum bellatulum*	1·40	1·30
860	20n. *Doritis pulcherrima*	2·75	2·50
861	25n. *Cymbidium giganteum*	4·25	3·25
862	35n. *Phalaenopsis mariae*	5·00	4·75

MS863 12 sheets, each 111×84 mm. (a) 30n. *Dendrobium aphyllum*; (b) 30n. *Dendrobium loddigesii*; (c) 30n. *Dendrobium margaritaceum*; (d) 30n. *Paphlopedilum haynaldianum*; (e) 30n. *Paphiopedilum niveum*; (f) 30n. *Phalaenopsis amabilis*; (g) 30n. *Phalaenopsis cornu-cervi*; (h) 30n*Phalaenopsis equestris*; (i) 30n. *Vanda alpine*; (j) 30n. *Vanda coerulescens*; (k) 30n. *Vanda cristata*; (l) 30n. *Vandopsis parishi* 50·00 50·00

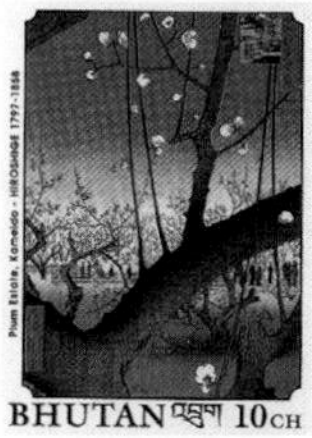
107 *Plum Estate, Kameido*

1990. Death of Emperor Hirohito and Accession of Emperor Akihito of Japan. *100 Famous Views of Edo* by Ando Hiroshige. Multicoloured.

864	10ch. Type **107**	10	10
865	20ch. *Yatsumi Bridge*	10	10
866	50ch. *Ayase River and Kanegafuchi*	10	10
867	75ch. *View of Shiba Coast*	10	10
868	1n. *Grandpa's Teahouse, Meguro*	15	15
869	2n. *Inside Kameido Tenjin Shrine*	25	25
870	6n. *Yoroi Ferry, Koami-cho*	90	80
871	7n. *Sakasai Ferry*	1·10	95
872	10n. *Fukagawa Lumberyards*	1·50	1·40
873	15n. *Suido Bridge and Surugadai*	2·40	2·10
874	20n. *Meguro Drum Bridge and Sunset Hill*	3·00	2·75
875	25n. *Atagoshita and Yabu Lane*	3·75	3·25

MS876 12 sheets, each 102×76 mm. (a) 25n. *The City Flourishing, Tanabata Festival*; (b) 25n. *Fukagawa Susaki and Jumantsubo*; (c) 25n. *Horikiri Iris Garden*; (d) 25n. *Komakata Hall and Azuma Bridge*; (e) 25n. *Minowa, Kanasugi, Mikawashima*; (f) 25n. *New Year's Eve Foxfires at the Changing Tree, Oji*; (g) 25n. *Nihonbashi, Clearing after Snow*; (h) 25n. *Sudden Shower over Shin-Ohashi Bridge and Atake*; (i) 25n. *Suijin Shrine and Massaki on the Sumida River*; (j) 25n. "Suruga-cho"; (k) 25n. *Towboats along the Yotsugi-dori Canal*; (l) 25n. *View to the North from Asukayama* 42·00 38·00

108 Thimphu Post Office

1990

877	**108**	1n. multicoloured	15	15

109 Giant Panda

1990. Mammals. Multicoloured.

878	50ch. Type **109**	10	10
879	1n. Giant panda in tree	15	15
880	2n. Giant panda with cub	30	30
881	3n. Giant panda (horiz)	50	45
882	4n. Giant panda eating (horiz)	65	60
883	5n. Tiger (horiz)	85	75
884	6n. Giant pandas pulling up bamboo (horiz)	1·00	90
885	7n. Giant panda and cub resting (horiz)	1·20	1·10
886	10n. Indian elephant (horiz)	1·60	1·50
887	15n. Giant panda beside fallen tree	2·50	2·20
888	20n. Indian muntjac (inscr "Barking deer") (horiz)	3·25	3·00
889	25n. Snow leopard (horiz)	4·00	3·50

MS890 12 sheets, each 100×73 mm. (a) 25n. Asiatic black bear; (b) 25n. Dhole (inscr "Asiatic wild dog"); (c) 25n. Clouded leopard; (d) 25n. Gaur; (e) 25n. Giant panda; (f) 25n. Golden cat; (g) 25n. Siberian musk deer (inscr "Himalayan"); (h) 25n. Redd deer (inscr "Himalayan shou"); (i) 25n. Pygmy hog; (j) 25n. Indian rhinoceros; (k) 25n. Sloth bear; (l) 25n. Wolf 45·00 45·00

110 Roim

1990. Religious Musical Instruments. Multicoloured.

891	10ch. Dungchen (large trumpets)	10	10
892	20ch. Dungkar (Indian chank shell)	10	10
893	30ch. Type **110**	10	10
894	50ch. Tinchag (cup cymbals)	10	10
895	1n. Dradu and drilbu (pellet drum and hand bell)	10	10
896	2n. Gya-ling (oboes)	20	15
897	2n.50 Nga (drum)	30	25
898	3n.50 Kang-dung (trumpets)	35	35

MS899 Two sheets, each 92×135 mm. (a) Nos. 891, 893, 895 and 898; (b) Nos. 892, 894 and 896/7 1·75 1·75

111 Penny Black and Bhutan 1962 2ch. Stamp

1990. "Stamp World London 90" International Stamp Exhibition. 150th Anniv of the Penny Black. Multicoloured.

900	50ch. Type **111**	10	10
901	1n. Oldenburg 1852 1/30th. stamp	15	15
902	2n. Bergedorf 1861 1½s. stamp	25	25
903	4n. German Democratic Republic 1949 50pf. stamp	50	45
904	5n. Brunswick 1852 1 sgr. stamp	60	55
905	6n. Basel 1845 2½r. stamp	85	75
906	8n. Geneva 1843 5c.+5c. stamp	1·10	1·00
907	10n. Zurich 1843 4r. stamp	1·40	1·30
908	15n. France 1849 20c. stamp	2·10	1·90
909	20n. Vatican City 1929 5c. stamp	2·75	2·50
910	25n. Israel 1948 3m. stamp	3·50	3·25
911	30n. Japan 1871 48m. stamp	4·25	3·75

MS912 12 sheets, each 106×76 mm. (a) 15n. Baden 1851 1k. stamp, 15n. Wurttemberg 1851 1k. stamp; (b) 15n. Germany 1872 3k. and 2g. stamps, 15n. Prussia 1850 6pf. stamp; (c) 15n. Hamburg 1859 ½s. stamp, 15n. North German Confederation 1868 ¼g. and 1k. stamps; (d) 15n. Heligoland 1867 ½ch. stamp, 15n. Hanover 1850 1ggr. stamp; (e) 15n. Schleswig-Holstein 1850 1s. stamp; 15n. Lubeck 1859 4s. stamp; (f) 15n. Mecklenburg-Schwerin 1856 4/4s. stamp, 15n. Mecklenburg-Strelitz 1864 ⅓sgr. stamp; (g) 15n. Thurn and Taxis (Northern District) 1852 ½sgr. stamp, 15n. Thurn and Taxis (Southern District) 1852 1k. stamp; (h) 30n. Bavaria 1849 1k. stamp; (i) 30n. West Berlin 1948 2pf. stamp; (j) 30n. Great Britain 1840 Penny Black; (k) 30n. Saxony 1850 3pf. stamp; (l) 30n. United States 1847 5c. stamp 48·00 48·00

Each value also depicts the Penny Black.
No. 901 is wrongly inscribed "Oldenberg".

112 Girls

1990. South Asian Association for Regional Co-operation Girl Child Year. Multicoloured.

913	50ch. Type **112**	20	20
914	20n. Girl	2·75	2·40

113 Temple of Artemis, Ephesus

1991. Wonders of the World. Designs featuring Walt Disney cartoon characters. Multicoloured.

915	1ch. Type **113**	10	10
916	2ch. Statue of Zeus, Olympia	10	10
917	3ch. Pyramids of Egypt	10	10
918	4ch. Lighthouse of Alexandria, Egypt	10	10
919	5ch. Mausoleum, Halicarnassus	10	10
920	10ch. Colossus of Rhodes	10	10
921	50ch. Hanging Gardens of Babylon	10	10
922	5n. Mauna Loa Volcanoes, Hawaii (horiz)	70	65
923	6n. Carlsbad Caverns, New Mexico (horiz)	90	80
924	10n. Rainbow Bridge National Monument, Utah (horiz)	1·50	1·40
925	15n. Grand Canyon, Colorado (horiz)	3·25	1·90
926	20n. Old Faithful, Yellowstone National Park, Wyoming (horiz)	2·75	2·50
927	25n. Sequoia National Park, California (horiz)	3·75	3·25
928	30n. Crater Lake and Wizard Island, Oregon (horiz)	4·50	4·00

MS929 14 sheets, each 127×101 mm. (a) 25n. Alcan Highway, Alaska and Canada (horiz); (b) 25n. Catacombs of Alexandria; (c) 25n. Sears Tower, Chicago, Illinois (horiz); (d) 25n. Great Wall of China (horiz); (e) 25n. St. Sophia's Mosque, Constantinople; (f) 25n. Porcelain Tower, Nanking, China (horiz); (g) 25n. Hoover Dam, Nevada; (h) 25n. Empire State Building, New York City; (i) 25n. Panama Canal (horiz); (j) 25n. Leaning Tower of Pisa; (k) 25n. Colosseum Rome; (l) 25n. Gateway Arch, St. Louis, Missouri; (m) 25n. Golden Gate Bridge, San Francisco (horiz); (n) 25n. Stonehenge 42·00 42·00

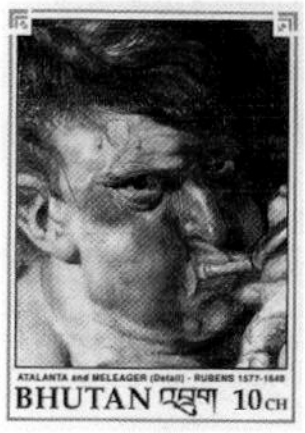
114 *Atalanta and Meleager* (detail)

1991. 350th Death Anniv (1990) of Peter Paul Rubens (painter). Multicoloured.

930	10ch. Type **114**	10	10
931	50ch. *The Fall of Phaeton* (detail)	10	10
932	1n. *Feast of Venus Verticordia* (detail)	15	15
933	2n. *Achilles slaying Hector* (detail)	35	30
934	3n. *Arachne punished by Minerva* (detail)	50	35
935	4n. *Jupiter receives Psyche on Olympus* (detail)	75	55
936	5n. *Atalanta and Meleager* (different detail)	90	85
937	6n. *Atalanta and Meleager* (different detail)	1·10	1·00
938	7n. *Venus in Vulcan's Furnace* (detail)	1·30	1·20
939	10n. *Atalanta and Meleager* (different detail)	1·70	1·60
940	20n. *Briseis returned to Achilles* (detail)	3·50	3·25
941	30n. *Mars and Rhea Sylvia* (detail)	5·00	4·50

MS942 12 sheets, each 72×101 mm (a/e) or 101×72 mm (f/l). (a) 25n. *Atlanta and Meleager*; (b) 25n. *Feast of Venus Verticordia*; (c) 25n. *Ganymede and the Eagle*; (d) 25n. *Jupiter receives Psyche on Olympus*; (e) 25n. *Venus shivering*; (f) 25n. *Adonis and Venus* (horiz); (g) 25n. *Arachne punished by Minerva* (horiz); (h) 25n. *Briseis returned to Achilles* (horiz); (i) 25n. *The Fall of the Titans* (horiz); (j) 25n. *Hero and Leander* (horiz); (k) 25n. *Mars and Rhea Sylvia* (horiz); (l) 25n. *The Origin of the Milky Way* (horiz) 48·00 48·00

115 *Cottages, Reminiscence of the North*

1991. Death Centenary (1990) of Vincent van Gogh (painter). Multicoloured.

943	10ch. Type **115**	10	10
944	50ch. *Head of a Peasant Woman with Dark Cap*	10	10
945	1n. *Portrait of a Woman in Blue*	15	15
946	2n. *Head of an Old Woman with White Cap (the Midwife)*	45	35
947	8n. *Vase with Hollyhocks*	1·20	1·10
948	10n. *Portrait of a Man with a Skull Cap*	1·40	1·30
949	12n. *Agostina Segatori sitting in the Cafe du Tambourin*	1·80	1·60
950	15n. *Vase with Daisies and Anemones*	2·20	2·00
951	18n. *Fritillaries in a Copper Vase*	2·75	2·40
952	20n. *Woman sitting in the Grass*	3·00	2·75
953	25n. *On the Outskirts of Paris* (horiz)	3·50	3·25
954	30n. *Chrysanthemums and Wild Flowers in a Vase*	4·25	3·75

MS955	12 sheets, each 76×101 mm (a/h) or 101×76 mm (i/l). (a) 30n. *Le Moulin de Blute-Fin*; (b) 30n. *Le Moulin de la Galette*; (c) 30n. *Le Moulin de la Galette* (with man in foreground); (d) 30n. *Poppies and Butterflies*; (e) 30n. *Trees in the Garden of St. Paul Hospital*; (f) 30n. *Vase with Peonies*; (g) 30n. *Vase with Red Poppies*; (h) 30n. *Vase with Zinnias*; (i) 30n. *Bowl with Sunflowers, Roses and Other Flowers* (horiz); (j) 30n. *Fishing in the Spring, Pont de Clichy* (horiz); (k) 30n. *Vase with Zinnias and Other Flowers* (horiz); (l) 30n. *Village Street in Auvers* (horiz)	48·00	48·00

116 Winning Uruguay Team, 1930

1991. World Cup Football Championship. Multicoloured.

956	50ch. Type **116**	10	10
957	1n. Italy, 1934	15	15
958	2n. Italy, 1938	25	20
959	3n. Uruguay, 1950	45	30
960	5n. West Germany, 1954	70	65
961	10n. Brazil, 1958	1·40	1·30
962	20n. Brazil, 1962	2·75	2·50
963	25n. England, 1966	3·50	3·25
964	29n. Brazil, 1970	4·00	3·50
965	30n. West Germany, 1974	4·25	3·75
966	31n. Argentina, 1978	4·25	3·75
967	32n. Italy, 1982	4·50	4·00
968	33n. Argentina, 1986	4·50	4·00
969	34n. West Germany, 1990	4·50	4·00
970	35n. Stadium, Los Angeles (venue for 1994 World Cup)	4·50	4·00
MS971	6 sheets, each 105×120 mm. (a) 30n. Roberto Baggio, Italy (vert); (b) 30n. Claudio Canniggia, Argentina (vert); (c) 30n. Paul Gascoigne, England (vert); (d) 30n. Lothar Matthaus, West Germany (vert); (e) 30n. Salvatore Schillaci, Italy (vert); (f) 30n. Peter Shilton, England	24·00	24·00

117 Bhutan and Japan State Flags

1991. "Phila Nippon '91" International Stamp Exhibition, Tokyo.

972	**117** 15n. multicoloured	2·10	1·80

118 Teachers, Pupils and Hemisphere

1992. "Education for All by Year 2000".

973	**118** 1n. multicoloured	10	10

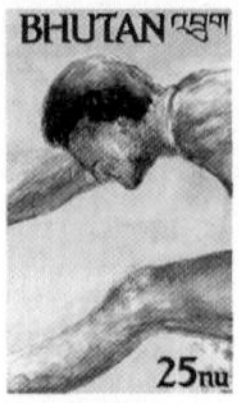

119 Hurdler

1992. Olympic Games, Barcelona. Multicoloured.

974	25n. Type **119**	3·25	3·25
975	25n. Body of hurdler	3·25	3·25
MS976	110×75 mm. 25n. Archery	4·75	4·75

Nos. 974/5 were issued together, *se-tenant*, forming a composite design.

120 *Santa Maria*

1992. 500th Anniv of Discovery of America by Columbus. Multicoloured.

977	15n. Type **120**	1·10	1·10
978	20n. Columbus	1·40	1·40
MS979	78×118 mm. 25n. As No. 978 but without inscription at top (27×43 mm)	2·00	2·00

121 Brandenburg Gate and rejoicing Couple

1992. Second Anniv of Reunification of Germany.

980	**121** 25n. multicoloured	1·80	1·80
MS981	110×82 mm. 25n. As No. 980 but without inscription at top (43×27 mm)	1·80	1·80

122 British Aerospace BAe 146 and Post Van

1992. 30th Anniv of Bhutan Postal Organization. Multicoloured.

982	1n. Type **122**	10	10
983	3n. Rural letter courier	25	25
984	5n. Emptying post box	40	40

123 Industry and Agriculture

1992. 20th Anniv of Accession of King Jigme Singye Wangchuck. Multicoloured.

985	1n. Type **123**	15	15
986	5n. British Aerospace RJ70 of National Airline	35	35
987	10n. House with water-pump	65	65
988	15n. King Jigme Singye Wangchuk	1·20	1·20
MS989	94×62 mm. 20n. King, flag and Bhutanese people (43×26 mm)	1·70	1·70

Nos. 985/8 were issued together, *se-tenant*, each horizontal pair within the block forming a composite design.

124 Dragon

1992. International Volunteer Day.

990	**124** 1n.50 multicoloured	15	15
991	**124** 9n. multicoloured	65	65
992	**124** 15n. multicoloured	1·20	1·20

125 *Meconopsis grandis*

1993. Medicinal Flowers. Designs showing varieties of the Asiatic Poppy. Multicoloured.

993	1n.50 Type **125**	15	15
994	7n. *Meconopsis* sp.	60	60
995	10n. *Meconopsis wallichii*	75	75
996	12n. *Meconopsis horridula*	1·00	1·00
997	20n. *Meconopsis discigera*	1·70	1·70
MS998	74×107 mm. 25n. *Meconopsis horridula* (different) (27×43 mm)	2·00	2·00

126 Rooster and Chinese Signs of the Zodiac

1993. New Year. Year of the Water Rooster. Sheet 89×89 mm.

MS999	**126** 25n. multicoloured	1·90	1·90

127 *The Love Letter* (Jean Honore Fragonard)

1993. Paintings. Multicoloured.

1000	1ch. Type **127** (postage)	15	15
1001	2ch. *The Writer* (Vittore Carpaccio)	15	15
1002	3ch. *Mademoiselle Lavergne* (Jean Etienne Liotard)	15	15
1003	5ch. *Portrait of Erasmus* (Hans Holbein)	15	15
1004	10ch. *Woman writing a Letter* (Gerard Terborch)	15	15
1005	15ch. Type **127**	15	15
1006	25ch. As No. 1001	15	15
1007	50ch. As No. 1002	15	15
1008	60ch. As No. 1003	15	15
1009	80ch. As No. 1004	15	15
1010	1n. Type **127**	15	15
1011	1n.25 As No. 1001	15	15
1012	2n. As No. 1002 (air)	15	15
1013	3n. As No. 1003	15	15
1014	6n. As No. 1004	15	15
MS1015	135×97 mm. As Nos. 1012/14 but with copper borders	1·70	1·70

128 Lesser Panda

1993. Environmental Protection. Multicoloured.

1016	7n. Type **128**	60	60
1017	10n. One-horned rhinoceros	85	85
1018	15n. Black-necked crane and blue poppy	1·20	1·20
1019	20n. Takin	1·50	1·50

Nos. 1016/19 were issued together, se-tenant, forming a composite design.

1993. "Taipei'93" International Stamp Exhibition, Taiwan. No. **MS**999 surch **TAIPEI'93 NU 30**.

MS1020	**126** 30n. on 25n. multicoloured	2·40	2·40

130 Namtheo-say

1993. Door Gods. Multicoloured.

1021	1n.50 Type **130**	10	15
1022	5n. Pha-ke-po	40	40
1023	10n. Chen-mi Jang	80	80
1024	15n. Yul-khor-sung	1·20	1·20

131 *Rhododendron mucronatum*

1994. Flowers. Multicoloured.

1025	1n. Type **131**	15	15
1026	1n.50 *Anemone rupicola*	15	15
1027	2n. *Polemonium coeruleum*	15	15
1028	2n.50 *Rosa marophylla*	15	15
1029	4n. *Paraquilegia microphylla*	35	35
1030	5n. *Aquilegia nivalis*	40	40
1031	6n. *Geranium wallichianum*	50	50
1032	7n. *Rhododendron campanulatum* (wrongly inscr "Rhodendron")	60	60
1033	9n. *Viola suavis*	75	75
1034	10n. *Cyananthus lobatus*	90	90
MS1035	126×86 mm. 13n. Lily (horiz)	1·00	1·00

132 Dog

1994. New Year. Year of the Dog. "Hong Kong '94" International Stamp Exhibition.

1036	**132** 11n.50 multicoloured	80	80
MS1037	118×178 mm. **132** 20n. multicoloured	1·50	1·50

133 Trophy and Mascot

1994. World Cup Football Championship, U.S.A.

1038	**133** 15n. multicoloured	80	80

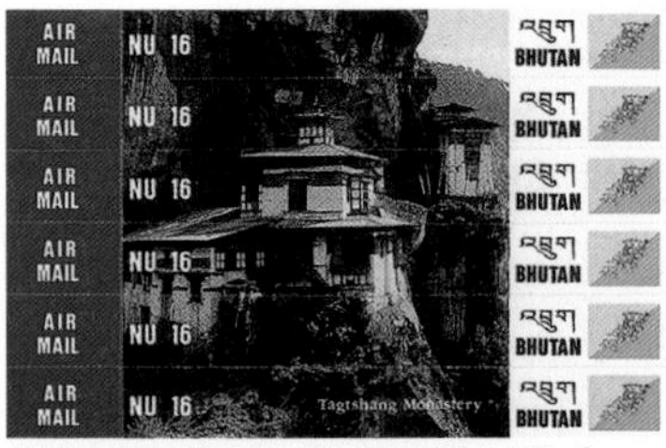

134 Tagtshang Monastery (image scaled to 57% of original size)

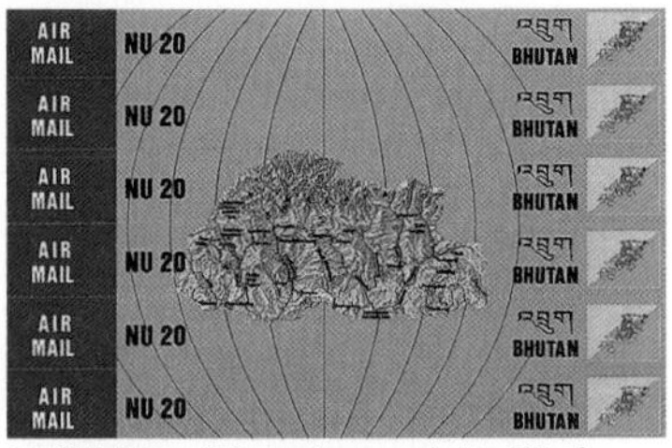

135 Relief Map of Bhutan (image scaled to 58% of original size)

1994. Air. Self-adhesive.

1039	**134** 16n. multicoloured	85	85
1040	**135** 20n. multicoloured	1·00	1·00

The individual stamps are peeled directly from the card backing. Each card contains six different designs with the same face value forming the composite designs illustrated. Each stamp is a horizontal strip with a label indicating the main class of mail covered by the rate at the left, separated by a vertical line of rouletting. The outer edges of the cards are imperforate.

136 Tower Bridge, London (centenary)

1994. Bridges. Sheet 160×101 mm containing T 136 and similar horiz design. Multicoloured.

MS1041	15n. Type **136**; 16n. *Wangdur Bridge, Bhutan* (Samuel Davies) (250th anniv)	1·60	1·60

137 Astronaut on Moon

1994. 25th Anniv of First Manned Moon Landing. Sheet 114×57 mm containing T **137** and similar horiz design. Multicoloured.

MS1042	30n. Type **137**; 36n. Space shuttle	3·50	3·50

138 Horseman with raised Sword

1994. 350th Anniv of Victory over Tibet-Mongol Army. Multicoloured.

1043	15n. Type **138**	80	80
1044	15n. Archers and hand-to-hand sword fighting	80	80
1045	15n. Horseman with insignia on helmet amongst infantry	80	80
1046	15n. Drummer, piper and troops	80	80

Nos. 1043/6 were issued together, *se-tenant*, forming a composite design of a battle scene and the Drugyel Dzong.

139 Paro Valley

1995. World Tourism Year. Sheet 111×92 mm containing T **139** and similar horiz designs. Multicoloured.

MS1047	1n.50 Type **139**; 5n. Chorton Kora; 10n. Thimphu Tshechu; 15n. Wangdue Tshechu	2·40	2·40

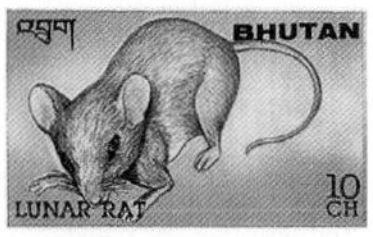

140 Lunar Rat

1995. New Year. Year of the Boar. Multicoloured.

1048	10ch. Type **140**	15	15
1049	20ch. Lunar ox	15	15
1050	30ch. Lunar tiger	15	15
1051	40ch. Lunar rabbit	15	15
1052	1n. Lunar dragon	15	15
1053	2n. Lunar snake	15	15
1054	3n. Lunar horse	15	15
1055	4n. Lunar sheep	15	15
1056	5n. Lunar monkey	15	15
1057	7n. Lunar rooster	25	25
1058	8n. Lunar dog	35	35
1059	9n. Lunar boar	40	40
MS1060	111×92 mm. 10n. Wood hogs	55	55

141 *Pleione praecox*

1995. Flowers. Multicoloured.

1061	9n. Type **141**	50	50
1062	10n. *Primula calderina*	60	60
1063	16n. *Primula whitei*	1·00	1·00
1064	18n. *Notholirion macrophyllum*	1·10	1·10

142 Human Resources Development

1995. 50th Anniv of UNO. Multicoloured.

1065	1n.50 Type **142**	15	15
1066	5n. Transport and Communications	35	35
1067	9n. Health and Population	50	50
1068	10n. Water and Sanitation	60	60
1069	11n.50 UN in Bhutan	65	65
1070	16n. Forestry and Environment	90	90
1071	18n. Peace and Security	1·00	1·00

143 Greater Pied Kingfisher ("Himalayan Pied Kingfisher")

1995. "Singapore '95" International Stamp Exhibition. Birds. Multicoloured.

1072	1n. Type **143**	15	15
1073	2n. Blyth's tragopan	15	15
1074	3n. Long-tailed minivets	15	15
1075	10n. Red junglefowl	60	60
1076	15n. Black-capped sibia	85	85
1077	20n. Red-billed chough	1·00	1·00
MS1078	73×97 mm. 20n. Black-necked crane	1·10	1·10

144 Making Paper

1995. Traditional Crafts. Multicoloured.

1079	1n. Type **144**	15	15
1080	2n. Religious painting	15	15
1081	3n. Clay sculpting	15	15
1082	10n. Weaving	60	60
1083	15n. Making boots	85	85
1084	20n. Carving wooden bowls	1·00	1·00
MS1085	121×82 mm. 20n. Decorative carvings on wooden buildings	1·00	1·00

145 Golden Langer

1996. New Year. Year of the Rat. Sheet 111×176 mm containing T **145** and similar square designs. Multicoloured.

MS1086	10n. Type **145**; 10n. Rat; 10n. Dragon	1·60	1·60

146 *The White Bird*

1996. Folk Tales. Multicoloured.

1087	1n. Type **146**	15	15
1088	2n. *Sing Sing Lhamo and the Moon*	15	15
1089	3n. *The Hoopoe*	15	15
1090	5n. *The Cloud Fairies*	35	35
1091	10n. *The Three Wishes*	60	60
1092	20n. *The Abominable Snowman*	1·10	1·10
MS1093	109×75 mm. 25n. As No. 1090	1·70	1·70

147 Blue Pansy

1996. Butterflies. Multicoloured.

1094	2n. Type **147**	15	15
1095	3n. Blue peacock	15	15
1096	5n. Great mormon	25	25
1097	10n. Fritillary	60	60
1098	15n. Blue duke	85	85
1099	25n. Brown gorgon	1·30	1·30
MS1100	Two sheets, each 108×75 mm. (a) 30n. Fivebar swordtail; (b) 30n. Xanthomelas	3·00	3·00

148 300n. Football Coin

1996. Olympic Games, Atlanta. Multicoloured.

1101	5n. Type **148**	25	25
1102	7n. 300n. basketball coin	40	40
1103	10n. 5s. judo coin	60	60
MS1104	102×80 mm. 15n. Archery	85	85

149 Standard Goods Locomotive, India

1996. Trains. Multicoloured.

1105	20n. Type **149**	1·00	1·00
1106	20n. Diesel-electric locomotive, Finland	1·00	1·00
1107	20n. Shunting tank locomotive, Russia	1·00	1·00
1108	20n. Alco PA-1 diesel-electric locomotive, U.S.A.	1·00	1·00
1109	20n. Class C11 passenger tank locomotive, Japan	1·00	1·00
1110	20n. Settebello high speed electric train, Italy	1·00	1·00
1111	20n. Tank locomotive No. 191, Chile	1·00	1·00
1112	20n. Pacific locomotive, France	1·00	1·00
1113	20n. Steam locomotive No. 10, Norway	1·00	1·00
1114	20n. Atlantic express locomotive, Germany	1·00	1·00
1115	20n. Express steam locomotive, Belgium	1·00	1·00
1116	20n. Type 4 diesel-electric locomotive, Great Britain	1·00	1·00
MS1117	Two sheets, each 96×66 mm. (a) 70n. *Hikari* express train, Series 200, Japan; (b) Class KD steam goods locomotive, Sweden	7·25	7·25

150 Penny Black

1996

1118	**150**	140n. gold and black	7·25	7·25

151 Vegard Ulvang, Norway

1997. Winter Olympic Gold Medallists. Multicoloured. (a) Without frame.

1119	10n. Type **151** (30km. cross-country skiing, 1992)	60	60
1120	15n. Kristi Yamaguchi, U.S.A. (women's figure skating, 1992)	85	85
1121	25n. Markus Wasmeier, Germany (men's super giant slalom, 1994)	1·50	1·50
1122	30n. Georg Hackl, Germany (luge, 1992)	1·70	1·70

(b) As T **151** but with black frame around design.

1123	15n. Andreas Ostler, West Germany (two-man bobsleighing, 1952)	80	80
1124	15n. East German team (four-man bobsleighing, 1984)	80	80
1125	15n. Stein Eriksen, Norway (men's giant slalom, 1952)	80	80
1126	15n. Alberto Tomba, Italy (men's giant slalom, 1988)	80	80
MS1127	Two sheets, each 106×76 mm. (a) 70n. Henri Oreiller, France (men's downhill skiing, 1948); (b) 70n. Swiss team (four-man bobsleighing, 1924)	7·50	7·50

152 Bee

1997. Insects and Arachnidae. Multicoloured.

1128	1ch. Type **152**	10	10
1129	2ch. *Neptunides polychromus* (beetle)	10	10
1130	3ch. *Conocephalus maculctus* (grasshopper)	10	10
1131	4ch. *Blattidae* sp. (beetle)	10	10
1132	5ch. Great diving beetle	10	10
1133	10ch. Hercules beetle	10	10
1134	15ch. Ladybird	10	10
1135	20ch. *Sarcophaga haemorrhoidalis* (fly)	10	10
1136	25ch. Stag beetle	10	10
1137	30ch. Caterpillar	10	10
1138	35ch. *Lycia hirtaria* (moth)	10	10
1139	40ch. *Clytarius pennatus* (beetle)	10	10
1140	45ch. *Ephemera denica* (mayfly)	10	10
1141	50ch. European field cricket	10	10
1142	60ch. Elephant hawk moth	10	10
1143	65ch. *Gerris* sp. (beetle)	10	10
1144	70ch. Banded agrion	10	10
1145	80ch. *Tachyta nana* (beetle)	10	10
1146	90ch. *Eurydema pulchra* (shieldbug)	10	10
1147	1n. *Hadrurus hirsutus* (scorpion)	10	10
1148	1n.50 *Vespa germanica* (wasp)	10	10
1149	2n. *Pyrops* sp. (beetle)	10	10
1150	2n.50 Praying mantis	10	10
1151	3n. *Araneus diadematus* (spider)	10	10
1152	3n.50 *Atrophaneura* sp. (butterfly)	10	10
MS1153	76×111 mm. 15n. Cockchafer (*Melolontha* sp.)	1·00	1·00

153 Polar Bears

1997. "Hong Kong '97" International Stamp Exhibition. Multicoloured.

1154	10n. Type **153**	55	55
1155	10n. Koalas (*Phascolarctos cinereus*)	55	55
1156	10n. Asiatic black bear (*Selenarctos thibetanus*)	55	55
1157	10n. Lesser panda (*Ailurus fulgens*)	55	55
MS1158	107×75 mm. 20n. Giant panda (*Ailuropoda melanoleuca*)	1·30	1·30

154 Rat

1997. New Year. Year of the Ox. Multicoloured.

1159	1ch. Type **154**	15	15
1160	2ch. Ox	15	15
1161	3ch. Tiger	15	15
1162	4ch. Rabbit	15	15
1163	90ch. Monkey	15	15
1164	5n. Dragon	25	25
1165	6n. Snake	35	35
1166	7n. Horse	40	40
1167	8n. Ram	50	50
1168	10n. Cock	65	65
1169	11n. Dog	75	75
1170	12n. Boar	85	85
MS1171	70×66 mm. 20n. Ox	2·75	2·75

155 Lynx

1997. Endangered Species. Multicoloured.

1172	10n. Type **155**	55	55
1173	10n. Lesser ("Red") panda (*Ailurus fulgens*)	55	55
1174	10n. Takin (*Budorcas taxicolor*)	55	55
1175	10n. Forest musk deer (*Moschus chrysogaster*)	55	55
1176	10n. Snow leopard (*Panthera uncia*)	55	55
1177	10n. Golden langur (*Presbytis geei*)	55	55
1178	10n. Tiger (*Pnthera tigris*)	55	55
1179	10n. Indian muntjac (*Muntiacus muntjak*)	55	55
1180	10n. Bobak marmot (*Marmota bobak*)	55	55
1181	10n. Dhole (*Cuon alpinis*) running	55	55
1182	10n. Dhole walking	55	55
1183	10n. Mother dhole nursing cubs	55	55
1184	10n. Two dhole	55	55
MS1185	Two sheets, each 106×76 mm. (a) 70n. Bharal (*Pseudois nayaur*); (b) 70n. Asiatic black bear (*Ursus thibetanus*)	7·50	7·50

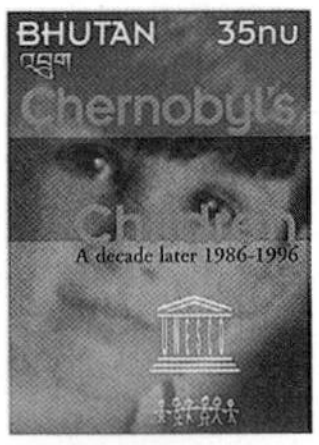

156 Child's Face and UNESCO Emblem

1997. Tenth Anniv of Chernobyl Nuclear Disaster.

1186	**156**	35n. multicoloured	1·90	1·90

157 Mount Huangshah, China

1997. 50th Anniv of UNESCO World Heritage Sites. Multicoloured.

1187	10n. Type **157**	65	65
1188	10n. Statue of Emperor Qin, China	65	65
1189	10n. Imperial bronze dragon, China	65	65
1190	10n. Pyramids, Tikal National Park, Guatemala	65	65
1191	10n. Fountain, Evora, Portugal	65	65
1192	10n. Forest path, Shirakami-Sanchi, Japan	65	65
1193	10n. View from Eiffel Tower, Paris, France	65	65
1194	10n. Wooden walkway, Valley Below the Falls, Croatia	65	65
1195	15n. Bamberg Cathedral, Germany	1·00	1·00
1196	15n. Aerial view of Bamberg	1·00	1·00
1197	15n. St. Michael's Church, Hildesheim, Germany	1·00	1·00
1198	15n. Potsdam Palace, Germany	1·00	1·00
1199	15n. Church, Potsdam	1·00	1·00
1200	15n. Waterfront, Lubeck, Germany	1·00	1·00
1201	15n. Quedlinberg, Germany	1·00	1·00
1202	15n. Benedictine church, Lorsch, Germany	1·00	1·00
MS1203	Two sheets, each 126×102 mm. (a) 60n. House, Goslar, Germany (horiz); (b) 60n. Comenzada Cathedral, Portugal (horiz)	6·25	6·25

158 Turkish Angora

1997. Domestic Animals. Mult. (a) Cats.

1204	10n. Type **158**	65	65
1205	15n. Oriental shorthair	90	90
1206	15n. Japanese bobtail	85	85
1207	15n. Ceylon	85	85
1208	15n. Exotic	85	85
1209	15n. Rex	85	85
1210	15n. Ragdoll	85	85
1211	15n. Russian blue	85	85
1212	20n. British shorthair	1·20	1·20
1213	25n. Burmese	1·40	1·40

(b) Dogs.

1214	10n. Dalmatian	65	65
1215	15n. Siberian husky	90	90
1216	20n. Saluki	1·20	1·20
1217	20n. Dandie Dinmont terrier	1·20	1·20
1218	20n. Chinese crested	1·20	1·20
1219	20n. Norwich terrier	1·20	1·20
1220	20n. Basset hound	1·20	1·20
1221	20n. Cardigan Welsh corgi	1·20	1·20
1222	20n. French bulldog	1·20	1·20
1223	25n. Shar-Pei	1·40	1·40
MS1224	Two sheets, each 76×106 mm. (a) 60n. Tokinese (cat); (b) 60n. Hovawart (dog)	6·75	6·75

Nos. 1206/11 and 1217/22 respectively were issued together, *se-tenant*, forming composite designs.

159 Stuart Pearce (England)

1997. World Cup Football Championship, France (1998). Black (Nos. 1225, 1231, 1235, 1237, 1241, 1243) or multicoloured (others).

1225	5n. Type **159**	35	35
1226	10n. Paul Gascoigne (England)	65	65
1227	10n. Diego Maradona (Argentina 1986) (horiz)	65	65
1228	10n. Carlos Alberto (Brazil 1970) (horiz)	65	65
1229	10n. Dunga (Brazil 1994) (horiz)	65	65
1230	10n. Bobby Moore (England 1966) (horiz)	65	65
1231	10n. Fritz Walter (West Germany 1954) (horiz)	65	65
1232	10n. Walter Matthaus (Germany 1990) (horiz)	65	65
1233	10n. Franz Beckenbauer (West Germany 1974) (horiz)	65	65
1234	10n. Daniel Passarella (Argentina 1978) (horiz)	65	65
1235	10n. Italy team, 1938 (horiz)	65	65
1236	10n. West Germany team, 1954 (horiz)	65	65
1237	10n. Uruguay team, 1958 (horiz)	65	65
1238	10n. England team, 1966 (horiz)	65	65
1239	10n. Argentina team, 1978 (horiz)	65	65
1240	10n. Brazil team, 1962 (horiz)	65	65
1241	10n. Italy team, 1934 (horiz)	65	65
1242	10n. Brazil team, 1970 (horiz)	65	65
1243	10n. Uruguay team, 1930 (horiz)	65	65
1244	10n. David Beckham (England)	1·00	1·00
1245	20n. Steve McManaman (England)	1·20	1·20
1246	25n. Tony Adams (England)	1·50	1·50
1247	30n. Paul Ince (England)	1·90	1·90
MS1248	Two sheets, each 102×127 mm. (a) 35n. Salvatore "Toto" Schillaci (Italy) (horiz); (b) 35n. Philippe Albert (Belgium)	4·75	4·75

160 Buddha in Lotus Position

1997. "Indepex '97" International Stamp Exhibition, New Delhi. 50th Anniv of Independence of India. Multicoloured.

1249	3n. Type **160**	15	15
1250	7n. Mahatma Gandhi with hands together	35	35
1251	10n. Gandhi (three-quarter face portrait)	50	50
1252	15n. Buddha with feet on footstool	65	65
MS1253	Two sheets, each 75×106 mm. (a) 15n. Buddha with right hand raised; (b) 15n. Gandhi carrying stick	1·70	1·70

161 Jawaharlal Nehru and King Jigme Dorji Wangchuck

1997. Int Friendship between India and Bhutan.

1254	**161** 3n. black and pink	15	15
MS1256	100×70 mm. 20n. multicoloured	2·30	2·30

DESIGNS: 10n. Prime Minister Rajiv Gandhi of India and King Jigme Singye Wangchuck. 76×34 mm—20n. President R Venkataraman of India and King Jigme Singye Wangchuck.

162 Tiger

1998. New Year. Year of the Tiger. T **162** and similar square designs. Multicoloured.

1257	3n. Type **162**	10	10
MS1258	Two sheets. (a) 95×95 mm. 3n. Type **162**; 5n. Lying down; 15n. Hunting; 17n. On rocky outcrop; (b) 114×81 mm. 20n. Head of tiger	2·75	2·75

163 Safe Motherhood and Anniversary Emblems

1998. 50th Anniv of WHO.

1259	**163**	3n. multicoloured	10	10
1260	**163**	10n. multicoloured	50	50
MS1261		100×60 mm. 15n. Safe Motherhood emblem (134×34 mm)	75	75

164 Mother Teresa

1998. Mother Teresa (founder of Missionaries of Charity) Commemoration. Multicoloured.

1262	10n. Type **164**	50	50
1263	10n. With Diana, Princess of Wales	50	50
1264	10n. Holding child	50	50
1265	10n. Holding baby	50	50
1266	10n. With Sisters	50	50
1267	10n. Smiling	50	50
1268	10n. Praying	50	50
1269	10n. With Pope John Paul II	50	50
1270	10n. Close-up of face	50	50
MS1271	150×122 mm. 25n. As No. 1263 but 39×46 mm; 25n. As No. 1269 but different colour background and 39×46 mm	2·00	2·00

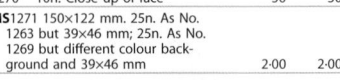

165 Red-billed Chough

1998. Birds. Multicoloured.

1272	10ch. Type **165**	15	15
1273	30ch. Great Indian hornbill ("Great Hornbill")	15	15
1274	50ch. Western Singing bush lark ("Singing Lark")	15	15
1275	70ch. Chestnut-flanked white-eye	15	15
1276	90ch. Magpie robin (wrongly inscr "Megpie-robin")	15	15
1277	1n. Mrs. Gould's sunbird	15	15
1278	2n. Long-tailed tailor bird ("Tailorbird")	15	15
1279	3n. Mallard ("Duck")	15	15
1280	5n. Great spotted cuckoo ("Spotted Cuckoo")	15	15
1281	7n. Severtzov's tit warbler ("Goldcrest")	15	15
1282	9n. Common mynah	15	15
1283	10n. Green cochoa	15	15
MS1284	75×118 mm. 15n. Turtle dove (40×29 mm)	90	90

166 Rabbit

1999. New Year. Year of the Rabbit. Multicoloured.

1285	4n. Type **166**	20	20
1286	16n. Rabbit on hillock	70	70
MS1287	83×114 mm. 20n. Rabbit beneath tree (34×34 mm)	1·00	1·00

167 Nuremberg

1999. "iBRA '99" International Stamp Exhibition, Nuremberg. Sheet 75×94 mm containing T **167** and similar square design. Multicoloured.

MS1288	35n. Type **167**; 40n. Exhibition emblem	1·00	1·00

168 King Wangchuck

1999. 25th Anniv of Coronation of King Jigme Singye Wangchuck. Multicoloured.

1289	25n. Type **168**	1·20	1·20
1290	25n. Facing left (yellow background)	1·20	1·20
1291	25n. Facing forwards (orange background)	1·20	1·20
1292	25n. With arm raised (green background)	1·20	1·20
MS1293	180×140 mm. 25n. King Wangchuk (magenta background)	4·25	4·25

169 Early German Steam Locomotive

1999. Trains. Multicoloured.

1294	5n. Type **169**	25	25
1295	10n. Electric locomotive	65	65
1296	10n. *Hikari* express train, Japan	60	60
1297	10n. Steam locomotive, South Africa, 1953	60	60
1298	10n. Super Chief locomotive, U.S.A., 1946	60	60
1299	10n. Magleus Magnet train, Japan, 1991	60	60
1300	10n. *Flying Scotsman*, Great Britain, 1992	60	60
1301	10n. Kodama locomotive, Japan, 1958	60	60
1302	10n. *Blue Train*, South Africa, 1969	60	60
1303	10n. Intercity train, Germany, 1960	60	60
1304	10n. ET 403 high speed electric locomotive, Germany, 1973	60	60
1305	10n. 4-4-0 steam locomotive, U.S.A., 1855	60	60
1306	10n. Beyer-Garratt steam locomotive, South Africa, 1954 (wrongly inscr "BAYER GARRATT")	60	60
1307	10n. Settebello locomotive, Italy, 1953	60	60
1308	15n. Pacific Class 01 steam locomotive, Germany	85	85
1309	15n. Neptune Express, Germany	85	85
1310	15n. 4-6-0 steam locomotive, Great Britain	85	85
1311	15n. Shovelnose Streamliner diesel locomotive, U.S.A.	85	85
1312	15n. Electric locomotive, Germany	85	85
1313	15n. Early steam locomotive, Germany	85	85
1314	15n. Union Pacific diesel locomotive, U.S.A.	85	85

1315 15n. 1881 Borsig steam locomotive, Germany 85 85
1316 15n. Borsig 4-6-4 diesel locomotive, Germany 85 85
1317 15n. Diesel-electric locomotive, France 85 85
1318 15n. Pennsylvania Railroad locomotive, U.S.A. 85 85
1319 15n. Steam locomotive, Germany 85 85
1320 15n. Amtrak locomotive, U.S.A. 85 85
1321 15n. 2-2-2 steam locomotive, Great Britain 85 85
1322 15n. P class steam locomotive, Denmark 85 85
1323 15n. Electric locomotive, France 85 85
1324 15n. First Japanese locomotive 85 85
1325 15n. 2-8-2 steam locomotive, Germany 85 85
1326 20n. Steam locomotive 1·20 1·20
1327 30n. Electric locomotive 1·70 1·70
MS1328 Two sheets, each 110×85 mm. (a) 80n. City of Los Angeles, U.S.A.; (b) 80n. Great Northern diesel-electric Streamliner locomotive, U.S.A 9·75 9·75

170 *Festive Dancers*

1999. 150th Death Anniv of Katsushika Hokusai (artist). Multicoloured.
1329 15n. Type **170** 75 75
1330 15n. *Drawings of Women* (woman reading) 75 75
1331 15n. *Festive Dancers* (man wearing pointed hat) 75 75
1332 15n. *Festive Dancers* (man looking up) 75 75
1333 15n. *Drawings of Women* (woman sitting on ground) 75 75
1334 15n. *Festive Dancers* (woman) 75 75
1335 15n. *Suspension Bridge between Hida and Etchu* 75 75
1336 15n. *Drawings of Women* (woman dressing hair) 75 75
1337 15n. *Exotic Beauty* 75 75
1338 15n. *The Poet Nakamaro in China* 75 75
1339 15n. *Drawings of Women* (woman rolling up sleeve) 75 75
1340 15n. *Chinese Poet in Snow* 75 75
1341 15n. *Mount Fuji seen above Mist on the Tama River* (horiz) 75 75
1342 15n. *Mount Fuji seen from Shichirigahama* (horiz) 75 75
1343 15n. *Sea Life* (turtle) (horiz) 75 75
1344 15n. *Sea Life* (fish) (horiz) 75 75
1345 15n. *Mount Fuji reflected in a Lake* (horiz) 75 75
1346 15n. *Mount Fuji seen through the Piers of Mannenbashi* (horiz) 75 75
MS1347 Three sheets (a) 100×71 mm 80n. *Peasants leading Oxen*; (b) 71×100 mm 80n. *The lotus Pedestal.* (c) 71×100 mm 870n. *Kusunoki Masahige* 15·00 15·00

171 Tyrannosaurus Rex

1999. Prehistoric Animals. Multicoloured.
1348 10n. Type **171** 60 60
1349 10n. Dimorphodon 60 60
1350 10n. Diplodocus 60 60
1351 10n. Pterodaustro 60 60
1352 10n. Tyrannosaurus Rex (different) 60 60
1353 10n. Edmontosaurus 60 60
1354 10n. Apatosaurus 60 60
1355 10n. Deinonychus 60 60
1356 10n. Hypsilophodon 60 60
1357 10n. Oviraptor 60 60
1358 10n. Stegosaurus beside lake 60 60
1359 10n. Head of Triceratops 60 60
1360 10n. Pterodactylus and Brachiosaurus 60 60
1361 10n. Pteranodon 60 60
1362 10n. Anurognathus and Tyrannosaurus Rex 60 60
1363 10n. Brachiosaurus 60 60
1364 10n. Corythosaurus 60 60
1365 10n. Iguanodon 60 60
1366 10n. Lesothosaurus 60 60
1367 10n. Allosaurus 60 60
1368 10n. Velociraptor 60 60
1369 10n. Triceratops in water 60 60
1370 10n. Stegosaurus in water 60 60
1371 10n. Compsognathus 60 60
1372 20n. Moeritherium 90 90
1373 20n. Platybelodon 90 90
1374 20n. Woolly mammoth 90 90
1375 20n. African elephant 90 90
1376 20n. Deinonychus 90 90
1377 20n. Dimorphodon 90 90
1378 20n. Archaeopteryx 90 90
1379 20n. Common pheasant ("Ring-necked Pheasant") 90 90
MS1380 Four sheets, each 110×85 mm. (a) 80n. Hoatzin (vert); (b) 80n. Icthyosaurus (wrongly inscr "Present Day Dolphin") (vert); (c) 80n. Triceratops (vert); (d) 80n. Pteranodon (wrongly inscr "Triceratops") 18·00 18·00

Nos. 1348/59 and 1360/71 were issued together, *se-tenant*, with the backgrounds forming a composite design.

172 Siberian Musk Deer

1999. "China '99" World Philatelic Exhibition, Peking. Animals. Multicoloured.
1381 20n. Type **172** 1·00 1·00
1382 20n. Takin (*Budorcas taxicolor*) 1·00 1·00
1383 20n. Bharal ("Blue sheep") (*Pseudois nayur*) (wrongly inscr "nayour") 1·00 1·00
1384 20n. Yak (*Bos gunniens*) 1·00 1·00
1385 20n. Common goral (*Nemorhaedus goral*) 1·00 1·00

173 Sara Orange-tip

1999. Butterflies. Multicoloured.
1386 5n. Type **173** 35 35
1387 10n. Pipe-vine swallowtail 60 60
1388 15n. Longwings 85 85
1389 20n. Viceroy 1·10 1·10
1390 20n. Frosted skipper 1·20 1·20
1391 20n. Fiery skipper 1·20 1·20
1392 20n. Banded hairstreak 1·20 1·20
1393 20n. Cloudless ("Clouded") sulphur 1·20 1·20
1394 20n. Milbert's tortoiseshell 1·20 1·20
1395 20n. Eastern tailed blue 1·20 1·20
1396 20n. Jamaican kite ("Zebra") swallowtail 1·20 1·20
1397 20n. Colorado hairstreak 1·20 1·20
1398 20n. Pink-edged sulphur 1·20 1·20
1399 20n. Barred sulphur (wrongly inscr "Fairy Yellow") 1·20 1·20
1400 20n. Red-spotted purple 1·20 1·20
1401 20n. Aphrodite 1·20 1·20
1402 25n. Silver-spotted skipper (vert) 1·40 1·40
1403 30n. Great spangled fritillary (vert) 1·70 1·70
1404 35n. Little copper (vert) 2·00 2·00
MS1405 Four sheets, each 98×68 mm. (a) 80n. Monarch (vert); (b) 80n. Checkered white; (c) 80n. Gulf fritillary (vert); (d) 80n. Grey hairstreak (vert) 14·50 14·50

Nos. 1390/95 and 1396/1401 were issued together, *se-tenant*, forming a composite design.

174 Chestnut-breasted Chlorophonia

1999. Birds. Multicoloured.
1406 15n. Type **174** 65 65
1407 15n. Yellow-faced amazon 65 65
1408 15n. White ibis 65 65
1409 15n. Parrotlet sp. ("Caique") 65 65
1410 15n. Green jay 65 65
1411 15n. Tufted coquette 65 65
1412 15n. Troupial 65 65
1413 15n. American purple gallinule ("Purple Gallinule") 65 65
1414 15n. Copper-rumped hummingbird 65 65
1415 15n. Great egret ("Common egret") 65 65
1416 15n. Rufous-browed pepper shrike 65 65
1417 15n. Glittering-throated emerald 65 65
1418 15n. Great kiskadee 65 65
1419 15n. Cuban green woodpecker 65 65
1420 15n. Scarlet ibis 65 65
1421 15n. Belted kingfisher 65 65
1422 15n. Barred antshrike 65 65
1423 15n. Brown-throated conure ("Caribbean Parakeet") 65 65
1424 15n. Rufous-tailed jacamar (vert) 65 65
1425 15n. Scarlet macaw (vert) 65 65
1426 15n. Channel-billed toucan (vert) 65 65
1427 15n. Louisiana heron ("Tri-colored heron") (vert) 65 65
1428 15n. St. Vincent amazon ("St. Vincent Parrot") (vert) 65 65
1429 15n. Blue-crowned motmot (vert) 65 65
1430 15n. Horned screamer (vert) 65 65
1431 15n. Grey plover ("Black-billed Plover") (vert) 65 65
1432 15n. Eastern meadowlark ("Common meadowlark") (vert) 65 65
MS1433 Three sheets, each 85×110 mm. (a) 80n. Military macaw (vert); (b) 80n. Toco toucan; (c) 80n. Red-billed scythebill (vert) 11·00 11·00

Nos. 1406/14, 1415/23 and 1424/32 were issued together, *se-tenant*, forming a composite design.

175 Yuri Gagarin (first person in space, 1961)

1999. 30th Anniv of First Manned Moon Landing. Multicoloured.
1434 20n. Type **175** 90 90
1435 20n. Alan Shepard (first American in space, 1961) 90 90
1436 20n. John Glenn (first American to orbit Earth, 1962) 90 90
1437 20n. Valentina Tereshkova (first woman in space, 1963) 90 90
1438 20n. Edward White (first American to walk in space, 1965) 90 90
1439 20n. Neil Armstrong (first person to set foot on Moon, 1969) 90 90
1440 20n. Neil Armstrong (wearing N.A.S.A. suit) 90 90
1441 20n. Michael Collins 90 90
1442 20n. Edwin (Buzz) Aldrin 90 90
1443 20n. *Columbia* (pointing upwards) 90 90
1444 20n. *Eagle* on lunar surface 90 90
1445 20n. Edwin Aldrin on lunar surface 90 90
1446 20n. North American X-15 rocket (1960) 90 90
1447 20n. Gemini 8 (1966) 90 90
1448 20n. Saturn V rocket (1969) 90 90
1449 20n. *Columbia* (pointing downwards) 90 90
1450 20n. *Eagle* above Moon 90 90
1451 20n. Edwin Aldrin descending ladder 90 90
MS1452 Three sheets. (a) 111×85 mm. 80n. Neil Armstrong (different); (b) 111×85 mm. 80n. Gemini 8 docking with Agena target vehicle (56×41 mm); (c) 85×111 mm. 80n. Apollo 11 command module landing in Pacific Ocean (vert) 11·00 11·00

Nos. 1434/9, 1440/5 and 1446/51 were issued together, *se-tenant* , forming a composite design.

176 Tortoiseshell Cat

1999. Animals. Multicoloured.
1453 5n. Type **176** 75 75
1454 5n. Man watching blue and white cat 75 75
1455 10n. Chinchilla golden longhair adult and kittens 1·40 1·40
1456 12n. Russian blue adult and kitten 65 65
1457 12n. Birman 65 65
1458 12n. Devon rex 65 65
1459 12n. Pewter longhair 65 65
1460 12n. Bombay 65 65
1461 12n. Sorrel somali 65 65
1462 12n. Red tabby manx 65 65
1463 12n. Blue smoke longhair 65 65
1464 12n. Oriental tabby shorthair adult and kitten 65 65
1465 12n. Australian silky terrier 65 65
1466 12n. Samoyed 65 65
1467 12n. Basset bleu de Gascogne 65 65
1468 12n. Bernese mountain dog 65 65
1469 12n. Pug 65 65
1470 12n. Bergamasco 65 65
1471 12n. Basenji 65 65
1472 12n. Wetterhoun 65 65
1473 12n. Drever 65 65
1474 12n. Przewalski horse 65 65
1475 12n. Shetland pony 65 65
1476 12n. Dutch gelderlander horse 65 65
1477 12n. Shire horse 65 65
1478 12n. Arab 65 65
1479 12n. Boulonnais 65 65
1480 12n. Falabella 65 65
1481 12n. Orlov trotter 65 65
1482 12n. Suffolk punch 65 65
1483 15n. Lipizzaner 65 65
1484 20n. Andalusian 1·20 1·20
1485 25n. Weimaraner (dog) 1·70 1·70
1486 30n. German shepherd dog 3·00 3·00
MS1487 Three sheets, each 115×91 mm. (a) 70n. Labrador retriever; (b) 70n. Norwegian forest cat; (c) 70n. Connemara horse 9·75 9·75

177 Bharal

1999. Animals and Birds of the Himalayas. Multicoloured.

(a) Animals.
1489 20n. Type **177** 90 90
1490 20n. Lynx 90 90
1491 20n. Rat snake 90 90
1492 20n. Indian elephant 90 90
1493 20n. Langur 90 90
1494 20n. Musk deer 90 90
1495 20n. Otter 90 90
1496 20n. Tibetan wolf 90 90
1497 20n. Himalayan black bear 90 90
1498 20n. Snow leopard 90 90
1499 20n. Flying squirrel 90 90
1500 20n. Red fox 90 90
1501 20n. Ibex 90 90
1502 20n. Takin 90 90
1503 20n. Agama lizard 90 90
1504 20n. Marmot 90 90
1505 20n. Red panda 90 90
1506 20n. Leopard cat 90 90
MS1507 Three sheets, each 78×118 mm. (a) 100n. Cobra; (b) 100n. Tiger; (c) 100n. Rhinoceros (wrongly inscr "Rhinoerous") 16·00 16·00

(b) Birds.
1508 20n. Red-crested pochard 90 90
1509 20n. Satyr tragopan 90 90
1510 20n. Lammergeier ("Lammergeier Vulture") 90 90
1511 20n. Kalij pheasant 90 90
1512 20n. Great Indian hornbill 90 90
1513 20n. White stork ("Stork") 90 90
1514 20n. Rufous-necked hornbill (wrongly inscr "Rofous") 90 90
1515 20n. Black drongo ("Drongo") 90 90
1516 20n. Himalayan monal pheasant 90 90
1517 20n. Black-necked crane 90 90
1518 20n. Little green bee-eater 90 90
1519 20n. Oriental ibis ("Ibis") 90 90
1520 20n. Crested lark 90 90
1521 20n. Ferruginous duck 90 90
1522 20n. Blood pheasant 90 90
1523 20n. White-crested laughing thrush ("Laughing Thrush") 90 90
1524 20n. Golden eagle 90 90
1525 20n. Siberian rubythroat 90 90
MS1526 Three sheets, each 78×118 mm. (a) 100n. Siberian rubythroat (different); (b) 100n. Black-naped monarch; (c) 100n. Mountain peacock pheasant 16·00 16·00

178 Elephant, Monkey, Rabbit and Bird (Four Friends)

1999. Year 2000.

1527	**178** 10n. multicoloured	60	60
1528	**178** 20n. multicoloured	1·10	1·10

179 Elegant Stink Horn

1999. Fungi. Multicoloured.

1529	20n. Type **179**	1·20	1·20
1530	20n. *Pholiota squarrosoides*	1·20	1·20
1531	20n. Scaly inky cap (*Coprinus quadrifidus*)	1·20	1·20
1532	20n. Golden spindles (*Clavulinopsis fusiformis*)	1·20	1·20
1533	20n. *Spathularia velutipes*	1·20	1·20
1534	20n. *Ganoderma lucidum*	1·20	1·20
1535	20n. *Microglossum rufum*	1·20	1·20
1536	20n. *Lactarius hygrophoroides*	1·20	1·20
1537	20n. *Lactarius speciosus complex*	1·20	1·20
1538	20n. *Calostoma cinnabarina*	1·20	1·20
1539	20n. *Clitocybe clavipes*	1·20	1·20
1540	20n. *Microstoma floccosa*	1·20	1·20
1541	20n. Frost's bolete (*Boletus frostii*)	1·20	1·20
1542	20n. Common morel (*Morchella esculenta*) (wrongly inscr "estculenta")	1·20	1·20
1543	20n. *Hypomyces lactifuorum*	1·20	1·20
1544	20n. *Polyporus auricularius*	1·20	1·20
1545	20n. *Cantharellus lateritius*	1·20	1·20
1546	20n. *Volvariella pusilla*	1·20	1·20
MS1547	Three sheets, each 78×118 mm. (a) 100n. *Pholiota aurivella*; (b) 100n. *Ramarai grandis*; (c) 100n. *Oudemansiella lucidum*	16·00	16·00

180 Green Dragon with Red Flames

2000. New Year. Year of the Dragon. Multicoloured.

1548	3n. Type **180**	15	15
1549	5n. Green dragon encircling moon	25	25
1550	8n. Dragon and symbols of Chinese zodiac	50	50
1552	12n. Brown dragon encircling moon	75	75
MS1553	90×130 mm. 15n. Dragon head (29×40 mm)	85	85

181 LZ-1 (first flight), 1900

2000. Centenary of First Zeppelin Flight. Multicoloured.

1554	25n. Type **181**	1·30	1·30
1555	25n. LZ-2, 1906	1·30	1·30
1556	25n. LZ-3 over hills (first flight, 1906)	1·30	1·30
1557	25n. LZ-127 *Graf Zeppelin* (first flight, 1928)	1·30	1·30
1558	25n. LZ-129 *Hindenberg* (first flight, 1936)	1·30	1·30
1559	25n. LZ-130 *Graf Zeppelin II* (first flight, 1938)	1·30	1·30
1560	25n. LZ-1 over hill with tree	1·30	1·30
1561	25n. LZ-2 over mountains	1·30	1·30
1562	25n. LZ-3 against sky	1·30	1·30
1563	25n. LZ-4 (first flight, 1908)	1·30	1·30
1564	25n. LZ-5 (first flight, 1909)	1·30	1·30
1565	25n. LZ-6 (formation of Deutsche Liftschiffahrts Aktien Gesallschaft (DELAG) (world's first airline), 1909)	1·30	1·30
1566	25n. LZ-1 over grassy hills, 1900	1·30	1·30
1567	25n. Z11 *Ersatz*, 1913	1·30	1·30
1568	25n. LZ-6 exiting hangar, 1909	1·30	1·30
1569	25n. LZ-10 *Schwabein* (first flight, 1911)	1·30	1·30
1570	25n. LZ-7 *Deutschland* (inscr "Ersatz Deutschland")	1·30	1·30
1571	25n. LZ-11 *Viktoria Luise*	1·30	1·30
MS1572	Three sheets, each 106×80 mm. (a) 80n. Ferdinand von Zeppelin wearing white cap (vert); (b) 80n. Zeppelin wearing cap (vert); (c) 80n. Zeppelin (vert)	12·50	12·50

182 Lunix III

2000. "WORLD STAMP EXPO 2000" International Stamp Exhibition, Anaheim, California. Space. Multicoloured.

1573	25n. Type **182**	1·30	1·30
1574	25n. Ranger 9	1·30	1·30
1575	25n. Lunar Orbiter	1·30	1·30
1576	25n. Lunar Prospector spacecraft	1·30	1·30
1577	25n. *Apollo 11* spacecraft	1·30	1·30
1578	25n. Selen satellite	1·30	1·30
1579	25n. Space shuttle *Challenger*	1·30	1·30
1580	25n. North American X-15 experimental rocket aircraft	1·30	1·30
1581	25n. Space shuttle *Buran*	1·30	1·30
1582	25n. Hermes (experimental space plane)	1·30	1·30
1583	25n. X-33 Venturi Star (reusable launch vehicle)	1·30	1·30
1584	25n. Hope (unmanned experimental spacecraft)	1·30	1·30
1585	25n. Victor Patsayev (cosmonaut)	1·30	1·30
1586	25n. Yladislоav Volkov (cosmonaut)	1·30	1·30
1587	25n. Georgi Dobrvolski (cosmonaut)	1·30	1·30
1588	25n. Virgil Grissom (astronaut)	1·30	1·30
1589	25n. Roger Chaffee (astronaut)	1·30	1·30
1590	25n. Edward White (astronaut)	1·30	1·30
MS1591	Three sheets. (a) 76×111 mm. 80n. Launch of space shuttle *Challenger* (vert); (b) 76×111 mm. 80n. Launch of space shuttle *Buran* (vert); (c) 116×85 mm. 80n. Edwin E. Aldrin on moon (first manned Moon landing, 1969) (vert)	12·50	12·50

183 Trashigang Dzong

2000. "EXPO 2000" World's Fair, Hanover, Germany (1st issue). Monasteries. Multicoloured.

1592	3n. Type **183**	15	15
1593	4n. Lhuentse Dzong	15	15
1594	6n. Gasa Dzong	25	25
1595	7n. Punakha Dzong	35	35
1596	10n. Trashichhoe Dzong	40	40
1597	20n. Paro Dzong	85	85
MS1598	157×98 mm. 15n. Roof (29×40 mm)	65	65

184 Snow Leopard

2000. "EXPO 2000" World's Fair, Hanover, Germany (2nd issue). Wildlife. Multicoloured.

1599	10n. Type **184**	40	40
1600	10n. Common raven ("Raven")	40	40
1601	10n. Golden langur	40	40
1602	10n. Rhododendron	40	40
1603	10n. Black-necked crane	40	40
1604	10n. Blue poppy	40	40

185 Jesse Owens (U.S.A.) (Berlin, 1936)

2000. Olympic Games, Sydney. Multicoloured.

1605	20n. Type **185**	1·00	1·00
1606	20n. Kayaking (modern games)	1·00	1·00
1607	20n. Fulton County Stadium, Atlanta, Georgia (1996 games)	1·00	1·00
1608	20n. Ancient Greek athlete	1·00	1·00

186 G. and R. Stephenson's *Rocket* (first steam locomotive)

2000. 175th Anniv of Opening of Stockton and Darlington Railway. Multicoloured.

1609	50n. Type **186**	2·50	2·50
1610	50n. Steam locomotive (opening of London and Birmingham railway, 1828)	2·50	2·50
1611	50n. Northumbrian locomotive, 1825	2·50	2·50
MS1612	118×79 mm. 100n. Inaugural run on Stockton and Darlington Railway, 1825 (56×42 mm)	4·00	4·00

187 Laird Commercial (biplane), 1929

2000. Airplanes. Multicoloured.

1613	25n. Type **187**	1·20	1·20
1614	25n. Ryan B-5 Brougham, 1927 (wrongly inscr "Broughm")	1·20	1·20
1615	25n. Cessna AW, 1928	1·20	1·20
1616	25n. Travel Air 4000 biplane, 1927	1·20	1·20
1617	25n. Fairchild F-71, 1927	1·20	1·20
1618	25n. Command Aire biplane, 1928	1·20	1·20
1619	25n. Waco YMF biplane, 1935	1·20	1·20
1620	25n. Piper J-4 Cub Coupe, 1938	1·20	1·20
1621	25n. Ryan ST-A, 1937	1·20	1·20
1622	25n. Spartan Executive, 1939	1·20	1·20
1623	25n. Luscombe 8, 1939	1·20	1·20
1624	25n. Stinson SR5 Reliant seaplane, 1935	1·20	1·20
1625	25n. Cessna 195 seaplane, 1949	1·20	1·20
1626	25n. Waco SRE biplane, 1940	1·20	1·20
1627	25n. Erco Ercope, 1948	1·20	1·20
1628	25n. Boeing Stearman biplane, 1941	1·20	1·20
1629	25n. Beech Staggerwing biplane, 1944	1·20	1·20
1630	25n. Republic Seabee, 1947	1·20	1·20
MS1631	Three sheets, each 77×108 mm. (a) 100n. Waco CSO seaplane, 1929; (b) 100n. Curtiss-Wright 19W, 1936; (c) 100n. Grumman G-44 Widgeon flying boat, 1941	12·00	12·00

188 *A Kind of Loving*, 1962

2000. Berlin Film Festival. Winners of Golden Bear Award. Multicoloured.

1632	25n. Type **188**	1·20	1·20
1633	25n. *Bushido Zankoku Monogatari*, 1963	1·20	1·20
1634	25n. *Hobson's Choice*, 1954	1·20	1·20
1635	25n. *El Lazarillo de Tormes*, 1960	1·20	1·20
1636	25n. *In the Name of the Father*, 1997	1·20	1·20
1637	25n. *Les Cousins*, 1959	1·20	1·20
MS1638	96×102 mm. 100n. *Die Ratten*, 1962	4·00	4·00

189 Einstein

2000. Albert Einstein—Time Magazine Man of the Century. Sheet 113×83 mm.

MS1639	**189** 100n. multicoloured	4·50	4·50

190 Aquinas

2000. 775th Birth Anniv of Thomas Aquinas (Catholic philosopher and theologian). Sheet 136×76 mm.

MS1640	**190** 25n.×4 multicoloured	4·00	4·00

191 Pierre de Coubertin

2000. New Millennium. Multicoloured. (a) Centenary of the Modern Olympic Games.

1641	25n. Type **191** (founder of modern games)	1·20	1·20
1642	25n. Hand holding baton (first modern Games, Athens, 1896)	1·20	1·20
1643	25n. Jesse Owen (Berlin, 1936)	1·20	1·20
1644	25n. Handprint and white dove (Munich, 1972)	1·20	1·20
1645	25n. Sydney Opera House (Sydney, 2000)	1·20	1·20
1646	25n. Children wearing T-shirts (Greece, 2004)	1·20	1·20

(b) Breakthroughs in Modern Medicine.

1647	25n. Albert Calmette (bacteriologist, joint discoverer of B.C.G. vaccine)	1·20	1·20
1648	25n. Camillo Colgi and S. Ramon y Cajal (discovery of the neurone)	1·20	1·20
1649	25n. Alexander Fleming (bacteriologist, discoverer of penicillin)	1·20	1·20
1650	25n. Jonas Salk (virologist, developer of polio vaccine)	1·20	1·20
1651	25n. Christiaan Barnard (surgeon, performed first human heart transplant)	1·20	1·20
1652	25n. Luc Mantagnier (A.I.D.S. research)	1·20	1·20

192 Paro Taktsang

2000. Sheet 86×49 mm.

MS1653	**192** 100n. multicoloured	4·00	4·00

193 Christopher Columbus

2000. Explorers. Two sheets, each 66×83 mm. Multicoloured.

MS1654	(a) 100n. Type **193**; (b) 100n. Captain James Cook	8·00	8·00

194 *Crinum amoenum*

2000. Flowers of the Himalayan Mountains. Multicoloured.

1655	25n. Type **194**	1·20	1·20
1656	25n. *Beaumontia grandiflora*	1·20	1·20
1657	25n. *Trachelospermum lucidum*	1·20	1·20
1658	25n. *Curcuma aromatica*	1·20	1·20
1659	25n. *Barleria cristata*	1·20	1·20
1660	25n. *Holmskioldia sanguinea*	1·20	1·20
1661	25n. *Meconopsis villosa*	1·20	1·20
1662	25n. *Salva hians*	1·20	1·20

1663	25n. *Caltha palustris*	1·20	1·20
1664	25n. *Anemone polyanthes*	1·20	1·20
1665	25n. *Cypripedium cordigerum*	1·20	1·20
1666	25n. *Cryptochilus luteus*	1·20	1·20
1667	25n. *Androsace globifera*	1·20	1·20
1668	25n. *Tanacetum atkinsonii*	1·20	1·20
1669	25n. *Aster stracheyi*	1·20	1·20
1670	25n. *Arenaria glanduligera*	1·20	1·20
1671	25n. *Sibbaldia purpurea*	1·20	1·20
1672	25n. *Saxifraga parnassifolia*	1·20	1·20

MS1673 Three sheets, each 68×98 mm. (a) 100n. *Dendrobium densiflorum* (vert); (b) 100n. *Rhododendron arboreum* (vert); (c) 100n. *Gypsophila cerastioides* 14·50 14·50

Nos. 1655/60, 1661/6 and 1667/72 respectively were issued together, se-tenant, forming a composite design.

195 *The Duke and Duchess of Osuna with their Children* (detail, Francisco de Goya)

2000. "Espana 2000" International Stamp Exhibition, Madrid. Prado Museum Exhibits. Multicoloured.

1674	25n. Type **195**	1·50	1·50
1675	25n. Young child (detail from *The Duke and Duchess of Osuna with their Children*)	1·50	1·50
1676	25n. Duke (detail from *The Duke and Duchess of Osuna with their Children*)	1·50	1·50
1677	25n. *Isidoro Maiquez* (Francisco de Goya)	1·50	1·50
1678	25n. *Dona Juana Galarza de Goicoechea* (Francisco de Goya)	1·50	1·50
1679	25n. *Ferdinand VII in an Encampment* (Francisco de Goya)	1·50	1·50
1680	25n. *Portrait of an Old Man* (Joos van Cleve)	1·50	1·50
1681	25n. *Mary Tudor* (Anthonis Mor)	1·50	1·50
1682	25n. *Portrait of a Man* (Jan van Scorel)	1·50	1·50
1683	25n. *The Court Jester Pejeron* (Anthonis Mor)	1·50	1·50
1684	25n. Elizabeth of France (Frans Pourbus the Younger)	1·50	1·50
1685	25n. *King James I* (Paul van Somer)	1·50	1·50
1686	25n. *The Empress Isabella of Portugal* (Titian)	1·50	1·50
1687	25n. *Lucrecia di Baccio del Fede, the Painter's Wife* (Andrea del Sarto)	1·50	1·50
1688	25n. *Self-Portrait* (Titian)	1·50	1·50
1689	25n. *Philip II* (Sofonisba Anguisciola)	1·50	1·50
1690	25n. *Portrait of a Doctor* (Lucia Anguisciola)	1·50	1·50
1691	25n. *Anna of Austria* (Sofonisba Anguisciola)	1·50	1·50

MS1692 Three sheets (a) 90×110 mm. 100n. Duchess and Duke (detail from *The Duke and Duchess of Osuna with their Children* (Francisco de Goya) (horiz); (b) 90×110 mm. 100n. *Charles V at Mühlberg* (Titian); (c) 110×90 mm. 100n. *The Relief of Genoa* (Antonio de Pereda) Set of 3 sheets 13·50 13·50

196 Butterfly

2000. "Indepex Asiana 2000" International Stamp Exhibition, Calcutta. Multicoloured.

1693	5n. Type **196**	15	15
1694	8n. Red jungle fowl	40	40
1695	10n. *Zinnia elegans*	50	50
1696	12n. Tiger	60	60

MS1697 144×84 mm. 15n. Spotted deer (28×34 mm) 65 65

197 Snake

2001. New Year. Year of the Snake. Multicoloured.

1698	3n. Type **197**	15	15
1699	20n. Snake	1·10	1·10

MS1700 135×135 mm. 3, 10n. As Type **197**; 15, 20n. As No. 1699 2·00 2·00

198 Snow Leopard (*Uncia uncia*)

2001. "Hong Kong 2001" International Stamp Exhibition. Nature Protection. Sheet 195×138 mm containing T **198** and similar horiz designs. Multicoloured.

MS1701 15n. Type **198**; 15n. Rufous-necked hornbill (*Aceros nipalensis*); 15n. Black-necked crane (*Grus nigricollis*); 15n. Tiger (*Panthera tigris*) 2·75 2·75

199 Working in Fields

2001. International Year of Volunteers. Multicoloured.

1702	3n. Type **199**	15	15
1703	4n. Planting crops	25	25
1704	10n. Children and bucket	50	50
1705	15n. Planting seeds and making compost	75	75

MS1706 170×120 mm. Nos. 1702/5 1·30 1·30

200 Chenrezig

2001. Buddhist Art, Taksang Monastery. Sheet 120×147 mm containing T **200** and similar vert designs. Multicoloured.

MS1707 10n. Type **200**; 15n. Guru Rimpoche; 20n. Sakyamuni 2·10 2·10

2001. Nos. 557/60 surch.

1708	4n. on 10ch. blue	40	40
1709	10n. on 25ch. red	50	50
1710	15n. on 50ch. violet	70	70
1711	20n. on 1n. brown	95	95

202 Snow Leopard's Head

2001. Snow Leopard (*Uncia uncia*). Sheet 172×140 mm containing T **202** and similar multicoloured design.

MS1712 10n.×4, each ×2, Type **202**; Two adults; Three juveniles; Crouched adult 4·00 4·00

203 Horse carrying Treasure Vase (Buddhist symbol)

2002. Year of the Horse. Multicoloured.

1713	20n. Type **203**	1·00	1·00
1714	20n. White horse	1·00	1·00

MS1715 94×94 mm. 25n. Horse and Dharma Wheel (horiz) 1·20 1·20

Nos. 1713/14 were issued together, *se-tenant* forming a composite design.

204 Teri gang

2002. International Year of Mountains. Sheet 144×105 mm containing T **204** and similar horiz designs. Multicoloured.

MS1716 20n. Type **204**; 20n. Tsenda gang; 20n. Jomolhari; 20n. Gange-heytag; 20n. Jitchudrake; 20n. Tse-rim Gang 5·75 5·75

205 *Rhomboda lanceolata*

2002. Orchids. Sheet 162×131 mm containing T **205** and similar vert designs. Multicoloured.

MS1717 10n. Type **205**; 10n. *Odontochilus lanceolatus*; 10n. *Zeuxine glandulosai*; 10n. *Goodyera schlechtendaliana*; 10n. *Anoectochilus lanceolatus*; 10n. *Goodyera hispida* 3·00 3·00

206 *Rhododendron niveum*

2002. Rhododendrons. Sheet 132×132 mm containing T **206** and similar square designs. Multicoloured.

MS1718 15n. Type **206**; 15n. *Rhododendron glaucophyllum*; 15n. *Rhododendron arboretum*; 15n. *Rhododendron grande*; 15n. *Rhododendron dalhousiae*; 15n. *Rhododendron barbatum* 4·00 4·00

207 Kapok Tree (*Bombax ceiba*)

2002. Medicinal Plants. Multicoloured.

1719	10n. Type **207**	25	25
1720	10n. Angel's trumpet (*Brugmansia suaveolens*)	25	25
1721	10n. Himalayan mayapple (*Podophyllum hexandrum*)	25	25
1722	10n. Himalayan pokeberry (*Photlacca acinosa*)	25	25

MS1723 85×106 mm. 10n.×4, Nos. 1719/22 1·20 1·20

208 Fireman and Flags

2002. "United We Stand".

1724	**208**	25n. multicoloured	60	60

209 Zinedine Zidane

2002. World Cup Football Championships, Japan and South Korea. Two sheets containing T **209** and similar vert designs. Multicoloured.

MS1725 (a) 167×118 mm. 25n. Type **209**; 25n. Michael Owen; 25n. Miyagi stadium, Japan; 25n. Cuauhtemoc Blanco (inscr "Cuahutemoc"); 25n. Gabriel Batistuta; 25n. Incheon stadium, South Korea; (b) 97×112 mm. 150n. Roberto Carlos 7·00 7·00

210 Queen Elizabeth

2002. Golden Jubilee of Queen Elizabeth II. Two sheets containing T **210** and similar square designs. Multicoloured.

MS1726 (a) 133×101 mm. 40n. Type **210**; 40n. Wearing green floral hat; 40n. With Duke of Edinburgh; 40n. Wearing white hat; (b) 79×108 mm. 90n. Wearing tiara 6·00 6·00

211 Ski Jumping

2002. Winter Olympic Games, Salt Lake City, USA. Sheet 89×120 mm containing T **211** and similar vert design. Multicoloured.

MS1727 50n. Type **211**; 50n. Cross country skiing 2·40 2·40

212 Lotus Flower

2002. United Nations Year of Eco-Tourism. Two sheets containing T **212** and similar vert designs. Multicoloured.

MS1728 (a) 117×75 mm. 50n. Type **212**; 50n. Northern jungle queen butterfly; 50n. Bengal tiger; (b) 72×95 mm. 90n. Peacock 5·75 5·75

213 Cub Scout

2002. World Scout Jamboree, Thailand. Two sheets containing T **213** and similar multicoloured designs.

MS1729 (a) 182×142 mm. 50n. Type **213**; 50n. Scouts of different nationalities; 50n. 1908 Scout; (b) 90×120 mm. 90n. Dan Beard (founder of American Boy Scouts) (vert) 5·75 5·75

214 Charles Lindbergh and *The Spirit of St Louis*

2002. 75th Anniv of First Solo Trans-Atlantic Flight. Two sheets containing T **214** and similar vert designs. Multicoloured.

MS1730 (a) 171×134 mm. 75n. Type **214**; 75n. Lindbergh; (b) 123×89 mm. 90n. Lindbergh (different) 5·75 5·75

215 Guar

2002. Flora and Fauna. Twelve sheets containing T **215** and similar horiz designs. Multicoloured.

MS1731 (a) 132×155 mm. 25n. Type **215**; 25n. Hog badger; 25n. Indian cobra; 25n. Leopard gecko; 25n. Gavial; 25n. Hispid hare; (b) 132×155 mm. 25n. Yellow-legged gull; 25n. Sand martin; 25n. Asian open-bill stork; 25n. White stork; 25n. Eurasian oystercatcher; 25n. Indian pitta; (c) 132×155 mm. 25n. Blue oak-leaf butterfly (inscr "Dead leaf butterfly") (Kalima horsfieldi); 25n. Golden birdwing (*Troides aeacus*); 25n. *Atrophaneura latrellei*; 25n. Kaiser-I-Hind (*Teinopalpus imperialis*); 25n. *Zeuxidia aurelius*; 25n. *Euploea dufresne*; (d) 137×158 mm. 25n. *Primula cawdoriana*; 25n. *Meconopsis aculeate*; 25n. *Primula wigramiana*; 25n. *Primula stuartii*; 25n. *Saxifraga andersonii*; 25n. *Rheum nobile*; (e) 133×153 mm. 25n. *Russula integra*; 25n. *Hydgrophorus marzuolus*; 25n. *Trichloma fulvum*; 25n. *Hypholoma fasciculare*; 25n. *Tricholoma populinum*; 25n. *Cortinarius orellanus*; (f) 136×161 mm. 25n. *Coelogyne rhodeana*; 25n. *Coelogyne virescens*; 25n. *Phalanopsis schilleriana*; 25n. *Angraecum eburneum*; 25n. *Dendrobium aureum*; 25n. *Dendrobium Ceasar*; (g) 89×92 mm. 90n. Esturine crocodile; (h) 89×94 mm. 90n. Mandarin duck; (i) 93×94 mm. 90n. *Portia philota*; (j) 103×101 mm. 90n. *Paris polyphylla*; (k) 101×101 mm. 90n. *Clathrus archeri*; (l) 99×100 mm. 90n. *Dendrobium chrysotoxum* 35·00 35·00

216 Elvis Presley

2003. Anniversaries in 2002. 25th Death Anniv of Elvis Presley (entertainer) (MS1732a/b). 85th Birth Anniv of John Fitzgerald Kennedy (president USA, 1961–1963) (MS1732c/d). 5th Death Anniv of Diana, Princess of Wales (MS1732e/f). Six sheets containing T **216** and similar vert designs. Multicoloured.

MS1732 Six sheets (a) 110×178 mm. 25n.×4, Type **216**; Holding guitar at waist; Singing into microphone; Seated holding guitar to side; (b) 195×131 mm. 25n.×6, Wearing shirt and kerchief; (c) 132×146 mm. 25n.×6, College graduate, 1935; Walking with John F. Kennedy Jr.; As Congressman, 1946; At the White House, 1961; With Jacqueline Kennedy on tennis court; Jacqueline Kennedy and children at John F. Kennedy's funeral; (d) 76×108 mm. 90n. Head and shoulders; (e) 134×118 mm. 25n.×4, Wearing earrings and red dress; Wearing ballgown; Wearing jacket and blouse; Wearing tiara; (f) 65×98 mm. 90n. Wearing hat with feathers 17·00 17·00

2003. No. 659 surch **8NU**.

1733 8n. on 75ch. multicoloured 20 20

218 Lamb

2003. Chinese New Year. ("Year of the Sheep"). Sheet 120×80 mm containing T **218** and similar multicoloured design.

MS1734 15n. Type **218**; 20n. Sheep's head (vert) 80 80

219 *Egret and Willow* (Suzuki Kitsu)

2003. Japanese Paintings. Six sheets containing T **219** and similar multicoloured designs.

MS1735 (a) 135×210 mm. 25n.×6, Type **219**; *White Cranes* (Ito Jakuchu); *Cranes* (Suzuki Kitsu); "*andarin Ducks amid Snow-covered Reeds* (Ito Jakuchu); *Rooster, Hen and Hydrangea* (Ito Jakuchu); *Hawk on Snow-covered Branch* (Shibara Zeshin); (b) 135×210 mm. 25n.×6, *Beauty reading Letter* (Utagawa Kunisada); *Two Beauties* (Katsukawa Shunsho); *Beauty arranging her Hai"* (Kaigetsudo Doshin); *Dancing* (Suzuki Kitsu); *Two Beauties* (Kitagawa Kikumaro); *Kambun Beauty*; (c) 159×140 mm. 25n.×6, Two seated men and one lying down (38×51 mm); Man holding fan, man holding lute and man facing left (38×51 mm); Man with raised arm and woman facing left (38×51 mm); Two men talking and two facing left (38×51 mm); Man wearing blue robe facing right and bald man (38×51 mm); Man with beard and two women (38×51 mm); (d) 90×90 mm. 90n. *Heads of Nine Beauties in a Roundel with Plum Blossom* (Hosoda Eishi); (e) 90×90 mm. *Hawk carrying Monkey* (Shibata Zeshin); (f) 92×92 mm. *Chrysanthemums by a Stream, with Rocks* (Ito Jakuchu) 17·00 17·00

The stamps of No. **MS**1735c form a composite design of "Thirty six Poets".

220 Lyonpo Sangay Ngedup

2003. Move for Health Walk (walk by Lyonpo Sangay Ngedup (Health Minister) from Trashigang to Thimphu). Sheet 120×80 mm.

MS1736 **220** 50n. multicoloured 1·20 1·20

221 Girl and Parrot

2003. Education for All. Sheet 70×109 mm containing T **221** and similar vert designs. Multicoloured.

MS1737 5n. Type **221**; 5n. Girl reading; 10n. Boy and girl carrying books; 20n. Girl holding football 1·00 1·00

222 Kalij Pheasant (*Lophura leucomelana*) (inscr "leucomelanus")

2003. Endangered Species. Birds. Sheet 69×100 mm containing T **222** and similar vert designs. Multicoloured.

MS1738 2n. Type **222**; 5n. Blyth's tragopan (*Tragopan blythii*); 8n. Satyr tragopan (*Tragopan satyra*); 15n. Himalayan monal pheasant (*Lophophorus impeyanus*) (inscr "impejanus") 70 70

223 Monkey

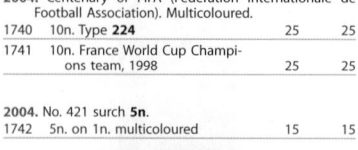

2004. New Year. Year of the Monkey. Sheet 95×130 mm containing T **223** and similar vert designs. Multicoloured.

MS1739 10n.×4, Type **223**; Facing left; With raised back legs; Family 1·00 1·00

The stamps and margin of No. **MS**1739 were issued together, *se-tenant*, forming a composite design.

224 Brazil World Cup Champions Team, 2002

2004. Centenary of FIFA (Federation Internationale de Football Association). Multicoloured.

1740 10n. Type **224** 25 25

1741 10n. France World Cup Champions team, 1998 25 25

2004. No. 421 surch **5n**.

1742 5n. on 1n. multicoloured 15 15

226 Traditional Ploughing

2004. 20th Anniv of Continuing Japanese Assistance with Food Production. Two sheets containing T **226** and similar multicoloured designs.

MS1743 (a) 155×105 mm. 5n.×6, Type **225**; Women transplanting; Traditional threshing; Modern ploughing; Modern transplanting; Modern threshing. (b) 130×85 mm. 30n. King Jigme Singe Wangchuk ploughing 1·50 1·50

The stamps and margin of No. **MS**1743a were issued together, *se-tenant*, forming a composite design.

227 Jungle Fowl

2005. New Year. "Year of the Rooster". Sheet 155×110 mm containing T **227** and similar horiz design. Multicoloured.

MS1744 15n. Type **227**; 20n. Domestic fowl 85 85

228 Dancer

2005. EXPO 2005 World Exposition, Aichi, Japan. Two sheets containing T **228** and similar vert designs. Multicoloured.

MS1745 126×201 mm. 10n. Type **228**; 10n. Dancer wearing skull mask; 20n. Dancer holding drum; 20n. Dancer wearing horned mask 1·50 1·50

MS1746 124×80 mm. 30n. Buddha (25×35 mm) 75 75

229 Pope John Paul II

2005. Pope John Paul II Commemoration. Multicoloured.

1747 15n. Type **229** 40 40

1747a 15n. As No. 1747 40 40

1747b 15n. As No. 1747 40 40

1747c 15n. As No. 1747 40 40

230 Locomotive P36 N 0097

2005. Bicentenary of Steam Locomotives (2004). Multicoloured.

1748–1751 30n.×4, Type **230**; Diesel locomotive VIA F 40 6428; InterRegio electric train, Amtrak 464 3·00 3·00

MS1752 100×71 mm. 85n. Locomotive P36N0032 (vert) 2·00 2·00

231 Guido Buchwald

2005. 75th Anniv of World Cup Football Championships. Multicoloured.

1753–1755 40n.×3, Type **231**; Mario Basler; Torsten Frings 3·00 3·00

MS1756 124×105 mm. 85n. Fredi Bobic 2·00 2·00

232 Linked Hands and Emblem

2005. Centenary of Rotary International. Sheet 95×113 mm.

MS1757 **232** 85n. multicoloured 2·00 2·00

232a Wachy Zam, Wangduephodrang

2005. Bridges. Sheet 200×160 mm containing T **232a** and similar horiz designs. Multicoloured.

MS1758 10n. Type **232a**; 10n. Chain bridge, Doksam; 10n. Wooden cantilevered bridge, Mishi, Paro; 20n. Mo Chu bridge, Punakha; 20n. Langjo bridge, Thimphu; 20n. Punatshang Chu bridge, Wangduephodrang 2·20 2·20

233 Children from Many Nations

2005. "My Dream of Peace One Day". Winning Designs in Children's Painting Competition. Multicoloured.

1759–1764 10n.×6, Type **233**; Candle of flags; Children holding jigsaw of family; Dove and light and dark hands holding globe; Hands holding children and dark globe releasing doves; Globe holding umbrella of flags 1·50 1·50

234 King Jigme Singye Wangchuck

2005. 50th Birth Anniv of King Jigme Singye Wangchuck. Sheet 216×163 mm containing T **234** and similar vert designs. Multicoloured.

MS1765 20n.×5 Type **234**; Standing on podium (inauguration) (39×87 mm); Speaking with microphone; Seated on throne; With women 2·60 2·60

The stamps of **MS**1765 share a composite background design.

234a Raven

2005. National Symbols. Sheet 200×160 mm containing T **234a** and similar square designs. Multicoloured.

MS1766 10n. Type **234a**; 10n. Takin (*Budorcas taxicolor*); 20n. Cypress tree; 20n. Blue poppy 1·30 1·30

235 St. Bernard

2006. New Year. Year of the Dog. Multicoloured.

1767	5n. Type **235**	15	15
1768	10n. Lhasa Apso (Inscr 'Apsoo')	25	25
1769	15n. Maltese terrier (inscr 'Maltese')	40	40
1770	20n. Papillion (inscr 'Papillon')	50	50
MS1771	125×105 mm. 5n. As No. 1767; 10n. As No. 1768; 15n. As No. 1769; 20n. As No. 1770; 25n. Husky (36×70 mm)	1·90	1·90

236 Jakur Dzong

2006. 50th Anniv of Europa Stamps. Multicoloured.

1772	150n. Type **236**	3·75	
1773	250n. Archery	6·25	
MS1774	100×72 mm. Nos. 1772/3	10·00	10·00

237 Female Fire Hog

2007. New Year. Year of the Pig. Multicoloured.

1775	20n. Type **237**	50	50
MS1776	93×120 mm. 25n. Pig (35×33 mm)	2·00	2·00

Nos. 1777/8 and Type **238** have been left for 'Year of the Rat', issued on 8 February 2008, not yet received.

No. **MS**1778 consists of a sleeve containing a CD ROM.

239 Ugyen Wangchuck (1907–1926)

2008. Centenary of Monarchy. Two sheets containing T **239** and similar multicoloured designs. Self-adhesive (**MS**1780) or ordinary gum (**MS**1779).

MS1779	170×122 mm. 5n. Type **239**; 10n. Jigme Wangchuck (1926–52); 15n. Jigme Dorji Wangchuck (1952–72); 20n. Jigme Singye Wangchuck (1972–2006); 25n. Jigme Khesar Namgyel Wangchuck (2006–)	1·80	1·80
MS1780	97×97 mm. 225n. Kings of Wangchuck dynasty	6·25	6·25

240 (Illustration reduced. Actual size 97×97 mm) (image scaled to 50% of original size)

2008. In Harmony with Nature. Sheet 97×97 mm. Self-adhesive.

MS1781	225n. **240** multicoloured	6·25	6·25

No. **MS**1781 consists of a sleeve containing a CD ROM.

241 Archer

2008. Olympic Games, Beijing. Sheet 130×130 mm containing T **241** and similar diamond shaped designs. Multicoloured.

MS1782	10n. Type **241**; 15n. Archer with leg raised; 25n. Auspicious symbols; 25n. Garuda in flight	1·80	1·80

242 Masked Dancers

2008. Bhutan's Participation at Smithsonian Folklife Festival. Three sheets containing T **242** and similar multicoloured designs.

MS1783	230×168 mm. 20n.×5, Type **242**; Archer; Ploughing; Dancers; Wood carving	3·50	3·50
MS1784	100×90 mm. 50n. Pavillion (38×50 mm)	1·80	1·80
MS1785	100×90 mm. 50n. Fireworks (50×38 mm)	1·80	1·80

243 Ox

2009. Chinese New Year

1786	20n. Type **243**	65	65
MS1787	162×210 mm. 30n. As Type **243** (40×30 mm)	1·10	1·10

244 Cantilever Bridge

2009. Punakha Dzong Bridge. Multicoloured.

1788	20n. Type **244**	65	65
MS1789	170×118 mm. 25n.×2, Bridge, left; Bridge, right	1·40	1·40

The stamps and margins of **MS**1789 form a composite design of the bridge and environs.

245 Eclipse (diamond ring effect)

2009. International Year of Astronomy. Multicoloured.

MS1790	25n.×2, Type **245**; Musicians and partial eclipse	1·70	1·70

246 Child leading Yaks carrying Gifted Rice from Japan

2009. 35th Anniv of World Food Programme in Bhutan

MS1791	200×119mm. 10n. Type **246**; 10n.Yaks carrying gifted rice from Saudi Arabia; 10n. Gifted rice in store; 10n. Cultivating hillside; 10n. People on track; 10n. New dwelling; 20n. Mother and child; 20n. Feeding children; 20n. Children studying	3·75	3·75
MS1792	100×75mm. 25n. Children holding red 'fill the cup' mugs (46×46mm)	90	90

247 Kushuthara

2009. Textiles. Multicoloured.

MS1793	20n.x4, Type **247**; Mentse Mathra; Lungserma; Yathra	2·75	2·75

248 Red Panda and Cub

2009. Red Panda (*Ailurus fulgens*). Multicoloured.

1794	20n. Type **248**	1·20	1·20
1795	20n. Facing left	1·20	1·20
1796	25n. Two pandas sleeping	1·40	1·40
1797	25n. Eating bamboo shoots	1·40	1·40

249 Tiger

2010. Chinese New Year. Year of the Tiger–Save the Tiger Campaign. Multicoloured.

MS1798	30n.×2, Type **249**; Laying facing right	1·90	1·90
MS1799	50n. Head and shoulders (vert)	1·60	1·60

250 National Memorial Chorten (stupa)

2010. World Health Day, 2010. Urbanization, a Challenge for Public Health. Multicoloured.

MS1800	10n.×6, Type **250**; Main street, Thimpu; Aerial view of Thimpu; Golf; New roadway; Clock tower and central square of Thimpu	2·20	2·20
MS1801	25n. New urban housing (50×38 mm)	1·50	1·50

251 Afghanistan

2010. 16th SAARC (South Asian Association for Regional Cooperation) Summit 2010, Bhutan. Multicoloured.

MS1802	200×150 mm. 10n.×8, Type **251**; Bangladesh; Bhutan; India; Maldives; Nepal; Pakistan; Sri Lnka	2·50	2·50
MS1803	148×100 mm. 25n. All members flags (51×40 mm)	1·50	1·50

252 King Jigme Dorji Wangchuck with Bow

2010. King Jigme Khesar Namgyel Wangchuck

MS1804	210×148 mm. 10n.×6, Type **252**; Throwing dart; Playing football with children; Playing basketball with children; In water, playing waterpolo; Riding mountain bike	2·20	2·20
MS1805	210×148 mm. 10n.×6, Greeting school children outside school; Seated in doorway with four children; Seated amogst children all with arms raised; Talking to children wearing grey; Greeting children from podium; With mother and child	2·20	2·20
MS1806	210×148 mm. 10n.×6, Clasping hands with monk; Crouched writing in book by firelight; Seated in doorway with family of four; Performing Namaste amongst crowd; Seated with family of five; Seated on earth bank with crowd	2·20	2·20
MS1807	101×145 mm. 20n. King Jigme Khesar Namgyel Wangchuck, head and shoulders (40×50 mm.)	3·50	3·50
MS1808	190×128 mm. 30n.×3, King Jigme Khesar Namgyel Wangchuck×3 (with gold, silver or bronze backgrounds) (38 mm (circular))	2·75	2·75

253 Desi Jigme Namgyel

2010. Wangchuck Dynasty. Multicoloured.

MS1809	15n.×6, Type **253;** Ugyen Wangchuck (1st king) (1907 - 1926); Jigme Wangchchuck (1926 - 1952); King Jigme Khesar Namgyel Wangchuck (2006 - present) (30×76 mm); Jigme Dorji Wangchuck (1952 - 1972) (45×30 mm); Jigme Singe Wangchuck (1972 - 2006) (45×30 mm)	2·50	2·50

254 Ashi Tsendu Lhamo Wangchuck

2010. Queens of Bhutan. Multicoloured.

MS1810	15n.×8, Type **254;** Ashi Phuntsho Choden Wangchuck; Ashi Pema Dechen Wangchuck; Ashi Kezang Choden Wangchuck; Ashi Dorji Wangma Wangchuck; Ashi Tshering Pem Wangchuck; Ashi Tshering Yangdon Wangchuck; Ashi Sangay Choden Wangchuck	2·75	2·75

255 Rabbit

2011. Chinese New Year. Year of the Rabbit. Sheet 100×150 mm

MS1811	**255** 25n. multicoloured	80	80

256 Cherry Blossom and *Meconopsis*

2011. 25th Anniv of Bhutan - Japan Diplomatic Relations. Multicoloured.

MS1812	20n.×4, Type **256**; Bridge; Cultivators; Apple orchard	2·50	2·50

257 King Jigme Dorji Wangchuck greeting Jawaharlal Nehru (prime minister of India)

2011. First Visit of Indian Prime Minister (Jawaharlal Nehru) to Bhutan. Multicoloured.

MS1813	120×170 mm. 10n.×4, Type **257**; Inspecting troops; Prime Minister Nehru and royal family;	1·40	1·40
MS1814	120×80 mm. 25n. Prime Minister Nehru riding yak (50×40 mm)	3·25	3·25

258 King Jigme Khesar Namgyel Wangchuck and Queen Jetsun Pema

2011. Wedding of King Jigme Khesar Namgyel Wangchuck to Jetsun Pema. Multicoloured.

MS1815 150×225 mm. 25n.×4, Type **258**; Jetsun Pema; As Type **258**, with trees as background; Jetsun Pema, with dark background	3·25	3·25
MS1816 122×82 mm. 50n. As Type **258**, orange-brown background (31×31 mm)	1·90	1·90
MS1817 115×77 mm. 50n. King Jigme Khesar Namgyel Wangchuck and Queen Jetsun Pema (44×65 mm)	1·90	1·90
MS1818 131×171 mm. 50n. Queen Jetsun Pema (41×65 mm)	1·90	1·90
MS1819 85×130 mm. 100n. King Jigme Khesar Namgyel Wangchuck and Queen Jetsun Pema with meconopsis and lotus flowers (50×72 mm)	3·50	3·50
MS1820 108×173 mm. 225n. King Jigme Khesar Namgyel Wangchuck and Queen Jetsun Pema (gold) (42×60 mm)	4·75	4·75

APPENDIX

The following stamps have either been issued in excess of postal needs or have not been available to the public in reasonable quantities at face value. Such stamps may later be given full listing if there is evidence of regular postal use.

1968

Bhutan Pheasants. 1, 2, 4, 8, 15ch., 2, 4, 5, 7, 9n.
Winter Olympic Games, Grenoble. Optd on 1966 Abominable Snowmen issue. 40ch., 1n.25, 3, 6n.
Butterflies (plastic-surfaced). Postage 15, 50ch., 1n.25, 2n.; Air 3, 4, 5, 6n.
Paintings (relief-printed). Postage 2, 4, 5, 10, 45, 80ch., 1n.05, 1n.40, 2, 3, 4, 5n.; Air 1n.50, 2n.50, 6, 8n.
Olympic Games, Mexico. 5, 45, 60, 80ch., 1n.05, 2, 3, 5n.
Human Rights Year. Die-stamped surch on unissued "Coins". 15ch. on 50n.p., 33ch. on 1r., 9n. on 3r.75.

1969

Flood Relief. Surch on 1968 Mexico Olympics issue. 5ch.+5ch., 80ch.+25ch., 2n.+50ch.
Fish (plastic-surfaced). Postage 15, 20, 30ch.; Air 5, 6, 7n.
Insects (plastic-surfaced). Postage 10, 75ch., 1n.25, 2n.; Air 3, 4, 5, 6n.
Admission of Bhutan to Universal Postal Union. 5, 10, 15, 45, 60ch., 1n.05, 1n.40, 4n.
5000 Years of Steel Industry. On steel foil. Postage 2, 5, 15, 45, 75ch., 1n.50, 1n.75, 2n.; Air 3, 4, 5, 6n.
Birds (plastic-surfaced). Postage 15, 50ch., 1n.25, 2n.; Air 3, 4, 5, 6n.
Buddhist Prayer Banners. On silk rayon. 15, 75ch., 2, 5, 6n.
Moon Landing of "Apollo 11" (plastic-surfaced). Postage 3, 5, 15, 20, 25, 45, 50ch., 1n.75; Air 3, 4, 5, 6n.

1970

Famous Paintings (plastic-surfaced). Postage 5, 10, 15ch., 2n.75; Air 3, 4, 5, 6n.
New U.P.U. Headquarters Building, Berne. 3, 10, 20ch., 2n.50.
Flower Paintings (relief-printed). Postage 2, 3, 5, 10, 15, 75ch., 1n., 1n.40; Air 80, 90ch., 1n.10, 1n.40, 1n.60, 1n.70, 3n., 3n.50.
Animals (plastic-surfaced). Postage 5, 10, 20, 25, 30, 40, 65, 75, 85ch.; Air 2, 3, 4, 5n.
Conquest of Space (plastic-surfaced). Postage 2, 5, 15, 25, 30, 50, 75ch., 1n.50; Air 2, 3, 6, 7n.

1971

History of Sculpture (plastic-moulded). Postage 10, 75ch., 1n.25, 2n.; Air 3, 4, 5, 6n.
Moon Vehicles (plastic-surfaced). Postage 10ch., 1n.70; Air 2n.50, 4n.
History of the Motor Car (plastic-surfaced). Postage 2, 5, 10, 15, 20, 30, 60, 75, 85ch., 1n., 1n.20, 1n.55, 1n.80, 2n., 2n.50; Air 4, 6, 7, 9, 10n.
Bhutan's Admission to United Nations. Postage 5, 10, 20ch., 3n.; Air 2n.50, 5, 6n.
60th Anniv of Boy Scout Movement. 10, 20, 50, 75ch., 2, 6n.
World Refugee Year. Optd on 1971 United Nations issue. Postage 5, 10, 20ch., 3n.; Air 2n.50, 5, 6n.

1972

Famous Paintings (relief-printed). Postage 15, 20, 90ch., 2n.50; Air 1n.70, 4n.60, 5n.40, 6n.
Famous Men (plastic-moulded). Postage 10, 15, 55ch.; Air 2, 6, 8n.
Olympic Games, Munich. Postage 10, 15, 20, 30, 45ch.; Air 35ch., 1n.35, 7n.
Space Flight of "Apollo 16" (plastic-surfaced). Postage 15, 20, 90ch., 2n.50; Air 1n.70, 4n.60, 5n.40, 6n.

1973

Dogs. 2, 3, 15, 20, 30, 99ch., 2n.50, 4n.
Roses (on scent-impregnated paper). Postage 15, 25, 30ch., 3n.; Air 6, 7n.
Moon Landing of "Apollo 17" (plastic-surfaced). Postage 10, 15, 55ch. 2n.; Air 7, 9n.
"Talking Stamps" (miniature records). Postage 10, 25ch., 1n.25, 7, 8n.; Air 3, 9n.
Death of King Jigme Dorji Wangchuck. Embossed on gold foil. Postage 10, 25ch., 3n.; Air 6, 8n.
Mushrooms. 15, 25, 30ch., 3, 6, 7n.
"Indipex 73" Stamp Exhibition, New Delhi. Postage 5, 10, 15, 25ch., 1n.25, 3n.; Air 5, 6n.

Pt. 1

BIAFRA

The Eastern Region of Nigeria declared its Independence on 30 May 1967 as the Republic of Biafra. Nigerian military operations against the breakaway Republic commenced in July 1967.

The Biafran postal service continued to use Nigerian stamps when supplies of these became low. In July 1967 "Postage Paid" cachets were used pending the issue of Nos. 1/3.

12 pence = 1 shilling; 20 shillings = 1 pound.

1 Map of Republic

1968. Independence. Multicoloured.

1		2d. Type **1**	10	70
2		4d. Arms, flag and date of Independence	10	70
3		1s. Mother and child (17×22 mm)	15	2·00

1968. Nos. 172/5 and 177/85 of Nigeria optd **SOVEREIGN BIAFRA** and arms.

4		½d. multicoloured (No. 172)	2·25	5·50
5		1d. multicoloured (No. 173)	3·50	8·50
6		1½d. multicoloured (No. 174)	12·00	17·00
7		2d. multicoloured (No. 175)	32·00	50·00
8		4d. multicoloured (No. 177)	19·00	50·00
9		6d. multicoloured (No. 178)	9·00	16·00
10		9d. blue and red (No. 179)	3·50	3·75
11		1s. multicoloured (No. 180)	65·00	£120
12		1s.3d. multicoloured (No. 181)	35·00	55·00
13		2s.6d. multicoloured (No. 182)	3·25	17·00
14		5s. multicoloured (No. 183)	3·75	16·00
15		10s. multicoloured (No. 184)	10·00	42·00
16		£1 multicoloured (No. 185)	10·00	42·00

The overprint on No. 15 does not include **SOVEREIGN**.

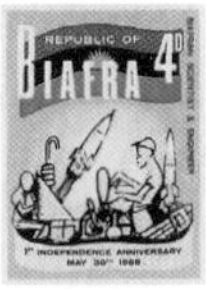

5 Flag and Scientist

1968. First Anniv of Independence. Multicoloured.

17		4d. Type **5**	20	20
18		1s. Victim of atrocity	20	30
19		2s.6d. Nurse and refugees	55	5·00
20		5s. Biafran arms and banknote	60	5·50
21		10s. Orphaned child	1·00	6·00

16 Child in Chains, and Globe

1969. Second Anniv of Independence. Multicoloured; frame colours given.

35	**16**	2d. orange	1·25	4·25
36	**16**	4d. red	1·25	4·25
37	**16**	1s. blue	1·75	7·50
38	**16**	2s.6d. green	2·00	15·00

17 Pope Paul VI, Africa, and Papal Arms

1969. Visit of Pope Paul to Africa. Multicoloured; background colours given.

39	**17**	4d. orange	70	3·00
40	-	6d. blue	85	7·00
41	-	9d. green	1·10	8·50
42	-	3s. mauve	2·75	15·00

DESIGNS: Pope Paul VI, map of Africa and 6d. Arms of Vatican; 9d. St. Peter's Basilica; 3s. Statue of St. Peter.

Pt. 1

BIJAWAR

A state of Central India. Now uses Indian stamps.

12 pies = 1 anna; 16 annas = 1 rupee.

1 Maharaja Sarwant Singh

1935

6	**1**	3p. brown	6·50	9·50
2	**1**	6p. red	8·50	6·50
3	**1**	9p. violet	12·00	7·00
4	**1**	1a. blue	14·00	6·50
5	**1**	2a. green	12·00	6·50

2 Maharaja Sarwant Singh

1937

11	**2**	4a. orange	12·00	£120
12	**2**	6a. lemon	21·00	£120
13	**2**	8a. green	22·00	£160
14	**2**	12a. blue	22·00	£170
15	**2**	1r. violet	45·00	£225

Pt. 5

BOHEMIA AND MORAVIA

Following the proclamation of Slovak Independence on 14 March, 1939, the Czech provinces of Bohemia and Moravia became a German Protectorate. The area was liberated in 1945 and returned to Czechoslovakia.

100 haleru = 1 koruna.

1939. Stamps of Czechoslovakia optd **BOHMEN u. MAHREN CECHY a MORAVA**.

1	**34**	5h. blue	55	2·40
2	**34**	10h. brown	55	2·40
3	**34**	20h. red	65	2·40
4	**34**	25h. green	30	4·00
5	**34**	30h. purple	55	2·40
6	**59**	40h. blue	4·25	9·75
7	**77**	50h. green	30	2·40
8	**60a**	60h. violet	4·25	11·50
9	**61**	1k. purple (No. 348)	80	4·00
10	**61**	1k. purple (No. 395)	65	2·40
11	-	1k.20 purple (No. 354)	3·75	9·75
12	**64**	1k.50 red	3·25	13·00
13	-	1k.60 green (No. 355a)	4·75	14·50
14	-	2k. green (No. 356)	1·60	13·00
15	-	2k.50 blue (No. 357)	3·75	9·75
16	-	3k. brown (No. 358)	3·75	13·00
17	**65**	4k. violet	5·75	14·50
18	-	5k. green (No. 361)	5·75	18·00
19	-	10k. blue (No. 362)	6·75	28·00

2 Linden Leaves and Buds

3 Karluv Tyn Castle

5 Zlin

1939

20	**2**	5h. blue	20	40
21	**2**	10h. brown	20	55
22	**2**	20h. red	20	40
23	**2**	25h. green	20	40
24	**2**	30h. purple	20	40
25	-	40h. blue	20	40
26	**3**	50h. green	20	40
27	-	60h. violet	20	40
28	-	1k. red	20	40
29	-	1k.20 purple	40	75
30	-	1k.50 red	20	40
31	-	2k. green	20	65
32	-	2k.50 blue	20	40
33	**5**	3k. mauve	20	40
34	-	4k. grey	20	55
35	-	5k. green	65	1·10
36	-	10k. blue	55	1·30
37	-	20k. brown	1·60	2·75

DESIGNS—As Type **3**: 40h. Svikov Castle; 60h. St. Barbara's Church, Kutna Hora; 1k. St. Vitus's Cathedral, Prague. As Type **5**—VERT: 1k.20, 1k.50, Brno Cathedral; 2k., 2k.50, Olomouc. HORIZ: 4k. Ironworks, Moravska-Ostrava; 5k., 10k., 20k. Karlsburg, Prague.

1940. As 1939 issue, but colours changed and new values.

38	**2**	30h. brown	20	20
39	**2**	40h. orange	20	20
40	**2**	50h. green	20	20
44	-	50h. green	30	30
41	**2**	60h. violet	20	20
42	**2**	80h. orange	30	30
45	-	80h. blue	20	40
43	**2**	1k. brown	30	30
46	-	1k.20 brown	40	30
47	-	1k.20 red	30	30
48	-	1k.50 pink	30	40
49	-	2k. green	30	30
50	-	2k. blue	30	40
51	-	2k.50 blue	65	75
52	-	3k. green	85	1·10
53	-	5k. green	30	30
54	-	6k. brown	30	75
55	-	8k. green	30	40
56	-	10k. blue	65	40
57	-	20k. brown	1·30	3·25

DESIGNS—As Type **3**: 50h. (No. 44), Neuhaus Castle; 80h. (No. 45), 3k. Pernstyn Castle; 1k.20 (No. 46), 2k.50, Brno Cathedral; 1k.20 (No. 47), St. Vitus's Cathedral, Prague; 1k.50 St. Barbara's Church, Kutna Hora; 2k. Pardubitz Castle. As Type **5**—HORIZ: 5k. Bridge at Beching; 6k. Samson Fountain, Budweis; 8k. Kremsier; 10k. Wallenstein Palace, Prague; 20k. Karlsburg, Prague.

6 Red Cross Nurse and Wounded Soldier

1940. Red Cross Relief Fund.

58	**6**	60h.+40h. blue	65	1·30
59	**6**	1k.20+80h. plum	65	1·30

7 Patient in Hospital

1941. Red Cross Relief Fund.

60	**7**	60h.+40h. blue	40	1·40
61	**7**	1k.20+80h. plum	40	1·40

8 Anton Dvorak

1941. Birth Centenary of Dvorak (composer).

62	**8**	60h. violet	40	75
63	**8**	1k.20 brown	40	75

9 Harvesting

10 Blast furnace, Pilsen

1941. Prague Fair.

64	**9**	30h. brown	20	55
65	**9**	60h. green	20	55
66	**10**	1k.20 plum	20	55
67	**10**	2k.50 blue	20	1·10

11 "Ständetheater", Prague

12 Mozart

1941. 150th Death Anniv of Mozart.

68	**11**	30h.+30h. brown	20	40
69	**11**	60h.+60h. green	20	40

70	**12**	1k.20+1k.20 red	20	40
71	**12**	2k.50+2k.50 blue	40	85

(13)

1942. Third Anniv of German Occupation. Optd with T **13**

72	1k.20 red (No. 47)	55	1·40
73	2k.50 blue (No. 51)	55	1·40

14 Adolf Hitler

1942. Hitler's 53rd Birthday.

74	**14**	30h.+20h. brown	20	40
75	**14**	60h.+40h. green	20	40
76	**14**	1k.20+80h. purple	20	40
77	**14**	2k.50+1k.50 blue	30	1·40

15 Adolf Hitler

1942. Various sizes.

78	**15**	10h. black	20	30
79	**15**	30h. brown	20	30
80	**15**	40h. blue	20	30
81	**15**	50h. green	20	30
82	**15**	60h. violet	20	30
83	**15**	80h. orange	20	30
84	**15**	1k. brown	20	30
85	**15**	1k.20 red	25	40
86	**15**	1k.50 red	25	40
87	**15**	1k.60 green	25	40
88	**15**	2k. blue	25	40
89	**15**	2k.40 brown	25	40
90	**15**	2k.50 blue	25	40
91	**15**	3k. olive	25	40
92	**15**	4k. purple	25	40
93	**15**	5k. green	25	40
94	**15**	6k. brown	25	55
95	**15**	8k. blue	25	55
96	**15**	10k. green	25	1·10
97	**15**	20k. violet	30	1·10
98	**15**	30k. red	55	2·50
99	**15**	50k. blue	1·10	3·25

SIZES—17½×21½ mm: 10h. to 80h.; 18½×21 mm: 1k. to 2k.40; 19×24 mm: 2k.50 to 8k.; 24×30 mm: 10k. to 50k.

16 Nurse and Patient

1942. Red Cross Relief Fund.

100	**16**	60h.+40h. blue	20	40
101	**16**	1k.20+80h. red	20	40

17 Mounted Postman

1943. Stamp Day.

102	**17**	60h. purple	25	75

18 Peter Parler

1943. Winter Relief Fund.

103	-	60h.+40h. violet	20	30
104	**18**	1k.20+80h. red	20	30
105	-	2k.50+1k.50 blue	20	30

DESIGNS: 60h. Charles IV; 2k.50, King John of Luxembourg.

19 Adolf Hitler

1943. Hitler's 54th Birthday.

106	**19**	60h.+1k.40 violet	20	85
107	**19**	1k.20+3k.80 red	20	85

20 Scene from "The Mastersingers of Nuremberg"

21 Richard Wagner

1943. 130th Birth Anniv of Wagner.

108	**20**	60h. violet	10	55
109	**21**	1k.20 red	10	55
110	-	2k.50 blue	10	55

DESIGN: 2k.50, Blacksmith scene from *Siegfried*.

22 Reinhard Heydrich

1943. First Death Anniv of Reinhard Heydrich (German Governor).

111	**22**	60h.+4k.40 black	50	2·10

23 Arms of Bohemia and Moravia and Red Cross

1943. Red Cross Relief Fund.

112	**23**	1k.20+8k.80 blk & red	30	65

24 National Costumes

25 Arms of Bohemia and Moravia

1944. Fifth Anniv of German Occupation.

113	**24**	1k.20+3k.80 red	20	40
114	**25**	4k.20+18k.80 brown	20	40
115	**24**	10k.+20k. blue	20	40

26 Adolf Hitler

1944. Hitler's 55th Birthday.

116	**26**	60h.+1k.40 brown	20	40
117	**26**	1k.20+3k.80 green	20	40

27 Smetana

1944. 60th Death Anniv of Bedrich Smetana (composer).

118	**27**	60h.+1k.40 green	20	40
119	**27**	1k.20+3k.80 red	20	40

28 St. Vitus's Cathedral, Prague

1944

120	**28**	1k.50 purple	20	40
121	**28**	2k.50 violet	20	55

29 Adolf Hitler

1944

122	**29**	4k.20 green	30	75

NEWSPAPER STAMPS

N6 Dove

1939. Imperf.

N38	**N6**	2h. brown	30	40
N39	**N6**	5h. blue	30	40
N40	**N6**	7h. red	30	40
N41	**N6**	9h. green	30	40
N42	**N6**	10h. red	30	40
N43	**N6**	12h. blue	30	40
N44	**N6**	20h. green	30	40
N45	**N6**	50h. brown	30	40
N46	**N6**	1k. green	30	55

1940. For bulk postings. No. N42 optd **GD-OT**.

N60	10h. red	25	75

N19 Dove

1943. Imperf.

N106	**N19**	2h. brown	10	20
N107	**N19**	5h. blue	10	20
N108	**N19**	7h. red	10	20
N109	**N19**	9h. green	10	20
N110	**N19**	10h. red	10	20
N111	**N19**	12h. blue	10	20
N112	**N19**	20h. green	10	20
N113	**N19**	50h. brown	10	20
N114	**N19**	1k. green	10	20

OFFICIAL STAMPS

O7 Numeral and Laurel Wreath

1941

O60	**O7**	30h. brown	20	20
O61	**O7**	40h. blue	20	20
O62	**O7**	50h. green	20	20
O63	**O7**	60h. green	20	20
O64	**O7**	80h. red	55	20
O65	**O7**	1k. brown	25	20
O66	**O7**	1k.20 red	25	20
O67	**O7**	1k.50 purple	40	20
O68	**O7**	2k. blue	40	20
O69	**O7**	3k. green	40	20
O70	**O7**	4k. purple	55	65
O71	**O7**	5k. yellow	1·30	1·30

O19 Eagle and Numeral

1943

O106	**O19**	30h. brown	20	85
O107	**O19**	40h. blue	20	85
O108	**O19**	50h. green	10	55
O109	**O19**	60h. violet	10	55
O110	**O19**	80h. red	10	55
O111	**O19**	1k. brown	10	55
O112	**O19**	1k.20 red	10	55
O113	**O19**	1k.50 brown	10	55
O114	**O19**	2k. blue	10	55
O115	**O19**	3k. green	10	55
O116	**O19**	4k. purple	10	55
O117	**O19**	5k. green	10	55

PERSONAL DELIVERY STAMPS

P6

1939

P38	**P6**	50h. blue	3·25	3·75
P39	**P6**	50h. red	2·10	4·25

POSTAGE DUE STAMPS

D6

1939

D38	**D 6**	5h. red	30	40
D39	**D 6**	10h. red	30	40
D40	**D 6**	20h. red	30	40
D41	**D 6**	30h. red	30	40
D42	**D 6**	40h. red	30	40
D43	**D 6**	50h. red	30	40
D44	**D 6**	60h. red	30	40
D45	**D 6**	80h. red	30	40
D46	**D 6**	1k. blue	30	55
D47	**D 6**	1k.20 blue	40	55
D48	**D 6**	2k. blue	1·30	1·60
D49	**D 6**	5k. blue	1·50	2·10
D50	**D 6**	10k. blue	2·10	2·75
D51	**D 6**	20k. blue	3·75	4·25

Pt. 20

BOLIVAR

One of the states of the Granadine Confederation. A department of Colombia from 1886, now uses Colombian stamps.

1863. 100 centavos = 1 peso.

1

1863. Imperf.

1	**1**	10c. green	£1700	£800
2	**1**	10c. red	39·00	37·00
3	**1**	1p. red	11·00	10·50

2

3

1872. Various frames. Imperf.

4	**2**	5c. blue	10·00	9·50
5	**3**	10c. mauve	10·00	9·50
6	-	20c. green	44·00	43·00
7	-	80c. red	90·00	85·00

6

7

8

1874. Imperf.

8	**6**	5c. blue	33·00	18·00
9	**7**	5c. blue	11·00	9·50
10	**8**	10c. mauve	5·50	4·75

9 Simon Bolivar

1879. Various frames. Dated "1879". White or blue paper. Perf.

14	**9**	5c. blue	45	45
12	**9**	10c. mauve	35	30
13	**9**	20c. red	45	45

1880. Various frames. Dated "1880". White or blue paper.

19	5c. blue	45	45
20	10c. mauve	55	55
21	20c. red	55	55
22	80c. green	3·25	3·25
23	1p. orange	3·50	3·50

10 Simon Bolivar

1882

30	**10**	5p. red and blue	1·00	85
31	**10**	10p. blue and purple	2·20	2·10

11 Simon Bolivar

1882. Various frames. Dated "1882".

32A	**11**	5c. blue	45	45
33A	**11**	10c. mauve	35	30
34A	**11**	20c. red	45	45
35A	**11**	80c. green	90	85
36A	**11**	1p. orange	90	85

1883. Various frames. Dated "1883".

37B	5c. blue	35	30
38B	10c. mauve	45	45
39B	20c. red	45	45
40B	80c. green	45	45
41A	1p. orange	3·00	3·00

1884. Various frames. Dated "1884".

42B	5c. blue	45	45
43B	10c. mauve	35	30
44B	20c. red	35	30
45B	80c. green	45	45
46B	1p. orange	45	45

1885. Various frames. Dated "1885".

47B	5c. blue	20	20
48B	10c. mauve	20	20
49B	20c. red	20	20
50B	80c. green	35	30
51B	1p. orange	45	45

12 Simon Bolivar

1891

56	**12**	1c. black	45	45
57	**12**	5c. orange	45	45
58	**12**	10c. red	45	45
59	**12**	20c. blue	90	85
60	**12**	50c. green	1·30	1·30
61	**12**	1p. violet	1·30	1·30

13 Simon Bolivar

1903. Various sizes and portraits. Imperf or perf. On paper of various colours.

63A	**13**	50c. green	90	85
64Ab	**13**	50c. blue	75	75
65A	**13**	50c. violet	6·00	6·00
67A	-	1p. red	90	85
68A	-	1p. green	2·20	2·20
69A	-	5p. red	90	85
70Ab	-	10p. blue	1·90	1·80
71A	-	10p. violet	5·00	4·75

PORTRAITS: 1p. Fernandez Madrid. 5p. Rodriguez Torices. 10p. Garcia de Toledo.

20 J. M. del Castillo

1904. Various portraits. Imperf or perf.

77A	**20**	5c. black	35	30
78A	-	10c. brown (M. Anguiano)	35	30
80A	-	20c. red (P.G. Ribon)	45	45

23

1904. Figures in various frames. Imperf.

81	**23**	½c. black	45	45
82	**23**	1c. blue (horiz)	75	75
83	**23**	2c. violet	90	85

ACKNOWLEDGEMENT OF RECEIPT STAMPS

AR19

1903. Imperf. On paper of various colours.

AR75A	**AR19**	20c. orange	1·90	1·80
AR76A	**AR19**	20c. blue	2·75	2·75

AR27

1904. Imperf.

AR85	**AR27**	2c. red	1·40	1·40

LATE FEE STAMPS

L18

1903. Imperf. On paper of various colours.

L73A	**L18**	20c. red	90	85
L74B	**L18**	20c. violet	90	85

REGISTRATION STAMPS

1879. As T **9** but additionally inscr "CERTIFICADA".

R17	**9**	40c. brown	45	45

1880. As previous issue dated "1880".

R28	40c. brown	45	45

1882. As T **11**, but additionally inscr "CERTIFICADA". Dated as shown.

R52B	**11**	40c. brown ("1882")	45	45
R53B	**11**	40c. brown ("1883")	45	45
R54B	**11**	40c. brown ("1884")	45	45
R55B	**11**	40c. brown ("1885")	45	45

R17

1903. Imperf. On paper of various colours.

R72A	**R17**	20c. orange	3·50	3·50

R26

1904. Imperf.

R84	**R26**	5c. black	2·30	2·30

Pt. 20

BOLIVIA

A republic of Central South America.

1867. 100 centavos = 1 boliviano.
1963. 100 centavos = 1 peso boliviano.
1963. Currency reform. 1000 (old) pesos = 1 (new) peso
1987. 100 centavos = 1 boliviano.

1 Condor

1867. Imperf.

3a	**1**	5c. green	2·50	5·00
10	**1**	5c. mauve	£200	£150
7	**1**	10c. brown	£180	£160
8	**1**	50c. yellow	28·00	39·00
11	**1**	50c. blue	£400	£350
9	**1**	100c. blue	43·00	95·00
12	**1**	100c. green	£170	£180

4 (9 Stars)

1868. Nine stars below Arms. Perf.

32	**4**	5c. green	22·00	12·50
33	**4**	10c. red	39·00	15·00
34	**4**	50c. blue	47·00	28·00
35	**4**	100c. orange	55·00	28·00
36	**4**	500c. black	£750	£750

1871. Eleven stars below Arms. Perf.

37	5c. green	15·00	7·50
38	10c. red	25·00	12·50
39	50c. blue	39·00	22·00
40	100c. orange	43·00	22·00
41	500c. black	£2250	£2250

7

1878. Perf.

42	**7**	5c. blue	9·50	3·25
43	**7**	10c. orange	8·75	2·40
44	**7**	20c. green	24·00	4·75
45	**7**	50c. red	£120	20·00

1887. Eleven stars below Arms. Roul.

46	**4**	1c. red	3·25	3·00
47	**4**	2c. violet	3·25	3·00
48	**4**	5c. blue	10·50	5·25
49	**4**	10c. orange	10·50	5·25

1890. Nine stars below Arms. Perf.

50	1c. red	2·75	1·30
58	2c. violet	7·00	4·00
52	5c. blue	5·75	1·40
53	10c. orange	14·00	1·40
54	20c. green	20·00	2·75
55	50c. red	9·00	2·50
56	100c. yellow	18·00	5·25

1893. Eleven stars below Arms. Perf.

59	5c. blue	8·50	2·75

11

1894

63	**11**	1c. bistre	2·00	1·80
64	**11**	2c. red	2·75	2·50
65	**11**	5c. green	2·00	1·80
66	**11**	10c. brown	2·00	1·80
67	**11**	20c. blue	8·00	5·75
68	**11**	50c. red	17·00	11·50
69	**11**	100c. red	40·00	29·00

12 Frias

13

1897

77	**12**	1c. green	2·10	1·50
78	-	2c. red (Linares)	3·00	2·50
79	-	5c. green (Murillo)	2·00	90
80	-	10c. purple (Monteagudo)	2·30	1·50
81	-	20c. black and red (J. Ballivian)	4·25	2·20
82	-	50c. orange (Sucre)	6·50	3·75
83	-	1b. blue (Bolivar)	8·00	5·25
84	**13**	2b. multicoloured	48·00	75·00

18 Sucre

1899

92	**18**	1c. blue	2·75	1·70
93	**18**	2c. red	2·50	1·70
94	**18**	5c. green	4·00	1·70
95	**18**	5c. red	2·75	90
96	**18**	10c. orange	3·75	1·70
97	**18**	20c. red	4·25	2·20
98	**18**	50c. brown	10·00	3·75
99	**18**	1b. lilac	3·25	3·50

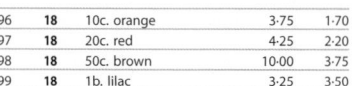

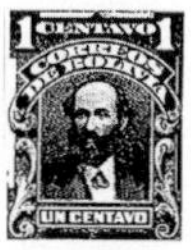

19 A. Ballivian

24

1901

100	**19**	1c. red	45	25
101	-	2c. green (Camacho)	55	35
102	-	5c. red (Campero)	55	35
103	-	10c. blue (J. Ballivian)	2·30	30
104	-	20c. black and purple (Santa Cruz)	1·30	30
105	**24**	2b. brown	7·00	4·00

25

26 Murillo

1909. Issued in La Paz. Centenary of Revolution of July, 1809. Centres in black.

110	**25**	5c. blue	16·00	12·50
111	**26**	10c. green	16·00	12·50
112	-	20c. orange (Lanza)	16·00	12·50
113	-	2b. red (Montes)	16·00	12·50

37 P. D. Murillo

1909. Centenary of Beginning of War of Independence, 1809–25.

115		1c. black and brown	65	40
116		2c. black and green	1·10	55
117	**37**	5c. black and red	1·10	45
118	-	10c. black and blue	1·30	35
119	-	20c. black and violet	1·30	55
120	-	50c. black and bistre	1·40	70
121	-	1b. black and brown	1·80	1·30
122	-	2b. black and brown	1·90	1·50

PORTRAITS: 1c. M. Betanzos. 2c. I. Warnes. 10c. B. Monteagudo. 20c. E. Arze. 50c. A. J. Sucre. 1b. S. Bolivar. 2b. M. Belgrano.

1910. Centenary of Liberation of Santa Cruz, Potosi and Cochabamba. Portraits as T **37**.

123	5c. black and green	55	25
124	10c. black and red	55	35
125	20c. black and blue	1·10	55

PORTRAITS: 5c. I. Warnes. 10c. M. Betanzos. 20c. E. Arze.

1911. Nos. 101 and 104 surch **5 Centavos 1911**.

127	5c. on 2c. green	65	35
128	5c. on 20c. black & purple	23·00	25·00

F8 Figure of Justice

1912. Stamps similar to Type **F8** optd **CORREOS 1912.** or surch also.

130	**F8**	2c. green	45	35
131	**F8**	5c. orange	75	55
132	**F8**	10c. red	1·50	70
129	**F8**	10c. on 1c. blue	75	35

1913. Portraits as 1901 and new types.

133	**19**	1c. pink	30	25
134	-	2c. red	30	25
135	-	5c. green	45	25
136	-	8c. yellow (Frias)	1·30	45
137	-	10c. grey	75	25
139	-	50c. purple (Sucre)	1·90	55
140	-	1b. blue (Bolivar)	3·25	1·50
141	**24**	2b. black	8·00	5·25

46 Monolith

47 Mt. Potosi

1916. Various sizes.

142	**46**	½c. brown	35	30
143	**47**	1c. green	45	30
144	-	2c. black and red	50	30
145	-	5c. blue	65	35
147	-	10c. blue and orange	1·60	25

DESIGNS—HORIZ: 2c. Lake Titicaca; 5c. Mt. Illimani; 10c. Parliament Building, La Paz.

51

1919

158a	**51**	1c. lake	30	15
158b	**51**	2c. violet	45	15
151	**51**	5c. green	65	10
152	**51**	10c. red	65	10
179	**51**	15c. blue	1·20	35
180	**51**	20c. blue	95	35
154	**51**	22c. blue	1·60	1·50
155	**51**	24c. violet	1·60	90
162	**51**	50c. orange	3·50	80
163	**51**	1b. brown	95	45
164	**51**	2b. brown	65	45

See also Nos. 194/206.

1923. Surch Habilitada and value.

165	5c. on 1c. lake	55	25
169	15c. on 10c. red	1·30	45
168	15c. on 22c. blue	95	45

54 Morane Saulnier Type P Airplane

1924. Air. Establishment of National Aviation School.

170	**54**	10c. black and red	55	45
171	**54**	15c. black and lake	2·10	1·70
172	**54**	25c. black and blue	1·10	80
173	**54**	50c. black and orange	1·80	1·40
174	-	1b. black and brown	2·30	1·90
175	-	2b. black and brown	4·50	4·00
176	-	5b. black and violet	6·50	6·25

Nos. 174/6 have a different view.

57 Andean Condor

1925. Centenary of Independence.

184		5c. red on green	1·10	90
185		10c. red on yellow	1·20	1·10
186		15c. red	85	45
187	**57**	25c. blue	1·90	80
188	-	50c. purple	1·60	80
189	-	1b. red	3·75	1·90
190	-	2b. yellow	4·75	2·75
191	-	5b. brown	5·00	3·00

DESIGNS—VERT: 5c. Torch of Freedom; 10c. Kantuta (national flower); 15c. Pres. B. Saavedra; 50c. Head of Liberty; 1b. Mounted archer; 5b. Marshal Sucre. HORIZ: 2b. Hermes.

1927. Surch **1927** and value.

192	**51**	5c. on 1c. lake	4·50	3·25
193	**51**	10c. on 24c. violet	4·50	3·25

1928

194	2c. yellow	55	35
195	3c. pink	75	70
196	4c. red	55	50
197	20c. olive	95	35
198	25c. blue	95	45
199	30c. violet	1·20	1·00
200	40c. orange	2·10	1·90
201	50c. brown	2·10	1·90
202	1b. red	2·50	1·90
203	2b. purple	3·75	3·25
204	3b. green	4·25	3·75
205	4b. lake	5·75	4·75
206	5b. brown	7·00	6·00

1928. Optd Octubre **1927** and star.

207	5c. green	35	20
208	10c. grey	45	20
209	15c. red	60	35

1928. Surch **15 cts. 1928.**

211	15c. on 20c. blue	13·00	13·00
213	15c. on 24c. violet	2·30	1·30
216	15c. on 50c. orange	1·80	1·00

66 "L.A.B." (Lloyd Aereo Boliviano)

1928. Air.

217	**66**	15c. green	3·25	2·10
218	**66**	20c. blue	5·25	4·25
219	**66**	35c. red	4·25	3·25

68 Andean Condor

1928

221	**68**	5c. green	2·30	30
222	-	10c. blue	45	20
223	-	15c. red	75	20

DESIGNS: 10c. Pres. Siles; 15c. Map of Bolivia.

1930. Stamps of 1913 and 1916 surch **R. S. 21-4 1930** and value.

224		0.01c. on 2c. (No. 134)	1·30	1·30
225		0.03c. on 2c. (No. 144)	1·60	1·40
226	**46**	25c. on ½c. brown	1·70	1·10
227	-	25c. on 2c. (No. 144)	1·80	1·10

1930. Air. Optd **CORREO AEREO R. S. 6-V-1930 or surch 5 Cts.** also.

228	**54**	5c. on 10c. black & red	11·50	13·00
229	**54**	10c. black and red	11·50	13·00
231	**54**	15c. black and lake	11·50	13·00
232	**54**	25c. black and blue	11·50	13·00
233	**54**	50c. black and orange	11·50	13·00
235	**54**	1b. black and brown	£225	£225

1930. *Graf Zeppelin* Air stamps. Stamps of 1928 surch **Z 1930** and value.

241	**66**	1b.50 on 15c. green	75·00	85·00
242	**66**	3b. on 20c. blue	75·00	85·00
243	**66**	6b. on 35c. red	£120	£130

75 Junkers F-13 over Bullock Cart

1930. Air.

244	**75**	5c. violet	1·90	1·10
245	-	15c. red	1·90	1·10
246	-	20c. yellow	1·50	95
247	**75**	35c. green	1·20	70
248	-	50c. blue	2·30	1·60
249	**75**	1b. brown	3·50	2·40
250	-	2b. red	4·50	3·25
251	**75**	3b. grey	7·00	4·50

DESIGN: 15, 20, 50c., 2b. Junkers F-13 seaplane over river boat.

77 Pres. Siles

78 Map of Bolivia

79 Marshal Sucre

1930

252	**77**	1c. brown	45	45
253	-	2c. green (Potosi)	2·10	75
254	-	5c. blue (Illimani)	2·10	30
255	-	10c. red (E. Abaroa)	2·10	30
256	**78**	15c. violet	2·10	30
257	**78**	35c. red	3·25	1·30
258	**78**	45c. orange	3·25	1·30
259	**79**	50c. slate	1·30	60
260	-	1b. brown (Bolivar)	1·90	1·50

80 Symbols of Revolution

1931. First Anniv of Revolution.

263	**80**	15c. red	3·75	65
264	**80**	50c. lilac	1·60	85

81

1932. Air.

265	**81**	5c. blue	3·50	2·75
266	**81**	10c. grey	1·90	1·50
267	**81**	15c. red	2·30	1·80
268	**81**	25c. orange	2·30	1·80
269	**81**	30c. green	1·60	90
270	**81**	50c. purple	3·50	2·75
271	**81**	1b. brown	3·50	2·75

1933. Surch **Habilitada D. S. 13-7-1933** and value.

273	**51**	5c. on 1b. red	95	55
274	**78**	15c. on 35c. red	55	55
275	**78**	15c. on 45c. orange	95	45
276	**51**	15c. on 50c. brown	1·90	45
277	**51**	25c. on 40c. orange	55	55

83

1933

278	**83**	2c. green	45	30
279	**83**	5c. blue	35	25
280	**83**	10c. red	75	45
281	**83**	15c. violet	55	30
282	**83**	25c. blue	1·10	85

84 M. Baptista

1935. Ex-President Baptista Commemoration.

283	**84**	15c. violet	75	30

85 Map of Bolivia

1935

284	**85**	2c. blue	45	20
285	**85**	3c. yellow	45	20
286	**85**	5c. green	45	20
287	**85**	5c. red	45	20
288	**85**	10c. brown	45	20
289	**85**	15c. blue	45	20
290	**85**	15c. red	45	20
291	**85**	20c. green	55	20
292	**85**	25c. blue	55	20
293	**85**	30c. red	1·10	45
294	**85**	40c. orange	1·10	30
295	**85**	50c. violet	1·10	20
296	**85**	1b. yellow	1·10	75
297	**85**	2b. brown	2·30	1·40

86 Fokker Super Universal

1935. Air.

298	**86**	5c. brown	20	20
299	**86**	10c. green	20	20
300	**86**	20c. violet	20	20
301	**86**	30c. blue	20	20
302	**86**	50c. orange	30	20
303	**86**	1b. brown	30	45
304	**86**	1½b. yellow	1·10	20
305	**86**	2b. red	1·10	20
306	**86**	5b. green	1·80	55
307	**86**	10b. brown	3·75	1·30

1937. Surch **Comunicaciones D.S. 25-2-37** and value in figures.

308	**83**	5c. on 2c. green	30	30
310	**83**	15c. on 25c. blue	45	45
311	**83**	30c. on 25c. blue	75	75
312	**51**	45c. on 1b. brown	85	85
313	**51**	1b. on 2b. purple	1·10	1·10
314	**83**	2b. on 25c. blue	1·10	1·10
315	**80**	3b. on 50c. lilac	1·50	1·50
316	**80**	5b. on 50c. lilac	2·30	2·30

1937. Air. Surch **Correo Aereo D. S. 25-2-37** and value in figures.

321	**75**	5c. on 35c. green	45	30
322	**66**	20c. on 35c. red	55	45
323	**66**	50c. on 35c. red	1·10	1·30
324	**66**	1b. on 35c. red	1·10	95
325	**54**	2b. on 50c. black & orge	1·70	1·40
317	-	3b. on 50c. pur (No. 188)	2·30	1·40
318	-	4b. on 1b. red (No. 189)	2·75	1·80
319	**57**	5b. on 2b. orange	3·75	2·10
320	**57**	10b. on 5b. sepia (No. 191)	7·00	4·50
326	**54**	12b. on 10c. black & red	9·00	6·50
327	**54**	15b. on 10c. black & red	9·00	3·75

89 Native School

92 Junkers Ju52/3m over Cornfield

1938

328	**89**	2c. red (postage)	85	65
329	-	10c. orange	95	45
330	-	15c. green	1·40	45
331	-	30c. yellow	1·70	55
332	-	45c. red	3·25	1·30
333	-	60c. violet	2·50	65
334	-	75c. blue	3·50	55
335	-	1b. brown	5·00	55
336	-	2b. buff	4·50	1·20

DESIGNS—VERT: 10c. Oil Wells; 15c. Industrial buildings; 30c. Pincers and torch; 75c. Indian and condor. HORIZ: 45c. Sucre-Camiri railway map; 60c. Natives and book; 1b. Machinery; 2b. Agriculture.

337		20c. red (air)	30	25
338		30c. grey	30	25
339		40c. yellow	30	25
340	**92**	50c. green	65	25
341	-	60c. blue	65	25
342	-	1b. red	85	25
343	-	2b. buff	1·60	30
344	-	3b. brown	1·60	30
345	-	5b. violet	2·30	55

DESIGNS—VERT: 20c. Mint, Potosi; 30c. Miner; 40c. Symbolical of women's suffrage; 1b. Pincers, torch and slogan; 3b. New Government emblem; 5b. Junkers aircraft over map of Bolivia. HORIZ: 60c. Airplane and monument; 2b. Airplane over river.

102 Llamas

103 Arms

1939

346	**102**	2c. green	75	55
347	**102**	4c. brown	75	55
348	**102**	5c. mauve	75	45
349	-	10c. black	95	55
350	-	15c. green	95	60
351	-	20c. green	95	45
352	**103**	25c. yellow	1·10	45
353	-	30c. blue	95	45
354	-	40c. red	2·10	55
355	-	45c. black	2·10	55
356	-	60c. red	2·10	85
357	-	75c. slate	3·25	85
358	-	90c. orange	3·75	85
359	-	1b. blue	3·75	85
360	-	2b. red	4·50	85
361	-	3b. violet	5·75	1·30
362	-	4b. brown	6·50	1·80
363	-	5b. purple	8·00	2·10

DESIGNS—HORIZ: 10, 15, 20c. Vicuna; 60, 75c. Mountain viscacha; 90c., 1b. Toco toucan; 2, 3b. Andean condor; 4, 5b. Jaguar. VERT: 40, 45c. Cocoi herons.

107 Virgin of Copacabana

1939. Air. Second National Eucharistic Congress. Inscr "II° CONGRESO EUCARISTICO NACIONAL".

364		5c. violet	75	45
365	**107**	30c. green	1·10	30
366	-	45c. blue	1·10	30
367	-	60c. red	1·10	50
368	-	75c. red	1·10	75
369	-	90c. blue	1·10	30
370	-	2b. brown	1·60	35
371	-	4b. mauve	2·75	55

372	**107**	5b. blue	6·50	1·10
373	-	10b. yellow	9·00	1·60

DESIGNS—TRIANGULAR: 5c., 10b. Allegory of the Light of Religion. VERT: 45c., 4b. The "Sacred Heart of Jesus"; 75c., 90c. S. Anthony of Padua. HORIZ: 60c., 2b. Facade of St. Francis's Church, La Paz.

111 Workman

1939. Obligatory Tax. Workers' Home Building Fund.

374	**111**	5c. violet	1·20	30

112 Flags of 21 American Republics

1940. 50th Anniv of Pan-American Union.

375	**112**	9b. red, blue & yellow	2·40	1·20

114 Urns of Murillo and Sagarnaga

1941. 130th Death Anniv of P. D. Murillo (patriot).

376	-	10c. purple	20	10
377	**114**	15c. green	30	10
378	-	45c. red	30	20
379	-	1b.05 blue	65	30

DESIGNS—VERT: 10c. Murillo statue; 1b.05 Murillo portrait. HORIZ: 45c. "Murillo dreaming in Prison".

117 Shadow of Aeroplane on Lake Titicaca

1941. Air.

380	**117**	10b. green	4·50	55
381	**117**	20b. blue	5·25	85
382	-	50b. mauve	10·50	1·40
383	-	100b. brown	24·00	8·50

DESIGN: 50, 100b. Andean condor over Mt. Illimani.

119 1867 and 1941 Issues

1942. First Students' Philatelic Exn, La Paz.

384	**119**	5c. mauve	75	65
385	**119**	10c. orange	75	65
386	**119**	20c. green	1·60	1·10
387	**119**	40c. red	2·00	1·30
388	**119**	90c. blue	3·75	1·60
389	**119**	1b. violet	4·75	2·50
390	**119**	10b. brown	16·00	13·00

120 "Union is Strength"

1942. Air. Chancellors' Meeting, Rio de Janeiro.

391	**120**	40c. red	45	30
392	**120**	50c. blue	45	30
393	**120**	1b. brown	1·70	1·10
394	**120**	5b. mauve	1·10	45
395	**120**	10b. purple	3·50	1·70

121 Mt. Potosi **122** Chaquiri Dam

1943. Mining Industry.

396	**121**	15c. brown	30	20
397	-	45c. blue	65	30
398	-	1b.25 purple	1·10	55
399	-	1b.50 green	80	55
400	-	2b. brown	1·10	55
401	**122**	2b.10 blue	85	75
402	-	3b. orange	3·50	1·40

DESIGNS—VERT: 45c. Quechisla (at foot of Mt. Chorolorque); 1b.25, Miner Drilling. HORIZ: 1b.50, Dam; 2b. Truck Convoy; 3b. Entrance to Pulacayo Mine.

125 Gen. Ballivian leading Cavalry Charge

1943. Centenary of Battle of Ingavi.

403	**125**	2c. green	30	10
404	**125**	3c. orange	30	10
405	**125**	25c. purple	45	15
406	**125**	45c. blue	55	20
407	**125**	3b. red	95	55
408	**125**	4b. purple	1·30	65
409	**125**	5b. sepia	1·50	85
MS409a Two sheets each 139×100 mm. Nos. 403/6 and Nos. 407/9			14·00	18·00
MS409b Do. Imperf			14·00	18·00

126 Gen. Ballivian and Trinidad Cathedral

1943. Centenary of Founding of El Beni. Centres in brown.

410	**126**	5c. green (postage)	30	15
411	**126**	10c. purple	35	20
412	**126**	30c. red	35	20
413	**126**	45c. blue	45	30
414	**126**	2b.10 orange	75	55
415	-	10c. violet (air)	30	15
416	-	20c. green	35	15
417	-	30c. red	45	20
418	-	3b. blue	65	30
419	-	5b. black	95	55

DESIGN: Nos. 415/19, Gen. Ballivian and mule convoy crossing bridge below airplane.

127 Trans. "Honour-Work-Law/All for the Country" **129** Allegory of "Flight"

1944. Revolution of 20th December, 1943.

420	**127**	20c. orange (postage)	20	10
421	**127**	20c. green	20	10
422	**127**	90c. blue	20	10
423	**127**	90c. red	20	10
424	-	1b. purple	25	10
425	-	2b.40 brown	30	20

DESIGN—VERT: 1b., 2b.40, Clasped hands and flag.

131 Posthorn and Envelope

1944. Obligatory Tax.

430	**131**	10c. red	1·10	30
432	**131**	10c. blue	1·10	30

Smaller Posthorn and Envelope.

469		10c. red	2·30	75
470		10c. yellow	2·30	75
471		10c. green	2·30	75
472		10c. brown	2·30	75

132 Douglas DC-2 and National Airways Route Map

1945. Air. Panagra Airways, 10th Anniv of First La Paz–Tacna Flight.

433	**132**	10c. red	20	15
434	**132**	50c. orange	25	15
435	**132**	90c. green	30	20
436	**132**	5b. blue	55	30
437	**132**	20b. brown	1·90	65

133 Lloyd-Aereo Boliviano Air Routes

1945. Air. 20th Anniv of First National Air Service.

438	**133**	20c. blue, orange & vio	20	10
439	**133**	30c. blue, orange & brn	20	10
440	**133**	50c. blue, orange & grn	20	10
441	**133**	90c. blue, orange & pur	20	10
442	**133**	2b. blue and orange	25	10
443	**133**	3b. blue, orange & red	30	20
444	**133**	4b. blue, orange & bistre	55	30

134 L. B. Vincenti and J. I. de Sanjines, Composers of National Anthem

1946. Centenary of National Anthem.

445	**134**	5c. black and mauve	10	10
446	**134**	10c. black and blue	10	10
447	**134**	15c. black and green	10	10
448	**134**	30c. brown and red	20	15
449	**134**	90c. brown and blue	20	15
450	**134**	2b. brown and black	75	55
MS450a Two sheets each 86×131 mm. (a) No. 448; (b) No. 450. Imperf. Each sold at 4b			7·00	7·00

1947. Surch **1947 Habilitada Bs. 1.40**.

451	1b.40 on 75c. blue (No. 334) (postage)	25	15
452	1b.40 on 75c. slate (No. 357)	25	15
455	1b.40 on 75c. red (No. 368) (air)	30	20

136 Seizure of Government Palace **137** Mt. Illimani

1947. Popular Revolution of 21 July 1946.

456	**136**	20c. green (postage)	10	10
457	**136**	50c. purple	10	10
458	**136**	1b.40 blue	10	10
459	**136**	3b.70 orange	20	10
460	**136**	4b. violet	30	20
461	**136**	10b. olive	95	45
462	**137**	1b. red (air)	10	10
463	**137**	1b.40 green	10	10
464	**137**	2b.50 blue	20	15
465	**137**	3b. orange	30	20
466	**137**	4b. mauve	45	20

138 Arms of Bolivia and Argentina

1947. Meeting of Presidents of Bolivia and Argentina.

467	**138**	1b.40 orange (postage)	45	25
468	**138**	2b.90 blue (air)	55	45

140 Cross and Child

1948. Third Inter-American Catholic Education Congress.

473	-	1b.40 bl & yell (postage)	45	10
474	**140**	2b. green and orange	55	20
475	-	3b. green and blue	85	25
476	-	5b. violet and orange	1·10	30
477	-	5b. brown and green	1·50	30
478	-	2b.50 orange & yell (air)	65	45
479	**140**	3b.70 red and buff	75	45
480	-	4b. mauve and blue	75	30
481	-	4b. blue and orange	75	25
482	-	13b.60 blue and green	95	45

DESIGNS: 1b.40, 2b.50, Christ the Redeemer, Monument; 3b., 4b. (No. 480), Don Bosco; 5b. (No. 476), 4b. (No. 481), Virgin of Copacabana; 5b. (No. 477), 13b.60, Pope Pius XII.

141 Map of S. America and Bolivian Auto Club Badge

1948. Pan-American Motor Race.

483	**141**	5b. blue & pink (postage)	2·30	75
484	**141**	10b. green & cream (air)	2·10	30

142 Posthorn, Globe and Pres. G. Pacheco

1950. 75th Anniv of U.P.U.

485	**142**	1b.40 blue (postage)	25	10
486	**142**	4b.20 red	30	10
487	**142**	1b.40 brown (air)	25	10
488	**142**	2b.50 orange	30	10
489	**142**	3b.30 purple	25	10

1950. Air. Surch **XV ANIVERSARIO PANAGRA 1935–1950** and value.

490	**132**	4b. on 10c. red	20	10
491	**132**	10b. on 20b. brown	55	35

1950. No. 379 surch **Bs. 2.- Habilitada D.S.6.VII.50**.

492	2b. on 1b.05 blue	45	20

145 Apparition at Potosi

1950. 400th Anniv of Apparition at El Potosi.

493	**145**	20c. violet	30	15
494	**145**	30c. orange	30	15
495	**145**	50c. purple	30	15
496	**145**	1b. red	30	15
497	**145**	2b. blue	35	15
498	**145**	6b. brown	45	15

146 Douglas DC-2

1950. Air. 25th Anniv of Lloyd Aereo Boliviano.

499	**146**	20c. orange	20	10
500	**146**	30c. violet	20	10
501	**146**	50c. green	20	10
502	**146**	1b. yellow	20	10
503	**146**	3b. blue	20	10
504	**146**	15b. red	65	20
505	**146**	50b. brown	1·90	65

1950. Air. Surch **Triunfo de la Democracia 24 de Sept. 49 Bs. 1.40.**

506	**137**	1b.40 on 3b. orange	30	30

148 UN Emblem and Globe

1950. Fith Anniv of UNO.

507	**148**	60c. blue (postage)	1·60	20
508	**148**	2b. green	2·10	30
509	**148**	3b.60 red (air)	75	20
510	**148**	4b.70 brown	95	20

150 St. Francis Gate

149 Gate of the Sun, Tiahuanacu

1951. Fourth Centenary of Founding of La Paz. Centres in black.

511	**149**	20c. green (postage)	20	10
512	**150**	30c. orange	20	10
513	**A**	40c. brown	20	10
514	**B**	50c. red	20	10
515	**C**	1b. purple	20	10
516	**D**	1b.40 violet	30	15
517	**E**	2b. purple	30	15
518	**F**	3b. mauve	45	20
519	**G**	5b. red	55	30
520	**H**	10b. sepia	1·10	45
MS520a Three sheets each 150×100 mm. Nos. 511/12, 520; 513, 516, 519; 514/15, 517/18			8·50	8·50
MS520b Do. Imperf			8·50	8·50
521	**149**	20c. red (air)	20	10
522	**150**	30c. violet	20	10
523	**A**	40c. slate	20	10
524	**B**	50c. green	20	10
525	**C**	1b. red	30	20
526	**D**	2b. orange	55	45
527	**E**	3b. blue	75	65
528	**F**	4b. red	80	65
529	**G**	5b. green	85	75
530	**H**	10b. brown	90	85
MS530a Three sheets each 150×100 mm. Nos. 521/2, 530; 523, 527, 529; 524/5, 526, 528			8·25	8·25
MS530b Do. Imperf			8·25	8·25

DESIGNS—HORIZ: As Type **149**: A, Camacho Avenue; B, Consistorial Palace; C, Legislative Palace; D, G.P.O. E, Arms; F, Pedro de la Casca authorizes plans of City; G, Founding the City; H, City Arms and Captain A. de Mendoza.

151 Tennis

1951. Sports. Centres in black.

531	-	20c. blue (postage)	20	10
532	**151**	50c. red	20	10
533	-	1b. purple	25	10
534	-	1b.40 yellow	30	20
535	-	2b. red	65	45
536	-	3b. brown	1·30	1·10
537	-	4b. blue	1·60	1·40
MS537a Two sheets each 150×100 mm. Nos. 531/2, 535/6; 533/4, 537			6·50	6·50
MS537b Do. Imperf			6·50	6·50
538		20c. violet (air)	30	10
539		30c. purple	45	15
540		50c. orange	75	20
541		1b. brown	75	20
542		2b.50 orange	1·20	45
543		3b. sepia	1·60	1·20
544		5b. red	3·25	2·30
MS544a 130×80 mm. Nos. 741/3			18·00	18·00
MS544b Do. Imperf			18·00	18·00

DESIGNS—Postage: 20c. Boxing; 1b. Diving; 1b.40, Football; 2b. Skiing; 3b. Pelota; 4b. Cycling. Air: 20c. Horse-jumping; 30c. Basketball; 50c. Fencing; 1b. Hurdling; 2b.50, Javelin; 3b. Relay race; 5b. La Paz Stadium.

152 Andean Condor and Flag

1951. 100th National Flag Anniv. Flag in red, yellow and green.

545	**152**	2b. green	10	10
546	**152**	3b.50c. blue	10	10
547	**152**	5b. violet	20	15
548	**152**	7b.50c. grey	55	20
549	**152**	15b. red	75	45
550	**152**	30b. brown	1·80	95

153 Posthorn and Envelope

1951. Obligatory Tax.

551	-	20c. orange	75	30
551b	-	20c. green	75	30
552	-	20c. blue	75	30
553	**153**	50c. green	85	30
553d	**153**	50c. red	85	30
553e	**153**	3b. green	85	30
553f	**153**	3b. bistre	95	75
553g	**153**	5b. violet	1·10	75

DESIGN: 20c. Condor over posthorn and envelope.

154 E. Abaroa

1952. 73rd Death Anniv of Abaroa (patriot).

554	**154**	80c. red (postage)	10	10
555	**154**	1b. orange	10	10
556	**154**	2b. green	20	10
557	**154**	5b. blue	65	20
558	**154**	10b. mauve	1·90	45
559	**154**	20b. brown	3·25	75
560	**154**	70c. red (air)	20	10
561	**154**	2b. yellow	45	20
562	**154**	3b. green	30	20
563	**154**	5b. blue	65	20
564	**154**	50b. purple	1·90	75
565	**154**	100b. black	3·25	1·60

155 Isabella the Catholic

1952. 500th Birth Anniv of Isabella the Catholic.

566	**155**	2b. blue (postage)	30	20
567	**155**	6b.30 red	55	25
568	**155**	50b. green (air)	95	30
569	**155**	100b. brown	45	35

156 Columbus Lighthouse

1952. Columbus Memorial Lighthouse. On tinted papers.

570	**156**	2b. blue (postage)	30	20
571	**156**	5b. red	85	65
572	**156**	9b. green	1·50	85
573	**156**	2b. purple (air)	25	20
574	**156**	3b.70 turquoise	25	20
575	**156**	4b.40 orange	30	20
576	**156**	20b. brown	65	30

157 Miner

1953. Nationalization of Mining Industry.

577	**157**	2b.50c. red	20	10
578	**157**	8b. violet	30	15

158 Villarroel, Paz Estenssoro and Siles Zuazo

159 Revolutionaries

1953. First Anniv of Revolution of April 9th, 1952.

579	**158**	50c. mauve (postage)	20	10
580	**158**	1b. red	20	10
581	**158**	2b. blue	20	10
582	**158**	3b. green	20	10
583	**158**	4b. yellow	20	10
584	**158**	5b. violet	30	20
585	**158**	3b.70 brown (air)	30	20
586	**158**	9b. red	30	20
587	**158**	10b. turquoise	30	20
588	**158**	16b. orange	30	20
589	**158**	40b. grey	65	20
590	**159**	6b. mauve	30	20
591	**159**	22b.50 brown	1·10	85

1953. Obligatory Tax. No. 551b and similar stamp surch 50 cts.

592	**158**	50c. on 20c. mauve	55	30
593	**158**	50c. on 20c. green	45	20

161

1954. Obligatory Tax.

594	**161**	1b. lake	1·30	30
595	**161**	1b. brown	30	30

162 Ear of Wheat and Map

1954. First National Agronomical Congress.

596	**162**	25b. blue	30	10
597	**162**	85b. brown	65	25

163 Pres. Paz Estenssoro embracing Indian

1954. Air. Third Inter-American Indigenous Congress.

598	**163**	20b. brown	20	10
599	**163**	100b. turquoise	80	10

1954. First Anniv of Agrarian Reform. As T **162**, but designs inscr "REFORMA AGRARIA".

600	5b. red (postage)	10	10
601	17b. turquoise	15	10
602	27b. mauve (air)	20	15
603	30b. orange	30	20
604	45b. purple	55	20
605	300b. green	2·30	45

DESIGNS—5b., 17b. Cow's head and map; 27b. to 300b. Indian peasant woman.

1955. Obligatory Tax. Nos. 553e and 553f surch **Bs. 5.— D. S. 21-IV-55.**

606	**153**	5b. on 3b. green	55	20
607	**153**	5b. on 3b. bistre	1·40	20

166 Refinery

167 Derricks

1955. Development of Petroleum Industry.

608	**166**	10b. blue (postage)	10	10
609	**166**	35b. red	15	10
610	**166**	40b. green	20	15
611	**166**	50b. purple	30	20
612	**166**	80b. brown	55	30
613	**167**	55b. blue (air)	20	10
614	**167**	70b. black	45	10
615	**167**	90b. green	55	15
616	**167**	500b. mauve	1·90	95
617	**167**	1000b. brown	3·25	1·90

168 Control Tower

169 Douglas DC-6B Aircraft

1957. Obligatory Tax. Airport Building Fund.

618	**168**	5b. blue	55	20
619	**169**	10b. green	45	20
620	**168**	5b. red	9·50	9·50
620b	**169**	20b. brown	55	30

DESIGNS: 5b. (No. 620), Douglas DC-6B over runway; 20b. Lockheed Constellation in flight.

1957. Currency revaluation. Founding of La Paz stamps of 1951 surch. Centres in black.

621	**F**	50b. on 3b. mauve (post)	10	10
622	**E**	100b. on 2b. purple	15	10
623	**C**	200b. on 1b. purple	20	10
624	**D**	300b. on 1b.40 violet	30	10
625	**149**	350b. on 20c. green	45	15
626	**A**	400b. on 40c. brown	45	15
627	**150**	600b. on 30c. orange	65	20
628	**B**	800b. on 50c. red	75	20
629	**H**	1000b. on 10b. sepia	75	25
630	**G**	2000b. on 5b. red	1·30	55
631	**E**	100b. on 3b. blue (air)	10	10
632	**D**	200b. on 2b. orange	15	10
633	**F**	500b. on 4b. red	20	10
634	**C**	600b. on 1b. red	25	15
635	**149**	700b. on 20c. red	55	20
636	**A**	800b. on 40c. slate	65	30
637	**150**	900b. on 30c. violet	75	20
638	**B**	1800b. on 50c. green	1·30	65
639	**G**	3000b. on 5b. green	1·70	1·20
640	**H**	5000b. on 10b. brown	3·25	2·10

172 Congress Buildings (Santiago de Chile and La Paz)

173 "Latin America" on Globe

1957. Seventh Latin-America Economic Congress, La Paz.

641	**172**	150b. bl & grey (postage)	10	10
642	**172**	350b. grey and brown	20	10
643	**172**	550b. sepia and blue	25	10
644	**172**	750b. green and red	35	15
645	**172**	900b. brown and green	55	20
646	**173**	700b. violet & lilac (air)	65	35
647	**173**	1200b. brown	70	45
648	**173**	1350b. red and mauve	1·10	65
649	**173**	2700b. olive and turq	1·90	90
650	**173**	4000b. violet and blue	3·75	1·50

174 Steam Train and Presidents of Bolivia and Argentina

1957. Yacuiba-Santa Cruz Railway Inauguration.

651	**174**	50b. orange (postage)	35	35
652	**174**	350b. blue and light blue	85	40
653	**174**	1000b. brown & cinna	1·90	60
654	**174**	600b. purple & pink (air)	80	40
655	**174**	700b. violet and blue	1·40	60
656	**174**	900b. green	1·90	45

175 Presidents and Flags of Bolivia and Mexico

1960. Visit of Mexican President to Bolivia.

657	**175**	350b. olive (postage)	30	10
658	**175**	600b. brown	45	20
659	**175**	1,500b. sepia	95	30
660	**175**	400b. red (air)	95	10
661	**175**	800b. blue	1·30	30
662	**175**	2,000b. green	1·90	75

The President's visit to Bolivia did not take place.

176 Indians and Mt. Illimani

177 "Gate of the Sun", Tiahuanacu

1960. Tourist Publicity.

663	**176**	500b. bistre (postage)	75	30
664	**176**	1000b. blue	1·40	45
665	**176**	2000b. sepia	3·25	75
666	**176**	4000b. green	5·75	3·75
667	**177**	3000b. grey (air)	3·25	1·70
668	**177**	5000b. orange	4·75	1·80
669	**177**	10,000b. purple	7·50	4·25
670	**177**	15,000b. violet	10·50	7·00

178 Refugees

179 "Uprooted Tree"

1960. World Refugee Year.

671	**178**	50b. brown (postage)	10	10
672	**178**	350b. purple	20	10
673	**178**	400b. blue	30	15
674	**178**	1000b. sepia	85	55
675	**178**	3000b. green	1·90	1·20
676	**179**	600b. blue (air)	55	20
677	**179**	700b. brown	55	30
678	**179**	900b. turquoise	65	35
679	**179**	1800b. violet	1·30	85
680	**179**	2000b. black	1·80	1·30

180 Jaime Laredo (violinist)

181 Jaime Laredo (violinist)

1960. Jaime Laredo Commem.

681	**180**	100b. green (postage)	30	10
682	**180**	350b. lake	65	10
683	**180**	500b. blue	75	15
684	**180**	1000b. brown	95	20
685	**180**	1500b. violet	1·80	55
686	**180**	5000b. black	5·75	1·60
687	**181**	600b. plum (air)	1·30	45
688	**181**	700b. olive	1·50	55
689	**181**	800b. brown	1·50	55
690	**181**	900b. blue	2·00	55
691	**181**	1800b. turquoise	2·30	1·60
692	**181**	4000b. grey	5·75	2·30

182 Rotary Emblem and Nurse with Children

1960. Founding of Children's Hospital by La Paz Rotary Club. Wheel in blue and yellow, foreground in yellow; background given.

693	**182**	350b. green (postage)	30	10
694	**182**	500b. sepia	45	10
695	**182**	600b. violet	65	15
696	**182**	1000b. grey	75	25
697	**182**	600b. brown (air)	75	45
698	**182**	1000b. olive	1·10	45
699	**182**	1800b. purple	1·50	75
700	**182**	5000b. black	4·75	2·10

183

1960. Air. Unissued stamp, surch as in T **183**.

701	**183**	1200b. on 10b. orange	1·30	95

184 Design from Gate of the Sun

1960. Unissued Tiahuanacu Excavation stamps surch as in T **184**. Gold backgrounds.

702	50b. on ½c. red	85	55
703	100b. on 1c. red	55	20
704	200b. on 2c. black	1·50	20
705	300b. on 5c. green	30	20
706	350b. on 10c. green	30	1·20
707	400b. on 15c. blue	55	20
708	500b. on 20c. red	55	20
709	500b. on 50c. red	65	20
710	600b. on 22½c. green	85	45
711	600b. on 60c. violet	95	55
712	700b. on 25c. violet	1·40	30
713	700b. on 1b. green	1·90	1·20
714	800b. on 30c. red	95	30
715	900b. on 40c. green	85	45
716	1000b. on 2b. blue	95	55
717	1800b. on 3b. grey	9·50	6·50
718	4000b. on 4b. grey	75·00	65·00
719	5000b. on 5b. grey	19·00	14·00

DESIGNS: Various gods, motifs and ornaments. SIZES: Nos. 702/6, As Type **184**. Nos. 707/17, As Type **184** but horiz. No. 718, 49×23 mm. No. 719, 50×52½ mm.

185 Flags of Argentina and Bolivia

1961. Air. Visit of Pres. Frondizi of Argentina.

720	**185**	4000b. multicoloured	1·40	1·30
721	-	6000b. sepia and green	2·10	1·70

DESIGN: 6000b. Presidents of Argentina and Bolivia.

186 Miguel de Cervantes (First Mayor of La Paz)

1961. M. de Cervantes Commem and 4th Centenary of Santa Cruz de la Sierra (1500b.).

722	**186**	600b. violet and ochre (postage)	65	30
723	-	1500b. blue and orange	1·20	45
724	-	1400b. brown & green (air)	85	30

DESIGNS: 1400b. Portrait as Type **186** (diamond shape, 30½×30½ mm); 1500b. Nuflo de Chaves (vert: as Type **186**).

See also Nos. 755/6.

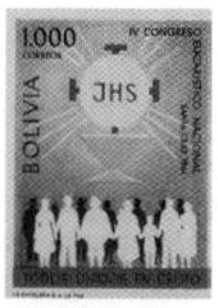

187 "United in Christ"

1962. Fourth National Eucharistic Congress, Santa Cruz.

725	**187**	1000b. yellow, red and green (postage)	85	45
726	-	1400b. yellow, pink and brown (air)	85	45

DESIGN: 1400b. Virgin of Cotoca.

1962. Nos. 671/80 surch.

727	**178**	600b. on 50b. brown (postage)	55	20
728	**178**	900b. on 350b. purple	60	20
729	**178**	1000b. on 400b. blue	65	25
730	**178**	2000b. on 1000b. brown	75	55
731	**178**	3500b. on 3000b. green	1·30	1·10
732	**179**	1200b. on 600b. blue (air)	1·20	55
733	**179**	1300b. on 700b. brown	1·20	55
734	**179**	1400b. on 900b. green	1·20	55
735	**179**	2800b. on 1800b. violet	1·90	75
736	**179**	3000b. on 2000b. black	1·90	1·10

189 Hibiscus

1962. Flowers in actual colours; background colours given.

737	**189**	200b. green (postage)	85	20
738	-	400b. brown	1·30	20
739	-	600b. deep blue	2·10	15
740	-	1000b. violet	3·00	45
741	-	100b. blue (air)	75	20
742	-	800b. green	1·40	30
743	-	1800b. violet	3·00	75
744	-	10,000b. deep blue	9·00	4·50
MS744a		130×80 mm. Nos. 741/3. Imperf	13·00	13·00

FLOWERS: Nos. 738, 740 Orchids; 739, St. James' lily; 741/4, Types of Kantuta (national flowers).

190 Infantry

1962. Armed Forces Commemoration.

745	**190**	400b. mult (postage)	10	10
746	-	500b. multicoloured	20	10
747	-	600b. multicoloured	30	15
748	-	2000b. multicoloured	85	55
749	-	600b. mult (air)	55	20
750	-	1200b. multicoloured	65	30
751	-	2000b. multicoloured	95	55
752	-	5000b. multicoloured	2·10	1·40

DESIGNS: No. 746, Cavalry; 747, Artillery; 748, Engineers; 749, Parachutists and aircraft; 750, 752, "Overseas Flights" (Lockheed Super Electra airplane over oxen-cart); 751, "Aerial Survey" (Douglas DC-3 airplane photographing ground).

191 Campaign Emblem

1962. Malaria Eradication.

753	**191**	600b. yellow, violet and lilac (postage)	65	45
754	-	2000b. yellow, green and blue (air)	2·00	95

DESIGN: 2000b. As No. 753 but with laurel wreath and inscription encircling emblem.

1962. Spanish Discoverers. As T **186** but inscribed "1548–1962".

755	600b. mauve on blue (postage)	45	20
756	1200b. brown on yellow (air)	65	30

PORTRAITS: 600b. A. de Mendoza. 1200b. P. de la Gasca.

192 Goal-Keeper diving to save Goal

1963. 21st South American Football Championships, La Paz. Multicoloured.

757	**192**	60c. Type **192** (postage)	75	15
758	**192**	1p. Goalkeeper saving ball (vert)	1·20	30
759	**192**	1p.40 Andean condor on football (vert) (air)	1·90	1·30
760	**192**	1p.80 Ball in corner of net (vert)	2·00	1·40

193 Globe and Emblem

1963. Freedom from Hunger.

761	**193**	60c. yellow, blue and indigo (postage)	55	15
762	-	1p.20 yellow, blue and myrtle (air)	1·30	1·20

DESIGN: 1p.20, Ear of wheat across Globe.

194 Alliance Emblem

1963. Air. "Alliance for Progress".

763	**194**	1p.20 green, blue & bis	1·30	1·20

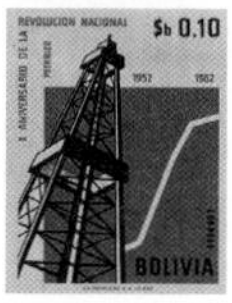

195 Oil Derrick

1963. Tenth Anniv of Revolution (1962).

764	**195**	10c. grn & brn (postage)	20	10
765	-	60c. sepia and orange	30	15
766	-	1p. yellow, violet & green	45	25
767	-	1p.20 pink, brown and grey (air)	65	30
768	-	1p.40 green and ochre	75	35
769	-	2p.80 buff and slate	1·60	1·40

DESIGNS: 60c. Map of Bolivia; 1p. Students; 1p.20, Ballot box and voters; 1p.40, Peasant breaking chain; 2p.80, Miners.

196 Flags of Bolivia and Peru

197 Marshal Santa Cruz

1966. Death Centenary of Marshal Santa Cruz.

770	**196**	10c. mult (postage)	20	10
771	**196**	60c. multicoloured	30	15
772	**196**	1p. multicoloured	55	30
773	**196**	2p. multicoloured	75	55
774	**197**	20c. blue (air)	20	10
775	**197**	60c. green	30	15
776	**197**	1p.20 brown	75	55
777	**197**	2p.80 black	1·30	1·10

198 Generals Barrientos and Ovando, Bolivian Map and Flag

1966. Co-Presidents Commemoration.

778	**198**	60c. mult (postage)	55	10
779	**198**	1p. multicoloured	65	15
780	**198**	2p.80 mult (air)	1·70	1·10
781	**198**	10p. multicoloured	3·75	1·40
MS782		136×83 mm. Nos. 778/81. Imperf	10·00	10·00

199 Needy Children

1966. Aid for Poor Children.

783	**199**	30c. brown, sepia and ochre (postage)	55	20
784	-	1p.40 black & blue (air)	2·50	65

DESIGN: 1p.40, Mother and needy children.

1966. Commemorative Issues. Various stamps surch with inscr (as given below) and value. (i) Red Cross Centenary. Surch Centenario de la Cruz Roja Internacional.

785	20c. on 150b. (No. 641) (post)	30	10
786	4p. on 4000b. (No. 650) (air)	2·10	1·60

(ii) General Azurduy de Padilla. Surch **Homenaje a la Generala J. Azurduy de Padilla**.

787	30c. on 550b. (No. 643)	45	20
788	2p.80 on 750b. (No. 644)	1·20	75

(iii) Air. Tupiza Cent. Surch **Centenario de Tupiza**.

789	60c. on 1350b. (No. 648)	75	30

(iv) Air. 25th Anniv of Bolivian Motor Club. Surch **XXV Aniversario Automovil Club Boliviano**.

790	2p.80 on 2700b. (No. 649)	3·25	2·30

(v) Air. Cochabamba Philatelic Society Anniv. Surch **Aniversario Centro Filatelico Cochabamba**.

791	1p.20 on 800b. (No. 742)	1·60	30
792	1p.20 on 1800b. (No. 743)	1·60	30

(vi) Rotary Help for Children's Hospital. Surch with value only. (a) Postage.

793	1p.60 on 350b. (No. 693)	1·20	75
794	2p.40 on 500b. (No. 694)	1·60	1·20

(b) Air.

795	1p.40 on 1000b. (No. 698)	85	75
796	1p.40 on 1800b. (No. 699)	85	75

(vii) 150th Anniv of Coronilla Heroines. Surch **CL Aniversario Heroinas Coronilla**. (a) Postage.

797	60c. on 350b. (No. 682)	75	20

(b) Air.

798	1p.20 on 800b. (No. 689)	1·20	75

(viii) Air. Centenary of Hymn La Paz. Surch **Centenario Himno Paceno**.

799	1p.40 on 4000b. (No. 692)	1·20	75

(ix) Air. 12th Anniv of Agrarian Reform. Surch **XII Aniversario Reforma Agraria**.

800	10c. on 27b. (No. 602)	30	20

(x) Air. 25th Anniv of Chaco Peace Settlement. Surch **XXV Aniversario Paz del Chaco**.

801	10c. on 55b. (No. 613)	30	20

(xi) Centenary of Rurrenabaque. Surch **Centenario de Rurrenabaque**.

802	1p. on 10b. brown	75	30

(xii) 25th Anniv of Busch Government. Surch **XXV Aniversario Gobierno Busch**.

803	20c. on 5b. red	30	20

(xiii) 20th Anniv of Villarroel Government. Surch **XX Aniversario Gob. Villarroel**.

804	60c. on 2b. green	45	20

(xiv) 25th Anniv of Pando Department. Surch **XXV Aniversario Dpto. Pando**. (a) Postage.

805	1p.60 on 50c. violet	75	30

(b) Air. Surch Aereo also.

806	1p.20 on 1b. blue	85	45

201 Sower

1967. 50th Anniv of Lions International. Multicoloured.

807	**201**	70c. Type **201** (postage)	55	20
808	**201**	2p. Lions emblem and Inca obelisks (horiz) (air)	1·30	95
MS809		129×80 mm. Nos. 807/8. Imperf	5·75	5·75

202 "Macheteros"

1968. Ninth Congress of the UPAE (Postal Union of the Americas and Spain). Bolivian Folklore. Designs showing costumed figures. Multicoloured.

810	**202**	30c. Type **202** (postage)	30	10
811	**202**	60c. "Chunchos"	45	20
812	**202**	1p. "Wiphala"	65	25
813	**202**	2p. "Diablada"	95	30
814	**202**	1p.20 "Pujllay" (air)	55	20
815	**202**	1p.40 "Ujusiris"	65	25
816	**202**	2p. "Morenada"	1·30	45
817	**202**	3p. "Auki-aukis"	1·70	55
MS818		Two sheets each 132×80 mm. Nos. 810/13 and 814/17. Imperf	27·00	27·00

203 Arms of Tarija

1968. 150th Anniv of Battle of the Tablada (1817).

819	**203**	20c. mult (postage)	20	10
820	**203**	30c. multicoloured	20	10
821	**203**	40c. multicoloured	30	10
822	**203**	60c. multicoloured	45	15
823	-	1p. multicoloured (air)	55	20
824	-	1p.20 multicoloured	65	20
825	-	2p. multicoloured	1·20	55
826	-	4p. multicoloured	1·70	85

DESIGNS: Nos. 823/6, Moto Mendez.

204 President G. Villarroel

1968. 400th Anniv of Cochabamba.

827	**204**	20c. brn & orge (postage)	80	20
828	**204**	30c. brown & turquoise	80	20
829	**204**	40c. brown and purple	80	20
830	**204**	50c. brown and green	80	20
831	**204**	1p. brown and bistre	95	20
832	-	1p.40 black & red (air)	1·10	45
833	-	3p. black and blue	1·50	55
834	-	4p. black and red	1·90	65
835	-	5p. black and green	2·40	65
836	-	10p. black and violet	4·25	1·30

DESIGN—HORIZ: 1p.40 to 10p. Similar portrait of President.

205 Painted Clay Cup

1968. 20th Anniv of UNESCO (1966).

837	**205**	20c. mult (postage)	40	10
838	**205**	60c. multicoloured	75	45
839	**205**	1p.20 black & blue (air)	75	45
840	**205**	2p.80 black and green	1·40	95

DESIGNS: Nos. 839/40, UNESCO emblem.

206 President J. F. Kennedy

1968. Fifth Death Anniv of John F. Kennedy (U.S. President).

841	**206**	10c. black & grn (postage)	30	10
842	**206**	4p. black and violet	2·10	2·10
843	**206**	1p. black and green (air)	40	20
844	**206**	10p. black and red	4·25	4·25
MS845		Two sheets each 131×80 mm. (a) No. 842; (b) No. 843. Imperf	9·50	9·50

207 ITU Emblem

1968. Centenary (1965) of ITU.

846	**207**	10c. black grey and yellow (postage)	30	10
847	**207**	60c. black, orange & bistre	55	30
848	**207**	1p.20 black, grey and yellow (air)	75	40
849	**207**	1p.40 black, blue & brn	85	30

208 Tennis Player

1968. South American Tennis Championships, La Paz.

850	**208**	10c. black, brown and grey (postage)	40	15
851	**208**	20c. black, brown & yell	40	15
852	**208**	30c. black, brown & blue	40	15
853	**208**	1p.40 black, brown and orange (air)	1·30	45
854	**208**	2p.80 black, brown & bl	2·40	95
MS855		Two sheets each 132×81 mm. (a) Nos. 850/2; (b) No. 853. Imperf	17·00	17·00

209 Unofficial 1r. Stamp of 1863

1963. Stamp Centenary.

856	**209**	10c. brown, black and green (postage)	90	15
857	**209**	30c. brown, black & blue	90	15
858	**209**	2p. brown, black & drab	90	15
859	-	1p.40 green, black and yellow (air)	1·30	70
860	-	2p.80 green, blk & pink	2·40	1·40
861	-	3p. green, black & lilac	2·40	1·40
MS862		Two sheets each 132×83 mm. (a) Nos. 856/8; (b) Nos. 859/61. Imperf	11·00	11·50

DESIGN: Nos. 859/61, First Bolivian stamp.

210 Rifle-shooting

1969. Olympic Games, Mexico (1968).

863	**210**	40c. black, red and orange (postage)	55	25
864	-	50c. black, red and green	55	25
865	-	60c. black, blue & green	55	25
866	-	1p.20 black, green and ochre (air)	70	50
867	-	2p.80 black, red & yell	1·40	1·00
868	-	5p. multicoloured	2·20	2·10
MS869		Two sheets each 131×81 mm. (a) Nos. 863/5; (b) Nos. 866/8	17·00	17·00

DESIGNS—HORIZ: 50c. Horse-jumping; 60c. Canoeing; 5p. Hurdling. VERT: 1p.20, Running; 2p.80, Throwing the discus.

211 F. D. Roosevelt

1969. Air. Franklin D. Roosevelt Commem.

870	**211**	5p. black, orange & brown	2·00	1·50

212 *Temensis laothoe violetta*

1970. Butterflies. Multicoloured.

871	5c. Type **212** (postage)	90	80
872	10c. *Papilio crassus*	1·80	1·60
873	20c. *Catagramma cynosura*	1·80	1·60
874	30c. *Eunica eurota flora*	1·80	1·60
875	80c. *Ituna phenarete*	1·80	1·60
876	1p. *Metamorpha dido wernichei* (air)	2·00	1·70
877	1p.80 *Heliconius felix*	2·75	2·40
878	2p.80 *Morpho casica*	3·75	3·50
879	3p. *Papilio yuracares*	4·00	3·50
880	4p. *Heliconsus melitus*	5·00	4·50
MS881	Two sheets each 132×80 mm. (a) Nos. 871/3; (b) Nos. 876/8. Imerf	29·00	29·00

213 Scout mountaineering

1970. Bolivian Scout Movement. Multicoloured.

882	**213**	5c. Type **213** (postage)	25	10
883	**213**	10c. Girl-scout planting shrub	25	10
884	**213**	50c. Scout laying bricks (air)	25	15
885	**213**	1p.20 Bolivian scout badge	55	45

214 President A. Ovando and Revolutionaries

1970. Obligatory Tax. Revolution and National Day.

886	**214**	20c. blk & red (postage)	65	25
887	**214**	30c. black & green (air)	65	25

DESIGN: 30c. Pres. Ovando, oil derricks and laurel sprig.

1970. "Exfilca 70" Stamp Exhibition, Caracas, Venezuela. No. 706 further surch **EXFILCA 70** and new value.

888	30c. on 350b. on 10c.	45	30

1970. Provisionals. Various stamps surch.

889	**178**	60c. on 900b. on 350b. (postage)	35	10
890	-	1p.20 on 1500b. (No. 723)	65	15
891	**185**	1p.20 on 4000b. (air)	45	15

217 Pres. G. Busch and Oil Derrick

1971. 32nd Death Anniv of President G. Busch and 25th Death Anniv of Pres. Villarroel.

892	**217**	20c. blk & lilac (postage)	65	25
893	-	30c. black and blue (air)	65	25

DESIGN: 30c. Pres. Villarroel and oil refinery.

218 *Amaryllis escobar uriae*

1971. Bolivian Flora. Multicoloured.

894	30c. Type **218** (postage)	35	15
895	40c. *Amaryllis evansae*	35	15
896	50c. *Amaryllis yungacensis* (vert)	55	25
897	2p. *Gymnocalycium chiquitanum* (vert)	1·40	55
898	1p.20 *Amaryllis pseudopardina* (air)	80	55
899	1p.40 *Rebutia kruegeri* (vert)	1·20	70
900	2p.80 *Lobivia pentlandii*	2·00	1·00
901	4p. *Rebutia tunariensis* (vert)	2·75	1·70
MS902	Two sheets each 130×80 mm. (a) Nos. 894/5, 898 and 900; (b) Nos. 896/7, 899 and 901. Imperf	27·00	27·00

219 Sica Sica Cathedral

1971. "Exfilima" Stamp Exhibition, Lima, Peru.

903	**219**	20c. multicoloured	45	25

220 Pres. H. Banzer

1972. "Bolivia's Development".

904	**220**	1p.20 multicoloured	1·80	25

221 Chiriwano de Achocalla Dance

1972. Folk Dances. Multicoloured.

905	20c. Type **221** (postage)	25	10
906	40c. Rueda Chapaca	45	15
907	60c. Kena-Kena	65	25

908	1p. Waca Thokori	80	30
909	1p.20 Kusillo (air)	70	25
910	1p.40 Taquirari	90	25

222 *Virgin and Child* (B. Bitti)

1972. Bolivian Paintings. Multicoloured.

911	10c. *The Washerwoman* (M. P. Holguin) (postage)	35	10
912	50c. *Coronation of the Virgin* (G. M. Berrio)	45	10
913	70c. *Arquebusier* (anon.)	65	10
914	80c. *St. Peter of Alcantara* (M. P. Holguin)	70	15
915	1p. Type **222**	1·00	20
916	1p.40 *Chola Pacena* (G. de Rojas) (air)	70	10
917	1p.50 *Adoration of the Kings* (G. Gamarra)	70	10
918	1p.60 *Pachamama Vision* (A. Borda)	70	10
919	2p. *Idol's Kiss* (G. de Rojas)	1·10	30

223 Tarija Cathedral

1972. "EXFILIBRA 72" Stamp Exhibition, Rio de Janeiro.

920	**223** 30c. multicoloured	45	15

224 National Arms

1972. Air.

921	**224** 4p. multicoloured	2·75	65

225 Santos Dumont and "14 bis"

1973. Air. Birth Centenary of Alberto Santos Dumont (aviation pioneer).

922	**225** 1p.40 black and yellow	90	40

226 *Echinocactus notocactus*

1973. Cacti. Multicoloured.

923	20c. Type **226** (postage)	55	25
924	40c. *Echinocactus lenninghaussii*	55	25
925	50c. *Mammillaria bocasana*	60	25
926	70c. *Echinocactus lenninghaussii* (different)	65	40
927	1p.20 *Mammillaria bocasana* (different) (air)	70	25
928	1p.90 *Opuntia cristata*	1·10	30
929	2p. *Echinocactus rebutia*	1·80	45

227 Power Station, Santa Isabel

1973. Bolivian Development Multicoloured.

930	10c. Type **227** (postage)	1·30	25
931	20c. Tin foundry	1·30	25
932	90c. Bismuth plant	1·50	30
933	1p. Gas plant	1·50	30
934	1p.40 Road bridge, Highways 1 and 4 (air)	2·50	40
935	2p. Inspection car crossing bridge, Al Beni	3·75	45

228 *Cattleya nobilior*

1974. Orchids. Multicoloured.

936	20c. Type **228** (postage)	1·30	25
937	50c. *Zygopetalum bolivianum*	1·30	25
938	1p. *Huntleya melagris*	1·30	25
939	2p.50 *Cattleya luteola* (horiz) (air)	2·30	40
940	3p.80 *Stanhopaea*	2·75	55
941	4p. *Catasetum* (horiz)	3·00	70
942	5p. *Maxillaria*	5·00	80

1974. Philatelic Exhibitions, 1975, 1976 and 1977. Four sheets each 130×80 mm showing reproductions of various stamps.

MS943	(a) Nos. 36, 911 and 942; (b) Nos. 36, 912 and 941; (c) Nos. 36, 914 and 939; (d) Nos. 36 and 921	16·00	16·00

See also No. **MS**954.

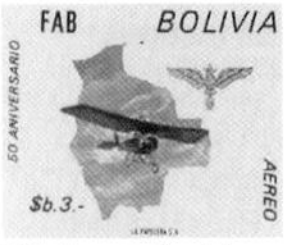

229 Morane Saulnier Type P and Emblem

1974. Air. 50th Anniv of Bolivian Air Force. Multicoloured.

944	3p. Type **229**	80	65
945	3p.80 Douglas DC-3 crossing Andes	1·30	80
946	4p.50 Triplane trainer and Morane Saulnier Paris I aircraft	1·30	80
947	8p. Col. Rafael Pabon and biplane fighter	2·00	1·60
948	15p. Jet airliner on "50"	4·25	2·50

230 General Sucre (after J. Wallpher)

1974. 150th Anniv of Battle of Avacucho.

949	**230** 5p. multicoloured	1·30	65

231 UPU and Exhibition Emblems

1974. Centenary of UPU and Expo UPU (Montevideo) and Prenfil UPU (Buenos Aires) Stamp Exhibitions.

950	**231** 3p.50 green, black & bl	1·20	45

232 Lions Emblem and Steles

1975. 50th Anniv of Lions International in Bolivia.

951	**232** 30c. multicoloured	45	40

233 Exhibition Emblem

1975. "Espana 75" International Stamp Exhibition, Madrid.

952	**233** 4p.50 multicoloured	95	40

234 Emblem of Meeting

1975. Cartagena Agreement. First Meeting of Postal Ministers, Quito, Ecuador.

953	**234** 2p.50 silver, violet & blk	80	30

1975. Philatelic Exhibitions 1975, 1976 and 1977. Four sheets as MS943.

MS954	(a) Nos. 36 and 950; (b) Nos. 36 and 951; (c) Nos. 36 and 952; (d) Nos. 36 and 953	17·00	17·00

235 Arms of Pando

1975. 150th Anniv of Republic (1st issue). Provincial Arms. Multicoloured.

955	20c. Type **235** (postage)	40	15
956	2p. Chuzuisaca	85	45
957	3p. Cochabamba	1·10	65
958	20c. Beni (air)	40	15
959	30c. Tarija	40	15
960	50c. Potosi	55	25
961	1p. Oruro	1·10	65
962	2p.50 Santa Cruz	2·00	1·30
963	3p. La Paz	2·00	1·30

See also Nos. 965/78.

236 Presidents Perez and Banzer

1975. Air. Visit of Pres. Perez of Venezuela.

964	**236** 3p. multicoloured	85	65

237 Pres. Victor Paz Estenssoro

1975. 150th Anniv of Republic (2nd issue).

965	30c. Type **237** (postage)	10	10
966	60c. Pres. Thomas Frias	15	10
966a	1p. Ismael Montes	25	15
967	2p.50 Aniceto Arce	65	25
968	7p. Bautista Saavedra	1·60	80
969	10p. Jose Manuel Pando	2·50	1·30
970	15p. Jose Maria Linares	3·25	1·60
971	50p. Simon Bolivar	12·50	8·75
972	50c. Rene Barrientos Ortuno (air)	15	10
973	2p. Francisco B. O'Connor	80	25
973a	3p.80 Gualberto Villaroel	80	65
974	4p.20 German Busch	1·30	80
975	4p.50 Pres. Hugo Banzer Suarez	1·30	80
976	20p. Jose Ballivian	5·00	3·25
977	30p. Pres. Andres de Santa Cruz	6·00	4·25
978	40p. Pres. Antonio Jose de Sucre	7·75	5·50

Nos. 965/70, 972/4 and 976/78 are smaller, 24×33 mm.

238 Laurel Wreath and LAB Emblem

1975. Air. 50th Anniv of Lloyd-Aereo Boliviano (national airline). Multicoloured.

979	1p. Type **238**	45	25
980	1p.50 Douglas DC-9 and L.A.B. route map (horiz)	70	35
981	2p. Guillermo Kyllmann (founder) and Junkers F-13 aircraft (horiz)	95	45

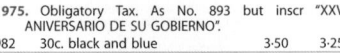

1975. Obligatory Tax. As No. 893 but inscr "XXV ANIVERSARIO DE SU GOBIERNO".

982	30c. black and blue	3·50	3·25

239 "EXFIVIA"

1975. "Exfivia 75". Stamp Exhibition.

983	**239** 3p. multicoloured	95	70

240 UPU Emblem

1975. Air. Centenary (1974) of UPU.

984	**240** 25p. multicoloured	3·50	3·25

241 Chiang Kai-shek

1976. First Death Anniv of President Chiang Kai-shek.

985	**241** 2p.50 multicoloured	3·50	1·30

242 Geological Hammer, Lamp and Map

1976. Bolivian Geological Institute.

986	**242** 4p. multicoloured	1·00	45

243 Naval Insignia

1976. Navy Day.

987	**243** 50c. multicoloured	45	30

244 Douglas DC-10 and Divided Roundel

1976. 50th Anniv of Lufthansa Airline.

988	**244** 3p. multicoloured	1·20	45

245 Bolivian Boy Scout and Badge

1976. 60th Anniv of Bolivian Boy Scouts.

989	**245** 1p. multicoloured	65	40

246 Battle Scene

1976. Bicentenary of American Revolution.

990	**246** 4p.50 multicoloured	1·70	80
MS991	130×81 mm. No. 990	20·00	20·00

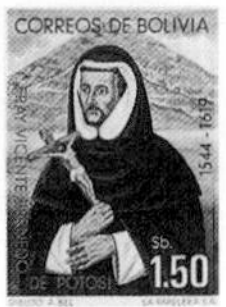

247 Brother Vicente Bernedo (missionary)

1976. Brother Vincente Bernedo Commemoration.

992	**247**	1p.50 multicoloured	40	25

248 Rainbow over La Paz, Police Handler with Dog

1976. 150th Anniv of Police Service.

993	**248**	2p.50 multicoloured	70	55

249 Bolivian Family

1976. National Census.

994	**249**	2p.50 multicoloured	65	45

250 Pedro Poveda (educator)

1976. Poveda Commemoration.

995	**250**	1p.50 multicoloured	45	25

251 Arms, Bolivar and Sucre

1976. International Bolivarian Societies Congress.

996	**251**	1p.50 multicoloured	80	40

252 "Numeral"

1976

997	**252**	20c. brown	30	10
998	**252**	1p. blue	55	25
999	**252**	1p.50 green	95	65

253 Boy and Girl

1977. Christmas 1976 and 50th Anniv of Inter-American Children's Institute.

1000	**253**	50c. multicoloured	30	10

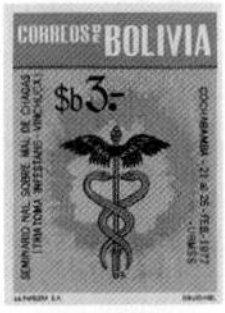

254 Caduceus

1977. National Seminar on "Chagas Disease".

1001	**254**	3p. multicoloured	85	25

255 Court Buildings, La Paz

1977. 150th Anniv of Bolivian Supreme Court. Multicoloured.

1002	2p.50 Type **255**	40	10
1003	4p. Dr. Manuel M. Urcullu, first President	55	10
1004	4p.50 Dr. Pantaleon Dalence, President, 1883–89	80	15

256 Tower and Map

1977. 90th Anniv of Oruro Club.

1005	**256**	3p. multicoloured	65	25

257 Newspaper Mastheads

1977. Bolivian Newspapers. Multicoloured.

1006	1p.50 Type **257**	30	10
1007	2p.50 *Ultima Hora* and Alfredo Alexander (horiz)	40	15
1008	3p. *El Diaro* and Jose Carrasco (horiz)	45	25
1009	4p. *Los Tiempos* and Demetrio Canelas	65	30
1010	5p.50 *Presencia*	80	25

258 Games Poster

1977. Eighth Bolivarian Games, La Paz.

1011	**258**	5p. multicoloured	85	30

259 Tin Miner and Mining Corporation Emblem

1977. 25th Anniv of Bolivian Mining Corporation.

1012	**259**	3p. multicoloured	85	25

260 Miners, Globe and Chemical Symbol for Tin

1977. International Tin Symposium, La Paz.

1013	**260**	6p. multicoloured	1·20	45

261 Map of Bolivia and Radio Masts

1977. 50th Anniv of Bolivian Radio.

1014	**261**	2p.50 multicoloured	65	40

1977. "Exfivia 77" Philatelic Exhibition, Cochabamba. No. 719 surch **EXFIVIA — 77 $b. 5.—**.

1015	5p. on 5,000b. on $b. 5 grey and gold	2·40	1·60

263 "Eye", Compass, Key and Law Book

1978. 50th Anniv of Audit Department.

1016	**263**	5p. multicoloured	85	25

264 Aesculapius Staff and Map of Andean Countries

1978. Fifth Meeting of Andean Countries' Health Ministers.

1017	**264**	2p. orange and black	45	25

265 Map of the Americas

1978. World Rheumatism Year (1977).

1018	**265**	2p.50 blue and red	65	25

266 Mt. Illimani

1978

1019	**266**	50c. green and blue	25	10
1020	-	1p. yellow and brown	25	10
1021	-	1p.50 grey and red	40	20

DESIGNS—HORIZ: 1p.50, Mt. Cerro de Potosi. VERT: 1p. Pre-Columbian monolith.

267 Central Bank

1978. 50th Anniv of Bank of Bolivia.

1022	**267**	7p. multicoloured	1·20	30

268 Jesus with Children

1979. International Year of the Child.

1023	**268**	8p. multicoloured	1·20	40

269 Antofagasta Cancellation

270 Antofagasta

1979. Centenary of Loss of Litoral Department to Chile.

1024	**269**	50c. brown and black	30	10
1025	-	1p. mauve and black	55	10
1026	-	1p.50 green and black	55	10
1027	**270**	5p.50 multicoloured	80	15
1028	-	6p.50 multicoloured	95	30
1029	-	7p. multicoloured	95	30
1030	-	8p. multicoloured	1·10	35
1031	-	10p. multicoloured	1·50	40

DESIGNS—HORIZ: 1p. La Chimba cancel; 1p.50, Mejillonos cancel. VERT: (As Type **270**). 6p.50, Woman in chains; 7p. Eduardo Arbaroa; 8p. Map of Department, 1876; 10p. Arms of Litoral.

271 Map and Radio Club Emblem

1979. Radio Club of Bolivia.

1032	**271**	3p. multicoloured	95	55

272 Runner and Games Emblem

1979. First "Southern Cross" Games. Multicoloured.

1033	6p.50 Type **272**	1·00	25
1034	10p. Gymnast	1·60	40

273 Bulgarian Stamp of 1879

1979. "Philaserdica 79" Philatelic Exhibition, Sofia, Bulgaria.

1035	**273**	2p.50 black, yellow and light yellow	45	30

274 "Exfilmar" Emblem

1979. "Exfilmar 79" Maritime Philatelic, Exhibition, La Paz.

1036	**274**	2p. blue, black and light blue	1·60	55

275 OAS Emblem and Map

1979. Ninth Congress of Organization of American States, La Paz.

1037	**275**	6p. multicoloured	95	30

276 Franz Tamayo (lawyer)

1979. Anniversaries and Events.

1038	**276**	2p.80 light grey, black and grey	45	40
1039	-	5p. multicoloured	80	25
1040	-	5p. multicoloured	80	25
1041	-	6p. multicoloured	95	40
1042	-	9p.50 multicoloured	2·75	80

DESIGNS—VERT: 2p.80, Type **276** (birth centenary); 5p. (No. 1039) U.N. emblem and delegates (18th CEPAL Sessions, La Paz); 5p. (No. 1042), Gastroenterological laboratory (Japanese health co-operation); 6p. Radio mast (50th anniv of national radio). HORIZ: 9p.50, Puerto Suarez iron ore deposits.

277 500c. Stamp of 1871, Exhibition Emblem and Flag

1980. "Exfilmar" Bolivian Maritime Stamp Exhibition, La Paz.

1043	**277**	4p. multicoloured	95	30

278 Juana Azurduy de Padilla

1980. Birth Bicentenary of Juana Azurduy de Padilla (Independence heroine).
1044 **278** 4p. multicoloured 65 30

279 Jean Baptiste de la Salle (founder)

1980. 300th Anniv of Brothers of Christian Schools.
1045 **279** 9p. multicoloured 1·40 55

280 "Victory in a Chariot", Emblem and Flags

1980. "Espamer 80" International Stamp Exhibition, Madrid.
1046 **280** 14p. multicoloured 2·00 55

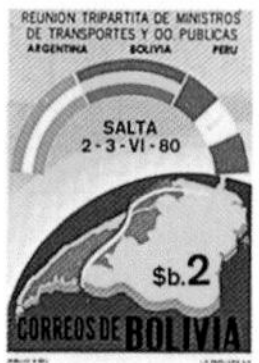

281 Flags over Map of South America

1980. Meeting of Public Works and Transport Ministers of Argentina, Bolivia and Peru.
1047 **281** 2p. multicoloured 85 15

282 Diesel Locomotive

1980. Inauguration of Santa Cruz-Trinidad Railway, Third Section.
1048 **282** 3p. multicoloured 55 25

283 Soldier and Citizen with Flag destroying Communism

1981. First Anniv of 17 July Revolution. Multicoloured.
1049 1p. Type **283** 6·00 7·25
1050 3p. Flag shattering hammer and sickle on map 6·00 7·25
1051 40p. Flag on map of Bolivia showing provinces 4·00 1·50
1052 50p. Rejoicing crowd (horiz) 5·75 1·20

284 Scarlet Macaw

1981. Macaws. Multicoloured.
1053 4p. Type **284** 65 25
1054 7p. Green-winged macaw 1·10 40
1055 8p. Blue and yellow macaw 1·30 45
1056 9p. Red-fronted macaw 1·40 50
1057 10p. Yellow-collared macaw 1·60 50
1058 12p. Hyacinth macaw 2·00 85
1059 15p. Military macaw 2·50 95
1060 20p. Chestnut-fronted macaw 3·25 1·20

285 Virgin and Child receiving Flower

1981. Christmas.
1061 **285** 1p. pink and red 15 10
1062 - 2p. light blue and blue 30 10
DESIGN: 2p. Child and star (horiz).
See also No. 1080.

286 Emblem

1982. 22nd American Air Force Commanders' Conference, Buenos Aires.
1063 **286** 14p. multicoloured 1·70 1·10

287 Cobija

1982. 75th Anniv of Cobija City.
1064 **287** 28p. multicoloured 45 30

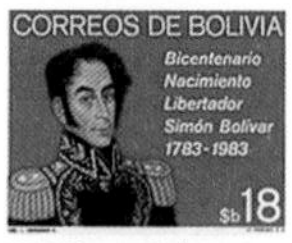

288 Simon Bolivar

1982. Birth Bicentenary of Simon Bolivar.
1065 **288** 18p. multicoloured 30 25

289 Dish Antenna

1982. World Communication Year.
1066 **289** 26p. multicoloured 45 30

290 Footballers

1982. World Cup Football Championship, Spain. Multicoloured.
1067 4p. Type **290** 25 10
1068 100p. "The Final Number" (Picasso) 2·00 1·20

291 Boy playing Football

1982. Bolivian Youth. Multicoloured.
1069 16p. Type **291** 1·10 45
1070 20p. Girl playing piano (horiz) 1·60 55

292 Harvesting

1982. China-Bolivian Agricultural Co-operation.
1071 **292** 30p. multicoloured 95 55

293 Flowers

1982. First Bolivian-Japanese Gastroenterological Days.
1072 **293** 22p. multicoloured 1·20 80

294 Bolivian Stamps

1982. Tenth Anniv of Bolivian Philatelic Federation.
1073 **294** 19p. multicoloured 1·30 45

295 Hernando Siles

1982. Birth Centenary of Hernando Siles (former President).
1074 **295** 20p. buff and brown 40 25

296 Baden-Powell

1982. 125th Birth Anniv of Lord Baden-Powell and 75th Anniv of Boy Scout Movement.
1075 **296** 5p. multicoloured 30 10

297 "Liberty", Cochabamba

1982. 25th Anniv of Cochabamba Philatelic Centre.
1076 **297** 3p. buff, black & blue 30 10

298 High Court, Cochabamba

1982. 150th Anniv of High Court, Cochabamba.
1077 **298** 10p. black, red and bronze 40 15

299 Virgin of Copacabana

1982. 400th Anniv of Enthronement of Virgin of Copacabana.
1078 **299** 13p. multicoloured 40 25

300 Puerto Busch Naval Base

1982. Navy Day.
1079 **300** 14p. multicoloured 40 25

1982. Christmas. Design as Type **285**, inscribed "NAVIDAD 1982".
1080 **285** 10p. grey and green 70 25

301 Footballer and Emblem

1983. TEnth American Youth Football Championships.
1081 **301** 50p. multicoloured 1·00 65

302 Sun Gate

1983. "Exfivia 83" Stamp Exhibition.
1082 **302** 150p. red 1·30 65

303 Presidents Figueiredo and Zuazo

1984. Visit of President of Brazil.
1083 **303** 150p. multicoloured 55 15

1984. Various stamps surch.
1084 **276** 40p. on 2p.80 light grey, black and grey 25 10
1085 - 60p. on 1p.50 green and black (1026) 25 10
1086 **265** 60p. on 2p.50 blue and red 25 10
1087 **274** 100p. on 2p. blue, black and light blue 40 25
1088 **174** 200p. on 350b. blue and light blue 80 30

1984. "Mladost 84" Youth Stamp Exn, Pleven, Bulgaria. No. 1035 surch.
1089 **273** 40p. on 2p.50 black, yellow and light yellow 25 10

306 *Simon Bolivar* (Mulato Gil de Quesada)

1984. Birth Bicentenary of Simon Bolivar. Multicoloured.
1090 50p. Type **306** 25 10
1091 200p. "Simon Bolivar entering La Paz" (Carmen Baptista) 70 30

1984. Various stamps surch.
1092 **297** 500p. on 3p. buff, black and blue (postage) 95 40
1093 **290** 1000p. on 4p. mult 2·00 95
1094 **285** 2000p. on 10p. grey and green 4·00 1·60
1095 **296** 5000p. on 5p. mult 9·50 4·00

308 Pedestrian walking in Road

1984. Road Safety Campaign. Multicoloured.
1096 - 10000p. on 3p.80 mult (No. 940) (air) 12·50 7·75
1097 80p. Type **308** 40 25
1098 120p. Police motorcyclist and patrol car 40 25

309 *Mendezs Birthplace* (Jorge Campos)

1984. Birth Bicentenary of Jose Eustaquio Mendez. Multicoloured.
1099 300p. Type **309** 25 10
1100 500p. "Battle of La Tablada" (M. Villegas) 30 10

310 Legs and Feet on Map and Bata Emblem

1984. World Footwear Festival. Multicoloured.
1101 100p. Type **310** 40 15
1102 200p. Legs and feet on map and Power emblem 40 15
1103 600p. Football and globes (World Cup, Mexico, 1986) (horiz) 45 15

311 Inca Postal Runner

1985
1104 **311** 11000p. blue 85 25

312 Vicuna

1985. Endangered Animals.
1105 **312** 23000p. brown and deep brown 1·20 55
1106 - 25000p. brown, blue and orange 45 30
1107 - 30000p. red and green 60 40
DESIGNS—VERT: 25000p. Andean condor; 30000p. Marsh deer.

313 National Work Education Service Emblem

1985. International Professional Education Year.
1108 **313** 2000p. blue and red 30 10

314 Hand with Syringe, Victim in Droplet and Campaign Emblem

1985. Anti-polio Campaign.
1109 **314** 20000p. blue and violet 40 25

315 Vicenta Juaristi Eguino

1985. Birth Bicentenary of Vicenta Juaristi Eguino (Independence heroine).
1110 **315** 300000p. multicoloured 95 55

316 U.N. Emblem

1985. 40th Anniv of U.N.O.
1111 **316** 1000000p. blue and gold 3·25 40

317 Emblem

1985. 75th Anniv of "The Strongest" Football Club.
1112 **317** 200000p. multicoloured 65 25

318 Emblem, Envelope and Posthorn

1986. Cent of Bolivian U.P.U. Membership.
1113 **318** 800000p. multicoloured 1·20 65

319 Bull and Rider

1986. 300th Anniv of Trinidad City.
1114 **319** 1400000p. multicoloured 2·00 1·20

1986. No. 1108 surch.
1115 **313** 200000p. on 2000p. blue and red 60 15
1116 **313** 5000000p. on 2000p. blue and red 6·00 3·25

321 Football as Globes

1986. World Cup Football Championship, Mexico.
1117 **321** 300000p. red and black 45 20
1118 - 550000p. multicoloured 80 45
1119 - 1000000p. black and green (horiz) 1·30 70
1120 - 2500000p. green & yell 4·00 1·40
DESIGNS—VERT: 550000p. Pique (mascot); 2500000p. Trophy. HORIZ: 1000000p. Azteca Stadium, Mexico City.

322 Alfonso Subieta Viaduct

1986. 25th Anniv of American Development Bank.
1121 **322** 400000p. blue 70 25

323 Envelope

1986. 50th Anniv of Society of Postmen.
1122 **323** 2000000p. brown 4·75 1·40

324 Emblem and Dove

1986. International Peace Year.
1123 **324** 200000p. green 50 20

325 Emblem

1986. International Youth Year (1985).
1124 **325** 150000p. red 35 20
1125 **325** 500000p. green 1·00 45
1126 - 3000000p. multicoloured 6·50 2·20
DESIGNS: 3000000p. Child clutching trophy and flag (25th anniv of Enrique Happ Sports Club, Cochabamba).

326 Zampa (after F. Diaz de Ortega)

1986. 50th Death Anniv of Friar Jose Antonio Zampa.
1127 **326** 400000p. multicoloured 95 45

327 1870 500c. Stamp

1986. 15th Anniv of Bolivian Philatelic Federation.
1128 **327** 600000p. brown 85 45

328 Refinery

1986. 50th Anniv of National Petroleum Refining Corporation.
1129 **328** 1000000p. multicoloured 1·90 1·10

329 Demon Mask

1987. Centenary of 10th February Society, Oruro.
1130 **329** 20c. multicoloured 95 25

330 Flags

1987. State Visit of President Richard von Weizsacker of German Federal Republic.
1131 **330** 30c. multicoloured 85 45

331 National Arms

1987. Visit of King Juan Carlos of Spain.
1132 **331** 60c. multicoloured 1·20 55

332 Andean ("Condor")

1987. Endangered Animals. Multicoloured.
1133 20c. Type **332** 70 25
1134 20c. Tapir 70 25
1135 30c. Vicuna (new-born) 95 35
1136 30c. Armadillo 95 35
1137 40c. Spectacled bear 1·30 45
1138 60c. Keel-billed toucans ("Tucan") 1·90 65

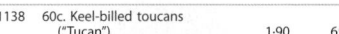

333 Modern View of Potosi

1987. "Exfivia 87" Stamp Exhibition, Potosi. Multicoloured.
1139 40c. Type **333** 80 45
1140 50c. 18th-century engraving of Potosi 1·90 55

334 *Nina* and Stern of *Santa Maria*

1987. "Espamer '87" Stamp Exhibition, La Coruna. Multicoloured.
1141 20c. Type **334** 45 25
1142 20c. *Pinta* and bow of *Santa Maria* 45 25
Nos. 1141/2 were printed together, *se-tenant*, forming a composite design.

335 Pan-pipes and Indian Flute

1987. Musical Instruments. Multicoloured.
1143 50c. Type **335** 1·10 45
1144 1b. Indian guitars 1·90 1·00

336 Carabuco Church

1988. Visit of Pope John Paul II. Multicoloured.
1145 20c. Type **336** 45 25
1146 20c. Tihuanacu church 45 25
1147 20c. Cathedral of the Kings, Beni 45 25
1148 30c. St. Joseph church, Chiquitos 70 25
1149 30c. St. Francis's church, Sucre 70 25
1150 40c. Cobija chapel (vert) 85 35
1151 50c. Cochabamba cathedral (vert) 1·10 35
1152 50c. Jayu Kcota church 1·10 35
1153 60c. St. Francis's Basilica, La Paz (vert) 1·30 45
1154 70c. Church of Jesus, Machaca 1·50 45
1155 70c. St. Lawrence's church, Potosi (vert) 1·50 45
1156 80c. Vallegrande church 1·70 65
1157 80c. Copacabana Virgin (vert) 1·70 65
1158 80c. "The Holy Family" (Peter Paul Rubens) (vert) 1·70 65
1159 1b.30 Concepcion church 2·75 1·10
1160 1b.30 Tarija cathedral (vert) 2·75 1·10
1161 1b.50 Pope and Arms of John Paul II and Bolivia 3·00 1·40

337 Handshake and Flags

1988. Visit of President Jose Sarney of Brazil.
1162 **337** 50c. multicoloured 85 45

338 St. John Bosco

1988. Death Centenary of St. John Bosco (founder of Salesian Brothers).

1163	**338**	30c. multicoloured	50	25

339 La Paz–Beni Steam Locomotive

1988. Centenary of Bolivian Railways.

1164	**339**	1b. multicoloured	2·30	80

340 Aguirre

1988. Death Cent of Nataniel Aguirre (writer).

1165	**340**	1b. black and brown	1·90	80

341 "Column of the Future" (Battle of Bahia Monument)

1988. 50th Anniv of Pando Department. Multicoloured.

1166	40c. Type **341**	75	25
1167	60c. Rubber production	1·00	45

342 Athlete

1988. Olympic Games, Seoul.

1168	**342**	1b.50 multicoloured	2·75	2·30

343 Mother Rosa Gattorno

1988. 88th Death Anniv of Mother Rosa Gattorno (Founder of the Daughters of St. Anne).

1169	**343**	80c. multicoloured	1·50	65

344 Bernardino de Cardenas

1988. 220th Death Anniv of Br. Bernardino de Cardenas (first Bishop of La Paz).

1170	**344**	70c. black and brown	1·30	60

345 Ministry Building

1988. Ministry of Transport and Communications.

1171	**345**	2b. black, green & red	3·50	1·70

346 Arms

1988. 50th Anniv of Army Communications Corps.

1172	**346**	70c. multicoloured	1·40	65

347 Rally Car

1988. 50th Anniv of Bolivian Automobile Club.

1173	**347**	1b.50 multicoloured	2·50	1·20

348 Microphone and Emblem

1989. 50th Anniv of Radio Fides.

1174	**348**	80c. multicoloured	1·30	65

349 Obverse and Reverse of 1852 Gold Cuartillo

1989. Coins.

1175	**349**	1b. multicoloured	1·80	70

350 "Bulgaria 89" Stamp Exhibition Emblem and Orchid

1989. Events and Plants. Multicoloured.

1176	50c. Type **350**	1·60	35
1177	60c. "Italia '90" World Cup football championship emblem and kantuta (national flower) (horiz)	1·90	45
1178	70c. "Albertville 1986" emblem and *Heliconia humilis*	2·30	55
1179	1b. Olympic Games, Barcelona emblem and *Hoffmanseggia*	3·00	80
1180	2b. Olympic Games, Seoul emblem and bromeliad	6·25	1·50

351 Birds

1989. Bicentenary of French Revolution.

1181	**351**	70c. multicoloured	1·40	55

352 Clock Tower and Steam Locomotive

1989. Centenary of Uyuni.

1182	**352**	30c. grey, black & blue	85	25

353 Federico Ahlfeld Waterfall, River Pauserna

1989. Noel Kempff Mercado National Park. Multicoloured.

1183	1b.50 Type **353**	3·00	1·20
1184	3b. Pampas deer	6·25	2·00

354 Making Metal Articles

1989. America. Tiahuanacu Culture. Multicoloured.

1185	50c. Type **354**	1·40	35
1186	1b. Kalasasaya Temple	2·75	70

355 Dr. Carlos Perez and Jaime Zamora

1989. Meeting of Presidents of Bolivia and Venezuela.

1187	**355**	2b. multicoloured	3·00	1·10

356 Cobija Arch

1989. World Heritage Site, Potosi. Multicoloured.

1188	60c. Type **356**	70	45
1189	80c. Mint	95	65

357 *Andean Lake* (Arturo Borda)

1989. Christmas. Paintings. Multicoloured.

1190	40c. Type **357**	85	25
1191	60c. *Virgin of the Roses* (anon)	1·30	35
1192	80c. *Conquistador* (Jorge de la Reza)	1·80	55
1193	1b. *Native Harmony* (Juan Rimsa)	2·40	65
1194	1b.50 *Woman with Pitcher* (Cecilio Guzman de Rojas)	3·25	1·10
1195	2b. *Flower of Tenderness* (Gil Imana)	4·25	1·40

358 Foot crushing Syringe

1990. Anti-drugs Campaign.

1196	**358**	80c. multicoloured	1·20	70

359 Map of Americas

1990. Centenary of Organization of American States.

1197	**359**	80c. blue and deep blue	1·20	45

360 Colonnade

1990. 450th Anniv of White City.

1198	**360**	1b.20 multicoloured	1·80	80

361 Penny Black, Sir Rowland Hill and Bolivian 5c. Condor Stamp

1990. 150th Anniv of the Penny Black.

1199	**361**	4b. multicoloured	6·25	2·40

362 Giuseppe Meaza Stadium, Milan

1990. World Cup Football Championship, Italy. Multicoloured.

1200	2b. Type **362**	2·50	1·40
1201	6b. Match scene	8·00	3·50

363 Emblem

1990. Cent of Bolivian Chamber of Commerce.

1202	**363**	50c. black, blue & gold	85	55

364 Satellite, Map and Globe

1990. Telecommunications Development Year.

1203	**364**	70c. multicoloured	1·00	70

365 Hall

1990. Centenary of Cochabamba Social Club.

1204	**365**	40c. multicoloured	65	35

366 Chipaya Village, Oruro

1990. America. Multicoloured.

1205	80c. Type **366**	4·00	45
1206	1b. Nevado Huayna, Cordillera Real (mountain) (vert)	4·75	65

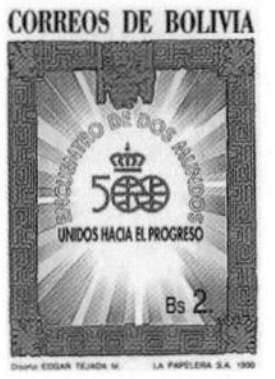

367 Emblem

1990. "Meeting of Two Worlds. United towards Progress". 500th Anniv (1992) of Discovery of America by Columbus.
1207 **367** 2b. multicoloured 2·50 1·20

368 Trees and Mountains

1990. 400th Anniv of Larecaja District.
1208 **368** 1b.20 multicoloured 1·50 70

369 Dove and German National Colours

1990. Unification of Germany.
1209 **369** 2b. multicoloured 2·75 1·10

370 Boys playing Football (Omar Espana)

1990. Christmas. Rights of the Child.
1210 **370** 50c. multicoloured 65 25

371 Arms of Bolivia and Ecuador

1990. Visit of Pres. Rodrigo Borja Cevallos of Ecuador.
1211 **371** 80c. multicoloured 1·50 55

372 Flags and Andes

1990. Fourth Andean Presidents' Council, La Paz.
1212 **372** 1b.50 multicoloured 2·10 70

373 Andes

1990. "Exfivia 90" National Stamp Exhibition.
1213 **373** 40c. blue 55 25

374 Arms of Bolivia and Mexico

1990. Visit of Pres. Carlos Salinas de Gortari of Mexico.
1214 **374** 60c. multicoloured 1·30 55

375 Emblem, Globe and Flags

1990. Express Mail Service.
1215 **375** 1b. multicoloured 1·30 45

376 Emblem

1991. 50th Anniv of Bolivian Radio Club.
1216 **376** 2b.40 multicoloured 2·75 1·10

377 Head of Bear

1991. The Spectacled Bear. Multicoloured.
1217 30c. Type **377** 1·90 45
1218 30c. Bear on branch 1·90 45
1219 30c. Bear and cub at water's edge 1·90 45
1220 30c. Bear and cubs on branches 1·90 45

378 National Museum of Archaeology

1991. "Espamer '91" Spain–Latin America Stamp Exhibition, Buenos Aires. Multicoloured.
1221 50c. Type **378** 55 20
1222 50c. National Art Museum 55 20
1223 1b. National Museum of Ethnography and Folklore 1·20 45

379 Map

1991. 56th Anniv of Ending of Chaco War and Beginning of Construction of "Heroes of Chaco" Road.
1224 **379** 60c. multicoloured 75 35

380 Statue of Our Lady of La Paz and Cathedral

1991. La Paz Cathedral.
1225 **380** 1b.20 multicoloured 1·90 65

381 Presidents Lacalle and Paz Zamora

1991. Meeting of Uruguayan and Bolivian Presidents.
1226 **381** 1b. multicoloured 1·10 45

382 Presidents Paz Zamora and Menem

1991. Meeting of Bolivian and Argentine Presidents.
1227 **382** 1b. multicoloured 1·10 45

383 "Exfivia 83", "87" and "90" Stamps

1991. 20th Anniv of Bolivian Philatelic Federation.
1228 **383** 70c. multicoloured 1·00 35

384 Presidents Fujimori and Paz Zamora

1991. Presidential Summit of Bolivia and Peru.
1229 **384** 50c. multicoloured 65 20

385 Route Map, Motor Cycle and Rally Car

1991. Pres. Jaime Paz Zamora National Grand Prix Motor Rally, Tarija-Cobija.
1230 **385** 50c. multicoloured 65 20

386 Data Retrieval Systems

1991. "Ecobol" Postal Security.
1231 **386** 1b.40 multicoloured 1·80 65

387 "First Discovery of Chuquiago" (Arturo Reque)

1991. America. Voyages of Discovery. Multicoloured.
1232 60c. Type **387** 2·10 35
1233 1b.20 "Foundation of City of Our Lady of La Paz" (J. Rimsa) (vert) 4·25 65

388 Stylized Figures and City Skyline

1991. National Population and Housing Census.
1234 **388** 50c. multicoloured 65 20

389 "Landscape" (Daniel Pena y Sarmiento)

1991. Christmas. Multicoloured.
1235 2b. Type **389** 2·50 80
1236 5b. "Fruit Seller" (Cecilio Guzman de Rojas) 6·25 2·00
1237 15b. "Native Mother" (Crespo Gastelu) 18·00 5·50

390 Camp-site and Emblem

1992. 75th Anniv (1990) of Bolivian Scout Movement and Los Andes Jamboree, Cochabamba.
1238 **390** 1b.20 multicoloured 1·60 80

391 Simon Bolivar

1992. "Exfilbo 92" National Stamp Exhibition, La Paz.
1239 **391** 1b.20 deep brown, brown and stone 1·60 80

392 Raising Flag

1992. Creation of Bolivian Free Zone in Ilo, Peru. Multicoloured.
1240 1b.20 Type **392** 1·40 80
1241 1b.50 Presidents Fujimori (Peru) and Paz Zamora (horiz) 1·60 90
1242 1b.80 Beach at Ilo (horiz) 2·10 1·00

393 Logotype of Pavilion

1992. "Expo '92" World's Fair, Seville, and "Granada '92" Int Stamp Exhibition. Multicoloured.
1243 30c. Type **393** 40 30
1244 50c. Columbus's fleet 70 40

394 Rotary International Emblem and Prize

1992. Rotary Club Miraflores District 4690 "Illimani de Oro" Prize.
1245 **394** 90c. gold, blue & black 1·20 70

395 School and Perez

1992. Birth Centenary of Elizardo Perez (founder of Ayllu School, Warisata).
1246 **395** 60c. blue, black & yellow 80 40

396 Government Palace

1992. UNESCO World Heritage Site, Sucre.
1247 **396** 50c. multicoloured 1·30 30

397 Mario Martinez Guzman

1992. Olympic Games, Barcelona.

1248	**397**	1b.50 multicoloured	2·00	1·00

398 Front Page

1992. 25th Anniv of *Los Tiempos* (newspaper).

1249	**398**	50c. multicoloured	70	40

399 Canoeing

1992. First International River Bermejo Canoeing Championship.

1250	**399**	1b.20 multicoloured	2·00	90

400 Columbus leaving Palos (after Bejarano)

1992. America. 500th Anniv of Discovery of America by Columbus.

1251	**400**	60c. brown and black	1·20	50
1252	-	2b. multicoloured	4·25	1·50

DESIGN—HORIZ: 2b. "Columbus meeting the Caribisis Tribe" (Luis Vergara).

401 Football Match

1992. World Cup Football Championship, U.S.A. (1994).

1253	**401**	1b.20 multicoloured	2·50	1·00

402 "Chenopodium quinoa"

1992. 50th Anniv of Interamerican Institute for Agricultural Co-operation.

1254	**402**	1b.20 multicoloured	1·90	90

403 University Arms and Minerals

1992. Cent of Oruro Technical University.

1255	**403**	50c. multicoloured	70	40

404 Mascots

1992. 12th Bolivarian Games, Cochabamba and Santa Cruz (1st issue).

1256	**404**	2b. multicoloured	2·75	1·20

See also No. 1271.

405 Cayman

1992. Ecology and Conservation. Multicoloured.

1257	20c. Type **405**	20	10
1258	50c. Spotted cavy	70	20
1259	1b. Chinchilla	1·40	60
1260	2b. Anteater	2·75	1·20
1261	3b. Jaguar	4·25	1·80
1262	4b. Long-tailed sylph ("Picaflor") (vert)	5·75	2·50
1263	5b. Piranhas	7·75	3·25

Each stamp also bears the emblem of an anniversary or event.

406 Battle Scene

1992. 150th Anniv of Battle of Ingavi.

1264	**406**	1b.20 brown and black	2·75	70

407 Man following Star in Boat

1992. Christmas. Multicoloured.

1265	1b.20 Type **407**	1·60	60
1266	2b.50 Star over church	3·50	1·30
1267	6b. Infant in manger and church	8·25	3·25

408 Nicolas Copernicus (450th death anniv)

1993. Astronomy.

1268	-	50c. multicoloured	70	40
1269	**408**	2b. black	2·75	1·00

DESIGN—HORIZ: 50c. Santa Ana International Astronomical Observatory, Tarija (10th anniv (1992)).

409 Mother Nazaria (after Victor Eusebio Choque)

1993. Beatification (1992) of Mother Nazaria Ignacia March Meza.

1270	**409**	60c. multicoloured	1·10	40

410 Pictograms and Flags of Ecuador, Venezuela, Peru, Bolivia, Colombia and Panama

1993. 12th Bolivarian Games, Cochabamba and Santa Cruz (2nd issue).

1271	**410**	2b.30 multicoloured	2·75	1·20

411 Bolivia 1962 10000b. Kantuta and Brazil 90r. "Bull's Eye" Stamps

1993. 150th Anniv of First Brazilian Stamps.

1272	**411**	2b.30 multicoloured	2·75	1·20

412 *Morpho* sp.

1993. Butterflies. Multicoloured.

1273	60c. Type **412**	1·10	30
1274	60c. *Archaeoprepona demophon*	1·10	30
1275	80c. *Papilio* sp.	1·50	40
1276	80c. Orion (*Historis odius*)	1·50	40
1277	80c. Mexican fritillary (*Euptoieta hegesia*)	1·50	40
1278	1b.80 *Morpho deidamia*	3·25	90
1279	1b.80 Orange swallowtail (*Papilio thoas*)	3·25	90
1280	1b.80 Monarch (*Danaus plexippus*)	3·25	90
1281	2b.30 Scarlet emperor (*Anaea marthesia*)	4·25	1·20
1282	2b.30 *Caligo* sp.	4·25	1·20
1283	2b.30 *Rothschildia* sp.	4·25	1·20
1284	2b.70 *Heliconius* sp.	5·00	1·40
1285	2b.70 *Marpesia corinna*	5·00	1·40
1286	2b.70 *Prepona chromus*	5·00	1·40
1287	3b.50 Rusty-tipped page (*Siproeta epaphus*)	6·75	1·90
1288	3b.50 *Heliconius* sp.	6·75	1·90

413 "Eternal Father" (wood statuette, Gaspar de la Cueva)

1993

1289	**413**	1b.80 multicoloured	2·75	90

414 "Virgin of Urkupina"

1993. 400th Anniv of Quillacollo.

1290	**414**	50c. multicoloured	1·10	40

415 Student, Machinery and Emblem

1993. 50th Anniv (1992) of Pedro Domingo Murillo Technical College.

1291	**415**	60c. multicoloured	70	30

416 Owl (painting, Chuquisaca)

1993. Cave Art. Multicoloured.

1292	80c. Type **416**	2·30	40
1293	80c. Animals (painting, Cochabamba)	2·30	40
1294	80c. Geometric patterns (engraving, Chuquisaca) (vert)	2·30	40
1295	80c. Sun (engraving, Beni) (vert)	2·30	40
1296	80c. Llama (painting, Oruro)	2·30	40
1297	80c. Human figure (engraving, Potosi)	2·30	40
1298	80c. Church and tower (painting, La Paz) (vert)	2·30	40
1299	80c. Warrior (engraving, Tarija) (vert)	2·30	40
1300	80c. Religious mask (engraving, Santa Cruz) (vert)	2·30	40

417 Common Squirrel-monkeys

1993. America. Endangered Animals. Multicoloured.

1301	80c. Type **417**	1·40	40
1302	2b.30 Ocelot	3·25	1·20

418 Emblems and Map

1993. 90th Anniv (1992) of Pan-American Health Organization. Anti-AIDS Campaign.

1303	**418**	80c. multicoloured	1·00	40

419 Yolanda Bedregal (poet)

1993. Personalities. Each brown.

1304	50c. Type **419**	50	30
1305	70c. Simon Martinic (President of Cochabamba Philatelic Centre)	80	40
1306	90c. Eugenio von Boeck (politician and President of Bolivian Philatelic Federation)	1·00	45
1307	1b. Marina Nunez del Prado (sculptor)	1·10	50

420 *Virgin with Child and Saints* (anonymous)

1993. Christmas. Multicoloured.

1308	2b.30 *Adoration of the Shepherds* (Leonardo Flores)	5·00	1·20
1309	3b.50 Type **420**	8·25	1·80
1310	6b. *Virgin of the Milk* (Melchor Perez de Holguin)	13·50	3·00

421 Riberalta Square

1994. Centenary of Riberalta.

1311	**421**	2b. multicoloured	2·40	1·00

422 *Population and Our World* (Mayari Rodriguez)

1994. Second Prize-winning Design (6–8 year group) in United Nations Fund for Population Activities International Design Contest.

1312	**422**	2b.30 multicoloured	3·75	1·20

423 Sanchez de Lozada

1994. Presidency of Gonzalo Sanchez de Lozada.

1313	**423**	2b. multicoloured	2·40	1·00
1314	**423**	2b.30 multicoloured	2·75	1·20

424 Mascot

1994. World Cup Football Championship, U.S.A. Multicoloured.

1315	80c. Type **424**	1·00	40
1316	1b.80 Bolivia v Uruguay	2·20	90
1317	2b.30 Bolivia v Venezuela	2·75	1·20
1318	2b.50 Bolivian team (left half)	2·75	1·30
1319	2b.50 Bolivian team (right half)	2·75	1·30
1320	2b.70 Bolivia v Ecuador	3·00	1·40
1321	3b.50 Bolivia v Brazil	4·50	1·80

Nos. 1318/19 were issued together, se-tenant, forming a composite design.

425 Child

1994. S.O.S. Children's Villages.

1322	**425**	2b.70 multicoloured	3·00	1·30

426 St. Peter's Church and Mgr. Jorge Manrique Hurtado (Archbishop, 1967–87)

1994. 50th Anniv (1993) of Archdiocese of La Paz. Multicoloured.

1323	1b.80 Type **426**	2·75	90
1324	2b. Church of the Sacred Heart of Mary and Mgr. Abel Antezana y Rojas (first Archbishop, 1943–67) (vert)	3·25	1·00
1325	3b.50 Santo Domingo Church and Mgr. Luis Sainz Hinojosa (Archbishop since 1987) (vert)	6·00	1·70

427 *Buddleja coriacea*

1994. Environmental Protection. Trees. Multicoloured.

1326	60c. Type **427**	65	30
1327	1b.80 *Bertholletia exelsa*	1·90	90
1328	2b. *Schinus molle* (horiz)	2·20	1·00
1329	2b.70 *Polylepis racemosa*	2·75	1·30
1330	3b. *Tabebuia chrysantha*	3·25	1·50
1331	3b.50 *Erythrina falcata* (horiz)	3·75	1·70

428 Paz

1994. Dr. Victor Paz Estenssoro (former President).

1332	**428**	2b. multicoloured	2·20	90

429 Tramcar and Mail Van

1994. America. Postal Transport. Multicoloured.

1333	1b. Type **429**	1·10	40
1334	5b. Boeing 747 and ox cart	5·50	2·30

430 Coral Tree

1994. 300th Anniv of San Borja.

1335	**430**	1b.60 multicoloured	1·70	70

431 Diagram of Eclipse

1994. Solar Eclipse.

1336	**431**	3b.50 multicoloured	3·75	1·50

432 1894 100c. Stamp

1994. Centenary of Arms Issue of 1894.

1337	**432**	1b.80 multicoloured	1·90	80

433 Col. Marzana and Soldiers

1994. 62nd Anniv of Defence of Fort Boqueron.

1338	**433**	80c. multicoloured	90	30

434 *Delicate Flower of Tarija*

1994. Christmas. Pastels of children by Maria Susana Castillo. Multicoloured.

1339	2b. Type **434**	3·50	90
1340	5b. "Child of the High Plateau"	8·75	2·30
1341	20b. "Shoot of the Bolivian East"	25·00	9·25

435 Emblem

1994. Pan-American Scout Jamboree, Cochabamba.

1342	**435**	1b.80 multicoloured	1·90	90

436 Sucre

1995. Birth Bicentenary of General Antonio Jose de Sucre. Multicoloured.

1343	1b.80 Type **436**	2·30	90
1344	3b.50 Sucre and national colours	4·75	1·70

437 Santa Ana Cathedral

1995. Centenary (1994) of Yacuma Province, Beni Department.

1345	**437**	1b.90 multicoloured	2·40	1·00
1346	**437**	2b.90 multicoloured	3·50	1·50

438 "Holy Virgin of Copacabana", Sanctuary and Franciscans

1995. Centenary of Franciscan Presence at Copacabana Sanctuary.

1347	**438**	60c. multicoloured	1·00	35
1348	**438**	80c. multicoloured	1·40	55

439 Anniversary Emblem

1995. 25th Anniv of Andean Development Corporation.

1349	**439**	2b.40 multicoloured	2·75	1·30

440 Paraguay and Bolivia Flags (Chaco Peace Treaty, 1938)

1995. Visit of President Juan Carlos Wasmosy of Paraguay and 169th Anniv (1994) of Republic of Bolivia.

1350	**440**	2b. multicoloured	2·00	1·10

441 Montenegro

1995. 50th Anniv of Publication of "Nationalism and Colonialism" by Carlos Montenegro.

1351	**441**	1b.20 black and pink	2·75	65

442 Digging Potatoes

1995. 50th Anniv of FAO.

1352	**442**	1b. multicoloured	2·00	55

443 Anniversary Emblem

1995. 50th Anniv of UNO.

1353	**443**	2b.90 dp blue, gold & bl	2·40	1·70

444 Andean Condor ("Condor")

1995. America. Endangered Species. Multicoloured.

1354	5b. Type **444**	4·50	2·75
1355	5b. Llamas	4·50	2·75

Nos. 1354/5 were issued together, *se-tenant*, forming a composite design.

445 Airbus Industrie A320

1995. 50th Anniv (1994) of ICAO.

1356	**445**	50c. multicoloured	90	45

446 Stone Head

1995. Archaeology. Samaipata Temple, Florida. Multicoloured.

1357	1b. Type **446**	90	55
1358	1b.90 Stone head (different)	1·70	1·10
1359	2b. Excavation and stone head	1·70	1·10
1360	2b.40 Entrance and animal-shaped vessel	2·00	1·30

Nos. 1357/60 were issued together, *se-tenant*, forming a composite design.

447 Brewery Complex

1995. Centenary of Taquina Brewery.

1361	**447**	1b. multicoloured	2·40	55

448 *The Annunciation* (Cima da Conegliano)

1995. Christmas. Multicoloured.

1362	1b.20 Type **448**	1·30	65
1363	3b. "The Nativity" (Hans Baldung)	3·25	1·70
1364	3b.50 "Adoration of the Wise Men" (altarpiece, Rogier van der Weyden)	4·00	2·00

449 Jose de Sanjines (lyricist)

1995. 150th Anniv of National Anthem. Multicoloured.

1365		1b. Type **449**	90	55
1366		2b. Benedetto Vincenti (composer)	1·70	1·10

Nos. 1365/6 were issued together, *se-tenant*, forming a composite design.

450 Flats, Villarroel, Factories, Road and Railway

1996. 50th Anniv of Decree for Abolition of Enforced Amerindian Labour. Multicoloured.

1367		1b.90 Type **450**	1·70	1·10
1368		2b.90 Pres. Gualberto Villarroel addressing Congress and freed workers	2·40	1·70

Nos. 1367/8 were issued together, *se-tenant*, forming a composite design.

1996. Various stamps surch.

1369	-	50c. on 3000000p. multicoloured (No. 1126) (postage)	45	35
1370	**265**	60c. on 2p.50 blue and red	90	40
1371	**313**	60c. on 5000000p. on 2000p. blue and red (No. 1116)	55	35
1372	**319**	60c. on 1400000p. mult	55	35
1373	**319**	1b. on 2500000p. green and yellow (No. 1120)	90	55
1374	**311**	1b.50 on 11000p. blue	1·30	90
1375	**312**	2b.50 on 23000p. brown and sepia	2·20	1·40
1376	**316**	3b. on 1000000p. blue and gold	2·40	1·70
1377	**272**	3b.50 on 6p.50 mult	3·25	2·00
1378	**279**	3b.50 on 9p. mult	3·25	2·00
1379	**323**	3b.50 on 2000000p. brown	3·25	2·00
1380	**298**	20b. on 10p. black, purple and bronze	19·00	11·00
1381	**299**	20b. on 13p. mult	19·00	11·00
1382	-	3b.80 on 3p.80 mult (No. 945) (air)	3·25	2·10
1383	-	20b. on 3p.80 mult (No. 973a)	19·00	11·00

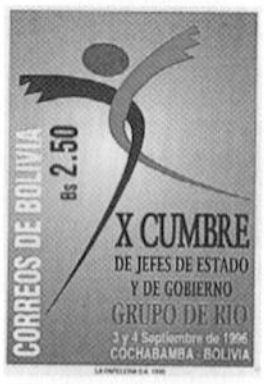

452 Summit Emblem

1996. Tenth Rio Group Summit Meeting, Cochabamba. Multicoloured.

1384		2b.50 Type **452**	2·10	1·30
1385		3b.50 Rio Group emblem	2·75	2·00

453 Summit Emblem

1996. Summit of the Americas on Sustainable Development, Santa Cruz de la Sierra.

1386	**453**	2b.50 multicoloured	2·10	1·30
1387	**453**	5b. multicoloured	4·25	2·75

454 Facade

1996. National Bank.

1388	**454**	50c. black and blue	55	35

455 De Lemoine

1996. 220th Birth Anniv of Jose Joaquin de Lemoine (first postal administrator).

1389	**455**	1b. brown and stone	1·20	65

456 Family

1997. CARE (Co-operative for American Relief Everywhere). Multicoloured.

1390		60c. Type **456** (20th anniv in Bolivia)	55	35
1391		70c. Hands cradling globe (50th anniv) (vert)	65	45

457 Musicians playing Piccolo and Saxophone

1997. 50th Anniv of National Symphony Orchestra. *Overture* by G. Rodo Boulanger. Multicoloured.

1392		1b.50 Type **457**	1·40	1·00
1393		2b. Musicians playing violin and cello	1·90	1·20

Nos. 1392/3 were issued together, *se-tenant*, forming a composite design of the complete painting.

458 Casa Dorada (cultural centre)

1997. Tarija. Multicoloured.

1394		50c. Type **458**	45	35
1395		60c. Entre Rios Church and musician	55	40
1396		80c. Narrows of San Luis (horiz)	85	60
1397		1b. Memorial to the Fallen of the Chaco War (territorial dispute with Paraguay) (horiz)	1·10	90
1398		3b. Virgin and shrine of Chaguaya (horiz)	3·25	2·75
1399		20b. Birthplace and statue of Jose Eustaquio Mendez (Independence hero), San Lorenzo (horiz)	20·00	18·00

459 La Glorieta, Sucre

1997. Chuquisaca. Multicoloured.

1400		60c. Type **459**	55	45
1401		1b. Government Palace, Sucre (vert)	90	75
1402		1b.50 Footprints and drawing of dinosaur	1·40	1·20
1403		1b.50 Interior of House of Freedom	1·40	1·20
1404		2b. Man playing traditional wind instrument (vert)	2·00	1·50
1405		3b. Statue of Juana Azurduy de Padilla (Independence heroine) (vert)	2·75	2·50

460 Miners' Monument

1997. Oruro. Multicoloured.

1406		50c. Type **460**	55	45
1407		60c. Demon carnival mask	85	55
1408		1b. Vigin of the Cave (statue)	1·10	90
1409		1b.50 Sajama (volcano) (horiz)	1·40	1·10
1410		2b.50 Chipaya child and belfry	2·40	2·20
1411		3b. Moreno (Raul Shaw) (singer and musician) (horiz)	2·75	2·50

461 Pres. Gonzalo Sanchez de Lozada of Bolivia and Pres. Chirac

1997. Visit to Bolivia of President Jacques Chirac of France.

1412	**461**	4b. multicoloured	4·00	3·25

462 Children playing (Pamela G. Villarroel)

1997. 50th Anniv of UNICEF Children's Drawings. Multicoloured.

1413		50c. Type **462**	55	45
1414		90c. Boy leaping across clifftop (Lidia Acapa)	1·00	90
1415		1b. Children of different races on top of world (Gabriela Philco)	1·20	1·00
1416		2b.50 Children and swing (Jessica Grundy)	2·75	2·40

463 St. John Bosco (founder)

1997. Centenary of Salesian Brothers in Bolivia. Multicoloured.

1417		1b.50 Type **463**	1·40	1·20
1418		2b. Church and statue of Bosco with child	2·00	1·70

464 Chulumani

1997. La Paz. Multicoloured.

1419		50c. Type **464**	45	35
1420		80c. Inca stone monolith	75	65
1421		1b.50 La Paz and Mt. Illimani	1·40	1·30
1422		2b. Gate of the Sun, Tiahuanaco (horiz)	2·00	1·90
1423		2b.50 Dancers	2·40	2·30
1424		10b. *Virgin of Copacabana* and balsa raft on Lake Titicaca (horiz)	10·00	9·75

465 Emblem

1997. Football Events. Multicoloured.

1425		3b. Type **465** (America Cup Latin-American Football Championship, Bolivia)	2·75	2·75
1426		5b. Eiffel Tower and trophy (World Cup Football Championship, France (1998) Eliminating Rounds)	5·00	4·75

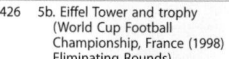

466 Parliamentary Session and Building

1997. National Congress.

1427	**466**	1b. multicoloured	90	75

467 Valley

1997. America. Traditional Costumes. Multicoloured.

1428		5b. Type **467**	5·00	4·75
1429		15b. Eastern region	14·50	14·00

468 Members Flags and Southern Cross

1997. Sixth Anniv of Mercosur (South American Common Market).

1430	**468**	3b. multicoloured	2·75	2·75

469 "Virgin of the Hill" (anon)

1997. Christmas. Multicoloured.

1431		2b. Type **469**	2·40	2·20
1432		5b. "Virgin of the Milk" (anon)	5·50	5·00
1433		10b. "Holy Family" (Melchor Perez Holguin)	11·00	10·00

470 Diana, Princess of Wales

1997. Diana, Princess of Wales Commemoration. Multicoloured.

1434		2b. Type **470**	2·20	2·00
1435		3b. Diana, Princess of Wales beside minefield warning sign (horiz)	2·75	2·50

471 Presidents of Boliva and Spain

1998. State Visit of Prime Minister Jose Maria Aznar of Spain.

1436	**471**	6b. multicoloured	5·50	5·00

472 Juan Munoz Reyes (President) and Medallion

1998. 75th Anniv of Bolivian Engineers' Association.

1437	**472**	3b.50 multicoloured	3·25	2·75

473 Linked Arms and Globe

1998. 70th Anniv of Rotary International in Bolivia.

1438	**473**	5b. multicoloured	4·75	4·25

474 Delivering Letter, 1998

1998. America. The Postman. Multicoloured.

1439	3b. Type **474**	2·75	2·50
1440	4b. Postmen on parade, 1942 (horiz)	3·75	3·25

475 Werner Guttentag Tichauer (35th anniv of his bibliography)

1998. Anniversaries.

1441	**475**	1b.50 brown	1·30	1·10
1442	-	2b. green	1·90	1·60
1443	-	3b.50 black	3·25	2·75

DESIGNS—VERT: 2b. Martin Cardenas Hermosa (botanist, birth centenary (1999)); 3b. Adrian Patino Carpio (composer, 47th death anniv).

476 Amazon Water-lily

1998. Beni. Multicoloured.

1444	50c. Type **476**	35	30
1445	1b. *Callandria* sp.	90	75
1446	1b.50 White tajibo tree (vert)	1·30	1·10
1447	3b.50 Ceremonial mask	3·25	2·75
1448	5b. European otter	4·75	4·00
1449	7b. King vulture ("Tropical Condor")	6·50	5·75

477 River Acre

1998. Pando. Multicoloured.

1450	50c. Type **477**	45	40
1451	1b. Pale-throated sloth (vert)	90	75
1452	1b.50 Arroyo Bahia (vert)	1·30	1·10
1453	4b. Boa constrictor	3·50	3·00
1454	5b. Capybara with young	4·50	3·75
1455	7b. Palm trees, Cobija (vert)	6·00	5·25

478 Rural Activities and First Lady

1998. America. Women. Multicoloured.

1456	1b.50 Type **478**	1·30	1·10
1457	2b. First Lady, girl at blackboard and woman using computer	1·80	1·50

Nos. 1456/7 were issued together, *se-tenant*, forming a composite design.

479 Town Arms and Church

1998. 450th Anniv of La Paz.

1458	**479**	2b. multicoloured	2·10	1·80

480 Emblem

1998. 50th Anniv of Organization of American States.

1459	**480**	3b.50 blue and yellow	3·00	2·75

481 Magnifying Glass and 1998 7b. Stamp

1998. "Espamer 98" Stamp Exhibition, Buenos Aires and 25th Anniv of Bolivian Philatelic Federation.

1460	**481**	2b. multicoloured	1·80	1·50

482 "People going to Church" (Kathia Lucuy Saenz)

1998. Christmas. Multicoloured.

1461	2b. Type **482**	1·70	1·40
1462	6b. Pope John Paul II (vert)	4·75	4·00
1463	7b. Pope John Paul II with Mother Teresa (vert)	5·50	4·75

483 U.P.U. Monument, Berne

1999. 125th Anniv of Universal Postal Union.

1464	**483**	3b.50 multicoloured	2·75	2·50

484 Statue of Football Player

1999. 75th Anniv of Cochabamba Football Association.

1465	**484**	5b. multicoloured	4·75	4·25

485 Red Cross Lorries at Earthquake Site

1999. 50th Anniv of Geneva Conventions.

1466	**485**	5b. multicoloured	4·00	3·50

486 Bernardo Guarachi and Mt. Everest

1999. First Ascent (1998) of Mt. Everest by a Bolivian.

1467	**486**	6b. multicoloured	5·50	4·75

487 Winners on Podium

1999. 30th Anniv of First Special Olympics. Multicoloured.

1468	2b. Type **487**	1·70	1·40
1469	2b.50 Athletes on race track and winners on podium	2·00	1·70

488 Golden Palace

1999. Centenary of Japanese Immigration to Bolivia. Multicoloured.

1470	3b. Type **488**	2·40	2·10
1471	6b. View over lake and flags (vert)	5·00	4·25

489 Children dancing

1999. Anti-drugs Campaign.

1472	**489**	3b.50 multicoloured	2·75	2·40

490 Route Map and Presidents Hugo Banzer Suarez of Bolivia and Fernando Cardoso of Brazil

1999. Inauguration of Gas Pipeline from Santa Cruz, Bolivia, to Campinas, Brazil. Multicoloured.

1473	3b. Type **490**	2·40	2·10
1474	6b. Presidents Hugo Banzer Suarez and Fernando Cardoso embracing	4·75	3·75

491 Village Scene

1999. 50th Anniv of SOS Children's Villages.

1475	**491**	3b.50 multicoloured	2·75	2·40

492 *Hacia la Gloria* (directed Rau Duran, Mario Camacho and Jose Jimenez)

1999. Centenary of Motion Pictures in Bolivia. Multicoloured.

1476	50c. Type **492**	35	30
1477	50c. *Jonah and the Pink Whale* (dir. J. Carlos Valdivia)	35	30
1478	1b. *Wara Wara* (dir. Jose Velasco)	65	55
1479	1b. *Vuelve Sebastiana* (dir. Jorge Ruiz)	65	55
1480	3b. *The Chaco Campaign* (dir. Juan Penaranda, Jose Velasco and Mario Camacho)	2·10	1·80
1481	3b. *The Watershed* (dir. Jorge Ruiz)	2·10	1·80
1482	6b. *Yawar Mallku* (dir. Jorge Sanjines)	4·25	3·50
1483	6b. *Mi Socio* (dir. Paolo Agazzi)	4·25	3·50
MS1484	180×80 mm. Nos. 1476/83	14·50	14·00

493 International Lions Emblem

1999. 50th Anniv (1998) of La Paz Lions Club.

1485	**493**	3b.50 multicoloured	2·75	2·40

494 Mt. Tunari

1999. Cochabamba. Multicoloured.

1486	50c. Type **494**	35	30
1487	1b. Forest, Cochabamba Valley	65	55
1488	2b. Omereque vase and fertility goddess (vert)	1·40	1·20
1489	3b. Totora	2·10	1·80
1490	5b. Teofilo Vargas Candia (composer) and music score (vert)	3·50	3·00
1491	6b. "Christ of Harmony" (mountain-top statue) (vert)	4·25	3·50

495 Tarapaya Lagoon (Inca spa)

1999. Potosi. Multicoloured.

1492	50c. Type **495**	35	30
1493	1b. First republican coins, minted in 1827 (horiz)	65	55
1494	2b. Mt. Chorolque (horiz)	1·40	1·20
1495	3b. Green Lagoon (horiz)	2·10	1·80
1496	5b. "The Mestizo sitting on a Trunk" (Teofilo Loaiza)	3·50	3·00
1497	6b. Alfredo Dominguez Romeo (Tupiceno singer)	4·25	3·50

496 Globe with Children, Fish, Flower, Pencil, Heart and Stars

1999. America. A New Millennium without Arms. Multicoloured.

1498	3b.50 Type **496**	2·40	2·10
1499	3b.50 Globe emerging from flower	2·40	2·10

497 Children from S.O.S. Childrens Village

1999. Christmas. Multicoloured.

1500	2b. Type **497**	1·30	1·10
1501	6b. "The Birth of Jesus" (Gaspar Miguel de Berrios) (vert)	4·00	3·50
1502	7b. "Our Family in the World" (Omar Medina) (vert)	5·00	4·25

498 Ugarte

2000. Fifth Death Anniv of Victor Agustin Ugarte (football player).

1503	**498**	3b. grey, green and yellow	2·20	1·90

499 El Arenal Park

2000. Santa Cruz. Multicoloured.

1504	50c. Type **499**	35	30
1505	1b. Ox cart	75	65
1506	2b. Raul Otero Reiche, Gabriel Rene Moreno and Hernando Sanabria Fernandez (writers)	1·50	1·30
1507	3b. Cotoca Virgin (statue) (vert)	2·20	1·90
1508	5b. Anthropomorphic vase (vert)	4·00	3·50
1509	6b. Bush dog	4·75	4·00

500 "The Village of Serinhaem in Brazil" (Frans Post)

2000. 500th Anniv of Discovery of Brazil.

1510	**500**	5b. multicoloured	3·75	3·25

501 Granado

2000. Javier del Granado (poet) Commemoration.

1511	**501**	3b. grey, blue and red	3·00	2·75

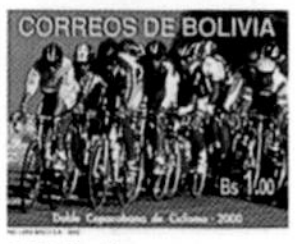

502 Cyclists

2000. "Double Copacabana" Cycle Race.

1512	**502**	1b. multicoloured	65	55
1513	-	3b. multicoloured	2·20	1·90
1514	-	5b. multicoloured	3·75	3·25
1515	-	7b. multicoloured	5·00	4·25

DESIGNS: 3b. to 7b. Various race scenes.

503 Oriental Clay Figure

2000. National Archaeology Museum Exhibits. Each brown and gold.

1516	50c. Type **503**	35	30
1517	50c. Clay figure, Potosi	35	30
1518	70c. Oriental clay head, Beni	55	45
1519	90c. Clay vase, Tarija	65	55
1520	1b. Clay head, Oruro	70	60
1521	1b. Yampara clay urn	70	60
1522	3b. Inca wood carving	2·20	1·90
1523	5b. Oriental anthropomorphic vase	3·75	3·25
1524	20b. Tiwanaku clay mask	15·00	14·00

504 Male and Female Symbols in Red Vortex

2000. America. Anti-AIDS Campaign. Multicoloured.

1525	3b.50 Type **504**	2·75	2·50
1526	3b.50 Couple walking through wall	2·75	2·50

505 Soldier's Head and Bird on Laurel Wreath

2000. Centenary of Maximiliano Parades Military School.

1527	**505**	2b.50 multicoloured	2·20	1·90

506 *Self-portrait*

2000. Birth Centenary of Cecilio Guzman de Rojas (artist). Showing paintings. Multicoloured.

1528	1b. Type **506**	75	65
1529	2b.50 *Triumph of Nature* (horiz)	2·20	1·90
1530	5b. *Andina*	4·50	3·75
1531	6b. *Students Quarrel* (horiz)	5·00	4·25

507 Crowd and Brandenburg Gate

2000. 50th Anniv of German Federal Republic.

1532	**507**	6b. multicoloured	5·00	4·25

508 San Francisco Basilica, La Paz

2000. Holy Year 2000. Bolivian Episcopal Conference. Multicoloured.

1533	4b. Type **508**	3·25	2·75
1534	6b. Stalks of grain breaking through barbed-wire	5·00	4·25

509 Waterfall and Statue

2000. New Millennium.

1535	**509**	5b. multicoloured	4·00	3·50

510 Archangel Gabriel

2000. Christmas. Showing 17th-century paintings of Angels from Calamarca Church. Multicoloured.

1536	3b. Type **510**	2·20	1·90
1537	5b. Angel of Virtue	4·50	3·75
1538	10b. Angel with ear of corn	7·75	6·50

511 Painting of John the Baptist and Emblem

2000. 900th Anniv of Sovereign Military Order of St. John.

1539	**511**	6b. multicoloured	4·75	4·00

512 Lobster Claw (*Heliconia rostrata*)

2001. Patriotic Symbols. Multicoloured.

1540	10b. Type **512** (designated national flower, 1990)	7·75	6·50
1541	20b. *Periphrangus dependens* (designated national flower 1924)	15·00	13·00
1542	30b. First Bolivian coat of arms (adopted 1825)	22·00	19·00
1543	50b. Second Bolivian coat of arms (adopted 1826)	40·00	34·00
1544	100b. Present day Bolivian coat of arms (adopted 1851)	75·00	65·00

513 Map and Stars of European Union and Map of Bolivia

2001. 25th Anniv of Co-operation between Bolivia and European Union.

1550	**513**	6b. multicoloured	4·75	4·00

514 Statue of Justice, Lion and Portico

2001. 171st Anniv of Faculty of Law and Political Sciences, Universidad de Mayor of San Andres, La Paz.

1551	**514**	6b. multicoloured	4·75	4·00

515 Temple of San Francisco, Potosi

2001. America. UNESCO World Heritage Sites. Multicoloured.

1552	1b.50 Type **515**	1·20	1·00
1553	5b. "Fraile" and "Ponce" (monoliths) (horiz)	4·25	3·50

516 Man carrying Envelopes up Stairs

2001. Philately. Each green.

1554	50c. Type **516**	35	30
1555	1b. Boy with six stamps	75	65
1556	1b.50 Man with glasses and stamp album	1·20	1·00
1557	2b. Child wearing hat, and three stamps	1·50	1·30
1558	2b.50 Humanized stamp lying in tray	2·00	1·70

517 Devil's Molar (mountain)

2001

1559	**517**	1b.50 multicoloured	1·20	1·00

518 Family

2001. National Census. Multicoloured.

1560	1b. Type **518**	90	75
1561	1b.50 People surrounding wheelchair user	1·20	1·00
1562	1b.50 Aboriginal woman and people of different races	1·20	1·00
1563	2b.50 People of different races	2·00	1·70
1564	3b. Children	2·40	2·10

519 Silver Spot (*Dione juno*)

2001. Butterflies and Insects. Multicoloured.

1565	1b. Type **519**	75	65
1566	1b. *Orthoptera* sp.	75	65
1567	1b.50 Bamboo page (*Philaethria dido*)	1·20	1·00
1568	2b.50 Jewel butterfly (*Diaethria clymena*) (inscr "Diathria clymene")	2·00	1·70
1569	2b.50 *Mantis religiosa*	2·00	1·70
1570	3b. *Tropidacris latreillei*	2·40	2·10
1571	4b. Hercules beetle (*Dynastes hercules*) (inscr "Escarabajo Hercule")	3·25	2·75
1572	5b. *Arctiidae* sp.	4·25	3·50
1573	5b. *Acrocinus longimanus*	4·25	3·50
1574	5b. *Lucanidae* sp.	4·25	3·50
1575	6b. *Morpho godarti*	4·75	4·25
1576	6b. *Caligo idomeneus* ("inscr idomineus")	4·75	4·25

520 Map of Americas and Emblem

2001. 21st Inter-America Scout Conference, Cochabamba.

1577	**520**	3b.50 multicoloured	2·75	2·50

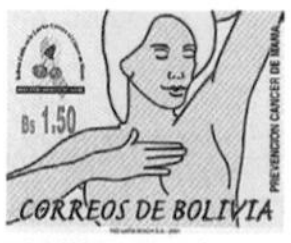

521 Woman and Emblem

2001. Breast Cancer Prevention Campaign.

1578	**521**	1b.50 multicoloured	1·20	1·00

522 St. Mary Magdalen

2001. Christmas. Showing sculptures by Gaspar of La Cueva from Convent of San Francisco, Potosi. Multicoloured.

1579	3b. Type **522**	2·40	2·10
1580	5b. St. Apolonia	4·25	3·50
1581	10b. St. Teresa of Avila	8·25	7·00

523 Portrait and Casa La Laertad, Sucre

2001. Joaquin Gantier Valda Commemoration.

1582	**523**	4b. multicoloured	3·25	2·75

524 Flags and Hands enclosing Farmer, Mother, Child and Doctor

2001. 25th Anniv of Co-operation between Bolivia and Belgium.

1583	**524**	6b. multicoloured	4·75	4·25

525 Aerial Photograph and Bridge

2002. Bolivia–Peru Presidential Summit. Multicoloured.

1584	50c. Type **525**	45	40
1585	3b. Aerial photograph and bridge (different)	2·40	2·10

526 Charangos (guitars) and Musical Score

2001. Birth Centenary of Mauro Nunez (musician). Multicoloured.

1586	1b. Type **526**	90	75
1587	6b. Mauro Nunez	4·75	4·25

527 Dancers with Horned Head-dresses (Diablada)

2001. Cultural Heritage. Oruro Carnival. Multicoloured.

1588	50c. Type **527**	45	40
1589	1b.50 Female dancer (Morenada)	1·10	95
1590	2b.50 Female dancers and man in embroidered clothes (Caporales)	1·80	1·50
1591	5b. Male dancers in multicoloured head-dresses (Tobas)	3·50	3·00
1592	7b. Woman dancer in elaborate hat and yellow skirt (Suri Sikuri) (vert)	5·00	4·25
1593	7b. Dancers wearing bonnets (Pujllay) (vert)	5·00	4·25

2002. Butterflies and Insects (2nd series). As T **519**. Multicoloured.

1594	3b. White-tailed page (*Urania leilus*)	2·40	2·10
1595	3b. *Tropidacris latreilli*	2·40	2·10
1596	3b. *Papilio cresphontes macho*	2·40	2·10
1597	3b. Longhorn beetle (*Acrocinus longimanus*)	2·40	2·10
1598	3b. *Prepona buckleyana*	2·40	2·10
1599	3b. *Thysannia agripyna cramer* (left wings)	2·40	2·10
1600	3b. *Thysannia agripyna cramer* (right wings)	2·40	2·10
1601	3b. *Lucanus verde* (inscr "Lucano")	2·40	2·10
1602	3b. Butterfly (inscr "Nymphalidae")	2·40	2·10
1603	3b. *Escarabajo hercule*	2·40	2·10
1604	3b. Butterfly (different) (inscr "Heliconinae")	2·40	2·10
1605	3b. Grasshopper (inscr "Orthopterdae")	2·40	2·10

Nos. 1599/1600 were issued in se-tenant pairs within the sheet, each pair forming a composite design.

528 "El Kusillo" (folk character)

2002. Third International Theatre Festival, La Paz.

1606	**528** 3b. multicoloured	2·40	2·10

529 Mountain Viscachas (rodent), Potosi

2002. International Year of Mountains and Eco-tourism. Multicoloured.

1607	80c. Type **529**	65	55
1608	1b. Polylepis (tree), Cochabamba (vert)	90	75
1609	1b.50 Huayna Potosi mountains, La Paz	1·30	1·10
1610	2b.50 Payachatas mountains, Oruro	2·20	1·90
1611	2b.50 Sajama mountain, Oruro (vert)	2·20	1·90

530 Anniversary Emblem and Rainbow

2002. Centenary of Pan-American Health Organization.

1612	**530** 3b. multicoloured	2·40	2·10

531 Gunnar Mendoza

2002. Dr. Gunnar Mendoza (scientist) Commemoration.

1613	**531** 4b. multicoloured	3·00	2·75

532 Gates Learget 25 over Mountains

2002. 50th Anniv of Military Aviation College, Gemán Busch. Multicoloured.

1614	4b. Type **532**	3·00	2·75
1615	5b. Acrobatic aeroplanes (vert)	4·00	3·50
1616	6b. Three helicopters	4·75	4·00

533 Orinoco Goose (*Neochen jubata*)

2002. Day of Natural Resources. Multicoloured.

1617	50c. Type **533** (CEFILCO philatelic association)	45	40
1618	4b. Orange-breasted falcon (*Falco deiroleucus*) (30th anniv of Bolivian philatelic federation)	3·25	2·75
1619	6b. Black-bodied woodpecker (*Dryocopus schulzi*) (PHILAKOREA 2002)	4·75	4·25

534 Thousand Year old Cedar Tree and Church Tower

2002. 400th Anniv of Sucre Monastery.

1620	**534** 4b. multicoloured	3·00	2·75

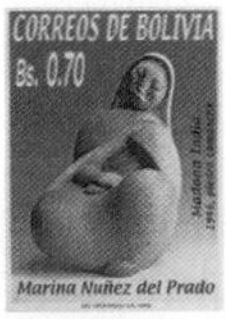

535 Indian Madonna

2002. Twentieth-century Art. Multicoloured.

1621	70c. Type **535** (sculpture, Marina Nunez del Prado)	55	45
1622	70c. Mountain (painting, Maria Luisa Pachero)	55	45
1623	80c. Indian mother (sculpture, Marina Nunez del Prado)	65	55
1624	80c. *Cordillera* (painting, Maria Luisa Pachero)	65	55
1625	5b. Venus Negra (sculpture, Marina Nunez del Prado)	4·00	3·50
1626	5b. *Cerros* (painting, Maria Luisa Pachero) (horiz)	4·00	3·50

536 Potosi and Armando Alba Zambrana

2002. Birth Centenary (2001) of Armando Alba Zambrana (historian).

1627	**536** 3b. multicoloured	2·40	2·10

537 Couple wearing Traditional Costume

2002. Birth Bicentenary of Alcide d'Orbigny (naturalist and palaeontologist). Multicoloured.

1628	1b. Type **537**	75	65
1629	4b. Boat on river (horiz)	3·00	2·75
1630	6b. Alcide d'Orbigny	4·75	4·00

538 Teacher and Pupils

2002. America. Education and Literacy Campaign. Multicoloured.

1631	1b. Type **538**	65	55
1632	2b.50 Indigenous children and computer	1·50	1·30

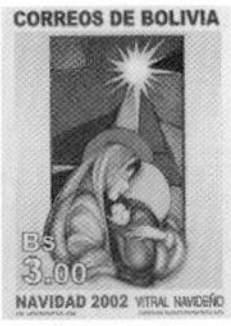

539 Mary and Jesus

2002. Christmas. Multicoloured.

1633	3b. Type **539**	1·70	1·40
1634	5b. Nativity	2·75	2·40
1635	6b. *The Adoration of the Kings* (painting, 18th-century)	3·25	2·75

540 Apolinar Camacho

2003. First Death Anniv of Apolinar Camacho (composer).

1636	**540** 2b.50 multicoloured	1·40	1·20

541 Soldier (statue)

2003. Centenary of Battle of Bahia. Multicoloured.

1637	50c. Type **541**	35	30
1638	1b. Three soldiers (statue)	55	45

542 Anniversary Emblem

2003. 25th Anniv of Culture of Peace Month (UN peace initiative). Bolivian Permanent Assembly of Human Rights.

1639	**542** 6b. ultramarine	3·25	2·75

543 Currency and Bank Emblem

2003. 75th Anniv of Central Bank.

1640	**543** 4b. multicoloured	2·20	1·90

544 Court Emblem

2003. Fifth Anniv of Sucre Constitutional Court.

1641	**544** 1b.50 multicoloured	90	75

545 Quinoa (*Chenopodium quinoa*)

2003. America. Flora and Fauna Multicoloured.

1642	50c. Type **545**	3·25	2·75
1643	1b. Llama	3·75	3·25

546 Anniversary Emblem

2003. Centenary of Panama Republic.

1644	**546** 7b. multicoloured	3·75	3·25

547 Porfirio Diaz Machicao, Rosendo Villalobos and Monsignor Juan Quiros (writers)

2003. 75th Anniv of Language Academy.

1645	**547** 6b. multicoloured	3·25	2·75

548 Flags and Latin America

2003. Latin American, Spanish and Portuguese Heads of Government Conference, Santa Cruz. Multicoloured.

1646	6b. Type **548**	3·25	2·75
1647	6b. Eastern globe and flags	3·25	2·75

Nos. 1646/7 were issued together, se-tenant, forming a composite design.

549 Virgin of Guadeloupe (Brother Diego de Ocana)

2003. 450th Anniv of La Plata Archdiocese.

1648	**549** 6b. multicoloured	3·25	2·75

550 *Adoration of the Shepherds* (Leonardo Flores) (Templo de Calamarca, La Paz)

2003. Christmas. Multicoloured.

1649	1b.50 Type **550**	90	75
1650	6b. *Adoration of the Shepherds* (Bernardo Bitti) (Cathedral museum, Sucre)	3·25	2·75
1651	7b. *Adoration of the Shepherds* (Melchor Perez de Holguin) (Santa Teresa museum, Potosi) (horiz)	3·75	3·25

551 Pope John Paul II

2004. 25th Anniv of Pontificate of Pope John Paul II. Multicoloured.

1652	1b. Type **551**	55	45
1653	1b.50 Seated facing right (painting)	90	75
1654	5b. Giving blessing to native Bolivians	2·75	2·40
1655	6b. Wearing gold cope	3·25	2·75
1656	7b. Seated facing left	3·75	3·25
MS1657	150×110 mm. 10b.×2, Mary of Copacabana and balsa boat on the Lake Titicaca; Santa Tersa de Avila (statue) (Gaspar de la Cueva)	11·00	10·50

552 Girl and Rainbow

2004. Tenth Anniv of ARCO IRIS Foundation (street children's charitable organization).

1658	**552**	1b.80 multicoloured	1·40	1·20

553 Battle Scene (painting)

2004. 25th Anniv of Military History Academy.

1659	**553**	1b. multicoloured	55	45

554 Athens, 2004 Emblem, Rifle Shooting, Gymnastics and Judo

2004. Olympic Games, Athens. Multicoloured.

1660	1b.50 Type **554**	90	75
1661	7b. Emblem, running and swimming	3·75	3·25

555 Holy Family

2004. Christmas. Multicoloured.

1662	1b.50 Type **555**	90	75
1663	3b. Child praying	2·40	2·10
1664	6b. Candle	3·25	2·75

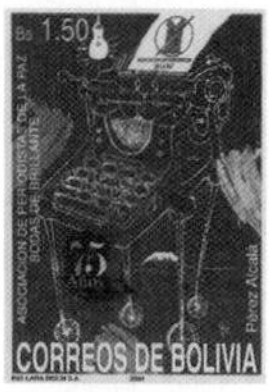

556 Typewriter on Wheels

2004. 75th Anniv of La Paz Journalists' Association.

1665	**556**	1b.50 multicoloured	90	75

2015

557 Palm

2004. America. Environmental Protection. Multicoloured.

1666	5b. Type **557**	2·75	2·40
1667	6b. Parrots (Gilka Wara Libermann)	3·25	2·75

558 Map of Bolivia and Emblems

2005. Centenary of Rotary International (charitable organization). Multicoloured.

1668	3b. Type **558**	2·40	2·10
1669	3b. Paul Harris (founder), "100" and emblem	2·40	2·10

Nos. 1668/9 were issued together, *se-tenant*, forming a composite design.

559 Water Pipe Outflow and Beach

2005. Environmental Projects. Multicoloured.

1670	5b. Type **559** (Pras Pando (water project))	2·75	2·40
1671	6b. Seedling, European Union and Bolivian Flags (PRAEDAC (programme to support alternate development)) (vert)	3·25	2·75

560 Striped Cloth

2005. Cultural Heritage. Textiles. Multicoloured.

1672	50c. Type **560**	45	40
1673	1b. Horizontal stripes and dark bands	55	45
1674	1b.50 Vertical decorated stripes and red bands	90	75
1675	6b. Wide black bands	3·25	2·75
1676	6b. Two decorated squares (horiz)	3·25	2·75

561 Otto Felipe Braun

2005. 80th Anniv of Colegio Mariscal Braun, La Paz.

1677	**561**	6b. multicoloured	3·25	2·75

562 *Harpia harpyja*

2005. Birds. Multicoloured.

1678	1b. Type **562** (Interexpo '05, Dominican Republic)	55	45
1679	1b.50 *Penelope dabbenei* (35th anniv of Filatelica Boliviana)	90	75
1680	7b. *Aulacorhynchus coeruleicinctus* (Washington 2006)	3·75	3·25

563 Pope John Paul II and Children

2005. Pope John Paul II Commemoration (1681) and Inauguration of Pope Benedict XVI (1682). Multicoloured.

1681	5b. Type **563**	2·75	2·40
1682	5b. Pope Benedict XVI (vert)	2·75	2·40

564 Sail Ship

2005. The Pacific War of 1879–1884.

1683	**564**	5b. multicoloured	2·75	2·40

565 Don Quixote riding Rocinante

2005. 400th Anniv of the Publication of *Don Quixote de la Mancha* by Miguel de Cervantes.

1684	**565**	4b. multicoloured	2·20	1·90

566 Mother and Child

2005. America. Struggle against Poverty. Multicoloured.

1685	6b. Type **566**	3·25	2·75
1686	7b. Fisherman and fleshless fish	3·75	3·25

567 Idelfonso Murguia

2005. 184th Anniv of Infanteria Colorado Regiment (presidential escort).

1687	**567**	2b. multicoloured	1·50	1·30

568 Flamingos in Flight

2005. Tourism.

1688	**568**	6b. multicoloured	3·25	2·75

569 Two-toed Sloth

2005. 20th Anniv of LIDEMA (conservation group).

1689	**569**	6b. multicoloured	3·25	2·75

570 1863 Un-issued 2r. Stamps

2005. Stamp Day. Sheet 91×110 mm containing T **570** and similar horiz designs. Multicoloured.

MS1690	2r.×3, Type **570**; 1924 5b. stamp; British 1840 Penny Black (1st stamp) and Brazil 1843 30r. ("Olho de Boi" ("Bull's Eye")) stamp; 4r.×3, 1867 5c. stamps (1st Bolivian stamps); 1930 3b. surch on 20c. ("Graf Zeppelin") stamp; 1987 60c. stamp	14·50	14·00

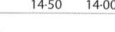

571 Three Wise Men

2005. Christmas. Multicoloured.

1691	1b.50 Type **571**	90	75
1692	3b. Holy family	1·70	1·40

2006. Nos. 1119, 1115 and No. 1119 surch.

1693	1b. on 1000000p. black and green	65	55
1694	2b. on 550000 multicoloured	1·40	1·20
1695	2b.50 on 1000000 multicoloured	2·30	2·00

575 School Building, 1906

2006. Centenary of Engineering University.

1696	**575**	6b. multicoloured	3·25	2·75

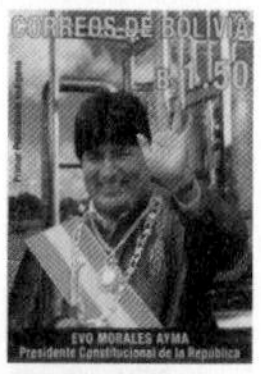

576 President Morales

2006. Election of President Juan Evo Morales Ayma (Evo Morales) (first indigenous South American President. Multicoloured.

1697	1b.50 Type **576**	90	75
1698	5b. At inauguration	2·75	2·40
1699	6b. Wearing tribal dress	3·25	2·75

577 Red Cross Worker

2006. Bolivian Red Cross.

1700	**577**	5b. multicoloured	2·75	2·40

578 Inca Messenger and Envelopes

2006. 15th Anniv of ECOBOL.

1701	**578**	1b. green	55	45
1702	**578**	1b.50 ultramarine	90	75

579 Boy Scouts at Exfivia 75

2006. Stamp Collectors' Day. Sheet 90×105 mm containing T **579** and similar horiz designs. Multicoloured.

MS1703 1b.50 Type **579**; 1b.50 Stamp album; 1b.50 Bird stamps of Boliva and Honduras; 6b. Exfilmar 80; 6b. Ship stamps of Bolivia and Iceland; 6b. Floral stamps of Bolivia and Dominican Republic 15·00 14·00

580 Legislative Palace and Second Adapted National Flag of 1851

2006. Flags. Multicoloured.

1704	1b.50 Type **580**	55	45
1705	5b. Liberty House and first adapted national flag of 1826	2·75	2·40
1706	6b. Liberty House and first national flag of 1825	3·25	2·75

581 Friar and Donkey

2006. 400th Anniv of Franciscan Order in Tarija. Multicoloured.

1707	2b. Type **581**	1·40	1·20
1708	2b. Early church	1·40	1·20
1709	6b. Basilica interior (vert)	3·25	2·75
1710	6b. "La Inmaulada" (vert)	3·25	2·75

582 *14-bis*

2006. Centenary of First Flight by Alberto Santos Dumont.

1711	**582**	1b.50 multicoloured	90	75

583 Sajama National Park

2006. 400th Anniv of Oruro.

1712	**583**	4b. multicoloured	2·20	1·90

584 9 February Avenue

2006. Centenary of Bahia Harbour. Multicoloured.

1713	1b. Type **584**	55	45
1714	1b.50 German Busch Plaza	90	75
1715	2b.50 Tree (vert)	2·20	1·90
1716	3b. Potosi Plaza	2·40	2·10
1717	4b. Bahia Pando river	2·75	2·30
1718	6b. Friendship Bridge	3·25	2·75
1719	7b. Port Avenue (vert)	3·75	3·25

585 Vicuna

2006. Endangered Species. Multicoloured.

1720	1b. Type **585**	55	45
1721	1b.50 Head of Yacare caiman (Caiman yacare) (horiz)	90	75
1722	5b. Yacare caiman (horiz)	2·75	2·40
1723	7b. Vicuna (horiz)	3·75	3·25

586 Area damaged by Mining

2006. International Year of Deserts and Desertification. Multicoloured.

1724	1b.50 Type **586**	90	75
1725	2b. Erosion, Tolomosa river basin	1·40	1·20
1726	3b. Terraces	2·40	2·10
1727	4b. Erosion, Caranavi	2·75	2·30

587 Low Energy Bulb as Flower

2006. America. Energy Conservation. Multicoloured.

1728	3b. Type **587**	2·40	2·10
1729	4b. Light bulb containing cash	2·75	2·30

588 Virgin of Roses

2006. Christmas. Multicoloured.

1730	4b. Type **588**	2·75	2·30
1731	5b. Adoration of the Magi	3·00	2·50
1732	6b. Adoration of the shepherds	3·25	2·75

589 Rocks (astronomical observatory)

2006. Manco Kapac. Multicoloured.

1733	5b. Type **589**	3·00	2·50
1734	6b. Copacabana Temple	3·25	2·75
1735	7b. Boat on lake	3·75	3·25

590 Toucan

2006. Birds of Pando. Multicoloured.

1736	2b.50 Type **590**	1·40	1·20
1737	6b. Inscr "Pajaro azul"	3·25	2·75

591 Helmeted Curassow (inscr "Pavichi cresta azul")

2006. Birds of Santa Cruz. Multicoloured.

1738	3b.50 Type **591**	2·75	2·40
1739	7b. Harpy eagle (inscr "Aguila arpia")	3·75	3·25

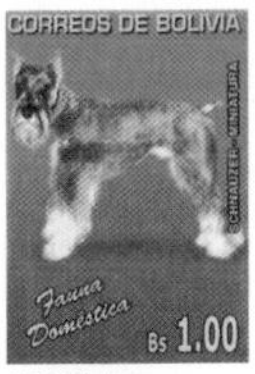

592 Miniature Schnauzer

2006. Dogs. Multicoloured.

1740	1b. Type **592**	90	75
1741	2b. Husky	1·40	1·20
1742	3b. American boxer	2·40	2·10
1743	4b. Inscr "Criollo"	2·75	2·40

593 14 September Plaza

2007. 'Latin America and Caribbean Lions' Forum, Cochabamba, Bolivia.

1744	**593**	6b. multicoloured	3·25	2·75

594 Map of Europe

2007. 50th Anniv of Treaty of Rome. Multicoloured.

1745	3b.50 Type **594**	2·75	2·30
1746	7b. Flag of stars	3·75	3·25

Nos. 1745/6 were issued together, *se-tenant*, forming a composite design.

595 Philatelic Magazines

2007. 50th Anniv of Philatelic Association. Multicoloured.

1747	50c. Type **595**	45	40
1748	1b. Arnold Glaeser (first president) and overprinted stamp	90	75
1749	2b.50 Simon Martinic and stamp catalogue	2·00	1·70
1750	3b. Franz Steimbach and Oscar Roca	2·40	2·10
1751	3b.50 Cathedral and 'Heroinas de la Coronilla' monument	2·75	2·30
1752	6b. 'Christ of the Concord' (statue) and Cathedral, Cochabamba	3·25	2·75

Nos. 1751/2 were issued together, se-tenant, forming a composite design.

596 Charango

2007. Cultural Heritage. Multicoloured.

1753	4b. Type **596**	2·75	2·40
1754	6b. Charango (different)	3·25	2·75

597 Emblem and '90'

2007. 90th Anniv of Bolivian Red Cross.

1755	**597**	2b.50 multicoloured	2·00	1·70

598 Francis Harrington (missionary and institute founder)

2007. Centenary of American Institute.

1756	**598**	7b.50 multicoloured	4·25	3·50

599 Cog, Map and Emblems

2007. 75th Anniv of Chamber of Commerce. Multicoloured.

1757	9b. Type **599**	5·00	4·25
1758	12b. '75 Anos', emblems and cog	6·50	5·75

599a *Ara ararauna* (blue and gold macaw)

2007. Birds. Multicoloured.

1758a	5b.50 Type **599a**	3·00	2·75
1758b	7b.50 *Porphyrula martinica* (purple gallinule)	4·25	3·50

600 Jaguar

2007. Santa Cruz Zoo. Multicoloured.

1759	6b. Type **600**	3·25	2·75
1760	9b. Puma	5·00	4·25

601 Emblems

2007. Heads of the American Air Force Conference, Santa Cruz, Bolivia.

1761	**601**	10b.50 multicoloured	6·00	5·25

602 Andean Condor (inscr 'Opisthocomus hoazin')

2007. Birds of La Paz. Multicoloured.

1762	4b. Type **602**	2·75	2·40
1763	5b.50 Andean cock-of-the rock (*Rupicola peruviana*) (inscr "Tunqui") (horiz)	3·00	2·75

603 Robert Baden Powell (founder)

2007. Centenary of World Scouting. Multicoloured.

1764		7b.50 Type **603**	4·25	3·50
1765		8b.50 Emblem (vert)	4·75	4·00

604 *Cyclarhis guyanensis*

2007. Birds. Multicoloured.

1766		3b.50 Type **604**	2·75	2·30
1767		4b. *Egretta alba* (vert)	2·75	2·40
1767a		5b.50 *Ramphastos toco*	3·00	2·75
1769		6b.50 *Bubo virgianus* (vert)	3·50	3·00
1770		6b.50 *Trogon melanurus* (vert)	3·50	3·00
1771		6b.50 *Falco sparverius*	3·50	3·00
1772		6b.50 *Hymantopus mexicanus* (vert)	3·50	3·00
1774		7b.50 *Platalea ajaja*	4·25	3·50
1774a		7b.50 *Opisthocomus hoazin*	4·25	3·50
1775		8b.50 *Sarcoramphus papa*	4·75	4·00
1776		8b.50 *Momotus momta*	4·75	4·00
1777		9b. *Tinamotis pentlandii* (vert)	5·00	4·25
1778		9b. *Chlorostilbon aureoventris* (vert)	5·00	4·25
1779		10b.50 *Ardea cocoi* (vert)	5·75	5·00

Nos. 1768 and 1773 have been left for stamps not yet received.

605 Signature

2007. 40th Death Anniv of Ernesto (Che) Guevara (resistance fighter). Multicoloured.

1780		30b. Type **605**	22·00	19·00
1781		50b. Images of Che Guevara (vert)	40·00	34·00

606 North American F-86 Sabres on Runway

2007. 50th Anniv of Bolivian Airforce. Multicoloured.

1782		7b.50 Type **606**	4·25	3·50
1783		9b. Aircraft in flight	5·00	4·25

607 Globe and Aircraft

2007. International Day of Civil Aviation. Multicoloured

1784		6b.50 Type **607**	3·50	3·00
1785		8b.50 Map and aircraft	4·75	4·00

608 School Pupils

2007. America. Education for All. Multicoloured.

1786		3b. Type **608**	2·40	2·10
1787		5b. Siembra, siembra no import que otro.....etc	3·00	2·50
1788		6b. Mother and child reading	3·25	2·75
1789		9b. Girl and flowers	5·00	4·25

609 Syncline, Maragua

2007. Tourism. Multicoloured.

1790		2b. Type **609**	1·40	1·20
1791		2b.50 Fescue, Pasto Iro	2·00	1·70
1792		3b.50 Trees in lake	2·75	2·30
1793		5b. Beni river lake	3·00	2·50
1794		5b.50 Manuripi river	3·25	2·75
1795		5b.50 Serranias de Tarija valley	3·25	2·75
1796		5b.50 Zongo valley	3·25	2·75
1797		7b.50 Orthon river	4·25	3·50
1798		7b.50 Tornado in Sajama valley (vert)	4·25	3·50
1799		9b. Bridge over Pilcomayo river	5·00	4·25
1800		9b. Cactus, Isla del Pescador (vert)	5·00	4·25
1801		10b. Chapare river valley	5·50	4·75
1802		10b.50 Salar de Uyuni (world's largest salt flat)	5·75	5·00
1803		10b.50 *Trichocereus camarguensis*	5·75	5·00
1804		20b. Caiman lake	10·00	8·50
1805		30b. Zongo (vert)	12·00	10·50
1806		50b. Plaza Sucre	17·00	14·00
1807		100b. Acoiris waterfall (vert)	22·00	19·00

610 *Holy Family* (Luca Cambiasso)

2007. Christmas. Multicoloured.

1808		3b.50 Type **610**	2·75	2·30
1809		4b. *Adoration of the Shepherds* (Pieter Aersten)	2·75	2·40
1810		6b.50 *The Nativity* (Gregoria Gamarra)	3·50	3·00

611 Globe as Post Box

2008. World Post Day.

1811	**611**	1b. multicoloured	90	75

612 Christ, Map and People

2008. 50th Anniv of ECOBOL (Episcopal social welfare commission). Multicoloured.

1812		10b. Type **612**	5·50	4·75
1813		15b. Indigenous inhabitants (vert)	8·25	7·00

613 Church

2008. Jesuit Church, Santa Cruz. Multicoloured.

1814		5b. Type **613**	3·00	2·50
1815		9b. Church, veranda and tower	5·00	4·25

614 '80' enclosing Emblem

2008. 80th Anniv (2007) of Rotary Club, Cochabamba.

1816	**614**	20b. multicoloured	10·00	8·50

615 Justice and Court Building

2008. 150th Anniv (2005) of High Court of Justice.

1817	**615**	20b. multicoloured	10·00	8·50

616 Centenary Emblem

2008. Centenary of 'The Strongest' Football Club. Multicoloured.

1818		1b.50 Type **616**	1·20	1·00
1819		2b.50 Arms	2·00	1·70
1820		5b.50 Model of *Quinteros*	3·25	2·75
1821		6b.50 Founding team	3·50	3·00

617 Pope Benedict XVI

2008. Pope Benedict XVI. Multicoloured.

1822		12b. Type **617**	6·50	5·75
1823		15b. Wearing cope	8·25	7·00

618 Stadium and Football

2008. Football—No Veto for Altitude.

1824	**618**	3b. multicoloured	2·40	2·10

619 Clock Tower

2008. Sucre 2009–Bicentenary of Independence. Multicoloured.

1825		1b.50 Type **619**	1·20	1·00
1826		5b.50 Bell tower	3·25	2·75
1827		7b.50 Clock tower and '25 de Mayo'	4·25	3·50
1828		9b. White tower	5·00	4·25

620 Emblem

2008. 80th Anniv of Supervision of Banks and Financial Institutions. Multicoloured.

1829		3b. Type **620**	2·40	2·10
1830		7b. Building facade (vert)	3·75	3·25

621 MA 60 in Flight

2008. Air Force—Incorporation of Xian Y7-MA 60. Multicoloured.

1831		1b.50 Type **621**	1·20	1·00
1832		9b. On ground	5·00	4·25

622 Luk'i Negra

2008. International Year of the Potato. Multicoloured.

1833		1b.50 Type **622**	1·20	1·00
1834		5b.50 Sani Imilla	3·25	2·75
1835		7b.50 Saq'ampaya	4·25	3·50
1836		10b.50 Waych'a	5·75	4·50

623 Emblem

2009. First Anniv of Nationalization of ENTEL (telecom company). Multicoloured.

1837		2b. Type **623**	1·10	85
1838		3b. Men and women (horiz)	2·40	2·10

624 Children and Rainbow

2009. 15th Anniv of Fundacion Arcoiris (Rainbow Foundation) (charity for abandoned children).

1839	**624**	5b. multicoloured	2·75	2·20

625 Building Facade

2009. Centenary of Mariscal Sucre National University.

1840	**625**	3b. multicoloured	2·40	2·10

626 Detainees

2009. Freedom for Cuban Five.

1841	**626**	7b.50 multicoloured	4·25	3·50

627 Children

2009. 50th Anniv of Inter-American Development Bank (IDB).

1842	**627**	5b. multicoloured	3·25	2·75

628 Rebels

2009. Bicentenary of Bolivian Liberation.

1843	**628**	2b. multicoloured	1·10	85

629 Building Facade

2009. 80th (2011) Anniv of School for Indigenous Pupils, Warisate.

1844	**629**	2b.50 multicoloured	2·00	1·70

630 Institute of Bacteriology Building

2009. Centenary of National Institute of Health Laboratories (INLASA).

1845	**630**	1b.50 multicoloured	1·20	1·00

631 Building Facade

2009. Centenary of Venezuela National High School.

1846	**631**	3b. multicoloured	2·40	2·10

632 Palm Tree and Building

2009. 50th Anniv of Enrique Lindemann B Educational Unit.

1847	**632**	3b.50 multicoloured	2·50	2·20

633 Bernardo Guarachi

2009. Tenth Anniv of Bernardo Guarachi's Ascent of Mount Everest (first Bolivian ascent). Multicoloured.

1848	50c. Type **633**		40	30
1849	7b. Wearing mountain equipment (horiz)		3·75	3·25

634 Elderly Couple

2009. Centenary of San Ramon Nursing Home.

1850	**634**	2b. multicoloured	1·10	85

635 Games Emblem

2009. Sucre 2009. Multicoloured.

1851	1b.50 Type **635**		1·20	1·10
1852	9b. Emblem (different)		4·75	4·50

636 Jacks

2009. America. Games. Multicoloured.

1853	1b. Type **636**		80	75
1854	7b. Kite flying		3·75	3·50

637 Bromeliad

2009. 38th Anniv of Philatelic Federation.

1855	**637**	3b.50 multicoloured	2·50	2·20

638 Holy Family

2009. Christmas. Multicoloured.

1856	7b. Type **638**		3·75	3·50
1857	9b. Infant Jesus		4·75	4·50

639 Pres Evo Morales Ayma

2010. Second Term of President Evo Morales Ayma. Multicoloured.

1858	1b.50 Type **639**		80	60
1859	9b. Wearing presidential sash and formal dress		1·40	1·20

640 Bi-plane (Potez 25 F-AJDZ) and Part of Envelope

2010. 80th Anniv of First Aeropostale Flight from the Pyrenees to Andes

1860	**640**	9b. multicoloured	2·00	1·80

641 Nevado Chacaltaya Glacier showing Ice Shrinkage

2010. Global Warming Awareness Campaign. Multicoloured.

1861	2b.50 Type **641**		95	70
1862	10b. Nevado Chacaltaya before ice shrinkage		1·90	1·70

642 Tupac Katari and Bartolina Sisa

2010. Tupac Katari and his Wife, Bartolina Sisa (Aymara anti-colonial rebels) Commemoration

1863	**642**	1b.50 reddish brown	45	30

643 Pepino

2010. Folklore. Multicoloured.

1864	1b. Type **643**		35	20
1865	2b. Moreno		80	60
1866	9b. Chuncho		3·25	2·75
1867	10b. Kusillo		4·00	3·50

644 Table set with Food for the Dead (All Saints)

2010. Traditions. Multicoloured.

1868	1b.50 Type **644**		80	60
1869	10b.50 Ekeko, God of Abundance and Wealth		1·40	1·20

645 Flowers

2010. Flowers. Multicoloured.

1870	1b.50 Type **645**		70	50
1871	1b.50 Flowers, butterfly on pink flower at right		70	50

Nos. 1870/1 were printed, *se-tenant*, each pair forming a composite design.

646 Rainer and José Luis Ibsen

2010. Rainer Ibsen Cárdenas and José Luis Ibsen Peña (disappeared) Commemoration

1872	**646**	3b. multicoloured	70	50

647 Tank, Modern Military Equipment and Soldiers

2010. Bicentenary of National Army. Multicoloured.

1873	3b.50 Type **647**		1·30	1·00
1874	9b. Personalities and scene from early battle		3·25	2·75

648 Footballer, Cyclist and Games Emblem

2010. Youth Olympic Games, Singapore. Multicoloured.

1875	2b. Type **648**		80	60
1876	9b. Swimmer, runner and games emblem		3·25	2·75

649 Revolutionary Statue, Cochabamba and Grupo Bicentenario Emblem

2010. Bicentenary of Latin American Freedom from Colonialism (1st issue)

1877	**649**	9b. multicoloured	3·25	2·75

650 Oxen, Basilica Menor de San Lorenzo, Santa Cruz and Grupo Bicentenario Emblem

2010. Bicentenary of Latin American Freedom from Colonialism (2nd issue)

1878	**650**	5b. multicoloured	2·10	1·80

651 Andean Condor (national bird)

2010. America. Multicoloured.

1879	2b.50 Type **651**		1·30	1·00
1880	5b. Patuju (national flower)		2·00	1·80

Nos. 1879/80 were printed, *se-tenant*, each pair forming a composite design.

652 EMI Building

2010. 60th Anniv of Military School of Engineering (EMI)

1881	**652**	7b. multicoloured	2·60	2·40

653 Adult Education

2010. 30th Anniv of JICA (Japan International Cooperation Agency) in Bolivia. Multicoloured.

1882	1b. Type **653**		35	25
1883	1b.50 Children and teacher		50	30
1884	3b. Drilling for water and children at stand pipe		1·30	1·00
1885	9b. Martial arts class		3·25	2·75

654 Building

2010. Bicentenary of Potosinos

1886	**654**	3b.50 multicoloured	1·40	1·10

655 *Puya raimondii*

2010. Endangered Species. Multicoloured.

1887	1b. Type **655**		35	25
1888	2b. *Leopardus jacobita* (Andean mountain cat) (horiz)		70	50
1889	2b.50 *Atelopus tricolor* (three-coloured harlequin toad) (horiz)		1·00	75
1890	3b.50 *Anairetes alpinus* (ash-breasted tit-tyrant) (horiz)		1·40	1·10

656 Pan Pipe Players (wooden carving)

2010. Birth Centenary of Fausto Aoiz Vilaseca (artist)

1891	**656**	2b. multicoloured	75	55

657 Angel (Baroque sculpture)

2010. Christmas. Multicoloured.

1892	3b. Type **657**	1·10	90
1893	9b. The Nativity (18th century painting) (horiz)	3·25	2·75

658 Jaime Gutierrez

2011. Jaime Alfonso Escalante Gutierrez (educator) Commemoration

1894	**658**	2b. multicoloured	70	50

659 Orange

2011. Fruit. Multicoloured.

1895	1b.50 Type **659**	45	35
1896	5b.50 Mango	1·60	1·40
1897	7b.50 Papaya	2·75	2·40
1898	9b. Avocado	3·25	2·75
1899	10b.50 Banana	3·50	3·00

660 *Chenopodium quinoa*

2011. Cereals. Multicoloured.

1900	1b. Type **660**	35	25
1901	2b. *Amaranthus*	70	50
1902	2b.50 *Chenopodium pallidicaule*	80	70
1903	5b. *Lupinus mutabilis*	1·50	1·30

661 BOA Airliner

2011. BOA Aviation (Boliviana de Aviacion) (state-owned airline)

1904	**661**	3b. multicoloured	1·10	90

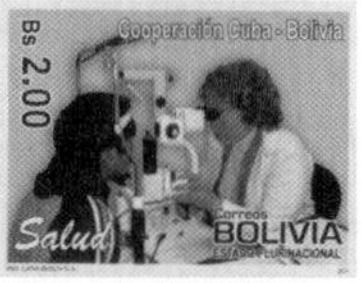

662 Eye Test (health)

2011. Bolivia - Cuba Cooperation. Multicoloured.

1905	2b. Type **662**	70	50
1906	2b.50 Dove and faces (solidarity with Cuba) (vert)	80	70
1907	3b. Indigenous woman and Cuban teacher (education)	1·10	90

663 Container Transport (Paraguay Waterway Paraná)

2011. Tenth Anniv of RIBB (Bolivian International Registration of Ships). Multicoloured.

1908	1b.50 Type **663**	45	35
1909	9b. Multi-purpose naval ship	3·25	2·75

664 Emblem

2011. Blood Donation Day

1910	**664**	3b. multicoloured	1·30	1·10

665 Anniversary Emblem

2011. Centenary of UPAEP

1911	**665**	9b. multicoloured	3·25	2·75

666 *Orestias agssii*

2011. Endangered Species. Fish. Multicoloured.

1912	1b. Type **666**	35	25
1913	1b.50 *Cichla pleiozona*	45	35
1914	3b. *Colossoma macropomum*	1·10	90
1915	9b. *Orestias luteus*	3·25	2·75

667 Graph, Equation and Stylised People

2011. 75th Anniv of National Institute of Statistics

1916	**667**	9b. multicoloured	3·25	2·75

668 UPAEP Emblem and Mailbox from 'Jose Joaquin Lemoine' Postal Museum

2011. America. Mailboxes. Multicoloured.

1917	1b.50 Type **668**	45	35
1918	9b. Emblem and mailbox from 'Jose Joaquin Lemoine' Postal Museum (different)	3·25	2·76

669 Star, Girl and Christmas Tree (Sarah Laura Zalles Azeñas)

2011. Christmas. Children's Drawings. Multicoloured.

1919	1b. Type **669**	35	25
1920	9b. Children, Christmas tree and map of South America (Adriana Nahir Peñaloza Cusi) (horiz)	3·25	2·75

670 Symbols of Human Rights

2011. Human Rights Day

1921	**670**	9b. multicoloured	3·25	2·75

671 *Bertholletia excelsa* (Brazil nut tree)

2011. International Year of Forests. Multicoloured.

1922	2b.50 Type **671**	80	70
1923	3b. *Swietenia macrophylla*	1·10	90

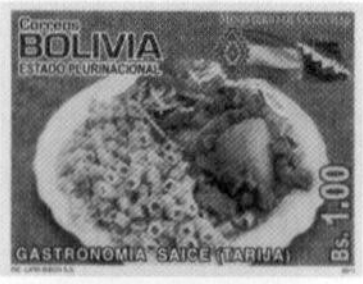

672 Saice Tarajeno

2011. Gastronomy. Multicoloured.

1924	1b. Type **672**	35	25
1925	1b.50 Majao camba	45	35
1926	2b.50 Silpancho cochabambino	80	70
1927	9b. Plato paceno	3·25	2·75

673 Coca Leaf Products

2011. Coca Leaf. Multicoloured.

1928	50c. Type **673**	20	15
1929	9b. Coca leaves on plant (vert)	3·25	2·75

674 Workers carrying Pipeline

2011. 75th Anniv of Yacimientos Petrolíferos Fiscales Bolivianos (YPFB) (state owned petroleum corporation). Multicoloured.

1930	50c. Type **674**	20	15
1931	9b. Dionisio Foianini (founder) and oil drill (vert)	3·25	2·75

POSTAGE DUE STAMPS

D81

1931

D265	**D81**	5c. blue	1·60	2·30
D266	**D81**	10c. red	1·80	2·50
D267	**D81**	15c. yellow	2·75	3·50
D268	**D81**	30c. green	2·75	3·50
D269	**D81**	40c. violet	4·00	5·50
D270	**D81**	50c. sepia	5·75	7·00

D93 "Youth"

1938. Triangular designs.

D346	**D93**	5c. red	75	75
D347	-	10c. green	75	75
D348	-	30c. blue	75	75

DESIGNS: 10c. Torch of Knowledge; 30c. Date and Symbol of 17 May 1936 Revolution.

129 Allegory of "Flight"

1944

426	**129**	40c. mauve (air)	20	10
427	-	1b. violet	25	10
428	-	1b.50 green	25	10
429	-	2b.50 blue	65	30

DESIGN—HORIZ: 1b.50, 2b.50, Lockheed 10 Electra air-plane and sun.

Pt. 1

BOPHUTHATSWANA

The republic of Bophuthatswana was established on 6 December 1977 as one of the "black homelands" constructed from the territory of the Republic of South Africa.

Although this independence did not receive international political recognition we are satisfied that the stamps had "de facto" acceptance as valid for the carriage of mail outside Bophuthatswana.

Bophuthatswana was formally re-incorporated into South Africa on 27 April 1994.

100 cents = 1 rand.

1 Hand releasing Dove

1977. Independence. Multicoloured.

1	4c. Type **1**	25	25
2	10c. Leopard (national emblem)	50	40
3	15c. Coat of arms	75	1·00
4	20c. National flag	1·25	1·40

2 African Buffalo

1977. Tribal Totems. Multicoloured.

5a	1c. Type **2**	15	20
6a	2c. Bush pig	25	20
7a	3c. Chacma baboon	15	20
8a	4c. Leopard	20	10
9a	5c. Crocodile	20	10
10	6c. Savanna monkey	20	10
11a	7c. Lion	30	15
12a	8c. Spotted hyena	20	15
13	9c. Cape porcupine	20	15
14	10c. Aardvark	20	10
15	15c. Tilapia (fish)	1·00	15
16	20c. Hunting dog	25	20
17	25c. Common duiker	30	30
18	30c. African elephant	1·00	35
19	50c. Python	50	40
20	1r. Hippopotamus	1·00	1·00
21	2r. Greater kudu	70	1·50

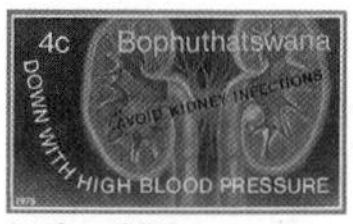

3 Infected Kidney

1978. World Hypertension Month. Multicoloured.

22	4c. Type **3**	50	25
23	10c. Heart and spoon of salt	70	70
24	15c. Spoon reflecting skull, knife and fork	1·25	1·25

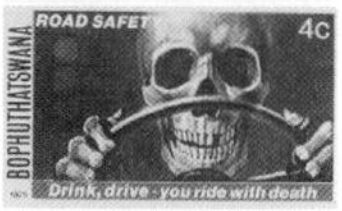

4 Skull behind Steering Wheel of Car

1978. Road Safety. Multicoloured.

25	4c. Type **4**	70	40
26	10c. Child knocked off tricycle	90	80
27	15c. Pedestrian stepping in front of car	1·00	1·10
28	20c. Cyclist ignoring stop sign	1·40	1·75

5 Cutting slabs of Travertine

1978. Semi-precious Stones. Multicoloured.

29	4c. Type **5**	65	25
30	10c. Polishing travertine	1·25	85
31	15c. Sorting semi-precious stones	1·50	1·25
32	20c. Factory at Taung	2·25	1·60

6 Wright Flyer I

1978. 75th Anniv of First Powered Flight by Wright Brothers.

33	**6**	10c. black, blue and red	1·00	1·00
34	-	15c. black, blue and red	1·40	1·50

DESIGN: 15c. Orville and Wilbur Wright.

7 Pres. Lucas M. Mangope

1978. 1st Anniv of Independence. Multicoloured.

35	4c. Type **7**	25	20
36	15c. Full face portrait of President	75	60

8 Drying Germinated Wheat Sorghum

1978. Sorghum Beer-making. Multicoloured.

37	4c. Type **8**	20	20
38	15c. Cooking the ground grain	50	70
39	20c. Sieving the liquid	60	75
40	25c. Drinking the beer	65	1·00

9 Kallie Knoetze (South Africa)

1979. Knoetze–Tate Boxing Match. Multicoloured.

41	15c. Type **9**	55	75
42	15c. John Tate (U.S.A.)	55	75

10 Emblem and Drawing of Local Fable (Hendrick Sebapo)

1979. International Year of the Child. Children's Drawings of Local Fables. Multicoloured.

43	4c. Type **10**	20	20
44	15c. Family with animals (Daisy Morapedi)	25	25
45	20c. Man's head and landscape (Peter Tladi)	35	35
46	25c. Old man, boy and donkey (Hendrick Sebapo)	45	60

11 Miner and Molten Platinum

1979. Platinum Industry.

47	**11**	4c. multicoloured	25	10
48	-	15c. multicoloured	35	30
49	-	20c. multicoloured	45	45
50	-	25c. black and grey	60	65

DESIGNS: 15c. Platinum granules and industrial use; 20c. Telecommunications satellite; 25c. Jewellery.

12 Cattle

1979. Agriculture. Multicoloured.

51	5c. Type **12**	20	20
52	15c. Picking cotton	25	25
53	20c. Scientist examining maize	30	30
54	25c. Catch of fish	35	35

13 Cigarettes forming Cross

1979. Anti-smoking Campaign.

55	**13**	5c. multicoloured	40	20

14 *Landolphia capensis*

1980. Edible Wild Fruits. Multicoloured.

56	5c. Type **14**	15	15
57	10c. *Vangueria infausta*	30	30
58	15c. *Bequaertiodendron magalismontanum*	40	40
59	20c. *Sclerocarya caffra*	55	55

15 Pied Babbler

1980. Birds. Multicoloured.

60	5c. Type **15**	25	20
61	10c. Carmine bee eater	35	35
62	15c. Shaft-tailed whydah	50	60
63	20c. Brown parrot ("Meyer's Parrot")	55	65

16 Sun City Hotel

1980. Tourism. Sun City. Multicoloured.

64	5c. Type **16**	10	15
65	10c. Gary Player Country Club	40	30
66	15c. Casino	45	50
67	20c. Extravaganza	50	70

17 Deaf Child

1981. Int Year of Disabled Persons. Multicoloured.

68	5c. Type **17**	15	10
69	15c. Blind child	30	20
70	20c. Archer in wheelchair	45	35
71	25c. Tuberculosis X-ray	60	60

18 "Behold the Lamb of God ..."

1981. Easter. Multicoloured.

72	5c. Type **18**	10	10
73	15c. Bread ("I am the bread of life")	25	25
74	20c. Shepherd ("I am the good shepherd")	35	35
75	25c. Wheatfield ("Unless a grain of wheat falls into the earth and dies ...")	45	45

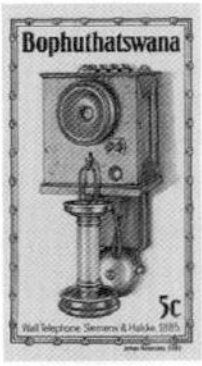

19 Siemens and Halske Wall Telephone, 1885

1981. History of the Telephone (1st series). Multicoloured.

76	5c. Type **19**	10	10
77	15c. Ericsson telephone, 1895	25	25
78	20c. Hasler telephone, 1900	35	35
79	25c. Mix and Genest wall telephone, 1904	45	45

See also Nos. 92/5, 108/11 and 146/9.

20 *Themeda triandra*

1981. Indigenous Grasses (1st series). Multicoloured.

80	5c. Type **20**	10	10
81	15c. "Rhynchelytrum repens"	20	25
82	20c. "Eragrostis capensis"	20	30
83	25c. "Monocymbium ceresiiforme"	30	45

See also Nos. 116/19.

21 Boy Scout

1982. 75th Anniv of Boy Scout Movement. Multicoloured.

84	5c. Type **21**	15	10
85	15c. Mafeking siege stamps	30	35
86	20c. Original cadet	30	40
87	25c. Lord Baden-Powell	35	45

22 Jesus arriving at Bethany (John 12:1)

1982. Easter. Multicoloured.

88	15c. Type **22**	25	25
89	20c. Jesus sending disciples for donkey (Matthew 21:1,2)	25	30
90	25c. Disciples taking donkey (Mark 11:5,6)	30	40
91	30c. Disciples with donkey and foal (Matthew 21:7)	30	45

23 Ericsson Telephone, 1878

1982. History of the Telephone (2nd series). Multicoloured.

92	8c. Type **23**	15	10
93	15c. Ericsson telephone, 1885	20	20
94	20c. Ericsson telephone, 1893	20	20
95	25c. Siemens and Halske telephone, 1898	30	30

24 Old Parliament Building

1982. Fifth Anniv of Independence. Multicoloured.

96	8c. Type **24**	10	10
97	15c. New government offices	20	20
98	20c. University, Mmabatho	25	25
99	25c. Civic Centre, Mmabatho	30	30

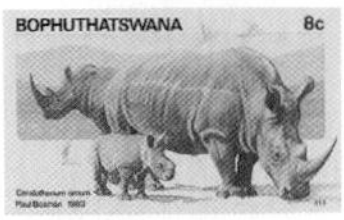

25 White Rhinoceros

1983. Pilanesberg Nature Reserve. Multicoloured.

100	8c. Type **25**	30	10
101	20c. Common zebras	40	30
102	25c. Sable antelope	40	35
103	40c. Hartebeest	60	60

26 Disciples bringing Donkeys to Jesus (Matthew 21:7)

1983. Easter. Palm Sunday. Multicoloured.

104	8c. Type **26**	10	10
105	20c. Jesus stroking colt (Mark 11:7)	30	30
106	25c. Jesus enters Jerusalem on donkey (Matthew 21:8)	35	35
107	40c. Crowd welcoming Jesus (Mark 11:9)	60	60

1983. History of the Telephone (3rd series). As T **19**. Multicoloured.

108	10c. A.T.M. table telephone c. 1920	15	10
109	20c. A/S Elektrisk wall telephone, c. 1900	25	30
110	25c. Ericsson wall telephone c. 1900	30	35
111	40c. Ericsson wall telephone c. 1900 (different)	40	60

27 Kori Bustard

1983. Birds of the Veld. Multicoloured.

112	10c. Type **27**	30	20
113	20c. Black bustard ("Black Korhaan")	45	45
114	25c. Crested bustard ("Red-crested Korhaan")	55	55
115	40c. Denhan's ("Stanley Bustard")	70	80

1984. Indigenous Grasses (2nd series). As T **20.** Multicoloured.

116	10c. *Panicum maximum*	15	10
117	20c. *Hyparrhenia dregeana*	20	20
118	25c. *Cenchrus ciliaris*	25	35
119	40c. *Urochloa brachyura*	50	70

28 Money-lenders in the Temple (Mark 11:11)

1984. Easter. Multicoloured.

120	10c. Type **28**	15	10
121	20c. Jesus driving the money-lenders from the Temple (Mark 11:15)	25	20
122	25c. Jesus and fig tree (Matthew 21:9)	30	35
123	40c. The withering of the fig tree (Matthew 21:9)	40	70

29 Car Upholstery, Ga-Rankuwa

1984. Industries. Multicoloured.

124	1c. Textile mill	10	10
125	2c. Sewing sacks, Selosesha	10	10
126	3c. Ceramic tiles, Babelegi	10	10
127	4c. Sheepskin car seat covers	10	10
128	5c. Crossbow manufacture	15	10
129	6c. Automobile parts, Babelegi	15	10
130	7c. Hosiery, Babelegi	15	10
131	8c. Specialised bicycle factory, Babelegi	30	10
132	9c. Lawn mower assembly line	30	15
133	10c. Dress factory, Thaba 'Nchu	20	10
134	11c. Molten platinum	60	20
135	12c. Type **29**	40	15
136	14c. Maize mill, Mafeking	50	15
137	15c. Plastic bags, Babelegi	25	15
137b	16c. Brick factory, Mmabatho	60	15
137c	18c. Cutlery manufacturing, Mogwase	60	15
138	20c. Men's clothing, Babelegi	25	15
138b	21c. Welding bus chassis	50	50
138c	21c. Fitting engine to bus chassis	50	50

138d	21c. Bus body construction	50	50
138e	21c. Spraying and finishing bus	50	50
138f	21c. Finished bus	50	50
139	25c. Chromium plating pram parts	30	20
140	30c. Spray painting metal beds	40	25
141	50c. Milk processing plant	50	40
142	1r. Modern printing works	60	75
143	2r. Industrial complex, Babelegi	1·00	2·50

1984. History of the Telephone (4th series). As T **19.** Multicoloured.

146	11c. Schuchhardt table telephone, 1905	15	10
147	20c. Siemens wall telephone, 1925	25	20
148	25c. Ericsson table telephone, 1900	30	30
149	30c. Oki table telephone, 1930	40	50

30 Yellow-throated Plated Lizard

1984. Lizards. Multicoloured.

150	11c. Type **30**	20	10
151	25c. Transvaal girdled lizard	25	30
152	30c. Ocellated sand lizard	25	40
153	45c. Bibron's thick-toed gecko	40	60

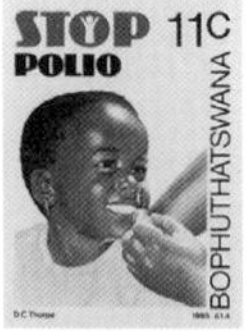

31 Giving Oral Vaccine against Polio

1985. Health. Multicoloured.

154	11c. Type **31**	40	10
155	25c. Vaccinating against measles	50	30
156	30c. Examining child for diphtheria	55	40
157	50c. Examining child for whooping cough	80	90

32 Chief Montshiwa of Barolong booRatshidi

1985. Centenary of Mafeking.

158	**32**	11c. black, grey and orange	20	10
159	-	25c. black, grey and blue	40	30

DESIGN: 25c. Sir Charles Warren.

33 The Sick flock to Jesus in the Temple (Matthew, 21:41)

1985. Easter. Multicoloured.

160	12c. Type **33**	20	10
161	25c. Jesus cures the sick (Matthew 21:14)	30	20
162	30c. Children praising Jesus (Matthew 21:15)	35	30
163	50c. Community leaders discussing Jesus's acceptance of praise (Matthew 21:15, 16)	50	60

34 "Faurea saligna" and planting Sapling

1985. Tree Conservation. Multicoloured.

164	12c. Type **34**	20	10
165	25c. "Boscia albitrunca" and kudu	25	20
166	30c. "Erythrina lysistemon" and mariqua sunbird	35	30
167	50c. "Bequaertiondendron magalismontanum" and bee	55	50

35 Jesus at Mary and Martha's, Bethany (John 12:2)

1986. Easter. Multicoloured.

168	12c. Type **35**	25	10
169	20c. Mary anointing Jesus's feet (John 12:3)	30	20
170	25c. Mary drying Jesus's feet with her hair (John 12:3)	35	25
171	30c. Disciple condemns Mary for anointing Jesus's head with oil (Matthew 26:7)	45	50

36 *Wesleyan Mission Station and Residence of Moroka, Chief of the Barolong, 1834* (C. D. Bell)

1986. Paintings of Thaba 'Nchu. Multicoloured.

172	14c. Type **36**	40	15
173	20c. *James Archbell's Congregation, 1834* (Charles Davidson Bell)	60	60
174	25c. *Mission Station at Thaba 'Nchu, 1850* (Thomas Baines)	65	80

37 Farmer using Tractor (agricultural development)

1986. Temisano Development Project. Multicoloured.

175	14c. Type **37**	20	10
176	20c. Children at school (community development)	30	20
177	25c. Repairing engine (training)	35	30
178	30c. Grain elevator (secondary industries)	50	50

38 Stewardesses and Cessna Citation II

1986. "B.O.P." Airways. Multicoloured.

179	14c. Type **38**	25	10
180	20c. Passengers disembarking from Boeing 707	40	20
181	25c. Mmabatho International Airport	50	35
182	30c. Cessna Citation II	60	50

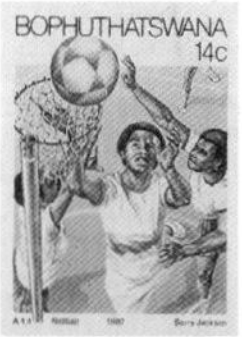

39 Netball

1987. Sports. Multicoloured.

183	14c. Type **39**	20	15
184	20c. Tennis	30	30
185	25c. Football	30	30
186	30c. Athletics	45	50

40 *Berkheya zeyheri*

1987. Wild Flowers. Multicoloured.

187	16c. Type **40**	25	15
188	20c. *Plumbago auriculata*	35	35
189	25c. *Pterodiscus speciosus*	35	35
190	30c. *Gazania krebsiana*	40	50

41 E. M. Mokgoko Farmer Training Centre

1987. Tertiary Education. Multicoloured.

191	16c. Type **41**	20	15
192	20c. Main lecture block, University of Bophuthatswana	30	35
193	25c. Manpower Centre	30	35
194	30c. Hotel Training School	30	50

42 Posts

1987. Tenth Anniv of Independence. Communications. Multicoloured.

195	16c. Type **42**	25	15
196	30c. Telephone	35	35
197	40c. Radio	35	35
198	50c. Television	40	50

43 Jesus entering Jerusalem on Donkey (John 12:12–14)

1988. Easter. Multicoloured.

199	16c. Type **43**	25	15
200	30c. Judas negotiating with chief priests (Mark 14:10–11)	35	35
201	40c. Jesus washing the disciples' feet (John 13:5)	35	35
202	50c. Jesus handing bread to Judas (John 13:26)	40	50

44 Environment Education

1988. National Parks Board. Multicoloured.

203	16c. Type **44**	25	15
204	30c. Rhinoceros (Conservation)	40	40
205	40c. Catering workers	40	40
206	50c. Cheetahs (Tourism)	55	65

45 Sunflowers

1988. Crops. Multicoloured.

207	16c. Type **45**	25	15
208	30c. Peanuts	35	35
209	40c. Cotton	45	45
210	50c. Cabbages	60	60

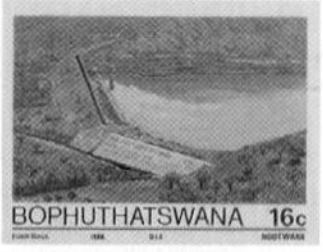

46 Ngotwane Dam

1988. Dams. Multicoloured.

211	16c. Type **46**	30	20
212	30c. Groothoek Dam	50	50
213	40c. Sehujwane Dam	50	50
214	50c. Molatedi Dam	70	70

47 The Last Supper (Matthew 26:26)

1989. Easter. Multicoloured.

215	16c. Type **47**	40	20
216	30c. Jesus praying in Garden of Gethsemane (Matthew 26:39)	60	55
217	40c. Judas kissing Jesus (Mark 14:45)	70	70
218	50c. Peter severing ear of High Priest's slave (John 18:10)	85	1·00

48 Cock (Thembi Atong)

1989. Children's Art. Designs depicting winning entries in National Children's Day Art Competition.

219	18c. Type **48**	30	20
220	30c. Traditional thatched hut (Muhammad Mahri)	40	40
221	40c. Airplane, telephone wires and houses (Tshepo Mashokwi)	45	45
222	50c. City scene (Miles Brown)	50	60

49 Black-shouldered Kite

1989. Birds of Prey. Paintings by Claude Finch-Davies. Multicoloured.

223	18c. Type **49**	1·25	30
224	30c. Pale chanting goshawk	1·40	75
225	40c. Lesser kestrel	1·60	1·10
226	50c. Short-toed eagle	1·75	1·50

50 Bilobial House

1989. Traditional Houses. Multicoloured.

227	18c. Type **50**	25	20
228	30c. House with courtyards at front and side	35	35
229	40c. House with conical roof	35	35
230	50c. House with rounded roof	40	50

51 Early Learning Schemes

1990. Community Services. Multicoloured.

231	18c. Type **51**	25	20
232	30c. Clinics	35	35
233	40c. Libraries	35	35
234	50c. Hospitals	40	45

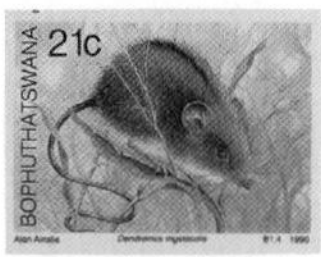

52 Lesser Climbing Mouse

1990. Small Mammals. Multicoloured.

235	21c. Type **52**	30	20
236	30c. Zorilla	40	40
237	40c. Transvaal elephant shrew	60	60
238	50c. Large-toothed rock hyrax	80	85

53 Variegated Sandgrouse

1990. Sandgrouse. Paintings by Claude Finch-Davies. Multicoloured.

239	21c. Type **53**	90	30
240	35c. Double-banded sandgrouse	1·10	75
241	40c. Namaqua sandgrouse	1·10	90
242	50c. Yellow-throated sandgrouse	1·40	1·40

54 Basketry

1990. Traditional Crafts. Multicoloured.

243	21c. Type **54**	40	20
244	35c. Training	60	60
245	40c. Beer making	60	65
246	50c. Pottery	65	75

55 Sud Aviation SE3130 Alouette II Helicopter

1990. Bophuthatswana Air Force. Multicoloured.

247	21c. Type **55**	1·40	1·10
248	21c. MBB-Kawasaki BK-117 helicopter	1·40	1·10
249	21c. Pilatus PC-7 turbo trainer	1·40	1·10
250	21c. Pilatus PC-6	1·40	1·10
251	21c. CASA C-212 Aviocar	1·40	1·10

56 Wild Custard Apple

1991. Edible Wild Fruit. Multicoloured.

252	21c. Type **56**	50	25
253	35c. Spine-leaved monkey orange	65	70
254	40c. Sycamore fig	70	75
255	50c. Kei apple	85	95

57 Arrest of Jesus (Mark 14:46)

1991. Easter. Multicoloured.

256	21c. Type **57**	45	25
257	35c. First trial by the Sanhedrin (Mark 14:53)	60	55
258	40c. Assault and derision of Jesus after sentence (Mark 14:65)	70	70
259	50c. Servant girl recognizing Peter (Mark 14:67)	75	90

58 Class 7A Locomotive No. 350, 1897

1991. Steam Locomotives. Multicoloured.

260	25c. Class 6A locomotive No. 194, 1897, trucks and caboose (71×25 mm)	95	55
261	40c. Type **58**	1·25	85
262	50c. Double-boiler Class 6Z locomotives pulling Cecil Rhodes's funeral train (71×25 mm)	1·40	1·25
263	60c. Class 8 locomotive at Mafeking station, 1904	1·50	1·75

59 Caneiro Chart, 1502

1991. Old Maps (1st series). Multicoloured.

264	25c. Type **59**	1·10	40
265	40c. Cantino Chart, 1502	1·50	95
266	50c. Giovanni Contarini's map, 1506	1·75	1·40
267	60c. Martin Waldseemuller's map, 1507	1·75	1·90

See also Nos. 268/71 and 297/300.

60 Fracanzano Map, 1508

1992. Old Maps (2nd series). Multicoloured.

268	27c. Type **60**	1·10	40
269	45c. Martin Waldseemuller's map (from edition of Ptolemy), 1513	1·50	95
270	65c. Section of Waldseemuller's woodcut "Carta Marina Navigatora Portugallan Navigationes", 1516	1·75	1·50
271	85c. Map from Laurent Fries's *Geographia*, 1522	1·75	2·00

61 Delivery of Jesus to Pilate (Mark 15:1)

1992. Easter. Multicoloured.

272	27c. Type **61**	25	20
273	45c. Scourging of Jesus (Mark 15:15)	40	40
274	65c. Placing crown of thorns on Jesus's head (Mark 15:17–18)	50	70
275	85c. Soldiers mocking Jesus (Mark 15:19)	60	90

62 Sweet Thorn

1992. Acacia Trees. Multicoloured.

276	35c. Type **62**	30	25
277	70c. Camel thorn	50	60
278	90c. Umbrella thorn	60	80
279	1r.05 Black thorn	70	1·00

63 View of Palace across Lake

1992. The Lost City Complex, Sun City. Mulicoloured.

280	35c. Type **63**	40	45
281	35c. Palace facade	40	45
282	35c. Palace porte cochere	40	45
283	35c. Palace lobby	40	45
284	35c. Tusk Bar, Palace	40	45

64 Light Sussex

1993. Chickens. Multicoloured.

285	35c. Type **64**	40	25
286	70c. Rhode Island red	55	50
287	90c. Brown leghorn	60	80
288	1r.05 White leghorn	70	1·10

65 Pilate offering Release of Barabbas (Luke 23:25)

1993. Easter. Multicoloured.

289	35c. Type **65**	60	30
290	70c. Jesus falling under cross (John 19:17)	95	75
291	90c. Simon of Cyrene carrying cross (Mark 15:21)	1·25	1·25
292	1r.05 Jesus being nailed to cross (Mark 15:23)	1·40	1·75

66 Mafeking Locomotive Shed, 1933

1993. Steam Locomotives (2nd series). Multicoloured.

293	45c. Type **66**	65	55
294	65c. Rhodesian Railways steam locomotive No. 5, 1901 (34×25 mm)	75	65
295	85c. Class 16B locomotive pulling "White Train" during visit of Prince George, 1934	95	95
296	1r.05 Class 19D locomotive, 1923 (34×25 mm)	1·25	1·40
MS297	127×113 mm. Nos. 293/6	2·75	3·25

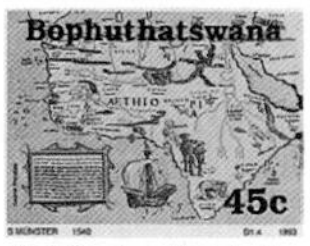

67 Sebastian Munster's Map (from edition of Ptolemy), 1540

1993. Old Maps (3rd series). Multicoloured.

298	45c. Type **67**	50	50
299	65c. Jacopo Gastaldi's map, 1564	65	65
300	85c. Map from Mercator's "Atlas", 1595	75	90
301	1r.05 Map from Ortelius's "Theatrum Orbis Terrarum", 1570	90	1·25

68 Crucifixion (Luke 23:33)

1994. Easter. Multicoloured.

302	35c. Type **68**	65	45
303	65c. Soldiers and Jews mocking Jesus (Luke 23:35–36)	95	80
304	85c. Soldier offering Jesus vinegar (Luke 23:36)	1·10	1·25
305	1r.05 Jesus on cross and charge notice (Luke 23:38)	1·60	1·75

Pt. 2, Pt. 3

BOSNIA AND HERZEGOVINA

Turkish provinces administered by Austria from 1878 and annexed by her in 1908. In 1928 it became part of Yugoslavia.

In 1992 Bosnia and Herzegovina declared itself independent. Hostilities subsequently broke out between the Croat, Moslem and Serbian inhabitants, which ultimately led to the establishment of three de facto administrations: the mainly Moslem Bosnian government, based in Sarajevo ; the Croats in Mostar; and the Serbian Republic in Pale. Under the Dayton Agreement in November 1995 the Republic was split between a Moslem-Croat Federation and the Serbian Republic.

A. Austro-Hungarian Military Post.
1879. 100 kreuzer = 1 gulden.
1900. 100 heller = 1 krone.
1993. 100 paras = 1 dinar.
2002. 100 cents = 1 euro.

B. Independent Republic.
I. Sarajevo Government.
1993. 100 paras = 1 dinar.
1997. 100 fennig = 1 mark.

II. Croatian Posts.
1993. 100 paras = 1 Croatian dinar.
1994. 100 lipa = 1 kuna.
1999. 100 feninga (f) = 1 marka (m).

Republika Srpska.
1992. 100 paras = 1 dinar.
1998. 100 fennig = 1 mark.

A. AUSTRO-HUNGARIAN MILITARY POST

1 Value at top

1879

106	**1**	½k. black	28·00	30·00
135	**1**	1k. grey	6·50	1·50
136	**1**	2k. yellow	4·00	65
137	**1**	3k. green	6·50	1·60
146	**1**	5k. red	6·50	80
139	**1**	10k. blue	9·25	1·20
140	**1**	15k. brown	8·25	4·50
141	**1**	20k. green	9·00	5·25
142	**1**	25k. purple	10·50	8·50

2 Value at bottom

1900

148	**2**	1h. black	45	15
149	**2**	2h. grey	45	15
151	**2**	3h. yellow	45	15
152	**2**	5h. green	40	10
154	**2**	6h. brown	60	20
155	**2**	10h. red	40	10
156	**2**	20h. pink	£225	11·00
158	**2**	25h. blue	1·70	40
160	**2**	40h. orange	£325	16·00
161	**2**	50h. purple	1·20	80
173	**2**	30h. brown	£325	11·00

Larger stamps with value in each corner.

162	1k. red	1·50	60
163	2k. blue	2·40	1·90
164	5k. green	5·00	5·75

1901. Black figures of value.

177	20h. pink and black	75	55
178	30h. brown and black	75	55
180	35h. blue and black	1·20	85
181	40h. orange and black	85	85
182	45h. turquoise and black	95	85

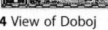

4 View of Doboj

5 In the Carshija (business quarter) Sarajevo

1906

186A	**4**	1h. black	15	15
187A	-	2h. violet	15	15
188A	-	3h. yellow	15	15
189A	-	5h. green	40	10
190A	-	6h. brown	25	30
191A	-	10h. red	45	10
192A	-	20h. brown	95	45
193A	-	25h. blue	2·30	1·60
194A	-	30h. green	2·30	80
195A	-	35h. green	2·30	80
196A	-	40h. orange	2·30	80
197A	-	45h. red	2·30	1·60
198A	-	50h. brown	2·30	1·60
199A	**5**	1k. red	7·00	3·75
200A	-	2k. green	7·75	16·00
201A	-	5k. blue	6·25	9·75

DESIGNS—As Type **4**: 2h. Mostar; 3h. The old castle, Jajce; 5h. Naretva pass and Prenz Planina; 6h. Valley of the Rama; 10h. Valley of the Vrbas; 20h. Old Bridge, Mostar; 25h. The Begova Djamia (Bey's Mosque), Sarajevo; 30h. Post by beast of burden; 35h. Village and lake, Jezero; 40h. Mail wagon; 45h. Bazaar at Sarajevo; 50h. Post car. As Type **5**: 2k. St. Luke's Campanile at Jajce; 5k. Emperor Francis Joseph I.

See also Nos. 359/61.

1910. 80th Birthday of Francis Joseph I. As stamps of 1906 but with date-label at foot.

343	1h. black	70	40
344	2h. violet	70	40
345	3h. yellow	70	40
346	5h. green	75	40
347	6h. brown	1·00	40
348	10h. red	80	15
349	20h. brown	2·50	2·30
350	25h. blue	4·25	3·75
351	30h. green	4·00	3·75
352	35h. green	4·00	3·75
353	40h. orange	4·00	4·50
354	45h. red	6·00	7·25
355	50h. brown	7·50	7·25
356	1k. red	7·50	7·75
357	2k. green	31·00	29·00
358	5k. blue	3·25	9·75

1912. As T **4** (new values and views).

359	12h. blue	5·50	6·50
360	60h. grey	3·00	5·50
361	72h. red	14·50	27·00

DESIGNS: 12h. Jajce; 60h. Konjica; 72h. Vishegrad.

25 Francis Joseph I

26 Francis Joseph I

1912. Various frames. Nos. 378/82 are larger (27×22 mm).

362	**25**	1h. olive	40	15
363	**25**	2h. blue	40	15
364	**25**	3h. lake	40	15
365	**25**	5h. green	40	15
366	**25**	6h. black	40	15
367	**25**	10h. red	40	15
368	**25**	12h. green	55	35
369	**25**	20h. brown	5·00	20
370	**25**	25h. blue	2·50	20
371	**25**	30h. red	2·50	20
372	**26**	35h. green	2·50	20
373	**26**	40h. violet	8·00	20
374	**26**	45h. brown	5·00	35
375	**26**	50h. blue	3·50	20
376	**26**	60h. brown	2·50	20
377	**26**	72h. blue	5·00	5·25
378	**25**	1k. brown on cream	15·00	65
379	**25**	2k. blue on blue	9·00	85
380	**26**	3k. red on green	12·00	11·50
381	**26**	5k. lilac and grey	25·00	29·00
382	**26**	10k. blue on grey	£100	£130

1914. Nos. 189 and 191 surch **1914.** and new value.

383	7h. on 5h. green	60	75
384	12h. on 10h. red	60	75

1915. Nos. 189 and 191 surch **1915.** and new value.

385	7h. on 5h. green	11·00	16·00
386	12h. on 10h. red	40	55

1915. Surch **1915.** and new value.

387	**25**	7h. on 5h. green	85	1·20
388	**25**	12h. on 10h. red	1·90	3·50

1916. Surch **1916.** and new value.

389	7h. on 5h. green	80	80
390	12h. on 10h. red	80	1·00

31

1916. War Invalids' Fund.

391	**31**	5h. (+2h.) green	1·10	1·80
392	-	10h. (+2h.) purple	1·70	2·40

DESIGN: 10h. Blind soldier and girl.
See also Nos. 434/5.

33 Francis Joseph I

34 Francis Joseph I

1916

393	**33**	3h. black	45	35
394	**33**	5h. olive	60	60
395	**33**	6h. violet	60	60
396	**33**	10h. bistre	2·50	3·00
397	**33**	12h. grey	75	95
398	**33**	15h. red	50	25
399	**33**	20h. brown	90	95
400	**33**	25h. blue	80	95
401	**33**	30h. green	80	95
402	**33**	40h. red	80	95
403	**33**	50h. green	80	95
404	**33**	60h. lake	80	95
405	**33**	80h. brown	2·00	80
406	**33**	90h. purple	2·00	1·40
407	**34**	2k. red on yellow	1·20	2·75
408	**34**	3k. green on blue	1·60	4·00
409	**34**	4k. red on green	7·00	16·00
410	**34**	10k. violet on grey	28·00	38·00

1917. War Widows' Fund. Optd **WITWEN-UND WAISENWOCHE 1917.**

411	**33**	10h. (+2h.) bistre	25	35
412	**33**	15h. (+2h.) pink	25	35

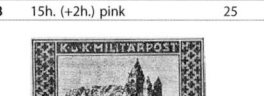

36 Design for Memorial Church, Sarajevo

1917. Assassination of Archduke Ferdinand. Fund for Memorial Church at Sarajevo.

413	**36**	10h. (+2h.) black	25	40
414	-	15h. (+2h.) red	25	40
415	-	40h. (+2h.) blue	25	40

PORTRAITS—HORIZ: 40h. Francis Ferdinand and Sophie. VERT: 15h. Archduke Francis Ferdinand.

39 Emperor Charles

1917

416	**39**	3h. grey	40	30
417	**39**	5h. olive	25	25
418	**39**	6h. violet	1·00	90
419	**39**	10h. brown	40	15
420	**39**	12h. blue	1·10	90
421	**39**	15h. red	25	15
422	**39**	20h. brown	50	25
423	**39**	25h. blue	1·60	80
424	**39**	30h. green	70	40
425	**39**	40h. bistre	60	40
426	**39**	50h. green	1·60	80
427	**39**	60h. red	1·60	80
428	**39**	80h. blue	90	55
429	**39**	90h. lilac	2·00	1·80
430	-	2k. red on yellow	1·50	80
431	-	3k. green on blue	21·00	29·00
432	-	4k. red on green	8·00	20·00
433	-	10k. violet on grey	4·00	21·00

The kronen values are larger (25×25 mm) and with different border.

1918. War Invalids' Fund.

434		10h. (+2h.) green (as No. 392)	1·30	1·70
435	**31**	15h. (+2h.) brown	1·30	1·70

40 Emperor Charles

1918. Emperor's Welfare Fund.

436	**40**	10h. (+10h.) green	80	1·20
437	-	15h. (+10h.) brown	80	1·20
438	**40**	40h. (+10h.) purple	80	1·20

DESIGN—15h. Empress Zita.

1918. Optd **1918.**

439	-	2h. violet (No. 344)	90	2·30
440	**25**	2h. blue	90	1·80

NEWSPAPER STAMPS

N27 Girl in Bosnian Costume

1913. Imperf.

N383	**N27**	2h. blue	65	1·10
N384	**N27**	6h. mauve	2·30	3·50
N385	**N27**	10h. red	2·75	3·50
N386	**N27**	20h. green	3·00	3·75

For these stamps perforated see Yugoslavia, Nos. 25 to 28.

N35 Mercury

1916. For Express.

N411	**N35**	2h. red	55	65
N412	**N35**	5h. green	80	1·00

POSTAGE DUE STAMPS

D4

1904. Imperf. or perf.

D183	**D4**	1h. black, red & yellow	1·20	30
D184	**D4**	2h. black, red & yellow	1·20	30
D185	**D4**	3h. black, red & yellow	1·20	30
D186	**D4**	4h. black, red & yellow	1·20	30
D187	**D4**	5h. black, red & yellow	5·75	30
D188	**D4**	6h. black, red & yellow	1·20	30
D189	**D4**	7h. black, red & yellow	8·25	4·00
D190	**D4**	8h. black, red & yellow	8·25	1·90
D191	**D4**	10h. black, red & yellow	1·60	30
D192	**D4**	15h. black, red & yellow	1·60	30
D193	**D4**	20h. black, red & yellow	11·00	40
D194	**D4**	50h. black, red & yellow	5·50	80
D195	**D4**	200h. black, red & grn	27·00	2·75

D35

1916

D411	**D35**	2h. red	60	1·20
D412	**D35**	4h. red	75	1·20
D413	**D35**	5h. red	1·20	1·20
D414	**D35**	6h. red	55	1·40
D415	**D35**	10h. red	80	1·20
D416	**D35**	15h. red	6·25	9·00
D417	**D35**	20h. red	80	1·40
D418	**D35**	25h. red	2·75	3·50
D419	**D35**	30h. red	2·75	3·50
D420	**D35**	40h. red	31·00	22·00
D421	**D35**	50h. red	70·00	65·00
D422	**D35**	1k. blue	4·00	11·50
D423	**D35**	3k. blue	16·00	43·00

B. Independent Republic.

I. SARAJEVO GOVERNMENT

The following issues were used for postal purposes in those areas controlled by the Sarajevo government.

50 State Arms

1993. Imperf.

450	**50**	100d. blue, lemon & yellow	10	10
451	**50**	500d. blue, yellow & pink	15	15
452	**50**	1000d. ultramarine, yellow and blue	20	20
453	**50**	5000d. blue, yellow & grn	85	85

454 **50** 10000d. blue, lemon & yell 1·70 1·70
455 **50** 20000d. blue, yellow & bis 3·25 3·25
456 **50** 50000d. blue, yellow & grey 8·75 8·75

51 Games Emblem

1994. Tenth Anniv of Winter Olympic Games, Sarajevo. Imperf.
457 **51** 50000d. black and orange 1·20 1·20
MS458 78×65 mm. 100000d. black, orange and lilac; 200000d. black, orange and lilac 9·75 9·75
DESIGNS: 45×27 mm—100000d. Four-man bobsleigh; 200000d. Ice hockey.

52 Koran Illustration

1995. Bairam Festival. Sheet 105×50 mm containing T **52** and similar horiz design. Multicoloured.
MS459 400d. Type **52**; 600d. Koran illustration (different) 11·00 11·00

53 Facade

1995. Sarajevo Head Post Office. Multicoloured.
460 10d. Type **53** 10 10
461 20d. Interior 20 20
462 30d. As No. 461 25 25
463 35d. Before conflict 35 35
464 50d. As No. 463 55 55
465 100d. Present day 1·20 1·20
466 200d. As No. 465 2·40 2·40

54 Historical Map, 10th–15th Centuries

1995. Bosnian History. Multicoloured.
467 35d. Type **54** 55 55
468 100d. 15th-century Bogomil tomb, Oplicici (vert) 1·30 1·30
469 200d. Arms of Kotromanic Dynasty (14th-15th centuries) (vert) 2·40 2·40
470 300d. Charter by Ban Kulin of Bosnia, 1189 3·50 3·50

55 Postman and Globe

1995. World Post Day.
471 **55** 100d. multicoloured 1·10 1·10

56 Dove with Olive Branch

1995. Europa. Peace and Freedom.
472 **56** 200d. multicoloured 3·50 3·50

57 Children and Buildings (A. Softic)

1995. Children's Week.
473 **57** 100d. multicoloured 1·40 1·40

58 Tramcar, 1895

1995. Centenary of Sarajevo Electric Tram System.
474 **58** 200d. multicoloured 2·75 2·75

59 *Simphyandra hofmannii*

1995. Flowers. Multicoloured.
475 100d. Type **59** 1·60 1·60
476 200d. Turk's-head lily 2·75 2·75

60 Dalmatian Barbel Gudgeon

1995. Fish. Multicoloured.
477 100d. Type **60** 1·60 1·60
478 200d. Adriatic minnow 2·75 2·75

61 Kozija Bridge, Sarajevo

1995. Bridges. Multicoloured.
479 20d. Type **61** 20 20
480 30d. Arslanagica Bridge, Trebinje 35 35
481 35d. Latinska Bridge, Sarajevo 45 45
482 50d. Old bridge, Mostar 55 55
483 100d. Visegrad 1·10 1·10

62 Visiting Friends

1995. Christmas. Multicoloured.
484 100d. Type **62** 1·10 1·10
485 200d. Madonna and Child (vert) 2·20 2·20

63 Queen Jelena of Bosnia and Tomb (600th death anniv)

1995. Multicoloured.
486 30d. Type **63** 35 35
487 35d. Husein Kapetan Gradascevic "Dragon of Bosnia" (leader of 1831 uprising against Turkey) 45 45
488 100d. Mirza Safvet Basagic (125th death anniv) (horiz) 1·10 1·10

64 Places of Worship and Graveyards

1995. Religious Pluralism.
489 **64** 35d. multicoloured 80 80

65 Stadium and Sports

1995. Destruction of Olympic Stadium, Sarajevo. Multicoloured.
490 35d. Type **65** 45 45
491 100d. Stadium ablaze (vert) 1·60 1·60

66 Bahrija Hadzic (opera singer)

1996. Europa. Famous Women. Multicoloured.
492 80d. Type **66** 1·30 1·30
493 120d. Nasiha Hadzic (children's writer and radio presenter) 2·00 2·00

67 Child's Handprint

1996. 50th Anniv of UNICEF. Multicoloured.
494 50d. Child stepping on landmine (P. Mirna and K. Princes) 55 55
495 150d. Type **67** 1·60 1·60

68 Bobovac Castle

1996
496 **68** 35d. black, blue and violet 60 60

69 Roofed Fountain and Extract from Holy Koran

1996. Bairam Festival.
497 **69** 80d. multicoloured 1·10 1·10

70 Town Hall

1996. Centenary of Sarajevo Town Hall.
498 **70** 80d. multicoloured 1·10 1·10

71 Hands on Computer Keyboard and Title Page of *Bosanki Prijatelj*

1996. 150th Anniv of Journalists' Association.
499 **71** 100d. multicoloured 1·30 1·30

72 Essen

1996. Essen 96, International Stamp Fair, Essen.
500 **72** 200d. multicoloured 2·50 2·50

73 Running

1996. Centenary of Modern Olympic Games and Olympic Games, Atlanta. Multicoloured.
501 30d. Type **73** 35 35
502 35d. Games emblem 40 40
503 80d. Torch bearer and Olympic flag 85 85
504 120d. Pierre de Coubertin (founder) 1·30 1·30
Nos. 501/4 were issued together, *se-tenant*, with the backgrounds forming a composite design of athletes.

74 *Campanula hercegovina*

1996. Flowers. Multicoloured.
505 30d. Type **74** 40 40
506 35d. *Iris bosniaca* 45 45

75 Barak

1996. Dogs. Multicoloured.
507 35d. Type **75** 45 45
508 80d. Tornjak 85 85

76 Globe, Telephone and Alexander Bell

1996. Anniversaries. Multicoloured.
509 80d. Type **76** (120th anniv of Bell's invention of telephone) 1·00 1·00
510 120d. 1910 50h. stamp (cent of post car in Bosnia and Herzegovina) 1·40 1·40

77 Charter with Seal

1996. Granting of Privileges to Dubrovnik by Ban Stepan II Kotromanic, 1333.
511 **77** 100d. multicoloured 1·20 1·20

78 Hot-air Balloons

1996. SOS Children's Village, Sarajevo.
512 **78** 100d. multicoloured 1·20 1·20

79 Muslim Costume of Bjelasnice

1996. Traditional Costumes. Multicoloured.
513 50d. Type **79** 55 55
514 80d. Croatian 1·10 1·10
515 100d. Muslim costume of Sarajevo 1·60 1·60

80 Bogomil Soldier

1996. Military Uniforms. Multicoloured.

516	35d. Type **80**	45	45
517	80d. Austro-Hungarian rifleman	85	85
518	100d. Turkish light cavalryman	1·10	1·10
519	120d. Medieval Bosnian king	1·40	1·40

81 Mosque

1996. Winter Festival, Sarajevo.

520	**81**	100d. multicoloured	1·20	1·20

82 Map and State Arms

1996. Bosnia Day.

521	**82**	120d. multicoloured	1·40	1·40

83 Crowd around Baby Jesus

1996. Christmas.

522	**83**	100d. multicoloured	1·30	1·30

84 Pope John Paul II

1996. Papal Visit.

523	**84**	500d. multicoloured	7·25	7·25

85 Palaeolithic Rock Carving, Badanj

1997. Archaeological Finds. Multicoloured.

524	35d. Type **85**	45	45
525	50d. Neolithic ceramic head, Butmir	65	65
526	80d. Bronze Age "birds" wagon, Glasinac	1·10	1·10
MS527	100×72 mm. 100, 120d. Walls of Illyrian town of Daorson (composite design)	2·75	2·75

86 Ferhad Pasha Mosque, Banja Luka

1997. Bairam Festival.

528	**86**	200d. multicoloured	2·50	2·50

87 *Clown* (Martina Nokto)

1997. Children's Week.

529	**87**	100d. multicoloured	1·20	1·20

88 Komadina

1997. 72nd Death Anniv of Mujaga Komadina (developer and Mayor of Mostar).

530	**88**	100d. multicoloured	1·20	1·20

89 Trojan Warriors and Map

1997. Europa. Tales and Legends. Multicoloured.

531	100d. Type **89** (theory of Roberto Prays)	1·60	1·60
532	120d. Man on prayer-mat and castle (*The Miraculous Spring of Ajvatovica*)	1·70	1·70

90 *Rainbow Warrior*

1997. 26th Anniv of Greenpeace (environmental organization). Designs showing the *Rainbow Warrior*. Multicoloured.

533	35d. Type **90**	45	45
534	80d. inscr "Dorreboom"	85	85
535	100d. inscr "Beltra"	1·20	1·20
536	120d. inscr "Morgan"	1·40	1·40

91 Open Air Cinema, Sarajevo

1997. Third International Film Festival, Sarajevo.

537	**91**	110d. multicoloured	1·20	1·20

92 Games Emblem

1997. Mediterranean Games, Bari. Multicoloured.

538	40d. Type **92**	45	45
539	130d. Boxing, basketball and kick boxing	1·40	1·40

93 Diagram of Electrons

1997. Anniversaries and Event. Multicoloured.

540	40d. Type **93** (centenary of discovery of electrons)	75	75
541	110d. Vasco da Gama (navigator) and map (500th anniv of science of navigation) (vert)	1·60	1·60
542	130d. Airmail envelope and airplane (Stamp Day)	1·80	1·80
543	150d. Steam locomotive "Bosna" (125th anniv of railway in Bosnia and Herzegovina)	2·00	2·00

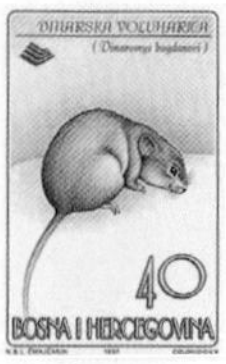

94 Vole

1997. Flora and Fauna. Multicoloured.

544	40d. Type **94**	55	55
545	40d. *Oxytropis prenja*	55	55
546	80d. Alpine newt	1·10	1·10
547	110d. *Dianthus freynii*	1·60	1·60

95 Map and Flags

1997. International Peace Day. Multicoloured.

548	50d. Type **95**	55	55
549	60d. Flags and right half of globe showing Europe and Africa	65	65
550	70d. Flags and left half of globe showing the Americas	75	75
551	110d. Map and flags (including U.S.A. and U.K.)	1·20	1·20

Nos. 548/51 were issued together, *se-tenant*, Nos. 549/50 forming a composite design.

96 House with Attic

1997. Architecture. Multicoloured.

552	40d. Type **96**	45	45
553	50d. Tiled stove and door	55	55
554	130d. Three-storey house	1·40	1·40

97 Sarajevo in 1697 and 1997

1997. 300th Anniv of Great Fire of Sarajevo.

555	**97**	110d. multicoloured	2·40	2·40

98 Augustin Tin Ujevic

1997. Personalities. Multicoloured.

556	1m.30 Type **98** (lyricist and essayist)	1·30	1·30
557	2m. Zaim Imanovic (singer) (vert)	2·20	2·20

99 Sarajevo and Corps Emblem

1997. Contribution of Italian Pioneer Corps in Reconstruction of Sarajevo.

558	**99**	1m.40 multicoloured	1·60	1·60

100 Diana, Princess of Wales, and Roses

1997. Diana, Princess of Wales, Commem.

559	**100**	2m.50 multicoloured	5·50	5·50

101 *Gnijezdo* (Fikret Libovac)

1997. Art. Multicoloured.

560	35f. Type **101**	35	35
561	80f. *Sarajevo Library* (sculpture, Nusret Pasic)	85	85

102 Youth Builders Emblem attached to Route Map

1997. 50th Anniv of Samac-Sarajevo Railway.

562	**102**	35f. multicoloured	45	45

103 Nativity (icon)

1997. Religious Events. Multicoloured.

563	50f. Type **103** (Orthodox Christmas)	65	65
564	1m.10 Wreath on door (Christmas)	1·30	1·30
565	1m.10 Pupils before teacher (14th-century miniature) (Haggadah)	1·30	1·30

104 Giant Slalom, Luge, Two-man Bobsleigh and Speed Skating

1998. Winter Olympic Games, Nagano, Japan. Sheet 78×60 mm containing T **104** and similar vert design. Multicoloured.

MS566	35f. Type **104**; 1m. Games emblem	1·60	1·60

105 Mosque Fountain

1998. Bairam Festival.

567	**105**	1m. multicoloured	1·10	1·10

106 Zvornik

1998. Old Fortified Towns. Multicoloured.

568	35f. Type **106**	55	55
569	70f. Bihac	1·10	1·10
570	1m. Pocitelj	1·40	1·40
571	1m.20 Gradacac	1·60	1·60

107 Muradbegovic

1998. Birth Centenary of Ahmed Muradbegovic (dramatist and actor-director).

572	**107**	1m.50 multicoloured	1·60	1·60

108 Branislav Djurdjev

1998. Former Presidents of the University of Arts and Science. Multicoloured.

573	40f. Type **108**	45	45
574	70f. Alojz Benac	75	75
575	1m.30 Edhem Camo	1·40	1·40

109 White Storks

1998. Endangered Species. The White Stork. Multicoloured.

576	70f. Type **109**	1·10	1·10
577	90f. Two storks flying	1·40	1·40
578	1m.10 Two adult storks on nest	1·50	1·50
579	1m.30 Adult stork with young	1·60	1·60

110 International Theatre Festival, Sarajevo

1998. Europa. National Festivals.

580	**110**	1m.10 multicoloured	2·75	2·75

111 Footballs

1998. World Cup Football Championship, France. Multicoloured.

581	50f. Type **111**	55	55
582	1m. Map of Bosnia and ball	1·10	1·10
583	1m.50 Asim Ferhatovic Hase (footballer)	1·60	1·60

112 Emblem

1998. International League of Humanists World Congress, Sarajevo. Sheet 104×61 mm containing T **112** and two labels.

MS584 **112** 2m. multicoloured 2·20 2·20

113 Common Morel

1998. Fungi. Multicoloured.

585	50f. Type **113**	55	55
586	80f. Chanterelle	85	85
587	1m.10 Edible mushroom	1·20	1·20
588	1m.35 Caesar's mushroom	1·40	1·40

114 Tunnel

1998. Fifth Anniv of Sarajevo's Supply Tunnels.

589	**114**	1m.10 multicoloured	1·10	1·10

115 Eiffel Tower and Underground Train

1998. Paris Metro.

590	**115**	2m. multicoloured	2·20	2·20

116 Henri Dunant (founder of Red Cross)

1998. Anti-tuberculosis Week.

591	**116**	50f. multicoloured	55	55

117 Vesna Misanovic

1998. Bosnian and Herzegovina Chess Teams. Sheet 109×88 mm containing T **117** and similar horiz designs. Multicoloured.

MS592 20f. Type **117** (silver medal, tenth European Team championship, Debrecen, 1992); 40f. Men's team (silver medal winners, 31st Chess Olympiad, Moscow, 1994); 60f. Women's team (32nd Chess Olympiad, Yerevan, 1996); 80f. National team (11th European Team championship, Pula, 1997) 2·20 2·20

118 Travnik

1998. Old Towns.

593	**118**	5f. black and green	10	10
597	-	38f. black and brown	45	45

DESIGN: 38f. Sarajevo.

119 Postal Workers in New Uniforms

1998. World Post Day.

605	**119**	1m. multicoloured	1·10	1·10

120 Lutes

1998. Musical Instruments.

606	**120**	80f. multicoloured	85	85

121 *The Creation of Adam* (detail of fresco on ceiling of Sistine Chapel, Michelangelo)

1998. World Disabled Day.

607	**121**	1m. multicoloured	1·60	1·60

122 Bjelasnica Mountain Range

1998

608	**122**	1m. multicoloured	1·10	1·10

123 People

1998. 50th Anniv of Universal Declaration of Human Rights.

609	**123**	1m.35 multicoloured	1·60	1·60

124 Christmas Tree (Lamija Pehilj)

1998. Christmas and New Year. Multicoloured.

610	1m. Type **124**	1·10	1·10
611	1m.50 Father Andeo Zvizdovic	1·60	1·60

125 Sarajevo University and *Proportion of Man* (Leonardo da Vinci)

1999. Anniversaries. Multicoloured.

612	40f. Type **125** (50th anniv)	45	45
613	40f. Sarajevo High School (120th anniv) (horiz)	45	45

126 Feral Rock Pigeons

1999. Flora and Fauna. Multicoloured.

614	80f. Type **126**	1·10	1·10
615	1m.10 *Knautia sarajevensis*	1·60	1·60

127 Astronaut, Earth and Moon

1999. 30th Anniv of First Manned Moon Landing.

616	**127**	2m. multicoloured	2·20	2·20

128 Slapovi Une

1999. Europa. Parks and Gardens.

617	**128**	2m. multicoloured	3·25	3·25

129 Gorazde

1999

618	**129**	40f. multicoloured	45	45

130 Children playing Football in Sun (Pranjkovic Nenad)

1999. Children's Week.

619	**130**	50f. multicoloured	55	55

131 House

1999. World Environment Day.

620	**131**	80f. multicoloured	85	85

132 Church, Mosque and Emblem

1999. Philexfrance 99, International Stamp Exhibition, Paris, France.

621	**132**	2m. multicoloured	2·20	2·20

133 Sarajevo on Stamp

1999. 120th Anniv of First Bosnia and Herzegovina Stamps.

622	**133**	1m. multicoloured	1·10	1·10

134 Letters encircling Globe and Telephones

1999. 125th Anniv of Universal Postal Union.

623	**134**	1m.50 multicoloured	1·60	1·60

135 Tuzlait from Tuoanj

1999. Minerals. Multicoloured.

624		40f. Type **135**	45	45
625		60f. Siderit from Vitez	65	65
626		1m.20 Hijelofan from Busovaca	1·30	1·30
627		1m.80 Quartz from Srebrenica (vert)	2·00	2·00

136 Dove and Cathedral

1999. Southern Europe Stability Pact, Sarajevo.

628	**136**	2m. multicoloured	2·20	2·20

137 Kursum Medresa, Sarajevo, 1537 (site of library)

1999. Gazi-Husref Library. Multicoloured.

629		1m. Type **137**	1·10	1·10
630		1m.10 Miniature from Hval Codex, 1404	1·20	1·20

138 Koran, 1550

1999

631	**138**	1m.50 multicoloured	1·60	1·60

139 X-Ray and Thermal Image of Hands

1999. Centenary of Radiology in Bosnia and Herzegovina.

632	**139**	90f. multicoloured	1·00	1·00

140 Kresevljakovic

1999. 40th Death Anniv of Hamdija Kresvljakovic (historian).

633	**140**	1m.30 multicoloured	1·40	1·40

141 Chess Emblems and Stars

1999. 15th European Chess Clubs Championship Final, Bugojno.

634	**141**	1m.10 multicoloured	1·20	1·20

142 Twipsy (exhibition mascot)

1999. Expo 2000, World's Fair, Hanover, Germany.

635	**142**	1m. multicoloured	1·10	1·10

143 Painting (Afan Ramic)

1999

636	**143**	1m.20 multicoloured	1·30	1·30

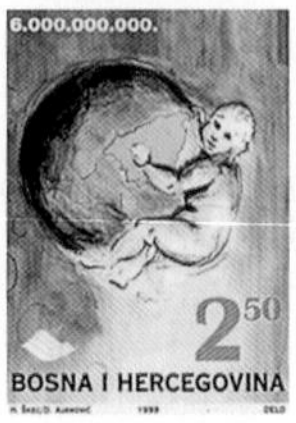

144 Globe and Baby

1999. Birth of World's Six Billionth Inhabitant in Sarajevo.

637	**144**	2m.50 multicoloured	2·75	2·75

145 Bjelasnica Observatory

1999. 105th Anniv of Bjelsnica Meteorological Observatory. Sheet 100×60 mm.

MS638	**145**	1m.10 multicoloured	1·20	1·20

146 Philharmonic Orchestra Building, Sarajevo

1999. International Music Festival, Sarajevo.

639	**146**	40f. black and red	45	45
640	-	1m.10 multicoloured	1·20	1·20

DESIGN: 1m.10, Festival poster.

147 Woman

2000. Bairam Festival.

641	**147**	1m.10 multicoloured	1·20	1·20

148 Map of Bosnia and Herzegovina and Emblem

2000. Olympic Games, Sydney. Sheet 104×72 mm containing T **148** and similar horiz design. Multicoloured.

MS642	1m.30 Type **148**; 1m.70 Map of Australia and stylised sailing boats	3·25	3·25

149 Spaho

2000. 60th (1999) Death Anniv of Mehmed Spaho (politician).

643	**149**	1m. multicoloured	1·10	1·10

150 Morse Apparatus

2000. 50th Anniv of Amateur Radio in Bosnia and Herzegovina.

644	**150**	1m.50 multicoloured	1·60	1·60

151 Illuminated Manuscript

2000. 50th Anniv of Institute of Oriental Studies, Sarajevo University.

645	**151**	2m. multicoloured	2·20	2·20

152 Boracko River

2000. 15th Anniv of Emerald River Nature Protection Organization. Multicoloured.

646		40f. Type **152**	65	65
647		1m. Figure of woman and river (vert)	1·70	1·70

153 Scorpionfish

2000. Greenpeace (environmental organization). Sheet 100×72 mm containing T **153** and similar horiz design. Multicoloured.

MS648	50f. Type **153**; 60f. Crayfish; 90f. Crimson anemone; 1m.50 Wreck of *Rainbow Warrior* (campaign ship)	3·75	3·75

154 Griffon Vulture

2000. Birds. Multicoloured.

649		1m. Type **154**	1·10	1·10
650		1m.50 White spoonbill	1·60	1·60

155 "Building Europe"

2000. Europa.

651	**155**	2m. multicoloured	3·00	3·00

156 Count Ferdinand von Zeppelin and *LZ*-1

2000. Centenary of 1st Zeppelin Flight.

652	**156**	1m.50 multicoloured	1·60	1·60

157 Zenica

2000. Towns. Multicoloured.

653		50f. Type **157**	55	55
654		1m. Mostar	1·10	1·10
655		1m.10 Bihac	1·20	1·20
656		1m.50 Tuzla (vert)	1·60	1·60

158 Millennium

2000. New Millennium. Sheet 100×72 mm containing T **158** and similar multicoloured design.

MS657	80f. Type **158**; 1m.20, Millennium (57×57 mm)	2·20	2·20

159 Vranduk

2000. Towns. Multicoloured.

658		1m.30 Type **159**	1·50	1·50
659		1m.50 Franciscan Abbey, Kraljeva Sutjeska	1·70	1·70

160 Tom Sawyer, Huckleberry Finn (characters) and Twain

2000. *The Adventures of Tom Sawyer* (children's book by Mark Twain).

660	**160**	1m.50 multicoloured	1·60	1·60

161 *People walking* (Ismet Mujezinovic)

2000. Paintings. Multicoloured.

661		60f. Type **161**	65	65
662		80f. *Trees* (Ivo Seremet)	85	85

162 Children and Globe

2000. International Children's Week.

663	**162**	1m.60 multicoloured	1·70	1·70

163 Refugees

2000. 50th Anniv of United Nations Commissioner for Refugees.

664	**163**	1m. multicoloured	1·10	1·10

164 Tesanj

2001. Towns. Multicoloured.

665		10f. Type **164**	10	10
666		20f. Bugojno (horiz)	20	20
667		30f. Konjic (horiz)	35	35
668		35f. Zivinice (horiz)	45	45
669		2m. Cazin (horiz)	2·20	2·20

165 Horse wearing Skirt

2001. Thelma (cartoon character). Sheet 125×170 mm containing T **165** and similar vert designs. Multicoloured.

MS670 30f. Type **165**; 30f. Bear chased by bees; 30f. Cat and boot; 30f. Thelma wet from watering can; 30f. Roast turkey 1·60 1·60

166 Kingfisher (*Alcedo athinis*)

2001. Fauna. Multicoloured.

671		90f. Type **166**	1·30	1·30
672		1m.10 Bohemian waxwing (*Bombycilla garrulous*)	1·40	1·40
673		1m.10 Serbian work horse (*Equus caballus*)	1·40	1·40
674		1m.90 Head of Serbian horse	2·40	2·40

167 Disney

2001. Birth Centenary of Walt Disney (film maker).

675	**167**	1m.10 multicoloured	1·20	1·20

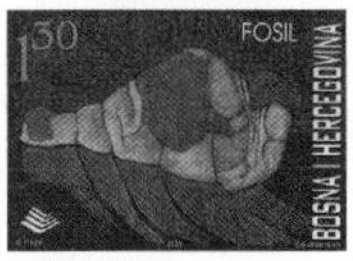

168 Sea Snail

2001. Fossils. Multicoloured.

676		1m.30 Type **168**	1·40	1·40
677		1m.80 Ammonite	1·80	1·80

169 Land and Sea Sports

2001. 14th Mediterranean Games, Tunis.

678	**169**	1m.30 multicoloured	1·40	1·40

170 Swans on Lake

2001. Europa. Water Resources. Sheet 60×81 mm.

MS679 **170** 2m. multicoloured 3·25 3·25

171 Building

2001. Adil Zulfikarpasic Foundation Bosniak Institute (inter-denominational foundation). Sheet 81×50 mm.

MS680 **171** 1m.10 multicoloured 1·20 1·20

172 Balic

2001. Emir Balic (bridge diving competition winner). Sheet 66×47 mm.

MS681 **172** 2m. multicoloured 2·20 2·20

173 Ferrari 625 F1 (1954)

2001. Ferrari Racing Cars. Multicoloured.

682		40f. Type **173**	45	45
683		60f. Ferrari 312 B (1970)	65	65
684		1m.30 Ferrari 312 T3 (1978)	1·40	1·40
685		1m.70 Ferrari 126 C3 (1983)	1·80	1·80

174 Zeljeznicar, Sarajevo Football Team

2001. National Football Champions, 2001.

686	**174**	1m. multicoloured	1·20	1·20

175 Ink Well, Quill Pen, Medal and Dove

2001. Centenary of First Nobel Prize.

687	**175**	1m.50 multicoloured	1·70	1·70

176 Charlie Chaplin

2001. Charlie Chaplin Commemoration.

688	**176**	1m.60 multicoloured	1·90	1·90

177 *Traces* (Edin Numankadic)

2001. Art. Multicoloured.

689		80f. Type **177**	1·20	1·20
690		2m. *David* (detail) (sculpture)	2·30	2·30

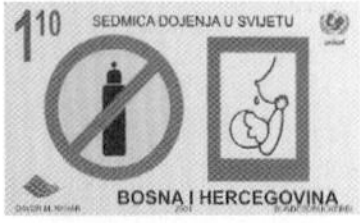

178 Feeding Bottle enclosed in Stop Sign and Baby at Breast

2001. International Breastfeeding Week.

691	**178**	1m.10 multicoloured	1·40	1·40

179 Acropolis, Castle and Pyramid

2001. United Nations Year of Dialogue Among Civilizations.

692	**179**	1m.30 multicoloured	1·60	1·60

180 Horse-drawn Tram

2001. Posteurop Plenary, Sarajevo.

693	**180**	1m.10 multicoloured	1·40	1·40

181 Alija Bejtic and Monument

2001. 20th Death Anniv of Alija Bejtic (cultural historian).

694	**181**	80f. multicoloured	95	95

182 Albert Einstein and Formula

2001. 80th Anniv of Albert Einstein's Nobel Prize for Physics (photoelectric effect).

695	**182**	1m.50 multicoloured	1·70	1·70

183 Davorin Popovic

2002. First Death Anniv of Davorin Popovic (musician).

696	**183**	38f. multicoloured	60	60

184 Bridge, Figure and Books

2002. 350th Birth Anniv of Mustafa Ejubovic (Sejh Jujo) (writer).

697	**184**	1m. multicoloured	1·20	1·20

185 Juraj Neidhardt

2002. Birth Centenary (2001) of Juraj Neidhardt (architect).

698	**185**	1m. multicoloured	1·20	1·20

186 Sevala Zidzic

2002. Birth Centenary (2003) of Sevala Zidzic (first female Bosnian doctor).

699	**186**	1m.30 multicoloured	1·70	1·70

187 Skier

2002. Sarajevo's Candidacy for Winter Olympic Games, 2010.

700	**187**	1m.50 multicoloured	1·80	1·80

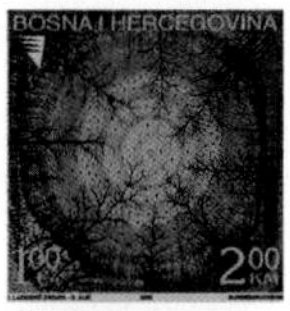

188 Trees

2002. International Earth Day.

701	**188**	2m. multicoloured	2·40	2·40

189 Scout Camp

2002. 80th Anniv of Bosnian Scouts.

702	**189**	1m. multicoloured	1·20	1·20

190 Gentian (*Gentiana dinarica*)

2002. Flora. Multicoloured.

703		1m. Type **190**	1·40	1·40
704		1m.50 Aquilegia (*Aquilegia dinarica*)	2·20	2·20

191 *War and Peace* (Asad Nuhanovic)

2002. Tenth Anniv of Independence.

705	**191**	2m.50 multicoloured	3·50	3·50

192 Apollo (*Parnassius Apollo*)

2002. Butterflies. Multicoloured.

706		1m.50 Type **192**	1·80	1·80
707		2m.50 Scarce swallowtail (*Iphiclides podalirius*)	3·50	3·50

193 Firemen fighting Fire

2002. 120th Anniv of Sarajevo Fire Brigades. Sheet 68×48 mm.

MS708	**193**	2m.20 multicoloured	3·00	3·00

194 Clown

2002. Europa. Circus.

709	**194**	2m.50 multicoloured	3·50	3·50

195 Boy wearing Gag

2002. Letter Writing Campaign. Sheet 120×105 mm containing T **195** and similar vert designs showing scenes from *Young Philatelists* (animated film). Multicoloured.

MS710 40f. Type **195**; 40f. Boy with burnt face; 40f. Boy hit by frying pan; 40f. Boy hit by hammer; 40f. Boy hit with saucepan lids		3·25	3·25

196 Cevapcici (traditional dish)

2002

711	**196**	1m.10 multicoloured	1·70	1·70

197 Galley

2002. Roman Ships. Sheet 90×54 mm containing T **197** and similar horiz design. Multicoloured.

MS712 1m.20 Type **197**; 1m.80 Galleon		4·00	4·00

198 White Water Rafting

2002. 30th Anniv of Una International Regatta.

713	**198**	1m.30 multicoloured	1·90	1·90

199 Association Emblem

2002. Centenary of Napredak (Croatian cultural association).

714	**199**	1m. multicoloured	1·50	1·50

200 Mountaineer and Hut

2002. 110th Anniv of Mountaineering Association.

715	**200**	1m. multicoloured	1·50	1·50

201 Synagogue

2002. Centenary of Ashkenazi Synagogue, Sarajevo.

716	**201**	2m. multicoloured	3·00	3·00

202 Metal Worker

2002. Traditional Crafts. Sheet 110×75 mm containing T **202** and similar horiz designs. Multicoloured.

MS717 80f. Type **202**; 1m.10 Leather worker; 1m 20 Filigree jewellery; 1m.30 Lace work		6·50	6·50

203 Bosnia and Herzegovina Flag

2002

718	**203**	1m. multicoloured	1·50	1·50

204 Coin and Map of Europe

2002. "The Euro" (European currency).

719	**204**	2m. multicoloured	3·00	3·00

205 Tvrtka I Coin (1376-1391)

2002. Old Coins.

720	**205**	20f. grey, red and black	25	25
721	-	30f. green, red and black	40	40
722	-	50f. blue, red and black	65	65

DESIGNS: 20f. Type **205**; 30f. Stepana Tomasa coin (1443-1461); 50f. Stepana Tomasevita coin (1461-1463).

206 Mother and Child Institute, Sarajevo

2002

723	**206**	38f. multicoloured	65	65

207 Horse's Head

2002. Art. Multicoloured.

724	40f. Type **207**	65	65
725	1m.10 Portrait of a woman (25×42 mm)	1·70	1·70
726	1m.50 Sculpture and portrait of two women (42×25 mm)	2·30	2·30

208 Mak Dizdar

2002. 85th Birth Anniv of Mak Dizdar (poet).

727	**208**	1m. multicoloured	1·50	1·50

209 Emaciated Man

2002. Anti-Drugs Campaign.

728	**209**	1m. multicoloured	25	25

210 Josip Stadler

2003. 160th Birth Anniv of Josip Stadler (first archbishop).

729	**210**	50f. multicoloured	65	65

A stamp of the same design was issued by Bosnia and Herzegovina Croatian Posts.

211 Musician

2003. Centenary of Bosnian Cultural Union "Preporod".

730	**211**	1m. multicoloured	1·30	1·30

212 Stylized Skier

2003. European Nordic Skiing Competition, Sarajevo (2006).

731	**212**	1m. multicoloured	1·30	1·30

213 "Mother and Child"

2003. Birth Centenary of Omer Mujadzic (artist).

732	**213**	70f. multicoloured	1·10	1·00

214 Svetozar Zimonjic

2003. 75th Birth Anniv of Svetozar Zimonjic (president of Sciences and Arts Academy).

733	**214**	90f. multicoloured	1·30	1·30

215 Edelweiss (*Leontopodium alpinium*)

2003. Flowers. Multicoloured.

734	90f. Type **215**	1·30	1·30
735	90f. Yellow gentian (*Gentiana symphyandra*)	1·30	1·30

216 Team Members

2003. National Volleyball Team—World Champions, 2002.

736	**216**	1m. multicoloured	1·70	1·50

217 Butterflies

2003. Europa. Poster Art.

737	**217**	1m. multicoloured	4·25	3·75

218 Pope John Paul II and Ivan Merz

2003. Second Visit of Pope John Paul II.

738	**218**	1m.50 multicoloured	2·50	2·30

A stamp of the same design was issued by Bosnia and Herzegovina Croatian Posts.

219 Stylized DNA

2003. 50th Anniv of the Discovery of DNA (genetic material).

739	**219**	50f. multicoloured	75	65

220 Man on Rooftop

2003. Letter Writing Campaign. Sheet 116×73 mm containing T **220** and similar horiz designs showing scenes from *The Sleep of Monsters* (graphic novel by Enki Bilal). Multicoloured.

MS740 50f.×4, Type **220**; Flying taxi; Man and woman (37×25 mm); Faces (37×25 mm)		3·00	2·75

221 Arches, Cekrelci Muslihudin Mosque

2003. Architecture. Multicoloured.

741	1m. Type **221**	2·30	2·30
742	2m. Hajji Sinan Dervish Convent, Sarajevo (30×30 mm)	4·75	4·75

222 *Skakavac Waterfall* (Helena Skec)

2003

743	**222**	1m.50 multicoloured	3·50	3·50

223 Children

2003. Children's Week. Ordinary gum or Self-adhesive gum.

744	**223**	50f. multicoloured	1·00	1·00

224 Alija Izetbegovic

2003. Alija Izetbegovic (first president) Commemoration. Sheet 68×52 mm.

MS746 **224**	2m. multicoloured	4·75	4·75

225 Lamps and Clock

2003. 90th Anniv of Post Building, Sarajevo. Sheet 80×65 mm.

MS747 **225**	3m. multicoloured	7·00	7·00

226 Chamois (*Rupicapra rupicapra*)

2003. Fauna. Multicoloured.

748	30f. Type **226**	80	80
749	50f. Grizzly bear (*Ursus arctos*)	1·20	1·20

227 *Plemenitas II* (Dzevad Hozo)

2003

750	**227**	10f. multicoloured	1·00	1·00

228 Sleigh and Hands holding Present

2003. Christmas.

751	**228**	20f. multicoloured	1·00	1·00

229 Orville and Wilbur Wright and Wright *Flyer I*

2003. Centenary of Powered Flight.

752	**229**	1m. multicoloured	2·40	2·40

230 Allegorical Painting

2003. 65th Birth Anniv of Ibrahim Ljubovic (artist).

753	**230**	1m.50 multicoloured	3·75	3·75

231 Bird

2004. Bayram Festival.

754	**231**	50f. multicoloured	1·30	1·30

232 Kulin on Horseback

2004. 800th Anniv of Reign of Kulin Ban (king).

755	**232**	50f. multicoloured	1·20	1·20

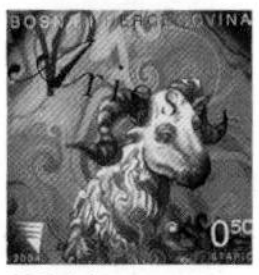

233 Aries

2004. Western Zodiac. Multicoloured. (a) Self-adhesive.

756	50f. Type **233**	95	95
757	50f. Taurus	95	95
758	50f. Gemini	95	95
759	50f. Cancer	95	95
760	50f. Leo	95	95
761	50f. Virgo	95	95
762	50f. Libra	95	95
763	50f. Scorpio	95	95
764	50f. Sagittarius	95	95
765	50f. Capricorn	95	95
766	50f. Aquarius	95	95
767	50f. Pisces	95	95

(b) Ordinary gum.

MS768	200×130 mm. 50f.×12, Nos. 756/67	14·00	14·00

234 Hearts

2004. St. Valentine's Day.

769	**234**	2m. multicoloured	4·75	4·75

235 Gloved Hand holding Torch

2004. 20th Anniv of Winter Olympics, Sarajevo.

770	**235**	1m.50 multicoloured	3·50	3·50

236 Jajce

2004. Towns. Multicoloured.. Multicoloured..

770a	10f. Breko (horiz)	40	40
771	20f. Type **236**	60	60
771a	20f. Livno (horiz)	60	60
771b	30f. Vissoko	80	80
772	50f. Jablanica (horiz)	1·20	1·20
771c	1m. Sanski Most	2·30	2·30
773	2m. Stolac (horiz)	4·75	4·75
774	4m. Gradacac	9·25	9·25
775	5m. Fojinca (horiz)	11·50	11·50

237 *Cattleya intermedia*

2004. Orchids. Multicoloured.

780	1m.50 Type **237**	4·00	4·00
781	2m. *Brassavola*	5·00	5·00

Nos. 780/1 were issued in *se-tenant* pairs within the sheet and were impregnated with the scent of orchid.

238 *Aloe barbardensis*

2004. Succulents. Multicoloured.

782	1m.50 Type **238**	4·00	4·00
783	2m. *Carnegiea gigantean*	5·00	5·00

239 Centenary Emblem

2004. Centenary of FIFA (Federation Internationale de Football Association).

784	**239**	2m. multicoloured	4·75	4·75

240 Alarm Clock on Skis

2004. Europa. Holidays. Multicoloured.

785	1m. Type **240**	2·30	2·30
786	1m.50 Alarm clocks on beach	3·50	3·50

241 Speech Bubbles

2004. European Youth Peace Conference, Sarajevo.

787	**241**	1m.50 multicoloured	3·75	3·75

242 Clown holding Balloons

2004. Greetings Stamps. Multicoloured.

788	50f. Type **242** (birthday)	95	95
789	1m. Bride and bridegroom (wedding)	3·25	3·25

243 Bee on Flower

2004. Bees. Sheet 100×50 mm containing T **243** and similar horiz design. Multicoloured.

MS790	2m.×2, Type **243**; Flying bee	8·75	8·75

244 *Old Bridge, Mostar* (painting)

2004. Reconstruction of Mostar Bridge. Multicoloured.

791	50f. Type **244**	1·20	1·20
792	100f. Bridge (different)	2·30	2·30
MS793	287×110 mm. Nos. 791/2	3·50	3·50

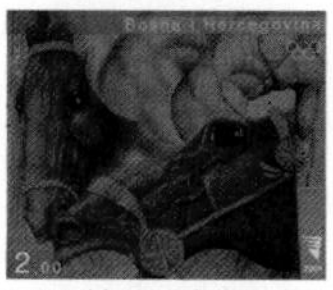

245 Athlete and Horses' Heads

2004. Olympic Games, Athens. Sheet 101×71 mm.

MS794 **245**	2m. multicoloured	4·75	4·75

246 "10" in Lights

2004. Tenth International Film Festival, Sarajevo.

795	**246**	1m.50 vermilion, yellow and black	3·50	3·50

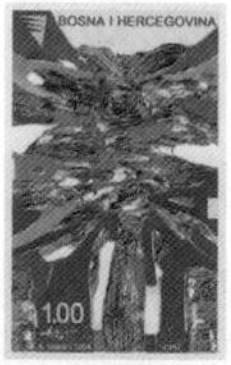

247 Abstract

2004. New Year.

796	**247**	1m. multicoloured	2·30	2·30

248 Svrzo House (18th-century Ottoman house)

2004. Cultural Heritage. Houses. Multicoloured.

797	1m. Type **248**	2·40	2·40
798	1m. Despic house (Serbian merchant's house)	2·40	2·40

249 Emblem, "50" and "@"

2004. 50th Anniv of European Cultural Convention.

799	**249**	1m.50 multicoloured	3·50	3·50

250 *Prozori* (window) (Safet Zec)

2004. Art.
800 **250** 2m. multicoloured 4·75 4·75

251 Nikola Sop

2004. Birth Centenary of Nikola Sop (writer).
801 **251** 3m. multicoloured 7·00 7·00

252 Auditorium

2005. 50th Anniv of Chamber Theatre 55.
802 **252** 40f. multicoloured 1·00 1·00

253 Dam

2005. 50th Anniv of Jablanica Hydroelectric Power Plant.
803 **253** 60f. multicoloured 1·40 1·40

254 Electric Tram

2005. 110th Anniv of Electrification and First Electric Tram.
804 **254** 2m. multicoloured 4·75 4·75

255 Izet Sarajlic

2005. 75th Birth Anniv of Izet Sarajlic (writer).
805 **255** 1m. multicoloured 2·30 2·30

256 Hasan Kickic

2005. Birth Centenary of Hasan Kickic (writer).
806 **256** 1m.50 multicoloured 3·50 3·50

257 *Rosa damascene*

2005. Roses. Multicoloured.
807 80f. Type **257** 1·60 1·60
808 1m.20 *Rosa alba* 2·30 2·30

258 Baklava

2005. Europa. Gastronomy. Multicoloured.
809 2m. Type **258** 3·50 3·50
810 2m. Sogon Dolma (stuffed onions) 3·50 3·50
MS811 115×88 mm. Nos. 809/10 7·00 7·00

The stamps and margin of No. **MS**811 form a composite design of a table laid with food.

259 Partridge (inscr "Tatro urogallus")

2005. Fauna. Multicoloured.
812 2m. Type **259** 3·50 3·50
813 3m. Beaver (*Castor fiber*) 5·25 5·25

260 Sportsmen

2005. Mediterranean Games, Almeria.
814 **260** 1m. multicoloured 1·80 1·80

261 Composers and Building Facade

2005. 50th Anniv of Sarajevo Music Academy.
815 **261** 1m. multicoloured 1·80 1·80

262 Grieving Women

2005. Tenth Anniv of Srebrenica Massacre.
816 **262** 1m. multicoloured 1·80 1·80

263 Sarajevo and Doha

2005
817 **263** 2m. multicoloured 3·50 3·50

A stamp of the same design was issued by Qatar.

264 Emblem and Post Van (EMS)

2005. Postal Service. Multicoloured.
818 10f. Type **264** 45 45
819 20f. Emblem and sorter (hybrid mail) 60 60
820 30f. Emblem and "IZBOR JE VAS!" (door to door) 75 75
821 50f. Emblem and pigeons (philately) 1·00 1·00

265 *Pyrus communis*

2005. Fruit. Multicoloured.
822 1m. Type **265** 2·10 2·10
823 1m.50 Orange (inscr "Orange carica") 3·25 3·25
824 2m. *Ficus carica* 4·25 4·25
825 2m.50 *Prunus domestica* 5·25 5·25
826 5m. Cherry (inscr "Prunus avium") 10·50 10·50

266 Column and Garden (Hakija Kulenovic)

2005. Birth Centenary of Hakija Kulenovic (artist).
827 **266** 2m. multicoloured 4·75 4·75

267 Dogs and Girl

2005. Youth Stamps. Sheet 96×72 mm containing T **267** and similar vert design. Multicoloured.
MS828 50f.×2, Type **267**; Hedgehog windsurfing 2·40 2·40

268 Trade Union Building

2005. Centenary of Trade Unions.
829 **268** 1m. multicoloured 2·40 2·40

269 Stylized Buildings

2005. Plehan Monastery.
830 **269** 1m. multicoloured 2·40 2·40

270 Aladza Mosque, Foca

2005. Cultural Heritage. Multicoloured.
831 1m. Type **270** 2·40 2·40
832 1m. Zitomislici Monastery 2·40 2·40

271 King Tvrtko Kotromanic

2005. History. Bogomils. Multicoloured.
833 50f. Type **271** 1·20 1·20
834 50f. Kulin Ban 1·20 1·20
835 1m. Burning man (Inquisition) (stone plaque) 2·30 2·30
836 2m. Eugene IV's Papal Bull (1439) 4·75 4·75

272 Decorated Salon

2005. Bosnia Institute. Multicoloured.
837 70f. Type **272** 1·60 1·60
838 4m. Exhibition 9·25 9·25

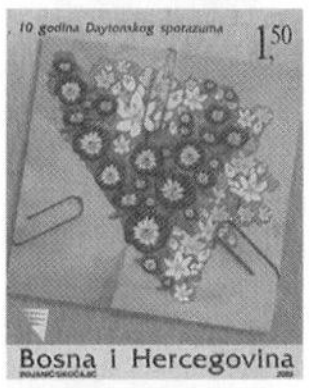

273 Flowers over map

2005. 10th Anniv of Dayton Agreement.
839 **273** 1m.50 multicoloured 3·50 3·50

274 Emblem

2005. 60th Anniv of End of World War II.
840 **274** 1m. multicoloured 2·40 2·40

275 Members' Flags and Globe (left)

2005. 50th Anniv of Europa Stamps. Multicoloured.
841 3m. Type **275** 5·00 5·00
842 3m. Globe (right) and members flags 5·00 5·00
843 3m. Euro coin and map of Europe 5·00 5·00
844 3m. Stars and 1999 chess championships emblem 5·00 5·00
MS845 104×76 mm. Nos. 841/4 19·00 19·00

Nos. 841/2 were issued together, *se-tenant*, forming a composite design.

276 Faces

2005. World Vision. People with Special Needs Week.
846 **276** 50f. multicoloured 1·60 1·60

277 Slalom Skier

2006. Winter Olympic Games, Turin. Sheet 88×77 mm containing T **277** and similar horiz design. Multicoloured.
MS847 1m. Type **277**; 2m. Speed skaters 7·00 7·00

278 Treskavica Mountains, Trnovo

2006. Tourism. Multicoloured.
848 1m. Type **278** 2·30 2·30
849 1m. Rafting, Goradzde (vert) 2·30 2·30

279 Mercedes Benz 500K Cabriolet B, 1935

2006. Cars. Sheet 104×76 mm containing T **279** and similar horiz designs. Multicoloured.

MS850 50f.×2 Type **279**; Dodge D11 Graber Cabriolet, 1939; 1m. Mercedes Benz SS Schwarzer, 1929; 2m. Bugatti T 57 Ventoux, 1939	9·50	9·50

280 Crowd

2006. Europa. Integration. Multicoloured.

851	2m. Type **280**	5·00	5·00
852	2m. Crowd (different)	5·00	5·00
MS853	115×87 mm. 2m.×2, As Type **280**; As No. 852	16·00	16·00

281 *Formica rufa*

2006. Fauna and Flora. Multicoloured.

854	1m.50 Type **281**	3·50	3·50
855	3m. *Sarcosphaera crassa*	7·00	7·00

282 Prisoners and Barbed Wire

2006. Prisoner of War Day.

856	**282**	1m. multicoloured	2·40	2·40

283 Gallery Facade

2006. 60th Anniv of National Art Gallery.

857	**283**	1m. multicoloured	2·40	2·40

284 Illustration from *Zenidba nosaca Samuela*

2006. Isak Samokovlija (writer) Commemoration.

858	**284**	1m. multicoloured	2·40	2·40

284a Mohamed Kadic

2006. Birth Centenaries. Multicoloured.

858a	1m. Type **284a**	2·40	2·40
858b	1m. Mustafa Kamaric	2·40	2·40

285 Team Members

2006. Football Event and Anniversary. Multicoloured.

859	1m. Type **285** (60th anniv of Sarajevo Football Club)	2·40	2·40
860	3m. Player, globe and flags (World Cup Football Championship, Germany)	7·00	7·00

286 Potatoes

2006. Vegetables. Multicoloured.

861	10f. Type **286**	60	60
862	20f. Cauliflower	80	80
863	30f. Savoy cabbage	95	95
864	40f. Green cabbage	1·20	1·20
865	1m. Carrots	2·50	2·50

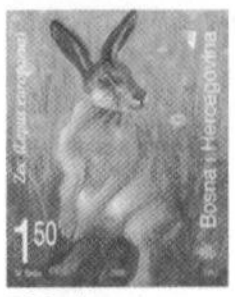
286a *Lepus europaeus*

2006. Fauna. Multicoloured.

866	1m.50 Type **286a**	3·50	3·50
867	2m. *Capreolus capreolus*	4·75	4·75
868	2m.50 *Anas* (mallard) (horiz)	5·75	5·75
869	4m. *Vulpes vulpes*	9·25	9·25
870	5m. *Canis lupus* (horiz)	11·50	11·50

287 Emblem

2006. European Junior Table Tennis Championship.

871	**287**	1m. multicoloured	2·40	2·40

288 Basilica, Breza

2006. Cultural—Historical Heritage. Multicoloured.

872	1m. Type **288**	2·40	2·40
873	1m. Semiz Ali Pasha's Mosque, Praca (vert)	2·40	2·40

289 Orange Bird

2006. Youth Philately. Sheet 115×88 mm containing T **289** and similar vert design. Multicoloured.

MS874	50f.×2, Type **289**; Yellow bird	4·75	4·75

290 Girl

2006. Children's Week. Stop Violence against Children Campaign. Self-adhesive.

875	**290**	50f. multicoloured	1·20	1·20

291 School Building

2006. 300th Anniv of Muslim Secondary School, Travnik.

876	**291**	1m. multicoloured	2·40	2·40

292 Vladimir Prelog (Chemistry, 1975)

2006. Nobel Prize Winners. Multicoloured.

877	1m. Type **292**	2·40	2·40
878	2m.50 Iro Andric (Literature, 1961)	5·75	5·75

293 Emblem

2006. 30th Anniv of Tuzli University.

879	**293**	1m. multicoloured	2·40	2·40

294 Museum Exhibits

2006

880	**294**	1m. multicoloured	2·40	2·40

295 Steam Locomotive

2006. Railways. Multicoloured.

881	50f. Type **295**	1·20	1·20
882	1m. Modern locomotive	2·40	2·40

296 Sheep

2007. Domestic Animals. Multicoloured.

883	10f. Type **296**	60	60
884	20f. Goat	80	80
885	30f. Cow	95	95
886	40f. Donkey	1·20	1·20
887	70f. Horse (42×35 mm)	1·90	1·90
888	1m. Cat (42×35 mm)	2·40	2·40

297 Arms

2007. 60th Anniv of National Opera Theatre.

889	**297**	50f. multicoloured	1·30	1·30

298 Scouts

2007. Europa. Centenary of Scouting. Multicoloured.

890	2m. Type **298**	4·75	4·75
891	2m. Scouts by campfire	4·75	4·75

299 Prokos Lake

2007. Tourism.

892	**299**	2m.50 multicoloured	6·00	6·00

300 *Knautia travnicensis*

2007. Fauna and Flora. Multicoloured.

893	80f. Type **300**	1·70	1·70
894	1m.20 *Sciurus vulgaris* (squirrel) (horiz)	3·00	3·00

301 Kozarac

2007. Tourism.

895	**301**	1m. multicoloured	2·40	2·40

302 Building Facade

2007. 140th Anniv of Cazin Madrasah (Islamic school).

896	**302**	2m. multicoloured	4·75	4·75

302a Fountain, Tuzla

2007. Fountains. Multicoloured.

897	1m.50 Type **302a**	3·50	3·50
898	2m. Mostar	4·75	4·75
899	2m.50 Sanski Most	5·75	5·75
900	4m. Sebilj, Sarajevo (horiz)	9·25	9·25
901	5m. Fountain, Bey's Mosque	11·50	11·50

303 Masthead

2007. Centenary of Gajret Periodical.

902	**303**	1m. multicoloured	2·40	2·40

304 Courtyard

2007. 30th Anniv of Islamic Science Faculty, Sarajevo.

903	**304**	2m. multicoloured	4·75	4·75

305 Front Elevation

2007. Gazi Husrev-Begova Library.

904	**305**	1m.50 multicoloured	3·50	3·50

306 *Landscape* (Ismet Rizvic)

2007. Art. Multicoloured.

905		1m. Pocitelj Visual Art Colony	2·40	2·40
906		1m.50 Type **306**	3·50	3·50

307 '140' and Stylised Building

2007. 140th Anniv of Abdulah Nakas Hospital.

907	**307**	1m.50 red and silver	3·50	3·50

308 Bear Figurine

2007. Museum Exhibit.

908	**308**	1m. multicoloured	2·40	2·40

309 Buildings and Karel Parik

2007. 150th Birth Anniv of Karel Parik (architect).

909	**309**	2m.50 multicoloured	6·00	6·00

310 Combatants

2007. Karate.

910	**310**	1m. multicoloured	2·40	2·40

311 *Self Portrait* (Zuko Dzumhur)

2007. Zuko Dzumhur (artist, writer and caricaturist).

911	**311**	1m. multicoloured	2·40	2·40

312 Building Facade

2007. 60th Anniv of Medical Faculty of Sarajevo University.

912	**312**	1m. multicoloured	2·40	2·40

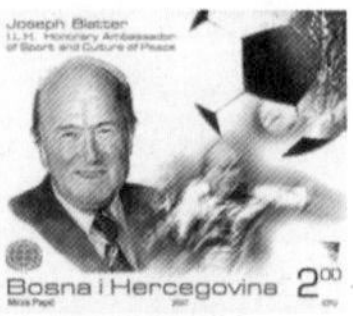

313 Joseph Blatter

2007. Honorary Ambassadors for Sport and Culture of Peace. Multicoloured.

913		2m. Type **313**	4·50	4·50
914		2m. Juan Antonio Samaranch (41×27 mm)	4·50	4·50

314 Heart (Amira Halilovic)

2007. Ecology. Children's Drawings. Multicoloured.

915		50f. Type **314**	1·30	1·30
916		50f. Couple holding globe (Maida Hasanic)	1·30	1·30
MS916a		75×95 mm. Nos. 915/16	2·50	2·50

315 Fortress, Samobor

2007. Cultural Heritage.

917	**315**	1m. multicoloured	2·40	2·40

316 Meat Pie

2007. Gastronomy.

918	**316**	2m. multicoloured	4·75	4·75

317 Stegosaurus

2007. Pre-History. Dinosaurs.

919	**317**	2m. multicoloured	5·00	5·00

318 Laika

2007. 50th Anniv of Space Exploration.

920	**318**	3m. multicoloured	7·00	7·00

319 Emblem

2007. 60th Anniv of University Sports Association.

921	**319**	50f. multicoloured	1·40	1·40

320 Player

2007. 60th Anniv of Bosnia Handball Club.

922	**320**	50f. multicoloured	1·30	1·30

321 Emblem

2008. 95th Anniv of Merhamet (Muslim charitable society).

923	**321**	70f. multicoloured	1·80	1·80

321a College Campus (image scaled to 56% of original size)

2008. 35th Anniv of College of Pharmacy.

923a	**321a**	2m. multicoloured	4·75	4·75

322 Bosanska Krupa

2008. Tourism. Multicoloured.

924		70f. Type **322**	4·75	4·75
925		1m. Velika Kladusa (horiz)	7·00	7·00

323 Shish-Kebab

2008. Gastronomy. Multicoloured.

926		1m. Type **323**	2·40	2·40
927		2m. Stuffed apple	4·75	4·75

324 Building Facade

2008. 50th Anniv of Blood Transfusion Service.

928	**324**	1m.50 multicoloured	3·50	3·50

325 Woman

2008. Centenary of International Women's Day.

929	**325**	2m. multicoloured	4·75	4·75

326 Candle, Quill and Letter

2008. Europa. The Letter. Multicoloured.

930		2m. Type **326**	4·75	4·75
931		3m. Postcard and hand holding pen	7·00	7·00
MS932		88×115 mm. Nos. 930/1	11·50	11·50

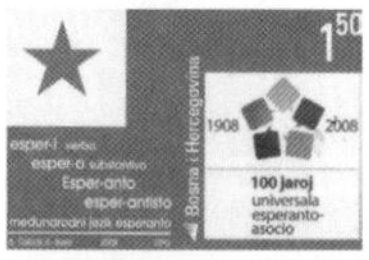

327 Emblem

2008. Centenary of Esperanto.

933	**327**	1m.50 multicoloured	3·50	3·50

328 Anniversary Emblem

2008. 60th Anniv of Shooting Club, Sarajevo.

934	**328**	1m.50 multicoloured	3·50	3·50

329 Judo

2008. Olympic Games, Beijing. Multicoloured.

935		1m. Type **329**	1·80	1·80
936		1m.50 Shot put and athletics	3·50	3·50

330 Oural-3 (M-66)

2008. Motorcycles. Multicoloured.

937		1m.50 Type **330**	3·50	3·50
938		1m.50 Jawa Trail 90	3·50	3·50

331 Vjetrenica Cave

2008. World Heritage Site.

939	**331**	1m. multicoloured	2·40	2·40

332 Signing

2008. Bosnia Hergovina–European Union Stabilization and Association Agreement.

940	**332**	70f. multicoloured	1·80	1·80

333 *Nymphaea alba*

2008. Flora and Fauna. Multicoloured.

941		1m.50 Type **333**	3·50	3·50
942		2m. *Rana esculenta*	4·75	4·75

334 Krivaja Villa, Zavidovici

2008. Cultural Heritage (1st issue).

943	**334**	2m.50 multicoloured	5·75	5·75

335 Musalla (place of prayer), Kamengrad

2008. Cultural Heritage (2nd issue). Multicoloured.

944		1m. Type **335**	2·40	2·40
945		1m.50 Ostrovica (horiz)	3·50	3·50

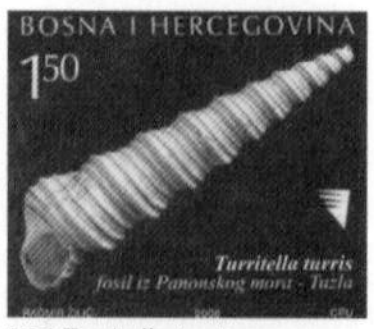

336 Turritella turris

2008. Fossils.

946	**336**	1m.50 multicoloured	3·50	3·50

337 Stylized Symbols of Kuwait and Bosnia Herzgovina (image scaled to 54% of original size)

2008. Bosnia Herzgovina–Kuwait Relations.

947	**337**	3m. multicoloured	7·00	7·00

338 Skier

2008. 80th Anniv of Sarajevo Ski Club.
948 **338** 2m. multicoloured 4·75 4·75

339 Lynx

2008. Flora and Fauna. Multicoloured.

949	5f. Type **339**	1·30	1·30
950	70f. Goshawk (*Accipiter gentilis*)	1·80	1·80
951	70f. Conifer and fields (horiz)	1·80	1·80
952	70f. Birch grove (horiz)	1·80	1·80
953	70f. Conifers and snow-covered chalet (horiz)	1·80	1·80
954	5m. Owl	11·50	11·50

340 Family

2009. International Day of Missing Persons.
955 **340** 20f. black and scarlet 45 45

341 *Hirundo rustica* (barn swallow)

2009
956 **341** 70f. multicoloured 1·80 1·80

342 Documents (image scaled to 37% of original size)

2009. Cultural Heritage. Historical Archives.
957 **342** 70f. multicoloured 1·80 1·80

343 Building Facade

2009. 60th Anniv of Arkus–Seljo Academic Cultural Centre, University of Sarajevo.
958 **343** 1m. multicoloured 2·40 2·40

344 Emblem

2009. 60th Anniv Council of Europe.
959 **344** 1m. multicoloured 2·40 2·40

345 Coffee

2009. Bosnian Gastronomy.
960 **345** 1m. multicoloured 2·40 2·40

346 Museum Emblem

2009. 60th Anniv of Sarajevo Museum.
961 **346** 1m. multicoloured 2·40 2·40

347 Runners

2009. IAAF World Athletics Championships–Berlin 2009. Multicoloured.

962	1m.50 Type **347**	3·50	3·50
963	2m. Stylized figures	4·50	4·50
MS964	106×50 mm. Nos. 962/3	8·00	8·00

348 Charles Darwin and Progression of Humanoids

2009. Birth Bicentenary of Charles Darwin (naturalist and evolutionary theorist).
965 **348** 2m. multicoloured 4·50 4·50

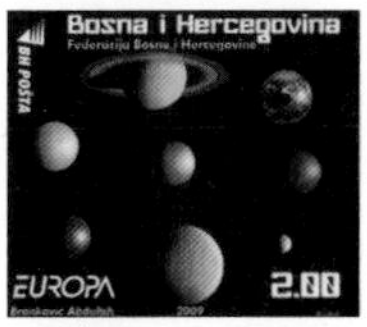

349 Planets

2009. Europa. Astronomy. Multicoloured.

966	2m. Type **349**	4·50	4·50
967	3m. Satellite	7·00	7·00
MS968	114×90 mm. Nos. 966/7	11·50	11·50

350 Family Group

2009. Children's Week.
969 **350** 70f. multicoloured 1·80 1·80

350a Building Facade and Justice

2009. 130th Anniv of Canton Tribunal, Sarajevo.
969a **350a** 1m. multicoloured 2·40 2·40

351 *Viola wittrockiana*

2009. Pansy.
970 **351** 1m. multicoloured 2·40 2·40

352 Gazi Husrev-beg Mosque, Sarajevo and Selimiye Mosque, Edirne

2009. BH Post Sarajevo and Turkish Post Co-operation.
971 **352** 2m. multicoloured 5·00 5·00

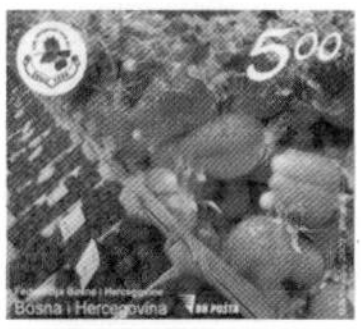

353 Strawberries

2009. Days of Berrylike Fruits Festival, Celic.
972 **353** 5m. multicoloured 11·50 11·50

354 Hands

2009. Sign Language.
973 **354** 1m.50 multicoloured 3·50 3·50

355 St Francis of Assissi

2009. 800th Anniv of Franciscan Order.
974 **355** 1m.50 multicoloured 3·50 3·50

356 Building Facade

2009. Centenary of Franciscan Theology Study Centre.
975 **356** 1m. multicoloured 2·40 2·40

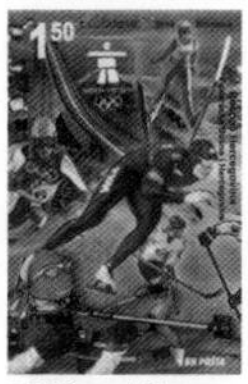

357 Speed Skater and Athletes

2010. Winter Olympic Games, Vancouver. Multicoloured.
MS976 1m.50 Type **357**; 2m. Bobsleigh and other athletes 8·50 8·50

358 Old Town, Srebrenik

2010. Cultural Heritage. Multicoloured.

977	1m. Old Town and Castle, Ostrozac	2·20	2·20
978	70f. Type **358**	2·75	2·75

359 *Taxus baccata* (yew)

2010. Trees. Multicoloured.

979	1m. Type **359**	3·50	3·50
980	1m. *Aesculus hippocastanum* (horse chestnut)	4·50	4·50

360 *Cynus olor* (mute swan)

2010. Water Bird
MS981 **360** 2m. multicoloured 5·50 5·50

361 Wounded Chief watched over by his Sisters

2010. Ballad of Hasanaginica
982 **361** 1m. multicoloured 2·75 2·75

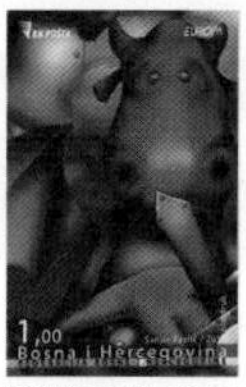

362 Noch the little Dragon

2010. Europa. Multicoloured.

983	1m. Type **362**	3·00	3·00
984	1m.50 Little Blu	4·00	4·00
MS985	67×103 mm. Nos. 982/3	7·00	7·00

Nos. 983/4 were printed, *se-tenant*, forming a composite design.

363 Knight on Horseback (image scaled to 55% of original size)

2010. 500th Anniv of Ajvatovica (Prusac)
986 **363** 1m.50 multicoloured 3·50 3·50

364 Robert Alexander Schumann

2010. Composers' Birth Bicentenaries. Multicoloured.

987	1m. Type **364**	3·00	3·00
988	1m.50 Fryderyk Franciszek (Frédéric) Chopin	3·50	3·50

365 Branches

2011. Europa. Forests. Multicoloured.

989	2m.50 Type **365**	9·00	9·00
990	2m.50 Tree trunk	9·00	9·00
MS991	73×115 mm. Nos. 989/90	18·00	18·00

366 *Gentiana jasnae*

2011. Flora. Gentian
992 **366** 2m. multicoloured 6·00 6·00

367 Yuri Gagarin

2011. 50th Anniv of First Manned Space Flight. Sheet 80×60 mm

MS993	**367**	2m. multicoloured	6·00	6·00

368 368 Virgin Mary (statue), St James Church, Hand holding Rose and Christ (image scaled to 55% of original size)

2011. Medjugorje

994	**368**	2m.50 multicoloured	9·00	9·00

369 *Passer domesticus* (House Sparrow)

2011. Birds. House Sparrow. Sheet 80×60 mm

MS995	**369**	2m.50 multicoloured	9·00	9·00

370 Coat of Arms

2011. Herceg Stjepan's Coat of Arms

996	**370**	1m. multicoloured	3·00	3·00

371 AIDS Ribbon

2011. 30th Anniv of AIDS Prevention Campaign

997	**371**	70f. scarlet-vermilion and black	2·75	2·75

372 Boats (image scaled to 55% of original size)

2011. Hutovo Blato Nature Reserve

998	**372**	70f. multicoloured	2·75	2·75

373 *Astacus astacus*

Fauna. European Crayfish

999	**373**	1m.50 multicoloured	4·00	4·00

374 Skender Kulenović

2011. Personalities. Writers. Multicoloured.

1000		1m. Type **374**	3·00	3·00
1001		1m.50 Meša Selimović	4·00	4·00

II. CROATIAN POSTS

Issues made by the Croat administration in Mostar.

C1 Statue and Church

1993. Sanctuary of Our Lady Queen of Peace Shrine, Medugorje.

C1	**C1**	2000d. multicoloured	1·20	1·20

C2 Silvije Kranjcevic (poet)

1993. Multicoloured.. Multicoloured..

C2		200d. Type **C2**	20	20
C3		500d. Jajce	35	35
C4		1000d. Mostar (horiz)	75	75

C3 Medieval Gravestone

1993. 250th Anniv of Census in Bosnia and Herzegovina.

C5	**C3**	100d. multicoloured	40	40

C4 "Madonna of the Grand Duke" (Raphael)

1993. Christmas.

C6	**C4**	6000d. multicoloured	2·30	2·30

C5 *Uplands in Bloom*

1993. Europa. Contemporary Art. Paintings by Gabrijel Jurkic. Multicoloured.

C7		3500d. Type **C5**	4·75	4·75
C8		5000d. *Wild Poppy*	5·25	5·25

C6 Kravica Waterfall

1993

C9	**C6**	3000d. multicoloured	1·30	1·30

C7 Hrvoje (from *Hrvoje's Missal* by Butko)

1993. 577th Death Anniv of Hrvoje Vukcic Hrvatinic, Duke of Split, Viceroy of Dalmatia and Croatia and Grand Duke of Bosnia.

C10	**C7**	1500d. multicoloured	80	80

C8 Plehan Monastery

1993

C11	**C8**	2200d. multicoloured	85	85

C9 Arms

1994. Proclamation (August 1993) of Croatian Community of Herceg Bosna.

C12	**C9**	10000d. multicoloured	4·00	4·00

C10 Bronze Cross, Rama-Scit (Mile Blazevic)

1994

C13	**C10**	2m.80 multicoloured	1·20	1·20

C 11 *Campanula hercegovina*

1994. Flora and Fauna. Multicoloured.

C14		3m.80 Type **C11**	1·60	1·60
C15		4m. Mountain dog	1·70	1·70

C 12 Hutova Swamp

1994

C16	**C12**	80f. multicoloured	45	45

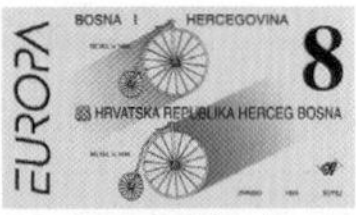

C 13 Penny Farthing Bicycles

1994. Europa. Discoveries and Inventions. Multicoloures.

C17		8m. Type **C13**	4·75	4·75
C18		10m. Mercedes cars, 1901	5·75	5·75

C14 Views of Town and Fortress

1994. 550th Anniv of First Written Record of Ljubuski.

C19	**C14**	1m. multicoloured	50	50

C15 Hospital and Christ

1994. Second Anniv of Dr. Nikolic Franciscan Hospital, Nova Bila.

C20	**C15**	5m. multicoloured	2·00	2·00

C16 Anniversary Emblem

1995. 50th Anniv of UNO. Self-adhesive. Rouletted.

C21	**C16**	1m.50 blue, red & black	60	60

C17 Crib

1995. Christmas.

C22	**C17**	5m.40 multicoloured	2·20	2·20

C18 Franciscan Monastery, Kraljeva Sutjeska

1995

C23	**C18**	3m. multicoloured	1·20	1·20

C 19 Srebrenica

1995. Towns. Multicoloured.

C24		2m. Type **C19**	70	70
C25		4m. Franciscan Monastery, Mostar	1·40	1·40

C20 Christ on the Cross

1995. Europa. Peace and Freedom.

C26	**C20**	6m.50 multicoloured	23·00	23·00

C21 Statue and Church

1996. 15th Anniv of Sanctuary of Our Lady Queen of Peace Shrine, Medugorje.

C27	**C21**	10m. multicoloured	4·75	4·75

C22 Queen Katarina Kosaca Kotromanic

1996. Europa. Famous Women.

C28	**C22**	2m.40 multicoloured	1·90	1·90

C23 Monastery

1996. 150th Anniv of Franciscan Monastery and Church, Siroki Brijeg.

C29	**C23**	1m.40 multicoloured	55	55

C24 Virgin Mary

1996. Self-adhesive.

C30	**C24**	2m. mult (postage)	60	60
C31	**C24**	9m. multicoloured (air)	3·00	3·00

1996. Taipeh '96, International Stamp Exn. Nos. C30/1 surch **1.10** and emblem.

C32		1m.10 on 2m. mult (postage)	45	45
C33		1m.10 on 9m. mult (air)	45	45

C26 *Madonna and Child* (anon)

1996. Christmas.
C34 **C26** 2m.20 multicoloured 90 90

C 27 St. George and the Dragon

1997. Europa. Tales and Legends. Mult.
C35 2m. Type **C27** 95 95
C36 5m. Zeus as bull and Europa (39×34 mm) 2·10 2·10

C28 Pope John Paul II

1997. Papal Visit.
C37 **C28** 3m.60 multicoloured 1·50 1·50
MSC38 90×100 mm. No. 37×4 6·00 6·00

C29 Chapel, Samatorje, Gorica

1997
C39 **C29** 1m.40 multicoloured 55 55

C30 Purple Heron

1997. Flora and Fauna. Multicoloured.
C40 1m. Type **C30** 60 60
C41 2m.40 *Symphyandra hofmannii* (orchid) 1·00 1·00

C31 *Birth of Christ* (fresco, Giotto)

1997. Christmas.
C42 **C31** 1m.40 multicoloured 55 55

C32 Cats

1998. Europa. Animated Film Festival.
C43 **C32** 6m.50 multicoloured 4·50 4·50

C33 Seal

1998. 550th Anniv of Herzegovina.
C44 **C33** 2m.30 red, black and gold 90 90

C34 Livno

1998. 1100th Anniv of Livno.
C45 **C34** 1m.20 multicoloured 55 55

C35 *Sibiraea croatica*

1998
C46 **C35** 1m.40 multicoloured 80 80

C36 Griffon Vulture

1998
C47 **C36** 2m.40 multicoloured 1·10 1·10

C37 Adoration of the Wise Men

1998. Christmas.
C48 **C37** 5m.40 multicoloured 2·20 2·20

C38 Woman, Posavina Region

1999. Regional Costumes.
C49 **C38** 40f. multicoloured 55 55

C39 Ruins of Bobovac

1999. Old Towns.
C50 **C39** 10f. multicoloured 25 25

C40 Simic

1999. Birth Centenary (1998) of Antun Simic (writer).
C51 **C40** 30f. multicoloured 55 55

C41 Blidinje Nature Park

1999. Europa. Parks and Gardens.
C52 **C41** 1m.50 multicoloured 4·00 4·00

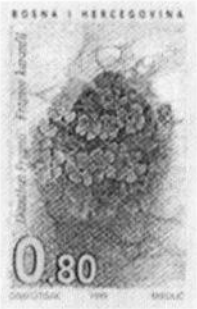

C42 *Dianthus freynii*

1999
C53 **C42** 80f. multicoloured 1·30 1·30

C43 Pine Marten

1999
C54 **C43** 40f. multicoloured 55 55

C44 Gradina Osanici, Stolac

1999. Archaeology.
C55 **C44** 10f. multicoloured 25 25

C45 The Nativity (mosaic)

1999. Christmas.
C56 **C45** 30f. multicoloured 55 55

C46 Sop

2000. 96th Birth Anniv of Nikola Sop (poet).
C57 **C46** 40f. multicoloured 60 60

C47 Emblem

2000. World Health Day.
C58 **C47** 40f. multicoloured 60 60

C48 Ceramic Doves

2000. Europa.
C59 **C48** 1m.80 multicoloured 4·00 4·00

C49 Chess Board and Emblem

2000. 40th Anniv of Bosnian Chess Association. Chess Events in 2000. Multicoloured.
C60 80f. Type **C49** (30th Chess Olympiad, Sarajevo) 1·30 1·30
C61 80f. Octopus holding pawn and emblem (16th European Chess Club Cup, Neum) 1·30 1·30

C50 Brother Karaula

2000. Birth Bicentenary of Brother Lovro Karaula.
C62 **C50** 80f. multicoloured 1·30 1·30

C51 Oak Tree (*Quercus sessilis*)

2000. Chestnut Oak of Siroki Brijeg.
C63 **C51** 1m.50 multicoloured 2·20 2·20

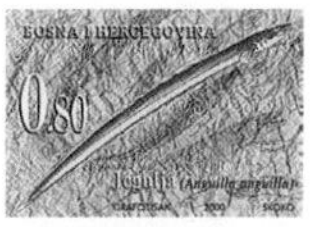

C52 European Eel (*Anguilla anguilla*)

2000
C64 **C52** 80f. multicoloured 1·30 1·30

C53 Franciscan Monastery, Tomislavgrad

2000
C65 **C53** 1m.50 multicoloured 2·20 2·20

C54 Woman and Patterned Cloth

2000. Traditional Costume from Kraljeve Sutjeske.
C66 **C54** 40f. multicoloured 80 80

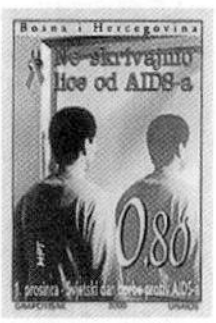

C55 Man and Reflection

2000. A.I.D.S. Awareness Campaign.
C67 **C55** 80f. multicoloured 1·30 1·30

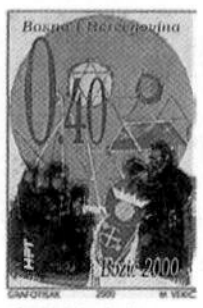

C56 Nativity

2000. Christmas.
C68 **C56** 40f. multicoloured 65 65

C57 *Chondrostoma phoxinus*

2001. Fishes. Multicoloured.
C69 30f. Type **C57** 40 40
C70 1m.50 *Salmo marmoratus* 2·20 2·20

C58 Tihaljina Spring

2001. Europa. Water Resources. Multicoloured.

C71		1m.10 Type **C58**	2·00	2·00
C72		1m.80 Pliva Waterfall	3·25	3·25

C59 Petar Zrinski

2001. 330th Death Anniversaries. Multicoloured.

C73		40f. Type **C59**	60	60
C74		40f. Fran Krsto Frankopan	60	60

C60 16th-century Galley Ship

2001

C75	**C60**	1m.80 multicoloured	2·75	2·75

C61 Boat, Neretva River Valley

2001

C76	**C61**	80f. multicoloured	1·30	1·30

C62 Queen of Peace of Medugorje

2001. 20th Anniv of Medugorje. Sheet 90×65 mm.

MSC77	**C62**	3m.80 multicoloured	5·25	5·25

C63 Our Lady of Kondzilo (17th-century painting)

2001

C78	**C63**	80f. multicoloured	1·30	1·30

C64 Binary Digits

2001. 50th Anniv of Computers. Each black and red.

C79		40f. Type **C64**	65	65
C80		40f. Binary forming "50"	65	65

C65 Mars, Globe and Sisyphus pushing Stone

2001. Millennium.

C81	**C65**	1m.50 multicoloured	2·00	2·00

C66 Father Slavko Barbaric

2001. First Death Anniv of Father Slavko Barbaric.

C82	**C66**	80f. multicoloured	1·30	1·30

C67 Minnie and Mickey Mouse (Danijela Nedic)

2001. Birth Centenary of Walt Disney (film maker).

C83	**C67**	1m.50 multicoloured	2·40	2·40

C68 Nativity

2001. Christmas.

C84	**C68**	40f. multicoloured	65	65

C69 Alfred Nobel

2001. Centenary of the Nobel Prize.

C85	**C69**	1m.80 multicoloured	3·00	3·00

C70 Skier

2002. Winter Olympic Games, Salt Lake City, U.S.A.

C86	**C70**	80f. multicoloured	1·40	1·40

C71 Vran Mountain

2002. International Year of Mountains.

C87	**C71**	40f. multicoloured	70	70

C72 Bridge over River Neretva, Mostar

2002. 550th Anniv of First Written Record of Mostar.

C88	**C72**	30f. multicoloured	55	55

C73 Clown, Lion and Mouse

2002. Europa. Circus. Multicoloured.

C89		80f. Type **C73**	2·10	2·00
C90		1m.50 Big Top and clowns	3·50	3·50

C74 Leonardo da Vinci and Designs

2002. 550th Birth Anniv of Leonardo da Vinci (artist and designer).

C91	**C74**	40f. brown and agate	70	70

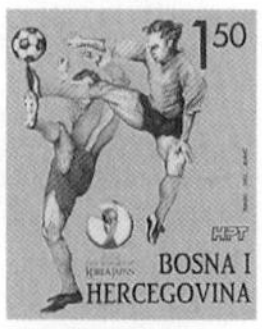

C75 Players and Football

2002. World Cup Football Championships, Japan and South Korea.

C92	**C75**	1m.50 multicoloured	2·50	2·40

C76 Father Buntic and Children

2002. 60th Death Anniv of Father Didak Buntic (humanitarian).

C93	**C76**	80f. multicoloured	1·40	1·40

C77 Inscribed Tablet

2002. 11th-century Inscribed Tablet, Humac.

C94	**C77**	40f. multicoloured	70	70

C78 Marilyn Monroe

2002. 40th Death Anniv of Marilyn Monroe (actor).

C95	**C78**	40f. multicoloured	70	70

C79 Elvis Presley

2002. 25th Death Anniv of Elvis Presley (entertainer).

C96	**C79**	1m.50 multicoloured	2·50	2·40

C80 Transmitter Tower

2002. 50th Anniv of Television.

C97	**C80**	1m.50 multicoloured	2·50	2·40

C81 1905 Postcard

2002. Stamp Day.

C98	**C81**	80f. multicoloured	1·40	1·40

C82 1929 Calendar

2002. Centenary of "Naprodak" (cultural association).

C99	**C82**	40f. multicoloured	70	70

C83 Stylized Player

2002. European Bowling Championships, Grude.

C100	**C83**	1m.50 multicoloured	2·50	2·40

C84 *Viola beckiana*

2002. Flowers.

C101	**C84**	30f. multicoloured	55	55

C85 Red Admiral (*Vanessa atalanta*)

2002. Butterflies.

C102	**C85**	80f. multicoloured	1·40	1·40

C86 Madonna and Child (painting, Bernardino Luini)

2002. Christmas.

C103	**C86**	40f. multicoloured	70	70

C87 School Buildings

2002. 120th Anniv of Society of Jesuits High School, Travnik.

C104	**C87**	80f. multicoloured	1·40	1·40

C88 Josip Stadler

2003. 160th Birth Anniv of Josip Stadler (first archbishop of Vrhbosna)

C105	**C88**	50f. multicoloured	85	85

C89 Sirokom Brijegu High School

2003

C106	**C89**	40f. multicoloured	80	80

C90 Key Box and Letter Holder

2003. Europa. Poster Art.

C107	**C90**	1m.80 multicoloured	4·75	4·75

C91 Figures

2003. 800th Anniv of the Abjuration at Bilino Polje.
C108 **C91** 50f. multicoloured 95 95

C92 Mary and Angels

2003. Tenth Anniv of HP Mostar
C109 **C92** 980f. multicoloured 1·60 1·60

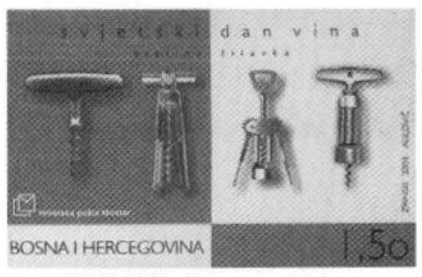

C93 Corkscrews

2003. World Wine Day.
C110 **C93** 1m.50 multicoloured 2·75 2·75

C94 *Oxytropis prenja*

2003. Flora and Fauna. Multicoloured.
C111 50f. Type **C94** 95 95
C112 2m. Rock partridge (*Alectoris graeca*) 3·75 3·75

C95 Pope John Paul II and Ivan Merz

2003. 2nd Visit of Pope John Paul II.
C113 **C95** 1m.50 multicoloured 2·75 2·75

C96 Crucifix

2003. 440th Birth Anniv of Matija Divkovic (writer).
C114 **C96** 3m.80 multicoloured 7·00 7·00

C97 Woman wearing Folk Costume, Rama

2003. Cultural Heritage. Multicoloured.
C115 50f. Type **C97** 95 95
C116 70f. Jewellery, Neum (horiz) 1·20 1·20

C98 Summit Cross

2003. 70th Anniv of Summit Cross on Krizevac Mountain.
C117 **C98** 80f. multicoloured 1·60 1·60

C99 Stjepan Kotromanic

2003. 650th Death Anniv of Stjepan Kotromanic (King of Bosnia).
C118 **C99** 20f. multicoloured 45 45

C100 Tele-printer

2003. World Post Day.
C119 **C100** 1m.50 black and red 3·25 3·25

C101 Quill and Inkwell

2003. Birth Bicentenary of Alberto Fortis (writer).
C120 **C101** 50f. multicoloured 1·00 1·00

C102 Car and Bicycle

2003. Children.
C121 **C102** 1m. multicoloured 2·10 2·10

C103 Nativity

2003. Christmas.
C122 **C103** 50f. multicoloured 1·00 1·00

C104 "100"

2003. Centenary of Powered Flight.
C123 **C104** 2m. multicoloured 4·25 4·25

C105 Emblem

2004. International Investment Conference.
C124 **C105** 5m. silver 11·50 11·50

C106 Hearts

2004. St. Valentine's Day.
C125 **C106** 10f. multicoloured 1·00 1·00

C107 Albert Einstein

2004. 125th Birth Anniv of Albert Einstein (physicist).
C126 **C107** 50f. multicoloured 1·30 1·30

C108 Decorated Hand

2004. Tattooing.
C127 **C108** 50f. multicoloured 1·30 1·30

C109 *Aquilegia dinarica*

2004. Flora and Fauna
C128 1m. Type **C109** 2·40 2·40
C129 1m.50 *Salamandra atra prenjensis* (horiz) 3·50 3·50

C110 Skis and Snow Scene

2004. Europa. Holidays. Multicoloured.
C130 1m.50 Type **C110** 3·75 3·75
C131 2m. Flippers and Beach Scene 4·75 4·75

C111 Andrije Kacica Miosica

2004. 300th Birth Anniv of Andrije Kacica Miosica (writer and theologian).
C132 **C111** 70f. yellow and brown 1·80 1·80

C112 Ball and Boots

2004. European Football Championship 2004, Portugal.
C133 **C112** 2m. multicoloured 5·00 5·00

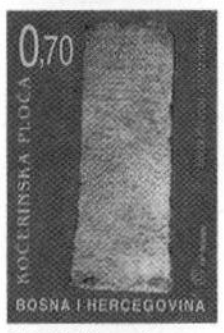

C113 Kocerin Tablet (carved stone), Siroki Brijeg (c.1404)

2004
C134 **C113** 70f. multicoloured 1·50 1·50

C114 Footprint

2004. 35th Anniv of First Landing on Moon.
C135 **C114** 1m. multicoloured 2·50 2·50

C115 Old Bridge, Mostar

2004. Reconstruction of Mostar Bridge.
C136 **C115** 50f. multicoloured 1·30 1·30

C116 Water Wheel, Buna

2004
C137 **C116** 1m. Multicoloured 2·50 2·50

C117 Envelope and Earth

2004. World Post Day.
C138 **C117** 1m.50 multicoloured 3·75 3·75

C118 Money Box and Hippopotamus

2004. World Savings Day.
C139 **C118** 50f. multicoloured 1·30 1·30

C119 Karl Friedrich Benz

2004. 160th Birth Anniv of Karl Friedrich Benz (German motor pioneer).
C140 **C119** 1m.50 multicoloured 3·75 3·75

C120 Mary and Joseph

2004. Christmas. Multicoloured.
C141 50f. Type **C120** 1·30 1·30
C142 1m. Postman carrying present 2·50 2·50

C121 Woman wearing Folk Costume, Kupres

2005. Cultural Heritage.
C143 **C121** 1m.50 multicoloured 3·75 3·75

C122 *Gentiana dinarica*

2005. Flora. Multicoloured.
C144 50f. Type **C122** 1·30 1·30
C145 50f. *Petteria ramentacea* 1·30 1·30

C123 Little Egret (*Egretta garzetta*)

2005. Birds. Multicoloured.
C146 1m. Type **C123** 2·50 2·50
C147 1m. Black-winged stilt (*Himantopus himantopus*) 2·50 2·50
C148 1m. Kingfisher (*Alcedo atthis*) 2·50 2·50

C149 1m. European bee eater (*Merops apiaster*) 2·50 2·50

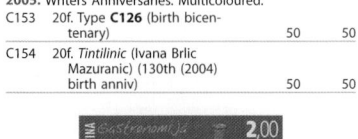

C124 Early Footballers

2005. Centenary of CSC Zrinjski Sports Club. Multicoloured.
C150 3m. Type **C124** 7·25 7·25
C151 3m. Modern footballers 7·25 7·25

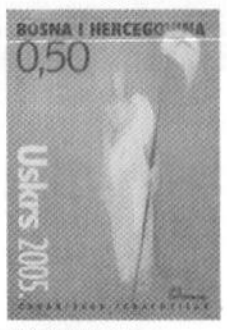

C125 Figure holding Flag

2005. Easter.
C152 **C125** 50f. multicoloured 1·30 1·30

C126 *Thumbelina* (Hans Christian Andersen)

2005. Writers Anniversaries. Multicoloured.
C153 20f. Type **C126** (birth bicentenary) 50 50
C154 20f. *Tintilinic* (Ivana Brlic Mazuranic) (130th (2004) birth anniv) 50 50

C127 Bread, Grapes, Wine, Nuts and Soft Cheese

2005. Europa. Gastronomy. Multicoloured.
C155 2m. Type **C127** 5·00 5·00
C156 2m. Bread, garlic, meats, glass and flagon 5·00 5·00

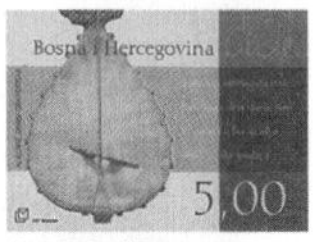

C128 Gusle

2005. Musical Instruments.
C157 **C128** 5m. multicoloured 12·50 12·50

C129 Vjetrenica Cave

2005. International Day of Water.
C158 **C129** 1m. multicoloured 2·50 2·50

C130 Steam Locomotive

2005. 120th Anniv of Metkovic—Mostar Railway.
C159 **C130** 50f. multicoloured 1·30 1·30

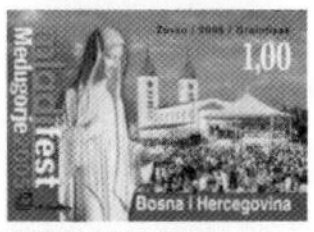

C131 Virgin Mary (statue) and Crowds

2005. Medjugorje Youth Festival.
C160 **C131** 1m. multicoloured 2·50 2·50

C132 Father Grgo Martic

2005. Birth Centenary of Father Grgo Martic.
C161 **C132** 1m. multicoloured 2·50 2·50

C133 Trumpet

2005. International Music Day.
C162 **C133** 50f. multicoloured 1·00 1·00

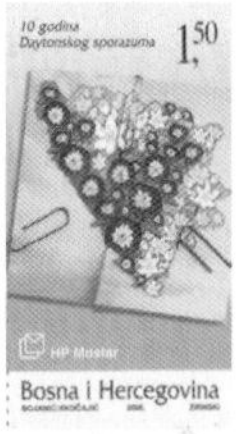

C134 Flowers over map

2005. Tenth Anniv of Dayton Agreement.
C163 **C134** 1m.50 multicoloured 3·75 3·75

C135 Slavko Barbaric

2005. Fifth Death Anniv of Slavko Barbaric (writer).
C164 **C135** 1m. multicoloured 2·50 2·50

C136 Mary and Jesus

2005. Christmas. Multicoloured.
C165 50f. Type **C136** 1·30 1·30
C166 50f. Tree 1·30 1·30

C137 "50"

2005. 50th Anniv of Europa Stamps. Multicoloured.
C167 2m. Type **C137** 3·75 3·75
C168 2m. Sunflowers and envelope 3·75 3·75
C169 2m. Map and 2003 1k.80 stamp (No. C107) 3·75 3·75
C170 2m. European flags 3·75 3·75
MSC171 90×100 mm. Nos. 167/70 20·00 20·00

C138 Lake and Bearded Tit

2006. International Swamp Protection Day.
C172 **C138** 1m. multicoloured 2·50 2·50

C139 Faces

2006. Europa. Integration. Multicoloured.
C173 2m. Type **C139** 5·00 5·00
C174 2m. "Integration" 5·00 5·00

C140 Sunflower and Globe

2006. Earth Day.
C175 **C140** 1m. multicoloured 2·50 2·50

C141 Paper Birds

2006. World Press Freedom Day.
C176 **C141** 50f. multicoloured 1·30 1·30

C142 Cable

2006. World Telecommunications Day.
C177 **C142** 1m. multicoloured 2·50 2·50

C143 Queen of Peace (statue) and Church

2006. 25th Anniv of Medugorje. Multicoloured.
C178 1m. Type **C143** 2·40 2·40
C179 1m. Statue with multicoloured halo amongst rocks 2·40 2·40
C180 1m. Cross, Krizevac Hill and statue 2·40 2·40
C181 1m. Statue (detail) and church 2·40 2·40
C182 1m. Stylized church and crowd 2·40 2·40

C144 Church

2006. 150th Anniv of Uzdol Parish.
C183 **C144** 50f. multicoloured 1·30 1·30

C145 Nikola Tesla

2006. 150th Birth Anniv of Nikola Tesla (engineer).
C184 **C145** 2m. multicoloured 5·00 5·00

C146 Archer and Stag

2006. Stecci (medieval tombstones).
C185 **C146** 20f. multicoloured 1·00 1·00

C147 Car

2006. Car Free Day.
C186 **C147** 1m. black, vermilion and yellow 2·50 2·50

C148 Crucifix from Woman's Rosary, Franciscan Monastery, Humac

2006
C187 **C148** 5m. multicoloured 12·50 12·50

C149 *Upupa epops* (hoopoe)

2006. Birds of Hutovo. Multicoloured.
C188 70f. Type **C149** 1·80 1·80
C189 70f. *Alauda arvensis* (skylark) 1·80 1·80
Nos. C190/1 have been left for additions to this set.

C150 *Papaver kerneri*

2006. Flora. Multicoloured.
C192 20f. Type **C150** 50 50
C193 20f. *Cerastium dinaricum* 50 50

C151 Door with Wreath

2006. Christmas and New Year. Multicoloured.
C194 50f. Type C **151** 1·30 1·30
C195 1m. Grass and candles 2·50 2·50

C152 Hearts and Birds

2007. St. Valentine's Day.
C196 **C152** 10f. multicoloured 1·00 1·00

C153 Head of Dog

2007. Dogs. Tornjak. Multicoloured.
C197 70f. Type **C153** 1·70 1·70
C198 70f. Head of dog, black markings 1·70 1·70
C199 70f. Dog with black markings 1·70 1·70
C200 70f. Dog with brown markings 1·70 1·70

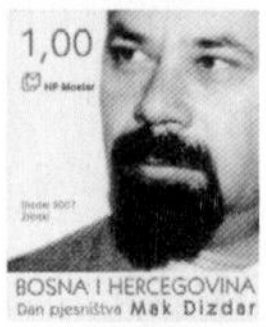

C154 Mak Dizdar

2007. 90th Birth Anniv of Mehmedalija Mak Dizdar (poet).
C201 **C154** 1m. multicoloured 2·50 2·50

C155 Clasped Hands

2007. Europa. Centenary of Scouting. Multicoloured.
C202 3m. Type **C155** 6·75 6·75
C203 3m. Reef knot 6·75 6·75

C156 *Sorbus domestica*

2007. Tree Day. Sheet 68×91 mm.
MSC204 **C156** 2k.10 multicoloured 5·25 5·25

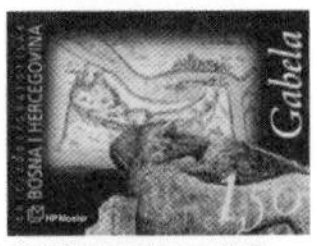

C157 Lion (bas relief) and Map

2007. Gabela Archaeological Site, Capljina.
C205 **C157** 1m.50 multicoloured 3·75 3·75

C158 Iris

2007. *Iris Illyrica*. Multicoloured.
C206 2m. Type **C158** 5·00 5·00
MSC207 61×80 mm. 3k. Iris and trireme (24×58 mm) 7·75 7·75

C159 Virgin Mary (statue)

2007. Medugorje. Multicoloured.
C208 1m. Type **C159** 2·40 2·40
C209 1m. Hands holding rosary 2·40 2·40
C210 1m. Virgin Mary and pilgrims 2·40 2·40
C211 1m. Bronze statue of Friar 2·40 2·40
C212 1m. Virgin Mary (statue) and tower 2·40 2·40

C160 Friar Marko Dobretic

2007. 300th Birth Anniv of Friar Marko Dobretic.
C213 **C160** 60f. multicoloured 1·50 1·50

C161 Duke Vlatko's Tombstone, Boljuni Necropolis

2007. Cultural Heritage Day.
C214 **C161** 20f. multicoloured 1·00 1·00

C162 Emblem

2007. World Bowling Championship, Grude.
C215 **C162** 5m. black and scarlet 12·50 12·50

C163 Hemp and Spindle

2007. Ethnological Treasures.
C216 **C163** 70f. multicoloured 1·80 1·80

C164 *Fulica atra* (coot)

2007. Birds. Multicoloured.
C217 2m. Type **C164** 3·75 3·75
C218 2m. *Anas platyrhynchos* (mallard) 3·75 3·75
C219 2m. *Anas crecca* (common teal) 3·75 3·75
C220 2m. *Streptopelia turtur* (turtle dove) 3·75 3·75

C165 *Gentiana lutea*

2007. Flora of Blidinje Park. Multicoloured.
C221 3m. Type **C165** 7·75 7·75
MSC222 80×60 mm. 3k. *Vaccinium vitis-idaea* 7·75 7·75

The stamp and margins **MS**C222 form a composite design.

C166 Candles

2007. Christmas. Multicoloured.
C223 50f. Type **C166** 1·30 1·30
C224 70f. Decorated trees and doorway 1·90 1·90

C167 Friar Andeo Kraljevic

2007. Birth Bicentenary of Friar Ivan (Andeo) Kraljevic.
C225 **C167** 1m. multicoloured 2·75 2·75

C168 Chick and Flowers

2008. Easter.
C226 **C168** 70f. multicoloured 1·90 1·90

C169 Piano Keys

2008. Tenth Anniv of Matica Hrvatska (cultural institution)'s Festival Week.
C227 **C169** 10f. black and vermilion 1·00 1·00

C170 Hand holding Envelope as Paper Aeroplane

2008. Europa. The Letter. Multicoloured.
C228 3m. Type **C170** 7·00 7·00
C229 3m. Pen nib 7·00 7·00

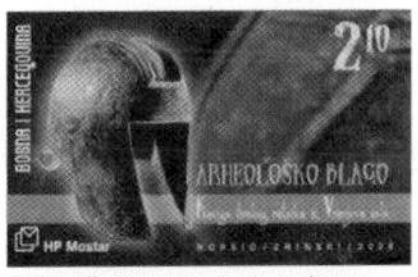

C171 Illyrian Warrior's Helmet, Vranjevo Selo

2008. Archaeology.
C230 **C171** 2m.10 multicoloured 6·00 6·00

C172 Grave of Mosha Danon, Rabbi of Sarajevo

2008. International Day of Diversity.
C231 **C172** 1m.50 multicoloured 4·25 4·25

C173 *Achillea millefolium* (milfoil)

2008. Myth and Flora. Andrija Simic and Milfoil. Sheet 80×60 mm.
MSC232 **C173** multicoloured 8·25 8·25

C174 Virgin Mary, Girl and Dove

2008. Medugorje. Multicoloured.
C233 1m. Type **C174** 2·75 2·75
C234 1m. Church of St. Jacob 2·75 2·75
C235 1m. Page, crucified Christ and praying hands 2·75 2·75
C236 1m. Virgin Mary (statue) 2·75 2·75
C237 1m. Summit Cross 2·75 2·75

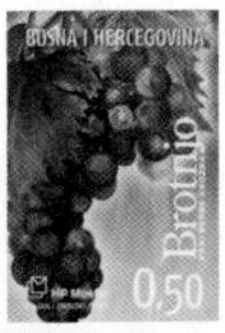

C175 Grapes

2008. Vintage Days in Brotnjo, 2008. Multicoloured.
C238 50f. Type **C175** 1·30 1·30
C239 70f. White grapes 2·20 2·20

C176 Building

2008. Zaostrog Monastery.
C240 **C176** 1m. multicoloured 3·00 3·00

C177 Tobacco Cutter

2008. Cultural Heritage. Ethnological Treasures. Avan (tobacco cutter).
C241 **C177** 2m. multicoloured 3·75 3·75

C178 Zepce

2008. 550th Anniv of Zepce.
C242 **C178** 1m.50 multicoloured 4·50 4·50

C179 Tubers

2008. International Year of the Potato. Multicoloured.
C243 50f. Type **C179** 1·75 1·75
MSC244 80×60 mm. 5m. Flowers 14·00 14·00

C180 *Falco tinnunculus* (Kestrel)

2008. Birds. Multicoloured.
C245 1m.50 Type **C180** 90 90
C246 1m.50 *Circactus gallicus* (short-toed eagle) 90 90
C247 1m.50 *Bubo bubo* (eagle owl) 90 90
C248 1m.50 *Accipiter gentilis* (goshawk) 90 90

C181 Leo Petrovic

2008. Father Leo Petrovic (professor of theology) Commemoration.
C249 **C181** 1m. multicoloured 9·25 9·25

C182 Gingerbread Man

2008. Christmas. Multicoloured.
C250 70f. Type **C182** 6·50 6·50
C251 70f. Bow 6·50 6·50

C183 Early Players

2008. 60th Anniv of Siroki Brijeg Football Club. Multicoloured.
C252 70f. Type **C183** 6·50 6·50
MSC253 80×60 mm. 2m.10 Modern players (35×30 mm) 18·00 18·00

C184 Woman holding Daffodil

2009. Daffodil Day (breast cancer awareness day).

C254 **C184** 20f. magenta and chrome yellow 1·00 1·00

C185 Waterfall, River Pliva

2009. International Water Day. Watermills in Pliva Lakes. Multicoloured.

C255 70f. Type **C185** 1·70 1·70
C256 70f. Watermills 1·70 1·70

C186 '60'

2009. 60th Anniv of Council of Europe and European Court of Human Rights. Each new blue and lemon.

C257 1m.50 Type **C186** 4·50 4·50
C258 1m.50 Court of Human Rights building (horiz) 4·50 4·50

C187 Earth and Planets

2009. Europa. Astronomy. Multicoloured.

C259 3m. Type **C187** 9·00 9·00
C260 3m. Telescope and planets 9·00 9·00

C188 Arms of Herzeg Stipan Vukcic Kosaca

2009. Archaeology.

C261 **C188** 1m.50 multicoloured 4·50 4·50

C189 *Tanacetum balsamita* (costamary)

2009. Myths and Flora. Multicoloured.

C262 2m.10 Type **C189** 4·00 4·00
MSC263 80×60 mm. 2m.10 Girl and flowers 4·00 4·00

C190 Building Facade

2009. 150th Anniv of Franciscan Monastery, Guca Gora.

C264 **C190** 70f. multicoloured 1·70 1·70

C191 Church of St. Jacob

2009. Medjugorje. Multicoloured.

C265 1m. Type **C191** 90 90
C266 1m. Summit Cross 90 90
C267 1m. Crucified Christ 90 90
C268 1m. Virgin Mary and Church of St. Jacob 90 90
C269 1m. Virgin Mary 90 90

C192 Festival Emblem

2009. Tenth Mediterranean Film Festival.

C270 **C192** 70f. multicoloured 1·70 1·70

C193 Chapel Entrance

2009. 800th Anniv of Franciscan Order.

C271 1m. multicoloured 1·20 1·20
C272 – 1m. deep brown 1·20 1·20

DESIGNS: Type C **193**; C272 Franciscan waist cord.

C194 Decorated Chest

2009. Stamp Day. Ethnological Treasures.

C273 **C194** 70f. multicoloured 1·70 1·70

C195 Monastery

2009. 150th Anniv Franciscan Monastery, Gorica Livno.

C274 **C195** 60f. multicoloured 1·70 1·70

C196 *Nycticorax nycticorax* (black-crowned night heron)

2009. Birds of Hutovo Blato. Multicoloured.

C275 1m.50 Type **C196** 1·20 1·20
C276 1m.50 *Cuculus canorus* (cuckoo) 1·20 1·20
C277 1m.50 *Coturnix coturnix* (quail) 1·20 1·20
C278 1m.50 *Rallus aquaticus* (water rail) 1·20 1·20

C197 Flowers and Fruit

2009. *Prunus domestica* (plum). Multicoloured.

C279 5m. Type **C197** 11·50 11·50
MSC280 65×65 mm. 5m. Fruit 11·50 11·50

C198 Candles

2009. Christmas. Multicoloured.

C281 70f. Type **C198** 1·70 1·70
C282 70f. Heart shaped cushion and parcels 1·70 1·70

C199 Maple Leaf

2010. Winter Olympic Games, Vancouver. Multicoloured.

C283 70f. multicoloured 1·60 1·70
C284 1m.50 bright scarlet, black and gold 2·10 2·10

Designs: 70f. Type **C199**; 1m.50 Stylized maple leaf on skis

C200 Carnations

2010. Centenary of International Women's Day

C284a **C200** 20f. multicoloured 1·00 1·00

C201 Friar Martin Nedic

2010. Birth Bicentenary of Friar Martin Nedić (builder of monastery and church in Tolisa)

C285 **C201** 2m.10 multicoloured 4·25 4·25

C202 Open Book, Stylized Child standing on Rainbow and Kite

2010. Europa. Multicoloured.

C286 3m. Type **C202** 5·75 5·75
C287 3m. Stylized child standing on open book holding windmill 5·75 5·75

C203 Cave Entrance and Pintadera

2010. Archeological Heritage

C288 **C203** 1m.50 multicoloured 3·25 3·25

C204 Linden Flower and Leaf

2010. Myths and Flora

MSC289 **C204** 5m. multicoloured 8·25 8·25

C205 Virgin Mary

2010. Medjugorje. Multicoloured.

C290 1m. Type **C205** 2·10 2·10
C291 1m. Summit Cross 2·10 2·10
C292 1m. Hand holding rosary 2·10 2·10
C293 1m. Virgin Mary (head and shoulders) 2·10 2·10
C294 1m. Pilgrims and flags 2·10 2·10

C206 Lighthouse and Emblem

2010. General Assembly of Matrix Croatica

C295 **C206** 1m. scarlet-vermilion and black 2·10 2·10

C207 Mother Teresa and Child

2010. Birth Centenary of Agnes Gonxha Bojaxhiu (Mother Teresa) (founder of Missionaries of Charity in Calcutta)

C296 **C207** 2m.10 bright ultramarine 4·25 4·25

C208 Prokoško Lake

2010. Environmental Protection. Multicoloured.

C297 1m. Type **C208** 2·10 2·10
C298 1m. *Triturus alpestris reiseri* (newt) 2·10 2·10

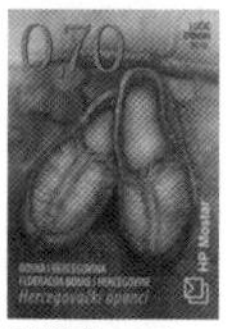

C209 Peasant Shoes

2010. Ethnological Treasures

C299 **C209** 70f. multicoloured 1·60 1·60

C210 Balkan Green Lizard

2010. Balkan Green Lizard (*Lacerta trilineata*). Multicoloured.

C300 50f. Type **C210** 1·40 1·40
C301 50f. Basking on rock 1·40 1·40
C302 50f. Climbing tree 1·40 1·40
C303 50f. Juvenile (brown striped) 1·40 1·40

C211 Fly Agaric (*Amanita muscaria*)

2010. Fungi. Multicoloured.

C304 2m.10 Type **C211** 4·25 4·25
C305 2m.10 Puffball (*Lycoperdon perlatum*) 4·25 4·25

C212 Slavko Barbaric

2010. Tenth Death Anniv of Fr. Slavko Barbaric

C306 **C212** 1m. multicoloured 2·10 2·10

C213 Rocking Horse Tree Decoration

2010. Christmas and New Year. Multicoloured.

C307	70f. Type **C213**	1·70	1·70
C308	70f. Angel	1·70	1·70

C214 Text and Book

2011. 400th Anniv of First Printed Book in National Language

C309	**C214**	70f. multicoloured	1·70	1·70

C215 Wind sock

2011. World Meteorological Day

C310	**C215**	20f. multicoloured	60	60

C216 Symbols of Easter

2011. Easter

C311	**C216**	70f. brown and black	1·80	2·80

C217 Coniferous Forest

2011. Europa. Forests. Multicoloured.

C312	3m. Type **C217**	5·75	5·75
C313	3m. Decdiduous forest in autumn	5·75	5·75

C218 Yuri Gagarin

2011. 50th Anniv of First Manned Space Flight

C314	**C218**	10f. multicoloured	1·00	1·00

C219 Floor Plan

2011. Archaeological Treasures. Early Christian Basilica in Cim

C315	**C219**	1m.50 multicoloured	2·25	2·25

C220 Symbols of Science

2011. 300th Birth Anniv of Josip Rudjer Boskovic (physicist, mathematician, astronomer, geodesist, poet, philosopher, engineer and diplomat)

C316	**C220**	2m.10 multicoloured	4·25	4·25

C221 Hawthorn

2011. Myths and Flora. Sheet 80×60 mm

MSC317	**C221**	5m. multicoloured	10·25	19·25

C222 Virgin Mary (head and shoulders)

2011. Medjugorje. Multicoloured.

C318	1m. Type **C222**	2·10	2·10
C319	1m. Crucified Christ	2·10	2·10
C320	1m. Virgin Mary and Church of St. Jacob	2·10	2·10
C321	1m. Summit Cross and rosary	2·10	2·10

C223 St. Anthony

2011. St. Anthony of Padua Commemoration

C322	**C223**	1m. multicoloured	2·10	2·10

C224 Cyclist

2011. World Bicycle Day

C323	**C224**	70f. green	1·70	1·70

C225 Parish Church

2011. Centenary of Skopaljska Gracanica Parish

C324	**C225**	50f. multicoloured	1·50	1·50

C226 Martyrs of Drina

2011. Martyrs of Drina

C325	**C226**	70f. multicoloured	1·70	1·70

C227 Golinjevo Fibulae (clasps)

2011. Post Day. Fibulae

C326	**C227**	1m. black and carmine-vermilion	2·10	2·10

C228 Fridtjof Nansen

2011. 150th Birth Anniv of Fridtjof Nansen (polar explorer, politician and diplomat)

C327	**C228**	1m.50 multicoloured	4·50	4·50

III. REPUBLIKA SRPSKA

Issued by the Serb administration based in Pale.

30 ═══

Република
Српска

(S1)

1992. Nos. 2587/98 of Yugoslavia surch as Type B.

S1	5d. on 10p. violet and green	1·10	1·10
S2	30d. on 3d. blue and red	£140	£140
S3a	50d. on 40p. green & purple	1·10	1·10
S4	60d. on 20p. red and yellow	1·20	1·20
S5	60d. on 30p. green & orange	1·20	1·20
S6	100d. on 1d. blue and purple	1·20	1·20
S7a	100d. on 2d. blue and red	1·20	1·20
S8	100d. on 3d. blue and red	1·20	1·20
S9a	300d. on 5d. ultram & blue	1·50	1·50
S10	500d. on 50p. green & violet	1·50	1·50
S11	500d. on 60p. mauve & red	1·50	1·50

S2 Stringed Instrument

1993. Dated "1992".

S12	**S2**	10d. black and yellow	4·50	4·50
S13	**S2**	20d. black and blue	20	20
S14	**S2**	30d. black and pink	50	50
S15	-	50d. black and red	60	60
S16	-	100d. black and red	1·50	1·50
S17	-	500d. black and blue	3·00	3·00

DESIGNS—VERT: 50, 100d. Coat of arms. HORIZ: 500d. Monastery.

1993. Dated "1993".

S18	**S2**	5000d. black and lilac	10	10
S19	**S2**	6000d. black and yellow	20	20
S20	**S2**	10000d. black and blue	3·50	3·50
S21	-	20000d. black and red	95	95
S22	-	30000d. black and red	1·50	1·50
S23	-	50000d. black and lilac	1·50	1·50

DESIGNS—VERT: 20000, 30000d. Coat of arms. HORIZ: 50000d. Monastery.

референдум 15-16. 05. '93.

7500 ═══

(S3)

1993. Referendum. Nos. S15/16 surch as Type **S3**.

S24	7500d. on 50d. black and red	2·00	2·00
S25	7500d. on 100d. black and red	2·00	2·00
S26	9000d. on 50d. black and red	2·75	2·75

S4 Symbol of St. John the Evangelist

1993. No value expressed.

S27	**S4**	A red	70	70

No. S27 was sold at the rate for internal letters.

S5 Icon of St. Stefan

1994. Republic Day.

S28	**S5**	1d. multicoloured	7·00	7·00

S6 King Petar I

1994. 150th Birth Anniv of King Petar I of Serbia.

S29	**S6**	80p. sepia and brown	3·50	3·50

S7 Banja Luka

1994. 500th Anniv of Banja Luka.

S30	**S7**	1d.20 multicoloured	4·00	4·00

1994. Issued at Doboj. Surch with letter. (a) On Nos. S13/16.

S31	**S2**	A on 20d. black and blue	
S32	**S2**	R on 20d. black and blue	
S33	**S2**	R on 30d. black and pink	
S34	-	R on 50d. black and red	
S35	-	R on 100d. black and red	

(b) On Nos. S18/19 and S21/2.

S36	**S2**	R on 5000d. black and lilac
S37	**S2**	R on 6000d. black and yellow
S38	-	A on 20000d. black and red
S39	-	R on 20000d. black and red
S40	-	R on 30000d. black and red

Stamps surcharged "A" were sold at the current rate for internal letters and those surcharged "R" at the rate for internal registered letters. The "R" on No. S32 is reversed.

S9 *Madonna and Child* (icon)

1994. Cajnicka Church.

S41	**S9**	1d. multicoloured	3·50	3·50

1994. Nos. S18/20 and S23 surch (Nos. S42/3 with letter).

S42	**S2**	A on 5000d. black & lilac	2·00	2·00
S43	**S2**	R on 6000d. black & yell	2·00	2·00
S44	**S2**	40p. on 10000d. blk & bl	2·00	2·00
S45	-	2d. on 50000d. black and lilac	2·00	2·00

No. S42 was sold at the current rate for internal letters and No. S43, which shows the surcharge as the cyrillic letter resembling "P", at the rate for internal registered letters.

S11 Tavna Monastery

1994. Monasteries. Multicoloured.

S46	60p. Type S **11**	2·00	2·00
S47	1d. Mostanica (horiz)	3·00	3·00
S48	1d.20 Zitomislic	3·50	3·50

S12 *Aquilegia dinarica*

1996. Nature Protection. Multicoloured.

S49	1d.20 Type **S12**	2·00	2·00
S50	1d.20 *Edraianthus niveus* (plant)	2·00	2·00
S51	1d.20 Shore lark	2·00	2·00
S52	1d.20 *Dinaromys bogdanovi* (dormouse)	2·00	2·00

1996. Nos. S14/16, S19 and S22 surch.

S53	**S2**	70p. on 30d. black and pink	60	60
S54	-	1d. on 100d. black & red	70	70
S55	-	2d. on 30000d. blk & red	1·30	1·30
S56	-	3d. on 50d. black and red	1·90	1·90
S57	**S2**	5d. on 6000d. black and yellow	3·25	3·25

S14 Relay Station, Mt. Kozara

1996

S58	**S14**	A green and bistre	25	25
S59	-	R purple and brown	60	60
S60	-	1d.20 violet and blue	65	65
S61	-	2d. lilac and mauve	1·30	1·30
S62	-	5d. purple and blue	2·75	2·75
S63	-	10d. brown and sepia	5·75	5·75

DESIGNS—VERT: R, Kraljica relay station, Mt. Ozren; 2d. Relay station, Mt. Romanija; 5d. Stolice relay station, Mt. Maljevica. HORIZ: 1d.20, Bridge over river Drina at Srbinje; 10d. Bridge at Visegrad.

No. S58 was sold at the current rate for an internal letter and No. S59 at the rate for an internal registered letter.

S15 Orthodox Church, Bascarsiji

1997

S64	**S15**	2d.50 multicoloured	1·40	1·40

S16 Pupin

1997. 62nd Death Anniv of Michael Pupin (physicist and inventor).

S65	**S16**	2d.50 multicoloured	1·40	1·40

S17 *Primula kitaibeliana*

1997. Flowers. Multicoloured.

S66	3d.20 Type **S17**	1·50	1·50
S67	3d.20 *Pedicularis hoermanniana*	1·50	1·50
S68	3d.20 *Knautia sarajevensis*	1·50	1·50
S69	3d.20 *Oxytropis campestris*	1·50	1·50

S18 Robert Koch

1997. Obligatory Tax. Anti-tuberculosis Week. Self-adhesive.

S70	**S18**	15f. red and blue	45	45

S19 Branko Copic

1997. Writers. Each mauve and yellow.

S71	A (60p.) Type **S19**	35	35
S72	R (90p.) Jovan Ducic	60	60
S73	1d.50 Mesa Selimovic	60	60
S74	3d. Aleksa Santic	1·40	1·40
S75	5d. Petar Kocic	2·30	2·30
S76	10d. Ivo Andric	4·75	4·75

S20 European Otter

1997. Nature Protection. Multicoloured.

S77	2d.50 Type **S20**	60	60
S78	4d.50 Roe deer	1·70	1·70
S79	6d.50 Brown bear	3·50	3·50

S21 Two Queens

1997. Europa. Tales and Legends. Multicoloured.

S80	2d.50 Type **S21**	9·25	9·25
S81	6d.50 Prince on horseback	20·00	20·00

S22 Diana, Princess of Wales

1998. Diana, Princess of Wales Commemoration.

S82	**S22**	3d.50 multicoloured ("DIANA" in Roman alphabet)	5·75	5·75
S83	**S22**	3d.50 multicoloured ("DIANA" in Cyrillic alphabet)	5·75	5·75

S23 Cross and Globe

1998. Obligatory Tax. Red Cross. Self-adhesive.

S84	**S23**	90f. red, blue and ultram	1·20	1·20

S24 Brazil

1998. World Cup Football Championship, France. Showing flags and players of countries in final rounds. Multicoloured.

S85	90f. Type **S24**	1·90	1·90
S86	90f. Morocco	1·90	1·90
S87	90f. Norway	1·90	1·90
S88	90f. Scotland	1·90	1·90
S89	90f. Italy	1·90	1·90
S90	90f. Chile	1·90	1·90
S91	90f. Austria	1·90	1·90
S92	90f. Cameroun	1·90	1·90
S93	90f. France	1·90	1·90
S94	90f. Saudi Arabia	1·90	1·90
S95	90f. Denmark	1·90	1·90
S96	90f. South Africa	1·90	1·90
S97	90f. Spain	1·90	1·90
S98	90f. Nigeria	1·90	1·90
S99	90f. Paraguay	1·90	1·90
S100	90f. Bulgaria	1·90	1·90
S101	90f. Netherlands	1·90	1·90
S102	90f. Belgium	1·90	1·90
S103	90f. Mexico	1·90	1·90
S104	90f. South Korea	1·90	1·90
S105	90f. Germany	1·90	1·90
S106	90f. United States of America	1·90	1·90
S107	90f. Yugoslavia	1·90	1·90
S108	90f. Iran	1·90	1·90
S109	90f. Romania	1·90	1·90
S110	90f. England (U.K. flag)	1·90	1·90
S111	90f. Tunisia	1·90	1·90
S112	90f. Colombia	1·90	1·90
S113	90f. Argentina	1·90	1·90
S114	90f. Jamaica	1·90	1·90
S115	90f. Croatia	1·90	1·90
S116	90f. Japan	1·90	1·90

S25 Couple and Musical Instrument

1998. Europa. National Festivals. Multicoloured.

S117	7m.50 Type **S25**	9·25	9·25
S118	7m.50 Couple from Neretva and musical instrument	9·25	9·25

S26 Family walking in Countryside

1998. Obligatory Tax. Anti-tuberculosis Week.

S119	**S26**	75f. multicoloured	1·20	1·20

S27 St. Pantelejmon

1998. 800th Anniv of Hilandar Monastery. Icons. Multicoloured.

S120	50f. Type **S27**	80	80
S121	70f. Jesus Christ	1·20	1·20
S122	1m.70 St. Nikola	2·50	2·50
S123	2m. St. John of Rila	3·00	3·00

S28 Bijelijna

1999. Towns. Multicoloured. (a) With face value.

S124	15f. Type **S28**	25	25
S125	20f. Sokolac	35	35
S126	75f. Prijedor	1·20	1·20
S127	2m. Brcko	3·00	3·00
S128	4m.50 Zvornik	6·50	6·50
S129	10m. Doboj	15·00	15·00

(b) Face value expressed by letter.

S130	A (50f.) Banja Luka	70	70
S131	R (1m.) Trebinje	1·50	1·50

No. S130 was sold at the current rate for an internal letter and No. S131 at the rate for an internal registered letter.

S29 Avions de Transport Regional ATR 72 over Lake

1999. Founding of Air Srpska (state airline). Multicoloured.

S132	50f. Type **S29**	70	70
S133	50f. Airliner above clouds	70	70
S134	75f. Airliner over beach	1·20	1·20
S135	1m.50 Airliner over lake (different)	2·20	2·20

S30 Table Tennis Ball as Globe

1999. International Table Tennis Championships, Belgrade. Multicoloured.

S136	1m. Type **S30**	1·70	1·70
S137	2m. Table tennis table, bat and ball	3·50	3·50

S31 Kozara National Park

1999. Europa. National Parks. Multicoloured.

S138	1m.50 Type **S31**	75·00	75·00
S139	2m. Perucica National Park	75·00	75·00

S32 Open Hands

1999. Obligatory Tax. Red Cross.

S140	**S32**	10f. multicoloured	45	45

S33 Manuscript

1999. 780th Anniv of Bosnia and Herzegovina Archbishopric (S142, S144/8) and 480th Anniv of Garazole Printing Works (S141, S143). Mult.

S141	50f. Type **S33**	70	70
S142	50f. Dobrun Monastery	70	70
S143	50f. "G"	70	70
S144	50f. Zhitomislib Monastery	70	70
S145	50f. Gomionitsa Monastery	70	70
S146	50f. Madonna and Child with angels and prophets (icon, 1578)	70	70
S147	50f. St. Nicolas (icon)	70	70
S148	50f. Wise Men (icon)	70	70

S34 Brown Trout

1999. Fish. Multicoloured.

S149	50f. Type **S34**	6·75	1·20
S150	50f. Lake trout (*Salmo trutta morpha lacustris*)	1·20	1·20
S151	75f. Huchen	1·70	1·70
S152	1m. European grayling	2·30	2·30

S35 Lunar Module on Moon's Surface

1999. 30th Anniv of First Manned Landing on Moon. Multicoloured.

S153	1m. Type **S35**	1·90	1·90
S154	2m. Astronaut on Moon	3·00	3·00

S36 Pencil and Emblem

1999. 125th Anniv of Universal Postal Union. Multicoloured

S155	75f. Type **S36**	1·20	1·20
S156	1m.25 Earth and emblem	2·00	2·00

S36a Roadway to '2000'

1999. Obligatory Tax. Tuberculosis Week. Ordinary or self adhesive gum.

S156a	10f. Type **S36a**

S37 Madonna and Child

1999. Art. Icons. Multicoloured.

S157	50f. Type **S37**	75	75
S158	50f. Madonna, Cajnice	75	75
S159	50f. Madonna Pelagonitisa	75	75
S160	50f. Holy Kirjak Otselnik	75	75
S161	50f. Pieta	75	75
S162	50f. Entry of Christ into Jerusalem	75	75
S163	50f. St. Jovan	75	75
S164	50f. Sava and Simeon	75	75

S38 Ancient Egyptians

1999. Millennium (1st series). Sheet 137×86 mm containing Type **S38** and similar horiz designs. Multicoloured.

MSS170 50f.×5, Type **S38**; Inventions for time keeping; Iron working; Invention of steam engines; Transport; 1m. Space exploration. 10·00 10·00

S39 Postal Stage-Coach during Austro-Hungarian Occupation

1999. 135th Anniv of Postal Service. Multicoloured.

S171 50f. Type **S39** 75 75

MSS172 55×70 mm. 3m. Tatar postmen crossing bridge during Turkish regency 80·00 80·00

S40 Fresco of St. Simeon (Stefan Nemanja) holding Studenica Monastery

2000. 800th Death Anniv of Stefan Nemanja (Stephen II).

S173 **S40** 1m.50 multicoloured 2·20 2·20

S41 *Prunus domestica* (plum)

2000. Trees. Multicoloured.

S174 1m. Type **S41** 1·50 1·50

S175 2m. *Corylus avellana* (hazel) 3·00 3·00

S42 Bridge, Sepk

2000. Bridges on Drina River. Multicoloured.

S176 1m. Type **S42** 1·60 1·60

S177 1m. Pavlovica Bridge, Bijeljina 1·60 1·60

S178 1m. Stag and iron bridge, Bratunac 1·60 1·60

S179 1m. Train crossing bridge, Zvornik 1·60 1·60

S43 Jovan Ducic

2000. Jovan Ducic (writer) Commemoration.

S180 **S43** 20f. multicoloured 35 35

S44 Construction of Europe

2000. Europa. Construction of Europe. Multicoloured.

S181 1m.50 Type **S44** 70·00 70·00

S182 2m.50 Children and stars 80·00 80·00

S45 Girl

2000. Obligatory Tax. Red Cross Week. Multicoloured. (a) Ordinary gum.

S183 10f. Type **S45** 50 50

S183a 10f. Symbols of care (30×41 mm) 50 50

(b) Self-adhesive.

S183b 50f. As No. 183a (20×30 mm) 50 50

S46 Basilica, Banja Luka (destroyed in 1941)

2000. Centenary of Banja Luka Province.

S184 **S46** 1m.50 multicoloured 2·20 2·20

S47 Footballers

2000. Euro 2000–European Football Championships, Belgium and the Netherlands. Multicoloured.

S185 1m. Type **S47** 1·50 1·50

S186 2m. Footballers (different) 3·00 3·00

MSS187 66×83 mm. 6m. Netherlands and Belgium flags as map and footballers (35×42 mm) 12·50 12·50

S48 Leaders of Herzegovina Uprising

2000. 125th Anniv of Herzegovina Rebellion (Nevesinje uprising).

S188 **S48** 1m.50 multicoloured 2·40 2·40

S49 Outline of Australia and Hurdling

2000. Olympic Games, Sydney. Multicoloured.

S189 50f. Type **S49** 75 75

S190 50f. Australia and volleyball 75 75

S191 50f. Australia and basketball 75 75

S192 50f. Australia and handball 75 75

MSS193 71×98 mm. 2m. Australia, emu and kangaroo 3·00 3·00

No. **MS**S193 also contains a stamp size label showing Sydney Opera House and Olympic Stadium, the whole forming a composite design.

S50 Toddler

2000. Obligatory Tax. Tuberculosis Week. Multicoloured. (a) Ordinary gum.

S194 10f. Type **S50** 50 50

(b) Self-adhesive.

S195 1m. As Type **S50** (20×30 mm) 50 50

S51 Locomotive, 1848

2000. 175th Anniv of Railways. Multicoloured.

S196 50f. Type **S51** 2·50 2·50

S197 50f. Steam locomotive, 1865 2·50 2·50

S198 50f. Steam locomotive, 1930 2·50 2·50

S199 1m. Electric locomotive, 1990 3·75 3·75

S52 *Leontopodium alpinum* (edelweiss)

2000. European Nature Protection. Multicoloured.

S200 1m. Type **S52** 1·50 1·50

S201 2m. *Proteus anguinus* (olm) (horiz) 3·00 3·00

S53 Columbus discovering America

2000. Millennium (2nd series). Two sheets, each 140×86 mm containing Type **S53** and similar horiz designs. Multicoloured.

MSS202 (a) 50f.×6, Type **S53**; Discovery of glass, iron and steel; First printing press; Industrial revolution; James Watt and steam engine; Hubble telescope and satellite (space exploration). (b) 3m. Exploration by sea (105×55 mm) 9·25 9·25

Nos. **MS**S202a/b were issued in a folder.

S54 The Assumption of Mary (fresco)

2000. Icons and Frescoes. Multicoloured.

S203 50f. Type **S54** 75 75

S204 50f. Entry of Christ into Jerusalem (icon) 75 75

S205 1m. Madonna with Child and Angels (icon) 1·50 1·50

S206 1m. Christos Pantocrator (ceiling fresco) 1·50 1·50

S55 Alexander Graham Bell and Development of Telephones

2001. 125th Anniv of Telephony.

S207 **S55** 1m. multicoloured 1·50 1·50

S56 Yuri Gagarin and *Vostok 1*

2001. 40th Anniv of First Manned Space Flight. Multicoloured.

S208 1m. Type **S56** 1·50 1·50

MSS209 86×66 mm. 3m. Yuri Gagarin, take off and first flight orbit (53×34 mm) 8·75 8·75

S57 Vlado Milosevic

2001. Birth Centenary of Vlado Milosevic (composer and ethnomusicologist).

S210 **S57** 50f. multicoloured 75 75

S58 Waterfall, Sutjeska River

2001. Europa. Water Conservation. Multicoloured.

S211 1m. Type **S58** 2·75 2·75

S212 2m. Turjanica river 5·50 5·50

59 *Maniola jurtina*

2001. Butterflies. Multicoloured.

S213 50f. Type **S59** 75 75

S214 50f. *Pyrgus malvae* 75 75

S215 1m. *Papilio machaon* 1·50 1·50

S216 1m. *Lycaena phlaeas* inscr 'Lycaena pylaeas' 1·50 1·50

S60 Women's Costumes, Popovo

2001. Traditional Costumes. Multicoloured.

S217 50f. Type **S60** 75 75

S218 50f. Bridal costume, Zmijanje 75 75

S219 1m. Woman's costume, Bileca mountains 1·50 1·50

S220 1m. Two women, Lijevce 1·50 1·50

S61 Combatants

2001. Republic of Srpska–Karate World Champion, 2001.

S221 **S61** 1m.50 multicoloured 2·20 2·20

S62 Old Castle, Kostajnica

2001. Towns. Multicoloured.

S222 25f. Type **S62** 35 35

S223 A (50f.) As No. S130 (24×22 mm) 75 75

S224 1m. Square with monument dedicated to war victims, Srbinje 1·50 1·50

No. S225 is vacant.

S63 Emblem

2001. Obligatory Tax. Anti-Tuberculosis Week.

S226 **S63** 10f. multicoloured 50 50

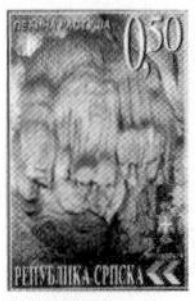

S64 Rastusa Cave, Teslic

2001. Caves. Multicoloured.

S227 50f. Type **S64** 75 75

S228 50f. Vagan cave, Vitorog 75 75

S229	50f. Pavlova cave, Petrovo	75	75
S230	50f. Orlovaca cave, Pale	75	75
S231	50f. Ledana cave, Bobija	75	75
S232	50f. Hole, Podovi plateau	75	75

S65 Alfred Nobel (founder)

2001. Centenary of Nobel Prizes. Multicoloured.

S233	1m. Type **S65**	1·50	1·50
S234	2m. Ivo Andric (winner of Nobel prize for Literature, 1961)	3·00	3·00

S66 Klinje Lake, Gacko

2001. European Nature Protection. Multicoloured.

S235	1m. Type **S66**	1·50	1·50
S236	1m. Bardaca Lake, Srbac	1·50	1·50

S67 *Still Life with Parrot* (Jovan Bijelic)

2001. Art. Multicoloured.

S237	50f. Type **S67**	75	75
S238	50f. *Djerdap* (Todor Svrakic)	75	75
S239	50f. *Suburb of Belgrade* (Kosta Hakman)	75	75
S240	50f. *Adela* (Miodrag Vujacic Mirski) (vert)	75	75

S68 Birth of Christ (icon, Studenica Monastery)

2001. Christmas.

S 241	**S68**	1m. multicoloured	1·50	1·50

S69 Player and Club Badge

2001. 75th Anniv of Borac Football Club.

S242	**S69**	1m.50 multicoloured	2·20	2·20

S70 National Arms

2002. Tenth Anniv of Republic Srpska. Multicoloured.

S243	50f. Type **S70**	80	80
S243a	1m. National flag (horiz)	1·60	1·60
MSS243b	71×64 mm. 2m. Map (42×35 mm)	3·25	3·25

S71 Hand gripping Cobra

2002. Fight against Terrorism. Multicoloured.

S244	1m. Type **S71**	1·60	1·60
MSS244a	68×76 mm. 2m. Eyes enclosed in globe	3·25	3·25

S72 Ski Jump

2002. Winter Olympic Games, Salt Lake City. Multicoloured.

S245	50f. Type **S72**	80	80
S246	1m. Two man bobsleigh	1·60	1·60

S73 Seated Woman with Cultural Symbols

2002. Centenary of Prosvjeta Cultural Association.

S247	**S73**	1m. multicoloured	1·60	1·60

S74 Vasilije Ostroski Church, Sarajevo

2002. Towns. Multicoloured.

S248	50f. Type **S74**	80	80
S249	2m. Oil Refinery, Srpski Brod (horiz)	3·25	32·00

S75 Charles Lindbergh and *Spirit of St. Louis*

2002. 75th Anniv of First Trans-Atlantic Flight.

S250	**S75**	1m. multicoloured	1·60	1·60

S76 Horses and Clown

2002. Europa. Circus. Multicoloured.

S251	1m. Type **S76**	1·60	1·60
S252	1m.50 Elephants	2·40	2·40

S76a Rescue Workers

2002. Obligatory Tax. Red Cross Week. Multicoloured. (a) Ordinary gum.

S252a	10f. Type **S76a**	55	55

(b) Self-adhesive.

S252b	50f. As Type **S76a** plus emblem	55	55

S77 Footballers

2002. World Cup Football Championships, Japan and South Korea.Multicoloured.

S253	50f. Type **S77**	80	80
S254	1m. Footballers (different)	1·60	1·60

S78 Slatina

2002. Spas. Multicoloured.

S255	25f. Type **S78**	40	40
S256	50f. Mljecanica	80	80
S257	75f. Vilina Vlas	1·30	1·30
S258	1m. Laktasi	1·70	1·70
S259	1m.50 Vrucica	2·50	2·50
S260	5m. Dvorovi	8·75	8·75

S79 Greek-Illyrian Helmet (4th—5th century BC)

2002. Museum Exhibits. Multicoloured.

S261	50f. Type **S79**	85	85
S262	50f. Murano glass cup	85	85
S263	1m. Headstone of Grd (12th century parish priest) (horiz)	1·70	1·70
S264	1m. Silver bracelet (4th–5th century BC) (horiz)	1·70	1·70

S79a Waterfall and Lungs as Forest

2002. Obligatory Tax. Tuberculosis Week. Multicoloured. (a) Ordinary gum.

S264a	10f. Type **S79a**	55	55

(b) Self-adhesive.

S264b	50f. As Type **S79a** (20×30 mm)	55	55

S80 *Boletus regius*

2002. Fungi. Multicoloured.

S265	50f. Type **S80**	85	85
S266	50f. *Macrolepiota procera*	85	85
S267	1m. *Amanita caesarea*	1·70	1·70
S268	1m. *Craterellus cornucopoides*	1·70	1·70

S81 Maglic Mountain

2002. European Nature Protection. Multicoloured.

S269	50f. Type **S81**	85	85
S269a	1m. Klekovaca Mountain	1·70	1·70

S82 *Petar Popovic Pecija* (Spiro Bocaric) (1933)

2002. Art. Multicoloured.

S270	50f. Type **S82**	85	85
S271	50f. *Black Lake beneath Durmitor* (Lazar Drljaca) (1935) (horiz)	85	85
S272	1m. *Zembilj Street* (Branko Sotra) (1937) (horiz)	1·70	1·70
S273	1m. *Birds and Landscape* (Milan Sovilj) (2000) (horiz)	1·70	1·70

S83 *Vrbas Canyon* (scene from film by Spiro Bocaric) (1937)

2003. Centenary of First Film shown in Republic Srpska. Sheet 92×73 mm.

MSS274	**S83** 3m. multicoloured	5·00	5·00

S84 Alekse Santic

2003. 135th Birth Anniv of Alekse Santic (writer).

S275	**S84**	1m. multicoloured	1·80	1·80

S85 Crucifixion, Sretenje Monastery

2003. Easter. Multicoloured.

S276	50f. Type **S85**	90	90
S277	1m. Resurrection (painting, Altarpiece, Eisenheim by Matias Greenwald)	1·80	1·80

S86 Everest Peaks

2003. 50th Anniv of First Ascent of Mount Everest. Sheet 82×58 mm containing Type **S86** and similar vert design. Multicoloured.

MSS278	1m.50 Type **S86**; 1m.50 Mountaineer through magnifying glass	7·25	7·25

The stamps and margin of **MS**S278 form a composite design.

S87 Aviation Poster

2003. Europa. Poster Art. Multicoloured.

S279	1m. Type **S87**	1·80	1·80
S280	1m.50 Naval poster	2·75	2·75

S87a Transfusion Equipment and Family

2003. Obligatory Tax. Red Cross Week.
S280a **S87a** 10f. multicoloured 60 60

S88 Arab

2003. Horses. Multicoloured.
S281 50f. Type **S88** 90 90
S282 50f. Lipizzaner 90 90
S283 1m. Inscr 'Bosanko' 1·80 1·80
S284 1m. Inscr 'Posavatz' 1·80 1·80

S89 Pope John Paul II

2003. Second Visit of Pope John Paul II to Bosnia Hercegovina. Multicoloured.
S285 1m.50 Type **S89** 8·25 8·25
S285a 1m.50 Pope John Paul II and Ivan Merz (Croatian lay academic, beatified by Pope John-Paul II on Sunday, June 22, 2003 at Banja Luka) (horiz) 3·00 3·00

Stamps of the same design as No. S285a were issued by Bosnia Herzegovina (Sarajevo) and Bosnia Herzegovina (Croatia).

S90 Medal of Honour

2003. Medals. Multicoloured.
S286 50f. Type **S90** 1·00 1·00
S287 1m. Njegos I medal 2·00 2·00

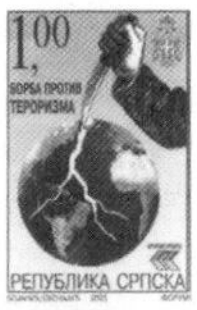

S91 Dagger piercing Globe

2003. Fight against Terrorism.
S288 **S91** 1m. multicoloured 2·00 2·00

S91a 'Stop TB'

2003. Obligatoery Tax. Tuberculosis Week. (a) Ordinary gum.
S288a **S91a** 10f. multicoloured 65 65

(b) Self-adhesive.
S288b 50f. As No. S288a (30×20 mm) 65 65

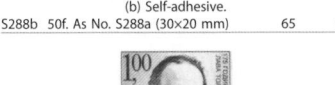

S92 Leo Tolstoy

2003. 175th Birth Anniv of Count Lev Nikolayevich (Leo) Tolstoy (writer, pacifist, Christian anarchist and educational reformer).
S289 **S92** 1m. multicoloured 2·10 2·10

S93 Ugar River Canyon

2003. European Nature Protection. Multicoloured.
S290 50f. Type **S93** 1·10 1·10
S291 1m. Drina River canyon 2·10 2·10

S94 *St. Sava and Martyr Varvara* (Radul)

2003. Religious Art. Multicoloured.
S292 50f. Type **S94** 1·30 1·30
S293 50f. *St. Lazar* (Andrej Raicevic) 1·30 1·30
S294 1m. *Coronation of Madonna with Saints* (Dimitrije Bacevic) 2·75 2·75
S295 1m. *Deisis* (intercession of Madonna and Jovan Pretaca) 2·75 2·75

S95 Child and Snowman

2003. Christmas and New Year. Multicoloured.
S296 50f. Type **S95** 1·30 1·30
S297 1m. Santa Claus and reindeer 2·75 2·75

S96 Wright Brothers and *Wright Flyer I*

2003. Centenary of Powered Flight. Multicoloured.
S298 50f. Type **S96** 1·30 1·30
S299 1m. Ferdinand von Zeppelin and air ship LZ 127 *Graf Zeppelin* 2·75 2·75

S97 *Oath of Rebels* (bas relief, memorial fountain, Orasac)

2004. Bicentenary of First Serbian Uprising. Sheet 78×62 mm containing Type **S97** and similar vert design. Multicoloured.
MSS300 1m.50×2, Type **S97**; *Oath of Rebels* (right) 8·00 8·00

The stamps of **MS**S300 form a composite design.

S98 Early Greek Chariot Race

2004. Olympic Games, Athens. Sheet 100×60 mm containing Type **S98** and similar vert design. Multicoloured.
MSS301 1m.50×2, Type **S98**; Early Greek chariot race (right) 8·50 8·50

The stamps of **MS**S301 form a composite design.

S99 Albert Einstein

2004. 125th Birth Anniv of Albert Einstein (physicist and 1921–Nobel Prize winner).
S302 **S99** 1m.50 multicoloured 4·25 4·25

S100 Risen Christ

2004. Easter. Multicoloured.
S303 50f. Type **S100** 1·40 1·40
S304 1m. Risen Christ (different) 2·75 2·75

S101 Canoeing

2004. Europa. Holidays. Multicoloured.
S305 50f. Type **S101** 2·75 2·75
S306 1m. Hang-gliding 4·25 4·25

S102 Hands holding Blood Droplet as Gift

2004. Obligatory Tax. Red Cross.
S307 **S102** 10f. multicoloured 1·00 1·00

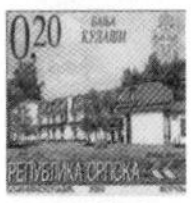

S103 Kulasi

2004. Spas.
S308 **S103** 20f. multicoloured 1·00 1·00

S104 Milutina Milankovica

2004. 125th Birth Anniv of Milutina Milankovica (scientist).
S309 **S104** 1m. multicoloured 2·75 2·75

S105 Football and Map

2004. European Football Championships, Portugal.
S310 **S105** 1m.50 multicoloured 4·25 4·25

S106 Discus Thrower, Games Emblem and Temple Ruins

2004. Olympic Games, Greece. Multicoloured.
S311 50f. Type **S106** 1·40 1·40
S312 50f. Hurdler, ruins and early runners 1·40 1·40
S313 1m. Early and modern runners and temple ruins 2·75 2·75
S314 1m. Runners and charioteers 2·75 2·75

S107 *Arctostaphylos uva* (bear ears)

2004. European Nature Protection. Multicoloured.
S315 50f. Type **S107** 1·40 1·40
S316 1m. *Monticola saxatilis* (rufous-tailed rock thrush) 2·75 2·75

S107a Stylized Lung

2004. Obligatory Tax. Tuberculosis Week. (a) Ordinary gum.
S316a **S107a** 10f. multicoloured 1·00 1·00

(b) Self-adhesive.
S316b 10f. As Type **S107a** (20×30 mm) 1·00 1·00

S108 Antimonite

2004. Minerals. Multicoloured
S317 50f. Type **S108** 1·40 1·40
S318 50f. Pyrites 1·40 1·40
S319 1m. Sphalerite 2·75 2·75
S320 1m. Quartz 2·75 2·75

S109 Mihajlo Pupin

2004. 150th Birth Anniv of Mihajlo Pupin (scientist).
S321 **S109** 1m. multicoloured 2·75 2·75

S110 Child, Grenade and Pigeons

2004. Struggle against Terrorism.
S322 **S110** 1m. multicoloured 2·75 2·75

S110a *Digitalis grandiflora*

2004. Flora. Multicoloured.
S322a 50f. Type **S110a** 1·40 1·40
S322b 50f. *Arnica montana* 1·40 1·40
S322c 1m. *Rosa pendulina* 2·75 2·75
S322d 1m. *Gentiana lutea* 2·75 2·75

S111 Mljecanica near Kozarska Dubica

2004. Spas. Multicoloured.
S323 50f. Type **S111** 1·40 1·40
S324 1m. Laktasi 2·75 2·75

S112 The Nativity (icon)

2004. Christmas.
S325 **S112** 1m. multicoloured 2·75 2·75

S113 *Serbian Peasant from Semberija*

2005. Art. Paintings by Milenko Atanackovic. Multicoloured.
S326 50f. Type **S113** 1·40 1·40
S327 1m. *Beledija–Old Community* (horiz) 2·75 2·75

S114 Janj River

2005. International Day of Water Protection.
S328 **S114** 1m. multicoloured 2·75 2·75

S115 Traditional Hearth

2005. Europa. Gastronomy. Multicoloured.
S329 1m. Type **S115** 2·75 2·75
S330 1m.50 Table laid with food 4·25 4·25

S116 *The Christ Guardian* (icon), Church of Madonna, Ljeviska

2005. Easter.
S331 **S116** 50f. multicoloured 1·50 1·50

S117 Pope John Paul II

2005. Pope John Paul II Commemoration. Multicoloured.
S332 1m.50 Type **S117** 4·25 4·25
MSS333 56×49 mm. 5m. St. Peters Basilica and Pope John Paul II 14·00 14·00

S118 Emblem

2005. Obligatory Tax. Red Cross. Self-adhesive.
S334 **S118** 10f. vermilion and black 1·00 1·00

S119 *Vipera berus berus*

2005. Snakes. Multicoloured.
S335 50f. Type **S119** 1·40 1·40
S336 50f. *Vipera ursinii* 1·40 1·40
S337 1m. *Vipera berus bosniensis* 2·75 2·75
S338 1m. *Vipera ammodytes* 2·75 2·75

S120 Castle

2005. 50th Anniv of Disneyland Theme Park, Florida. Multicoloured.
S339 50f. Type **S120** 1·40 1·40
S340 1m. houses 2·75 2·75

S121 Fighting Bulls, Grmec

2005. Traditions.
S341 **S121** 1m.50 multicoloured 4·25 4·25

S122 *Prasuma Perucica*

2005. 50th Anniv of Europa Stamps. Multicoloured.
S342 1m.95 Type **S122** 5·50 5·50
S343 1m.95 Rafting, Odmor 5·50 5·50
S344 1m.95 Mostar bridge 5·50 5·50
S345 1m.95 Drina river 5·50 5·50

S123 Landscape and Lungs

2005. Obligatory Tax. Anti-Tuberculosis Week.
S346 **S123** 10f. multicoloured 1·00 1·00

S124 Balls and Belgrade Arena

2005. European Basketball Championship, Belgrade. Multicoloured, colour wash given.
S347 **S124** 50f. lilac 1·40 1·40
S348 **S124** 50f. yellow 1·40 1·40
S349 **S124** 50f. green 1·40 1·40
S350 **S124** 50f. lilac 1·40 1·40
S351 **S124** 50f. blue 1·40 1·40

S125 National Museum

2005. 75th Anniversaries. Multicoloured.
S352 1m. Type **S125** 2·75 2·75
S353 1m. National Theatre (horiz) 2·75 2·75

S126 Tunnel, Sargan

2005. Tourism. Makra Gora Railway, Visegard. Sheet 101×54 mm containing Type **S126** and similar vert design. Multicoloured.
MSS354 50f. Type **S126**; 1m. Station, Makra Gora 4·25 4·25
The stamps and margin of **MS**S354 form a composite design.

S127 *Bleriot XI*

2005. Centenary of International Aviation Federation (FAI).
S355 **S127** 1m.50 multicoloured 4·25 4·25

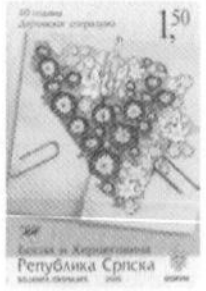

S128 Flowers over map

2005. Tenth Anniv of Dayton Agreement.
S356 **S128** 1m.50 multicoloured 4·25 4·25

S129 Guber

2005. Spas.
S357 **S129** 50f. multicoloured 1·40 1·40

S130 *Crex crex* (corncrake)

2005. European Nature Protection. Birds. Multicoloured.
S358 50f. Type **S130** 1·40 1·40
S359 1m. *Platalea leucorodia* (spoonbill) 2·75 2·75

S131 Monument to Victims

2005. 60th Anniv of Liberation of Jasenovac Concentration Camp.
S360 **S131** 50f. multicoloured 1·40 1·40

S132 Mozart

2006. 250th Birth Anniv of Wolfgang Amadeus Mozart (composer and musician).
S361 **S132** 1m.50 multicoloured 4·25 4·25

S133 Branke Sotre

2006. Birth Centenary of Branke Sotre (artist).
S362 **S133** 1m. multicoloured 2·75 2·75

S134 Biathlete

2006. Winter Olympic Games, Turin. Multicoloured.
S363 50f. Type **S134** 1·40 1·40
S364 1m. Alpine skier 2·75 2·75

S135 Kulasi

2006. Spas.
S365 **S135** 20f. multicoloured 1·00 1·00
No. S365 is as No. S308 but redrawn.

S136 Inscr "Saxifraga prenja"

2006. Flora. Multicoloured.
S366 50f. Type **S136** 1·40 1·40
S367 50f. *Asperula hercegovina* 1·40 1·40
S368 1m. *Campanula hercegovina* 2·75 2·75
S369 1m. Inscr "Oxtropis prenja" 2·75 2·75

S137 Basket of Eggs

2006. Easter.
S370 **S137** 70f. multicoloured 2·10 2·10

S138 *Tear* (Luja Kajkut)

2006. Europa. Integration. Multicoloured.
S371 1m. Type **S138** 2·75 2·75
S372 1m.50 "Country Dance" (Milica Popic) 4·25 4·25

S139 Emblem

2005. Obligatory Tax. Red Cross.
S373 **S139** 20f. multicoloured 1·00 1·00

S140 Legs and Ball

2006. World Cup Football Championship, Germany. Multicoloured.
S374 50f. Type **S140** 1·40 1·40
S375 1m. Stadium and ball 2·75 2·75
MSS376 65×49 mm. 3m.German player and ball 8·25 8·25

S141 Runner

2006. Tenth Anniv of Vidovdan Road Race.
S377 **S141** 1m. multicoloured 2·75 2·75

S142 Nikola Tesla

2006. 150th Birth Anniv of Nikola Tesla (engineer) (1st issue). Sheet 66×60 mm.
MSS378 1m.50 multicoloured 4·25 4·25
The stamps and margin of **MS**S378 form a composite design.
See also No. S385.

S143 "CTOH TB"

2006. Obligatory Tax. Anti-Tuberculosis Week.

S379	**S143** 20f. multicoloured	1·00	1·00

S144 *Tetrao urogallus* (capercaille)

2006. European Nature Protection. Multicoloured.

S380	50f. Type **S144**	1·40	1·40
S381	1m. *Rupicapra rupicapra* (chamois)	2·75	2·75

No. S382 and Type S **145** have been left for "50th Anniv of Children's Theatre", issued on 14 October 2006, not yet received.

S146 Buckle

2006. Museum Exhibits. Multicoloured.

S383	1m. Type **S146**	2·75	2·75
S384	1m. Curved buckle with red stones	2·75	2·75

S147 Nikola Tesla

2006. 150th Birth Anniv of Nikola Tesla (engineer) (2nd issue).

S385	**S147** 70f. multicoloured	2·10	2·10

S148 Johann von Goethe

2007. 175th Birth Anniv of Johann Wolfgang von Goethe (polymath).

S386	**S148** 1m.50 multicoloured	4·25	4·25

S149 Decorated Egg

2007. Easter.

S387	**S149** 70f. multicoloured	2·10	2·10

S150 Study for Isabella d'Este

2007. 555th Birth Anniv of Leonardo da Vinci (artist and polymath). Multicoloured.

S388	70f. Type **S150**	2·10	2·10
S389	1m. Study for The Last Supper	2·75	2·75

S151 Campsite

2007. Europa. Centenary of Scouting. Multicoloured. (a) 26×41 mm.

S390	1m. Type **S151**	2·75	2·75
S391	1m.50 Scouts	4·25	4·25

(b) Size 35×45 mm.

S392	1m. As Type **S151**, with pink upper edge	2·75	2·75
S393	1m. As Type S **151**, with pink lower edge 'EUROPA 100 JAHRE PFADFINDERBEWEGUNG'	2·75	2·75
S394	1m. As Type S **151** with pink lower edge 'EUROPA 100 ANS DU SCOUTISME'	2·75	2·75
S395	1m.50 As No. S 391, with pink upper edge	4·25	4·25
S396	1m.50 As No. S 391, with pink upper edge 'EUROPA 100 YEARS OF SCOUTING'	4·25	4·25
S397	1m.50 As No. S 391, with pink lower edge	4·25	4·25

S152 Clasped Hands

2007. Obligatory Tax. Red Cross.

S398	**S152** 20f. multicoloured	1·00	1·00

S153 Liplje Monastery

2007. Monasteries. Multicoloured.

S399	70f. Type **S153**	1·90	1·90
S400	1m. Dobricevo	2·75	2·75

S154 Koarac

2007. Cities. Multicoloured.

S401	20f. Type **S154**	70	70
S402	20f. Derventa	70	70
S403	20f. Prijedor	70	70
S404	20f. Laktasi	70	70
S405	20f. Foca	70	70
S406	20f. Bijelijina	70	70
S407	70f. Srebrenica	2·10	2·10
S408	1m.50 Sipovo	4·25	4·25
S409	1m.50 Mrkonjic Grad	4·25	4·25
S410	2m. Trebinje	5·50	5·50
S411	5m. Zvornik	14·00	14·00

S155 Serbian Tri-colour Hound

2007. Dogs. Multicoloured.

S412	70f. Type **S155**	2·10	2·10
S413	70f. Istarski Ostrodlaki gonic (rough coated scent hound)	2·10	2·10
S414	70f. Srpski odbrambeni pas (Serbian guard dog)	2·10	2·10
S415	70f. Tornak (sheep dog)	2·10	2·10

S156 Orthodox Church and Old Post Office

2007. Centenary of Post Office, Obudovac.

S416	**S156** 10f. multicoloured	1·00	1·00

S157 Ban Milosavljevic (statue)

2007. 125th Birth Anniv of Ban Svetislav Milosavljevic (leader 1930–33).

S417	**S157** 1m.50 multicoloured	4·25	4·25

S158 Apple containing People

2007. Obligatory Tax. Anti-Tuberculosis Week.

S418	**S158** 20f. multicoloured	1·20	1·20

S159 Early Racquet and Balls

2007. Centenary of Banja Luca Tennis Club. Sheet 83×58 mm containing Type **S159** and similar horiz design. Multicoloured.

MSS419	1m.×2 Type **S159**; Modern racquet and ball	5·50	5·50

The stamps and margin of **MS**S419 form a composite design.

S160 Sputnik and Globe

2007. 50th Anniv of Space Exploration.

S420	**S160** 1m.50 multicoloured	4·25	4·25

S161 *Picea abies*

2007. European Nature Protection. Conifers. Multicoloured.

S421	70f. Type **S161**	1·90	1·90
S422	1m. *Picea omorica*	2·75	2·75

S162 Post Office Building

2008. 125th Anniv of Samac Post Office.

S422a	**S162** 1m.40 multicoloured	4·25	4·25

S163 *Self Portrait*

2008. 155th Birth Anniv of Vincent Van Gogh (artist).

S423	**S163** 1m.50 multicoloured	4·25	4·25

S164 Player's Foot and Ball

2008. Euro 2008–European Football Championships, Austria and Switzerland. Sheet 82×60 mm containing Type **S164** and similar vert design. Multicoloured.

MSS424	1m.40×2, Type **S164**; Ball and red and white boot	8·25	8·25

The stamps and margins of **MS**S424 form a composite design.

S165 Quill and Ink Pot

2008. Europa. The Letter. Multicoloured.

S425	1m. Type **S165**	2·75	2·75
S426	2m. Hand holding pencil	5·50	5·50
MSS427	108×82 mm. Nos. S425/6, each×3	26·00	26·00

S166 Hands

2008. Obligatory Tax. Red Cross.

S428	**166** 20f. multicoloured	1·20	1·20

S167 Children and Microphone

2008. 15th Children's Song Festival, Djurdjerdan.

S429	**S167** 1m.50 multicoloured	4·25	4·25

S168 Post Van

2008. Personal Stamps. Multicoloured. Self-adhesive.

S430	70f. Type **S168**	2·10	2·10
S431	70f. Post box (vert)	2·10	2·10
S432	70f. Hand stamp (vert)	2·10	2·10
S433	70f. Post horn	2·10	2·10

S169 Festival Mascot as Postman

2008. Banja Luka International Festival.

S434	**S169** 1m.50 multicoloured	4·25	4·25

S170 *Gyromitra esculenta*

2008. Poisonous Fungi. Multicoloured.

S435	70f. Type **S170**	2·10	2·10
S436	70f. *Amanita muscaria*	2·10	2·10
S437	70f. *Amanita pantherina*	2·10	2·10
S438	70f. *Amanita phalloides*	2·10	2·10

S171 Charles Darwin

2008. 150th Anniv of Publication of *On the Origin of Species* by Charles Darwin.

S439	**S171** 1m.50 multicoloured	4·25	4·25

S172 *Gentiana verna*

2008. Flowers. Multicoloured.

S440	50f. Type **S172**	1·60	1·60
S441	1m.50 *Galanthus nivalis* (vert)	4·75	4·75
S442	2m. *Viola odorata*	6·25	6·25
S443	5m. *Centaurea cyanus*	16·00	16·00

S173 High Jump and National Stadium

2008. Olympic Games, Beijing. Multicoloured.

S444	70f. Type **S173**	2·40	2·40
S445	2m.10 Swimmer and National Aquatic Center, Beijing	6·50	6·50
MSS446	3m.10 Gymnast	10·00	10·00

No. S447 is vacant.

S174 *Ciconia ciconia* (white stork)

2008. European Nature Protection. Birds. Multicoloured.

S448	1m. Type **S174**	3·25	3·25
S449	1m. *Strix aluco* (Eurasian tawny owl)	3·25	3·25

S175 Tvrdos

2008. Monasteries. Multicoloured.

S450	1m. Type **S175**	3·25	3·25
S451	1m. Gracanica	3·25	3·25

S175a Flowers

2008. Obligatory Tax. Tuberculosis Week.

S451a	**S 175a** 20f. multicoloured	1·20	1·20

S176 Milan Jelic

2008. Milan Jelic (president 2006–7) Commemoration. Sheet 87×63 mm.

MSS452	multicoloured	6·50	6·50

S177 Train and Travellers

2008. 125th Anniv of Orient Express.

S453	**S177** 1m.40 multicoloured	4·20	4·25

S178 Alfred Nobel

2008. 175th Birth Anniv of Alfred Nobel (chemist, engineer, inventor of dynamite and instituted Nobel Prizes).

S454	**S178** 1m.50 multicoloured	4·75	4·75

S179 Jovan Zmaj

2008. 125th Birth Anniv of Jovan Jovanovic Zmaj (writer).

S455	**S179** 1m.50 multicoloured	4·25	4·25

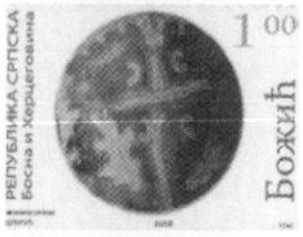

S180 Celebratory Loaf of Bread

2008. Christmas.

S456	**S180** 1m. multicoloured	3·00	3·00

S181 Vucko (games mascot)

2009. 25th Anniv of Winter Olympic Games, Sarajevo.

S457	**S181** 1m.50 multicolured	4·75	4·75

S182 Amerigo Vespucci

2009. Explorers. Multicoloured.

S458	70f. Type **S182**	2·10	2·10
S459	1m.50 Marco Polo	4·75	4·75

S183 Triceratops

2009. Dinosaurs. Multicoloured.

S460	70f. Type **S183**	2·10	2·10
S461	1m.50 Diplodocus	4·75	4·75

S184 Court of Human Rights Building

2009. 50th Anniv of European Court of Human Rights (S462) or 60th Anniv of Council of Europe (S463). Multicoloured.

S462	1m. Type **S184**	3·75	3·75
S463	1m.50 Council of Europe Building	4·75	4·75

Nos. S464/6 and Type S **185** are left for Animals, issued on 15 April 2009, not yet received.

Nos. S467/9 and Type S **186** are left for Europa. Astronomy, issued on 23 April 2009, not yet received.

S187 Globe and Red Cross Flag

2009. Obligatory Tax.150th Anniv of Red Cross.

S470	**S187** 20f. multicoloured	1·00	1·00

Nos. S471 and Type S **188** are left for World Rafting Championship, issued on 15 May 2009, not yet received.

S189 Paje Jovanovic

2009. 150th Birth Anniv of Paje Jovanovic (artist).

S472	**S189** 1m.50 multicoloured	4·25	4·25

S190 Self and Other Portraits

2009. 125th Birth Anniv of Amedeo Clemente Modigliani (artist).

S473	**S190** 1m.50 multicoloured	4·25	4·25

S191 Siamese

2009. Cats. Multicoloured.

S474	70f. Type **S191**	2·10	2·10
S475	70f. Tabby	2·10	2·10
S476	70f. Russian Blue	2·10	2·10
S477	70f. Persian	2·10	2·10

S192 Dragonfly

2009. Insects. Multicoloured.

S478	1m. Type **S192**	2·75	2·75
S479	1m. Ladybird	2·75	2·75
S480	1m. Staghorn beetle	2·75	2·75

S193 Robert Koch (bacteriologist, Nobel Prize Winner for Physiology or Medicine, 1905)

2009. Obligatory Tax. Tuberculosis Week.

S481	**S193** 20f. multicoloured	4·75	4·75

S194 Zvornik

2009. Castles. Multicoloured.

S482	70f. Type **S194**	2·10	2·10
S483	1m. Banja Luka	3·25	3·25

S195 Locomotive SKODA 1937

2009. Narrow Gauge. Multicoloured.

S484	70f. Type **S195**	2·10	2·10
S485	70f. Locomotive RAMA	2·10	2·10
S486	80f. Locomotive JZ 83-057	2·75	2·75
S487	80f. Locomotive UNRRA 22	2·75	2·75

S196 Citroen 2 CV

2009. Classic Cars. Multicoloured.

S488	70f. Type **S196**	2·10	2·10
S489	70f. Fiat Cinquecento	2·10	2·10
S490	80f. Volkswagen Beetle	2·75	2·75

S197 Snowman

2009. Christmas and New Year. Multicoloured.

S491	60f. Type **S197**	1·70	1·70
S492	60f. Santa Claus	1·70	1·70

S198 Badger

2009. Fauna

S493	**S198** 20f. multicoloured	75	75

S199 Bridge and Tower

2010. 600th Anniv of Zvornik

S494	**S199** 70f. multicoloured		

S200 Games Emblem and Luge

2010. Winter Olympic Games, Vancouver. Multicoloured.

S495	70f. Type **S200**	1·60	1·60
S496	1m.50 Ice dance	3·25	3·25

S201 Frédéric Chopin

2010. Birth Bicentenary of Frédéric François Chopin (composer)

S497	**S201** 1m.50 multicocloured	4·75	4·75

No. S498 and Type S **202** are left for Birth Centenary of Mesa Selimovic, issued on 26 April 2010, not yet received.

Nos. S499/501 and Type S **203** are left for Europa, issued on 7 May 2010, not yet received.

204 Player's Legs

2010. World Cup Football Championships, South Africa. Multicoloured.

S502	1m.50 Type **S204**	4·25	4·25
S503	1m.50 No. 11 player with arms wide spread	4·25	£425

S205 Hedgehog

2010. Fauna. Multicoloured.

S504	10f. Type **S205**	2·10	2·10
S505	50f. Wild boar	2·10	2·10
S506	90f. Wolf	2·10	2·10
S507	1m. Brown bear	2·10	2·10

S206 Sword (yataghan)

2010. Weaponry. Multicoloured.

S508	1m.80 Type **S206**	6·25	6·25
S509	2m. Flintlock pistol	6·50	6·50
S510	5m. Iron mace	14·50	14·50

S207 *Rhododendron hirsutum*

2010. Flora. Multicoloured.

S511	70f. Type **S207**	2·30	2·30
S512	70f. *Edraianthus sutjeski* (inscr 'Edrainthus Sutjeski')	2·30	2·30
S513	70f. *Trollius europaeus*	2·30	2·30
S514	70f. *Pancicia serbica*	2·30	2·30

S208 Figures (bas-relief)

2010. Cultural Heritage. Multicoloured.

S515	70f. Type **S208**	1·60	1·60
S516	1m.50 Inscribed tablet	3·25	3·25

S209 Trumpets and Trumpeter

2010. 50th Anniv of Trumpet Festival, Guca

S517	**S209**	1m.50 multicoloured	4·75	4·75

S210 Empty Silhouette

2010. Day of Missing and Fallen Persons

S518	**S210**	90f. scarlet-vermilion and black	2·75	2·75

Nos. S519/20 and Type S **211** are left for Nature Protection, issued on 23 September 2010, not yet received.

S212 '80' wearing Hats

2010. 80th Anniv of National Museum

S521	**S212**	90f. multicoloured	6·25	6·25

S213 St. Nicholas and Stocking

2010. Christmas

S522	**S213**	1m. multicoloured	3·25	3·25

No. S523 and Type **S214** are left for 400th Birth Anniv of St. Vasilije, issued on 28 December 2010, not yet received.

No. S524/5 and Type **S215** are left for Museum Exhibits, issued on 24 January 2011, not yet received.

No. S526 and Type **S216** are left for 120th Birth Anniv of Milan Budmir, issued on 11 February 2011, not yet received.

S217 Marie Curie and Chemistry Equipment

2011. Centenary of Marie Curie's Nobel Prize for Chemistry

S527	**S217**	1m.50 multicoloured	2·10	2·10

S213 Woodpecker, Deer, Fawn and Hare

2011. Europa. Forests. Multicoloured.

S528	1m. Type **S218**	2·10	2·10
S529	2m. Owl, fox and bear in coniferous woodland	4·25	4·25
MSS530	131×90 mm. 1m. As Type S**218** (35×45 mm) (imperf at foot); 1m. As Type S**218** (35×45 mm) (imperf at top); 1m. As Type S**218** (47×45 mm) (imperf at foot and right vertical side); 2m. As No. S529 (35×45 mm) (imperf at top); 2m. As S529 (35×45 mm) (imperf at foot); 2m. As S529 (47×45 mm) (imperf at top and right vertical side)	20·00	20·00

No. S531/4 and Type **S2**19 are left for Fauna, issued on 20 April 2011, not yet received.

S220 Red Cross

2011. OBLIGATORY TAX. Red Cross Week

(a) Sheet stamp

S535	**S220**	20f. multicoloured	80	80

(b) Coil Stamp

S535a	**S220**	20f. multicoloured	80	80

Nos. S536/9 and Type **S221** are left for Birds, issued on 10 May 2011, not yet received.

S222 Books

2011. 75th Anniv of National Library and University

S540	**S222**	90f. multicoloured	2·75	2·75

No. S541 and Type **S223** are left for Canoeing Championship, issued on 7 June 2011, not yet received.

S224 Crown and Saint

2011. Illuminated Letters from Miroslav's Gospel. Multicoloured.

S542	1m.50 Type **S224**	3·75	3·75
S543	2m.30 Figure leading multicoloured animal	4·75	4·75
S544	5m. Two birds	14·00	14·00

S225 Emblem

2011. International Year of Youth

S545	**S225**	90f. multicoloured	2·75	2·75

S226 Locomotive DHL 720-001

2011. Locomotives. Multicoloured.

SS546	90f. Type S**226**	2·75	2·75
SS547	90f. DHL 740-108	2·75	2·75
SS548	90f. DIVIV 801	2·75	2·75
SS549	90f. DIVIV 802	2·75	2·75
MSSS550	80×58 mm. 3m. DHL L45H-096	8·25	8·25

Pt. 1

BOTSWANA

Formerly Bechuanaland Protectorate, attained independence on 30 September 1966, and changed its name to Botswana.

1966. 100 cents = 1 rand.
1976. 100 thebe = 1 pula.

47 National Assembly Building

1966. Independence. Multicoloured.

202	2½c. Type **47**	15	10
203	5c. Abattoir, Lobatsi	20	10
204	15c. National Airways Douglas DC-3	65	20
205	35c. State House, Gaberones	40	30

1966. Nos. 168/81 of Bechuanaland optd **REPUBLIC OF BOTSWANA**.

206	**28**	1c. multicoloured	25	10
207	-	2c. orange, black and olive	30	1·75
208	-	2½c. multicoloured	30	10
209	-	3½c. multicoloured	1·25	40
210	-	5c. multicoloured	1·50	1·50
211	-	7½c. multicoloured	50	1·75
212	-	10c. multicoloured	1·00	20
213	-	12½c. multicoloured	2·00	3·00
214	-	20c. brown and drab	20	1·00
215	-	25c. sepia and lemon	20	2·00
216	-	35c. blue and orange	30	2·50
217	-	50c. sepia and olive	20	70
218	-	1r. black and brown	40	1·25
219	-	2r. brown and turquoise	60	2·75

52 Golden Oriole

1967. Multicoloured.

220	1c. Type **52**	30	15
221	2c. Hoopoe ("African Hoopoe")	60	70
222	3c. Groundscraper thrush	55	10
223	4c. Cordon-bleu ("Blue Waxbill")	55	10
224	5c. Secretary bird	55	10
225	7c. Southern yellow-billed hornbill ("Yellow-billed Hornbill")	60	1·00
226	10c. Burchell's gonolek ("Crimson-breasted Shrike")	60	15
227	15c. Malachite kingfisher	8·00	3·00
228	20c. African fish eagle ("Fish Eagle")	8·00	2·00
229	25c. Go-away bird ("Grey Loerie")	4·00	1·50
230	35c. Scimitar-bill	6·00	2·75
231	50c. Comb duck ("Knob-Billed Duck")	2·75	2·75
232	1r. Levaillant's barbet ("Crested Barbet")	5·00	3·50
233	2r. Didric cuckoo ("Diederick Cuckoo")	7·00	17·00

66 Students and University

1967. First Conferment of University Degrees.

234	**66**	3c. sepia, blue and orange	10	10
235	**66**	7c. sepia, blue and turquoise	10	10
236	**66**	15c. sepia, blue and red	10	10
237	**66**	35c. sepia, blue and violet	20	20

67 Bushbuck

1967. Chobe Game Reserve. Multicoloured.

238	3c. Type **67**	10	20
239	7c. Sable Antelope	15	30
240	35c. Fishing on the Chobe River	90	1·10

70 Arms of Botswana and Human Rights Emblem

1968. Human Rights Year.

241	**70**	3c. multicoloured	10	10
242	-	15c. multicoloured	25	45
243	-	25c. multicoloured	25	60

The designs of Nos. 242/3 are similar, but are arranged differently.

73 Eland and Giraffe Rock Paintings, Tsodilo Hills

1968. Opening of National Museum and Art Gallery. Multicoloured.

244	3c. Type **73**	20	20
245	7c. Girl wearing ceremonial beads (31×48 mm)	25	40
246	10c. "Baobab Trees" (Thomas Baines)	25	30
247	15c. National Museum and art gallery (72×19 mm)	40	1·50
MS248	132×82 mm. Nos. 244/7	1·00	2·25

77 African Family, and Star over Village

1968. Christmas.

249	**77**	1c. multicoloured	10	10
250	**77**	2c. multicoloured	10	10
251	**77**	5c. multicoloured	10	10
252	**77**	25c. multicoloured	15	50

78 Scout, Lion and Badge in frame

1969. 22nd World Scout Conference, Helsinki. Multuicoloured.

253	3c. Type **78**	30	30
254	15c. Scouts cooking over open fire (vert)	35	1·00
255	25c. Scouts around camp fire	35	1·00

81 Woman, Child and Christmas Star

1969. Christmas.

256	**81**	1c. blue and brown	10	10
257	**81**	2c. olive and brown	10	10
258	**81**	4c. yellow and brown	10	10
259	**81**	35c. brown and violet	20	20
MS260		86×128 mm. Nos. 256/9	70	1·10

82 Diamond Treatment Plant, Orapa

1970. Developing Botswana. Multicoloured.

261	3c. Type **82**	80	20
262	7c. Copper-nickel mining	1·00	20
263	10c. Copper-nickel mine, Selebi-Pikwe (horiz)	1·25	15
264	35c. Orapa Diamond mine and diamonds (horiz)	3·00	1·25

83 Mr. Micawber (*David Copperfield*)

1970. Death Centenary of Charles Dickens. Multicoloured.

265	3c. Type **83**	25	10
266	7c. Scrooge (*A Christmas Carol*)	25	10
267	15c. Fagin (*Oliver Twist*)	45	40
268	25c. Bill Sykes (*Oliver Twist*)	70	60
MS269	114×81 mm. Nos. 265/8	2·75	4·00

84 U.N. Building and Emblem

1970. 25th Anniv of United Nations.

270	**84**	15c. blue, brown and silver	70	30

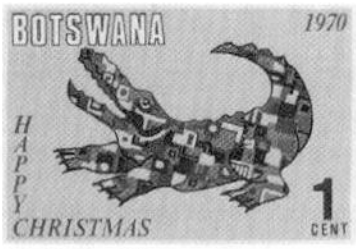

85 Crocodile

1970. Christmas. Multicoloured.

271	1c. Type **85**	10	10
272	2c. Giraffe	10	10
273	7c. Elephant	15	15
274	25c. Rhinoceros	60	80
MS275	128×90 mm. Nos. 271/4	1·00	3·00

86 Sorghum

1971. Important Crops. Multicoloured.

276	3c. Type **86**	15	10
277	7c. Millet	20	10
278	10c. Maize	20	10
279	35c. Groundnuts	70	1·00

87 Map and Head of Cow

1971. Fifth Anniv of Independence.

280	**87**	3c. black, brown and green	10	10
281	-	4c. black, light blue and blue	10	10
282	-	7c. black and orange	20	15
283	-	10c. multicoloured	20	15
284	-	20c. multicoloured	55	2·50

DESIGNS: 4c. Map and cogs; 7c. Map and common zebra; 10c. Map and sorghum stalk crossed by tusk; 20c. Arms and map of Botswana.

88 King bringing Gift of Gold

1971. Christmas. Multicoloured.

285	2c. Type **88**	10	10
286	3c. King bringing frankincense	10	10
287	7c. King bringing myrrh	10	10
288	20c. Three Kings behold the star	35	65
MS289	85×128 mm. Nos. 285/8	1·00	3·50

89 Orion

1972. "Night Sky".

290	**89**	3c. blue, black and red	1·00	40
291	-	7c. blue, black and yellow	1·25	85
292	-	10c. green, black and orange	1·40	1·00
293	-	20c. blue, black and green	2·00	3·50

CONSTELLATIONS: 7c. The Scorpion; 10c. The Centaur; 20c. The Cross.

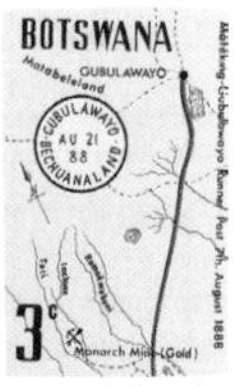

90 Postmark and Map

1972. Mafeking-Gubulawayo Runner Post. Multicoloured.

294	3c. Type **90**	30	10
295	4c. Bechuanaland stamp and map	30	35
296	7c. Runners and map	45	50
297	20c. Mafeking postmark and map	1·10	1·50
MS298	84×216 mm. Nos. 294/7 vertically *se-tenant*, forming a composite map design	11·00	15·00

For these designs with changed inscription see Nos. 652/5.

91 Cross, Map and Bells

1972. Christmas. Each with Cross and Map. Multicoloured.

299	2c. Type **91**	10	75
300	3c. Cross, map and candle	10	10
301	7c. Cross, map and Christmas tree	15	25
302	20c. Cross, map, star and holly	40	85
MS303	96×119 mm. Nos. 299/302	1·25	3·50

92 Thor

1973. Centenary of I.M.O./W.M.O. Norse Myths. Multicoloured.

304	3c. Type **92**	20	10
305	4c. Sun God's chariot (horiz)	25	15
306	7c. Ymir, the frost giant	30	15
307	20c. Odin and Sleipnir (horiz)	75	70

93 Livingstone and River Scene

1973. Death Centenary of Dr. Livingstone. Multicoloured.

308	3c. Type **93**	20	10
309	20c. Livingstone meeting Stanley	90	90

94 Donkey and Foal at Village Trough

1973. Christmas. Multicoloured.

310	3c. Type **94**	10	10
311	4c. Shepherd and flock (horiz)	10	10
312	7c. Mother and Child	10	10
313	20c. Kgotla meeting (horiz)	40	85

95 Gaborone Campus

1974. Tenth Anniv of University of Botswana, Lesotho and Swaziland. Multicoloured.

314	3c. Type **95**	10	10
315	7c. Kwaluseni Campus	10	10
316	20c. Roma Campus	15	20
317	35c. Map and flags of the three countries	20	35

96 Methods of Mail Transport

1974. Centenary of U.P.U. Multicoloured.

318	2c. Type **96**	55	35
319	3c. Post Office, Palapye, circa 1889	55	35
320	7c. Bechuanaland Police Camel Post, circa 1900	95	70
321	20c. Hawker Siddeley H.S.748 and de Havilland D.H.9 mail planes of 1920 and 1974	2·75	2·50

97 Amethyst

1974. Botswana Minerals. Multicoloured.

322	1c. Type **97**	60	2·50
323	2c. Agate-"Botswana Pink"	60	2·50
324	3c. Quartz	65	80
325	4c. Copper nickel	70	60
326	5c. Moss agate	70	1·00
327	7c. Agate	80	1·25
328	10c. Stilbite	1·60	65
329	15c. Moshaneng banded marble	2·00	4·00
330	20c. Gem diamonds	4·00	4·50
331	25c. Chrysotile	5·00	2·50
332	35c. Jasper	5·00	5·50
333	50c. Moss quartz	4·50	7·00
334	1r. Citrine	7·50	10·00
335	2r. Chalcopyrite	20·00	20·00

98 *Stapelia variegata*

1974. Christmas. Multicoloured.

336	2c. Type **98**	20	40
337	7c. *Hibiscus lunarifolius*	30	20
338	15c. *Ceratotheca triloba*	45	1·00
339	20c. *Nerine laticoma*	60	1·25
MS340	85×130 mm. Nos. 336/9	2·00	4·25

99 President Sir Seretse Khama

1975. Tenth Anniv of Self-Government.

341	**99**	4c. multicoloured	10	10
342	**99**	10c. multicoloured	15	10
343	**99**	20c. multicoloured	25	25
344	**99**	35c. multicoloured	45	50
MS345		93×130 mm. Nos. 341/4	1·00	1·50

100 Ostrich

1975. Rock Paintings, Tsodilo Hills. Multicoloured.

346	4c. Type **100**	60	10
347	10c. White rhinoceros	1·00	10
348	25c. Spotted hyena	2·00	55
349	35c. Scorpion	2·00	1·10
MS350	150×150 mm. Nos. 346/9	12·00	7·50

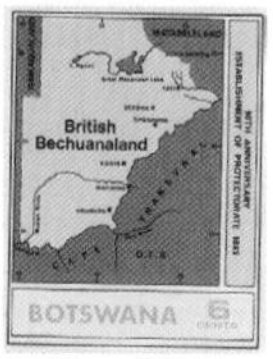

101 Map of British Bechuanaland, 1885

1975. Anniversaries. Multicoloured.

351	6c. Type **101**	30	20
352	10c. Chief Khama, 1875	40	15
353	25c. Chiefs Sebele, Bathoen and Khama, 1895 (horiz)	80	75

EVENTS: 6c. 90th anniv of Protectorate; 10c. Centenary of Khama's accession; 25c. 80th anniv of Chiefs' visit to London.

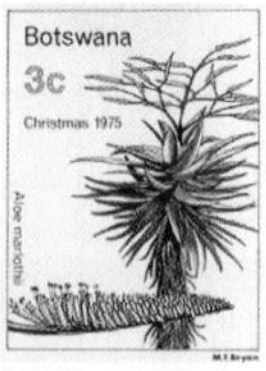

102 *Aloe marlothii*

1975. Christmas. Aloes. Multicoloured.

354	3c. Type **102**	20	10
355	10c. *Aloe lutescens*	40	20
356	15c. *Aloe zebrina*	60	1·50
357	25c. *Aloe littoralis*	75	2·50

103 Drum

1976. Traditional Musical Instruments. Multicoloured.

358	4c. Type **103**	15	10
359	10c. Hand piano	20	10
360	15c. Segankuru (violin)	25	50
361	25c. Kudu signal horn	30	1·25

104 One Pula Note

1976. First National Currency. Multicoloured.

362	4c. Type **104**	15	10
363	10c. Two pula note	20	10
364	15c. Five pula note	35	20
365	25c. Ten pula note	45	45
MS366	163×107 mm. Nos. 362/5	1·00	3·50

1976. Nos. 322/35 surch in new currency.

367	1t. on 1c. multicoloured	2·00	70
368	2t. on 2c. multicoloured	2·00	1·75
369	3t. on 3c. multicoloured	1·50	60

370	4t. on 4c. multicoloured	2·50	40
371	5t. on 5c. multicoloured	2·50	40
372	7t. on 7c. multicoloured	1·25	2·75
373	10t. on 10c. multicoloured	1·25	80
374	15t. on 15c. multicoloured	4·25	3·25
375	20t. on 20c. multicoloured	7·50	80
376	25t. on 25c. multicoloured	5·00	1·25
377	35t. on 35c. multicoloured	4·00	5·00
378	50t. on 50c. multicoloured	5·50	9·00
379	1p. on 1r. multicoloured	6·00	9·50
380	2p. on 2r. multicoloured	8·00	11·00

106 Botswana Cattle

1976. Tenth Anniv of Independence. Multicoloured.

381	4t. Type **106**	15	10
382	10t. Antelope, Okavango Delta (vert)	20	10
383	15t. School and pupils	20	40
384	25t. Rural weaving (vert)	20	50
385	35t. Miner (vert)	75	85

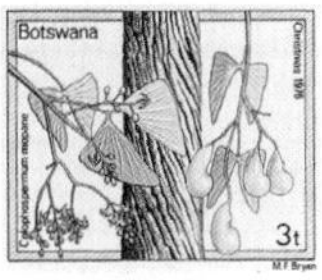

107 *Colophospermum mopane*

1976. Christmas. Trees. Multicoloured.

386	3t. Type **107**	15	10
387	4t. *Baikiaea plurijuga*	15	10
388	10t. *Sterculia rogersii*	20	10
389	25t. *Acacia nilotica*	45	50
390	40t. *Kigelia africana*	75	1·25

108 Coronation Coach

1977. Silver Jubilee. Multicoloured.

391	4t. The Queen and Sir Seretse Khama	10	10
392	25t. Type **108**	20	15
393	40t. The Recognition	35	90

109 African Clawless Otter

1977. Diminishing Species. Multicoloured.

394	3t. Type **109**	4·25	40
395	4t. Serval	4·25	40
396	10t. Bat-eared fox	4·75	40
397	25t. Temminck's ground pangolin	11·00	2·00
398	40t. Brown hyena	13·00	7·50

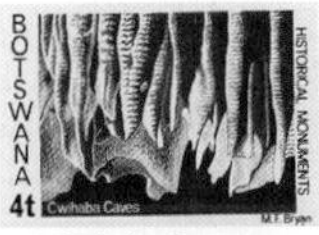

110 Cwihaba Caves

1977. Historical Monuments. Multicoloured.

399	4t. Type **110**	20	10
400	5t. Khama Memorial	20	10
401	15t. Green's Tree	30	40
402	20t. Mmajojo Ruins	30	45
403	25t. Ancient morabaraba board	30	50
404	35t. Matsieng's footprint	40	60
MS405	154×105 mm. Nos. 399/404	2·50	3·25

111 *Hypoxis nitida*

1977. Christmas. Lilies. Multicoloured.

406	3t. Type **111**	15	10
407	5t. *Haemanthus magnificus*	15	10
408	10t. *Boophane disticha*	20	10
409	25t. *Vellozia retinervis*	40	55
410	40t. *Ammocharis coranica*	55	1·25

112 Black Bustard

1978. Birds. Multicoloured.

411	1t. Type **112**	70	1·25
412	2t. Marabou stork	90	1·25
413	3t. Green wood hoopoe ("Red Billed Hoopoe")	70	85
414	4t. Carmine bee eater	2·00	1·00
415	5t. African jacana	1·00	40
416	7t. African paradise flycatcher ("Paradise Flycatcher")	1·00	3·00
417	10t. Bennett's woodpecker	2·00	60
418	15t. Red bishop	1·50	3·00
419	20t. Crowned plover	1·75	2·00
420	25t. Giant kingfisher	70	3·00
421	30t. White-faced whistling duck ("White-faced Duck")	70	70
422	35t. Green-backed heron	70	3·25
423	45t. Black-headed heron	1·00	3·00
424	50t. Spotted eagle owl	5·00	4·50
425	1p. Gabar goshawk	2·50	4·50
426	2p. Martial eagle	3·00	8·00
427	5p. Saddle-bill stork	5·50	16·00

113 Tawana making Kaross

1978. Okavango Delta. Multicoloured.

428	4t. Type **113**	10	30
429	5t. Tribe localities	10	10
430	15t. Bushman collecting roots	25	40
431	20t. Herero woman milking	35	70
432	25t. Yei poling "mokoro" (canoe)	40	60
433	35t. Mbukushu fishing	45	1·75
MS434	150×98 mm. Nos. 428/33	1·50	3·75

114 *Caralluma lutea*

1978. Christmas. Flowers. Multicoloured.

435	5t. Type **114**	35	10
436	10t. *Hoodia lugardii*	50	15
437	15t. *Ipomoea transvaalensis*	90	55
438	25t. *Ansellia gigantea*	1·10	70

115 Sip Well

1979. Water Development. Multicoloured.

439	3t. Type **115**	10	10
440	5t. Watering pit	10	10
441	10t. Hand dug well	15	10
442	22t. Windmill	20	30
443	50t. Drilling rig truck	40	55

116 Pottery

1979. Handicrafts. Multicoloured.

444	5t. Type **116**	10	10
445	10t. Clay modelling	10	10
446	25t. Basketry	20	25
447	40t. Beadwork	40	50
MS448	123×96 mm. Nos. 444/7	1·00	2·50

117 British Bechuanaland 1885 1d. Stamp and Sir Rowland Hill

1979. Death Centenary of Sir Rowland Hill. Multicoloured.

449	5t. Type **117**	20	10
450	25t. Bechuanaland Protectorate 1932 2d. stamp	45	50
451	45t. 1967 Hoopoe 2c. definitive stamp	55	1·25

118 Children Playing

1979. International Year of the Child. Multicoloured.

452	5t. Type **118**	20	10
453	10t. Child playing with doll (vert)	30	20

119 *Ximenia caffra*

1979. Christmas. Flowers. Multicoloured.

454	5t. Type **119**	10	10
455	10t. *Sclerocarya caffra*	20	20
456	15t. *Hexalobus monopetalus*	35	35
457	25t. *Ficus soldanella*	45	45

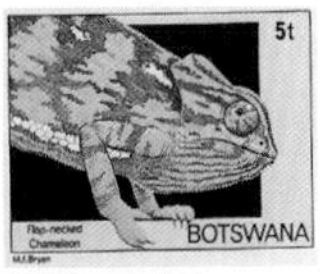

120 Flap-necked Chameleon

1980. Reptiles. Multicoloured.

458	5t. Type **120**	30	10
459	10t. Leopard tortoise	30	15
460	25t. Puff adder	50	65
461	40t. White-throated monitor	60	2·50

121 Rock Breaking

1980. Early Mining. Multicoloured.

462	5t. Type **121**	25	15
463	10t. Ore hoisting	30	15
464	15t. Ore transport	70	60
465	20t. Ore crushing	75	90
466	25t. Smelting	80	90
467	35t. Tool and products	1·00	1·75

122 "Chiwele and the Giant"

1980. Folktales. Multicoloured.

468	5t. Type **122**	10	10
469	10t. "Kgori is not deceived" (vert)	15	10
470	30t. "Nyambi's wife and Crocodile" (vert)	45	45
471	45t. "Clever Hare" (horiz)	60	60

The 10t. and 30t. are 28×37 mm and the 45t. 44×27 mm.

123 Game watching, Makgadikgadi Pans

1980. World Tourism Conference, Manila.

472	**123**	5t. multicoloured	45	20

124 *Acacia gerrardii*

1980. Christmas. Multicoloured.

473	6t. Type **124**	10	10
474	1t. *Acacia nilotica*	20	10
475	25t. *Acacia erubescens*	45	30
476	40t. *Dichrostachys cinerea*	70	70

125 Heinrich von Stephan and Botswana 3d. and 3c. U.P.U. Stamps

1981. 150th Birth Anniv of Heinrich von Stephan (founder of Universal Postal Union). Multicoloured.

477	6t. Type **125**	50	30
478	20t. 6d. and 7c. U.P.U. stamps	1·25	2·25

126 *Anax imperator* (dragonfly)

1981. Insects. Multicoloured.

479	6t. Type **126**	15	10
480	7t. *Sphodromantis gastrica* (mantid)	15	20
481	10t. *Zonocerus elegans* (grass-hopper)	15	20
482	20t. *Kheper nigroaeneus* (beetle)	25	50
483	30t. *Papilio demodocus* (butterfly)	35	70
484	45t. *Acanthocampa belina* (moth larva)	40	1·10
MS485	180×89 mm. Nos. 479/84	3·00	8·50

127 Camphill Community Rankoromane, Otse

1981. International Year for Disabled Persons. Multicoloured.

486	6t. Type **127**	20	10
487	20t. Resource Centre for the Blind, Mochudi	55	35
488	30t. Tlamelong Rehabilitation Centre, Tlokweng	75	45

128 Woman reading Letter

1981. Literacy Programme. Multicoloured.

489	6t. Type **128**	20	10
490	7t. Man filling in form	20	15
491	20t. Boy reading newspaper	60	35
492	30t. Child being taught to read	80	45

129 Sir Seretse Khama and Building

1981. First Death Anniv of Sir Seretse Khama (former President). Multicoloured.

493	6t. Type **129**	15	10
494	10t. Seretse Khama and building (different)	25	15
495	30t. Seretse Khama and Botswana flag	40	45
496	45t. Seretse Khama and building (different)	55	70

1981. Nos. 417 and 422 surch.

497	25t. on 35t. Green-backed heron	2·50	2·00
498	30t. on 10t. Bennett's woodpecker	2·50	2·00

131 Traditional Ploughing

1981. Cattle Industry. Multicoloured.

499	6t. Type **131**	10	10
500	20t. Agricultural show	30	50
501	30t. Botswana Meat Commission	35	60
502	45t. Vaccine Institute, Botswana	50	1·00

132 *Nymphaea caerulea*

1981. Christmas. Flowers. Multicoloured.

503	6t. Type **132**	20	10
504	10t. *Nymphoides indica*	25	10
505	25t. *Nymphaea lotus*	60	90
506	40t. *Ottelia kunenensis*	80	2·25

133 *Cattle Post Scene* (Boitumelo Golaakwena)

1982. Children's Art. Multicoloured.

507	6t. Type **133**	40	10
508	10t. *Kgotla Meeting* (Reginald Klinck)	50	15
509	30t. *Village Water Supply* (Keronemang Matswiri)	1·75	1·25
510	45t. *With the Crops* (Kennedy Balemoge)	1·75	3·00

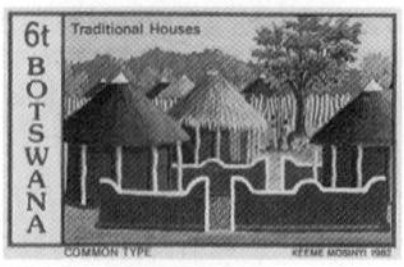

134 Common Type

1982. Traditional House. Multicoloured.

511	6t. Type **134**	40	15
512	10t. Kgatleng type	50	15
513	30t. North Eastern type	2·00	1·10
514	45t. Sarwa type	2·00	3·00

135 African Masked Weaver

1982. Birds. Multicoloured.

515	1t. Type **135**	80	1·75
516	2t. Miombo double-collared sunbird ("Lesser double-collared Sunbird")	90	1·75
517	3t. Red-throated bee eater	1·00	1·75
518	4t. Ostrich	1·00	1·75
519	5t. Grey-headed gull	1·00	1·75
520	6t. African pygmy ("Pygmy Goose")	1·00	40
521	7t. Cattle egret	1·00	15
522	8t. Lanner falcon	2·50	1·75
523	10t. Yellow-billed stork	1·00	20
524	15t. Red-billed pintail ("Red-billed Teal") (horiz)	2·75	25
525	20t. Barn owl (horiz)	5·50	3·50
526	25t. Hammerkop ("Hammerkop") (horiz)	3·25	70
527	30t. South African stilt ("Stilt") (horiz)	3·75	90
528	35t. Blacksmith plover (horiz)	3·75	80
529	45t. Senegal wattled plover ("Watted Plover") (horiz)	3·75	1·75
530	50t. Helmeted guineafowl ("Crowned Guineafowl") (horiz)	4·75	2·50
531	1p. Cape vulture (horiz)	9·00	12·00
532	2p. Augur buzzard (horiz)	11·00	17·00

136 *Coprinus comatus*

1982. Christmas. Fungi. Multicoloured.

533	7t. Type **136**	2·50	20
534	15t. *Lactarius deliciosus*	3·75	65
535	35t. *Amanita pantherina*	6·00	2·00
536	50t. *Boletus edulis*	7·50	8·00

137 President Quett Masire

1983. Commonwealth Day. Multicoloured.

537	7t. Type **137**	10	10
538	15t. Native dancers	15	20
539	35t. Melbourne conference centre	45	55
540	45t. Meeting of Heads of State, Melbourne	55	80

138 Wattled Crane

1983. Endangered Species. Multicoloured.

541	7t. Type **138**	3·00	55
542	15t. *Aloe lutescens*	2·50	80
543	35t. Roan antelope	3·00	3·25
544	50t. Ivory palm	3·50	7·00

139 Wooden Spoons

1983. Traditional Artifacts. Multicoloured.

545	7t. Type **139**	25	10
546	15t. Personal ornaments	45	30
547	35t. Ox-hide milk bag	75	65
548	50t. Decorated knives	1·00	1·10
MS549	115×102 mm. Nos. 545×8	4·25	5·00

140 *Pantala flavescens*

1983. Christmas. Dragonflies. Multicoloured.

550	6t. Type **140**	85	10
551	15t. *Anax imperator*	1·75	50
552	25t. *Trithemis arteriosa*	2·00	85
553	45t. *Chlorolestes elegans*	2·75	4·75

141 Sorting Diamonds

1984. Mining Industry. Multicoloured.

554	7t. Type **141**	2·00	50
555	15t. Lime kiln	2·00	75
556	35t. Copper-nickel smelter plant (vert)	3·25	3·25
557	60t. Stockpiled coal (vert)	3·75	10·00

142 Riding Cattle

1984. Traditional Transport. Multicoloured.

558	7t. Type **142**	20	10
559	25t. Sledge	65	60
560	35t. Wagon	85	1·50
561	50t. Two-wheeled donkey cart	1·25	4·50

143 Avro 504 Aircraft

1984. 40th Anniv of International Civil Aviation Organization. Multicoloured.

562	7t. Type **143**	75	20
563	10t. Westland Wessex trimotor	1·00	35
564	15t. Junkers Ju 52/3m	1·40	95
565	25t. de Havilland Dominie	2·00	1·75
566	35t. Douglas DC-3 *Wenala*	2·25	3·50
567	50t. Fokker Friendship	2·50	7·00

144 *Papilio demodocus*

1984. Christmas. Butterflies. Multicoloured.

568	7t. Type **144**	2·00	30
569	25t. *Byblia anvatara*	3·25	1·50
570	35t. *Danaus chrysippus*	3·50	3·00
571	50t. *Graphium taboranus*	4·75	11·00

No. 570 is incorrectly inscr "Hypolimnas misippus".

145 Seswaa (meat dish)

1985. Fifth Anniv of Southern African Development Co-ordination Conference. Traditional Foods. Multicoloured.

572	7t. Type **145**	50	10
573	15t. Bogobe (cereal porridge)	75	35
574	25t. Madila (soured coagulated cow's milk)	1·00	55
575	50t. Phane (caterpillars)	1·50	2·25
MS576	117×103 mm. Nos. 572/5	7·00	10·00

146 1885 British Bechuanaland Overprint on Cape of Good Hope ½d.

1985. Centenary of First Bechuanaland Stamps.

577	**146**	7t. black, grey and red	1·00	20
578	-	15t. black, brown yell	1·75	50
579	-	25t. black and red	2·25	80
580	-	35t. black, blue and gold	2·50	2·00
581	-	50t. multicoloured	2·75	3·75

DESIGNS—VERT: 15t. 1897 Bechuanaland Protectorate overprint on G.B. 3d.; 25t. Bechuanaland Protectorate 1932 1d. definitive. HORIZ: 35t. Bechuanaland 1965 Internal Self-Government 5c.; 50t. Botswana 1966 Independence 2½c.

147 Bechuanaland Border Police, 1885–95

1985. Centenary of Botswana Police. Multicoloured.

582	7t. Type **147**	2·25	50
583	10t. Bechuanaland Mounted Police, 1895–1902	2·50	50
584	25t. Bechuanaland Protectorate Police, 1903–66	3·50	2·00
585	50t. Botswana Police, from 1966	5·50	7·50

148 *Cucumis metuliferus*

1985. Christmas. Edible Wild Cucumbers. Multicoloured.

586	7t. Type **148**	1·25	10
587	15t. *Acanthosicyos naudinianus*	2·25	70
588	25t. *Coccinia sessifolia*	3·50	1·25
589	50t. *Momordica balsamina*	5·00	9·50

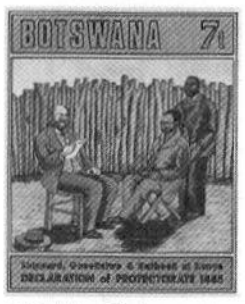

149 Mr. Shippard and Chief Gaseitsiwe of the Bangwaketse

1985. Centenary of Declaration of Bechuanaland Protectorate. Multicoloured.

590	7t. Type **149**	35	10
591	15t. Sir Charles Warren and Chief Sechele of the Bakwena	70	45
592	25t. Revd. Mackenzie and Chief Khama of the Bamangwato	1·25	85
593	50t. Map showing Protectorate	2·75	6·50
MS594	130×133 mm. Nos. 590/3	13·00	15·00

150 Halley's Comet over Serowe

1986. Appearance of Halley's Comet. Multicoloured.

595	7t. Type **150**	80	15
596	15t. Comet over Bobonong at sunset	1·50	70
597	35t. Comet over Gomare at dawn	2·00	1·50
598	50t. Comet over Thamaga and Letlhakeng	2·25	3·75

151 Milk Bag

1986. Traditional Milk Containers. Multicoloured.

599	8t. Type **151**	30	10
600	15t. Clay pot and calabashes	45	30
601	35t. Wooden milk bucket	75	65
602	50t. Milk churn	1·00	1·40

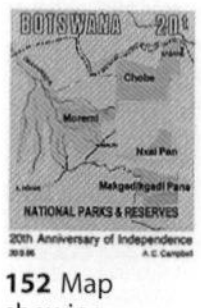

152 Map showing National Parks and Reserves

1986. 20th Anniv of Independence. Sheet 100×120 mm. Multicoloured.

MS603	20t. Type **152**; 20t. Morupule power station; 20t. Cattle breeding in Kgalagadi; 20t. National Assembly Building	3·75	2·50

153 *Ludwigia stogonifera*

1986. Christmas. Flowers of Okavango. Multicoloured.

604	8t. Type **153**	1·25	10
605	15t. *Sopubia mannii*	2·25	1·10
606	35t. *Commelina diffusa*	3·50	3·00
607	50t. *Hibiscus diversifolius*	4·00	12·00

154 Divining

1987. Traditional Medicine. Multicoloured.

608	8t. Type **154**	80	10
609	15t. Lightning prevention	1·50	80
610	35t. Rain making	2·25	2·50
611	50t. Blood letting	2·75	8·50

1987. Nos. 520, 523 and 530 surch.

612	3t. on 6t. African pygmy goose	1·75	75
613	5t. on 10t. Yellow-billed stork	1·75	1·25
614	20t. on 50t. Helmeted guineafowl (horiz)	3·25	1·40

156 Oral Rehydration Therapy

1987. UNICEF Child Survival Campaign. Multicoloured.

615	8t. Type **156**	35	10
616	15t. Growth monitoring	60	55
617	35t. Immunization	1·25	2·00
618	50t. Breast feeding	1·50	5·00

157 Cape Fox

1987. Animals of Botswana. Multicoloured.

619	1t. Type **157**	10	1·25
620	2t. Lechwe	50	1·75
621	3t. Zebra	15	1·25
622	4t. Duiker	15	1·75
623	5t. Banded mongoose	20	1·75
624	6t. Rusty-spotted genet	20	1·75
625	8t. Hedgehog	30	10
626	10t. Scrub hare	30	10
627	12t. Hippopotamus	4·00	4·00
628	15t. Suricate	2·50	2·25
629	20t. Caracal	70	65
630	25t. Steenbok	70	1·50
631	30t. Gemsbok	1·50	1·50
632	35t. Square-lipped rhinoceros	2·50	3·00
633	40t. Mountain reedbuck	1·75	1·50
634	50t. Rock dassie	90	1·75
635	1p. Giraffe	2·50	4·00
636	2p. Tsessebe	2·50	5·50
637	3p. Side-striped jackal	3·75	8·00
638	5p. Hartebeest	6·00	9·00

158 *Cyperus articulatus*

1987. Christmas. Grasses and Sedges of Okavango. Multicoloured.

639	8t. Type **158**	40	10
640	15t. Broomgrass	60	40
641	30t. *Cyperus alopurcides*	1·25	75
642	1p. Bulrush sedge	2·50	5·75
MS643	88×99 mm. Nos. 639/42	4·25	5·75

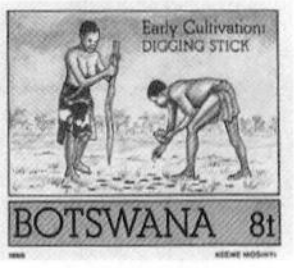

159 Planting Seeds with Digging Stick

1988. Early Cultivation. Multicoloured.

644	8t. Type **159**	40	10
645	15t. Using iron hoe	60	35
646	35t. Wooden ox-drawn plough	1·00	1·00
647	50t. Villagers working in lesotlas communal field	1·40	2·00

160 Red Lechwe at Water-hole

1988. Red Lechwe. Multicoloured.

648	10t. Type **160**	90	15
649	15t. Red lechwe and early morning sun	1·75	65
650	35t. Female and calf	2·50	1·75
651	75t. Herd on the move	3·75	8·50

161 Gubulawayo Postmark and Route Southwards to Tati

1988. Cent of Mafeking–Gubalawayo Runner Post. Designs as Nos. 294/7, but redrawn smaller with changed inscriptions as in T **161**. Multicoloured.

652	10t. Type **161**	35	10
653	15t. Bechuanaland 1888 6d. on 6d. stamp and route from Tati southwards	55	30
654	30t. Runners and twin routes south from Shoshong	95	75
655	60t. Mafeking postmark and routes to Bechuanaland and Transvaal	1·60	2·75
MS656	81×151 mm. Nos. 652/5 vertically se-tenant, forming a composite map design	9·00	9·50

162 Pope John Paul II and Outline Map of Botswana

1988. Visit of Pope John Paul II. Multicoloured.

657	10t. Type **162**	2·00	20
658	15t. Pope John Paul II	2·25	30
659	30t. Pope giving blessing and outline map	2·75	70
660	80t. Pope John Paul II (different)	3·50	4·00

163 National Museum and Art Gallery, Gaborone

1988. 20th Anniv of National Museum and Art Gallery, Gaborone. Multicoloured.

661	8t. Type **163**	15	10
662	15t. Pottery	20	25
663	30t. Blacksmith's buffalo bellows	35	40
664	60c. Children and land rover mobile museum van	70	1·00

164 *Grewia flava*

1988. Flowering Plants of South-eastern Botswana. Multicoloured.

665	8t. Type **164**	20	10
666	15t. *Cienfuegosia digitata*	30	25
667	40t. *Solanum seaforthianum*	60	55
668	75t. *Carissa bispinosa*	1·00	1·40

165 Basket Granary

1989. Traditional Grain Storage. Multicoloured.

669	8t. Type **165**	75	10
670	15t. Large letlole granary	1·25	40
671	30t. Pot granary	2·00	60
672	60t. Two types of serala	2·75	2·25

166 Female with Eggs

1989. Slaty Egret. Multicoloured.

673	8t. Type **166**	55	15
674	15t. Chicks in nest	75	40
675	30t. In flight	1·00	75
676	60t. Pair building nest	1·40	2·25
MS677	119×89 mm. Nos. 673/6	3·25	3·75

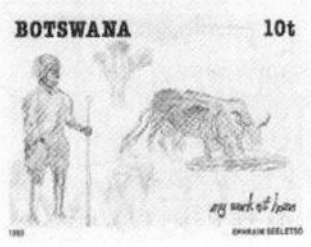

167 *My Work at Home* (Ephraim Seeletso)

1989. Children's Paintings. Multicoloured.

678	10t. Type **167**	35	10
679	15t. *My Favourite Game* (hopscotch) (Neelma Bhatia) (vert)	50	35
680	30t. *My Favourite Toy* (clay animals) (Thabo Habana)	75	70
681	1p. *My School Day* (Thabo Olesitse)	2·00	3·25

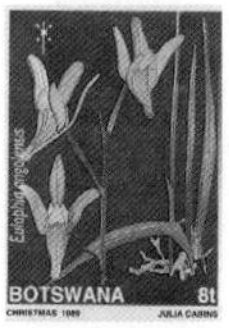

168 *Eulophia angolensis*

1989. Christmas. Orchids. Multicoloured.

682	8t. Type **168**	90	10
683	15t. *Eulophia hereroensis*	1·50	60
684	30t. *Eulophia speciosa*	2·00	1·00
685	60t. *Eulophia petersii*	3·50	7·00

169 Bechuanaland 1965 New Constitution 25c. Stamp (25th anniv of Self-Government)

1990. Anniversaries.

686	**169**	8t. multicoloured	70	15
687	-	15t. multicoloured	75	50
688	-	30t. multicoloured	3·75	1·60
689	-	60t. black, blue and yellow	3·75	7·00

DESIGNS: 15t. Casting vote in ballot box (25th anniv of First Elections); 30t. Outline map and flags of Southern Africa Development Co-ordination Conference countries (10th anniv); 60t. Penny Black (150th anniv of first postage stamp).

1990. Nos. 619, 624 and 627 surch.

690	10t. on 1t. Type **157**	60	20
691	20t. on 6t. Rusty-spotted genet	1·00	80
692	50t. on 12t. Hippopotamus	3·50	3·50

171 Telephone Engineer

1990. Stamp World London 90, International Stamp Exhibition. Multicoloured.

693	8t. Type **171**	35	10
694	15t. Transmission pylon	65	40
695	30t. Public telephone	1·00	75
696	2p. Testing circuit board	3·00	6·50

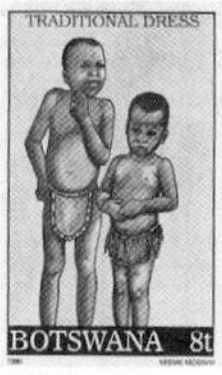

172 Young Children

1990. Traditional Dress. Multicoloured.

697	8t. Type **172**	45	10
698	15t. Young woman	80	40
699	30t. Adult man	1·40	70
700	2p. Adult woman	3·50	6·50
MS701	104×150 mm. Nos. 697/700	8·00	10·00

173 *Acacia nigrescens*

1990. Christmas. Flowering Trees. Multicoloured.

702	8t. Type **173**	60	10
703	15t. *Peltophorum africanum*	95	35
704	30t. *Burkea africana*	1·75	75
705	2p. *Pterocarpus angolensis*	3·75	7·50

174 Children running in front of Hatchback

1990. First National Road Safety Day. Multicoloured.

706	8t. Type **174**	2·50	30
707	15t. Careless overtaking	3·00	1·00
708	30t. Cattle on road	3·75	2·75

175 Cattle

1991. Rock Paintings. Multicoloured.

709	8t. Type **175**	2·25	40
710	15t. Cattle, drying frames and tree	2·75	85
711	30t. Animal hides	3·25	1·50
712	2p. Family herding cattle	6·00	10·00

176 Children

1991. National Census. Multicoloured.

713	8t. Type **176**	1·50	20
714a	15t. Village	2·00	55
715	30t. School	2·25	1·00
716	2p. Hospital	8·00	11·00

177 Tourists viewing Elephants

1991. African Tourism Year. Okavango Delta. Multicoloured.

717	8t. Type **177**	1·75	70
718	15t. Crocodiles basking on river bank	2·00	90
719	35t. Fish eagles and de Havilland D.H.C.7 Dash Seven aircraft	4·25	3·25
720	2p. Okavango wildlife (26×44 mm)	6·00	9·00

178 *Harpagophytum procumbens*

1991. Christmas. Seed Pods. Multicoloured.

721	8t. Type **178**	60	10
722	15t. *Tylosema esculentum*	1·00	40
723	30t. *Abrus precatorius*	1·75	80
724	2p. *Kigelia africana*	4·50	8·50

1992. Nos. 621, 624 and 627 surch.

725	8t. on 12t. Hippopotamus	1·50	70
726	10t. on 12t. Hippopotamus	1·50	70
727	25t. on 6t. Rusty-spotted genet	1·25	1·50
728	40t. on 3t. Zebra	2·25	4·00

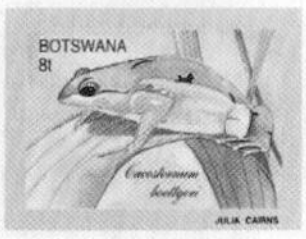

179 *Cacosternum boettgeri*

1992. Climbing Frogs. Multicoloured.

729	8t. Type **179**	75	30
730	10t. *Hyperolius marmoratus angolensis* (vert)	75	30
731	40t. *Bufo fenoulheti*	2·50	1·50
732	1p. *Hyperolius* sp. (vert)	5·00	7·00

180 Air-conditioned Carriages

1992. Deluxe Railway Service. Multicoloured.

733	10t. Type **180**	1·50	40
734	25t. Diesel locomotive No. BD001 (vert)	2·25	80
735	40t. Carriage interior (vert)	2·50	1·25
736	2p. Diesel locomotive No. BD028	3·75	7·50
MS737	127×127 mm. Nos. 733/6	13·00	13·00

181 Cheetah

1992. Animals. Multicoloured.

738	1t. Type **181**	40	2·00
739	2t. Spring hare	40	2·00
740	4t. Blackfooted cat	50	2·00
741	5t. Striped mouse	50	1·75
742	10t. Oribi	65	10
743	12t. Pangolin	1·25	3·00
744	15t. Aardwolf	1·25	40
745	20t. Warthog	1·25	40
746	25t. Ground squirrel	1·25	20
747	35t. Honey badger	1·50	30
748	40t. Common mole rat	1·50	30
749	45t. Wild dog	1·50	30
750	50t. Water mongoose	1·50	35
751	80t. Klipspringer	2·50	2·50
752	1p. Lesser bushbaby	2·50	2·50
753	2p. Bushveld elephant shrew	3·50	4·50
754	5p. Zorilla	5·50	8·00
755	10p. Vervet monkey	8·00	12·00

182 Boxing

1992. Olympic Games, Barcelona. Multicoloured.

756	10t. Type **182**	60	10
757	50t. Running	1·50	50
758	1p. Boxing (different)	2·00	2·50
759	2p. Running (different)	2·50	5·00
MS760	87×117 mm. Nos. 756/9	6·00	8·00

183 *Adiantum incisum*

1992. Christmas. Ferns. Multicoloured.

761	10t. Type **183**	40	10
762	25t. *Actiniopteris radiata*	70	35
763	40t. *Ceratopteris cornuta*	1·00	55
764	1p.50 *Pellaea calomelanos*	3·00	7·00

184 Helping Blind Person (Lions Club International)

1993. Charitable Organizations in Botswana. Multicoloured.

765	10t. Type **184**	80	20
766	15t. Nurse carrying child (Red Cross Society) (horiz)	90	40
767	25t. Woman watering seedling (Ecumenical Decade)	90	50
768	35t. Deaf children (Round Table) (horiz)	1·25	1·50
769	40t. Crowd of people (Rotary International)	1·25	1·75
770	50t. Hands at prayer (Botswana Christian Council) (horiz)	1·50	2·50

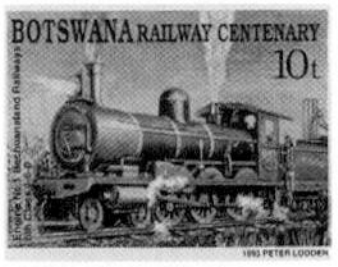

185 Bechuanaland Railways Class "6" Locomotive No. 1

1993. Railway Centenary. Multicoloured.

771	10t. Type **185**	75	40
772	40t. Class "19" locomotive No. 317	1·40	75
773	50t. Class "12" locomotive No. 256	1·40	90
774	1p.50 Class "7" locomotive No. 71	2·00	5·00
MS775	190×100 mm. Nos. 771/4	5·00	7·00

186 Long-crested Eagle

1993. Endangered Eagles. Multicoloured.

776	10t. Type **186**	70	35
777	25t. Short-toed eagle ("Snake eagle")	1·25	65
778	50t. Bateleur ("Bateleur Eagle")	1·60	1·75
779	1p.50 Secretary bird	2·50	6·50

187 *Aloe zebrina*

1993. Christmas. Flora. Multicoloured.

780	12t. Type **187**	40	10
781	25t. *Croton megalobotrys*	60	25
782	50t. *Boophane disticha*	85	70
783	1p. *Euphoria davyi*	1·25	3·50

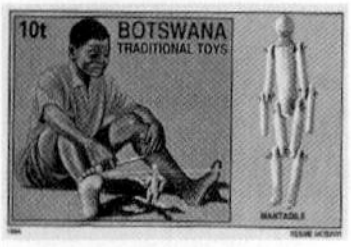

188 Boy with String Puppet

1994. Traditional Toys. Multicoloured.

784	10t. Type **188**	20	10
785	40t. Boys with clay cattle	45	30
786	50t. Boy with spinner	50	50
787	1p. Girls playing in make-believe houses	1·10	3·00

189 Interior of Control Tower, Gaborone Airport

1994. 50th Anniv of I.C.A.O. Multicoloured.

788	10t. Type **189**	40	10
789	25t. Crash fire tender	75	40
790	40t. Loading supplies onto airliner (vert)	1·00	85
791	50t. Control tower, Gaborone (vert)	1·00	1·75

1994. No. 743 surch **10t.**

792	10t. on 12t. Pangolin	8·50	75

191 Lesser Flamingos at Sua Pan

1994. Environment Protection. Makgadikgadi Pans. Multicoloured.

793	10t. Type **191**	1·00	40
794	35t. Baobab trees (horiz)	50	40
795	50t. Zebra and palm trees	65	80
796	2p. Map of area (horiz)	3·00	6·00

192 *Ziziphus mucronata*

1994. Christmas. Edible Fruits. Multicoloured.

797	10t. Type **192**	25	10
798	25t. *Strychnos cocculoides*	40	30
799	40t. *Bauhinia petersiana*	60	70
800	50t. *Schinziphyton rautoneii*	70	1·40

193 Fisherman with Bow and Arrow

1995. Traditional Fishing. Multicoloured.

801	15t. Type **193**	35	20
802	40t. Men in canoe and boy with fishing rod	60	45
803	65t. Fisherman with net	80	90
804	80t. Fisherman with basket fish trap	1·00	2·00

194 Boys watering Horses (FAO)

1995. 50th Anniv of United Nations. Multicoloured.

805	20t. Type **194**	20	10
806	50t. Schoolchildren queueing for soup (WFP)	35	30
807	80t. Policeman conducting census (UNDP)	1·00	1·00
808	1p. Weighing baby (UNICEF)	70	2·00

195 Brown Hyena

1995. Endangered Species. Brown Hyena. Multicoloured.

809	20t. Type **195**	45	60
810	50t. Pair of hyenas	65	75
811	80t. Hyena stealing ostrich eggs	1·10	1·50
812	1p. Adult hyena and cubs	1·25	2·25

196 *Adenia glauca*

1995. Christmas. Plants. Multicoloured.

813	20t. Type **196**	35	10
814	50t. *Pterodiscus ngamicus*	60	30
815	80t. *Sesamothamnus lugardii*	1·00	1·00
816	1p. *Fockea multiflora*	1·10	2·00

1996. Nos. 738/40 surch.

817	20t. on 2t. Spring hare	1·00	30
818	30t. on 1t. Type **181**	1·25	30
819	70t. on 4t. Blackfooted cat	2·00	3·25

198 Spears

1996. Traditional Weapons. Multicoloured.

820	20t. Type **198**	20	10
821	50t. Axes	35	30
822	80t. Shield and knobkerries	55	65
823	1p. Knives and sheaths	60	1·50

199 Child with Basic Radio

1996. Centenary of Radio. Multicoloured.

824	20t. Type **199**	25	10
825	50t. Radio Botswana's mobile transmitter	40	30
826	80t. Police radio control	1·50	1·10
827	1p. Listening to radio	70	1·75

200 Olympic Flame, Rings and Wreath

1996. Centenary of Modern Olympic Games. Multicoloured.

828	20t. Type **200**	40	10
829	50t. Pierre de Coubertin (founder of modern Olympics)	60	30
830	80t. Map of Botswana with flags and athletes	1·50	1·00
831	1p. Ruins of ancient stadium at Olympia	1·00	1·60

201 Family Planning Class (Botswana Family Welfare Association)

1996. Local Charities. Multicoloured.

832	20t. Type **201**	20	10
833	30t. Blind workers (Pudulogong Rehabilitation Centre)	20	15
834	50t. Collecting seeds (Forestry Association of Botswana)	30	30
835	70t. Secretarial class (YWCA)	40	70
836	80t. Children's day centre (Botswana Council of Women)	50	80
837	1p. Children's village, Tlokweng (S.O.S. Children's village)	60	1·50

202 *Adansonia digitata* Leaf and Blossom

1996. Christmas. Parts of Life Cycle for *Adansonia digitata*. Multicoloured.

838	20t. Type **202**	25	10
839	50t. Fruit	40	25
840	80t. Tree in leaf	60	75
841	1p. Tree with bare branches	70	1·60

203 Tati Hotel

1997. Francistown Centenary. Multicoloured.

842	20t. Type **203**	15	10
843	50t. Railway Station	75	35
844	80t. Company Manager's House	60	80
845	1p. Monarch Mine	1·00	1·60

204 Steam Locomotive, Bechuanaland Railway, 1897

1997. Railway Centenary. Multicoloured.

846	35t. Type **204**	40	20
847	50t. Elephants crossing railway line	60	35
848	80t. First locomotive in Bechuanaland, 1897	70	45
849	1p. Beyer-Garratt type steam locomotive No. 352	75	75
850	2p. Diesel locomotive No. BD339	1·00	1·75
851	2p.50 Fantuzzi container stacker	1·25	2·25

205 Pel's Fishing Owl

1997. Birds. Multicoloured.

852	5t. Type **205**	70	1·25
853	10t. African harrier hawk ("Gymnogene") (horiz)	70	1·25
854	15t. Brown parrot ("Meyer's Parrot")	75	1·25
855	20t. Harlequin quail (horiz)	80	1·25
856	25t. Mariqua sunbird ("Marico Sunbird") (horiz)	80	1·25
857	30t. Kurrichane thrush (horiz)	85	1·25
858	40t. Paradise sparrow ("Red-headed Finch")	90	80
859	50t. Red-billed buffalo weaver ("Buffalo Weaver")	1·00	50
860	60t. Sacred ibis (horiz)	1·25	1·00
861	70t. Cape shoveler (horiz)	1·25	1·00
862	80t. Black-throated honeyguide ("Greater Honeyguide") (horiz)	1·25	1·00
863	1p. Woodland kingfisher (horiz)	1·50	1·00
864	1p.25 Purple heron	2·00	1·75
865	1p.50 Yelllow-billed oxpecker (horiz)	2·00	2·25
866	2p. Shaft-tailed whydah	2·25	2·50
867	2p.50 White stork	2·75	3·00
868	5p. Ovampo sparrow hawk ("Sparrowhawk")	4·00	4·50
869	10p. Spotted crake	6·50	8·00

No. 861 is inscribed "Shoveller" in error.

1997. Golden Wedding of Queen Elizabeth and Prince Philip. As T **173** of Ascension. Multicoloured.

870	35t. Prince Philip with carriage	20	55
871	35t. Queen Elizabeth with binoculars	20	55
872	2p. Queen Elizabeth with horse team	90	1·50
873	2p. Prince Philip and horse	90	1·50
874	2p.50 Queen Elizabeth and Prince Philip	1·10	1·50
875	2p.50 Princess Anne and Prince Edward	1·10	1·50
MS876	110×70 mm. 10p. Queen Elizabeth and Prince Philip in landau (horiz)	4·00	5·50

206 *Combretum zeyheri*

1997. Christmas. Plants. Multicoloured.

877	35t. Type **206**	45	10
878	1p. *Combretum apiculatum*	1·00	35
879	2p. *Combretum molle*	1·75	1·90
880	2p.50 *Combretum imberbe*	2·00	2·75

207 Baobab Trees

1998. Tourism (1st series). Multicoloured.

881	35t. Type **207**	25	15
882	1p. Crocodile	50	45
883	2p. Stalactites (vert)	95	1·10
884	2p.50 Tourists and rock paintings (vert)	1·25	1·60

See also Nos. 899/902.

1998. Diana, Princess of Wales Commemoration. As T **223a** of Bahamas. Multicoloured.

885	35t. Princess Diana, 1990	25	15
886	1p. In green hat, 1992	40	35
887	2p. In white blouse, 1993	75	1·10
888	2p.50 With crowd, Cambridge, 1993	90	1·50
MS889	145×70 mm. As Nos. 885/8, but each with a face value of 2p.50	3·00	3·75

208 *Village Life* (tapestry)

1998. Botswana Weavers. Multicoloured.

890	35t. Type **208**	30	15
891	55t. Weaver dyeing threads	40	20
892	1p. *African Wildlife* (tapestry)	1·40	1·00
893	2p. Weaver at loom	1·50	2·25
MS894	68×58 mm. 2p.50, *Elephants* (tapestry) (horiz)	3·00	3·75

209 *Ficus ingens*

1998. Christmas. Plants. Multicoloured.

895	35t. Type **209**	45	10
896	55t. *Ficus pygmaea*	65	20
897	1p. *Ficus abutilifolia*	1·25	55
898	2p.50 *Ficus sycomorus*	2·00	3·00

1999. Tourism (2nd series). As T **207**. Multicoloured.

899	35t. Rock painting of men and cattle	85	25
900	55t. Expedition at Salt Pan	1·25	30
901	1p. Rock painting of elephant and antelope (vert)	1·50	1·40
902	2p. Tourists under Baobab tree (vert)	1·60	2·50

210 Road Map

1999. Southern African Development Community Day. Sheet 77×84 mm.

MS903	**210** 5p. multicoloured	3·75	4·00

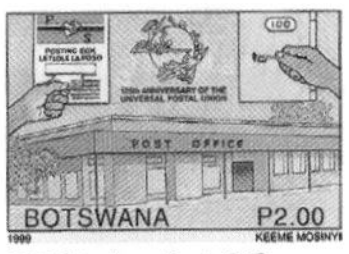

211 Modern Post Office

1999. 125th Anniv of Universal Postal Union.

904	**211** 2p. multicoloured	2·00	2·00

212 Mpule Kwelagobe winning contest

1999. Mpule Kwelagobe ("Miss Universe 1999"). Multicoloured.

905	35t. Type **212**	35	10
906	1p. In traditional dress (horiz)	75	30
907	2p. In traditional dancing costume with lion	1·10	60
908	2p.50 Wearing "Botswana" sash (horiz)	1·25	75
909	15p. With leopard in background (horiz)	7·00	12·00
MS910	175×80 mm. Nos. 905/9	9·50	12·00

213 Saddle-bill Stork and Limpopo River

2000. Scenic Rivers. Multicoloured.

911	35t. Type **213**	60	20
912	1p. Hippopotamuses in water lilies (vert)	1·00	60
913	2p. African skimmer and makoro (dugout canoe)	1·75	1·75
914	2p.50 African elephant at sunset, Chobe River (vert)	2·00	2·50

214 Mopane Moth

2000. Moths. Multicoloured.

915	35t. Type **214**	15	10
916	70t. Wild silk moth	25	20
917	1p. Crimson speckled footman ("Tiger Moth")	35	30
918	2p. African lunar moth	65	60
919	15p. Speckled emperor moth	4·75	9·00
MS920	175×135 mm. Nos. 915/19	7·50	10·00

No. **MS**920 is in the shape of a moth.

215 Mother reading Medicine Label with Child ("Protect Your Children")

2000. United Nations Literacy Decade. Multicoloured.

921	35t. Type **215**	20	10
922	70t. Adult literacy class ("Never Too Old To Learn")	30	20
923	2p. Man smoking next to petrol pump ("Be Aware Of Danger")	75	1·10
924	2p.50 Man at Automatic Teller Machine ("Be Independent")	90	2·00

216 Pres. Sir Seretse Khama

2000. Chiefs and Presidents.

925	**216**	35t. black, red and gold	50	10
926	-	1p. multicoloured	75	40
927	-	2p. multicoloured	1·25	1·40
928	-	2p.50 multicoloured	1·50	2·25

DESIGNS—HORIZ (60×40 mm): 35t. Chiefs Sebele I of Bakwena, Bathoen I of Bangwaketse and Khama III of Bangato, 1895. VERT (as T **216**): 2p. Pres. Sir Ketumile Masire; 2p.50, Pres. Festus Mogae.

217 Doctor giving Eye Test

2000. Airborne Medical Service. Multicoloured.

929	35t. Type **217**	30	10
930	1p. Medical team and family	65	40
931	2p. Aircraft over canoes	1·25	1·40
932	2p.50 Donkeys and mule cart on airstrip	1·50	2·25

218 Hippopotamus

2000. Wetlands (1st series). Okavango Delta. Multicoloured.

933	35t. Type **218**	50	20
934	1p. Tiger fish and tilapia	55	30
935	1p.75 Painted reed frog and wattled crane (vert)	1·50	1·50
936	2p. Pels fishing owl and vervet monkey (vert)	1·75	1·75
937	2p.50 Nile crocodile, Sitatunga and red lechwe	1·75	1·75
MS938	175×80 mm. Nos. 933/7	6·50	6·50

See also Nos. 958/62, 994/**MS**999 and 1009/**MS**1014.

2001. HONG KONG 2001 Stamp Exhibition. No. **MS**938 overprinted with exhibition logo on sheet margin.

MS939	175×80 mm. Nos. 933/7	6·00	7·00

219 Diamonds

2001. Diamonds. Multicoloured. Self-adhesive.

940	35t. Type **219**	70	35
941	1p.75 J.C.B. in open-cast mine	1·75	2·00
942	2p. Quality inspector	2·00	2·25
943	2p.50 Diamonds in jewellery	2·50	3·00

220 African Pygmy Falcon

2001. Kgalagadi Transfrontier Wildlife Park. Joint Issue with South Africa. Multicoloured.

944	35t. Type **220**	1·50	45
945	1p. Leopard	1·00	75
946	2p. Gemsbok	1·60	2·25
947	2p.50 Bat-eared fox	1·60	2·25
MS948	115×80 mm. Nos. 945 and 947	2·50	3·00

221 Shallow Basket

2001. Traditional Baskets. Multicoloured.

949	35t. Type **221**	20	15
950	1p. Tall basket	35	25
951	2p. Woman weaving basket	60	85
952	2p.50 Spherical basket	65	95
MS953	177×92 mm. Nos. 949/52	2·00	3·50

222 Boys by River at Sunset

2001. Scenic Skies. Multicoloured.

954	50t. Type **222**	35	15
955	1p. Woman with baby at sunset	60	25
956	2p. Girls carrying firewood at sunset	90	75
957	10p. Traditional village at sunset near huts	3·50	4·50

2001. Wetlands (2nd series). Chobe River. As T **218**. Multicoloured.

958	50t. Water monitor and carmine bee-eater	65	20
959	1p.75 Buffalo	75	60
960	2p. Savanna baboons (vert)	90	1·00
961	2p.50 Lion (vert)	1·10	1·40
962	3p. African elephants in river	2·25	2·25
MS963	175×80 mm. Nos. 958/62	5·00	5·00

223 Black Mamba

2002. Snakes. Multicoloured.

964	50t. Type **223**	45	15
965	1p.75 Spitting cobra (vert)	70	45
966	2p.50 Puff adder	80	1·40
967	3p. Boomslang (vert)	1·00	1·75

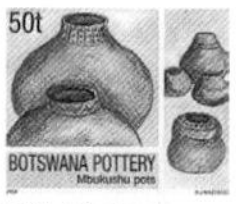

224 Mbukushu Pots

2002. Botswana Pottery. Multicoloured.

968	50t. Type **224**	45	10
969	2p. Sekgatla pots	80	75
970	2p.50 Setswana pots	90	1·10
971	3p. Kalanga pots	1·10	1·50

225 Queen Elizabeth in Evening Dress and Commonwealth Emblem

2002. Golden Jubilee. Multicoloured.

972	55t. Type **225**	65	15
973	2p.75 Queen Elizabeth with bouquet (vert)	1·75	2·00

226 Tree Squirrel

2002. Mammals. Multicoloured.

974	5t. Type **226**	10	30
975	10t. Black-backed jackal	15	30
976	20t. African wild cat	20	40
977	30t. Slender mongoose (horiz)	30	40
978	40t. African civet (horiz)	50	50
979	55t. Elephant	1·75	50
980	90t. Reedbuck	60	50
981	1p. Kudu	70	50
982	1p.45 Waterbuck	1·00	1·00
983	1p.95 Sable (horiz)	1·50	1·50
984	2p.20 Sitatunga (horiz)	1·50	1·50
985	2p.75 Porcupine (horiz)	1·50	1·50
986	3p.30 Serval (horiz)	1·60	1·75
987	4p. Antbear (horiz)	2·00	2·50
988	5p. Bushpig (horiz)	2·25	2·75
989	15p. Chakma baboon	5·00	7·00

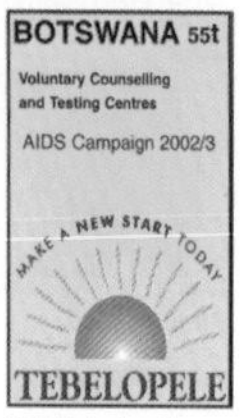

227 Tebelopele (counselling and testing centres) Symbol

2002. AIDS Awareness. Multicoloured.

990	55t. Type **227**	60	15
991	1p.10 AIDS ribbon and mother and baby badge	1·10	40
992	2p.75 Hands and male gender symbol	1·75	2·25
993	3p.30 Orphans with foster parent	1·90	2·50

2002. Wetlands (3rd series). The Makgadikgadi Pans. As T **218**. Multicoloured.

994	55t. Aardwolf	50	15
995	1p.10 Blue wildebeest and zebra	1·00	30
996	2p.50 Zebra (vert)	1·75	1·40
997	2p.75 Flamingo (vert)	2·25	2·50
998	3p.30 Pelican in flight	2·50	3·00
MS999	175×80 mm. Nos. 994/8	7·25	8·00

228 Lentswe la Baratani ("Hill of Lovers")

2003. Natural Places of Interest. Multicoloured.

1000	55t. Type **228**	35	15
1001	2p.20 Sand dunes	1·00	90
1002	2p.75 Moremi Waterfalls (vert)	1·50	2·00
1003	3p.30 Gcwihaba Cave	1·75	2·50

229 Ngwale

2003. Beetles. Multicoloured.

1004	55t. Type **229**	40	15
1005	2p.20 Kgomo-ya-buru	1·10	80
1006	2p.75 Kgomo-ya-pula	1·40	1·75
1007	3p.30 Lebitse	1·75	2·25
MS1008	69×59 mm. 5p.50 Kgaladuwa	5·00	5·50

2003. Wetlands (4th series). The Limpopo River. As Type **218**. Multicoloured.

1009	55t. Giraffe	70	35
1010	1p.45 Black eagle and Nile crocodile (vert)	1·50	85
1011	2p.50 Ostrich (vert)	2·00	1·50
1012	2p.75 Klipspringer	1·60	1·75
1013	3p.30 Serval cat	1·90	2·25
MS1014	175×80 mm. Nos. 1010/13	7·00	8·00

230 San People with Birds (Cg'Ose Ntcox'o)

2004. Kuru Art Project. Multicoloured.

1015	55t. Type **230**	35	20
1016	1p.45 Tree with gum (Nxaedom Qhomatca)	75	55
1017	2p.75 Tree with berries (Nxaedom Qhomatca)	1·10	1·60
1018	3p.30 Snake (Qgoma Ncokg'o)	1·50	2·00

231 Masimo (working the land)

2004. Traditional Life Styles. Multicoloured.

1019	80t. Type **231**	50	25
1020	2p.10 Kgotla (village meeting place)	1·25	85
1021	3p.90 Moraka (cattle post)	1·75	2·25
1022	4p.70 Legae (compound within village)	2·25	3·00

232 Child posting Letter

2004. World Post Day. Multicoloured.

1023	80t. Type **232**	45	25
1024	2p.10 Children sharing a letter	1·00	85
1025	3p.90 Post man	1·60	2·25
1206	4p.70 Woman reading letter	2·00	2·50

233 Peregrine Falcon (Angola)

2004. First Joint Issue of Southern Africa Postal Operators Association Members. Sheet 170×95 mm containing T **233** and similar hexagonal designs showing national birds of Association members. Multicoloured.

MS1027	40t. Type **233**; 50t. Two African Fish Eagles in flight (Zambia); 60t. Two African fish eagles perched (Zimbabwe); 70t. Bar-tailed trogon (Malawi) (inscribed "apaloderma vittatum"); 80t. Purple-crested turaco ("Lourie") (Swaziland); 1p. African fish eagle (Namibia); 2p. Stanley ("Blue") crane (South Africa); 5p. Cattle egret (Botswana)	13·00	14·00

The 70t. value stamp is not inscribed with the country of which the bird is a national symbol. Miniature sheets of similar designs were also issued by Namibia, Zimbabwe, Angola, Swaziland, South Africa, Malawi and Zambia.

234 *Pterodiscus speciosus*

2004. Christmas. Flowers. Multicoloured.

1028	80t. Type **234**	50	25
1029	2p.10 *Bulbine narcissifolia*	95	60
1030	3p.90 *Bulbiana hypogea*	1·75	2·25
1031	4p.70 *Hibiscus micranthus*	2·25	3·00

235 Blackbeard's Store, Phalatswe

2005. Historical Buildings. Multicoloured.

1032	80t. Type **235**	45	25
1033	2p.10 Primary School	85	60
1034	3p.90 Telegraph Office, Phalatswe	1·60	2·25
1035	4p.70 Magistrate's Court, Phalatswe	2·00	3·00

236 Cowpeas ("beans")

2005. Edible Crops. Multicoloured.

1036	80t. Type **236**	40	20
1037	2p.10 Pearl millet	80	55
1038	3p.90 Sorghum	1·40	2·25
1039	4p.70 Watermelon	1·75	3·00

237 Black-footed Cat with Prey

2005. Endangered Species. Black-footed Cat (*Felis nigripes*). Multicoloured.

1040	80t. Type **237**	45	20
1041	2p.10 Black-footed cat	85	60
1042	3p.90 With cub	1·60	2·00
1043	4p.70 In close-up	2·00	2·75
MS1044	160×185 mm. Nos. 1040/3, ×2	7·00	8·50

238 Namaqua Dove

2005. Christmas. Doves and Pigeons. Multicoloured.

1045	80t. Type **238**	50	20
1046	2p.10 Red-eyed dove	95	60
1047	3p.90 Laughing doves (pair)	1·75	2·25
1048	4p.70 Green pigeons (pair)	2·25	3·00

2006. Nos. 690 and 693 surch

1048a	80t. on 90t. Reedbuck	75	35
1048b	2p.10 on 1p.95 Sable (horiz)	1·25	1·25

239 Nembwe

2006. Okavango Fish. Multicoloured.

1049	80t. Type **239**	50	40
1050	2p.10 Tiger fish	1·25	80
1051	3p.90 Pike	1·75	2·00
1052	4p.70 Spotted squeaker	2·25	2·75

240 Oxen

2006. Tswana Cattle. Multicoloured.

1053	1p.10 Type **240**	40	35
1054	2p.60 Cows and calves	85	75
1055	4p.10 Bulls	1·25	2·00
1056	4p.90 Horn shapes	1·50	2·25

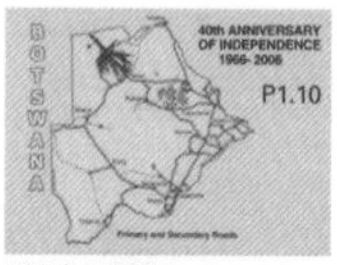

241 Road Map

2006. 40th Anniv of Independence. Showing maps of Botswana. Multicoloured.

1057	1p.10 Type **241**	75	45
1058	2p.60 Population distribution	95	90
1059	4p.10 Mines and coal resources	2·50	2·50
1060	4p.90 National parks and game reserves	2·75	3·00

242 *Hyphaene petersiana*

2006. Christmas. Trees. Multicoloured.

1062	1p.10 Type **242**	45	30
1063	2p.60 *Phoenix reclinata*	1·00	70
1064	4p.10 *Hyphaene petersiana*	1·50	2·00
1065	4p.90 *Phoenix reclinata*	1·75	2·50

243 Pied Kingfisher

2007. Kingfishers. Multicoloured.

1066	1p.10 Type **243**	60	45
1067	2p.60 Malachite kingfisher	1·40	1·00
1068	4p.10 Woodland kingfisher	2·00	2·25
1069	4p.90 Brown-hooded kingfisher	2·50	3·00

244 *Chlorophyllum molybdites* (false parasol)

2007. Fungi. Multicoloured.

1070	1p.10 Type **244**	40	30
1071	2p.60 *Phlebopus sudanicus* (bushveld bolete)	90	80
1072	4p.10 *Ganoderma lucidum* (laquered bracket fungus)	1·50	1·75
1073	4p.90 *Geastrum triplex* (collared earthstar)	1·75	2·00

245 Nyala (pair) (Malawi)

2007. Second Joint Issue of Southern Africa Postal Operators Association Members. Designs showing national animals of association members. Multicoloured.

1074	1p.10 Type **245**	40	30
1075	2p.60 Nyala (Zimbabwe)	90	80
1076	4p.10 Oryx (Namibia)	1·50	1·75
1077	4p.90 African buffalo (Zambia)	1·75	2·00
1078	5p.50 Burchell's zebra (Botswana)	2·25	2·50
MS1079	135×170 mm. Nos. 1074/9	7·00	7·50

Miniature sheets containing similar designs were also issued by Malawi, Namibia, Zambia and Zimbabwe. Zambia also issued sheet stamps.

246 Students and Tutor (University of Botswana Library)

2007. 25th Anniv of University of Botswana. Multicoloured.

1080	1p.10 Type **246**	35	30
1081	2p.60 Farmers and Sir Seretse Khama (first Botswana President) (BUCA campus appeal)	75	70
1082	4p.10 Researcher, village and wetland (Okavango Research)	1·25	1·50
1083	4p.90 Students and university buildings ('Infrastructure; old and new')	1·75	2·00

247 Mimosa Sapphire (*Iolaus mimosae mimosae*)

2007. Butterflies. Multicoloured.

1084	10t. Type **247**	10	10
1085	20t. Bushveld orange-tip (*Colotis pallene*)	10	10
1086	30t. African monarch (*Danaus chrysippus aegyptius*)	10	10
1087	40t. Common black-eye (*Gonatomyrina gorgias gorgias*)	15	20
1088	50t. Brown playboy (*Virachola antalus*)	25	30
1089	1p. Sapphire (*Lolaus silas*)	50	55
1090	(1p.10) Scarlet tip (*Colotis* (C) *danae annae*)	55	60
1091	2p. Large blue emperor (*Charaxes bohemani*)	65	70
1092	(2p.60) Dwarf blue (*Oraidium barberae*))	70	75
1093	3p. Apricot playboy (*Virachola dinochares*)	80	85
1094	4p. Blue pansy (*Junonia oenone oenone*)	90	95
1095	5p. Black-striped hairtail (*Anthene amarah amarah*)	1·10	1·25
1096	10p. Natal barred blue (*Spindasis natalensis*)	2·25	2·40
1097	20p. Foxy charaxes (*C. jasius saturnus*)	4·50	4·75

No. 1090 was inscr 'Standard Postage A' and sold for 1p.10. No. 1092 was inscr 'Standard Postage B' and sold for 2p.60.

248 Traditional Dancer (Boitshepo Lesego)

2008. Artists in Botswana. Designs showing winning entries in stamp design competition. Multicoloured.

1098	1p.10 Type **248**	35	30
1099	2p.60 Baobab tree (Philip Huebsch)	75	70
1100	4p.10 Girl playing with dolls (Giel Kgamane)	1·25	1·40
1101	4p.90 Donkeys tired after hard work (Tineni Kepaletswe) (horiz)	1·60	2·00
1102	5p.50 Donkeys in the city (Andrew Jones) (horiz)	1·90	2·40

249 Hunter and Guide facing Bull Elephant

2008. Elephants in Botswana. Multicoloured.

1103	1p.10 Type **249**	75	45
1104	2p.60 Tourists photographing female elephant with baby from dugout canoe	1·50	90
1105	4p.10 Villagers chasing crop raiding elephant	2·25	2·25
1106	4p.90 Elephant-back safari in Okavango Delta	2·50	2·75

250 Athletes

2008. Olympic Games, Athens. Multicoloured.

1107	1p.10 Type **250**	45	40
1108	2p.60 Boxers	80	85

251 Pitse Ya Naga Launch

2008. 40th Anniv of Botswana National Museum. Multicoloured.

1109	1p.10 Type **251**	35	30
1110	2p.60 Botanical Garden (vert)	65	60
1111	4p.10 New Museum Galleries	1·25	1·25
1112	4p.90 Rock painting, Tsodilo Hills	1·60	2·00
1113	5p.50 Official opening (vert)	1·75	2·25

252 Address Plaque for The No. 1 Ladies Detective Agency and Precious Ramotswe

2008. Events of Botswana 2008. Multicoloured.

1114	4p.10 Type **252** (Botswana Movie Premiere of *The No. 1 Ladies Detective Agency*)	1·25	1·25
1115	4p.90 Heart within heart (launch of Heart Foundation) (vert)	1·60	1·75
1116	5p.50 DTC Building (launch of Diamond Trading Company Botswana)	1·90	2·25

253 *Gymnopleurus humanus* (small green dung beetle)

2008. Beetles of Botswana. Multicoloured.

1117	1p.10 Type **253**	60	40
1118	2p.60 *Cheilomenes lunata* (lunate ladybird)	1·25	90
1119	4p.10 *Pachnoda sinuata* (garden fruit chafer)	1·75	1·90
1120	4p.90 *Eleodes* sp. (darkling beetle)	2·00	2·25

254 Lesser Flamingo

2009. Endangered Birds of Botswana. Multicoloured.

1121	1p.10 Type **254**	55	40
1122	2p.60 Grey crowned crane (horiz)	1·25	90
1123	4p.10 Wattled crane (horiz)	1·60	1·75
1124	4p.90 Blue crane (horiz)	1·90	2·25

255 Boy and Girl reading ('Education')

2009. Children of Botswana

1125	1p.10 Type **255**	45	40
1126	2p.60 Boy washing hands under tap ('Sanitation') (vert)	90	80
1127	4p.10 Giving girl oral vaccine ('Inoculation') (vert)	1·50	1·60
1128	4p.90 Woman with children ('Orphan Care')	1·75	2·00

256 Southern Cross over Tsodilo World Heritage Site and Giraffes

2009. Night Skies. Multicoloured.

1129	1p.10 Type **256**	45	40
1130	2p.60 Meteorite over Okavango Delta and Ju/'hoansi firing arrows	90	80
1131	4p.10 Moon, Jupiter and Venus over central Kalahari and three Setswana women	1·50	1·60
1132	4p.90 Solar eclipse over Setswana village and trickster lion from Naro story	1·75	2·00

257 Honey Bee alighting on Flower

2010. Honey Bees. Multicoloured.

1133	1p.10 Type **257**	35	30
1134	2p.60 Two bees on honeycomb	75	70
1135	4p.10 Bee's nest in tree	1·25	1·40
1136	4p.90 Bee gathering pollen from flower	1·60	1·75

258 Player, Football, Botswana Flag and Zakumi Mascot

2010. Third Joint Issue of Southern Africa Postal Operators Association Members. World Cup Football Championship, South Africa. Multicoloured.

1137	1p.10 Type **258**	10	10
1138	2p.60 Namibia	70	75
1139	3p. South Africa	80	85
1140	4p. Zimbabwe	90	95
1141	4p.10 Malawi	1·00	1·10
1142	4p.90 Swaziland	1·40	1·50
1143	5p.50 Mauritius	1·50	1·75
1144	6p.60 Lesotho	1·75	1·90
1145	8p.20 Zambia	2·25	2·40
MS1146	188×167 mm. As Nos. 1137/45 but with gold foil background	9·25	10·00

Stamps from **MS**1146 have a shiny gold background; the sheet stamps have a matt gold background.

Similar designs were issued by Lesotho, Malawi, Mauritius, Namibia, South Africa, Swaziland, Zambia and Zimbabwe.

259 Family watching Television ('Coal for National Power Grid')

2010. Energy Sources and Uses. Multicoloured.

1147	2p.60 Type **259**	70	75
1148	4p.10 Woman using mobile phone and solar panel ('Solar Power Voltaic Panels')	1·00	1·10
1149	5p.50 Diesel locomotive	1·50	1·75
1150	6p.10 Compact fluorescent light bulb ('CFLs Save Money and Energy') (horiz)	1·75	1·90

POSTAGE DUE STAMPS

1967. Nos. D10/12 of Bechuanaland optd **REPUBLIC OF BOTSWANA**.

D13	**D1**	1c. red	15	1·75
D14	**D1**	2c. violet	15	1·75
D15	**D1**	5c. green	20	1·75

D 5 African Elephant

1971

D16	**D5**	1c. red	1·10	3·25
D17	**D5**	2c. violet	1·40	3·50
D18	**D5**	6c. brown	1·75	5·50
D19	**D5**	14c. green	2·00	7·50

D 6 Common Zebra

1977

D25a	**D6**	1t. black and red	60	1·25
D26a	**D6**	2t. black and green	60	1·25
D27a	**D6**	4t. black and red	60	1·25
D28a	**D6**	10t. black and blue	60	1·25
D29a	**D6**	16t. black and brown	70	1·50

Pt. 20

BOYACA

One of the states of the Granadine Confederation. A Department of Colombia from 1886, now uses Colombian stamps.

100 centavos = 1 peso.

1 Mendoza Perez

1899. Imperf or perf.

1	**1**	5c. green	1·20	1·20

2

6 Battle of Boyaca Monument

1903. Imperf or perf.

3A	**2**	10c. grey	35	30
4B	**2**	10c. blue	4·00	3·75
12	-	10c. orange	35	30
5A	**2**	20c. brown	45	45
5Aa	**2**	20c. lake	45	45
6B	-	50c. turquoise	45	45
8A	-	1p. red	45	45
9B	-	1p. red	4·00	3·75
10B	**6**	5p. black on red	1·50	1·50
11A	-	10p. black on buff	1·50	1·50

DESIGNS—As Type **2**: 10c. orange, Building; 50c. Gen. Pinzon; 1p. Figure of value. As Type **6**: 10p. Pres. Marroquin.

Pt. 20

BRAZIL

A country in the N.E. of S. America. Portuguese settlement, 1500. Kingdom, 1815. Empire, 1822. Republic from 1889.

1843. 1000 reis = 1 milreis.
1942. 100 centavos = 1 cruzeiro.
1986. 100 centavos = 1 cruzado.
1990. 100 centavos = 1 cruzeiro.
1994. 100 centavos = 1 real.
2008. 1st PCC = 1st porte Commercials.

1 "Bull's Eye"

1843. Imperf.

4	**1**	30r. black	£1900	£275
5	**1**	60r. black	£375	£150
6	**1**	90r. black	£1800	£750

2

1844. Imperf.

10B	**2**	10r. black	70·00	13·50
11B	**2**	30r. black	90·00	20·00
12B	**2**	60r. black	70·00	13·50
13B	**2**	90r. black	£550	70·00
14B	**2**	180r. black	£2500	£900
15B	**2**	300r. black	£3750	£1200
16B	**2**	600r. black	£3500	£1400

3

1850. Imperf.

17A	**3**	10r. black	28·00	38·00
18A	**3**	20r. black	85·00	£110
19A	**3**	30r. black	11·00	3·25
20A	**3**	60r. black	11·00	2·75
21A	**3**	90r. black	95·00	13·00
22A	**3**	180r. black	95·00	60·00
23A	**3**	300r. black	£375	65·00
24A	**3**	600r. black	£425	£100

4

1854. Imperf.

25		10r. blue	13·50	13·00
26		30r. blue	37·00	55·00
27	**4**	280r. red	£160	£110
28	**4**	430r. yellow	£250	£150

5

6

17 Emperor Dom Pedro II

1866. Various frames, but in T **5** the Emperor has a dark beard. Perf or roul.

43	**5**	10r. red	13·50	5·50
44a	**6**	20r. purple	24·00	3·25
45	**5**	50r. blue	34·00	2·75
46a	**5**	80r. purple	£170	19·00
47	**5**	100r. green	£534	1·70
55	**6**	200r. black	95·00	8·50
56	**5**	500r. orange	£225	40·00
67	**17**	300r. green and orange	95·00	23·00

12

13

1878. Various frames, but in T **13** the Emperor's beard is white. Roulette.

57	**12**	10r. red	13·50	3·25
58	**13**	20r. mauve	19·00	2·75
59	**12**	50r. blue	30·00	5·00
60	**12**	80r. red	32·00	11·00
61	**12**	100r. green	32·00	1·40
62	**12**	200r. black	£160	19·00
63	**12**	260r. brown	95·00	25·00
64	**12**	300r. brown	95·00	6·50
65	**12**	700r. red	£190	90·00
66	**12**	1000r. grey	£200	42·00

21

1881. Various frames. Perf.

71	**21**	10r. black	15·00	32·00
72	**21**	10r. orange	3·75	3·25
73	**21**	50r. blue	46·00	4·75
74	**21**	100r. olive	55·00	4·50
77a	**21**	100r. lilac	70·00	7·00
75a	**21**	200r. red	60·00	15·00

No. 77 is inscr "CORREIO".

27 Pedro II

1884

81	**27**	100r. lilac	£110	3·75

25

26

29

30 Southern Cross

31

32

33 Entrance to Bay of Rio de Janeiro

1884

78	**25**	20r. green	46·00	4·50
80	**26**	50r. blue	44·00	6·50
83	**29**	100r. lilac	95·00	2·30
84	**30**	300r. blue	£325	37·00
85a	**31**	500r. olive	£180	18·00
86	**32**	700r. lilac	£100	£150
87	**33**	1000r. blue	£375	£150

35 Southern Cross

1890

97a	**35**	20r. green	3·00	1·80
89	**35**	50r. green	6·00	1·70
110a	**35**	100r. purple	50·00	2·00
91	**35**	200r. violet	13·00	2·30
92	**35**	300r. blue	£120	15·00
100	**35**	300r. slate	£120	8·00
93	**35**	500r. buff	20·00	13·00
94	**35**	500r. grey	20·00	10·50
95	**35**	700r. brown	28·00	32·00
96	**35**	1000r. yellow	24·00	4·75

37 Head of Liberty

1891

111d	**37**	100r. red and blue	39·00	1·70

38 Head of Liberty

1893

114	**38**	100r. red	70·00	1·50

39 Sugar-loaf Mountain

41 Head of Liberty

43 Head of Mercury

1894

124	**39**	10r. blue and red	2·40	85
125	**39**	20r. blue and orange	1·60	55
126	**39**	50r. blue	9·50	2·75
232	**39**	50r. green	17·00	95
127	**41**	100r. black and red	8·00	60
239	**41**	100r. red	17·00	55
128	**41**	200r. black and orange	1·20	45
234	**41**	200r. blue	20·00	55
129	**41**	300r. black and green	17·00	70
153	**41**	500r. black and blue	35·00	2·50
131a	**41**	700r. black and mauve	20·00	2·20
132	**43**	1000r. mauve and green	65·00	2·00
133	**43**	2000r. purple and grey	75·00	18·00

1897. As T **39** but inscr "REIS REIS" instead of "DEZ REIS".

165	**43**	10r. blue and red	1·40	55

1898. Newspaper stamps of 1889 surch 1898 between value twice in figures.

168	**N34**	100r. on 50r. orange	2·40	50·00
169	**N34**	200r. on 100r. mauve	4·25	1·40
170	**N34**	300r. on 200r. black	4·25	1·40
171	**N34**	500r. on 300r. red	7·50	5·50
172	**N34**	700r. on 500r. orange	7·75	11·50
173	**N34**	700r. on 500r. green	9·50	2·30
174	**N34**	1000r. on 700r. orange	39·00	32·00
175	**N34**	1000r. on 700r. blue	27·00	17·00
176	**N34**	2000r. on 1000r. orange	33·00	17·00
177	**N34**	2000r. on 1000r. brown	24·00	6·75

1898. Newspaper stamp of 1890 surch **200** over 1898.

181	**N37**	200r. on 100r. mauve	11·00	5·00

1898. Newspaper stamps of 1890 surch **1898** over new value.

182	**N38**	20r. on 10r. blue	3·25	6·00
183	**N38**	50r. on 20r. green	8·50	10·00
184	**N38**	100r. on 50r. green	18·00	20·00

1899. Postage stamps of 1890 surch **1899** over new value.

194	**35**	50r. on 20r. green	1·40	2·00
195	**35**	100r. on 50r. green	1·40	2·00
196	**35**	300r. on 200r. violet	5·25	8·00
190	**35**	500r. on 300r. blue	12·50	5·00
190b	**35**	500r. on 300r. slate	12·50	5·00
191	**35**	700r. on 500r. buff	17·00	4·00
192a	**35**	1,000r. on 700r. brown	12·50	4·00
193	**35**	2,000r. on 1,000r. yellow	42·00	3·00

50 Discovery of Brazil

52 Emancipation of Slaves

1900. 400th Anniv of Discovery of Brazil.

226	**50**	100r. red	7·25	5·75
227	-	200r. green and yellow	7·25	5·75
228	**52**	500r. blue	7·25	5·75
229	-	700r. green	7·25	5·75

DESIGNS—HORIZ: 200r. Declaration of Independence. VERT: 700r. Allegory of Republic.

56 Pan-American Congress

1906

259a	**56**	100r. red	39·00	23·00
259b	**56**	200r. blue	95·00	10·50

57 Aristides Lobo

61 Liberty

1906

260	**57**	10r. grey	1·10	25
261	-	20r. violet	65	15
262	-	50r. green	1·10	25
264	-	100r. red	1·40	15
265	-	200r. blue	2·40	25
267	-	300r. brown	3·75	75
268	-	400r. olive	35·00	2·30
269	-	500r. violet	7·00	65
272	-	600r. olive	1·10	35
273	-	700r. brown	7·00	3·50
274	**61**	1000r. red	39·00	1·10
275	-	1000r. green	4·75	45
276	-	1000r. grey	28·00	75
277a	**61**	2000r. green	7·00	70
278	**61**	2000r. blue	14·00	45
279	**61**	5000r. pink	10·00	1·90
280	-	5000r. brown	55·00	8·50
281	-	10000r. brown	9·50	2·30

PORTRAITS: 20r. B. Constant. 50r. A. Cabral. 100r. Wandendkolk. 200r. D. da Fonseca. 300r. F. Peixoto. 400r., 600r. P. de Moraes. 500r. C. Salles. 700r., 5000r. (No. 280) R. Alves. 1000r. (Nos. 275/6) B. do Rio Branco. 10000r. N. Pecanha.

64 King Carlos and Pres. Affonso Penna and Emblems of Portuguese-Brazilian Amity

1908. Centenary of Opening of Brazilian Ports to Foreign Commerce.

282	**64**	100r. red	10·50	1·10

65 Emblems of Peace, Commerce and Industry

1908. National Exhibition, Rio de Janeiro.

283	**65**	100r. red	23·00	1·70

66 Bonifacio, San Martin, Hidalgo, Washington, O'Higgins, Bolivar

1909. Pan-American Congress, Rio de Janeiro.

284	**66**	200r. blue	10·50	1·00

67 Cape Frio

1915. 300th Anniv of Discovery of Cape Frio.

285	**67**	100r. turquoise on yellow	4·75	3·75

69 Bay of Guajara

1916. 300th Anniv of City of Belem.

286	**69**	100r. red	10·50	5·25

70 Revolutionary Flag

1917. Centenary of Pernambuco Revolution.

287	**70**	100r. blue	17·00	7·50

71 Liberty

72 Liberty

74 Inscr "BRAZIL"

1918. Various frames.

288A	**71**	10r. brown	60	30
289A	**71**	20r. violet	60	30
290A	**71**	25r. grey	60	30
291B	**71**	50r. green	1·70	60
292A	**72**	100r. red	2·00	30
293B	**72**	200r. blue	7·25	60
294A	**72**	300r. orange	23·00	3·75
295A	**72**	500r. purple	23·00	3·75
296B	**72**	600r. orange	3·00	9·50
297	**74**	1000r. blue	8·00	30
298	**74**	2000r. brown	35·00	8·50
299	**74**	5000r. lilac	10·00	8·50
300a	**74**	10,000r. red	11·00	1·10

77 Steam Locomotive

78 "Industry"

79 "Agriculture"

80 "Aviation"

81 Mercury

82 "Shipping"

1920. T **74** inscr "BRASIL".

317	**77**	10r. purple	35	25
387A	**80**	10r. brown	20	15
318	**77**	20r. grey	35	25
388A	**80**	20r. violet	20	15
389A	**78**	25r. purple	20	15
354	**79**	40r. brown	60	35
306	**78**	50r. green	1·10	45
355	**78**	50r. brown	90	35
390	**80**	50r. purple	20	15
391	**80**	50r. green	20	15
308	**79**	80r. green	35	2·20
309	**80**	100r. red	3·75	45
367	**80**	100r. green	45	20
392A	**80**	100r. orange	35	15
420	**80**	100r. yellow	2·00	30
311	**80**	150r. violet	1·30	25
312	**80**	200r. blue	6·00	45
330	**80**	200r. red	30	10
383	**80**	200r. green	3·25	85
333	**81**	300r. red	25	15
394A	**81**	300r. green	70	15
405	**81**	300r. grey	20	15
335	**81**	400r. orange	55	40
406	**81**	400r. blue	25	20
385	**81**	500r. blue	1·70	25
407	**81**	500r. brown	4·00	15
341	**82**	600r. orange	2·50	45
397	**81**	600r. brown	4·00	15
422	**81**	600r. orange	6·00	30
409	**81**	700r. violet	4·25	15
342	**82**	1000r. purple	6·75	30
410	**81**	1000r. blue	12·00	35
362d	**74**	2000r. blue	7·00	40
411	**74**	2000r. violet	32·00	1·40
363	**74**	5000r. brown	20·00	5·25
364	**74**	10000r. purple	21·00	1·00

93 King Albert and Pres. Pessoa

1920. Visit of King of the Belgians.

431	**93**	100r. red	90	85

94 Declaration of Ypiranga

1922. Centenary of Independence.

432	**94**	100r. blue	3·75	75
433	-	200r. red	6·50	50
434	-	300r. green	6·50	50

DESIGNS: 200r. Dom Pedro I and J. Bonifacio; 300r. National Exn. and Pres. Pessoa.

97 Brazilian Army entering Bahia

1923. Centenary of Capture of Bahia from the Portuguese.

435	**97**	200r. red	10·50	6·50

98 Arms of the Confederation

1924. Centenary of Confederation of the Equator.

436	**98**	200r. multicoloured	4·00	2·50

99 Ruy Barbosa

1927

438a	**99**	1000r. red	2·75	55

100 "Justice"

1927. Centenary of Law Courses.

439	**100**	100r. blue	1·00	55
440	-	200r. red	90	40

DESIGN: 200r. Map and Balances.

1928. Air. Official stamps of 1913, Type **O67**, surch **SERVICO AEREO** and new value. Centres in black.

441	50r. on 10r. grey	45	30
442	200r. on 1000r. brown	2·40	4·75
443	200r. on 2000r. brown	1·40	11·00
444	200r. on 5000r. bistre	1·60	1·40
445	300r. on 500r. yellow	1·60	2·30
446	300r. on 600r. purple	85	85
447	500r. on 50r. grey	1·60	75
448	1000r. on 20r. olive	1·20	25
449	2000r. on 100r. red	2·75	1·90
450	2000r. on 200r. blue	3·50	1·90
451	2000r. on 10,000r. black	3·25	70
452	5000r. on 20,000r. blue	9·25	4·25
453	5000r. on 50,000r. green	9·25	4·25
454	5000r. on 100,000r. red	31·00	32·00
455	10,000r. on 500,000r. brown	35·00	23·00
456	10,000r. on 1,000,000r. sepia	33·00	30·00

104 Liberty holding Coffee Leaves

1928. Bicent of Introduction of the Coffee Plant.

457	**104**	100r. green	1·60	65
458	**104**	200r. red	1·00	50
459	**104**	300r. black	8·75	40

1928. Official stamps of 1919 surch.

460	**O77**	700r. on 500r. orange	7·50	7·00
461	**O77**	1000r. on 100r. red	4·50	50
462	**O77**	2000r. on 200r. blue	6·25	1·00
463	**O77**	5000r. on 50r. green	7·25	1·50
464	**O77**	10,000r. on 10r. brown	27·00	1·90

106 Ruy Barbosa

1929

465	**106**	5000r. blue	19·00	90

108 Santos Dumonts Airship 'No. 6'

109 Santos Dumont

1929. Air.

469	-	50r. green	30	25
470	**108**	200r. red	1·40	15
471	-	300r. blue	2·00	15
472	-	500r. purple	2·50	15
473	-	1000r. brown	8·50	30
479	-	2000r. green	12·50	50
480	-	5000r. red	14·50	1·30
481a	**109**	10,000r. grey	9·00	1·30

DESIGNS: 50r. De Gusmao's monument; 300r. A. Severo's airship "*Pax*; 500r. Santos Dumont's biplane *14 bi*"; 1000r. R. de Barros's flying boat *Jahu*; 2000r. De Gusmao; 5000r. A. Severo.

110

1930. Air.

486	**110**	3000r. violet	2·20	1·80

112

1930. Fourth Pan-American Architectural Congress.

487	-	100r. turquoise	2·40	1·30
488	**112**	200r. grey	4·25	95
489	-	300r. red	6·50	1·70

DESIGNS: 100r. Sun rays inscr "ARCHITECTOS"; 300r. Architrave and Southern Cross.

113 G. Vargas and J. Pessoa – "Redemption of Brazil"

114 O. Aranha – "What is the matter?"

1931. Charity. Revolution of 3 October 1930.

490	**113**	10r.+10r. blue	20	10·00
491	**113**	20r.+20r. brown	20	7·50
492	**114**	50r.+50r. green, red and yellow	20	35
493	**113**	100r.+50r. orange	45	40
494	**113**	200r.+100r. green	45	40
495	-	300r.+150r. mult	45	40
496	**113**	400r.+200r. red	1·50	1·20
497	**113**	500r.+250r. blue	1·40	90
498	**113**	600r.+300r. purple	90	10·50
499	**113**	700r.+350r. mult	1·70	85
500	**114**	1$+500r. green, red and yellow	3·00	45
501	-	2$+1$ grey and red	12·50	80
502	-	5$+2$ 500r. black & red	31·00	12·00
503	-	10$+5$ green & yellow	75·00	22·00

DESIGNS: 300r., 700r. as Type **113**, but portraits in circles and frames altered. Milreis values as Type **114** with different portraits and frames.

1931. No. 333 surch **1931 200 Reis**.

507	**81**	200r. on 300r. red	45	25

1931. Zeppelin Air Stamps. Surch **ZEPPELIN** and value.

508	**108**	2$500 on 200r. red (No. 470)	27·00	24·00
511	**106**	3$500 on 5000r. blue (No. 468b)	28·00	27·00
509	-	5$000 on 300r. blue (No. 471)	35·00	32·00
512	**74**	7$000 on 10,000r. red (No. 364)	28·00	27·00

1931. Air. No. 486 surch **2.500 REIS**.

510	**110**	2500r. on 3000r. violet	24·00	23·00

121 Brazil

1932. 400th Anniv of Colonization of Sao Vicente.

513	**121**	20r. purple	25	40
514	-	100r. black	55	45
515	-	200r. violet	1·10	25
516	-	600r. brown	1·90	1·90
517	-	700r. blue	3·50	2·75

DESIGNS: 100r. Natives; 200r. M. Afonso de Souza; 600r. King John III of Portugal; 700r. Founding of Sao Vicente.

125 Soldier and Flag

130 "Justice"

1932. Sao Paulo Revolutionary Government issue.

518		100r. brown	55	2·75
519	**125**	200r. red	45	95
520	-	300r. green	2·75	5·00
521	-	400r. blue	9·25	10·50
522	-	500r. sepia	11·00	10·50
523	-	600r. red	11·00	10·50
524	**125**	700r. violet	5·00	10·50
525	-	1000r. orange	2·40	10·50
526	-	2000r. brown	21·00	28·00
527	-	5000r. green	24·00	48·00
528	**130**	10,000r. purple	29·00	55·00

DESIGNS—As Type **125**: 100, 500r. Map of Brazil; 300r., 600r. Symbolical of freedom, etc., 400, 1000r. Soldier in tin helmet. As Type **130**: 2000r. "LEX" and sword; 5000r. "Justice" and soldiers with bayonets.

131 Campo Bello Square and Memorial. Vassouras

1933. Centenary of Vassouras.

529	**131**	200r. red	1·30	1·10

132 Flag and Dornier Wal Flying Boat

1933. Air.

532	**132**	3500r. blue, green & yell	4·00	2·00

1933. Surch **200 REIS**.

536	**81**	200r. on 300r. red	55	50

134 Flag of the Race

1933. 441st Anniv of Departure of Columbus from Polos.

537	**134**	200r. red	1·00	90

135 Christian Symbols

1933. First Eucharistic Congress, Sao Salvador.

538	**135**	200r. red	1·00	90

136 From Santos Dumont Statue, St. Cloud

1933. Obligatory Tax for Airport Fund.

539	**136**	100r. purple	75	25

137 Faith and Energy

1933

540	**137**	200r. red	60	20
543	**137**	200r. violet	1·40	30

138 "Republic" and Flags

1933. Visit of Pres. Justo of Argentina.

545	**138**	200r. blue	55	55
546	**138**	400r. green	1·80	1·70
547	**138**	600r. red	6·50	9·00
548	**138**	1000r. violet	9·25	6·50

139 Santos Dumont Statue, St. Cloud

1934. First National Aviation Congress, Sao Paulo.

549	**139**	200r. blue	1·10	1·00

140 Exhibition Building

1934. Seventh International Sample Fair, Rio de Janeiro.

550	**140**	200r. brown	65	55
551	**140**	400r. red	2·75	2·75
552	**140**	700r. blue	2·75	1·90
553	**140**	1000r. orange	7·75	1·30

141 Brazilian Stamp of 1844

1934. National Philatelic Exhibition, Rio. Imperf.

555	**141**	200r.+100r. purple	1·80	5·50
556	**141**	300r.+100r. red	1·80	5·50
557	**141**	700r.+100r. blue	10·50	46·00
558	**141**	1000r.+100r. black	10·50	46·00

142 Christ of Mt. Corcovado

1934. Visit of Cardinal Pacelli.

559	**142**	300r. red	5·50	5·50
560	**142**	700r. blue	22·00	22·00

143 Jose de Anchieta

1934. 400th Anniv of Founding of Sao Paulo by Anchieta.

561	**143**	200r. brown	90	75
562	**143**	300r. violet	65	55
563	**143**	700c. blue	4·00	4·00
564	**143**	1000r. green	7·75	1·70

145 "Brazil" and "Uruguay"

1935. Visit of President Terra of Uruguay.

565	-	200r. orange	1·30	75
566	**145**	300r. yellow	1·70	1·40
567	**145**	700r. blue	6·50	8·75
568	-	1000r. violet	17·00	8·75

DESIGN—HORIZ: 200, 1000r. Female figures as in Type **145** and bridge.

146 Town of Igarassu

1935. 400th Anniv of Founding of Pernambuco.

569	**146**	200r. brown and red	2·00	1·30
570	**146**	300r. olive and violet	2·00	1·10

147 Nurse and Patient

1935. Third Pan-American Red Cross Conference.

571	**147**	200r.+100r. violet	2·40	2·40
572	**147**	300r.+100r. brown	2·40	2·00
573	**147**	700r.+100r. blue	17·00	14·50

149 Gen. da Silva

1935. Cent of Farroupilha "Ragged Revolution".

574	-	200r. black	1·80	1·80
575	-	300r. red	1·80	1·10
576	**149**	700r. blue	5·00	8·75
577	-	1000r. violet	6·00	5·50

DESIGNS: 200, 300r. Mounted Gaucho; 1000r. Marshal Caxias.

151 Gavea

1935. Children's Day.

578	**151**	300r. violet and brown	3·50	2·75
579	**151**	300r. turquoise and black	3·50	2·75
580	**151**	300r. blue and green	3·50	2·75
581	**151**	300r. black and red	3·50	2·75

152 Federal District Coat of Arms

1935. Eighth International Fair.

582	**152**	200r. blue	5·00	5·25

153 Coutinho's ship *Gloria*, 1535

1935. 400th Anniv of Colonization of State of Espirito Santo.

583	**153**	300r. red	3·25	1·40
584	-	700r. blue	7·25	4·25

DESIGN—VERT: 700r. Arms of Coutinho.

154a Viscount Cairu

1936. Death Centenary of Cairu.

585	**154a**	1200r. violet	12·00	8·75

155 Cameta

1936. Tercentenary of Founding of Cameta.

586	**155**	200r. buff	2·20	2·00
587	**155**	500r. green	2·20	1·10

156 Coin Press

1936. Numismatic Congress, Sao Paulo.

588	**156**	300r. brown	2·00	2·00

157 Scales of Justice

1936. First National Juridical Congress, Rio.

589	**157**	300r. red	2·40	90

158 A. Carlos Gomes

159 *Il* Guarany

1936. Birth Centenary of C. Gomes (composer).

590	**158**	300r. red	1·10	1·10
591	**158**	300r. brown	1·10	1·10
592	**159**	700r. blue	4·50	2·75
593	**159**	700r. buff	5·00	4·00

1936. Ninth International Sample Fair, Rio. As T **152** with inscription and date altered.

594	**152**	200r. red	1·50	90

160 Congress Seal

1936. Second National Eucharistic Congress, Belo Horizonte.

595	**160**	300r. multicoloured	1·40	90

161 Botafogo Bay

1937. Birth Centenary of Dr. Francisco Pereira Passos.

596	**161**	700r. blue	1·80	1·20
597	**161**	700r. black	1·80	1·20

162 Esperanto Star and National Flags

1937. Ninth Brazilian Esperanto Congress, Rio de Janeiro.

598	**162**	300r. green	1·90	1·00

163 Bay of Rio de Janeiro

1937. Second S. American Radio Conference.

599	**163**	300r. black and orange	1·10	1·10
600	**163**	700r. brown and blue	3·00	1·10

164 Globe

1937. Golden Jubilee of Esperanto.

601	**164**	300r. green	1·80	1·00

166 Iguazu Falls

1937. Tourist Propaganda.

602	-	200r. blue and brown	1·30	1·30
603	-	300r. green and orange	1·30	1·30
604	**166**	1000r. brown and sepia	4·00	2·75
605	-	2000r. red and green	17·00	18·00
606	**166**	5000r. green and black	33·00	33·00
607	-	10,000r. blue and red	65·00	65·00

DESIGNS—HORIZ: 200, 2000r. Monroe Palace, Rio. VERT: 300, 10,000r. Botanical Gardens, Rio.

168 J. Da Silva Paes

1937. Bicent of Founding of Rio Grande do Sul.

608	**168**	300r. blue	1·30	65

169 Eagle and Shield

1937. 150th Anniv of U.S. Constitution.

609	**169**	400r. blue	1·90	90

170 Coffee

1938. Coffee Propaganda.

610	**170**	1200r. multicoloured	7·75	65

171 "Grito" Memorial

1938. Commemoration of Abortive Proclamation of Republic.

611	**171**	400r. brown	1·30	65

172 Arms of Olinda

1938. Fourthth Centenary of Olinda.

612	**172**	400r. violet	1·10	55

173 Couto de Magalhaes

1938. Birth Centenary of De Magalhaes.

613	**173**	400r. green	1·00	55

174 National Archives

1938. Centenary of Founding of National Archives.

614	**174**	400r. brown	1·00	55

174a Rowland Hill

1938. Brazilian International Philatelic Exhibition (BRAPEX), Rio de Janeiro. T **174a** repeated ten times in sheet together with exhibition emblem.

MS614a 117×118 mm. 400r. green		30·00	35·00

174b President Vargas

1938. First Anniv of Constitution issued by President Vargas. T **174b** repeated ten times in sheet together with star emblem.

MS614b 115×138 mm. 400r. blue		33·00	33·00

175 Rio de Janeiro

1939

615	**175**	1200r. purple	2·75	20

176 Santos

1939. Centenary of Santos City.

616	**176**	400r. blue	65	45

177 Chalice-vine and Cup-of-gold Blossoms

1939. First S. American Botanical Congress, Rio.

617	**177**	400r. green	2·10	45

178 Seal of Congress

1939. Third National Eucharistic Congress, Recife.

618	**178**	400r. red	65	65

179 Duke of Caxias

1939. Soldiers' Day.

619	**179**	400r. blue	65	65

180 Washington

1939. New York World's Fair. Inscr "FEIRA MUNDIAL DE NOVA YORK".

620	**180**	400r. orange	90	45
621	-	800r. green	45	35
622	-	1200r. red	1·00	35
623	-	1600r. blue	1·00	45

DESIGNS—HORIZ: 1200r. Grover Cleveland. VERT: 800r. Dom Pedro II; 1m. Water lily; 1600r. Statue of Liberty, Rio de Janeiro; 5m. Bust of Pres. Vargas; 10m. Relief map of Brazil.

184 Benjamin Constant

1939. 50th Anniv of Constitution.

624	**184**	400r. green	1·10	75
625	-	800r. black	75	65
626	-	1200r. brown	1·20	75

DESIGNS—VERT: 800r. Marshal da Fonseca. HORIZ: 1200r. Marshal da Fonseca and Pres. Vargas.

188 Child and Southern Cross

1940. Child Welfare.

627		100r.+100r. violet	1·30	1·30
628		200r.+100r. blue	1·80	1·80
629	**188**	400r.+200r. olive	1·30	1·10
630	-	1200r.+400r. red	5·50	2·40

DESIGNS: 100r. Three Wise Men; 200r. Angel and Child; 1200r. Mother and Child.

189 Roosevelt, Vargas and American Continents

1940. 50th Anniv of Pan-American Union.

631	**189**	400r. blue	1·30	75

190 Map of Brazil

1940. Ninth National Geographical Congress, Florianopolis.

632	**190**	400r. red	65	65

191 Water Lily

192 Map of Brazil

1940. New York World's Fair (2nd issue). No gum.

633	**191**	1m. violet	1·80	1·80
634	—	5m. red (Pres. Vargas)	13·00	10·50
635	**192**	10m. blue	15·00	5·00

MS635a Three sheets each 127×147 mm. Nos. 633/5 each in block of ten		£375	£500

1940. Birth Centenary of Machado de Assis (poet and novelist). As T **173** but portrait of de Assis, dated "1839–1939".

636	400r. black	90	45

193 Two Workers

1940. Bicentenary of Colonization of Porto Alegre.

637	**193**	400r. green	75	45

194 Acclaiming King John IV of Portugal

1940. Centenaries of Portugal (1140–1640-1940) (1st issue).

638	**194**	1200r. grey	3·25	55

See also Nos. 642/5.

195 Brazilian Flags and Head of Liberty

1940. Tenth Anniv of Govt. of President Vargas.

639B	**195**	400r. purple	90	35

196 Date of Fifth Census

197 Globe showing Spotlight on Brazil

1941. Fifth General Census.

640a	**196**	400r. blue & red (postage)	45	20
641	**197**	1200r. brown (air)	4·75	90

199 Father Antonio Vieira

1941. Centenaries of Portugal (2nd issue).

642B	-	200r. pink	35	20
643B	**199**	400r. blue	35	10
644B	-	800r. violet	55	35
645B	-	5400r. green	2·75	75

DESIGNS—VERT: 200r. Alfonso Henriques; 800r. Governor-Gen. Benevides. HORIZ: 5,400r. Carmona and Vargas.

202 Father Jose Anchieta

1941. 400th Anniv of Order of Jesuits.

646	**202**	1m. violet	2·20	1·30

205 Oil Wells

210 Count of Porto Alegre

1941. Value in reis.

647A	**205**	10r. orange	55	40
648A	**205**	20r. olive	55	40
649A	**205**	50r. brown	55	40
650A	**205**	100r. turquoise	65	40
651B	-	200r. brown	2·00	65
652A	-	300r. red	65	40
653B	-	400r. blue	65	45
654A	-	500r. red	75	40
655B	-	600r. violet	90	55
656A	-	700r. red	65	40
657B	-	1000r. grey	3·25	65
658B	-	1200r. blue	4·00	65
659A	-	2000r. purple	6·00	65
660B	-	5000r. blue	7·75	65
661B	**210**	10,000r. red	17·00	2·75
662A	-	20,000r. brown	20·00	2·00
663D	-	50m. red	29·00	5·50
664D	-	100m. blue	2·00	6·50

DESIGNS: 200r. to 500r. Wheat harvesting machinery; 600r. to 1200r. Smelting works; 2000r. "Commerce"; 5000r. Marshal F. Peixoto; 20,000r. Admiral Maurity; 50m. "Armed Forces"; 100m. Pres. Vargas.

For stamps with values in centavos and cruzeiros see Nos. 751, etc.

213 Amador Bueno

1941. 300th Anniv of Amador Bueno as King of Sao Paulo.

665	**213**	400r. black	1·10	65

214 Brazilian Air Force Emblem

1941. Aviation Week.

666	**214**	5400r. green	6·00	4·50

1941. Air. Fourth Anniv of President Vargas's New Constitution. Optd **AEREO "10 Nov." 937-941.**

667a	5400r. green (No. 645)	3·75	1·75

215 Indo-Brazilian Cow

1942. Second Agriculture and Cattle Show, Uberaba.

668	**215**	200r. blue	1·00	65
669	**215**	400r. brown	90	60

216 Bernardino de Campos

1942. Birth Centenaries of B. de Campos and P. de Morais (lawyers and statesmen).

670	**216**	1000r. red	2·20	1·40
671	-	1200r. blue	7·25	65

PORTRAIT: 1200r. Prudente de Morais.

217 Torch of Learning

1942. 8th National Education Congress, Goiania.

672	**217**	400r. brown	90	55

218 Map of Brazil showing Goiania

1942. Founding of Goiania City.

673	**218**	400r. violet	90	55

219 Congressional Seal

1942. Fourth National Eucharistic Congress, Sao Paulo.

674	**219**	400r. brown	1·10	40

1942. Air. Fifth Anniv of President Vargas's New Constitution. No. 645 surch **AEREO "10 Nov." 937-942** and value.

675a	5cr.40 on 5400r. green	4·50	2·40

221 Tributaries of R. Amazon

1943. 400th Anniv of Discovery of River Amazon.

676	**221**	40c. brown	75	70

222 Early Brazilian Stamp

1943. Centenary of Petropolis.

677	**222**	40c. violet	1·10	60

223 Memorial Tablet

1943. Air. Visit of Pres. Morinigo of Paraguay.

678	**223**	1cr.20 blue	3·25	2·20

224 Map of S. America showing Brazil and Bolivia

1943. Air. Visit of President Penaranda of Bolivia.

679	**224**	1cr.20 multicoloured	2·75	1·70

225 "Bulls-eye"

1943. Centenary of First Brazilian Postage Stamps. (a) Postage. Imperf.

680	**225**	30c. black	1·10	1·00
681	**225**	60c. black	1·20	45
682	**225**	90c. black	75	75

MS682a 127×95 mm. Nos. 680/2. No gum. Imperf 29·00 33·00

226

(b) Air. Perf.

683	**226**	1cr. black and yellow	4·50	3·25
684	**226**	2cr. black and green	6·00	3·25
685	**226**	5cr. black and red	7·25	4·50

MS685a 155×155 mm. Nos. 683/5. Imperf. No gum 75·00 75·00

227 Book of the Law

1943. Air. Inter-American Advocates Conference.

686	**227**	1cr.20 red and brown	1·70	65

228 Ubaldino do Amaral

1943. Birth Centenary of Ubaldino do Amaral.

687	**228**	40c. grey	1·00	20

229 Indo-Brazilian Cow

1943. Ninth Cattle Show, Bahia.

688	**229**	40c. brown	1·40	90

230 Justice and Seal

1943. Centenary of Institute of Brazilian Lawyers.

689a	**230**	2cr. red	1·50	90

231 Santa Casa de Misericordia Hospital

1943. 400th Anniv of Santa Casa de Misericordia de Santos.

690	**231**	1cr. blue	90	65

232 Barbosa Rodrigues

1943. Birth Centenary of B. Rodrigues (botanist).

691	**232**	40c. green	90	45

233 Pedro Americo

1943. Birth Centenary of Pedro Americo (artist and author).

692	**233**	40c. brown	1·10	45

1944. Air. No. 629 surch. **AEREO** and value.

693	**188**	20c. on 400r.+200r.	1·80	1·00
694	**188**	40c. on 400r.+200r.	2·75	1·00
695	**188**	60c. on 400r.+200r.	4·00	70
696	**188**	1cr. on 400r.+200r.	6·25	1·00
697	**188**	1cr.20 on 400r.+200r.	6·00	65

235 Gen. Carneiro and Defenders of Lapa

1944. 50th Anniv of Siege of Lapa.

698	**235**	1cr.20c. red	1·50	75

236 Baron do Rio Branco

1944. Inauguration of Monument to Baron do Rio Branco.

699	**236**	1cr. blue	1·00	65

237 Duke of Caxias

1944. Centenary of Pacification of Revolutionary Uprising of 1842.

700	**237**	1cr.20 green and yellow	1·60	65

238 Emblems of YMCA

1944. Centenary of YMCA.

701	**238**	40c. blue, red and yellow	65	35

239 Rio Grande Chamber of Commerce

1944. Centenary of Founding of Rio Grande Chamber of Commerce.

702	**239**	40c. brown	70	35

240 "Bartolomeo de Gusmao and the Aerostat" (Bernardino de Souza Pereira)

1944. Air. Air Week.

703	**240**	1cr.20 red	75	45

241 Ribeiro de Andrada

1945. Death Centenary of M. de Andrada (statesman).

704	**241**	40c. blue	90	20

242 Meeting between Caxias and Canabarro

1945. Centenary of Pacification of Rio Grande do Sul.

705	**242**	40c. blue	90	20

244 L. L. Zamenhof

1945. Tenth Brazilian Esperanto Congress, Rio de Janeiro.

706	-	40c. green (postage)	1·20	65
707	**244**	1cr.20 brown (air)	90	55

DESIGN: 40c. Woman and map.

247 Baron do Rio Branco (statesman)

1945. Birth Centenary of Baron do Rio Branco.

708	-	40c. blue (postage)	1·20	55
709	-	1cr.20 purple (air)	75	55
710	**247**	5cr. purple	2·10	90

DESIGNS—HORIZ: 40c. Bookplate. VERT: 1cr.20, S. America.

248 "Glory"

250 "Co-operation"

1945. Victory of Allied Nations in Europe. Roul.

711	-	20c. violet	55	20
712	**248**	40c. red	55	20
713	-	1cr. orange	1·10	55
714	-	2cr. blue	2·75	65
715	**250**	5cr. green	5·50	90

SYMBOLICAL DESIGNS—VERT: 20c. Tranquility (inscr "SAUDADE"). HORIZ: 1cr. "Victory" (inscr "VITORIA"); 2cr. "Peace" (inscr "PAZ").

251 F. M. da Silva

1945. 150th Birth Anniv of Francisco Manoel da Silva (composer of Brazilian National Anthem).

716	**251**	40c. red	1·30	60

252 Bahia Institute

1945. 50th Anniv of Founding of Bahia Institute of Geography and History.

717	**252**	40c. blue	2·00	35

253 Shoulder Flash

255 "V" Sign and Flashes

1945. Return of Brazilian Expeditionary Force.

718	**253**	20c. blue, red and green	55	45
719	-	40c. multicoloured	55	45
720	-	1cr. multicoloured	1·50	90

721	-	2cr. multicoloured	2·20	1·30
722	**255**	5cr. multicoloured	6·50	1·50

DESIGNS (embodying shoulder flashes) As Type **253**: 40c. B.E.F. flash. As Type **255**. HORIZ: 1cr. U.S.A. flag; 2cr. Brazilian flag.

256 Wireless Mast and Map

1945. Third Inter-American Radio Communication Conference.

723	**256**	1cr.20 black	1·40	20

257 Admiral Saldanha da Gama

1946. Birth Centenary of Admiral S. da Gama.

724	**257**	40c. grey	90	1·40

258 Princess Isabel d'Orleans-Braganza

1946. Birth Centenary of Princess Isabel d'Orleans-Braganza.

725	**258**	40c. black	90	1·90

260 Lockheed 14 Super Electra over Bay of Rio de Janiero

261 P.O., Rio de Janeiro

1946. Fifth Postal Union. Congress of the Americas and Spain.

726	-	40c. orange and black	55	45
727	**260**	1cr.30 orange and green	75	75
728	**260**	1cr.70 orange and red	75	75
729	**261**	2cr. blue and slate	1·10	45
730	**260**	2cr.20 orange and blue	1·10	1·10
731	**261**	5cr. blue and brown	5·50	1·90
732	**261**	10cr. blue and violet	6·00	1·10

DESIGN (25×37 mm): 40c. Post-horn, V and envelope.

262 Proposed Columbus Lighthouse

1946. Construction of Columbus Lighthouse, Dominican Republic.

733	**262**	5cr. blue	17·00	3·75

263 "Liberty"

1946. New Constitution.

734	**263**	40c. grey	55	35

264 Orchid

1946. Fourth National Exn of Orchids, Rio de Janeiro.

735	**264**	40c. blue, red and yellow	1·20	35

265 Gen. A. E. Gomes Carneiro

1946. Birth Centenary of Gen. A. E. Gomes Carneiro.

736	**265**	40c. green	55	10

266 Academy of Arts

1946. 50th Anniv of Brazilian Academy of Arts.

737	**266**	40c. blue	65	45

267 Antonio de Castro Alves

1947. Birth Centenary of Castro Alves (poet).

738	**267**	40c. turquoise	55	10

268 Pres. Gonzalez

1947. Visit of Chilean President.

739	**268**	40c. brown	55	10

269 "Peace and Security"

270 "Dove of Peace"

1947. Inter-American Defence Conference, Rio de Janeiro.

740	**269**	1cr.20 blue (postage)	55	45
741	**270**	2cr.20 green (air)	75	55

271 Pres. Truman, Map of S. America and Statue of Liberty

1947. Visit of President Truman.

742	**271**	40c. blue	65	10

272 Pres. Enrico Gaspar Dutra

1947. Commemorating Pres. Dutra.

743	**272**	20c. green (postage)	20	10
744	**272**	40c. red	35	10
745	**272**	1cr.20 blue	65	10
MS746a		130×75 mm. Nos. 743/5. No gum. Imperf (air)	£110	£130

273 Woman and Child

1947. Children's Week. First Brazilian Infant Welfare Convention and Paediatrics.

747	**273**	40c. blue	65	10

274 Icarus

1947. Obligatory Tax. "Week of the Wing" Aviation Fund.

748	**274**	40c.+10c. orange	75	20

275 Santos Dumont Monument, St. Cloud, France

1947. Air. Homage to Santos Dumont (aviation pioneer).

749	**275**	1cr.20c. brown & green	1·10	55

276 Arms of Belo Horizonte

1947. 50th Anniv of Founding of City of Belo Horizonte.

750	**276**	1cr.20c. red	90	10

1947. As postage stamps of 1941, but values in centavos or cruzeiros.

751	**205**	2c. olive	35	10
752	**205**	5c. brown	35	10
753	**205**	10c. turquoise	45	10
754	-	20c. brown (No. 651)	55	10
755	-	30c. red (No. 652)	1·40	20
756	-	40c. blue (No. 653)	55	10
757	-	50c. red (No. 654)	1·40	20
758	-	60c. violet (No. 655)	2·20	20
759	-	70c. red (No. 656)	1·00	20
760	-	1cr. grey (No. 657)	4·50	20
761	-	1cr.20 blue (No. 658)	5·50	20
762	-	2cr. purple (No. 659)	7·75	20
763	-	5cr. blue (No. 660)	19·00	20
764	**210**	10cr. red	14·50	20
765	-	20cr. brown (No. 662)	26·00	20
766a	-	50cr. red (No. 663)	31·00	5·50

277 Rio de Janeiro and Rotary Emblem

1948. Air. 39th Rotary Congress Rio de Janeiro.

769	**277**	1cr.20 red	1·10	90
770	**277**	3cr.80 violet	2·20	95

278 Globe

279 Quitandinha Hotel

1948. International Industrial and Commercial Exhibition, Quitandinha.

771	**278**	40c. grn & mve (postage)	65	30
772	**279**	1cr.20 brown (air)	55	55
773	**279**	3cr.80 violet	1·40	65

280 Arms of Paranagua

1948. Tercentenary of Founding of Paranagua.

774	**280**	5cr. brown	4·50	1·10

281 Girl Reading

1948. National Children's Campaign.

775	**281**	40c. green	55	20

282 Three Muses (after Henrique Bernardelli)

1948. Air. Centenary of National School of Music.

776	**282**	1cr.20 blue	1·40	35

283 President Berres

1948. Air. Visit of Uruguayan President.

777	**283**	1cr.70 blue	75	35

284 Merino Ram

1948. Air. International Livestock Show, Bage.

778	**284**	1cr.20 orange	1·70	65

285 Congress Seal

1948. Air. Fifth National Eucharistic Congress, Porto Alegre.

779	**285**	1cr.20 purple	75	35

286 "Tiradentes" (trans. "Tooth-puller")

1948. Birth Bicentenary of A. J. J. da Silva Xavier (patriot).

780	**286**	40c. orange	55	20

287 Crab and Globe

1948. Anti-cancer Campaign.

781	**287**	40c. purple	55	55

288 Adult Student

1949. Campaign for Adult Education.

782	**288**	60c. purple	55	10

289 Battle of Guararapes

1949. 300th Anniv of Second Battle of Guararapes.

783	**289**	60c. blue (postage)	2·20	1·10
784	-	1cr.20 pink (air)	3·25	1·70

DESIGN: 1cr.20, View of Guararapes.

290 St. Francis of Paula Church

1949. Bicentenary of Ouro Fino.

785	**290**	60c. brown	65	35
MS785a 70×89 mm. No. 785. Imperf			75·00	65·00

291 Father Nobrega

292 De Souza meeting Indians

1949. Fourth Centenary of Founding of Bahia. (a) Postage. Imperf.

786	**291**	60c. violet	65	35

(b) Air. Perf.

787	**292**	1cr.20 blue	75	40

293 Franklin D. Roosevelt

1949. Air. Homage to Franklin D. Roosevelt. Imperf.

788	**293**	3cr.80 blue	2·20	1·50
MS788a 85×110 mm. No. 788			39·00	46·00

294 Douglas DC-3 and Air Force Badge

1949. Homage to Brazilian Air Force. Imperf.

789	**294**	60c. violet	55	10

295 Joaquim Nabuco

1949. Air. Birth Centenary of J. Nabuco (lawyer and author).

790	**295**	3cr.80 purple	1·70	45

296 "Revelation"

1949. First Sacerdotal Vocational Congress, Bahia.

791	**296**	60c. purple	65	20

297 Globe

1949. 75th Anniv of UPU.

792	**297**	1cr.50 blue	90	10

298 Ruy Barbosa

1949. Birth Centenary of Ruy Barbosa (statesman).

793	**298**	1cr.20 red	1·40	45

299 Cardinal Arcoverde

1950. Birth Centenary of Cardinal Joaquim Arcoverde.

794	**299**	60c. pink	75	15

300 "Agriculture and Industry"

1950. 75th Anniv of Arrival of Italian Immigrants.

795	**300**	60c. red	65	10

301 Virgin of the Globe

1950. Centenary of Establishment of Daughters of Charity of St. Vincent de Paul.

796	**301**	60c. blue and black	55	10

302 Globe and Footballers

303 Stadium

1950. Fourth World Football Championship, Rio de Janeiro.

797	**302**	60c. grey & bl (postage)	1·90	55
798	**303**	1cr.20 orange and blue (air)	2·10	90
799	-	5cr.80 yellow, green and blue	6·50	1·10

DESIGN—VERT: 5cr.80 Linesman and flag.

304 Three Heads, Map and Graph

305 Line of People and Map

1950. Sixth Brazilian Census, 1950.

800	**304**	60c. red (postage)	55	10
801	**305**	1cr.20 brown (air)	85	20

306 Oswaldo Cruz

1950. Fifth International Microbiological Congress. Rio de Janeiro.

802	**306**	60c. brown	90	10

307 Blumenau and Itajai River

1950. Centenary of Founding of Blumenau.

803	**307**	60c. pink	90	10

308 Government Offices

1950. Centenary of Amazon Province.

804	**308**	60c. red	65	10

309 Arms

1950. Centenary of Juiz de Fora City.

805	**309**	60c. red	75	35

310 P.O. Building, Recife

1951. Inauguration of Head Post Office, Pernambuco Province.

806	**310**	60c. red	65	10
807	**310**	1cr.20 red	70	10

311 Arms of Joinville

1951. Centenary of Founding of Joinville.

808	**311**	60c. brown	70	15

312 S. Romero

1951. Birth Centenary of Sylvio Romero (poet).

809	**312**	60c. brown	90	10

313 De La Salle

1951. Birth Tricentenary of Jean-Baptiste de la Salle (educational reformer).

810	**313**	60c. blue	65	10

314 Heart and Flowers

1951. Mothers' Day.

811	**314**	60c. purple	1·00	55

315 J. Caetano and Stage

1951. First Brazilian Theatrical Congress.

812	**315**	60c. blue	65	10

316 O. A. Derby

1951. Birth Centenary of Derby (geologist).

813	**316**	2cr. slate	1·00	55

317 Crucifix and Congregation

1951. Fourth Inter-American Catholic Education Congress, Rio de Janeiro.

814	**317**	60c. brown and buff	65	10

318 E. P. Martins and Map

1951. 29th Anniv of First Rio–New York Flight.

815	**318**	3cr.80 brown & lemon	3·75	75

319 Penha Convent

1951. 400th Anniv of Founding of Vitoria.

816	**319**	60c. brown and buff	75	15

320 Santos Dumont and Boys with Model Aircraft

1951. "Week of the Wing" and 50th Anniv of Santos Dumont's Flight over Paris.

817	**320**	60c. brn & orge (postage)	1·00	35
818	-	3cr.80 violet (air)	3·25	45

DESIGN: 3cr.80, "Ballon No. 6" airship over Eiffel Tower.

321 Wheat Harvesters

1951. Wheat Festival, Bage.

819	**321**	60c. green and grey	90	75

322 Bible and Map

1951. Bible Day.

820	**322**	1cr.20 brown	1·30	65

323 Isabella the Catholic

1952. 500th Birth Anniv of Isabella the Catholic.

821	**323**	3cr.80 blue	1·60	55

324 Henrique Oswald

1952. Birth Centenary of Henrique Oswald (composer).

822	**324**	60c. brown	65	10

325 Map and Symbol of Labour

1952. Fifth Conf of American Members of I.L.O.

823	**325**	1cr.50 red	65	10

326 Dr. L. Cardoso

1952. Birth Centenary of Cardoso (scientist) and 4th Brazilian Homoeopathic Congress, Porto Alegre.

824	**326**	60c. blue	75	35

327 Gen. da Fonseca

1952. Centenary of Telegraphs in Brazil.

825	**327**	2cr.40 red	1·00	20
826	-	5cr. blue	5·00	35
827	-	10cr. turquoise	5·00	35

PORTRAITS—VERT: 5cr. Baron de Capanema. 10cr. E. de Queiros.

328 L. de Albuquerque

1952. Bicentenary of Mato Grosso City.

828	**328**	1cr.20 violet	65	10

329 Olympic Flame and Athletes

1952. 50th Anniv of Fluminense Football Club.

829	**329**	1cr.20 blue	1·50	75

330 Councillor J. A. Saraiva

1952. Centenary of Terezina City.

830	**330**	60c. mauve	65	10

331 Emperor Dom Pedro II

1952. Stamp Day and Second Philatelic Exhibition, Sao Paulo.

831	**331**	60c. black and blue	65	10

332 Globe, Staff and Rio de Janeiro Bay

1952. Second American Congress of Industrial Medicine.

832	**332**	3cr.80 green and brown	1·90	65

333 Dove, Globe and Flags

1952. United Nations Day.

833	**333**	3cr.80 blue	2·10	65

334 Compasses and Modern Buildings, Sao Paulo

1952. City Planning Day.

834	**334**	60c. yellow, green & blue	65	10

335 D. A. Feijo (Statesman)

1952. Homage to D. A. Feijo.

835	**335**	60c. brown	75	10

336 Father Damien

1952. Obligatory Tax. Leprosy Research Fund.

836	**336**	10c. brown	90	35
837	**336**	10c. green	40	15

337 R. Bernardelli

1952. Birth Centenary of Bernardelli (sculptor).

838	**337**	60c. blue	65	10

338 Arms of Sao Paulo and Settler

339 "Expansion"

1953. 400th Anniv of Sao Paulo (1st issue).

839	**338**	1cr.20 black and brown	2·20	55
840	-	2cr. green and yellow	4·50	55
841	-	2cr.80 brown and orange	3·25	35
842	**339**	3cr.80 brown and green	3·25	35
843	**339**	5cr.80 blue and green	2·10	35

DESIGNS—VERT: (Inscr as Type **339**): 2cr. Coffee blossom and berries; 2cr.80, Monk planting tree.

See also Nos. 875/9.

340

1953. Sixth Brazilian Accountancy Congress, Port Alegre.

844	**340**	1cr.20 brown	65	10

341 J. Ramalho

1953. Fourth Centenary of Santo Andre.

845	**341**	60c. blue	65	10

342 A. Reis and Plan of Belo Horizonte

1953. Birth Centenary of A. Reis (engineer).

846	**342**	1cr.20 brown	65	10

343 *Almirante Saldanha* (cadet ship)

1953. Fourth Voyage of Circumnavigation by Training Ship *Almirante Saldanha*.

847	**343**	1cr.50 blue	1·00	35

344 Viscount de Itaborahy

1953. Centenary of Bank of Brazil.

848	**344**	1cr.20 violet	65	10

345 Lamp and Rio-Petropolis Highway

1953. Tenth Int Nursing Congress, Petropolis.

849	**345**	1cr.20 grey	65	10

346 Bay of Rio de Janeiro

1953. Fourth World Conference of Young Baptists.

850	**346**	3cr.80c. turquoise	1·00	35

347 Ministry of Health and Education

1953. Stamp Day and First National Philatelic Exhibition of Education, Rio de Janeiro.

851	**347**	1cr.20 turquoise	65	10

348 Arms and Map

1953. Centenary of Jau City.

852	**348**	1cr.20 violet	65	10

349 Maria Quiteria de Jesus

1953. Death Centenary of Maria Quiteria de Jesus.

853	**349**	60c. blue	40	10

350 Pres. Odria

1953. Visit of President of Peru.

854	**350**	1cr.40 purple	65	10

351 Caxias leading Troops

1953. 150th Birth Anniv of Duke of Caxias.

855	**351**	60c. turquoise	40	15
856	-	1cr.20 purple	90	15
857	-	1cr.70 blue	90	15
858	-	3cr.80 brown	2·10	20
859	-	5cr.80 violet	1·30	20

DESIGNS: 1cr.20, Tomb; 1cr.70, 5cr.80, Portrait of Caxias; 3cr.80, Coat of arms.

352 Quill-pen and Map

1953. Fifth National Congress of Journalists, Curitiba.

860	**352**	60c. blue	65	20

353 H. Hora

1953. Birth Centenary of H. Hora (painter).

861	**353**	60c. purple and orange	65	10

354 President Somoza

1953. Visit of President Somoza of Nicaragua.

862	**354**	1cr.40 purple	65	20

355 A. de Saint-Hilaire

1953. Death Centenary of A. de Saint-Hilaire (explorer and botanist).

863	**355**	1cr.20 lake	75	30

356 J. do Patrocinio and "Spirit of Emancipation" (after R. Amoedo)

1953. Death Centenary of J. do Patrocinio (slavery abolitionist).

864	**356**	60c. slate	65	20

357 Clock Tower, Crato

1953. Centenary of Crato City.

865	**357**	60c. green	65	20

358 C. de Abreu

1953. Birth Centenary of Abreu (historian).

866	**358**	60c. blue	40	10
867	**358**	5cr. violet	2·40	35

359 "Justice"

1953. 50th Anniv of Treaty of Petropolis.

868	**359**	60c. blue	65	10
869	**359**	1cr.20 purple	65	10

360 Harvesting

1953. Third National Wheat Festival, Erechim.

870	**360**	60c. turquoise	65	10

361 Teacher and Pupils

1953. First National Congress of Elementary Schoolteachers, Salvador.

871	**361**	60c. red	65	20

362 Porters with Trays of Coffee Beans

1953. Centenary of State of Parana.

872a	-	2cr. brown and black	1·90	55
873	**362**	5cr. orange and black	3·00	55

DESIGN: 2cr. Portrait of Z. de Gois e Vasconcellos.

363 A. de Gusmao

1954. Death Bicentenary of Gusmao (statesman).

874	**363**	1cr.20 purple	75	30

364 Growth of Sao Paulo

365 Sao Paulo and Arms

1954. 400th Anniv of Sao Paulo (2nd issue).

875	**364**	1cr.20 brown	2·10	90
876	-	2cr. mauve	3·25	65
877	-	2cr.80 violet	3·75	55
878	**365**	3cr.80 green	4·50	55
879	**365**	5cr.80 red	4·50	55

DESIGNS—VERT: 2cr. Priest, pioneer and Indian; 2cr.80, J. de Anchieta.

366 J. F. Vieira, A. V. de Negreiros, A. F. Camarao and H. Dias

1954. 300th Anniv of Recovery from the Dutch of Pernambuco.

880	**366**	1cr.20 blue	90	35

367 Sao Paulo and Allegorical Figure

1954. Tenth International Congress of Scientific Organization, Sao Paulo.

881	**367**	1cr.50 purple	75	35

368 Grapes and Winejar

1954. Grape Festival, Rio Grande do Sul.

882	**368**	40c. lake	65	20

369 Immigrants' Monument

1954. Immigrants' Monument, Caxias do Sul.

883	**369**	60c. violet	65	20

370 "Baronesa", 1852 (first locomotive used in Brazil)

1954. Centenary of Brazilian Railways.

884	**370**	40c. red	1·30	40

371 Pres. Chamoun

1954. Visit of President of Lebanon.

885	**371**	1cr.50 lake	75	30

372 Sao Jose College, Rio de Janeiro

373 Vel Marcelino Champagnat

1954. 50th Anniv of Marists in Brazil.

886	**372**	60c. violet	50	20
887	**373**	1cr.20 blue	50	20

374 Apolonia Pinto

1954. Birth Centenary of Apolonia Pinto (actress).

888	**374**	1cr.20 green	65	20

375 Admiral Tamandare

1954. Portraits.

889	**375**	2c. blue	35	20
890	**375**	5c. red	35	10
891	**375**	10c. green	35	10
892	-	20c. red	35	15
893	-	30c. slate	55	10
894	-	40c. red	1·00	20
895	-	50c. lilac	1·30	20
896	-	60c. turquoise	50	15
897	-	90c. salmon	1·00	20
904a	-	1cr. brown	1·90	55
899	-	1cr.50 blue	35	10
904b	-	2cr. green	2·75	55
904c	-	5cr. purple	8·50	35
902	-	10cr. green	2·50	30
903	-	20cr. red	2·50	30
904	-	50cr. blue	15·00	30

PORTRAITS—20, 30, 40c. O. Cruz; 50c. to 90c. J. Murtinho; 1cr., 1cr.50, 2cr. Duke of Caxias; 5, 10cr., R. Barbosa; 20, 50cr. J. Bonifacio.

376 Boy Scout

1954. International Scout Encampment, Sao Paulo.

905	**376**	1cr.20 blue	1·60	35

377 B. Fernandes

1954. Tercentenary of Sorocaba City.

906	**377**	60c. red	75	20

378 Cardinal Piazza

1954. Visit of Cardinal Piazza (Papal Legate).

907	**378**	4cr.20 red	1·60	35

379 Virgin and Map

1954. Marian Year. Inscr "ANO MARIANO".

908	**379**	60c. lake	90	30
909	-	1cr.20 blue	1·10	45

DESIGN: 1cr.20, Virgin and globe.

No. 909 also commemorates the Centenary of the Proclamation of the Dogma of the Immaculate Conception.

380 Benjamin Constant and Braille Book

1954. Centenary of Education for the Blind in Brazil.

910	**380**	60c. green	65	15

381 River Battle of Riachuelo

382 Admiral Barroso

1954. 150th Birth Anniv of Admiral Barroso.

911	**381**	40c. brown	75	20
912	**382**	60c. violet	50	20

383 S. Hahnemann (physician)

1954. First World Congress of Homoeopathy.

913	**383**	2cr.70 green	75	35

446 Brazil on Globe

1958. Int Investments Conference, Belo Horizonte.
986 **446** 2cr.50 brown 75 20

447 Tiradentes Palace, Rio de Janeiro

1958. 47th Inter-Parliamentary Union Conf.
987 **447** 2cr.50 brown 75 20

448 J. B. Brandao (statesman)

1958. Centenary of Julio Buend Brandão.
988 **448** 2cr.50 brown 75 20

449 Dawn Palace, Brasilia

1958. Construction of Presidential Palace.
989 **449** 2cr.50 blue 75 20

450 Freighters

1958. Govt Aid for Brazilian Merchant Navy.
990 **450** 2cr.50 blue 75 20

451 J. C. da Silva

1958. Birth Centenary of J. C. Da Silva (author).
991 **451** 2cr.50 brown 75 20

452 Pres. Gronchi

1958. Visit of President of Italy.
992 **452** 7cr. blue 1·50 45

453 Archers

1958. Tenth Spring Games, Rio de Janeiro.
993 **453** 2cr.50 orange 1·10 35

454 Old People within Hour-glass

1958. Old People's Day.
994 **454** 2cr.50 lake 75 20

455 Machado de Assis (writer)

1958. 50th Death Anniv of Machado de Assis.
995 **455** 2cr.50 brown 75 20

456 Pres. Vargas with oily Hand

1958. Fifth Anniv of State Petroleum Law.
996 **456** 2cr.50 blue 75 20

457 Globe showing Brazil and the Americas

1958. Seventh Inter-American Municipalities Congress, Rio de Janeiro.
997 **457** 2cr.50 blue 75 20

458 Gen. L. Sodre

1958. Birth Centenary of L. Sodre.
998 **458** 3cr.30 green 75 20

459 UN Emblem

1958. Tenth Anniv of Human Rights Declaration.
999 **459** 2cr.50 blue 75 20

460 Footballer

1959. World Football Cup Victory, 1958.
1000 **460** 3cr.30 brown & green 1·10 45

461 Map and Railway Line

1959. Centenary of Opening of Patos-Campina Grande Railway.
1001 **461** 2cr.50 brown 75 20

462 Pres. Sukarno

1959. Visit of President of Indonesia.
1002 **462** 2cr.50 blue 75 20

463 Basketball Player

1959. Air. World Basketball Championships 1959.
1003 **463** 3cr.30 brown & blue 1·00 20

464 King John VI of Portugal

1959
1004 **464** 2cr.50 red 75 20

465 Polo Players

1959. Children's Games.
1005 **465** 2cr.50 brown 75 20

466 Dockside Scene

1959. Rehabilitation of National Ports Law.
1006 **466** 2cr.50 green 75 20

467 Church Organ, Diamantina

1959. Bicentenary of Carmelite Order in Brazil.
1007 **467** 3cr.30 lake 75 20

468 Dom J. S. de Souza (First Archbishop)

1959. Birth Centenary of Archbishop of Diamantina.
1008 **468** 2cr.50 brown 75 20

469 Sugar-loaf Mountain and Road

1959. 11th International Roads Congress.
1009 **469** 3cr.30 blue and green 75 20

470 Londrina and Parana

1959. 25th Anniv of Londrina.
1010 **470** 2cr.50 green 75 20

471 Putting the Shot

1959. Spring Games.
1011 **471** 2cr.50 mauve 75 20

472 Daedalus

1959. Air. Aviation Week.
1012 **472** 3cr.30 blue 75 20

473 Globe and "Snipe" Class Yachts

1959. World Sailing Championships, Porto Alegre.
1013 **473** 6cr.50 green 75 20

474 Lusignan Cross and Arms of Salvador, Bahia

1959. Fourth International Brazilian–Portuguese Study Conference, Bahia University.
1014 **474** 6cr.50 blue 75 20

475 Gunpowder Factory

1959. 50th Anniv of President Vargas Gunpowder Factory.
1015 **475** 3cr.30 brown 75 20

476

1959. Thanksgiving Day.
1016 **476** 2cr.50 blue 75 20

477 Sud Aviation SE 210 Caravelle

1959. Air. Inauguration of "Caravelle" Airliners by Brazilian National Airlines.
1017 **477** 6cr.50 blue 75 20

478 Burning Bush

1959. Centenary of Presbyterian Work in Brazil.
1018 **478** 3cr.30 green 75 20

479 P. da Silva and *Schistosoma mansoni*

1959. 50th Anniv of Discovery and Identification of *Schistosoma mansoni* (fluke).
1019 **479** 2cr.50 purple 1·50 45

480 L. de Matos and Church

1960. Birth Centenary of Luiz de Matos (Christian evangelist).
1020 **480** 3cr.30 brown 75 20

481 Pres. Lopez Mateos of Mexico

1960. Air. Visit of Mexican President.
1021 **481** 6cr.50 brown 75 20

482 Pres. Eisenhower

1960. Air. Visit of United States President.
1022 **482** 6cr.50 brown 75 20

483 Dr. L. Zamenhof

1960. Birth Centenary of L. Zamenhof (inventor of Esperanto).
1023 **483** 6cr.50 green 75 20

484 Adel Pinto (engineer)

1960. Birth Centenary of Adel Pinto.
1024 **484** 11cr.50 red 1·00 35

485 "Care of Refugees"

1960. Air. World Refugee Year.
1025 **485** 6cr.50 blue 75 20

486 Plan of Brasilia

1960. Inauguration of Brasilia as Capital.

1026	-	2cr.50 green (postage)	75	35
1027	-	3cr.30 violet (air)	50	20
1028	-	4cr. blue	2·10	45
1029	-	6cr.50 mauve	50	20
1030	**486**	11cr.50 brown	50	20

1960. Birthday of Pres. Kubitschek.
MS1031 110×52 mm. 27cr. Orange (postage) 2·20 1·90

DESIGNS—Outlines representing: HORIZ: 2cr.50 President's Palace of the Plateau; 3cr.30 Parliament Buildings; 4cr. Cathedral; 11cr.50, 27cr. T **486**. VERT: 6cr.50 Tower.

487 Congress Emblem

1960. Air. Seventh Nat Eucharistic Congress, Curitiba.
1032 **487** 3cr.30 mauve 75 20

488 Congress Emblem, Sugar-loaf Mountain and Cross

1960. Air. Tenth Baptist World Alliance Congress, Rio de Janeiro.
1033 **488** 6cr.50 blue 75 20

489 Boy Scout

1960. Air. 50th Anniv of Scouting in Brazil.
1034 **489** 3cr.30 orange 75 20

490 "Agriculture"

1960. Cent of Brazilian Ministry of Agriculture.
1035 **490** 2cr.50 brown 75 20

491 Caravel

1960. Air. Fifth Death Centenary of Prince Henry the Navigator.
1036 **491** 6cr.50 black 75 20

492 P. de Frontin

1960. Birth Centenary of Paulo de Frontin (engineer).
1037 **492** 2cr.50 orange 75 20

493 Locomotive Piston Gear

1960. Tenth Pan-American Railways Congress.
1038 **493** 2cr.50 blue 1·50 55

494 Athlete

1960. 12th Spring Games.
1039 **494** 2cr.50 turquoise 75 20

495

1960. World Volleyball Championships.
1040 **495** 11cr. blue 25 10

496 Maria Bueno in play

1960. Air. Maria Bueno's Wimbledon Tennis Victories, 1959–60.
1041 **496** 6cr. brown 75 20

497 Exhibition Emblem

1960. International Industrial and Commercial Exhibition, Rio de Janeiro.
1042 **497** 2cr.50 brown & yellow 75 20

498 War Memorial, Rio de Janeiro

1960. Air. Return of Ashes of World War II Heroes from Italy.
1043 **498** 3cr.30 lake 75 20

499 Pylon and Map

1961. Air. Inauguration of Tres Marias Hydro-electric Station.
1044 **499** 3cr.30 mauve 75 20

500 Emperor Haile Selassie

1961. Visit of Emperor of Ethiopia.
1045 **500** 2cr.50 brown 75 20

501 Sacred Book and Map of Brazil

1961. 50th Anniv of Sacre-Coeur de Marie College.
1046 **501** 2cr.50 blue 75 20

502 Map of Guanabara State

1961. Promulgation of Guanabara Constitution.
1047 **502** 7cr.50 brown 75 20

503 Arms of Academy

1961. 150th Anniv of Agulhas Negras Military Academy.

1048	**503**	2cr.50 green	65	15
1049	-	3cr.30 red	65	15

DESIGN: 3cr.30, Military cap and sabre.

504 "Spanning the Atlantic Ocean"

1961. Visit of Foreign Minister to Senegal.
1050 **504** 27cr. blue 90 35

505 View of Ouro Preto

1961. 250th Anniv of Ouro Preto.
1051 **505** 1cr. orange 75 20

506 Arsenal, Rio de Janeiro

1961. 150th Anniv of Rio de Janeiro Arsenal.
1052 **506** 5cr. brown 75 20

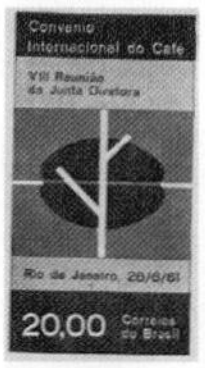
507 Coffee Plant

1961. Int Coffee Convention, Rio de Janeiro.
1053 **507** 20cr. brown 3·00 30

508 Tagore

1960. Birth Centenary of Rabindranath Tagore (poet).

1054	**508**	10cr. mauve	75	10

509 280r. Stamp of 1861 and Map of France

1961. "Goat's Eyes" Stamp Centenary.

1055	**509**	10cr. red	2·00	10
1056	-	20cr. orange	6·25	10

DESIGN: 20cr. 430r. stamp and map of the Netherlands.

510 Cloudburst

1962. World Meteorological Day.

1057	**510**	10cr. brown	2·30	55

511 Pinnacle, Rope and Haversack

1962. 50th Anniv of First Ascent of "Finger of God" Mountain.

1058	**511**	8cr. green	80	25

512 Dr. G. Vianna and parasites

1962. 50th Anniv of Vianna's Cure for Leishman's Disease.

1059	**512**	8cr. blue	70	25

513 Campaign Emblem

1962. Air. Malaria Eradication.

1060	**513**	21cr. blue	70	25

514 Henrique Dias (patriot)

1962. 300th Death Anniv of Henrique Dias.

1061	**514**	10cr. purple	80	30

515 Metric Measure

1962. Cent of Brazil's Adoption of Metric System.

1062	**515**	100cr. red	1·40	10

516 "Snipe" Sailing-boats

1962. 13th "Snipe" Class Sailing Championships, Rio de Janeiro.

1063	**516**	8cr. turquoise	70	25

517 J. Mesquita and Newspaper *O Estado de Sao Paulo*

1962. Birth Centenary of Mesquita (journalist and founder of *O Estado de Sao Paulo*).

1064	**517**	8cr. bistre	95	25

518 Empress Leopoldina

1962. 140th Anniv of Independence.

1065	**518**	8cr. mauve	70	25

519 Brasilia

1962. 51st Interparliamentary Conference, Brasilia.

1066	**519**	10cr. orange	80	40

520 Foundry Ladle

1962. Inauguration of "Usiminas" (national iron and steel foundry).

1067	**520**	8cr. orange	70	25

521 UPAE Emblem

1962. 50th Anniv of Postal Union of the Americas and Spain.

1068	**521**	8cr. mauve	70	25

522 Emblems of Industry

1962. Tenth Anniv of National Bank.

1069	**522**	10cr. turquoise	70	25

523 Q. Bocaiuva

1962. 50th Death Anniv of Q. Bocaiuva (journalist and patriot).

1070	**523**	8cr. brown	80	40

524 Footballer

1962. Brazil's Victory in World Football Championships, 1962.

1071	**524**	10cr. turquoise	1·30	15

525 Carrier Pigeon

1962. Tercentenary of Brazilian Posts.

1072	**525**	8cr. multicoloured	70	25
MS1072a 145×58 mm. **525** 100cr. multicoloured			4·75	4·25

526 Dr. S. Neiva (first Brazilian P.M.G.)

1963

1073	**526**	8cr. violet	70	15
1073a	-	30cr. turquoise (Euclides da Cunha)	3·75	15
1073b	-	50cr. brown (Prof. A. Moreira da Costa Lima)	2·75	15
1073c	-	100cr. blue (G. Dias)	1·10	15
1073d	-	200cr. red (Tiradentes)	5·75	15
1073e	-	500cr. brown (Emperor Pedro I)	40·00	40
1073f	-	1000cr. blue (Emperor Pedro II)	£100	1·00

527 Rockets and Dish Aerial

1963. Int Aeronautics and Space Exn, Sao Paulo.

1074	**527**	21cr. blue	70	15

528 Cross

1963. Ecumenical Council, Vatican City.

1075	**528**	8cr. purple	70	25

529 "abc" Symbol

1963. National Education Week.

1076	**529**	8cr. blue	70	25

530 Basketball

1963. Fourth World Basketball Championships.

1077	**530**	8cr. mauve	70	10

531 Torch Emblem

1963. Fourth Pan-American Games, Sao Paulo.

1078	**531**	10cr. red	90	15

532 "OEA" and Map

1963. 15th Anniv of Organization of American States.

1079	**532**	10cr. orange	90	40

533 J. B. de Andrada e Silva

1963. Birth Bicentenary of Jose B. de Andrada e Silva ("Father of Independence").

1080	**533**	8cr. bistre	70	15

534 Campaign Emblem

1963. Freedom from Hunger.

1081	**534**	10cr. blue	90	40

535 Centenary Emblem

1963. Red Cross Centenary.

1082	**535**	8cr. red and yellow	70	15

536 J. Caetano

1963. Death Centenary of Joao Caetano (actor).

1083	**536**	8cr. black	70	15

537 "Atomic" Development

1963. First Anniv of National Nuclear Energy Commission.
1084 **537** 10cr. mauve 70 10

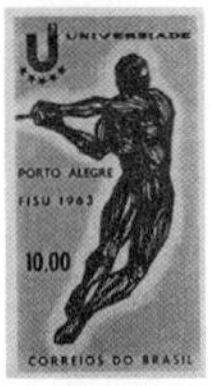

538 Throwing the Hammer

1963. International Students' Games, Porto Alegre.
1085 **538** 10cr. black and grey 1·40 40

539 Pres. Tito

1963. Visit of President Tito of Yugoslavia.
1086 **539** 80cr. drab 1·70 55

540 Cross and Map

1963. Eigth Int Leprology Congress, Rio de Janeiro.
1087 **540** 8cr. turquoise 70 15

541 Petroleum Installations

1963. Tenth Anniv of National Petroleum Industry.
1088 **541** 8cr. green 70 15

542 "Jogos da Primavera"

1963. Spring Games.
1089 **542** 8cr. yellow 70 15

543 A. Borges de Medeiros

1963. Birth Centenary of A. Borges de Medeiros (politician).
1090 **543** 8cr. brown 70 15

544 Bridge of Sao Joao del Rey

1963. 250th Anniv of Sao Joao del Rey.
1091 **544** 8cr. blue 70 15

545 Dr. A. Alvim

1963. Birth Cent of Dr. Alvaro Alvim (scientist).
1092 **545** 8cr. slate 70 15

546 Viscount de Maua

1963. 150th Birth Anniv of Viscount de Maua (builder of Santos–Jundiai Railway).
1093 **546** 8cr. mauve 70 15

547 Cactus

1964. Tenth Anniv of North-East Bank.
1094 **547** 8cr. green 70 15

548 C. Netto

1964. Birth Centenary of Coelho Netto (author).
1095 **548** 8cr. violet 70 15

549 L. Muller

1964. Birth Cent of Lauro Muller (patriot).
1096 **549** 8cr. red 70 15

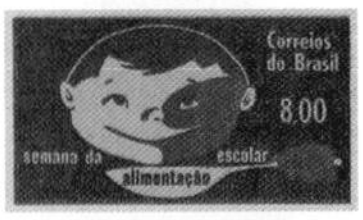

550 Child with Spoon

1964. Schoolchildren's Nourishment Week.
1097 **550** 8cr. yellow and brown 70 15

551 "Chalice" (carved rock), Vila Velha, Parana

1964. Tourism.
1098 **551** 80cr. red 90 15

552 A. Kardec (author)

1964. Cent of Spiritual Code, "O Evangelho".
1099 **552** 30cr. green 1·60 40

553 Pres. Lubke

1964. Visit of Pres. Lubke of West Germany.
1100 **553** 100cr. brown 1·70 45

554 Pope John XXIII

1964. Pope John Commemoration.
1101 **554** 20cr. lake 70 15

555 Pres. Senghor

1964. Visit of Pres. Senghor of Senegal.
1102 **555** 20cr. sepia 70 15

556 "Visit Rio de Janeiro"

1964. 400th Anniv (1965) of Rio de Janeiro.

1103	**556**	15cr. blue and orange	90	45
1104	-	30cr. red and blue	80	15
1105	-	30cr. black and blue	80	40
1106	-	35cr. black and orange	55	30
1107	-	100cr. brn & grn on yell	70	30
1108	-	200cr. red and green	5·75	25

MS1109 Two sheets 129×76 mm. containing stamps similar to Nos. 1103, 1107/8 each in brown (sold at 320cr.) and 132×78 mm containing stamps similar to Nos. 1104/6 each in orange (sold at 100cr.) 22·00 24·00

DESIGNS: As Type **556**—HORIZ: 30cr. (No. 1105), Tramway viaduct; 200cr. Copacabana Beach. VERT: 35cr. Estacio de Sa's statue; 100cr. Church of Our Lady of the Rock. SMALLER (24½×37 mm): 30cr. (No. 1104), Statue of St. Sebastian.

558 Pres. De Gaulle

1964. Visit of Pres. De Gaulle.
1110 **558** 100cr. brown 1·00 15

559 Pres. Kennedy

1964. Pres. Kennedy Commemoration.
1111 **559** 100cr. black 70 30

560 Nahum (statue)

1964. 150th Death Anniv of A. F. Lisboa (sculptor).
1112 **560** 10cr. black 70 15

561 Cross and Sword

1965. Fisrst Anniv of Democratic Revolution.
1113 **561** 120cr. grey 80 30

562 V. Brazil (scientist)

1965. Birth Cent of Vital Brazil.
1114 **562** 120cr. orange 80 30

563 Shah of Iran

1965. Visit of Shah of Iran.
1115 **563** 120cr. red 70 15

564 Marshal Rondon and Map

1965. Birth Cent of Marshal C. M. da S. Rondon.
1116 **564** 30cr. purple 70 15

565 Lions Emblem

1965. Brazilian Lions Clubs National Convention, Rio de Janeiro.
1117 **565** 35cr. black and lilac 70 15

566 I.T.U. Emblem and Symbols

1965. I.T.U. Centenary.
1118 **566** 120cr. green and yellow 90 15

567 E. Pessoa

1965. Birth Centenary of Epitacio Pessoa.
1119 **567** 35cr. slate 70 15

568 Barrosos Statue

1965. Centenary of Naval Battle of Riachuelo.
1120 **568** 30cr. blue 70 15

569 Author and Heroine

1965. Centenary of Publication of Jose de Alencar's *Iracema*.
1121 **569** 30cr. purple 70 15

570 Sir Winston Churchill

1965. Winston Churchill Commemoration.
1122 **570** 200cr. slate 1·80 25

571 Scout Badge and Emblem of Rio's 400th Anniv

1965. First Pan-American Scout Jamboree, Rio de Janeiro.
1123 **571** 30r. multicoloured 80 30

572 ICY Emblem

1965. International Co-operation Year.
1124 **572** 120cr. black and blue 70 15

573 L. Correia

1965. Birth Centenary of Leoncia Correia (poet).
1125 **573** 35cr. green 70 15

574 Exhibition Emblem

1965. Sao Paulo Biennale (Art Exn).
1126 **574** 30cr. red 70 15

575 President Saragat

1965. Visit of President of Italy.
1127 **575** 100cr. green on pink 70 15

576 Grand Duke and Duchess of Luxembourg

1965. Visit of Grand Duke and Duchess of Luxembourg.
1128 **576** 100cr. brown 70 15

577 Curtiss Fledgling on Map

1965. Aviation Week and Third Philatelic Exn.
1129 **577** 35cr. blue 70 15

578 OEA Emblem

1965. Inter-American Conference, Rio de Janeiro.
1130 **578** 100cr. black and blue 70 15

579 King Baudouin and Queen Fabiola

1965. Visit of King and Queen of the Belgians.
1131 **579** 100cr. slate 80 15

580 Coffee Beans

1965. Brazilian Coffee.
1132 **580** 30cr. brown on cream 90 15

581 F. A. Varnhagen

1965. Air. 150th Birth Anniv of Francisco Varnhagen (historian).
1133 **581** 45cr. brown 70 15

582 Emblem and Map

1966. Air. Fifth Anniv of "Alliance for Progress".
1134 **582** 120cr. blue & turquoise 1·40 15

583 Sister and Globe

1966. Air. Centenary of Dorothean Sisters Educational Work in Brazil.
1135 **583** 35cr. violet 70 15

584 Loading Ore at Quayside

1966. Inauguration of Rio Doce Iron-ore Terminal Tubarao, Espirito Santo.
1136 **584** 110cr. black and bistre 80 30

585 "Steel"

1966. Silver Jubilee of National Steel Company.
1137 **585** 30cr. black on orange 70 15

586 Prof. Rocha Lima

1966. 50th Anniv of Professor Lima's Discovery of the Characteristics of *Rickettsia prowazeki* (cause of typhus fever).
1138 **586** 30cr. turquoise 1·10 40

587 Battle Scene

1966. Centenary of Battle of Tuiuti.
1139 **587** 30cr. green 90 15

588 "The Sacred Face"

1966. Air. "Concilio Vaticano II".
1140 **588** 45cr. brown 70 15

589 Mariz e Barros

1966. Air. Death Centenary of Commander Mariz e Barros.
1141 **589** 35cr. brown 70 15

590 Decade Symbol

1966. International Hydrological Decade.
1142 **590** 100cr. blue and brown 90 15

591 Pres. Shazar

1966. Visit of President Shazar of Israel.
1143 **591** 100cr. blue 80 40

592 *Youth*

1966. Air. Birth Centenary of Eliseu Visconti (painter).
1144 **592** 120cr. brown 1·10 40

593 Imperial Academy of Fine Arts

1966. 150th Anniv of French Art Mission's Arrival in Brazil.
1145 **593** 100cr. brown 2·20 25

594 Military Service Emblem

1966. New Military Service Law.
1146 **594** 30cr. blue and yellow 70 15
MS1147 111×53 mm. No. 1146. No gum (sold at 100cr.) 2·30 2·40

595 R. Dario

1966. 50th Death Anniv of Ruben Dario (Nicaraguan poet).
1148 **595** 100cr. purple 70 15

596 Santarem Candlestick

1966. Centenary of Goeldi Museum.
1149 **596** 30cr. brown on salmon 70 15

597 Arms of Santa Cruz do Sul

1966. First National Tobacco Exn, Santa Cruz.
1150 **597** 30cr. green 70 15

598 UNESCO Emblem

1966. 20th Anniv of UNESCO.

1151	**598**	120cr. black	2·20	45
MS1152 110×52 mm. No. 1151. No gum (sold at 150cr.)			5·75	5·50

599 Capt. A. C. Pinto and Map

1966. Bicentenary of Arrival of Captain A. C. Pinto.

1153	**599**	30cr. red	70	15

600 Lusignan Cross and Southern Cross

1966. Lubrapex 1966 Stamp Exn, Rio de Janeiro.

1154	**600**	100cr. green	80	30

601 Madonna and Child

1966. Christmas.

1155	**601**	30cr. green	70	15
1156	-	35cr. blue and orange	70	15
1157	-	150cr. pink and blue	6·75	6·75

DESIGN—DIAMOND(34×34 mm). 35cr. Madonna and child (different). VERT (46×103 mm). 150cr. As 35cr. inscr "Pax Hominibus" but not "Brazil Correio".

602 Arms of Laguna

1967. Centenary of Laguna Postal and Telegraphic Agency.

1158	**602**	60cr. sepia	70	15

603 Grota Funda Viaduct and 1866 Viaduct

1967. Centenary of Santos–Jundiai Railway.

1159	**603**	50cr. orange	1·50	25

604 Polish Cross and "Black Madonna"

1967. Polish Millennium.

1160	**604**	50cr. red, blue & yellow	1·30	30

605 Research Rocket

1967. World Meteorological Day.

1161	**605**	50cr. black and blue	1·70	25

606 Anita Garibaldi

1967

1162	-	1c. blue	55	10
1163	-	2c. red	55	10
1164	-	3c. green	55	10
1165	**606**	5c. black	1·00	15
1166	-	6c. brown	1·00	15
1167	-	10c. green	3·00	40

PORTRAITS: 1c. Mother Angelica. 2c. Marilia de Dirceu. 3c. Dr. R. Lobato. 6c. Ana Neri. 10c. Darci Vargas.

607 "VARIG 40 Years"

1967. 40th Anniv of Varig Airlines.

1171	**607**	6c. black and blue	80	25

608 Lions Emblem and Globes

1967. 50th Anniv of Lions International.

1172	**608**	6c. green	80	25
MS1173 130×80 mm. No. 1172. Imperf (sold at 15c.)			7·50	7·50

609 "Madonna and Child"

1967. Mothers' Day.

1174	**609**	5c. violet	80	25
MS1175 130×76 mm. **609** 15c. violet. Imperf			7·50	7·50

610 Prince Akihito and Princess Michiko

1967. Visit of Crown Prince and Princess of Japan.

1176	**610**	10c. black and red	80	25

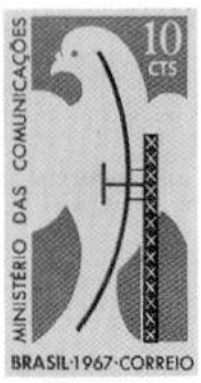

611 Radar Aerial and Pigeon

1967. Inauguration of Communications Ministry, Brasilia.

1177	**611**	10c. black and mauve	70	15

612 Brother Vicente do Salvador

1967. 400th Birth Anniv of Brother Vicente do Salvador (founder of Franciscan Brotherhood, Rio de Janeiro).

1178	**612**	5c. brown	70	15

613 Emblem and Members

1967. National 4-S ("4-H") Clubs Day.

1179	**613**	5c. green and black	70	15

614 Mobius Symbol

1967. Sixth Brazilian Mathematical Congress. Rio de Janeiro.

1180	**614**	5c. black and blue	70	15

615 Dorado (fish) and "Waves"

1967. Bicentenary of Piracicaba.

1181	**615**	5c. black and blue	80	25

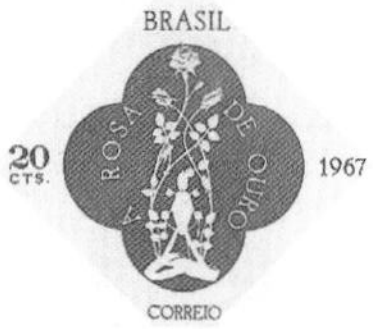

616 Papal Arms and "Golden Rose"

1967. Pope Paul VI's "Golden Rose" Offering to Our Lady of Fatima.

1182	**616**	20c. mauve and yellow	2·75	80

617 General A. de Sampaio

1967. Gen. Sampaio Commemoration.

1183	**617**	5c. blue	70	15

618 King Olav of Norway

1967. Visit of King Olav.

1184	**618**	10c. brown	70	15

619 Sun and Rio de Janeiro

1967. Meeting of International Monetary Fund, Rio de Janeiro.

1185	**619**	10c. black and red	70	15

620 N. Pecanha (statesman)

1967. Birth Centenary of Nilo Pecanha.

1186	**620**	5c. purple	70	15

621 Our Lady of the Apparition and Basilica

1967. 250th Anniv of Discovery of Statue of Our Lady of the Apparition.

1187	**621**	5c. blue and ochre	80	25
MS1188 80×130 mm. **621** 5c. and 10c. each blue and ochre. Imperf			10·50	10·50

No. **MS**1188 was issued for Christmas.

622 "Song Bird"

1967. International Song Festival.

1189	**622**	20c. multicoloured	1·40	80

623 Balloon, Rocket and Airplane

1967. Aviation Week.

1190	**623**	10c. blue	1·40	55
MS1191 131×76 mm. **623** 15c. blue. Imperf			17·00	17·00

624 Pres. Venceslau Braz

1967

1192	-	10c. blue	70	15
1193	-	20c. brown	2·20	15
1195	**624**	50c. black	11·00	40
1198	-	1cr. purple	17·00	40
1199	-	2cr. green	3·50	25

Portraits of Brazilian Presidents: 10c. Arthur Bernardes. 20c. Campos Salles. 1cr. Washington Luiz. 2cr. Castello Branco.

625 Rio Carnival

1967. International Tourist Year.

1200 **625** 10c. multicoloured 80 25

MS1201 76×130 mm. **625** 15c. multicoloured. Imperf 10·50 11·00

626 Sailor, Anchor and *Almirante Tamandare* (cruiser)

1967. Navy Week.

1202 **626** 10c. blue 80 25

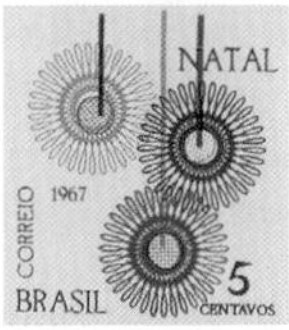

627 Christmas Decorations

1967. Christmas.

1203 **627** 5c. multicoloured 70 15

628 O. Bilac (poet), Aircraft, Tank and Aircraft Carrier *Minas Gerais*

1967. Reservists Day.

1204 **628** 5c. blue and yellow 80 25

629 J. Rodrigues de Carvalho

1967. Birth Centenary of Jose Rodriques de Carvalho (jurist and writer).

1205 **629** 10c. green 70 15

630 O. Rangel

1968. Birth Centenary of Orlando Rangel (chemist).

1206 **630** 5c. black and blue 1·00 45

631 Madonna and Diver

1968. 250th Anniv of Paranagua Underwater Exploration.

1207 **631** 10c. green and slate 1·00 45

632 Map of Free Zone

1968. Manaus Free Zone.

1208 **632** 10c. red, green and yellow 1·00 45

633 Human Rights Emblem

1968. 20th Anniv of Declaration of Human Rights.

1209 **633** 10c. red and blue 1·00 45

634 Paul Harris

1968. Birth Centenary of Paul Harris (founder of Rotary International).

1210 **634** 20c. brown and green 3·00 1·40

GUM. All the following issues to No.1425 are without gum, except where otherwise stated.

635 College Arms

1968. Centenary of St. Luiz College. With gum.

1211 **635** 10c. gold, blue and red 1·60 70

636 Cabral and his Fleet, 1500

1968. 500th Birth Anniv of Pedro Cabral (discoverer of Brazil).

1212 **636** 10c. multicoloured 2·30 85

1213 - 20c. multicoloured 2·50 1·20

DESIGN: 20c. *The First Mass* (C. Portinari).

637 *Maternity* (after H. Bernardeli)

1968. Mother's Day.

1214 **637** 5c. multicoloured 1·00 45

638 Harpy Eagle

1968. 150th Anniv of National Museum. With gum.

1215 **638** 20c. black and blue 9·75 1·20

639 Women of Brazil and Japan

1968. Inauguration of "VARIG" Brazil–Japan Air Service.

1216 **639** 10c. multicoloured 1·70 80

640 Horse-racing

1968. Centenary of Brazilian Jockey Club.

1217 **640** 10c. multicoloured 1·00 45

641 Musician Wren

1968. Birds.

1218 - 10c. multicoloured 2·30 55

1219 **641** 20c. brown, green & bl 2·50 55

1220 - 50c. multicoloured 5·75 1·10

DESIGNS—VERT: 10c. Red-crested cardinal; 50c. Royal flycatcher.

642 Ancient Post-box

1968. Stamp Day. With gum.

1221 **642** 5c. black, green & yellow 70 15

643 Marshal E. Luiz Mallet

1968. E. Luiz Mallet Commemoration. With gum.

1222 **643** 10c. lilac 70 15

644 Map of South America

1968. Visit of Chilean President. With gum.

1223 **644** 10c. orange 70 15

645 Lyceum Badge

1968. Centenary of Portuguese Literacy Lyceum (High School). With gum.

1224 **645** 5c. green and pink 70 15

646 Map and Telex Tape

1968. "Telex Service for 25th City (Curitiba)". With gum.

1225 **646** 20c. green and yellow 1·40 45

647 "Cock" shaped as Treble Clef

1968. Third Int Song Festival, Rio de Janeiro.

1227 **647** 6c. multicoloured 80 30

648 Soldiers on Medallion

1968. Eighth American Armed Forces Conference.

1226 **648** 5c. black and blue 1·40 55

649 "Petrobras" Refinery

1968. 15th Anniv of National Petroleum Industry.

1228 **649** 6c. multicoloured 1·30 80

650 Boy walking towards Rising Sun

1968. UNICEF.

1229 **650** 5c. black and blue 90 45

1230 - 10c. black, red & blue 1·10 45

1231 - 20c. multicoloured 1·40 45

DESIGNS—HORIZ: 10c. Hand protecting child. VERT: 20c. Young girl in plaits.

651 Children with Books

1968. Book Week.

1232 **651** 5c. multicoloured 80 25

652 WHO Emblem and Flags

1968. 20th Anniv of WHO.

1233 **652** 20c. multicoloured 1·70 70

653 J. B. Debret (painter)

1968. Birth Bicentenary of Jean Baptiste Debret (1st issue).

1234 **653** 10c. black and yellow 1·00 45

See Nos. 1273/4.

654 Queen Elizabeth II

1968. State Visit of Queen Elizabeth II.
1235 **654** 70c. multicoloured 4·50 2·00

655 Brazilian Flag

1968. Brazilian Flag Day.
1236 **655** 10c. multicoloured 1·10 55

656 F. Braga and part of "Hymn of National Flag"

1968. Birth Cent of Francisco Braga (composer).
1237 **656** 5c. purple 1·10 45

657 Clasped Hands

1968. Blood Donors' Day.
1238 **657** 5c. red, black and blue 70 25

1968. Obligatory Tax. Leprosy Research Fund. Revalued currency. With gum.
1239 **388** 5c. green 2·10 85
1240 **388** 5c. red 80 25

658 Steam Locomotive No. 1 *Maria Fumaca*, 1868

1968. Centenary of Sao Paulo Railway.
1241 **658** 5c. multicoloured 2·75 95

659 Angelus Bell

1968. Christmas. Multicoloured.
1242 5c. Type **659** 80 25
1243 6c. Father Christmas giving present 80 25

660 F.A.V. Caldas Jr

1968. Birth Centenary of Francisco Caldas Junior (founder of *Correio do Povo* newspaper).
1244 **660** 10c. black, pink & red 70 20

661 Reservists Emblem and Memorial

1968. Reservists' Day. With gum.
1245 **661** 5c. green and brown 1·00 40

662 Dish Aerial

1969. Inauguration of Satellite Communications System.
1246 **662** 30c. black and blue 2·10 1·10

663 Viscount do Rio Branco

1969. 150th Birth Anniv of Viscount do Rio Branco.
1247 **663** 5c. sepia and drab 80 30

664 St. Gabriel

1969. St. Gabriel's Day (Patron Saint of Telecommunications).
1248 **664** 5c. multicoloured 1·10 40

665 Shoemaker's Last and Globe

1969. Fourth Int Shoe Fair, Novo, Hamburgo.
1249 **665** 5c. multicoloured 70 30

666 Kardec and Monument

1969. Death Centenary of "Allan Kardec" (Professor H. Rivail) (French educationalist and spiritualist).
1250 **666** 5c. brown and green 80 30

667 Men of Three Races and Arms of Cuiaba

1969. 250th Anniv of Cuiaba (capital of Mato Grosso state).
1251 **667** 5c. multicoloured 80 30

668 Mint and Banknote Pattern

1969. Opening of New State Mint Printing Works.
1252 **668** 5c. bistre and orange 1·30 70

669 Society Emblem and Stamps

1969. 50th Anniv of Sao Paulo Philatelic Society.
1253 **669** 5c. multicoloured 80 30

670 "Our Lady of Santana" (statue)

1969. Mothers' Day.
1254 **670** 5c. multicoloured 1·40 80

671 ILO Emblem

1969. 50th Anniv of ILO. With gum.
1255 **671** 5c. gold and red 70 25

672 Diving Platform and Swimming Pool

1969. 40th Anniv of Cearense Water Sports Club, Fortaleza.
1256 **672** 20c. black, green & brn 1·70 85

673 *Mother and Child at Window* (after Di Cavalcanti)

1969. Tenth Art Exhibition Biennale, Sao Paulo. Multicoloured.
1257 10c. Type **673** 1·80 45
1258 20c. Modern sculpture (F. Leirner) 1·80 1·00
1259 50c. *Sunset in Brasilia* (D. di Prete) 4·50 2·50
1260 1cr. *Angelfish* (A. Martins) 4·00 2·00

No. 1258 is square, size 33×33 mm and Nos. 1259/60 vertical, size 33×53 mm.

674 Freshwater Angelfish

1969. ACAPI Fish Preservation and Development Campaign.
1261 20c. Type **674** 1·70 80

MS1262 134×100 mm. Four designs each 38×22 mm. 10c. Tetra; 15c. Piranha; 20c. *Megalamphodus megalopterus*; 30c. Black tetra 17·00 17·00

675 I. O. Teles de Manezes (founder)

1969. Centenary of Spiritualist Press. With gum.
1263 **675** 50c. green and orange 3·00 2·00

676 Postman delivering Letter

1969. Stamp Day. With gum.
1264 **676** 30c. blue 2·75 1·70

677 General Fragoso

1969. Birth Centenary of General Tasso Fragoso. With gum.
1265 **677** 20c. green 2·30 95

678 Map of Army Bases

1969. Army Week. Multicoloured.
1266 10c. Type **678** 1·40 60
1267 20c. Monument and railway bridge (39×22 mm) 2·30 1·00

679 Jupia Dam

1969. Inauguration of Jupia Dam.
1268 **679** 20c. multicoloured 1·70 1·00

680 Mahatma Gandhi and Spinning-wheel

1969. Birth Centenary of Mahatma Gandhi.
1269 **680** 20c. black and yellow 1·20 60

681 Alberto Santos Dumont, "Ballon No. 6", Eiffel Tower and Moon Landing

1969. First Man on the Moon and Santos Dumont's Flight (1906). Commemoration.
1270 **681** 50c. multicoloured 4·25 1·90

682 Smelting Plant

1969. Expansion of USIMINAS Steel Consortium.

1271	**682**	20c. multicoloured	1·30	85

683 Steel Furnace

1969. 25th Anniv of ACESITA Steel Works.

1272	**683**	10c. multicoloured	1·30	85

684 *The Water Cart* (after Debrot)

1969. Birth Centenary of J. B. Debret (painter) (2nd issue). Multicoloured. No. 1274 dated "1970".

1273	20c. Type **684**	3·00	95
1274	30c. *Street Scene*	3·00	1·90

685 Exhibition Emblem

1969. "Abuexpo 69" Stamp Exn.

1275	**685**	10c. multicoloured	1·10	35

686 Embraer Bandeirante Airplane

1969. Brazilian Aeronautical Industry Expansion Year.

1276	**686**	50c. multicoloured	7·00	2·50

687 Pele scoring Goal

1969. Footballer Pele's 1,000th Goal.

1277	**687**	10c. multicoloured	1·30	95
MS1278		81×120 mm. **687** 75c. multi-coloured. Imperf	12·00	7·00

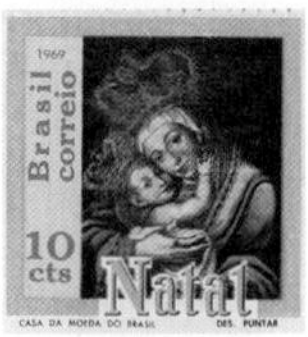

688 *Madonna and Child* (painted panel)

1969. Christmas.

1279	**688**	10c. multicoloured	1·20	35
MS1280		137×102 mm. **688** 75c. multi-coloured. Imperf	32·00	30·00

689 *Pernambuco* (destroyer) and *Bahia* (submarine)

1969. Navy Day. With gum.

1281	**689**	5c. blue	1·10	45

690 Dr. H. Blumenau

1969. 150th Birth Anniv of Dr. Hermann Blumenau (German immigrant leader). With gum.

1282	**690**	20c. green	2·20	80

691 Carnival Dancers

1969. Carioca Carnival, Rio de Janeiro (1970). Multicoloured.

1283	5c. Type **691**	1·10	60
1284	10c. Samba dancers (horiz)	1·10	60
1285	20c. Clowns (horiz)	1·30	80
1286	30c. Confetti and mask	7·00	5·25
1287	50c. Tambourine-player	7·00	4·75

692 Carlos Gomes conducting

1970. Centenary of Opera *O. Guarani* by A. Carlos Gomes.

1288	**692**	20c. multicoloured	1·70	80

693 Monastery

1970. 400th Anniv of Penha Monastery, Vilha Velha.

1289	**693**	20c. multicoloured	85	35

694 National Assembly Building

1970. Tenth Anniv of Brasilia. Multicoloured.

1290	20c. Type **694**	2·50	1·40
1291	50c. Reflecting Pool	6·00	3·50
1292	1cr. Presidential Palace	6·00	3·50

695 Emblem on Map

1970. Rondon Project (students' practical training scheme).

1293	**695**	50c. multicoloured	6·50	7·00

696 Marshal Osorio and Arms

1970. Opening of Marshal Osorio Historical Park.

1294	**696**	20c. multicoloured	4·25	1·90

697 *Madonna and Child* (San Antonio Monastery)

1970. Mothers' Day.

1295	**697**	20c. multicoloured	1·20	80

698 Brasilia Cathedral (stylized)

1970. Eighth National Eucharistic Congress, Brasilia. With gum.

1296	**698**	20c. green	85	45

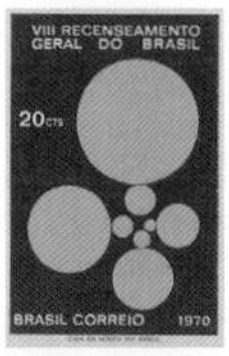

699 Census Symbol

1970. Eigth National Census.

1297	**699**	20c. yellow and green	1·70	1·70

700 Jules Rimet Cup, and Map

1970. World Cup Football Championships Mexico.

1298	**700**	50c. black, gold & blue	2·40	2·20

701 Statue of Christ

1970. Marist Students. Sixth World Congress.

1299	**701**	50c. multicoloured	7·00	6·50

702 Bellini and Swedish Flag (1958)

1970. Brazil's Third Victory in World Cup Football Championships. Multicoloured.

1300	1cr. Type **702**	4·75	3·50
1301	2cr. Garrincha and Chilean flag (1962)	9·25	3·50
1302	3cr. Pele and Mexican flag (1970)	7·75	2·50

703 Pandia Calogeras

1970. Birth Centenary of Pandia Calogeras (author and politician).

1303	**703**	20c. green	1·40	95

704 Brazilian Forces Badges and Map

1970. 25th Anniv of World War II. Victory.

1304	**704**	20c. multicoloured	1·30	95

705 *The Annunciation* (Cassio M'Boy)

1970. St. Gabriel's Day (Patron Saint of Telecommunications).

1305	**705**	20c. multicoloured	3·00	1·90

706 Boy in Library

1970. Book Week.

1306	**706**	20c. multicoloured	3·00	1·90

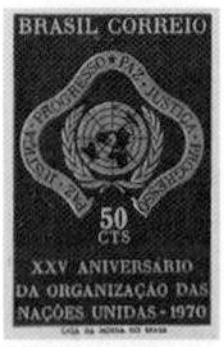

707 U.N. Emblem

1970. 25th Anniv of United Nations.

1307	**707**	50c. blue, silver & ultram	3·00	2·30

708 *Rio de Janeiro, circa 1820*

1970. Third Brazilian–Portuguese Stamp Exhibition Lubrapex 70, Rio de Janeiro.

1308	**708**	20c. multicoloured	3·00	1·50
1309	-	50c. brown and black	7·00	3·00
1310	-	1cr. multicoloured	7·25	4·50
MS1311		60×80 mm. **708** 1cr. multicol-oured. Imperf	24·00	26·00

DESIGNS: 50c. Post Office Symbol; 1cr. Rio de Janeiro (modern view).

709 *The Holy Family* (C. Portinari)

1970. Christmas.

1312	**709**	50c. multicoloured	3·00	3·00
MS1313		107×52 mm. **709** 1cr. multicoloured. Imper	42·00	45·00

710 *Graca Aranha* (destroyer)

1970. Navy Day.

1314	**710**	20c. multicoloured	3·00	1·70

711 Congress Emblem

1971. Third Inter-American Housing Congress, Rio de Janeiro.

1315	**711**	50c. red and black	3·75	4·00

712 Links and Globe

1971. Racial Equality Year.

1316	**712**	20c. multicoloured	1·80	1·10

713 *Morpho melacheilus*

1971. Butterflies. Multicoloured.

1317	20c. Type **713**	2·40	1·40
1318	1cr. *Papilio thoas brasiliensis*	10·50	7·50

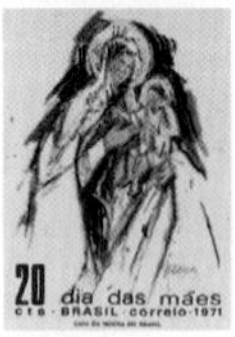

714 Madonna and Child

1971. Mothers' Day.

1319	**714**	20c. multicoloured	2·10	90

715 Hands reaching for Ball

1971. Sixth Women's Basketball World Championships.

1320	**715**	70c. multicoloured	4·25	2·20

716 Eastern Part of Highway Map

1971. Trans-Amazon Highway Project. Multicoloured.

1321	40c. Type **716**	12·00	6·00
1322	1cr. Western part of Highway Map	12·00	9·75

Nos. 1321/2 were issued together *se-tenant*, forming a composite design.

717 *Head of Man* (V. M. Lima)

1971. Stamp Day. Multicoloured.

1323	40c. Type **717**	4·25	1·80
1324	1cr. *Arab Violinist* (Pedro Americo)	9·50	3·75

718 General Caxias and Map

1971. Army Week.

1325	**718**	20c. red and green	1·30	1·40

719 Anita Garibaldi

1971. 150th Birth Anniv of Anita Garibaldi.

1326	**719**	20c. multicoloured	1·30	90

720 Xavante and Santos Dumont's Biplane *14 bis*

1971. First Flight of Embraer Xavante Jet Fighter.

1327	**720**	40c. multicoloured	4·25	1·70

721 Flags of Central American Republics

1971. 150th Anniv of Central American Republics' Independence.

1328	**721**	40c. multicoloured	3·00	1·40

722 Exhibition Emblem

1971. Franca 71 Industrial, Technical and Scientific Exhibition, Sao Paulo.

1329	**722**	1cr.30 multicoloured	4·25	2·50

723 *The Black Mother* (L. de Albuquerque)

1971. Centenary of Slaves Emancipation Law.

1330	**723**	40c. multicoloured	2·00	1·10

724 Archangel Gabriel

1971. St. Gabriel's Day (Patron Saint of Communications).

1331	**724**	40c. multicoloured	1·90	1·50

725 *Couple on Bridge* (Marisa da Silva Chaves)

1971. Children's Day. Multicoloured.

1332	35c. Type **725**	1·40	1·00
1333	45c. *Couple on Riverbank* (Mary Rosa e Silva)	3·00	1·00
1334	60c. *Girl in Hat* (Teresa A. P. Ferreira)	1·40	1·00

726 *Laelia purpurata Werkhauserii superba*

1971. Brazilian Orchids.

1335	**726**	40c. multicoloured	5·25	2·30

727 Eunice Weaver

1971. Obligatory Tax. Leprosy Research Fund.

1336	**727**	10c. green	1·70	55
1337	**727**	10c. purple	60	20

728 "25 Senac"

1971. 25th Annivs of SENAC (apprenticeship scheme) and SESC (workers' social service).

1338	**728**	20c. blue and black	3·00	2·30
1339	-	40c. orange and black	3·00	2·30

DESIGN: 40c. As Type **728**, but inscribed "25 SESC".

729 *Parati* (gunboat)

1971. Navy Day.

1340	**729**	20c. multicoloured	2·00	1·20

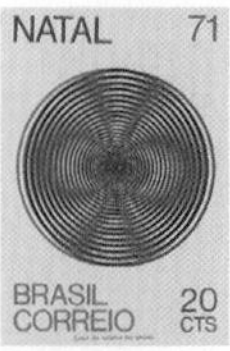

730 Cruciform Symbol

1971. Christmas.

1341	**730**	20c. lilac, red and blue	1·00	80
1342	**730**	75c. black on silver	2·10	6·25
1343	**730**	1cr.30 multicoloured	10·50	4·75

731 Washing Bomfim Church

1972. Tourism. Multicoloured.

1344	20c. Type **731**	3·75	1·70
1345	40c. Cogwheel and grapes (Grape Festival, Rio Grande do Sul)	5·75	1·20
1346	75c. Nazareth Festival procession, Belem	6·00	5·50
1347	1cr.30 Street scene (Winter Festival of Ouro Preto)	13·00	5·75

732 Pres. Lanusse

1972. Visit of President Lanusse of Argentina.

1348	**732**	40c. multicoloured	4·75	5·75

733 Presidents Castello Branco, Costa e Silva and Medici

1972. Eighth Anniv of 1964 Revolution.

1349	**733**	20c. multicoloured	3·00	1·40

734 Post Office Symbol

1972

1350	**734**	20c. brown	4·75	30

735 Pres. Tomas

1972. Visit of Pres. Tomas of Portugal.

1351	**735**	75c. multicoloured	4·75	3·75

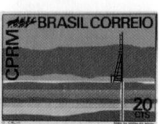

736 Exploratory Borehole (C.P.R.M.)

1972. Mineral Resources. Multicoloured.

1352	20c. Type **736**	3·00	1·20
1353	40c. Oil rig (PETROBRAS) (vert)	7·25	1·90
1354	75c. Power station and dam (ELECTROBRAS)	3·25	3·25
1355	1cr.30 Iron ore production (Vale do Rio Doce Co.)	7·25	3·25

737 *Female Nude* (1922 Catalogue cover by Di. Cavalcanti)

1972. 50th Anniv of First Modern Art Week, Sao Paulo. Sheet 79×111 mm. With gum.

MS1356	**737**	1cr. black and carmine	70·00	65·00

738 Postman and Map (Post Office)

1972. Communications. Multicoloured.

1357	35c. Type **738**	3·25	85
1358	45c. Microwave Transmitter (Telecommunications) (vert)	3·50	3·50
1359	60c. Symbol and diagram of Amazon microwave system	3·50	2·75
1360	70c. Worker and route map (Amazon Basin development)	4·50	2·75

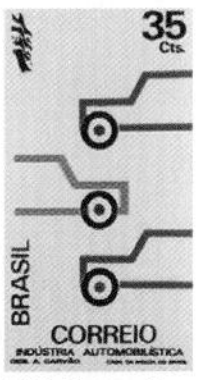

739 Motor Cars

1972. Major Industries.

1361	**739**	35c. orange, red & black	2·50	1·20
1362	-	45c. multicoloured	2·50	1·40
1363	-	70c. multicoloured	2·50	1·20

DESIGNS—HORIZ: 45c. Three hulls (Shipbuilding); 70c. Metal Blocks (Iron and Steel Industry).

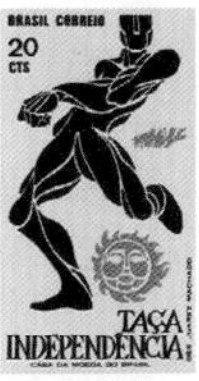

740 Footballer (Independence Cup Championships)

1972. Sports and Pastimes.

1364	**740**	20c. black and brown	2·40	1·20
1365	-	75c. black and red	4·25	6·50
1366	-	1cr.30 black and blue	8·00	6·50

DESIGNS: 75c. Treble clef in open mouth ("Popular Music"); 1cr.30, Hand grasping plastic ("Plastic Arts").

741 Diego Homem's Map of Brazil, 1568

1972. EXFILBRA 72 Fourth International Stamp Exhibition, Rio de Janeiro. Multicoloured.

1367	70c. Type **741**	1·30	1·20
1368	1cr. Nicolau Visscher's Map of Americas, c. 1652	18·00	2·30
1369	2cr. Lopo Homem's World Map, 1519	8·75	3·50
MS1370	125×89 mm. 1cr. *Declaration of Ypiranga* (Pedro Americo) (horiz)	10·50	11·00

742 Figurehead, Sao Francisco River

1972. Brazilian Folklore. Multicoloured.

1371	45c. Type **742**	2·10	85
1372	60c. Fandango, Rio Grande do Sul	3·25	2·75
1373	75c. Capoeira (game), Bahia	70	65
1374	1cr.15 Karaja statuette	1·40	1·30
1375	1cr.30 *Bumba-Meu-Boi* (folk play)	10·00	3·75

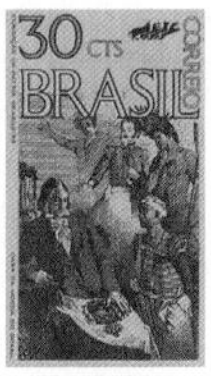

743 *Institution of Brazilian Flag*

1972. 150th Anniv of Independence.

1376	**743**	30c. green and yellow	3·00	2·75
1377	-	70c. mauve and pink	2·40	1·80
1378	-	1cr. red and brown	14·50	2·75
1379	-	2cr. black and brown	7·50	2·75
1380	-	3cr.50 black and grey	14·00	7·00

DESIGNS—HORIZ: 70c. *Proclamation of Emperor Pedro I* (lithograph after Debret); 2cr. Commemorative gold coin of Pedro I; 3cr.50, Declaration of Ypiranga monument. VERT: 1cr. *Emperor Pedro I* (H. J. da Silva).

744 Numeral and P.T.T. Symbol

745 Scroll

1972

1383	**744**	5c. orange	55	20
1384	**744**	10c. brown	80	20
1394	**744**	15c. blue	45	10
1385	**744**	20c. blue	80	20
1396	**744**	25c. brown	55	30
1386	**744**	30c. red	90	20
1387	**744**	40c. green	45	20
1388	**744**	50c. green	70	20
1398	**744**	70c. purple	70	10
1389	**745**	1cr. purple	1·00	20
1390	**745**	2cr. blue	1·60	20
1391	**745**	4cr. orange and lilac	3·50	20
1392	**745**	5cr. brown, cinnamon and red	5·25	20
1393	**745**	10cr. green, brown & blk	11·00	65

Nos. 1392/3 have a background of multiple P.T.T. symbols.

746 Fittipaldi in Racing Car

1972. Emerson Fittipaldi's Victory in Formula 1 World Motor-racing Championship. Sheet 122×87 mm.

MS1411	**746**	2cr. multicoloured	22·00	25·00

747 Writing Hand and People ("Mobral" Literacy Campaign)

1972. Social Development. Multicoloured.

1412	10c. Type **747**	45	55
1413	20c. Graph and people (National Census Cent)	2·50	1·70
1414	1cr. House in hand (Pension Fund system)	17·00	65
1415	2cr. Workers and factory (Gross National Product)	4·75	1·70

748 Legislative Building, Brasilia

1972. National Congress Building, Brasilia.

1416	**748**	1cr. black, orange & bl	20·00	11·00

749 Pottery Crib

1972. Christmas.

1417	**749**	20c. black and brown	2·10	1·20

750 Farm-worker and Pension Book (Rural Social Security Scheme)

1972. Government Services.

1418	**750**	10c. black, orange & bl	1·30	1·20
1419	-	10c. multicoloured	2·50	2·30
1420	-	70c. black, brown & red	18·00	7·00
1421	-	2cr. multicoloured	29·00	12·50

DESIGNS—VERT: 70c. Dr. Oswald Cruz, public health pioneer (birth cent.). HORIZ: 10c. (No. 1419), Children and traffic lights (Transport system development); 2cr. Bull, fish and produce (Agricultural exports).

751 Brazilian Expeditionary Force Monument

1972. Armed Forces' Day.

1422	**751**	10c. black, purple & brn	3·75	2·50
1423	-	30c. multicoloured	3·75	2·50
1424	-	30c. multicoloured	3·75	2·50
1425	-	30c. black, brn & lilac	3·75	2·50

DESIGNS: No. 1423, Sail-training ship (Navy); No. 1424, Trooper (Army); No. 1425, Dassault Mirage IIIC jet fighter (Air Force).

GUM. All the following issues are with gum, except where otherwise stated.

752 Emblem and Cogwheels

1973. 50th Anniv of Rotary in Brazil.

1426	**752**	1cr. blue, lt blue & yell	4·00	3·50

753 Swimming

1973. Sporting Events.

1427	**753**	40c. brown and blue	80	75
1428	-	40c. red and green	5·50	2·10
1429	-	40c. brown and purple	1·70	1·60

DESIGNS AND EVENTS—HORIZ: No. 1427, ("Latin Cup" Swimming Championships); No. 1428, Gymnast (Olympic Festival of Gymnastics, Rio de Janeiro). VERT: No. 1429, Volleyball player (Internation Volleyball Championships, Rio de Janeiro).

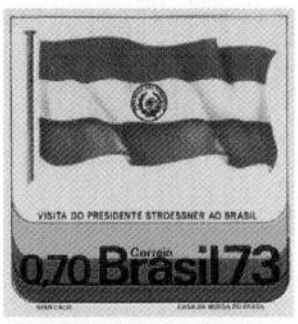

754 Paraguayan Flag

1973. Visit of Pres. Stroessner of Paraguay.

1430	**754**	70c. multicoloured	4·00	2·75

755 "Communications"

1973. Inauguration of Ministry of Communications Building, Brasilia.

1431	**755**	70c. multicoloured	1·90	1·60

756 Neptune and Map

1973. Inauguration of "Bracan I" Underwater Cable, Recife to Canary Islands.

1432	**756**	1cr. multicoloured	9·75	7·00

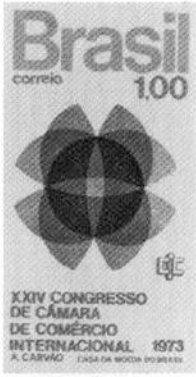

757 Congress Emblem

1973. 24th Int Chamber of Commerce Congress.

1433	**757**	1cr. purple and orange	9·50	7·00

758 Swallow-tailed Manakin and *Acacia decurrens*

1973. Tropical Birds and Plants. Multicoloured.

1434	20c. Type **758**	2·75	75
1435	20c. Troupial and *Cereus peruvianus*	2·75	75
1436	20c. Brazilian ruby and *Tecoma umbellata*	2·75	75

759 "Tourism"

1973. National Tourism Year.

1437	**759**	70c. multicoloured	2·50	1·90

760 "Caboclo" Festival Cart

1973. Anniversaries. Multicoloured.

1438	20c. Type **760**	1·80	75
1439	20c. Arariboia (Indian chief)	1·80	75
1440	20c. Convention delegates	1·80	75
1441	20c. *The Graciosa Road*	1·80	75

EVENTS: No. 1438, 150th anniv of Liberation Day; 1439, 400th anniv of Niteroi; 1440, Cent of Itu Convention; 1441, Cent of Nhundiaquara highway.

761 "Institute of Space Research"

1973. Scientific Research Institute. Multicoloured.

1442	20c. Type **761**	90	65
1443	70c. "Federal Engineering School", Itajuba	6·25	2·30
1444	1cr. "Institute for Pure and Applied Mechanics"	8·00	2·30

762 Santos Dumont and Biplane *14 bis*

1973. Birth Centenary of Alberto Santos Dumont (aviation pioneer).

1445	**762**	20c. brown, grn & lt grn	2·20	55
1446	-	70c. brown, red & yellow	4·50	2·75
1447	-	2cr. brown, ultram & bl	5·25	2·75

DESIGNS: 70c. Airship *Ballon No. 6*; 2cr. Monoplane No. 20 *Demoiselle*.

763 Map of the World

1973. Stamp Day.

1448	**763**	40c. black and red	5·75	4·75
1449	-	40c. black and red	5·75	4·75

The design of No. 1449 differs from Type **763** in that the red portion is to the top and right, instead of to the top and left.

764 G. Dias

1973. 150th Birth Anniv of Goncalves Dias (poet).

1450	**764**	40c. black and violet	2·10	85

See also Nos. 1459 and 1477.

765 Copernicus and "Sun-god"

1973. 500th Birth Anniv of Nicholas Copernicus (astronomer). Sheet 125×87 mm.

MS1451	**765** 1cr. multicoloured	14·00	13·00

766 Festival Banner

1973. National Folklore Festival.

1452	**766**	40c. multicoloured	2·10	1·20

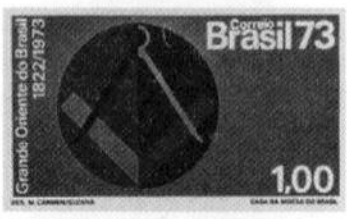

767 Masonic Emblems

1973. 150th Anniv of Masonic Grand Orient Lodge of Brazil.

1453	**767**	1cr. blue	6·75	4·25

768 Fire Protection

1973. National Protection Campaign. Multicoloured.

1454	40c. Type **768**	1·80	85
1455	40c. Cross and cornice (cultural protection)	1·80	85
1456	40c. Winged emblem (protection in flight)	1·80	85
1457	40c. Leaf (protection of nature)	1·80	85

769 St. Gabriel and Papal Bull

1973. First National Exhibition of Religious Philately, Rio de Janeiro. Sheet 125×87 mm.

MS1458	**769** 1cr. black and ochre	17·00	18·00

1973. Birth Centenary of St. Theresa of Lisieux. As T **764**.

1459	2cr. brown and orange	8·50	5·75

DESIGN: Portrait of St. Theresa.

770 M. Lobato and *Emilia*

1973. Monteiro Lobato's Children's Stories. Multicoloured.

1460	40c. Type **770**	1·90	1·20
1461	40c. "Aunt Nastasia"	1·90	1·20
1462	40c. "Nazarinho", "Pedrinho" and "Quindim"	1·90	1·20
1463	40c. "Visconde de Sabugosa"	1·90	1·20
1464	40c. "Dona Benta"	1·90	1·20

771 Father J. M. Nunes Garcia

1973. "The Baroque Age". Multicoloured.

1465	40c. Wood carving, Church of St. Francia, Bahia	70	65
1466	40c. *Prophet Isaiah* (detail, sculpture by Aleijadinho)	70	65
1467	70c. Type **771**	3·75	3·25
1468	1cr. Portal, Church of Conceicao da Praia	16·00	7·00
1469	2cr. *Glorification of Holy Virgin*, ceiling, St. Francis Assisi Church, Ouro Preto	8·50	7·00

772 Early Telephone and Modern Instruments

1973. 50th Anniv of Brazilian Telephone Company.

1470	**772**	40c. multicoloured	80	65

773 *Angel* (J. Kopke)

1973. Christmas.

1471	**773**	40c. multicoloured	80	65

774 *Gailora* (river steamboat)

1973. Brazilian Boats. Multicoloured.

1472	40c. Type **774**	80	65
1473	70c. *Regatao* (river trading boat)	2·75	2·50
1474	1cr. *Jangada* (coastal raft)	9·75	4·50
1475	2cr. *Saveiro* (passenger boat)	9·75	4·50

775 Scales of Justice

1973. Judiciary Power.

1476	**775**	40c. violet and mauve	1·40	65

1973. Birth Centenary of Placido de Castro. As T **764**.

1477	40c. black and red	1·70	85

DESIGN: Portrait of Castro.

776 Scarlet Ibis and "Victoria Regia" Lilies

1973. Brazilian Flora and Fauna. Multicoloured.

1478	40c. Type **776**	2·50	45
1479	70c. Jaguar and Indian tulip	7·50	3·75
1480	1cr. Scarlet macaw and palm	9·75	45
1481	2cr. Greater rhea and mulunga plant	16·00	6·00

777 Saci Perere (goblin)

1974. Brazilian Folk Tales. Multicoloured.

1482	40c. Type **777**	90	55
1483	80c. Zumbi (warrior)	1·80	1·30
1484	1cr. Chico Rei (African king)	4·00	1·10
1485	1cr.30 Little black boy of the pasture (32×33 mm)	6·25	1·90
1486	2cr.50 Iara, queen of the waters (32×33 mm)	21·00	5·75

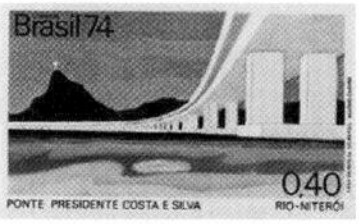

778 View of Bridge

1974. Inauguration of President Costa e Silva (Rio de Janeiro–Niteroi) Bridge.

1487	**778**	40c. multicoloured	1·70	65

779 "Press"

1974. Brazilian Communications Pioneers.

1488	**779**	40c. red, blue & bistre	1·10	65
1489	-	40c. brown, blue & bistre	1·10	65
1490	-	40c. blue, pink & brown	1·10	65

DESIGNS AND EVENTS: No. 1488, Birth bicentenary of Hipolito da Costa (founder of newspaper *Correio Brasiliense*, 1808); 1489, *Radio waves* (Edgar R. Pinto, founder of Radio Sociedade do Rio de Janeiro, 1923); 1490, *Television screen* (F. de Assis Chateaubriand, founder of first T.V. station, Sao Paulo, 1950).

780 "Construction"

1974. Tenth Anniv of March Revolution.

1491	**780**	40c. multicoloured	1·70	95

781 Christ of the Andes

1974. Birth Cent of G. Marconi (radio pioneer).

1492	**781**	2cr.50 multicoloured	11·50	6·50

782 Heads of Three Races

1974. Ethnical Origins and Immigration. Multicoloured.

1493	40c. Type **782**	80	65
1494	40c. Heads of many races	45	45
1495	2cr.50 German immigration	8·50	3·50
1496	2cr.50 Italian immigration	12·50	3·50
1497	2cr.50 Japanese immigration	3·00	2·10

783 Artwork and Stamp-printing Press

1974. State Mint.

1498	**783**	80c. multicoloured	2·50	45

784 Sete Cidades National Park

1974. Tourism. Multicoloured.

1499	40c. Type **784**	1·80	1·20
1500	80c. Ruins of church of St. Michael of the Missions	1·80	1·20

785 Footballer

1974. World Cup Football Championship, West Germany. Sheet 125×87 mm.

MS1501	**785** 2cr.50 multicoloured	9·75	9·75

See also No. 1506.

786 Caraca College

1974. Bicentenary of Caraca College.

1502	**786**	40c. multicoloured	1·30	85

787 Wave Pattern

1974. Third Brazilian Telecommunications Congress, Brasilia.

1503	**787**	40c. black and blue	70	65

788 Fernao Dias Paes

1974. 300th Anniv of Paes Expedition.

1504	**788**	20c. multicoloured	70	65

1974. Visit of President Alvarez of Mexico. As T **754**. Multicoloured.

1505	80c. Mexican Flag	6·25	2·30

789 Flags and Crowd in Stadium

1974. World Cup Football Championship, West Germany (2nd issue).

1506	**789**	40c. multicoloured	1·30	1·20

790 Braille "Eye" and Emblem

1974. Fifth General Assembly of World Council for Welfare of the Blind. Sheet 127×90 mm.

MS1507	**790**	1cr.30 multicoloured	2·30	3·25

791 *Pederneiras* (after J. Carlos)

1974. Birth Centenary of Raul Pederneiras (lawyer, author and artist).

1508	**791**	40c. black & yell on brn	70	65

792 Emblem and Seascape

1974. 13th Int Union of Building Societies and Savings Associations Congress, Rio de Janeiro.

1509	**792**	1cr.30 multicoloured	3·50	2·00

793 *Five Women of Guaratingueta* (E di Cavalcanti)

1974. Lubrapex 74 Stamp Exhibition, Sao Paulo (1st issue). Sheet 87×126 mm.

MS1510	**793**	2cr. multicoloured	6·75	10·50

See also No. 1522.

794 "UPU" on World Map

1974. Centenary of UPU.

1511	**794**	2cr.50 black and blue	11·50	3·75

795 Aruak Hammock

1974. "Popular Culture".

1512	**795**	50c. purple	4·50	85
1513	-	50c. light blue and blue	5·75	85
1514	-	50c. brown, red & yellow	1·40	85
1515	-	50c. brown and yellow	1·80	85

DESIGNS—SQUARE: No. 1513, Bilro Lace. VERT: (24×37 mm), No. 1514, Guitar player (folk literature); 1515, Horseman (statuette by Vitalino).

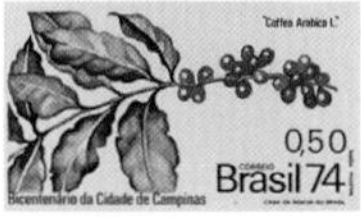

796 Coffee Beans

1974. Bicentenary of City of Campinas.

1516	**796**	50c. multicoloured	2·30	1·30

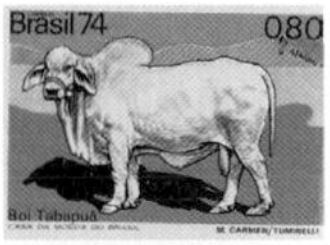

797 Hornless Tabapua

1974. Domestic Animals. Multicoloured.

1517	80c. Type **797**	2·50	1·50
1518	1cr.30 Creole horse	2·40	1·50
1519	2cr.50 Brazilian mastiff	16·00	4·50

798 Ilha Solteira Dam

1974. Ilha Solteira Hydro-electric Power Project.

1520	**798**	50c. brown, grey & yell	3·50	1·20

799 Herald Angel

1974. Christmas.

1521	**799**	50c. multicoloured	1·70	65

800 *The Girls* (Carlos Reis)

1974. Lubrapex 74 Stamp Exhibition, Sao Paulo (2nd issue).

1522	**800**	1cr.30 multicoloured	1·70	1·20

801 "Justice for Juveniles"

1974. 50th Anniv of Brazilian Juvenile Court.

1523	**801**	90c. multicoloured	70	65

802 Athlete

1974. 50th Anniv of Sao Silvestre Long-distance Race.

1524	**802**	3cr.30 multicoloured	1·80	1·70

803 Mounted Newsvendor and Newspaper Masthead

1975. Centenary of Newspaper *O Estado de S. Paulo*.

1525	**803**	50c. multicoloured	3·00	1·70

804 Industrial Complex, Sao Paulo

1975. Economic Resources.

1526	**804**	50c. yellow and blue	3·25	85
1527	-	1cr.40 yellow & brown	1·40	85
1528	-	4cr.50 yellow & black	11·00	85

DESIGNS: 1cr.40 Rubber industry, Acre; 4cr.50, Manganese industry, Amapa.

805 Santa Cruz Fortress, Rio de Janeiro

1975. Colonial Forts. Each brown on yellow.

1529	50c. Type **805**	70	45
1530	50c. Reis Magos Fort, Rio Grande do Norte	1·30	55
1531	50c. Monte Serrat Fort, Bahia	2·30	55
1532	90c. Nossa Senhora dos Remedios Fort, Fernando de Noronha	70	45

806 "Palafita" House, Amazonas

1975. Brazilian Architecture. Multicoloured.

1533	50c. Modern Architecture, Brasilia	2·75	2·50
1534	50c. Modern Architecture, Brasilia (yellow line at left)	19·00	11·50
1535	1cr. Type **806**	1·90	45
1536	1cr.40 Indian hut, Rondonia (yellow line at left)	4·25	4·00
1537	1cr.40 As No. 1536 but yellow line at right	1·10	1·00
1538	3cr.30 "Enxaimel" house, Santa Catarina (yellow line at right)	1·80	1·70
1539	3cr.30 As No. 1538 but yellow line at left	8·00	7·50

807 Oscar (*Astronotus ocellatus*)

1975. Freshwater Fish. Multicoloured.

1540	50c. Type **807**	3·75	45
1541	50c. South American pufferfish (*Colomesus psitacus*)	90	85
1542	50c. Tail-spot livebearer (*Phallocerus caudimaculatus*)	90	85
1543	50c. Red discus (*Symphysodon discus*)	1·40	55

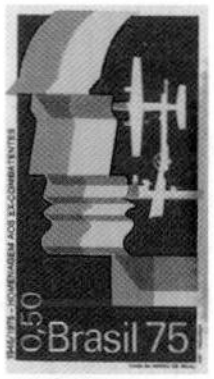

808 Flags forming Serviceman's Head

1975. Honouring Ex-Servicemen of Second World War.

1544	**808**	50c. multicoloured	90	65

809 Brazilian Pines

1975. Fauna and Flora Preservation. Multicoloured.

1545	70c. Type **809**	4·00	75
1546	1cr. Giant otter (vert)	2·50	1·10
1547	3cr.30 Marsh cayman	2·50	1·10

810 Inga Carved Stone, from Paraiba

1975. Archaeology. Multicoloured.

1548	70c. Type **810**	1·40	85
1549	1cr. Marajoara pot from Para	80	75
1550	1cr. Fossilized garfish from Ceara (horiz)	80	75

811 Statue of the Virgin Mary

1975. Holy Year. 300th Anniv of Franciscan Province of Our Lady of the Immaculate Conception.

1551	**811**	3cr.30 multicoloured	2·50	1·60

812 Ministry of Communications Building, Rio de Janeiro

1975. Stamp Day.

1552	**812**	70c. red	1·70	65

813 "Congada" Sword Dance, Minas Gerais

1975. Folk Dances. Multicoloured.

1553	70c. Type **813**	90	75
1554	70c. "Frevo" umbrella dance, Pernambuco	90	75
1555	70c. "Warrior" dance, Alagoas	90	75

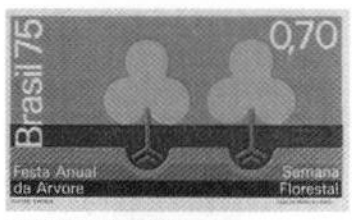

814 Stylized Trees

1975. Tree Festival.

1556	**814**	70c. multicoloured	70	55

815 Dish Aerial and Globe

1975. Inauguration of Tangua Satellite Telecommunications Station.

1557	**815**	3cr.30 multicoloured	1·70	1·60

816 Woman holding Globe

1975. International Women's Year.

1558	**816**	3cr.30 multicoloured	2·50	1·40

817 Tile, Balcony Rail and Memorial Column, Alcantara

1975. Historic Towns. Multicoloured.

1559		70c. Type **817**	1·50	95
1560		70c. Belfry, weather vane and jug, Goias (26×38 mm)	1·50	95
1561		70c. Sao Francisco Convent, Sao Cristovao (40×22 mm)	1·50	95

818 Crowd welcoming Walking Book

1975. Day of the Book.

1562	**818**	70c. multicoloured	55	55

819 ASTA Emblem and Arrows

1975. 45th American Society of Travel Agents Congress.

1563	**819**	70c. multicoloured	55	55

820 Two Angels

1975. Christmas.

1564	**820**	70c. brown and red	55	45

821 Aerial, and Map of America

1975. Second International Telecommunications Conference, Rio de Janeiro.

1565	**821**	5cr.20 multicoloured	7·50	4·50

822 Friar Nicodemus

1975. Obligatory Tax. Leprosy Research Fund.

1566	**822**	10c. brown	35	30

823 People in front of Cross

1975. Thanksgiving Day.

1567	**823**	70c. turquoise and blue	90	85

824 Emperor Pedro II in Naval Uniform (after P. P. da Silva Manuel)

1975. 150th Birth Anniv of Emperor Pedro II.

1568	**824**	70c. brown	2·10	95

825 Sal Stone Beach, Piaui

1975. Tourism. Multicoloured.

1569		70c. Type **825**	70	65
1570		70c. Guarapari Beach, Espirito Santo	70	65
1571		70c. Torres Cliffs Rio Grande do Sul	70	65

826 Triple Jump

1975. Seventh Pan-American Games, Santo Domingo, Dominican Republic.

1572	**826**	1cr.60 turquoise & black	70	65

827 UN Emblem and HQ Building, New York

1975. 30th Anniv of United Nations.

1573	**827**	1cr.30 violet on blue	55	55

828 Light Bulbs and House

1976. "Preservation of Fuel Resources". Multicoloured.

1574		70c. Type **828**	70	45
1575		70c. Drops of petrol and car	70	45

829 Concorde

1976. Concorde's First Commercial Flight, Paris–Rio de Janeiro.

1576	**829**	5cr.20 black and grey	1·30	75

830 Pinheiro's Nautical Map of 1776

1976. Centenary of Hydrographical and Navigational Directorate. Sheet 88×124 mm.

MS1577	**830**	70c. multicoloured	2·75	2·75

831 Early and Modern Telephone Equipment

1976. Telephone Centenary.

1578	**831**	5cr.20 black & orange	1·90	1·20

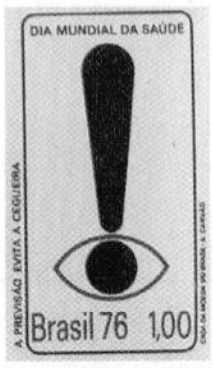

832 "Eye"-part of Exclamation Mark

1976. World Health Day.

1579	**832**	1cr. red, brown & violet	1·30	1·20

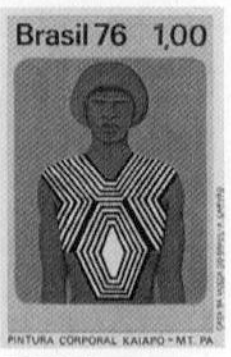

833 Kaiapo Body-painting

1976. Brazil's Indigenous Culture. Multicoloured.

1580		1cr. Type **833**	45	30
1581		1cr. Bakairi ceremonial mask	45	30
1582		1cr. Karaja feather head-dress	45	30

834 Itamaraty Palace, Brasilia

1976. Diplomats' Day.

1583	**834**	1cr. multicoloured	1·90	1·40

835 *The Sprinkler* (3D composition by J. Tarcisio)

1976. Modern Brazilian Art. Multicoloured.

1584		1cr. Type **835**	55	45
1585		1cr. *Beribboned Fingers* (P. Checcacci) (horiz)	55	45

836 Basketball

1976. Olympic Games, Montreal.

1586	**836**	1cr. black and green	45	45
1587	-	1cr.40 black and blue	45	45
1588	-	5cr.20 black and orange	1·60	1·30

DESIGNS: 1cr.40, Olympic yachts; 5cr.20, Judo.

837 Golden Lion-Tamarin

1976. Nature Protection. Multicoloured.

1589		1cr. Type **837**	1·40	45
1590		1cr. Orchid (*Acacallis cyanea*)	1·40	45

838 Cine Camera on Screen

1976. Brazilian Cinematograph Industry.

1591	**838**	1cr. multicoloured	55	55

839 Ox-cart Driver

1976

1592	**839**	10c. red	45	20
1593	-	15c. brown	70	30
1594	-	20c. blue	45	10
1595	-	30c. red	45	10
1596	-	40c. orange	55	20
1597a	-	50c. brown	45	20
1598	-	70c. black	55	20
1599	-	80c. green	1·90	30
1600a	-	1cr. black	45	20
1601	-	1cr.10 purple	45	10
1602	-	1cr.30 red	55	10
1603a	-	1cr.80 violet	55	20
1604a	-	2cr. brown	1·10	30
1605	-	2cr.50 brown	55	20
1605a	-	3cr.20 blue	55	20
1606a	-	5cr. lilac	4·50	55
1607	-	7cr. violet	8·00	30
1608a	-	10cr. green	4·50	55
1609	-	15cr. green	2·75	30
1610	-	20cr. blue	6·75	30
1611	-	21cr. purple	1·60	30
1612	-	27cr. brown	1·60	55

DESIGNS—HORIZ: 20c. Pirogue fisherman; 40c. Cowboy; 3cr.20, Sao Francisco boatman; 27cr. Muleteer. VERT: 15c. Bahia woman; 30c. Rubber gatherer; 50c. Gaucho; 70c. Women breaking Babacu chestnuts; 80c. Gold-washer; 1cr. Banana gatherer; 1cr.10, Grape harvester; 1cr.30, Coffee harvester; 1cr.80, Carnauba cutter; 2cr. Potter; 2cr.50, Basket maker; 5cr. Sugar-cane cutter; 7cr. Salt worker; 10cr. Fisherman; 15cr. Coconut vendor; 20cr. Lace maker; 21cr. Ramie cutter.

840 Neon Tetra (*Paracheirodon innesi*)

1976. Brazilian Freshwater Fish. Multicoloured.

1613		1cr. Type **840**	1·40	85
1614		1cr. Splash tetra (*Copeina arnoldi*)	1·40	85
1615		1cr. Prochilodus (*Prochilodus insignis*)	1·40	85
1616		1cr. Spotted pike cichlid (*Crenicichla lepidota*)	1·40	85
1617		1cr. Bottle-nosed catfish (*Ageneiosus* sp.)	1·40	85
1618		1cr. Reticulated corydoras (*Corydoras reticulatus*)	1·40	85

841 Santa Marta Lighthouse

1976. 300th Anniv of Laguna.

1619	**841**	1cr. blue	45	20

842 Postage Stamps as Magic Carpet

1976. Stamp Day.

1620	**842**	1cr. multicoloured	55	30

843 Oil Lamp and Profile

1976. 50th Anniv of Brazilian Nursing Assn.

1621	**843**	1cr. multicoloured	55	30

844 Puppet Soldier

1976. Mamulengo Puppet Theatre. Multicoloured.

1622		1cr. Type **844**	45	20
1623		1cr.30 Puppet girl	45	20
1624		1cr.60 Finger puppets (horiz)	45	20

845 Winner's Medal

1976. 27th International Military Athletics Championships, Rio de Janeiro.

1625	**845**	5cr.20 multicoloured	1·70	1·20

846 Family within "House"

1976. SESC and SENAC National Organizations for Appenticeship and Welfare.

1626	**846**	1cr. blue	55	20

847 Rotten Tree

1976. Conservation of the Environment.

1627	**847**	1cr. multicoloured	55	20

848 Electron Orbits and Atomic Agency Emblem

1976. 20th International Atomic Energy Conference, Rio de Janeiro.

1628	**848**	5cr.20 multicoloured	1·70	1·20

849 Underground Train

1976. Inauguration of Sao Paulo Underground Railway.

1629	**849**	1cr.60 multicoloured	80	30

850 St. Francis

1976. 750th Death Anniv of St. Francis of Assisi.

1630	**850**	5cr.20 multicoloured	1·70	85

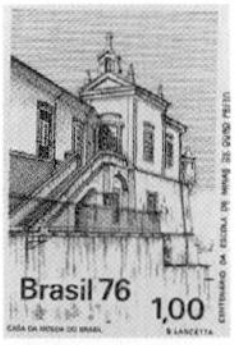

851 School Building

1976. Centenary of Ouro Preto Mining School.

1631	**851**	1cr. violet	90	1·10

852 *Three Kings* (J. A. da Silva)

1976. Christmas. Multicoloured.

1632	80c. Type **852**	70	45
1633	80c. *Father Christmas* (T. Onivaldo Cogo)	70	45
1634	80c. *Nativity Scene* (R. Yabe)	70	45
1635	80c. *Angels* (E. Folchini)	70	45
1636	80c. *Nativity* (A.L. Cintra)	70	45

853 Section of Brazilian 30,000-reis Banknote

1976. Opening of Bank of Brazil's Thousandth Branch at Barra do Bugres. Sheet 125×88 mm.

MS1637	**853**	80c. multicoloured	1·70	2·75

854 *Our Lady of Monte Serrat* (Friar A. da Piedade)

1976. Brazilian Sculpture. Multicoloured.

1638	80c. Type **854**	45	45
1639	5cr. *St. Joseph* (unknown artist) (25×37 mm)	1·60	85
1640	5cr.60 *The Dance* (J. Bernardelli) (square)	1·60	85
1641	6cr.50 *The Caravel* (B. Giorgi) (As 5cr.)	1·60	85

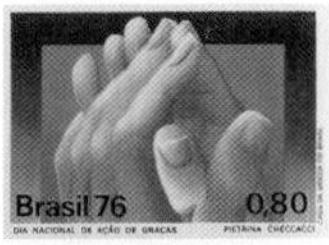

855 Hands in Prayer

1976. Thanksgiving Day.

1642	**855**	80c. multicoloured	70	45

856 Sailor of 1840

1976. Brazilian Navy Commemoration. Multicoloured.

1643	80c. Type **856**	70	30
1644	2cr. Marine of 1808	90	55

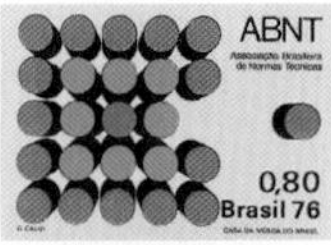

857 "Natural Resources"

1976. Brazilian Bureau of Standards.

1645	**857**	80c. multicoloured	55	30

858 *Wheel of Life* (wood-carving, G. T. de Oliveira)

1977. Second World Black and African Festival of Arts and Culture, Lagos (Nigeria). Multicoloured.

1646	5cr. Type **858**	1·40	75
1647	5cr.60 *The Beggar* (wood-carving, A. dos Santos)	1·40	75
1648	6cr.50 Benin pectoral mask	2·75	85

859 Airport Layout

1977. Inauguration of Operation of International Airport, Rio de Janeiro.

1649	**859**	6c.50 multicoloured	2·10	1·40

860 Seminar Emblem

1977. Sixth InterAmerican Budget Seminar.

1650	**860**	1cr.10 turq, bl & stone	1·90	45

861 Salicylic Acid Crystals

1977. World Rheumatism Year.

1651	**861**	1cr.10 multicoloured	70	30

862 Emblem of Lions Clubs

1977. 25th Anniv of Brazilian Lions Clubs.

1652	**862**	1cr.10 multicoloured	70	30

863 H. Villa-Lobos and Music

1977. Brazilian Composers. Multicoloured.

1653	1cr.10 Type **863**	45	10
1654	1cr.10 Chiquinha Gonzaga and guitar	45	10
1655	1cr.10 Noel Rosa and guitar	45	10

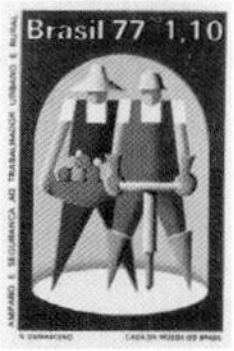

864 Rural and Urban Workers

1977. Industrial Protection and Safety. Multicoloured.

1656	1cr.10 Type **864**	45	10
1657	1cr.10 Laboratory vessels	45	10

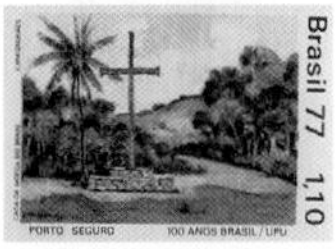

865 Memorial, Porto Seguro

1977. Centenary of UPU Membership. Views of Porto Seguro. Multicoloured.

1658	1cr.10 Type **865**	35	10
1659	5cr. Beach	2·75	65
1660	5cr.60 Old houses	1·50	65
1661	6cr.50 Post Office	2·00	65

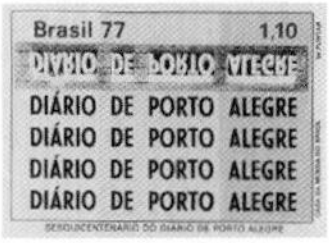

866 Newspaper Title in Linotype and Print

1977. 150th Anniv of Brazilian Newspaper *Diario de Porto Allegre*.

1662	**866**	1cr.10 black & purple	55	30

867 Blue Whale

1977. Fauna Preservation.

1663	**867**	1cr.30 multicoloured	3·50	45

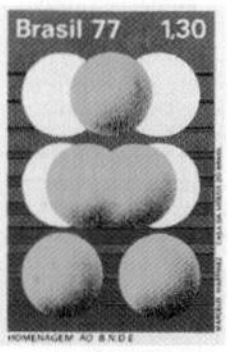

868 "Cell System"

1977. 25th Anniv of National Economic Development Bank.

1664	**868**	1cr.30 multicoloured	55	30

869 Locomotive leaving Tunnel

1977. Centenary of Rio de Janeiro–Sao Paulo Railway.

1665	**869**	1c.30 black	1·10	45

870 Goliath Conch

1977. Brazilian Molluscs. Multicoloured.

1666	1cr.30 Type **870**	1·40	45
1667	1cr.30 Thin-bladed murex (*Murex tenuivaricosus*)	1·40	45
1668	1cr.30 Helmet vase (*Vasum cassiforme*)	1·40	45

871 Caduceus

1977. Third International Congress of Odontology.

1669	**871**	1cr.30 brown, bis & orge	45	20

872 Masonic Symbols

1977. 50th Anniv of Brazilian Grand Masonic Lodge.

1670	**872**	1cr.30 blue, dp bl & blk	55	30

873 "Sailboat"

1977. Stamp Day.

1671	**873**	1cr.30 multicoloured	45	20

874 Law Proclamation

1977. 150th Anniv of Juridical Courses.

1672	**874**	1cr.30 multicoloured	55	30

875 "Cavalhada" (horsemen)

1977. Folklore. Multicoloured.

1673	1cr.30 Type **875**	45	20
1674	1cr.30 Horseman with flag	45	20
1675	1cr.30 Jousting (horiz)	45	20

876 Doubloon

1977. Brazilian Colonial Coins. Multicoloured.

1676	1cr.30 Type **876**	45	20
1677	1cr.30 Pataca	45	20
1678	1cr.30 Vintem	45	20

877 Toy Windmill

1977. National Day.

1679	**877**	1cr.30 multicoloured	55	30

878 *Neoregelia carolinae*

1977. Nature Conservation.

1680	**878**	1cr.30 multicoloured	55	30

879 Pen, Pencil and Writing

1977. 150th Anniv of Official Elementary Schooling.

1681	**879**	1cr.30 multicoloured	55	30

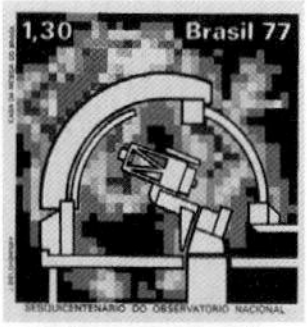

880 Observatory and Electrochromograph of Supernova

1977. 150th Anniv of National Observatory.

1682	**880**	1cr.30 multicoloured	70	35

881 Airship *Pax*

1977. Aviation Anniversaries. Multicoloured.

1683	1cr.30 Type **881**	80	55
1684	1cr.30 Savoia Marchetti flying boat *Jahu*	80	55

ANNIVERSARIES: No. 1683, 75th anniv of *Pax* flight; 1684, 50th anniv of *Jahu* South Atlantic crossing.

882 Text from *O Guarani* and Ceci

1977. Day of the Book and Jose de Alencar Commemoration.

1685	**882**	1cr.30 multicoloured	55	20

883 Radio Waves

1977. Amateur Radio Operators' Day.

1686	**883**	1cr.30 multicoloured	55	20

884 Nativity (in carved gourd)

1977. Christmas. Multicoloured.

1687	1cr.30 Type **884**	55	20
1688	2cr. The Annunciation	70	30
1689	5cr. Nativity	1·50	45

885 Emerald

1977. Portucale 77 Thematic Stamp Exhibition. Multicoloured.

1690	1cr.30 Type **885**	70	45
1691	1cr.30 Topaz	70	45
1692	1cr.30 Aquamarine	70	45

886 Angel holding Cornucopia

1977. Thanksgiving Day.

1693	**886**	1cr.30 multicoloured	55	30

887 Curtiss Fledgling Douglas DC-3 and Badge (National Airmail Service)

1977. National Integration. Multicoloured.

1694	1cr.30 Type **887**	70	45
1695	1cr.30 Amazon River naval patrol boat and badge (Amazon Fleet)	70	45
1696	1cr.30 Train crossing bridge and badges (Engineering Corps and Railway Battalion)	70	45

888 Douglas DC-10 and Varig Airline Emblems

1977. 50th Anniv of Varig State Airline.

1697	**888**	1cr.30 black, lt bl & bl	55	30

889 Sts. Cosmus and Damian Church, Igaracu

1977. Regional Architecture, Churches. Multicoloured.

1698	2cr.70 Type **889**	70	30
1699	7cr.50 St. Bento Monastery Church, Rio de Janeiro	2·10	75
1700	8cr.50 St. Francis Assisi Church, Ouro Preto	2·20	85
1701	9cr.50 St. Anthony Convent Church, Joao Pessoa	2·75	95

890 Woman with Wheat Sheaf

1977. Diplomats' Day.

1702	**890**	1cr.30 multicoloured	55	30

891 Scene from *Fosca* and Carlos Gomes (composer)

1978. Bicentenary of La Scala Opera House, Milan, and Carlos Gomes Commemoration.

1703	**891**	1cr.80 multicoloured	45	20

892 Foot kicking Ball

1978. World Cup Football Championship, Argentina. Multicoloured.

1704	1cr.80 Type **892**	70	20
1705	1cr.80 Ball in net	70	20
1706	1cr.80 Stylized player with cup	70	20

893 "Postal Efficiency"

1978. Postal Staff College.

1707	**893**	1cr.80 multicoloured	55	30

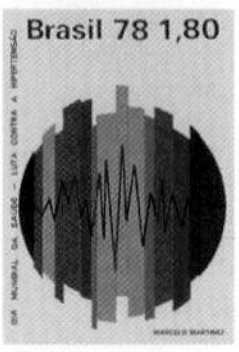

894 Electrocardiogram

1978. World Hypertension Month.

1708	**894**	1cr.80 multicoloured	55	30

895 World Map and Antenna

1978. World Telecommunications Day.

1709	**895**	1cr.80 multicoloured	55	30

896 Saffron Finch

1978. Birds. Multicoloured.

1710	7cr.50 Type **896**	2·30	85
1711	8cr.50 Banded cotinga	2·40	1·10
1712	9cr.50 Seven-coloured tanager	2·75	1·30

897 *Discussing the Opening Speech* (G. Mondin)

1978. 85th Anniv of Union Court of Audit.

1713	**897**	1cr.80 multicoloured	55	30

898 Post and Telegraph Headquarters, Brasilia

1978. Opening of Post and Telegraph Headquarters.

1714	**898**	1cr.80 multicoloured	55	45

1978. Brapex III Third Brazilian Philatelic Exhibition. Sheet 70×90 mm.

MS1715	**898**	7cr. 50 multicoloured	2·30	3·25

899 President Geisel

1978. President Geisel Commemoration.

1716	**899**	1cr.80 olive	55	30

900 Savoia Marchetti S-64 and Map

1978. 50th Anniv of South Atlantic Flight by del Prete and Ferrarin.

1717	**900**	1cr.80 multicoloured	55	30

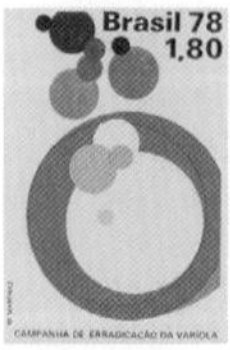

901 "Smallpox"

1978. Global Eradication of Smallpox.

1718	**901**	1cr.80 multicoloured	55	30

902 10r. Pedro II "White Beard" Stamp of 1878

1978. Stamp Day.

1719	**902**	1cr.80 multicoloured	45	20

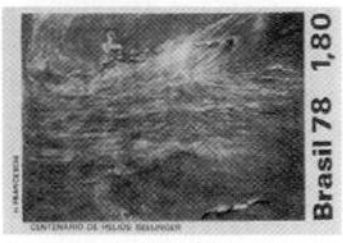

903 *Jangadeiros*

1978. Birth Centenary of Helios Seelinger (painter).

1720	**903**	1cr.80 multicoloured	55	30

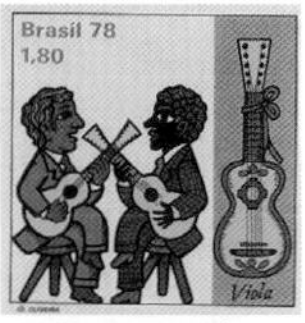

904 Musicians with Violas

1978. Folk Musicians. Multicoloured.

1721	1cr.80 Type **904**	45	20
1722	1cr.80 Two fife players	45	20
1723	1cr.80 Berimbau players	45	20

905 Children playing Football

1978. National Week.

1724	**905**	1cr.80 multicoloured	55	30

906 Patio de Colegio Church

1978. Restoration of Patio de Colegio Church, Sao Paulo.

1725	**906**	1cr.80 brown	55	30

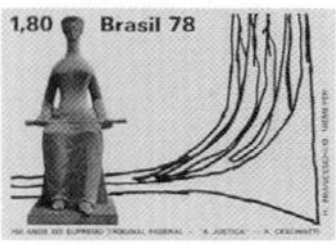

907 *Justice* (A. Ceschiatti)

1978. 150th Anniv of Federal Supreme Court.

1726	**907**	1cr.80 black and bistre	55	30

908 Ipe (flowering tree)

1978. Environment Protection. Iguacu Falls National Park. Multicoloured.

1727	1cr.80 Type **908**	55	30
1728	1cr.80 Iguacu Falls	55	30

909 Stages of Intelsat Assembly

1978. Third Assembly. Users of Intelsat Telecommunications Satellite.

1729	**909**	1cr.80 multicoloured	55	30

910 Flag of the Order of Christ

1978. Lubrapex 78 Stamp Exhibition. Flags. Multicoloured.

1730	1cr.80 Type **910**	1·30	1·10
1731	1cr.80 Principality of Brazil	1·30	1·10
1732	1cr.80 United Kingdom of Brazil	1·30	1·10
1733	8cr.50 Empire of Brazil	1·30	1·10
1734	8cr.50 National Flag of Brazil	1·30	1·10

911 Postal Tramcar

1978. 18th U.P.U. Congress, Rio de Janeiro.

1735	**911**	1cr.80 brown, blk & bl	1·50	65
1736	-	1cr.80 brown, blk & bl	1·50	65
1737	-	1cr.80 grey, blk & rose	1·50	65
1738	-	7cr.50 grey, blk & rose	1·80	85
1739	-	8cr.50 brown, blk & grn	2·10	95
1740	-	9cr.50 brown, blk & grn	2·30	1·10

DESIGNS: No. 1736, Post container truck; 1737, Post van, 1914; 1738, Travelling post office; 1739, Mail coach; 1740, Mule caravan.

912 Gaucho

1978. Day of the Book and J. Guimaraes Rosa Commemoration.

1741	**912**	1cr.80 multicoloured	45	30

913 *Morro de Santo Antonio* (Nicolas Antoine Taunay)

1978. Landscape Paintings. Multicoloured.

1742	1cr.80 Type **913**	45	30
1743	1cr.80 *View of Pernambuco* (Frans Post)	45	30
1744	1cr.80 *Morro de Castelo* (Victor Meirelles)	45	30
1745	1cr.80 *Landscape at Sabara* (Alberto da Veiga Guignard)	45	30

914 Angel with Lute

1978. Christmas. Multicoloured.

1746	1cr.80 Type **914**	45	30
1747	1cr.80 Angel with lyre	45	30
1748	1cr.80 Angel with trumpet	45	30

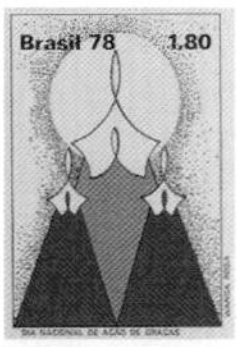

915 "Thanksgiving"

1978. Thanksgiving Day.

1749	**915**	1cr.80 ochre, blk & red	55	30

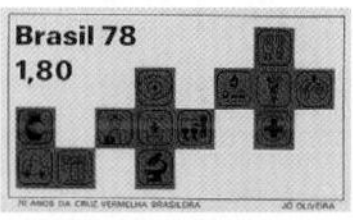

916 Red Cross Services

1978. 70th Anniv of Brazilian Red Cross.

1750	**916**	1cr.80 red and black	55	30

917 Peace Theatre, Belem

1978. Brazilian Theatres. Multicoloured.

1751	10cr.50 Type **917**	1·50	55
1752	12cr. Jose de Alencar Theatre, Fortaleza	1·60	65
1753	12cr.50 Rio de Janeiro Municipal Theatre	1·90	75

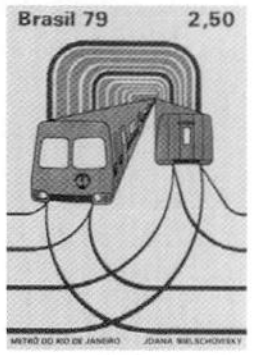

918 Underground Trains

1979. Inauguration of Rio de Janeiro Underground Railway.

1754	**918**	2cr.50 multicoloured	1·10	45

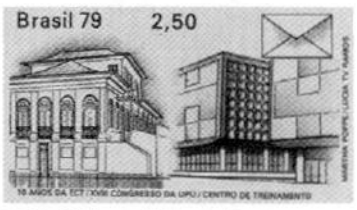

919 Old and New Post Offices

1979. Tenth Anniv of Post & Telegraph Department and 18th U.P.U. Congress (2nd issue). Multicoloured.

1755	2cr.50 Type **919**	55	30
1756	2cr.50 Mail boxes	55	30
1757	2cr.50 Mail sorting	55	30
1758	2cr.50 Mail planes	55	30
1759	2cr.50 Telegraph and telex machines	55	30
1760	2cr.50 Postmen	55	30

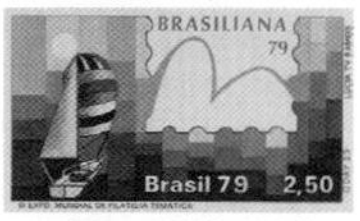

920 "O'Day 23" Class Yacht

1979. Brasiliana 79 3rd World Thematic Stamp Exhibition (1st issue). Multicoloured.

1761	2cr.50 Type **920**	70	55
1762	10cr.50 "Penguin" class dinghy	1·40	75
1763	12cr. "Hobie Cat" class catamaran	1·60	65
1764	12cr.50 "Snipe" class dinghy	1·90	75

See Nos. 1773/6 and 1785/90.

921 Joao Bolinha (characters from children's story)

1979. Children's Book Day.

1765	**921**	2cr.50 multicoloured	55	30

922 *Victoria amazonica*

1979. 18th U.P.U. Congress (3rd issue). Amazon National Park. Multicoloured.

1766	10cr.50 Type **922**	1·60	85
1767	12cr. Amazon manatee	1·80	1·10
1768	12cr.50 Tortoise	1·90	1·20

923 Bank Emblem

1979. 25th Anniv of Northeast Bank of Brazil.

1769	**923**	2cr.50 multicoloured	55	30

924 Physicians and Patient (15th cent woodcut)

1979. 150th Anniv of National Academy of Medicine.

1770	**924**	2cr.50 yellow and black	55	30

925 Clover with Hearts as Leaves

1979. 35th Brazilian Cardiology Congress.

1771	**925**	2cr.50 multicoloured	55	30

926 Hotel Nacional, Rio de Janeiro

1979. Brasiliana 79 (2nd issue). Sheet 87×124 mm.

MS1772	**926**	12cr.50 multicoloured	2·30	2·50

927 *Cithaerias aurora*

1979. Brasiliana 79 (2nd issue). Butterflies. Multicoloured.

1773	2cr.50 Type **927**	45	20
1774	10cr.50 *Evenus regalis*	1·70	45
1775	12cr. *Caligo eurilochus*	1·70	65
1776	12cr.50 *Diaethria clymena janeira*	1·90	75

928 Embraer Xingu

1979. Tenth Anniv of Brazilian Aeronautical Industry.

1777	**928**	2cr.50 dp blue and blue	55	30

929 Globe illuminating Land

1979. National Week.

1778	**929**	3cr.20 blue, green & yell	55	30

930 Our Lady Aparecida

1979. 75th Anniv of Coronation of Our Lady Aparecida.

1779	**930**	2cr.50 multicoloured	55	30

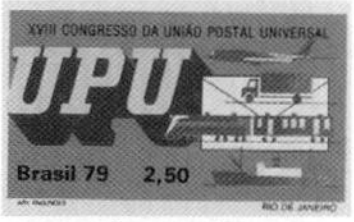

931 Envelope and Transport

1979. 18th UPU Congress, Rio de Janeiro (4th issue). Multicoloured.

1780	2cr.50 Type **931**	55	30
1781	2cr.50 Post Office emblems	55	30
1782	10cr.50 Globe	1·10	95
1783	12cr. Flags of Brazil and UPU	1·60	1·30
1784	12cr.50 UPU emblem	1·80	1·50

932 *Igreja da Gloria*

1979. Brasiliana 79 Third World Thematic Stamp Exhibition (3rd issue). Paintings by Leandro Joaquim. Multicoloured.

1785	2cr.50 Type **932**	45	30
1786	12cr. *Fishing on Guanabara Bay*	1·40	1·10
1787	12cr.50 *Boqueirao Lake and Carioca Arches*	1·60	1·30

933 Pyramid Fountain, Rio de Janeiro

1979. Brasiliana 79 (4th issue). 1st International Exhibition of Classical Philately. Fountains.

1788	**933**	2cr.50 black, grn & emer	45	30
1789	-	10cr.50 black, turq & bl	1·00	75
1790	-	12cr. black, red and pink	1·40	1·10

DESIGNS—VERT: 12cr. Boa Vista, Recife. HORIZ: 10cr.50, Marilia Fountain, Ouro Preto.

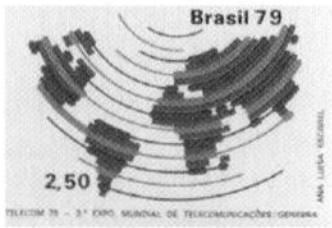

934 World Map

1979. Third World Telecommunications Exhibition, Geneva.

1791	**934**	2cr.50 multicoloured	55	30

935 "UPU" and Emblem

1979. UPU Day.

1792	**935**	2cr.50 multicoloured	55	45
1793	**935**	10cr.50 multicoloured	1·30	1·10
1794	**935**	12cr. multicoloured	1·40	1·20
1795	**935**	12cr.50 multicoloured	1·60	1·30

936 "Peteca" (shuttlecock)

1979. International Year of the Child. Multicoloured.

1796	2cr.50 Type **936**	55	45
1797	3cr.20 Spinning top	70	55
1798	3cr.20 Jumping Jack	70	55
1799	3cr.20 Rag doll	70	55

937 *The Birth of Jesus*

1979. Christmas. Tiles from the Church of Our Lady of Health and Glory, Salvador. Multicoloured.

1800	3cr.20 Type **937**	55	30
1801	3cr.20 *Adoration of the Kings*	55	30
1802	3cr.20 *The Boy Jesus among the Doctors*	55	30

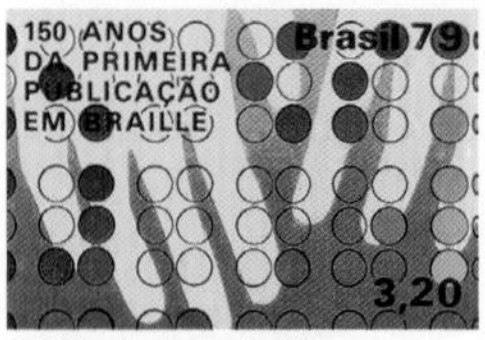

938 Hands reading Braille

1979. 150th Anniv of First Braille Publication. Sheet 127×88 mm.

MS1803	**938** 3cr. 20 multicoloured	1·10	1·10

939 Woman with Wheat

1979. Thanksgiving Day.

1804	**939**	3cr.20 multicoloured	55	30

940 Steel Mill

1979. 25th Anniv of Cosipa Steel Works, Sao Paulo.

1805	**940**	3cr.20 multicoloured	55	30

941 Plant within Raindrop

1980. Energy Conservation. Multicoloured.

1806	3cr.20 Type **941**	55	30
1807	17cr.+7cr. Sun and lightbulb	2·75	1·30
1808	20cr.+8cr. Windmill and lightbulb	3·50	1·60
1809	21cr.+9cr. Dam and lightbulb	4·75	1·70

942 Coal Trucks

1980. Coal Industry.

1810	**942**	4cr. black, orge & red	55	30

943 Coconuts

1980

1811	**943**	2cr. brown	25	10
1812	-	3cr. red	35	10
1813	-	4cr. orange	55	10
1814	-	5cr. violet	25	10
1815	-	7cr. orange	55	20
1816	-	10cr. green	25	10
1817	-	12cr. green	45	20
1818	-	15cr. brown	25	10
1819	-	17cr. red	55	20
1820	-	20cr. brown	25	10
1821	-	24cr. orange	2·30	20
1822	-	30cr. black	2·50	30
1823	-	34cr. brown	9·75	1·50
1824	-	38cr. red	3·50	85
1825	-	42cr. green	17·00	1·70
1825a	-	45cr. brown	25	10
1826	-	50cr. orange	55	20
1826a	-	57cr. brown	2·50	1·80
1826b	-	65cr. purple	45	20
1827	-	66cr. violet	13·50	1·90
1827a	-	80cr. red	1·10	95
1828	-	100cr. brown	4·75	30
1828a	-	120cr. blue	1·30	30
1829	-	140cr. red	8·00	95
1829a	-	150cr. green	70	20
1830	-	200cr. green	2·30	30
1830a	-	300cr. purple	2·50	45
1831	-	500cr. brown	2·50	45
1832	-	800cr. green	2·75	45
1833	-	1000cr. olive	2·75	45
1834	-	2000cr. orange	2·75	55

DESIGNS: 3cr. Mangoes; 4cr. Corn; 5cr. Onions; 7cr. Oranges; 10cr. Passion fruit; 12cr. Pineapple; 15cr. Bananas; 17cr. Guarana; 20cr. Sugar cane; 24cr. Bee and honeycomb; 30cr. Silkworm and mulberry; 34cr. Cocoa beans; 38cr. Coffee; 42cr. Soya bean; 45cr. Manioc; 50cr. Wheat; 57cr. Peanuts; 65cr. Rubber; 66cr. Grapes; 80cr. Brazil nuts; 100cr. Cashews; 120cr. Rice; 140cr. Tomatoes; 150cr. Eucalyptus; 200cr. Castor-oil bean; 300cr. Parana pine; 500cr. Cotton; 800cr. Carnauba palm; 1000cr. Babassu palm; 2000cr. Sunflower.

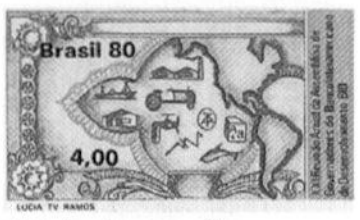

944 Banknote with Development Symbols

1980. 21st Inter-American Bank of Development Directors' Annual Assembly Meeting, Rio de Janeiro.

1836	**944**	4cr. blue, brown & blk	55	30

945 Tapirape Mask

1980. Indian Art. Ritual Masks. Multicoloured.

1837	4cr. Type **945**	55	30
1838	4cr. Tukuna mask (vert)	55	30
1839	4cr. Kanela mask (vert)	55	30

946 Geometric Head

1980. 30th Anniv of Brazilian Television.

1840	**946**	4cr. multicoloured	55	30

947 *Duke of Caxias* (after Miranda Junior)

1980. Death Centenary of Duke de Caxias (General and statesman).

1841	**947**	4cr. multicoloured	55	30

948 *The Labourer* (Candido Portinari)

1980. Art in Brazilian Museums. Multicoloured.

1842	24cr. Type **948**	2·50	1·20
1843	28cr. *Mademoiselle Pogany* (statuette, Constantin Brancusi)	2·75	1·30
1844	30cr. *The Glass of Water* (A. de Figueiredo)	4·00	1·50

MUSEUMS. 24cr. Sao Paulo Museum of Art. 28cr. Rio de Janeiro Museum of Modern Art. 30cr. Rio de Janeiro Museum of Fine Art.

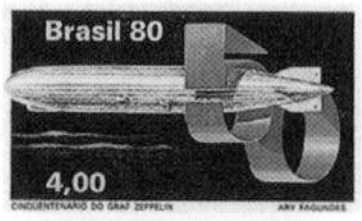

949 *Graf Zeppelin* flying through "50"

1980. 0th Annivs of "*Graf Zeppelin* and First South Atlantic Air Mail Flight.

1845	**949**	4cr. black, blue & violet	1·00	45
1846	-	4cr. multicoloured	1·00	45

DESIGN: No. 1846, Latecoere seaplane *Comte de la Vaulx*.

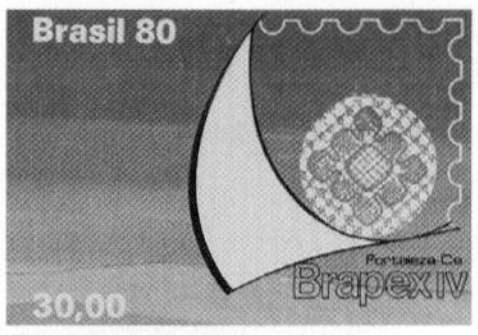

950 Sail and Bone-lace "Sun"

1980. Brapex IV National Stamp Exhibition, Fortaleza. Sheet 125×87 mm.

MS1847	**950** 30cr. multicoloured	2·30	3·25

951 Pope John Paul II and Fortaleza Cathedral

1980. Papal Visit and 10th National Eucharistic Congress. Pope John Paul II and cathedrals. Multicoloured.

1848	4cr. Type **951**	55	30
1849	4cr. St. Peter's, Rome (horiz)	55	30
1850	24cr. Apericida (horiz)	1·90	75
1851	28cr. Rio de Janeiro (horiz)	2·10	85
1852	30cr. Brasilia (horiz)	3·75	95

952 Shooting

1980. Olympic Games, Moscow. Multicoloured.

1853	4cr. Type **952**	55	30
1854	4cr. Cycling	55	30
1855	4cr. Rowing	55	30

953 Classroom

1980. Rondon Project (voluntary student work in rural areas).

1856	**953**	4cr. multicoloured	55	30

954 Helen Keller and Anne Sullivan

1980. Birth Centenary of Helen Keller, and 4th Brazilian Congress on Prevention of Blindness, Belo Horizonte.

1857	**954**	4cr. multicoloured	55	30

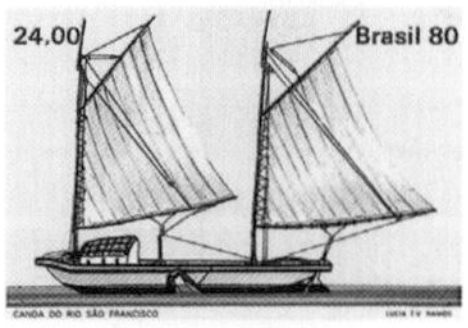

955 Sao Francisco River Canoe

1980. Stamp Day. Sheet 125×86 mm.

MS1858	**955** 24cr. multicoloured	2·30	2·40

956 Houses and Microscope

1980. National Health Day. Campaign against Chagas Disease (barber bug fever).

1859	**956**	4cr. multicoloured	55	30

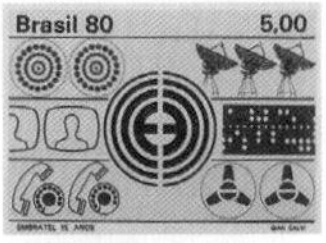
957 Communications Equipment

1980. 15th Anniv of National Telecommunications System.

1860	**957**	5cr. stone, blue & green	55	30

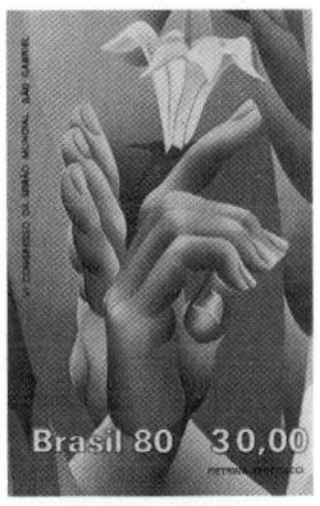
958 Hands with Lily

1980. Sixth World Union of St. Gabriel (Religious Philately Federation) Congress, Sao Paulo. Sheet 124×86 mm.

MS1861 **958**	30cr. multicoloured	2·30	2·30

959 *Cattleya amethysto-glossa*

1980. Espamer 80 International Stamp Exhibition, Madrid. Orchids. Multicoloured.

1862	5cr. Type **959**	55	30
1863	5cr. *Laelia cinnabarina*	55	30
1864	24cr. *Zygopetalum crinitum*	2·30	1·20
1865	28cr. *Laelia tenebrosa*	2·30	1·20

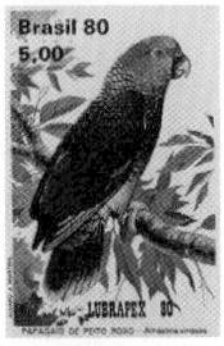
960 Vinaceous Amazon

1980. Lubrapex 80 Portuguese–Brazilian Stamp Exhibition, Lisbon. Parrots. Multicoloured.

1866	5cr. Type **960**	80	50
1867	5cr. Red-tailed amazon	80	50
1868	28cr. Red-spectacled amazon	5·25	2·10
1869	28cr. Brown backed parrotlet	5·25	2·10

961 Captain Rodrigo (fictional character)

1980. Book Day and Erico Verissimo (writer). Commemoration.

1870	**961**	5cr. multicoloured	55	30

962 Flight into Egypt

1980. Christmas.

1871	**962**	5cr. multicoloured	55	30

963 Wave-form

1980. Inauguration of Telecommunications Centre for Research and Development, Campanas City.

1872	**963**	5cr. multicoloured	70	30

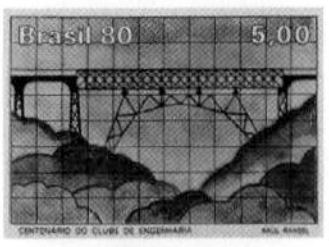
964 Carvalho Viaduct, Paranagua–Curitiba Railway Line

1980. Centenary of Engineering Club.

1873	**964**	5cr. multicoloured	80	35

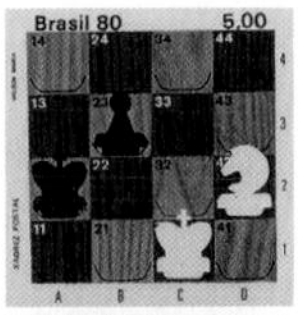
965 Postal Chessboard

1980. Postal Chess.

1874	**965**	5cr. multicoloured	70	45

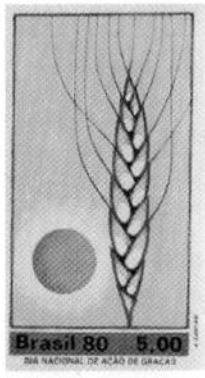
966 Sun and Wheat

1980. Thanksgiving Day.

1875	**966**	5cr. multicoloured	55	30

967 Father Anchieta writing Poem in Sand

1980. Beatification of Father Jose de Anchieta.

1876	**967**	5cr. multicoloured	55	30

968 Christ on the Mount of Olives

1980. 250th Birth Anniv of Antonio Lisboa (Aleijadinho) (sculptor). Wood sculptures of Christ's head. Multicoloured.

1877	5cr. Type **968**	70	45
1878	5cr. The Arrest in the Garden	70	45
1879	5cr. Flagellation	70	45
1880	5cr. Wearing Crown of Thorns	70	45
1881	5cr. Carrying the cross	70	45
1882	5cr. Crucifixion	70	45

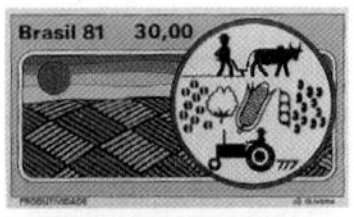
969 Agricultural Produce

1981. Agricultural Development. Multicoloured.

1883	30cr. Type **969**	2·75	65
1884	35cr. Shopping	2·30	65
1885	40cr. Exporting	2·30	65

970 Scout sitting by Camp Fire

1981. Fourth Pan-American Jamboree. Multicoloured.

1886	5cr. Type **970**	55	10
1887	5cr. Troop cooking	55	10
1888	5cr. Scout with totem pole	55	10

971 First-class Mailman (Empire period)

1981. 50th Anniv of Integrated Post Office and Telegraph Department (DCT). Sheet 99×70 mm containing T **971** and similar vert designs. Multicoloured.

MS1889	30cr. Type **971**; 35cr. DCT mailman; 40cr. Telegraph messenger (first republic)	8·50	8·50

972 *The Hunter and the Jaguar*

1981. Death Centenary of Felix Emile, Baron of Tauny (artist). Sheet 70×90 mm.

MS1890 **972**	30cr. multicoloured	3·00	3·25

973 Lima Barreto and Rio de Janeiro Street Scene

1981. Birth Centenary of Lima Barreto (author).

1891	**973**	7cr. multicoloured	60	25

974 Tupi-Guarani Ceramic Funeral Urn

1981. Artefacts from Brazilian Museums. Multicoloured.

1892	7cr. Type **974** (Archaeology and Popular Arts Museum, Paranagua)	60	25
1893	7cr. Marajoara "tanga" ceramic loincloth (Emilio Goeldi Museum, Para)	60	25
1894	7cr. Maraca tribe funeral urn (National Museum, Rio de Janeiro)	60	25

975 Ruby-topaz Hummingbird

1981. Hummingbirds. Multicoloured.

1895	7cr. Type **975**	1·70	55
1896	7cr. Horned sungem	1·70	55
1897	7cr. Frilled coquette	1·70	55
1898	7cr. Planalto hermit	1·70	55

976 Hands and Cogwheels

1981. 72nd Int Rotary Convention, Sao Paulo.

1899	**976**	7cr. red and black	45	45
1900	-	35cr. multicoloured	2·20	1·60

DESIGN: 35cr. Head and cogwheels.

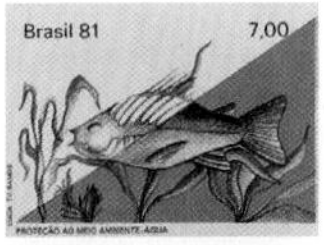
977 "Protection of the Water"

1981. Environment Protection. Multicoloured.

1901	7cr. Type **977**	70	20
1902	7cr. "Protection of the forests"	70	20
1903	7cr. "Protection of the air"	70	20
1904	7cr. "Protection of the soil"	70	20

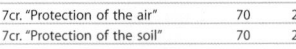

978 Curtiss Fledgling

1981. 50th Anniv of National Air Mail Service.

1905	**978**	7cr. multicoloured	1·00	45

979 Locomotive *Colonel Church* and Map of Railway

1981. 50th Anniv of Madeira–Mamore Railway Nationalization.

1906	**979**	7cr. multicoloured	1·40	55

980 Esperanto Star and Arches of Alvorada Governmental Palace, Brasilia

1981. 66th World Esperanto Congress, Brasilia.

1907	**980**	7cr. green, grey & black	45	20

981 Pedro II and 50r. "Small Head" Stamp

1981. Centenary of Pedro II "Small Head" Stamps.

1908	**981**	50cr. brown, blk & bl	2·75	55
1909	-	55cr. mauve and green	2·75	55
1910	-	60cr. blue, black & orge	2·75	55

DESIGNS: 55cr. Pedro II and 100r. "Small Head" stamp; 60r. Pedro II and 200r. "Small Head" stamp.

982 Military Institute of Engineering

1981. 50th Anniv of Military Institute of Engineering.

1911	**982**	12cr. multicoloured	45	30

983 Caboclinhos Folkdance

1981. Festivities. Multicoloured.

1912	50cr. Type **983**	1·90	55
1913	55cr. Marujada folk festival	1·90	55
1914	60cr. Resado parade	1·90	55

984 Sun and Erect, Drooping, and Supported Flowers

1981. International Year of Disabled Persons.

1915	**984**	12cr. multicoloured	45	10

985 *Dalechampia capero-niodes*

1981. Flowers of the Central Plateau. Multicoloured.

1916	12cr. Type **985**	1·10	45

1917 12cr. *Palicourea rigida* 1·10 45
1918 12cr. *Eremanthus sphaerocephalus* (vert) 1·10 45
1919 12cr. *Cassia clausseni* (vert) 1·10 45

986 Image of Our Lady of Nazareth

1981. Festival of Our Lady of Nazareth, Belem.
1920 **986** 12cr. multicoloured 45 30

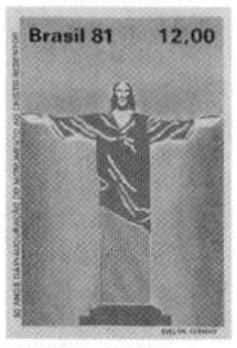

987 Christ the Redeemer Monument

1981. 50th Anniv of Christ the Redeemer Monument, Rio de Janeiro.
1921 **987** 12cr. multicoloured 45 30

988 Farmhands seeding the Land

1981. World Food Day.
1922 **988** 12cr. multicoloured 45 30

989 Santos Dumont and Biplane *14 bis* landing at Paris

1981. 75th Anniv of Santos Dumont's First Powered Flight.
1923 **989** 60cr. multicoloured 2·20 65

990 Friar Santos Rita Durao, Title Page and Scene from *Caramuru*

1981. Book Day and Bicentenary of Publication of Epic Poem *Caramuru*.
1924 **990** 12cr. multicoloured 45 30

991 Crib, Juazeiro de Norte (Cica)

1981. Christmas. Various designs showing Cribs. Multicoloured.
1925 12cr. Type **991** 45 30
1926 50cr. Caruaru (Vitalino Filho) 2·75 45
1927 55cr. Sao Jose dos Campos (Eugenia) (vert) 2·75 45
1928 60cr. Taubate (Candida) (vert) 2·75 55

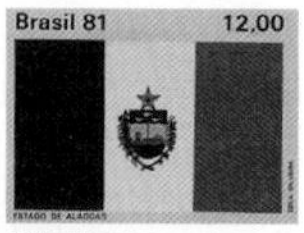

992 Alagoas

1981. State Flags (1st series). Multicoloured.
1929 12cr. Type **992** 55 55
1930 12cr. Bahia 55 55
1931 12cr. Federal District 55 55
1932 12cr. Pernambuco 55 55
1933 12cr. Sergipe 55 55

See also Nos. 1988/92, 2051/5, 2113/17, 2204/7 and 3043/4.

993 Girls with Wheat

1981. Thanksgiving Day.
1934 **993** 12cr. multicoloured 45 30

994 Heads and Symbols of Occupations

1981. 50th Anniv of Ministry of Labour.
1935 **994** 12cr. multicoloured 55 30

995 Federal Engineering School, Itajuba

1981. Birth Centenary of Theodomiro Carneiro Santiago (founder of Federal Engineering School).
1936 **995** 15cr. green and mauve 90 45

996 Musician of Police Military Band and Headquarters

1981. 150th Anniv of Sao Paulo Military Police. Multicoloured.
1937 12cr. Type **996** 45 10
1938 12cr. Lancers of Ninth of July Regiment, Mounted Police 45 10

997 Army Library "Ex Libris"

1981. Centenary of Army Library.
1939 **997** 12cr. multicoloured 45 30

998 Envelope and "Bull's Eye" Stamp

1981. 50th Anniv of Philatelic Club of Brazil. Sheet 89×69 mm.
MS1940 **998** 180cr. bistre, blue and black 9·75 9·75

999 Brigadier Eduardo Gomes

1982. Brigadier Eduardo Gomes Commem.
1941 **999** 12cr. blue and black 70 45

1000 Lage, Coal Trucks, *Ita* freighter and HL-1 Airplane

1981. Birth Cent of Henrique Lage (industrialist).
1942 **1000** 17cr. multicoloured 1·60 45

1001 Tackle

1982. World Cup Football Championship, Spain. Multicoloured.
1943 75cr. Type **1001** 2·30 65
1944 80cr. Kicking ball 2·30 65
1945 85cr. Goalkeeper 2·30 65
MS1946 125×87 mm. 100cr.×3. As Nos. 1943/5. Imperf 8·00 8·00

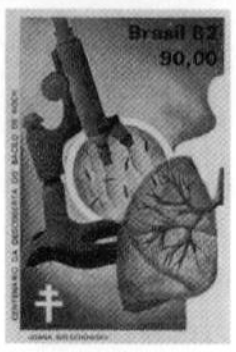

1002 Microscope, Bacillus and Lung

1982. Centenary of Robert Koch's Discovery of Tubercle Bacillus. Multicoloured.
1947 90cr. Type **1002** 5·25 1·90
1948 100cr. Flasks, tablets, syringe, bacillus and lung 5·25 1·90

1003 *Laelia purpurata*

1982. Brapex V National Stamp Exhibition, Santa Catarina. Sheet 100×70 mm containing T **1003** and similar vert designs showing orchids. Multicoloured.
MS1949 75cr. Type **1003**; 80cr. *Oncidium flexuosum*; 85cr. *Cleistes revolute* 13·50 13·50

1004 Oil Rig Workers

1982. Birth Centenary of Monteiro Lobato (writer).
1950 **1004** 17cr. multicoloured 55 30

1005 St. Vincent de Paul

1982. 400th Birth Anniv of St. Vincent de Paul.
1951 **1005** 17cr. multicoloured 55 30

1006 Fifth Fall

1982. Guaira's Seven Falls. Multicoloured.
1952 17cr. Type **1006** 55 30
1953 21cr. Seventh fall 70 45

1007 Envelope, Telephone, Antenna and Postcode

1982. 15th Anniv of Ministry of Communications.
1954 **1007** 21cr. multicoloured 65 35

1008 The Old Arsenal (National Historical Museum)

1982. 50th Anniv of Museology Course.
1955 **1008** 17cr. black and pink 65 35

1009 Cogwheels and Ore Mountains

1982. 40th Anniv of Vale do Rio Doce Company.
1956 **1009** 17cr. multicoloured 65 35

1010 Martim Afonso de Souza proclaiming Sao Vicente a Town

1982. 450th Anniv of Sao Vicente.
1957 **1010** 17cr. multicoloured 70 45

1011 Giant Anteater

1982. Animals. Multicoloured.
1958 17cr. Type **1011** 1·30 45
1959 21cr. Maned wolf 1·40 50
1960 30cr. Pampas deer 3·75 55

1012 Film and "Golden Palm"

1982. 20th Anniv of "Golden Palm" Film Award to "The Given World".
1961 **1012** 17cr. multicoloured 55 30

1013 Obelisk with Reliefs illustrating Verses by Guilherme de Almeida

1982. 50th Anniv of Sao Paulo Revolutionary Government. Sheet 70×100 mm.
MS1962 **1013** 140cr. black and blue 5·25 5·25

1014 Church of Our Lady of O, Sabara

1982. Baroque-style Architecture in Minas Gerais. Multicoloured.
1963 17cr. Type **1014** 90 20
1964 17cr. Church of Our Lady of Carmo, Mariana (horiz) 90 20
1965 17cr. Church of Our Lady of Rosary, Diamantina (horiz) 90 20

1015 St. Francis of Assisi

1982. 800th Birth Anniv of St. Francis of Assisi.

1966	**1015**	21cr. multicoloured	55	30

1016 "Large Head" Stamp of 1882

1982. Centenary of Pedro II "Large Head" Stamps.

1967	**1016**	21cr. yellow, brn & blk	55	30

1017 Amazon River and Hands holding Seedling, Screw and Coin

1982. Manaus Free Trade Zone.

1968	**1017**	75cr. multicoloured	2·10	65

1018 Lord Baden-Powell

1982. 125th Birth Anniv of Lord Baden Powell and 75th Anniv of Boy Scout Movement. Sheet 100×70 mm containing T **1018** and similar vert design. Multicoloured.

MS1969 85cr. Type **1018**; 185cr. Scout saluting 10·50 10·50

1019 Xango

1982. Orixas Religious Costumes. Multicoloured.

1970	20cr. Type **1019**	50	10
1971	20cr. Iemanja	50	10
1972	20cr. Oxumare	50	10

1020 XII Florin

1982. Tenth Anniv of Brazilian Central Bank Values Museum. Multicoloured.

1973	25cr. Type **1020**	55	30
1974	25cr. Pedro I Coronation piece	55	30

1021 *Ipiranga Cry* (Dom Pedro proclaiming independence)

1982. Independence Week.

1975	**1021**	25cr. multicoloured	90	55

1022 St. Theresa of Jesus

1982. 400th Death Anniv of St. Theresa of Jesus.

1976	**1022**	85cr. multicoloured	2·40	55

1023 Musical Instrument Maker

1982. Lubrapex 82 Brazilian–Portuguese Stamp Exhibition, Curitiba. The Paranaense Fandango. Multicoloured.

1977	75cr. Type **1023**	2·00	1·10
1978	80cr. Dancers	2·00	1·10
1979	85cr. Musicians	2·00	1·10
MS1980	100×70 mm. Nos. 1977/9	8·00	8·00

1024 Embraer Tucano Trainers

1982. Aeronautical Industry Day.

1981	**1024**	24cr. multicoloured	55	25

1025 Bastos Tigre and Verse from *Saudade*

1982. Day of the Book and Birth Centenary of Bastos Tigre (poet).

1982	**1025**	24cr. multicoloured	55	30

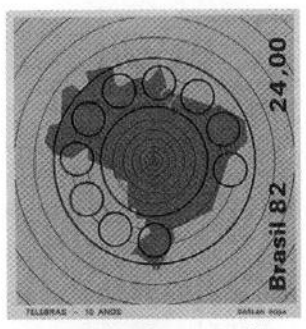

1026 Telephone Dial on Map of Brazil

1982. TEnth Anniv of Telebras (Brazilian Telecommunications Corporation).

1983	**1026**	24cr. multicoloured	55	30

1027 *Nativity* (C.S. Miyaba)

1982. Christmas. Children's Paintings. Multicoloured.

1984	24cr. Type **1027**	2·10	10
1985	24cr. *Choir of Angels* (N. N. Aleluia)	2·10	10
1986	30cr. *Holy Family* (F. T. Filho)	2·10	20
1987	30cr. *"ativity with Angel* (N. Arand)	2·10	20

1982. State Flags (2nd series). As T **992**. Multicoloured.

1988	24cr. Ceara	2·30	65
1989	24cr. Espirito Santo	2·30	65
1990	24cr. Paraiba	2·30	65
1991	24cr. Rio Grande do Norte	2·30	65
1992	24cr. Rondonia	2·30	65

1028 "Germination"

1982. Thanksgiving Day.

1993	**1028**	24cr. multicoloured	90	20

1029 *Efeta* (S. Tempel)

1982. The Hard of Hearing.

1994	**1029**	24cr. multicoloured	70	45

1030 *Benjamin Constant* (cadet ship)

1982. Bicentenary of Naval Academy. Multicoloured.

1995	24cr. Type **1030**	1·10	45
1996	24cr. *Almirante Saldanha* (cadet ship)	1·10	45
1997	24cr. *Brasil* (training frigate)	1·10	45

1031 300r. Stamp of 1845

1982. Brasiliana 83 International Stamp Exhibition, Rio de Janeiro (1st issue). Sheet 99×69 mm.

MS1998 **1031** 200cr. black, ochre and blue 8·50 8·50

See Also Nos. 1999/2002, 2029/**MS**2032 and **MS**2033.

1032 Samba Parade Drummers

1983. Brasiliana 83 International Stamp Exhibition, Rio de Janeiro. Carnival. Multicoloured.

1999	24cr. Type **1032**	1·10	45
2000	130cr. Masked clowns	4·00	1·10
2001	140cr. Dancer	4·00	1·10
2002	150cr. Indian	4·00	1·10

1033 Support Ship *Barao de Teffe* in Antarctic

1983. First Brazilian Antarctic Expedition.

2003	**1033**	150cr. multicoloured	4·50	1·20

1034 Woman with Ballot Paper

1983. 50th Anniv of Women's Suffrage in Brazil.

2004	**1034**	130cr. multicoloured	2·75	95

1035 Itaipu Dam

1983. Itaipu Brazilian–Paraguayan Hydro-electric Project.

2005	**1035**	140cr. multicoloured	4·50	85

1036 Luther

1983. 500th Birth Anniv of Martin Luther (Protestant reformer).

2006	**1036**	150cr. deep green, green and black	3·50	65

1037 Microscope and Crab

1983. Cancer Prevention. 30th Anniv of Antonio Prudente Foundation and A.C. Camargo Hospital. Multicoloured.

2007	30cr. Type **1037**	50	45
2008	38cr. Antonio Prudente, hospital and crab	50	45

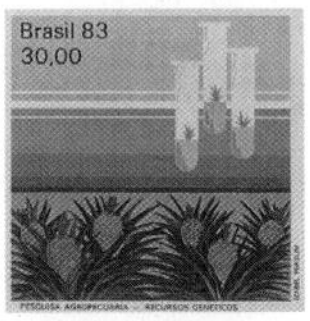

1038 Tissue Culture

1983. Agricultural Research. Multicoloured.

2009	30cr. Type **1038**	50	10
2010	30cr. Brazilian wild chestnut tree	50	10
2011	38cr. Tropical soya beans	55	15

1039 Friar Rogerio Neuhaus before Altar

1983. Cent of Ordination of Friar Rogerio Neuhaus.

2012	**1039**	30cr. multicoloured	50	10

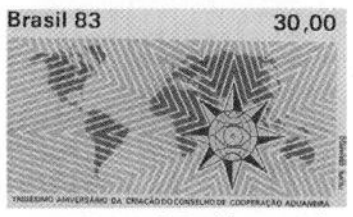

1040 Council Emblem and World Map

1983. 30th Anniv of Customs Co-operation Council.

2013	**1040**	30cr. multicoloured	50	10

1041 Satellite

1983. World Communications Year.

2014	**1041**	250cr. multicoloured	4·75	1·40

1042 Toco Toucan

1983. Toucans. Multicoloured.

2015	30cr. Type **1042**	1·10	35
2016	185cr. Red-billed toucan	4·00	1·10
2017	205cr. Red-breasted toucan	4·25	1·20
2018	215cr. Channel-billed toucan	4·50	1·30

1043 *The Resurrection*

1983. 500th Birth Anniv of Raphael (artist). Sheet 70×90 mm.

MS2019 **1043** 250cr. multicoloured 6·75 7·00

1044 Baldwin Locomotive No. 1, 1881

1983. Locomotives. Multicoloured.

2020	30cr. Type **1044**	95	55
2021	30cr. Hohenzollern locomotive No. 980, 1875	95	55
2022	38cr. Locomotive No. 1 *Maria Fumaca*, 1868	95	55

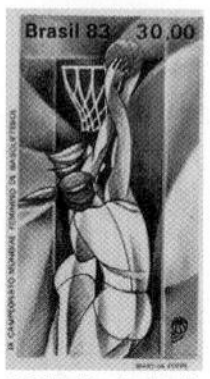
1045 Basketball Players

1983. Ninth Women's World Basketball Championship, Sao Paulo.

2023	30cr. Type **1045**	45	10
2024	30cr. Basketball players (different)	45	10

1046 *Bolivar* (after Tito Salas)

1983. Birth Bicentenary of Simon Bolivar.

2025	**1046** 30cr. multicoloured	45	10

1047 Boy with Kite and Boy waiting for Polio Vaccination

1983. Polio and Measles Vaccination Campaign. Multicoloured.

2026	30cr. Type **1047**	50	20
2027	30cr. Girl on bicycle and girl receiving measles vaccination	50	20

1048 Minerva and Computer Punched Tape

1983. 20th Anniv of Post-graduate Master's Programmes in Engineering.

2028	**1048** 30cr. light brown, blue and brown	50	20

1049 30r. "Bulls Eye" Stamp and Rio de Janeiro Bay

1983. Brasiliana 83 International Stamp Exhibition, Rio de Janeiro. 140th Anniv of "Bull's Eye" Stamps.

2029	**1049** 185cr. black and blue	2·50	85
2030	- 205cr. black and blue	2·50	85
2031	- 215cr. black and violet	2·50	85
MS2032	100×70 mm. 185cr., 205cr., 215cr. each black and blue	20·00	21·00

DESIGNS: Nos. 2030/1, As Type **1049** but showing 60r. and 90r. "Bull's-Eye" stamp respectively; No. **MS**2032, "Bull's-Eye" stamp on each value as for Nos. 2029/31, and composite design of Rio de Janeiro Bay across the three.

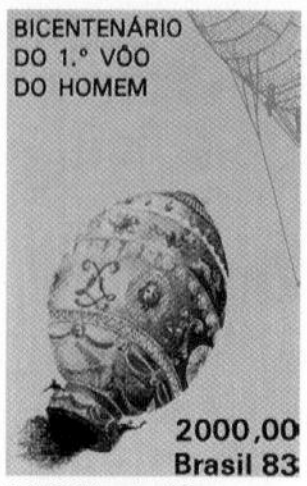
1050 Montgolfier Balloon

1983. Brasiliana 83 International Stamp Exhibition, Rio de Janeiro (4th issue). Five sheets 105×149 mm (a, d) or 149×105 mm (others), each containing design as T **1050**. Multicoloured.

MS2033	Five sheets (a) 2000cr. Type **1050** (Bicentenary of manned flight); (b) 2000cr. Racing car (Formula 1 champions 1972, 1974, 1981); (c) 2000cr. "Tornado" and "Class 470" sailing dinghies (Olympic sailing champion, 1980); (d) 2000cr. Triple jumper (Olympic triple jump champions, 1952, 1956); (e) 2000cr. World Cup and footballer (World Cup champions, 1958, 1962, 1970)	£225	£225

1051 *The First Mass in Brazil*

1983. 150th Birth Anniv (1982) of Victor Meireles (artist). Sheet 100×70 mm.

MS2034	**1051** 250cr. multicoloured	7·00	7·00

1052 Embracer EMB-120 Brasilia

1983. Brazilian Aeronautics Industry.

2035	**1052** 30cr. multicoloured	50	20

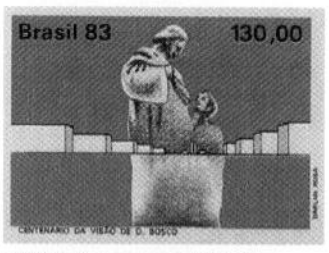
1053 Bosco and State Departments Esplanade, Brasilia

1983. Dom Bosco's Dream of Brazil.

2036	**1053** 130cr. multicoloured	1·60	45

1054 *Council of State decides on Independence* (detail, Georgina de Albuquerque)

1983. National Week.

2037	**1054** 50cr. multicoloured	75	35

1055 Iron and Steel Production

1983. Tenth Anniv of Siderbras (Brazilian Steel Corporation).

2038	**1055** 45cr. multicoloured	65	15

1056 *Pilosocereus gounellei*

1983. Cacti. Multicoloured.

2039	45cr. Type **1056**	1·30	35
2040	45cr. *Melocactus bahiensis*	1·30	35
2041	57cr. *Cereus jamacari*	1·50	35

1057 Monstrance

1983. 50th Anniv of National Eucharistic Congress.

2042	**1057** 45cr. multicoloured	1·00	35

1058 Mouth and Wheat

1983. 20th Anniv of World Food Programme. Fishery Resources. Multicoloured.

2043	45cr. Type **1058**	1·30	20
2044	57cr. Fish and fishing pirogue	2·50	45

1059 Telegraph Key and Praca da Republica, Rio de Janeiro

1983. Death Centenary of Louis Breguet (telegraph pioneer). Sheet 70×99 mm.

MS2045	**1059** 376cr. multicoloured	11·50	11·50

1060 *Our Lady of Angels* (wood, Franisco Xavier de Brito)

1983. Christmas. Statues of the Madonna. Multicoloured.

2046	45cr. Type **1060**	1·30	35
2047	315cr. *Our Lady of Birth*	3·50	1·20
2048	335cr. *Our Lady of Joy* (fired clay, Agostinho de Jesus)	3·50	1·30
2049	345cr. *Our Lady of Presentation*	3·50	1·40

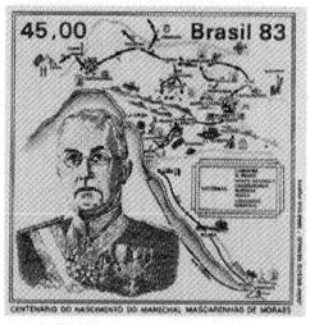
1061 Moraes and Map of Italian Campaign

1983. Birth Centenary of Marshal Mascarenhas de Moraes.

2050	**1061** 45cr. pink, green & pur	50	20

1983. State Flags (3rd series). As Type **992**. Multicoloured.

2051	45cr. Amazonas	1·00	55
2052	45cr. Goias	1·00	55
2053	45cr. Rio de Janeiro	1·00	55
2054	45cr. Mato Grosso do Sul	1·00	55
2055	45cr. Parana	1·00	55

1062 Praying Figure and Wheat

1983. Thanksgiving Day.

2056	**1062** 45cr. multicoloured	75	35

1063 Friar Vincente Borgard

1983. Obligatory Tax. Anti-leprosy Week.

2057	**1063** 10cr. brown	3·25	1·60

1064 Montgolfier Balloon

1983. Bicentenary of Manned Flight.

2058	**1064** 345cr. multicoloured	10·00	3·00

1065 Indian, Portuguese Navigator and Negro

1984. 50th Anniv of Publication of *Masters and Slaves* by Gilberto Freyre.

2059	**1065** 45cr. multicoloured	50	35

1066 Crystal Palace

1984. Centenary of Crystal Palace, Petropolis.

2060	**1066** 45cr. multicoloured	50	35

1067 *Monument of the Flags*, Sao Paulo

1984. 90th Birth Anniv of Victor Brecheret (sculptor). Sheet 100×70 mm.

MS2061	**1067** 805cr. multicoloured	4·50	4·50

1068 *Don Afonso* (sail/steam warship) and Figurehead

1984. Cent of Naval Oceanographic Museum.

2062	**1068** 620cr. multicoloured	3·25	1·10

1069 Manacled Hands and Beached Fishing Pirogue

1984. Centenary of Abolition of Slavery in Ceara and Amazonas. Multicoloured.

2063	585cr. Type **1069**	2·30	60
2064	610cr. Emancipated slave	2·40	65

1070 King Carl XVI Gustaf and Pres. Figueiredo

1984. Visit of King of Sweden. Sheet 98×69 mm.

MS2065	**1070** 2105cr. multicoloured	8·25	8·25

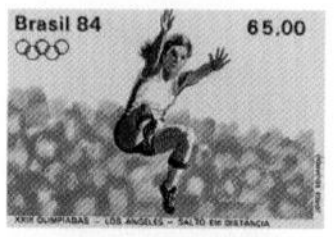
1071 Long Jumping

1984. Olympic Games, Los Angeles. Multicoloured.

2066	65cr. Type **1071**	1·30	45
2067	65cr. 100 metres	1·30	45
2068	65cr. Relay	1·30	45
2069	585cr. Pole vaulting	1·50	75
2070	610cr. High jumping	1·50	75
2071	620cr. Hurdling	1·50	75

1072 Oil Rigs and Blast Furnace

1984. Birth Cent (1983) of Getulio Vargas (President 1930–45 and 1951–54). Multicoloured.

2072	65cr. Type **1072**	50	10
2073	65cr. Ballot boxes and symbols of professions and trades	50	10
2074	65cr. Sugar refinery and electricity pylons	50	10

1073 Pedro Alvares Cabral

1984. Espana 84 International Stamp Exhibition, Madrid. Explorers. Multicoloured.

2075	65cr. Type **1073**	75	20
2076	610cr. Christopher Columbus	3·25	65

1074 Heads and Map of Americas

1984. Eighth Pan-American Surety Association General Assembly.

2077	**1074**	65cr. multicoloured	50	35

1075 Chinese Painting

1984. Lubrapex 84 Brazilian-Portuguese Stamp Exhibition, Lisbon.

2078	**1075**	65cr. multicoloured	50	35
2079	-	585cr. multicoloured	2·00	75
2080	-	610cr. multicoloured	2·10	1·00
2081	-	620cr. multicoloured	2·30	1·00

DESIGNS: 585 to 620cr. Chinese paintings from Mariana Cathedral.

1076 FIFA Emblem

1984. 80th Anniv of International Federation of Football Associations. Sheet 98×68 mm.

MS2082 **1076**	2115cr. mult	7·50	7·50

1077 Marsh Deer and Great Egret

1984. Mato Grosso Flood Plain. Multicoloured.

2083	65cr. Type **1077**	1·30	45
2084	65cr. Jaguar, capybara and rose-ate spoonbill	1·30	45
2085	80cr. Alligator, jabiru and red-cowled cardinals	1·40	55

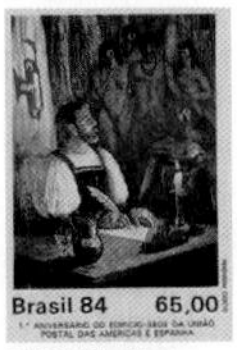

1078 *The First Letter Sent from Brazil* (Guido Mondin)

1984. First Anniv of Postal Union of the Americas and Spain H.Q., Montevideo, Uruguay.

2086	**1078**	65cr. multicoloured	50	20

1079 Route Map and Dornier Wal Flying Boat

1984. 50th Anniv of First Trans-Oceanic Air Route. Multicoloured.

2087	610cr. Type **1079**	2·50	1·00
2088	620cr. Support ship "Westfalen" and Dornier Wal	2·75	1·10

1080 Mother and Baby

1984. Wildlife Preservation. Woolley Spider Monkey. Multicoloured.

2089	65cr. Type **1080**	2·50	75
2090	80cr. Monkey in tree	1·90	75

1081 Murrah Buffaloes

1984. Marajo Island Water Buffaloes. Designs showing different races. Multicoloured.

2091	65cr. Type **1081**	1·30	35
2092	65cr. Carabao buffaloes	1·30	35
2093	65cr. Mediterranean buffaloes	1·30	35

Nos. 2091/3 were issued together, *se-tenant*, forming a composite design.

1082 Headquarters, Salvador

1984. 150th Anniv of Economic Bank.

2094	**1082**	65cr. multicoloured	25	10

1083 Da Luz Station, Sao Paulo

1984. Preservation of Historic Railway Stations. Multicoloured.

2095	65cr. Type **1083**	1·30	35
2096	65cr. Japeri station Rio de Janeiro	1·30	35
2097	80cr. Sao Joao del Rei station, Minas Gerais	1·30	35

1084 Girl Guide

1984. 65th Anniv of Girl Guides Movement in Brazil. Sheet 99×69 mm.

MS2098 **1084**	585cr. multicoloured	6·25	6·25

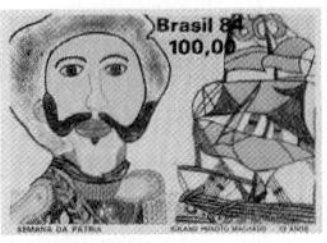

1086 *Pedro I* (Solano Peixoto Machado)

1984. 20th Anniv of National Housing Bank.

2099	**1085**	65cr. multicoloured	50	20

1085 Roof protecting Couple

1984. National Week. Designs showing children's paintings. Multicoloured.

2100	100cr. Type **1086**	40	10
2101	100cr. Girl painting word "BRASIL" (Juruce Maria Klein)	40	10
2102	100cr. Children of different races under rainbow (Priscela Barreto da Fonseca Bara)	40	10
2103	100cr. Caravels (Carlos Peixoto Mangueira)	40	10

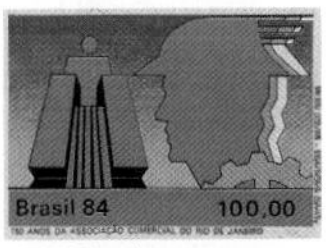

1087 Headquarters, Mercury and Cogwheel

1984. 150th Anniv of Rio de Janeiro Commercial Association.

2104	**1087**	100cr. multicoloured	50	20

1088 Pedro I

1984. 150th Death Anniv of Emperor Pedro I.

2105	**1088**	1000cr. multicoloured	4·50	2·40

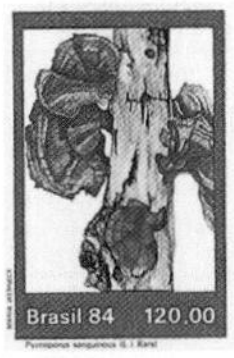

1089 *Pycnoporus sanguineus*

1984. Fungi. Multicoloured.

2106	120cr. Type **1089**	75	30
2107	1050cr. *Calvatia* sp.	3·25	1·00
2108	1080cr. *Pleurotus* sp. (horiz)	3·25	1·00

1090 Child stepping from Open Book

1984. Book Day. Children's Literature.

2109	**1090**	120cr. multicoloured	65	10

1091 New State Mint and 17th-century Minter

1984. Inauguration of New State Mint, Santa Cruz, Rio de Janeiro.

2110	**1091**	120cr. blue & deep blue	65	10

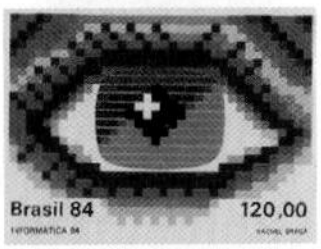

1092 Computer Image of Eye

1984. Informatica 84 17th National Information Congress and Fourth International Informatics Fair, Rio de Janeiro.

2111	**1092**	120cr. multicoloured	65	10

1093 Sculpture by Bruno Giorgi and Flags

1984. 14th General Assembly of Organization of American States, Brasilia.

2112	**1093**	120cr. multicoloured	65	10

1984. State Flags (4th series). As T **992**.

2113	120cr. red, black & buff	1·00	65
2114	120cr. multicoloured	1·00	65
2115	120cr. multicoloured	1·00	65
2116	120cr. multicoloured	1·00	65
2117	120cr. multicoloured	1·00	65

DESIGNS: No. 2113, Minas Gerais; 2114, Mato Grosso; 2115, Piaui; 2116, Maranhao; 2117, Santa Catarina.

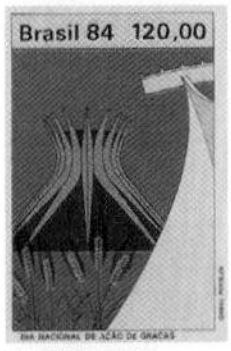

1094 Brasilia Cathedral and Wheat

1984. Thanksgiving Day.

2118	**1094**	120cr. multicoloured	65	10

1095 Father Bento Dias Pacheco

1984. Obligatory Tax. Anti-leprosy Week.

2119	**1095**	30cr. blue	75	35

See also Nos. 2208, 2263 and 2291.

1096 *Nativity* (Djanira da Mota e Silva)

1984. Christmas. Paintings from Federal Savings Bank collection. Multicoloured.

2120	120cr. Type **1096**	45	20
2121	120cr. *Virgin and Child* (Glauco Rodrigues)	45	20
2122	1050cr. *Flight into Egypt* (Paul Garfunkel)	2·50	75
2123	1080cr. *Nativity* (Emiliano Augusto di Cavalcanti)	2·50	75

1097 Airbus Industrie A300

1984. 40th Anniv of I.C.A.O.

2124	**1097**	120cr. multicoloured	65	20

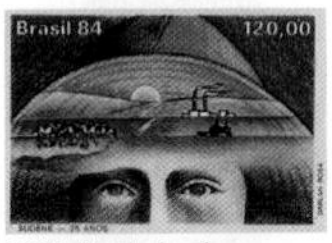

1098 Symbols of Agriculture and Industry on Hat

1984. 25th Anniv of North-east Development Office.

2125	**1098**	120cr. multicoloured	50	20

1099 *Virgin of Safe Journeys Church* (detail)

1985. 77th Death Anniv of Emilio Rouede (artist).
2126 **1099** 120cr. multicoloured 50 20

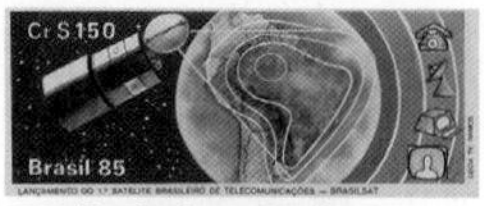

1100 "Brasilsat" over Brazil

1985. Launch of "Brasilsat" (first Brazilian telecommunications satellite).
2127 **1100** 150cr. multicoloured 50 20

1101 Electric Trains and Plan of Port Alegre Station

1985. Inauguration of Metropolitan Surface Railway, Recife and Porto Alegre.
2128 **1101** 200cr. multicoloured 1·30 35

1102 Butternut Tree

1985. Opening of Botanical Gardens, Brasilia.
2129 **1102** 200cr. multicoloured 75 10

1103 Parachutist

1985. 40th Anniv of Military Parachuting.
2130 **1103** 200cr. multicoloured 75 10

1104 Map, Temperature Graph and Weather Scenes

1985. National Climate Programme.
2131 **1104** 500cr. multicoloured 80 20

1105 Campolina

1985. Brazilian Horses. Multicoloured.
2132 1000cr. Type **1105** 2·10 55
2133 1500cr. Marajoara 2·75 65
2134 1500cr. Mangalarga pacer 2·75 65

1106 Ouro Preto

1985. UNESCO World Heritage Sites. Multicoloured.
2135 220cr. Type **1106** 40 10
2136 220cr. Sao Miguel das Missoes 40 10
2137 220cr. Olinda 40 10

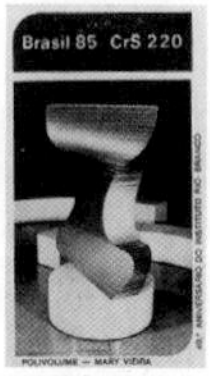

1107
Polyvolume
(Mary Vieira)

1985. 40th Anniv of Rio-Branco Institute (diplomatic training academy).
2138 **1107** 220cr. multicoloured 50 10

1108 National Theatre

1985. 25th Anniv of Brasilia. Multicoloured.
2139 220cr. Type **1108** 50 10
2140 220cr. Catetinho (home of former President Juscelino Keubitschek) and memorial 50 10

1109 Rondon and Morse Telegraph

1985. 120th Birth Anniv of Marshal Candido Mariano da Silva Rondon (military engineer and explorer).
2141 **1109** 220cr. multicoloured 50 10

1110 Fontoura and Pharmaceutical Equipment

1985. Birth Centenary of Candido Fontoura (pharmacist).
2142 **1110** 220cr. multicoloured 50 10

1111 Lizards

1985. Rock Paintings. Multicoloured.
2143 300cr. Type **1111** 40 20
2144 300cr. Deer 40 20
2145 2000cr. Various animals 1·80 1·00
MS2146 100×70 mm. Nos. 2143/5 4·00 4·00

Nos. **MS**2146 is inscribed for Brapex VI national stamp exhibition, Belo Horizonte.

1112 Numeral

1113 Numeral

1985
2147 **1112** 50cr. red 30 10
2148 **1112** 100cr. purple 30 10
2149 **1112** 150cr. lilac 30 10
2150 **1112** 200cr. blue 30 10
2151 **1112** 220cr. green 1·10 55
2152 **1112** 300cr. blue 30 10
2153 **1112** 500cr. black 40 20
2154 **1113** 1000cr. brown 30 10
2155 **1113** 2000cr. green 40 20
2156 **1113** 3000cr. lilac 45 20
2157 **1113** 5000cr. brown 2·20 20

1114 Common Noddies

1985. National Marine Park, Abrolhos. Multicolored.
2168 220cr. Type **1114** 1·20 40
2169 220cr. Magnificent frigate birds and blue-faced booby 1·20 40
2170 220cr. Blue-faced boobies and red-billed tropic bird 1·20 40
2171 2000cr. Grey plovers 3·50 75

1115
Breast-feeding

1985. United Nations Children's Fund Child Survival Campaign. Multicoloured.
2172 220cr. Type **1115** 35 15
2173 220cr. Growth chart and oral rehydration 35 15

1116 Bell 47J Ranger Helicopter rescuing Man, *Brasil* (corvette) and Diver

1985. International Sea Search and Rescue Convention, Rio de Janeiro.
2174 **1116** 220cr. multicoloured 60 40

1117 World Cup and Ball

1985. World Cup Football Championship, Mexico (1986) (1st issue). Sheet 70×99 mm.
MS2175 **1117** 2000cr. mult 8·25 8·25

See also No.**MS**2213.

1118 Children holding Hands

1985. International Youth Year.
2176 **1118** 220cr. multicoloured 45 25

1119 Hands holding Host

1985. 11th Nat Eucharistic Congress, Aparecida.
2177 **1119** 2000cr. multicoloured 1·70 75

1120 Scene from *Mineiro Blood*, Camera and Mauro

1985. 60th Anniv of Humberto Mauro's Cataguases Cycle of Films.
2178 **1120** 300cr. multicoloured 45 25

1121 Escola e Sacro Museum

1985. 400th Anniv of Paraiba State.
2179 **1121** 330cr. multicoloured 45 25

1122
Inconfidencia Museum, Ouro Preto

1985. Museums. Multicoloured.
2180 300cr. Type **1122** 35 15
2181 300cr. Historical and Diplomatic Museum Itamaraty 35 15

1123 *Cabano*
(Guido Mondin)

1985. 150th Anniv of Cabanagem Insurrection, Belem City.
2182 **1123** 330cr. multicoloured 45 25

1124 Aeritalia/Aermacchi AM-X Fighter

1985. AM-X (military airplane) Project.
2183 **1124** 330cr. multicoloured 45 25

1125 Captain and Crossbowman (early 16th century)

1985. Military Dress. Multicoloured.
2184 300cr. Type **1125** 45 25
2185 300cr. Arquebusier and sergeant (late 16th cent) 45 25
2186 300cr. Musketeer and pikeman (early 17th century) 45 25
2187 300cr. Mulatto fusilier and pikeman with scimitar (early 17th century) 45 25

1126 *Farroupilha Rebels*
(Guido Mondin)

1985. 150th Anniv of Farroupilha Revolution.
2188 **1126** 330cr. multicoloured 45 25

1127 Itaimbezinho Canyon

1985. Aparados da Serra National Park. Multicoloured.
2189 3100cr. Type **1127** 2·00 55
2190 3320cr. Mountain range 2·00 55
2191 3480cr. Pine forest 2·00 55

1128 Neves and Brasilia Buildings

1985. Tancredo Neves (President-elect) Commem.
2192 **1128** 330cr. black & orange 45 25

1129 "FEB" on Envelope

1985. 40th Anniv (1984) of Brazilian Expeditionary Force Postal Service.
2193 **1129** 500cr. multicoloured 45 25

1130 *Especuladora*, 1835

1985. 150th Anniv of Rio de Janeiro–Niteroi Ferry Service. Multicoloured.

2194	500cr. Type **1130**	60	30
2195	500cr. *Segunda*, 1862	60	30
2196	500cr. *Terceira*, 1911	60	30
2197	500cr. *Urca*, 1981	60	30

1131 Muniz M-7

1985. 50th Anniv of Muniz M-7 Biplane's Maiden Flight.

2198	**1131**	500cr. multicoloured	45	25

1132 Dove Emblem and Stylized Flags

1985. 40th Anniv of UNO.

2199	**1132**	500cr. multicoloured	45	25

1133 Front Page of First Edition

1985. 160th Anniv of *Pernambuco Daily News*.

2200	**1133**	500cr. multicoloured	45	25

1134 Adoration

1985. Christmas. Multicoloured.

2201	500cr. Type **1134**	45	25
2202	500cr. Adoration of the Magi	45	25
2203	500cr. Flight into Egypt	45	25

1985. State Flags (5th series). As T **992**. Multicoloured.

2204	500cr. Para	55	25
2205	500cr. Rio Grande do Sul	55	25
2206	500cr. Acre	55	25
2207	500cr. Sao Paulo	55	25

1985. Obligatory Tax. Anti-leprosy Week.

2208	**1095**	100cr. red	55	35

1135 Child holding Wheat

1985. Thanksgiving Day.

2209	**1135**	500cr. multicoloured	45	25

1136 Transport, Mined Ore and Trees

1985. Carajas Development Programme.

2210	**1136**	500cr. multicoloured	45	25

1137 Gusmao and Balloons

1985. 300th Birth Anniv of Bartolomeu Lourenco de Gusmao (inventor).

2211	**1137**	500cr. multicoloured	45	25

1138 *The Trees*

1985. Birth Centenary of Antonio Francisco da Costa e Silva (poet).

2212	**1138**	500cr. multicoloured	45	25

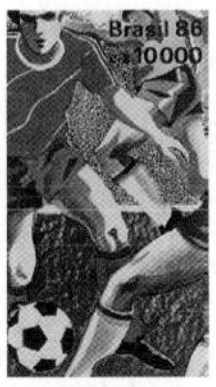

1139 Footballers

1986. World Cup Football Championship, Mexico (2nd issue) and Lubrepex 86 Brazilian—Portuguese Stamp Exhibition, Rio de Janeiro (1st issue). Sheet 69×99 mm.

MS2213	**1139**	10000cr. multicoloured	6·00	6·00

See also Nos. 2260/**MS**2262.

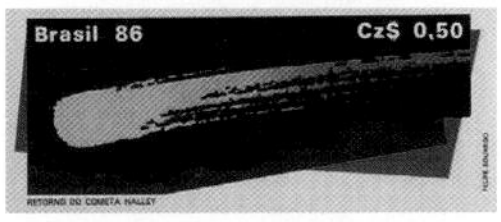

1140 Comet

1986. Appearance of Halley's Comet.

2214	**1140**	50c. multicoloured	45	25

1141 Flags and Station

1986. Second Anniv of Commander Ferraz Antarctic Station.

2215	**1141**	50c. multicoloured	45	25

1142 Symbols of Industry, Agriculture and Commerce

1986. Labour Day.

2216	**1142**	50c. multicoloured	45	25

1143 *Maternity*

1986. 50th Death Anniv of Henrique Bernardelli (artist).

2217	**1143**	50c. multicoloured	45	25

1144 Broken Chain Links as Birds

1986. 25th Anniv of Amnesty International.

2218	**1144**	50c. multicoloured	45	25

1145 *Pyrrhopyge ruficauda*

1986. Butterflies. Multicoloured.

2219	50c. Type **1145**	85	35
2220	50c. *Pierriballia mandela molione*	85	35
2221	50c. *Prepona eugenes diluta*	85	35

1146 Gomes Peri, and Score of *O Guarani*

1986. 150th Birth Anniv of Antonio Carlos Gomes (composer).

2222	**1146**	50c. multicoloured	45	25

1147 Man in Safety Harness

1986. Prevention of Industrial Accidents.

2223	**1147**	50c. multicoloured	45	25

1148 "Black Beard" 10r. Stamp

1986. Stamp Day. 120th Anniv of Pedro II Black Beard Stamps and 75th Anniv of Brazilian Philatelic Society. Sheet 69×99 mm.

MS2224	**1148**	5cz. red and ochre	2·00	2·00

1149 Garcia D'Avilas House Chapel, Nazare de Mata

1986

2225	**1149**	10c. green	35	10
2226	-	20c. blue	35	10
2228	-	50c. orange	1·10	25
2230	-	1cz. brown	35	10
2231	-	2cz. red	45	10
2233	-	5cz. green	1·30	25
2235	-	10cz. blue	1·10	25
2236	-	20cz. red	1·50	25
2238	-	50cz. orange	2·75	25
2240	-	100cz. green	2·75	25
2241	-	200cz. blue	2·75	25
2242	-	500cz. brown	3·50	80

DESIGNS—HORIZ: 20c. Church of Our Lady of the Assumptiom, Anchieta; 50c. Reis Magos Fortress, Natal; 1cz. Pelourinho, Alcantara; 2cz. St. Francis's Monastery, Olinda; 5cz. St. Anthony's Chapel, Sao Roque; 10cz. St Lawrence of the Indians Church, Niteroi; 20cz. Principe da Beira Fortress, Costa Marques, Rondobua; 100cz. Church of Our Lady of Sorrows, Campanha; 200cz. Counting House, Ouro Preto; 500cz. Customs building, Belem. VERT: 50cz. Church of the Good Jesus, Matasinhos.

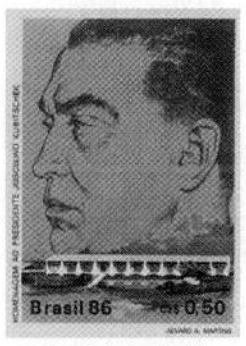

1150 Kubitschek and Alvorada Palace

1986. Tenth Death Anniv of Juscelino Kubitschek (President 1956–61).

2244	**1150**	50c. multicoloured	45	25

1151 Mangabeira and Itamaraty Palace, Rio de Janeiro

1986. Birth Cent of Octavio Mangabeira (politician).

2245	**1151**	50c. multicoloured	45	25

1152 Congress Emblem and Sao Paulo

1986. Eighth World Gastroenterology Congress, Sao Paulo.

2246	**1152**	50c. multicoloured	45	25

1153 Microphone and Radio Waves

1986. 50th Annivs. of National Radio and Education and Culture Ministry Radio.

2247	**1153**	50c. multicoloured	45	25

1154 *Peace* (detail, Candido Portinari)

1986. International Peace Year.

2248	**1154**	50c. multicoloured	45	25

1155 *Urera mitis*

1986. Flowers. Multicoloured.

2249	50c. Type **1155**	35	15
2250	6cz.50 *Couroupita guyanensis*	1·70	45
2251	6cz.90 Mountain ebony (horiz)	1·80	45

1156 Simoes Filho and Newspaper

1986. Birth Centenary of Ernesto Simoes Filho (politician and founder of *A Tarde*).

2252	**1156**	50c. multicoloured	45	25

1157 Title Page of Gregorio de Matto's MS

1986. Book Day. Poets' Birth Anniversaries.

2253	**1157**	50c. brown & lt brown	45	25
2254	-	50c. green and red	45	25

DESIGNS: No. 2253, Type **1157** (350th anniv); 2254, Manuel Bandeira and last verse of *I'll Return to Pasargada* (centenary).

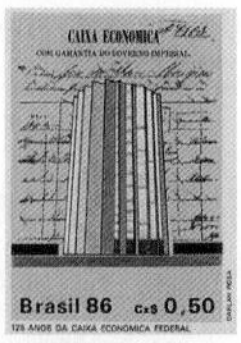

1158 Head Office, Brasilia

1986. 125th Anniv of Federal Savings Bank.
2255 **1158** 50c. multicoloured 45 25

1159 Birds around Baby lying in Nest

1986. Christmas. Multicoloured.
2256 50c. Type **1159** 60 25
2257 6cz.50 Birds around tree with Christmas decorations 2·20 55
2258 7cz.30 Birds wearing Santa Claus caps 2·20 70

1160 Rocha on Strip of Film

1986. Fifth Death Anniv of Glauber Rocha (film producer).
2259 **1160** 50c. multicoloured 45 25

1161 *History of Empress Porcina*

1986. Lubrapex 86 Brazilian–Portuguese Stamp Exhibition, Rio de Janeiro. Design showing scenes from Cordel Literature. Multicoloured.
2260 6cz.90 Type **1161** 1·40 70
2261 6cz.90 *Romance of the Mysterious Peacock* 1·40 70
MS2262 70×100 mm. Nos. 2260/2 4·25 4·25

1986. Obligatory Tax. Anti-leprosy Week.
2263 **1095** 10c. brown 35 25

1162 Lieutenant Commander, 1930

1986. Military Uniforms. Multicoloured.
2264 50c. Type **1162** 35 25
2265 50c. Military Aviation flight lieutenant, 1930 35 25

1163 *Graf Zeppelin* over Hangar

1986. 50th Anniv of Bartolomeu de Gusmao Airport, Santa Cruz.
2266 **1163** 1cz. multicoloured 45 35

1164 Museum

1987. 50th Anniv of National Fine Arts Museum, Rio de Janeiro.
2267 **1164** 1cz. multicoloured 45 35

1165 Villa-Lobos conducting and Musical Motifs

1987. Birth Cent of Heitor Villa-Lobos (composer).
2268 **1165** 1cz.50 multicoloured 55 35

1166 Flag, Lockheed C-130 Hercules Aircraft and Antarctic Landscape

1987. Air Force Participation in Brazilian Antarctic Programme.
2269 **1166** 1cz. multicoloured 95 25

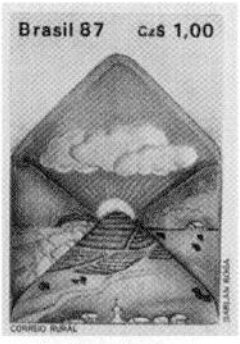

1167 Landscape on Open Envelope (Rural Post Office Network)

1987. Special Mail Services. Multicoloured.
2270 1cz. Type **1167** 45 35
2271 1cz. Satchel and globe (International Express Mail Service) 45 35

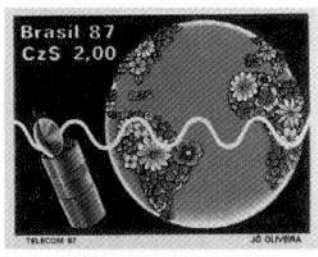

1168 "Brasilsat" Satellite, Radio Wave and Globe

1987. Telecom 87 World Telecommunications Exhibition, Geneva.
2272 **1168** 2cz. multicoloured 45 35

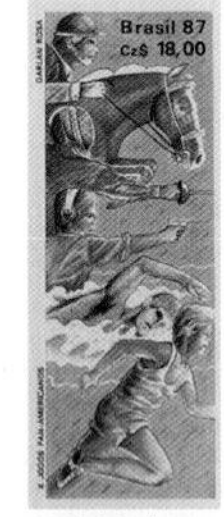

1169 Modern Pentathlon

1987. Tenth Pan-American Games, Indianapolis, U.S.A.
2273 **1169** 18cz. multicoloured 3·00 1·10

1170 Hawksbill Turtle

1987. Endangered Animals. Multicoloured.
2274 2cz. Type **1170** 85 45
2275 2cz. Right whale 85 45

1171 Old and New Court Buildings and Symbol of Justice

1987. 40th Anniv of Federal Appeal Court.
2276 **1171** 2cz. multicoloured 45 35

1172 Arms

1987. Centenary of Military Club.
2277 **1172** 3cz. multicoloured 60 35

1173 Institute and Foodstuffs

1987. Centenary of Agronomic Institute, Campinas.
2278 **1173** 2cz. multicoloured 45 35

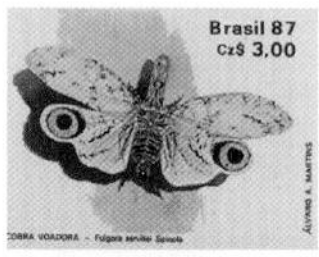

1174 *Fulgora servillei*

1987. 50th Anniv of Brazilian Entomology Society. Multicoloured.
2279 3cz. Type **1174** 85 35
2280 3cz. *Zoolea lopiceps* 85 35

1175 Features of Northern and North-east Regions

1987. National Tourism Year. Multicoloured.
2281 3cz. Type **1175** 45 35
2282 3cz. Features of mid-west, south-east and south regions 45 35

1176 Main Tower

1987. 150th Anniv of Royal Portuguese Reading Cabinet, Rio de Janeiro.
2283 **1176** 30cz. green and red 2·20 1·70

1177 International Sport Club (1975, 1976, 1979)

1987. Brazilian Football Championship Gold Cup Winners (1st series). Designs showing footballers and Club emblems.
2284 **1177** 3cz. red, black & yellow 45 25
2285 - 3cz. red, yellow & black 45 25
2286 - 3cz. multicoloured 45 25
2287 - 3cz. red, black & yellow 45 25

DESIGNS: No. 2285, Sao Paulo Football Club (1977, 1986); 2286, Guarani Football Club (1978); 2287, Regatas do Flamengo Club (1980, 1982, 1983).

See also Nos. 2322/5, 2398 and 2408.

1178 St. Francis's Church and Tiled Column

1987. 400th Anniv of St. Francis's Monastery, Salvador.
2288 **1178** 4cz. multicoloured 45 35

1179 Almeida and Scenes from *A Bagaceira*

1987. Birth Centenary of Jose Americo de Almeida (writer).
2289 **1179** 4cz. multicoloured 35 25

1180 Barra do Picao

1987. 450th Anniv of Recife.
2290 **1180** 5cz. multicoloured 35 10

1987. Obligatory Tax. Anti-leprosy Week.
2291 **1095** 30cz. green 35 25

1181 Rainbow, Dove and Open Hands

1987. Thanksgiving Day.
2292 **1181** 5cz. multicoloured 35 25

1182 Angels

1987. Christmas. Multicoloured.
2293 6cz. Type **1182** 45 35
2294 6cz. Dancers on stage 45 35
2295 6cz. Shepherd playing flute 45 35

1183 Bernardo Pereira de Vasconcelos (founder) and Pedro II

1987. 150th Anniv of Pedro II School, Rio de Janeiro.
2296 **1183** 6cz. yellow, blk & red 45 35

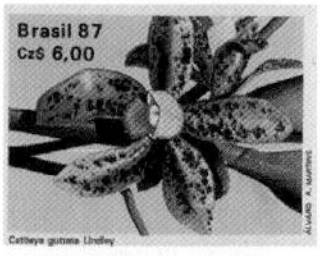

1184 *Cattleya guttata*

1987. 50th Anniv of Brazilian Orchid Growers Society. Multicoloured.
2297 6cz. Type **1184** 85 25
2298 6cz. *Laelia lobata* 85 25

1185 Statue and Fatima Basilica, Portugal

1987. Marian Year. Visit to Brazil of Statue of Our Lady of Fatima.
2299 **1185** 50cz. multicoloured 3·00 2·30

1186 Sousa, Indians and Fauna

1987. 400th Anniv of *Descriptive Treaties of Brazil* by Gabriel Soares de Sousa.
2300 **1186** 7cz. multicoloured 45 35

1187 Page from Book of Gregorian Chants and Computer Terminal

1988. 150th Anniv of National Archives.
2301 **1187** 7cz. multicoloured 45 35

1188 National Colours, Caravel and Modern Ship

1988. 180th Anniv of Opening of Brazilian Ports to Free Trade.
2302 **1188** 7cz. multicoloured 45 35

1189 Microscope and Map

1988. Antarctic Research. Sheet 99×69 mm.
MS2303 **1189** 80cz. multicoloured 4·25 4·25

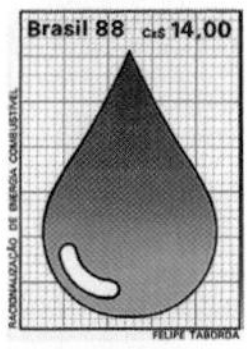

1190 Petrol Droplet

1988. Energy Conservation. Multicoloured.
2304 14cz. Type **1190** 45 35
2305 14cz. Flash of electricity 45 35

1191 Williams-Honda Racing Car and Flag

1988. Nelson Piquet's Third Formula 1 Motor Racing World Championship Title (1987). Sheet 99×69 mm.
MS2306 **1191** 300cz. multicoloured 9·50 9·50

1192 Bonifacio and Emblems of his Life

1988. 150th Death Anniv of Jose Bonifacio de Andrada e Silva (scientist, writer and *Patriarch of the Independence*).
2307 **1192** 20cz. multicoloured 60 45

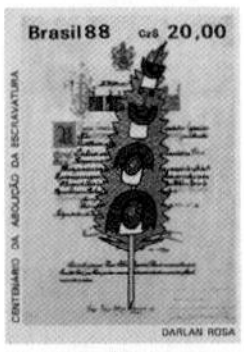

1193 Quill Pen on Page of Aurea Law

1988. Centenary of Abolition of Slavery. Multicoloured.
2308 20cz. Type **1193** 45 35
2309 50cz. Norris map of Africa, 1773, slave ship and plan of trading routes 1·30 1·00

1194 Church of the Good Jesus of Matosinhos

1988. UNESCO World Heritage Sites. Multicoloured.
2310 20cz. Type **1194** 45 35
2311 50cz. Brasilia 1·30 90
2312 100cz. Pelourinho, Salvador 2·40 1·80

1195 Concentric Circles on Map of Americas

1988. Americas Telecom 88 Telecommunications Exhibition, Rio de Janeiro.
2313 **1195** 50cz. multicoloured 1·90 90

1196 *Kasato Maru* (first immigrant ship) and Japanese Family

1988. 80th Anniv of Japanese Immigration into Brazil.
2314 **1196** 100cz. multicoloured 1·90 1·00

1197 Postal Authority Emblem

1988. No value expressed.
2315 **1197** (–) blue 1·40 25

No. 2315 was valid for use at the current first class inland letter rate. It could not be used to pay postage to foreign countries.

1198 Judo

1988. Olympic Games, Seoul.
2316 **1198** 20cz. multicoloured 1·10 25

1199 Giant Anteater

1988. Endangered Mammals. Multicoloured.
2317 20cz. Type **1199** 60 35
2318 50cz. Thin-spined porcupine 95 45
2319 100cz. Bush dog 2·00 1·10

1200 *Motherland* (Pedro Bruno)

1988. Stamp Day. Brasiliana 89 International Stamp Exhibition. Sheet 98×69 mm.
MS2320 **1200** 250cz. multicoloured 6·50 6·50

1201 Industrial Symbols

1988. 50th Anniv of National Confederation of Industry.
2321 **1201** 50cz. multicoloured 60 35

1988. Brazilian Football Championship Gold Cup Winners (2nd series). As T **1177**. Multicoloured.
2322 50cz. Sport Club do Recife (1987) 45 25
2323 50cz. Coritiba Football Club (1985) 45 25
2324 100cz. Gremio Football Porto Alegrense (1981) 70 35
2325 200cz. Fluminense Football Club (1984) 1·20 80

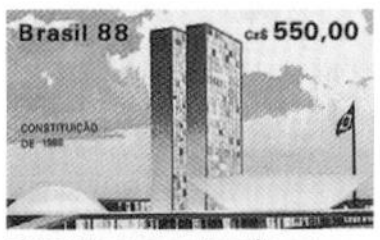

1202 Congress, Brasilia

1988. Promulgation of 1998 Consitution. Sheet 99×69 mm.
MS2326 **1202** 550cz. multicoloured 5·00 5·00

1203 Raul Pompeia and Lines from *O Ateneu*

1988. Book Day. Centenaries of Publication of *O Ateneu* and *Verses*. Multicoloured.
2327 50cz. Type **1203** 40 25
2328 100cz. Olavo Bilac and lines from "Verses" 55 30

1204 Church

1988. Christmas. Origami by Marcia Bloch. Multicoloured.
2329 50cz. Type **1204** 60 35
2330 100cz. Nativity 70 35
2331 200cz. Santa Claus and parcels 1·40 80

1205 Father Santiago Uchoa

1988. Obligatory Tax. Anti-leprosy Week.
2332 **1205** 1cz.30 brown 45 25

See also Nos. 2614 and 2686.

1206 Mate and Rodeo Rider

1988. Abrafex Argentine–Brazilian Stamp Exhibition, Buenos Aires.
2333 **1206** 400cz. multicoloured 3·00 1·00

1207 Hatchetfish (*Gasteropelecus* sp.)

1988. Freshwater Fish. Multicoloured.
2334 55cz. Type **1207** 35 35
2335 55cz. Black arawana (*Osteoglossum ferreira*) 35 35
2336 55cz. Green moenkhausia (*Moenkhausia* sp.) 35 35
2337 55cz. Pearlfish (*Xavantei*) 35 35
2338 55cz. Armoured bristlemouth catfish (*Ancistrus hoplogenys*) 35 35
2339 55cz. Emerald catfish (*Brochis splendens*) 35 35

1208 Red-tailed Amazon

1988. Brapex VII National Stamp Exhibition, Sao Paulo. Conservation of Jurelia. Sheet 99×68 mm containing T **1208** and similar vert designs. Multicoloured.
MS2340 100cz. Type **1208**; 250cz. "Vriesia ensiformis" (bromelia); 400cz. Great egret 17·00 17·00

1209 Dish Aerials

1988. Tenth Anniv of Ansat 10 (first Brazilian dish aerial), Macapa.
2341 **1209** 70cz. multicoloured 35 35

1210 "Four Arts"

1988. Establishment of National Foundation of Scenic Arts.
2342 **1210** 70cz. multicoloured 45 35

1211 Court Building

1989. 380th Anniv of Bahia Court of Justice.
2343 **1211** 25c. multicoloured 95 55

1212 Library Building and Detail of Main Door

1989. Public Library Year. 178th Anniv of First Public Library, Bahia.
2344 **1212** 25c. multicoloured 95 55

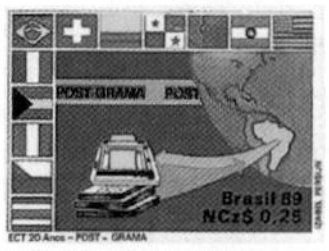

1213 Facsimile Machine

1989. 20th Anniv of Post and Telegraph Department. Postal Services. Multicoloured.
2345 25c. Type **1213** 85 55
2346 25c. Hand holding parcel (Express Mail Service) 85 55
2347 25c. Airbus Industrie 300 airplane on runway (SEDEX express parcel service) 85 55
2348 25c. Putting coin in savings box (CEF postal savings) 85 55

1214 Senna

1989. Aryton Senna's Formula 1 Motor Racing World Championship Title (1988). Sheet 99×69 mm.
MS2349 **1214** 2cz. multicoloured 15·00 15·00

1215 Emblem

1989. "Our Nature" Programme.

2350	**1215** 25c. multicoloured	70	45

1216 Hand reaching for Symbol of Freedom

1989. Bicentenary of Inconfidencia Mineira (independence movement). Multicoloured.

2351	30c. Type **1216**	60	35
2352	30c. Man's profile and colonial buildings	60	35
2353	40c. Baroque buildings in disarray	95	45

1217 School

1989. Centenary of Rio de Janeiro Military School.

2354	**1217** 50c. multicoloured	1·10	70

1218 *Pavonia alnifolia*

1989. Endangered Plants. Multicoloured.

2355	50c. Type **1218**	1·40	1·00
2356	1cz. *Worsleya rayneri* (vert)	3·00	2·20
2357	1cz.50 *Heliconia farinosa* (vert)	4·25	3·50

1219 Barreto and Pedro II Square, Recife Law School

1989. 150th Birth Anniv of Tobias Barreto (writer).

2358	**1219** 50c. multicoloured	1·50	90

1220 *Quiabentia zehntneri*

1989. Flowers. Currency expressed as "NCz $". Multicoloured.

2359	10c. *Dichorisandra* sp.	35	25
2360	20c. Type **1220**	45	25
2361	50c. *Bougainvillea glabra*	95	30
2363	1cz. *Impatiens* sp.	2·10	40
2364	2cz. *Chorisia crispiflora* (vert)	70	25
2366	5cz. *Hibiscus trilineatus*	70	30

See also Nos. 2413/24.

1221 Shooting of "Revistinha"

1989. 20th Anniv of TV Cultura.

2371	**1221** 50c. multicoloured	1·40	90

1222 Postal Authority Emblem

1989. No value expressed.

2372	**1222** (–) blue and orange	1·40	30

No. 2372 was sold at the current rate for first class internal postage.

1223 Brasilia T.V. Tower and Microlight

1989. Aerosports and 80th Anniv of Santos Dumont's Flight in *Demoiselle*. Multicoloured.

2373	50c. Type **1223**	95	80
2374	1cz.50 Eiffel Tower and *Demoiselle*	3·25	2·20

1224 *Largo da Carioca* (detail, Nicolas Antoine Taunay)

1989. Philexfrance 89 International Stamp Exhibition, Paris and Bicentenary of French Revolution. Sheet 99×69 mm.

MS2375	**1224** 3cz. multicoloured	6·00	6·00

1225 Tourmaline

1989. Precious Stones. Multicoloured.

2376	50c. Type **1225**	95	55
2377	1cz.50 Amethyst	2·40	1·80

1226 Imperial Palace, Rio de Janeiro

1989. Stamp Day. Brasiliana 89 International Stamp Exhibition, Rio de Janeiro. Sheet 99×69 mm.

MS2378	**1226** 5cz. multicoloured	7·75	7·75

1227 Rainbow and Association H.Q. Mercury

1989. 150th Anniv of Pernambuco Trade Assn.

2379	**1227** 50c. multicoloured	85	55

1228 Pioneers' Names and 19th-century to Modern Photographs

1989. International Photography Year.

2380	**1228** 1cz.50 multicoloured	2·40	1·70

1229 Power Station

1989. Centenary of Marmelos-o Power Station (first South American hydro-electric power station).

2381	**1229** 50c. multicoloured	70	45

1230 Hebrew Volute

1989. Molluscs. Multicoloured.

2382	50c. Type **1230**	35	25
2383	1cz. Matthew's morum	85	45
2384	1cz.50 Travasso's ancilla	1·20	70

1231 Muiraquita

1989. America. Pre-Columbian Artefacts. Multicoloured.

2385	1cz. Type **1231**	95	6·75
2386	4cz. Caryatid vase (horiz)	3·75	2·75

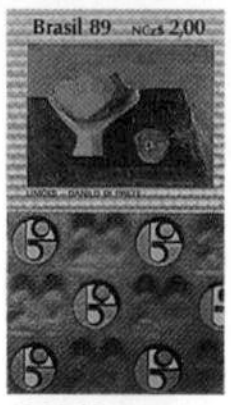

1232 *Limoes* (Danilo di Prete)

1989. 20th International Biennial Art Exhibition, Sao Paulo. Sheet 99×79 mm containing T **1232** and similar vert designs. Multicoloured.

MS2387	2cz. Type **1232**; 3cz. *O Indio e a Suacuaoara* (sculpture, Brecheret); 5cz. Francisco Matarazzo (exhibition founder)	7·75	7·75

1233 Casimiro de Abreu

1989. Book Day. Writers' Birth Annivs. Multicoloured.

2388	1cz. Type **1233** (150th anniv)	1·10	80
2389	1cz. Machado de Assis (150th anniv)	1·10	80
2390	1cz. Cora Coralina (cent)	1·10	80

1234 Postal Authority Emblem

1989. No value expressed. Burelage in second colour.

2391	**1234** (–) red and orange	4·50	1·90

No. 2391 was sold at the current rate for first class international postage.

1235 Police Emblem

1989. 25th Anniv of Federal Police Department.

2392	**1235** 1cz. multicoloured	60	35

1236 *Deodoro presents the Flag of the Republic* (detail, anon)

1989. Centenary of Proclamation of Republic. Sheet 98×68 mm.

MS2393	**1236** 15cz. multicoloured	8·75	8·75

1237 Angel

1989. Christmas. Multicoloured.

2394	70c. Type **1237**	35	35
2395	1cz. Nativity	45	35

1238 Candle Flame as Dove

1989. Thanksgiving Day.

2396	**1238** 1cz. multicoloured	45	35

1239 Fr. Damien de Veuster

1989. Obligatory Tax. Anti-leprosy Week.

2397	**1239** 2c. red	35	25

See also Nos. 2458, 2509 and 2565.

1989. Football Clubs. As T **1177**. Multicoloured.

2398	50c. Bahia Sports Club	45	35

1240 *The Yellow Man*

1989. Birth Cent of Anita Malfatti (painter).

2399	**1240** 1cz. multicoloured	45	35

1241 Archive and Proclamation by Bento Goncalves

1990. Cent of Bahia State Public Archive.

2400	**1241** 2cz. multicoloured	60	35

1242 *Mimosa caesalpiniifolia*

1990. 40th Anniv of Brazilian Botanical Society. Multicoloured.

2401	2cz. Type **1242**	45	35
2402	13cz. *Caesalpinia echinata*	2·75	2·20

1243 Cathedral of St. John the Baptist, Santa Cruz do Sul

1990. Churches. Multicoloured.

2403	2cz. Type **1243**	35	25
2404	3cz. Our Lady of Victory Church, Oeiras (horiz)	60	35
2405	5cz. Our Lady of the Rosary Church, Ouro Preto	85	55

1244 Sailing Barque and Modern Container Ship

1990. Cent of Lloyd Brasileiro Navigation Company.

2406	**1244** 3cz. multicoloured	45	25

1245 Chinstrap Penguins and Map

1990. Brazilian Antarctic Programme. Sheet 98×68 mm.

MS2407	**1245** 20cz. multicoloured	3·75	3·75

1990. Brazilian Football Clubs As T **1177**. Multicoloured.

2408	10cz. Vasco da Gama Regatas Club	95	80

1246 Collor and Newspaper Mastheads

1990. Birth Cent of Lindolfo Collor (journalist).

2409	**1246**	20cz. multicoloured	1·90	1·40

1247 Sarney

1990. Tribute to Jose Sarney (retiring President).

2410	**1247**	20cz. blue	2·00	1·40

1248 Gold Coin, Anniversary Emblem and Bank Headquarters, Brasilia

1990. 25th Anniv of Brazil Central Bank.

2411	**1248**	20cr. multicoloured	1·80	90

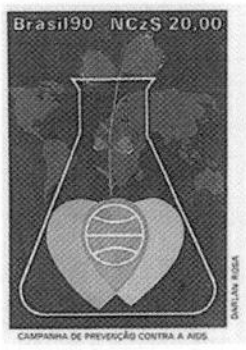

1249 Hearts sprouting in Flask

1990. World Health Day. Anti-AIDS Campaign.

2412	**1249**	20cr. multicoloured	1·90	90

1990. Flowers. As T **1220** but with currency expressed as "Cr$".

2413	1cr. *Impatiens* sp.	25	10
2414	2cr. *Chorisia crispiflora* (vert)	25	10
2415	5cr. *Hibiscus trilineatus*	25	10
2417	10cr. *Tibouchina granulosa* (vert)	35	25
2418	20cr. *Cassia micranthera* (vert)	60	35
2419	50cr. *Tibouchina mutabillis* (vert)	70	45
2420	50cr. *Clitoria fairchildiana* (vert)	70	45
2421	50cr. *Tibouchina mutabilis* (vert)	60	35
2422	100cr. *Erythrina crista-galli* (vert)	1·30	55
2423	200cr. *Jacaranda mimosifolia* (vert)	2·20	1·10
2424	500cr. *Caesalpinia peltophoroides* (vert)	3·50	1·80
2424a	1000cr. *Pachira aquatica* (vert)	45	25
2424b	2000cr. *Hibiscus pernambucensis* (vert)	60	25
2424c	5000cr. *Triplaris surinamensis* (vert)	1·40	60
2424d	10000cr. *Tabebuia heptaphylia* (vert)	3·00	1·20
2424e	20000cr. *Erythrina speciosa* (vert)	3·75	1·40

1250 Amazon Post Launch

1990. River Post Network.

2425	**1250**	20cr. multicoloured	1·90	1·00

1251 Emperor Pedro LL and 30r. "Bull's-Eye"

1990. Stamp World London 90 International Stamp Exhibition and 150th Anniv of Penny Black. Sheet 100×70 mm containing T **1251** and similar vert design, each black and lemon.

MS2426	20cz. Type **1251**; 100cr. Queen Victoria and Penny Black	8·25	8·25

1252 Map and Emblem

1990. World Cup Football Championship, Italy. Sheet 69×99 mm.

MS2427	**1252** 120cr. multicoloured	8·75	8·75

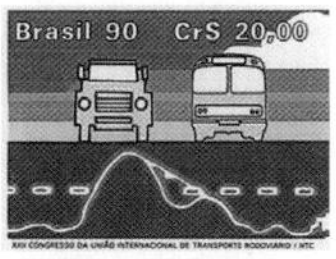

1253 Truck and Coach

1990. 22nd World Congress of Int Road Transport Union, Rio de Janeiro. Multicoloured.

2428	20cr. Type **1253**	1·30	90
2429	80cr. Volkswagen transporter van and car	1·90	1·40

Nos. 2428/29 were printed together, *se-tenant*, forming a composite design.

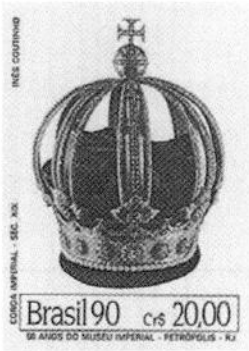

1254 Imperial Crown (Imperial Museum, Petropolis)

1990. Museum 50th Anniversaries. Multicoloured.

2430	20cr. Type **1254**	1·40	90
2431	20cr. *Our Lady of the Immaculate Conception* (woodcarving) (Missionary Museum, Sao Miguel das Missoes)	1·40	90

1990. Creation of State of Tocantins. As T **992**, showing state flag.

2432	20cr. yellow, blue and black	1·40	90

1255 Service Building. Hildebrand Theodolite and Map of Rio de Janeiro

1990. Centenary of Army Geographic Service.

2433	**1255**	20cr. multicoloured	1·40	90

1256 Adhemar Gonzaga (producer)

1990. Brazilian Film Industry. Each maroon and purple.

2434	25cr. Type **1256**	1·20	70
2435	25cr. Carmen Miranda (actress)	1·20	70
2436	25cr. Carmen Santos (actress)	1·20	70
2437	25cr. Oscarito (actor)	1·20	70

1257 Aerial View of House

1990. Fifth Anniv of France–Brazil House, Rio de Janeiro.

2438	**1257**	50cr. multicoloured	3·00	2·50

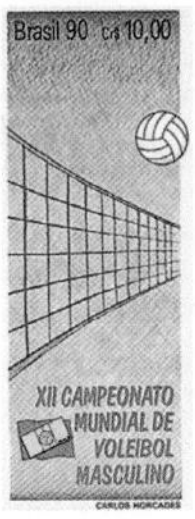

1258 Ball and Net

1990. 12th World Men's Volleyball Championship, Brazil.

2439	**1258**	10cr. multicoloured	85	45

1259 Embraer/FMA Vector

1990. Aeronautics Industry.

2440	**1259**	10cr. multicoloured	85	45

1260 Globe, Pencil and Alphabet

1990. International Literacy Year.

2441	**1260**	10cr. multicoloured	85	45

1261 Institute

1990. Cent of Granbery Institute, Juiz de Fora.

2442	**1261**	13cr. multicoloured	95	55

1262 Map, Track and Diesel Locomotive

1990. 18th Pan-American Railways Congress, Rio de Janeiro.

2443	**1262**	95cr. multicoloured	4·25	2·75

1263 Satellite and Computer Communication

1990. 25th Anniv of Embratel (Telecommunications Enterprise).

2444	**1263**	13cr. multicoloured	95	55

1264 "Bathers" (Alfredo Ceschiatti)

1990. Lubrapex 90 Brazilian–Portuguese Stamp Exhibition, Brasilia. Brasilia Sculptures. Multicoloured.

2445	25cr. Type **1264**	1·20	90
2446	25cr. *Warriors* (Bruno Giorgi)	1·20	90
2447	100cr. *St. John* (Ceschiatti)	2·50	1·80
2448	100cr. *Justice* (Ceschiatti)	2·50	1·80
MS2449	150×89 mm. Nos. 2445/8	12·00	12·00

1265 *Bromelia antiacantha*

1990. America. 500th Anniv of Discovery of America by Columbus. Praia do Sul Nature Reserve. Multicoloured.

2450	15cr. Type **1265**	95	55
2451	105cr. Wooded shoreline of Lagoa do Sul	4·75	3·50

Nos. 2450/1 were printed together, *se-tenant*, forming a composite design.

1266 Oswald de Andrade (birth centenary) and Illustration from *Anthropophagic Manifesto*

1990. Book Day. Anniversaries. Multicoloured.

2452	15cr. Type **1266**	85	55
2453	15cr. Guilherme de Almeida (birth cent) and illustration of *Geek Songs*	85	55
2454	15cr. National Library (180th anniv) and illuminated book	85	55

1267 Emblem and Tribunal Offices, Brasilia

1990. Centenary of National Accounts Tribunal.

2455	**1267**	15cr. multicoloured	85	55

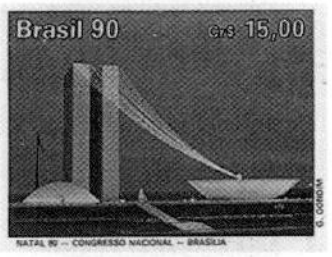

1268 National Congress Building

1990. Christmas. Brasilia Lights. Multicoloured.

2456	15cr. Type **1268**	85	55
2457	15cr. Television Tower	85	55

1990. Obligatory Tax. Anti-Leprosy Week. As No. 2397 but value and colour changed.

2458	**1239**	50c. blue	35	25

1269 Fingers touching across Map of Americas

1990. Centenary of Organization of American States.

2459	**1269**	15cr. multicoloured	45	25

1270 "Nike Apache" Rocket on Launch Pad

1990. 25th Anniv of Launch of "Nike Apache" Rocket.

2460	**1270**	15cr. multicoloured	45	25

1271 Sao Cristovao City

1990. 400th Anniv of Colonization of Sergipe State.
2461 **1271** 15cr. multicoloured 45 25

1272 Gymnasts

1991. World Congress on Physical Education, Sports and Recreation, Foz do Iguacu.
2462 **1272** 17cr. multicoloured 55 25

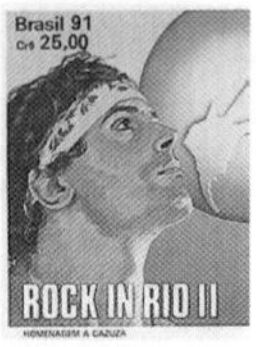

1273 Cazuza

1991. "Rock in Rio" Concert. Multicoloured.
2463 25cr. Type **1273** 95 55
2464 185cr. Raul Seixas 3·50 90

Nos. 2463/4 were printed together, *se-tenant*, forming a composite design.

1274 Aeritalia/Aermacchi AM-X and Republic Thunderbolt

1991. 50th Anniv of Aeronautics Ministry.
2465 **1274** 17cr. multicoloured 55 35

1275 Effigies of Day Woman and Midnight Man, Olinda

1991. Carnival. Multicoloured.
2466 25cr. Type **1275** 35 30
2467 30cr. Electric trio on truck, Salvador 40 35
2468 280cr. Samba dancers, Rio de Janeiro 5·25 4·00

1276 Antarctic Wildlife

1991. Visit of President Collor to Antarctica.
2469 **1276** 300cr. multicoloured 4·25 2·30

1277 Hang-gliders

1991. Eighth World Free Flight Championships, Governador Valadares.
2470 **1277** 36cr. multicoloured 85 55

1278 Yachting

1991. 11th Pan-American Games, Cuba, and Olympic Games, Barcelona (1992). Mult.
2471 36cr. Type **1278** 70 45
2472 36cr. Rowing 70 45
2473 300cr. Swimming 4·75 3·75

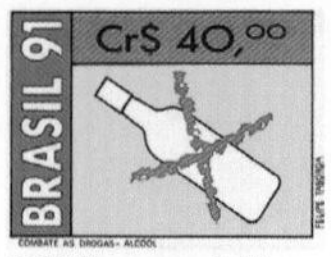

1279 Cross over Bottle (alcoholism)

1991. Anti-addiction Campaign. Multicoloured.
2474 40cr. Type **1279** 85 55
2475 40cr. Cross over cigarette (smoking) 85 55
2476 40cr. Cross over syringe (drug abuse) 85 55

1280 Old and Present Offices and Mastheads

1991. Cent of *Jornal do Brasil* (newspaper).
2477 **1280** 40cr. multicoloured 85 55

1281 Yanomami Youth in Ceremonial Paint

1991. Indian Culture. The Yanomami. Multicoloured.
2478 40cr. Type **1281** 70 55
2479 400cr. Hunter (horiz) 7·00 5·25

1282 Orinoco Goose

1991. United Nations Conference on Environment and Development.
2480 **1282** 45cr. multicoloured 85 55

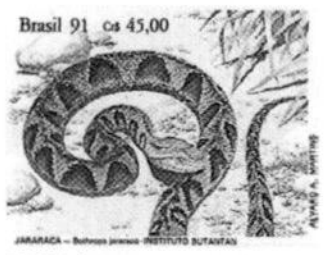

1283 Jararaca

1991. 90th Anniv of Butantan Institute (2481/2) and 173rd Anniv of National Museum (others). Multicoloured.
2481 45cr. Type **1283** 70 45
2482 45cr. Green tree boa 70 45
2483 45cr. Theropoda (dinosaurs) 70 45
2484 350cr. Sauropoda (dinosaurs) 4·25 3·00

1284 National Flag

1991. No value expressed.
2485a **1284** (–) multicoloured 45 25

1285 Early Steam Pump and Santos City 6th Fire Group's Headquarters

1991. Fire Fighting.
2486 **1285** 45cr. multicoloured 60 45

1286 Pedra Pintada, Boa Vista, Roraima

1991. Tourism. Centenaries of Boa Vista (1990) and Teresopolis. Multicoloured.
2487 45cr. Type **1286** 60 45
2488 350cr. God's Finger, Teresopolis, Rio de Janeiro 2·75 2·10

1287 Welder, "Justice" and Farmer

1991. 50th Anniv of Labour Justice Legal System.
2489 **1287** 45cr. multicoloured 60 45

1288 Folklore Characters, Singers and Mota

1991. Fifth International Festival of Folklore and Birth Centenary of Leonardo Mota (folklorist).
2490 **1288** 45cr. red, ochre & black 60 45

1289 Jose Basilio da Gama (poet)

1991. Writers' Birth Anniversaries. Multicoloured.
2491 45cr. Type **1289** (250th anniv) 55 40
2492 50cr. Luis Nicolau Fagundes Varela (poet, 150th anniv) 60 45
2493 50cr. Jackson de Figueiredo (essayist and philosopher, centenary) 60 45

1290 Pope John Paul II

1991. Papal Visit and 12th National Eucharistic Congress, Natal. Multicoloured.
2494 50cr. Type **1290** 60 45
2495 400cr. Congress emblem 1·80 1·10

Nos. 2494/5 were issued together, *se-tenant*, forming a composite design.

1291 *The Constitutional Commitment* (Aurelio de Figueiredo)

1991. Centenary of 1891 Constitution.
2496 **1291** 50cr. multicoloured 85 35

1292 Exhibition Emblem and dish Aerial

1991. Telecom 91 International Telecommuni- cations Exhibition, Geneva.
2497 **1292** 50cr. multicoloured 85 35

1293 Ferdinand Magellan

1991. America. Voyages of Discovery. Multicoloured.
2498 50cr. Type **1293** 85 35
2499 400cr. Francisco de Orellana on River Amazon 2·75 2·10

1294 White-vented Violetear and *Cattleya warneri*

1991. Brapex 91 National Stamp Exhibition, Vitoria. Humming Birds and Orchids in Mata Atlantica Forest. Multicoloured.
2500 50cr. Type **1294** 60 35
2501 65cr. Glittering-bellied emerald and *Rodriguezia venusta* 70 45
2502 65cr. Brazilian ruby and *Zygopetalum intermedium* 70 45
MS2503 99×69 mm. 50cr. White-vented violetear and *Cattelya warneri*; 50cr. Glittering-bellied emerald and tree trunk; 500cr. *Rodriguezia venusta* and Brazilian ruby 12·00 12·00

1295 *Self-portrait III*

1991. Birth Centenary of Lasar Segall (artist).
2504 **1295** 400cr. multicoloured 1·80 75

1296 Agricultural Projects

1991. Centenary of Bureau of Agriculture and Provision, Sao Paulo.
2505 **1296** 70cr. multicoloured 60 35

1297 Dr. Manuel Ferraz de Campos Salles (President, 1898–1902)

1991. 150th Birth Anniversaries. Multicoloured.
2506 70cr. Type **1297** 60 35
2507 90cr. Dr. Prudente de Moraes (President, 1894–98) and Catete Palace, Rio de Janeiro (former Executive Headquarters) 70 45

Nos. 2506/7 were issued together, *se-tenant*, forming a composite design.

1298 Madonna and Child

1991. Christmas.
2508 **1298** 70cr. multicoloured 1·20 35

1991. Obligatory Tax. Anti-leprosy Week.
2509 **1239** 3cr. green 35 25

1299 Hand holding Prayer Book

1991. Thanksgiving Day.
2510 **1299** 70cr. multicoloured 60 35

1300 Pedro II

1991. 150th Anniv of Coronation and Death Centenary of Emperor Pedro II. Sheet 99×69 mm containing T **1300** and similar vert design. Multicoloured.
MS2511 80cr. Type **1300**; 800cr. Pedro II at coronation 4·75 4·75

1301 Policeman in Historic Uniform and Tobias de Aguiar Battalion Building, Sao Paulo

1991. Military Police.
2512 **1301** 80cr. multicoloured 60 35

1302 First Baptist Church, Niteroi (centenary)

1992. Church Anniversaries. Multicoloured.
2513 250cr. Type **1302** 1·30 45
2514 250cr. Presbyterian Cathedral, Rio de Janeiro (130th anniv) 1·30 45

1303 Afranio Costa (silver, free pistol)

1992. Olympic Games, Barcelona (1st issue). 1920 Olympics Shooting Medal Winners. Multicoloured.
2515 300cr. Type **1303** 1·80 85
2516 2500cr. Guilherme Paraense (gold, 30 m revolver) 14·00 3·50
See also No. 2526.

1304 Old and Modern Views of Port

1992. Centenary of Port of Santos.
2517 **1304** 300cr. multicoloured 1·10 55

1305 White-tailed Tropic Birds

1992. Second United Nations Conference on Environment and Development, Rio de Janeiro (1st issue). Multicoloured.
2518 400cr. Type **1305** 1·20 55
2519 2500cr. Spinner dolphins 4·25 2·00
See also Nos. 2532/5, 2536/8, 2539/42 and 2543/6.

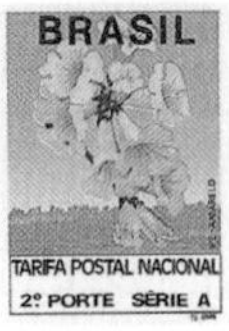

1306 Ipe

1992. No value expressed.
2520 **1306** (–) multicoloured 2·30 25
No. 2520 was valid for use at the second class inland letter rate.

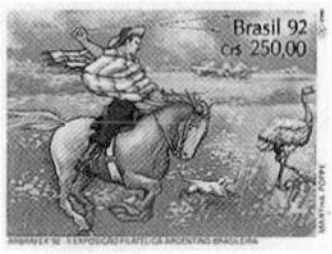

1307 Hunting using Boleadeira

1992. Abrafex '92 Argentinian–Brazilian Stamp Exhibition, Porto Alegre. Multicoloured.
2521 250cr. Type **1307** 70 55
2522 250cr. Traditional folk dancing 70 55
2523 250cr. Horse and cart 70 55
2524 1000cr. Rounding-up cattle 1·40 1·10
MS2525 150×89 mm. 250cr. As No. 2522; 250cr. As No. 2523; 500cr. Type **1307**; 1500cr. As No. 2524 8·75 8·75

1308 Sportsmen on Globe

1992. Olympic Games, Barcelona (2nd issue).
2526 **1308** 300cr. multicoloured 60 35

1309 Tiradentes (sculpture, Bruno Giorgi)

1992. Death Bicentenary of Joaquim Jose da Silvaxavier (Independence fighter). Sheet 98×68 mm.
MS2527 **1309** 3500cr. mult 6·50 6·50

1310 Columbus's Fleet

1992. America. 500th Anniv of Discovery of America by Columbus. Multicoloured.
2528 500cr. Type **1310** 70 45
2529 3500cr. Columbus, route map and quadrant 3·75 2·30
Nos. 2528/9 were issued together, *se-tenant*, forming a composite design.

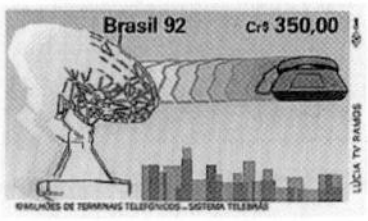

1311 Dish Aerial, Telephone and City

1992. Installation of 10,000,000th Telephone Line in Brazil.
2530 **1311** 350cr. multicoloured 70 35

1312 Sailing Canoes

1992. Lubrapex 92 Brazilian–Portuguese Stamp Exhibition, Lisbon. Bicentenary of *Philosophical Journey* by Alexandre Rodrigues Ferreira. Sheet 148×88 mm containing T **1312** and similar horiz designs.
MS2531 500cr., 1000cr., 2500cr. Composite design of watercolour by Jose Freire showing arrival of expedition's ship at Vila de Cameta 6·75 6·75

1313 Hercule Florence (botanist)

1992. Second UN Conference on Environment and Development (2nd issue). 170th Anniv of Langsdorff Expedition. Multicoloured.
2532 500cr. Type **1313** 60 45
2533 500cr. Aime-Adrien Taunay (ethnographer) and Amerindians 60 45
2534 500cr. Johann Moritz Rugendas (zoologist) 60 45
2535 3000cr. Gregory Ivanovich Langsdorff and route map 3·75 2·50

1314 Urban and Rural Symbols

1992. Second UN Conference on Environment and Development (3rd issue). Multicoloured.
2536 450cr. Type **1314** 45 35
2537 450cr. Flags of Sweden (host of first conference) and Brazil around globe 45 35
2538 3000cr. Globe, map, flora and fauna 3·75 2·50

1315 Monica sitting by Waterfall

1992. Second UN Conference on Environment and Development (4th issue). Ecology. Designs showing cartoon characters. Multicoloured.
2539 500cr. Type **1315** 70 35
2540 500cr. Cebolinha in canoe 70 35
2541 500cr. Cascao photographing wildlife 70 35
2542 500cr. Magali picking wild fruit 70 35
Nos. 2539/42 were issued together, *se-tenant*, forming a composite design.

1316 *Nidularium innocentii*

1992. Second UN Conference on Environment and Development (5th issue). 3rd Anniv of Margaret Mee Brazilian Botanical Foundation. Flower paintings by Margaret Mee. Multicoloured.
2543 600cr. Type **1316** 85 55
2544 600cr. *Canistrum exiguum* 85 55
2545 700cr. *Nidularium rubens* 90 65
2546 700cr. *Canistrum cyathiforme* 90 65

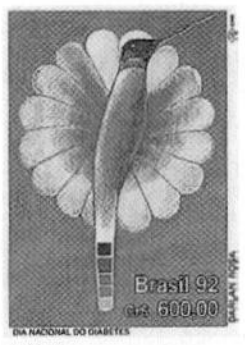

1317 Humming-bird's Wings forming Flower

1992. National Diabetes Day.
2547 **1317** 600cr. multicoloured 85 35

1318 Training Tower and First Manual Pump

1992. Centenary of Joinville Volunteer Fire Service.
2548 **1318** 550cr. multicoloured 60 35

1319 Animals, Cave Paintings and Map of Piaui State

1992. 13th Anniv of Capivara Mountain National Park. Multicoloured.
2549 550cr. Type **1319** 60 35
2550 550cr. Canyons and map of Brazil 60 35
Nos. 2549/50 were issued together, *se-tenant*, forming a composite design.

1320 Projects within Flask

1992. 24th Anniv of Financing Agency for Studies and Projects.
2551 **1320** 550cr. multicoloured 60 35

1321 Students at Work

1992. 50th Anniv of National Industrial Training Service.
2552 **1321** 650cr. multicoloured 60 55

1322 Santa Cruz Fortress, Anhatomirim Island

1992. Santa Catarina Fortresses. Multicoloured.
2553 650cr. Type **1322** 60 45
2554 3000cr. Santo Antonio Fort, Ratones Grande island 2·20 1·80

1323 Masonic Emblem and Palace, Brasilia

1992. 170th Anniv of Grande Oriente (Federation of Brazil's Freemasonry Lodges).
2555 **1323** 650cr. multicoloured 60 35

1324 Profiles of Child and Man forming Hourglass

1992. 50th Anniv of Brazilian Legion of Assistance.
2556 **1324** 650cr. multicoloured 60 35

1325 Medical Equipment and Patients

1992. Sarah Locomotor Hospital, Brasilia.
2557 **1325** 800cr. multicoloured 60 45

1326 Menotti del Picchia

1992. Book Day. Writers' Birth Centenaries. Multicoloured.
2558 900cr. Type **1326** 60 45
2559 900cr. Graciliano Ramos 60 45
2560 1000cr. Assis Chateaubriand (journalist) (horiz) 65 50

1327 Meridian Circle, Map, Cruls and Tent

1992. Centenary of Luiz Cruls's Exploration of Central Plateau.
2561 **1327** 900cr. multicoloured 60 45

1328 Productivity Graph on Flag

1992. Second Anniv of Brazilian Quality and Productivity Programme.
2562 **1328** 1200cr. multicoloured 55 35

1329 Pepino Beach, Rio de Janeiro

1992. Year of Tourism in the Americas. Sheet 70×100 mm containing T **1329** and similar horiz design. Multicoloured.
MS2563 1200cr. Type **1329**; 9000cr. Sugar Loaf, Rio de Janeiro 3·75 3·75

1330 Father Christmas

1992. Christmas. No value expressed.
2564 **1330** (–) multicoloured 75 45

1992. Obligatory Tax. Anti-leprosy Week.
2565 **1239** 30cr. brown 65 55

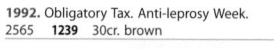

1331 Sister Dulce, Patients and Lacerda Lift, Salvador

1993. Sister Dulce (founder of Santo Antonio Hospital and Simoes Filho Educational Centre) Commemoration.
2566 **1331** 3500cr. multicoloured 40 25

1332 Diving

1993. South American Water Sports Championships, Goiania. Sheet 69×99 mm containing T **1332** and similar horiz designs. Multicoloured.
MS2567 3500cr. Type **1332**; 3500cr. Synchronized swimming; 25000cr. Water polo 5·25 3·25

1333 Tube Station, Pine Trees and Church of the Third Order of St. Francis of Assisi and Stigmata

1993. 300th Anniv of Curitiba.
2568 **1333** 4500cr. multicoloured 75 70

1334 Heart dripping Blood onto Flowers

1993. Health and Preservation of Life. Multicoloured.
2569 4500cr. Type **1334** (blood donation) 50 35
2570 4500cr. Crab attacking healthy cell (anti-cancer campaign) 50 35
2571 4500cr. Rainbow, head and encephalogram (mental health) 50 35

1335 *Night with the Geniuses of Study and Love*

1993. 150th Birth Anniv of Pedro Americo (painter). Multicoloured.
2572 5500cr. Type **1335** 65 45
2573 36000cr. *David and Abizag* (horiz) 4·50 2·75
2574 36000cr. *A Carioca* 4·50 2·75

1336 Flag

1993. No value expressed. Self-adhesive. Die-cut.
2575 **1336** (–) blue, yellow & grn 2·10 55

No. 2575 was valid for use at the current first class inland letter rate. It could not be used to pay postage to foreign countries.

1337 *Dynastes hercules*

1993. World Environment Day. Beetles. Multicoloured.
2576 8000cr. Type **1337** 65 45
2577 55000cr. *Batus barbicornis* 3·00 2·75

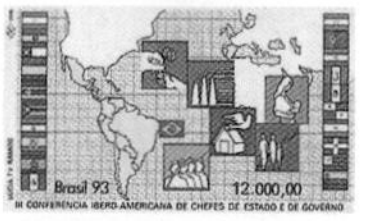

1338 Map, Flags and Discussion Themes

1993. Third Iberian–American Summit Conference, Salvador.
2578 **1338** 12000cr. multicoloured 75 35

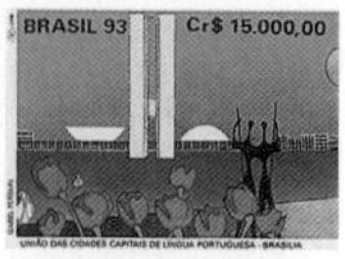

1339 Lake, Congress Building and *Os Candangos* (statue), Brasilia

1993. Union of Portuguese-speaking Capital Cities. Multicoloured.
2579 15000cr. Type **1339** 40 25
2580 71000cr. Copacabana beach and "Christ the Redeemer" (statue), Rio de Janeiro 2·10 1·30

Nos. 2579/80 were issued together, *se-tenant*, forming a composite design.

1340 30r. "Bulls Eye" Stamp

1993. 150th Anniv of First Brazilian Stamps (1st issue) and Brasiliana 93 International Stamp Exhibition, Rio de Janeiro. Each black, red and yellow.
2581 30000cr. Type **1340** 90 45
2582 60000cr.60r. "Bull's Eye" stamp 1·90 1·10
2583 90000cr.90r. "Bull's Eye" stamp 2·50 1·60
MS2584 132×99 mm. As Nos. 2581/3 but without engraver's name and commemorative inscription 15·00 15·00

See also Nos. 2585/8.

1341 Cebolinha designing Stamp

1993. 150th Anniv of First Brazilian Stamps (2nd issue). No value expressed. Cartoon characters. Multicoloured.
2585 (–) Type **1341** 75 25
2586 (–) Cascao as King and 30r. "Bull's Eye" stamp 75 25
2587 (–) Monica writing letter and 60r. "Bull's Eye" stamp 75 25
2588 (–) Magali receiving letter and 90r. "Bull's Eye" stamp 75 25

Nos. 2585/8 were issued together, *se-tenant*, forming a composite design.

Nos. 2585/8 were valid for use at the current first class inland letter rate. They could not be used to pay postage to other countries.

1342 Imperial Palace (former postal H.Q.), Rio de Janeiro

1993. 330th Anniv of Postal Service. Multicoloured.
2589 20000cr. Type **1342** 65 35
2590 20000cr. Petropolis post office 65 35
2591 20000cr. Main post office, Rio de Janeiro 65 35
2592 20000cr. Niteroi post office 65 35

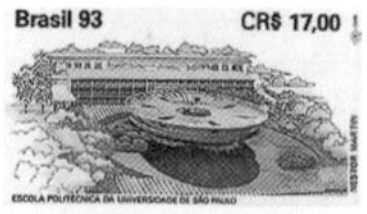

1343 Polytechnic School, Sao Paulo University

1993. Engineering Schools. Multicoloured.
2593 17cr. Type **1343** (centenary, 1994) 90 55
2594 17cr. Old and new engineering schools, Rio de Janeiro Federal University (bicent, 1992) 90 55

1344 Forest Mound and Tools

1993. Preservation of Archaeological Sites. Mult.
2595 17cr. Type **1344** 65 45
2596 17cr. Coastal mound, shells and tools 65 45

1345 Guimaraes and National Congress

1993. Ulysses Guimaraes (politician).
2597 **1346** 22cr. Multicoloured. 65 55

1346 Hands holding Candles and Rope around Statue

1993. Bicentenary of Procession of "Virgin of Nazareth", Belem.
2598 22cr. multicoloured 65 55

1347 Hyacinth Macaw, Glaucous Macaw and Indige Macaw

1993. America. Endangered Macaws. Multicoloured.
2599 22cr. Type **1347** 75 45
2600 130cr. Spix's macaw 2·50 75

1348 Vinicius de Moraes

1993. Composers' Anniversaries. Multicoloured.
2601 22cr. Type **1348** (80th birth anniv) 40 25
2602 22cr. Alfredo da Rocha Vianna (pseud. Pixinguinha) and score of *Carinhoso* (20th death anniv) 40 25

1349 Liberty

1993. No value expressed.
2603 **1349** (–) blue, turq & yell 5·00 4·50

No. 2603 was sold at the current rate for first class international postage.

1350 Mario de Andrade

1993. Book Day. Writers' Birth Centenaries. Multicoloured.
2604 30cr. Type **1350** 40 25
2605 30cr. Alceu Amoroso Lima (pseud. Tristao de Athayde) 40 25
2606 30cr. Gilka Machado (poet) 40 25

1351 Knot

1993. 40th Anniv of Brazil–Portugal Consultation and Friendship Treaty.

2607 **1351** 30cr. multicoloured 50 25

1352 Nho-Quim

1993. Second International Comic Strip Biennial. No value expressed. Multicoloured.

2608 (-) Type **1352** 1·00 35
2609 (-) Benjamin (Louneiro) 1·00 35
2610 (-) Lamparina 1·00 35
2611 (-) Reco-Reco, Bolao and Azeitona (Luiz Sa) 1·00 35

See note below Nos. 2585/8.

1353 Diagram and *Tamoio* (submarine)

1993. Launch of First Brazilian-built Submarine.

2612 **1353** 240cr. multicoloured 3·25 2·75

1354 Nativity

1993. Christmas. No value expressed.

2613 **1354** (-) multicoloured 1·30 85

See note below Nos. 2585/8.

1993. Obligatory Tax. Anti-leprosy Week.

2614 **1205** 50c. blue 40 25

1355 Republic P-47 Thunderbolt Fighters over Tarquinia Camp, Italy

1993. 50th Anniv of Formation of 1st Fighter Group, Brazilian Expeditionary Force.

2615 **1355** 42cr. multicoloured 90 55

1356 Flag

1994. No value expressed. Self-adhesive. Imperf.

2616 **1356** (-) blue, yellow & green 1·20 70

See note below Nos. 2585/8.

1357 Foundation of Republican Memory, Convent and Cloisters

1994. 340th Anniv of Convent of Merces (now Cultural Centre), Sao Luis.

2617 **1357** 58cr. multicoloured 65 35

1358 "Mae Menininha"

1994. Birth Centenary of Mae Menininha do Gantois (Escolastica Maria da Conceiao Nazare).

2618 **1358** 80cr. multicoloured 75 70

1359 Olympic Rings and Rower

1994. Centenaries of International Olympic Committee and Rowing Federation, Rio Grande do Sul. No value expressed.

2619 **1359** (-) multicoloured 4·00 2·30

See note below No. 2603.

1360 Blue and White Swallow

1994. Birds. Multicoloured.

2620 10cr. Type **1360** 65 10
2621 20cr. Roadside hawk 65 10
2622 50cr. Rufous-bellied thrush 65 10
2623 100cr. Ruddy ground dove 65 10
2624 200cr. Southern lapwing 65 10
2625 500cr. Rufous-collared sparrow 1·90 35

See after Nos. 2649/61.

1361 Map and Prince Henry

1994. 600th Birth Anniv of Prince Henry the Navigator.

2626 **1361** 635cr. multicoloured 5·00 2·50

1362 Bicycle

1994. America. Postal Vehicles. Multicoloured.

2627 110cr. Type **1362** 65 35
2628 635cr. Post motor cycle 5·75 1·70

1363 Statue, Grain Store and Chapel of Help, Juazeiro do Norte

1994. 150th Anniv of Birth of Father Cicero Romao Batista. With service indicator.

2629 **1363** (-) multicoloured 1·20 85

See note below Nos. 2585/8.

1364 Sabin and Children

1994. First Death Anniv of Albert Sabin (developer of oral polio vaccine).

2630 **1364** 160cr. multicoloured 1·00 55

1365 Castello Branco and Brasilia

1994. Carlos Castello Branco (journalist).

2631 **1365** 160cr. multicoloured 1·00 55

1366 *Euterpe oleracea*

1994. Birth Bicentenary of Karl Friedrich Phillip von Martius (botanist). With service indicator. Multicoloured. (a) Inscr "1. PORTE NACIONAL".

2632 (-) Type **1366** 1·30 55
2633 (-) *Jacaranda paucifoliolata* 1·30 55

(b) Inscr "1. PORTE INTERNACIONAL TAXE PERCUE".

2634 (-) *Barbacenia tomentosa* 3·50 1·70

Nos. 2632/3 were for use at the current first class inland letter rate and Nos. 2634 for first class international postage.

1367 "Brazil"

1994. With service indicator. (a) Size 21×28 mm. Self-adhesive. Rouletted. (i) PRINTED MATTER. Inscr "1. PORTE IMPRESSO CATEGORIA II".

2635 **1367** (-) blue 55 45

(ii) INLAND POSTAGE. Inscr "3. PORTE NACIONAL".

2636 (3rd) red 1·00 75

(b) INLAND POSTAGE. Inscr "PORTE NACIONAL". Size 26×35 mm.

2637 (4th) green 2·00 1·50
2638 (5th) red 4·00 2·75

Nos. 2635/8 were valid for internal use in the category described.

1368 Brazilian Player wearing "100"

1994. Centenary of Football in Brazil and World Cup Football Championship, U.S.A. With service indicator.

2639 **1368** (-) multicoloured 3·75 2·50

See note below No. 2603.

1369 Emperor Tamarin (*Saguinus imperator*)

1994. Endangered Mammals. With service indicator. Multicoloured.

2640 (-) Type **1369** 1·10 50
2641 (-) Bare-faced tamarin (*Saguinus bicolor*) 1·10 50
2642 (-) Golden lion tamarin (*Leontopithecus rosalia*) 1·10 50

See note below Nos. 2585/8.

1370 Book and Disks

1994. 46th International Book Fair, Frankfurt, Germany. Sheet 99×69 mm.

MS2643 **1370** (-) multicoloured 4·25 4·25

No. **MS**2643 was sold at the currant rate for first class international postage.

1371 Pencils Crossing over Fingerprint

1994. Ten Year Education Plan. With service indicator. Multicoloured.

2644 (-) Type **1371** (literacy campaign) 1·20 55
2645 (-) PRONAICA pencil and school (National Programme of Integral Care to Children and Teenagers) 1·20 55
2646 (-) Lecture scene and graph (increase in qualified teachers) 1·20 55
2647 (-) Pencil and "lecturers" on television (distance learning by video) 1·20 55

See note below Nos. 2585/8.

1372 Map of the Americas (Bartholomeu Velho, 1561) and Treaty Boundaries

1994. 500th Anniv of the Treaty of Tordesillas (defining Portuguese and Spainish spheres of influence). Sheet 67×99 mm.

MS2648 **1372** (-) multicoloured 4·00 4·00

No. **MS**2648 was sold at the currant rate for first class international postage.

1994. Birds. As T **1360** but with value expressed as "R$". Multicoloured.

2649 1c. Type **1360** 45 15
2650 2c. As No. 2621 45 15
2652 5c. As No. 2622 45 15
2654 10c. As No. 2623 45 15
2655 15c. Saffron finch 80 45
2656 20c. As No. 2624 1·00 50
2657 22c. Fork-tailed fly-catcher 80 50
2658 50c. As No. 2625 3·00 1·30
2661 1r. Rufous hornero 5·25 2·50

1373 Edgard Santos (founder of Bahia University)

1994. Anniversaries. With service indicator. Multicoloured.

2662 (-) Type **1373** (birth centenary) 1·30 65
2663 (-) Oswaldo Aranha (politician, birth centenary) 1·30 65
2664 (-) Otto Lara Resende (author and journalist, 2nd death anniv) 1·30 65

See note below Nos. 2585/8.

1374 *Petrobras X* (drilling platform), Campos Basin. Rio de Janeiro

1994. 40th Anniv of Petrobras (state oil company).

2665 **1374** 12c. multicoloured 80 50

1375 17th century Coin Production

1994. 300th Anniv of Brazilian Mint.

2666 **1375** 12c. multicoloured 80 65

1376 Loaf of Bread

1994. Campaign against Famine and Misery. With service indicator.

2667 **1376** (-) multicoloured 1·20 65
2668 - (-) black and blue 1·20 65

DESIGN: No. 2668, Fish.

See note below Nos. 2585/8.

1377 Writing with Quill and Scales of Justice

1994. 150th Anniv of Brazilian Lawyers Institute.
2669 **1377** 12c. multicoloured 80 65

1378 Family within Heart

1994. International Year of the Family.
2670 **1378** 84c. multicoloured 5·25 4·00

1379 Hospital, White Stork and Babies forming "1000000"

1994. Centenary of Sao Paulo Maternity Hospital. Its Millionth Birth.
2671 **1379** 12c. multicoloured 85 65

1380 Celestino performing and "Maternal Heart" (record sleeve)

1994. Birth Centenary of Vicente Celestino (singer).
2672 **1380** 12c. multicoloured 1·30 50

1381 Fernando de Azevedo (educationist)

1994. Writers' Birth Anniversaries. Multicoloured.
2673 12c. Type **1381** (cent) 65 40
2674 12c. Tomas Antonio Gonzaga (poet, 250th) 65 40

1382 "Joao and Maria" (*Hansel and Gretel*)

1994. Centenary of Publication of *Fairy Tales* by Alberto Figueiredo Pimentel (first Brazilian children's book). Multicoloured.
2675 12c. Type **1382** 85 65
2676 12c. "Dona Baratinha" (*Little Mrs Cockroach*) 85 65
2677 84c. *Puss in Boots* 3·50 2·40
2678 84c. *Tom* Thumb 3·50 2·40

1383 St. Clare, St. Damian's Convent and Statue of St. Francis

1994. 800th Birth Anniv of St. Clare of Assisi (founder of order of Poor Clares).
2679 **1383** 12c. multicoloured 65 40

1384 McLaren–Honda F1 Racing Car and Brazilian Flag

1994. Ayrton Senna (racing driver) Commemoration. Multicoloured.
2680 12c. Type **1384** 1·10 60
2681 12c. Senna and crowd waving farewell 1·10 60
2682 84c. Brazilian and chequered flags, racing cars and Senna giving victory salute 3·50 2·20

Nos. 2680/2 were issued together, *se-tenant*, forming a composite design.

1385 Books and Globe

1994. Centenary of Historical and Geographical Institute, Sao Paulo.
2683 **1385** 12c. multicoloured 65 50

1386 Adoniran Barbosa and "11 o'Clock Train"

1994. Composers. Multicoloured.
2684 12c. Type **1386** 65 50
2685 12c. Score of "The Sea" (Dorival Caymmi) 65 50

1994. Obligatory Tax. Anti-Leprosy Week.
2686 **1205** 1c. purple 40 25

1387 Maggot wearing Santa Claus Hat in Apple

1994. Christmas. Multicoloured.
2687 12c. Type **1387** 55 40
2688 12c. Carol singers 55 40
2689 12c. Boy smoking pipe and letter in boot 55 40
2690 84c. Boy wearing saucepan on head and Santa Claus cloak 3·75 2·30

1388 Trophy

1994. Brazil, World Cup Football Championship (U.S.A.) Winners. Sheet 100×69 mm.
MS2691 **1388** 2r.14 multicoloured 10·50 10·00

1389 Pasteur

1995. Death Centenary of Louis Pasteur (chemist).
2692 **1389** 84c. multicoloured 4·00 3·25

1390 Duke of Caxias and Soldiers

1995. 150th Anniv of Peace of Ponche Verde (pacification of Farroupilha Revolution) (2693) and 50th Anniv of Battle of Monte Castello (2694). Multicoloured.
2693 12c. Type **1390** 65 40
2694 12c. Soldier, Brazilian flag and battle scene 65 40

1391 Pres. Franco

1995. Itamar Franco (President 1992–94).
2695 **1391** 12c. multicoloured 65 40

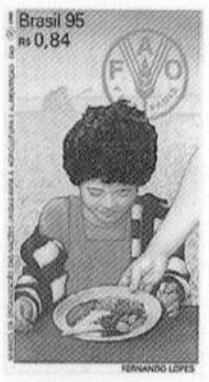
1392 Meal before Child

1995. 50th Anniv of F.A.O.
2696 **1392** 84c. multicoloured 4·00 3·25

1393 Alexandre de Gusmao (diplomat)

1995. Birth Anniversaries. Multicoloured.
2697 12c. Type **1393** (300th anniv) 65 40
2698 12c. Visconde (Viscount) de Jequitinhonha (lawyer, bicent (1994)) 65 40
2699 15c. Barao (Baron) do Rio Branco (diplomat, 150th anniv) 65 40

1394 Guglielmo Marconi and his Transmitter

1995. Centenary of First Radio Transmission.
2700 **1394** 84c. multicoloured 4·00 3·25

1395 Ipe-amarelo and Cherry Blossom

1995. Centenary of Brazil–Japan Friendship Treaty.
2701 **1395** 84c. multicoloured 4·00 3·25

1396 Solitary Tinamou (*Tinamus solitarius*)

1995. Birds. Multicoloured.
2702 12c. Type **1396** 1·00 50
2703 12c. Razor-billed curassow (*Mitu mitu*) 1·00 50

1397 St. John's Party, Campina Grande

1995. June Festivals. Multicoloured.
2704 12c. Type **1397** 65 40
2705 12c. Country wedding, Caruaru 65 40

1398 St. Antony holding Child Jesus (painting, Vieira Lusitano)

1995. 800th Birth Anniv of St. Antony of Padua.
2706 **1398** 84c. multicoloured 4·25 3·25

1399 Lumiere Brothers and Early Projection Equipment

1995. Centenary of Motion Pictures. Sheet 99×70 mm.
MS2707 **1399** 2r.14 multicoloured 10·50 10·00

1400 Laurel and "Republic"

1995. First Anniv of Real Currency.
2708 **1400** 12c. brown, green & blk 65 40

1401 Player, Net and Anniversary Emblem

1995. Centenary of Volleyball.
2709 **1401** 15c. multicoloured 1·10 65

1402 Angaturama limai

1995. 14th Brazilian Palaeontology Society Congress, Uberaba. Dinosaurs. Multicoloured.
2710 15c. Type **1402** 65 45
2711 1r.50 Titanosaurus 3·25 3·00

1403 Crash Test Dummies in Car

1995. Road Safety Campaign. Multicoloured.
2712 12c. Type **1403** 65 50
2713 71c. Car crashing into glass of whisky 4·00 2·75

1404 *Calathea burle-marxii*

1995. Singapore '95 International Stamp Exhibition. Tenth Anniv of Donation to Nation by Roberto Burle Marx of his Botanical Collection. Multicoloured.
2714 15c. Type **1404** 20 15
2715 15c. "Vellozia burle-marxii" 20 15
2716 1r.50 "Heliconia aemygdiana" 2·00 1·75

1405 Paratroopers and Lockheed C-130 Hercules

1995. 50th Anniv of Parachutist Infantry Brigade.
2717 **1405** 15c. multicoloured 80 65

1406 Paulista Museum and "Fernao Dias Paes Leme" (statue, Luigi Brizzolara)

1995. Centenary of Paulista Museum of the University of Sao Paulo.
2718 **1406** 15c. multicoloured 80 65

1407 Olinda

1995. Lighthouses. Multicoloured.

2719	15c. Type **1407**	80	65
2720	15c. Sao Joao	80	65
2721	15c. Santo Antonio da Barra	80	65

1408 Scarlet Ibis and Stoat catching Fish

1995. Lubrapex 95 Brazilian–Portuguese Stamp Exhibition, Sao Paulo. Fauna of the Tiete River Valley. Multicoloured.

2722	15c. Type **1408**	80	65
2723	84c. Great egret flying over canoe	4·00	2·50
MS2724	125×185 mm. 1r.50×2 Motifs as in Nos. 2722/3 forming a composite design	14·50	14·50

1409 X-Ray of Hand

1995. 150th Birth Anniv of Wilhelm Rontgen and Centenary of his Discovery of X-Rays.

2725	**1409**	84c. multicoloured	4·25	3·25

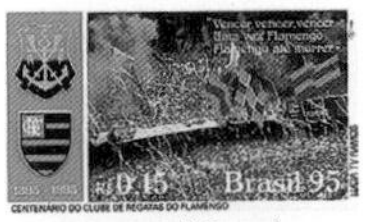

1410 Arms and Crowd

1995. Centenary of Flamengo Regatta Club.

2726	**1410**	15c. multicoloured	95	65

1411 Fungi and Alligator

1995. America. Environmental Protection. Multicoloured.

2727	15c. Type **1411**	80	65
2728	84c. Black-necked swans on lake	3·50	2·40

Nos. 2727/8 were issued together, *se-tenant*, forming a composite design.

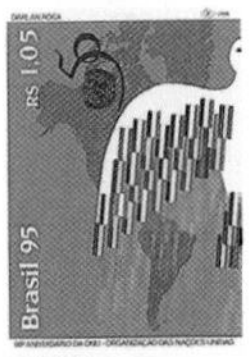

1412 Dove over World Map (left detail)

1995. 50th Anniv of U.N.O. Multicoloured.

2729	1r.05 Type **1412**	4·50	4·25
2730	1r.05 Dove over world map (right detail)	4·50	4·25

Nos. 2729/30 were issued together, *se-tenant*, forming a composite design.

1413 Jose Maria Eca de Queiroz

1995. Book Day. Writers' Anniversaries. Multicoloured.

2731	15c. Type **1413** (150th birth)	65	50
2732	15c. Rubem Braga (5th death)	65	50
2733	23c. Carlos Drummond de Andrade (8th death)	1·10	65

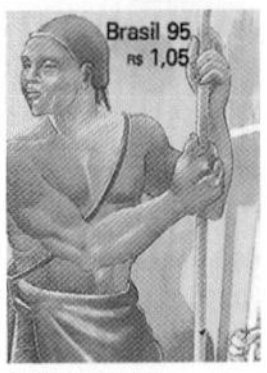

1414 Zumbi

1995. 300th Death Anniv of Zumbi (leader of Palmares (autonomous state formed by rebelled slaves)). Sheet 100×69 mm.

2734	**1414**	1r.05 multicoloured	5·00	5·00

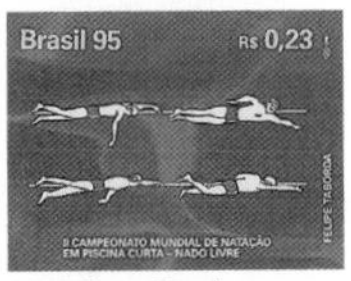

1415 Front Crawl (Freestyle)

1995. 11th World Short-course Swimming Championships, Rio de Janeiro. Multicoloured.

2735	23c. Type **1415**	95	65
2736	23c. Backstroke	95	65
2737	23c. Butterfly	95	65
2738	23c. Breaststroke	95	65

Nos. 2735/8 were issued together, *se-tenant*, forming a composite design of a swimming pool.

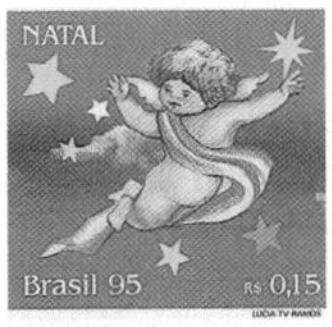

1416 Cherub

1995. Christmas. Multicoloured.

2739	15c. Type **1416**	80	50
2740	23c. Cherub (different)	95	65

Nos. 2739/40 were issued together, *se-tenant*, forming a composite design.

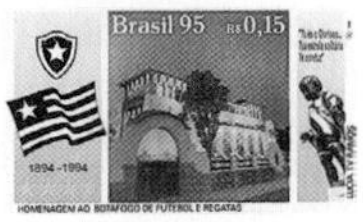

1417 Flag, Former Headquarters and *Manequinho* (statue)

1995. Centenary (1994) of Botafogo Football and Regatta Club.

2741	**1417**	15c. multicoloured	80	65

1418 Computer, Mouse and Masthead

1995. 170th Anniv of *Diario de Pernambuco* (newspaper).

2742	**1418**	23c. multicoloured	95	65

1419 Theatre Dome

1996. Centenary of Amazon Theatre, Manaus. Sheet 98×69 mm.

MS2743	**1419**	1r.23 multicoloured	6·00	6·00

1420 Prestes Maia and Sao Paulo

1996. Birth Centenary of Francisco Prestes Maia (Mayor of Sao Paulo).

2744	**1420**	18c. multicoloured	80	40

1421 Bornhausen and Santa Catarina

1996. Birth Centenary of Irineu Bornhausen (Governor of State of Santa Catarina).

2745	**1421**	27c. multicoloured	1·00	65

1422 *Ouro Preto Landscape* (Alberto da Veiga Guignard)

1996. Artists' Birth Centenaries. Multicoloured.

2746	15c. Type **1422**	60	40
2747	15c. *Boat with Little Flags and Birds* (Alfredo Volpi)	60	40

1423 Doll

1996. 50th Anniv of United Nations Children's Fund. Campaign against Sexual Abuse.

2748	**1423**	23c. multicoloured	1·00	50

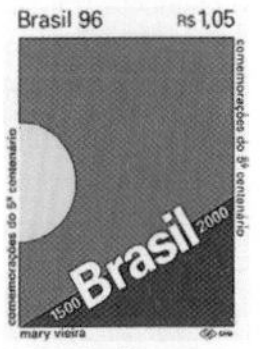

1424 Anniversary Emblem

1996. 500th Anniv (2000) of Discovery of Brazil by the Portuguese.

2749	**1424**	1r.05 multicoloured	3·75	2·50

1425 Pinheiro da Silva and National Congress

1996. Birth Centenary of Israel Pinheiro da Silva (politician).

2750	**1425**	18c. multicoloured	85	50

1426 Pantanal

1996. Tourism. Multicoloured. Self-adhesive. Imperf (backing paper rouletted).

2751	23c. Amazon River	1·00	65
2752	23c. Type **1426**	1·00	65
2753	23c. Jangada raft	1·00	65
2754	23c. *The Sugarloaf*, Guanabara Bay	1·00	65
2755	23c. Iguazu Falls	1·00	65

1427 Crimson Topaz

1996. Espamer 96 Spanish and Latin-American Stamp Exhibition, Seville, Spain. Hummingbirds. Multicoloured.

2756	15c. Type **1427**	85	40
2757	1r.05 Black-breasted plover-crest	5·00	2·50
2758	1r.15 Swallow-tailed hummingbird	5·00	2·50

1428 Marathon Runners

1996. Cent of Modern Olympic Games. Multicoloured.

2759	18c. Type **1428**	60	40
2760	23c. Gymnastics	65	50
2761	1r.05 Swimming	2·75	2·50
2762	1r.05 Beach volleyball	2·75	2·50

1429 Cave Entrance

1996. National Heritage. Caverns. Sheet 99×68 mm.

MS2763	**1429**	2r.68 multicoloured	9·50	9·50

1430 Dish Aerial, Satellite over Earth and Sports

1996. Americas Telecom 96 International Telecommunications Exn, Rio de Janeiro.

2764	**1430**	1r.05 multicoloured	4·00	2·50

1431 Sun and Raindrop replenishing Dry Tree

1996. World Anti-desertification Day. Sheet 70×96 mm.

MS2765	**1431**	1r.23 multicoloured	5·50	5·50

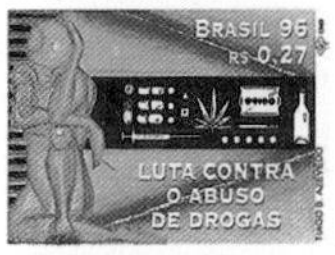

1432 Addict and Drugs

1996. Anti-drug Abuse Campaign.

2766	**1432**	27c. multicoloured	3·50	1·10

1433 Coloured Pencils

1996. Education Year.

2767	**1433**	23c. multicoloured	95	50

1434 Princess Isabel and Aurea Law

1996. 150th Birth Anniv of Princess Isabel the Redeemer.

2768	**1434**	18c. multicoloured	80	40

The Aurea Law abolished slavery in Brazil.

1435 Gomes and Peace Theatre

1996. Death Centenary of Carlos Gomes (opera composer).

2769	**1435**	50c. multicoloured	2·10	1·10

1436 *Cattleya eldorado*

1996. 15th International Orchid Conference, Rio de Janeiro. Multicoloured.

2770	15c. Type **1436**	1·30	45
2771	15c. *Cattleya loddigesii*	1·30	45
2772	15c. *Promenaea stapellioides*	1·30	45

1437 Melania and Maximino and Virgin Mary

1996. 150th Anniv of Apparition of Our Lady at La Salette, France.

2773	**1437**	1r. multicoloured	3·25	2·75

1438 Cuca

1996. BRAPEX 96 National Stamp Exhibition, Recife. Folk Legends. Sheet 72×100 mm containing T **1438** and similar horiz designs. Multicoloured.

MS2774	23c. Type **1438**; 1r.05 Boitata; 1r.15 Caipora	7·50	7·50

1439 *Marilyn Monroe* (Andy Warhol)

1996. 23rd International Biennale, Sao Paulo. Paintings. Multicoloured.

2775	55c. Type **1439**	1·40	1·00
2776	55c. *The Scream* (Edvard Munch)	1·40	1·00
2777	55c. *Mirror for the red Room* (Louise Bourgeois)	1·40	1·00
2778	55c. *Lent* (Pablo Picasso)	1·40	1·00

1440 Emblem

1996. Defenders of Nature (environmental organization).

2779	**1440**	10r. multicoloured	14·50	12·00

1441 Vaqueiro

1996. America. Traditional Costumes. Multicoloured.

2780	50c. Type **1441**	1·60	1·10
2781	1r. Baiana (seller of beancakes)	3·25	2·30

1442 Poinsettia and Lighted Candle

1996. Christmas.

2782	**1442**	(–) multicoloured	1·40	50

See second note below No. 2588.

1443 *Melindrosa* (cover of 1931 *O Cruzeiro* magazine)

1996. 46th Death Anniv of Jose Carlos (caricaturist).

2783	**1443**	(–) multicoloured	1·40	50

See second note below No. 2588.

1444 Ipiranga Monument

1996. Tourism. Multicoloured. Self-adhesive. Imperf (backing paper rouletted).

2784	(–) Type **1444**	80	55
2785	(–) Hercilio Luz Bridge	80	55
2786	(–) National Congress building	80	55
2787	(–) Pelourinho	80	55
2788	(–) Ver-o-Peso market	80	55

Nos. 2784/8 were valid for use at the current first stage inland letter rate.

1445 Campaign Emblem and Guanabara Bay

1997. Bid by Rio de Janeiro for 2004 Olympic Games.

2789	**1445**	(–) multicoloured	4·25	2·75

No. 2789 was valid for use at the current first stage international letter rate.

1446 Postman and Letter Recipients

1997. America. The Postman.

2790	**1446**	(–) multicoloured	1·30	60

No. 2790 was valid for use at the current first stage inland letter rate.

1447 Alves, Flogging and Salvador Harbour

1997. 150th Birth Anniv of Antonio de Castro Alves (poet).

2791	**1447**	15c. multicoloured	65	40

1448 *Tamandare* (after Miranda Junior) and *Rescue of 'Ocean Monarch'* by Don *Afonso* (Samuel Walters)

1997. Death Centenary of Marquis of Tamandare (naval reformer).

2792	**1448**	23c. multicoloured	65	50

1449 "Joy, Joy"

1997. Winning Entry in "Art on Stamps" Competition.

2793	**1449**	15c. multicoloured	4·25	65

1450 Globe in Glass of Water

1997. World Water Day.

2794	**1450**	1r.05 multicoloured	3·25	2·50

1451 Embraer EMB-145

1997. Brazilian Aircraft. Multicoloured. Self-adhesive. Imperf (backing paper rouletted).

2795	15c. Type **1451**	40	25
2796	15c. Aeritalia/Aermacchi AM-X jet fighter	40	25
2797	15c. Embraer EMB-312 H Super Tucano	40	25
2798	15c. Embraer EMB-120 Brasilia	40	25
2799	15c. Embraer EMB-312 Tucano trainer	40	25

1452 Red Ribbon inside Condom

1997. Family Health Association (A.S.F.) Anti-AIDS Campaign.

2810	**1452**	23c. multicoloured	75	45

1453 Traditional Weapons and Tribesmen

1997. Indian Cultures. Sheet 70×100 mm.

MS2811	**1453**	1r.15 multicoloured	3·50	3·25

1454 Emblem

1997. 500th Anniv (2000) of Discovery of Brazil by the Portuguese.

2812	**1454**	1r.05 multicoloured	3·25	2·50

1455 Pixinguinha

1997. Birth Centenary of Pixinguinha (musician).

2813	**1455**	15c. multicoloured	45	40

1456 Landmark

1997. Centenary of Brazilian Sovereignty of Trinidade Island. Sheet 99×68 mm.

MS2814	**1456**	1r.23 multicoloured	4·00	3·75

1457 Inscription

1997. "Human Rights, Rights of All".

2815	**1457**	18c. black and red	65	40

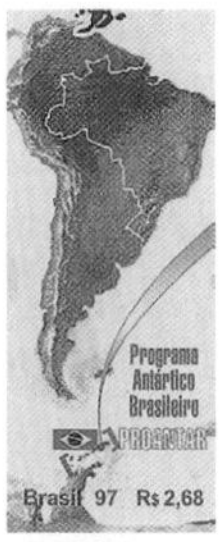

1458 Map

1997. Brazilian Antarctic Programme. Sheet 69×99 mm.

MS2816	**1458**	2r.68 multicoloured	8·75	8·25

1459 Melon

1997. Fruits. Self-adhesive. (a) Imperf (backing paper rouletted). (i) With service indicator.

2817	**1459**	(–) red and green	55	50

(ii) With face values.

2818	1c. yellow, orange & grn	15	15
2819	2c. yellow, brown & blk	15	15
2820	5c. orange, yellow & blk	15	15
2821	10c. yellow, brown & grn	25	25
2822	20c. yellow, red & green	55	50

(b) Die-cut wavy edge.

2823	1c. yellow, orange & grn	15	15
2824	10c. yellow, brown & grn	15	15
2825	20c. lt green, grn & blk	55	50
2826	22c. red, purple & green	55	40
2827	27c. orange, brown and green	65	65
2828	40c. multicoloured	80	75
2829	50c. multicoloured	80	75
2830	51c. green, lt grn & brn	1·30	1·30
2831	80c. red, green & yellow	2·10	2·00
2832	82c. lt grn, grn & dp grn	2·10	2·00
2833	1r. red, green & yellow	2·75	1·60

DESIGNS—HORIZ: Nos. 2818, 2823, Oranges; 2819, Bananas; 2820, Mango. VERT: Nos. 2821, 2824, Pineapple; 2822, Cashew nuts; 2825, Sugar-apple; 2826, Grapes; 2827, Cupuacu; 2828, Soursop; 2829, Suriname cherry ("Pitanga"); 2830, Coconut; 2831, Apples; 2832, Limes; 2833, Strawberries.

No. 2817 was valid for use at the current first stage inland letter rate.

1460 Mahogany (*Swietenia macropylla*)

1997. World Environment Day. Amazon Flora and Fauna. Multicoloured.

2836	27c. Type **1460**	80	65
2837	27c. Arapaima (55×22 mm)	80	65

1461 Antonio Vieira in Pulpit

1997. Death Anniversaries of Missionaries to Brazil. Multicoloured.

2838 1r.05 Type **1461** (300th) 2·75 2·50
2839 1r.05 Indian children and Jose de Auchieta (400th) 2·75 2·50

1462 Parnaiba Delta and Sculpture (Mestre Dezinho)

1997. Tourism. With service indicator. Mult.

2840 (–) Type **1462** 2·75 2·50
2841 (–) Lencois Maranhenses National Park and costume 2·75 2·50

Nos. 2840/1 were valid for use at the current rate for first class international postage.

1463 Blue-black Grassquit

1997. Birds. Multicoloured. Self-adhesive. Imperf (backing paper rouletted). (a) With service indicator.

2842 (–) Type **1463** 95 90

(b) With face value.

2843 22c. Social flycatcher ("Vermilion-crowned Flycatcher") 55 50

No. 2842 was valid for use at the current first stage inland letter rate.

1464 Academy

1998. Centenary of Brazilian Literature Academy.

2850 **1464** 22c. multicoloured 95 50

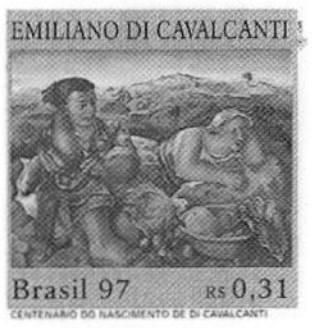

1465 *Gipsies* (Di Cavalcanti)

1997. Birth Centenary of Emiliano di Cavalcanti (artist).

2851 **1465** 31c. multicoloured 85 75

1466 Pope John Paul II, "Christ the Redeemer" and Family

1997. Second World Meeting of Pope with Families, Rio de Janeiro.

2852 **1466** 1r.20 multicoloured 4·75 3·00

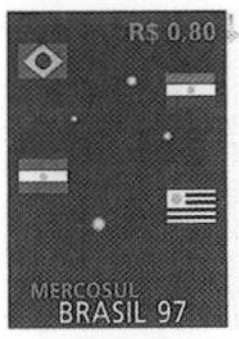

1467 Flags of Member Countries

1997. Mercosur (South American Common Market).

2853 **1467** 80c. multicoloured 2·75 1·90

1468 Antonio Conselheiro (religious leader)

1997. Centenary of End of Canudos War.

2854 **1468** 22c. multicoloured 70 50

1469 Mercosur Members starred on Map of South America

1997. 25th Anniv of Telebras.

2855 **1469** 80c. multicoloured 3·25 1·90

1470 Lorenzo Fernandez and Score of *Sonata Breve*

1997. Composers' Birth Centenaries. Each black and gold.

2856 22c. Type **1470** 70 50
2857 22c. Francisco Mignone and score of *Second Brazilian Fantasia* 70 50

1471 "Our Good Mother" and Blackboard with Marist Motto

1997. Centenary of Marist Brothers in Brazil.

2858 **1471** 22c. multicoloured 70 50

1472 Angel playing Trumpet

1997. Christmas.

2859 **1472** 22c. multicoloured 70 50

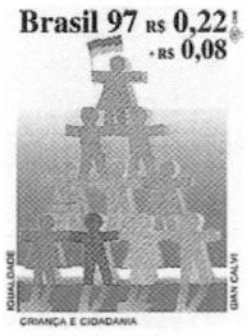

1473 'Equality' (Gian Calvi)

1997. Children and Citizenship. Multicoloured.

2860 22c.+8c. Type **1473** 85 75
2861 22c.+8c. "Love and Tenderness" (Alcy Linares) 85 75
2862 22c.+8c. "Admission to School" (Ziraldo) 85 75
2863 22c.+8c. "Healthy Pregnancy" (Claudio Martins) 85 75
2864 22c.+8c. "Being Happy" (Cica Fittipaldi) 85 75
2865 22c.+8c. "Work for Parents, School for Children" (Roger Mello) 85 75
2866 22c.+8c. "Breast-feeding" (Angela Lago) 85 75
2867 22c.+8c. "Civil Registration" (Mauricio de Sousa) 85 75
2868 22c.+8c. "Integration of the Handicapped" (Nelson Cruz) 85 75
2869 22c.+8c. "Presence of Parents during Illness" (Eliardo Franca) 85 75
2870 22c.+8c. "Quality of Teaching" (Graca Lima) 85 75
2871 22c.+8c. "Safe Delivery" (Eva Furnari) 85 75
2872 22c.+8c. "Family and Community Life" (Gerson Conforti) 85 75
2873 22c.+8c. "Music playing" (Ana Raquel) 85 75
2874 22c.+8c. "Respect and Dignity" (Helena Alexandrino) 85 75
2875 22c.+8c. "Summary of Children's Statute" (Darlan Rosa) 85 75

1474 Children and Globe

1997. Education and Citizenship.

2876 **1474** 31c. blue and yellow 1·00 75

1475 Belo Horizonte at Night

1997. Centenary of Belo Horizonte.

2877 **1475** 31c. multicoloured 1·00 75

1476 Outline Map and Books (Education)

1997. Citizens' Rights. Multicoloured. Self-adhesive.

2878 22c. Type **1476** 1·40 50
2879 22c. Map and hand holding labour card (work) 1·40 50
2880 22c. Map and fruit (agriculture) 1·40 50
2881 22c. Map and stethoscope (health) 1·40 50
2882 22c. Clapper-board and paint brush (culture) 1·40 50

1477 Alexandrite

1998. Minerals. Multicoloured.

2883 22c. Type **1477** 85 50
2884 22c. Chrysoberyl cat's-eye 85 50
2885 22c. Indicolite 85 50

1478 Elis Regina (singer)

1998. America. Famous Women. Multicoloured.

2886 22c. Type **1478** 70 50
2887 22c. Clementina de Jesus (singer) 70 50
2888 22c. Dulcina de Moraes (actress) 70 50
2889 22c. Clarice Lispector (writer) 70 50

1479 Pupils

1998. Education. Multicoloured.

2890 31c. Type **1479** (universal schooling) 85 75
2891 31c. Teacher (teacher appraisal) 85 75

Nos. 2390/1 were issued together, *se-tenant*, forming a composite design of a classroom.

1480 Cruze Sousa

1998. Death Centenary of Joao da Cruze Sousa (poet).

2892 **1480** 36c. multicoloured 1·10 90

1481 Map, 1519

1998. 500th Anniv (2000) of Discovery of Brazil by the Portuguese. Multicoloured.

2893 1r.05 Type **1481** 2·75 2·50
2894 1r.05 Galleon 2·75 2·50

Nos. 2893/4 were issued together, *se-tenant*, forming a composite design.

1482 Woman Caring for Elderly Man

1998. Voluntary Work. Multicoloured.

2895 31c. Type **1482** 85 75
2896 31c. Woman caring for child 85 75
2897 31c. Fighting forest fire 85 75
2898 31c. Adult's and child's hands 85 75

Nos. 2895/8 were issued together, *se-tenant*, forming a composite design.

1483 Clown

1998. Circus. Multicoloured.

2899 31c. Type **1483** 85 75
2900 31c. Clown resting on stick 85 75
2901 31c. Clown (left half) and outside of Big Top 85 75
2902 31c. Clown (right half) and inside of Big Top 85 75

Nos. 2899/2902 were issued together, *se-tenant*, forming a composite design.

1484 Turtle

1998. Expo '98 World's Fair, Lisbon. International Year of the Ocean. Multicoloured.

2903 31c. Type **1484** 85 75
2904 31c. Tail of whale 85 75
2905 31c. Barracuda 85 75
2906 31c. Jellyfish and fishes 85 75
2907 31c. Diver and school of fishes 85 75
2908 31c. Two dolphins 85 75
2909 31c. Angelfish (brown spotted fish) 85 75
2910 31c. Two whales 85 75
2911 31c. Two long-nosed butterflyfishes (with black stripe across eye) 85 75
2912 31c. Sea perch (red and yellow fish) 85 75
2913 31c. Manatee 85 75
2914 31c. Seabream (blue, yellow and white fish) 85 75
2915 31c. Emperor angelfish and coral 85 75
2916 31c. School of snappers (blue and yellow striped fishes) 85 75
2917 31c. Flying gurnard 85 75
2918 31c. Manta ray 85 75
2919 31c. Two butterflyfishes (black and green fishes) 85 75
2920 31c. Pipefish 85 75
2921 31c. Moray eel 85 75
2922 31c. Angelfish (blue, yellow and black) and coral 85 75
2923 31c. Red and yellow fish, starfish and coral 85 75
2924 31c. Crab and coral 85 75
2925 31c. Snapper and coral 85 75
2926 31c. Seahorse and coral 85 75

Nos. 2903/26 were issued together, *se-tenant*, forming a composite design.

1485 Ball breaking Net (Antonio Henrique Amaral)

1998. World Cup Football Championship, France. Designs depicting football art by named artists. Multicoloured.

2927	22c. Type **1485**	55	50
2928	22c. Aldemir Martins	55	50
2929	22c. Glauco Rodrigues	55	50
2930	22c. Marcia Grostein	55	50
2931	22c. Claudio Tozzi	55	50
2932	22c. Zelio Alves Pinto	55	50
2933	22c. Guto Lacaz	55	50
2934	22c. Antonio Peticov	55	50
2935	22c. Cildo Meireles	55	50
2936	22c. Mauricio Nogueira Lima	55	50
2937	22c. Roberto Magalhaes	55	50
2938	22c. Luiz Zerbine	55	50
2939	22c. Maciej Babinski (horiz)	55	50
2940	22c. Wesley Duke Lee (horiz)	55	50
2941	22c. Joao Camara (horiz)	55	50
2942	22c. Jose Zaragoza (horiz)	55	50
2943	22c. Mario Gruber (horiz)	55	50
2944	22c. Nelson Leirner (horiz)	55	50
2945	22c. Carlos Vergara (horiz)	55	50
2946	22c. Tomoshige Kusuno (horiz)	55	50
2947	22c. Gregorio Gruber (horiz)	55	50
2948	22c. Jose Roberto Aguilar (horiz)	55	50
2949	22c. Ivald Granato (horiz)	55	50
2950	22c. Leda Catunda (horiz)	55	50

1486 Bean Casserole and Vegetables

1998. Cultural Dishes.

2951	**1486**	31c. multicoloured	1·00	75

1487 *Araucaria angustifolia*

1998. Environmental Protection. Multicoloured.

2952	22c. Type **1487**	95	50
2953	22c. Azure jay (*Cyanocorax caeruleus*)	95	50

Nos. 2952/3 were issued together, *se-tenant*, forming a composite design.

1488 *Tapajo*

1998. Launching of Submarine *Tapajo*.

2954	**1488**	51c. multicoloured	1·40	1·30

1489 Bust of Queiroz and College Building

1998. Death Centenary of Luiz de Queiroz (founder of Agricultural College, Piracicaba).

2955	**1489**	36c. multicoloured	1·00	90

1490 Statue of St. Benedict and Monastery

1998. 400th Anniv of St. Benedict's Monastery, Sao Paulo.

2956	**1490**	22c. multicoloured	85	50

1491 Santos-Dumont and his First Balloon "Brasil"

1998. Aviation. Aircraft Designs by Alberto Santos-Dumont (aviator). Multicoloured.

2957	31c. Type **1491**	85	75
2958	31c. Santos-Dumont and Dirigible *No. 1*	85	75

1492 Early Film of Guanabara Bay

1998. Centenary (1997) of Brazilian Cinema. Multicoloured.

2959	31c. Type **1492**	85	75
2960	31c. Taciana Reis (actress) in *Limite* (dir. Mario Peixoto, 1912)	85	75
2961	31c. Grande Otela and Oscarito in *A Dupla do Barulho* (dir. Carlos Manga, 1953) (inscr "Chanchada")	85	75
2962	31c. Mazzaropi (actor) and film titles (Vera Cruz film company)	85	75
2963	31c. Glauber Rocha (director) (*New Cinema*)	85	75
2964	31c. Titles of prize-winning films, 1962–98	85	75

1493 Andrade, Entrance to St. Antony's Church (Tiradentes) and Church of Our Lady of the Rosary (Ouro Preto)

1998. Birth Centenary of Rodrigo Melo Franco de Andrade (founder of Federal Institution for Preservation of the National Historic and Artistic Patrimony).

2965	**1493**	51c. multicoloured	1·40	1·10

1494 Cascudo and Folk Characters

1998. Birth Centenary of Luis da Camara Cascudo (writer).

2966	**1494**	22c. multicoloured	90	50

1495 Fencing

1998. 42nd World Aeronautical Pentathlon Championships, Natal. Multicoloured.

2967	22c. Type **1495**	90	50
2968	22c. Running	90	50
2969	22c. Swimming	90	50
2970	22c. Shooting	90	50
2971	22c. Basketball	90	50

1496 Missionary Cross and St. Michael of the Missions Church

1998. Mercosur. Missions.

2972	**1496**	80c. multicoloured	2·30	1·50

1497 *Untitled Work* (Jose Leonilson) (Biennale emblem)

1998. 24th Art Biennale, Sao Paulo. Paintings. Multicoloured.

2973	31c. Type **1497**	85	65
2974	31c. *Tapuia Dance* (Albert von Eckhout)	85	65
2975	31c. *The Schoolboy* (Vincent van Gogh) (vert)	85	65
2976	31c. *Portrait of Michel Leiris* (Francis Bacon) (vert)	85	65
2977	31c. *The King's Museum* (Rene Magritte) (vert)	85	65
2978	31c. *Urutu* (Tarsila do Amaral)	85	65
2979	31c. *Facade with Arcs, Circle and Fascia* (Alfredo Volpi) (vert)	85	65
2980	31c. *The Raft of the Medusa* (Asger Jorn)	85	65

1498 "Citizenship" (Erika Albuquerque)

1998. Child and Citizenship.

2981	**1498**	22c. multicoloured	85	40

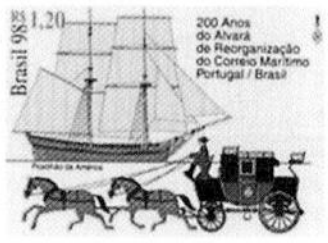

1499 Mail Coach and *Postilhao da America* (brigantine)

1998. Bicentenary of Reorganization of Maritime Mail Service between Portugal and Brazil.

2982	**1499**	1r.20 multicoloured	2·75	2·50

1500 *D. Pedro I* (Simplicio Rodrigues da Sa), Crown and Sceptre

1998. Birth Bicentenary of Emperor Pedro I.

2983	**1500**	22c. multicoloured	80	40

1501 Mangoes and Glasses of Juice

1998. Frisco (fruit juice) Publicity Campaign. Self-adhesive.

2984	**1501**	36c. multicoloured	4·00	2·75

1502 *Solanum lycocarpum*

1998. Cerrado Flowers. Multicoloured.

2985	31c. Type **1502**	80	65
2986	31c. *Cattleya walkeriana*	80	65
2987	31c. *Kielmeyera coriacea*	80	65

1503 Mother Teresa (founder of Missionaries of Charity)

1998. Peace and Fraternity. Multicoloured.

2988	31c. Type **1503**	80	65
2989	31c. Friar Galvao (first Brazilian to be beatified, 1998)	80	65
2990	31c. Betinho (Herbert Jose de Souza)	80	65
2991	31c. Friar Damiao	80	65

Nos. 2988/91 were issued together, *se-tenant*, forming a central composite design of the Earth.

1504 Sergio Motta and Headquarters, Brasilia

1998. First Anniv of National Telecommunications Agency.

2992	**1504**	31c. multicoloured	95	65

Motta was Minister of Communications when the agency was established.

1505 Tiles and Church of Our Lady of Fatima, Brasilia

1998. Christmas.

2993	**1505**	22c. multicoloured	90	40

1506 Moxoto Goat

1998. Domestic Animals. Mult. Self-adhesive.

2994	22c. Type **1506**	60	35
2995	22c. North-eastern donkey	60	35
2996	22c. Junqueira ox	60	35
2997	22c. Brazilian terrier (vert)	60	35
2998	22c. Brazilian shorthair (vert)	60	35

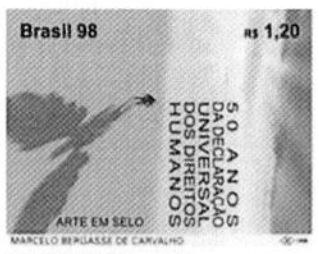

1507 Man casting Winged Shadow

1998. 50th Anniv of Universal Declaration of Human Rights.

2999	**1507**	1r.20 multicoloured	4·00	1·90

1508 Mother Luiza Lighthouse, Natal

1999. 400th Annivs of Natal (1999) and of Wise Men's Fortress (1998). Multicoloured.

3000	31c. Type **1508**	1·00	40
3001	31c. Wise Men's Fortress, Natal (horiz)	1·00	40

1509 Extent of Economic Zone, Satellite and Belmonte Lighthouse

1999. Evaluation Programme of Sustainable Potential of Living Resources in the Exclusive Economic Zone (REVIZEE). Multicoloured.

3002	31c. Type **1509** (Sao Pedro and Sao Paulo Archipelago Research Programme)	65	40
3003	31c. Blue-faced booby on buoy	65	40
3004	31c. *Riobaldo* (research ship)	65	40
3005	31c. Turtle	65	40
3006	31c. Dolphin	65	40
3007	31c. Diver	65	40

Nos. 3002/7 were issued together, *se-tenant*, forming a composite design.

No. 3004 includes the emblem of "Australia 99" International Stamp Exhibition, Melbourne.

1510 Stamp Vending Machines of 1940s and 1998

1999. 125th Anniv of Universal Postal Union. Multicoloured.

3008	31c. Type **1510**	65	40
3009	31c. Postal products vending machines of 1906 and 1998	65	40
3010	31c. Postboxes of 1870 and 1973	65	40
3011	31c. Brazilian Quality and Productivity Programme silver award to Rio Grande postal region, 1998	65	40

Nos. 3008/11 were issued together, *se-tenant*, forming a composite design of the U.P.U. emblem.

1511 Lacerda Lift, Barra Lighthouse and Church of Our Lady of the Rosary

1999. 450th Anniv of Salvador.

3012	**1511**	1r.05 multicoloured	3·50	1·60

1512 Footprint, Iguanodon, Stegosaurus and Allosaurus

1999. iBRA 99 International Stamp Exhibition, Nuremberg, Germany. Valley of the Dinosaurs, Sousa.

3013	**1512**	1r.05 multicoloured	2·75	1·90

1513 Fortress

1999. 415th Anniv of St. Amaro of Barra Grande Fortress, Guaruja.

3014	**1513**	22c. multicoloured	75	40

1514 Children of Various Races

1999. 500th Anniv (2000) of Discovery of Brazil (4th issue). Sheet 69×99 mm.

MS3015 **1514**	2r.68 multicoloured	6·25	6·25

1515 Embracer EMB-110 Bandeirante, Emblem, Dove and Globe

1999. 30th Anniv of 6th Air Transportation Squadron.

3016	**1515**	51c. multicoloured	1·60	90

1516 Banner and Revellers

1999. Feast of the Holy Spirit, Planaltina.

3017	**1516**	22c. multicoloured	70	40

1517 Ouro Preto

1999. Philexfrance 99 International Stamp Exhibition. World Heritage Sites. Sheet 70×110 containing T **1517** and similar horiz designs. Multicoloured.

MS3018	1r.05 Type **1517**; 1r.05 Olinda; 1r.05 Sao Lius	7·00	7·00

1518 Symbols of Computer Science, Chemistry, Engineering, Metallurgy and Geology

1999. Centenary of Institute for Technological Research, Sao Paulo.

3019	**1518**	36c. multicoloured	95	50

1519 Santos-Dumont and Ballon No. 3

1999. Centenary of Flight of Alberto Santos-Dumont's Airship Ballon No. 3.

3020	**1519**	1r.20 multicoloured	3·50	1·80

1520 Anteater and Emblem

1999. National Campaign for Prevention and Combat of Forest Fires (PREVFOGO). Mult. Self-adhesive.

3021	51c. Type **1520**	1·10	75
3022	51c. Flower and IBAMA emblem	1·10	75
3023	51c. Leaf and IBAMA emblem	1·10	75
3024	51c. Burnt tree trunk and PREVFOGO emblem	1·10	75

Nos. 3021/4 were issued together, *se-tenant*, forming a composite design of a map and flames.

Nos. 3021/4 are also impregnated with the scent of burnt wood.

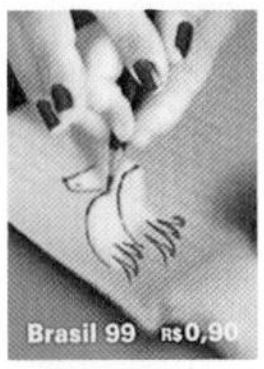

1521 Hands drawing Dove

1999. America. A New Millennium without Arms. Sheet 109×69 mm containing T **1521** and similar vert design. Multicoloured.

MS3025	90c. Type **1521**; 90c. Overturned tank	4·25	4·25

1522 Stitched Heart

1999. 20th Anniv of Political Amnesty in Brazil.

3026	**1522**	22c. multicoloured	65	25

1523 Joaquim Nabuco (politician)

1999. 150th Birth Anniversaries. Multicoloured.

3027	22c. Type **1523**	65	25
3028	31c. Rui Barbosa (politician)	80	40

1524 Dorado

1999. China '99 International Stamp Exhibition, Peking. Fishes. Multicoloured.

3029	22c. Type **1524**	30	25
3030	31c. *Brycon microlepis*	45	40
3031	36c. *Acestrorhynchus pantaneiro*	65	50
3032	51c. Tetra "*Hyphessobrycon eques*"	95	75
3033	80c. *Rineloricaria* sp.	1·40	1·10
3034	90c. *Leporinus macrocephalus*	1·60	1·30
3035	1r.05 *Abramites* sp.	1·90	1·50
3036	1r.20 Bristle-mouthed catfish	2·20	1·80

Nos. 3029/36 were issued together, *se-tenant*, with the backgrounds forming a composite design.

No. 3036 also includes a hologram of the exhibition emblem.

1525 Open Book and Flags of Member Countries

1999. Mercosur. The Book.

3037	**1525**	80c. multicoloured	2·50	1·30

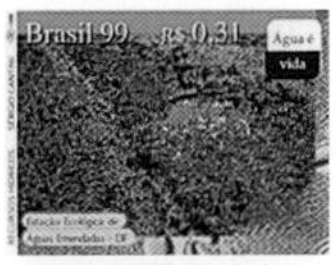

1526 Aguas Emendadas Ecological Station

1999. Water Resources. Multicoloured.

3038	31c. Type **1526**	50	40
3039	31c. House and jetty	50	40
3040	31c. Cedro Dam	50	40
3041	31c. Oros Dam	50	40

Nos. 3038/41 were issued together, *se-tenant*, forming a composite design of a whirlpool.

1527 "Ex Libris" (Eliseu Visconti)

1999. National Library, Rio de Janeiro.

3042	**1527**	22c. multicoloured	55	25

1999. State Flags (6th series). As T **992**.

3043	31c. Amapa	65	50
3044	36c. Roraima	65	50

1528 Piano and Woman

1999. Fifth Death Anniv of Antonio Carlos Jobim (composer).

3045	**1528**	31c. multicoloured	65	50

1529 The Annunciation

1999. Christmas. Birth Bimillenary of Jesus Christ. Multicoloured.

3046	22c. Type **1529**	35	25
3047	22c. Adoration of the Magi	35	25
3048	22c. Presentation of Jesus in the Temple	35	25
3049	22c. Baptism of Jesus by John the Baptist	35	25
3050	22c. Jesus and the Twelve Apostles	35	25
3051	22c. Death and resurrection of Jesus	35	25

1530 Open Book and Globe

1999. New Middle School Education Programme.

3052	**1530**	31c. multicoloured	70	50

1531 Itamaraty Palace, Rio de Janeiro

1999. Centenary of Installation of Ministry of Foreign Relations Headquarters in Itamaraty Palace, Rio de Janeiro.

3053	**1531**	1r.05 brown and stone	2·75	1·60

1532 Buildings and Trees (Milena Karoline Ribeiro Reis)

2000. "Stampin the Future". Winning Entries in Children's International Painting Competition. Multicoloured.

3054	22c.+8c. Type **1532**	65	50
3055	22c.+8c. Globe, sun, trees, children and whale (Caio Ferreira Guimaraes de Oliveira)	65	50
3056	22c.+8c. Woman with globe on dress (Clarissa Cazane)	65	50
3057	22c.+8c. Children hugging globe (Jonas Sampaio de Freitas)	65	50

1533 "2000"

2000. New Millennium.

3058	**1533**	90c. multicoloured	2·00	1·50

1534 Map of South America and Children holding Books

2000. National School Book Programme.

3059	**1534**	31c. multicoloured	85	65

1535 Ada Rogato

2000. Women Aviators. Multicoloured.

3060	22c. Type **1535**	50	40
3061	22c. Thereza de Marzo	50	40
3062	22c. Anesia Pinheiro	50	40

1536 Moqueca Capixaba

2000. Cultural Dishes. Multicoloured.

3063	1r.05 Type **1536**	2·75	2·10
3064	1r.05 Moqueca baiana	2·75	2·10

1537 Freyre and Institute Facade

2000. Birth Centenary of Gilberto Freyre (writer).

3065	**1537**	36c. multicoloured	1·00	75

1538 Painting and Emblem

2000. 500th Anniv of the Discovery of Brazil.

3066	**1538**	51c. multicoloured	1·30	1·00

1539 Natives

2000. 500th Anniv of the Discovery of Brazil. Multicoloured.

3067	31c. Type **1539**	85	65
3068	31c. Natives watching ships	85	65
3069	31c. Sailors in rigging	85	65
3070	31c. Ships sails and natives	85	65

1540 Sailing Ship and Brazilian Flag

2000. 500th Anniv of the Discovery of Brazil. Multicoloured.

3071	45c. Type **1540**	1·30	1·00
3072	45c. Man dressed in red suit, pineapple and telephone dial	1·30	1·00
3073	45c. Red-spectacled amazon and silhouettes of sailing ships	1·30	1·00
3074	45c. Four babies	1·30	1·00
3075	45c. Go-kart, Formula 1 racing car and Ayrton Senna	1·30	1·00
3076	45c. Sloth, Toco toucan, crocodile, penguin and tiger	1·30	1·00
3077	45c. Outline of Brazil and compass roses	1·30	1·00
3078	45c. Peace dove	1·30	1·00
3079	45c. Child with decorated face	1·30	1·00
3080	45c. "500" emblem	1·30	1·00
3081	45c. Man wearing feather headdress	1·30	1·00
3082	45c. Man in boat, sails and town (Nataly M. N. Moriya)	1·30	1·00
3083	45c. Wristwatch, balloon, Alberto Santos-Dumont and his biplane *14 bis*	1·30	1·00
3084	45c. Sailing ship and document (first report of discovery)	1·30	1·00
3085	45c. Jules Rimet Cup and World Cup trophies, player, football and year dates (Brazilian victories in World Cup Football Championship)	1·30	1·00
3086	45c. Hand writing, street lights and fireworks	1·30	1·00
3087	45c. Banners and Brazilian flag forming cow	1·30	1·00
3088	45c. Golden conure perched on branch	1·30	1·00
3089	45c. Bakairi masks	1·30	1·00
3090	45c. Globe, ship and emblem	1·30	1·00

1541 Globe and Map of Brazil

2000. Second Anniv of BrazilTradeNet (business information web site).

3091	**1541**	27c. multicoloured	65	50

1542 Turtle, Scarlet Macaw and Map

2000. National Coastal Management Programme (GERCO).

3092	**1542**	40c. multicoloured	1·00	75

1543 Waterfall and Detail of Map

2000. EXPO 2000 World's Fair, Hanover, Germany and 31st International Geologic Congress, Rio de Janeiro. Sheet 109×69 mm containing T **1543** and similar vert design. Multicoloured.

MS3093	1r.30 Type **1543**; 1r.30 Map of Brazil; 1r.30 Gold ingot and minerals	10·00	10·00

1544 Cruz, Students and Building Facade

2000. Centenary of the Oswaldo Cruz Foundation (medical research institution).

3094	**1544**	40c. multicoloured	1·00	75

1545 Mask, Musical Instruments and Jewellery

2000. Africa Day.

3095	**1545**	1r.10 multicoloured	2·75	2·10

1546 Klink in Rowing Boat and Portion of Globe showing Route

2000. Voyages by Amyr Klink (navigator). Multicoloured.

3096	1r. Type **1546** (first South Atlantic crossing by rowing boat (1984))	2·75	2·00
3097	1r. *Paratii* (polar sailing boat) in Antarctica and portion of globe showing route (first single-handed circumnavigation of Antarctica (1999))	2·75	2·00

Nos. 3096/7 were issued together, *se-tenant*, forming a composite design.

1547 Flag, Buildings, Map and City Arms

2000. 150th Anniv of Juiz de Fora.

3098	**1547**	60c. multicoloured	1·70	1·30

1548 Hang Gliding

2000. Outdoor Pursuits. Multicoloured. Self-adhesive.

3099	27c. Type **1548**	65	50
3100	27c. Surfing	65	50
3101	40c. Rock climbing	1·00	75
3102	40c. Skateboarding	1·00	75

1549 Forest

2000. Environmental Protection. Multicoloured.

3103	40c. Type **1549**	1·20	90
3104	40c. Oncilla standing on branch in forest	1·20	90
3105	40c. Vegetation, adult oncilla and head of kitten	1·20	90
3106	40c. Vegetation, adult oncilla and body of kitten	1·20	90

Nos. 3103/6 were issued together, *se-tenant*, forming a composite design.

1550 *Cisne Branco* (full-rigged cadet ship)

2000. Brazilian Navy. Cadet Ships. Multicoloured.

3107	27c. Type **1550**	85	65
3108	27c. *Brasil* (cadet frigate)	85	65

1551 *Oswaldo Cruz* (hospital ship) and Birds

2000. Environment Protection. Sheet 137×84 mm.

MS3109	**1551** 1r.50 multicoloured	4·25	4·25

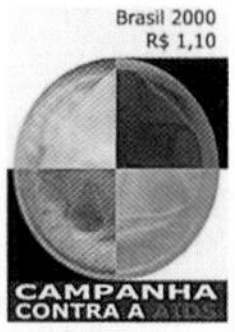

1552 Emblem

2000. America. Health Campaigns. Sheet 84×137 mm containing T **1552** and similar vert design. Multicoloured.

MS3110	1r.10 Type **1552** (anti-AIDS); 1r.10 Glasses, pills, needles and Marijuana leaves (national anti-drugs week)	6·00	6·00

1553 Teixeira, Carneiro Ribeiro Education Center, Salvador and Pupils

2000. Birth Centenary of Anisio Teixeira (education reformer).

3111	**1553**	45c. multicoloured	1·30	1·00

1554 Child walking to School

2000. Tenth Anniv of the Children and Teenagers Statute (3112) and 15th Anniv of National Movement of Street Boys and Girls (3113). Multicoloured.

3112	27c. Type **1554**	85	65
3113	40c. Rainbow with girl and boy holding star	1·20	90

1555 Capanema

2000. Birth Centenary of Gustavo Capanema Filho (politician).

3114	**1555**	60c. multicoloured	1·70	1·30

1556 Television and Hand writing in Notebook

2000. Fifth Anniv of Telecourse 2000 (educational television programme).

3115	**1556**	27c. multicoloured	85	65

1557 Campos

2000. Birth Centenary of Milton Campos (politician and lawyer).

3116	**1557**	1r. multicoloured	2·75	2·10

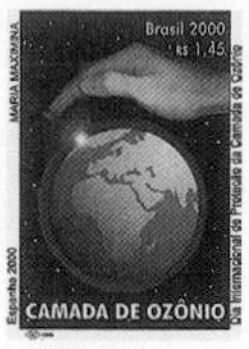

1558 Hand protecting Globe

2000. World Day for Protection of the Ozone Layer.

3117	**1558**	1r.45 multicoloured	3·75	3·00

1559 Archery

2000. Olympic Games, Sydney. Multicoloured.

3118	40c. Type **1559**	1·00	75
3119	40c. Beach volleyball	1·00	75
3120	40c. Boxing	1·00	75
3121	40c. Football	1·00	75
3122	40c. Canoeing	1·00	75
3123	40c. Handball	1·00	75
3124	40c. Diving	1·00	75
3125	40c. Rhythmic gymnastics	1·00	75
3126	40c. Badminton	1·00	75
3127	40c. Swimming	1·00	75
3128	40c. Hurdling	1·00	75
3129	40c. Pentathlon	1·00	75
3130	40c. Basketball	1·00	75
3131	40c. Tennis	1·00	75
3132	40c. Marathon	1·00	75
3133	40c. High-jump	1·00	75
3134	40c. Long-distance running	1·00	75
3135	40c. Triple jump	1·00	75
3136	40c. Triathlon	1·00	75
3137	40c. Sailing	1·00	75
3138	40c. Pommel horse (gymnastics)	1·00	75
3139	40c. Weightlifting	1·00	75
3140	40c. Discus	1·00	75
3141	40c. Rings (gymnastics)	1·00	75
3142	40c. Athletics	1·00	75
3143	40c. Javelin	1·00	75
3144	40c. Artistic gymnastics	1·00	75
3145	40c. Hockey	1·00	75
3146	40c. Volleyball	1·00	75
3147	40c. Synchronized swimming	1·00	75
3148	40c. Judo	1·00	75
3149	40c. Wrestling	1·00	75
3150	40c. Cycling	1·00	75
3151	40c. Rowing	1·00	75
3152	40c. Parallel bars (gymnastics)	1·00	75
3153	40c. Horse riding	1·00	75
3154	40c. Pole vault	1·00	75
3155	40c. Fencing	1·00	75
3156	40c. Rifle shooting	1·00	75
3157	40c. Taekwondo	1·00	75

1560 Surgeon and Electrocardiogram Graph

2000. Organ Donation. Multicoloured.

3158	1r.50 Type **1560**	4·00	3·00
3159	1r.50 Hands holding heart	4·00	3·00

Nos. 3158/9 were issued together, *se-tenant*, each pair forming a composite design.

1561 Brazilian Clovis Mask

2000. Brazil–China Joint Issue. 25th Anniv of Diplomatic Relations between Brazil and China. Multicoloured.

3160	27c. Type **1561**	65	50
3161	27c. Chinese Monkey King puppet	65	50

1562 Chico Landi and Ferrari 125 Formula 1 Racing Car

2000. Motor Racing Personalities. Multicoloured.

3162	1r.30 Type **1562**	3·25	2·40

3163 1r.45 Ayrton Senna and Formula 1 racing car 3·50 2·75

1563 Embraer EMB 145 AEW

2000. Brazilian Aircraft. Multicoloured. Self-adhesive.

3164	27c. Type **1563**	65	50
3165	27c. Super Tucano	65	50
3166	27c. Embraer AMX-T	65	50
3167	27c. Embraer ERJ 135	65	50
3168	27c. Embraer ERJ 170	65	50
3169	27c. Embraer ERJ 145	65	50
3170	27c. Embraer ERJ 190	65	50
3171	27c. Embraer EMB 145 RS/MP	65	50
3172	27c. Embraer ERJ 140	65	50
3173	27c. Embraer EMB 120	65	50

1564 Hand reaching for Star

2000. Christmas. Multicoloured.

3174	27c. Type **1564**	65	50
3175	27c. Mary and Jesus	65	50
3176	27c. Family and fishes	65	50
3177	27c. Jesus pointing to his heart	65	50
3178	27c. Trees, Globe and open hand	65	50
3179	27c. Jesus and Globe	65	50

Nos. 3174/5, 3176/7 and 3178/9 respectively were issued together, *se-tenant*, forming a composite design.

1565 Conductor's Baton and Music Score

2000. Light and Sound Shows.
3180 **1565** 1r.30 multicoloured 3·25 2·50

1566 Maps and Baron Rio Branco

2000. Centenary of Arbitration Ruling setting Boundary between Brazil and French Guiana.
3181 **1566** 40c. multicoloured 1·00 75

1567 Three Wise Men, Chalice and Dove

2001. New Millennium. Multicoloured.

3182	40c. Type **1567**	1·00	75
3183	1r.30 Star of David, Menorah, scroll and stone tablets	3·25	2·50
3184	1r.30 Minaret, dome and Holy Kaaba	3·25	2·50
MS3185	68×113 mm. As Nos. 3182/4	7·50	7·50

No. **MS**3185 also has a barcode at the bottom of the sheet, separated from the miniature sheet by a line of rouletting.

1568 Map of Americas, Flags, Emblems and Waterfall

2001. 11th Pan American Scout Jamboree, Foz do Iguacu. Multicoloured.

3186	1r.10 Type **1568**	2·75	2·10
3187	1r.10 Waterfall, canoeists and emblems	2·75	2·10

Nos. 3186/7 were issued together, se-tenant, forming a composite design.

1569 Snake and Chinese Zodiac

2001. HONG KONG 2001 Stamp Exhibition. New Year. Year of the Snake.
3188 **1569** 1r.45 multicoloured 3·75 3·00

1570 *Dirphya* sp. and Institute

2001. Centenary of Butantan Institute (vaccine research centre), Sao Paulo. Venomous Animals. Sheet 115×155 mm containing T **1570** and similar horiz designs showing Institute building. Multicoloured.

3189	40c. Type **1570**	1·00	85
3190	40c. Puss caterpillar (*Megalopyge* sp.)	1·00	85
3191	40c. *Phoneutria* sp.	1·00	85
3192	40c. Brown scorpion (*Tityus bahiensis*)	1·00	85
3193	40c. Brazilian rattle snake (*Crotalus durissus*)	1·00	85
3194	40c. Coral snake (*Micrurus corallinus*)	1·00	85
3195	40c. Bushmaster (*Lachesis muta*)	1·00	85
3196	40c. Jararaca (*Bothrops jacaraca*)	1·00	85

1571 Old and Modern Printing Methods

2001. Publishing.
3197 **1571** 27c. multicoloured 65 55

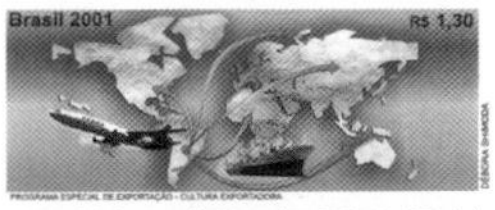

1572 McDonnell Douglas DC-10, World Map and Ship

2001. Exports.
3198 **1572** 1r.30 multicoloured 3·00 2·50

1573 Books and Library Facade

2001. 190th Anniv of National Library, Rio de Janeiro.
3199 **1573** 27c. multicoloured 65 55

1574 Man, Microscope and Emblem

2001. Brazilian Council for Scientific and Technological Development (CNPq).
3200 **1574** 40c. blue 85 70

1575 Footballer and Emblem

2001. 89th Anniv of Santos Football Club.
3201 **1575** 1r. multicoloured 2·20 1·80

1576 Children

2001. International Decade for a Culture of Peace.
3202 **1576** 1r.10 multicoloured 2·50 2·10

1577 Mendes and Halfeld Street

2001. Birth Centenary of Muriles Mendes (poet).
3203 **1577** 40c. multicoloured 85 70

1578 Building Facade and View of Town

2001. Centenary of Minas Gerais Trade Association.
3204 **1578** 40c. multicoloured 85 70

1579 Sunflower and No-Smoking Signs

2001. World No-Smoking Day.
3205 **1579** 40c. multicoloured 85 70

1580 Do Rego and Illustrations from his Novels

2001. Birth Centenary of Jose Lins do Rego (writer).
3206 **1580** 60c. multicoloured 1·20 1·00

1581 Hyacinth Macaw (*Anodorhynchus hyacinthinus*)

2001. Birds. Sheet 106×149 mm containing T **1581** and similar vert designs. Multicoloured.
MS3207 1r.30 Type **1581**; 1r.30 Sun conure (*Aratinga solititialis auricapilla*); 1r.30 Blue-throated conure (*Pyrrhura cruentata*); 1r.30 Yellow-faced amazon (*Amazona xanthops*) 10·00 10·00

1582 Sobrinho

2001. First Death Anniv of Alexandre Jose Barbosa Lima Sobrinho (journalist).
3208 **1582** 40c. multicoloured 85 70

1583 Jericoacoara Beach, Ceara

2001. Beaches. Multicoloured.

3209	40c. Type **1583**	85	70
3210	40c. Ponta Negra beach, Rio Grande do Norte	85	70
3211	40c. Rosa beach, Santa Catarina	85	70

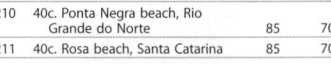

1584 Romi-Isetta, 1959 (½-size illustration)

2001. Cars. Sheet 159×115 mm containing T **1584** and similar horiz designs. Multicoloured.
MS3212 1r.10 Type **1584**; 1r.10 DKW-Vemag, 1965; 1r.10 Renault Gordini, 1962; 1r.10 Fusca-Volkswagen 1200, 1959; 1r.10 Simca Chambord, 1964; 1r.10 Aero Willys, 1961 13·00 13·00

1585 Sayao

2001. Birth Centenary of Bernado Sayao (politician and construction pioneer).
3213 **1585** 60c. multicoloured 1·20 1·00

1586 Eleazar de Carvalho, Musical Notation and Musicians

2001. Eleazar de Carvalho (composer and conductor) Commemoration.
3214 **1586** 45c. multicoloured 1·00 85

1587 Racquet and Ball

2001. Roland Garros Tennis Championship. Sheet 70×112 mm.
MS3215 **1587** 1r.30 multicoloured 2·75 2·75

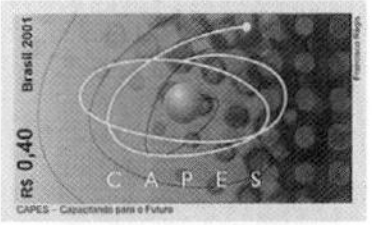

1588 Emblem

2001. 50th Anniv of CAPES (training fund).
3216 **1588** 40c. multicoloured 85 70

1589 Buildings, Symbols of Justice and Pedro Alexio

2001. Birth Centenary of Pedro Alexio (Judge and politician).
3217 **1589** 55c. multicoloured 1·20 1·00

1590 Player and Ball

2001. Vasco da Gama Football Club.
3218 **1590** 70c. multicoloured 1·50 1·30

1591 Figure enclosing Map of Brazil (½-size illustration)

2001. Fifth Anniv of Solidarity Council. Multicoloured.
3219 55c. Type **1591** 1·20 1·00
3220 55c. Map enclosing figure 1·20 1·00

Nos. 3219/20 were issued together, *se-tenant*, forming a composite design.

1592 Player and Ball

2001. Palmeiras Football Club.
3221 **1592** 70c. multicoloured 1·50 1·30

1593 Emblem

2001. World Conference on Racism, Durban, South Africa.
3222 **1593** 1r.30 multicoloured 2·75 2·30

1594 Player and Ball

2001. Gremio Football Porto Algrense (football club).
3223 **1594** 70c. multicoloured 1·50 1·30

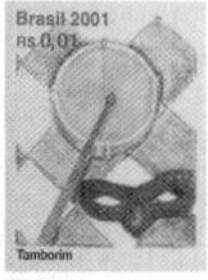

1595 Tambourine

2001. Musical Instruments. Multicoloured. Self-adhesive.
3224 1c. Type **1595** 15 15
3224a 1c. Conga drum 15 15
3225 5c. Saxophone 15 15
3225a 5c. Snare drum 15 15
3226 10c. Cavaquinho (guitar) 15 15
3226a 10c. Trumpet 15 15
3227 20c. Clarinet 35 30
3228 40c. Flute 85 70
3229 45c. Mandolin 90 80
3230 50c. Fiddle 1·00 85
3230a 50c. Tambourine 1·00 85
3231 55c. Viola (guitar) 1·20 1·00
3232 60c. Zabumba 1·30 1·10
3233 70c. Viola Caipira (guitar) 1·50 1·30
3234 70c. Rattle 1·50 1·30
3235 80c. Xylophone 1·70 1·40
3236 1r. Trombone 2·20 1·80
3236a 1r. Berimbau 2·20 1·80

1596 Clóvis Beviláqua

2001. Clóvis Beviláqua (lawyer) Commemoration.
3250 **1596** 55c. multicoloured 1·20 1·00

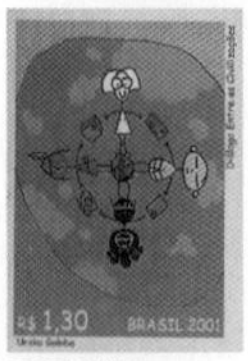

1597 Children encircling Globe

2001. United Nations Year of Dialogue among Civilizations.
3251 **1597** 1r.30 multicoloured 2·75 2·30

1598 Map of Brazil and Jewish and Dutch Flags

2001. 365th Anniv of First Jewish Synagogue in Recife.
3252 **1598** 1r.30 multicoloured 2·75 2·30

1599 Junkers F13 Passenger Aircraft

2001. Commercial Aircraft. Sheet 107×149 mm containing T **1599** and similar horiz designs. Multicoloured.
MS3253 55c. Type **1599**; 55c. Douglas DC-3/C47; 55c. Dornier Do-J Wal flying boat; 55c. Lockheed Constellation; 55c. Convair CV 340; 55c. Caravelle V1-R jet airliner 6·50 6·50

1600 Cecíla Meireles

2001. Birth Centenary of Cecíla Meireles (writer).
3254 **1600** 55c. multicoloured 1·20 1·00

1601 Aleijadinho (sculptor) and Bom Jesus de Matosinhos Sanctuary

2001. America. UNESCO World Heritage Sites.
3255 **1601** 1r.30 multicoloured 2·75 2·30

1602 Madalena Caramuru and Page

2001. Madalena Caramuru (first literate Brazilian woman) Commemoration.
3256 **1602** 55c. multicoloured 1·20 1·00

1603 Face, Gavel, Book and Dove

2001. National Black Awareness Day.
3257 **1603** 40c. multicoloured 85 70

1604 Caiman (*Caiman crocodilus*) and Roseate Spoonbill (*Platalea ajaja*) (inscr "*Plataleia*")

2001. Flora and Fauna. Multicoloured. Self-adhesive.
3258 55c. Type **1604** 1·20 1·00
3259 55c. American darter (*Anhinga anhinga*) 1·20 1·00
3260 55c. Cocoi heron (*Ardea cocoi*) 1·20 1·00
3261 55c. Jabiru (*Ephippiorhynchus mycteria*) (inscr "Jabiru") 1·20 1·00
3262 55c. *Pseudoplatystoma fasciatum* (fish) 1·20 1·00
3263 55c. *Leporinus macrocephalus* (fish) 1·20 1·00
3264 55c. Capybara (*Hydrochoerus hydrochaeris*) (inscr "hydrochoeris") 1·20 1·00
3265 55c. Southern coati (*Nasua nasua*) 1·20 1·00
3266 55c. Water hyacinth (*Eichornia crassipes*) 1·20 1·00
3267 55c. Purple gallinule (*Porphyrula martinica*) 1·20 1·00

1605 Three Kings and Holy Family

2001. Christmas.
3268 **1605** 40c. multicoloured 85 70

1606 Emblem, Player and Football

2001. Libertadores da America Football Championship Winners (1st issue). Flamengo Football Club (1981).
3269 **1606** 1r. multicoloured 2·00 1·70

See also No. 3275.

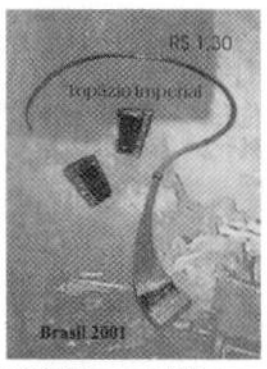

1607 Imperial Topaz Necklace and Earrings

2001. Jewellery. Sheet 101×70 mm containing T **1607** and similar vert design. Multicoloured.
MS3270 1r.30 Type **1607**; 1r.30 Garnet ring 5·50 5·50

No. **MS**3270 was issued with a strip containing a barcode separated by a line of rouletting.

1608 Stylized Eye, Mouth, Hand and Ear

2001. International Day of the Disabled.
3271 **1608** 1r.45 multicoloured 3·00 2·50

1609 Cup of Coffee and Beans

2001. Coffee.
3272 **1609** 1r.30 multicoloured 2·75 2·40

1610 *Copocabana*

2001. Merchant Ships. Multicoloured.
3273 55c. Type **1610** 1·20 1·00
3274 55c. *Flamengo* 1·20 1·00

Nos. 3273/4 were issued together, *se-tenant*, forming a composite design.

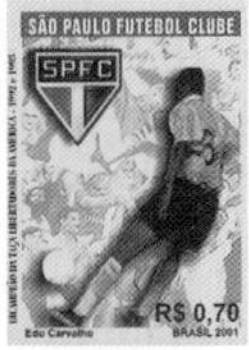

1611 Emblem, Player and Football

2001. Libertadores da America Football Championship Winners (2nd issue). Sao Paulo Football Club (1992 and 1993).
3275 **1611** 70c. multicoloured 1·50 1·30

1612 Water Hyacinth (*Eichornia crassipes*)

2001. Mercosur. Flora.
3276 **1612** 1r. multicoloured 2·00 1·70

1613 Chinese Zodiac and Horse

2002. New Year. Year of the Horse.
3277 **1613** 1r.45 multicoloured 3·00 2·50

1614 Alpine skier

2002. Winter Olympic Games, Salt Lake City, USA. Multicoloured.
3278 1r.10 Type **1614** 2·30 2·00
3279 1r.10 Cross country skier 2·30 2·00
3280 1r.10 Luge 2·30 2·00
3281 1r.10 Bobsled 2·30 2·00

Nos. 3278/81 were issued together, *se-tenant*, forming a composite design.

1615 Brasilia and Lucio Costa

2002. Birth Centenary of Lucio Costa (architect).
3282 **1615** 55c. multicoloured 1·20 1·00

1616 Women encircling Globe

2002. International Women's Day.
3283 **1616** 40c. multicoloured 85 70

1617 View of City from River

2002. 150th Anniv of Sao Jose do Rio Preto.
3284 **1617** 40c. multicoloured 85 70

1618 Brasilia and Juscelino Kubitschek

2002. Birth Centenary of Juscelino Kubitschek (president, 1956–61).
3285 **1618** 55c. multicoloured 1·20 1·00

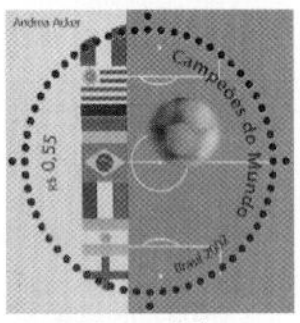

1619 Winners' Flags and Football

2002. World Cup Football Championship, Japan and South Korea. Multicoloured.

3286	55c. Type **1619**	1·00	85
3287	55c. Footballer	1·00	85

1620 School Children and Alphabet

2002. Education. Multicoloured.

3288	40c. Type **1620**	85	70
3289	40c. Computer, globe and alphabet	85	70

1621 Josemaria Escriva

2002. Birth Centenary of Josemaria Escriva de Balaguer (founder of Opus Dei (religious organization)).

3290	**1621**	55c. multicoloured	1·20	1·00

1622 North American T6

2002. Smoke Air Squadron (air force display team). Sheet 105×150 mm containing T **1622** and similar horiz designs. Multicoloured.

MS3291 55c. ×6, Type **1622**; T-24 Fouga Magister; Neiva T-25 Universal (inscr "T-25 Universal"); Two Embraer EMB-312 Tucano (inscr "T-27 Tucano") and plateau; T-27 Tucano and heart-shape; T-27 Tucano over forest 6·50 6·50

1623 Boy wearing Crown, Girls carrying Banners and Boy with Sword

2002. Cavalhadinha (children's festival). Multicoloured.

3292	40c. Type **1623**	85	70
3293	40c. Boys riding hobby horses	85	70
3294	40c. Children wearing masks	85	70
3295	40c. Musicians and drinks vendor	85	70

1624 Cannonball Tree (*Couroupita guianensis*)

2002. Self-adhesive.

3296	**1624**	55c. multicoloured	1·00	85

1625 Coral and Fish

2002. Coral Reefs. Sheet 105×150 mm containing T **1625** and similar square designs. Multicoloured.

MS3297 40c. ×4, Type **1625**; Seahorse; Corals and fish; Fish and starfish 2·75 2·75

1626 Building Facade

2002. 150th Anniv of Sisterhood of Charity Hospital, Curitiba.

3298	**1626**	70c. multicoloured	1·00	85

1627 Jules Rimet and World Cup Trophies

2002. Brasil, Football World Cup Championship Winners (1958, 1962, 1970, 1994, 2002).

3299	**1627**	55c. multicoloured	1·20	1·00

1628 White-browed Guan (*Penelope jacucaca*)

2002. Conservation of North Eastern Caatinga Region. Sheet 70×111 mm.

MS3300 **1628** 1r.10 multicoloured 1·50 1·60

1629 Footballer and Emblem

2002. Centenary of Santos Football Club.

3301	**1629**	55c. multicoloured	65	55

1630 House Facade

2002. "The Enchanted House" Museum (house of Alberto Santos Dumont (aviation pioneer)), Rio De Janeiro. Sheet containing T **1630** and similar square design. Multicoloured.

MS3302 1r. ×2, Type **1630**; Alberto Santos Dumont 2·75 2·75

1631 Radar, Airplane, Boy, Animals and Birds

2002. SIVAM (environmental monitoring of Amazon project).

3303	**1631**	1r.10 multicoloured	1·50	1·30

1632 Families enclosed in Wheel

2002. Crianca Esperanca (Hope of the Child) Awareness Campaign. Multicoloured.

3304	(1st Porto) Type **1632** (child development)	85	70
3305	(1st Porto) Children playing (eradication of child labour)	85	70

1633 Jorge Amado

2002. First Death Anniv of Jorge Amado (writer).

3306	**1633**	40c. multicoloured	50	45

1634 Rio Branco Palace, Xapuri Village and Placido de Castro (revolutionary leader)

2002. Centenary of Acre River Revolution.

3307	**1634**	50c. multicoloured	65	55

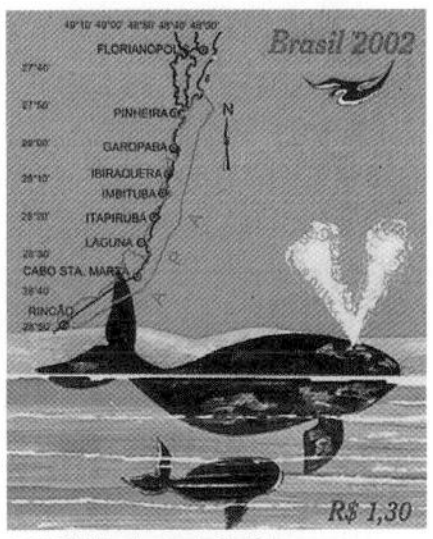

1635 Whale and Calf

2002. Southern Right Whale Habitat Protection Project. Sheet 71×112 mm.

MS3308 **1635** 1r.30. multicoloured 1·70 1·70

1636 Rivers

2002. Watershed of Negro and Solimoes Rivers, Manaus.

3309	**1636**	45c. multicoloured	50	45

1637 Adhelmar Ferreira da Silva

2002. First Death Anniv of Adhelmar Ferreira da Silva (Olympic triple jump champion).

3310	**1637**	40c. multicoloured	50	45

1638 Yamaha 125cc. (1974) and YZF-R1

2002. Motorcycles. Sheet 105×149 mm containing T **1638** and similar horiz designs. Multicoloured.

MS3311 60c.×6 Type **1638**; Honda CB100 (1976) and CG125 Titan; Suzuki 1952 model and GSX-R1000; First Triumph model (1902) and Datona 955i; BMW R32 and R 1200C; First Harley Davidson model (1903) and V-Rod 4·25 4·25

1639 Steam Locomotive *Baroneza* (1852)

2002. Trains. Multicoloured.

3312	55c. Type **1639**	65	55
3313	55c. Locomotive *Zeze Leoni* (1922)	65	55

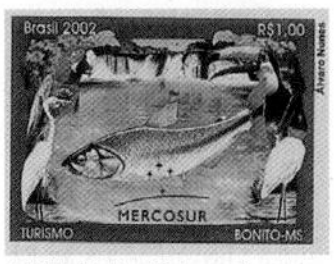

1640 Birds, Fish and Waterfall

2002. Mercosur (South American Common Market).

3314	**1640**	1r. multicoloured	1·40	1·20

1641 Itabira, Carlos Drummond de Andrade and Rio de Janeiro

2002. Birth Centenary of Carlos Drummond de Andrade (writer).

3315	**1641**	55c. multicoloured	80	70

1642 Fingerprint, Book, Globe and Figure Child

2002. America. Education and Literacy Campaign.

3316	**1642**	1r.30 multicoloured	1·80	1·60

1643 Map and Building

2002. National Archives.

3317	**1643**	40c. multicoloured	60	50

1644 Sergio Motta (founder) and Centre Building

2002. Sergio Motta Cultural Centre.

3318	**1644**	45c. multicoloured	60	50

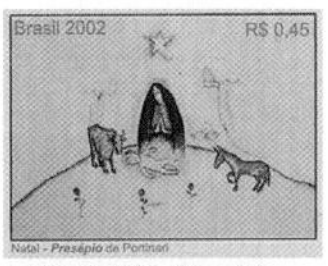

1645 *Nativity* (Candido Portinari)

2002. Christmas.

3319	**1645**	45c. multicoloured	60	50

1646 "80"

2002. 80th Anniv of Social Security.

3320	**1646**	45c. multicoloured	60	50

1647 *Dancing Tapuia*

2002. Art. Paintings by Albert Eckhout. Paintings. Multicoloured.

3321	45c. Type **1647**	80	70
3322	45c. *Mameluca*	80	70
3323	45c. *Tapuia Man*	80	70
3324	45c. *Tupi Man*	80	70
3325	45c. *Negro*	80	70
3326	45c. *Tupi Woman*	80	70
3327	45c. *West African Woman and Child*	80	70
3328	45c. *Mestizo Man*	80	70

1648 Marajoara Pots, Brazil

2002. Centenary of Brazil–Iran Diplomatic Relations. Multicoloured.

3329	60c. Type **1648**	1·00	85
3330	60c. Iranian decorated pots	1·00	85

Stamps of a similar design were issued by Iran.

1649 Anniversary Emblem

2003. 80th Anniv of Rotary Club (charitable organization).
3331 **1649** 60c. multicoloured 1·00 85

1650 Salto do Itiquira, Formosa

2003. International Day of Freshwater. Waterfalls. Multicoloured.
3332 45c. Type **1650** 80 70
3333 45c. Salto do Rio Preto, Alto Paraiso 80 70

1651 Winnowing and Building

2003. Coffee Production. Sheet 70×110 mm containing T **1651** and similar square design. Multicoloured.
MS3334 1r.×2, Type **1651**; Buildings, planting and picking 3·25 3·25

1652 Flag, Hands, Dove and Map

2003. Timor Leste Independence.
3335 **1652** 1r.45 multicoloured 2·40 2·10

1653 *Macrosiphonia velame*

2003. America. Flora and Fauna. Sheet 107×150 mm containing T **1653** and similar square designs. Multicoloured.
MS3336 60c.×6, Type **1653**; *Lychnophora ericoides*; *Lafoensia pacari*; *Tabebuia impetiginosa*;*Xylopia aromatica*; *Himatanthus obovatus* 5·00 5·00

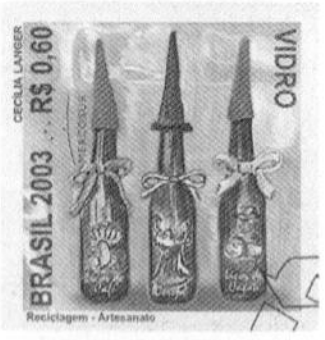

1654 Decorated Bottles

2003. Mercosur. Recycling. Multicoloured.
3337 60c. Type **1654** 1·00 85
3338 60c. Paper dolls 1·00 85
3339 60c. Plastic flower pot 1·00 85
3340 60c. Decorated metal box 1·00 85

1655 Saint Inacio, College Building and Students

2003. Centenary of St. Inacio College, Rio de Janeiro.
3341 **1655** 60c. multicoloured 1·00 85

1656 Pluft and Maribel

2003. Pluft (cartoon character created by Maria Clara Machado).
3342 **1656** 80c. multicoloured 1·20 1·00

1657 Sail Boat on Beach

2003. Centenary of Ceara State.
3343 **1657** 70c. multicoloured 1·20 1·00

1658 Album, Tweezers and Stamps

2003. Philately. Sheet 110×71 mm containing T **1658** and similar square design. Multicoloured.
MS3344 1r.30×2, Type **1658**; Portuguese 25r. stamp 4·25 4·25

1659 Dolphins

2003. 500th Anniv of Fernando de Noronha Island. Sheet 69×100 mm.
MS3345 **1659** 2r.90 multicoloured 4·50 4·50

1660 Emblem, Buildings and Antonio Maria Zaccaria (founder)

2003. Centenary of Barnabite Priests in Brazil.
3346 **1660** 45c. multicoloured 80 70

1661 Duke of Caxias and Battle Scene

2003. Birth Bicentenary of Luis Alves de Lima y Silva, Duke of Caxias.
3347 **1661** 60c. multicoloured 1·00 85

1662 Self-Portrait

2003. Birth Centenary of Candido Potinari (artist).
3348 **1662** 80l. multicoloured 1·40 1·20

1663 Stop Sign enclosing Bottle

2003. Traffic Code Awareness. Multicoloured. Self-adhesive.
3349 (50c.) Type **1663** 80 70
3350 (74c.) Triangular traffic sign enclosing dove 1·20 1·00

1664 Club Emblem

2003. Centenary of Gremio Football Porto Alegrense.
3351 **1664** 60c. multicoloured 90 80

1665 Locomotive

2003. Preservation of Railways.
3352 **1665** 74c. multicoloured 1·20 1·00

1666 Kite Flying

2003. Children's Games. Multicoloured.
3353 50c. Type **1666** 80 70
3354 50c. Ball games 80 70
3355 50c. Skipping 80 70
3356 50c. Hula hoop 80 70

1667 Campaign Emblem

2003. Zero Hunger Campaign.
3357 **1667** 50c. multicoloured 80 70

1668 Grapes, Bridge and Mask

2003. Export Campaign. Sheet 110×69 mm.
MS3358 **1668** 1r.30 multicoloured 2·00 2·00

1669 Decorated Tree

2003. Christmas. Self-adhesive.
3359 **1669** 50c. multicoloured 80 70
3360 **1669** 50c. multicoloured 80 70

Sao Paulo Art Critcs Trophy and Auditing Court (building)

2003. Marcantonio Vilaca Cultural Space.
3361 **1670** 74c. multicoloured 1·20 1·00

1671 Ary Barroso and Maracana Stadium

2003. Birth Centenary of Ary Barroso (conductor and sports commentator).
3362 **1671** 1r.50 multicoloured 2·40 2·10

1672 Palacio des Arcos, Cadeia Velha and New Congress Building, Rio de Janeiro

2003. 180th Anniv of National Congress.
3363 **1672** 74c. multicoloured 1·20 1·00

1673 Para-glider over Sao Conrado, Rio de Janeiro

2003. Adventurous Sports.
3364 **1673** 75c. multicoloured 1·20 1·00

1674 Cedar Lebanon

2003. 60th Anniv of Diplomatic Relations with Lebanon.
3365 **1674** 1r.75 multicoloured 2·75 2·40

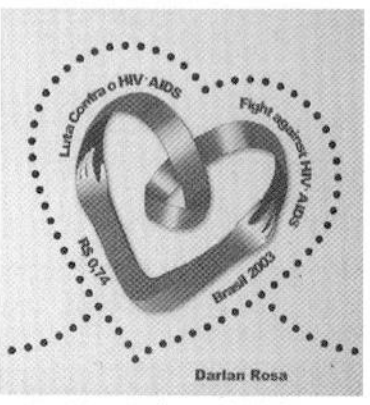

1675 Heart-shaped Ribbon and Hands

2003. AIDS Awareness Campaign.
3366 **1675** 74c. multicoloured 1·20 1·00

2003. Birth Centenary of Candido Potinari. Lost Paintings (1st issue). As T **1662**. Black. Self-adhesive.
3367 74c. *Menino de Brodoski* 1·20 1·00
3368 75c. *Cangaceiro* 1·20 1·00
See also Nos. 3382/6.

1676 Capistrano de Abreu

2003. 150th Birth Anniv of Capistrano de Abreu (historian and ethnographer).
3369 **1676** 50c. multicoloured 80 70

1677 Fernando Henrique Cardoso

2003. Fernando Henrique Cardoso (38th president).
3370 **1677** 74c. multicoloured 1·20 1·00

1678 Archangel St. Michael Chapel, Sao Paulo

2004. Cultural Heritage. Sheet 100×70 mm. Litho.
MS3371 **1678** 1r.50 multicoloured 2·20 2·20

1679 Faces

2004. 450th Anniv of Sao Paulo. Multicoloured.

3372		74c. Type **1679**	1·20	1·00
3373		74c. Buildings surrounding roadway	1·20	1·00
3374		74c. Park and city buildings	1·20	1·00
3375		74c. "450"	1·20	1·00

1680 Dom Vicente Scherer

2004. Birth Centenary of Cardinal Vicente Scherer.

3376	**1680**	50c. multicoloured	80	70

1681 Musicians and Dancers

2004. Lapa District, Rio de Janeiro.

3377	**1681**	75c. multicoloured	1·20	1·00

1682 Scarlet Ibis (*Eudocimus ruber*)

2004

3378	**1682**	74c. multicoloured	1·20	1·00

1683 Figure holding Water Droplet

2004. Mercosur. Water Conservation Campaign.

3379	**1683**	1r.20 multicoloured	1·80	1·60

1684 Orlando Villas Boas

2004. 90th Birth Anniv of Orlando Villas Boas (joint founder Xingu National Park and Nobel Peace Prize winner).

3380	**1684**	74c. multicoloured	1·20	1·00

1685 Anniversary Emblem

2004. Centenary of FIFA (Federation Internationale de Football Association).

3381	**1685**	1r.60 multicoloured	2·50	2·30

2004. Birth Centenary of Candido Potinari. Lost Paintings (2nd issue). As T **1662**. Self-adhesive.

3382		55c. multicoloured	90	80
3383		80c. multicoloured	1·20	1·00
3384		95c. multicoloured	1·50	1·30
3385		1r.15 black	1·70	1·50
3386		1r.50 multicoloured	2·40	2·10

DESIGNS: 55c. *Negrinha*; 80c. *Duas Criancas*; 95c. *Menino Sentado e Carneiro*; 1r.15 *Comosicao*; 1r.50 *Marcel Gontrau.*

1686 Emblem

2004. 92nd International Labour Conference (ILO).

3387	**1686**	50c. multicoloured	80	70

1687 Roseate Spoonbill (*Ajaia ajaja*)

2004. Mangrove Swamps and Tidal Zones Preservation. Sheet 149×105 mm containing T **1687** and similar horiz designs. Multicoloured.

MS3388		1r.60×5, Type **1687**; Great kiskadee (*Pitangus sulphuratus*); *Chasmagnathus granulate; Aramides mangle; Goniopsis cruentata*	10·50	10·50

1688 Runner holding Olympic Torch

2004. Olympic Games, Athens. Multicoloured.

3389		1r.60 Type **1688**	2·50	2·30
3390		1r.60 Athens 2004 emblem	2·50	2·30
3391		1r.60 Dinghies and catamarans	2·50	2·30
3392		1r.60 Runner	2·50	2·30

1689 Senhor Bom Jesus do Bonfim Church, Salvador

2004. Cultural Heritage.

3393	**1689**	74c. multicoloured	1·20	1·00

1690 Caprichoso Bull

2004. Parintins Festival. Multicoloured.

3394		74c. Type **1690**	1·20	1·00
3395		74c. Garantido bull	1·20	1·00

Nos. 3394/5 were issued together, *se-tenant*, forming a composite design.

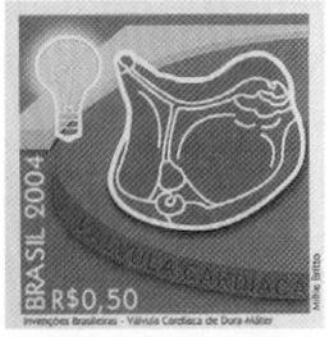

1691 Dura-Mater Artificial Heart Valve

2004. Brazilian Inventions. Multicoloured.

3396		50c. Type **1691**	80	70
3397		50c. Telephone caller identification (BINA)	80	70
3398		50c. Telephone cards	80	70

1692 Map of South America, Satellite and Brazilian and Chinese Flags as Clasped Hands

2004. CBER-2 (Brazilian—Chinese satellite).

3399	**1692**	1r.75 multicoloured	2·75	2·40

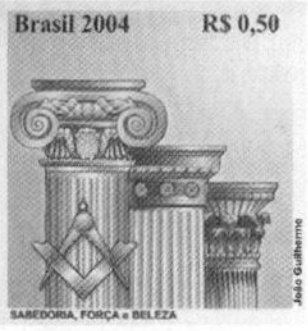

1693 Columns, Square and Compass

2004. Masonic Philatelic Association.

3400		50c. Type **1693**	80	70
3401		50c. Stone mason	80	70
3402		50c. Jacob's ladder	80	70
3403		50c. Masonic tools	80	70

1694 Nelson Rodrigues

2004. Nelson Rodrigues (writer) Commemoration.

3404	**1694**	50c. multicoloured	80	70

1695 FAB Emblem, Republic P-47 Thunderbolt and Campaign Medals

2004. World War II. Multicoloured.

3405		50c. Type **1695** (Italian air campaign)	80	70
3406		50c. Navy emblem, destroyer and campaign medals (South Atlantic campaign)	80	70
3407		50c. FEB emblem, soldiers and campaign medals (Italian land campaign)	80	70
3408		50c. Soldier reading letter	80	70

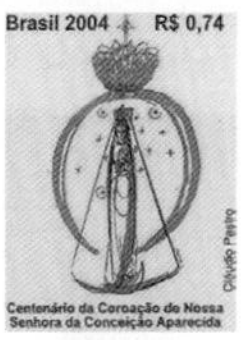

1696 Crowned Halo enclosing Statue

2004. Centenary of Coronation of Our Lady of Immaculate Conception ("Aparecida").

3409	**1696**	74c. multicoloured	1·20	1·00

1697 Allan Kardec

2004. Birth Bicentenary of Allan Kardec (writer).

3410	**1697**	1r.60 multicoloured	2·50	2·30

1698 Father Christmas

2004. Christmas. Self-adhesive.

3411	**1698**	1st class (50c.) multicoloured	80	70

No. 3406 was for use on internal non-commercial mail weighing 20 grams or less.

1699 Post Office Building (museum)

2004. Porto Alegre Museum and Archive.

3412	**1699**	50c. multicoloured	80	70

1700 *Cyperus articulatus*

2004. Aromatic Plants.

3413	**1700**	1r.60 multicoloured	2·50	2·30

1701 Buildings and Statue

2004. Pampulha Architectural Complex.

3414	**1701**	80c. multicoloured	1·30	1·10

1702 Cat, Art, Textiles and Nise da Silveira

2005. Birth Centenary of Nise da Silveira (psychiatrist).

3415	**1702**	55c. multicoloured	90	80

1703 Rotary Emblem and Faces

2005. Centenary of Rotary International (charitable organization).

3416	**1703**	1r.45 multicoloured	2·40	2·10

1704 Fruit on Tree

2005. Cupacu (*Theobrome grandiflorum*). Sheet 70×111 mm containing T **1704** and similar square design. Multicoloured.

MS3417		1r.90×2, Type **1704**; Open fruit	6·00	6·00

1705 Brazilian and Lebanese Trees and Flags

2005. Lebanese Immigration to Brazil.

3418	**1705**	1r.75 multicoloured	2·75	2·40

1706 Museum Building

2005. Oscar Niemeyer Museum.

3419	**1706**	80c. multicoloured	1·30	1·10

1707 Pope John Paul II

2005. Pope John Paul II Commemoration.

3420	**1707**	80c. multicoloured	1·30	1·10

1708 Circle and Arrows

2005. World Information Society Summit, Tunis. Sheet 86×128 mm containing T **1708** and similar horiz designs. Multicoloured.

MS3421 80c.×3, Type **1708**; Figure enclosed in circle; Envelope contained in circle	3·50	3·50

The stamps and margins of No. **MS**3421 form a composite design.

1709 Dancers (contemporary dance)

2005. Brazil Year in France. Multicoloured.

3422	80c. Type **1709**	1·30	1·10
3423	80c. Pankararu Indians (indigenous art)	1·30	1·10
3424	80c. Pato no Tucupi (gastronomy)	1·30	1·10
3425	80c. Choro musicians (music)	1·30	1·10
3426	80c. String of pages (literature)	1·30	1·10
3427	80c. Vivaldo Lima Stadium (architecture)	1·30	1·10

1710 Erico Verissimo

2005. Birth Centenary of Erico Verissimo (writer).

3428	**1710**	1r.25 multicoloured	1·90	1·60

1711 Mario Quintana

2005. Birth Centenary (2006) of Mario Quintana (writer).

3429	**1711**	80c. green	1·30	1·10

1712 Woman, Water Barrel, Cistern, Boy and Workmen

2005. America. Water Cisterns.

3430	**1712**	80c. multicoloured	1·30	1·10

1713 Emblem

2005. 19th Congress of America, Spain and Portugal Postal Union. Self-adhesive.

3431	**1713**	(80c.) multicoloured	1·30	1·10

1714 Gold panning, Route and Caravan

2005. Tourism. Estrada Real (road from Diamantina to Parati and Rio De Janeiro). Multicoloured.

3432	80c. Type **1714**	1·30	1·10
3433	80c. Hikers	1·30	1·10
3434	80c. Horse riders	1·30	1·10

Nos. 3432/4 were issued together, *se-tenant*, forming a composite design.

1715 Dancer

2005. Samba (dance).

3435	**1715**	55c. multicoloured	90	80

1716 Brazilian Flag and Samba Dancers

2005. National Dances. Multicoloured.

3436	80c. Type **1716**	1·30	1·10
3437	80c. Cuban flag and Son dancers	1·30	1·10

Stamps of a similar design were issued by Cuba.

1717 Sao Francisco River

2005

3438	**1717**	80c. multicoloured	1·30	1·10

1718 School Building

2005. Centenary of Command and General Staff School.

3439	**1718**	80c. multicoloured	1·30	1·10

1719 "ABC"

2005. Teachers' Day. Self-adhesive.

3440	**1719**	(1st porte) multicoloured	90	80

1720 Bell

2005. Christmas (1st issue). Self-adhesive.

3441	**1720**	(1st porte) multicoloured	90	80

See also No. **MS**3444.

1721 Referee and Players

2005. Women's Football.

3442	**1721**	85c. multicoloured	1·40	1·20

1722 Fish Leaping (*Salminus maxillosus*)

2005. Piracema (fish reproduction). Sheet 101×71 mm.

MS3443	**1722**	3r.10 multicoloured	5·00	5·00

1723 *Adoration of Shepherds* (Oscar Pereira da Silva)

2005. Christmas (2nd issue). Sheet 71×111 mm.

MS3444	**1723**	2r.90 multicoloured	4·50	4·50

1724 Light *Luna* (Fernando Prado)

2005. Brazilian Design. Multicoloured.

3445	85c. Type **1724**	1·40	1·20
3446	85c. Ventilator "Spirit" (Indio da Costa design)	1·40	1·20
3447	85c. Chair "Corallo" (Hemberto and Fernando Corallo)	1·40	1·20
3448	85c. Table "Bandeirola" (Ivan Rezende)	1·40	1·20

1725 Hans Christian Andersen and *The Ugly Duckling*

2005. Birth Bicentenary of Hans Christian Andersen (writer).

3449	**1725**	55c. multicoloured	90	80

1726 Dressmaker

2005. Professions. Multicoloured. Self-adhesive.

3450	5c. Type **1726**	20	15
3451	20c. Cobbler	40	35
3452	85c. Shoe shine	1·40	1·20

1727 Sambista

2005. Urban Art. Multicoloured.

3453	55c. Type **1727**	90	80
3454	55c. Boy in pipe	90	80
3455	55c. Graffiti artist (horiz)	90	80

1728 Santos-Dumont Biplane *14 bis*

2005. Centenarian Mission (Brazilian astronaut, Marcos Pontes's flight on Soyuz rocket to International Space Station). Multicoloured.

3456	85c. Type **1728**	1·40	1·20
3457	85c. "Soyuz"	1·40	1·20
3458	85c. International Space Station	1·40	1·20

Nos. 3456/8 were issued together, *se-tenant*, forming a composite design.

1729 Emblem

2006. World Cup Football Championship, Germany.

3459	**1729**	85c. multicoloured	1·40	1·20

1730 Bidu Sayao

2006. Balduina de Oliveira Sayao (Bidu Sayao) (opera singer) Commemoration.

3460	**1730**	55c. multicoloured	90	80

1731 World Map and Faces

2006. International Day of Cultural Diversity.

3461	**1731**	1r.90 multicoloured	3·25	2·75

1732 Emblem

2006. RIO 2007—15th Pan American Games. Self-adhesive.

3462	**1732**	(1st Porte) multicoloured	1·40	1·20

1733 Stylized Athlete

2006. Brazilian Paralympics Committee.

3463	**1733**	1r.35 multicoloured	2·00	1·70

1734 Viola de Cocho

2006. Mercosur. Musical Instruments.

3464	**1734**	55c. multicoloured	90	80

1735 Rhea, Emas National Park

2006. National Parks. Multicoloured. Self-adhesive.

3465	85c. Type **1735**	1·40	1·20
3466	85c. Uakari monkey, Sustainable Development Reserve, Mamiraua	1·40	1·20
3467	85c. Maned wolf, Chapada dos Veadeiros National Park	1·40	1·20
3468	85c. Squirrel, Itatiaia National Park	1·40	1·20

2006. Urban Art (2nd issue). Sheet 111×70 mm containing vert designs as T **1727**. Multicoloured.

MS3468a 1r.60×2, As No. 3454; As No. 3455	5·00	5·00

1735a Leaves and Fruit

2006. Cajueiro (cashew nut tree). Sheet 111×70 mm.
MS3468b **1735a** 2r.90 multicoloured 4·50 4·50

No. **MS**3468b was cut round in the shape of a tree.

1736 Fernando de Noronha Archipelago

2006. Tourism.
3469 **1736** 2r.50 multicoloured 3·50 3·00

1737 Santos-Dumont *14-bis*

2006. Centenary of Flight of Santos-Dumont 14-bis.
3470 **1737** (90c.) multicoloured 1·40 1·20

1738 Star, House and Mail Box

2006. Christmas (1st issue). Self-adhesive.
3471 **1738** (1st Porte) multicoloured 1·00 85

2006. Professions. As T **1726**. Multicoloured. Self-adhesive.
3471a 1c. Popcorn seller 20 15
3471b 1r. Manicurist 1·75 1·75

1739 The Magi

2006. Christmas (2nd issue). Sheet 111×70 mm containing T **1739** and similar multicoloured designs.
MS3472 1r.60×3, Type **1739** Angel (36×40 mm) (arched): Holy family 7·00 7·00

1740 Hydro-electric Dam and Street Lighting

2006. America. Energy Conservation.
3473 **1740** 1r.75 multicoloured 2·75 2·40

1741 *Isurus oxyrinchus* and *Sphyrna lewini*

2006. Sharks. Sheet 70×111 mm containing T **1741** and similar square design. Multicoloured.
MS3474 1r.90×2, Type **1741** *Mustelus schmitti* 6·00 6·00

1742 Diving

2007. Pan American Games, Rio de Janeiro. Multicoloured. Self-adhesive.
3477 (1º Porte Carta Comercial) Type **1742** 1·20 1·00
3478 (1º Porte Carta Comercial) Swimming 1·20 1·00
3479 (1º Porte Carta Comercial) Synchronised Swimming 1·20 1·00
3480 (1º Porte Carta Comercial) Futsal 1·20 1·00
3481 (1º Porte Carta Comercial) Water polo 1·20 1·00

1743 Carimbo

2007. Dances. Multicoloured.
3482 (1º Porte Carta Comercial) Type **1743** 90 80
3483 (1º Porte Carta Comercial) Frevo 90 80

1744 Research Vessel

2007. International Polar Year. Multicoloured.
3484 (1º Porte Carta Comercial) Type **1744** 1·40 1·20
3485 (1º Porte Carta Comercial) Ferraz research station 1·40 1·20
3486 (1º Porte Carta Comercial) Penguin and map of Antarctica 1·40 1·20

Nos. 3484/6 were issued together, *setenant*, forming a composite design.

1745 First Church of Our Lady of Assumption

2007. Jose de Anchieta (Jesuit missionary) Commemoration. Multicoloured.
3487 90c. Type **1745** 1·40 1·20
3488 90c. Founding of Espirito Santo 1·40 1·20
3489 90c. Metropolitan Cathedral of Vitoria 1·40 1·20

Nos. 3487/9 were issued together, setenant, forming a composite design.

1746 Estadio Olimpico Edgard Proenca (Mangueirao), Belem

2007. Stadia. Multicoloured.
3490 60c. Type **1746** 1·00 85
3491 60c. Estadio Municipal Paulo Machado de Carvalho, Pacaembu 1·00 85
3492 90c. Estadio Serra Dourada, Goiania 1·50 1·30
3493 2r.60 Estadio Jornalista Mario Filho (Maracana), Rio de Janeiro 4·00 3·50

1747 JK Bridge

2007. Mercosul. National Architecture.
3494 **1747** (1º porte Carta Comercial) mult 1·50 1·30

1748 Robert Baden-Powell

2007. Centenary of Scouting.
3495 **1748** 2r. multicoloured 3·25 3·00

1749 Pope Benedict XVI

2007. Pope Benedict XVI Visit to Brazil.
3496 **1749** 90c. multicoloured 1·50 1·30

1750 *Cochlespira elongate*

2007. Shells. Sheet 126×84 mm containing T **1750** and similar vert designs. Multicoloured.
MS3497 2r.×3, Type **1750** *Charonia variegata*; *Chicoreus* 9·75 9·75

The stamps and margins of **MS**3497 form a composite design of a seashore.

1751 *My New Accordion* (Napachie Pootoogook)

2007. 140th Anniv of Brazil–Canada Diplomatic Relations.
3498 **1751** 90c. multicoloured 1·50 1·30

1752 *Rio Pardo* and Giuseppe Garibaldi

2007. Birth Bicentenary of Giuseppe Garibaldi (soldier and nationalist). Multicoloured.
3499 1r.40 Type **1752** 2·20 1·90
3500 1r.40 On horseback 2·20 1·90

Stamps of a similar design were issued by Uruguay.

1753 Metro Locomotive

2007. Transport. Multicoloured.
3501 1r.40 Type **1753** 2·20 1·90
3502 1r.45 Steam locomotive No. 1 *Baroneza* 2·30 2·00
3503 1r.90 Tram, Bonde Santa Teresa 3·25 2·75

1754 Teofilo Ottoni

2007. Birth Bicentenary of Teofilo Benedict Ottoni (politician and journalist).
3504 **1754** 60c. multicoloured 1·00 85

1755 Children, Computers and 'abc'

2007. America. Education for All.
3505 **1755** 60c. multicoloured 1·00 85

1756 Inscr 'High &; Magic'

2007. Roses. Sheet 85×128 mm containing T **1756** and similar vert designs.
MS3506 2r.60×3, Type **1756**; Inscr 'Caballero'; Inscr 'Avalanche' 12·00 12·00

The stamps and margins of **MS**3506 form a composite design.

1757 Giraffes

2007. Zoological Fauna. Multicoloured.
3507 60c. Type **1757** 1·00 85
3508 60c. Tiger 1·00 85
3509 60c. Elephant 1·00 85
3510 60c. Lion 1·00 85
3511 60c. Chimpanzees 1·00 85
3512 60c. Macaw 1·00 85

1758 Candles

2007. Christmas. Multicoloured. Self-adhesive.
3513 1st (porte nao-Comercial) Type **1758** 1·50 1·30
3514 1st (porte Comercial) The Nativity 1·50 1·30

1759 King Joao VI

2008. Bicentenary of Portuguese Royal Family's Arrival in Brazil (1st issue). Multicoloured.
3515 2r. Type **1759** 3·25 2·75
3516 2r. Royal Family and Entourage 3·25 2·75

Nos. 3515/16 were issued together, *se-tenant*, forming a composite design.

Stamps of the same design were issued by Portugal.

1760 Ships (opening of ports to friendly nations)

2008. Bicentenary of Portuguese Royal Family's Arrival in Brazil (2nd issue). Bicentenary of External Relations. Multicoloured.
3517 1st Porte Carta Comercial Type 1760 3·00 2·50
3518 1st Porte Carta Comercial Globe (foreign trade) 3·00 2·50

No. 3519 is left for stamp not yet received.

1761 Dancer and Musicians (Tambor de Crioula)

2008. America. National Festivals. Self-adhesive.

3520 **1761** 1st Porte Carta Nao Comercial multicoloured 3·00 2·50

1762 UFRJ Faculty of Medicine

2008. Bicentenary of Portuguese Royal Family's Arrival in Brazil (3rd issue). Bicentenary of Faculties of Medicine. Multicoloured.

3521 1st Porte Carta Nao Comercial Type **1762** 3·00 2·50

3522 1st Porte Carta Nao Comercial Bahia Faculty of Medicine 3·00 2·50

1763 Stylized figures and Map as Jigsaw

2008. National Conference on Youth. Self-adhesive.

3523 **1763** 1st Porte Carta Nao Comercial multicoloured 3·00 2·50

1764 Transport Ship, Helicopter and Soldiers

2008. Bicentenary of Portuguese Royal Family's Arrival in Brazil (4th issue). Bicentenary of Naval Fusiliers Corps.

3524 **1764** 1st Porte Carta Comercial multicoloured 3·00 2·50

1765 Museum of Contemporary Art, Niteroi

2008. Designs by Oscar Niemeyer (architect). Sheet 112×72 mm containing T **1765** and similar vert design. Black, ultramarine and vermilion.

MS3525 2r.60×2, Type **1765**; Latin America Memorial 7·75 7·75

1766 Building and *A Justica* (Alfredo Ceschiatti)

2008. Bicentenary of Portuguese Royal Family's Arrival in Brazil (5th issue). Bicentenary of Independent Judiciary.

3526 **1766** 1st Porte Carta Comercial multicoloured 3·00 2·50

1767 Flag and 'Justice'

2008. Bicentenary of Portuguese Royal Family's Arrival in Brazil (6th issue). Bicentenary of Supreme Military Court.

3527 **1767** 1st Porte Carta Comercial multicoloured 3·00 2·50

1768 Headquarters and Gustavo de Lacerda (founder)

2008. Centenary of Press Association.

3528 **1768** 1st Porte Carta Comercial multicoloured 3·00 2·50

1769 Dom Pedro I (first ruler of independent Brazil)

2008. National Heroes. Multicoloured.

3529 1st Porte Carta Comercial Type **1769** 3·00 2·50

3530 1st Porte Carta Comercial Marechal Deodoro da Foncesca (first president of Republic of Brazil) 3·00 2·50

3531 1st Porte Carta Comercial Luís Alves de Lima e Silva, Duke of Caxias (military leader, statesman and Prime Minister) 3·00 2·50

3532 1st Porte Carta Comercial Admiral Francisco Manuel Barroso da Silva (commander of victorious Brazilian Navy at Battle of Riachuelo) 3·00 2·50

3533 1st Porte Carta Comercial Joaquim Marques Lisbon, Admiral Tamandare 3·00 2·50

3534 1st Porte Carta Comercial Jose Bonifacio de Andrada e Silva (statesman and naturalist) 3·00 2·50

3535 1st Porte Carta Comercial Alberto Santos-Dumont (aviation pioneer) 3·00 2·50

3536 1st Porte Carta Comercial Zumbi dos Palmares (last leaders of Quilombo dos Palmares (runaway and free-born Black African slaves community)) 3·00 2·50

3537 1st Porte Carta Comercial Joaquim Jose da Silva Xavier (Triadentes) (nationalist) 3·00 2·50

3538 1st Porte Carta Comercial Placido de Castro 3·00 2·50

1770 Policeman

2008. Bicentenary of Portuguese Royal Family's Arrival in Brazil (7th issue). Bicentenary of Civil Police (horiz) or bicentenary of Dragoons (vert). Multicoloured.

3539 1st Porte Carta Comercial Type **1770** 3·00 2·50

3540 1st Porte Carta Comercial Cavalry (vert) 3·00 2·50

1771 Printing Press, Print and Building

2008. Bicentenary of Portuguese Royal Family's Arrival in Brazil (8th issue). Bicentenary of National Press.

3541 **1771** 1st Porte Carta Comercial multicoloured 3·00 2·50

1772 *Tangara cayana* (burnished-buff tanager)

2008. Serra do Japi—São Paulo Natural Heritage. Sheet 111×70 mm containing T **1772** and similar horiz design. Multicoloured.

MS3542 2r.×2, Type **1772**; *Consul fabius drurii* 5·50 5·50

The stamps and margins of **MS**3542 form a composite design.

1773 *Lippia alba* and *Copaifera lucens*

2008. Bicentenary of Portuguese Royal Family's Arrival in Brazil (9th issue). Bicentenary of Botanic Garden.

3543 **1773** 1st Porte Carta Comercial multicoloured 3·00 2·50

1774 Ship

2008. Centenary of Japanese Immigration. Sheet 128×86 mm containing T **1774** and similar vert design. Multicoloured.

MS3544 3r.50×2, Type **1774**; Flags and origami 14·00 14·00

The stamps and margins of **MS**3544 form a composite design.

1775 Mer de Glace

2008. Landscapes. Multicoloured.

3545 2r. Type **1775** 3·25 2·75

3546 2r. Serra do Araca 3·25 2·75

Nos. 3545/6 were issued together, *se-tenant*, forming a composite design.

Stamps of a similar design were issued by France.

1776 Joao Guimaraes Rosa and Scene from *Grande Sertão: Veredas*

2008. Birth Centenary of Joao Guimaraes Rosa (writer).

3547 **1776** 60c. multicoloured 1·00 85

No. 3547 is embossed with Braille characters.

1777 Headquarters

2008. Bicentenary of Portuguese Royal Family's Arrival in Brazil (10th issue). Bicentenary of Ministry of Finance.

3548 **1777** 1st Porte Carta Comercial multicoloured 3·00 2·50

1778 Gymnastics

2008. Olympic Games, Beijing. Multicoloured.

3549 65c. Type **1778** 1·10 90

3550 65c. Equestrian 1·10 90

3551 65c. Swimming 1·10 90

3552 65c. Games emblem 1·10 90

1779 Cozido Completo and Quindim

2008. Bicentenary of Portuguese Royal Family's Arrival in Brazil (11th issue). Brazilian Portuguese Cuisine.

3553 **1779** 90c. multicoloured 1·50 1·30

1780 *Lontra longicaudis* (American river otter)

2008. Endangered Species. Multicoloured.

3554 1r. Type **1780** 1·50 1·30

3555 1r. *Trichechus inunguis* (Amazonian manatee) 1·50 1·30

3556 1r. *Pteronura brasiliensis* (giant otter) 1·50 1·30

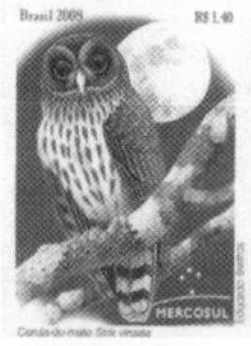

1781 *Strix virgata* (mottled owl)

2008. Mercosul. Birds. Multicoloured.

3557 1r.40 Type **1781** 2·20 1·90

3558 1r.40 *Celeus obrieni* (Kaempfer's woodpecker) 2·20 1·90

1782 Nativity

2008. Christmas. Multicoloured. Self adhesive.

3559 1st Porte Carta Nao Comercial Type **1782** (800th anniv of Franciscans) 3·00 2·50

3560 1st Porte Carta Comercial San Antonio (400th anniv of Santo Antonio convent) 3·00 2·50

Nos. 3559/60 were for use on mail up to 20g., No. 3559 was originally on sale for 65c. and No. 3560 for 1r.

1783 Map and Symbols of Post

2008. Bicentenary of Portuguese Royal Family's Arrival in Brazil (9th issue). Bicentenary of Postal Provision.

3561 **1783** 1r. multicoloured 2·75 2·20

1784 Louis Braille

2009. Birth Bicentenary of Louis Braille (inventor of Braille writing for the blind).

3562 **1784** 2r.20 multicoloured 3·25 2·50

No. 3562 is embossed with Braille writing.

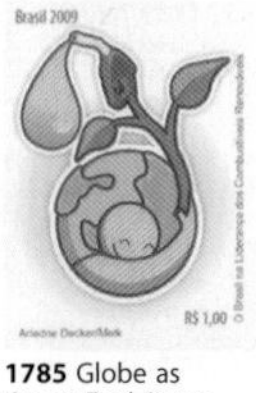

1785 Globe as Green Fuel Pump

2009. Brazil–Leader in Renewable Fuel Production. Self-adhesive.

3563 **1785** 1r. multicoloured 1·50 1·20

1786 Ox

2009. Chinese New Year. Year of the Ox.

3564 **1786** 2r.35 multicoloured 3·50 2·75

1787 Sao Simao Dam, Paranaiba River

2009. Natural Heritage. Rivers. Centenary of Meteorological Office. Two sheets, 112×70 mm, containing T **1787** and similar horiz design. Multicoloured.

MS3565 2r.60 Type **1787** 4·00 3·25

MS3566 3r.85 *Cichla mirianae* (Amazon peacock bass) 5·75 4·50

1788 Dom Helder Camara

2009. Birth Centenary of Dom Helder Camara

3567 **1788** 1r. multicoloured 70 55

1789 *Hydrurga leptonyx* (leopard seal)

2009. Preserve Polar Regions and Glaciers. Multicoloured.

3568 1r. Type **1789** 1·50 1·20

3569 1r. *Ursus maritimus* (polar bear) 1·50 1·20

No. 3567 and Type **1788** are left for Birth Centenary of Dom Helder Camara, issued on 7 February 2009, not yet received.

Nos. 3568/9, were printed, *se-tenant*, each pair forming a composite design.

1789a Postman holding Letter

2009. Postal Services (1st issue). Multicoloured.

3569a 65c. Type **1789a** 1·20 90

3569b 1r. Hand holding telegram 1·70 1·20

1790 Emblem

2009. Centenary of Sports Club International.

3570 **1790** 1r. multicoloured 1·50 1·20

1791 *Aechmea disticantha*, Atlantic Forest and Sao Pedro de Alcantara Cathedral

2009. Brazil–Thailand Diplomatic Relations. Multicoloured.

3571 2r.35 Type **1791** 3·50 2·75

3572 2r.35 *Rhynchostylis gigantea* and Dusit Maha Prasat Palace (Grand Palace) 3·50 2·75

1792 Books, Tower Blocks and Kahlil Gibran (writer)

2009. Brazil–Lebanon Diplomatic Relations. Beirut–World Book Capital, 2009.

3573 **1792** 2r.35 multicoloured 3·50 2·75

1793 Musicians and Dancers

2009. Capoeira and Craft of the Masters of Capoeira. Self-adhesive.

3574 **1793** 65c. multicoloured 1·00 80

1794 Justice and Building Facade

2009. Escola Judicial Desembargador Edesio Fernandes (Judge Edesio Fernandes judicial school).

3575 **1794** 1r. multicoloured 1·50 1·20

1795 *Soyuz*

2009. Brazil–Russia Diplomatic Relations. Co-operation in Space.

3576 **1795** 2r.35 multicoloured 3·50 2·75

1796 Theatre Facade

2009. Centenary of Rio de Janeiro Municipal Theatre.

3577 **1796** 1st Porte Carta Comercial multicoloured 3·00 2·50

1797 Anniversary Emblem

2009. Bicentenary of Royal Charter.

3578 **1797** 1r. multicoloured 1·50 1·20

1798 *Vitis labrusca*

2009. Mercosul. Exports. Fruit. Multicoloured.

3579 1st PCC Type **1798** 3·50 2·50

3580 1st PCC *Prunus persica* (peach) 3·00 2·50

3581 1st PCC *Prunus salicina* (Japanese plum) 3·00 2·50

3582 1st PCC *Malpighia glabra* (Barbados cherry) 3·00 2·50

3583 1st PCC *Vitus labrusca* (white grapes) 3·00 2·50

3584 1st PCC *Fragaria×ananassa* (strawberry) 3·00 2·50

3585 1st PCC *Pasiflora edulis* (passion fruit) 3·00 2·50

3586 1st PCC *Vitis* (black grapes) 3·00 2·50

3587 1st PCC *Ficus carica* (fig) 3·00 2·50

3588 1st PCC *Diospyros kaki* (persimmon) 3·00 2·50

1st PCC=Porte Carte Comercial

1799 Mauricio de Nassau

2009. Dutch Presence in Brazil. Sheet 105×148 mm containing T **1799** and similar vert designs. Multicoloured.

MS3589 2r.20×6, Type **1799**; *Zutphen*; Dutch pipes; Palacio de Friburgo, Santo Antônio, Recife; Palacio do Campo das Princesas (state administrative headquarters), Santo Antônio, Recife; Rua Aurora 6·50 6·50

1800 Marbles

2009. America. Games. Multicoloured.

3590 1r. Type **1800** 1·50 1·20

3591 1r. Dominoes 1·50 1·20

3592 1r. Chess 1·50 1·20

3593 1r. Table tennis 1·50 1·20

1801 '100', Symbols of Education and Map showing Centres

2009. Centenary of Federal Network of Professional Technical Education.

3594 **1801** 1st PCC multicoloured 3·00 2·50

1802 Lookouts of Sao Luis

2009. Lookouts of Sao Luis

3595 **1802** 1st PCC multicoloured 3·00 2·50

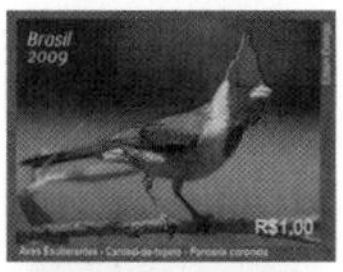

1803 *Paroaria coronata* (red-crested cardinal)

2009. Brightly Coloured Birds. Multicoloured.

MS3596 1r.×6, Type **1803**; *Rupicola rupicola* (cock-of-the-rock); *Chlorophonia cyanea* (blue-naped chlorophonia); *Porphyrospiza caerulescens* (yellow-billed blue finch); *Tangara cyanocephala* (red-necked tanager); *Amblyramphus holosericeus* (scarlet-headed blackbird) 5·25 5·25

1804 Carmen Miranda

2009. Brazil–Portugal Diplomatic Relations

3597 **1804** 2r.20 multicoloured 2·20 1·70

Nos. 3599/600 and Type **1806** are left for Postal Services, issued on 9 October 2009, not yet received.

1805 Carmen Miranda

2009. Brazil–France Diplomatic Relations. Year of France in Brazil. Multicoloured.

MS3598 2r.20×2, Type **1805**; Amerindian (Claude Levi-Strauss (anthropologist)) 4·25 4·25

The stamps and margins of **MS**3598 form a composite design.

2009. Postal Services (2nd issue). Multicoloured.

3599 1st Mail bag (inscr 'MALOTE') (vert) 1·10 80

3600 1st Motorcycle delivery (inscr 'SEDEX') 1·10 80

1807 Club Emblem

2009. Centenary of Coritiba Football Club

3601 **1807** 1r.05 multicoloured 1·70 1·20

1808 Garland

2009. Christmas (1st issue)

3602 **1808** 1st PCC multicoloured 1·70 1·20

1809 Roadside Crib

2009. Christmas (2nd issue). Multicoloured.

3603 1st PCC Type **1809** 1·70 1·20

3604 1st PCC The Nativity 1·70 1·20

3605 1st PCC Crib festooned with lights, amongst trees 1·70 1·20

3606 1st PCC Ceramic crib showing The Nativity and Magi 1·70 1·20

3607 1st PCC Thatched crib showing Magi, Infant Jesus, Mary and sheep 1·70 1·20

3608 1st PCC Ceramic crib showing Holy Family, shepherd holding child, cow and donkey 1·70 1·20

1810 Angel

2009. Christmas (3rd issue). Multicoloured.

MS3609 2r.70×2, Type **1810**; Angel facing left 5·75 5·75

The stamps and margins of **MS**3609 form a composite design.

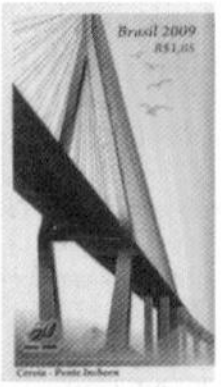

1811 Incheon Bridge, South Korea

2009. Brazil–South Korea Diplomatic Relations. Multicoloured.

3610 1r.05 Type **1811** 1·70 1·20

3611 1r.05 Octávio Frias de Oliveira bridge, Brazil 1·70 1·20

Nos. 3610/11 were printed, *se-tenant*, each pair forming a composite design.

1812 Brazil Player

2009. Brazil–Hong Kong Diplomatic Relations. Multicoloured.

3612	1r.05 Type **1812**	1·70	1·20
3613	1r.05 Brazilian player (different)	1·70	1·20
3614	1r.05 Hong Kong player	1·70	1·20
3615	1r.05 Hong Kong goalkeeper	1·70	1·70

Nos. 3612/15 were printed, *se-tenant*, forming a composite design.

Stamps of a similar design were issued by Hong Kong.

1813 Runners

2010. Race of Kings (road race from Cuiabá–Mato Grosso).

3616	**1813**	70c. multicoloured	1·10	80

1814 Pres. Tancredo Neves

2010. Birth Centenary of Tancredo de Almeida Neves (politician and president March–April 1985 (who died before inauguration))

3617	**1814**	1r.05 multicoloured	1·70	1·20

1815 Zilda Arns

2010. Mercosur. Decade of Culture of Peace. Zilda Arns (founder and worker of Children's Pastoral, Brazilian church-based organisation (who died Haitian earthquake, 2010)) Commemoration

3618	**1815**	1r.45 multicoloured	2·40	2·00

1816 Chico Xavier

2010. Birth Centenary of Francisco Cândido Xavier (Chico Xavier) (spritism medium)

3619	**1816**	1st PCC multicoloured	3·00	2·50

1817 Memorial JK (memorial to President Juscelino Kubitschek)

2010. 50th Anniv of Brasilia as National Capital. Multicoloured.

3620	1st PCC Type **1817**	3·00	2·50
3621	1st PCC *Dois Candangos* (two labourers)	3·00	2·50
3622	1st PCC Cathedral of Brasília (horiz)	3·00	2·50
3623	1st PCC Igrejinha de Fátima (little chapel of Fatima) (horiz)	3·00	2·50
3624	1st PCC Sculpture (by Alfredo Ceschiatti), Palacio da Alvorada (Oscar Niemeyer, architect)	3·00	2·50
3625	1st PCC National Congress Building and Ipe Amarelo (national flower)	3·00	2·50

1818 Monastery Façade

2010. Religious Architecture and Festivals

3626	**1818**	1st PCC multicoloured	3·00	2·50

1819 Amerigo Vespucci and Caravel

2010. Brazil–Italy Diplomatic Relations. Multicoloured.

MS3627	2r.40×2, Type **1819**; In old age	4·25	4·25

The stamps and margins of **MS**3627 form a composite design.

1820 'RIO 2011' and Games Emblem

2010. Rio 2011, Fifth International Military Games, Rio de Janeiro

3628	**1820**	2r. multicoloured	3·00	2·50

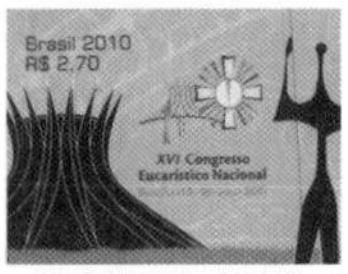

1821 Cathedral of Brasilia, Congress Emblem and Dois Candangos (two labourers)

2010. 50th Anniv of Brasilia as National Capital. Multicoloured.

MS3629	2r.70×2, Type **1821**; *Dois Candangos* (two labourers), *Memorial JK* and Catetinho (first official residence of the President in new capital)	5·50	5·50

The stamps and margins of **MS**3629 form a composite design.

2010. Religious Architecture and Festivals

3630	**1822**	1r.10 multicoloured	1·70	1·20

1823 The Holy Trinity, Mary, Shrine of Divine Eternal Father Basilica and Ox Cart

2010. Religious Architecture and Festivals

3631	**1823**	70c. multicoloured	1·40	1·00

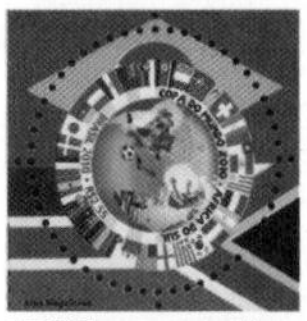

1824 Flags surrounding Stylized Players

2010. World Cup Football Championships, South Africa

3632	**1824**	2r.55 multicoloured	4·25	3·75

1825 Peter Lund and Cave at Lagoa Santa

2010. Peter Wilhelm Lund ('father' of Brazilian paleontology and discoverer of Pleistocene era remains at Lagoa Santa) Commemoration

3633	**1825**	1r.50 multicoloured	1·70	1·20

1826 Abu Simbel Temples, Nubia

2010. Brazil–Egypt Diplomatic Relationships

3634	**1826**	1r.05 multicoloured	1·70	1·20

1827 Rio de Janeiro, Brazil and Maalula, Syria

2010. Brazil–Syria Diplomatic Relationships

3635	**1827**	2r. multicoloured	2·20	1·70

No. 3636 is vacant.

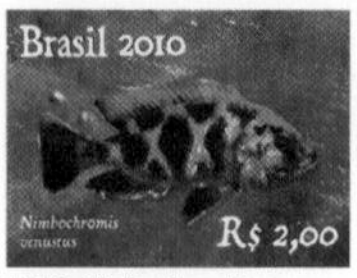

1828 *Nimbochromis venustrus*

2010. Brazil–Malawi Diplomatic Relationships. Multicoloured.

MS3637	2r.×3, Type **1828**; *A. jacobfreibergi eureka*; *Cynotilapia*	6·50	6·50

1829 Clock Tower and Village Skyline

2010. Paranapiacaba, Santo André (company town for employees of São Paulo Railway, privately owned British company)

3638	**1829**	1r.05 multicoloured	1·70	1·20

1830 '150 ANOS' and Stylized Fields

2010. 150th Anniv of Ministry of Agriculture

2639	**1830**	1r.05 multicoloured	1·70	1·20

1831 Barao de Maua (transport pioneer)

2010. 150th Anniv of Ministry of Transport

3640	**1831**	1r.05 multicoloured	1·70	1·20

1832 *Gossyplum hirsutum*

2010. Textile Plants. Multicoloured.

3641	2r. Type **1832**	2·20	1·70
3642	2r. *Cocos nucifera* (coir)	2·20	1·70
3643	2r. *Corchorus capsularis* (jute)	2·20	1·70
3644	2r. *Agave sisalana* (sisal)	2·20	1·70

1833 Player and Club Emblem

2010. Centenary of Corinthians Paulista Sports Club

3645	**1833**	8r.30 multicoloured	5·25	4·25

No. 3645 and Type **1833** are left for Centenary of Sport Club issued on 1 September 2010, not yet received.

1834 Arms

2010. America. Patriotic Symbols. Multicoloured.

3646	1r.05 Type **1834**	1·70	1·20
3647	1r.05 Flag	1·70	1·20
3648	1r.05 Seal	1·70	1·20
3649	1r.05 National anthem score	1·70	1·20

1835 Symbols of Tourism

2010. Association of Government Printers Conference

3650	**1835**	2r. multicoloured	2·10	1·70

1836 Tomatoes on the Vine

2010. International Year of Biodiversity

MS3651	2r.40×2, Type **1836**; Growing salad vegetables	4·25	4·25

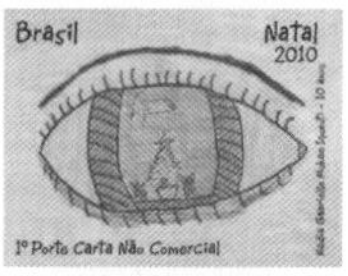

1837 Eye enclosing Tree, Presents and Star (Nadia Gabrielle Mukae Iqueuti)

2010. Christmas. Childrens' Drawings (Nos. 3652/3)

(a) Self-adhesive

3652	1st PCNC Type **1837**	65	50
3653	1st PCC The Nativity (Maria Elisa Alcántata da Cruz)	85	70

(b) Ordinary gum

MS3654	70×110 mm. 2r.70 The Holy Family (38×38 mm)	2·20	2·20

1838 Leopard

2010. Brazil - Zambia Diplomatic Relations. Multicoloured.

3654a	1r.05 Type **1838**	85	70
3655	1r.05 Victoria Falls	85	70
3656	1r.05 Lion	85	70
3657	1r.05 Buffalo	85	70
3658	1r.05 Rhinoceros	85	70
3659	1r.05 Elephant	85	70

Nos. 3654a/9 were printed, *se-tenant*, in blocks of six stamps within the sheet, each block forming a composite design.

1839 *Lonchorhina aurita*

2010. Bats. Multicoloured.

3660	2r. Type **1839**	2·10	1·70
3661	2r. *Artibeus gnomus*	2·10	1·70
3662	2r. *Platyrrhinus helleri*	2·10	1·70
3663	2r. *Lonchophylla dekeyseri*	2·10	1·70

1840 Pres. Lula

2011. President Luiz Inácio Lula da Silva

3664	**1840**	2r. multicoloured	2·10	1·70

1841 'CAIXA' and Map

2011. 150th Anniv of Federal Savings Bank (CAIXA)

3665	**1841**	1st PCC multicoloured	3·00	3·25

1842 Father de Moura

2011. Father Roberto Landell de Moura (priest and inventor who demonstrated a radio broadcast of human voice on June 3, 1900) Commemoration

3666	**1842**	1st PCC multicoloured	3·00	2·50

1843 Anniversary Emblem

2011. Centenary of Postal Union of the Americas, Spain and Portugal (UPAEP)

3667	**1843**	1r.25 multicoloured	3·25	2·75

1844 Emblem

2011. Centenary of Guarani Football Club

3668	**1844**	1st PCC multicoloured	85	70

1845 St. Francis of Assisi Church, Our Lady of Mount Carmel Church, Partial View of Mariana painted in Blue (in style of Mestre Athayde, painter born in Mariana), *Maria Smoke* (locomotive), Mariana Pillory and Town Hall

2011. Historic Cities. 300th Anniv of Mariana

3669	**1845**	1r.10 multicoloured	85	70

1846 Gates of Military Academy of Agulhas Negras, Colours of Brazilian Flag, Coat of Arms, 'AMAN 200 Anos', Marlins Caxias and Shako

2011. Bicentenary of Military Academy (AMAN)

3670	**1846**	1r.10 multicoloured	85	70

1847 Julio Prestes Station

2011. Railway Stations

(a) Ordinary gum

3671	1r.10 Type **1847**	85	70
3672	1r.10 Luz Station	85	70

(b) Self-adhesive

3673	1r.10 Brazil Central Station, Rio de Janeiro (vert)	85	70

1848 Itaipu Hydroelectric Plant, Parana River and Bicentenary of Paraguay Independence Emblem

2011. Brazil - Paraguay Diplomatic Relations. Bicentenary of Paraguay Independence

3674	**1848**	1r.10 multicoloured	85	70

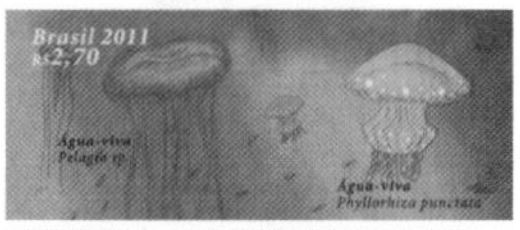

1849 *Pelagia* and *Phyllorhyza punctata* (jellyfish)

2011. Marine Fauna. Philanippon 2011, International Philatelic Exhibition, Yokohama. Multicoloured.

MS3675	2r.70×4, Type **1849**; *Sepioteuthis sepioidea* (squid); *Octopus insularis*; *Oreaster reticulatus* (starfish)	7·50	7·50

1850 *Tangara seledon* (green-headed tanager) and *Hadrolaelia lobata*

2011. Tijuca National Park. Multicoloured.

MS3676	5r.×2, Type **1850**; *Thalurania glaucopis* (violet-capped wood-nymph (hummingbird)) and *Coendou insidiosus* (hedgehog)	3·75	3·75

1851 Elderly Couple sheltering under Umbrella

2011. International Network for the Prevention of Violence Against the Elderly Day

3677	**1851**	1r.10 multicoloured	85	70

1852 Bowl (used for gold extraction), Gold Bar, Houses with Carmo Church, Itacolomi Peak, Joaquim Jose da Silva Xavier (statue), Tiradentes Monument and Town

2011. Historic Cities. 300th Anniv of Ouro Preto

3678	**1852**	1r.10 multicoloured	85	70

1853 Bicentenary Emblem

2011. Bicentenary of Commercial Association of Bahia

3679	**1853**	1r.10 multicoloured	85	70

1854 Paulo Gracindo

2011. Mercosur. Birth Centenary of Pelopidas Gracindo Brandao Guimaraes (Paulo Gracindo) (actor)

3680	**1854**	1r.85 multicoloured	1·50	1·20

1855 Gold Museum, Gold Exhibits, Interior of Municipal Theatre (blue), Nossa Senhora do Ó Church, Sculpture (Aleijadinho), Church of Our Lady of Mount Carmel and City Hall

2011. Historic Cities. 300th Anniv of Sabara

3681	**1855**	1r.10 multicoloured	85	70

No. **MS**3682 and Type **1856** are left for Folklore, issued on 23 July 2011, not yet received.

No. 3683 and Type **1857** are left for Brazil - Ukraine Diplomatic Relations, issued on 24 August 2011, not yet received.

1858 Spanish Soldiers, First and Third Order of Carmel Churches, Mogi das Cruzes (blue), Dove, Tea House, Cocuera (built by Kazuo Hanaoka), Obelisk and City Hall

2011. Historic Cities. 400th Anniv of Mogi das Cruzes

3684	**1858**	1r.10 multicoloured	85	70

1859 Theatre Façade

2011. Centenary of Municipal Theatre, São Paulo

3685	**1859**	2r. multicoloured	1·70	1·40

EXPRESS STAMP

1930. Surch 1000 REIS EXPRESSO and bars.

E490	**66**	1000r. on 200r. blue	6·25	2·30

NEWSPAPER STAMPS

N34

1889. Roul.

N88	**N34**	10r. orange	4·75	4·50
N89	**N34**	20r. orange	9·25	11·50
N90	**N34**	50r. orange	15·00	9·00
N91	**N34**	100r. orange	6·00	4·50
N92	**N34**	200r. orange	4·75	2·30
N93	**N34**	300r. orange	4·75	2·30
N94	**N34**	500r. orange	33·00	13·00
N95	**N34**	700r. orange	4·75	15·00
N96	**N34**	1000r. orange	4·75	15·00

1889. Roul.

N97	10r. green	2·20	80
N98	20r. green	2·20	80
N99	50r. buff	2·75	1·40
N100	100r. mauve	3·75	2·00
N101	200r. black	3·50	2·10
N102	300r. red	14·50	11·00
N103	500r. green	60·00	60·00
N104	700r. blue	32·00	37·00
N105	1000r. brown	14·50	34·00

N37

1890. Perf.

N111	**N37**	10r. blue	19·00	11·50
N112	**N37**	20r. green	60·00	18·00
N113	**N37**	100r. mauve	21·00	15·00

N38 Southern Cross and Sugar-loaf Mountain

1890. Perf.

N119	**N38**	10r. blue	6·25	2·75
N123a	**N38**	20r. green	5·00	80
N127	**N38**	50r. green	18·00	10·00

OFFICIAL STAMPS

O64 Pres. Affonso Penna

1906. Various frames.

O282	**O64**	10r. green & orange	1·00	30
O283	**O64**	20r. green & orange	1·20	30
O284	**O64**	50r. green & orange	1·70	30
O285	**O64**	100r. green & orange	1·00	30
O286	**O64**	200r. green & orange	1·20	30
O287	**O64**	300r. green & orange	3·75	65
O288	**O64**	400r. green & orange	8·00	2·75
O289	**O64**	500r. green & orange	4·25	1·70
O290	**O64**	700r. green & orange	5·00	4·00
O291	**O64**	1000r. green & orange	4·00	1·30
O292	**O64**	2000r. green & orange	6·50	2·30
O293	**O64**	5000r. green & orange	12·50	1·60
O294	**O64**	10000r. green & orange	12·50	1·50

O67 Pres. Hermes de Fonseca

1913. Various frames.

O295	**O67**	10r. black and grey	40	60
O296	**O67**	20r. black and olive	40	60
O297	**O67**	50r. black and grey	40	60
O298	**O67**	100r. black and red	90	40
O299	**O67**	200r. black and blue	1·50	40
O300	**O67**	500r. black & yellow	3·50	50
O301	**O67**	600r. black & purple	4·25	2·75
O302	**O67**	1000r. black & brown	5·00	1·50
O303	**O67**	2000r. black & brown	7·50	1·50
O304	**O67**	5000r. black & bistre	9·75	3·75
O305	**O67**	10000r. black	16·00	8·50
O306	**O67**	20000r. black & blue	30·00	29·00
O307	**O67**	50000r. black & green	55·00	60·00
O308	**O67**	100000r. black & red	£200	£200
O309	**O67**	500000r. black & brn	£350	£350
O310	**O67**	1000000r. black & brn	£375	£375

O77 Pres. Wenceslao Braz

1919

O311	**O77**	10r. brown	45	4·50
O312	**O77**	50r. green	1·20	1·40
O313	**O77**	100r. red	2·10	90
O314	**O77**	200r. blue	3·50	90
O315	**O77**	500r. orange	9·25	24·00

POSTAGE DUE STAMPS

D34

1889. Roul.

D88	**D34**	10r. red	2·75	2·10
D89	**D34**	20r. red	4·50	2·75
D90	**D34**	50r. red	7·75	5·75
D91	**D34**	100r. red	2·75	2·10
D92	**D34**	200r. red	90·00	21·00
D93	**D34**	300r. red	9·25	11·50
D94	**D34**	500r. red	9·25	11·50
D95	**D34**	700r. red	15·00	21·00
D96	**D34**	1000r. red	15·00	15·00

1890. Roul.

D97	10r. orange	90	45
D98	20r. blue	90	45
D99	50r. olive	2·00	45
D100	200r. red	9·25	85
D101	300r. green	4·50	2·10
D102	500r. grey	6·00	4·25
D103	700r. violet	7·25	11·50
D104	1000r. purple	8·75	7·50

D45

1895. Perf.

D172	**D45**	10r. blue	2·10	1·40
D173	**D45**	20r. green	8·75	3·25
D174	**D45**	50r. green	11·00	6·00
D175	**D45**	100r. red	7·25	1·40
D176b	**D45**	200r. lilac	5·50	3·50
D177	**D45**	300r. blue	4·00	2·50
D178	**D45**	2000r. brown	18·00	17·00

D64

1906

D282	**D64**	10r. slate	25	25
D283	**D64**	20r. violet	25	25
D284	**D64**	50r. green	30	25
D285	**D64**	100r. red	2·00	65
D286	**D64**	200r. blue	1·10	30
D287	**D64**	300r. grey	40	65
D288	**D64**	400r. green	1·30	1·00
D289	**D64**	500r. lilac	40·00	38·00
D290	**D64**	600r. purple	1·40	3·25
D291	**D64**	700r. brown	35·00	32·00
D292	**D64**	1000r. red	1·60	3·50
D293	**D64**	2000r. green	5·25	6·00
D294	**D64**	5000r. brown	1·60	23·00

D77

1919

D345	**D77**	5r. brown	25	25
D403	**D77**	10r. mauve	15	15
D365	**D77**	20r. olive	45	5·00
D404	**D77**	20r. black	15	15
D405	**D77**	50r. green	20	15
D375	**D77**	100r. red	1·00	95
D407	**D77**	200r. blue	30	20
D408	**D77**	400r. brown	1·40	1·40
D350	**D77**	600r. orange	65	55
D401	**D77**	600r. violet	25	15
D409	**D77**	1000r. turquoise	50	40
D411	**D77**	5000r. blue	90	70
D439	**D77**	2000r. brown	1·60	1·50

Pt. 7

BREMEN

A free city of the Hanseatic League, situated on the R. Weser in northern Germany. Joined the North German Confederation in 1868.

72 grote = 1 thaler (internal).
22 grote = 10 silbergroschen (overseas mail)

1

1855. Imperf.

1	**1**	3g. black on blue	£275	£425

2

3

1856. Imperf.

3	**2**	5g. black on red	£200	£425
4	**2**	7g. black on yellow	£325	£950
5	**3**	5sg. green	£200	£475

4

5

1861. Zigzag roulette or perf.

17	**4**	2g. orange	£130	£425
19	**1**	3g. black on blue	£110	£400
20	**2**	5g. black on red	£170	£400
21	**2**	7g. black on yellow	£200	£6000
22	**5**	10g. black	£250	£1500
24	**3**	5sg. green	£700	£275

Pt. 1

BRITISH ANTARCTIC TERRITORY

Constituted in 1962 comprising territories south of latitude 60°S., from the former Falkland Island Dependencies.

1963. 12 pence = 1 shilling; 20 shillings = 1 pound.
1971. 100 (new) pence = 1 pound.

1 M.V. *Kista Dan*

1963

1	**1**	½d. blue	1·25	1·75
2	-	1d. brown	1·25	80
3	-	1½d. red and purple	1·25	1·50
4	-	2d. purple	1·50	80
5	-	2½d. myrtle	3·25	1·25
6	-	3d. turquoise	3·75	1·50
7	-	4d. sepia	2·75	1·50
8	-	6d. olive and blue	4·75	2·50
9	-	9d. green	3·50	2·00
10	-	1s. turquoise	4·25	1·50
11	-	2s. violet and brown	20·00	10·00
12	-	2s.6d. blue	22·00	15·00
13	-	5s. orange and red	22·00	19·00
14	-	10s. blue and green	45·00	26·00
15	-	£1 black and blue	48·00	48·00
15a	-	£1 red and black	£130	£120

DESIGNS: 1d. Manhauling; 1½d. Muskeg (tractor); 2d. Skiing; 2½d. de Havilland D.H.C.2 Beaver (aircraft); 3d. R.R.S. *John Biscoe II* 4d. Camp scene; 6d. H.M.S. *Protector*; 9d. Sledging; 1s. de Havilland D.H.C.3 Otter (aircraft); 2s. Huskies; 2s.6d. Westland Whirlwind helicopter; 5s. Snocat (tractor); 10s. R.R.S. *Shackleton*; £1 (No. 15), Antarctic map; £1 (No. 15a), H.M.S. *Endurance I*.

1966. Churchill Commemoration. As T **38** of Antigua.

16	½d. blue	80	3·25
17	1d. green	3·25	3·25
18	1s. brown	23·00	6·50
19	2s. violet	25·00	7·00

17 Lemaire Channel and Icebergs

1969. 25th Anniv of Continuous Scientific Work.

20	**17**	3½d. black, blue and ultram	2·50	3·00
21	-	6d. multicoloured	1·00	2·50
22	-	1s. black, blue and red	1·00	2·00
23	-	2s. black, orange and turquoise	1·00	3·00

DESIGNS: 6d. Radio Sonde balloon; 1s. Muskeg pulling tent equipment; 2s. Surveyors with theodolite.

1971. Decimal Currency. Nos. 1/14 surch.

24	½p. on ½d. blue	60	3·00
25	1p. on 1d. brown	1·00	90
26	1½p. on 1½d. red and purple	1·25	75
27	2p. on 2d. purple	1·25	40
28	2½p. on 2½d. green	3·00	2·25
29	3p. on 3d. blue	2·50	75
30	4p. on 4d. brown	2·25	75
31	5p. on 6d. green and blue	4·75	3·50
32	6p. on 9d. green	14·00	8·50
33	7½p. on 1s. blue	14·00	8·50
34	10p. on 2s. violet and brown	14·00	12·00
35	15p. on 2s.6d. blue	15·00	12·00
36	25p. on 5s. orange and red	15·00	15·00
37	50p. on 10s. blue and green	18·00	25·00

19 Setting up Camp, Graham Land

1971. Tenth Anniv of Antarctic Treaty. Multicoloured.

38	1½p. Type **19**	6·00	5·50
39	4p. Snow petrels	16·00	8·00
40	5p. Weddell seals	9·50	8·00
41	10p. Adelie penguins	22·00	9·00

Nos. 38/41 each include Antarctic map and Queen Elizabeth in their design.

1972. Royal Silver Wedding. As T **52** of Ascension, but with Kerguelen fur seals and Emperor penguins in background.

42	5p. brown	2·00	3·00
43	10p. green	2·00	3·00

21 James Cook and H.M.S. *Resolution*

1973. Multicoloured.

64a	½p. Type **21**	1·00	2·50
65	1p. Thaddeus von Bellingshausen and *Vostok*	60	2·25
66	1½p. James Weddell and *Jane*	60	2·25
67	2p. John Biscoe and *Tula*	1·50	2·50
48	2½p. J. S. C. Dumont d'Urville and *L'Astrolabe*	1·50	1·75
49	3p. James Clark Ross and H.M.S. *Erebus*	1·00	1·75
50	4p. C. A. Larsen and *Jason*	1·00	1·75
51	5p. Adrien de Gerlache and *Belgica*	1·00	1·75
52	6p. Otto Nordenskjold and *Antarctic*	1·25	3·50
53	7½p. W. S. Bruce and *Scotia*	1·25	3·50
74a	10p. Jean-Baptiste Charcot and *Pourquoi Pas?*	50	3·00
75	15p. Ernest Shackleton and *Endurance*	1·25	2·75
76	25p. Hubert Wilkins and Lockheed Vega *San Francisco*	1·00	1·50
77b	50p. Lincoln Ellsworth and Northrop Gamma *Polar Star*	85	2·75
78	£1 John Rymill and *Penola*	2·75	2·00

The 25p. and 50p. show aircraft; the rest show ships.

1973. Royal Wedding. As T **47** of Anguilla. Background colour given. Multicoloured.

59	5p. brown	40	20
60	15p. blue	70	30

22 Churchill and Churchill Peninsula, B.A.T.

1974. Birth Centenary of Sir Winston Churchill. Multicoloured.

61	5p. Type **22**	1·75	1·75
62	15p. Churchill and *Trepassey*	2·00	2·25
MS63	114×88 mm. Nos. 61/2	8·50	8·50

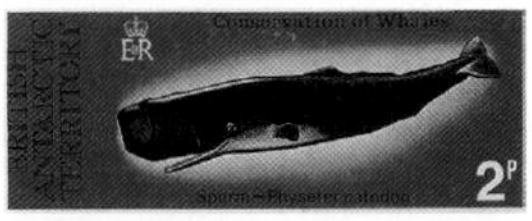
23 Sperm Whale

1977. Whale Conservation. Multicoloured.

79	2p. Type **23**	5·50	3·00
80	8p. Fin whale	6·50	3·50
81	11p. Humpback whale	7·00	3·50
82	25p. Blue whale	7·50	4·50

24 The Queen before Taking the Oath

1977. Silver Jubilee. Multicoloured.

83	6p. Prince Philip's visit, 1956/7	70	40
84	11p. The Coronation Oath	80	50
85	33p. Type **24**	1·00	65

25 Emperor Penguin

1978. 25th Anniv of Coronation.

86	-	25p. green, deep green and silver	60	1·00
87	-	25p. multicoloured	60	1·00
88	**25**	25p. green, deep green and silver	60	1·00

DESIGNS: No. 86, Black Bull of Clarence; 87, Queen Elizabeth II.

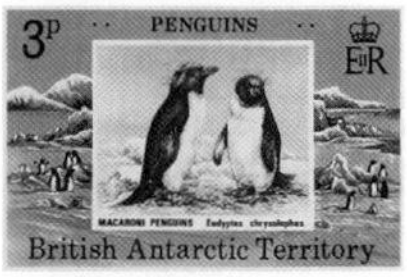

26 Macaroni Penguins

1979. Penguins. Multicoloured.

89	3p. Type **26**	9·00	11·00
90	8p. Gentoo penguins	2·00	2·75
91	11p. Adelie penguins	2·50	3·25
92	25p. Emperor penguins	3·50	4·25

27 Sir John Barrow and *Tula*

1980. 150th Anniv of Royal Geographical Society. Former Presidents. Multicoloured.

93	3p. Type **27**	15	15
94	7p. Sir Clement Markham and *Discovery*	15	25
95	11p. Lord Curzon and whaleboat *James Caird*	20	30
96	15p. Sir William Goodenough	20	35
97	22p. Sir James Wordie	25	55
98	30p. Sir Raymond Priestley	30	65

28 Map of Antarctic

1981. 20th Anniv of Antarctic Treaty.

99	**28**	10p. black, blue and light blue	30	70
100	-	13p. black, blue and green	35	80
101	-	25p. black, blue and mauve	40	90
102	-	26p. black, brown and red	40	90

DESIGNS: 13p. Conservation research ("scientific co-operation"); 25p. Satellite image mapping ("technical co-operation"); 26p. Global geophysics ("scientific co-operation").

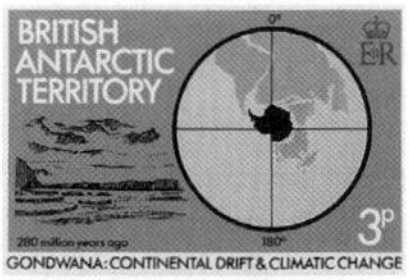

29 Map of Gondwana 280 million years ago and Contemporary Landscape Scene

1982. Gondwana – Continental Drift and Climatic Change. Maps of Gondwana showing position of continents, and contemporary landscapes. Multicoloured.

103	3p. Type **29**	20	40
104	6p. 260 million years ago	20	50
105	10p. 230 million years ago	25	60
106	13p. 175 million years ago	30	70
107	25p. 50 million years ago	35	75
108	26p. Present day	35	75

30 British Antarctic Territory Coat of Arms

1982. 21st Birthday of Princess of Wales. Multicoloured.

109	5p. Type **30**	15	30
110	17p. Princess of Wales (detail of painting by Bryan Organ)	35	60
111	37p. Wedding ceremony	50	90
112	50p. Formal portrait	90	1·25

31 Leopard Seal

1983. Tenth Anniv of Antarctic Seal Conservation Convention. Multicoloured.

113	5p. Type **31**	25	40
114	10p. Weddell seals	30	45
115	13p. Southern elephant seals	30	50
116	17p. Kerguelen fur seals	30	60
117	25p. Ross seals	30	70
118	34p. Crabeater seals	35	95

32 de Havilland Twin Otter 200/300

1983. Bicentenary of Manned Flight. Multicoloured.

119	5p. Type **32**	25	30
120	13p. de Havilland DHC-3 Twin Otter	35	45
121	17p. Consolidated PBY-5A Canso amphibian	45	60
122	50p. Lockheed Vega *San Francisco*	70	1·25

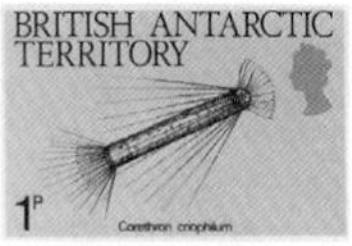

33 *Corethron criophilum*

1984. Marine Life. Multicoloured.

123	1p. Type **33**	60	1·75
124	2p. *Desmonema gaudichaudi*	65	1·75
125	3p. *Tomopteris carpenteri*	65	1·75
126	4p. *Pareuchaeta antarctica*	70	1·75
127	5p. *Antarctomysis maxima*	70	1·75
128	6p. *Antarcturus signiensis*	70	1·75
129	7p. *Serolis cornuta*	70	1·75
130	8p. *Parathemisto gaudichaudii*	70	1·75
131	9p. *Bovallia gigantea*	70	1·75
132	10p. *Euphausia superba*	70	1·75
133	15p. *Colossendeis australis*	70	1·75
134	20p. *Todarodes sagittatus*	75	1·75
135	25p. Antarctic rockcod	80	1·75
136	50p. Black-finned icefish	1·25	2·00
137	£1 Crabeater seal	1·75	2·50
138	£3 Antarctic marine food chain	5·00	6·50

34 M.Y. *Penola* in Stella Creek

1985. 50th Anniv of British Graham Land Expedition. Multicoloured.

139	7p. Type **34**	40	75
140	22p. Northern Base, Winter Island	70	1·40
141	27p. de Havilland DH.83 Fox Moth at Southern Base, Barry Island	80	1·60
142	54p. Dog Team, near Ablation Point, George VI Sound	1·50	2·25

35 Robert McCormick and South Polar Skua

1985. Early Naturalists. Multicoloured.

143	7p. Type **35**	80	1·25
144	22p. Sir Joseph Dalton Hooker and *Deschampsia antarctica*	1·25	2·50
145	27p. Jean Rene C. Quoy and hourglass dolphin	1·25	2·50
146	54p. James Weddell and Weddell seal	1·75	3·50

36 Dr. Edmond Halley

1986. Appearance of Halley's Comet. Multicoloured.

147	7p. Type **36**	75	1·25
148	22p. Halley Station, Antarctica	1·00	2·25
149	27p. *Halley's Comet, 1531* (from Peter Apian woodcut, 1532)	1·25	2·50
150	44p. "Giotto" spacecraft	2·25	4·50

37 Snow Crystal

1986. 50th Anniv of International Glaciological Society. Snow Crystals.

151	**37**	10p. light blue and blue	40	75
152	-	24p. green and deep green	50	1·40
153	-	29p. mauve and deep mauve	60	1·50
154	-	58p. blue and violet	80	2·50

38 Captain Scott, 1904

1987. 75th Anniv of Captain Scott's Arrival at South Pole. Multicoloured.

155	10p. Type **38**	55	95
156	24p. Hut Point and *Discovery* Ross Island, 1902–4	90	2·00
157	29p. Cape Evans Hut, 1911–13	1·00	2·25
158	58p. Scott's expedition at South Pole, 1912	1·50	3·00

39 IGY Logo

1987. 30th Anniv of International Geophysical Year.

159	**39**	10p. black and green	30	75
160	-	24p. multicoloured	50	1·40
161	-	29p. multicoloured	60	1·75
162	-	58p. multicoloured	1·10	2·50

DESIGNS: 24p. Port Lockroy; 29p. Argentine Islands; 58p. Halley Bay.

40 Aurora over South Ice Plateau Station

1988. 30th Anniv of Commonwealth Trans-Antarctic Expedition. Multicoloured.

163	10p. Type **40**	30	75
164	24p. de Havilland Canada DHC-3 Otter at Theron Mountains	50	1·25
165	29p. Seismic ice-depth sounding	60	1·40
166	58p. "Sno-cat" over crevasse	1·00	2·00

41 *Xanthoria elegans*

1989. Lichens. Multicoloured.

167	10p. Type **41**	90	1·00
168	24p. *Usnea aurantiaco-atra*	1·60	2·00
169	29p. *Cladonia chlorophaea*	1·75	2·25
170	58p. *Umbilicaria antarctica*	2·50	3·25

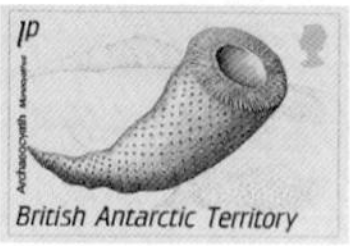

42 *Monocyathus* (archaeocyath)

1990. Fossils. Multicoloured.

171	1p. Type **42**	1·25	1·50
172	2p. *Lingulella* (brachiopod)	1·25	1·50
173	3p. *Triplagnoslus* (trilobite)	1·25	1·50
174	4p. *Lyriaspis* (trilobite)	1·50	1·50
175	5p. *Glossopteris* leaf (gymnosperm)	1·50	1·50
176	6p. *Gonatosorus* (fern)	1·50	1·60
177	7p. *Belemnopsis aucklandica* (belemnite)	1·50	1·60
178	8p. *Sanmartinoceras africanum insignicostatum* (ammonite)	1·50	1·60
179	9p. *Pinna antarctica* (mussel)	1·50	1·60
180	10p. *Aucellina andina* (mussel)	1·50	1·60
181	20p. *Pterotrigonia malagninoi* (mussel)	2·00	2·25
182	25p. *Perissoptera* (conch shell)	2·00	2·25
183	50p. *Ainoceras* sp. (ammonite)	2·75	3·50
184	£1 *Gunnarites zinsmeisteri* (ammonite)	3·75	4·75
185	£3 *Hoploparia* (crayfish)	7·50	8·50

1990. 90th Birthday of Queen Elizabeth the Queen Mother. As T **134** of Ascension.

186	26p. multicoloured	1·25	2·00
187	£1 black and brown	2·50	3·50

DESIGNS: 29×36 mm: 26p. Wedding of Prince Albert and Lady Elizabeth Bowes-Lyon, 1923. 29×37 mm: £1 The Royal Family, 1940.

43 Late Cretaceous Forest and Southern Beech Fossil

1991. Age of the Dinosaurs. Multicoloured.

188	12p. Type **43**	1·25	1·25
189	26p. Hypsilophodont dinosaurs and skull	2·00	2·25
190	31p. Frilled sharks and tooth	2·25	2·50
191	62p. Mosasaur, plesiosaur, and mosasaur vertebra	3·50	4·00

44 Launching Meteorological Balloon, Halley IV Station

1991. Discovery of Antarctic Ozone Hole. Multicoloured.

192	12p. Type **44**	90	1·75
193	26p. Measuring ozone with Dobson spectrophotometer	1·60	2·75
194	31p. Satellite map showing ozone hole	1·90	3·00
195	62p. Lockheed ER-2 aircraft and graph of chlorine monoxide and ozone levels	3·25	5·50

45 Researching Dry Valley

1991. 30th Anniv of Antarctic Treaty.

196	**45**	12p. multicoloured	90	90
197	-	26p. multicoloured	1·60	1·75
198	-	31p. black and green	1·75	1·90
199	-	62p. multicoloured	3·00	3·25

DESIGNS: 26p. Relief map of ice sheet; 31p. BIOMASS logo; 62p. Ross seal.

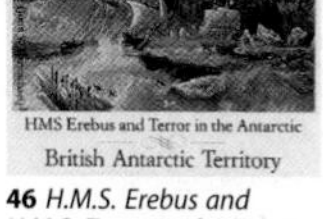

46 *H.M.S. Erebus and H.M.S. Terror in the Antarctic* (J. Carmichael)

1991. Maiden Voyage of *James Clark Ross* (research ship). Multicoloured.

200	12p. Type **46**	90	1·50
201	26p. Launch of *James Clark Ross*	1·60	2·50
202	31p. *James Clark Ross* in Antarctica	1·75	2·75
203	62p. Scientific research	3·00	3·75

1991. Birth Bicentenary of Michael Faraday (scientist). Nos. 200/3 additionally inscr "200th Anniversary M. Faraday 1791–1867".

204	12p. Type **46**	90	1·75
205	26p. Launch of *James Clark Ross*	1·60	2·75
206	31p. *James Clark Ross* in Antarctica	1·75	3·00
207	62p. Scientific research	3·00	4·50

47 Ross Seals

1992. Endangered Species. Seals and Penguins. Multicoloured.

208	4p. Type **47**	1·25	1·25
209	5p. Adelie penguins	1·25	1·25
210	7p. Weddell seal with pup	1·25	1·25
211	29p. Emperor penguins with chicks	2·50	2·25
212	34p. Crabeater seals with pup	1·75	2·25
213	68p. Bearded penguins ("Chinstrap Penguin") with young	2·50	2·75

48 Sun Pillar at Faraday

1992. Lower Atmospheric Phenomena. Multicoloured.

214	14p. Type **48**	80	1·50
215	29p. Halo over iceberg	1·40	1·90
216	34p. Lee Wave cloud	1·75	2·25
217	68p. Nacreous clouds	2·75	4·00

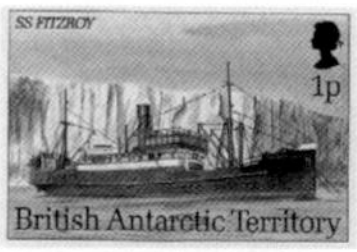

49 *Fitzroy* (mail and supply ship)

1993. Antarctic Ships. Multicoloured.

218	1p. Type **49**	2·25	2·75
219	2p. *William Scoresby* (research ship)	2·50	2·75
220	3p. *Eagle* (sealer)	2·50	2·75
221	4p. *Trepassey* (supply ship)	2·50	2·75
222	5p. *John Biscoe I* (research ship)	2·50	3·00
223	10p. *Norsel* (supply ship)	2·75	3·00
224	20p. H.M.S. *Protector* (ice patrol ship)	4·00	4·00
225	30p. *Oluf Sven* (supply ship)	4·50	4·50
226	50p. *John Biscoe II* and *Shackleton* (research ships)	5·50	6·00
227	£1 *Tottan* (supply ship)	7·00	8·00
228	£3 *Perla Dan* (supply ship)	11·00	12·00
229	£5 H.M.S. *Endurance I* (ice patrol ship)	15·00	16·00

1994. "Hong Kong '94", International Stamp Exhibition. Nos. 240/5 optd **HONG KONG '94** and emblem.

230	15p. Type **51**	1·10	1·50
231	24p. de Havilland Turbo Beaver III aircraft	1·60	2·00
232	31p. de Havilland Otter aircraft and dog team	1·75	2·50
233	36p. de Havilland Twin Otter 200/300 aircraft and dog team	1·90	2·75
234	62p. de Havilland Dash Seven aircraft over landing strip, Rothera Point	2·75	3·25
235	72p. de Havilland Dash Seven aircraft on runway	2·75	3·50

50 Bransfield House Post Office, Port Lockroy

1994. 50th Anniv of Operation Tabarin. Multicoloured.

236	15p. Type **50**	1·00	1·50
237	31p. Survey team, Hope Bay	1·60	2·00
238	36p. Dog team, Hope Bay	2·50	2·50
239	72p. *Fitzroy* (supply ship) and H.M.S. *William Scoresby* (minesweeper)	3·25	4·50

51 Huskies and Sledge

1994. Forms of Transportation. Multicoloured.

240	15p. Type **51**	70	80
241	24p. de Havilland Turbo Beaver III aircraft	90	1·00
242	31p. de Havilland Otter aircraft and dog team	1·00	1·10
243	36p. de Havilland Twin Otter 200/300 aircraft and dog team	1·10	1·40
244	62p. de Havilland Dash Seven aircraft over landing strip, Rothera Point	2·00	2·50
245	72p. de Havilland Dash Seven aircraft on runway	2·00	2·75

52 Capt. James Cook and H.M.S. *Resolution*

1994. Antarctic Heritage Fund. Multicoloured.

246	17p.+3p. Type **52**	2·50	3·25
247	35p.+15p. Sir James Clark Ross with H.M.S. *Erebus* and H.M.S. *Terror*	2·75	3·50
248	40p.+10p. Capt. Robert Falcon Scott and interior of hut	2·75	3·50
249	76p.+4p. Sir Ernest Shackleton and *Endurance*	3·75	4·75

53 Pair of Crabeater Seals

1994. Antarctic Food Chain. Multicoloured.

250	35p. Type **53**	2·25	3·00
251	35p. Blue whale	2·25	3·00
252	35p. Wandering albatross	2·25	3·00
253	35p. Mackerel icefish	2·25	3·00
254	35p. Krill	2·25	3·00
255	35p. Seven star flying squid	2·25	3·00

54 Hauberg Mountains

1995. Geological Structures. Multicoloured.

256	17p. Type **54**	1·75	2·00
257	35p. Arrowsmith Peninsula	2·50	2·75
258	40p. Colbert Mountains	2·75	3·00
259	76p. Succession Cliffs	4·00	5·75

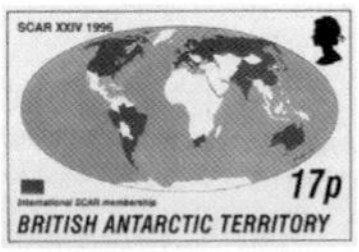

55 World Map showing Member Countries

1996. 24th Meeting of Scientific Committee on Antarctic Research. Multicoloured.

260	17p. Type **55**	1·00	1·50
261	35p. Scientist analysing ice samples	1·75	2·00
262	40p. Releasing balloon	2·00	2·25
263	76p. Antarctic research ship catching marine life	2·75	4·00
MS264	100×90 mm. £1 S.C.A.R. logo	6·50	8·50

56 Killer Whales

1996. Whales. Multicoloured.

265	17p. Type **56**	80	1·25
266	35p. Sperm whales	1·40	1·75
267	40p. Minke whales	1·60	2·00
268	76p. Blue whale and calf	2·50	3·25
MS269	105×82 mm. £1 Humpback whale	4·00	4·25

1996. 70th Birthday of Queen Elizabeth II. As T **165** of Ascension, each incorporating a different photograph of the Queen. Multicoloured.

270	17p. At premiere of *Chaplin*, Leicester Square, 1992	1·00	1·25
271	35p. At Buckingham Palace dinner, 1991	1·50	1·60
272	40p. In Aberdeen, 1993	1·75	1·75
273	76p. At Royal Military School of Music, 1990	2·25	3·75

1997. "HONG KONG '97" International Stamp Exhibition. Sheet 130×90 mm, containing design as No. 226. Multicoloured.

MS274	50p. *John Biscoe II* and *Shackleton* (research ships)	1·75	2·25

1997. Return of Hong Kong to China. Sheet 130×90 mm containing design as No. 227, but with "1997" imprint date.

MS275	£1 *Tottan*	2·75	3·75

57 Chinstrap Penguins sledging

1997. Christmas. Multicoloured.

276	17p. Type **57**	2·25	1·50
277	35p. Emperor penguins carol singing	2·75	2·25
278	40p. Adelie penguins throwing snowballs	3·00	2·50
279	76p. Gentoo penguins ice-skating	4·25	5·50

1998. Diana, Princess of Wales Commemoration. Sheet 145×70 mm, containing vert designs as T **177** of Ascension. Multicoloured.

MS280	35p. Wearing sunglasses; 35p. Wearing round-necked white blouse, 1993; 35p. Wearing white blouse and jacket, 1990; 35p. Wearing green jacket, 1992 (sold at £1.40+20p. charity premium)	2·50	2·50

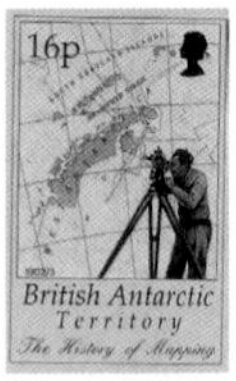

58 Chart of South Shetland Islands (Swedish South Polar Expedition, 1902–3)

1998. History of Mapping in Antarctica. Multicoloured.

281	16p. Type **58**	2·50	2·00
282	30p. Map of Antarctic Peninsula (1949)	3·00	2·50
283	35p. Map of Antarctic Peninsula (1964)	3·25	2·75
284	40p. Map of Antarctic Peninsula from Landsat (1981)	3·25	3·25
285	65p. Map of Antarctic Peninsula from satellite (1995)	4·50	6·00

59 Antarctic Explorer and H.M.S. *Erebus*, 1843

1998. Antarctic Clothing. Multicoloured.

286	30p. Type **59**	3·50	2·25
287	35p. Explorer with dog, and *Discovery I*, 1900	4·00	2·25
288	40p. Surveyor, and *Fitzroy*, 1943	4·00	2·50
289	65p. Scientist with Adelie penguins, and *James Clark Ross*, 1998	5·50	6·50

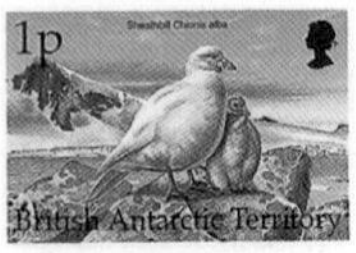

60 Snowy Sheathbill

1998. Antarctic Birds. Multicoloured.

290	1p. Type **60**	3·50	2·50
291	2p. Dove prion ("Antarctic Prion")	2·25	2·50
292	5p. Adelie penguin	2·25	2·50
293	10p. Emperor penguin	2·25	2·50
294	20p. Antarctic tern	2·50	2·50
295	30p. Black-bellied storm petrel	2·50	2·50
296	35p. Southern fulmar ("Antarctic Fulmar")	2·75	2·75
297	40p. Blue-eyed cormorant ("Blue-eyed Shag")	2·75	3·00
298	50p. South polar skua ("McCormick's Skua")	3·00	3·25
299	£1 Southern black-backed gull ("Kelp Gull")	5·00	6·00
300	£3 Wilson's storm petrel	9·50	11·00
301	£5 Antactic skua ("Brown Skua")	13·00	15·00

61 Mackerel Icefish

1999. Fish of the Southern Ocean. Multicoloured.

302	10p. Type **61**	2·00	2·00
303	20p. Blenny rockcod ("Toothfish")	2·50	2·50
304	25p. Borch	2·50	2·50
305	50p. Marbled rockcod ("Marbled notothen")	4·00	4·00
306	80p. Bernacchi's rockcod ("Bernach")	6·50	7·50

62 Map showing Crustal Microplates of West Antarctica

1999. British Antarctic Survey Discoveries. Multicoloured.

307	15p. Type **62**	3·00	2·25
308	30p. Testing lead levels in ice	3·50	3·00
309	35p. Decolopodid sea spider (Gigantism in marine invertebrates) (horiz)	3·50	3·00
310	40p. Scientist operating Dobson Spectrophotometer for testing ozone layer (horiz)	3·50	3·50
311	70p. Radar antenna (aurora electric field research) (horiz)	5·50	6·50

63 Wreck of *Endurance*

2000. Shackleton's Trans-Antarctic Expedition, 1914–17, Commemoration. Multicoloured.

312	35p. Type **63**	5·00	3·75
313	40p. Ocean Camp on ice	5·00	3·75
314	65p. Launching *James Caird* from Elephant Island	9·00	10·00

64 Iceberg and Opening Bars

2000. Composition of Antarctic Symphony by Sir Peter Maxwell Davies. Multicoloured.

315	37p. Type **64**	4·50	4·50
316	37p. Stern of *James Clark Ross* and pack ice	4·50	4·50
317	43p. de Havilland Canada DH-6 Twin Otter and camp on Jones Ice Self	5·00	5·00
318	43p. Frozen sea	5·00	5·00

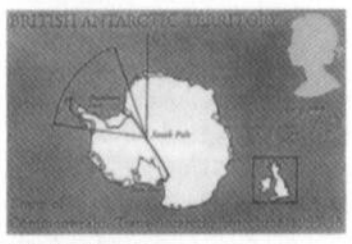

65 Route of Commonwealth Trans-Antarctic Expedition, 1955–58

2000. "Heroic Age of Antarctica" (1st series). Commonwealth Trans-Antarctic Expedition, 1955–8. Multicoloured.

319	37p. Type **65**	8·50	7·00
320	37p. Expedition at South Pole, 1958	8·50	7·00
321	37p. *Magga Dan* (Antarctic supply ship)	8·50	7·00
322	37p. "Sno-cat" repair camp	8·50	7·00
323	37p. "Sno-cat" over crevasse	8·50	7·00
324	37p. Seismic explosion	8·50	7·00

See also Nos. 333/8 and 351/6.

66 *Bransfield* unloading "Sno-cat", Halley

2000. Survey Ships. Multicoloured.

325	20p. Type **66**	4·00	2·50
326	33p. *Ernest Shackelton* unloading supplies into *Tula*	6·00	4·00
327	37p. *Bransfield* in the ice (horiz)	6·00	4·00
328	43p. *Ernest Shackleton* with Westland Lynx helicopter (horiz)	7·50	7·00

67 Tourists at Port Lockroy

2001. Restoration of Port Lockroy Base. Multicoloured.

329	33p. Type **67**	4·00	2·50
330	37p. Port Lockroy and cruise ship	4·00	2·50
331	43p. Port Lockroy huts in 1945	4·50	2·75
332	65p. Interior of Port Lockroy laboratory in 1945	7·50	7·00

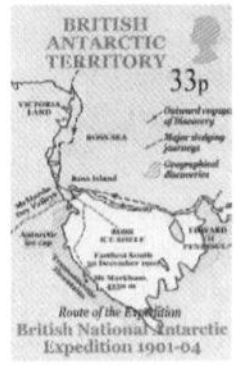

68 Map of Ross Sea Area

2001. "Heroic Age of Antarctica" (2nd series). Captain Scott's 1901–04 Expedition. Multicoloured.

333	33p. Type **68**	2·25	2·25
334	37p. Captain Robert F. Scott	2·50	2·50
335	43p. First Antarctic balloon ascent, 1902 (horiz)	3·00	3·00
336	65p. *Emperor Penguin chick* (drawing by Edward Wilson)	4·00	4·00
337	70p. Shackleton, Scott and Wilson and most southerly camp, 1902 (horiz)	4·00	4·00
338	80p. *Discovery I* trapped in ice off Hut Point (horiz)	4·50	4·50

2002. Golden Jubilee. As T **200** of Ascension.

339	20p. black, mauve and gold	1·50	1·50
340	37p. multicoloured	1·75	1·75
341	43p. black, mauve and gold	2·00	2·00
342	50p multicoloured	2·50	3·25
MS343	162×95 mm. Nos. 339/42 and 50p. multicoloured	8·50	10·00

DESIGNS—HORIZ: 20p. Princess Elizabeth and Princess Margaret making radio broadcast, 1940; 37p. Queen Elizabeth in Garter robes, 1998; 43p. Queen Elizabeth at Balmoral, 1952; 50p. Queen Elizabeth in London, 1996. VERT (38×51 mm)—50p. Queen Elizabeth after Annigoni.

Designs as Nos. 339/42 in No. **MS**343 omit the gold frame around each stamp and the "Golden Jubilee 1952–2002" inscription.

2002. Queen Elizabeth the Queen Mother Commemoration. As T **202** of Ascension.

344	40p. black, gold and purple	1·50	1·50
345	45p. multicoloured	1·50	1·50
MS346	145×70 mm. 70p. black and gold; 95p. multicoloured	7·50	7·50

DESIGNS: 40p. Lady Elizabeth Bowes-Lyon, 1913; 45p. Queen Mother on her birthday, 1996; 70p. Queen Elizabeth at niece's wedding, London, 1951; 95p. Queen Mother at Cheltenham Races, 1999.

Designs in No. **MS**346 omit the "1900–2002" inscription and the coloured frame.

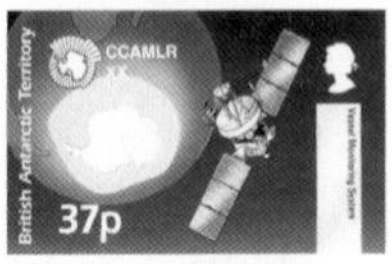

69 Satellite and Antarctica

2002. 20th Anniv of Commission for Conservation of Antarctic Marine Living Resources (CCAMLR). Multicoloured.

347	37p. Type **69**	3·50	3·75

348	37p. Trawler and wandering albatross	3·50	3·75
349	37p. Icefish, toothfish and crabeater seal	3·50	3·75
350	37p. Krill and phytoplankton	3·50	3·75

2002. "Heroic Age of Antarctica" (3rd series). Scottish National Antarctic Expedition, 1902–04. As T **68** but horiz. Multicoloured.

351	30p. Map of Weddell Sea	4·00	3·25
352	40p. Piper Gilbert Kerr and emperor penguin (horiz)	4·50	4·00
353	45p. *Scotia* (expedition ship)	4·50	4·00
354	70p. Weather station and meteorologist (horiz)	5·00	5·50
355	95p. William Speirs Bruce	6·00	6·50
356	£1 Omond House, Laurie Island (horiz)	6·00	7·00

2003. 50th Anniv of Coronation. As T **206** of Ascension. Multicoloured.

357	40p. Coronation Coach in procession	2·50	2·00
358	45p. Queen Elizabeth II with Prince Charles on Buckingham Palace balcony	2·50	2·00
MS359	95×115 mm. 95p. As 40p.; 95p. As 45p.	8·50	7·50

Nos. 357/8 have scarlet frame; stamps from **MS**359 have no frame and country name in mauve panel.

2003. As T **207** of Ascension.

360	£2 multicoloured	6·00	6·00

70 Blue Whale

2003. Endangered Species. Blue Whale. Multicoloured.

361	40p. Type **70**	1·50	1·50
362	45p. Tail fluke	1·50	1·50
363	45p. Two blue whales	1·50	1·50
364	70p. Two blue whales at surface	2·00	2·00

71 Emperor Penguins

2003. Penguins of the Antarctic (1st series). Multicoloured.

365	(–) Type **71**	3·00	3·00
366	(–) Head of macaroni penguin	3·00	3·00
367	(–) Gentoo penguin	3·00	3·00
368	(–) Pair of adelie penguins	3·00	3·00
369	(–) Chinstrap penguin	3·00	3·00
370	(–) Gentoo penguin chick	3·00	3·00
371	(–) Emperor penguins (different)	3·00	3·00
372	(–) Chinstrap penguin chick	3·00	3·00
373	(–) Group of adelie penguins	3·00	3·00
374	(–) Gentoo penguin and chick	3·00	3·00
375	(–) Pair of macaroni penguins	3·00	3·00
376	(–) Emperor penguin chick	3·00	3·00

Nos. 365/76, inscribed "AIRMAIL POSTCARD", were initially sold at 40p.

See also Nos. 424/47 and 474/485.

72 Base G, Admiralty Bay

2003. Research Bases and Postmarks. Multicoloured.

377	1p. Type **72**	1·00	1·50
378	2p. Base B, Deception Island	1·00	1·50
379	5p. Base D, Hope Bay	1·25	1·75
380	22p. Base F, Argentine Islands	2·25	2·00
381	25p. Base E, Stonington Island	2·25	2·00
382	40p. Base A, Port Lockroy	2·75	2·50
383	45p. Base H, Signy	2·75	2·50
384	50p. Base N, Anvers Island	2·75	2·50
385	95p. Base P, Rothera	5·00	5·00
386	£1 Base T, Adelaide Island	5·00	5·00
387	£3 Base Y, Horseshoe Island	13·00	13·00
388	£5 Base Z, Halley Bay	18·00	18·00

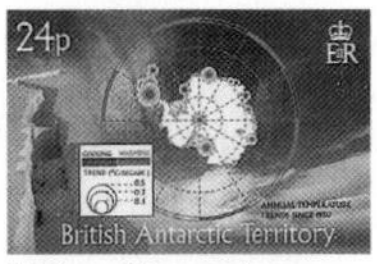

73 Annual Temperature Trends since 1950

2004. Climate Change. Multicoloured.

389	24p. Type **73**	2·00	2·00
390	24p. Larsen ice shelf	2·00	2·00
391	42p. Ice core measurements	2·75	2·75
392	42p. Ice core drilling	2·75	2·75
393	50p. Rise in air temperatures at Faraday Station	3·50	3·50
394	50p. Antarctic pearlwort	3·50	3·50

74 Pintado ("Cape") Petrel

2005. Birdlife International. Petrels. Multicoloured.

395	25p. Type **74**	3·00	1·10
396	42p. Snow petrel	3·75	1·50
397	75p. Wilson's storm petrel	5·50	4·00
398	£1 Antarctic petrel	6·50	5·00
MS399	170×85 mm. 50p.×6 Southern giant petrel and glaciers; Southern giant petrel in flight (from side); Head of Southern giant petrel; Southern giant petrel standing over chick; Southern giant petrel roosting with chick; Southern giant petrel chick	22·00	20·00

75 *Endurance* 1914–15 (three masted barque)

2005. *Endurance*. Multicoloured.

400	42p. Type **75**	4·00	2·00
401	50p. HMS *Endurance*, 1968–90 (ice patrol and hydrographic survey ship)	5·50	3·25
402	£1 HMS *Endurance*, 1991 (class 1A1 ice-breaker ship)	9·00	6·50

76 Deception Island from the South East

2005. 50th Anniv of FIDASE (Falkland Islands and Dependencies Aerial Survey Expedition, 1955–7). Multicoloured.

403	45p. Type **76**	2·25	2·25
404	55p. Hunting Lodge, Deception Island	2·50	2·50
405	80p. Bell 47D helicopter with perspex bubble and flotation landing gear	6·00	6·00
406	£1 Canso flying boat	6·00	6·00

77 Samson, Shakespeare and Surley

2005. Shackleton Expedition (1914—16) Dogs. Multicoloured.

407	45p. Type **77**	4·00	3·00
408	45p. Tom Crean holding puppies (vert)	4·00	3·00
409	55p. Dogs outside ice kennels and HMS *Endurance*	5·00	3·25
410	£1 Sled dog team training on sea ice and HMS *Endurance* (vert)	8·00	8·50

78 Faber Maunsell's Winning Concept Design

2005. Halley VI Research Station International Design Competition. Multicoloured.

411	45p. Type **78**	2·50	2·50
412	45p. Buro Happold concept design	2·50	2·50
413	55p. Hopkins concept design	2·75	2·75
414	80p. Laws building at Halley V Research Station	5·00	6·00

79 Sea and Icebergs (Erica Currie)

2006. ATCM XXIX Edinburgh (Tristan da Cunha) 2006 Stamp Design Competition. Children's Paintings. Multicoloured.

415	45p. Type **79**	2·00	2·00
416	45p. Penguins and icebergs (Meghan Joyce)	2·00	2·00
417	55p. Icebreaker (Lorna MacDonald)	2·25	2·25
418	£1 Penguin wearing Union Jack (Danielle Dalgleish)	4·25	5·00

2006. 80th Birthday of Queen Elizabeth II. As T **223** of Ascension. Multicoloured.

419	45p. Princess Elizabeth	2·25	2·00
420	55p. Queen wearing diadem, c. 1952	2·50	2·25
421	80p. Wearing red hat	3·50	3·50
422	£1 In evening dress	3·75	3·75
MS423	144×75 mm. Nos. 420/1	5·50	5·50

Stamps from **MS**423 do not have white borders.

2006. Penguins of the Antarctic (2nd series). As T **71**. Multicoloured. (a) Ordinary gum.

424	(–) Chinstrap penguin chick	2·00	2·00
425	(–) Head of emperor penguin	2·00	2·00
426	(–) Adelie penguin with wings outstretched	2·00	2·00
427	(–) Head of chinstrap penguin	2·00	2·00
428	(–) Macaroni penguin	2·00	2·00
429	(–) Gentoo penguin feeding chick	2·00	2·00
430	(–) Emperor penguin chick	2·00	2·00
431	(–) Adelie penguin on nest	2·00	2·00
432	(–) Emperor penguin	2·00	2·00
433	(–) Gentoo penguin	2·00	2·00
434	(–) Adelie penguin feeding chick	2·00	2·00
435	(–) Two emperor penguin chicks	2·00	2·00

(b) Self-adhesive. Size 24×29 mm.

436	(–) As No. 424	1·75	2·25
437	(–) As No. 425	1·75	2·25
438	(–) As No. 426	1·75	2·25
439	(–) As No. 430	1·75	2·25
440	(–) As No. 431	1·75	2·25
441	(–) As No. 432	1·75	2·25
442	(–) As No. 427	1·75	2·25
443	(–) As No. 428	1·75	2·25
444	(–) As No. 429	1·75	2·25
445	(–) As No. 433	1·75	2·25
446	(–) As No. 434	1·75	2·25
447	(–) As No. 435	1·75	2·25

Nos. 424/47 are inscribed "AIRMAIL POSTCARD" and were sold at 50p. each.

80 Elephant Seals

2006. Seals. Multicoloured.

448	25p. Type **80**	1·50	1·50
449	50p. Crabeater seals	2·25	2·25
450	60p. Weddell seals	2·50	2·75
451	£1.05 Leopard seal	4·00	5·00

81 *Marseniopsis molle* (sea lemon)

2007. Marine Invertebrates. Multicoloured.

452	25p. Type **81**	1·75	1·50
453	50p. *Isotealia antarctica* (Antarctic sea anemone)	2·75	2·75
454	60p. *Decolopoda australis* (sea spider)	3·00	3·25
455	£1.05 *Odontaster validus* (sea star)	5·50	6·50

82 Pinnacle Iceberg

2007. Icebergs. Multicoloured.

456	25p. Type **82**	1·75	1·50
457	50p. Pinnacle and tabular icebergs and ice floes at sunset	2·75	2·75
458	60p. Wedge iceberg	3·00	3·25
459	£1.05 Tabular iceberg and ice floes	5·50	6·50

83 Aerial View of Antarctica

2007. International Polar Year 2007–2008. Circular sheet 97×97 mm.

MS460	**83** £2 multicoloured	7·00	10·00

84 James Weddell, *Jane* and *Beaufoy*

2008. Explorers and Ships. Multicoloured.

461	1p. Type **84**	20	30
462	2p. Sir James Clark Ross, *Erebus* and *Terror*	35	40
463	5p. Neil Alison Mackintosh and *Discovery II*	55	65
464	27p. Sir Douglas Mawson and *Discovery*	1·25	1·00
465	55p. Captain James Cook and *Resolution*	2·50	2·00
466	65p. Carsten Egeberg Borchgrevink and *Southern Cross*	2·50	2·50
467	65p. Dr. William Speirs Bruce and *Scotia*	2·50	2·50
468	65p. Captain Robert Falcon Scott and *Discovery*	2·50	2·50
469	65p. Sir Ernest Shackleton and *Endurance*	2·50	2·50
470	£1.10 John Riddoch Rymill and *Penola*	4·25	4·50
471	£2.50 Captain Victor Marchesi and *William Scoresby*	8·25	8·50
472	£5 Sir Vivian Fuchs and *Magga Dan*	16·00	16·00
MS473	110×80 mm. As Nos. 466/9 but inscr 'AIRMAIL LETTER'	9·00	10·00

No. **MS**473 was sold for £2.60.

2008. Penguins of the Antarctic (3rd series). As T **71**. Multicoloured.

474	(–) Head of chinstrap penguin	3·00	3·00
475	(–) Gentoo penguin and two chicks	3·00	3·00
476	(–) Head of macaroni penguin, calling with beak open	3·00	3·00
477	(–) Chinstrap penguin, calling, with beak open and wings and tail raised	3·00	3·00
478	(–) Two emperor penguins	3·00	3·00
479	(–) Adelie penguin	3·00	3·00
480	(–) Chinstrap penguin, walking with wings outstretched	3·00	3·00
481	(–) Head of gentoo penguin, calling with beak open	3·00	3·00
482	(–) Macaroni penguin	3·00	3·00
483	(–) Emperor penguin with chick	3·00	3·00
484	(–) Two adelie penguins	3·00	3·00
485	(–) Emperor penguin chick	3·00	3·00

Nos. 474/85, inscribed 'AIRMAIL POSTCARD' and were sold at 55p. each.

85 *Lophosoria cupulatus*, Snow Island

2008. Fossil Ferns. Designs showing map of Antarctica and fossil ferns. Multicoloured.

486	55p. Type **85**	3·00	2·00
487	65p. cf. *Cladophlebis oblonga*, Alexander Island	3·50	2·50
488	£1.10 *Pachypteris indica*, Snow Island	6·00	6·50

489	£1.10 *Aculea acicularis*, Alexander Island	6·00	6·50

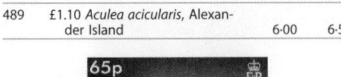

86 Aurora Australis

2008. Aurora Australis. Multicoloured.

490	65p. Type **86**	3·50	3·50
491	65p. Blue aurora	3·50	3·50
492	65p. Red aurora	3·50	3·50
493	65p. Turquoise-blue aurora	3·50	3·50
494	65p. Green and white aurora	3·50	3·50

87 Fairey Seafox

2009. Centenary of Naval Aviation. Multicoloured.

495	10p. Type **87**	80	1·00
496	10p. Westland Lynx helicopter	80	1·00
497	90p. Supermarine Walrus	5·00	5·50
498	90p. Westland Wasp helicopter	5·00	5·50
MS499	110×70 mm. £2 HMA No. 1 *Mayfly* (airship)	10·50	11·50

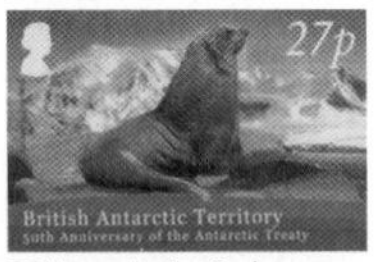

88 Antarctic Fur Seal

2009. 50th Anniv of the Antarctic Treaty. Multicoloured. .

500	27p. Type **88**	1·10	1·25
501	27p. Humpback whale	1·10	1·25
502	55p. Southern giant petrel	2·00	1·75
503	55p. Gentoo penguin	2·00	1·75
504	65p. Giant squid	2·50	2·00
505	65p. Jellyfish	2·50	2·00

Nos. 500/1, 502/3 and 504/5 were each printed together, *se-tenant*, as horizontal pairs in sheets of 24 (2 panes 2×6 with horizontal gutter), each pair forming a composite background design.

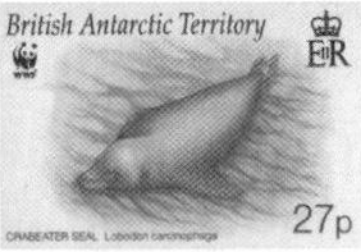

89 Crabeater Seal

2009. Endangered Species. Crabeater Seal (*Lobodon carcinophaga*). Multicoloured.

506	27p. Type **89**	1·25	1·00
507	65p. Crabeater seal (close-up of head)	2·50	2·00
508	£1.10 Two crabeater seals	4·25	4·50
509	£1.50 Crabeater seal (swimming to right)	6·00	6·25

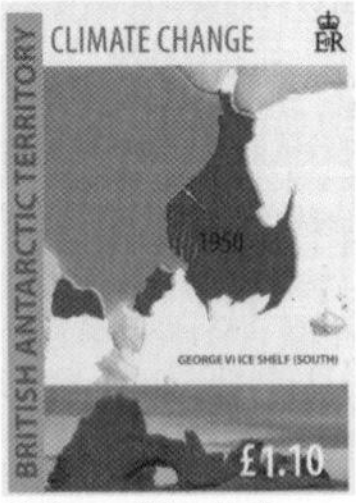

90 George VI Ice Shelf (South)

2009. Climate Change. Sheet 165×130 mm containing T **90** and similar vert designs showing the extent of Antarctic ice shelves in 1950 and today. Multicoloured.

MS510	£1.10×4 Type **90**; Larsen B Ice Shelf; Wilkins Ice Shelf; Larsen C Ice Shelf	18·00	18·00

91 Button Worm

2010. Marine Biodiversity. Multicoloured.

511	27p. Type **91**	90	90
512	27p. Amphipod	90	90
513	27p. Polychaete worm	90	90
514	27p. Sponge	90	90
MS515	140×95 mm. £1.15×4 Solitary coral; Amphipod (different); Comb jelly; Basket star (all 36×36 mm)	14·00	14·00

92 *Terra Nova* on the Horizon

2010. Centenary of the British Antarctic Expedition (1910–13). Each black and grey.

516	27p. Type **92**	90	90
517	27p. Expedition ponies	90	90
518	27p. Cavern in the iceberg	90	90
519	27p. The 'Tenements' bunks in Winterquarters Hut	90	90
520	27p. Captain Scott's birthday dinner	90	90
521	27p. Observing at the weather station	90	90
522	27p. Captain Scott writing in his journal	90	90
523	27p. *Terra Nova* in the ice	90	90
524	60p. *Terra Nova* in harbour	1·40	1·40
525	60p. Lieut. Rennick leading pony	1·40	1·40
526	60p. The Matterhorn Berg	1·40	1·40
527	60p. Nelson at work in the lab	1·40	1·40
528	60p. Captain Scott on skis	1·40	1·40
529	60p. Chris (dog) and the gramophone	1·40	1·40
530	60p. Motor and load passing Inaccessible Island	1·40	1·40
531	60p. The polar party at the South Pole	1·40	1·40

93 South Polar Skua

2010. Antarctic Birds. Multicoloured.

532	27p. Type **93**	90	90
533	27p. Adélie penguin	90	9·90
533	70p. Grey-headed albatross	2·10	2·10
535	70p. Emperor penguin	2·10	2·10
536	£1.15 Kelp gull	4·00	4·00
537	£1.15 Antarctic petrel	4·00	4·00

94 *James Clark Ross* en route to Signy Research Station, South Shetland Islands, 2007

2011. Research Ships. Multicoloured.

(a) Ordinary paper

538	(60p.) Type **94**	1·40	1·40
539	(60p.) RRS *Bransfield* loading outbound cargo from Halley Research Station	1·40	1·40
540	(60p.) RRS *Bransfield* alongside wharf at Rothera Research Station	1·40	1·40
541	(60p.) RRS *Ernest Shackleton* tied up against sea ice on the Brunt Ice Shelf	1·40	1·40
542	(60p.) RRS *Ernest Shackleton* (against Brunt Ice Shelf) and RRS *James Clark Ross*	1·40	1·40
543	(60p.) RRS *James Clark Ross* leaving Rothera Research Station, January 1998	1·40	1·40
MS544	100×80 mm. £1.15 Penguin and RRS *James Clark Ross* (20th anniv of maiden Antarctic voyage) (36×36 mm)	3·75	3·75

(b) Self-adhesive coil stamps. Size 36×25 mm

545	(60p.) As Type **94**	1·40	1·40
546	(60p.) As No. 539	1·40	1·40
547	(60p.) As No. 540	1·40	1·40
548	(60p.) As No. 541	1·40	1·40
549	(60p.) As No. 542	1·40	1·40
550	(60p.) As No. 543	1·40	1·40

Nos. 538/43 and 545/50 were all inscr 'AIRMAL POSTCARD' and originally sold for 60p. each.

95 Fur Seal

2011. BBC *Frozen Planet*. Multicoloured.

551	27p. Type **95**	90	90
552	27p. Elephant seal	90	90
553	27p. Crabeater seal	90	90
554	27p. Leopard seal	90	90
555	27p. Killer whale (dorsal fin and upper body above water)	90	90
556	27p. Killer whales (one with head above water)	90	90
557	27p. Humpback whales	90	90
558	27p. Two killer whales (dorsal fins and upper bodies above water)	90	90
559	60p. Gentoo penguin and chick	2·00	2·00
560	60p. Gentoo penguin and two chicks	2·00	2·00
561	60p. Adelie penguins adult and chicks	2·00	2·00
562	60p. Adelie penguin feeding chick	2·00	2·00
563	60p. Gentoo penguin chick	2·00	2·00
564	60p. Gentoo penguin moulting and boat	2·00	2·00
565	60p. Adelie penguins leaping onto ice	2·00	2·00
566	60p. Chinstrap penguin	2·00	2·00

96 Winterquarters Hut and Camp

2011. Antarctic Science. Multicoloured.

MS567	174×122 mm. 27p.×8 Type **96**; Bonner Laboratory at Rothera Research Station; Expedition members launching balloon with instruments to record temperature and pressure, 1910-13 (vert); Modern scientist launching helium filled balloon to take daily meteorological records, Halley Research Station (vert); Expedition members taking samples at stern of *Terra Nova* (vert); Sampling waters of Bellingshausen Sea from RRS *James Clark Ross* using CTD (conductivity, temperature, depth) device (vert); Expedition members on skiis; Divers on RIB (rigid inflatable boat), Rothera Research Station	7·25	7·25
MS568	165×80 mm. 70p.x4 de Havilland Canada Dash-7 in flight; Geologist testing hot water drill on the Rutford Ice Stream; Meteorologist checking Met screen at Rothera Point; Piggott Space Science building, Halley Research Station (all 36×36 mm)	9·50	9·50
MS569	165×80 mm. £1.15×4 Surgeon Dr. Edward Atkinson conducting experiments; Dr. George Simpson taking observations at weather station; Dr. Simpson's laboratory in Winterquarters Hut; Charles Wright (expedition physicist and glaciologist) with transit (instrument used for observation of star positions), (all British Antarctic Expedition 1910-13, all 36×36 mm)	15·00	15·00

Pt. 1

BRITISH COLUMBIA AND VANCOUVER ISLAND

Former British colonies, now a Western province of the Dominion of Canada, whose stamps are now used.

1860. 12 pence = 1 shilling; 20 shillings = 1 pound.
1865. 100 cents = 1 dollar.

1

1860. Imperf or perf.

2	1	2½d. pink	£425	£200

VANCOUVER ISLAND

2

1865. Imperf or perf. Various frames.

13	2	5c. red	£350	£200
14	-	10c. blue	£250	£170

BRITISH COLUMBIA

4 Emblems of United Kingdom

1865

22	4	3d. blue	£110	85·00

1868. Surch in words or figures and words.

28	2c. brown	£170	£140
29	5c. red	£225	£160
24	10c. red	£900	£700
31	25c. yellow	£250	£160
26	50c. mauve	£800	£700
27	$1 green	£1300	£1400

Pt. 1

BRITISH COMMONWEALTH OCCUPATION OF JAPAN

Stamps used by British Commonwealth Occupation Forces, 1946–49.

12 pence = 1 shilling; 20 shillings = 1 pound.

1946. Stamps of Australia optd **B.C.O.F. JAPAN 1946**.

J1	27	½d. orange	7·00	11·00
J2	46	1d. purple	6·00	7·00
J3	31	3d. brown	2·75	4·50
J4	-	6d. brown (No. 189a)	26·00	20·00
J5	-	1s. green (No. 191)	18·00	22·00
J6	1	2s. red	45·00	65·00
J7a	38	5s. red	£110	£170

Pt. 1

BRITISH EAST AFRICA

Now incorporated in Kenya and Uganda.

16 annas = 100 cents = 1 rupee.

1890. Stamps of Great Britain (1881) surch **BRITISH EAST AFRICA COMPANY** and value in annas.

1	57	½a. on 1d. lilac	£275	£200
2	73	1a. on 2d. green and red	£500	£275
3	78	4a. on 5d. purple and blue	£550	£300

3 Arms of the Company

1890. Nos. 16/19 are larger (24×25 mm).

4b	3	½a. brown	70	8·50
5	3	1a. green	8·00	12·00
6	3	2a. red	4·50	5·00
7c	3	2½a. black on yellow	4·75	6·00
8a	3	3a. black on red	2·25	12·00
9	3	4a. brown	2·50	11·00
11a	3	4½a. purple	2·50	17·00
29	3	5a. black on blue	1·25	10·00
30	3	7½a. black	1·25	16·00
12	3	8a. blue	5·50	9·50
13	3	8a. grey	£275	£225
14	3	1r. red	6·00	9·00
15	3	1r. grey	£225	£225
16	-	2r. red	14·00	45·00
17	-	3r. purple	11·00	50·00
18	-	4r. blue	12·00	50·00
19	-	5r. green	30·00	70·00

1891. With handstamped or pen surcharges. Initialled in black.

20	½a. on 2a. red	£9500	£950
31	½a. on 3a. black on red	£425	50·00
32	1a. on 3a. black on red	£7000	£3750
26	1a. on 4a. brown	£8500	£1700

1894. Surch in words and figures.

27	5a. on 8a. blue	75·00	90·00
28	7½a. on 1r. red	75·00	90·00

1895. Optd **BRITISH EAST AFRICA**.

33	½a. brown	80·00	30·00
34	1a. green	£200	£120
35	2a. red	£200	£100
36	2½a. black on yellow	£200	60·00
37	3a. black on red	95·00	55·00
38	4a. brown	65·00	40·00
39	4½a. purple	£200	£100
40	5a. black on blue	£300	£150
41	7½a. black	£140	85·00

42		8a. blue	£100	80·00
43		1r. red	65·00	55·00
44	-	2r. red	£475	£300
45	-	3r. purple	£225	£140
46	-	4r. blue	£200	£170
47	-	5r. green	£450	£300

1895. Surch with large **2½**.

48	3	2½a. on 4½a. purple	£200	85·00

1895. Stamps of India (Queen Victoria) optd **British East Africa**.

49	23	½a. turquoise	7·00	5·50
50	-	1a. purple	6·50	6·00
51	-	1½a. brown	4·25	4·00
52	-	2a. blue	8·00	3·00
53	-	2a.6p. green	12·00	2·50
54	-	3a. orange	20·00	11·00
55a	-	4a. green (No. 96)	28·00	25·00
56	-	6a. brown (No. 80)	50·00	50·00
57c	-	8a. mauve	30·00	55·00
58	-	12a. purple on red	22·00	35·00
59	-	1r. grey (No. 101)	£100	65·00
60	37	1r. green and red	48·00	£130
61	38	2r. red and orange	£120	£180
62	38	3r. brown and green	£140	£190
63	38	5r. blue and violet	£150	£190

1895. No. 51 surch with small **2½**.

64	2½ on 1½a. brown	£110	50·00

11

1896

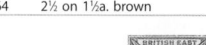

65	11	½a. green	5·00	80
66	11	1a. red	13·00	40
67	11	2a. brown	10·00	7·00
68	11	2½a. blue	16·00	2·00
69	11	3a. grey	8·50	12·00
70	11	4a. green	8·00	4·00
71	11	4½a. yellow	15·00	16·00
72	11	5a. brown	8·00	7·00
73	11	7½a. mauve	9·00	23·00
74	11	8a. grey	9·50	7·00
75	11	1r. blue	75·00	26·00
76	11	2r. orange	65·00	30·00
77	11	3r. violet	65·00	35·00
78	11	4r. red	60·00	75·00
79	11	5r. brown	60·00	42·00

1897. Stamps of Zanzibar, 1896, optd **British East Africa**.

80	13	½a. green and red	60·00	50·00
81	13	1a. blue and red	£100	95·00
82	13	2a. brown and red	45·00	22·00
83	13	4½a. orange and red	60·00	30·00
84	13	5a. brown and red	65·00	42·00
85	13	7½a. mauve and red	65·00	45·00

1897. As last, surch **2½**.

86	2½ on 1a. blue and red	£130	70·00
89	2½ on 3a. grey and red	£130	65·00

1897. As Type **11**, but larger.

92a	1r. blue	£100	50·00
93	2r. orange	£130	£130
94	3r. violet	£170	£180
95	4r. red	£475	£550
96	5r. brown	£425	£500
97	10r. brown	£425	£550
98	20r. green	£950	£2000
99	50r. mauve	£2000	

Pt. 1

BRITISH FORCES IN EGYPT

SPECIAL SEALS AND STAMPS FOR THE USE OF BRITISH FORCES IN EGYPT

A. SEALS

A1

1932. (a) Inscr "POSTAL SEAL".

A1	A1	1p. blue and red	95·00	4·50

(b) Inscr "LETTER SEAL".

A2	1p. blue and red	48·00	85

A2

1932. Christmas Seals.

A3	A2	3m. black on blue	50·00	70·00
A4	A2	3m. lake	7·50	50·00
A5	A2	3m. blue	7·00	30·00
A6a	A2	3m. red	11·00	29·00

A3

1934

A8	A3	1p. green	5·50	5·00
A9	A3	1p. red	4·50	4·00

1935. Silver Jubilee. Optd **JUBILEE COMMEMORATION 1935**.

A10	1p. blue	£275	£180

1935. Provisional Christmas Seal. Surch **Xmas 1935 3 Milliemes**.

A11	3m. on 1p. red	16·00	70·00

B. POSTAGE STAMPS

A6 King Fuad 1

1936

A12	A6	3m. green	1·00	2·00
A13	A6	10m. red	7·50	10

A7 King Farouk

1939

A14	A7	3m. green	6·00	9·00
A15	A7	10m. red	8·00	10

Pt. 1

BRITISH GUIANA

Situated on the N.E. coast of S. America. A British colony granted full internal self-government in August 1951. Attained independence on 26 May 1966, when the country was renamed Guyana.

100 cents = 1 dollar.

1

1850. Imperf.

1	1	2c. black on red	-	£225000
2	1	4c. black on orange	£60000	£10000
4	1	8c. black on green	£40000	£9000
5	1	12c. black on blue	£17000	£6500

Prices are for used stamps cut round. Stamps cut square are worth much more.

2

1852. Imperf.

9	2	1c. black on magenta	£9500	£4250
10	2	4c. black on blue	£17000	£9000

3 Seal of the Colony

1853. Imperf.

12	3	1c. red	£4500	£1600
20	3	4c. blue	£1500	£550

6

1856. Imperf.

23	6	1c. black on magenta	†	-
24	6	4c. black on magenta	-	£11000
25	6	4c. black on blue	£38000	£16000

7

9

1860. Perf.

29	7	1c. pink	£3000	£275
40	7	1c. brown	£425	£110
85	7	1c. black	20·00	8·00
87	7	2c. orange	50·00	4·75
89	7	4c. blue	£130	13·00
92	9	6c. blue	£180	35·00
95	7	8c. red	£250	35·00
98	7	12c. lilac	£250	23·00
99	7	12c. grey	£250	25·00
64	7	24c. green	£325	50·00
79	9	24c. green	£200	13·00
82	9	48c. red	£350	70·00

The prices quoted for Nos. 29/82 are for fine copies with four margins. Medium specimens can be supplied at much lower rates.

10

1862. Various borders. Roul.

116	10	1c. black on red	£4750	£750
119	10	2c. black on yellow	£4750	£400
122	10	4c. black on blue	£5000	£850

The above prices are for stamps signed in the centre by the Postmaster. Unsigned stamps are worth considerably less.

16

1876

126	16	1c. grey	2·75	1·40
171	16	2c. orange	45·00	15
172	16	4c. blue	£100	5·00
173	16	6c. brown	5·00	6·50
174	16	8c. red	£110	40
131	16	12c. violet	70·00	1·75
132	16	24c. green	75·00	3·25
133	16	48c. brown	£150	42·00
134	16	96c. olive	£475	£250

1878. Optd with thick horiz or horiz and vert bars. (a) On postage stamps.

137		1c. on 6c. brown	45·00	£120
141	9	1c. on 6c. blue	£200	75·00

(b) On official stamps of 1875 and 1877.

138	7	1c. black	£250	75·00
139	16	1c. grey	£200	70·00
140	16	2c. orange	£400	70·00
144	16	4c. blue	£375	£110
145	16	6c. brown	£550	£110
146	7	8c. red	£4000	£350
148	16	8c. red	£500	£120

1881. Surch with figure. Old value barred out in ink. (a) On postage stamps.

152	9	"1" on 48c. red	45·00	5·00
149		"1" on 96c. olive	4·50	9·00
150		"2" on 96c. olive	14·00	17·00

(b) On stamps optd **OFFICIAL**.

153	7	"1" on 12c. lilac	£140	75·00
154	16	"1" on 48c. brown	£190	£130
155	16	"2" on 12c. violet	85·00	48·00
157	16	"2" on 24c. green	95·00	55·00

26

1882

162	26	1c. black on red	65·00	30·00
165	26	2c. black on yellow	85·00	50·00

Each stamp is perforated with the word "SPECIMEN".

1888. T **16** without value in bottom tablet, surch **INLAND REVENUE** and value.

175	16	1c. purple	2·75	20
176	16	2c. purple	2·00	2·00
177	16	3c. purple	1·25	20
178	16	4c. purple	12·00	30
179	16	6c. purple	13·00	5·00
180	16	8c. purple	1·50	30
181	16	10c. purple	6·00	2·50
182	16	20c. purple	22·00	20·00
183	16	40c. purple	35·00	29·00
184	16	72c. purple	70·00	65·00
185	16	$1 green	£475	£600
186	16	$2 green	£250	£275
187	16	$3 green	£250	£275
188	16	$4 green	£550	£700
189	16	$5 green	£350	£375

1889. No. 176 surch with additional **2**.

192	"2" on 2c. purple	4·75	15

30

1889

193	30	1c. purple and grey	7·00	3·25
213	30	1c. green	75	10
194	30	2c. purple and orange	4·50	10
234	30	2c. purple and red	3·25	30
241a	30	2c. purple & black on red	4·50	10
253a	30	2c. red	8·50	10
195	30	4c. purple and blue	4·50	3·75
254	30	4c. brown and purple	2·50	1·25
214	30	5c. blue	3·25	10
243a	30	5c. purple & blue on blue	3·50	6·50
198	30	6c. purple and brown	7·00	22·00
236	30	6c. black and blue	7·00	11·00
256	30	6c. grey and black	13·00	7·00
199	30	8c. purple and red	15·00	3·75
215	30	8c. purple and black	6·00	1·75
200a	30	12c. purple and mauve	8·50	4·00
257	30	12c. orange and purple	4·00	5·50
246a	30	24c. purple and green	3·75	4·75
202	30	48c. purple and red	26·00	11·00
247a	30	48c. grey and brown	14·00	24·00
248a	30	60c. green and red	14·00	95·00
203	30	72c. purple and brown	28·00	50·00
205	30	96c. purple and red	65·00	70·00
250	30	96c. black & red on yellow	35·00	45·00

1890. Nos. 185/8 surch **ONE CENT**.

207	16	1 cent on $1 green	2·25	35
208	16	1 cent on $2 green	2·00	60
209	16	1 cent on $3 green	2·50	1·25
210	16	1 cent on $4 green	4·50	10·00

32 Mount Roraima

33 Kaieteur Falls

1898. Jubilee.

216	32	1c. black and red	8·00	2·25
217	33	2c. brown and blue	30·00	4·25
219w	32	5c. green and brown	45·00	5·00
220	33	10c. black and red	25·00	27·00
221	32	15c. brown and blue	30·00	23·00

1899. Nos. 219/21 surch **TWO CENTS**.

222		2c. on 5c. green and brown	3·25	3·00
223	33	2c. on 10c. black and red	3·50	2·25
224	32	2c. on 15c. brown and blue	3·50	1·25

1905. T **30** but inscr "REVENUE", optd **POSTAGE AND REVENUE**.

251	30	$2.40 green and violet	£190	£425

37

1913

259a	37	1c. green	1·75	25
260	37	2c. red	1·50	10
274	37	2c. violet	2·50	10
261b	37	4c. brown and purple	3·75	25
262	37	5c. blue	1·75	1·00
263	37	6c. grey and black	3·00	2·00
276	37	6c. blue	3·00	30
264	37	12c. orange and violet	1·25	1·00
278	37	24c. purple and green	2·00	4·50
279	37	48c. grey and purple	9·50	3·50
280	37	60c. green and red	10·00	50·00

281	**37**	72c. purple and brown	32·00	75·00
269a	**37**	96c. black and red on yellow	26·00	48·00

1918. Optd **WAR TAX**.

271	2c. red	1·50	15

39 Ploughing a Rice Field

40 Indian shooting Fish

41 Kaieteur Falls

42 Public Buildings, Georgetown

1931. Centenary of County Union.

283	**39**	1c. green	2·50	1·25
284	**40**	2c. brown	2·00	10
285	**41**	4c. red	2·25	45
286	**42**	6c. blue	2·25	1·25
287	**41**	$1 violet	48·00	55·00

43 Ploughing a Rice Field

44 Gold Mining

1934

288	**43**	1c. green	60	2·00
289	**40**	2c. brown	1·50	1·75
290	**44**	3c. red	30	10
291	**41**	4c. violet	2·00	3·50
292	-	6c. blue	4·50	7·00
293	-	12c. orange	20	20
294	-	24c. purple	3·50	11·00
295	-	48c. black	8·50	9·00
296	**41**	50c. green	12·00	20·00
297	-	60c. brown	26·00	28·00
298	-	72c. purple	1·25	2·25
299	-	96c. black	29·00	32·00
300	-	$1 violet	45·00	42·00

DESIGNS—HORIZ: 6c. Shooting logs over falls; 12c. Stabroek Market; 24c. Sugar canes in punts; 48c. Forest road; 60c. Victoria Regia lilies; 72c. Mount Roraima; $1 Botanical Gardens. VERT: 96c. Sir Walter Raleigh and his son.

The 2c., 4c. and 50c. are without the dates shown in Types **40/44** and the 12, 48, 72 and 96c. have no portrait.

1935. Silver Jubilee. As T **13** of Antigua.

301	2c. blue and grey	30	20
302	6c. brown and blue	2·00	5·00
303	12c. green and blue	8·50	8·50
304	24c. grey and purple	13·00	16·00

1937. Coronation. As T **2** of Aden.

305	2c. brown	15	10
306	4c. grey	50	60
307	6c. blue	60	2·00

53 South America

1938. Designs as for same values of 1934 issue (except where indicated) but with portrait of King George VI (as in T **53**) where portrait of King George V previously appeared.

308a	**43**	1c. green	30	10
309a	-	2c. violet (As 4c.)	45	10
310b	**53**	4c. red and black	50	15
311	-	6c. blue (As 2c.)	70	10
312a	-	24c. green	3·00	10
313a	-	36c. violet (As 4c.)	3·00	30
314	-	48c. orange	60	50
315	-	60c. brown (As 6c.)	18·00	9·50
316	-	96c. purple	9·00	2·75
317	-	$1 violet	24·00	35
318	-	$2 purple (As 72c.)	15·00	25·00
319	-	$3 brown	38·00	35·00

DESIGN—HORIZ: $3 Victoria Regia lilies.

1946. Victory. As T **9** of Aden.

320	3c. red	10	40
321	6c. blue	75	85

1948. Silver Wedding. As T **10/11** of Aden.

322	3c. red	10	40
323	$3 brown	22·00	26·00

1949. UPU. As T **20/23** of Antigua.

324	4c. red	10	50
325	6c. blue	1·75	1·75
326	12c. orange	15	50
327	24c. green	15	70

1951. Inauguration of BWI University College. As T **24/25** of Antigua.

328	3c. black and red	30	50
329	6c. black and blue	30	65

1953. Coronation. As T **13** of Aden.

330	4c. black and red	30	10

55 G.P.O., Georgetown

1954

331	**55**	1c. black	20	10
332	-	2c. myrtle	20	10
333	-	3c. olive and brown	3·50	20
334	-	4c. violet	1·75	10
335	-	5c. red and black	1·75	10
336	-	6c. green	1·00	10
337	-	8c. blue	55	20
338a	-	12c. black and brown	1·25	10
360	-	24c. black and orange	4·00	10
361	-	36c. red and black	60	60
341a	-	48c. blue and brown	1·00	1·00
342	-	72c. red and green	16·00	2·75
364	-	$1 multicoloured	7·00	90
344	-	$2 mauve	25·00	8·50
345	-	$5 blue and black	22·00	32·00

DESIGNS—HORIZ: 2c. Botanical Gardens; 3c. *Victoria Regia* lilies; 5c. Map of Caribbean; 6c. Rice combine-harvester; 8c. Sugar cane entering factory; 24c. Bauxite mining; 36c. Mount Roraima; $1 Channel-billed toucan; $2 Dredging gold. VERT: 4c. Amerindian shooting fish; 12c. Felling greenheart; 48c. Kaieteur Falls; 72c. Arapaima (fish); $5 Arms of British Guiana.

70

1961. History and Culture Week.

346	**70**	5c. sepia and red	20	10
347	**70**	6c. sepia and green	20	15
348	**70**	30c. sepia and orange	45	45

1963. Freedom from Hunger. As T **28** of Aden.

349	20c. violet	30	10

1963. Centenary of Red Cross. As T **33** of Antigua.

350	5c. red and black	20	20
351	20c. red and blue	55	35

71 Weightlifting

1964. Olympic Games, Tokyo.

367	**71**	5c. orange	10	10
368	**71**	8c. blue	15	35
369	**71**	25c. mauve	25	40

1965. Centenary of ITU. As T **36** of Antigua.

370	5c. green and olive	10	15
371	25c. blue and mauve	20	15

1965. ICY. As T **37** of Antigua.

372	5c. purple and turquoise	15	10
373	25c. green and lavender	30	20

72 St George's Cathedral, Georgetown

1966. Churchill Commemoration.

374	**72**	5c. black, red and gold	1·00	10
375	**72**	25c. black, blue and gold	2·25	50

1966. Royal Visit. As T **39** of Antigua.

376	3c. black and blue	75	15
377	25c. black and mauve	1·50	60

OFFICIAL STAMPS

1875. Optd **OFFICIAL**.

O1	**7**	1c. black	65·00	23·00
O2	**7**	2c. orange	£225	14·00
O3	**7**	8c. red	£350	£130
O4	**7**	12c. lilac	£3250	£500
O5	**9**	24c. green	£2500	£250

1877. Optd **OFFICIAL**.

O6	**16**	1c. grey	£275	65·00
O7	**16**	2c. orange	£130	15·00
O8	**16**	4c. blue	£110	24·00
O9	**16**	6c. brown	£5500	£600
O10	**16**	8c. red	£2000	£450

POSTAGE DUE STAMPS

1940. As Type D **1** of Barbados, but inscr "BRITISH GUIANA".

D1	1c. green	6·50	10·00
D2a	2c. black	4·50	8·00
D3	4c. blue	30	12·00
D4	12c. red	35·00	6·00

For later issues see **GUYANA**.

Pt. 1

BRITISH HONDURAS

A British colony on the East coast of Central America. Self-government was granted on 1 January 1964. The country was renamed Belize from 1 June 1973.

1866. 12 pence = 1 shilling; 20 shillings = 1 pound.
1888. 100 cents = 1 dollar.

1

1866

17	**1**	1d. blue	75·00	22·00
18	**1**	1d. red	23·00	13·00
13	**1**	3d. brown	£170	25·00
20	**1**	4d. mauve	95·00	4·75
21	**1**	6d. yellow	£275	£225
9	**1**	6d. red	£450	55·00
16	**1**	1s. green	£325	13·00
22	**1**	1s. grey	£250	£160

1888. Surch as **2 CENTS**.

36	1c. on 1d. green	80	1·50
37	2c. on 1d. red	60	2·25
25	2c. on 6d. red	£190	£170
38	3c. on 3d. brown	3·50	1·40
39	6c. on 3d. blue	4·75	23·00
40	10c. on 4d. mauve	23·00	50
41	20c. on 6d. yellow	18·00	14·00
42	50c. on 1s. grey	35·00	85·00

1888. No. 42 surch **TWO**.

35	"TWO" on 50c. on 1s. grey	55·00	95·00

1891. No. 40 surch **6** and bar.

44	6c. on 10c. on 4d. mauve	1·75	1·50

1891. Nos. 38 and 39 surch.

49	"FIVE" on 3c. on 3d. brown	1·25	1·40
50	"15" on 6c. on 3d. blue	13·00	28·00

8

1891

51	**8**	1c. green	2·50	1·25
52	**8**	2c. red	4·00	20
53	**8**	3c. brown	9·50	4·00
54	**8**	5c. blue	12·00	75
55	**8**	5c. black and blue on blue	19·00	2·75
56	**8**	6c. blue	13·00	2·00
57	**8**	10c. mauve and green (A)	14·00	15·00
58	**8**	10c. purple and green (B)	11·00	7·50
59	**8**	12c. lilac and green	2·50	3·25
60	**8**	24c. yellow and blue	6·00	21·00
61	**8**	25c. brown and green	85·00	£130
62	**8**	50c. green and red	28·00	65·00
63	**8**	$1 green and red	95·00	£150
64	**8**	$2 green and blue	£150	£200
65	**8**	$5 green and black	£325	£425

NOTE: 10c. (A) inscr "POSTAGE POSTAGE"; (B) inscr "POSTAGE & REVENUE".

1899. Optd **REVENUE**.

66		5c. blue	25·00	2·50
67		10c. mauve and green	15·00	18·00
68		25c. brown and green	3·75	38·00
69	**1**	50c. on 1s. grey	£225	£375

14

1902

84a	**14**	1c. green	2·75	2·25
85a	**14**	2c. purple and black on red	1·75	20
96	**14**	2c. red	14·00	10
86	**14**	5c. black and blue on blue	1·75	20
97	**14**	5c. blue	2·50	10
87	**14**	10c. purple and green	4·00	16·00
83	**14**	20c. purple	12·00	17·00
89	**14**	25c. purple and orange	9·50	55·00
100	**14**	25c. black on green	6·50	45·00
90	**14**	50c. green and red	24·00	90·00
91	**14**	$1 green and red	70·00	£100
92	**14**	$2 green and blue	£150	£200
93	**14**	$5 green and black	£350	£400

16

1913

101	**16**	1c. green	4·00	1·50
102	**16**	2c. red	5·00	1·00
103	**16**	3c. orange	1·25	20
104	**16**	5c. blue	2·25	85
105	**16**	10c. purple and green	4·50	6·50
106	**16**	25c. black on green	1·25	12·00
107	**16**	50c. purple and blue on blue	26·00	15·00
108	**16**	$1 black and red	27·00	65·00
109	**16**	$2 purple and green	85·00	£100
110	**16**	$5 purple and black on red	£250	£300

1915. Optd with pattern of wavy lines.

111a	1c. green	50	19·00
112	2c. red	3·50	50
113	5c. blue	30	6·00

1916. Optd **WAR**.

114	1c. green (No. 111a)	10	2·75
119	1c. green (No. 101)	20	30
120	3c. orange (No. 103)	80	3·25

21

1921. Peace.

121	**21**	2c. red	4·75	50

1921. As No. 121 but without word "PEACE".

123	4c. grey	12·00	50

22

1922

126	**22**	1c. green	16·00	6·50
127	**22**	2c. brown	1·50	1·50
128	**22**	2c. red	9·00	1·50
129	**22**	3c. orange	32·00	4·00
130	**22**	4c. grey	19·00	85
131	**22**	5c. blue	1·50	55
132	**22**	10c. purple and olive	3·75	30
133	**22**	25c. black on green	2·00	8·50
134	**22**	50c. purple and blue on blue	6·00	16·00
136	**22**	$1 black and red	18·00	26·00
137	**22**	$2 green and purple	48·00	£120
125	**22**	$5 purple and black on red	£225	£275

1932. Optd **BELIZE RELIEF FUND PLUS** and value.

138	1c.+1c. green	2·50	14·00
139	2c.+2c. red	2·50	14·00
140	3c.+3c. orange	2·50	28·00
141	4c.+4c. grey	15·00	30·00
142	5c.+5c. blue	6·50	14·00

1935. Silver Jubilee. As T **13** of Antigua.

143	3c. blue and black	2·00	50
144	4c. green and blue	4·50	4·00
145	5c. brown and blue	2·00	2·50
146	25c. grey and purple	7·50	9·00

1937. Coronation. As T **2** of Aden.

147	3c. orange	30	30
148	4c. grey	70	30
149	5c. blue	80	1·90

24 Maya figures

1938

150	**24**	1c. purple and green	70	1·50
151	-	2c. black and red	1·25	1·00
152	-	3c. purple and brown	2·00	1·75
153	-	4c. black and green	1·50	70
154	-	5c. purple and blue	3·25	1·75
155	-	10c. green and brown	4·00	60
156	-	15c. brown and blue	7·00	1·50
157	-	25c. blue and green	4·50	2·00
158	-	50c. black and purple	25·00	4·50
159	-	$1 red and olive	45·00	10·00
160	-	$2 blue and purple	50·00	28·00
161	-	$5 red and brown	48·00	42·00

DESIGNS—VERT: 2c. Chicle tapping; 3c. Cohune palm; $1 Court House, Belize; $2 Mahogany felling; $5 Arms of Colony. HORIZ: 4c. Local products; 5c. Grapefruit; 10c. Mahogany logs in river; 15c. Sergeant's Cay; 25c. Dorey; 50c. Chicle industry.

1946. Victory. As T **9** of Aden.

162	3c. brown	10	20
163	5c. blue	10	20

1948. Silver Wedding. As T **10** and **11** of Aden.

164	4c. green	15	60
165	$5 brown	24·00	50·00

36 Island of Saint George's Cay

1949. 150th Anniv of Battle of Saint George's Cay.

166	**36**	1c. blue and green	20	1·25
167	**36**	3c. blue and brown	20	1·50
168	**36**	4c. olive and violet	20	1·75
169	-	5c. brown and blue	1·90	75
170	-	10c. green and brown	1·90	30
171	-	15c. green and blue	1·90	30

DESIGNS: 5, 10 and 15c. H.M.S. *Merlin*.

1949. U.P.U. As T **20/23** of Antigua.

172	4c. green	30	75
173	5c. blue	1·50	50
174	10c. brown	40	3·50
175	25c. blue	35	50

1951. Inauguration of B.W.I. University College. As T **24/25** of Antigua.

176	3c. violet and brown	45	1·50
177	10c. green and brown	45	30

1953. Coronation. As T **13** of Aden.

178	4c. black and green	50	30

39 Baird's Tapir

49 Mountain Orchid

1953

179	-	1c. green and black	10	40
180a	**39**	2c. brown and black	2·00	30
181a	-	3c. lilac and mauve	20	10
182	-	4c. brown and green	1·50	30
183	-	5c. olive and red	30	20
184a	-	10c. slate and blue	50	10
185	-	15c. green and violet	50	10
186	-	25c. blue and brown	6·50	3·75
187	-	50c. brown and purple	17·00	4·00
188	-	$1 slate and brown	10·00	5·00
189	-	$2 red and grey	10·00	4·50
190	**49**	$5 purple and slate	48·00	17·00

DESIGNS—HORIZ: 1c. Arms of British Honduras; 3c. Mace and Legislative Council Chamber; 4c. Pine industry; 5c. Spiny lobster; 10c. Stanley Field Airport; 15c. Maya frieze, Xunantunich; 25c. *Morpho peleides* (butterfly); $1 Nine-banded armadillo; $2 Hawkesworth Bridge. VERT: 50c. Maya indian.

50 *Belize from Fort George, 1842* (C. J. Hullmandel)

1960. Post Office Centenary.

191	**50**	2c. green	45	1·25
192	-	10c. red	45	10
193	-	15c. blue	45	35

DESIGNS: 10c. Public seals, 1860 and 1960; 15c. Tamarind tree, Newtown Barracks.

1961. New Constitution. Stamps of 1953 optd **NEW CONSTITUTION 1960**.

194	**39**	2c. brown and black	25	40
195	-	3c. lilac and mauve	30	40
196	-	10c. slate and blue	30	10
197	-	15c. green and violet	30	20

1962. Hurricane Hattie Relief Fund. Stamps of 1953 optd **HURRICANE HATTIE**.

198	1c. green and black	10	65
199	10c. slate and blue	30	10
200	25c. blue and brown	1·75	80
201	50c. brown and purple	75	1·00

55 Great Curassow

1962. Birds in natural colours; portrait and inscr in black; background colours given.

239	**55**	1c. yellow	10	50
240	-	2c. grey	30	1·00
204	-	3c. green	4·25	3·25
241	-	4c. grey	2·25	2·00
242	-	5c. buff	40	10
243	-	10c. stone	40	10
244	-	15c. stone	40	10
209	-	25c. slate	4·50	30
210	-	50c. grey	6·00	35
211	-	$1 blue	9·00	2·00
212	-	$2 stone	23·00	5·50
213	-	$5 grey	28·00	16·00

BIRDS: 2c. Red-legged honeycreeper; 3c. Northern jacana ("American Jacana"); 4c. Great kiskadee; 5c. Scarlet-rumped tanager; 10c. Scarlet macaw; 15c. Slaty-tailed trogon ("Massena Trogon"); 25c. Red-footed booby; 50c. Keel-billed toucan; $1 Magnificent frigate bird; $2 Rufous-tailed jacamar; $5 Montezuma oropendola.

1963. Freedom from Hunger. As T **28** of Aden.

214	22c. green	30	15

1963. Centenary of Red Cross. As T **33** of Antigua.

215	4c. red and black	20	1·25
216	22c. red and blue	40	1·25

1964. New Constitution. Nos. 202, 204, 205, 207 and 209 optd **SELF GOVERNMENT 1964**.

217	**55**	1c. yellow	10	30
218	-	3c. green	45	30
219	-	4c. pale grey	45	30
220	-	10c. stone	45	10
221	-	25c. slate	55	30

1965. Centenary of I.T.U. As T **36** of Antigua.

222	2c. red and green	10	10
223	50c. yellow and purple	35	25

1965. I.C.Y. As T **37** of Antigua.

224	1c. purple and turquoise	10	15
225	22c. green and lavender	20	15

1966. Churchill Commemoration. As T **38** of Antigua.

226	1c. blue	10	75
227	4c. green	55	10
228	22c. brown	85	10
229	25c. violet	1·00	45

1966. Dedication of new Capital Site. Nos. 202, 204/5 207 and 209 optd **DEDICATION OF SITE NEW CAPITAL 9th OCTOBER 1965**.

230	**55**	1c. yellow	10	40
231	-	3c. green	55	40
232	-	4c. grey	55	40
233	-	10c. stone	55	10
234	-	25c. slate	75	35

58 Citrus Grove

1966. Stamp Centenary. Multicoloured.

235	5c. Type **58**	10	10
236	10c. Half Moon Cay	10	10
237	22c. Hidden Valley Falls	10	10
238	25c. Maya ruins, Xunantunich	15	45

59 Sailfish

1967. International Tourist Year.

246	**59**	5c. blue, black and yellow	20	30
247	-	10c. brown, black and red	20	10
248	-	22c. orange, black and green	35	10
249	-	25c. blue, black and yellow	35	60

DESIGNS: 10c. Red brocket; 22c. Jaguar; 25c. Atlantic tarpon.

60 *Schomburgkia tibicinis*

1968. 20th Anniv of Economic Commission for Latin America. Orchids. Multicoloured.

250	5c. Type **60**	20	15
251	10c. *Maxillaria tenuifolia*	25	10
252	22c. *Bletia purpurea*	30	10
253	25c. *Sobralia macrantha*	40	20

61 Monument Belizean Patriots

1968. Human Rights Year. Multicoloured.

254	22c. Type **61**	15	10
255	50c. Monument at site of new capital	15	20

63 Spotted Jewfish

1968. Wildlife.

276	-	½c. multicoloured and blue	10	10
277	-	½c. multicoloured and yellow	2·50	1·00
256	**63**	1c. black, brown and yellow	30	10
257	-	2c. black, green and yellow	10	10
258	-	3c. black, brown and lilac	20	10
259	-	4c. multicoloured	15	1·25
260	-	5c. black and red	15	1·25
261	-	10c. multicoloured	15	10
262	-	15c. multicoloured	2·00	20
263	-	25c. multicoloured	30	20
264	-	50c. multicoloured	70	1·25
265	-	$1 multicoloured	2·50	1·25
266	-	$2 multicoloured	2·50	2·00
278	-	$5 multicoloured	2·50	10·00

DESIGNS: ½c. (Nos. 276 and 277) Mozambique mouthbrooder ("Crana"); 2c. White-lipped peccary; 3c. Misty grouper; 4c. Collared anteater; 5c. Bonefish; 10c. Paca; 15c. Dolphin; 25c. Kinkajou; 50c. Mutton snapper; $1 Tayra; $2 Great barracuda; $5 Puma.

64 *Rhyncholaelia digbyana*

1969. Orchids of Belize (1st series). Multicoloured.

268	5c. Type **64**	60	20
269	10c. *Cattleya bowringiana*	65	15
270	22c. *Lycaste cochleatum*	95	15
271	25c. *Coryanthes speciosum*	1·10	1·10

See also Nos. 287/90.

65 Ziricote Tree

1969. Indigenous Hardwoods (1st series). Multicoloured.

272	5c. Type **65**	10	20
273	10c. Rosewood	10	10
274	22c. Mayflower	20	10
275	25c. Mahogany	20	45

See also Nos. 291/4, 315/18 and 333/7.

66 *The Virgin and Child* (Bellini)

1969. Christmas. Paintings. Multicoloured.

279	5c. Type **66**	10	10
280	15c. Type **66**	10	10
281	22c. *The Adoration of the Magi* (Veronese)	10	10
282	25c. As No. 281	10	20

1970. Population Census. Nos. 260/3 optd **POPULATION CENSUS 1970**.

283	5c. multicoloured	10	10
284	10c. multicoloured	15	10
285	15c. multicoloured	20	10
286	25c. multicoloured	20	15

1970. Orchids of Belize (2nd series). As T **64**. Multicoloured.

287	5c. Black orchid	35	15
288	15c. White butterfly orchid	50	10
289	22c. Swan orchid	70	10
290	25c. Butterfly orchid	70	40

69 Santa Maria

1970. Indigenous Hardwoods (2nd series). Multicoloured.

291	5c. Type **69**	25	10
292	15c. Nargusta	40	10
293	22c. Cedar	45	10
294	25c. Sapodilla	45	35

70 *The Nativity* (A. Hughes)

1970. Christmas. Multicoloured.

295	½c. Type **70**	10	10
296	5c. *The Mystic Nativity* (Botticelli)	10	10
297	10c. Type **70**	15	10
298	15c. As 5c.	25	10
299	22c. Type **70**	30	10
300	50c. As 5c.	40	85

71 Legislative Assembly House

1971. Establishment of New Capital, Belmopan. Multicoloured.

301	5c. Old capital, Belize	10	10
302	10c. Government Plaza	10	10
303	15c. Type **71**	10	10

304	22c. Magistrates' Court	15	10
305	25c. Police H.Q	15	15
306	50c. New G.P.O	25	40

The 5c. and 10c. are larger, 60×22 mm.

72 *Tabebuia chrysantha*

1971. Easter. Flowers. Multicoloured.

307	½c. Type **72**	10	10
308	5c. *Hymenocallis littorallis*	10	10
309	10c. *Hippeastrum equestre*	10	10
310	15c. Type **72**	20	10
311	22c. As 5c.	20	10
312	25c. As 10c.	20	30

1971. Racial Equality Year. Nos. 261 and 264 optd **RACIAL EQUALITY YEAR–1971**.

313	10c. multicoloured	25	10
314	50c. multicoloured	55	20

74 Tubroos

1971. Indigenous Hardwoods (3rd series). Multicoloured.

315	5c. Type **74**	60	10
316	15c. Yemeri	80	30
317	26c. Billywebb	1·10	35
318	50c. Logwood	1·75	4·25
MS319	96×171 mm. Nos. 315/18	3·50	7·50

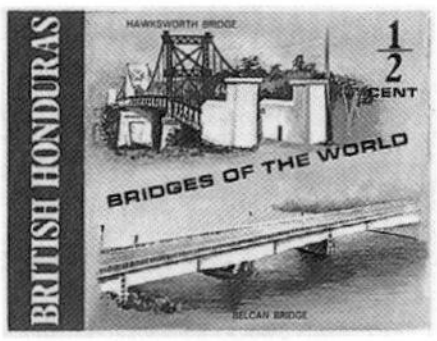

75 Hawksworth and Belcan Bridges

1971. Bridges of the World. Multicoloured.

320	½c. Type **75**	10	20
321	5c. Narrows Bridge, N.Y. and Quebec Bridge	30	15
322	26c. London Bridge (1871) and reconstructed, Arizona (1971)	80	15
323	50c. Belize Mexican Bridge and Swing Bridge	1·00	1·25

76 *Petrae volubis*

1972. Easter. Wild Flowers. Multicoloured.

324	6c. Type **76**	15	10
325	15c. Yemeri	25	30
326	26c. Mayflower	50	45
327	50c. Tiger's Claw	80	1·40

77 Seated Figure

1972. Mayan Artefacts. Multicoloured.

328	3c. Type **77**	25	10
329	6c. Priest in "dancing" pose	25	10
330	16c. Sun God's head (horiz)	50	15
331	26c. Priest and Sun God	70	20
332	50c. Full-front figure	1·40	3·75

78 Banak

1972. Indigenous Hardwoods (4th series). Multicoloured.

333	3c. Type **78**	25	10
334	5c. Quamwood	25	10
335	16c. Waika Chewstick	55	15
336	26c. Mamee-Apple	75	25
337	50c. My Lady	1·60	3·25

1972. Royal Silver Wedding. As T **52** of Ascension, but with Orchids of Belize in background.

341	26c. green	25	10
342	50c. violet	40	65

80 Baron Bliss Day

1973. Festivals of Belize. Multicoloured.

343	3c. Type **80**	15	10
344	10c. Labour Day	15	10
345	26c. Carib Settlement Day	30	10
346	50c. Pan American Day	50	85

POSTAGE DUES

D1

1923

D1	**D1**	1c. black	2·25	13·00
D4	**D1**	2c. black	2·75	6·50
D5	**D1**	4c. black	1·25	6·50

For later issues see **BELIZE**.

Pt. 1

BRITISH INDIAN OCEAN TERRITORY

A Crown Colony, established 8 November 1965, comprising the Chagos Archipelago (previously administered by Mauritius) and Aldabra, Farquhar and Desroches, previously administered by Seychelles to which country they were returned on 29 June 1976.

The Chagos Archipelago has no indigenous population, but stamps were provided from 1990 for use by civilian workers at the U.S. Navy base on Diego Garcia.

1968. 100 cents = 1 rupee.
1990. 100 pence = 1 pound.

1968. Nos 196/200, 202/4 and 206/12 of Seychelles optd **B.I.O.T.**

1	**24**	5c. multicoloured	1·00	1·50
2	-	10c. multicoloured	10	15
3	-	15c. multicoloured	25	20
4	-	20c. multicoloured	20	15
5	-	25c. multicoloured	20	15
6	-	40c. multicoloured	20	20
7	-	45c. multicoloured	20	30
8	-	50c. multicoloured	20	30
9	-	75c. multicoloured	1·50	35
10	-	1r. multicoloured	1·50	35
11	-	1r.50 multicoloured	1·75	1·50
12	-	2r.25 multicoloured	3·00	3·75
13	-	3r.50 multicoloured	3·00	4·50
14	-	5r. multicoloured	10·00	6·50
15	-	10r. multicoloured	20·00	15·00

2 Lascar

1968. Marine Life. Multicoloured.

16	5c. Type **2**	1·00	2·25
17	10c. Smooth hammerhead (vert)	30	1·25
18	15c. Tiger shark	30	1·50
19	20c. Spotted eagle ray ("Bat ray")	30	1·00
20	25c. Yellow-finned butterflyfish and ear-spot angelfish (vert)	80	1·00
20a	30c. Robber crab	3·50	2·75
21	40c. Blue-finned trevalley ("Caranx")	2·25	40
22	45c. Crocodile needlefish ("Garfish") (vert)	2·25	2·50
23	50c. Pickhandle barracuda	2·25	30
23a	60c. Spotted pebble crab	3·50	3·25
24	75c. Indian Ocean steep-headed parrotfish	2·50	2·25
24a	85c. Rainbow runner ("Dorade")	4·50	3·00
25	1r. Giant hermit crab	1·75	35
26	1r.50 Parrotfish ("Humphead")	2·50	3·00
27	2r.25 Yellow-edged lyre-tail and Aredate grouper ("Rock cod")	12·00	10·00
28	3r.50 Black marlin	4·00	3·75
29	5r. black, green and blue (Whale shark) (vert)	21·00	14·00
30	10r. Lionfish	6·00	6·50

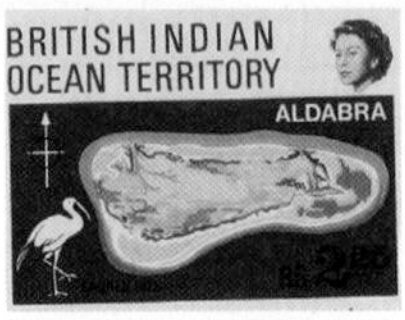

3 Sacred Ibis and Aldabra Coral Atoll

1969. Coral Atolls.

31	**3**	2r.25 multicoloured	1·75	1·00

4 Outrigger Canoe

1969. Ships of the Islands. Multicoloured.

32	45c. Type **4**	55	75
33	75c. Pirogue	55	80
34	1r. M.V. *Nordvaer*	60	90
35	1r.50 *Isle of Farquhar*	65	1·00

5 Giant Land Tortoise

1971. Aldabra Nature Reserve. Multicoloured.

36	45c. Type **5**	2·50	2·50
37	75c. Aldabra lily	3·00	2·50
38	1r. Aldabra tree snail	3·50	2·75
39	1r.50 Western reef heron ("Dimorphic Egrets")	12·00	10·00

6 Arms of Royal Society and White-throated Rail

1971. Opening of Royal Society Research Station, Aldabra.

40	**6**	3r.50 multicoloured	15·00	10·00

7 Staghorn Coral

1972. Coral. Multicoloured.

41	40c. Type **7**	3·50	4·00
42	60c. Brain coral	4·00	4·25
43	1r. Mushroom coral	4·00	4·25
44	1r.75 Organ pipe coral	5·00	6·50

1972. Royal Silver Wedding. As T **52** of Ascension, but with White-throated rail and Sacred ibis in background.

45	95c. green	50	40
46	1r.50 violet	50	40

9 *Christ on the Cross*

1973. Easter. Multicoloured.

47	45c. Type **9**	20	40
48	75c. *Joseph and Nicodemus burying Jesus*	30	55
49	1r. Type **9**	30	60
50	1r.50 As 75c.	30	70
MS51	126×110 mm. Nos. 47/50	1·00	4·00

10 Upsidedown Jellyfish

1973. Wildlife (1st series). Multicoloured.

53	50c. Type **10**	3·50	3·00
54	1r. *Hypolimnas misippus* and *Belenois aldabrensis* (butterflies)	4·00	3·00
55	1r.50 *Nephila madagascarienis* (spider)	4·25	3·00

See also Nos. 58/61, 77/80 and 86/9.

11 M.V. *Nordvaer*

1974. Fiifth Anniv of *Nordvaer* Travelling Post Office. Multicoloured.

56	85c. Type **11**	85	75
57	2r.50 *Nordvaer* off shore	1·40	1·25

12 Red-cloud Auger and Subulat Auger

1974. Wildlife (2nd series). Shells. Multicoloured.

58	45c. Type **12**	2·25	1·25
59	75c. Great green turban	2·50	1·50
60	1r. Strawberry drupe	2·75	1·75
61	1r.50 Bull-mouth helmet	3·00	2·00

13 Aldabra Drongo

1975. Birds. Multicoloured.

62	5c. Type **13**	1·25	2·75
63	10c. Black coucal ("Malagasy Coucal")	1·25	2·75
64	20c. Mascarene fody ("Red-Headed Forest Foddy")	1·25	2·75
65	25c. White tern	1·25	2·75
66	30c. Crested tern	1·25	2·75
67	40c. Brown booby	1·25	2·75
68	50c. Common noddy ("Noddy Tern") (horiz)	1·25	3·00
69	60c. Grey heron	1·25	3·00
70	65c. Blue-faced booby (horiz)	1·25	3·00
71	95c. Madagascar white eye ("Malagasy White-eye") (horiz)	1·25	3·00
72	1r. Green-backed heron (horiz)	1·25	3·00
73	1r.75 Lesser frigate bird (horiz)	2·00	5·00
74	3r.50 White-tailed tropic bird (horiz)	3·25	6·00
75	5r. Souimanga sunbird (horiz)	3·00	5·00
76	10r. Madagascar turtle dove ("Malagasy Turtle Dove") (horiz)	5·00	9·00

14 *Grewia salicifolia*

1975. Wildlife (3rd series). Seashore Plants. Multicoloured.

77	50c. Type **14**	50	1·25
78	65c. *Cassia aldabrensis*	55	1·40
79	1r. *Hypoestes aldabrensis*	65	1·50
80	1r.60 *Euphorbia pyrifolia*	80	1·60

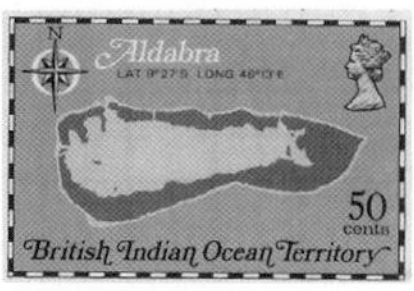

15 Map of Aldabra

1975. Tenth Anniv of Territory. Maps. Multicoloured.

81	50c. Type **15**	80	65
82	1r. Desroches	95	85
83	1r.50 Farquhar	1·10	1·00
84	2r. Diego Garcia	1·25	1·25
MS85	147×147 mm. Nos. 81/4	7·00	14·00

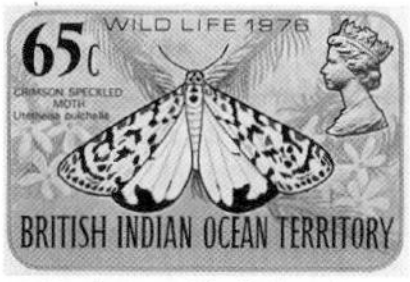

16 *Utetheisa pulchella* (moth)

1976. Wildlife (4th series). Multicoloured.

86	65c. Type **16**	60	1·10
87	1r.20 *Dysdercus fasciatus* (bug)	75	1·25
88	1r.50 *Sphex torridus* (wasp)	80	1·40
89	2r. *Oryctes rhinoceros* (beetle)	85	1·40

17 White-tailed Tropic Bird

1990. Birds. Multicoloured.

90	15p. Type **17**	1·10	2·00
91	20p. Madagascar turtle dove ("Turtle Dove")	1·25	2·00
92	24p. Great frigate bird ("Greater Frigate")	1·40	2·00
93	30p. Green-backed heron ("Little Green Heron")	1·50	2·25
94	34p. Great sand plover ("Greater Sand Plover")	1·60	2·25
95	41p. Crab plover	1·75	2·50
96	45p. Crested tern	4·50	2·50
97	54p. Lesser crested tern	2·25	3·00
98	62p. White tern ("Fairy Tern")	2·25	3·00
99	71p. Red-footed booby	2·25	3·00
100	80p. Common mynah ("Indian Mynah")	2·50	3·25
101	£1 Madagascar red fody ("Madagascar Fody")	3·25	3·50

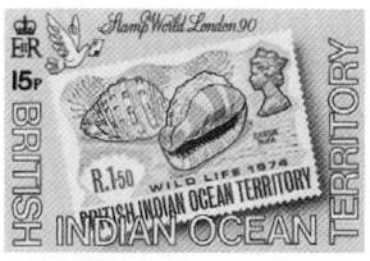

18 1974 Wildlife 1r.50 Stamp

1990. "Stamp World London 90" International Stamp Exhibition. Multicoloured.

102	15p. Type **18**	4·50	3·25
103	20p. 1976 Wildlife 2r. stamp	5·00	3·50
104	34p. 1975 Diego Garcia map 2r. stamp	8·50	5·50
105	54p. 1969 "Nordvaer" 1r. stamp	10·00	7·50

1990. 90th Birthday of Queen Elizabeth the Queen Mother. As T **34** of Ascension.

106	24p. multicoloured	3·50	3·50
107	£1 black and ochre	6·50	6·50

DESIGNS—21×36 mm: Lady Elizabeth Bowes-Lyon, 1923. 29×37 mm: £1 Queen Elizabeth and her daughters, 1940.

19 Territory Flag

1990. 25th Anniv of British Indian Ocean Territory. Multicoloured.

108	20p. Type **19**	4·00	4·50
109	24p. Coat of arms	4·00	4·50
MS110	63×99 mm. £1 map of Chagos Archipelago	9·50	12·00

20 Postman emptying Pillar Box

1991. British Indian Ocean Territory Administration. Multicoloured.

111	20p. Type **20**	1·50	2·50
112	24p. Commissioner inspecting guard of Royal Marines	1·75	2·50
113	34p. Policeman outside station	3·50	4·50
114	54p. Customs officers boarding yacht	4·25	6·00

21 *Experiment* (E.I.C. survey brig), 1786

1991. Visiting Ships. Multicoloured.

115	20p. Type **21**	2·00	3·00
116	24p. *Pickering* (American brig), 1819	2·25	3·25
117	34p. *Emden* (German cruiser), 1914	3·00	4·25
118	54p. H.M.S. *Edinburgh* (destroyer), 1988	3·75	5·50

1992. 40th Anniv of Queen Elizabeth II's Accession. As T **143** of Ascension. Multicoloured.

119	15p. Catholic chapel, Diego Garcia	1·75	1·40
120	20p. Planter's house, Diego Garcia	2·00	1·60
121	24p. Railway tracks on wharf, Diego Garcia	4·50	2·25
122	34p. Three portraits of Queen Elizabeth	3·50	2·50
123	54p. Queen Elizabeth II	3·50	2·75

22 R.A.F. Consolidated PBY-5 Catalina (flying boat)

1992. Visiting Aircraft. Multicoloured.

124	20p. Type **22**	1·50	2·50
125	24p. R.A.F. Hawker Siddeley Nimrod M.R.2 (maritime reconnaissance aircraft)	1·75	2·50
126	34p. Lockheed P-3 Orion (transport aircraft)	2·50	3·25
127	54p. U.S.A.A.F. Boeing B-52 Stratofortress (heavy bomber)	3·00	4·50

23 *The Mystical Marriage of St. Catherine* (Correggio)

1992. Christmas. Religious Paintings. Multicoloured.

128	5p. Type **23**	70	80
129	24p. *Madonna* (anon)	1·25	1·60
130	34p. *Madonna* (anon) (different)	1·40	2·25
131	54p. *The Birth of Jesus* (Kaspar Jele)	1·75	3·50

24 Coconut Crab and Rock

1993. Endangered Species. Coconut Crab. Multicoloured.

132	10p. Type **24**	1·25	1·25
133	10p. Crab on beach	1·25	1·25
134	10p. Two crabs	1·25	1·25
135	15p. Crab climbing coconut tree	1·50	1·50

1993. 75th Anniv of Royal Air Force. As T **149** of Ascension. Multicoloured.

136	20p. Vickers Virginia Mk X	1·00	1·50
137	24p. Bristol Bulldog IIA	1·10	1·50
138	34p. Short S.25 Sunderland Mk III	1·25	2·00
139	54p. Bristol Blenheim Mk IV	2·00	3·25
MS140	110×77 mm. 20p. Douglas DC-3 Dakota; 20p. Gloster G.41 Javelin; 20p. Blackburn Beverley C1; 20p. Vickers VC-10	7·50	8·00

25 *Stachytarpheta urticifolia*

1993. Christmas. Flowers. Multicoloured.

141	20p. Type **25**	80	1·50
142	24p. *Ipomea pes-caprae*	80	1·50
143	34p. *Sida pusilla*	1·10	2·25
144	54p. *Catharanthus roseus*	1·75	3·50

1994. "Hong Kong '94" International Stamp Exhibition. Nos. 92 and 101 optd **HONG KONG '94** and emblem.

145	24p. Great frigate bird ("Greater Frigate")	5·00	3·00
146	£1 Madagascar red fody ("Madagascar Fody")	6·50	7·50

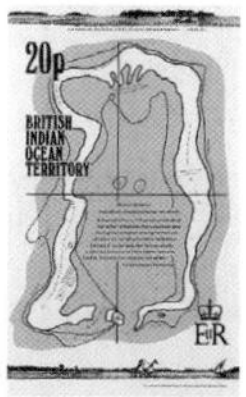

26 Forrest's Map of Diego Garcia, 1778

1994. 18th-century Maps. Each black and blue.

147	20p. Type **26**	70	1·50
148	24p. Blair's plan of Diego Garcia harbour, 1786–87	75	1·60
149	34p. Blair's chart of Chagos Archipelago, 1786–87	80	1·75
150	44p. Plan of part of Diego Garcia, 1774	90	1·90
151	54p. Fontaine's plan of Diego Garcia, 1770	1·10	2·00

27 *Junonia villida*

1994. Butterflies. Multicoloured.

152	24p. Type **27**	1·50	1·75
153	30p. *Petrelaea dana*	1·75	2·50
154	56p. *Hypolimnas misippus*	2·75	4·00

28 Short-tailed Nurse Sharks

1994. Sharks. Multicoloured.

155	15p. Type **28**	4·25	3·50
156	20p. Silver-tipped sharks	4·25	3·50
157	24p. Black-finned reef shark	4·25	3·50
158	30p. Oceanic white-tipped sharks	4·75	4·00
159	35p. Black-tipped shark	5·00	4·50
160	41p. Smooth hammerhead	5·00	4·50
161	46p. Sickle-finned lemon shark	5·00	4·50
162	55p. White-tipped reef shark	6·00	5·50
163	65p. Tiger sharks	6·50	5·50
164	74p. Indian sand tiger	6·50	6·00
165	80p. Great hammerhead	6·50	6·00
166	£1 Great white shark	7·50	7·00

1995. 50th Anniv of End of Second World War. As T **161** of Ascension. Multicoloured.

167	20p. Military cemetery	1·75	1·75
168	24p. Rusty 6-inch naval gun at Cannon Point	2·00	1·75
169	30p. Short S.25 Sunderland flying boat	2·25	2·25
170	56p. H.M.I.S. *Clive* (sloop)	3·50	3·75
MS171	75×85 mm. £1 Reverse of 1939–45 War Medal (vert)	2·50	3·00

29 Dolphin (fish)

1995. Gamefish. Multicoloured.

172	20p. Type **29**	1·75	1·60
173	24p. Sailfish	1·90	1·60
174	30p. Wahoo	2·50	2·50
175	56p. Striped marlin	3·50	3·75

30 *Terebra crenulata*

1996. Sea Shells. Multicoloured.

176	20p. Type **30**	1·25	1·50
177	24p. *Bursa bufonia*	1·25	1·50
178	30p. *Nassarius papillosus*	1·75	2·00
179	56p. *Lopha cristagalli*	3·00	3·25

1996. 70th Birthday of Queen Elizabeth II. As T **165** of Ascension, each incorporating a different photograph of the Queen. Multicoloured.

180	20p. View of lagoon from south	90	1·00
181	24p. Manager's House, Peros Banhos	1·00	1·00
182	30p. Wireless hut, Peros Banhos	1·25	1·40
183	56p. Sunset	1·75	2·00
MS184	64×66 mm. £1 Queen Elizabeth II	3·25	3·50

31 Loggerhead Turtle

1996. Turtles. Multicoloured.

185	20p. Type **31**	1·00	1·25
186	24p. Leatherback turtle	1·10	1·25
187	30p. Hawksbill turtle	1·40	1·60
188	56p. Green turtle	2·00	2·50

32 Commissioner's Representative (naval officer)

1996. Uniforms. Multicoloured.

189	20p. Type **32**	1·00	1·10
190	24p. Royal Marine officer	1·10	1·10
191	30p. Royal Marine in battle-dress	1·50	1·75
192	56p. Police officers	2·25	2·75

1997. "HONG KONG '97" International Stamp Exhibition. Sheet 130×90 mm, containing design as No. 163. Multicoloured.

MS193	65p. Tiger sharks	2·00	2·75

1997. Return of Hong Kong to China. Sheet 130×90 mm, containing design as No. 164, but with "1997" imprint date.

MS194	74p. Indian sand tiger	2·75	3·50

1997. Golden Wedding of Queen Elizabeth and Prince Philip. As T **173** of Ascension. Multicoloured.

195	20p. Queen Elizabeth at Bristol, 1994	1·60	1·75
196	20p. Prince Philip competing in Royal Windsor Horse Show, 1996	1·60	1·75
197	24p. Queen Elizabeth in phaeton, Trooping the Colour, 1987	1·60	1·75
198	24p. Prince Philip	1·60	1·75
199	30p. Queen Elizabeth and Prince Philip with Land Rover	1·60	1·75
200	30p. Queen Elizabeth at Balmoral	1·60	1·75
MS201	110×71 mm. £1.50, Queen Elizabeth and Prince Philip in landau (horiz)	9·00	9·50

Nos. 195/6, 197/8 and 199/20 respectively were printed together, *se-tenant*, with the backgrounds forming a compsite design.

33 H.M.S. *Richmond* (frigate) and H.M.S. *Beaver* (frigate)

1997. Exercise Ocean Wave. Multicoloured.

202	24p. Type **33**	2·00	1·75
203	24p. H.M.S. *Illustrious* (aircraft carrier) launching BAe (Hawker) Sea Harrier	2·00	1·75
204	24p. H.M.S. *Beaver*	2·00	1·75
205	24p. Royal Yacht *Britannia*, R.F.A. *Sir Percival* and H.M.S. *Beaver*	2·00	1·75
206	24p. Royal Yacht *Britannia*	2·00	1·75
207	24p. H.M.S. *Richmond*, H.M.S. *Beaver* and H.M.S. *Gloucester* (destroyer)	2·00	1·75
208	24p. H.M.S. *Richmond*	2·00	1·75
209	24p. Aerial view of H.M.S. *Illustrious*	2·00	1·75
210	24p. H.M.S. *Gloucester* (wrongly inscr "Sheffield")	2·00	1·75
211	24p. H.M.S. *Trenchant* (submarine) and R.F.A. *Diligence*	2·00	1·75
212	24p. R.F.A. *Fort George* replenishing H.M.S. *Illustrious* and H.M.S. *Gloucester*	2·00	1·75
213	24p. Aerial view of H.M.S. *Richmond*, H.M.S. *Beaver* and H.M.S. *Gloucester*	2·00	1·75

1998. Diana, Princess of Wales Commemoration. Sheet 145×70 mm, containing vert designs as T **177** of Ascension. Multicoloured.

MS214	26p. Wearing patterned jacket, 1993; 26p. Wearing heart-shaped earrings, 1988; 34p. Wearing cream jacket, 1993; 60p. Wearing blue blouse, 1982 (sold at £1.46 + 20p. charity premium)	2·50	3·75

1998. 80th Anniv of the Royal Air Force. As T **178** of Ascension. Multicoloured.

215	26p. Blackburn Iris	1·25	1·10
216	34p. Gloster Gamecock	1·50	1·40
217	60p. North American SF-86 Sabre F.4	2·50	2·50
218	80p. Avro Type **694** Lincoln	3·00	3·00
MS219	110×77 mm. 34p. Sopwith Baby (seaplane); 34p. Martinsyde Elephant; 34p. de Havilland Tiger Moth; 34p. North American Mustang III	6·00	7·50

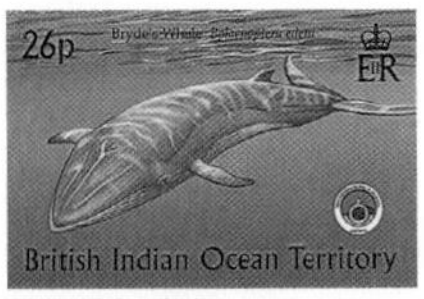

34 Bryde's Whale

1998. International Year of the Ocean. Multicoloured.

220	26p. Type **34**	2·50	2·50
221	26p. Striped dolphin	2·50	2·50
222	34p. Pilot whale	2·50	2·50
223	34p. Spinner dolphin	2·50	2·50

35 *Westminster* (East Indiaman), 1837

1999. Ships. Multicoloured.

224	2p. Type **35**	50	1·00
225	15p. *Sao Cristovao* (Spanish galleon), 1589	1·50	1·25
226	20p. *Sea Witch* (U.S. clipper), 1849	1·50	1·25
227	26p. H.M.S. *Royal George* (ship of the line), 1778	1·75	1·25
228	34p. *Cutty Sark* (clipper), 1883	2·75	1·75
229	60p. *Mentor* (East Indiaman), 1789	3·50	3·50
230	80p. H.M.S. *Trinculo* (brig), 1809	3·75	4·00
231	£1 *Enterprise* (paddle-steamer), 1825	4·75	5·00
232	£1.15 *Confiance* (French privateer), 1800	5·00	5·50
233	£2 *Kent* (East Indiaman), 1820	8·00	9·00

36 *Cutty Sark* (clipper)

1999. "Australia '99" World Stamp Exhibition, Melbourne. Sheet 150×75 mm, containing T **36** and similar horiz design. Multicoloured.

MS234	60p. Type **36**; 60p. *Thermopylae* (clipper)	6·00	8·00

37 Field Vole (Colin Sargent)

2000. "The Stamp Show 2000", International Stamp Exhibition, London. "Shoot a Stamp" Competition Winners. Sheet 150×100 mm, containing T **37** and similar vert designs. Multicoloured.

MS235	26p. Type **37**; 34p. Atlantic puffin (P. J. Royal); 55p. Red fox (Jim Wilson); £1 European robin ("Robin") (Harry Smith)	10·00	11·00

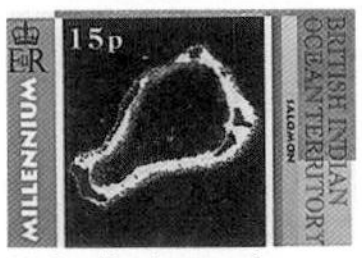

38 Satellite Image of Salomon Island

2000. New Millennium. Satellite Images of Islands. Multicoloured.

236	15p. Type **38**	1·60	1·60
237	20p. Egmont	1·75	1·75
238	60p. Blenheim Reef	2·75	3·00
239	80p. Diego Garcia	3·00	3·25

39 Queen Elizabeth the Queen Mother

2000. Queen Elizabeth the Queen Mother's 100th Birthday. Multicoloured.

240	26p. Type **39**	1·40	1·40
241	34p. Wearing green hat and outfit	1·40	1·40
MS242	113×88 mm. 55p. In blue hat and outfit	4·75	5·50

40 *Delonix regia*

2000. Christmas Flowers. Multicoloured.

243	26p. Type **40**	1·75	1·75
244	34p. *Barringtonia asiatica*	2·00	2·00
245	60p. *Zephyranthes rosea*	3·50	4·00

2000. "HONG KONG 2001" Stamp Exhibition. Sheet 150×90 mm, containing T **41** and similar design showing butterfly. Multicoloured.

MS246	26p. Type **41**; 34p. *Junonia villida chagoensis*	3·00	3·50

42 H.M.S. *Turbulent*

2001. Centenary of Royal Navy Submarine Service. Multicoloured (except Nos. 248 and 250).

247	26p. Type **42**	1·75	2·00
248	26p. H.M.S. *Churchill* (grey and black)	1·75	2·00
249	34p. H.M.S. *Resolution*	2·00	2·50
250	34p. H.M.S. *Vanguard*	2·00	2·50
251	60p. H.M.S. *Otter* (73×27 mm)	2·50	3·00
252	60p. H.M.S. *Oberon* (73×27 mm) (grey and black)	2·50	3·00

43 Cushion Star

2001. Endangered Species. Seastars. Multicoloured.

253	15p. Type **43**	1·25	1·25
254	26p. Azure sea star	1·75	1·50
255	34p. Crown-of-Thorns	1·90	1·75
256	56p. Banded bubble star	3·00	3·50

44 *Scadoxus multiflora*

2001. Plants (1st series). Flowers. Multicoloured.

257	26p. Type **44**	1·75	1·75
258	34p. *Striga asiatica*	2·00	2·00
MS259	173×78 mm. Nos. 257/8 and 10p. *Catharanthus roseus* (horiz); 60p. *Argusia argentea* (horiz); 70p. *Euphorbia cyathophora* (horiz)	5·50	6·50

In No. **MS**259 the 60p. is inscribed "argentia" in error.

45 Crab Plovers on Beach

2001. Birdlife World Bird Festival. Crab Plovers. Sheet 175×80 mm, containing T **45** and similar multicoloured designs.

MS260	50p. Type **45**; 50p. Crab plover catching crab (vert); 50p. Head of crab plover (vert); 50p. Crab plovers in flight; 50p. Crab plover standing on one leg	7·50	8·50

2002. Golden Jubilee. As T **200** of Ascension.

261	10p. brown, blue and gold	1·00	1·00
262	25p. multicoloured	1·50	1·50
263	35p. black, blue and gold	1·75	1·75
264	55p. multicoloured	2·50	2·75
MS265	162×95 mm. Nos. 261/4 and 75p. multicoloured	6·50	7·00

DESIGNS—HORIZ: 10p. Princess Elizabeth in pantomime, Windsor, 1943; 25p. Queen Elizabeth in floral hat, 1967; 35p. Princess Elizabeth and Prince Philip on their engagement, 1947; 55p. Queen Elizabeth in evening dress. VERT (38×51 mm)—75p. Queen Elizabeth after Annigoni.

Designs as Nos. 261/4 in No. **MS**265 omit the gold frame around each stamp and the "Golden Jubilee 1952–2002" inscription.

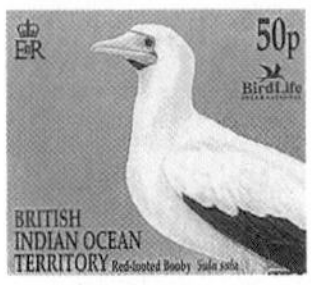

46 Adult Red-footed Booby

2002. Birdlife International. Red-footed Booby. Sheet 175×80 mm, containing T **46** and similar multicoloured designs.

MS266	50p. Type **46**; 50p. Head of dark morph red-footed booby; 50p. Adult bird in flight (vert); 50p. Dark morph on nest (vert); 50p. Fledgling on nest	8·50	10·00

2002. Queen Elizabeth the Queen Mother Commemoration. As T **202** of Ascension.

267	26p. brown, gold and purple	1·25	1·00
268	£1 multicoloured	2·75	3·00
MS269	145×70 mm. £1 black and gold; £1 multicoloured	7·00	8·00

DESIGNS: 26p. Lady Elizabeth Bowes-Lyon, 1921; £1 (No. 268) Queen Mother, 1986; £1 brownish black and gold (No. **MS**269) Queen Elizabeth at garden party, 1951; £1 multicoloured (No. **MS**269) Queen Mother at Cheltenham Races, 1994.

Designs in No. **MS**269 omit the "1900–2002" inscription and the coloured frame.

47 Microgoby

2002. Tenth Anniv of Friends of Chagos (conservation association). Reef Fish. Multicoloured.

270	2p. Type **47**	45	70
271	15p. Angel fish	1·25	1·25
272	26p. Surgeonfish	1·50	1·50
273	34p. Trunkfish	1·75	1·75
274	58p. Soldierfish	2·75	3·25
275	£1 Chagos anemonefish	5·00	6·00

48 *Halgerda tesselata*

2003. Sea Slugs. Multicoloured.

276	2p. Type **48**	40	70
277	15p. *Notodoris minor*	90	90
278	26p. *Nembrotha lineolata*	1·10	1·10
279	50p. *Chromodoris quadricolor*	2·00	2·50
280	76p. *Glossodoris cincta*	2·75	3·50
281	£1.10 *Chromodoris cf leopardus*	3·50	4·50

2003. 50th Anniv of Coronation. As T **206** of Ascension. Multicoloured.

282	£1 Queen Elizabeth II wearing Imperial State Crown in Coronation Coach	3·50	3·75
283	£2 Queen with members of Royal Family in Coronation robes	6·50	7·50
MS284	95×115 mm. £1 As No. 282; £2 As No. 283	10·00	11·00

Nos. 282/3 have red frame; stamps from **MS**284 have no frame and country name in mauve panel.

2003. As T **207** of Ascension.

285	£2.50 black, pink and red	7·00	7·50

2003. 21st Birthday of Prince William of Wales. As T **208** of Ascension. Multicoloured.

286	50p. Prince William at Cirencester Polo Club	2·25	2·25
287	£1 With Prince Charles on skiing holiday and at Cirencester Polo Club	3·75	3·00

2003. Centenary of Powered Flight. As Type **209** of Ascension. Multicoloured.

288	34p. Avro Type 683 Lancaster	2·00	2·00
289	34p. de Havilland D.H.98 Mosquito	2·00	2·00
290	58p. Hawker Hurricane	3·00	3·00
291	58p. Supermarine Spitfire	3·00	3·00
292	76p. Vickers-Armstrong Wellington	3·50	3·50
293	76p. Lockheed C-130 Hercules	3·50	3·50
MS294	233×85 mm. 26p. Boeing E-3A Sentry AWACS; 26p. Boeing B-17 Flying Fortress; 26p. Lockheed P-3 Orion; 26p. Consolidated B-24 Liberator; 26p. Lockheed C-141 StarLifter; 26p. Supermarine Walrus; 26p. Short S.25 Sunderland (flying boat); 26p. Supermarine Stranraer; 26p. PBY Catalina; 26p. Supermarine Sea Otter	10·00	12·00

49 *Pacific Marlin* (fisheries patrol ship)

2004. Fisheries Patrol. Multicoloured.

MS295	150×110 mm. 34p. Type **49**; 34p. Marlin; 58p. Skipjack tuna; 58p. Yellowfin tuna; 76p. Swordfish; 76p. Bigeye tuna	12·00	13·00

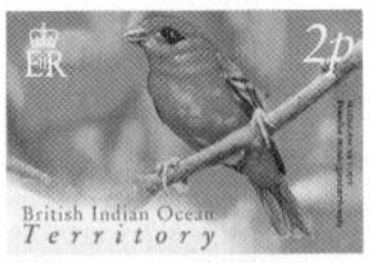

50 Madagascar Red Fody ("Madagascar Fody")

2004. Birds. Multicoloured.

296	2p. Type **50**	50	85
297	14p. Zebra dove ("Barred Ground Dove")	1·25	1·25
298	20p. Common mynah ("Indian Mynah")	1·50	1·25
299	26p. Cattle egret	1·75	1·25
300	34p. White tern ("Fairy Tern")	2·00	1·40
301	58p. Blue-faced booby ("Masked Booby")	2·75	2·75
302	76p. Great frigate bird	4·00	4·00
303	80p. White-tailed tropic bird	4·00	4·00
304	£1.10 Green-backed heron ("Little Green Heron")	5·00	5·50
305	£1.34 Pacific golden plover	6·00	7·00
306	£1.48 Garganey ("Garganey Teal")	6·50	7·50
307	£2.50 Bar-tailed godwit	9·50	11·00

51 Coconut Crab

2004. Crabs. Multicoloured.

308	26p. Type **51**	1·10	80
309	34p. Land crab	1·40	1·00
310	76p. Rock crab	3·00	3·25
311	£1.10 Ghost crab	4·00	5·00

52 Two Hawksbill Turtle Babies

2005. Turtles. Multicoloured.

312	26p. Type **52**	1·50	1·50
313	26p. Baby Green turtle	1·50	1·50
314	34p. Adult Hawksbill turtle	2·00	2·00
315	34p. Adult Green turtle	2·00	2·00
316	76p. Hawksbill turtle swimming	3·50	3·50
317	£1.10 Green turtle swimming	4·50	4·50
MS318	90×63 mm. £1.70 As No. 317	6·50	7·50

No. **MS**318 commemorates the Turtle Cove Clean-up operation sponsored by Cable and Wireless.

2005. Bicentenary of Battle of Trafalgar (1st issue). As T **216** of Ascension. Multicoloured.

319	26p. Tower Sea Service Pistol, 1796	1·40	1·40
320	26p. HMS *Phoebe*	1·40	1·40
321	34p. Boatswain RN, 1805	1·75	1·75
322	34p. HMS *Harrier*	1·75	1·75
323	76p. Portrait of Admiral Nelson	3·25	3·75
324	76p. HMS *Victory* (horiz)	3·25	3·75
MS325	120×79 mm. £1.10 HMS *Minotaur*; £1.10 HMS *Spartiate*	7·50	8·50

No. 324 contains traces of powdered wood from HMS *Victory*.

See also Nos. 344/6.

53 HMAS *Wollongong*, September 1942

2005. 60th Anniv of the End of World War II. "Route to Victory". As T **53**. Multicoloured.

326	26p. Type **53**	1·00	1·00
327	26p. *Ondina* (Dutch tanker) and HMS *Bengal* attacked by Japanese surface raiders, 11 November 1942	1·00	1·00
328	26p. HMS *Pathfinder* (arrived at Diego Garcia, 4 April 1944)	1·00	1·00
329	26p. HMS *Lossie* (rescued survivors from Australian freighter *Nellore*, 29 June 1944)	1·00	1·00
330	26p. US Liberty Ship *Jean Nicolet* (sunk by Japanese, 2 July 1944)	1·00	1·00
331	34p. General Douglas MacArthur and landing party wading ashore	1·40	1·40
332	34p. General Bernard Montgomery and tanks in North African desert	1·40	1·40
333	34p. General George Patton and tanks	1·40	1·40
334	34p. Winston Churchill and St. Paul's Cathedral	1·40	1·40
335	34p. US Pres. Franklin Roosevelt and steelworks	1·40	1·40

54 Blacktip Reef Shark

2005. Sharks and Rays. Multicoloured.

336	26p. Type **54**	1·00	1·00
337	26p. Grey reef shark	1·00	1·00
338	34p. Silvertip shark	1·40	1·40
339	34p. Tawny nurse shark	1·40	1·40
340	34p. Spotted eagle ray	1·40	1·40
341	34p. Manta ray	1·40	1·40
342	76p. Porcupine ray	2·75	3·00
343	£2 Feathertail stingray	7·00	8·00

2005. Bicentenary of the Battle of Trafalgar (2nd issue). As T **220** of Ascension. Multicoloured.

344	26p. HMS *Victory*	1·25	1·00
345	34p. Ships engaged in battle (horiz)	1·75	1·50
346	£2 Admiral Lord Nelson	7·00	8·50

55 Crab on Beach

2005. 40th Anniv of British Indian Ocean Territory. T **55** and similar vert designs. Multicoloured.

MS347	205×129 mm. 34p. Type **55**; 34p. Two hermit crabs on beach; 34p. Blue-faced boobies at nest; 34p. Outline map of Indian Ocean and lesser frigate bird; 34p. Pair of imperial angelfish; 34p. Pair of racoon butterflyfish; 34p. Moorish idol (fish); 34p. Outline map of British Indian Ocean Territory and turtle	12·00	14·00

The stamps within No. **MS**347 form a composite background design showing a beach and coral reef.

2006. 80th Birthday of Queen Elizabeth II. As T **223** of Ascension. Multicoloured.

348	26p. Princess Elizabeth	1·25	1·00
349	34p. Queen Elizabeth II, c. 1952	1·75	1·50
350	76p. Wearing tiara	3·00	3·50
351	£1.10 Wearing headscarf	3·50	4·00
MS352	144×75 mm. £1 As No. 349; £1 As No. 350	7·00	8·00

56 Dusky Angelfish

2006. Marine Life (1st series). Angelfish. Sheet 205×129 mm containing T **56** and similar horiz designs. Multicoloured.

MS353	26p. Type **56**; 26p. Two-spined angelfish; 26p. Bicolour angelfish; 34p. Orangeback angelfish; 34p. Emperor angelfish; £2 Threespot angelfish	14·00	15·00

The stamps and margins of No. **MS**353 form a composite design showing a coral reef.

See also Nos. **MS**354, **MS**356 and **MS**372.

2006. Marine Life (2nd series). Butterflyfish. Sheet 205×129 mm containing horiz designs as T **56**. Multicoloured.

MS354	26p. Melon butterflyfish; 26p. Raccoon butterflyfish; 26p. Scrawled butterflyfish; 34p. Longnose butterflyfish; 34p. Threadfin butterflyfish; £2 Masked bannerfish	14·00	15·00

The stamps and margins of No. **MS**354 form a composite design showing a coral reef.

57 Great Frigatebird

2006. BirdLife International. Barton Point Nature Reserve. Sheet 170×85 mm containing T **57** and similar horiz designs. Multicoloured.

MS355	26p. Type **57**; 26p. Black-naped tern; 26p. Yellow-billed tropicbird; 26p. White tern; 26p. Brown noddy; £2 Red-footed booby	14·00	15·00

The stamps within No. **MS**355 form a composite design.

2007. Marine Life (3rd series). Parrotfish. Sheet 205×129 mm containing horiz designs as T **56**. Multicoloured.

MS356	54p. Common parrotfish; 54p. Daisy parrotfish; 54p. Bicolour parrotfish; 54p. Bridled parrotfish; 90p. Indian Ocean steephead parrotfish; 90p. Ember parrotfish	14·00	16·00

The stamps and margins of No. **MS**356 form a composite design showing a coral reef.

58 Princess Elizabeth and Lt. Philip Mountbatten, c. 1947

2007. Diamond Wedding of Queen Elizabeth II and Duke of Edinburgh. Multicoloured.

357	54p. Type **58**	1·60	1·60
358	54p. Wedding procession and crowds, 1949	1·60	1·60
359	90p. Princess Elizabeth and Lt. Philip Mountbatten arm in arm, c. 1947	3·00	3·00
360	90p. Wedding ceremony, 1949	3·00	3·00
MS361	125×85 mm. £2.14 Princess Elizabeth and Lt. Philip Mountbatten, c. 1947 (42×56 mm)	8·00	8·50

59 Charles Darwin and Beach with Tropic Bird, Terns and Turtle

2007. 125th Death Anniv of Charles Darwin. Multicoloured.

362	54p. Type **59**	2·00	2·00
363	54p. HMS *Beagle*	2·00	2·00
364	90p. Turtles	3·75	3·75
365	90p. Coral reef	3·75	3·75

60 Pomarine Skua pursuing Tropic Bird

2007. BirdLife International. Pomarine Skua (*Stercorarius pomarinus*). Multicoloured.

366	54p. Type **60**	2·25	2·25
367	54p. Pomarine skua pursuing booby	2·25	2·25
368	54p. Pair of pomarine skuas in flight	2·25	2·25
369	54p. Pair of pomarine skuas on beach	2·25	2·25
370	90p. Pomarine skua pursuing terns	4·00	4·00
371	90p. Pomarine skua on sea	4·00	4·00

2008. Marine Life (4th series). Damselfish. Sheet 205×129 mm containing horiz designs as T **56**. Multicoloured.

MS372	54p. *Chrysiptera unimaculata* (onespot demoiselle); 54p. *Abudefdufseptemfasciatus* (banded sergeant); 54p. *Plectroglyphidodon johnstonianus* (Johnston Island damsel); 54p. *Amphiprion chagosensis* (Chagos anemonefish); 90p. *Chromisatripectoralis* (black-axil chromis); 90p. *Pomacentrus caeruleus* (caerulean damsel)	9·50	10·00

The stamps and margins of No. **MS**372 form a composite design showing a coral reef.

61 Royal Marines

2008. Military Uniforms. Multicoloured.

373	27p. Type 61	1·40	1·40
374	27p. Royal Engineers	1·40	1·40
375	54p. Sepoys, East India Company Army	2·25	2·25
376	54p. Officer, East India Company Army	2·25	2·25
377	54p. Artillery Corps	2·25	2·25
378	54p. Sergeant, Royal Military Police	2·25	2·25

62 Avro 504

2008. 90th Anniv of the Royal Air Force. Multicoloured.

379	27p. Type **62**	1·25	1·25
380	27p. Short Sunderland	1·25	1·25
381	27p. de Havilland Mosquito	1·25	1·25
382	27p. Vickers VC10	1·25	1·25
383	54p. English Electric Canberra	2·00	2·00
MS384	70×110 mm. £1.72 King George V, Marshal of the RAF (vert). Wmk inverted	9·50	10·00

63 Pte Harry Lamin, 1918

2008. 90th Anniv of the End of World War I. Designs showing soldiers and their letters home. Multicoloured.

385	50p. Type **63**	2·00	2·25
386	50p. Second Lt. Eric Heaton, 1916	2·00	2·25
387	50p. Pte Dennis Harry Wilson, 1917	2·00	2·25
388	50p. Second Lt. Eric Rose, 1917	2·00	2·25
389	50p. Sgt.-Major Francis Proud, 1915	2·00	2·25
390	50p. Second Lt. Charles Roberts, 1917	2·00	2·25
MS391	110×70 mm. £1 UK Overseas Territories Wreath of Remembrance	3·75	4·25

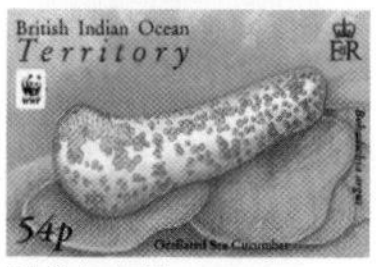

64 *Bohadschia argus* (ocellated sea cucumber)

2008. Endangered Species. Sea Cucumbers. Multicoloured.

392	54p. Type **64**	2·75	2·75
393	54p. *Thelenota ananas* (pineapple sea cucumber)	2·75	2·75
394	90p. *Pearsonothuria graeffei* (Graeffe's sea cucumber)	4·00	4·00
395	90p. *Stichopus chloronotus* (dark green sea cucumber)	4·00	4·00

65 HMS *Endeavour* (Cook)

2009. Seafaring and Exploration. Multicoloured.

396	54p. Type **65**	2·75	2·75
397	54p. HMS *Victory* (Nelson)	2·75	2·75
398	54p. HMS *Beagle* (Darwin)	2·75	2·75
399	54p. SS *Windsor Castle* (landing of Captain Raymond, Diego Garcia, 1884)	2·75	2·75
400	54p. SMS *Fürst Bismarck* (German armoured cruiser, 1900)	2·75	2·75
401	54p. HMS *Edinburgh* (1983)	2·75	2·75
MS402	110×70 mm. £1.30 Vasco da Gama (Portuguese navigator, sighted Chagos Archipelago, early 16th century) (vert)	6·00	6·50

2009. Centenary of Naval Aviation. Multicoloured (except **MS**407).

403	27p. Short S.38	1·75	1·75
404	27p. Sopwith Pup	1·75	1·75
405	54p. Supermarine Scimitar	3·00	3·00
406	54p. Westland Wessex helicopter	3·00	3·00
MS407	110×70 mm. £1.72 Sqn. Cdr. E. H. Dunning landing aircraft on HMS *Furious*, 1917 (black, deep ultramarine and rosine)	10·00	11·00

2009. International Year of Astronomy. 40th Anniv of First Moon Landing. Multicoloured.

408	54p. Development of early rockets *Corporal* and *Private*	2·50	2·50
409	54p. *Flying Bedstead*, 1964	2·50	2·50
410	54p. Apollo Launch Site, 1969	2·50	2·50
411	54p. Space Transportation System 71 launch, 1995	2·50	2·50
412	90p. ESA Columbus Laboratory STS 122, 2008	4·00	4·00
MS413	100×80 mm. £1.50 *Savoring the Moment* (astronaut Jack Schmitt on Moon) (Alan Bean) (39×59 mm)	6·50	7·00

66 Two Band Anemonefish (*Amphiprion bicinctus*)

2009. Fish, Fauna, Flora and Coves. Multicoloured.

414	1p. Type **66**	10	10

415	2p. Angelfish (*Centropyge bicolor*)	15	15
416	5p. Royal poinciana (*Delonix regia*)	25	25
417	12p. Beach morning glory (*Ipomoea pes-caprae*)	55	55
418	27p. Bay cedar (*Suriana maritima*)	1·25	1·25
419	45p. Scaevola bush (*Scaevola taccada*)	2·00	2·00
420	54p. Madagascan red fody (*Foudia madagascariensis*)	2·50	2·50
421	90p. Greater frigatebird (*Fregata minor*)	4·00	4·00
422	£1.30 Sharks Cove	5·00	5·00
423	£1.72 Turtle Cove	6·25	6·25
424	£2.64 Hawksbill turtle	8·75	8·75
425	£3.02 Sicklefin lemon shark (*Negaprion acutidens*)	11·00	11·00
MS426	194×134 mm. Nos. 414/25	38·00	38·00

67 *Lentinus* sp.

2009. Fungi. Multicoloured.

427	54p. Type **67**	2·50	2·50
428	54p. *Entoloma* sp.	2·50	2·50
429	90p. *Leucocoprinus* sp.	4·00	4·00
430	90p. *Pycnoporus* sp.	4·00	4·00

68 Hugh Dowding

2010. 70th Anniv of the Battle of Britain. Aces and Leaders. Multicoloured.

431	50p. Type **68**	2·50	2·50
432	50p. Bob Stanford-Tuck	2·50	2·50
433	50p. Ginger Lacey	2·50	2·50
434	50p. Eric Lock	2·50	2·50
435	50p. Mike Crossley	2·50	2·50
436	50p. Bob Doe	2·50	2·50
MS437	110×70mm. $1.50 Sir Douglas Bader	6·00	6·50

69 Great Britain George V 1934 1½d. Stamp

2010. London 2010 Festival of Stamps and Centenary of Accession of King George V

MS438	**69** £1.50 multicoloured	6·00	6·50

70 Archer and Mounted Knight, Battle of Hastings, 1066

2010. Great Battles. Multicoloured.

439	50p. Type **70**	2·00	2·00
440	50p. Mounted knight carrying standard and archers, Battle of Agincourt, 1415	2·00	2·00
441	50p. Mounted knights, Battle of Bosworth, 1485	2·00	2·00
442	50p. Cavalry, Battle of Naseby, 1645	2·00	2·00
443	50p. Soldiers, Battle of Culloden, 1746	2·00	2·00
444	50p. Duke of Wellington on horseback and soldiers, Battle of Waterloo, 1815	2·00	2·00
445	50p. Soldiers and cavalryman, Battle of Alma, 1854	2·00	2·00
446	50p. British soldiers, Battle of Rorke's Drift, 1879	2·00	2·00
447	50p. Soldiers, Siege of Mafeking, 1899	2·00	2·00
448	50p. Soldiers, Battle of the Somme, 1916	2·00	2·00
449	50p. Soldiers, Battle of El Alamein, 1942	2·00	2·00
450	50p. Normandy Landings, 1944	2·00	2·00

Nos. 439/50 were each printed in sheetlets of six stamps with enlarged illustrated margins.

2011. Queen Elizabeth II and Prince Philip 'A Lifetime of Service'. Multicoloured.

451	54p. Queen Elizabeth II, c. 1952	1·75	1·75
452	54p. Queen Elizabeth II and Prince Philip (black/white photo), c. 1972	1·75	1·75
453	54p. Queen Elizabeth II and Prince Philip, c. 1955	1·75	1·75
454	54p. Queen Elizabeth II and Prince Philip (seen in profile), c. 2010	1·75	1·75
455	54p. Queen Elizabeth II and Prince Philip, c. 1970	1·75	1·75
456	54p. Prince Philip, c. 1955	1·75	1·75
MS457	174×163 mm. Nos. 451/6 and three stamp-size labels	10·50	10·50
MS458	110×70 mm. £3.02 Queen Elizabeth II and Prince Philip, c. 2007	10·50	10·50

71 Prince William and Miss Catherine Middleton

2011. Royal Wedding (1st issue)

MS459	**71** £3 multicoloured	11·00	11·00

2011. Royal Wedding (2nd issue). Multicoloured.

460	54p. Duke and Duchess of Cambridge waving from State Landau	1·90	1·90
461	54p. Duke and Duchess of Cambridge kissing on Buckingham Palace balcony (vert)	1·90	1·90
462	90p. Duke and Duchess of Cambridge at Westminster Abbey after wedding ceremony (vert)	2·75	2·75
463	90p. Leaving Buckingham Palace in car with 'JUST WED' numberplate	2·75	2·75

72 Field of Poppies, Flanders

2011. 90th Anniv of the Royal British Legion. Multicoloured.

464	50p. Type **72**	1·75	1·75
465	50p. Silhouette of soldier and war memorials	1·75	1·75
466	50p. War graves	1·75	1·75
467	50p. Poppy Appeal	1·75	1·75
468	50p. Aircraft dropping poppies	1·75	1·75
469	50p. Ex-servicemen wearing medals	1·75	1·75
470	50p. Wooden remembrance crosses with poppies	1·75	1·75
471	50p. Festival of Remembrance	1·75	1·75
MS472	94×64 mm. £1.50 Remembrance Day service	5·25	5·25

73 Queen Elizabeth II, c. 1970

2012. Diamond Jubilee. Multicoloured.

473	54p. Type **73**	1·90	1·90
474	54p. Queen Elizabeth II wearing blue hat, c. 1975	1·90	1·90
475	54p. Queen Elizabeth II wearing red, c. 1980	1·90	1·90
476	54p. Queen Elizabeth II wearing tiara, pendant and pearl earrings. c. 1955 (colour photo)	1·90	1·90
477	54p. Queen Elizabeth II wearing tiara, c. 1955 (black/white photo)	1·90	1·90
478	54p. Queen Elizabeth II, c. 2005	1·90	1·90
MS479	174×164 mm. Nos. 473/8 and three stamp-size labels	10·25	10·25
MS480	110×70 mm. £3.02 Queen Elizabeth II wearing red cardigan and pearl necklace, c. 1975	16·00	16·00

PARCEL POST STAMPS

2002. Tenth Anniv of Friends of Chagos (conservation association). Reef Fish. Sheet 115×95 mm, containing horiz design as T **47**. Multicoloured.

PMS1	£1.90 Parrotfish	11·00	12·00

Pt. 1

BRITISH LEVANT

Stamps used at British post offices in the Turkish Empire. These offices closed in 1914. The stamps were again in use after 1918, during the British Occupation of Turkey.

Stamps of Great Britain surcharged or overprinted.

40 paras = 1 piastre.

A. BRITISH POST OFFICES IN TURKISH EMPIRE I. TURKISH CURRENCY

1885. Queen Victoria stamps surch in **PARAS** or **PIASTRES**.

1	**64**	40pa. on 2½d. lilac	£130	1·25
4	**74**	40pa. on 2½d. purple on blue	14·00	10
7	**71**	40pa. on ½d. red	£425	£100
2	**62**	80pa. on 5d. green	£225	9·50
5	**78**	80pa. on 5d. purple & blue	18·00	30
6	**81**	4pi. on 10d. purple and red	42·00	8·00
3a	**58**	12pi. on 2s.6d. lilac	60·00	26·00

1902. King Edward VII stamps surch in **PARAS** or **PIASTRES**.

29	-	30pa. on 1½d. purple & grn	6·50	55
8	**83**	40pa. on 2½d. blue	22·00	10
9	-	80pa. on 5d. purple and blue	14·00	2·00
13	**83**	1pi. on 2½d. blue	25·00	10
30	-	2pi. on 5d. purple and blue	23·00	3·25
10	-	4pi. on 10d. purple and red	20·00	4·00
21	-	5pi. on 1s. green and red	4·25	16·00
11	-	12pi. on 2s.6d. purple	38·00	38·00
12	-	24pi. on 5s. red	32·00	42·00

1906. Surch **1 Piastre**.

15	1pi. on 2d. green and red	£1400	£650

1909. King Edward VII stamps surch in **PIASTRE PARAS**.

17	-	1pi. 10pa. on 3d. pur on yell	12·00	50·00
18	-	1pi. 30pa. on 4d. grn & brn	5·00	18·00
19	-	1pi. 30pa. on 4d. orange	22·00	70·00
20	**83**	2pi. 20pa. on 6d. purple	26·00	70·00

1910. King Edward VII stamps surch in **PIASTRES**.

22	-	1¼pi. on 3d. purple on yellow	65	1·00
23	-	1¾pi. on 4d. orange	50	60
24	**83**	2½pi. on 6d. purple	2·50	65

1913. King George V stamps surch.

35	**105**	30pa. on 1½d. brown	3·50	14·00
41	**105**	30pa. on ½d. green	75	16·00
36a	**104**	1pi. on 2½d. blue	13·00	15
37	**106**	1¼pi. on 3d. violet	8·00	4·25
42	**104**	1½pi. on 1d. red	1·75	1·50
38	**106**	1¾pi. on 4d. grey-green	3·50	8·00
43	**104**	3¾pi. on 2½d. blue	1·25	25
39	**108**	4pi. on 10d. blue	10·00	27·00
44	**106**	4½pi. on 3d. violet	2·00	3·75
40	**108**	5pi. on 1s. brown	42·00	60·00
45	**107**	7½pi. on 5d. brown	50	10
46	**108**	15pi. on 10d. blue	70	15
47	**108**	18¾pi. on 1s. brown	4·25	4·25
48	**109**	45pi. on 2s.6d. brown	20·00	45·00
49	**109**	90pi. on 5s. red	25·00	30·00
50	**109**	180pi. on 10s. blue	45·00	40·00

II. BRITISH CURRENCY

1905. King Edward VII stamps optd **LEVANT**.

L1	**83**	½d. green	8·50	15
L2	**83**	1d. red	14·00	15
L3	-	1½d. purple and green	6·00	2·25
L4a	-	2d. green and red	3·75	8·00
L5	**83**	2½d. blue	8·50	20·00
L6	-	3d. purple and yellow	7·00	12·00
L7	-	4d. green and brown	9·50	70·00
L8	-	5d. purple and blue	16·00	38·00
L9	**83**	6d. purple	12·00	25·00
L10	**83**	1s. green and red	42·00	50·00

1911. King George V stamps optd **LEVANT**.

L12	**98**	½d. green	2·25	2·75
L14	**101**	½d. green	2·25	20
L16	**105**	½d. green	1·75	3·25
L13	**99**	1d. red	50	8·00
L15	**102**	1d. red	2·25	1·60
L17	**104**	1d. red	30	7·50
L18	**106**	2d. orange	2·50	40·00
L19	**106**	3d. violet	7·50	10·00
L20	**106**	4d. green	5·00	21·00
L21	**107**	5d. brown	12·00	28·00
L22a	**107**	6d. purple	29·00	8·50
L23	**108**	1s. brown	18·00	8·50
L24	**109**	2s.6d. brown	38·00	95·00

B. BRITISH FIELD OFFICE IN SALONICA

1916. King George V stamps of Great Britain optd **Levant**.

S1	**105**	½d. green	70·00	£325
S2	**104**	1d. red	70·00	£325
S3	**106**	2d. orange	£190	£450
S4	**106**	3d. violet	£160	£450
S5	**106**	4d. green	£190	£450
S6	**107**	6d. purple	£100	£400
S7	**108**	9d. black	£400	£750
S8	**108**	1s. brown	£350	£650

The above stamps were optd at Salonica during the war of 1914–18.

Pt. 1

BRITISH OCCUPATION OF ITALIAN COLONIES

Issues for use in Italian colonies occupied by British Forces. Middle East Forces overprints were used in Cyrenaica, Dodecanese Islands, Eritrea, Italian Somaliland and Tripolitania.

Middle East Forces.
12 pence = 1 shilling; 20 shillings = 1 pound.

Cyrenaica.
10 milliemes = 1 piastre; 20 shillings = 1 pound.

Eritrea.
100 cents = 1 shilling.

MIDDLE EAST FORCES

1942. Stamps of Great Britain optd **M.E.F.**

M11	**128**	1d. red	1·50	10
M12	**128**	2d. orange	2·00	1·25
M13	**128**	2½d. blue	1·75	10
M4	**128**	3d. violet	2·00	30
M5	**129**	5d. brown	2·00	30
M16	**129**	6d. purple	40	10
M17	**130**	9d. olive	85	10
M18	**130**	1s. brown	50	10
M19	**131**	2s.6d. green	7·00	1·00
M20	**131**	5s. red	26·00	17·00
M21	**131**	10s. blue (No. 478a)	38·00	10·00

PRICES. Our prices for Nos. M1/21 in used condition are for stamps with identifiable postmarks of the territories in which they were issued. These stamps were also used in the United Kingdom with official sanction, from the summer of 1950 onwards, and with U.K. postmarks are worth about 25 per cent less.

POSTAGE DUE STAMPS

1942. Postage Due stamps of Great Britain optd **M.E.F.**

MD1	**D1**	½d. green	30	13·00
MD2	**D1**	1d. red	30	1·75
MD3	**D1**	2d. black	1·75	1·25
MD4	**D1**	3d. violet	50	4·25
MD5	**D1**	1s. blue	3·75	13·00

CYRENAICA

24 Mounted Warrior

25 Mounted Warrior

1950

136	**24**	1m. brown	4·00	7·50
137	**24**	2m. red	4·00	7·50
138	**24**	3m. yellow	4·00	6·50
139	**24**	4m. green	4·00	7·50
140	**24**	5m. grey	4·00	6·50
141	**24**	8m. orange	4·00	3·50
142	**24**	10m. violet	4·00	2·50
143	**24**	12m. red	4·00	3·00
144	**24**	20m. blue	4·00	2·50
145	**25**	50m. blue and brown	14·00	9·00
146	**25**	100m. red and black	22·00	11·00
147	**25**	200m. violet and blue	30·00	32·00
148	**25**	500m. yellow and green	55·00	80·00

POSTAGE DUE STAMPS

D26

1950

D149	**D26**	2m. brown	60·00	£110
D150	**D26**	4m. green	60·00	£110
D151	**D26**	8m. red	60·00	£120
D152	**D26**	10m. orange	60·00	£120
D153	**D26**	20m. yellow	60·00	£140
D154	**D26**	40m. blue	60·00	£180
D155	**D26**	100m. black	60·00	£200

ERITREA BRITISH MILITARY ADMINISTRATION

1948. Stamps of Great Britain surch **B.M.A. ERITREA** and value in cents or shillings.

E1	**128**	5c. on ½d. green	2·75	65
E2	**128**	10c. on 1d. red	2·00	2·75
E3	**128**	20c. on 2d. orange	2·75	2·25
E4	**128**	25c. on 2½d. blue	2·00	60
E5	**128**	30c. on 3d. violet	2·25	4·50
E6	**129**	40c. on 5d. brown	2·75	4·25
E7	**129**	50c. on 6d. purple	2·00	1·00
E7a	**130**	65c. on 8d. red	7·00	2·00
E8	**130**	75c. on 9d. olive	3·50	75
E9	**130**	1s. on 1s. brown	2·50	50
E10	**131**	2s.50 on 2s.6d. green	10·00	10·00
E11	**131**	5s. on 5s. red	12·00	24·00
E12	-	10s. on 10s. blue (No. 478a)	26·00	24·00

BRITISH ADMINISTRATION

1950. Stamps of Great Britain surch **B.A. ERITREA** and value in cents or shillings.

E13	**128**	5c. on ½d. green	1·50	8·00
E26	**128**	5c. on ½d. orange	1·75	2·50
E14	**128**	10c. on 1d. red	40	3·00
E27	**128**	10c. on 1d. blue	1·50	75
E15	**128**	20c. on 2d. orange	1·00	80
E28	**128**	20c. on 2d. brown	1·75	30
E16	**128**	25c. on 2½d. blue	1·00	60
E29	**128**	25c. on 2½d. red	1·75	30
E17	**128**	30c. on 3d. violet	40	2·25
E18	**129**	40c. on 5d. brown	2·50	1·75
E19	**129**	50c. on 6d. purple	40	20
E20	**130**	65c. on 8d. red	5·50	1·50
E21	**130**	75c. on 9d. olive	1·50	25
E22	**130**	1s. on 1s. brown	40	15
E23	**131**	2s.50 on 2s.6d. green	9·00	5·00
E24	**131**	5s. on 5s. red	9·00	12·00
E25	-	10s. on 10s. blue (No. 478a)	75·00	70·00

1951. Nos. 509/11 of Great Britain surch **B.A. ERITREA** and value in cents and shillings.

E30	**147**	2s.50 on 2s.6d. green	21·00	30·00
E31	-	5s. on 5s. red	23·00	30·00
E32	-	10s. on 10s. blue	27·00	32·00

POSTAGE DUE STAMPS

1948. Postage Due stamps of Great Britain surch **B.M.A ERITREA** and new value in cents and shillings.

ED1	**D1**	5c. on ½d. green	10·00	22·00
ED2	**D1**	10c. on 1d. red	10·00	24·00
ED3	**D1**	20c. on 2d. black	17·00	16·00
ED4	**D1**	30c. on 3d. violet	13·00	17·00
ED5	**D1**	1s. on 1s. blue	21·00	32·00

1950. Postage Due stamps of Great Britain surch **B.A. ERITREA** and new value in cents or shillings.

ED6	5c. on ½d. green	16·00	60·00
ED7	10c. on 1d. red	16·00	21·00
ED8	20c. on 2d. black	16·00	25·00
ED9	30c. on 3d. violet	20·00	42·00
ED10	1s. on 1s. blue	21·00	42·00

SOMALIA BRITISH OCCUPATION

1943. Stamps of Great Britain optd **E.A.F.** (East African Forces).

S1	**128**	1d. red	1·50	1·25
S2	**128**	2d. orange	1·75	1·75
S3	**128**	2½d. blue	2·00	3·50
S4	**128**	3d. violet	1·75	15
S5	**129**	5d. brown	2·50	40
S6	**129**	6d. purple	2·25	1·50
S7	**130**	9d. olive	2·75	3·50
S8	**130**	1s. brown	3·75	15
S9	**131**	2s.6d. green	28·00	14·00

PRICES. Our prices for Nos. S1/9 in used condition are for stamps with identifiable postmarks of the territories in which they were issued. These stamps were also used in the United Kingdom with official sanction, from the summer of 1950, and with U.K. postmarks are worth about 25 per cent less.

BRITISH MILITARY ADMINISTRATION

1948. Stamps of Great Britain surch **B.M.A. SOMALIA** and new value in cents and shillings.

S10	**128**	5c. on ½d. green	1·25	2·00
S11	**128**	15c. on 1½d. brown	1·75	15·00
S12	**128**	20c. on 2d. orange	3·00	5·00
S13	**128**	25c. on 2½d. blue	2·25	4·50
S14	**128**	30c. on 3d. violet	2·25	9·00
S15	**129**	40c. on 5d. brown	1·25	20
S16	**129**	50c. on 6d. purple	50	2·00
S17	**130**	75c. on 9d. olive	2·00	26·00
S18	**130**	1s. on 1s. brown	1·25	20
S19	**131**	2s.50 on 2s.6d. green	7·00	25·00
S20	**131**	5s. on 5s. red	18·00	60·00

BRITISH ADMINISTRATION

1950. Stamps of Great Britain surch **B.A. SOMALIA** and value in cents and shillings.

S21	**128**	5c. on ½d. green	20	3·00
S22	**128**	15c. on 1½d. brown	75	17·00
S23	**128**	20c. on 2d. orange	75	7·50
S24	**128**	25c. on 2½d. blue	50	12·00
S25	**128**	30c. on 3d. violet	1·25	8·00
S26	**129**	40c. on 5d. brown	55	1·25
S27	**129**	50c. on 6d. purple	50	1·00
S28	**130**	75c. on 9d. olive	2·00	10·00
S29	**130**	1s. on 1s. brown	60	1·50
S30	**131**	2s.50 on 2s.6d. green	6·00	30·00
S31	**131**	5s. on 5s. red	17·00	50·00

TRIPOLITANIA BRITISH MILITARY ADMINISTRATION

1948. Stamps of Great Britain surch **B.M.A. TRIPOLITANIA** and value in **M.A.L.** (Military Administration lire).

T1	**128**	1l. on ½d. green	1·00	3·50
T2	**128**	2l. on 1d. red	50	15
T3	**128**	3l. on 1½d. brown	50	50
T4	**128**	4l. on 2d. orange	50	70
T5	**128**	5l. on 2½d. blue	50	20
T6	**128**	6l. on 3d. violet	50	40
T7	**129**	10l. on 5d. brown	50	15
T8	**129**	12l. on 6d. purple	50	20
T9	**130**	18l. on 9d. olive	1·25	1·50
T10	**130**	24l. on 1s. brown	2·25	2·50
T11	**131**	60l. on 2s.6d. green	8·00	16·00
T12	**131**	120l. on 5s. red	27·00	28·00
T13	**131**	240l. on 10s. blue (No. 478a)	30·00	£140

BRITISH ADMINISTRATION

1950. As Nos. **T1/13** but surch **B.A. TRIPOLITANIA** and value in **M.A.L.**

T14	**128**	1l. on ½d. green	5·50	13·00
T27	**128**	1l. on ½d. orange	30	9·00
T15	**128**	2l. on 1d. red	4·50	40
T28	**128**	2l. on 1d. blue	30	1·00
T16	**128**	3l. on 1½d. brown	3·50	13·00
T29	**128**	3l. on 1½d. green	30	8·00
T17	**128**	4l. on 2d. orange	4·00	4·50
T30	**128**	4l. on 2d. brown	30	1·25
T18	**128**	5l. on 2½d. blue	2·00	70
T31	**128**	5l. on 2½d. red	30	7·50
T19	**128**	6l. on 3d. violet	3·25	3·25
T20	**129**	10l. on 5d. brown	3·25	4·00
T21	**129**	12l. on 6d. purple	4·50	50
T22	**130**	18l. on 9d. olive	7·00	2·75
T23	**130**	24l. on 1s. brown	6·50	3·75
T24	**131**	60l. on 2s.6d. green	15·00	12·00
T25	**131**	120l. on 5s. red	32·00	35·00
T26	-	240l. on 10s. blue (No. 478a)	50·00	85·00

1951. Nos. 509/11 of Great Britain surch **B.A. TRIPOLITANIA** and value in **M.A.L.**

T32	**147**	60l. on 2s.6d. green	17·00	35·00
T33	-	120l. on 5s. red	17·00	35·00
T34	-	240l. on 10s. blue	50·00	80·00

POSTAGE DUE STAMPS

1948. Postage Due stamps of Great Britain surch **B.M.A. TRIPOLITANIA** and value in **M.A.L.**

TD1	**D1**	1l. on ½d. green	5·50	65·00
TD2	**D1**	2l. on 1d. red	2·50	55·00
TD3	**D1**	4l. on 2d. black	13·00	50·00
TD4	**D1**	6l. on 3d. violet	7·50	26·00
TD5	**D1**	24l. on 1s. blue	29·00	£110

1950. As Nos. **TD1/5** but surch **B.A. TRIPOLITANIA** and value in **M.A.L.**

TD6	1l. on ½d. green	14·00	£100
TD7	2l. on 1d. red	9·00	29·00
TD8	4l. on 2d. black	10·00	45·00
TD9	6l. on 3d. violet	19·00	80·00
TD10	24l. on 1s. blue	55·00	£170

Pt. 1

BRITISH POST OFFICES IN CHINA

Stamps for use in Wei Hai Wei, and the neighbouring islands, leased to Great Britain from 1898 to 1 October 1930, when they were returned to China. The stamps were also used in the Treaty Ports from 1917 until 1922.

100 cents = 1 dollar.

1917. Stamps of Hong Kong (King George V) optd **CHINA**.

18	**24**	1c. brown	3·00	5·50
19	**24**	2c. green	7·00	2·25
3	**24**	4c. red	9·50	1·75
4	**24**	6c. orange	8·50	1·00
5	**24**	8c. grey	15·00	1·25
6	**24**	10c. blue	16·00	30
7	**24**	12c. purple on yellow	18·00	9·00
8	**24**	20c. purple and olive	24·00	1·50
9	**24**	25c. purple	11·00	15·00
11	**24**	30c. purple and orange	48·00	8·50
12b	**24**	50c. black on green	50·00	5·50
13	**24**	$1 purple and blue on blue	80·00	2·50
14	**24**	$2 red and black	£225	75·00
15	**24**	$3 green and purple	£950	£250
16	**24**	$5 green and red on green	£350	£325
17	**24**	$10 purple and black on red	£950	£650

Pt. 1

BRITISH POST OFFICES IN CRETE

40 paras = 1 piastre.

B1

1898

B1	**B1**	20pa. violet	£425	£225

B2

1898

B2	**B2**	10pa. blue	9·50	23·00
B4	**B2**	10pa. brown	11·00	30·00
B3	**B2**	20pa. green	18·00	21·00
B5	**B2**	20pa. red	20·00	18·00

Pt. 1

BRITISH POST OFFICES IN SIAM

Used at Bangkok.

100 cents = 1 dollar.

1882. Stamps of Straits Settlements optd **B** on issue of 1867.

1	**19**	32c. on 2a. yellow	£35000	

On issues of 1867 to 1883.

14	**5**	2c. brown	£650	£375
15	**5**	2c. red	70·00	50·00
13	**9**	2c. on 32c. red (No. 60)	£3500	£3500
16	**5**	4c. red	£750	£350
17	**5**	4c. brown	95·00	80·00
4	**18**	5c. brown	£425	£475
18	**18**	5c. blue	£325	£190
5	**5**	6c. lilac	£300	£140
20	**5**	8c. orange	£200	70·00
21	**19**	10c. grey	£200	90·00
8	**5**	12c. blue	£1100	£500
22	**5**	12c. purple	£350	£160
9	**5**	24c. green	£750	£160
10	**8**	30c. red	£45000	£30000
11	**9**	96c. grey	£7500	£3000

Pt. 1

BRITISH POST AGENCIES IN EASTERN ARABIA

British stamps surcharged for use in parts of the Perisian Gulf.

The stamps were used in Muscat from 1 April 1948 to 29 April 1966; in Dubai from 1 April 1948 to 6 January 1961; In Qatar: Doho from August 1950, Umm Said from February 1956 to 31 March 1957; and in Abu Dhabi from 30 March 1963 (Das Islandfrom December 1960) to 29 March 1964.

Nos 21/2 were placed on sale in Kuwait Post Offices in 1951 and from February to November 1953 due to shortages of stamps "KUWAIT" overprinted. Isolated examples of other values can be found comercially used from Bahrain and Kuwait.

1948. 12 pies = 1 anna; 16 annas = 1 rupee.
1957. 100 naya paise = 1 rupee.

Stamps of Great Britain surch in Indian currency.

1948. King George VI.

16	**128**	½a. on ½d. green	2·75	7·50
35	**128**	½a. on ½d. orange	70	9·00
17	**128**	1a. on 1d. red	3·00	30
36	**128**	1a. on 1d. blue	30	7·50
18	**128**	1½a. on 1½d. brown	16·00	7·00
37	**128**	1½a. on 1½d. green	18·00	40·00
19	**128**	2a. on 2d. orange	2·00	3·25
38	**128**	2a. on 2d. brown	30	8·50
20	**128**	2½a. on 2½d. blue	3·50	8·00
39	**128**	2½a. on 2½d. red	30	16·00
21	**128**	3a. on 3d. violet	3·50	10
40	**129**	4a. on 4d. blue	1·00	3·50
22	**129**	6a. on 6d. purple	4·00	10
23	**130**	1r. on 1s. brown	4·50	60
24	**131**	2r. on 2s.6d. green	10·00	50·00

1948. Royal Silver Wedding.

25	**137**	2½a. on 2½d. blue	2·75	5·00
26	**138**	15r. on £1 blue	25·00	35·00

1948. Olympic Games.

27	**139**	2½a. on 2½d. blue	45	2·50
28	**140**	3a. on 3d. violet	55	2·50
29	-	6a. on 6d. purple	65	2·75
30	-	1r. on 1s. brown	1·40	4·00

1949. 75th Anniv of U.P.U.

31	**143**	2½a. on 2½d. blue	60	3·00
32	**144**	3a. on 3d. violet	60	4·00
33	-	6a. on 6d. purple	60	2·75
34	-	1r. on 1s. brown	2·25	7·00

1951. Pictorial.

41	**147**	2r. on 2s.6d. green	42·00	7·00

1952. Queen Elizabeth.

42	**154**	½a. on ½d. orange	10	2·25
43	**154**	1a. on 1d. blue	10	2·25
44	**154**	1½a. on 1½d. green	10	2·25
45	**154**	2a. on 2d. brown	20	10
46	**155**	2½a. on 2½d. red	10	10
47	**155**	3a. on 3d. lilac	20	1·25
48	**155**	4a. on 4d. blue	2·50	4·00
49	**157**	6a. on 6d. purple	35	10
50	**160**	12a. on 1s.3d. green	7·50	30
51	**160**	1r. on 1s.6d. blue	2·25	10

1953. Coronation.

52	**161**	2½a. on 2½d. red	1·75	3·50
53	-	4a. on 4d. blue	1·75	1·00
54	**163**	12a. on 1s.3d. green	3·00	1·00
55	-	1r. on 1s.6d. blue	3·25	50

1955. Pictorials.

56	**166**	2r. on 2s.6d. brown	9·00	70
57	-	5r. on 5s. red	10·00	2·25

1957. Value in naye paise. Queen Elizabeth II stamps surch **NP** twice (once only on 75n.p.) and value.

79	**157**	1n.p. on 5d. brown	10	20
80	**154**	3n.p. on ½d. orange	55	80
81	**154**	5n.p. on 1d. blue	1·75	3·50
67	**154**	6n.p. on 1d. blue	20	2·75
68	**154**	9n.p. on 1½d. green	50	2·50
83	**154**	10n.p. on 1½d. green	1·00	2·75
69	**154**	12n.p. on 2d. brown	30	2·75
85	**155**	15n.p. on 2½d. red	25	10
71	**155**	20n.p. on 3d. lilac	20	10
72	**155**	25n.p. on 4d. blue	70	8·50
87	**155**	30n.p. on 4½d. brown	40	50
73	**157**	40n.p. on 6d. purple	30	10
89	**158**	50n.p. on 9d. olive	1·00	2·50
75	**160**	75n.p. on 1s.3d. green	2·75	40
91	**159**	1r. on 1s.6d. blue	29·00	9·00
92	**166**	2r. on 2s.6d. brown	14·00	50·00
93	**166**	5r. on 5s. red	30·00	60·00

DESIGN: No. 93 Caernarvon Castle.

1957. World Scout Jubilee Jamboree.

76	**170**	15n.p. on 2½d. red	35	85
77	**171**	25n.p. on 4d. blue	35	85
78	-	75n.p. on 3d. green	40	85

Pt. 1

BRITISH VIRGIN ISLANDS

A group of the Leeward Islands, Br. W. Indies. Used general issues for Leeward Islands concurrently with Virgin Islands stamps until 1 July 1956. A Crown Colony.

1951. 100 cents = 1 West Indian dollar.
1962. 100 cents = 1 U.S. dollar.

1 St. Ursula

2

3

4

1866

1	**1**	1d. green	45·00	60·00
16	**3**	4d. red	42·00	60·00
7	**2**	6d. red	60·00	90·00
11	**4**	1s. black and red	£275	£375

No. 11 has a double-lined frame.

1867. With heavy coloured border.

19	**4**	1s. black and red	70·00	80·00

6

1880

26	**6**	½d. yellow	85·00	85·00
27	**6**	½d. green	6·50	13·00
24	**6**	1d. green	75·00	90·00
29	**6**	1d. red	38·00	40·00
25	**6**	2½d. brown	£110	£130
31	**6**	2½d. blue	2·75	16·00

1887

32	**1**	1d. red	3·75	9·00
35	**3**	4d. brown	35·00	65·00
39	**2**	6d. violet	19·00	50·00
41	**4**	1s. brown	45·00	70·00

1888. No. 18 surch **4D**.

42	4d. on 1s. black and red	£130	£160

8

1899

43	**8**	½d. green	3·75	55
44	**8**	1d. red	5·00	2·50
45	**8**	2½d. blue	12·00	2·75
46	**8**	4d. brown	4·00	18·00
47	**8**	6d. violet	6·50	3·00
48	**8**	7d. green	12·00	6·00
49	**8**	1s. yellow	22·00	35·00
50	**8**	5s. blue	75·00	85·00

9

1904

54	**9**	½d. purple and green	1·00	40
55	**9**	1d. purple and red	2·50	35
56	**9**	2d. purple and brown	7·50	3·50
57	**9**	2½d. purple and blue	3·25	2·00
58	**9**	3d. purple and black	4·25	2·50
59	**9**	6d. purple and brown	3·50	2·50
60	**9**	1s. green and red	6·00	5·00
61	**9**	2s.6d. green and black	35·00	55·00
62	**9**	5s. green and blue	48·00	70·00

11

1913

69	**11**	½d. green	3·75	6·00
70a	**11**	1d. red	2·25	14·00
71	**11**	2d. grey	5·50	28·00
72	**11**	2½d. blue	7·00	9·00
73	**11**	3d. purple on yellow	2·75	6·50
74	**11**	6d. purple	8·00	17·00
75	**11**	1s. black on green	3·25	9·00
76	**11**	2s.6d. black and red on blue	50·00	55·00
77	**11**	5s. green and red on yellow	45·00	£130

1917. Optd **WAR STAMP**.

78c	1d. red	30	3·75
79a	3d. purple on yellow	3·25	14·00

14

1922

86	**14**	½d. green	85	2·75
87	**14**	1d. red	60	60
88	**14**	1d. violet	1·25	5·00
91	**14**	1½d. red	2·00	1·50
92	**14**	2d. grey	1·25	6·00
94	**14**	2½d. orange	1·25	1·75
95	**14**	2½d. blue	11·00	3·50
96	**14**	3d. purple on yellow	2·25	11·00
97	**14**	5d. purple and olive	5·50	45·00
98	**14**	6d. purple	1·75	6·50
83	**14**	1s. black on green	75	14·00
84	**14**	2s.6d. black and red on blue	5·50	11·00
101	**14**	5s. green and red on yellow	19·00	70·00

1935. Silver Jubilee. As T **13** of Antigua.

103	1d. blue and red	1·25	8·00
104	1½d. blue and grey	1·25	7·00
105	2½d. brown and blue	3·75	6·50
106	1s. grey and purple	19·00	35·00

1937. Coronation. As T **2** of Aden.

107	1d. red	1·00	3·25
108	1½d. brown	75	3·00
109	2½d. blue	60	1·50

15 King George VI and Badge of Colony

1938

110a	**15**	½d. green	1·50	1·00
111a	**15**	1d. red	2·50	1·75
112a	**15**	1½d. brown	2·75	1·75
113a	**15**	2d. grey	2·75	1·75
114a	**15**	2½d. blue	3·50	2·75
115a	**15**	3d. orange	2·25	1·00
116a	**15**	6d. mauve	6·00	2·25
117a	**15**	1s. brown	4·00	2·25
118a	**15**	2s.6d. brown	17·00	7·50
119a	**15**	5s. red	17·00	6·50
120	**15**	10s. blue	8·50	9·50
121	**15**	£1 black	10·00	24·00

1946. Victory. As T **9** of Aden.

122	1½d. brown	10	10
123	3d. orange	10	60

1949. Silver Wedding. As T **10/11** of Aden.

124	2½d. blue	10	10
125	£1 grey	16·00	21·00

1949. 75th Anniv of U.P.U. As T **20/23** of Antigua.

126	2½d. blue	30	2·25
127	3d. orange	1·50	2·50
128	6d. mauve	45	40
129	1s. olive	35	50

1951. Inauguration of B.W.I. University College. As T **24/25** of Antigua.

130	3c. black and red	40	2·50
131	12c. black and violet	60	1·75

16 Map

1951. Restoration of Legislative Council.

132	**16**	6c. orange	50	1·50
133	**16**	12c. purple	1·00	50
134	**16**	24c. olive	70	1·00
135	**16**	$1.20 red	2·25	1·00

18 Map of Jost Van Dyke

1952

136	-	1c. black	80	3·50
137	**18**	2c. green	70	30
138	-	3c. black and brown	80	2·50
139	-	4c. red	70	2·75
140	-	5c. red and black	1·50	50
141	-	8c. blue	1·00	2·00
142	-	12c. violet	1·00	2·00
143	-	24c. brown	70	50
144	-	60c. green and blue	5·00	11·00
145	-	$1.20 black and blue	5·50	12·00
146	-	$2.40 green and brown	16·00	17·00
147	-	$4.80 blue and red	18·00	20·00

DESIGNS—VERT: 1c. Sombrero lighthouse; 24c. Badge of Presidency. HORIZ—VIEWS: 3c. Sheep industry; 5c. Cattle industry; 60c. Dead Man's Chest (Is); $1.20, Sir Francis Drake Channel; $2.40, Road Town. HORIZ—MAPS: 4c. Anegada Island; 8c. Virgin Gorda Island; 12c. Tortola Island; $4.80, Virgin Islands.

1953. Coronation. As T **13** of Aden.

148	2c. black and green	30	1·25

29 Map of Tortola

30 Virgin Island Sloop

1956

149	**29**	½c. black and purple	1·25	30
150	-	1c. turquoise and slate	1·50	1·25
151	-	2c. red and black	30	10
152	-	3c. blue and olive	30	30
153	-	4c. brown and turquoise	70	30
154	-	5c. black	50	10
155	-	8c. orange and blue	2·00	40
156	-	12c. blue and red	4·00	75
157	-	24c. green and brown	1·00	65
158	-	60c. blue and orange	8·50	8·00
159	-	$1.20 green and red	4·00	9·50
160	**30**	$2.40 yellow and purple	42·00	13·00
161	-	$4.80 sepia and turquoise	42·00	13·00

DESIGNS—HORIZ: As Type **29**: 1c. Virgin Islands sloop; 2c. Nelthrop Red Poll bull; 3c. Road Harbour; 4c. Mountain travel; 5c. Badge of the Presidency; 8c. Beach scene; 12c. Boat launching; 24c. White cedar tree; 60c. Skipjack tuna ("Bonito"); $1.20, Treasury Square Coronation celebrations. As Type **30**: $4.80, Magnificent frigate bird ("Man-o'-War Bird").

1962. New Currency. Nos. 149/53, 155/61 surch in U.S. Currency.

162	**29**	1c. on ½c. black and purple	30	10
163	-	2c. on 1c. turq & vio	1·75	10
164	-	3c. on 2c. red and black	70	10
165	-	4c. on 3c. blue and olive	30	10
166	-	5c. on 4c. brown & turq	30	10
167	-	8c. on 8c. orange and blue	30	10
168	-	10c. on 12c. blue and red	2·00	10
169	-	12c. on 24c. green & brn	30	10
170	-	25c. on 60c. blue and orange	2·75	45
171	-	70c. on $1.20 green and red	35	45
172	**30**	$1.40 on $2.40 yellow and purple	9·50	4·50
173	-	$2.80 on $4.80 sepia & turq	9·50	4·50

1963. Freedom from Hunger. As T **28** of Aden.

174	25c. violet	20	10

1963. Centenary of Red Cross. As T **33** of Antigua.

175	2c. red and black	15	20
176	25c. red and blue	50	20

1964. 400th Birth Anniv of Shakespeare. As T **34** of Antigua.

177	10c. blue	20	10

43 Skipjack Tuna

44 Soper's Hole

1964

178	**43**	1c. blue and olive	30	2·00
179	**44**	2c. olive and red	15	30
180	**44**	3c. sepia and turquoise	4·75	2·25
181	-	4c. black and red	80	3·00
182	-	5c. black and green	1·75	2·25
183	-	6c. black and orange	30	85
184	-	8c. black and mauve	30	50
185	-	10c. lake and lilac	6·00	1·00
186	-	12c. green and blue	2·50	3·25
187	-	15c. green and black	1·50	2·75
188	-	25c. green and purple	11·00	2·50
189	-	70c. black and brown	4·25	8·50
190	-	$1 green and brown	3·00	2·00
191	-	$1.40 blue and red	24·00	11·00
192	-	$2.80 black and purple	26·00	12·00

DESIGNS—HORIZ (As Type **43**): 2c. Soper's Hole; 3c. Brown pelican; 4c. Dead Man's Chest; 5c. Road Harbour; 6c. Fallen Jerusalem; 8c. The Baths, Virgin Gorda; 10c. Map of Virgiin Islands; 12c. *Youth of Tortola* (Tortola–St Thomas ferry); 15c. The Towers, Tortola; 25c. Beef Island Airfield. VERT (As Type **44**): $1 Virgin Gorda: $1.40, Yachts at anchor. (27½×37½ mm): $2.80, Badge of the Colony.

1965. Centenary of I.T.U. As T **36** of Antigua.

193	4c. yellow and turquoise	20	10
194	25c. blue and buff	45	20

1965. I.C.Y. As T **37** of Antigua.

195	1c. purple and turquoise	10	15
196	25c. green and lavender	30	15

1966. Churchill Commemoration. As T **38** of Antigua.

197	1c. blue	10	40
198	2c. green	35	40
199	10c. brown	75	10
200	25c. violet	1·40	25

1966. Royal Visit. As T **39** of Antigua.

201	4c. black and blue	40	10
202	70c. black and mauve	1·40	45

58 *Atrato I* (paddle-steamer), 1866

1966. Stamp Centenary. Multicoloured.

203	5c. Type **58**	35	10
204	10c. 1d. and 6d. stamps of 1866	35	10
205	25c. Mail transport, Beef Island, and 6d. stamp of 1866	55	10
206	60c. Landing mail at Roadtown, 1866 and 1d. stamp of 1866	1·00	2·50

1966. Nos. 189 and 191/2 surch.

207	**44**	50c. on 70c. blk & brn	1·25	90
208	-	$1.50 on $1.40 blue and red	2·25	2·00
209	-	$3 on $2.80 black and purple	2·25	2·75

1966. 20th Anniv of UNESCO. As T **54/6** of Antigua.

210	2c. multicoloured	10	10
211	12c. yellow, violet and olive	30	10
212	60c. black, purple and orange	1·00	45

63 Map of Virgin Islands

1967. New Constitution.

213	**63**	2c. multicoloured	10	10
214	**63**	10c. multicoloured	15	10
215	**63**	25c. multicoloured	15	10
216	**63**	$1 multicoloured	55	40

64 *Mercury* (cable ship) and Bermuda–Tortola Link

1967. Inauguration of Bermuda–Tortola Telephone Service. Multicoloured.

217	4c. Type **64**	30	10
218	10c. Chalwell Telecommunications Station	20	10
219	50c. *Mercury* (cable ship)	60	30

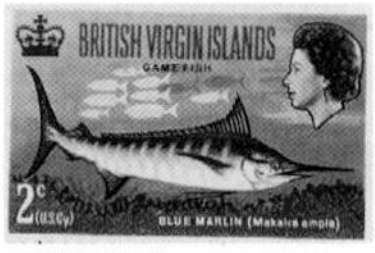

67 Blue Marlin

1968. Game Fishing. Multicoloured.

220	2c. Type **67**	10	1·00
221	10c. Cobia	25	10
222	25c. Wahoo	55	10
223	40c. Fishing launch and map	85	85

1968. Human Rights Year. Nos. 185 and 188 optd **1968 INTERNATIONAL YEAR FOR HUMAN RIGHTS**.

224	10c. lake and lilac	20	10
225	25c. green and purple	30	40

72 Dr. Martin Luther King, Bible, Sword and Armour Gauntlet

1968. Martin Luther King Commemoration.

226	**72**	4c. multicoloured	25	20
227	**72**	25c. multicoloured	40	40

73 de Havilland Canada DH-6 Twin Otter 100

1968. Opening of Beef Island Airport Extension. Multicoloured.

228		2c. Type **73**	25	1·25
229		10c. Hawker Siddeley H.S.748 airliner	40	10
230		25c. de Havilland Canada DH-114 Heron 2 airplane	45	10
231		$1 Royal Engineers' cap badge	50	2·00

77 Long John Silver and Jim Hawkins

1969. 75th Death Anniv of Robert Louis Stevenson. Scenes from *Treasure Island*.

232	**77**	4c. blue, yellow and red	20	15
233	-	10c. multicoloured	20	10
234	-	40c. brown, black and blue	25	30
235	-	$1 multicoloured	45	1·00

DESIGNS—HORIZ: 10c. Jim Hawkins escaping from the pirates; $1 Treasure trove. VERT: 40c. The fight with Israel Hands.

82 Yachts in Road Harbour, Tortola

1969. Tourism. Multicoloured.

236		2c. Tourist and yellow-finned grouper (fish)	15	50
237		10c. Type **82**	30	10
238		20c. Sun-bathing at Virgin Gorda National Park	40	20
239		$1 Tourist and Pipe Organ cactus at Virgin Gorda	90	1·50

Nos. 236 and 239 are vert.

85 Carib Canoe

1970

240	**85**	½c. buff, brown and sepia	10	1·50
241	-	1c. blue and green	15	75
242	-	2c. orange, brown and slate	40	1·00
243	-	3c. red, blue and sepia	30	1·25
244	-	4c. turquoise, blue & brn	30	50
245	-	5c. green, pink and black	30	10
246	-	6c. violet, mauve and green	40	2·25
247	-	8c. green, yellow and sepia	50	6·00
248	-	10c. blue and brown	50	15
249	-	12c. yellow, red and brown	65	1·50
250	-	15c. green, orange and brown	6·00	85
251	-	25c. green, blue and purple	4·00	1·75
252	-	50c. mauve, green and brown	3·25	1·50
253	-	$1 salmon, green and brown	4·00	3·75
254	-	$2 buff, slate and grey	8·50	7·00
255	-	$3 ochre, blue and sepia	2·75	4·50
256	-	$5 violet and grey	2·75	5·00

DESIGNS: 1c. *Santa Maria* (Columbus's flagship); 2c. *Elizabeth Bonaventure* (Drake's flagship); 3c. Dutch buccaneer, c. 1660; 4c. *Thetis*, 1827 (after etching by E. W. Cooke); 5c. Henry Morgan's ship (17th-century); 6c. H.M.S. *Boreas* (Captain Nelson, 1784); 8c. H.M.S. *Eclair*, 1804; 10c. H.M.S. *Formidable*, 1782; 12c. H.M.S. *Nymph*, 1778; 15c. *Windsor Castle* (sailing packet) engaging *Jeune Richard* (French brig), 1807; 25c. H.M.S. *Astrea*, 1808; 50c. Wreck of R.M.S. *Rhone*, 1867; $1 Tortola sloop; $2 H.M.S. *Frobisher*; $3 *Booker Viking* (cargo liner), 1967; $5 Hydrofoil *Sun Arrow*.

102 *A Tale of Two Cities*

1970. Death Centenary of Charles Dickens.

257	**102**	5c. black, red and grey	25	1·00
258	-	10c. black, blue and green	35	10
259	-	25c. black, green and yellow	50	25

DESIGNS: 10c. *Oliver Twist*; 25c. *Great Expectations*.

103 Hospital Visit

1970. Centenary of British Red Cross. Multicoloured.

260		4c. Type **103**	20	45
261		10c. First Aid class	20	10
262		25c. Red Cross and coat of arms	50	55

104 Mary Read

1970. Pirates. Multicoloured.

263		½c. Type **104**	10	15
264		10c. George Lowther	30	10
265		30c. Edward Teach (Blackbeard)	60	25
266		60c. Henry Morgan	80	1·00

105 Children and "UNICEF"

1971. 25th Anniv of UNICEF.

267	**105**	15c. multicoloured	10	10
268	**105**	30c. multicoloured	20	25

1972. Royal Visit of Princess Margaret. Nos 244 and 251 optd **VISIT OF H.R.H. THE PRINCESS MARGARET 1972 1972.**

269		4c. blue, light blue and brown	40	15
270		25c. green, blue and plum	60	45

107 Seaman of 1800

1972. "Interpex" Stamp Exhibition, New York. Naval Uniforms. Multicoloured.

271		½c. Type **107**	10	40
272		10c. Boatswain, 1787–1807	35	10
273		30c. Captain, 1795–1812	85	55
274		60c. Admiral, 1787–95	1·25	2·75

1972. Royal Silver Wedding. As T **52** of Ascension, but with sailfish and *Sir Winston Churchill* (cadet schooner) in background.

275		15c. blue	25	15
276		25c. blue	25	15

109 Blue Marlin

1972. Game Fish. Multicoloured.

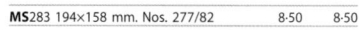

277		½c. Type **109**	15	1·40
278		½c. Wahoo	15	1·40
279		15c. Yellow-finned tuna ("Allison tuna")	65	25
280		25c. White marlin	75	30
281		50c. Sailfish	1·25	1·50
282		$1 Dolphin	2·00	2·50
MS283		194×158 mm. Nos. 277/82	8·50	8·50

110 J. C. Lettsom

1973. "Interpex 1973" (Quakers). Multicoloured.

284		½c. Type **110**	10	15
285		10c. Lettsom House (horiz)	15	10
286		15c. Dr. W. Thornton	20	10
287		30c. Dr. Thornton and Capitol, Washington (horiz)	25	20
288		$1 William Penn (horiz)	60	1·10

111 Green-throated Carib and Antillean Crested Hummingbird

1973. First Issue of Coinage. Coins and local scenery. Multicoloured.

289		1c. Type **111**	10	30
290		5c. "Zenaida Dove" (5c. coin)	60	10
291		10c. "Ringed Kingfisher" (10c. coin)	75	10
292		25c. "Mangrove Cuckoo" (25c. coin)	95	15
293		50c. "Brown Pelican" (50c. coin)	1·10	1·00
294		$1 "Magnificent Frigate-bird ($1 coin)	1·40	2·00

1973. Royal Wedding. As T **47** of Anguilla. Multicoloured. Background colours given.

301		5c. brown	10	10
302		50c. blue	20	20

112 *Virgin and Child* (Pintoricchio)

1973. Christmas. Multicoloured.

303		½c. Type **112**	10	10
304		3c. *Virgin and Child* (Lorenzo di Credi)	10	10
305		25c. *Virgin and Child* (Crivelli)	15	10
306		50c. *Virgin and Child with St. John* (Luini)	30	40

113 Crest of the *Canopus* (French)

1974. "Interpex 1974". Naval Crests. Multicoloured.

307		5c. Type **113**	15	10
308		18c. U.S.S. *Saginaw*	25	25
309		25c. H.M.S. *Rothesay*	25	30
310		50c. H.M.C.S. *Ottawa*	45	60
MS311		196×128 mm. Nos. 307/10	1·25	4·50

114 Christopher Columbus

1974. Historical Figures.

312	**114**	5c. orange and black	20	10
313	-	10c. blue and black	20	10
314	-	25c. violet and black	25	25
315	-	40c. brown and deep brown	45	75
MS316		84×119 mm. Nos. 312/15	1·00	2·25

PORTRAITS: 10c. Sir Walter Raleigh; 25c. Sir Martin Frobisher; 40c. Sir Francis Drake.

115 Atlantic Trumpet Triton

1974. Seashells. Multicoloured.

317		5c. Type **115**	30	15
318		18c. West Indian murex	50	30
319		25c. Bleeding tooth	60	35
320		75c. Virgin Islands latirus	1·25	2·25
MS321		146×95 mm. Nos. 317/20	3·00	6·50

116 Churchill and St. Mary, Aldermanbury, London

1974. Birth Centenary of Sir Winston Churchill. Multicoloured.

322		10c. Type **116**	15	10
323		50c. St. Mary, Fulton, Missouri	35	50
MS324		141×108 mm. Nos. 322/3	80	1·40

117 H.M.S. *Boreas*

1975. "Interpex 1975" Stamp Exhibition, New York. Ships' Figure-heads. Multicoloured.

325		5c. Type **117**	20	10
326		18c. *Golden Hind*	50	15
327		40c. H.M.S. *Superb*	50	25
328		85c. H.M.S. *Formidable*	1·00	1·50
MS329		192×127 mm. Nos. 325/8	1·75	8·00

118 Rock Beauty

1975. Fish. Multicoloured.

330		½c. Type **118**	15	50
331		1c. Long-spined squirrelfish	40	2·75
332		3c. Queen triggerfish	1·00	2·75
333		5c. Blue angelfish	30	20
334		8c. Stoplight parrotfish	30	25
335		10c. Queen angelfish	30	25
336		12c. Nassau grouper	40	30
337		13c. Blue tang	40	30
338		15c. Sergeant major	40	35
339		18c. Spotted jewfish	80	1·50
340		20c. Bluehead wrasse	60	80
341		25c. Grey angelfish	1·00	60
342		60c. Glass-eyed snapper	1·25	2·25
343		$1 Blue chromis	1·75	1·75
344		$2.50 French angelfish	2·00	4·50
345		$3 Queen parrotfish	2·50	4·50
346		$5 Four-eyed butterflyfish	2·75	6·00

119 St. George's Parish School (first meeting-place, 1950)

1975. 25th Anniv of Restoration of Legislative Council. Multicoloured.

347		5c. Type **119**	10	10
348		25c. Legislative Council Building	20	10
349		40c. Mace and gavel	25	15
350		75c. Commemorative scroll	35	65

120 Copper Mine Point

1976. Historic Sites. Multicoloured.

351	5c. Type **120**	10	10
352	18c. Pleasant Valley	20	10
353	50c. Callwood Distillery	40	30
354	75c. The Dungeon	60	65

121 Massachusetts Brig *Hazard*

1976. Bicentenary of American Revolution. Multicoloured.

355	8c. Type **121**	30	15
356	22c. American privateer *Spy*	45	20
357	40c. *Raleigh* (American frigate)	55	60
358	75c. Frigate *Alliance* and H.M.S. *Trepassy*	80	1·25
MS359	114×89 mm. Nos. 355/8	2·75	11·00

122 Government House, Tortola

1976. Fifth Anniv of Friendship Day with U.S. Virgin Islands. Multicoloured.

360	8c. Type **122**	10	10
361	15c. Government House, St. Croix (vert)	10	10
362	30c. Flags (vert)	15	10
363	75c. Government seals	50	40

123 Royal Visit, 1966

1977. Silver Jubilee. Multicoloured.

364	8c. Type **123**	10	10
365	30c. The Holy Bible	15	15
366	60c. Presentation of Holy Bible	25	40

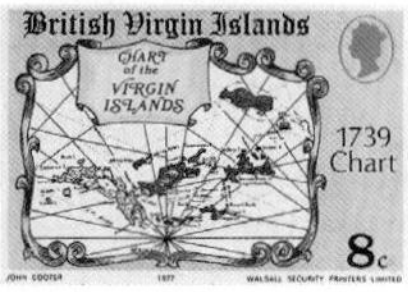

124 Chart of 1739

1977. 18th-century Maps. Multicoloured.

367	8c. Type **124**	40	10
368	22c. French map, 1758	55	30
369	30c. Map from English and Danish surveys, 1775	65	65
370	75c. Map of 1779	85	1·50

1977. Royal Visit. As Nos. 364/6 inscr "SILVER JUBILEE ROYAL VISIT".

371	5c. Type **123**	10	10
372	25c. The Holy Bible	20	10
373	50c. Presentation of Holy Bible	35	25

125 Divers checking Equipment

1978. Tourism. Multicoloured.

374	½c. Type **125**	10	10
375	5c. Cup coral on wreck of *Rhone*	20	10
376	8c. Sponge formation on wreck of *Rhone*	25	10
377	22c. Cup coral and sponges	45	15
378	30c. Sponges inside cave	60	20
379	75c. Marine life	90	85

126 Fire Coral

1978. Corals. Multicoloured.

380	8c. Type **126**	25	15
381	15c. Staghorn coral	40	30
382	40c. Brain coral	75	85
383	75c. Elkhorn coral	1·50	1·60

127 Iguana

1978. 25th Anniv of Coronation.

384	-	50c. brown, green and silver	20	40
385	-	50c. multicoloured	20	40
386	**127**	50c. brown, green and silver	20	40

DESIGNS: No. 384, Plantagenet Falcon; 385, Queen Elizabeth II.

128 Lignum Vitae

1978. Flowering Trees. Multicoloured.

387	8c. Type **128**	15	10
388	22c. Ginger Thomas	20	15
389	40c. Dog almond	30	20
390	75c. White cedar	45	70
MS391	131×95 mm. Nos. 387/90	1·00	3·00

129 *Eurema lisa*

1978. Butterflies. Multicoloured.

392	5c. Type **129**	25	10
393	22c. *Agraulis vanillae*	40	20
394	30c. *Heliconius charithonia*	1·10	30
395	75c. *Hemiargus hanno*	1·40	1·25
MS396	159×113 mm. No. 392×6 and No. 393×3	2·50	5·50

130 Spiny Lobster

1978. Wildlife Conservation. Multicoloured.

397	5c. Type **130**	15	10
398	15c. Large iguana (vert)	25	10
399	22c. Hawksbill turtle	40	15
400	75c. Black coral (vert)	75	90
MS401	130×153 mm. Nos. 397/400	1·40	3·75

131 Strawberry Cactus

1979. Native Cacti. Multicoloured.

402	½c. Type **131**	10	10
403	5c. Snowy cactus	15	10
404	13c. Barrel cactus	20	20
405	22c. Tree cactus	25	35
406	30c. Prickly pear	30	40
407	75c. Dildo cactus	40	1·00

132 West Indian Girl

1979. International Year of the Child. Multicoloured.

408	5c. Type **132**	10	10
409	10c. African boy	10	10
410	13c. Asian girl	10	10
411	$1 European boy	50	85
MS412	91×114 mm. Nos. 408/11	70	1·50

133 1956 Road Harbour 3c. Definitive Stamp

1979. Death Centenary of Sir Rowland Hill.

413	**133**	5c. dp blue, blue & green	10	10
414	-	13c. blue and mauve	10	10
415	-	75c. blue and purple	45	50
MS416		37×91 mm. $1 blue and red	70	1·25

DESIGNS (39×27 mm)—13c. 1880 2½d. red-brown; 75c. Great Britain 1910 unissued 2d. Tyrian plum. (40×28 mm)—$1 1867 1s. "Missing Virgin" error.

134 Pencil Urchin

1979. Marine Life. Multicoloured.

417	½c. Calcified algae	40	2·75
418	1c. Purple-tipped sea anemone	55	2·75
419	3c. Common starfish	1·00	2·75
420	5c. Type **134**	1·25	2·25
421	8c. Atlantic trumpet triton	1·25	1·75
422	10c. Christmas tree worms	30	1·25
423a	13c. Flamingo tongue snail	1·50	75
424	15c. Spider crab	40	1·00
425	18c. Sea squirts	2·00	4·25
426	20c. True tulip	55	1·50
427	25c. Rooster-tail conch	1·25	4·00
428	30c. West Indian fighting conch	2·50	1·50
429	60c. Mangrove crab	1·50	3·00
430	$1 Coral polyps	1·25	4·25
431	$2.50 Peppermint shrimp	1·25	4·00
432	$3 West Indian murex	1·25	4·50
433	$5 Carpet anemone	1·75	5·50

135 Rotary Athletics Meeting, Tortola

1980. 75th Anniv of Rotary International. Multicoloured.

434	8c. Type **135**	10	10
435	22c. Paul P. Harris (founder)	15	10
436	60c. Mount Saga, Tortola ("Creation of National Park")	30	40
437	$1 Rotary anniversary emblem	55	75
MS438	149×148 mm. Nos. 434/7	1·00	3·75

136 Brown Booby

1980. "London 1980" International Stamp Exhibition. Birds. Multicoloured.

439	20c. Type **136**	20	20
440	25c. Magnificent frigate bird	25	25
441	50c. White-tailed tropic bird	40	40
442	75c. Brown pelican	55	55
MS443	152×130 mm. Nos. 439/42	1·25	2·25

1980. Caribbean Commonwealth Parliamentary Association Meeting, Tortola. Nos. 414/15 optd **CARIBBEAN COMMONWEALTH PARLIAMENTARY ASSOCIATION MEETING TORTOLA 11–19 JULY 1980.**

444	13c. blue and red	15	10
445	75c. deep blue and blue	40	40

138 Sir Francis Drake

1980. Sir Francis Drake Commemoration. Multicoloured.

446	8c. Type **138**	60	10
447	15c. Queen Elizabeth I	80	15
448	30c. Drake receiving knighthood	1·00	30
449	75c. *Golden Hind* and coat of arms	1·90	1·25
MS450	171×121 mm. Nos. 446/9	3·75	6·50

139 Jost Van Dyke

1980. Island Profiles. Multicoloured.

451	2c. Type **139**	10	10
452	5c. Peter Island	10	10
453	13c. Virgin Gorda	15	10
454	22c. Anegada	20	10
455	30c. Norman Island	25	15
456	$1 Tortola	70	1·00
MS457	95×88 mm. No. 456	85	1·50

140 Dancing Lady

1981. Flowers. Multicoloured.

458	5c. Type **140**	10	10
459	20c. Love in the mist	15	15
460	22c. *Pitcairnia angustifolia*	15	15
461	75c. Dutchman's pipe	35	65
462	$1 Maiden apple	35	80

141 Wedding Bouquet from British Virgin Islands

1981. Royal Wedding. Multicoloured.

463	10c. Type **141**	10	10
464	35c. Prince Charles and Queen Elizabeth the Queen Mother in Garter robes	20	15
465	$1.25 Prince Charles and Lady Diana Spencer	60	80

142 Stamp Collecting

1981. 25th Anniv of Duke of Edinburgh Award Scheme. Multicoloured.

466	10c. Type **142**	10	10
467	15c. Athletics	10	10
468	50c. Camping	25	25
469	$1 Duke of Edinburgh	40	45

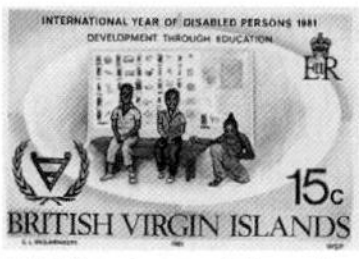

143 "Development through Education"

1981. International Year for Disabled Persons. Multicoloured.

470	15c. Type **143**	15	15
471	20c. Fort Charlotte Children's Centre	15	20
472	30c. "Developing cultural awareness"	20	30
473	$1 Fort Charlotte Children's Centre (different)	60	1·25

144 Detail from *The Adoration of the Shepherds* (Rubens)

1981. Christmas.

474	**144** 5c. multicoloured	15	10
475	- 15c. multicoloured	25	10
476	- 30c. multicoloured	45	15
477	- $1 multicoloured	1·10	1·10
MS478	117×90 mm. 50c. multicoloured (horiz)	2·00	1·00

DESIGNS: 15c. to $1 Further details from *The Adoration of the Shepherds* by Rubens.

145 Green-throated Caribs and Erythrina

1982. Hummingbirds. Multicoloured.

479	15c. Type **145**	50	15
480	30c. Green-throated carib and bougainvillea	60	45
481	35c. Antillean crested hummingbirds and *granadilla passiflora*	70	55
482	$1.25 Antillean crested hummingbirds and hibiscus	1·75	3·00

146 "People caring for People"

1982. Tenth Anniv of Lions Club of Tortola. Multicoloured.

483	10c. Type **146**	15	10
484	20c. Tortola Headquarters	20	15
485	30c. "We Serve"	25	15
486	$1.50 "Lions" symbol	60	1·00
MS487	124×102 mm. Nos. 483/6	1·75	4·25

147 Princess at Victoria and Albert Museum, November, 1981

1982. 21st Birthday of Princess of Wales. Multicoloured.

488	10c. British Virgin Islands coat of arms	15	10
489	35c. Type **147**	25	15
490	50c. Bride and groom proceeding into Vestry	35	35
491	$1.50 Formal portrait	80	1·10

148 Douglas DC-3

1982. Tenth Anniv of Air BVI. Multicoloured.

492	10c. Type **148**	45	15
493	15c. Britten-Norman BN-2 Islander	60	20
494	60c. Hawker Siddeley H.S.748	1·10	75
495	75c. Runway scene	1·25	90

149 Scouts raising Flag

1982. 75th Anniv of Boy Scout Movement and 50th Anniv of Scouting in B.V.I. Multicoloured.

496	8c. Type **149**	20	10
497	20c. Cub Scout	30	25
498	50c. Sea Scout	40	55
499	$1 First camp, Brownsea Island, and portrait of Lord Baden-Powell	70	1·50

150 Legislature in Session

1983. Commonwealth Day. Multicoloured.

500	10c. Type **150**	10	10
501	30c. Tourism	25	20
502	35c. Satellite view of Earth showing Virgin Islands	25	25
503	75c. B.V.I. and Commonwealth flags	70	90

151 Florence Nightingale

1983. Nursing Week. Multicoloured.

504	10c. Type **151**	60	15
505	30c. Staff nurse and assistant nurse	1·00	45
506	60c. Public Health nurses testing blood pressure (horiz)	1·90	1·25
507	75c. Peebles Hospital (horiz)	1·90	1·75

152 Frame Construction

1983. Traditional Boat-building. Multicoloured.

508	15c. Type **152**	25	25
509	25c. Planking	30	45
510	50c. Launching	50	80
511	$1 Maiden voyage	65	1·75
MS512	127×101 mm. Nos. 508/11	1·50	3·75

153 Grumman G21 Goose Amphibian

1983. Bicentenary of Manned Flight. Multicoloured.

513	10c. Type **153**	20	15
514	30c. Riley Turbo Skyliner	45	45
515	60c. Embraer EMB-110 Bandeirante	65	85
516	$1.25 Hawker Siddeley H.S.748	90	1·60

154 *Madonna and Child with the Infant Baptist*

1983. Christmas. 500th Birth Anniv of Raphael. Multicoloured.

517	8c. Type **154**	10	10
518	15c. *La Belle Jardiniere*	20	15
519	50c. *Madonna del Granduca*	50	60
520	$1 *The Terranuova Madonna*	90	1·10
MS521	108×101 mm. Nos. 517/20	2·25	3·50

155 Local Tournament

1984. 60th Anniv of International Chess Federation. Multicoloured.

522	10c. Type **155**	1·00	40
523	35c. Staunton king, rook and pawn (vert)	2·00	1·50
524	75c. Karpov's winning position against Jakobsen in 1980 Olympiad (vert)	3·75	4·25
525	$1 B.V.I. Gold Medal won by Bill Hook at 1980 Chess Olympiad	4·25	5·50

156 Port Purcell

1984. 250th Anniv of *Lloyd's List* (newspaper). Multicoloured.

526	15c. Type **156**	35	30
527	25c. Boeing 747-100	60	50
528	50c. Wreck of *Rhone* (mail steamer), 1867	1·00	95
529	$1 *Booker Viking* (cargo liner)	1·75	1·60

157 Mail Ship *Boyne*, Boeing 747-100 and U.P.U. Logo

1984. Universal Postal Union Congress, Hamburg. Sheet 90×69 mm.

MS530	**157** $1 blue and black	2·25	2·50

158 Running

1984. Olympic Games, Los Angeles. Multicoloured.

531	15c. Type **158**	40	40
532	15c. Runner	40	40
533	20c. Wind-surfing	40	45
534	20c. Surfer	40	45
535	30c. Sailing	45	65
536	30c. Yacht	45	65
MS537	97×69 mm. Torch-bearer	1·50	1·90

159 Steel Band

1984. 150th Anniv of Abolition of Slavery. Multicoloured.

538	10c. Type **159**	30	35
539	10c. Dancing girls	30	35
540	10c. Men in traditional costumes	30	35
541	10c. Girl in traditional costumes	30	35
542	10c. Festival Queen	30	35
543	30c. Green and yellow dinghies	45	50
544	30c. Blue and red dinghies	45	50
545	30c. White and blue dinghies	45	50
546	30c. Red and yellow dinghies	45	50
547	30c. Blue and white dinghies	45	50

DESIGNS: Various aspects of Emancipation Festival.

Nos. 543/7 form a composite design, the sail colours of the dinghies being described.

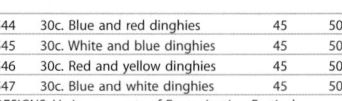

160 Sloop

1984. Boats. Multicoloured.

548	10c. Type **160**	40	20
549	35c. Fishing boat	60	65
550	60c. Schooner	75	1·25
551	75c. Cargo boat	75	1·60
MS552	125×90 mm. Nos. 548/51	1·50	4·00

161 One Cent Coin and Aerial View

1985. New Coinage. Coins and Local Scenery. Multicoloured.

553	1c. Type **161**	10	10
554	5c. Five cent coin and boulders on beach	10	10
555	10c. Ten cent coin and scuba diving	20	20
556	25c. Twenty-five cent coin and yachts	45	50
557	50c. Fifty cent coin and jetty	90	1·25
558	$1 One dollar coin and beach at night	1·75	2·25
MS559	103×159 mm. Nos. 553/8	3·00	7·00

162 Red-billed Tropic Bird

1985. Birds of the British Virgin Islands. Multicoloured.

560	1c. Type **162**	1·25	2·50
561	2c. Yellow-crowned night heron ("Night Gaulin")	1·25	2·50
562	5c. Mangrove cuckoo ("Rain Bird")	1·75	2·00
563	8c. Northern mockingbird ("Mockingbird")	1·75	3·00
564	10c. Grey kingbird ("Chinchary")	2·00	75
565	12c. Red-necked pigeon ("Wild Pigeon")	2·25	1·50
649	15c. Least bittern ("Bittlin")	2·75	1·50
567	18c. Smooth-billed ani ("Black Witch")	3·00	3·00
651	20c. Clapper rail ("Pond Shakey")	2·75	1·75
652	25c. American kestrel ("Killy-killy")	2·75	1·75
570	30c. Pearly-eyed thrasher ("Thrushie")	2·75	1·75
654	35c. Bridled quail dove ("Marmi Dove")	2·75	1·25
572	40c. Green-backed heron ("Little Gaulin")	3·25	1·75
573	50c. Scaly-breasted ground dove ("Ground Dove")	3·50	3·50
574	60c. Little blue heron ("Blue Gaulin")	4·00	5·00
658	$1 Audubon's shearwater ("Pimleco")	5·00	6·00
576	$2 Blue-faced booby ("White Booby")	5·50	8·50
577	$3 Cattle egret ("Cow Bird")	7·50	13·00
578	$5 Zenaida dove ("Turtle Dove")	9·00	15·00

163 The Queen Mother at Festival of Remembrance

1985. Life and Times of Queen Elizabeth the Queen Mother. Multicoloured.

580A	10c. At Victoria Palace Theatre, 1984	10	20
582A	25c. Opening Celia Johnson Theatre, 1985	15	40
584A	50c. At the Tate Gallery, 1983	20	70
586A	75c. Unveiling Mountbatten Statue, 1983	25	1·00
MS587A	85×114 mm. $1 At Columbia University; $1 At a Wedding, St. Margaret's, Westminster, 1983	85	4·00

579B	10c. Type **163**	2·75	2·75
B581	25c. At the engagement of the Prince of Wales, 1981	2·75	2·75
B583	50c. The Queen Mother on her 82nd birthday	3·25	3·25
B585	75c. At the Royal Smithfield Show, 1983	3·25	3·25

164 Seaside Sparrow

1985. Birth Bicentenary of John J. Audubon (ornithologist). Designs showing original paintings. Multicoloured.

588	5c. Type **164**	30	20
589	30c. Passenger pigeon	40	70
590	50c. Yellow-breasted chat	45	1·75
591	$1 American kestrel	50	2·75

165 S.V. *Flying Cloud*

1986. Visiting Cruise Ships. Multicoloured.

592	35c. Type **165**	80	85
593	50c. M.V. *Newport Clipper*	1·10	1·50
594	75c. M.V. *Cunard Countess*	1·10	2·50
595	$1 M.V. *Sea Goddess*	1·25	3·00

1986. Inaugural Flight of Miami–Beef Island Air Service. Nos 581/2 and 585/6 optd **MIAMI B.V.I. INAUGURAL FLIGHT**.

596A	25c. At the engagement of the Prince of Wales, 1981	40	50
597A	25c. Opening Celia Johnson Theatre, 1985	40	50
598A	75c. At the Royal Smithfield Show, 1983	1·25	1·50
599A	75c. Unveiling Mountbatten statue, 1983	1·25	1·50

167 Queen Elizabeth II in 1958

1986. 60th Birthday of Queen Elizabeth II. Multicoloured.

600	12c. Type **167**	15	20
601	35c. At a Maundy Service	20	45
602	$1.50 Queen Elizabeth	45	1·75
603	$2 During a visit to Canberra, 1982 (vert)	60	2·25
MS604	85×115 mm. $3 Queen with bouquet	3·50	6·00

168 Miss Sarah Ferguson

1986. Royal Wedding. Multicoloured.

605	35c. Type **168**	30	70
606	35c. Prince Andrew and Miss Sarah Ferguson	30	70
607	$1 Prince Andrew in morning dress (horiz)	50	1·25
608	$1 Miss Sarah Ferguson (different) (horiz)	50	1·25
MS609	115×85 mm. $4 Duke and Duchess of York in carriage after wedding (horiz)	2·00	6·00

169 Harvesting Sugar Cane

1986. History of Rum Making. Multicoloured.

610	12c. Type **169**	1·50	45
611	40c. Bringing sugar cane to mill	1·75	1·25
612	60c. Rum distillery	2·25	3·50
613	$1 Delivering barrels of rum to ship	5·50	6·50
MS614	115×84 mm. $2 Royal Navy rum issue	6·50	8·50

170 *Sentinel*

1986. 20th Anniv of Cable and Wireless Caribbean Headquarters, Tortola. Cable Ships. Multicoloured.

615	35c. Type **170**	60	80
616	35c. *Retriever* (1961)	60	80
617	60c. *Cable Enterprise* (1964)	75	1·50
618	60c. *Mercury* (1962)	75	1·50
619	75c. *Recorder* (1955)	75	1·75
620	75c. *Pacific Guardian* (1984)	75	1·75
621	$1 *Great Eastern* (1860's)	80	2·00
622	$1 *Cable Venture* (1977)	80	2·00
MS623	Four sheets, each 102×131 mm. (a) 40c. × 2 As 35c. (b) 50c. × 2 As 60c. (c) 80c. × 2 As 75c. (d) $1.50 × 2 As $1 Set of 4 sheets	5·00	12·00

1986. Centenary of Statue of Liberty. T **17** and similar vert views of Statue in separate miniature sheets. Multicoloured.

MS624	Nine sheets, each 85×115 mm. 50c.; 75c.; 90c.; $1; $1.25; $1.50; $1.75; $2; $2.50 Set of 9 sheets	4·25	11·00

172 18th-century Spanish Galleon

1987. Shipwrecks. Multicoloured.

625	12c. Type **172**	2·50	55
626	35c. H.M.S. *Astrea* (frigate), 1808	3·75	1·40
627	75c. *Rhone* (mail steamer), 1867	5·50	4·50
628	$1.50 *Captain Rokos* (freighter), 1929	8·00	11·00
MS629	85×65 mm. $1.50, *Volvart*, 1819	16·00	15·00

173 Outline Map and Flag of Montserrat

1987. 11th Meeting of Organization of Eastern Caribbean States. Each showing map and flag. Multicoloured.

630	10c. Type **173**	70	70
631	15c. Grenada	80	75
632	20c. Dominica	85	80
633	25c. St. Kitts-Nevis	90	1·00
634	35c. St. Vincent and Grenadines	1·40	1·00
635	50c. British Virgin Islands	2·00	2·50
636	75c. Antigua and Barbuda	2·25	3·25
637	$1 St. Lucia	2·75	3·50

174 Spider Lily

1987. Opening of Botanical Gardens. Multicoloured.

638	12c. Type **174**	80	35
639	35c. Barrel cactus	1·75	1·00
640	$1 Wild plantain	2·75	3·25
641	$1.50 Little butterfly orchid	8·00	8·50
MS642	139×104 mm. $2.50, White cedar	3·75	6·00

175 Early Mail Packet and 1867 1s. Stamp

1987. Bicentenary of Postal Services. Multicoloured.

662	10c. Type **175**	1·75	80
663	20c. Map and 1899 1d. stamp	2·50	1·40
664	35c. Road Town Post Office and Customs House, c. 1913, and 1847 4d. stamp	2·50	1·75
665	$1.50 Piper PA-23 Apache mail plane and 1964 25c. definitive	8·00	11·00
MS666	70×60 mm. $2.50, Mail ship, 1880's, and 1880 1d.	6·00	9·50

1988. 500th Birth Anniv of Titian (artist). As T **238** of Antigua. Multicoloured.

667	10c. *Salome*	65	55
668	12c. *Man with the Glove*	70	60
669	20c. *Fabrizio Salvaresio*	90	80
670	25c. *Daughter of Roberto Strozzi*	1·00	90
671	40c. *Pope Julius II*	1·60	2·00
672	50c. *Bishop Ludovico Beccadelli*	1·75	2·00
673	60c. *King Philip II*	1·90	2·50
674	$1 *Empress Isabella of Portugal*	2·50	2·75
MS675	Two sheets, each 110×95 mm. (a) $2 *Emperor Charles V at Muhlberg* (detail). (b) $2 *Pope Paul III and his Grandsons* (detail) Set of 2 sheets	17·00	14·00

176 de Havilland Canada DHC-5 Transporter over Sir Francis Drake Channel and Staunton Pawn

1988. First British Virgin Islands Open Chess Tournament. Multicoloured.

676	35c. Type **176**	4·75	1·50
677	$1 Jose Capablanca (former World Champion) and Staunton king	9·50	8·50
MS678	109×81 mm. $2 Chess match	10·00	11·00

177 Hurdling

1988. Olympic Games, Seoul. Multicoloured.

679	12c. Type **177**	35	25
680	20c. Windsurfing	60	45
681	75c. Basketball	3·75	3·25
682	$1 Tennis	3·75	3·75
MS683	71×102 mm. $2 Athletics	3·00	4·50

178 Swimmer ("Don't Swim Alone")

1988. 125th Anniv of International Red Cross.

684	**178**	12c. black, red and blue	1·75	40
685	-	30c. black, red and blue	2·50	80
686	-	60c. black, red and blue	3·75	3·00
687	-	$1 black, red and blue	4·50	4·00
MS688		68×96 mm. 50c. × 4 black and red	5·00	6·50

DESIGNS—HORIZ: 30c. Swimmers ("No swimming during electrical storms"); 60c. Beach picnic ("Don't eat before swimming"); $1 Boat and equipment ("Proper equipment for boating"). VERT: 50c.×4 Recovery position, clearing airway, mouth-to-mouth resuscitation, cardiac massage.

179 Princess Alexandra

1988. Visit of Princess Alexandra. Designs showing different portraits.

689	**179**	40c. multicoloured	2·75	75
690	-	$1.50 multicoloured	6·00	4·75
MS691		102×98 mm. $2 multicoloured	5·00	6·50

180 Brown Pelican in Flight

1988. Wildlife (1st series). Aquatic Birds. Multicoloured.

692	10c. Type **180**	1·60	50
693	12c. Brown pelican perched on post	1·60	55
694	15c. Brown pelican	1·75	1·10
695	35c. Brown pelican swallowing fish	2·75	3·00
MS696	106×76 mm. $2 Common shoveler (horiz)	12·00	9·00

No. **MS**696 is without the W.W.F. logo.

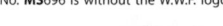

181 Anegada Rock Iguana

1988. Wildlife (2nd series). Endangered Species. Multicoloured.

697	20c. Type **181**	1·50	75
698	40c. Virgin Gorda dwarf gecko	1·75	1·40
699	60c. Hawksbill turtle	2·75	3·50
700	$1 Humpback whale	7·50	8·00
MS701	106×77 mm. $2 Trunk turtle (vert)	7·00	8·50

182 Yachts at Start

1989. Spring Regatta. Multicoloured.

702	12c. Type **182**	45	40
703	40c. Yacht tacking (horiz)	1·00	1·00
704	75c. Yachts at sunset	1·60	2·50
705	$1 Yachts rounding buoy (horiz)	2·00	2·75
MS706	83×69 mm. $2 Yacht under full sail	5·50	7·00

1989. 500th Anniv (1992) of Discovery of America by Columbus (1st issue). Pre-Columbian Arawak Society. As T **247** of Antigua. Multicoloured.

707	10c. Arawak in hammock	70	45
708	20c. Making fire	1·00	50
709	25c. Making implements	1·00	60
710	$1.50 Arawak family	4·50	7·00
MS711	85×70 mm. $2 Religious ceremony	9·00	11·00

See also Nos. 741/5, 793/7 and 818/26.

183 "Apollo II" Emblem

1989. 20th Anniv of First Manned Landing on the Moon. Multicoloured.

712	15c. Type **183**	1·25	60
713	30c. Edwin Aldrin deploying scientific experiments	2·25	1·00
714	65c. Aldrin and U.S. flag on Moon	3·00	4·00
715	$1 "Apollo II" capsule after splashdown	4·00	4·25
MS716	102×77 mm. $2 Neil Armstrong (38×50 mm)	9·50	10·50

184 Black Harry and Nathaniel Gilbert preaching to Slaves

1989. Bicentenary of Methodist Church in British Virgin Islands. Multicoloured.

717	12c. Type **184**	1·00	50
718	25c. Methodist school exercise book	1·40	75
719	35c. East End Methodist Church, 1810	1·60	85
720	$1.25 Reverend John Wesley (founder of Methodism) and church youth choir	3·25	6·50
MS721	100×69 mm. $2 Dr. Thomas Cole	4·75	9·00

185 Player tackling

1989. World Cup Football Championship, Italy, 1990. Multicoloured.

722	5c. Type **185**	80	80
723	10c. Player dribbling ball	80	80
724	20c. Two players chasing ball	1·50	80
725	$1.75 Goalkeeper diving for ball	7·00	7·50
MS726	100×70 mm. $2 British Virgin Islands team captain	8·50	11·00

186 Princess Alexandra and Sunset House

1990. "Stamp World London 90" International Stamp Exhibition. Royal Visitors. Multicoloured.

727	50c. Type **186**	4·50	4·50
728	50c. Princess Margaret and Government House	4·50	4·50
729	50c. Hon. Angus Ogilvy and Little Dix Bay Hotel	4·50	4·50
730	50c. Princess Diana with Princes William and Henry and Necker Island Resort	4·50	4·50
MS731	89×80 mm. $2 Royal Yacht *Britannia*	15·00	15·00

187 Audubon's Shearwater

1990. Birds. Multicoloured.

732	5c. Type **187**	1·75	1·75
733	12c. Red-necked pigeon	2·25	60
734	20c. Moorhen ("Common Gallinule")	2·50	60
735	25c. Green-backed heron ("Green Heron")	2·50	60
736	40c. Yellow warbler	2·75	1·50
737	60c. Smooth-billed ani	3·00	2·75
738	$1 Antillean crested hummingbird	3·00	3·25
739	$1.25 Black-faced grassquit	3·00	4·50
MS740	Two sheets, each 98×70 mm. (a) $2 Royal tern egg (vert) (b) $2 Red-billed tropicbird egg (vert) Set of 2 sheets	11·00	7·00

1990. 500th Anniv (1992) of Discovery of America by Columbus (2nd issue). New World Natural History–Fishes. As T **260** of Antigua. Multicoloured.

741	10c. Blue tang (horiz)	1·50	60
742	35c. Glass-eyed snapper (horiz)	2·50	70
743	50c. Slippery dick (horiz)	3·00	3·50
744	$1 Porkfish (horiz)	4·50	4·75
MS745	100×70 mm. $2 Yellow-tailed snapper	5·00	6·50

188 Queen Elizabeth the Queen Mother

1990. 90th Birthday of Queen Elizabeth the Queen Mother.

746	**188**	12c. multicoloured	50	25
747	-	25c. multicoloured	90	55
748	-	60c. multicoloured	1·75	2·25
749	-	$1 multicoloured	2·00	2·50
MS750		75×75 mm. $2 multicoloured	2·75	2·75

DESIGNS: 25, 60c., $2 Recent photographs.

189 Footballers

1990. World Cup Football Championship, Italy.

751	**189**	12c. multicoloured	60	40
752	-	20c. multicoloured	90	50
753	-	50c. multicoloured	1·75	2·00
754	-	$1.25 multicoloured	2·50	3·75
MS755		91×76 mm. $2 multicoloured	4·50	4·50

DESIGNS: 20, 50c., $2, Footballers.

190 Judo

1990. Olympic Games, Barcelona (1992). Multicoloured.

756	12c. Type **190**	1·50	45
757	40c. Yachting	2·25	1·60
758	60c. Hurdling	2·75	3·75
759	$1 Show jumping	4·50	4·50
MS760	78×105 mm. $2 Windsurfing	4·50	4·00

191 Tree-fern, Sage Mountain National Park

1991. 30th Anniv of National Parks Trust. Multicoloured.

761	10c. Type **191**	1·00	1·25
762	25c. Coppermine ruins, Virgin Gorda (horiz)	1·75	80
763	35c. Ruined windmill, Mt. Healthy	1·75	80
764	$2 The Baths (rock formation), Virgin Gorda (horiz)	9·50	12·00

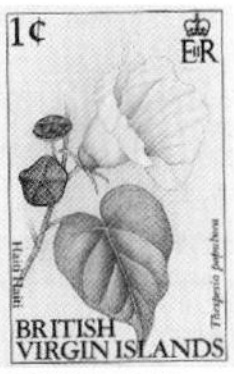

192 Haiti Haiti

1991. Flowers. Multicoloured.

765	1c. Type **192**	20	1·50
766	2c. Lobster claw	20	1·50
767	5c. Frangipani	20	1·50
887	10c. Autograph tree	50	1·40
769	12c. Yellow allamanda	40	30
889	15c. Lantana	65	40
771	20c. Jerusalem thorn	50	30
772	25c. Turk's cap	55	40
892	30c. Swamp immortelle	70	50
893	35c. White cedar	85	55
775	40c. Mahoe tree	75	65
895	45c. Pinguin	95	80
896	50c. Christmas orchid	2·25	2·00
778	70c. Lignum vitae	1·10	2·00
779	$1 African tulip tree	1·25	2·00
899	$2 Beach morning glory	3·00	5·50
781	$3 Organ pipe cactus	4·00	7·00
901	$5 Tall ground orchid	8·50	13·00
783	$10 Ground orchid	17·00	22·00

193 *Phoebis sennae*

1991. Butterflies. Multicoloured.

784	5c. Type **193**	1·00	1·50
785	10c. *Dryas iulia*	1·25	1·50
786	15c. *Junonia evarete*	1·75	75
787	20c. *Dione vanillae*	1·75	1·00
788	25c. *Battus polydamus*	1·75	1·00
789	30c. *Eurema lisa*	1·90	1·00
790	35c. *Heliconius charitonius*	1·90	1·10
791	$1.50 *Siproeta stelenes*	4·75	7·00
MS792	Two sheets. (a) 77×117 mm. $2 *Danaus plexippus* (horiz). (b) 117×77 mm. $2 *Biblis hyperia* (horiz) Set of 2 sheets	14·00	15·00

1991. 500th Anniv (1992) of Discovery of America by Columbus (3rd issue). History of Exploration. As T **277** of Antigua. Multicoloured.

793	12c. multicoloured	2·00	50
794	50c. multicoloured	3·75	2·00
795	75c. multicoloured	4·50	3·25
796	$1 multicoloured	5·00	4·00
MS797	105×76 mm. $2 black and orange	9·50	9·50

DESIGNS—HORIZ: 12c. *Vitoria* in Pacific (Magellan 1519–21); 50c. La Salle on the Mississippi, 1682; 75c. John Cabot landing in Nova Scotia, 1497–98; $1 Cartier discovering the St. Lawrence, 1534. VERT: $2 *Santa Maria* (woodcut).

1991. Death Centenary (1990) of Vincent Van Gogh (artist). As T **278** of Antigua. Multicoloured.

798	15c. *Cottage with Decrepit Barn and Stooping Woman* (horiz)	1·25	50
799	30c. *Paul Gauguin's Armchair*	1·75	80
800	75c. *Breton Women* (horiz)	3·00	3·00
801	$1 *Vase with Red Gladioli*	3·50	3·50
MS802	103×81 mm. $2 *Dance Hall in Arles* (detail) (horiz)	13·00	14·00

1991. Christmas. Religious Paintings by Quinten Massys. As T **291** of Antigua. Multicoloured.

803	15c. *The Virgin and Child Enthroned* (detail)	1·25	25
804	30c. *The Virgin and Child Enthroned* (different detail)	2·00	50
805	60c. *Adoration of the Magi* (detail)	3·50	3·75
806	$1 *Virgin in Adoration*	3·75	4·00
MS807	Two sheets, each 102×127 mm. (a) $2 *The Virgin standing with Angels*. (b) $2 *The Adoration of the Magi* Set of 2 sheets	16·00	18·00

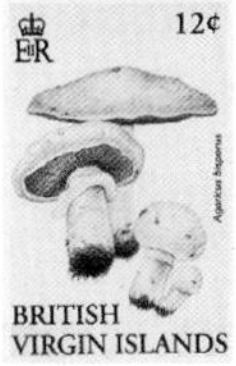

194 *Agaricus bisporus*

1992. Fungi. Multicoloured.

808	12c. Type **194**	1·50	55
809	30c. *Lentinula edodes* (horiz)	2·25	85
810	45c. *Hygocybe acutoconica*	2·25	1·00
811	$1 *Gymnopilus chrysopellus* (horiz)	4·00	6·00
MS812	94×68 mm. $2 *Pleurotous ostreatus* (horiz)	12·00	13·00

1992. 40th Anniv of Queen Elizabeth II's Accession. As T **288** of Antigua. Multicoloured.

813	12c. Little Dix Bay, Virgin Gorda	1·25	30
814	25c. Deadchest Bay, Peter Island	2·75	90
815	60c. Pond Bay, Virgin Gorda	2·75	2·50
816	$1 Cane Garden Bay, Tortola	3·00	3·00
MS817	75×97 mm. $2 Long Bay, Beef Island	9·50	10·00

195 Queen Isabella of Spain

1992. 500th Anniv of Discovery of America by Columbus (4th issue). Multicoloured.

818	10c. Type **195**	90	1·00
819	15c. Fleet of Columbus (horiz)	1·60	1·00
820	20c. Arms awarded to Columbus	1·60	1·25
821	30c. Landing Monument, Watling Island and Columbus's signature (horiz)	1·60	1·00
822	45c. Christopher Columbus	2·25	1·40
823	50c. Landing in New World and Spanish royal standard (horiz)	2·25	2·25
824	70c. Convent at La Rabida	2·50	3·50
825	$1.50 Replica of *Santa Maria* and Caribbean Pavilion, New York World's Fair (horiz)	3·75	5·50
MS826	Two sheets. (a) 116×86 mm. $2 Ships of second voyage at Virgin, Gorda (horiz). (b) 86×116 mm. $2 De la Cosa's map of New World (horiz) Set of 2 sheets	15·00	17·00

196 Basketball

1992. Olympic Games, Barcelona. Multicoloured.

827	15c. Type **196**	2·50	75
828	30c. Tennis	2·50	90
829	60c. Volleyball	2·75	3·00
830	$1 Football	3·00	3·75
MS831	100×70 mm. $2 Olympic flame	12·00	14·00

197 Issuing Social Security Cheque

1993. 25th Anniv of Ministerial Government. Multicoloured.

832	12c. Type **197**	40	40
833	15c. Map of British Virgin Islands	1·25	70
834	45c. Administration building	80	70
835	$1.30 International currency abbreviations	2·25	4·25

198 Cruising Yacht and Swimmers, The Baths, Virgin Gorda

1993. Tourism. Multicoloured.

836	15c. Type **198**	1·50	50
837	30c. Cruising yacht under sail (vert)	1·75	60
838	60c. Scuba diving	2·50	2·75
839	$1 Cruising yacht at anchor and snorklers (vert)	2·75	3·25
MS840	79×108 mm. $1 *Promenade* (trimaran) (vert); $1 Scuba diving (different) (vert)	7·50	8·50

1993. 40th Anniv of Coronation. As T **307** of Antigua.

841	12c. multicoloured	90	1·25
842	45c. multicoloured	1·25	1·50
843	60c. grey and black	1·40	1·75
844	$1 multicoloured	1·60	1·90

DESIGNS: 12c. Queen Elizabeth II at Coronation (photograph by Cecil Beaton); 45c. Orb; 60c. Queen with Prince Philip, Queen Mother and Princess Margaret, 1953; $1 Queen Elizabeth II on official visit.

200 Columbus with King Ferdinand and Queen Isabella

1993. 500th Anniv of Discovery of Virgin Islands by Columbus. Multicoloured.

846	3c. Type **200**	25	80
847	12c. Columbus's ship leaving port	70	40
848	15c. Blessing the fleet	75	45
849	25c. Arms and flag of B.V.I.	85	60
850	30c. Columbus and *Santa Maria*	1·00	70
851	45c. Ships of second voyage	1·25	95
852	60c. Columbus in ship's boat	1·75	2·50
853	$1 Landing of Columbus	2·25	2·75
MS854	Two sheets, each 120×80 mm. (a) $2 Amerindians sighting fleet. (b) $2 Christopher Columbus and ships Set of 2 sheets	13·00	14·00

201 Library Services Publications

1993. 50th Anniv of Secondary Education and Library Services. Multicoloured.

855	5c. Type **201**	65	1·50
856	10c. Secondary school sports	3·00	1·50
857	15c. Stanley Nibbs (school teacher) (vert)	1·25	80
858	20c. Mobile library	1·75	80
859	30c. Dr. Norwell Harrigan (adminstrator and lecturer) (vert)	1·75	80
860	35c. Children in library	1·75	80
861	70c. Commemorative inscription on book	2·50	3·50
862	$1 B.V.I. High School	2·75	3·50

202 Anegada Ground Iguana

1994. Endangered Species. Anegada Ground Iguana.

863	**202**	5c. multicoloured	90	1·25
864	-	10c. multicoloured	90	1·25
865	-	15c. multicoloured	1·00	75
866	-	45c. multicoloured	1·60	1·50
MS867		106×77 mm. $2 multicoloured	5·00	6·00

DESIGNS: 10c. to $2 Different iguanas.

No. **MS**867 does not carry the W.W.F. Panda emblem.

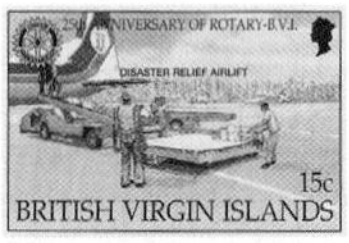

203 Loading Disaster Relief HS748 Aircraft

1994. Centenary of Rotary International in B.V.I. Multicoloured.

868	15c. Type **203**	35	35
869	45c. Training children in marine safety	85	85
870	50c. Donated operating table	90	1·00
871	90c. Paul Harris (founder) and emblem	1·60	2·50

1994. 25th Anniv of First Manned Moon Landing. As T **326** of Antigua. Multicoloured.

872	50c. Anniversary logo	2·00	2·25
873	50c. Lunar landing training vehicle	2·00	2·25
874	50c. Launch of "Apollo 11"	2·00	2·25
875	50c. Lunar module "Eagle" in flight	2·00	2·25
876	50c. Moon's surface	2·00	2·25
877	50c. Neil Armstrong (astronaut) taking first step	2·00	2·25
MS878	106×76 mm. $2 Signatures and mission logo	14·00	14·00

204 Argentina v. Netherlands, 1978

1994. World Cup Football Championship, U.S.A. Previous Winners. Multicoloured.

879	15c. Type **204**	1·25	50
880	35c. Italy v. West Germany, 1982	2·00	70
881	50c. Argentina v. West Germany, 1986	2·75	2·25
882	$1.30 West Germany v. Argentina, 1990	4·50	6·50
MS883	74×101 mm. $2 U.S. flag and World Cup trophy (horiz)	12·00	14·00

1995. 50th Anniv of United Nations. As T **213** of Bahamas. Multicoloured.

903	15c. Peugeot P4 all-purpose field cars	45	40
904	30c. Foden medium road tanker	75	60
905	45c. SISU all-terrain vehicle	1·00	90
906	$2 Westland Lynx AH7 helicopter	3·75	5·50

205 Pair of Juvenile Greater Flamingos

1995. Anegada Flamingos Restoration Project. Multicoloured.

907	15c. Type **205**	85	50
908	20c. Pair of adults	85	55
909	60c. Adult feeding	1·40	2·00
910	$1.45 Adult feeding chick	2·50	4·00
MS911	80×70 mm. $2 Chicks	6·50	7·00

206 *Tortola House with Christmas Tree* (Maureen Walters)

1995. Christmas. Children's Paintings. Multicoloured.

912	12c. Type **206**	1·75	30
913	50c. *Father Christmas in Rowing Boat* (Collin Collins)	3·00	1·40
914	70c. *Christmas Tree and Gifts* (Clare Wassell)	3·25	2·75
915	$1.30 *Peace Dove* (Nicholas Scott)	4·50	6·50

207 Seine Fishing

1996. Island Profiles (1st series). Jost Van Dyke. Multicoloured.

916	15c. Type **207**	1·50	40
917	35c. Sandy Spit	1·75	55
918	90c. Map	4·00	3·50
919	$1.50 Foxy's Regatta	4·25	6·50

See also Nos. 1003/6 and 1105/10.

1996. 70th Birthday of Queen Elizabeth II. As T **165** of Ascension, each incorporating a different photograph of the Queen. Multicoloured.

920	10c. Government House, Tortola	30	20
921	30c. Legislative Council Building	65	55
922	45c. Liner in Road Harbour	1·50	70
923	$1.50 Map of British Virgin Islands	3·25	5·00
MS924	63×65 mm. $2 Queen Elizabeth II	3·00	3·75

208 Hurdling

1996. Centenary of Modern Olympic Games. Multicoloured.

925	20c. Type **208**	45	30
926	35c. Volley ball	70	60
927	50c. Swimming	1·10	1·75
928	$1 Yachting	2·00	2·75

209 Mercedes-Benz 500 K A, Cabriolet 1934

1996. "CAPEX '96" International Stamp Exhibition, Toronto. Early Motor Cars. Multicoloured.

929	15c. Type **209**	45	30
930	40c. Citroen 12 Traction saloon, 1934	1·00	70
931	60c. Cadillac V-8 Sport Phaeton, 1932	1·25	1·75
932	$1.35 Rolls Royce Phantom II saloon, 1934	2·75	4·00
MS933	79×62 mm. $2 Ford Sport Coupe, 1932	3·25	4·25

210 Children with Computer

1996. 50th Anniv of UNICEF. Multicoloured.

934	10c. Type **210**	40	40
935	15c. Carnival costume	50	50
936	30c. Children on Scales of Justice	80	80
937	45c. Children on beach	1·25	1·25

211 Young Rainbows in Art Class

1996. 75th Anniv of Guiding in the British Virgin Islands. Multicoloured.

938	10c. Type **211**	20	20
939	15c. Brownies serving meals	30	25
940	30c. Guides around campfire	50	45
941	45c. Rangers on parade	65	60
942	$2 Lady Baden-Powell	2·75	4·00

212 Spanish Mackerel

1997. Game Fishes. Multicoloured.

943	1c. Type **212**	10	50
944	10c. Wahoo	25	80
945	15c. Great barracuda	55	40
946	20c. Tarpon	90	40
947	25c. Tiger shark	90	50
948	35c. Sailfish	90	40
949	40c. Dolphin	1·50	75
950	50c. Black-finned tuna	1·50	90
951	60c. Yellow-finned tuna	1·50	90
952	75c. King mackerel ("Kingfish")	1·75	1·25
953	$1.50 White marlin	3·25	3·25
954	$1.85 Amberjack	4·00	3·50
955	$2 Atlantic bonito	4·50	4·50
956	$5 Bonefish	9·00	10·00
957	$10 Blue marlin	16·00	19·00

1997. "HONG KONG '97" International Stamp Exhibition. Sheet 130×90 mm, containing design as No. 953, but with "1997" imprint date. Multicoloured.

MS958	$1.50, White marlin	2·25	2·75

1997. Golden Wedding of Queen Elizabeth and Prince Philip. As T **173** of Ascension. Multicoloured.

959	30c. Prince Philip with horse	70	1·00
960	30c. Queen Elizabeth at Windsor, 1989	70	1·00
961	45c. Queen in phaeton, Trooping the Colour	90	1·25
962	45c. Prince Philip in Scots Guards uniform	90	1·25
963	70c. Queen Elizabeth and Prince Philip at the Derby, 1993	1·25	1·60
964	70c. Prince Charles playing polo, Mexico, 1993	1·25	1·60
MS965	110×70 mm. $2 Queen Elizabeth and Prince Philip in landau (horiz)	3·25	4·00

213 Fiddler Crab

1997. Crabs. Multicoloured.

966	12c. Type **213**	65	50
967	15c. Coral crab	70	50
968	35c. Blue crab	1·10	60
969	$1 Giant hermit crab	2·00	3·00
MS970	76×67 mm. $2 Arrow crab	3·50	4·50

214 *Psychilis macconnelliae*

1997. Orchids of the World. Multicoloured.

971	20c. Type **214**	1·25	1·25
972	50c. *Tolumnia prionochila*	1·40	1·40
973	60c. *Tetramicra canaliculata*	1·40	1·40
974	75c. *Liparis elata*	1·50	1·50
MS975	59×79 mm. $2 *Dendrobium crumenatum* (vert)	3·25	4·25

215 Sir Francis Drake and Signature

1997. 420th Anniv of Drake's Circumnavigation of the World. Multicoloured.

976	40c. Type **215**	1·75	1·75
977	40c. Drake's coat of arms	1·75	1·75
978	40c. Queen Elizabeth I and signature	1·75	1·75
979	40c. *Christopher* and *Marigold*	1·75	1·75
980	40c. *Golden Hind*	1·75	1·75
981	40c. *Swan*	1·75	1·75
982	40c. *Cacafuego* (Spanish galleon)	1·75	1·75
983	40c. *Elizabeth*	1·75	1·75
984	40c. *Maria* (Spanish merchant ship)	1·75	1·75
985	40c. Drake's astrolabe	1·75	1·75
986	40c. *Golden Hind's* figurehead	1·75	1·75
987	40c. Compass rose	1·75	1·75
MS988	96×76 mm. $2 *Sir Francis Drake* (ketch)	3·75	4·50

Nos. 976/87 were printed together, *se-tenant*, with the backgrounds forming a composite map of Drake's route.

1998. Diana, Princess of Wales Commemoration. Sheet 145×70 mm, containing vert designs as T **177** of Ascension. Multicoloured.

MS989	15c. Wearing pink jacket, 1992; 45c. Holding child, 1991; 70c. Laughing, 1991; $1 Wearing high-collared blouse, 1986 (sold at $2.30 + 20c. charity premium)	2·50	4·00

1998. 80th Anniv of Royal Air Force. As T **178** of Ascension. Multicoloured.

990	20c. Fairey IIIF (seaplane)	60	40
991	35c. Supermarine Scapa (flying boat)	85	50
992	50c. Westland Sea King H.A.R. (helicopter)	1·40	1·10
993	$1.50 BAe Harrier GR7	2·50	3·25
MS994	110×77 mm. 75c. Curtiss H.16 (flying boat); 75c. Curtiss JN-4A; 75c. Bell Airacobra; 75c. Boulton-Paul Defiant	6·50	7·00

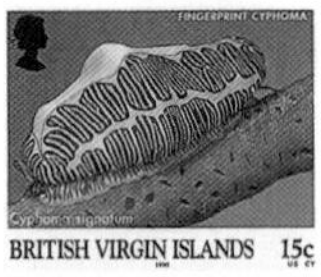

216 Fingerprint Cyphoma

1998. Marine Life. Multicoloured.

995	15c. Type **216**	1·00	50
996	30c. Long-spined sea urchin	1·25	55
997	45c. Split crown feather duster worm	1·60	70
998	$1 Upside down jelly	2·50	3·75
MS999	77×56 mm. $2 Giant anemone	4·75	5·00

217 *Carnival Reveller* (Rebecca Peck)

1998. Festival. Children's Paintings. Multicoloured.

1000	30c. Type **217**	1·25	50
1001	45c. *Leader of a Troupe* (Jehiah Maduro)	1·50	65
1002	$1.30 *Steel Pans* (Rebecca McKenzie) (horiz)	3·50	5·00

218 Salt Pond

1998. Island Profiles (2nd series). Salt Island. Multicoloured.

1003	12c. Type **218**	1·50	70
1004	30c. Wreck of "Rhone" (mail steamer)	2·00	75
1005	70c. Traditional house	1·75	2·25

1006	$1.45 Salt Island from the air	3·25	4·50
MS1007	118×78 mm. $2 Collecting salt	7·00	8·00

219 Business Studies, Woodwork and Technology Students

1998. Anniversaries. Multicoloured.

1008	5c. Type **219**	25	75
1009	15c. Comprehensive school band	45	40
1010	30c. Chapel, Mona Campus, Jamaica	60	50
1011	45c. Anniversary plaque and University arms	75	70
1012	50c. Dr. John Coakley Lettsom and map of Little Jost Van Dyke	1·00	1·25
1013	$1 The Medical Society of London building and arms	1·50	2·50

EVENTS: 5, 15c. 30th anniv of Comprehensive Education in B.V.I.; 30, 45c. 50th anniv of University of West Indies; 50c., $1 250th anniv of Medical Society of London.

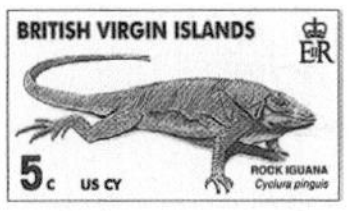

220 Rock Iguana

1999. Lizards. Multicoloured.

1014	5c. Type **220**	30	65
1015	35c. Pygmy gecko	85	45
1016	60c. Slippery back skink	1·50	1·50
1017	$1.50 Wood slave gecko	2·25	3·50
MS1018	100×70 mm. 75c. Doctor lizard; 75c. Yellow-bellied lizard; 75c. Man lizard; 75c. Ground lizard	5·00	6·00

1999. Royal Wedding. As T **185** of Ascension. Multicoloured.

1019	20c. Photographs of Prince Edward and Miss Sophie Rhys-Jones	1·00	40
1020	$3 Engagement photograph	4·75	6·00

1999. 30th Anniv of First Manned Landing on Moon. As T **186** of Ascension. Multicoloured.

1021	10c. "Apollo 11" on launch pad	45	60
1022	40c. Firing of second stage rockets	1·00	65
1023	50c. Lunar module on Moon	1·10	1·00
1024	$2 Astronauts transfer to command module	3·00	4·50
MS1025	90×80 mm. $2.50, Earth as seen from moon (circular, 40 mm diam)	3·75	4·50

221 Sunrise Tellin

1999. Sea Shells. Multicoloured.

1026A	5c. Type **221**	65	90
1027A	10c. King helmet	65	90
1028A	25c. Measle cowrie	80	1·00
1029A	35c. West Indian top shell	85	1·00
1030A	75c. Zigzag scallop	1·25	1·50
1031A	$1 West Indian fighting conch	1·25	1·50

Nos. 1026A/31A were printed together, *se-tenant*, with the backgrounds forming a composite design.

222 Zion Hill Methodist Church

1999. Christmas. Church Buildings. Multicoloured.

1032	20c. Type **222**	45	35
1033	35c. Seventh Day Adventist Church, Fat Hogs Bay, 1982	60	45
1034	50c. Ruins of St. Phillip's Anglican Church, Kingstown	85	1·00
1035	$1 St. William's Catholic Church, Road Town	1·60	2·75

223 King Henry VII

2000. "Stamp Show 2000" International Stamp Exhibition, London. Kings and Queens of England. Multicoloured.

1036	60c. Type **223**	1·10	1·25
1037	60c. Lady Jane Grey	1·10	1·25
1038	60c. King Charles I	1·10	1·25
1039	60c. King William III	1·10	1·25
1040	60c. King George III	1·10	1·25
1041	60c. King Edward VII	1·10	1·25

2000. 18th Birthday of Prince William. As T **191** of Ascension. Multicoloured.

1042	20c. Prince William as baby (horiz)	60	35
1043	40c. Prince William playing with ball, 1984	90	60
1044	50c. Skiing in British Columbia, 1998	1·25	1·00
1045	$1 In evening dress, 1997 (horiz)	2·00	2·75
MS1046	175×95 mm. 60c. Prince William in 1999 (horiz) and Nos. 1042/5	8·50	8·50

224 Duchess of York, 1920s

2000. 100th Birthday of Queen Elizabeth the Queen Mother. Multicoloured.

1047	15c. Type **224**	50	25
1048	35c. As Queen Mother in 1957	1·00	1·50
1049	70c. In evening dress, 1970	1·50	1·75
1050	$1.50 With family on 99th birthday	2·50	3·25

225 Red Hibiscus

2000. Flowers. Multicoloured.

1051	10c. Type **225**	40	50
1052	15c. Pink oleander	45	50
1053	35c. Yellow bell	1·00	55
1054	50c. Yellow and white frangipani	1·25	1·00
1055	75c. Flamboyant	1·75	2·25
1056	$2 Bougainvillea	3·50	5·00

226 Sunday Morning Well (Site of Emancipation Proclamation)

2000. New Millennium. Multicoloured.

1057	5c. Type **226**	15	50
1058	20c. Nurse Mary Louise Davies M.B.E.	45	35
1059	30c. Cheyney University, U.S.A.	60	45
1060	45c. Enid Leona Scatliffe (former chief education officer)	80	70
1061	50c. H. Lavity Stoutt Community College	90	1·00
1062	$1 Sir J. Olva Georges	1·60	2·25
MS1063	69×59 mm. $2 Private Samuel Hodge's Victoria Cross (vert)	3·75	4·50

227 Dr. Q. William Osborne and Arnando Scatliffe

2000. 50th Anniv of Restoration of Legislative Council. Multicoloured.

1064	10c. Type **227**	25	50
1065	15c. H. Robinson O'Neal and A. Austin Henley	35	50
1066	20c. Wilfred W. Smith and John C. Brudenell-Bruce	45	50
1067	35c. Howard R. Penn and I. G. Fonseca	65	55
1068	50c. Carlton L. de Castro and Theodolph H. Faulkner	90	1·00
1069	60c. Willard W. Wheatley (Chief Minister, 1971–79)	1·25	1·50
1070	$1 H. Lavity Stoutt (Chief Minister, 1967–71, 1979–83 and 1986–95)	1·60	2·25

2001. "HONG KONG 2001" Stamp Exhibition. Sheet 150×90 mm, containing T **228** and similar horiz design showing dove. Multicoloured.

MS1071	50c. Type **41**; 50c. Bar-tailed cuckoo dove	3·50	4·50

229 H.M.S.*Wistaria* (sloop), 1923–30

2001. Royal Navy Ships connected to British Virgin Islands (1st series). Multicoloured.

1072	35c. Type **229**	1·50	55
1073	50c. H.M.S. *Dundee* (sloop), 1934–35	1·75	90
1074	60c. H.M.S. *Eurydice* (frigate), 1787	1·75	1·60
1075	75c. H.M.S. *Pegasus* (frigate), 1787	2·00	1·90
1076	$1 H.M.S. *Astrea* (frigate), 1807	2·75	2·75
1077	$1.50 Royal Yacht *Britannia*, 1966	4·00	5·00

See also Nos. 1101/4.

230 Fridtjof Nansen (Peace Prize, 1922)

2001. Centenary of Nobel Prize. Multicoloured.

1078	10c. Type **230**	70	1·00
1079	20c. Albert Einstein (Physics Prize,1921)	80	60
1080	25c. Sir Arthur Lewis (Economic Sciences Prize, 1979)	70	60
1081	40c. Saint-John Perse (Literature Prize, 1960)	80	80
1082	70c. Mother Teresa (Peace Prize, 1979)	6·00	3·50
1083	$2 Christian Lous Lange (Peace Prize, 1921)	3·75	5·00

2002. Golden Jubilee. As T **200** of Ascension.

1084	15c. brown, mauve and gold	70	25
1085	50c. multicoloured	1·25	1·00
1086	60c. multicoloured	1·25	1·40
1087	75c. multicoloured	1·50	1·75
MS1088	162×95 mm. Nos. 1084/7 and $1 multicoloured	8·00	9·00

DESIGNS—HORIZ: 15c. Princess Elizabeth in A.T.S. uniform, changing wheel; 50c. Queen Elizabeth in fur hat, 1977; 60c. Queen Elizabeth carrying bouquet; 75c. Queen Elizabeth at banquet, Prague, 1996. VERT (38×51 mm)—$1 Queen Elizabeth after Annigoni.

Designs as Nos. 1084/7 in No. **MS**1088 omit the gold frame around each stamp and the "Golden Jubilee 1952–2002" inscription.

231 Estuarine Crocodile

2002. Reptiles. Multicoloured.

1089	5c. Type **231**	30	75
1090	20c. Reticulated python	60	45
1091	30c. Komodo dragon	80	50
1092	40c. Boa constrictor	95	70
1093	$1 Dwarf caiman	2·25	2·50
1094	$2 *Sphaerodactylus parthenopion* (gecko)	4·00	5·00
MS1095	89×68 mm. $1.50, Head of *Sphaerodactylus parthenopion* on finger	3·75	4·50

2002. Queen Elizabeth the Queen Mother Commemoration. As T **202** of Ascension.

1096	20c. brown, gold and purple	45	30
1097	60c. multicoloured	1·25	1·00
1098	$2 black, gold and purple	3·50	3·75
1099	$3 multicoloured	4·75	5·50
MS1100	145×70 mm. Nos. 1098/9	8·50	9·50

DESIGNS—20c. Duchess of York, 1920s; 60c. Queen Mother at Somerset House, 2000; $2 Lady Elizabeth Bowes-Lyon, 1920; $3 Queen Mother inspecting guard of honour.

Designs as Nos. 1098/9 in No. **MS**1100 omit the "1900–2002" inscription and the coloured frame.

2002. Royal Navy Ships connected to British Virgin Islands (2nd series). As T **229**. Multicoloured.

1101	20c. H.M.S. *Invincible* (ship of the line) re-capturing H.M.S. *Argo* (frigate), 1783	85	55
1102	35c. H.M.S. *Boreas* and H.M.S. *Solebay* (sailing frigates)	1·50	60
1103	50c. H.M.S. *Coventry* (frigate)	1·75	1·25
1104	$3 H.M.S. *Argyll* (frigate)	7·50	9·00

2002. Island Profiles (3rd series). Virgin Gorda. As T **218**. Multicoloured.

1105	5c. Spring Bay	30	75
1106	40c. Devils Bay	1·00	55
1107	60c. The Baths	1·40	1·00
1108	75c. St. Thomas Bay	1·50	1·50
1109	$1 Savannah and Pond Bay	1·75	2·00
1110	$2 Trunk Bay	3·50	5·00

232 Young West Indian Whistling Duck and Nest

2002. Birdlife International (1st series). West Indian Whistling Duck. Multicoloured.

1111	10c. Type **232**	40	65
1112	35c. Adult bird on rock (vert)	1·00	55
1113	40c. Adult bird landing on water (vert)	1·00	70
1114	70c. Two adult birds	1·50	2·00
MS1115	175×80 mm. Nos. 1111/14 and $2 Head of duck	6·00	7·00

See also Nos. 167/76.

233 200 Metres Race

2003. Anniversaries and Events. Multicoloured.

1116	10c. Type **233**	50	70
1117	10c. Indoor cycling	50	70
1118	35c. Laser class dinghy racing	75	75
1119	35c. Women's long-jumping	75	75
1120	50c. Bareboat class yachts	1·00	1·25
1121	50c. Racing cruiser class yachts	1·00	1·25
1122	$1.35 Carlos and Esme Downing (founders)	2·00	2·25
1123	$1.35 Copies of newspaper and anniversary logo	2·00	2·25

ANNIVERSARIES AND EVENTS: 10c. Commonwealth Games, 2002; 35c. 20th anniv of British Virgin Islands' admission to Olympic Games; 50c. 30th anniv of Spring Regatta; $1.35, 40th anniv of *The Island Sun* (newspaper).

2003. 50th Anniv of Coronation. A T **206** of Ascension. Multicoloured.

1124	15c. Queen Elizabeth II	75	30
1125	$5 Queen and Royal Family on Buckingham Palace balcony	8·50	9·00
MS1126	95×115 mm. As Nos. 1124/5	8·00	8·50

Nos. 1124/5 have red frame; stamps from **MS**1126 have no frame and country name in mauve panel.

2003. As T **207** of Ascension.

1127	$5 black, bistre and brown	5·25	6·00

2003. 21st Birthday of Prince William of Wales. As T **208** of Ascension. (a) Multicoloured.

1128	50c. Prince William at Tidworth and Beaufort Polo Clubs, 2002	1·00	75
1129	$2 Playing polo, 2002 and at Holyrood House, 2001	4·00	4·25

(b) As Nos. 1128/9 but with grey frame.

1130	50c. As No. 1128	1·00	75
1131	$2 As No. 1129	4·00	4·25

2003. Centenary of Powered Flight. As T **209** of Ascension. Multicoloured.

1132	15c. Douglas DC-4	70	50
1133	20c. Boeing Stearman Kaydet	75	50
1134	35c. North American B-25J Mitchell	1·00	50
1135	40c. McDonnell Douglas F-4B Phantom	1·10	60
1136	70c. Boeing-Vertol CH-47 Chinook helicopter	2·00	1·75
1137	$2 Hughes AH-64 Apache helicopter	4·25	5·50

234 Townsmen under Arcades

2003. Christmas. *Stories from the Life of St. Ursula: Arrival of the English Ambassadors* by Carpaccio. Multicoloured.

1138	20c. Type **234**	60	25
1139	40c. English ambassadors	1·00	50
1140	$2.50 King Maurus of Brittany	4·50	6·00
MS1141	172×87 mm. $1 King Maurus receiving English ambassadors (35×35 mm) and Nos. 1138/40	7·50	8·50

Nos. 1138/40 show details of the painting and No. **MS**1141 the complete painting.

2004. Game Fish. Designs as Nos. 945/6 and 948/9. Self-adhesive. Size 23×19 mm.

1142	15c. Great barracuda	15	20
1143	20c. Tarpon	25	30
1144	35c. Sailfish	40	45
1145	40c. Dolphin	45	50

235 Pomegranate

2004. Local Fruits. Multicoloured.

1146	1c. Hog plum	10	30
1147	10c. Coco plum	20	30
1148	15c. Type **235**	30	30
1149	20c. Cashew	40	30
1150	25c. Sugar apple	60	45
1151	35c. Tamarind	70	45
1152	40c. Soursop	75	50
1153	50c. Mango	85	65
1154	60c. Papaya	1·25	75
1155	75c. Custard apple	1·50	1·25
1156	$1 Otaheite gooseberry	2·00	2·00
1157	$1.50 Guava	3·00	3·25
1158	$2 Guavaberry	4·00	4·25
1159	$5 Mamee apple	8·50	10·00
1160	$10 Passion fruit	15·00	17·00

236 Festival Parade

2004. Golden Jubilee of Island Festival. Multicoloured.

1161	10c. Type **236**	30	50
1162	60c. Horse racing	1·75	1·00
1163	$1 Canoeing	2·00	2·00
1164	$2 Festival queen	3·75	4·75

237 Women's Football

2004. Centenary of FIFA (Federation Internationale de Football Association) and Olympic Games, Athens. Multicoloured.

1165	75c. Type **237**	1·40	1·40
1166	$1 Sprinting	1·75	1·75

238 Black and White Warbler

2005. Birdlife International (2nd series). Caribbean Endemic Bird Festival. Multicoloured.

1167	5c. Type **238**	60	70
1168	10c. Prairie warbler	80	1·00
1169	15c. Yellow-rumped warbler	1·00	1·25
1170	25c. Worm-eating warbler	1·25	50
1171	35c. Yellow warbler	1·25	70
1172	40c. Black-throated warbler	1·50	2·00
1173	50c. Prothonotary warbler	1·50	1·50
1174	60c. Cape May warbler	2·25	3·00
1175	75c. Parula warbler (inscr "Northern Parula")	2·50	3·25
1176	$2.75 Palm warbler	5·50	6·50

2005. Pope John Paul II Commemoration. As T **219** of Ascension.

1177	75c. multicoloured	2·25	2·00

239 Virgin Islands Tree Boa

2005. Endangered Species. Virgin Islands Tree Boa (*Epicrates monensis grant*). Multicoloured.

1178	20c. Type **239**	75	55
1179	30c. Boa in plant (facing left)	1·00	60
1180	70c. On leafy branch	2·00	2·00
1181	$1.05 In foliage (facing right)	2·75	3·50

2005. Bicentenary of the Battle of Trafalgar. As T **220** of Ascension. Multicoloured.

1182	5c. HMS *Colossus* in action before breaking the line	75	75
1183	25c. HMS *Boreas* off British Virgin Islands, 1787	1·75	75
1184	75c. *HMS Victory* (Francis Smitheman)	3·50	2·50
1185	$3 Admiral Lord Nelson (vert)	8·50	10·00
MS1186	120×79 mm. $2.50 HMS *Colossus* firing (44×44 mm)	9·00	10·00

240 Mr. Joshua Smith (first director of Social Security)

2005. Anniversaries. Multicoloured.

1187	20c. Type **240** (25th anniv of Social Security)	60	55
1188	40c. Transmitter on mast and world map (40th anniv of Radio Station ZBVI)	1·50	1·00
1189	50c. Control tower (25th anniv of Beef Island airstrip)	2·00	1·50
1190	$1 Emblem (Centenary of Rotary International)	2·50	3·50

241 Decorated Century Plant

2005. Christmas. Plants and Flowers. Multicoloured.

1191	15c. Type **241**	65	30
1192	35c. Poinsettia (horiz)	1·25	70
1193	60c. Decorated ink-berry in pot	1·75	1·25
1194	$2.50 Snow-on-the-mountain (horiz)	5·50	7·50

2006. 80th Birthday of Queen Elizabeth II. As T **223** of Ascension. Multicoloured.

1195	15c. Princess Elizabeth in Girl Guide uniform	75	30
1196	75c. Queen Elizabeth II wearing white hat and green and white jacket	2·00	1·25
1197	$1.50 Wearing drop earrings	3·50	4·25
1198	$2 Wearing pale mauve hat and jacket	4·75	6·00
MS1199	144×75 mm. $1.50 As No. 1196; $2 As No. 1197	8·00	9·00

Stamps from **MS**1199 do not have white borders.

242 New Red Cross Headquarters, Virgin Gorda

2007. Red Cross Buildings. Multicoloured.

1200	20c. Type **242**	75	80
1201	$3 Former Red Cross building	4·50	5·00

2008. 90th Anniv of the Royal Air Force. As T **63** of British Indian Ocean Territory. Multicoloured.

1202	18c. Supermarine Spitfire	60	50
1203	20c. Avro Lancaster	75	50
1204	35c. Douglas C-47 Dakota	1·25	55
1205	60c. Handley Page Halifax	2·25	1·75
1206	$1.75 Westland Lysander	4·75	6·00
MS1207	110×70 mm. $2.50 Spitfire patrolling D-Day beaches	6·00	6·50

243 Diana, Princess of Wales

2008. Tenth Death Anniv of Diana, Princess of Wales. Multicoloured.

1208	60c. Type **243**	1·00	1·00
MS1209	120×85 mm. $3.50 Wearing red sleeveless dress (42×57 mm)	6·00	7·00

244 Shield

2008. 300th Birth Anniv of Charles Wesley (2007). Multicoloured.

1210	20c. Type **244**	60	40
1211	50c. Rev. Charles Wesley	1·25	1·25
1212	$1.75 Rev. Charles Wesley (in half profile)	3·00	4·00

245 Athlete running

2008. Olympic Games, Beijing. Multicoloured.

1213	15c. Type **245**	30	30
1214	18c. Yachting	35	35
1215	20c. Athlete in race	40	40
1216	$1 Dinghy sailing	2·25	2·75

246 Mace and Mace Head

2008. Ministerial Government. Multicoloured.

1217	18c. Type **246**	35	25
1218	35c. Facade and entrance of House of Assembly	70	55
1219	60c. Henry O. Creque and Ivan Dawson (legislators)	1·40	1·50
1220	$2 Paul Wattley and Terrance B. Lettsome (legislators)	3·75	5·00

247 Sanctuary Wood Cemetery, Ypres, Belgium

2008. 90th Anniv of the End of World War I. Multicoloured.

1221	75c. Type **247**	1·60	1·75
1222	80c. Poppies growing on Somme Battlefield, France (horiz)	1·75	2·00
1223	90c. Lone Pine Cemetery, Gallipoli (horiz)	2·00	2·25
1224	$1 War Memorial, Vauquois, France	2·25	2·50
1225	$1.15 Thiepval Memorial, France (horiz)	2·50	2·75
1226	$1.25 Menin Gate, Ypres, Belgium (horiz)	2·50	2·75
MS1227	110×70 mm. $2 UK Overseas Territories Wreath of Remembrance	4·00	4·50

248 Climbing Pandanus (*Freycinetia cumingiana*)

2009. J. R. O'Neal Botanic Gardens, Road Town, Tortola. Multicoloured.

1228	20c. Type **248**	50	45
1229	35c. True aloe (*Aloe vera*)	85	65
1230	50c. Crown of thorns (*Euphorbia milii*)	1·50	1·50
1231	$1 Red-eared slider (*Trachemys scripta elegans*) (terrapin)	2·25	2·75
MS1232	64×90 mm. $2.50 Fountain and royal palms	4·50	5·50

2009. Seafaring and Exploration. As T **65** of British Indian Ocean Territory. Multicoloured.

1233	15c. HMS *Ark Royal* (English galleon)	70	60
1234	20c. *Whydah* (three masted ship of galley design)	70	60
1235	60c. *Santa Maria* (Columbus)	1·75	1·40
1236	70c. RMS *Rhone* (steam packet)	1·90	1·90
1237	90c. *Golden Hind* (Drake)	2·50	2·25
1238	$1.95 HMY *Britannia* (royal yacht)	4·50	5·00
MS1239	110×70 mm. $2 Christopher Columbus	8·00	8·00

249 Lt. Robert Hampton Gray, 9 August 1945

2009. Centenary of Naval Aviation. Designs showing Victoria Cross holders and aircraft. Multicoloured.

1240	18c. Type **249**	60	60
1241	35c. Lt. Cdr. (A) Eugene Esmonde, 12 February 1942	1·25	1·00
1242	60c. Flt. SLt. Rex Warneford, 7 June 1915	2·25	2·25
1243	90c. Sqn. Cdr. Richard Bell Davies, 19 November 1915	3·00	3·75
MS1244	110×70 mm. $2 Airplane on deck of HMS *Illustrious*, Taranto, 1940	5·50	6·00

2009. International Year of Astronomy. 40th Anniv of First Moon Landing. As T **214** of Bermuda. Multicoloured.

1245	50c. Goddard Rocket Shop, Roswell, 1940	1·50	1·75
1246	75c. Vertol VZ-2, 1960	1·75	2·00
1247	$1 Apollo 11, 1969	2·10	2·50
1248	$1.25 Space Transportation System 126, 2008	2·50	2·75
1249	$2.30 Docking procedure, International Space Station	3·00	3·50
MS1250	100×80 mm. $3 *Tuning in Earth* (Dave Scott pointing antenna at Earth and Jim Irwin loading Lunar Rover) (Alan Bean) (39×59 mm)	6·00	7·00

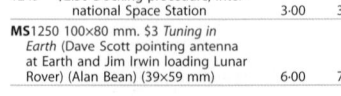

250 Turtle

2010. Coral Reefs

1251	20c. Type **250**	50	50
1252	35c. Fish	65	55
1253	50c. Seahorse (vert)	1·50	1·50
1254	60c. Conch shell (vert)	1·60	1·60
1255	$1.50 Coral reef	3·75	4·50

251 Mr. John E. George (sub-postmaster)

2010. North Sound Post Office. Multicoloured.

1256	20c. Type **251**	90	90
1257	50c. New North Sound Sub Post Office (horiz)	1·60	1·60
1258	$2 Old North Sound Sub Post Office (horiz)	4·50	5·50

252 Church Bell

2010. Bicentenary of East End Methodist Church. Multicoloured.

1259	20c. Type **252**	60	50
1260	50c. East End Methodist Church, 2010	1·75	1·60
1261	60c. East End Methodist Church, 1977	2·00	1·90
1262	$2 East End Methodist Church in early 19th century	5·00	6·00

253 Dinghy sailing

2011. Sailability BVI (sailing programme for the disabled). Multicoloured.

1263	5c. Type **253**	15	25
1264	20c. Two sailors in dinghy with red sails	70	50
1265	25c. Two sailors in blue dinghy	75	65
1266	40c. Arrival of Geoff Holt (quadriplegic transatlantic sailor) in Tortola, 2010	1·40	1·25
1267	50c. Geoff Holt on board yacht *Impossible Dream*, arm raised in triumph	1·60	1·60
1268	$1.50 Geoff Holt on board yacht *Impossible Dream*, arm raised in triumph	4·00	5·00

254 J24 Keel Boat racing, 2000

2011. 40th Anniv of British Virgin Islands Spring Regatta. Multicoloured.

1269	15c. Type **254**	60	45
1270	35c. Mixed fleet (vert), 1980s	1·50	1·00
1271	50c. Yachts flying spinnakers, 1990s	1·90	1·90
1272	$2 Clubhouse and moored dinghies, 1970s	4·00	5·00

255 William and Miss Catherine Middleton

2011. Royal Wedding

MS1273	**255** $5 multicoloured	7·50	8·00

OFFICIAL STAMPS

1985. Nos. 418/21 and 423/33 optd **OFFICIAL**.

O1	1c. Purple-tipped sea anemone	30	1·25
O2	3c. Common starfish	45	1·25
O3	5c. Type **134**	45	45
O4	8c. Triton's trumpet (shell)	55	60
O5	13c. Flamingo tongue snail	80	75
O6	15c. Spider crab	85	70
O7	18c. Sea squirts	90	1·75
O8	20c. True tulip (shell)	90	80
O9	25c. Rooster tail conch (shell)	1·25	2·00
O10	30c. Fighting conch (shell)	1·40	1·00
O11	60c. Mangrove crab	2·00	2·50
O12	$1 Coral polyps	3·00	3·75
O13	$2.50 Peppermint shrimp	4·50	9·00
O14	$3 West Indian murex (shell)	5·50	10·00
O15	$5 Carpet anemone	7·50	10·00

1986. Nos. 560/78 optd **OFFICIAL**.

O16	1c. Type **162**	60	1·75
O17	2c. Yellow-crowned night heron	40	1·75
O18	5c. Mangrove cuckoo	1·25	2·00
O19	8c. Northern mockingbird	55	2·75
O20	10c. Grey kingbird	1·25	2·00
O21	12c. Red-necked pigeon	70	40
O22	15c. Least bittern	1·50	40
O23	18c. Smooth-billed ani	70	75
O24	20c. Clipper rail	1·50	1·00
O25	25c. American kestrel	1·50	1·00
O26	30c. Pearly-eyed thrasher	1·50	1·00
O27	35c. Bridled quail dove	1·50	1·00
O28	40c. Green-backed heron	1·25	1·00
O29	50c. Scaly-breasted ground dove	1·40	1·75
O30	60c. Little blue heron	1·50	2·50
O31	$1 Audubon's shearwater	2·25	3·50
O32	$2 Blue-faced booby	2·50	4·00
O33	$3 Cattle egret	6·00	7·50
O34	$5 Zenaida dove	8·00	10·00

1991. Nos. 767/8, 771, 773/9 and 781 optd **OFFICIAL**.

O35	5c. Frangipani	60	1·50
O36	10c. Autograph tree	60	1·50
O37	20c. Jerusalem thorn	80	65
O38	30c. Swamp immortelle	1·00	65
O39	35c. White cedar	1·00	65
O40	40c. Mahoe tree	1·25	85
O41	45c. Pinguin	1·25	85
O42	50c. Christmas orchid	2·00	1·25
O43	70c. Lignum vitae	2·00	2·50
O44	$1 African tulip tree	2·00	2·75
O45	$3 Organ pipe cactus	5·00	7·50

Pt. 1

BRUNEI

A Sultanate on the North Coast of Borneo.

100 cents = 1 dollar.

1 Star and Local Scene

1895

1	1	½c. brown	5·50	20·00
2	1	1c. brown	5·00	15·00
3	1	2c. black	4·50	16·00
4	1	3c. blue	5·00	14·00
5	1	5c. green	6·50	17·00
6	1	8c. purple	6·50	45·00
7	1	10c. red	8·00	42·00
8	1	25c. green	80·00	£100
9	1	50c. green	24·00	£100
10	1	$1 green	26·00	£120

1906. Stamps of Labuan optd **BRUNEI**. or surch also.

11	18	1c. black and purple	45·00	55·00
12	18	2c. on 3c. black and brown	6·00	18·00
13	18	2c. on 8c. black and orange	27·00	80·00
14	18	3c. black and brown	38·00	85·00
15	18	4c. on 12c. black and yellow	6·50	5·00
16	18	5c. on 16c. green and brown	48·00	75·00
17	18	8c. black and orange	13·00	32·00
18	18	10c. on 16c. green and brown	6·50	22·00
19	18	25c. on 16c. green and brown	£110	£120
20	18	30c. on 16c. green and brown	£110	£120
21	18	50c. on 16c. green and brown	£120	£130
22	18	$1 on 8c. black and orange	£120	£130

5 View on Brunei River

1907

23	5	1c. black and green	2·25	11·00
24	5	2c. black and red	2·50	3·75
25	5	3c. black and brown	10·00	22·00
26	5	4c. black and mauve	7·50	8·00
27	5	5c. black and blue	50·00	90·00
28	5	8c. black and orange	7·50	23·00
29	5	10c. black and green	4·50	5·00
30	5	25c. blue and brown	32·00	48·00
31	5	30c. violet and black	28·00	22·00
32	5	50c. green and brown	15·00	22·00
33	5	$1 red and grey	60·00	90·00

1908

35	1c. green	60	2·00
60	1c. black	1·00	75
79	1c. brown	50	2·00
36	2c. black and brown	4·25	1·25
61	2c. brown	1·00	9·50
62	2c. green	2·00	1·00
80	2c. grey	60	7·50
37	3c. red	6·50	1·25
63	3c. green	1·50	6·50
64	4c. purple	1·50	1·25
65	4c. orange	2·00	1·00
40	5c. black and orange	7·00	7·00
67	5c. grey	21·00	12·00
68	5c. brown	21·00	1·00
82	5c. orange	80	2·00
41	8c. blue and indigo	7·00	11·00
71	8c. blue	6·00	5·00
72	8c. black	16·00	75
84	8c. red	50	2·00
42	10c. purple on yellow	5·50	1·75
85	10c. violet	2·25	30
86	15c. blue	1·75	70
87	25c. purple	2·75	2·00
44	30c. purple and yellow	12·00	15·00
88	30c. black and orange	2·50	1·00
77	50c. black on green	16·00	15·00
89	50c. black	5·50	1·25
46	$1 black and red on blue	26·00	48·00
90	$1 black and red	12·00	2·00
47	$5 red on green	£180	£275
91	$5 green and orange	19·00	24·00
92	$10 black and purple	90·00	30·00
48	$25 black on red	£600	£1100

1922. Optd **MALAYA- BORNEO EXHIBITION. 1922**.

51	1c. green	10·00	50·00
52	2c. black and brown	10·00	50·00
53	3c. red	11·00	55·00
54	4c. red	17·00	55·00
55	5c. orange	22·00	60·00
56	10c. purple on yellow	8·00	60·00
57	25c. lilac	14·00	80·00
58	50c. black on green	45·00	£150
59	$1 black and red on blue	75·00	£190

7 Native Houses, Water Village

1924

81	7	3c. green	1·50	6·50
70	7	6c. red	9·50	11·00
83	7	6c. black	1·00	5·00
74	7	12c. blue	4·50	9·00

8 Sultan Ahmed Tajudin and Water Village

1949. Silver Jubilee of H.H. the Sultan.

93	8	8c. black and red	1·25	1·25
94	8	25c. purple and orange	1·25	1·60
95	8	50c. black and blue	1·25	1·60

1949. 75th Anniv of UPU. As T **20/23** of Antigua.

96	8c. red	1·00	2·25
97	15c. blue	3·50	1·50
98	25c. mauve	1·00	1·50
99	50c. black	1·00	1·25

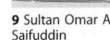

9 Sultan Omar Ali Saifuddin

1952. Dollar values as T **8**, but with arms instead of portrait inset.

100	9	1c. black	10	50
101	9	2c. black and orange	10	50
102	9	3c. black and lake	15	30
103	9	4c. black and green	20	20
104	9	6c. black and grey	1·25	10
123	9	8c. black and red	1·00	10
106	9	10c. black and sepia	20	10
125	9	12c. black and violet	1·50	10
126	9	15c. black and blue	55	10
109	9	25c. black and purple	2·50	10
110	9	50c. black and blue	5·00	10
111	9	$1 black and green (horiz)	1·50	1·40
112	9	$2 black and red (horiz)	5·00	3·00
113	9	$5 black and purple (horiz)	29·00	11·00

11 Brunei Mosque and Sultan Omar

1958. Opening of the Brunei Mosque.

114	11	8c. black and green	20	65
115	11	15c. black and red	25	15
116	11	35c. black and lilac	30	90

12 "Protein Foods"

1963. Freedom from Hunger.

117	12	12c. sepia	2·75	1·00

13 ITU Emblem

1965. Centenary of ITU.

132	13	4c. mauve and brown	35	10
133	13	75c. yellow and green	1·00	75

14 ICY Emblem

1965. International Co-operation Year.

134	14	4c. purple and turquoise	20	10
135	14	15c. green and lavender	55	35

15 Sir Winston Churchill and St. Paul's Cathedral in Wartime

1966. Churchill Commemoration. Designs in black, red and gold and with backgrounds in colours given.

136	15	3c. blue	30	2·00
137	15	10c. green	1·50	20
138	15	15c. brown	1·75	35
139	15	75c. violet	4·25	3·50

16 Footballer's Legs, Ball and Jules Rimet Cup

1966. World Cup Football Championships.

140	16	4c. multicoloured	20	15
141	16	75c. multicoloured	80	60

17 WHO Building

1966. Inauguration of WHO Headquarters, Geneva.

142	17	12c. black, green and blue	40	65

143	17	25c. black, purple and ochre	60	1·25

18 "Education"

1966. 20th Anniv of UNESCO.

144	**18**	4c. multicoloured	35	10
145	-	15c. yellow, violet and olive	75	50
146	-	75c. black, purple and orange	2·50	6·00

DESIGNS: 15c. "Science"; 75c. "Culture".

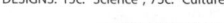

21 Religious Headquarters Building

1967. 1400th Anniv of Revelation of the Koran.

147	**21**	4c. multicoloured	10	10
148	**21**	10c. multicoloured	15	10
149	-	25c. multicoloured	20	30
150	-	50c. multicoloured	35	1·50

Nos. 149/50 have sprigs of laurel flanking the main design (which has a smaller circle) in place of flagpoles.

22 Sultan of Brunei, Mosque and Flags

1968. Installation of Y.T.M. Seri Paduka Duli Pengiran Temenggong. Multicoloured.

151	4c. Type **22**	15	80
152	12c. Sultan of Brunei, Mosque and Flags (different) (horiz)	40	1·60
153	25c. Type **22**	55	2·00

23 Sultan of Brunei

1968. Birthday of Sultan.

154	**23**	4c. multicoloured	10	50
155	**23**	12c. multicoloured	20	85
156	**23**	25c. multicoloured	30	1·40

24 Sultan of Brunei

1968. Coronation of Sultan of Brunei.

157	4c. multicoloured	15	25
158	12c. multicoloured	25	50
159	25c. multicoloured	40	75

25 New Building and Sultan's Portrait

1968. Opening of Hall of Language and Literature Bureau. Multicoloured.

160	10c. Type **25**	20	1·75
161	15c. New Building and Sultan's portrait (48½×22 mm)	20	35
162	30c. As 15c.	45	90

27 Human Rights Emblem and struggling Man

1968. Human Rights Year.

163	**27**	12c. black, yellow and green	10	20
164	**27**	25c. black, yellow and blue	15	25
165	**27**	75c. black, yellow and purple	45	1·75

28 Sultan of Brunei and WHO Emblem

1968. 20th Anniv of World Health Organization.

166	**28**	4c. yellow, black and blue	30	30
167	**28**	15c. yellow, black and violet	55	65
168	**28**	25c. yellow, black and olive	65	1·25

29 Deep Sea Oil-Rig, Sultan of Brunei and inset portrait of Pengiran Di-Gadong

1969. Installation (9th May, 1968) of Pengiran Shar-bandar as Y.T.M. Seri Paduka Duli Pengiran Di-Gadong Sahibol Mal.

169	**29**	12c. multicoloured	85	50
170	**29**	40c. multicoloured	1·25	2·00
171	**29**	50c. multicoloured	1·25	2·00

30 Aerial View of Parliament Buildings

1969. Opening of Royal Audience Hall and Legislative Council Chamber.

172	**30**	12c. multicoloured	20	25
173	**30**	25c. multicoloured	30	45
174	-	50c. red and violet	60	3·50

DESIGN: 50c. Elevation of new buildings.

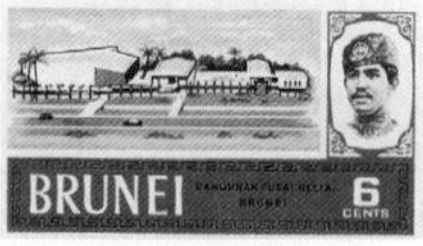
32 Youth Centre and Sultan's Portrait

1969. Opening of New Youth Centre.

175	**32**	6c. multicoloured	20	1·00
176	**32**	10c. multicoloured	25	10
177	**32**	30c. multicoloured	70	1·00

33 Soldier, Sultan and Badge

1971. Tenth Anniv of Royal Brunei Malay Regiment. Multicoloured.

178	10c. Type **33**	80	30
179	15c. Bell 205 Iroquois helicopter, Sultan and badge (horiz)	1·75	70
180	75c. "Pahlawan" (patrol boat), Sultan and badge (horiz)	3·25	7·00

34 Badge, and Officer in Full-dress Uniform

1971. 50th Anniv of Royal Brunei Police Force. Multicoloured.

181	10c. Type **34**	50	30
182	15c. Badge and Patrol constable	60	90
183	50c. Badge and Traffic constable	1·10	6·00

35 Perdana Wazir, Sultan of Brunei and View of Water Village

1971. Installation of the Yang Teramat Mulia as the Perdana Wazir.

184	**35**	15c. multicoloured	40	50
185	-	25c. multicoloured	70	1·00
186	-	50c. multicoloured	1·40	5·00

Nos. 185/6 show various views of Brunei Town.

36 Pottery

1972. Opening of Brunei Museum. Multicoloured.

187	10c. Type **36**	30	10
188	12c. Straw-work	40	20
189	15c. Leather-work	45	20
190	25c. Gold-work	1·25	1·25
191	50c. Museum Building (58×21 mm)	2·25	5·50

37 Modern Building, Queen Elizabeth and Sultan of Brunei

1972. Royal Visit. Each design with portrait of Queen and Sultan. Multicoloured.

192	10c. Type **37**	70	20
193	15c. Native houses	95	55
194	25c. Mosque	2·00	1·60
195	50c. Royal Assembly Hall	3·75	7·00

38 Secretariat Building

1972. Renaming of Brunei Town as Bandar Seri Begawan.

196	**38**	10c. multicoloured	20	15
197	-	15c. green, yellow and black	25	15
198	-	25c. blue, yellow and black	45	50
199	-	50c. red, blue and black	75	2·25

VIEWS: 15c. Darul Hana Palace; 25c. Old Brunei Town; 50c. Town and Water Village.

39 Blackburn Beverley C1 parachuting Supplies

1972. Opening of R.A.F. Museum, Hendon. Multicoloured.

200	25c. Type **39**	1·75	1·25
201	75c. Blackburn Beverley C1 landing	3·25	4·75

1972. Royal Silver Wedding. As T **52** of Ascension, but with girl with traditional flower-pot, and boy with bowl and pipe in background.

210	12c. red	10	10
211	75c. green	20	50

41 Interpol H.Q., Paris

1973. 50th Anniv of Interpol.

212	**41**	25c. green, purple and black	1·50	1·25
213	-	50c. blue, ultram & red	1·50	1·25

DESIGN: 50c. Different view of the H.Q.

42 Sultan, Princess Anne and Captain Phillips

1973. Royal Wedding.

214	**42**	25c. multicoloured	15	10
215	**42**	50c. multicoloured	15	25

43 Churchill Painting

1973. Opening of Churchill Memorial Building. Multicoloured.

216	12c. Type **43**	10	20
217	50c. Churchill statue	30	1·40

44 Sultan Sir Hassanal Bolkiah Mu'izzaddin Waddaulah

1975. Multicoloured. Background colours given.

218	**44**	4c. green	20	20
219	**44**	5c. blue	20	30
220	**44**	6c. green	3·25	6·50
221	**44**	10c. lilac	30	10
222	**44**	15c. brown	2·50	40
223	**44**	20c. stone	30	20
224	**44**	25c. green	40	15
225	**44**	30c. blue	40	15
226	**44**	35c. grey	40	20
227	**44**	40c. purple	40	20
228	**44**	50c. brown	40	20
229	**44**	75c. green	60	3·50
256	**44**	$1 orange	1·50	3·50
231	**44**	$2 yellow	2·25	11·00
232	**44**	$5 silver	3·00	18·00
233	**44**	$10 gold	5·00	32·00

45 Aerial View of Airport

1974. Inauguration of Brunei International Airport. Multicoloured.

234	50c. Type **45**	1·25	1·00
235	75c. Sultan in Army uniform, and airport (48×36 mm)	1·50	1·50

46 U.P.U. Emblem and Sultan

1974. Centenary of Universal Postal Union.

236	**46**	12c. multicoloured	20	20

237	46	50c. multicoloured	40	1·40
238	46	75c. multicoloured	50	1·75

47 Sir Winston Churchill

1974. Birth Centenary of Sir Winston Churchill.

239	47	12c. black, blue and gold	25	20
240	-	75c. black, green and gold	45	1·40

DESIGN: 75c. Churchill smoking cigar (profile).

48 Boeing 737 and R.B.A. Crest

1975. Inauguration of Royal Brunei Airlines. Multicoloured.

241	12c. Type **48**	1·00	25
242	35c. Boeing 737 over Bandar Seri Begawan Mosque	1·75	1·75
243	75c. Boeing 737 in flight	2·50	4·00

1976. Surch **10 sen**.

263	44	10c. on 6c. brown	1·75	1·75

50 Royal Coat of Arms

1977. Silver Jubilee. Multicoloured.

264	10c. Type **50**	15	15
265	20c. Imperial State Crown	20	20
266	75c. Queen Elizabeth (portrait by Annigoni)	45	60

51 The Moment of Crowning

1978. 25th Anniv of Coronation. Multicoloured.

267	10c. Type **51**	15	10
268	20c. Queen in Coronation regalia	20	20
269	75c. Queen's departure from Abbey	55	80

52 Royal Crest

1978. Tenth Anniv of Coronation of Sultan.

270	52	10c. black, red and yellow	20	10
271	-	20c. multicoloured	40	25
272	-	75c. multicoloured	1·10	3·50
MS273		182×77 mm. Nos. 270/2	12·00	16·00

DESIGNS: 20c. Coronation; 75c. Sultan's Crown.

53 Human Rights Emblem and Struggling Man

1978. Human Rights Year.

274	53	10c. black, yellow and red	15	10
275	53	20c. black, yellow and violet	20	35
276	53	75c. black, yellow and bistre	40	2·50

Type **53** is similar to the design used for the previous Human Rights issue in 1968.

54 Smiling Children

1979. International Year of the Child.

277	54	10c. multicoloured	20	10
278	-	$1 black and green	80	2·50

DESIGN: $1 I.Y.C. emblem.

55 Earth Satellite Station

1979. Telisai Earth Satellite Station. Multicoloured.

279	10c. Type **55**	20	15
280	20c. Satellite and antenna	30	40
281	75c. Television camera, telex machine and telephone	60	2·75

56 Hegira Symbol

1979. Moslem Year 1400 A.H. Commemoration.

282	56	10c. black, yellow and green	10	15
283	56	20c. black, yellow and blue	15	30
284	56	75c. black, yellow and lilac	45	2·25
MS285		178×200 mm. Nos. 282/4	3·00	7·50

57 Installation Ceremony

1980. First Anniv of Prince Sufri Bolkiah's Installation as First Wazir. Multicoloured. Blue borders.

286	10c. Type **57**	15	10
287	75c. Prince Sufri	85	2·25

1980. First Anniv of Prince Jefri Bolkiah's Installation as Second Wazir. Designs similar to T **57**. Multicoloured. Green borders.

288	10c. Installation ceremony	15	10
289	75c. Prince Jefri	85	2·25

58 Royal Umbrella and Sash

1981. Royal Regalia (1st series). Multicoloured.

290	10c. Type **58**	20	15
291	15c. Sword and Shield	35	25
292	20c. Lance and Sheath	40	40
293	30c. Betel Leaf Container	60	1·25
294	50c. Coronation Crown (39×22 mm)	1·25	5·00
MS295	98×142 mm. Nos. 290/4	5·00	8·00

See Nos. 298/303, 314/19 and 320/5.

59 ITU and WHO Emblems

1981. World Telecommunications and Health Day.

296	59	10c. black and red	50	25
297	59	75c. black, blue and violet	2·25	5·00

60 Shield and Broadsword

1981. Royal Regalia (2nd series). Multicoloured.

298	10c. Type **60**	10	10
299	15c. Blunderbuss and Pouch	20	20
300	20c. Crossed Lances and Sash	30	30
301	30c. Sword, Shield and Sash	40	75
302	50c. Forked Lance	60	2·50
303	75c. Royal Drum (29×45 mm)	80	4·50

61 Prince Charles as Colonel of the Welsh Guards

1981. Royal Wedding. Multicoloured.

304	10c. Wedding bouquet from Brunei	15	15
305	$1 Type **61**	35	1·50
306	$2 Prince Charles and Lady Diana Spencer	50	2·50

62 Fishing

1981. World Food Day. Multicoloured.

307	10c. Type **62**	50	15
308	$1 Farm produce and machinery	4·50	7·50

63 Blind Man and Braille Alphabet

1981. International Year for Disabled Persons. Multicoloured.

309	10c. Type **63**	65	20
310	20c. Deaf people and sign language	1·50	80
311	75c. Disabled person and wheelchairs	3·00	6·75

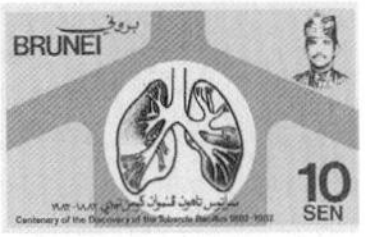

64 Drawing of Infected Lungs

1982. Centenary of Robert Koch's Discovery of Tubercle Bacillus. Multicoloured.

312	10c. Type **64**	50	25
313	75c. Magnified tubercle bacillus and microscope	3·00	6·50

1982. Royal Regalia (3rd series). As T **60**. Multicoloured.

314	10c. Ceremonial Ornament	10	10
315	15c. Silver Betel Caddy	20	20
316	20c. Traditional Flowerpot	25	30
317	30c. Solitary Candle	50	90
318	50c. Golden Pipe	70	2·50
319	75c. Royal Chin Support (28×45 mm)	90	4·00

1982. Royal Regalia (4th series). As T **60**. Multicoloured.

320	10c. Royal Mace	25	10
321	15c. Ceremonial Shield and Spears	35	30
322	20c. Embroidered Ornament	45	40
323	30c. Golden-tasseled Cushion	75	1·50
324	50c. Ceremonial Dagger and Sheath	1·25	3·50
325	75c. Religious Mace (28×45 mm)	1·60	4·50

65 Brunei Flag

1983. Commonwealth Day.

326	65	10c. multicoloured	15	80
327	-	20c. blue, black and buff	20	90
328	-	75c. blue, black and green	45	1·40
329	-	$2 blue, black and yellow	1·10	2·00

DESIGNS: 20c. Brunei Mosque; 75c. Machinery; $2 Sultan of Brunei.

66 "Postal Service"

1983. World Communications Year.

330	66	10c. multicoloured	15	10
331	-	75c. yellow, brown and black	60	75
332	-	$2 multicoloured	1·75	2·25

DESIGNS: 75c. "Telephone Service"; $2 "Communications".

67 Football

1983. Official Opening of the National Hassanal Bolkiah Stadium. Multicoloured.

333	10c. Type **67**	55	15
334	75c. Athletics	2·25	1·50
335	$1 View of stadium (44×27 mm)	2·75	4·00

68 Fishermen and Crustacea

1983. Fishery Resources. Multicoloured.

336	10c. Type **68**	1·50	15
337	50c. Fishermen with net	3·75	1·50
338	75c. Fishing trawler	4·00	4·25
339	$1 Fishing with hook and tackle	4·25	4·75

69 Royal Assembly Hall

1984. Independence.

340	69	10c. brown and orange	20	10
341	-	20c. pink and red	30	20

342	-	35c. pink and purple	60	60
343	-	50c. light blue and blue	1·75	1·25
344	-	75c. light green and green	1·75	2·00
345	-	$1 grey and brown	2·00	2·50
346	-	$3 multicoloured	7·00	10·00
MS347		150×120 mm. Nos. 340/6	12·00	16·00
MS348		Two sheets, each 150×120 mm, containing 4 stamps (34×69 mm). (a) 25c. × 4 grey-black and new blue (Signing of the Brunei Constitution). (b) 25c. × 4 multicoloured (Signing of Brunei–U.K. Friendship Agreement) Set of 2 sheets	2·25	4·50

DESIGNS—34×25 mm: 20c. Government Secretariat Building; 35c. New Supreme Court; 50c. Natural gas well; 75c. Omar Ali Saifuddin Mosque; $1 Sultan's Palace. 68×24 mm: $3 Brunei flag and map of South-East Asia.

70 Natural Forests and Enrichment Planting

1984. Forestry Resources. Multicoloured.

349	10c. Type **70**	1·00	25
350	50c. Forests and water resources	2·50	2·25
351	75c. Recreation forests	3·25	4·50
352	$1 Forests and wildlife	4·75	6·00

71 Sultan Omar Saiffuddin 50c. Stamp of 1952

1984. "Philakorea" International Stamp Exhibition, Seoul. Multicoloured.

353	10c. Type **71**	50	15
354	75c. Brunei River view 10c. stamp of 1907	1·50	2·25
355	$2 Star and view ½c. stamp of 1895	2·50	6·50
MS356	Three sheets, 117×100 mm, each containing one stamp as Nos. 353/5 Set of 3 sheets	3·75	7·00

72 United Nations Emblem

1985. Admission of Brunei to World Organizations (1st issue).

357	**72**	50c. black, gold and blue	50	70
358	-	50c. multicoloured	50	70
359	-	50c. multicoloured	50	70
360	-	50c. multicoloured	50	70
MS361		110×151 mm. Nos. 357/60	4·00	4·00

DESIGNS: No. 358, Islamic Conference Organization logo; 359, Commonwealth logo; 360, A.S.E.A.N. emblem.

See also Nos. 383/7.

73 Young People and Brunei Flag

1985. International Youth Year. Multicoloured.

362	10c. Type **73**	2·00	30
363	75c. Young people at work	5·50	7·00
364	$1 Young people serving the community	6·00	7·50

74 Palestinian Emblem

1985. International Palestinian Solidarity Day.

365	**74**	10c. multicoloured	2·25	20
366	**74**	50c. multicoloured	4·75	1·50
367	**74**	$1 multicoloured	6·50	3·75

75 Early and Modern Scout Uniforms

1985. National Scout Jamboree. Multicoloured.

368	10c. Type **75**	60	10
369	20c. Scout on tower signalling with flag	90	40
370	$2 Jamboree emblem	2·75	3·25

76 Sultan Sir Hassanal Bolkiah Mu'izzaddin Waddaulah

1985

371	**76**	10c. multicoloured	30	10
372	**76**	15c. multicoloured	30	10
373	**76**	20c. multicoloured	40	10
374	**76**	25c. multicoloured	40	15
375	**76**	35c. multicoloured	55	20
376	**76**	40c. multicoloured	60	25
377	**76**	50c. multicoloured	70	35
378	**76**	75c. multicoloured	90	50
379	**76**	$1 multicoloured	1·25	70
380	**76**	$2 multicoloured	2·75	1·75
381	**76**	$5 multicoloured	4·25	5·00
382	**76**	$10 multicoloured	8·00	11·00

Nos. 379/82 are larger, size 32×39 mm.

1986. Admission of Brunei to World Organizations (2nd issue). As T **72**.

383	50c. black, gold and green	50	60
384	50c. black, gold and mauve	50	60
385	50c. black, gold and red	50	60
386	50c. black, gold and blue	50	60
MS387	105×155 mm. Nos. 383/6	1·50	4·00

DESIGNS: No. 383, World Meteorological Organ-ization emblem; 384, International Tele-communication Union emblem; 385, Universal Postal Union emblem; 386, International Civil Aviation Organization emblem.

78 Soldiers on Assault Course and Bell 205 UH-1H Iroquois Helicopter

1986. 25th Anniv of Brunei Armed Forces. Multicoloured.

388	10c. Type **78**	4·25	4·25
389	20c. Operating computer	4·50	4·50
390	50c. Anti-aircraft missile, MBB-Bolkow Bo 150L helicopter and missile boat	6·00	6·00
391	75c. Army, commanders and parade	6·50	6·50

Nos. 388/91 were printed together, *se-tenant*, forming a composite design.

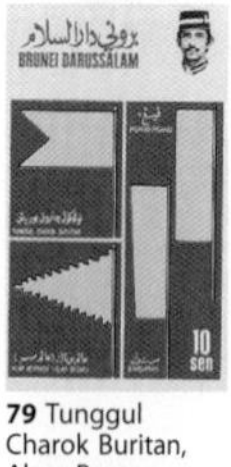

79 Tunggul Charok Buritan, Alam Bernaga (Alam Besar), Pisang-Pisang and Sandaran

1986. Royal Ensigns (1st series).

392	**79**	10c. black, yellow and red	30	10
393	-	75c. multicoloured	1·10	1·10
394	-	$2 black, yellow and green	2·25	2·75

DESIGNS: 75c. Ula-Ula Besar, Sumbu Layang and Payong Haram; $2 Panji-Panji, Chogan Istiadat (Chogan Di-Raja) and Chogan Ugama.

1986. Royal Ensigns (2nd series). As T **79**.

395	10c. multicoloured	30	10
396	75c. black, red and yellow	1·10	1·10
397	$2 multicoloured	2·25	2·75

DESIGNS: 10c. Dadap, Tunggul Kawan, Ambal, Payong Ubor-Ubor, Sapu-Sapu Ayeng and Rawai Lidah; 75c. Payong Tinggi and Payong Ubor-Ubor Tiga Ringkat; $2 Lambang Duli Yang Maha Mulia and Mahligai.

80 Stylized Peace Doves

1986. International Peace Year. Multicoloured.

398	50c. Type **80**	75	75
399	75c. Stylized hands and "1986"	1·00	1·10
400	$1 International Peace Year emblem and arms of Brunei	1·25	1·50

81 Drug Addict in Cage and Syringe (poster by Othman bin Ramboh)

1987. National Anti-drug Campaign. Children's Posters. Multicoloured.

401	10c. Type **81**	1·50	35
402	75c. Drug addict and noose (Arman bin Mohd. Zaman)	3·00	4·25
403	$1 Blindfolded drug addict and noose (Abidin bin Hj. Rashid)	3·50	5·50

82 Cannon ("badil")

1987. Brassware (1st series). Multicoloured.

404	50c. Type **82**	50	50
405	50c. Lamp ("pelita")	50	50
406	50c. Betel container ("langguai")	50	50
407	50c. Water jug ("kiri")	50	50

See also Nos. 434/7.

83 Map showing Member Countries

1987. 20th Anniv of Association of South East Asian Nations. Multicoloured.

408	20c. Type **83**	35	20
409	50c. Dates and figures "20"	60	50
410	$1 Flags of member states	1·25	1·25

84 Brunei Citizens

1987. 25th Anniv (1986) of Language and Literature Bureau. Multicoloured.

411	10c. Type **84**	50	40
412	50c. Flame emblem and hands holding open book	1·00	75
413	$2 Scenes of village life	1·75	2·00

Nos. 411/13 were printed together, *se-tenant*, forming a composite design taken from a mural.

85 *Artocarpus odoratissima*

1987. Local Fruit (1st series). Multicoloured.

414	50c. Type **85**	75	70
415	50c. *Canarium odontophyllum mig*	75	70
416	50c. *Litsea garciae*	75	70
417	50c. *Mangifera foetida lour*	75	70

See also Nos. 421/4, 459/62, 480/2 and 525/8.

86 Modern House

1987. International Year of Shelter for the Homeless.

418	**86**	50c. multicoloured	40	50
419	-	75c. multicoloured	55	65
420	-	$1 multicoloured	80	90

DESIGNS: 75c., $1 Modern Brunei housing projects.

1988. Local Fruits (2nd series). As T **85**. Multicoloured.

421	50c. *Durio spp*	95	1·25
422	50c. *Durio oxleyanus*	95	1·25
423	50c. *Durio graveolens* (blue background)	95	1·25
424	50c. *Durio graveolens* (white background)	95	1·25

87 Wooden Lathe

1988. Opening of Malay Technology Museum. Multicoloured.

425	10c. Type **87**	15	10
426	75c. Crushing sugar cane	55	70
427	$1 Bird scarer	70	85

88 Patterned Cloth

1988. Handwoven Material (1st series). Multicoloured.

428	10c. Type **88**	10	10
429	20c. Jong Sarat cloth	15	15
430	25c. Si Pugut cloth	20	25
431	40c. Si Pugut Bunga Berlapis cloth	30	35
432	75c. Si Lobang Bangsi Bunga Belitang Kipas cloth	55	80
MS433	105×204 mm. Nos. 428/32	3·00	4·50

See also Nos. 442/7.

1988. Brassware (2nd series). As T **82**. Multicoloured.

434	50c. Lidded two-handled pot ("periok")	60	75
435	50c. Candlestick ("lampong")	60	75
436	50c. Shallow circular dish with stand ("gangsa")	60	75
437	50c. Repousse box with lid ("celapa")	60	75

89 Sultan reading Proclamation

1988. 20th Anniv of Sultan's Coronation. Multicoloured.

438	20c. Type **89**	25	15
439	75c. Sultan reading from Koran	1·00	60
440	$2 In Coronation robes (26×63 mm)	2·25	1·60
MS441	164×125 mm. Nos. 438/40	3·00	2·50

1988. Handwoven Material (2nd series). As T **88**. Multicoloured.

442	10c. Beragi cloth	15	10
443	20c. Bertabur cloth	20	20
444	25c. Sukma Indra cloth	25	35
445	40c. Si Pugut Bunga cloth	40	75
446	75c. Beragi Si Lobang Bangsi Bunga Cendera Kesuma cloth	75	1·40
MS447	150×204 mm. Nos. 442/6	3·50	4·50

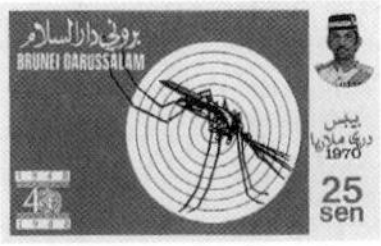

90 Malaria-carrying Mosquito

1988. 40th Anniv of WHO. Multicoloured.

448	25c. Type **90**	1·25	30
449	35c. Man with insecticide spray and sample on slide	1·40	45
450	$2 Microscope and magnified malaria cells	3·25	2·00

91 Sultan and Council of Ministers

1989. Fifth Anniv of National Day. Multicoloured.

451	20c. Type **91**	15	10
452	30c. Guard of honour	20	15
453	60c. Firework display (27×55 mm)	45	40
454	$2 Congregation in mosque	1·50	1·75
MS455	164×124 mm. Nos. 451/4	2·25	2·75

92 Dove escaping from Cage

1989. "Freedom of Palestine". Multicoloured.

456	20c. Type **92**	50	20
457	75c. Map and Palestinian flag	2·00	1·25
458	$1 Dome of the Rock, Jerusalem	2·75	1·50

1989. Local Fruit (3rd series). As T **85**. Multicoloured.

459	60c. *Daemonorops fissa*	2·00	2·50
460	60c. *Eleiodoxa conferta*	2·00	2·50
461	60c. *Salacca zalacca*	2·00	2·50
462	60c. *Calamus ornatus*	2·00	2·50

93 Oil Pump

1989. 60th Anniv of Brunei Oil and Gas Industry. Multicoloured.

463	20c. Type **93**	2·50	30
464	60c. Loading tanker	4·00	2·25
465	90c. Oil well at sunset	4·50	3·00
466	$1 Pipe laying	4·75	3·00
467	$2 Oil terminal	8·00	9·00

94 Museum Building and Exhibits

1990. 25th Anniv of Brunei Museum. Multicoloured.

468	30c. Type **94**	1·50	70
469	60c. Official opening, 1965	2·25	2·25
470	$1 Brunei Museum	3·00	4·00

95 Letters from Malay Alphabet

1990. International Literacy Year. Multicoloured.

471	15c. Type **95**	80	40
472	90c. English alphabet	3·50	4·25
473	$1 Literacy Year emblem and letters	3·50	4·25

96 Tarsier in Tree

1990. Endangered Species. Western Tarsier. Multicoloured.

474	20c. Western Tarsier on branch	1·25	45
475	60c. Western Tarsier feeding	2·50	3·00
476	90c. Type **96**	3·50	4·50

97 Symbolic Family

1990. Worldwide Campaign against AIDS. Multicoloured.

477	20c. Type **97**	3·00	60
478	30c. Sources of infection	4·00	2·00
479	90c. "AIDS" headstone surrounded by skulls	9·50	8·50

1990. Local Fruit (4th series). As T **85**. Multicoloured.

480	60c. *Willoughbea* sp. (brown fruit)	3·00	3·75
481	60c. Ripe *Willoughbea* sp. (yellow fruit)	3·00	3·75
482	60c. *Willoughbea angustifolia*	3·00	3·75

98 Proboscis Monkey on Ground

1991. Endangered Species. Proboscis Monkey. Multicoloured.

483	15c. Type **98**	1·50	60
484	20c. Head of monkey	1·60	70
485	50c. Monkey sitting on branch	3·00	3·25
486	60c. Female monkey with baby climbing tree	3·25	3·75

99 Junior School Classes

1991. Teachers' Day. Multicoloured.

487	60c. Type **99**	2·25	2·50
488	90c. Secondary school class	2·75	3·50

100 Young Brunei Beauty

1991. Fish. Brunei Beauty. Multicoloured.

489	30c. Type **100**	1·50	85
490	60c. Female fish	2·50	4·00
491	$1 Male fish	3·00	4·75

101 Graduate with Family

1991. Happy Family Campaign. Multicoloured.

492	20c. Type **101**	70	50
493	60c. Mothers with children	1·75	2·00
494	90c. Family	2·00	3·25

102 Symbolic Heart and Trace

1992. World Health Day.

495	**102**	20c. multicoloured	2·25	50
496	-	50c. multicoloured	4·00	2·50
497	-	75c. multicoloured	6·00	6·50

DESIGNS: 50c., 70c. (48×27 mm) Heart and heartbeat trace.

103 Map of Cable System

1992. Launching of Singapore–Borneo–Philippines Fibre Optic Submarine Cable System. Multicoloured.

498	20c. Type **103**	3·00	50
499	30c. Diagram of Brunei connection	3·00	1·50
500	90c. Submarine cable	6·00	6·50

104 Modern Sculptures

1992. Visit ASEAN Year. Multicoloured.

501	20c. Type **104**	2·75	3·00
502	60c. Traditional martial arts	3·00	3·25
503	$1 Modern sculptures (different)	3·25	3·50

Nos. 501/3 were printed together, *se-tenant*, the backgrounds forming a composite design.

105 "ASEAN 25" and Logo

1992. 25th Anniv of ASEAN (Association of South East Asian Nations). Multicoloured.

504	20c. Type **105**	1·25	65
505	60c. Headquarters building	2·75	2·75
506	90c. National landmarks	3·50	4·50

106 Sultan in Procession

1992. 25th Anniv of Sultan's Accession. Multicoloured.

507	25c. Type **106**	1·50	2·00
508	25c. Brunei International Airport	1·50	2·00
509	25c. Sultan's Palace	1·50	2·00
510	25c. Docks and Brunei University	1·50	2·00
511	25c. Mosque	1·50	2·00

Nos. 507/11 were printed together, *se-tenant*, forming a composite design.

107 Crested Wood Partridge

1992. Birds (1st series). Multicoloured.

512	30c. Type **107**	1·00	50
513	60c. Asiatic paradise flycatcher ("Asian Paradise Flycatcher")	2·00	2·25
514	$1 Great argus pheasant	2·25	3·00

See also Nos. 515/17, 518/20, 575/7 and 602/5.

1993. Birds (2nd series). As T **107**. Multicoloured.

515	30c. Long-tailed parakeet	1·00	50
516	60c. Magpie robin	2·00	2·25
517	$1 Blue-crowned hanging parrot ("Malay Lorikeet")	2·50	3·00

1993. Birds (3rd series). As T **107**. Multicoloured.

518	30c. Chesnut-breasted malkoha	1·25	50
519	60c. White-rumped shama	2·25	2·50
520	$1 Black and red broadbill (vert)	3·00	3·50

108 National Flag and "10"

1994. Tenth Anniv of National Day. Multicoloured.

521	10c. Type **108**	1·25	1·25
522	20c. Symbolic hands	1·25	1·40
523	30c. Previous National Day symbols	1·40	1·50
524	60c. Coat of arms	1·75	1·90

1994. Local Fruit (5th issue). As T **85**, but each 36×26 mm. Multicoloured.

525	60c. *Nephelium mutabile*	85	1·40
526	60c. *Nephelium xerospermoides*	85	1·40
527	60c. *Nephelium spp*	85	1·40
528	60c. *Nephelium macrophyllum*	85	1·40

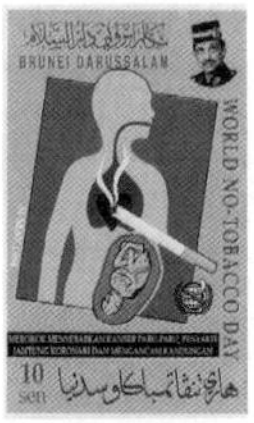

109 Cigarette burning Heart and Deformed Baby in Womb

1994. World No Tobacco Day. Multicoloured.

529	10c. Type **109**	40	20
530	15c. Symbols of smoking over crowd of people	40	20
531	$2 Globe crushing cigarettes	3·00	5·00

110 Raja Isteri (wife of Sultan in Guide uniform)

1994. 40th Anniv of Brunei Girl Guides' Association. Multicoloured.

532	40c. Type **110**	2·00	2·00
533	40c. Guide receiving award	2·00	2·00
534	40c. Guide reading	2·00	2·00
535	40c. Group of guides	2·00	2·00
536	40c. Guides erecting tent	2·00	2·00

111 Fokker F-27 Friendship on Runway

1994. 20th Anniv of Royal Brunei Airlines. Multicoloured.

537	10c. Type **111**	1·00	45
538	20c. Boeing 757 on runway	1·50	45
539	$1 Boeing 757 in the air	3·50	4·50

112 Malay Family

1994. International Day against Drug Abuse and Trafficking. Multicoloured.

540	20c. Type **112**	1·10	1·60
541	60c. Chinese family	1·40	1·90
542	$1 Doctor, police officers and members of youth organizations	1·75	2·50

Nos. 540/2 were printed together, *se-tenant*, forming a composite design.

113 Aerial View of City, 1970

1995. 25th Anniv of Bandar Seri Begawan. Multicoloured.

543	30c. Type **113**	1·50	45
544	50c. City in 1980	2·00	1·50
545	$1 City in 1990	2·75	4·00

114 United Nations General Assembly

1995. 50th Anniv of United Nations. Multicoloured.

546	20c. Type **114**	50	25
547	60c. Security Council in session	1·00	90
548	90c. United Nations Building, New York (27×44 mm)	1·50	2·50

115 Students in Laboratory

1995. Tenth Anniv of University of Brunei. Multicoloured.

549	30c. Type **115**	45	35
550	50c. University building	70	70
551	90c. Sultan visiting University	1·25	2·25

116 Police Officers

1996. 75th Anniv of Royal Brunei Police Force. Multicoloured.

552	25c. Type **116**	1·50	60
553	50c. Aspects of police work	2·00	1·50
554	75c. Sultan inspecting parade	2·50	3·50

117 Telephones

1996. World Telecommunications Day. Children's Paintings. Multicoloured.

555	20c. Type **117**	85	40
556	35c. Telephone dial and aspects of telecommunications	1·40	60
557	$1 Globe and aspects of telecommunications	3·50	4·00

118 Sultan and Crowd

1996. 50th Birthday of Sultan Hassanal Bolkiah Mu'izzaddin Waddaulah. Multicoloured.

558	50c. Type **118**	1·40	1·75
559	50c. Sultan in ceremonial dress	1·40	1·75
560	50c. Sultan receiving dignitaries at mosque	1·40	1·75
561	50c. Sultan with subjects	1·40	1·75
MS562	152×100 mm. $1 Sultan in ceremonial dress (different)	2·25	3·00

119 Sultan Hassanal Bolkiah Mu'izzaddin Waddaulah

1996

563	**119**	10c. multicoloured	20	10
564	**119**	15c. multicoloured	25	25
565	**119**	20c. multicoloured	30	25
566	**119**	30c. multicoloured	40	35
567	**119**	50c. multicoloured	70	50
568	**119**	60c. multicoloured	80	60
569	**119**	75c. multicoloured	1·00	70
570	**119**	90c. multicoloured	1·25	90
571	-	$1 multicoloured	1·50	1·00
572	-	$2 multicoloured	2·75	2·25
573	-	$5 multicoloured	6·50	6·50
574	-	$10 multicoloured	12·00	12·00

DESIGN—27×39 mm: $1 to $10 Sultan in ceremonial robes.

121 Black-naped Tern

1996. Birds (4th series). Sea Birds. Multicoloured.

575	20c. Type **121**	75	50
576	30c. Roseate tern	75	50
577	$1 Bridled tern	1·75	2·75

No. 576 is inscr "ROSLATE TERN" in error.

122 *Acanthus ebracteatus*

1997. Mangrove Flowers. Multicoloured.

578	20c. Type **122**	45	25
579	30c. *Lumnitzera littorea*	50	35
580	$1 *Nypa fruticans*	1·40	2·50

123 *Heterocentrotus mammillatus*

1997. Marine Life. Multicoloured.

581	60c. Type **123**	70	1·00
582	60c. *Linckia laevigata* (starfish)	70	1·00
583	60c. *Oxycomanthus bennetti* (plant)	70	1·00
584	60c. *Bohadschia argus* (sea slug)	70	1·00

124 Children and Sign Language

1998. Asian and Pacific Decade of Disabled Persons, 1993–2002. Multicoloured.

585	20c. Type **124**	55	25
586	50c. Woman typing and firework display	1·00	1·00
587	$1 Disabled athletes	1·75	2·50

125 Sultan performing Ceremonial Duties

1998. 30th Anniv of Coronation of Sultan Hassanal Bolkiah Mu'izzaddin Waddaulah. Multicoloured.

588	60c. Type **125**	1·00	50
589	90c. Sultan on Coronation throne	1·40	1·60
590	$1 Coronation parade	1·50	1·60
MS591	150×180 mm. Nos. 588/90	3·50	4·00

126 A.S.E.A.N. Architecture and Transport

1998. 30th Anniv of Association of South-east Asian Nations. Multicoloured.

592	30c. Type **126**	1·25	1·25
593	30c. Map of Brunei and city scenes	1·25	1·25
594	30c. Flags of member nations	1·25	1·25

127 Crown Prince at Desk

1998. Proclamation of Prince Al-Muhtadee Billah as Crown Prince. Multicoloured.

595	$1 Type **127**	1·00	1·00
596	$2 Crown Prince in military uniform	1·75	2·75
597	$3 Crown Prince's emblem	2·25	3·75
MS598	175×153 mm. Nos. 595/7.	5·50	7·00

128 Koran, Civil Servants and Handshake

1998. Fifth Anniv of Civil Service Day. Multicoloured.

599	30c. Type **128**	60	30
600	60c. Symbols of progress	1·00	75
601	90c. Civil servants at work	1·50	2·00

129 Blue-eared Kingfisher

1998. Birds (5th series). Kingfishers. Multicoloured.

602	20c. Type **129**	1·00	60
603	30c. River kingfisher ("Common Kingfisher")	1·25	60
604	60c. White-collared kingfisher	2·00	1·50
605	$1 Stork-billed kingfisher	2·50	3·00

130 Water Village, Bandar Seri Begawan

1999. 15th Anniv of National Day. Multicoloured.

606	20c. Type **130**	50	20
607	60c. Modern telecommunications and Boeing 757	1·50	1·10
608	90c. Aspects of modern Brunei	2·00	2·25
MS609	118×85 mm. Nos. 606/8	3·50	4·00

131 Rifle-shooting

1999. 20th South-east Asia Games, Brunei. Multicoloured.

610	20c. Type **131**	65	75
611	20c. Golf and tennis	65	75
612	20c. Boxing and judo	65	75
613	20c. Squash and table tennis	65	75
614	20c. Swimming and canoe racing	65	75
615	20c. Hockey and cycling	65	75
616	20c. Basketball and football	65	75
617	20c. High jumping, shot putting and running	65	75
618	20c. Snooker	65	75
619	20c. Bowling	65	75
MS620	110×73 mm. $1 Various sports	2·00	3·25

132 Clasped Hands and Globe

1999. 125th Anniv of Universal Postal Union. Multicoloured.

621	20c. Type **132**	60	25
622	30c. "125" and logos	70	30
623	75c. Aspects of postal service	1·50	2·25

133 Modern Building and Children using Computer

2000. New Millennium. Multicoloured.

624	20c. Type **133**	75	75
625	20c. Royal Palace, tree and people using computer	75	75
626	20c. Aerial view of mosque and factory	75	75
627	20c. Plan of Parterre Gardens	75	75
628	20c. Container ships and Boeing 757	75	75
629	20c. Satellite dish aerials	4·00	75
MS630	221×121 mm. Nos. 624/9	4·00	4·00

Nos. 624/9 were printed together, *se-tenant*, with the backgrounds forming a composite design.

134 Sultan Mohamed Jemal-ul-Alam and Traditional Buildings, 1901–20

2000. Brunei in the 20th Century. Multicoloured.

631	30c. Type **134**	1·00	1·00
632	30c. Sultan Ahmed Tajudin, oil well and Brunei police, 1921–40	1·00	1·00
633	30c. Signing of the Constitution and Brunei Mosque, 1941–60	1·00	1·00
634	30c. Oil installation, satellite dish, Boeing 757 of Royal Brunei Airlines and bank note, 1961–80	1·00	1·00

635	30c. Sultan on throne, international organisation emblems and crowd with trophy, 1981–99	1·00	1·00

135 Sultan Hashim Jalil-ul-Alam, 1885–1906

2000. The Sultans of Brunei. Multicoloured.

636	60c. Type **135**	1·40	1·40
637	60c. Sultan Mohamed Jemal-ul-Alam, 1906–24	1·40	1·40
638	60c. Sultan Ahmed Tajudin, 1924–50	1·40	1·40
639	60c. Sultan Omar Ali Saifuddin, 1950–67	1·40	1·40
640	60c. Sultan Hassanal Bolkiah, 1967	1·40	1·40
MS641	190×99 mm. Nos. 636/40	4·50	6·00

136 *Rafflesia pricei*

2000. Local Flowers. Multicoloured.

642	30c. Type **136**	75	30
643	50c. *Rhizanthes lowi*	1·25	1·25
644	60c. *Nepenthes rafflesiana*	1·40	1·40

137 Information Technology

2000. Asia–Pacific Economic Cooperation. Heads of Government Meeting. Multicoloured.

645	20c. Type **137**	70	70
646	30c. Small and medium businesses	70	95
647	60c. Tourism	1·75	1·75
MS648	150×108 mm. Nos. 645/7	3·00	3·50

138 Green Turtle

2000. Turtles. Multicoloured.

649	30c. Type **138**	1·00	1·00
650	30c. Hawksbill turtle	1·00	1·00
651	30c. Olive Ridley turtle	1·00	1·00

139 Tourist Canoe on River

2001. "Visit Brunei Year" (1st series). Multicoloured.

652	20c. Type **139**	1·25	75
653	30c. Traditional water village	1·25	75
654	60c. Carved building facade	2·25	2·75

See also Nos. 669/72.

140 Sultan in Army Uniform

2001. 55th Birthday of Sultan Hassanal Bolkiah Muizzaddin Waddaulah. Multicoloured.

655	55c. Type **140**	1·40	1·40
656	55c. Sultan in Air Force uniform	1·40	1·40
657	55c. Sultan in traditional dress	1·40	1·40
658	55c. Sultan in Army camouflage jacket	1·40	1·40
659	55c. Sultan in Navy uniform	1·40	1·40
MS660	100×75 mm. 55c. Sultan and Bandar Seri Begawan (40×71 mm)	2·25	2·50

141 First Aid Demonstration

2001. International Youth Camp. Multicoloured.

661	30c. Type **141**	1·00	1·00
662	30c. Brunei guides and tent demonstration	1·00	1·00
663	30c. Scouts with cooking pot	1·00	1·00
MS664	110×77 mm. Nos. 661/3	2·75	3·25

Nos. 661/3 were printed together, *se-tenant*, forming a composite design.

142 Islamic Regalia

2001. First Islamic International Exhibition, Brunei. Multicoloured.

665	20c. Type **142**	80	80
666	20c. Exhibition centre	80	80
667	20c. Computer communications	80	80
668	20c. Opening ceremony	80	80

143 Forest Walkway

2001. Visit Brunei (2nd series). Multicoloured.

669	20c. Type **143**	85	85
670	20c. Waterfall	85	85
671	20c. Jerudong Theme Park	85	85
672	20c. Footbridges across lake	85	85

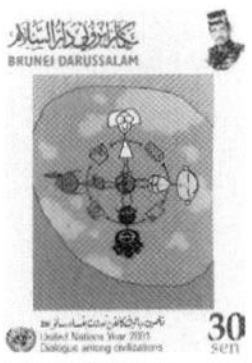

144 "Children encircling Globe" (Urska Golob)

2001. U.N. Year of Dialogue among Civilisations. Multicoloured.

673	30c. Type **144**	1·00	1·00
674	30c. Quotation marks illustrated with faces	1·00	1·00
675	30c. Cubist portrait and Japanese girl	1·00	1·00
676	30c. Coloured leaves	1·00	1·00

145 Male and Female Bulwer's Pheasants

2001. Endangered Species. Bulwer's Pheasant. Multicoloured.

677	30c. Type **145**	1·10	1·10
678	30c. Male pheasant	1·10	1·10
679	30c. Female pheasant with chicks	1·10	1·10
680	30c. Female pheasant	1·10	1·10

146 Early and Modern Telephone Systems

2002. 50th Anniv of Department of Telecommunications (JTB). Multicoloured.

681	50c. Type **146**	1·40	1·40
682	50c. JTB Golden Jubilee emblem	1·40	1·40
683	50c. Computer networks	1·40	1·40

147 50th Anniversary Logo

2002. 50th Anniv of Survey Department. Multicoloured.

684	50c. Type **147**	1·40	1·40
685	50c. Survey Department Offices	1·40	1·40
686	50c. Theodolite and thermal map	1·40	1·40

148 Modern Housing, Water Village

2002. Tenth Anniv of Yayasan Sultan Haji Hassanal Bolkiah Foundation. Multicoloured.

687	10c. Type **148**	50	50
688	10c. Mosque and interior	50	50
689	10c. School and computer class	50	50
690	10c. University of Brunei	50	50

149 Anti-Corruption Bureau Headquarters

2002. 20th Anniv of Anti-Corruption Bureau. Multicoloured.

691	20c. Type **149**	85	85
692	20c. Skyscrapers and mosque	85	85
693	20c. Anti-Corruption Bureau posters	85	85

150 *Melastoma malabathricum*

2003. Flowering Medicinal Plants. Multicoloured.

694	20c. Type **150**	80	80
695	20c. *Etlingera solaris*	80	80
696	20c. *Dillenia suffruticosa*	80	80
697	20c. *Costus speciosus*	80	80

151 Drums and Musicians

2003. ASEAN—Japan Exchange Year. Multicoloured.

698	20c. Type **151**	70	70
699	20c. Woodworker and handicrafts	70	70
700	20c. Exchange Year logo	70	70

152 Sultan of Brunei and UN Emblem

2004. 20th Anniv of National Day. Multicoloured.

701	20c. Type **152**	70	70
702	20c. In military uniform	70	70
703	20c. Reading speech at National Day celebration	70	70
704	20c. Emblem	70	70
MS705	185×140 mm. Nos. 701/4	2·75	3·00

153 Brunei 1895 ½c. Stamp

2004. Brunei Darussalam National Philatelic Society. Multicoloured.

706	25c. Type **153**	75	75
707	25c. Magnifying glass, perforation gauge, tweezers and stamps	75	75
708	25c. Postmarks, stamp catalogue and first day covers	75	75

154 Crown Prince Al-Muhtadee Billah Bolkiah and Sarah Salleh

2004. Royal Wedding.

709	**154** 99c. multicoloured	1·60	1·75

155 Sultan of Brunei and Jame'Asr Hassanal Bolkiah Mosque

2006. 60th Birthday of Sultan Hassanal Bolkiah Muizzaddin Waddaulah. Designs showing montage of images, all with portrait of Sultan at top right. Multicoloured (except $60), panel colours given.

710	60c. Type **155** (mauve)	1·00	1·00
711	60c. Sultan, palace and crowd with flags (red)	1·00	1·00
712	60c. Sultan and urban and agricultural scenes (yellow)	1·00	1·00
713	60c. Sultan speaking at 9th ASEAN–Japan Summit and at APEC 2000 (salmon)	1·00	1·00
714	60c. Sultan meeting woman (green)	1·00	1·00
715	60c. Sultan in military uniform (blue)	1·00	1·00
MS716	166×120 mm. Nos. 710/15	5·50	6·00
MS717	148×137 mm. $60 Montage of five black and white photographs of Sultan as young man, at Coronation, seated on throne and wearing crown and military uniform (black and grey) (99×90 mm)	42·00	48·00

156 General Post Office, Bandar Seri Begawan

157 Parcels and Letters travelling around Globe

2006. Centenary of Postal Services Department. Multicoloured. Litho. (a) T 156.

718	100c. Type **156**	1·40	1·60
719	100c. Kuala Belait Post Office	1·40	1·60
720	100c. Tutong Post Office at the District Office, Tutong	1·40	1·60
721	100c. Bangar Post Office at the District Office, Temburong	1·40	1·60
MS722	115×115 mm. Nos. 718/21	5·00	5·75

(b) T **157** and similar vert designs showing children's drawings.

MS723	95×145 mm. 100s.×6 Type **157**; Postman; Globe, letter, house and aircraft; Air mail letters, postbox and post office; Letters, globe and families in Brunei and China; Globe and national flags ('EVERYONE REACHING EVERYWHERE')	7·00	8·00

158 *Balistapus undulates* (orangestriped triggerfish)

2007. Marine Life. Multicoloured.

724	60c. Type **158**	1·25	1·25
725	60c. *Taenionotis triacanthus* (leaf scorpionfish)	1·25	1·25
MS726	100×70 mm. $1 *Nautilus pompilus* (chambered nautilus); $1 *Ostracion meleagris* (spotted boxfish)	3·50	3·50

Stamps in similar designs were issued by Malaysia.

159 Sultan Hassanal Bolkiah Mu'izzaddin Waddaulah

2007. Multicoloured.

727	**159**	10c. multicoloured	10	10
728	**159**	15c. multicoloured	20	20
729	**159**	20c. multicoloured	25	25
730	**159**	30c. multicoloured	35	35
731	**159**	50c. multicoloured	60	60
732	**159**	60c. multicoloured	70	70
733	**159**	75c. multicoloured	90	90
734	**159**	90c. multicoloured	1·10	1·10
735	–	$1 multicoloured	1·25	1·25
736	–	$2 multicoloured	2·40	2·40
737	–	$5 multicoloured	6·00	6·00
738	–	$10 multicoloured	12·00	12·00

Nos. 735/8 are as Type **159** but larger, 27×40 mm.

160 Bubungan Dua Belas

2007. Centenary of Bubungan Dua Belas, Bukit Subok. Multicoloured.

739	30s. Type **160**	90	35
740	60s. Bubungan Dua Belas (seen from above)	1·60	1·25
741	$1 Bubungan Dua Belas, 1907	2·50	3·00
MS742	150×90 mm. Nos. 739/41	4·50	4·75

Bubungan Dua Belas—House of 12 Roofs was the British High Commissioner's Residence.

Nos. 739/**MS**742, T **160** are left for 100 Years of Bubangan, issued 23 July 2007, not yet received.

161 Public Works Department Headquarters

2007. Centenary (2006) of Public Works Department. Multicoloured.

743	75c. Type **161**	1·00	1·25
744	75c. Engineers Office, (PWD Headquarters), Subok, 1906	1·00	1·25
745	75c. 100	1·00	1·25

162 Secretariat Building, Brunei

2007. 40th Anniv of ASEAN (Association of South-east Asian Nations). Ancient and Modern Architecture. Multicoloured.

746	20c. Type **162**	1·10	1·10
747	20c. Yangon Post Office, Myanmar	1·10	1·10
748	20c. National Museum of Cambodia	1·10	1·10
749	20c. Malacañang Palace, Philippines	1·10	1·10
750	20c. Fatahillah Museum, Jakarta, Indonesia	1·10	1·10
751	20c. National Museum of Singapore	1·10	1·10
752	20c. Lao Typical House	1·10	1·10
753	20c. Vimanmek Mansion, Bangkok, Thailand	1·10	1·10
754	20c. Malayan Railway Headquarters Building, Kuala Lumpur, Malaysia	1·10	1·10
755	20c. Presidential Palace, Hanoi, Vietnam	1·10	1·10

Similar designs were issued by the ten member countries, Indonesia, Malaysia, Philippines, Singapore, Thailand, Vietnam, Laos, Myanmar and Cambodia.

163 Istana Majlis

2008. Centenary of Transition of the Capital City from Kampung Air to Mainland. Multicoloured.

756	20c. Type **163**	60	40
757	30c. Istana Kota	70	40
758	60c. Bandar Brunei Mula-Mula Dirona di Darat, 1906	1·40	1·25
759	100c. Modern city of Bandar Seri Begawan	2·25	2·75
MS760	130×130 mm. Nos. 756/9	4·50	4·50

164 Sultan saluting

2008. 40th Anniv of Coronation of Sultan Hassanal Bolkiah Mu'izzaddin Waddaulah. Multicoloured.

761	40s. Type **164**	60	60
762	40s. Coronation ceremony	60	60
763	40s. Crowning of Sultan	60	60
764	40s. Crowned Sultan seated in chair	60	60
MS765	160×100 mm. Nos. 761/4	3·25	3·75
MS766	159×100 mm. $40 Crowned Sultan on throne and courtiers (44×69 mm)	35·00	40·00

165 Sultan Omar Ali Saifuddin outside Mosque, 1958

2008. 50th Anniv of Omar Ali Saifuddien Mosque. Multicoloured.

767	50c. Type **165**	85	85
768	50c. Sultan Hassanal Bolkiah Mu'izzadin Waddaulah	85	85
769	50c. Sultan and courtiers inside Mosque	85	85
770	50c. Aerial view of Mosque	85	85
MS771	150×80 mm. Noc. 767/70	3·00	3·50
MS772	199×110 mm. $50 Omar Ali Saifuddin Mosque (44×71 mm)	40·00	45·00

166 Scanner and Medical Staff

2008. Centenary of Health Services in Brunei. Multicoloured.

773	10c. Type **166**	25	25
774	10c. Nurse with mother and baby	25	25
775	$1 First government hospital in Brunei town	1·75	2·00

167 Montage of Buildings

2009. National Day Silver Jubilee (25th Anniv of Independence). Multicoloured, background colours given.

776	25c. Type **167**	55	55
777	25c. Montage of buildings (different) (bright green)	55	55
778	25c. Military parade, helicopter (on ground) and buildings (cerise)	55	55
779	25c. Montage of buildings (different) (pale yellow)	55	55
780	25c. Oil refinery, oil well, storage tanks and docks (lavender)	55	55
781	25c. Dancers and processions with national flags (bright purple)	55	55
782	25c. Women using mobile phone and laptop computer, modern buildings and airliner (reddish-brown)	55	55
783	25c. Anniversary emblem	55	55
784	25c. As Type **167** but blue border	55	55
785	25c. As No. 777 but blue border	55	55
786	25c. As No. 778 but blue border	55	55
787	25c. As No. 779 but blue border	55	55
788	25c. As No. 780 but blue border	55	55
789	25c. As No. 781 but blue border	55	55
790	25c. As No. 782 but blue border	55	55
791	25c. As No. 783 but blue border	55	55
MS792	180×140 mm. $25 Sultan Hassanal Bolkiah Mu'izzaddin Waddaulah, Sultan Omar Ali Saifuddin and Bandar Seri Begawan city (101×71 mm)	27·00	29·00

JAPANESE OCCUPATION OF BRUNEI

These stamps were valid throughout British Borneo (i.e. in Brunei, Labuan, North Borneo and Sarawak).

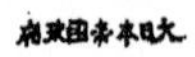

(1) ("Imperial Japanese Government")

1942. Stamps of Brunei optd with T **1**.

J1	**5**	1c. black	9·00	23·00
J2	**5**	2c. green	50·00	£110
J3	**5**	2c. orange	6·00	9·00
J4	**5**	3c. green	29·00	75·00
J5	**5**	4c. orange	4·00	13·00
J6	**5**	5c. brown	5·50	13·00
J7	**7**	6c. grey	40·00	£275
J8	**7**	6c. red	£550	£550
J9	**5**	8c. black	£750	£850
J10	**7**	8c. red	8·50	12·00
J11	**5**	10c. purple on yellow	10·00	26·00
J12	**7**	12c. blue	30·00	26·00
J13	**7**	15c. blue	23·00	26·00
J14	**5**	25c. lilac	26·00	50·00
J15	**5**	30c. purple and orange	95·00	£180
J16	**5**	50c. black on green	38·00	60·00
J17	**5**	$1 black and red on blue	55·00	70·00
J18	**5**	$5 red on green	£950	£3000
J19	**5**	$25 black on red	£950	£3000

(2) ("Imperial Japanese Postal Service $3")

1944. No. J1 surch with T **2**.

J20	$3 on 1c. black	£8500	£9000

Pt. 7

BRUNSWICK

Formerly a duchy of N. Germany. Joined North German Confederation in 1868.

30 silbergroschen = 1 thaler.

1

1852. Imperf.

1	**1**	1sg. red	£2750	£400
2	**1**	2sg. blue	£1900	£350
3	**1**	3sg. red	£1900	£350

1853. Imperf.

4	¼gg. black on brown	£1100	£350
5	⅓gg. black	£190	£425
15	½sg. black on green	32·00	£325
7	1sg. black on buff	£550	85·00
8	2sg. black on blue	£425	85·00
11	3sg. black on red	£750	£225

3

1857. Imperf.

12	**3**	4/4gg. black on brown	55·00	£130

1864. Rouletted.

22	**1**	⅓gg. black	£650	£3000
23	**1**	½sg. black on green	£275	£4250
24	**1**	1sg. black on yellow	£4250	£2000
25	**1**	1sg. yellow	£550	£190
26	**1**	2sg. black on blue	£550	£450
27	**1**	3sg. pink	£1100	£700

4

1865. Roul.

28	**4**	⅓g. black	37·00	£475
29	**4**	1g. red	3·25	70·00
32	**4**	2g. blue	11·50	£170
34	**4**	3g. brown	9·50	£200

Pt. 20

BUENOS AIRES

A province of the Argentine Republic. Issued its own stamps from 1858 to 1862.

8 reales = 1 peso.

P1 Paddle Steamer

1858. Imperf.

P13	**P1**	4r. brown	£225	£170
P17	**P1**	1 (IN) p. brown	£300	£250
P20	**P1**	1 (IN) p. blue	£120	£100
P25	**P1**	1 (TO) p. blue	£500	£250
P1	**P1**	2p. blue	£180	£100
P4	**P1**	3p. green	£1200	£650
P7	**P1**	4p. red	£3250	£1700
P10	**P1**	5p. yellow	£2500	£1100

P2 Head of Liberty

1859. Imperf.

P37	**P2**	4r. green on blue	£180	£100
P38	**P2**	1p. blue	15·00	9·00
P45	**P2**	1p. red	£140	65·00
P43	**P2**	2p. red	£200	£120
P48	**P2**	2p. blue	£225	55·00

Pt. 3

BULGARIA

Formerly a Turkish province; a principality under Turkish suzerainty from 1878 to 1908, when an independent kingdom was proclaimed. A People's Republic since 1946.

1879. 100 centimes = 1 franc.
1881. 100 stotinki = 1 lev.

1 Large Lion

1879. Value in centimes and franc.

1	**1**	5c. black and yellow	£225	75·00
3	**1**	10c. black and green	£1000	£200
5	**1**	25c. black and purple	£600	50·00
7	**1**	50c. black and blue	£850	£170
8	**1**	1f. black and red	£130	50·00

2 Large Lion

1881. Value in stotinki.

10	**2**	3s. red and grey	43·00	8·25
11	**2**	5s. black and yellow	43·00	8·25
14	**2**	10s. black and green	£250	26·00
15	**2**	15s. red and green	£250	26·00
18	**2**	25s. black and purple	£1000	£130
19	**2**	30s. blue and brown	43·00	21·00

See also No. 275/9.

A

B

C

D

1882

46		1s. violet (Type A)	38·00	12·50
48		1s. violet (Type C)	2·75	50
47		2s. green (Type B)	37·00	11·50
49		2s. green (Type D)	2·75	50
21		3s. orange and yellow	2·20	1·00
23		5s. green	16·00	1·60
26		10s. red	22·00	1·60
28		15s. purple and mauve	22·00	1·30
31		25s. blue	20·00	2·10
33		30s. lilac and green	21·00	1·90
34		50s. blue and red	21·00	1·90
50		1l. black and red	75·00	9·50

1884. Surch with large figure of value.

38	3 on 10s. red	£110	£100
43	5 on 30s. blue and brown	£110	£100
45	15 on 25s. blue	£200	£140
40	50 on 1f. black and red	£750	£475

7

1889

85	**7**	1s. mauve	20	20
88	**7**	2s. grey	1·30	1·00
89	**7**	3s. brown	55	50
90	**7**	5s. green	20	20
94	**7**	10s. red	1·60	1·00
96	**7**	15s. orange	1·10	50
100	**7**	25s. blue	1·10	50
58	**7**	30s. brown	18·00	1·00
59	**7**	50s. green	1·10	50
60	**7**	1l. red	1·10	1·00
83	**7**	2l. red and pink	4·25	3·25
84	**7**	3l. black and buff	6·50	7·25

1892. Surch **15**.

61		15 on 30s. brown	55·00	2·10

1895. Surch **01**.

74	**2a**	01 on 2s. green (No. 49)	1·60	50

11 Arms of Bulgaria

1896. Baptism of Prince Boris.

78	**11**	1s. green	55	30
79	**11**	5s. blue	55	30
81	**11**	15s. violet	65	50
82	**11**	25s. red	9·25	3·25

1901. Surch in figures.

101	**7**	5 on 3s. brown	2·75	2·10
103	**7**	10 on 50s. green	2·75	2·30

13 Cherry wood Cannon used against the Turks

1901. 25th Anniv of Uprising against Turkey.

104	**13**	5s. red	2·20	1·60
105	**13**	15s. green	2·20	1·60

14 Prince Ferdinand

1901

106	**14**	1s. black and purple	35	15
107	**14**	2s. blue and green	55	15
108	**14**	3s. black and orange	55	15
109	**14**	5s. brown and green	2·20	20
110	**14**	10s. brown and red	3·25	20
113	**14**	15s. black and lake	1·60	30
114	**14**	25s. black and blue	1·60	15
116	**14**	30s. black and brown	49·00	1·00
117	**14**	50s. brown and blue	2·20	30
118	**14**	1l. green and red	5·50	40
120	**14**	2l. black and red	11·00	1·60
123	**14**	3l. red and grey	16·00	7·25

16 Fighting at Shipka Pass

1902. 25th Anniv of Battle of Shipka Pass.

124	**16**	5s. red	3·25	1·00
125	**16**	10s. green	3·25	1·00
126	**16**	15s. blue	13·00	5·25

1903. Surch.

140	**15**	5 on 15s. black and red	3·25	2·10
141	**15**	10 on 15s. black and red	5·50	1·00
143	**15**	25 on 30s. black & brown	18·00	2·10

18 Ferdinand I in 1887 and 1907

1907. 20th Anniv of Prince Ferdinand's Accession.

132	**18**	5s. green	22·00	2·10
134	**18**	10s. brown	33·00	2·30
137	**18**	25s. blue	75·00	4·25

1909. Optd **1909**.

146	**7**	1s. mauve	2·20	95
149	**7**	5s. green	2·20	95

1909. Surch **1909** and new value.

151	5 on 30s. brown	3·75	65
153	10 on 15s. orange	3·75	1·30
156	10 on 50s. green	3·75	1·30

1910. Surch **1910** and new value.

157	**14**	1 on 3s. black and orange	8·75	2·10
158	**14**	5 on 15s. black and lake	2·20	1·60

23 King Asen Tower

24 Tsar in General's Uniform

25 Veliko Turnovo

1911

159	**23**	1s. green	35	15
182a	**23**	1s. slate	20	15
160	**24**	2s. black and red	35	15
161	**25**	3s. black and lake	85	15
162	-	5s. black and green	1·60	15
181	-	5s. purple and green	4·25	20
163	-	10s. black and red	2·75	20
181a	-	10s. sepia and brown	20	15
164	-	15s. bistre	8·25	30
183	-	15s. olive	70	15
165	-	25s. black and blue	55	15
166	-	30s. black and blue	8·25	30
182	-	30s. brown and olive	55	20
167	-	50s. black and yellow	43·00	50
168	-	1l. brown	20·00	30
169	-	2l. black and purple	3·75	1·30
170	-	3l. black and violet	22·00	7·75

DESIGNS—VERT: 5, 10, 25s., 1l. Portraits of Tsar Ferdinand. HORIZ: 15s. R. Isker; 30s. Rila Monastery; 50s. Tsars and Princes (after Ya. Veshin); 2l. Monastery of the Holy Trinity, Veliko Turnovo; 3l. Varna.

See also Nos. 229/30 and 236/7.

35 Tsar Ferdinand

1912. Tsar's Silver Jubilee.

171	**35**	5s. grey	5·50	2·10
172	**35**	10s. red	7·50	3·75
173	**35**	25s. blue	11·00	5·75

ОСВОБ. ВОЙНА

1912-1913

(36) "War of Liberation" 1912–13

1913. Victory over Turks. Stamps of 1911 optd as T **36**.

174	**23**	1s. green	55	20
175	**24**	2s. black and red	55	20
176	**25**	3s. black and lake	2·20	50
177	-	5s. black and green	55	20
178	-	10s. black and red	55	20
179	-	15s. bistre	3·25	1·60
180	-	25s. black and blue	8·75	2·50

1915. No. 165 surch **10 CT.** and bar.

180a	10s. on 25s. blk & blue	1·30	30

3
СТОТИНКИ
(37a)

1916. Red Cross Fund. Surch with T **37a**.

185	**7**	3s. on 1s. mauve	13·00	12·50

38

39 Bulgarian Peasant

45 Veles

46 Bulgarian Ploughman

1917. Liberation of Macedonia.

193	**45**	1s. grey	20	10
194	**46**	1s. green	20	10
186	**38**	5s. green	55	40
195	-	5s. green	20	10
187	**39**	15s. grey	20	20
188	-	25s. blue	20	20
189	-	30s. orange	20	30
190	-	50s. violet	1·10	85
191	-	2l. brown	1·10	85
192	-	3l. red	1·60	1·40

DESIGNS—As Type **45**: 5s. Monastery of St. John, Ohrid. As Type **38**: 25s. Soldier and Mt. Sonichka; 50s. Ohrid and Lake. As Type **39**: 30s. Nish. 2l. Demir Kapija; 3l. Gevgeli.

48 Tsar Ferdinand

1918. 30th Anniv of Tsar's Accession.

196	**48**	1s. slate	20	15
197	**48**	2s. brown	20	15
198	**48**	3s. blue	55	50
199	**48**	10s. red	55	50

49 Parliament Building

1919

201	**49**	1s. black	20	15
202	**49**	2s. olive	20	15

50 King Boris III

1919. First Anniv of Enthronement of King Boris III.

203	**50**	3s. red	20	15
204	**50**	5s. green	20	15
205	**50**	10s. red	20	15
206	**50**	15s. violet	20	15
207	**50**	25s. blue	20	15
208	**50**	30s. brown	20	15
209	**50**	50s. brown	20	15

ЗА НАШИТѢ ПЛѢННИЦИ 2½
(52)

ЗА НАШИТѢ ПЛѢННИЦИ 50
(53)

1920. Prisoners of War Fund. Surch as T **52/53**.

210	**49**	1 on 2s. olive	20	15
211	**50**	2½ on 5s. green	20	15
212	**50**	5 on 10s. red	20	15
213	**50**	7½ on 15s. violet	20	15
214	**50**	12½ on 25s. blue	20	15
215	**50**	15 on 30s. brown	20	15
216	**50**	25 on 50s. brown	20	15
217	-	50 on 1l. brown (No. 168)	55	30
218	-	1 on 2l. brown (No. 191)	55	50
219	-	1½ on 3l. red (No. 192)	1·60	1·00

54 Vazov's Birthplace at Sopot and Cherry-wood Cannon

55 "The Bear-fighter", character from *Under the Yoke*

1920. 70th Birth Anniv of Ivan Vazov (writer).

220	**54**	30s. red	20	15
221	**55**	50s. green	45	20
222	-	1l. sepia	75	50
223	-	2l. brown	2·20	1·30
224	-	3l. violet	2·75	1·80
225	-	5l. blue	3·75	2·30

DESIGNS—HORIZ: 1l. Ivan Vazov in 1870 and 1920; 3l. Vazov's Houses in Plovdiv and Sofia. VERT: 2l. Vazov; 5l. Father Paisii Khilendarski (historian).

59 Aleksandr Nevski Cathedral, Sofia

62 King Boris III

1921

226	59	10s. violet	20	15
227	-	20s. green	20	15
228	62	25s. blue	20	15
229	25	50s. orange	45	20
230	25	50s. blue	9·25	3·50
231	-	75s. violet	20	15
232	-	75s. blue	55	20
233	62	1l. red	55	20
234	62	1l. blue	45	15
235	-	2l. brown	1·60	20
236	-	3l. purple	1·60	20
237	-	5l. blue	8·75	40
238	62	10l. red	22·00	4·75

DESIGNS—HORIZ: 20s. Alexander II "The Liberator" Monument, Sofia; 75s. Shipka Pass Monastery; 5l. Rila Monastery. VERT: 2l. Harvester; 3l. King Asen Tower.

66 Tsar Ferdinand and Map

68 Mt. Shar

1921

239	66	10s. red	20	15
240	-	10s. red	20	15
241	68	10s. red	20	15
242	-	10s. mauve	20	15
243	-	20s. blue	85	20

DESIGNS—VERT: No. 240, Tsar Ferdinand. HORIZ: No. 242, Bridge over Vardar, at Skopje; 243, St. Clement's Monastery, Ohrid.

71 Bourchier in Bulgarian Costume

72 J. D. Bourchier

73 Rila Monastery, Bourchier's Resting-place

1921. James Bourchier ("Times" Correspondent) Commemoration.

244	71	10s. red	20	20
245	71	20s. orange	20	20
246	72	30s. grey	20	20
247	72	50s. lilac	20	20
248	72	1l. purple	55	20
249	73	1½l. green	55	40
250	73	2l. green	55	30
251	73	3l. blue	1·30	50
252	73	5l. red	2·40	1·20

1924. Surch.

253	49	10s. on 1s. black	20	15
254	D 37	10s. on 20s. orange	20	15
255	D 37	20s. on 5s. green	27·00	26·00
256	D 37	20s. on 10s. violet	8·25	7·75
257	D 37	20s. on 30s. orange	20	15
258	50	1l. on 5s. green	35	15
259	25	3l. on 50s. blue	1·10	30
260	62	6l. on 1l. red	2·20	65

77

78

79 King Boris III

81 Aleksandr Nevski Cathedral, Sofia

82 Harvesters

1925

261	77	10s. blue & red on rose	35	20
262	77	15s. orange & red on blue	35	20
263	77	30s. buff and black	35	20
264	78	50s. brown on green	35	20
265	79	1l. olive	1·00	20
266	79	1l. green	1·20	20
267	81	2l. green and buff	4·25	20
267a	79	2l. brown	1·60	20
268	82	4l. red and yellow	4·25	20

83 Proposed Rest-home, Verona

1925. Sunday Delivery Stamps.

268b	83	1l. black on green	11·00	30
268c	83	1l. brown	11·00	30
268d	83	1l. orange	16·00	50
268e	83	1l. pink	14·00	50
268f	83	1l. violet on red	16·00	50
268g	-	2l. green	1·60	30
268h	-	2l. violet	1·60	30
268i	-	5l. blue	17·00	1·30
268j	-	5l. red	17·00	1·30

DESIGN: 2, 5l., Proposed Sanatorium, Bankya.

85 St. Nedelya's Cathedral, Sofia after Bomb Outrage

1926

269	85	50s. black	35	20

86 C. Botev (poet)

1926. Botev Commemoration.

270	86	1l. green	1·30	50
271	86	2l. blue	2·75	50
272	86	4l. red	3·75	2·50

87

1926

273	87	6l. olive and blue	2·20	30
274	87	10l. brown and sepia	16·00	4·00

1927. As T **2** in new colours.

275	10s. red and green	20	20
276	15s. black and yellow	20	20
277	30s. slate and buff	20	20
278	30s. blue and buff	20	20
279	50s. black and red	20	20

1927. Air. Various stamps optd with Albatros biplane and No. 281 surch **1l** also.

281		1l. on 6l. green and blue	2·20	2·10
282	79	2l. brown	2·20	2·10
283	82	4l. red and yellow	3·25	2·10
284	87	10l. orange and brown	85·00	50·00

89 King Boris III

1928

285	89	1l. green	3·25	20
286	89	2l. brown	4·25	20

90 Saint Clement of Ohrid

1929. 50th Anniv of Liberation of Bulgaria and Millenary of Tsar Simeon.

287	90	10s. violet	30	10
288	-	15a. purple	30	10
289	-	30s. red	30	10
290	-	50s. green	75	20
291	-	1l. red	1·90	20
292	-	2l. blue	2·10	20
293	-	3l. green	5·25	1·00
294	-	4l. brown	9·50	40
295	-	5l. brown	7·25	1·00
296	-	6l. blue	9·25	2·50

PORTRAITS—23½x33½ mm: 15s. Konstantin Miladinov (poet and folklorist); 1l. Father Paisii Khilendarski (historian); 2l. Tsar Simeon; 4l. Vasil Levski (revolutionary); 5l. Georgi Benkovski (revolutionary); 6l. Tsar Alexander II of Russia, "The Liberator". 19x28½ mm: 30s. Georgi Rakovski (writer). 19x26 mm: 3l. Lyuben Karavelov (journalist).

98 Convalescent Home, Varna

1930. Sunday Delivery stamps.

297	98	1l. green and purple	18·00	30
298	98	1l. yellow and green	2·10	30
299	98	1l. brown and red	2·10	30

99

1930. Wedding of King Boris and Princess Giovanna of Italy.

300	99	1l. green	50	40
301	-	2l. purple	85	50
302	99	4l. red	85	50
303	-	6l. blue	1·00	55

DESIGN: 2, 6l. Portraits in separate ovals.

101 King Boris III

1931

304a	101	1l. green (A)	1·30	20
305	101	2l. red (A)	1·30	20
306	101	4l. orange (A)	1·80	20
308a	101	4l. orange (B)	1·00	20
307	101	6l. blue (A)	1·30	20
308b	101	6l. blue (B)	2·75	20
308c	101	7l. blue (B)	40	20
308d	101	10l. slate (B)	42·00	2·50
308	101	12l. brown (A)	1·00	30
308e	101	14l. brown (B)	95	50
308f	-	20l. brown & pur (B)	2·50	1·00

(A) Without coloured frame-lines at top and bottom; (B) with frame-lines.

The 20l. is 24½x33½ mm.

103 Gymnastics

1931. Balkan Olympic Games.

309	103	1l. green	3·25	1·50
326	103	1l. turquoise	4·25	4·00
310	-	2l. red	4·25	2·00
327	-	2l. blue	6·25	4·50
311	-	4l. red	9·50	2·50
328	-	4l. purple	10·50	5·50
312	-	6l. green	21·00	6·00
329	-	6l. red	21·00	10·00
313	-	10l. orange	42·00	15·00
330	-	10l. brown	£160	65·00
314	-	12l. blue	£130	40·00
331	-	12l. orange	£250	£100
315	-	50l. brown	£140	85·00
332	-	50l. red	£750	£750

DESIGNS—VERT (23x28 mm): 2l. Footballer; 4l. Horse-riding. As Type **103**—HORIZ: 6l. Fencing; 10l. Cycling. VERT: 12l. Diving; 50l. Spirit of Victory.

108

1931. Air.

316	108	1l. green	85	30
316a	108	1l. purple	50	20
317	108	2l. purple	85	30
317a	108	2l. green	65	30
318	108	6l. blue	1·00	50
318a	108	6l. red	1·60	60
319	108	12l. red	2·10	50
319a	108	12l. blue	1·80	70
320	108	20l. violet	2·10	1·00
321	108	30l. orange	4·25	2·00
322	108	50l. brown	5·75	3·50

109 Rila Monastery

1932. Air.

323	109	18l. green	£140	70·00
324	109	24l. red	95·00	45·00
325	109	28l. blue	50·00	35·00

1934. Surch **2.**

333	101	2 on 3l. olive	13·50	1·00

111 Defending the Pass

1934. Unveiling of Shipka Pass Memorial.

334A	111	1l. green	2·10	1·00
340A	111	1l. green	2·10	1·00
335A	-	2l. red	1·60	50
341A	-	2l. orange	1·60	50
336A	-	3l. brown	5·25	3·00
342A	-	3l. yellow	5·25	3·00
337A	-	4l. red	3·75	1·00
343A	-	4l. red	3·75	1·00
338A	-	7l. blue	7·25	3·50
344A	-	7l. light blue	7·25	3·50
339A	-	14l. purple	27·00	18·00
345	-	14l. bistre	27·00	18·00

DESIGNS—VERT: 2l. Shipka Memorial; 3, 7l. Veteran standard-bearer; 14l. Widow showing memorial to orphans. HORIZ: 4l. Bulgarian veteran.

113 Convalescent Home, Troyan

1935. Sunday Delivery stamps.

346	113	1l. red and brown	2·10	30
347	113	1l. blue and green	2·10	30
348	-	5l. blue and red	6·75	1·50

DESIGN: 5l. Convalescent Home, Bakya.

114 Capt. Georgi Mamarchef

1935. Centenary of Turnovo Insurrection.

349		1l. blue	3·25	80
350	114	2l. purple	3·25	1·20

DESIGN: 1l. Velcho Atanasov Dzhamdzhiyata.

115 Aleksandr Nevski Cathedral, Sofia

1935. Fifth Balkan Football Tournament.

351	-	1l. green	8·25	6·00
352	115	2l. grey	12·50	8·00
353	-	4l. red	16·00	10·00
354	-	7l. blue	29·00	20·00
355	-	14l. orange	26·00	20·00
356	-	50l. brown	£475	£400

DESIGNS—HORIZ: 1l. Match in progress at Yunak Stadium, Sofia; 4l. Footballers. VERT: 7l. Herald and Balkan map; 14l. Footballer and trophy; 50l. Trophy.

116 Girl Gymnast

1935. Eighth Bulgarian Gymnastic Tournament. Dated "12–14. VII. 1935".

357		1l. green	9·50	8·00
358		2l. blue	10·50	9·00
359	**116**	4l. red	13·50	11·00
360	-	7l. blue	16·00	16·00
361	-	14l. brown	16·00	15·00
362	-	50l. orange	£325	£250

DESIGNS—VERT: 1l. Parallel bars; 2l. Male gymnast in uniform; 7l. Pole vault; 50l. Athlete and lion. HORIZ: 14l. Yunak Stadium, Sofia.

117 Janos Hunyadi

1935. Unveiling of Monument to Ladislas III of Poland at Varna. Inscr "WARNEN CZYK(A)", etc.

363A	**117**	1l. orange	3·25	1·00
364B	-	2l. red	5·00	1·50
365A	-	4l. red	26·00	7·00
366A	-	7l. blue	4·75	1·90
367A	-	14l. green	4·75	1·80

DESIGNS—VERT: 2l. King Ladislas of Hungary enthroned (22×32 mm); 7l. King Ladislas in armour (20×31 mm). HORIZ: 4l. Varna Memorial (33×24 mm); 14l. Battle scene (30×25 mm).

118 Dimitur

1935. 67th Death Anniv of Khadzhi Dimitur (revolutionary).

368A		1l. green	3·25	1·00
369A	**118**	2l. brown	5·25	2·00
370A	-	4l. red	14·50	5·00
371A	-	7l. blue	21·00	9·00
372A	-	14l. orange	26·00	10·00

DESIGNS—VERT: 1l. Dimitur's monument at Sliven; 7l. Revolutionary group (dated 1868). HORIZ: 4l. Dimitur and Stefan Karadzha (revolutionary); 14l. Dimitur's birthplace at Sliven.

119

120

1936

373	**119**	10s. red	20	15
373a	**119**	15s. green	20	15
374	**120**	30s. red	30	15
374a	**120**	30s. brown	20	15
374b	**120**	30s. blue	20	15
375	**120**	50s. blue	30	15
375a	**120**	50s. red	30	15
375b	**120**	50s. green	20	15

121 Nesebur

1936. Slav Geographical and Ethnographical Congress, Sofia.

376	-	1l. violet	4·25	2·00
377	-	2l. blue	4·25	2·00
378	**121**	7l. blue	8·25	4·00

DESIGNS—25×34 mm: 1l. Meteorological Bureau, Mt. Musala; 23×34 mm: 2l. Peasant girl.

122 St. Cyril and St. Methodius

1937. Millenary of Introduction of Cyrillic Alphabet and Slavonic Liturgy.

379	**122**	1l. green	75	30
380	**122**	2l. purple	75	30
381	-	4l. red	85	30
382	**122**	7l. blue	4·25	2·20
383	-	14l. red	4·25	2·30

DESIGN: 4., 14l. The Saints Preaching.

124 Princess Marie Louise

1937

384	**124**	1l. green	75	20
385	**124**	2l. red	85	20
386	**124**	4l. red	85	50

125 King Boris III

1937. 19th Anniv of Accession.

387	**125**	2l. red	1·00	50

MS387a 76×115 mm. **125** 2l. (+18l.) ultramarine. Imperf. 10·50 20·00

126 Harvesting

1938. Agricultural Products.

388	**126**	10s. orange	20	10
389	**126**	10s. red	20	10
390	-	15s. red	50	10
391	-	15s. purple	50	10
392	-	30s. brown	40	10
393	-	30s. brown	45	10
394	-	50s. blue	95	10
395	-	50s. black	95	10
396	-	1l. green	1·00	10
397	-	1l. green	1·00	10
398	-	2l. red	1·00	20
399	-	2l. brown	1·00	20
400	-	3l. purple	2·10	1·00
401	-	3l. purple	2·10	1·00
402	-	4l. brown	1·60	50
403	-	4l. purple	1·60	50
404	-	7l. violet	3·25	1·00
405	-	7l. blue	3·25	1·00
406	-	14l. brown	5·25	2·00
407	-	14l. brown	5·25	2·00

DESIGNS—VERT: 15s. Sunflower; 30s. Wheat; 50s. Chickens and eggs; 1l. Grapes; 3l. Strawberries; 4l. Girl carrying grapes; 7l. Roses; 14l. Tobacco leaves. HORIZ: 2l. "Attar of Roses".

129 Prince Simeon

1938. First Birthday of Heir Apparent.

408	**129**	1l. green	30	20
409	**129**	2l. red	30	20
410	-	4l. red	40	25
411	**129**	7l. blue	1·60	80
412	-	14l. brown	1·60	80

DESIGN: 4, 14l. Another portrait.

131 King Boris III

1938. 20th Anniv of King's Accession. Portraits of King in various uniforms.

413	**131**	1l. green	25	20
414	-	2l. red	1·30	30
415	-	4l. brown	40	30
416	-	7l. blue	65	50
417	-	14l. mauve	65	50

132 Class 01 Steam Locomotive

1939. 50th Anniv of Bulgarian State Railways. Locomotive types dated "1888–1938".

418		1l. green	50	40
419	**132**	2l. brown	50	40
420	-	4l. orange	3·25	1·50
421	-	7l. blue	9·50	5·50

DESIGNS: 1l. First Locomotive in Bulgaria, 1866; 4l. Train crossing viaduct; 7l. King Boris as engine-driver.

133 P.O. Emblem

1939. 60th Anniv of Bulgarian P.O. Inscr "1879 1939".

422	**133**	1l. green	40	10
423	-	2l. red (G.P.O., Sofia)	50	15

135 Gymnast

1939. Yunak Gymnastic Society's Rally, Sofia.

424	**135**	1l. green	50	40
425	-	2l. red	50	40
426	-	4l. brown	1·00	50
427	-	7l. blue	3·25	1·50
428	-	14l. mauve	16·00	12·00

DESIGNS: 2l. Yunak badge; 4l. *The Discus-thrower* (statue by Miron); 7l. Rhythmic dancer; 14l. Athlete holding weight aloft.

Наводнението
1939
1+1
лева

(136) ("Inundation 1939")

1939. Sevlievo and Turnovo Floods Relief Fund. Surch as T **136** and value.

429	**39**	1l.+1l. on 15s. grey	20	45
430	**73**	2l.+1l. on 1½l. olive	30	50
431	**73**	4l.+2l. on 2l. green	35	60
432	**73**	7l.+4l. on 3l. blue	1·00	1·50
433	**73**	14l.+7l. on 5l. red	1·60	2·50

137 Mail Plane

1940. Air.

434	**137**	1l. green	20	15
435	-	2l. red	2·50	15
436	-	4l. orange	20	15
437	-	6l. blue	40	20
438	-	10l. brown	75	30
439	-	12l. brown	1·00	50
440	-	16l. violet	1·60	80
441	-	19l. blue	1·70	1·00
442	-	30l. mauve	2·50	1·50
443	-	45l. violet	6·75	3·75
444	-	70l. red	5·25	4·00
445	-	100l. blue	21·00	14·00

DESIGNS—VERT: Aircraft over: King Asen's Tower (2l.), Bachovo Monastery (4l.), Aleksandr Nevski Cathedral, Sofia (45l.), Shipka Pass Memorial (70l.); 10l. Airplane, mail train and express motor cycle; 30l. Airplane and swallow; 100l. Airplane and Royal cypher. HORIZ: 6l. Loading mails at aerodrome. Aircraft over: Sofia Palace (12l.), Mt. El Tepe (16l.), Rila Lakes and mountains (19l.).

138 King Boris III

1940

445a	**138**	1l. green	40	20
446	**138**	2l. red	50	20

139 First Bulgarian Postage Stamp

1940. Cent of First Adhesive Postage Stamp.

447	**139**	10l. olive	3·25	2·50
448	-	20l. blue	3·25	2·50

DESIGN: 20l. has scroll dated "1840–1940".

140 Grapes

141 Ploughing

142 King Boris III

1940

449	**140**	10s. orange	20	15
450	-	15s. blue	20	15
451	**141**	30s. brown	20	15
452	-	50s. violet	20	15
452a	-	50s. green	20	15
453	**142**	1l. green	20	15
454	**142**	2l. red	30	15
455	**142**	4l. orange	30	15
456	**142**	6l. violet	50	20
457	**142**	7l. blue	30	15
458	**142**	10l. green	50	20

DESIGNS—VERT: 15s. Beehive. HORIZ: 50s. Shepherd and flock.

143 Peasant Couple and King Boris

144 King Boris and Map of Dobrudja

1940. Recovery of Dobrudja from Rumania. Designs incorporating miniature portrait of King Boris.

464	**143**	1l. green	20	15
465	-	2l. red	30	20
466	**144**	4l. brown	50	30
467	**144**	7l. blue	1·00	80

DESIGN—VERT: 2l. Bulgarian flags and wheat-field.

145 Bee-keeping

1940. Agricultural Scenes.

468	-	10s. purple	20	15
469	-	10s. blue	20	15
470	-	15s. green	20	15
471	-	15s. olive	20	15
472	**145**	30s. orange	20	15
473	**145**	30s. green	20	15
474	-	50s. violet	20	15
475	-	50s. purple	20	15
476	-	3l. brown	85	20
477	-	3l. black	1·90	1·00
478	-	5l. brown	1·60	80
479	-	5l. blue	2·10	1·50

DESIGNS: 10s. Threshing; 15s. Ploughing with oxen; 50s. Picking apples; 3l. Shepherd; 5l. Cattle.

146 Pencko Slaveikov (poet)

147 St. Ivan Rilski

1940. National Relief.

480	**146**	1l. green	20	15
481	-	2l. red	20	15
482	**147**	3l. brown	25	20
483	-	4l. orange	30	20
484	-	7l. blue	2·10	1·50
485	-	10l. brown	3·25	2·00

DESIGNS: 2l. Bishop Sofronii of Vratsa; 4l. Marin Drinov (historian); 7l. Chernorisets Khratur (monk); 10l. Kolo Ficheto (writer).

148 Johannes Gutenberg
149 Nikola Karastoyanov

1940. 500th Anniv of Invention of Printing and Centenary of Bulgarian Printing.

486	**148**	1l. green	40	20
487	**149**	2l. brown	50	20

150 Botev
151 Arrival in Koslodui

1941. 65th Death Anniv of Khristo Botev (poet and revolutionary).

488	**150**	1l. green	20	20
489	**151**	2l. red	50	30
490	-	3l. brown	1·40	1·00

DESIGN—VERT: 3l. Botev Memorial Cross.

152 National History Museum

1941. Buildings in Sofia.

491	**152**	14l. brown	75	40
492	-	20l. green	85	50
493	-	50l. blue	3·75	2·00

DESIGNS: 20l. Tsarita Icanna Workers' Hospital; 50l. National Bank.

153 Thasos Island
154 Ohrid

1941. Reacquisition of Macedonia.

494		1l. green	20	15
495	**153**	2l. orange	20	15
496	-	2l. red	20	15
497	-	4l. brown	20	15
498	**154**	7l. blue	95	70

DESIGNS—VERT: 1l. Macedonian girl. HORIZ: 2l. (No. 496) King Boris and map dated "1941"; 4l. Poganovski Monastery.

155 Children on Beach

1942. Sunday Delivery. Inscr as in T **155**.

499	-	1l. green	20	15
500	**155**	2l. orange	30	20
501	-	5l. blue	1·00	40

DESIGNS: 1l. St. Konstantin Sanatorium, Varna; 5l. Sunbathing terrace, Bankya.

156 Bugler at Camp
157 Folk Dancers

1942. "Work and Joy". Inscr as at foot of T **157**.

502		1l. green	20	15
503		2l. red	30	15
504		4l. black	40	20
505	**156**	7l. blue	50	30
506	**157**	14l. brown	65	40

DESIGNS—VERT: 1l. Guitarist and accordion player; 2l. Camp orchestra; 4l. Hoisting the flag.

158 Wounded Soldier
159 Queen visiting Wounded

1942. War Invalids. Inscr as T **158/9**.

507	**158**	1l. green	20	15
508	-	2l. red	20	15
509	-	4l. orange	20	15
510	-	7l. blue	20	15
511	-	14l. brown	30	15
512	**159**	20l. black	65	20

DESIGNS—HORIZ: 2l. Soldier and family; 4l. First aid on battlefield; 7l. Widow and orphans at grave; 14l. Unknown Soldiers Memorial.

160 Khan Kubrat (ruled 595–642)

1942. Historical series.

513	**160**	10s. black	20	15
514	-	15s. blue	20	15
515	-	30s. mauve	20	15
516	-	50s. blue	20	15
517	-	1l. green	20	15
518	-	2l. red	20	15
519	-	3l. brown	20	15
520	-	4l. orange	20	15
521	-	5l. green	20	15
522	-	7l. blue	20	15
523	-	10l. black	20	15
524	-	14l. olive	40	20
525	-	20l. brown	1·00	70
526	-	30l. black	2·10	1·00

DESIGNS: 15s. Cavalry charge (Khan as parukh, 680–701); 30s. Equestrian statue of Khan Krum (803–814); 50s. Baptism of King Boris I; 1l. St. Naum's School; 2l. King Boris crowns his son, Tsar Simeon; 3l. Golden Era of Bulgarian literature; 4l. Trial of Bogomil Vasilii; 5l. Proclamation of Second Bulgarian Empire; 7l. Ivan Asen II (1214–81) at Tebizond; 10l. Expulsion of Eutimil Patriarch of Turnovo; 14l. Wandering minstrels; 20l. Father Paisii Khilendarski (historian); 30l. Shipka Pass Memorial.

161 King Boris III

1944. King Boris Mourning Issue. Portraits dated "1894–1943". Perf or imperf.

527A	**161**	1l. olive	20	20
528A	-	2l. brown	25	25
529A	-	4l. brown	30	30
530A	-	5l. violet	85	85
531A	-	7l. blue	1·00	1·00

163 King Simeon II

1944

532A	**163**	3l. orange	20	10

**ВСИЧКО
ЗА
ФРОНТА**
(164)

1945. "All for the Front". Parcel Post stamps optd as T **164** or surch also.

533	**P163**	1l. red	20	15
534	**P163**	4l. on 1l. red	20	15
535	**P163**	7l. purple	20	15
536	**P163**	20l. brown	30	15
537	**P163**	30l. purple	40	20
538	**P163**	50l. orange	75	50
539	**P163**	100l. blue	1·80	1·00

1945. Air. Optd with airplane or surch also.

540	**142**	1l. green	20	15
541	**142**	4l. orange	20	15
542	**P 163**	10l. on 100l. yellow	30	15
543	**P 163**	45l. on 100l. yellow	40	20
544	**P 163**	75l. on 100l. yellow	1·00	60
545	**P 163**	100l. yellow	1·30	90

Nos. 540/1 are perf; the rest imperf.

167

1945. Slav Congress. Perf or imperf.

546	**167**	4l. red	15	10
547	**167**	10l. blue	15	10
548	**167**	50l. red	40	30

СЪБИРАЙТЕ ВСЪКАКВИ ПАРЦАЛИ
(168) "Collect All Rags"

СЪБИРАЙТЕ СТАРО ЖЕЛЪЗО
(169) "Collect Old Iron"

СЪБИРАЙТЕ ХАРТИЕНИ ОТПАДЪЦИ
(170) "Collect Wastepaper"

1945. Salvage Campaign. Nos. 457/9 optd with T **168/70**.

549B	**142**	1l. green	30	40
550C	**142**	2l. red	1·30	40
551A	**142**	4l. orange	1·00	40

Prices are the same for these stamps with any one of the overprints illustrated.

171 Lion Rampant
172

1945. Lion Rampant, in various frames.

552	-	30s. green	25	15
553	-	50s. blue	25	15
554	**171**	1l. green	25	15
555	-	2l. brown	25	15
556	-	4l. blue	25	15
557	-	5l. violet	25	15
558	**172**	9l. grey	25	15
559	-	10l. blue	25	15
560	-	15l. brown	25	15
561	-	20l. black	50	15
562	-	20l. red	50	15

173 Chain-breaker

1945. Liberty Loan. Imperf.

563	**173**	50l. orange	30	15
564	**173**	50l. lake	30	15
565	-	100l. blue	40	20
566	-	100l. brown	40	20
567	-	150l. red	1·00	60
568	-	150l. green	1·00	60
569	-	200l. olive	1·30	80
570	-	200l. blue	1·30	80

MS570a Two blocks 88×123 mm, with the four values imperf (a) in brown-red and (b) in violet. Pair 16·00 24·00

DESIGNS: 100l. Hand holding coin; 150l. Water-mill; 200l. Coin and symbols of industry and agriculture.

174 "VE Day"

1945. "Victory in Europe".

571	**174**	10l. green and brown	20	15
572	**174**	50l. green and red	65	30

175
176

1945. First Anniv of Fatherland Front Coalition.

573	**175**	1l. olive	20	15
574	**175**	4l. blue	20	15
575	**175**	5l. mauve	20	15
576	**176**	10l. blue	20	15
577	**176**	20l. red	20	20
578	**175**	50l. green	1·00	60
579	**175**	100l. brown	1·30	1·00

177 Refugee Children
178 Red Cross Train

1946. Red Cross. Cross in red.

580	**177**	2l. olive	20	15
645d	**177**	2l. brown	15	15
581	-	4l. violet	20	15
645e	-	4l. black	15	15
582	**177**	10l. purple	20	15
645f	**177**	10l. green	20	20
583	-	20l. dark blue	20	15
645g	-	20l. light blue	50	50
584	-	30l. brown	30	20
645h	-	30l. green	65	60
585	**178**	35l. black	50	40
645i	**178**	35l. green	75	70
586	-	50l. purple	65	50
645j	-	50l. lake	1·00	1·00
587	**178**	100l. brown	2·10	1·80
645k	**178**	100l. blue	1·70	1·60

DESIGNS—HORIZ: 4l., 20l. Soldier on stretcher. VERT: 30l., 50l. Nurse and wounded soldier.

179 Postal Savings Emblem
180 Savings Bank-Note

1946. 50th Anniv of Savings Bank.

588	**179**	4l. red	20	15
589	**180**	10l. olive	20	15
590	-	20l. blue	20	15
591	-	50l. black	1·60	1·40

DESIGNS—VERT: 20l. Child filling money-box; 50l. Postal Savings Bank.

181 Arms of Russia and Bulgaria and Spray of Oak

1946. Bulgo-Russian Congress.

592	**181**	4l. red	10·00	10·00
593	**181**	4l. orange	20	20
594	**181**	20l. blue	10·00	10·00
595	**181**	20l. green	40	40

182 Lion Rampant

1946. Stamp Day. Imperf.

596	**182**	20l. blue	85	40

183
190

1946. Air. Inscr "PAR AVION".

597	**183**	1l. purple	25	15
598	**183**	2l. grey	25	15
599	-	4l. black	25	15
600	-	6l. blue	25	15
601	-	10l. green	25	15
602	-	12l. brown	25	15
603	-	16l. purple	25	15
604	-	19l. red	25	15
605	-	30l. orange	30	20
606	-	45l. green	65	25
607	-	75l. brown	95	30

608	190	100l. red	1·70	50
609	-	100l. grey	1·70	50

DESIGNS—23×18 mm: 4l. Bird carrying envelope; 100l. (No. 609), Airplane. 18×23 mm: 6l. Airplane and envelope; 10, 12, 19l. Wings and posthorn; 16l. Wings and envelope; 30l. Airplane; 45, 75l. Dove and posthorn.

192 Stamboliiski

1946. 23rd Death Anniv of Aleksandur Stamboliiski (Prime Minister 1919–23).

610	192	100l. orange	9·50	9·50

193 Flags of Albania, Bulgaria, Yugoslavia and Rumania

1946. Balkan Games.

611	193	100l. brown	1·80	1·80

195 Junkers Ju87B "Stuka" Dive Bombers

196 Artillery

1946. Military and Air Services.

612	-	2l. red	20	15
613	-	4l. grey	20	15
614	196	5l. red	20	15
615	195	6l. brown	20	15
616	-	9l. mauve	20	15
617	-	10l. violet	20	15
618	-	20l. blue	50	20
619	-	30l. orange	65	30
620	-	40l. olive	75	40
621	-	50l. green	95	70
622	-	60l. brown	1·30	80

DESIGNS—HORIZ: 2, 20l. Grenade thrower and machine-gunner; 9l. Building pontoon-bridge; 10, 30l. Cavalry charge; 40l. Supply column; 50l. Motor convoy; 60l. Tanks. VERT: 4l. Grenade thrower.

203 St. Ivan Rilski

1946. Death Millenary of St. Ivan Rilski.

623	203	1l. brown	20	15
624	-	4l. sepia	20	15
625	-	10l. green	30	20
626	-	20l. blue	50	25
627	-	50l. red	2·10	1·10

DESIGNS—HORIZ: 4l. Rila Monastery; 10l. Monastery entrance; 50l. Cloistered courtyard. VERT: 20l. Aerial view of Monastery.

208 "New Republic"

1946. Referendum.

628	208	4l. red	20	15
629	208	20l. blue	20	15
630	208	50l. brown	50	40

209 Assault

210 Ambuscade

1946. Partisan Activities.

631	209	1l. purple	20	15
632	210	4l. green	20	15
633	-	5l. brown	20	15
634	210	10l. red	20	15
635	209	20l. blue	50	20
636	-	30l. brown	65	30
637	-	50l. black	85	70

DESIGNS—VERT: 5l., 50l. Partisan riflemen; 30l. Partisan leader.

211 Nurse and Children

1947. Winter Relief.

638	211	1l. violet	20	15
639	-	4l. red	20	15
640	-	9l. olive	20	15
641	211	10l. grey	20	15
642	-	20l. blue	20	15
643	-	30l. brown	40	20
644	-	40l. red	50	40
645	211	50l. green	95	70

DESIGNS: 4l., 9l. Child carrying gifts; 20l., 40l. Hungry child; 30l. Destitute mother and child.

212a Partisans

1947. Anti-fascists of 1923, 1941 and 1944 Commem.

645a	-	10l. brown and orange	75	70
645b	212a	20l. dp blue & lt blue	75	70
645c	-	70l. brown and red	47·00	45·00

DESIGNS—HORIZ: 10l. Group of fighters; 70l. Soldier addressing crowd.

213 Olive Branch

214 Dove of Peace

1947. Peace.

646	213	4l. olive	20	15
647	214	10l. brown	20	20
648	214	20l. blue	50	50

"BULGARIA" is in Roman characters on the 20l.

215 "U.S.A." and "Bulgaria"

1947. Air. Stamp Day and New York International Philatelic Exhibition.

649	215	70l.+30l. brown	2·10	2·00

216 Esperanto Emblem and Map of Bulgaria

1947. 30th Esperanto Jubilee Congress, Sofia.

650	216	20l.+10l. purple & green	1·00	1·00

217 G.P.O., Sofia

218 National Theatre, Sofia

219 Parliament Building

220 President's Palace

221 G.P.O., Sofia

1947. Government Buildings. (a) T **217**.

651		1l. green	20	15

(b) T **218**.

652		50s. green	20	15
653		2l. red	20	15
654		4l. blue	20	15
655		9l. red	65	20

(c) T **219**.

656		50s. green	20	15
657		2l. blue	20	15
658		4l. blue	20	15
659		20l. blue	1·60	1·00

(d) T **220**.

660		1l. green	20	15

(e) T **221**.

661		1l. green	20	15
662		2l. red	20	15
663		4l. blue	20	15

222 Hydro-electric Power Station and Dam

223 Emblem of Industry

1947. Reconstruction.

664	222	4l. green	20	15
665	-	9l. brown (Miner)	30	25
666	223	20l. blue	40	35
667	-	40l. green (Motor plough)	1·30	1·20

224 Exhibition Building

225 Former Residence of the French Poet Lamartine

226 Rose and Grapes

1947. Plovdiv Fair. (a) Postage.

668	224	4l. red	15	10
669	225	9l. red	20	10
670	226	20l. blue	40	40

227 Airplane over City

(b) Air. Imperf.

671	227	40l. green	1·60	1·50

228 Cycle Racing

229 Basketball

1947. Balkan Games.

672	228	2l. lilac	75	40
673	229	4l. green	85	50
674	-	9l. brown	1·60	60
675	-	20l. blue	2·10	70
676	-	60l. red	4·75	3·25

DESIGNS—VERT: 9l. Chess; 20l. Football; 60l. Balkan flags.

231 V. E. Aprilov

1947. Death Cent of Vasil Aprilov (educationist).

677	231	40l. blue	85	50
678	-	4l. red	30	15

DESIGN: 4l. Another portrait of Aprilov.

233 Postman

1947. Postal Employees' Relief Fund.

679	233	4l.+2l. olive	15	15
680	-	10l.+5l. red	20	20
681	-	20l.+10l. blue	30	30
682	-	40l.+20l. brown	1·60	1·50

DESIGNS: 10l. Linesman; 20l. Telephonists; 40l. Wireless masts.

235 Geno Kirov

1947. Theatrical Artists' Benevolent Fund.

683	235	50s. brown	10	10
684	-	1l. green	10	10
685	-	2l. green	10	10
686	-	3l. blue	10	10
687	-	4l. red	10	10
688	-	5l. purple	10	10
689	-	9l.+5l. blue	20	15
690	-	10l.+6l. red	20	20
691	-	15l.+7l. violet	50	35
692	-	20l.+15l. blue	75	60
693	-	30l.+20l. purple	1·60	1·30

PORTRAITS: 1l. Zlotina Nedeva; 2l. Ivan Popov; 3l. Atanas Kirchev; 4l. Elena Snezhina; 5l. Stoyan Buchvarov; 9l. Khristo Ganchev; 10l. Adriana Budevska; 15l. Vasil Kirkov; 20l. Save Orgnyanov; 30l. Krustyn Sarafov.

236 "Rodina" (freighter)

1947. National Shipping Revival.

694	236	50l. blue	1·00	80

237 Worker and Flag

238 Worker and Globe

1948. Second General Workers' Union Congress.

695	237	4l. blue (postage)	20	10
696	238	60l. brown (air)	85	70

239

240

1948. Leisure and Culture.

697	239	4l. red	20	15
698	240	20l. blue	40	20
699	-	40l. green	75	40
700	-	60l. brown	1·30	80

DESIGNS—VERT: 40l. Workers' musical interlude; 60l. Sports girl.

241 Kikola Vaptsarov

1948. Poets.

701	**241**	4l. red on cream	20	15
702	-	9l. brown on cream	25	20
703	-	15l. purple on cream	30	25
704	-	20l. blue on cream	40	35
705	-	45l. green on cream	1·00	90

PORTRAITS: 9l. Peya Yavorov; 15l. Khristo Smirnenski; 20l. Ivan Vazov; 45l. Petko Slaveikov.

242 Petlyakov Pe-2 Bomber over Baldwin's Tower

1948. Air. Stamp Day.

706	**242**	50l. brown on cream	2·10	2·00

243 Soldier

244 Peasants and Soldiers

1948. Soviet Army Monument.

707	**243**	4l. red on cream	20	15
708	**244**	10l. green on cream	25	20
709	-	20l. blue on cream	50	40
710	-	60l. olive on cream	1·30	1·00

DESIGNS—HORIZ: 20l. Soldiers of 1878 and 1944. VERT: 60l. Stalin and Spassky Tower, Kremlin.

245 Malyovitsa Peak

1948. Bulgarian Health Resorts.

711		2l. red	20	15
712		3l. orange	20	15
713		4l. blue	20	15
714		10l. purple	40	20
715	**245**	20l. blue	1·60	30
716	-	20l. blue	2·30	60
717	**245**	5l. brown	75	15
718	-	15l. olive	1·00	15

DESIGNS: 2l. Bath, Gorna Banya; 3, 10l. Bath, Bankya; 4, 20l. (No. 716), Mineral bath, Sofia; 15l. Malyovitsa Peak.

246 Lion Emblem

1948

719	**246**	50s. orange	20	15
719a	**246**	50s. brown	20	15
720	**246**	1l. green	20	15
721	**246**	9l. black	50	30

247 Dimitur Blagoev

248 Youths marching

1948. 25th Anniv of September Uprising.

722	**247**	4l. brown	20	15
723	-	9l. orange	20	15
724	-	20l. blue	30	30
725	**248**	60l. brown	1·60	1·20

DESIGNS—VERT: 9l. Gabrit Genov. HORIZ: 20l. Bishop Andrei Monument.

249 Khristo Smirnenski

1948. 500th Birth Anniv of Smirnenski (poet and revolutionary).

726	**249**	4l. blue	20	15
727	**249**	16l. brown	40	20

250 Miner

1948

728	**250**	4l. blue	40	20

251 Battle of Grivitsa

1948. Treaty of Friendship with Rumania.

729	**251**	20l. blue (postage)	30	20
730	-	40l. black (air)	50	40
731	-	100l. mauve	1·30	1·20

DESIGNS: 40l. Parliament Buildings in Sofia and Bucharest; 100l. Projected Danube Bridge.

252 Botev's House, Kalofer

253 Botev

1948. Birth Centenary of Khristo Botev (poet and revolutionary).

732	**252**	1l. green	20	15
733	**253**	4l. brown	20	15
734	**253**	4l. purple	20	15
735	-	9l. violet	20	15
736	-	15l. brown	20	15
737a	-	20l. blue	40	20
738	-	40l. brown	75	50
739	-	50l. black	1·00	70

DESIGNS—HORIZ: 9l. River paddle-steamer "Radetski"; 15l. Village of Kalofer; 40l. Botev's mother and verse of poem. VERT: 20l. Botev in uniform; 50l. Quill, pistol and laurel wreath.

254 Lenin

1949. 25th Death Anniv of Lenin. Inscr "1924–1949".

740	**254**	4l. brown	30	20
741	-	20l. red	75	60

DESIGN—(27×37 mm): 20l. Lenin as an orator.

255 Road Construction

1949. National Youth Movement.

742	**255**	4l. red	20	15
743	-	5l. brown	40	20
744	-	9l. green	1·00	50
745	-	10l. violet	65	40
746	-	20l. blue	1·30	1·00
747	-	40l. brown	2·50	1·20

DESIGNS—HORIZ: 5l. Tunnel construction; 9l. Class 10 steam locomotive; 10l. Textile workers; 20l. Girl driving tractor; 40l. Workers in lorry.

256 Lisunov Li-2 over Pleven Mausoleum

1949. Air. Seventh Philatelic Congress, Pleven.

748	**256**	50l. bistre	5·75	5·00

257 G. Dimitrov

258 G. Dimitrov

1949. Death of Georgi Dimitrov (Prime Minister 1946–49).

749	**257**	4l. red	30	30
750	**258**	20l. blue	1·60	60

259 Hydro-electric Power Station

260 Symbols of Agriculture and Industry

1949. Five Year Industrial and Agricultural Plan.

751	**259**	4l. olive (postage)	20	15
752	-	9l. red	30	25
753	-	15l. violet	50	30
754	-	20l. blue	1·60	90
755	**260**	50l. brown (air)	4·50	2·00

DESIGNS—VERT: 9l. Cement works; 15l. Tractors in garage. HORIZ: 20l. Tractors in field.

261 Javelin and Grenade Throwing

262 Motor-cyclist and Tractor

1949. Physical Culture Campaign.

756	**261**	4l. red	75	40
757	-	9l. olive	2·10	90
758	**262**	20l. blue	3·25	1·70
759	-	50l. red	7·75	4·25

DESIGNS—HORIZ: 9l. Hurdling and leaping barbed-wire. VERT: 50l. Two athletes marching.

263 Globe

1949. Air. 75th Anniv of Universal Postal Union.

760	**263**	50l. blue	3·25	1·70

265 Guardsman with Dog

264 Guardsman and Peasant

1949. Frontier Guards.

761	**264**	4l. brown (postage)	50	40
762	-	20l. blue	1·60	1·40
763	**265**	60l. green (air)	4·75	4·00

DESIGN—VERT: 20l. Guardsman on coast.

266 Georgi Dimitrov (Prime Minister 1946–49)

267 "Unanimity"

1949. Fatherland Front.

764	**266**	4l. brown	20	15
765	**267**	9l. violet	85	50
766	-	20l. blue	95	60
767	-	50l. red	1·30	1·00

DESIGNS: 20l. Man and woman with wheelbarrow and spade; 50l. Young people marching with banners.

268 Zosif Stalin

1949. 70th Birthday of Stalin.

768	**268**	4l. orange	50	20
769	-	40l. red	1·60	1·10

DESIGN—VERT: (25×37 mm): 40l. Stalin as an orator.

269 Kharalampi Stoyanov

270 Strikers and Train

1950. 30th Anniv of Railway Strike.

770	**269**	4l. brown	50	20
771	**270**	20l. blue	65	30
772	-	60l. olive	1·00	80

DESIGN—VERT: 60l. Two workers and flag.

271 Miner

272 Class 48 Steam Shunting Locomotive

1950

773	**271**	1l. olive	15	10
773a	**271**	1l. violet	30	10
774	**272**	2l. black	1·00	30
774a	**272**	2l. brown	1·00	25
775	-	3l. blue	50	10
776a	-	4l. green	3·25	1·20
777	-	5l. red	65	10
778	-	9l. grey	40	15
779	-	10l. purple	30	10
780	-	15l. red	1·00	30
781	-	20l. blue	1·20	40

DESIGNS—VERT: 3l. Ship under construction; 10l. Power station; 15l., 20l. Woman in factory. HORIZ: 4l. Tractor; 5l., 9l. Threshing machines.

273 Kolarov

1950. Death of Vasil Kolarov (Prime Minister 1949–50). Inscr "1877–1950".

782	**273**	4l. brown	20	15
783	-	20l. blue	85	80

DESIGN—(27½×39½ mm): 20l. Portrait as Type **273**, but different frame.

274 Starislas Dospevski (self-portrait)

274a *In the Field* (Khristo Storclev)

1950. Painters and paintings.

784	**274**	1l. green	65	40
785	-	4l. orange	2·10	60
786	-	9l. brown	3·25	80
787	**274a**	15l. brown	4·50	1·00
788	**274a**	20l. blue	6·75	3·00
789	-	40l. brown	8·25	4·00
790	-	60l. orange	9·00	6·00

DESIGNS—VERT: 4l. King Kaloyan and Desislava; 9l. Nikolai Pavlovich; 40l. Statue of Debeyanov (Ivan Lazarov); 60l. *Peasant* (Vladimir Dimitrov the Master).

275 Ivan Vazov and Birthplace, Sopot

1950. Birth Centenary of Ivan Vazov (poet).

791	**275**	4l. olive	20	15

276a G. Dimitrov (statesman)

1950. First Death Anniv of Georgi Dimitrov.

792	-	50s. brown (postage)	40	15
793	-	50s. green	40	15
794	**276a**	1l. brown	50	20
795	-	2l. slate	50	20
796	-	4l. purple	1·00	30
797	-	9l. red	1·80	90
798	-	10l. red	2·50	1·20
799	-	15l. grey	2·50	1·20
800	-	20l. blue	4·25	2·50
801	-	40l. brown (air)	8·25	4·00

DESIGNS—HORIZ: 50s. green, Dimitrov and birthplace, Kovachevtsi; 2l. Dimitrov's house, Sofia; 15l. Dimitrov signing new constitution; 20l. Dimitrov; 40l. Mausoleum. VERT: 50s. brown, 4, 9, 10l. Dimitrov in various poses.

277 Runners

1950

802	**277**	4l. green	95	50
803	-	9l. brown (Cycling)	1·00	80
804	-	20l. blue (Putting the shot)	1·30	1·20
805	-	40l. purple (Volleyball)	3·25	2·50

278 Workers and Tractor

1950. Second National Peace Congress.

806	**278**	4l. red	20	15
807	-	20l. blue	95	60

DESIGN—VERT: 20l. Stalin on flag and three heads.

278b

1950. Arms designs.

807a		2l. brown	20	15
807b		3l. red	20	15
807c	**278b**	5l. red	20	15
807d	-	9l. blue	20	15

Although inscribed "OFFICIAL MAIL", the above were issued as regular postage stamps.

279 Children on Beach

1950. Sunday Delivery.

808		1l. green (Sanatorium)	20	15
809	**279**	2l. red	30	15
810	-	5l. orange (Sunbathing)	65	30
811	**279**	10l. blue	1·60	60

280 Molotov, Kolarov, Stalin and Dimitrov

281 Russian and Bulgarian Girls

1950. Second Anniv of Soviet–Bulgarian Treaty of Friendship.

812	**280**	4l. brown	20	15
813	-	9l. red	30	15
814	**281**	20l. blue	65	50
815	-	50l. green	3·25	1·20

DESIGNS—VERT: 9l. Spassky Tower and flags; 50l. Freighter and tractor.

282 Marshal Tolbukhin

1950. Honouring Marshal Tolbukhin.

816	**282**	4l. mauve	30	20
817	-	20l. blue	1·60	80

DESIGN—HORIZ: 20l. Bulgarians greeting Tolbukhin.

284 A. S. Popov

1951. 45th Death Anniv of Aleksandr Popov (radio pioneer).

818	**284**	4l. brown	75	30
819	**284**	20l. blue	1·40	70

286 Georgi Kirkov

1951. Anti-fascist Heroes.

823	-	1l. mauve	40	20
824	-	2l. plum	40	20
825	**286**	4l. red	40	20
826	-	9l. brown	1·20	60
827	-	15l. olive	2·50	1·10
828	-	20l. blue	2·50	1·50
829	-	50l. grey	6·25	2·20

PORTRAITS: 1l. Chankova, Adalbert Antonov-Malchika, Sasho Dimitrov and Lilyana Dimitrova; 2l. Stanke Dimitrov; 9l. Anton Ivanov; 15l. Mikhailov; 20l. Georgi Dimitrov at Leipzig; 50l. Nocho Ivanov and Acram Stoyahov.

285 First Bulgarian Truck

1951. National Occupations. (a) As T **285**.

820		1l. violet (Tractor)	20	10
821		2l. green (Steam-roller)	25	10
822	**285**	4l. brown	30	10

289 Embroidery

(b) As T **289**.

830	-	1l. brown (Tractor)	30	20
831	-	2l. violet (Steam-roller)	40	30
832	-	4l. brown (Truck)	75	60
833	**289**	9l. violet	1·30	80
834	-	15l. purple (Carpets)	2·30	1·50
835	-	20l. blue (Roses and Tobacco)	5·25	2·20
836	-	40l. green (Fruit)	7·75	3·25

The 9l. and 20l. are vert, the remainder horiz.

290 Turkish Attack

1951. 75th Anniv of April Uprising.

837	**290**	1l. brown	75	35
838	-	4l. green	85	40
839	-	9l. purple	1·30	1·00
840	-	20l. blue	1·90	1·50
841	-	40l. lake	2·50	2·00

DESIGNS—HORIZ: 4l. Proclamation of Uprising; 9l. Cannon and cavalry; 20l. Patriots in 1876 and 1944; 40l. Georgi Benkovsky and Georgi Dimitrov.

291 Dimitur Blagoev as Orator

1951. 60th Anniv of First Bulgarian Social Democratic Party Congress, Buzludzha.

842	**291**	1l. violet	30	20
843	**291**	4l. green	1·00	40
844	**291**	9l. purple	1·80	1·20

292 Babies in Creche

1951. Children's Day.

845	**292**	1l. brown	30	20
846	-	4l. purple	75	30
847	-	9l. green	1·60	60
848	-	20l. blue	3·25	2·00

DESIGNS: 4l. Children building models; 9l. Girl and children's play ground; 20l. Boy bugler and children marching.

293 Workers

1951. Third General Workers' Union Congress.

849	**293**	1l. black	20	15
850	-	4l. brown	30	20

DESIGN inscr "16 XII 1951"; 4l. Georgi Dimitrov and Valdo Chervenkov (Prime minister).

294 Labour medal (Obverse)

295 Labour medal (Reverse)

1952. Order of Labour.

851	**294**	1l. red	20	15
852	**295**	1l. brown	20	15
853	**294**	4l. green	20	15
854	**295**	4l. green	20	15
855	**294**	9l. violet	75	20
856	**295**	9l. blue	75	20

296 Vasil Kolarov Dam

1952

857	**296**	4s. green	20	15
858	**296**	12s. violet	30	15
859	**296**	16s. brown	40	15
860	**296**	44s. red	1·00	20
861	**296**	80s. blue	4·50	50

297 G. Dimitrov and Chemical Works

1952. 70th Birth Anniv of Georgi Dimitrov (statesman). Dated "1882–1952".

862	**297**	16s. brown	95	50
863	-	44s. brown	1·60	1·00
864	-	80s. blue	2·75	1·50

DESIGNS—HORIZ: 44s. Georgi Dimitrov (Prime minister 1946–49) and Prime minister Vulko Chervenkov. VERT: 80s. Full-face portrait of Georgi Dimitrov.

298 Republika Power Station

1952

866	**298**	16s. sepia	65	20
867	**298**	44s. purple	2·10	30

299 N. Vaptsarov (revolutionary)

1952. Tenth Death Anniv of Nikola Vaptsarov (poet and revolutionary).

869	**299**	16s. lake	95	70
870	-	44s. brown	1·90	1·70
871	-	80s. sepia	4·00	1·90

PORTRAITS: 44s. Facing bayonets; 80s. Full-face.

300 Congress Delegates

1952. 40th Anniv of First Workers' Social Democratic Youth League Congress.

872	**300**	2s. lake	20	15
873	-	16s. violet	40	30
874	-	44s. green	1·60	85
875	-	80s. sepia	2·50	1·90

DESIGNS: 16s. Young partisans; 44s. Factory and guards; 80s. Dimitrov addressing young workers.

301 Attack on Winter Palace, St. Petersburg

1952. 35th Anniv of Russian Revolution. Dated "1917 1952".

876	**301**	4s. lake	40	20
877	-	8s. green	50	30
878	-	16s. blue	1·20	40
879	-	44s. sepia	1·50	50
880	-	80s. olive	3·00	2·40

DESIGNS: 8s. Volga–Don canal; 16s. Dove and globe; 44s. Lenin and Stalin; 80s. Lenin, Stalin and Himlay hydro-electric station.

302

303 Vintagers and Grapes

1952. Wood Carvings depicting National Products.

881		2s. brown	20	15
882		8s. green	20	15
883		12s. brown	40	15
884		16s. purple	80	15
885	**302**	28s. green	1·10	20
886	-	44s. brown	1·50	30
887	**303**	80s. blue	1·70	40
888	**303**	1l. violet	4·00	60
889	**303**	4l. red	4·75	3·50

DESIGNS—VERT: 2s. Numeral in carved frame. HORIZ: 8s. Gift-offering to idol; 12s. Birds and grapes; 16s. Rose-gathering; 44s. "Attar of Roses".

304 V. Levski

1953. 80th Anniv of Execution of Vasil Levski (revolutionary).

890	**304**	16s. brown on cream	20	15
891	-	44s. brown on cream	60	30

DESIGN: 44s. Levski addressing crowd.

305 Russian Army Crossing R. Danube

1953. 75th Anniv of Liberation from Turkey.

892	**305**	8s. blue	30	20
893	-	16s. brown	40	20
894	-	44s. green	95	30
895	-	80s. lake	3·00	1·50
896	-	1l. black	3·50	3·00

DESIGNS—VERT: 16s. Battle of Shipka Pass. HORIZ: 44s. Peasants welcoming Russian soldiers; 80s. Bulgarians and Russians embracing; 1l. Shipka Pass memorial and Dimitrovgrad.

306 Mother and Children

1953. International Women's Day.

897	**306**	16s. blue	30	10
898	**306**	16s. green	30	10

307 Karl Marx

1953. 70th Death Anniv of Karl Marx.

899	**307**	16s. blue	30	20
900	-	44s. brown	70	50

DESIGN—VERT: 44s. Book "Das Kapital".

308 May Day Parade

1953. Labour Day.

901	**308**	16s. red	40	20

309 Stalin

1953. Death of Stalin.

902	**309**	16s. brown	80	30
903	**309**	16s. black	80	30

310 Goce Delcev (Macedonian revolutionary)

1953. 50th Anniv of Ilinden–Preobrazhenie Rising.

904	**310**	16s. brown	20	15
905	-	44s. violet	80	50
906	-	1l. purple	1·10	80

DESIGNS. 44s. Insurgents and flag facing left. HORIZ: 1l. Insurgents and flag facing right.

311 Soldier and Insurgents

1953. Army Day.

907	**311**	16s. red	50	20
908	-	44s. blue	95	30

DESIGN: 44s. Soldier, factories and combine-harvester.

312 Dimitur Blagoev

1953. 50th Anniv of Bulgarian Workers' Social Democratic Party.

909	**312**	16s. brown	50	30
910	-	44s. red	95	30

DESIGN: 44s. Dimitrov and Blagoev.

313 Georgi Dimitrov and Vasil Kolarov

1953. 30th Anniv of September Uprising.

911	**313**	8s. black	30	15
912	-	16s. brown	40	20
913	-	44s. red	1·30	60

DESIGNS: 16s. Insurgent and flag; 44s. Crowd of Insurgents.

314 Railway Viaduct

1953. Bulgarian–Russian Friendship.

914	**314**	8s. blue	20	15
915	-	16s. slate	30	20
916	-	44s. brown	80	40
917	-	80s. orange	95	70

DESIGNS—HORIZ: 16s. Welder and industrial plant; 80s. Combine-harvester. VERT: 44s. Iron foundry.

315 Dog Rose

1953. Medicinal Flowers.

918		2s. blue	20	15
919		4s. orange	20	15
920		8s. turquoise	20	15
921	**315**	12s. green	20	15
922	-	12s. red	20	15
923	-	16s. blue	50	20
924	-	16s. brown	50	20
925	-	20s. red	80	25
926	-	28s. green	85	30
927	-	40s. blue	95	50
928	-	44s. brown	1·50	60
929	-	80s. brown	2·40	1·10
930	-	1l. brown	6·75	1·90
931	-	2l. purple	9·75	4·00
MS931a 161×172 mm. Twelve values as above in green (sold at 6l.)			70·00	70·00

FLOWERS: 2s. Deadly nightshade; 4s. Thorn-apple; 8s. Sage; 16s. Great yellow gentian; 20s. Opium poppy; 28s. Peppermint; 40s. Bear-berry; 44s. Coltsfoot; 80s. Primula; 1l. Dandelion; 2l. Foxglove.

316 Vasil Kolarov Library

1953. 75th Anniv of Kolarov Library, Sofia.

932	**316**	44s. brown	60	40

317 Singer and Musician

1953. Amateur Theatricals.

933	**317**	16s. brown	30	15
934	-	44s. green	70	40

DESIGN: 44s. Folk-dancers.

318 Airplane over Mountains

1954. Air.

935	**318**	8s. green	20	15
936	-	12s. lake	20	15
937	-	16s. brown	20	15
938	-	20s. salmon	20	15
939	-	28s. blue	40	20
940	-	44s. purple	50	20
941	-	60s. brown	85	30
942	-	80s. green	95	40
943	-	1l. green	3·00	85
944	-	4l. blue	5·25	2·40

DESIGNS—VERT: 12s. Exhibition buildings, Plovdiv; 80s. Tirnovo; 4l. Partisans' Monument. HORIZ: 16s. Seaside promenade, Varna; 20s. Combine-harvester in cornfield; 28s. Rila Monastery; 44s. Studena hydro-electric barrage; 60s. Dimitrovgrad; 1l. Sofia University and equestrian statue.

319 Lenin and Stalin

1954. 30th Death Anniv of Lenin.

945	**319**	16s. brown	30	15
946	-	44s. lake	70	20
947	-	80s. blue	95	40
948	-	1l. green	1·90	1·20

DESIGNS—VERT: 44s. Lenin statue; 80s. Lenin–Stalin Mausoleum and Kremlin; 1l. Lenin.

320 Dimitur Blagoev and Crowd

1954. 30th Death Anniv of Blagoev.

949	**320**	16s. brown	20	10
950	-	44s. sepia	80	30

DESIGN: 44s. Blagoev writing at desk.

321 Dimitrov Speaking

1954. Fifth Death Anniv of Dimitrov.

951	**321**	44s. lake	50	30
952	-	80s. brown	95	70

DESIGN—HORIZ: 80s. Dimitrov and blast-furnace.

322 Class 10 Steam Locomotive

1954. Railway Workers' Day.

953	**322**	44s. turquoise	1·70	80
954	**322**	44s. black	1·70	80

323 Miner Operating Machinery

1954. Miners' Day.

955	**323**	44s. green	50	20

324 Marching Soldiers

1954. Tenth Anniv of Fatherland Front Government.

956	**324**	12s. lake	20	15
957	-	16s. red	20	15
958	-	28s. slate	30	20
959	-	44s. brown	60	25
960	-	80s. blue	1·30	50
961	-	1l. green	1·50	60

DESIGNS—VERT: 16s. Soldier and parents; 80s. Girl and boy pioneers; 1l. Dimitrov. HORIZ: 28s. Industrial plant; 44s. Dimitrov and workers.

325 Academy Building

1954. 85th Anniv of Academy of Sciences.

962	**325**	80s. black	1·50	80

326 Gymnast

1954. Sports. Cream paper.

963	**326**	16s. green	1·50	50
964	-	44s. red	1·60	95
965	-	80s. brown	3·50	1·90
966	-	2l. blue	5·25	4·00

DESIGNS—VERT: 44s. Wrestlers; 2l. Ski-jumper. HORIZ: 80s. Horse-jumper.

327 Velingrad Rest Home

1954. 50th Anniv of Trade Union Movement.

967	**327**	16s. green	30	20
968	-	44s. red	50	30
969	-	80s. blue	1·20	95

DESIGNS—VERT: 44s. Foundryman. HORIZ: 80s. Georgi Dimitrov, Dimitur Blagoev and Georgi Kirkov.

328 Geese

329 Communist Party Building

1955

970	**328**	2s. green	20	10
971	-	4s. olive	30	10
972	-	12s. brown	60	20
973	-	16s. brown	95	30
974	-	28s. blue	60	20
975	**329**	44s. red	11·50	3·50
976	-	80s. brown	1·50	50
977	-	1l. green	2·40	95

DESIGNS: 4s. Rooster and hens; 12s. Sow and piglets; 16s. Ewe and lambs; 28s. Telephone exchange; 80s. Flats; 1l. Cellulose factory.

330 Mill Girl

1955. International Women's Day.

978	**330**	12s. brown	10	10
979	-	16s. green	30	15
980	-	44s. blue	1·10	20
981	-	44s. red	1·10	20

DESIGNS—HORIZ: 16s. Girl feeding cattle. VERT: 44s. Mother and baby.

1955. As Nos. 820 and 822 surch **16 CT.**

981a		16s. on 1l. violet	20	10
982	**285**	16s. on 4l. brown	1·90	50

332 Rejoicing Crowds

1955. Labour Day.

983	**332**	16s. red	30	20
984	-	44s. blue	70	30

DESIGN: 44s. Three workers and globe.

333 St. Cyril and St. Methodius

1955. 1100th Anniv of First Bulgarian Literature. On cream paper.

985	**333**	4s. blue	20	15
986	-	8s. olive	20	15
987	-	16s. black	20	15
988	-	28s. red	50	40
989	-	44s. brown	80	50
990	-	80s. red	1·40	95
991	-	2l. black	3·50	2·10

DESIGNS: 8s. Monk writing; 16s. Early printing press; 28s. Khristo Botev (poet); 44s. Ivan Vazov (poet and novelist); 80s. Dimitur Blagoev (writer and editor) and books; 2l. Dimitur Blagoev Polygraphic Complex, Sofia.

334 Sergei Rumyantsev

1955. 30th Death Annivs of Bulgarian Poets. On cream paper.

992	**334**	12s. brown	40	20
993	-	16s. brown	50	30
994	-	44s. green	1·50	95

DESIGNS: 16s. Khristo Yusenov; 44s. Geo Milev.

335 F. Engels and Book

1955. 60th Death Anniv of Engels.

995	**335**	44s. brown on cream	95	80

336 Mother and Children

1955. World Mothers' Congress, Lausanne.

996	**336**	44s. lake on cream	95	80

337 "Youth of the World"

1955. Fifth World Youth Festival, Warsaw.

997	**337**	44s. blue on cream	95	80

338 Main Entrance in 1892

1955. 16th International Fair, Plovdiv.

998	**338**	4s. brown on cream	20	15
999	-	16s. red on cream	25	15
1000	-	44s. green on cream	50	20
1001	-	80s. cream	1·20	40

DESIGNS—VERT: 16s. Sculptured group; 80s. Fair poster. HORIZ: 44s. Fruit.

339 Friedrich Schiller (dramatist) (150th death anniv)

1955. Cultural Annivs. Writers. On cream paper.

1002	**339**	16s. brown	50	20
1003	-	44s. red	1·10	30
1004	-	60s. blue	1·40	40
1005	-	80s. black	1·70	60
1006	-	1l. purple	3·50	1·50
1007	-	2l. olive	4·50	3·00

PORTRAITS: 44s. Adam Mickiewicz (poet, death centenary); 60s. Hans Christian Andersen (150th birth anniv); 80s. Baron de Montesquieu (philosopher, death bicentenary); 1l. Miguel de Cervantes (350th anniv of publication of *Don Quixote*); 2l. Walt Whitman (poet) (centenary of publication of *Leaves of Grass*).

340 Industrial Plant

1955. Bulgarian–Russian Friendship. On cream paper.

1008	**340**	2s. slate	20	15
1009	-	4s. blue	20	15
1010	-	16s. green	60	20
1011	-	44s. brown	80	20
1012	-	80s. green	1·20	30
1013	-	1l. black	1·30	70

DESIGNS—HORIZ: 4s. Dam; 16s. Friendship railway bridge over River Danube between Ruse and Giurgiu (Rumania). VERT: 44s. Monument; 80s. Ivan-Michurin (botanist); 1l. Vladimir Mayakovsky (writer).

341 Emblem

1956. Centenary of Library Reading Rooms. On cream paper.

1014	**341**	12s. red	20	15
1015	-	16s. brown	30	20
1016	-	44s. myrtle	1·20	50

DESIGNS: 16s. K. Pshourka writing; 44s. B. Kiro reading.

342 Quinces

1956. Fruits.

1017	**342**	4s. red	2·10	30
1017a	**342**	4s. green	20	10
1018	-	8s. green (Pears)	95	30
1018a	-	8s. brown (Pears)	20	10
1019	-	16s. dark red (Apples)	1·70	40
1019a	-	16s. red (Apples)	60	20
1020	-	44s. violet (Grapes)	1·90	60
1020a	-	44s. ochre (Grapes)	1·20	30

343 Artillerymen

1956. 80th Anniv of April Uprising.

1021	**343**	16s. brown	40	40
1022	-	44s. green (Cavalry charge)	50	50

344 Blagoev and Birthplace at Zagovichane

1956. Birth Centenary of Dimitur Blagoev (socialist writer).

1023	**344**	44s. turquoise	1·50	95

345 Cherries

1956. Fruits.

1024	**345**	2s. lake	15	10
1025	-	12s. blue (Plums)	20	10
1026	-	28s. buff (Greengages)	40	30
1027	-	80s. red (Strawberries)	1·20	60

346 Football

1956. Olympic Games.

1028		4s. blue	60	20
1029		12s. red	70	25
1030		16s. brown	80	30
1031	**346**	44s. green	1·50	60
1032	-	80s. brown	2·40	1·30
1033	-	1l. lake	3·50	1·50

DESIGNS—VERT: 4s. Gymnastics; 12s. Throwing the discus; 80s. Basketball. HORIZ: 16s. Pole vaulting; 1l. Boxing.

347 Tobacco and Rose

1956. 17th International Fair, Plovdiv.

1034	**347**	44s. red	1·50	60
1035	**347**	44s. green	1·50	60

348 Gliders

1956. Air. 30th Anniv of Gliding Club.

1036	-	44s. blue	40	20
1037	-	60s. violet	50	30
1038	**348**	80s. green	1·50	95

DESIGNS: 44s. Launching glider; 60s. Glider over hangar.

349 National Theatre

1956. Centenary of National Theatre.

1039	**349**	16s. brown	30	20
1040	-	44s. turquoise	70	60

DESIGN: 44s. Dobri Voinikov and Sava Dobroplodni (dramatist).

350 Wolfgang Mozart (composer, birth bicent)

1956. Cultural Anniversaries.

1041		16s. olive	30	20
1042		20s. brown	50	20
1043	**350**	40s. red	70	25
1044	-	44s. brown	80	30
1045	-	60s. slate	95	35
1046	-	80s. brown	1·50	80
1047	-	1l. green	2·40	95
1048	-	2l. green	4·75	3·00

PORTRAITS: 16s. Benjamin Franklin (journalist and statesman, 150th birth anniv); 20s. Rembrandt (artist, 350th birth anniv); 44s. Heinrich Heine (poet, death centenary); 60s. George Bernard Shaw (dramatist, birth centenary); 80s. Fyodor Dostoevsky (novelist, 75th death anniv); 1l. Henrik Ibsen (dramatist, 50th death anniv); 2l. Pierre Curie (physicist, 50th death anniv).

351 Cyclists

1957. Tour of Egypt Cycle Race.

1049	**351**	80s. brown	1·50	70
1050	**351**	80s. turquoise	1·50	70

352 Woman with Microscope

1957. International Women's Day. Inscr as in T **352**.

1051	**352**	12s. blue	10	10
1052	-	16s. brown	30	15
1053	-	44s. green	60	30

DESIGNS: 16s. Woman and children; 44s. Woman feeding poultry.

353 *New Times*

1957. 60th Anniv of *New Times* (book).

1054	**353**	16s. red	40	20

354 Lisunov Li-2 Airliner

1957. Air. Tenth Anniv of Bulgarian Airways.

1055	**354**	80s. blue	1·50	50

355 St. Cyril and St. Methodius

1957. Centenary of Canonization of Saints Cyril and Methodius (founders of Cyrillic alphabet).

1056	**355**	44s. olive and buff	1·50	60

356 Basketball

1957. Tenth European Basketball Championships.

1057	**356**	44s. green	2·40	70

357 Girl in National Costume

1957. Sixth World Youth Festival, Moscow.

1058	**357**	44s. blue	80	30

358 G. Dimitrov

1957. 75th Birth Anniv of Georgi Dimitrov (statesman).

1059	**358**	44s. red	1·50	50

359 V. Levski

1957. 120th Birth Anniv of Vasil Levski (revolutionary).

1060	**359**	44s. green	95	30

360 View of Turnovo and Ludwig Zamenhof (inventor)

1957. 70th Anniv of Esperanto (invented language) and 50th Anniv of Bulgarian Esperanto Association.

1061	**360**	44s. green	1·50	50

361 Soldiers in Battle

1957. 80th Anniv of Liberation from Turkey.

1062	-	16s. green	20	10
1063	**361**	44s. brown	80	25

DESIGN: 16s. Old and young soldiers.

362 Woman Planting Tree

1957. Reafforestation Campaign.

1064	**362**	2s. green	20	15
1065	-	12s. brown	20	15
1066	-	16s. blue	20	15
1067	-	44s. turquoise	70	30
1068	-	80s. green	1·20	60

DESIGNS—HORIZ: 12s. Red deer in forest; 16s. Dam and trees; 44s. Polikarpov Po-2 biplane over forest; 80s. Trees and cornfield.

363 Two Hemispheres

1957. Fourth World TUC, Leipzig.

1069	**363**	44s. blue	80	30

364 Lenin

1957. 40th Anniv of Russian Revolution. Inscr "1917–1957".

1070	**364**	12s. brown	60	30
1071	-	16s. turquoise	1·30	80
1072	-	44s. blue	2·75	95
1073	-	60s. red	3·00	1·50
1074	-	80s. green	9·75	3·50

DESIGNS: 16s. Cruiser *Aurora*; 44s. Dove of Peace over Europe; 60s. Revolutionaries; 80s. Oil refinery.

365 Youth and Girl

1957. Tenth Anniv of Dimitrov National Youth Movement.

1075	**365**	16s. red	30	20

366 Partisans

1957. 15th Anniv of Fatherland Front.

1076	**366**	16s. brown	30	20

367 Mikhail Glinka (composer, death centenary)

1957. Cultural Celebrities.

1077	**367**	12s. brown	60	20
1078	-	16s. green	70	25
1079	-	40s. blue	1·60	30
1080	-	44s. brown	1·70	40
1081	-	60s. brown	1·90	80
1082	-	80s. purple	3·00	2·75

DESIGNS: 16s. Ion Comenius (educationist) (300th anniv of publication of *Didoetica Opera Omria*); 40s. Carl Linnaeus (botanist, 250th birth anniv); 44s. William Blake (writer, birth bicent); 60s. Carlo Goldoni (dramatist, 250th birth anniv); 80s. Auguste Comte (philosopher, death centenary).

368 Hotel Vasil, Kolarov

1958. Holiday Resorts.

1083		4s. blue	20	15
1084		8s. brown	20	15
1085		12s. green	20	15
1086	**368**	16s. green	20	15
1087	-	44s. turquoise	50	20
1088	-	60s. blue	80	30
1089	-	80s. brown	95	40
1090	-	1l. brown	1·20	50

DESIGNS—HORIZ: 4s. Skis and Pirin Mts; 8s. Old house in Koprivshtita; 12s. Hostel at Yelingrad; 44s. Hotel at Momin-Prokhod; 60s. Seaside hotel and peninsula, Nesebur; 80s. Beach scene, Varna; 1l. Modern hotels, Varna.

369 Brown Hare

1958. Forest Animals.

1091	**369**	2s. deep green & green	70	20
1092	-	12s. brown and green	1·20	30
1093	-	16s. brown and green	1·60	40
1094	-	44s. brown and blue	1·90	60
1095	-	80s. brown and ochre	2·40	80
1096	-	1l. brown and blue	3·00	1·20

DESIGNS—VERT: 12s. Roe doe. HORIZ: 16s. Red deer; 44s. Chamois; 80s. Brown bear; 1l. Wild boar.

370 Marx and Lenin

1958. Seventh Bulgarian Communist Party Congress. Inscr as in T **370**.

1097	**370**	12s. brown	50	20
1098	-	16s. red	80	30
1099	-	44s. blue	1·60	95

DESIGNS: 16s. Workers marching with banners; 44s. Lenin blast furnaces.

371 Wrestlers

1958. Wrestling Championships.

1100	**371**	60s. lake	2·10	1·50
1101	**371**	80s. sepia	2·40	1·90

372 Chessmen and "Oval Chessboard"

1958. Fifth World Students' Team Chess Championship, Varna.

1102	**372**	80s. green	11·50	10·50

373 Russian Pavilion

1958. 18th International Fair, Plovdiv.

1103	**373**	44s. red	95	70

374 Swimmer

1958. Bulgarian Students' Games.

1104	**374**	16s. blue	30	15
1105	-	28s. brown	60	20
1106	-	44s. green	85	50

DESIGNS: 28s. Dancer; 44s. Volleyball players at net.

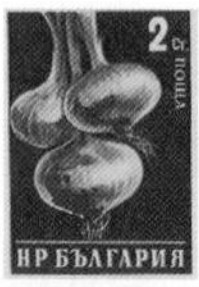

375 Onions

1958. "Agricultural Propaganda".

1107	**375**	2s. brown	20	15
1108	-	12s. lake (Garlic)	20	15
1109	-	16s. myrtle (Peppers)	30	20
1110	-	44s. red (Tomatoes)	50	25
1111	-	80s. green (Cucumbers)	1·20	40
1112	-	1l. violet (Aubergines)	1·60	50

376 Insurgent with Rifle

1958. 35th Anniv of September Uprising.

1113	**376**	16s. orange	50	30
1114	-	44s. lake	95	70

DESIGN—HORIZ: 44s. Insurgent helping wounded comrade.

377 Conference Emblem

1958. First World Trade Union's Young Workers' Conference, Prague.

1115	**377**	44s. blue	95	70

378 Exhibition Emblem

1958. Brussels International Exhibition.

1116	**378**	1l. blue and black	9·75	9·75

379 Sputnik over Globe

1958. Air. IGY.

1117	**379**	80s. turquoise	6·75	5·75

380 Running

1958. Balkan Games. Inscr "1958".

1118	**380**	16s. brown	85	40
1119	-	44s. olive	95	60
1120	-	60s. blue	1·60	70
1121	-	80s. green	1·90	95
1122	-	4l. lake	11·50	7·25

DESIGNS—HORIZ: 44s. Throwing the javelin; 60s. High-jumping; 80s. Hurdling. VERT: 4l. Putting the shot.

381 Young Gardeners

1958. Fourth Dimitrov National Youth Movement Congress. Inscr as in T 381.

1123	**381**	8s. green	20	15
1124	-	12s. brown	20	15
1125	-	16s. purple	20	15
1126	-	40s. blue	80	20
1127	-	44s. red	1·20	50

DESIGNS—HORIZ: 12s. Farm girl with cattle; 40s. Youth with wheel-barrow. VERT: 16s. Youth with pickaxe and girl with spade; 44s. Communist Party Building.

382 Smirnenski

1958. 60th Birth Anniv of Khristo Smirnenski (poet and revolutionary).

1128	**382**	16s. red	40	20

383 First Cosmic Rockets

1959. Air. Launching of First Cosmic Rocket.

1129	**383**	2l. brown and blue	9·75	9·75

384 Footballers

1959. Youth Football Games, Sofia.

1130	**384**	2l. brown on cream	3·50	2·40

385 UNESCO Headquarters, Paris

1959. Inauguration of UNESCO Headquarters Building.

1131	**385**	2l. purple on cream	3·50	2·40

386 Skier

1959. 40 Years of Skiing in Bulgaria.

1132	**386**	1l. blue on cream	2·40	95

1959. No. 1110 surch **45 CT.**

1133	45s. on 44s. red	1·50	50

388 Military Telegraph Linesman

1959. 80th Anniv of 1st Bulgarian Postage Stamps.

1134	**388**	12s. yellow and green	20	15
1135	-	16s. mauve and purple	50	20
1136	-	60s. yellow and brown	85	40
1137	-	80s. salmon and red	95	50
1138	-	1l. blue	2·40	60
1139	-	2l. brown	4·75	2·40
MS1139a 91×121 mm. 60s. (+4l.40) yellow and black (as 1136). Imperf			75·00	75·00
MS1139b 125×125 mm. Remaining values in different colours (sold at 5l.) Imperf			75·00	75·00

DESIGNS—HORIZ: 16s. 19th-century mail-coach; 80s. Early postal car; 2l. Striking railway workers. VERT: 60s. Bulgarian 1879 stamp; 1l. Radio tower.

389 Great Tits

1959. Birds.

1140	**389**	2s. slate and yellow	40	20
1141	-	8s. green and brown	70	30
1142	-	16s. sepia and brown	80	35
1143	-	45s. myrtle and brown	1·80	70
1144	-	60s. grey and blue	3·50	1·20
1145	-	80s. drab and turquoise	4·75	1·90

DESIGNS—HORIZ: 8s. Hoopoe; 60s. Rock partridge; 80s. European cuckoo. VERT: 16s. Great spotted woodpecker; 45s. Grey partridge.

390 Cotton-picking

1959. Five Year Plan.

1146		2s. brown	20	15
1147		4s. bistre	20	15
1148	**390**	5s. green	20	15
1149	-	10s. brown	20	15
1150	-	12s. brown	20	15
1151	-	15s. mauve	20	15
1152	-	16s. violet	20	15
1153	-	20s. orange	30	20
1154	-	25s. blue	30	20
1155	-	28s. green	40	20
1156	-	40s. blue	50	20
1157	-	45s. brown	50	20
1158	-	60s. red	95	40
1159	-	80s. olive	1·70	30
1160	-	1l. lake	95	50
1161	-	1l.25 blue	3·00	95
1162	-	2l. red	1·80	60

DESIGNS—HORIZ: 2s. Children at play; 10s. Dairymaid milking cow; 16s. Industrial plant; 20s. Combine-harvester; 40s. Hydro-electric barrage; 60s. Furnaceman; 1l.25, Machinist. VERT: 4s. Woman doctor examining child; 12s. Tobacco harvesting; 15s. Machinist; 25s. Power linesman; 28s. Tending sunflowers; 45s. Miner; 80s. Fruit-picker; 1l. Workers with symbols of agriculture and industry; 2l. Worker with banner.

391 Patriots

1959. 300th Anniv of Batak.

1163	**391**	16s. brown	50	20

392 Piper

1959. Spartacist Games. Inscr "1958–1959".

1164	**392**	4s. olive on cream	20	15
1165	-	12s. red on yellow	20	15
1166	-	16s. lake on salmon	30	20
1167	-	20s. blue on blue	50	25
1168	-	80s. green on green	1·50	60
1169	-	1l. brown on orange	1·60	1·10

DESIGNS—VERT: 12s. Gymnastics; 1l. Urn. HORIZ: 16s. Girls exercising with hoops; 20s. Dancers leaping; 80s. Ballet dancers.

393 Soldiers in Lorry

1959. 15th Anniv of Fatherland Front Government.

1170	**393**	12s. blue and red	20	15
1171	-	16s. black and red	20	15
1172	-	45s. blue and red	40	20
1173	-	60s. green and red	50	30
1174	-	80s. brown and red	80	40
1175	-	1l.25 brown and red	1·60	70

DESIGNS—HORIZ: 16s. Partisans meeting Red Army soldiers; 45s. Blast furnaces; 60s. Tanks; 80s. Combine-harvester in cornfield. VERT: 1l.25, Pioneers with banner.

394 Footballer

1959. 50th Anniv of Football in Bulgaria.

1176	**394**	1l.25 green on yellow	7·75	7·75

395 Tupolev Tu-104A Jetliner and Statue of Liberty

1959. Air. Visit of Nikita Khrushchev (Russian Prime Minister) to U.S.A.

1177	**395**	1l. pink and blue	4·00	4·00

396 Globe and Letter

1959. International Correspondence Week.

1178	**396**	45s. black and green	70	20
1179	-	1l.25 red, black & blue	1·30	50

DESIGN: 1l.25, Pigeon and letter.

397 Parachutist

1960. Third Voluntary Defence Congress.

1180	**397**	1l.25 cream & turquoise	3·50	1·60

398 N. Vaptsarov

1960. 50th Birth Anniv of Nikola Vaptsarov (poet and revolutionary).

1181	**398**	80s. brown and green	95	50

399 Dr. L. Zamenhof

1960. Birth Centenary of Dr. Ludwig Zamenhof (inventor of Esperanto).

1182	**399**	1l.25 green & lt green	1·50	95

400

1960. 50th Anniv of State Opera.

1183	**400**	80s. black and green	95	60
1184	-	1l.25 black and red	1·50	85

DESIGN: 1l.25, Lyre.

401 Track of Trajectory of "Lunik 3" around the Moon

1960. Flight of "Lunik 3".

1185	**401**	1l.25 green, yellow & bl	7·25	5·75

402 Skier

1960. Winter Olympic Games.

1186	**402**	2l. brown, blue & black	1·50	1·50

403 Vela Blagoeva

1960. 50th Anniv of International Women's Day. Inscr "1910–1960".

1187	**403**	16s. brown and pink	20	15
1188	-	28s. olive and yellow	20	15
1189	-	45s. green and olive	40	20
1190	-	60s. blue and light blue	50	30
1191	-	80s. brown and red	80	40
1192	-	1l.25 olive and ochre	95	80

PORTRAITS: 28s. Anna Maimunkowa; 45s. Vela Piskova; 60s. Rosa Luxemburg; 80s. Clara Zetkin; 1l.25, Nadezhda Krupskaya.

404 Lenin

1960. 90th Birth Anniv of Lenin.

1193	**404**	16s. flesh and brown	1·90	80
1194	-	45s. black and pink	3·50	1·60

DESIGN: 45s. "Lenin at Smolny" (writing in chair).

406 Basketball Players

1960. Seventh European Women's Basketball Championships.

1195	**406**	1l.25 black and yellow	1·90	95

407 Moon Rocket

1960. Air. Landing of Russian Rocket on Moon.

1196	**407**	1l.25 black, yellow & bl	7·25	5·75

408 Parachutist

1960. World Parachuting Championships, 1960.

1197	**408**	16s. blue and lilac	60	55
1198	-	1l.25 red and blue	3·00	1·20

DESIGN: 1l.25, Parachutes descending.

409 *Gentiana lutea*

1960. Flowers.

1199	**409**	2s. orange, grn & drab	20	15
1200	-	5s. red, green and yellow	80	20
1201	-	25s. orge, grn & salmon	85	25
1202	-	45s. mauve, grn & lilac	95	30
1203	-	60s. red, green and buff	1·50	40
1204	-	80s. blue, green & drab	1·90	1·50

FLOWERS: 5s. *Tulipa rhodopea*; 25s. *Lilium jankae*; 45s. *Rhododendron ponticum*; 60s. *Cypripedium calceolus*; 80s. *Haberlea rhodopenis*.

410 Football

1960. Olympic Games.

1205	**410**	8s. pink and brown	20	15
1206	-	12s. pink and violet	20	15
1207	-	16s. pink & turquoise	40	20
1208	-	45s. pink and purple	50	25
1209	-	80s. pink and blue	1·10	70
1210	-	2l. pink and green	1·50	95

DESIGNS: 12s. Wrestling; 16s. Weightlifting; 45s. Gymnastics; 80s. Canoeing; 2l. Running.

411 Racing Cyclists

1960. Tour of Bulgaria Cycle Race.

1211	**411**	1l. black, yellow & red	1·90	1·50

412 Globes

1960. 15th Anniv of WFTU.

1212	**412**	1l.25 cobalt and blue	95	60

413 Popov

1960. Birth Centenary of Alexsandr Popov (Russian radio pioneer).

1213	**413**	90s. black and blue	1·50	95

414 Y. Veshin

1960. Birth Centenary of Yavoslav Veshin (painter).

1214	**414**	1l. olive and yellow	5·75	3·00

415 U.N. Headquarters, New York

1961. 15th Anniv of UNO.

1215	**415**	1l. cream and brown	2·40	2·40

MS1215a 74×57 mm. **415** 1l. (+1l.) pink and green. Imperf 13·50 13·50

416 Boyana Church

1961. 700th Anniv of Boyana Murals (1959).

1216	**416**	60s. black, emer & grn	95	40
1217	-	80s. grn, cream & orange	1·50	50
1218	-	1l.25 red, cream & green	1·90	95

DESIGNS (Frescoes of): 80s. Theodor Tiron; 1l.25, Desislava.

417 Cosmic Rocket and Dogs Belda and Strelka

1961. Russian Cosmic Rocket Flight of August, 1960.

1219	**417**	1l.25 blue and red	6·75	6·75

419 Pleven Costume

1961. Provincial Costumes.

1220	-	12s. yellow, green & orge	20	10
1221	**419**	16s. brown, buff & lilac	20	10
1222	-	28s. red, black, & green	40	15
1223	-	45s. blue and red	80	20
1224	-	60s. yellow, blue & turq	1·10	30
1225	-	80s. red, green & yellow	1·30	70

COSTUMES: 12s. Kyustendil; 28s. Sliven; 45s. Sofia; 60s. Rhodope; 80c. Karnobat.

420 Clock Tower, Vratsa

1961. Museums and Monuments. Values and star in red.

1226	**420**	8s. green	20	15
1227	-	12s. violet	20	15
1228	-	16s. brown	20	15
1229	-	20s. blue	20	15
1230	-	28s. turquoise	30	20
1231	-	40s. brown	40	25
1232	-	45s. olive	50	30
1233	-	60s. slate	70	40
1234	-	80s. brown	1·20	50
1235	-	1l. turquoise	1·90	95

DESIGNS—As Type **420**. VERT: 12s. Clock Tower, Bansko; 20s. "Agushev" building, Mogilitsa (Smolensk). HORIZ: 28s. Oslekoff House, Koprivshtitsa; 40s. Pasha's House, Melnik. SQUARE (27×27 mm): 16s. Wine jug; 45s. Lion (bas-relief); 60s. "Horseman of Madara"; 80s. Fresco, Bachkovo Monastery; 1l. Coin of Tsar Konstantin-Asen (13th cent).

421 Dalmatian Pelican

1961. Birds.

1236		2s. turquoise, blk & red	25	15
1237	**421**	4s. orange, blk & grn	30	20
1238	-	16s. orange, brn & grn	40	30
1239	-	80s. yellow, brn & turq	3·00	1·10
1240	-	1l. yellow, sepia and blue	3·50	1·70
1241	-	2l. yellow, brown & blue	4·75	1·90

DESIGNS: 2s. White capercaillie; 16s. Common pheasant; 80s. Great bustard; 1l. Lammergeier; 2l. Hazel grouse.

422 "Communications and Transport"

1961. 50th Anniv of Transport Workers' Union.

1242	**422**	80s. green and black	95	50

423 Gagarin and Rocket

1961. World's First Manned Space Flight.

1243	**423**	4l. turquoise, blk & red	6·75	4·25

424 Shevchenko (Ukrainian poet)

1961. Death Centenary of Taras Shevchenko.

1244	**424**	1l. brown and green	6·25	4·25

425 Throwing the Discus

1961. World Students' Games. Values and inscr in black.

1245	-	4s. blue	20	15
1246	-	5s. red	20	15
1247	-	16s. olive	30	20
1248	**425**	45s. blue	50	30
1249	-	1l.25 brown	1·70	50
1250	-	2l. mauve	1·90	1·30

MS1250a 66×66 mm. 5l. blue, yellow and green (Sports Palace and inscriptions). Imperf 19·00 19·00

DESIGNS—VERT: 4s. Water polo; 2l. Basketball. HORIZ: 5s. Tennis; 16s. Fencing; 1l.25, Sports Palace, Sofia.

426 Short-snouted Seahorse

1961. Black Sea Fauna.

1251		2s. sepia and green	20	15
1252		12s. pink and blue	20	15
1253		16s. violet and blue	25	20
1254	**426**	45s. brown and blue	1·50	95
1255	-	1l. blue and green	4·00	1·50
1256	-	1l.25 brown and blue	4·75	2·40

DESIGNS—HORIZ: 2s. Mediterranean monk seal; 12s. Lung jellyfish; 16s. Common dolphins; 1l. Stellate sturgeons; 1l.25, Thorn-backed ray.

427 "Space" Dogs

1961. Air. Space Exploration.

1257	**427**	2l. slate and purple	5·75	4·25
1258	-	2l. blue, yellow & orange	10·50	6·75

DESIGN: No. 1258, "Venus" rocket in flight (24×41½ mm).

428 Dimitur Blagoev as Orator

1961. 70th Anniv of First Bulgarian Social Democratic Party Congress, Buzludzha.

1259	**428**	45s. red and cream	30	20
1260	**428**	80s. blue and pink	70	50
1261	**428**	2l. sepia and green	1·50	1·20

429 Hotel

1961. Tourist issue. Inscr in black; designs green. Background colours given.

1262	**429**	4s. green	10	10
1263	-	12s. blue (Hikers)	10	10
1264	-	16s. green (Tents)	20	15
1265	-	1l.25 bistre (Climber)	1·20	30

Nos. 1263/5 are vert.

430 *The Golden Girl*

1961. Bulgarian Fables.

1266	**430**	2s. multicoloured	20	15
1267	-	8s. grey, black & purple	20	15
1268	-	12s. pink, black & green	25	20
1269	-	16s. multicoloured	95	50
1270	-	45s. multicoloured	1·90	80
1271	-	80s. multicoloured	2·40	95

DESIGNS: 8s. Man and woman (*The Living Water*); 12s. Archer and dragon (*The Golden Apple*); 16s. Horseman (*Krali Marko*, national hero); 45s. Female archer on stag (*Samovila-Vila*, fairy); 80s. *Tom Thumb* and cockerel.

431 Major Titov in Space-suit

1961. Air. Second Russian Manned Space Flight.

1272	**431**	75s. flesh, blue & olive	4·00	3·00
1273	-	1l.25 pink, bl & violet	4·75	4·00

DESIGN: 1l.25, "Vostok-2" in flight.

432 *Amanita caesarea*

1961. Mushrooms.

1274	**432**	2s. red, bistre & black	20	15
1275	-	4s. brown, grn & blk	20	15
1276	-	12s. brown, bistre & blk	20	15
1277	-	16s. brown, mve & blk	20	20
1278	-	45s. multicoloured	30	30
1279	-	80s. orange, sepia & blk	80	60
1280	-	1l.25 lav, brn & blk	1·60	80
1281	-	2l. brown, bistre & black	2·10	1·90

MUSHROOMS: 4s. *Psalliota silvatica*; 12s. *Boletus elegans*; 16s. *Boletus edulis*; 45s. *Lactarius deliciosus*; 80s. *Lepiota procera*; 1l.25, *Pleurotus ostreatus*; 2l. *Armillariella mellea*.

433 Dimitur and Konstantin Miladinov (authors)

1961. Publication Centenary of "Bulgarian Popular Songs".

1282	**433**	1l.25 black and olive	1·50	95

1962. Surch. (A) Surch in one line; (B) in two lines.

1283	1s. on 10s. brown (1149)	20	15
1284	1s. on 12s. brown (1150)	20	15
1285	2s. on 15s. mauve (1151)	20	15
1286	2s. on 16s. violet (1152)	20	15
1287	2s. on 20s. orange (1153) (A)	20	15
1288	2s. on 20s. orange (1153) (B)	30	15
1289	3s. on 25s. blue (1154)	20	15
1290	3s. on 28s. green (1155)	20	15
1291	5s. on 44s. green (1087)	30	15
1292	5s. on 44s. red (1110)	30	15
1293	5s. on 45s. brown (1157)	40	20
1294	10s. on 1l. red (1160)	60	30
1295	20s. on 2l. red (1162)	1·20	70
1296	40s. on 4l. red (889)	3·00	1·50

436 Isker River

1962. Air.

1297	**436**	1s. blue and violet	20	15
1298	-	2s. blue and pink	20	15
1299	-	3s. brown and chestnut	20	20
1300	-	10s. black and bistre	60	25
1301	-	40s. black and green	2·30	1·10

DESIGNS: 2s. Yacht at Varna; 3s. Melnik; 10s. Turnovo; 40s. Pirin Mountains.

437 Freighter *Varna*

1962. Bulgarian Merchant Navy.

1302	**437**	1s. green and blue	20	10
1303	-	5s. light blue and green	50	15
1304	-	20s. violet and blue	1·30	50

SHIPS: 5s. Tanker *Komsomols*; 20s. Liner *Georgi Dimitrov*.

438 Rila Mountains

1962. Views.

1305	**438**	1s. turquoise	20	15
1306	-	2s. blue	20	15
1307	-	6s. turquoise	40	20
1308	-	8s. purple	60	30
1309	-	13s. green	1·20	70
1310	-	1l. deep green	6·75	1·90

VIEWS: 2s. Pirin Mts; 6s. Fishing boats, Nesebur; 8s. Danube shipping; 13s. Viden Castle; 1l. Rhodope Mts.

439 Georgi Dimitrov as Typesetter

1962. 80th Anniv of State Printing Office.

1311	**439**	2s. red, black & yellow	20	15
1312	-	13s. black, orange & yell	80	40

DESIGN: 13s. Emblem of Printing Office.

440 Pink Roses

1962. Bulgarian Roses. T **440** and similar designs.

1313	1s. pink, green and violet	20	15
1314	2s. red, green and buff	20	15
1315	3s. red, green and blue	40	20
1316	4s. yellow, turquoise & grn	60	25
1317	5s. pink, green and blue	95	30
1318	6s. red, green and turquoise	1·30	70
1319	8s. red, green and yellow	3·00	1·30
1320	13s. yellow, green and blue	5·25	3·75

441 "The World United against Malaria"

1962. Malaria Eradication.

1321	**441**	5s. yellow, black & brn	60	20
1322	-	20s. yellow, green & blk	1·80	80

DESIGN: 20s. Campaign emblem.

442 Lenin and Front Page of "Pravda"

1962. 50th Anniv of *Pravda* Newspaper.

1323	**442**	5s. blue, red and black	1·90	1·20

443 Text-book and Blackboard

1962. Bulgarian Teachers' Congress.

1324	**443**	5s. black, yellow & blue	50	20

444 Footballer

1962. World Football Championship, Chile.

1325	**444**	13s. brown, green & blk	1·90	95

445 Dimitrov

1962. 80th Birth Anniv of Georgi Dimitrov (Prime Minister 1946–49).

1326	**445**	2s. green	50	20
1327	**445**	5s. blue	95	40

446 Bishop

1962. 15th Chess Olympiad, Varna. Inscr "1962". Inscr in black.

1328	**446**	1s. green and grey	20	15
1329	-	2s. bistre and grey	30	20
1330	-	3s. purple and grey	40	25
1331	-	13s. orange and grey	1·90	80
1332	-	20s. blue and grey	2·50	1·50

MS1332a 76×66 mm. 20s. (+30s.) red and green (Chess pieces). Imperf 14·50 14·50

CHESS PIECES: 2s. Rook; 3s. Queen; 13s. Knight; 20s. Pawn.

XXXV КОНГРЕС
1962

13 =

(447)

1962. 35th Esperanto Congress, Burgas. Surch as T **447**.

1333	**360**	13s. on 44s. green	4·75	3·50

448 Festival Emblem

1962. World Youth Festival, Helsinki. Inscr "1962".

1334	**448**	5s. blue, pink and green	40	20
1335	-	13s. blue, purple & grey	1·10	30

DESIGN: 13s. Girl and emblem.

449 Ilyushin Il-18 Airliner

1962. Air. 13th Anniv of TABSO Airline.

1336	**449**	13s. blue, ultram & blk	1·50	50

450 Apollo

1962. Butterflies and Moths. Multicoloured.

1337	1s. Type **450**	20	15
1338	2s. Eastern festoon	25	15
1339	3s. Meleager's blue	30	15
1340	4s. Camberwell beauty	40	20
1341	5s. Crimson underwing	50	30
1342	6s. Hebe tiger moth	95	40
1343	10s. Danube clouded	3·50	1·30
1344	13s. Cardinal	4·75	2·40

451 K. E. Tsiolkovsky (scientist)

1962. Air. 13th International Astronautics Congress. Inscr "1962".

1345	**451**	5s. drab and green	4·75	1·90
1346	-	13s. blue and yellow	1·90	95

DESIGN: 13s. Moon rocket.

452 Combine Harvester

1962. Eight Bulgarian Communist Party Congress.

1347	**452**	1s. olive and turquoise	20	15
1348	-	2s. turquoise and blue	25	20
1349	-	3s. brown and red	30	20
1350	-	13s. sepia, red & purple	1·20	60

DESIGNS: 2s. Electric train; 3s. Steel furnace; 13s. Blagoev and Dimitrov.

453 Cover of *History of Bulgaria*

1962. Bicentenary of Paisii Khilendarski's *History of Bulgaria*.

1351	**453**	2s. black and olive	20	15
1352	-	5s. sepia and brown	50	20

DESIGN—HORIZ: 5s. Father Paisii at work on book.

454 Andrian Nikolaev and "Vostok 3"

1962. Air. First "Team" Manned Space Flight.

1353	**454**	1s. olive, blue and black	30	20
1354	-	2s. olive, green & black	70	30
1355	-	40s. pink, turquoise & blk	4·00	2·10

DESIGNS: 2s. Pavel Ropovich and "Vostok 4"; 40s. "Vostoks 3" and "4" in flight.

455 Parachutist

1963

1356A		1s. lake	20	10
1357A		1s. brown	20	10
1358A		1s. turquoise	20	10
1359A		1s. green	20	10
1360A	**455**	1s. blue	20	10

DESIGNS—VERT: No. 1356, State crest. HORIZ: No. 1357, Sofia University; 1358, "Vasil Levski" Stadium, Sofia; 1359, "The Camels" (archway), Hisar.

456 Aleko Konstantinov

1963. Birth Cent of Konstantinov (author).

1361	**456**	5s. green and red	50	30

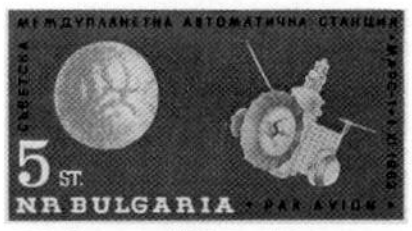

457 Mars and "Mars 1" Space Probe

1963. Air. Launching of Soviet Space Station "Mars 1".

1362	**457**	5s. multicoloured	95	50
1363	-	13s. turquoise, red & blk	1·90	95

DESIGN: 13s. Release of probe from rocket.

458 Orpheus Restaurant, "Sunny Beach"

1963. Black Sea Coast Resorts.

1364	**458**	1s. blue	20	15
1365a	-	2s. red	7·25	20
1366	-	3s. bistre	30	20
1367	-	5s. purple	50	20
1368	-	13s. turquoise	1·50	40
1369	-	20s. green	1·90	50

VIEWS "Sunny Beach": 5s. The Dunes Restaurant; 20s. Hotel. "Golden Sands"; 2s., 3s., 13s. Various hotels.

459 V. Levski

1963. 90th Anniv of Execution of Vasil Levski (revolutionary).

1370	**459**	13s. blue and yellow	1·90	75

460 Dimitrov, Boy and Girl

1963. Tenth Dimitrov Communist Youth League Congress, Sofia.

1371	**460**	2s. brown, red & black	20	15
1372	-	13s. brown, turq & blk	80	45

DESIGN: 13s. Girl and youth holding book and hammer aloft.

461 Eurasian Red Squirrel

1963. Woodland Animals.

1373	**461**	1s. brown, red and green on turquoise	20	15
1374	-	2s. blk, red & grn on yell	25	15
1375	-	3s. sep, red & ol on drab	30	20
1376	-	5s. brown, red and blue on violet	95	35
1377	-	13s. black, red and brown on pink	3·50	65
1378	-	20s. sepia, red and blue on blue	4·75	1·10

ANIMALS—HORIZ: 2s. East European hedgehog; 3s. Marbled polecat; 5s. Beech marten; 13s. Eurasian badger. VERT: 20s. European otter.

462 Wrestling

1963. 15th International Open Wrestling Championships, Sofia.

1379	**462**	5s. bistre and black	50	20
1380	-	20s. brown and black	1·50	85

DESIGN—HORIZ: 20s. As Type **462** but different hold.

463 Congress Emblem and Allegory

1963. World Women's Congress, Moscow.

1381	**463**	20s. blue and black	1·50	55

464 Esperanto Star and Sofia Arms

1963. 48th World Esperanto Congress, Sofia.

1382	**464**	13s. multicoloured	1·50	55

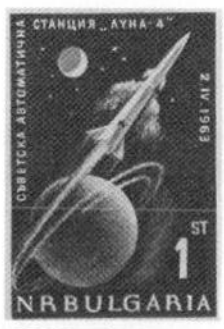

465 Rocket, Globe and Moon

1963. Launching of Soviet Moon Rocket "Luna 4". Inscr "2.IV.1963".

1383	**465**	1s. blue	20	10
1384	-	2s. purple	20	10
1385	-	3s. turquoise	20	10

DESIGNS: 2s. Tracking equipment; 3s. Sputniks.

466 Valery Bykovsky in Spacesuit

1963. Air. Second "Team" Manned Space Flights. Inscr "14. VI.1963".

1386	**466**	1s. turquoise and lilac	20	10
1387	-	2s. brown and yellow	30	15
1388	-	5s. red and light red	50	20
1389	-	20s.+10s. grn & lt bl	2·40	1·10

MS1389a 79×68 mm. 50s. purple and brown (Spassk Tower and Globe). Imperf 4·75 4·25

DESIGNS: 2s. Valentina Tereshkova in spacesuit; 5s. Globe; 20s. Bykovsky and Tereshkova.

1963. Europa Fair, Riccione. Nos. 1314/5 and 1318 (Roses) optd **MOSTRA EUROPEISTICA.1963 RICCIONE** and sailing boat motif or additionally surch.

1390	2s. red, green and buff	50	20
1391	5s. on 3s. red, green and blue	70	35
1392	13s. on 6s. red, green & turq	1·70	55

468 Relay-racing

1963. Balkan Games. Flags in red, yellow, blue, green and black.

1393	**468**	1s. green	10	10
1394	-	2s. violet	15	10
1395	-	3s. turquoise	20	15
1396	-	5s. red	95	20
1397	-	13s. brown	4·00	3·00

MS1397a 74×69 mm. 50s. black and green (as T **468**). Imperf 7·00 7·00

DESIGNS: 2s. Throwing the hammer; 3s. Long jumping; 5s. High jumping; 13s. Throwing the discus. Each design includes the flags of the competing countries.

469 Slavonic Scroll

1963. Fifth International Slav Congress, Sofia.

1398	**469**	5s. red, yellow & dp grn	50	20

470 Insurgents

1963. 40th Anniv of September Uprising.

1399	**470**	2s. black and red	30	15

471 *Aquilegia aurea*

1963. Nature Protection. Flowers in natural colours; background colours given.

1400	**471**	1s. turquoise	20	15
1401	-	2s. olive	20	15
1402	-	3s. yellow	20	15
1403	-	5s. blue	40	20
1404	-	6s. purple	50	35
1405	-	8s. light grey	95	45
1406	-	10s. mauve	1·90	85
1407	-	13s. olive	3·50	1·10

FLOWERS: 2s. Edelweiss; 3s. *Primula deorum*; 5s. White water-lily; 6s. Tulip; 8s. *Viola delphinantha*; 10s. Alpine clematis; 13s. *Anemone narcissiflora*.

472 Khristo Smirnenski

1963. 65th Birth Anniv of Smirnenski (poet and revolutionary).

1408	**472**	13s. black and lilac	95	45

473 Chariot Horses (wall-painting)

1963. Thracian Tombs, Kazanilk.

1409	**473**	1s. red, yellow and grey	20	15
1410	-	2s. violet, yellow & grey	20	15
1411	-	3s. turquiose, yell & grey	20	15
1412	-	5s. brown, yellow & grn	40	35
1413	-	13s. black, yellow & grn	1·10	55
1414	-	20s. red, yellow & green	1·90	85

DESIGNS (wall paintings on tombs): 2s. Chariot race; 3s. Flautists; 5s. Tray-bearer; 13s. Funeral feast; 20s. Seated woman.

474 Hemispheres and Centenary Emblem

1964. Centenary of Red Cross.

1415	**474**	1s. yellow, red & black	20	15
1416	-	2s. blue, red and black	20	15
1417	-	3s. multicoloured	20	15
1418	-	5s. turq, red & black	30	20
1419	-	13s. black, red & orange	1·30	55

DESIGNS: 2s. Blood donation; 3s. Bandaging wrist; 5s. Nurse; 13s. Henri Dunant.

475 Speed-skating

1964. Winter Olympic Games, Innsbruck.

1420	**475**	1s. indigo, brown & blue	20	15
1421	-	2s. olive, mauve & black	20	15
1422	-	3s. green, brown & blk	20	15
1423	-	5s. multicoloured	40	20
1424	-	10s. orange, blk & grey	80	45
1425	-	13s. mauve, violet & blk	95	55
MS1425a		64×67 mm. 50s. red, blue and grey (Girl skater). Imperf	6·50	6·50

DESIGNS: 2s. Figure skating; 3s. Cross-country skiing; 5s. Ski jumping. Ice hockey—10s. Goalkeeper; 13s. Players.

476 Head (2nd cent)

1964. 2500 Years of Bulgarian Art. Borders in grey.

1426	**476**	1s. turquoise and red	20	15
1427	-	2s. sepia and red	20	15
1428	-	3s. bistre and red	20	15
1429	-	5s. blue and red	30	20
1430	-	6s. brown and red	60	25
1431	-	8s. brown and red	85	35
1432	-	10s. olive and red	95	40
1433	-	13s. olive and red	1·20	1·00

DESIGNS: 2s. Horseman (1st to 4th cent); 3s. Jug (19th cent); 5s. Buckle (19th cent); 6s. Pot (19th cent); 8s. Angel (17th cent); 10s. Animals (8th to 10th cent); 13s. Peasant woman (20th cent).

477 *The Unborn Maid*

1964. Folk Tales. Multicoloured.

1434	1s. Type **477**	20	15
1435	2s. *Grandfather's Glove*	20	15
1436	3s. *The Big Turnip*	20	15
1437	5s. *The Wolf and the Seven Kids*	30	20
1438	8s. *Cunning Peter*	60	35
1439	13s. *The Loaf of Corn*	1·60	55

478 Turkish Lacewing (*Ascalaphus ottomanus*)

1964. Insects.

1440	**478**	1s. black, yellow & brn	20	15
1441	-	2s. black, ochre & turq	20	15
1442	-	3s. green, black & drab	25	20
1443	-	5s. violet, black & green	90	35
1444	-	13s. brown, black & vio	1·80	55
1445	-	20s. yellow, black & bl	3·00	75

DESIGNS—VERT: 2s. Thread lacewing fly (*Nemoptera coa*); 5s. Alpine longhorn beetle (*Rosalia alpina*); 13s. Cockchafer (*Anisoplia austriaca*). HORIZ: 3s. Cricket (*Saga natalia*); 20s. Hunting wasp (*Scolia flavitrons*).

479 Football

1964. 50th Anniv of Levski Physical Culture Association.

1446	2s. Type **479**	20	10
1447	13s. Handball	1·20	55
MS1447a	60×60 mm. 60s. green and yellow (Cup and Map of Europe). Imperf	4·50	4·25

480 Title Page and Petar Beron (author)

1964. 40th Anniv of First Bulgarian Primer.

1448	**480**	20s. black and brown	2·20	2·20

481 Stephenson's *Rocket*, 1829

1964. Railway Transport. Multicoloured.

1449	1s. Type **481**	20	15
1450	2s. Class 05 steam locomotive	20	15
1451	3s. German V.320.001 diesel locomotive	20	15
1452	5s. Electric locomotive	35	20
1453	8s. Class 05 steam locomotive and train on bridge	90	45
1454	13s. Class E41 electric train emerging from tunnel	1·30	1·10

482 Alsatian

1964. Dogs. Multicoloured.

1455	1s. Type **482**	20	15
1456	2s. Setter	25	15
1457	3s. Poodle	35	20
1458	4s. Pomeranian	45	25
1459	5s. St. Bernard	60	35
1460	6s. Fox terrier	90	55
1461	10s. Pointer	3·50	1·60
1462	13s. Dachshund	4·50	3·25

(483)

1964. Air. International Cosmic Exhibition, Riccione. No. 1386 surch with T 483 and No. 1387 surch as T **483**, but in Italian.

1463	**466**	10s. on 1s. turquoise and lilac	45	45
1464	-	20s. on 2s. brown & yell	1·30	65

484 Partisans and Flag

1964. 20th Anniv of Fatherland. Front Government. Flag in red.

1465	**484**	1s. blue and light blue	20	15
1466	-	2s. olive and bistre	20	15
1467	-	3s. lake and mauve	20	15
1468	-	4s. violet and lavender	20	15
1469	-	5s. brown and orange	20	15
1470	-	6s. blue and light blue	35	20
1471	-	8s. green and light green	70	35
1472	-	13s. brown and salmon	90	55

DESIGNS: 2s. Greeting Soviet troops; 3s. Soviet aid—arrival of goods; 4s. Industrial plant, Kremikovtzi; 5s. Combine-harvester; 6s. "Peace" campaigners; 8s. Soldier of National Guard; 3s. Blagoev and Dimitrov. All with flag as Type **484**.

(485)

1964. 21st Int Fair, Plovdiv. Surch with T **485**.

1473	20s. on 44s. ochre (No. 1020a)	1·80	75

486 Transport

1964. First National Stamp Exn, Sofia.

1474	**486**	20s. blue	1·60	1·10

487 Gymnastics

1964. Olympic Games, Tokyo. Rings and values in red.

1475	**487**	1s. green and light green	20	15
1476	-	2s. blue and lavender	20	15
1477	-	3s. blue and turquoise	20	15
1478	-	5s. violet and red	35	20
1479	-	13s. blue and light blue	1·20	35
1480	-	20s. green and buff	1·30	75
MS1480a		61×67 mm. 40s.+20s. ochre, red and blue (Rings, tracks etc.). Imperf	5·75	5·50

DESIGNS: 2s. Long-jump; 3s. Swimmer on starting block; 5s. Football; 13s. Volleyball; 20s. Wrestling.

488 Vratsata

1964. Landscapes.

1481	**488**	1s. green	20	15
1482	-	2s. brown	20	15
1483	-	3s. blue	20	15
1484	-	4s. brown	25	15
1485	-	5s. green	45	20
1486	-	6s. violet	70	35

DESIGNS: 2s. The Ritli; 3s. Maliovitsa; 4s. Broken Rocks; 5s. Erkyupria; 6s. Rhodope mountain pass.

489 Paper and Cellulose Factory, Bukovtsi

1964. Air. Industrial Buildings.

1487	**489**	8s. turquoise	45	15
1488	-	10s. purple	60	20
1489	-	13s. violet	70	25
1490	-	20s. blue	1·30	55
1491	-	40s. green	2·20	75

DESIGNS: 10s. Metal works, Plovdiv; 13s. Metallurgical works, Kremikovtzi; 20s. Petrol refinery, Burgas; 40s. Fertiliser factory, Stara-Zagora.

490 Rila Monastery

1964. Philatelic Exn for Franco–Bulgarian Amity.

1492	**490**	5s. black and drab	55	25
1493	-	13s. black and blue	1·30	65

DESIGN: 13s. Notre-Dame, Paris (inscr in French).

491 500-year-old Walnut

1964. Ancient Trees. Values and inscr in black.

1494	**491**	1s. brown	20	15
1495	-	2s. purple	20	15
1496	-	3s. sepia	20	15
1497	-	4s. blue	20	15
1498	-	10s. green	90	35
1499	-	13s. olive	1·30	45

TREES: 2s. Plane (1000 yrs.); 3s. Plane (600 yrs.); 4s. Poplar (800 yrs.); 10s. Oak (800 yrs.); 13s. Fir (1200 yrs.).

492

1964. Eighth Congress of Int Union of Students, Sofia.

1500	**492**	13s. black and blue	90	55

493 Bulgarian Veteran and Soviet Soldier (Sculpture by T. Zlatarev)

1965. 30 Years of Bulgarian–Russian Friendship.

1501	**493**	2s. red and black	45	20

494 "Gold Medal"

1965. Olympic Games, Tokyo (1964).

1502	**494**	20s. black, gold & brown	1·30	75

495 Vladimir Komarov

1965. Flight of "Voskhod 1". Multicoloured.

1503	1s. Type **495**	20	15
1504	2s. Konstantin Feoktistov	20	15
1505	5s. Boris Yegorov	25	20
1506	13s. The three astronauts	1·10	35
1507	20s. "Voskhod I"	1·30	55

496 Corn-cob

1965. Agricultural Products.

1508	**496**	1s. yellow	15	10
1509	-	2s. green	20	10
1510	-	3s. orange	25	10
1511	-	4s. olive	35	15
1512	-	5s. red	40	15
1513	-	10s. blue	45	20
1514	-	13s. bistre	1·30	35

DESIGNS: 2s. Ears of Wheat; 3s. Sunflowers; 4s. Sugar beet; 5s. Clover; 10s. Cotton; 13s. Tobacco.

497 "Victory against Fascism"

1965. 20th Anniv of "Victory of 9 May, 1945".

1515	**497**	5s. black, bistre & grey	20	10
1516	-	13s. blue, black & grey	70	45

DESIGN: 13s. Globes on dove ("Peace").

498 Northern Bullfinch

1965. Song Birds. Multicoloured.

1517	1s. Type **498**	20	15
1518	2s. Golden oriole	25	15
1519	3s. Rock thrush	35	15
1520	5s. Barn swallows	60	20
1521	8s. European roller	70	55
1522	10s. Eurasian goldfinch	2·50	90
1523	13s. Rose-coloured starling	2·75	1·70
1524	20s. Nightingale	3·75	3·50

499 Transport, Globe and Whale

1965. Fourth International Transport Conf, Sofia.

1525	**499**	13s. multicoloured	1·90	1·10

500 ICY Emblem

1965. International Co-operation Year.

1526	**500**	20s. orange, olive & blk	1·40	80

501 ITU Emblem and Symbols

1965. Centenary of ITU.

1527	**501**	20s. yellow, green & bl	1·40	80

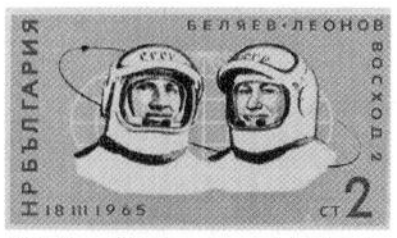

502 Pavel Belyaev and Aleksei Leonov

1965. "Voskhod 2" Space Flight.

1528	**502**	2s. purple, grn & drab	45	20
1529	-	20s. multicoloured	3·75	1·50

DESIGN: 20s. Leonov on space.

503 Common Stingray

1965. Fish. Borders in grey.

1530	**503**	1s. gold, black & orange	10	10
1531	-	2s. silver, indigo & blue	20	10
1532	-	3s. gold, black & green	30	15
1533	-	5s. gold, black and red	45	20
1534	-	10s. silver, blue & turq	2·00	1·00
1535	-	13s. gold, black & brown	2·50	1·30

Designs: 2s. Atlantic bonito; 3s. Brown scorpionfish; 5s. Tub gurnard; 10s. Mediterranean horse-mackerel; 13s. Black Sea turbot.

504 Marx and Lenin

1965. Organization of Socialist Countries' Postal Ministers' Conference, Peking.

1536	**504**	13s. brown and red	1·40	90

505 Film and Screen

1965. Balkan Film Festival. Varna.

1537	**505**	13s. black, silver & blue	95	35

506 Quinces

1965. Fruits.

1538	**506**	1s. orange	10	10
1539	-	2s. olive (Grapes)	10	10
1540	-	3s. bistre (Pears)	20	10
1541	-	4s. orange (Plums)	30	10
1542	-	5s. red (Strawberries)	35	20
1543	-	6s. brown (Walnuts)	45	35

507 Ballerina

1965. Ballet Competitions, Varna.

1544	**507**	5s. black and mauve	1·90	1·10

508 Dove, Emblem and Map

1965. "Balkanphila" Stamp Exhibition, Varna.

1545	**508**	1s. silver, blue & yellow	10	10
1546	-	2s. silver, violet & yellow	15	10
1547	-	3s. gold, green & yellow	30	20
1548	-	13s. gold, red & yellow	1·40	1·30
1549	-	20s. brown, blue & silver	1·90	1·70
MS1550		71×62 mm. 40s. gold and blue (T **508**). Imperf	4·25	4·00

DESIGNS: 2s. Yacht emblem; 3s. Stylised fish and flowers; 13s. Stylised sun, planet and rocket. LARGER (45×25½ mm): 20s. Cosmonauts Pavel Belyaev and Aleksei Leonov.

509 Escapers in Boat

1965. 40th Anniv of Political Prisoners' Escape from "Bolshevik Island".

1551	**509**	2s. black and slate	45	20

(510)

1965. National Folklore Competition. No. 1084 surch with T **510**.

1552	2s. on 8s. brown	2·20	2·20

511 Gymnast

1965. Balkan Games.

1553	**511**	1s. black and red	20	15
1554	-	2s. purple and black	20	15
1555	-	3s. purple, black & red	30	15
1556	-	5s. brown, black & red	30	20
1557	-	10s. purple, black & mve	1·00	45
1558	-	13s. purple and black	1·10	55

DESIGNS: 2s. Gymnastics on bars; 3s. Weight-lifting; 5s. Rally car and building; 10s. Basketball; 13s. Rally car and map.

512 Dressage

1965. Horsemanship.

1559	**512**	1s. plum, black & blue	20	15
1560	-	2s. brown, black & ochre	20	15
1561	-	3s. red, black and purple	20	15
1562	-	5s. brown and green	65	20
1563	-	10s. brown, blk & grey	2·75	1·30
1564	-	13s. brown, grn & buff	3·25	1·70
MS1565		80×80 mm. 40s.+20s. plum and grey (as 13s.). Imperf	6·00	5·50

DESIGNS: 5s. Horse-racing. Others, Horse-jumping (various).

513 Young Pioneers

1965. Dimitrov Septembrist Pioneers Organization.

1566	**513**	1s. green and turquoise	20	15
1567	-	2s. mauve and violet	20	15
1568	-	3s. bistre and olive	20	15
1569	-	5s. ochre and blue	30	20
1570	-	8s. orange and brown	95	45
1571	-	13s. violet and red	1·40	80

DESIGNS: 2s. Admitting recruit; 3s. Camp bugler; 5s. Flying model airplane; 8s. Girls singing; 13s. Young athlete.

514 Junkers Ju 52/3m over Turnovo

1965. Bulgarian Civil Aviation. Multicoloured.

1572	1s. Type **514**	20	15
1573	2s. Ilyushin Il-14M over Plovdiv	20	15
1574	3s. Mil Mi-4 helicopter over Dimitrovgrad	20	15
1575	5s. Tupolev Tu-104A over Ruse	35	20
1576	13s. Ilyushin Il-18 over Varna	1·10	45
1577	20s. Tupolev Tu-114 over Sofia	1·90	80

515 Women of N. and S. Bulgaria

1965. 80th Anniv of Union of North and South Bulgaria.

1578	**515**	13s. black and green	95	80

516 I.Q.S.Y. Emblem and Earth's Radiation Zones

1965. International Quiet Sun Year.

1579	**516**	1s. yellow, green & blue	20	15
1580	-	2s. multicoloured	20	15
1581	-	13s. multicoloured	1·20	45

DESIGNS (I.Q.S.Y. emblem and): 2s. Sun and solar flares; 13s. Total eclipse of the Sun.

517 "Spring Greetings"

1966. "Spring". National Folklore.

1582	**517**	1s. mauve, blue & drab	20	15
1583	-	2s. red, black and drab	20	15
1584	-	3s. violet, red and grey	20	15
1585	-	5s. red, violet and black	30	20
1586	-	8s. purple, brown & mve	55	30
1587	-	13s. mauve, black & bl	1·10	35

DESIGNS: 2s. Drummer; 3s. "Birds" (stylised); 5s. Folk dancer; 8s. Vase of flowers; 13s. Bagpiper.

518 Byala Bridge

1966. Ancient Monuments.

1588	**518**	1s. turquoise	20	15
1589	-	1s. green	20	15
1590	-	2s. green	20	15
1591	-	2s. purple	20	15
1592	-	8s. brown	55	20
1593	-	13s. blue	95	45

DESIGNS: No. 1589, Svilengrand Bridge; 1590, Fountain, Samokov; 1591, Ruins of Matochina Castle, Khaskovo; 1592, Cherven Castle, Ruse; 1593, Cafe, Bozhentsi, Gabrovo.

519 *Christ* (from fresco Boyana Church)

1966. "2,500 Years of Culture". Multicoloured.

1594	1s. Type **519**	3·75	3·25
1595	2s. *Destruction of the Idols* (from fresco, Boyana Church) (horiz)	35	35
1596	3s. Bachkovo Monastery	45	40
1597	4s. Zemen Monastery (horiz)	55	45

1598	5s. John the Baptist Church, Nesebur	65	55
1599	13s. *Nativity* (icon, Aleksandr Nevski Cathedral, Sofia)	95	1·00
1600	20s. *Virgin and Child* (icon, Archaeological Museum, Sofia)	1·40	1·10

520 *The First Gunshot* at Koprivshtitsa

1966. 90th Anniv of April Uprising.

1601	**520**	1s. black, brown & gold	20	15
1602	-	2s. black, red and gold	20	15
1603	-	3s. black, green & gold	20	15
1604	-	5s. black, blue & gold	25	15
1605	-	10s. black, purple & gold	65	20
1606	-	13s. black, violet & gold	75	55

DESIGNS: 2s. Georgi Benkovski and Todor Kableskov; 3s. "Showing the Flag" at Panagyurishte; 5s. Vasil Petleshkov and Tsanko Dyustabanov; 10s. Landing of Khristo Botev's detachment at Kozlodui; 13s. Panyot Volov and Zlarion Dragostinov.

521 Luna reaching for the Moon

1966. Moon Landing of "Luna 9". Sheet 70×50 mm.

MS1607	**521** 60s. silver, black and red	5·50	5·50

522 W.H.O. Building

1966. Inaug of W.H.O. Headquarters, Geneva.

1608	**522**	13s. blue and silver	1·10	55

523 Worker

1966. Sixth Trades Union Congress, Sofia.

1609	**523**	20s. black and pink	1·40	80

524 Indian Elephant

1966. Sofia Zoo Animals. Multicoloured.

1610	1s. Type **524**	20	15
1611	2s. Tiger	20	15
1612	3s. Chimpanzee	20	15
1613	4s. Ibex	30	20
1614	5s. Polar bear	95	35
1615	8s. Lion	1·10	55
1616	13s. American bison	3·25	1·70
1617	20s. Eastern grey kangaroo	4·25	2·20

525 Boy and Girl holding Banners

1966. Third Congress of Bulgarian Sports Federation.

1618	**525**	13s. blue, orge & cobalt	95	55

526 *Radetski* and Pioneer

1966. 90th Anniv of Khristo Botev's Seizure of River Paddle-steamer *Radetski*.

1619	**526**	2s. multicoloured	30	20

527 Standard-bearer Simov-Kuruto

1966. 90th Death Anniv of Nikola Simov-Kuruto (hero of the Uprising against Turkey).

1620	**527**	5s. multicoloured	45	20

528 Federation Emblem

1966. Seventh Int Youth Federation Assembly, Sofia.

1621	**528**	13s. blue and black	95	35

529 UNESCO Emblem

1966. 20th Anniv of UNESCO.

1622	**529**	20s. ochre, red & black	1·10	55

530 Footballer with Ball

531 Jules Rimet Cup

1966. World Cup Football Championships, London. (a) Showing players in action. Borders in grey.

1623	**530**	1s. black and brown	20	15
1624	-	2s. black and red	20	15
1625	-	5s. black and bistre	30	20
1626	-	13s. black and blue	85	45
1627	-	20s. black and blue	95	55

(b) Sheet 60×65½ mm. T **531**.

MS1628	50s. gold, cerise and grey	4·25	3·75

532 Wrestling

1966. Third Int Wrestling Championships, Sofia.

1629	**532**	13s. sepia, green & brn	95	55

533 Throwing the Javelin

1966. Third Republican Spartakiade.

1630	**533**	2s. green, red & yellow	20	15
1631	-	13s. green, red & yellow	75	40

DESIGN: 13s. Running.

534 Map of Balkans, Globe and UNESCO Emblem

1966. Int Balkan Studies Congress, Sofia.

1632	**534**	13s. green, pink & blue	95	55

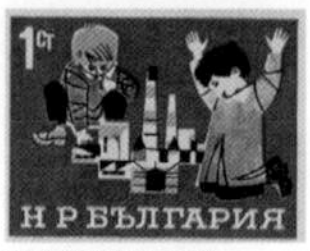

535 Children with Construction Toy

1966. Children's Day.

1633	**535**	1s. black, yellow & red	10	10
1634	-	2s. black, brown & grn	10	10
1635	-	3s. black, yellow & blue	20	15
1636	-	13s. black, mauve & bl	1·50	35

DESIGNS: 2s. Rabbit and Teddy Bear; 3s. Children as astronauts; 13s. Children with gardening equipment.

536 Yuri Gagarin and "Vostok 1"

1966. Russian Space Exploration.

1637	**536**	1s. slate and grey	10	10
1638	-	2s. purple and grey	10	10
1639	-	3s. brown and grey	10	10
1640	-	5s. lake and grey	20	10
1641	-	8s. blue and grey	35	20
1642	-	13s. turquoise and grey	1·10	35
1643	-	20s.+10s. vio & grey	1·90	65
MS1644		70×62½ mm. 30s.+10s. black, red and grey. Imperf	4·25	3·75

DESIGNS: 2s. German Titov and "Vostok 2"; 3s. Andrian Nikolaev, Povel Popovich and "Vostok 3" and "4"; 5s. Valentina Tereshkova, Vallery Bykovsky and "Vostok 5" and "6"; 8s. Vladimir Komarov, Boris Yegorov, Konstantin Feoktistov and "Voskhod 1"; 13s. Povel Belyaev, Aleksei Leonov and "Voskhod 2"; 20s. Gagarin, Leonov and Tereshkova; 30s. Rocket and globe.

537 St. Clement (14th-cent wood-carving)

1966. 1050th Death Anniv of St. Clement of Ohrid.

1645	**537**	5s. brown, red & drab	95	55

538 Metodi Shatorov

1966. Anti-fascist Fighters. Frames in gold; value in black.

1646	**538**	2s. violet and red	10	10
1647	-	3s. brown and mauve	20	10
1648	-	5s. blue and red	30	15
1649	-	10s. brown and orange	65	20
1650	-	13s. brown and red	75	35

PORTRAITS: 3s. Vladno Trichkov; 5s. Vulcho Ivanov; 10s. Rasko Daskalov; 13s. Gen. Vladimir Zaimov.

539 Georgi Dimitrov (statesman)

1966. Ninth Bulgarian Communist Party Congress, Sofia.

1651	**539**	2s. black and red	20	10
1652	-	20s. black, red and grey	1·70	45

DESIGN: 20s. Furnaceman and steelworks.

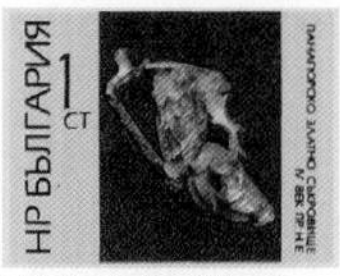

540 Deer's Head Vessel

1966. The Gold Treasures of Panagyurishte. Multicoloured.

1653	1s. Type **540**	20	15
1654	2s. Amazon	25	15
1655	3s. Ram	30	15
1656	5s. Plate	35	15
1657	6s. Venus	45	20
1658	8s. Roe-buck	95	35
1659	10s. Amazon (different)	1·10	45
1660	13s. Amphora	1·40	55
1661	20s. Goat	2·30	1·10

Except for the 5s. and 13s. the designs show vessels with animal heads.

541 Bansko Hotel

1966. Tourist Resorts.

1662	**541**	1s. blue	20	15
1663	-	2s. green (Belogradchik)	20	15
1664	-	2s. lake (Tryavna)	20	15
1665	-	20s. pur (Malovitsa, Rila)	1·10	45

542 Christmas Tree

1966. New Year. Multicoloured.

1666	2s. Type **542**	20	15
1667	13s. Money-box	85	45

543 Percho Slaveikov (poet)

1966. Cultural Celebrities.

1668	**543**	1s. bistre, blue & orange	20	15
1669	-	2s. brown, orge & grey	20	15
1670	-	3s. blue, bistre & orange	20	15
1671	-	5s. purple, drab & orge	30	20
1672	-	8s. grey, purple & blue	65	30
1673	-	13s. violet, blue & purple	75	35

CELEBRITIES. Writers (with pen emblem): 2s. Dimcho Debelyanov (poet); 3s. Petko Todorov. Painters (with brush emblem): 5s. Dimitur Dobrovich; 8s. Ivan Murkvichka; 13s. Iliya Beshkov.

544 Dahlias

1966. Flowers. Multicoloured.

1674	1s. Type **544**	15	10
1675	1s. Clematis	20	10
1676	2s. Poet's narcissus	25	10
1677	2s. Foxgloves	30	15
1678	3s. Snowdrops	45	20
1679	5s. Petunias	55	30
1680	13s. Tiger lilies	1·10	35
1681	20s. Canterbury bells	1·40	55

545 Common Pheasant

1967. Hunting. Multicoloured.

1682	1s. Type **545**	30	20
1683	2s. Chukar partridge	30	20
1684	3s. Grey partridge	35	20
1685	5s. Brown hare	95	45
1686	8s. Roe deer	2·50	90
1687	13s. Red deer	2·75	1·60

546 "Philately"

1967. Tenth Bulgarian Philatelic Federation Congress, Sofia.

1688	**546**	10s. yellow, black & grn	2·30	1·70

547 6th-cent B.C. Coin of Thrace

1967. Ancient Bulgarian Coins. Coins in silver on black background except 13s. (gold on black). Frame colours given.

1689	**547**	1s. brown	20	15
1690	-	2s. purple	20	15
1691	-	3s. green	20	15
1692	-	5s. brown	45	35
1693	-	13s. turquoise	1·40	90
1694	-	20s. violet	2·30	1·70

COINS—SQUARE: 2s. 2nd-cent B.C. Macedonian tetradrachm; 3s. 2nd-cent B.C. Odessos (Varna) tetradrachm; 5s. 4th-cent B.C. Macedonian coin of Philip II. HORIZ: (38×25 mm): 13s. Obverse and reverse of 4th cent B.C. coin of King Sevt (Thrace); 20s. Obverse and reverse of 5th-cent B.C. coin of Apollonia (Sozopol).

548 Partisans listening to radio

1967. 25th Anniv of Fatherland Front. Multicoloured.

1695	1s. Type **548**	20	15
1696	20s. Dimitrov speaking at rally	1·30	45

549 Nikola Kofardzhiev

1967. Anti-fascist Fighters.

1697	**549**	1s. red, black & blue	20	15
1698	-	2s. green, black & blue	20	15
1699	-	5s. brown, black & blue	20	15
1700	-	10s. blue, black & lilac	65	30
1701	-	13s. purple, black & grey	95	35

PORTRAITS: 2s. Petko Napetov; 5s. Petko Petkov; 10s. Emil Markov; 13s. Traicho Kostov.

550 "Cultural Development"

1967. First Cultural Conference, Sofia.

1702	**550**	13s. yellow, grn & gold	95	55

551 Angora Kitten

1967. Cats. Multicoloured.

1703	1s. Type **551**	20	15
1704	2s. Siamese (horiz)	30	15
1705	3s. Abyssinian	45	20
1706	5s. European black and white	1·50	35
1707	13s. Persian (horiz)	1·90	65
1708	20s. European tabby	2·30	1·70

552 "Golden Sands" Resort

1967. International Tourist Year. Multicoloured.

1709	13s. Type **552**	45	20
1710	20s. Pamporovo	95	45
1711	40s. Old Church, Nesebur	2·30	1·00

553 Scene from Iliev's Opera *The Master of Boyana*

1967. Third International Young Opera Singers' Competition, Sofia.

1712	**553**	5s. red, blue and grey	20	15
1713	-	13s. red, blue and grey	75	45

DESIGN—VERT: 13s. *Vocal Art* (song-bird on piano-keys).

554 G. Kirkov

1967. Birth Cent of Georgi Kirkov (patriot).

1714	**554**	2s. bistre and red	20	15

555 Roses and Distillery

1967. Economic Achievements. Multicoloured.

1715	1s. Type **555**	20	15
1716	1s. Chick and incubator	20	15
1717	2s. Cucumber and glass-houses	20	15
1718	2s. Lamb and farm building	20	15
1719	3s. Sunflower and oil-extraction plant	20	15
1720	4s. Pigs and piggery	25	15
1721	5s. Hops and vines	30	15
1722	6s. Grain and irrigation canals	35	15
1723	8s. Grapes and "Bulgar" tractor	40	15
1724	10s. Apples and tree	45	20
1725	13s. Honey bees and honey	95	45
1726	20s. Honey bee on flower, and hives	1·20	55

556 DKMS Emblem

1967. 11th Anniv of Dimitrov Communist Youth League.

1727	**556**	13s. black, red and blue	95	35

557 Map and Spassky Tower, Moscow Kremlin

1967. 50th Anniv of October Revolution.

1728	**557**	1s. multicoloured	20	15
1729	-	2s. olive and purple	20	15
1730	-	3s. violet and purple	20	15
1731	-	5s. red and purple	20	15
1732	-	13s. blue and purple	65	35
1733	-	20s. blue and purple	1·40	55

DESIGNS: 2s. Lenin directing revolutionaries; 3s. Revolutionaries; 5s. Marx, Engels and Lenin; 13s. Soviet oil refinery; 20s. "Molniya" satellite and Moon (Soviet space research).

558 Scenic "Fish" and Rod

1967. Seventh World Angling Championships, Varna.

1734	**558**	10s. multicoloured	75	45

559 Cross-country Skiing

1967. Winter Olympic Games, Grenoble (1968).

1735	**559**	1s. black, red & turq	20	15
1736	-	2s. black, bistre & blue	20	15
1737	-	3s. black, blue & purple	20	15
1738	-	5s. black, yellow & grn	30	20
1739	-	13s. black, buff & blue	1·40	45
1740	-	20s.+10s. mult	2·40	90

MS1741 98× 98 mm. (diamond) 40s.+10s. black, ochre and blue. Imperf — 3·75 — 3·25

DESIGNS: 2s. Ski jumping; 3s. Biathlon; 5s. Ice hockey; 13, 40s. Ice skating (pairs); 20s. Men's slalom.

560 Bogdan Peak, Sredna Mts

1967. Tourism. Mountain Peaks.

1742	**560**	1s. green and yellow	20	15
1743	-	2s. sepia and blue	20	15
1744	-	3s. indigo and blue	20	15
1745	-	5s. green and blue	30	15
1746	-	10s. brown and blue	40	20
1747	-	13s. black and blue	45	40
1748	-	20s. blue and purple	95	80

DESIGNS—HORIZ: 2s. Cherni Vruh, Vitosha; 5s. Persenk, Rhodopes; 10s. Botev, Stara-Planina; 20s. Vikhren, Pirin. VERT: 3s. Ruen, Osogovska Planina; 13s. Musala, Rila.

561 G. Rakovski

1967. Death Cent of G. Rakovski (revolutionary).

1749	**561**	13s. black and green	95	55

562 Yuri Gagarin, Valentina Tereshkova and Aleksei Leonov

1967. Space Exploration. Multicoloured.

1750	1s. Type **562**	20	15
1751	2s. John Glenn and Edward White	20	15
1752	5s. "Molniya 1"	30	20
1753	10s. "Gemini 6" and "7"	95	35
1754	13s. "Luna 13"	1·00	55
1755	20s. "Gemini 10" docking with "Agena"	1·20	1·10

563 Railway Bridge over Yantra River

1967. Views of Turnovo (ancient capital).

1756	**563**	1s. black, drab and blue	20	15
1757	-	2s. multicoloured	20	15
1758	-	3s. multicoloured	20	15
1759	-	5s. black, slate and red	45	25
1760	-	13s. multicoloured	75	35
1761	-	20s. black, orange & lav	95	55

DESIGNS: 2s. Hadji Nikola's Inn; 3s. Houses on hillside; 5s. Town and river; 13s. "House of the Monkeys"; 20s. Gurko street.

564 *The Ruchenitsa* (folk dance, from painting by Murkvichka)

1967. Belgian–Bulgarian "Painting and Philately" Exhibition, Brussels.

1762	**564**	20s. green and gold	1·90	1·70

565 *The Shepherd* (Zlatko Boyadzhiev)

1967. Paintings in the National Gallery, Sofia. Multicoloured.

1763	1s. Type **565**	10	10
1764	2s. *The Wedding* (Vladimir Dimitrov) (vert)	10	10
1765	3s. *The Partisans* Ilya Petrov (55×35 mm)	45	20
1766	5s. *Anastasia Penchovich* (Nikolai Pavlovich) (vert)	95	35
1767	13s. *Self-portrait* (Zakharii Zograf) (vert)	1·90	1·00
1768	20s. *Old Town of Plovdiv* (Tsanko Lavrenov)	2·30	1·10

MS1769 65×85 mm. 60s. *St. Clement of Ohrid* (Anton Mitov) — 6·75 — 6·75

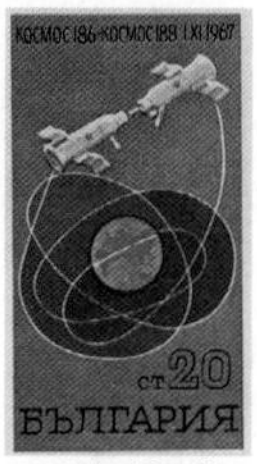

566 Linked Satellites "Cosmos 186" and "188"

1968. "Cosmic Activities". Multicoloured.

1770	20s. Type **566**	95	55
1771	40s. "Venus 4" and orbital diagram (horiz)	2·30	1·10

567 *Crossing the Danube* (Orenburgski)

1968. 90th Anniv of Liberation from Turkey. Paintings. Inscr and frames in black and gold; centre colours below.

1772	**567**	1s. green	20	15
1773	-	2s. blue	20	15
1774	-	3s. brown	20	15
1775	-	13s. blue	1·10	55
1776	-	20s. turquoise	1·40	65

DESIGNS—VERT: 2s. *Flag of Samara* (Veschin); 13s. *Battle of Orlovo Gnezdo* (Popov). HORIZ: 3s. *Battle of Pleven* (Orenburgski); 20s. *Greeting Russian Soldiers* (Goudienov).

568 Karl Marx

1968. 150th Birth Anniv of Karl Marx.

1777	**568**	13s. grey, red & black	95	35

569 Gorky

1968. Birth Cent of Maksim Gorky (writer).

1778	**569**	13s. green, orange & blk	95	35

570 Dancers

1968. Ninth World Youth and Students' Festival. Sofia. Multicoloured.

1779	2s. Type **570**		20	15
1780	5s. Running		20	15
1781	13s. "Doves"		85	35
1782	20s. "Youth" (symbolic design)		95	55
1783	40s. Bulgarian 5c. stamp of 1879 under magnifier and Globe		1·60	1·30

571 *Campanula alpina*

1968. Wild Flowers. Multicoloured.

1784	1s. Type **571**	20	15
1785	2s. Trumpet gentian	20	15
1786	3s. *Crocus veluchensis*	20	15
1787	5s. Siberian iris	45	20
1788	10s. Dog's-tooth violet	65	20
1789	13s. House leek	1·10	35
1790	20s. Burning bush	1·40	55

572 *The Unknown Hero* (Ran Bosilek)

1968. Bulgarian–Danish Stamp Exhibition. Fairy Tales. Multicoloured.

1791	13s. Type **572**	45	35
1792	20s. "The Witch and the Young Men" (Hans Andersen)	95	80

573 Memorial Temple, Shipka

1968. Bulgarian–West Berlin Stamp Exn.

1793	**573**	13s. multicoloured	95	55

574 Copper Rolling-mill, Medet

1968. Air.

1794	**574**	1l. red	3·25	80

575 Lake Smolyan

1968

1795	**575**	1s. green	20	15
1796	-	2s. myrtle	20	15
1797	-	3s. sepia	20	15
1798	-	8s. green	35	15
1799	-	10s. brown	40	20
1800	-	13s. olive	45	30
1801	-	40s. blue	1·40	35
1802	-	2l. brown	6·50	2·20

DESIGNS: 2s. River Ropotamo; 3s. Lomnitza Gorge, Erma River; 8s. River Isker; 10s. Cruise ship *Die Fregatte*; 13s. Cape Kaliakra; 40s. Sozopol; 2l. Mountain road, Kamchia River.

576 Gymnastics

1968. Olympic Games, Mexico.

1803	**576**	1s. black and red	20	15
1804	-	2s. black, brown & grey	20	15
1805	-	3s. black and mauve	20	15
1806	-	10s. black, yell & turq	65	20
1807	-	13s. black, pink & blue	1·40	55
1808	-	20s.+10s. grey, pk & bl	1·90	65

MS1809 74×76 mm. 50s.+10s. black, grey and blue. Imperf 4·75 4·50

DESIGNS: 2s. Horse-jumping; 3s. Fencing; 10s. Boxing; 13s. Throwing the discus; 20s. Rowing; 50s. Stadium and communications satellite.

577 Dimitur on Mt. Buzludzha, 1868

1968. Centenary of Exploits of Khadzhi Dimitur and Stefan Karadzha (revolutionaries).

1810	**577**	2s. brown and silver	20	10
1811	-	13s. green and gold	75	45

DESIGN: 13s. Dimitur and Karadzha.

578 Human Rights Emblem

1968. Human Rights Year.

1812	**578**	20s. gold and blue	1·10	55

579 Cinereous Black Vulture

1968. 80th Anniv of Sofia Zoo.

1813	**579**	1s. black, brown & blue	20	20
1814	-	2s. black, yellow & brn	25	20
1815	-	3s. black and green	30	20
1816	-	5s. black, yellow & red	65	35
1817	-	13s. black, bistre & grn	2·40	1·10
1818	-	20s. black, green & blue	3·25	1·70

DESIGNS: 2s. South African crowned crane; 3s. Common zebra; 5s. Leopard; 13s. Python; 20s. Crocodile.

580 Battle Scene

1968. 280th Anniv of Chiprovtsi Rising.

1819	**580**	13s. multicoloured	95	20

581 Caterpillar-hunter

1968. Insects.

1820	**581**	1s. green	30	10
1821	-	1s. brown	30	10
1822	-	1s. blue	30	10
1823	-	1s. brown	30	10
1824	-	1s. purple	30	10

DESIGNS—VERT: No. 1821, Stag beetle (*Lucanus cervus*); 1822, *Procerus scabrosus* (ground beetle). HORIZ: No. 1823, European rhinoceros beetle (*Oryctes nasicornis*); 1824, *Perisomena caecigena* (moth).

582 Flying Swans

1968. "Co-operation with Scandinavia".

1825		2s. ochre and green	1·90	1·70
1826	**582**	5s. blue, grey & black	1·90	1·70
1827	-	13s. purple and maroon	1·90	1·70
1828	-	20s. grey and violet	1·90	1·70

DESIGNS: 2s. Wooden flask; 13s. Rose; 20s. "Viking ship".

583 Congress Building and Emblem

1968. International Dental Congress, Varna.

1829	**583**	20s. gold, green and red	95	35

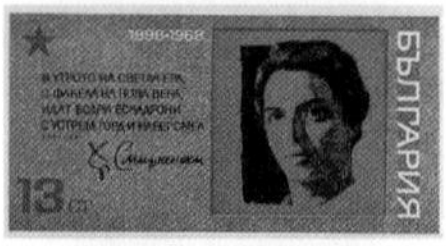

584 Smirnenski and Verse from *Red Squadrons*

1968. 70th Birth Anniv of Khristo Smirnenski (poet).

1830	**584**	13s. black, orange & gold	95	35

585 Dove with Letter

1968. National Stamp Exhibition, Sofia and 75th Anniv of "National Philately".

1831	**585**	20s. green	1·90	1·70

586 Dalmatian Pelican

1968. Srebirna Wildlife Reservation. Birds. Multicoloured.

1832	1s. Type **586**	35	20
1833	2s. Little egret	45	30
1834	3s. Great crested grebe	55	35
1835	5s. Common tern	65	45
1836	13s. White spoonbill	2·00	1·50
1837	20s. Glossy ibis	4·25	2·20

587 Silistra Costume

1968. Provincial Costumes. Multicoloured.

1838	1s. Type **587**	20	15
1839	2s. Lovech	20	15
1840	3s. Yamboi	20	15
1841	13s. Chirpan	75	35
1842	20s. Razgrad	1·10	65
1843	40s. Ikhtiman	2·40	90

588 *St. Arsenius* (icon)

1968. Rila Monastery. Icons and murals. Multicoloured.

1844	1s. Type **588**	20	15
1845	2s. *Carrying St. Ivan Rilski's Relics* (horiz)	20	15
1846	3s. *St. Michael torments the Rich Man's Soul*	30	20
1847	13s. *St. Ivan Rilski*	1·10	65
1848	20s. *Prophet Joel*	1·70	90
1849	40s. *St. George*	2·75	1·50

MS1850 100×74 mm. 1l. *Arrival of Relics at Rila Monastery*. Imperf 7·50 7·25

589 *Matricaria chamomilla*

1968. Medicinal Plants. Multicoloured.

1851	1s. Type **589**	20	15
1852	1s. "Mespilus oxyacantha"	20	15
1853	2s. Lily of the valley	20	15
1854	3s. Deadly nightshade	20	15
1855	5s. Common mallow	30	15
1856	10s. Yellow peasant's eye	65	20
1857	13s. Common poppy	75	35
1858	20s. Wild thyme	1·10	55

590 Silkworms and Spindles

1969. Silk Industry. Multicoloured.

1859	1s. Type **590**	20	15
1860	2s. Worm, cocoons and pattern	20	15
1861	3s. Cocoons and spinning wheel	20	15
1862	5s. Cocoons and pattern	20	15
1863	13s. Moth, cocoon and spindles	75	20
1864	20s. Moth, eggs and shuttle	1·10	35

591 *Death of Ivan Asen*

1969. Manasses Chronicle (1st series). Multicoloured.

1865	1s. Type **591**	20	15
1866	2s. *Emperor Nicephorus invading Bulgaria*	20	15
1867	3s. *Khan Krum's Feast*	20	15
1868	13s. *Prince Sviatoslav invading Bulgaria*	1·10	45
1869	20s. *The Russian invasion*	1·60	55
1870	40s. *Jesus Christ, Tsar Ivan Alexander and Constantine Manasses*	2·30	1·10

See also Nos. 1911/16.

592 *Saints Cyril and Methodius* (mural, Troyan Monastery)

1969. Saints Cyril and Methodius Commem.

1871	**592**	28s. multicoloured	1·90	1·10

593 Galleon

1969. Air. "SOFIA 1969" International Stamp Exhibition. Transport. Multicoloured.

1872	1s. Type **593**	20	15
1873	2s. Mail coach	20	15
1874	3s. Steam locomotive	20	15
1875	5s. Early motor-car	20	15
1876	10s. Montgolfier's balloon and Henri Giffard's steam-powered dirigible airship	35	20
1877	13s. Early flying machines	65	35
1878	20s. Modern aircraft	1·10	45
1879	40s. Rocket and planets	2·00	1·10

MS1880 57×55 mm. 1l. gold and orange. Imperf 4·75 4·50

DESIGN: 1l. Postal courier.

594 Posthorn Emblem

1969. 90th Anniv of Bulgarian Postal Services.

1881	**594**	2s. yellow and green	20	15
1882	-	13s. multicoloured	65	20
1883	-	20s. blue	1·10	55

DESIGNS: 13s. Bulgarian Stamps of 1879 and 1946; 20s. Post Office workers' strike, 1919.

595 I.L.O. Emblem

1969. 50th Anniv of I.L.O.

1884	**595**	13s. black and green	65	35

596 "Fox" and "Rabbit"

1969. Children's Book Week.

1885	**596**	1s. black, orange & grn	20	15
1886	-	2s. black, blue and red	20	15
1887	-	13s. black, olive & blue	75	35

DESIGNS: 2s. Boy with "hedgehog" and "squirrel"; 13s. *The Singing Lesson*.

597 Hand with Seedling

1969. "10,000,000 Hectares of New Forests".

1888	**597**	2s. black, green & purple	20	10

598 *St. George* (14th Century)

1969. Religious Art. Multicoloured.

1889	1s. Type **598**	20	15
1890	2s. *The Virgin and St. John Bogoslov* (14th century)	20	15
1891	3s. *Archangel Michael* (17th century)	20	15
1892	5s. *Three Saints* (17th century)	30	15
1893	8s. *Jesus Christ* (17th century)	35	15
1894	13s. *St. George and St. Dimitr* (19th century)	75	20
1895	20s. *Christ the Universal* (19th century)	95	45
1896	60s. *The Forty Martyrs* (19th century)	2·75	1·70
1897	80s. *The Transfiguration* (19th century)	3·75	2·20

MS1898 103×165 mm. 40s. ×4, *St. Dimitur* (17th-century) 9·25 9·00

599 Roman Coin

1969. "SOFIA 1969" International Stamp Exhibition. "Sofia Through the Ages".

1899	**599**	1s. silver, blue and gold	10	10
1900	-	2s. silver, green & gold	10	10
1901	-	3s. silver, lake and gold	10	10
1902	-	4s. silver, violet & gold	15	10
1903	-	5s. silver, purple & gold	20	10
1904	-	13s. silver, green & gold	45	15
1905	-	20s. silver, blue & gold	75	35
1906	-	40s. silver, red & gold	1·40	65

MS1907 78×72 mm. 1l. multicoloured. Imperf 6·50 5·50

DESIGNS: 2s. Roman coin showing Temple of Aesculapius; 3s. Church of St. Sophia; 4s. Boyana Church; 5s. Parliament Building; 13s. National Theatre; 20s. Aleksandr Nevski Cathedral; 40s. Sofia University. 44×44 mm. 1l. Arms.

600 St. George and the Dragon

1969. Int Philatelic Federation Congress, Sofia.

1908	**600**	40s. black, orange & sil	2·30	1·10

601 St. Cyril

1969. 1,100th Death Anniv of St. Cyril.

1909	**601**	2s. green & red on silver	20	10
1910	-	28s. blue & red on silver	1·60	65

DESIGN: 28s. St. Cyril and procession.

1969. Manasses Chronicle (2nd series). Designs as T **591**, but all horiz. Multicoloured.

1911	1s. *Nebuchadnezzar II and Balthasar of Babylon, Cyrus and Darius of Persia*	10	10
1912	2s. *Cambyses, Gyges and Darius of Persia*	10	10
1913	5s. *Prophet David and Tsar Ivan Alexander*	30	10
1914	13s. *Rout of the Byzantine Army, 811*	95	35
1915	20s. *Christening of Khan Boris*	1·90	45
1916	60s. *Tsar Simeon's attack on Constantinople*	2·75	1·90

602 Partisans

1969. 25th Anniv of Fatherland Front Government.

1917	**602**	1s. lilac, red and black	20	15
1918	-	2s. brown, red & black	20	15
1919	-	3s. green, red and black	20	15
1920	-	5s. brown, red & black	20	15
1921	-	13s. blue, red & black	65	20
1922	-	20s. multicoloured	1·20	55

DESIGNS: 2s. Combine-harvester; 3s. Dam; 5s. Folk singers; 13s. Petroleum refinery; 20s. Lenin, Dimitrov and flags.

603 Gymnastics

1969. Third Republican Spartakiad. Multicoloured.

1923	2s. Type **603**	20	10
1924	20s. Wrestling	95	65

604 "Construction" and soldier

1969. 25th Anniv of Army Engineers.

1925	**604**	6s. black and blue	30	15

605 T. Tserkovski

1969. Birth Cent of Tsanke Tserkovski (poet).

1926	**605**	13s. multicoloured	75	35

606 "Woman" (Roman Statue)

1969. 1,800th Anniv of Silistra.

1927	**606**	2s. grey, blue and silver	20	15
1928	-	13s. brown, grn & silver	1·00	45

DESIGN—HORIZ: 13s. "Wolf" (bronze statue).

607 Skipping-rope Exercise

1969. World Gymnastics Competition, Varna.

1929	**607**	1s. grey, blue and green	20	15
1930	-	2s. grey and blue	20	15
1931	-	3s. grey, green and emerald	20	15
1932	-	5s. grey, purple and red	20	15
1933	-	13s.+5s. grey, bl & red	1·10	55
1934	-	20s.+10s. grey, green and yellow	1·40	65

DESIGNS: 2s. Hoop exercise (pair); 3s. Hoop exercise (solo); 5s. Ball exercise (pair); 13s. Ball exercise (solo); 20s. Solo gymnast.

608 Marin Drinov (founder)

1969. Cent of Bulgarian Academy of Sciences.

1935	**608**	20s. black and red	95	45

609 *Neophit Rilski* (Zakharii Zograf)

1969. Paintings in National Gallery, Sofia. Multicoloured.

1936	1s. Type **609**	10	10
1937	2s. *German's Mother* (Vasil Stoilov)	20	10
1938	3s. *Workers' Family* (Neuko Balkanski) (horiz)	30	10
1939	4s. *Woman Dressing* (Ivan Nenov)	35	10
1940	5s. *Portrait of a Woman* (Nikolai Pavlovich)	45	20
1941	13s. *Krustyn Sarafov as Falstaff* (Dechko Uzunov)	95	30
1942	20s. *Artist's Wife* (N. Mikhailov) (horiz)	1·30	45
1943	20s. *Worker's Lunch* (Stoyan Sotirov) (horiz)	1·40	55
1944	40s. *Self-portrait* (Tseno Todorov) (horiz)	1·90	80

610 Pavel Banya

1969. Sanatoria.

1945	**610**	2s. blue	20	10
1946	-	5s. blue	20	10
1947	-	6s. green	35	10
1948	-	20s. green	75	35

SANATORIA: 5s. Khisar; 6s. Kotel; 20s. Narechen Polyclinic.

611 Deep-sea Trawler

1969. Ocean Fisheries.

1949	**611**	1s. grey and blue	20	15
1950	-	1s. green and black	20	15
1951	-	2s. violet and black	20	15
1952	-	3s. blue and black	20	15
1953	-	5s. mauve and black	30	20
1954	-	10s. grey and black	1·50	45
1955	-	13s. flesh, orange & blk	2·30	80
1956	-	20s. brown, ochre & blk	3·00	1·10

DESIGNS: 1s. (No. 1950), Cape hake; 2s. Atlantic horse-mackerel; 3s. South African pilchard; 5s. Large-eyed dentex; 10s. Chub mackerel; 13s. Senegal croaker; 20s. Vadigo.

612 Trapeze Act

1969. Circus. Multicoloured.

1957	1s. Type **612**	10	10
1958	2s. Acrobats	10	10
1959	3s. Balancing act with hoops	10	10
1960	5s. Juggler, and bear on cycle	20	10
1961	13s. Equestrian act	65	35
1962	20s. Clowns	1·40	55

613 V. Kubasov, Georgi Shonin and "Soyuz 6"

1970. Space Flights of "Soyuz 6, 7 and 8".

1963	**613**	1s. multicoloured	10	10
1964	-	2s. multicoloured	10	10
1965	-	3s. multicoloured	20	15
1966	-	28s. pink and blue	1·50	55

DESIGNS: 2s. Viktor Gorbacko, Vladislav Volkov, Anatoly Filipchenko and "Soyuz 7"; 3s. Aleksei Elseev, Vladimir Shatalov and "Soyuz 8"; 28s. Three "Soyuz" spacecraft in orbit.

614 Khan Asparerch and "Old-Bulgars" crossing the Danube, 679

1970. History of Bulgaria. Multicoloured.

1967	1s. Type **614**	20	15
1968	2s. Khan Krum and defeat of Emperor Nicephorus, 811	20	15
1969	3s. Conversion of Khan Boris I to Christianity, 865	20	15
1970	5s. Tsar Simeon and Battle of Akhelo, 917	30	15
1971	8s. Tsar Samuel and defeat of Byzantines, 976	35	15
1972	10s. Tsar Kaloyan and victory over Emperor Baldwin, 1205	55	20
1973	13s. Tsar Ivan Assen II and defeat of Komnine of Epirus, 1230	95	35
1974	20s. Coronation of Tsar Ivailo, 1277	1·40	55

615 Bulgarian Pavilion

1970. "Expo 70" World's Fair, Osaka, Japan (1st issue).

1975	**615**	20s. silver, yellow & brn	1·90	1·10

See Nos. 2009/12.

616 Footballers

1970. World Football Cup, Mexico.

1976	**616**	1s. multicoloured	10	10
1977	-	2s. multicoloured	10	10
1978	-	3s. multicoloured	10	10
1979	-	5s. multicoloured	20	15
1980	-	20s. multicoloured	1·60	55
1981	-	40s. multicoloured	2·00	75

MS1982 55×99 mm. 80s.+20s. multicoloured. Imperf 4·75 4·50

DESIGNS—HORIZ: 2s. to 40s. Various football scenes. VERT (45×69 mm.) 80s. Football and inscription.

617 Lenin

1970. Birth Cent of Lenin. Multicoloured.

1983	2s. Type **617**	20	15
1984	13s. Full-face portrait	75	35
1985	20s. Lenin writing	1·60	65

618 *Tephrocactus Alexanderi v. bruchi*

1970. Flowering Cacti. Multicoloured.

1986	1s. Type **618**	20	15
1987	2s. *Opuntia drummondii*	20	15
1988	3s. *Hatiora cilindrica*	20	15
1989	5s. *Gymnocalycium vatteri*	30	20
1990	8s. *Heliantho cereus grandiflorus*	45	35
1991	10s. *Neochilenia andreaeana*	2·20	80
1992	13s. *Peireskia vargasii v. longispina*	2·30	90
1993	20s. *Neobesseya rosiflora*	2·75	1·10

619 Rose

1970. Bulgarian Roses.

1994	**619**	1s. multicoloured	20	15
1995	-	2s. multicoloured	20	15
1996	-	3s. multicoloured	30	15
1997	-	4s. multicoloured	40	15
1998	-	5s. multicoloured	45	20
1999	-	13s. multicoloured	95	45
2000	-	20s. multicoloured	1·90	1·10
2001	-	28s. multicoloured	3·25	1·90

DESIGNS: 2s. to 28s. Various roses.

620 Union Badge

1970. 70th Anniv of Agricultural Union.

2002	**620**	20s. black, gold and red	1·40	45

621 Gold Bowl

1970. Gold Treasures of Thrace.

2003	**621**	1s. black, blue and gold	20	15
2004	-	2s. black, lilac and gold	20	15
2005	-	3s. black, red and gold	20	15
2006	-	5s. black, green & gold	30	20
2007	-	13s. black, orge & gold	1·40	55
2008	-	20s. black, violet & gold	1·90	1·10

DESIGNS: 2s. Three small bowls; 3s. Plain lid; 5s. Pear shaped ornaments; 13s. Large lid with pattern; 20s. Vase.

622 Rose and Woman with Baskets of Produce

1970. "Expo 70" World's Fair, Osaka, Japan (2nd issue). Multicoloured.

2009	1s. Type **622**	20	15
2010	2s. Three Dancers	20	15
2011	3s. Girl in National costume	20	15
2012	28s. Dancing couples	1·70	80

MS2013 75×90 mm. 40s. Bulgarian pavilion 1·90 1·90

623 UN Emblem

1970. 25th Anniv of United Nations.

2014	**623**	20s. gold and blue	95	55

624 I. Vasov

1970. 120th Birth Anniv of Ivan Vasov (poet).

2015	**624**	13s. blue	85	35

625 Edelweiss Sanatorium, Borovets

1970. Health Resorts.

2016	**625**	1s. green	20	15
2017	-	2s. olive	20	15
2018	-	4s. blue	20	15
2019	-	8s. blue	45	15
2020	-	10s. blue	65	20

DESIGNS: 2s. Panorama Hotel, Pamporovo; 4s. Yachts, Albena; 8s. Harbour scene, Rousalka; 10s. Shtastlivetsa Hotel, Mt. Vitosha.

626 Hungarian Retriever

1970. Dogs. Multicoloured.

2021	1s. Type **626**	20	15
2022	2s. Retriever (vert)	30	15
2023	3s. Great Dane (vert)	35	15
2024	4s. Boxer (vert)	45	20
2025	5s. Cocker spaniel (vert)	55	30
2026	13s. Dobermann pinscher (vert)	1·40	80
2027	20s. Scottish terrier (vert)	2·75	1·20
2028	28s. Russian hound	3·25	1·70

627 Fireman with Hose

1970. Fire Protection.

2029	**627**	1s. grey, yellow & black	20	10
2030	-	3s. red, grey and black	30	20

DESIGN. 3s. Fire-engine.

628 Congress Emblem

1970. Seventh World Sociological Congress, Varna.

2031	**628**	13s. multicoloured	75	20

629 Two Male Players

1970. World Volleyball Championships.

2032	**629**	2s. black and brown	20	15
2033	-	2s. orange, black & blue	20	15
2034	-	20s. yellow, black & grn	1·20	55
2035	-	20s. multicoloured	1·40	65

DESIGNS: No. 2033, Two female players; 2034, Male player; 2035, Female player.

630 Cyclists

1970. 20th Round-Bulgaria Cycle Race.

2036	**630**	20s. mauve, yellow & grn	95	55

631 Enrico Caruso and Scene from *Il Pagliacci*

1970. Opera Singers. Multicoloured.

2037	1s. Type **631**	20	15
2038	2s. Khristina Morfova and *The Bartered Bride*	20	15
2039	3s. Petur Raichev and *Tosca*	20	15
2040	10s. Tsvetana Tabakova and *The Flying Dutchman*	35	25
2041	13s. Katya Popova and *The Masters of Nuremberg*	45	35
2042	20s. Fyodor Chaliapin and *Boris Godunov*	2·30	1·30

632 Beethoven

1970. Birth Bicentenary of Ludwig von Beethoven (composer).

2043	**632**	28s. blue and purple	2·75	2·20

633 Ivan Asen II Coin

1970. Bulgarian Coins of the 14th century. Multicoloured.

2044	1s. Type **633**	20	15
2045	2s. Theodor Svetoslav	20	15
2046	3s. Mikhail Shishman	20	15
2047	13s. Ivan Alexander and Mikhail Asen	45	20
2048	20s. Ivan Sratsimir	1·40	45
2049	28s. Ivan Shishman (initials)	1·90	65

634 "Luna 16"

1970. Moon Mission of "Luna 16". Sheet 51×70 mm.

MS2050	**634**	1l. red, silver and blue	7·50	7·25

635 Engels

1970. 150th Birth Anniv of Friedrich Engels.

2051	**635**	13s. brown and red	95	55

636 Snow Crystal

1970. New Year.

2052	**636**	2s. multicoloured	20	10

637 "Lunokhod 1" on Moon

1970. Moon Mission of "Lunokhod 1". Sheet 60×72 mm.

MS2053	**637**	80s. silver, purple and blue	7·25	5·50

638 *Girl's Head* (Zheko Spiridonov)

1971. Modern Bulgarian Sculpture.

2054	**638**	1s. violet and gold	20	15
2055	-	2s. green and gold	20	15
2056	-	3s. brown and gold	20	15
2057	-	13s. green and gold	65	20
2058	-	20s. red and gold	1·30	45
2059	-	28s. brown and gold	1·40	65

MS2060 61×72 mm. 1l. chestnut and gold 4·75 4·75

SCULPTURES: 2s. *Third Class Carriage* (Ivan Funev); 3s. *Elin Pelin* (Marko Markov); 13s. *Nina* (Andrei Nikolov); 20s. *Kneeling Woman* (Yavorov monument, Ivan Lazarov); 28s. *Engineer* (Ivan Funev). 36½×41 mm. 1l. *Refugees* (Sekul Krimov).

639 Birds and Flowers

1971. Spring.

2061	**639**	1s. multicoloured	10	10
2062	-	2s. multicoloured	10	10
2063	-	3s. multicoloured	10	10
2064	-	5s. multicoloured	10	10
2065	-	13s. multicoloured	45	20
2066	-	20s. multicoloured	1·00	45

DESIGNS: 2s. to 20s. Various designs of birds and flowers similar to Type **639**.

640 *Khan Asparuch crossing Danube* (Boris Angelushev)

1971. Bulgarian History. Paintings. Multicoloured.

2067	2s. Type **640**	20	15
2068	3s. *Ivajlo in Turnovo* (Ilya Petrov)	20	15
2069	5s. *Cavalry Charge, Benkovski* (P. Morosov)	45	20
2070	8s. *Gen. Gzrko entering Sofia, 1878* (D. Gyudzhenov)	95	30
2071	28s. *Greeting Red Army* (Stefan Venev)	3·75	2·00
MS2072	137×131 mm. Nos. 2067/70	1·90	1·70

641 Running

1971. Second European Indoor Track and Field Championships. Multicoloured.

2073	2s. Type **641**	20	15
2074	20s. Putting the shot	1·90	55

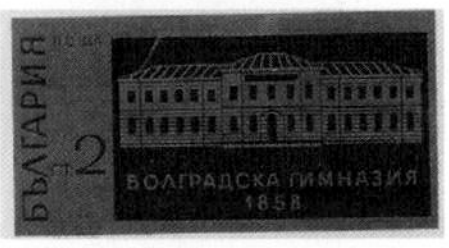
642 School Building

1971. Foundation of First Bulgarian Secondary School, Bolgrad.

2075	**642**	2s. green, brown & sil	20	15
2076	-	20s. violet, brown & sil	1·30	45

DESIGN: 20s. Dimitur Mutev, Prince Bogoridi and Sava Radulov (founders).

643 Communards

1971. Centenary of Paris Commune.

2077	**643**	20s. black and red	95	55

644 Georgi Dimitrov challenging Hermann Goering

1971. 20th Anniv of "Federation Internationale des Resistants".

2078	**644**	2s. multicoloured	20	15
2079	**644**	13s. multicoloured	1·40	55

645 Gagarin and Space Scenes

1971. Tenth Anniv of First Manned Space Flight. Sheet 80×53 mm.

MS2080	**645** 40s.+20s. multicoloured	4·75	4·00

646 G. Rakovski

1971. 150th Birth Anniv of Georgi Rakovski (politician and Revolutionary).

2081	**646**	13s. brown, cream & grn	75	20

647 Worker and Banner ("People's Progress")

1971. Tenth Bulgarian Communist Party Congress. Multicoloured.

2082	1s. Type **647**	20	15
2083	2s. Symbols of "Technical Progress" (horiz)	20	15
2084	12s. Men clasping hands ("Bulgarian-Soviet Friendship")	1·40	45

648 Pipkov and Music

1971. Birth Centenary of Panaiot Pipokov.

2085	**648**	13s. black, green & silver	95	55

649 "Three Races"

1971. Racial Equality Year.

2086	**649**	13s. multicoloured	95	55

650 Mammoth

1971. Prehistoric Animals. Multicoloured.

2087	1s. Type **650**	20	20
2088	2s. Bear (vert)	20	20
2089	3s. Hipparion	20	20
2090	13s. Mastodon	1·90	65
2091	20s. Dinotherium (vert)	2·75	1·70
2092	28s. Sabre-toothed tiger	3·25	2·20

651 Facade of Ancient Building

1971. Ancient Buildings of Koprivshtitsa.

2093	**651**	1s. green, brown & grn	10	10
2094	-	2s. brown, green & buff	10	10
2095	-	6s. violet, brown & blue	35	15
2096	-	13s. red, blue & orange	95	45

DESIGNS: 1s. to 13s. Different facades.

652 Weights Emblem on Map of Europe

1971. 30th European Weightlifting Championships, Sofia. Multicoloured.

2097	2s. Type **652**	20	15
2098	13s. Figures supporting weights	1·40	45

653 Frontier Guard and Dog

1971. 25th Anniv of Frontier Guards.

2099	**653**	2s. olive, green & turq	20	10

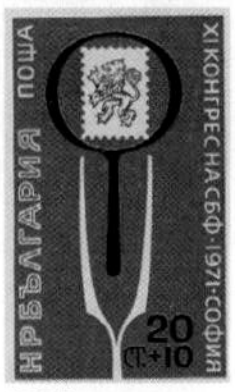
654 Tweezers, Magnifying Glass and "Stamp"

1971. Ninth Congress of Bulgarian Philatelic Federation.

2100	**654**	20s.+10s. brown, black and red	1·90	80

655 Congress Meeting (sculpture)

1971. 80th Anniv of Bulgarian Social Democratic Party Congress, Buzludzha.

2101	**655**	2s. green, cream and red	20	10

656 *Mother* (Ivan Nenov)

1971. Paintings from the National Art Gallery (1st series). Multicoloured.

2102	1s. Type **656**	20	15
2103	2s. *Lazorova* (Stefan Ivanov)	20	15
2104	3s. *Portrait of Yu. Kh.* (Kiril Tsonev)	35	20
2105	13s. *Portrait of a Lady* (Dechko Uzunov)	95	35
2106	30s. *Young Woman from Kalotina* (Vladimir Dimitrov)	1·40	80
2107	40s. *Goryanin* (Stryan Venev)	1·90	1·30

See also Nos. 2145/50.

657 Factory Botevgrad

1971. Industrial Buildings.

2108	**657**	1s. violet	10	10
2109	-	2s. red	10	10
2110	-	10s. violet	35	15
2111	-	13s. red	55	20
2112	-	40s. brown	1·90	45

DESIGNS—VERT: 2s. Petro-chemical plant, Pleven. HORIZ: 10s. Chemical works, Vratsa; 13s. "Maritsa-Istok" plant, Dimitrovgrad; 40s. Electronics factory, Sofia.

658 Free Style Wrestling

1971. European Wrestling Championships, Sofia.

2113	**658**	2s. green, black and blue	10	10
2114	-	13s. black, red and blue	95	45

DESIGN: 13s. Greco-Roman wrestling.

659 Posthorn Emblem

1971. Organization of Socialist Countries' Postal Administrations Congress.

2115	**659**	20s. gold and green	95	55

660 Entwined Ribbons

1971. 7th European Biochemical Congress, Varna.

2116	**660**	13s. red, brown & black	95	55

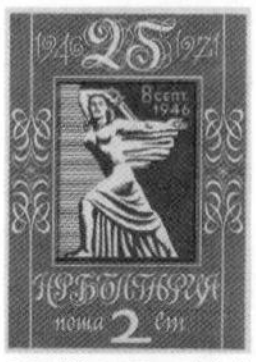
661 "New Republic" Statue

1971. 25th Anniv of People's Republic.

2117	**661**	2s. red, yellow and gold	10	10
2118	-	13s. green, red and gold	95	45

DESIGN: 13s. Bulgarian flag.

662 Cross-country Skiing

1971. Winter Olympic Games, Sapporo, Japan. Multicoloured.

2119	1s. Type **662**	20	15
2120	2s. Downhill skiing	20	15
2121	3s. Ski jumping	20	15
2122	4s. Figure skating	20	15
2123	13s. Ice hockey	95	65
2124	28s. Slalom skiing	1·90	1·10
MS2125	60×70 mm. 1l. Olympic flame and stadium	4·75	3·00

663 Brigade Members

1971. 25th Anniv of Youth Brigades Movement.

2126	**663**	2s. blue	20	10

664 UNESCO Emblem and Wreath

1971. 25th Anniv of UNESCO.

2127	**664**	20s. multicoloured	95	55

665 *The Footballer*

1971. Paintings by Kiril Tsonev. Multicoloured.

2128	1s. Type **665**	20	15
2129	2s. *Landscape* (horiz)	20	15
2130	3s. Self-portrait	30	20
2131	13s. *Lilies*	95	35
2132	20s. *Woodland Scene* (horiz)	1·40	65
2133	40s. *Portrait of a Young Woman*	1·90	90

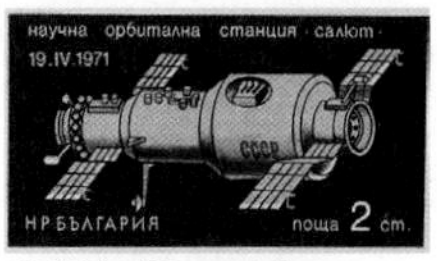
666 "Salyut" Space-station

1971. Space Flights of "Salyut" and "Soyuz 11". Multicoloured.

2134	2s. Type **666**	20	15
2135	13s. "Soyuz 11"	45	30
2136	40s. "Salyut" and "Soyuz 11" joined together	2·30	80

MS2137 70×74 mm. 80s. Cosmonauts G. Dobrovolsky, Vladislav Volkov and V. Patsaev (victims of "Soyuz 11" disaster). Imperf 3·25 2·75

667 *Vikhren* (ore carrier)

1972. "One Million Tons of Bulgarian Shipping".

2138	**667**	18s. lilac, red and black	1·40	55

668 Goce Delcev

1972. Birth Centenaries of Macedonian Revolutionaries.

2139	**668**	2s. black and red	10	10
2140	-	5s. black and green	20	10
2141	-	13s. black and yellow	65	35

PATRIOTS: 5s. Jan Sandanski (1972); 13s. Dume Gruev (1971).

669 Gymnast with Ball

1972. World Gymnastics Championships, Havana (Cuba). Multicoloured.

2142		13s. Type **669**	95	35
2143		18s. Gymnast with hoop	1·40	65

MS2144 61×74 mm. 70s. Team with hoops. Imperf 4·75 4·50

1972. Paintings in Bulgarian National Gallery (2nd series). As T **656** but horiz. Multicoloured.

2145	1s. *Melnik* (Petur Mladenov)	20	15
2146	2s. *Ploughman* (Pencho Georgiev)	20	15
2147	3s. *By the Death-bed* (Aleksandur Zhendov)	30	20
2148	13s. *Family* (Vladimir Dimitrov)	1·20	35
2149	20s. *Family* (Neuko Balkanski)	1·50	45
2150	40s. *Father Paisii* (Koyu Denchev)	1·70	55

670 Bulgarian Worker

1972. Seventh Bulgarian Trade Unions Congress.

2151	**670**	13s. multicoloured	65	20

671 *Singing Harvesters*

1972. 90th Birth Anniv of Vladimir Dimitrov, the Master (painter). Multicoloured.

2152	1s. Type **671**	20	15
2153	2s. *Farm Worker*	20	15
2154	3s. *Women Cultivators* (horiz)	30	15
2155	13s. *Peasant Girl* (horiz)	45	20
2156	20s. *My Mother*	1·40	90
2157	40s. Self-portrait	1·90	1·30

672 Heart and Tree Emblem

1972. World Heart Month.

2158	**672**	13s. multicoloured	1·40	80

673 St. Mark's Cathedral

1972. UNESCO "Save Venice" Campaign.

2159	**673**	2s. green, turquoise & bl	30	20
2160	-	13s. brown, violet & grn	1·20	55

DESIGN: 13s. Doge's Palace.

674 Dimitrov at Typesetting Desk

1972. 90th Birth Anniv of Georgi Dimitrov (statesman). Multicoloured.

2161	1s. Type **674**	20	15
2162	2s. Dimitrov leading uprising of 1923	20	15
2163	3s. Dimitrov at Leipzig Trial	20	15
2164	5s. Dimitrov addressing workers	20	15
2165	13s. Dimitrov with Bulgarian crowd	35	35
2166	18s. Addressing young people	45	45
2167	28s. Dimitrov with children	95	65
2168	40s. Dimitrov's mausoleum	1·90	1·00
2169	80s. Portrait head (green and gold)	5·50	2·10

MS2170 87×84 mm. As No. 2169, but centre in red and gold. Imperf 8·25 7·75

2173	80s. As No. 2169	11·00	11·00

No. 2173 has the centre in red and gold, and is imperforate.

675 "Lamp of Learning" and Quotation

1972. 250th Birth Anniv of Father Paisii Khilendurski (historian).

2171	**675**	2s. brown, green & gold	20	10
2172	-	13s. brown, grn & gold	1·20	45

DESIGN: 13s. Paisii writing.

676 Canoeing

1972. Olympic Games, Munich. Multicoloured.

2174	1s. Type **676**	20	15
2175	2s. Gymnastics	20	15
2176	3s. Swimming	20	15
2177	13s. Volleyball	45	35
2178	18s. Hurdling	95	55
2179	40s. Wrestling	1·90	1·10

MS2180 64×60 mm. 80s. Running track and sports. Imperf 4·75 4·50

677 Angel Kunchev

1972. Death Cent of Angel Kunchev (patriot).

2181	**677**	2s. mauve, gold & purple	20	15

678 "Golden Sands"

1972. Black Sea Resorts. Hotels. Multicoloured.

2182	1s. Type **678**	20	15
2183	2s. Druzhba	20	15
2184	3s. "Sunny Beach"	20	15
2185	13s. Primorsko	65	20
2186	28s. Rusalka	1·20	45
2187	40s. Albena	1·40	55

679 Canoeing (Bronze Medal)

1972. Bulgarian Medal Winners, Olympic Games, Munich. Multicoloured.

2188	1s. Type **679**	20	15
2189	2s. Long jumping (Silver Medal)	20	15
2190	3s. Boxing (Gold Medal)	20	15
2191	18s. Wrestling (Gold Medal)	1·40	45
2192	40s. Weightlifting (Gold Medal)	1·70	90

680 Subi Dimitrov

1972. Resistance Heroes. Multicoloured.

2193	1s. Type **680**	10	10
2194	2s. Tsvyatko Radoinov	10	10
2195	3s. Iordan Lyutibrodski	10	10
2196	5s. Mito Ganev	30	15
2197	13s. Nedelcho Nikolov	95	35

681 Commemorative Text

1972. 50th Anniv of U.S.S.R.

2198	**681**	13s. red, yellow & gold	75	35

682 *Lilium rhodopaeum*

1972. Protected Flowers. Multicoloured.

2199	1s. Type **682**	20	15
2200	2s. Marsh gentian	20	15
2201	3s. Sea lily	20	15
2202	4s. Globe flower	30	20
2203	18s. *Primula frondosa*	95	45
2204	23s. Pale pasque flower	1·40	65
2205	40s. "*Fritillaria stribrnyi*	1·90	1·00

СВЕТОВЕН ПЪРВЕНЕЦ
(683)

1972. "Bulgaria, World Weightlifting Champions". No. 2192 optd with T 683.

2206	40s. multicoloured	2·30	1·10

684 Dobri Chintulov

1972. 150th Birth Anniv of Dobri Chintulov (poet).

2207	**684**	2s. multicoloured	35	20

685 Forehead Ornament (19th-century)

1972. Antique Ornaments.

2208	**685**	1s. black and brown	20	15
2209	-	2s. black and green	20	15
2210	-	3s. black and blue	20	15
2211	-	8s. black and red	45	20
2212	-	23s. black and brown	1·20	55
2213	-	40s. black and violet	1·90	1·30

DESIGNS: 2s. Belt-buckle (19th-century); 3s. Amulet (18th-century); 8s. Pendant (18th-century); 23s. Earrings (14th-century); 40s. Necklace (18th-century).

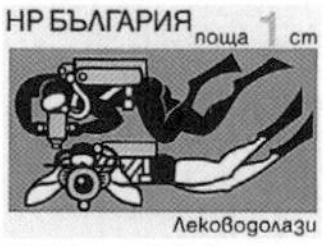

686 Divers with Cameras

1973. Underwater Research in the Black Sea.

2214	**686**	1s. black, yellow & blue	20	20
2215	-	2s. black, yellow & blue	20	20
2216	-	18s. black, yellow & blue	95	65
2217	-	40s. black, yellow & blue	1·90	80

MS2218 118×98 mm. 20s. ×4. Designs as Nos. 2214/17, but background colours changed (sold at 1l.) 8·75 8·50

DESIGNS—HORIZ: 2s. Divers with underwater research vessel "*Shelf 1*. VERT: 18s. Diver and *NIV 100* diving bell; 40s. Lifting balloon.

687 *The Hanging of Vasil Levski* (Boris Angelushev)

1973. Death Cent of Vasil Levski (patriot).

2219	**687**	2s. green and red	20	10
2220	-	20s. brown, cream & grn	1·70	80

DESIGN: 20s. "Vasil Levski" (Georgi Danchov).

688 Elhovo Mask

1973. Kukeris' Festival Masks. Multicoloured.

2221	1a. Type **688**	20	15
2222	2s. Breznik	20	15
2223	3s. Khisar	20	15
2224	13s. Radomir	65	35
2225	20s. Karnobat	95	65
2226	40s. Pernik	4·75	4·25

689 Copernicus

1973. 500th Birth Anniv of Copernicus.

2227	**689**	28s. purple, black & brn	2·30	1·60

1973. "Visit Bulgaria by Air". No. **MS**2072 surch with various airline emblems and new sheet value.

MS2228 137×131 mm. Nos. 2067/70 surch with new sheet value 1l. 30·00 30·00

690 Vietnamese "Girl"

1973. Vietnam Peace Treaty.

2229	**690**	18s. multicoloured	75	55

1973. "IBRA 73" Stamp Exhibition, Munich. No. MS1907 optd with **IBRA** and Olympic symbols in green.

MS2230 78×72 mm. 1l. multicoloured £140 £140

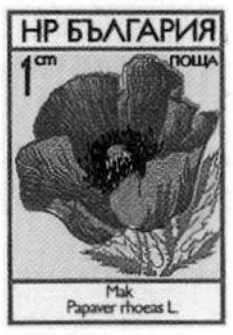

691 Common Poppy

1973. Wild Flowers. Multicoloured.

2231	1s. Type **691**	20	15
2232	2s. Ox-eye daisy	20	15
2233	3s. Peony	20	15
2234	13s. Cornflower	65	35
2235	18s. Corn cockle	6·50	4·50
2236	28s. Meadow buttercup	1·90	1·20

692 C. Botev (after T. Todorov)

1973. 125th Birth Anniv of Khristo Botev (poet and revolutionary).

2237	**692**	2s. yellow, brown & grn	20	15
2238	**692**	18s. grn, lt grn & bronze	1·40	1·10

693 Asen Khalachev and Insurgents

1973. 50th Anniv of June Uprising.

2239	**693**	1s. black, red and gold	10	10
2240	-	2s. black, orange & gold	10	10

DESIGN: 2s. *Wounded Worker* (illustration by Boris Angelushev to the poem "September" by Geo Milev).

694 Stamboliiski (from sculpture by A. Nikolov)

1973. 50th Death Anniv of Aleksandur Stamboliiski (Prime Minister 1919–23).

2241	**694**	18s. lt brn, brn & orge	65	55
2242	**694**	18s. orange	5·00	4·25

695 Muskrat

1973. Bulgarian Fauna. Multicoloured.

2243	1s. Type **695**	20	15
2244	2s. Racoon-dog	20	15
2245	3s. Mouflon (vert)	20	15
2246	12s. Fallow deer (vert)	65	45
2247	18s. European bison	1·90	1·10
2248	40s. Elk	6·50	4·25

696 Turnovo

1973. Air. Tourism. Views of Bulgarian Towns and Cities. Multicoloured.

2249	2s. Type **696**	20	15
2250	13s. Rusalka	65	25
2251	20s. Plovdiv	3·75	3·25
2252	28s. Sofia	95	85

697 Insurgents on the March (Boris Angelushev)

1973. 50th Anniv of September Uprising.

2253	**697**	2s. multicoloured	20	15
2254	-	5s. violet, pink & red	30	20
2255	-	13s. multicoloured	65	35
2256	-	18s. olive, cream & red	1·40	1·10

DESIGNS—HORIZ: 5s. *Armed Train* (Boris Angelushev). VERT: 13s. Patriotic poster by N. Mirchev. HORIZ: 18s. Georgi Dimitrov and Vasil Kolarov.

698 Congress Emblem

1973. Eight World Trade Union Congress, Varna.

2257	**698**	2s. multicoloured	20	20

699 "Sun" Emblem and Olympic Rings

1973. Olympic Congress, Varna. Multicoloured.

2258	13s. Type **699**	1·90	75
2259	28s. Lion Emblem of Bulgarian Olympic Committee (vert)	2·30	1·60
MS2260	61×77 mm. 80s. Footballers (40×25 mm)	6·00	5·50

700 *Prince Kaloyan*

1973. Fresco Portraits, Boyana Church. Multicoloured.

2261	1s. Type **700**	20	15
2262	2s. *Desislava*	20	15
2263	3s. *Saint*	30	20
2264	5s. *St. Eustratius*	55	25
2265	10s. *Tsar Constantine-Asen*	95	55
2266	13s. *Deacon Laurentius*	1·10	65
2267	18s. *Virgin Mary*	1·30	85
2268	20s. *St. Ephraim*	1·50	1·10
2269	28s. *Jesus Christ*	4·75	1·60
MS2270	56×76 mm. 80s. *Scribes*. Imperf	8·75	8·75

701 Smirnenski and Cavalry Charge

1973. 75th Birth Anniv of Khristo Smirnenski (poet and revolutionary).

2271	**701**	1s. blue, red and gold	20	10
2272	**701**	2s. blue, red and gold	45	20

702 Human Rights Emblem

1973. 25th Anniv of Declaration of Human Rights.

2273	**702**	13s. gold, red and blue	65	55

703 Tsar Todor Svetoslav meeting the Byzantine Embassy, 1307

1973. Bulgarian History. Multicoloured.

2274	1s. Type **703**	20	15
2275	2s. Tsar Mikhail Shishman in battle against Byzantines, 1328	20	15
2276	3s. Battle of Rosokastro, 1332 and Tsar Ivan Aleksandur	20	15
2277	4s. Defence of Turnovo, 1393 and Patriarch Evtimii	20	15
2278	5s. Tsar Ivan Shisman's attack on the Turks	30	20
2279	13s. Momchil attacks Turkish ships at Umur, 1344	65	35
2280	18s. Meeting of Tsar Ivan Sratsimir and Crusaders, 1396	95	45
2281	28s. Embassy of Empress Anne of Savoy meets Boyars Balik, Teodor and Dobrotitsa	2·30	1·60

704 "Finn" One-man Dinghy

1973. Sailing. Various Yachts. Multicoloured.

2282	1s. Type **704**	20	15
2283	2s. *Flying Dutchman* two-man dinghy	20	15
2284	3s. *Soling* yacht	20	15
2285	13s. *Tempest* dinghy	65	35
2286	20s. *470* two-man dinghy	95	65
2287	40s. *Tornado* catamaran	4·75	4·25

705 *Balchik* (Bercho Obreshkov)

1973. 25th Anniv of National Art Gallery, Sofia and 150th Birth Anniv of Stanislav Dospevski (painter). Multicoloured.

2288	1s. Type **705**	20	20
2289	2s. *Mother and Child* (Stryan Venev)	20	20
2290	3s. *Rest* (Tsenko Boyadzhiev)	20	20
2291	13s. *Vase with Flowers* (Siruk Skitnik) (vert)	75	35
2292	18s. *Mary Kuneva* (Iliya Petrov) (vert)	95	45
2293	40s. *Winter in Plovdiv* (Zlatyn Boyadzhiev) (vert)	4·25	3·75
MS2294	100×95 mm. 50s. *Domnika Lambreva* (S. Dospevski) (vert); 50s. *Self-portrait* (S. Dospevski) (vert)	6·00	4·25

706 Footballers and Emblem

1973. World Cup Football Championship, Munich (1974). Sheet 62×94 mm.

MS2295	**706** 28s. multicoloured (sold at 1l.)	6·50	6·50

707 Old Testament Scene (Wood-carving)

1974. Wood-Carvings from Rozhen Monastery.

2296	**707**	1s. dk brn, cream & brn	20	15
2297	-	2s. dk brn, cream & brn	20	15
2298	-	3s. dk brn, cream & brn	20	15
2299	-	5s. olive, cream & green	30	15
2300	-	8s. olive, cream & green	35	20
2301	-	13s. brown, cream and chestnut	55	40
2302	-	28s. brown, cream and chestnut	1·10	65

DESIGNS: Nos. 2296/8, *Passover Table*; 2299/2300, *Abraham and the Angel*; 2301/2, *The Expulsion from Eden*.

Nos. 2296/8, 2299/300 and 2301/2 form three composite designs.

708 *Lenin* (N. Mirchev)

1974. 50th Death Anniv of Lenin. Multicoloured.

2303	2s. Type **708**	20	15
2304	18s. *Lenin with Workers* (W. A. Serov)	95	65

709 *Blagoev addressing Meeting* (G. Kovachev)

1974. 50th Death Anniv of D. Blagoev (founder of Bulgarian Social Democratic Party).

2305	**709**	2s. multicoloured	20	15

710 Sheep

1974. Domestic Animals.

2306	**710**	1s. brown, buff & green	20	15
2307	-	2s. purple, violet & red	20	15
2308	-	3s. brown, pink & green	20	15
2309	-	5s. brown, buff & blue	20	15
2310	-	13s. black, blue and brown	1·10	35
2311	-	20s. brown, pink & blue	3·00	1·80

DESIGNS: 2s. Goat; 3s. Pig; 5s. Cow; 13s. Buffalo; 20s. Horse.

711 Social Economic Integration Emblem

1974. 25th Anniv of Council for Mutual Economic Aid.

2312	**711**	13s. multicoloured	75	55

712 Footballers

1974. World Cup Football Championship.

2313	**712**	1s. multicoloured	20	15
2314	-	2s. multicoloured	20	15
2315	-	3s. multicoloured	20	15
2316	-	13s. multicoloured	55	20
2317	-	28s. multicoloured	95	55
2318	-	40s. multicoloured	2·30	1·60
MS2319		66×78 mm. 1l. multicoloured (55×30 mm)	4·75	4·25

DESIGNS: Nos. 2314/19, Various designs similar to Type **712**.

713 Folk-singers

1974. Amateur Arts and Sports Festival. Multicoloured.

2320	1s. Type **713**	20	15
2321	2s. Folk-dancers	20	15
2322	3s. Piper and drummer	20	15
2323	5s. Wrestling	20	15
2324	13s. Athletics	95	85
2325	18s. Gymnastics	1·10	55

714 *Cosmic Research* (Penko Barnbov)

1974. "Mladost '74" Youth Stamp Exhibition, Sofia. Multicoloured.

2326	1s. Type **714**	15	10
2327	2s. *Salt Production* (Mariana Bliznakaa)	20	10
2328	3s. *Fire-dancer* (Detelina Lalova)	55	10
2329	28s. *Friendship Train* (Vanya Boyanova)	2·75	2·40
MS2330	70×70 mm. 60s. *Spring* (Vladimir Kunchev) (40×40 mm)	4·25	4·25

715 Motor-cars

1974. World Automobile Federation's Spring Congress, Sofia.

2331	**715**	13s. multicoloured	65	45

716 Period Architecture

1974. UNESCO Executive Council's 94th Session, Varna.

2332	**716**	18s. multicoloured	65	45

717 Chinese Aster

1974. Bulgarian Flowers. Multicoloured.

2333	1s. Type **717**	20	20
2334	2s. Mallow	20	20
2335	3s. Columbine	20	20
2336	18s. Tulip	95	35
2337	20s. Marigold	1·10	45
2338	28s. Pansy	2·75	1·80
MS2339	80×60 mm. 80s. Gaillarde (44×33 mm)	3·75	3·25

718 19th Century Post-boy

1974. Centenary of UPU.

2340	**718**	2s. violet & blk on orge	20	15
2341	-	18s. green & blk on orge	95	45
MS2342		80×58 mm. 28s. blue and orange (sold at 80st.)	3·25	3·25

DESIGN: 18s. First Bulgarian mail-coach; 20s. UPU emblem.

719 Young Pioneer and Komsomol Girl

1974. 30th Anniv of Dimitrov's Septembrist Pioneers Organization. Multicoloured.

2343	1s. Type **719**	15	10
2344	2s. Pioneer with doves	15	10
MS2345	60×84 mm. 60s. Emblem with portrait of Dimitrov (34×44 mm)	2·50	2·20

720 Communist Soldiers with Flag

1974. 30th Anniv of Fatherland Front Government. Multicoloured.

2346	1s. Type **720**	20	15
2347	2s. "Soviet Liberators"	20	15
2348	5s. "Industrialisation"	20	15
2349	13s. "Modern Agriculture"	55	20
2350	18s. "Science and Technology"	1·00	65

721 Stockholm and Emblems

1974. "Stockholm '74" International Stamp Exhibition. Sheet 65×72 mm.

MS2351	**721** 40s. blue, green and yellow	7·50	7·50

722 Gymnast on Beam

1974. 18th World Gymnastic Championships, Varna. Multicoloured.

2352	2s. Type **722**	15	10
2353	13s. Gymnast on horse	65	55

723 Doves on Script

1974. European Security and Co-operation Conference. Sheet 97×117 mm containing T **723** and similar vert designs.

MS2354	13s. yellow, blue and chestnut (T **723**); 13s. blue, mauve and chestnut (Map of Europe and script); 13s. green, blue and chestnut (Leaves on script); 13s. multicoloured (Commemorative text) (sold at 60s.)	3·50	3·50

724 Envelope with Arrow pointing to Postal Code

1974. Introduction of Postal Coding System (1 January 1975).

2355	**724**	2s. green, orange & blk	20	15

725 "Sourovachka" (twig decorated with coloured ribbons)

1974. New Year.

2356	**725**	2s. multicoloured	20	15

726 Icon of St. Theodor Stratilar

1974. Bulgarian History.

2357	**726**	1s. multicoloured	20	15
2358	-	2s. grey, mauve & black	20	15
2359	-	3s. grey, blue and black	20	15
2360	-	5s. grey, lilac and black	20	15
2361	-	8s. black, buff and brown	30	15
2362	-	13s. grey, green & black	45	20
2363	-	18s. black, gold & red	75	35
2364	-	28s. grey, blue & black	2·20	1·10

DESIGNS: 2s. Bronze medallion; 3s. Carved capital; 5s. Silver bowl of Sivin Jupan; 8s. Clay goblet; 13s. Lioness (torso); 18s. Gold tray; 28s. Double-headed eagle.

727 Apricot

1975. Fruit-tree Blossoms. Multicoloured.

2365	1s. Type **727**	20	15
2366	2s. Apple	20	15
2367	3s. Cherry	20	15
2368	19s. Pear	65	35
2369	28s. Peach	1·60	55

728 Peasant with Flag

1975. 75th Anniv of Bulgarian People's Agrarian Union. Sheet 104×95 mm containing T **728** and similar vert designs.

MS2370	2s. brown, orange and green; 5s. brown, orange and green; 13s. sepia, orange and green; 18s. chestnut, orange and green	1·60	1·60

DESIGNS: 5s. Rebels keeping watch during 1923 September uprising; 13s. Dancing; 18s. Woman harvesting fruit.

729 Spanish 6c. Stamp of 1850 and "Espana" Emblem

1975. "Espana 1975" International Stamp Exhibition, Madrid. Sheet 68×100 mm.

MS2371	**729** 40s. multicoloured	8·00	7·50

730 Star and Arrow

1975. 30th Anniv of "Victory in Europe" Day.

2372	**730**	2s. red, black & brown	20	15
2373	-	13s. black, brown & bl	75	35

DESIGNS: 13s. Peace dove and broken sword.

731 "Weights and Measures"

1975. Centenary of Metre Convention.

2374	**731**	13s. violet, black & silver	30	20

732 Tree and open Book

1975. 50th Anniv of Forestry School.

2375	**732**	2s. multicoloured	20	15

733 Michelangelo

1975. 500th Birth Anniv of Michelangelo.

2376	**733**	2s. purple and blue	20	15
2377	-	13s. violet and purple	55	35
2378	-	18s. brown and green	1·10	65
MS2379		70×84 mm. **733** 2s. green and red (sold at 60s.)	2·20	2·20

DESIGNS—HORIZ: Sculptures from Giuliano de Medici's tomb: 13s. *Night*; 18s. *Day*.

734 Festival Emblem

1975. Festival of Humour and Satire, Gabrovo.

2380	**734**	2s. multicoloured	20	15

735 Women's Head and Emblem

1975. International Women's Year.

2381	**735**	13s. multicoloured	45	20

736 Vasil and Sava Kokareshkov

1975. "Young Martyrs to Fascism".

2382	**736**	1s. black, green & gold	10	10
2383	-	2s. black, mauve & gold	10	10

2384	-	5s. black, red and gold	15	10
2385	-	13s. black, blue & gold	55	45

DESIGNS—HORIZ: 2s. Mitko Palauzov and Ivan Vasilev; 5s. Nikola Nakev and Stefcho Kraichev; 13s. Ivanka Pashkolouva and Detelina Mincheva.

737 *Mother feeding Child* (Jean Millet)

1975. World Graphics Exhibition, Sofia. Celebrated Drawings and Engravings. Multicoloured.

2386	1s. Type **737**	20	15
2387	2s. *Mourning a Dead Daughter* (Goya)	20	15
2388	3s. *The Reunion* (Iliya Beshkov)	20	15
2389	13s. *Seated Nude* (Auguste Renoir)	45	20
2390	20s. Man in a Fur Hat (Rembrandt)	65	55
2391	40s. *The Dream* (Horore Daumier) (horiz)	2·30	1·20
MS2392	80×95 mm. 1l. *Temptation* (Albrecht Durer) (37×53 mm)	3·75	3·25

738 Gabrovo Costume

1975. Women's Regional Costumes. Multicoloured.

2393	2s. Type **738**	20	15
2394	3s. Trun costume	20	15
2395	5s. Vidin costume	20	15
2396	13s. Goce Delcev costume	75	35
2397	18s. Ruse costume	1·70	55

739 *Bird* (manuscript illumination)

1975. Original Bulgarian Manuscripts. Multicoloured.

2398	1s. Type **739**	20	15
2399	2s. *Head*	20	15
2400	3s. Abstract design	20	15
2401	8s. *Pointing finger*	35	20
2402	13s. *Imaginary creature*	75	35
2403	18s. Abstract design	1·30	45

740 Ivan Vasov

1975. 125th Anniv of Ivan Vasov (writer). Multicoloured.

2404	2s. Type **740**	20	10
2405	13s. Vasov seated	55	20

741 "Soyuz" and Aleksei Leonov

1975. "Apollo"–"Soyuz" Space Link.

2406	**741**	13s. multicoloured	45	20
2407	-	18s. multicoloured	95	35
2408	-	28s. multicoloured	1·90	65
MS2409		76×84 mm. 1l. blue, grey and red	4·25	3·25

DESIGNS: 18s. "Apollo" and Thomas Stafford; 28s. The Link-up; 1l. "Apollo" and "Soyuz" after docking.

742 Ryukyu Sailing Boat, Map and Emblems

1975. International Exposition, Okinawa.

2410	**742**	13s. multicoloured	45	20

743 St. Cyril and St. Methodius

1975. "Balkanphila V" Stamp Exhibition, Sofia.

2411	**743**	2s. brown, lt brn & red	20	10
2412	-	13s. brown, lt brn & grn	55	20
MS2413		90×86 mm. 50s. sepia, brown and orange	2·20	2·20

DESIGNS—VERT: 13s. St. Constantine and St. Helene. HORIZ: 50s. Sophia Church, Sofia (53×43 mm.).

744 Footballer

1975. Eighth Inter-Toto (Football Pools) Congress, Varna.

2414	**744**	2s. multicoloured	20	15

745 Deaths-head Hawk Moth

1975. Hawk Moths. Multicoloured.

2415	1s. Type **745**	20	15
2416	2s. Oleander hawk moth	20	15
2417	3s. Eyed hawk moth	20	15
2418	10s. Mediterranean hawk moth	55	20
2419	13s. Elephant hawk moth	95	45
2420	18s. Broad-bordered bee hawk moth	1·90	75

746 UN Emblem

1975. 30th Anniv of UNO.

2421	**746**	13s. red, brown & black	45	20

747 Map of Europe on Peace Dove

1975. European Security and Co-operation Conference, Helsinki.

2422	**747**	18s. lilac, blue & yellow	85	85

748 D. Khristov

1975. Birth Cent of Dobri Khristov (composer).

2423	**748**	5s. brown, yellow & grn	20	10

749 Constantine's Rebellion against the Turks

1975. Bulgarian History. Multicoloured.

2424	1s. Type **749**	20	15
2425	2s. Vladislav III's campaign	20	15
2426	3s. Battle of Turnovo	20	15
2427	10s. Battle of Chiprovtsi	30	20
2428	13s. 17 th-century partisans	75	35
2429	18s. Return of banished peasants	1·00	55

750 "First Aid"

1975. 90th Anniv of Bulgarian Red Cross.

2430	**750**	2s. brown, black and red	15	10
2431	-	13s. green, black and red	55	20

DESIGN: 13s. "Peace and international Co-operation".

751 Ethnographical Museum, Plovdiv

1975. European Architectural Heritage Year.

2432	**751**	80s. brown, yellow & grn	2·75	2·75

752 Christmas Lanterns

1975. Christmas and New Year. Multicoloured.

2433	2s. Type **752**	20	10
2434	13s. Stylized peace dove	45	35

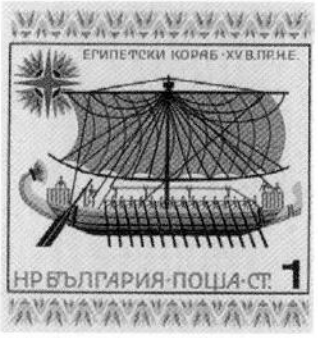

753 Egyptian Galley

1975. Historic Ships (1st series). Multicoloured.

2435	1s. Type **753**	10	10
2436	2s. Phoenician galley	10	10
2437	3s. Greek trireme	10	10
2438	5s. Roman galley	20	10
2439	13s. *Mora* (Norman ship)	55	35
2440	18s. Venetian galley	1·10	55

See also Nos. 2597/2602, 2864/9, 3286/91 and 3372/7.

754 Modern Articulated Tramcar

1976. 75th Anniv of Sofia Tramways. Multicoloured.

2441	2s. Type **754**	20	10
2442	13s. Early 20th-century tramcar	85	40

755 Skiing

1976. Winter Olympic Games, Innsbruck. Multicoloured.

2443	1s. Type **755**	20	15
2444	2s. Cross-country skiing (vert)	20	15
2445	2s. Ski jumping	20	15
2446	13s. Biathlon (vert)	55	35
2447	18s. Ice hockey (vert)	65	55
2448	18s. Speed skating (vert)	1·90	75
MS2449	70×80 mm. 80s. Ice skating (pairs) (30×55 mm)	3·25	2·75

756 Stylized Bird

1976. 11th Bulgarian Communists Party Congress. Multicoloured.

2450	2s. Type **756**	10	10
2451	5s. "1956–1976, Fulfilment of the Five Year Plans"	20	15
2452	13s. Hammer and Sickle	45	20
MS2453	55×65 mm. 50s. Georgi Dimitrov (Prime Minister and Party secretary-general, 1945–49) (33×43 mm)	1·90	1·60

757 Alexander Graham Bell and early Telephone

1976. Telephone Centenary.

2454	**757**	18s. lt brown, brn & pur	65	35

758 Mute Swan

1976. Waterfowl. Multicoloured.

2455	1s. Type **758**	20	15
2456	2s. Ruddy shelduck	20	15
2457	3s. Common shelduck	30	20
2458	5s. Garganey	1·10	35
2459	13s. Mallard	1·40	85
2460	18s. Red-crested pochard	3·75	2·75

759 Guerillas' Briefing

1976. Cent of April Uprising (1st issue). Multicoloured.

2461	1s. Type **759**	10	10
2462	2s. Peasants' briefing	10	10
2463	5s. Krishina, horse and guard	20	10
2464	13s. Rebels with cannon	55	35

See also Nos. 2529/33.

760 Kozlodui Atomic Energy Centre

1976. Modern Industrial Installations.

2465	**760**	5s. green	20	15
2466	-	8s. red	30	20
2467	-	10s. green	45	25
2468	-	13s. violet	55	30
2469	-	20s. green	75	35

DESIGNS: 8s. Bobaudol plant; 10s. Sviloza chemical works; 13s. Devaya chemical works; 20s. Sestvitro dam.

761 Guard with Patrol-dog

1976. 30th Anniv of Frontier Guards. Multicoloured.

2470	2s. Type **761**	20	15
2471	13s. Mounted guards	45	20

762 Worker with Spade

1976. 30th Anniv of Youth Brigades Movement.

2472	**762**	2s. multicoloured	20	15

763 Botev

1976. Death Cent of Khristo Botev (poet).

2473	**763**	13s. green and brown	65	35

764 "Martyrs of First Congress" (relief)

1976. 85th Anniv of 1st Bulgarian Social Democratic Party Congress, Buzludzha. Multicoloured.

2474	2s. Type **764**	15	10
2475	5s. Modern memorial, Buzludzha Peak	20	10

765 Dimitur Blagoev

1976. 120th Birth Anniv of Dimitur Blagoev (founder of Bulgarian Social Democratic Party).

2476	**765**	13s. black, red and gold	65	20

766 "Thematic Stamps"

1976. 12th Bulgarian Philatelic Federation Congress. Sheet 73×103 mm.

MS2477	**766** 50s. multicoloured	3·25	2·75

767 Children Playing

1976. Child Welfare.

2478	**767**	1s. multicoloured	20	15
2479	-	2s. multicoloured	20	15
2480	-	5s. multicoloured	20	15
2481	-	23s. multicoloured	95	55

DESIGNS: 2s. Girls with pram and boy on rocking horse; 5s. Playing ball; 23s. Dancing.

768 Wrestling

1976. Olympic Games, Montreal. Multicoloured.

2482	1s. Type **768**	20	15
2483	2s. Boxing (vert)	20	15
2484	3s. Weight-lifting (vert)	20	15
2485	13s. Canoeing (vert)	45	20
2486	18s. Gymnastics (vert)	65	35
2487	28s. Diving (vert)	1·00	55
2488	40s. Athletics (vert)	1·40	65
MS2489	70×80 mm. 1l. Weightlifting (vert)	3·25	3·25

769 Belt Buckle, Vidin

1976. Thracian Art (8th–4th Centuries B.C.). Multicoloured.

2490	1s. Type **769**	20	15
2491	2s. Brooch, Durzhanitsa	20	15
2492	3s. Mirror handle, Chukarka	20	15
2493	5s. Helmet cheek guard, Gurlo	20	15
2494	13s. Gold decoration, Orizovo	45	20
2495	18s. Decorated horse-harness, Brezovo	65	30
2496	20s. Greave, Mogilanska Mogila	85	35
2497	28s. Pendant, Bukovtsi	95	55

770 *Partisans at Night* (Petrov)

1976. Paintings by Iliya Petrov and Tsanko Lavrenov from the National Gallery. Multicoloured.

2498	2s. Type **770**	20	15
2499	5s. *Kurshum-Khan* (Lavrenov)	20	15
2500	13s. *Seated Woman* (Petrov)	45	20
2501	18s. *Boy seated in chair* (Petrov) (vert)	95	35
2502	28s. *Old Plovdiv* (Lavrenov) (vert)	1·10	45
MS2503	60×82 mm. 80s. *Self-portrait* (Petrov) (vert)	2·75	2·75

771 Weightlifting

1976. Gold Medal Winners, Montreal Olympic Games. Sheet 98×116 mm containing vert designs as T **771**, each with medal in red and gold.

MS2504	25s. yellow (T **771**); 25s. blue (rowing); 25s. green (running); 25s. red (wrestling)	3·25	3·25

772 Fish on line

1976. World Sports Fishing Congress, Varna.

2505	**772**	5s. multicoloured	30	20

773 *The Pianist*

1976. 75th Birth Anniv of Alex Jhendov (caricaturist).

2506	**773**	2s. dp grn, cream & grn	10	10
2507	-	5s. dp violet, vio & lilac	30	15
2508	-	13s. black, pink & red	45	20

DESIGNS: 5s. *Trick or Treat*; 13s. *The Leader*.

774 St. Theodor

1976. Zemen Monastery. Frescoes. Multicoloured.

2509	2s. Type **774**	20	15
2510	3s. St. Paul and Apostle	20	15
2511	5s. St. Joachim	30	15
2512	13s. Prophet Melchisadek	55	20
2513	19s. St. Porphyrus	75	35
2514	28s. Queen Doya	95	45
MS2515	60×76 mm. 1l. Holy Communion	3·25	3·25

775 Legal Document

1976. 25th Anniv of State Archives.

2516	**775**	5s. multicoloured	30	20

776 Horse Chestnut

1976. Plants. Multicoloured.

2517	1s. Type **776**	20	15
2518	2s. Shrubby cinquefoil	20	15
2519	5s. Holly	20	15
2520	8s. Yew	30	20
2521	13s. *Daphne pontica*	45	35
2522	23s. Judas tree	1·20	55

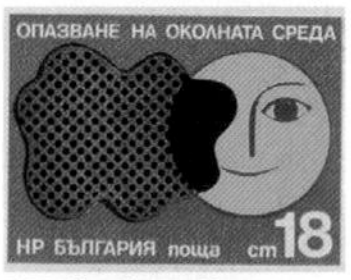

777 Cloud over Sun

1976. Protection of the Environment. Multicoloured.

2523	2s. Cloud over tree	20	15
2524	18s. Type **777**	65	35

778 Dimitur Polyanov

1976. Birth Cent of Dimitur Polyanov (poet).

2525	**778**	2s. lilac and orange	20	15

779 Congress Emblem

1976. 33rd Bulgarian People's Agrarian Union Congress. Multicoloured.

2526	2s. Type **779**	20	10
2527	13s. Flags	55	35

780 Warrior with Horses (vase painting)

1976. 30th Anniv of United Nations Educational Scientific and Cultural Organization. Sheet 71×81 mm.

MS2528	**780** 50s. multicoloured	2·75	2·75

781 *Khristo Botev* (Zlatyu Boyadzhiev)

1976. Centenary of April Uprising (2nd issue). Multicoloured.

2529	1s. Type **781**	20	15
2530	2s. *Partisan carrying Cherrywood Cannon* (Iliya Petrov)	20	15
2531	3s. *Necklace of Immortality* (Dechko Uzunov)	20	15
2532	13s. *April 1876* (Georgi Popov)	45	20
2533	18s. *Partisans* (Stoyan Venev)	75	45
MS2534	45×82 mm. 60s. *The Oath* (Svetlin Rusev)	2·20	2·20

782 Tobacco Workers

1976. 70th Birth Anniv of Veselin Staikov (artist). Multicoloured.

2535	1s. Type **782**	10	10
2536	2s. *Melnik*	15	10
2537	13s. *Boat Builders*	55	25

783 "Snowflake"

1976. New Year.

2538	**783**	2s. multicoloured	20	10

784 Zakhari Stojanov

1976. 125th Birth Anniv of Zakhari Stojanov (writer).

2539	**784**	2s. brown, red and gold	20	10

785 Bronze Coin of Septimus Severus

1977. Roman Coins struck in Serdica. Multicoloured.

2540	1s. Type **785**	20	15
2541	2s. Bronze coin of Caracalla	20	15
2542	13s. Bronze coin of Caracalla (diff.)	30	20
2543	18s. Bronze coin of Caracalla (diff.)	55	35
2544	23s. Copper coin of Diocletian	95	55

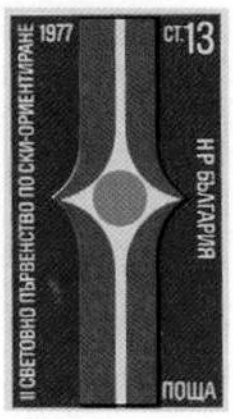

786 Championships Emblem

1977. World Ski-orienteering Championships.

2545	**786**	13s. blue, red & ultram	55	20

787 Congress Emblem

1977. Fifth Congress of Bulgarian Tourist Associations.

2546	**787**	2s. multicoloured	20	10

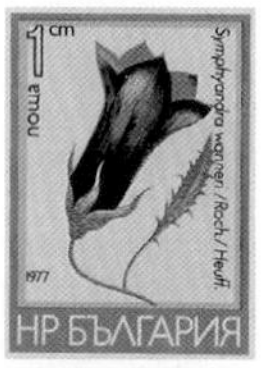

788 "Symphyandra wanneri"

1977. Mountain Flowers. Multicoloured.

2547	1s. Type **788**	20	15
2548	2s. *Petcovia orphanidea*	20	15
2549	3s. *Campanula lanatre*	20	15
2550	13s. *Campanula scutellata*	55	35
2551	43s. Nettle-leaved bellflower	1·90	75

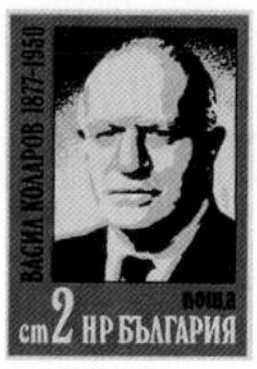

789 V. Kolarov

1977. Birth Centenary of Vasil Kolarov (Prime Minister 1949–50).

2552	**789**	2s. grey, black & blue	20	10

790 Congress Emblem

1977. Eighth Bulgarian Trade Unions Congress.

2553	**790**	2s. multicoloured	20	10

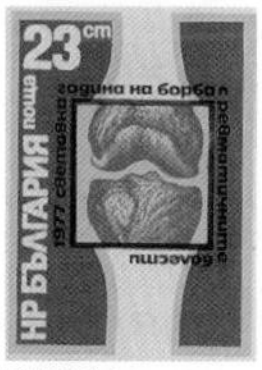

791 Joint

1977. World Rheumatism Year.

2554	**791**	23s. multicoloured	95	55

792 Wrestling

1977. World University Games, Sofia. Multicoloured.

2555	2s. Type **792**	20	20
2556	13s. Running	45	25
2557	23s. Handball	85	45
2558	43s. Gymnastics	1·40	85

793 Ivan Vazov National Theatre

1977. Buildings in Sofia. Pale brown backgrounds.

2559	**793**	12s. red	35	20
2560	-	13s. brown	45	25
2561	-	23s. blue	75	35
2562	-	30s. green	1·10	45
2563	-	80s. violet	1·90	1·20
2564	-	1l. brown	2·40	1·50

DESIGNS: 13s. Party Building; 23s. People's Army Building; 30s. Clement of Ohrid University; 80s. National Art Gallery; 1l. National Assembly Building.

794 Congress Emblem

1977. 13th Dimitrov Communist Youth League Congress.

2565	**794**	2s. red, green and gold	20	10

795 *St. Nicholas* Nesebur

1977. Bulgarian Icons. Multicoloured.

2566	1s. Type **795**	20	15
2567	2s. *Old Testament Trinity*, Sofia	20	15
2568	3s. *The Royal Gates*, Veliko Turnovo	20	15
2569	5s. *Deisis*, Nesebur	20	15
2570	13s. *St. Nicholas*, Elena	45	20
2571	23s. *The Presentation of the Blessed Virgin*, Rila Monastery	75	35
2572	35s. *The Virgin Mary with Infant*, Varna	1·10	75
2573	40s. *St. Demetrius on Horseback*, Provadya	2·40	1·10
MS2574	100×99 mm. 1l. *The Twelve Festival Days*, Rila Monastery. Imperf	4·25	3·25

796 Wolf

1977. Wild Animals. Multicoloured.

2575	1s. Type **796**	20	15
2576	2s. Red fox	20	15
2577	10s. Weasel	45	20
2578	13s. Wild cat	65	55
2579	23s. Golden jackal	1·90	1·10

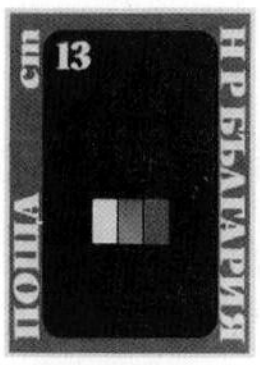

797 Congress Emblem

1977. Third Bulgarian Culture Congress.

2580	**797**	13s. multicoloured	45	20

798 *Crafty Peter riding a Donkey* (drawing by Iliya Beshkov)

1977. 11th Festival of Humour and Satire, Gabrovo.

2581	**798**	2s. multicoloured	20	10

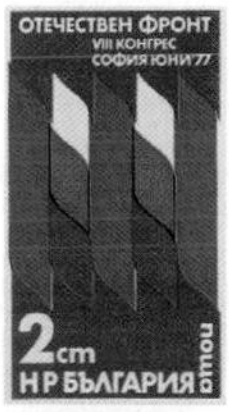

799 Congress Emblem

1977. Eighth Congress of the Popular Front, Sofia.

2582	**799**	2s. multicoloured	20	10

800 Newspaper Masthead

1977. Centenary of Bulgarian Daily Press.

2583	**800**	2s. multicoloured	20	10

801 St. Cyril

1977. 1150th Birth Anniv of St. Cyril. Sheet 106×87 mm.

MS2584	**801**	1l. multicoloured	3·75	3·75

802 Conference Emblem

1977. International Writers Conference, Sofia.

2585	**802**	23s. blue, lt blue & grn	1·40	1·10

803 Map of Europe

1977. 21st Congress of European Organization for Quality Control, Varna.

2586	**803**	23s. multicoloured	95	55

804 Basketball

1977. Women's European Basketball Championships.

2587	**804**	23s. multicoloured	95	55

805 Weightlifter

1977. World Junior Weightlifting Championships.

2588	**805**	13s. multicoloured	45	20

806 Georgi Dimitrov

1977. 95th Birth Anniv of Georgi Dimitrov (statesman).

2589	**806**	13s. brown and red	65	35

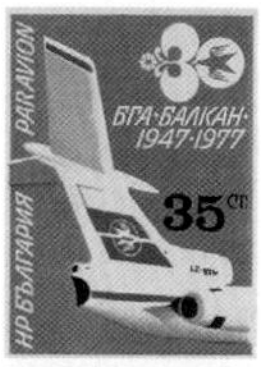

807 Tail Section of Tupolev Tu-154

1977. Air. 30th Anniv of Bulgarian Airline "Balkanair".

2590	**807**	35s. multicoloured	1·70	85

808 Games Emblem

1977. World University Games, Sofia (2nd issue). Sheet 84×76 mm.

MS2591	**808**	1l. multicoloured	3·25	2·75

809 T.V. Towers, Berlin and Sofia

1977. "Sozphilex 77" Stamp Exhibition, East Berlin.

2592	**809**	25s. blue and deep blue	95	55

810 Elin Pelin alias Dimitur Stoyanov (writer)

1977. Writers and Painters.

2593	**810**	2s. brown and gold	20	20
2594	-	5s. olive and gold	20	20
2595	-	13s. red and gold	35	25
2596	-	23s. blue and gold	1·10	55

DESIGNS: 5s. Peyu Yavorov (poet); 13s. Boris Angelushev (painter and illustrator); 23s. Iseno Todorov (painter).

1977. Historic Ships (2nd series). As T **753**. Multicoloured.

2597	1s. Hansa Kogge	20	15
2598	2s. *Santa Maria*	20	15
2599	3s. Drake's *Golden Hind*	20	15
2600	12s. Carrack *Santa Catherina*	40	20
2601	13s. *La Couronne* (French galleon)	45	25
2602	43s. Mediterranean galley	1·90	65

811 Women Canoeists

1977. World Canoe Championships.

2603	**811**	2s. blue and yellow	20	15
2604	-	23s. blue and turquoise	95	45

DESIGN: 23s. Men canoeists.

812 Balloon over Plovdiv

1977. Air. 85th Anniv "Panair". International Aviation Exhibition, Plovdiv.

2605	**812**	25s. orange, yell & brn	95	55

813 Presidents Zhivkov and Brezhnev

1977. Soviet–Bulgarian Friendship.

2606	**813**	18s. brown, red & gold	55	45

814 Conference Building

1977. 64th International Parliamentary Conference, Sofia.

2607	**814**	23s. green, pink and red	95	45

815 Newspaper Mastheads

1977. 50th Anniv of Official Newspaper "Rabotnichesko Delo" (Workers' Press).

2608	**815**	2s. red, green and grey	20	10

816 *The Union of Earth and Water*

1977. 400th Birth Anniv of Rubens. Multicoloured.

2609	13s. Type **816**	55	20
2610	23s. *Venus and Adonis* (detail)	1·10	1·10
2611	40s. *Amorous Shepherd* (detail)	2·20	1·60
MS2612	71×87 mm. 1l. *Portrait of a Chambermaid*	4·75	3·75

817 Cossack with Bulgarian Child (Angelushev)

1977. Centenary of Liberation from Turkey. (1978). Posters.

2613	**817**	2s. multicoloured	30	15
2614	-	13s. green, blue & red	45	20
2615	-	23s. blue, red & green	85	45
2616	-	25s. multicoloured	95	50

DESIGNS: 13s. Bugler (Cheklarov); 23s. Mars (god of war) and Russian soldiers (Petrov); 25s. Flag of Russian Imperial Army.

818 Albena, Black Sea

1977. Tourism.

2617	**818**	35s. blue, turq & brn	1·30	55
2618	-	43s. yellow, grn & blue	1·40	65

DESIGN: 43s. Rila Monastery.

819 Dr. Nikolai Pirogov (Russian surgeon)

1977. Cent of Dr. Pirogov's Visit to Bulgaria.

2619	**819**	13s. brown, buff & grn	45	35

820 Space walking

1977. Air. 20th Anniv of First Artificial Satellite. Multicoloured.

2620	12s. Type **820**	45	20
2621	25s. Space probe over Mars	95	45
2622	35s. Space probe "Venus-4" over Venus	1·40	55

821 Soviet Emblems and Decree

1977. 60th Anniv of Russian Revolution.

2623	**821**	2s. red, black & stone	30	20
2624	-	13s. red and purple	55	25
2625	-	23s. red and violet	1·00	35

DESIGNS: 13s. Lenin; 23s. "1977" as flame.

822 Diesel Train on Bridge

1977. 50th Anniv of Transport, Bridges and Highways Organization.

2626	**822**	13s. yellow, green & olive	75	55

1977. 150th Birth Anniv of Petko Ratshev Slaveikov (poet). As T **810**.

2627	8s. brown and gold	30	20

824 Decorative Initials of New Year Greeting

1977. New Year. Multicoloured.

2628	2s. Type **824**	20	10
2629	13s. "Fireworks"	45	15

825 Footballer

1978. World Cup Football Championship, Argentina. Multicoloured.

2630	13s. Type **825**	45	35
2631	23s. Shooting the ball	1·40	85
MS2632	77×61 mm. 50s. Tackle for ball	2·50	2·20

826 Baba Vida Fortress, Vidin

1977. Air. "The Danube – European River". Multicoloured.

2633	25s. Type **826**	75	55
2634	35s. Friendship Bridge	1·40	1·20

827 Television Mast, Moscow

1978. 20th Anniv of Organization of Socialist Postal Administrations (O.S.S.).

2635	**827**	13s. multicoloured	45	20

828 Shipka Monument

1978. Centenary of Liberation from Turkey (2nd issue). Sheet 55×73 mm.

MS2636	**828**	50s. multicoloured	1·60	1·60

829 Red Cross in Laurel Wreath

1978. Centenary of Bulgarian Red Cross.

2637	**829**	25s. red, brown & blue	95	55

830 "XXX" formed from Bulgarian and Russian National Colours

1978. 30th Anniv of Bulgarian–Soviet Friendship.

2638	**830**	2s. multicoloured	20	15

831 Leo Tolstoy (Russian writer)

1978. Famous Personalities.

2639	**831**	2s. green and yellow	30	15
2640	-	5s. brown and bistre	30	15
2641	-	13s. green and mauve	35	20
2642	-	23s. brown and grey	40	35
2643	-	25s. brown and green	45	40
2644	-	35s. violet and blue	1·40	55

DESIGNS: 5s. Fyodor Dostoevsky (Russian writer); 13s. Ivan Turgenev (Russian writer); 23s. Vassily Vereshchagin (Russian artist); 25s. Giuseppe Garibaldi (Italian patriot); 35s. Victor Hugo (French writer).

832 Nikolai Roerich (artist)

1978. Nikolai Roerich Exhibition, Sofia.

2645	**832**	8s. brown, green & red	45	20

833 Bulgarian Flag and Red Star

1978. Communist Party National Conference, Sofia.

2646	**833**	2s. multicoloured	20	10

834 Goddess

1978. "Philaserdica 79" International Stamp Exhibition (1st issue). Ancient Ceramics. Multicoloured.

2647	2s. Type **834**	20	15
2648	5s. Mask with beard	20	15
2649	13s. Decorated vase	45	20
2650	23s. Vase with scallop design	75	65
2651	35s. Head of Silenus	1·10	1·10
2652	53s. Cockerel	4·00	1·60

See also Nos. 2674/9, 2714/18, 2721/5 and 2753/4.

835 "Spirit of Nature"

1978. Birth Cent of Andrei Nikolov (sculptor).

2653	**835**	13s. blue, mauve & vio	45	20

836 Heart and Arrows

1978. World Hypertension Month.

2654	**836**	23s. red, orange & grey	95	45

837 "Kor Karoli" and Map of Route

1978. Georgi Georgiev's World Voyage.

2655	**837**	23s. blue, mauve & grn	1·90	85

838 Doves

1978. 11th World Youth and Students' Festival, Havana.

2656	**838**	13s. multicoloured	45	20

839 *Portrait of a Young Man* (Durer)

1978. Paintings. Multicoloured.

2657	13s. Type **839**	30	20
2658	23s. *Bathsheba at the Fountain* (Rubens)	45	35
2659	25s. *Signor de Moret* (Hans Holbein the Younger)	55	40
2660	35s. *Self portrait with Saskia* (Rembrandt)	75	45
2661	43s. *Lady in Mourning* (Tintoretto)	95	55
2662	60s. *Old Man with a Beard* (Rembrandt)	1·20	75
2663	80s. *Man in Armour* (Van Dyck)	2·75	1·80

840 *Fritillaria stribrnyi*

1978. Flowers. Multicoloured.

2664	1s. Type **840**	20	15
2665	2s. *Fritillaria drenovskyi*	20	15
2666	3s. *Lilium rhodopaeum*	20	15
2667	13s. *Tulipa urumoffii*	45	20
2668	23s. *Lilium jankae*	55	35
2669	43s. *Tulipa rhodopaea*	1·90	1·10

841 Varna

1978. 63rd Esperanto Congress, Varna.

2670	**841**	13s. orange, red & green	75	45

842 Delcev

1978. 75th Death Anniv of Goce Delcev (Macedonian revolutionary).

2671	**842**	13s. multicoloured	55	20

843 Freedom Fighters

1978. 75th Anniv of Ilinden-Preobrazhenie Rising.

2672	**843**	5s. black and red	20	10

844 *The Sleeping Venus*

1978. World Masters of Art. Sheet 71×71 mm. Imperf.

MS2673	**844**	1l. multicoloured	2·20	2·20

845 *Market* (Noiden Petkov)

1978. "Philaserdica 79" International Stamp Exhibition (2nd issue). Paintings of Sofia. Multicoloured.

2674	2s. Type **845**	20	20
2675	5s. *View of Sofia* (Euril Stoichev)	20	20
2676	13s. *View of Sofia* (Boris Ivanov)	30	20
2677	23s. *Tolbukhin Boulevard* (Nikola Tanev)	75	35
2678	35s. *National Theatre* (Nikola Petrov)	85	45
2679	53s. *Market* (Anton Mitov)	95	85
MS2679a	186×106 mm. Nos. 2674/9	7·00	7·00

846 Black Woodpecker

1978. Woodpeckers. Multicoloured.

2680	1s. Type **846**	20	15
2681	2s. Syrian woodpecker	20	15
2682	3s. Three-toed woodpecker	20	15
2683	13s. Middle-spotted woodpecker	95	55
2684	23s. Lesser spotted woodpecker	1·40	75
2685	43s. Green woodpecker	3·75	2·40

847 Ivan Vazov National Theatre, Sofia

1978. "Praga 78" and "Philaserdica 79" International Stamp Exhibitions. Sheet 153×110 mm containing T **847** and similar horiz designs. Multicoloured.

MS2686	(a) 40s. Type **847**; (b) 40s. Festival Hall, Sofia; (c) 40s. Charles Bridge, Prague; (d) 40s. Belvedere Palace, Prague	3·25	3·25

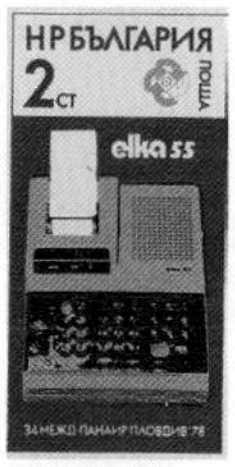

848 "Elka 55" Computer

1978. Plovdiv International Fair.

2687	**848**	2s. multicoloured	20	10

849 *September 1923* (Boris Angelushev)

1978. 55th Anniv of September Uprising.

2688	**849**	2s. red and brown	20	10

850 Khristo Danov

1978. 150th Birth Anniv of Khristo Danov (first Bulgarian publisher).

2689	**850**	2s. orange and lake	20	10

851 *The People of Vladaya* (Todor Panayotov)

1978. 60th Anniv of Vladaya Mutiny.

2690	**851**	2s. lilac, brown and red	20	10

852 Hands supporting Rainbow

1978. International Anti-apartheid Year.

2691	**852**	13s. multicoloured	45	20

853 Pipeline and Flags

1978. Inauguration of Orenburg–U.S.S.R. Natural Gas Pipeline.

2692	**853**	13s. multicoloured	45	20

854 Acrobats

1978. Third World Sports Acrobatics Championships, Sofia.

2693	**854**	13s. multicoloured	45	20

855 Salvador Allende

1978. 70th Birth Anniv of Salvador Allende (Chilean politician).

2694	**855**	13s. brown and red	45	20

856 Human Rights Emblem

1978. 30th Anniv of Declaration of Human Rights.

2695	**856**	23s. yellow, red & blue	95	55

857 *Levski and Matei Mitkaloto* (Kalina Taseva)

1978. History of Bulgaria. Paintings. Multicoloured.

2696	1s. Type **857**	20	15
2697	2s. *Give Strength to my Arm* (Zlatyu Boyadzhiev)	20	15
2698	3s. *Rumena Voevoda* (Nikola Mirchev) (horiz)	20	15
2699	13s. *Kolya Ficheto* (Elza Goeva)	45	35
2700	23s. *A Family of the National Revival Period* (Naiden Petkov)	1·00	65

858 Tourist Home, Plovdiv

1978. European Architectural Heritage. Multicoloured.

2701	43s. Type **858**	1·50	55
2702	43s. Tower of the Prince, Rila Monastery	1·50	55

859 *Geroi Plevny* and Route Map

1978. Opening of the Varna–Ilichovsk Ferry Service.

2703	**859**	13s. blue, red & green	45	35

860 Mosaic Bird (Santa Sofia Church)

1978. "Bulgaria 78" National Stamp Exhibition, Sofia.

2704	**860**	5s. multicoloured	35	20

861 Monument to St. Clement of Ohrid (university patron) (Lyubemir Dalcher)

1978. 90th Anniv of Sofia University.

2705	**861**	2s. lilac, black & green	20	10

862 Nikola Karastoyanov

1978. Birth Bicentenary of Nikola Karastoyanov (first Bulgarian printer).

2706	**862**	2s. brn, yell & chestnut	35	20

863 Initial from 13th Century Bible Manuscript

1978. Centenary of Cyril and Methodius People's Library. Multicoloured.

2707	2s. Type **863**	20	15
2708	13s. Monk writing (from a 1567 manuscript)	45	20
2709	23s. Decorated page from 16th-century manuscript Bible	85	45
MS2710	63×94 mm. 80s. Seated saint with attendant (from 13th century manuscript Bible)	2·20	2·20

864 Ballet Dancers

1978. 50th Anniv of Bulgarian Ballet.

2711	**864**	13s. green, mauve & lav	45	35

865 Tree of Birds

1978. New Year. Multicoloured.

2712	2s. Type **865**	20	10
2713	13s. Posthorn	30	15

866 1961 Communist Congress Stamp

1978. "Philaserdica 79" International Stamp Exhibition (3rd issue) and Bulgarian Stamp Centenary (1st issue).

2714	-	2s. red and green	20	15
2715	-	13s. claret and blue	20	15
2716	-	23s. green and mauve	30	20
2717	**866**	35s. grey and blue	95	45
2718	-	53s. green and red	1·70	65
MS2719 62×87 mm. 1l. black, yellow and green			2·20	2·20

DESIGNS—HORIZ: 2s. 1901 "Cherrywood Cannon" stamp; 13s. 1946 "New Republic" stamp; 23s. 1957 Canonisation of St. Cyril and St. Methodius stamp; 1l. First Bulgarian stamp. VERT: 53s. 1962 Dimitrov stamp.

See also Nos. 2721/5 and **MS**2755.

867 Council Building, Moscow and Flags

1979. 30th Anniv of Council of Mutual Economic Aid.

2720	**867**	13s. multicoloured	45	20

1979. "Philaserdica 79" Int Stamp Exn (4th issue) and Bulgarian Stamp Cent (2nd issue). As Nos. 2714/18 but inscr "1979" and colours changed.

2721	-	2s. red and blue	20	15
2722	-	13s. claret and green	45	20
2723	-	23s. green, yellow & red	55	35
2724	**866**	35s. grey and red	95	45
2725	-	53s. brown and violet	1·20	65

868 National Bank

1979. Centenary of Bulgarian National Bank.

2726	**868**	2s. grey and yellow	20	10

868a

1979. Coil stamps.

2726a	**868a**	2s. blue	10	10
2726b	**868a**	5s. red	20	10

The 5s. is as T **868a** but different pattern.

869 Stamboliiski

1979. Birth Centenary of Alexandur Stamboliiski (Prime Minister 1919–23).

2727	**869**	2s. brown and yellow	20	10

870 Child's Head as Flower

1979. International Year of the Child.

2728	**870**	23s. multicoloured	95	45

871 Profiles

1979. Eighth World Congress for the Deaf, Varna.

2729	**871**	13s. green and blue	45	20

872 "75" and Emblem

1979. 75th Anniv of Bulgarian Trade Unions.

2730	**872**	2s. green and orange	20	10

873 Soviet War Memorial

1979. Centenary of Sofia as Capital of Bulgaria. Sheet 106×105 mm containing T **873** and similar vert designs. Multicoloured.

MS2731 2s. Type **873**, 5s. Mother and child (sculpture); 13, 23, 25s. Bas-relief from monument to the Liberators of 1876	2·20	2·20

The 13, 23 and 25s. values form a composite design.

874 Rocket

1979. Soviet–Bulgarian Space Flight. Multicoloured.

2732	2s. Georgi Ivanov (horiz)	20	15
2733	12s. Type **874**	35	20
2734	13s. Nikolai Rukavishnikov and Ivanov (horiz)	75	25
2735	25s. Link-up with "Salyut" space station (horiz)	95	45
2736	35s. Capsule descending by parachute	1·10	55
MS2737 67×86 mm. 1l. Globe and orbiting space craft (horiz)		2·75	2·75

875 Carrier Pigeon and Tupolev Tu-154 Jet

1979. Centenary of Bulgarian Post and Telegraph Services. Multicoloured.

2738	2s. Type **875**	20	15
2739	5s. Old and new telephones	20	15
2740	13s. Morse key and teleprinter	45	20
2741	23s. Old radio transmitter and aerials	65	35
2742	35s. T.V. tower and satellite	95	45
MS2743 64×69 mm. 50s. Ground receiving station (38×28 mm)		2·75	2·75

876 Running

1979. Olympic Games. Moscow (1980) (1st issue). Athletics. Multicoloured.

2744	2s. Type **876**	30	25
2745	13s. Pole vault (horiz)	65	55
2746	25s. Discus	1·10	75
2747	35s. Hurdles (horiz)	1·40	1·10
2748	43s. High jump (horiz)	1·90	1·30
2749	1l. Long jump	2·75	2·20
MS2750 90×65 mm. 2l. Shot put		9·75	9·75

See also Nos. 2773/**MS**2779, 2803/**MS**2809, 2816/**MS**2822, 2834/**MS**2840 and 2851/**MS**2857.

877 Thracian Gold Leaf Collar

1979. 48th International Philatelic Federation Congress, Sofia. Sheet 77×86 mm.

MS2751 **877** 1l. multicoloured	4·50	4·50

878 First Bulgarian Stamp and 1975 European Security Conference Stamp

1979. "Philaserdica 79" International Exhibition, Sofia (5th issue). Sheet 63×61 mm.

MS2752 **878** 1l. multicoloured	7·50	7·50

879 Hotel Vitosha-New Otani

1979. "Philaserdica 79" International Stamp Exhibition, Sofia (5th issue) and Bulgaria Day.

2753	**879**	2s. pink and blue	20	10

880 *Good Morning, Little Brother* (illus by Kukuliev of folktale)

1979. "Philaserdica 79" International Stamp Exhibition, Sofia (6th issue) and Bulgarian–Russian Friendship Day.

2754	**880**	2s. multicoloured	20	10

881 First Bulgarian Stamp

1979. Centenary of First Bulgarian Stamp (3rd issue). Sheet 91×121 mm.

MS2755 **881** 5s. multicoloured	60·00	60·00

882 *Man on Donkey* (Boris Angelushev)

1979. 12th Festival of Humour and Satire, Grabovo.

2756	**882**	2s. multicoloured	20	15

883 *Four Women*

1979. 450th Death Anniv of Albrecht Durer (artist). Multicoloured.

2757	13s. Type **883**	20	20
2758	23s. *Three Peasants Talking*	55	35
2759	25s. *The Cook and his Wife*	75	45
2760	35s. *Portrait of Eobanus Hessus*	1·10	65
MS2761 80×81 mm. 80s. *Rhinoceros* (horiz). Imperf		2·20	2·20

884 Clocktower, Byala Cherkva

1979. Air. Clocktowers (1st series). Multicoloured.

2762	13s. Type **884**	35	20
2763	23s. Botevgrad	45	35
2764	25s. Pazardzhik	55	45
2765	35s. Gabrovo	65	65
2766	53s. Tryavna	1·40	1·10

See also Nos. 2891/5.

885 Petko Todorov (birth centenary)

1979. Bulgarian Writers.

2767	**885**	2s. black, brown & yell	25	20
2768	-	2s. green and yellow	25	20
2769	-	2s. red and yellow	25	20

DESIGNS: No. 2768, Dimitur Dimov (70th birth anniv); 2769, Stefan Kostov (birth cent).

886 Congress Emblem

1979. 18th Congress of International Theatrical Institute, Sofia.

2770	**886**	13s. cobalt, blue & black	35	20

887 House of Journalists, Varna

1979. 20th Anniv of House of Journalists (holiday home), Varna.

2771	**887**	8s. orange, black & blue	20	10

888 Children of Different Races

1979. "Banners for Peace" Children's Meeting, Sofia.

2772	**888**	2s. multicoloured	20	10

889 Parallel Bars

1979. Olympic Games, Moscow (1980) (2nd issue). Gymnastics. Multicoloured.

2773	2s. Type **889**	30	25
2774	13s. Horse exercise (horiz)	55	35
2775	25s. Rings exercise	75	55
2776	35s. Beam exercise	95	85
2777	43s. Uneven bars	1·40	1·20
2778	1l. Floor exercise	2·75	2·40
MS2779	65×88 mm. 2l. Horizontal bars	9·75	9·75

890 *Virgin and Child* (Nesebur)

1979. Icons of the Virgin and Child. Multicoloured.

2780	13s. Type **890**	45	20
2781	23s. Nesebur (diff)	55	35
2782	35s. Sozopol	65	45
2783	43s. Sozopol (diff)	75	65
2784	53s. Samokov	1·40	1·10

891 Anton Bezenshek

1979. Centenary of Bulgarian Stenography.

2785	**891**	2s. yellow and grey	20	10

892 Mountaineer

1979. 50th Anniv of Bulgarian Alpine Club.

2786	**892**	2s. multicoloured	20	10

893 Commemorative Inscription

1979. Centenary of Bulgarian Public Health Services.

2787	**893**	2s. black, silver & green	20	20

894 Rocket and Flowers

1979. 35th Anniv of Fatherland Front Government. Multicoloured.

2788	2s. Type **894**	10	10
2789	5s. Russian and Bulgarian flags	15	10
2790	13s. "35" in national colours	35	20

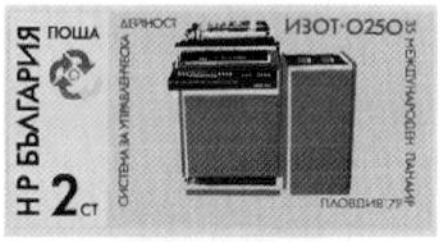

895 "IZOT–0250" Computer

1979. 35th Plovdiv Fair.

2791	**895**	2s. multicoloured	20	10

896 Games Emblem

1979. World University Games, Mexico.

2792	**896**	5s. red, yellow and blue	20	10

897 Footballer

1979. 50th Anniv of DFS Lokomotiv Football Team.

2793	**897**	2s. red and black	20	10

898 Lyuben Karavelov

1979. Death Centenary of Lyuben Karavelov (newspaper editor and President of Bulgarian Revolutionary Committee).

2794	**898**	2s. green and blue	20	10

899 Cross-country Skiing

1979. Winter Olympic Games, Lake Placid (1980).

2795	**899**	2s. red, purple and black	20	15
2796	-	13s. orange, blue & blk	35	20
2797	-	23s. turquoise, blue and black	65	35
2798	-	43s. purple, turq & blk	1·70	55
MS2799		68×77 mm. 1l. green, blue and black. Imperf	3·25	3·25

DESIGNS: 13s. Speed skating; 23s. Skiing; 43s. Luge; 1l. Skiing (different).

900 *Woman from Thrace*

1979. 80th Birth Anniv of Dechko Uzunov (artist). Multicoloured.

2800	12s. *Figure in Red*	35	15
2801	13s. Type **900**	35	20
2802	23s. *Composition II*	1·10	65

901 Canoeing (Canadian pairs)

1979. Olympic Games, Moscow (1980) (3rd issue). Water Sports. Multicoloured.

2803	2s. Type **901**	35	35
2804	13s. Swimming (freestyle)	65	55
2805	25s. Swimming (backstroke) (horiz)	1·10	75
2806	35s. Kayak (horiz)	1·40	1·10
2807	43s. Diving	1·90	1·30
2808	1l. Springboard diving	2·75	2·20
MS2809	64×88 mm. 2l. Water polo	9·75	9·75

902 Nikola Vaptsarov

1979. 70th Birth Anniv of Nikola Vaptsarov (writer).

2810	**902**	2s. pink and red	30	20

903 *Dawn in Plovdiv* (Ioan Leviev)

1979. History of Bulgaria. Paintings. Multicoloured.

2811	2s. *The First Socialists* (Boyan Petrov) (horiz)	20	15
2812	13s. *Dimitur Blagoev as Editor of "Rabotnik"* (Dimitur Gyvdzhenov) (horiz)	35	20
2813	25s. *Workers' Party March* (Stoyan Sotirov) (horiz)	75	45
2814	35s. Type **903**	1·10	85

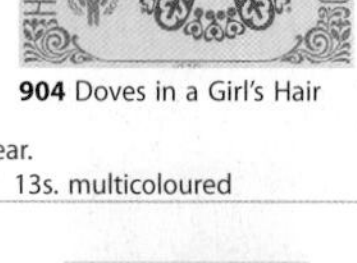

904 Doves in a Girl's Hair

1979. New Year.

2815	**904**	13s. multicoloured	35	20

905 Shooting

1979. Olympic Games, Moscow (1980) (4th issue). Multicoloured.

2816	2s. Type **905**	35	25
2817	13s. Judo (horiz)	65	55
2818	25s. Wrestling (horiz)	1·10	85
2819	35s. Archery	1·40	1·10
2820	43s. Fencing (horiz)	1·90	1·20
2821	1l. Fencing (different)	2·75	2·20
MS2822	65×89 mm. 2l. Boxing	9·75	9·75

906 Procession with Relics of Saints

1979. Frescoes of Saints Cyril and Methodius in St. Clement's Basilica, Rome. Multicoloured.

2823	2s. Type **906**	20	15
2824	13s. Cyril and Methodius received by Pope Adrian II	30	20
2825	23s. Burial of Cyril the Philosopher	55	35
2826	25s. St. Cyril	75	45
2827	35s. St. Methodius	1·10	65

907 Television Screen showing Emblem

1979. 25th Anniv of Bulgarian Television.

2828	**907**	5s. blue and deep blue	30	20

908 Puppet of Krali Marko (national hero)

1980. 50th Anniv of International Puppet Theatre Organization (UNIMA).

2829	**908**	2s. multicoloured	20	10

909 Thracian Rider (3rd-cent votive tablet)

1980. Centenary of National Archaeological Museum, Sofia.

2830	**909**	2s. brown, gold & purple	20	10
2831	-	13s. brown, gold & grn	35	20

DESIGN: 13s. Grave stele of Deines (5th–6th cent).

910 *Meeting of Lenin and Dimitrov* (Aleksandur Poplilov)

1980. 110th Birth Anniv of Lenin.

2832	**910**	13s. multicoloured	35	20

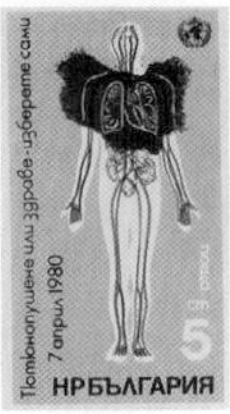

911 Diagram of Blood Circulation and Lungs obscured by Smoke

1980. World Health Day. Anti-smoking Campaign.

2833	**911**	5s. multicoloured	20	10

912 Basketball

1980. Olympic Games, Moscow (5th issue). Multicoloured.

2834	2s. Type **912**	35	25
2835	13s. Football	65	55
2836	25s. Hockey	1·10	75
2837	35s. Cycling	1·40	1·10
2838	43s. Handball	1·90	1·30
2839	1l. Volleyball	2·75	2·20
MS2840	66×90 mm. 2s. Weightlifting	9·75	9·75

913 Emblem, Cosmonauts and Space Station

1980. "Intercosmos" Space Programme. Sheet 111×102 mm.

MS2841 **913** 50s. multicoloured	2·20	2·20

914 Penyo Penev

1980. 50th Birth Anniv of Penyo Penev (poet).

2842	**914**	5s. brown, red & turq	30	20

915 Penny Black

1980. "London 1980" International Stamp Exhibition.

2843	**915**	25s. black and red	1·10	75

916 Dimitur Khv. Chorbadzhuski-Chudomir (self-portrait)

1980. 90th Birth Anniv of Dimitur Khv. Chorbadzhuski-Chudomir (artist).

2844	**916**	5s. pink, brown & turq	20	10
2845	-	13s. black, blue & turq	35	35

DESIGN: 13s. "Our People".

917 Nikolai Gyaurov

1980. 50th Birth Anniv of Nikolai Gyaurov (opera singer).

2846	**917**	5s. yellow, brown & grn	30	20

918 Soviet Soldiers raising Flag on Berlin Reichstag

1980. 35th Anniv of "Victory in Europe" Day.

2847	**918**	5s. gold, brown & black	20	10
2848	-	13s. gold, brown & black	35	20

DESIGN: 13s. Soviet Army memorial, Berlin–Treptow.

919 Open Book and Sun

1980. 75th Anniv Bulgarian Teachers' Union.

2849	**919**	5s. purple and yellow	20	10

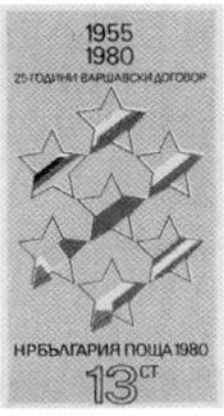

920 Stars representing Member Countries

1980. 25th Anniv of Warsaw Pact.

2850	**920**	13s. multicoloured	45	20

921 Greek Girl with Olympic Flame

1980. Olympic Games, Moscow (6th issue). Multicoloured.

2851	2s. Type **921**	35	25
2852	13s. Spartacus monument, Sandanski	65	55
2853	25s. Liberation monument, Sofia (detail)	1·10	85
2854	35s. Liberation monument, Plovdiv	1·40	1·00
2855	43s. Liberation monument, Shipka Pass	1·90	1·30
2856	1l. Liberation monument, Ruse	2·75	2·20
MS2857	66×92 mm. 2l. Athlete with Olympic flame, Moscow	9·75	9·75

922 Ballerina

1980. Tenth International Ballet Competition, Varna.

2858	**922**	13s. multicoloured	45	20

923 Europa Hotel, Sofia

1980. Hotels. Multicoloured.

2859	23s. Type **923**	55	35
2860	23s. Bulgaria Hotel, Burgas (vert)	55	35
2861	23s. Plovdiv Hotel, Plovdiv	55	35
2862	23s. Riga Hotel, Ruse (vert)	55	35
2863	23s. Varna Hotel, Prazhba	55	35

1980. Historic Ships (3rd series). As T **753**. Multicoloured.

2864	5s. Hansa kogge *Jesus of Lubeck*	20	15
2865	8s. Roman galley	30	15
2866	13s. Galleon *Eagle*	35	20
2867	23s. *Mayflower*	55	35
2868	35s. Maltese galleon	1·00	45
2869	53s. Galleon *Royal Louis*	1·50	1·10

924 Parachute Descent

1980. 15th World Parachute Championships, Kazanluk. Multicoloured.

2870	13s. Type **924**	35	20
2871	25s. Parachutist in free fall	75	35

925 Clown and Children

1980. First Anniv of "Banners for Peace" Children's Meeting. Multicoloured.

2872	3s. Type **925**	20	15
2873	5s. "Cosmonauts in Spaceship" (vert)	20	15
2874	8s. "Picnic"	20	15
2875	13s. "Children with Ices"	30	20
2876	25s. "Children with Cat" (vert)	45	35
2877	35s. "Crowd"	1·00	45
2878	43s. "Banners for Peace" monument (vert)	1·50	65

926 Assembly Emblem

1980. Assembly of Peoples' Parliament for Peace, Sofia.

2879	**926**	25s. multicoloured	55	45

927 Iordan Iovkov

1980. Birth Centenary of Iordan Iovkov (writer).

2880	**927**	5s. multicoloured	30	25

928 Yakovlev Yak-24 Helicopter, Missile Launcher and Tank

1980. Bulgarian Armed Forces. Multicoloured.

2881	3s. Type **928**	10	10
2882	5s. Mikoyan Gurevich MiG-21 bomber, radar antennae and missile transporter	20	15
2883	8s. Mil Mi-24 helicopter, missile boat and landing ship *Ropucha*	35	20

929 Computer

1980. 36th Plovdiv Fair.

2884	**929**	5s. multicoloured	20	10

930 *Virgin and Child with St. Anne*

1980. Paintings by Leonardo da Vinci. Multicoloured.

2885	5s. Type **930**	20	15
2886	8s. Angel (detail, *The Annunciation*)	20	15
2887	13s. Virgin (detail, *The Annunciation*)	35	20
2888	25s. *Adoration of the Kings* (detail)	65	45
2889	35s. *Woman with Ermine*	1·10	55
MS2890	57×80 mm. 50s. *Mona Lisa*. Imperf	1·60	1·60

1980. Air. Clocktowers (2nd series). As T **884**. Multicoloured.

2891	13s. Byala	35	20
2892	23s. Razgrad	45	35
2893	25s. Karnobat	55	45
2894	35s. Sevlievo	95	55
2895	53s. Berkovitsa	1·90	85

931 *Parodia saint-pieana*

1980. Cacti. Multicoloured.

2896	5s. Type **931**	20	15
2897	13s. *Echinopsis bridgesii*	35	20
2898	25s. *Echinocereus purpureus*	75	45
2899	35s. *Opuntia bispinosa*	1·10	85
2900	53s. *Mamillopsis senilis*	2·30	1·10

932 UN Building and Bulgarian Arms

1980. 25th Anniv of United Nations Membership. Sheet 64×86 mm.

MS2901 **932** 60s. multicoloured	4·25	4·25

933 Wild Horse

1980. Horses. Multicoloured.

2902	3s. Type **933**	20	35
2903	5s. Tarpan	20	35
2904	13s. Arabian	55	55
2905	23s. Anglo-Arabian	1·50	1·10
2906	35s. Draught horse	3·25	2·75

934 Vasil Stoin

1980. Birth Centenary of Vasil Stoin (collector of folk songs).

2907	**934**	5s. violet, yellow & gold	20	10

935 Armorial Lion

1980. New Year. 1300th Anniv of Bulgarian State. Multicoloured.

2908	5s. Type **935**	20	10
2909	13s. Dish and dates "681–1981"	35	15

936 Red Star

1980. 12th Bulgarian Communist Party Congress (1st issue).

2910	**936**	5s. yellow and red	20	10

See also Nos. 2920/2.

937 Cross-country Skier

1981. World Ski-racing Championship, Velingrad.

2911	**937**	43s. orange, blue & blk	1·10	65

938 Midland Hawthorn (*Crataegus oxpacantha*)

1981. Useful Plants. Multicoloured.

2912	3s. Type **938**	20	15
2913	5s. Perforate St. John's wort (*Hypericum perforatum*)	20	15
2914	13s. Elder (*Sambucus nigra*)	45	20
2915	25s. Dewberry (*Rubus caesius*)	85	35
2916	35s. Lime (*Tilia argentea*)	1·00	55
2917	43s. Dog rose (*Rosa canina*)	1·60	1·10

939 Skier

1981. Alpine Skiing World Championships, Borovets.

2918	**939**	43s. yellow, black & blue	1·10	65

940 Nuclear Traces

1981. 25th Anniv of Nuclear Research Institute, Dubna, U.S.S.R.

2919	**940**	13s. black and silver	35	15

941 "XII" formed from Flag

1981. 12th Bulgarian Communist Party Congress (2nd issue).

2920	**941**	5s. multicoloured	20	15
2921	-	13s. red, black and blue	35	20
2922	-	23s. red, black and blue	65	55
MS2923		68×86 mm. 50s. multicoloured	1·60	1·60

DESIGNS: 13s. Stars; 23s. Computer tape; 50s. Georgi Dimitrov and Dimitur Blagoev.

942 Palace of Culture

1981. Opening of Palace of Culture, Sofia.

2924	**942**	5s. dp green, grn & red	20	10

943 *Self-portrait*

1981. 170th Birth Anniv (1980) of Zakharu Zograf (artist). Multicoloured.

2925	5s. Type **943**	20	15
2926	13s. *Portrait of Khristionia Zografska*	45	20
2927	23s. *The Transfiguration* (icon from Preobrazhenie Monastery)	75	35
2928	25s. *Doomsday* (detail) (horiz)	95	55
2929	35s. *Doomsday* (detail – different) (horiz)	1·40	1·10

944 Squacco Heron

1981. Birds. Multicoloured.

2930	5s. Type **944**	20	15
2931	8s. Eurasian bittern	45	20
2932	13s. Cattle egret	65	35
2933	25s. Great egret	1·50	65
2934	53s. Black stork	2·75	1·60

945 Liner *Georgi Dimitrov*

1981. Centenary of Bulgarian Shipbuilding. Multicoloured.

2935	35s. Type **945**	95	35
2936	43s. Freighter *Petimata of RMS*	1·40	55
2937	53s. Tanker *Khan Asparuch*	1·90	85

946 Hofburg Palace, Vienna

1981. "WIPA 1981" International Stamp Exhibition, Vienna.

2938	**946**	35s. crimson, red & green	95	65

947 "XXXIV"

1981. 34th Bulgarian People's Agrarian Union Congress.

2939	**947**	5s. multicoloured	20	15
2940	-	8s. orange, black & blue	30	20
2941	-	13s. multicoloured	55	35

DESIGNS: 8s. Flags; 13s. Bulgarian Communist Party and Agrarian Union flags.

948 Wild Cat

1981. International Hunting Exhibition, Plovdiv.

2942	**948**	5s. stone, black & brown	20	15
2943	-	13s. black, brn & stone	45	20
2944	-	23s. brown, blk & orge	95	45
2945	-	25s. black, brown & mve	1·10	55
2946	-	35s. lt brown, blk & brn	1·50	65
2947	-	53s. brown, blk & grn	2·30	1·10
MS2948		78×103 mm. 1l. brown, black and green (52×42 mm)	3·25	3·25

DESIGNS: 13s. Wild boar; 23s. Mouflon; 25s. Chamois; 35s. Roebuck; 53s. Fallow deer; 1l. Red deer.

949 *Crafty Peter* (sculpture, Georgi Chapkanov)

1981. Festival of Humour and Satire, Gabrovo.

2949	**949**	5s. multicoloured	20	10

950 Bulgarian Arms and UNESCO Emblem

1981. 25th Anniv of UNESCO Membership.

2950	**950**	13s. multicoloured	35	20

951 Deutsche Flugzeugwerke D.F.W. C.V. Biplane

1981. Air. Aircraft. Multicoloured.

2951	5s. Type **951**	20	15
2952	12s. LAS-7 monoplane	30	15
2953	25s. LAS-8 monoplane	75	45
2954	35s. DAR-1 biplane	95	55
2955	45s. DAR-3 biplane	1·10	85
2956	55s. DAR-9 biplane	1·40	1·10

952 "Eye"

1981. Centenary of State Statistical Office.

2957	**952**	5s. multicoloured	20	10

953 Veliko Tirnovo Hotel

1981. Hotels.

2958	**953**	23s. multicoloured	55	35

954 *Flying Figure*

1981. 90th Anniv of First Bulgarian Social Democratic Party Congress, Buzludzha. Sculptures by Velichko Minekov.

2959	**954**	5s. blue, black and green	20	15
2960	-	13s. brown, blk & orge	35	20

DESIGN: 13s. *Advancing Female*.

955 Animal-shaped Dish

1981. Golden Treasure of Old St. Nicholas. Multicoloured.

2961	5s. Type **955**	20	15
2962	13s. Jug with decorated neck	35	20
2963	23s. Jug with loop pattern	55	45
2964	25s. Jug with bird pattern	75	55
2965	35s. Decorated vase	95	75
2966	53s. Decorated dish	1·90	1·30

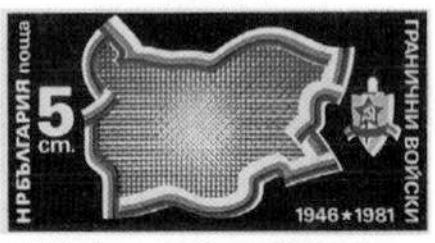

956 Badge and Map of Bulgaria

1981. 35th Anniv of Frontier Guards.

2967	**956**	5s. multicoloured	20	10

957 Saints Cyril and Methodius (9th century)

1981. 1300th Anniv of Bulgarian State.

2968	-	5s. green and grey	20	15
2969	**957**	5s. brown and yellow	20	15
2970	-	8s. violet and lilac	20	15
2971	-	12s. mauve and purple	30	15
2972	-	13s. purple and brown	35	15
2973	-	13s. green and black	35	15
2974	-	16s. green & deep green	45	20
2975	-	23s. black and blue	65	35
2976	-	25s. green and light green	75	45
2977	-	35s. brown and light brown	1·00	55
2978	-	41s. red and pink	1·20	65
2979	-	43s. red and pink	1·20	65
2980	-	53s. dp brown and brown	1·30	70
2981	-	55s. dp green and green	1·40	75
MS2982		Two sheets, each 83×74 mm. (a) 50s. grey and green; (b) 1l. brown, black and brown	5·00	5·00

DESIGNS: No. 2968, Madara horsemen (8th century); 2970, Plan of Round Church at Veliki Preslav (10th century); 2971, Four Evangelists of King Ivan, 1356; 2972, Column of Ivan Asen II (13th century); 2973, Manasiev Chronicle (14th century); 2974, Rising of April 1876; 2975, Arrival of Russian liberation troops; 2976, Foundation ceremony of Bulgarian Social Democratic Party, 1891; 2977, Rising of September 1923; 2978, Formation of Fatherland Front Government, 9 September 1944; 2979, Bulgarian Communist Party Congress, 1948; 50s. Bas-relief of lion at Stara Zagora (10th century); 2980, 10th Communist Party Congress, 1971; 2981, Kremikovski metallurgical combine; 1l. Leonid Brezhnev and Todor Yovkov.

958 Volleyball Players

1981. European Volleyball Championships.

2983	**958**	13s. red, blue and black	35	20

959 *Pegasus* (bronze sculpture)

1981. Day of the Word.

2984	**959**	5s. green	20	10

960 Loaf of Bread

1981. World Food Day.

2985	**960**	13s. brown, black & grn	35	20

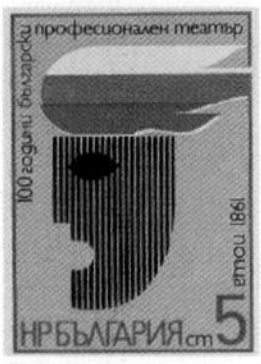

961 Mask

1981. Cent of Bulgarian Professional Theatre.

2986	**961**	5s. multicoloured	20	15

962 Examples of Bulgarian Art

1981. Cultural Heritage Day.

2987	**962**	13s. green and brown	95	20

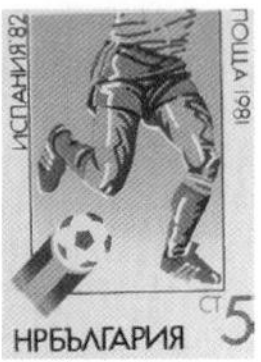

963 Footballer

1981. World Cup Football Championship, Spain (1982). Multicoloured.

2988	5s. Type **963**	20	15
2989	13s. Heading ball	30	20
2990	43s. Saving a goal	95	65
2991	53s. Running with ball	1·10	1·00

964 Dove encircled by Barbed Wire

1981. Anti-apartheid Campaign.

2992	**964**	5s. red, black and yellow	20	10

1981. 13th Bulgarian Philatelic Federation Congress. Sheet 51×72 mm containing design as T **962** but inscr "XIII KONGRES NA SBF SOFIYA" at foot.

MS2993	60s. blue and red	9·25	8·25

965 *Mother* (Lilyann Ruseva)

1981. 35th Anniv of UNICEF. Various designs showing mother and child paintings by named artists. Multicoloured.

2994	53s. Type **965**	1·70	55
2995	53s. *Bulgarian Madonna* (Vasil Stoilov)	1·70	55
2996	53s. *Village Madonna* (Ivan Milev)	1·70	55
2997	53s. *Mother* (Vladimir Dimitrov)	1·70	55

966 8th Century Ceramic from Pliska

1981. New Year. Multicoloured.

2998	5s. Armorial lion	20	10
2999	13s. Type **966**	35	15

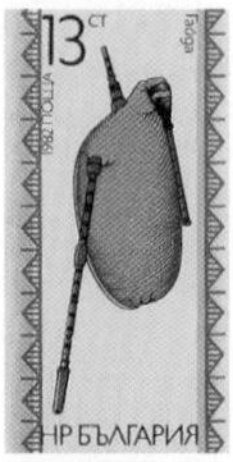

967 Bagpipes

1982. Musical Instruments. Multicoloured.

3000	13s. Type **967**	30	20
3001	25s. Single and double flutes	55	25
3002	30s. Rebec	65	35
3003	35s. Flute and pipe	75	45
3004	44s. Mandolin	1·50	55

968 Open Book

1982. 125th Anniv of Public Libraries.

3005	**968**	5s. green	20	10

969 *Sofia Plains*

1982. Birth Centenary of Nikola Petrov (artist).

3006	5s. Type **969**	20	15
3007	13s. *Girl Embroidering*	35	20
3008	30s. *Fields of Peshtera*	1·00	55

970 Womans' Head and Dove

1982. International Decade for Women. Sheet 66×76 mm.

MS3009	**970**	1l. multicoloured	2·75	2·75

971 *Peasant Woman*

1982. Birth Centenary of Valadimir Dimitrov (artist). Multicoloured.

3010	5s. Figures in a landscape (horiz)	20	15
3011	8s. Town and harbour (horiz)	20	15
3012	13s. Town scene (horiz)	45	20
3013	25s. *Reapers*	55	35
3014	30s. Woman and child	65	45
3015	35s. Type **971**	95	50
MS3016	65×58 mm. 50s. *Self-portrait* (horiz)	1·60	1·60

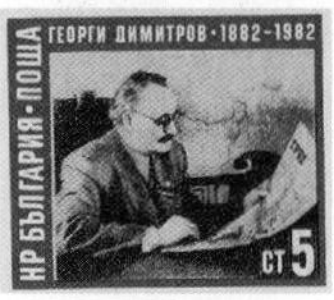

972 Georgi Dimitrov

1982. Ninth Bulgarian Trade Unions Congress, Sofia.

3017	**972**	5s. lt brn, dp brn & brn	10	10
3018	-	5s. brown and blue	20	10

DESIGN: No. 3018, Palace of Culture, Sofia.

973 Summer Snowflake

1982. Medicinal Plants. Multicoloured.

3019	3s. Type **973**	20	15
3020	5s. Chicory	20	15
3021	8s. Rosebay willowherb	30	15
3022	13s. Solomon's seal	45	20
3023	25s. Sweet violet	85	35
3024	35s. *Ficaria verna*	1·40	55

974 Russian Space Station

1982. 25th Anniv of First Soviet Artificial Satellite.

3025	**974**	13s. multicoloured	35	20

975 Georgi Dimitrov

1982. "Sozphilex '82" Stamp Exhibition, Veliko, Tirnovo. Sheet 61×82 mm.

MS3026	**975**	50s. red and black	3·25	3·25

976 Dimitrov and Congress Emblem

1982. 14th Dimitrov Communist Youth League Congress, Sofia.

3027	**976**	5s. blue, red & yellow	20	10

977 First French and Bulgarian Stamps

1982. "Philexfrance 82" International Stamp Exhibition, Paris.

3028	**977**	42s. multicoloured	95	55

978 Abstract with Birds

1982. Alafrangi Frescoes from 19th-century Houses.

3029	**978**	5s. multicoloured	20	15
3030	-	13s. multicoloured	30	20
3031	-	25s. multicoloured	45	35
3032	-	30s. multicoloured	55	45
3033	-	42s. multicoloured	95	55
3034	-	60s. multicoloured	1·90	65

DESIGNS: 13s. to 60s. Various flower and bird patterns.

During 1982 sets were issued for World Cup Football Championship, Spain (5, 13, 30s.), Tenth Anniv of First European Security and Co-operation Conference (5, 13, 25, 30s.), World Cup Results (5, 13, 30s.) and 10th Anniv (1983) of European Security and Co-operation Conference, Helsinki (5, 13, 25, 30s.). Supplies and distribution of these stamps were restricted and it is understood they were not available at face value.

979 Georgi Dimitrov

1982. Birth Centenary of Georgi Dimitrov (statesman). Sheet 76×52 mm.

MS3035	**979**	50s. multicoloured	1·60	1·60

980 Georgi Dimitrov

1982. Ninth Fatherland Front Congress, Sofia.

3036	**980**	5s. multicoloured	20	10

981 Airplane

1982. 35th Anniv of Balkanair (state airline).

3037	**981**	42s. blue, green & red	1·00	65

982 Atomic Bomb Mushroom-cloud

1982. Nuclear Disarmament Campaign.

3038	**982**	13s. multicoloured	45	20

983 Lyudmila Zhivkova

1982. 40th Birth Anniv of Lyudmila Zhivkova (founder of "Banners for Peace" Children's Meetings).

3039	**983**	5s. multicoloured	20	10
3040	**983**	13s. multicoloured	35	15
MS3041	62×67 mm. **983**	1l. multi-coloured	2·20	2·20

984 Emblem

1982. Tenth Anniv of U.N. Environment Programme.

3042	**984**	13s. green and blue	35	20

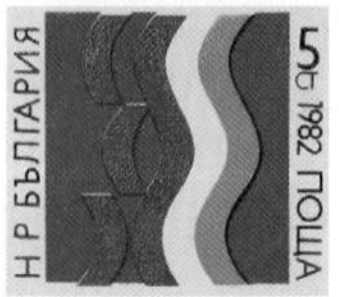

985 Wave Pattern

1982. Fifth Bulgarian Painters' Association Congress.

3043	**985**	5s. multicoloured	25	20

986 Child Musicians

1982. Second "Banners for Peace" Children's Meeting (1st issue). Children's Paintings. Multicoloured.

3044	3s. Type **986**	10	10
3045	5s. Children skating	20	10
3046	8s. Adults, children and flowers	30	15
3047	13s. Children with flags	35	20
MS3048	70×110 mm. 50s. Children in "Sun" balloon (vert)	2·20	2·20

See also Nos. 3057/**MS**3063.

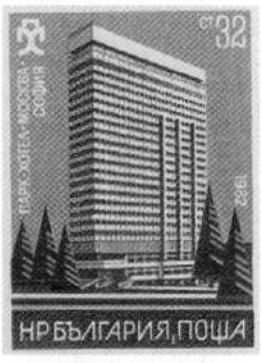

987 Moscow Park Hotel, Sofia

1982. Hotels. Multicoloured.

3049	32s. Type **987**	85	45
3050	32s. Black Sea Hotel, Varna	85	45

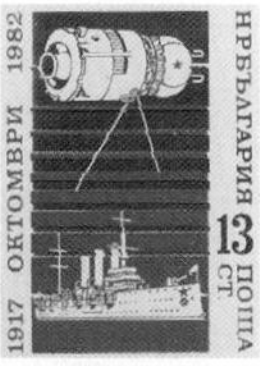

988 Cruiser "Aurora" and Satellite

1982. 65th Anniv of Russian October Revolution.

3051	**988** 13s. red and blue	35	25

989 Hammer and Sickle

1982. 60th Anniv of U.S.S.R.

3052	**989** 13s. red, gold & violet	35	20

990 *The Piano*

1982. Birth Cent of Pablo Picasso (artist). Multicoloured.

3053	13s. Type **990**	45	25
3054	30s. *Portrait of Jacqueline*	65	55
3055	42s. *Maternity*	1·40	85
MS3056	61×79 mm. 1l. *Self-portrait*	2·75	2·75

991 Boy and Girl

1982. Second "Banners for Peace" Children's Meeting (2nd issue). Multicoloured.

3057	3s. Type **991**	20	15
3058	5s. Market place	20	15
3059	8s. Children in fancy dress (vert)	20	15
3060	13s. Chickens (vert)	35	20
3061	25s. Interlocking heads	75	35
3062	30s. Lion	85	45
MS3063	70×109 mm. 50s. Boy and girl in garden (vert). Perf or imperf	2·20	2·20

992 Lions

1982. New Year. Multicoloured.

3064	5s. Type **992**	20	10
3065	13s. Decorated letters	35	15

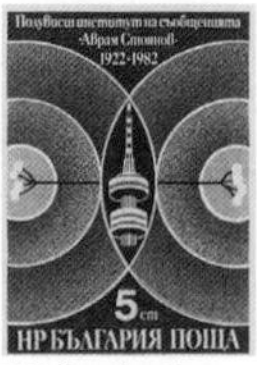

993 Broadcasting Tower

1982. 60th Anniv of Avram Stoyanov Broadcasting Institute.

3066	**993** 5s. blue	20	15

994 Dr. Robert Koch

1982. Cent of Discovery of Tubercle Bacillus.

3067	**994** 25s. brown and green	65	35

995 Simon Bolivar

1982. Birth Anniversaries.

3068	**995** 30s. green and grey	75	45
3069	- 30s. yellow and brown	75	45

DESIGN: No. 3068, Type **995** (bicent); 3069, Rabindranath Tagore (philosopher, 120th anniv).

996 Vasil Levski

1983. 110th Death Anniv of Vasil Levski (revolutionary).

3070	**996** 5s. brown & green	20	10

997 Skier

1983. "Universiade 83" University Games, Sofia.

3071	**997** 30s. multicoloured	75	45

998 Northern Pike

1983. Freshwater Fishes. Multicoloured.

3072	3s. Type **998**	20	15
3073	5s. Beluga sturgeon	20	15
3074	13s. Chub	35	20
3075	25s. Zander	75	35
3076	30s. Wels	85	45
3077	42s. Brown trout	2·40	55

999 Karl Marx

1983. Death Centenary of Karl Marx.

3078	**999** 13s. red, purple & yellow	45	20

1000 Hasek and Illustrations from *The Good Soldier Schweik*

1983. Birth Centenary of Jaroslav Hasek (Czech writer).

3079	**1000** 13s. brown, grey & grn	35	20

1001 Martin Luther

1983. 500th Birth Anniv of Martin Luther (Protestant reformer).

3080	**1001** 13s. grey, black & brn	45	20

1002 Figures forming Initials

1983. 55th Anniv of Young Workers' Union.

3081	**1002** 5s. red, black & orange	20	15

1003 Khaskovo Costume

1983. Folk Costumes. Multicoloured.

3082	5s. Type **1003**	25	15
3083	8s. Pernik	30	15
3084	13s. Burgas	35	20
3085	25s. Tolbukhin	75	35
3086	30s. Blagoevgrad	85	45
3087	42s. Topolovgrad	2·40	55

1004 Old Man feeding a Chicken

1983. Sixth International Festival of Humour and Satire, Gabrovo.

3088	**1004** 5s. multicoloured	20	10

During 1983 sets were issued for European Security and Co-operation Conference, Budapest (5, 13, 25, 30s.), Olympic Games, Los Angeles (5, 13, 30, 42s.), Winter Olympic Games, Sarajevo (horiz designs, 5, 13, 30, 42s.) and European Security and Co-operation Conference, Madrid (5, 13, 30, 42s.). Supplies and distribution of these stamps were restricted, and it is understood they were not available at face value.

1005 Smirnenski

1983. 85th Birth Anniv of Khristo Smirnenski (poet).

3089	**1005** 5s. red, brown & yellow	20	20

1006 Emblem

1983. 17th Int Geodesy Federation Congress.

3090	**1006** 30s. green, blue & yell	65	45

1007 Stylized Houses

1983. "Interarch 83" World Architecture Biennale, Sofia.

3091	**1007** 30s. multicoloured	75	45

1008 Staunton Chessmen on Map of Europe

1983. Eighth European Chess Team Championship, Plovdiv.

3092	**1008** 13s. multicoloured	45	20

1009 Brazilian and Bulgarian Football Stamps

1983. "Brasiliana 83" International Stamp Exhibition, Rio de Janeiro. Sheet 73×103 mm.

MS3093	**1009** 1l. green, brown and gold	2·75	2·75

1010 Valentina Tereshkova

1983. Air. 20th Anniv of First Woman in Space. Sheet 121×75 mm containing T **1010** and similar vert design, each blue and brown.

MS3094	50s. Type **1010**; 50s. Svetlana Savitskaya, 1982, cosmonaut	3·25	3·25

1011 Television Mast, Tolbukhin

1983. Air. World Communications Year.

3095	**1011** 5s. blue and red	20	15
3096	- 13s. mauve and red	35	20
3097	- 30s. yellow and red	55	35

DESIGNS: 13s. Postwoman; 30s. Radio tower, Mount Botev.

1012 Lenin addressing Congress

1983. 80th Anniv of Second Russian Social Democratic Workers' Party Congress.

3098	**1012** 5s. pur, dp pur & yell	20	10

1013 Pistol and Dagger on Book

1983. 80th Anniv of Ilinden-Preobrazhenie Rising.

3099	**1013** 5s. yellow and green	20	10

1014 Crystals and Hammers within Gearwheels

1983. 30th Anniv of Mining and Geology Institute, Sofia.
3100 **1014** 5s. grey, purple & blue 20 10

1015 Georgi Dimitrov and Revolution Scenes

1983. 60th Anniv of September Uprising. Multicoloured.
3101 5s. Type **1015** 20 10
3102 13s. Wreath and revolution scenes 35 15

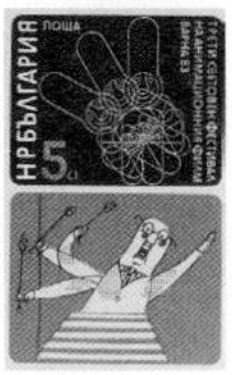

1016 Animated Drawings

1983. Third Animated Film Festival, Varna.
3103 **1016** 5s. multicoloured 20 10

1017 Angora

1983. Cats. Multicoloured.
3104 5s. Type **1017** 25 20
3105 13s. Siamese 45 20
3106 20s. Abyssinian (vert) 65 35
3107 25s. European 95 45
3108 30s. Persian (vert) 1·10 65
3109 42s. Khmer 1·90 1·10

1018 Richard Trevithick's Locomotive, 1803

1983. Locomotives (1st series). Multicoloured.
3110 5s. Type **1018** 20 10
3111 13s. John Blenkinsop's rack locomotive *Prince Royal*, 1810 45 35
3112 42s. William Hedley's *Puffing Billy*, 1813–14 2·00 1·10
3113 60s. Stephenson locomotive *Adler*, 1835, Germany 3·25 1·60
See also Nos. 3159/63.

1019 Liberation Monument, Plovdiv

1983. 90th Anniv of Bulgarian Philatelic Federation and Fourth National Stamp Exhibition, Plovdiv. Sheet 65×79 mm.
MS3114 **1019** 50s. grey, blue and red 1·60 1·60

1020 Mask and Laurel as Lyre

1983. 75th Anniv of National Opera, Sofia.
3115 **1020** 5s. red, black & gold 20 10

1021 Ioan Kukuzel

1983. Bulgarian Composers.
3116 **1021** 5s. yellow, brown & grn 20 15
3117 - 8s. yellow, brown & red 20 15
3118 - 13s. yellow, brown and green 30 20
3119 - 20s. yellow, brown & bl 35 25
3120 - 25s. yellow, brn & grey 45 35
3121 - 30s. yell, dp brn & brn 55 45
DESIGNS: 8s. Georgi Atanasov; 13s. Petko Stainov; 20s. Veselin Stoyanov; 25s. Lyubomir Pipkov; 30s. Pancho Vladigerov.

1022 Snowflake

1983. New Year.
3122 **1022** 5s. green, blue & gold 20 10

1023 *Angelo Donni*

1983. 500th Birth Anniv of Raphael (artist). Multicoloured.
3123 5s. Type **1023** 20 15
3124 13s. *Portrait of a Cardinal* 35 20
3125 30s. *Baldassare Castiglioni* 45 45
3126 42s. *Woman with a Veil* 95 55
MS3127 59×98 mm. 1l. *Sistine Madonna* 2·40 2·40

1024 Eurasian Common Shrew

1983. Protected Mammals. Multicoloured.
3128 12s. Type **1024** 45 35
3129 13s. Greater horseshoe bat 65 35
3130 20s. Common long-eared bat 1·00 45
3131 30s. Forest dormouse 1·60 65
3132 42s. Fat dormouse 3·25 1·10

1025 Karavelov

1984. 150th Birth Anniv of Lyuben Karavelov (poet).
3133 **1025** 5s. blue, bistre & brn 20 10

During 1984 sets were issued for European Confidence- and Security-building Measures and Disarmament Conference, Stockholm (5, 13, 30, 42s.) and Winter Olympic Games, Sarajevo (vert designs, 5, 13, 30, 42s.). Supplies and distribution of these stamps were restricted and it is understood that they were not available at face value.

1026 Mendeleev and Formulae

1984. 150th Birth Anniv of Dmitry Mendeleev (chemist).
3134 **1026** 13s. multicoloured 35 20

1027 Bulk Carrier "Gen. Vl. Zaimov"

1984. Ships. Multicoloured.
3135 5s. Type **1027** 20 10
3136 13s. Tanker *Mesta* 35 15
3137 25s. Tanker *Veleka* 65 35
3138 32s. Train ferry *Geroite na Odesa* 80 45
3139 42s. Bulk carrier *Rozhen* 1·40 55

1028 World Cup Stamps

1984. "Espana 84" International Stamp Exhibition, Madrid. Sheet 89×110 mm.
MS3140 **1028** 2l. multicoloured 8·25 8·25

1029 Pigeon with Letter over Globe

1984. "Mladost '84" Youth Stamp Exhibition, Pleven (1st issue).
3141 **1029** 5s. multicoloured 20 10
See also Nos. 3171/2.

1030 Wild Cherries

1984. Fruits. Multicoloured.
3142 5s. Type **1030** 20 15
3143 8s. Wild strawberries 20 15
3144 13s. Dewberries 35 20
3145 20s. Raspberries 55 35
3146 42s. Medlars 1·70 55

1031 *Vitosha Conference* (K. Buyukliiski and P. Petrov)

1984. 60th Anniv of Bulgarian Communist Party Conference, Vitosha.
3147 **1031** 5s. purple, brn & red 20 10

1032 Security Conference 1980 13s. Stamp

1984. Fifth International Stamp Fair, Essen. Sheet 94×147 mm containing T **1032** and similar horiz design. Multicoloured.
MS3148 1l.50, Type **1032**; 1l.50, Security Conference 35s. stamp 8·75 8·75

1033 Athletes and Doves

1984. Sixth Republican Spartakiad.
3149 **1033** 13s. multicoloured 35 20

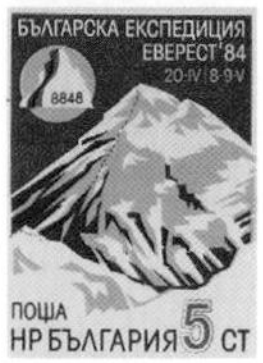

1034 Mt. Everest

1984. Bulgarian Expedition to Mt. Everest.
3150 **1034** 5s. multicoloured 20 10

1035 Kogge

1984. Universal Postal Union Congress Philatelic Salon, Hamburg. Sheet 100×107 mm.
MS3151 **1035** 3l. multicoloured 7·50 7·50

1036 Drummer

1984. Sixth Amateur Performers Festival.
3152 **1036** 5s. multicoloured 20 10

1037 Seal

1984. 50 Years of Bulgarian–U.S.S.R. Diplomatic Relations.
3153 **1037** 13s. multicoloured 35 20

1038 Feral Rock Pigeon

1984. Pigeons and Doves. Multicoloured.
3154 5s. Type **1038** 20 10
3155 13s. Stock pigeon 35 20
3156 20s. Wood pigeon 55 35
3157 30s. Turtle dove 95 45
3158 42s. Domestic pigeon 1·20 55

1984. Locomotives (2nd series). As T **1018**. Multicoloured.
3159 13s. *Best Friend of Charleston*, 1830, U.S.A. 35 20
3160 25s. *Saxonia*, 1836, Saxony 65 35
3161 30s. *Lafayette*, 1837, U.S.A. 85 45
3162 42s. *Borsig*, 1841, Germany 1·20 60
3163 60s. *Philadelphia*, 1843, U.S.A. 2·00 85

1039 Production Quality Emblem

1984. 40th Anniv of Fatherland Front Government.
3164 **1039** 5s. red, lt green & green 20 15

3165	-	20s. red and violet	55	25
3166	-	30s. red and blue	85	45

DESIGNS: 20s. Monument to Soviet Army, Sofia; 30s. Figure nine and star.

1040 *Boy with Harmonica*

1984. Paintings by Nenko Balkanski. Multicoloured.

3167	5s. Type **1040**	20	15
3168	30s. *Window in Paris*	85	45
3169	42s. *Portrait of Two Women* (horiz)	1·60	55
MS3170	65×110 mm. 1l. *Self-portrait*	2·75	2·75

1041 Mausoleum of Russian Soldiers

1984. "Mladost '84" Youth Stamp Exhibition, Pleven (2nd issue).

3171	**1041**	5s. multicoloured	20	10
3172	-	13s. black, grn & red	35	15

DESIGN: 13s. Panorama building.

1042 Pioneers saluting

1984. 40th Anniv of Dimitrov Septembrist Pioneers Organization.

3173	**1042**	5s. multicoloured	20	10

1043 Vaptsarov (after D. Nikolov)

1984. 75th Birth Anniv of Nikola I. Vaptsarov (poet).

3174	**1043**	5s. yellow and red	20	10

1044 Goalkeeper saving Goal

1984. 75th Anniv of Bulgarian Football.

3175	**1044**	42s. multicoloured	95	55

1045 Profiles

1984. "Miadost '84" Youth Stamp Exhibition, Pleven (3rd issue). Sheet 50×76 mm.

MS3176	**1045** 50s. multicoloured	1·60	1·60

1046 Devil's Bridge, R. Arda

1984. Bridges. Multicoloured.

3177	5s. Type **1046**	30	20
3178	13s. Kolo Ficheto Bridge, Byala	55	45
3179	30s. Asparukhov Bridge, Varna	95	85
3180	42s. Bebresh Bridge, Botevgrad	2·00	1·50

1047 Olympic Emblem

1984. 90th Anniv of International Olympic Committee.

3181	**1047**	13s. multicoloured	35	20

1048 Moon and "Luna I", "II" and "III"

1984. 25th Anniv of First Moon Rocket. Sheet 79×57 mm.

MS3182	**1048** 1l. multicoloured	3·25	3·25

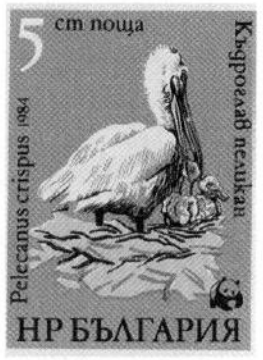

1049 Dalmatian Pelican with Chicks

1984. Wildlife Protection. Dalmatian Pelican.

3183	**1049**	5s. multicoloured	45	20
3184	-	13s. lav, blk & brn	95	45
3185	-	20s. multicoloured	1·40	1·10
3186	-	32s. multicoloured	3·25	1·60

DESIGNS: 13s. Two pelicans; 20s. Pelican on water; 32s. Pelican in flight.

1050 Anton Ivanov

1984. Birth Cent of Anton Ivanov (revolutionary).

3187	**1050**	5s. yell, brn & red	20	10

1051 Girl's Profile with Text as Hair

1984. 70th Anniv of Bulgarian Women's Socialist Movement.

3188	**1051**	5s. multicoloured	20	10

1052 Snezhanka Television Tower

1984. Television Towers.

3189	**1052**	5s. blue, green & mve	20	15
3190	-	1l. brown, mauve & bis	2·30	1·10

DESIGN: 1l. Orelek television tower.

1053 Birds and Posthorns

1984. New Year. Multicoloured.

3191	5s. Type **1053**	20	10
3192	13s. Decorative pattern	35	15

1054 *September Nights*

1984. 80th Birth Anniv of Stoyan Venev (artist). Multicoloured.

3193	5s. Type **1054**	20	15
3194	30s. *Man with Three Orders*	85	45
3195	42s. *The Hero*	1·40	55

1055 Peacock (butterfly)

1984. Butterflies. Multicoloured.

3196	13s. Type **1055**	35	20
3197	25s. Swallowtail	65	35
3198	30s. Great banded grayling	85	45
3199	42s. Orange-tip	1·20	55
3200	60s. Red admiral	2·00	75
MS3201	75×60 mm. 1l. Poplar admiral (*Limenitis populi*)	2·75	2·75

1056 Augusto Sandino

1984. 50th Death Anniv of Augusto Sandino (Nicaraguan revolutionary).

3202	**1056**	13s. black, red & yell	35	20

1057 Tupolev Tu-154 Jetliner

1984. 40th Anniv of ICAO.

3203	**1057**	42s. multicoloured	95	55

1058 *The Three Graces* (detail)

1984. 500th Birth Anniv (1983) of Raphael (artist) (2nd issue). Multicoloured.

3204	5s. Type **1058**	25	20
3205	13s. *Cupid and the Three Graces* (detail)	30	25
3206	30s. *Original Sin* (detail)	65	45
3207	42s. *La Fornarina*	1·30	50
MS3208	106×95 mm. 1l. *Galatea* (detail)	2·50	2·50

1059 *Sofia*

1984. Maiden Voyage of Danube Cruise Ship *Sofia*.

3209	**1059**	13s. dp blue, blue & yell	35	20

1060 Eastern Hog-nosed Skunk

1985. Mammals.

3210	**1060**	13s. black, blue & orge	30	15
3211	-	25s. black, brown & grn	65	35
3212	-	30s. black, brown & yell	75	40
3213	-	42s. multicoloured	1·10	55
3214	-	60s. multicoloured	1·90	85

DESIGNS: 25s. Banded linsang; 30s. Zorilla; 42s. Banded palm civet; 60s. Broad-striped galidia.

1061 Nikolai Liliev

1985. Birth Centenary of Nikolai Liliev (poet).

3215	**1061**	30s. lt brn, brn & gold	65	45

1062 Tsvyatko Radoinov

1985. 90th Birth Anniv of Tsvyatko Radoinov (resistance fighter).

3216	**1062**	5s. brown and red	20	10

1063 Asen Zlatarov

1985. Birth Cent. of Asen Zlatarov (biochemist).

3217	**1063**	5s. purple, yellow & grn	20	10

1064 Research Ship *Akademik*

1985. 13th General Assembley and 125th Anniv of Intergovernmental Oceanographic Commission. Sheet 90×60 mm.

MS3218	**1064** 80s. multicoloured	2·20	2·20

1065 Lenin Monument, Sofia

1985. 115th Birth Anniv of Lenin. Sheet 55×87 mm.

MS3219	**1065** 50s. multicoloured	1·30	1·30

1066 Olive Branch and Sword Blade

1985. 30th Anniv of Warsaw Pact.

3220	**1066**	13s. multicoloured	30	20

1067 Bach

1985. Composers.

3221	**1067**	42s. blue and red	1·40	65
3222	-	42s. violet and green	1·40	65
3223	-	42s. yellow, brn & orge	1·40	65
3224	-	42s. yellow, brn & red	1·40	65
3225	-	42s. yellow, grn & blue	1·40	65
3226	-	42s. yellow, red & grn	1·40	65

DESIGNS: No. 3222, Mozart; 3223, Tchaikovsky; 3224, Modest Petrovich Musorgsky; 3225, Giuseppe Verdi; 3226, Filip Kutev.

1068 Girl with Birds

1985. Third "Banners for Peace" Children's Meeting, Sofia. Multicoloured.

3227	5s. Type **1068**	20	15
3228	8s. Children painting	20	15
3229	13s. Girl among flowers	30	20
3230	20s. Children at market stall	45	25
3231	25s. Circle of children	55	35
3232	30s. Nurse	65	45
MS3233	70×110 mm. 50st. Children dancing (vert). Perf or imperf	2·20	2·20

1069 St. Methodius

1985. 1100th Death Anniv of St. Methodius.

3234	**1069**	13s. multicoloured	65	35

1070 Soldiers and Nazi Flags

1985. 40th Anniv of V.E. ("Victory in Europe") Day. Multicoloured.

3235	5s. Type **1070**	20	15
3236	13s. 11th Infantry parade, Sofia	35	25
3237	30s. Soviet soldier with orphan	75	35
MS3238	90×123 mm. 50s. Soldier raising Soviet flag	1·60	1·60

1071 Woman carrying Child and Man on Donkey

1985. Seventh International Festival of Humour and Satire, Gabrovo.

3239	**1071**	13s. black, yell & red	30	20

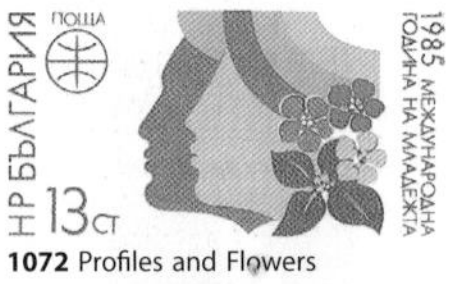

1072 Profiles and Flowers

1985. International Youth Year.

3240	**1072**	13s. multicoloured	30	20

1073 Ivan Vazov

1985. 135th Birth Anniv of Ivan Vazov (poet).

3241	**1073**	5s. brown and stone	20	10

1074 Monument to Unknown Soldiers and City Arms

1985. Millenary of Khaskovo.

3242	**1074**	5s. multicoloured	20	10

1075 Festival Emblem

1985. 12th World Youth and Students' Festival, Moscow.

3243	**1075**	13s. multicoloured	30	20

1076 Indira Gandhi

1985. Indira Gandhi (Indian Prime Minister) Commemoration.

3244	**1076**	30s. brown, orge & yell	65	35

1077 Vasil E. Aprilov (founder)

1985. 150th Anniv of New Bulgarian School, Gabrovo.

3245	**1077**	5s. blue, purple & grn	20	10

1078 Congress Emblem

1985. 36th International Shorthand and Typing Federation Congress ("Intersteno"), Sofia.

3246	**1078**	13s. multicoloured	30	20

1079 Alexandr Nevski Cathedral, Sofia

1985. Sixth General Assembly of World Tourism Organization, Sofia.

3247	**1079**	42s. green, blue & orge	95	55

1080 State Arms and UN Flag

1985. 40th Anniv of UNO (3248) and 30th Anniv of Bulgaria's Membership (3249). Multicoloured.

3248	13s. Dove around UN emblem	30	20
3249	13s. Type **1080**	30	20

1081 Rosa "Trakijka"

1985. Roses. Multicoloured.

3250	5s. "Rosa damascena"	20	15
3251	13s. Type **1081**	30	20
3252	20s. "Radiman"	45	25
3253	30s. "Marista"	55	35
3254	42s. "Valentina"	95	45
3255	60s. "Maria"	1·40	55

1082 Peace Dove

1985. Tenth Anniv of European Security and Co-operation Conference, Helsinski.

3256	**1082**	13s. multicoloured	30	20

1083 Water Polo

1985. European Swimming Championships, Sofia. Multicoloured.

3257	5s. Butterfly stroke (horiz)	20	15
3258	13s. Type **1083**	30	20
3259	42s. Diving	1·10	55
3260	60s. Synchronized swimming (horiz)	1·90	75

1084 Edelweiss

1985. 90th Anniv of Bulgarian Tourist Organization.

3261	**1084**	5s. multicoloured	20	10

1085 State Arms

1985. Cent of Union of E. Roumelia and Bulgaria.

3262	**1085**	5s. black, orge & green	20	10

1086 Footballers

1985. World Cup Football Championship, Mexico (1986) (1st issue).

3263	**1086**	5s. multicoloured	20	15
3264	-	13s. multicoloured	30	20
3265	-	30s. multicoloured	65	45
3266	-	42s. multicoloured	1·40	55
MS3267		54×76 mm. 1l. multicoloured (horiz)	2·30	2·30

DESIGNS: 13s. to 1l. Various footballers.
See also Nos. 3346/**MS**3352.

1087 Computer Picture of Boy

1985. International Young Inventors' Exhibition, Plovdiv. Multicoloured.

3268	5s. Type **1087**	20	15
3269	13s. Computer picture of youth	30	20
3270	30s. Computer picture of cosmonaut	75	35

1088 St. John's Church, Nesebur

1985. 40th Anniv of UNESCO. Multicoloured.

3271	5s. Type **1088**	20	15
3272	13s. Rila Monastery	30	20
3273	35s. Soldier (fresco, Ivanovo Rock Church)	95	45
3274	42s. Archangel Gabriel (fresco, Boyana Church)	1·10	55
3275	60s. Thracian woman (fresco, Kazanlak tomb)	1·90	75
MS3276	100×83 mm. 1l. Madara horseman (horiz). Imperf	2·20	2·20

1089 Lyudmila Zhivkova Palace of Culture

1985. 23rd United Nations Educational, Scientific and Cultural Organization General Session, Sofia. Sheet 62×95 mm.

MS3277	**1089**	1l. multicoloured	2·20	2·20

1090 Colosseum, Rome

1985. "Italia '85" International Stamp Exhibition, Rome.

3278	**1090**	42s. multicoloured	95	55

1091 "Gladiolus"

1985. Flowers.

3279	**1091**	5s. pink and red	20	15
3280	-	5s. blue and light blue	20	15
3281	-	5s. lt violet & violet	20	15
3282	-	8s. light blue and blue	20	15
3283	-	8s. orange and red	20	15
3284	-	32s. orange and brown	65	35

DESIGNS: No. 3280, Garden iris; 3281, Dwarf morning glory; 3282, Morning glory; 3283, *Anemone coronaria*; 3284, Golden-rayed lily.

1092 St. Methodius

1985. Cultural Congress of European Security and Co-operation Conference, Budapest. Sheet 105×93 mm containing T 1092 and similar vert designs. Multicoloured.

MS3285	50s. St. Cyril; 50s. Map of Europe; 50s. Type **1092**	4·25	4·25

1985. Historic Ships (4th series). As T **753**. Multicoloured.

3286	5s. 17th-century Dutch fly	20	10
3287	12s. *Sovereign of the Seas* (English galleon)	30	15
3288	20s. Mediterranean polacca	45	20
3289	25s. *Prince Royal* (English warship)	55	35
3290	42s. Xebec	1·00	65
3291	60s. 17th-century English warship	1·90	75

1093 Cologne Cathedral

1985. "Philatelia '85" International Stamp Exhibition, Cologne. Sheet 109×56 mm containing T **1093** and similar vert design, each black, blue and red.

MS3292	30s. Type **1093**; 30s. Alexandr Nevski Cathedral, Sofia	1·60	1·60

1094 Bacho Kiro

1985. Revolutionaries.

3293	**1094**	5s. light brown, brown and blue	20	10
3294	-	5s. green, purple & brown	20	10

DESIGN: No. 3294, Georgi S. Rakovski.

1095 Hands, Sword and Bible

1985. 150th Anniv of Turnovo Uprising.

3295	**1095**	13s. brown, blue & pur	30	20

1096 *1185 Revolution* (G. Bogdanov)

1985. 800th Anniv of Liberation from Byzantine Empire. Multicoloured.

3296	5s. Type **1096**	20	15
3297	13s. *1185 Revolution* (Al. Terziev)	35	20
3298	30s. *Battle of Klakotnitsa, 1230* (B. Grigorov and M. Ganovski)	45	35
3299	42s. *Veliko Turnovo* (Ts. Lavrenov)	1·40	55
MS3300	74×80 mm. 1l. Church of St. Dimitrius, Veliko Turnovo (38×28 mm). Imperf	2·20	2·20

1097 Emblem

1985. "Bralkanfila '85" Stamp Exhibition, Vratsa. Sheet 55×80 mm.

MS3301 **1097**	40s. blue, black and deep blue	1·10	1·10

1098 Emblem and Globe

1985. International Development Programme for Posts and Telecommunications.

3302	**1098**	13s. multicoloured	30	20

1099 Popov

1985. 70th Birth Anniv of Anton Popov (revolutionary).

3303	**1099**	5s. red	20	10

1100 Doves around Snowflake

1985. New Year. Multicoloured.

3304	5s. Type **1100**	20	10
3305	13s. Circle of stylized doves	30	15

1101 Pointer and Chukar Partridge

1985. Hunting Dogs. Multicoloured.

3306	5s. Type **1101**	20	20
3307	8s. Irish setter and common pochard	25	20
3308	13s. English setter and mallard	30	20
3309	20s. Cocker spaniel and Eurasian woodcock	35	25
3310	25s. German pointer and rabbit	55	35
3311	30s. Bulgarian bloodhound and boar	75	40
3312	42s. Dachshund and fox	1·50	55

1102 Person in Wheelchair and Runners

1985. International Year of Disabled Persons (1984).

3313	**1102**	5s. multicoloured	20	10

1103 Georgi Dimitrov (statesman)

1985. 50th Anniv of 7th Communist International Congress, Moscow.

3314	**1103**	13s. red	35	20

1104 Emblem within "40"

1986. 40th Anniv of UNICEF.

3315	**1104**	13s. blue, gold & black	35	20

1105 Blagoev

1986. 130th Birth Anniv of Dimitur Blagoev (founder of Bulgarian Social Democratic Party).

3316	**1105**	5s. purple and orange	20	10

1106 Hands and Dove within Laurel Wreath

1986. International Peace Year.

3317	**1106**	5s. multicoloured	20	10

1107 *Dactylorhiza romana*

1986. Orchids. Multicoloured.

3318	5s. Type **1107**	20	15
3319	13s. *Epipactis palustris*	30	20
3320	30s. *Ophrys cornuta*	40	25
3321	32s. *Limodorum abrotivum*	45	35
3322	42s. *Cypripedium calceolus*	85	45
3323	60s. *Orchis papilionacea*	1·40	55

1108 Angora Rabbit

1986. Rabbits.

3324	-	5s. grey, black & brown	20	15
3325	**1108**	25s. red and black	45	20
3326	-	30s. brown, yell & blk	55	25
3327	-	32s. orange and black	65	35
3328	-	42s. red and black	85	45
3329	-	60s. blue and black	1·40	55

DESIGNS: 5s. French grey; 30s. English lop-eared; 32s. Belgian; 42s. English spotted; 60s. Dutch black and white rabbit.

1109 Front Page and Ivan Bogorov

1986. 140th Anniv of *Bulgarian Eagle*.

3330	**1109**	5s. multicoloured	20	10

1110 Neptune and Comet Position, 1980

1986. Appearance of Halley's Comet. Sheet 120×114 mm containing T **1110** and similar horiz designs, each violet, blue and yellow.

MS3331	25s. Type **1110**; 25s. Sun, Earth, Mars, Saturn and comet positions, 1985 and 1910/86; 25s. Uranus and comet positions, 1960, 1926, 1948 and 1970; 25s. Jupiter and comet position, 1911	2·20	2·20

1111 Bashev

1986. 50th Birth Anniv (1985) of Vladimir Bashev (poet).

3332	**1111**	5s. blue & light blue	20	10

1112 Wave Pattern

1986. 13th Bulgarian Communist Party Congress.

3333	**1112**	5s. blue, green and red	10	15
3334	-	8s. blue and red	25	15
3335	-	13s. blue, red & lt blue	30	20
MS3336		60×77 mm. 50s. multicoloured	1·00	1·10

DESIGNS: 8s. Printed circuit as tail of shooting star; 13s. Computer picture of man; 50s. Steel construction tower.

1113 "Vostok I"

1986. 25th Anniv of First Man in Space. Sheet 105×100 mm containing T **1113** and similar horiz design, each deep blue and blue.

MS3337	50s. Type **1113**; 50s. Yuri Gagarin	2·20	2·20

1114 Monument, Panagyurishte

1986. 110th Anniv of April Uprising.

3338	**1114**	5s. black, stone and green	20	10
3339	-	13s. black, stone & red	30	15

DESIGN: 13s. Statue of Khristo Botev, Vratsa.

1115 Gymnast

1986. 75th Anniv of Levski-Spartak Sports Club. Sheet 81×65 mm. Imperf.

MS3340 **1115**	50s. multicoloured	1·00	1·10

1116 Stylized Ear of Wheat

1986. 35th Bulgarian People's Agrarian Union Congress.

3341	**1116**	5s. gold, orange & blk	10	10
3342	-	8s. gold, blue and black	20	10
3343	-	13s. multicoloured	30	15

DESIGNS: 8s. Stylized ear of wheat on globe; 13s. Flags.

1117 Transport Systems

1986. Socialist Countries' Transport Ministers Conference.

3344	**1117**	13s. multicoloured	30	20

1118 Emblem

1986. 17th International Book Fair, Sofia.

3345	**1118**	13s. grey, red and black	30	20

1119 Player with Ball

1986. World Cup Football Championship, Mexico (2nd issue). Multicoloured.

3346	5s. Type **1119**	20	15
3347	13s. Player tackling (horiz)	30	20
3348	20s. Player heading ball (horiz)	35	25
3349	30s. Player kicking ball (horiz)	65	35
3350	42s. Goalkeeper (horiz)	95	45
3351	60s. Player with trophy	1·50	65
MS3352	95×75 mm. 1l. Azteca Stadium (42×31 mm)	2·20	2·20

1120 Square Brooch

1986. Treasures of Preslav. Multicoloured.

3353	5s. Type **1120**	20	15
3354	13s. Pendant (vert)	30	20
3355	20s. Wheel-shaped pendant	35	25
3356	30s. Breast plate decorated with birds and chalice	65	35
3357	42s. Pear-shaped pendant (vert)	95	45
3358	60s. Enamelled cockerel on gold base	1·40	55

1121 Fencers with Sabres

1986. World Fencing Championships, Sofia. Multicoloured.

3359	5s. Type **1121**	20	10
3360	13s. Fencers	30	15
3361	25s. Fencers with rapiers	55	35

1122 Stockholm Town Hall

1986. "Stockholmia 86" International Stamp Exn.

3362	**1122**	42s. brn, red & dp red	75	65

1123 White Stork (*Ciconia ciconia*)

1986. Nature Protection. Sheet 138×90 mm containing T **1123** and similar vert designs. Multicoloured.

MS3363 30s. Type **1132**; 30s. Yellow water-lily (*Nuphar lutea*); 30s. Fire salamander (*Salamandra salamandra*); 30s. White water-lily (*Nymphaea alba*) 5·00 4·25

1124 Arms and Parliament Building, Sofia

1986. 40th Anniv of People's Republic.

3364	**1124**	5s. green, red & lt grn	20	10

1125 Posthorn

1986. 15th Organization of Socialist Countries' Postal Administrations Session, Sofia.

3365	**1125**	13s. multicoloured	30	20

1126 "All Pull Together"

1986. 40th Anniv of Voluntary Brigades.

3366	**1126**	5s. multicoloured	20	10

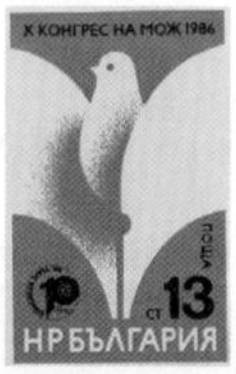
1127 Dove and Book as Pen Nib

1986. Tenth International Journalists Association Congress, Sofia.

3367	**1127**	13s. blue & deep blue	30	20

1128 Wrestlers

1986. 75th Anniv of Levski-Spartak Sports Club.

3368	**1128**	5s. multicoloured	20	10

1129 Saints Cyril and Methodius with Disciples (fresco)

1986. 1100th Anniv of Arrival in Bulgaria of Pupils of Saints Cyril and Methodius.

3369	**1129**	13s. brown and buff	30	20

1130 Old and Modern Telephones

1986. Centenary of Telephone in Bulgaria.

3370	**1130**	5s. multicoloured	20	10

1131 Weightlifter

1986. World Weightlifting Championships, Sofia.

3371	**1131**	13s. multicoloured	30	20

1986. Historic Ships (5th series). 18th-century ships. As T **753**. Multicoloured.

3372	5s. *King of Prussia*	10	10
3373	13s. Indiaman	20	15
3374	25s. Xebec	45	25
3375	30s. *Sv. Paul*	55	35
3376	32s. Topsail schooner	65	45
3377	42s. *Victory*	1·40	55

1132 (image scaled to 47% of original size)

1986. European Security and Co-operation Conference Review Meeting, Vienna. Sheet 109×86 mm containing T **1132** and similar vert designs.

MS3378 50s. olive, orange and green; 50s. green, orange and blue (Vienna Town Hall); 50s. multicoloured (United Nations Centre, Vienna) 4·25 4·25

1133 Silver Jug decorated with Seated Woman

1986. 14th Congress of Bulgarian Philatelic Federation and 60th Anniv of International Philatelic Federation. Repousse work found at Rogozen.

3379	**1133**	10s. grey, black & bl	30	20
3380	-	10s. green, blk & red	30	20

DESIGN: No. 3380, Silver jug decorated with sphinx.

1134 Doves between Pine Branches

1986. New Year.

3381	**1134**	5s. red, green and blue	20	10
3382	-	13s. mauve, blue & vio	30	20

DESIGN: 13s. Fireworks and snowflakes.

1135 Earphones as "60" on Globe

1986. 60th Anniv of Bulgarian Amateur Radio.

3383	**1135**	13s. multicoloured	30	20

1136 *The Walnut Tree* (Danail Dechev)

1986. 90th Anniv of Sofia Art Academy. Modern Paintings. Sheet 146×102 mm containing T **1136** and similar horiz designs. Multicoloured.

MS3384 25s. Type **1136**; 25s. *Resistance Fighters and Soldiers* (Iliya Beshkov); 30s. *Melnik* (Veselin Staikov); 30s. *The Olive Grove* (Kiril Tsonev) 3·25 3·25

1137 Gen. Augusto Sandino and Flag

1988. 25th Anniv of Sandinista National Liberation Front of Nicaragua.

3385	**1137**	13s. multicoloured	30	20

1138 Dimitur and Konstantin Miladinov (authors)

1986. 125th Anniv of "Bulgarian Popular Songs".

3386	**1138**	10s. blue, brn & red	20	10

1139 Pencho Slaveikov (poet)

1986. Writers' Birth Annivs. Multicoloured.

3387	5s. Type **1139** (125th anniv)	20	10
3388	5s. Stoyan Mikhailovski (130th anniv)	20	10
3389	8s. Nikola Atanasov (dramatist) (centenary)	20	10
3390	8s. Ran Bosilek (children's author) (centenary)	20	10

1140 Raiko Daskalov

1986. Birth Cent of Raiko Daskalov (politician).

3391	**1140**	5s. brown	20	10

1141 *Girl with Fruit*

1986. 500th Birth Anniv of Titian (painter). Multicoloured.

3392	5s. Type **1141**	20	15
3393	13s. *Flora*	30	15
3394	20s. *Lucretia and Tarquin*	35	20
3395	30s. Caiphas and Mary Magdalene	50	25
3396	32s. *Toilette of Venus* (detail)	55	35
3397	42s. *Self-portrait*	1·10	45
MS3398	105×75 mm. 1l. *Danae* (32×54 mm)	3·00	2·75

1142 Fiat, 1905

1986. Racing Cars.

3399	**1142**	5s. brown, red & black	20	15
3400	-	10s. red, orange & blk	20	15
3401	-	25s. green, red & black	45	20
3402	-	32s. brown, red & blk	55	35
3403	-	40s. violet, red & black	95	40
3404	-	42s. grey, black and red	1·20	45

DESIGNS: 10s. Bugatti, 1928; 25s. Mercedes, 1936; 32s. Ferrari, 1952; 40s. Lotus, 1985; 42s. Maclaren, 1986.

1143 Steam Locomotive

1987. 120th Anniv of Ruse–Varna Railway.

3405	**1143**	5s. multicoloured	20	20

1144 Debelyanov

1987. Birth Cent of Dimcho Debelyanov (poet).

3406	**1144**	5s. dp blue, yellow & bl	20	10

1145 Lazarus Ludwig Zamenhof (inventor)

1987. Centenary of Esperanto (invented language).

3407	**1145**	13s. blue, yellow & grn	30	20

1146 The Blusher

1987. Edible Fungi. Multicoloured.

3408	5s. Type **1146**	20	15
3409	20s. Royal boletus	30	20
3410	30s. Red-capped scaber stalk	45	35
3411	32s. Shaggy ink cap	65	40
3412	40s. Bare-toothed russula	75	45
3413	60s. Chanterelle	85	55

1147 Worker

1987. Tenth Trade Unions Congress, Sofia.

3414	**1147**	5s. violet and red	20	10

1148 Silver-gilt Plate with Design of Hercules and Auge

1987. Treasure of Rogozen. Multicoloured.

3415	5s. Type **1148**	20	15
3416	8s. Silver-gilt jug with design of lioness attacking stag	20	15
3417	20s. Silver-gilt plate with quatrefoil design	30	20
3418	30s. Silver-gilt jug with design of horse rider	35	25
3419	32s. Silver-gilt pot with palm design	45	30
3420	42s. Silver jug with chariot and horses design	55	35

1149 Ludmila Zhivkova Featival Complex, Varna

1987. Modern Architecture. Sheet 107×100 mm containing T **1149** and similar horiz designs. Multicoloured.

MS3421 30s. Type **1149**; 30s. Ministry of Foreign Affairs building, Sofia; 30s. Interpred building, Sofia; 30s. Hotel, Sandanski — 2·20 — 2·20

1150 Wrestlers

1987. 30th European Freestyle Wrestling Championships, Turnovo.

3422	**1150**	5s. lilac, red and violet	10	10
3423	-	13s. dp blue, red & blue	20	10

DESIGNS: 13st. Wrestlers (different).

1151 Totem Pole

1987. "Capex '87" International Stamp Exhibition, Toronto.

3424	**1151**	42s. multicoloured	75	45

1152 "X" and Flags

1987. Tenth Fatherland Front Congress.

3425	**1152**	5s. green, orange & bl	20	10

1153 Georgi Dimitrov and Profiles

1987. 15th Dimitrov Communist Youth League Congress.

3426	**1153**	5s. purple, green & red	20	10

1154 Mask

1987. Eighth International Festival of Humour and Satire, Gabrovo.

3427	**1154**	13s. multicoloured	30	20

1155 Mastheads

1987. 60th Anniv of *Rabotnichesko Delo* (newspaper).

3428	**1155**	5s. red and black	20	10

1156 Mariya Gigova

1987. 13th World Rhythmic Gymnastics Championships, Varna.

3429	**1156**	5s. blue and yellow	20	15
3430	-	8s. red and yellow	20	15
3431	-	13s. blue and stone	30	20
3432	-	25s. red and yellow	45	25
3433	-	30s. black and yellow	55	30
3434	-	42s. mauve and yellow	75	35

MS3435 78×87 mm. 1l. violet and ochre — 2·20 — 2·20

DESIGNS: 8s. Iliana Raeva; 13s. Aneliya Ralenkova; 25s. Dilyana Georgieva; 30s. Liliya Ignatova; 42s. Bianka Panova; 1l. Neshka Robeva.

1157 Man breaking Chains around Globe and Kolarov

1987. 110th Birth Anniv of Vasil Kolarov (Prime Minister 1949–50).

3436	**1157**	5s. multicoloured	20	10

1158 Stela Blagoeva

1987. Birth Centenary of Stela Blagoeva.

3437	**1158**	5s. brown and pink	20	20

1159 Levski

1987. 150th Birth Anniv of Vasil Levski (revolutionary).

3438	**1159**	5s. brown and green	10	10
3439	-	13s. green and brown	20	10

DESIGN: 13s. Levski and Bulgarian Revolutionary Central Committee emblem.

1160 Roe Deer

1987. Stags. Multicoloured.

3440	5s. Type **1160**	20	15
3441	10s. Elk (horiz)	20	15
3442	32s. Fallow deer	55	25
3443	40s. Sika deer	65	35
3444	42s. Red deer (horiz)	75	45
3445	60s. Reindeer	1·00	55

MS3445a 145×131 mm. Nos. 3340/5. Imperf — 3·75 — 3·75

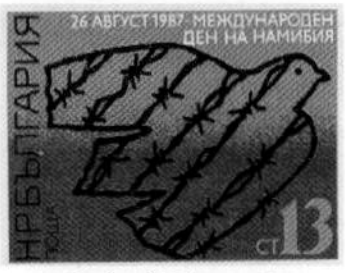

1161 Barbed Wire as Dove

1987. International Namibia Day.

3446	**1161**	13s. black, red & orge	25	10

1162 Kirkov

1987. 120th Birth Anniv of Georgi Kirkov (pseudonym Maistora) (politician).

3447	**1162**	5s. red and pink	20	10

1163 *Phacelia tanacetifolia*

1987. Flowers. Multicoloured.

3448	5s. Type **1163**	20	15
3449	10s. Sunflower	20	15
3450	30s. False acacia	50	30
3451	32s. Dutch lavender	55	35
3452	42s. Small-leaved lime	75	45
3453	60s. *Onobrychis sativa*	1·10	55

1164 Mil Mi-8 Helicopter, Tupolev Tu-154 and Antonov An-12 Aircraft

1987. 40th Anniv of Balkanair.

3454	**1164**	25s. multicoloured	55	20

1165 1879 5c. Stamp

1987. "Bulgaria '89" International Stamp Exhibition, Sofia (1st issue).

3455	**1165**	13s. multicoloured	20	10

See also Nos. 3569, 3579/82 and 3602/5.

1166 Copenhagen Town Hall

1987. "Hafnia '87" International Stamp Exhibition, Copenhagen.

3456	**1166**	42s. multicoloured	75	55

1167 *Portrait of Girl* (Stefan Ivanov)

1987. Paintings in Sofia National Gallery. Multicoloured.

3457	5s. Type **1167**	20	15
3458	8s. *Woman carrying Grapes* (Bencho Obreshkov)	20	15
3459	20s. *Portrait of a Woman wearing a Straw Hat* (David Perez)	35	20
3460	25s. *Women listening to Marimba* (Kiril Tsonev)	45	30
3461	32s. *Boy with Harmonica* (Nenko Balkanski)	65	35
3462	60s. *Rumyana* (Vasil Stoilov)	1·20	55

1168 Battle Scene

1987. 75th Anniv of Balkan War.

3463	**1168**	5s. black, stone and red	20	10

1169 Emblem

1987. 30th Anniv of International Atomic Energy Agency.

3464	**1169**	13s. blue, green and red	35	20

1170 Mastheads

1987. 95th Anniv of *Rabotnik*, 90th Anniv of *Rabotnicheski Vestnik* and 60th Anniv of *Rabotnichesko Delo* (newspapers).

3465	**1170**	5s. red, blue and gold	20	10

1171 Winter Wren

1987. Birds. Multicoloured.

3466	5s. Type **1171**	20	15
3467	13s. Yellowhammer	20	15
3468	20s. Eurasian nuthatch	45	20
3469	30s. Blackbird	65	35
3470	42s. Hawfinch	1·00	45
3471	60s. White-throated dipper	1·40	55

1172 "Vega" Automatic Space Station

1987. 30th Anniv of Soviet Space Exploration. Sheet 98×98 mm containing T **1172** and similar horiz design.

MS3472 50s. blue, orange and purple (Type **1172**); 50s. deep blue, blue and purple ("Soyuz" spacecraft docking with "Mir" space station) — 2·75 — 2·75

1173 Lenin and Revolutionary

1987. 70th Anniv of Russian Revolution.

3473	**1173**	5s. purple and red	10	10
3474	-	13s. blue and red	20	10

DESIGN: 13s. Lenin and cosmonaut.

1174 Biathlon

1987. Winter Olympic Games, Calgary. Multicoloured.

3475	5s. Type **1174**	20	15
3476	13s. Slalom	20	15
3477	30s. Figure skating (women's)	55	35

3478	42s. Four-man bobsleigh	85	55
MS3479	65×87 mm. 1l. Ice hockey	2·20	2·20

1175 "Socfilex" Emblem within Folk-design Ornament

1987. New Year. Multicoloured.

3480	5s. Type **1175**	10	10
3481	13s. Emblem within flower ornament	20	10

1176 Helsinki Conference Centre

1987. European Security and Co-operation Conference Review Meeting, Vienna. Sheet 140×100 mm containing T **1176** and similar vert designs.

MS3482	50s. lavender, brown and red; 50s. multicoloured (Map of Europe); 50s. multicoloured (Vienna Conference Centre)	5·00	5·00

1177 Kabakchiev

1988. 110th Birth Anniv of Khristo Kabakchiev (Communist Party official).

3483	**1177**	5s. multicoloured	20	10

1178 *Scilla bythynica*

1988. Marsh Flowers. Multicoloured.

3484	5s. Type **1178**	10	10
3485	10s. *Geum rhodopaeum*	15	10
3486	13s. *Caltha polypetala*	20	10
3487	25s. Fringed water-lily	45	20
3488	30s. *Cortusa matthioli*	55	30
3489	42s. Water soldier	65	45

1179 Commander on Horseback

1988. 110th Anniv of Liberation from Turkey. Multicoloured.

3490	5s. Type **1179**	10	10
3491	13s. Soldiers	20	10

1180 Emblem

1988. Public Sector Workers' 8th International Congress, Sofia.

3492	**1180**	13s. multicoloured	20	10

1181 *Yantra*, 1888

1988. Centenary of State Railways. Locomotives. Multicoloured.

3493	5s. Type **1181**	15	10
3494	13s. *Khristo Botev*, 1905	20	15
3495	25s. Steam locomotive No. 807, 1918	55	20
3496	32s. Class 46 steam locomotive, 1943	65	35
3497	42s. Diesel locomotive, 1964	85	45
3498	60s. Electric locomotive, 1979	1·40	55

1182 Ivan Nedyalkov (Shablin)

1988. Post Office Anti-fascist Heroes.

3499	**1182**	5s. light brown and brown	10	10
3500	-	8s. grey and blue	10	10
3501	-	10s. green and olive	15	10
3502	-	13s. pink and red	20	10

DESIGNS: 8s. Delcho Spasov; 10s. Nikola Ganchev (Gudzho); 13s. Ganka Rasheva (Boika).

1183 Traikov

1988. 90th Birth Anniv of Georgi Traikov (politician).

3503	**1183**	5s. orange and brown	20	10

1184 Red Cross, Red Crescent and Globe

1988. 125th Anniv of International Red Cross.

3504	**1184**	13s. multicoloured	20	10

1185 Girl

1988. Fourth "Banners for Peace" Children's Meeting, Sofia. Children's paintings. Multicoloured.

3505	5s. Type **1185**	10	10
3506	8s. Artist at work	20	10
3507	13s. Circus (horiz)	35	15
3508	20s. Kite flying (horiz)	45	20
3509	32s. Accordion player	55	30
3510	42s. Cosmonaut	65	35
MS3511	86×90 mm. 50s. Emblem with film frame (Youth Film Festival) (horiz)	1·10	1·10

1186 Marx

1988. 170th Birth Anniv of Karl Marx.

3512	**1186**	13s. red, black & yellow	20	10

1187 Herring Gull

1988. Birds. Multicoloured.

3513	5s. Type **1187**	20	10
3514	5s. White stork	20	10
3515	8s. Grey heron	40	15
3516	8s. Carrion crow	40	15
3517	10s. Northern goshawk	55	20
3518	42s. Eagle owl	1·60	45

1188 African Elephant

1988. Centenary of Sofia Zoo. Multicoloured.

3519	5s. Type **1188**	10	10
3520	13s. White rhinoceros	20	10
3521	25s. Hunting dog	55	20
3522	30s. Eastern white pelican	65	35
3523	32s. Abyssinian ground hornbill	75	45
3524	42s. Snowy owl	1·00	65

1189 "Soyuz TM" Spacecraft, Flags and Globe

1988. Second Soviet–Bulgarian Space Flight. Multicoloured.

3525	5s. Type **1189**	10	10
3526	13s. Rocket on globe	20	10

1190 Young Inventor

1988. International Young Inventors' Exhibition, Plovdiv.

3527	**1190**	13s. multicoloured	20	10

1191 1856 Handstamp of Russian Duchy of Finland

1988. "Finlandia '88" International Stamp Exhibition, Helsinki.

3528	**1191**	30s. blue and red	45	35

1192 Player taking Corner Kick

1988. Eighth European Football Championship, West Germany. Multicoloured.

3529	5s. Type **1192**	10	10
3530	13s. Goalkeeper and player	20	15
3531	30s. Referee and player	65	35
3532	42s. Player with trophy	85	45
MS3533	90×69 mm. 1l. Stadium (horiz)	2·20	2·20

1193 *Portrait of Child*

1988. Second Death Anniv of Dechko Uzunov (painter). Multicoloured.

3534	5s. Type **1193**	10	10
3535	13s. *Portrait of Mariya Vasileva*	35	15
3536	30s. *Self-portrait*	65	20

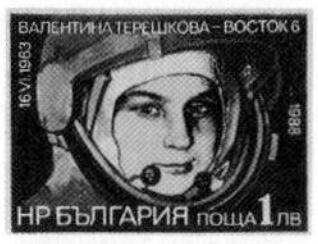

1194 Valentina Tereshkova

1988. 25th Anniv of First Woman in Space. Sheet 87×56 mm.

MS3537	**1194**	1l. pink and blue	2·20	2·20

1195 *St. John*

1988. Icons from Kurdzhali. Multicoloured.

3538	5s. Type **1195**	20	10
3539	8s. *St. George and Dragon*	20	10

1196 High Jumping

1988. Olympic Games, Seoul. Multicoloured.

3540	5s. Type **1196**	10	10
3541	13s. Weightlifting	20	10
3542	30s. Wrestling	55	30
3543	42s. Gymnastics	85	35
MS3544	115×75 mm. 1l. Volleyball	2·20	2·20

1197 Dimitur and Karadzha

1988. 120th Death Anniv of Khadzhi Dimitur and Stefan Karadzha (revolutionaries).

3545	**1197**	5s. green, black & brn	20	10

1198 Magazines

1988. 30th Anniv of *Problems of Peace and Socialism* (magazine).

3546	**1198**	13s. multicoloured	20	10

1199 *The Dead Tree* (Roland Udo)

1988. Paintings in Lyudmila Zhivkova Art Gallery. Multicoloured.

3547	30s. Type **1199**	55	35
3548	30s. *Algiers Harbour* (Albert Marque)	55	35
3549	30s. *Portrait of Hermine David* (Jule Pasquin)	55	35
3550	30s. *Madonna and Child with two Saints* (Giovanni Rosso)	55	35

1200 University Building

1988. Centenary of St. Clement of Ohrid University, Sofia.

3551	**1200**	5s. black, yellow & grn	20	10

1201 Czechoslovakia 1918 Stamp Design

1988. "Praga '88" International Stamp Exhibition, Prague.

3552	**1201**	25s. red and blue	45	35

1202 Korea 1884 5m. Stamp

1988. "Olymphilex '88" Olympic Stamps Exhibition, Seoul.

3553	**1202**	62s. red and green	1·30	1·10

1203 Anniversary Emblem

1988. 25th Anniv of Kremikovtsi Steel Mills.

3554	**1203**	5s. violet, red and blue	20	10

1204 Parliament Building, Sofia, and Map

1988. 80th Interparliamentary Conference, Sofia.

3555	**1204**	13s. blue and red	35	15

1205 Chalice, Glinena

1988. Kurdzhali Culture. Multicoloured.

3556	5s. Type **1205**	20	10
3557	8s. Part of ruined fortifications, Perperikon (vert)	20	10

1206 Soldiers

1988. 300th Anniv of Chiprovtsi Rising.

3558	**1206**	5s. multicoloured	20	10

1207 Brown Bear

1988. Bears. Multicoloured.

3559	5s. Type **1207**	10	10
3560	8s. Polar bear	10	10
3561	13s. Sloth bear	20	10
3562	20s. Sun bear	45	20
3563	32s. Asiatic black bear	65	30
3564	42s. Spectacled bear	1·10	35

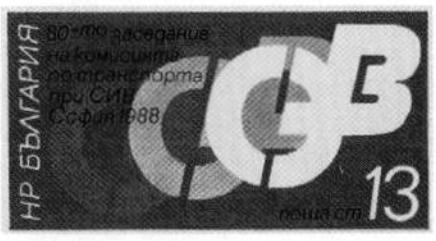

1208 Emblem

1988. 80th Council of Mutual Economic Aid Transport Commission Meeting, Sofia.

3565	**1208**	13s. red and black	35	15

1209 Emblem

1988. World Ecoforum.

3566	**1209**	20s. multicoloured	45	20

1210 Amphitheatre, Plovdiv

1988. "Plovdiv '88" National Stamp Exhibition.

3567	**1210**	5s. multicoloured	20	10

1211 Transmission Towers

1988. 25th Anniv of Radio and Television.

3568	**1211**	5s. green, blue & brown	20	10

1212 1879 5c. Stamp

1988. "Bulgaria '89" International Stamp Exhibition (2nd issue).

3569	**1212**	42s. orange, blk & mve	65	55

1213 *Ruse* (river boat)

1988. 40th Anniv of Danube Commission. Sheet 104×124 mm containing T **1213** and similar horiz design. Multicoloured.

MS3570	1l. Type **1213**; 1l. *Al. Stamboliiski* (river cruiser)	4·25	4·50

1214 Children and Cars

1988. Road Safety Campaign.

3571	**1214**	5s. multicoloured	20	10

1215 Rila Hotel, Borovets

1988. Hotels. Multicoloured.

3572	5s. Type **1215**	20	15
3573	8s. Pirin Hotel, Bansko	20	15
3574	13s. Shtastlivetsa Hotel, Vitosha	35	20
3575	30s. Perelik Hotel, Pamporovo	55	30

1216 Tree Decoration

1988. New Year. Multicoloured.

3576	5s. Type **1216**	10	10
3577	13s. "Bulgaria '89" emblem, tree and decorations	20	10

1217 Space Shuttle "Buran"

1988. Energiya–Buran Space Flight. Sheet 102×67 mm.

MS3578	**1217**	1l. blue	2·20	2·00

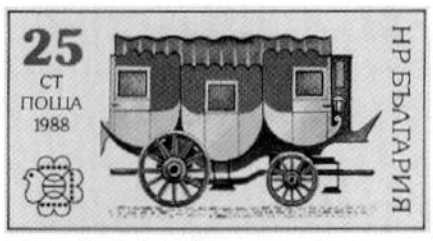

1218 Mail Coach

1988. "Bulgaria '89" International Stamp Exhibition, Sofia (3rd issue). Mail Transport. Multicoloured.

3579	25s. Type **1218**	55	20
3580	25s. Paddle-steamer	55	20
3581	25s. Lorry	55	20
3582	25s. Biplane	55	20

1219 India 1947 1½a. Independence Stamp

1989. "India 89" International Stamp Exhibition, New Delhi.

3583	**1219**	62s. green and orange	1·10	90

1220 France 1850 10c. Ceres Stamp

1989. "Philexfrance '89" International Stamp Exhibition, Paris.

3584	**1220**	42s. brown and blue	65	55

1221 Slalom

1989. "Sofia '89" University Winter Games, Sofia. Sheet 84×142 mm containing T **1221** and similar vert designs. Multicoloured. Imperf.

MS3585	25s. Type **1221**; 25s. Ice hockey; 25s. Biathlon; 25s. Speed skating	2·20	2·20

1222 Don Quixote (sculpture, House of Humour and Satire)

1989. International Festival of Humour and Satire, Gabrovo.

3586	**1222**	13s. multicoloured	35	15

1223 *Ramonda serbica*

1989. Flowers. Multicoloured.

3587	5s. Type **1223**	10	10
3588	10s. *Paeonia maskula*	20	10
3589	25s. *Viola perinensis*	45	20
3590	30s. *Dracunculus vulgaris*	55	35
3591	42s. *Tulipa splendens*	85	45
3592	60s. *Rindera umbellata*	1·10	55

1224 Common Noctule Bat

1989. Bats. Multicoloured.

3593	5s. Type **1224**	20	15
3594	13s. Greater horseshoe bat	35	20
3595	30s. Large mouse-eared bat	1·10	45
3596	42s. Particoloured frosted bat	1·60	1·30

1225 Stamboliiski

1989. 110th Birth Anniv of Aleksandur Stamboliiski (Prime Minister 1919–23).

3597	**1225**	5s. black and orange	20	10

1226 Launch of "Soyuz 33"

1989. Tenth Anniv of Soviet–Bulgarian Space Flight. Sheet 130×90 mm containing T **1226** and similar vert design. Multicoloured.

MS3598	50s. Type **1226**; 50s. Cosmonauts Nicolai Rukavishnikov and Georgi Ivanov	2·20	2·20

1227 Young Inventor

1989. International Young Inventors' Exhibition, Plovdiv.

3599	**1227**	5s. multicoloured	20	10

1228 Stanke Dimitrov-Marek (Party activist)

1989. Birth Centenaries.

3600	**1228**	5s. red and black	20	10
3601	-	5s. red and black	20	10

DESIGN: No. 3601, Petko Yenev (revolutionary).

1229 *John the Baptist* (Toma Vishanov)

1989. "Bulgaria '89" International Stamp Exhibition, Sofia (4th issue). Icons. Multicoloured.

3602	30s. Type **1229**	55	20
3603	30s. *St. Dimitur* (Ivan Terziev)	55	20
3604	30s. *Archangel Michael* (Dimitur Molerov)	55	20
3605	30s. *Madonna and Child* (Toma Vishanov)	55	20

1230 Fax Machine and Woman reading letter

1989. 110th Anniv of Bulgarian Post and Telegraph Services. Multicoloured.

3606	5s. Type **1230**	20	15
3607	8s. Telex machine and old telegraph machine	20	15
3608	35s. Modern and old telephones	65	45
3609	42s. Dish aerial and old radio	85	55

1231 *Nike in Quadriga* (relief)

1989. 58th International Philatelic Federation Congress, Sofia. Sheet 87×120 mm.

MS3610	**1231** 1l. multicoloured	2·20	2·20

1232 A. P. Aleksandrov, A. Ya. Solovov and V. P. Savinikh

1989. Air. "Soyuz TM5" Soviet-Bulgarian Space Flight.

3611	**1232** 13s. multicoloured	35	20

1233 Party Programme

1989. 70th Anniv of First Bulgarian Communist Party Congress, Sofia.

3612	**1233** 5s. blk, red & dp red	20	10

1234 Sofronii Vrachanski (250th anniv)

1989. Writers' Birth Anniversaries.

3613	**1234** 5s. green, brown & blk	20	10
3614	- 5s. green, brown & blk	20	10

DESIGN: No. 3614, Iliya Bluskov (150th anniv).

1235 Birds

1989. Bicentenary of French Revolution. Each black, red and blue.

3615	13s. Type **1235**	35	15
3616	30s. Jean-Paul Marat	55	20
3617	42s. Robespierre	75	35

1236 Gymnastics

1989. Seventh Friendly Armies Summer Spartakiad. Multicoloured.

3618	5s. Type **1236**	10	10
3619	13s. Show jumping	35	15
3620	30s. Long jumping	55	20
3621	42s. Shooting	75	45

1237 Aprilov

1989. Birth Bicent of Vasil Aprilov (educationist).

3622	**1237** 8s. lt blue, blue & blk	20	10

1238 Zagorchinov

1989. Birth Centenary of Stoyan Zagorchinov (writer).

3623	**1238** 10s. turq, brown & blk	20	10

1239 Woman in Kayak

1989. Canoeing and Kayak Championships, Plovdiv. Multicoloured.

3624	13s. Type **1239**	35	20
3625	30s. Man in kayak	75	35

1240 Felix Nadar taking Photograph from his Balloon *Le Geant* (1863) and Airship *Graf Zeppelin* over Alexsandr Nevski Cathedral, Sofia

1989. 150th Anniv of Photography.

3626	**1240** 42s. black, stone & yell	1·10	45

1241 Lammergeier and Lynx

1989. Centenary of Natural History Museum.

3627	**1241** 13s. multicoloured	35	30

1242 Soldiers

1989. 45th Anniv of Fatherland Front Government. Multicoloured.

3628	5s. Type **1242**	10	10
3629	8s. Welcoming officers	10	10
3630	13s. Crowd of youths	35	15

1243 Lyubomir Dardzhikov

1989. 48th Death Anniversaries of Post Office War Heroes. Multicoloured.

3631	5s. Type **1243**	10	10
3632	8s. Ivan Bankov Dobrev	10	10
3633	13s. Nestor Antonov	35	15

1244 Yasenov

1989. Birth Cent of Khisto Yasenov (writer).

3634	**1244** 8s. grey, brown & blk	20	10

1245 Lorry leaving Weighbridge

1989. 21st Transport Congress, Sofia.

3635	**1245** 42s. blue & deep blue	1·10	65

1246 Nehru

1989. Birth Centenary of Jawaharlal Nehru (Indian statesman).

3636	**1246** 13s. yellow, brn & blk	35	20

1247 Cranes flying

1989. Ecology Congress of European Security and Co-operation Conference, Sofia. Sheet 130×85 mm containing T **1247** and similar vert design. Multicoloured.

MS3637	50s. Type **1247**; 1l. Cranes flying (different)	4·25	4·50

1248 Javelin Sand Boa

1989. Snakes. Multicoloured.

3638	5s. Type **1248**	10	10
3639	10s. Aesculapian snake	20	15
3640	25s. Leopard snake	55	35
3641	30s. Four-lined rat snake	65	45
3642	42s. Cat snake	1·00	55
3643	60s. Whip snake	1·30	65

1249 Tiger and Balloon of Flags

1989. Young Inventors' Exhibition, Plovdiv.

3644	**1249** 13s. multicoloured	35	20

1250 Boy on Skateboard

1989. Children's Games. Sheet 100×120 mm containing T **1250** and similar vert designs. Multicoloured.

MS3645	30s.+15s. Type **1250**; 30s.+15s. Girl with ball and doll; 30s.+15s. Girl jumping over ropes; 30s.+15s. Boy with toy train	3·75	4·00

1251 Goalkeeper saving Ball

1989. World Cup Football Championship, Italy (1990) (1st issue). Multicoloured.

3646	5s. Type **1251**	10	10
3647	13s. Player tackling	20	10
3648	30s. Player heading ball	55	35
3649	42s. Player kicking ball	1·30	55
MS3650	109×54 mm. 50s. Player tackling; 50s. Players	2·20	2·00

See also Nos. 3675/**MS**3679.

1252 Gliders

1989. 82nd International Airsports Federation General Conference, Varna. Aerial Sports. Multicoloured.

3651	5s. Type **1252**	10	10
3652	13s. Hang gliding	35	20
3653	30s. Parachutist landing	75	40
3654	42s. Free falling parachutist	85	45

1253 Children on Road Crossing

1989. Road Safety.

3655	**1253** 5s. multicoloured	20	10

1254 Santa Claus's Sleigh

1989. New Year. Multicoloured.

3656	5s. Type **1254**	20	15
3657	13s. Snowman	35	20

1255 European Shorthair

1989. Cats.

3658	**1255** 5s. black and yellow	20	15
3659	- 5s. black and grey	20	15
3660	- 8s. black and yellow	20	15
3661	- 10s. black & brown	35	20
3662	- 10s. black and blue	35	20
3663	- 13s. black and red	45	25

DESIGNS—HORIZ: No. 3659, Persian; 3660, European shorthair (different); 3662, Persian (different). VERT: No. 3661, Persian (different); 3663, Siamese.

1256 Christopher Columbus and *Santa Maria*

1990. Navigators and their Ships. Multicoloured.

3664	5s. Type **1256**	20	20
3665	8s. Vasco da Gama and *Sao Gabriel*	20	20
3666	13s. Ferdinand Magellan and *Vitoria*	25	20
3667	32s. Francis Drake and *Golden Hind*	65	45
3668	42s. Henry Hudson and *Discoverie*	1·00	55
3669	60s. James Cook and H.M.S. *Endeavour*	1·30	65

1257 Banner

1990. Centenary of Esperanto (invented language) in Bulgaria.

3670	**1257**	10s. stone, green & blk	20	10

1258 *Portrait of Madeleine Rono* (Maurice Brianchon)

1990. Paintings. Multicoloured.

3671	30s. Type **1258**	75	45
3672	30s. *Still Life* (Suzanne Valadon)	75	45
3673	30s. *Portrait of a Woman* (Moise Kisling)	75	45
3674	30s. *Portrait of a Woman* (Giovanni Boltraffio)	75	45

1259 Players

1990. World Cup Football Championship, Italy.

3675	**1259**	5s. multicoloured	20	15
3676	-	13s. multicoloured	35	20
3677	-	30s. multicoloured	65	35
3678	-	42s. multicoloured	1·10	45

MS3679 80×125 mm. 2×50s. multicoloured 2·75 2·50

DESIGNS: 13 to 50s. Various match scenes.

1260 Bavaria 1849 1k. Stamp

1990. "Essen 90" International Stamp Fair.

3680	**1260**	42s. black and red	85	80

1261 Penny Black

1990. "Stamp World London 90" International Stamp Exhibition. Sheet 90×140 mm containing T **1261** and similar horiz design.

MS3681 50s. black and blue (Type **1261**); 50s. black and red (Sir Rowland Hill (instigator of postage stamps)) 2·20 2·10

1262 "100" and Rainbow

1990. Centenary of Co-operative Farming.

3682	**1262**	5s. multicoloured	20	10

1263 *Elderly Couple at Rest*

1990. Birth Centenary of Dimitur Chorbadzhiiski-Chudomir (artist).

3683	**1263**	5s. multicoloured	20	10

1264 Map

1990. Centenary of Labour Day.

3684	**1264**	10s. multicoloured	20	15

1265 Emblem

1990. 125th Anniv of ITU.

3685	**1265**	20s. blue, red & black	55	35

1266 Belgium 1849 10c. "Epaulettes" Stamp

1990. "Belgica 90" International Stamp Exhibition, Brussels.

3686	**1266**	30s. brown and green	65	55

1267 Lamartine and his House

1990. Birth Bicentenary of Alphonse de Lamartine (poet).

3687	**1267**	20s. multicoloured	55	35

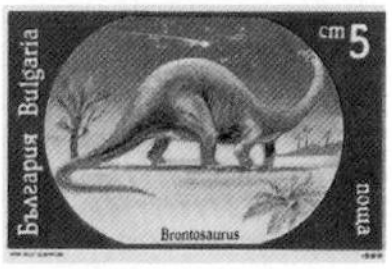

1268 Brontosaurus

1990. Prehistoric Animals. Multicoloured.

3688	5s. Type **1268**	20	15
3689	8s. Stegosaurus	20	15
3690	13s. Edaphosaurus	35	20
3691	25s. Rhamphorhynchus	65	45
3692	32s. Protoceratops	85	55
3693	42s. Triceratops	1·30	65

1269 Swimming

1990. Olympic Games, Barcelona (1992) (1st issue). Multicoloured.

3694	5s. Type **1269**	10	10
3695	13s. Handball	35	20
3696	30s. Hurdling	65	40
3697	42s. Cycling	1·10	45

MS3698 77×117 mm. 50s. Tennis player serving; 50s. Tennis player waiting to receive ball 2·75 2·20

See also Nos. 3840/**MS**3844.

1270 Southern Festoon

1990. Butterflies and Moths. Multicoloured.

3699	5s. Type **1270**	20	15
3700	10s. Jersey tiger moth	20	15
3701	20s. Willow-herb hawk moth	45	20
3702	30s. Striped hawk moth	65	45
3703	42s. *Thecla betulae*	75	65
3704	60s. Cynthia's fritillary	1·30	90

1271 Airbus Industrie A310 Jetliner

1990. Aircraft. Multicoloured.

3705	5s. Type **1271**	20	15
3706	10s. Tupolev Tu-204	20	15
3707	25s. Concorde	55	35
3708	30s. Douglas DC-9	60	40
3709	42s. Ilyushin Il-86	75	55
3710	60s. Boeing 747-300/400	1·30	90

No. 3705 is wrongly inscribed Airbus "A300".

1272 Iosif I

1990. 150th Birth Anniv of Exarch Iosif I.

3711	**1272**	5s. mauve, black & grn	20	10

1273 Road and UN Emblem within Triangles

1990. International Road Safety Year.

3712	**1273**	5s. multicoloured	20	10

1274 Putting the Shot

1990. "Olymphilex '90" Olympic Stamps Exhibition, Varna. Multicoloured.

3713	5s. Type **1274**	20	15
3714	13s. Throwing the discus	20	15
3715	42s. Throwing the hammer	75	55
3716	60s. Throwing the javelin	1·10	90

1275 "Sputnik" (first artificial satellite, 1957)

1990. Space Research. Multicoloured.

3717	5s. Type **1275**	10	10
3718	8s. "Vostok" and Yuri Gagarin (first manned flight, 1961)	20	15
3719	10s. Aleksei Leonov spacewalking from "Voskhod 2" (first spacewalk, 1965)	25	20
3720	20s. "Soyuz"–"Apollo" link, 1975	45	35
3721	42s. Space shuttle "Columbia", 1981	1·10	55
3722	60s. Space probe "Galileo"	1·30	90

MS3723 90×71 mm. 1l. Neil Armstrong from "Apollo 11" on lunar surface (first manned moon landing, 1969) (28×53 mm) 2·20 2·20

1276 St. Clement of Ohrid

1990. 1150th Birth Anniv of St. Clement of Ohrid.

3724	**1276**	5s. brown, black & grn	20	10

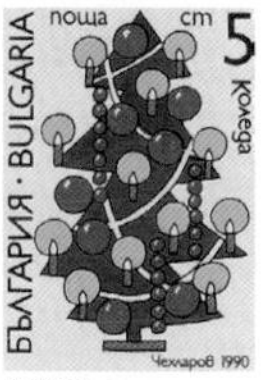

1277 Tree

1990. Christmas. Multicoloured.

3725	5s. Type **1277**	20	10
3726	20s. Father Christmas	45	20

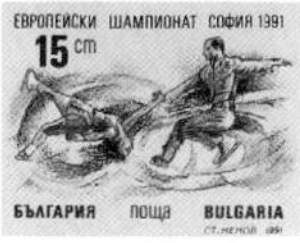

1278 Skaters

1991. European Figure Skating Championships, Sofia.

3727	**1278**	15s. multicoloured	35	20

1279 Chicken

1991. Farm Animals.

3728	-	20s. brown and black	20	10
3729	-	25s. blue and black	20	10
3730	**1279**	30s. brown and black	20	10
3731	-	40s. brown and black	35	20
3732	-	62s. green and black	55	45
3733	-	86s. red and black	75	45
3734	-	95s. mauve and black	80	50
3735	-	1l. brown and black	85	55
3736	-	2l. green and black	1·60	1·10
3737	-	5l. violet and black	2·75	2·00
3738	-	10l. blue and black	5·00	2·75

DESIGNS: 20s. Sheep; 25s. Goose; 40s. Horse; 62, 95s. Billy goat; 86s. Sow; 1l. Donkey; 2l. Bull; 5l. Common turkey; 10l. Cow.

1280 Death Cap

1991. Fungi. Multicoloured.

3746	5s. Type **1280**	10	10
3747	10s. *Amanita verna*	25	20
3748	20s. Panther cap	25	20
3749	32s. Fly agaric	35	25
3750	42s. Beefsteak morel	45	35
3751	60s. Satan's mushroom	1·20	50

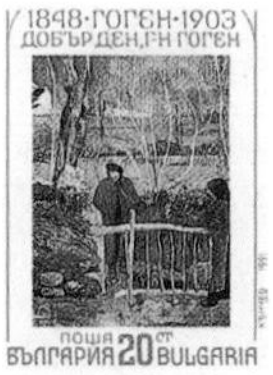

1281 *Good Day* (Paul Gauguin)

1991. Paintings. Multicoloured.

3752	20s. Type **1281**	25	20
3753	43s. *Madame Dobini* (Edgar Degas)	35	25
3754	62s. *Peasant Woman* (Camille Pissarro)	60	35
3755	67s. *Woman with Black hair* (Edouard Manet)	70	50

3756		80s. *Blue Vase* (Paul Cezanne)	1·00	70
3757		2l. *Madame Samari* (Pierre Auguste Renoir)	2·00	1·10
MS3758		65×90 mm. 3l. *Self-portrait* (Vincent van Gogh)	3·00	3·00

1282 Map

1991. 700th Anniv of Swiss Confederation.

3759	**1282**	62s. red and violet	70	50

1283 Postman on Bicycle, Envelopes and Paper

1991. 100 Years of Philatelic Publications in Bulgaria.

3760	**1283**	30s. multicoloured	35	25

1284 "Meteosat" Weather Satellite

1991. Europa. Europe in Space. Multicoloured.

3761		43s. Type **1284**	1·20	60
3762		62s. "Ariane" rocket	1·70	85

1285 Przewalski's Horse

1991. Horses. Multicoloured.

3763		5s. Type **1285**	25	20
3764		10s. Tarpan	25	20
3765		25s. Black arab	30	25
3766		35s. White arab	35	30
3767		42s. Shetland pony	45	35
3768		60s. Draught horse	1·20	60

1286 "Expo '91"

1991. "Expo '91" Exhibition, Plovdiv.

3769	**1286**	30s. multicoloured	35	25

1287 Mozart

1991. Death Bicentenary of Wolfgang Amadeus Mozart (composer).

3770	**1287**	62s. multicoloured	70	50

1288 Astronaut and Rear of Space Shuttle "Columbia"

1991. Space Shuttles. Multicoloured.

3771		12s. Type **1288**	15	10
3772		32s. Satellite and "Challenger"	25	20
3773		50s. "Discovery" and satellite	45	25
3774		86s. Satellite and "Atlantis" (vert)	60	35
3775		1l.50 Launch of "Buran" (vert)	1·40	60
3776		2l. Satellite and "Atlantis" (vert)	1·70	60
MS3777		86×74 mm. 3l. Earth, "Atlantis" and Moon	3·00	3·00

1289 Luge

1991. Winter Olympic Games, Albertville (1992). Multicoloured.

3778		30s. Type **1289**	35	25
3779		43s. Skiing	45	30
3780		67s. Ski jumping	70	50
3781		2l. Biathlon	2·30	1·40
MS3782		128×86 mm. 3l. Two-man bobsleigh	3·00	3·00

1290 Sheraton Hotel Balkan, Sofia

1991

3783	**1290**	62s. multicoloured	60	50

1291 Japanese Chin

1991. Dogs. Multicoloured.

3784		30s. Type **1291**	25	25
3785		43s. Chihuahua	35	25
3786		62s. Miniature pinscher	45	30
3787		80s. Yorkshire terrier	60	35
3788		1l. Mexican hairless	80	60
3789		3l. Pug	2·30	1·20

1292 Arms

1991. "Philatelia '91" Stamp Fair, Cologne.

3790	**1292**	86s. multicoloured	70	60

1293 Brandenburg Gate

1991. Bicentenary of Brandenburg Gate, Berlin. Sheet 90×70 mm.

MS3791	**1293**	4l. green and blue	3·00	2·75

1294 Japan 1871 48mon "Dragon" Stamp

1991. "Phila Nippon '91" International Stamp Exhibition, Tokyo.

3792	**1294**	62s. black, brown & bl	45	35

1295 Early Steam Locomotive and Tender

1991. 125th Anniv of the Railway in Bulgaria. Multicoloured.

3793		30s. Type **1295**	35	25
3794		30s. Early six-wheeled carriage	35	25

1296 Ball ascending to Basket

1991. Centenary of Basketball. Multicoloured.

3795		43s. Type **1296**	35	20
3796		62s. Ball level with basket mouth	45	25
3797		90s. Ball entering basket	60	35
3798		1l. Ball in basket	70	50

1297 *Christ carrying the Cross*

1991. 450th Birth Anniv of El Greco (painter). Multicoloured.

3799		43s. Type **1297**	25	15
3800		50s. *Holy Family with St. Anna*	30	20
3801		60s. *St. John of the Cross and St. John the Evangelist*	45	25
3802		62s. *St. Andrew and St. Francis*	60	30
3803		1l. *Holy Family with Magdalene*	70	35
3804		2l. *Cardinal Fernando Nino de Guevara*	1·20	50
MS3805		68×86 mm. 3l. Detail of *Holy Family with St. Anna* (different) (39×50 mm)	2·10	1·40

1298 Snowman, Moon, Candle, Bell and Heart

1991. Christmas. Multicoloured.

3806		30s. Type **1298**	25	15
3807		62s. Star, clover, angel, house and Christmas tree	45	25

1299 Small Pasque Flower

1991. Medicinal Plants. Multicoloured.

3808		30s.(+15s.) Pale pasque flower	15	10
3809		40s. Type **1299**	25	10
3810		55s. *Pulsatilla halleri*	30	15
3811		60s. *Aquilegia nigricans*	35	20
3812		1l. Sea buckthorn	60	25
3813		2l. Blackcurrant	1·20	50

No. 3808 includes a *se-tenant* premium-carrying label for 15s. inscribed "ACTION 2000. For Environment Protection".

1300 Greenland Seals

1991. Marine Mammals. Multicoloured.

3814		30s. Type **1300**	15	10
3815		43s. Killer whales	25	15
3816		62s. Walruses	30	20
3817		68s. Bottle-nosed dolphins	35	25
3818		1l. Mediterranean monk seals	60	35
3819		2l. Common porpoises	1·20	50

1301 Synagogue

1992. 500th Anniv of Jewish Settlement in Bulgaria.

3820	**1301**	1l. multicoloured	60	25

1302 Rossini, *The Barber of Seville* and Figaro

1992. Birth Bicentenary of Gioacchino Rossini (composer).

3821	**1302**	50s. multicoloured	35	20

1303 Plan of Fair

1992. Centenary of Plovdiv Fair.

3822	**1303**	1l. black and stone	60	25

1304 Volvo "740"

1992. Motor Cars. Multicoloured.

3823		30s. Type **1304**	25	10
3824		45s. Ford "Escort"	30	15
3825		50s. Fiat "Croma"	35	20
3826		50s. Mercedes Benz "600"	35	20
3827		1l. Peugeot "605"	80	25
3828		2l. B.M.W. "316"	1·40	50

1305 Amerigo Vespucci

1992. Explorers. Multicoloured.

3829		50s. Type **1305**	25	20
3830		50s. Francisco de Orellana	25	20
3831		1l. Ferdinand Magellan	70	35
3832		1l. Jimenez de Quesada	70	35
3833		2l. Sir Francis Drake	1·20	55
3834		3l. Pedro de Valdivia	1·70	60
MS3835		121×83 mm. 4l. Christopher Columbus	3·00	2·50

1306 Granada

1992. "Granada '92" Int Stamp Exhibition.

3836	**1306**	62s. multicoloured	35	25

1307 *Santa Maria*

1992. Europa. 500th Anniv of Discovery of America by Columbus. Multicoloured.

3837		1l. Type **1307**	1·70	60
3838		2l. Christopher Columbus	3·00	85

Nos. 3837/8 were issued together, *se-tenant*, forming a composite design.

1308 House

1992. S.O.S. Children's Village.

3839	**1308**	1l. multicoloured	70	25

1309 Long Jumping

1992. Olympic Games, Barcelona (2nd issue). Multicoloured.

3840	50s. Type **1309**	35	20
3841	50s. Swimming	35	20
3842	1l. High jumping	60	35
3843	3l. Gymnastics	1·90	60
MS3844	52×75 mm. 4l. Olympic Torch (vert)	2·30	1·80

1310 1902 Laurin and Klement Motor Cycle

1992. Motor Cycles. Multicoloured.

3845	30s. Type **1310**	25	10
3846	50s. 1928 Puch "200 Luxus"	35	15
3847	50s. 1931 Norton "CS 1"	35	15
3848	70s. 1950 Harley Davidson	45	20
3849	1l. 1986 Gilera "SP 01"	70	25
3850	2l. 1990 BMW "K 1"	1·40	50

1311 Genoa

1992. "Genova '92" International Thematic Stamp Exhibition.

3851	**1311**	1l. multicoloured	70	25

1312 Grasshopper

1992. Insects. Multicoloured.

3852	1l. Four-spotted libellula	10	10
3853	2l. *Raphidia notata*	35	20
3854	3l. Type **1312**	80	25
3855	4l. Stag beetle	1·20	35
3856	5l. Fire bug	1·40	50
3857	7l. Ant	2·30	1·20
3858	20l. Wasp	5·75	1·80
3859	50l. Praying mantis	14·00	3·50

1313 Silhouette of Head on Town Plan

1992. 50th Anniv of Institute of Architecture and Building.

3862	**1313**	1l. red and black	70	25

1314 Oak

1992. Trees. Multicoloured.

3863	50s. Type **1314**	20	15
3864	50s. Horse chestnut	20	15
3865	1l. Oak	60	25
3866	1l. Macedonian pine	60	25
3867	2l. Maple	1·40	35
3868	3l. Pear	1·70	60

1315 Embroidered Flower

1992. Centenary of Folk Museum, Sofia.

3869	**1315**	1l. multicoloured	70	25

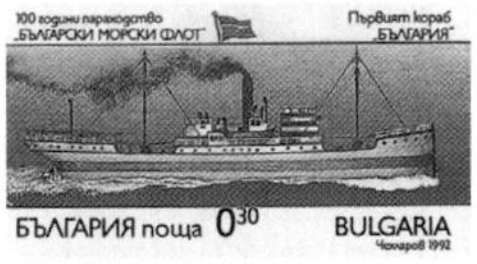

1316 *Bulgaria* (freighter)

1992. Centenary of National Shipping Fleet. Multicoloured.

3870	30s. Type **1316**	10	10
3871	50s. *Kastor* (tanker)	25	15
3872	1l. *Geroite na Sebastopol* (train ferry)	70	25
3873	2l. *Aleko Konstantinov* (tanker)	1·20	50
3874	2l. *Bulgaria* (tanker)	1·20	50
3875	3l. *Varna* (container ship)	1·90	70

1317 Council Emblem

1992. Admission to Council of Europe.

3876	**1317**	7l. multicoloured	4·75	2·40

1318 Family exercising on Beach

1992. Fourth World Sport for All Congress, Varna. Sheet 58×75 mm.

MS3877 **1318**	4l. multicoloured	2·50	2·50

1319 *Santa Claus* (Ani Bacheva)

1992. Christmas. Children's Drawings. Multicoloured.

3878	1l. Type **1319**	60	25
3879	7l. "Madonna and Child" (Georgi Petkov)	3·75	1·60

1320 Leopard

1992. Big Cats. Multicoloured.

3880	50s. Type **1320**	35	10
3881	50s. Cheetah	35	10
3882	1l. Jaguar	70	25
3883	2l. Puma	1·40	60
3884	2l. Tiger	1·40	60
3885	3l. Lion	1·70	70

1321 Cricket

1992. Sport. Multicoloured.

3886	50s. Type **1321**	35	15
3887	50s. Baseball	35	15
3888	1l. Pony and trap racing	70	25
3889	1l. Polo	70	25
3890	2l. Hockey	1·40	60
3891	3l. American football	1·70	70

1322 Tengmalm's Owl

1992. Owls. Multicoloured.

3892	30s. Type **1322**	25	15
3893	50s. Tawny owl (horiz)	35	15
3894	1l. Long-eared owl	70	25
3895	2l. Short-eared owl	1·40	60
3896	2l. Eurasian scops owl (horiz)	1·40	60
3897	3l. Barn owl	2·10	70

1323 *Khan Kubrat* (Dimitur Gyudzhenov)

1992. Historical Paintings. Multicoloured.

3898	50s. Type **1323**	35	15
3899	1l. *Khan Asparukh* (Nikolai Pavlovich)	70	25
3900	2l. *Khan Terval at Tsarigrad* (Dimitur Panchev)	1·20	60
3901	3l. *Prince Boris* (Nikolai Pavlovich)	1·90	95
MS3902	75×90 mm. 4l. *The Warrior* (Mito Ganovski) (vert)	2·50	2·50

1324 Sculpted Head

1993. Centenary of National Archaeological Museum, Sofia.

3903	**1324**	1l. multicoloured	70	25

1325 Shooting

1993. "Borovets '93" Biathlon Championship. Multicoloured.

3904	1l. Type **1325**	70	35
3905	7l. Cross-country skiing	4·75	2·00

1326 Rilski

1993. Birth Bicentenary of Neofit Rilski (compiler of Bulgarian grammar and dictionary).

3906	**1326**	1l. bistre and red	70	25

1327 *Morning* (sculpture, Georgi Chapkunov)

1993. Europa. Contemporary Art. Multicoloured.

3907	3l. Type **1327**	1·70	60
3908	8l. *Composition* (D. Buyukliiski)	3·00	1·80

1328 Veil-tailed Goldfish

1993. Fish. Multicoloured.

3909	1l. Type **1328**	25	15
3910	2l. Yucatan sail-finned molly	45	20
3911	3l. Two-striped lyretail	70	25
3912	3l. Freshwater angelfish	70	25
3913	4l. Red discus	1·00	35
3914	8l. Pearl gourami	2·10	70

1329 Apple

1993. Fruits. Multicoloured.

3915	1l. Type **1329**	25	10
3916	2l. Peach	45	15
3917	2l. Pear	45	15
3918	3l. Quince	70	25
3919	5l. Pomegranate	1·40	35
3920	7l. Fig	2·10	60

1330 Monteverdi

1993. 350th Death Anniv of Claudio Monteverdi (composer).

3921	**1330**	1l. green, yellow & red	25	15

1331 High Jumping

1993. Int Games for the Deaf, Sofia. Multicoloured.

3922	1l. Type **1331**	25	15
3923	2l. Swimming	45	20
3924	3l. Cycling	80	25
3925	4l. Tennis	85	35
MS3926	86×75 mm. 5l. Football	1·20	1·20

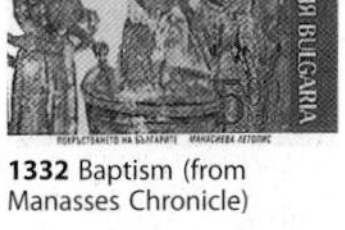

1332 Baptism (from Manasses Chronicle)

1993. 1100th Anniv of Preslav and Introduction of Cyrillic Script. Sheet 113×110 mm containing T **1332** and similar horiz designs. Multicoloured.

MS3927	5l. Type **1332**; 5l. Prince Boris I (after Dimitur Gyudzhenov); 5l. Tsar Simeon I (after Dimitur Gyudzhenov); 5l. Cavalry charge (after Manasses Chronicle)	4·75	4·75

1333 Prince Alexander

1993. Death Centenary of Prince Alexander I.

3928	**1333**	3l. multicoloured	70	25

1334 Tchaikovsky

1993. Death Centenary of Pyotr Tchaikovsky (composer).

3929	**1334**	3l. multicoloured	70	25

1335 Crossbow

1993. Weapons. Multicoloured.

3930	1l. Type **1335**	25	15
3931	2l. 18th-century flintlock pistol	45	20
3932	3l. Revolver	70	25
3933	3l. Luger pistol	70	25
3934	5l. Mauser rifle	1·30	40
3935	7l. Kalashnikov assault rifle	1·90	70

1336 Newton

1993. 350th Birth Anniv of Sir Isaac Newton (mathematician).

3936	**1336**	1l. multicoloured	25	15

1337 "100" on Stamps and Globe

1993. Centenary of Bulgarian Philately.

3937	**1337**	1l. multicoloured	25	15

1338 "Ecology" in Cyrillic Script

1993. Ecology. Multicoloured.

3938	1l. Type **1338**	25	15
3939	7l. "Ecology" in English	1·90	60

1339 Mallard

1993. Hunting. Multicoloured.

3940	1l. Type **1339**	15	10
3941	1l. Common pheasant	15	10
3942	2l. Red fox	35	20
3943	3l. Roe deer	60	25
3944	6l. European brown hare	1·20	50
3945	8l. Wild boar	1·70	70

1340 "Taurus", "Gemini" and "Cancer"

1993. Christmas. Signs of the Zodiac. Multicoloured.

3946	1l. Type **1340**	10	10
3947	1l. "Leo", "Virgo" and "Libra"	10	10
3948	7l. "Aquarius", "Pisces" and "Aries"	1·40	50
3949	7l. "Scorpio", "Sagittarius" and "Capricorn"	1·40	50

Nos. 3946/7 and 3948/9 were each issued together, *se-tenant*; when placed together the four stamps form a composite design.

1341 Sofia Costume

1993. Costumes. Multicoloured.

3950	1l. Type **1341**	25	10
3951	1l. Plovdiv	25	10
3952	2l. Belograd	35	15
3953	3l. Oryakhovo	45	20
3954	3l. Shumen	45	20
3955	8l. Kurdzhali	1·40	60

1342 Freestyle Skiing

1994. Winter Olympic Games, Lillehammer, Norway. Multicoloured.

3956	1l. Type **1342**	10	10
3957	2l. Speed skating	35	15
3958	3l. Two-man luge	60	20
3959	4l. Ice hockey	95	25
MS3960	59×90 mm. 3l. multicoloured	95	95

1343 *Self-portrait* and *Tsar Simeon*

1994. Death Centenary of Nikolai Pavlovich (artist).

3961	**1343**	3l. multicoloured	60	25

1344 Plesiosaurus

1994. Prehistoric Animals. Multicoloured.

3962	2l. Type **1344**	35	10
3963	3l. Archaeopteryx	60	20
3964	3l. Iguanodon	60	20
3965	4l. Edmontonia	80	25
3966	5l. Styracosaurus	95	35
3967	7l. Tyrannosaurus	1·40	50

1345 Players (Chile, 1962)

1994. World Cup Football Championship, U.S.A. Multicoloured.

3968	3l. Type **1345**	60	25
3969	6l. Players (England, 1966)	1·20	35
3970	7l. Goalkeeper making save (Mexico, 1970)	1·30	50
3971	9l. Player kicking (West Germany, 1974)	1·60	70
MS3972	90×123 mm. 5l. Player punching air (Mexico, 1986) (vert); 5l. Player tackling (U.S.A., 1994)	2·50	2·50

1346 Photoelectric Analysis (Georgi Nadzhakov)

1994. Europa. Discoveries. Multicoloured.

3973	3l. Type **1346**	1·20	60
3974	15l. Cardiogram and heart (Prof. Ivan Mitev)	4·00	1·80

1347 Khristov

1994. 80th Birth Anniv of Boris Khristov (actor).

3975	**1347**	3l. multicoloured	60	25

1348 Sleeping Hamster

1994. The Common Hamster. Multicoloured.

3976	3l. Type **1348**	60	25
3977	7l. Hamster looking out of burrow	1·00	60
3978	10l. Hamster sitting up in grass	1·70	85
3979	15l. Hamster approaching berry	2·50	1·30

1349 Space Shuttle, Satellite and Dish Aerial

1994. North Atlantic Co-operation Council (North Atlantic Treaty Organization and Warsaw Pact members).

3980	**1349**	3l. multicoloured	60	35

1350 Baron Pierre de Coubertin (founder of modern games)

1994. Cent of International Olympic Committee.

3981	**1350**	3l. multicoloured	60	35

1351 *Christ Pantocrator*

1994. Icons. Multicoloured.

3982	2l. Type **1351**	25	10
3983	3l. *Raising of Lazarus*	45	20
3984	5l. *Passion of Christ*	60	25
3985	7l. *Archangel Michael*	1·20	50
3986	8l. *Sts. Cyril and Methodius*	1·40	60
3987	15l. *Madonna Enthroned*	3·00	70

1352 Vechernik

1994. Christmas. Breads. Multicoloured.

3988	3l. Type **1352**	60	25
3989	15l. Bogovitsa	3·00	1·60

1353 "Golden Showers"

1994. Roses. Multicoloured.

3990	2l. Type **1353**	35	10
3991	3l. "Caen Peace Monument"	60	25
3992	5l. "Theresa of Lisieux"	95	35
3993	7l. "Zambra 93"	1·40	60
3994	10l. "Gustave Courbet"	2·00	65
3995	15l. "Honore de Balzac"	3·00	1·20

БЪЛГАРИЯ - С БРОНЗОВИ МЕДАЛИ

(1354)

1994. Bulgaria's Fourth Place in World Cup Football Championship. No. MS3972 overprinted with T **1354** in margin.

MS3996	90×123 mm. 5l. multicoloured; 5l. multicoloured	22·00	22·00

1355 "AM/ASES", 1912

1994. Trams. Multicoloured.

3997	1l. Type **1355**	10	10
3998	2l. "AM/ASES", 1928	35	15
3999	3l. "M.A.N./AEG", 1931	60	25
4000	5l. "D.T.O.", 1942	95	35
4001	8l. Republika, 1951	1·70	70
4002	10l. Kosmonavt articulated tramcar set, 1961	2·10	85

1356 Petleshkov and Flag

1995. 150th Birth Anniv of Vasil Petleshkov (leader of 1876 April uprising).

4003	**1356**	3l. multicoloured	60	35

1357 Daisy growing through Cracked Helmet

1995. Europa. Peace and Freedom. Multicoloured.

4004	3l. Type **1357**	1·20	60
4005	15l. Dove with olive branch on rifle barrel	4·00	1·80

1358 Player

1995. Centenary of Volleyball. Sheet 92×75 mm containing T **1358** and similar multicoloured design.

MS4006	10l. Type **1358**; 15l. Player hitting ball (vert)	4·25	4·25

1359 Sea Lily (*Pancratium martimum*)

1995. European Nature Conservation Year. Sheet 70×99 mm containing T **1359** and similar horiz design. Multicoloured.

MS4007	10l. Type **1359**; 15l. Imperial Eagle (*Aquila heliaca*)	5·50	5·50

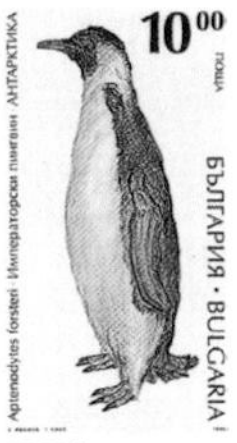

1360 Emperor Penguin

1995. Antarctic Animals. Multicoloured.

4008	1l. Shrimp (horiz)	15	10
4009	2l. Ice fish (horiz)	35	15
4010	3l. Sperm whale (horiz)	45	25
4011	5l. Weddell's seal (horiz)	80	35
4012	8l. South polar skua (horiz)	1·40	70
4013	10l. Type **1360**	1·70	85

1361 Stambolov

1995. Death Cent of Stefan Stambolov (politician).

4014	**1361**	3l. multicoloured	60	35

1362 Pole Vaulting

1995. Olympic Games, Atlanta (1996) (1st issue). Multicoloured.

4015	3l. Type **1362**	45	15
4016	7l. High jumping	1·20	50
4017	10l. Long jumping	1·70	60
4018	15l. Triple jumping	2·50	85

See also Nos. 4083/6.

1363 Pea

1995. Food Plants. Multicoloured.

4019	2l. Type **1363**	25	15
4020	3l. Chickpea	45	25
4021	3l. Soya bean	45	25
4022	4l. Spinach	70	35
4023	5l. Peanut	80	50
4024	15l. Lentil	2·30	85

1364 "100"

1995. Centenary of Organized Tourism.

4025	**1364**	1l. multicoloured	60	25

1365 *Ivan Nikolov-Zograf*

1995. Birth Centenary of Vasil Zakhariev (painter).

4026	**1365**	2l. multicoloured	35	15
4027	-	3l. multicoloured	60	25
4028	-	5l. black, brown & grn	95	50
4029	-	10l. multicoloured	1·70	95

DESIGNS: 3l. *Rila Monastery*; 5l. *Self-portrait*; 10l. *Raspberry Collectors*.

1366 "Dove-Hands" holding Globe

1995. 50th Anniv of UNO.

4030	**1366**	3l. multicoloured	60	25

1367 Polikarpov Po-2 Biplane

1995. Aircraft. Multicoloured.

4031	3l. Type **1367**	45	25
4032	5l. Lisunov Li-2 airliner	80	35
4033	7l. Junkers Ju 52	1·20	60
4034	10l. Focke Wulf FW58	1·70	70

1368 Charlie Chaplin and Mickey Mouse

1995. Centenary of Motion Pictures. Multicoloured.

4035	2l. Type **1368**	35	15
4036	3l. Marilyn Monroe and Marlene Dietrich	45	25
4037	5l. Nikolai Cherkasov and Humphrey Bogart	60	30
4038	8l. Sophia Loren and Liza Minelli	1·50	35
4039	10l. Gerard Philipe and Toshiro Mifune	1·70	50
4040	15l. Katya Paskaleva and Nevena Kokanova	2·30	85

1369 Agate

1995. Minerals. Multicoloured.

4041	1l. Type **1369**	15	10
4042	2l. Sphalerite	35	15
4043	5l. Calcite	95	25
4044	7l. Quartz	1·20	30
4045	8l. Pyromorphite	1·40	35
4046	10l. Almandine	1·90	60

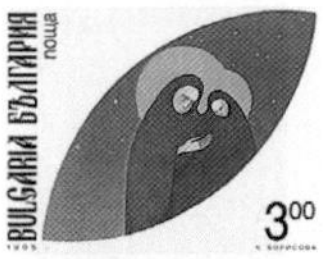

1370 Mary and Joseph

1995. Christmas. Multicoloured.

4047	3l. Type **1370**	60	25
4048	15l. Three wise men approaching stable	2·30	1·30

1371 *Polynesian Woman with Fruit*

1996. Birth Centenary of Kiril Tsonev (painter).

4049	**1371**	3l. multicoloured	60	25

1372 Luther (after Lucas Cranach the elder)

1996. 450th Death Anniv of Martin Luther (Protestant reformer).

4050	**1372**	3l. multicoloured	60	25

1373 Preobrazhenie

1996. Monasteries.

4051	**1373**	3l. green	15	10
4052	-	5l. red	35	20
4053	-	10l. blue	45	25
4054	-	20l. orange	1·20	50
4055	-	25l. brown	1·40	70
4056	-	40l. purple	2·30	1·20

DESIGNS: 5l. Arapov; 10l. Dryanovo; 20l. Bachkov; 25l. Troyan; 40l. Zograf.

1374 Bulgarian National Bank

1996. Fifth Anniv of European Reconstruction and Development Bank.

4063	**1374**	7l. green, red and blue	60	35
4064	-	30l. blue, red & purple	2·30	85

DESIGN: 30l. Palace of Culture, Sofia.

1375 Yew

1996. Conifers. Multicoloured.

4065	5l. Type **1375**	25	10
4066	8l. Silver fir	45	20
4067	10l. Norway spruce	60	25
4068	20l. Scots pine	1·20	35
4069	25l. *Pinus heldreichii*	1·40	50
4070	40l. Juniper	2·30	1·20

1376 Battle Scene and Mourning Women

1996. 120th Anniversaries. Multicoloured.

4071	10l. Type **1376** (April uprising)	60	25
4072	40l. Khristo Botev and script (poet, death anniv) (horiz)	2·30	1·20

1377 Modern Officer's Parade Uniform

1996. Military Uniforms. Multicoloured.

4073	5l. Type **1377**	20	10
4074	8l. Second World War combat uniform	30	15
4075	10l. Balkan War uniform	40	20
4076	20l. Guard officer's ceremonial uniform	95	50
4077	25l. Serbo-Bulgarian War officer's uniform	1·20	60
4078	40l. Russo-Turkish War soldier's uniform	1·70	1·20

1378 Monument

1996. 50th Anniv of the Republic.

4079	**1378**	10l. multicoloured	60	35

1379 Elisaveta Bagryana (poet)

1996. Europa. Famous Women. Multicoloured.

4080	10l. Type **1379**	2·30	1·20
4081	40l. Katya Popova (opera singer)	3·00	1·80

1380 Player

1996. European Football Championship, England. Sheet 71×86 mm containing T **1380** and similar vert design. Multicoloured.

MS4082	10l. Type **1380**; 15l. Player (different)	2·50	2·50

1381 Nikola Stanchev (wrestling, Melbourne 1956)

1996. Olympic Games, Atlanta (2nd issue). Bulgarian Medal Winners. Multicoloured.

4083	5l. Type **1381**	20	10
4084	8l. Boris Georgiev (boxing, Helsinki 1952)	45	20
4085	10l. Ivanka Khristova (putting the shot, Montreal 1976)	70	25
4086	25l. Z. Iordanova and S. Otsetova (double sculls, Montreal 1976)	1·50	60
MS4087	89×68 mm. 15l. Olympic Stadium, Athens, 1896	1·70	1·70

1382 *The Letter* (detail)

1996. 250th Birth Anniv of Francisco Goya (painter). Multicoloured.

4088	5l. Detail of fresco	20	10
4089	8l. Type **1382**	60	35
4090	26l. *3rd of May 1808 in Madrid* (detail)	1·50	70
4091	40l. *Neighbours on a Balcony* (detail)	2·30	1·20
MS4092	99×73 mm. 10l. *Clothed Maja* (50×26 mm); 15l. *Naked Maja* (50×26 mm)	1·70	1·70

1383 Water Flea

1996. Aquatic Life. Multicoloured.

4093	5l. Type **1383**	20	10
4094	10l. Common water louse	45	20
4095	12l. European river crayfish	60	25
4096	25l. Prawn	1·00	35
4097	30l. *Cumella limicola*	1·20	60
4098	40l. Mediterranean shore crab	3·00	1·20

1384 St. Ivan

1996. 1050th Death Anniv of Ivan Rilski (founder of Rila Monastery). Sheet 56×87 mm.

MS4099	**1384**	10l. multicoloured	1·00	1·00

1385 Tryavna

1996. Houses.

4100	**1385**	10l. brown and stone	35	15
4101	-	15l. red and yellow	45	20
4102	-	30l. green and yellow	95	50
4103	-	50l. violet and mauve	1·60	85
4104	-	60l. green and lt green	2·10	1·20
4105	-	100l. ultramarine & bl	3·25	1·80

DESIGNS: 15l. Nesebur; 30l. Tryavna (different); 50l. Koprivshtitsa; 60l. Plovdiv; 100l. Koprivshtitsa (different).

1386 *Philadelphia*, 1836

1996. Steam Locomotives. Multicoloured.

4106	5l. Type **1386**	25	20
4107	10l. *Jenny Lind*, 1847	60	25
4108	12l. *Liverpool*, 1848	70	35
4109	26l. *Anglet*, 1876	1·50	70

1387 Anniversary Emblem and Academy

1996. Centenary of National Arts Academy.

4110	**1387**	15l. black and yellow	95	35

1388 Sword and Miniature from *Chronicle of Ivan Skilitsa*

1996. 1100th Anniv of Tsar Simeon's Victory over the Turks. Multicoloured.

4111	10l. Type **1388**	60	25
4112	40l. Dagger and right-hand detail of miniature	2·30	1·20

Nos. 4111/12 were issued together, *se-tenant*, forming a composite design.

1389 Fishes and Diver (Dilyana Lokmadzhieva)

1996. 50th Anniv of UNICEF. Children's Paintings. Multicoloured.

4113	7l. Type **1389**	45	25
4114	15l. Circus (Velislava Dimitrova)	95	50
4115	20l. Man and artist's pallet (Miglena Nikolova)	1·30	60
4116	60l. Family meal (Darena Dencheva)	3·75	1·90

1390 Christmas Tree

1996. Christmas. Multicoloured.

4117	15l. Type **1390**	80	35
4118	60l. Star over basilica and Christmas tree	3·50	1·80

1391 *Zograf Monastery*

1996. Birth Centenary of Tsanko Lavrenov (painter).

4119	**1391**	15l. multicoloured	80	35

1392 Pointer

1997. Puppies. Multicoloured.

4120	5l. Type **1392**	25	25
4121	7l. Chow chow	35	20
4122	25l. Carakachan dog	1·20	60
4123	50l. Basset hound	2·30	1·20

1393 Bell

1997. 150th Birth Anniv of Alexander Graham Bell (telephone pioneer).

4124	**1393**	30l. multicoloured	95	50

1394 Man drinking

1997. Birth Centenary of Ivan Milev (painter). Murals from Kazaluk. Multicoloured.

4125	5l. Type **1394**	20	15
4126	15l. Woman praying	45	25
4127	30l. Reaper	60	50
4128	60l. Mother and child	1·70	95

1395 Lady March (symbol of spring)

1997. Europa. Tales and Legends. Multicoloured.

4129	120l. Type **1395**	3·00	1·20
4130	600l. St. George (national symbol)	2·30	1·20

1396 Kisimov in Character

1997. Birth Cent of Konstantin Kisimov (actor).

4131	**1396**	120l. multicoloured	25	25

1397 Von Stephan

1997. Death Centenary of Heinrich von Stephan (founder of U.P.U.).

4132	**1397**	60l. multicoloured	25	25

1398 Old Town, Nesebur

1997. Historic Sights.

4133	**1398**	80l. brown and black	10	10
4134	-	200l. violet and black	25	10
4135	-	300l. yellow and black	35	25
4136	-	500l. green and black	60	35
4137	-	600l. yellow and black	80	50
4138	-	1000l. orange and black	1·40	85

DESIGNS: 200l. Sculpture, Ivanovski Church; 300l. Christ (detail of icon), Boyana Church; 500l. Horseman (stone relief), Madara; 600l. Figure of woman (carving from sarcophagus), Sveshary; 1000l. Tomb decoration, Kazanlak.

1399 Gaetano Donizetti

1997. Composers' Anniversaries. Multicoloured.

4139	120l. Type **1399** (birth bicentenary)	45	35
4140	120l. Franz Schubert (birth bicentenary)	45	35
4141	120l. Felix Mendelssohn-Bartholdy (150th death anniv)	45	35
4142	120l. Johannes Brahms (death centenary)	45	35

1400 *Trifolium rubens*

1997. Flowers in the Red Book. Multicoloured.

4143	80l. Type **1400**	25	10
4144	100l. *Tulipa hageri*	35	10
4145	120l. *Inula spiraeifolia*	35	25
4146	200l. Thin-leafed peony	80	35

1401 Anniversary Emblem

1997. 50th Anniv of Civil Aviation.

4147	**1401**	120l. multicoloured	35	25

1402 Georgiev

1997. Death Centenary of Evlogii Georgiev.

4148	**1402**	120l. multicoloured	35	25

1403 Show Jumping and Running

1997. World Modern Pentathlon Championship, Sofia. Multicoloured.

4149	60l. Type **1403**	35	10
4150	80l. Fencing and swimming	35	25
4151	100l. Running and fencing	45	25
4152	120l. Shooting and swimming	60	35
4153	200l. Show jumping and shooting	70	50

1404 St. Basil's Cathedral

1997. 850th Anniv of Moscow and "Moskva 97" International Stamp Exhibition. Sheet 87×96 mm.

MS4154	**1404**	120l. multicoloured	80	60

1405 D 2500 M Boat Engine

1997. Centenary of Diesel Engine. Multicoloured.

4155	80l. Type **1405**	35	10
4156	100l. D 2900 T tractor engine	50	25
4157	120l. D 3900 A truck engine	60	35
4158	200l. D 2500 K fork-lift truck engine	1·00	50

1406 Goddess with Mural Crown

1997. 43rd General Assembly of Atlantic Club, Sofia.

4159	**1406**	120l. mve, bl & ultram	50	35
4160	-	120l. grn, bl & ultram	50	35
4161	-	120l. brn, bl & ultram	50	35
4162	-	120l. vio, bl & ultram	50	35

DESIGNS: No. 4160, Eagle on globe; 4161, Venue; 4162, Venue (different).

1407 Cervantes and Don Quixote with Sancho

1997. 450th Birth Anniv of Miguel de Cervantes (writer).

4163	**1407**	120l. multicoloured	50	25

1408 Raztsvetnikov

1997. Birth Centenary of Asen Raztsvetnikov (writer and translator).

4164	**1408**	120l. multicoloured	50	25

1409 Fragment of Tombstone

1997. Millenary of Coronation of Tsar Samuel. Multicoloured.

4165	120l. Type **1409**	50	25
4166	600l. Tsar Samuel and knights in battle	2·40	1·20

1410 Star and Houses forming Christmas Tree

1997. Christmas. Multicoloured.

4167	120l. Type **1410**	50	25
4168	600l. Stable with Christmas tree roof	2·20	1·20

1411 Speed Skating

1997. Winter Olympic Games, Nagano, Japan (1998). Multicoloured.

4169	60l. Type **1411**	25	10
4170	80l. Skiing	35	20
4171	120l. Shooting (biathlon)	50	25
4172	600l. Ice skating	3·00	1·90

1412 Radiometric System R-400

1997. 25th Anniv of Bulgarian Space Experiments. Sheet 87×68 mm.

MS4173	**1412** 120l. multicoloured	1·20	1·20

1413 State Arms

1997

4174	**1413** 120l. multicoloured	40	25

1414 Botev (after B. Petrov)

1998. 150th Birth and 120th Death (1996) Anniv of Khristo Botev (poet and revolutionary).

4175	**1414** 120l. multicoloured	40	25

1415 Brecht

1998. Birth Cent of Bertolt Brecht (playwright).

4176	**1415** 120l. multicoloured	40	25

1416 Arrows

1998. Cent of Bulgarian Telegraph Agency.

4177	**1416** 120l. multicoloured	40	25

1417 Barn Swallow at Window

1998. 120th Birth Anniv of Aleksandur Bozhinov (children's illustrator). Multicoloured.

4178	120l. Type **1417**	40	15
4179	120l. Blackbird with backpack on branch	40	15
4180	120l. Father Frost and children	40	15
4181	120l. Maiden Rositsa in field holding hands up to rain	40	15

1418 Tsar Alexander II

1998. 120th Anniv of Liberation from Turkey. Multicoloured.

4182	120l. Type **1418**	40	15
4183	600l. Independence monument, Ruse	2·00	95

1419 Christ ascending and Hare pulling Cart of Eggs

1998. Easter.

4184	**1419** 120l. multicoloured	40	25

1420 Torch Bearer

1998. 75th Anniv of Bulgarian Olympic Committee.

4185	**1420** 120l. multicoloured	40	25

1421 Map of Participating Countries

1998. Phare International Programme for Telecommunications and Post.

4186	**1421** 120l. multicoloured	40	25

1422 Girls in Folk Costumes

1998. Europa. National Festivals. Multicoloured.

4187	120l. Type **1422**	1·40	70
4188	600l. Boys wearing dance masks	3·50	2·75

ПЪРВИ
ЗЛАТЕН МЕДАЛ
ЗА БЪЛГАРИЯ

Е. ДАФОВСКА

(1423)

1998. Winning of Gold Medal in 15km Biathlon by Ekaterina Dafovska at Winter Olympic Games, Nagano. No. 4171 optd with T **1423**.

4189	120l. multicoloured	4·00	4·00

1424 *Dante and Virgil in Hell*

1998. Birth Bicentenary of Eugene Delacroix (artist).

4190	**1424** 120l. multicoloured	40	25

1425 Footballer and Club Badge

1998. 50th Anniv of TsSKA Football Club.

4191	**1425** 120l. multicoloured	40	25

1426 European Tabby

1998. Cats. Multicoloured.

4192	60l. Type **1426**	15	10
4193	80l. Siamese	25	15
4194	120l. Exotic shorthair	40	25
4195	600l. Birman	2·20	1·10

1427 *Oh, You are Jealous!*

1998. 150th Birth Anniv of Paul Gauguin (artist).

4196	**1427** 120l. multicoloured	40	25

1428 Khilendarski-Bozveli

1998. 150th Death Anniv of Neofit Khilendarski-Bozveli (priest and writer).

4197	**1428** 120l. multicoloured	40	25

1429 Tackling

1998. World Cup Football Championship, France. Multicoloured.

4198	60l. Type **1429**	15	10
4199	80l. Players competing for ball	25	15
4200	120l. Players and ball	40	25
4201	600l. Goalkeeper	2·20	1·10
MS4202	68 ×91 mm. 120l. Lion, ball and Eiffel Tower	1·40	1·40

1430 A. Aleksandrov

1998. Tenth Anniv of Second Soviet–Bulgarian Space Flight.

4203	**1430** 120l. multicoloured	55	25

1431 Vasco da Gama

1998. "Expo '98" World's Fair, Lisbon. 500th Anniv of Vasco da Gama's Voyage to India. Multicoloured.

4204	600l. Type **1431**	2·30	70
4205	600l. *Sao Gabriel* (Vasco da Gama's ship)	2·30	70

Nos. 4204/5 were issued together, *se-tenant*, forming a composite design.

1432 Focke Wolf FW 61, 1937

1998. Helicopters. Multicoloured.

4206	80l. Type **1432**	25	10
4207	100l. Sikorsky R-4, 1943	40	15
4208	120l. Mil Mi-V12, 1970	55	25
4209	200l. McDonnell-Douglas MD-900, 1995	80	40

1433 Mediterranean Monk Seal (*Monachus monachus*)

1998. International Year of the Ocean. Sheet 67×88 mm.

MS4210	**1433** 120l. multicoloured	4·75	4·75

1434 Talev

1998. Birth Centenary of Dimitur Talev (writer).

4211	**1434** 180l. multicoloured	70	40

1435 Aleksandur Malinov (Prime Minister, 1931)

1998. 90th Anniv of Independence.

4212	**1435** 180l. black, blue & yell	70	40

1436 *Limenitis redukta* and *Ligularia sibirica*

1998. Butterflies and Flowers. Multicoloured.

4213	60l. Type **1436**	10	10
4214	180l. Painted lady and *Anthemis macrantha*	70	25
4215	200l. Red admiral and *Trachelium jacquinii*	80	40
4216	600l. *Anthocharis gruneri* and *Geranium tuberosum*	2·20	1·20

1437 Smirnenski

1998. Birth Cent of Khristo Smirnenski (writer).

4217	**1437** 180l. multicoloured	70	40

1438 Silhouette of Man

1998. 50th Anniv of Universal Declaration of Human Rights.

4218	**1438** 180l. multicoloured	70	40

1439 Bruno

1998. 450th Birth Anniv of Giordano Bruno (scholar).

4219	**1439**	180l. multicoloured	70	40

1440 Man diving through Heart ("I Love You")

1998. Greetings Stamps. Multicoloured.

4220	180l. Type **1440**	70	40
4221	180l. Making wine (holiday) (vert)	70	40
4222	180l. Man in chalice (birthday) (vert)	70	40
4223	180l. Waiter serving wine (name day) (vert)	70	40

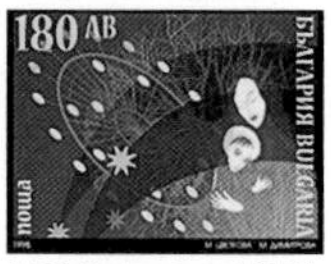

1441 Madonna and Child

1998. Christmas.

4224	**1441**	180l. multicoloured	70	40

1442 Geshov

1999. 150th Birth Anniv of Ivan Evstratiev Geshov (politician).

4225	**1442**	180l. multicoloured	70	40

1443 National Assembly Building, Sofia

1999. 120th Anniv of Third Bulgarian State. Multicoloured.

4226	180l. Type **1443**	70	40
4227	180l. Council of Ministers	70	40
4228	180l. Statue of Justice (Supreme Court of Appeal)	70	40
4229	180l. Coins (National Bank)	70	40
4230	180l. Army	70	40
4231	180l. Lion emblem of Sofia and lamp post	70	40

1444 Georgi Karakashev (stage designer) and Set of *Kismet*

1999. Birth Centenaries. Multicoloured.

4232	180l. Type **1444**	55	25
4233	200l. Bencho Obreshkov (artist) and *Lodki*	70	35
4234	300l. Score and Asen Naidenov (conductor of Sofia Opera)	80	40
4235	600l. Pancho Vladigerov (composer) and score of *Vardar*	1·90	95

1445 Rainbow Lory (*Trichoglossus haematodus*)

1999. "Bulgaria '99" European Stamp Exhibition. Parrots. Sheet 100×110 mm containing T **1445** and similar vert designs. Multicoloured.

MS4236	600l. Type **1445**; 600l. Eastern rosella; 600l. Budgerigar; 600l. Green-winged macaw	12·00	12·00

1446 Sun and Emblem

1999. 50th Anniv of North Atlantic Treaty Organization.

4237	**1446**	180l. multicoloured	55	25

1447 Decorated Eggs

1999. Easter.

4238	**1447**	180l. multicoloured	55	25

1448 Red-crested Pochard and Ropotamo Reserve

1999. Europa. Parks and Gardens. Multicoloured.

4239	180l. Type **1448**	95	40
4240	600l. Central Balkan National Park	2·40	2·00

1449 Albrecht Durer (self-portrait) and Nuremberg

1999. "iBRA '99" International Stamp Exhibition, Nuremberg, Germany.

4241	**1449**	600l. multicoloured	2·00	95

1450 Anniversary Emblem

1999. 50th Anniv of Council of Europe.

4242	**1450**	180l. multicoloured	1·40	70

1451 Honore de Balzac (novelist)

1999. Birth Anniversaries. Multicoloured.

4243	180l. Type **1451** (bicentenary)	55	15
4244	200l. Johann Wolfgang von Goethe (poet and playwright) (250th anniv)	95	25
4245	300l. Aleksandr Pushkin (poet) (bicentenary)	1·10	55
4246	600l. Diego de Silva Velazquez (painter) (400th anniv)	2·00	95

1452 Penny Farthing

1999. Bicycles. Multicoloured.

4247	180l. Type **1452**	55	10
4248	200l. Road racing bicycles	70	15
4249	300l. Track racing bicycles	1·10	40
4250	600l. Mountain bike	2·00	70

1453 St. Cyril and Methodius

1999. "Bulgaria '99" European Stamp Exhibition, Sofia. 19th-century Icons of Sts. Cyril and Methodius. Sheet 100×110 mm containing T **1453** and similar vert designs. Multicoloured.

MS4251	600l. Type **1453**; 600l. St. Cyril with scroll and staff and St. Methodius; 600l. Sts. Cyril and Methodius with scrolls; 600l. St. Cyril with crucifix, St. Methodius and Christ	11·00	11·00

1454 Sopot Monastery Fountain

1999. Fountains.

4252	**1454**	1st. light brown	15	10
4254	-	8st. green and black	15	10
4255	-	10st. deep brown	40	10
4257	-	18st. light blue	55	15
4258	-	20st. bright blue	55	25
4260	-	60st. brown and black	1·80	40

DESIGNS: 8st. Peacock Fountain, Karlovo; 10st. Peev Fountain, Kopivshtitsa; 18st. Sandanski Fountain; 20st. Eagle Owl Fountain, Karlovo; 60st. Fountain, Sokolski Monastery.

1455 *Oxytropis urumovii*

1999. "Bulgaria '99" European Stamp Exhibition, Sofia (2nd issue). Flowers in Pirin National Park. Sheet 109×100 mm containing T **1455** and similar horiz designs. Multicoloured.

MS4265	60st. Type **1455**; 60st. Bellflower; 60st. Iris; 60st. Spotted gentian	13·50	13·50

1456 Cracked Green Russula

1999. Fungi. Multicoloured.

4266	10st. Type **1456**	40	10
4267	18st. Field mushroom	55	15
4268	20st. *Hygrophorus russula*	80	25
4269	60st. Wood blewit	2·20	55

1457 Diagram of path of Eclipse

1999. Solar Eclipse (11 Aug 1999). Sheet 90×90 mm.

MS4270	**1457**	20st. multicoloured	2·00	2·00

1458 Four-leaved Clover

1999. Centenary of Organized Peasant Movement.

4271	**1458**	18st. multicoloured	40	25

1459 1884 25st. Postage Due Stamp

1999. "Bulgaria '99" European Stamp Exhibition, Sofia (3rd issue). 125th Anniv of Universal Postal Union. Sheet 110×102 mm containing T **1459** and similar vert deisgns. Multicoloured.

MS4272	60st. Type **1459**; 60st. Dove and hand with letter; 60st. Globe and left half of messenger; 60st. Right half of messenger with letter and globe	11·00	11·00

1460 Lesser Grey Shrike

1999. Song Birds and their Eggs. Multicoloured.

4273	8st. Type **1460**	25	10
4274	18st. Mistle thrush	55	15
4275	20st. Dunnock	70	25
4276	60st. Ortolan bunting	1·90	80

1461 Greek Tortoise

1999. Reptiles. Multicoloured.

4277	10st. Type **1461**	40	10
4278	18st. Swamp turtle	55	15
4279	30st. Hermann's tortoise	95	40
4280	60st. Caspian turtle	1·90	80

1462 Boxing (16 medals)

1999. Bulgarian Olympic Medal Winning Sports. Multicoloured.

4281	10st. Type **1462**	40	10
4282	20st. High jumping (17 medals)	70	25
4283	30st. Weightlifting (31 medals)	95	40
4284	60st. Wrestling (60 medals)	1·90	80

1463 Police Light and Emblem

1999. Tenth European Police Conference.

4285	**1463**	18st. multicoloured	40	25

1464 Jug

1999. Gold Artefacts from Panagyurishte.

4286	**1464**	2st. brown and green	10	10
4287	-	3st. brown and green	10	10
4288	-	5st. brown and blue	10	10
4289	-	30st. brown and violet	70	25
4290	-	1l. brown and red	2·40	1·40

DESIGNS: 3st. Human figures around top of drinking horn; 5st. Bottom of chamois-shaped drinking horn; 30st. Decorated handle and spout; 1l. Head-shaped jug.

1465 Virgin and Child

1999. Christmas. Religious Icons. Multicoloured.

4291		18st. Type **1465**	40	25
4292		60st. Jesus Christ	1·80	80

1466 Scout beside Fire

1999. Scouts. Multicoloured.

4293		10st. Type **1466**	40	15
4294		18st. Scout helping child	55	25
4295		30st. Scout saluting	80	40
4296		60st. Girl and boy scouts	1·60	80

1467 Emblem

1999. "Expo 2005" World's Fair, Aichi, Japan.

4297	**1467**	18st. multicoloured	55	25

1468 Emblem and Flag

2000. Bulgarian Membership of European Union.

4298	**1468**	18st. multicoloured	1·40	70

1469 White Stork (*Ciconia ciconia*)

2000. Endangered Species. Sheet 80×60 mm.

MS4299	**1469**	60st. multicoloured	2·75	2·75

1470 Peter Beron and Scientific Instruments

2000. Birth Anniversaries. Multicoloured.

4300		10st. Type **1470** (scientist, bicentenary)	40	15
4301		20st. Zakhari Stoyanov (writer, 150th anniv)	70	25
4302		50st. Kolyo Ficheto (architect, bicentenary)	1·40	55

1471 Madonna and Child with Circuit Board

2000. Europa. Multicoloured.

4303		18st. Type **1471**	1·40	70
4304		60st. Madonna and Child (Leonardo da Vinci) with circuit board	2·75	2·50

1472 Judo

2000. Olympic Games, Sydney. Multicoloured.

4305		10st. Type **1472**	25	10
4306		18st. Tennis	40	15
4307		20st. Pistol shooting	55	25
4308		60st. Long jump	1·60	80

1473 *Puss in Boots* (Charles Perrault)

2000. Children's Fairytales. Multicoloured.

4309		18st. Type **1473**	55	40
4310		18st. *Little Red Riding Hood* (Brothers Grimm)	55	40
4311		18st. *Thumbelina* (Hans Christian Andersen)	55	40

1474 *Friends* (detail) (Assen Vasiliev)

2000. Artists Birth Centenaries. Art. Multicoloured.

4312		18st. Type **1474**	55	25
4313		18st. *All Soul's Day* (detail) (Pencho Georgiev)	55	25
4314		18st. *Veliko Tunovo* (detail) (Ivan Khristov)	55	25
4315		18st. *At the Fountain* (sculpture) (detail) (Ivan Funev)	55	25

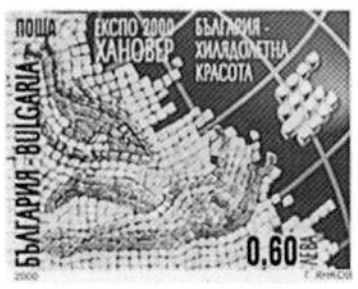

1475 Roman Mosaic (detail), Stara Zagora

2000. "EXPO 2000" World's Fair, Hanover, Germany.

4316	**1475**	60st. multicoloured	1·80	70

1476 Johannes Gutenberg (inventor of printing) and Printed Characters

2000. Anniversaries. Multicoloured.

4317		10st. Type **1476** (600th birth anniv)	25	10
4318		18st. Johann Sebastian Bach (composer, 250th death anniv)	40	15
4319		20st. Guy de Maupassant (writer, 150th birth anniv)	70	25
4320		60st. Antoine de Saint-Exupery (writer and aviator, birth centenary)	2·00	55

1477 *La Jeune* (Lebardy-Juillot airship) and Eiffel Tower, 1903

2000. Centenary of First Zeppelin Flight. Airship Development. Multicoloured.

4321		10st. Type **1477**	25	10
4322		18st. LZ-13 *Hansa* (Zeppelin airship) over Cologne	40	15
4323		20st. N-1 *Norge* over Rome	70	25
4324		60st. *Graf Zeppelin* over Sofia	2·00	80

1478 Vazov and Text

2000. 150th Birth Anniv of Ivan Vazov (writer).

4325	**1478**	18st. multicoloured	55	25

1479 Letter "e" with Hands

2000. 25th Anniv of Organization for Security and Co-operation in Europe. Helsinki Final Act (establishing governing principles). Sheet 68×72 mm containing T **1479** and similar horiz design. Multicoloured.

MS4326	20st. Type **1479**; 20st. Three "e's"	2·75	2·00

1480 St. Atanasii Church, Startsevo

2000. Churches.

4327	**1480**	22st. black and blue	55	10
4328	-	24st. black and mauve	70	15
4329	-	50st. black and yellow	1·40	40
4330	-	65st. black and green	1·80	70
4331	-	3l. black and orange	6·75	2·75
4332	-	5l. black and rose	11·00	4·75

DESIGNS: 24st. St. Clement of Orhid, Sofia; 50st. Mary of the Ascension, Sofia; 65st. St. Nedelya, Nedelino; 3l. Mary of the Ascension, Sofia (different), Sofia; 5l. Mary of the Ascension, Pamporovo.

1481 Ibex (*Capra ibex*)

2000. Animals. Multicoloured.

4333		10st. Type **1481**	25	10
4334		22st. Argali (*Ovis ammon*)	55	20
4335		30st. European bison (*Bison bonasus*)	70	25
4336		65st. Yak (*Bos grunniens*)	1·90	55

1482 Field Gladiolus (*Gladiolus segetum*)

2000. Spring Flowers. Multicoloured.

4337		10st. Type **1482**	25	10
4338		22st. Liverwort (*Hepatica nobilis*)	55	20
4339		30st. Pheasant's eye (*Adonis vernalis*)	80	25
4340		65st. Peacock anemone (*Anemone pavonina*)	1·90	55

1483 Crowd and Emblem

2000. 50th Anniv of European Convention on Human Rights.

4341	**1483**	65st. multicoloured	2·00	1·40

1484 Order of Gallantry, 1880

2000. Medals. Multicoloured.

4342		12st. Type **1484**	25	10
4343		22st. Order of St. Aleksandu, 1882	70	20
4344		30st. Order of Merit, 1891	80	25
4345		65st. Order of Cyril and Methodius, 1909	2·00	55

1485 Prince Boris-Mihail

2000. Bimillenary of Christianity. Multicoloured.

4346		22st. Type **1485**	70	25
4347		22st. St. Sofroni Vrachanski	70	25
4348		65st. Mary and Child (detail)	2·00	55
4349		65st. Antim I	2·00	55

1486 Seal

2000. 120th Anniv of Supreme Audit Office.

4350	**1486**	22st. multicoloured	70	25

1487 Microchip, Planets and *The Proportions of Man* (Leonardo DaVinci)

2001. New Millennium.

4351	**1487**	22st. multicoloured	70	25

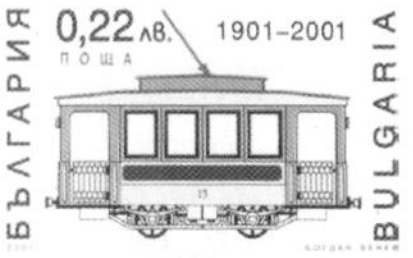

1488 Tram

2001. Centenary of the Electrification of Bulgarian Transport. Multicoloured.

4352		22st. Type **1488**	70	25
4353		65st. Train carriages	2·00	55

1489 Muscat Grapes and Evsinograd Palace

2001. Viticulture. Multicoloured.

4354		12st. Type **1489**	25	10
4355		22st. Gumza grapes and Baba Vida Fortress	70	20
4356		30st. Shiroka Melnishka Loza grapes and Melnik Winery	80	25
4357		65st. Mavrud grapes and Asenova Krepost Fortress	2·00	55

1490 "@" and Microcircuits

2001. Information Technology. Sheet 82×95 mm containing T **1490** and similar horiz design. Multicoloured.

MS4358	Type **1490**; 65st. John Atanasoff (computer pioneer) and ABC	34·00	34·00

1491 Southern Europe and Emblem

2001. Tenth Anniv of the Atlantic Club of Bulgaria. Sheet 87×67 mm.
MS4359 **1491** 65st. multicoloured 5·50 4·00

1492 Eagle and Lakes, Rila

2001. Europa. Water Resources. Multicoloured.
4360 22st. Type **1492** 1·40 1·10
4361 65st. Cave and waterfall, Rhodope 26·00 23·00

1493 Building, Bridge and Kableschkov

2001. 125th Anniv of the April Uprising and 150th Birth Anniv of Todor Kableschkov (revolutionary leader).
4362 **1493** 22st. multicoloured 70 40

1494 Juvenile Egyptian Vulture in Flight

2001. Endangered Species. Egyptian Vulture (*Neophron percnopterus*). Multicoloured.
4363 12st. Type **1494** 40 10
4364 22st. Juvenile landing 70 25
4365 30st. Adult and chick 80 40
4366 65st. Adult and eggs 1·90 55

1495 Georgi (Gundy) Asparuchov (footballer)

2001. Sportsmen. Multicoloured.
4367 22st. Type **1495** 70 40
4368 30st. Dancho (Dan) Kolev (wrestler) 80 50
4369 65st. Gen. Krum Lekarski (equestrian) 1·90 1·10

1496 Rainbow and People

2001. 50th Anniv United Nations High Commissioner for Refugees.
4370 **1496** 65st. multicoloured 1·90 65

1497 Alexander Zhendov

2001. Artists Birth Centenaries. Multicoloured.
4371 22st. Type **1497** 70 40
4372 65st. Ilya Beshkov 2·00 1·20

1498 Court Seal

2001. Tenth Anniv of Constitutional Court.
4373 **1498** 25st. multicoloured 70 40

1499 Flags

2001. North Atlantic Treaty Organization Summit, Sofia. Sheet 116×111 mm containing T 1499 and similar horiz designs.
MS4374 12st. Type **1499**; 24st. Streamer of flags; 25st. Flags in upper right semi-circle; 65st. Flags in upper left semi-circle 3·00 2·00

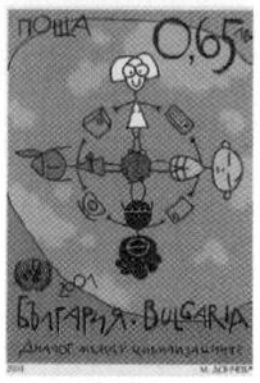
1500 Children encircling Globe

2001. United Nations Year of Dialogue among Civilizations.
4375 **1500** 65st. multicoloured 1·80 80

1501 Black Sea Turbot (*Scopthalmus maeoticus*)

2001. International Day for the Protection of the Black Sea. Sheet 73×91 mm.
MS4376 **1501** 65st. multicoloured 1·30 1·10

1502 The Nativity

2001. Christmas.
4377 **1502** 25st. multicoloured 70 40

1503 Cape Shabla Lighthouse

2001. Lighthouses.
4378 **1503** 25st. red and green 70 40
4379 - 32st. blue and yellow 80 50
DESIGN: 32st. Kaliakra Cape lighthouse.

1504 Monastery Buildings

2001. Zographu Monastery, Mount Athos. Sheet 85×105 mm containing T **1504** and similar horiz design. Multicoloured.
MS4380 25st. Type **1504**; 65st. Icon 2·75 2·00

1505 Father Christmas (from film by Al. Zahariev)

2001. Bulgarian Animation.
4381 **1505** 25c. multicoloured 80 50

1506 Vincenzo Bellini

2001. Birth Bicentenary of Vincenzo Bellini (composer).
4382 **1506** 25st. multicoloured 80 50

1507 Crowd and Ancient Calendar

2001. Founders of Bulgarian State (1st series). Multicoloured.
4383 10st. Type **1507** 25 10
4384 25st. Khans, Kubrat and Asparuh 80 50
4385 30st. Khans, Krum and Omurtag 95 55
4386 65st. King Boris and Tsar Simeon 2·00 1·20
See also Nos. 4427/7, 4456/9, 4511/14, 4559/62 and 4610/13.

1508 "€" Symbol and Stars

2002. The Euro (European currency).
4387 **1508** 65st. multicoloured 2·00 1·20

1509 Matches

2002. 50th Anniv of United Nations Disarmament Commission.
4388 **1509** 25st. multicoloured 80 50

1510 Limestone Arch

2002. "BALKANMAX '02" International Stamp Exhibition. Sheet 95×87 mm containing T **1510** and similar vert design. Multicoloured.
MS4389 25st. Type **1510**; 65st. Long-legged buzzard (*Buteo rufinus*) 34·00 33·00

1511 Figure Skater

2002. Winter Olympic Games, Salt Lake City. Multicoloured.
4390 25st. Type **1511** 80 50
4391 65st. Speed skater 2·00 1·20

1512 Station Building and Bearded Penguins

2002. Tenth National Antarctic Expedition.
4392 **1512** 25st. multicoloured 80 50

1513 Performing Elephant

2002. Europa. Circus. Multicoloured.
4393 25st. Type **1513** 95 55
4394 65st. Clown 2·40 1·50

1514 Veselin Stojano

2002. Birth Centenaries. Multicoloured.
4395 25st. Type **514** (composer) 80 50
4396 65st. Angel Karaliechev (writer) 95 55

1515 *Illustrated Landscape* (Vasil Barakov)

2002. Art. Multicoloured.
4397 10st. Type **1515** 25 10
4398 25st. Book illustration from *Under the Yoke* (novel by Ivan Vazov) (Boris Angulshev) (horiz) 80 50
4399 65st. *The Balcony and Canary* (Ivan Nenov) 2·00 1·20

1516 Stefan Kanchev

2002. First Death Annivs of Stamp Designers. Multicoloured.
4400 25st. Type **1516** 80 50
4401 65st. Alex Popilov 2·00 1·20

1517 Melon (*Cucumis melo*)

2002. Fruits. Multicoloured.
4402 10st. Type **1517** 40 25
4403 25st. Watermelon (*Citrullus lanatus*) 80 50
4404 27st. Pumpkin (*Cucurbita pepo*) 90 55
4405 65st. Calabash (*Lagenaria siceraria*) 2·00 1·20

1518 Cock Bird

2002. Poultry. Multicoloured.
4406 10st. Type **1518** 40 25
4407 20st. Leghorn pair (horiz) 70 40
4408 25st. Two cocks fighting (horiz) 80 50
4409 65st. Plymouth rock pair (inscr "Plimouth Rock") 2·00 1·20

1519 Pope John Paul II and Monument to Cyril & Methodius

2002. Pope John Paul II's Visit to Bulgaria.
4410 **1519** 65st. multicoloured 2·00 1·20

1520 Chess Pieces

2002. Sheet 91×71 mm containing T **1520** and similar vert design.

MS4411 25st. brown, cinnamon and black (Type **1520**); 65st. multicoloured (Hand holding pawn)	2·75	2·00

1521 Flag and Stars

2002. Tenth Anniv of Bulgaria's Admission to Council of Europe.

4412	**1521**	25st. multicoloured	80	50

1522 Rabbit

2002. Woodcarvings by Peter Kuschlev.

4413	**1522**	6st. brown and black	15	10
4414	-	12st. orange and black	40	25
4415	-	36st. green and black	1·10	65
4416	-	44st. pink and black	1·40	80

DESIGNS: 12st. Deer; 36st. Bird; 44st. Boar.

1523 *Marie-Luisa* (1st ocean-going liner)

2002. Merchant Ships. Multicoloured.

4417	12st. Type **1523**	40	25
4418	36st. *Persenk* (cargo ship)	1·10	65
4419	49st. *Kaliakra* (sail training ship)	1·60	1·00
4420	65st. *Sofia* (container ship)	2·00	1·20

1524 Father Christmas and Sun

2002. Christmas.

4421	**1524**	36st. multicoloured	1·10	65

1525 Flag and NATO Emblem

2002. Bulgaria's Participation in NATO Conference, Prague. Sheet 85×65 mm.

MS4422 **1525** 65st. multicoloured	4·00	3·00

1526 Paper Bird

2002. 30th Anniv of Security and Co-operation in Europe Conference. Sheet 85×60 mm.

MS4423 **1526** 65st. multicoloured	3·50	2·75

1527 Tsar Samuil

2002. Founders of Bulgarian State (2nd series). Multicoloured.

4424	18st. Type **1527**	55	35
4425	36st. Tsars Peter II and Assen	1·10	65
4426	49st. Tsar Kaloyan	1·40	80
4427	65st. Tsar Ivan Assen II	1·90	1·10

1528 Exhibition Emblem

2003. Europalia Cultural Exhibition, Belgium.

4428	**1528**	65st. multicoloured	2·00	1·20

1529 *Rose Pickers* (Stoyan Sotirov)

2003. Artists' Birth Centenaries. Multicoloured.

4429	18st. Type **1529**	55	35
4430	36st. *The Blind Fiddler* (Illya Petrov)	1·10	65
4431	65st. *Swineherd* (Zlatyo Boyadjiev)	1·90	1·10

1530 Space Construction surrounding Earth

2003. Space Exploration. Sheet 104×85 mm.

MS4432 **1530** 65st. multicoloured	2·75	2·00

1531 Statue of Russian and Bulgarian Soldiers

2003. 125th Anniv of Bulgarian State.

4433	**1531**	36st. multicoloured	1·10	65

1532 Exarch Stefan I, Menorah Candlestick and Dimitar Peshev

2003. 60th Anniv of Rescue of Bulgarian Jews.

4434	**1532**	36st. multicoloured	1·10	65

1533 Silhouettes of Birds and Woman

2003. Europa. Poster Art. Multicoloured.

4435	36st. Type **1533**	1·10	65
4436	65st. Chicken, legs and farm animals	1·90	1·10

1534 *Vase with Fifteen Sunflowers*

2003. 150th Birth Anniv of Vincent van Gogh (artist). Sheet 70×90 mm.

MS4437 **1534** 65st. multicoloured	1·90	1·50

1535 Pterodactylus

2003. Dinosaurs. Multicoloured.

4438	30st. Type **1535**	80	50
4439	36st. Gorgosaurus	1·10	65
4440	49st. Mesosaurus	1·50	90
4441	65st. Monoclonius	1·90	1·10

1536 *Nymphoides Peltata*

2003. Water Plants (1st issue). Multicoloured.

4442	**1536**	36st. multicoloured	1·10	65

See also Nos. 4447/50.

1537 Honey Bee (*Apis mellifera*)

2003. Bees. Multicoloured.

4443	20st. Type **1537**	55	35
4444	30st. *Anthidium manicatum*	80	50
4445	36st. Bumble bee (*Bombus subterraneus*)	95	55
4446	65st. Blue carpenter bee (*Xylocopa violacea*)	1·80	1·10

1538 *Butomus umbellatus*

2003. Water Plants (2nd issue). Multicoloured.

4447	20st. Type **1538**	55	35
4448	36st. *Sagirraria sagittifolia*	1·10	65
4449	50st. *Menyanthes trifoliate*	1·50	90
4450	65st. *Iris pseudoacorus*	1·90	1·10

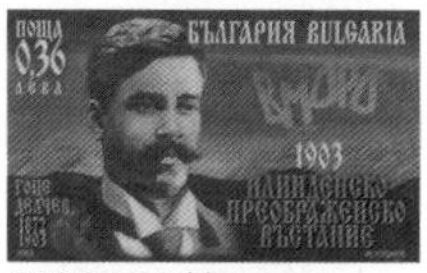

1539 Gotze Delchev

2003. Death Centenary of Gotze Delchev (revolutionary). Centenary of Macedonian Uprising.

4451	**1539**	36st. multicoloured	1·10	65

1540 Mountains

2003. International Year of Mountains.

4452	**1540**	65st. multicoloured	6·00	4·50

1541 Bulgarian and USA Flags as Bowtie

2003. Centenary of Bulgaria—USA Diplomatic Relations.

4453	**1541**	65st. multicoloured	1·90	1·10

1542 John Atanasoff

2003. Birth Centenary of John Atanasoff (computer pioneer).

4454	**1542**	65st. multicoloured	1·90	1·10

1543 Pawn and Buildings

2003. European Chess Championship, Plovdiv.

4455	**1543**	65st. multicoloured	1·90	1·10

1544 Tsar Ivan Alexander

2003. Founders of Bulgarian State (3rd series). Multicoloured.

4456	30st. Type **1544**	80	50
4457	45st. Despot Dobrotitsa	1·20	75
4458	65st. Tsar Ivan Shishman	1·90	1·10
4459	89st. Tsar Ivan Sratsimir	2·20	1·30

1545 Taekwondo

2003. 80th Anniv of National Olympic Committee. Multicoloured.

4460	20st. Type **1545**	55	35
4461	36st. Mountain biking	1·10	65
4462	50st. Softball	1·50	90
4463	65st. Canoe slalom	1·90	1·10

1546 Father Christmas

2003. Christmas.

4464	**1546**	65st. multicoloured	1·90	1·10

1547 Carriage and Man wearing Top Hat

2003. Carriages. Multicoloured.

4465	30st. Type **1547**	80	50
4466	36st. Closed carriage with woman passenger	1·10	65
4467	50st. State coach, woman and dog	1·50	90
4468	65st. Couple and large carriage	1·90	1·10

1548 FIFA Centenary Emblem

2003. Centenary of FIFA (Federation Internationale de Football Association). Multicoloured.

4469	20st. Type **1548**	55	35
4470	25st. Early players	70	40
4471	36st. Early players and rules	1·10	65
4472	50st. FIFA fair play trophy (vert)	1·40	80
4473	65st. FIFA world player trophy (vert)	1·90	1·10

1549 Eye, Square, Compass and Statue

2003. Tenth Anniv of Re-establishment of Masonic Activity in Bulgaria.

4474	**1549** 80st. multicoloured	2·20	1·30

1550 *Noctua tertia*

2004. Moths. Multicoloured.

4475	40st. Type **1550**	1·10	65
4476	45st. *Rethera komarovi*	1·20	75
4477	55st. *Symtomis marjana*	1·50	90
4478	80st. *Arctia caja*	2·20	1·30

1551 Mask

2004. SERVA, International Masquerade Festival, Pernik.

4479	**1551** 80st. multicoloured	2·20	1·40

1552 OSCE Emblem and Bridge

2004. Bulgaria, Chair of Organization for Security and Co-operation in Europe.

4480	**1552** 80st. multicoloured	2·10	1·30

1553 Theatre Facade

2004. Centenary of Ivan Vazov National Theatre, Sofia.

4481	**1553** 45st. multicoloured	1·30	80

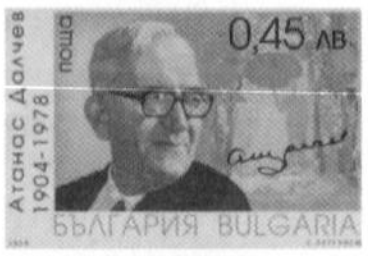

1554 Atanas Dalchev

2004. Birth Centenaries. Multicoloured.

4482	45st. Type **1554** (poet)	1·30	80
4483	80st. Lubomir Pipkov (composer)	2·20	1·40

1555 NATO Emblem and National Colours

2004. Accession to Full Membership of NATO.

4484	**1555** 80st. multicoloured	2·75	1·80

1556 Georgi Ivanov

2004. 25th Anniv of First Bulgarian in Space. Sheet 84×68 mm.

MS4485	**1556** 80st. multicoloured	2·20	1·90

1557 Cover of Document

2004. 125th Anniv of Turnovska Constitution and Restoration of Bulgarian State. Sheet 86×67 mm.

MS4486	**1557** 45st. multicoloured	7·00	5·25

1558 Globe surmounted by Mortar Board

2004. "Bulgarian Dream" (graduate assistance) Programme.

4487	**1558** 45st. multicoloured	1·30	80

1559 Salvador Dali (sculpture)

2004. Birth Centenary of Salvador Dali (artist). Sheet 85×65 mm.

MS4488	**1559** 80st. multicoloured	4·25	3·50

1560 Luben Dimitrov (sculptor) and Boris Ivanov (cinema director)

2004. Birth Centenaries. Multicoloured.

4489	45st. Type **1560**	1·40	90
4490	80st. Vassil Stoilov and Stoyan Venev (artists)	2·20	1·40

1561 Mountains and Skiers

2004. Europa. Holidays. Multicoloured.

4491	45st. Type **1561**	1·40	90
4492	80st. Beach scene	2·20	1·40

1562 Christo Stoychkov

2004. Bulgarian Footballers. Multicoloured.

4493	45st. Type **1562**	1·40	90
4494	45st. Georgi Asparuchov	1·40	90
4495	45st. Krassimir Balakov	1·40	90
4496	45st. Nikola Kotkov	1·40	90

1563 Footballer and Ball

2004. European Football Championship 2004, Portugal. Sheet 85×67 mm.

MS4497	**1563** 80st. multicoloured	2·20	1·90

1564 Seal

2004. 125th Anniv of Bulgaria—Austria Diplomatic Relations.

4498	**1564** 80st. multicoloured	2·20	1·40

1565 Lion (statue), Flag and Document

2004. 125th Anniv of Ministry of Interior.

4499	**1565** 45st. multicoloured	1·40	90

1566a De Dion Button Post Car (1905)

2004. 125th Anniv of Postal Service. Sheet 93×80 mm.

MS4500	**1566a** 45st. multicoloured	7·00	5·75

No. **MS**4500 contains a se-tenant stamps size label, which with the stamp forms a composite design.

1567 Red Kite (*Milvus milvus*)

2004. Endangered Species. Preservation of the Black Sea. Sheet 86×86 mm containing T **1567** and similar horiz design. Multicoloured.

MS4501	45st. Type **1567**; 80st. *Blennius ocellaris*	3·75	3·00

1568 Runner holding Torch and Olympic Flame (Berlin, 1936)

2004. Olympic Games, Athens 2004. Designs showing runner and Olympic flame. Multicoloured.

4502	10st. Type **1568**	30	20
4503	20st. Munich, 1972	55	35
4504	45st. Moscow, 1980	1·40	90
4505	80st. Athens, 2004	2·20	1·40

1569 *Krum* (steamer)

2004. 125th Anniv of Bulgarian Navy. Multicoloured.

4506	10st. Type **1569**	30	20
4507	25st. *Druski* (torpedo boat)	70	45
4508	45st. *Christo Botev* (minesweeper)	1·40	90
4509	80st. *Smeli* (frigate)	2·20	1·40

1570 Square and Compass

2004. 125th Anniv of Bulgarian Masonic Movement.

4510	**1570** 45st. multicoloured	7·00	5·25

1571 Patriarch Ephtimius Turnovski

2004. Founders of Bulgarian State (4th series). Multicoloured.

4511	10st. Type **1571**	30	20
4512	20st. Kniaz Fruzhin and Kniaz Constantine	70	45
4513	45st. Georgi Peyachevich and Peter Partchevich	1·40	90
4514	80st. Piessii Hilendarski	2·50	1·60

1572 *Polyporus squamosus*

2004. Fungi. Sheet 125×93 mm containing T **1572** and similar horiz designs. Multicoloured.

MS4515	10st. Type **1572**; 20st. *Fomes fomentarius*; 45st. *Piptoporus betulinus*; 80st. *Laetiporus sulphurous*	5·00	3·75

1573 Two Sturgeon

2004. Sturgeon (*Huso huso*). Multicoloured.

4516	80st. Type **1573**	2·50	1·60
4517	80st. From below	2·50	1·60
4518	80st. Looking down	2·50	1·60
4519	80st. Eating	2·50	1·60

1574 Father Christmas

2004. Christmas.

4520	**1574** 45st. multicoloured	1·40	90

1575 Hands

2004. 12th Organization for Security and Co-operation in Europe (OSCE) Council, Sofia. Sheet 84×67 mm.

MS4521	80st. multicoloured	2·10	1·90

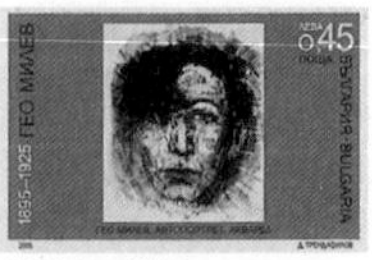

1576 Geo Milev

2005. Birth Centenary of Georghi Milev Kassabov (Geo Milev) (writer and revolutionary).

4522	**1576** 45st. multicoloured	1·50	1·10

1577 Emblem

2005. Centenary of Rotary International (charitable organization).
4523 **1577** 80st. multicoloured 2·40 1·70

1578 Charlie Chaplin in *Gold Rush* (1925)

2005. History of Cinema. Sheet 88×118 mm containing T **1578** and similar vert designs. Multicoloured.
MS4524 10st. Type **1578**; 20st. Scene from *Battleship Potemkin (Bronenoset Potemkin)* (1925); 45st. Marlene Dietrich in *Blue Angel (Der Blaue Engel)* (1930); 80st. Vassil Ghendov in *Bulgarian is a Gallant Man* (first Bulgarian film) 4·75 4·25

1579 *The Monument* (lithograph) (Nickolai Pavlovitch)

2005. 135th Anniv of Exarchate (independent Bulgarian ecclesiastical organisation). Sheet 68×88 mm.
MS4525 **1579** 45st. multicoloured 2·20 1·80

1580 European Stars and Bulgarian Flag

2005. Volunteers for Europe (educational campaign).
4526 **1580** 80st. multicoloured 2·40 1·70

1581 Panayot Hitov and Philip Totyo

2005. 175th Birth Anniv of Panayot Hitov and Philip Totyo (revolutionaries).
4527 **1581** 45st. multicoloured 1·50 1·10

1582 Robert Peary

2005. Polar Explorers. Sheet 64×95 mm containing T **1582** and similar horiz design. Multicoloured.
MS4528 45st. Type **1582** (American) (North Pole, 1909); 80st. Rual Admundsen (Norwegian) (South Pole, 1911) 3·75 3·25

1583 Peugeot (1936)

2005. Fire Engines. Sheet 136×77 mm containing T **1583** and similar horiz design. Multicoloured.
MS4529 10st. Type **1583**; 20st. Mercedes (1935); 45st. Magirus (1934); 80st. Renault (1925) 4·75 4·00

1584 Hans Christian Andersen

2005. Birth Bicentenary of Hans Christian Andersen (writer). Sheet 87×78 mm.
MS4530 **1584** 80st. multicoloured 2·40 2·00

1585 Hand holding Scroll

2005. Cyrillic Alphabet. Sheet 88×59 mm.
MS4531 **1585** 80st. multicoloured 2·40 2·00

1586 Electric Locomotive 46

2005. Railways. Multicoloured.
4532 45st. Type **1586** 1·50 1·10
4533 80st. Modern locomotive DMV 10 7·25 5·50

1587 *Radetski* (revolutionary ship) (Georgi Dimov)

2005. Children's Painting.
4534 **1587** 45st. multicoloured 1·50 1·10

1588 Blinis

2005. Europa. Gastronomy. Multicoloured.
4535 45st. Type **1588** 1·50 1·10
4536 80st. Bread, kebab and tomatoes 2·40 1·70

1589 Stylized Figures

2005. 50th Anniv of Europa—CEPT Postage Stamps.
4537 **1589** 45st. violet, green and black 1·50 1·10
4538 - 80st. blue, magenta and black 2·40 1·70
DESIGNS: 45st. Type **1589**; 80st. Square of figures.

1590 *Cordulegaster bidentata*

2005. Dragonflies. Multicoloured.
4539 10st. Type **1590** 30 20
4540 20st. *Erythromma najas* (horiz) 60 45
4541 45st. *Sympetrum pedemontanum* (horiz) 1·30 1·00
4542 80st. *Brachytron pratense* 2·50 1·80

1591 Elias Canetti

2005. Birth Centenary of Elias Canetti (writer).
4543 **1591** 80st. multicoloured 2·50 1·80

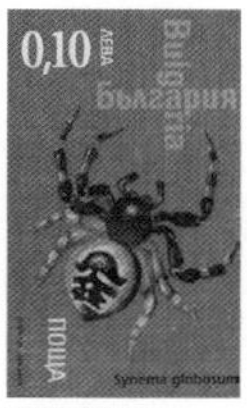

1592 *Synema globosum*

2005. Spiders. Multicoloured.
4544 10st. Type **1592** 30 20
4545 20st. *Argiope bruennichi* 60 45
4546 45st. *Eresus cinnaberinus* 1·30 1·00
4547 80st. *Araneus diadematus* 2·50 1·80

1593 Flag as Tree Bark

2005. 110th Anniv of Organized Tourism.
4548 **1593** 45st. multicoloured 1·20 90

1594 Map

2005. 120th Anniv of Unification of Bulgaria.
4549 **1594** 45st. multicoloured 1·20 90

1595 Girl wearing Traditional Costume, Sofia

2005. Women's Traditional Costumes. Multicoloured.
4550 20st. Type **1595** 50 40
4551 25st. Pleven 70 55
4552 45st. Sliven 1·20 90
4553 80st. Stara Zagora 2·00 1·60

1596 Stamen Grigoroff (discoverer)

2005. Centenary of Discovery of Lactobacillus bulgaricus Grigoroff (yoghurt bacilli) (1st issue). Sheet 94×81 mm.
MS4554 **1596** 80st. multicoloured 2·20 1·70
See also **MS**4557.

1597 Chess Board and Antoaneta Steffanova (Women's World Chess Champion)

2005. Chess.
4555 **1597** 80st. multicoloured 2·00 1·60

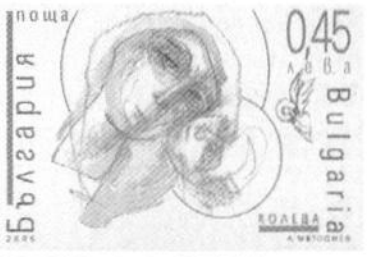

1598 Virgin and Child

2005. Christmas.
4556 **1598** 45st. multicoloured 1·20 90

1599 Stamen Grigoroff (discoverer)

2005. Centenary of Discovery of Lactobacillus bulgaricus Grigoroff (yoghurt bacilli) (2nd issue). Sheet 94×81 mm. Imperf.
MS4557 **1599** 80st. multicoloured 20·00 18·00
The design of **MS**4557 is as Type **1596** with the addition of an owl in the top right corner. The sheets include a perforated number.

1600 Stylized Couple

2005. 50th Anniv of Membership of United Nations. Sheet 86×88 mm.
4558 **1600** 80st. multicoloured 2·20 1·70

1601 Patriarchs Illarion Makariopolski and Antim I

2005. Founders of Bulgarian State (5th series).
4559 **1601** 10st. chocolate and green 35 25
4560 - 20st. brown and green 50 40
4561 - 45st. claret and green 1·20 90
4562 - 80st. purple and green 2·00 1·60
DESIGNS: 10st. Type **1601**; 20st. Georgi Rakovski and Vassil Levski; 45st. Luben Karavelov and Christo Botev; 80st. Panayot Volov and Pavel Bobekov.

1602 *Rosa pendulina*

2006. Roses. Multicoloured.
4563 54st. Type **1602** 1·40 1·10
4564 1l.50 *Rosa gallica* 3·75 3·00
4565 2l. *Rosa spinosissima* 5·00 4·00
4566 10l. *Rosa arvensis* 24·00 18·00

1603 Mozart

2006. 250th Birth Anniv of Wolfgang Amadeus Mozart.
4567 **1603** 1l. multicoloured 8·50 8·00

1604 Ellin Pellin (writer)

2006. 115th Anniv of National Philatelic Press. Bulgarian Philatelists. Multicoloured.

4568	35st. Type **1604**	85	80
4569	55st. Lazar Dobritch (circus artiste)	1·40	1·20
4570	60st. Boris Christov (opera singer)	1·50	1·30
4571	1l. Bogomil Nonev (writer)	2·50	2·10

1605 Snowboarder

2006. Winter Olympic Games, Turin. Sheet 86×118 mm containing T **1605** and similar vert design. Multicoloured.

MS4572 55st. Type **1605**; 1l. Ice dancers 4·00 3·75

1606 Sextant

2006. Tenth Anniv of Bulgarian Antarctic Cartography. Sheet 86×69 mm.

MS4573 **1606** 1l. multicoloured 2·50 2·20

1607 Ship (15th Century manuscript)

2006. 610th Anniv of Battle at Nikopol.

4574 **1607** 1l.50 multicoloured 3·50 2·75

1608 *Martes martes*

2006. Ecology. Sheet 86×118 mm containing T **1608** and similar horiz design. Multicoloured.

MS4575 55st. Type **1608**; 1l.50 *Ursus arctos* 4·75 4·25

1609 Stylized Figure and Stars

2006. Europa. Integration. Multicoloured.

4576	55st. Type **1609**	1·70	1·30
4577	1l. Star as flower	3·50	2·75

1610 Emblem

2006. Meeting of NATO Foreign Ministers, Sofia. Sheet 87×70 mm.

MS4578 **1610** 1l.50 multicoloured 3·50 3·25

1611 Mastheads

2006. 70th Anniv of *Trud* Newspaper.

4579 **1611** 55st. multicoloured 2·50 2·00

1612 Vesselin Topalov

2006. Vesselin Topalov—World Chess Champion. Sheet 87×71 mm.

MS4580 **1612** 1l.50 multicoloured 3·50 3·25

No. **MS**4580 also exist imperforate.

1613 Building Facade

2006. 25th Anniv of National Palace of Culture.

4581 **1613** 55st. multicoloured 1·70 1·50

1614 *Circus aeruginosus*

2006. Raptors. Multicoloured.

4582	10st. Type **1614**	35	25
4583	35st. *Circus cyaneus*	85	65
4584	55st. *Circus macrourus*	1·20	90
4585	1l. *Circus pygargus*	2·75	2·10

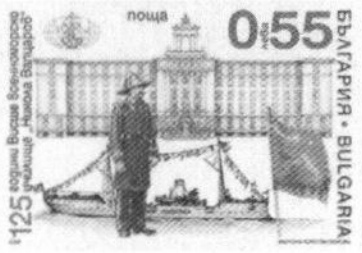
1615 Building Facade, Ship and Sailor

2006. 125th Anniv of Nikola Vaptsarov Naval Academy, Varna.

4586 **1615** 55st. multicoloured 1·20 90

1616 Players

2006. World Cup Football Championship, Germany. Sheet 87×87 mm.

MS4587 **1616** 1l. multicoloured 2·20 2·00

1617 Emblem

2006. 50th Anniv of Bulgaria in UNESCO.

4588 **1617** 1l. multicoloured 2·20 1·70

1618 Gena Dimitrova

2006. 65th Birth Anniv and First Death Anniv of Gena Dimitrova (opera singer).

4589 **1618** 1l. multicoloured 2·20 1·70

1619 *Saponaria strajensis*

2006. Flora. Multicoloured.

4590	10st. Type **1619**	35	25
4591	35st. *Trachystemon orientalis*	85	65
4592	55st. *Hypericum calycinum*	1·20	90
4593	1l. *Rhododendron ponticum*	2·75	2·10

1620 Rover Maestro

2006. Bulgaria Automobile Industry. Multicoloured.

4594	10st. Type **1620**	35	25
4595	35st. Moskovitch	85	65
4596	55st. Bulgaralpine	1·20	90
4597	1l. Bulgarrnault	2·75	2·10

1621 *Return of the Prodigal Son*

2006. 400th Birth Anniv of Rembrandt Harmenszoon van Rijn. Sheet 65×84 mm.

MS4598 **1621** 1l. multicoloured 2·75 2·40

1622 *All Soul's Day* (Ivan Murkvitchka)

2006. Art Anniversaries. Multicoloured.

4599	10st. Type **1622** (150th birth anniv)	35	25
4600	35st. *Sozopol—Houses* (Vesselin Statkov) (birth centenary)	1·00	80
4601	55st. *Sofia in Winter* (Nikola Petrov) (90th death anniv)	1·50	1·20
4602	1l. *T. Popova* (John Popov) (birth centenary)	2·75	2·10

1623 Competitors

2006. World Sambo Championship, Sofia.

4603 **1623** 55st. multicoloured 1·50 1·20

1624 Post Van

2006. Post Europ. Sheet 85×75 mm.

MS4604 **1624** 1l. multicoloured 15·00 14·50

1625 Angel

2006. Christmas.

4605 **1625** 55st. multicoloured 1·50 1·20

1626 Ballot Box and Flags

2006. Bulgaria and Romania's Membership of European Union. Multicoloured.

4606	55st. Type **1626**	1·50	1·20
4607	1l.50 "EU"	4·00	3·25

MS4608 97×87 mm. Nos. 4606/7 5·75 5·50

Stamps of a similar design were issued by Romania.

1627 Peter Dimkov

2006. 120th Birth Anniv of Peter Dimkov (naturopath).

4609 **1627** 55st. multicoloured 1·50 1·20

1628 Generals Danail Nikolaev and Racho Petrov

2006. Founders of Bulgarian State (6th series). Multicoloured.

4610	10st. Type **1628**	35	25
4611	35st. Petko Karavelov and Marin Drinov	1·00	80
4612	55st. Konstantin Stoylov and Stephan Stambolov	1·50	1·20
4613	1l. Prince Albert I of Bulgaria	2·75	2·10

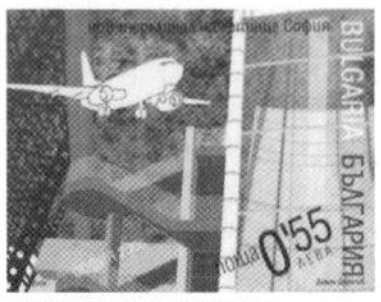
1629 Boeing 737 and Terminal Building

2006. New Airport Terminal, Sofia. Sheet 87×72 mm.

MS4614 **1629** 55st. multicoloured 1·50 1·30

1631 Emilian Stanev

2007. Birth Centenary of Nikola Stoyanov Stanev (Emilian Stanev) (writer).

4616 **1631** 55st. multicoloured 1·40 1·10

1632 Flags as Stars

2007. 50th Anniv of Treaty of Rome.

4617 **1632** 1l. multicoloured 2·50 2·00

1633 Ivan Dimov

2007. Theatre Personalities. Multicoloured.

4618	10st. Type **1633**	35	25
4619	55st. Sava Ognyanov	1·40	1·10
4620	1l. Krustyo Sarfov	2·50	2·00

1634 Sputnik

2007. 50th Anniv of First Manmade Satellite. Sheet 87×56 mm.

MS4621 **1634** 1l. multicoloured 2·50 2·40

1635 Campfire

2007. Europa. Centenary of Scouting. Multicoloured. (a) Size 39×28 mm.

4622	55st. Type **1635**	1·40	1·10
4623	1l.50 Route finding	3·75	3·00

(b) Size 31×23 mm.

4624	1l. As Type **1635**	1·40	1·10
4625	1l. As No. 4623	3·75	3·00

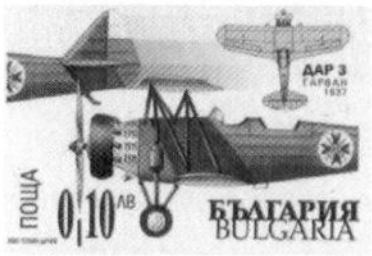

1636 DAR-3 Garvan II (1937)

2007. Military Aircraft. Multicoloured.

4626	10st. Type **1636**	35	25
4627	35st. DAR-9 Siniger (1939)	85	65
4628	55st. Kaproni Bulgarski KB-6 Papagal (1939)	1·40	1·10
4629	1l. Kaproni Bulgarski KB-11A Fanzan	2·50	2·00

1637 Boris I

2007. 1100th Death Anniv of Knyaz (Prince) Boris I (Michael).

4630	**1637**	55st. multicoloured	1·40	1·10

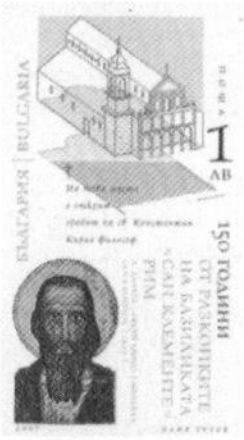

1637a Basilica and Saint Cyril

2007. 150th Anniv of Excavation of San Clement Basilica, Rome.

4630a	**1637a**	1l. multicoloured	2·75	2·10

1638 Dimcho Debelyanov

2007. Birth Anniversaries. Multicoloured.

4631	10st. Type **1638** (poet) (120th)	35	25
4632	35st. Nenko Balkanski (artist) (centenary)	85	65
4633	55st. Vera Lukova (artist) (centenary)	1·20	90
4634	1l. Theodor Trayanov (poet) (125th)	2·75	2·10

1639 St. Spass Monastery, Lozenski

2007. Monasteries. Multicoloured.

4635	63st. Type **1639**	1·70	1·30
4636	75st. St. Mina, Obradovski	2·00	1·60
4637	1l.20 St. George the Victor, Kremikovski	3·25	2·50
4638	2l.20 Three Saints, Chepinski	6·00	4·50

1640 Symbols of Transport

2007. International Transport Forum, Sofia.

4639	**1640**	1l. multicoloured	2·75	2·10

1641 Presidents of Bulgaria and Azerbaijan

2007. 15th Anniv of Bulgaria–Azerbaijan Diplomatic Relations. Sheet 86×64 mm.

MS4640 **1641**	1l. multicoloured	2·75	2·50

1642 *Onosma thracica*

2007. Flora. Multicoloured.

4641	10st. Type **1642**	35	25
4642	45st. *Astracantha aitosensis*	1·20	90
4643	55st. *Veronica krumovii*	1·50	1·20
4644	1l. *Verbascum adrianopolitanum*	2·75	2·10

1643 Vassal Levski

2007. 170th Birth Anniv of Vassal Levski (revolutionary leader).

4645	**1643**	55st. multicoloured	1·50	1·20

1644 Sailor

2007. Junior World Sailing Championship–Olympian Class 470, Burgas.

4646	**1644**	1l. multicoloured	2·75	2·10

1645 Lt. Colonel Pavel Kalitin (painting) and *Battle at Stara Zagora* (Nikola Kozhuharov)

2007. 130th Anniv of Battle at Stara Zagora.

4647	**1645**	55st. multicoloured	1·50	1·20

1646 Players

2007. Rugby. 50th (2005) Anniv of Locomotiv Rugby Club, Sofia. World Rugby Championship–2007, France.

4648	**1646**	55st. multicoloured	1·50	1·20

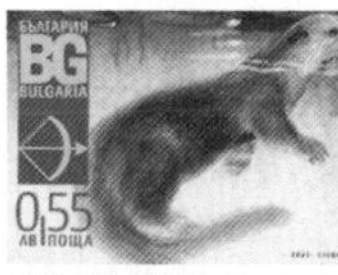

1647 *Lutra lutra* (otter)

2007. Ecology. 15th Anniv of Ropotamo Reserve. Sheet 85×85 mm containing T **1647** and similar horiz design. Multicoloured.

MS4649 55st. Type **1647**; 1l. *Haliaeetus albicilla* (white tailed eagle) 4·25 4·00

The stamps and margins of **MS**4549 form a composite design.

1648 *Alcedo atthis* (kingfisher)

2007. Endangered Species. Birds. Sheet 97×130 mm containing T **1648** and similar horiz design. Multicoloured.

MS4650 10st. Type **1648**; 35st. *Tichodroma muraria* (wall creeper); 55st. *Bombycilla garrulous* (waxwing); 1l. *Phoenicopterus ruber* (flamingo) 5·50 5·25

1649 Emblem

2007. Tenth Anniv Grand Lodge of the Ancient Freemasons.

4651	**1649**	55st. multicoloured	1·50	1·20

1650 Centre Building

2007. Inauguration of Exchange and Sorting Centre, Sofia. Sheet 87×63 mm.

MS4652 **1650**	55st. multicoloured	1·50	1·40

1651 Ivan Hadjiski

2007. Birth Centenary of Ivan Hadjiski (social psychologist).

4653	**1651**	55st. multicoloured	1·50	1·20

1652 Woman holding Offerings

2007. Christmas.

4654	**1652**	55st. multicoloured	1·50	1·20

1653 Rumyana Neykova (European 2000m. skiff rowing champion)

2007. Women Sports Personalities. Multicoloured.

4655	10st. Type **1653**	35	25
4656	35st. Stanka Zlateva (World freestyle wrestling champion)	85	65
4657	1l. Stefka Kostadinova (World record high jump (30.8.1987))	2·75	2·10

1654 '100' and Soldier

2007. Centenary of Military Reconnaissance.

4658	**1654**	55st. multicoloured	1·50	1·20

1655 Hristo Botev

2008. Birth Centenary of Hristo Botev (poet and revolutionary).

4659	**1655**	55st. multicoloured	1·50	1·20

1656 Polar Bear

2008. International Polar Year. 20th Anniv of Bulgarian Antarctic Expedition. Sheet 115×85 mm containing T **1656** and similar horiz design. Multicoloured.

MS4660 55st. Type **1656**; 1l. Skua stealing penguin chick 4·25 4·00

The stamps and margins of **MS**4660 form a composite design.

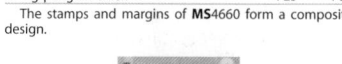

1657 Volleyball Player

2008. Olympic Games, Beijing. Sheet 88×109 mm containing T **1657** and similar vert design. Multicoloured.

MS4661 55st. Type **1657**; 1l. Two players 4·25 4·00

The stamps of **MS**4661 form a composite design of a volley ball match.

1658 Arms of Bulgaria

2008. 130th Anniv of San Stefano Peace Treaty (treaty between Russia and the Ottoman Empire at the end of the Russo-Turkish War (setting up an autonomous self-governing tributary principality of Bulgaria)).

4662	**1658**	55st. multicoloured	1·50	1·20

1659 Envelope as Postman

2008. Europa. The Letter. Multicoloured (background colour given).

4663	55st. Type **1659**	1·50	1·20
4664	55st. As Type **1659** (purple)	1·50	1·20
4665	1l. Envelope as pigeon (blue)	2·75	2·10
4666	1l. As No. 4665 (yellow)	2·75	2·10

1660 Captain Dimiter Spissarevski

2008. History of Military Aviation. Pilots' Birth Anniversaries. Multicoloured.

4667 55st. Type **1660** (90th birth anniv) 1·50 1·20

4668 1l. General Stoyan Stoyanov (95th birth anniv) 2·75 2·10

Nos. 4667/8 were issued together, *se-tenant*, forming a composite design.

1661 *Women from the Rhodopes* (Boris Kotsev)

2008. Artists' Birth Centenaries. Multicoloured.

4669 10st. Type **1661** 35 25

4670 35st. *Nude* (Eliezer Alsheh) 85 65

4671 55st. *Nude* (Vera Nedova) 1·50 1·20

4672 1l. *Maritsa* (Assen Peykov) 2·75 2·10

1662 Club Members

2008. 60th Anniv of CSKA Central Sports Club. Sheet 90×58 mm.

MS4673 **1662** 55st. multicoloured 1·70 1·60

1663 White-headed Marmoset (*Callithrix geoffroyi*)

2008. 120th Anniv of Zoological Gardens, Sofia. Two sheets containing T **1663** and similar vert designs. Multicoloured.

MS4674 (a) 126×130 mm. 10st. Type **1663**; 20st. Hippopotamus (*Hippopotamus amphibius*); 35st. Bactrian camel (*Camelus bactrianus*); 55st. Meerkat (*Suricata suricatta*); 60st. Blue-and-yellow macaw (*Ara ararauna*); 1l. Eurasian lynx (*Lynx lynx*); (b) 66×85 mm. 55st. Merrkat (*Suricata suricatta*). Imperf 7·25 7·25

1664 Alexander Alexandrov

2008. 20th Anniv of Alexander Alexandrov's Flight in Orbital Space Station MIR. Sheet 85×61 mm.

MS4675 **1664** 1l. multicoloured 2·75 2·75

1665 BMW R12 Single Carb, 1935

2008. 70th Anniv of Union of Bulgarian Philatelists.

4676 **1665** 60st. multicoloured 1·70 1·30

MS4677 106×92 mm. 60st. As Type **1665**. Imperf 1·90 1·90

1666 *Canis aureus* (golden jackal)

2008. Strandja Nature Park. Sheet 104×79 mm containing T **1666** and similar multicoloured design.

MS4678 60st. Type **1666**; 1l.50 *Aquila pomarina* (lesser spotted eagle) (vert) 5·50 5·50

The stamps and margins of **MS**4678 form a composite design.

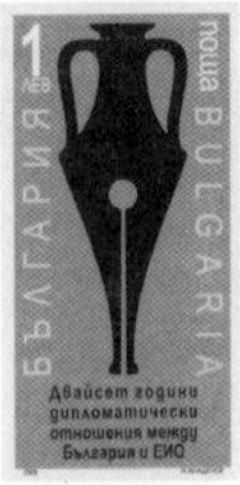

1667

2008. 20th Anniv of Bulgaria—European Economic Community.

4679 **1667** 1l. black and yellow 2·75 2·10

1668 Wagons Lits (sleeping car)

2008. 125th Anniv of Orient Express. Multicoloured.

4680 60st. Type **1668** 1·70 1·30

4681 1l.50 Steg Wien locomotive No. 5 3·75 3·00

The stamps also show the arms of cities enroute and the emblems of the Orient Express (60st.) or the Bulgarian State Railways (1l.50).

1669 Nikola and Dimitar Petkov

2008. Birth Anniversaries of Dimitar Petkov (Prime Minister 1906–1907) (150th) and Nikola Petkov (politician, son of Dimitar Petkov and leader of Bulgarian Agrarian National Union) (115th).

4682 **1669** 60st. multicoloured 1·70 1·30

1670 Tsar Ferdinand

2008. Centenary of Proclamation of Independence. Sheet 48×87 mm.

MS4683 **1670** 60st. multicoloured 1·90 1·90

1671 Arms of the Templars

2008. 700th Anniv (2007) of Disbanding of Knights Templar (Order of the Temple) by King Philip IV of France.

4684 **1671** 1l. multicoloured 2·75 2·10

1672 Race Car (2008)

2008. Ferrari Racing Cars. Multicoloured.

4685 60st. Type **1672** 1·70 1·30

4686 1l. Race car (1952) 2·75 2·10

MS4687 As No. 4685. Imperf 1·90 1·90

1673 Arms

2008. 130th Anniv of Bulgarian Red Cross Societies.

4688 **1673** 60st. multicoloured 1·70 1·30

1674 Virgin Mary, Rila Monastery (12th–century)

2008. Bulgarian Icons. Multicoloured.

4689 50st. Type **1674** 1·40 1·10

4690 60st. Virgin and Child, Troyan Monastery (18th–century) 1·70 1·30

4691 1l. Virgin and Child, Bachkovo Monastery (14th–century) 2·75 2·10

MS4691a 112×73 mm. As No. 4690. Imperf 1·70 1·70

1675 Virgin and Child

2008. Christmas.

4692 **1675** 60st. multicoloured 1·70 1·30

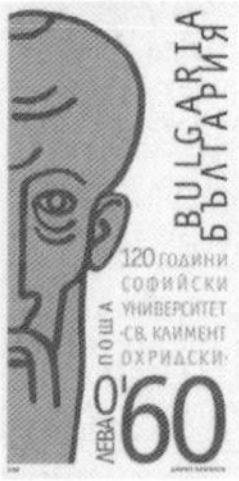

1676 Saint Clement of Ohrid (St. Kliment Ohridski)

2008. 120th Anniv of Sofia University St. Kliment Ohridski.

4693 **1676** 60st multicoloured 1·70 1·30

1677 Andranik Ozanyan (Armenian general in Balkan Wars of Independence)

2008. Nationalist Liberation Movements of Bulgaria and Armenia. Multicoloured.

4694 60st. Type **1677** 1·70 1·30

4695 1l.50 Peyo Yavorov (Bulgarian poet and revolutionary) 2·75 2·10

1678 Emblem

2009. Bulgaria 2009–European Philatelic Exhibition.

4696 **1678** 60st. multicoloured 1·70 1·30

1679 Abraham Lincoln

2009. Birth Bicentenaries. T **1679** and similar horiz designs. Each green,olive and brown-olive.

4697 10st. Type **1679** (pres of USA) 35 25

4698 50st. Nikolai Gogol (writer) 1·40 1·10

4699 60st. Charles Darwin (naturalist) 1·70 1·30

4700 1l. Edgar Allan Poe (writer) 2·75 2·10

MS4701 55x105mm. 60st. Charles Darwin (different). Imperf 1·70 1·70

1680 *Scolopax rusticola* (Eurasian woodcock)

2009. Ecology–Balkan Mountains. Multicoloured.

4702 60st. Type **1680** 1·70 1·30

4703 1l. *Monticola saxatilis* (rufous-tailed rock thrush) 2·75 2·10

MS4704 106×85 mm. As Nos. 4702/3. Imperf 5·50 5·50

Nos. 4702/3 were printed together, *se-tenant*, forming a composite design.

Stamps of a similar design were issued by Serbia.

1681 Amethyst

2009. 120th Anniv of National Natural Science Museum.

4705 **1681** 60st. multicoloured 1·70 1·30

MS4706 87x61mm. 60st As Type **1681.** Imperf 1·70 1·70

1682 Hagia Sofia Church and St. Alexander Nevsky Cathedral

2009. 130th Anniv of Sofia as Capital of Bulgaria.

4707 **1682** 60st. multicoloured 1·70 1·30

1683 Penguins and Narwhal

2009. Preserve Polar Regions and Glaciers. Sheet 127×63 mm containing T **1683** and similar horiz design. Multicoloured.

MS4708 60st. Type **1683**; 1l.50 Polar bear, elephant seal and white-tailed eagle 5·50 5·50

1684 Flags as '60'

2009. 60th Anniv of NATO (4708). 5th Anniv of Bulgaria's Membership of NATO (4709). Multicoloured.

4709 60st. Type **1684** 1·70 1·30

4710 1l.50 Bulgarian flag as '5' 2·75 2·10

1685 Bicycle

2009. Bicycles. Multicoloured.

4711 10st. Type **1685** 35 25

4712 50st. Purple cycle 1·40 1·10

4713 60st. Penny farthing cycles 1·70 1·30

4714 1l. Early pedal-less cycle 2·75 2·10

MS4715 130x71mm 60st As No. 4714. Imperf 170170 1·70 1·70

Nos. 4711/14 were printed together, *se-tenant*, forming a composite design.

1686 Georgi Ivanov

2009. 30th Anniv of Space Flight of First Bulgarian Cosmonaut. Sheet 93×93 mm.

MS4716 **1686** 60st. multicoloured 1·70 1·30

1687 Arms (1879)

2009. 130th Anniv of Restoration of State. Sheet 105×84 mm containing T **1687** and similar horiz design. Multicoloured.

MS4717 60st. Type **1687**; 1l. Arms (1997) 4·50 4·50

1688 *Rathbunia alamosensis*

2009. Cacti. Multicoloured.

4718 10st. Type **1688** 35 25

4719 50st. *Mammillaria pseudoperbella* 1·40 1·10

4720 60st. *Obregonia degenerii* 1·70 1·30

4721 1l.50 Inscr 'Astrophitum mayas' 2·75 2·10

MS4722 71×108 mm. 60t. As No. 4720. Imperf 1·70 1·70

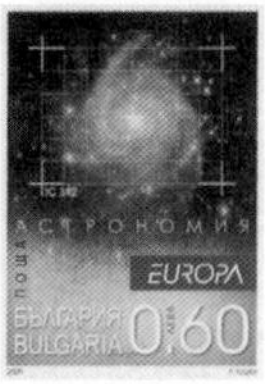

1689 Spiral Galaxy IC 342

2009. Europa. Astronomy. Multicoloured.

4723 60st. Type **1689** 1·70 1·30

4724 1l.50 Andromeda Galaxy (M 31) 2·75 2·10

MS4725 112×90 mm. Size 29×39 mm. 60st.×2, As 4725×2; 1l.50×2, As No. 4726×2 9·00 9·00

4726 60st. As Type **1689** 1·70 1·30

4727 1l.50 As No. 4724 (Andromeda Galaxy (M 31)) 2·75 2·10

1690 Members Flags surrounding Euro

2009. Tenth Anniv of Euro Currency.

4728 **1690** 1l. multicoloured 2·75 2·10

1691 *Landscape* (Vassil Ivanov) (birth centenary)

2009. Artists' Anniversaries. Multicoloured.

4729 10st. Type **1691** 35 25

4730 50st. *Three Vases* (Georgi Kolarov) (birth centenary) 1·40 1·10

4731 60st *The Black Sea* (Alexander Mutaffov) (130th birth anniv) 1·70 1·30

4732 1l. *Cast Shadows* (Konstantine Sturkelov) (120th birth anniv) 2·75 2·10

1692 Fan

2009. 80th Anniv of Locomotive Sofia Sports Club.

4733 **1692** 60st. multicoloured 1·70 1·30

1693 *Bubo bubo* (Eurasian eagle owl)

2009. Owls. Multicoloured.

4734 10st. Type **1693** 35 25

4735 50st. *Athene noctua* (Little owl) 1·40 1·10

4736 60st. *Strix uralensis* (Ural owl) 1·70 1·30

4737 1l.50 *Glaucidium passerinum* (Eurasian pygmy owl) 2·75 2·10

1694 Motorcycle and Rider

2009. SuperMoto European Championship. Sheet 96×85 mm.

MS4738 **1694** **60st.**multicoloured 1·70 1·70

1695 Petko Voivoda

2009. 165th Birth Anniv of Petko Voivoda (nationalist).

4739 **1695** 60st. multicoloured 1·70 1·30

1696 Todor Burmov (first Minister for Internal Affairs)

2009. 130th Anniv of Ministry of Internal Affairs.

4740 **1696** 60st. multicoloured 1·70 1·30

1697 Airmail Envelope

2009. 130th Anniv of Bulgarian Communications. Sheet 97×117 mm containing T 1697 and similar horiz design. Multicoloured.

MS4741 60st. Type **1697**; 1l. Telephone 4·50 4·50

1698 Neil Armstrong and Lunar Module

2009. 40th Anniv of First Moon Landing. Sheet 101×84 mm.

MS4742 **1698** 60st. multicoloured 1·70 1·70

No. **MS**4742 was also issued overprinted for Bulgaria 2009.

1699 Symbols of Science

2009. 140th of National Academy of Science.

4743 **1699** 60st. multicoloured 1·70 1·30

1700 Flags as Pen and Ink

2009. 130th Anniv of Bulgaria–Italy Diplomatic Relations. Sheet 101×71 mm.

MS4744 **1700** 1l. multicoloured 2·75 2·10

1701 Flags and Rose

2009. 130th Anniv of First Bulgarian Diplomatic Relations. Sheet 113×113 mm.

MS4745 **1701** 1l. multicoloured 2·75 2·10

1702 Anniversary Cake enclosed in TV Screen

2009. 50th Anniv of National Television.

4746 **1702** 60st. multicoloured 2·75 2·10

1703 Fokker E. III Monoplane and Marko Parvanov (Bulgarian gunner)

2009. History of Bulgarian Military Aviation. Multicoloured.

4747 60st. Type **1703** 1·70 1·30

4748 1l. Assen Jordanoff (aircraft designer) and Jordanov-1 2·75 2·10

Nos. 4747/8 were printed, *se-tenant*, forming a composite design.

1704 Virgin and Child

2009. Christmas.

4749 **1704** 60st. multicoloured 1·70 1·30

1705 Nikola Vaptsarov

2009. Birth Centenary of Nikola Vaptsarov (poet, communist and revolutionary).

4750 **1705** 60st. multicoloured 1·70 1·30

1706 Dimitar Milandinov

2010. Birth Bicentenary of Dimitar Milandinov (poet and folklorist).

4751 **1706** 60st. multicoloured 1·70 1·30

1707 Headset and Microphone

2010. 75th Anniv of Bulgarian National Radio.

4752 **1707** 60st. multicoloured 1·70 1·30

1708 Luge

2010. Winter Olympic Games, Vancouver. Sheet 98×90 mm containing T **1708** and similar horiz design. Multicoloured.

MS4753 60st. Type **1708**; 1l. Snowboarder 4·50 4·50

1709 Frederic Chopin

2010. Birth Bicentenary of Frederic Chopin (composer).

4754 **1709** 1l. multicoloured 2·75 2·10

1710 *Paeonia suffruticosa var. rockii*

2010. Peonies. Sheet 80×86 mm containing T **1710** and similar vert design. Multicoloured.

MS4755 60st×2, Type **1710**; *Paeonia officinalis 'Rubra Plena'* 3·50 3·50

1711 General Georgi Vazov (1860-1934)

2010. 150th Birth Annivs of Bulgarian Commanders. Sheet 113×102 mm containing T **1711** and similar horiz designs. Multicoloured.

MS4756 60st.×5, Type **1711**; General Ivan Fichev (1860-1931); General Stilian Kovachev (1860-1939); Colonel Vladimir Serafimov (1860-1934); General Dimitar Geshev (1860-1922) 8·50 8·50

1712 Chess Pieces

2010. World Chess Championship Match 2010 between Viswanathan Anand (winner) and Veselin Topalov. Sheet 69×85 mm.
MS4757 **1712** 1l. ochre, black and light grey 2·75 2·10

1713 House and Hedgehog

2010. Europa. Multicoloured.

4758	60st Type **1713**	1·80	1·40
4759	60st. As Type **1713** (29×39 mm)	1·80	1·40
4760	Hare and fairy carrying lantern	3·00	2·40
4761	1l.50 Hare and fairy carrying lantern	3·00	2·40
MS4762	106×85 mm. 60st. As Type **1713**; 1l.50 As No. 4760	4·75	4·75

The stamps of No. **MS**4762 have no white borders and, with the margins form a composite design.

1714 Dragon and Shanghai Skyline

2010. Expo 2010, Shanghai

4762a	**1714** 1l.40 multicoloured	1·80	1·40
MS4763	113×74 mm 1l.40×4, Type **1714**×4	9·50	9·50

1714a Flag

2010. Centenary of Bulgaria–Spain Diplomatic Relations
4764 **1714a** 1l. multicoloured 1·80 1·40

1715 Bird, Mouse and Whale

2010. International Year of Biodiversity
MS4765 78x60 mm. **1715** 1l.50 multicoloured 2·75 2·75

1715a Bulgarian Shepherd Dog

2010. Balkan Dogs
MS4765a **1715a** 60st. multicoloured 1·80 1·40

1716 Emanuil Manolov

2010. Composers Anniversaries. Multicoloured.

4766	1l. Type **1716** (150th birth anniv)	2·75	2·10
4767	1l. Robert Schumann (birth bicentenary)	2·75	2·10

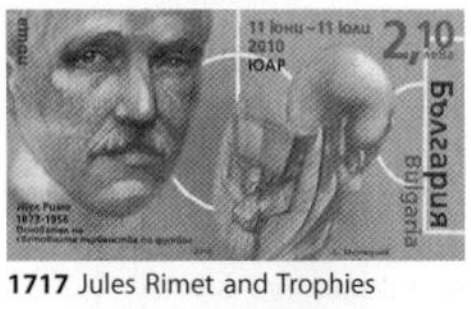
1717 Jules Rimet and Trophies

2010. World Cup Football Championships, South Africa
MS4768 **1717** 79x55 mm. 2l.10 multicoloured 5·50 5·50

1718 St. Procopius

2010. Death Bicentenary of St. Procopius of Varna
4769 **1718** 60st. multicoloured 1·80 1·40

1719 Manoeuvres (1899)

2010. 150th Birth Anniv of Yaroslav Veshin (Czech artist). Multicoloured.

4770	1l. Type **1719**	2·75	2·10
4771	1l. *Return from Market*(1898)	2·75	2·10

1720 Summer and Autumn (Les Saisons (1900))

2010. 150th Birth Anniv of Alphonse (Alfons) Maria Mucha (Czech artist). Multicoloured.
MS4772 1l.×2, Type **1720**; Winter and Spring (*Les Saisons* (1900)) 5·50 5·50

1721 Athletes, Emblem and Book

2010. Youth Olympic Games, Singapore 2010
4773 **1721** 1l.40 multicoloured 3·00 2·40

1722 Entwined Tree Trunks

2010. 125th Anniv of Bulgaria's Reunification
4774 **1722** 60st. multicoloured 1·80 1·40

1723 Magirus Feuerwehrwerke Fire-fighting Appliance

2010. History of the Fire Fighting
MS4775 **1723** 102x71 mm. 65st. multicoloured 1·90 1·90

1724 Giant Panda (*Ailuropoda melanoleuca*)

2010. Pandas. Multicoloured.
MS4776 95x126 mm. 10st. Type **1724**; 60st. Giant panda seated; 1l. Red panda (*Ailurus fulgens*); 1l.50 Red panda, head and shoulders 6·00 6·00

1725 Jak-23

2010. 60th Anniv of Military Jet Aviation. Multicoloured.

4777	50st. Type **1725**	1·60	1·10
4778	65st. Mikoyan-Gurevich type MiG-15	1·90	1·50
4779	1l. Mikoyan MiG-29	2·75	2·10

1726 Santa wearing Spectacles

2010. Christmas
4780 **1726** 65st. multicoloured 1·90 1·50

1727 Female Figures from Thracian Tomb of Svestari

2010. Regions. Multicoloured.
MS4781 85x113 mm. 10st. Type **1727**; 50st. Balchik Palace; 65st. Srebarna Nature Reserve; 1l. Pobiti Kamani rock formations 4·75 4·75

1728 Self-Portrait

2010. Birth Bicentenary of Zahari Hristovich Dimitrov (Zahari Zograf) (artist)
MS4782 61x70 mm. **1728** 1l.50 multicoloured 3·00 3·00

1729 San Cristobal Cathedral, Havana

2010. 50th Anniv of Bulgaria–Cuba Diplomatic Relations. Multicoloured.

4783	65c. Type **1729**	1·90	1·50
4784	1l.40 St. Alexander Nevsky Cathedral, Sofia	3·00	2·40

Stamps of a similar design were issued by Cuba

1730 Griffon Vulture

2010. Balkanfila 2010 International Stamp Exhibition, Plovdiv
MS4785 88x78 mm. **1730** 65st. multicoloured 1·90 1·90

1731 *Hydrurga leptonyx* (leopard seal)

2011. Antarctica
4786 **1731** 58st. black and scarlet-vermilion 1·80 1·40

1732 Princess Clementine and Soldiers

2011. 125th Anniv of 9th Plovdiv Infantry Regiment
4787 **1732** 65st. multicoloured 1·90 1·50

1733 Vanga

2011. Birth Centenary of Vangelia Pandeva Dimitrova (Vanga) (blind mystic, healer and herbalist)
4788 **1733** 65st. multicoloured 1·90 1·50

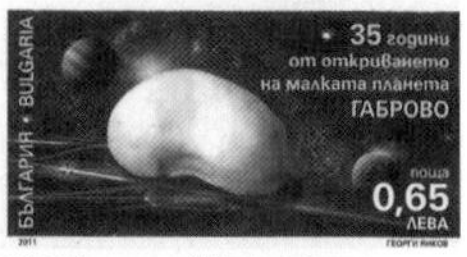
1734 Space and Haricot Bean

2011. Day of Humor and Joke (April Fool's Day)
4789 **1734** 65st. multicoloured 1·90 1·50

No. 4789 has a *se-tenant* stamp size label attached at right which, with the stamp forms a composite design of planets and space.

1735 Politicians

2011. 20th Anniv of Atlantic Club of Bulgaria
MS2790 87x78 mm. **1735** 1l. multi-coloured 2·75 2·75

1736 Yuri Gagarin

2011. 50th Anniv of First Manned Space Flight. Multicoloured.
MS4791 83x103 mm. 65st. Type **1736**; 1l.50 *Venera 1* 5·25 5·25

1737 Capreolus capreolus (roe deer) in Snow

2011. Europa. Forests. Multicoloured.

4792	65st. Type **1737**	2·00	1·60
4793	1l.50 *Scolopax rusticola* (woodcock)	3·25	2·50
MS4794	106×85 mm. Nos. 4792/3	5·25	5·25

1738 Emperor Galerius

2011. 1700th Anniv of Serdica Edict of Religious Tolerance, issued by Roman Emperor Galerius. Sheet 102×65 mm

MS4795	1738	65st. multicoloured	2·00	2·00

1739 Emblem

2011. 20th Anniv of Commission on Protection of Competition

4796	1739	65st. multicoloured	2·00	1·60

1740 Rabbit as Newspaper Boy

2011. 120th Anniv of Philatelic Press. Sheet 91×81 mm

MS4797	1740	65st. multicoloured	2·00	1·60
MS4797a	1740	65st. multicoloured		

1741 Bear and Woodpecker

2011. Regions. North-Central Bulgaria. Multicoloured.

MS4798	65st Type **1741**; 65st. Coin and church; 1l. Castle; 1l. Woman knitting and textiles	10·50	1·50

1742 *Stizostedion lucioperca, Esox lucius, Hucho hucho* and *Aspius aspius*

2011. Museum of the Danube Fishing, Tutrakan. Multicoloured.

MS4799	65st. Type **1742**; 65st. *Abramis brama, Ctenopharyngodon idella, Cyprinus carpio* and *Carassius carassius*; 1l. *Acipenser ruthenus*; 1l. *Siurus glanis* and *Loto lota*	10·50	10·00

1743 Mounted Soldiers

2011. 1200th Anniv of Khan Krum Victory at Varbitsa Pass

4800	1743	65st. multicoloured	2·00	1·60

1744 *Rhodophyllus sinuatus*

2011. Poisonous Fungi. Multicoloured.

MS4801	65st. Type **1744**; 65st. *Inocybe patouillardii*; 1l. *Russula emetica*; 1l. *Omphalotus olearius*	10·50	10·50

1745 Tall Ship

2011. Tall Ships Regatta, 2011. Sheet 90×66 mm

MS4802	1745	1l. multicoloured	2·75	2·10

1746 Fridtjof Nansen

2011. 150th Birth Anniv of Fridtjof Wedel-Jarlsberg Nansen (explorer, humanitarian and winner of 1922 Nobel Peace Prize). Sheet 103×77 mm

MS4803	1746	1l. multicoloured	2·75	2·75

1747 Franz Liszt

2011. Birth Bicentenary of Franz Liszt (Liszt Ferenc)

4804	1747	1l. multicoloured	2·75	2·10

1748 William Gladstone

2011. 145th Anniv of First Railway in Bulgaria. Multicoloured.

MS4805	65st. Type **1748**; 1l. Early carriage; 1l.50 Early steam locomotive	8·00	8·00

1749 Laika

2011. Dogs in Space. Multicoloured.

MS4806	65st. Type **1749**; 65st. Belka and Strlka; 1l. Chernushka; 1l. Zvezdochka	7·50	7·50

1750 Can-AM Renegade 800

2011. Peter Tsenkov and Todor Hristov, First Bulgarians to Compete in Dakar Rally

4807	1750	1l.50 multicoloured	3·25	2·50

1751 *Scomber scombrus* (Atlantic mackerel)

2011. International Day of Black Sea. Multicoloured.

MS4808	1l.×2, Type **1751**; *Mytilus galloprovincialis* (blue mussel)	5·50	5·50

1752 Yosif Tsankov

2011. Birth Centenary of Yosif Tsankov

4809	1752	65st. multicoloured	2·00	1·60

1753 '65' as Snowman

2011. Christmas

4810	1753	65st. multicoloured	2·00	1·60

1754 '120', Medical Bag and Building

2011. 120th Anniv of Military Medical Academy, Sofia

4811	1754	65st. multicoloured	2·00	1·60

1755 Garden Flowers

2012. Garden Flowers. Multicoloured.

4812	65st. Type **1755**	2·00	1·60
4813	1l. Flowers (different) (vert)	2·75	2·20

1756 Cross

2012. 700th Anniv of disbanding of Order of the Temple (Knights Templar) by Pope Clement V

4814	1756	65st. black and scarlet-vermilion	2·00	2·60

1757 Anton Mitov

2012. Personalities. Multicoloured.

4815	65st. Type **1757** (artist) (150th birth anniv)	2·00	1·60
4816	65st. Dimcho Debelyanov (writer) (125th birth anniv)	2·00	1·60
4817	1l. Petya Dubarova (writer) (50th birth anniv)	2·75	2·20
4818	1l. Yana Yazova (writer) (birth centenary)	2·75	2·20

1758 Baldwin Tower, Tsarevets Fortress

2012. Europa. Visit Bulgaria. Multicoloured.

4819	65st. Type **1758**	2·00	1·60
4820	1l. Patriarchial Cathedral, Tsarevets	2·75	2·20
MS4821	85×126 mm. Nos. 4819/20	9·50	9·50

1759 Gentoo Penguins (*Pygoscelis papua*) and Bulgarian Flag

2012. 20th Bulgarian Antarctic Expedition

4822	1l.40 Type **1759**	3·25	2·50

No. 4823 is left for imperforate miniature sheet, not yet received.

1760 *Titanic* at Night

2012. Centenary of *Titanic*. Sheet 100×50 mm

MS4824	1760	1l.40 multicoloured	3·25	3·25

1761 Albatros D. II Aircraft

2012. Centenary of Bulgarian Aviation in Balkan War. Battle of Edirne

4825	1761	65st. multicoloured	2·00	1·60

1762 Parashkev Hadjiev

2012. Birth Centenary of Parashkev Hadjiev (composer)

4826	1762	65st. multicoloured	2·00	1·60

1763 Anniversary Emblem

2012. 20th Anniv of Bulgaria's Membership of Council of Europe

4827	1763	1l. multicoloured	2·75	2·20

EXPRESS STAMPS

E137 Express Delivery Van

1939

E429	-	5l. blue	1·80	45
E430	E137	6l. brown	85	40
E431	-	7l. brown	1·30	40
E432	E137	8l. red	1·60	50
E433	-	20l. red	2·50	1·20

DESIGNS—VERT: 5l., 20l. Bicycle messenger; 7l. Motorcyclist and sidecar.

OFFICIAL STAMPS

O158

1942

O507	O158	10s. green	10	10
O508	O158	30s. orange	10	10
O509	O158	50s. brown	10	10
O510	-	1l. blue	10	10
O511	-	2l. green	15	10
O534	-	2l. red	1·40	50
O512	-	3l. mauve	20	10
O513	-	4l. pink	30	15
O514	-	5l. red	50	20

The 1l. to 5l. are larger (19×23 mm).

O177

1945. Arms designs. Imperf or perf.

O580B		1l. mauve	10	10
O581B	O 177	2l. green	10	10
O582B	-	3l. brown	10	10

O583B	-	4l. blue	10	10
O584B	-	5l. red	10	10

PARCEL POST STAMPS

P153 Weighing Machine

P154 Loading Motor Lorry

1941

P494	**P153**	1l. green	15	10
P495	**A**	2l. red	15	10
P496	**P 154**	3l. brown	15	10
P497	**B**	4l. orange	15	10
P498	**P 153**	5l. blue	15	10
P506	**P 153**	5l. green	20	15
P499	**B**	6l. purple	15	10
P507	**B**	6l. brown	20	15
P500	**P 153**	7l. blue	15	10
P508	**P 153**	7l. sepia	20	15
P501	**P 154**	8l. turquoise	20	10
P509	**P 154**	8l. green	20	15
P502	**A**	9l. olive	30	15
P503	**B**	10l. orange	40	15
P504	**P 154**	20l. violet	65	20
P505	**A**	30l. black	1·50	30

DESIGNS—HORIZ: A, Loading mall coach; B, Motor-cycle combination.

P163

1944. Imperf.

P532	**P163**	1l. red	20	15
P533	**P163**	3l. green	20	15
P534	**P163**	5l. green	20	15
P535	**P163**	7l. mauve	20	15
P536	**P163**	10l. blue	20	15
P537	**P163**	20l. brown	20	15
P538	**P163**	30l. purple	40	20
P539	**P163**	50l. orange	75	50
P540	**P163**	100l. blue	1·40	80

POSTAGE DUE STAMPS

D7

1884. Perf.

D75	**D7**	5s. orange	55·00	7·75
D54	**D7**	25s. lake	27·00	7·75
D55	**D7**	50s. blue	27·00	23·00

1886. Imperf.

D50	5s. orange	£550	26·00
D51	25s. lake	£800	23·00
D52a	50s. blue	33·00	26·00

1893. Surch with bar and **30**.

D78d	30s. on 50s. blue (perf)	49·00	16·00
D79	30s. on 50s. blue (imperf)	43·00	16·00

D12

1896. Perf.

D83	**D12**	5s. orange	27·00	4·25
D84	**D12**	10s. violet	16·00	3·75
D85	**D12**	30s. green	13·00	3·25

D16

1901

D124	**D16**	5s. red	1·10	50
D125	**D16**	10s. green	2·20	65
D126	**D16**	20s. blue	16·00	65
D127	**D16**	30s. red	5·50	70
D128	**D16**	50s. orange	14·00	12·50

D37

1915

D200	**D37**	5s. green	55	10
D240	**D37**	10s. violet	20	10
D202	**D37**	20s. red	55	20
D241	**D37**	20s. orange	20	10
D203a	**D37**	30s. red	55	20
D242	**D37**	50s. blue	20	10
D243	**D37**	1l. green	55	10
D244	**D37**	2l. red	55	20
D245	**D37**	3l. brown	1·10	40

D110

1932

D326	**D110**	1l. bistre	2·10	1·30
D327	**D110**	2l. red	2·10	1·30
D328	**D110**	6l. purple	4·75	1·50

D111

D112

1933

D333	**D111**	20s. sepia	20	10
D334	**D111**	40s. blue	20	10
D335	**D111**	80s. red	20	10
D336	**D 112**	1l. brown	1·00	60
D337	**D 112**	2l. olive	1·00	90
D338	**D 112**	6l. violet	50	40
D339	**D 112**	14l. blue	75	60

1947. As Type D **112**, but larger (18×24 mm).

D646	1l. brown	20	20
D647	2l. red	30	30
D648	8l. orange	20	20
D649	20l. blue	75	30

D293

1951

D849	**D293**	1l. brown	20	15
D850	**D293**	2l. purple	30	15
D851	**D293**	8l. orange	65	50
D852	**D293**	20l. blue	1·70	1·30

Pt. 3

BULGARIAN OCCUPATION OF ROMANIA

100 stotinki = 1 leva.

(DOBRUJA DISTRICT)

(1)

1916. Bulgarian stamps of 1911 optd with T **1**.

1	**23**	1s. grey	25	25
2	-	5s. brown and green	4·75	3·00
3	-	10s. sepia and brown	45	35
4	-	25s. black and blue	45	35

Pt. 1

BUNDI

A state of Rajasthan, India. Now uses Indian stamps.

12 pies = 1 anna; 16 annas = 1 rupee.

3 Native Dagger

1894. Imperf.

12	**3**	½a. grey	6·50	5·50
13	**3**	1a. red	5·50	5·50
14	**3**	2a. green	18·00	22·00
8	**3**	4a. green	90·00	£130
15	**3**	8a. red	24·00	26·00
16a	**3**	1r. yellow on blue	24·00	35·00

1898. As T **3**, but with dagger point to left.

17a	4a. green	27·00	32·00

11 Raja protecting Sacred Cows

1914. Roul or perf.

26	**11**	¼a. blue	1·90	4·25
38	**11**	½a. black	3·25	4·75
28	**11**	1a. red	4·00	15·00
20a	**11**	2a. green	5·00	9·00
30	**11**	2½a. yellow	11·00	30·00
31	**11**	3a. brown	11·00	60·00
32	**11**	4a. green	4·00	55·00
33a	**11**	6a. blue	7·00	£140
42	**11**	8a. orange	9·00	80·00
43	**11**	10a. olive	17·00	£130
44	**11**	12a. green	18·00	£130
25	**11**	1r. lilac	35·00	£140
46	**11**	2r. brown and black	95·00	£225
47	**11**	3r. blue and brown	£170	£300
48	**11**	4r. green and red	£325	£400
49	**11**	5r. red and green	£325	£400

20

1941. Perf.

79	**20**	3p. blue	3·25	6·50
80	**20**	6p. blue	6·50	11·00
81	**20**	1a. red	8·50	13·00
82	**20**	2a. brown	9·00	23·00
83	**20**	4a. green	16·00	70·00
84	**20**	8a. green	21·00	£300
85	**20**	1r. blue	48·00	£400

21 Maharao Rajah Bahadur Singh

1947

86	**21**	¼a. green	2·25	48·00
87	**21**	½a. violet	2·00	38·00
88	**21**	1a. green	2·00	40·00
89	-	2a. red	2·00	85·00
90	-	4a. orange	2·50	£100
91	-	8a. blue	3·25	
92	-	1r. brown	18·00	

DESIGNS: 2, 4a. Rajah in Indian dress; 8a., 1r. View of Bundi.

OFFICIAL STAMPS

बूंदी

सरविस

(O1)

1915. Optd as Type **O1**.

O6A	¼a. blue	1·60
O16Aa	½a. black	75
O8A	1a. red	4·50
O18A	2a. green	11·00
O2A	2½a. yellow	6·00
O3A	3a. brown	5·50
O19A	4a. green	14·00
O11A	6a. blue	15·00
O20A	8a. orange	15·00
O21A	10a. olive	80·00
O22A	12a. green	60·00
O5A	1r. lilac	75·00
O24A	2r. brown and black	£400
O25A	3r. blue and brown	£275
O26A	4r green and red	£300
O27A	5r. red and green	£325

1915. Optd **BUNDI SERVICE**.

O6B	**11**	¼a. blue	2·50
O16B	**11**	½a. black	3·50
O8Bb	**11**	1a. red	18·00
O18B	**11**	2a. green	24·00
O2B	**11**	2½a. yellow	21·00
O3B	**11**	3a. brown	23·00
O19B	**11**	4a. green	95·00
O11B	**11**	6a. blue	£325
O20B	**11**	8a. orange	40·00
O21B	**11**	10a. olive	£120
O22B	**11**	12a. green	£140
O5B	**11**	1r. lilac	80·00
O24B	**11**	2r. brown and black	£200
O25B	**11**	3r. blue and brown	£225
O26B	**11**	4r. green and red	£300
O27B	**11**	5r. red and green	£325

Prices for Nos. O2/27 are for unused examples. Used examples are generally worth a small premium over the prices quoted.

1941. Optd **SERVICE**.

O53	**20**	3p. blue	8·00	19·00
O54	**20**	6p. blue	19·00	19·00
O55	**20**	1a. red	16·00	16·00
O56	**20**	2a. brown	22·00	15·00
O57	**20**	4a. green	65·00	£150
O58	**20**	8a. green	£225	£700
O59	**20**	1r. blue	£300	£800

For later issues see **RAJASTHAN**.

Pt. 12

BURKINA FASO

A country in W. Africa, formerly known as Upper Volta. The name was changed in August 1984.

100 centimes = 1 franc.

249 *Graphium pylades*

1984. Air. Butterflies. Multicoloured.

738	10f. Type **249**	30	10
739	120f. *Hyploimnas misippus*	1·30	55
740	400f. *Danaus chrysippus*	4·25	2·10
741	450f. *Papilio demodocus*	5·00	2·30

250 Soldier with Gun

1984. First Anniv of Captain Thomas Sankara's Presidency. Multicoloured.

742	90f. Type **250**	39·00
743	120f. Capt. Sankara and crowd	55·00

1984. Aid for the Sahel. No. 682 of Upper Volta optd **BURKINA FASO Aide au Sahel 84**.

743a	100f. multicoloured

1985. Nos. 716/21 of Upper Volta optd **BURKINA FASO**.

744	25f. Type **246** (postage)	45	20
745	185f. "Pterocarpus lucens"	2·75	1·50
746	200f. "Phlebopus colossus sudanicus"	3·75	1·70
747	250f. "Cosmos sulphureus"	4·50	2·10
748	300f. "Trametes versicolor" (air)	4·75	2·40
749	400f. "Ganoderma lucidum"	6·50	3·25

252 National Flag

1985. National Symbols. Multicoloured.

750	5f. Type **252** (postage)	40	20
751	15f. National arms (vert)	45	25
752	90f. Maps of Africa and Burkina Faso	1·80	90
753	120f. Type **252** (air)	1·60	80
754	150f. As No. 751	2·20	1·00
755	185f. As No. 752	2·50	1·20

253 Footballers and Statue

1985. World Cup Football Championship, Mexico.

756	**253**	25f. mult (postage)	40	10
757	-	45f. multicoloured	55	20
758	-	90f. multicoloured	1·10	35
759	-	100f. multicoloured (air)	1·20	30
760	-	150f. multicoloured	1·40	55
761	-	200f. mult (horiz)	1·90	85
762	-	250f. mult (horiz)	2·50	1·10
MS763		78×77 mm. 500f. multicoloured (horiz)	5·50	1·30

DESIGNS: 45f. to 500f. Mexican statues and various footballing scenes.

254 Children playing and Boy

1985. Air "Philexafrique" International Stamp Exhibition, Lome, Togo (1st issue). Multicoloured.

764	200f. Type **254**	2·00	1·20
765	200f. Solar panels, transmission mast, windmill, dish aerial and tree	2·00	1·20

See also Nos. 839/40.

255 G. A. Long's Steam Tricycle

1985. Centenary of Motor Cycle. Multicoloured.

766	50f. Type **255** (postage)	90	20
767	75f. Pope	1·10	25
768	80f. Manet	1·60	35
769	100f. Ducati (air)	95	30
770	150f. Jawa	1·60	55
771	200f. Honda	2·20	85
772	250f. B.M.W.	2·75	1·10

256 *Chamaeleon dilepis*

1985. Reptiles and Amphibians. Multicoloured.

773	5f. Type **256** (postage)	25	15
774	15f. *Agama stellio*	70	15
775	33f. *Lacerta lepida* (horiz)	1·10	15
776	85f. *Hiperolius marmoratus* (horiz)	1·70	30
777	100f. *Echis leucogaster* (horiz) (air)	1·40	30
778	150f. *Kinixys erosa* (horiz)	2·10	50
779	250f. *Python regius* (horiz)	3·25	70

257 Benz *Victoria*, 1893

1985. Motor Cars and Aircraft. Multicoloured.

780	5f. Type **257** (postage)	20	10
781	25f. Peugeot "174", 1927	45	10
782	45f. Bleriot XI airplane	60	10
783	50f. Breguet 14T biplane	60	10
784	500f. Bugatti "Napoleon T41 Royale" (air)	5·25	1·30
785	500f. Airbus Industrie A300	4·25	1·30
786	600f. Mercedes-Benz "540 K", 1938	5·25	1·70
787	600f. Airbus Industrie A300	5·25	1·70
MS788	100×68 mm. 1000f. Louis Bleriot and Bleriot XI, Karl Benz and early Benz motor car	8·50	3·50

258 Wood Duck

1985. Birth Bicentenary of John J. Audubon (ornithologist). Multicoloured.

789	60f. Type **258** (postage)	60	20
790	100f. Northern mockingbird	90	40
791	300f. Northern oriole	3·00	90
792	400f. White-breasted nuthatch	3·50	1·20
793	500f. Common flicker (air)	4·25	1·30
794	600f. Rough-legged buzzard	5·25	1·60
MS795	73×83 mm. 1000f. White-crowned pigeon	9·00	3·50

259 Young Lady Elizabeth Bowes-Lyon on Pony

1985. 85th Birthday of Queen Elizabeth the Queen Mother. Multicoloured.

796	75f. Type **259** (postage)	80	35
797	85f. Marriage of Lady Elizabeth Bowes-Lyon and Albert, Duke of York	80	35
798	500f. Duke and Duchess of York with Princess Elizabeth (air)	4·00	1·30
799	600f. Royal family in Coronation robes	5·25	1·60
MS800	104×64 mm. 1000f. Queen Elizabeth the Queen Mother at christening of Prince William of Wales	8·50	3·50

260 Gaucho on Piebald Horse

1985. "Argentina '85" International Stamp Exhibition, Buenos Aires. Horses. Multicoloured.

801	25f. Type **260** (postage)	45	10
802	45f. Gaucho on horse	75	25
803	90f. Rodeo rider	1·30	40
804	100f. Rider hunting gazelle (air)	1·00	35
805	150f. Horses and gauchos at camp fire	1·50	55
806	200f. Horse and man sitting on steps	2·10	85
807	250f. Riding contest	2·75	1·10
MS808	100×89 mm. 500f. Foal (39×31 mm)	7·50	3·00

261 Electric Locomotive No. 105-30 and Tank Wagon

1985. Trains. Multicoloured.

809	50f. Type **261** (postage)	80	10
810	75f. Diesel shunting locomotive	1·00	25
811	80f. Diesel passenger locomotive	1·30	25
812	100f. Diesel railcar (air)	1·10	10
813	150f. Diesel locomotive No. 6093	1·60	30
814	200f. Diesel railcar No. 105	2·10	40
815	250f. Diesel locomotive pulling passenger train	2·75	55

262 Pot (Tikare)

1985. Handicrafts. Multicoloured.

816	10f. Type **262** (postage)	25	10
817	40f. Pot with lid decorated with birds (P. Bazega)	70	20
818	90f. Bronze statuette of mother with child (Ouagadougou)	1·40	35
819	120f. Bronze statuette of drummer (Ouagadougou) (air)	2·10	50

263 *Pholiota mutabilis*

1985. Fungi. Multicoloured.

820	15f. Type **263** (postage)	20	10
821	20f. *Hypholoma (nematoloma) fasciculare*	20	10
822	30f. *Ixocomus granulatus*	40	20
823	60f. *Agaricus campestris*	90	15
824	80f. *Trachypus scaber*	1·40	50
825	250f. *Marasmius scorodonius*	3·75	1·50
826	150f. *Armillaria mellea* (air)	2·75	70

264 *Virgin and Child*

1985. "Italia '85" International Stamp Exhibition, Rome. Paintings by Botticelli. Multicoloured.

827	25f. Type **264** (postage)	50	10
828	45f. *Portrait of an Unknown Man*	90	20
829	90f. *Mars and Venus*	1·60	40
830	100f. *Birth of Venus* (air)	1·20	50
831	150f. *Allegory of Calumny*	1·40	65
832	200f. *Pallas and the Centaur*	2·50	85
833	250f. *Allegory of Spring*	3·25	1·10
MS834	71×91 mm. 500f. *Virgin of the Pomegranate* (31×39 mm)	5·00	2·00

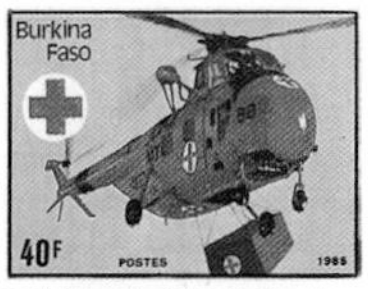

265 Sikorsky S-55 Helicopter

1985. Red Cross. Multicoloured.

835	40f. Type **265** (postage)	1·70	35
836	85f. Ambulance	3·00	50
837	150f. Henri Dunant (founder) (vert) (air)	2·30	65
838	250f. Nurse attending patient (vert)	3·75	1·10

266 Transport and Communications (development)

1985. Air. "Philexafrique" International Stamp Exhibition, Lome, Togo (2nd issue). Multicoloured.

839	250f. Type **266**	3·50	1·50
840	250f. Youth activities (youth)	3·50	1·50

267 Girls drumming and clapping

1986. Dodo Carnival. Multicoloured.

841	20f. Type **267**	10	10
842	25f. Masked lion dancers	25	10
843	40f. Masked stick dancers and drummers	45	15
844	45f. Stick dancers with elaborate headdresses	55	20
845	90f. Masked elephant dancer	1·20	45
846	90f. Animal dancers	1·20	45

268 Mother breast-feeding Baby

1986. Child Survival Campaign.

847	**268**	90f. multicoloured	1·10	50

269 Couple carrying Rail

1986. Railway Construction. Multicoloured.

848	90f. Type **269** (postage)	85	35
849	120f. Laying tracks	1·00	45
850	185f. Workers waving to passing train	1·50	65
851	500f. *Inauguration of First German Railway* (Heim) (air)	4·25	2·00
MS852	90×68 mm. 1000f. Experimental inter-city train and diesel locomotive series 290	8·50	3·50

Nos. 851/**MS**852 commemorate the 150th Anniv of German railways.

270 Columbus before King of Portugal, and *Nina*

1986. 480th Death Anniv of Christopher Columbus (explorer). Multicoloured.

853	250f. Type **270** (postage)	2·50	70
854	300f. *Santa Maria* and Columbus with astrolabe	2·75	90
855	400f. Columbus imprisoned and *Santa Maria*	3·75	1·10
856	450f. Landing at San Salvador and *Pinta* (air)	4·25	1·80
MS857	90×68 mm. 1000f. Fleet leaving Palos	8·50	2·10

271 Village and First Aid Post

1986. "Health For All by Year 2000". Multicoloured.

858	90f. Type **271**	95	35
859	100f. Man receiving first aid (26×36 mm)	95	45
860	120f. People queuing for vaccinations (26×36 mm)	1·30	50

272 "Phryneta aurocinta"

1986. Insects. Multicoloured.

861	15f. Type **272**	25	10
862	20f. *Sternocera interrupta*	35	10
863	40f. *Prosoprocera lactator*	80	30
864	45f. *Gonimbrasia hecate*	90	35
865	85f. *Charaxes epijasius*	1·40	60

273 Woman feeding Child and Fresh Foods

1986. Gobi Health Strategy. Multicoloured.

866	30f. Type **273**	40	10
867	60f. Ingredients of oral rehydration therapy	70	30
868	90f. Mother holding child for vaccination	1·00	45
869	120f. Doctor weighing child	1·50	55

274 UPU Emblem on Dove

1986. World Post Day.

870	**274**	120f. multicoloured	1·30	55

275 Emblem

1986. International Peace Year.

871	**275**	90f. blue	1·20	55

276 Namende Dancers

1986. National Bobo Culture Week. Multicoloured.

872	10f. Type **276**	25	10
873	25f. Mouhoun dancers	50	10
874	90f. Houet dancer	1·10	45
875	105f. Seno musicians	1·10	50
876	120f. Ganzourgou dancers	1·70	60

277 Warthog

1986. Wildlife. Multicoloured.

877	50f. Type **277**	70	20
878	65f. Spotted hyena	80	30
879	90f. Antelope	1·20	35
880	100f. Red-fronted gazelle	1·20	45
881	120f. Harnessed antelope	1·30	55
882	145f. Hartebeest	1·80	65
883	500f. Kob	5·75	2·20

278 Peul

1986. Traditional Hairstyles. Multicoloured.

884	35f. Type **278**	35	10
885	75f. Dafing	80	35
886	90f. Peul (different)	1·30	45
887	120f. Mossi	1·60	60
888	185f. Peul (different)	2·30	90

279 Charlie Chaplin within Film Frame (10th death anniv)

1987. Tenth Fespaco Film Festival.

889	-	90f. mauve, black & brn	1·10	60
890	-	120f. multicoloured	2·20	85
891	**279**	185f. multicoloured	3·25	1·40

DESIGNS: 90f. Camera on map in film frame; 120f. Cameraman and soundman (60th anniv of first talking film *The Jazz Singer*).

280 Woman trimming Rug

1987. International Women's Day.

892	**280**	90f. multicoloured	1·00	45

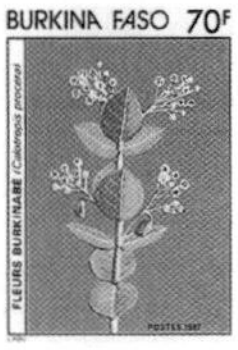

281 *Calotripis procera*

1987. Flowers. Multicoloured.

893	70f. Type **281**	80	30
894	75f. *Acacia seyal*	80	30
895	85f. *Parkia biglobosa*	1·00	50
896	90f. *Sterospernum kunthianum*	1·00	50
897	100f. *Dichrostachys cinerea*	1·40	55
898	300f. *Combretum paniculatum*	3·50	1·30

282 High Jumping

1987. Olympic Games, Seoul (1988). 50th Death Anniv of Pierre de Coubertin (founder of modern Olympic Games). Multicoloured.

899	75f. Type **282**	80	40
900	85f. Tennis (vert)	90	40
901	90f. Ski jumping	95	55
902	100f. Football	1·00	55
903	145f. Running	1·40	70
904	350f. Pierre de Coubertin and tennis game (vert)	3·50	1·70

283 Follereau and Doctor treating Patient

1987. Anti-leprosy Campaign. 10th Death Anniv of Raoul Follereau (pioneer). Multicoloured.

905	90f. Type **283**	1·10	45
906	100f. Laboratory technicians	1·30	45
907	120f. Gerhard Hansen (discoverer of bacillus)	1·50	55
908	300f. Follereau kissing patient	3·50	1·50

284 Woman sweeping

1987. World Environment Day. Multicoloured.

909	90f. Type **284**	1·00	60
910	145f. Emblem	1·50	75

285 Globe in Envelope

1987. World Post Day.

911	**285**	90f. multicoloured	1·00	55

286 Luthuli and Open Book

1987. Anti-Apartheid Campaign. 20th Death Anniv of Albert John Luthuli (anti-apartheid campaigner). Multicoloured.

912	90f. Barbed wire and apartheid victims	1·00	45
913	100f. Type **286**	1·10	45

287 Dagari

1987. Traditional Costumes. Multicoloured.

914	10f. Type **287**	10	10
915	30f. Peul	25	10
916	90f. Mossi (female)	85	45
917	200f. Senoufo	1·60	90
918	500f. Mossi (male)	5·00	2·30

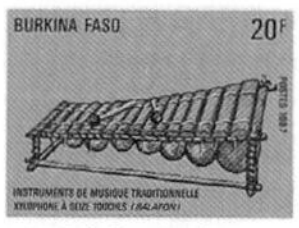

288 Balafon (16 key xylophone)

1987. Traditional Music Instruments. Multicoloured.

919	20f. Type **288**	25	10
920	25f. Kunde en more (3 stringed lute) (vert)	25	20
921	35f. Tiahoun en bwaba (zither)	40	25
922	90f. Jembe en dioula (conical drum)	90	45
923	1000f. Bendre en more (calabash drum) (vert)	9·75	4·50

289 Dwellings

1987. International Year of Shelter for the Homeless.

924	**289**	90f. multicoloured	1·00	45

290 Small Industrial Units

1987. Five Year Plan for Popular Development. Multicoloured.

925	40f. Type **290**	35	10
926	55f. Management of dams	60	25
927	60f. Village community building primary school	60	25
928	90f. Bus (Transport and communications)	1·00	35
929	100f. National education: literacy campaign	1·00	55
930	120f. Intensive cattle farming	1·30	55

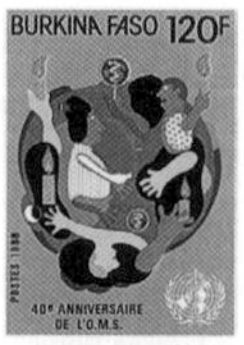

291 People with Candles

1988. 40th Anniv of WHO.

931	**291**	120f. multicoloured	1·30	45

292 Exhibition Emblem and Games Mascot

1988. Olympic Games, Seoul, and "Olymphilex '88" Olympic Stamps Exhibition, Rome (932). Multicoloured.

932	30f. Type **292**	30	10
933	160f. Olympic flame (vert)	1·50	60
934	175f. Football	1·70	70
935	235f. Volleyball (vert)	2·30	1·10
936	450f. Basketball (vert)	4·25	2·00
MS937	115×100 mm. 500f. 1500 metres race (36×48 mm)	5·75	5·25

293 Houet "Sparrow Hawk" Mask

1988. Masks. Multicoloured.

938	10f. Type **293**	10	10
939	20f. Ouillo "Young Girls" mask	30	25
940	30f. Houet "Hartebeest" mask	40	25
941	40f. Mouhoun "Blacksmith" mask	45	25
942	120f. Ouri "Nanny" mask	1·30	45
943	175f. Ouri "Bat" mask (horiz)	1·80	75

294 Kieriba Jug

1988. Handicrafts. Multicoloured.

944	5f. Type **294**	10	10
945	15f. Mossi basket (horiz)	10	10
946	25f. Gurunsi chair (horiz)	25	10
947	30f. Bissa basket (horiz)	25	20
948	45f. Ouagadougou hide box (horiz)	45	20
949	85f. Ouagadougou bronze statuette	75	40
950	120f. Ouagadougou hide travelling bag (horiz)	1·10	55

295 Envelopes forming Map

1988. World Post Day.

951	**295**	120f. blue, black & yellow	1·10	45

296 White-collared Kingfisher

1988. Aquatic Wildlife. Multicoloured.

952	70f. Type **296**	60	25
953	100f. Elephantfish	1·00	40
954	120f. Frog	1·40	45
955	160f. White-faced whistling duck	1·60	70

297 Mohammed Ali Jinnah (first Pakistan Governor-General)

1988. Death Anniversaries. Multicoloured.

956	80f. Type **297** (40th anniv) (postage)	75	40
957	120f. Mahatma Gandhi (Indian human rights activist, 40th anniv)	1·10	55
958	160f. John Fitzgerald Kennedy (U.S. President, 25th anniv)	1·70	70

959	235f. Martin Luther King (human rights activist, 20th anniv) (air)	2·10	1·10

298 Shepherds adoring Child

1988. Christmas. Stained Glass Windows. Multicoloured.

960	120f. Type **298**	1·20	40
961	160f. Wise men presenting gifts to Child	1·40	70
962	450f. Virgin and Child	4·00	1·80
963	1000f. Flight into Egypt	8·50	4·50

299 Satellite and Globe

1989. 20th Anniv of FESPACO Film Festival. Multicoloured.

964	75f. Type **299** (postage)	1·70	40
965	500f. Ababacar Samb Makharam (air)	6·25	2·75
966	500f. Jean Michel Tchissoukou	6·25	2·75
967	500f. Paulin Soumanou Vieyra	6·25	2·75
MS968	114×85 mm. As Nos. 965/7 but with anniversary inscriptions and values in gold	21·00	19·00

300 WHO and Aids Emblems

1989. Campaign against AIDS.

969	**300** 120f. multicoloured	1·10	55

301 *Oath of the Tennis Court* (Jacques Louis David) (½-size illustration)

1989. Air. "Philexfrance 89" International Stamp Exhibition, Paris, and Bicentenary of French Revolution. Multicoloured.

970	150f. Type **301**	1·40	80
971	200f. *Storming of the Bastille* (Thevenin)	2·00	1·20
972	600f. *Rouget de Lisle singing La Marseillaise* (Pils)	6·25	3·50

302 Map and Tractor

1989. 30th Anniv of Council of Unity.

973	**302** 75f. multicoloured	75	40

303 *Striga generioides*

1989. Parasitic Plants. Multicoloured.

974	20f. Type **303**	25	10
975	50f. *Striga hermonthica*	45	25
976	235f. *Striga aspera*	2·10	1·10
977	450f. *Alectra vogelii*	4·00	1·80

304 Sahel Dog

1989. Dogs. Multicoloured.

978	35f. Type **304**	45	25
979	50f. Young dog	55	25
980	60f. Hunting dog	80	35
981	350f. Guard dog	3·50	1·80

305 Statue

1989. Solidarity with Palestinian People.

982	**305** 120f. multicoloured	1·20	45

1989. Nos. 647/9 of Upper Volta optd **BURKINA FASO**.

983	**229** 90f. multicoloured	80	30
984	**229** 120f. multicoloured	1·00	40
985	**229** 170f. multicoloured	1·50	60

307 Pilgrims at Shrine of Our Lady of Yagma

1990. Visit of Pope John Paul II. Multicoloured.

986	120f. Type **307**	1·20	55
987	160f. Pope and crowd	1·70	90

308 Mail Steamer, Globe and Penny Black

1990. 150th Anniv of Penny Black and "Stamp World London 90" International Stamp exhibition. Multicoloured.

988	120f. Type **308**	1·20	55
MS989	70×80 mm. 500f. Penny Black and early mail steamers (vert)	4·25	4·00

309 Goalkeeper catching Ball

1990. World Cup Football Championship, Italy. Multicoloured.

990	30f. Type **309**	35	25
991	150f. Footballers	1·60	70
MS992	72×65 mm. 1000f. Footballers and "1990"	8·50	8·25

310 *Cantharellus cibarius*

1990. Fungi. Multicoloured.

993	10f. Type **310**	20	20
994	15f. *Psalliota bispora*	25	20
995	60f. *Amanita caesarea*	85	60
996	190f. *Boletus badius*	2·75	1·50
MS997	77×108 mm. 75f.×4 As Nos. 993/6	4·75	4·00

311 Open Book

1990. International Literacy Year.

998	**311** 40f. multicoloured	45	20
999	**311** 130f. multicoloured	1·20	55

312 Maps, Emblem and Native Artefacts

1990. Second International Salon of Arts and Crafts, Ouagadougou. Multicoloured.

1000	35f. Type **312**	25	20
1001	45f. Pottery (horiz)	40	20
1002	270f. Cane chair	2·20	1·10

313 De Gaulle

1990. Birth Centenary of Charles de Gaulle (French statesman).

1003	**313** 200f. multicoloured	2·00	90

314 Quartz

1991. Rocks. Multicoloured.

1004	20f. Type **314**	25	10
1005	50f. Granite	70	40
1006	280f. Amphibolite	2·75	1·70

315 Hand Holding Cigarette, Syringe and Tablets

1991. Anti-drugs Campaign.

1007	**315** 130f. multicoloured	1·10	65

316 Film and Landscape

1991. 12th "Fepaco 91" Pan-African Cinema and Television Festival. Multicoloured.

1008	150f. Type **316**	1·70	90
MS1009	77×108 mm. 1000f. *Stallion of Yennenga* (Festival Grand Prix statuette)	12·00	12·00

317 Morse and Key

1991. Birth Bicentenary of Samuel Morse (inventor of signalling system).

1010	**317** 200f. multicoloured	1·80	1·10

318 Traditional Hairstyle

1991

1011	**318** 5f. multicoloured	10	10
1012	**318** 10f. multicoloured	10	10
1013	**318** 25f. multicoloured	10	10
1014	**318** 50f. multicoloured	20	10
1018	**318** 130f. multicoloured	1·10	25
1019	**318** 150f. multicoloured	1·40	60
1020	**318** 200f. multicoloured	1·70	85
1021	**318** 330f. multicoloured	2·20	75

319 *Grewia tenax*

1991. Flowers. Multicoloured.

1025	5f. Type **319**	10	10
1026	15f. *Hymenocardia acide*	10	10
1027	60f. *Cassia sieberiana* (vert)	70	30
1028	100f. *Adenium obesum*	90	55
1029	300f. *Mitragyna inermis*	2·75	1·60

320 Warba

1991. Dance Costumes. Multicoloured.

1030	75f. Type **320**	85	40
1031	130f. Wiskamba	1·20	70
1032	280f. Pa-Zenin	3·00	1·60

321 Pillar Box and Globe

1991. World Post Day.

1033	**321** 130f. multicoloured	1·20	55

322 Cake Tin

1992. Cooking Utensils. Multicoloured.

1034	45f. Type **322**	70	65
1035	130f. Cooking pot (vert)	1·40	70
1036	310f. Pestle and mortar (vert)	2·75	1·40
1037	500f. Ladle and bowl	4·75	2·10

323 Yousouf Fofana

1992. African Nations Cup Football Championship, Senegal. Multicoloured.

1038	50f. Type **323**	50	30
1039	100f. Francois-Jules Bocande	1·00	70
MS1040	98×93 mm. 500f. Stadium and trophy	4·75	4·50

324 Disabled Man at Potter's Wheel

1992. U.N. Decade of the Handicapped.

1041	**324**	100f. multicoloured	90	55

325 Child and Cardiograph

1992. World Health Day. "Health in Rhythm with the Heart".

1042	**325**	330f. multicoloured	3·50	1·80

326 Columbus and *Santa Maria*

1992. "Genova '92" International Thematic Stamp Exhibition and 500th Anniv of Discovery of America by Columbus. Multicoloured.

1043	50f. Type **326**	70	30
1044	150f. Amerindians watching Columbus's fleet off San Salvador	2·10	90
MS1045	129×91 mm. 350f. Route map of first voyage (51×30 mm)	4·75	3·50

327 *Dysdercus voelkeri* (fire bug) on Cotton Boll

1992. Insects. Multicoloured.

1046	20f. Type **327**	25	10
1047	40f. *Rhizopertha dominica* (beetle) on leaf	50	30
1048	85f. *Orthetrum microstigma* (dragonfly) on stem	1·20	50
1049	500f. Honey bee on flower	5·25	2·50

328 Crib

1992. Christmas. Multicoloured.

1050	10f. Type **328**	10	10
1051	130f. Children decorating crib	1·30	65
1052	1000f. Boy with Christmas card	9·50	5·25

329 Film Makers' Monument

1993. 13th "Fespaco" Pan-African Film Festival, Ouagadougou. Multicoloured.

1053	250f. Type **329**	2·50	1·50
1054	750f. Douta Seck (comedian) (horiz)	7·50	4·50

330 Yellow-billed Stork

1993. Birds. Multicoloured.

1055	100f. Type **330**	95	60
1056	200f. Marabou stork	2·00	1·20
1057	500f. Saddle-bill stork	5·00	2·75
MS1058	120×82 mm. Nos. 1046/8 (sold at 1200f.)	14·50	11·00

331 Statue of Liberty, Globe and Ball

1993. World Cup Football Championship, U.S.A. (1994). Multicoloured.

1059	500f. Type **331**	5·00	2·50
1060	1000f. Players, map of world and U.S. flag	9·75	5·50

332 Peterbilt Canadian Hauler and Diesel Locomotive Type BB 852, France

1993. Centenary of Invention of Diesel Engine.

1061	**332**	1000f. multicoloured	9·50	5·25

333 *Saba senegalensis*

1993. Wild Fruits. Multicoloured.

1062	150f. Type **333**	1·60	80
1063	300f. Karite (horiz)	3·00	1·60
1064	600f. Baobab	6·50	3·25

334 Flowers, "Stamps" and Sights of Paris

1993. First European Stamp Salon, Flower Gardens, Paris (1994). Multicoloured.

1065	400f. Type **334**	4·50	2·30
1066	650f. "Stamps", sights of Paris, daffodils and irises	5·75	3·75

335 Peulh Copper Hair Ornament

1993. Jewellery. Multicoloured.

1067	200f. Type **335**	1·80	1·10
1068	250f. Mossi agate necklace (vert)	2·20	1·30
1069	500f. Gourounsi copper bracelet	4·50	2·50

336 Gazelle

1993. The Red-fronted Gazelle. Multicoloured.

1070	30f. Type **336**	1·00	35
1071	40f. Two gazelle	1·00	40
1072	60f. Two gazelle (different)	2·00	75
1073	100f. Gazelle	4·00	1·30
MS1074	110×89 mm. Nos. 1061/4 (sold at 400f.)	6·25	6·00

337 Woodland Kingfisher

1994. Kingfishers. Multicoloured.

1075	600f. Type **337**	4·75	2·75
1076	1200f. Striped kingfisher	9·50	5·50
MS1077	84×72 mm. 2000f. African pygmy kingfisher	15·00	13·50

338 Players

1994. World Cup Football Championship, United States. Multicoloured.

1078	1000f. Type **338**	6·00	2·75
1079	1800f. Goalkeeper saving ball	9·00	4·50
MS1080	84×72 mm. No. 1079 (sold at 2000f.)	9·75	9·25

339 Dog with Puppy

1994. First European Stamp Salon, Flower Gardens, Paris, France.

1081	**339**	1500f. multicoloured	6·75	4·00
MS1082		82×80 mm. No. 1081 (sold at 2000f.)	9·75	9·25

340 Astronaut planting Flag on Moon

1994. 25th Anniv of First Manned Moon Landing. Multicoloured.

1083	750f. Type **340**	3·75	2·10
1084	750f. Landing module on Moon	3·75	2·10

Nos. 1083/4 were issued together, se-tenant, forming a composite design.

341 Guinea Sorrel

1994. Vegetables. Multicoloured.

1085	40f. Type **341**	35	10
1086	45f. Aubergine	35	10
1087	75f. Aubergine	35	20
1088	100f. Okra	60	30

342 Pig

1994. Domestic Animals. Multicoloured.

1089	150f. Type **342**	80	45
1090	1000f. Goat (vert)	4·75	2·75
1091	1500f. Sheep	7·00	3·00

343 Pierre de Coubertin (founder) and Anniversary Emblem

1994. Centenary of Int Olympic Committee.

1092	**343**	320f. multicoloured	1·60	90

344 Donkey Rider

1995. 20th Anniv of World Tourism Organization. Multicoloured.

1093	150f. Type **344**	80	65
1094	350f. Bobo-Dioulasso railway station (horiz)	1·50	90
1095	450f. Great Mosque, Bani (horiz)	2·00	1·20
1096	650f. Roan antelope and map (horiz)	2·75	1·70

345 Crocodile

1995. Multicoloured, colour of frame given.

1097	**345**	10f. brown	10	10
1098	**345**	20f. mauve	10	10
1099	**345**	25f. brown	10	10
1100	**345**	30f. green	10	10
1101	**345**	40f. purple	10	10
1102	**345**	50f. grey	10	10
1103	**345**	75f. purple	25	10
1104	**345**	100f. brown	40	10
1105	**345**	150f. green	55	35
1106	**345**	175f. blue	75	40
1107	**345**	250f. brown	90	60
1108	**345**	400f. green	1·40	1·00

346 *Rabi* (dir. Gaston Kabore)

1995. "Fespaco 95" Pan-African Film Festival and Centenary of Motion Pictures. Multicoloured.

1109	150f. Type **346**	80	50
1110	250f. *Tila* (Idrissa Ouedraogo)	95	65

347 Elvis Presley in "Loving You"

1995. Entertainers. Multicoloured.

1111	300f. Type **347**	1·40	80
1112	400f. Marilyn Monroe	1·80	1·10
1113	500f. Elvis Presley in *Jailhouse Rock*	2·30	1·40
1114	650f. Marilyn Monroe in *Asphalt Jungle*	2·75	1·80
1115	750f. Marilyn Monroe in *Niagara*	3·00	2·10
1116	1000f. Elvis Presley in *Blue Hawaii*	4·50	3·00
MS1117	Two sheets. (a) 123×95 mm. 1500f. Marilyn Monroe in *The Seven Year Itch* (41×48 mm). (b) 137×89 mm. 1500f. Marilyn Monroe and Elvis Presley (60th birth anniv of Presley (50×41 mm)) Set of 2 sheets	13·00	12·50

348 Common Gonolek

1995. Birds. Multicoloured.

1118	450f. Type **348**	2·00	1·00
1119	600f. Red-cheeked cordon-bleu	3·00	1·50
1120	750f. Golden bishop	3·50	2·10
MS1121	80×120 mm. Nos. 1118/20 (sold at 2000f.)	8·75	8·25

349 Hissing Sand Snake

1995. Reptiles. Multicoloured.

1122	450f. Type **349**	2·50	1·50
1123	500f. Sand python	2·50	1·60
1124	1500f. Tortoise	7·50	4·50

350 Basketball

1995. Olympic Games, Atlanta (1996). Multicoloured.

1125	150f. Type **350**	55	30
1126	250f. Baseball	95	55
1127	650f. Tennis	2·20	1·40
1128	750f. Table tennis	3·25	1·80
MS1129	127×89 mm. 1500f. Dressage (35×50 mm)	6·50	6·25

351 Juan Manuel Fangio (racing driver)

1995. Sportsmen. Multicoloured.

1130	300f. Type **351**	3·75	95
1131	400f. Andre Agassi (tennis player)	1·40	90
1132	500f. Ayrton Senna (racing driver)	2·00	1·10
1133	1000f. Michael Schumacher (racing driver)	3·75	2·10
MS1134	146×112 mm. 1500f. Enzo Ferrari, Formula 1 racing car and Ferrari F40 sports car (56×48 mm)	13·00	8·75

352 Children and Christmas Tree

1995. Christmas. Multicoloured.

1135	150f. Type **352**	75	55
1136	450f. Grotto, Yagma	2·20	1·50
1137	500f. Flight into Egypt	2·50	1·60
1138	1000f. Adoration of the Wise Men	4·50	3·00

353 Headquarters Building, New York

1995. 50th Anniv of United Nations. Multicoloured.

1139	500f. Type **353**	2·20	1·70
1140	1000f. Village council under tree with superimposed U.N. emblem (vert)	4·25	3·00

354 Mossi Type

1995. Traditional Houses. Multicoloured.

1141	70f. Type **354**	25	10
1142	100f. Kassena type	45	25
1143	200f. Roro type	90	35
1144	250f. Peulh type	1·10	55

Nos.1145/8 and Type **355** are left for Christmas, issued on 18 Dec 1995, not yet received.

Nos.1149/50 and Type **356** are left for 50th Anniv of UN, issued on 20 Dec 1995, not yet received.

357 Les Etalons (national team) Emblem

1996. African Cup of Nations Football Championships. Multicoloured.

1151	150f.+25f. Type **357**	80	35
1152	250f.+25f. Player and map of Africa	1·40	65
MS1153	90×84mm. 150f. + 25f. As Type **357**	2·75	1·30

The premium was for the benefit of national sport

358 *Panthera leo* (lions)

1996. Big Cats. Multicoloured.

1154	100f. Type **358**	60	25
1155	150f. *Acinonyx jubatus* (cheetah)	85	30
1156	175f. *Lynx caracal* (caracal)	1·00	40
1157	250f. *Panthera pardus* (leopard)	1·60	70

Nos.1158/9 and Type **359** are left for France–Africa Summit, issued 1996, not yet received.

360 Orchid

1996. Orchids. Multicoloured.

1160	100f. Type **360**	85	45
1161	175f. Yellow orchid	1·30	70
1162	250f. Red and pink orchid	1·90	90
1163	300f. Lime green and dark pink orchid	2·30	1·10

Nos. 1164/5 and Type **361** are left for FESPACO Film Festival, issued 5 February 1997, not yet received.

Nos. 1166/9 and Type **362** are left for Fauna, issued 20 March 1997, not yet received.

No. 1170 and Type **363** are left for Death Centenary of H. von Stephan, issued 8 April 1997, not yet received.

Nos. 1171/4 and Type **364** are left for Masks, issued 20 May 1997, not yet received.

Nos. 1175/8 and Type **365** are left for Ceramics, issued 11 September 1997, not yet received.

Nos. 1179/83 and Type **366** are left for Fish, issued 20 November 1997, not yet received.

Nos. 1184/7 and Type **367** are left for African Football, issued 20 January 1998, not yet received.

Nos. 1188/91 and Type **368** are left for Traditional Costumes, issued 20 February 1998, not yet received.

Nos. 1192/3 and Type **369** are left for 20th Anniv of Agricultural Development Fund, issued 20 March 1998, not yet received.

Nos. 1194/7 and Type **370** are left for Endangered Species, issued 20 May 1998, not yet received.

Nos. 1198/9 and Type **371** are left for Organization for African Unity Summit, issued 20 May 1998, not yet received.

372 White-winged Triller

1998. Birds. Multicoloured.

1200	5f. Type **372**	15	10
1201	10f. (Arabian) Golden sparrow	15	10
1202	100f. American goldfinch	55	30
1203	170f. Red-legged thrush	95	45
1204	260f. Willow warbler	1·70	85
1205	425f. Blue grosbeak	2·75	1·90
MS1206	106×152 mm. 260f.×9, Bank swallow (sand martin); Kirtland's warbler; Long-tailed minivet; Blue-grey gnatcatcher; Reed bunting; Black-collared apalis; American robin; Cape longclaw; Wood thrush	11·50	3·35
MS1207	106×152 mm. 425f.×9, Song sparrow; Dartford warbler; Eastern bluebird; Rock thrush; Northern mockingbird; Northern cardinal; Eurasian goldfinch; Varied thrush; Northern oriole	17·00	5·75
MS1208	84×110 mm. 1500f. Golden whistler (horiz)	7·25	2·50
MS1209	110×84 mm. 1500f. Swallow	7·25	2·50

Nos.1210 and Type **373** are left for 40th Anniv of Council of Entente, issued 5 May 1999, not yet received.

374 Family of Lions

1999. Lions

1211	**374**	170f. multicoloured	75	30
1212	**374**	260f. multicoloured	95	40
1213	**374**	425f. multicoloured	2·00	85
1214	**374**	530f. multicoloured	2·30	1·10
1215	**374**	590f. multicoloured	4·25	2·00

375 Kitten and Butterfly

1999. Pets. Multicoloured.

1216	5f. Type **375**	10	10
1217	10f. Two chinchilla kittens (horiz)	15	10
1218	20f. Yorkshire terriers (horiz)	25	15
1219	25f. Cocker spaniels (horiz)	35	25
MS1220	105×110 mm. Vert: 260f.×6, Afghan hound puppy; Wire fox terrier; Pug; Dalmatian; Boston terrier; Cocker spaniel	5·75	2·30
MS1221	157×88 mm. Horiz: 530f.×6, American wire-haired kitten; Tabby; Burmese blue and frog; Abyssian; Burmese lilac lying down; Siamese playing with string	13·00	8·00
MS1222	97×79 mm. 1000f. Flowers and two labrador retriever puppies	4·25	2·60
MS1223	105×80 mm. 1000f. Labrador retriever puppy	4·25	2·60
MS1224	110×85 mm. 1000f. Persian tabby (horiz)	4·25	2·60
MS1225	82×110 mm. 1000f. Japanese bobtail kitten	4·25	2·60

376 Gelderlander

1999. Domestic Animals. Multicoloured.

1226	170f. Type **376**	60	25
1227	170f. Trait lourd horse	60	25
1228	170f. Vladimir heavy draft horse	60	25
1229	170f. Percheron horse	60	25
1230	170f. Sumba pony	60	25
1231	170f. Dartmoor pony	60	25
1232	425f. French bulldog	2·10	60
1233	425f. Bernese dog	2·10	60
1234	425f. Griffon dog	2·10	60
1235	425f. King Charles spaniel	2·10	60
1236	425f. Miniature Spitz dog	2·10	60
1237	425f. Yorkshire terrier	2·10	60
1238	590f. American wire-haired cat	3·00	1·20
1239	590f. Japanese bob-tail cats	3·00	1·20
1240	590f. Himalayan cat	3·00	1·20
1241	590f. LaPerm cat	3·00	1·20
1242	590f. Lilac point Siamese cat and kitten	3·00	1·20
1243	590f. Norwegian forest cat	3·00	1·20
MS1244	76×106 mm. 1000f. Shetland pony leaning over stable door (vert)	4·25	3·00
MS1245	106×78 mm. 1000f. Japanese bobtail cat (vert)	4·25	3·00
MS1246	107×77 mm. 1000f. Basset hound (vert)	4·00	3·25

377 *Portland*

1999. Historic Ships. Multicoloured.

MS1247	135×97 mm. 170f.×3, Type **377**; *Goethe*; *Fulton*	2·25	1·10
MS1248	104×76 mm. 1000f. *Grand Voiler*	4·25	2·00
MS1249	104×76 mm. 1000f. *Batavia*	8·25	4·25

378 Sukhoi Su-24

1999. Aviation. Multicoloured.

MS1250	145×95 mm. 425f.×6, Type **378**; Yakolev Yak-38; Tupolev *Blackjack*; Antonov An-26; Antonov An-22 Antheus (inscr 'Anteus'); Antonov An-124	10·50	6·00
MS1251	76×105 mm. 1000f. Ilyushin Il-76 T (57×42 mm)	4·25	2·75

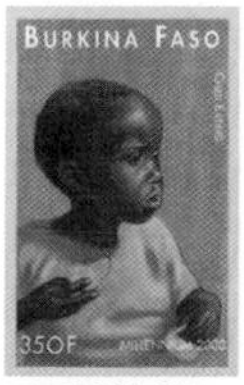

379 Child holding Food

1999. Millennium 2000

1252	350f. multicoloured	1·40	80

APPENDIX

The following stamps have either been issued in excess of postal needs or have not been available to the public in reasonable quantities at face value. Such stamps may later be given full listing if there is evidence of regular postal use.

1985

85th Birthday of Queen Elizabeth the Queen Mother. 1500f.

1996

Fungi. 150f., 250f., 300f., 400f., 500f., 650f., 1000f.
Fungi. 175f., 250f., 300f., 450f.
Entertainers. 150f., 250f., 300f., 400f., 500f., 650f., 1000f.
Butterflies and Insects. 100f., 150f., 175f., 250f.
Butterflies. 150f., 250f., 450f., 600f.
Insects. 25f., 75f., 300f., 400f.
Andre Agassi Olympic Gold Medal. 400f.
Endangered Birds. 500f., 750f., 1000f., 1500f.

1997

Princess Diana. 260f., 425f.×2, 590f.
Mother Teresa. 260f.

1998

Butterflies. 170f.×9
Christmas. 100f., 170f., 260f., 425f., 530f.
Football World Cup. 50f., 150f., 250f., 450f.

Pt. 1, Pt. 21

BURMA

A territory in the east of India, which was granted independence by the British in 1948. From May 1990 it was known as Myanmar.

Burma.
1937. 12 pies = 1 anna; 16 annas = 1 rupee.
1953. 100 pyas = 1 kyat.

Japanese Occupation of Burma.
1942. 12 pies = 1 anna; 16 annas = 1 rupee.
1942. 100 cents = 1 rupee.

1937. Stamps of India (King George V) optd **BURMA**.

1	**55**	3p. grey	2·00	10
3	**80**	9p. green	1·00	10
2	**79**	½a. green	1·00	10
4	**81**	1a. brown	4·00	10
5	**59**	2a. red	1·00	10
6	**61**	2½a. orange	75	10
7	**62**	3a. red	4·00	30
8	**83**	3½a. blue	6·00	10
9	**63**	4a. olive	1·00	10
10	**64**	6a. bistre	1·00	35
11	**65**	8a. mauve	3·50	10
12	**66**	12a. red	12·00	3·00
13	**67**	1r. brown and green	55·00	4·75
14	**67**	2r. red and orange	42·00	26·00
15	**67**	5r. blue and violet	50·00	27·00
16	**67**	10r. green and red	£200	90·00
17	**67**	15r. blue and olive	£700	£190
18	**67**	25r. orange and blue	£1200	£475

2 King George VI and "Chinthes"

3 King George VI and "Nagas"

4 "Karaweik" (royal barge)

8 King George VI and Peacock

1938. King George VI.

18b	**2**	1p. orange	3·25	1·75
19	**2**	3p. violet	30	3·00
20	**2**	6p. blue	50	10
21	**2**	9p. green	1·75	1·50
22	**3**	1a. brown	30	10
23	**3**	1½a. green	1·00	3·50
24	**3**	2a. red	3·00	1·00
25	**4**	2a.6p. red	15·00	3·50
26	-	3a. mauve	15·00	3·50
27	-	3a.6p. blue	3·75	9·00
28	**3**	4a. blue	3·50	20
29	-	8a. green	4·00	55
30	**8**	1r. purple and blue	4·00	1·00
31	**8**	2r. brown and purple	23·00	5·00
32	-	5r. violet and red	75·00	55·00
33	-	10r. brown and green	80·00	85·00

DESIGNS—HORIZ: As Type **4**: 3a. Burma teak; 3a.6p. Burma rice; 8a. River Irrawaddy. VERT: As Type **3**: 5, 10r. King George VI and "Nats".

1940. Cent of First Adhesive Postage Stamp. Surch **COMMEMORATION POSTAGE STAMP 6th MAY 1840 ONE ANNA 1A** and value in native characters.

34	**4**	1a. on 2a.6p. red	4·00	2·00

For Japanese issues see "Japanese Occupation of Burma".

1945. British Military Administration. Stamps of 1938 optd **MILY ADMN**.

35	**2**	1p. orange	10	10
36	**2**	3p. violet	20	2·00
37	**2**	6p. blue	20	30
38	**2**	9p. green	30	1·75
39	**3**	1a. brown	20	10
40	**3**	1½a. green	20	15
41	**3**	2a. red	20	15
42	**4**	2a.6p. red	2·25	3·50
43	-	3a. mauve	1·50	20
44	-	3a.6p. blue	20	70
45	**3**	4a. blue	20	70
46	-	8a. green	20	1·75
47	**8**	1r. purple and blue	50	50
48	**8**	2r. brown and purple	50	1·50
49	-	5r. violet and red	50	1·50
50	-	10r. brown and green	50	1·50

1946. British Civil Administration. As 1938, but colours changed.

51	**2**	3p. brown	15	4·00
52	**2**	6p. violet	20	30
53	**2**	9p. green	1·50	6·50
54	**3**	1a. blue	55	20
55	**3**	1½a. orange	30	10
56	**3**	2a. red	30	50
57	**4**	2a.6p. blue	2·75	7·50
57a	-	3a. blue	6·50	10·00
57b	-	3a.6p. black and blue	3·00	5·00
58	**3**	4a. purple	70	1·50
59	-	8a. mauve	1·75	7·00
60	**8**	1r. violet and mauve	3·00	3·50
61	**8**	2r. brown and orange	8·50	7·00
62	-	5r. green and brown	10·00	28·00
63	-	10r. red and violet	22·00	40·00

14 Burman

1946. Victory.

64	**14**	9p. green	20	20
65	-	1½a. violet (Burmese woman)	20	10
66	-	2a. red (Chinthe)	20	10
67	-	3a.6p. (Elephant)	50	20

ကြားဖြတ်
အစိုးရ။

(18) Trans. "Interim Government"

1947. Stamps of 1946 opt with T **18** or with larger opt on large stamps.

68	**2**	3p. brown	1·75	70
69	**2**	6p. violet	20	30
70	**2**	9p. green	20	30
71	**3**	1a. blue	20	30
72	**3**	1½a. orange	2·75	10
73	**3**	2a. red	30	15
74	**4**	2a.6p. blue	1·75	1·00
75	-	3a. blue	2·50	1·75
76	-	3a.6p. black and blue	2·50	3·25
77	**3**	4a. purple	1·75	30
78	-	8a. mauve	1·75	3·25
79	**8**	1r. violet and mauve	9·00	3·25
80	**8**	2r. brown and orange	9·00	9·50
81	-	5r. green and brown	9·00	7·50
82	-	10r. red and violet	6·50	7·50

20 Gen. Aung San, Chinthe and Map of Burma

1948. Independence Day.

83	**20**	½a. green	10	10
84	**20**	1a. pink	10	10
85	**20**	2a. red	20	15
86	**20**	3½a. blue	25	15
87	**20**	8a. brown	25	25

21 Martyrs' Memorial

1948. First Anniv of Murder of Aung San and his Ministers.

88	**21**	3p. blue	10	10
89	**21**	6p. green	10	10
90	**21**	9p. red	10	10
91	**21**	1a. violet	10	10
92	**21**	2a. mauve	10	10
93	**21**	3½a. green	10	10
94	**21**	4a. brown	20	10
95	**21**	8a. red	20	15
96	**21**	12a. purple	25	15
97	**21**	1r. green	45	25
98	**21**	2r. blue	90	50
99	**21**	5r. brown	2·00	1·30

22 Playing Cane-ball

25 Bell, Mingun Pagoda

27 Transplanting Rice

28 Lion Throne

1949. First Anniv of Independence.

100	**22**	3p. blue	1·10	25
120	**22**	3p. orange	20	10
101	-	6p. green	20	10
121	-	6p. purple	10	10
102	-	9p. red	20	10
122	-	9p. blue	10	10
103	**25**	1a. red	20	10
123	**25**	1a. blue	10	10
104	-	2a. orange	20	10
124	-	2a. green	35	15
105	**27**	2a.6p. mauve	20	15
125	**27**	2a.6p. green	35	15
106	-	3a. violet	20	15
126	-	3a. red	20	15
107	-	3a.6p. green	25	15
127	-	3a.6p. orange	20	15
108	-	4a. brown	25	15
128	-	4a. red	20	15
109	-	8a. red	35	15
129	-	8a. blue	35	20
110	**28**	1r. green	65	15
130	**28**	1r. violet	50	55
111	**28**	2r. blue	1·50	45
131	**28**	2r. green	1·10	60
112	**28**	5r. brown	3·00	1·40
132	**28**	5r. blue	3·25	1·70
113	**28**	10r. orange	5·50	2·20
133	**28**	10r. blue	6·25	4·25

DESIGNS—As Type **22**: 6p. Dancer; 9p. Girl playing saung-gaut (string instrument); 2a. Hintha (legendary bird). As Type **25**: 4a. Elephant hauling log. As Type **27**: 3a. Girl weaving; 3a.6p. Royal Palace; 8a. Ploughing paddy field with oxen.

See also Nos. 137/50.

29 UPU Monument, Berne

1949. 75th Anniv of UPU.

114	**29**	2a. orange	25	25
115	**29**	3½a. green	25	15
116	**29**	6a. violet	35	25
117	**29**	8a. red	45	45
118	**29**	12½a. blue	90	60
119	**29**	1r. green	1·10	85

30 Independence Monument, Rangoon, and Map

1953. Fifth Anniv of Independence.

134	**30**	14p. green (22×18 mm)	20	10
135	**30**	20p. red (36½×26½ mm)	25	15
136	**30**	25p. blue (36½×26½ mm)	45	15

1954. New Currency. As 1949 issue but values in pyas and kyats.

137	**22**	1p. orange	70	10
138	-	2p. purple (as 6p.)	10	10
139	-	3p. blue (as 9p.)	10	10
140	**25**	5p. blue	10	10
141	**27**	10p. green	10	10
142	-	15p. green (as 2a.)	25	10
143	-	20p. red (as 3a.)	20	10
144	-	25p. orange (as 3a.6p.)	20	15
145	-	30p. red (as 4a.)	25	15
146	-	50p. blue (as 8a.)	25	15
147	**28**	1k. violet	80	25
148	**28**	2k. green	1·50	45
149	**28**	5k. blue	4·25	80
150	**28**	10k. blue	7·75	1·40

31 Sangiti Mahapasana Rock Cave in Grounds of Kaba-Aye Pagoda

1954. Sixth Buddhist Council, Rangoon.

151	-	10p. blue	10	10
152	-	15p. purple	15	15
153	**31**	35p. brown	25	25
154	-	50p. green	45	25
155	-	1k. red	95	50
156	-	2k. violet	1·60	1·10

DESIGNS: 10p. Rock caves and Songha of Cambodia; 15p. Buddhist priests and Kuthodaw Pagoda, Mandalay; 50p. Rock cave and Songha of Thailand; 1k. Rock cave and Songha of Ceylon; 2k. Rock cave and Songha of Laos.

32 Fifth Buddhist Council Monuments

1956. Buddha Jayanti.

157	**32**	20p. green and blue	15	15
158	-	40p. green and blue	35	25
159	-	60p. yellow and green	45	35
160	-	1k.25 blue and yellow	95	80

DESIGNS: 40p. Thatbyinnyu Pagoda, Pagan; 60p. Shwedagan Pagoda, Rangoon; 1k.25, Sangiti Mahapasana Rock Cave and Kaba-Aye Pagoda, Rangoon (venue of 6th Buddhist Council).

မြန္တလာ-နှစ်တရာ
၁၂၂၁-၁၃၂၁
15 P ၁၅ပြား

(33) "Mandalay Town—100 Years/1221–1321"

1959. Centenary of Mandalay. No. 144 surch with T **33** and Nos. 147/8 with two-line opt only.

161		15p. on 25p. orange	25	15
162	**28**	1k. violet	85	80
163	**28**	2k. green	1·70	1·20

1961. No. 134 surch as right-hand characters in third line of T **33**.

164	**30**	15p. on 14p. green	60	25

35 Torch-bearer in Rangoon

1961. Second South-East Asia Peninsula Games, Rangoon.

165	**35**	15p. blue and red	40	25
166	-	25p. green and brown	1·50	50
167	-	50p. mauve and blue	1·60	1·00
168	-	1k. yellow and green	3·50	2·00

DESIGNS—VERT: 25p. Contestants; 50p. Women sprinting in Aung San Stadium, Rangoon. HORIZ: 1k. Contestants.

36 Children at Play

1961. 15th Anniv of UNICEF.

169	**36**	15p. red and pink	1·50	40

37 Flag and Map

1963. First Anniv of Military Coup by General Ne Win.

170	**37**	15p. red	1·50	65

1963. Freedom from Hunger. Nos. 141 and 146 optd **FREEDOM FROM HUNGER**.

171	**27**	10p. green	1·00	80
172	-	50p. blue	3·00	2·00

အလုပ်သမားနေ့
၁၉၆၃

(39)

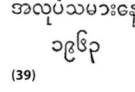

1963. Labour Day. No. 143 optd with T 39.

173		20p. red	65	35

40 White-browed Fantail

1964. Burmese Birds (1st series).

174	**40**	1p. black	25	15
175	**40**	2p. red	75	30
176	**40**	3p. green	75	30
177	-	5p. blue	75	30
178	-	10p. brown	80	35
179	-	15p. green	1·20	50
180	-	20p. brown and red	1·60	60
181	-	25p. brown and yellow	2·00	75
182	-	50p. blue and red	4·00	1·50
183	-	1k. blue, yellow & grey	7·50	2·00
184	-	2k. blue, green and red	16·00	4·00
185	-	5k. multicoloured	35·00	10·00

BIRDS—22×26 mm: 5 to 15p. Indian roller. 27×37 mm: 25p. Crested serpent eagle. 50p. Sarus crane. 1k. Indian pied hornbill. 5k. Green peafowl. 35½×25 mm: 20p. Red-whiskered bulbul. 37×27 mm: 2k. Kalij pheasant.

See also Nos. 195/206.

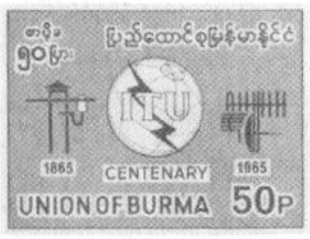

41 ITU Emblem and Symbols

1965. Centenary of ITU.

186	**41**	20p. mauve	90	40
187	**41**	50p. green (34×24½ mm)	1·10	80

42 ICY Emblem

1965. International Co-operation Year.

188	**42**	5p. blue	25	15
189	**42**	10p. brown	45	25
190	**42**	15p. olive	1·40	60

43 Harvesting

1966. Peasants' Day.

191	**43**	15p. multicoloured	1·50	40

44 Cogwheel and Hammer

1967. May Day.

192	**44**	15p. yellow, black & blue	1·75	40

45 Aung San and Agricultural Cultivation

1968. 20th Anniv of Independence.

193	**45**	15p. multicoloured	2·20	50

46 Burma Pearls

1968. Burmese Gems, Jades and Pearls Emporium, Rangoon.

194	**46**	15p. ultram, blue & yell	3·00	1·00

1968. Burmese Birds (2nd series). Designs and colours as Nos. 174/85 but formats and sizes changed.

195	**40**	1p. black	80	35
196	**40**	2p. red	75	35
197	**40**	3p. green	75	35
198	-	5p. blue	75	35
199	-	10p. brown	1·00	45
200	-	15p. yellow	1·50	50
201	-	20p. brown and red	2·20	75
202	-	25p. brown and yellow	2·60	95
203	-	50p. blue and red	4·50	1·40
204	-	1k. blue, yellow & grey	10·00	3·00
205	-	2k. blue, green and red	20·00	6·00
206	-	5k. multicoloured	45·00	18·00

NEW SIZES—21×17 mm: 1, 2, 3p. 39×21 mm: 20p., 2k. 23×28 mm: 5, 10, 15p. 21×39 mm: 25, 50p., 1, 5k.

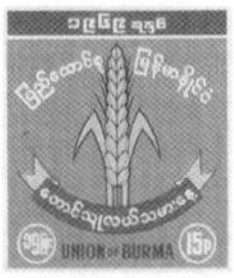

47 Spike of Paddy

1969. Peasants' Day.

218	**47**	15p. yellow, blue & green	2·00	40

48 ILO Emblem

1969. 50th Anniv of ILO.

219	**48**	15p. gold and green	40	30
220	**48**	50p. gold and red	1·90	80

49 Football

1969. Fifth South-East Asian Peninsula Games, Rangoon.

221	**49**	15p. multicoloured	80	40
222	-	25p. multicoloured	90	40
223	-	50p. multicoloured	1·80	80
224	-	1k. black, green & blue	3·50	1·50

DESIGNS—HORIZ: 25p. Running. VERT: 50p. Weightlifting; 1k. Volleyball.

50 Marchers with Independence, Resistance and Union Flags

1970. 25th Anniv of Burmese Armed Forces.

225	**50**	15p. multicoloured	2·00	40

51 "Peace and Progress"

1970. 25th Anniv of United Nations.

226	**51**	15p. multicoloured	2·00	40

52 Boycott Declaration and Marchers

1970. National Day and 50th Anniv of University Boycott. Multicoloured.

227		15p. Type **52**	45	25
228		25p. Students on boycott march	85	50
229		50p. Banner and demonstrators	2·00	75

53 Burmese Workers

1971. First Burmese Socialist Programme Party Congress. Multicoloured.

230		5p. Type **53**	25	20
231		15p. Burmese races and flags	45	50
232		25p. Hands holding scroll	1·25	65
233		50p. Party flag	1·75	85
MS234		179×127 mm. Nos. 230/3. Imperf	18·00	18·00

54 Child drinking Milk

1971. 25th Anniv of UNICEF. Multicoloured.

235		15p. Type **54**	1·00	35
236		50p. Marionettes	2·75	1·30

55 Aung San and Independence Monument, Panglong

1972. 25th Anniv of Independence. Multicoloured.

237		15p. Type **55**	45	30
238		50p. Aung San and Burmese in national costumes	1·40	45
239		1k. Flag and map (vert)	2·75	1·20

56 Burmese and Stars

1972. Tenth Anniv of Revolutionary Council.

240	**56**	15p. multicoloured	1·00	45

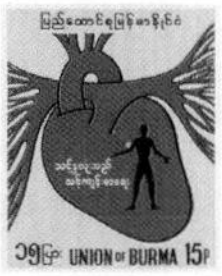

57 Human Heart

1972. World Health Day.

241	**57**	15p. red, black & yellow	2·00	65

58 Ethnic Groups

1973. National Census.

242	**58**	15p. multicoloured	80	40

59 Casting Vote

1973. National Constitutional Referendum.

243	**59**	5p. red and black	15	10
244	-	10p. multicoloured	15	10
245	-	15p. multicoloured	15	10

DESIGNS—HORIZ: 10p. Voter supporting map. VERT: 15p. Burmese with ballot papers.

60 Open-air Meeting

1974. Opening of 1st Pyithu Hluttaw (People's Assembly). Multicoloured.

246		15p. Burmese flags, 1752–1974 (80×26 mm)	40	25
247		50p. Type **60**	1·00	45
248		1k. Burmese badge	1·80	1·00

61 UPU Emblem and Carrier Pigeon

1974. Centenary of Universal Postal Union. Multicoloured.

249		15p. Type **61**	60	35
250		20p. Woman reading letter (vert)	70	35
251		50p. UPU emblem on "stamps" (vert)	1·20	65
252		1k. Stylized doll (vert)	2·50	1·20
253		2k. Postman delivering letter to family	5·00	1·80

62 Kachin Couple

63 Bamar Couple

1974. Burmese Costumes. Inscr "SOCIALIST REPUBLIC OF THE UNION OF BURMA".

254	**62**	1p. mauve	25	25
255	**62**	3p. brown and mauve	30	20
256	**62**	5p. violet and mauve	35	20
257	**62**	10p. blue	45	20
258	**62**	15p. green and light green	55	20
259	**63**	20p. black, brown & blue	95	35
260	-	50p. violet, brown & ochre	2·40	80
261	-	1k. violet, mauve & black	4·75	1·80
262	-	5k. multicoloured	20·00	8·00

DESIGNS—As Type **62**: 3p. Kayah girl; 5p. Kayin couple and bronze drum; 15p. Chin couple. As Type **63**: 50p. Mon woman; 1k. Rakhine woman; 5k. Musician.

For 15, 50p. and 1k. stamps in these designs, but inscr "UNION OF BURMA", see Nos. 309/11.

64 Woman on Globe and IWY Emblem

1975. International Women's Year.

263	**64**	50p. black and green	1·25	60
264	-	2k. black and blue	4·50	2·30

DESIGN—VERT: 2k. Globe on flower and IWY emblem.

65 Burmese and Flag

1976. Constitution Day.

265	**65**	20p. black and blue	60	30
266	-	50p. brown and blue	1·10	70
267	-	1k. multicoloured	2·20	1·20

DESIGNS—As Type **65**: 50p. Burmese with banners and flag. 57×21 mm: 1k. Map of Burma, Burmese and flag.

66 Emblem and Burmese Learning Alphabet

1976. International Literacy Year.

268	**66**	10p. brown and red	35	30
269	-	15p. turquoise, grn & blk	55	30
270	-	50p. blue, orange & black	2·00	90
271	-	1k. multicoloured	3·60	2·00

DESIGNS—HORIZ: 15p. Abacus and open books. 50p. Emblem. VERT: 1k. Emblem, open book and globe.

67 Early Train and Ox-cart

1977. Centenary of Railway.

272		15p. green, black & mauve	7·25	1·50
273	**67**	20p. multicoloured	2·00	80
274	-	25p. multicoloured	3·00	1·00
275	-	50p. multicoloured	4·75	1·90
276	-	1k. multicoloured	11·00	3·50

DESIGNS—26×17 mm: 15p. Early steam locomotive. As Type **67**—HORIZ: 25p. Diesel locomotive DD1517, steam train and railway station; 50p. Ava railway bridge over River Irrawaddy. VERT: Diesel train emerging from tunnel.

68 Karaweik Hall

1978

277	**68**	50p. brown	2·60	1·60
278	-	1k. multicoloured	85	60

DESIGN—79½×25 mm: 1k. Side view of Karaweik Hall.

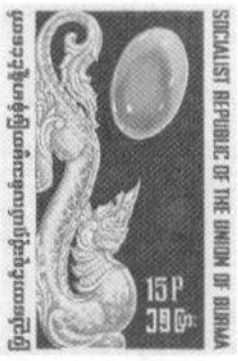

69 Jade Naga and Gem

1979. 16th Gem Emporium.

279	**69**	15p. green and turquoise	15	10
280	-	20p. blue, yellow & mauve	1·40	40
281	-	50p. blue, brown & green	3·75	1·00
282	-	1k. multicoloured	7·50	1·75

DESIGNS—As T **69**: 20p. Hintha (legendary bird) holding pearl in beak; 50p. Hand holding pearl and amethyst pendant. 55×20 mm: 1k. Gold jewel-studded dragon.

70 "Intelsat IV" Satellite over Burma

1979. Introduction of Satellite Communications System.

283	**70**	25p. multicoloured	25	15

71 IYC Emblem on Map of Burma

1979. International Year of the Child.

284	**71**	25p. orange and blue	1·25	50
285	**71**	50p. red and violet	2·50	1·00

72 Weather Balloon

1980. World Meteorological Day.

286	**72**	25p. blue, yellow & black	1·00	40
287	-	50p. green, black and red	2·00	80

DESIGN: 50p. Meteorological satellite and WMO emblem.

73 Weightlifting

1980. Olympic Games, Moscow.

288	**73**	20p. green, orange & blk	45	25
289	-	50p. black, orange and red	1·20	50
290	-	1k. black, orange and blue	2·75	1·20

DESIGNS: 50p. Boxing; 1k. Football.

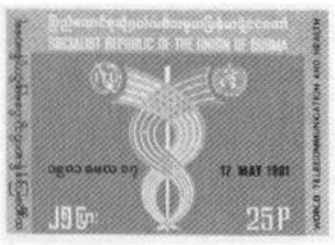

74 ITU and WHO Emblems with Ribbons forming Caduceus

1981. World Telecommunications Day.

291	**74**	25p. orange and black	1·50	35

75 Livestock and Vegetables

1981. World Food Day. Multicoloured.

292	25p. Type **75**	70	35
293	50p. Farm produce and farmer holding wheat	1·60	55
294	1k. Globe and stylized bird	2·60	90

76 Athletes and Person in Wheelchair

1981. International Year of Disabled Persons.

295	**76**	25p. multicoloured	2·00	60

77 Telephone, Satellite and Antenna

1983. World Communications Year.

296	**77**	15p. blue and black	60	30
297	**77**	25p. mauve and black	1·00	40
298	**77**	50p. green, black and red	2·30	90
299	**77**	1k. brown, black & green	4·50	1·80

78 Fish and Globe

1983. World Food Day.

300	**78**	15p. yellow, blue & black	65	45
301	**78**	25p. orange, green & black	1·30	75
302	**78**	50p. green, yellow & black	2·60	1·50
303	**78**	1k. blue, yellow and black	5·00	3·00

79 Globe and Log

1984. World Food Day.

304	**79**	15p. blue, yellow & black	50	35
305	**79**	25p. violet, yellow & black	1·00	60
306	**79**	50p. green, pink and black	2·00	1·20
307	**79**	1k. mauve, yellow & black	4·50	3·00

80 Potted Plant

1985. International Youth Year.

308	**80**	15p. multicoloured	1·40	35

1989. As Nos. 258/9 and 260/1 but inscr "UNION OF BURMA".

309	**62**	15p. dp green & green	40	35
310	-	50p. violet and brown	90	70
311	-	1k. violet, mauve & black	1·70	1·40

Examples of No. 309a, which have been prepared several years earlier but not issued, were inadvertently supplied to Shan State post office in July 1995. Subsequently a limited quantity were sold to philatelists in Yangon.

OFFICIAL STAMPS

1937. Stamps of India (King George V) optd **BURMA SERVICE**.

O1	**55**	3p. grey	4·25	10
O3	**80**	9p. green	5·00	2·00
O2	**79**	½a. green	17·00	10
O4	**81**	1a. brown	9·00	10
O5	**59**	2a. red	18·00	45
O6	**61**	2½a. orange	8·50	3·50
O7	**63**	4a. olive	9·00	10
O8	**64**	6a. bistre	9·50	17·00
O9	**65**	8a. mauve	8·50	3·50
O10	**66**	12a. red	9·00	14·00
O11	**67**	1r. brown and green	25·00	11·00
O12	**67**	2r. red and orange	50·00	70·00
O13	**67**	5r. blue and violet	£180	75·00
O14	**67**	10r. green and red	£450	£250

1939. Stamps of 1938 optd **SERVICE**.

O15	**2**	3p. violet	20	20
O16	**2**	6p. blue	20	20
O17	**2**	9p. green	4·00	6·50
O18	**3**	1a. brown	20	15
O19	**3**	1½a. green	3·50	3·25
O20	**3**	2a. red	1·25	20
O21	**4**	2a.6p. red	26·00	21·00
O22	**3**	4a. blue	4·50	2·25
O23	-	8a. green (No. 29)	17·00	4·00
O24	**8**	1r. purple and blue	16·00	5·50
O25	**8**	2r. brown and purple	32·00	18·00
O26	-	5r. violet and red (No. 32)	26·00	42·00
O27	-	10r. brown and green (No. 33)	£130	48·00

1946. Stamps of 1946 optd **SERVICE**.

O28	**2**	3p. brown	3·75	6·00
O29	**2**	6p. violet	2·75	2·25
O30	**2**	9p. green	1·75	6·50
O31	**3**	1a. blue	30	2·00
O32	**3**	1½a. orange	1·50	20
O33	**3**	2a. red	30	2·00
O34	**4**	2a.6p. blue	3·25	12·00
O35	**3**	4a. purple	1·00	70
O36	-	8a. mauve (No. 59)	5·00	7·00
O37	**8**	1r. violet and mauve	3·00	10·00
O38	**8**	2r. brown and orange	8·50	50·00
O39	-	5r. green and brown (No. 62)	20·00	65·00
O40	-	10r. red and violet (No. 63)	20·00	75·00

1947. Interim Government. Nos. O28 etc., optd with T **18** or with large overprint on larger stamps.

O41	**2**	3p. brown	3·00	40
O42	**2**	6p. violet	4·75	10
O43	**2**	9p. green	7·00	90
O44	**3**	1a. blue	7·00	80
O45	**3**	1½a. orange	12·00	30
O46	**3**	2a. red	7·00	15
O47	**4**	2a.6p. blue	32·00	20·00
O48	**3**	4a. purple	25·00	40
O49	-	8a. mauve	25·00	4·00
O50	**8**	1r. violet and mauve	17·00	3·50
O51	**8**	2r. brown and orange	18·00	20·00
O52	-	5r. green and brown	19·00	22·00
O53	-	10r. red and violet	19·00	35·00

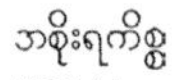

(O29) (size of opt varies)

1949. First Anniv of Independence. Nos. 100/4 and 107/113 optd as Type **O29**.

O114	**22**	3p. blue	55	15
O115	-	6p. green	10	10
O116	-	9p. red	10	10
O117	**25**	1a. red	10	10
O118	-	2a. orange	20	15
O119	-	3a.6p. green	20	15
O120	-	4a. brown	20	15
O121	-	8a. red	20	15
O122	**28**	1r. green	55	25
O123	**28**	2r. blue	90	45
O124	**28**	5r. brown	2·40	1·70
O125	**28**	10r. orange	6·00	4·25

1954. Nos. 137/40 and 142/50 optd as Type **O29**.

O151	**22**	1p. orange	55	15
O152	-	2p. purple	20	15
O153	-	3p. blue	20	15
O154	**25**	5p. blue	20	15
O155	-	15p. green	20	15
O156	-	20p. red	20	15
O157	-	25p. orange	20	15
O158	-	30p. red	20	15
O159	-	50p. blue	20	15
O160	**28**	1k. violet	65	15
O161	**28**	2k. green	1·50	35
O162	**28**	5k. blue	3·00	95
O163	**28**	10k. blue	6·50	3·00

1964. No. 139 optd **Service**.

O174	3p. blue	12·00	8·50

1965. Nos. 174/7 and 179/85 optd as Type **O29**.

O196	**40**	1p. black	15	15
O197	**40**	2p. red	25	25
O198	**40**	3p. green	25	25
O199	-	5p. blue	35	25
O200	-	15p. green	35	25
O201	-	20p. brown and red	70	60
O202	-	25p. brown and yellow	80	70
O203	-	50p. blue and red	1·40	85
O204	-	1k. blue, yellow & grey	4·00	1·10
O205	-	2k. blue, green & red	5·25	1·90
O206	-	5k. multicoloured	15·00	13·00

1968. Nos. 195/8 and 200/6 optd as Type **O29**.

O207	1p. black	15	15
O208	2p. red	15	15
O209	3p. green	15	15
O210	5p. blue	25	15
O211	15p. green	25	15
O212	20p. brown and red	25	15
O213	25p. brown and yellow	45	15
O214	50p. blue and red	85	45
O215	1k. blue, yellow and grey	1·30	1·10
O216	2k. blue, green and red	2·75	2·30
O217	5k. multicoloured	6·50	5·75

For later issues see **MYANMAR**.

JAPANESE OCCUPATION OF BURMA

Note.—There are various types of the Peacock overprint. Our prices, as usual in this Catalogue, are for the cheapest type.

(1)

(3)

1942. Postage stamps of Burma of 1937 (India types) optd as T **1**.

J22	**55**	3p. grey	4·00	23·00
J23	**80**	9p. green	27·00	70·00
J24	**59**	2a. red	£120	£200
J2	**83**	3½a. blue	80·00	

1942. Official stamp of Burma of 1937 (India type) optd as T **1**.

J3	**64**	6a. bistre	80·00	

1942. Postage stamps of Burma, 1938, optd as T **1** or with T **3** (rupee values).

J25	**1**	1p. orange	£225	£350
J12	**1**	3p. violet	20·00	75·00
J27	**1**	6p. blue	25·00	55·00
J14	**1**	9p. green	25·00	70·00
J29	**3**	1a. brown	9·00	42·00
J30	**3**	1½a. green	23·00	70·00
J16	**3**	2a. red	26·00	85·00
J17	**3**	4a. blue	55·00	£110
J18	**8**	1r. purple and blue	£425	£700
J19	**8**	2r. brown and purple	£225	£475

1942. Official stamps of Burma of 1939 optd with T **1**.

J7	**1**	3p. violet	38·00	90·00
J8	**1**	6p. blue	25·00	65·00
J9	**3**	1a. brown	26·00	55·00
J35	**3**	1½a. green	£180	£325
J10	**3**	2a. red	35·00	£100
J11	**3**	4a. blue	35·00	80·00

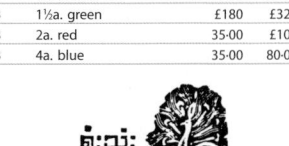

(6a) ("Yon Thon" = "Office Use")

1942. Official stamp of Burma of 1939 optd with T **6a**.

J44	8a. green (No. O23)	£100	£250

7

1942. Yano Seal.

J45	**7**	(1a.) red	50·00	70·00

8 Farmer

1942

J46	**8**	1a. red	21·00	23·00

1942. Stamps of Japan surch in annas or rupees.

J47	-	¼a. on 1s. brown (No. 314)	45·00	50·00
J48	**83**	½a. on 2s. red	55·00	50·00
J49	-	¾a. on 3s. green (No. 316)	80·00	80·00
J50	-	1a. on 5s. purple (No. 396)	80·00	70·00
J51	-	3a. on 7s. green (No. 320)	£130	£150
J52	-	4a. on 4s. green (No. 317)	60·00	65·00
J53	-	8a. on 8s. violet (No. 321)	£150	£150
J54	-	1r. on 10s. red (No. 322)	27·00	32·00
J55	-	2r. on 20s. blue (No. 325)	55·00	55·00
J56	-	5r. on 30s. blue (No. 327)	17·00	27·00

1942. No. 386 of Japan commemorating the fall of Singapore, surch in figures.

J56g	4a. on 4s.+2s. green and red	£180	£190

1942. Handstamped **5 C.**

J57	**5**	5c. on 1a. red (No. J46)	24·00	28·00

1942. Nos. J47/53 with anna surcharges obliterated, and handstamped with new values in figures.

J58	-	1c. on ¼a. on 1s. brown	55·00	55·00

J59	**84**	2c. on ½a. on 2s. red	55·00	55·00
J60	-	3c. on ¾a. on 3s. green	60·00	60·00
J61	-	5c. on 1a. on 5s. red	85·00	65·00
J62	-	10c. on 3a. on 7s. green	£160	£140
J63	-	15c. on 4a. on 4s. green	50·00	55·00
J64	-	20c. on 8a. on 8s. violet	£850	£650

1942. Stamps of Japan surch in cents.

J65		1c. on 1s. brown (No. 314)	35·00	20·00
J66	**83**	2c. on 2s. red	60·00	40·00
J67	-	3c. on 3s. green (No. 316)	95·00	65·00
J68	-	5c. on 5s. purple (No. 396)	95·00	55·00
J69	-	10c. on 7s. green (No. 320)	£130	80·00
J70	-	15c. on 4s. green (No. 317)	27·00	27·00
J71	-	20c. on 8s. violet (No. 321)	£200	95·00

14 Burma State Crest

1943. Perf or imperf.

J72	**14**	5c. red	26·00	30·00

15 Farmer

1943

J73a	**15**	1c. orange	4·25	9·00
J74	**15**	2c. green	1·00	1·00
J75	**15**	3c. blue	4·25	1·00
J77	**15**	5c. red	3·50	7·00
J78	**15**	10c. brown	8·50	8·50
J79	**15**	15c. mauve	30	4·00
J80	**15**	20c. lilac	30	1·00
J81	**15**	30c. green	50	2·50

16 Soldier carving word "Independence"

17 Rejoicing Peasant

(18) Boy with National Flag

1943. Independence Day. Perf or roul.

J85	**16**	1c. orange	1·25	1·75
J86	**17**	3c. blue	2·50	3·50
J87	**18**	5c. red	3·25	3·75

19 Burmese Woman

20 Elephant carrying Log

21 Watch Tower Mandalay

1943

J88	**19**	1c. orange	20·00	15·00
J89	**19**	2c. green	50	2·00
J90	**19**	3c. violet	50	2·25
J91	**20**	5c. red	75	60
J92	**20**	10c. blue	2·00	1·10
J93	**20**	15c. orange	1·00	3·00
J94	**20**	20c. green	1·00	1·75
J95	**20**	30c. brown	1·00	2·00
J96	**21**	1r. orange	30	2·00
J97	**21**	2r. violet	30	2·25

22 Playing Cane-ball

23 Shan Woman

1943. Shan States issue.

J98	**22**	1c. brown	40·00	48·00
J99	**22**	2c. green	45·00	48·00
J100	**22**	3c. violet	6·50	14·00
J101	**22**	5c. blue	2·75	8·50
J102	**23**	10c. blue	16·00	18·00
J103	**23**	20c. red	42·00	22·00
J104	**23**	30c. brown	25·00	65·00

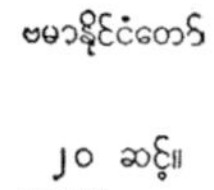

(24) "Burma State" and value

1944. Optd with T **24**.

J105	**22**	1c. brown	4·50	8·50
J106	**22**	2c. green	60	5·50
J107	**22**	3c. violet	2·25	7·00
J108	**22**	5c. blue	2·50	3·25
J109	**23**	10c. blue	3·25	2·00
J110	**23**	20c. red	65	1·50
J111	**23**	30c. brown	1·00	1·75

Pt. 12

BURUNDI

Once part of the Belgian territory, Ruanda-Urundi. Independent on 1 July 1962, when a monarchy was established. After a revolution in 1967 Burundi became a republic.

100 centimes = 1 franc.

1962. Stamps of Ruanda-Urundi optd Royaume du Burundi and bar or surch also. (a) Flowers. (Nos. 178 etc.).

1		25c. multicoloured	25	20
2		40c. multicoloured	25	20
3		60c. multicoloured	35	35
4		1f.25 multicoloured	16·00	16·00
5		1f.50 multicoloured	60	60
6		5f. multicoloured	1·10	90
7		7f. multicoloured	1·75	1·40
8		10f. multicoloured	2·50	2·25

(b) Animals (Nos. 203/14).

9		10c. black, red and brown	10	10
10		20c. black and green	10	10
11		40c. black, olive and mauve	10	10
12		50c. brown, yellow & green	10	10
13		1f. black, blue and brown	10	10
14		1f.50 black and orange	10	10
15		2f. black, brown and turq	10	10
16		3f. black, red and brown	10	10
17		3f.50 on 3f. black, red & brn	10	10
18a		4f. on 10f. multicoloured	20	20
19		5f. multicoloured	20	20
20		6f.50 brown, yellow and red	20	20
21		8f. black, mauve and blue	35	25
23		10f. multicoloured	50	30

(c) Animals (Nos. 229/30).

24	**25**	20f. multicoloured	1·60	60
25	-	50f. multicoloured	1·90	1·10

10 King Mwambutsa IV and Royal Drummers

1962. Independence. Inscr "1.7.1962".

26	**10**	50c. sepia and lake	10	10
27	**A**	1f. green, red & deep green	10	10
28	**B**	2f. sepia and olive	10	10
29	**10**	3f. sepia and red	10	10
30	**A**	4f. green, red and blue	15	10
31	**B**	8f. sepia and violet	30	15
32	**10**	10f. sepia and green	40	15
33	**A**	20f. green, red and sepia	45	20
34	**B**	50f. sepia and mauve	1·25	45

DESIGNS—VERT: A, Burundi flag and arms. HORIZ: B, King and outline map of Burundi.

1962. Dag Hammarskjold Commem. No. 222 of Ruanda-Urundi surch **HOMMAGE A DAG HAMMARSKJOLD ROYAUME DU BURUNDI** and new value. U.N. emblem and wavy pattern at foot. Inscr in French or Flemish.

35		3f.50 on 3f. salmon and blue	35	35
36		6f.50 on 3f. salmon and blue	65	45
37		10f. on 3f. salmon and blue	1·25	1·10

1962. Malaria Eradication. As Nos. 31 and 34 but colours changed and with campaign emblem superimposed on map.

38		8f. sepia, turquoise & bistre	55	35
39		50f. sepia, turquoise & olive	1·40	35

12 Prince Louis Rwagasore

1963. Prince Rwagasore Memorial and Stadium Fund.

40	**12**	50c.+25c. violet	10	10
41	-	1f.+50c. blue and orange	10	10
42	-	1f.50+75c. vio & bistre	10	10
43	**12**	3f.50+1f.50 mauve	20	10
44	-	5f.+2f. blue and pink	20	10
45	-	6f.50+3f. violet & olive	25	10

DESIGNS—HORIZ: 1f., 5f. Prince and stadium; 1f.50, 6f.50 Prince and memorial.

13 "Sowing"

1963. Freedom from Hunger.

46	**13**	4f. purple and olive	15	15
47	**13**	8f. purple and olive	20	15
48	**13**	15f. purple and green	35	15

1963. "Peaceful Uses of Outer Space" Nos. 28 and 34 optd **UTILISATIONS PACIFIQUES DE L'ESPACE** around globe encircled by rocket.

49	**B**	2f. sepia and olive	2·25	2·25
50	**B**	50f. sepia and mauve	3·50	3·50

1963. First Anniv of Independence. Nos. 30/3 but with colours changed and optd **Premier Anniversaire**.

51	**A**	4f. green, red and olive	20	10
52	**B**	8f. sepia and orange	30	10
53	**10**	10f. sepia and mauve	40	20
54	**A**	20f. green, red and grey	90	30

1963. Nos. 27 and 33 surch.

55		6f.50 on 1f. green, red and deep green	55	10
56		15f. on 20f. grn, red & sepia	85	35

17 Globe and Red Cross Flag

1963. Centenary of Red Cross.

57	**17**	4f. green, red and grey	20	10
58	**17**	8f. brown, red and grey	40	20
59	**17**	10f. blue, red and grey	50	20
60	**17**	20f. violet, red and grey	1·10	40
MS60a		90×140 mm. Nos. 57/60 in new colours, each with **+2f.** surcharge in black. Imperf	3·50	3·50

IMPERF STAMPS. Many Burundi stamps from No. 61 onwards exist imperf from limited printings and/or miniature sheets.

18 "1962" and UNESCO Emblem

1963. First Anniv of Admission to UNO. Emblems and values in black.

61	**18**	4f. olive and yellow	15	10
62	-	8f. blue and lilac	25	10
63	-	10f. violet and blue	40	10
64	-	20f. green and yellow	65	20
65	-	50f. brown and ochre	1·75	35
MS65a		111×74 mm. Nos. 64/5 but with emblems changed. Imperf	4·25	4·25

EMBLEMS: 8f. ITU; 10f. WMO; 20f. UPU, 50f. FAO; **MS**65a 20f. FAO; 50f. WMO.

19 UNESCO Emblem and Scales of Justice

1963. 15th Anniv of Declaration of Human Rights.

66	**19**	50c. blk, blue and pink	10	10
67	-	1f.50 black, blue & orange	10	10
68	-	3f.50 black, green & brown	15	10
69	-	6f.50 black, green and lilac	25	10
70	-	10f. black, bistre and blue	40	15
71	-	20f. multicoloured	70	25

DESIGNS: 3f.50, 6f.50, Scroll; 10f., 20f. Lincoln.

20 Ice-hockey

1964. Winter Olympic Games, Innsbruck.

72	**20**	50c. black, gold and olive	15	10
73	-	3f.50 black, gold & brown	20	10
74	-	6f.50 black, gold and grey	45	20
75	-	10f. black, gold and grey	90	35
76	-	20f. black, gold and bistre	2·10	65
MS76a		122×85 mm. 10f.+5f. and 20f.+5f. (as Nos. 75/6 but in new colours). Perf or imperf	4·25	1·30

DESIGNS: 3f.50, Figure-skating; 6f.50, Olympic flame; 10f. Speed-skating; 20f. Skiing (slalom).

21 Hippopotamus

1964. Burundi Animals. Multicoloured. (i) Postage. (a) Size as T **21**.

77		50c. Impala	10	10
78		1f. Type **21**	10	10
79		1f.50 Giraffe	10	10
80		2f. African buffalo	20	10
81		3f. Common zebra	20	10
82		3f.50 Waterbuck	20	10

(b) Size 16×42½ mm or 42½×26 mm.

83		4f. Impala	25	10
84		5f. Hippopotamus	30	10
85		6f.50 Common zebra	30	10
86		8f. African buffalo	55	20
87		10f. Giraffe	60	20
88		15f. Waterbuck	85	30

(c) Size 53½×33½ mm.

89		20f. Cheetah	1·50	40
90		50f. African elephant	4·00	65
91		100f. Lion	6·50	1·10

(ii) Air. Inscr "POSTE AERIENNE" and optd with gold border. (a) Size 26×42½ mm or 42½×26 mm.

92		6f. Common zebra	35	10
93		8f. African buffalo	60	10
94		10f. Impala	70	10
95		14f. Hippopotamus	85	15
96		15f. Waterbuck	1·40	35

(b) Size 53½×33½ mm.

97		20f. Cheetah	1·75	40
98		50f. African elephant	4·00	90

The impala, giraffe and waterbuck stamps are all vert. designs, and the remainder are horiz.

22 Burundi Dancer

1964. World's Fair, New York (1st series). Gold backgrounds.

99	**22**	50c. multicoloured	10	10
100	-	1f. multicoloured	10	10
101	-	4f. multicoloured	15	10
102	-	6f.50 multicoloured	20	10
103	-	10f. multicoloured	40	15
104	-	15f. multicoloured	70	20
105	-	20f. multicoloured	90	30
MS105a 120×100 mm. Nos. 103/5. Perf or imperf			3·50	3·50

DESIGNS: 1f. to 20f. Various dancers and drummers as Type **22**.

See also Nos. 175/**MS**81a.

23 Pope Paul and King Mwambutsa IV

1964. Canonization of 22 African Martyrs. Inscriptions in gold.

106	**23**	50c. lake and blue	15	10
107	-	1f. blue and purple	15	10
108	-	4f. sepia and mauve	25	10
109	-	8f. brown and red	40	15
110	-	14f. brown and turquoise	40	20
111	**23**	20f. green and red	65	40

DESIGNS—VERT: 1f., 8f. Group of martyrs. HORIZ: 4f., 14f., Pope John XXIII and King Mwambutsa IV.

24 Putting the Shot

1964. Olympic Games, Tokyo. Inscr "TOKYO 1964". Multicoloured.

112	50c. Type **24**	10	10
113	1f. Throwing the discus	10	10
114	3f. Swimming (horiz)	10	10
115	4f. Relay-racing	10	10
116	6f.50 Throwing the javelin	30	20
117	8f. Hurdling (horiz)	35	20
118	10f. Long-jumping (horiz)	40	20
119	14f. High-diving	55	20
120	18f. High-jumping (horiz)	65	35
121	20f. Gymnastics (horiz)	85	35
MS121a 115×71 mm. 18f.+2f. and 20f.+5f. (as Nos. 120/1). Perf or imperf		3·25	3·25

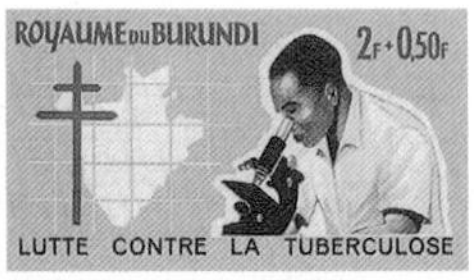

25 Scientist, Map and Emblem

1965. Anti-T.B. Campaign. Country name, values and Lorraine Cross in red.

122	**25**	2f.+50c. sepia and drab	10	10
123	**25**	4f.+1f.50 green & pink	25	10
124	**25**	5f.+2f.50 violet & buff	30	15
125	**25**	8f.+3f. blue and grey	40	20
126	**25**	10f.+5f. red and green	55	30
MS126a 100×71 mm. 10f.+10f. sepia and olive. Perf or imperf			1·10	1·10

26 Purple Swamphen

1965. Birds. Multicoloured. (i) Postage. (a) Size as T **26**.

127	50c. Type **26**	10	10
128	1f. Little bee eater	10	10
129	1f.50 Secretary bird	10	10
130	2f. Painted stork	20	10
131	3f. Congo peafowl	25	10
132	3f.50 African darter	30	10
	(b) Size 26×42½ mm.		
133	4f. Type **26**	40	10
134	5f. Little bee eater	50	15
135	6f.50 Secretary bird	60	15
136	8f. Painted stork	60	15
137	10f. Congo peafowl	70	15
138	15f. African darter	85	25
	(c) Size 33½×53 mm.		
139	20f. Saddle-bill stork	1·25	25
140	50f. Abyssinian ground hornbill	2·40	50
141	100f. South African crowned crane	4·00	90
	(ii) Air. Inscr "POSTE AERIENNE". Optd with gold border. (a) Size 26×42½ mm.		
142	6f. Secretary bird	50	10
143	8f. African darter	60	15
144	10f. Congo peafowl	70	15
145	14f. Little bee eater	75	20
146	15f. Painted stork	85	20
	(b) Size 33½×53 mm.		
147	20f. Saddle-bill stork	1·25	30
148	50f. Abyssinian ground hornbill	2·25	80
149	75f. Martial eagle	2·50	1·00
150	130f. Lesser flamingo	4·75	1·60

27 "Relay" Satellite and Telegraph Key

1965. Centenary of ITU. Multicoloured.

151	1f. Type **27**	10	10
152	3f. "Telstar 1" and hand telephone	10	10
153	4f. "Lunik 3" and wall telephone	10	10
154	6f.50 Weather satellite and tracking station	15	10
155	8f. "Telstar 2" and headphones	15	15
156	10f. "Sputnik" and radar scanner	20	15
157	14f. "Syncom" and aerial	30	20
158	20f. "Pioneer 5" space probe and radio aerial	35	30
MS158a 121×85 mm. Nos. 156 and 158. Perf or imperf		2·50	2·50

28 Arms (reverse of 10f. coin)

1965. First Independence Anniv Gold Coinage Commem. Circular designs on gold foil, backed with multicoloured patterned paper. Imperf. (i) Postage. (a) 10f. coin. Diameter 1½ in.

159	**28**	2f.+50c. red & yellow	15	15
160	-	4f.+50c. blue & red	20	20
		(b) 25f. coin. Diameter 1¾ in.		
161	**28**	6f.+50c. orange & grey	50	30
162	-	8f.+50c. blue & purple	60	60
		(c) 50f. coin. Diameter 2½ in.		
163	**28**	12f.+50c. green & purple	60	60
164	-	15f.+50c. green & lilac	65	65
		(d) 100f. coin. Diameter 258in.		
165	**28**	25f.+50c. blue and flesh	1·25	1·25
166	-	40f.+50c. mauve & brn	1·75	1·75
		(ii) Air. (a) 10f. coin. Diameter 1½ in.		
167	**28**	3f.+1f. violet & lavender	30	30
168	-	5f.+1f. red & turquoise	40	40
		(b) 25f. coin. Diameter 1¾ in.		
169	**28**	11f.+1f. purple & yellow	60	60
170	-	14f.+1f. green and red	60	60
		(c) 50f. coin. Diameter 2½ in.		
171	**28**	20f.+1f. black and blue	85	85
172	-	30f.+1f. red and orange	1·10	1·10
		(d) 100f. coin. Diameter 2¾ in.		
173	**28**	50f.+1f. violet and blue	1·25	1·25
174	-	100f.+1f. purple & mve	3·00	3·00

DESIGNS: The 4, 5, 8, 14, 15, 30, 40 and 100f. each show the obverse side of the coin (King Mwambutsa IV).

1965. Worlds Fair, New York (2nd series). As Nos. 99/105, but with silver backgrounds.

175	**22**	50c. multicoloured	10	10
176	-	1f. multicoloured	10	10
177	-	4f. multicoloured	15	10
178	-	6f.50 multicoloured	25	10
179	-	10f. multicoloured	45	20
180	-	15f. multicoloured	55	30
181	-	20f. multicoloured	70	35
MS181a 120×100 mm. Nos. 179/81. perf or imperf			2·50	2·50

29 Globe and ICY Emblem

1965. International Co-operation Year. Multicoloured.

182	1f. Type **29**	10	10
183	4f. Map of Africa and cogwheel emblem of UN Science and Technology Conference	15	10
184	8f. Map of South-East Asia and Colombo Plan emblem	20	10
185	10f. Globe and UN emblem	25	10
186	18f. Map of Americas and "Alliance for Progress" emblem	40	10
187	25f. Map of Europe and CEPT emblems	60	30
188	40f. Space map and satellite (UN—"Peaceful Uses of Outer Space")	1·00	50
MS188a 100×100 mm. 18f. (Map of Africa and UN emblem); 25f. and 40f. (similar to Nos. 187/8). Perf or imperf		2·60	2·60

30 Prince Rwagasore and Memorial

1966. Prince Rwagasore and Pres. Kennedy Commemoration.

189	**30**	4f.+1f. brown and blue	20	10
190	-	10f.+1f. blue, brn & grn	30	10
191	-	20f.+2f. green and lilac	65	15
192	-	40f.+2f. brown & green	75	30
MS193 75×90 mm. 20f.+5f. and 40f.+5f. (as Nos. 189 and 191). Perf or imperf			2·25	2·50

DESIGNS—HORIZ: 10f. Prince Rwagasore and Pres. Kennedy; 20f. Pres. Kennedy and memorial library. VERT: 40f. King Mwambutsa at Pres. Kennedy's grave.

31 Protea

1966. Flowers. Multicoloured. (i) Postage. (a) Size as T **31**.

194	50c. Type **31**	15	10
195	1f. Crossandra	15	10
196	1f.50 Ansellia	15	10
197	2f. Thunbergia	15	10
198	3f. Schizoglossum	25	10
199	3f.50 Dissotis	25	10
	(b) Size 41×41 mm.		
200	4f. Type **31**	25	10
201	5f. Crossandra	35	10
202	6f.50 Ansellia	45	10
203	8f. Thunbergia	65	10
204	10f. Schizoglossum	70	10
205	15f. Dissotis	85	10
	(c) Size 50×50 mm.		
206	20f. Type **31**	1·10	15
207	50f. Gazania	2·50	35
208	100f. Hibiscus	4·00	55
209	150f. Markhamia	6·25	75
	(ii) Air. (a) Size 41×41 mm.		
210	6f. Dissotis	25	15
211	8f. Crossandra	35	15
212	10f. Ansellia	35	15
213	14f. Thunbergia	40	15
214	15f. Schizoglossum	40	15
	(b) Size 50×50 mm.		
215	20f. Gazania	65	20
216	50f. Type **31**	1·75	40
217	75f. Hibiscus	2·50	1·00
218	130f. Markhamia	3·75	1·40

32 UNESCO

33

1966. 20th Anniv of UNESCO.

MS219 Three sheets, each 201×127 mm, each containing single stamps (Type **32**) with se-tenant label inscribed in English or French and an adjoining block of six stamps (3×2) as Type **33**, forming a composite design of the mural tapestry hanging in the U.N. General Assembly building, New York. (a) Postage: Two sheets 1f.50×7 and 4f.×7. (b) Air. One sheet 14f.×7 multicoloured Set of 3 sheets	6·00

1967. Fourth Anniv of Independence (1966).

MS220 Four unissued sheets, diamond-shaped, 200×200 mm, each containing eight "Flower" stamps as Type **31** but with values and corresponding designs changed, and centre se-tenant label showing "Flag", "Map", "Arms" or "Flower" emblem. Values: 6, 7, 8, 10, 14, 15, 20 and 50f. Multicoloured. Stamps and sheet margins have the original inscriptions obliterated by the overprint **REPUBLIQUE DU BURUNDI** in black on gold panels Set of 4 sheets	11·00

1967. Various stamps optd. (i) Nos. 127, etc. (Birds) optd **REPUBLIQUE DU BURUNDI** and bar. (a) Postage.

221	50c. multicoloured	1·60	25
222	1f.50 multicoloured	35	25
223	3f.50 multicoloured	45	35
224	5f. multicoloured	60	45
225	6f.50 multicoloured	60	65
226	8f. multicoloured	70	80
227	10f. multicoloured	80	80
228	15f. multicoloured	1·10	1·25
229	20f. multicoloured	2·75	1·75
230	50f. multicoloured	5·25	3·75
231	100f. multicoloured	8·50	7·00
	(b) Air.		
232	6f. multicoloured	55	25
233	8f. multicoloured	70	40
234	10f. multicoloured	85	65
235	14f. multicoloured	1·10	65
236	15f. multicoloured	1·25	80
237	20f. multicoloured	1·75	95
238	50f. multicoloured	6·25	2·75
239	75f. multicoloured	8·50	3·50
240	130f. multicoloured	12·00	5·75

(ii) Nos. 194, etc. (Flowers) optd as Nos. 221, etc., but with two bars. (a) Postage.

241	50c. multicoloured	15	15
242	1f. multicoloured	15	15
243	1f.50 multicoloured	15	15
244	2f. multicoloured	15	15
245	3f. multicoloured	20	15
246	3f.50 multicoloured	30	15
247	4f. multicoloured	1·90	15

248	5f. multicoloured	50	20
249	6f.50 multicoloured	45	30
250	8f. multicoloured	45	30
251	10f. multicoloured	60	40
252	15f. multicoloured	75	45
253	50f. multicoloured	3·75	65
254	100f. multicoloured	9·00	2·50
255	150f. multicoloured	8·50	9·25

(b) Air.

256	6f. multicoloured	20	15
257	8f. multicoloured	30	15
258	10f. multicoloured	35	15
259	14f. multicoloured	45	30
260	15f. multicoloured	55	30
261	20f. multicoloured	1·75	40
262	50f. multicoloured	3·75	65
263	75f. multicoloured	5·75	90
264	130f. multicoloured	5·75	1·50

35 Sir Winston Churchill and St. Paul's Cathedral

1967. Churchill Commemoration. Multicoloured.

265	4f.+1f. Type **35** (postage)	30	10
266	15f.+2f. Churchill and Tower of London	50	25
267	20f.+3f. Big Ben and Boadicea Statue, Westminster	60	35
MS268	80×80 mm. 50f.+5f. Sir Winston Churchill (57×57 mm) (air). Perf or imperf	3·00	3·00

36 Egyptian Mouthbrooder

1967. Fish. Multicoloured. (a) Postage. (i) Size as T **36**.

269	50c. Type **36**	15	20
270	1f. Spotted climbing-perch	15	20
271	1f.50 Six-banded lyretail	15	20
272	2f. Congo tetra	15	20
273	3f. Jewel cichlid	15	20
274	3f.50 Spotted mouthbrooder	15	20

(ii) Size 53½×27 mm.

275	4f. Type **36**	50	20
276	5f. As 1f.	50	20
277	6f.50. As 1f.50	65	20
278	8f. As 2f.	65	20
279	10f. As 3f.	1·00	20
280	15f. As 3f.50	1·10	20

(iii) Size 63½×31½ mm.

281	20f. Type **36**	1·90	30
282	50f. Dusky snakehead	3·50	50
283	100f. Red-tailed notho	7·50	75
284	150f. African tetra	7·50	1·10

(b) Air. (i) Size 50×23 mm.

285	6f. Type **36**	30	20
286	8f. As 1f.	45	20
287	10f. As 1f.50	55	20
288	14f. As 2f.	65	20
289	15f. As 3f.	80	20

(ii) Size 59×27 mm.

290	20f. As 3f.50	95	20
291	50f. As 50f. (No. 282)	4·75	30
292	75f. As 100f.	6·00	50
293	130f. As 150f.	11·00	1·00

37 Baule Ancestral Figures

1967. "African Art". Multicoloured.

294	50c. Type **37** (postage)	10	10
295	1f. "Master of Buli's" carved seat	10	10
296	1f.50 Karumba antelope's head	10	10
297	2f. Bobo buffalo's head	10	10
298	4f. Guma-Goffa funeral figures	15	10
299	10f. Bakoutou "spirit" (carving) (air)	30	20
300	14f. Bamum sultan's throne	40	20
301	17f. Bebin bronze head	45	20
302	24f. Statue of 109th Bakouba king	55	30
303	26f. Burundi basketwork and lances	60	35

1967. 50th Anniv of Lions International. Nos. 265/**MS**268 optd **1917 1967** and emblem.

304	4f.+1f. multicoloured	50	20
305	15f.+2f. multicoloured	80	35
306	20f.+3f. multicoloured	95	35
MS307	80×80 mm. 50f.+5f. multicoloured (air) Perf or imperf	4·25	4·25

39 Lord Baden-Powell (founder)

1967. 60th Anniv of Scout Movement and World Scout Jamboree, Idaho. Multicoloured.

308	50c. Scouts climbing (postage)	20	10
309	1f. Scouts preparing meal	20	10
310	1f.50 Type **39**	20	10
311	2f. Two scouts	20	10
312	4f. Giving first aid	30	10
313	10f. As 50c. (air)	60	15
314	14f. As 1f.	70	15
315	17f. Type **39**	85	15
316	24f. As 2f.	1·10	35
317	26f. As 4f.	1·25	40

40 *The Gleaners* (Millet)

1967. World Fair, Montreal. Multicoloured.

318	4f. Type **40**	15	10
319	8f. *The Water-carrier of Seville* (Velasquez)	15	10
320	14f. *The Triumph of Neptune and Amphitrite* (Poussin)	35	15
321	18f. *Acrobat with a ball* (Picasso)	35	15
322	25f. *Margaret van Eyck* (Van Eyck)	95	25
323	40f. *St. Peter denying Christ* (Rembrandt)	1·10	50
MS324	105×105 mm. Nos. 322/3. Perf or imperf	3·25	3·25

41 Boeing 707

1967. Air. Opening of Bujumbura Airport. Aircraft and inscr in black and silver.

325	41	10f. green	40	10
326	-	14f. yellow	65	20
327	-	17f. blue	95	20
328	-	26f. purple	1·60	30

AIRCRAFT: 14f. Boeing 727-100 over lakes. 17f. Vickers Super VC-10 over lake. 26f. Boeing 727 over Bujumbura Airport.

42 Pres. Micombero and Flag

1967. First Anniv of Republic. Multicoloured.

329	5f. Type **42**	25	10
330	14f. Memorial and Arms	35	15
331	20f. View of Bujumbura and Arms	50	20
332	30f. "Place de la Revolution" and President Micombero	90	30

43 *The Adoration of the Shepherds* (J. B. Mayno)

1967. Christmas. Religious Paintings. Multicoloured.

333	1f. Type **43**	10	10
334	4f. *The Holy Family* (A. van Dyck)	15	10
335	14f. *The Nativity* (Maitre de Moulins)	40	20
336	26f. *Madonna and Child* (C. Crivelli)	75	30
MS337	120×120 mm. Nos. 333/6	4·25	4·25

44 Burundi Scouts

1968. Air. 20th Anniv of Burundi Scouts and 60th Anniv of Scout Movement. Diamond-shaped sheet containing T 44 and similar design. Multicoloured.

MS338	142×142 mm. 24f. and 26f. with two se-tenant labels depicting Lord Baden-Powell and scouting activities	2·25	2·25

DESIGN: 26f. Burundi scouts practising first-aid.

45 Downhill Skiing

1968. Winter Olympic Games, Grenoble. Multicoloured.

339	5f. Type **45**	20	10
340	10f. Ice-hockey	25	10
341	14f. Figure-skating	40	10
342	17f. Bobsleighing	50	10
343	26f. Ski-jumping	65	10
344	40f. Speed-skating	1·10	25
345	60f. Olympic torch	1·75	30
MS346	129×82 mm. Nos. 344/5. Perf or imperf	2·75	2·75

46 *Portrait of a Young Man* (Botticelli)

1968. Famous Paintings. Multicoloured.

347	1f.50 Type **46** (postage)	10	10
348	2f. *La Maja Vestida* (Goya) (horiz)	10	10
349	4f. *The Lacemaker* (Vermeer)	15	10
350	17f. *Woman and Cat* (Renoir) (air)	40	20
351	24f. *"The Jewish Bride* (Rembrandt) (horiz)	55	30
352	26f. *Pope Innocent X* (Velasquez)	80	40

47 Module landing on Moon

1968. Space Exploration. Multicoloured.

353	4f. Type **47** (postage)	20	10
354	6f. Russian cosmonaut in Space	30	10
355	8f. Weather satellite	30	10
356	10f. American astronaut in Space	45	15
357	14f. Type **47** (air)	40	15
358	18f. As 6f.	50	15
359	25f. As 8f.	80	25
360	40f. As 10f.	1·10	40
MS361	109×82 mm. 25f. Type **47**; 40f. Weather satellite. Perf or imperf	2·40	2·40

48 *Salamis aethiops*

1968. Butterflies. Multicoloured. (a) Postage. (i) Size 30½×34 mm.

362	50c. Type **48**	15	15
363	1f. *Graphium ridleyanus*	20	15
364	1f.50 *Cymothoe*	25	15
365	2f. *Charaxes eupale*	35	15
366	3f. *Papilio bromius*	40	15
367	3f.50 *Teracolus annae*	50	15

(ii) Size 34×38 mm.

368	4f. Type **48**	50	15
369	5f. As 1f.	50	15
370	6f.50 As 1f.50	60	15
371	8f. As 2f.	90	20
372	10f. As 3f.	1·10	20
373	15f. As 3f.50	1·40	25

(iii) Size 41×46 mm.

374	20f. Type **48**	2·50	30
375	50f. *Papilio zenobia*	4·50	75
376	100f. *Danais chrysippus*	8·25	1·25
377	150f. *Salamis temora*	14·00	2·10

(b) Air. With gold frames. (i) Size 33×37 mm.

378	6f. As 3f.50	50	15
379	8f. As 1f.	55	15
380	10f. As 1f.50	60	15
381	14f. As 2f.	70	20
382	15f. As 3f.	1·00	20

(ii) Size 39×44 mm.

383	20f. As 50f. (No. 375)	2·40	25
384	50f. Type **48**	5·50	50
385	75f. As 100f.	6·75	90
386	130f. As 150f.	12·50	1·10

49 *Woman by the Manzanares* (Goya)

1968. International Letter-writing Week. Multicoloured.

387	4f. Type **49** (postage)	25	10
388	7f. *Reading a Letter* (De Hooch)	35	10
389	11f. *Woman reading a Letter* (Terborch)	40	10
390	14f. *Man writing a Letter* (Metsu)	45	10
391	17f. *The Letter* (Fragonard) (air)	60	10
392	26f. *Young Woman reading Letter* (Vermeer)	80	20
393	40f. *Folding a Letter* (Vlgee-Lebruni)	90	25
394	50f. *Mademoiselle Lavergne* (Liotard)	95	35
MS395	103×120 mm. Nos. 393/4 (without "POSTE AERIENNE" inscr). Perf or imperf	2·00	2·00

50 Football

1968. Olympic Games, Mexico. Multicoloured.

396	4f. Type **50** (postage)	25	10
397	7f. Basketball	30	10
398	13f. High jumping	35	10
399	24f. Relay racing	55	20
400	40f. Throwing the javelin	1·25	40
401	10f. Putting the shot (air)	25	15
402	17f. Running	45	15
403	26f. Throwing the hammer	70	25
404	50f. Hurdling	1·40	45
405	75f. Long jumping	2·25	60
MS406	95×85 mm. Nos. 404/5 (without "POSTE AERIENNE" inscr). Perf or imperf	6·00	6·00

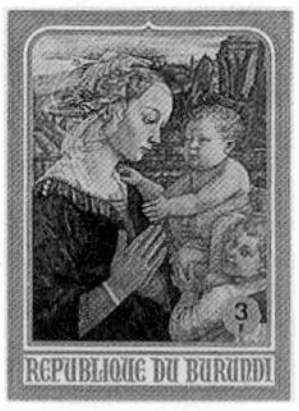

51 *Virgin and Child* (Lippi)

1968. Christmas. Paintings. Multicoloured.

407	3f. Type **51** (postage)	20	10
408	5f. *The Magnificat* (Botticelli)	25	10
409	6f. *Virgin and Child* (Durer)	40	10
410	11f. *Virgin and Child* (Raphael)	40	10
411	10f. *Madonna* (Correggio) (air)	25	10
412	14f. *The Nativity* (Baroccio)	35	15
413	17f. *The Holy Family* (El Greco)	55	20
414	26f. *Adoration of the Magi* (Maino)	75	35
MS415	Two sheets each 120×120 mm. (a) Nos. 407/10; (b) Nos. 411/14. Perf or imperf	2·75	2·75

52 WHO Emblem and Map

1969. 20th Anniv of World Health Organization Operation in Africa.

416	**52**	5f. multicoloured	15	10
417	**52**	6f. multicoloured	20	10
418	**52**	11f. multicoloured	25	15

53 Hand holding Flame

1969. Air. Human Rights Year.

419	**53**	10f. multicoloured	35	10
420	**53**	14f. multicoloured	45	10
421	**53**	26f. multicoloured	65	25

1969. Space Flight of "Apollo 8". Nos. 407/14 optd ***VOL DE NOEL APOLLO 8*** and space module.

422	3f. multicoloured (postage)	15	10
423	5f. multicoloured	25	10
424	6f. multicoloured	40	10
425	11f. multicoloured	50	20
426	10f. multicoloured (air)	30	15
427	14f. multicoloured	35	20
428	17f. multicoloured	55	25
429	26f. multicoloured	70	35

55 Map showing African Members

1969. Fifth Anniv of Yaounde Agreement between Common Market Countries and African-Malagasy Economic Community. Multicoloured.

430	5f. Type **55**	20	10
431	14f. Ploughing with tractor	40	15
432	17f. Teacher and pupil	55	20
433	26f. Maps of Africa and Europe (horiz)	75	25

56 *Resurrection* (Isenmann)

1969. Easter. Multicoloured.

434	11f. Type **56**	30	10
435	14f. *Resurrection* (Caron)	40	15
436	17f. *Noli me Tangere* (Schongauer)	45	20
437	26f. *Resurrection* (El Greco)	75	30
MS438	102×125 mm. Nos. 434/7. Perf or imperf	1·50	1·60

57 Potter

1969. 50th Anniv of ILO. Multicoloured.

439	3f. Type **57**	10	10
440	5f. Farm workers	10	10
441	7f. Foundry worker	25	10
442	10f. Harvester	25	15

58 Nurse and Patient

1969. 50th Anniv of League of Red Cross Societies. Multicoloured.

443	4f.+1f. Type **58** (postage)	15	10
444	7f.+1f. Stretcher bearers	35	10
445	11f.+1f. Operating theatre	50	15
446	17f.+1f. Blood bank	60	25
447	26f.+3f. Laboratory (air)	75	25
448	40f.+3f. Red Cross truck in African village	1·10	45
449	50f.+3f. Nurse and woman patient	1·60	50
MS450	90×97 mm. Nos. 447/9 (without "POSTE AERIENNE" inscr). Perf or imperf	3·50	3·50

59 Steel Works

1969. Fifth Anniv of African Development Bank. Multicoloured.

451	10f. Type **59**	30	30
452	17f. Broadcaster	50	50
453	30f. Language laboratory	70	70
454	50f. Tractor and harrow	1·25	1·25
MS455	103×125 mm. Nos. 451/4. Perf or imperf	2·50	2·50

60 Pope Paul VI

1969. First Papal Visit to Africa. Multicoloured.

456	3f.+2f. Type **60**	15	10
457	5f.+2f. Pope Paul and map of Africa (horiz)	30	10
458	10f.+2f. Pope Paul and African flags (horiz)	30	10
459	14f.+2f. Pope Paul and the Vatican (horiz)	55	10
460	17f.+2f. Type **60**	60	10
461	40f.+2f. Pope Paul and Uganda Martyrs (horiz)	1·25	30
462	50f.+2f. Pope Paul enthroned (horiz)	1·60	35
MS463	80×103 mm. As Nos. 461/2 but face values 40f.+5f. and 50f.+5f. Perf or imperf	2·75	2·75

61 *Girl reading Letter* (Vermeer)

1969. International Letter-writing Week. Multicoloured.

464	4f. Type **61**	15	10
465	7f. *Graziella* (Renoir)	20	10
466	14f. *Woman writing a Letter* (Terborch)	30	10
467	26f. *Galileo* (unknown painter)	55	15
468	40f. *Beethoven* (unknown painter)	1·10	35
MS469	133×75 mm. Nos. 467/8. Perf or imperf	2·10	2·10

62 Blast-off

1969. First Man on the Moon. Multicoloured.

470	4f. Type **62** (postage)	30	10
471	6f.50 Rocket in Space	40	10
472	7f. Separation of lunar module	50	10
473	14f. Module landing on Moon	80	15
474	17f. Command module in orbit	1·10	25
475	26f. Astronaut descending ladder (air)	1·25	20
476	40f. Astronaut on Moon's surface	2·00	25
477	50f. Module in sea	3·00	45
MS478	140×90 mm. 26f. As 14f.; 40f. As 26f.; 50f. As 40f. Perf or imperf	6·25	6·25

63 *Adoration of the Magi* (detail, Rubens)

1969. Christmas. Multicoloured.

479	5f. Type **63** (postage)	15	10
480	6f. *Virgin and Child with St. John* (Romano)	15	10
481	10f. *Madonna of the Magnificat* (Botticelli)	40	15
482	17f. *Virgin and Child* (Garofalo) (horiz) (air)	60	15
483	26f. *Madonna and Child* (Negretti) (horiz)	80	20
484	50f. *Virgin and Child* (Barbarelli) (horiz)	1·60	35
MS485	Two sheets (a) 110×85 mm. Nos. 479/81; (b) 85×110 mm. Nos. 482/4. Perf or imperf Set of 2 sheets	3·75	1·10

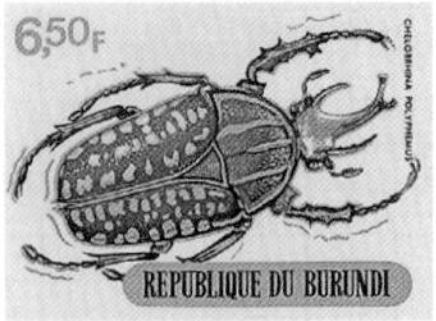

64 *Chelorrhina polyphemus*

1970. Beetles. Multicoloured. (a) Postage. (i) Size 39×28 mm.

486	50c. *Sternotomis bohemani*	20	10
487	1f. *Tetralobus flabellicornis*	20	10
488	1f.50 Type **64**	20	10
489	2f. *Brachytritus hieroglyphicus*	20	10
490	3f. *Goliathus goliathus*	20	10
491	3f.50 *Homoderus mellyi*	30	10

(ii) Size 46×32 mm.

492	4f. As 50c.	45	10
493	5f. As 1f.	65	10
494	6f. Type **64**	65	10
495	8f. As 2f.	65	10
496	10f. As 3f.	70	10
497	15f. As 3f.50	1·10	15

(iii) Size 62×36 mm.

498	20f. As 50c.	1·50	30
499	50f. *Stephanorrhina guttata*	4·00	40
500	100f. *Phyllocnema viridocostata*	6·75	85
501	150f. *Mecynorrhina oberthueri*	8·25	1·60

(b) Air. (i) Size 46×32 mm.

502	6f. As 3f.50	35	10
503	8f. As 1f.	45	10
504	10f. Type **64**	60	15
505	14f. As 2f.	70	15
506	15f. As 3f.	75	20

(ii) Size 52×36 mm.

507	20f. As 50f. (No. 499)	1·25	25
508	50f. As 50c.	4·00	35
509	75f. As 100f.	5·00	55
510	130f. As 150f.	8·00	80

65 *Jesus Condemned to Death*

1970. Easter. *The Stations of the Cross* (Carredano). Multicoloured.

511	1f. Type **65** (postage)	10	10
512	1f.50 *Carrying the Cross*	10	10
513	2f. *Jesus falls for the First Time*	10	10
514	3f. *Jesus meets His Mother*	10	10
515	3f.50 *Simon of Cyrene takes the Cross*	15	10
516	4f. *Veronica wipes the face of Christ*	15	10
517	5f. *Jesus falls for the Second Time*	15	10
518	8f. *The Women of Jerusalem* (air)	20	10
519	10f. *Jesus falls for the Third Time*	25	15
520	14f. *Christ stripped*	30	25
521	15f. *Jesus nailed to the Cross*	40	25
522	18f. *The Crucifixion*	40	30
523	20f. *Descent from the Cross*	50	30
524	50f. *Christ laid in the Tomb*	1·25	45
MS525	Two sheets each 155×125 mm. (a) Nos. 511/17; (b) Nos. 518/24	4·00	2·50

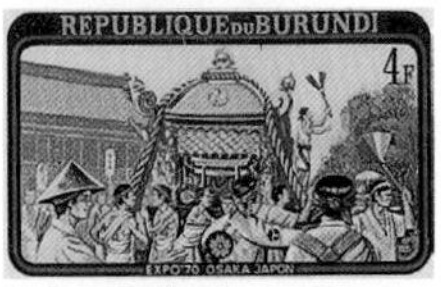

66 Japanese Parade

1970. World Fair, Osaka, Japan (EXPO '70). Multicoloured.

526	4f. Type **66**	15	10
527	6f.50 Exhibition site from the air	75	15
528	7f. African pavilions	20	10
529	14f. Pagoda (vert)	30	10

530	26f. Recording pavilion and pool	60	15
531	40f. Tower of the Sun (vert)	1·00	30
532	50f. National flags (vert)	1·25	35
MS533	105×80 mm. As Nos. 531/2 with additional "POSTE AERIENNE" inscr. Perf or imperf	2·25	65

67 Burundi Cow

1970. Source of the Nile. Multicoloured.

534	7f. Any design (postage)	95	30
535	14f. Any design (air)	1·25	30

Nos. 534 and 535 were each issued in se-tenant sheets of 18 stamps as Type **67**, showing map sections, animals and birds, forming a map of the Nile from Cairo to Burundi.

68 Common Redstart

1970. Birds. Multicoloured. (a) Postage. Size 44×33 mm or 33×44 mm.

536	2f. Great grey shrike (vert)	25	10
537	2f. Common starling (vert)	25	10
538	2f. Yellow wagtail (vert)	25	10
539	2f. Sand martin (vert)	25	10
540	3f. Winter wren	60	10
541	3f. Firecrest	60	10
542	3f. Eurasian sky lark	60	10
543	3f. Crested lark	60	10
544	3f.50 Woodchat shrike (vert)	65	10
545	3f.50 Rock thrush (vert)	65	10
546	3f.50 Black redstarts (vert)	65	10
547	3f.50 Ring ousel (vert)	65	10
548	4f. Type **68**	95	10
549	4f. Dunnock	95	10
550	4f. Grey wagtail	95	10
551	4f. Meadow pipit	95	10
552	5f. Hoopoe (vert)	1·25	15
553	5f. Pied flycatcher (vert)	1·25	15
554	5f. Great reed warbler (vert)	1·25	15
555	5f. River kingfisher (vert)	1·25	15
556	6f.50 House martin	1·40	20
557	6f.50 Sedge warbler	1·40	20
558	6f.50 Fieldfare	1·40	20
559	6f.50 Golden oriole	1·40	20

(b) Air. Size 52×44 mm or 44×52 mm.

560	8f. As No. 536	1·50	20
561	8f. As No. 537	1·50	20
562	8f. As No. 538	1·50	20
563	8f. As No. 539	1·50	20
564	10f. As No. 540	1·75	25
565	10f. As No. 541	1·75	25
566	10f. As No. 542	1·75	25
567	10f. As No. 543	1·75	25
568	14f. As No. 544	1·75	25
569	14f. As No. 545	1·75	25
570	14f. As No. 546	1·75	25
571	14f. As No. 547	1·75	25
572	20f. Type **68**	2·10	30
573	20f. As No. 549	2·10	30
574	20f. As No. 550	2·10	30
575	20f. As No. 551	2·10	30
576	30f. As No. 552	2·25	30
577	30f. As No. 553	2·25	30
578	30f. As No. 554	2·25	30
579	30f. As No. 555	2·25	30
580	50f. As No. 556	3·75	30
581	50f. As No. 557	3·75	30
582	50f. As No. 558	3·75	30
583	50f. As No. 559	3·75	30

69 Library

1970. International Educational Year. Multicoloured.

584	3f. Type **69**	10	10
585	5f. Examination	15	10
586	7f. Experiments in the laboratory	25	10
587	10f. Students with electron microscope	30	10

70 United Nations Building, New York

1970. Air. 25th Anniv of United Nations. Multicoloured.

588	7f. Type **70**	25	10
589	11f. Security Council in session	30	10
590	26f. Paul VI and U Thant	70	20
591	40f. U.N. and National flags	1·00	30
MS592	125×80 mm. As Nos. 590/1 but without "POSTE AERIENNE" inscr. Perf or imperf	1·70	50

71 Pres. Micombero and Wife

1970. Fourth Anniv of Republic. Multicoloured

593	4f. Type **71**	10	10
594	7f. Pres. Micombero and flag	25	10
595	11f. Revolution Memorial	35	15
MS596	125×142 mm. Nos. 593/5 (air). Perf or imperf	70	35

72 King Baudouin and Queen Fabiola

1970. Air. Visit of King and Queen of the Belgians. Each brown, purple and gold.

597	6f. Type **72**	65	15
598	20f. Pres. Micombero and King Baudouin	1·50	40
599	40f. Pres. Micombero in evening dress	3·00	70
MS600	143×117 mm. As Nos. 597/9 but with "POSTE AERIENNE" inscr omitted. Perf or imperf	5·00	1·25

73 *Adoration of the Magi* (Durer)

1970. Christmas. Multicoloured.

601	6f.50+1f. Type **73** (postage)	50	15
602	11f.+1f. *The Virgin of the Eucharist* (Botticelli)	60	25
603	20f.+1f. *The Holy Family* (El Greco)	90	30
604	14f.+3f. *The Adoration of the Magi* (Velasquez) (air)	50	25
605	26f.+3f. *The Holy Family* (Van Cleve)	85	40
606	40f.+3f. *Virgin and Child* (Van der Weyden)	1·40	60
MS607	Two sheets each 135×75 mm. (a) Nos. 601/3; (b) Nos. 604/6. Perf or imperf	4·75	2·00

74 Lenin in Discussion

1970. Birth Cent of Lenin. Each brown and gold.

608	3f.50 Type **74**	20	15
609	5f. Lenin addressing Soviet	30	15
610	6f.50 Lenin with soldier and sailor	40	15
611	15f. Lenin speaking to crowd	60	25
612	50f. Lenin	2·00	55

75 Lion

1971. African Animals (1st series). Multicoloured. (a) Postage. Size 38×38 mm.

613	1f. Type **75**	35	10
614	1f. African buffalo	35	10
615	1f. Hippopotamus	35	10
616	1f. Giraffe	35	10
617	2f. Topi	50	15
618	2f. Black rhinoceros	50	15
619	2f. Common zebra	50	15
620	2f. Leopard	50	15
621	3f. Grant's gazelle	85	25
622	3f. Cheetah	85	25
623	3f. African white-backed vultures	85	25
624	3f. Okapi	85	25
625	5f. Chimpanzee	1·00	25
626	5f. African elephant	1·00	25
627	5f. Spotted hyena	1·00	25
628	5f. Gemsbok	1·00	25
629	6f. Gorilla	1·40	25
630	6f. Blue wildebeest	1·40	25
631	6f. Warthog	1·40	25
632	6f. Hunting dog	1·40	25
633	11f. Sable antelope	2·25	30
634	11f. Caracal	2·25	30
635	11f. Ostriches	2·25	30
636	11f. Bongo	2·25	30

(b) Air. Size 44×44 mm.

637	10f. Type **75**	70	35
638	10f. As No. 614	70	35
639	10f. As No. 615	70	35
640	10f. As No. 616	70	35
641	14f. As No. 617	80	40
642	14f. As No. 618	80	40
643	14f. As No. 619	80	40
644	14f. As No. 620	80	40
645	17f. As No. 621	90	40
646	17f. As No. 622	90	40
647	17f. As No. 623	90	40
648	17f. As No. 624	90	40
649	24f. As No. 625	1·50	55
650	24f. As No. 626	1·50	55
651	24f. As No. 627	1·50	55
652	24f. As No. 628	1·50	55
653	26f. As No. 629	1·50	55
654	26f. As No. 630	1·50	55
655	26f. As No. 631	1·50	55
656	26f. As No. 632	1·50	55
657	31f. As No. 633	1·60	70
658	31f. As No. 634	1·60	70
659	31f. As No. 635	1·60	70
660	31f. As No. 636	1·60	70

See also Nos. 1028/75, 1178/1225 and 1385/97.

76 *The Resurrection* (Il Sodoma)

1971. Easter. Multicoloured.

661	3f. Type **76** (postage)	15	10
662	6f. *The Resurrection* (Del Castagno)	30	10
663	11f. *Noli Me Tangere* (Correggio)	45	15
664	14f. *The Resurrection* (Borrassa) (air)	50	20
665	17f. *The Resurrection* (Della Francesca)	65	20
666	26f. *The Resurrection* (Pleydenwyurff)	85	30
MS667	Two sheets each 117×84 mm. (a) Nos. 661/3; (b) Nos. 664/6. Colours changed. Perf or imperf	3·00	1·10

1971. Air. United Nations Campaigns. Nos. 637/48 optd or surch. (a) Optd **LUTTE CONTRE LE RACISME ET LA DISCRIMINATION RACIALE** and Racial Equality Year emblem.

668	10f. multicoloured	90	15
669	10f. multicoloured	90	15
670	10f. multicoloured	90	15
671	10f. multicoloured	90	15

(b) Surch **LUTTE CONTRE L'ANALPHABETISME, UNESCO** emblem and premium (Campaign against Illiteracy).

672	14f.+2f. multicoloured	1·40	25
673	14f.+2f. multicoloured	1·40	25
674	14f.+2f. multicoloured	1·40	25
675	14f.+2f. multicoloured	1·40	25

(c) Surch **AIDE INTERNATIONALE AUX REFUGIES**, emblem and premium (Int Help for Refugees).

676	17f.+1f. multicoloured	2·25	40
677	17f.+1f. multicoloured	2·25	40
678	17f.+1f. multicoloured	2·25	40
679	17f.+1f. multicoloured	2·25	40

1971. Air. Olympic Commems. Nos. 653/56 surch. (a) Surch **75eme ANNIVERSAIRE DES JEUX OLYMPIQUES MODERNES (1896–1971)**, Olympic rings and premium.

680	26f.+1f. multicoloured	1·25	35
681	26f.+1f. multicoloured	1·25	35
682	26f.+1f. multicoloured	1·25	35
683	26f.+1f. multicoloured	1·25	35

(b) Surch **JEUX PRE-OLYMPIQUES MUNICH 1972**, rings and premium (Olympic Games, Munich (1972)).

684	31f.+1f. multicoloured	2·25	1·10
685	31f.+1f. multicoloured	2·25	1·10
686	31f.+1f. multicoloured	2·25	1·10
687	31f.+1f. multicoloured	2·25	1·10

79 *Venetian Girl*

1971. International Letter-writing Week. Paintings by Durer. Multicoloured.

688	6f. Type **79**	30	30
689	11f. *Jerome Holzschuhers*	35	35
690	14f. *Emperor Maximilian*	40	40
691	17f. Altar painting, Paumgartner	65	65
692	26f. *The Halle Madonna*	80	80
693	31f. Self-portrait	1·00	1·00
MS694	137×80 mm. As Nos. 692/3 (air). Perf or imperf	1·80	1·80

1971. Sixth Congress of International Institute of French Law, Bujumbura. Nos. 668/693 optd **VIeme CONGRES DE L'INSTITUT INTERNATIONAL DE DROIT D'EXPRESSION FRANCAISE**.

695	6f. multicoloured	30	10
696	11f. multicoloured	35	10
697	14f. multicoloured	45	20
698	17f. multicoloured	65	20
699	26f. multicoloured	75	25
700	31f. multicoloured	1·00	25
MS701	137×80 mm. No. **MS**694. Perf or imperf	1·50	1·50

81 *The Virgin and Child* (Il Perugino)

1971. Christmas. Paintings of Virgin and Child by following artists. Multicoloured.

702	3f. Type **81** (postage)	15	10
703	5f. Del Sarto	25	10
704	6f. Morales	50	10

705	14f. Da Conegliano (air)	55	15
706	17f. Lippi	60	20
707	31f. Leonardo da Vinci	1·10	45
MS708	Two sheets each 125×80 mm. (a) Nos. 702/4; (b) Nos. 705/7	3·00	1·10

1971. 25th Anniv of UNICEF. Nos. 702/7 surch **UNICEF XXVe ANNIVERSAIRE 1946–1971**, emblem and premium.

709	3f.+1f. mult (postage)	30	10
710	5f.+1f. multicoloured	50	20
711	6f.+1f. multicoloured	60	30
712	14f.+1f. mult (air)	40	20
713	17f.+1f. multicoloured	95	25
714	31f.+1f. multicoloured	1·50	45
MS715	Two sheets each 125×80 mm. No. **MS**708 surch with 2f. premium on each stamp in the sheets	3·00	3·00

83 *Archangel Michael* (icon, St. Mark's)

1971. UNESCO "Save Venice" Campaign. Multicoloured.

716	3f.+1f. Type **83** (postage)	25	10
717	5f.+1f. *La Polenta* (Longhi)	35	15
718	6f.+1f. *Gossip* (Longhi)	35	15
719	11f.+1f. *Diana's Bath* (Pittoni)	45	25
720	10f.+1f. Casa d'Oro (air)	45	10
721	17f.+1f. Doge's Palace	65	15
722	24f.+1f. St. John and St. Paul Church	90	25
723	31f.+1f. *Doge's Palace and Piazzetta* (Canaletto)	2·00	40
MS724	Two sheets each 115×132 mm. (a) Nos. 716/19; (b) Nos. 720/3. Each design in sheet has a 2f. premium. Perf or imperf	5·25	1·50

84 "Lunar Orbiter"

1972. Conquest of Space. Multicoloured.

725	6f. Type **84**	15	15
726	11f. "Vostok" spaceship	40	15
727	14f. "Luna 1"	45	30
728	17f. First Man on Moon	65	30
729	26f. "Soyuz 11" space flight	80	40
730	40f. "Lunar Rover"	1·60	95
MS731	135×135 mm. Nos. 725/30 with additional inscr (air)	4·00	2·25

85 Slalom skiing

1972. Winter Olympic Games, Sapporo, Japan. Multicoloured.

732	5f. Type **85**	15	10
733	6f. Pair skating	20	10
734	11f. Figure-skating	35	10
735	14f. Ski-jumping	35	20
736	17f. Ice-hockey	50	20
737	24f. Speed skating	60	25
738	26f. Ski-bobbing	60	25
739	31f. Downhill skiing	75	25
740	50f. Bobsleighing	1·50	35
MS741	107×127 mm. As Nos. 738/40. Perf or imperf (air)	2·75	85

86 *Ecce Homo* (Metzys)

1972. Easter. Paintings. Multicoloured.

742	3f.50 Type **86**	20	10
743	6f.50 *The Crucifixion* (Rubens)	30	10
744	10f. *The Descent from the Cross* (Portormo)	40	10
745	18f. *Pieta* (Gallegos)	70	15
746	27f. *The Trinity* (El Greco)	1·40	30
MS747	111×160 mm. Nos. 742/6. Perf or imperf	3·00	75

87 Gymnastics

1972. Olympic Games, Munich. Multicoloured.

748	5f. Type **87** (postage)	20	10
749	6f. Throwing the javelin	20	10
750	11f. Fencing	35	15
751	14f. Cycling	50	20
752	17f. Pole-vaulting	75	20
753	24f. Weightlifting (air)	65	25
754	26f. Hurdling	90	25
755	31f. Throwing the discus	1·40	40
756	40f. Football	1·50	50
MS757	123×75 mm. Nos. 755/6 without "POSTE AERIENNE" inscr	3·00	90

88 Prince Rwagasore, Pres. Micombero and Drummers

1972. Tenth Anniv of Independence. Multicoloured.

758	5f. Type **88** (postage)	15	10
759	7f. Rwagasore, Micombero and map	25	10
760	13f. Pres. Micombero and Burundi flag	40	15
761	15f. Type **65** (air)	30	15
762	18f. As 7f.	35	15
763	27f. As 13f.	60	30
MS764	Two sheets each 147×80 mm. (a) Nos. 758/60; (b) Nos. 761/3	2·10	95

1972. Christmas. Madonna and Child paintings by artists given below. Multicoloured.

765	5f. Type **89** (postage)	30	10
766	10f. Raphael	50	10
767	15f. Botticelli	75	15
768	18f. S. Mainardi (air)	50	15
769	27f. H. Memling	1·00	25
770	40f. Lotto	1·50	40
MS771	Two sheets each 128×82 mm. (a) Nos. 765/7; (b) Nos. 768/70	4·50	1·10

90 *Platycoryne crocea*

1972. Orchids. Multicoloured.

772	50c. Type **90** (postage)	30	15
773	1f. *Cattleya trianaei*	30	15
774	2f. *Eulophia cucullata*	30	15
775	3f. *Cymbidium hamsey*	30	15
776	4f. *Thelymitra pauciflora*	30	15
777	5f. *Miltassia*	30	15
778	6f. *Miltonia*	1·25	15
779	7f. Type **90**	1·25	15
780	8f. As 1f.	1·40	15
781	9f. As 2f.	1·40	20
782	10f. As 3f.	1·90	20
783	13f. As 4f. (air)	1·25	15
784	14f. As 5f.	1·25	15
785	15f. As 6f.	1·60	20
786	18f. Type **90**	1·60	20
787	20f. As 1f.	1·60	25
788	27f. As 2f.	2·75	30
789	36f. As 3f.	4·50	40

Nos. 779/89 are size 53×53 mm.

1972. Christmas Charity. Nos. 765/770 surch.

790	5f.+1f. mult (postage)	35	15
791	10f.+1f. multicoloured	65	20
792	15f.+1f. multicoloured	75	25
793	18f.+1f. multicoloured (air)	60	20
794	27f.+1f. multicoloured	90	25
795	40f.+1f. multicoloured	1·50	45
MS796	Two sheets as **MS**771 with 2f. premium surch on each stamp	4·50	1·10

92 H. M. Stanley

1973. Centenary of Stanley/Livingstone African Exploration. Multicoloured.

797	5f. Type **92** (postage)	20	10
798	7f. Expedition bearers	25	10
799	13f. Stanley directing foray	45	15
800	15f. Dr. Livingstone (air)	35	20
801	18f. Stanley meets Livingstone	55	20
802	27f. Stanley conferring with Livingstone	1·00	30
MS803	100×141 mm. Nos. 800/2. Perf or imperf	1·90	70

93 *The Scourging* (Caravaggio)

1973. Easter. Multicoloured.

804	5f. Type **93** (postage)	15	10
805	7f. *Crucifixion* (Van der Weyden)	25	10
806	13f. *The Deposition* (Raphael)	50	15
807	15f. *Christ bound to the Pillar* (Guido Reni) (air)	45	25
808	18f. *Crucifixion* (M. Grunewald)	70	25
809	27f. *The Descent from the Cross* (Caravaggio)	1·10	30
MS810	Two sheets each 121×74 mm. (a) Nos. 804/6; (b) Nos. 807/9	3·00	1·10

94 Interpol Emblem

1973. 50th Anniv of Interpol. Multicoloured.

811	5f. Type **94** (postage)	25	10
812	10f. Burundi flag	40	10
813	18f. Interpol H.Q., Paris	60	15
814	27f. As 5f. (air)	75	25
815	40f. As 10f.	1·25	35

95 Capricorn, Aquarius and Pisces

1973. 500th Birth Anniv of Copernicus.

816	**95**	3f. gold, red and black (postage)	20	10
817	-	3f. gold, red and black	20	10
818	-	3f. gold, red and black	20	10
819	-	3f. gold, red and black	20	10
820	-	5f. multicoloured	30	10
821	-	5f. multicoloured	30	10
822	-	5f. multicoloured	30	10
823	-	5f. multicoloured	30	10
824	-	7f. multicoloured	40	10
825	-	7f. multicoloured	40	10
826	-	7f. multicoloured	40	10
827	-	7f. multicoloured	40	10
828	-	13f. multicoloured	60	10
829	-	13f. multicoloured	60	10
830	-	13f. multicoloured	60	10
831	-	13f. multicoloured	60	10
832	-	15f. multicoloured (air)	40	15
833	-	15f. multicoloured	40	15
834	-	15f. multicoloured	40	15
835	-	15f. multicoloured	40	15
836	-	18f. multicoloured	55	15
837	-	18f. multicoloured	55	15
838	-	18f. multicoloured	55	15
839	-	18f. multicoloured	55	15
840	-	27f. multicoloured	95	25
841	-	27f. multicoloured	95	25
842	-	27f. multicoloured	95	25
843	-	27f. multicoloured	95	25
844	-	36f. multicoloured	2·10	40
845	-	36f. multicoloured	2·10	40
846	-	36f. multicoloured	2·10	40
847	-	36f. multicoloured	2·10	40
MS848		Two sheets each 137×147 mm. (a) Nos. 816/31; (b) Nos. 832/47	20·00	10·00

DESIGNS: No. 816, Type **95**; 817, Aries, Taurus and Gemini; 818, Cancer, Leo and Virgo; 819, Libra, Scorpio and Sagittarius; 820/23, Greek and Roman Gods; 824/7, Ptolemy and Ptolemaic System; 828/31, Copernicus and Solar System; 823/5, Copernicus, Earth, Pluto and Jupiter; 836/39, Copernicus, Venus, Saturn and Mars; 840/43, Copernicus, Uranus, Neptune and Mercury; 844/7, Earth and spacecraft.

The four designs of each value were issued se-tenant in blocks of four within the sheet, forming composite designs.

96 *Protea cynaroides*

1973. Flora and Butterflies. Multicoloured.

849	1f. Type **96** (postage)	70	15
850	1f. *Precis octavia*	70	15
851	1f. *Epiphora bauhiniae*	70	15
852	1f. *Gazania longiscapa*	70	15
853	2f. *Kniphofia* – "Royal Standard"	70	15
854	2f. *Cymothoe coccinata hew*	1·00	20
855	2f. "*Nudaurelia zambesina*	1·00	20
856	2f. *Freesia refracta*	1·00	15
857	3f. *Calotis eupompe*	1·00	20
858	3f. Narcissus	1·00	15
859	3f. *Cineraria hybrida*	1·00	15
860	3f. *Cyrestis camillus*	1·00	20
861	5f. *Iris tingitana*	1·40	15
862	5f. *Papilio demodocus*	2·10	20
863	5f. *Catopsilia avelaneda*	2·10	20
864	5f. *Nerine sarniensis*	1·40	15
865	6f. *Hypolimnas dexithea*	2·10	20
866	6f. *Zantedeschia tropicalis*	1·40	15
867	6f. *Sandersonia aurantiaca*	1·40	15
868	6f. *Drurya antimachus*	2·10	20
869	11f. *Nymphaea capensis*	1·75	20
870	11f. *Pandoriana pandora*	2·75	25
871	11f. *Precis orythia*	2·75	25
872	11f. *Pelargonium domesticum*–"Aztec"	1·75	20
873	10f. Type **96** (air)	50	10
874	10f. As No. 850	90	10
875	10f. As No. 851	90	10
876	10f. As No. 852	50	10
877	14f. As No. 853	60	10
878	14f. As No. 854	1·00	20
879	14f. As No. 855	1·00	20
880	14f. As No. 856	40	15
881	17f. As No. 857	1·25	25
882	17f. As No. 858	90	20
883	17f. As No. 859	90	20
884	17f. As No. 860	1·25	25
885	24f. As No. 861	1·40	25
886	24f. As No. 862	1·75	30
887	24f. As No. 863	1·75	30
888	24f. As No. 864	1·10	25
889	26f. As No. 865	1·75	30
890	26f. As No. 866	1·10	30
891	26f. As No. 867	1·10	30
892	26f. As No. 868	1·75	30
893	31f. As No. 869	1·25	35
894	31f. As No. 870	1·90	45
895	31f. As No. 871	1·90	45

896	31f. As No. 872	1·25	35

Nos. 849, 852/3, 856, 858/9, 861, 864, 866/7, 869, 872, 876/7, 880, 882/3, 885, 888, 890/1, 893 and 896 depict flora and the remainder butterflies.

The four designs of each value were issued se-tenant in blocks of four within the sheet, forming composite designs.

97 *Virgin and Child* (G. Bellini)

1973. Christmas. Various paintings of the Virgin and Child by artists listed below. Multicoloured.

897	5f. Type **97** (postage)	45	10
898	10f. Van Eyck	55	15
899	15f. G. A. Boltraffio	75	20
900	18f. Raphael (air)	35	10
901	27f. P. Perugino	1·10	30
902	40f. Titian	1·60	40
MS903	Two sheets each 144×78 mm. (a) Nos. 897/9; (b) Nos. 900/2	4·75	1·25

1973. Christmas Charity. Nos. 897/902 surch.

904	**97**	5f.+1f. mult (postage)	50	15
905	-	10f.+1f. multicoloured	80	20
906	-	15f.+1f. multicoloured	95	25
907	-	18f.+1f. mult (air)	70	15
908	-	27f.+1f. multicoloured	1·10	35
909	-	40f.+1f. multicoloured	1·60	50
MS910		Two sheets as **MS**903 with 2f. premium surch on each stamp	4·75	1·25

98 *The Pieta* (Veronese)

1974. Easter. Religious Paintings. Multicoloured.

911	5f. Type **98**	15	10
912	10f. *The Virgin and St. John* (Van der Weyden)	30	15
913	18f. *The Crucifixion* (Van der Weyden)	60	20
914	27f. *The Entombment* (Titian)	85	30
915	40f. *The Pieta* (El Greco)	2·10	50
MS916	145×120 mm. Nos. 911/15	4·00	1·25

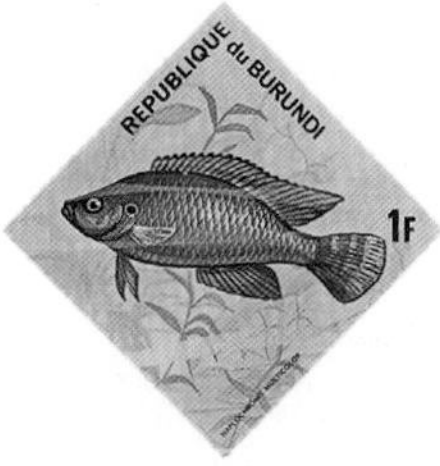

99 Egyptian Mouthbrooder (*Haplochromis multicolor*)

1974. Fish. Multicoloured.

917	1f. Type **99** (postage)	55	10
918	1f. Spotted mouthbrooder (*Tropheus duboisi*)	55	10
919	1f. Freshwater butterfly-fish (*Pantodon buchholzi*)	55	10
920	1f. Six-banded distichodus (*Distichodus sexfasciatus*)	55	10
921	2f. Rainbow krib (*Pelmatochromis kribensis*)	55	10
922	2f. African leaf-fish (*Polycentropsis abbreviata*)	55	10
923	2f. Three-lined tetra (*Nannaethiops tritaeniatus*)	55	10
924	2f. Jewel cichlid (*Hemichromis bimaculatus*)	55	10
925	3f. Spotted climbing-perch (*Ctenopoma acutirostre*)	55	10
926	3f. African mouthbrooder (*Tilapia melanopleura*)	55	10
927	3f. Angel squeaker (*Synodontis angelicus*)	55	10
928	3f. Two-striped lyretail (*Aphyosemion bivittatum*)	55	10
929	5f. Diamond fingerfish (*Monodactylus argenteus*)	90	10
930	5f. Regal angelfish (*Pygoplites diacanthus*)	90	10
931	5f. Moorish idol (*Zanclus canescens*)	90	10
932	5f. Peacock hind (*Cephalopholis argus*) and surgeonfish	90	10
933	6f. Bigeye (*Priacanthus arenatus*)	2·75	10
934	6f. Rainbow parrotfish (*Scarus guacamaia*) and French angelfish	2·75	10
935	6f. French angelfish (*Pomacanthus arcuatus*)	2·75	10
936	6f. John dory (*Zeus faber*)	2·75	10
937	11f. Scribbled cowfish (*Lactophrys quadricornis*)	3·00	20
938	11f. Ocean surgeonfish (*Acanthurus bahianus*)	3·00	20
939	11f. Queen triggerfish (*Balistes vetula*)	3·00	20
940	11f. Queen angelfish (*Holocanthus ciliaris*)	3·00	20
941	10f. Type **99** (air)	45	10
942	10f. As No. 918	45	10
943	10f. As No. 919	45	10
944	10f. As No. 920	45	10
945	14f. As No. 921	95	10
946	14f. As No. 922	95	10
947	14f. As No. 923	95	10
948	14f. As No. 924	95	10
949	17f. As No. 925	95	10
950	17f. As No. 926	95	10
951	17f. As No. 927	95	10
952	17f. As No. 928	95	10
953	24f. As No. 929	2·10	10
954	24f. As No. 930	2·10	10
955	24f. As No. 931	2·10	10
956	24f. As No. 932	2·10	10
957	26f. As No. 933	3·00	20
958	26f. As No. 934	3·00	20
959	26f. As No. 935	3·00	20
960	26f. As No. 936	3·00	20
961	31f. As No. 937	3·75	30
962	31f. As No. 938	3·75	30
963	31f. As No. 939	3·75	30
964	31f. As No. 940	3·75	30

The four designs of each value are arranged together in *se-tenant* blocks of four within the sheet, forming composite designs.

100 Footballers and World Cup Trophy

1974. World Cup Football Championships.

965	**100**	5f. mult (postage)	25	10
966	-	6f. multicoloured	30	10
967	-	11f. multicoloured	40	20
968	-	14f. multicoloured	50	25
969	-	17f. multicoloured	55	25
970	-	20f. multicoloured (air)	70	35
971	-	26f. multicoloured	90	45
972	-	40f. multicoloured	1·40	60
MS973		88×142 mm. As Nos. 970/2 but without airmail inscriptions	3·00	1·40

DESIGNS: Nos. 966/72, Football scenes as Type **100**.

101 Burundi Flag

1974. Centenary of UPU. Multicoloured.

974	6f. Type **101** (postage)	20	10
975	6f. Burundi P.T.T. Building	20	10
976	11f. Postmen carrying letters	30	10
977	11f. Postmen carrying letters	30	10
978	14f. UPU Monument	1·25	70
979	14f. Mail transport	1·25	70
980	17f. Burundi on map	55	10
981	17f. Dove and letter	55	10
982	24f. Type **101** (air)	80	20
983	24f. As No. 975	80	20
984	26f. As No. 976	1·10	30
985	26f. As No. 977	1·10	30
986	31f. As No. 978	2·75	1·10
987	31f. As No. 979	2·75	1·10
988	40f. As No. 980	3·50	45
989	40f. As No. 981	3·50	45
MS990	Two sheets each 96×164 mm. (a) Nos. 974/81; (b) Nos. 982/9	20·00	6·00

The two designs in each denomination were arranged together in *se-tenant* pairs within the sheet, each pair forming a composite design.

102 *St. Ildefonse writing a letter* (El Greco)

1974. International Letter-writing Week. Multicoloured.

991	6f. Type **102**	30	15
992	11f. *Lady sealing a letter* (Chardin)	50	20
993	14f. *Titus at desk* (Rembrandt)	55	30
994	17f. *The Love-letter* (Vermeer)	60	30
995	26f. *The Merchant G. Gisze* (Holbein)	65	50
996	31f. *A. Lenoir* (David)	90	55
MS997	95×105 mm. Nos. 955/6	1·50	1·00

103 *Virgin and Child* (Van Orley)

1974. Christmas. Showing Virgin and Child paintings by artists named. Multicoloured.

998	5f. Type **103** (postage)	25	10
999	10f. Hans Memling	45	15
1000	15f. Botticelli	1·00	20
1001	18f. Hans Memling (different) (air)	35	20
1002	27f. F. Lippi	1·10	35
1003	40f. L. di Gredi	1·50	45
MS1004	Two sheets each 126×89 mm. (a) Nos. 998/1000; (b) Nos. 1001/3	4·50	1·50

1974. Christmas Charity. Nos. 998/1003 surch.

1005	**103**	5f.+1f. mult (postage)	30	10
1006	-	10f.+1f. multicoloured	40	25
1007	-	15f.+1f. multicoloured	1·10	30
1008	-	18f.+1f. mult (air)	55	20
1009	-	27f.+1f. multicoloured	85	35
1010	-	40f.+1f. multicoloured	1·60	45
MS1011		Two sheets as **MS**1004 with 2f. premium on each stamp	4·50	1·50

104 "Apollo" Spacecraft with Docking Tunnel

1975. "Apollo–Soyuz" Space Project. Multicoloured.

1012	26f. Type **104** (postage)	45	30
1013	26f. Leonov and Kubasov	45	30
1014	26f. "Soyuz" Spacecraft	45	30
1015	26f. Slayton, Brand and Stafford	45	30
1016	31f. "Soyuz" launch	55	40
1017	31f. "Apollo" and "Soyuz" spacecraft	55	40
1018	31f. "Apollo" third stage separation	55	40
1019	31f. Slayton, Brand, Stafford, Leonov and Kubasov	55	40
1020	27f. Type **104** (air)	60	45
1021	27f. As No. 1012	60	45
1022	27f. As No. 1013	60	45
1023	27f. As No. 1014	60	45
1024	40f. As No. 1015	80	60
1025	40f. As No. 1016	80	60
1026	40f. As No. 1017	80	60
1027	40f. As No. 1018	80	60

The four designs in each value were issued together in *se-tenant* blocks of four within the sheet.

105 Addax

1975. African Animals (2nd series). Multicoloured.

1028	1f. Type **105** (postage)	40	15
1029	1f. Roan antelope	40	15
1030	1f. Nyala	40	15
1031	1f. White rhinoceros	40	15
1032	2f. Mandrill	40	15
1033	2f. Eland	40	15
1034	2f. Salt's dik-dik	40	15
1035	2f. Thomson's gazelles	40	15
1036	3f. African claw-less otter	55	15
1037	3f. Bohar reedbuck	55	15
1038	3f. African civet	55	15
1039	3f. African buffalo	55	15
1040	5f. Black wildebeest	55	15
1041	5f. African asses	55	15
1042	5f. Angolan black and white colobus	55	15
1043	5f. Gerenuk	55	15
1044	6f. Addra gazelle	95	20
1045	6f. Black-backed jackal	95	20
1046	6f. Sitatungas	95	20
1047	6f. Banded duiker	95	20
1048	11f. Fennec fox	1·40	20
1049	11f. Lesser kudus	1·40	20
1050	11f. Blesbok	1·40	20
1051	11f. Serval	1·40	20
1052	10f. Type **105** (air)	60	10
1053	10f. As No. 1029	60	10
1054	10f. As No. 1030	60	10
1055	10f. As No. 1031	60	10
1056	14f. As No. 1032	70	15
1057	14f. As No. 1033	70	15
1058	14f. As No. 1034	70	15
1059	14f. As No. 1035	70	15
1060	17f. As No. 1036	1·10	15
1061	17f. As No. 1037	1·10	15
1062	17f. As No. 1038	1·10	15
1063	17f. As No. 1039	1·10	15
1064	24f. As No. 1040	1·75	20
1065	24f. As No. 1041	1·75	20
1066	24f. As No. 1042	1·75	20
1067	24f. As No. 1043	1·75	20
1068	26f. As No. 1044	1·90	20
1069	26f. As No. 1045	1·90	20
1070	26f. As No. 1046	1·90	20
1071	26f. As No. 1047	1·90	20
1072	31f. As No. 1048	2·25	25
1073	31f. As No. 1049	2·25	25
1074	31f. As No. 1050	2·25	25
1075	31f. As No. 1051	2·25	25

The four designs in each value were issued together in horiz. *se-tenant* strips within the sheet, forming composite designs.

1975. Air. International Women's Year. Nos. 1052/9 optd **ANNEE INTERNATIONALE DE LA FEMME**.

1076	**105**	10f. multicoloured	80	50
1077	-	10f. multicoloured	80	50
1078	-	10f. multicoloured	80	50
1079	-	10f. multicoloured	80	50
1080	-	14f. multicoloured	1·40	60
1081	-	14f. multicoloured	1·40	60
1082	-	14f. multicoloured	1·40	60
1083	-	14f. multicoloured	1·40	60

1975. Air. 30th Anniv of United Nations. Nos. 1068/75 optd **30eme ANNIVERSAIRE DES NATIONS UNIES**.

1084	26f. multicoloured	1·40	1·25
1085	26f. multicoloured	1·40	1·25
1086	26f. multicoloured	1·40	1·25
1087	26f. multicoloured	1·40	1·25
1088	31f. multicoloured	2·25	2·00
1089	31f. multicoloured	2·25	2·00
1090	31f. multicoloured	2·25	2·00
1091	31f. multicoloured	2·25	2·00

108 *Jonah*

1975. Christmas. 500th Birth Anniv of Michaelangelo. Multicoloured.

1092	5f. Type **108** (postage)	25	10
1093	5f. "Libyan Sibyl"	25	10
1094	13f. "Daniel"	90	10
1095	13f. "Cumaean Sybil"	90	10
1096	27f. "Isaiah"	1·25	15
1097	27f. "Delphic Sybil" (different)	1·25	15

1098	18f. "Zachariah" (air)	90	10
1099	18f. "Joel"	90	10
1100	31f. "Erythraean Sybil"	1·60	30
1101	31f. "Ezekiel"	1·60	30
1102	40f. "Persian Sybil"	2·00	35
1103	40f. "Jeremiah"	2·00	35
MS1104	Two sheets each 138×111 mm. (a) Nos. 1092/7; (b) Nos. 1098/1103	14·00	2·25

1975. Christmas Charity. Nos. 1092/1103 surch +1F.

1105	**108** 5f.+1f. mult (postage)	45	10
1106	- 5f.+1f. multicoloured	45	10
1107	- 13f.+1f. multicoloured	75	10
1108	- 13f.+1f. multicoloured	75	10
1109	- 27f.+1f. multicoloured	1·25	15
1110	- 27f.+1f. multicoloured	1·25	15
1111	- 18f.+1f. mult (air)	1·00	10
1112	- 18f.+1f. multicoloured	1·00	10
1113	- 31f.+1f. multicoloured	1·60	30
1114	- 31f.+1f. multicoloured	1·60	30
1115	- 40f.+1f. multicoloured	1·90	35
1116	- 40f.+1f. multicoloured	1·90	35
MS1117	Two sheets as **MS**1104 with 2f. premium on each stamp	14·00	2·25

110 Speed Skating

1976. Winter Olympic Games, Innsbruck. Mult.

1118	17f. Type **110** (postage)	45	20
1119	24f. Figure-skating	50	20
1120	26f. Two-man bobsleigh	60	20
1121	31f. Cross-country skiing	70	30
1122	18f. Ski-jumping (air)	40	25
1123	36f. Skiing (slalom)	1·50	40
1124	50f. Ice-hockey	1·60	60
MS1125	Two sheets (a) 101×101 mm. Nos. 1118/21; (b) 131×131 mm. Nos. 1122/4	5·75	2·10

111 Basketball

1976. Olympic Games, Montreal. Multicoloured.

1126	14f. Type **111** (postage)	40	30
1127	14f. Pole-vaulting	40	30
1128	17f. Running	60	45
1129	17f. Football	60	45
1130	28f. As No. 1127	90	65
1131	28f. As No. 1128	90	65
1132	40f. As No. 1129	1·50	1·10
1133	40f. Type **111**	1·50	1·10
1134	27f. Hurdling (air)	90	65
1135	27f. High-jumping (horiz)	90	65
1136	31f. Gymnastics (horiz)	1·25	90
1137	31f. As No. 1134 (horiz)	1·25	90
1138	50f. As No. 1135 (horiz)	1·90	1·40
1139	50f. As No. 1136 (horiz)	1·90	1·40
MS1140	Two sheets. (a) 115×120 mm. 14f. Football; 17f. Pole vault; 28f. Basketball; 40f. Running (postage). (b) 99×120 mm. 27f. Gymnastics; 31f. High jump; 50f. Hurdles (air)	7·00	5·50

112 *Battle of Bunker Hill* (detail, John Trumbull)

1976. Air. Bicent of American Revolution. Multicoloured.

1141	18f. Type **112**	55	15
1142	18f. As Type **112**	55	15
1143	26f. Franklin, Jefferson and John Adams	75	25
1144	26f. As No. 1143	75	25
1145	36f. *Signing of Declaration of Independence* (Trumbull)	1·25	35
1146	36f. As No. 1145	1·25	35
MS1147	101×148 mm. Nos. 1141/6	5·00	1·50

The two designs of each value form composite pictures. Type **112** is the left-hand portion of the painting.

113 *Virgin and Child* (Dirk Bouts)

1976. Christmas. Multicoloured.

1148	5f. Type **113** (postage)	35	10
1149	13f. *Virgin of the Trees* (Bellini)	65	10
1150	27f. *Virgin and Child* (C. Crivelli)	1·00	25
1151	18f. *Virgin and Child* with St. Anne (Leonardo) (air)	80	30
1152	31f. *Holy Family with Lamb* (Raphael)	1·10	60
1153	40f. *Virgin with Basket* (Correggio)	1·60	70
MS1154	Two sheets each 122×80 mm. (a) Nos. 1148/50; (b) Nos. 1151/3	5·50	2·00

1976. Christmas Charity. Nos. 1148/53 surch **+1F**.

1155	**113** 5f.+1f. mult (postage)	25	10
1156	- 13f.+1f. multicoloured	70	30
1157	- 27f.+1f. multicoloured	1·10	50
1158	- 18f.+1f. mult (air)	60	30
1159	- 31f.+1f. multicoloured	1·00	45
1160	- 40f.+1f. multicoloured	1·90	65
MS1161	Two sheets as **MS**1154 with 2f. premium on each stamp	5·50	2·00

115 *The Ascent of Calvary* (Rubens)

1977. Easter. 400th Birth Anniv of Peter Paul Rubens. Multicoloured.

1162	10f. Type **115**	35	25
1163	21f. *Christ Crucified*	95	70
1164	27f. *The Descent from the Cross*	1·10	80
1165	35f. *The Deposition*	1·50	1·10
MS1166	111×85 mm. As Nos. 1162/5 (air)	4·00	2·70

116 Alexander Graham Bell

1977. Telephone Centenary and World Telecommunications Day. Multicoloured.

1167	10f. Type **116** (postage)	25	15
1168	10f. Satellite, Globe and telephones	25	15
1169	17f. Switchboard operator and wall telephone	45	30
1170	17f. Satellite transmitting to Earth	45	30
1171	26f. A. G. Bell and first telephone	80	60
1172	26f. Satellites circling Globe, and videophone	80	60
1173	18f. Type **116** (air)	40	30
1174	18f. As No. 1172	40	30
1175	36f. As No. 1169	1·10	80
1176	36f. As No. 1168	1·10	80
MS1177	120×135 mm. 10f. As No. 1171; 17f. Type **116**; 26f. As No. 1168; 18f. As No. 1170; 36f. As No. 1172	3·25	2·00

117 Kobs

1977. African Animals (3rd series). Multicoloured.

1178	2f. Type **117** (postage)	75	20
1179	2f. Marabou storks	75	20
1180	2f. Blue wildebeest	75	20
1181	2f. Bush pig	75	20
1182	5f. Grevy's zebras	85	20
1183	5f. Whale-headed stork	85	20
1184	5f. Striped hyenas	85	20
1185	5f. Pygmy chimpanzee	85	20
1186	8f. Greater flamingoes	95	20
1187	8f. Nile crocodiles	95	20
1188	8f. Green tree snake	95	20
1189	8f. Greater kudus	95	20
1190	11f. Large-toothed rock hyrax	1·00	20
1191	11f. Cobra	1·00	20
1192	11f. Golden jackals	1·00	20
1193	11f. Verreaux eagles	1·00	20
1194	21f. Ratel	1·25	30
1195	21f. Bushbuck	1·25	30
1196	21f. Secretary bird	1·25	30
1197	21f. Klipspringer	1·25	30
1198	27f. Bat-eared fox	1·60	30
1199	27f. African elephants	1·60	30
1200	27f. Vulturine guineafowl	1·60	30
1201	27f. Impalas	1·60	30
1202	9f. Type **117** (air)	60	25
1203	9f. As No. 1179	60	25
1204	9f. As No. 1180	60	25
1205	9f. As No. 1181	60	25
1206	13f. As No. 1182	85	30
1207	13f. As No. 1183	85	30
1208	13f. As No. 1184	85	30
1209	13f. As No. 1185	85	30
1210	30f. As No. 1186	1·25	50
1211	30f. As No. 1187	1·25	50
1212	30f. As No. 1188	1·25	50
1213	30f. As No. 1189	1·25	50
1214	35f. As No. 1190	1·40	60
1215	35f. As No. 1191	1·40	60
1216	35f. As No. 1192	1·40	60
1217	35f. As No. 1193	1·40	60
1218	54f. As No. 1194	2·40	70
1219	54f. As No. 1195	2·40	70
1220	54f. As No. 1196	2·40	70
1221	54f. As No. 1197	2·40	70
1222	70f. As No. 1198	3·25	85
1223	70f. As No. 1199	3·25	85
1224	70f. As No. 1200	3·25	85
1225	70f. As No. 1201	3·25	85

The four designs in each value were issued together *se-tenant* in horizontal strips within the sheet, forming composite designs.

118 *The Man of Iron* (Grimm)

1977. Fairy Tales. Multicoloured.

1226	5f. Type **118**	20	10
1227	5f. *Snow White and Rose Red* (Grimm)	20	10
1228	5f. *The Goose Girl* (Grimm)	20	10
1229	5f. *The Two Wanderers* (Grimm)	20	10
1230	11f. *The Hermit and the Bear* (Aesop)	60	10
1231	11f. *The Fox and the Stork* (Aesop)	60	10
1232	11f. *The Litigious Cats* (Aesop)	60	10
1233	11f. *The Blind and the Lame* (Aesop)	60	10
1234	14f. *The Ice Maiden* (Andersen)	70	10
1235	14f. *The Old House* (Andersen)	70	10
1236	14f. *The Princess and the Pea* (Andersen)	70	10
1237	14f. *The Elder Tree Mother* (Andersen)	70	10
1238	17f. *Hen with the Golden Egg* (La Fontaine)	80	15
1239	17f. *The Wolf Turned Shepherd* (La Fontaine)	80	15
1240	17f. *The Oyster and Litigants* (La Fontaine)	80	15
1241	17f. *The Wolf and the Lamb* (La Fontaine)	80	15
1242	26f. *Jack and the Beanstalk* (traditional)	1·60	25
1243	26f. *Alice in Wonderland* (Lewis Carroll)	1·60	25
1244	26f. *Three Heads in the Well* (traditional)	1·60	25
1245	26f. *Tales of Mother Goose* (traditional)	1·60	25

119 UN General Assembly and UN 3c. Stamp, 1954

1977. 25th Anniv of United Nations Postal Administration. Multicoloured.

1246	8f. Type **119** (postage)	40	30
1247	8f. UN 4c. stamp, 1957	40	30
1248	8f. UN 3c. stamp, 1954 (FAO)	40	30
1249	8f. UN 1½c. stamp, 1951	40	30
1250	10f. Security Council and UN 8c. red, 1954	50	35
1251	10f. UN 8c. green, 1956	50	35
1252	10f. UN 8c. black, 1955	50	35
1253	10f. UN 7c. stamp, 1959	50	35
1254	21f. Meeting hall and UN 3c. grey, 1956	80	60
1255	21f. UN 8c. stamp, 1956	80	60
1256	21f. UN 3c. brown, 1953	80	60
1257	21f. UN 3c. green, 1952	80	60
1258	24f. Building by night and UN 4c. red, 1957 (air)	80	60
1259	24f. UN 8c. brn & grn, 1960	80	60
1260	24f. UN 8c. green, 1955	80	60
1261	24f. UN 8c. red, 1955	80	60
1262	27f. Aerial view of UN 8c. red, 1957	90	65
1263	27f. UN 3c. stamp, 1953	90	65
1264	27f. UN 8c. green, 1954	90	65
1265	27f. UN 8c. brown, 1956	90	65
1266	35f. UN Building by day and UN 5c. stamp, 1959	1·40	1·00
1267	35f. UN 3c. stamp, 1962	1·40	1·00
1268	35f. UN 3c. bl & pur, 1951	1·40	1·00
1269	35f. UN 1c. stamp, 1951	1·40	1·00
MS1270	Two sheets each 127×76 mm. (a) 8f. As No. 1253; 10f. As No. 1255; 21f. As No. 1248. (b) 24f. As No. 1263; 27f. As No. 1266; 35f. As No. 1260	4·75	3·30

The four designs in each value were issued together in se-tenant blocks of four, each design in the block having the same background.

120 *Virgin and Child* (Jean Lambardos)

1977. Christmas. Paintings of Virgin and Child by artists named. Multicoloured.

1271	5f. Type **120** (postage)	15	10
1272	13f. Melides Toscano	65	50
1273	27f. Emmanuel Tzanes	95	70
1274	18f. Master of Moulins (air)	50	35
1275	31f. Lorenzo di Credi	1·00	75
1276	40f. Palma the Elder	1·25	90
MS1277	Two sheets each 130×72 mm. (a) Nos. 1271/3. (b) Nos. 1274/6	4·50	3·25

121 Cruiser *Aurora* and Russian 5r. Stamp, 1922

1977. 60th Anniv of Russian Revolution. Multicoloured.

1278	5f. Type **121**	40	10
1279	5f. Russia S.G. 455	40	10
1280	5f. Russia S.G. 1392	40	10
1281	5f. Russia S.G. 199	40	10
1282	8f. Decemberists' Square, Leningrad and Russia S.G. 983	25	10
1283	8f. Russia S.G. 2122	25	10
1284	8f. Russia S.G. 1041	25	10
1285	8f. Russia S.G. 2653	25	10
1286	11f. Pokrovski Cathedral, Moscow and Russia S.G. 3929	45	10
1287	11f. Russia S.G. 3540	45	10
1288	11f. Russia S.G. 3468	45	10
1289	11f. Russia S.G. 3921	45	10
1290	13f. May Day celebrations, Moscow and Russia S.G. 4518	60	15

1291	13f. Russia S.G. 3585	60	15
1292	13f. Russia S.G. 3024	60	15
1293	13f. Russia S.G. 2471	60	15

The four designs in each value were issued in *se-tenant* blocks of four, each design in the block having the same background.

122 Tanker Unloading (Commerce)

1977. 15th Anniv of Independence. Multicoloured.

1294	1f. Type **122**	20	15
1295	5f. Assembling electric armatures (Economy)	20	15
1296	11f. Native dancers (Tourism)	30	20
1297	14f. Picking coffee (Agriculture)	45	30
1298	17f. National Palace, Bujumbura	55	40

1977. Christmas Charity. Nos. 1271/6 surch **+1F**.

1299	**120**	5f.+1f. mult (postage)	30	15
1300	-	13f.+1f. multicoloured	65	20
1301	-	27f.+1f. multicoloured	95	45
1302	-	18f.+1f. mult (air)	65	25
1303	-	31f.+1f. multicoloured	1·00	45
1304	-	40f.+1f. multicoloured	1·60	60
MS1305		Two sheets as **MS**1277 with 2f. premium on each stamp	4·75	3·50

123 *Madonna and Child* (Solario)

1979. Christmas (1978). Paintings of Virgin and Child by named artists. Multicoloured.

1306	13f. Rubens	85	85
1307	17f. Type **123**	90	90
1308	27f. Tiepolo	1·40	1·40
1309	31f. Gerard David	1·60	1·60
1310	40f. Bellini	2·00	2·00
MS1311	114×120 mm. Nos. 1306/10 (air)	6·75	6·75

1979. Christmas Charity. Nos. 1306/10 surch **+1F**.

1312	-	13f.+1f. multicoloured	85	85
1313	**123**	17f.+1f. multicoloured	90	90
1314	-	27f.+1f. multicoloured	1·40	1·40
1315	-	31f.+1f. multicoloured	1·60	1·60
1316	-	40f.+1f. multicoloured	2·00	2·00
MS1317		As **MS**1311 with 2f. premium on each stamp	6·75	6·75

124 Abyssinian Ground Hornbill

1979. Birds. Multicoloured.

1318	1f. Type **124** (postage)	1·10	60
1319	2f. African darter	1·10	60
1320	3f. Little bee eater	1·10	60
1321	5f. Lesser flamingo	1·50	80
1322	8f. Congo peafowl	1·90	1·10
1323	10f. Purple swamphen	2·10	1·25
1324	20f. Martial eagle	2·40	1·40
1325	27f. Painted stork	3·00	1·75
1326	50f. Saddle-bill stork	4·75	2·50
1327	6f. Type **124** (air)	1·75	1·00
1328	13f. As No. 1319	2·10	1·25
1329	18f. As No. 1320	2·40	1·40
1330	26f. As No. 1321	2·75	1·60
1331	31f. As No. 1322	3·00	1·60
1332	36f. As No. 1323	3·00	1·75
1333	40f. As No. 1324	3·75	2·10
1334	54f. As No. 1325	4·00	2·40
1335	70f. As No. 1326	5·25	3·00

125 Mother and Child

1979. International Year of the Child. Multicoloured.

1336	10f. Type **125**	90	90
1337	20f. Baby	1·40	1·40
1338	27f. Child with doll	1·50	1·50
1339	50f. S.O.S. village, Gitega	2·00	2·00
MS1340	131×85 mm. Nos. 1336/9 additionally inscr "+ 2f."	6·25	6·25

126 *Virgin and Child* (Raffaellino Del Garbo)

1979. Christmas. Virgin and Child paintings by named artists. Multicoloured.

1341	20f. Type **126**	90	90
1342	27f. Giovanni Penni	1·10	1·10
1343	31f. Giulio Romano	1·25	1·25
1344	50f. Detail of *Adoration of the Shepherds* (Jacopo Bassano)	1·75	1·75
MS1345	85×110 mm. Nos. 1341/4 (air)	5·00	5·00

127 Sir Rowland Hill and Penny Black

1979. Death Centenary of Sir Rowland Hill. Multicoloured.

1346	20f. Type **127**	80	80
1347	27f. German East Africa 25p. stamp and Ruanda-Urundi 5c. stamp	95	95
1348	31f. Burundi 1f.25 and 50f. stamps of 1962	1·10	1·10
1349	40f. 4f. (1962) and 14f. (1969) stamps of Burundi	1·25	1·25
1350	60f. Heinrich von Stephan (founder of UPU) and Burundi 14f. UPU stamps of 1974	6·75	3·00
MS1351	110×105 mm. Nos. 1346/50	11·00	7·00

1979. Christmas Charity. Nos. 1341/4 additionally inscr with premium.

1352	20f.+1f. multicoloured	65	65
1353	27f.+1f. multicoloured	1·40	1·40
1354	31f.+1f. multicoloured	1·60	1·60
1355	50f.+1f. multicoloured	2·10	2·10
MS1356	85×110 mm. As **MS**1345 with 2f. premium on each stamp (air)	11·00	7·00

1980. As Nos. 1318/19 and 1321/3 but new values. (a) With copper frames.

1356a	5f. Abyssinian ground hornbill
1356b	10f. African darter
1356c	40f. Lesser flamingo
1356d	45f. Congo peafowl
1356e	50f. Purple swamphen

(b) With grey-green frames.

1356f	5f. As No. 1356a
1356g	10f. As No. 1356b
1356h	40f. As No. 1356c
1356i	45f. As No. 1356d
1356j	50f. As No. 1356e

128 Approaching Hurdle (110 m Hurdles, Thomas Munkelt)

1980. Olympic Medal Winners. Multicoloured.

1357	20f. Type **128**	95	95
1358	20f. Jumping hurdle	95	95
1359	20f. Completing jump	95	95
1360	30f. Discus—beginning to throw	1·40	1·40
1361	30f. Continuing throw	1·40	1·40
1362	30f. Releasing discus	1·40	1·40
1363	40f. Football—running for goal (Czechoslovakia)	1·50	1·50
1364	40f. Kicking ball	1·50	1·50
1365	40f. Saving ball	1·50	1·50
MS1366	145×111 mm. As Nos. 1357/65	8·75	8·75

129 *The Virgin and Child* (Sebastiano Mainardi)

1980. Christmas. Multicoloured.

1367	10f. Type **129**	90	90
1368	30f. *Doni Tondo* (Michelangelo)	1·50	1·50
1369	40f. *The Virgin and Child* (Piero di Cosimo)	2·10	2·10
1370	45f. *The Holy Family* (Fra Bartolomeo)	2·25	2·25
MS1371	134×103 mm. As Nos. 1367/70 (air)	6·75	6·75

130 Congress Emblem

1980. First National Party Congress, Uprona.

1372	**130**	10f. multicoloured	30	30
1373	**130**	40f. multicoloured	1·50	1·50
1374	**130**	45f. multicoloured	1·60	1·60
MS1375		108×68 mm. As Nos. 1372/4 (air)	3·25	3·25

1981. Christmas Charity. Nos. 1367/70 additionally inscr with premium.

1376	10f.+1f. multicoloured	75	75
1377	30f.+1f. multicoloured	1·75	1·75
1378	40f.+1f. multicoloured	2·25	2·25
1379	50f.+1f. multicoloured	2·50	2·50
MS1380	134×103 mm. As Nos. 1376/9 but each stamp with 2f. premium (air)	7·25	7·25

131 Kepler and Dish Aerial

1981. 350th Death Anniv of Johannes Kepler (astronomer). First Earth Satellite Station in Burundi. Multicoloured.

1381	10f. Type **131**	60	60
1382	40f. Satellite and antenna	1·50	1·50
1383	45f. Satellite (different) and antenna	1·90	1·90
MS1384	78×108 mm. Nos. 1381/3	3·50	3·50

132 Giraffes

1982. African Animals (4th series). Multicoloured.

1385	2f. Lion	4·75	2·10
1386	3f. Type **132**	4·75	2·10
1387	5f. Black rhinoceros	4·75	2·10
1388	10f. African buffalo	15·00	6·75
1389	20f. African elephant	23·00	11·50
1390	25f. Hippopotamus	26·00	12·50
1391	30f. Common zebra	30·00	14·50
1392	50f. Warthog	55·00	26·00
1393	60f. Eland	70·00	32·00
1394	65f. Black-backed jackal	85·00	40·00
1395	70f. Cheetah	95·00	45·00
1396	75f. Blue Wildebeest	£100	48·00
1397	85f. Spotted hyena	£120	60·00

1983. Animal Protection Year. Nos. 1385/97 optd with World Wildlife Fund Emblem.

1398	2f. Type **131**	5·00	4·25
1399	3f. Giraffe	5·00	4·25
1400	5f. Black rhinoceros	5·00	4·25
1401	10f. African buffalo	14·00	13·00
1402	20f. African elephant	23·00	20·00
1403	25f. Hippopotamus	26·00	24·00
1404	30f. Common zebra	28·00	25·00
1405	50f. Warthog	55·00	48·00
1406	60f. Eland	70·00	60·00
1407	65f. Jackal (*Canis mesomelas*)	80·00	75·00
1408	70f. Cheetah	95·00	80·00
1409	75f. Blue wildebeest	£100	90·00
1410	85f. Spotted Hyena	£120	£110

133 Flag and National Party Emblem

1983. 20th Anniv (1982) of Independence. Multicoloured.

1411	10f. Type **133**	65	65
1412	25f. Flag and arms	1·00	1·00
1413	30f. Flag and map of Africa	1·10	1·10
1414	50f. Flag and emblem	1·50	1·50
1415	65f. Flag and President Bagaza	2·00	2·00

134 *Virgin and Child* (Lucas Signorelli)

1983. Christmas. Multicoloured.

1416	10f. Type **134**	1·10	1·10
1417	25f. E. Murillo	1·50	1·50
1418	30f. Carlo Crivelli	1·75	1·75
1419	50f. Nicolas Poussin	2·40	2·40
MS1420	106×151 mm. As Nos. 1416/19, but with green backgrounds	6·75	6·75

DESIGNS: Virgin and Child paintings by named artists.

1983. Christmas Charity. Nos. 1416/19 additionally inscr with premium.

1421	10f.+1f. multicoloured	1·10	1·10
1422	25f.+1f. multicoloured	1·50	1·50
1423	30f.+1f. multicoloured	1·75	1·75
1424	50f.+1f. multicoloured	2·40	2·40
MS1425	106×151 mm. As **MS**1420 with 2f. premium on each stamp (air)	6·75	6·75

Nos. 1421/4 have green backgrounds; stamps on **MS**1425 have carmine backgrounds.

135 *Papilio zalmoxis*

1984. Butterflies. Multicoloured.

1426	5f. Type **135**	2·00	85
1427	5f. *Cymothoe coccinata*	2·00	85
1428	10f. *Papilio antimachus*	4·75	2·10
1429	10f. *Asterope pechueli*	4·75	2·10
1430	30f. *Bebearia mardania*	9·25	4·00
1431	30f. *Papilio hesperus*	9·25	4·00
1432	35f. *Euphaedra perseis*	12·00	5·25
1433	35f. *Euphaedra neophron*	12·00	5·25
1434	65f. *Pseudacraea striata*	22·00	9·75
1435	65f. *Euphaedra imperialis*	22·00	9·75

136 Stamps of German East Africa and Belgian Occupation

1984. 19th U.P.U. Congress, Hamburg. Multicoloured.

1436	10f. Type **136**	65	65
1437	30f. 1962 Burundi overprinted stamps	1·10	1·10
1438	35f. 1969 14f. Letter-writing Week and 1982 30f. Zebra stamps	1·25	1·25
1439	65f. Heinrich von Stephan (founder of UPU) and 1974 14f. UPU Centenary stamps	18·00	11·50
MS1440	147×84 mm. As Nos. 1436/9 but each 39×31 mm (air)	21·00	15·00

137 Jesse Owens (runner)

1984. Olympic Games, Los Angeles. Multicoloured.

1441	10f. Type **137**	1·10	1·10

1442	30f. Rafer Johnson (discus thrower)	1·60	1·60
1443	35f. Bob Beamon (long jumper)	1·75	1·75
1444	65f. K. Keino (sprinter)	2·25	2·25
MS1445	119×99 mm. As Nos. 1441/4 but some colours changed (air)	6·75	6·75

138 *Virgin and Child* (Botticelli)

1984. Christmas. Multicoloured.

1446	10f. "Rest on the Flight into Egypt" (Murillo)	30	30
1447	25f. *Virgin and Child* (R. del Garbo)	1·10	1·10
1448	30f. Type **138**	1·60	1·60
1449	50f. *Adoration of the Shepherds* (J. Bassano)	2·00	2·00
MS1450	125×92 mm. As Nos. 1446/9 but some colours changed. Olive border	5·00	5·00

1984. Christmas Charity. As Nos. 1446/49 but with additional premium.

1451	10f.+1f. multicoloured	30	30
1452	25f.+1f. multicoloured	1·10	1·10
1453	30f.+1f. multicoloured	1·60	1·60
1454	50f.+1f. multicoloured	2·00	2·00
MS1455	125×92 mm. As No. **MS**1450 with 2f. premium on each stamp (air)	5·00	5·00

139 Thunbergia

1986. Flowers. Multicoloured.

1456	2f. Type **139** (postage)	1·40	80
1457	3f. African violets	1·40	80
1458	5f. *Clivia*	1·40	80
1459	10f. *Cassia*	1·40	80
1460	20f. Bird of Paradise flower	2·50	1·60
1461	35f. *Gloriosa*	4·50	3·00
1462	70f. Type **139** (air)	2·50	2·10
1463	75f. As No. 1457	2·75	2·25
1464	80f. As No. 1458	2·75	2·40
1465	85f. As No. 1459	3·25	2·75
1466	100f. As No. 1460	3·50	2·75
1467	150f. As No. 1461	6·00	5·00

140 Bombs as Flats

1987. International Peace Year (1986). Multicoloured.

1468	10f. Type **140**	20	20
1469	20f. Molecular diagrams as flower	40	40
1470	30f. Clasped hands across globe	1·10	1·10
1471	40f. Chicks in split globe	1·25	1·25
MS1472	85×120 mm. Nos. 1468/71	3·00	3·00

141 Map, Airplane and Emblem

1987. Tenth Anniv of Great Lakes Countries Economic Community. Multicoloured.

1473	5f. Type **141**	55	55
1474	10f. Map, ear of wheat, cog-wheel and emblem	65	65
1475	15f. Map, factory and emblem	75	75
1476	25f. Map, electricity pylons and emblem	1·60	1·60
1477	35f. Map, flags and emblem	2·25	2·25
MS1478	117×114 mm. Nos. 1473/7 plus label	5·75	5·75

142 Leaves and Sticks Shelter

1988. International Year of Shelter for the Homeless (1987). Multicoloured.

1479	10f. Type **142**	55	55
1480	20f. People living in concrete pipes	70	70
1481	80f. Boys mixing mortar	1·50	1·50
1482	150f. Boys with model house	3·00	3·00
MS1483	124×100 mm. Nos. 1479/82	5·75	5·75

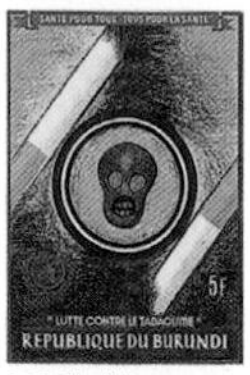

143 Skull between Cigarettes

1989. Anti-smoking Campaign. Multicoloured.

1484	5f. Type **143**	70	70
1485	20f. Cigarettes, lungs and skull	1·40	1·40
1486	80f. Cigarettes piercing skull	2·25	2·25
MS1487	120×80 mm. Nos. 1484/6	4·25	4·25

No. **MS**1487 also shows World Health Organization 40th Anniv emblem.

1989. Various stamps surch.

1487b	20f. on 3f. mult (No. 1457)	70	70
1487c	80f. on 30f. mult (No. 1430)	2·00	2·00
1487d	80f. on 30f. mult (No. 1431)	2·00	2·00
1487e	80f. on 35f. mult (No. 1432)	2·00	2·00
1487f	80f. on 35f. mult (No. 1433)	2·00	2·00
1487g	85f. on 65f. mult (No. 1435)		

144 Pope John Paul II

1990. Papal Visit.

1488	**144**	5f. multicoloured	45	45
1489	**144**	10f. multicoloured	45	45
1490	**144**	20f. multicoloured	70	70
1491	**144**	30f. multicoloured	70	70
1492	**144**	50f. multicoloured	1·40	1·40
1493	**144**	80f. multicoloured	2·00	2·00

145 Hippopotamus

1991. Animals. Multicoloured.

1495	5f. Type **145**	1·10	75
1496	10f. Hen and cockerel	1·10	75
1497	20f. Lion	1·10	75
1498	30f. Elephant	1·10	1·10
1499	50f. Helmet guineafowl (*Pintade*)	3·00	2·25
1500	80f. Crocodile	4·50	3·25
MS1501	109×123 mm. Nos. 1495/1500	16·00	8·75

146 Drummer

1992. Traditional Dancing. Multicoloured.

1502	15f. Type **146**	25	25
1503	30f. Men dancing	40	40
1504	115f. Group of drummers (horiz)	1·90	1·90
1505	200f. Men dancing in fields (horiz)	3·25	3·25
MS1506	120×105 mm. Nos. 1502/5	5·75	5·75

147 *Impatiens petersiana*

1992. Flowers. Multicoloured.

1507	15f. Type **147**	90	65
1508	20f. *Lachenalia aloides* "Nelsonii"	90	65
1509	30f. Egyptian lotus	1·40	1·00
1510	50f. Kaffir lily	3·00	2·25
MS1511	105×120 mm. Nos. 1507/10	6·25	4·50

148 Pigtail Macaque

1992. Air. Animals. Multicoloured.

1512	100f. Type **148**	2·40	1·75
1513	115f. Grevy's zebra	2·75	2·10
1514	200f. Ox	4·00	3·00
1515	220f. Eastern white pelican	5·00	3·75
MS1516	105×120 mm. Nos. 1512/15	14·00	10·00

149 People holding Hands and Flag

1992. 30th Anniv of Independence. Multicoloured.

1517	30f. Type **149**	20	20
1518	85f. State flag	80	80
1519	110f. Independence monument (vert)	1·10	1·10
1520	115f. As No. 1518	1·10	1·10
1521	120f. Map (vert)	1·40	1·40
1522	140f. Type **149**	1·50	1·50
1523	200f. As No. 1519	2·10	2·10
1524	250f. As No. 1521	2·75	2·75

150 *Russula ingens*

1992. Fungi. Multicoloured.

1525	10f. Type **150**	15	15
1526	15f. *Russula brunneorigida*	20	20
1527	20f. *Amanita zambiana*	25	30
1528	30f. *Russula subfistulosa*	40	45
1529	75f. *Russula meleagris*	90	95
1530	85f. As No. 1529	1·00	1·10
1531	100f. *Russula immaculata*	1·25	1·25
1532	110f. Type **150**	1·40	1·40
1533	115f. As No. 1526	1·40	1·40
1534	120f. *Russula sejuncta*	1·40	1·60
1535	130f. As No. 1534	1·50	1·60
1536	250f. *Afroboletus luteolus*	3·00	3·25

151 Columbus's Fleet, Treasure and Globes

1992. 500th Anniv of Discovery of America by Columbus. Multicoloured.

1541	200f. Type **151**	2·00	2·00
1542	400f. American produce, globes and Columbus's fleet	4·25	4·25

152 Serval

1992. The Serval. Multicoloured.

1543	30f. Type **152**	60	50
1544	130f. Pair sitting and crouching	2·40	2·00
1545	200f. Pair, one standing over the other	3·75	3·00
1546	220f. Heads of pair	4·00	3·50

153 Running

1992. Olympic Games, Barcelona. Multicoloured.

1547	130f. Type **153**	1·50	1·50
1548	500f. Hurdling	5·25	5·25

154 Emblems

1992. International Nutrition Conference, Rome. Multicoloured.

1549	200f. Type **154**	2·00	2·00
1550	220f. Woman's face made from vegetables (G. Arcimbolo)	2·40	2·40

155 Horsemen

1992. Christmas. Details of *Adoration of the Magi* by Gentile da Fabriano. Multicoloured.

1551	100f. Type **155**	90	90
1552	130f. Three Kings	1·10	1·10
1553	250f. Holy family	2·50	2·50
MS1554	109×91 mm. Nos. 1551/3 (sold at 580f.)	4·50	4·50

156 Flags of Member Countries and European Community Emblem

1993. European Single Market. Multicoloured.

1555	130f. Type **156**	1·25	1·25
1556	500f. Europe shaking hands with Africa	5·00	5·00

157 Indonongo

1993. Musical Instruments. Multicoloured.

1557	200f. Type **157**	2·00	2·00
1558	220f. Ingoma (drum)	2·25	2·25
1559	250f. Ikembe (xylophone)	2·50	2·50
1560	300f. Umuduri (musical bow)	3·25	3·25

158 Broad Blue-banded Swallowtail

1993. Butterflies. Multicoloured.

1561	130f. Type **158**	1·50	1·25
1562	200f. Green charaxes	2·40	2·10
1563	250f. Migratory glider	3·00	2·50
1564	300f. Red swallowtail	3·75	3·50
MS1565	84×123 mm. Nos. 1561/4 (sold at 980f.)	10·00	9·00

159 Players, Stadium, United States Flag and Statue of Liberty

1993. World Cup Football Championship, U.S.A. (1994). Multicoloured.

1566	130f. Type **159**	1·25	1·25
1567	200f. Players, stadium, United States flag and Golden Gate Bridge	2·50	2·50

160 Cattle

1993. Domestic Animals. Multicoloured.

1568	100f. Type **160**	1·00	1·00
1569	120f. Sheep	1·10	1·10
1570	130f. Pigs	1·25	1·25
1571	250f. Goats	2·50	2·50

161 Woman with Baby and Two Men

1993. Christmas. Each orange and black.

1572	100f. Type **161**	1·25	1·25
1573	130f. Nativity	1·50	1·50
1574	250f. Woman with baby and three men	3·00	3·00
MS1575	127×82 mm. Nos. 1572/4 (sold at 580f.)	5·75	5·75

162 Elvis Presley

1994. Entertainers. Multicoloured.

1576	60f. Type **162**	30	30
1577	115f. Mick Jagger	55	55
1578	120f. John Lennon	60	60
1579	200f. Michael Jackson	1·00	1·00
MS1580	80×114 mm. Nos. 1576/9	2·40	2·40

163 "The Discus Thrower" (statue)

1994. Centenary of International Olympic Committee.

1581	**163**	150f. multicoloured	75	75

164 Pres. Buyoya handing over Baton of Power to Pres. Ndadaye

1994. First Anniv of First Multi-party Elections in Burundi. Multicoloured.

1582	30f.+10f. Type **164**	20	20
1583	110f.+10f. Pres. Ndadaye (first elected President) giving inauguration speech	60	60
1584	115f.+10f. Arms on map	60	60
1585	120f.+10f. Warrior on map	65	65

165 Madonna, China

1994. Christmas. Multicoloured.

1586	115f. Type **165**	55	55
1587	120f. Madonna, Japan	60	60
1588	250f. Black Virgin, Poland	1·25	1·25
MS1589	80×118 mm. No. 1588	1·25	1·25

166 Emblem and Earth

1995. 50th Anniversaries. Multicoloured.

1590	115f. Type **166** (FAO)	55	55
1591	120f. UNO emblems and dove	60	60

167 *Cassia didymobotrya*

1995. Flowers. Multicoloured.

1592	15f. Type **167**	15	15
1593	20f. *Mitragyna rubrostipulosa*	15	15
1594	30f. *Phytolacca dodecandra*	25	20
1595	85f. *Acanthus pubescens*	65	60
1596	100f. *Bulbophyllum comatum*	80	75
1597	110f. "*Angraecum evrardianum*	90	80
1598	115f. *Eulophia burundiensis*	90	80
1599	120f. *Habenaria adolphii*	1·00	90

168 Otraca Bus

1995. Transport. Multicoloured.

1600	30f. Type **168**	15	15
1601	115f. Transintra lorry	65	65
1602	120f. Lake ferry	90	70
1603	250f. Air Burundi Beeck King Air	1·40	1·40

169 Boy with Panga

1995. Christmas. Multicoloured.

1604	100f. Type **169**	55	55
1605	130f. Boy with sheaf of wheat	75	75
1606	250f. Mother and children	1·40	1·40
MS1607	126×82 mm. Nos. 1604/6 (sold at 580f.)	5·75	5·75

170 Venuste Niyongabo

1996. Olympic Games, Atlanta. Runners. Multicoloured.

1608	130f. Type **170** (5000 m gold medal winner)	40	40
1609	500f. Arthemon Hatungimana	1·50	1·50

171 Hadada Ibis

1996. Birds. Multicoloured.

1610	15f. Type **171**	25	25
1611	20f. Egyptian goose	25	25
1612	30f. African fish eagle	25	25
1613	120f. Goliath heron	75	75
1614	165f. South African crowned crane	1·00	1·00
1615	220f. African jacana	1·40	1·40

172 Marlier's Julie

1996. Fish of Lake Tanganyika. Multicoloured.

1616	30f. Type **172**	25	20
1617	115f. *Cyphotilapia frontosa*	75	60
1618	120f. *Lamprologus brichardi*	75	60
1619	250f. Stone squeaker	1·50	1·25
MS1620	108×108 mm. Nos. 1616/19 (sold at 615f.)	6·00	6·00

173 Children

1998. 50th Anniv of S.O.S Children's Villages. Multicoloured.

1621	100f. Type **173**	25	25
1622	250f. Flags, "50" and children waving	65	65
1623	270f. Children dancing around flag	70	70

174 Madonna and Child

1999. Christmas (1996–98). Multicoloured.

1624	100f. Type **174** (1996)	25	25
1625	130f. Madonna and Child (different) (1997)	30	30
1626	250f. Madonna and Child (different) (1998)	65	65
MS1627	125×82 mm. Nos. 1624/6 (sold at 580f.)	5·75	5·75

175 Diana, Princess of Wales

1999. Second Death Anniv of Diana, Princess of Wales.

1628	**175**	100f. multicoloured	20	20
1629	**175**	250f. multicoloured	20	20
1630	**175**	300f. multicoloured	50	50

176 Danny Kaye (entertainer) holding African Baby

2000. New Millennium. "A World Free from Hunger".

1631	**176**	350f. multicoloured	60	60

Pt. 1

BUSHIRE

An Iranina seaport. Stamps issued during the British occupation in the 1914-18 War.

20 chahis = 1 kran, 10 krans = 1 toman

1915. Portrait stamps of Iran (1911) optd **BUSHIRE Under British Occupation**.

1	**57**	1ch. orange and green	70·00	75·00
2	**57**	2ch. brown and red	70·00	65·00
3	**57**	3ch. green and grey	85·00	85·00
4	**57**	5ch. red and brown	£475	£425
5	**57**	6ch. lake and green	70·00	48·00
6	**57**	9ch. lilac and brown	70·00	85·00
7	**57**	10ch. brown and red	75·00	80·00
8	**57**	12ch. blue and green	90·00	85·00
9	**57**	24ch. green and purple	£170	95·00
10	**57**	1kr. red and blue	£160	55·00
11	**57**	2kr. red and green	£425	£300
12	**57**	3kr. black and lilac	£350	£350
13	**57**	5kr. blue and red	£275	£225
14	**57**	10kr. red and brown	£250	£200

1915. Coronation issue of Iran optd **BUSHIRE Under British Occupation**.

15	**66**	1ch. blue and red	£700	£550
16	**66**	2ch. red and blue	£11000	£11000
17	**66**	3ch. green	£800	£800
18	**66**	5ch. red	£10000	£10000
19	**66**	6ch. red and green	£8500	£8500
20	**66**	9ch. violet and brown	£1300	£1000
21	**66**	10ch. brown and green	£1900	£1900
22	**66**	12ch. blue	£2250	£2250
23	**66**	24ch. black and brown	£900	£700
24	**67**	1kr. black, brown and silver	£900	£850
25	**67**	2kr. red, blue and silver	£850	£900
26	**67**	3kr. black, lilac and silver	£950	£950
27	**67**	5kr. slate, brown and silver	£900	£950
28	-	1t. black, violet and gold	£800	£800
29	-	3t. red, lake and gold	£6500	£6000

Pt. 1

BUSSAHIR (BASHAHR)

A state in the Punjab, India. Now uses Indian stamps.

12 pies = 1 anna; 16 annas = 1 rupee.

1

1895. Various frames. Imperf, perf or roul.

9	**1**	¼a. pink	95·00	£130
10	**1**	½a. grey	25·00	£160
11	**1**	1a. red	25·00	£100
12	**1**	2a. yellow	35·00	£100
13	**1**	4a. violet	32·00	£100
14	**1**	8a. brown	25·00	£120
15	**1**	12a. green	85·00	£140
16	**1**	1r. blue	55·00	£130

1896. Similar types, but inscriptions on white ground and inscr "POSTAGE" instead of "STAMP".

27	¼a. violet	23·00	23·00
37	¼a. red	5·00	15·00
25	½a. blue	15·00	24·00
26	1a. olive	22·00	50·00
32	1a. red	5·00	18·00
41	2a. yellow	75·00	95·00
36	4a. red	75·00	£150

Pt. 1

CAICOS ISLANDS

Separate issues for these islands, part of the Turks and Caicos Islands group, appeared from 1981 to 1985.

100 cents = 1 dollar.

1981. Nos. 514, 518, 520, 523 and 525/7 of Turks and Caicos Islands optd **CAICOS ISLANDS**.

1	1c. Indigo hamlet	15	15
2	5c. Spanish grunt	20	20
3	8c. Four-eyed butterflyfish	20	20
4	20c. Queen angelfish	35	30
5	50c. Royal gramma ("Fairy Basslet")	40	1·00
6	$1 Fin-spot wrasse	60	1·75
7	$2 Stoplight parrotfish	1·10	3·25

1981. Royal Wedding. Nos. 653/6 of Turks and Caicos Islands optd. (A) **Caicos Islands**.

8A	35c. Prince Charles and Lady Diana Spencer	20	25
9A	65c. Kensington Palace	30	40
10A	90c. Prince Charles as Colonel of the Welsh Guards	40	50
MS11A	96×82 mm. $2 Glass Coach	1·00	2·00

(B) **CAICOS ISLANDS**.

8B	35c. Prince Charles and Lady Diana Spencer	30	70
9B	65c. Kensington Palace	40	1·00
10B	90c. Prince Charles as Colonel of the Welsh Guards	50	1·50
MS11B	96×82 mm. $2 Glass Coach	1·00	2·50

1981. Royal Wedding. As Nos. 657/9 of Turks and Caicos Islands, but each inscr "Caicos Islands". Multicoloured. Self-adhesive.

12	20c. Lady Diana Spencer	30	40
13	$1 Prince Charles	80	1·25
14	$2 Prince Charles and Lady Diana Spencer	4·00	5·50

4 Queen or Pink Conch and Lobster Fishing, South Caicos

1983. Multicoloured.

15	8c. Type **4**	1·50	85
16	10c. Hawksbill turtle, East Caicos	1·75	1·00
17	20c. Arawak Indians and idol, Middle Caicos	1·75	1·00
18	35c. Boat-building, North Caicos	2·00	1·50
19	50c. Marine biologist at work, Pine Cay	3·00	2·25
20	95c. Boeing 707 airliner at new airport, Providenciales	5·50	3·00
21	$1.10 Columbus's *Pinta*, West Caicos	5·50	3·00
22	$2 Fort George Cay	3·75	4·75
23	$3 Pirates Anne Bonny and Calico Jack at Parrot Cay	6·00	4·75

5 Goofy and Patch

1983. Christmas. Multicoloured.

30	1c. Type **5**	10	30
31	1c. Chip and Dale	10	30
32	2c. Morty	10	30
33	2c. Morty and Ferdie	10	30
34	3c. Goofy and Louie	10	30
35	3c. Donald Duck, Huey, Dewey and Louie	10	30
36	50c. Uncle Scrooge	4·00	3·25
37	70c. Mickey Mouse and Ferdie	4·25	3·75
38	$1.10 Pinocchio, Jiminy Cricket and Figaro	5·00	4·50
MS39	126×101 mm. $2 Morty and Ferdie	3·75	3·50

6 *Leda and the Swan*

1984. 500th Birth Anniv of Raphael. Multicoloured.

40	35c. Type **6**	75	50
41	50c. *Study of Apollo for Parnassus*	1·00	70
42	95c. *Study of two figures for the battle of Ostia*	2·00	1·25
43	$1.10 *Study for the Madonna of the Goldfinch*	2·00	1·50
MS44	71×100 mm. $2.50, *The Garvagh Madonna*	3·00	3·25

7 High Jumping

1984. Olympic Games, Los Angeles.

45	**7**	4c. multicoloured	10	10
46	-	25c. multicoloured	30	20
47	-	65c. black, deep blue and blue	1·75	50
48	-	$1.10 multicoloured	1·25	85
MS49		105×75 mm. $2 multicoloured	2·25	3·00

DESIGNS—VERT: 25c. Archery; 65c. Cycling; $1.10, Football. HORIZ: $2.50, Show jumping.

8 Horace Horsecollar and Clarabelle Cow

1984. Easter. Walt Disney Cartoon Characters. Multicoloured.

50	35c. Type **8**	1·40	60
51	45c. Mickey and Minnie Mouse, and Chip	1·50	75
52	75c. Gyro Gearloose, Chip 'n Dale	1·90	1·25
53	85c. Mickey Mouse, Chip 'n Dale	1·90	1·40
MS54	127×101 mm. $2.20, Donald Duck	5·50	3·75

1984. Universal Postal Union Congress Hamburg. Nos. 20/1 optd **UNIVERSAL POSTAL UNION 1874-1984** and emblem.

55	95c. Boeing 707 airliner at new airport, Providenciales	1·00	1·25
56	$1.10 Columbus's "Pinta", West Caicos	1·25	1·50

1984. "Ausipex" International Stamp Exhibition, Melbourne. No. 22 optd **AUSIPEX 1984**.

57	$2 Fort George Cay	2·40	2·50

11 Seamen sighting American Manatees

1984. 492nd Anniv of Columbus's First Landfall. Multicoloured.

58	10c. Type **11**	1·00	80
59	70c. Columbus's fleet	3·75	3·25
60	$1 First landing in the West Indies	4·25	3·75
MS61	99×69 mm. $2 Fleet of Columbus (different)	2·75	3·00

12 Donald Duck and Mickey Mouse with Father Christmas

1984. Christmas. Walt Disney Cartoon Characters. Multicoloured.

62	20c. Type **12**	1·50	85
63	35c. Donald Duck opening refrigerator	1·75	1·00
64	50c. Mickey Mouse, Donald Duck and toy train	2·50	2·25
65	75c. Donald Duck and parcels	3·00	3·00
66	$1.10 Donald Duck and carol singers	3·25	3·25
MS67	127×102 mm. $2 Donald Duck as Christmas tree	3·75	4·00

13 Thick-billed Vireo

1985. Birth Bicentenary of John J. Audubon (ornithologist). Multicoloured.

68	20c. Type **13**	1·75	70
69	35c. Black-faced grassquit	2·00	95
70	50c. Pearly-eyed thrasher	2·25	1·50
71	$1 Greater Antillean bullfinch	2·75	2·50
MS72	100×70 mm. $2 Striped-headed tanager	3·50	3·50

14 Two Children learning to Read and Write (Education)

1985. International Youth Year. 40th Anniv of United Nations. Multicoloured.

73	16c. Type **14**	20	25
74	35c. Two children on playground swings (Health)	50	55
75	70c. Boy and girl (Love)	1·00	1·10
76	90c. Three children (Peace)	1·25	1·40
MS77	101×71 mm. $2 Child, dove carrying ears of wheat and map of the Americas	2·75	3·25

15 Douglas DC-3 on Ground

1985. 40th Anniv of International Civil Aviation Organization. Multicoloured.

78	35c. Type **15**	3·00	55
79	75c. Convair CV 440 Metropolitan	4·00	1·40
80	90c. Britten Norman Islander	4·00	1·60
MS81	100×70 mm. $2.20, Hand-gliding over the Caicos Islands	3·00	3·25

16 The Queen Mother visiting Foundation for the Disabled, Leatherhead

1985. Life and Times of Queen Elizabeth the Queen Mother. Multicoloured.

82	35c. Type **16**	1·25	55
83	65c. With Princess Anne (horiz)	1·75	95
84	95c. At Epsom, 1961	2·25	1·60
MS85	56×85 mm. $2 Visiting Royal Hospital, Chelsea	4·75	3·00

1985. 150th Birth Anniv of Mark Twain (author). Designs as T **118** of Anguilla, showing Walt Disney cartoon characters in scenes from *Tom Sawyer, Detective*. Multicoloured.

86	8c. Huckleberry Finn (Goofy) and Tom Sawyer (Mickey Mouse) reading reward notice	60	20
87	35c. Huck and Tom meeting Jake Dunlap	1·75	65
88	95c. Huck and Tom spying on Jubiter Dunlap	3·25	2·00
89	$1.10 Huck and Tom with hound (Pluto)	3·25	2·25
MS90	127×101 mm. Tom unmasking Jubiter Dunlap	4·75	4·25

1985. Birth Bicentenaries of Grimm Brothers (folklorists). Designs as T **119** of Anguilla, showing Walt Disney cartoon characters in scenes from *Six Soldiers of Fortune*. Multicoloured.

91	16c. The Soldier (Donald Duck) with his meagre pay	1·75	30
92	25c. The Soldier meeting the Strong Man (Horace Horsecollar)	2·00	45
93	65c. The Soldier meeting the Marksman (Mickey Mouse)	3·50	1·25
94	$1.35 The Fast Runner (Goofy) winning the race against the Princess (Daisy Duck)	4·25	2·25
MS95	126×101 mm. $2 The Soldier and the Strong Man with sack of gold	4·75	4·00

Pt. 21

CAMBODIA

A kingdom in south-east Asia.

From 1887 Cambodia was part of the Union of Indo-China. In 1949 it became an Associated State of the French Union, in 1953 it attained sovereign independence and in 1955 it left the Union.

Following the introduction of a republican constitution in 1970 the name of the country was changed to Khmer Republic and in 1975 to Kampuchea.

In 1989 it reverted to the name of Cambodia. Under a new constitution in 1993 it became a parliamentary monarchy.

1951. 100 cents = 1 piastre.
1955. 100 cents = 1 riel.

1 "Apsara" or Dancing Nymph

2 Throne Room, Phnom-Penh

3 King Norodom Sihanouk

1951

1	**1**	10c. green and deep green	50	3·50
2	**1**	20c. brown and red	45	1·50
3	**1**	30c. blue and violet	55	60
4	**1**	40c. blue and ultramarine	1·10	90
5	**2**	50c. green and deep green	95	85
6	**3**	80c. green and blue	1·70	4·25
7	**2**	1p. violet and blue	1·30	45
8	**3**	1p.10 red and lake	2·10	4·25
9	**1**	1p.50 red and lake	2·00	1·40
10	**2**	1p.50 blue and indigo	2·10	2·30
11	**3**	1p.50 brown and chocolate	2·10	1·80
12	**3**	1p.90 blue and indigo	3·75	6·00
13	**2**	2p. brown and red	2·75	75
14	**3**	3p. brown and red	4·25	2·30
15	**1**	5p. violet and blue	12·50	5·75
16	**2**	10p. blue and violet	13·50	10·50
17	**3**	15p. violet and deep violet	28·00	45·00
MS17a		Three sheets, each 130×90 mm. Nos. 15/17. Price for 3 sheets	£120	£100

1952. Students' Aid Fund. Surch **AIDE A L'ETUDIANT** and premium.

18		1p.10+40c. red and lake	3·50	13·00
19		1p.90+60c. blue & indigo	3·50	13·00
20		3p.+1p. brown and red	3·50	13·00
21	**1**	5p.+2p. violet and blue	3·75	13·00

5 "Kinnari"

1953. Air.

22	**5**	50c. green	1·10	2·10
23	**5**	3p. red	2·00	1·80
24	**5**	3p.30 violet	2·50	5·25
25	**5**	4p. blue and brown	2·75	1·20
26	**5**	5p.10 ochre, red and brown	4·00	6·75
27	**5**	6p.50 purple and brown	3·75	8·75
28	**5**	9p. green and mauve	5·00	13·00
29	**5**	11p.50 multicoloured	9·75	18·00

30	5	30p. ochre, brown and green	16·00	26·00
MS30a		Three sheets, each 129×100 mm. Nos. 22, 24, 26 and 30 (sold at 50p.); Nos. 23, 25 and 29 (sold at 25p.); Nos. 27/8 (sold at 20p.) Price for 3 sheets	£180	£160

6 Arms of Cambodia

7 "Postal Transport"

1954

31	-	10c. red	1·20	1·80
32	-	20c. green	1·40	50
33	-	30c. blue	1·40	2·10
34	-	40c. violet	1·40	85
35	-	50c. purple	1·40	25
36	-	70c. brown	1·60	3·25
37	-	1p. violet	1·70	1·80
38	-	1p.50 red	1·70	60
39	6	2p. red	1·30	45
40	6	2p.50 green	1·60	60
41	7	2p.50 green	2·50	2·10
42	6	3p. blue	2·10	1·70
43	7	4p. sepia	3·25	2·75
44	6	4p.50 violet	2·75	1·80
45	7	5p. red	3·50	2·50
46	6	6p. brown	3·00	2·50
47	7	10p. violet	4·00	2·75
48	7	15p. blue	5·00	5·00
49	-	20p. blue	11·50	5·75
50	-	30p. green	18·00	9·75
MS50a		Three sheets, each 120×20 mm. Nos. 31/5 (sold at 2p.); Nos. 39/40, 42, 44 and 46 (sold at 20p.); Nos. 41, 43, 45 and 47/8 (sold at 40p.) and one sheet 160×92 mm containing Nos. 36/8 and 49/50 (sold at 60p.) Price for 4 sheets	£150	£140

DESIGNS—VERT: 10c. to 50c. View of Phnom Daun Penah. HORIZ: 70c. 1, 1p.50, 20, 30p. East Gate, Temple of Angkor.

8 King Norodom Suramarit

1955

51		50c. blue	25	20
52	8	50c. violet	35	30
53	8	1r. red	40	30
54	8	2r. blue	70	45
55	-	2r.50 brown	1·00	35
56	-	4r. green	1·40	45
57	-	6r. lake	1·90	1·20
58	8	7r. brown	2·30	1·40
59	-	15r. lilac	3·25	1·20
60	8	20r. green	4·75	4·25

PORTRAIT: Nos. 51, 55/7 and 59, Queen Kossamak.

For stamps as Nos. 58 and 60, but with black border, see Nos. 101/2.

9 King and Queen of Cambodia

1955. Coronation (1st issue).

61	9	1r.50 sepia and brown	75	45
62	9	2r. black and blue	75	55
63	9	3r. red and orange	95	30
64	9	5r. black and green	1·50	55
65	9	10r. purple and violet	2·50	55

See Nos. 66/71.

10 King Norodom Suramarit

1956. Coronation (2nd issue).

66	10	2r. red	1·10	2·30
67	-	3r. blue	1·60	3·25
68	-	5r. green	2·40	4·50
69	10	10r. green	6·25	9·25
70	10	30r. violet	13·00	22·00
71	-	50r. purple	25·00	25·00

PORTRAIT—VERT: 3, 5, 50r. Queen of Cambodia.

11 Prince Sihanouk, Flags and Globe

1957. First Anniv of Admission of Cambodia to UNO.

72	11	2r. red, blue and green	1·20	90
73	11	4r.50 blue	1·20	90
74	11	8r.50 red	1·20	90

12

1957. 2,500th Anniv of Buddhism. (a) With premiums.

75	12	1r.50+50c. bis, red & bl	1·40	1·80
76	12	6r.50+1r.50 bis, red & pur	2·10	2·75
77	12	8r.+2r. bistre, red & blue	3·50	4·50

(b) Colours changed and premiums omitted.

78		1r.50 red	1·30	1·00
79		6r.50 violet	1·50	1·20
80		8r. green	1·50	1·50

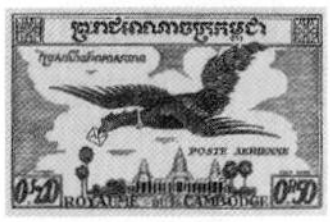

13 Mythological Bird

1957. Air.

81	13	50c. lake	35	10
82	13	1r. green	60	10
83	13	4r. blue	1·80	45
84	13	50r. red	7·50	2·75
85	13	100r. red, green and blue	13·00	5·00
MS85a		160×92 mm. Nos. 81/5 (sold at 160r.)	13·00	28·00

14 King Ang Duong

1958. King Ang Duong Commemoration.

86	14	1r.50 brown and violet	55	45
87	14	5r. bistre and black	70	65
88	14	10r. sepia and purple	1·40	90
MS88a		156×92 mm. Nos. 86/8 (sold at 25r.)	6·00	5·00

15 King Norodom I

1958. King Norodom I Commemoration.

89	15	2r. brown and blue	60	35
90	15	6r. green and orange	85	55
91	15	15r. brown and green	1·70	1·10
MS91a		156×92 mm. Nos. 89/91 (sold at 32r.)	6·00	4·50

16 Children

1959. Children's World Friendship.

92	16	20c. purple	25	35
93	16	50c. blue	45	45
94	16	80c. red	90	85

1959. Red Cross Fund. Nos. 92/4 surch with red cross and premium.

95		20c.+20c. purple	30	45
96		50c.+30c. blue	65	65
97		80c.+50c. red	1·30	1·20

18 Prince Sihanouk, Plan of Port and Freighter

1960. Inauguration of Sihanoukville Port.

98	18	2r. sepia and red	55	55
99	18	5r. brown and blue	55	65
100	18	20r. blue and violet	2·00	2·00

1960. King Norodom Suramarit Mourning issue. Nos. 58 and 60 reissued with black border.

101	8	7r. brown and black	3·00	4·25
102	8	20r. green and black	3·00	4·25

19 Sacred Plough in Procession

1960. Festival of the Sacred Furrow.

103	19	1r. purple	60	45
104	19	2r. brown	75	65
105	19	3r. green	1·20	90

20 Child and Book ("Education")

1960. "Works of the Five Year Plan".

106	20	2r. brown, blue and green	50	30
107	-	3r. green and brown	65	35
108	-	4r. violet, green and pink	65	45
109	-	6r. brown, orange & green	75	55
110	-	10r. blue, green and bistre	1·80	1·10
111	-	25r. red and lake	3·75	2·20
MS111a		Two sheets, each 150×100 mm. Nos. 106, 109 and 111 (sold at 42r.); Nos. 107/8 and 110 (sold at 23r.) Price for 2 sheets	5·25	6·50

DESIGNS—HORIZ: 3r. Chhouksar Barrage ("Irrigation"); 6r. Carpenter and huts ("Construction"); 10r. Rice-field ("Agriculture"). VERT: 4r. Industrial scene and books ("National balance-sheet"); 25r. Anointing children ("Child welfare").

21 Flag and Dove of Peace

1961. Peace. Flag in red and blue.

112	21	1r.50 green and brown	30	45
113	21	5r. red	45	65
114	21	7r. blue and green	60	90
MS114a		147×93 mm. Nos. 112/14 (sold at 16r.)	20·00	11·00
MS114b		as MS114a but stamps in new colours (sold at 20r.)	4·00	11·00

23 Frangipani

1961. Cambodian Flowers.

115	23	2r. yellow, green & mauve	50	55
116	-	5r. mauve, green and blue	80	1·10
117	-	10r. red, green and blue	2·30	2·00
MS117a		130×100 mm. Nos. 115/17 (sold at 20r.)	7·00	7·00

FLOWERS: 5r. Oleander. 10r. Amaryllis.

24 "Rama" (from temple door, Baphoun)

1961. Cambodian Soldiers Commemoration.

118	24	1r. mauve	50	20
118a	24	2r. blue	1·90	1·80
119	24	3r. green	85	30
120	24	6r. orange	1·00	45
MS120a		150×85 mm. Nos. 118/20 (sold at 12r.)	3·25	3·25

25 Prince Norodom Sihanouk and Independence Monument

1961. Independence Monument.

121	25	2r. green (postage)	80	35
122	25	4r. sepia	80	45
123	25	7r. multicoloured (air)	75	75
124	25	30r. red, blue and green	2·30	2·30
125	25	50r. multicoloured	3·50	3·75
MS125a		Two sheets, each 150×85 mm. Nos. 121/2 (sold at 10r.); Nos. 123/5 (sold at 100r.). Price for 2 sheets	15·00	11·00

1961. Sixth World Buddhist Conference. Optd **VIe CONFERENCE MONDIALE BOUDDHIQUE 12-11-1961.**

126	6	2p.50 (2r.50) green	90	55
127	6	4p.50 (4r.50) violet	1·40	85

27 Power Station (Czech Aid)

1962. Foreign Aid Programme.

128	27	2r. lake and red	30	20
129	-	3r. brown, green and blue	35	20
130	-	4r. brown, red and blue	35	30
131	-	5r. purple and green	55	35
132	-	6r. brown and blue	1·00	35
MS132a		150×85 mm. Nos. 128/32 (sold at 25r.)	7·50	5·00

DESIGNS: 3r. Motorway (American Aid); 4r. Textile Factory (Chinese Aid); 5r. Friendship Hospital (Soviet Aid); 6r. Airport (French Aid).

28 Campaign Emblem

1962. Malaria Eradication.

133	28	2r. purple and brown	35	30
134	28	4r. green and brown	40	35
135	28	6r. violet and bistre	35	45

29 Curucmas

1962. Cambodian Fruits (1st issue).

136	29	2r. yellow and brown	45	45
137	-	4r. green and turquoise	65	55
138	-	6r. red, green and blue	75	85
MS138a		150×85 mm. Nos. 136/8 (sold at 15r.)	6·00	3·75

FRUITS: 4r. Lychees. 6r. Mangosteens.

1962. Cambodian Fruits (2nd issue).

139		2r. brown and green	75	35
140		5r. green and brown	1·10	55
141		9r. brown and green	1·30	75

DESIGNS—VERT: 2r. Pineapples. 5r. Sugar-cane. 9r. "Bread" trees.

1962. Surch.

142	16	50c. on 80c. red	55	35
150	-	3r. on 2r.50 brn (No. 55)	75	45

1962. Inauguration of Independence Monument. Surch **INAUGURATION DU MONUMENT** and new value.

143	**25**	3r. on 2r. green (postage)	55	35
144	**25**	12r. on 7r. mult (air)	1·50	1·00

32 Campaign Emblem, Corn and Maize

1963. Freedom from Hunger.

145	**32**	3r. chestnut, brown & blue	50	45
146	**32**	6r. chestnut, brown & blue	50	45

33 Temple Preah Vihear

1963. Reunification of Preah Vihear Temple with Cambodia.

147	**33**	3r. brown, purple & green	40	35
148	**33**	6r. green, orange and blue	70	55
149	**33**	15r. brown, blue & green	1·10	90

35 Kep sur Mer

1963. Cambodian Resorts. Multicoloured.

151	3r. Koh Tonsay (vert)	40	30
152	7r. Popokvil (waterfall) (vert)	65	35
153	20r. Type **35**	2·10	90

1963. Red Cross Centenary. Surch 1863 1963 **CENTENAIRE DE LA CROIX-ROUGE** and premium.

154	**28**	4r.+40c. green & brown	65	75
155	**28**	6r.+60c. violet & bistre	1·00	1·10

37 Scales of Justice

1963. 15th Anniv of Declaration of Human Rights.

156	**37**	1r. green, red and blue	40	45
157	**37**	3r. red, blue and green	70	55
158	**37**	12r. blue, green and red	1·30	1·30

38 Kouprey

1964. Wild Animal Protection.

159	**38**	50c. brown, green & chest	85	35
160	**38**	3r. brown, chestnut & grn	1·20	55
161	**38**	6r. brown, blue and green	1·80	1·10

39 Black-billed Magpie

1964. Birds.

162	**39**	3r. blue, green and indigo	1·10	65
163	-	6r. orange, purple & blue	1·80	1·00
164	-	12r. green and purple	3·25	2·00

BIRDS: 6r. River kingfisher. 12r. Grey heron.

40 "Hanuman"

1964. Air.

165	**40**	5r. mauve, brown & blue	65	45
166	**40**	10r. bistre, mauve & green	1·00	55
167	**40**	20r. bistre, violet and blue	1·70	1·10
168	**40**	40r. bistre, blue and red	3·75	2·00
169	**40**	80r. orange, green & purple	6·00	5·00

1964. Air Olympic Games, Tokyo. Surch **JEUX OLYMPIQUES TOKYO-1964**, Olympic rings and value.

170	3r. on 5r. mve, brn and bl	60	35
171	6r. on 10r. bis, mve & grn	1·00	55
172	9r. on 20r. bistre, vio & bl	1·10	90
173	12r. on 40r. bis, bl & red	2·30	1·40

42 Airline Emblem

1964. Eighth Anniv of Royal Air Cambodia.

174	**42**	1r.50 red and violet	25	20
175	**42**	3r. red and blue	45	30
176	**42**	7r.50 red and blue	90	45

43 Prince Norodom Sihanouk

1964. Tenth Anniv of Foundation of Sangkum (Popular Socialist Community).

177	**43**	2r. violet	45	30
178	**43**	3r. brown	60	35
179	**43**	10r. blue	1·20	75

44 Weaving

1965. Native Handicrafts.

180	**44**	1r. violet, brown & bistre	30	30
181	-	3r. brown, green & purple	55	35
182	-	5r. red, purple and green	85	75

DESIGNS: 3r. Engraving. 5r. Basket-making.

1965. Indo-Chinese People's Conference. Nos. 178/9 optd **CONFERENCE DES PEUPLES INDOCHINOIS.**

183	**43**	3r. brown	45	45
184	**43**	10r. blue	70	65

46 ITU Emblem and Symbols

1965. Centenary of ITU.

185	**46**	3r. bistre and green	35	35
186	**46**	4r. blue and red	45	55
187	**46**	10r. purple and violet	75	75

47 Cotton

1965. Industrial Plants. Multicoloured.

188	1r.50 Type **47**	45	30
189	3r. Groundnuts	70	35
190	7r.50 Coconut palms	1·10	75

48 Preah Ko

1966. Cambodian Temples.

191	**48**	3r. green, turquoise & brn	75	45
192	-	5r. brown, green & purple	95	55
193	-	7r. brown, green & ochre	1·30	65
194	-	9r. purple, green and blue	2·20	90
195	-	12r. red, green & verm	2·75	1·60

TEMPLES: 5r. Baksei Chamkrong, 7r. Banteay Srei, 9r. Angkor Vat. 12r. Bayon.

49 WHO Building

1966. Inaug of WHO Headquarters, Geneva.

196	**49**	2r. multicoloured	30	20
197	**49**	3r. multicoloured	35	30
198	**49**	5r. multicoloured	60	45

50 Tree-planting

1966. Tree Day.

199	**50**	1r. brown, green & dp brn	25	30
200	**50**	3r. brown, green & orange	40	35
201	**50**	7r. brown, green and grey	70	45

51 UNESCO Emblem

1966. 20th Anniv of UNESCO.

202	**51**	3r. multicoloured	35	30
203	**51**	7r. multicoloured	45	55

52 Stadium

1966. "Ganefo" Games, Phnom Penh.

204	**52**	3r. blue	15	20
205	-	4r. green	20	35
206	-	7r. red	30	55
207	-	10r. brown	40	75

DESIGNS: 4r., 7r., 10r. Various bas-reliefs of ancient sports from Angkor Vat.

53 Wild Boar

1967. Fauna.

208	**53**	3r. black, green and blue	70	45
209	-	5r. multicoloured	80	75
210	-	7r. multicoloured	1·30	1·10

FAUNA—VERT: 5r. Hog-deer. HORIZ: 7r. Indian elephant.

1967. International Tourist Year. Nos. 191/2, 194/5 and 149 optd **ANNEE INTERNATIONALE DU TOURISME 1967.**

211	**48**	3r. green, turquoise & brn	65	45
212	**48**	5r. brown, green & purple	75	45
213	-	9r. purple, green and blue	1·10	75
214	-	12r. red, green & verm	1·30	90
215	**33**	15r. brown, blue & green	1·60	1·10

1967. Millenary of Banteay Srei Temple. No. 193 optd **MILLENAIRE DE BANTEAY SREI 967–1967.**

216	7r. brown, green and ochre	1·10	45

56 Ballet Dancer

1967. Cambodian Royal Ballet. Designs showing ballet dancers.

217	**56**	1r. orange	30	35
218	-	3r. blue	65	35
219	-	5r. blue	85	45
220	-	7r. red	1·30	65
221	-	10r. multicoloured	1·70	90

1967. Int Literacy Day. Surch **Journee Internationale de l'Alphabetisation 8-9-67** and new value.

222	**37**	6r. on 12r. blue, grn & red	70	35
223	**15**	7r. on 15r. brown & green	85	55

58 Decade Emblem

1967. International Hydrological Decade.

224	**58**	1r. orange, blue and black	20	20
225	**58**	6r. orange, blue and violet	40	35
226	**58**	10r. orange, lt green & grn	60	55

59 Royal University of Kompong-Cham

1968. Cambodian Universities and Institutes.

227	**59**	4r. purple, blue & brown	40	30
228	-	6r. brown, green and blue	55	35
229	-	9r. brown, green and blue	75	45

DESIGNS: 6r. "Khmero-Soviet Friendship" Higher Technical Institute; 9r. Sangkum Reaster Niyum University Centre.

60 Doctor tending child

1968. 20th Anniv of WHO.

230	**60**	3r. blue	45	30
231	-	7r. blue	65	45

DESIGN: 7r. Man using insecticide.

61 Stadium

1968. Olympic Games, Mexico.

232	**61**	1r. brown, green and red	40	30
233	-	2r. brown, red and blue	45	35
234	-	3r. brown, blue and purple	55	35
235	-	5r. violet	60	35
236	-	7r.50 brown, green & red	85	45

DESIGNS—HORIZ: 2r. Wrestling; 3r. Cycling. VERT: 5r. Boxing; 7r.50, Runner with torch.

62 Stretcher-party

1968. Cambodian Red Cross Fortnight.

237	**62**	3r. red, green and blue	70	30

63 Prince Norodom Sihanouk

1968. 15th Anniv of Independence.

238	63	7r. violet, green and blue	45	45
239	-	8r. brown, green and blue	45	65

DESIGN: 8r. Soldiers wading through stream.

64 Human Rights Emblem and Prince Norodom Sihanouk

1968. Human Rights Year.

240	64	3r. blue	30	20
241	64	5r. purple	65	30
242	64	7r. black, orange & green	95	45

65 ILO Emblem

1969. 50th Anniv of ILO.

243	65	3r. blue	25	20
244	65	6r. red	40	30
245	65	9r. green	65	45

66 Red Cross Emblems around Globe

1969. 50th Anniv of League of Red Cross Societies.

246	66	1r. multicoloured	30	20
247	66	3r. multicoloured	40	30
248	66	10r. multicoloured	85	45

67 Golden Birdwing

1969. Butterflies.

249	67	3r. black, yellow & violet	1·40	55
250	-	4r. black, green & verm	1·40	85
251	-	8r. black, orange & green	1·80	1·40

DESIGNS: 4r. Tailed jay. 8r. Orange tiger.

68 Diesel Train and Route Map

1969. Opening of Phnom Penh–Sihanoukville Railway.

252	68	3r. multicoloured	30	30
253	-	6r. brown, black & green	45	30
254	-	8r. black	75	35
255	-	9r. blue, turquoise & grn	85	45

DESIGNS: 6r. Phnom Penh Station; 8r. Diesel locomotive and Kampor Station; 9r. Steam locomotive at Sihanoukville Station.

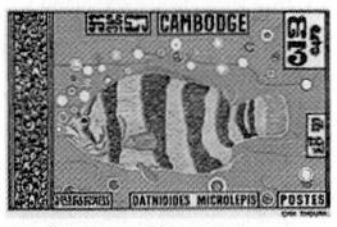

69 Siamese Tigerfish

1970. Fish. Multicoloured.

256	3r. Type **69**	75	65
257	7r. Marbled sleeper	1·50	1·10
258	9r. Chevron snakehead	2·40	1·50

70 Vat Tepthidaram

1970. Buddhist Monasteries in Cambodia. Multicoloured.

259	2r. Type **70**	40	30
260	3r. Vat Maniratanaram (horiz)	45	30
261	6r. Vat Patumavati (horiz)	85	35
262	8r. Vat Unnalom (horiz)	1·60	45

71 Dish Aerial and Open Book

1970. World Telecommunications Day.

263	71	3r. multicoloured	15	20
264	71	4r. multicoloured	25	20
265	71	9r. multicoloured	40	35

72 New Headquarters Building

1970. Opening of New UPU Headquarters Building, Berne.

266	72	1r. multicoloured	20	10
267	72	3r. multicoloured	30	10
268	72	4r. multicoloured	55	10
269	72	10r. multicoloured	1·10	35

73 *Nelumbium speciosum*

1970. Aquatic Plants. Multicoloured.

270	3r. Type **73**	40	55
271	4r. *Eichhornia crassipes*	60	55
272	13r. *Nymphea lotus*	1·10	85

74 "Banteay-srei" (bas-relief)

1970. World Meteorological Day.

273	74	3r. red and green	30	10
274	74	4r. red, green and blue	45	30
275	74	7r. green, blue and black	60	55

75 Rocket, Dove and Globe

1970. 25th Anniv of United Nations.

276	75	3r. multicoloured	25	20
277	75	5r. multicoloured	45	35
278	75	10r. multicoloured	65	55

76 IEY Emblem

1970. International Education Year.

279	76	1r. blue	15	10
280	76	3r. purple	20	10
281	76	8r. green	50	35

77 Samdech Chuon Nath

1971. Second Death Anniv of Samdech Chuon-Nath (Khmer language scholar).

282	77	3r. multicoloured	25	10
283	77	8r. multicoloured	60	30
284	77	9r. multicoloured	75	45

For issues between 1971 and 1989 see under KHMER REPUBLIC and KAMPUCHEA in volume 3.

203 17th-century Coach

1989. Coaches. Multicoloured.

1020	2r. Type **203**	10	10
1021	3r. Paris–Lyon coach, 1720	15	10
1022	5r. Mail coach, 1793	25	10
1023	10r. Light mail coach, 1805	55	20
1024	15r. Royal mail coach	80	30
1025	20r. Russian mail coach	95	35
1026	35r. Paris–Lille coupe, 1837 (vert)	1·90	55
MS1027	60×84 mm. 45r. Royal messenger coach, 1815 (31×39 mm)	4·25	90

No. **MS**1027 commemorates "Philexfrance '89" International Stamp Exhibition, Paris.

204 *Papilio zagreus*

1989. "Brasiliana 89" International Stamp Exhibition, Rio de Janeiro. Butterflies. Multicoloured.

1028	2r. Type **204**	10	10
1029	3r. *Morpho catenarius*	15	10
1030	5r. *Morpho aega*	25	10
1031	10r. *Callithea sapphira* ("wrongly inscr "saphhira")	50	10
1032	15r. *Catagramma sorana*	75	20
1033	20r. *Pierella nereis*	95	20
1034	35r. *Papilio brasiliensis*	1·90	20
MS1035	100×66 mm. 45r. *Thecla marsyas* (39×31 mm)	5·25	90

205 Pirogue

1989. Khmer Culture. Multicoloured.

1036	3r. Type **205**	20	10
1037	12r. Pirogue (two sets of oars)	80	35
1038	30r. Pirogue with cabin	2·10	90

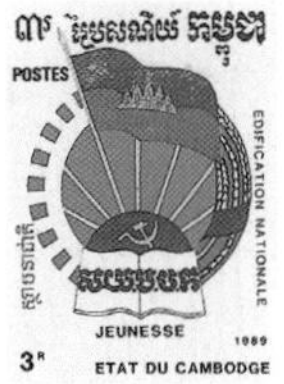

206 Youth

1989. National Development. Multicoloured.

1039	3r. Type **206**	20	10
1040	12r. Trade unions emblem (horiz)	60	20
1041	30r. National Front emblem (horiz)	1·70	75

207 Goalkeeper

1990. World Cup Football Championship, Italy. Multicoloured.

1042	2r. Type **207**	10	10
1043	3r. Dribbling ball	15	10
1044	5r. Controlling ball with thigh	25	10
1045	10r. Running with ball	55	10
1046	15r. Shooting	80	20
1047	20r. Tackling	95	20
1048	35r. Tackling (different)	1·90	20
MS1049	94×75 mm. 45r. Players (31×39 mm)	4·25	90

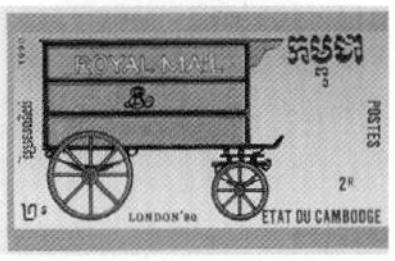

208 Two-horse Postal Van

1990. "Stamp World London 90" International Stamp Exhibition. Royal Mail Horse-drawn Transport. Multicoloured.

1050	2r. Type **208**	10	10
1051	3r. One-horse cart	10	10
1052	5r. Rural post office cart	15	10
1053	10r. Rural post office van	25	10
1054	15r. Local post office van	40	20
1055	20r. Parcel-post cart	55	20
1056	35r. Two-horse wagon	1·10	20
MS1057	69×80 mm. 45r. Rural one-horse van (39×31 mm)	4·25	90

209 Rice Grains

1990. Cultivation of Rice. Multicoloured.

1058	3r. Type **209**	20	10
1059	12r. Transporting rice (horiz)	80	35
1060	30r. Threshing rice	2·10	90

210 Shooting

1990. Olympic Games, Barcelona (1992) (1st issue). Multicoloured.

1061	2r. Type **210**	10	10
1062	3r. Putting the shot	15	10
1063	5r. Weightlifting	25	10
1064	10r. Boxing	55	10
1065	15r. Pole vaulting	80	20
1066	20r. Basketball	1·10	20
1067	35r. Fencing	1·90	20
MS1068	83×70 mm. 45r. Gymnastics (31×37 mm)	4·25	90

See also Nos. 1163/**MS**1170, 1208/**MS**1213 and 1241/**MS**1246.

211 Four-man Bobsleighing

1990. Winter Olympic Games, Albertville (1992) (1st issue). Multicoloured.

1069	2r. Type **211**	10	10
1070	3r. Speed skating	15	10
1071	5r. Figure skating	20	10
1072	10r. Ice hockey	45	10
1073	15r. Biathlon	70	20
1074	20r. Lugeing	90	20
1075	35r. Ski jumping	1·70	20
MS1076	64×104 mm. Ice hockey goalkeeper (31×38 mm)	4·25	90

See also Nos. 1152/**MS**1159.

212 Facade of Banteay Srei

1990. Khmer Culture. Multicoloured.

1077	3r. Type **212**	20	10
1078	12r. Ox-carts (12th-century relief)	80	35
1079	30r. Banon ruins (36×21 mm)	2·10	90

213 *Zizina oxleyi*

1990. "New Zealand 1990" International Stamp Exhibition, Auckland. Butterflies. Multicoloured.

1080	2r. Type **213**	10	10
1081	3r. *Cupha prosope*	10	10
1082	5r. *Heteronympha merope*	15	10
1083	10r. *Dodonidia helmsi*	30	20
1084	15r. *Argirophenga antipodum*	55	20
1085	20r. *Tysonotis danis*	80	20
1086	35r. *Pyrameis gonnarilla*	1·20	30
MS1087	76×65 mm. 45r. *Pyrameis itea* (39×31 mm)	5·75	1·10

214 "Vostok"

1990. Spacecraft. Multicoloured.

1088	2r. Type **214**	10	10
1089	3r. "Soyuz"	10	10
1090	5r. Satellite	15	10
1091	10r. "Luna 10"	35	20
1092	15r. "Mars 1"	55	30
1093	20r. "Venus 3"	70	35
1094	35r. "Mir" space station	1·10	75
MS1095	92×72 mm. 45r. "Energiya" and space shuttle "Burn" (31×39 mm)	5·25	90

215 Poodle

1990. Dogs. Multicoloured.

1096	20c. Type **215**	20	10
1097	80c. Shetland sheepdog	20	10
1098	3r. Samoyede	45	10
1099	6r. Springer spaniel	85	10
1100	10r. Wire-haired fox terrier	1·10	20
1101	15r. Afghan hound	1·70	20
1102	25r. Dalmatian	2·30	20
MS1103	95×83 mm. Burmese mountain dog (39×31 mm)	4·25	90

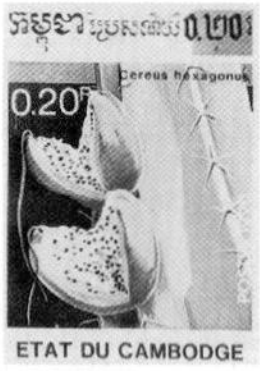

216 *Cereus hexagonus*

1990. Cacti. Multicoloured.

1104	20c. Type **216**	10	10
1105	80c. *Arthrocereus rondonianus*	10	10
1106	3r. *Matucana multicolor*	15	10
1107	6r. *Hildewintera aureispina*	25	10
1108	10r. *Opuntia retrosa*	50	20
1109	15r. *Erdisia tenuicula*	75	20
1110	25r. *Mamillaria yaquensis*	1·10	20

217 Learning to Write

1990. International Literacy Year.

1111	**217**	3r. black and blue	15	10
1112	**217**	12r. black and yellow	1·10	35
1113	**217**	30r. black and pink	3·50	90

218 English Nef, 1200

1990. Ships. Multicoloured.

1114	20c. Type **218**	20	10
1115	80c. 16th-century Spanish galleon	30	10
1116	3r. Dutch jacht, 1627	45	10
1117	6r. *La Couronne* (French galleon), 1638	85	10
1118	10r. Dumont d'Urville's ship *L'Astrolabe*, 1826	1·10	20
1119	15r. *Louisiane* (steamer), 1864	1·90	20
1120	25r. Clipper, 1900 (vert)	2·30	20
MS1121	97×80 mm. 45r. 19th-century merchant brig (31×39 mm)	4·75	90

No. 1118 is wrongly inscribed "d'Uville".

219 Phnom-Penh–Kampong Som Railway

1990. National Development. Multicoloured.

1122	3r. Type **219**	30	10
1123	12r. Port, Kampong Som	1·30	35
1124	30r. Fishing boats, Kampong Som	3·75	90

220 Sacre-Coeur de Montmartre and White Bishop

1990. "Paris '90" World Chess Championship, Paris. Multicoloured.

1125	2r. Type **220**	20	10
1126	3r. "The Horse Trainer" (statue) and white knight	30	10
1127	5r. "Victory of Samothrace" (statue) and white queen	45	10
1128	10r. Azay-le-Rideau Chateau and white rook	95	20
1129	15r. "The Dance" (statue) and white pawn	1·40	30
1130	20r. Eiffel Tower and white king	1·90	35
1131	35r. Arc de Triomphe and black chessmen	3·25	55
MS1132	91×58 mm. 45r. White chessmen (39×31 mm)	5·25	1·10

221 Columbus

1990. 500th Anniv (1992) of Discovery of America by Columbus (1st issue). Multicoloured.

1133	2r. Type **221**	30	10
1134	3r. Queen Isabella's jewel-chest	45	10
1135	5r. Queen Isabella the Catholic	55	10
1136	10r. *Santa Maria* (flagship)	95	10
1137	15r. Juan de la Cosa	1·40	10
1138	20r. Monument to Columbus	1·90	20
1139	35r. Devin Pyramid, Yucatan	3·50	20
MS1140	79×60 mm. 45r. Christopher Columbus (31×39 mm)	5·25	90

See also Nos. 1186/**MS**1193.

222 Tyre Factory

1991. National Festival. Multicoloured.

1141	100r. Type **222**	55	20
1142	300r. Rural hospital	2·10	90
1143	500r. Freshwater fishing (27×40 mm)	3·25	1·20

223 Tackle

1991. World Cup Football Championship, U.S.A. (1994) (1st issue).

1144	**223**	5r. multicoloured	15	10
1145	-	25r. multicoloured	15	10
1146	-	70r. multicoloured	35	10
1147	-	100r. multicoloured	40	10
1148	-	200r. multicoloured	75	20
1149	-	400r. multicoloured	1·50	20
1150	-	1000r. multicoloured	3·50	20
MS1151		85×93 mm. 900r. multicoloured	5·25	90

DESIGNS: 25r. to 1000r. Different footballing scenes.

See also Nos. 1220/**MS**1225, 1317/**MS**1322 and 1381/**MS**1386.

224 Speed Skating

1991. Winter Olympic Games, Albertville (1992) (2nd issue). Multicoloured.

1152	5r. Type **224**	20	10
1153	25r. Slalom skiing	30	10
1154	70r. Ice hockey	55	10
1155	100r. Bobsleighing	65	10
1156	200r. Freestyle skiing	1·30	20
1157	400r. Ice skating	2·50	20
1158	1000r. Downhill skiing	3·75	20
MS1159	87×62 mm. 900r. Ski jumping (31×39 mm)	5·25	90

225 *Torso of Vishnu Reclining* (11th cent)

1991. Sculpture. Multicoloured.

1160	100r. *Garuda* (Koh Ker, 10th century)	35	20
1161	300r. Type **225**	1·10	90
1162	500r. *Reclining Nandin* (7th century)	1·90	1·10

226 Pole Vaulting

1991. Olympic Games, Barcelona (1992) (2nd issue). Multicoloured.

1163	5r. Type **226**	20	10
1164	25r. Table tennis	30	10
1165	70r. Running	45	10
1166	100r. Wrestling	55	10
1167	200r. Gymnastics (bars)	95	20
1168	400r. Tennis	1·80	20
1169	1000r. Boxing	4·25	20
MS1170	78×73 mm. 900r. Gymnastics (beam) (31×39 mm)	5·25	90

227 Douglas DC-10-30

1991. Airplanes. Multicoloured.

1171	5r. Type **227**	15	10
1172	25r. McDonnell Douglas MD-11	20	10
1173	70r. Ilyushin Il-96-300	30	10
1174	100r. Airbus Industrie A310	40	10
1175	200r. Yakovlev Yak-42	80	20
1176	400r. Tupolev Tu-154	1·50	20
1177	1000r. Douglas DC-9	3·75	20

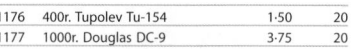

228 Diaguita Funerary Urn, Catamarca

1991. "Espamer '91" Iberia–Latin America Stamp Exhibition, Buenos Aires. Multicoloured.

1178	5r. Bareales glass pot, Catamarca (horiz)	15	10
1179	25r. Type **228**	20	10
1180	70r. Quiroga urn, Tucuman	30	10
1181	100r. Round glass pot, Santiago del Estero (horiz)	45	10
1182	200r. Pitcher, Santiago del Estero (horiz)	85	20
1183	400r. Diaguita funerary urn, Tucuman	1·60	20
1184	1000r. Bareales funerary urn, Catamarca (horiz)	4·00	20
MS1185	80×65 mm. 900r. Funerary urn, Catamarce (36×27 mm)	5·25	90

229 *Pinta*

1991. 500th Anniv (1992) of Discovery of America by Columbus (2nd issue). Each brown, stone and black.

1186	5r. Type **229**	20	10
1187	25r. *Nina*	30	10
1188	70r. *Santa Maria*	55	10
1189	100r. Landing at Guanahani, 1492 (horiz)	65	10
1190	200r. Meeting of two cultures (horiz)	1·30	20
1191	400r. La Navidad (first European settlement in America) (horiz)	2·50	20
1192	1000r. Amerindian village (horiz)	5·75	20
MS1193	84×59 mm. Columbus (39×31 mm)	5·75	90

230 *Neptis pryeri*

1991. "Phila Nippon '91" International Stamp Exhibition, Tokyo. Butterflies. Multicoloured.

1194	5r. Type **230**	15	10
1195	25r. *Papilio xuthus*	15	10
1196	70r. Common map butterfly	10	10
1197	100r. *Argynnis anadiomene*	40	10
1198	200r. *Lethe marginalis*	75	20
1199	400r. *Artopoetes pryeri*	95	20
1200	1000r. African monarch	3·50	20
MS1201	73×57 mm 900r. *Ochlodes subhyalina* (39×31 mm)	5·25	1·10

231 Coastal Fishing Port

1991. National Development. Food Industry. Multicoloured.

1202	100r. Type **231**	50	45
1203	300r. Preparing palm sugar (29×40 mm)	1·40	90
1204	500r. Picking peppers	2·40	1·20

232 Chakdomuk Costumes

1992. National Festival. Traditional Costumes. Multicoloured.

1205	150r. Type **232**	50	20
1206	350r. Longvek	1·40	30
1207	1000r. Angkor	2·50	45

233 Wrestling

1992. Olympic Games, Barcelona (3rd issue). Multicoloured.

1208	5r. Type **233**	15	10
1209	15r. Football	15	10
1210	80r. Weightlifting	20	10
1211	400r. Archery	1·00	30
1212	1500r. Gymnastics	3·50	35
MS1213	79×59 mm. 1000r. show jumping (31×39 mm)	4·25	90

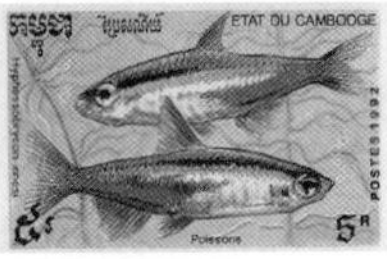

234 Neon Tetra

1992. Fish. Multicoloured.

1214	5r. Type **234**	15	10
1215	15r. Siamese fighting fish	15	10
1216	80r. Kaiser tetra	20	10
1217	400r. Dwarf gourami	1·00	30
1218	1500r. Port hoplo	3·50	35
MS1219	80×65 mm. 1000r. Freshwater angelfish (39×31 mm)	4·25	90

235 Germany v. Columbia

1992. World Cup Football Championship, U.S.A. (1994) (2nd issue). Multicoloured.

1220	5r. Type **235**	15	10
1221	15r. Netherlands player (horiz)	15	10
1222	80r. Uruguay v. C.I.S. (ex-Soviet states)	20	10
1223	400r. Cameroun v. Yugoslavia	1·00	30
1224	1500r. Italy v. Sweden	3·50	35
MS1225	75×51 mm. 1000r. Shot at goal (39×31 mm)	4·25	90

236 Monument

1992. Khmer Culture. 19th-century Architecture. Multicoloured.

1226	150r. Type **236**	55	35
1227	350r. Stupa	1·30	85
1228	1000r. Mandapa library	3·50	2·00

237 Motor Car

1992. 540th Birth Anniv (1992) of Leonardo da Vinci (artist and inventor). Multicoloured.

1229	5r. Type **237**	20	10
1230	15r. Container ship	20	10
1231	80r. Helicopter	30	10
1232	400r. Scuba diver	1·50	30
1233	1500r. Parachutists (vert)	4·75	35
MS1234	79×59 mm. 1000r. Da Vinci and drawing of "Flying Man" (31×39 mm)	4·75	90

238 Juan de la Cierva and Autogyro

1992. "Expo '92" World's Fair, Seville. Inventors. Multicoloured (except MS1240).

1235	5r. Type **238**	20	10
1236	15r. Thomas Edison and electric light bulb	20	10
1237	80r. Samuel Morse and Morse telegraph	30	10
1238	400r. Narciso Monturiol and "Ictineo" (early submarine)	1·40	30
1239	1500r. Alexander Graham Bell and early telephone	2·75	35
MS1240	83×62 mm.1000r. pink and black (Robert Fulton (steamship)) (31×39 mm)	4·75	90

239 Weightlifting

1992. Olympic Games, Barcelona (4th issue). Multicoloured.

1241	5r. Type **239**	20	10
1242	15r. Boxing	20	10
1243	80r. Basketball	30	10
1244	400r. Running	1·40	30
1245	1500r. Water polo	4·75	35
MS1246	71×75 mm. 1000r. Gymnastics (39×31 mm)	4·50	90

240 Palm Trees

1992. Environmental Protection. Multicoloured.

1247	5r. Couple on riverside	20	10
1248	15r. Pagoda	20	10
1249	80r. Type **240**	30	10
1250	400r. Boy riding water buffalo	1·40	30
1251	1500r. Swimming in river	4·75	35
MS1252	100×71 mm. 1000r. Angkor Wat (39×31 mm)	4·50	90

241 Louis de Bougainville and *La Boudeuse*

1992. "Genova '92" International Thematic Stamp Exhibition, Genoa. Multicoloured.

1253	5r. Type **241**	20	10
1254	15r. James Cook and H.M.S. *Endeavour*	30	10
1255	80r. Charles Darwin and H.M.S. *Beagle*	45	10
1256	400r. Jacques Cousteau and *Calypso*	1·50	30
1257	1500r. *Kon Tiki* (replica of balsa raft)	5·25	35
MS1258	80×65 mm. 1000r. Christopher Columbus (28×36 mm)	4·50	90

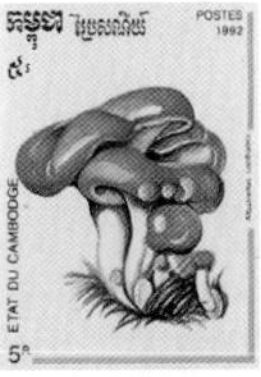

242 *Albatrellus confluens*

1992. Fungi. Multicoloured.

1259	5r. Type **242**	15	10
1260	15r. Scarlet-stemmed boletus	20	10
1261	80r. Verdigris agaric	25	10
1262	400r. *Telamonia armillata*	1·00	30
1263	1500r. Goaty smell cortinarius	3·75	35

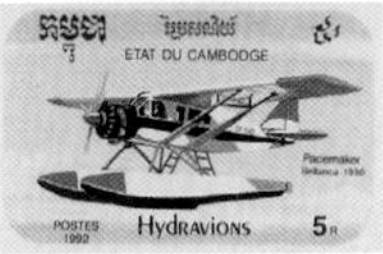

243 Bellanca Pacemaker Seaplane, 1930

1992. Aircraft. Multicoloured.

1264	5r. Type **243**	20	10
1265	15r. Canadair CL-215 fire-fighting amphibian, 1965	20	10
1266	80r. Grumman G-21 Goose amphibian, 1937	30	10
1267	400r. Grumman SA-6 Sealand flying boat, 1947	1·30	30
1268	1500r. Short S.23 Empire "C" Class flying boat, 1936	4·50	35
MS1269	80×60 mm. Grumman G-44 Widgeon, 1940 (31×39 mm)	4·50	90

244 Dish Aerial

1992. National Development. Multicoloured.

1270	150r. Type **244**	55	20
1271	350r. Dish aerial, flags and satellite	1·30	30
1272	1000r. Hotel Cambodiana	4·00	45

245 Sociological Institute

1993. National Festival. Multicoloured.

1273	50r. Type **245**	45	20
1274	450r. Motel Cambodiana	1·40	30
1275	1000r. Theatre, Bassac	4·00	45

246 Bottle-nosed Dolphin and Submarine

1993. Wildlife and Technology. Multicoloured.

1276	150r. Type **246**	55	10
1277	200r. Supersonic jet airplane and peregrine falcon	65	20
1278	250r. Eurasian beaver and dam	75	20
1279	500r. Satellite and natterer's bat	2·00	20
1280	900r. Rufous humming-bird and helicopter	3·00	30

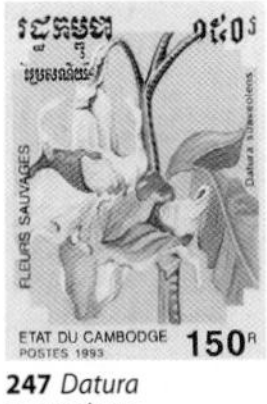

247 *Datura suaveolens*

1993. Wild Flowers. Multicoloured.

1281	150r. Type **247**	55	10
1282	200r. *Convolvulus tricolor*	65	20
1283	250r. "Hippeastrum" hybrid	75	20
1284	500r. "Camellia" hybrid	1·90	20
1285	900r. *Lilium speciosum*	3·00	30
MS1286	75×50 mm. 1000t. Various flowers (31×39 mm)	4·50	1·10

248 Vihear Temple

1993. Khmer Culture. Multicoloured.

1287	50r. Sculpture of ox	45	20
1288	450r. Type **248**	1·30	75
1289	1000r. Offering to Buddha	3·75	1·70

249 Philippine Flying Lemur

1993. Animals. Multicoloured.

1290	150r. Type **249**	55	20
1291	200r. Red giant flying squirrel	65	20
1292	250r. Fringed gecko	75	30
1293	500r. Wallace's flying frog	2·00	35
1294	900r. Flying lizard	3·00	65

250 *Symbrenthia hypselis*

1993. "Brasiliana '93" International Stamp Exhibition, Rio de Janeiro. Butterflies. Multicoloured.

1295	250r. Type **250**	75	20
1296	350r. *Sithon nedymond*	1·30	20
1297	600r. *Geitoneura minyas*	1·90	30
1298	800r. *Argyreus hyperbius*	2·40	35
1299	1000r. *Argyrophenga antipodum*	3·25	65
MS1300	82×52 mm. 1500r. *Parage schakra* (39×31 mm)	5·75	1·10

251 Armed Cambodians reporting to U.N. Base

1993. United Nations Transitional Authority in Cambodia Pacification Programme. Each black and blue.

1301	150r. Type **251**	55	10
1302	200r. Military camp	65	20
1303	250r. Surrender of arms	75	20
1304	500r. Vocational training	1·70	20
1305	900r. Liberation	2·75	30
MS1306	54×84 mm. 1000r. Return to homes (31×39 mm)	4·75	1·10

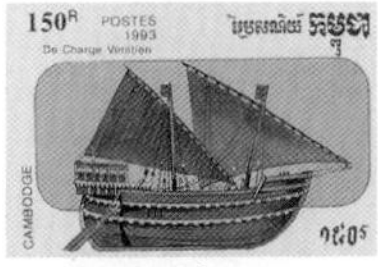

252 Venetian Felucca

1993. Sailing Ships. Multicoloured.

1307	150r. Type **252**	40	10
1308	200r. Phoenician galley	50	20
1309	250r. Egyptian merchantman	65	20
1310	500r. Genoese merchantman	1·50	20
1311	900r. English merchantman	2·40	30

253 Santos-Dumont, Eiffel Tower and "Ballon No. 6", 1901

1993. 120th Birth Anniv of Alberto Santos-Dumont (aviator). Multicoloured.

1312	150r. Type **253**	55	10
1313	200r. *14 bis* (biplane), 1906 (horiz)	65	20
1314	250r. *Demoiselle* (monoplane), 1909 (horiz)	75	20
1315	500r. Embraer EMB-201 A (horiz)	2·00	20
1316	900r. Embraer EMB-111 (horiz)	3·00	30

254 Footballer

1993. World Cup Football Championship, U.S.A. (1994) (3rd issue).

1317	**254**	250r. multicoloured	75	10
1318	-	350r. multicoloured	1·30	20
1319	-	600r. multicoloured	1·90	20
1320	-	800r. multicoloured	2·40	20
1321	-	1000r. mult (vert)	3·25	30
MS1322		60×85 mm. 1500r. multicoloured (39×31 mm)	5·75	1·10

DESIGNS: 350r. to 1500r. Various footballing scenes.

255 European Wigeon

1993. "Bangkok 1993" International Stamp Exhibition, Thailand. Ducks. Multicoloured.

1323	250r. Type **255**	75	20
1324	350r. Baikal teal	1·30	30
1325	600r. Mandarin	1·90	35
1326	800r. Wood duck	2·40	65
1327	1000r. Harlequin duck	3·25	85
MS1328	63×89 mm. 1500tr. Head of mandarin (39×31 mm)	5·75	90

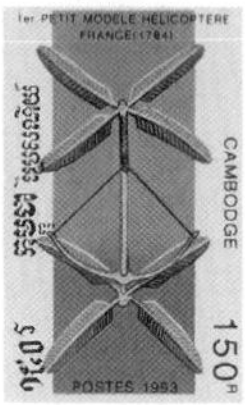
256 First Helicopter Model, France, 1784

1993. Vertical Take-off Aircraft. Multicoloured.

1329	150r. Type **256**	55	10
1330	200r. Model of steam helicopter, 1863	65	20
1331	250r. New York–Atlanta–Miami autogyro flight, 1927 (horiz)	75	20
1332	500r. Sikorsky helicopter, 1943 (horiz)	1·70	20
1333	900r. French vertical take-off jet	3·00	30
MS1334	90×49 mm. 1000r. Juan de la Clerva's C.4, 1923 (first practical autogyro)	4·75	90

257 *Cnaphalocrosis medinalis*

1993. National Development. Harmful Insects. Multicoloured.

1335	50r. Type **257**	30	20
1336	450r. Brown leaf-hopper	1·50	20
1337	500r. *Scirpophaga incertulas*	1·70	30
1338	1000r. Stalk-eyed fly	3·50	30
MS1339	89×90 mm. 1000r. *Leptocorisa oratorius* (31×39 mm)	4·75	90

258 Ministry of Posts and Telecommunications

1993. 40th Anniv of Independence.

1340	**258**	300r. multicoloured	1·10	30
1341	-	500r. multicoloured	1·70	65
1342	-	700r. blue. red & black	2·50	90

DESIGNS—VERT: 500r. Independence monument. HORIZ: 700r. National flag.

259 Boy with Pony

1993. Figurines by M. J. Hummel. Multicoloured.

1343	50r. Type **259**	20	10
1344	100r. Girl and pram	55	10
1345	150r. Girl bathing doll	75	10
1346	200r. Girl holding doll	95	20
1347	250r. Boys playing	1·20	20
1348	300r. Girls pulling boy in cart	1·50	30
1349	350r. Girls playing ring-o-roses	1·70	35
1350	600r. Boys with stick and drum	2·75	55

260 Figure Skating

1994. Winter Olympic Games, Lillehammer, Norway. Multicoloured.

1351	150r. Type **260**	45	10
1352	250r. Two-man luge (horiz)	75	20
1353	400r. Skiing (horiz)	1·30	20
1354	700r. Biathlon (horiz)	2·30	20
1355	1000r. Speed skating	3·25	30
MS1356	85×60 mm. 1500r. Curling (31×39 mm)	5·75	90

261 Opel 4/12 Laubfrosch two-seater, 1924

1994. Motor Cars. Multicoloured.

1357	150r. Type **261**	55	10
1358	200r. Mercedes 35 h.p. four-seater, 1901	65	20
1359	250r. Ford Model "T" Tudor sedan, 1927	75	20
1360	500r. Rolls Royce 40/50 Silver Ghost tourer, 1907	1·70	20
1361	900r. Hutton racing car, 1908	2·75	30
MS1362	80×60 mm 1000r. Duesenberg model J phaeton, 1931 (31×39 mm)	4·50	90

262 Gymnastics

1994. Olympic Games, Atlanta (1996) (1st issue). Multicoloured.

1363	150r. Type **262**	45	10
1364	200r. Football	65	10
1365	250r. Throwing the javelin	75	20
1366	300r. Canoeing	85	20
1367	600r. Running	1·90	20
1368	1000r. Diving (horiz)	3·50	20
MS1369	79×63 mm. 1500r. Show jumping (31×39 mm)	5·75	90

See also Nos. 1437/**MS**1442 and 1495/**MS**1501.

263 Siva and Uma (10th century, Banteay Srei)

1994. Khmer Culture. Statues. Multicoloured.

1370	300r. Type **263**	1·10	55
1371	500r. Vishnu (6th cent, Tvol Dai-Buon)	1·90	90
1372	700r. King Jayavarman VII (12th–13th century, Krol Romeas Angkor)	2·75	1·30

264 Olympic Flag

1994. Centenary of International Olympic Committee. Multicoloured.

1373	100r. Type **264**	30	10
1374	300r. Flag and torch	1·10	45
1375	600r. Flag and Pierre de Coubertin (reviver of modern Olympic Games)	2·30	85

265 Mesonyx

1994. Prehistoric Animals. Multicoloured.

1376	150r. Type **265**	55	20
1377	250r. Doedicurus	85	30
1378	400r. Mylodon	1·50	45
1379	700r. Uintatherium	2·50	55
1380	1000r. Hyrachyus	3·50	85

266 Players

1994. World Cup Football Championship, U.S.A. (4th issue).

1381	**266**	150r. multicoloured	45	10
1382	-	250r. multicoloured	75	20
1383	-	400r. multicoloured	1·30	20
1384	-	700r. multicoloured	2·30	20
1385	-	1000r. multicoloured	3·25	30
MS1386		58×78 mm. 1500r. multicoloured	5·75	90

DESIGNS: 250r. to 1500r. Various footballing scenes.

267 "Soldiers in Combat"

1994. Tourism. Statues in Public Gardens. Multicoloured.

1387	300r. "Stag and Hind"	1·30	45
1388	500r. Type **267**	1·90	90
1389	700r. "Lions"	2·75	1·40

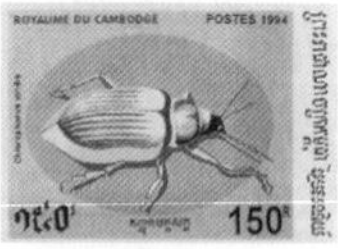
268 *Chlorophanus viridis*

1994. Beetles. Multicoloured.

1390	150r. Type **268**	55	10
1391	200r. *Chrysochroa fulgidissima*	65	20
1392	250r. *Lytta vesicatoria*	75	20
1393	500r. *Purpuricenus kaehleri*	2·00	45
1394	900r. Herculese beetle	3·00	75
MS1395	69×50 mm. *Timarcha tenebricosa* (31×39 mm)	4·75	90

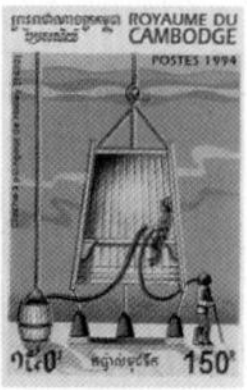
269 Halley's Diving-bell, 1690

1994. Submarines. Multicoloured.

1396	150r. Type **269**	55	10
1397	200r. *Gimnote*, 1886 (horiz)	65	20
1398	250r. *Peral* (Spain), 1888 (horiz)	75	20
1399	500r. *Nautilus* (first nuclear-powered submarine), 1954 (horiz)	2·00	20
1400	900r. *Trieste* (bathyscaphe), 1953 (horiz)	3·00	30
MS1401	80×70 mm. 1000r. Narciso Monturiol's submarine *Ictineo*, 1885 (39×31 mm)	4·75	90

270 Francois-Andre Philidor, 1795

1994. Chess Champions. Multicoloured.

1402	150r. Type **270**	55	10
1403	200r. Mahe de la Bourdonnais, 1821	65	20
1404	250r. Karl Anderssen, 1851	75	20
1405	500r. Paul Morphy, 1858	2·00	45
1406	900r. Wilhelm Steinitz, 1866	3·00	75
MS1407	90×50 mm. 1000r. Emanual Lasker, 1894 (31×38 mm)	4·50	1·10

271 Sikorsky S-42 Flying Boat

1994. Aircraft. Multicoloured.

1408	150r. Type **271**	55	10
1409	200r. Vought-Sikorsky VS-300A helicopter prototype	65	20
1410	250r. Sikorsky S-37 biplane	75	20
1411	500r. Sikorsky S-35 biplane	2·00	20
1412	900r. Sikorsky S-43 amphibian	3·00	30
MS1413	80×50 mm. 1500r. Sikorsky Ilya Muroments (80th Anniv of first multi-engined airplane) (39×31 mm)	4·50	90

272 Penduline Tit

1994. Birds. Multicoloured.

1414	150r. Type **272**	45	10
1415	250r. Bearded reedling	75	20
1416	400r. Little bunting	1·40	20
1417	700r. Cirl bunting	2·40	45
1418	1000r. Goldcrest	3·50	75
MS1419	60×90 mm. 1500r. African pitta (31×39)	5·75	1·40

273 Postal Service Float

1994. National Independence Festival. Multicoloured.

1420	300r. Type **273**	1·10	45
1421	500r. Soldiers marching	1·60	90
1422	700r. Women's army units on parade	2·50	1·40

274 Chruoi Changwar Bridge

1994. National Development. Multicoloured.

1423	300r. Type **274**	85	30
1424	500r. Olympique Commercial Centre	1·50	45
1425	700r. Sakyamony Chedei Temple	1·90	65

275 Psittacosaurus

1995. Prehistoric Animals. Multicoloured.

1426	100r. Type **275**	20	10
1427	200r. Protoceratops	45	20
1428	300r. Montanoceraptors	65	20
1429	400r. Centrosaurus	1·40	30
1430	700r. Styracosaurus	2·30	35
1431	800r. Triceratops	3·00	55

276 Orange-tip

1995. Butterflies. Multicoloured.

1432	100r. Type **276**	20	10
1433	200r. Scarce swallowtail	65	20
1434	300r. Dark green fritillary	95	20
1435	600r. Red admiral	1·40	20
1436	800r. Peacock	2·10	30

277 Swimming

1995. Olympic Games, Atlanta (1996) (2nd issue). Multicoloured.

1437	100r. Type **277**	30	10
1438	200r. Callisthenics (vert)	65	20
1439	400r. Basketball (vert)	1·20	20
1440	800r. Football (vert)	2·75	20
1441	1000r. Cycling (vert)	3·25	30
MS1442	48×69 mm. 1500r. Running (31×39 mm)	3·75	90

278 Death Cap

1995. Fungi. Multicoloured.

1443	100r. Type **278**	30	10
1444	200r. Chanterelle	75	20
1445	300r. Honey fungus	1·10	20
1446	600r. Field mushroom	1·80	20
1447	800r. Fly agaric	2·40	30

279 Kneeling Ascetic

1995. Khmer Culture. Statues. Multicoloured.

1448	300r. Type **279**	85	30
1449	500r. Parasurama	1·50	45
1450	700r. Shiva	1·90	65

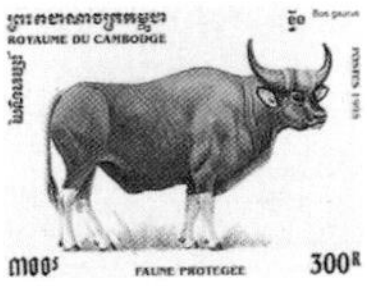
280 Gaur

1995. Protected Animals. Multicoloured.

1451	300r. Type **280**	85	20
1452	500r. Kouprey (vert)	1·50	30
1453	700r. Saurus crane (vert)	1·90	45

281 Black-capped Lory

1995. Parrot Family. Multicoloured.

1454	100r. Type **281**	30	10
1455	200r. Princess parrot	65	20
1456	400r. Eclectus parrot	1·20	20
1457	800r. Scarlet macaw	2·75	20
1458	1000r. Budgerigar	3·25	30
MS1459	52×81 mm. 1500r. Yellow-headed amazon (30×38 mm)	4·75	90

282 Bird (sculpture)

1995. Tourism. Public Gardens. Multicoloured.

1460	300r. Type **282**	85	30
1461	500r. Water feature	1·50	45
1462	700r. Mythical figures (sculpture)	1·60	65

283 Richard Trevithick's Locomotive, 1804

1995. Steam Locomotives. Multicoloured.

1463	100r. Type **283**	20	10
1464	200r. G. and R. Stephenson's *Rocket*, 1829	75	20
1465	300r. George Stephenson's *Locomotion*, 1825	1·10	20
1466	600r. *Lafayette*, 1837	1·70	45
1467	800r. *Best Friend of Charleston*, 1830	2·10	75
MS1468	74×59 mm. 1000r. George Stephenson (inventor of steam locomotive) (31×38 mm)	3·25	1·50

284 Bristol Type 142 Blenheim Mk II Bomber

1995. Second World War Planes. Multicoloured.

1469	100r. Type **284**	20	10
1470	200r. North American B-25B Mitchell bomber (horiz)	75	20
1471	300r. Avro Type 652 Anson Mk I general purpose plane (horiz)	1·10	20
1472	600r. Avro Manchester bomber (horiz)	1·70	20
1473	800r. Consolidated B-24 Liberator bomber (horiz)	2·10	30
MS1474	81×49 mm. 1000r. Boeing B-17 Flying Fortress bomber (31×38 mm)	3·25	90

285 Gathering Crops

1995. 50th Anniv of FAO. Multicoloured.

1475	300r. Type **285**	55	30
1476	500r. Transplanting crops	1·10	45
1477	700r. Paddy field	1·60	65

286 Bridge

1995. 50th Anniv of UNO. Preah Kunlorng Bridge. Multicoloured.

1478	300r. Type **286**	55	30
1479	500r. People on bridge	1·10	45
1480	700r. Closer view of bridge	1·60	65

287 Queen Monineath

1995. National Independence. Multicoloured.

1481	700r. Type **287**	2·10	65
1482	800r. King Norodom Sihanouk	2·75	75

288 Pennant Coralfish

1995. Fish. Multicoloured.

1483	100r. Type **288**	30	10
1484	200r. Copper-banded butterflyfish	65	20
1485	400r. Crown anemonefish	1·20	20
1486	800r. Palette surgeonfish	2·75	20
1487	1000r. Queen angelfish	2·10	30
MS1488	85×50 mm. win-spotted wrasse	4·75	90

289 Post Office Building

1995. Cent of Head Post Office, Phnom Penh.

1489	**289**	300r. multicoloured	85	30
1490	**289**	500r. multicoloured	1·60	45
1491	**289**	700r. multicoloured	2·30	65

290 Independence Monument

1995. 40th Anniv of Admission of Cambodia to United Nations Organization. Multicoloured.

1492	300r. Type **290**	55	30
1493	400r. Angkor Wat	1·10	45
1494	800r. U.N. emblem and national flag (vert)	1·60	65

291 Tennis

1996. Olympic Games, Atlanta (3rd issue). Multicoloured.

1495	100r. Type **291**	10	10
1496	200r. Volleyball	25	10
1497	300r. Football	45	20
1498	500r. Running	60	20
1499	900r. Baseball	1·10	20
1500	1000r. Basketball	1·10	20
MS1501	64×94 mm. 1500r. Windsurfing (28×38 mm)	3·25	90

292 Kep State Chalet

1996

1502	**292**	50r. blue and black	20	10
1503	-	100r. red and black	20	10
1504	-	200r. yellow and black	20	10
1505	-	500r. blue and black	55	20
1506	-	800r. mauve and black	95	30
1507	-	1000r. yellow and black	1·30	45
1508	-	1500r. green and black	1·90	65

DESIGNS—HORIZ: 100r. Power station; 200r. Wheelchair; 500r. Handicapped basketball team; 1000r. Kep beach; 1500r. Serpent Island. VERT: 800r. Man making crutches.

293 European Wild Cat

1996. Wild Cats. Multicoloured.

1509	100r. *Felis libyca* (vert)	20	10
1510	200r. Type **293**	35	10
1511	300r. Caracal	50	20
1512	500r. Geoffroy's cat	80	20
1513	900r. Black-footed cat	1·20	20
1514	1000r. Flat-headed cat	1·40	20

294 Player dribbling Ball

1996. World Cup Football Championship, France (1998) (1st issue). Multicoloured.

1515	**294**	100r. multicoloured	30	10
1516	-	200r. multicoloured	45	10
1517	-	300r. multicoloured	75	20
1518	-	500r. multicoloured	1·30	20
1519	-	900r. multicoloured	2·30	20
1520	-	1000r. mult (horiz)	2·75	20
MS1521		65×79 mm. 1500r. multicoloured (31×38 mm)	4·75	90

DESIGNS: 200r. to 1500r. Different players.

See also Nos. 1613/**MS**1619 and 1726/**MS**1732.

295 Tusmukh

1996. Khmer Culture. Multicoloured.

1522	100r. Type **295**	20	10
1523	300r. Ream Iso	1·30	45
1524	900r. Isei	2·20	85

296 Pacific Steam Locomotive No. 620, Finland

1996. Railway Locomotives. Multicoloured.

1525	100r. Type **296**	10	10
1526	200r. GNR steam locomotive No. 261, Great Britain	10	10
1527	300r. Steam tank locomotive, 1930	30	20
1528	500r. Steam tank locomotive No. 1362, 1914	40	20
1529	900r. LMS Turbomotive No. 6202, 1930, Great Britain	55	20
1530	1000r. Locomotive *Snake*, 1884, New Zealand	75	20
MS1531	80×55 mm. 1500r. Canadian Pacific train with Vistadome observation car (39×31 mm)	4·75	90

No. **MS**1531 commemorates "CEPEX '96" International Stamp Exhibition, Toronto.

297 White-rumped Shama

1996. Birds. Multicoloured.

1532	100r. Type **297**	30	10
1533	200r. Pekin robin	45	10
1534	300r. Varied tit	75	20

1535	500r. Black-naped oriole	1·30	20
1536	900r. Japanese bush warbler	2·30	20
1537	1000r. Blue and white flycatcher	2·75	20

298 Rhythmic Gymnastics

1996. "Olymphilex '96" Olympic Stamps Exhibition, Atlanta, U.S.A. Multicoloured.

1538	100r. Type **298**	20	10
1539	200r. Judo	30	10
1540	300r. High jumping	55	20
1541	500r. Wrestling	1·10	20
1542	900r. Weightlifting	1·90	20
1543	1000r. Football	2·30	20
MS1544	84×55 mm. 1500r. Diving (31×39 mm)	3·75	90

299 Douglas M-2, 1926

1996. Biplanes. Multicoloured.

1545	100r. Type **299**	30	10
1546	200r. Pitcairn PS-5 Mailwing, 1926	45	10
1547	300r. Boeing 40-B, 1928	75	20
1548	500r. Potez 25. 1925	1·30	20
1549	900r. Stearman C-3MB, 1927	2·30	20
1550	1000r. de Havilland D.H.4. 1918	2·75	20
MS1551	80×60 mm. 1500r. Standar JR-1B, 1918 (39×30 mm)	4·75	90

300 Aspara

1996. Tonle Bati Temple Ruins.

1552	**300**	50r. black and yellow	20	10
1553	-	100r. black and blue	20	10
1554	-	200r. black and brown	45	10
1555	-	500r. black and blue	75	20
1556	-	800r. black and green	1·10	30
1557	-	1000r. black and green	1·40	45
1558	-	1500r. black and bistre	2·30	65

DESIGNS—VERT: 100r. Aspara (different); 200r. Aspara (different); 800r. Taprum Temple; 1000r. Grandmother Peou Temple. HORIZ: 500r. Reliefs on wall; 1500r. Overall view of Tonle Bati.

301 Coelophysis

1996. Prehistoric Animals. Multicoloured.

1559	50r. Type **301**	10	10
1560	100r. Euparkeria	10	10
1561	150r. Plateosaurus	30	10
1562	200r. Herrerasaurus	50	10
1563	250r. Dilophosaurus	55	10
1564	300r. Tuojiangosaurus	70	10
1565	350r. Camarasaurus	1·10	20
1566	400r. Ceratosaurus	1·30	20
1567	500r. Espinosaurio	1·50	30
1568	700r. Ouranosaurus	2·00	35
1569	800r. Avimimus	2·50	55
1570	1200r. Deinonychus	3·50	65

Nos. 1559/62, 1563/6 and 1567/70 respectively were issued together, *se-tenant*, each sheetlet containing a composite design of a globe.

302 Jose Raul Capablanca (1921–27)

1996. World Chess Champions. Multicoloured.

1571	100r. Type **302**	30	10
1572	200r. Aleksandr Alekhine (1927–35, 1937–46)	45	10
1573	300r. Vasily Vasilevich Smyslov (1957–58)	75	20
1574	500r. Mikhail Nekhemyevich Tal (1960–61)	1·30	20
1575	900r. Robert Fischer (1972–75)	2·30	20
1576	1000r. Anatoly Karpov (1975–85)	2·75	20
MS1577	70×87 mm. 1500r. Garry Kasparov (1985–2000) (31×38 mm)	4·75	90

303 Brown Bear

1996. Mammals and their Young. Multicoloured.

1578	100r. Type **303**	30	10
1579	200r. Lion	45	10
1580	300r. Malayan tapir	65	20
1581	500r. Bactrian camel	1·30	20
1582	900r. Ibex (vert)	2·10	20
1583	1000r. Californian sealion (vert)	2·75	20

304 Rough Collie

1996. Dogs. Multicoloured.

1584	200r. Type **304**	45	10
1585	300r. Labrador retriever	65	20
1586	500r. Dobermann pinscher	1·30	20
1587	900r. German shepherd	2·10	20
1588	1000r. Boxer	2·40	30

305 Chinese Junk

1996. Ships. Multicoloured.

1589	200r. Type **305**	45	10
1590	300r. Phoenician warship, 1500–1000 B.C.	65	20
1591	500r. Roman war galley, 264–241 B.C.	1·30	20
1592	900r. 19th-century full-rigged ship	2·10	20
1593	1000r. *Sirius* (paddle- steamer), 1838	2·40	30
MS1594	90×60 mm. 1500r. *Great Eastern* (cable ship and paddle-steamer), 1858 (39×31 mm)	4·75	90

306 Silver Pagoda, Phnom Penh

1996. 45th Anniv of Cambodian Membership of Universal Postal Union.

1595	**306**	200r. multicoloured	55	20
1596	**306**	400r. multicoloured	1·10	35
1597	**306**	900r. multicoloured	2·10	85

307 Environmental Vessel and Helicopter

1996. 25th Anniv of Greenpeace (environmental organization). Multicoloured.

1598	200r. Type **307**	75	10
1599	300r. Float-helicopter hovering over motor launch	1·40	20
1600	500r. Helicopter on deck and motor launches	2·10	30
1601	900r. Helicopter with two bar-rels suspended beneath	3·75	35
MS1602	111×90 mm. 10000r. Float-helicopter (31×39 mm)	4·75	90

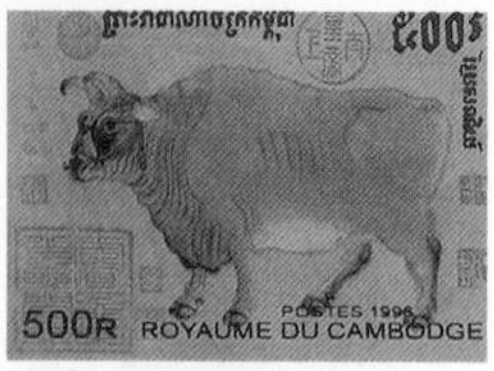

308 Ox

1996. New Year. Year of the Ox. Details of painting by Han Huang. Multicoloured.

1603	500r. Type **308**	65	20
1604	500r. Ox with head turned to right (upright horns)	65	20
1605	500r. Brown and white ox with head up ("handlebar" horns)	65	20
1606	500r. Ox with head in bush ("ram's" horns)	65	20

309 Dam, Phnom Kaun Sat

1996. Tenth International United Nations Volunteers Day. Multicoloured.

1607	100r. Type **309**	30	10
1608	500r. Canal, O Angkrung	1·40	45
1609	900r. Canal, Chrey Krem	2·50	85

310 Architect's Model of Reservoir

1996. 43rd Anniv of Independence. Water Management. Multicoloured.

1610	100r. Type **310**	30	10
1611	500r. Reservoir	1·40	45
1612	900r. Reservoir (different)	2·50	85

311 Players

1997. World Cup Football Championship, France (1998) (2nd issue).

1613	**311**	100r. multicoloured	30	10
1614	-	200r. multicoloured	45	10
1615	-	300r. multicoloured	75	20
1616	-	500r. multicoloured	1·30	20
1617	-	900r. multicoloured	2·30	20
1618	-	1000r. multicoloured	2·75	20
MS1619		99×68 mm. 2000r. multicoloured (39×31 mm)	4·75	90

DESIGNS: 200r. to 2000r. Different footballing scenes.

312 Two Elephants

1997. The Indian Elephant. Multicoloured.

1620	300r. Type **312**	30	10
1621	500r. Group of three	55	20
1622	900r. Elephants fighting	1·10	30
1623	1000r. Adult and calf	1·30	35

314 Horse-drawn Water Pump, 1731

1997. Fire Engines. Multicoloured.

1630	200r. Type **314**	30	10
1631	500r. Putnam horse-drawn water pump, 1863	45	10
1632	900r. Merryweather horse-drawn engine, 1894	65	20
1633	1000r. Shand Mason Co horse-drawn water pump, 1901	85	20
1634	1500r. Maxin Motor Co automatic pump, 1949	1·30	20
1635	4000r. Merryweather exhaust pump, 1950	3·50	20
MS1636	106×87 mm. 5400r. Mack Truck Co. mechanical ladder, 1953 (39×31 mm)	4·75	90

315 Statue on Plinth

1997. Angkor Wat.

1637	**315**	300r. black and red	30	10
1638	-	300r. black and blue	30	10
1639	-	800r. black and green	65	10
1640	-	1500r. black & brown	1·30	10
1641	-	1700r. black & orange	1·50	20
1642	-	2500r. black and blue	1·90	20
1643	-	3000r. black & green	2·50	20

DESIGNS—VERT: No. 1638, Statue in wall recess; 1639, Walled courtyard; 1640, Decorative panel with two figures. HORIZ: No. 1641, Rectangular gateway; 1642, Statues and arched gateway; 1643, Stupa and ruins.

316 Steller's Eider

1997. Aquatic Birds. Multicoloured.

1644	200r. Type **316**	10	10
1645	500r. Egyptian goose	25	10
1646	900r. American wigeon	40	20
1647	1000r. Falcated teal	45	20
1648	1500r. Surf scoter	65	20
1649	4000r. Blue-winged teal	1·90	20
MS1650	95×75 mm. 5400r. Baikal teal (31×39 mm)	4·75	90

317 Von Stephan

1997. Death Centenary of Heinrich von Stephan (founder of UPU).

1651	**317**	500r. blue & dp blue	45	20
1652	**317**	1500r. green and olive	1·30	30
1653	**317**	2000r. yellow & green	1·80	45

318 Main Entrance

1997. Khmer Culture. Banteay Srei Temple. Multicoloured.

1654	500r. Type **318**	45	20
1655	1500r. Main and side entrances	1·30	30
1656	2000r. Courtyard	1·80	45

319 Birman

1997. Cats. Multicoloured.

1657	200r. Type **319**	30	10
1658	500r. Exotic shorthair	45	10
1659	900r. Persian	65	20
1660	1000r. Turkish van	85	20
1661	1500r. American shorthair	1·30	20
1662	4000r. Scottish fold	3·50	20
MS1663	90×70 mm. 5400r. Sphinx (31×39 mm)	3·75	90

320 No. 488 S.W.R. Loco British Rail No. 30583

1997. Steam Railway Locomotives. Multicoloured.

1664	200r. Type **320**	30	10
1665	500r. *Frederick Smith*	45	10
1666	900r. No. 3131	65	20
1667	1000r. London Transport No. L44, Great Britain	85	20
1668	1500r. LNER No. 1711, Great Britain	1·30	20
1669	4000r. No. 60523 *Chateau du Soleil*	3·50	20
MS1670	76×60 mm. 5400r. LNER No. 2006, Great Britain	4·25	90

321 Shar-pei

1997. Dogs. Multicoloured.

1671	200r. Type **321**	30	10
1672	500r. Chin-chin	45	10
1673	900r. Pekingese	55	20
1674	1000r. Chow-chow (vert)	65	20
1675	1500r. Pug (vert)	1·30	20
1676	4000r. Akita (vert)	3·50	20
MS1677	111×88 mm. 5400r. Chinese crested (vert)	3·75	90

322 Qunalom Temple

1997. 30th Anniv of Association of South East Asian Nations. Multicoloured.

1678	500r. Type **322**	45	20
1679	1500r. Royal Palace	1·30	30
1680	2000r. National Museum	1·80	45

323 15th-century Caravelle

1997. Sailing Ships. Multicoloured.

1681	200r. Type **323**	30	10
1682	500r. Spanish galleon	45	10
1683	900r. *Great Harry* (British galleon)	65	20
1684	1000r. *La Couronne* (French galleon)	85	20
1685	1500r. 18th-century East Indiaman	1·30	20
1686	4000r. 19th-century clipper	3·50	20
MS1687	94×68 mm. 5400r. H.M.S. *Victory* (Nelson)	4·25	90

324 Public Garden

1997. Public Gardens (Nos. 1688/91) and Tuk Chha Canal (others).

1688	**324**	300r. green and black	30	10
1689	-	300r. red and black	30	10
1690	-	800r. yellow and black	65	10
1691	-	1500r. orange and black	1·30	10
1692	-	1700r. pink and black	1·50	20
1693	-	2500r. blue and black	1·90	20
1694	-	3000r. blue and black	2·50	20

DESIGNS—HORIZ: 300r. Statue at intersection of paths; 300r. Hedging in triangular bed; 1500r. Tree and statue of lion; 1700r. View along canal; 2500r. View across canal; 3000r. Closed lock gates. VERT: 800r. Mounted bowl.

325 Satan's Mushroom

1997. Fungi. Multicoloured.

1695	200r. Type **325**	30	10
1696	500r. *Amanita regalis*	45	10
1697	900r. *Morchella semilibera*	65	20
1698	1000r. *Gomphus clavatus*	85	20
1699	1500r. *Hygrophorus hypothejus*	1·30	20
1700	4000r. *Albatrellus confluens*	3·50	20
MS1701	110×89 mm. 5400r. Red-cracked boletus	4·75	90

326 Peaceful Fightingfish (*Betta imbellis*) and Siamese Fightingfish (*Betta splendens*)

1997. Fish. Multicoloured.

1702	200r. Type **326**	20	10
1703	500r. Banded gourami	25	10
1704	900r. Rosy barbs	40	20
1705	1000r. Paradise fish	55	20
1706	1500r. *Epalzeorhynchos frenatus*	1·00	20
1707	4000r. *Capoeta tetrazona*	2·10	20
MS1708	96×72 mm. 5400r. Harlequin fish	4·75	90

327 Kampot Post Office

1997. 44th Anniv of Independence. Multicoloured.

1709	1000r. Type **327**	85	30
1710	3000r. Prey Veng Post Office	2·75	65

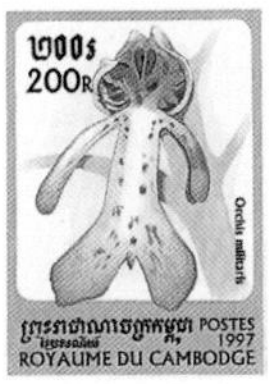

328 *Orchis militaris*

1997. Orchids. Multicoloured.

1711	200r. Type **328**	20	10
1712	500r. *Orchiaceras bivonae*	30	10
1713	900r. *Orchiaceras spuria*	50	20
1714	1000r. *Gymnadenia conopsea*	60	20
1715	1500r. *"Perapias neglecta*	1·30	20
1716	4000r. *"Pseudorhiza bruniana"*	2·75	20
MS1717	70×90 mm. 5400r. *Dactylodenia wintonii*	4·75	90

329 In black Jacket

1997. Diana, Princess of Wales Commemoration. Multicoloured.

1718	100r. Type **329**	15	10
1719	200r. In black dress	15	10
1720	300r. In blue jacket	15	10
1721	500r. Close-up of Princess in visor	30	10
1722	1000r. In mine-protection clothing	50	10
1723	1500r. With Elizabeth Dole	85	10
1724	2000r. Holding landmine	1·20	20
1725	2500r. With Mother Teresa and Sisters of Charity	1·40	20

330 Player with Ball

1998. World Cup Football Championship, France (3rd issue).

1726	**330**	200r. multicoloured	15	10
1727	-	500r. multicoloured	25	10
1728	-	900r. multicoloured	45	20
1729	-	1000r. multicoloured	55	20
1730	-	1500r. multicoloured	80	20
1731	-	4000r. multicoloured	2·30	20
MS1732		110×90 mm. 5400r. multicoloured (39×31 mm)	3·25	90

DESIGNS: 500r. to 5400r. Different footballing scenes.

331 Suorprat Gateway

1998. Temple Ruins.

1733	**331**	300r. orange and black	20	10
1734	-	500r. pink and black	30	10
1735	-	1200r. orange and black	45	10
1736	-	1500r. orange and black	65	10
1737	-	1700r. blue and black	75	20
1738	-	2000r. green and black	95	20
1739	-	3000r. lilac and black	1·50	20

DESIGNS—HORIZ: No. 1734, Kumlung wall; 1735, Bapuon entrance; 1737, Prerup; 1738, Preah Khan. VERT: No. 1736, Palilai; 1739, Bayon.

332 Tiger Cub

1998. New Year. Year of the Tiger. Multicoloured.

1740	200r. Type **332**	20	10
1741	500r. Tiger and cubs	30	10
1742	990r. Tiger on alert	45	20
1743	1000r. Tiger washing itself (horiz)	55	20
1744	1500r. Tiger lying in grass (horiz)	80	20
1745	4000r. Tiger snarling (horiz)	2·30	20
MS1746	120×90 mm. 5400r. Tiger on rock (31×30 mm)	3·25	90

333 Oakland, Antioch and Eastern Electric Locomotive No. 105

1998. Railway Locomotives. Multicoloured.

1747	200r. Type **333**	20	10
1748	500r. New York, Westchester and electric locomotive No. 1	45	10
1749	900r. Spokane and Inland electric locomotive No. MII	55	20
1750	1000r. International Railway electric locomotive	75	20
1751	1500r. British Columbia Electric Railway locomotive No. 823	1·10	20
1752	4000r. Southern Pacific electric locomotive No. 200	3·00	20
MS1753	88×94 mm. Storage battery locomotive (vert triangle)	3·75	90

334 Rottweiler

1998. Dogs. Multicoloured.

1754	200r. Type **334**	15	10
1755	500r. Beauceron	35	10
1756	900r. Boxer	50	20
1757	1000r. Siberian husky	60	20
1758	1500r. Welsh Pembroke corgi	85	20
1759	4000r. Basset hound	2·30	20
MS1760	110×89 mm. Schnauzer (28×37½ mm)	3·75	90

335 Stag Beetle

1998. Beetles. Multicoloured.

1761	200r. Type **335**	20	10
1762	500r. *Carabus auronitens* (ground beetle)	45	10
1763	900r. Alpine longhorn beetle	65	20
1764	1000r. *Geotrupes* (dor beetle)	75	20
1765	1500r. *Megasoma elephas*	1·10	20
1766	4000r. *Chalcosoma*	2·75	20
MS1767	110×90 mm. 5400r. *Leptura rubra* (longhorn beetle)	3·75	90

336 Prerup Temple

1998. Khmer Culture. Multicoloured.

1768	500r. Type **336**	30	20
1769	1500r. Bayon Temple	75	30
1770	2000r. Angkor Vat	1·10	45

337 Cutter

1998. Ships. Multicoloured.

1771	200r. Type **337**	20	10
1772	500r. *Britannia* (mail paddle-steamer, 1840)	45	10
1773	900r. Viking longship, Gokstad	65	20
1774	1000r. *Great Britain* (steam/sail)	75	20
1775	1500r. Medieval coasting nau	1·10	20
1776	4000r. Full-rigged ship (inscr "Fregate")	2·75	20
MS1777	110×91 mm. 5400r. *Tartane* (fishing boat) (39×31 mm)	3·75	90

338 Scottish Fold

1998. Domestic Cats. Multicoloured.

1778	200r. Type **338**	15	10
1779	500r. Ragdoll	35	10
1780	900r. Cymric	50	20
1781	1000r. Devon rex	60	20
1782	1500r. American curl	85	20
1783	4000r. Sphinx	2·30	20
MS1784	90×108 mm. 5400r. Japanese bobtail (39×31 mm)	3·75	90

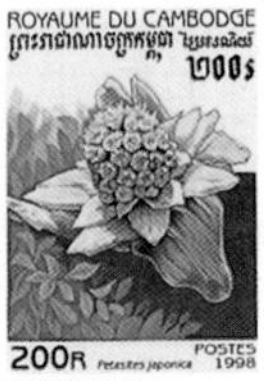

339 *Petasites japonica*

1998. Flowers. Multicoloured.

1785	200r. Type **339**	15	10
1786	500r. *Gentiana triflora*	30	10
1787	900r. *Doronicum cordatum*	50	20
1788	1000r. *Scabiosa japonica*	55	20
1789	1500r. *Magnolia sieboldii*	75	20
1790	4000r. *Erythronium japonica*	2·30	20
MS1791	90×101 mm. China aster (30×36 mm)	3·25	90

340 *Baptism of Christ* (Gerard David)

1998. "Italia 98" International Stamp Exhibition, Milan. Paintings. Multicoloured.

1792	200r. Type **340**	20	10
1793	500r. *Madonna of Martin van Niuwenhoven* (Hans Memling)	30	10
1794	900r. *Baptism of Christ* (Hendrich Holtzius)	55	20
1795	1000r. *Christ with the Cross* (Luis de Morales)	65	20
1796	1500r. *Elias in the Desert* (Dirk Bouts)	95	20
1797	4000r. *The Virgin* (Petrus Christus)	2·75	20
MS1798	87×107 mm. *The Immaculate Conception* (Bartolome Murillo) (39×31 mm)	3·75	90

There are errors of spelling in some of the inscriptions.

341 *Phyciodes tharos*

1998. Butterflies. Multicoloured.

1799	200r. Type **341**	20	10
1800	500r. *Pararge megera*	30	10
1801	900r. Monarch	55	20
1802	1000r. Apollo	65	20
1803	1500r. Swallowtail	95	20
1804	4000r. *Eumenis semele*	2·75	20
MS1805	91×110 mm. 5400r. Blue morpho (39×31 mm)	3·75	90

342 Post Box, 1997

1998. World Post Day. Multicoloured.

1806	1000r. Type **342**	55	30
1807	3000r. Wall-mounted post box, 1951	1·40	65

343 Big-Headed Turtle

1998. Tortoise and Turtles. Multicoloured.

1808	200r. Type **343**	15	10
1809	500r. Green turtle	25	10
1810	900r. American soft-shelled turtle	40	20
1811	1000r. Hawksbill turtle	50	20
1812	1500r. Aldabra tortoise	70	20
1813	4000r. Leatherback sea turtle	2·00	20
MS1814	5400r. Matamata turtle (39×31 mm)	3·25	90

344 Bayon Dance

1998. 45th Anniv of Independence. Multicoloured.

1815	500r. Type **344**	35	20
1816	1500r. Bayon dance (different)	85	30
1817	2000r. Bayon dance (different)	1·20	45

345 Cheetah

1998. Big Cats. Multicoloured.

1818	200r. Type **345**	15	10
1819	500r. Snow leopard	25	10
1820	900r. Ocelot	40	20
1821	1000r. Leopard	50	20
1822	1500r. Serval	70	20
1823	4000r. Jaguar	2·00	20
MS1824	90×109 mm. 5400r. Tiger (31×39 mm)	3·25	90

346 Rabbit

1999. New Year. Year of the Rabbit. Multicoloured. Showing rabbits.

1825	200r. Type **346**	30	10
1826	500r. Facing left	45	10
1827	900r. Sitting in bush	75	20
1828	1000r. Sitting on rock	85	20
1829	1500r. Sitting upright	1·40	20
1830	4000r. Head looking out from grass (vert)	3·75	20
MS1831	110×84 mm. 5400r. Rabbit (39×31 mm)	3·75	90

347 Foster and Rastik's *Stourbridge Lion*, 1829, U.S.A.

1999. Steam Railway Locomotives. Multicoloured.

1832	200r. Type **347**	20	10
1833	500r. *Atlantic*, 1832	30	10
1834	900r. No. 035, 1934	45	20
1835	1000r. Daniel Gooch's *Iron Duke*, 1847, Great Britain	60	20
1836	1500r. *4-6-0*	95	20
1837	4000r. *4-4-2*	2·50	20
MS1838	84×109 mm. 5400r. *Fire Fly*, 1840, *Great Britain* (39×31 mm)	3·75	90

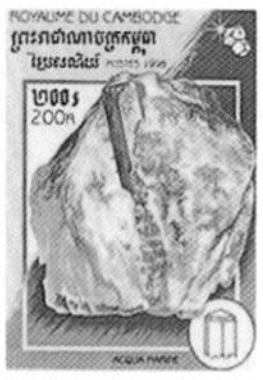

348 Aquamarine

1999. Minerals. Multicoloured.

1839	200r. Type **348**	10	10
1840	500r. Cat's eye	20	10
1841	900r. Malachite	35	20
1842	1000r. Emerald	45	20
1843	1500r. Turquoise	65	20
1844	4000r. Ruby	1·80	20
MS1845	107×88 mm. 5400r. Diamond (39×31 mm)	3·75	90

349 Alsatian

1999. Dogs. Multicoloured.

1846	200r. Type **349**	20	10
1847	500r. Shih tzu (horiz)	30	10
1848	900r. Tibetan spaniel (horiz)	50	20
1849	1000r. Ainu-ken	55	20
1850	1500r. Lhassa apso (horiz)	90	20
1851	4000r. Tibetan terrier (horiz)	2·50	20
MS1852	109×88 mm. 5400r. Tosa inu (31×39 mm)	3·75	90

350 La Rapide steam carriage, 1881

1999. Cars. Multicoloured.

1853	200r. Type **350**	15	10
1854	500r. Duryea motor buggy, 1895	25	10
1855	900r. Marius Barbarou voiturette, 1898	40	20
1856	1000r. Panhard and Levassor voiturette, 1898	50	20
1857	1500r. Mercedes-Benz Tonneau, 1901	70	20
1858	4000r. Ford model sedan, 1915	2·00	20
MS1859	108×86 mm. 5400r. Marcus, 1875 (39×31 mm)	3·75	90

351 Ragdoll

1999. Cats. Multicoloured.

1860	200r. Type **351**	20	10
1861	500r. Russian blue	25	10
1862	900r. Bombay	50	20
1863	1000r. Siamese	55	20
1864	1500r. Oriental shorthair	95	20
1865	4000r. Somali	2·50	20
MS1866	84×109 mm. 5400r. Egyptian mau (31×38 mm)	3·75	90

352 Dragon Bridge

1999. Khmer Culture. Multicoloured.

1867	500r. Type **352**	25	20
1868	1500r. Temple of 100 Columns, Kratie	80	30
1869	2000r. Krapum Chhouk, Kratie	1·20	45

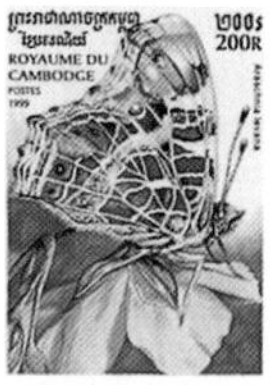

353 *Araschnia levana*

1999. Butterflies. Multicoloured.

1870	200r. Type **353**	20	10
1871	500r. Painted lady (horiz)	25	10
1872	900r. *Clossiana euphrosyne*	50	20
1873	1000r. *Coenonympha hero*	55	20
1874	1500r. Apollo (horiz)	90	20
1875	4000r. *Plebejus argus*	2·50	20
MS1876	109×90 mm. 5400r. Purple-edged copper (31×39 mm)	3·75	90

354 Saurornitholestes

1999. Prehistoric Animals. Multicoloured.

1877	200r. Type **354**	15	10
1878	500r. Prenocephale	20	10
1879	900r. Wuerhosaurus	40	20
1880	1000r. Muttaburrasaurus	45	20
1881	1500r. Shantungosaurus	70	20
1882	4000r. Microceratops	2·10	20
MS1883	111×84 mm. 5400r. Daspletosaurus	3·75	90

355 *Flabellina affinis*

1999. Molluscs. Multicoloured.

1884	200r. Type **355**	20	10
1885	500r. *Octopus macropus*	30	10
1886	900r. *Helix hortensis*	55	20
1887	1000r. *Lima hians*	65	20
1888	1500r. *Arion empiricorum*	95	20
1889	4000r. Swan mussel	2·75	20
MS1890	110×84 mm. 5400r. *Eledone aldrovandii*	3·75	90

356 *Flowers in a Vase* (Henri Fantin-Latour)

1999. "Philexfrance 99" International Stamp Exhibition, Paris. Paintings. Multicoloured.

1891	200r. Type **356**	30	10
1892	500r. *Fruit* (Paul Cezanne)	45	10
1893	900r. *Table and Chairs* (Andre Derain)	75	20
1894	1000r. *Vase on a Table* (Henri Matisse)	85	20
1895	1500r. *Tulips and Marquerites* (Othon Friesz)	1·40	20
1896	4000r. *Still Life with Tapestry* (Matisse)	3·75	20
MS1897	107×84 mm. 5400r. *Still Life with Tapestry*(detail) (Cezanne)	3·75	90

357 Prasat Neak Poan

1999. Temples.

1898	**357**	100r. blue and black	20	10
1899	-	300r. red and black	20	10
1900	-	500r. grn & blk (vert)	30	10
1901	-	1400r. green and black	85	10
1902	-	1600r. mauve and black	95	20
1903	-	1800r. vio & blk (vert)	1·10	20
1904	-	1900r. brown and black	1·20	20

DESIGNS: 300r. Statue, Neak Poan; 500r. Banteay Srey; 1400r. Banteay Samre; 1600r. Banteay Srey; 1800r. Bas-relief, Angkor Vat; 1900r. Brasat Takeo.

358 Pagoda, Tongzhou

1999. "China 1999" International Stamp Exhibition, Peking. Multicoloured.

1905	200r. Type **358**	20	10
1906	500r. Pagoda, Tianning Temple	30	10
1907	900r. Pagoda, Summer Palace	75	10
1908	900r. Pagoda, Blue Cloud Temple	75	10
1909	1000r. White pagoda, Bei Hai	75	10
1910	1000r. Pagoda, Scented Hill	75	10
1911	1500r. Pagoda, Yunju Temple	1·30	20
1912	4000r. White pagoda, Miaoying Temple	3·25	20

359 *Cymbidium insigne*

1999. Orchids. Multicoloured.

1913	200r. Type **359**	20	10
1914	500r. *Papilionanthe teres*	30	10
1915	900r. *Panisea uniflora*	55	20
1916	1000r. *Euanthe sanderiana*	65	20
1917	1500r. *Dendrobium trigonopus*	95	20
1918	4000r. *Vanda coerulea*	2·75	20
MS1919	109×80 mm. 5400r. *Paphiopedilum callosum* (26×36 mm)	3·75	90

360 Northern Bullfinch

1999. Birds. Multicoloured.

1920	200r. Type **360**	30	10

1921	500r. Hawfinch	45	10
1922	900r. Western greenfinch	75	20
1923	1000r. Yellow warbler	85	20
1924	1500r. Great grey shrike	1·40	20
1925	4000r. Blue tit	3·75	20
MS1926	109×85 mm. 5400r. European robin (39×30 mm)	3·75	90

361 Emblem

1999. 46th Anniv of Independence. Multicoloured.

1927	500r. Type **361**	30	20
1928	1500r. People with symbols of transport and industry	75	30
1929	2000r. People queueing to vote	1·10	45

362 Tiger Barbs

1999. Fish. Multicoloured.

1930	200r. Type **362**	30	10
1931	500r. Rainbow shark minnow	45	10
1932	900r. Clown rasbora	75	20
1933	1000r. Orange-spotted cichlid	85	20
1934	1500r. Crescent betta	1·40	20
1935	4000r. Honey gourami	3·75	20
MS1936	109×84 mm. Eyespot puffer-fish (39×31 mm)	3·75	90

363 Harpy Eagle

1999. Birds of Prey. Multicoloured.

1937	200r. Type **363**	30	10
1938	500r. Bateleur (vert)	45	10
1939	900r. Egyptian vulture (vert)	75	20
1940	1000r. Peregrine falcon (vert)	85	20
1941	1500r. Red-tailed hawk (vert)	1·40	20
1942	4000r. American bald eagle	3·75	20
MS1943	109×85 mm. 5400r. Red kite (31×39 mm)	3·75	90

364 Mail Carriage and Globe

1999. 125th Anniv of Universal Postal Union.

1944	**364**	1600r. multicoloured	1·60	90

365 Giant Panda

1999. Mammals. Multicoloured.

1945	200r. Type **365**	20	10
1946	500r. Yak	30	10
1947	900r. Chinese water deer	55	20
1948	1000r. Eurasian water shrew (horiz)	65	20
1949	1500r. European otter (horiz)	95	20
1950	4000r. Tiger (horiz)	2·75	20
MS1951	110×81 mm. 5400r. Pere David's deer (39×31 mm)	3·75	90

366 Coral Snake

1999. Snakes. Multicoloured.

1952	200r. Type **366**	30	10
1953	500r. Rainbow boa	45	10
1954	900r. Yellow anaconda	75	20
1955	1000r. Southern ring-necked snake	85	20
1956	1500r. Harlequin snake	1·40	20
1957	4000r. Eastern tiger snake	3·75	20
MS1958	107×81 mm. 5400r. Green python (36×28 mm)	3·75	90

367 Dragon

2000. New Year. Year of the Dragon.

1959	**367**	200r. multicoloured	30	10
1960	-	500r. red, buff and black	45	10
1961	-	900r. multicoloured	75	20
1962	-	1000r. multicoloured	85	20
1963	-	1500r. multicoloured	1·40	20
1964	-	4000r. multicoloured	3·75	20
MS1965		86×110 mm. 4500r. multi-coloured	3·25	90

DESIGNS: 500r. Dragon enclosed in circle; 900r. Green dragon with red flames; 1000r. Heraldic dragon; 1500r. Red dragon with blue extremities; 4000r. Blue dragon with yellow flames; 4500r. Dragon's head (32×40 mm).

368 Iguanodon

2000. Dinosaurs. Multicoloured.

1966	200r. Type **368**	20	10
1967	500r. Euoplocepalus	30	10
1968	900r. Diplosaurus	55	20
1969	1000r. Diplodocus	65	20
1970	1500r. Stegoceras	95	20
1971	4000r. Stegosaurus	2·75	20
MS1972	110×85 mm. 4500r. Brachiosaurus (32×40 mm)	3·75	90

369 Ground Beetle (*Calosoma sycophanta*)

2000. Insects. Multicoloured.

1973	200r. Type **369**	30	10
1974	500r. European rhinoceros beetle (*Oryctes nasicornis*)	45	10
1975	900r. *Diochrysa fastuosa*	75	20
1976	1000r. *Blaps gigas*	85	20
1977	1500r. Green tiger beetle (*Cincindela campestris*)	1·40	20
1978	4000r. *Cissistes cephalotes*	3·75	20
MS1979	107×85 mm. 4500r. Scarab beetle (*Scarabaeus aegyptiorum*) (40×32 mm)	3·25	90

370 Box Turtle (*Cuora amboinensis*)

2000. "Bangkok 2000" International Stamp Exhibition. Turtles and Tortoise. Multicoloured.

1980	200r. Type **370**	30	10
1981	500r. Yellow box turtle (*Cuora flavomarginata*)	45	10
1982	900r. Black-breasted leaf turtle (*Geoemyda spengleri*) (horiz)	75	20
1983	1000r. Impressed tortoise (*Manouria (Geochelone) impressa*) (horiz)	85	20
1984	1500r. Reeves' turtle (*Chinemys reevesi*) (horiz)	1·40	20
1985	4000r. Spiny turtle (*Heosemys spinosa*) (horiz)	3·75	20
MS1986	111×86 mm. 4500r. Annadal's turtle (*Hieremys annandalei*) (horiz) (40×32 mm)	3·25	90

371 Ox-cart carrying Rice

2000. Rice Cultivation.

1987	**371**	100r. green and black	20	10
1988	-	300r. blue and black	30	10
1989	-	500r. mauve and black	45	10
1990	-	1400r. blue and black	1·10	10
1991	-	1600r. brown and black	1·50	20
1992	-	1900r. brown and black	1·80	20
1993	-	2200r. red and black	2·10	20

DESIGNS: 300r. Harrowing; 500r. Threshing; 1400r. Winnowing; 1600r. Planting; 1900r. Ploughing; 2200r. Binding sheaves.

372 *Jules Petiet* Steam Locomotive

2000. Locomotives. "WIPA 2000" International Stamp Exhibition, Vienna (MS2000). Multicoloured.

1994	200r. Type **372**	30	10
1995	500r. *Longue Chaudiere* steam locomotive, 1891	45	10
1996	900r. *Le Grand Chocolats* steam locomotive	65	20
1997	1000r. *Glehn du Busquet* steam locomotive, 1891	85	20
1998	1500r. *Le Pendule Francais* diesel locomotive	1·30	20
1999	4000r. TGV 001 locomotive, 1976	3·50	20
MS2000	110×86 mm. 4500r. "Le Shuttle" in tunnel (80×32 mm)	3·25	90

373 Fly Agaric (*Amanita muscaria*)

2000. Fungi. Multicoloured.

2001	200r. Type **373**	20	10
2002	500r. Panther cap (*Amanita pantherina*)	30	10
2003	900r. *Clitocybe olearia*	55	20
2004	1000r. *Lactarius scrobiculatus*	65	20
2005	1500r. *Scleroderma vulgare*	95	20
2006	4000r. *Amanita verna*	2·75	20
MS2007	110×86 mm. 4500r. Death cap (*Amanita phalloides*) (32×40 mm)	3·75	90

374 *Betta unimaculata* and *Betta pugnax*

2000. Fighting Fish. Multicoloured.

2008	200r. Type **374**	10	10
2009	500r. *Betta macrostoma* and *Betta taeniata*	30	10
2010	900r. *Betta foerschi* and *Betta imbellis*	65	20
2011	1000r. *Betta tessyae* and *Betta picta*	65	20
2012	1500r. *Betta edithae* and *Betta bellica*	95	20
2013	4000r. *Betta smaragdina*	2·75	20
MS2014	110×85 mm. 4500r. Siamese fighting fish (*Betta splendens*) (40×32 mm)	3·25	90

375 Woman in Arched Alcove (stone carving)

2000. Khmer Cultural Heritage. Each brown and black.

2015	500r. Type **375**	30	20
2016	1000r. Woman in flowered head-dress in rectangula bas-relief	75	30
2017	2000r. Woman with right arm raised in arche bas-relief	1·10	45

376 Galapagos Albatross (*Diomedea irrorata*)

2000. Sea Birds. Multicoloured.

2018	200r. Type **376**	30	10
2019	500r. Kentish plover (*Charadrius alexandrinus*) (vert)	45	10
2020	900r. Blue-footed booby (*Sula nebouxii*)	65	20
2021	1000r. Common tern (*Sterna hirundo*)	85	20
2022	1500r. Herring gull (*Larus argentatus*) (vert)	1·30	20
2023	4000r. Whiskered tern (*Chlidonias hybrida*)	3·50	20
MS2024	108×83 mm. 4500r. Gannet (*Sula (Morus) bassana*)	3·25	90

377 *Cypripedium macranthum*

2000. Orchids. Multicoloured.

2025	200r. Type **377**	30	10
2026	500r. *Vandopsis gigantean*	45	10
2027	900r. *Calypso bulbosa*	65	20
2028	1000r. *Vanda luzonica*	85	20
2029	1500r. *Paphiopedilum villosum*	1·30	20
2030	4000r. *Vanda merrillii*	3·50	20
MS2031	81×107 mm. 4500r. *Paphiopedilum Victoria*	3·25	90

378 Rowers in Large Canoe

2000. Tourism. Multicoloured.

2032	500r. Type **378**	30	20
2033	1500r. Front of decorated canoe	75	30
2034	2000r. Temple, elephant and dancer	1·10	45

379 Weightlifting

2000. Sports. Multicoloured.

2035	200r. Type **379**	20	10
2036	500r. Gymnastics	45	10
2037	900r. Baseball	55	20
2038	1000r. Tennis	65	20
2039	1500r. Basketball	1·10	20
2040	4000r. High jump	2·75	20
MS2041	110×85 mm. 4500r. Running	3·00	90

380 Metz DLK 23-6

2000. Fire Engines. Multicoloured.

2042	200r. Type **380**	20	20
2043	500r. Iveco-Magirus SLF 24/100	45	35
2044	900r. Metz SLF 7000 WS	55	45
2045	1000r. Iveco-Magirus TLF 24/50	65	55
2046	1500r. Saval-Konenburg RFF-11.000	1·10	90
2047	4000r. Metz TLF 24/50	2·75	2·30

MS2048	110×85 mm. 4500r. Metz TLF 16/25	6·50	5·50

381 Smooth Haired Dachshund

2000. Dachshunds. Multicoloured.

2049	200r. Type **381**	20	10
2050	500r. Wire haired	45	10
2051	900r. Long haired	55	20
2052	1000r. Two smooth haired	65	20
2053	1500r. Mother and pups	1·10	20
2054	4000r. Two puppies	2·75	20
MS2055	117×86 mm. 4500r. Head of wire haired (32×40 mm)	3·00	90

382 Rover 12 C (1912)

2000. Cars. Espana 2000 International Stamp Exhibition, Madrid. Multicoloured.

2056	200r. Type **382**	20	10
2057	500r. Austin 30 CV (1907)	45	10
2058	900r. Rolls-Royce Silver Ghost (1909)	55	20
2059	1000r. Graham Paige (1929)	65	20
2060	1500r. Austin 12 (1937)	1·10	20
2061	4000r. Mercedes-Benz 300SL (1957)	2·75	20
MS2062	110×86 mm. 4500r. MG (1936) (40×32 mm)	3·00	90

383 18th-century Korean Painting and Two Kittens

2000. Cats. Multicoloured.

2063	200r. Type **383**	20	10
2064	500r. 18th-century Portuguese tiles and tabby cat	45	10
2065	900r. Satsuma ceramic cat and two cats	55	20
2066	1000r. Goddess Basset (Egyptian) and mother cat and kittens	65	20
2067	1500r. Goddess Freya (engraving) and tortoiseshell cat	1·10	20
2068	4000r. Japanese painting and Manx cat	2·75	20
MS2069	110×86 mm. 4500r. Leaping cat (40×32 mm)	3·00	90

384 Flowers, Monument and Flag

2000. 47th Anniv of Independence. Multicoloured.

2070	500r. Type **384**	30	20
2071	1500r. Dove, monument and flag	75	30
2072	2000r. Flag, monument and crowd	1·10	45

385 *The Courageous Little Tailor*

2000. Children's Stories. Multicoloured.

2073	200r. Type **385**	20	10
2074	500r. *Tom Thumb*	45	10
2075	900r. *Thumbelina*	50	20
2076	1000r. *Pinocchio (horiz)*	65	20
2077	1500r. *The Crayfish (horiz)*	1·10	20
2078	4000r. *Peter Pan (horiz)*	2·75	20
MS2079	110×85 mm. 4500r. *Pied Piper of Hamelin* (32×40 mm)	3·00	90

386 Wattled Starling (*Creatophora cinera*)

2000. Birds. Multicoloured.

2080	200r. Type **386**	20	10
2081	500r. Common starling (*Sturnus vulgaris*)	45	10
2082	900r. Pekin robin (*Leiothrix lutea*)	55	20
2083	1000r. Guianian cock of the rock (*Rupicola rupicola*)	85	20
2084	1500r. Alpine accentor (*Prunella collaris*)	1·10	20
2085	4000r. Bearded reedling (*Panurus biarmicus*) (inscr "biarnicus")	2·75	20
MS2086	85×110 mm. 4500r. Inscr *Muscicapula pallipes* (32×40 mm)	3·00	90

387 Johannes Gutenberg (invention of printing press)

2001. Millennium. Multicoloured.

2087	200r. Type **387**	20	10
2088	500r. Michael Faraday (discovery of electricity)	45	10
2089	900r. Samuel Morse (invention of Morse code)	55	20
2090	1000r. Alexander Bell (invention of telephone)	65	20
2091	1500r. Enrico Fermi (discovery of nuclear fission)	1·10	20
2092	4000r. Edward Roberts (invention of personal computer)	2·75	20
MS2093	86×112 mm. 5400r. Christopher Columbus (discovery of America) (40×32 mm); 5400r. Neil Armstrong (first moon walk) (40×32 mm)	7·50	90

388 Snake Head

2001. Year of the Snake. Multicoloured.

2094	200r. Type **388**	20	10
2095	500r. Two snakes entwined	45	10
2096	900r. Snake entwined with moon	55	20
2097	1000r. Entwined snakes (*different*)	65	20
2098	1500r. Snake encircling moon	1·10	20
2099	4000r. Three snakes' heads	2·75	20
MS2100	110×86 mm. 5400r. Snake head (*different*) (40×32 mm)	3·75	90

389 Sandou Ladder Transport (1910)

2001. Fire Engines. Multicoloured.

2101	200r. Type **389**	20	10
2102	500r. Gallo ladder transport (1899)	45	10
2103	900r. Merry Weather appliance (1950)	55	20
2104	1000r. Merry Weather ambulance (1940)	65	20
2105	1500r. Man-Metz appliance (1972)	1·10	20
2106	4000r. Roman diesel appliance (1970)	2·75	20
MS2107	111×87 mm. 5400r. Metropolitan steam engine (1898) (40×32 mm).	3·75	90

390 Puff Ball (*Lycoperdon perlatum*)

2001. Fungi. Multicoloured.

2108	200r. Type **390**	20	10
2109	500r. *Trametes versicolor*	45	10
2110	900r. *Hypholoma sublaterium* (inscr "Hipholoma")	55	20
2111	1000r. Fly agaric (*Amanita muscaria*)	65	20
2112	1500r. *Lycoperdon umbrinum*	1·10	20
2113	4000r. *Cortinarius orellanus*	2·75	20
MS2114	111×84 mm. 5400r. Death cap (*Amanita phalloides*) (32×40 mm)	3·75	90

391 Preah Vihear

2001. Temples.

2115	**391**	200r. blue and black	20	10
2116	-	300r. red and black	30	10
2117	-	600r. green and black	45	10
2118	-	1000r. orange and black	65	10
2119	-	1500r. green and black	95	20
2120	-	1700r. violet and black	1·20	20
2121	-	2200r. brown and black	1·40	20

DESIGNS: 300r. Thonmanom; 600r. Tasom; 1000r. Kravan; 1500r. Takeo; 1700r. Mebon; 2200r. Banteay Kdei.

392 Angkor Wat

2001. Third Anniv of Day of Khmer Culture. Showing bas-reliefs. Multicoloured.

2122	500r. Type **392**	30	20
2123	1500r. Bayon Temple	1·10	30
2124	2000r. Bayon Temple (different)	1·40	45

393 Large Tortoiseshell (*Nymphalis polychloros*)

2001. Butterflies. Belgica 2001 International Stamp Exhibition, Brussels. Multicoloured.

2125	200r. Type **393**	20	10
2126	500r. *Cethosia hypsea*	45	10
2127	900r. *Papilio palinurus*	55	20
2128	1000r. Lesser purple emperor (*Apatua ilia*)	65	20
2129	1500r. Clipper (*Parthenos Sylvia*)	1·10	20
2130	4000r. *Morpho grandensis*	2·75	20
MS2131	111×85 mm. 5400r. *Heliconius melpomene* (40×32 mm)	3·75	90

394 Gary Cooper

2001. Cinema Actors. Multicoloured.

2132	200r. Type **394**	20	10
2133	500r. Marlene Dietrich	45	10
2134	900r. Walt Disney	55	20
2135	1000r. Clark Gable	65	20
2136	1500r. Jeanette Macdonald	1·10	20
2137	4000r. Melvyn Douglas	2·75	20
MS2138	86×111 mm. 5400r. Rudolf Valentino (32×40 mm); 5400r. Marilyn Monroe (32×40 mm)	7·50	90

395 TVR M series (1972)

2001. Cars. Multicoloured.

2139	200r. Type **395**	20	10
2140	500r. Ferrari 410 (1956)	45	10
2141	900r. Peugeot 405 (1995)	55	20
2142	1000r. Fiat 8VZ (1953)	65	20
2143	1500r. Citroen Xsara (1997)	1·10	20
2144	4000r. Renault Espace (1997)	2·75	20
MS2145	111×85 mm. 5400r. Ferrari 250 GT (1963) (40×32 mm)	3·75	90

396 Bayon Temple

2001. Tourism. Bayon Temple. Multicoloured.

2146	500r. Type **396**	30	30
2147	1500r. Faces and monument	1·10	90
2148	2000r. Face and trees	1·40	1·20

397 Steam Locomotive 4-6-0

2001. Trains. Philanippon '01 International Stamp Exhibition, Tokyo. Multicoloured.

2149	200r. Type **397**	20	20
2150	500r. Steam locomotive 4-6-4	45	35
2151	900r. Steam locomotive 4-4-0	55	45
2152	1000r. Steam locomotive 4-6-4	65	55
2153	1500r. Locomotive 4-6-2	1·10	90
2154	4000r. Locomotive 4-8-2	2·75	2·30
MS2155	110×84 mm. 5400r. Steam locomotive 2-8-2 (40×32 mm).	3·75	3·25

398 Emperor Penguin (*Aptenodytes forsteri*)

2001. Penguins. Multicoloured.

2156	200r. Type **398**	20	20
2157	500r. Jackass penguin (*Spheniscus demersus*)	45	35
2158	900r. Humboldt penguin (*Spheniscus humboldti*)	55	45
2159	1000r. Rockhopper penguin (*Eudypes crestatus*) (inscr "cristatus")	65	55
2160	1500r. King penguin (*Aptenodytes patagonica*)	1·10	90
2161	4000r. Bearded penguin (*Pygocelis Antarctica*)	2·75	2·30
MS2162	108×83 mm. 5400r. Gentoo penguin (*Pygoscelis papua*) (40×32 mm)	3·75	3·25

399 Singapura

2001. Cats. Multicoloured.

2163	200r. Type **399**	10	10
2164	500r. Cymric	30	30
2165	900r. Exotic short haired (inscr "shirthair")	65	55
2166	1000r. Ragdoll	65	55
2167	1500r. Manx	1·10	90
2168	4000r. Somali	2·75	2·40
MS2169	110×85 mm. 5400r. Egyptian mau (40×32 mm)	3·75	3·25

400 Khleng Chak

2001. Traditional Kites. Multicoloured.

2170	300r. Type **400**	20	20
2171	500r. Khleng Kanton	30	30
2172	1000r. Khleng Phnong	55	45
2173	1500r. Khleng KaunMorn	1·10	90
2174	3000r. Khleng Me Ambao	2·10	1·80

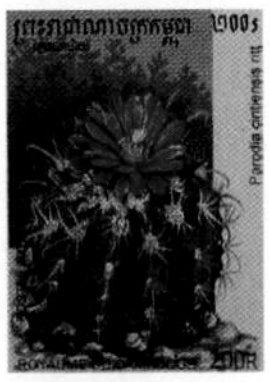

401 *Parodia cintiensis*

2001. Cacti. Multicoloured.

2175	200r. Type **401**	10	10
2176	500r. *Astrophytum asterias*	30	30
2177	900r. *Parodia faustiana*	65	55
2178	1000r. *Coryphantha sulcolanata*	65	55
2179	1500r. *Neochilenia hankena*	1·10	90
2180	4000r. *Mammillaria boolii* (inscr "Mamillaria")	2·75	2·40
MS2181	110×85 mm. 5400r. *Mammillaria* inscr "Mamilleria swinglei" (32×40 mm)	3·75	3·25

402 Fishing Dance

2001. Dances. Multicoloured.

2182	500r. Type **402**	30	30
2183	1500r. Red fish dance	1·10	90
2184	2000r. Dance of Apsara	1·50	1·30

403 Timber Wolf (*Canis occidentalis*)

2001. Wolves and Foxes. Multicoloured.

2185	200r. Type **403**	20	20
2186	500r. Alaska tundra wolf (*Canis tundrorum*)	45	30
2187	900r. Fox (inscr "Vulpes fulvas")	55	45
2188	1000r. Coyote (*Canis latrans*)	65	55
2189	1500r. Fennec fox (*Vulpes zerda*)	1·10	90
2190	4000r. Arctic fox (*Alopex lagopus*)	2·75	2·30
MS2191	112×87 mm. 5400r. Iberian wolf (*Canis signatus*) (40×32 mm)	3·75	3·25

404 *Australopithecus anamensis*

2001. Prehistoric Man. Multicoloured.

2192	100r. Type **404**	10	10
2193	200r. *Australopithecus afarensis*	20	20
2194	300r. *Australopithecus africanus*	20	20
2195	500r. *Australopithecus rudolfensis*	30	30
2196	500r. *Australopithecus boisei*	30	30
2197	1000r. *Homo habilis*	65	55
2198	1500r. *Homo erectus*	1·10	90
2199	4000r. *Homo sapiens neanderthalensis* (inscr "nesnderthalensis")	2·75	2·40
MS2200	110×85 mm. 5400r. *Homo sapiens sapiens* (40×32 mm)	3·75	3·25

404a World Cup Champions (1934)

2001. Italian Football. Multicoloured.

2200a	200r. Type **404a**	20	15
2200b	500r. World Cup champions (1938)	30	25
2200c	900r. European Cup champions (1968)	55	45
2200d	1000r. World Cup champions (1982)	65	50
2200e	1500r. World Cup qualifying team (2002)	1·10	90
2200f	4000r. Federazione Italiana Giuoco Calcio emblem	2·75	2·40

404b Castle (18th-century)

2001. Chess. Multicoloured.

2200g	200r. Type **404b**	20	15
2200h	500r. Pawn (19th-century)	30	25
2200i	900r. King (19th-century)	55	45
2200j	1000r. Bishop (17th-century)	65	50
2200k	1500r. Queen (17th-century)	1·10	90
2200l	4000r. Knight (20th-century) 2.74	2·40	
MS2200m	112×87 mm. 5400r. King (16th-century) (40×32 mm)	3·75	3·25

405 Preah Vihear Temple

2002. Tenth Anniv of ASEAN (Association of South East Asian Nations) Post. Temples. Multicoloured.

2201	500r. Type **405**	30	25
2202	1000r. Preah Ko	55	40
2203	1500r. Banteay Srei	1·10	85
2204	2500r. Bayon	1·80	1·40
2205	3500r. Ankor Wat	2·20	1·70

406 Bridge No. 26, Route 6A

2003. Japanese Grant Aid. Multicoloured.

2206	100r. Type **406**	15	10
2207	200r. Bridge No. 25, Route 6A	30	25
2208	400r. Chroy Changvar bridge	45	35
2209	800r. Kazuna bridge	60	45
2210	3500r. Monument	3·00	2·40

407 Ox Cart carrying supplies

2003. 140th Anniv of Red Cross and Red Crescent. Multicoloured.

2211	100r. Type **407**	25	20
2212	200r. Red Cross worker (vert)	25	20
2213	300r. Queen Norodom Monineath Sihanouk and young men	30	25
2214	400r. Queen greeting young woman in crowd	30	25
2215	500r. Queen and man	30	25
2216	700r. Queen greeting older woman in crowd	40	30
2217	800r. Queen presenting cloth	65	45
2218	1000r. Woman with shaved head and Queen	65	45
2219	1900r. Queen and M. Bun Rany Hun Sen (pres. of Cambodian Red Cross) (vert)	1·20	95
2220	2100r. M. Bun Rany Hun Sen and Red Cross worker (vert)	1·20	95
2221	4000r. Queen and M. Bun Rany Hun Sen holding baby	2·50	2·00

408 Sugar Palm Tree

2003. Sugar Palm. Multicoloured.

2222	300r. Type **408**	30	25
2223	500r. Female flower	30	25
2224	700r. Male flower	40	30
2225	1500r. Fruit	1·10	85

409 Ankor Wat, Cambodia

2003. 50th Anniv of China–Cambodia Diplomatic Relations. Multicoloured.

2226	2000r. Type **409**	1·20	95
2227	2000r. Great Wall, China	1·20	95

410 Conference Emblem

2003. 36th ASEAN Ministerial Meeting and Tenth ASEAN Regional Forum, Phnom Penh. Multicoloured.

2228	400r. Type **410**	40	30
2229	500r. Dancer (Apsara dance)	50	40
2230	600r. Seated dancer	55	45
2231	1600r. Two seated dancers	1·30	1·00
2232	1900r. Two dancers (Temonorom dance)	1·50	1·20

411 King Norodom Sihanouk and Map

2003. 50th Anniv of Independence. King Norodom Sihanouk. Multicoloured.

2233	200r. Type **411**	25	20
2234	400r. With soldiers (vert)	40	30
2235	500r. Seated (vert)	50	40
2236	800r. With arm extended (vert)	55	45
2237	1000r. Saluting (vert)	65	50
2238	2000r. Independence monument and King Norodom Sihanouk (vert)	1·20	95
2239	5000r. Wearing suit	3·50	2·70

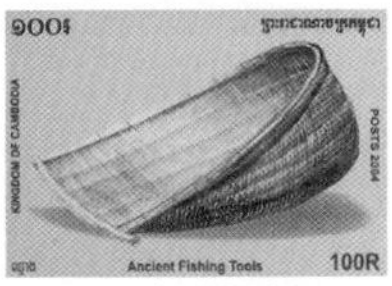

412 Scoop-shaped Fishing Basket

2004. Fishing Tools. Multicoloured.

2240	100r. Type **412**	20	10
2241	200r. Narrow basket	30	20
2242	800r. Cylindrical basket	40	25
2243	1700r. Goblet-shaped basket (vert)	90	55
2244	2200r. Cylindrical basket with baffles (vert)	1·10	70
MS2245	85×110 mm. 2000r. Child and basket (vert)	1·10	1·10

413 Bayon Sculpture

2004. Day of Khmer Culture. Multicoloured.

2246	100r. Type **413**	20	10
2247	200r. Banteay Srei sculpture	30	20
2248	400r. Banteay Srei sculpture (detail)	40	25
2249	800r. Bayon sculpture (different) (vert)	55	35
2250	3500r. Banteay Srei sculpture (detail) (different) (vert)	1·50	90
MS2251	110×85 mm. 2000r. As No. 2250 with design enlarged (vert)	1·10	1·10

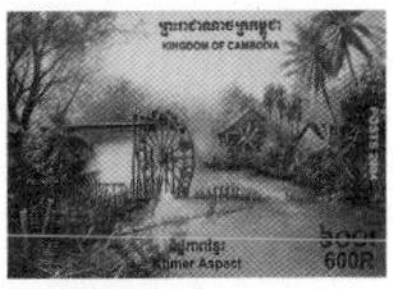

414 Waterwheel

2004. Tourism. Landscapes. Multicoloured.

2252	600r. Type **414**	30	20
2253	900r. Paddy fields	50	30
2254	2000r. River and palms	1·10	70
MS2255	110×85 mm. 2000r. Ox cart	1·10	1·10

415 Two Dancers

2004. Tepmonorum Dance. Multicoloured.

2256	400r. Type **415**	40	30
2257	1000r. Two dancers wearing blue outfits	65	50
2258	2100r. Two female dancers	1·30	1·00
MS2259	110×85 mm. 2000r. As No. 2259 with design enlarged	1·20	1·20

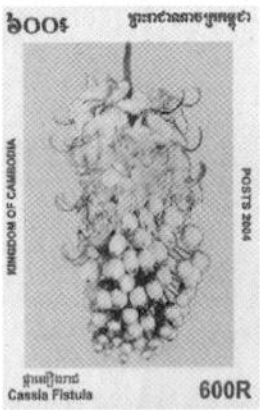

416 *Cassia fistula*

2004. Flowers. Multicoloured.

2260	600r. Type **416**	35	25
2261	700r. *Butea monosperma*	40	30
2262	900r. *Couroupita quianensis*	55	40
2263	1000r. *Delonix regia* (horiz)	65	50
2264	1800r. *Lagerstroemia floribunda*	1·00	80
MS2265	110×85 mm. 2000r. *Lagerstroemia floribunda* (horiz)	1·20	1·20

417 Preah Khan

2004. Tourism. Temples. Multicoloured.

2266	200r. Type **417**	20	10
2267	500r. Pre Rup	25	15
2268	600r. Banteay Samre	30	20
2269	1600r. Bayon	80	50
2270	1900r. Ankor Wat	90	55
MS2271	110×85 mm. 2000r. Stone head, Bayon (vert)	1·10	1·10

418 King Norodom Sihamoni

2004. Coronation of King Norodom Sihamoni. Multicoloured.

2272	100r. Type **418**	20	10
2273	400r. With monks	30	20
2274	500r. Planting tree	35	20
2275	600r. King Norodom Sihamoni (portrait)	40	25
2276	700r. With crowd, greeting child (horiz)	45	30
2277	900r. Greeting men in uniform (horiz)	50	35
2278	2100r. Releasing dove (horiz)	95	55
2279	2200r. With young men (horiz)	1·10	70
2280	4000r. King Norodom Sihamoni and temple (horiz)	1·70	1·10

419 Anniversary Emblem

2005. 50th Anniv of Cambodian Red Cross Society. Multicoloured.

2281	400r. Type **419**	15	10
2282	700r. Signing book (horiz)	30	20
2283	800r. Lok Chumteav Bun Rany Hun Sen (president) dispensing aid (horiz)	35	20
2284	1900r. Queen Mother Norodom Monineath Sihanouk dispensing aid (horiz)	1·00	60
2285	2100r. Lok Chumteav Bun Rany Hun Sen presenting certificate to volunteer (horiz)	1·10	65
2286	2200r. King Norodom Sihamoni and Queen Mother Norodom Monineath Sihanouk on dais (horiz)	1·20	70

420 Aspara Dance

2005. Traditional Dance. Aspara Dance. Multicoloured.

2287	800r. Type **420**	35	20
2288	900r. Gold skirt, facing right	40	30
2289	1400r. Blue skirt, facing left	55	35
2290	1600r. Cream skirt, leg raised	95	55
2291	2000r. Chequered skirt, facing left	1·10	65

421 Banteay Kdei

2005. Cultural Heritage. Multicoloured.

2292	500r. Type **421**	20	10
2293	700r. Elephant terrace, Angkor Thom	30	20
2294	1000r. Thommanon temple, Angkor	50	30
2295	2000r. Ta Prohm temple, Angkor	1·10	65
2296	2500r. Angkor Wat	1·30	80

422 *Nymphaea*

2005. Flowers. *Nymphaea*. Multicoloured.

2297	100r. Type **422**	20	10
2298	500r. Cream flower	35	20
2299	1200r. Blue flower	70	40
2300	2000r. Yellow flower	1·40	85
2301	2500r. Pink flower	1·60	1·00
MS2302	110×85 mm. 4000r. Basket of deep pink flowers (horiz)	2·30	2·30

Nos. 2303/8 and Type **423** are left for Fish issued on 5 September 2005, not yet received.

424 King Norodom Sihamoni

2005. First Anniv of Coronation of Preah Karuna Preah Bat Sâmdech Preah Bâromneath Norodom Sihamoni, King of Cambodia

2309	**424** 500r. multicoloured	40	25
2310	**424** 1500r. multicoloured	70	40
2311	**424** 2200r. multicoloured	1·10	65

425 Woman holding Scoop

2006. Khmer Cultural Heritage. Weaving. Multicoloured.

2312	100r. Type **425**	20	10
2313	800r. Dye pots	45	30
2314	1500r. Woman seated at frame	70	40
2315	2200r. Woman winding yarn	1·20	75
2316	3500r. Woman weaving blue cloth	1·90	1·10
MS2317	110×85 mm. 5400r. Woman seated at loom weaving pink cloth (horiz)	2·50	2·50

426 *Sousa chinensis* (Chinese white dolphin)

2006. Aquatic Mammals. Multicoloured.

2318	500r. Type **426**	40	30
2319	900r. *Neophocaena phocaenoides* (finless porpoise)	55	35
2320	1400r. *Delphinus capensis tropicalis* (Arabian long-beaked common dolphin) (insc 'Dolphinus')	70	45
2321	2100r. *Stenella longirrostris roseiventris* (dwarf spinner dolphin)	1·40	85
2322	3500r. *Tusiops aduncus* (Indo-Pacific bottlenose dolphin)	2·10	1·30

Nos. 2324/8 are left for single stamps not yet received.

427 Hanuman and Mermaid, Princess Sovanna Maccha

2006. *The Reamker* (Cambodian epic poem). Khmer Dance Theatre

MS2329	110×85 mm. 5400r. Type **427**	4·00	4·00

Nos. 2330/5 and Type **428** are left for Elephants issued on 15 May 2006, not yet received.

429 Chhai Yaim

2006. Dance. Multicoloured.

2336	600r. Type **429**	35	20
2337	1900r. Buffalo sacrifice	1·00	60
2338	2200r. inscr 'Mouth Organ Dance'	1·10	65
2339	3500r. Rice harvest	1·70	1·10

Nos. 2340/5 and Type **430** are left for Birds issued on 8 November 2006, not yet received.

431 Couple and No. 1 Emblem

2006. HIV/AIDS Prevention. '100% Condom Use' (Population Services International (PSI) Number One, condom social marketing programme). Multicoloured.

2346	300r. Type **431**	25	15
2347	500r. Rickshaw (cyclo) driver	35	20
2348	2200r. Water Festival	1·10	65

Nos. 2349/54 and Type **432** are left for National Asia-Pacific Leadership Forum Champion (APLF) on HIV/AIDS in Cambodia issued on 5 January 2007, not yet received.

Nos. 2355/9 and Type **433** are left for 40th Anniv of Cambodia - Vietnam Diplomatic Relations issued on 24 June 2007, not yet received

434 Temple and Anniversary Emblem

2007. 25th Anniv of Handicap International

2360	**434** 1000r. multicoloured	65	40
2361	**434** 1500r. multicoloured	95	55

Nos. 2362/6 and Type **435** are left for 40th Anniv of ASEAN - Dance, issued on 8 August 2007, not yet recieved.

436 Secretariat Building, Bandar Seri Begawan, Brunei Darussalam

2007. Architecture. 40th Anniv of ASEAN (Association of South-East Asian Nations). Multicoloured.

2367	1000r. Type **436**	35	20
2368	1000r. National Museum, Cambodia	35	20
2369	1000r. Fatahillah Museum, Jakarta	35	20
2370	1000r. Traditional house, Laos	35	20
2371	1000r. Railway Headquarters Building, Malaysia	35	20
2372	1000r. Yangon Post Office, Union of Myanmar	35	20
2373	1000r. Malacanang Palace, Manila	35	20
2374	1000r. National Museum, Singapore	35	20
2375	1000r. Vimanmek Mansion, Bangkok, Thailand	35	20
2376	1000r. Presidential Palace, Hanoi, Vietnam	35	20

Nos. 2377/82 and Type **437** are left for Aquatic Plants, issued on 30 June 2008, not yet received.

438 Tian'anmen (Gate of Heavenly Peace), Beijing, China (inscr 'Tian An Men Rostrum')

2008. 50th Anniv of Cambodia - China Friendship. Multicoloured.

2383	2000r. Type **438**	70	40
2384	2000r. Royal Palace, Phnom Penh, Cambodia	70	40

439 Dancer

2008. Dances. Robam Jun Por (best wishes/blessings). Multicoloured.

2385	600r. Type **439**	20	10
2386	1000r. Dancer facing left, right hand raised (mauve)	35	20
2387	1700r. Dancer holding cup in right hand (light green)	60	30
2388	1800r. Dancer right leg and left arm raised (new blue)	65	35
2389	1900r. Dancer kneeling with cup in left hand (new blue)	65	35
MS2390	98×75 mm. 6000r. Dancer with Angkor Wat in background	2·25	1·25

440 Temple Walls

2008. Cultural Heritage. Temple of Preah Vihear (1st series). Multicoloured.

2391	600r. Type **440**	20	10
2392	700r. Steps, rocks, tree and temple walls	20	10
2393	1000r. Entrance gate	35	20
2394	2000r. Trees and wallswith pediments	70	40
2395	3000r. Ruins against the sky and flag	1·00	70

441 Woman decorating Pot

2008. Khmer Cultural Heritage. Pottery. Multicoloured.

2396	100r. Type **441**	10	10
2397	700r. Woman building large pot by hand	25	15
2398	1900r. Woman seated decorating inscised pot	65	35
2399	2000r. Woman holding wooden implement to impress design on pot	70	40
2400	2200r. Woman raising pot on wheel	75	45
MS2401	110×85 mm. 6000r. Ox cart carrying pots	2·00	1·25

442 Children in Class and playing Football

2009. 30th Anniv of Victory Day. Multicoloured.

2402	100r. Type **442**	10	10
2403	200r. Ox cart and agricultural scenes	15	15
2404	1500r. Factory workers, power lines, refinery and dam	65	30
2405	2200r. Symbols of communication	75	45
2406	2500r. Symbols of transport	80	50
2407	2800r. Symbols of cultural heritage	95	65
2408	3000r. Flag and anniversary emblem (vert)	1·00	70

443 Temple

2009. Cultural Heritage. Temple of Preah Vihear (2nd series). Multicoloured.

2409	300r. Type **443**	10	10
2410	800r. Walls, entrances with pediments	30	25
2411	1600r. Multi-headed serpents	60	35
2412	1800r. Ruins against the sky	65	35
2413	2800r. Aerial view of Preah Vihear	90	65
MS2414	111×75 mm. 6000r. Temple of Preah Vihear	2·00	1·25

444 Plough

2010. Ancient Agricultural Tools. Multicoloured.

2415	300r. Type **444**	10	10
2416	1200r. Rake-shaped harrow	40	25
2417	1700r. Roller	60	30
2418	1800r. Pedal-driven chain pump	65	35
2419	2800r. Cart	90	65
MS2420	90×70 mm. 6000r. Woman working pedal-driven chain pump (vert)	2·00	1·25

No. 2421 and Type **445** are left for 50th Anniv of Cambodia - Cuba Diplomatic Relations, issued on 15 April 2010, not yet received.

446 Globe as Face and Rubbish

2010. Combat Climate Change. Multicoloured.

2421	200r. Type **446**	10	10
2422	800r. Watering can, hand enclosing globe and cars under water	30	25
2423	1400r. Globe opened to reveal green field and tree	55	35
2424	1700r. Egg timer enclosing icebergs draining into factory	60	35
2425	3000r. Forest and hands enclosing tree	1·00	70
MS2426	110×70 mm. 6000r. Cars under water (as detail of No. 2423)	2·00	1·25

447 Anniversary Emblem

2010. 60th Anniv of Cambodia - USA Diplomatic Relations

2427	**447**	2800r. multicoloured	2·00	1·25

448 Condoms

2011. 30th Anniv of Discovery of AIDS. Multicoloured.

2428	1000r. Type **448**	35	20
2429	1500r. Couple and child	55	35
2430	2800r. Young people in club	90	65
2431	4000r. Pair of green doves	1·40	1·00

EXPRESS MAIL STAMPS

E313 Bohemian Waxwing

1997. Birds. Multicoloured.

E1624	600r. Type E **313**	1·10	45
E1625	900r. Great grey shrike	1·30	65
E1626	1000r. Eurasian tree sparrow	1·80	75
E1627	2000r. Black redstart	3·50	1·70
E1628	2500r. Reed bunting	4·75	2·00
E1629	3000r. Ortolan bunting	5·25	2·50

POSTAGE DUE STAMPS

D13

1957

D81	**D13**	10c. red, blue & black	20	20
D82	**D13**	50c. red, blue & black	55	45
D83	**D13**	1r. red, blue & black	85	75
D84	**D13**	3r. red, blue & black	1·10	90
D85	**D13**	5r. red, blue & black	1·80	1·60

Pt. 1

CAMEROON

Former German colony occupied by British and French troops during 1914–16. The territory was divided between them and the two areas were administered under League of Nations mandates from 1922, converted into United Nations trusteeships in 1946.

The British section was administered as part of Nigeria until 1960, when a plebiscite was held. The northern area voted to join Nigeria and the southern part joined the newly-independent Cameroun Republic (formerly the French trust territory). In November 1995 this republic joined the Commonwealth.

12 pence = 1 shilling;
20 shillings = 1 pound.

I. CAMEROONS EXPEDITIONARY FORCE

1915. "Yacht" key-types of German Kamerun surch **C.E.F.** and value in English currency.

B1	N	½d. on 3pf. brown	13·00	55·00
B2	N	½d. on 5pf. green	6·00	9·50
B3	N	1d. on 10pf. red	1·25	9·50
B4	N	2d. on 20pf. blue	3·50	22·00
B5	N	2½d. on 25pf. black and red on yellow	15·00	55·00
B6	N	3d. on 30pf. black and orange on buff	13·00	60·00
B7	N	4d. on 40pf. black and red	13·00	60·00
B8	N	6d. on 50pf. black and purple on buff	13·00	60·00
B9	N	8d. on 80pf. black and red on rose	13·00	60·00
B10	O	1s. on 1m. red	£190	£850
B11	O	2s. on 2m. blue	£200	£900
B12	O	3s. on 3m. black	£200	£900
B13	O	5s. on 5m. red and black	£250	£950

II. CAMEROONS TRUST TERRITORY

Issue used in the British trusteeship from October 1960 to June 1961 in the northern are and until Spetember 1961 in the southern area, when they joined with Nigeria nad the Cameroun Republic respectively.

1960. Stamps of Nigeria of 1953 optd **CAMEROONS U.K.T.T.**

T1	**18**	½d. black and orange	10	2·00
T2	-	1d. black and green	10	70
T3	-	1½d. green	10	20
T4	-	2d. grey	60	3·00
T5	-	3d. black and lilac	20	10
T6	-	4d. black and blue	20	2·50
T7	-	6d. brown and black	30	20
T8	-	1s. black and purple	30	10
T9	**26**	2s.6d. black and green	1·50	1·00
T10	-	5s. black and orange	2·00	3·50
T11	-	10s. black and brown	3·00	7·00
T12	**29**	£1 black and violet	14·00	29·00

III. REPUBLIC OF CAMEROON

The Republic of Cameroon joined the Commonwealth on 1 November 1995 and issues from that date will be listed below, when examples and information have been received.

PRICES: Prices shown for used stamps of Cameroon are somewhat tentative, but have been compiled with the assistance of collectors of these issues. Unused stamps for this period are scarce to rare and, when offered, can command very high prices. Under the cirumstances it has been decided not to quote unused prices at the present time, but we hope to be able to add these in a future edition of this catalogue.

418 Athlete holding Olympic Rings ('Records du monde')

1996. Olympic Games, Atlanta. Multicoloured.

1186	125f. Type **418**		65
1187	250f. As No. 1186 but inscr 'Records olympiques' (vert)		1·40

419 Conference Emblem

1996. 32nd Conference of Heads of State of Organisation of African Unity, Yaounde.

1188	**419**	125f. multicoloured		1·25
1189	**419**	200f. multicoloured (1997)		1·10
1190	**419**	250f. multicoloured (1997)		1·40
1191	–	410f. multicoloured (vert)		1·90

Imprint dates: '1996' Nos. 1188, 1191; '1997' Nos. 1188a, 1189, 1190.

420 Emblem

1997

1192	**420**	500f. multicoloured		15·00

No. 1192 was originally produced to pay fees for opening a Cameroon Postal Savings Bank account, but has been found used on mail.

421 Pineapple

1998. Tourism. Multicoloured.

1193	100f. Type **421**		2·50
1194	125f. Type **421**		2·50
1195	150f. Coffee		3·00
1196	175f. Crowned crane		6·00
1197	200f. Mandrill		1·10
1198	250f. As No. 1195		1·40
1199	410f. As No. 1196		1·90

422 *Lanius* sp. (bird)

1998

1200	**422**	125f. multicoloured		65

423 World Cup Trophy, Emblem and Cameroon Flag

1998. Fourth Participation of Cameroon in World Cup Football, France. Multicoloured.

1201	125f. Type **423**		2·50
1202	250f. Football and map containing national colours (horiz)		2·75

424 Emblem

1998. 50th Anniv of Declaration of Human Rights.

1203	**424**	370f. multicoloured		3·50

425 Flags and Africa on Globe

1999. CEMAC Conference, Yaounde. Multicoloured.

1204	125f. Flags (different) and Africa on globe		8·00
1205	225f. Type **425**		2·50

426 National Symbols

2000. National Symbols. Multicoloured.

1206	125f. Type **426**		65
1207	200f. Outline map enclosing Cameroon scenes (vert)		1·10
1208	250f. Airplane over landscape with wild animals (vert)		1·40

427 Congress Centre, Yaounde

2001. 30th Anniv of Co-operation between Cameroon and People's Republic of China.

1209	**427**	125f. multicoloured		1·25

428 Chantal Biya with Baby

2001. Chantal Biya Foundation. Multicoloured.

1210	125f. Type **428**		2·50
1211	250f. Baby in uterus and emblems		1·25
MS1212	110×90 mm. Nos. 1210/11		

429 Lion, National Flags and Football

2002. World Cup Football, Japan and South Korea. Multicoloured.

1213	125f. Type **429**		1·25
1214	250f. Pres. Paul Biya, lion and Africa Cup (horiz)		2·75
MS1215	Circular 96×96 mm. No. 1213; As No. 1214 but square		

430 Emblem

2002. 71st General Assembly of Interpol, Yaounde.

1216	**430**	125f. multicoloured		1·25
MS1217		91×120 mm. No. 1216		

431 Pres. Biya, Japanese Prime Minister Koizumi and Primary School Mfandena 2, Yaoundé)

2005. Co-operation between Cameroon and Japan.

1218	**431**	100f. multicoloured		1·25
1219	**431**	125f. multicoloured		1·25
1220	**431**	200f. multicoloured		2·25
1221	**431**	250f. multicoloured		2·75
1222	**431**	370f. multicoloured		3·50
1223	**431**	410f. multicoloured		3·75
1224	**431**	500f. multicoloured		4·50
1225	**431**	1000f. multicoloured		7·50

Pt. 6, Pt. 7, Pt. 12

CAMEROUN

Territory in western Africa which became a German Protectorate in 1884. During 1914-16 it was occupied by Allied troops and in 1922 Britain and France were granted separate United Nations mandates.

In 1960 the French trust territory became an independent republic and, following a plebiscite, in September 1961 the southern part of the area under British control joined the Cameroun Republic. In November 1995 the republic joined the Commonwealth.

A. German Colony of Kamerun.
100 pfennig = 1 mark.

B. French Administration of Cameroun.
100 centimes = 1 franc.

A. GERMAN COLONY OF KAMERUN

1897. Stamps of Germany optd **Kamerun**.

K1a	**8**	3pf. brown	12·50	21·00
K2	**8**	5pf. green	7·50	10·50
K3	**9**	10pf. red	5·25	6·25
K4	**9**	20pf. blue	5·25	9·50
K5	**9**	25pf. orange	23·00	55·00
K6a	**9**	50pf. brown	18·00	34·00

1900. "Yacht" key-types inscr "KAMERUN".

K7	N	3pf. brown	1·70	2·10
K21	N	5pf. green	1·10	2·10
K22	N	10pf. red	3·25	2·10
K10	N	20pf. blue	30·00	3·00
K11	N	25pf. black & red on yell	1·90	6·75
K12	N	30pf. black & orge on buff	2·50	5·75
K13	N	40pf. black and red	2·50	5·25
K14	N	50pf. black & pur on buff	2·50	8·00
K15	N	80pf. black & red on rose	3·25	13·50
K16	O	1m. red	85·00	95·00
K17	O	2m. blue	6·75	95·00
K18	O	3m. black	6·75	£150
K19	O	5m. red and black	£200	£650

B. FRENCH ADMINISTRATION OF CAMEROUN

1915. Stamps of Gabon with inscription "AFRIQUE EQUATORIALE-GABON" optd **Corps Expeditionnaire Franco-Anglais CAMEROUN**.

1	**7**	1c. brown and orange	£100	60·00
2	**7**	2c. black and brown	£170	£170
3	**7**	4c. violet and blue	£170	£170
4	**7**	5c. olive and green	37·00	33·00
5	**7**	10c. red and lake (on No. 37 of Gabon)	39·00	22·00
6	**7**	20c. brown and violet	£170	£190
7	**8**	25c. brown and blue	70·00	60·00
8	**8**	30c. red and grey	£170	£190
9	**8**	35c. green and violet	70·00	55·00
10	**8**	40c. blue and brown	£170	£190
11	**8**	45c. violet and red	£170	£190
12	**8**	50c. grey and green	£170	£190
13	**8**	75c. brown and orange	£180	£200
14	**9**	1f. yellow and brown	£190	£200
15	**9**	2f. brown and red	£200	£225

1916. Optd **Occupation Francaise du Cameroun**. (a) On stamps of Middle Congo.

16	**1**	1c. olive and brown	£100	£110
17	**1**	2c. violet and brown	£100	£110
18	**1**	4c. blue and brown	£100	£110
19	**1**	5c. green and blue	50·00	50·00
20	**2**	35c. brown and blue	£120	90·00
21	**2**	45c. violet and orange	£100	£100

(b) On stamps of French Congo

22	**6**	15c. violet and green	£110	£110
23	**8**	20c. green and red	£120	£110
24	**8**	30c. red and yellow	£100	90·00
25	**8**	40c. brown and green	70·00	£100
26	**8**	50c. violet and lilac	£110	£100
27	**8**	75c. purple and orange	£100	80·00
28	-	1f. drab and grey (48)	£120	£120
29	-	2f. red and brown (49)	£120	£120

1916. Stamps of Middle Congo optd **CAMEROUN Occupation Francaise**.

30	**1**	1c. olive and brown	35	3·25
31	**1**	2c. violet and brown	65	3·25
32	**1**	4c. blue and brown	75	3·25
33	**1**	5c. green and blue	90	2·40
34	**1**	10c. red and blue	1·20	2·75
34a	**1**	15c. purple and red	3·00	4·50
35	**1**	20c. brown and blue	1·70	3·50
36	**2**	25c. blue and green	1·00	1·30
37	**2**	30c. pink and green	2·00	2·75
38	**2**	35c. brown and blue	1·70	3·50
39	**2**	40c. green and brown	2·00	4·75
40	**2**	45c. violet and orange	2·75	5·50
41	**2**	50c. green and orange	2·75	4·50
42	**2**	75c. brown and blue	2·50	6·00
43	**3**	1f. green and violet	2·30	3·50
44	**3**	2f. violet and green	8·75	16·00
45	**3**	5f. blue and pink	13·00	33·00

1921. Stamps of Middle Congo (colours changed) optd **CAMEROUN**.

46	**1**	1c. orange and green	20	5·50
47	**1**	2c. red and brown	20	5·75
48	**1**	4c. green and grey	45	6·25
49	**1**	5c. orange and red	45	3·25
50	**1**	10c. light green and green	90	3·75
51	**1**	15c. orange and blue	1·50	6·25
52	**1**	20c. grey and purple	2·00	5·00
53	**2**	25c. orange and grey	1·90	2·00
54	**2**	30c. red and carmine	1·50	5·50
55	**2**	35c. blue and grey	2·00	5·50
56	**2**	40c. orange and green	1·90	5·50
57	**2**	45c. red and brown	1·30	5·00
58	**2**	50c. ultramarine and blue	1·10	3·50
59	**2**	75c. green and purple	1·30	6·00
60	**3**	1f. orange and grey	3·25	6·50
61	**3**	2f. red and green	7·75	18·00
62	**3**	5f. grey and red	8·75	33·00

1924. Stamps of 1921 surch.

63	**1**	25c. on 15c. orange & blue	1·20	7·75
64	**3**	25c. on 2f. red and green	1·80	7·75
65	**3**	25c. on 5f. grey and red	1·50	8·25
66	**2**	"65" on 45c. red and brown	2·20	8·75
67	**2**	"85" on 75c. green & red	3·25	9·00

5 Cattle fording River

1925

68	**5**	1c. mauve and olive	20	3·75
69	**5**	2c. green & red on green	35	2·50
70	**5**	4c. black and blue	45	3·25
71	**5**	5c. mauve and yellow	40	40
72	**5**	10c. orange & pur on yell	1·30	90
73	**5**	15c. green	2·75	5·50
88	**5**	15c. red and lilac	1·00	3·00
74	**A**	20c. brown and olive	1·70	5·75
89	**A**	20c. green	1·10	3·25
90	**A**	20c. brown and red	65	25
75	**A**	25c. black and green	1·40	55
76	**A**	30c. red and green	1·30	1·20
91	**A**	30c. green and olive	1·10	1·30
77	**A**	35c. black and brown	1·80	7·00
91a	**A**	35c. green	4·50	5·75
78	**A**	40c. violet and orange	4·00	3·25
79	**A**	45c. red	1·00	5·50
92	**A**	45c. brown and mauve	3·25	3·50
80	**A**	50c. red and green	3·00	45
93	**A**	55c. red and blue	5·00	8·25
81	**A**	60c. black and mauve	2·50	5·25
94	**A**	60c. red	1·30	6·00
82	**A**	65c. brown and blue	3·00	90
83	**A**	75c. blue	1·70	3·00
95	**A**	75c. mauve and brown	1·30	1·40
95a	**A**	80c. brown and red	2·00	7·75
84	**A**	85c. blue and red	1·40	3·25
96	**A**	90c. red	3·50	3·50
85	**B**	1f. brown and blue	2·20	6·50
97	**B**	1f. blue	1·70	1·40
98	**B**	1f. mauve and brown	2·00	2·75
99	**B**	1f. brown and green	4·00	2·10
100	**B**	1f.10 brown and red	4·50	11·50
100a	**B**	1f.25 blue and brown	12·00	11·50
101	**B**	1f.50 blue	3·00	95
101a	**B**	1f.75 red and brown	2·30	1·90
101b	**B**	1f.75 blue	11·50	16·00
86	**B**	2f. orange and olive	4·50	1·10
102	**B**	3f. mauve and brown	5·00	2·50
87	**B**	5f. black & brown on bl	5·25	1·50
103	**B**	10f. mauve and orange	12·00	9·00
104	**B**	20f. green and red	30·00	21·00

DESIGNS—VERT: A, Tapping rubber-trees. HORIZ: B, Liana suspension bridge.

1926. Surch with new value.

105	1f.25 on 1f. blue	1·80	6·00

1931. "Colonial Exhibition" key-types inscribed "CAMEROUN".

106	**E**	40c. green	5·25	9·25
107	**F**	50c. mauve	5·50	9·00
108	**G**	90c. orange	6·25	8·75
109	**H**	1f.50 blue	6·25	6·75

14 Sailing Ships

1937. Paris International Exhibition. Inscr "EXPOSITION INTERNATIONALE PARIS 1937".

110	-	20c. violet	2·30	6·75
111	**14**	30c. green	2·50	6·50
112	-	40c. red	1·80	6·25
113	-	50c. brown & deep brown	2·30	3·50
114	-	90c. red	2·10	5·50
115	-	1f.50 blue	2·00	6·25

MS115a 120×100 mm. 163f. red and agate 10·50 31·00

DESIGNS—VERT: 20c. Allegory of Commerce; 50c. Allegory of Agriculture. HORIZ: 40c. Berber, Negress and Annamite; 90c. France extends torch of Civilization; 1f.50, Diane de Poitiers.

19 Pierre and Marie Curie

1938. International Anti-cancer Fund.

116	**19**	1f.75+50c. blue	10·50	33·00

20

1939. New York World's Fair.

117	**20**	1f.25 red	2·30	6·75
118	**20**	2f.25 blue	2·75	6·75

21 Lamido Woman

1939

119	**21**	2c. black	30	5·25
120	**21**	3c. mauve	40	5·25
121	**21**	4c. blue	75	5·25
122	**21**	5c. brown	60	5·25
123	**21**	10c. green	65	4·75
124	**21**	15c. red	90	6·50
125	**21**	20c. purple	95	6·50
126	**A**	25c. black	1·40	4·75
127	**A**	30c. orange	85	6·50
128	**A**	40c. blue	85	5·25
129	**A**	45c. green	2·10	8·50
130	**A**	50c. brown	1·10	4·00
131	**A**	60c. blue	1·50	7·25
132	**A**	70c. purple	3·00	8·75
133	**B**	80c. blue	3·50	10·50
134	**B**	90c. blue	2·10	2·30
135	**B**	1f. red	3·25	4·25
135a	**B**	1f. brown	1·90	3·25
136	**B**	1f.25 red	4·50	16·00
137	**B**	1f.40 orange	2·75	8·00
138	**B**	1f.50 brown	1·70	3·00
139	**B**	1f.60 brown	2·75	8·25
140	**B**	1f.75 blue	2·20	4·00
141	**B**	2f. green	1·90	2·30
142	**B**	2f.25 blue	2·50	4·75
143	**B**	2f.50 purple	3·25	4·00
144	**B**	3f. violet	1·70	2·50
145	**C**	5f. brown	2·40	2·75
146	**C**	10f. purple	2·40	5·75
147	**C**	20f. green	4·00	6·50

DESIGNS—VERT: A, Banyo Waterfall; C, African boatman. HORIZ: B, African elephants.

25 Storming the Bastille

1939. 150th Anniv of Revolution.

148	**25**	45c.+25c. green	10·00	22·00
149	**25**	70c.+30c. brown	10·00	22·00
150	**25**	90c.+35c. orange	10·00	27·00
151	**25**	1f.25+1f. red	10·00	28·00
152	**25**	2f.25+2f. blue	12·00	33·00

1940. Adherence to General de Gaulle. Optd **CAMEROUN FRANCAIS 27-8-40**.

153	**21**	2c. black	90	1·60
154	**21**	3c. mauve	90	3·25
155	**21**	4c. blue	55	1·70
156	**21**	5c. brown	7·75	7·50
157	**21**	10c. green	75	1·60
158	**21**	15c. red	1·40	5·50
159	**21**	20c. purple	26·00	23·00
160	**A**	25c. black	1·10	95
161	**A**	30c. orange	22·00	23·00
162	**A**	40c. blue	6·00	4·75
163	**A**	45c. green	1·80	2·00
164	-	50c. red & green (No. 80)	90	1·20
165	**A**	60c. blue	6·75	9·75
166	**A**	70c. purple	1·80	1·90
167	**B**	80c. blue	7·25	4·00
168	**B**	90c. blue	55	80
169	**20**	1f.25 red	4·50	5·00
170	**B**	1f.25 red	85	90
171	**B**	1f.40 orange	1·40	2·20
172	**B**	1f.50 brown	70	1·00
173	**B**	1f.60 brown	1·00	1·40
174	**B**	1f.75 blue	85	1·30
175	**20**	2f.25 blue	3·50	3·50
176	**B**	2f.25 blue	70	1·10
177	**B**	2f.50 purple	70	55
178	-	5f. black and brown on blue (No. 87)	19·00	6·50
179	**C**	5f. brown	24·00	5·50
180	-	10f. mve & orge (No. 103)	28·00	7·75
181	**C**	10f. purple	80·00	75·00
182	-	20f. green & red (No. 104)	65·00	11·00
183	**C**	20f. green	£160	£200

1940. War Relief Fund. Nos. 100a, 101a and 86 surch **OEUVRES DE GUERRE** and premium.

184	1f.25+2f. blue and brown	37·00	46·00
185	1f.75+3f. red and brown	37·00	46·00
186	2f.+5f. orange and olive	27·00	30·00

1940. Spitfire Fund. Nos. 126, 129, 131/2 surch +5 **Frs. SPITFIRE**.

187	**A**	25c.+5f. black	£120	£120
188	**A**	45c.+5f. green	£120	£120
189	**A**	60c.+5f. blue	£130	£130
190	**A**	70c.+5f. purple	£130	£130

1941. Spitfire Fund. Surch **SPITFIRE+10 fr. General de GAULLE**.

190a	**20**	1f.25+10f. red	£120	£130
190b	**20**	2f.25+10f. blue	£120	£130

29b Sikorsky S-43 over Map

29c Sikorsky S-43 Amphibian

1941. Air.

190c	**29b**	25c. red	1·00	7·00
190d	**29b**	50c. green	75	7·00
190e	**29b**	1f. purple	2·50	7·00
190f	**29c**	2f. olive	1·50	4·75
190g	**29c**	3f. brown	1·70	5·00
190h	**29c**	4f. blue	1·30	5·00
190i	**29c**	6f. myrtle	1·50	4·25
190j	**29c**	7f. purple	1·40	4·25
190k	**29c**	12f. orange	7·25	16·00
190l	**29c**	20f. red	4·50	8·50
190m	-	50f. blue	4·75	8·50

DESIGN: 50f. Latecoere 631 flying boat over harbour.

1941. Laquintinie Hospital Fund. Surch **+10 Frs. AMBULANCE LAQUINTINIE**.

191	**20**	1f.25+10f. red	41·00	47·00
192	**20**	2f.25+10f. blue	50·00	47·00

31 Cross of Lorraine, Sword and Shield

32 Fairey FC-1

1942. Free French Issue.

193	**31**	5c. brown (postage)	15	1·90
194	**31**	10c. blue	15	60
195	**31**	25c. green	15	70
196	**31**	30c. red	40	70
197	**31**	40c. green	50	60
198	**31**	80c. purple	60	95
199	**31**	1f. mauve	90	55
200	**31**	1f.50 red	80	45
201	**31**	2f. black	85	55
202	**31**	2f.50 blue	60	70
203	**31**	4f. violet	60	1·20
204	**31**	5f. yellow	90	1·40
205	**31**	10f. brown	65	45
206	**31**	20f. green	95	1·20
207	**32**	1f. orange (air)	1·30	5·50
208	**32**	1f.50 red	2·00	6·25
209	**32**	5f. purple	1·20	6·25
210	**32**	10f. black	1·40	6·75
211	**32**	25f. blue	2·00	6·75
212	**32**	50f. green	2·75	4·00
213	**32**	100f. red	2·30	4·25

1943. Surch **Valmy+100 frs**.

213a	-	1f.25+100f. blue and brown (No. 100a)	13·00	65·00
213b	**20**	1f.25+100f. red	10·50	65·00
213c	-	1f.25+100f. red (No. 136)	33·00	65·00
213d	-	1f.50+100f. brown (No. 138)	20·00	65·00
213e	**20**	2f.25+100f. blue	18·00	65·00

33

1944. Mutual Aid and Red Cross Funds.

214	**33**	5f.+20f. red	85	11·00

1945. Surch.

215	**31**	50c. on 5c. brown	1·30	7·00
216	**31**	60c. on 5c. brown	55	7·00
217	**31**	70c. on 5c. brown	65	7·25
218	**31**	1f.20 on 5c. brown	1·00	7·25
219	**31**	2f.40 on 25c. green	1·00	2·75
220	**31**	3f. on 25c. green	1·10	3·25
221	**31**	4f.50 on 25c. green	1·70	8·75
222	**31**	15f. on 2f.50 blue	1·40	8·25

34 Felix Eboue

1945

223	**34**	2f. black	45	2·30
224	**34**	25f. green	90	5·50

35 "Victory"

1946. Air. Victory.

225	**35**	8f. purple	70	2·30

36 Chad

1946. Air. From Chad to the Rhine. Inscr "DU TCHAD AU RHIN".

226	**36**	5f. blue	2·50	8·25
227	-	10f. purple	1·70	8·25
228	-	15f. red	2·00	8·25
229	-	20f. blue	2·10	8·25
230	-	25f. brown	3·00	8·25
231	-	50f. black	2·75	8·50

DESIGNS: 10f. Koufra; 15f. Mareth; 20f. Normandy; 25f. Paris; 50f. Strasbourg.

37 Zebu and Herdsman

45 Aeroplane, African and Mask

1946

232	**37**	10c. green (postage)	25	2·10
233	**37**	30c. orange	25	4·00
234	**37**	40c. blue	25	5·75
235	-	50c. sepia	70	1·40
236	-	60c. purple	90	5·50
237	-	80c. brown	90	6·00
238	-	1f. orange	1·10	30
239	-	1f.20 green	1·50	6·50
240	-	1f.50 red	2·75	3·25
241	-	2f. black	90	30
242	-	3f. red	2·40	35
243	-	3f.60 red	2·30	6·75
244	-	4f. blue	1·10	30
245	-	5f. red	2·20	70
246	-	6f. blue	2·20	55
247	-	10f. green	1·60	30
248	-	15f. blue	2·75	85
249	-	20f. green	3·25	1·00
250	-	25f. black	2·75	1·80
251	-	50f. green (air)	2·75	1·30
252	-	100f. brown	3·50	2·50
253	**45**	200f. olive	6·25	5·00

DESIGNS—VERT: 50c. to 80c. Tikar women; 1f. to 1f.50, Africans carrying bananas; 2f. to 4f. Bowman; 5f. to 10f. Lamido horsemen; 15f. to 25f. Native head. HORIZ: 50f. Birds over mountains; 100f. African horsemen and Dewoitine D-333 trimotor airplane.

46 People of Five Races, Lockheed Constellation Airplane and Globe

1949. Air. 75th Anniv of UPU.

254	**46**	25f. multicoloured	4·00	7·50

47 Doctor and Patient

1950. Colonial Welfare Fund.

255	**47**	10f.+2f. green & turq	5·25	15·00

48 Military Medal

1952. Military Medal Centenary.

256	**48**	15f. red, yellow and green	5·50	5·00

49 Porters Carrying Bananas

50 Transporting Logs

1953

257	**49**	8f. violet, orange and purple (postage)	65	25
258	**49**	15f. brown, yellow & red	2·50	55
259	-	40f. brown, pink & choc	2·00	70
260	**50**	50f. ol, brn & sep (air)	5·00	90
261	-	100f. sepia, brown & turq	13·00	1·80
262	-	200f. brown, blue & grn	15·00	7·00
262a	-	500f. indigo, blue and lilac	28·00	17·00

DESIGNS—As Type **49**: 40f. Woman gathering coffee. As Type **50**: HORIZ: 100f. Airplane over giraffes; 200f. Freighters, Douala Port. VERT: 500f. Sud Ouest Corse II over Piton d'Humsiki.

51 Edea Barrage

1953. Air. Opening of Edea Barrage.

263	**51**	15f. blue, lake and brown	2·75	1·00

52 "D-Day"

1954. Air. Tenth Anniv of Liberation.

264	**52**	15f. green and turquoise	7·75	6·50

53 Dr. Jamot and Students

1954. Air. 75th Birthday of Dr. Jamot (physician).

265	**53**	15f. brown, blue & green	5·25	7·25

54 Native Cattle

1956. Economic and Social Development Fund. Inscr "F.I.D.E.S.".

266	**54**	5f. brown and sepia	55	30
267	-	15f. turq, blue & black	1·40	45
268	-	20f. turquoise and blue	1·20	75
269	-	25f. blue	1·80	90

DESIGNS: 15f. R. Wouri bridge; 20f. Technical education; 25f. Mobile medical unit.

55 Coffee

1956

270	**55**	15f. vermilion and red	50	30

56 Woman, Child and Flag

1958. First Anniv of First Cameroun Govt.

271	**56**	20f. multicoloured	55	35

57 "Human Rights"

1958. 30th Anniv of Declaration of Human Rights.

272	**57**	20f. brown and red	1·20	2·50

58 "Randia malleifera"

1958. Tropical Flora.

273	**58**	20f. multicoloured	1·10	55

59 Loading Bananas on Ship at Douala

1959

274	**59**	20f. multicoloured	1·00	35
275	-	25f. green, brn & pur	1·20	90

DESIGN—VERT: 25f. Bunch of bananas and native bearers in jungle path.

C. INDEPENDENT REPUBLIC

60 Prime Minister A. Ahidjo

1960. Proclamation of Independence. Inscr "1 ER JANVIER 1960".

276		20f. multicoloured	80	25
277	**60**	25f. green, bistre & black	80	25

DESIGN: 20f. Cameroun flag and map.

61 "Uprooted Tree"

1960. World Refugee Year.

278	**61**	30f. green, blue and brown	1·10	55

62 CCTA Emblem

1960. Tenth Anniv of African Technical Co-operation Commission.

279	**62**	50f. black and purple	1·60	80

63 Map and Flag

1961. Red Cross Fund. Flag in green, red and yellow; cross in red; background colours given.

280	**63**	20f.+5f. green and red	1·20	95
281	**63**	25f.+10f. red and green	1·50	1·20
282	**63**	30f.+15f. red and green	2·10	1·60

64 U.N. Headquarters, Emblem and Cameroun Flag

1961. Admission to UNO. Flag in green, red and yellow; emblem in blue, buildings and inscr in colours given.

283	**64**	15f. brown and green	50	30
284	**64**	25f. green and blue	75	40
285	**64**	85f. purple, blue and red	2·30	1·40

1961. Surch **REPUBLIQUE FEDERALE** and value in Sterling currency.

286	-	½d. on 1f. orange (238) (postage)	45	25
287	-	1d. on 2f. black (241)	45	40
288	**54**	1½d. on 5f. brown & sepia	55	45
289	-	2d. on 10f. green (247)	1·00	70
290	-	3d. on 15f. turquoise, indigo and black (267)	1·30	70
291	-	4d. on 15f. vermilion and red (270)	1·50	90
292	-	6d. on 20f. mult (274)	2·10	1·30
293	**60**	1s. on 25f. grn, bis & blk	3·00	2·20
294a	**61**	2s.6d. on 30f. green, blue and brown	5·50	5·00
295a	-	5s. on 100r. sepia, brown and turquoise (264) (air)	10·00	9·50
296a	-	10s. on 200f. brown, blue and green (265)	20·00	19·00
297a	-	£1 on 500f. indigo, blue and lilac (253a)	34·00	32·00

The above were for use in the former British Cameroon Trust Territory pending the introduction of the Cameroun franc.

66 Pres. Ahidjo and Prime Minister Foncha

1962. Reunification. (a) T **66**.

298	20f. brown and violet		
299	25f. brown and green		
300	60f. green and red		

(b) T **66** surch in Sterling currency.

301	3d. on 20f. brown & violet		
302	6d. on 25f. brown and green		
303	2s.6d. on 60f. green and red		

68 Lions International Badge, Doctor and Leper

1962. World Leprosy Day. Lions International Relief Fund.

304	**68**	20f.+5f. purple & brown	75	70
305	**68**	25f.+10f. purple & blue	95	90
306	**68**	50f.+15f. purple & green	1·80	1·60

69 European, African and Boeing 707 Airliners

1962. Air. Foundation of "Air Afrique" Airline.

307	**69**	25f. purple, violet & grn	1·00	50

70 Campaign Emblem

1962. Malaria Eradication.

308	**70**	25f.+5f. mauve	1·00	80

71 Giraffes and Waza Camp

1962. (a) Postage. Animals.

309	**A**	50c. sepia, blue & turquoise	10	10
310	**B**	1f. black, turquoise & orge	10	10
311	**C**	1f.50 brown, sage & blk	20	10
312	**D**	2f. black, blue and green	20	20
313	**C**	3f. brown, orange & purple	20	20
314	**B**	4f. sepia, green & turq	25	20
315	**D**	5f. purple, green & brown	35	20
316	**A**	6f. sepia, blue and lemon	45	25
317	**E**	8f. blue, red and green	95	70
318	**F**	10f. black, orange & blue	75	25
319	**A**	15f. brown, blue & turq	1·40	45
320	**71**	20f. brown and grey	95	45
321	**F**	25f. brown, yellow & grn	2·75	1·00
322	**E**	30f. black, blue & brown	3·00	1·10
323	**71**	40f. lake and green	6·50	2·10

(b) Air.

324	50f. brown, myrtle & blue	95	70
325	100f. multicoloured	4·75	1·50
326	200f. black, brn & turq	8·00	2·40
327	500f. buff, purple and blue	11·00	3·75

DESIGNS—HORIZ: As Type **71**: A, Moustached monkey; B, African elephant and Ntem Falls; C, Kob, Dschang; D, Hippopotamus, Hippo Camp; E, African manatee, Lake Ossa; F, Buffalo, Batoun Region. (48×27 mm): 50f. Cocotiers Hotel, Douala; 100f. *Cymothoe sangaris* (butterfly); 200f. Ostriches; 500f. Kapsikis, Mokolo (landscape).

72 Union Flag

1962. First Anniv of Union of African and Malagasy States. Flag in green, red and gold.

328	**72**	30f. brown	2·00	90

73 Map and View

1962. First Anniv of Reunification.

329	**73**	9f. bistre, violet & brown	35	25
330	**73**	18f. red, green and blue	45	40
331	-	20f. bistre, blue and purple	60	40
332	-	25f. orange, sepia & blue	60	45
333	-	50f. blue, sepia and red	1·50	90

DESIGNS: 20f., 25f. Sunrise over Cameroun; 50f. Commemorative scroll.

74 "The School Under the Tree"

1962. Literacy and Popular Education Plan.

334	**74**	20f. red, yellow and green	1·00	50

75 Globe and "Telstar"

1963. First Trans-Atlantic Television Satellite Link.

335	**75**	1f. ol, vio & blue (postage)	20	10
336	**75**	2f. lake, green and blue	30	25
337	**75**	3f. olive, purple and green	30	25
338	**75**	25f. blue and green	1·00	1·00
339	**75**	100f. brown and green (air) (48×27 mm)	2·30	1·40

76 Globe and Emblem

1963. Freedom from Hunger.

340	**76**	18f.+5f. blue, brn & grn	90	50
341	**76**	25f.+5f. green & brown	1·30	60

77 VHF Station, Mt. Bankolo, Yaounde

1963. Inauguration of Doala–Yaounde VHF Radio Service.

342	**77**	15f. mult (postage)	45	30
343	-	20f. multicoloured	60	45
344	-	100f. multicoloured (air)	2·30	1·40

DESIGNS: 20f. Aerials and control panel; 100f. Edea relay station (26×44 mm).

78 "Centre regional ..."

1963. Inauguration of UNESCO Regional Schoolbooks Production Centre, Yaounde.

345	**78**	20f. red, black and green	45	25
346	**78**	25f. red, black and orange	55	25
347	**78**	100f. red, black and gold	2·00	1·10

1963. Air. African and Malagasian Posts and Telecommunications Union. As T **18** of Central African Republic.

348	85f. multicoloured	2·20	1·50

80 Pres. Ahidjo

1963. Second Anniv of Reunification. Multicoloured.

349	9f. Type **80**	40	30
350	18f. Map and flag	60	30
351	20f. Type **80**	75	40

1963. Air. Inauguration of "DC-8" Service. As T **11** of Congo Republic.

352	50f. multicoloured	1·30	60

82 Globe and Scales of Justice

1963. 15th Anniv of Declaration of Human Rights.

353	**82**	9f. brown, black and blue	40	25
354	**82**	18f. red, black and green	55	25
355	**82**	25f. green, black & red	75	35
356	**82**	75f. blue, black & yellow	1·80	95

83 Lion

1964. Waza National Park.

357	**83**	10f. bistre green & brown	1·40	45
358	**83**	25f. bistre and green	2·00	85

84 Football Stadium, Yaounde

1964. Tropics Cup. Inscr as in T **84**.

359	**84**	10f. brown, turquoise & grn	45	25
360	-	18f. green, red and violet	60	40
361	-	30f. blue, brown and black	1·00	60

DESIGNS: 18f. Sports Equipment; 30f. Stadium Entrance. Yaounde.

85 Palace of Justice, Yaounde

1964. First Anniv of European–African Economic Convention. Multicoloured.

362	15f. Type **85**	1·20	70
363	40f. Sun, moon and economic emblems (vert)	2·30	1·40

86 Olympic Flame and Hurdling

1964. Olympic Games, Toyko.

364	**86**	9f. red, blk & grn (postage)	1·70	1·40
365	-	10f. brown, violet and red	2·20	1·40
366	-	300f. turquoise, brown and red (air)	8·25	4·75
MS366a		168×100 mm. Nos. 364/66 (air)	14·50	14·50

DESIGNS—VERT: 10f. Running. HORIZ: 300f. Wrestling.

87 Ntem Falls

1964. Folklore and Tourism.

367		9f. red, blue & grn (postage)	55	25
368		18f. blue, brown and red	75	45
369	**87**	20f. drab, green and red	90	45
370	-	25f. red, brown & orange	1·40	75
371	-	50f. brown, grn & bl (air)	1·20	70
372	-	250f. sepia, grn & brn	11·00	3·75

DESIGNS—As Type **87**. VERT: 9f. Bamileke dance costume; 18f. Bamenda dance mask. HORIZ: 25f. Fulani horseman. LARGER (43×27½ mm): 50f. View of Kribi and Longji; 250f. Black rhinoceros.

88 Co-operation

1964. French, African and Malagasy Co-operation.

373	**88**	18f. brown, green and blue	95	40
374	**88**	30f. brown, turq & brn	1·40	55

89 Pres. Kennedy

1964. Air. Pres. Kennedy Commem.

375	**89**	100f. sepia, grn & apple	2·30	2·20
MS375a	**89**	129×90 mm. Block of four	9·00	9·00

90 Inscription recording laying of First Rail

1965. Opening of Mbanga–Kumba Railway.

376	**90**	12f. indigo, green and blue	95	50
377	-	20f. yellow, green and red	2·50	1·00

DESIGN—HORIZ: (36×22 mm): 20f. Series BB500 diesel locomotive.

91 Abraham Lincoln

1965. Air. Death Centenary of Abraham Lincoln.

378	**91**	100f. multicoloured	2·30	1·60

92 Ambulance and First Aid Post

1965. Cameroun Red Cross.

379	**92**	25f. yellow, green and red	75	30
380	-	50f. brown, red and grey	1·50	55

DESIGN—VERT: 50f. Nurse and child.

93 "Syncom" and ITU Emblem

1965. Air. Centenary of ITU.

381	**93**	70f. black, blue and red	1·60	85

94 Churchill giving "V" Sign

1965. Air. Churchill Commem. Multicoloured.

382	12f. Type **94**	1·20	70
383	18f. Churchill, oak spray and cruiser "De Grasse"	1·20	70

95 "Map" Savings Bank

1965. Federal Postal Savings Bank.

384	**95**	9f. yellow, red and green	40	25
385	-	15f. brown, green & blue	55	25
386	-	20f. brown, chest & turq	60	40

DESIGNS—HORIZ: (48×27 mm): 15f. Savings Bank building. VERT: (27×48 mm): 20f. "Cocoa-bean" savings bank.

96 Africa Cup and Players

1965. Winning of Africa Cup by Oryx Football Club.

387	**96**	9f. brown, yellow and red	75	35
388	**96**	20f. blue, yellow and red	1·50	55

97 Map of Europe and Africa

1965. "Europafrique".

389	**97**	5f. red, lilac and black	30	25
390	-	40f. multicoloured	1·30	80

DESIGN: 40f. Yaounde Conference.

98 UPU Monument, Berne and Doves

1965. Fifth Anniv of Admission to UPU.

391	**98**	30f. purple and red	80	60

99 ICY Emblem

1965. International Co-operation Year.

392	**99**	10f. red & blue (postage)	45	35
393	**99**	100f. blue and red (air)	2·30	1·00

100 Pres. Ahidjo and Government House

1965. Re-election of Pres. Ahidjo. Multicoloured.

394		9f. Pres. Ahidjo wearing hat, and Government House (vert)	30	10
395		18f. Type **100**	45	20
396		20f. As 9f.	55	25
397		25f. Type **100**	85	45

101 Musgum Huts, Pouss

1965. Folklore and Tourism.

398	**101**	9f. green, brown and red (postage)	40	25
399	-	18f. brown, green & blue	45	25
400	-	20f. brown and blue	95	40
401	-	25f. grey, lake and green	95	40
402	-	50f. brown, blue and green (48×27 mm) (air)	2·20	80

DESIGNS—HORIZ: 18f. Great Calao's dance (N. Cameroons); 25f. National Tourist office, Yaounde; 50f. Racing pirogue on Sanaga River, Edea. VERT: 20f. Sultan's palace gate Foumban.

102 "Vostok 6"

1966. Air. Spacecraft.

403	**102**	50f. green and red	95	55
404	-	100f. blue and purple	2·10	90
405	-	200f. violet and blue	3·75	2·20
406	-	500f. blue and indigo	8·75	4·50

DESIGNS: 100f. "Gemini 4", and White in space; 200f. "Gemini 5"; 500f. "Gemini 6" and "Gemini 7" making rendezvous.

103 Mountain's Hotel, Buea

1966. Cameroun Hotels.

407	**103**	9f. bistre, green and red (postage)	35	25
408	-	20f. black, green & blue	45	25
409	-	35f. red, brown & green	95	55
410	**103**	18f. black, grn & bl (air)	45	25
411	-	25f. indigo, red and blue	65	45
412	-	50f. brown, orange & grn	2·40	1·10
413	-	60f. brown, green & blue	1·40	75
414	-	85f. blue, red and green	1·80	85
415	-	100f. purple, blue & grn	2·75	1·20
416	-	150f. orange, brn & blue	3·50	1·60

HOTELS—HORIZ: 20f. Deputies, Yaounde. 25f. Akwa Palace, Douala. 35f. Dschang. 50f. Terminus, Yaounde. 60f. Imperial, Yaounde. 85f. Independence, Yaounde. 150f. Huts, Waza Camp. VERT: 100f. Hunting Lodge, Mora.

104 Foumban Bas-relief

1966. World Festival of Negro Arts, Dakar.

417	**104**	9f. black and red	75	25
418	-	18f. purple, brn and grn	75	30
419	-	20f. brown, blue & violet	1·00	40
420	-	25f. brown and plum	1·20	40

DESIGNS—VERT: 18f. Ekoi mask; 20f. Bamileke statue. HORIZ: 25f. Bamoun stool.

105 WHO Headquarters, Geneva

1966. U.N. Agency Buildings.

421	**105**	50f. lake, blue and yellow	1·20	70
422	-	50f. yellow, blue & green	55	25

DESIGN: No. 422, ITU Headquarters, Geneva.

106 *Phaeomeria magnifica*

1966. Flowers. Multicoloured. (a) Postage. Size as T **106**.

423		9f. Type **106**	60	25
424		15f. *Strelitzia reginae*	95	25
425		18f. *Hibiscus schizopetalus x rosa-sinensis*	75	25
426		20f. *Antigonon leptopus*	75	25

(b) Air. Size 26×45½ mm.

427		25f. *Hibiscus mutabilis* ("Caprice des dames")	75	25
428		50f. *Delonix regia*	1·50	30
429		100f. *Bougainvillea glabra*	3·00	60
430		200f. *Thevetia peruviana*	4·50	1·60
431		250f. *Hippeastrum equestre*	5·50	2·10

For stamps as Type **106** but showing fruits, see Nos. 463/71.

107 Mobile Gendarmerie

1966. Air. Cameroun Armed Forces.

432	**107**	20f. blue, brown & plum	55	25
433	-	25f. green, violet & brown	55	25
434	-	60f. indigo, green & blue	1·80	80
435	-	100f. blue, red & purple	2·75	1·20

DESIGNS: 25f. Paratrooper; 60f. Gunboat *Vigilant*; 100f. Dassault MD-315 Flamant airplane.

108 Wembley Stadium

1966. Air. World Cup Football Championship.

436	**108**	50f. green, blue and red	1·40	55
437	-	200f. red, blue and green	4·50	2·20

DESIGN: 200f. Footballers.

109 Douglas DC-8F Jet Trader and "Air Afrique" Emblem

1966. Air. Inauguration of DC-8 Air Service.

438	**109**	25f. grey, black & purple	80	45

110 U.N. General Assembly

1966. Sixth Anniv of Admission to U.N.

439	**110**	50f. purple, green & blue	90	25
440	-	100f. blue, brown & green	1·90	85

DESIGN—VERT: 100f. Africans encircling U.N. emblem within figure "6".

111 1st Minister's Residency, Buea (side view)

1966. Fifth Anniv of Cameroun's Reunification. Multicoloured.

441		9f. Type **111**	40	25
442		18f. Prime Minister's Residency, Yaounde (front view)	50	25
443		20f. As 18f. but side view	55	45
444		25f. As Type **111** but front view	85	45

112 Learning to Write

1966. 20th Anniv of UNESCO and UNICEF.

445	**112**	50f. brown, purple & blue	1·30	60
446	-	50f. black, blue & purple	1·30	60

DESIGN: No. 446. Cameroun children.

113 Buea Cathedral

1966. Air. Religious Buildings.

447	**113**	18f. purple, blue & green	45	25
448	-	25f. violet, brown & green	55	25
449	-	30f. lake, green & purple	75	40
450	-	60f. green, red & turquoise	1·40	70

BUILDINGS: 25f. Yaounde Cathedral. 30f. Orthodox Church, Yaounde. 60f. Garoua Mosque.

114 Proclamation

1967. Seventh Anniv of Independence.

451	**114**	20f. red, green & yellow	2·00	1·10

115 Map of Africa, Railway Lines and Signals

1967. Fifth African and Malagasy Railway Technicians Conference, Yaounde. Multicoloured.

452		20f. Type **115**	2·30	1·00
453		20f. Map of Africa and diesel train	3·25	1·40

116 Lions Emblem and Jungle

1967. 50th Anniv of Lions International. Multicoloured.

454		50f. Type **116**	95	55
455		100f. Lions emblem and palms	2·00	1·20

117 Aircraft and ICAO Emblem

1967. International Civil Aviation Organization.

456	**117**	50f. multicoloured	1·30	60

118 Dove and IAEA Emblem

1967. International Atomic Energy Agency.

457	**118**	50f. blue and green	1·30	60

119 Rotary Banner and Emblem

1967. Tenth Anniv of Cameroun Branch, Rotary Int.

458	**119**	25f. red, gold and blue	1·20	55

120 "Pioneer A"

1967. Air. "Conquest of the Moon".

459	**120**	25f. green, brown & blue	45	25
460	-	50f. violet, purple & grn	90	40
461	-	100f. purple, brown & bl	2·30	90
462	-	250f. purple, grey and brown	5·00	2·75

DESIGNS: 50f. "Ranger 6"; 100f. "Luna 9"; 250f. "Luna 10".

121 Grapefruit

1967. Fruits. Multicoloured.

463		1f. Type **121**	10	10

464	2f. Papaw	10	10
465	3f. Custard-apple	25	25
466	4f. Breadfruit	25	25
467	5f. Coconut	35	25
468	6f. Mango	45	25
469	8f. Avocado	95	30
470	10f. Pineapple	1·50	45
471	30f. Bananas	3·50	1·50

122 Sanaga Waterfalls

1967. International Tourist Year.

472	**122**	30f. multicoloured	80	35

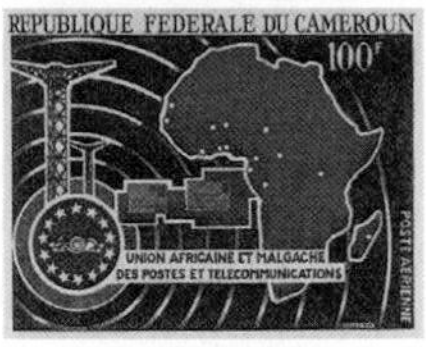

123 Map, Letters and Pylons

1967. Air. Fifth Anniv of African and Malagasy Posts and Telecommunications Union (UAMPT).

473	**123**	100f. pur, lake & turq	2·20	95

124 Harvesting Coconuts (carved box)

1967. Cameroun Art.

474	**124**	10f. brown, red and blue	35	25
475	-	20f. brown, green & yell	50	30
476	-	30f. brown, red & green	90	45
477	-	100f. brown, red & grn	2·30	95

DESIGNS (Carved boxes): 20f. Lion-hunting; 30f. Harvesting coconuts (different); 100f. Carved chest.

125 Crossed Skis

1967. Air. Winter Olympic Games, Grenoble.

478	**125**	30f. brown and blue	1·50	85

126 Cameroun Exhibit

1967. Air. World Fair, Montreal.

479	**126**	50f. brown, chest & pur	95	40
480	-	100f. brown, purple & grn	3·00	1·10
481	-	200f. green, purple & brn	4·25	2·20

DESIGNS: 100f. Totem poles; 200f. African pavilion.

For No. 481 optd **PREMIER HOMME SUR LA LUNE 20 JUILLET 1969/FIRST MAN LANDING ON MOON 20 JULY 1969** see note below Nos. 512/17.

127 Chancellor Adenauer and Cologne Cathedral

1967. Air. Adenauer Commem. Multicoloured.

482		30f. Type **127**	95	40
483		70f. Adenauer and Chancellor's residence, Bonn	2·00	70

128 Arms of the Republic

1968. Eighth Anniv of Independence.

484	**128**	30f. multicoloured	1·00	50

129 Pres. Ahidjo and King Faisal of Saudi Arabia

1968. Air. Pres. Ahidjo's Pilgrimage to Mecca and Visit to the Vatican. Multicoloured.

485		30f. Type **129**	85	45
486		60f. Pope Paul VI greeting Pres. Ahidjo	2·10	70

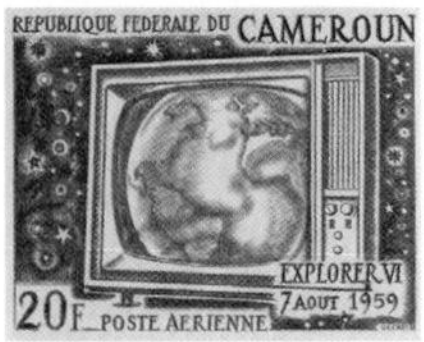

130 "Explorer VI" (televised picture of Earth)

1968. Air. Telecommunications Satellites.

487	**130**	20f. grey, red and blue	50	25
488	-	30f. blue, indigo and red	80	45
489	-	40f. green, red & plum	1·10	50

DESIGNS: 30f. "Molnya"; 40f. "Molnya" (televised picture of Earth).

131 Douala Port

1968. Air. Five-year Development Plan.

490		20f. blue, red and green	55	30
491		30f. blue, green & brown	4·50	1·80
492		30f. blue, brown & green	1·00	50
493		40f. brown, green & turq	1·00	40
494	**131**	60f. purple, indigo & blue	2·50	1·00

DESIGNS—VERT: 20f. Steel forge; 30f. (No. 491), "Transcamerounais" express train leaving tunnel; 30f. (No. 492), Tea-harvesting; 40f. Rubber-tapping.

132 Spiny Lobster

1968. Fish and Crustaceans.

495	**132**	5f. green, brown & violet	20	20
496	-	10f. slate, brown & blue	30	20
497	-	15f. brown, chest & pur	65	20
498	-	20f. brown and blue	75	20
499	-	25f. blue, brown and green	1·10	55
500	-	30f. brown, blue and red	1·50	55
501	-	40f. blue, brown & orge	1·70	70
502	-	50f. red, slate and green	2·50	85
503	-	55f. purple, brown & blue	3·25	1·20
504	-	60f. blue, purple & green	5·25	1·60

DESIGNS—HORIZ: 10f. Freshwater crayfish; 15f. Nile mouthbrooder; 20f. Sole. 25f. Northern pike; 30f. Swimming crab; 55f. Dusky snakehead; 60f. Capitaine threadfin. VERT: 40f. African spadefish; 50f. Prawn.

133 Refinery and Tanker

1968. Inauguration of Petroleum Refinery, Port Gentil, Gabon.

505	**133**	30f. multicoloured	1·20	45

134 Boxing

1968. Air. Olympic Games, Mexico.

506	**134**	30f. brown, green & emer	75	35
507	-	50f. brown, red & green	1·30	60
508	-	60f. brown, blue & green	1·50	70
MS509		131×101 mm. Nos. 506/8	4·50	4·50

DESIGNS: 50f. Long-jumping; 60f. Gymnastics.

135 Human Rights Emblem

1968. Human Rights Year.

510	**135**	15f. blue & orge (postage)	60	25
511	**135**	30f. green & purple (air)	75	40

136 Mahatma Gandhi and Map of India

1968. Air. "Apostles of Peace".

512	**136**	30f. black, yellow & blue	55	45
513	-	30f. black and blue	55	45
514	-	40f. black and pink	95	75
515	-	60f. black and lilac	1·20	75
516	-	70f. black, blue & buff	1·30	90
517	-	70f. black and green	1·30	90
MS518		122×162 mm. Nos. 512, 514/15 and 517	7·50	7·50

PORTRAITS: No. 513, Martin Luther King. No. 514, J. F. Kennedy. No. 515, R. F. Kennedy. No. 516, Gandhi (full-face). No. 517, Martin Luther King (half-length).

During 1969, Nos. 481 and 512/17 were issued optd **PREMIER HOMME SUR LA LUNE 20 JUILLET 1969/ FIRST MAN LANDING ON MOON 20 JULY 1969** in very limited quantities.

137 *The Letter* (A. Cambon)

1968. Air. "Philexafrique" Stamp Exhibition, Abidjan (in 1969). (1st issue).

519	**137**	100f. multicoloured	3·25	2·50

138 Wouri Bridge and 1f. stamp of 1925

1969. Air. "Philexafrique" Stamp Exhibition, Abidjan, Ivory Coast (2nd issue).

520	**138**	50f. blue, olive and green	3·25	2·10

139 President Ahidjo

1969. Ninth Anniv of Independence.

521	**139**	30f. multicoloured	80	30

140 Vat of Chocolate

1969. Chocolate Industry Development.

522	**140**	15f. blue, brown and red	45	25
523	-	30f. brown, choc & grn	75	40
524	-	50f. red, green & bistre	1·00	55

DESIGNS—HORIZ: 30f. Chocolate factory. VERT: 50f. Making confectionery.

141 *Caladium bicolor*

1969. Air. Third Int Flower Show, Paris. Multicoloured.

525		30f. Type **141**	80	55
526		50f. *Aristolochia elegans*	1·70	80
527		100f. *Gloriosa simplex*	3·50	1·50

142 Reproduction Symbol

1969. Abbia Arts and Folklore.

528	**142**	5f. purple, turq & blue	30	20
529	-	10f. orange, olive & blue	45	20
530	-	15f. indigo, red & blue	45	25
531	-	30f. green, brown & blue	95	40
532	-	70f. red, green and blue	1·70	85

DESIGNS—HORIZ: 10f. "Two Toucans"; 30f. "Vulture attacking Monkey". VERT: 15f. Forest Symbol; 70f. Oliphant-player.

143 Post Office, Douala

1969. Air. New Post Office Buildings.

533	**143**	30f. brown, blue & green	55	25
534	-	50f. red, slate & turquoise	95	45
535	-	100f. brown and turquoise	1·80	85

DESIGNS: 50f. G.P.O., Buea; 100f. G.P.O., Bafoussam.

144 *Coronation of Napoleon* (David)

1969. Air. Birth Bicent of Napoleon Bonaparte.

536	**144**	30f. multicoloured	1·20	70
537	-	1,000f. gold	42·00	40·00

DESIGN: 1,000f. *Napoleon crossing the Alps*. No. 537 is embossed on gold foil.

145 Kumba Station

1969. Opening of Mbanga–Kumba Railway. Multicoloured.

538		30f. Type **145**	1·10	55
539		50f. Diesel train on bridge over River Mungo (vert)	2·75	1·00

146 Bank Emblem

1969. Fifth Anniv of African Development Bank.

540	**146**	30f. brown, green & vio	80	40

1969. Air. Negro Writers. Portrait designs as T **136**.

541		15f. brown and blue	45	25
542		30f. brown and purple	75	25
543		30f. brown and yellow	75	25
544		50f. brown and green	95	45
545		50f. brown and agate	95	45
546		100f. brown and yellow	1·90	1·10
MS547		115×125 mm. Nos. 541/6	7·25	7·25

DESIGNS—VERT: No. 541, Dr. P. Mars (Haiti); No. 542, W. Dubois (U.S.A.); No. 543, A. Cesaire (Martinique); No. 544, M. Garvey (Jamaica); No. 545, L. Hughes (U.S.A.); No. 546, R. Maran (Martinique).

148 I.L.O. Emblem

1969. Air. 50th Anniv of I.L.O.

548	**148**	30f. black and turquoise	70	40
549	**148**	50f. black and mauve	1·30	60

149 Astronauts and "Apollo 11" in Sea

1969. Air. First Man on the Moon. Multicoloured.

550		200f. Type **149**	4·75	2·20
551		500f. Astronaut and module on Moon	11·50	4·50

150 Airplane, Map and Airport

1969. Tenth Anniv of Aerial Navigation Security Agency for Africa and Madagascar (ASECNA).

552	**150**	100f. green	1·80	85

151 President Ahidjo, Arms and Map

1970. Air. Tenth Anniv of Independence.

553	**151**	1,000f. gold & mult	25·00	23·00

No. 553 is embossed on gold foil.

152 Mont Febe Hotel, Yaounde

1970. Air. Tourism.

554	**152**	30f. grey, green & brn	80	30

153 Lenin

1970. Air. Birth Centenary of Lenin.

555	**153**	50f. brown and yellow	1·90	75

154 *Lantana camara*

1970. African Climbing Plants. Multicoloured.

556		15f. Type **154** (postage)	45	25
557		30f. *Passiflora quadrangularis*	1·00	40
558		50f. *Cleome speciosa* (air)	1·50	70
559		100f. *Mussaenda erythrophylla*	3·00	1·40

155 Lions' Emblem and Map of Africa

1970. Air. 13th Congress of Lions International District 403, Yaounde.

560	**155**	100f. multicoloured	2·20	95

156 New UPU HQ.

1970. New UPU Headquarters Building, Berne.

561	**156**	30f. green, violet & blue	90	25
562	**156**	50f. blue, red and grey	1·30	40

157 U.N. Emblem and Stylized Doves

1970. Air. 25th Anniv of United Nations.

563	**157**	30f. brown and orange	90	45
564	-	50f. indigo and blue	1·30	65

DESIGN—VERT: 50f. U.N. emblem and stylized dove.

158 Fermenting Vats

1970. Brewing Industry.

565	**158**	15f. brown, green & grey	45	25
566	-	30f. red, brown and blue	90	40

DESIGN: 30f. Storage tanks.

159 Japanese Pavilion

1970. Air. Expo 70.

567	**159**	50f. blue, red and green	95	55
568	-	100f. red, blue and green	2·00	90
569	-	150f. brown, slate & blue	3·50	1·60

DESIGNS—VERT: 100f. Expo Emblem and Map of Japan. HORIZ: 150f. Australian Pavilion.

160 Gen. De Gaulle in Tropical Kit

1970. Air. "Homage to General De Gaulle".

570	**160**	100f. brown, blue & grn	3·00	1·60
571	-	200f. blue, green & brn	5·50	2·50

DESIGN: 200f. Gen. De Gaulle in military uniform.

Nos. 570/1 were issued together as a triptych, separated by a stamp-size label showing maps of France and Cameroun.

161 Aztec Stadium, Mexico City

1970. Air. World Cup Football Championship, Mexico. Multicoloured.

572		50f. Type **161**	95	55
573		100f. Mexican team	2·00	1·10
574		200f. Pele and Brazilian team with World Cup (vert)	3·50	1·90

162 Dancers

1970. Ozila Dancers.

575	**162**	30f. red, orange & grn	1·20	45
576	**162**	50f. red, brown & scar	2·40	95

163 Doll in National Costume

1970. Cameroun Dolls.

577	**163**	10f. green, black & red	65	45
578	**163**	15f. red, green & yellow	75	55
579	**163**	30f. brown, green & blk	1·60	70

164 Beethoven (after Stieler)

1970. Air. Birth Bicent of Beethoven.

580	**164**	250f. multicoloured	5·25	2·75

1970. Air. Rembrandt Paintings. As T **144**. Multicoloured.

581		70f. *Christ at Emmaus*	1·50	60
582		150f. *The Anatomy Lesson*	2·50	1·30

166 "Industry and Agriculture"

1970. "Europafrique" Economic Community.

583	**166**	30f. multicoloured	80	40

167 Bust of Dickens

1970. Air. Death Centenary of Charles Dickens.

584	**167**	40f. brown and red	95	35
585	-	50f. multicoloured	1·10	55
586	-	100f. multicoloured	1·90	1·10

DESIGNS: 50f. Characters from David Copperfield; 100f. Dickens writing.

1971. Air. De Gaulle Memorial Issue. Nos. 570/1 optd **IN MEMORIAM 1890-1970**.

587	**160**	100f. brown, blue & grn	3·00	1·40
588	-	200f. blue, green & brn	5·50	2·30

169 University Buildings

1971. Inauguration of Federal University, Yaounde.

589	**169**	50f. green, blue & brown	1·00	45

170 Presidents Ahidjo and Pompidou

1971. Visit of Pres. Pompidou of France.

590	**170**	30f. multicoloured	1·50	70

171 "Cameroun Youth"

1971. Fifth National Youth Festival.

591	**171**	30f. multicoloured	80	45

172 Timber Yard, Douala

1971. Air. Industrial Expansion.

592	**172**	40f. brown, green & red	55	25
593	-	70f. brown, green and blue	1·20	50
594	-	100f. red, blue & green	1·60	70

DESIGNS—VERT: 70f. "Alucam" aluminium plant, Edea. HORIZ: 100f. Mbakaou Dam.

173 *Gerbera hybrida*

1971. Flowers. Multicoloured.

595		20f. Type **173**	65	40
596		40f. *Opuntia polyantha*	1·50	55
597		50f. *Hemerocallis hybrida*	1·90	70

For similar designs inscr "United Republic of Cameroon" etc., see Nos. 648/52.

174 "World Races"

1971. Racial Equality Year. Multicoloured.

598		20f. Type **174**	50	25
599		30f. Hands of four races clasping globe	75	25

175 Crowned Cranes, Camp de Waza

1971. Landscapes.

600	**175**	10f. blue, red and green	1·70	45
601	-	20f. red, brown & green	1·10	45
602	-	30f. green, blue & brown	1·10	45

DESIGNS: 20f. African pirogue; 30f. Sanaga River.

176 Relay-racing

1971. Air. 75th Anniv of Modern Olympic Games.

603	**176**	30f. blue, red and brown	60	30
604	-	50f. purple and blue	85	40
605	-	100f. black, green & red	1·70	70

DESIGNS—VERT: 50f. Olympic runner with torch. HORIZ: 100f. Throwing the discus.

177 *Villalba* (deep-sea trawler)

1971. Air. Fishing Industry.

606	**177**	30f. brown, green & blue	95	50
607	-	40f. purple, blue & green	1·00	70
608	-	70f. brown, red and blue	1·90	90
609	-	150f. multicoloured	4·75	1·90

DESIGNS: 40f. Traditional fishing method, Northern Cameroun; 70f. Fish quay, Douala; 150f. Shrimp-boats, Douala.

178 Peace Palace, The Hague

1971. 25th Anniv of International Court of Justice, The Hague.

610	**178**	50f. brown, blue & green	90	35

179 1916 French Occupation 20c. and 1914–18 War Memorial, Yaounde

1971. Air. "Philatecam 71" Stamp Exhibition, Yaounde (1st issue).

611	**179**	20f. brown, ochre & grn	50	25
612	-	25f. brown, green & blue	60	25
613	-	40f. green, grey & brown	95	25
614	-	50f. multicoloured	1·10	45
615	-	100f. green, brown & orge	2·10	85

DESIGNS: 25f. 1954 15f. Jamot stamp and memorial; 40f. 1965 25f. Tourist Office stamp and public buildings, Yaounde; 50f. German stamp and Imperial German postal emblem; 100f. 1915 Expeditionary Force optd, error, and Expeditionary Force memorial.

See also No. 620.

180 Rope Bridge

1971. "Rural Life". Multicoloured.

616		40f. Type **180**	1·40	45
617		45f. Local market (horiz)	1·40	45

181 Bamoun Horseman (carving)

1971. Cameroun Carving.

618	**181**	10f. brown and yellow	45	20
619	-	15f. brown and yellow	45	25

DESIGN: 15f. Fetish statuette.

182 Pres. Ahidjo, Flag and "Reunification" Road

1971. Air. "Philatecam 71" Stamp Exhibition, Yaounde (2nd issue).

620	**182**	250f. multicoloured	6·00	4·25

183 Satellite and Globe

1971. Pan-African Telecommunications Network.

621	**183**	40f. multicoloured	80	50

184 UAMPT Headquarters, Brazzaville and Carved Stool

1971. Air. Tenth Anniv of African and Malagasy Posts and Telecommunications Union.

622	**184**	100f. multicoloured	1·90	85

185 Children acclaiming Emblem

1971. 25th Anniv of UNICEF.

623	**185**	40f. purple, blue & slate	85	25
624	-	50f. red, green and blue	1·00	50

DESIGN—VERT: 50f. Ear of Wheat and Emblem.

186 *The Annunciation* (Fra Angelico)

1971. Air. Christmas. Paintings. Multicoloured.

625		40f. Type **186**	55	25
626		45f. *Virgin and Child* (Del Sarto)	80	45
627		150f. *The Holy Family with the Lamb* (detail Raphael) (vert)	3·25	1·20

187 Cabin, South-Central Region

1972. Traditional Cameroun Houses. Multicoloured.

628		10f. Type **187**	30	25
629		15f. Adamaoua round house	50	25

188 Airline Emblem

1972. Air. Cameroun Airlines' Inaugural Flight.

630	**188**	50f. multicoloured	80	25

189 Giraffe and Palm Tree

1972. Festival of Youth. Multicoloured.

631		2f. Type **189**	30	10
632		5f. Domestic scene	30	10
633		10f. Blacksmith (horiz)	30	20
634		15f. Women	30	20

190 Africa Cup

1972. African Football Cup Championship. Multicoloured.

635		20f. Type **190**	65	25
636		40f. Players with ball (horiz)	85	40
637		45f. Team captains	1·40	55

191 *St. Mark's Square and Doge's Palace* (detail-Caffi)

1972. Air. UNESCO "Save Venice" Campaign. Multicoloured.

638		40f. Type **191**	75	40
639		100f. *Regatta on the Grand Canal* (detail – Canaletto)	2·00	70
640		200f. *Regatta on the Grand Canal* (detail – Canaletto) (different)	4·00	1·40

192 Assembly Building, Yaounde

1972. 110th Session of Inter-Parliamentary Council, Yaounde.

641	**192**	40f. multicoloured	80	40

193 Horseman, North Cameroun

1972. Traditional Life and Folklore. Multicoloured.

642		15f. Type **193**	40	20
643		20f. Bororo woman (vert)	50	20
644		40f. Wouri River and Mt. Cameroun	1·80	55

194 Pataiev, Dobrovolsky and Volkov

1972. Air. "Soyuz 11" Cosmonauts. Memorial Issue.

645	**194**	50f. multicoloured	90	50

195 U.N. Building, New York, Gate of Heavenly Peace, Peking and Chinese Flag

1972. Air. Admission of Chinese People's Republic to U.N.

646	**195**	50f. multicoloured	2·75	70

196 Chemistry Laboratory, Federal University

1972. Pres. Ahidjo Prize.

647	**196**	40f. red, green & purple	80	50

1972. Flowers. As T **173**, but inscr "UNITED REPUBLIC OF CAMEROON", etc. Multicoloured.

648		40f. "Solanum macranthum"	85	30
649		40f. *Solanum macranthum*	1·00	25
650		45f. *Hoya carnosa*	1·00	50
651		45f. *Cassia alata*	1·20	30
652		50f. *Crinum sanderianum*	1·50	40

197 Swimming

1972. Air. Olympic Games, Munich.

653	**197**	50f. green, brown & lake	95	45
654	-	50f. brown, blue and sepia	95	45
655	-	200f. lake, grey & purple	3·75	1·70
MS656		140×100 mm. As Nos. 653/5 but colours changed; 50f. brown, violet and blue; 50f. brown, blue and purple; 200f. brown and blue	6·50	6·50

DESIGNS—HORIZ: No. 655, Horse-jumping. VERT: No. 654, Boxing.

198 *Charaxes ameliae*

1972. Butterflies. Multicoloured.

657		40f. Type **198**	3·00	90
658		45f. *Papiliotynderaeus*	4·25	1·30

1972. No. 471 surch.

659		40f. on 30f. multicoloured	1·00	50

1972. Air. Olympic Gold Medal Winners. Nos. 653/5 optd as listed below.

660		50f. green, brown and red	95	45
661		50f. brown, blue and sepia	95	45
662		200f. lake, grey and purple	3·75	1·70

OVERPRINTS: No. 660, **NATATION MARK SPITZ 7 MEDAILLES D'OR**. No. 661, **SUPER-WELTER KOTTYSCH MEDAILLE D'OR**. No. 662, **CONCOURS COMPLET MEADE MEDAILLE D'OR**.

201 Great Blue Turacos

1972. Birds. Multicoloured.

663		10f. Type **201**	1·20	45
664		45f. Red-faced lovebirds (horiz)	2·75	1·10

202 *The Virgin with Angels* (Cimabue)

1972. Air. Christmas. Multicoloured.

665		45f. Type **202**	1·00	45
666		140f. *The Madonna of the Rose Arbour* (S. Lochner)	2·75	1·60

203 St. Theresa

1973. Air. Birth Centenary of St. Theresa of Lisieux.

667	**203**	45f. blue, brown & violet	75	25
668	-	100f. mauve, brown, & bl	1·70	70

DESIGN: 100f. Lisieux Basilica.

204 Emperor Haile Selassie and "Africa Hall", Addis Ababa

1973. Air. 80th Birthday of Emperor Haile Selassie of Ethiopia.

669	**204**	45f. multicoloured	90	50

205 Cotton Cultivation, North Cameroun

1973. Third Five Year Plan. Multicoloured.

670	5f. Type **205**	20	10
671	10f. Cacao pods, South-central region	30	10
672	15f. Forestry, South-eastern area	50	20
673	20f. Coffee plant, West Cameroun	1·00	25
674	45f. Tea-picking, West Cameroun	2·20	40

206 "Food for All"

1973. Air. Tenth Anniv of World Food Programme.

675	**206**	45f. multicoloured	80	45

207 Human Hearts

1973. Air. 25th Anniv of W.H.O.

676	**207**	50f. red and blue	90	45

208 Pres. Ahidjo, Map, Flag and Cameroun Stamp

1973. First Anniv of United Republic. Multicoloured.

677	10f. Type **208** (postage)	65	25
678	20f. Pres. Ahidjo, proclamation and stamp	1·00	50
679	45f. Pres. Ahidjo, map of Cameroun rivers and stamp (air)	85	25
680	70f. Significant dates on Cameroun flag	1·10	65

209 Mask

1973. Bamoun Masks.

681	**209**	5f. black, brown & green	10	10
682	-	10f. brown, black & purple	30	10
683	-	45f. brown, black & red	75	40
684	-	100f. brown, black & blue	1·90	70

DESIGNS: 10f., 45f., 100f., as Type **209**, but different masks.

210 Dr. G. A. Hansen

1973. Centenary of Hansen's Identification of Leprosy Bacillus.

685	**210**	45f. blue, lt blue & brown	1·70	70

211 Scout Emblem and Flags

1973. Air. Admission of Cameroun to 24th World Scout Conference.

686	**211**	40f. multicoloured	85	35
687	**211**	45f. multicoloured	1·20	50
688	**211**	100f. multicoloured	2·50	80

1973. African Solidarity "Drought Relief". No. 670 surch **100F. SECHERESSE SOLIDARITE AFRICAINE**.

689	**205**	100f. on 5f. multicoloured	1·70	1·20

213 Folk-dancers

1973. Folklore Dances of South-west Cameroun. Multicoloured.

690	10f. Type **213**	20	10
691	25f. Dancer in plumed hat	55	20
692	45f. Dancers with "totem"	1·10	30

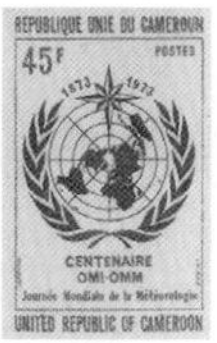

214 WMO Emblem

1973. Centenary of WMO.

693	**214**	45f. blue and green	1·50	40

215 Garoua Party H.Q. Building

1973. Seventh Anniv of Cameroun National Union.

694	**215**	40f. multicoloured	80	45

216 Crane with Letter and Telecommunications Emblem

1973. 12th Anniv of UAMPT.

695	**216**	100f. blue, lt blue & green	1·70	75

217 African Mask and Old Town Hall, Brussels

1973. Air. African Fortnight, Brussels.

696	**217**	40f. brown and purple	80	45

218 Avocado

1973. Cameroun Fruits. Multicoloured.

697	10f. Type **218**	60	25
698	20f. Mango	75	30
699	45f. Plum	1·70	65
700	50f. Custard-apple	2·10	80

219 Map of Africa

1973. Air. Aid for Handicapped Children.

701	**219**	40f. red, brown & green	80	50

220 Kirdi Village

1973. Cameroun Villages.

702	**220**	15f. black, green & brown	35	20
703	-	45f. brown, red & orange	85	45
704	-	50f. black, green & orange	1·00	55

DESIGNS: 45f. Mabas village. 50f. Fishing village.

221 Earth Station

1973. Air. Inauguration of Satellite Earth Station, Zamengoe.

705	**221**	100f. brown, blue & grn	1·40	75

222 *The Madonna with Chancellor Rolin* (Van Eyck)

1973. Air. Christmas. Multicoloured.

706	45f. Type **222**	1·00	55
707	140f. *The Nativity* (Federico Fiori–Il Barocci)	2·75	1·70

223 Handclasp on Map of Africa

1974. Tenth Anniv of Organization of African Unity.

708	**223**	40f. blue, red and green	55	25
709	**223**	45f. green, blue and red	65	25

224 Mill-worker

1974. C.I.C.A.M. Industrial Complex.

710	**224**	45f. brown, green & red	80	25

225 Bilinga Carved Panel (detail)

1974. Cameroun Art.

711	**225**	10f. brown and green	30	25
712	-	40f. brown and red	85	25
713	-	45f. red and blue	1·00	45

DESIGNS: 40f. Tubinga carving (detail); 45f. Acajou Ngollon carved panel (detail).

1974. No. 469 surch.

714	40f. on 8f. multicoloured	80	35

227 Cameroun Cow

1974. Cattle-raising in North Cameroun. Multicoloured.

715	40f. Type **227** (postage)	1·20	50
716	45f. Cattle in pen (air)	1·20	50

228 Route-map and Track

1974. Trans-Cameroun Railway. Inauguration of Yaounde–Ngaoundere Line.

717	**228**	5f. brown, blue & green	45	25
718	-	20f. brown, blue & violet	95	40
719	-	40f. red, blue & green	1·80	80
720	-	100f. green, blue & brown	3·00	1·40

DESIGNS—HORIZ: 20f. Laying track; 100f. Railway bridge over Djerem River. VERT: 40f. Welding rails.

229 Sir Winston Churchill

1974. Air. Birth Cent of Sir Winston Churchill.

721	**229**	100f. black, red & blue	1·60	75

230 Footballer and City Crests

1974. Air. World Cup Football Championship.

722	**230**	45f. orange, slate & grey	80	25
723	-	100f. orange, slate & grey	1·40	70
724	-	200f. blue, orange & blk	3·00	1·70

DESIGNS: 100f. Goalkeeper and city crests; 200f. World Cup.

1974. Air. West Germany's Victory in World Cup Football Championship. Nos. 722/4 optd **7th JULY 1974 R.F.A. 2 HOLLANDE 1 7 JUILLET 1974**.

725	**230**	45f. orange, slate & grey	75	25
726	-	100f. orange, slate & grey	1·30	70
727	-	200f. blue, orange & blk	2·75	1·70

232 UPU Emblem and Hands with Letters

1974. Centenary of Universal Postal Union.

728	**232**	40f. red, blue and green (postage)	90	45
729	-	100f. green, vio & bl (air)	1·70	85
730	-	200f. green, red and blue	2·75	1·70

DESIGNS: 100f. Cameroun UPU headquarters stamps of 1970; 200f. Cameroun UPU 75th anniv stamps of 1949.

233 Copernicus and Solar System

1974. Air. 500th Birth Anniv (1973) of Copernicus.

731	**233**	250f. blue, red & brown	4·00	2·30

234 Modern Chess Pieces

1974. Air. Chess Olympics, Nice.

732	**234**	100f. multicoloured	4·00	1·60

235 African Mask and "Arphila" Emblem

1974. Air. "Arphila 75" Stamp Exhibition, Paris.

733	**235**	50f. brown and red	60	45

236 African Leaders, UDEAC HQ and Flags

1974. Tenth Anniv of Central African Customs and Economics Union.

734	**236**	40f. mult (postage)	1·40	70
735	-	100f. multicoloured (air)	1·80	75

DESIGN: 100f. Similar to Type **236**.

1974. No. 717 surch **100F 10 DECEMBRE 1974**.

736	**228**	100f. on 5f. brn, bl & grn	1·90	1·10

238 "Apollo" Emblem, Astronaut, Module and Astronaut's Boots

1974. Air. Fifth Anniv of 1st Landing on Moon.

737	**238**	200f. brown, red & blue	3·25	1·70

1974. Christmas. As T **222**. Multicoloured.

738	40f. *Virgin of Autumn* (15th-century sculpture)	95	45
739	45f. *Virgin and Child* (Luis de Morales)	1·20	60

239 De Gaulle and Eboue

1975. Air. 30th Anniv of Felix Eboue ("Free French" leader).

740	**239**	45f. multicoloured	1·70	70
741	**239**	200f. multicoloured	6·00	2·75

240 *Celosia cristata*

1975. Flowers of North Cameroun. Multicoloured.

742	5f. Type **240**	20	20
743	40f. *Costus spectabilis*	1·20	40
744	45f. *Mussaenda erythrophylla*	1·40	50

241 Fish and Fishing-boat

1975. Offshore Fishing.

745	**241**	40f. brown, blue & choc	1·90	70
746	-	45f. brown, bistre & blue	1·90	70

DESIGN: 45f. Fishing-boat and fish in net.

242 Afo Akom Statue

1975

747	**242**	40f. multicoloured	50	25
748	**242**	45f. multicoloured	75	45
749	**242**	200f. multicoloured	2·50	1·60

243 *Polypore* (fungus)

1975. Natural History. Multicoloured.

750	15f. Type **243**	75·00	2·10
751	40f. *Nymphalis Chrysalis*	45·00	95

244 View of Building

1975. Inaug of New Ministry of Posts Building.

752	**244**	40f. blue, green & brown	65	25
753	**244**	45f. brown, green & blue	90	50

245 Presbyterian Church, Elat

1975. Churches and Mosque.

754	**245**	40f. brown, blue & black	45	25
755	-	40f. brown, blue & slate	45	25
756	-	45f. brown, green & blk	55	25

DESIGNS: No. 755, Foumban Mosque; No. 756, Catholic Church, Ngaoundere.

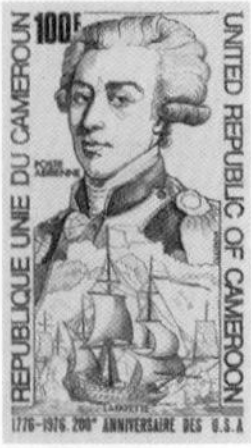

246 Marquis de Lafayette (after Chappel) and Naval Battle

1975. Air. Bicent (1976) of American Revolution.

757	**246**	100f. blue, turq & brn	2·10	1·10
758	-	140f. blue, brown & green	2·30	1·10
759	-	500f. green, brown & blue	7·25	2·50

DESIGNS: 140f. George Washington (after Stuart) and Continental Infantry (after Ogden); 500f. Benjamin Franklin (after Peale and Nee) and Boston.

247 Harvesting Maize

1975. "Green Revolution". Multicoloured.

760	40f. Type **247**	75	25
761	40f. Ploughing with oxen (horiz)	75	25

248 *The Burning Bush* (N. Froment)

1975. Air. Christmas. Multicoloured.

762	50f. Type **248**	85	50
763	500f. *Adoration of the Magi* (Gentile da Fabriano) (horiz)	7·25	5·25

249 Tracking Aerial

1976. Inauguration of Satellite Monitoring Station, Zamengoe. Multicoloured.

764	40f. Type **249**	50	25
765	100f. Close-up of tracking aerial (vert)	1·20	50

250 Porcelain Rose

1976. Flowers. Multicoloured.

766	40f. Type **250**	90	25
767	50f. Flower of North Cameroun	1·40	35

251 Concorde

1976. Air. Concorde's First Commercial Flight, Paris to Rio de Janeiro.

768	**251**	500f. multicoloured	5·25	2·75
MS769		130×93 mm. No. 768	7·75	7·75

252 Masked Dancer

1976. Cameroun Dances. Multicoloured.

770	40f. Type **252** (postage)	80	50
771	50f. Drummers and two dancers (air)	60	25
772	100f. Female dancer	1·20	50

253 Telephone Exchange

1976. Air. Telephone Centenary.

773	**253**	50f. multicoloured	85	55

254 Young Men Building House

1976. Tenth Anniv of National Youth Day. Multicoloured.

774	40f. Type **254**	45	25
775	45f. Gathering palm leaves	50	25

255 Dr. Adenauer and Cologne Cathedral

1976. Birth Centenary of Dr. Konrad Adenauer (Statesman).

776	**255**	100f. multicoloured	95	45

256 *Adoration of the Shepherds* (Charles Le Brun)

1976. Air. Christmas.. Multicoloured.

777	30f. Type **256**	80	35
778	60f. *Adoration of the Magi* (Rubens)	1·00	45
779	70f. *Virgin and Child* (Bellini)	1·30	60
780	500f. *The New-born* (G. de la Tour)	8·50	4·75
MS781	149×119 mm. Nos. 777/80	12·50	12·50

257 Pres. Ahidjo and Douala Party H.Q.

1976. Tenth Anniv of Cameroun National Union. Multicoloured.

782	50f. Type **257**	45	20
783	50f. Pres. Ahidjo and Yaounde Party H.Q.	45	20

258 Bamoun Copper Pipe

1977. Second World Festival of Negro Arts, Nigeria. Multicoloured.

784		50f. Type **258** (postage)	75	30
785		60f. Traditional chief on throne (sculpture) (air)	1·10	45

259 Crowned Cranes ("Crown-Cranes")

1977. Cameroun Birds. Multicoloured.

786		30f. Ostrich	2·50	70
787		50f. Type **259**	2·75	80

260 *Christ on the Cross* (Issenheim Altarpiece, Mathias Grunewald)

1977. Air. Easter. Multicoloured.

788		50f. Type **260**	95	30
789		125f. *Christ on the Cross* (Veslasquez) (vert)	1·50	75
790		150f. *The Entombment* (Titian)	2·50	1·10
MS791		210×115 mm. Nos. 788/90	7·00	7·00

261 Lions Club Emblem

1977. Air. 19th Congress of Douala Lions Club.

792	**261**	250f. multicoloured	3·50	2·10

262 Rotary Club Emblem, Mountain and Road

1977. Air. 20th Anniv of Douala Rotary Club.

793	**262**	60f. red and blue	75	45

263 Jean Mermoz and Seaplane "Comte de la Vaulx"

1977. Air. History of Aviation.

794	**263**	50f. blue, orange & brown	95	40
795	-	60f. purple and orange	95	55
796	-	80f. lake and blue	1·20	55
797	-	100f. green and yellow	1·60	80
798	-	300f. blue, red & purple	5·25	2·50
799	-	500f. purple, grn & plum	7·75	4·50
MS800		Two sheets (a) 170×100 mm. Nos. 794/6; (b) 190×100 mm. Nos. 797/9	20·00	20·00

DESIGNS—VERT: 60f. Antoine de Saint-Exupery and Latecoere 2b. HORIZ: 80f. Maryse Bastie and Caudron C-635 Simoun; 100f. Sikorski S-43 amphibian (1st airmail, Marignane–Douala, 1937); 300f. Concorde; 500f. Charles Lindbergh and *Spirit of St. Louis*.

1977. Air. Tenth Anniv of International French Language Council. As T **204** of Benin.

801		70f. multicoloured	1·40	1·10

264 Cameroun 40f. and Basle 2½r. Stamps

1977. "Jufilex" Stamp Exhibition, Berne.

802	**264**	50f. multicoloured	95	45
803	-	70f. green, black & brown	1·30	60
804	-	100f. multicoloured	2·10	95

DESIGNS: 70f. Zurich 4r. and Kamerun 1m. stamps; 100f. Geneva 5+5c. and Cameroun 20f. stamps.

265 Stafford and "Apollo" Rocket

1977. U.S.A.–U.S.S.R. Space Co-operation. Multicoloured.

805		40f. Type **265** (postage)	45	25
806		60f. Leonov and "Soyuz" rocket	65	25
807		100f. Brand and "Apollo" space vehicle (air)	95	45
808		250f. "Apollo–Soyuz" link-up	2·30	1·10
809		350f. Kubasov and "Soyuz" vehicle	3·25	1·50
MS810		120×81 mm. 500f. Slayton and space handshake	5·00	5·00

266 Luge Sledging

1977. Winter Olympics, Innsbruck. Multicoloured.

811		40f. Type **266** (postage)	1·10	45
812		50f. Ski-jumping	1·70	45
813		140f. Ski-marathon (air)	1·20	60
814		200f. Ice-hockey	1·80	85
815		350f. Figure-skating	3·25	1·50
MS816		116×77 mm. 500f. Slalom	5·00	5·00

1977. Palestinian Welfare. No. 765 optd **Au bien-etre des familles des martyrs et des combattants pour la liberte de la Palestine. To the Welfare of the families of martyrs and freedom fighters of Palestine.**

817		100f. multicoloured	95	55

268 Mao Tse-tung and Great Wall of China

1977. First Death Anniv of Mao Tse-tung.

818	**268**	100f. brown and green	2·75	90

269 Knee Joint

1977. Air. World Rheumatism Year.

819	**269**	70f. brown, red & blue	75	30

1977. Air. First Paris–New York Commercial Flight of Concorde. Nos. 798 and 768 optd **PREMIER VOL PARIS-NEW YORK FIRST FLIGHT PARIS-NEW YORK 22 nov. 1977 — 22nd Nov. 1977.**

820	-	300f. blue, red & purple	3·25	1·60
821	**251**	500f. multicoloured	5·00	2·50

271 *The Nativity* (Albrecht Altdorfer)

1977. Christmas. Multicoloured.

822		30f. Type **271** (postage)	55	25
823		50f. *Madonna of the Grand Duke* (Raphael)	1·10	40
824		60f. *Virgin and Child with Four Saints* (Bellini) (horiz) (air)	1·00	45
825		400f. *Adoration of the Shepherds* (G. de la Tour) (horiz)	5·00	2·50

272 Club Flag and Rotary Emblem

1978. 20th Anniv of Yaounde Rotary Club.

826	**272**	50f. multicoloured	75	30

273 Pres. Ahidjo, Flag and Map

1978. New Cameroun Flag. Multicoloured.

827		50f. Type **273** (postage)	90	30
828		60f. President, Flag and arms (air)	75	30

274 *Cardioglossa escalerae*

1978. Cameroun Frogs. Multicoloured.

829		50f. Type **274** (postage)	1·40	55
830		60f. *Cardioglossa elegans*	2·10	80
831		100f. *Cardioglossa trifasciata* (air)	3·00	1·20

275 *L'Arlesienne* (Van Gogh)

1978. Air. Paintings. Multicoloured.

832		200f. Type **275**	4·50	1·80
833		200f. *Deposition of Christ* (Durer)	3·50	1·10

276 Raoul Follereau and Leprosy Distribution Map

1978. Air. World Leprosy Day.

834	**276**	100f. multicoloured	1·20	55

277 Capt. Cook and the Siege of Quebec

1978. Air. 250th Birth Anniv of Capt. James Cook.

835	**277**	100f. green, blue & lilac	2·10	90
836	-	250f. brown, red and lilac	4·75	2·00

DESIGN: 250f. Capt. Cook, H.M.S. *Adventure* and H.M.S. *Resolution*.

278 Footballers

1978. Air. World Cup Football Championship, Argentina. Multicoloured.

837		100f. Argentinian Team (horiz)	1·00	45
838		200f. Type **278**	2·00	95
839		1000f. Football illuminating globe	10·00	5·50

279 Jules Verne and scene from *From the Earth to the Moon*

1978. 150th Birth Anniv of Jules Verne (novelist). Multicoloured.

840		250f. Type **279** (postage)	2·30	80
841		400f. Portrait and *20,000 Leagues under the Sea* (horiz) (air)	4·00	1·60

280 *Hypolimnas salmacis*

1978. Butterflies. Multicoloured.

842		20f. Type **280**	1·40	65
843		25f. *Euxanthe trajanus*	1·80	65
844		30f. *Euphaedra cyparissa*	2·50	65

281 Planting Trees

1978. Protection against Saharan Encroachment.

845	**281**	10f. multicoloured	30	10
846	**281**	15f. multicoloured	35	10

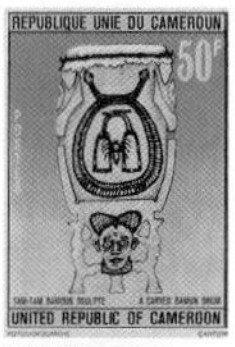

282 Carved Bamoun Drum

1978. Musical Instruments. Multicoloured.

847		50f. Type **282** (postage)	45	25
848		60f. Gueguerou (horiz)	80	40
849		100f. Mvet Zither (air)	1·20	50

283 Presidents of Cameroun and France with Independence Monument, Douala

1978. Visit of President Giscard d'Estaing.

850	**283**	60f. multicoloured	1·40	80

284 African, Human Rights Charter and Emblem

1979. 30th Anniv of Declaration of Human Rights.

851	**284**	5f. mult (postage)	30	10
852	**284**	500f. multicoloured (air)	6·00	2·75

See also No. 1070.

285 Lions Emblem and Map of Cameroun

1979. Air. Lions International Congress.

853	**285**	60f. multicoloured	75	40

286 Globe, Emblem and Waving Children

1979. International Year of the Child.

854	**286**	50f. multicoloured	75	25

287 Penny Black, Rowland Hill and German Cameroun 10pf. Stamp

1979. Air. Death Cent of Sir Rowland Hill.

855	**287**	100f. black, red & turq	1·20	60

288 Black Rhinoceros

1979. Endangered Animals (1st series). Multicoloured.

856	50f. Type **288**	1·30	35
857	60f. Giraffe (vert)	1·70	45
858	60f. Gorilla	1·70	45
859	100f. African elephant (vert)	2·75	65
860	100f. Leopard	2·75	65

See also Nos. 891/2, 904/6, 975/7, 939/40 and 1007/8.

289 "Telecom 79"

1979. Air. Third World Telecommunications Exhibition, Geneva.

861	**289**	100f. orange, blue & grey	1·20	60

290 Pope John Paul II

1979. Air. Popes.

862	**290**	100f. blue, violet & grn	2·30	80
863	-	100f. brown, red & green	2·30	80
864	-	100f. chestnut, olive & grn	2·30	80

DESIGNS: No. 863, Pope John Paul I. No. 864, Pope Paul VI.

291 Dr. Jamot, Map and *Glossina palpalis*

1979. Birth Centenary of Dr. Eugene Jamot (discoverer of sleeping sickness cure).

865	**291**	50f. brown, blue and red	2·75	70

292 *The Annunciation* (Fra Filippo Lippi)

1979. Christmas. Multicoloured.

866	10f. Type **292**	10	10
867	50f. *Rest during the Flight into Egypt* (Antwerp Master)	45	10
868	60f. *The Nativity* (Kalkar)	80	25
869	60f. *The Flight into Egypt* (Kalkar)	80	25
870	100f. *The Nativity* (Boticelli)	1·60	45

293 "Double Eagle II" and Balloonists

1979. Air. First Atlantic Crossing by Balloon. Multicoloured.

871	500f. Type **293**	5·25	2·00
872	500f. *Double Eagle II* over Atlantic and balloonists in basket	5·25	2·00

294 *Piper capense*

1979. Medicinal Plants. Multicoloured.

873	50f. Type **294**	1·10	25
874	60f. *Pteridium aquilinum*	1·30	25

295 Pres. Ahidjo, Map, Independence Stamp and Arms

1980. 20th Anniv of Independence.

875	**295**	50f. multicoloured	60	25

296 Congress Building

1980. Third Ordinary Congress of Cameroun National Union, Bafoussam.

876	**296**	50f. multicoloured	60	25

297 Globe

1980. 75th Anniv of Rotary International. Multicoloured.

877	200f. Type **297**	2·20	90
878	200f. Map of Cameroun	2·20	90
MS879	179×140 mm. Nos. 877/8 plus 8 labels	5·00	5·00

298 Voacanga Fruit and Seeds

1980. Medicinal Plants. Multicoloured.

880	50f. Type **298**	65	10
881	60f. Voacanga tree	75	10
882	100f. Voacanga flowers	1·10	25

299 *Dissotis perkinsiae*

1980. Flowers. Multicoloured.

883	50f. Type **299**	70	10
884	60f. *Brillantaisia* sp.	1·00	20
885	100f. *Clerodendron splendens*	1·70	45

300 Ka'aba, Mecca

1980. 1350th Anniv of Mohammed's Occupation of Mecca.

886	**300**	50f. multicoloured	95	40

301 Ice Skating

1980. Air. Olympic Games, Moscow and Lake Placid.

887	-	100f. brown and ochre	95	45
888	**301**	150f. brown and blue	1·30	60
889	-	200f. brown and green	2·00	75
890	-	300f. brown and red	2·50	1·30

DESIGNS: 100f. Running; 200f. Throwing the Javelin; 300f. Wrestling.

302 Crocodile

1980. Endangered Animals (2nd series). Multicoloured.

891	200f. Type **302**	3·00	80
892	300f. Kob	4·00	1·30

303 Bororo Girls and Roumsiki Peak

1980. Tourism. Multicoloured.

893	50f. Type **303**	55	25
894	60f. Dschang tourist centre	55	25

304 Banana Trees

1981. Bertona Agricultural Research Station. Multicoloured.

895	50f. Type **304**	65	10
896	60f. Cattle in watering hole	85	25

305 Girl on Crutches

1981. Int Year of Disabled People. Multicoloured.

897	60f. Type **305**	55	25
898	150f. Boy in wheelchair	1·40	65

306 Camair Headquarters, Douala

1981. Tenth Anniv of Cameroun Airlines. Multiicoloured.

899	100f. Type **306**	95	35
900	200f. Boeing 747 "Mount Cameroun"	2·00	75
901	300f. Douala International Airport	3·00	1·10

307 Presentation African Club Champions Cup

1981. Football Victories of Cameroun Clubs. Multicoloured.

902	60f. Type **307**	95	45
903	60f. Cup presentation (African Cup Winner's Cup)	95	45

308 African Buffalo

1981. Endangered Animals (3rd series). Multicoloured.

904	50f. Type **308**	1·50	45
905	50f. Cameroun tortoise	1·50	45
906	100f. Long-tailed pangolin	3·00	50

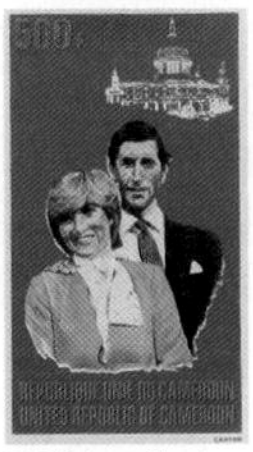

309 Prince Charles, Lady Diana Spencer and St. Paul's Cathedral

1981. Wedding of Prince of Wales. Multicoloured.
907 500f. Type **309** 4·50 1·90
908 500f. Prince Charles, Lady Diana and Royal Coach 4·50 1·90
MS909 145×94 mm. Nos. 907/8 10·00 10·00

310 Bafoussam–Bamenda Road

1981. Tourism.
910 **310** 50f. multicoloured 55 25

311 Yuri Gagarin and "Vostok 1"

1981. 20th Anniv of First Men in Space. Multicoloured.
911 500f. Type **311** 5·00 1·70
912 500f. Alan Shepard and "Freedom 7" 5·00 1·70

312 *Cam Iroko* (freighter) in Harbour

1981. Cameroun Shipping Lines.
913 **312** 60f. multicoloured 95 40

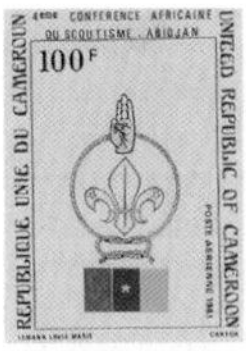

313 Scout Salute and Badge within Knotted Rope, and National Flag

1981. Air. Fourth African Scouting Conference, Abidjan. Multicoloured.
914 100f. Type **313** 95 40
915 500f. Saluting Girl Guide 4·50 1·80

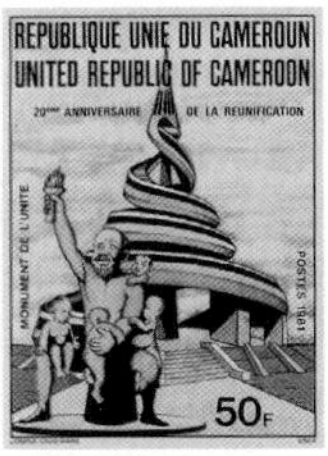

314 Unity Monument

1981. 20th Anniv of Reunification.
916 **314** 50f. multicoloured 60 25

315 *L'Estaque* (Cezanne)

1981. Air. Paintings. Multicoloured.
917 500f. Type **315** 6·00 1·80
918 500f. *Guernica* (detail) (Picasso) 6·00 1·80

316 *Virgin and Child* (detail of San Zeno altarpiece, Mantegna)

1981. Air. Christmas. Paintings. Multicoloured.
919 50f. "Virgin and Child" (detail, *The Burning Bush*) (Nicholas Froment) 45 10
920 60f. Type **316** 60 25
921 400f. *The Flight into Egypt* (Giotto) (horiz) 3·50 1·30
MS922 190×111 mm. Nos. 919/21 7·75 7·75

317 *Voacanga thouarsii*

1981. Medicinal Plants. Multicoloured.
923 60f. Type **317** 1·00 35
924 70f. *Cassia alata* 1·30 50

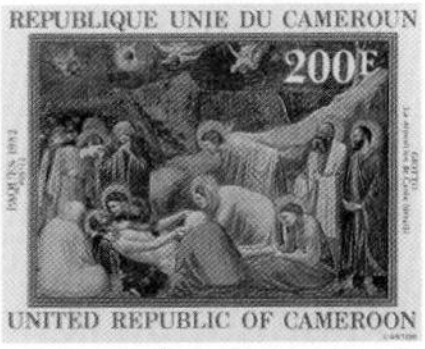

318 *Descent from the Cross* (detail, Giotto)

1982. Easter. Paintings. Multicoloured.
925 100f. *Christ in the Garden of Olives* (Eugene Delacroix) 1·00 30
926 200f. Type **318** 1·90 70
927 250f. *Pieta in the Countryside* (Bellini) 2·30 80

319 Carving, Giraffes and Map

1982. "Philexfrance 82" International Stamp Exhibition, Paris.
928 **319** 90f. multicoloured 1·50 35

320 Clay Water Jug

1982. Local Handicrafts. Multicoloured.
929 60f. Python-skin handbag 60 25
930 70f. Type **320** 80 25

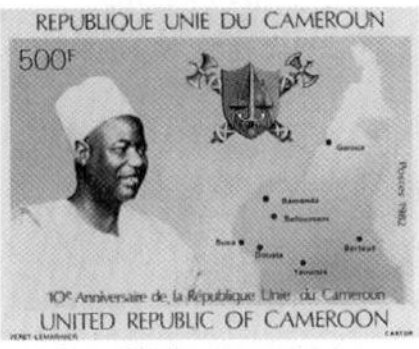

321 Pres. Ahidjo, Map and Arms

1982. Tenth Anniv of United Republic.
931 **321** 500f. multicoloured 5·25 1·70

322 Douala Town Hall

1982. Town Halls. Multicoloured.
932 40f. Type **322** 45 10
933 60f. Yaounde town hall 60 25

See also No. 1139.

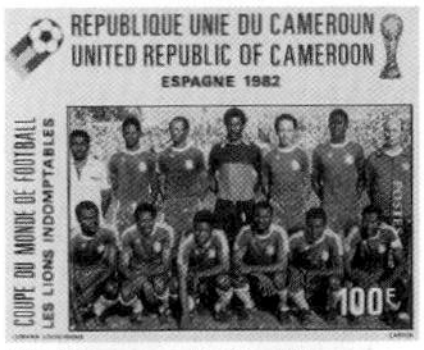

323 Cameroun Football Team

1982. World Cup Football Championship, Spain. Multicoloured.
934 100f. Type **323** 1·50 45
935 200f. Cameroun and Algerian teams 3·00 75
936 300f. Nkono Thomas, Cameroun goalkeeper 4·50 1·00
937 400f. Cameroun team (different) 6·00 1·50
MS938 216×95 mm. No. 937×2 15·00 15·00

324 Bongo

1982. Endangered Animals (4th series). Multicoloured.
939 200f. Type **324** 3·00 80
940 300f. Black colobus 4·25 1·30

325 Cameroun Mountain Francolin ("Perdrix")

1982. Birds. Multicoloured.
941 10f. Type **325** 1·80 35
942 15f. Red-eyed dove ("Tourterelle") 2·10 60
943 20f. Barn swallow ("Hirondelle") 3·00 80

See also No. 1071.

326 Scouts round Campfire

1982. 75th Anniv of Boy Scout Movement. Multicoloured.
944 200f. Type **326** 2·30 80
945 400f. Lord Baden-Powell 4·00 1·60

327 ITU Emblem

1982. ITU Delegates' Conference, Nairobi.
946 **327** 70f. multicoloured 75 25

328 Nyasoso Chapel

1982. 25th Anniv of Presbyterian Church. Multicoloured.
947 45f. Buea Chapel 50 25
948 60f. Type **328** 75 25

329 World Cup, Footballers and Globe

1982. World Cup Football Championship Result.
949 **329** 500f. multicoloured 5·25 2·20
950 **329** 1000f. multicoloured 10·50 3·50

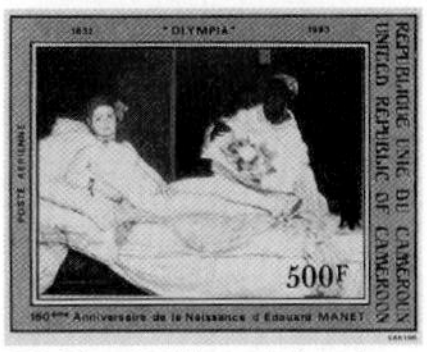

330 *Olympia* (Edouard Manet)

1982. Air. Artists' Anniversaries. Multicoloured.
951 500f. Type **330** (150th birth anniv) 5·50 2·10
952 500f. *Still-life* (Georges Braque, birth centenary) 5·50 2·10

331 Council Headquarters, Brussels

1983. 30th Anniv of Customs Co-operation Council. Multicoloured.
953 250f. Type **331** 2·30 1·10
954 250f. Council emblem 2·30 1·10

332 Yaounde University Hospital

1983. Second Yaounde Medical Days.
955 **332** 60f. multicoloured 75 25
956 **332** 70f. multicoloured 95 25

333 Pres. Kennedy

1983. Air. 20th Death Anniv of John F. Kennedy (U.S. President).
957 **333** 500f. multicoloured 5·00 2·20

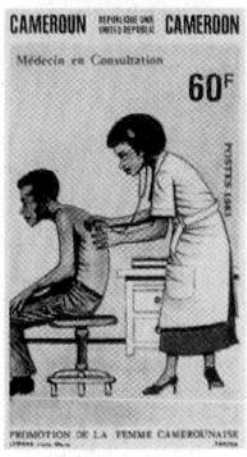

334 Woman Doctor

1983. Cameroun Women. Multicoloured.

958	60f. Type **334**	75	25
959	70f. Woman lawyer	75	25

335 Lions Emblem and Map

1983. Air. District 403 of Lions International Convention, Douala.

960	**335**	70f. multicoloured	65	25
961	**335**	150f. multicoloured	1·10	65

336 Bafoussam Town Hall

1983. Town Halls. Multicoloured.

962	60f. Type **336**	65	25
963	70f. Garoua town hall	75	25

337 President Biya and National Flag

1983. 11th Anniv of United Republic. Multicoloured.

964	60f. Type **337**	55	20
965	70f. Pres. Biya and national arms	75	25

338 Container Ship and Buoy

1983. 25th Anniv of IMO.

966	**338**	500f. multicoloured	5·00	2·10

339 Martial Eagle ("L'Aigle Martial")

1983. Birds. Multicoloured.

967	25f. Type **339**	1·10	45
968	30f. Rufous-breasted sparrow hawk ("L'Epervier")	1·50	60
969	50f. Purple heron ("Le Heron Pourpre")	2·75	80

See also Nos. 1157 and 1169.

340 Bread Mask ("Wery-Nwen-Nto")

1983. Cameroun Artists. Multicoloured.

970	60f. Type **340**	75	20
971	70f. Basket with lid ("Chechia Bamoun")	95	25

341 Mobile Rural Post Office

1983. World Communications Year. Multicoloured.

972	90f. Type **341**	95	30
973	150f. Radio operator with morse key	1·50	50
974	250f. Tom-tom drums	2·75	85

342 African Civet

1983. Endangered Animals (5th series). Multicoloued.

975	200f. Type **342**	2·75	75
976	200f. Gorilla	2·75	75
977	350f. Guinea-pig (vert)	4·50	1·50

See also No. 1170.

343 *Jeanne d'Aragon* (Raphael)

1983. Air. Paintings. Multicoloured.

978	500f. Type **343**	5·50	1·90
979	500f. *Massacre of Scio* (Delacroix)	5·50	1·90

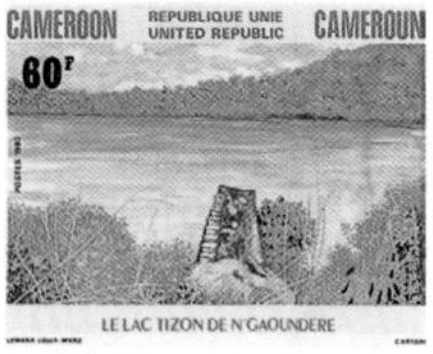

344 Lake Tizon

1983. Landscapes. Multicoloured.

980	60f. Type **344**	55	20
981	70f. Mount Cameroun in eruption	75	25

345 Boy and Girl holding Hands

1983. 35th Anniv of Declaration of Human Rights.

982	**345**	60f. multicoloured	55	20
983	**345**	70f. multicoloured	75	20

346 Christmas Tree

1983. Christmas. Multicoloured.

984	60f. Type **346**	50	20
985	200f. Stained-glass window, Yaounde Cathedral	1·80	75
986	500f. Statue of angel, Reims Cathedral	4·75	1·70
987	500f. *The Rest on the Flight into Egypt* (Philipp Otto Runge) (horiz)	4·75	1·70
MS988	140×89 mm. Nos. 985/7	12·00	12·00

348 *Pieta* (G. Hernandez)

1984. Air. Easter. Multicoloured.

992	200f. Type **348**	2·00	75
993	500f. *Martyrdom of St. John the Evangelist* (C. le Brun)	5·00	2·20
MS994	160×104 mm. Nos. 992/3	8·25	8·25

349 Urban Council Building, Bamenda

1984. Town Halls. Multicoloured.

995	60f. Type **349**	60	25
996	70f. Mbalmayo	75	35

350 High Jump

1984. Air. Olympic Games, Los Angeles. Multicoloured.

997	100f. Type **350**	95	40
998	150f. Volleyball	1·40	60
999	250f. Basketball	2·30	90
1000	500f. Cycling	4·50	1·80

351 Running with Ball

1984. Air. European Football Championship. Multicoloured.

1001	250f. Type **351**	2·30	90
1002	250f. Heading ball	2·30	45
1003	500f. Tackle	4·50	1·80
MS1004	130×85 mm. As Nos. 1001/3, but with the background colours different	11·00	11·00

352 Catholic Church, Zoetele

1984. Churches. Multicoloured.

1005	60f. Type **352**	55	25
1006	70f. Marie Gocker Protestant Church, Yaounde	75	40

353 Antelope

1984. Endangered Animals (6th series). Multicoloured.

1007	250f. Type **353**	3·50	1·10
1008	250f. Wild boar	3·50	1·10

354 Pres. Biya and Arms

1984. Air. President's Oath-taking Ceremony. (a) Inscr in French.

1009	**354**	60f. multicoloured	45	25
1010	**354**	70f. multicoloured	55	25
1011	**354**	200f. multicoloured	2·00	70

(b) Inscr in English.

1012	60f. multicoloured	50	25
1013	70f. multicoloured	75	25
1014	200f. multicoloured	2·00	70

355 *Diana Bathing* (Watteau)

1984. Air. Anniversaries. Multicoloured.

1015	500f. Type **355** (300th birth anniv) (wrongly inscr "1624")	5·75	1·90
1016	500f. Diderot (encyclopaedist, death bicentenary)	5·75	1·90

1984. Air. Olympic Games Medal Winners. Nos. 997/1000 optd.

1017	100f. **MOEGENBURG (R.F.A.) 11-08-84**	95	50
1018	150f. **U.S.A. 11-08-84**	1·40	70
1019	250f. **YOUGOSLAVIE 9-08-84**	2·30	1·10
1020	500f. **GORSKI (U.S.A.) 3-08-84**	4·50	2·20

357 Nightingale ("Le Rossignol")

1984. Birds. Multicoloured.

1021	60f. Type **357**	3·00	80
1022	60f. Ruppell's griffon ("Le Vautour")	3·00	80

See also No. 1158.

358 Neil Armstrong

1984. Air. 15th Anniv of First Man on the Moon. Multicoloured.

1023	500f. Type **358**	5·00	1·90
1024	500f. Launching of "Apollo 12"	5·00	1·90

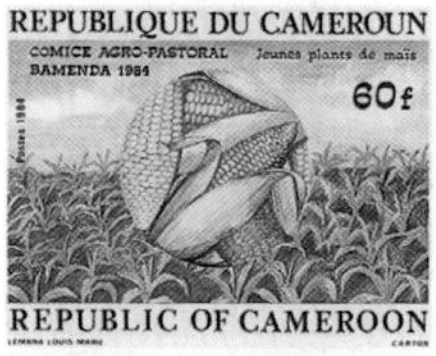

359 Maize and Young Plants

1984. Agro-pastoral Fair. Bamenda. Multicoloured.

1025	60f. Type **359**	65	25
1026	70f. Zebus	75	30
1027	300f. Potatoes	3·50	1·30

360 Anniversary Emblem

1984. 40th Anniv of ICAO.

1028	-	200f. multicoloured	1·90	90
1029	**360**	200f. blue & deep blue	1·90	90
1030	-	300f. multicoloured	2·75	1·40
1031	-	300f. multicoloured	3·50	1·50

DESIGNS: No. 1028, "Icarus" (Hans Herni); 1030, Cameroun Airlines Boeing 737; 1031, "Solar Princess" (Sadiou Diouf).

361 Wrestling

1985. "Olymphilex '85" International Thematic Stamps Exhibition, Lausanne.

1032	**361**	150f. multicoloured	1·50	70

362 Balafons (xylophone)

1985. Musical Instruments. Multicoloured.

1033	60f. Type **362**	65	20
1034	70f. Mvet (stringed instrument)	85	30
1035	100f. Flute	1·40	40

363 Intelcam Headquarters, Yaounde

1985. 20th Anniv of Int Telecommunications Satellite Consortium.

1036	-	125f. black, orange & bl	1·70	60
1037	**363**	200f. multicoloured	2·20	90

DESIGN: 125f. "Intelsat V" satellite.

365 U.N. Emblem and Headquarters

1985. 40th Anniv of UNO.

1038	**365**	250f. multicoloured	2·50	1·00
1039	**365**	500f. multicoloured	5·00	2·00

366 French and Cameroun Flags and Presidents

1985. President Mitterrand of France's Visit to Cameroun.

(a) Inscr "Mitterand" in error.

1040	**366**	60f. multicoloured		
1041	**366**	70f. multicoloured		

(b) Inscr corrected to "Mitterrand".

1041a	60f. multicoloured	1·40	45
1041b	70f. multicoloured	1·40	45

367 UNICEF Emblem

1985. Child Survival Campaign.

1042	**367**	60f. black, blue & yell	65	25
1043	-	300f. multicoloured	3·00	1·30

DESIGN: Doctor inoculating babies.

368 Lake Barumbi, Kumba

1985. Landscapes. Multicoloured.

1044	60f. Type **368**	80	25
1045	70f. Pygmy village, Bonando	80	30
1046	150f. River Cameroun	1·60	65

369 Ebolowa Town Hall

1985. Town Halls. Multicoloured.

1047	60f. Type **369**	55	25
1048	60f. Ngaoundere town hall	55	25

370 Pope John Paul II

1985. Papal Visit to Cameroun. Multicoloured.

1049	60f. Type **370**	1·00	40
1050	70f. Pope John Paul II holding crucifix	1·30	70
1051	200f. Pres. Biya and Pope John Paul II	3·50	1·70
MS1052	137×100 mm. Nos. 1049/51	6·75	6·75

371 Porcupine

1985. Animals. Multicoloured.

1053	125f. Type **371**	1·40	55
1054	200f. Squirrel	2·20	90
1055	350f. Greater cane rat	3·75	1·60

372 Wooden Mask

1985. Cameroun Art (1st series). Multicoloured.

1056	60f. Type **372**	65	20
1057	70f. Wooden mask (different)	80	30
1058	100f. Men using pestle and mortar (wooden bas-relief)	1·40	75

See also Nos. 1081/3.

373 *Tomb of Henri Claude d'Harcourt* (detail)

1985. Air. Death Anniversaries. Multicoloured.

1059	500f. Type **373** (bicentenary Jean Baptiste Pigalle (sculptor))	5·75	2·30
1060	500f. Louis Pasteur (bacteriologist, 90th anniv) (after Edelfelt)	5·75	2·30

374 Yellow-casqued Hornbill ("Le Toucan")

1985. Birds. Multicoloured.

1061	140f. Type **374**	2·00	70
1062	150f. Cock	2·10	70
1063	200f. European robins ("Le Rouge-gorge")	3·00	1·10

See also No. 1156.

375 Child's Toys

1985. Air. Christmas. Multicoloured.

1064	250f. Type **375**	2·30	1·00
1065	300f. Akono church	2·75	1·30
1066	400f. Christmas crib	3·25	1·70
1067	500f. *The Virgin of the Blue Diadem* (Raphael)	5·00	2·30

376 Emblem, Flag and Volunteers

1986. 25th Anniv of American Peace Corps in Cameroun.

1068	**376**	70f. multicoloured	75	30
1069	**376**	100f. multicoloured	1·00	45

1986. As Nos. 851 and 941 but inscr "Republique du Cameroun/Republic of Cameroon".

1070	**284**	5f. multicoloured	25	10
1071	**325**	10f. multicoloured	45	10

377 *Virgin Mary* (Pierre Prud'hon)

1986. Easter. Multicoloured.

1072	210f. Type **377**	2·00	95
1073	350f. *Stoning of St. Stephen* (Van Scorel)	3·00	1·50

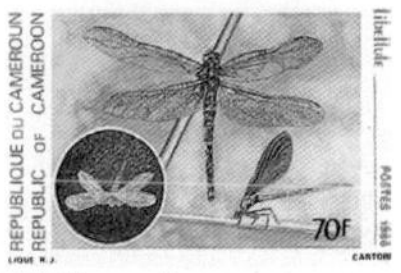

378 "Anax sp."

1986. Insects. Multicoloured.

1074	70f. Type **378**	1·20	45
1075	70f. Bee on flower (vert)	1·30	50
1076	100f. Grasshopper	1·90	70

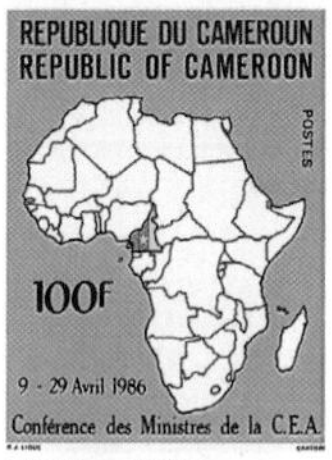

379 Map of Africa

1986. Economic Commission for Africa Ministers' Conference. Multicoloured.

1077	100f. Type **379**	1·00	55
1078	175f. Members' flags	2·10	85

380 Azteca Stadium

1986. Air. World Cup Football Championship, Mexico. Multicoloured.

1079	300f. Type **380**	2·75	1·40
1080	400f. Mexico team	3·75	1·70

1986. Cameroun Art (2nd series). As T **372**. Multicoloured.

1081	70f. Copper Statuette	65	30
1082	100f. Wooden ash-tray	95	35
1083	130f. Wooden horseman	1·70	55

381 Queen Elizabeth

1986. 60th Birthday of Queen Elizabeth II. Multicoloured.

1084	100f. Type **381**	1·10	50
1085	175f. Queen and President Biya	1·60	80
1086	210f. Queen Elizabeth (different)	2·10	1·00

382 President Biya

1986. First Anniv of Cameroun Republic Democratic Party. Multicoloured.

1087	70f. Type **382**	80	30
1088	70f. Bamenda Party headquarters (horiz)	80	30
1089	100f. President Biya making speech	1·00	40

383 Argentine Team

1986. Air. World Cup Football Championship Winners.

1090	**383**	250f. multicoloured	3·00	1·40

384 Mask Dancer with Sword

1986. Traditional Dances of North-west Kwem. Multicoloured.

1091	100f. Type **384**	1·00	55
1092	130f. Mask dancer with rattle	1·40	70

385 Cheetah

1986. Endangered Animals (7th series). Multicoloured.

1093	300f. Type **385**	3·25	1·50
1094	300f. Varan	3·25	1·50

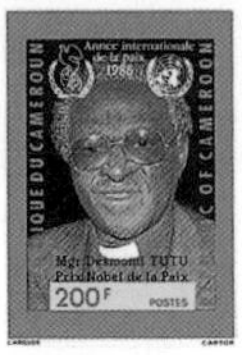

386 Bishop Desmond Tutu (Nobel Peace Prize Winner)

1986. International Peace Year. Multicoloured.

1095	175f. Type **386**	1·90	80
1096	200f. Type **386**	2·10	95
1097	250f. I.P.Y. and U.N. emblems	2·40	1·20

387 Pierre Curie (physicist)

1986. Air. Death Anniversaries. Multicoloured.

1098	500f. Type **387** (80th anniv)	6·75	2·50
1099	500f. Jean Mermoz and *Arc en Ciel* (aviation pioneer, 50th anniv)	6·75	2·50

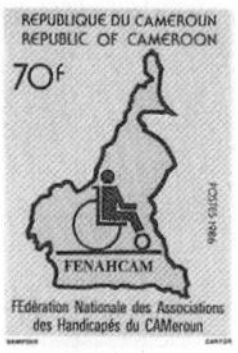

388 Emblem

1986. National Federation of Cameroun Handicapped Associations.

1100	**388** 70f. yellow and red	70	25

389 Man holding Syringe and National Flag "Umbrella" over Woman and Child

1986. African Vaccination Year.

1101	70f. Type **389**	85	30
1102	100f. Flag behind woman holding child being immunised	1·00	45

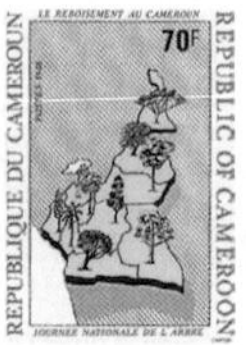

390 Trees on Map

1986. National Tree Day.

1103	70f. Type **390**	85	30
1104	100f. Hands holding clump of earth and seedling	1·00	45

391 Loading Palm Nuts onto Trailer at Dibombari

1986. Agricultural Development. Multicoloured.

1105	70f. Type **391**	85	30
1106	70f. Payment for produce harvested	85	30
1107	200f. Pineapple plantation	1·90	90

392 *Antestiopsis lineaticollis intricata*

1987. Harmful Insects. Multicoloured.

1108	70f. Type **392**	1·10	45
1109	100f. "Distantiella theobroma"	1·60	65

393 Millet

1987. Agricultural Show, Maroua. Multicoloured.

1110	70f. Type **393**	85	30
1111	100f. Cotton	1·00	45
1112	150f. Cattle	1·50	80

394 Shot-putting

1987. Fourth All-Africa Games, Kenya. Multicoloured.

1113	100f. Type **394**	95	40
1114	140f. Pole-vaulting	1·40	60

395 Drill Baboon

1988. Endangered Mammals. Drill Baboon. Multicoloured.

1115	30f. Type **395**	1·80	80
1116	40f. Adult baboons	2·00	90
1117	70f. Young baboon	2·50	1·50
1118	100f. Mother with baby	4·75	2·10

396 National Assembly Building

1989. Centenary of Interparliamentary Union.

1119	**396** 50f. multicoloured	55	15

397 Cameroun and Argentine Players

1990. World Cup Football Championship, Italy. Multicoloured.

1120	200f. Type **397**	1·80	75
1121	250f. Cameroun player and match scene	2·20	1·10
1122	250f. Cameroun winning goal	2·20	1·10
1123	300f. Cameroun first eleven	2·75	1·40
MS1124	108×77 mm. Nos. 1120/3	10·00	10·00

1990. Nos. 1062 and 1093 surch.

1125	- 20f. on 150f. multicoloured	1·90	20
1126	**385** 70f. on 300f. multicoloured	6·25	35

399 Milla and Match Scene

1990. Roger Milla, 4th Best Player in World Cup.

1127	**399** 500f. multicoloured	5·25	2·75
MS1128	108×76 mm. No. 1125	8·50	8·50

400 Anniversary Emblem

1990. 40th Anniv of United Nations Development Programme.

1129	**400** 50f. multicoloured	55	25

401 UNESCO and ILY Emblems

1990. International Literacy Year.

1130	**401** 200f. black, lt blue & bl	1·90	80

402 Arms and Pres. Paul Biya

1991. 30th Anniv (1990) of Independence. Multicoloured.

1131	150f. Type **402**	1·60	70
1132	1000f. Flag, city and 1960 20f. Independence stamp	9·75	4·50
MS1133	164×99 mm. Nos. 1131/2	12·00	12·00

403 Treating Cacao Plantation

1991. Unissued stamps (for Ebolowa Agricultural Show) with bars over inscr and surch **125F**. Multicoloured.

1134	125f. on 70f. Type **403**	95	45
1135	125f. on 100f. Sheep	1·30	75

The stamps without surcharge were sold only by the Paris agency.

405 Snake on National Colours and Map

1991. Anti-AIDS Campaign. Multicoloured.

1137	15f. Type **405**	10	10
1138	25f. Youth pushing back "AIDS" in French and English (horiz)	40	10

See also Nos. 1171/2.

1991. As No. 932 but inscr "Republic du Cameroun / Republic of Cameroun".

1139	**322** 40f. multicoloured	45	10

406 Oribi

1991. Sovereign Military Order of Malta Child Survival Project. Antelopes. Multicoloured.

1140	125f.+10f. Type **406**	1·80	1·10
1141	250f.+20f. Waterbucks	2·75	2·20
MS1142	144×90 mm. Nos. 1140/1	6·25	6·25

407 Serle's Bush Shrike ("La Pie Grieche du Mont-kupe")

1991. Birds. Multicoloured.

1143	70f. Type **407**	75	45
1144	70f. Grey-necked bald crow ("Le Picathartes Chauve ") (horiz)	75	45
1145	300f. As No. 1144	2·75	1·60
1146	350f. Type **407**	3·50	1·60
MS1147	108×80 mm. Nos. 144/5	7·75	7·75

408 African Elephant

1991. Animals. Multicoloured.

1148	125f. Type **408**	1·50	70
1149	250f. Buffalo	2·75	1·60
MS1150	120×80 mm. Nos. 1148/9	6·25	6·25

409 Mvolye Church

1991. Centenary (1990) of Catholic Church in Cameroun. Multicoloured.

1151	125f. Type **409**	1·40	70
1152	250f. Akono church	2·40	1·50
MS1153	108×80 mm. Nos. 1151/2	4·00	4·00

410 Emblems

1991. Seventh African Group Meeting of Int Savings Banks Institute, Yaounde.

1154	**410** 250f. multicoloured	2·40	1·20
MS1155	107×80 mm. No. 1154	2·75	2·75

1992. Birds. As previous designs but with values changed. Multicoloured.

1156	125f. As No. 1063	1·40	50
1157	200f. As No. 968	2·00	85
1158	350f. Type **357**	3·50	1·50

411 Columbus's Fleet

1992. 500th Anniv of Discovery of America by Columbus. Multicoloured.

1159	125f. Type **411**	1·40	70
1160	250f. Columbus kneeling on beach	2·50	1·40
1161	400f. Meeting Amerindians	3·75	2·10
1162	500f. Fleet crossing the Atlantic	5·25	3·00

412 Mbappe Lepe (footballer)

1992. Cameroun Football. Multicoloured.

1163	125f. Type **412**	1·30	70
1164	250f. League emblem	2·50	1·50
1165	400f. National Football Federation emblem (horiz)	3·75	2·10
1166	500f. Ahmadou Ahidjo Stadium, Yaounde (horiz)	5·50	3·00

See also Nos. 1173/5.

413 Crocodile

1993. Endangered Animals. Mult. Self-adhesive.

1167	125f. Type **413**	1·40	70
1168	250f. Kob (vert)	2·40	1·40

1993. As Nos. 967 and 975 but inscr "REPUBLIQUE DU CAMEROUN REPUBLIC OF CAMEROON" and with values changed.

1169	**339** 370f. multicoloured	3·50	1·80
1170	**342** 410f. multicoloured	4·25	2·10

1993. Anti-AIDS Campaign. As Nos. 1137/8 but values changed. Multicoloured.

1171	100f. Type **405**	1·00	60
1172	175f. As No. 1138	1·90	1·00

1993. As Nos. 1163/5 but values changed.

1173	10f. As No. 1165		
1174	25f. As No. 1164		
1175	50f. Type **412**		

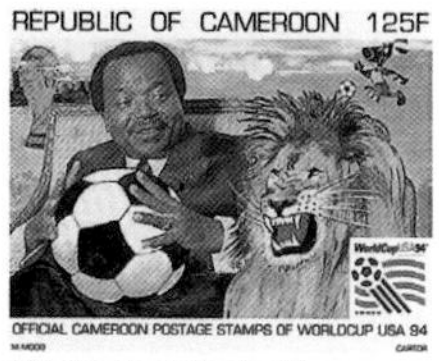

414 President Biya holding Football and Lion (national team mascot)

1994. World Cup Football Championship, United States. Multicoloured.

1176	125f. Type **414**	85	45
1177	250f. Emblem, lion, player and map of Cameroun	1·40	75
1178	450f. Players, ball showing world map, national flag and trophy	2·50	1·50
1179	500f. Eagle and lion supporting ball	3·00	1·70
MS1180	120×100 mm. Nos. 1176/9	13·00	13·00

415 Grey Parrot

1995

1181	**415**	125f. multicoloured	1·30	45

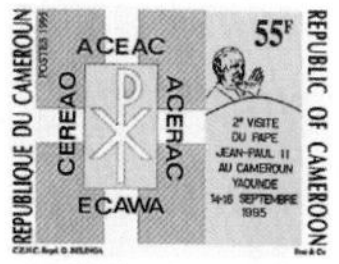

416 Chi-rho, Cross and Pope John Paul II

1995. Second Papal Visit.

1182	**416**	55f. black, pink & yell	35	25
1183	-	125f. multicoloured	85	35

DESIGN: 125f. Pope and open book.

417 Anniversary Emblem and Dove carrying Branch

1995. 50th Anniv of UNO Multicoloured.

1184	200f. Type **417**	1·20	55
1185	250f. Anniversary emblem and figures joining hands	1·50	75

MILITARY FRANK STAMP

Cameroun joined the Commonwealth on 1 November 1995.

M78 Arms and Crossed Swords

1963. No value indicated.

M1	**M78**	(–) lake	3·00	3·25

POSTAGE DUE STAMPS

D8 Felling Mahogany Tree

1925

D88	**D8**	2c. black and blue	40	3·75
D89	**D8**	4c. purple and olive	40	3·00
D90	**D8**	5c. black and lilac	80	3·75
D91	**D8**	10c. black and red	80	4·50
D92	**D8**	15c. black and grey	1·00	4·25
D93	**D8**	20c. black and olive	1·70	4·75
D94	**D8**	25c. black and yellow	1·60	5·75
D95	**D8**	30c. orange and blue	1·60	5·75
D96	**D8**	50c. black and brown	1·90	5·75
D97	**D8**	60c. red and green	2·00	6·50
D98	**D8**	1f. green & red on grn	2·30	1·70
D99	**D8**	2f. mauve and red	4·00	8·25
D100	**D8**	3f. blue and brown	7·25	10·50

D25 African Idols

1939

D148	**D25**	5c. purple	45	4·50
D149	**D25**	10c. blue	55	5·00
D150	**D25**	15c. red	35	4·50
D151	**D25**	20c. brown	35	4·50
D152	**D25**	30c. blue	35	3·25
D153	**D25**	50c. green	40	4·50
D154	**D25**	60c. purple	55	4·50
D155	**D25**	1f. violet	90	3·25
D156	**D25**	2f. orange	1·00	5·00
D157	**D25**	3f. blue	1·10	6·00

D46

1947

D254	**D46**	10c. red	25	4·50
D255	**D46**	30c. orange	25	4·75
D256	**D46**	50c. black	25	4·75
D257	**D46**	1f. red	70	4·50
D258	**D46**	2f. green	2·10	5·00
D259	**D46**	3f. mauve	2·10	5·25
D260	**D46**	4f. blue	1·80	4·25
D261	**D46**	5f. brown	1·70	4·75
D262	**D46**	10f. blue	2·10	3·00
D263	**D46**	20f. sepia	2·75	4·50

D77 *Hibiscus rosa sinensis*

1963. Flowers. Multicoloured.

D342	50c. Type D **77**	10	50
D343	50c. *Erythrine*	10	50
D344	1f. *Plumeria lutea*	10	50
D345	1f. *Ipomoea* sp.	10	50
D346	1f.50 *Grinum* sp.	10	50
D347	1f.50 *Hoodia gordonii*	10	50
D348	2f. *Ochna*	20	60
D349	2f. *Gloriosa*	20	60
D350	5f. *Costus spectabilis*	20	60
D351	5f. *Bougainvillea spectabilis*	20	60
D352	10f. *Delonix regia*	55	55
D353	10f. *Haemanthus*	55	55
D354	20f. *Titanopsis*	1·30	1·20
D355	20f. *Ophthalmophyllum*	1·30	1·20
D356	40f. *Zingiberacee*	2·00	1·80
D357	40f. *Amorphophalus*	2·00	1·80

No post 1995 issues, see West Africa catalogue.

Cameroun joined the Commonwealth on 1 November 1995.

Pt. 1

CANADA

A British dominion consisting of the former province of Canada with British Columbia, New Brunswick, Newfoundland, Nova Scotia and Prince Edward Island.

1851. 12 pence = 1 shilling (Canadian).
1859. 100 cents = 1 dollar.

COLONY OF CANADA

1 Beaver

2 Prince Albert

3

4

5

6 Jacques Cartier

1851. Imperf

17	**4**	½d. red	£950	£550
5	**1**	3d. red	£2250	£200
9	**2**	6d. purple	£38000	£1000
12	**5**	7½d. green	£11000	£2250
14	**6**	10d. blue	£11000	£1500
4	**3**	12d. black	£170000	£100000

1858. Perf.

25		½d. red	£4250	£950
26	**1**	3d. red	£11000	£350
27a	**2**	6d. purple	£16000	£3750

1859. Values in cents. Perf.

29	**4**	1c. red	£400	48·00
44	**4**	2c. red	£600	£170
31	**1**	5c. red	£425	17·00
36	**2**	10c. brown	£1300	80·00
38	**2**	10c. purple	£1400	80·00
40	**5**	12½c. green	£1100	70·00
42	**6**	17c. blue	£1500	95·00

DOMINION OF CANADA

13

14

1868. Various frames.

54	**13**	½c. black	75·00	60·00
55	**14**	1c. brown	£500	60·00
56a	**14**	1c. yellow	£1000	90·00
57	**14**	2c. green	£650	48·00
49	**14**	3c. red	£1400	35·00
63	**14**	5c. green	£850	85·00
59b	**14**	6c. brown	£1200	60·00
60	**14**	12½c. blue	£900	60·00
69	**14**	15c. blue	£170	32·00
70	**14**	15c. purple	70·00	19·00

21

27

1870. Various frames.

101	**27**	½c. black	19·00	11·00
75	**21**	1c. yellow	40·00	2·25
104	**21**	2c. green	55·00	3·50
105	**21**	3c. red	50·00	1·50
106	**21**	5c. grey	£100	1·75
107	**21**	6c. brown	48·00	15·00
117	-	8c. grey	£170	8·50
120	-	8c. purple	£110	8·50
111	**21**	10c. pink	£250	35·00

On 8c. head is to left.

28

1893

115	**28**	20c. red	£250	65·00
116	**28**	50c. blue	£275	45·00

30

1897. Jubilee.

121	**30**	½c. black	70·00	70·00
122	**30**	1c. orange	12·00	5·50
124	**30**	2c. green	21·00	9·00
126	**30**	3c. red	12·00	2·25
128	**30**	5c. blue	48·00	15·00
129	**30**	6c. brown	£120	£110
130	**30**	8c. violet	48·00	35·00
131	**30**	10c. purple	80·00	65·00
132	**30**	15c. slate	£130	£110
133	**30**	20c. red	£130	£100
134	**30**	50c. blue	£180	£110
136	**30**	$1 lake	£550	£500
137	**30**	$2 violet	£950	£400
138	**30**	$3 bistre	£1300	£750
139	**30**	$4 violet	£1200	£650
140	**30**	$5 green	£1200	£650

31

1897. Maple-leaves in four corners.

141	**31**	½c. black	14·00	7·00
143	**31**	1c. green	25·00	90
144	**31**	2c. violet	22·00	1·50
145	**31**	3c. red	45·00	2·25
146	**31**	5c. blue	70·00	2·75
147	**31**	6c. brown	60·00	30·00
148	**31**	8c. orange	85·00	8·00
149	**31**	10c. purple	£140	55·00

1898. As T **31** but figures in lower corners.

150	½c. black	7·00	1·10
151	1c. green	28·00	1·00
154	2c. purple	27·00	30
155	2c. red	38·00	30
156	3c. red	75·00	1·00
157	5c. blue	£110	4·00
159	6c. brown	£100	65·00
160	7c. yellow	70·00	23·00
162	8c. orange	£120	42·00
163	10c. purple	£170	14·00
165	20c. green	£300	50·00

33

1898. Imperial Penny Postage.

166	**33**	2c. black, red and lavender	30·00	6·50

1899. Surch **2 CENTS**.

171	2c. on 3c. red (No. 145)	22·00	8·00
172	2c. on 3c. red (No. 156)	19·00	4·25

35 King Edward VII

1903

175	**35**	1c. green	30·00	50
176	**35**	2c. red	20·00	50
178	**35**	5c. blue	90·00	2·50
180	**35**	7c. olive	80·00	2·75
182	**35**	10c. purple	£160	22·00
185	**35**	20c. olive	£300	30·00
187	**35**	50c. violet	£450	£110

36 King George V and Queen Mary, when Prince and Princess of Wales

1908. Tercententary of Quebec. Dated "1608 1908".

188	**36**	½c. brown	4·75	3·50
189	-	1c. green	26·00	2·75
190	-	2c. red	25·00	1·00
191	-	5c. blue	65·00	32·00
192	-	7c. olive	90·00	65·00
193	-	10c. violet	£100	85·00
194	-	15c. orange	£120	95·00
195	-	20c. brown	£160	£130

DESIGNS: 1c. Cartier and Champlain; 2c. King Edward VII and Queen Alexandra; 5c. Champlain's House in Quebec; 7c. Generals Montcalm and Wolfe; 10c. Quebec in 1700; 15c. Champlain's departure for the West; 20c. Cartier's arrival before Quebec.

44

1912

196	**44**	1c. green	9·50	50
200	**44**	2c. red	8·50	50
205	**44**	3c. brown	6·00	50
205b	**44**	5c. blue	65·00	75
209	**44**	7c. yellow	24·00	3·00
210	**44**	10c. purple	95·00	2·75
212	**44**	20c. olive	42·00	1·50
215	**44**	50c. sepia	50·00	3·75

See also Nos. 246/55.

1915. Optd **WAR TAX** diagonally.

225	5c. blue	£120	£200
226	20c. olive	60·00	£100
227	50c. sepia	£130	£170

46

1915

228	**46**	1c. green	8·00	50
229	**46**	2c. red	25·00	2·50

47

1916

233	**47**	2c.+1c. red	50·00	2·25
239	**47**	2c.+1c. brown	5·50	50

48 Quebec Conference, 1864, from painting *The Fathers of the Confederation* by Robert Harris

1917. 50th Anniv of Confederation.

244	**48**	3c. brown	22·00	3·25

1922

246	**44**	1c. yellow	3·00	60
247	**44**	2c. green	2·25	10
248	**44**	3c. red	3·75	10
249	**44**	4c. yellow	8·00	3·50
250	**44**	5c. violet	5·00	1·75
251	**44**	7c. brown	12·00	9·00
252	**44**	8c. blue	22·00	11·00
253	**44**	10c. blue	15·00	3·25
254	**44**	10c. brown	25·00	4·00
255	**44**	$1 orange	55·00	9·50

1926. Surch **2 CENTS** in one line.

264	2c. on 3c. red	50·00	60·00

1926. Surch **2 CENTS** in two lines.

265	2c. on 3c. red	17·00	27·00

51 Sir J. A. Macdonald

52 "The Fathers of the Confederation"

1927. 60th Anniv of Confederation. I. Commemoration Issue. Dated "1867–1927".

266	**51**	1c. orange	2·50	1·50
267	**52**	2c. green	2·25	30
268	-	3c. red	9·50	5·00
269	-	5c. violet	5·50	4·25
270	-	12c. blue	29·00	7·00

DESIGNS—HORIZ: As Type **52**: 3c. Parliament Buildings, Ottawa; 12c. Map of Canada, 1867–1927. VERT: As Type **51**: 5c. Sir W. Laurier.

56 Darcy McGee

57 Sir W. Laurier and Sir J. A. Macdonald

II. Historical Issue.

271	**56**	5c. violet	3·00	2·50
272	**57**	12c. green	17·00	4·50
273	-	20c. red	17·00	13·00

DESIGN—As Type **57**: 20c. R. Baldwin and L. H. Lafontaine.

59

1928. Air.

274	**59**	5c. brown	8·00	5·00

60 King George V

61 Mount Hurd and Indian Totem Poles

1928

275	**60**	1c. orange	2·75	2·50
276	**60**	2c. green	1·25	20
277	**60**	3c. lake	19·00	22·00
278	**60**	4c. bistre	13·00	10·00
279	**60**	5c. violet	6·50	5·50
280	**60**	8c. blue	7·50	7·50
281	**61**	10c. green	8·50	2·25
282	-	12c. black	26·00	17·00
283	-	20c. lake	35·00	17·00
284	-	50c. blue	£150	50·00
285	-	$1 olive	£150	80·00

DESIGNS—HORIZ: 12c. Quebec Bridge; 20c. Harvesting with horses; 50c. *Bluenose* (fishing schooner); $1 Parliament Buildings, Ottawa.

66

67 Parliamentary Library, Ottawa

68 The Old Citadel, Quebec

1930

288	**66**	1c. orange	1·75	1·25
289	**66**	1c. green	2·50	10
290	**66**	2c. green	1·75	10
291	**66**	2c. red	2·25	3·00
292b	**66**	2c. brown	1·50	10
293	**66**	3c. red	1·75	10
294	**66**	4c. yellow	10·00	4·50
295	**66**	5c. violet	2·75	7·00
296	**66**	5c. blue	5·50	20
297	**66**	8c. blue	11·00	16·00
298	**66**	8c. orange	7·50	5·50
299	**67**	10c. olive	21·00	1·50
300	**68**	12c. black	14·00	5·50
325	**68**	13c. violet	70·00	2·25
301	-	20c. red	22·00	2·00
302	-	50c. blue	90·00	17·00
303	-	$1 olive	£120	32·00

DESIGNS—HORIZ: 20c. Harvesting with tractor; 50c. Acadian Memorial Church, Grand Pre, Nova Scotia; $1 Mount Edith Cavell.

72 Mercury and Western Hemisphere

1930. Air.

310	**72**	5c. brown	25·00	24·00

73 Sir Georges Etienne Cartier

1931

312	**73**	10c. green	13·00	20

1932. Air. Surch **6** and bars.

313	**59**	6c. on 5c. brown	3·00	2·50

1932. Surch **3** between bars.

314a	**66**	3c. on 2c. red	1·00	60

76 King George V

77 Duke of Windsor when Prince of Wales

78 Allegory of British Empire

1932. Ottawa Conference. (a) Postage.

315	**76**	3c. red	70	80
316	**77**	5c. blue	13·00	5·00
317	**78**	13c. green	13·00	6·00

(b) Air. **Surch 6 6 OTTAWA CONFERENCE 1932.**

318	**72**	6c. on 5c. brown	14·00	21·00

80 King George V

1932

319	**80**	1c. green	60	10
320	**80**	2c. brown	70	10
321b	**80**	3c. red	85	10
322	**80**	4c. brown	45·00	12·00
323	**80**	5c. blue	12·00	10
324	**80**	8c. orange	35·00	4·25

81 Parliament Buildings, Ottawa

1933. UPU Congress (Preliminary Meeting).

329	**81**	5c. blue	10·00	3·00

1933. Optd **WORLD'S GRAIN EXHIBITION & CONFERENCE REGINA 1933.**

330	20c. red (No. 295)	19·00	9·50

83 S.S. *Royal William* (after S. Skillett)

1933. Cent of First Transatlantic Steamboat Crossing.

331	**83**	5c. blue	20·00	4·00

84 Jacques Cartier approaching Land

1934. Fourth-century of Discovery of Canada.

332	**84**	3c. blue	6·00	1·50

85 U.E.L. Statue, Hamilton

1934. 150th Anniv of Arrival of United Empire Loyalists.

333	**85**	10c. olive	12·00	8·00

86 Seal of New Brunswick

1934. 150th Anniv of New Brunswick.

334	**86**	2c. brown	1·50	3·50

87 Queen Elizabeth II when Princess

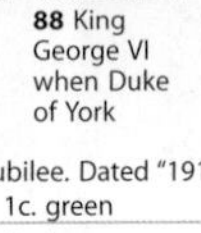

88 King George VI when Duke of York

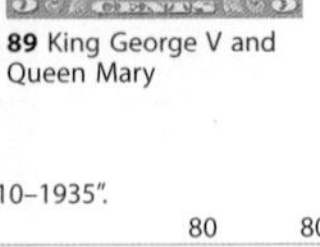

89 King George V and Queen Mary

1935. Silver Jubilee. Dated "1910–1935".

335	**87**	1c. green	80	80
336	**88**	2c. brown	70	80
337	**89**	3c. red	3·25	1·50
338	-	5c. blue	5·50	8·00
339	-	10c. green	10·00	9·50
340	-	13c. blue	11·00	9·50

DESIGNS—VERT: 5c. Duke of Windsor when Prince of Wales. HORIZ: 10c. Windsor Castle; 13c. Royal Yacht *Britannia*.

93 King George V

94 Royal Canadian Mounted Policeman

1935

341	**93**	1c. green	1·75	10
342	**93**	2c. brown	1·75	10
343	**93**	3c. red	1·75	10
344	**93**	4c. yellow	3·50	2·75
345	**93**	5c. blue	3·50	10
346	**93**	8c. orange	4·25	5·00
347	**94**	10c. red	6·50	50
348	-	13c. purple	7·50	65
349	-	20c. green	25·00	1·50
350	-	50c. violet	25·00	7·00
351	-	$1 blue	40·00	11·00

DESIGNS—HORIZ: 13c. Confederation, Charlottetown, 1864; 20c. Niagara Falls; 50c. Parliament Buildings, Victoria, B.C.; $1 Champlain Monument, Quebec.

99 Daedalus

1935. Air.

355	**99**	6c. brown	3·25	1·00

100 King George VI and Queen Elizabeth

1937. Coronation.

356	**100**	3c. red	1·75	1·50

101 King George VI

102 Memorial Chamber Parliament Buildings, Ottawa

104 Fort Garry Gate, Winnipeg

1937

357	**101**	1c. green	2·00	10
358	**101**	2c. brown	2·75	10
359	**101**	3c. red	1·75	10
360	**101**	4c. yellow	5·50	1·75
361	**101**	5c. blue	6·50	10
362	**101**	8c. orange	6·50	3·75
363	**102**	10c. red	5·00	60
364	-	13c. blue	30·00	2·75
365	**104**	20c. brown	25·00	2·75
366	-	50c. green	50·00	16·00
367	-	$1 violet	65·00	16·00

DESIGNS—HORIZ: 13c. Halifax Harbour; 50c. Vancouver Harbour; $1 Chateau de Ramezay, Montreal.

107 Fairchild 45-80 Sekani Seaplane over *Distributor* on Mackenzie River

1938. Air.

371	**107**	6c. blue	18·00	2·25

108 Queen Elizabeth II when Princess and Princess Margaret

1939. Royal Visit.

372	**108**	1c. black and green	2·50	25
373	-	2c. black and brown	3·00	2·00
374	-	3c. black and red	2·00	25

DESIGNS—HORIZ: 3c. King George VI and Queen Elizabeth. VERT: 2c. National War Memorial, Ottawa.

111 King George VI in Naval Uniform

112 King George VI in Military Uniform

114 Grain Elevator

115 Farm Scene

121 Air Training Camp

1942. War Effort.

375	**111**	1c. green (postage)	1·50	10
376	**112**	2c. brown	1·75	10
377	-	3c. red	1·25	60
378	-	3c. purple	1·25	10
379	**114**	4c. grey	5·50	2·75
380	**112**	4c. red	70	10
381	**111**	5c. blue	3·00	10
382	**115**	8c. brown	5·50	1·00
383	-	10c. brown	13·00	10
384	-	13c. green	10·00	9·50
385	-	14c. green	27·00	1·00
386	-	20c. brown	21·00	45
387	-	50c. violet	26·00	7·00
388	-	$1 blue	48·00	11·00
399	**121**	6c. blue (air)	30·00	13·00
400	**121**	7c. blue	4·75	50

DESIGNS—As Type **112**: 3c. King George VI. As Type **121**. VERT: 10c. Parliament Buildings. HORIZ: 13, 14c. Ram tank; 20c. Corvette; 50c. Munitions factory; $1 H.M.S. *Cossack* (destroyer).

122 Ontario Farm Scene

1946. Re-conversion to Peace.

401	**122**	8c. brown (postage)	2·25	2·75
402	-	10c. green	2·75	10
403	-	14c. sepia	6·00	3·25
404	-	20c. grey	3·50	10
405	-	50c. green	16·00	6·50
406	-	$1 purple	27·00	6·50
407	-	7c. blue (air)	6·00	40

DESIGNS: 10c. Great Bear Lake; 14c. St. Maurice River power station; 20c. Combine harvester; 50c. Lumbering in British Columbia; $1 *Abegweit* (train ferry); 7c. Canada geese in flight.

129 Alexander Graham Bell and "Fame"

1947. Birth Centenary of Graham Bell (inventor of the telephone).

408	**129**	4c. blue	15	50

130 "Canadian Citizenship"

1947. Advent of Canadian Citizenship and 80th Anniv of Confederation.

409	**130**	4c. blue	10	40

131 Queen Elizabeth II when Princess

1948. Princess Elizabeth's Wedding.

410	**131**	4c. blue	15	15

132 Queen Victoria. Parliament Building, Ottawa, and King George VI

1948. Centenary of Responsible Government.

411	**132**	4c. grey	10	10

133 Cabot's Ship *Matthew*

1949. Entry of Newfoundland into Canadian Confederation.

412	**133**	4c. green	30	10

134 *Founding of Halifax, 1749* (after C. W. Jeffries)

1949. Halifax Bicentenary.

413	**134**	4c. violet	45	10

135 King George VI

1949. Portraits of King George VI.

414	**135**	1c. green	50	10
415	-	2c. sepia	2·25	45
415a	-	2c. green	2·50	10
416	-	3c. purple	30	10
417	-	4c. red	20	10
418	-	5c. blue	2·50	60

1950. As Nos. 414 and 416/18 but without "POSTES POSTAGE".

424	1c. green	70	1·00
425	2c. sepia	70	4·25
426	3c. purple	70	65
427	4c. red	70	20
428	5c. blue	70	2·25

141 Oil Wells in Alberta

142 Drying Furs

1950

432	**142**	10c. purple	4·50	10
441	-	20c. grey	2·50	10
431	**141**	50c. green	6·00	1·00
433	-	$1 blue	45·00	6·00

DESIGNS: 20c. Forestry products; $1 Fisherman.

145 Mackenzie King

1951. Canadian Prime Ministers.

434		3c. green (Borden)	20	1·50
444	-	3c. purple (Abbott)	35	75
435	**145**	4c. red	60	15
445	-	4c. red (A. Mackenzie)	25	35
475	-	4c. violet (Thompson)	20	75
483	-	4c. violet (Bennett)	20	60
476	-	5c. blue (Bowell)	20	50
484	-	5c. blue (Tupper)	20	10

146 Mail Trains, 1851 and 1951

149 Reproduction of 3d., 1851

1951. Centenary of First Canadian Postage Stamp. Dated "1851 1951".

436	**146**	4c. black	75	10
437	-	5c. violet	2·00	3·00
438	-	7c. blue	75	1·75
439	**149**	15c. red	1·60	10

DESIGNS—As Type **146**: 5c. *City of Toronto* and S.S. *Prince George*; 7c. Mail coach and Canadair DC-4M North Star airplane.

150 Queen Elizabeth II when Princess and Duke of Edinburgh

1951. Royal Visit.

440	**150**	4c. violet	20	30

152 Red Cross Emblem

1952. 18th Int Red Cross Conf, Toronto.

442	**152**	4c. red and blue	15	10

153 Canada Goose

1952

443	**153**	7c. blue	1·25	10

154 Pacific Coast Indian House and Totem Pole

160 Textile Industry

164 Northern Gannet

165 Eskimo Hunter

1953

477	**165**	10c. brown	1·25	10
474	**164**	15c. black	1·25	10
488	-	20c. green	60	10
489	-	25c. red	70	10
462	**160**	50c. green	1·75	10
446	**154**	$1 black	3·25	20

DESIGNS (As Type **160**)—HORIZ: 20c. Pulp and paper industry. VERT: 25c. Chemical industry.

155 Polar Bear

1953. National Wild Life Week.

447	**155**	2c. blue	15	10
448	-	3c. sepia (Elk)	15	70
449	-	4c. slate (American bighorn)	15	10

158 Queen Elizabeth II

1953

450	**158**	1c. brown	10	10
451	**158**	2c. green	15	10
452	**158**	3c. red	15	15
453	**158**	4c. violet	20	10
454	**158**	5c. blue	25	10

159 Queen Elizabeth II

1953. Coronation.

461	**159**	4c. violet	10	10

161

1954

463	**161**	1c. brown	10	10
464	**161**	2c. green	20	10
465	**161**	3c. red	1·00	10
466	**161**	4c. violet	30	10
467	**161**	5c. blue	30	10
468	**161**	6c. orange	1·75	55

1954. National Wild Life Week. As T **155**.

472	4c. slate (Walrus)	45	20
473	5c. blue (American beaver)	35	10

166 Musk-ox

167 Whooping Cranes

1955. National Wild Life Week.

478	**166**	4c. violet	30	10
479	**167**	5c. blue	1·00	20

168 Dove and Torch

1955. Tenth Anniv of ICAO.

480	**168**	5c. blue	35	20

169 Pioneer Settlers

1955. 50th Anniv of Alberta and Saskatchewan Provinces.

481	**169**	5c. blue	20	25

170 Scout Badge and Globe

1955. Eighth World Scout Jamboree.

482	**170**	5c. brown and green	30	10

173 Ice-hockey Players

1956. Ice-hockey Commemoration.

485	**173**	5c. blue	20	20

1956. National Wild Life Week. As T **155**.

486	4c. violet (Reindeer)	20	15
487	5c. blue (Mountain goat)	20	10

178

1956. Fire Prevention Week.

490	**178**	5c. red and black	30	10

179 Fishing

1957. Outdoor Recreation.

491	**179**	5c. blue	40	10
492	-	5c. blue	40	10
493	-	5c. blue	40	10
494	-	5c. blue	40	10

DESIGNS: No. 492, Swimming; 493, Hunting; 494, Skiing.

183 White-billed Diver

1957. National Wild Life Week.

495	**183**	5c. black	50	20

184 Thompson with Sextant, and North American Map

1957. Death Cent of David Thompson (explorer).

496	**184**	5c. blue	45	30

185 Parliament Buildings, Ottawa

1957. 14th UPU Congress, Ottawa.

497	**185**	5c. slate	15	10
498	-	15c. slate	55	1·75

DESIGNS—HORIZ (33½×22 mm): 15c. Globe within post-horn.

187 Miner

1957. Mining Industry.

499	**187**	5c. black	35	20

188 Queen Elizabeth II and Duke of Edinburgh

1957. Royal Visit.

500	**188**	5c. black	30	10

189 "A Free Press"

1958. The Canadian Press.

501	**189**	5c. black	20	70

190 Microscope

1958. International Geophysical Year.

502	**190**	5c. blue	20	10

191 Miner panning for Gold

1958. Centenary of British Columbia.

503	**191**	5c. turquoise	20	10

192 La Verendrye statue

1958. La Verendrye (explorer) Commemoration.

504	**192**	5c. blue	20	10

193 Samuel de Champlain and Heights of Quebec

1958. 350th Anniv of Founding of Quebec by Samuel de Champlain.

505	**193**	5c. brown and green	30	10

194 Nurse

1958. National Health.

506	**194**	5c. purple	30	10

195 "Petroleum 1858–1958"

1958. Centenary of Canadian Oil Industry.

507	**195**	5c. red and olive	30	10

196 Speaker's Chair and Mace

1958. Bicentenary of First Elected Assembly.

508	**196**	5c. slate	30	10

197 John McCurdy's Biplane *Silver Dart*

1959. 50th Anniv of First Flight of the *Silver Dart* in Canada.

509	**197**	5c. black and blue	30	10

198 Globe showing NATO Countries

1959. Tenth Anniv of NATO.

510	**198**	5c. blue	40	10

199

1959. "Associated Country Women of the World" Commemoration.

511	**199**	5c. black and olive	15	10

200 Queen Elizabeth II

1959. Royal Visit.

512	**200**	5c. red	30	10

201 Maple Leaf linked with American Eagle

1959. Opening of St. Lawrence Seaway.

513	**201**	5c. blue and red	20	10

202 Maple Leaves

1959. Bicentenary of Battle of Quebec.

514	**202**	5c. green and red	30	10

203 Girl Guides Badge

1960. Golden Jubilee of Canadian Girl Guides Movement.

515	**203**	5c. blue and brown	20	10

204 Dollard des Ormeaux

1960. Tercent of Battle of Long Sault.

516	**204**	5c. blue and brown	20	10

205 Surveyor, Bulldozer and Compass Rose

1961. Northern Development.

517	**205**	5c. green and red	15	10

206 E. Pauline Johnson

1961. Birth Centenary of E. Pauline Johnson (Mohawk poetess).

518	**206**	5c. green and red	15	10

207 Arthur Meighen (statesman)

1961. Arthur Meighen Commemoration.

519	**207**	5c. blue	15	10

208 Engineers and Dam

1961. Colombo Plan.

520	**208**	5c. brown and blue	30	10

209 "Resources for Tomorrow"

1961. Natural Resources.

521	**209**	5c. green and brown	15	10

210 "Education"

1962. Education Year.

522	**210**	5c. black and brown	15	10

211 Lord Selkirk and Farmer

1962. 150th Anniv of Red River Settlement.

523	**211**	5c. brown and green	20	10

212 Talon bestowing Gifts on Married Couple

1962. Jean Talon Commemoration.

524	**212**	5c. blue	20	10

213 British Columbia and Vancouver Island 2½d. Stamp of 1860, and Parliament Buildings, B.C.

1962. Centenary of Victoria, B.C.

525	**213**	5c. red and black	30	10

1962

214 Highway (map version) and Provincial Arms

1962. Opening of Trans-Canada Highway.

526	**214**	5c. black and brown	15	20

215 Queen Elizabeth II and Wheat (agriculture) Symbol

1962. Different symbols in top left corner.

527	**215**	1c. brown	10	10
528	-	2c. green	15	20
529	-	3c. violet	15	10
530	-	4c. red	20	10
531	-	5c. blue	50	10

SYMBOLS: 1c. Crystals (Mining); 2c. Tree (Forestry); 3c. Fish (Fisheries); 4c. Electricity pylon (Industrial power); 5c. Wheat (Agriculture).

216 Sir Casimir Gzowski

1963. 150th Birth Anniv of Sir Casimir Gzowski (engineer).

535	**216**	5c. purple	15	10

217 "Export Trade"

1963

536	**217**	$1 red	4·75	2·00

218 Frobisher and barque "Gabriel"

1963. Sir Martin Frobisher Commemoration.

537	**218**	5c. blue	30	10

219 Horseman and Map

1963. Bicent of Quebec–Trois-Rivieres–Montreal Postal Service.

538	**219**	5c. brown and green	15	25

220 Canada Geese

221 Douglas DC-9 Airliner and Uplands Airport, Ottawa

1963

540	**221**	7c. blue	35	70
540a	**221**	8c. blue	50	50
539	**220**	15c. blue	1·00	10

222 "Peace on Earth"

1964. "Peace".

541	**222**	5c. ochre, blue & turq	15	10

223 Maple Leaves

1964. "Canadian Unity".

542	**223**	5c. lake and blue	10	10

224 White Trillium and Arms of Ontario

1964. Provincial Badges.

543	**224**	5c. green, brown and orange	40	20
544	-	5c. green, brown and yellow	40	20
545	-	5c. red, green and violet	30	20
546	-	5c. blue, red and green	30	20
547	-	5c. purple, green and brown	30	20
548	-	5c. brown, green and mauve	30	20
549	-	5c. lilac, green and purple	50	20
550	-	5c. green, yellow and red	30	20
551	-	5c. sepia, orange and green	30	20
552	-	5c. black, red and green	30	20
553	-	5c. drab, green and yellow	30	20
554	-	5c. blue, green and red	30	20
555	-	5c. red and blue	30	20

FLOWERS AND ARMS OF: No. 544, Madonna Lily, Quebec; 545, Purple Violet, New Brunswick; 546, Mayflower, Nova Scotia; 547, Dogwood, British Columbia; 548, Prairie Crocus, Manitoba; 549, Lady's Slipper, Prince Edward Island; 550, Wild Rose, Alberta; 551, Prairie Lily, Saskatchewan; 552, Pitcher Plant, Newfoundland; 553, Mountain Avens, Northwest Territories; 554, Fireweed, Yukon Territory; 555, Maple Leaf, Canada.

1964. Surch **8**.

556	**221**	8c. on 7c. blue	15	15

238 Fathers of the Confederation Memorial, Charlottetown

1964. Centenary of Charlottetown Conference.

557	**238**	5c. black	10	10

239 Maple Leaf and Hand with Quill Pen

1964. Centenary of Quebec Conference.

558	**239**	5c. red and brown	15	10

240 Queen Elizabeth II

1964. Royal Visit.

559	**240**	5c. purple	15	10

241 "Canadian Family"

1964. Christmas.

560	**241**	3c. red	10	10
561	**241**	5c. blue	10	10

242 "Co-operation"

1965. International Co-operation Year.

562	**242**	5c. green	35	10

243 Sir W. Grenfell

1965. Birth Centenary of Sir Wilfred Grenfell (missionary).

563	**243**	5c. green	20	10

244 National Flag

1965. Inauguration of National Flag.

564	**244**	5c. red and blue	15	10

245 Sir Winston Churchill

1965. Churchill Commemoration.

565	**245**	5c. brown	15	10

246 Peace Tower, Parliament Buildings, Ottawa

1965. Inter-Parliamentary Union Conference, Ottawa.

566	**246**	5c. green	10	10

247 Parliament Buildings, Ottawa, 1865

1965. Centenary of Proclamation of Ottawa as Capital.

567	**247**	5c. brown	10	10

248 "Gold, Frankincense and Myrrh"

1965. Christmas.

568	**248**	3c. green	10	10
569	**248**	5c. blue	10	10

249 "Alouette 2" over Canada

1966. Launching of Canadian Satellite, "Alouette 2".

570	**249**	5c. blue	15	10

250 La Salle

1966. 300th Anniv of La Salle's Arrival in Canada.

571	**250**	5c. green	15	10

251 Road Signs

1966. Highway Safety.

572	**251**	5c. yellow, blue and black	15	10

252 Canadian Delegation and Houses of Parliament

1966. Centenary of London Conference.

573	**252**	5c. brown	10	10

253 Douglas Point Nuclear Power Station

1966. Peaceful Uses of Atomic Energy.

574	**253**	5c. blue	10	10

254 Parliamentary Library, Ottawa

1966. Commonwealth Parliamentary Association Conference, Ottawa.

575	**254**	5c. purple	10	10

255 *Praying Hands*, after Durer

1966. Christmas.

576	**255**	3c. red	10	10
577	**255**	5c. orange	10	10

256 Flags and Canada on Globe

1967. Canadian Centennial.

578	**256**	5c. red and blue	10	10

257 Queen Elizabeth, Northern Lights and Dog-team

262 "Alaska Highway" (A. Y. Jackson)

1967

579	**257**	1c. brown	10	10
580	-	2c. green	10	20
581	-	3c. purple	30	50
582	-	4c. red	20	10
583	-	5c. blue	20	10
601	-	6c. red	45	10
607	-	6c. black	30	10
609	-	7c. green	30	70
584	**262**	8c. purple	25	1·00
610	-	8c. black	30	10
585	-	10c. olive	25	10
586	-	15c. purple	30	10
587	-	20c. blue	1·60	10
588	-	25c. green	1·50	10
589	-	50c. brown	1·50	10
590	-	$1 red	1·50	1·25

DESIGNS—As Type **257**: 2c. Totem pole; 3c. Combine-harvester and oil derrick; 4c. Ship in lock; 5c., Harbour scene; 6c., 7c. "Transport"; 8c. (No. 610), Library of Parliament. As Type **262**: 10c. *The Jack Pine* (T. Thomson); 15c. *Bylot Island* (L. Harris); 20c. *Quebec Ferry* (J. W. Morrice); 25c. *The Solemn Land* (J. E. H. MacDonald); 50c. *Summer's Stores* (Grain elevators, J. Ensor); $1 *Oilfield* (near Edmonton, H. G. Glyde).

269 Canadian Pavilion

1967. World Fair, Montreal.

611	**269**	5c. blue and red	10	10

270 Allegory of "Womanhood" on Ballot-box

1967. 50th Anniv of Women's Franchise.

612	**270**	5c. purple and black	10	10

271 Queen Elizabeth II and Centennial Emblem

1967. Royal Visit.

613	**271**	5c. plum and brown	15	10

272 Athlete

1967. Pan-American Games, Winnipeg.

614	**272**	5c. red	10	10

273 "World News"

1967. 50th Anniv of Canadian Press.

615	**273**	5c. blue	10	10

274 Governor-General Vanier

1967. Vanier Commemoration.

616	**274**	5c. black	10	10

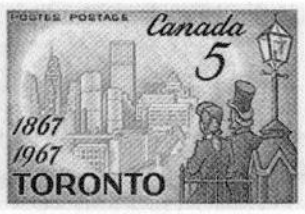

275 People of 1867, and Toronto, 1967

1967. Cent of Toronto as Capital City of Ontario.

617	**275**	5c. green and red	10	10

276 Carol Singers

1967. Christmas.

618	**276**	3c. red	10	10
619	**276**	5c. green	10	10

277 Grey Jays

1968. Wild Life.

620	**277**	5c. multicoloured	30	10

See also Nos. 638/40.

278 Weather Map and Instruments

1968. 20th Anniv of First Meteorological Readings.

621	**278**	5c. multicoloured	15	10

279 Narwhal

1968. Wild Life.

622	**279**	5c. multicoloured	15	10

280 Globe, Maple Leaf and Rain Gauge

1968. International Hydrological Decade.

623	**280**	5c. multicoloured	15	10

281 The *Nonsuch*

1968. 300th Anniv of Voyage of the *Nonsuch*.

624	**281**	5c. multicoloured	20	10

282 Lacrosse Players

1968. Lacrosse.

625	**282**	5c. multicoloured	15	10

283 Front Page of *The Globe*, George Brown and Legislative Building

1968. 150th Birth Anniv of George Brown (politician and journalist).

626	**283**	5c. multicoloured	10	10

284 H. Bourassa (politician and journalist)

1968. Birth Centenary of Henri Bourassa.

627	**284**	5c. black, red and cream	10	10

285 John McCrae, Battlefield and First Lines of *In Flanders Fields*

1968. 50th Death Anniv of John McCrae (soldier and poet).

628	**285**	5c. multicoloured	10	10

286 Armistice Monument, Vimy

1968. 50th Anniv of 1918 Armistice.

629	**286**	15c. black	30	40

287 Eskimo Family (carving)

1968. Christmas.

630	**287**	5c. black and blue	10	10
631	-	6c. black and ochre	10	10

DESIGN: 6c. *Mother and Child* (carving).

289 Curling

1969. Curling.

632	**289**	6c. black, blue and red	15	20

290 Vincent Massey

1969. Vincent Massey, First Canadian-born Governor-General.

633	**290**	6c. sepia and ochre	10	10

291 *Return from the Harvest Field* (Suzor-Cote)

1969. Birth Centenary of Marc Aurele de Foy Suzor-Cote (painter).

634	**291**	50c. multicoloured	1·50	2·75

292 Globe and Tools

1969. 50th Anniv of I.L.O.

635	**292**	6c. green	10	10

293 Vickers Vimy Aircraft over Atlantic Ocean

1969. 50th Anniv of 1st Non-stop Transatlantic Flight.

636	**293**	15c. brown, green and blue	40	55

294 *Sir William Osler* (J. S. Sargent)

1969. 50th Death Anniv of Sir William Osler (physician).

637	**294**	6c. blue and brown	20	10

295 White-throated Sparrow

1969. Birds. Multicoloured.

638	6c. Type **295**	25	10
639	10c. Savannah sparrow ("Ipswich Sparrow") (horiz)	35	1·10
640	25c. Hermit thrush (horiz)	1·10	3·75

298 Flags of Winter and Summer Games

1969. Canadian Games.

641	**298**	6c. green, red and blue	10	10

299 Outline of Prince Edward Island showing Charlottetown

1969. Bicentenary of Charlottetown as Capital of Prince Edward Island.

642	**299**	6c. brown, black and blue	20	20

300 Sir Isaac Brock and Memorial Column

1969. Birth Bicentenary of Sir Isaac Brock.

643	**300**	6c. orange, bistre and brown	10	10

301 Children of the World in Prayer

1969. Christmas.

644	**301**	5c. multicoloured	10	10
645	**301**	6c. multicoloured	10	10

302 Stephen Butler Leacock, Mask and "Mariposa"

1969. Birth Centenary of Stephen Butler Leacock (humorist).

646	**302**	6c. multicoloured	10	10

303 Symbolic Cross-roads

1970. Centenary of Manitoba.

647	**303**	6c. blue, yellow and red	15	10

304 "Enchanted Owl" (Kenojuak)

1970. Centenary of Northwest Territories.

648	**304**	6c. red and black	10	10

305 Microscopic View of Inside of Leaf

1970. International Biological Programme.

649	**305**	6c. green, yellow and blue	15	10

306 Expo 67 Emblem and stylized Cherry Blossom

1970. World Fair, Osaka. Multicoloured.

650	25c. Type **306** (red)	1·50	2·25
651	25c. Dogwood (violet)	1·50	2·25
652	25c. White trillium (green)	1·50	2·25
653	25c. White garden lily (blue)	1·50	2·25

NOTE: Each stamp shows a stylized cherry blossom, in a different colour, given above in brackets.

310 Henry Kelsey

1970. 300th Birth Anniv of Henry Kelsey (explorer).

654	**310**	6c. multicoloured	10	10

311 "Towards Unification"

1970. 25th Anniv of UNO.

655	**311**	10c. blue	75	1·50
656	**311**	15c. mauve and lilac	75	50

312 Louis Riel (Metis leader)

1970. Louis Riel Commemoration.

657	**312**	6c. blue and red	10	10

313 Mackenzie's Inscription, Dean Channel

1970. Sir Alexander Mackenzie (explorer).

658	**313**	6c. brown	15	10

314 Sir Oliver Mowat (statesman)

1970. Sir Oliver Mowat Commemoration.

659	**314**	6c. red and black	10	10

315 *Isles of Spruce* (A. Lismer)

1970. 50th Anniv of "Group of Seven" (artists).

660	**315**	6c. multicoloured	10	10

316 *Horse-drawn Sleigh* (D. Niskala)

1970. Christmas. Children's Drawings. Multicoloured.

661	5c. Type **316**	30	20
662	5c. *Stable and Star of Bethlehem* (L. Wilson)	30	20
663	5c. *Snowmen* (M. Lecompte)	30	20
664	5c. *Skiing* (D. Durham)	30	20
665	5c. *Santa Claus* (A. Martin)	30	20
666	6c. *Santa Claus* (E. Bhattacharya)	30	20
667	6c. *Christ in Manger* (J. McKinney)	30	20
668	6c. *Toy Shop* (N. Whateley)	30	20
669	6c. *Christmas Tree* (J. Pomperleau)	30	20
670	6c. *Church* (J. McMillan)	30	20
671	10c. *Christ in Manger* (C. Fortier) (37×20 mm)	25	30
672	15c. *Trees and Sledge* (J. Dojcak) (37×20 mm)	35	60

328 Sir Donald A. Smith

1970. 150th Birth Anniv of Sir Donald Alexander Smith.

673	**328**	6c. yellow, brown and green	15	10

329 *Big Raven* (E. Carr)

1971. Birth Centenary of Emily Carr (painter).

674	**329**	6c. multicoloured	20	30

330 Laboratory Equipment

1971. 50th Anniv of Discovery of Insulin.

675	**330**	6c. multicoloured	30	30

331 "The Atom"

1971. Birth Centenary of Lord Rutherford (scientist).

676	**331**	6c. yellow, red and brown	20	20

332 Maple "Keys"

1971. "The Maple Leaf in Four Seasons". Multicoloured.

677	6c. Type **332** (spring)	20	20
678	6c. Green leaves (summer)	20	20
679	7c. Autumn leaves	20	20
680	7c. Withered leaves and snow (winter)	20	20

333 Louis Papineau

1971. Death Centenary of Louis-Joseph Papineau (politician).

681	**333**	6c. multicoloured	15	25

334 Chart of Coppermine River

1971. Bicentenary of Samuel Hearne's Expedition to the Coppermine River.

682	**334**	6c. red, brown and buff	40	40

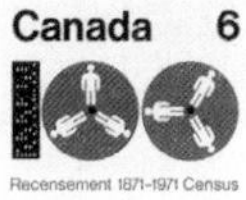

335 "People" and Computer Tapes

1971. Centenary of first Canadian Census.

683	**335**	6c. blue, red and black	30	20

336 Maple Leaves

1971. Radio Canada International.

684	**336**	15c. red, yellow and black	50	1·50

337 "B. C."

1971. Centenary of British Columbia's Entry into the Confederation.

685	**337**	7c. multicoloured	15	10

338 *Indian Encampment on Lake Huron* (Kane)

1971. Death Centenary of Paul Kane (painter).

686	**338**	7c. multicoloured	20	10

339 "Snowflake"

1971. Christmas.

687	**339**	6c. blue	10	10
688	**339**	7c. green	15	10
689	-	10c. silver and red	50	1·25
690	-	15c. silver, purple and lavender	65	2·00

DESIGN: 10c., 15c. "Snowflake" design similar to Type **339** but square (26×26 mm).

340 Pierre Laporte (Quebec Cabinet Minister)

1971. First Anniv of Assassination of Pierre Laporte.

691	**340**	7c. black on buff	15	10

341 Skaters

1972. World Figure Skating Championships, Calgary.

692	**341**	8c. purple	15	20

342 J. A. MacDonald

343 Forest, Central Canada

344 Vancouver

1972

693	**342**	1c. orange	10	30
694	-	2c. green	10	10
695	-	3c. brown	10	50
696	-	4c. black	10	50
697	-	5c. mauve	10	10
698	-	6c. red	10	50
699	-	7c. brown	40	50
700	-	8c. blue	15	10
701	-	10c. red	75	10
702a	**343**	10c. green, turquoise and orange	40	15
703b	-	15c. blue and brown	1·25	10
704a	-	20c. orange, violet and blue	1·50	10
705b	-	25c. ultram and blue	1·00	10
706	-	50c. green, blue and brown	1·00	30
709a	**344**	$1 multicoloured	85	70
708	-	$2 multicoloured	1·50	2·00

DESIGNS—As Type **342** (1 to 7c. show Canadian Prime Ministers): 2c. W. Laurier; 3c. R. Borden; 4c. W. L. Mackenzie King; 5c. R. B. Bennett; 6c. L. B. Pearson; 7c. Louis St. Laurent; 8, 10c. Queen Elizabeth II. As Type **343**: 15c. American bighorn; 20c. Prairie landscape from the air; 25c. Polar bears; 50c. Seashore, Eastern Canada. As Type **344**: $2 Quebec.

345 Heart

1972. World Health Day.

719	**345**	8c. red	30	10

346 Frontenac and Fort Saint-Louis, Quebec

1972. 300th Anniv of Governor Frontenac's Appointment to New France.

720	**346**	8c. red, brown and blue	15	15

347 Plains Indians' Artefacts

347a Buffalo Chase

1972. Canadian Indians. (a) Horiz designs showing Artefacts as T 347 or Scenes from Indian Life as T **347a**.

721	**347**	8c. multicoloured	40	10
722	**347a**	8c. brown, yellow & blk	40	10
723	-	8c. multicoloured	40	10
724	-	8c. multicoloured	40	10
725	-	8c. multicoloured	40	10
726	-	8c. brown, yellow & blk	40	10
727	-	8c. multicoloured	40	10
728	-	8c. multicoloured	40	10
729	-	10c. multicoloured	40	20
730	-	10c. red, brown and black	40	20

TRIBES: Nos. 721/2, Plains Indians; Nos. 723/4, Algonkians; Nos. 725/6, Pacific Coast Indians; Nos. 727/8, Subarctic Indians; Nos. 729/30, Iroquoians.

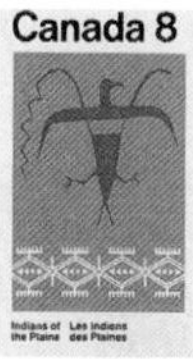

348 Thunderbird and Tribal Pattern

348a Dancer in Ceremonial Costume

(b) Vert designs showing Thunderbird and pattern as T **348** or Costumes as T **348a**.

731	**348**	8c. orange, red and black	40	15
732	**348a**	8c. multicoloured	40	15
733	-	8c. red, violet and black	40	10
734	-	8c. green, brown and black	40	10
735	-	8c. red and black	40	10
736	-	8c. multicoloured	40	10
737	-	8c. green, brown and black	40	10
738	-	8c. multicoloured	40	10
739	-	10c. brown, orange & blk	40	20
740	-	10c. multicoloured	40	20

TRIBES: Nos. 731/2, Plains Indians; Nos. 733/4, Algonkians; Nos. 735/6, Pacific Coast Indians; Nos. 737/8, Subarctic Indians; Nos. 739/40, Iroquoians.

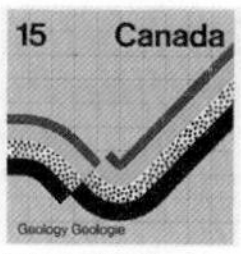

349 Earth's Crust

1972. Earth Sciences.

741		15c. multicoloured	1·10	1·90
742		15c. grey, blue and black	1·10	1·90
743	**349**	15c. multicoloured	1·10	1·90
744	-	15c. green, orange and black	1·10	1·90

DESIGNS AND EVENTS: No. 741 Photogrammetric surveying (12th Congress of International Society of Photogrammetry); No. 742 "Siegfried" lines (6th Conference of Int Cartographic Association); No. 743 (24th International Geological Congress); No. 744 Diagram of village at road-intersection (22nd Int Geographical Congress).

350 Candles

1972. Christmas. Multicoloured.

745	6c. Type **350**	15	10
746	8c. Type **350**	15	10
747	10c. Candles with fruits and pine boughs (horiz)	50	1·25
748	15c. Candles with prayer-book, caskets and vase (horiz)	60	2·00

Nos. 747/8 are size 36×20 mm.

351 *The Blacksmith's Shop* (Krieghoff)

1972. Death Centenary of Cornelius Krieghoff (painter).

749	**351**	8c. multicoloured	30	15

352 F. de Montmorency-Laval

1973. 350th Birth Anniv of Monsignor de Laval (1st Bishop of Quebec).

750	**352**	8c. blue, gold and silver	20	40

353 Commissioner French and Route of the March West

1973. Centenary of Royal Canadian Mounted Police.

751	**353**	8c. brown, orange and red	35	20
752	-	10c. multicoloured	1·00	1·25
753	-	15c. multicoloured	2·25	2·00

DESIGNS: 10c. Spectrograph; 15c. Mounted policeman.

354 Jeanne Mance

1973. 300th Death Anniv of Jeanne Mance (nurse).

754	**354**	8c. multicoloured	20	40

355 Joseph Howe

1973. Death Centenary of Joseph Howe (Nova Scotian politician).

755	**355**	8c. gold and black	20	40

356 *Mist Fantasy* (MacDonald)

1973. Birth Cent of J. E. H. MacDonald (artist).

756	**356**	15c. multicoloured	30	55

357 Oaks and Harbour

1973. Centenary of Prince Edward Island's Entry into the Confederation.

757	**357**	8c. orange and red	20	30

358 Scottish Settlers

1973. Bicentenary of Arrival of Scottish Settlers at Pictou, Nova Scotia.

758	**358**	8c. multicoloured	25	20

359 Queen Elizabeth II

1973. Royal Visit and Commonwealth Heads of Government Meeting, Ottawa.

759	**359**	8c. multicoloured	25	20
760	**359**	15c. multicoloured	80	1·50

360 Nellie McClung

1973. Birth Centenary of Nellie McClung (feminist).

761	**360**	8c. multicoloured	20	50

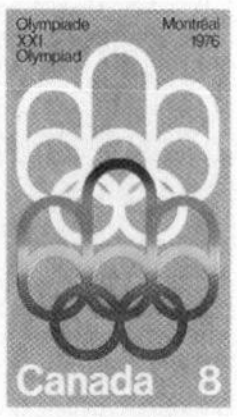

361 Emblem of 1976 Olympics

1973. 1976 Olympic Games, Montreal (1st issue).

762	**361**	8c. multicoloured	25	15
763	**361**	15c. multicoloured	45	1·25

See also Nos. 768/71, 772/4, 786/9, 798/802, 809/11, 814/16, 829/32, 833/7 and 842/4.

362 Ice-skate

1973. Christmas. Multicoloured.

764	6c. Type **362**	15	10
765	8c. Bird decoration	15	10
766	10c. Santa Claus (20×36 mm)	50	1·10
767	15c. Shepherd (20×36 mm)	60	1·50

363 Diving

1974. 1976 Olympic Games, Montreal. (2nd issue). "Summer Activities". Each blue.

768	8c. Type **363**	30	50
769	8c. "Jogging"	30	50
770	8c. Cycling	30	50
771	8c. Hiking	30	50

1974. 1976 Olympic Games, Montreal. (3rd issue). As T **361** but smaller (20×36½ mm).

772	8c.+2c. multicoloured	25	45
773	10c.+5c. multicoloured	40	1·00
774	15c.+5c. multicoloured	45	1·40

364 Winnipeg Signpost, 1872

1974. Winnipeg Centennial.

775	**364**	8c. multicoloured	20	15

365 Postmaster and Customer

1974. Centenary of Canadian Letter Carrier Delivery Service. Multicoloured.

776	8c. Type **365**	50	80
777	8c. Postman collecting mail	50	80
778	8c. Mail handler	50	80
779	8c. Mail sorters	50	80
780	8c. Postman making delivery	50	80
781	8c. Rural delivery by car	50	80

366 "Canada's Contribution to Agriculture"

1974. Centenary of "Agricultural Education". Ontario Agricultural College.

782	**366**	8c. multicoloured	20	20

367 Telephone Development

1974. Centenary of Invention of Telephone by Alexander Graham Bell.

783	**367**	8c. multicoloured	20	20

368 Bicycle Wheel

1974. World Cycling Championships, Montreal.

784	**368**	8c. black, red and silver	20	30

369 Mennonite Settlers

1974. Centenary of Arrival of Mennonites in Manitoba.

785	**369**	8c. multicoloured	20	20

1974. 1976 Olympic Games, Montreal (4th issue). "Winter Activities". As T **363**. Each red.

786	8c. Snow-shoeing	55	60
787	8c. Skiing	55	60
788	8c. Skating	55	60
789	8c. Curling	55	60

370 Mercury, Winged Horses and UPU Emblem

1974. Centenary of UPU.

790	**370**	8c. violet, red and blue	15	15
791	**370**	15c. red, violet and blue	50	1·50

371 *The Nativity* (J. P. Lemieux)

1974. Christmas. Multicoloured.

792	6c. Type **371**	10	10
793	8c. *Skaters in Hull* (H. Masson) (34×31 mm)	10	10
794	10c. *The Ice Cone, Montmorency Falls* (R. C. Todd)	30	75
795	15c. *Village in the Laurentian Mountains* (C. A. Gagnon)	35	1·10

372 Marconi and St. John's Harbour, Newfoundland

1974. Birth Centenary of Guglielmo Marconi (radio pioneer).

796	**372**	8c. multicoloured	20	20

373 Merritt and Welland Canal

1974. William Merritt Commemoration.

797	**373**	8c. multicoloured	20	30

374 Swimming

1975. 1976 Olympic Games, Montreal (5th issue). Multicoloured.

798	8c.+2c. Type **374**	45	65
799	10c.+5c. Rowing	60	1·25
800	15c.+5c. Sailing	70	1·40

375 "The Sprinter"

1975. 1976 Olympic Games, Montreal (6th issue). Multicoloured.

801	$1 Type **375**	1·25	2·00
802	$2 "The Diver" (vert)	1·75	3·50

376 *Anne of Green Gables* (Lucy Maud Montgomery)

1975. Canadian Writers (1st series). Multicoloured.

803	8c. Type **376**	30	10
804	8c. *Maria Chapdelaine* (Louis Hemon)	30	10

See also Nos. 846/7, 940/1 and 1085/6.

377 Marguerite Bourgeoys (founder of the Order of Notre Dame)

378 S. D. Chown (founder of United Church of Canada)

1975. Canadian Celebrities.

805	**377**	8c. multicoloured	60	40
806	-	8c. multicoloured	60	40
807	**378**	8c. multicoloured	30	75
808	-	8c. multicoloured	30	75

DESIGNS—As Type **377**: No. 806, Alphonse Desjardins (leader of Credit Union movement). As Type **378**: No. 808, Dr. J. Cook (first moderator of Presbyterian Church in Canada).

379 Pole-vaulting

1975. 1976 Olympics (7th issue). Multicoloured.

809	20c. Type **379**	40	50
810	25c. Marathon-running	55	80
811	50c. Hurdling	70	1·25

380 *Untamed* (photo by Walt Petrigo)

1975. Centenary of Calgary.

812	**380**	8c. multicoloured	30	30

381 I. W. Y. Symbol

1975. International Women's Year.

813	**381**	8c. grey, brown and black	30	30

382 Fencing

1975. Olympic Games, Montreal (1976) (8th issue). Multicoloured.

814	8c.+2c. Type **382**	35	75
815	10c.+5c. Boxing	45	1·50
816	15c.+5c. Judo	55	1·75

383 "Justice-Justitia" (statue by W. S. Allward)

1975. Centenary of Canadian Supreme Court.

817	**383**	8c. multicoloured	20	30

384 *William D. Lawrence* (full-rigged ship)

1975. Canadian Ships (1st series). Coastal Vessels.

818	**384**	8c. brown and black	70	75
819	-	8c. green and black	70	75
820	-	8c. green and black	70	75
821	-	8c. brown and black	70	75

DESIGNS: No. 819, *Neptune* (steamer); 820, *Beaver* (paddle-steamer); 821, *Quadra* (steamer).

See also Nos. 851/4, 902/5 and 931/4.

385 *Santa Claus* (G. Kelly)

1975. Christmas. Multicoloured.

822	6c. Type **385**	15	10
823	6c. "Skater" (B. Cawsey)	15	10
824	8c. "Child" (D. Hebert)	15	10
825	8c. "Family" (L. Caldwell)	15	10
826	10c. "Gift" (D. Lovely)	30	50
827	15c. "Trees" (R. Kowalski) (horiz)	40	75

386 Text, Badge and Bugle

1975. 50th Anniv of Royal Canadian Legion.

828	**386**	8c. multicoloured	20	20

387 Basketball

1976. Olympic Games, Montreal (9th issue). Mult.

829	8c.+2c. Type **387**	1·50	1·00
830	10c.+5c. Gymnastics	60	1·40
831	20c.+5c. Soccer	70	1·60

388 Games Symbol and Snow Crystal

1976. 12th Winter Olympic Games, Innsbruck.

832	**388**	20c. multicoloured	20	40

389 "Communications Arts"

1976. Olympic Games, Montreal (10th issue). Multicoloured.

833	20c. Type **389**	40	25
834	25c. Handicrafts	65	75
835	50c. Performing Arts	95	1·60

390 Place Ville Marie and Notre-Dame Church

1976. Olympic Games, Montreal (11th issue). Multicoloured.

836	$1 Type **390**	2·25	4·50
837	$2 Olympic stadium and flags	2·75	5·50

391 Flower and Urban Sprawl

1976. HABITAT. U.N. Conference on Human Settlements, Vancouver.

838	**391**	20c. multicoloured	20	30

392 Benjamin Franklin and Map

1976. Bicentenary of American Revolution.

839	**392**	10c. multicoloured	20	35

393 Wing Parade before Mackenzie Building

1976. Centenary of Royal Military College. Multicoloured.

840	8c. Colour party and Memorial Arch	25	30
841	8c. Type **393**	25	30

394 Transfer of Olympic Flame by Satellite

1976. Olympic Games, Montreal (12th issue). Multicoloured.

842	8c. Type **394**	20	10
843	20c. Carrying the Olympic flag	45	60
844	25c. Athletes with medals	45	85

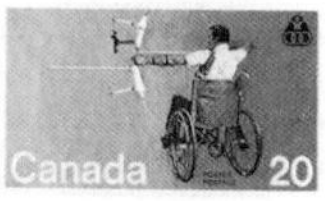

395 Archer

1976. Disabled Olympics.

845	**395**	20c. multicoloured	20	30

396 *Sam McGee* (Robert W. Service)

1976. Canadian Writers (2nd series). Multicoloured.

846	8c. Type **396**	15	40
847	8c. *Le Survenant* (Germaine Guevremont)	15	40

397 *Nativity* (F. Mayer)

1976. Christmas. Stained-glass Windows. Mult.

848	8c. Type **397**	10	10
849	10c. *Nativity* (G. Maile & Son)	10	10
850	20c. *Nativity* (Yvonne Williams)	20	60

398 *Northcote* (paddle-steamer)

1976. Canadian Ships (2nd series). Inland Vessels.

851	**398**	10c. lt brown, brn & blk	45	60
852	-	10c. blue and black	45	60
853	-	10c. blue and black	45	60
854	-	10c. lt green, green & blk	45	60

DESIGNS: No. 852, *Passport* (paddle-steamer); 853, *Chicora* (paddle-steamer); 854, *Athabasca* (steamer).

399 Queen Elizabeth II

1977. Silver Jubilee.

855	**399**	25c. multicoloured	30	50

400 Bottle Gentian

401 Queen Elizabeth II (bas-relief by J. Huta)

402 Houses of Parliament

403 Trembling Aspen

404 Prairie Town Main Street

405 Fundy National Park

1977.

856	**400**	1c. multicoloured	10	20
870	**402**	1c. blue	1·25	3·25
857	-	2c. multicoloured	10	10
858	-	3c. multicoloured	10	10
859	-	4c. multicoloured	10	10
860	-	5c. multicoloured	10	10
871	**402**	5c. lilac	50	1·25
861	-	10c. multicoloured	15	10
866	-	12c. multicoloured	15	60
867	**401**	12c. blue, grey and black	15	10
872	**402**	12c. blue	70	30
868	**401**	14c. red, grey and black	20	10
873	**402**	14c. red	15	10
866a	-	15c. multicoloured	15	15
875	**403**	15c. multicoloured	15	10
869	**401**	17c. black, grey and green	50	10
874	**402**	17c. green	30	10
876	-	20c. multicoloured	15	10
877	-	25c. multicoloured	15	10
869b	**401**	30c. dp pur, grey & pur	70	1·25
878	-	30c. multicoloured	20	10
869c	**401**	32c. black, grey and blue	50	1·25
879	-	35c. multicoloured	25	10
883	**404**	50c. multicoloured	85	1·00
883b	-	60c. multicoloured	65	80
881	-	75c. multicoloured	1·00	1·50
882	-	80c. multicoloured	85	1·25
884	**405**	$1 multicoloured	70	50
884b	-	$1 multicoloured	85	45
884c	-	$1.50 multicoloured	1·75	2·75
885	-	$2 multicoloured	1·00	45
885c	-	$2 multicoloured	4·75	2·00
885d	-	$5 multicoloured	3·00	3·00
885e	-	$5 multicoloured	8·00	4·50

DESIGN—As Type **400**: 2c. Red columbine; 3c. Canada lily; 4c. Hepatica; 5c. Shooting star; 10c. Franklin's lady's slipper orchid. 12c. Jewel-weed; 15c. (No. 866a) Canada violet. As Type **403**: 20c. Douglas fir; 25c. Sugar maple; 30c. Red oak; 35c. White pine. As Type **404**: 60c. Ontario City street; 75c. Eastern City street; 80c. Maritimes street. As Type **405**: $1 Glacier; $1.50, Waterton Lakes; $2 (No. 885) Kluane; $2 (No. 885c) Banff; $5 (No. 885d) Point Pelee; $5 (No. 885e) La Maurice.

406 Puma

1977. Endangered Wildlife (1st series).

886	**406**	12c. multicoloured	20	20

See also Nos. 906, 936/7, 976/7 and 1006/7.

407 "April in Algonquin Park"

1977. Birth Centenary of Tom Thomson (painter). Multicoloured.

887	12c. Type **407**	15	20
888	12c. *Autumn Birches*	15	20

408 Crown and Lion

1977. Anniversaries. Multicoloured.

889	12c. Type **408**	15	25
890	12c. Order of Canada	15	25

EVENTS: No. 889, 25th anniv of First Canadian-born Governor-General; No. 890, 10th anniv of Order of Canada.

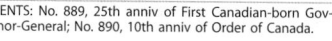

409 Peace Bridge, Niagara River

1977. 50th Anniv of Opening of Peace Bridge.

891	**409**	12c. multicoloured	15	15

410 Sir Sandford Fleming (engineer)

1977. Famous Canadians.

892	**410**	12c. blue	30	30
893	-	12c. brown	30	30

DESIGN: No. 893, Joseph E. Bernier (explorer) and *Arctic* (survey ship).

411 Peace Tower, Parliament Buildings, Ottawa

1977. 23rd Commonwealth Parliamentary Conference.

894	**411**	25c. multicoloured	20	30

412 Hunter Braves following Star

1977. Christmas. Canada's first carol *Jesous Ahatonhia.* Multicoloured.

895	10c. Type **412**	10	10
896	12c. Angelic choir	10	10
897	25c. Christ Child and *Chiefs from afar*	20	45

413 Seal Hunter (soapstone sculpture)

1977. Canadian Eskimos ("Inuits") (1st series). Hunting. Multicoloured.

898	12c. Type **413**	35	35
899	12c. Fishing with spear	35	35
900	12c. Disguised archer	35	35
901	12c. Walrus hunting	35	35

See also Nos. 924/7, 958/61 and 989/92.

414 *Pinky* (fishing boat)

1977. Canadian Ships (3rd series). Sailing Craft. Multicoloured.

902	12c. Type **414**	20	35
903	12c. *Malahat* (schooner)	20	35
904	12c. Tern schooner	20	35
905	12c. Mackinaw boat	20	35

415 Peregrine Falcon

1978. Endangered Wildlife (2nd series).

906	**415**	12c. multicoloured	30	20

416 Pair of 1851 12d. Black Stamps

1978. "CAPEX '78" International Philatelic Exhibition, Toronto.

907	**416**	12c. black and sepia	10	10
914	-	14c. blue, lt grey & grey	15	10
915	-	30c. red, lt grey and grey	25	40
916	-	$1.25 violet, lt grey & grey	70	1·50
MS917		101×96 mm. Nos. 914/16	1·25	2·50

DESIGNS: 14c. Pair of 1855 10d. Cartier stamps; 30c. Pair of 1857 ½d. red stamps; $1.25, Pair of 1851 6d. Prince Albert stamps.

417 Games Emblem

1978. 11th Commonwealth Games, Edmonton (1st issue). Multicoloured.

908	14c. Type **417**	10	10
909	30c. Badminton	20	60

See also Nos. 918/21.

418 *Captain Cook* (Nathaniel Dance)

1978. Bicentenary of Cook's Third Voyage. Multicoloured.

910	14c. Type **418**	20	20
911	14c. *Nootka Sound* (J. Webber)	20	20

419 Hardrock Silver Mine, Cobalt, Ontario

1978. Resources Development. Multicoloured.

912	14c. Type **419**	15	20
913	14c. Giant excavators, Athabasca Tar Sands	15	20

1978. 11th Commonwealth Games, Edmonton (2nd issue). As T **417**. Multicoloured.

918	14c. Games stadium	20	20
919	14c. Running	20	20
920	30c. Alberta legislature building	50	50
921	30c. Bowls	50	50

420 Princes' Gate (Exhibition entrance)

1978. Centenary of National Exhibition.

922	**420**	14c. multicoloured	15	30

421 Marguerite d'Youville

1978. Marguerite d'Youville (founder of Grey Nuns) Commemoration.

923	**421**	14c. multicoloured	15	30

1978. Canadian Eskimos ("Inuits") (2nd series). Travel. As T **413**. Multicoloured.

924	14c. *Woman on foot* (painting by Pitseolak)	30	40
925	14c. *Migration* (soapstone sculpture of sailing umiak by Joe Talurinili)	30	40
926	14c. *Aeroplane* (stonecut and stencil print by Pudlo)	30	40
927	14c. *Dogteam and dogsled* (ivory sculpture by Abraham Kingmeatook)	30	40

422 *Madonna of the Flowering Pea* (Cologne School)

1978. Christmas. Paintings. Multicoloured.

928	12c. Type **422**	10	10
929	14c. *The Virgin and Child with St. Anthony and Donor* (detail, Hans Memling)	10	10
930	30c. *The Virgin and Child* (Jacopo di Cione)	25	90

423 *Chief Justice Robinson* (paddle-steamer)

1978. Canadian Ships (4th series). Ice Vessels. Multicoloured.

931	14c. Type **423**	45	65
932	14c. *St. Roch* (steamer)	45	65
933	14c. *Northern Light* (steamer)	45	65
934	14c. *Labrador* (steamer)	45	65

424 Carnival Revellers

1978. Quebec Carnival.

935	**424**	14c. multicoloured	20	20

425 Eastern Spiny Soft-shelled Turtle

1979. Endangered Wildlife (3rd series). Multicoloured.

936	17c. Type **425**	20	10
937	35c. Bowhead whale	90	90

426 Knotted Ribbon round Woman's Finger

1979. Postal Code Publicity. Multicoloured.

938	17c. Type **426**	20	15
939	17c. Knotted string around man's finger	20	15

427 Scene from *Fruits of the Earth* by Frederick Philip Grove

1979. Canadian Writers (3rd series). Multicoloured.

940	17c. Type **427**	15	15
941	17c. Scene from *Le Vaisseau d'Or* by Emile Nelligan	15	15

428 Charles-Michel de Salaberry (military hero)

1979. Famous Canadians. Multicoloured.

942	17c. Type **428**	25	15
943	17c. John By (engineer)	25	15

429 Ontario

1979. Canada Day. Flags. Multicoloured.

944a	17c. Type **429**	25	40
944b	17c. Quebec	25	40
944c	17c. Nova Scotia	25	40
944d	17c. New Brunswick	25	40
944e	17c. Manitoba	25	40
944f	17c. British Columbia	25	40
944g	17c. Prince Edward Island	25	40
944h	17c. Saskatchewan	25	40
944i	17c. Alberta	25	40
944j	17c. Newfoundland	25	40
944k	17c. Northwest Territories	25	40
944l	17c. Yukon Territory	25	40

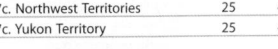

430 Paddling Kayak

1979. Canoe-Kayak Championships.

956	**430**	17c. multicoloured	15	30

431 Hockey Players

1979. Women's Field Hockey Championships, Vancouver.

957	**431**	17c. black, yellow and green	15	30

1979. Canadian Eskimos (3rd series). Shelter and the Community. As T **413**. Multicoloured.

958	17c. *Summer Tent* (print by Kiakshuk)	15	40
959	17c. *Five Eskimos building an Igloo* (soapstone sculpture by Abraham)	15	40
960	17c. *The Dance* (print by Kalvak)	15	40
961	17c. *Inuit drum dance* (soapstone sculptures by Madeleine Isserkut and Jean Mapsalak)	15	40

432 Toy Train

1979. Christmas. Multicoloured.

962	15c. Type **432**	10	10
963	17c. Hobby-horse	10	10
964	35c. Rag doll (vert)	25	1·00

433 *Child watering Tree of Life* (painting by Marie-Annick Viatour)

1979. International Year of the Child.

965	**433**	17c. multicoloured	15	30

434 Canadair CL-215

1979. Canadian Aircraft (1st series). Flying Boats. Multicoloured.

966	17c. Type **434**	25	20
967	17c. Curtiss HS-2L	25	20
968	35c. Vickers Vedette	65	65
969	35c. Consolidated Canso	65	65

See also Nos. 996/9, 1026/9 and 1050/3.

435 Map of Arctic Islands

1980. Centenary of Arctic Islands Acquisition.

970	**435**	17c. multicoloured	15	30

436 Skier

1980. Winter Olympic Games, Lake Placid.

971	**436**	35c. multicoloured	55	85

437 *A Meeting of the School Trustees* (Robert Harris)

1980. Centenary of Royal Canadian Academy of Arts. Multicoloured.

972	17c. Type **437**	25	20
973	17c. *Inspiration* (Philippe Hebert)	25	20
974	35c. *Sunrise on the Saguenay* (Lucius O'Brien)	50	55
975	35c. Thomas Fuller's design sketch for the original Parliament Buildings	50	55

438 Canadian Whitefish

1980. Endangered Wildlife (4th series). Multicoloured.

976	17c. Type **438**	30	15
977	17c. Prairie chicken	30	15

439 Garden Flowers

1980. International Flower Show, Montreal.

978	**439**	17c. multicoloured	15	20

440 "Helping Hand"

1980. Rehabilitation.

979	**440**	17c. gold and blue	15	20

441 Opening Bars of *O Canada*

1980. Centenary of *O Canada* (national song). Multicoloured.

980	17c. Type **441**	15	15
981	17c. Calixa Lavallee (composer), Adolphe-Basile Routhier (original writer) and Robert Stanley Weir (writer of English version)	15	15

442 John G. Diefenbaker (statesman)

1980. John G. Diefenbaker Commemoration.

982	**442**	17c. blue	15	20

443 Emma Albani (singer)

1980. Famous Canadians. Multicoloured.

983	17c. Type **443**	15	25
984	17c. Healey Willan (composer)	15	25
985	17c. Ned Hanlan (oarsman) (horiz)	15	15

444 Alberta

1980. 75th Anniv of Alberta and Saskatchewan Provinces. Multicoloured.

986	17c. Type **444**	15	15
987	17c. Saskatchewan	15	15

445 Uraninite Molecular Structure

1980. Uranium Resources.

988	**445**	35c. multicoloured	30	30

1980. Canadian Eskimos ("Inuits") (4th series). Spirits. As T 413. Multicoloured.

989	17c. *Return of the Sun* (print, Kenojouak)	20	15
990	17c. *Sedna* (sculpture, Ashoona Kiawak)	20	15
991	35c. *Shaman* (print, Simon Tookoome)	35	55
992	35c. *Bird Spirit* (sculpture, Doris Hagiolok)	35	55

446 *Christmas Morning* (J. S. Hallam)

1980. Christmas. Multicoloured.

993	15c. Type **446**	10	10
994	17c. *Sleigh Ride* (Frank Hennessy)	15	10
995	35c. *McGill Cab Stand* (Kathleen Morris)	30	1·40

447 Avro (Canada) CF-100 Canuck Mk 5

1980. Canadian Aircraft (2nd series). Multicoloured.

996	17c. Type **447**	40	20
997	17c. Avro Type 683 Lancaster	40	20
998	35c. Curtiss JN-4 Canuck biplane	60	65
999	35c. Hawker Hurricane Mk I	60	65

448 Emmanuel-Persillier Lachapelle

1980. Dr. E.-P. Lachapelle (founder, Notre-Dame Hospital, Montreal) Commemoration.

1000	**448**	17c. brown, deep brown and blue	15	15

449 Mandora (18th century)

1981. "The Look of Music" Exhibition, Vancouver.

1001	**449**	17c. multicoloured	15	15

450 Henrietta Edwards

1981. Feminists. Multicoloured.

1002	17c. Type **450**	30	30
1003	17c. Louise McKinney	30	30
1004	17c. Idola Saint-Jean	30	30
1005	17c. Emily Stowe	30	30

451 Vancouver Marmot

1981. Endangered Wildlife (5th series). Multicoloured.

1006	17c. Type **451**	15	10
1007	35c. American bison	35	30

452 Kateri Tekakwitha

1981. 17th-century Canadian Women. Statues by Emile Brunet.

1008	**452**	17c. brown and green	15	20
1009	-	17c. deep blue and blue	15	20

DESIGN: No. 1009, Marie de l'Incarnation.

453 *Self Portrait* (Frederick H. Varley)

1981. Canadian Paintings. Multicoloured.

1010	17c. Type **453**	20	10
1011	17c. *At Baie Saint-Paul* (Marc-Aurele Fortin) (horiz)	20	10
1012	35c. *Untitled No 6* (Paul-Emile Borduas)	40	45

454 Canada in 1867

1981. Canada Day. Maps showing evolution of Canada from Confederation to present day. Multicoloured.

1013	17c. Type **454**	15	20
1014	17c. Canada in 1873	15	20
1015	17c. Canada in 1905	15	20
1016	17c. Canada since 1949	15	20

455 Frere Marie-Victorin

1981. Canadian Botanists. Multicoloured.

1017	17c. Type **455**	20	30
1018	17c. John Macoun	20	30

456 The Montreal Rose

1981. Montreal Flower Show.

1019	**456**	17c. multicoloured	15	20

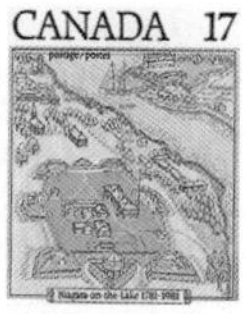

457 Drawing of Niagara-on-the-Lake

1981. Bicentenary of Niagara-on-the-Lake (town).

1020	**457**	17c. multicoloured	15	20

458 Acadian Community

1981. Centenary of First Acadia (community) Convention.

1021	**458**	17c. multicoloured	15	20

459 Aaron R. Mosher

1981. Birth Centenary of Aaron R. Mosher (founder of Canadian Labour Congress).

1022	**459**	17c. multicoloured	15	20

460 Christmas Tree, 1781

1981. Christmas. Bicentenary of First Illuminated Christmas Tree in Canada.

1023	15c. Type **460**	20	15
1024	15c. Christmas Tree, 1881	20	15
1025	15c. Christmas Tree, 1981	20	15

461 de Havilland Tiger Moth

1981. Canadian Aircraft (3rd series). Multicoloured.

1026	17c. Type **461**	25	15
1027	17c. Canadair CL-41 Tutor jet trainer	25	15
1028	35c. Avro (Canada) CF-102 jet airliner	45	40
1029	35c. de Havilland DHC-7 Dash 7	45	40

462 Canadian Maple Leaf Emblem

1981

1030a	**462**	A (30c.) red	20	45

No. 1030a was printed before a new first class domestic letter rate had been agreed, "A" representing the face value of the stamp, later decided to be 30c.

1982. As T **462** but including face values.

1033	5c. purple	10	20
1033d	8c. blue	1·75	2·50
1034	10c. green	1·50	2·25
1032	30c. red, grey and blue	30	60
1036	30c. red	35	40
1032b	32c. red, brown and stone	45	45
1036b	32c. red	1·50	2·50

463 1851 3d. Stamp

1982. "Canada 82" International Philatelic Youth Exhibition, Toronto. Stamps on Stamps. Mult.

1037	30c. Type **463**	30	30
1038	30c. 1908 Centenary of Quebec 15c. commemorative	30	30
1039	35c. 1935 10c. R.C.M.P	30	50
1040	35c. 1928 10c.	30	50
1041	60c. 1929 50c.	60	1·00
MS1042	159×108 mm. Nos. 1037/41	2·25	3·75

464 Jules Leger

1982. Jules Leger (politician) Commemoration.

1043	**464**	30c. multicoloured	20	20

465 Stylized drawing of Terry Fox

1982. Cancer victim Terry Fox's "Marathon of Hope" (Trans-Canada fund-raising run) Commemoration.

1044	**465**	30c. multicoloured	20	20

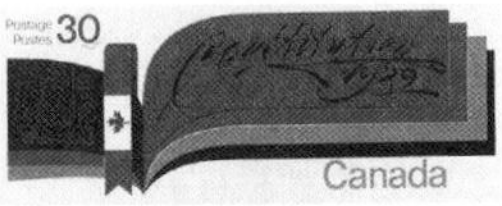

466 Stylized Open Book

1982. Patriation of Constitution.

1045	**466**	30c. multicoloured	20	20

467 Male and Female Salvationists with Street Scene

1982. Centenary of Salvation Army in Canada.

1046	**467**	30c. multicoloured	20	20

468 *The Highway near Kluane Lake* (Yukon Territory) (Jackson)

1982. Canada Day. Paintings of Canadian Landscapes. Multicoloured.

1047a	30c. Type **468**	35	40
1047b	30c. *Street Scene, Montreal* (Quebec) (Hebert)	35	40
1047c	30c. *Breakwater* (Newfoundland) (Pratt)	35	40
1047d	30c. *Along Great Slave Lake* (Northwest Territories) (Richard)	35	40
1047e	30c. *Till Hill* (Prince Edward Island) (Lamb)	35	40
1047f	30c. *Family and Rainstorm* (Nova Scotia) (Colville)	35	40
1047g	30c. *Brown Shadows* (Saskatchewan) (Knowles)	35	40
1047h	30c. *The Red Brick House* (Ontario) (Milne)	35	40
1047i	30c. *Campus Gates* (New Brunswick) (Bobak)	35	40
1047j	30c. *Prairie Town—Early Morning* (Alberta) (Kerr)	35	40
1047k	30c. *Totems at Ninstints* (British Columbia) (Plaskett)	35	40
1047l	30c. *Doc Snider's House* (Manitoba) (Fitzgerald)	35	40

469 Regina Legislative Building

1982. Centenary of Regina.

1048	**469**	30c. multicoloured	20	20

470 Finish of Race

1982. Centenary of Royal Canadian Henley Regatta.

1049	**470**	30c. multicoloured	20	25

471 Fairchild FC-2W1

1982. Canadian Aircraft (4th series). Bush Aircraft. Multicoloured.

1050	30c. Type **471**	35	20
1051	30c. de Havilland DHC-2 Beaver	35	20
1052	60c. Fokker Super Universal	65	85
1053	60c. Noorduyn Norseman	65	85

472 Decoy

1982. Heritage Artefacts.

1054	**472**	1c. black, lt brn and brn	10	10
1055	-	2c. black, blue and green	10	10
1056	-	3c. black and deep blue	10	10
1057	-	5c. black, pink and brown	10	10
1058	-	10c. black, blue & turq	10	10
1059	-	20c. black, lt brn & brn	20	10
1060	-	25c. multicoloured	1·25	10
1061	-	37c. black, grn & dp grn	45	70
1062	-	39c. black, grey and violet	1·75	2·00
1063	-	42c. multicoloured	2·25	1·00
1064	-	48c. dp brn, brn & pink	50	40
1065	-	50c. black, lt blue & blue	1·75	20
1066	-	55c. multicoloured	2·00	30
1067	-	64c. dp grey, blk & grey	60	35
1068	-	68c. black, lt brn & brn	1·75	50
1069	-	72c. multicoloured	2·00	35

DESIGNS—VERT: 2c. Fishing spear; 3c. Stable lantern; 5c. Bucket; 10c. Weathercock; 20c. Skates; 25c. Butter stamp. HORIZ: 37c. Plough; 39c. Settle-bed; 42c. Linen chest; 48c. Cradle; 50c. Sleigh; 55c. Iron kettle; 64c. Kitchen stove; 68c. Spinning wheel; 72c. Hand-drawn cart.

475 Mary, Joseph and Baby Jesus

1982. Christmas. Nativity Scenes.

1080	30c. Type **475**	20	10
1081	35c. The Shepherds	25	60
1082	60c. The Three Wise Men	45	1·50

476 Globes forming Symbolic Designs

1983. World Communications Year.

1083	**476**	32c. multicoloured	30	30

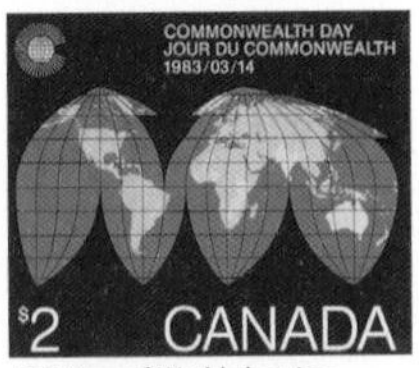

477 Map of World showing Canada

1983. Commonwealth Day.

1084	**477**	$2 multicoloured	2·00	3·25

478 Scene from Novel *Angeline de Montbrun* by *Laure Conan* (Felicite Angers)

1983. Canadian Writers (4th series).

1085	32c. Type **478**	40	90
1086	32c. Woodcut illustrating *Seagulls* (poem by E. J. Pratt)	40	90

479 St. John Ambulance Badge and "100"

1983. Centenary of St. John Ambulance in Canada.

1087	**479**	32c. red, yellow and brown	30	30

480 Victory Pictogram

1983. "Universiade 83" World University Games, Edmonton.

1088	**480**	32c. multicoloured	25	15
1089	**480**	64c. multicoloured	50	70

481 Fort William, Ontario

1983. Canada Day. Forts (1st series). Multicoloured.

1090	32c. Fort Henry, Ontario (44×22 mm)	55	80
1091	32c. Type **481**	55	80
1092	32c. Fort Rodd Hill, British Columbia	55	80
1093	32c. Fort Wellington, Ontario (28×22 mm)	55	80
1094	32c. Fort Prince of Wales, Manitoba (28×22 mm)	55	80
1095	32c. Halifax Citadel, Nova Scotia (44×22 mm)	55	80
1096	32c. Fort Chambly, Quebec	55	80
1097	32c. Fort No. 1, Point Levis, Quebec	55	80
1098	32c. Coteau-du-Lac Fort, Quebec (28×22 mm)	55	80
1099	32c. Fort Beausejour, New Brunswick (28×22 mm)	55	80

See also Nos. 1163/72.

482 Scouting Poster by Marc Fournier (aged 21)

1983. Scouting in Canada (75th Anniv) and 15th World Scout Jamboree, Alberta.

1100	**482**	32c. multicoloured	30	30

483 Cross Symbol

1983. Sixth Assembly of the World Council of Churches, Vancouver.

1101	**483**	32c. green and lilac	30	20

484 Sir Humphrey Gilbert (founder)

1983. 400th Anniv of Newfoundland.

1102	**484**	32c. multicoloured	30	30

485 "NICKEL" Deposits

1983. Cent of Discovery of Sudbury Nickel Deposits.

1103	**485**	32c. multicoloured	30	30

486 Josiah Henson and Escaping Slaves

1983. 19th-century Social Reformers. Multicoloured.

1104	32c. Type **486**	35	50
1105	32c. Father Antoine Labelle and rural village (32×26 mm)	35	50

487 Robert Stephenson's Locomotive *Dorchester*, 1836

1983. Railway Locomotives (1st series). Multicoloured.

1106	32c. Type **487**	1·00	1·00
1107	32c. Locomotive *Toronto*, 1853	1·00	1·00
1108	37c. Timothy Hackworth's locomotive *Samson*, 1838	1·00	1·00
1109	64c. Western Canadian Railway locomotive *Adam Brown*, 1855	1·60	2·50

See also Nos. 1132/5, 1185/8 and 1223/6.

488 School Coat of Arms

1983. Centenary of Dalhousie Law School.

1110	**488**	32c. multicoloured	30	40

489 City Church

1983. Christmas. Churches. Multicoloured.

1111	32c. Type **489**	30	10
1112	37c. Family walking to church	40	90
1113	64c. Country chapel	1·00	2·00

490 Royal Canadian Regiment and British Columbia Regiment

1983. Canadian Army Regiments. Multicoloured.

1114	32c. Type **490**	75	1·25
1115	32c. Royal Winnipeg Rifles and Royal Canadian Dragoons	75	1·25

491 Gold Mine in Prospecting Pan

1984. 50th Anniv of Yellowknife.

1116	**491**	32c. multicoloured	30	30

492 Montreal Symphony Orchestra

1983. 50th Anniv of Montreal Symphony Orchestra.

1117	**492**	32c. multicoloured	35	30

493 Jacques Cartier

1984. 450th Anniv of Jacques Cartier's Voyage to Canada.

1118	**493**	32c. multicoloured	40	30

494 U.S.C.S. *Eagle*

1984. Tall Ships Visit.

1119	**494**	32c. multicoloured	35	30

495 Service Medal

1984. 75th Anniv of Canadian Red Cross Society.

1120	**495**	32c. multicoloured	35	40

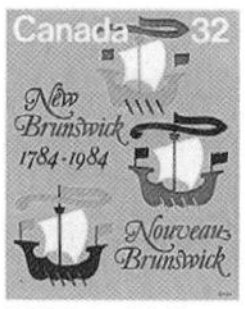

496 Oared Galleys

1984. Bicentenary of New Brunswick.

1121	**496**	32c. multicoloured	35	30

497 St. Lawrence Seaway

1984. 25th Anniv of St. Lawrence Seaway.

1122	**497**	32c. multicoloured	45	30

498 *New Brunswick*

1984. Canada Day. Paintings by Jean Paul Lemieux. Multicoloured.

1123a	32c. Type **498**	50	60
1123b	32c. *British Columbia*	50	60
1123c	32c. *Northwest Territories*	50	60
1123d	32c. *Quebec*	50	60
1123e	32c. *Manitoba*	50	60
1123f	32c. *Alberta*	50	60
1123g	32c. *Prince Edward Island*	50	60
1123h	32c. *Saskatchewan*	50	60
1123i	32c. *Nova Scotia* (vert)	50	60
1123j	32c. *Yukon Territory*	50	60
1123k	32c. *Newfoundland*	50	60
1123l	32c. *Ontario* (vert)	50	60

The captions on the Northwest Territories and Yukon Territory paintings were transposed at the design stage.

499 Loyalists of 1784

1984. Bicentenary of Arrival of United Empire Loyalists.

1124	**499**	32c. multicoloured	30	30

500 St. John's Basilica

1984. Bicentenary of Roman Catholic Church in Newfoundland.

1125	**500**	32c. multicoloured	30	25

501 Coat of Arms of Pope John Paul II

1984. Papal Visit.

1126	**501**	32c. multicoloured	40	20
1127	**501**	64c. multicoloured	85	1·10

502 Louisbourg Lighthouse, 1734

1984. Canadian Lighthouse (1st series). Multicoloured.

1128	32c. Type **502**	1·75	1·75
1129	32c. Fisgard Lighthouse, 1860	1·75	1·75
1130	32c. Ile Verte Lighthouse, 1809	1·75	1·75
1131	32c. Gibraltar Point Lighthouse, 1808	1·75	1·75

See also Nos. 1176/9.

503 Great Western Railway Locomotive *Scotia*, 1860

1984. Railway Locomotives (2nd series). Multicoloured.

1132	32c. Type **503**	1·40	1·40
1133	32c. Northern Pacific Railroad locomotive *Countess of Dufferin*, 1872	1·40	1·40
1134	37c. Grand Trunk Railway Class E3 locomotive, 1886	1·40	1·60
1135	64c. Canadian Pacific Class D10a steam locomotive	2·00	2·75
MS1136	153×104 mm. As Nos. 1132/5, but with background colour changed from green to blue	5·50	6·50

No. **MS**1136 commemorates "CANADA '84" National Stamp Exhibition, Montreal.

See also Nos. 1185/8 and 1223/6.

504 *The Annunciation* (Jean Dallaire)

1984. Christmas. Religious Paintings. Multicoloured.

1137	32c. Type **504**	40	10
1138	37c. *The Three Kings* (Simone Bouchard)	70	1·00
1139	64c. *Snow in Bethlehem* (David Milne)	90	1·75

505 Pilots of 1914–18, 1939–45 and 1984

1984. 60th Anniv of Royal Canadian Air Force.

1140	**505**	32c. multicoloured	35	30

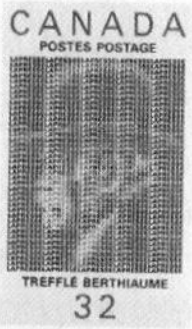

506 Treffle Berthiaume (editor)

1984. Centenary of *La Presse* (newspaper).

1141	**506**	32c. brown, red & lt brn	35	30

507 Heart and Arrow

1985. International Youth Year.

1142	**507**	32c. multicoloured	30	30

508 Astronaut in Space, and Planet Earth

1985. Canadian Space Programme.

1143	**508**	32c. multicoloured	40	30

509 Emily Murphy

1985. Women's Rights Activists. Multicoloured.

1144	32c. Type **509**	40	90
1145	32c. Therese Casgrain	40	90

510 Gabriel Dumont (Metis leader) and Battle of Batoche, 1885

1985. Centenary of the North-West Rebellion.

1146	**510**	32c. blue, red and grey	30	30

511 Rear View, Parliament Building, Ottawa

512 Queen Elizabeth II

512a Queen Elizabeth II in 1984 (from photo by Karsh)

1985

1147b	-	1c. green	1·00	80
1148	-	2c. green	25	1·50
1149	-	5c. brown	75	1·75
1150a	-	6c. brown	70	50
1150b	-	6c. purple	2·50	1·00
1151	**511**	34c. black	2·25	2·75
1155	**511**	34c. multicoloured	60	10
1158	**511**	34c. brown	2·25	3·00
1161	**512**	34c. black and blue	1·40	30
1152	**511**	36c. purple	4·00	5·00
1156a	**511**	36c. multicoloured	30	45
1159	**511**	36c. red	2·25	55
1162	**512**	36c. purple	2·75	1·10
1153	**511**	37c. blue	1·75	30
1157	-	37c. multicoloured	85	10
1162a	**512a**	37c. multicoloured	3·50	10
1154	**511**	38c. blue	2·75	1·25
1157c	-	38c. multicoloured	65	10
1160b	**511**	38c. green	50	30
1162b	**512a**	38c. multicoloured	1·50	20
1162c	**512a**	39c. multicoloured	1·00	20
1162d	**512a**	40c. multicoloured	1·00	20
1162e	**512a**	42c. multicoloured	1·00	40
1162f	**512a**	43c. multicoloured	1·25	80
1162g	**512a**	45c. multicoloured	2·50	80
1162h	**512a**	46c. multicoloured	1·00	45
1162i	**512a**	47c. multicoloured	1·00	60

DESIGNS: 1, 5, 6c. (1150b) East Block, Parliament Building; 2, 6c. (1150a) West Block, Parliament Building; 37c. (1157) Front view, Parliament Building; 38c. (1157c) Side view, Parliament Building.

1985. Canada Day. Forts (2nd series). As T **481**. Multicoloured.

1163	34c. Lower Fort Garry, Manitoba	50	60
1164	34c. Fort Anne, Nova Scotia	50	60
1165	34c. Fort York, Ontario	50	60
1166	34c. Castle Hill, Newfoundland	50	60
1167	34c. Fort Whoop Up, Alberta	50	60
1168	34c. Fort Erie, Ontario	50	60
1169	34c. Fort Walsh, Saskatchewan	50	60
1170	34c. Fort Lennox, Quebec	50	60
1171	34c. York Redoubt, Nova Scotia	50	60
1172	34c. Fort Frederick, Ontario	50	60

Nos. 1163 and 1168 measure 44×22 mm and Nos. 1166/7 and 1171/2 28×22 mm.

513 Louis Hebert (apothecary)

1985. 45th International Pharmaceutical Sciences Congress of Pharmaceutical Federation, Montreal.

1173	**513**	34c. multicoloured	45	45

514 Parliament Buildings and Map of World

1985. 74th Conference of Inter-Parliamentary Union, Ottawa.

1174	**514**	34c. multicoloured	45	45

515 Guide and Brownie Saluting

1985. 75th Anniv of Girl Guide Movement.

1175	**515**	34c. multicoloured	45	35

516 Sisters Islets Lighthouse

1985. Canadian Lighthouses (2nd series). Multicoloured.

1176	34c. Type **516**	2·00	2·00
1177	34c. Pelee Passage Lighthouse	2·00	2·00
1178	34c. Haut-fond Prince Lighthouse	2·00	2·00
1179	34c. Rose Blanche Lighthouse, Cains Island	2·00	2·00
MS1180	190×90 mm. Nos. 1176/9	7·50	8·00

No. **MS**1180 publicises "Capex 87" International Stamp Exhibition, Toronto.

517 Santa Claus in Reindeer-drawn Sleigh

1985. Christmas. Santa Claus Parade. Multicoloured.

1181	32c. Canada Post's parade float	60	85
1182	34c. Type **517**	70	20
1183	39c. Acrobats and horse-drawn carriage	1·00	1·25
1184	68c. Christmas tree, pudding and goose on float	1·90	2·50

1985. Steam Railway Locomotives (3rd series). As T **503**. Multicoloured.

1185	34c. Grand Trunk Railway Class K2	1·25	1·75
1186	34c. Canadian Pacific Class P2a	1·25	1·75
1187	39c. Canadian Northern Class O10a	1·25	1·50
1188	68c. Canadian Govt Railway Class H4D	2·00	2·75

518 Naval Personnel of 1910, 1939–45 and 1985

1985. 75th Anniv of Royal Canadian Navy.

1189	**518**	34c. multicoloured	65	65

519 *The Old Holton House, Montreal* (James Wilson Morrice)

1985. 125th Anniv of Montreal Museum of Fine Arts.

1190	**519**	34c. multicoloured	40	50

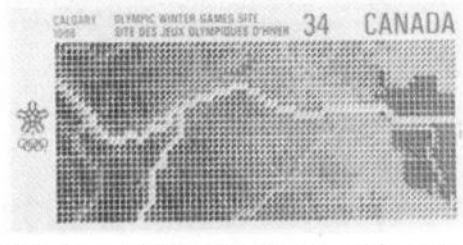

520 Map of Alberta showing Olympic Sites

1986. Winter Olympic Games, Calgary (1988) (1st issue).

1191	**520**	34c. multicoloured	40	50

See also Nos. 1216/17, 1236/7, 1258/9 and 1281/4.

521 Canada Pavilion

1986. "Expo '86" World Fair, Vancouver (1st issue). Multicoloured.

1192	34p. Type **521**	1·25	50
1193	39p. Early telephone, dish aerial and satellite	2·00	3·25

See also Nos. 1196/7.

522 Molly Brant

1986. 250th Birth Anniv of Molly Brant (Iroquois leader).

1194	**522**	34c. multicoloured	40	50

523 Aubert de Gaspe and Scene from *Les Anciens Canadiens*

1986. Birth Bicentenary of Philippe Aubert de Gaspe (author).

1195	**523**	34c. multicoloured	40	50

1986. "Expo '86" World Fair, Vancouver (2nd issue). As T **521**. Multicoloured.

1196	34c. Expo Centre, Vancouver (vert)	70	50
1197	68c. Early and modern trains	1·40	3·25

524 Canadian Field Post Office and Cancellation, 1944

1986. 75th Anniv of Canadian Forces Postal Service.

1198	**524**	34c. multicoloured	60	60

525 Great Blue Heron

1986. Birds of Canada. Multicoloured.

1199	34c. Type **525**	1·75	2·25
1200	34c. Snow goose	1·75	2·25
1201	34c. Great horned owl	1·75	2·25
1202	34c. Spruce grouse	1·75	2·25

526 Railway Rotary Snowplough

1986. Canada Day. Science and Technology. Canadian Inventions (1st series). Multicoloured.

1203	34c. Type **526**	1·75	2·25
1204	34c. Space shuttle "Challenger" launching satellite with Canadarm	1·75	2·25
1205	34c. Pilot wearing anti-gravity flight suit and Supermarine Spitfire	1·75	2·25
1206	34c. Variable-pitch propeller and Avro 504 airplane	1·75	2·25

See also Nos. 1241/4 and 1292/5.

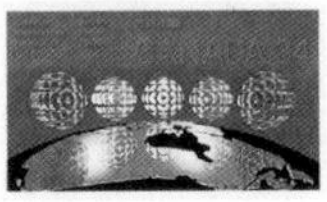

527 C.B.C. Logos over Map of Canada

1986. 50th Anniv of Canadian Broadcasting Corporation.

1207	**527**	34c. multicoloured	40	50

528 Ice Age Artefacts, Tools and Settlement

1986. Exploration of Canada (1st series). Discoverers. Multicoloured.

1208	34c. Type **528**	1·50	2·00
1209	34c. Viking ships	1·50	2·00
1210	34c. John Cabot's *Matthew*, 1497, compass and Arctic char (fish)	1·50	2·00
1211	34c. Henry Hudson cast adrift, 1611	1·50	2·00
MS1212	119×84 mm. Nos. 1208/11	5·50	7·50

No. **MS**1212 publicises "Capex '87" International Stamp Exhibition, Toronto.

See also Nos. 1232/5, 1285/8 and 1319/22.

529 Crowfoot (Blackfoot Chief) and Indian Village

1986. Founders of the Canadian West. Multicoloured.

1213	34c. Type **529**	80	1·00
1214	34c. James Macleod of the North West Mounted Police and Fort Macleod	80	1·00

530 Peace Dove and Globe

1986. International Peace Year.

1215	**530**	34c. multicoloured	60	60

531 Ice Hockey

1986. Winter Olympic Games, Calgary (1988) (2nd issue). Multicoloured.

1216	34c. Type **531**	1·75	1·75
1217	34c. Biathlon	1·75	1·75

532 Angel with Crown

1986. Christmas. Multicoloured.

1218	29c. Angel singing carol (36×22 mm)	65	35
1219	34c. Type **532**	60	25
1220	39c. Angel playing lute	1·00	1·60
1221	68c. Angel with ribbon	1·75	3·00

533 John Molson with Theatre Royal, Montreal, *Accomodation* (paddle-steamer) and Railway Train

1986. 150th Death Anniv of John Molson (businessman).

1222	**533**	34c. multicoloured	1·25	75

1986. Railway Locomotives (4th series). As T **503** but size 60×22 mm. Multicoloured.

1223	34c. Canadian National Class V-1-a diesel locomotive No. 9000	1·90	1·90
1224	34c. Canadian Pacific Class T1a steam locomotive No. 9000	1·90	1·90
1225	39c. Canadian National Class U-2-a steam locomotive	1·90	1·00
1226	68c. Canadian Pacific Class H1c steam locomotive No. 2850	2·50	3·50

534 Toronto's First Post Office

1987. "Capex '87" International Stamp Exhibition, Toronto. Post Offices.

1227	34c. Type **534**	60	20
1228	36c. Nelson-Miramichi, New Brunswick	65	45
1229	42c. Saint-Ours, Quebec	70	65
1230	72c. Battleford, Saskatchewan	1·00	1·25
MS1231	155×92 mm. 36c. As No. 1227 and Nos. 1228/30, but main inscr in green	3·25	2·75

535 Etienne Brule exploring Lake Superior

1987. Exploration of Canada (2nd series). Pioneers of New France. Multicoloured.

1232	34c. Type **535**	1·75	2·00
1233	34c. Radisson and Des Groseilliers with British and French flags	1·75	2·00
1234	34c. Jolliet and Father Marquette on the Mississippi	1·75	2·00
1235	34c. Jesuit missionary preaching to Indians	1·75	2·00

1987. Winter Olympic Games, Calgary (1988) (3rd issue). As T **531**. Multicoloured.

1236	36c. Speed skating	50	40
1237	42c. Bobsleighing	75	60

536 Volunteer Activities

1987. National Volunteer Week.

1238	**536**	36c. multicoloured	30	35

537 Canadian Coat of Arms

1987. Fifth Anniv of Canadian Charter of Rights and Freedoms.

1239	**537**	36c. multicoloured	75	35

538 Steel Girder, Gear Wheel and Microchip

1987. Centenary of Engineering Institute of Canada.

1240	**538**	36c. multicoloured	75	40

539 R. A. Fessenden (AM Radio)

1987. Canada Day. Science and Technology. Canadian Inventors (2nd series). Multicoloured.

1241	36c. Type **539**	1·25	1·75
1242	36c. C. Fenerty (newsprint pulp)	1·25	1·75
1243	36c. G.-E. Desbarats and W. Leggo (half-tone engraving)	1·25	1·75
1244	36c. F. N. Gisborne (first North American undersea telegraph)	1·25	1·75

540 *Segwun*

1987. Canadian Steamships. Multicoloured.

1245	36c. Type **540**	1·75	2·50
1246	36c. *Princess Marguerite* (52×22 mm)	1·75	2·50

541 Figurehead from *Hamilton*, 1813

1987. Historic Shipwrecks. Multicoloured.

1247	36c. Type **541**	1·50	2·00
1248	36c. Hull of *San Juan*, 1565	1·50	2·00
1249	36c. Wheel from *Breadalbane*, 1853	1·50	2·00
1250	36c. Bell from *Ericsson*, 1892	1·50	2·00

542 Air Canada Boeing 767-200 and Globe

1987. 50th Anniv of Air Canada.

1251	**542**	36c. multicoloured	1·00	35

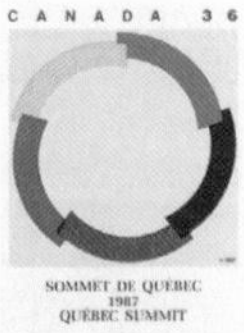

543 Summit Symbol

1987. Second Int Francophone Summit, Quebec.

1252	**543**	36c. multicoloured	30	35

544 Commonwealth Symbol

1987. Commonwealth Heads of Government Meeting, Vancouver.

1253	**544**	36c. multicoloured	35	40

545 Poinsettia

1987. Christmas. Christmas Plants. Multicoloured.

1254	31c. Decorated Christmas tree and presents (36×20 mm)	90	50
1255	36c. Type **545**	40	20
1256	42c. Holly wreath	1·25	50
1257	72c. Mistletoe and decorated tree	1·75	80

1987. Winter Olympic Games, Calgary (1988) (4th issue). As T **531**. Multicoloured.

1258	36c. Cross-country skiing	90	75
1259	36c. Ski-jumping	90	75

546 Football, Grey Cup and Spectators

1987. 75th Grey Cup Final (Canadian football championship), Vancouver.

1260	**546**	36c. multicoloured	35	40

547 Flying Squirrel

1988. Canadian Mammals and Architecture. Multicoloured. (a) As T **547**.

1261	1c. Type **547**	10	10
1262	2c. Porcupine	10	10
1263	3c. Muskrat	10	10
1264	5c. Varying hare	10	10
1265	6c. Red fox	10	10
1266	10c. Striped skunk	10	10
1267	25c. American beaver	30	15
1268	43c. Lynx (26×20 mm)	1·40	1·25
1269	44c. Walrus (27×21 mm)	1·40	20
1270	45c. Pronghorn (27×21 mm)	50	40
1270c	46c. Wolverine (27×21 mm)	1·50	1·50
1271	57c. Killer whale (26×20 mm)	2·00	55
1272	59c. Musk ox (27×21 mm)	3·50	2·75
1273	61c. Wolf (27×21 mm)	70	1·25
1273b	63c. Harbour porpoise (27×21 mm)	2·00	2·50
1274	74c. Wapiti (26×20 mm)	1·60	50
1275	76c. Brown bear (27×21 mm)	2·50	50
1276	78c. White whale (27×21 mm)	1·00	55
1276c	80c. Peary caribou (27×21 mm)	1·00	60

548a Runnymede Library, Toronto

(b) As T **548a**.

1277	$1 Type **548a**	1·50	30
1278	$2 McAdam Railway Station, New Brunswick	2·25	50
1279	$5 Bonsecours Market, Montreal	4·75	4·00

1988. Winter Olympic Games, Calgary (5th issue). As T **531**. Multicoloured.

1281	37c. Slalom skiing	85	50
1282	37c. Curling	85	50
1283	43c. Figure skating	85	45
1284	74c. Luge	1·40	80

549 Trade Goods, Blackfoot Encampment and Page from Anthony Henday's Journal

1988. Exploration of Canada (3rd series). Explorers of the West. Multicoloured.

1285	37c. Type **549**	1·00	70
1286	37c. Discovery and map of George Vancouver's voyage	1·00	70
1287	37c. Simon Fraser's expedition portaging canoes	1·00	70
1288	37c. John Palliser's surveying equipment and view of prairie	1·00	70

550 *The Young Reader* (Ozias Leduc)

1988. Canadian Art (1st series).

1289	**550**	50c. multicoloured	70	70

See also Nos. 1327, 1384, 1421, 1504, 1539, 1589, 1629, 1681, 1721, 1825, 1912, 2011, 2097 and 2133.

551 Mallard landing on Marsh

1988. Wildlife and Habitat Conservation. Multicoloured.

1290	37c. Type **551**	1·00	50
1291	37c. Moose feeding in marsh	1·00	50

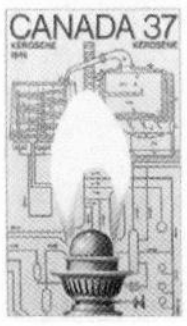

552 Kerosene Lamp and Diagram of Distillation Plant

1988. Canada Day. Science and Technology. Canadian Inventions (3rd series). Multicoloured.

1292	37c. Type **552**	1·00	1·00
1293	37c. Ears of Marquis wheat	1·00	1·00
1294	37c. Electron microscope and magnified image	1·00	1·00
1295	37c. Patient under "Cobalt 60" cancer therapy	1·00	1·00

553 *Papilio brevicauda*

1988. Canadian Butterflies. Multicoloured.

1296	37c. Type **553**	80	1·00
1297	37c. *Lycaeides idas*	80	1·00
1298	37c. *Oeneis macounii*	80	1·00
1299	37c. *Papilio glaucus*	80	1·00

554 St. John's Harbour Entrance and Skyline

1988. Centenary of Incorporation of St. John's, Newfoundland.

1300	**554**	37c. multicoloured	35	40

555 Club Members working on Forestry Project and Rural Scene

1988. 75th Anniv of 4-H Clubs.

1301	**555**	37c. multicoloured	35	40

556 Saint-Maurice Ironworks

1988. 250th Anniv of Saint-Maurice Ironworks, Quebec.

1302	**556**	37c. black, orange & brn	40	40

557 Tahltan Bear Dog

1988. Canadian Dogs. Multicoloured.

1303	37c. Type **557**	1·25	1·40
1304	37c. Nova Scotia duck tolling retriever	1·25	1·40
1305	37c. Canadian eskimo dog	1·25	1·40
1306	37c. Newfoundland	1·25	1·40

558 Baseball, Glove and Pitch

1988. 150th Anniv of Baseball in Canada. Multicoloured.

1307	**558**	37c. multicoloured	35	40

559 Virgin with Inset of Holy Child

1988. Christmas. Icons. Multicoloured.

1308	32c. Holy Family (36×21 mm)	45	55
1309	37c. Type **559**	45	20
1310	43c. Virgin and Child	50	45
1311	74c. Virgin and Child (different)	90	75

On No. 1308 the left-hand third of the design area is taken up by the bar code.

No. 1309 also commemorates the millennium of Ukrainian Christianity.

560 Bishop Inglis and Nova Scotia Church

1988. Bicentenary of Consecration of Charles Inglis (first Canadian Anglican bishop) (1987).

1312	**560**	37c. multicoloured	35	40

561 Frances Ann Hopkins and *Canoe manned by Voyageurs*

1988. 150th Birth Anniv of Frances Anne Hopkins (artist).

1313	**561**	37c. multicoloured	35	40

562 Angus Walters and *Bluenose* (yacht)

1988. 20th Death Anniv of Angus Walters (yachtsman).

1314	**562**	37c. multicoloured	40	40

563 Chipewyan Canoe

1989. Small Craft of Canada (1st series). Native Canoes. Multicoloured.

1315	38c. Type **563**	90	70
1316	38c. Haida canoe	90	70
1317	38c. Inuit kayak	90	70
1318	38c. Micmac canoe	90	70

See also Nos. 1377/80 and 1428/31.

564 Matonabbee and Hearne's Expedition

1989. Exploration of Canada (4th issue). Explorers of the North. Multicoloured.

1319	38c. Type **564**	1·25	75
1320	38c. Relics of Franklin's expedition and White Ensign	1·25	75
1321	38c. Joseph Tyrell's compass, hammer and fossil	1·25	75
1322	38c. Vilhjalmur Stefansson, camera on tripod and sledge dog team	1·25	75

565 Construction of Victoria Bridge, Montreal and William Notman

1989. Canada Day. "150 Years of Canadian Photography". Designs showing early photographs and photographers. Multicoloured.

1323	38c. Type **565**	85	85
1324	38c. Plains Indian village and W. Hanson Boorne	85	85
1325	38c. Horse-drawn sleigh and Alexander Henderson	85	85
1326	38c. Quebec street scene and Jules-Ernest Livernois	85	85

566 Tsimshian Ceremonial Frontlet, c. 1900

1989. Canadian Art (2nd series).

1327	**566**	50c. multicoloured	1·00	60

567 Canadian Flag and Forest

1989. Self-adhesive. Multicoloured.

1328	38c. Type **567**	1·50	2·75
1328b	39c. Canadian flag and prairie	1·50	2·75
1328c	40c. Canadian flag and sea	1·75	1·75
1328d	42c. Canadian flag over mountains	2·00	3·00
1328e	43c. Canadian flag over lake	1·75	2·50

568 Archibald Lampman

1989. Canadian Poets. Multicoloured.

1329	38c. Type **568**	1·25	1·40
1330	38c. Louis-Honore Frechette	1·25	1·40

569 *Clavulinopsis fusiformis*

1989. Mushrooms. Multicoloured.

1331	38c. Type **569**	70	1·00
1332	38c. *Boletus mirabilis*	70	1·00
1333	38c. *Cantharellus cinnabarinus*	70	1·00
1334	38c. *Morchella esculenta*	70	1·00

570 Night Patrol, Korea

1989. 75th Anniv of Canadian Regiments. Multicoloured.

1335	38c. Type **570** (Princess Patricia's Canadian Light Infantry)	1·75	1·75
1336	38c. Trench raid, France, 1914–18 (Royal 22e Regiment)	1·75	1·75

571 Globe in Box

1989. Canada Export Trade Month.

1337	**571**	38c. multicoloured	40	45

572 Film Director

1989. Arts and Entertainment.

1338	**572**	38c. brown, dp brn & vio	1·00	1·25
1339	-	38c. brown, dp brn & grn	1·00	1·25
1340	-	38c. brown, dp brn & mve	1·00	1·25
1341	-	38c. brown, dp brn & bl	1·00	1·25

DESIGNS: No. 1339, Actors; No. 1340, Dancers; No. 1341, Musicians.

573 "now II (Lawren S. Harris)

1989. Christmas. Paintings of Winter Landscapes. Multicoloured.

1342	33c. *Champ-de-Mars, Winter* (William Brymner) (35×21 mm)	1·00	65
1343	38c. *Bend in the Gosselin River* (Marc-Aurele Suzor-Cote) (21×35 mm)	40	25
1344	44c. Type **573**	65	50
1345	76c. *Ste. Agnes* (A. H. Robinson)	1·40	85

On No. 1342 the left-hand third of the design area is taken up by a bar code.

574 Canadians listening to Declaration of War, 1939

1989. 50th Anniv of Outbreak of Second World War (1st issue).

1346	**574**	38c. black, silver & pur	1·10	1·25
1347	-	38c. black, silver and grey	1·10	1·25
1348	-	38c. black, silver and green	1·10	1·25
1349	-	38c. black, silver and blue	1·10	1·25

DESIGNS: No. 1347, Army mobilization; No. 1348, British Commonwealth air crew training; No. 1349, North Atlantic convoy.

See also Nos. 1409/12, 1456/9, 1521/4, 1576/9, 1621/4, and 1625/8.

575 Canadian Flag

576

1989

1350	**575**	1c. multicoloured	20	1·00
1351	-	5c. multicoloured	40	30
1352	-	39c. multicoloured	1·40	2·25
1354	**576**	39c. multicoloured	70	10
1360	-	39c. purple	60	75
1353	-	40c. multicoloured	2·00	2·75
1355	-	40c. multicoloured	80	10
1361	-	40c. blue	40	60
1356	-	42c. multicoloured	1·00	15
1362	-	42c. red	40	60
1357	-	43c. multicoloured	1·00	1·50
1363	-	43c. green	1·50	2·25
1358d	-	45c. multicoloured	1·00	1·00
1364	-	45c. green	65	1·50
1359	-	46c. multicoloured	1·10	65
1365	-	46c. red	60	1·25
1367	-	47c. multicoloured	1·00	75
1368	-	48c. multicoloured	80	1·50
1369	-	49c. multicoloured	1·10	1·50
1370	-	50c. multicoloured	1·10	1·25
1371	-	50c. multicoloured	1·10	1·25
1372	-	50c. multicoloured	1·10	1·25
1373	-	50c. multicoloured	1·10	1·25
1374	-	50c. multicoloured	1·10	1·25
1374a	-	51c. multicoloured	1·00	1·25
1374b	-	51c. multicoloured	1·00	1·25
1374c	-	51c. multicoloured	1·00	1·25
1374d	-	51c. multicoloured	1·00	1·25
1374e	-	51c. multicoloured	1·00	1·25

DESIGNS: Nos. 1351/3, 1360/5, As T **575** but different folds in flag. As T **576**: No. 1355, Flag over forest; 1356, Flag over mountains; 1357, Flag over prairie; 1358d, Flag and skyscraper; 1359, Flag and iceberg; 1367, Flag and inukshuk (Inuit cairn); 1368, Flag in front of Canada Post Headquarters, Ottawa, Flag and Edmonton; 1370, Broadway Bridge, Saskatoon; 1371, Durrell, South Twillingate Island; 1372, Shannon Falls, Squamish; 1373, Church of Saint-Hilaire, Quebec; 1374, Cruise boat and skyline, Toronto; 1374a, Winter scene near New Glasgow, Prince Edward Island; 1374b, Bridge, Bouctouche, New Brunswick; 1374c, Wind turbines, Pincher Creek, Alberta; 1374d, Southwest bastion, Lower Fort Garry National Historic Site, Manitoba; 1374e, Dogsled, St. Elias Mountains, Yukon.

No. 1359 comes with ordinary or self-adhesive gum and 1367/9 and 1370/4e are self-adhesive.

577 Norman Bethune in 1937 and performing Operation, Montreal

1990. Birth Centenary of Dr. Norman Bethune (surgeon). Multicoloured.

1375	39c. Type **577**	1·75	2·25
1376	39c. Bethune in 1939, and treating wounded Chinese soldiers	1·75	2·25

1990. Small Craft of Canada (2nd series). Early Work Boats. As T **563**. Multicoloured.

1377	39c. Fishing dory	1·10	1·50
1378	39c. Logging pointer	1·10	1·50
1379	39c. York boat	1·10	1·50
1380	39c. North canoe	1·10	1·50

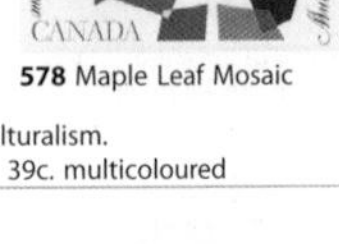

578 Maple Leaf Mosaic

1990. Multiculturalism.

1381	**578**	39c. multicoloured	35	40

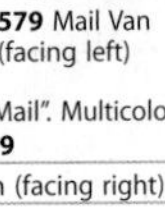

579 Mail Van (facing left)

1990. "Moving the Mail". Multicoloured.

1382	39c. Type **579**	75	75
1383	39c. Mail van (facing right)	75	75

1990. Canadian Art (3rd series). As T **550**. Multicoloured.

1384	50c. *The West Wind* (Tom Thomson)	1·00	1·00

580 Amerindian and Inuit Dolls

1990. Dolls. Multicoloured.

1385	39c. Type **580**	1·25	1·50
1386	39c. 19th-century settlers' dolls	1·25	1·50
1387	39c. Commerical dolls, 1917–36	1·25	1·50
1388	39c. Commercial dolls, 1940–60	1·25	1·50

581 Canadian Flag and Fireworks

1990. Canada Day.

1389	**581**	39c. multicoloured	50	50

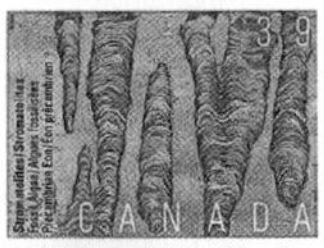

582 *Stromatolites* (fossil algae)

1990. Prehistoric Canada (1st series). Primitive Life. Multicoloured.

1390	39c. Type **582**	1·25	1·50
1391	39c. *Opabinia regalis* (soft invertebrate)	1·25	1·50
1392	39c. *Paradoxides davidis* (trilobite)	1·25	1·50
1393	39c. *Eurypterus remipes* (sea scorpion)	1·25	1·50

See also Nos. 1417/20, 1568/71 and 1613/16.

583 Acadian Forest

1990. Canadian Forests. Multicoloured.

1394	39c. Type **583**	80	70
1395	39c. Great Lakes–St. Lawrence forest	80	70
1396	39c. Pacific Coast forest	80	70
1397	39c. Boreal forest	80	70

584 Clouds and Rainbow

1990. 150th Anniv of Weather Observing in Canada.

1398	**584**	39c. multicoloured	60	50

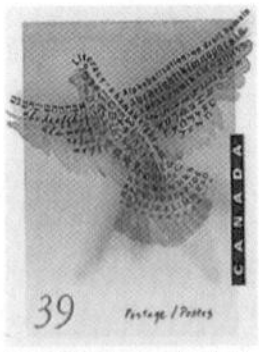

585 "Alphabet" Bird

1990. International Literacy Year.

1399	**585**	39c. multicoloured	40	50

586 Sasquatch

1990. Legendary Creatures. Multicoloured.

1400	39c. Type **586**	1·25	1·50
1401	39c. Kraken	1·25	1·50
1402	39c. Werewolf	1·25	1·50
1403	39c. Ogopogo	1·25	1·50

587 Agnes Macphail

1990. Birth Centenary of Agnes Macphail (first woman elected to Parliament).

1404	**587**	39c. multicoloured	40	50

588 *Virgin Mary with Christ Child and St. John the Baptist* (Norval Morrisseau)

1990. Christmas. Native Art.

1405	-	34c. multicoloured	65	55
1406	**588**	39c. multicoloured	30	20
1407	-	45c. multicoloured	35	45
1408	-	78c. black, red and grey	70	75

DESIGNS—35×21 mm: 34c. *Rebirth* (Jackson Beardy). As T **588**: 45c. *Mother and Child* (Inuit sculpture, Cape Dorset); 78c. *Children of the Raven* (Bill Reid).

No. 1405 includes a bar code in the design.

1990. 50th Anniv of Second World War (2nd issue). As T **574**.

1409	39c. black, silver and green	2·00	2·00
1410	39c. black, silver and brown	2·00	2·00
1411	39c. black, silver and brown	2·00	2·00
1412	39c. black, silver and mauve	2·00	2·00

DESIGNS: No. 1409, Canadian family at home, 1940; 1410, Packing parcels for the troops; 1411, Harvesting; 1412, Testing anti-gravity flying suit.

589 Jennie Trout (first woman physician) and Women's Medical College, Kingston

1991. Medical Pioneers. Multicoloured.

1413	40c. Type **589**	1·10	90
1414	40c. Wilder Penfield (neurosurgeon) and Montreal Neurological Institute	1·10	90
1415	40c. Frederick Banting (discoverer of insulin) and University of Toronto medical faculty	1·10	90
1416	40c. Harold Griffith (anesthesiologist) and Queen Elizabeth Hospital, Montreal	1·10	90

1991. Prehistoric Canada (2nd series). Primitive Vertebrates. As T **582**. Multicoloured.

1417	40c. Foord's crossopt (*Eusthenopteron foordi*) (fish fossil)	2·25	2·50
1418	40c. *Hylonomus lyelli* (land reptile)	2·25	2·50
1419	40c. Fossil conodonts (fossil teeth)	2·25	2·50
1420	40c. *Archaeopteris halliana* (early tree)	2·25	2·50

1991. Canadian Art (4th series). As T **550**. Multicoloured.

1421	50c. *Forest, British Columbia* (Emily Carr)	1·25	1·75

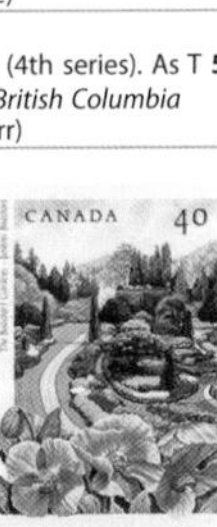

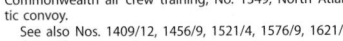

590 Blue Poppies and Butchart Gardens, Victoria

1991. Public Gardens. Multicoloured.

1422	40c. Type **590**	70	70
1423	40c. Marigolds and International Peace Garden, Boissevain	70	70
1424	40c. Lilac and Royal Botanical Gardens, Hamilton	70	70
1425	40c. Roses and Montreal Botanical Gardens	70	70

1426	40c. Rhododendrons and Halifax Public Gardens	70	70

591 Maple Leaf

1991. Canada Day.

1427	**591**	40c. multicoloured	50	60

1991. Small Craft of Canada (3rd series). As T **563**. Multicoloured.

1428	40c. Verchere rowboat	1·40	1·40
1429	40c. Touring kayak	1·40	1·40
1430	40c. Sailing dinghy	1·40	1·40
1431	40c. Cedar strip canoe	1·40	1·40

592 South Nahanni River

1991. Canadian Rivers (1st series). Multicoloured.

1432	40c. Type **592**	1·00	1·40
1433	40c. Athabasca River	1·00	1·40
1434	40c. Boundary Waters, Voyageur Waterway	1·00	1·40
1435	40c. Jacques-Cartier River	1·00	1·40
1436	40c. Main River	1·00	1·40

See also Nos. 1492/6, 1558/62 and 1584/8.

593 *Leaving Europe*

1991. Centenary of Ukrainian Immigration. Panels from *The Ukrainian Pioneer* by William Kurelek. Multicoloured.

1437	40c. Type **593**	80	85
1438	40c. *Canadian Winter*	80	85
1439	40c. *Clearing the Land*	80	85
1440	40c. *Harvest*	80	85

594 Ski Patrol rescuing Climber

1991. Emergency Services. Multicoloured.

1441	40c. Type **594**	2·25	2·25
1442	40c. Police at road traffic accident	2·25	2·25
1443	40c. Firemen on extending ladder	2·25	2·25
1444	40c. Boeing-Vertol Chinook rescue helicopter and *Spindrift* (lifeboat)	2·25	2·25

595 *The Witched Canoe*

1991. Canadian Folktales. Multicoloured.

1445	40c. Type **595**	1·40	95
1446	40c. *The Orphan Boy*	1·40	95
1447	40c. *Chinook*	1·40	95
1448	40c. *Buried Treasure*	1·40	95

596 Grant Hall Tower

1991. 150th Anniv of Queen's University, Kingston.

1449	**596**	40c. multicoloured	1·10	1·00

597 North American Santa Claus

1991. Christmas. Multicoloured.

1450	35c. British Father Christmas (35×21 mm)	1·00	1·00
1451	40c. Type **597**	1·00	20
1452	46c. French Bonhomme Noel	1·25	1·60
1453	80c. Dutch Sinterklaas	2·00	3·75

598 Players jumping for Ball

1991. Basketball Centenary. Multicoloured.

1454	40c. Type **598**	1·50	75
MS1455	155×90 mm. 40c. Type **598**, but with shorter inscr below face value; 46c. Player taking shot; 80c. Player challenging opponent	6·50	6·00

1991. 50th Anniv of Second World War (3rd issue). As T **574**.

1456	40c. black, silver and blue	2·00	2·00
1457	40c. black, silver and brown	2·00	2·00
1458	40c. black, silver and lilac	2·00	2·00
1459	40c. black, silver and brown	2·00	2·00

DESIGNS: No. 1456, Women's services, 1941; 1457, Armament factory; 1458, Cadets and veterans, 1459, Defence of Hong Kong.

599 Blueberry

600 McIntosh Apple

600a Court House, Yorktown

1991. Multicoloured. (a) Edible Berries. As T **599**.

1460	1c. Type **599**	10	10
1461	2c. Wild strawberry	10	10
1462	3c. Black crowberry	50	10
1463	5c. Rose hip	10	10
1464	6c. Black raspberry	10	10
1465	10c. Kinnikinnick	10	10
1466	25c. Saskatoon berry	25	25

(b) Fruit and Nut Trees. As T **600**.

1467	48c. Type **600**	50	35
1468	49c. Delicious apple	2·50	1·00
1469	50c. Snow apple	1·50	1·00
1470	52c. Grauenstein apple	1·60	50
1471	65c. Black walnut	1·75	50
1472	67c. Beaked hazelnut	1·75	1·25
1473	69c. Shagbark hickory	2·75	1·25
1474	71c. American chestnut	3·00	1·00
1475	84c. Stanley plum	1·00	75
1476	86c. Bartlett pear	2·75	1·00
1477	88c. Westcot apricot	1·75	1·60
1478	90c. Elberta peach	1·60	1·00

(c) Architecture. As T **600a**.

1479b	$1 Type **600a**	2·75	1·00
1480b	$2 Provincial Normal School, Truro	3·50	1·60
1481	$5 Public Library, Victoria	7·00	4·75

601 Ski Jumping

1992. Winter Olympic Games, Albertville. Mulicoloured.

1482	42c. Type **601**	1·25	1·25
1483	42c. Figure skating	1·25	1·25
1484	42c. Ice hockey	1·25	1·25
1485	42c. Bobsleighing	1·25	1·25
1486	42c. Alpine skiing	1·25	1·25

602 Ville-Marie in 17th Century

1992. "CANADA 92" International Youth Stamp Exhibition, Montreal. Multicoloured.

1487	42c. Type **602**	1·50	1·50
1488	42c. Modern Montreal	1·50	1·50
1489	48c. Compass rose, snow shoe and crow's nest of Cartier's ship *Grande Hermine*	2·25	1·25
1490	84c. Atlantic map, Aztec "calendar stone" and navigational instrument	3·50	4·50
MS1491	181×120 mm. Nos. 1487/90	8·00	8·00

1992. Canadian Rivers (2nd series). As T **592** but horiz. Multicoloured.

1492	42c. Margaree River	1·50	1·50
1493	42c. West (Eliot) River	1·50	1·50
1494	42c. Ottawa River	1·50	1·50
1495	42c. Niagara River	1·50	1·50
1496	42c. South Saskatchewan River	1·50	1·50

603 Road Bed Construction and Route Map

1992. 50th Anniv of Alaska Highway.

1497	**603**	42c. multicoloured	1·50	70

1992. Olympic Games, Barcelona. As T **601**. Multicoloured.

1498	42c. Gymnastics	1·10	1·25
1499	42c. Athletics	1·10	1·25
1500	42c. Diving	1·10	1·25
1501	42c. Cycling	1·10	1·25
1502	42c. Swimming	1·10	1·25

604 *Quebec, Patrimoine Mondial* (A. Dumas)

1992. Canada Day. Paintings. Multicoloured.

1503a	42c. Type **604**	1·50	1·75
1503b	42c. *Christie Passage, Hurst Island, British Columbia* (E. J. Hughes)	1·50	1·75
1503c	42c. *Toronto, Landmarks of Time* (Ontario) (V. McIndoe)	1·50	1·75
1503d	42c. *Near the Forks* (Manitoba) (S. Gouthro)	1·50	1·75
1503e	42c. *Off Cape St. Francis* (Newfoundland) (R. Shepherd)	1·50	1·75
1503f	42c. *Crowd at City Hall* (New Brunswick) (Molly Bobak)	1·50	1·75
1503g	42c. *Across the Tracks to Shop* (Alberta) (Janet Mitchell)	1·50	1·75
1503h	42c. *Cove Scene* (Nova Scotia) (J. Norris)	1·50	1·75
1503i	42c. *Untitled* (Saskatchewan) (D. Thauberger)	1·50	1·75
1503j	42c. *Town Life* (Yukon) (T. Harrison)	1·50	1·75
1503k	42c. *Country Scene* (Prince Edward Island) (Erica Rutherford)	1·50	1·75
1503l	42c. *Playing on an Igloo* (Northwest Territories) (Agnes Nanogak)	1·50	1·75

1992. Canadian Art (5th series). As T **550**. Multicoloured.

1504	50c. *Red Nasturtiums* (David Milne)	1·25	1·40

605 Jerry Potts (scout)

1992. Folk Heroes. Multicoloured.

1505	42c. Type **605**	1·25	1·50
1506	42c. Capt. William Jackman and wreck of *Sea Clipper*, 1867	1·25	1·50
1507	42c. Laura Secord (messenger)	1·25	1·50
1508	42c. Jos Montferrand (lumberjack)	1·25	1·50

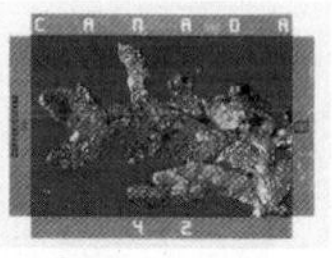

606 Copper

1992. 150th Anniv of Geological Survey of Canada. Minerals. Multicoloured.

1509	42c. Type **606**	1·75	2·00
1510	42c. Sodalite	1·75	2·00
1511	42c. Gold	1·75	2·00
1512	42c. Galena	1·75	2·00
1513	42c. Grossular	1·75	2·00

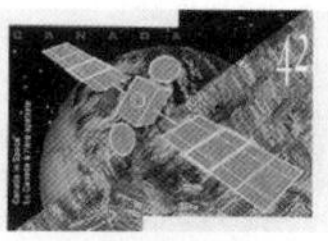

607 Satellite and Photographs from Space

1992. Canadian Space Programme. Multicoloured.

1514	42c. Type **607**	1·25	1·75
1515	42c. Space shuttle over Canada (hologram) (32×26 mm)	1·25	1·75

608 Babe Siebert, Skates and Stick

1992. 75th Anniv of National Ice Hockey League. Multicoloured.

1516	42c. Type **608**	1·60	1·75
1517	42c. Claude Provost, Terry Sawchuck and team badges	1·60	1·75
1518	42c. Hockey mask, gloves and modern player	1·60	1·75

609 Companion of the Order of Canada Insignia

1992. 25th Anniv of the Order of Canada and Daniel Roland Michener (former Governor-General) Commemoration. Multicoloured.

1519	42c. Type **609**	1·40	1·75
1520	42c. Daniel Roland Michener	1·40	1·75

1992. 50th Anniv of Second World War (4th issue). As T **574**.

1521	42c. black, silver & brown	2·25	2·50
1522	42c. black, silver & green	2·25	2·50
1523	42c. black, silver & brown	2·25	2·50
1524	42c. black, silver and blue	2·25	2·50

DESIGNS: No. 1521, Reporters and soldier, 1942; 1522, Consolidated Liberator bombers over Newfoundland; 1523 Dieppe raid; 1524, U-boat sinking merchant ship.

610 Estonian Jouluvana

1992. Christmas. Multicoloured.

1525	37c. North American Santa Claus (35×21 mm)	1·10	80
1526	42c. Type **610**	40	20
1527	48c. Italian La Befana	1·50	2·25
1528	84c. German Weihnachtsmann	2·25	3·25

611 Adelaide Hoodless (women's movement pioneer)

1993. Prominent Canadian Women. Multicoloured.

1529	43c. Type **611**	1·10	1·50
1530	43c. Marie-Josephine Gerin-Lajoie (social reformer)	1·10	1·50
1531	43c. Pitseolak Ashoona (Inuit artist)	1·10	1·50
1532	43c. Helen Kinnear (lawyer)	1·10	1·50

612 Ice Hockey Players with Cup

1993. Centenary of Stanley Cup.

1533	**612**	43c. multicoloured	1·00	60

613 Coverlet, New Brunswick

1993. Hand-crafted Textiles. Multicoloured.

1534	43c. Type **613**	1·50	2·00
1535	43c. Pieced quilt, Ontario	1·50	2·00
1536	43c. Doukhobor bedcover, Saskatchewan	1·50	2·00
1537	43c. Ceremonial robe, Kwakwaka'wakw	1·50	2·00
1538	43c. Boutonne coverlet, Quebec	1·50	2·00

1993. Canadian Art (6th series). As T **550**. Multicoloured.

1539	86c. *The Owl* (Kenojuak Ashevak)	2·25	3·25

614 Empress Hotel, Victoria

1993. Historic Hotels. Multicoloured.

1540	43c. Type **614**	60	1·10
1541	43c. Banff Springs Hotel	60	1·10
1542	43c. Royal York Hotel, Toronto	60	1·10
1543	43c. Le Chateau Frontenac, Quebec	60	1·10
1544	43c. Algonquin Hotel, St. Andrews	60	1·10

615 Algonquin Park, Ontario

1993. Canada Day. Provincial and Territorial Parks. Multicoloured.

1545	43c. Type **615**	70	80
1546	43c. De La Gaspesie Park, Quebec	70	80
1547	43c. Cedar Dunes Park, Prince Edward Island	70	80
1548	43c. Cape St. Mary's Seabird Reserve, Newfoundland	70	80
1549	43c. Mount Robson Park, British Columbia	70	80
1550	43c. Writing-on-Stone Park, Alberta	70	80
1551	43c. Spruce Woods Park, Manitoba	70	80
1552	43c. Herschel Island Park, Yukon	70	80
1553	43c. Cypress Hills Park, Saskatchewan	70	80
1554	43c. The Rocks Park, New Brunswick	70	80
1555	43c. Blomidon Park, Nova Scotia	70	80
1556	43c. Katannilik Park, Northwest Territories	70	80

616 Toronto Skyscrapers

1993. Bicentenary of Toronto.

1557	**616**	43c. multicoloured	1·00	70

1993. Canadian Rivers (3rd series). As T **592**. Multicoloured.

1558	43c. Fraser River	80	1·10
1559	43c. Yukon River	80	1·10
1560	43c. Red River	80	1·10
1561	43c. St. Lawrence River	80	1·10
1562	43c. St. John River	80	1·10

617 Taylor's Steam Buggy, 1867

1993. Historic Automobiles (1st issue). Sheet 177×125 mm, containing T **617** and similar horiz designs. Multicoloured.

MS1563	43c. Type **617**; 43c. Russel Model L touring car, 1908; 49c. Ford Model T touring car, 1914 (43×22 mm); 49c. Studebaker Champion Deluxe Starlight coupe, 1950 (43×22 mm); 86c. McLaughlin-Buick 28–496 special, 1928 (43×22 mm); 86c. Gray-Dort 25 SM luxury sedan, 1923 (43×22 mm)	7·50	8·00

See also Nos. **MS**1611, **MS**1636 and **MS**1683/4.

618 The Alberta Homesteader

1993. Folk Songs. Multicoloured.

1564	43c. Type **618**	70	1·00
1565	43c. *Les Raftmans* (Quebec)	70	1·00
1566	43c. *I'se the B'y that Builds the Boat* (Newfoundland)	70	1·00
1567	43c. *Onkwa:ri Tenhanonniahkwe* (Mohawk Indian)	70	1·00

1993. Prehistoric Canada (3rd series). Dinosaurs. As T **582** but 40×28 mm. Multicoloured.

1568	43c. Massospondylus	80	80
1569	43c. Stryacosaurus	80	80
1570	43c. Albertosaurus	80	80
1571	43c. Platecarpus	80	80

619 Polish Swiety Mikolaj

1993. Christmas. Multicoloured.

1572	38c. North American Santa Claus (35×22 mm)	90	90
1573	43c. Type **619**	55	20
1574	49c. Russian Ded Moroz	1·10	1·40
1575	86c. Australian Father Christmas	1·90	2·75

1993. 50th Anniv of Second World War (5th issue). As T **574**.

1576	43c. black, silver and green	2·25	2·25
1577	43c. black, silver and blue	2·25	2·25
1578	43c. black, silver and blue	2·25	2·25
1579	43c. black, silver and brown	2·25	2·25

DESIGNS: No. 1576, Loading munitions for Russia, 1943; No. 1577, Loading bombs on Avro Lancaster; No. 1578, Escorts attacking U-boat; No. 1579, Infantry advancing, Italy.

620 (face value at right)

1994. Self-adhesive Greetings stamps. Mult.

1580	43c. Type **620**	1·00	1·00
1581	43c. As Type **620** but face value at left	1·00	1·00

It was intended that the sender should insert an appropriate greetings label into the circular space on each stamp before use.

For 45c. values in this design see Nos. 1654/5.

621 Jeanne Sauve

1994. Jeanne Sauve (former Governor-General) Commemoration.

1582	**621**	43c. multicoloured	60	60

622 Timothy Eaton, Toronto Store of 1869 and Merchandise

1994. 125th Anniv of T. Eaton Company Ltd (department store group).

1583	**622**	43c. multicoloured	55	75

1994. Canadian Rivers (4th series). As T **592**, but horiz. Multicoloured.

1584	43c. Saguenay River	80	90
1585	43c. French River	80	90
1586	43c. Mackenzie River	80	90
1587	43c. Churchill River	80	90
1588	43c. Columbia River	80	90

1994. Canadian Art (7th series). As T **550**. Multicoloured.

1589	88c. *Vera* (detail) (Frederick Varley)	1·50	2·00

623 Lawn Bowls

1994. 15th Commonwealth Games, Victoria. Multicoloured.

1590	43c. Type **623**	50	70
1591	43c. Lacrosse	50	70
1592	43c. Wheelchair race	50	70
1593	43c. High jumping	50	70
1594	50c. Diving	50	55
1595	88c. Cycling	2·25	2·00

624 Mother and Baby

1994. International Year of the Family. Sheet 178×134 mm, containing T **624** and similar vert designs. Multicoloured.

MS1596	43c. Type **624**; 43c. Family outing; 43c. Grandmother and granddaughter; 43c. Computer class; 43c. Play group, nurse with patient and female lawyer	3·00	3·50

625 Big Leaf Maple Tree

1994. Canada Day. Maple Trees. Multicoloured.

1597	43c. Type **625**	80	90
1598	43c. Sugar maple	80	90
1599	43c. Silver maple	80	90
1600	43c. Striped maple	80	90
1601	43c. Norway maple	80	90
1602	43c. Manitoba maple	80	90
1603	43c. Black maple	80	90
1604	43c. Douglas maple	80	90
1605	43c. Mountain maple	80	90
1606	43c. Vine maple	80	90
1607	43c. Hedge maple	80	90
1608	43c. Red maple	80	90

626 Billy Bishop (fighter ace) and Nieuport 17

1994. Birth Centenaries. Multicoloured.

1609	43c. Type **626**	1·00	1·25
1610	43c. Mary Travers ("La Bolduc") (singer) and musicians	1·00	1·25

1994. Historic Automobiles (2nd issue). Sheet 177×125 mm, containing horiz designs as T **617**. Multicoloured.

MS1611	43c. Ford Model F60L-AMB military ambulance, 1942–43; 43c. Winnipeg police wagon, 1925; 50c. Sicard snowblower, 1927 (43×22 mm); 50c. Bickle Chieftain fire engine, 1936 (43×22 mm); 88c. St. John Railway Company tramcar No. 40, 1894 (51×22 mm), 88c. Motor Coach Industries Courier 50 Skyview coach, 1950 (51×22 mm)	10·00	10·00

No. **MS**1611 was sold in a protective pack.

627 Symbolic Aircraft, Radar Screen and Clouds

1994. 50th Anniv of ICAO.

1612	**627**	43c. multicoloured	1·00	70

1994. Prehistoric Canada (4th series). Mammals. As T **582**, but 40×28 mm. Multicoloured.

1613	43c. Coryphodon	2·00	2·00
1614	43c. Megacerops	2·00	2·00
1615	43c. Arctodus simus (bear)	2·00	2·00
1616	43c. Mammuthus primigenius (mammoth)	2·00	2·00

628 Carol Singing around Christmas Tree

1994. Christmas. Multicoloured.

1617	(–)c. Carol singer (35×21 mm)	65	75
1618	43c. Type **628**	50	20
1619	50c. Choir (vert)	1·00	1·40
1620	88c. Couple carol singing in snow (vert)	2·25	3·25

No. 1617 is without face value, but was intended for use as a 38c. on internal greetings cards posted before 31 January 1995. The design shows a barcode at left.

1994. 50th Anniv of Second World War (6th issue). As T **574**.

1621	43c. black, silver and green	2·25	2·25
1622	43c. black, silver and red	2·25	2·25
1623	43c. black, silver and blue	2·25	2·25
1624	43c. black, silver and grey	2·25	2·25

DESIGNS: No. 1621, D-Day landings, Normandy; No. 1622, Canadian artillery, Normandy; No. 1623, Hawker Typhoons on patrol; No. 1624, Canadian infantry and disabled German self-propelled gun, Walcheren.

1995. 50th Anniv of Second World War (7th issue). As T **574**.

1625	43c. black, silver and purple	2·25	2·25
1626	43c. black, silver and brown	2·25	2·25
1627	43c. black, silver and green	2·25	2·25
1628	43c. black, silver and blue	2·25	2·25

DESIGNS: No. 1625, Returning troop ship; 1626, Canadian P.O.W.s celebrating freedom; 1627, Canadian tank liberating Dutch town; 1628, Parachute drop in support of Rhine Crossing.

1995. Canadian Art (8th series). As T **550**. Multicoloured.

1629	88c. *Floraison* (Alfred Pellan)	1·50	2·25

629 Flag and Lake

1995. 30th Anniv of National Flag. No face value.

1630	**629**	(43c.) multicoloured	1·00	50

630 Louisbourg Harbour

1995. 275th Anniv of Fortress of Louisbourg. Multicoloured.

1631	(43c.) Type **630**	70	80
1632	(43c.) Barracks (32×29 mm)	70	80
1633	(43c.) King's Bastion (40×29 mm)	70	80
1634	(43c.) Site of King's Garden, convent and hospital (56×29 mm)	70	80
1635	(43c.) Site of coastal fortifications	70	80

1995. Historic Automobiles (3rd issue). Sheet 177×125 mm, containing horiz designs as T **617**. Multicoloured.

MS1636 43c. Cockshutt "30" farm tractor, 1950; 43c. Bombadier "Ski-Doo Olympique 335" snowmobile, 1970; 50c. Bombadier "B-12 CS" multi-passenger snowmobile, 1948 (43×22 mm); 50c. Gotfredson "Model 20" farm truck, 1924 (43×22 mm); 88c. Robin-Nodwell "RN 110" tracked carrier, 1962 (43×22 mm); 88c. Massey-Harris "No. 21" self-propelled combine-harvester, 1942 (43×22 mm) 7·00 7·50

No. **MS**1636 was sold in a protective pack.

631 Banff Springs Golf Club, Alberta

1995. Centenaries of Canadian Amateur Golf Championship and of the Royal Canadian Golf Association. Multicoloured.

1637	43c. Type **631**	80	80
1638	43c. Riverside Country Club, New Brunswick	80	80
1639	43c. Glen Abbey Golf Club, Ontario	80	80
1640	43c. Victoria Golf Club, British Columbia	80	80
1641	43c. Royal Montreal Golf Club, Quebec	80	80

632 *October Gold* (Franklin Carmichael)

1995. Canada Day. 75th Anniv of *Group of Seven* (artists). Miniature sheets, each 180×80 mm, containing square designs as T 632. Multicoloured.

MS1642a 43c. Type **632**; 43c. *From the North Shore, Lake Superior* (Lawren Harris); 43c. *Evening, Les Eboulements, Quebec* (A. Jackson) 3·00 3·50

MS1642b 43c. *Serenity, Lake of the Woods* (Frank Johnston); 43c. *A September Gale, Georgian Bay* (Arthur Lismer); 43c. *Falls, Montreal River* (J. E. H. MacDonald); 43c. *Open Window* (Frederick Varley) 3·00 3·50

MS1642c 43c. *Mill Houses* (Alfred Casson); 43c. *Pembina Valley* (Lionel FitzGerald); 43c. *The Lumberjack* (Edwin Holgate) 3·00 3·50

The three sheets were sold together in an envelope which also includes a small descriptive booklet.

633 Academy Building and Ship Plan

1995. Centenary of Lunenburg Academy.

1643	**633**	43c. multicoloured	50	45

634 Aspects of Manitoba

1995. 125th Anniv of Manitoba as Canadian Province.

1644	**634**	43c. multicoloured	50	45

635 Monarch Butterfly

1995. Migratory Wildlife. Multicoloured.

1645	45c. Type **635**	1·10	1·40
1646	45c. Belted kingfisher*	1·10	1·40
1647	45c. Belted kingfisher*	1·10	1·40
1648	45c. Pintail	1·10	1·40
1649	45c. Hoary bat	1·10	1·40

*No. 1646: Inscr "aune migratrice" in error. No. 1647: Inscr corrected to "faune migratrice".

636 Quebec Railway Bridge

1995. 20th World Road Congress, Montreal. Bridges. Multicoloured.

1650	45c. Type **636**	2·25	2·25
1651	45c. 401-403-410 Interchange, Mississauga	2·25	2·25
1652	45c. Hartland Bridge, New Brunswick	2·25	2·25
1653	45c. Alex Fraser Bridge, British Columbia	2·25	2·25

1995. Self-adhesive Greetings stamps. As T **620**. Multicoloured. Imperf.

1654	45c. Face value at right	60	75
1655	45c. Face value at left	60	75

It is intended the sender should insert an appropriate greetings label into the circular space on each stamp before use.

637 Mountain, Baffin Island, Polar Bear and Caribou

1995. 50th Anniv of Arctic Institute of North America. Multicoloured.

1656	45c. Type **637**	1·00	1·25
1657	45c. Arctic poppy, Auyuittuq National Park and cargo canoe	1·00	1·25
1658	45c. Inuk man and igloo	1·00	1·25
1659	45c. Ogilvie Mountains, dog team and ski-equipped airplane	1·00	1·25
1660	45c. Inuit children	1·00	1·25

638 Superman

1995. Comic Book Superheroes. Multicoloured.

1661	45c. Type **638**	80	90
1662	45c. Johnny Canuck	80	90
1663	45c. Nelvana	80	90
1664	45c. Captain Canuck	80	90
1665	45c. Fleur de Lys	80	90

639 Prime Minister MacKenzie King signing U.N. Charter, 1945

1995. 50th Anniv of United Nations.

1666	**639**	45c. multicoloured	75	50

640 *The Nativity*

1995. Christmas. Sculptured Capitals from Ste.-Anne-de-Beaupre Basilica designed by Emile Brunet (Nos. 1668/70). Multicoloured.

1667	40c. Sprig of holly (35×22 mm)	85	70
1668	45c. Type **640**	50	20
1669	52c. *The Annunciation*	1·60	1·60
1670	90c. *The Flight to Egypt*	2·25	2·75

641 World Map and Emblem

1995. 25th Anniv of La Francophonie and The Agency for Cultural and Technical Co-operation.

1671	**641**	45c. multicoloured	60	50

642 Concentration Camp Victims, Uniform and Identity Card

1995. 50th Anniv of the End of The Holocaust.

1672	**642**	45c. multicoloured	70	50

643 American Kestrel

1996. Birds (1st series). Multicoloured.

1673	45c. Type **643**	1·90	1·75
1674	45c. Atlantic puffin	1·90	1·75
1675	45c. Pileated woodpecker	1·90	1·75
1676	45c. Ruby-throated hummingbird	1·90	1·75

See also Nos. 1717/20, 1779/82, 1865/8, 1974/7 and 2058/61.

644 *Louis R. Desmarais* (tanker), Three-dimensional Map and Radar Screen

1996. High Technology Industries. Multicoloured.

1677	45c. Type **644**	65	1·00
1678	45c. Canadair Challenger 601-3R, jet engine and navigational aid	65	1·00
1679	45c. Map of North America and eye	65	1·00
1680	45c. Genetic engineering experiment and Canola (plant)	65	1·00

1996. Canadian Art (9th series). As T **550**. Multicoloured.

1681	90c. *The Spirit of Haida Gwaii* (sculpture) (Bill Reid)	1·40	2·25

645 *One World, One Hope* (Joe Average)

1996. 11th International Conference on AIDS, Vancouver.

1682	**645**	45c. multicoloured	70	70

1996. Historic Automobiles (4th issue). Sheet 177×125 mm, containing horiz designs as T **617**. Multicoloured.

MS1683 45c. Still Motor Co electric van, 1899; 45c. Waterous Engine Works steam roller, 1914; 52c. International D.35 delivery truck, 1938; 52c. Champion road grader, 1936; 90c. White Model WA 122 articulated lorry, 1947 (51×22 mm); 90c. Hayes HDX 45-115 logging truck, 1975 (51×22 mm) 7·50 8·00

No. **MS**1683 also includes the "CAPEX '96" International Stamp Exhibition logo on the sheet margin and was sold in a protective pack.

1996. "CAPEX '96" International Stamp Exhibitiion, Toronto. Sheet 368×182 mm, containing horiz designs as Nos. **MS**1563, **MS**1611, **MS**1636 and MS1683, but with different face values, and one new design (45c.).

MS1684 5c. Bombadier "Ski–Doo Olympique 335" snowmobile, 1970; 5c. Cockshutt "30" farm tractor, 1950; 5c. Type **617**; 5c. Ford "Model F160L-AMB" military ambulance, 1942; 5c. Still Motor Co electric van, 1895; 5c. International "D.35" delivery truck, 1936; 5c. Russel "Model L" touring car, 1908; 5c. Winnipeg police wagon, 1925; 5c. Waterous Engine Works steam roller, 1914; 5c. Champion road grader, 1936; 10c. White "Model WA 122" articulated lorry, 1947 (51×22 mm); 10c. St. John Railway Company tramcar, 1894 (51×22 mm); 10c. Hayes "HDX 45-115" logging truck, 1975 (51×22 mm); 10c. Motor Couch Industries "Courier 50 Skyview" coach, 1950 (51×22 mm); 20c. Ford "Model T" touring car, 1914 (43×22 mm); 20c. McLaughlin-Buick "28-496 special", 1928 (43×22 mm); 20c. Bombadier "B-12 CS" multi-passenger snowmobile, 1948 (43×22 mm); 20c. Robin-Nodwell "RN 110" tracked carrier, 1962 (43×22 mm); 20c. Studebaker "Champion Deluxe Starlight" coupe, 1950 (43×22 mm); 20c. Gray-Dort "25 SM" luxury sedan, 1923 (43×22 mm); 20c. Gotfredson "Model 20" farm truck, 1924 (43×22 mm); 20c. Massey-Harris "No. 21" self-propelled combine-harvester, 1942 (43×22 mm); 20c. Bickle "Chieftain" fire engine, 1936 (43×22 mm); 20c. Sicard snowblower, 1927 (43×22 mm); 45c. Bricklin "SV-1" sports car, 1975 (51×22 mm) 8·00 9·00

The price quoted for No. **MS**1684 is for a folded example.

646 Skookum Jim Mason and Bonanza Creek

1996. Centenary of Yukon Gold Rush. Multicoloured.

1685	45c. Type **646**	80	1·00
1686	45c. Prospector and boats on Lake Laberge	80	1·00
1687	45c. Superintendent Sam Steele (N.W.M.P.) and U.S.A.–Canada border	80	1·00
1688	45c. Dawson saloon	80	1·00
1689	45c. Miner with rocker box and sluice	80	1·00

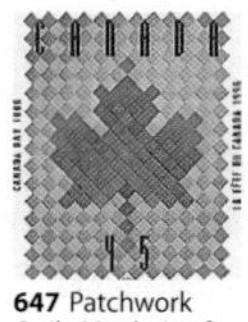

647 Patchwork Quilt Maple Leaf

1996. Canada Day. Self-adhesive. Imperf.

1690	**647**	45c. multicoloured	1·00	60

648 Ethel Catherwood (high jump), 1928

1996. Canadian Olympic Gold Medal Winners. Multicoloured.

1691	45c. Type **648**	70	85
1692	45c. Etienne Desmarteau (56lb weight throw), 1904	70	85
1693	45c. Fanny Rosenfeld (400 m relay), 1928	70	85
1694	45c. Gerald Ouellette (small bore rifle, prone), 1956	70	85
1695	45c. Percy Williams (100 and 200 m), 1928	70	85

649 Indian Totems, City Skyline, Forest and Mountains

1996. 125th Anniv of British Columbia.

1696	**649**	45c. multicoloured	50	50

650 Canadian Heraldic Symbols

1996. 22nd International Congress of Genealogical and Heraldic Sciences, Ottawa.

1697	**650**	45c. multicoloured	50	50

651 *L'Arivee d'un Train en Gare* (1896)

1996. Centenary of Cinema. Two sheets, each 180×100 mm, containing T **651** and similar vert designs. Multicoloured. Self-adhesive.

MS1698a	45c. Type **651**; 45c. *God's Country* (1919); 45c. "Hen Hop" (1942); 45c.*Pour la Suite du Monde* (1963); 45c. *Goin' Down the Road* (1970).	4·25	4·75
MS1698b	45c. "Mon Oncle Antoine" (1971); 45c. *The Apprenticeship of Duddy Kravitz* (1974); 45c. *Les Ordres* (1974); 45c. *Les Bons Debarras* (1980); 45c. *The Grey Fox* (1982)	4·25	4·75

The two sheets were sold together in an envelope with a descriptive booklet.

652 Interlocking Jigsaw Pieces and Hands

1996. Literacy Campaign.

1699	**652**	45c.+5c. mult	85	1·00

653 Edouard Montpetit and Montreal University

1996. Edouard Montpetit (academic) Commem.

1700	**653**	45c. multicoloured	50	50

654 Winnie and Lt. Colebourn, 1914

1996. Stamp Collecting Month. Winnie the Pooh. Multicoloured.

1701	45c. Type **654**	1·75	1·50
1702	45c. Christopher Robin Milne and teddy bear, 1925	1·75	1·50
1703	45c. Illustration from *Winnie the Pooh*, 1926	1·75	1·50
1704	45c. Winnie the Pooh at Walt Disney World, 1996	1·75	1·50
MS1705	152×112 mm. Nos 1701/4	6·25	6·50

655 Margaret Laurence

1996. Canadian Authors.

1706	**655**	45c. multicoloured	80	1·40
1707	-	45c. black, grey and red	80	1·40
1708	-	45c. multicoloured	80	1·40
1709	-	45c. multicoloured	80	1·40
1710	-	45c. multicoloured	80	1·40

DESIGNS: No. 1707, Donald G. Creighton; 1708, Gabrielle Roy; 1709, Felix-Antoine Savard; 1710, Thomas C. Haliburton.

656 Children tobogganing

1996. Christmas. 50th Anniv of UNICEF. Multicoloured.

1711	45c. Type **656**	50	20
1712	52c. Father Christmas skiing	70	1·00
1713a	90c. Couple ice-skating	1·25	2·00

657 Head of Ox

1997. Chinese New Year ("Year of the Ox").

1714	**657**	45c. multicoloured	85	90
MS1715		155×75 mm. Nos. 1714×2	2·00	2·50

No. **MS**1715 is an extended fan shape with overall measurements as quoted.

1997. "HONG KONG '97" International Stamp Exhibition. As No. **MS**1715, but with exhibition logo added to the sheet margin in gold.

MS1716	155×75 mm. No. 1714×2	6·50	7·50

1997. Birds (2nd series). As T **643**. Multicoloured.

1717	45c. Mountain bluebird	1·25	1·40
1718	45c. Western grebe	1·25	1·40
1719	45c. Northern gannet	1·25	1·40
1720	45c. Scarlet tanager	1·25	1·40

1997. Canadian Art (10th series). As T **550**. Multicoloured.

1721	90c. *York Boat on Lake Winnipeg, 1930* (Walter Phillips)	1·50	2·25

658 Man and Boy with Bike, and A. J. and J. W. Billes (company founders)

1997. 75th Anniv of the Canadian Tire Corporation.

1722	**658**	45c. multicoloured	80	70

659 Abbe Charles-Emile Gadbois

1997. Abbe Charles-Emile Gadbois (musicologist) Commemoration.

1723	**659**	45c. multicoloured	60	50

660 Blue Poppy

1997. "Quebec in Bloom" International Floral Festival.

1724	**660**	45c. multicoloured	75	55

661 Nurse attending Patient

1997. Centenary of Victorian Order of Nurses.

1725	**661**	45c. multicoloured	1·25	50

662 Osgoode Hall and Seal of Law School

1997. Bicentenary of Law Society of Upper Canada.

1726	**662**	45c. multicoloured	75	50

663 Great White Shark

1997. Ocean Fishes. Multicoloured.

1727	45c. Type **663**	1·00	1·25
1728	45c. Pacific halibut	1·00	1·25
1729	45c. Common sturgeon	1·00	1·25
1730	45c. Blue-finned tuna	1·00	1·25

664 Lighthouse and Confederation Bridge

1997. Opening of Confederation Bridge, Northumberland Strait. Multicoloured.

1731	45c. Type **664**	1·40	1·00
1732	45c. Confederation Bridge and great blue heron	1·40	1·00

665 Gilles Villeneuve in Ferrari T-3

1997. 15th Death Anniv of Gilles Villeneuve (racing car driver). Multicoloured.

1733	45c. Type **665**	1·00	60
1734	90c. Villeneuve in Ferrari T-4	2·00	2·25
MS1735	203×115 mm. Nos. 1733/4 each × 4	8·00	8·00

666 Globe and the *Matthew*

1997. 500th Anniv of John Cabot's Discovery of North America.

1736	**666**	45c. multicoloured	1·00	55

667 Sea to Sky Highway, British Columbia, and Skier

1997. Scenic Highways (1st series). Multicoloured.

1737	45c. Type **667**	1·25	1·40
1738	45c. Cabot Trail, Nova Scotia, and rug-making	1·25	1·40
1739	45c. Wine route, Ontario, and glasses of wine	1·25	1·40
1740	45c. Highway 34, Saskatchewan, and cowboy	1·25	1·40

See also Nos. 1810/13 and 1876/9.

668 Kettle, Ski-bike, Lounger and Plastic Cases

1997. 20th Congress of International Council of Societies for Industrial Design.

1741	**668**	45c. multicoloured	60	50

669 Caber Thrower, Bagpiper, Drummer and Highland Dancer

1997. 50th Anniv of Glengarry Highland Games, Ontario.

1742	**669**	45c. multicoloured	1·00	50

670 Knights of Columbus Emblem

1997. Centenary of Knights of Columbus (welfare charity) in Canada.

1743	**670**	45c. multicoloured	50	50

671 Postal and Telephone Workers with PTTI Emblem

1997. 28th World Congress of Postal, Telegraph and Telephone International Staff Federation, Montreal.

1744	**671**	45c. multicoloured	50	50

672 CYAP Logo

1997. Canada's Year of Asia Pacific.

1745	**672**	45c. multicoloured	1·00	50

673 Paul Henderson celebrating Goal

1997. 25th Anniv of Canada–U.S.S.R. Ice Hockey Series. Multicoloured.

1746	45c. Type **673**	1·25	1·25
1747	45c. Canadian team celebrating	1·25	1·25

674 Martha Black

1997. Federal Politicians. Multicoloured.

1748	45c. Type **674**	70	1·00
1749	45c. Lionel Chevrier	70	1·00
1750	45c. Judy LaMarsh	70	1·00
1751	45c. Real Caouette	70	1·00

675 Vampire and Bat

1997. The Supernatural. Centenary of Publication of Bram Stoker's *Dracula*. Multicoloured.

1752	45c. Type **675**	65	85
1753	45c. Werewolf	65	85
1754	45c. Ghost	65	85
1755	45c. Goblin	65	85

676 Grizzly Bear

1997. Fauna. Multicoloured.

1756	$1 Great northern diver ("Loon") (47×39 mm) (27.10.98)	1·00	90
1757	$1 White-tailed deer (47×39 mm) (20.10.05)	1·50	1·50
1758	$1 Atlantic walrus (47×39 mm) (20.10.05)	1·50	1·50
1759	$2 Polar bear (47×39 mm) (27.10.98)	2·25	1·75
1760	$2 Peregrine falcon (47×39 mm) (19.12.05)	2·25	2·50
1761	$2 Sable Island horse (mare and foal) (47×39 mm) (19.12.05)	2·25	2·50
1762	$5 Moose (19.12.03)	8·00	7·00
1762b	$8 Type **676**	9·00	9·00
1762c	$10 Blue whale (128×49 mm) (4.10.2010)	9·00	9·00
MS1762d	Two sheets, each 155×130 mm. (a) Nos. 1757/8, each ×2. (b) Nos. 1760/1, each ×2	15·00	17·00

677 *Our Lady of the Rosary* (detail, Holy Rosary Cathedral, Vancouver)

1997. Christmas. Stained Glass Windows. Multicoloured.

1763a	45c. Type **677**	50	40
1764	52c. *Nativity* (detail, Leith United Church, Ontario)	60	65
1765	90c. *Life of the Blessed Virgin* (detail, St. Stephen's Ukrainian Catholic Church, Calgary)	1·00	1·40

678 Livestock and Produce

1997. 75th Anniv of Royal Agricultural Winter Fair, Toronto.

1766	**678**	45c. multicoloured	1·50	55

679 Tiger

1998. Chinese New Year ("Year of the Tiger").

1767	**679**	45c. multicoloured	60	50
MS1768		130×110 mm. As No. 1767×2	1·25	1·50

No. **MS**1768 is diamond-shaped with overall measurements as quoted.

680 John Robarts (Ontario, 1961–71)

1998. Canadian Provincial Premiers. Multicoloured.

1769	45c. Type **680**	65	75
1770	45c. Jean Lesage (Quebec, 1960–66)	65	75
1771	45c. John McNair (New Brunswick, 1940–52)	65	75
1772	45c. Tommy Douglas (Saskatchewan, 1944–61)	65	75
1773	45c. Joseph Smallwood (Newfoundland, 1949–72)	65	75
1774	45c. Angus MacDonald (Nova Scotia, 1933–40, 1945–54)	65	75
1775	45c. W. A. C. Bennett (British Columbia, 1960–66)	65	75
1776	45c. Ernest Manning (Alberta, 1943–68)	65	75
1777	45c. John Bracken (Manitoba, 1922–43)	65	75
1778	45c. J. Walter Jones (Prince Edward Island, 1943–53)	65	75

1998. Birds (3rd series). As T **643**. Multicoloured.

1779	45c. Hairy woodpecker	1·40	1·25
1780	45c. Great crested flycatcher	1·40	1·25
1781	45c. Eastern screech owl	1·40	1·25
1782	45c. Rosy finch ("Gray-crowned Rosy-finch")	1·40	1·25

681 Maple Leaf

1998. Self-adhesive Automatic Cash Machine Stamps. Imperf.

1783	**681**	45c. multicoloured	45	40

For stamps in this design, but without "POSTAGE POSTES" at top left see Nos. 1836/40.

682 Coquihalla Orange Fly

1998. Fishing Flies. Multicoloured.

1784	45c. Type **682**	90	90
1785	45c. Steelhead Bee	90	90
1786	45c. Dark Montreal	90	90
1787	45c. Lady Amherst	90	90
1788	45c. Coho Blue	90	90
1789	45c. Cosseboom Special	90	90

683 Mineral Excavation, Oil Rig and Pickaxe

1998. Centenary of Canadian Institute of Mining, Metallurgy and Petroleum.

1790	**683**	45c. multicoloured	70	50

684 1898 2c. Imperial Penny Postage Stamp and Postmaster General Sir William Mulock

1998. Centenary of Imperial Penny Postage.

1791	**684**	45c. multicoloured	1·00	55

685 Two Sumo Wrestlers

1998. First Canadian Sumo Basho (tournament), Vancouver. Multicoloured.

1792	45c. Type **685**	65	75
1793	45c. Sumo wrestler in ceremonial ritual	65	75
MS1794	84×152 mm. Nos. 1792/3	1·25	1·50

686 St. Peters Canal, Nova Scotia

1998. Canadian Canals. Multicoloured.

1795	45c. Type **686**	1·10	1·25
1796	45c. St. Ours Canal, Quebec	1·10	1·25
1797	45c. Port Carling Lock, Ontario	1·10	1·25
1798	45c. Lock on Rideau Canal, Ontario	1·10	1·25
1799	45c. Towers and platform of Peterborough Lift Lock, Trent–Severn Waterway, Ontario	1·10	1·25
1800	45c. Chambly Canal, Quebec	1·10	1·25
1801	45c. Lachine Canal, Quebec	1·10	1·25
1802	45c. Rideau Canal in winter, Ontario	1·10	1·25
1803	45c. Boat on Big Chute incline railway, Trent–Severn Waterway, Ontario	1·10	1·25
1804	45c. Sault Ste. Marie Canal, Ontario	1·10	1·25

687 Staff of Aesculapius and Cross

1998. Canadian Health Professionals.

1805	**687**	45c. multicoloured	1·00	55

688 Policeman of 1873 and Visit to Indian Village

1998. 125th Anniv of Royal Canadian Mounted Police. Multicoloured.

1806	45c. Type **688**	90	75
1807	45c. Policewoman of 1998 and aspects of modern law enforcement	90	75
MS1808	160×102 mm. Nos. 1806/7	1·75	1·90

689 William J. Roue (designer) and *Bluenose* (schooner)

1998. William James Roue (naval architect) Commemoration.

1809	**689**	45c. multicoloured	70	50

1998. Scenic Highways (2nd series). As T **667**. Multicoloured.

1810	45c. Dempster Highway, Yukon, and caribou	65	75
1811	45c. Dinosaur Trail, Alberta, and skeleton	65	75
1812	45c. River Valley Drive, New Brunswick, and fern	65	75
1813	45c. Blue Heron Route, Prince Edward Island, and lobster	65	75

690 *Painting* (Jean-Paul Riopelle)

1998. 50th Anniv of *Refus Global* (manifesto of The Automatistes group of artists). Multicoloured. Self-adhesive. Imperf.

1814	45c. Type **690**	1·10	1·10
1815	45c. *La derniere campagne de Napoleon* (Fernand Leduc) (37×31½ mm)	1·10	1·10
1816	45c. *Jet fuligineux sur noir torture* (Jean-Paul Mousseau)	1·10	1·10
1817	45c. *Le fond du garde-robe* (Pierre Gauvreau) (29½×42 mm)	1·10	1·10
1818	45c. *Joie lacustre* (Paul-Emile Borduas)	1·10	1·10
1819	45c. *Seafarers Union* (Marcelle Ferron) (36×34 mm)	1·10	1·10
1820	45c. *Le tumulte a la machoire crispee* (Marcel Barbeau) (36×34 mm)	1·10	1·10

691 Napoleon-Alexandre Comeau (naturalist)

1998. Legendary Canadians. Multicoloured.

1821	45c. Type **691**	55	75
1822	45c. Phyllis Munday (mountaineer)	55	75
1823	45c. Bill Mason (film-maker)	55	75
1824	45c. Harry Red Foster (sports commentator)	55	75

1998. Canadian Art (11th series). As T **550**. Multicoloured.

1825	90c. *The Farmer's Family* (Bruno Bobak)	1·00	1·60

692 Indian Wigwam

1998. Canadian Houses. Multicoloured.

1826	45c. Type **692**	50	70
1827	45c. Settler sod hut	50	70
1828	45c. Maison Saint-Gabriel (17th-century farmhouse), Quebec	50	70
1829	45c. Queen Anne style brick house, Ontario	50	70
1830	45c. Terrace of town houses	50	70
1831	45c. Prefabricated house	50	70
1832	45c. Veterans' houses	50	70
1833	45c. Modern bungalow	50	70
1834	45c. Healthy House, Toronto	50	70

693 University of Ottawa

1998. 150th Anniv of University of Ottawa.

1835	**693**	45c. multicoloured	50	50

1998. As T **681**, but without "POSTAGE POSTES" at top left. Self-adhesive gum, imperf (46c.) or ordinary gum, perf (others).

1839	**681**	45c. multicoloured	1·25	1·25
1840	**681**	46c. multicoloured	1·00	1·25
1836	**681**	55c. multicoloured	1·75	1·75
1837	**681**	73c. multicoloured	1·25	1·40
1838	**681**	95c. multicoloured	2·25	2·25

694 Performing Animals

1998. Canadian Circus. Multicoloured.

1851	45c. Type **694**	1·25	1·25
1852	45c. Flying trapeze and acrobat on horseback	1·25	1·25
1853	45c. Lion tamer	1·25	1·25
1854	45c. Acrobats and trapeze artists	1·25	1·25
MS1855	133×133 mm. Nos. 1851/4	4·00	4·50

695 John Peters Humphrey (author of original Declaration draft)

1998. 50th Anniv of Universal Declaration of Human Rights.

1856	**695**	45c. multicoloured	50	50

696 H.M.C.S. *Sackville* (corvette)

1998. 75th Anniv of Canadian Naval Reserve. Multicoloured.

1857	45c. Type **696**	80	90
1858	45c. H.M.C.S. *Shawinigan* (coastal defence vessel)	80	90

697 Angel blowing Trumpet

1998. Christmas. Statues of Angels. Multicoloured.

1859	45c. Type **697**	50	20
1860b	52c. Adoring Angel	85	75
1861b	90c. Angel at prayer	1·60	2·00

698 Rabbit

1999. Chinese New Year ("Year of the Rabbit").

1862	**698**	46c. multicoloured	50	50

MS1863 Circular 100 mm diam. **698** 95c. mult (40×40 mm) 1·75 2·25

No. **MS**1863 also exists with the "CHINA '99" World Stamp Exhibition, Beijing, logo overprinted in gold on the top of the margin.

699 Stylized Mask and Curtain

1999. 50th Anniv of Le Theatre du Rideau Vert.

1864	**699**	46c. multicoloured	50	50

1999. Birds (4th series). As T **643**. Multicoloured. Ordinary or self-adhesive gum.

1865	46c. Northern goshawk	85	85
1866	46c. Red-winged blackbird	85	85
1867	46c. American goldfinch	85	85
1868	46c. Sandhill crane	85	85

700 "The Raven and the First Men" (B. Reid) and The Great Hall

1999. 50th Anniv of University of British Columbia Museum of Anthropology.

1873	**700**	46c. multicoloured	50	50

701 *Marco Polo* (full-rigged ship)

1999. Canada–Australia Joint Issue. *Marco Polo* (emigrant ship).

1874	**701**	46c. multicoloured	50	50

MS1875 160×95 mm. 85c. As No. 1728 of Australia. 46c. Type **701**. (No. **MS**1875 was sold at $1.25 in Canada) 1·75 2·00

No. **MS**1875 includes the "Australia '99" emblem on the sheet margin and was postally valid in Canada to the value of 46c.

The same miniature sheet was also available in Australia.

1999. Scenic Highways (3rd series). As T **667**. Multicoloured.

1876	46c. Route 132, Quebec, and hang-glider	75	85
1877	46c. Yellowhead Highway, Manitoba, and bison	75	85
1878	46c. Dempster Highway, Northwest Territories, and Indian village elder	75	85
1879	46c. The Discovery Trail, Newfoundland, and whale's tailfin	75	85

702 Inuit Children and Landscape

1999. Creation of Nunavut Territory.

1880	**702**	46c. multicoloured	50	50

703 Elderly Couple on Country Path

1999. International Year of Older Persons.

1881	**703**	46c. multicoloured	50	50

704 Khanda (Sikh symbol)

1999. Centenary of Sikhs in Canada.

1882	**704**	46c. multicoloured	50	50

705 *Arethusa bulbosa* (orchid)

1999. 16th World Orchid Conference, Vancouver. Multicoloured.

1883	46c. Type **705**	75	75
1884	46c. *Amerorchis rotundifolia*	75	75
1885	46c. *Cypripedium pubescens*	75	75
1886	46c. *Platanthera psycodes*	75	75

706 Bookbinding

1999. Traditional Trades. Multicoloured. (a) Ordinary gum.

1887	1c. Type **706**	10	10
1888	2c. Decorative ironwork	10	10
1889	3c. Glass-blowing	10	10
1890	4c. Oyster farming	10	10
1891	5c. Weaving	10	10
1892	9c. Quilting	10	10
1893	10c. Wood carving	10	15
1894	25c. Leatherworking	20	25

(b) Self-adhesive.

1895	65c. Jewellery making (horiz)	50	55
1896	77c. Basket weaving (horiz)	1·50	1·50
1897	$1.25 Wood-carving (horiz)	1·00	1·10

707 *Northern Dancer* (racehorse)

1999. Canadian Horses. Multicoloured. Ordinary or self-adhesive gum.

1903	46c. Type **707**	80	80
1904	46c. *Kingsway Skoal* (rodeo horse)	80	80
1905	46c. *Big Ben* (show jumper)	80	80
1906	46c. *Armbro Flight* (trotter)	80	80

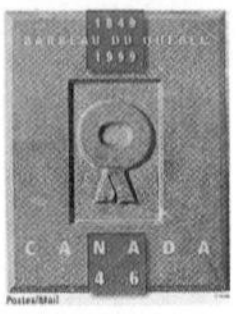

708 Logo engraved on Limestone

1999. 150th Anniv of Barreau du Quebec (Quebec lawyers' association).

1911	**708**	46c. multicoloured	50	50

1999. Canadian Art (12th series). As T **550**. Multicoloured.

1912	95c. *Coq licorne* (Jean Dallaire)	1·25	1·75

709 Athletics

1999. 13th Pan-American Games, Winnipeg. Multicoloured.

1913	46c. Type **709**	85	90
1914	46c. Cycling	85	90
1915	46c. Swimming	85	90
1916	46c. Football	85	90

1999. "China '99" International Stamp Exhibition, Beijing. Sheet 78×133 mm, containing Nos. 1883/6. Multicoloured.

MS1917 46c. Type **705**; 46c. *Amerorchis rotundifolia*; 46c. *Cypripedium pubescens*; 46c. *Platanthera psycodes* 2·25 2·75

710 Female Rower

1999. 23rd World Rowing Championships, St. Catharines.

1918	**710**	46c. multicoloured	50	50

711 UPU Emblem and World Map

1999. 125th Anniv of Universal Postal Union.

1919	**711**	46c. multicoloured	75	50

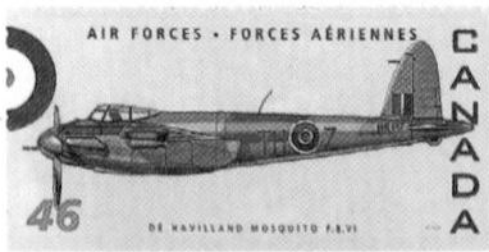

712 de Havilland Mosquito F.B. VI

1999. 75th Anniv of Canadian Air Force. Multicoloured.

1920	46c. Type **712**	75	85
1921	46c. Sopwith F.1 Camel	75	85
1922	46c. de Havilland Canada DHC-3 Otter	75	85
1923	46c. de Havilland Canada CC-108 Caribou	75	85
1924	46c. Canadair CL-28 Argus Mk 2	75	85
1925	46c. Canadair (North American) F-86 Sabre 6	75	85
1926	46c. McDonnell Douglas CF-18	75	85
1927	46c. Sopwith 5.F.1 Dolphin	75	85
1928	46c. Armstrong Whitworth Siskin IIIA	75	85
1929	46c. Canadian Vickers (Northrop) Delta II	75	85
1930	46c. Sikorsky CH-124A Sea King helicopter	75	85
1931	46c. Vickers-Armstrong Wellington Mk II	75	85
1932	46c. Avro Anson Mk I	75	85
1933	46c. Canadair (Lockheed) CF-104G Starfighter	75	85
1934	46c. Burgess-Dunne	75	85
1935	46c. Avro 504K	75	85

713 Fokker DR-1

1999. 50th Anniv of Canadian International Air Show. Multicoloured.

1936	46c. Type **713**	85	90
1937	46c. H101 Salto glider	85	90
1938	46c. de Havilland DH100 Vampire Mk III	85	90
1939	46c. Wing walker on Stearman A-75	85	90

Nos. 1936/9 were printed together, se-tenant, forming a composite design which includes a nine-plane Snowbird formation of Canadair CT114 Tutor in the background.

714 NATO Emblem and National Flags

1999. 50th Anniv of North Atlantic Treaty Organization.

1940	**714**	46c. multicoloured	1·00	50

715 Man ploughing on Book

1999. Centenary of Frontier College (workers' education organization).

1941	**715**	46c. multicoloured	50	50

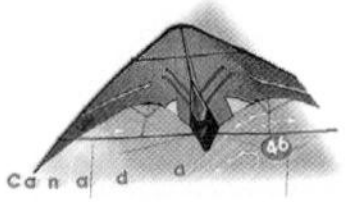

716 Master Control Sports Kite

1999. Stamp Collecting Month. Kites. Multicoloured.

1942	46c. Type **716**	55	65
1943	46c. Indian Garden Flying Carpet (irregular rectangle, 35½×32 mm)	55	65
1944	46c. Gibson Girl box kite (horiz, 38½×25 mm)	55	65
1945	46c. Dragon Centipede (oval, 39×29 mm)	55	65

717 Boy holding Dove

1999. New Millennium. Three sheets, each 108×108 mm, containing T **717** and similar square designs in blocks of 4. Self-adhesive.

MS1946 – 46c.×4 multicoloured	2·00	2·50
MS1947 **717** 55c.×4 multicoloured	4·50	4·75
MS1948 – 95c.×4 brown	3·75	4·50

DESIGNS: 46c. Holographic image of dove in flight; 95c. Dove with olive branch.

718 Angel playing Drum

1999. Christmas. Victorian Angels. Multicoloured.

1949	46c. Type **718**	60	20
1950	55c. Angel with toys	80	50
1951	95c. Angel with star	1·40	2·25

719 Portia White (singer)

1999. Millennium Collection (1st series). Entertainment and Arts. Miniature sheets, each 108×112 mm, containing T **719** and similar vert designs. Multicoloured.

MS1952 46c. Type **719**; 46c. Glenn Gould (pianist); 46c. Guy Lombardo (conductor of *Royal Canadians*); 46c. Félix Leclerc (musician, playwright and actor) 2·25 2·75

MS1952/5 Set of 4 sheets 8·00 10·00

MS1953 46c. Artists looking at painting (Royal Canadian Academy of Arts); 46c. Cloud, stave and pencil marks (The Canada Council); 46c. Man with video camera (National Film Board of Canada); 46c. Newsreader (Canadian Broadcasting Corporation) 2·25 2·75

MS1954 46c. Calgary Stampede; 46c. Circus performers; 46c. Ice hockey (Hockey Night); 46c. Goalkeeper (Ice hockey live from The Forum) 2·25 2·75

MS1955 46c. IMAX cinema; 46c. Computer image (Softimage); 46c. Ted Rogers Sr (*Plugging in the Radio*); 46c. Sir William Stephenson (inventor of radio facsimile system) 2·25 2·75

See also Nos. **MS**1959/62, **MS**1969/73 and **MS**1982/5.

720 Millennium Partnership Programme Logo

2000. Canada Millennium Partnership Programme.

1956 **720** 46c. red, green and blue 50 50

721 Chinese Dragon

2000. Chinese New Year ("Year of the Dragon").

1957 **721** 46c. multicoloured 50 50

MS1958 150×85 mm. **721** 90c. multicoloured 1·25 1·50

2000. Millennium Collection (2nd series). Charities, Medical Pioneers, Peacekeepers and Social Reforms. Miniature sheets, each 108×112 mm, containing vert designs as T **719**. Multicoloured.

MS1959 46c. Providing equipment (Canadian International Development Agency); 46c. Dr. Lucille Teasdale (medical missionary); 46c. Terry Fox (Marathon of Hope); 46c. Delivering meal (Meals on Wheels) 2·25 2·50

MS1959/62 Set of 4 sheets 8·00 9·00

MS1960 46c. Sir Frederick Banting (discovery of insulin); 46c. Armand Frappier (developer of BCG vaccine); 46c. Dr. Hans Selye (research into stress); 46c. *Dr. Maude Abbott* (pathologist) (M. Bell Eastlake) 2·25 2·50

MS1961 46c. Senator Raoul Dandurand (diplomat); 46c. Pauline Vanier and Elizabeth Smellie (nursing pioneers); 46c. Lester B. Pearson (diplomat); 46c. One-legged man (Ottawa Convention on Banning Landmines) 2·25 2·50

MS1962 46c. Nun and surgeon (medical care); 46c. *Women are persons* (sculpture by Barbara Paterson) (Appointment of women senators); 46c. Alphonse and Dorimène Desjardins (People's bank movement); 46c. Father Moses Coady (Adult education pioneer) 2·25 2·50

722 Wayne Gretzky (ice-hockey player)

2000. 50th National Hockey League All-Star Game. Multicoloured.

1963 46c. Type **722** 80 80

1964 46c. Gordie Howe (No. 9 in white jersey) 80 80

1965 46c. Maurice Richard (No. 9 in blue and red jersey) 80 80

1966 46c. Doug Harvey (No. 2) 80 80

1967 46c. Bobby Orr (No. 4) 80 80

1968 46c. Jacques Plante (No. 1) 80 80

See also Nos. 2052/7, 2118/23, 2178/3, 2250/5 and 2316/27.

2000. Millennium Collection (3rd series). First Inhabitants, Great Thinkers, Culture and Literary Legends, and Charitable Foundations. Miniature sheets, each 108×112 mm, containing vert designs as T **719**. Multicoloured.

MS1969 46c. Pontiac (Ottawa chief); 46c. Tom Longboat (long-distance runner); 46c. *Inuit Shaman* (sculpture by Paul Toolooktook); 46c. Shaman and patient (Indian medicine) 2·25 2·50

MS1969/73 Set of 5 sheets 10·00 11·00

MS1970 46c. Prof. Marshall McLuhan (media philosopher); 46c. Northrop Frye (literary critic); 46c. Roger Lemelin (novelist); 46c. Prof. Hilda Marion Neatby (educator) 2·25 2·50

MS1971 46c. Bow of Viking longship (L'Anse aux Meadows World Heritage Site); 46c. Immigrant family (Pier 21 monument); 46c. Neptune mask (Neptune Theatre, Halifax); 46c. Auditorium and actor (The Stratford Festival) 2·25 2·50

MS1972 46c. W. O. Mitchell (writer); 46c. Gratien Gélinas (actor, producer and playwright); 46c. Text and fountain pen (Cercle du Livre de France); 46c. Harlequin and roses (Harlequin Books) 2·25 2·50

MS1973 46c. Hart Massey (Massey Foundation); 46c. Izaak Walton Killam and Dorothy Killam; 46f. Eric Lafferty Harvie (Glenbow Foundation); 46c. Macdonald Stewart Foundation 2·25 2·50

2000. Birds (5th series). As T **643**. Multicoloured. Ordinary or self-adhesive gum.

1974 46c. Canadian warbler 85 90

1975 46c. Osprey 85 90

1976 46c. Pacific diver ("Pacific Loon") 85 90

1977 46c. Blue jay 85 90

2000. Millennium Collection (4th series). Canadian Agriculture, Commerce and Technology. Miniature sheets, each 108×112 mm, containing vert designs as T **719**. Multicoloured.

MS1982 46c. Sir Charles Saunders (developer of Marquis wheat); 46c. Baby (Pablum baby food); 46c. Dr. Archibald Gowanlock Huntsman (frozen fish pioneer); 46c. Oven chips and field of potatoes (McCain Frozen Foods) 2·25 2·50

MS1982/5 Set of 4 sheets 8·00 9·00

MS1983 46c. Early trader and Indian (Hudson's Bay Company); 46c. Satellite over earth (Bell Canada Enterprises); 46c. Jos. Louis biscuits and Vachon family (Vachon Family Bakery); 46c. Bread and eggs (George Weston Limited) 2·25 2·50

MS1984 46c. George Klein and cog wheels (inventor of electric wheelchair and micro-surgical staple gun); 46c. Abraham Gesner (developer of kerosene); 46c. Alexander Graham Bell (inventor of telephone); 46c. Joseph-Armand Bombadier (inventor of snowmobile) 2·25 2·50

MS1985 46c. Workers and steam locomotive (Rogers Pass rail tunnel); 46c. Manic 5 dam (Manicouagan River hydro-electric project); 46c. Mobile Servicing System for International Space Station (Canadian Space Program); 46c. CN Tower (World's tallest building) 2·25 2·50

723 Judges and Supreme Court Building

2000. 125th Anniv of Supreme Court of Canada.

1986 **723** 46c. multicoloured 50 50

724 Lethbridge Bridge, Synthetic Rubber Plant, X-ray of Heart Pacemaker and Microwave Radio System

2000. 75th Anniv of Ceremony for Calling of an Engineer.

1987 **724** 46c. multicoloured 50 50

Each vertical pair completes the engineer's ring as shown on Type **274**.

725

2000. "Picture Postage" Greetings Stamps. Self-adhesive.

1988 **725** 46c. multicoloured 50 50

No. 1988 was issued to include appropriate greetings labels which could be inserted into the rectangular space on each stamp.

See also Nos. 2045 and 2099.

726 Coastal-style Mailboxes in Autumn

2000. Traditional Rural Mailboxes. Multicoloured.

1989 46c. Type **726** 75 75

1990 46c. House and cow-shaped mailboxes in springtime 75 75

1991 46c. Tractor-shaped mailbox in summertime 75 75

1992 46c. Barn and duck-shaped mailboxes in winter 75 75

727 Gorge and Fir Tree

2000. Canadian Rivers and Lakes. Multicoloured. Self-adhesive.

1993 55c. Type **727** 60 65

1994 55c. Lake and water lilies 60 65

1995 55c. Glacier and reflected mountains 60 65

1996 55c. Estuary and aerial view 60 65

1997 55c. Waterfall and forest edge 60 65

1998 95c. Iceberg and mountain river 95 1·10

1999 95c. Rapids and waterfall 95 1·10

2000 95c. Moraine and river 95 1·10

2001 95c. Shallows and waves on lake 95 1·10

2002 95c. Forest sloping to waters edge and tree 95 1·10

728 Queen Elizabeth the Queen Mother with Roses

2000. Queen Elizabeth the Queen Mother's 100th Birthday.

2003 **728** 95c. multicoloured 1·40 1·40

729 Teenager with Two Children

2000. Centenary of Boys and Girls Clubs of Canada.

2004 **729** 46c. multicoloured 50 50

730 Clouds over Rockies and Symbol

2000. 57th General Conference Session of Seventh-day Adventist Church, Toronto.

2005 **730** 46c. multicoloured 50 50

731 *Space Travellers and Canadian Flag* (Rosalie Anne Nardelli)

2000. "Stampin' the Future" (children's stamp design competition). Multicoloured.

2006 46c. Type **731** 60 70

2007 46c. *Travelling to the Moon* (Sarah Lutgen) 60 70

2008 46c. *Astronauts in shuttle* (Andrew Wright) 60 70

2009 46c. *Children completing Canada as jigsaw* (Christine Weera) 60 70

MS2010 114×90 mm. Nos. 2006/9 2·40 3·00

2000. Canadian Art (13th series). As T **550**. Mult.

2011 95c. *The Artist at Niagara, 1858* (Cornelius Krieghoff) 1·25 1·75

732 Tall Ships, Halifax Harbour

2000. Tall Ships Race. Multicoloured. Self-adhesive.

2012 46c. Type **732** 75 85

2013 46c. Tall ships, Halifax Harbour (face value top right) 75 85

Nos. 2012/13 are arranged as five *se-tenant* pairs on a background photograph of Halifax Harbour.

733 Workers, Factory and Transport

2000. Centenary of Department of Labour.

2014 **733** 46c. multicoloured 50 50

734 Petro-Canada Sign, Oil Rig and Consumers

2000. 25th Anniv of Petro-Canada (oil company). Self-adhesive.

2015 **734** 46c. multicoloured 75 50

735 Narwhal

2000. Whales. Multicoloured.

2016 46c. Type **735** 1·40 1·40

2017 46c. Blue whale (*Balaenoptera musculus*) 1·40 1·40

2018 46c. Bowhead whale (*Balaena mysticetus*) 1·40 1·40

2019 46c. White whales (*Delphinapterus leucas*) 1·40 1·40

Nos. 2016/19 were printed together, *se-tenant*, with the backgrounds forming an overall composite design.

736

2000. "Picture Postage" Christmas Greetings. Self-adhesive.

2020 **736** 46c. multicoloured 50 50

See also Nos. 2045/9 and 2099/103.

737 *The Nativity* (Susie Matthias)

2000. Christmas. Religious Paintings by Mouth and Foot Artists. Multicoloured.

2021 46c. Type **737** 50 20

2022 55c. *The Nativity and Christmas Star* (Michael Guillemette) 65 60

2023 95c. *Mary and Joseph journeying to Bethlehem* (David Allan Carter) 1·25 1·90

738 Lieut.-Col. Sam Steele, Lord Strathcona's Horse

2000. Canadian Regiments. Multicoloured.

2024	46c. Type **738**	75	75
2025	46c. Drummer, Voltigeurs de Quebec	75	75

739 Red Fox

2000. Wildlife. Multicoloured.

2026	60c. Type **739**	65	75
2027	75c. Grey wolf	1·25	1·25
2028	$1.05 White-tailed deer	1·10	1·25

740 Maple Leaves

740a Maple Leaves and Key

740b Red Maple Leaf and Stem

2000. Self-adhesive coil stamp.

2029	**740**	47c. multicoloured	1·00	1·00
2030	**740**	48c. multicoloured	1·00	1·00
2031	**740a**	49c. multicoloured	1·00	1·00
2032	**740b**	80c. multicoloured	1·10	1·10
2036	**740b**	$1.40 multicoloured (green leaf)	1·90	1·90

2000. "Picture Postage" Greetings Stamps. As T **725** and **736**. Multicoloured. Self-adhesive.

2045	47c. Type **725**	55	60
2046	47c. Type **736**	55	60
2047	47c. Roses frame	55	60
2048	47c. Mahogany frame	55	60
2049	47c. Silver frame	55	60

741 Green Jade Snake

2001. Chinese New Year. ("Year of the Snake").

2050	**741**	47c. multicoloured	50	50
MS2051		112×75 mm. $1.05, Brown jade snake	1·25	1·60

2001. National Hockey League. All-Star Game Players (2nd series). As T **722**. Multicoloured.

2052	47c. Jean Beliveau (wearing No. 4)	75	75
2053	47c. Terry Sawchuk (on one knee)	75	75
2054	47c. Eddie Shore (wearing No. 2)	75	75
2055	47c. Denis Potvin (wearing No. 5)	75	75
2056	47c. Bobby Hull (wearing No. 9)	75	75
2057	47c. Syl Apps (in Toronto jersey)	75	75

See also Nos. 2118/23 and 2178/83.

2001. Birds (6th series). As T **643**. Multicoloured. Ordinary or self-adhesive gum.

2058	47c. Golden eagle	75	75
2059	47c. Arctic tern	75	75
2060	47c. Rock ptarmigan	75	75
2061	47c. Lapland bunting ("Lapland Longspur")	75	75

742 Highjumping

2001. Fourth Francophonie Games. Multicoloured.

2066	47c. Type **742**	70	70
2067	47c. Folk dancing	70	70

743 Ice Dancing

2001. World Figure Skating Championships, Vancouver. Multicoloured.

2068	47c. Type **743**	80	80
2069	47c. Pairs	80	80
2070	47c. Men's singles	80	80
2071	47c. Women's singles	80	80

744 3d. Beaver Stamp of 1851

2001. 150th Anniv of the Canadian Postal Service.

2072	**744**	47c. multicoloured	1·00	1·00

745 Toronto Blue Jay Emblem, Maple Leaf and Baseball

2001. 25th Season of the Toronto Blue Jays (baseball team). Self-adhesive.

2073	**745**	47c. multicoloured	60	70

746 North and South America on Globe

2001. Summit of the Americas, Quebec.

2074	**746**	47c. multicoloured	1·00	50

747 Butchart Gardens, British Columbia

2001. Tourist Attractions (1st series). Multicoloured. Self-adhesive.

2075	60c. Type **747**	95	1·10
2076	60c. Apple Blossom Festival, Nova Scotia	95	1·10
2077	60c. White Pass and Yukon Route	95	1·10
2078	60c. Sugar Bushes, Quebec	95	1·10
2079	60c. Court House, Niagra-on-the-Lake, Ontario	95	1·10
2080	$1.05 The Forks, Winnipeg, Manitoba	1·40	1·60
2081	$1.05 Barkerville, British Colombia	1·40	1·60
2082	$1.05 Canadian Tulip Festival, Ontario	1·40	1·60
2083	$1.05 Auyuittuq National Park, Nunavut	1·40	1·60
2084	$1.05 Signal Hill, St. John's, Newfoundland	1·40	1·60

See also Nos. 2143/52, 2205/14 and 2257/61.

748 Christ on Palm Sunday and Khachkar (stone cross)

2001. 1700th Anniv of Armenian Church.

2085	**748**	47c. multicoloured	60	70

749 Cadets, Mackenzie Building and Military Equipment

2001. 125th Anniv of Royal Military College of Canada.

2086	**749**	47c. multicoloured	70	45

750 Pole-vaulting

2001. Eighth International Amateur Athletic Federation World Championships, Edmonton. Multicoloured.

2087	47c. Type **750**	80	1·00
2088	47c. Sprinting	80	1·00

751 *Pierre Trudeau* (Myfanwy Pavelic)

2001. Pierre Trudeau (former Prime Minister) Commemoration.

2089	**751**	47c. multicoloured	60	45
MS2090		128×155 mm. No. 2090×4	2·00	2·25

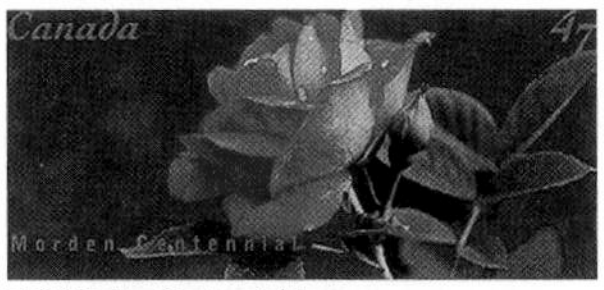

752 *Morden Centennial* Rose

2001. Canadian Roses. Multicoloured. Self-adhesive.

2091	47c. Type **752**	1·00	1·10
2092	47c. *Agnes*	1·00	1·10
2093	47c. *Champlain*	1·00	1·10
2094	47c. *Canadian White Star*	1·00	1·10
MS2095	145×90 mm. Nos. 2091/4	3·50	4·00

753 Ottawa Chief Hassaki addressing Peace Delegates

2001. 300th Anniv of Great Peace Treaty of Montreal between American Indians and New France.

2096	**753**	47c. multicoloured	60	70

2001. Canadian Art (14th series). As T **550**. Multicoloured.

2097	$1.05 *The Space Between Columns 21 (Italian)* (Jack Shadbolt)	1·40	1·75

754 Clown juggling with Crutches and Handicapped Boy

2001. The Shriners (charitable organization) Commemoration.

2098	**754**	47c. multicoloured	60	45

755 Toys and Flowers

2001. "Picture Postage" Greetings Stamps. Frames as Nos. 2045/7 and 2049, but each inscr "Domestic Lettermail Postes-lettres du regime interieur". Multicoloured. Self-adhesive.

2099	As Type **725**	60	60
2100	As Type **736**	60	60
2101	Type **755**	60	60
2102	Roses frame	60	60
2103	Silver frame	60	60

756 Jean Gascon and Jean-Louis Roux (founders of Theatre du Nouveau Monde, Montreal)

2001. Theatre Anniversaries. Multicoloured.

2104	47c. Type **756** (50th anniv)	65	80
2105	47c. Ambrose Small (founder of Grand Theatre, London, Ontario) (centenary)	65	80

757 Hot Air Balloons

2001. Stamp Collecting Month. Hot Air Balloons. Multicoloured, background colours given below. Self-adhesive.

2106	47c. Type **757** (green background)	80	90
2107	47c. Balloons with lavender background	80	90
2108	47c. Balloons with mauve background	80	90
2109	47c. Balloons with bistre background	80	90

758 Horse-drawn Sleigh and Christmas Lights

2001. Christmas. Festive Lights. Multicoloured.

2110	47c. Type **758**	70	20
2111	60c. Ice skaters and Christmas lights	1·00	1·00
2112	$1.05 Children with snowman and Christmas lights	1·40	1·90

759 Pattern of Ys Logo

2001. 150th Anniv of YMCA in Canada.

2113	**759**	47c. multicoloured	70	45

760 Statues from Canadian War Memorial, Ottawa and Badge

2001. 75th Anniv of Royal Canadian Legion.

2114	**760**	47c. multicoloured	70	45

761 Queen Elizabeth II and Maple Leaf

2002. Golden Jubilee.

2115	**761**	48c. multicoloured	70	45

762 Horse and Bamboo Leaves

2002. Chinese New Year ("Year of the Horse"). Multicoloured.

2116	**762**	48c. multicoloured	60	45
MS2117		102×102 mm. $1.25, Horse and peach blossom	1·40	1·75

2002. National Hockey League. All-Star Game Players (3rd series). As T **722**. Multicoloured.

2118	48c. Tim Horton (wearing Maple Leaf No. 7 jersey)	1·00	1·00
2119	48c. Guy Lafleur (wearing Canadiens No. 10 jersey)	1·00	1·00
2120	48c. Howie Morenz (wearing Canadiens jersey and brown gloves)	1·00	1·00
2121	48c. Glenn Hall (wearing Chicago Blackhawks jersey)	1·00	1·00
2122	48c. Red Kelly (wearing Maple Leaf No. 4 jersey)	1·00	1·00
2123	48c. Phil Esposito (wearing Boston Bruins No. 7 jersey)	1·00	1·00

763 Speed Skating

2002. Winter Olympic Games, Salt Lake City. Multicoloured.

2124	48c. Type **763**	75	85
2125	48c. Curling	75	85
2126	48c. Aerial skiing	75	85
2127	48c. Women's ice hockey	75	85

764 Lion Symbol of Governor General and Rideau Hall, Ottawa

2002. 50th Anniv of First Canadian Governor-General.

2128	**764**	48c. multicoloured	60	45

765 University of Manitoba (125th Anniv)

2002. Canadian Universities' Anniversaries (1st issue). Multicoloured.

2129	48c. Type **765**	85	85
2130	48c. Universite Laval, Quebec (150th anniv of charter)	85	85
2131	48c. Trinity College, Toronto (150th anniv of foundation)	85	85
2132	48c. Saint Mary's University, Halifax (bicent)	85	85

See also Nos. 2190/1, 2271/2, 2333/7, 2419, 2487 and 2544/5.

2002. Canadian Art (15th series). As T **550**. Multicoloured.

2133	$1.25 *Church and Horse* (Alex Colville)	1·40	1·60

766 *City of Vancouver* Tulip and Vancouver Skyline

2002. 50th Canadian Tulip Festival, Ottawa. Tulips. Multicoloured. Self-adhesive.

2134	48c. Type **766**	70	85
2135	48c. *Monte Carlo* and Dows Lake tulip beds	70	85
2136	48c. *Ottawa* and National War Memorial	70	85
2137	48c. *The Bishop* and Ottawa Hospital	70	85

767 *Dendronepthea gigantea* and *Dendronepthea* (coral)

2002. Canada–Hong Kong Joint Issue. Corals. Multicoloured.

2138	48c. Type **767**	70	85
2139	48c. *Tubastrea, Echinogorgia* and island	70	85
2140	48c. North Atlantic pink tree coral, Pacific orange cup and North Pacific horn coral	70	85
2141	48c. North Atlantic giant orange tree coral and black coral	70	85
MS2142	161×87 mm. Nos. 2138/41	2·25	3·00

2002. Tourist Attractions (2nd series). As T **747**. Multicoloured. Self-adhesive.

2143	65c. Yukon Quest Sled Dog Race	1·00	1·10
2144	65c. Icefields Parkway, Alberta	1·00	1·10
2145	65c. Train in Agawa Canyon, Northern Ontario	1·00	1·10
2146	65c. Old Port, Montreal	1·00	1·10
2147	65c. Saw mill, Kings Landing, New Brunswick	1·00	1·10
2148	$1.25 Northern Lights, Northwest Territories	1·75	2·00
2149	$1.25 Stanley Park, British Columbia	1·75	2·00
2150	$1.25 Head-Smashed-In Buffalo Jump, Alberta	1·75	2·00
2151	$1.25 Saguenay Fjord, Quebec	1·75	2·00
2152	$1.25 Lighthouse, Peggy's Cove, Nova Scotia	1·75	2·00

768 *Embacle* (Charles Daudelin)

2002. Sculptures. Multicoloured.

2153	48c. Type **768**	60	70
2154	48c. *Lumberjacks* (Leo Mol)	60	70

769 1899 Queen Victoria 2c. Stamp, Stonewall Post Office and Postmark

2002. Centenary of Canadian Postmasters and Assistants Association.

2155	**769**	48c. multicoloured	60	70

770 World Youth Day Logo

2002. 17th World Youth Day, Toronto. Self-adhesive.

2156	**770**	48c. multicoloured	60	70

2002. "Amphilex 2002" International Stamp Exhibition, Amsterdam. Ordinary gum.

MS2157	160×97 mm. As Nos. 2134/7	2·25	2·75

771 Hands gripping Rope and P.S.I. Logo

2002. Public Services International World Congress, Ottawa.

2158	**771**	48c. multicoloured	60	45

772 Tree in Four Seasons

2002. 75th Anniv of Public Pensions.

2159	**772**	48c. multicoloured	60	45

773 Mount Elbrus, Russia

2002. International Year of Mountains. Multicoloured. Self-adhesive.

2160	48c. Type **773**	70	85
2161	48c. Puncak Jaya, Indonesia	70	85
2162	48c. Mount Everest, Nepal	70	85
2163	48c. Mount Kilimanjaro, Tanzania	70	85
2164	48c. Vinson Massif, Antarctica	70	85
2165	48c. Mount Aconcagua, Argentina	70	85
2166	48c. Mount McKinley, U.S.A.	70	85
2167	48c. Mount Logan, Canada	70	85

774 Teacher writing on Board

2002. World Teachers' Day.

2168	**774**	48c. multicoloured	60	45

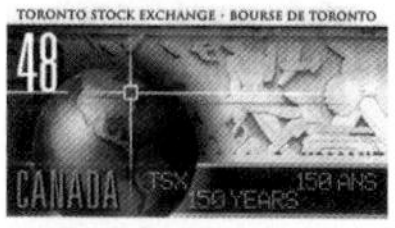

775 Frieze from Toronto Stock Exchange and Globe

2002. 150th Anniv of Toronto Stock Exchange.

2169	**775**	48c. multicoloured	60	45

776 Sir Sandford Fleming, Map of Canada and *Iris* (cable ship)

2002. Communications Centenaries. Multicoloured.

2170	48c. Type **776** (opening of Pacific Cable)	65	75
2171	48c. Guglielmo Marconi, Map of Canada and wireless equipment (first Transatlantic radio message)	65	75

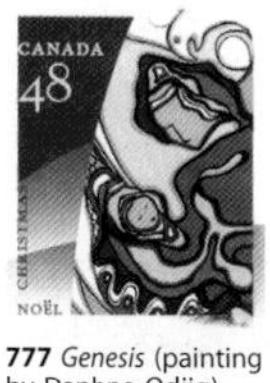

777 *Genesis* (painting by Daphne Odjig)

2002. Christmas. Aboriginal Art. Multicoloured.

2172	48c. Type **777**	55	20
2173	65c. *Winter Travel* (painting by Cecil Youngfox)	70	70
2174	$1.25 *Mary and Child* (sculpture by Irene Katak Angutitaq)	1·25	1·75

778 Conductor's Hands and Original Orchestra

2002. Centenary of Quebec Symphony Orchestra.

2175	**778**	48c. multicoloured	1·00	45

779 Sculpture of Ram's Head

2003. Chinese New Year ("Year of the Ram"). Multicoloured.

2176	48c. Type **779**	60	45
MS2177	125×103 mm. $1.25 Sculpture of goat's head (33×57 mm)	1·25	1·50

2003. National Hockey League. All-Star Game Players (4th series). As T **722**. Multicoloured. Ordinary or self-adhesive.

2178	48c. Frank Mahovlich (wearing Maple Leaf No. 27 jersey)	80	90
2179	48c. Raymond Bourque (wearing Boston Bruins No. 77 jersey)	80	90
2180	48c. Serge Savard (wearing Canadiens No. 18 jersey)	80	90
2181	48c. Stan Mikita (wearing Chicago Blackhawks No. 21 jersey)	80	90
2182	48c. Mike Bossy (wearing New York Islanders No. 22 jersey)	80	90
2183	48c. Bill Durnan (wearing Canadiens jersey and brown gloves)	80	90

779a Bishop's University, Quebec (150th anniv of university status)

2003. Canadian Universities' Anniversaries (2nd issue). Multicoloured.

2190	48c. Bishop's University, Quebec (150th anniv of university status)	70	75
2191	48c. University of Western Ontario, London (125th anniv)	70	75
2192	48c. St. Francis Xavier University, Nova Scotia (150th Anniv)	70	75
2193	48c. Macdonald Institute, University of Guelph, Ontana (centenary)	70	75
2194	48c. Universite de Montreal (125th anniv)	70	75

780 Leach's Storm Petrel

2003. Bird Paintings by John Audubon (1st series). Multicoloured. Ordinary gum.

2195	48c. Type **780**	85	85
2196	48c. Brent goose ("Brant")	85	85
2197	48c. Great cormorant	85	85
2198	48c. Common murre	85	85

(b) Self-adhesive.

2199	65c. Gyrfalcon (vert)	2·00	2·50

See also Nos. 2274/8 and 2340/4.

781 Ranger looking through Binoculars

2003. 60th Anniv of Canadian Rangers.

2200	**781**	48c. multicoloured	70	45

782 Greek Figure with Dove

2003. 75th Anniv of American Hellenic Educational Progressive Association in Canada.
2201 **782** 48c. multicoloured 70 45

783 Firefighter carrying Boy and Burning Buildings

2003. Volunteer Firefighters.
2202 **783** 48c. multicoloured 1·25 65

784 Queen Elizabeth II

2003. 50th Anniv of Coronation.
2203 **784** 48c. multicoloured 1·00 55

785 Quebec City (c. 1703) Seal and Excerpt from Letter

2003. Pedro da Silva (first official courier of New France).
2204 **785** 48c. multicoloured 70 55

2003. Tourist Attractions (3rd series). As T **747**. Multicoloured. Self-adhesive.

2205	65c. Wilberforce Falls, Nunavut	1·10	1·40
2206	65c. Inside Passage, British Columbia	1·10	1·40
2207	65c. Royal Canadian Mounted Police Depot Division, Regina, Saskatchewan	1·10	1·40
2208	65c. Casa Loma, Toronto	1·10	1·40
2209	65c. Gatineau Park, Quebec	1·10	1·40
2210	$1.25 Dragon boat race, Vancouver	1·75	1·90
2211	$1.25 Polar bear, Churchill, Manitoba	1·75	1·90
2212	$1.25 Niagara Falls, Ontario	1·75	1·90
2213	$1.25 Magdalen Islands, Quebec	1·75	1·90
2214	$1.25 Province House, Charlottetown, Prince Edward Island	1·75	1·90

2003. Vancouver's Successful Bid for Winter Olympic Games, 2010. No. 1368 (Canadian flag definitive) optd **VANCOUVER 2010**.
2215 48c. multicoloured 80 80

787 Mountains and Sea

2003. Canada–Alaska Cruise "Picture Postage". Multicoloured. Self-adhesive.

2216	(–) Type **787**	3·75	4·50
2217	(–) Tail fin of whale, mountains and sea	3·75	4·50

788 Assembly Logo

2003. Tenth Lutheran World Federation Assembly, Winnipeg.
2218 **788** 48c. multicoloured 70 55

789 Canadian F-86 Sabre Fighter Plane, Sailors and Infantrymen

2003. 50th Anniv of Signing of Korea Armistice.
2219 **789** 48c. multicoloured 70 55

790 Anne Hebert

2003. 50th Anniv of National Library of Canada. Showing authors and portions of their handwritten text. Multicoloured.

2220	48c. Type **790**	80	85
2221	48c. Hector de Saint-Denys Garneau	80	85
2222	48c. Morley Callaghan	80	85
2223	48c. Susanna Moodie and Catharine Parr Traill	80	85

791 Cyclists in Road Race

2003. World Road Cycling Championships, Hamilton, Ontario.
2224 **791** 48c. multicoloured 1·10 70

792 Marc Garneau

2003. Stamp Collecting Month. Canadian Astronauts. Multicoloured. Self-adhesive.

2225	48c. Type **792**	85	1·00
2226	48c. Roberta Bondar	85	1·00
2227	48c. Steve MacLean	85	1·00
2228	48c. Chris Hadfield	85	1·00
2229	48c. Robert Thirsk	85	1·00
2230	48c. Bjarni Tryggvason	85	1·00
2231	48c. Dave Williams	85	1·00
2232	48c. Julie Payette	85	1·00

793 Maple Leaves, Canada

2003. National Emblems. Multicoloured.

2233	48c. Type **793**	1·00	1·00
2234	48c. Cassis fistula flowers, Thailand	1·00	1·00
MS2235	120×96 mm. Nos. 2233/4	2·00	2·25

No. **MS**2235 commemorates Bangkok 2003 International Stamp Exhibition, Thailand.

Stamps of the same designs were issued by Thailand.

794 White Birds

2003. 80th Birth Anniv of Jean-Paul Riopelle (painter and sculptor). T **794** and similar horiz designs showing details from fresco *L'Hommage a Rosa Luxemburg*. Multicoloured.

MS2236 178×244 mm. 48c. Type **794**; 48c. Two white herons and white birds; 48c. Flying bird, flower and three white birds in cameo; 48c. Grouse on moor, white bird and sun; 48c. Two flying white birds in cameo and silhouette of falcon; 48c. Two white birds and cameo of flying duck 4·00 5·00

MS2237 159×95 mm. $1.25 Eggs and bird silhouette 2·00 2·50

795 Ice Skates and Wrapped Presents

2003. Christmas. Multicoloured.

2238	48c. Type **795**	70	55
2239	65c. Teddy bear and wrapped presents	1·25	1·50
2240	$1.25 Toy duck on wheels and wrapped presents	1·90	2·50

796 Queen Elizabeth II, 2002

2003. Self-adhesive.

2241	**796**	49c. black, mauve and scarlet	1·10	80
2242	**796**	50c. multicoloured	70	80

797 Monkey King on Cloud

2004. Chinese New Year ("Year of the Monkey"). Showing scenes from *Journey to the West* by Wu Ch'eng-en. Multicoloured.

2247	49c. Type **797**	1·00	70
MS2248	115×82 mm. $1.40 Monkey on road to India	1·90	2·25

2004. Hong Kong 2004 International Stamp Exhibition. No. **MS**2248 optd Hong Kong Stamp Expo 2004 and exhibition emblem in gold on sheet margin.
MS2249 115×82 mm. $1.40 Monkey on road to India 1·90 2·25

2004. National Hockey League. All-Star Players (5th series). As T **722**. Multicoloured. Ordinary or self-adhesive gum.

2250	49c. Larry Robinson (wearing Canadiens jersey)	1·40	1·40
2251	49c. Marcel Dionne (wearing Los Angeles Kings jersey)	1·40	1·40
2252	49c. Ted Lindsay (wearing Detroit Red Wings jersey)	1·40	1·40
2253	49c. Johnny Bower (wearing Toronto Maple Leafs goal keeper kit)	1·40	1·40
2254	49c. Brad Park (wearing New York Rangers jersey)	1·40	1·40
2255	49c. Milt Schmidt (wearing Boston Bruins jersey)	1·40	1·40

798 Bonhomme (Snowman), Quebec Winter Carnival

2004. Tourist Attractions (4th series). Multicoloured. Self-adhesive. Imperf.

2257	49c. Type **798**	1·25	1·40
2258	49c. St. Joseph's Oratory	1·25	1·40
2259	49c. Audience at International Jazz Festival, Montreal	1·25	1·40
2260	49c. People watching Traversee Internationale du Lac St-Jean	1·25	1·40
2261	49c. People at Canadian National Exhibition and Prince's Gate	1·25	1·40

799 Governor General Ramon Hnatyshyn

2004. 70th Birth Anniv of Governor General Ramon Hnatyshyn.
2262 **799** 49c. multicoloured 70 70

800 *Fram* (polar research ship)

2004. 150th Birth Anniv of Otto Sverdrup (polar explorer). Each purple and buff.

2263	49c. Type **800**	1·50	70
MS2264	166×60 mm. $1.40 As No. 2263 plus two labels	2·25	2·50

Stamps of similar designs were issued by Greenland and Norway.

801 Silhouettes of Cadets

2004. 125th Anniv of Royal Canadian Army Cadets. Self-adhesive. Imperf.
2265 **801** 49c. multicoloured 1·25 1·00

802 Subway Train, Toronto

2004. Light Rail Urban Transit. Multicoloured.

2266	49c. Type **802**	1·50	1·50
2267	49c. TransLink SkyTrain, Vancouver	1·50	1·50
2268	49c. Metro train, Montreal	1·50	1·50
2269	49c. CTrain, Calgary	1·50	1·50

803 Canadian Map and Employee

2004. 40th Anniv of Home Hardware (co-operative business). Self-adhesive.
2270 **803** 49c. multicoloured 90 90

2004. Canadian Universities Anniversaries (3rd series). As T **779a**. Multicoloured.

2271	49c. University of Sherbrooke (50th anniv)	90	90
2272	49c. University of Prince Edward Island (bicent)	90	90

804 Teddy Bears

2004. Centenary of Montreal Children's Hospital. Self-adhesive.
2273 **804** 49c. multicoloured 90 90

805 Ruby-crowned kinglet

2004. Bird Paintings by John Audubon (2nd series). Multicoloured. (a) Ordinary gum.

2274	49c. Type **805**	85	85
2275	49c. White-winged crossbill	85	85
2276	49c. Bohemian waxwing	85	85
2277	49c. Boreal chickadee	85	85

(b) Self-adhesive. Imperf.
2278 80c. Lincoln's sparrow 2·00 2·25

806 Sir Samuel Cunard

2004. Sir Samuel Cunard and Sir Hugh Allan (founders of transatlantic mail service) Commemorations. Multicoloured. Self-adhesive.

2279	49c. Type **806**	80	1·00
2280	49c. Sir Hugh Allan	80	1·00

Nos. 2279/80 were printed together, *se-tenant*, forming a composite design.

806a Butterfly on Flower

2004. "Write me...Ring me" Greetings Stamps. Multicoloured.

2280a	Type **806a**	2·00	2·00
2280b	Two young children at beach	2·00	2·00
2280c	Red rose	2·00	2·00
2280d	Pug (dog)	2·00	2·00

Nos. 2280a/d are inscribed "Domestic Lettermail" (initial value was 49c.).

807 Soldiers storming Juno Beach, Normandy

2004. 60th Anniv of D-Day Landings.

2281	**807**	49c. multicoloured	1·25	80

808 Pierre Dugua de Mons

2004. 400th Anniv of First French Settlement in Acadia, St. Croix Island (1st issue).

2282	**808**	49c. ochre, blue and orange	80	70

See also No. 2361, 2400 and 2508.

809 Spyros Louis (Greek athlete) and Marathon Runner

2004. Olympic Games, Athens, Greece. Multicoloured.

2283	49c. Type **809**	1·50	1·50
2284	49c. Girls playing football	1·50	1·50

810 Golfer and Trophy from Early Tournament

2004. Canadian Open Golf Championship. Multicoloured. Self-adhesive.

2285	49c. Type **810**	1·00	1·25
2286	49c. Golfer and trophy from modern tournament	1·00	1·25

811 Segmented Heart

2004. 50th Anniv of Montreal Heart Institute. Self-adhesive.

2287	**811**	49c. multicoloured	80	1·00

812 Goldfish in Bowl

2004. Pets. Multicoloured. Self-adhesive. Imperf.

2288	49c. Type **812**	1·10	1·25
2289	49c. Two cats on chair	1·10	1·25
2290	49c. Child with rabbit	1·10	1·25
2291	49c. Child with dog	1·10	1·25

813 Gerhard Herzberg (Chemistry, 1971)

2004. Nobel Chemistry Prize Winners. Multicoloured.

2292	49c. Type **813**	90	1·00
2293	49c. Michael Smith (Chemistry, 1993)	90	1·00

814 Maple Leaf in Photo Album Frame

2004. Picture Postage. Multicoloured. Self-adhesive.

2294	(49c.) Type **814**	90	1·00
2295	(49c.) Maple leaf in silver frame	90	1·00

Nos. 2294/2295 were both inscribed "Domestic Postage Paid" and sold for 49c.

815 Victoria Cross (embossed)

2004. 150th Anniv of First Canadian Recipient of the Victoria Cross. Multicoloured.

2296	49c. Type **815**	1·10	1·25
2297	49c. Victoria Cross and signature of Queen Elizabeth II	1·10	1·25

Nos. 2296/7 were printed together as sheetlets of 16 around a central illustration and the names of 94 Canadians who have received the Victoria Cross.

816 *Self-portrait*, 1974

2004. "Art Canada". Birth Centenary of Jean Paul Lemieux (artist). Multicoloured.

2298	49c. Type **816**	1·00	85
MS2299	150×86 mm. 49c. Type **815**; 80c. *A June Wedding*, 1972 (53×34 mm); $1.40 *Summer*, 1959 (64×31 mm)	4·50	5·00

817 Santa in his Sleigh and Reindeer

2004. Christmas. Multicoloured. Self-adhesive.

2300	49c. Type **817**	1·00	45
2301	80c. Santa sitting in a Cadillac and towing a house	1·60	2·00
2302	$1.40 Santa driving a train	2·50	3·00

818 Red Calla Lily

2004. Flowers. Multicoloured. (1st series) Self-adhesive.

2303	50c. Type **818**	70	80
2304	51c. Red bergamot	70	55
2305	85c. Yellow calla lily	1·00	1·25
2306	89c. Lady's slipper orchids	1·25	1·25
2307	$1.05 Pink fairy slipper orchids	1·50	1·60
2308	$1.45 purple Dutch iris	1·90	2·00
2309	$1.49 Himalayan blue poppies	1·90	2·00

Nos. 2305/9 come imperf.
See also Nos. 2470/**MS**2477 and 2530/**MS**2537.

819 Rooster facing East (right)

2005. Chinese New Year ("Year of the Rooster"). 35th Anniv of Diplomatic Relations with China (**MS**2315b). T **819** and similar multicoloured designs.

2314	50c. Type **819**	1·00	60
MS2315	Two sheets, each 105×82 mm. (a) $1.45 Rooster facing west (left) (40×41 mm). (b) $1.45 As No. **MS**2315a.	2·50	3·00

Nos. **MS**2315a/b both have a barcode tab attached at foot.

2004. National Hockey League. All-Star Game Players (6th series). As T **722**. Multicoloured. Ordinary or self-adhesive gum.

2316	50c. Henri Richard (wearing Habs jersey)	1·40	1·40
2317	50c. Grant Fuhr (wearing Oilers goal keeper kit)	1·40	1·40
2318	50c. Allan Stanley (wearing Toronto Maple Leafs jersey)	1·40	1·40
2319	50c. Pierre Pilote (wearing Chicago Black Hawks jersey)	1·40	1·40
2320	50c. Bryan Trottier (wearing New York Islanders jersey)	1·40	1·40
2321	50c. John Bucyk (wearing Boston Bruins jersey)	1·40	1·40

820 Alevin Fishing Fly

2005. Fishing Flies. Multicoloured. (a) Ordinary gum.

MS2328	190×112 mm. 50c.×4 Type **820**; Jock Scott; P.E.I. Fly; Mickey Finn	3·00	3·25

(b) Self-adhesive.

2329	50c. Type **820**	1·25	1·25
2330	50c. Jock Scott	1·25	1·25
2331	50c. Mickey Finn	1·25	1·25
2332	50c. P.E.I. Fly	1·25	1·25

2005. Canadian Universities Anniversaries (4th series). As T **779a** (No. 2190). Multicoloured.

2333	50c. Nova Scotia Agricultural College	80	75

821 Inukshuk of Five Rocks

2005. Expo 2005 International Exhibition, Aichi, Japan.

2335	**821**	50c. multicoloured	70	50

822 Yellow Daffodils

2005. Daffodils. Multicoloured. (a) Self-adhesive.

2336	50c. Type **822**	90	90
2337	50c. White daffodils with yellow trumpets	90	90

(b) Ordinary gum.

MS2338	120×80 mm. Nos. 2336/7	1·25	1·60

No. **MS**2338 also commemorates Pacific Explorer 2005 World Stamp Expo Exhibition, Sydney, Australia.

823 TD Bank Building of c.1900, Cashier and TD Tower, Toronto

2005. 150th Anniv of TD Bank Financial Group. Self-adhesive.

2339	**823**	50c. multicoloured	80	80

824 Horned Lark

2005. Bird Paintings by John Audubon (3rd series). Multicoloured. (a) Ordinary gum.

2340	50c. Type **824**	1·25	1·25
2341	50c. Piping plover	1·25	1·25
2342	50c. Stilt sandpiper	1·25	1·25
2343	50c. Willow ptarmigan	1·25	1·25

(b) Size 45×35 mm. Self-adhesive. Imperf.

2344	85c. Double-crested cormorant	1·90	2·25

825 Jacques Cartier Bridge, Montreal, Quebec

2005. Bridges. Multicoloured. Self-adhesive.

2345	50c. Type **825**	75	1·00
2346	50c. Souris Swinging Bridge, Manitoba	75	1·00
2347	50c. Angus L. Macdonald Bridge, Halifax, Nova Scotia	75	1·00
2348	50c. Canso Causeway, Nova Scotia	75	1·00

826 Magazine Covers of 1911, 1954, 1962 and 1917

2005. Centenary of Maclean's Magazine.

2349	**826**	50c. multicoloured	60	50

827 Saskatoon Berries and Osprey, Waterton Lakes National Park, Alberta, Canada

2005. Biosphere Reserves. Multicoloured.

2350	50c. Type **827**	1·10	1·10
2351	50c. Red Deer stags, Killarney National Park, Ireland	1·10	1·10
MS2352	120×70 mm. Nos. 2350/1	2·10	2·40

Stamps in similar designs were issued by Ireland.

828 Sailor Lookout, Canadian Navy Corvette and Survivors in Lifeboat

2005. 60th Anniv of Battle of the Atlantic.

2353	**828**	50c. multicoloured	1·00	60

829 Candle, Silhouettes, Memorial Cross GRV and New Museum Building

2005. Opening of New Canadian War Museum Building, Ottawa. Self-adhesive.

2354	**829**	50c. multicoloured	70	70

830 *Down in the Laurentides*

2005. "Art Canada". 150th Birth Anniv of Homer Watson (artist). Paintings. Multicoloured.

2355	50c. Type **830**	70	50
MS2356	150×87 mm. 50c. Type **830**; 85c. *The Flood Gate* (53×39 mm)	1·10	1·40

No. **MS**2356 also commemorates the 125th anniversary of the National Gallery of Canada.

831 Volunteer with Search Dog, Crashed Aircraft and Satellite

2005. Search and Rescue. Sheet 260×170 mm containing T **831** and similar vert designs. Multicoloured.

MS2357	50c.×2 Type **831**; 50c.×2 Rescuers, crew in life raft and sinking ship; 50c.×2 Seaman winched into helicopter and float plane; 50c.×2 Mountain rescue team with stretcher and satellite	6·50	6·50

832 Ellen Fairclough and Parliament Buildings, Ottawa

2005. Birth Centenary of Ellen Fairclough (first woman federal cabinet minister).

2358	**832**	50c. multicoloured	70	50

833 Diver spinning in mid-air

2005. 11th FINA (Federation Internationale de Natation) World Championships, Montreal. Multicoloured.

2359	50c. Type **833**	75	90
2360	50c. Swimmer in butterfly stroke	75	90

834 Port-Royal, 1605 (from drawing by Samuel de Champlain)

2005. French Settlement in North America (2nd issue). 400th Anniv of Founding of Port-Royal, Nova Scotia.

2361	**834**	50c. multicoloured	70	55

835 Chemicals Plant, Calgary Skyline, Mount Grassi and Railway Line

2005. Centenary of Alberta Province. Self-adhesive.

2362	**835**	50c. multicoloured	70	55

The backing paper is illustrated with four different scenes, each running across two stamps: Calgary Stampede; Jasper Avenue, Edmonton, 1963; Lake Minnewanka, Banff; and oil refinery of c. 1912.

836 Woman with Arms outstretched, Sunflowers and Legislature Building, Regina

2005. Centenary of Saskatchewan.

2363	**836**	50c. multicoloured	70	55

837 1930 50c. Acadian Memorial Church Stamp and Acadian Flag

2005. 250th Anniv of Deportation of French Settlers from Acadia (Nova Scotia) to British Colonies of North America.

2364	**837**	50c. multicoloured	80	60

838 Oscar Peterson

2005. 80th Birthday of Oscar Peterson (jazz composer and musician).

2365	**838**	50c. multicoloured	1·00	50
MS2366		112×116 mm. No. 2365×4	3·50	4·25

839 Children playing and discarded Leg Braces

2005. 50th Anniv of Mass Polio Vaccination in Canada.

2367	**839**	50c. multicoloured	70	50

840 Wall climbing

2005. Youth Sports. Multicoloured. Self-adhesive.

2368	50c. Type **840**	60	70
2369	50c. Skateboarding	60	70
2370	50c. Mountain biking	60	70
2371	50c. Snowboarding	60	70

841 *Puma concolor* (cougar)

2005. 35th Anniv of Canada—China Diplomatic Relations. Carnivores. Multicoloured.

2372	50c. Type **841**	60	70
2373	50c. *Panthera pardus orientalis* (Amur leopard)	60	70
MS2374	108×58 mm. Nos. 2372/3	1·25	1·60

Stamps of the same design were issued by China (People's Republic).

842 Snowman

2005. Christmas (1st issue). Self-adhesive.

2375	**842**	50c. multicoloured	70	50

843 Creche by Michel Forest

2005. Christmas (2nd issue). Showing Christmas creches. Multicoloured. Self-adhesive.

2376	50c. Type **843**	70	50
2377	85c. Creche with aboriginal figures by Keena (31×39 mm)	1·40	2·00
2378	$1.45 Creche by Sylvia Daoust (27×40 mm)	2·25	3·00

844 Chow

2006. Chinese New Year ("Year of the Dog"). Multicoloured.

2379	51c. Type **844**	60	60
MS2380	129×106 mm. $1.49 Chow with puppy	2·50	3·00

845 Queen Elizabeth II, Ottawa, 2002

2006. 80th Birthday of Queen Elizabeth II (1st issue). Self-adhesive.

2381	**845**	51c. multicoloured	70	70

See also No. **MS**2392.

846 Team Pursuit Speed Skating

2006. Winter Olympic Games, Turin, Italy. Multicoloured.

2382	51c. Type **846**	75	75
2383	51c. Skeleton (sled)	75	75

847 Trilliums and Black-throated Blue Warbler (Shade Garden)

2006. Gardens. Multicoloured. Self-adhesive.

2384	51c. Type **847**	1·25	1·25
2385	51c. Purple coneflowers and American painted lady butterfly (flower garden)	1·25	1·25
2386	51c. Water lilies and green darner dragonfly	1·25	1·25
2387	51c. Rock garden and blue-spotted salamander	1·25	1·25

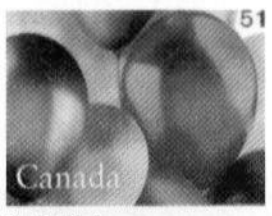

848 Balloons

2006. Greetings Stamp. Self-adhesive.

2388	**848**	51c. multicoloured	75	75

849 *The Field of Rapeseed*

2006. "Art Canada". Paintings by Dorothy Knowles. Multicoloured.

2389	51c. Type **849**	75	50
MS2390	150×87 mm. 51c. Type **849**; 89c. *North Saskatchewan River* (42×51 mm)	2·25	2·75

850 Hands enclosing Globe

2006. 50th Anniv of Canadian Labour Congress.

2391	**850**	51c. multicoloured	70	50

2006. 80th Birthday of Queen Elizabeth II (2nd issue). Sheet 125×75 mm. Multicoloured.

MS2392	$1.49×2 As Type **845** but 39×31 mm	4·75	5·50

851 Colophon emerging from Book

2006. Centenary of McClelland & Stewart (publishing house). Self-adhesive.

2393	**851**	51c. blue and silver	1·40	1·25

852 Mid 19th-Century Transformation Mask and Other Exhibits

2006. 150th Anniv of Canadian Museum of Civilization, Gatineau, Quebec. Self-adhesive.

2394	**852**	89c. multicoloured	1·75	2·25

853 Lorne Greene

2006. Canadians in Hollywood. Multicoloured. (a) Self-adhesive.

2395	51c. Type **853**	75	85
2396	51c. Fay Wray	75	85
2397	51c. Mary Pickford	75	85
2398	51c. John Candy	75	85

(b) Ordinary gum.

MS2399	180×63 mm. As Nos. 2395/8	3·25	3·75

854 Champlain's Ship

2006. French Settlement in North America (3rd issue). 400th Anniv of Samuel de Champlain's Survey of East Coast of North America.

2400	51c. ×2 Type **854**	70	50
MS2401	204×146 mm. 51c. Type **854**; 39c.×2, As Type **2879** of USA	1·00	1·25

No. **MS**2401 also commemorates Washington 2006 International Stamp Exhibition.

A self-adhesive stamp in the same design and an identical miniature sheet were also issued by the United States.

855 Girl watching Beluga Whale

2006. 50th Anniv of Vancouver Aquarium. Self-adhesive.

2402	**855**	51c. multicoloured	70	60

856 Pilot and Snowbirds

2006. 35th Anniv of Snowbirds Demonstration Team (431 Squadron). Multicoloured.

2403	51c. Type **856**	1·25	1·25
2404	51c. Snowbirds and emblem	1·25	1·25
MS2405	130×65 mm. Nos. 2403/4	2·50	2·50

857 James White (Chief Geographer), Proportional Dividers and Modern Map

2006. Centenary of *The Atlas of Canada*.

2406	**857**	51c. multicoloured	1·25	1·00

858 Player and Event Tickets

2006. World Lacrosse Championships, London, Ontario. Self-adhesive.

2407	**858**	51c. multicoloured	70	70

859 Early and Modern Climbers

2006. Centenary of the Alpine Club of Canada. Self-adhesive.

2408	**859**	51c. multicoloured	1·00	85

860 Barrow's Goldeneye

2006. Duck Decoys. Multicoloured.

2409	51c. Type **860**	1·10	1·10
2410	51c. Mallard (decoy with white ring around neck)	1·10	1·10
2411	51c. Black duck (plain brown decoy)	1·10	1·10
2412	51c. Red-breasted merganser (black and white decoy with red bill)	1·10	1·10
MS2413	130×145 mm. Nos. 2409/12	4·00	4·25

861 "g" as Beaver enclosing "50"

2006. 50th Anniv of the Society of Graphic Designers of Canada.

2414	**861**	51c. multicoloured	70	50

862 Glasses of Wine

2006. Canadian Wine and Cheese. Multicoloured. Self-adhesive.

2415	51c. Type **862**	80	90
2416	51c. Wine taster (horiz as Type **862**)	80	90
2417	51c. Canadian cheeses (wedge-shaped, 36×38 mm)	80	90
2418	51c. Serving cheese platter at fromagerie (wedge-shaped, 36×38 mm)	80	90

2006. Canadian Universities Anniversaries (5th series). Vert design as T **779a** (No. 2190). Multicoloured.

2419	51c. Macdonald College, Sainte-Anne-de-Bellevue, Quebec (centenary)	1·00	85

863 Newfoundland Marten

2006. Endangered Species (1st series). Multicoloured. (a) Self-adhesive.

2420	51c. Type **863**	1·10	1·10
2421	51c. Blotched tiger salamander	1·10	1·10
2422	51c. Blue racer	1·10	1·10
2423	51c. Swift fox	1·10	1·10

(b) Ordinary gum. Size 48×24 mm.

MS2424	160×74 mm. Nos. 2420/3	4·00	4·50

See also Nos. 2511/**MS**2515.

864 Maureen Forrester and Place des Arts, Montréal

2006. Canadian Opera Singers. Multicoloured.

2425	51c. Type **864**	1·10	1·10
2426	51c. Raoul Jobin and Palais Garnier, Paris	1·10	1·10
2427	51c. Leopold Simoneau, Pierrette Alarie and Opera-Comique, France	1·10	1·10
2428	51c. Jon Vickers and La Scala, Milan	1·10	1·10
2429	51c. Edward Johnson and Metropolitan Opera Company, New York	1·10	1·10

865 *Madonna and Child* (detail) (Antoine-Sebastien Falardeau)

2006. Christmas (1st issue). Self-adhesive.

2430	**865**	51c. multicoloured	85	55

866 *Snowman* (Yvonne McKague Housser)

2006. Christmas (2nd issue). Showing Christmas cards from 1931 *Painters of Canada* series. Multicoloured. Self-adhesive.

2431	51c. Type **866**	85	55
2432	89c. *Winter Joys* (J. E. Sampson)	1·75	2·25
2433	$1.49 *Contemplation* (Edwin Holgate)	2·25	3·25

867 Ice Fields and Fjord, Sirmilik National Park, Nunavut

2006. (a) Self-adhesive stamps inscr "P" instead of face value. Each showing Canadian flag. Multicoloured.

2434	(51c.) Type **867**	1·10	1·25
2435	(51c.) Coast and ancient trees, Chemainus, British Columbia	1·10	1·25
2436	(51c.) Polar bears, Churchill, Manitoba	1·10	1·25
2437	(51c.) Lighthouse at Bras d'Or Lake, Nova Scotia	1·10	1·25
2438	(51c.) Tuktut Nogait National Park, Northwest Territories	1·10	1·25
2439	(52c.) Sambra Island lighthouse, Nove Scotia (red and white striped)	1·40	1·40
2440	(52c.) Point Clark lighthouse, (trees at left)(above cliff) Ontario	1·40	1·40
2441	(52c.) Cap-des-Rosiers lighthouse, Quebec	1·40	1·40
2442	(52c.) Warren Landing lighthouse, Manitoba (in sandunes)	1·40	1·40
2443	(52c.) Pachena Point lighthouse, and keepers house, British Coloumbia	1·40	1·40
2444	(52c.) Pachena Point Lighthouse and part of keeper's house (at right)	1·40	1·40
2445	(57c.) Watson's Mill (three storey stone building), Manotick, Ontario	1·40	1·40
2446	(57c.) Keremeos Grist Mill (wooden building with waterwheel at left), British Columbia	1·40	1·40
2447	(57c.) Old stone Mill National Historic Site (four storey stone building with red doors), Delta, Ontario	1·40	1·40
2448	(57c.) Riordon Grist Mill (two storey stone building), Caraquet, New Brunswick	1·40	1·40
2449	(57c.) Cornell Mill (weir at right), Stanbridge East, Quebec	1·40	1·40

(b) Ordinary gum

MS2450	130x70 mm. As Nos. 2445/9 (ordinary gum)	6·25	7·00

Nos. 2434/8 were inscribed "P" and initially sold for 51c. each and Nos. 2439/43 were inscribed 'P' and initially sold for 52c. each and nos 2445/9 were all inscribed 'P' and initially sold for 57c.

868 Queen Elizabeth II, 2005

2006. Self-adhesive. Multicoloured.

2464	(51c.) Type **868**	90	90
2465	(52c.) Queen Elizabeth II, Saskatoon, 2005	1·00	1·00
2466	(54c.) Queen Elizabeth in Canada, 19 May 2005 (red background)	1·25	1·25
2467	(57c.) Queen Elizabeth II (wearing deep blue jacket and hat)	1·40	1·40
2467	(57c.) Queen Elizabeth II (wearing deep blue jacket and hat)	1·40	1·40

No. 2464 was inscribed 'P' and initially sold for 51c., and No. 2465 was inscribed 'P' and initially sold for 52c. No. 2466, in scribed 'P', and intially sold for 54c.No. 2467 inscribed 'P', was intiailly sold for 57c.

869 Spotted coralroot

2006. Flowers (2nd series). Multicoloured. Self-adhesive.

2470	**869**	(51c.) Spotted coralroot	60	35
2471	**869**	93c. Flat-leaved bladderwort	1·10	1·25
2472	**869**	$1.10 Marsh skullcap	1·25	1·50
2473	**869**	$1.55 Little larkspur	1·75	2·25

(b) Self-adhesive.

2474	93c. Flat-leaved bladderwort	1·10	1·25
2475	$1.10 Marsh skullcap	1·25	1·50
2476	$1.55 Little larkspur	1·75	2·25

(c) Ordinary gum.

MS2477	120×72 mm. As Nos. 2470/3	6·00	7·00

No. 2470 was inscribed "P" and initially sold for 51c. each.

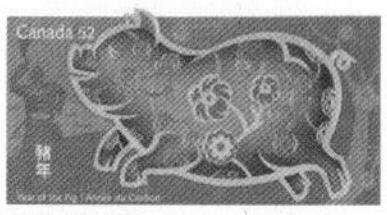

870 Pig

2007. Chinese New Year ("Year of the Pig"). Multicoloured.

2478	52c. Type **870**	1·25	60
MS2479	98×97 mm. $1.55 Pig (running to right)	2·25	2·75

No. 2479 is cut in a lantern shape.

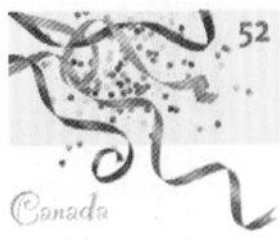

871 Ribbons and Confetti

2007. Greetings Stamp. Self-adhesive.

2480	**871**	52c. multicoloured	85	1·00

872 King Eider (*Somateria spectabilis*)

2007. International Polar Year. Multicoloured.

2481	52c. Type **872**	1·50	1·50
2482	52c. *Crossota millsaeare* (deep-sea jellyfish)	1·50	1·50
MS2483	105×70 mm. Nos. 2481/2	3·00	3·00

873 *Syringa vulgaris* "Princess Alexandra"

2007. Lilacs. Multicoloured. (a) Self-adhesive.

2484	52c. Type **873**	90	90
2485	52c. *Syringa×prestoniae* "Isabella"	90	90

(b) Ordinary gum.

MS2486	128×80 mm. As Nos. 2484/5	1·75	2·00

2007. Canadian Universities' Anniversaries (6th issue). As T **779a** (No. 2190). Multicoloured. Self-adhesive.

2487	52c. HEC (Ecole des hautes etudes commerciales), Montreal (centenary)	85	85
2488	52c. University of Saskatchewan	85	85

874 *Jelly Shelf*

2007. "Art Canada". Paintings by Mary Pratt. Multicoloured.

2489	52c. Type **874**	75	50
MS2490	150×87 mm. 52c. Type **874**; $1.55 *Iceberg in the North Atlantic* (62×40 mm)	3·00	3·50

875 Parliament Buildings, Ottawa, 2007 and Lumberers Regatta, 1860

2007. 150th Anniv of Ottawa as Capital of Canada. Self-adhesive.

2491	**875**	52c. multicoloured	1·00	85

(b) Ordinary gum.

MS2492	102×102 mm. 52c. As No. 2491; $1.55 As No. 2491	3·50	3·75

876 University of Lethbridge (Arthur Erickson), 1971

2007. Centenary of Royal Architectural Institute of Canada. Multicoloured.

2493 52c. Type **876** 1·00 1·00
2494 52c. St. Mary's Church (Douglas Cardinal), 1969 1·00 1·00
2495 52c. Ontario Science Centre (Raymond Moriyama), 1969 1·00 1·00
2496 52c. National Gallery of Canada (Moshe Safdie), 1988 1·00 1·00

877 Capt. George Vancouver

2007. 250th Birth Anniv of Captain George Vancouver (explorer of west coast of North America).

2497 **877** $1.55 multicoloured 2·50 2·50
MS2498 70×120 mm. **877** $1.55 multicoloured 2·50 3·00

878 Official U-20 World Cup Football and Canadian Team in Action

2007. FIFA U-20 World Cup, Canada.

2499 **878** 52c. multicoloured 1·00 85

879 Gordon Lightfoot

2007. Canadian Recording Artists (1st series). Multicoloured. (a) Self-adhesive.

2500 52c. Type **879** 1·00 1·10
2501 52c. Joni Mitchell 1·00 1·10
2502 52c. Anne Murray 1·00 1·10
2503 52c. Paul Anka 1·00 1·10

(b) Ordinary gum.

MS2504 Circular 105×105 mm. As Nos. 2500/3 3·25 4·00

880 Sunrise over Alexander Bay, Terra Nova National Park, Newfoundland

2007. 50th Anniv of Terra Nova National Park, Newfoundland. Self-adhesive.

2505 **880** 52c. multicoloured 1·00 1·00

881 Jasper National Park

2007. Centenary of Jasper National Park, Alberta. Self-adhesive.

2506 **881** 52c. multicoloured 1·00 1·00

882 Scouts forming Emblem

2007. Centenary of Scouting. Self-adhesive.

2507 **882** 52c. multicoloured 1·25 1·00

883 Membertou (Grand Chief of the Mi'kmaq) and French Settlement, Port Royal

2007. French Settlement in North America (4th issue). Chief Membertou.

2508 **883** 52c. multicoloured 1·00 85

884 Founding Members and Registry Roll

2007. Centenary of the Law Society of Saskatchewan.

2509 **884** 52c. multicoloured 1·00 1·00

885 Books, Photograph of James Muir Gavel (first President)

2007. Centenary of the Law Society of Alberta.

2510 **885** 52c. multicoloured 1·00 85

2007. Endangered Species (2nd series). As T **863**. Multicoloured. (a) Self-adhesive.

2511 52c. North Atlantic right whale 1·40 1·40
2512 52c. Northern cricket frog 1·40 1·40
2513 52c. White sturgeon 1·40 1·40
2514 52c. Leatherback turtle 1·40 1·40

(b) Ordinary gum. Size 48×24 mm.

MS2515 160×75 mm. As Nos. 2511/14 5·00 5·00

886 *Hippodamia convergens* and (convergent lady beetle)

2007. Beneficial Insects. . Multicoloured.

2516 1c. Type **886** 10 10
2517 2c. *Danaus plexippus* (monarch butterfly caterpilliar) 10 10
2518 3c. *Chrysopa oculata* (golden-eyed lacewing) 10 10
2518a 4c. *Polistes fuscatus* (paper wasp) 10 10
2519 5c. *Bombus polaris* (northern bumblebee) 10 10
2519a 6c. *Zelus luridus* (assassin bug) 15 10
2519b 7c. *Oncopeltus fasciatus* (large milkweed bug) 20 15
2519c 8c. *Chauliognathus marginatus* (margined leatherwing) 25 20
2519d 9c. *Chrysochus auratus* (dog-bane beetle) 25 20
2520 10c. *Aeshna canadensis* (Canada darner dragonfly) 25 20
2521 25c. *Hyalophora cecropia* (cecropia moth) 50 40
MS2522 133×58 mm. Nos. 2516/21 1·00 1·25
MS2523 133×58 mm. Nos. 2518*a* and 2519*a*/*d* 1·00 1·25

887 Reindeer

2007. Christmas (1st issue). Self-adhesive.

2526 **887** (52c.) multicoloured 1·00 85

No. 2526 was inscribed 'P' and initially sold for 52c.

888 Nativity ('HOPE')

2007. Christmas (2nd issue). Multicoloured. Self-adhesive.

2527 (52c.) Type **888** 1·00 85
2528 93c. Angel playing trumpet ('JOY') 2·00 2·50
2529 $1.55 Dove ('PEACE') 2·75 3·25

No. 2527 was inscribed 'P' and initially sold for 52c.

889 *Odontioda* Island Red

2007. Flowers (3rd series). Canadian Hybrid Orchids. Multicoloured. (a) Self-adhesive.

2530 (52c.) Type **889** 1·00 85
2531 96c. *Potinara* Janet Elizabeth 'Fire Dancer' 1·75 1·75
2532 $1.15 *Laeliocattleya* Memoria Evelyn Light 1·90 1·90
2533 $1.60 *Masdevallia* Kaleidoscope 'Conni' 2·75 3·00

(b) Ordinary gum.

MS2537 120×72 mm. As Nos. 2530/3 7·50 8·50

No. 2530 was inscribed 'P' and sold for 52c.

890 Rat Bride

2008. Chinese New Year ('Year of the Rat'). Multicoloured.

2538 52c. Type **890** 1·25 1·00
MS2539 130×100 mm. $1.60 Rat groom 2·75 3·25

891 Fireworks

2008. Greetings Stamp. Self-adhesive.

2540 **891** (52c.) multicoloured 1·25 1·25

No. 2540 was inscribed 'P' and initially sold for 52c.

892 *Paeonia lactiflora* 'Elgin'

2008. Peonies. Multicoloured. (a) Self-adhesive.

2541 52c. Type **892** 1·00 1·00
2542 52c. *Paeonia lactiflora* 'Coral 'n Gold' 1·00 1·00

(b) Ordinary gum.

MS2543 120×84 mm. As Nos. 2541/2 2·00 2·25

893 Dentistry Building, University of Alberta (centenary)

2008. Canadian Universities' Anniversaries (7th issue). Multicoloured. Self-adhesive.

2544 52c. Type **893** 1·00 1·00
2545 52c. Walter C. Koerner Library, University of British Columbia (centenary) 1·00 1·00

894 Ice Hockey Players

2008. International Ice Hockey Federation World Championship, Halifax and Quebec. Self-adhesive.

2546 **894** 52c. multicoloured 1·00 1·00

895 Guide Dog at Work

2008. Guide Dogs. Self-adhesive.

2547 **895** 52c. multicoloured 1·40 1·40

No. 2547 it has the face value in Braille.

896 Welder working on Pipeline

2008. Oil and Gas Industry. Multicoloured. Self-adhesive.

2548 52c. Type **896** 1·10 1·10
2549 52c. James Miller Williams (drilled first Canadian oil well, 1858) and Charles Tripp (developed bitumen deposits of southwest Ontario, 1850s) 1·10 1·10

897 Samuel de Champlain's Ship, Native Canoe and New Settlement of Quebec, 1608

2008. French Settlement in North America (5th issue). 400th Anniv of City of Quebec. Fluorescent frame.

2550 **897** 52c. multicoloured 1·00 90

A stamp in a similar design was issued by France.

898 Self-portrait

2008. Art Canada. Birth Centenary of Yousuf Karsh (portrait photographer). Multicoloured. (a) Ordinary gum.

2551 52c. Type **898** 1·00 90
MS2552 150×87 mm. 52c. Type **898**; 96c. Audrey Hepburn; $1.60 Winston Churchill 5·25 6·00

(b) Self-adhesive.

2553 96c. Audrey Hepburn 2·00 2·50
2554 $1.60 Winston Churchill 3·50 4·00

899 50 Cent Coin, 1908

2008. Centenary of the Royal Canadian Mint.

2555 **899** 52c. multicoloured 1·00 90

900 Nurse

2008. Centenary of Canadian Nurses Association. Self-adhesive.

2556 **900** 52c. multicoloured 1·10 1·10

901 Anne

2008. Centenary of Publication of *Anne of Green Gables* by Lucy Maud Montgomery. Multicoloured. (a) Self-adhesive.

2557 52c. Type **901** 1·00 1·00
2558 52c. Green Gables (house), Cavendish, Prince Edward Island 1·00 1·00

(b) Ordinary gum.

MS2559 124×72 mm. As Nos. 2557/8 1·75 2·00

2008. Canadians in Hollywood (2nd series). As T **853**. Multicoloured. (a) Self-adhesive.

2560 52c. Norma Shearer 1·25 1·25
2561 52c. Chief Dan George 1·25 1·25
2562 52c. Marie Dressler 1·25 1·25
2563 52c. Raymond Burr 1·25 1·25

(b) Ordinary gum.

MS2564	136×77 mm. As Nos. 2560/3	4·00	4·50

902 Athlete and Canadian Flag

2008. Olympic Games, Beijing. Self-adhesive.

2565	**902**	52c. multicoloured	1·40	1·40

903 Lifeguard and Water Rescue

2008. Centenary of Lifesaving Society. Self-adhesive.

2566	**903**	52c. multicoloured	1·00	1·00

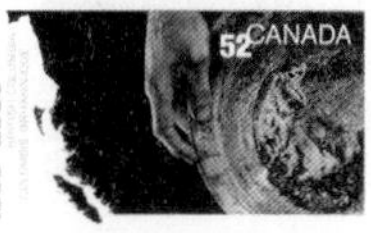

904 Panning for Gold

2008. 150th Anniv of British Columbia.

2567	**904**	52c. multicoloured	1·40	1·00

905 McLaughlin Buick, c. 1912 and Sam McLaughlin

2008. Sam McLaughlin (founder of McLaughlin Motor Car Company and philanthropist) Commemoration.

2568	**905**	52c. multicoloured	1·00	85

2008. Endangered Species (3rd series). As T **863**. Multicoloured. (a) Self-adhesive.

2569	52c. Prothonotary warbler	1·40	1·40
2570	52c. Taylor's checkerspot (butterfly)	1·40	1·40
2571	52c. Roseate tern	1·40	1·40
2572	52c. Burrowing owl	1·40	1·40

(b) Ordinary gum. Size 48×24 mm.

MS2573	160×75 mm. As Nos. 2569/72	5·00	5·50

906 Woman with Megaphone

2008. Mental Health. Self-adhesive.

2574	**906**	(52c.)+10c. multicoloured	1·25	1·40

No. 2574 was inscribed 'P+10' and initially sold for 52c. plus a 10c. surcharge for the Canada Post Foundation for Mental Health.

907 Québec City Skyline

2008. 12th Francophone Summit, Quebec.

2575	**907**	52c. multicoloured	1·00	85

908 Infant Jesus (creche figure by Antonio Caruso)

2008. Christmas (1st issue). Self-adhesive.

2576	**908**	(52c.) multicoloured	1·10	85

No. 2576 was inscribed 'P' and was initially valid for 52c.

909 Child making Snow Angels

2008. Christmas (2nd issue). Winter Fun. Showing children. (a) Self-adhesive.

2577	(52c.) Type **909**	1·10	85
2578	96c. Child skiing	1·90	2·25
2579	$1.60 Child tobogganing	3·00	3·50

(b) Ordinary gum.

MS2580	102×72 mm. As Nos. 2577/9	5·50	6·50

No. 2577 was inscribed 'P' and was initially valid for 52c.

910 Ox

2009. Chinese New Year. Year of the Ox. Multicoloured.

2581	(54c.) Type **910**	1·40	1·00
MS2582	40×140 mm. $1.65 Earthenware cooking pot by Shu-Hwei Kao	3·25	3·75

No. 2581 was inscribed 'P' and initially sold for 54c. It has a background flower pattern which extends over the stamps and sheet margins.

2009. China 2009 World Stamp Exhibition. No. MS2582 optd with **CHINA 2009** logo in gold on the sheet margin.

MS2583	40×140 mm. $1.65 Earthenware cooking pot by Shu-Hwei Kao	3·25	3·75

911 Freestyle Skiing

2009. Winter Olympic Games, Vancouver, 2010 (1st issue). Olympic Sports. Multicoloured. (a) Self-adhesive.

2584	(54c.) Type **911**	1·40	1·40
2585	(54c.) Snowboarding	1·40	1·40
2586	(54c.) Ice sledge hockey	1·40	1·40
2587	(54c.) Bobsleigh	1·40	1·40
2588	(54c.) Curling	1·40	1·40

(b) Ordinary gum.

MS2589	140×82 mm. As Nos. 2584/8	5·75	6·25

Nos. 2584/8 and stamps from **MS**2589 were all inscribed 'P' and initially sold for 54c. each.

912 Vancouver 2010 Winter Olympic Games Emblem

2009. Winter Olympic Games, Vancouver, 2010 (2nd issue). Mascots and Emblems. Multicoloured. (a) Self-adhesive.

2590	(54c.) Type **912**	1·00	1·25
2591	(54c.) Vancouver 2010 Paralympic Games emblem	1·00	1·25
2592	98c. Miga skiing	2·00	2·25
2593	$1.18 Sumi curling (12 Feb)	2·25	2·75
2594	$1.65 Quatchi playing ice hockey	3·25	3·75

(b) Ordinary gum.

MS2598	140×82 mm. As Nos. 2590/4	9·00	10·00

Nos. 2590/1 were initially sold for 54c. each.

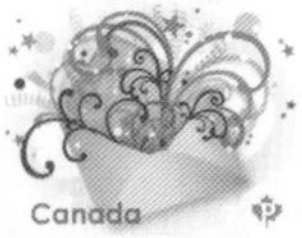

913 Stylized Ribbons, Fireworks and Confetti bursting from Envelope

2009. Greetings Stamp. 'Celebrate'. Self-adhesive.

2599	**913**	(54c.) multicoloured	1·10	1·00

No. 2599, inscribed 'P', was initially sold for 54c.

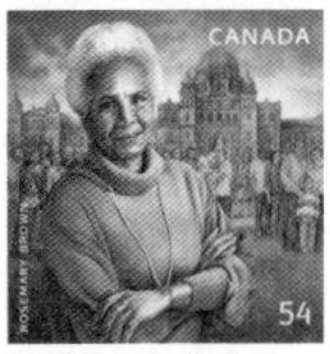

914 Rosemary Brown (civil rights campaigner) and BC Legislative Building

2009. Black History Month. Multicoloured.

2600	54c. Type **914**	1·00	1·25
2601	54c. Abraham Doras Shadd (holding lantern) and runaway slaves	1·00	1·25

915 Flight of *Silver Dart*, Bras d'Or Lake, Nova Scotia, 23 February 1909

2009. Centenary of First Powered Flight in Canada. Self-adhesive.

2602	**915**	(54c.) multicoloured	1·50	1·00

916 White Rhododendron with Pink Buds

2009. Rhododendrons. Multicoloured. (a) Self-adhesive.

2603	54c. Type **916**	1·10	1·25
2604	54c. Deep pink rhododendron	1·10	1·25

(b) Ordinary gum.

MS2605	120×74 mm. As Nos. 2603/4	2·00	2·50

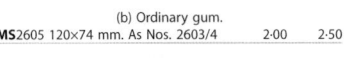

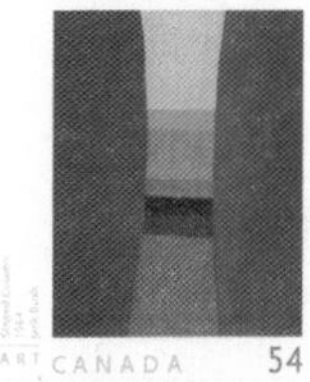

917 *Striped Column* (Jack Bush), 1964

2009. Art Canada. Birth Centenary of Jack Bush (artist). Design showing paintings. Multicoloured.

2606	54c. Type **917**	1·00	85
MS2607	150×87 mm. No. 2606; Chopsticks, 1977 (57×23 mm)	4·00	4·50

918 Horsehead Nebula and Dominion Astrophysical Observatory, Saanich, BC

2009. International Year of Astronomy. Multicoloured. (a) Self-adhesive.

2608	54c. Type **918**	1·10	1·25
2609	54c. Eagle Nebula and Canada-France-Hawaii Telescope, Mauna Kea, Hawaii	1·10	1·25

(b) Ordinary gum.

MS2610	101×90 mm. As Nos. 2608/9 but 30×40 mm	2·00	2·50

919 Polar Bear

2009. Preserve the Polar Regions and Glaciers. Multicoloured.

2611	54c. Type **919**	1·25	1·25
2612	54c. Arctic tern	1·25	1·25
MS2613	120×80 mm. Nos. 2611/12	2·50	2·50

920 Canadian Horse

2009. Canadian Horse and Newfoundland Pony. Multicoloured. Self-adhesive.

2614	54c. Type **920**	1·40	1·40
2615	54c. Newfoundland Pony	1·40	1·40

Nos. 2614/2615 form a composite background design.

921 Canadian Flag and Globe

2009. Centenary of Department of Foreign Affairs and International Trade.

2616	**921**	54c. multicoloured	1·25	1·00

922 Niagara Falls in 1909 and 2009

2009. Centenary of the Boundary Waters Treaty.

2617	**922**	54c. multicoloured	1·00	85

923 Robert Charlebois

2009. Canadian Recording Artists (2nd series). Multicoloured. (a) Self-adhesive.

2618	54c. Type **923**	80	90
2619	54c. Edith Butler	80	90
2620	54c. Stompin' Tom Connors	80	90
2621	54c. Bryan Adams	80	90

(b) Ordinary gum.

MS2622	Circular 105×105 mm. As Nos. 2618/21	4·00	4·50

924 Mr. PG, Prince George, British Columbia

2009. Roadside Attractions. Multicoloured. (a) Self-adhesive.

2623	54c. Type **924**	1·40	1·50
2624	54c. Sign Post Forest, Watson Lake, Yukon	1·40	1·50
2625	54c. Inukshuk (stone giant), Hay River, Northwest Territories	1·40	1·50
2626	54c. Pysanka (giant Easter egg), Vegreville, Alberta	1·40	1·50

(b) Ordinary gum.

MS2627	98×109 mm. As Nos. 2623/6	4·00	5·00

925 Captain Bartlett with Sextant and *Roosevelt* in the Canadian Arctic

2009. Captain Robert Abram 'Bob' Bartlett (Arctic explorer, ice captain and scientist) Commemoration.

2628	**925**	54c. multicoloured	1·25	85

No. 2628 commemorates the centenary of Capt. Bartlett's attempt to reach the North Pole.

926 Five-pin Bowling

2009. Canadian Inventions. Sports. Multicoloured. Self-adhesive.

2629	54c. Type **926**	1·25	1·40
2630	54c. Ringette	1·25	1·40
2631	54c. Lacrosse	1·25	1·40
2632	54c. Basketball	1·25	1·40

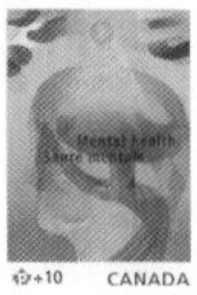

927 Tree and River inside Human Head and Sun breaking through Clouds

2009. Mental Health. Self-adhesive.

2633	**927**	(54c.)+10c. multicoloured	1·25	1·40

No. 2633 was inscr 'P+10' and was initially valid for 54c. plus a 10c. surcharge for the Canada Post Foundation for Mental Health.

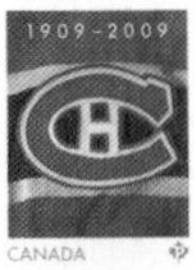

928 Detail from Maurice Richard's Hockey Sweater

929 Maurice Richard, 19 October 1957

2009. Centenary of Montreal Canadiens (ice hockey team). Multicoloured. Self-adhesive. (a)

2634	**928**	(54c.) multicoloured	1·25	1·25

(b) Sheet 130×100 mm containing T929 and similar horiz designs showing 500th goals of famous players.

MS2635	$3 Type **929**; Jean Beliveau, 11 February 1971; Guy Lafleur, 20 December 1983	18·00	20·00

No. 2634 was inscribed 'P' and originally valid for 54c.

The stamps within No. **MS**2635 are based on digital clips and use Motionstamp technology to show action replays of goals.

930 Two Soldiers (detail from National War Memorial, Ottawa)

2009. 'Lest We Forget'. (a) Self-adhesive.

2636	**930**	(54c.) multicoloured	1·10	1·10

(b) Ordinary gum.

MS2637	108×60 mm. As Type **930**×2	2·50	3·00

No. 2636 and the stamps within **MS**2637 were all inscr 'P' and were originally valid for 54c.

MS2637 was originally sold for $1.08.

931 Madonna and Infant Jesus

2009. Christmas (1st issue). Showing creche figures by Antonio Caruso. Multicoloured. (a) Self-adhesive.

2638	(54c.) Type **931**	1·25	95
2639	98c. Magi with gift	2·00	2·50
2640	$1.65 Shepherd carrying lamb	3·25	4·00

(b) Ordinary gum.

MS2641	150×100 mm. As Nos. 2576 and 2638/40	7·00	8·00

No. 2638 was inscr 'P' and was originally valid for 54c.

932 Christmas Tree

2009. Christmas (2nd issue). Self-adhesive.

2642	**932**	(54c.) multicoloured	1·10	85

No. 2642 was inscribed 'P' and was initially valid for 54c.

933 Tiger Seal

2010. Chinese New Year. Year of the Tiger.

2643	(54c.) Type **933**	1·25	1·00
MS2644	40×140 mm. 170c. Tiger's head seal	3·50	4·00

934 Striped Coralroot (*Corallorhiza striata*)

2010. Flowers (4th series). Wild Orchids. Multicoloured. (a) Self-adhesive coil stamps.

2645	(57c.) Type **934**	1·10	95
2646	$1 Giant helleborine (*Epipactis gigantea*)	2·25	2·00
2647	$1.22 Rose pogonia (*Pogonia ophioglossoides*)	2·40	2·75
2648	$1.70 Grass pink (*Calopogon tuberosus*)	3·50	3·75

(b) Self-adhesive.

2649	$1 As No. 2646	2·50	2·75
2650	$1.22 As No. 2647	2·75	3·25
2651	$1.70 As No. 2648	4·00	4·50

(c) Ordinary gum.

MS2652	120×72 mm. As Nos. 2645/8	9·25	9·75

No. 2645 was inscribed 'P' and originally sold for 57c.

935 Whistler, British Columbia

2010. Olympic Winter Games, Vancouver (3rd issue). Multicoloured. (a) Self-adhesive.

2653	57c. Type **935**	1·40	1·40
2654	57c. Vancouver	1·40	1·40

(b) Ordinary gum.

MS2655	141×83 mm. As Nos. 2653/4	2·75	3·25

936 William Hall, V.C. in 1900 and HMS *Shannon*

2010. Black History Month.

2656	**936**	57c. multicoloured	1·50	1·10

937 *Romeo LeBlanc* (Christan Nicholson)

2010. Romeo LeBlanc (former Minister of Fisheries and Governor General of Canada 1995–9) Commemoration.

2657	**937**	57c. multicoloured	1·25	1·10

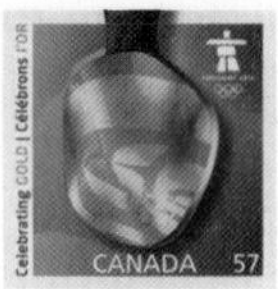

938 Vancouver 2010 Olympic Gold Medal

2010. Olympic Winter Games, Vancouver (4th issue). Canada's First Olympic Gold on Canadian Soil. (a) Self-adhesive.

2658	**938**	57c. multicoloured	1·40	1·25

(b) Ordinary gum.

MS2659	150×60 mm. As Type **938**×2	2·50	2·75

939 Child with Painted Face, Bobsleigh and Speed Skaters

2010. Olympic Winter Games, Vancouver (5th issue). Multicoloured. (a) Self-adhesive.

2660	57c. Type **939**	1·40	1·40
2661	57c. Child with painted face, Chandra Crawford with gold medal (Turin 2006) and skiers	1·40	1·40

(b) Ordinary gum.

MS2662	134×60 mm. As Nos. 2660/1	2·50	2·75

940 African Violet 'Decelles' Avalanche'

2010. African Violets. Multicoloured. (a) Self-adhesive.

2663	(57c.) Type **940**	1·40	1·40
2664	(57c.) African violet 'Picasso' (violet and white flowers)	1·40	1·40

(b) Ordinary gum.

MS2665	120×82 mm. As Nos. 2663/4	2·50	2·75

Nos. 2663/4 and the stamps within **MS**2665 were all inscr 'P' and were originally valid for 57c.

MS2665 was originally sold for $1.14.

941 Figures forming Maple Leaf and Star of David

2010. Canada–Israel, 60 Years of Friendship. Self-adhesive.

2666	**941**	$1.70 rosine, new blue and brownish grey	4·25	4·50

A similar design was issued by Israel,

942 *Tee Yee Neen Ho Ga Row*

2010. Four Indian Kings paintings by John Verelst. Multicoloured.

2667	57c. Type **942**	1·60	1·60
2668	57c. *Sa Ga Yeath Qua Pieth Tow*	1·60	1·60
2669	57c. *Ho Nee Yeath Taw No Row*	1·60	1·60
2670	57c. *Etow Oh Koam*	1·60	1·60
MS2671	168×75 mm. Nos. 2667/70	5·75	5·75

The portraits show representatives of the Iroquois and Algonquin nations who travelled to London in 1710 for an audience with Queen Anne.

2010. London 2010 Festival of Stamps. No. **MS**2671 optd with **LONDON 2010 FESTIVAL OF STAMPS** logo on the sheet margin.

MS2672	168×75 mm. Nos. 2667/70	5·00	5·50

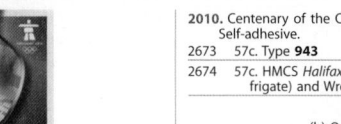

943 HMCS *Niobe* and Sailor, c. 1910

2010. Centenary of the Canadian Navy. Multicoloured. (a) Self-adhesive.

2673	57c. Type **943**	1·40	1·40
2674	57c. HMCS *Halifax* (modern frigate) and Wren	1·40	1·40

(b) Ordinary gum.

MS2675	108×64 mm. As Nos. 2673/4	2·75	3·00

944 Harbour Porpoise (Phocoena phocoena)

2010. . Each black, dull ultramarine and turquoise-blue.

2676	57c. Type **944**	1·40	1·40
2677	57c. Sea otter (*Enhydra lutris*	1·40	1·40
MS2678	105×69 mm. As Nos. 2676/7	2·50	2·75

Stamps of a similar design were issued by Sweden.

945 *Selasphorus rufus* (hummingbird) (Wing Yan Tam)

2010. Canadian Geographic's Wildlife Photography of the Year

(a) Self-adhesive. Die-cut perf 13

2679	57c. Type **945**	1·40	1·40
2680	57c. *Tachycineta bicolor* (tree swallows) (Mark Bradley)	1·40	1·40
2681	57c. *Tettigoniidae* (katydid) (Julie Bazinet) (vert)	1·40	1·40
2682	57c. *Ardea herodias* (great blue heron) (Martin Cooper) (vert)	1·40	1·40
2683	57c. *Vulpes vulpes* (red fox) (Ben Boulter) (vert)	1·40	1·40

(b) Ordinary gum. P 12½×13

MS2684	150×100 mm. As Nos. 2679/83	6·25	6·75

946 Man wearing Rotary Vest

2010. Centenary of Rotary International

2685	**946**	57c. multicoloured	1·40	1·40

947 *Rollande*, 1929

2010. Art Canada. Multicoloured.

2686	57c. Type **947**	1·25	1·10
MS2687	150×87 mm. 57c. Type **947**; $1.70 *At the Theatre*, 1928 (42×40 mm)	5·50	6·00

2010. Roadside Attractions (2nd series)

(a) Self-adhesive

2688	(57c.) The Coffee Pot, David-son, SK	1·40	1·40
2689	(57c.) Happy Rock, Gladstone, Manitoba	1·40	1·40
2690	(57c.) Goose, Wawa, Ontario	1·40	1·40
2691	(57c.) Puffin, Longue-Pointe-de-Mingan, Quebec	1·40	1·40

(b) Ordinary gum

MS2692	99×109 mm. As Nos. 2688/91	5·00	5·00

Nos. 2688/91 and the stamps within **MS**2692 were all inscr 'P' and were originally valid for 57c.

948 Guides

2010. Centenary of Girl Guides of Canada

2693	**948**	(57c.) multicoloured	1·40	1·40

No. 2693 was inscr 'P' and was originally valid for 57c.

949 Coins, Glass and Amber Trading Beads and 17th-century Map of Avalon Peninsula, Newfoundland

2010. 400th Anniv of Cupids, Newfoundland (first English settlement in Canada)

2694 **949** 57c. multicoloured 1·25 1·10

950 Immigrant Boy, Boy ploughing and SS *Sardinian*

2010. 'Home Children' (British orphaned and abandoned children sent to Canada)

2695 **950** 57c. multicoloured 1·25 1·10

951 Mental Health Patient on Road to Recovery

2010. Mental Health

2696 **951** (57c.)+10c. multicoloured 1·40 1·40

No. 2696 was inscr 'P+10' and was initially valid for 57c. plus a 10c. surcharge for the Canada Post Foundation for Mental Health.

952 Our Lady of the Night (sculpture by Antonio Caruso)

2010. Christmas (1st issue)

2697 **952** (57c.) multicoloured 1·25 1·10

953 Red Baubles

2010. Christmas (2nd issue). Multicoloured.

(a) Self-adhesive

2698 (57c.) Type **953** 1·25 1·10
2699 $1 Blue baubles 2·40 2·25
2700 $1.70 Pink baubles 3·75 3·50

(b) Ordinary gum

MS2701 116×60 mm. As Nos. 2698/700 7·50 7·75

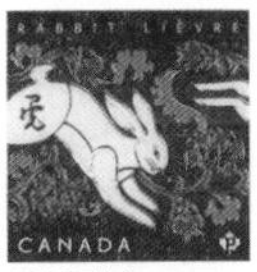

954 Rabbit

2011. Chinese New Year. Year of the Rabbit. Multicoloured.

2702 (59c.) Type **954** 1·25 1·10
MS2703 140x40mm. $1.75 Two rabbits (on medallion) 3·75 3·50

955 Arctic Hares

2011. Young Wildlife. Multicoloured.

(a) Self-adhesive coil stamps

2704 (59c.) Type **955** 1·25 1·10
2705 $1.03 Red fox cub 2·25 2·10
2706 $1.25 Two Canada geese goslings 2·75 2·50
2707 $1.75 Polar bear cub 3·75 3·50

(b) Self-adhesive

2708 $1.03 As No. 2705 2·25 2·10
2709 $1.25 As No. 2706 2·75 2·50
2710 $1.75 As No. 2707 3·75 3·50

(c) Ordinary gum

MS2711 120×72 mm. As Nos. 2704/7 10·00 9·50

No. 2704 was inscribed 'P' and originally sold for 59c.
Nos. 2712/27 are left for additions to this definitive series.

956 Canadian Flag on Soldier's Uniform and Helicopter lifting Supplies

2011. 'Canadian Pride'. Multicoloured.

(a) Self-adhesive booklet stamps

2728 (59c.) Type **956** 1·25 1·10
2729 (59c.) Canadian flag on hot air balloon 1·25 1·10
2730 (59c.) Canadian flag on search and rescue uniform and ship 1·25 1·10
2731 (59c.) Canadian flag on Canadarm 1·25 1·10
2732 (59c.) Canadian flag on back-pack and Colosseum, Rome 1·25 1·10

(b) Ordinary gum

MS2749 148×70 mm. As Nos. 2728/32 6·25 6·00

Nos. 2728/32 and the stamps within **MS**2749 were all inscr 'P' and originally valid for 59c. each.
Nos. 2733/48 are left for additions to this definitive series.

957 Carrie Best (journalist and civil rights campaigner)

2011. Black History Month. Multicoloured.

2750 59c. Type **957** 1·25 1·10
2751 59c. Fergie (Ferguson) Jenkins (baseball pitcher) 1·25 1·10

958 Wrapped Gift

2011. Greetings Stamp. 'Celebration'

2752 **958** (59c.) multicoloured 1·25 1·10

No. 2752, inscribed 'P', was initially valid for 59c.

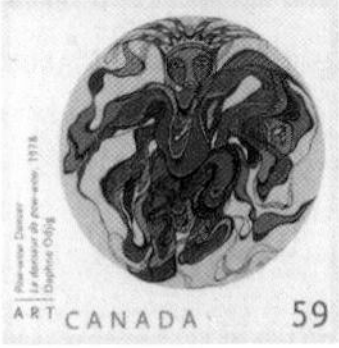

959 *Pow-wow Dancer*, 1978

2011. Art Canada. Paintings by Daphne Odjig

(a) Ordinary gum

2753 59c. Type **959** 1·25 1·10
MS2754 150×87 mm. 59c. Type **959**; $1.03 *Pow-wow*, 1969 (32×39 mm); $1.75 *Spiritual Renewal*, 1984 (55×39 mm) 7·50 7·25

(b) Self-adhesive

2755 $1.03 *Pow-wow*, 1969 (32×39 mm) 2·25 2·10
2756 $1.75 *Spiritual Renewal*, 1984 (55×39 mm) 3·75 3·50

960 Sunflower 'Prado Red'

961 Sunflower 'Sunbright'

2011. Sunflowers (*Helianthus annuus*)

(a) Coil stamps. Horiz designs as T **960**. Self-adhesive.

2757 (59c.) Type **960** 1·40 1·25
2758 (59c.) Sunflower 'Sunbright' 1·40 1·25

(b) Booklet stamps. Vert designs as T **961**. Self-adhesive

2759 (59c.) Sunflower 'Prado Red' 1·40 1·25
2760 (59c.) Type **961** 1·40 1·20

(c) Ordinary gum. Sheet 120×84 mm containing T **961** and similar vert design

MS2761 (59c.) Sunflower 'Prado Red'; (59c.) As Type **961** 2·50 2·25

Nos. 2757/60 and the stamps within **MS**2761 were all inscr 'P' and were originally valid for 59c.

962 Ram's Head

2011. Signs of the Zodiac. Multicoloured.

(a) Self-adhesive

2762 (59c.) Type **962** 1·40 1·25
2763 (59c.) Taurus (21.4.11) 1·40 1·25
2764 (59c.) Gemini (20.5.11) 1·40 1·25
2765 (59c.) Cancer (22.6.11) 1·40 1·25

(b) Ordinary gum

MS2774 128×128 mm. As Nos. 2762/5 (21.4.11) 5·50 5·00

Nos. 2762/5 and the stamps within **MS**2774 were all inscr P' and were originally valid for 59c.
Nos. 2666/73 and 2775/6 are left for additions to this series.

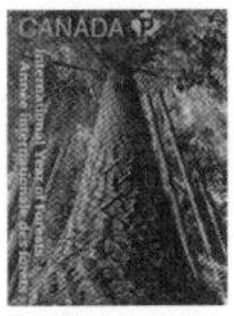

963 Tree

2011. International Year of Forests. Multicoloured.

(a) Self-adhesive

2777 (59c.) Type **963** 1·25 1·10
2778 (59c.) Forest floor with fungi 1·25 1·10

(b) Ordinary gum

MS2779 70×125 mm. As Nos. 2777/8 2·50 2·25

Nos. 2777/8 and the stamps within **MS**2779 form a composite design showing forest trees and undergrowth.
Nos. 2777/8 and the stamps within **MS**2779 were all inscr 'P' and were originally valid for 59c.

964 Prince William and Miss Catherine Middleton, November 2010

2011. Royal Wedding (1st issue). Multicoloured.

(a) Ordinary paper

2780 (59c.) Type **964** 1·25 1·10
2781 $1.75 Prince William and Miss Catherine Middleton embracing, November 2010 3·75 3·50
MS2782 120×83 mm. Nos. 2780/1 5·00 4·75
MS2783 As No. **MS**2782 but with gold crown on upper left sheet margin 5·00 4·75

(b) Self-adhesive

2784 (59c.) As Type **964** 1·40 1·25
2785 $1.75 As No. 2768 4·00 3·75

Nos. 2780 and 2784 were both inscr 'P' and originally valid for 59c.

965 Mail Barrel rigged with Sail and Rudder, Magdalen Islands, 1910

2011. Methods of Mail Delivery. Multicoloured.

2786 59c. Type **965** 1·25 1·10
2787 59c. Dog sled carrying mail in winter, northern Canada 1·25 1·10

Nos. 2786/7 were printed together, *se-tenant*, each pair forming a composite design.

966 Hiker, Moose and Eagle in Mountain Landscape

2011. Centenary of Parks Canada

2788 **966** 59c. multicoloured 1·40 1·25

967 Concrete Tower of Burrard Bridge, Vancouver

2011. Art Déco. Multicoloured.

(a) Self-adhesive

2789 (59c.) Type **967** 1·40 1·25
2790 (59c.) Wall of Cormier House with stone carving, Montreal 1·40 1·25
2791 (59c.) R. C. Harris Water Treatment Plant, Toronto 1·40 1·25
2792 (59c.) Detail from Supreme Court of Canada, Ottawa 1·40 1·25
2793 (59c.) Dominion Building, Regina 1·40 1·25

(b) Ordinary gum

MS2794 127×84 mm. As Nos. 2789/93 6·50 6·25

Nos. 2789/93 and the stamps within **MS**2794 were all inscr 'P' and were originally valid for 59c.

968 Duke and Duchess of Cambridge in State Landau

2011. Royal Wedding (2nd issue)

(a) Self-adhesive

2795 **968** (59c.) multicoloured 1·40 1·25

(b) Ordinary gum

MS2796 120×84 mm. As Type **968**×2 (sheet margin showing Westminster Abbey) 3·00 2·75
MS2797 120×84 mm. As Type **968**×2 (sheet margin showing Parliament Buildings, Canada and optd with gold maple leaf and 'Royal Tour 2011 From June 30 to July 8' in English and French) 3·00 2·75

No. 2795 and the stamps within **MS**2796/7 were inscr 'P' and were originally valid for 59c.

969 Ginette Reno

2011. Canadian Recording Artists (3rd series). Multicoloured.

(a) Self-adhesive

2798 (59c.) Type **969** 1·40 1·25
2799 (59c.) Bruce Cockburn 1·40 1·25
2800 (59c.) Robbie Robertson 1·40 1·25
2801 (59c.) Kate and Anna McGarrigle 1·40 1·25

(b) Ordinary gum

2802 (59c.) As Type **969** 1·40 1·25
2803 (59c.) As No. 2799 1·40 1·25
2804 (59c.) As No. 2800 1·40 1·25
2805 (59c.) As No. 2801 1·40 1·25
MS2806 Circular 105×105 mm. As Nos. 2798/801 10·00 9·50

Nos. 2798/5 and the stamps within **MS**2806 were all inscr 'P' and were originally valid for 59c.

2011. Roadside Attractions (3rd series). Multicoloured.

(a) Self-adhesive

2807 (59c.) The World's Largest Lobster, Shediac, New Brunswick 1·40 1·25
2808 (59c.) The Wild Blueberry, Oxford, Nova Scotia 1·40 1·25

2809	(59c.) The Big Potato, O'Leary, Prince Edward Island	1·40	1·25
2810	(59c.) The Giant Squid, Glover's Harbour, Newfoundland	1·40	1·25

(b) Ordinary gum

MS2811	98×109 mm. As Nos. 2807/10	6·50	6·25

Nos. 2807/10 and the stamps within **MS**2811 were all inscr 'P' and were originally valid for 59c.

970 *Miss Supertest III*

2011. *Miss Supertest III* (hydroplane, winner of Harmsworth Trophy 1959, 1960 and 1961) . Multicoloured.

(a) Self-adhesive

2812	(59c.) Type **970**	1·40	1·25

(b) Ordinary paper

MS2813	132×70 mm. As Type **970**; $1.75 *Miss Supertest III* in race	5·00	5·25

No. 2812 and the left-hand stamp within **MS**2813 were inscr 'P' and were originally valid for 59c.

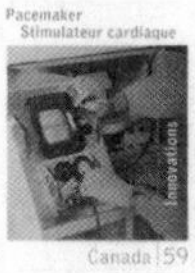

971 Cardiac Pacemaker

2011. Canadian Innovations. Multicoloured.

2814	59c. Type **971**	1·40	1·25
2815	59c. BlackBerry	1·40	1·25
2816	59c. Electric oven	1·40	1·25
2817	59c. Electric wheelchair	1·40	1·24

972 *The Puzzle* (Miriane Majeau)

2011. Mental Health. Multicoloured.

(a) Self-adhesive

2818	(59c.) Type **972**	1·50	1·40

(b) Ordinary gum

MS2819	118×100 mm. As Type **972**×2	3·25	3·00

No. 2818 and the stamps within **MS**2819 were inscr 'P+10' and were initially valid for 59c. plus a 10c. surcharge for the Canada Foundation for Mental Health.

973 Dr. John Charles Polanyi (Nobel Prize for Chemistry, 1986)

2011. International Year of Chemistry

2820	**973**	(59c.) multicoloured	1·25	1·10

No. 2820 was inscr 'P' and was originally valid for 59c.

974 Angel appearing to Joseph

2011. Christmas (1st issue). Stained-glass Windows from the Cathedral of the Immaculate Conception, Kingston, Ontario. Multicoloured.

(a) Self-adhesive

2821	(59c.) Type **974**	1·25	1·10
2822	$1.03 Nativity	2·25	2·10
2823	$1.75 Epiphany	3·75	3·50

(b) Ordinary gum

MS2824	105×60 mm. As Nos. 2821/3	7·25	7·50

975 Holly

2011. Christmas (2nd issue)

2825	**975**	(59c.) multicoloured	1·25	1·10

No. 2825 was inscr 'P' and was originally valid for 59c.

OFFICIAL STAMPS

1949. Optd **O.H.M.S.**

O162	**111**	1c. green (postage)	4·50	6·00
O163	**112**	2c. brown	12·00	12·00
O164	-	3c. purple (No. 378)	3·75	4·50
O165	**112**	4c. red	4·50	4·50
O171	-	7c. blue (No. 407) (air)	24·00	11·00
O166	-	10c. green (No. 402)	7·00	15
O167	-	14c. sepia (No. 403)	12·00	6·50
O168	-	20c. grey (No. 404)	12·00	1·00
O169	-	50c. green (No. 405)	£170	£140
O170	-	$1 purple (No. 406)	45·00	65·00

1949. Optd **O.H.M.S.**

O172	**135**	1c. green	4·50	3·00
O173	-	2c. sepia (No. 415)	3·50	3·50
O174	-	3c. purple (No. 416)	2·75	3·00
O175	-	4c. red (No. 417)	2·75	35
O176	-	5c. blue (No. 418)	7·50	2·75
O177	**141**	50c. green	42·00	45·00

1950. Optd **G.**

O178	**135**	1c. green (postage)	1·50	10
O179	-	2c. sepia (No. 415)	5·00	5·50
O180	-	2c. green (No. 415a)	1·75	10
O181	-	3c. purple (No. 416)	2·25	10
O183	-	4c. red (No. 417)	3·00	60
O184	-	5c. blue (No. 418)	6·00	2·25
O190	-	7c. blue (No. 407) (air)	24·00	15·00
O193	**153**	7c. blue	2·00	3·50
O185	-	10c. green (No. 402)	3·00	10
O191	**142**	10c. purple	4·00	1·00
O186	-	14c. sepia (No. 403)	23·00	12·00
O187	-	20c. grey (No. 404)	50·00	1·00
O194	-	20c. grey (No. 441)	2·00	20
O188	**141**	50c. green	17·00	23·00
O189	-	$1 purple (No. 406)	80·00	80·00
O192	-	$1 blue (No. 433)	80·00	85·00

1953. First Queen Elizabeth II stamps optd **G.**

O196	**158**	1c. brown	15	10
O197	**158**	2c. green	20	10
O198	**158**	3c. red	20	10
O199	**158**	4c. violet	30	10
O200	**158**	5c. blue	30	10

1953. Pictorial stamps optd **G.**

O206	**165**	10c. brown	70	80
O207	-	20c. green (No. 488)	3·25	30
O201	**160**	50c. green	3·25	4·25
O195	**154**	$1 black	8·00	15·00

1955. Second Queen Elizabeth II stamps optd **G.**

O202	**161**	1c. brown	65	20
O203	**161**	2c. green	15	20
O204	**161**	4c. violet	40	1·00
O205	**161**	5c. blue	15	10

1963. Third Queen Elizabeth II stamps optd **G.**

O208	**215**	1c. brown	50	5·50
O209	**215**	2c. green	60	5·50
O210	**215**	4c. red	60	2·25
O211	**215**	5c. blue	50	2·50

OFFICIAL SPECIAL DELIVERY STAMPS

1950. Optd **O.H.M.S.**

OS20	10c. green (No. S15)	17·00	32·00

1950. Optd **G.**

OS21	10c. green (No. S15)	26·00	30·00

POSTAGE DUE STAMPS

D1

1906

D1	**D1**	1c. violet	10·00	2·75
D3	**D1**	2c. violet	30·00	1·00
D5	**D1**	4c. violet	48·00	55·00
D7	**D1**	5c. violet	42·00	4·50
D8	**D1**	10c. violet	32·00	24·00

D2

1930

D9	**D2**	1c. violet	8·50	11·00
D10	**D2**	2c. violet	7·50	2·25
D11	**D2**	4c. violet	15·00	6·50
D12	**D2**	5c. violet	16·00	38·00
D13	**D2**	10c. violet	65·00	38·00

D3

1933

D14	**D3**	1c. violet	12·00	17·00
D15	**D3**	2c. violet	9·00	5·00
D16	**D3**	4c. violet	16·00	15·00
D17	**D3**	10c. violet	28·00	45·00

D4

1935

D18	**D4**	1c. violet	80	10
D19	**D4**	2c. violet	3·75	10
D20	**D4**	3c. violet	6·00	5·00
D21	**D4**	4c. violet	1·50	10
D22	**D4**	5c. violet	6·00	4·75
D23	**D4**	6c. violet	2·00	3·00
D24	**D4**	10c. violet	70	10

D5

1967. (a) Size 21×17½ mm.

D25	**D5**	1c. red	1·75	4·50
D26	**D5**	2c. red	1·00	1·00
D27	**D5**	3c. red	2·25	5·50
D28	**D5**	4c. red	2·75	1·25
D29	**D5**	5c. red	4·25	6·00
D30	**D5**	6c. red	1·60	3·75
D31	**D5**	10c. red	2·00	2·50

(b) Size 19½×16 mm.

D32	1c. red	1·00	30
D33	2c. red	1·00	3·00
D34	3c. red	3·25	5·00
D35	4c. red	1·00	60
D36a	5c. red	30	2·00
D37	6c. red	2·75	3·75
D38	8c. red	30	45
D39	10c. red	40	45
D40	12c. red	30	50
D41	16c. red	4·75	5·50
D42	20c. red	30	1·25
D43	24c. red	30	1·50
D44	50c. red	40	2·00

REGISTRATION STAMPS

R1

1875

R1	**R1**	2c. orange	60·00	1·00
R6	**R1**	5c. green	85·00	1·25
R9	**R1**	8c. blue	£400	£275

SPECIAL DELIVERY STAMPS

S1

1898

S2	**S1**	10c. green	60·00	13·00

S2

1922

S4	**S2**	20c. red	40·00	6·50

S3 Mail-carrying, 1867 and 1927

1927. 60th Anniv of Confederation.

S5	**S3**	20c. orange	12·00	14·00

S4

1930

S6	**S4**	20c. red	42·00	7·00

1932. As Type **S4**, but inscr "CENTS" instead of "TWENTY CENTS".

S7	20c. red	45·00	18·00

S5 Allegory of Progress

1935

S8	**S5**	20c. red	4·75	5·00

S6 Canadian Coat of Arms

1938

S9	**S6**	10c. green	21·00	4·00
S10	**S6**	20c. red	40·00	28·00

1939. Surch 10 10 and bars.

S11	10c. on 20c. red	10·00	18·00

S8 Coat of Arms and Flags

S9 Lockheed L.18 Lodestar

1942

S12	**S8**	10c. green (postage)	10·00	30
S13	**S9**	16c. blue (air)	6·00	45
S14	**S9**	17c. blue	4·50	55

1946

S15	10c. green (postage)	9·00	60
S16	17c. blue (air)	4·50	8·50

DESIGNS: 10c. As Type S **8** but with wreath of leaves; 17c. As Type S **9** but with Canadair DC-4M North Star airplane.

Pt. 22

CANAL ZONE

Territory adjacent to the Panama Canal leased by the U.S.A. from the Republic of Panama. The U.S. Canal Zone postal service closed on 30 September 1979.

1904. 100 centavos = 1 peso.
1906. 100 centesimos = 1 balboa.
1924. 100 cents = 1 dollar (U.S.).

1904. Stamps of Panama (with PANAMA optd twice) optd **CANAL ZONE** horiz in one line.

1	**5**	2c. red (No. 54)	£450	£350
2	**5**	5c. blue (No. 55)	£275	£180
3	**5**	10c. orange (No. 56)	£375	£225

1904. Stamps of the United States of 1902 optd CANAL **ZONE PANAMA**.

4	**103**	1c. green	36·00	20·00
5	**117**	2c. red	27·00	25·00
6	**107**	5c. blue	£100	60·00
7	**109**	8c. violet	£160	95·00
8	**110**	10c. brown	£140	80·00

1904. 1905 stamps optd **CANAL ZONE** in two lines.

9	**38**	1c. green	3·25	2·30
10	**38**	2c. red	5·00	3·00

1904. Stamps with PANAMA optd twice, optd **CANAL ZONE** in two lines or surch also.

11	**5**	2c. red (No. 54)	7·75	5·50
12	**5**	5c. blue (No. 55)	8·75	4·00
14	**5**	8c. on 50c. brown (No. 65)	35·00	25·00
13	**5**	10c. orange (No. 56)	23·00	13·50

1906. 1892 stamps surch PANAMA on both sides and **CANAL ZONE** and new value in centre between bars.

19	1c. on 20c. violet (No. 64)	2·20	1·70
22	2c. on 1p. red (No. 66)	3·00	3·00

1906. 1906 stamps optd **CANAL ZONE** vert.

26	**42**	1c. black and green	2·75	1·20
27	**43**	2c. black and red	3·50	1·50
28	**45**	5c. black and blue	6·50	2·50
29	**46**	8c. black and purple	23·00	8·75
30	**47**	10c. black and violet	22·00	8·75

1909. 1909 stamps optd **CANAL ZONE** vert.

35	**48**	1c. black and green	4·25	1·40
36	**49**	2c. black and red	5·00	1·50
37	**51**	5c. black and blue	19·00	4·25
38	**52**	8c. black and purple	13·00	6·50
43	**53**	10c. black and purple	55·00	9·25

1911. Surch **CANAL ZONE 10 cts.**

53	**38**	10c. on 13c. grey	6·50	2·50

1914. Optd **CANAL ZONE** vert.

54	10c. grey	55·00	13·50

1915. 1915 and 1918 stamps optd **CANAL ZONE** vert.

55	1c. black and green (No. 162)	11·00	7·00
56	2c. black and red (No. 163)	13·00	4·75
57	5c. black and blue (No. 166)	12·00	6·25
58	10c. black & orange (No. 167)	25·00	12·00
59	12c. black & violet (No. 178)	19·00	5·50
60	15c. black & blue (No. 179)	55·00	27·00
61	24c. black & brown (No. 180)	46·00	15·00
62	50c. black & orange (No. 181)	£300	£170
63	1b. black & violet (No. 182)	£190	70·00

1921. 1921 stamps optd **CANAL ZONE** vert.

64	**65**	1c. green	4·25	1·60
65	-	2c. red (No. 186)	3·25	1·40
66	**68**	5c. blue	12·00	3·75
67	-	10c. violet (No. 191)	20·00	8·25
68	-	15c. blue (No. 192)	55·00	19·00
69	-	24c. sepia (No. 194)	75·00	25·00
70	-	50c. black (No. 195)	£160	£100

1924. 1924 stamps optd **CANAL ZONE** vert.

72	**72**	1c. green	11·00	5·00
73	**72**	2c. red	8·25	3·00

1924. Stamps of the United States of 1922 optd **CANAL ZONE** horiz.

74	½c. sepia (No. 559)	1·90	80
75	1c. green (No. 602)	2·00	1·10
76	1½c. brown (No. 603)	2·75	1·90
103	2c. red (No. 604)	2·75	1·40
87	3c. violet (No. 638a)	4·00	3·50
88	5c. blue (No. 640)	5·00	3·25
106	10c. orange (No. 645)	19·00	11·00
90	12c. purple (No. 693)	25·00	15·00
141	14c. blue (No. 695)	5·00	3·75
92	15c. grey (No. 696)	8·25	5·00
93	17c. black (No. 697)	5·00	3·25
94	20c. red (No. 698)	8·00	3·50
95	30c. sepia (No. 700)	6·25	4·00
84	50c. mauve (No. 701)	85·00	49·00
97	$1 brown (No. 579)	£150	60·00

1926. Liberty Bell stamp of United States optd **CANAL ZONE**.

101	**177**	2c. red	5·50	4·25

22 Gen. Gorgas

24 Panama Canal under Construction

1928

107	**22**	1c. green	25	10
108	-	2c. red	25	10
109	**24**	5c. blue	1·10	45
110	-	10c. orange	25	20
111	-	12c. purple	80	65
112	-	14c. blue	95	75
113	-	15c. grey	45	35
114	-	20c. brown	65	20
115	-	30c. black	95	75
116	-	50c. mauve	1·60	70

PORTRAITS: 2c. Gen. Goethals. 10c. H. F. Hodges. 12c. Col. Gaillard. 14c. Gen. Sibert. 15c. Jackson Smith. 20c. Admiral Rousseau. 30c. Col. S. B. Williamson. 50c. Governor Blackburn.

1929. Air. Stamps of 1928 surch **AIR MAIL** and value.

124	-	10c. on 50c. mauve	9·25	6·50
117	**22**	15c. on 1c. green	8·75	6·00
125	-	20c. on 2c. red	5·25	1·60
119	-	25c. on 2c. red	3·75	2·20

36 Steamer, Panama Canal

1931. Air.

126	**36**	4c. purple	80	70
127	**36**	5c. green	65	35
128	**36**	6c. brown	80	40
129	**36**	10c. orange	1·10	40
130	**36**	15c. blue	1·40	40
131	**36**	20c. violet	2·20	40
132	**36**	30c. red	5·00	1·10
133	**36**	40c. yellow	3·75	1·20
134	**36**	$1 black	9·75	1·70

1933. No. 720 of United States optd **CANAL ZONE**.

140	3c. violet	3·00	35

38 Gen. Goethals

1934. 20th Anniv of Opening of Panama Canal.

142	**38**	3c. violet	25	20

45 Balboa (before construction)

1939. 25th Anniv of Opening of Panama Canal and 10th Anniv of Canal Zone Airmail Service. (a) Postage. As T **45**. Inscr "25TH ANNIVERSARY 1939 OPENING PANAMA CANAL 1914".

149	**45**	1c. green	70	35
150	-	2c. red	75	40
151	-	3c. violet	75	25
152	-	5c. blue	1·70	1·40
153	-	6c. orange	3·25	3·25
154	-	7c. black	3·50	3·25
155	-	8c. green	5·50	3·75
156	-	10c. blue	3·75	5·50
157	-	11c. green	8·75	8·75
158	-	12c. purple	9·25	8·25
159	-	14c. violet	9·25	8·25
160	-	15c. olive	13·00	6·50
161	-	18c. red	11·00	9·25
162	-	20c. brown	16·00	8·25
163	-	25c. orange	20·00	19·00
164	-	50c. purple	31·00	6·50

DESIGNS: 2c. Balboa (after construction); 3c., 5c. Gaillard Cut; 6c., 7c. Bas Obispo; 8c., 10c. Gatun Locks; 11c., 12c. Canal Channel; 14c., 15c. Gamboa; 18c., 20c. Pedro Miguel Locks; 25c.50c. Gatun Spillway.

(b) Air. Inscr "TENTH ANNIVERSARY AIR MAIL" and "25TH ANNIVERSARY OPENING PANAMA CANAL".

143	5c. black	4·25	2·50
144	10c. violet	3·75	3·25
145	15c. brown	5·50	1·10
146	25c. blue	14·00	8·75
147	30c. red	15·00	8·50
148	$1 green	38·00	30·00

DESIGNS—HORIZ: As Type **45**: 5c. Douglas DC-3 airplane over Sosa Hill; 10c. Douglas DC-3 airplane, Sikorsky S-42A flying boat and map of Central America; 15c. Sikorsky S-42A and Fort Amador; 25c. Sikorsky S-42A at Cristobal Harbour, Manzanillo Island; 30c. Sikorsky S-42A over Culebra Cut. $1 Sikorsky S-42A and palm trees.

1939. Stamps of United States (1938) optd **CANAL ZONE.**

165	**276**	½c. orange	20	10
166	-	1½c. brown (No. 801)	20	10

67 John F. Stevens

1946. Portraits.

188		½c. red (Davis)	45	25
189		1½c. brown (Magoon)	45	25
190		2c. red (Theodore Roosevelt)	20	20
191	**67**	5c. blue	40	20
192	-	25c. green (Wallace)	95	60

69 Northern Coati and Barro Colorado Island

1948. 25th Anniv of Establishment of Canal Zone Biological Area.

194	**69**	10c. black	1·90	85

70 Arriving at Chagres on the Atlantic Side

1949. Centenary of the Gold Rush.

195	**70**	3c. blue	70	25
196	-	6c. violet	70	35
197	-	12c. green	1·90	1·00
198	-	18c. mauve	2·20	1·60

DESIGNS: 6c. *Up the Chagres River to Las Cruces*"; 12c. *Las Cruces Trail to Panama*; 18c. *Leaving Panama for San Francisco*.

74 Western Hemisphere

1951. Air.

199	**74**	4c. purple	80	40
200	**74**	5c. green	1·10	65
201	**74**	6c. brown	55	25
202	**74**	7c. olive	1·10	50
210	**74**	8c. red	80	35
203	**74**	10c. orange	1·00	40
204	**74**	15c. purple	5·50	3·00
205	**74**	21c. blue	8·25	4·25
206	**74**	25c. yellow	13·00	3·00
207	**74**	31c. red	8·25	4·00
208	**74**	35c. blue	8·75	3·00
209	**74**	80c. black	5·00	1·60

75 Labourers in Gaillard Cut

1951. West Indian Panama Canal Labourers.

211	**75**	10c. red	3·25	1·60

76 Locomotive *Nueva Granada*, 1852

1955. Centenary of Panama Railway.

212	**76**	3c. violet	1·10	65

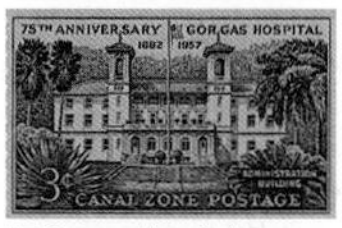

77 Gorgas Hospital

1957. 75th Anniv of Gorgas Hospital.

213	**77**	3c. black on green	50	40

78 *Ancon II* (liner)

1958

214	**78**	4c. turquoise	45	35

79 Roosevelt Medal and Map of Canal Zone

1958. Birth Centenary of Theodore Roosevelt.

215	**79**	4c. brown	65	35

80 "First Class" Scout Badge

1960. 50th Anniv of American Boy Scout Movement.

216	**80**	4c. ochre, red and blue	60	45

81 Administration Building, Balboa

1960

217	**81**	4c. purple	20	20

82 U.S. Army Caribbean School Crest

1961. Air.

221	**82**	15c. blue and red	1·90	80

83 Girl Scout Badge and Camp on Lake Gatun

1962. 50th Anniv of U.S. Girl Scout Movement.

222	**83**	4c. ochre, green and blue	45	35

84 Campaign Emblem and Mosquito

1962. Air. Malaria Eradication.

223	**84**	7c. black on yellow	55	45

85 Thatcher Ferry Bridge

1962. Opening of Thatcher Ferry Bridge.

224	**85**	4c. black and silver	40	25

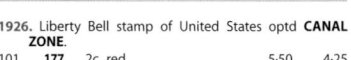

86 Torch of Progress

1963. Air. "Alliance for Progress".

225	**86**	15c. blue, green and black	1·60	95

87 Cristobal

1964. Air. 50th Anniv of Panama Canal.

226	**87**	6c. black and green	65	40
227	-	8c. black and red	65	40
228	-	15c. black and blue	1·40	80
229	-	20c. black and purple	1·70	1·10
230	-	30c. black and brown	3·00	2·50
231	-	80c. black and bistre	4·75	3·25

DESIGNS: 8c. Gatun Locks; 15c. Madden Dam; 20c. Gaillard Cut; 30c. Miraflores Locks; 80c. Balboa.

93 Seal and Jetliner

1965. Air.

232	**93**	6c. black and green	55	35
233	**93**	8c. black and red	50	20
234	**93**	10c. black and orange	40	20
235	**93**	11c. black and green	40	20
236	**93**	13c. black and green	95	25
237	**93**	15c. black and blue	80	20
238	**93**	20c. black and violet	85	35
239	**93**	22c. black and violet	1·20	2·20
240	**93**	25c. black and green	85	75
241	**93**	30c. black and brown	1·20	35
242	**93**	35c. black and red	1·40	2·20
243	**93**	80c. black and ochre	2·75	80

94 Goethal's Memorial, Balboa

1968

244	**94**	6c. blue and green	35	35
245	-	8c. multicoloured	40	20

DESIGN: 8c. Fort San Lorenzo.

96 Dredger *Cascadas*

1976

249	**96**	13c. black, green & blue	40	20

97 Electric Towing Locomotive

1978

251	**97**	15c. green and deep green	45	20

OFFICIAL STAMPS

1941. Air. Optd **OFFICIAL PANAMA CANAL**.

O167	**36**	5c. green	6·00	1·60
O168	**36**	6c. brown	13·00	5·50
O169	**36**	10c. orange	9·25	3·75
O170	**36**	15c. blue	12·00	4·25
O171	**36**	20c. violet	14·00	7·75
O172	**36**	30c. red	20·00	9·75
O173	**36**	40c. yellow	19·00	8·75
O174	**36**	$1 black	22·00	13·00

1941. Optd **OFFICIAL PANAMA CANAL**.

O180	**22**	1c. green	2·20	45
O181	**38**	3c. violet	4·00	80
O182	**24**	5c. blue	£1100	55·00
O183	-	10c. orange	8·25	2·20
O184	-	15c. grey (No. 113)	14·00	3·25
O185	-	20c. brown (No. 114)	16·00	3·75
O186	-	50c. mauve (No. 116)	41·00	9·75

67 John F. Stevens

1947. No. 192 optd **OFFICIAL PANAMA CANAL**.

O193	**67**	5c. blue	9·75	3·25

POSTAGE DUE STAMPS

1914. Postage Due stamps of United States of 1894 optd **CANAL ZONE** diag.

D55	**D87**	1c. red	95·00	22·00
D56	**D87**	2c. red	£275	47·00
D57	**D87**	10c. red	£1100	44·00

1915. Postage Due stamps of Panama of 1915 optd **CANAL ZONE** vert.

D59	**D58**	1c. brown	13·50	5·50
D60	-	2c. brown	£250	19·00
D61	-	10c. brown	55·00	11·00

1915. Postage Due stamps of Panama of 1915 surch **CANAL ZONE** vert and value in figures.

D62	**D58**	1c. on 1c. brown	£120	16·00
D63	-	2c. on 2c. brown	27·00	8·25
D66	-	4c. on 4c. brown	38·00	16·00
D64	-	10c. on 10c. brown	25·00	5·50

1925. Postage Due stamps of United States of 1894 optd **CANAL ZONE** horiz in two lines.

D92	**D87**	1c. red	8·75	3·25
D93	**D87**	2c. red	16·00	4·25
D94	**D87**	10c. red	£160	22·00

1925. Stamps of Canal Zone of 1924 optd **POSTAGE DUE**.

D89	1c. green (No. 75)	£100	16·00
D90	2c. red (No. 103)	25·00	7·75
D91	10c. orange (No. 106)	55·00	12·00

1929. No. 109 surch **POSTAGE DUE** and value and bars.

D120	**24**	1c. on 5c. blue	5·00	2·50
D121	**24**	2c. on 5c. blue	8·75	3·25
D122	**24**	5c. on 5c. blue	8·75	3·50
D123	**24**	10c. on 5c. blue	8·75	3·50

D37 Canal Zone Shield

1932

D135	**D37**	1c. red	20	20
D136	**D37**	2c. red	20	20
D137	**D37**	5c. red	40	20
D138	**D37**	10c. red	1·50	1·60
D139	**D37**	15c. red	1·20	1·10

Pt. 17

CANTON

A treaty port in S. China. Stamps issued at the French Indo-Chinese P.O., which was closed in 1922.

1901. 100 centimes = 1 franc.
1919. 100 cents = 1 piastre.

Stamps of Indo-China overprinted or surcharged.

CANTON
州廣
(1)

1901. "Tablet" key-type, optd with T **1**. The Chinese characters represent "Canton" and are therefore the same on every value.

1	**D**	1c. black and blue	1·50	2·00
2	**D**	2c. brown on yellow	2·00	2·75
3	**D**	4c. brown on grey	3·50	3·00
4	**D**	5c. green	1·80	2·00
6	**D**	10c. black on lilac	5·50	9·25
7	**D**	15c. blue	3·75	4·50
8	**D**	15c. grey	7·50	5·00
9	**D**	20c. red on green	18·00	25·00
10	**D**	25c. black on pink	14·00	10·00
11	**D**	30c. brown on drab	28·00	60·00
12	**D**	40c. red on yellow	55·00	65·00
13	**D**	50c. red on rose	38·00	65·00
14	**D**	75c. brown on orange	50·00	95·00
15	**D**	1f. green	70·00	75·00
16	**D**	5f. mauve on lilac	£250	£250

1903. "Tablet" key-type, surch. as T **1**. The Chinese characters indicate the value and therefore differ for each value.

17	1c. black on blue	3·00	8·25
18	2c. brown on yellow	6·00	8·00
19	4c. brown on grey	4·00	9·25
20	5c. green	3·00	9·25
21	10c. red	3·00	8·75
22	15c. grey	3·50	4·00
23	20c. red on green	15·00	34·00
24	25c. blue	7·50	14·00
25	25c. black on pink	13·00	14·50
26	30c. brown on drab	50·00	55·00
27	40c. red on yellow	75·00	80·00
28	50c. red on rose	£350	£325
29	50c. brown on blue	85·00	95·00
30	75c. brown on orange	£110	95·00
31	1f. green	80·00	90·00
32	5f. mauve on lilac	£100	95·00

1906. Surch **CANTON** (letters without serifs) and value in Chinese.

33	**8**	1c. green	2·00	4·75
34	**8**	2c. purple on yellow	1·60	2·75
35	**8**	4c. mauve on blue	1·50	2·50
36	**8**	5c. green	1·80	2·50
37	**8**	10c. red	4·50	4·75
38	**8**	15c. brown on blue	5·00	8·50
39	**8**	20c. red on green	3·50	6·50
40	**8**	25c. blue	3·75	3·00
41	**8**	30c. brown on cream	5·50	14·00
42	**8**	35c. black on yellow	2·75	6·50
43	**8**	40c. black on grey	7·00	16·00
44	**8**	50c. brown on cream	9·25	18·00
45	**D**	75c. brown on orange	75·00	95·00
46	**8**	1f. green	16·00	36·00
47	**8**	2f. brown on yellow	38·00	75·00
48	**D**	5f. mauve on lilac	£100	£120
49	**8**	10f. red on green	75·00	£120

1908. 1907 stamps surch **CANTON** and value in Chinese.

50	**10**	1c. black and brown	1·00	50
51	**10**	2c. black and brown	80	75
52	**10**	4c. black and blue	1·20	1·80
53	**10**	5c. black and green	1·40	80
54	**10**	10c. black and red	2·50	1·00
55	**10**	15c. black and violet	4·00	3·00
56	**11**	20c. black and violet	4·75	5·00
57	**11**	25c. black and blue	7·25	1·00
58	**11**	30c. black and brown	9·00	7·25
59	**11**	35c. black and green	10·00	7·50
60	**11**	40c. black and brown	20·00	7·75
61	**11**	50c. black and red	21·00	5·00
62	**12**	75c. black and orange	19·00	9·50
63	-	1f. black and red	40·00	22·00
64	-	2f. black and green	60·00	70·00
65	-	5f. black and blue	75·00	70·00
66	-	10f. black and violet	£120	£120

1919. As last, but additionally surch.

67	**10**	$\frac{2}{5}$c. on 1c. black and brown	90	4·50
68	**10**	$\frac{4}{5}$c. on 2c. black and brown	75	1·90
69	**10**	1$\frac{3}{5}$c. on 4c. black and blue	1·30	2·75
70	**10**	2c. on 5c. black and green	2·00	85
71	**10**	4c. on 10c. black and red	1·80	1·40
72	**10**	6c. on 15c. black & violet	2·50	1·40
73	**11**	8c. on 20c. black & violet	2·75	2·50
74	**11**	10c. on 25c. black & blue	6·50	45
75	**11**	12c. on 30c. black & brown	3·75	1·80
76	**11**	14c. on 35c. black & green	90	75
77	**11**	16c. on 40c. black & brown	2·00	1·80
78	**11**	20c. on 50c. black and red	4·50	45
79	**12**	30c. on 75c. black & orange	4·00	75
80	-	40c. on 1f. black and red	21·00	10·00
81	-	80c. on 2f. black and green	28·00	21·00
82	-	2p. on 5f. black and blue	16·00	40·00
83	-	4p. on 10f. black & violet	12·00	46·00

Pt. 9

CAPE JUBY

Former Spanish possession on the N.W. coast of Africa, ceded to Morocco in 1958.

100 centimos = 1 peseta.

1916. Stamps of Rio de Oro surch **CABO JUBI** and value.

1	**12**	5c. on 4p. red	£250	27·00
2	**12**	10c. on 10p. violet	55·00	27·00
3	**12**	15c. on 50c. brown	55·00	27·00
4	**12**	40c. on 1p. lilac	90·00	37·00

1919. Stamps of Spain optd **CABO JUBY**.

5	**38a**	$\frac{1}{4}$c. green	20	20
18	**66**	1c. green (imperf)	28·00	18·00
6	**64**	2c. brown	20	20
7	**64**	5c. green	70	45
8	**64**	10c. red	90	65
9	**64**	15c. yellow	3·75	3·50
10	**64**	20c. green	24·00	23·00
19	**64**	20c. violet	£140	47·00
11	**64**	25c. blue	3·50	1·80
12	**64**	30c. green	3·50	1·80
13	**64**	40c. orange	3·50	1·40
14	**64**	50c. blue	4·50	3·50
15	**64**	1p. red	12·00	11·00
16	**64**	4p. purple	50·00	50·00
17	**64**	10p. orange	70·00	70·00

1925. Stamps of Spain optd **CABO JUBY**.

19a	**68**	2c. green	£375	
20	**68**	5c. purple	5·50	4·25
21	**68**	10c. green	16·00	4·25
22	**68**	20c. violet	32·00	14·50

1926. As Red Cross stamps of Spain of 1926 optd **CABO-JUBY**.

23	**70**	1c. orange	17·00	17·00
24	-	2c. red	17·00	17·00
25	-	5c. brown	4·25	4·25
26	-	10c. green	2·10	2·10
27	**70**	15c. violet	1·50	1·50
28	-	20c. purple	1·50	1·50
29	**71**	25c. red	1·50	1·50
30	**70**	30c. green	1·50	1·50
31	-	40c. blue	50	50
32	-	50c. red	50	50
33	-	1p. red	50	50
34	-	4p. bistre	1·90	1·90
35	**71**	10p. violet	4·50	4·50

1929. Seville and Barcelona Exhibition stamps of Spain (Nos. 504/14) optd **CABO JUBY**.

36	-	5c. red	50	70
37	-	10c. green	50	70
38	**83**	15c. blue	50	70
39	**84**	20c. violet	50	70
40	**83**	25c. red	50	70
41	-	30c. brown	50	70
42	-	40c. blue	50	70
43	**84**	50c. orange	60	90
44	-	1p. grey	24·00	34·00
45	-	4p. red	35·00	55·00
46	-	10p. brown	35·00	55·00

1934. Stamps of Spanish Morocco optd **Cabo Juby**. (a) Stamps of 1928.

47	**11**	1c. red	1·90	1·40
48	**11**	2c. violet	4·25	2·75
49	**11**	5c. blue	4·25	2·75
50	**11**	10c. green	10·50	8·25
51	**11**	15c. brown	25·00	18·00
52	**12**	25c. red	4·25	2·75
53	-	1p. green	42·00	33·00
54	-	2p.50 purple	£100	70·00
55	-	4p. blue	£120	95·00

(b) Stamps of 1933.

56	**14**	1c. red	45	35
57	-	10c. green	2·75	2·10
58	**14**	20c. black	9·50	6·25
59	-	30c. red	9·50	6·25
60	**15**	40c. blue	31·00	25·00
61	**15**	50c. orange	60·00	47·00

1935. Stamps of Spanish Morocco of 1933 optd **CABO JUBY**.

62	**14**	1c. red	20	10
63	-	2c. green	60	50
64	-	5c. mauve	2·40	1·70
65	-	10c. green	16·00	11·00
66	-	15c. yellow	5·50	4·25
67	**14**	20c. black	5·50	4·25
68	-	25c. red	70·00	47·00
73	-	25c. violet	5·25	5·25
74	-	30c. red	5·25	5·25
75	-	40c. orange	7·50	7·50
76	-	50c. blue	15·00	15·00
77	-	60c. green	20·00	20·00
69	-	1p. grey	10·50	7·00
78	-	2p. brown	£110	£110
70	-	2p.50 brown	37·00	27·00
71	-	4p. green	60·00	45·00
72	-	5p. black	50·00	36·00

1937. First Anniv of Civil War. Nos. 184/99 of Spanish Morocco optd **CABO JUBY**.

79	1c. blue	50	50
80	2c. brown	50	50
81	5c. mauve	50	50
82	10c. green	50	50
83	15c. blue	50	50
84	20c. purple	50	50
85	25c. mauve	50	50
86	30c. red	50	50
87	40c. orange	1·50	1·50
88	50c. blue	1·50	1·50
89	60c. green	1·50	1·50
90	1p. violet	1·50	1·50
91	2p. blue	£110	£110
92	2p.50 black	£110	£110
93	4p. brown	£110	£110
94	10p. black	£110	£110

1938. Air. Nos. 203/12 of Spanish Morocco optd **CABO JUBY**.

95	5c. brown	20	20
96	10c. green	20	20
97	25c. red	20	20
98	40c. blue	3·75	3·75
99	50c. mauve	20	20
100	75c. blue	20	20
101	1p. brown	20	20
102	1p.50 violet	2·50	2·50
103	2p. red	5·50	5·50
104	3p. black	15·00	15·00

1939. As Nos. 213/16 of Spanish Morocco optd **CABO JUBY**.

105		5c. red	55	55
106		10c. green	55	55
107		15c. purple	55	55
108		20c. blue	55	55

1940. Nos. 217/32 of Spanish Morocco, but without "ZONA" on back, optd **CABO JUBY**.

109		1c. brown	15	15
110		2c. green	15	15
111		5c. blue	15	15
112		10c. mauve	15	15
113		15c. green	15	15
114		20c. violet	15	15
115		25c. brown	15	15
116		30c. green	15	15
117		40c. green	60	60
118		45c. red	60	60
119		50c. brown	60	60
120		75c. blue	2·00	2·00
121		1p. brown and blue	4·25	4·25
122		2p.50 green and brown	12·50	12·50
123		5p. brown and purple	12·50	12·50
124		10p. brown & deep brown	35·00	35·00

1942. Air. Nos. 258/62 of Spanish Morocco, but without "Z" opt and inscr **CABO JUBY**.

125		5c. blue	15	15
126		10c. brown	15	15
127		15c. green	15	15
128		90c. pink	55	55
129		5p. black	1·80	1·80

1944. Nos. 269/82 (agricultural scenes) of Spanish Morocco optd **CABO JUBY**.

130	-	1c. blue and brown	15	15
131	-	2c. light green & green	15	15
132	26	5c. green and brown	15	15
133	-	10c. orange and blue	15	15
134	-	15c. light green & green	15	15
135	-	20c. black and purple	15	15
136	-	25c. brown and blue	15	15
137	-	30c. blue and green	15	15
138	-	40c. purple and brown	15	15
139	26	50c. brown and blue	15	15
140	-	75c. blue and green	1·40	1·40
141	-	1p. brown and blue	1·40	1·40
142	-	2p.50 blue and black	4·00	4·00
143	-	10p. black and orange	27·00	27·00

1946. Nos. 285/94 (craftsmen) of Spanish Morocco optd **CABO JUBY**.

144		1c. brown and purple	25	25
145	27	2c. violet and green	25	25
146	-	10c. blue and orange	25	25
147	27	15c. green and blue	25	25
148	-	25c. blue and green	25	25
149	-	40c. brown and blue	25	25
150	27	45c. red and black	30	30
151	-	1p. blue and green	2·20	2·20
152	-	2p.50 green and orange	6·50	6·50
153	-	10p. grey and blue	20·00	20·00

1948. Nos. 307/17 (transport and commerce) of Spanish Morocco, but without "Z" on back, optd **CABO JUBY**.

154	30	2c. brown and violet	25	25
155	-	5c. violet and purple	25	25
156	-	15c. green and blue	25	25
157	-	25c. green and black	25	25
158	-	35c. black and blue	25	25
159	-	50c. violet and red	25	25
160	-	70c. blue and green	25	25
161	-	90c. green and mauve	25	25
162	-	1p. violet and blue	35	35
163	30	2p.50 green and purple	2·00	2·00
164	-	10p. blue and black	6·00	6·00

EXPRESS LETTER STAMPS

1919. Express letter stamp of Spain optd **CABO JUBY**.

E18	E53	20c. red	3·50	3·50

1926. Red Cross stamp. As Express letter stamp of Spain optd **CABO-JUBY**.

E36	E77	20c. black and blue	4·50	4·50

1934. Stamp of Spanish Morocco optd **Cabo Juby**.

E62	E12	20c. black	10·50	10·50

1935. Stamp of Spanish Morocco optd **CABO JUBY**.

E79	E16	20c. red	5·25	5·25

1937. No. E200 of Spanish Morocco optd **CABO JUBY**.

E95	E19	20c. red	1·50	1·50

1940. No. E233 of Spanish Morocco optd **CABO JUBY**.

E125	E21	25c. red	55	55

Pt. 1

CAPE OF GOOD HOPE

Formerly a British Colony, later the southern-most province of the Union of South Africa.

12 pence = 1 shilling;
20 shillings = 1 pound.

1 'Hope'

1853. Imperf.

18	1	1d. red	£250	£275
19	1	4d. blue	£225	£100
20	1	6d. lilac	£350	£475
8b	1	1s. green	£400	£550

3

1861. Imperf.

13	3	1d. red	£17000	£2750
14	3	4d. blue	£25000	£1900

4 'Hope' seated with vine and ram (with outer frame)

1864. With outer frame line. Perf.

23a	4	1d. red	£110	32·00
24	4	4d. blue	£160	4·50
52a	4	6d. purple	18·00	20
53a	4	1s. green	£150	50

6 (no outer frame line)

1868. Surch.

32		1d. on 6d. violet	£650	£130
33		1d. on 1s. green	£120	65·00
34	6	3d. on 4d. blue	£150	2·00
27		4d. on 6d. violet	£450	18·00

1880. No outer frame line.

48		½d. black	9·00	10
49		1d. red	12·00	10
36		3d. pink	£300	35·00
43		3d. purple	10·00	1·75
51		4d. blue	21·00	50
54		5s. orange	£150	8·50

1880. Surch **THREEPENCE**.

35		3d. on 4d. pink	£100	3·00

1880. Surch **3**.

37		"3" on 3d. pink	£110	1·75

1882. Surch **One Half-penny**.

47		½d. on 3d. purple	50·00	6·00

1882

61		½d. green	1·50	50
62		2d. brown	2·75	2·75
56		2½d. olive	20·00	10
63a		2½d. blue	10·00	10
64		3d. mauve	16·00	1·00
65		4d. olive	9·00	3·75
66		1s. green	90·00	7·50
67		1s. yellow	16·00	3·00

On the 2½d. stamps the value is in a white square at upper right-hand corner as well as at foot.

1891. Surch **2½d.**

55a		2½d. on 3d. mauve	7·00	20

1893. Surch **ONE PENNY**.

57a		1d. on 2d. brown	5·00	50

17 'Hope' standing. Table Bay in background

1893

58	17	½d. green	7·50	20
59a	17	1d. red	3·00	10
60	17	3d. mauve	6·00	2·75

18 Table Mountain and Bay and Arms of the colony

1900

69	18	1d. red	7·00	10

19

1902. Various frames.

70	19	½d. green	2·50	10
71	19	1d. red	2·50	10
72	19	2d. brown	20·00	80
73	19	2½d. blue	4·25	10·00
74	19	3d. purple	14·00	1·25
75	19	4d. green	17·00	65
76	19	6d. mauve	26·00	30
77	19	1s. yellow	18·00	1·25
78	19	5s. orange	£140	25·00

Pt. 9, Pt. 12

CAPE VERDE ISLANDS

Islands in the Atlantic. Formerly Portuguese; became independent on 5 July 1975.

1877. 1000 reis = 1 milreis.
1913. 100 centavos = 1 escudo.

1877. "Crown" key-type inscr "CABO VERDE".

1	P	5r. black	3·50	2·30
2a	P	10r. yellow	20·00	11·00
18	P	10r. green	3·00	2·30
3	P	20r. bistre	2·40	1·60
19	P	20r. red	5·75	4·00
4	P	25r. pink	2·40	1·60
20	P	25r. lilac	4·25	3·25
5	P	40r. blue	95·00	60·00
21	P	40r. yellow	4·25	2·25
15	P	50r. green	£300	£140
22	P	50r. blue	8·25	6·25
7b	P	100r. lilac	6·75	3·50
8	P	200r. orange	5·25	4·00
9b	P	300r. brown	6·25	5·25

1886. "Embossed" key-type inscr "PROVINCIA DE CABO-VERDE".

33	Q	5r. black	4·75	3·25
34	Q	10r. green	4·75	3·50
35	Q	20r. red	8·75	5·50
26	Q	25r. mauve	8·75	5·75
27	Q	40r. brown	8·75	3·50
28	Q	50r. blue	8·75	3·50
29	Q	100r. brown	8·75	5·00
30	Q	200r. lilac	19·00	11·00
31	Q	300r. orange	22·00	4·50

1894. "Figures" key-type inscr "CABO-VERDE".

37	R	5r. orange	1·70	1·40
38	R	10r. mauve	1·70	1·40
39	R	15r. brown	4·00	2·75
40	R	20r. lilac	4·00	2·75
41	R	25r. green	3·50	2·30
42	R	50r. blue	3·50	2·30
51	R	75r. red	12·00	6·25
43	R	80r. green	34·00	27·00
44	R	100r. brown on buff	9·75	5·50
58	R	150r. red on rose	34·00	29·00
59	R	200r. blue on blue	34·00	29·00
46	R	300r. blue on buff	39·00	18·00

1898. "King Carlos" key-type inscr "CABO VERDE".

60	S	2½r. grey	40	35
61	S	5r. orange	55	35
62	S	10r. green	55	35
63	S	15r. brown	5·72	2·10
111	S	15r. green	2·20	1·50
64	S	20r. lilac	1·70	95
65	S	25r. green	3·50	1·30
112	S	25r. red	1·20	25
66	S	50r. blue	3·50	1·60
113	S	50r. brown	4·50	3·00
114	S	65r. blue	29·00	18·00
67	S	75r. red	9·00	3·50
115	S	75r. purple	4·00	2·75
68	S	80r. mauve	9·00	3·50
69	S	100r. blue on blue	3·50	1·90
116	S	115r. brown on pink	18·00	12·00
117	S	130r. brown on yellow	19·00	12·00
70	S	150r. brown on yellow	9·00	5·25
71	S	200r. purple on pink	4·25	3·00
72	S	300r. blue on pink	10·50	5·25
118	S	400r. blue on yellow	20·00	12·50
73	S	500r. black on blue	10·50	5·25
74	S	700r. mauve on yellow	30·00	19·00

1902. Key-types of Cape Verde Is. surch.

119	S	50r. on 65r. blue	4·75	3·75
75	Q	65r. on 5r. black	5·75	4·00
78	R	65r. on 10r. mauve	7·25	4·00
79	R	65r. on 20r. lilac	7·25	4·00
80	R	65r. on 100r. brn on buff	9·25	5·50
76	Q	65r. on 200r. lilac	5·75	4·00
77	Q	65r. on 300r. orange	5·75	4·00
85	R	115r. on 5r. orange	4·25	3·25
82	Q	115r. on 10r. green	5·75	4·00
83	Q	115r. on 20r. red	5·75	4·00
87	R	115r. on 25r. green	3·00	2·30
88	R	115r. on 150r. red on rose	8·75	6·75
90	Q	130r. on 50r. blue	5·75	4·00
93	R	130r. on 75r. red	4·25	3·25
96	R	130r. on 80r. green	3·50	2·20
92	Q	130r. on 100r. brown	5·75	4·00
97	R	130r. on 200r. blue on blue	3·75	2·75
106	V	400r. on 2½r. brown	1·70	1·60
98	Q	400r. on 25r. mauve	3·00	2·75
99	Q	400r. on 40r. brown	5·75	5·00
101	R	400r. on 50r. blue	5·75	3·25
103	R	400r. on 300r. blue on buff	2·75	1·80

1902. "King Carlos" key-type of Cape Verde Is. optd **PROVISORIO**.

107		15r. brown	1·90	1·30
108		25r. green	1·90	1·30
109		50r. blue	1·90	1·30
110		75r. red	3·75	2·75

1911. "King Carlos" key-type of Cape Verde Is. optd **REPUBLICA**.

120		2½r. grey	35	30
121		5r. orange	35	30
122		10r. green	1·20	95
123		15r. green	1·00	50
124		20r. lilac	1·70	95
125		25r. red	1·00	50
126		50r. brown	10·50	7·25
127		75r. purple	1·60	95
128		100r. blue on blue	1·60	95
129		115r. brown on pink	1·60	95
130		130r. brown on yellow	1·60	95
131		200r. purple on pink	8·00	4·75
132		400r. blue on yellow	4·00	1·40
133		500r. black on blue	4·00	1·40
134		700r. mauve on yellow	4·00	1·40

1912. "King Manoel" key-type inscr "CABO VERDE" and optd **REPUBLICA**.

135	T	2½r. lilac	25	25
136	T	5r. black	25	25
137	T	10r. green	50	45
138	T	20r. red	3·00	1·60
139	T	25r. brown	50	25
140	T	50r. blue	5·75	4·00
141	T	75r. brown	1·30	1·20
142	T	100r. brown on green	1·30	1·20
143	T	200r. green on pink	2·10	1·20
144	T	300r. black on blue	2·10	1·20
145	T	400r. blue and black	4·50	3·50
146	T	500r. brown and olive	4·50	3·50

1913. Surch. **REPUBLICA CABO VERDE** and new value on "Vasco da Gama" issues of (a) Portuguese Colonies.

147		¼c. on 2½r. green	1·60	80
148		½c. on 5r. red	1·60	80
149		1c. on 10r. purple	1·60	80
150		2½c. on 25r. green	1·10	50
151		5c. on 50r. blue	2·20	1·80
152		7½c. on 75r. brown	4·50	3·50
153		10c. on 100r. brown	2·20	2·20
154		15c. on 150r. bistre	3·00	3·00

(b) Macao.

155		¼c. on ½a. green	1·60	1·00
156		½c. on 1a. red	1·60	1·00
157		1c. on 2a. purple	1·60	1·00
158		2½c. on 4a. green	1·60	1·00
159		5c. on 8a. blue	8·50	7·50
160		7½c. on 12a. brown	6·75	3·00
161		10c. on 16a. brown	2·75	2·00
162		15c. on 24a. bistre	7·25	4·00

(c) Timor.

163		¼c. on ½a. green	1·60	1·00
164		½c. on 1a. red	1·60	1·00
165		1c. on 2a. purple	1·60	1·00

166	2½c. on 4a. green	1·60	1·00
167	5c. on 8a. blue	8·75	7·00
168	7½c. on 12a. brown	6·75	3·75
169	10c. on 16a. brown	2·75	2·00
170	15c. on 24a. bistre	5·50	3·00

1913. Stamps of 1902 optd **REPUBLICA**.

171	S	75r. red (No. 110)	6·75	4·75
192	R	115r. on 5r. (No. 85)	1·70	95
193	Q	115r. on 10r. (No. 82)	3·00	1·90
195	Q	115r. on 20r. (No. 83)	3·25	2·10
198	R	115r. on 25r. (No. 87)	3·00	1·90
200	R	115r. on 150r. (No. 88)	1·00	95
201	Q	130r. on 50r. (No. 90)	3·00	1·60
202	R	130r. on 75r. (No. 93)	3·00	1·20
204	R	130r. on 80r. (No. 96)	3·00	1·20
206	Q	130r. on 100r. (No. 92)	2·00	1·20
208	R	130r. on 200r. (No. 97)	2·00	1·20

1914. "Ceres" key-type inscr "CABO VERDE". Name and value in black.

219	U	¼c. green	35	30
220	U	½c. black	35	30
221	U	1c. green	35	30
222	U	1½c. brown	35	30
223	U	2c. red	35	30
224	U	2c. grey	40	30
180	U	2½c. violet	75	65
214	U	2½c. mauve	35	30
215	U	3c. orange	30	25
216	U	4c. red	30	25
228	U	4½c. grey	40	40
229	U	5c. blue	45	40
230	U	6c. mauve	40	40
231	U	7c. blue	40	40
232	U	7½c. brown	40	40
233	U	8c. grey	75	55
234	U	10c. red	40	40
235	U	12c. green	70	65
236	U	15c. pink	40	40
237	U	20c. green	40	40
238	U	24c. blue	1·20	95
239	U	25c. brown	1·20	95
188	U	30c. brown on green	5·75	3·75
240	U	30c. green	55	50
189	U	40c. brown on pink	3·25	2·75
241	U	40c. turquoise	55	50
190	U	50c. orange on orange	4·00	2·75
242	U	50c. mauve	1·00	80
243	U	60c. blue	1·40	1·00
244	U	60c. red	1·60	95
245	U	80c. red	5·00	1·40
191	U	1e. green on blue	4·00	3·00
246	U	1e. pink	5·75	3·00
247	U	1e. blue	6·25	3·75
248	U	2e. purple	5·75	3·00
249	U	5e. brown	10·50	7·25
250	U	10e. pink	24·00	14·50
251	U	20e. green	65·00	49·00

1921. Nos. 153/4 surch.

252	2c. on 15c. on 150r. brown	2·75	1·90
253	4c. on 10c. on 100r. brown	3·25	3·00

1921. No. 69 surch **6 c. REPUBLICA**.

254	S	6c. on 100r. blue on blue	3·25	2·50

1921. Charity Tax stamp of Portuguese Colonies (General issues) optd **CABO VERDE CORREIOS** or surch also.

255	¼ on 1c. green	60	40
256	½c. on 1c. green	75	55
257	1c. green	1·10	85

1922. Provisionals of 1913 surch **$04**.

260	R	4c. on 130r. on 75r. red (No. 202)	80	60
262	R	4c. on 130r. on 80r. green (No. 204)	1·10	85
265	R	4c. on 130r. on 200r. blue (No. 208)	1·10	90

1925. Provisional stamps of 1902 surch **Republica 40 C**.

267	V	40c. on 400r. on 2½r. brown (No. 106)	1·10	90
268	R	40c. on 400r. on 300r. blue on buff (No. 103)	1·10	90

1931. No. 245 surch **70 C**.

269	U	70c. on 80c. red	29·00	11·00

1934. As T **17** of Angola (new "Ceres" type).

270	17	1c. brown	20	15
271	17	5c. sepia	20	15
272	17	10c. mauve	20	15
273	17	15c. black	30	25
274	17	20c. grey	30	25
275	17	30c. green	30	25
276	17	40c. red	30	25
277	17	45c. blue	1·20	95
278	17	50c. brown	1·00	65
279	17	60c. olive	1·00	65
280	17	70c. brown	1·00	65
281	17	80c. green	1·00	65
282	17	85c. red	4·50	3·00
283	17	1e. red	3·00	50
284	17	1e.40 blue	4·00	3·75
285	17	2e. mauve	5·25	3·00
286	17	5e. green	23·00	5·75
287	17	10e. brown	36·00	21·00
288	17	20e. orange	70·00	28·00

1938. As Nos. 383/409 of Angola.

289	1c. olive (postage)	25	20
290	5c. brown	25	20
291	10c. red	25	20
292	15c. purple	1·10	95
293	20c. slate	50	30
294	30c. purple	50	20
295	35c. green	50	30
296	40c. brown	50	30
297	50c. mauve	50	30
298	60c. black	50	30
299	70c. violet	50	30
300	80c. orange	50	30
301	1e. red	80	30
302	1e.75 blue	2·10	80
303	2e. green	4·00	2·30
304	5e. olive	9·25	2·30
305	10e. blue	14·50	3·00
306	20e. brown	49·00	6·00
307	10c. red (air)	85	70
308	20c. violet	85	70
309	50c. orange	85	70
310	1e. blue	85	70
311	2e. red	2·00	1·10
312	3e. green	2·75	1·90
313	5e. brown	8·00	2·75
314	9e. red	13·00	4·75
315	10e. mauve	14·50	6·25

14 Route of President's Tour

1939. Pres. Carmona's 2nd Colonial Tour.

316	14	80c. violet on mauve	4·50	3·00
317	14	1e.75 blue on blue	37·00	27·00
318	14	20e. brown on cream	75·00	25·00

1948. Nos. 276 and 294 surch.

319	10c. on 30c. purple	1·80	1·00
320	25c. on 40c. red	1·90	1·00

16 Machado Point, Sao Vicente

17 Ribeira Brava, Sao Nicolau

1948

321	16	5c. purple and bistre	50	40
322	-	10c. green and light green	50	40
323	17	50c. purple and lilac	1·00	40
324	-	1e. purple	3·75	1·70
325	-	1e.75 blue and green	4·50	2·40
326	-	2e. brown and ochre	10·50	3·00
327	-	5e. green and yellow	21·00	5·75
328	-	10e. red and orange	34·00	19·00
329	-	20e. violet and buff	85·00	36·00

DESIGNS—VERT: 10c. Ribeira Grande. HORIZ: 1e. Porto Grande, Sao Vicente; 1e.75, 5e. Mindelo, Sao Vicente; 2e. Joao de Evora beach, Sao Vicente; 10e. Volcano, Fogo; 20e. Paul.

1948. Honouring the Statue of Our Lady of Fatima. As T **33** of Angola.

330	50c. blue	13·00	8·50

1949. 75th Anniv of U.P.U. As T **39** of Angola.

331	1e. mauve	10·50	5·00

1950. Holy Year. As T **41/2** of Angola.

332	1e. brown	1·20	65
333	2e. blue	4·75	2·75

1951. Surch with figures and bars over old value.

334	10c. on 35c. (No. 295)	65	55
335	20c. on 70c. (No. 299)	85	65
336	40c. on 70c. (No. 299)	1·00	65
337	50c. on 80c. (No. 300)	1·00	65
338	1e. on 1e.75 (No. 302)	1·10	65
339	2e. on 10e. (No. 305)	5·25	2·10

1951. Termination of Holy Year. As T **44** of Angola.

340	2e. violet and mauve	1·50	1·00

1952. No. 302 surch with figures and cross over old values.

341	10c. on 1e.75 blue	1·30	1·20
342	20c. on 1e.75 blue	1·30	1·20
343	50c. on 1e.75 blue	6·25	6·00
344	1e. on 1e.75 blue	75	20
345	1e.50 on 1e.75 blue	75	20

20 Map, c. 1471

21 V. Dias and G. de Cintra

1952. Portuguese Navigators as T **20/21**. Multicoloured.

346	5c. Type **20**	20	20
347	10c. Type **21**	20	20
348	30c. D. Afonso and A. Fernandes	20	20
349	50c. Lancarote and S. da Costa	20	20
350	1e. D. Gomes and A. da Nola	20	20
351	2e. Princes Fernando and Henry the Navigator	1·40	20
352	3e. A. Goncalves and D. Dias	12·00	1·90
353	5e. A. Goncalves Baldaia and J. Fernandes	4·00	95
354	10e. D. Eanes da Gra and A. de Freitas	8·00	2·30
355	20e. Map, 1502	14·50	2·75

22 Doctor giving Injection

1952. First Tropical Medicine Congress, Lisbon.

356	22	20c. black and green	75	55

23 Facade of Monastery

1953. Missionary Art Exhibition.

357	23	10c. brown and olive	20	20
358	23	50c. violet and salmon	95	45
359	23	1e. green and orange	2·30	1·40

1953. Portuguese Stamp Centenary. As T **48** of Angola.

360	50c. multicoloured	1·90	1·30

1954. Fourth Cent of Sao Paulo. As T **49** of Angola.

361	1e. black, green and buff	85	65

24 Arms of Cape Verde Is. and Portuguese Guinea

1955. Presidential Visit.

362	24	1e. multicoloured	55	40
363	24	1e.60c. multicoloured	1·30	1·10

25 Arms of Praia

1958. Centenary of City of Praia. Multicoloured.

364	25	1e. on yellow	65	55
365	25	2e.50 on salmon	1·30	1·10

1958. Brussels International Exn. As T **55** of Angola.

366	2e. multicoloured	95	45

1958. Sixth International Congress of Tropical Medicine. As T **56** of Angola. Multicoloured.

367	3c. "Aloe vera" (plant)	5·75	2·75

26 Prince Henry the Navigator

1960. 500th Death Anniv of Prince Henry the Navigator.

368	26	2e. multicoloured	1·40	1·40

27 Antonio da Nola

1960. 500th Anniv of Colonization of Cape Verde Islands. Multicoloured.

369	1e. Type **27**	95	55
370	2e.50 Diogo Gomes	2·30	1·20

28 "Education"

1960. Tenth Anniv of African Technical Co-operation Commission.

371	28	2e.50 multicoloured	1·40	85

29 Arms of Praia

1961. Urban Arms. As T **29**. Arms multicoloured; inscriptions in red and green; background colours given.

372	5c. buff	30	20
373	15c. blue	30	20
374	20c. yellow	30	20
375	30c. lilac	30	20
376	1e. green	75	20
377	2e. lemon	75	20
378	2e.50 pink	1·10	50
379	3e. brown	1·80	65
380	5e. blue	1·80	65
381	7e.50 olive	1·90	1·10
382	15e. mauve	2·75	1·10
383	30e. yellow	7·25	3·00

ARMS: 15c. Nova Sintra. 20c. Ribeira Brava. 30c. Assomada. 1e. Maio. 2e. Mindelo. 2e.50 Santa Maria. 3e. Pombas. 5e. Sal-Rei. 7e.50, Tarrafal. 15e. Maria Pia. 30e. San Felipe.

1962. Sports. As T **62** of Angola. Multicoloured.

384	50c. Throwing the javelin	40	30
385	1e. Discus thrower	1·10	40
386	1e.50 Batsman (cricket)	75	45
387	2e.50 Boxing	1·10	55
388	4e.50 Hurdler	1·90	1·30
389	12e.50 Golfers	3·50	2·75

1962. Malaria Eradication. Mosquito design as T **63** of Angola. Multicoloured.

390	2e.50 *Anopheles pretoriensis*	1·50	1·20

1963. Tenth Anniv of T.A.P. Airline. As T **69** of Angola.

391	2e.50 multicoloured	1·10	85

1964. Centenary of National Overseas Bank. As T **71** of Angola but portrait of J. da S. M. Leal.

392	1e.50 multicoloured	1·10	85

1965. Centenary of I.T.U. As T **73** of Angola.

393	2e.50 multicoloured	2·30	1·70

30 Militia Regiment Drummer, 1806

1965. Portuguese Military Uniforms. Multicoloured.

394	50c. Type **30**	40	30
395	1e. Militiaman, 1806	55	30
396	1e.50 Infantry Grenadiers officers, 1833	70	55
397	2e.50 Infantry grenadier, 1833	1·40	45
398	3e. Cavalry officer, 1834	2·75	65
399	4e. Infantry grenadier, 1835	1·30	65
400	5e. Artillery officer, 1848	1·40	65
401	10e. Infantry drum-major, 1856	3·25	2·10

1966. 40th Anniv of National Revolution. As T **77** of Angola, but showing different building. Multicoloured.

402	1e. Dr A. Moreira's Academy and Public Assistance Building	65	55

1967. Centenary of Military Naval Association. As T **79** of Angola. Multicoloured.
403 1e. F. da Costa and gunboat *Mandovy* 85 65
404 1e. 50 C. Araujo and mine-sweeper *Augusto Castilho* 1·30 1·00

1967. 50th Anniv of Fatima Apparitions. As T **80** of Angola. Multicoloured.
405 1e. Image of Virgin Mary 40 30

33 President Tomas

1968. Visit of President Tomas of Portugal.
406 **33** 1e. multicoloured 40 30

1968. 500th Birth Anniv of Pedro Cabral (explorer). As T **84** of Angola. Multicoloured.
407 1e. Cantino's map, 1502 95 85
408 1e.50 Pedro Alvares Cabral (vert) 1·50 95

34 Port of Sao Vicente

1968. "Produce of Cape Verde Islands". Multicoloured.
409 50c. Type **34** 30 20
410 1e. Purgueira (*Tatrophus curcus*) (vert) 45 25
411 1e.50 Groundnuts (vert) 45 25
412 2e.50 Castor-oil plant (vert) 45 25
413 3e.50 Inhame (*Dioscorea alata*) (vert) 45 25
414 4e. Date palm (vert) 45 25
415 4e.50 Goiabeira (*Psidium guajava*) (vert) 75 30
416 5e. Tamarind (vert) 1·10 40
417 10e. Manioc (vert) 1·50 75
418 30e. Girl of Cape Verde (vert) 3·50 2·75

1969. Birth Centenary of Admiral Gago Coutinho. As T **86** of Angola. Multicoloured.
419 30c. Fairey IIID seaplane *Lusitania* and map of Lisbon-Rio flight (vert) 30 20

1969. 500th Birth Anniv of Vasco da Gama (explorer). Multicoloured. As T **87** of Angola.
420 1e.50 Vasco da Gama (vert) 40 30

1969. Centenary of Overseas Administrative Reforms. As T **88** of Angola.
421 2e. multicoloured 40 30

1969. 500th Birth Anniv of King Manoel I. As T **89** of Angola. Multicoloured.
422 3e. Manoel I 55 40

1970. Birth Centenary of Marshal Carmona. As T **91** of Angola. Multicoloured.
423 2e.50 Half-length portrait 55 40

35 Desalination Installation

1971. Inauguration of Desalination Plant, Mindelo.
424 **35** 4e. multicoloured 1·30 1·00

1972. 400th Anniv of Camoens' *Lusiad* (epic poem). As T **96** of Angola. Multicoloured.
425 5e. Galleons at Cape Verde 65 30

1972. Olympic Games, Munich. As T **97** of Angola. Multicoloured.
426 4e. Basketball and boxing 65 30

1972. 50th Anniv of First Flight Lisbon–Rio de Janeiro. As T **98** of Angola. Multicoloured.
427 3e.50 Fairey IIID seaplane *Lusitania* near Sao Vicente 65 30

1973. Centenary of I.M.O./W.M.O. As Type **99** of Angola.
428 2e.50 multicoloured 65 30

1975. Independence. No. 407 optd **INDEPENDENCIA 5-Julho-75.**
430 1e. multicoloured 1·00 60

37 Cabral, Flag and People

1975. Third Anniv of Amilcar Cabral's Assassination.
431 **37** 5e. multicoloured 1·25 75

38 Islanders with Broken Shackles

1976. First Anniv of Independence.
432 **38** 50c. multicoloured 40 25
433 **38** 3e. multicoloured 15 10
434 **38** 15e. multicoloured 40 20
435 **38** 50e. multicoloured 1·25 65
MS436 150×110 mm. Nos. 432/5 10·00 7·50

1976. Nos. 428, 424 and 415 optd **REPUBLICA DE**.
437 **38** 2e.50 multicoloured (No. 428) 1·00 50
438 **38** 4e. multicoloured (No. 424) 30·00 10·00
439 **38** 4e.50 multicoloured (No. 415) 4·50 2·75

40 Cabral and Map

1976. 20th Anniv of PAIGC (Revolutionary Party).
440 **40** 1e. multicoloured 75 40

41 Map of Islands

1977. Red Cross.
441 **41** 50c. multicoloured 1·00 60

42 Printed Circuit

1977. International Telecommunications Day.
442 **42** 5e.50 orange, brown and black 40 25

43 Ashtray on Stand

1977. Craftsmanship in Coconut. Multicoloured.
443 20c. Type **43** 10 10
444 30c. Ornamental bell 10 10
445 50c. Lamp 10 10
446 1e. Nativity 10 10
447 1e.50 Desk lamp 15 10
448 5e. Storage jar 50 25
449 10e. Container with hinged lid 1·00 50
450 20e. Tobacco jar 2·00 1·00
451 30e. Stringed instrument 3·00 1·50

44 5r. Stamp, 1877

1977. Centenary of First Cape Verde Stamps.
452 **44** 4e. multicoloured 1·00 60
453 **44** 8e. multicoloured 2·00 1·20

45 Congress Emblem

1977. Third PAIGC Congress, Bissau.
454 **45** 3e.50 multicoloured 2·00 1·20

1978. No. 419 surch **3$00**.
455 3e. on 30c. multicoloured 4·00 2·00

47 Microwave Antenna

1978. Tenth World Telecommunications Day.
456 **47** 3e.50 multicoloured 40 20

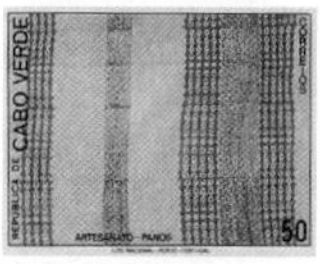

48 Textile Pattern

1978. Handicrafts. Multicoloured.
457 50c. Type **48** 10 10
458 1e.50 Carpet runner and map of Islands 30 15
459 2e. Woven ribbon and map of Islands 40 20
460 3e. Shoulder bag and map of Islands 55 30
461 10e. Woven Cushions (vert) 1·80 1·00

49 Map of Africa

1978. International Anti-Apartheid Year.
462 **49** 4e.50 multicoloured 1·20 75

50 Freighter *Cabo Verde*

1978. First Cape Verde Merchant Ship.
463 **50** 1e. multicoloured 80 30

51 Human Rights Emblem

1978. 30th Anniv of Declaration of Human Rights.
464 **51** 1e.50 multicoloured 60 40
465 **51** 2e. multicoloured 80 50

52 Children with Flowers

1979. International Year of the Child. Multicoloured.
466 1e.50 Children with balloons and flags 60 30
467 3e.50 Type **52** 1·20 1·40

53 Monument

1979. 20th Anniv of Pindjiguiti Massacre.
468 **53** 4e.50 multicoloured 15 10

54 Poster

1979. First National Youth Week.
469 **54** 3e.50 multicoloured 80 35

55 Mindelo

1980. Centenary of Mindelo City.
470 **55** 4e. multicoloured 55 15

56 Family, Graph and Map

1980. First Population and Housing Census.
471 **56** 3e.50 multicoloured 65 35
472 **56** 4e.50 multicoloured 80 45

57 National Flag

1980. Fifth Anniv of Independence (1st issue).
473 **57** 4e. multicoloured 75 40
See also Nos. 481/3.

58 Running

1980. Olympic Games, Moscow. Multicoloured.
474 1e. Type **58** 10 10
475 2e.50 Boxing 10 10
476 3e. Basketball 10 10
477 4e. Volleyball 30 15
478 20e. Swimming 50 90
479 50e. Tennis 3·75 2·30
MS480 98×67 mm. 30e. Football (horiz) 10·00 7·50

59 Stylized Bird

1980. Fifth Anniv of Independence (2nd issue).

481	**59**	4e. multicoloured	40	25
482	**59**	7e. multicoloured	75	45
483	**59**	11e. multicoloured	1·20	80

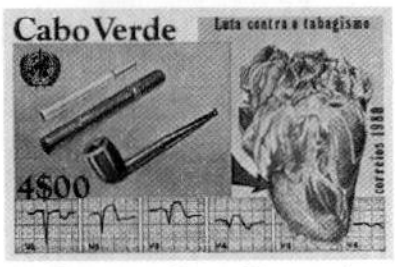

60 Cigarette, Cigar, Pipe and Diseased Heart

1980. World Health Day. Anti-smoking Campaign. Multicoloured.

484	4e. Type **60**	1·00	45
485	7e. Healthy lungs plus smoking equals diseased lungs	1·50	75

61 Albacore

1980. Marine Life. Multicoloured.

486	50c. Type **61**	10	10
487	4e.50 Atlantic horse-mackerel	30	15
488	8e. Mediterranean moray	50	45
489	10e. Brown meagre	70	35
490	12e. Skipjack tuna	80	40
491	50e. Blue shark	3·25	1·80

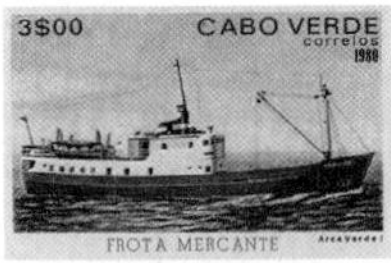

62 *Area Verdel*

1980. Freighters. Multicoloured.

492	3e. Type **62**	30	20
493	5e.50 *Ilha do Maio*	60	20
494	7e.50 *Ilha de Komo*	80	40
495	9e. *Boa Vista*	1·00	50
496	12e. *Santo Antao*	1·40	65
497	30e. *Santiago*	3·25	1·80

63 *Lochnera rosea*

1980. Flowers. Multicoloured.

498	50c. Type **63**	10	10
499	4e.50 *Poinciana regia Bojer*	40	20
500	8e. *Mirabilis jalapa*	85	45
501	10e. *Nerium oleander*	25	10
502	12e. *Bougainvillea litoralis*	1·00	55
503	30e. *Hibiscus rosa sinenis*	2·50	1·25

64 Desert Scene and Hands holding plant

1981. Desert Erosion Prevention. Multicoloured.

504	4e.50 Type **64**	70	35
505	10e.50 Hands caring for plant and river scene	1·60	80

65 Map, Flag, and "Official Bulletin" announcing Constitution

1981. Sixth Anniv of Constitution.

506	**65**	4e.50 multicoloured	1·50	70

66 Austrian Winter Olympics Stamps of 1975

1981. WIPA 1981 International Stamp Exhibition, Vienna. Sheet 107×62 mm.

MS507	**66** 50e. multicoloured	3·75	3·75

67 Antenna

1981. Telecommunications. Multicoloured.

508	4e.50 Type **67**	40	20
509	8e. Dish antenna	75	35
510	20e. Dish antenna and satellite	1·80	90

68 Disabled Person in Wheelchair and IYDP Emblem

1981. International Year of Disabled Persons.

511	**68**	4e.50 multicoloured	75	30

69 Moorhens

1981. Birds. Multicoloured.

512	1e. Little egret (vert)	20	15
513	4e.50 Barn owl (vert)	40	20
514	8e. Grey-headed kingfisher (vert)	90	30
515	10e. Type **69**	2·30	1·10
516	12e. Helmet guineafowls	2·50	1·30
MS517	79×54 mm. 50e. Raza Island lark (*Alauda razae*) (vert)	9·00	5·00

70 Map showing Member States

1982. CILSS Congress, Praia.

518	**70**	11e.50 multicoloured	55	50

71 Tackle

1982. "Amilcar Cabral" Football Cup Competition. Multicoloured.

519	4e.50 Type **71**	55	15
520	7e.50 Running with ball	95	35
521	11e.50 Goalmouth scene	1·40	65

72 Militiawomen

1982. First Anniv of Cape Verde Women's Organization. Multicoloured.

522	4e.50 Type **72**	30	15
523	8e. Women farmers	94	40
524	12e. Nursery teacher	1·30	70

73 Footballers

1982. World Cup Football Championship, Spain.

525	**73**	1e.50 multicoloured	15	10
526	-	4e.50 multicoloured	40	25
527	-	8e. multicoloured	80	40
528	-	10e.50 multicoloured	1·00	60
529	-	12e. multicoloured	1·20	65
530	-	20e. multicoloured	2·00	1·10
MS531		82×96 mm. 50e. multicoloured (29×37 mm)	4·75	2·75

DESIGNS: 4e.50 to 50e. Various footballing scenes.

74 *Morrissey-Ernestina*

1982. Return of Schooner *Morrissey-Ernestina*.

532	**74**	12e. multicoloured	2·50	1·50

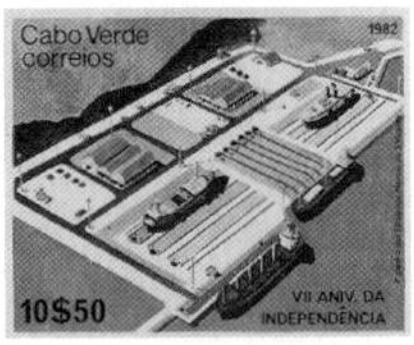

75 San Vicente Shipyard

1982. Seventh Anniv of Independence.

533	**75**	10e.50 multicoloured	2·00	1·00

76 *Hypolimnas misippus*

1982. Butterflies. Multicoloured.

534	2e. Type **76**	30	15
535	4e.50 *Melanitis lede*	70	30
536	8e. *Catopsilia florella*	1·30	60
537	10e.50 *Colias electo*	1·60	75
538	11e.50 *Danaus chrysippus*	1·80	80
539	12e. *Papilio demodecus*	2·00	85

77 Amilcar Cabral

1983. Amilcar Cabral Symposium.

540	**77**	7e. multicoloured	80	65
541	**77**	10e.50 multicoloured	1·30	1·00

78 Francisco Xavier de Cruz (composer)

1983. Composers and Poets. Multicoloured.

543	7e. Type **78**	1·00	60
544	14e. Eugenio Tavares (poet)	2·00	1·30

79 "World Communications Network"

1983. World Communications Year.

545	**79**	13e. multicoloured	1·50	75

80 Cape Verde Cone

1983. Shells. Multicoloured.

546	50c. Type **80**	10	10
547	1e. *Conus decoratus*	15	15
548	3e. *Conus salreiensis*	40	25
549	10e. *Conus verdensis*	1·40	1·40
550	50e. *Conus cuneolus*	6·50	3·50

81 Arch and Cross

1983. 450th Anniv of Christianity in Cape Verde Islands.

551	**81**	7e. multicoloured	1·40	1·30

82 Auster D5/160 Husky

1984. 40th Anniv of ICAO. Multicoloured.

552	50c. Type **82**	25	10
553	2e. de Havilland Dove	30	15
554	10e. Hawker Siddeley HS748	90	60
555	13e. de Havilland Dragon Rapide	1·20	95
556	20e. de Havilland Twin Otter	1·80	1·50
557	50e. Britten-Norman Islander	4·75	3·50

83 Families, Houses and Emblems as Balloons

1984. National Solidarity Campaign.

558	**83**	6e.50 multicoloured	1·20	50
559	**83**	13e.50 multicoloured	2·30	1·20

84 Figure rising from Nautilus Shell

1985. Second Cape Verde Womens' Organization Conference.

560	**84**	8e. multicoloured	1·30	1·00

85 Emblem

1985. Tenth Anniv of Independence.

561	**85**	8e. multicoloured	1·40	95
562	**85**	12e. multicoloured	2·00	1·40

87 "Steamer"

1985

564	**87**	30e. on 10c. multicoloured	22·00	22·00
MS565 Three sheets, each 190×260 mm. (a) 50e. As No. 564 but ship upper structure red×4; (b) 50e. As No. 564 but ship upper structure yellow×4; (c) 50e. As No. 564 but ship upper structure green×4			£375	

88 *Mabuya vaillanti*

1986. Endangered Reptiles. Multicoloured.

566	8e. Type **88**	4·50	2·50
567	10e. *Tarentola gigas brancoensis*	5·50	3·25
568	15e. *Tarentola gigas gigas*	8·00	4·75
569	30e. *Hemidactylus bouvieri*	16·00	10·00
MS570 130×60 mm. 50e. Type **88**; 50e. As No. 569		25·00	20·00

89 Food in Pot over Fire

1986. World Food Day. Multicoloured.

571	8e. Type **89**	45	35
572	12e. Women pounding food in mortar	70	55
573	15e. Woman rolling flat bread with stone	1·00	70

90 Dove and Olive Branch

1986. International Peace Year.

574	**90**	12e. multicoloured	65	35
575	**90**	30e. multicoloured	1·70	85

91 Family Planning and Child Health Centre, Praia, and Woman breast-feeding Baby

1987. Child Survival Campaign. Multicoloured.

576	8e. Type **91**	40	30
577	10e. Assomada SOS children's village	50	35
578	12e. Family planning clinic, Mindelo, and nurse with child	60	45
579	16e. Children's home, Mindelo, and nurse with baby	80	55
580	100e. Calouste Gulbenkian kindergarten, Praia, and child writing	4·75	3·50

92 Mindelo City

1987. Tourism. Multicoloured.

581	1e. Type **92**	20	10
582	2e.50 Santo Antao island	25	15
583	5e. Fogo island	30	20
584	8e. Pillory, Velha City	50	25
585	10e. Boa Entrada valley, Santiago island	60	30
586	12e. Fishing boats, Santiago	75	40
587	100e. Furna harbour, Brava island	6·00	3·00

93 *Carvalho* (schooner)

1987. Sailing Ships. Multicoloured.

588	**93**	12e. black, mauve & blue	80	50
589	-	16e. black, blue & mauve	1·00	85
590	-	50e. black, blue & dp blue	3·00	2·50
MS591 105×105 mm 60e.×2, black, brown and violet			7·25	6·25

DESIGNS: 16e. *Nauta*; 50e. *Maria Sony*; 60e. *Madalan*.

94 Emblem

1987. Second National Development Plan.

592	**94**	8e. multicoloured	1·00	50

95 Moths on Stem

1988. Crop Protection. Multicoloured.

593	50c. Type **95**	10	10
594	2e. Caterpillars on plant treated with bio-insecticides	20	15
595	9e. Use of imported predators	75	45
596	13e. Use of imported predatorial insects	1·10	60
597	16e. Locust on stem	1·40	80
598	19e. Damaged wood	1·60	90
MS599 115×70 mm. 50e. Agricultural Research Institute (41×30 mm)		4·00	4·50

96 17th-century Dutch Map

1988. Antique Maps of Cape Verde Islands. Multicoloured.

600	1e. Type **96**	55	30
601	2e.50 18th-cent Belgian map	90	50
602	4e.50 18th-cent French map	1·10	65
603	9e.50 18th-cent English map	1·30	80
604	19e.50 19th-cent English map	1·60	1·00
605	20e. 18th-cent French map (vert)	2·30	1·30

97 Church of the Abbot of the Holy Shelter, Tarrafal, Santiago

1988. Churches. Multicoloured.

606	5e. Type **97**	30	20
607	8e. Church of Our Lady of Light, Maio	50	30
608	10e. Church of the Nazarene, Praia, Santiago	65	35
609	12e. Church of Our Lady of the Rosary, Sao Nicolau	80	40
610	15e. Church of the Nazarene, Mindelo, Sao Vicente	1·10	50
611	20e. Church of Our Lady of Grace, Praia, Santiago	1·40	1·30

98 Boy filling Tin with Water

1988. Water Economy Campaign.

612	**98**	12e. multicoloured	80	50

99 Red Cross Workers

1988. 125th Anniv of Red Cross Movement.

613	**99**	7e. multicoloured	75	40

100 Group of Youths and Pres. Pereira

1988. Third Congress of African Party for the Independence of Cape Verde. Multicoloured.

614	7e. Type **100**	30	20
615	10e.50 Pres. Pereira and Perez de Cuellar (U.N. Secretary-General)	50	30
616	30e. Emblem and Pres. Pereira	1·40	80
MS617 130×90 mm. 100e. As No. 616		4·75	4·00

101 Handball

1988. Olympic Games, Seoul. Multicoloured.

618	12e. Type **101**	85	60
619	15e. Tennis	1·10	80
620	20e. Football	1·50	1·10
621	30e. Boxing	2·00	1·70
MS622 130×90 mm. 50e. Long jump		3·00	3·00

102 Hot-air Balloon *Pro Juventute*

1989. Second Pro Juventute Congress.

623	**102**	30e. multicoloured	1·50	75

103 Silva

1989. Death Centenary of Roberto Duarte Silva (chemist).

624	**103**	12e.50 multicoloured	1·50	75

104 *Liberty guiding the People* (Eugene Delacroix)

1989. Bicentenary of French Revolution.

625	**104**	20e. multicoloured	90	50
626	**104**	24e. multicoloured	1·20	60
627	**104**	25e. multicoloured	1·20	65
MS628 120×76 mm. 100e. multicoloured			4·75	4·00

DESIGNS: 29×37 mm. 100e. Detail of Arc de Triomphe, Paris.

No. **MS**628 also commemorates "Philexfrance 89" International Stamp Exhibition.

105 Anniversary Emblem

1989. Centenary of Interparliamentary Union. Multicoloured.

629	2e. Type **105**	20	10
630	4e. Dove	30	20
631	13e. National Assembly building	90	65

106 Fonte Lima Women firing Pots

1989. Traditional Pottery. Multicoloured.

632	13e. Type **106**	50	35
633	20e. Terra di Monti women and children arranging pots to bake in sun (vert)	85	55
634	24e. Terra di Monti woman shaping pot	1·00	65
635	25e. Fonte Lima women kneading clay (vert)	1·10	70

107 Boy and Truck

1989. Christmas. Home-made Toys. Multicoloured.

636	1e. Type **107**	25	25
637	6e. Boy with car on waste ground	35	30
638	8e. Boy with truck on pavement	50	35
639	11e.50 Boys with various vehicles	1·00	50
640	18e. Boys and sit-on scooter	1·50	90
641	100e. Boy with boat	5·00	4·50

108 Pope John Paul II

1990. Papal Visit.

642	**108**	13e. multicoloured	1·00	50
643	**108**	20e. multicoloured	1·00	50
MS644 110 mm. 200e. multicoloured			6·50	6·00

DESIGN: 200e. Pope wearing mitre.

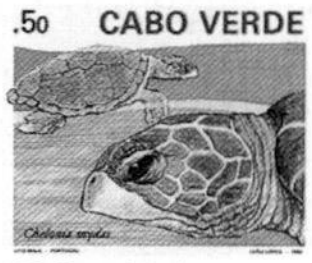

109 Green Turtles

1990. Turtles. Multicoloured.

645	50c. Type **109**	15	10
646	1e. Leatherback turtles	20	10
647	5e. Olive ridley turtles	45	25
648	10e. Loggerhead turtles	90	60
649	42e. Hawksbill turtles	3·50	2·50

110 Footballers

1990. World Cup Football Championship, Italy.

650	**110**	4e. multicoloured	15	10
651	-	7e.50 multicoloured	20	10
652	-	8e. multicoloured	25	10
653	-	100e. multicoloured	3·00	2·00
MS654 87×54 mm. 100e. multicoloured			4·00	2·50

DESIGNS: 7e.50 to 100e. Different footballing scenes.

111 Face

1990. First Congress of Cape Verde Women's Movement.

655	**111**	9e. multicoloured	50	30

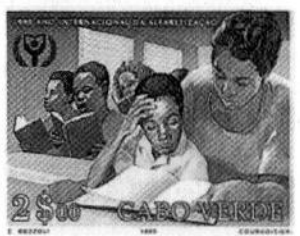

112 Teacher helping Boy to Read

1990. International Literacy Year. Multicoloured.

656	2e. Type **112**	20	10
657	3e. Teacher with adult class	25	15
658	15e. Teacher with flash-card	80	50
659	19e. Adult student pointing to letters on blackboard	1·10	70

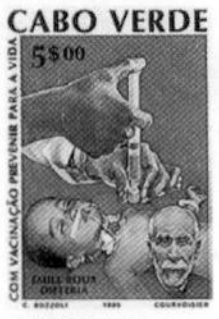

113 Diphtheria Treatment and Emile Roux (pioneer of antitoxic method)

1990. Vaccination Campaign. Multicoloured.

660	5e. Type **113**	75	30
661	13e. Tuberculosis vaccination and Robert Koch (discoverer of tubercle bacillus)	1·40	75
662	20e. Tetanus vaccination and Gaston Ramon	2·30	1·30
663	24e. Poliomyelitis oral vaccination and Jonas Edward Salk (discoverer of vaccine)	2·50	1·50

114 Musician on Bull's Back

1990. Traditional Stories. Multicoloured.

664	50c. Type **114**	10	10
665	2e.50 Fisherman and mermaid ("Joao Piquinote")	20	15
666	12e. Girl and snake	90	50
667	25e. Couple and eggs ("Ti Lobo, Ti Lobo")	1·80	1·00

115 World Map and Beam destroying AIDS Virus

1991. Anti-AIDS Campaign. Multicoloured.

668	13e. Type **115**	2·40	1·80
669	24e. Beam, AIDS virus and "SIDA"	4·50	3·35

116 Fishing Boat at Sea and Fishermen on Shore

1991. Fishing Industry. Multicoloured.

670	10e. Type **116**	60	45
671	24e. Fisherman removing hook from fish	1·50	1·20
672	25e. Fishing boats	1·60	1·20
673	50e. Fishermen taking in lines	3·25	2·30

117 Our Lady of the Rosary Church

1991. Tourism. Ruins of Ribeira Grande, Santiago Island. Multicoloured.

674	12e.50 Type **117**	75	50
675	15e. Se Cathedral	90	75
676	20e. Sao Filipe fortress	1·30	1·00
677	30e. St. Francis's Convent	1·80	1·50
MS678	81×79 mm. 100e. Pillory (vert)	5·25	5·25

118 *Lavandula rotundifolia*

1991. Medicinal Plants. Multicoloured.

679	10e. Type **118**	45	30
680	15e. *Micromeria forbesii*	70	50
681	21e. *Sarcostemma daltonii*	90	70
682	24e. *Periploca chevalieri*	1·10	80
683	30e. *Echium hypertropicum*	1·30	1·10
684	35e. *Erysimum caboverdeanum*	1·50	1·20

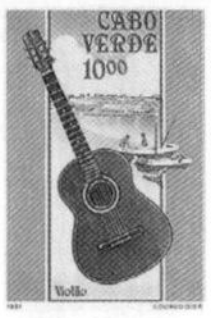

119 Guitar

1991. Musical Instruments. Multicoloured.

685	10e. Type **119**	50	40
686	20e. Violin	1·00	80
687	29e. Guitar with five double strings	1·40	1·20
688	47e. Cimboa	2·30	1·90
MS689	97×82 mm. (a) 60e. Accordian (horiz)	3·50	2·50

120 Crib (Tito Livio Goncalves)

1991. Christmas. Multicoloured.

690	31e. Type **120**	1·00	90
691	50e. Fonte-Lima crib	1·60	1·50

121 Rose Apples

1992. Tropical Fruits. Multicoloured.

692	16e. Type **121**	80	60
693	25e. Mangoes	1·30	1·10
694	31e. Cashews	1·50	1·40
695	32e. Avocados	1·60	1·50

122 Ships anchored in Bay

1992. 500th Anniv of Discovery of America by Columbus. Columbus's Landings in Cape Verde Islands. Multicoloured.

696	40e. Type **122**	2·50	2·00
697	40e. Caravel	2·50	2·00
MS698	130×63 mm. Nos. 696/7 (sold at 150e.)	9·50	7·50

123 Alhambra, Granada

1992. Granada 92 International Stamp Exhibition, Spain. Sheet 135×95 mm.

MS699	**123** 50e. multicoloured (sold at 150e.)	8·00	8·00

124 Throwing the Javelin

1992. Olympic Games, Barcelona. Multicoloured.

700	16e. Type **124**	60	40
701	20e. Weightlifting	80	65
702	32e. Pole vaulting	1·30	1·00
703	40e. Putting the shot	1·50	1·30
MS704	98×71 mm. 100e. Gymnastics (26×32 m)	3·75	3·75

125 Oxen and Sugar Cane

1992. Production of Molasses. Multicoloured.

705	19e. Type **125**	85	45
706	20e. Crushing cane	90	75
707	37e. Feeding cane into mill	1·70	1·60
708	38e. Cooking molasses	1·80	1·70

126 Cat

1992. Domestic Animals. Multicoloured.

709	16e. Type **126**	75	25
710	31e. Chickens	1·50	1·30
711	32e. Dog (vert)	1·50	1·40
712	50e. Horse	2·30	2·00

127 *Tubastrea aurea*

1993. Corals. Multicoloured.

713	5e. Type **127**	20	15
714	31e. *Corallium rubrum*	1·20	1·00
715	37e. *Porites porites*	1·80	1·60
716	50e. *Millepora alcicornis*	£180	1·60

128 *Praia Harbour, Santiago Island, 1806*

1993. Brasilliana 93 International Stamp Exhibition, Rio de Janeiro, and union of Portuguese-speaking Capital Cities. Sheet 118×75 mm.

MS717	**128** 100e. multicoloured	5·50	4·50

129 King Ferdinand and Queen Isabella of Spain and Pope Alexander VI

1993. 500th Annivs of Pope Alexander VI's Bulls (on Portuguese and Spanish spheres of influence) and of Treaty of Tordesillas. Multicoloured.

718	37e. Type **129**	1·10	95
719	37e. King Joao II of Portugal and Pope Julius II	1·10	95
720	38e. Astrolabe, quill and left-half of globe	1·20	1·00
721	38e. Map of Iberian Peninsula and right-half of globe with Cape Verde Islands highlighted	1·20	1·00

Stamps of the same value were issued together in *se-tenant* pairs, each pair forming a composite design.

130 *Palinurus charlestoni*

1993. Lobsters. Multicoloured.

722	2e. Type **130**	25	20
723	10e. Brown lobster	60	50
724	17e. Royal lobster	1·00	90
725	38e. Stone lobster	2·30	2·00
MS726	110×70 mm.100e. Royal lobster on seabed (51×36 mm)	5·75	5·75

131 Cory's Shearwater

1993. Nature Reserves. Multicoloured.

727	10e. Type **131** (Branco and Raso Islets)	80	70
728	30e. Brown booby (De Cima and Raso Islets)	2·50	2·00
729	40e. Magnificent frigate bird (Curral Velho and Baluarte Islets)	3·50	2·50
730	41e. Red-billed tropic bird (Raso and De Cima Islets)	3·75	2·75

132 Rose

1993. Flowers. Multicoloured.

731	5e. Type **132**	25	20
732	30e. Bird of Paradise flower	1·30	1·10
733	37e. Sweet William	1·60	1·40
734	50e. Cactus dahlia	1·90	1·80

1994. Hong Kong 94 International Stamp Exhibition,. Sheet 110×70 mm. Multicoloured.

MS735	No. 729 (sold at 150e.)	9·00	9·00

133 Map and Prince Henry

1994. 600th Birth Anniv of Prince Henry the Navigator.

736	**133** 37e. multicoloured	2·75	2·00

134 Players and Giants Stadium, New York

1994. World Cup Football Championship, U.S.A. Multicoloured.

737	1e. Type **134**	40	10
738	20e. Referee showing red card and Rose Bowl, Los Angeles	80	55
739	37e. Scoring goal and Foxboro Stadium, Boston	1·50	1·00
740	38e. Linesman raising flag and Silverdome, Detroit	1·60	1·10
MS741	110×70 mm. 100e. Tackle and RFK Stadium, Washington D.C	4·50	3·00

135 Sand Tiger

1994. Sharks. Multicoloured.

742	21e. Type **135**	1·30	1·20
743	27e. Black-tipped shark	1·60	1·50
744	37e. Whale shark	2·30	2·10
745	38e. Velvet belly	2·50	2·20

136 "Prata" Bananas

1994. Bananas. Multicoloured.

746	12e. Type **136**	70	40
747	16e. "Pao" bananas (horiz)	90	55
748	30e. "Ana roberta" bananas	1·60	1·00
749	40e. "Roxa" bananas	2·30	1·30
MS750	64×82 mm. 100e. "Prata" bananas on tree (27×40 mm) (sold at 150e.)	8·00	5·00

No. **MS**750 commemorates Philakorea 1994 International and Singpex 94 stamp exhibitions.

137 Fontes Pereira de Melo

1994. Lighthouses. Multicoloured.

751	2e. Type **137**	50	40
752	37e. Morro Negro	2·50	2·30

753	38e. D. Amelia (vert)	2·75	2·50
754	50e. D. Maria Pia (vert)	8·50	3·00

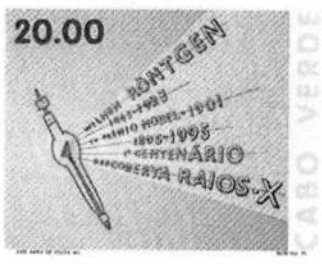

138 X-Ray Tube and Dates

1995. Centenary of Discovery of X-Rays by Wilhelm Rontgen.

755	**138** 20e. multicoloured	1·50	1·30
756	**138** 37e. multicoloured	2·75	2·50
MS757	Sheet 142×95 mm. Nos. 755/6 (sold at 100e.)	7·00	7·00

139 Child with Tuna

1995. 50th Anniv of FAO. Multicoloured.

758	37e. Type **139**	2·20	2·20
759	38e. Globe and wheat ear	2·40	2·40

140 Wire-haired Fox Terrier and *Two Foxhounds and Fox Terrier* (John Emms)

1995. Dogs. Heads of dogs and paintings. Multicoloured.

760	1e. Type **140**	20	20
761	10e. Cavalier King Charles and *Shooting Over Dogs* (Richard Ansdell)	15	10
762	40e. German shepherd and rough collies	2·30	1·60
763	50e. Bearded collie and *Hounds at Full Cry* (Thomas Blinks)	2·75	2·00

141 Communications

1995. 20th Anniv of Independence.

764	**141** 37e. multicoloured	1·30	1·00

142 Sweet William (*Dianthus barbatus*)

1995. Singapore 95 International Stamp Exhibition. Sheet 110×70 mm.

MS765	**142** 37e. multicoloured (sold at 150e.)	7·00	7·00

143 Horse Race

1995. St. Philip's Flag Festival, Fogo. Multicoloured.

766	2e. Type **143**	20	20
767	10e. Preparing for horse race	25	25
768	37e. Preparing food and clapping to music	95	85
769	40e. Crowd watching final horse race	1·10	95

144 Grasshopper playing Guitar

1995. Childrens' Stories. 300th Death Anniv of Jean de La Fontaine (writer). Scenes from *The Ant and the Grasshopper*. Multicoloured.

770	10e. Type **144**	25	20
771	25e. Grasshopper in snowstorm looking through ants' window	60	55
772	38e. Ant laying-in supplies for winter	90	80
773	45e. Ants welcoming grasshopper into their home	1·10	1·00

145 *Sonchus daltonii*

1996. Endangered Flowers. Multicoloured.

774	20e. Type **145**	65	60
775	37e. *Echium vulcanorum*	1·20	1·00
776	38e. *Nauplius smithii*	1·30	1·10
777	50e. *Campanula jacobaea*	1·60	1·40

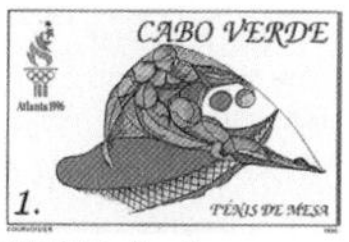

146 Table Tennis

1996. Olympic Games, Atlanta. Multicoloured.

778	1e. Type **146**	25	40
779	37e. Gymnastics	1·40	1·40
780	100e. Athletics	1·50	75

147 Student (Education of Girls)

1996. 50th Anniv of UNICEF. Multicoloured.

781	20e. Type **147**	1·50	75
782	40e. Mother kissing child (Right to Love)	80	75

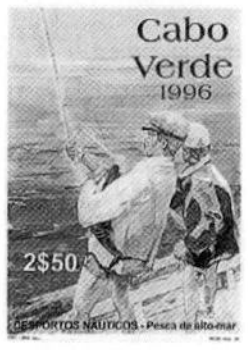

148 Deep Sea Fishing

1996. Water Sports. Multicoloured.

783	2e.50 Type **148**	50	25
784	10e. Sailboard	5·00	45
785	22e.50 Jet skiing	1·10	1·00
786	100e. Surfing (horiz)	4·75	4·50
MS787	155×110 mm. 100e. Fish (scuba diving) (78×60 mm)	5·25	5·00

1997. Nos. 582 and 650/1 surch.

788	3e. on 2e.50 multicoloured	50	50
789	37e. on 4e. multicoloured	5·00	5·00
790	38e. on 7e.50 multicoloured	5·00	5·00

150 State Arms

1997. National Symbols. Multicoloured.

791	25e. Type **150**	80	70
792	37e. National anthem	1·20	1·00
793	50e. State flag	1·50	1·30

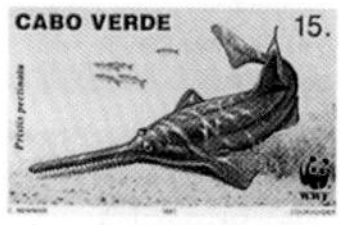

151 Small-toothed Sawfish

1997. The Small-toothed Sawfish. Multicoloured.

794	15e. Type **151**	70	70
795	15e. Underside of sawfish	70	70
796	15e. Sawfish and school of fishes	70	70
797	15e. Two sawfishes	20	10

152 Fish and Dolphins

1997. Oceans. Multicoloured.

798	45e. Type **152**	1·50	1·50
799	45e. Mermaid and merman	1·50	1·50
800	45e. Fishes, eel, coral and sunken gate	1·50	1·50

Nos. 798/800 were issued together, *se-tenant*, forming a composite design.

153 Yellow-finned Tuna

1997. Tuna. Multicoloured.

801	13e. Type **153**	50	45
802	21e. Big-eyed tuna	80	75
803	41e. Little tuna	1·60	1·50
804	45e. Skipjack tuna	1·80	1·60

154 Players chasing Ball

1998. World Cup Football Championship, France. Multicoloured.

805	10e. Type **154**	40	20
806	30e. Ball in net (vert)	1·10	80
807	45e. Player with ball (vert)	1·60	1·10
808	50e. Globe, football and trophy	1·80	1·30

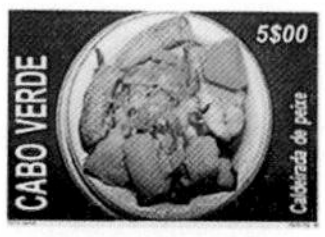

155 Fish Dish

1998. Local Cuisine.

809	**155** 5e. multicoloured	30	30
810	- 25e. multicoloured	1·30	1·30
811	- 35e. multicoloured	1·80	1·80
812	- 40e. multicoloured	2·00	2·00

DESIGNS: 25e. to 40e. Different food dishes.

156 Navigators reading Books and Banana Tree

1998. 500th Anniv (1997) of Vasco da Gama's Expedition to India. Multicoloured.

813	50e. Type **156**	1·80	1·80
814	50e. Seaman with sword and couple	1·80	1·80
815	50e. Compass rose and Portuguese galleon in harbour	1·80	1·80

Nos. 813/15 were issued together, *se-tenant*, forming a composite design.

157 Brava Island Costume

1998. Local Women's Costumes. Multicoloured.

816	10e. Type **157**	25	25
817	18e. Fogo Island	75	60
818	30e. Boa Vista Island	1·30	1·20
819	50e. Santiago Island	2·00	1·90

158 *Byblia ilithyia*

1999. Butterflies and Moths. Multicoloured.

820	5e. Type **158**	25	25
821	10e. *Aganais speciosa*	30	30
822	20e. Crimson-speckled moth	80	75
823	30e. Painted lady	35	15
824	50e. Cabbage looper	1·90	1·80
825	100e. *Grammodes congenita*	3·75	3·50
MS826	114×68 mm. No. 822/3	3·75	3·75

159 Concorde in Flight

1999. 30th Anniv of Concorde (supersonic airplane). Multicoloured.

827	30e. Type **159**	2·75	2·75
828	50e. Concorde on airport apron	4·50	4·50

160 Alain Gerbault (solo yachtsman) and Mindelo Harbour

1999. "Philexfrance 99" International Stamp Exhibition, Paris, France. Multicoloured.

829	30e. Type **160**	3·00	3·00
830	50e. Roberto Duarte Silva (chemist) and Eiffel Tower, Paris	3·00	3·00
MS831	155×79 mm. Nos. 829/30 (sold at 100e.)	7·00	7·00

161 Globe in Envelope and UPU Emblem

1999. 125th Anniv of Universal Postal Union. Multicoloured.

832	30e. Type **161**	2·30	22·30
833	50e. Paper airplanes	3·50	3·50

Nos. 832/3 are not inscribed with the country name.

162 Cola Sanjon Dance

1999. Local Dances. Multicoloured.

834	10e. Type **162**	35	35
835	30e. Contradanca	1·00	1·00
836	50e. Desfile de Tabanca (horiz)	1·80	1·70
837	100e. Batuque (horiz)	3·50	3·25

163 Globe, Open Book and Hourglass

2000. New Millennium. Multicoloured.

838	40e. Type **163**	2·30	2·30
839	50e. "2000" (horiz)	2·50	2·50

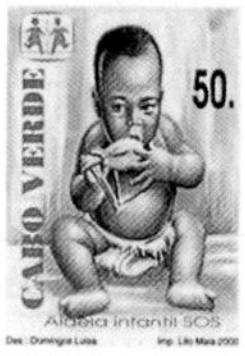

164 Baby

2000. 50th Anniv (1999) of S.O.S. Children's Villages. Multicoloured.

840	50e. Type **164**	1·80	1·60
841	100e. Child and emblem (horiz)	3·50	3·25

165 "25" and Emblem

2000. 25th Anniv of Independence.

842	**165** 50e. multicoloured	1·50	1·50

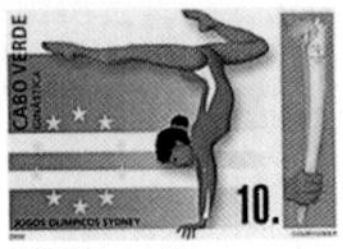

166 Gymnastics

2000. Olympic Games, Sydney. Multicoloured.

843	10e. Type **166**	35	30
844	40e. Taekwondo	1·00	90
845	50e. Athletics	1·50	1·40
MS846	70×120 mm. Nos. 843/5	3·00	3·00

167 Dragon Tree

2000. Dragon Tree.

847	**167** 5e. green	25	25
848	**167** 40e. red	1·30	80
849	**167** 60e. brown	2·00	1·30

168 Students (left-hand detail)

2000. 134th Anniv of the Liceu de Sao Nicolau Seminary. Multicoloured.

850	60e. Type **168**	2·00	1·90
851	60e. Students (right-hand detail)	2·00	1·90
852	60e. Jose Alves Feio, Jose Julio Dias (co-founders) and Antonio Jose de Oliveira Boucas (Principal) (56×26 mm)	70	35

Nos. 850/2 were issued together, *se-tenant*, forming a composite design.

169 White Sea Bream (*Diplodus sargus*)

2001. Fish. Multicoloured.

853	10e. Type **169**	50	50
854	22e. *Diplodus prayensis*	1·10	1·00
855	28e. Marmora sea bream (*Lithognathus mormyrus*)	1·40	1·30
856	48e. *Diplodus fasciatus*	2·30	2·10
857	60e. *Diplodus puntazzo*	2·75	2·50

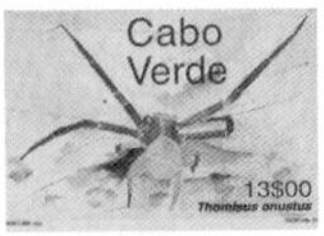

170 *Thomisus onustus*

2001. Spiders. Multicoloured.

858	13e. Type **170**	65	65
859	16e. *Scytodes velutina*	75	70
860	40e. *Hersiliola simony*	2·00	1·80
861	100e. *Loxosceles rufescens*	4·75	4·50

171 *Acacia albida*

2001. Trees. Multicoloured.

862	50e. Type **171**	2·10	2·00
863	60e. *Ficus sycomorus*	2·50	2·30

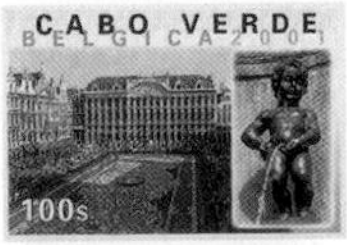

172 Grand Place, Brussels and Fountain

2001. "Belgica 2001" International Stamp Exhibition, Brussels. Sheet 116×86 mm.

MS864	**172** 100e. multicoloured	4·00	4·00

173 *Artemisia gorgonum* (inscr "Artimisia")

2001. Plants (1st series). Multicoloured.

865	20e. Type **173**	70	65
866	27e. *Globularia amygdalifolia*	90	85
867	47e.50 *Sidereoxylon marginata* (horiz)	1·60	1·50
868	50e. *Umbilicus schmidtii* (horiz)	1·70	1·70
869	60e. *Verbascum cystolithicum*	2·10	1·90
870	100e. *Limonium lobinii*	3·50	3·25

See also Nos. 873/6.

174 Children encircling Globe

2001. United Nations Year of Dialogue among Civilizations.

871	**174** 60e. multicoloured	2·00	2·00

175 Antonio Goncalves

2001. Birth Centenary of Antonio Aurelio Goncalves (writer).

872	**175** 100e. multicoloured	3·25	3·00

2002. Plants (2nd series). As T **173**. Multicoloured.

873	10e. *Euphorbia tuckeyana* (inscr "tuckeyna") (*horiz*)	35	35
874	50e. *Limonium*	1·80	1·60
875	60e. *Aeonium gorgoneum*	2·00	1·90
876	100e. *Polycarpaea gayi*	3·50	3·25

176 Player heading Ball into Goal

2002. World Cup Football Championship, Japan and South Korea. Multicoloured.

877	60e. Type **176**	2·00	1·80
878	100e. Player kicking ball towards goal	3·25	3·00

177 Two Adult Turtles

2002. Marine Turtles (*Caretta caretta*). Multicoloured.

879	10e. Type **177**	45	40
880	20e. Laying eggs	80	75
881	30e. Young emerging from sand	1·30	1·20
882	60e. Young crawling towards sea	2·60	2·50
883	100e. Adult swimming	4·25	4·00
MS884	150×110 mm. 100e. Adult on beach (80×61 mm)	4·25	4·25

178 Basket from St. Nicholas Island

2002. Traditional Baskets. Multicoloured.

885	20e. Type **178**	70	65
886	33e. From St. Anthony Island	1·20	1·10
887	60e. From Santiago Island	2·10	2·00
888	100e. From Boa Vista Island	3·50	3·25

179 Carlos Alberto Silva Martins (Katchass) (musician)

2003. Poets and Musicians. Multicoloured.

889	12e. Type **179**	50	45
890	20e. Jorge Monteiro (Jotamonte) (composer)	75	70
891	32e. Luís Rendall (composer)	1·20	1·00
892	47e.50 Jorge Barbosa (poet)	1·80	1·70
893	60e. Januario Leite (poet)	2·20	2·10
894	100e. Jose Lopes (poet)	3·75	3·50

180 Cesaria Evora

2003. Cesaria Evora (singer) Commemoration. Multicoloured.

895	60e. Type **180**	2·30	2·00
896	100e. Cesaria Evora (different)	3·75	3·50
MS897	85×115 mm. 200e. Cesaria Evora's legs (51×38 mm)	7·75	7·25

MS897 forms a composite design of Cesaria Evora singing.

181 Purple Heron (*Ardea purpurea bournei*)

2003. Herons and Egrets. Multicoloured.

898	10e. Type **181**	80	70
899	27e. Grey heron (*Ardea cinerea*)	1·10	1·00
900	42e. Cattle egret (*Bubulcus ibis*)	1·80	1·60
901	60e. Little egret (*Egretta garzeta*)	2·50	2·25

182 Scout

2003. Scouting. Multicoloured.

902	60e. Type **182** (13th anniv of Scouts Association)	2·30	2·00
903	100e. Scout with raised hand (3rd anniv of Catholic Scouts Corps)	3·50	3·25

183 Blue Whale (*Balaenoptera musculus*)

2003. Marine Mammals. Multicoloured.

904	10e. Type **183**	65	60
905	20e. Sperm whale (*Physeter macrocephalus*)	1·30	1·30
906	50e. Humpback whale (*Megaptera novaeangliae*)	3·25	3·00
907	60e. Pilot whale (*Globicephala macrorhynchus*)	4·00	3·75

184 CAMS 51-F (biplane flying boat) at Calheta de Sao Martinho

2003. 75th Anniv of First Postal Hydroplane Base, Calheta de Sao Martinho. Multicoloured.

908	10e. Type **184**	65	60
909	42e. Paulin Paris (1st pilot) and route	2·75	2·50
910	60e. Route and CAMS 51-F	3·75	3·50
MS911	100×54 mm. 100e. As No. 908 but with design enlarged (57×33 mm)	4·75	4·50

185 Pope John Paul II and Child

2003. 25th Anniv of the Pontificate of Pope John Paul II. Multicoloured.

912	30e. Type **185**	1·90	1·50
913	60e. Pope John Paul II and ships (horiz)	3·50	3·50
MS914	83×64 mm. 100e. Pope John Paul II blessing crucifix	6·00	6·00

186 Mahogany (*Khaya senegalensis*)

2004. Trees. Multicoloured.

915	20e. Type **186**	90	80
916	27e. Black thorn (*Acacia nilotica*)	1·30	1·10
917	60e. Ceiba (*Ceiba pentandra*)	2·50	2·40
918	100e. Palm (*Phoenix atlantica*)	4·25	4·00

187 Windmill

2004. Ecological Energy Production.

919	**187** 20e. blue	80	70
920	**187** 60e. magenta	2·50	2·20
921	**187** 100e. green	4·00	3·75

188 Taekwondo

2004. Olympic Games, Athens. Multicoloured.

922	10e. Type **188**	60	50
923	60e. Gymnastics	2·50	2·30
924	100e. Boxing (horiz)	4·00	3·75

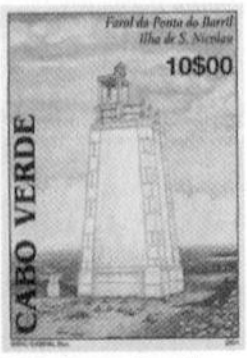

189 Ponta Barril, Sao Nicolau

2004. Lighthouses. Multicoloured.

925	10e. Type **189**	60	50
926	30e. Ponta Jalunga, Brava	1·80	1·50
927	40e. Dom Luis, Sao Vicente (horiz)	2·25	2·00
928	50e. Ponta Preta, Santiago (horiz)	3·00	2·75

190 House with Veranda

2004. Fogo Island's Historic Houses. Multicoloured.

929		20e. Type **190**	80	75
930		40e. House with veranda, bay window and wall with gate	2·00	1·75
931		50e. Three storied house	2·50	2·25
932		60e. Pink house	3·25	3·73

191 Wall-mounted Telephone

2004. Twentieth-century Telephones. Multicoloured.

933		10e. Type **191**	1·00	75
934		40e. Early windup handset	1·50	1·50
935		60e. Candlestick telephone	2·30	2·00
936		100e. Bakelite telephone	3·75	3·00

192 *storia storia*

2005. Stories. Multicoloured.

937		10e. Type **192**	75	35
938		20e. *era um vez!*	1·30	60
939		30e. *sapatinha ribera baxu*	1·50	1·00
940		60e. *Quem ki sabi mas conta midjor*	75	45

193 Amilcar Cabral (freedom fighter)

2005. 30th Anniv of Independence.

941	**193**	60e. multicoloured	3·50	3·00

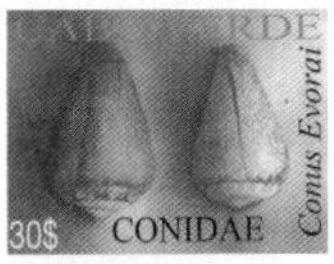

194 *Conus evorai*

2005. Shells. Multicoloured.

942		30e. Type **194**	1·30	90
943		40e. *Harpa doris*	2·00	1·80
944		50e. *Strombus lotus*	2·50	2·25
945		60e. *Phyllonotus duplex*	3·00	2·75

195 *Passer iagoensis*

2005. Birds. Multicoloured.

946		19e. Type **195**	1·40	1·00
947		42e. *Estrilda astrid*	1·80	1·50
948		44e. *Passer domesticus*	2·00	1·80
949		55e. *Acrocephalus brevipennis*	2·50	2·25

196 Emblem

2005. World Information Society Summit, Tunis.

950	**196**	60e. multicoloured	4·00	3·50

197 Tobacco Pipes

2005. Artefacts. Multicoloured.

951		5e. Type **197**	50	50
952		10e. Spy glass, ornate stand and decorated box	75	75
953		30e. Cannon	2·75	2·50
954		60e. Astrolabe	5·50	2·25
MS955		115×85 mm. 100e. Shackles (80×60 mm)	7·50	7·50

CHARITY TAX STAMPS

Used on certain days of the year as an additional postal tax on internal letters. Other values in some of the types were for use on telegrams only. The proceeds were devoted to public charities. If one was not affixed in addition to the ordinary postage, postage due stamps were used to collect the deficiency and the fine.

1925. As Marquis de Pombal issue of Portugal but inscr "CABO VERDE".

C266	**C73**	15c. violet	1·40	1·40
C267	-	15c. violet	1·40	1·40
C268	**C 75**	15c. violet	1·40	1·40

C16 St. Isabel

1948

C321	**C16**	50c. green	4·75	3·00
C322	**C16**	1e. red	9·25	3·75

1959. Surch.

C368		50c. on 1e. red	55	30

1959. Colours changed.

C369		50c. mauve	2·40	1·40
C370		1e. blue	2·40	1·40

C31

1967

C406	**C31**	30c. multicoloured	40	40
C407	**C31**	50c. mult (purple panel)	85	85
C408	**C31**	50c. mult (red panel)	65	65
C409	**C31**	1e. mult (brown panel)	95	95
C410	**C31**	1e. mult (purple panel)	95	95

C32

1968. Pharmaceutical Tax stamps surch as in Type **C32**.

C411a	**C32**	50c. on 1c. black, orange and green	1·50	1·10
C412c	**C32**	50c. on 2c. black, orange and green	70	40
C413	**C32**	50c. on 3c. black, orange and green	1·20	65
C414	**C32**	50c. on 5c. black, orange and green	1·20	65
C415	**C32**	50c. on 10c. black, orange and green	1·40	1·10
C416	**C32**	1e. on 1c. black, orange and green	3·00	2·20
C417a	**C32**	1e. on 2c. black, orange and green	2·10	1·70

NEWSPAPER STAMP

1893. "Newspaper" key-type inscr "CABO VERDE".

N37	**V**	2½r. brown	1·70	80

POSTAGE DUE STAMPS

1904. "Due" key-type inscr "CABO VERDE".

D119	**W**	5r. green	65	40
D120	**W**	10r. grey	65	40
D121	**W**	20r. brown	80	50
D122	**W**	30r. orange	2·00	50
D123	**W**	50r. brown	80	45
D124	**W**	60r. brown	15·00	5·25
D125	**W**	100r. mauve	3·00	1·60
D126	**W**	130r. blue	3·00	1·30
D127	**W**	200r. red	2·75	2·40
D128	**W**	500r. lilac	8·00	4·00

1911. Nos. D119/28 optd **REPUBLICA**.

D135		5r. green	45	30
D136		10r. grey	45	35
D137		20r. brown	55	35
D138		30r. orange	55	35
D139		50r. brown	1·00	60
D140		60r. brown	1·00	60
D141		100r. mauve	1·00	60
D142		130r. blue	1·20	95
D143		200r. red	3·25	2·20
D144		500r. lilac	4·00	3·50

1921. "Due" key-type inscr "CABO VERDE" with currency in centavos.

D252		½c. green	40	30
D253		1c. slate	40	30
D254		2c. brown	40	30
D255		3c. orange	40	30
D256		5c. brown	40	30
D257		6c. brown	40	30
D258		10c. mauve	40	30
D259		13c. blue	80	70
D260		20c. red	90	80
D261		50c. grey	2·50	1·80

1925. As Nos. C266/8, optd **MULTA**.

D266	**C73**	30c. violet	96	85
D267	-	30c. violet	95	85
D268	**C75**	30c. violet	95	85

1952. As Type **D45** of Angola, but inscr "CABO VERDE". Numerals in red; name in black.

D356		10c. brown and grey	30	30
D357		30c. black, blue & mauve	30	30
D358		50c. blue, green & yellow	30	30
D359		1e. blue and pale blue	30	30
D360		2e. brown and orange	40	40
D361		5e. green and grey	1·20	1·20

Pt. 4

CARABISCH NEDERLAND (CARIBBEAN NETHERLANDS)

A Netherlands colony consisting of two groups of islands in the Caribbean Sea, N. of Venezuela. Later part of Netherlands Antilles. On 10th October 2010 Bonaire, Saba and Sint Eustatius, as Caribbean Netherlands, became special municipalities of the Netherlands

100 cents = 1 gulden.

1 Saba, Bonaire and Sint Eustatius islands, Arms and Queen Beatrix of Netherlands

2010. Constitutional Reform

1	**1**	111c. multicoloured	3·50	3·50

Pt. 7

CAROLINE ISLANDS

A group of islands in the Pacific Ocean, formerly a German protectorate; under Japanese mandate after 1918. Now under United States trusteeship.

100 pfennig = 1 mark.

1899. Stamps of Germany optd **Karolinen**.

7	**8**	3pf. brown	15·00	17·00
8	**8**	5pf. green	21·00	21·00
9	**9**	10pf. red	21·00	23·00
10	**9**	20pf. blue	27·00	34·00
11	**9**	25pf. orange	65·00	75·00
12	**9**	50pf. brown	65·00	75·00

1901. "Yacht" key-types inscr "KAROLINEN".

13	**N**	3pf. brown	1·30	2·10
14	**N**	5pf. green	1·30	2·50
15	**N**	10pf. red	1·30	5·75
16	**N**	20pf. blue	1·50	10·50
17	**N**	25f. black & red on yellow	1·80	17·00
18	**N**	30pf. black & orge on buff	1·80	17·00
19	**N**	40pf. black and red	1·80	19·00
20	**N**	50pf. black & pur on buff	2·30	26·00
21	**N**	80pf. black & red on rose	3·50	30·00
22	**O**	1m. red	5·25	75·00
23	**O**	2m. blue	8·50	£110
24	**O**	3m. black	11·50	£180
25	**O**	5m. red and black	£190	£650

1910. No. 13 surch **5 Pf.**

26	**N**	5pf. on 3pf. brown		£7500

Pt. 3

CASTELROSSO

One of the Aegean Is. Occupied by the French Navy on 27 December 1915. The French withdrew in August 1921 and, after a period of Italian Naval administration, the island was included in the Dodecanese territory.

A. French Occupation.
100 centimes = 1 franc = 4 piastres.

B. Italian Occupation.
100 centesimi = 1 lira.

A. FRENCH OCCUPATION

1920. Stamps of 1902–20 of French Post Offices in Turkish Empire optd **B. N. F. CASTELLORIZO.**

F1	**A**	1c. grey	60·00	60·00
F2	**A**	2c. purple	60·00	60·00
F3	**A**	3c. red	60·00	60·00
F4	**A**	5c. green	75·00	70·00
F5	**B**	10c. red	75·00	70·00
F6	**B**	15c. red	£110	£100
F7	**B**	20c. brown	£120	£120
F9	**B**	30c. lilac	£130	£130
F10	**C**	40c. red and blue	£225	£225
F8	**B**	1pi. on 20c. blue	£120	£120
F11	**C**	2pi. on 50c. brown & lilac	£250	£250
F12	**C**	4pi. on 1f. red & green	£325	£325
F13	**C**	20pi. on 5f. blue & brown	£900	£850

1920. Optd **O. N. F. Castellorizo.** (a) On stamps of 1902–20 of French Post Offices in Turkish Empire.

F14	**A**	1c. grey	50·00	50·00
F15	**A**	2c. purple	50·00	50·00
F16	**A**	3c. red	50·00	50·00
F17	**A**	5c. green	50·00	50·00
F18	**B**	10c. red	55·00	55·00
F19	**B**	15c. red	65·00	65·00
F20	**B**	20c. brown	£130	£130
F22	**B**	30c. lilac	£120	£120
F23	**C**	40c. red and blue	£120	£120
F21	**B**	1pi. on 25c. blue	£130	£120
F24	**C**	2pi. on 50c. brown & lilac	£120	£120
F25	**C**	4pi. on 1f. red and green	£150	£150
F26	**C**	20pi. on 5f. blue & brown	£550	£500

(b) On Nos. 334 and 341 of France.

F27	**18**	10c. red	55·00	32·00
F28	**18**	25c. blue	55·00	32·00

1920. Stamps of France optd **O F CASTELLORISO.**

F29		5c. green	£300	£275
F30		10c. red	£300	£275
F31		20c. red	£300	£275
F32		25c. blue	£300	£275
F33	**13**	50c. brown and lilac	£1600	£1600
F34	**13**	1f. red and green	£1600	£1600

B. ITALIAN OCCUPATION

1922. Stamps of Italy optd **CASTELROSSO.**

15	**37**	5c. green	2·20	27·00
16	**37**	10c. red	2·20	27·00
17	**37**	15c. grey	2·20	38·00
18	**41**	20c. orange	2·20	38·00
19	**39**	25c. blue	2·20	30·00
20	**39**	40c. brown	2·20	30·00
21	**39**	50c. violet	2·20	38·00
22	**39**	60c. red	2·20	43·00
23	**39**	85c. brown	2·75	55·00
24	**34**	1l. brown and green	2·75	55·00

2

1923

10	**2**	5c. green	4·00	18·00
11	**2**	10c. red	4·00	18·00
12	**2**	25c. blue	4·00	18·00
13	**2**	50c. purple	4·00	18·00
14	**2**	1l. brown	4·00	18·00

1930. Ferrucci stamps of Italy optd **CASTELROSSO.**

25	**114**	20c. violet	8·50	7·50
26	-	25c. green (No. 283)	8·50	13·00
27	-	50c. black (as No. 284)	8·50	7·50
28	-	1l.25 blue (No. 285)	8·50	15·00
29	-	5l.+2l. red (as No. 286)	39·00	75·00

1932. Garibaldi stamps of Italy optd **CASTELROSSO.**

30		10c. brown	34·00	55·00
31	**128**	20c. brown	34·00	55·00
32	-	25c. green	34·00	55·00
33	**128**	30c. blue	34·00	55·00
34	-	50c. purple	34·00	55·00
35	-	75c. red	34·00	55·00
36	-	1l.25 blue	34·00	55·00

37	-	1l.75+25c. brown	34·00	55·00
38	-	2l.55+50c. red	34·00	55·00
39	-	5l.+1l. violet	34·00	55·00

Pt. 20

CAUCA

A State of Colombia, reduced to a Department in 1886, now uses Colombian stamps.

100 centavos = 1 peso.

2

1902. Imperf.

2	**2**	10c. black on red	6·00	5·75
3	**2**	20c. black on orange	4·00	3·75

Pt. 16

CAVALLA (KAVALLA)

French P.O. in a former Turkish port, now closed.

100 centimes = 1 franc.
40 paras = 1 piastre.

1893. Stamps of France optd **Cavalle** or surch also in figures and words.

41	**10**	5c. green	19·00	36·00
43	**10**	10c. black on lilac	12·00	13·00
45	**10**	15c. blue	50·00	28·00
46	**10**	1pi. on 25c. black on pink	21·00	4·50
47	**10**	2pi. on 50c. red	80·00	46·00
48	**10**	4pi. on 1f. green	£110	70·00
49	**10**	8pi. on 2f. brown on blue	£120	£130

1902. "Blanc", "Mouchon" and "Merson" key-types inscr "CAVALLE". The four higher values surch also.

50	**A**	5c. green	2·75	2·30
51	**B**	10c. red	3·75	2·75
52	**B**	15c. red	13·00	12·00
53	**B**	15c. orange	4·50	2·75
54	**B**	1pi. on 25c. blue	4·25	2·50
55	**C**	2pi. on 50c. brown & lilac	6·00	4·00
56	**C**	4pi. on 1f. red and green	7·25	5·50
57	**C**	8pi. on 2f. lilac and brown	22·00	13·00

Pt. 1

CAYES OF BELIZE

A chain of several hundred islands, coral atolls, reefs and sandbanks stretching along the eastern seaboard of Belize. The following issues for the Cayes of Belize fall outside the criteria for full listing as detailed on page viii.

100 cents = 1 dollar

APPENDIX

1984

Marine Life, Map and Views, 1, 2, 5, 10, 15, 25, 75c., $3, $5.
250th Anniv of *Lloyd's List* (newspaper). 25, 75c., $1, $2.
Olympic Games, Los Angeles. 10, 15, 75c., $2.
90th Anniv of "Caye Service" Local Stamps. 10, 15, 75c., $2.

1985

Birth Bicent of John J. Audubon (ornithologist). 25, 75c., $1, $3.
Shipwrecks. $1×4.

Pt. 1

CAYMAN ISLANDS

A group of islands in the British West Indies. A dependency of Jamaica until August 1962, when it became a Crown Colony.

1900. 12 pence = 1 shilling; 20 shillings = 1 pound.
1969. 100 cents = 1 Jamaican dollar.

1

1900

1a	**1**	½d. green	12·00	21·00
2	**1**	1d. red	13·00	3·50

2

1902

8	**2**	½d. green	10·00	13·00
4	**2**	1d. red	10·00	9·50
10	**2**	2½d. blue	10·00	4·50
13	**2**	4d. brown and blue	35·00	60·00
11	**2**	6d. brown	18·00	38·00
14	**2**	6d. olive and red	38·00	75·00
12	**2**	1s. orange	29·00	48·00
15	**2**	1s. violet and green	60·00	85·00
16	**2**	5s. orange and green	£200	£325

1907. Surch **One Halfpenny**.

17	½d. on 1d. red	55·00	85·00

1907. Surch.

18	½d. on 5s. orange and green	£300	£450
19	1d. on 5s. orange and green	£275	£400
35	2½d. on 4d. brown and blue	£1800	£3500

11

8

1907

38	**11**	¼d. brown	4·00	50
25	**8**	½d. green	3·75	4·00
26	**8**	1d. red	1·75	75
27	**8**	2½d. blue	5·00	2·50
28	**8**	3d. purple on yellow	3·25	2·75
29	**8**	4d. black and red on yellow	60·00	75·00
30	**8**	6d. purple	22·00	35·00
31	**8**	1s. black on green	9·00	22·00
32	**8**	5s. green and red on yellow	38·00	70·00
34	**8**	10s. green and red on green	£180	£250

12

1912

40	**12**	¼d. brown	1·00	40
41	**12**	½d. green	2·75	5·00
42	**12**	1d. red	3·25	2·50
43	**12**	2d. grey	1·00	10·00
44	**12**	2½d. blue	6·00	9·50
45a	**12**	3d. purple on yellow	3·50	8·00
46	**12**	4d. black and red on yellow	1·00	10·00
47	**12**	6d. purple	3·75	7·50
48b	**12**	1s. black on green	3·50	3·50
49	**12**	2s. purple and blue on blue	12·00	65·00
50	**12**	3s. green and violet	19·00	75·00
51	**12**	5s. green and red on yellow	80·00	£170
52b	**12**	10s. green and red on green	£110	£170

1917. Surch **1½d** with **WAR STAMP**. in two lines.

54	1½d. on 2½d. blue	1·75	6·00

1917. Optd or surch as last, but with **WAR STAMP** in one line and without full point.

57	½d. green	60	2·50
58	1½d. on 2d. grey	4·25	7·50
56	1½d. on 2½d. blue	30	60
59	1½d. on 2½d. orange	80	1·25

19

1921

69	**19**	¼d. brown	50	1·50
70	**19**	½d. green	50	30
71	**19**	1d. red	1·40	85
72	**19**	1½d. brown	1·75	30
73	**19**	2d. grey	1·75	4·00
74	**19**	2½d. blue	50	50
75	**19**	3d. purple on yellow	2·25	4·00
62	**19**	4d. red on yellow	1·00	4·25
76	**19**	4½d. green	3·25	3·00
77	**19**	6d. red	5·50	35·00
63	**19**	1s. black on green	1·25	9·50
80	**19**	2s. violet on blue	14·00	27·00
81	**19**	3s. violet	23·00	16·00
82	**19**	5s. green on yellow	25·00	55·00
83	**19**	10s. red on green	70·00	£100

20 Kings William IV and George V

1932. Centenary of "Assembly of Justices and Vestry".

84	**20**	¼d. brown	1·50	1·00
85	**20**	½d. green	2·75	9·00
86	**20**	1d. red	2·75	13·00
87	**20**	1½d. orange	2·75	2·75
88	**20**	2d. grey	2·75	3·50
89	**20**	2½d. blue	2·75	1·50
90	**20**	3d. green	7·00	5·50
91	**20**	6d. purple	10·00	23·00
92	**20**	1s. black and brown	17·00	32·00
93	**20**	2s. black and blue	50·00	85·00
94	**20**	5s. black and green	£100	£150
95	**20**	10s. black and red	£325	£425

21 Cayman Islands

1935

96	**21**	¼d. black and brown	50	1·00
97	-	½d. blue and green	1·00	1·00
98	-	1d. blue and red	4·00	2·25
99	-	1½d. black and orange	1·50	1·75
100	-	2d. blue and purple	3·75	1·10
101	-	2½d. blue and black	3·25	1·25
102	**21**	3d. black and green	2·50	3·00
103	-	6d. purple and black	8·50	4·00
104	-	1s. blue and orange	6·00	6·50
105	-	2s. blue and black	48·00	35·00
106	-	5s. green and black	60·00	60·00
107	-	10s. black and red	95·00	£100

DESIGNS—HORIZ: ½, 2d., 1s. Cat boat; 1d., 2s. Red-footed boobys ("Booby-birds"); 2½, 6d., 5s. Hawksbill turtles. VERT: 1½d., 10s. Queen or pink conch shells and coconut palms.

1935. Silver Jubilee. As T **13** of Antigua.

108	½d. black and green	15	1·00
109	2½d. brown and blue	5·00	1·00
110	6d. blue and olive	1·50	7·00
111	1s. grey and purple	11·00	9·50

1937. Coronation. As T **2** of Aden.

112	½d. green	30	1·90
113	1d. red	50	20
114	2½d. blue	95	40

26 Beach View

29 Hawksbill Turtles

1938

115a	**26**	¼d. orange	10	65
116	-	½d. green	1·00	55
117	-	1d. red	30	75
118	**26**	1½d. black	30	10
119a	**29**	2d. violet	60	30
120	-	2½d. blue	40	20
120a	-	2½d. orange	3·50	50
121	-	3d. orange	40	15
121a	-	3d. blue	3·00	30
122a	**29**	6d. olive	3·25	1·25
123	-	1s. brown	6·50	1·50
124a	**26**	2s. green	25·00	9·00
125	-	5s. red	38·00	15·00
126	**29**	10s. brown	30·00	9·00

DESIGNS—HORIZ: ½d., 1s. Caribbean dolphin; 1d., 3d. Map of Islands; 2½d., 5s. *Rembro* (schooner).

1946. Victory. As T **9** of Aden.

127	1½d. black	40	40
128	3d. yellow	40	40

1948. Silver Wedding. As T **10/11** of Aden.

129	½d. green	10	1·00
130	10s. blue	24·00	30·00

1949. U.P.U. As T **20/25** of Antigua.

131	2½d. orange	30	1·00
132	3d. blue	1·50	2·25
133	6d. olive	60	2·25
134	1s. brown	60	50

31 Cat Boat

1950

135	**31**	¼d. blue and red	15	60
136	-	½d. violet and green	15	1·25
137	-	1d. olive and blue	60	75
138	-	1½d. green and brown	40	75
139	-	2d. violet and red	1·25	1·50
140	-	2½d. blue and black	1·25	60
141	-	3d. green and blue	1·40	1·50
142	-	6d. brown and blue	2·00	1·25
143	-	9d. red and green	13·00	2·00
144	-	1s. brown and orange	3·25	2·75
145	-	2s. violet and purple	14·00	11·00
146	-	5s. olive and violet	24·00	7·00
147	-	10s. black and red	29·00	22·00

DESIGNS: ½d. Coconut grove, Cayman Brac; 1d. Green turtle; 1½d. Making thatch rope; 2d. Cayman seamen; 2½d. Map; 3d. Parrotfish; 6d. Bluff, Cayman Brac; 9d. Georgetown Harbour. 1s. Turtle in "crawl"; 2s. *Ziroma* (schooner); 5s. Boat-building; 10s. Government offices, Grand Cayman.

44 South Sound Lighthouse, Grand Cayman

1953. As 1950 issue but with portrait of Queen Elizabeth II as in T **44**.

148	¼d. blue and red	1·00	50
149	½d. violet and green	75	50
150	1d. olive and blue	70	40
151	1½d. green and brown	60	20
152	2d. violet and red	3·00	85
153	2½d. blue and black	3·50	80
154	3d. green and blue	4·00	60
155	4d. black and blue	2·00	40
156	6d. brown and blue	1·75	30
157	9d. red and green	7·50	30
158	1s. brown and orange	3·75	20
159	2s. violet and purple	13·00	9·00
160	5s. olive and violet	15·00	8·00
161	10s. black and red	22·00	8·00
161a	£1 blue	42·00	12·00

Portrait faces right on ¼d., 2d., 2½d., 4d., 1s. and 10s. values and left on others. The £1 shows a larger portrait of the Queen (vert).

1953. Coronation. As T **13** of Aden.

162	1d. black and green	30	2·00

46 Arms of the Cayman Islands

1959. New Constitution.

163	**46**	2½d. black and blue	45	2·50
164	**46**	1s. black and orange	55	50

48 Cat Boat

1962. Portraits as in T **48**.

165	-	¼d. green and red	55	1·00
166	**48**	1d. black and olive	80	20
167	-	1½d. yellow and purple	2·75	80
168	-	2d. blue and brown	1·00	30
169	-	2½d. violet and turquoise	85	1·00
170	-	3d. blue and red	30	10
171	-	4d. green and purple	3·50	60
172	-	6d. turquoise and sepia	3·25	30
173	**48**	9d. blue and purple	3·75	40
174	-	1s. sepia and red	1·50	10
175	-	1s.3d. turquoise and brown	6·00	2·25
176	-	1s.9d. turquoise and violet	19·00	1·25
177	-	5s. plum and green	12·00	14·00
178	-	10s. olive and blue	21·00	14·00
179	-	£1 red and black	21·00	27·00

DESIGNS—VERT: ¼d. Cuban amazon ("Cayman Parrot"); 9d. Angler with king mackerel; 10s. Arms; £1 Queen Elizabeth II. HORIZ: 1½d. *Schomburgkia thomsoniana* (orchid); 2d. Cayman Islands map; 2½d. Fisherman casting net; 3d. West Bay Beach; 4d. Green turtle; 6d. *Lydia E. Wilson* (schooner), 1s Iguana; 1s.3d. Swimming pool, Cayman Brac; 1s.9d. Water sports; 5s. Fort George.

1963. Freedom from Hunger. As T **28** of Aden.

180	1s.9d. red	30	15

1963. Centenary of Red Cross. As T **33** of Antigua.

181	1d. red and black	30	75
182	1s.9d. red and blue	70	1·75

1964. 400th Birth Anniv of Shakespeare. As T **34** of Antigua.

183	6d. purple	20	10

1965. Centenary of ITU. As T **36** of Antigua.

184	1d. blue and purple	15	10
185	1s.3d. purple and green	55	45

1965. ICY. As T **37** of Antigua.

186	1d. purple and turquoise	20	10
187	1s. green and lavender	60	25

1966. Churchill Commemoration. As T **38** of Antigua.

188	¼d. blue	10	2·25
189	1d. green	60	15
190	1s. brown	1·50	15
191	1s.9d. violet	1·60	75

1966. Royal Visit. As T **39** of Antigua.

192	1d. black and blue	75	35
193	1s.9d. black and mauve	2·75	1·50

1966. World Cup Football Championship. As T **40** of Antigua.

194	1½d. multicoloured	15	10
195	1s.9d. multicoloured	50	25

1966. Inauguration of WHO Headquarters, Geneva. As T **41** of Antigua.

196	2d. black, green and blue	65	15
197	1s.3d. black, purple and ochre	1·60	60

62 Telephone and Map

1966. International Telephone Links.

198	**62**	4d. multicoloured	20	20
199	**62**	9d. multicoloured	20	30

1966. 20th Anniv of UNESCO. As T **54/6** of Antigua.

200	1d. multicoloured	15	10
201	1s.9d. yellow, violet and olive	60	10
202	5s. black, purple and orange	1·50	70

63 B.A.C One Eleven 200/400 Airliner over *Ziroma* (Cayman schooner)

1966. Opening of Cayman Jet Service.

203	**63**	1s. black, blue and green	35	30
204	**63**	1s.9d. purple, blue and green	40	35

64 Water-skiing

1967. International Tourist Year. Multicoloured.

205	4d. Type **64**	35	10
206	6d. Skin diving	35	30
207	1s. Sport fishing	35	30
208	1s.9d. Sailing	40	75

68 Former Slaves and Emblem

1968. Human Rights Year.

209	**68**	3d. green, black and gold	10	10
210	**68**	9d. brown, gold and green	10	10
211	**68**	5s. ultram, gold and green	30	90

69 Long-jumping

1968. Olympic Games, Mexico. Multicoloured.

212	1s. Type **69**	15	10
213	1s.3d. High-jumping	20	25
214	2s. Pole-vaulting	20	75

72 *The Adoration of the Shepherds* (Fabritius)

1968. Christmas. Multicoloured.

215	¼d. Type **72***	10	20
221	¼d. Type **72***	10	20
216	1d. *The Adoration of the Shepherds* (Rembrandt)	10	10
217	6d. Type **72**	15	10
218	8d. As 1d.	15	15
219	1s.3d. Type **72**	20	25
220	2s. As 1d.	25	35

*No. 215 has a brown background and No. 221 a bright purple one.

74 Grand Cayman Thrush ("Cayman Thrush")

1969. Multicoloured

222	¼d. Type **74**	10	75
223	1d. Brahmin cattle	10	10
224	2d. Blowholes on the coast	10	10
225	2½d. Map of Grand Cayman	15	10
226	3d. Georgetown scene	10	10
227	4d. Royal Poinciana	15	10
228	6d. Cayman Brac and Little Cayman on chart	20	10
229	8d. Motor vessels at berth	25	10
230	1s. Basket-making	15	10
231	1s.3d. Beach scene	35	1·00
232	1s.6d. Straw-rope making	35	1·00
233	2s. Great barracuda	1·25	80
234	4s. Government House	35	80
235	10s. Arms of the Cayman Islands (vert)	1·00	1·50
236	£1 black, ochre and red (Queen Elizabeth II) (vert)	1·25	2·00

1969. Decimal Currency. Nos. 222/36 surch **C-DAY 8th September 1969.** Multicoloured.

238	**74**	¼c. on ¼d.	10	75
239	-	1c. on 1d.	10	10
240	-	2c. on 2d.	10	10
241	-	3c. on 4d.	10	10
242	-	4c. on 2½d.	10	10
243	-	5c. on 6d.	10	10
244	-	7c. on 8d.	10	10
245	-	8c. on 3d.	15	10
246	-	10c. on 1s.	25	10
247	-	12c. on 1s.3d.	35	1·75
248	-	15c. on 1s.6d.	45	1·50
249	-	20c. on 2s.	1·25	1·75
250	-	40c. on 4s.	45	85
251	-	$1 on 10s.	1·00	2·50
252	-	$2 on £1	1·50	3·25

90 *Madonna and Child* (Vivarini)

1969. Christmas. Multicoloured. Background colours given.

253	**90**	¼c. red	10	10
254	**90**	¼c. mauve	10	10
255	**90**	¼c. green	10	10
256	**90**	¼c. blue	10	10
257	-	1c. blue	10	10
258	**90**	5c. red	10	10
259	-	7c. green	10	10
260	**90**	12c. green	15	15
261	-	20c. purple	20	25

DESIGNS: 1c., 7c., 20c. *The Adoration of the Kings* (Gossaert).

92 *Noli me tangere* (Titian)

1970. Easter. Multicoloured; frame colours given.

262	**92**	¼c. red	10	10
263	**92**	¼c. green	10	10
264	**92**	¼c. brown	10	10
265	**92**	¼c. violet	10	10
266	**92**	10c. blue	35	10
267	**92**	12c. brown	40	10
268	**92**	40c. plum	55	60

93 Barnaby (*Barnaby Rudge*)

1970. Death Centenary of Charles Dickens.

269	**93**	1c. black, green and yellow	10	10
270	-	12c. black, brown and red	35	10
271	-	20c. black, brown and gold	40	10
272	-	40c. black, ultram & blue	45	25

DESIGNS: 12c. Sairey Gamp (*Martin Chuzzlewit*); 20c. Mr. Micawber and David (*David Copperfield*); 40c. The "Marchioness" (*The Old Curiosity Shop*).

97 Grand Cayman Thrush ("Cayman Thrush")

1970. Decimal Currency. Designs as Nos. 222/36, but with values inscribed in decimal currency as in T **97**.

273	¼c. multicoloured	65	30
274	1c. multicoloured	10	10
275	2c. multicoloured	10	10
276	3c. multicoloured	20	10
277	4c. multicoloured	20	10
278	5c. multicoloured	35	10
279	7c. multicoloured	30	10
280	8c. multicoloured	30	10
281	10c. multicoloured	30	10
282	12c. multicoloured	90	1·00
283	15c. multicoloured	1·25	4·00
284	20c. multicoloured	3·25	1·25
285	40c. multicoloured	85	75
286	$1 multicoloured	1·25	4·75
287	$2 black, ochre and red	2·00	4·75

98 The Three Wise Men

1970. Christmas.

288	**98**	¼c. green, grey and emerald	10	10
289	-	1c. black, yellow and green	10	10
290	**98**	5c. grey, orange and red	10	10
291	-	10c. black, yellow and red	10	10
292	**98**	12c. grey, green and blue	15	10
293	-	20c. black, yellow and green	20	15

DESIGN: 1, 10, 20c. Nativity scene and Globe.

100 Grand Cayman Terrapin

1971. Turtles. Multicoloured.

294	5c. Type **100**	30	25
295	7c. Green turtle	35	25
296	12c. Hawksbill turtle	55	30
297	20c. Turtle farm	1·00	1·40

101 *Dendrophylax fawcettii*

1971. Orchids. Multicoloured.

298	¼c. Type **101**	10	1·25
299	2c. *Schomburgkia thomsoniana*	60	90
300	10c. *Vanilla claviculata*	2·25	50
301	40c. *Oncidium variegatum*	4·50	3·50

102 *Adoration of the Kings* (French 15th century)

1971. Christmas. Multicoloured.

302	¼c. Type **102**	10	10
303	1c. *The Nativity* (Parisian, 14th century)	10	10
304	5c. *Adoration of the Magi* (Burgundian, 15th century)	10	10
305	12c. Type **102**	20	15
306	15c. As 1c.	20	25
307	20c. As 5c.	25	35
MS308	113×115 mm. Nos. 302/7	1·25	2·25

103 Turtle and Telephone Cable

1972. Co-axial Telephone Cable.

309	**103**	2c. multicoloured	10	10
310	**103**	10c. multicoloured	15	10
311	**103**	40c. multicoloured	30	40

104 Court House Building

1972. New Government Buildings. Multicoloured.

312	5c. Type **104**	10	10
313	15c. Legislative Assembly Building	10	10
314	25c. Type **104**	15	15
315	40c. As 15c.	20	30
MS316	121×108 mm. Nos. 312/15	50	2·00

1972. Royal Silver Wedding. As T **52** of Ascension but with Hawksbill Turtle and Queen or Pink Conch in background.

317	12c. violet	15	10
318	30c. green	15	20

106 $1 Coin and Note

1972. First Issue of Currency. Multicoloured.

319	3c. Type **106**	20	10

320	6c. $5 Coin and note	20	70
321	15c. $10 Coin and note	60	30
322	25c. $25 Coin and note	80	45
MS323	128×107 mm. Nos. 319/22	3·50	3·25

107 *The Way of Sorrow*

1973. Easter. Stained-glass Windows. Multicoloured.

324	10c. Type **107**	15	10
325	12c. *Christ Resurrected*	20	10
326	20c. *The Last Supper* (horiz)	25	15
327	30c. *Christ on the Cross* (horiz)	30	25
MS328	122×105 mm. Nos. 324/7 (imperf)	1·00	1·60

108 *The Nativity* (Sforza Book of Hours)

1973. Christmas.

329	**108** 3c. multicoloured	10	10
330	- 5c. multicoloured	10	10
331	**108** 9c. multicoloured	15	10
332	- 12c. multicoloured	15	10
333	**108** 15c. multicoloured	15	15
334	- 25c. multicoloured	20	25

DESIGN: 5, 12, 25c. *The Adoration of the Magi* (Breviary of Queen Isabella).

1973. Royal Wedding. As T **47** of Anguilla. Background colour given. Multicoloured.

335	10c. green	10	10
336	30c. mauve	15	10

109 White-winged Dove

1974. Birds (1st series). Multicoloured.

337	3c. Type **109**	2·00	30
338	10c. Vitelline warbler	2·75	30
339	12c. Antillean grackle ("Greater Antilliean Grackle")	2·75	30
340	20c. Great red-bellied woodpecker ("West Indian Red-bellied Woodpecker")	4·25	80
341	30c. Stripe-headed tanager	5·50	1·50
342	50c. Yucatan vireo	7·00	5·50

See also Nos. 383/8.

110 Old School Building

1974. 25th Anniv of University of West Indies. Multicoloured.

343	12c. Type **110**	10	10
344	20c. New Comprehensive School	15	20
345	30c. Creative Arts Centre, Mona	15	60

111 Hermit Crab and Staghorn Coral

1974. Size 41½×27 mm or 27×41½ mm. Multicoloured.

346	1c. Type **111**	3·50	1·25
347	3c. Treasure-chest and lion's paw	3·50	75
348	4c. Treasure and spotted scorpionfish	50	70
349	5c. Flintlock pistol and brain coral	3·00	75
350	6c. Blackbeard and green turtle	35	2·25
366	8c. As 9c.	2·50	8·50
351	9c. Jewelled pomander and porkfish	4·00	11·00
352	10c. Spiny lobster and treasure	4·50	80
353	12c. Jewelled sword and dagger and sea-fan	35	2·00
354	15c. Cabrit's murex and treasure	45	1·25
417	20c. Queen or pink conch and treasure	3·50	3·00
356	25c. Hogfish and treasure	45	70
357	40c. Gold chalice and seawhip	4·00	1·25
358	$1 Coat of arms (vert)	2·75	3·25
419	$2 Queen Elizabeth II (vert)	8·50	6·50

For smaller designs see Nos. 445/52.

112 Sea Captain and Ship (Shipbuilding)

1974. Local Industries. Multicoloured.

360	8c. Type **112**	30	10
361	12c. Thatcher and cottage	25	10
362	20c. Farmer and plantation	25	20
MS363	92×132 mm. Nos. 360/2	1·50	3·25

113 Arms of Cinque Ports and Lord Warden's Flag

1974. Birth Centenary of Sir Winston Churchill. Multicoloured.

380	12c. Type **113**	15	10
381	50c. Churchill's coat of arms	45	70
MS382	98×86 mm. Nos. 380/1	60	1·60

1975. Birds (2nd series). As T **109**. Multicoloured.

383	3c. Common flicker ("Yellow-shafted Flicker")	70	50
384	10c. Black-billed whistling duck ("West Indian Tree Duck")	1·25	50
385	12c. Yellow warbler	1·40	65
386	20c. White-bellied dove	2·00	2·00
387	30c. Magnificent frigate bird	3·25	4·25
388	50c. Cuban amazon ("Cayman Amazon")	3·75	12·00

114 "The Crucifixion"

1975. Easter. French Pastoral Staffs.

389	**114** 15c. multicoloured	10	20
390	- 35c. multicoloured	20	45
MS391	128×98 mm. Nos, 389/90	65	2·75

DESIGN: 35c. Pastoral staff similar to Type **114**.

115 Israel Hands

1975. Pirates. Multicoloured.

392	10c. Type **115**	35	15
393	12c. John Fenn	35	30
394	20c. Thomas Anstis	60	50
395	30c. Edward Low	65	1·50

1975. Christmas.*Virgin and Child with Angels*. As T **114**.

396	12c. multicoloured	10	10
397	50c. multicoloured	30	30
MS398	113×85 mm. Nos. 396/7	1·00	3·00

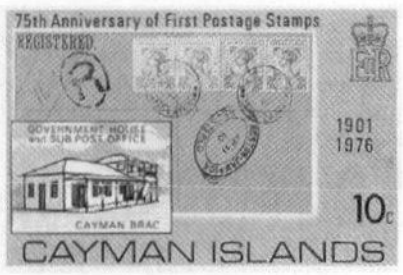

116 Registered Cover, Government House and Sub-Post Office

1975. 75th Anniv of First Cayman Islands Postage Stamp. Multicoloured.

399	10c. Type **116**	15	10
400	20c. ½d. stamp and 1890–94 postmark	20	15
401	30c. 1d. stamp and 1908 surcharge	30	25
402	50c. ½d. and 1d. stamps	45	65
MS403	117×147 mm. Nos. 399/402	2·50	3·00

117 Seals of Georgia, Delaware and New Hampshire

1976. Bicentenary of American Revolution. Mulicoloured.

404	10c. Type **117**	40	15
405	15c. Carolina, New Jersey and Maryland seals	55	20
406	20c. Virginia, Rhode Island and Massachusetts seals	65	25
407	25c. New York, Connecticut and North Carolina seals	65	35
408	30c. Pennsylvania seal, Liberty Bell and U.S. Great Seal	70	40
MS409	166×124 mm. Nos. 404/8	4·00	8·50

118 "470" Dinghies

1976. Olympic Games, Montreal. Multicoloured.

410	20c. Type **118**	40	10
411	50c. Racing dinghy	70	50

119 Queen Elizabeth II and Westminster Abbey

1977. Silver Jubilee. Multicoloured.

427	8c. The Prince of Wales' visit, 1973	10	20
428	30c. Type **119**	15	40
429	50c. Preparation for the Anointing (horiz)	30	75

120 Scuba Diving

1977. Tourism. Multicoloured.

430	5c. Type **120**	15	10
431	10c. Exploring a wreck	20	10
432	20c. Royal gramma ("Fairy basslet") (fish)	55	20
433	25c. Sergeant major (fish)	65	35
MS434	146×89 mm. Nos. 430/3	2·00	4·50

121 *Composia fidelissima* (moth)

1977. Butterflies and Moth. Multicoloured.

435	5c. Type **121**	75	20
436	8c. *Heliconius charithonia*	85	20
437	10c. *Danaus gilippus*	85	20
438	15c. *Agraulis vanillae*	1·25	45
439	20c. *Junonia evarete*	1·25	45
440	30c. *Anartia jatrophae*	1·50	70

122 Cruise Liner *Southward*

1978. New Harbour and Cruise Ships. Multicoloured.

441	3c. Type **122**	40	10
442	5c. Cruise liner *Renaissance*	40	10
443	30c. New harbour (vert)	90	25
444	50c. Cruise liner *Daphne* (vert)	1·25	65

1978. As Nos. 346/7, 349, 352, 417, 357/8 and 419, but designs smaller, 40×26 mm or 26×40 mm.

445	1c. Type **111**	1·00	1·25
446	3c. Treasure chest and lion's paw	80	50
447	5c. Flintlock pistol and brain coral	1·50	2·00
448	10c. Spiny lobster and treasure	1·25	60
449	20c. Queen or pink conch and treasure	2·25	1·00
450	40c. Gold chalice and seawhip	13·00	18·00
451	$1 Coat of arms (vert)	20·00	5·50
452	$2 Queen Elizabeth II (vert)	4·00	20·00

123 *The Crucifixion* (Durer)

1978. Easter and 450th Death Anniv of Durer.

459	**123** 10c. mauve and black	30	10
460	- 15c. yellow and black	40	15
461	- 20c. turquoise and black	50	20
462	- 30c. lilac and black	60	35
MS463	120×108 mm. Nos. 459/62	4·25	6·50

DESIGNS: 15c. *Christ at Emmaus*; 20c. *The Entry into Jerusalem*; 30c. *Christ washing Peter's Feet*.

124 "Explorers" Singing Game

1978. Third International Council Meeting of Girls' Brigade. Multicoloured.

464	3c. Type **124**	20	10
465	10c. Colour party	25	10
466	20c. Girls and Duke of Edinburgh Award interests	40	20
467	50c. Girls using domestic skills	70	80

125 Yale of Beaufort

1978. 25th Anniv of Coronation.

468	**125** 30c. green, mauve and silver	20	25
469	- 30c. multicoloured	20	25
470	- 30c. green, mauve and silver	20	25

DESIGNS: No. 469, Queen Elizabeth II; 470, Barn owl.

126 Four-eyed Butterflyfish

1978. Fish (1st series). Multicoloured.

471	3c. Type **126**	25	10
472	5c. Grey angelfish	30	10
473	10c. Squirrelfish	45	10

474	15c. Queen parrotfish	60	30
475	20c. Spanish hogfish	70	35
476	30c. Queen angelfish	80	50

127 Lockheed L.18 Lodestar

1979. 25th Anniv of Owen Roberts Airfield. Multicoloured.

477	3c. Type **127**	30	15
478	5c. Consolidated PBY-5A Catalina amphibian	30	15
479	10c. Vickers Viking 1B	35	15
480	15c. B.A.C. One Eleven 455 on tarmac	65	25
481	20c. Piper PA-31 Cheyenne II, Bell 47G Trooper helicopter and Hawker Siddeley H.S.125	75	35
482	30c. B.A.C. One Eleven 475 over airfield	1·00	50

128 Trumpetfish

1979. Fish (2nd series). Multicoloured.

483	1c. Type **128**	10	10
484	3c. Nassau grouper	25	10
485	5c. French angelfish	25	10
486	10c. Schoolmaster snapper	35	10
487	20c. Banded butterflyfish	55	25
488	50c. Black-barred soldierfish	1·00	70

129 1900 1d. Stamp

1979. Death Centenary of Sir Rowland Hill.

489 **129**	5c. black, carmine and blue	10	10
490 -	10c. multicoloured	15	10
491 -	20c. multicoloured	20	25
MS492	138×90 mm. 50c. mult	55	65

DESIGNS: 10c. Great Britain 1902 3d. purple on lemon; 20c. 1955 £1 blue.

130 The Holy Family and Angels

1979. Christmas. Multicoloured.

493	10c. Type **130**	15	10
494	20c. Angels appearing to Shepherds	25	10
495	30c. Nativity	30	20
496	40c. The Magi	40	30

131 Local Rotary Project

1980. 75th Anniv of Rotary International.

497 **131**	20c. blue, black and yellow	20	15
498 -	30c. blue, black and yellow	25	20
499 -	50c. blue, yellow and black	35	30

DESIGNS—VERT: 30c. Paul P. Harris (founder); 50c. Rotary anniversary emblem.

132 Walking Mail Carrier

1980. "London 1980" International Stamp Exhibition. Multicoloured.

500	5c. Type **132**	10	10
501	10c. Delivering mail by cat boat	15	10
502	15c. Mounted mail carrier	20	10
503	30c. Horse-drawn wagonette	25	15
504	40c. Postman on bicycle	35	15
505	$1 Motor transport	45	55

133 Queen Elizabeth the Queen Mother at the Derby, 1976

1980. 80th Birthday of the Queen Mother.

506 **133**	20c. multicoloured	20	25

134 American Thorny Oyster

1980. Shells (1st series). Multicoloured.

507	5c. Type **134**	25	10
508	10c. West Indian murex	30	10
509	30c. Angular triton	45	40
510	50c. Caribbean vase	70	80

See also Nos. 565/8 and 582/5.

135 *Lantana camara*

1980. Flowers (1st series). Multicoloured.

511	5c. Type **135**	15	10
512	15c. *Bauhinia variegata*	20	10
513	30c. *Hibiscus* hybrid	25	10
514	$1 *Crinum amabile* ("Milk and Wine Lily")	50	90

See also Nos. 541/4.

136 Juvenile Tarpon and Fire Sponge

1980. Multicoloured

515A	3c. Type **136**	1·00	2·50
516B	5c. Flat tree or mangrove-root oyster	1·25	80
517A	10c. Mangrove crab	50	1·50
518A	15c. Lizard and *Phyciodes phaon* (butterfly)	1·00	1·75
519A	20c. Louisiana heron (Tricoloured Heron)	1·50	2·25
520A	30c. Red mangrove flower	70	1·00
521A	40c. Red mangrove seeds	75	1·00
522A	50c. Waterhouse's leaf-nosed bat	1·25	1·50
523A	$1 Black-crowned night heron	4·50	5·00
524A	$2 Coat of arms	1·25	3·75
525A	$4 Queen Elizabeth II	2·00	4·25

137 Eucharist

1981. Easter. Multicoloured.

526	3c. Type **137**	10	10
527	10c. Crown of thorns	10	10
528	20c. Crucifix	15	10
529	$1 Lord Jesus Christ	50	60

138 Wood Slave

1981. Reptiles and Amphibians. Multicoloured.

530	20c. Type **138**	25	20
531	30c. Cayman iguana	30	35
532	40c. Lion lizard	40	45
533	50c. Terrapin ("Hickatee")	45	55

139 Prince Charles

1981. Royal Wedding. Multicoloured.

534	20c. Wedding bouquet from Cayman Islands	15	10
535	30c. Type **139**	20	10
536	$1 Prince Charles and Lady Diana Spencer	50	75

140 Disabled Scuba Divers

1981. Int Year for Disabled Persons. Multicoloured.

537	5c. Type **140**	10	10
538	15c. Old school for the handicapped	25	20
539	20c. New school for the handicapped	30	25
540	$1 Disabled people in wheelchairs by the sea	1·25	85

1981. Flowers (2nd series). As T **135**. Multicoloured.

541	3c. *Bougainvillea spectabilis*	10	10
542	10c. Morning Glory	15	10
543	20c. *Hippeastrum equestre* (Wild amaryllis)	25	25
544	$1 *Cordia sebestena*	1·00	1·75

141 Dr. Robert Koch and Microscope

1982. Centenary of Robert Koch's Discovery of Tubercle Bacillus. Multicoloured.

545	15c. Type **141**	25	25
546	30c. Koch looking through microscope (vert)	45	45
547	40c. Microscope (vert)	70	70
548	50c. Dr. Robert Koch (vert)	80	80

142 Bride and Groom walking down Aisle

1982. 21st Birthday of Princess of Wales. Multicoloured.

549	20c. Cayman Islands coat of arms	20	25
550	30c. Lady Diana Spencer in London, June, 1981	60	45
551	40c. Type **142**	60	65
552	50c. Formal portrait	2·25	1·00

143 Pitching Tent

1982. 75th Anniv of Boy Scout Movement. Multicoloured.

553	3c. Type **143**	15	10
554	20c. Scouts camping	40	40
555	30c. Cub Scouts and Leaders	60	55
556	50c. Boating skills	80	85

144 *Madonna and Child with the Infant Baptist*

1982. Christmas. Raphael Paintings. Multicoloured.

557	3c. Type **144**	10	10
558	10c. *Madonna of the Tower*	20	20
559	20c. *Ansidei Madonna*	35	35
560	30c. *Madonna and Child*	50	50

145 Mace

1982. 150th Anniv of Representative Government. Multicoloured.

561	3c. Type **145**	10	20
562	10c. Old Courthouse	20	20
563	20c. Commonwealth Parliamentary Association coat of arms	35	45
564	30c. Legislative Assembly building	50	90

1983. Shells (2nd series). As T **134**. Multicoloured.

565	5c. Colourful Atlantic moon	15	30
566	10c. King helmet	25	30
567	20c. Rooster-tail conch	30	40
568	$1 Reticulated cowrie-helmet	50	4·00

146 Legislative Building, Cayman Brac

1983. Royal Visit. Multicoloured.

569	20c. Type **146**	45	35
570	30c. Legislative Building, Grand Cayman	60	50
571	50c. Duke of Edinburgh (vert)	1·25	90
572	$1 Queen Elizabeth II (vert)	2·00	2·00
MS573	113×94 mm. Nos. 569/72	6·50	4·25

147 Satellite View of Earth

1983. Commonwealth Day. Multicoloured.

574	3c. Type **147**	20	15
575	15c. Cayman Islands and Commonwealth flags	50	40
576	20c. Fishing	50	40
577	40c. Portrait of Queen Elizabeth II	75	80

148 MRCU Cessna Ag Wagon

1983. Bicentenary of Manned Flight. Multicoloured.

578	3c. Type **148**	60	50
579	10c. Consolidated PBY-5A Catalina amphibian	65	50
580	20c. Boeing 727-200	1·25	1·50
581	40c. Hawker Siddeley H.S.748	1·75	3·75

1984. Shells (3rd series). As T **134**. Multicoloured.

582	3c. Florida moon	70	40
583	10c. Austin's cone	80	40
584	30c. Leaning dwarf triton	2·25	2·75
585	50c. Filose or threaded turban	2·50	4·25

149 *Song of Norway* (cruise liner)

1984. 250th Anniv of *Lloyd's List* (newspaper). Multicoloured.

586	5c. Type **149**	55	20
587	10c. View of old harbour	55	25
588	25c. Wreck of *Ridgefield* (freighter)	1·10	1·00
589	50c. *Goldfield* (schooner)	2·00	2·75
MS590	105×75 mm. $1 *Goldfield* (schooner) (different)	2·10	2·25

1984. Universal Postal Union Congress, Hamburg. No. 589 optd **UPU CONGRESS HAMBURG 1984**.

591	50c. Schooner *Goldfield*	1·50	2·00

151 Snowy Egret

1984. Birds of the Cayman Islands (1st series). Multicoloured.

592	5c. Type **151**	1·00	75
593	10c. Bananaquit	1·00	75
594	35c. Belted kingfisher ("Kingfisher")	3·25	2·50
595	$1 Brown booby	6·00	11·00

See also Nos. 627/30.

152 Couple on Beach at Sunset

1984. Christmas. Local Festivities. Multicoloured.

596	5c. Type **152**	85	1·50
597	5c. Family and schooner	85	1·50
598	5c. Carol singers	85	1·50
599	5c. East End bonfire	85	1·50
600	25c. Yachts	1·25	1·50
601	25c. Father Christmas in power-boat	1·25	1·50
602	25c. Children on beach	1·25	1·50
603	25c. Beach party	1·25	1·50
MS604	59×79 mm. $1 As No. 599, but larger 27×41 mm	4·00	4·50

Nos. 596/9 and 600/3 were each printed together, *se-tenant*, the four designs of each value forming a composite picture of a beach scene at night (5c.) or in the daytime (25c.).

153 *Schomburgkia thomsoniana* (var. minor)

1985. Orchids. Multicoloured.

605	5c. Type **153**	1·00	30
606	10c. *Schomburgkia thomsoniana*	1·00	30
607	25c. *Encyclia plicata*	2·50	1·00
608	50c. *Dendrophylax fawcettii*	3·75	3·00

154 Freighter Aground

1985. Shipwrecks. Multicoloured.

609	5c. Type **154**	90	50
610	25c. Submerged sailing ship	2·75	1·25
611	35c. Wrecked trawler	3·00	2·50
612	40c. Submerged wreck on its side	3·25	3·50

155 Athletics

1985. International Youth Year. Multicoloured.

613	5c. Type **155**	25	25
614	15c. Students in library	40	30
615	25c. Football (vert)	75	55
616	50c. Netball (vert)	1·75	2·50

156 Morse Key (1935)

1985. 50th Anniv of Telecommunications System. Multicoloured.

617	5c. Type **156**	45	70
618	10c. Hand cranked telephone	50	70
619	25c. Tropospheric scatter dish (1966)	1·50	80
620	50c. Earth station dish aerial (1979)	2·50	5·00

1986. 60th Birthday of Queen Elizabeth II. As T **110** of Ascension. Multicoloured.

621	5c. Princess Elizabeth at wedding of Lady May Cambridge, 1931	10	30
622	10c. In Norway, 1955	15	30
623	25c. Queen inspecting Royal Cayman Islands Police, 1983	1·50	75
624	50c. During Gulf tour, 1979	75	2·00
625	$1 At Crown Agents Head Office, London, 1983	1·10	2·75

157 Magnificent Frigate Bird

1986. Birds of the Cayman Islands (2nd series). Multicoloured.

627	10c. Type **157**	1·75	1·00
628	25c. Black-billed whistling duck ("West Indian Whistling Duck") (vert)	2·25	1·40
629	35c. La Sagra's flycatcher (vert)	2·50	2·50
630	40c. Yellow-faced grassquit	3·00	5·00

1986. Royal Wedding. As T **112** of Ascension. Multicoloured.

633	5c. Prince Andrew and Miss Sarah Ferguson	40	25
634	50c. Prince Andrew aboard H.M.S. *Brazen*	1·60	2·25

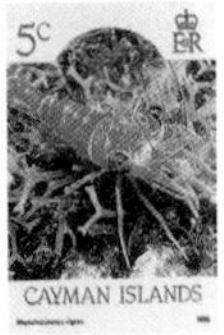

158 Red Coral Shrimp

1986. Marine Life. Multicoloured.

635	5c. Type **158**	40	1·00
636	10c. Yellow crinoid	40	50
637	15c. Hermit crab	35	60
638	20c. Tube dwelling anemone	35	1·75
639	25c. Christmas tree worm	45	2·50
640	35c. Porcupinefish	70	2·75
641	50c. Orangeball anemone	80	4·50
642	60c. Basket starfish	3·50	9·00
643	75c. Flamingo tongue	10·00	11·00
644	$1 Sea anemone	1·10	2·50
645	$2 Diamond blenny	1·25	4·75
646	$4 Rough file shell	2·00	6·50

159 Golf

1987. Tourism. Multicoloured.

647	10c. Type **159**	2·50	1·25
648	15c. Sailing	2·50	1·25
649	25c. Snorkelling	2·50	1·25
650	35c. Paragliding	2·75	2·00
651	$1 Game fishing	5·50	11·00

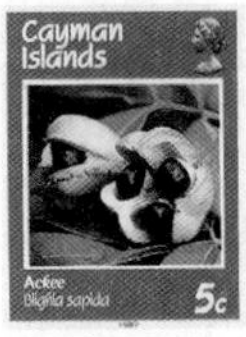

160 Ackee

1987. Cayman Islands Fruits. Multicoloured.

652	5c. Type **160**	75	1·25
653	25c. Breadfruit	2·00	55
654	35c. Pawpaw	2·00	70
655	$1 Soursop	4·50	8·00

161 Lion Lizard

1987. Lizards. Multicoloured.

656	10c. Type **161**	2·25	65
657	50c. Iguana	4·50	3·50
658	$1 Anole	5·50	7·00

162 Poinsettia

1987. Flowers. Multicoloured.

659	5c. Type **162**	65	45
660	25c. Periwinkle	1·75	75
661	35c. Yellow allamanda	1·90	1·10
662	75c. Blood lily	3·50	4·50

163 *Hemiargus ammon* and *Strymon martialis*

1988. Butterflies. Multicoloured.

663	5c. Type **163**	1·25	65
664	25c. *Phocides pigmalion*	2·50	85
665	50c. *Anaea troglodyta*	4·00	3·75
666	$1 *Papilio andraemon*	5·00	5·00

164 Green-backed Heron

1988. Herons. Multicoloured.

667	5c. Type **164**	1·25	65
668	25c. Louisiana heron	2·25	85
669	50c. Yellow-crowned night heron	3·00	3·00
670	$1 Little blue heron	3·50	4·25

165 Cycling

1988. Olympic Games, Seoul. Multicoloured.

671	10c. Type **165**	3·00	1·00
672	50c. Cayman Airways Boeing 727 airliner and national team	4·00	3·25
673	$1 "470" dinghy	4·00	4·25
MS674	53×60 mm. $1 Tennis	4·00	3·00

166 Princess Alexandra

1988. Visit of Princess Alexandra. Multicoloured.

675	5c. Type **166**	1·75	1·00
676	$1 Princess Alexandra in evening dress	7·50	6·50

167 George Town Post Office, and Cayman Postmark on Jamaica 1d., 1889

1989. Centenary of Cayman Islands Postal Service. Multicoloured.

677	**167**	5c. multicoloured	85	1·00
678	-	25c. green, black and blue	2·00	1·00
679	-	35c. multicoloured	2·00	1·25
680	-	$1 multicoloured	8·00	9·50

DESIGNS: 25c. *Orinoco* (mail steamer) and 1900 ½d. stamp; 35c. G.P.O., Grand Cayman and "London 1980" $1 stamp; $1 Cayman Airways B.A.C. One Eleven 200/400 airplane and 1966 1s. Jet Service stamp.

168 Captain Bligh ashore in West Indies

1989. Captain Bligh's Second Breadfruit Voyage, 1791–93. Multicoloured.

681	50c. Type **168**	5·00	5·00
682	50c. H.M.S. *Providence* (sloop) at anchor	5·00	5·00
683	50c. Breadfruit in tubs and H.M.S. *Assistant* (transport)	5·00	5·00
684	50c. Sailors moving tubs of breadfruit	5·00	5·00
685	50c. Midshipman and stores	5·00	5·00

Nos. 681/5 were printed together, *se-tenant*, forming a composite design.

169 Panton House

1989. Architecture. Designs showing George Town buildings. Multicoloured.

686	5c. Type **169**	75	1·00
687	10c. Town hall and clock tower	75	1·00
688	25c. Old Court House	1·40	60
689	35c. Elmslie Memorial Church	1·60	75
690	$1 Post Office	3·50	6·50

170 Map of Grand Cayman, 1773, and Surveying Instruments

1989. Island Maps and Survey Ships. Multicoloured.

691	5c. Type **170**	2·00	1·50
692	25c. Map of Cayman Islands, 1956, and surveying instruments	4·25	1·25
693	50c. H.M.S. *Mutine*, 1914	6·00	5·50
694	$1 H.M.S. *Vidal*, 1956	9·00	11·00

171 French Angelfish

1990. Angelfishes. Multicoloured.

707	10c. Type **171**	1·25	70
708	25c. Grey angelfish	2·25	90
709	50c. Queen angelfish	3·50	4·25
710	$1 Rock beauty	5·50	8·00

1990. 90th Birthday of Queen Elizabeth the Queen Mother. As T **134** of Ascension.

711	50c. multicoloured	1·25	2·25
712	$1 black and blue	2·75	4·00

DESIGNS—21×36 mm: 50c. Silver Wedding photograph, 1948. 29×37 mm: $1 King George VI and Queen Elizabeth with Winston Churchill, 1940.

172 *Danaus eresimus*

1990. "Expo 90" International Garden and Greenery Exhibition, Osaka. Butterflies. Multicoloured.

713	5c. Type **172**	65	60
714	25c. *Brephidium exilis*	1·50	1·10
715	35c. *Phyciodes phaon*	1·75	1·25
716	$1 *Agraulis vanillae*	4·00	6·50

173 Goes Weather Satellite

1991. International Decade for Natural Disaster Reduction. Multicoloured.

717	5c. Type **173**	80	70
718	30c. Meteorologist tracking hurricane	2·00	1·10
719	40c. Damaged buildings	2·25	1·25
720	$1 U.S. Dept of Commerce weather reconnaisance Lockheed WP-3D Orion	5·00	8·00

174 Angels and *Datura candida*

1991. Christmas. Multicoloured.

721	5c. Type **174**	80	80
722	30c. Mary and Joseph going to Bethlehem and *Allamanda cathartica*	2·00	60
723	40c. Adoration of the Kings and *Euphorbia pulcherrima*	2·25	1·10
724	60c. Holy Family and *Guaiacum officinale*	3·25	6·00

175 Coconut Palm

1991. Island Scenes. Multicoloured.

725	5c. Type **175**	50	50
726	15c. Beach scene (horiz)	1·75	50
727	20c. Poincianas in bloom (horiz)	70	35
728	30c. Blowholes (horiz)	1·75	50
729	40c. Police band (horiz)	2·50	1·40
730	50c. *Song of Norway* (liner) at George Town	2·00	1·40
731	60c. The Bluff, Cayman Brac (horiz)	1·75	2·25
732	80c. Coat of arms	1·50	2·50
733	90c. View of Hell (horiz)	1·60	2·50
734	$1 Game fishing (horiz)	3·25	2·50
735	$2 *Nieuw Amsterdam* (1983) and *Holiday* (liners) in harbour	8·00	7·50
736	$8 Queen Elizabeth II	16·00	19·00

1992. 40th Anniv of Queen Elizabeth II's Accession. As T **143** of Ascension. Multicoloured.

737	5c. Caymans' house	30	30
738	20c. Sunset over islands	1·00	50
739	30c. Beach	1·10	65
740	40c. Three portraits of Queen Elizabeth	1·10	1·00
741	$1 Queen Elizabeth II	2·00	3·50

176 Single Cyclist

1992. Olympic Games, Barcelona. Cycling. Multicoloured.

742	15c. Type **176**	1·75	65
743	40c. Two cyclists	2·50	1·50
744	60c. Cyclist's legs	3·00	3·25
745	$1 Two pursuit cyclists	3·75	4·50

177 Woman and Donkey with Panniers

1992. Island Heritage. Multicoloured.

746	5c. Type **177**	50	50
747	30c. Fisherman weaving net	1·25	85
748	40c. Maypole dancing	1·50	1·10
749	60c. Basket making	2·50	3·50
750	$1 Cooking on caboose	3·00	4·50

178 Yellow Stingray

1993. Rays. Multicoloured.

751	5c. Type **178**	70	60
752	30c. Southern stingray	1·75	1·25
753	40c. Spotted eagle-ray	2·00	1·50
754	$1 Manta	4·25	5·50

179 Turtle and Sailing Dinghies

1993. Tourism. Multicoloured.

755	15c. Type **179**	1·50	1·75
756	15c. Tourist boat, fishing launch and scuba diver	1·50	1·75
757	15c. Golf	1·50	1·75
758	15c. Tennis	1·50	1·75
759	15c. Pirates and ship	1·50	1·75
760	30c. Liner, tourist launch and yacht	1·75	1·90
761	30c. George Town street	1·75	1·90
762	30c. Tourist submarine	1·75	1·90
763	30c. Motor scooter riders and cyclist	1·75	1·90
764	30c. Cayman Airways Boeing 737 airliners	1·75	1·90

180 Cuban Amazon with Wings spread

1993. Endangered Species. Cuban Amazon ("Grand Cayman Parrot"). Multicoloured.

765	5c. Type **180**	85	1·50
766	5c. On branch with wings folded	85	1·50
767	30c. Head of parrot	2·25	2·50
768	30c. Pair of parrots	2·25	2·50

181 *Ionopsis utricularioides* and Manger

1993. Christmas. Orchids. Multicoloured.

769	5c. Type **181**	1·25	75
770	40c. *Encyclia cochleata* and shepherd	2·75	85
771	60c. *Vanilla pompona* and wise men	3·75	4·00
772	$1 *Oncidium caymanense* and Virgin Mary	4·75	7·00

182 Queen Angelfish

1994. "Hong Kong '94" International Stamp Exhibition. Reef Life. Sheet 121×85 mm, containing T **182** and similar vert designs. Multicoloured.

MS773	60c. Type **182**; 60c. Diver with porkfish and short-finned hogfish; 60c. Rock beauty and Royal gramma; 60c. French angelfish and Banded butterflyfish	8·50	9·50

183 Flags of Great Britain and Cayman Islands

1994. Royal Visit. Multicoloured.

774	5c. Type **183**	2·00	1·25
775	15c. Royal Yacht *Britannia*	3·00	1·00
776	30c. Queen Elizabeth II	3·00	1·25
777	$2 Queen Elizabeth and Prince Philip disembarking	9·00	12·00

184 Black-billed Whistling Duck

1994. Black-billed Whistling Duck ("West Indian Whistling Duck"). Multicoloured.

778	5c. Type **184**	1·50	1·00
779	15c. Duck landing on water (horiz)	2·25	75
780	20c. Duck preening (horiz)	2·25	80
781	80c. Duck flapping wings	4·50	5·50
782	$1 Adult and duckling	5·00	6·50
MS783	71×45 mm. $1 As No. 782, but including Cayman Islands National Trust symbol	7·00	8·00

185 *Electrostrymon angelia*

1994. Butterflies. Multicoloured.

784	10c. Type **185**	1·00	1·50
785	10c. *Eumaeus atala*	1·00	1·50
786	$1 *Eurema daira*	4·75	5·00
787	$1 *Urbanus dorantes*	4·75	5·00

186 H.M.S. *Convert* (frigate)

1994. Bicentenary of Wreck of Ten Sail off Grand Cayman. Multicoloured.

788	10c. Type **186**	55	55
789	10c. Merchant brig and full-rigged ship	55	55
790	15c. Full-rigged ship near rock	75	50
791	20c. Long boat leaving full-rigged ship	85	55
792	$2 Merchant brig	4·50	7·50

187 Young Green Turtles

1995. Sea Turtles. Multicoloured.

793	10c. Type **187**	55	45
794	20c. Kemp's ridley turtle	80	55
795	25c. Hawksbill turtle	90	60
796	30c. Leatherback turtle	95	70
797	$1.30 Loggerhead turtle	3·50	4·75
798	$2 Pacific ridley turtles	4·50	6·00
MS799	167×94 mm. Nos. 793/8	10·00	11·50

188 Running

1995. CARIFTA and IAAF Games, George Town. Multicoloured.

800	10c. Type **188**	60	40
801	20c. High jumping	90	70
802	30c. Javelin throwing	1·25	80
803	$1.30 Yachting	4·25	6·00
MS804	100×70 mm. $2 Athletes with medals	6·50	7·50

1995. 50th Anniv of End of Second World War. As T **161** of Ascension. Multicoloured.

805	10c. Members of Cayman Home Guard	70	55
806	25c. *Comayagua* (freighter)	1·75	85
807	40c. U-boat *U125*	2·00	1·50
808	$1 U.S. Navy L-3 airship	3·75	6·00
MS809	75×85 mm. $1.30, Reverse of 1939–45 War Medal (vert)	2·50	3·00

189 Queen Elizabeth the Queen Mother

1995. 95th Birthday of Queen Elizabeth the Queen Mother. Sheet 70×90 mm.

MS810	**189** $4 multicoloured	8·50	9·50

190 Ox and Christ Child

1995. Christmas. Nativity Animals. Multicoloured.

811	10c. Type **190**	70	30
812	20c. Sheep and lamb	1·25	45
813	30c. Donkey	2·00	60
814	$2 Camels	8·00	10·00
MS815	160×75 mm. Nos. 811/14	11·00	11·00

191 Sea Grape

1996. Wild Fruit. Multicoloured.

816	10c. Type **191**	50	40
817	25c. Guava	1·00	50
818	40c. West Indian cherry	1·50	80
819	$1 Tamarind	2·75	4·50

192 "Laser" Dinghy

1996. Centenary of Modern Olympic Games. Multicoloured.

820	10c. Type **192**	55	40
821	20c. Sailboarding	85	60
822	30c. "Finn" dinghy	1·00	80
823	$2 Running	4·25	7·00

193 Guitar and Score of National Song

1996. National Identity. Multicoloured.

824	10c. Type **193**	35	40
825	20c. Cayman Airways Boeing 737-200	1·25	40
826	25c. Queen Elizabeth opening Legislative Assembly	75	50
827	30c. Seven Mile Beach	75	55
828	40c. Scuba diver and stingrays	1·00	75
829	60c. Children at turtle farm	2·00	1·10
830	80c. Cuban amazon ("Cayman Parrot") (national bird)	3·00	2·25
831	90c. Silver thatch palm (national tree)	1·75	2·25
832	$1 Cayman Islands flag	3·75	2·50
833	$2 Wild Banana Orchid (national flower)	5·50	5·50
834	$4 Cayman Islands coat of arms	9·00	13·00
835	$6 Cayman Islands currency	11·00	15·00

194 *Christmas Time on North Church Street* (Joanne Sibley)

1996. Christmas. Paintings. Multicoloured.

836	10c. Type **194**	40	30
837	25c. *Gone Fishing* (Lois Brezinsky)	70	50
838	30c. *Claus Encounters* (John Doak)	80	70
839	$2 *A Caymanian Christmas* (Debbie van der Bol)	4·00	6·50

1997. "HONG KONG '97" International Stamp Exhibition. Sheet 130×90 mm, containing design as No. 830 with "1997" imprint date. Multicoloured.

MS840	80c. Cuban amazon ("Cayman Parrot")	1·75	2·00

1997. Golden Wedding of Queen Elizabeth and Prince Philip. As T **173** of Ascension. Multicoloured.

841	10c. Queen Elizabeth	1·10	1·40
842	10c. Prince Philip and Prince Charles at Trooping the Colour	1·10	1·40
843	30c. Prince William horse riding, 1989	1·75	1·90
844	30c. Queen Elizabeth and Prince Philip at Royal Ascot	1·75	1·90
845	40c. Prince Philip at the Brighton Driving Trials	1·90	2·00
846	40c. Queen Elizabeth at Windsor Horse Show, 1993	1·90	2·00
MS847	110×70 mm. $1 Queen Elizabeth and Prince Philip in landau (horiz)	5·50	5·50

195 Children accessing Internet

1997. Telecommunications. Multicoloured.

848	10c. Type **195**	35	25
849	25c. Cable & Wireless cable ship	70	45
850	30c. New area code "345" on children's T-shirts	75	60
851	60c. Satellite dish	1·50	2·50

196 Santa in Hammock

1997. Christmas. Multicoloured.

852	10c. Type **196**	35	25
853	30c. Santa with children on the Bluff	65	45
854	40c. Santa playing golf	1·50	80
855	$1 Santa scuba diving	2·00	3·50

1998. Diana, Princess of Wales Commemoration. As T **177** of Ascension. Multicoloured.

856	10c. Wearing gold earrings, 1997	40	30
857	20c. Wearing black hat	70	90
MS858	145×70 mm. 10c. As No. 856; 20c. As No. 857; 40c. With bouquet, 1995; $1 Wearing black and white blouse, 1983 (sold at $1.70 + 30c. charity premium)	2·75	4·00

1998. 80th Anniv of the Royal Air Force. As T **178** of Ascension. Multicoloured.

859	10c. Hawker Horsley	60	70
860	20c. Fairey Hendon	75	80
861	25c. Hawker Siddeley Gnat	85	90
862	30c. Hawker Siddeley Dominie	95	1·00
MS863	110×77 mm. 40c. Airco D.H.9; 60c. Spad 13 Scout; 80c. Airspeed Oxford; $1 Martin Baltimore	5·50	6·50

197 Black-billed Whistling Duck ("West Indian Whistling Duck")

1998. Birds. Multicoloured.

864	10c. Type **197**	1·25	60
865	20c. Magnificent frigate bird ("Magnificant Frigatbird")	1·75	60
866	60c. Red-footed booby	2·75	3·00
867	$1 Cuban amazon ("Grand Cayman Parrot")	3·50	4·25

198 Santa at the Blowholes

1998. Christmas. Multicoloured.

868	10c. Type **198**	30	30
869	30c. Santa diving on wreck of *Capt. Keith Tibbetts*	75	60
870	40c. Santa at Pedro Castle	90	75
871	60c. Santa arriving on Little Cayman	1·75	2·50

199 *They Rolled the Stone Away* (Miss Lassie)

1999. Easter. Paintings by Miss Lassie (Gladwyn Bush). Multicoloured.

884	10c. Type **199**	30	35
885	20c. *Ascension* (vert)	60	70
886	30c. *The World Praying for Peace*	75	85
887	40c. *Calvary* (vert)	95	1·10

200 *Cayman House* (Jessica Cranston)

1999. Vision 2008 Project. Children's Paintings. Multicoloured.

888	10c. Type **200**	40	20
889	30c. *Coral Reef* (Sarah Hetley)	1·00	55
890	40c. *Fisherman on North Sound* (Sarah Cuff)	1·10	70
891	$2 *Three Fish and a Turtle* (Ryan Martinez)	4·25	6·50

1999. Royal Wedding. As T **185** of Ascension. Multicoloured.

892	10c. Photographs of Prince Edward and Miss Sophie Rhys-Jones	50	30
893	$2 Engagement photograph	3·75	4·75

1999. 30th Anniv of First Manned Landing on Moon. As T **186** of Ascension. Multicoloured.

894	10c. Coastguard cutter on patrol during launch	45	35
895	25c. Firing of third stage rockets	80	60
896	30c. Buzz Aldrin descending to Moon's surface	85	65
897	60c. Jettisoning of lunar module	1·40	2·25
MS898	90×80 mm. $1.50, Earth as seen from Moon (circular, 40 mm diam)	3·25	3·50

1999. "Queen Elizabeth the Queen Mother's Century". As T **187** of Ascension. Multicoloured.

899	10c. Visiting anti-aircraft battery, London, 1940	45	40
900	20c. With children on her 94th birthday, 1994	65	65
901	30c. With Prince Charles and Prince William, 1997	80	90
902	40c. Reviewing Chelsea Pensioners, 1986	90	1·00
MS903	145×70 mm. $1.50, Duchess of York with Princess Elizabeth, 1926, and Royal Wedding, 1923	2·50	3·00

201 1969 Christmas ¼c. Stamp

1999. Christmas. Designs showing previous Christmas stamps. Multicoloured.

904	10c. Type **201**	40	25
905	30c. 1984 Christmas 5c.	70	50
906	40c. 1997 Christmas 10c.	85	65
907	$1 1979 Christmas 20c. (horiz)	1·90	2·50
MS908	111×100 mm. Nos. 904/7	3·50	3·50

2000. "Stamp Show 2000" International Stamp Exhibition, London. Kings and Queens of England. As T **223** of British Virgin Islands. Multicoloured.

909	10c. King Henry VII	60	70
910	40c. King Henry VIII	1·40	1·75
911	40c. Queen Mary I	1·40	1·75
912	40c. King Charles II	1·40	1·75
913	40c. Queen Anne	1·40	1·75
914	40c. King George IV	1·40	1·75
915	40c. King George V	1·40	1·75

202 Ernie fishing from Rubber Ring

2000. "Sesame Street" (children's T.V. programme). Multicoloured.

916	10c. Type **202**	25	35
917	20c. Grover flying	40	50
918	20c. Zoe in airplane	40	50
919	20c. Oscar the Grouch in balloon	40	50
920	20c. The Count on motorbike	40	50
921	20c. Big Bird rollerskating	40	50
922	20c. Cookie Monster heading for Cookie Factory	40	50
923	20c. Type **202**	40	50
924	20c. Bert in rowing boat	40	50
925	20c. Elmo snorkeling	40	50
926	30c. As No. 920	55	55
MS927	139×86 mm. 20c. Elmo with stamps	1·00	1·00

Nos. 917/25 were printed together, *se-tenant*, with the backgrounds forming a composite design.

2000. 18th Birthday of Prince William. As T 191 of Ascension. Multicoloured.

928	10c. Prince William in 1999 (horiz)	50	40
929	20c. In evening dress, 1997 (horiz)	75	60
930	30c. At Muick Falls, 1997	90	80
931	40c. In uniform of Parachute Regiment, 1986	1·25	1·25
MS932	175×95 mm. $1 As baby with toy mouse (horiz) and Nos. 928/31	7·50	7·50

203 Green Turtle

2000. Marine Life. Multicoloured.

933	10c. Type **203**	55	45
934	20c. Queen angel fish	80	50
935	30c. Sleeping parrotfish	1·10	65
936	$1 Green moray eel	3·50	4·50

204 Boy thinking about Drugs and Fitness

2000. National Drugs Council. Multicoloured.

937	10c. Type **204**	60	35
938	15c. Rainbow, sun, clouds and "ez2B Drug Free"	85	35
939	30c. Musicians dancing	1·40	65
940	$2 Hammock between two palm trees	5·00	8·00

205 Children on Beach ("Backing Sand")

2000. Christmas. Traditional Customs. Multicoloured.

941	10c. Type **205**	85	50
942	30c. Christmas dinner	2·00	80
943	40c. Yard dance	2·25	85
944	60c. Conch shell borders	2·75	3·25

206 Woman on Beach

2001. United Nations Women's Human Rights Campaign.

945	**206**	10c. multicoloured	60	60

207 Red Mangrove Cay

2001. Cayman Brac Tourism Project. Multicoloured.

946	15c. Type **207**	1·10	75
947	20c. Peter's Cave (vert)	1·25	80
948	25c. Bight Road steps (vert)	1·40	90
949	30c. Westerly Ponds	1·50	1·00
950	40c. Aerial view of Spot Bay	1·75	1·40
951	60c. The Marshes	2·75	3·50

208 Work of National Council of Voluntary Organizations

2001. Non-Profit Organizations. Multicoloured.

952	15c. Type **208**	80	65
953	20c. Pet welfare (Cayman Humane Society)	1·75	1·00
954	25c. Stick figures (Red Cross and Red Crescent)	1·75	1·50
955	30c. Pink flowers (Cayman Islands Cancer Society) (vert)	1·75	1·50
956	40c. Women's silhouettes and insignia (Lions Club Breast Cancer Awareness Campaign) (vert)	1·90	1·75
MS957	145×95 mm. Nos. 952/6 (sold at $1.80)	7·50	8·00

No. **MS**957 was sold at $1.80 which included a 50c. donation to the featured organisations.

209 Children walking Home

2001. Transportation. Multicoloured.

958	15c. Type **209**	70	60
959	15c. Boy on donkey	70	60

960	20c. Bananas by canoe	70	45
961	25c. Horse and buggy	1·00	55
962	30c. Catboats fishing	1·00	55
963	40c. Schooner	1·25	65
964	60c. Police cyclist (vert)	2·50	1·50
965	80c. Lady drivers	2·00	1·75
966	90c. Launching *Cimboco* (motor coaster) (vert)	2·50	2·00
967	$1 Amphibian aircraft	2·75	2·25
968	$4 Container ship	8·50	9·00
969	$10 Boeing 767 airliner	18·00	20·00

210 Father Christmas on Scooter with Children, Cayman Brac

2001. Christmas. Multicoloured.

970	15c. Type **210**	1·00	55
971	30c. Father Christmas on eagle ray, Little Cayman	1·40	80
972	40c. Father Christmas in catboat, Grand Cayman	1·60	1·10
973	60c. Father Christmas parasailing over Grand Cayman	2·40	3·00

211 Statue of Liberty, U.S. and Cayman Flags

2002. In Remembrance. Victims of Terrorist Attacks on U.S.A. (11 September 2001).

974	**211**	$1 multicoloured	3·00	3·50

2002. Golden Jubilee. As T **200** of Ascension.

975	15c. grey, blue and gold	50	40
976	20c. multicoloured	65	40
977	30c. black, blue and gold	80	60
978	80c. multicoloured	2·00	2·25
MS979	162×95 mm. Nos. 975/8 and $1 multicoloured	7·00	7·00

DESIGNS—HORIZ: 15c. Princess Elizabeth as young child; 20c. Queen Elizabeth in evening dress, 1976; 30c. Princess Elizabeth and Princess Margaret as Girl Guides, 1942; 80c. Queen Elizabeth at Newbury, 1996. VERT (38×51 mm)—$1 Queen Elizabeth after Annigoni.

Designs as Nos. 975/8 in No. **MS**979 omit the gold frame around each stamp and the "Golden Jubilee 1952–2002" inscription.

212 Snoopy painting Woodstock at Cayman Brac Bluff

2002. "A Cayman Vacation". Peanuts (cartoon characters by Charles Schulz). Multicoloured.

980	15c. Type **212**	75	65
981	20c. Charlie Brown and Sally at Hell Post Office, Grand Cayman	80	65
982	25c. Peppermint Patty and Marcie on beach, Little Cayman	85	75
983	30c. Snoopy as Red Baron and Boeing 737-200 over Grand Cayman	1·10	85
984	40c. Linus and Snoopy at Point of Sand, Little Cayman	1·40	1·10
985	60c. Charlie Brown playing golf at The Links, Grand Cayman	2·25	3·00
MS986	230×160 mm. Nos. 980/5	6·50	7·00

No. **MS**986 is die-cut in the shape of a suitcase.

213 Cayman Islands Footballers

2002. World Cup Football Championship, Japan and Korea and 35th Anniv of Cayman Islands Football Association.

987	**213**	30c. multicoloured	1·50	1·25
988	**213**	40c. multicoloured	1·50	1·25

2002. Queen Elizabeth the Queen Mother Commemoration. As T **202** of Ascension.

989	15c. black, gold and purple	80	30
990	30c. multicoloured	1·25	60
991	40c. black, gold and purple	1·50	1·00
992	$1 multicoloured	2·75	3·75
MS993	145×70 mm. Nos. 991/2	5·00	6·00

DESIGNS: 15c. Queen Elizabeth at Red Corss and St. John's summer fair, London, 1943; 30c. Queen Mother at Royal Caledonian School, Bushey; 40c. Duchess of York in 1936; $1 Queen Mother at film premiere in 1989.

Designs in No. **MS**993 omit the "1900–2002" inscription and the coloured frame.

214 Angel Gabriel appearing to Virgin Mary

2002. Christmas. Multicoloured.

994	15c. Type **214**	60	55
995	20c. Mary and Joseph travelling to Bethlehem	70	55
996	30c. The Holy Family	85	60
997	40c. Angel appearing to shepherds	1·00	90
998	60c. Three Wise Men	1·60	2·50
MS999	234×195 mm. Nos. 994/8	4·25	5·00

215 Catalina Flying Boat, North Sound, Grand Cayman

2002. 50th Anniv of Cayman Islands. Aviation. Multicoloured.

1000	15c. Type **215**	1·10	75
1001	20c. Grand Cayman Airport, 1952	1·25	75
1002	25c. Cayman Brac Airways AC 50	1·25	80
1003	30c. Cayman Airways Boeing 737	1·40	85
1004	40c. British Airways Concorde at Grand Cayman, 1984	2·00	1·50
1005	$1.30 Island Air DHC 6 Twin Otter on Little Cayman	4·50	5·50

216 Skipping

2003. Children's Games. Multicoloured.

1006	15c. Type **216**	80	60
1007	20c. Maypole dancing	90	60
1008	25c. Gig	1·00	70
1009	30c. Hopscotch	1·10	70
1010	$1 Marbles	3·00	4·00

2003. 50th Anniv of Coronation. As T **206** of Ascension. Multicoloured.

1011	15c. Queen Elizabeth II wearing Imperial State Crown	75	35
1012	$2 Newly crowned Queen flanked by Bishops of Durham and Bath & Wells	4·25	5·00
MS1013	95×115 mm. 20c. As 15c.; $4 As $2	9·00	10·00

Nos. 1011/12 have red frames; stamps from **MS**1013 have no frame and country name in mauve panel.

2003. As T **207** of Ascension.

1014	$4 black, red and violet	8·00	8·50

2003. 21st Birthday of Prince William of Wales. As T **208** of Ascension. Multicoloured.

1015	15c. Prince William at Tidworth Polo Club, 2002 and on Raleigh International Expedition, 2000	70	35
1016	40c. At Golden Jubilee church service, 2002 and Queen Mother's 101st birthday, 2001	1·25	60
1017	80c. At Queen Mother's 101st birthday and at Holyrood House, 2001	2·25	3·00
1018	$1 At Eton College and at Christmas Day church service in 2000	2·25	3·00

217 Turtles hatching

2003. 500th Anniv of Discovery of Cayman Islands. Multicoloured.

1019	15c. Type **217**	80	65
1020	20c. Old waterfront, George Town, 1975	1·00	75
1021	20c. *Santa Maria* (Columbus) and turtle	1·25	80
1022	25c. Nassau grouper (fish) and corals	1·25	80
1023	30c. *Kirk-B* (Cayman Brac schooner)	1·40	80
1024	40c. George Town harbour	1·40	85
1025	60c. Musical instruments	1·50	1·40
1026	80c. Smokewood tree and ghost orchids	2·25	2·25
1027	90c. Little Cayman Baptist Church	2·25	2·50
1028	$1 Loading thatch rope onto *Caymania*	2·75	3·00
1029	$1.30 Children's dance troupe	3·25	4·50
1030	$2 Cayman Parliament in session	4·25	6·00
MS1031	216×151 mm. Nos. 1019/30	21·00	23·00

218 Bell and "Merry Christmas"

2003. Christmas. Multicoloured.

1032	15c. Type **218**	85	55
1033	20c. Christmas wreath and "Celebrate with Family"	95	55
1034	30c. Gold star, angel and "Happy New Year"	1·25	60
1035	40c. Christmas lights and "Happy Holidays"	1·50	70
1036	60c. Poinsettias and "Seasons Greetings"	2·00	2·75

219 Female and Calf

2003. Endangered Species. Short-finned Pilot Whale. Multicoloured.

1037	15c. Type **219**	1·40	75
1038	20c. Four pilot whales	1·50	90
1039	30c. Two pilot whales at surface	1·75	1·10
1040	40c. Short-finned pilot whale	2·50	1·90

220 *Lady Slater*

2004. Centenary of Shipping Registry. Multicoloured.

1041	15c. Type **220**	85	55
1042	20c. *Seanostrum*	95	70
1043	30c. *Kirk Pride*	1·40	1·00
1044	$1 *Boadicea*	4·25	5·50

221 *Jesus carrying His Cross* (Carole Mayer)

2004. Easter. Multicoloured.

1045	15c. Type **221**	75	40
1046	30c. *The Ascension* (Natasha Claire Kozaily)	1·25	1·00

222 Swimming

2004. Olympic Games, Athens, Greece. Multicoloured.

1047	15c. Type **222**	75	40
1048	40c. Sprinting	1·25	75
1049	60c. Long jump	1·90	1·60
1050	80c. Two Cayman Islands swimmers	2·40	3·00

223 Blue Iguana

2004. Blue Iguana. Multicoloured.

1051	15c. Type **223**	75	60
1052	20c. Baby iguana hatching from egg	85	60
1053	25c. Four iguanas	95	70
1054	30c. Baby iguana on finger	1·10	70
1055	40c. Iguana with open mouth	1·25	80
1056	90c. Eye of iguana	2·75	3·50
MS1057	104×58 mm. 60c. Iguana on rock facing right; 80c. Iguana on rock facing left	4·50	5·00

2005. Bicentenary of Battle of Trafalgar. As T **216** of Ascension. Multicoloured.

1058	15c. HMS *Victory* (horiz)	1·00	70
1059	20c. HMS *Tonnant* tangling into bow of *Algesiras* (horiz)	1·10	70
1060	25c. Flint cannon lock and linstock (horiz)	1·10	80
1061	60c. Boatswain's Mate RN (horiz)	1·75	1·25
1062	$1 Portrait of Admiral Nelson	2·75	3·00
1063	$2 HMS *Orion* in action against *Intrepide* (horiz)	5·00	6·00
MS1064	120×79 mm. 60c. *Pluton*; $2 HMS *Tonnant*	6·00	7·00

No. 1058 contains traces of powdered wood from HMS *Victory*.

224 Rotary Emblem

2005. Centenary of Rotary International.

1065	**224**	15c. multicoloured	70	60
1066	-	30c. ultramarine, black and grey	1·10	1·00

DESIGN: 30c. Polio Plus and Rotary emblems.

225 *Myrmecophila purpurea*

2005. Orchids. Multicoloured.

1067	15c. Type **225**	75	55
1068	20c. *Prosthechea boothiana*	80	55
1069	30c. *Tolumnia calochila* (vert)	90	60
1070	40c. *Encyclia phoenicia*	1·10	80
1071	80c. *Prosthechea cochleata* (vert)	2·00	2·50
MS1072	80×52 mm. $1.50 *Encyclia kingsii*	4·00	4·50

2005. Pope John Paul II Commemoration. As T **219** of Ascension.

1073	30c. multicoloured	1·75	1·25

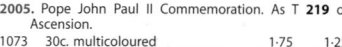

226 The Queen (butterfly)

2005. Butterflies. Multicoloured. (a) Ordinary gum.

1074	15c. Type **226**	70	60
1075	20c. Mexican fritillary	75	65
1076	25c. Malachite	80	70
1077	30c. Cayman crescent spot	85	70
1078	40c. Cloudless sulphur	1·10	80
1079	90c. Swallowtail	2·25	3·00

(b) Self-adhesive. Size 29×24 mm.

1080	15c. Type **226**	70	80
1081	20c. Mexican fritillary	75	85
1082	30c. Cayman crescent spot	90	1·10

227 Angels

2005. Christmas. Multicoloured.

1083	15c. Type **227**	60	40
1084	30c. Three Wise Men (horiz)	80	50
1085	40c. Holy Family	1·00	75
1086	60c. Shepherds (horiz)	1·40	1·75
MS1087	156×106 mm. Nos. 1083/6	3·50	3·50

228 Wash Wood (*Jacquinia keyensis*)

2006. Trees. Multicoloured.

1088	15c. Type **228**	70	50
1089	20c. Red mangrove (*Rhizophora mangle*)	80	60
1090	30c. Ironwood (*Chionanthus caymanensis*)	90	60
1091	60c. West Indian cedar (*Cedrela odorata*)	1·75	1·40
1092	$2 Spanish elm (*Cordia gerascanthus*)	4·50	5·50

2006. 80th Birthday of Queen Elizabeth II. As T **223** of Ascension. Multicoloured.

1093	15c. Princess Elizabeth as young child	80	50
1094	40c. Queen Elizabeth in uniform, c. 1952	1·50	80
1095	$1 Wearing tiara	2·25	2·50
1096	$2 Wearing white blouse	4·25	4·75
MS1097	144×75 mm. As Nos. 1094/5, but without white borders	8·00	8·50

229 Hawksbill Turtle

2006. Cayman's Aquatic Treasures. Multicoloured. (a) Ordinary gum.

1098	25c. Type **229**	1·00	90
1099	25c. Grey angelfish	1·00	90
1100	60c. Queen angelfish (vert)	2·00	1·75
1101	75c. Diamond blenny	2·25	2·50
1102	$1 Spotted drum (juvenile) (vert)	3·00	3·50
MS1103	145×95 mm. As Nos. 1098/102	8·00	8·50

(b) Size 29×24 mm. Self-adhesive.

1104	25c. As Type **229**	90	1·10
1105	25c. As No. 1099	90	1·10
1106	60c. As No. 1100	1·75	2·00
1107	75c. As No. 1101	1·90	2·50

Stamps from **MS**1103 do not have white borders.

230 Bananaquit

2006. Birds (1st series). Multicoloured.

1108	25c. Type **230**	75	15
1109	50c. Vitelline warbler	1·40	90
1110	75c. Cuban Amazon ("Grand Cayman Parrot")	1·75	1·25
1111	80c. White-bellied dove ("Caribbean Dove")	1·75	1·25
1112	$1 Caribbean elaenia	2·00	1·75
1113	$1.50 Great red-bellied woodpecker ("West Indian Woodpecker")	3·00	3·00
1114	$1.60 Thick-billed vireo	3·25	3·25
1115	$2 Common flicker ("Northern Flicker")	4·00	4·25
1116	$4 Cuban bullfinch	8·00	8·50
1117	$5 Stripe-headed tanager ("Western spindalis")	9·00	9·50
1118	$10 Loggerhead kingbird	17·00	18·00
1119	$20 Red-legged thrush	30·00	32·00

See also Nos. 1124/6.

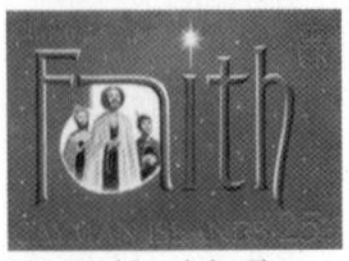

231 "Faith" and the Three Magi

2006. Christmas. Multicoloured.

1120	25c. Type **231**	75	30
1121	75c. "Hope" and prophet speaking of the Messiah	1·90	1·75
1122	80c. "Joy" and angel	1·90	1·75
1123	$1 "Love" and Mary with baby Jesus	2·00	2·50

232 Bananaquit

2007. Birds (2nd series). Designs as Nos. 1108, and 1110/11 but each 30×25 mm with redrawn inscriptions. Self-adhesive.

1124	25c. Type **232**	1·10	1·40
1125	75c. Cuban amazon ('GRAND CAYMAN PARROT')	2·25	2·75
1126	80c. White-bellied dove ('CARIBBEAN DOVE')	2·25	2·75

233 Brac Reef Dock

2007. Cayman Islands Scenes. Multicoloured.

1127	20c. Type **233**	70	50
1128	25c. Waterfront, Hog Sty Bay, George Town, Grand Cayman	75	60
1129	30c. East End blowholes, Grand Cayman Island (vert)	80	60
1130	40c. Man lying in hammock on beach at sunset (vert)	1·10	75
1131	75c. Poinciana flowers	2·00	2·50
1132	$1 Driftwood on shore, Little Cayman Island	2·25	2·75

2007. Centenary of Scouting. As T **281** of Bahamas. Multicoloured.

1133	25c. Early Wolf Cubs with their flag	75	50
1134	75c. Modern Cub Scouts after Remembrance Day Parade, 2006	2·00	2·00
1135	80c. Scouts camping	2·00	2·00
1136	$1 Drill team, Remembrance Day Parade, 2005	2·25	2·50
MS1137	90×65 mm. 50c. Cayman Islands scouts in opening ceremony of 13th Caribbean Scout Jamboree, Jamaica, 2006 (vert); $1.50 Lord Baden-Powell (vert)	3·75	4·00

2007. Diamond Wedding of Queen Elizabeth II and Duke of Edinburgh. As T **58** of British Indian Ocean Territory. Multicoloured.

1138	50c. Princess Elizabeth alighting from car and Lt. Philip Mountbatten, c. 1949	1·40	1·10
1139	75c. Princess Elizabeth wearing tiara and wedding veil, 1949	2·00	2·00
1140	80c. Queen Elizabeth the Queen Mother and Princess-es Elizabeth and Margaret	2·00	2·00
1141	$1 Princess Elizabeth and Duke of Edinburgh in procession down Westminster Abbey aisle on wedding day, 1949	2·25	2·50
MS1142	125×85 mm. $2 Princess Elizabeth and Lt. Philip Mountbatten, c. 1949 (42×56 mm)	4·25	4·75

234 Nativity

2007. Christmas. Stained glass windows. Multicoloured.

1143	25c. Type **234**	75	50
1144	50c. Jesus Christ	1·40	1·00
1145	75c. Jesus with disciples	1·75	1·40
1146	80c. Peace dove	1·75	1·75
1147	$1 The Cross	2·25	2·25
1148	$1.50 Shepherd with lamb	3·25	4·00

235 Beach at Sunset and Turtles ('Hello')

2008. Greetings Stamps. Multicoloured. (a) Ordinary gum.

1149	20c. Type **235**	60	65
1150	20c. Crossed fingers and horseshoes ('Good Luck')	60	65
1151	20c. Balloons and stars ('Congratulations')	60	65
1152	20c. Invitation and fireworks ('You're Invited')	60	65
1153	20c. Fountain pen and flowers ('Best Wishes')	60	65
1154	20c. Cupid and hearts ('Love')	60	65
1155	25c. Type **235**	60	65
1156	25c. As No. 1150	60	65
1157	25c. As No. 1151	60	65
1158	25c. As No. 1152	60	65
1159	25c. As No. 1153	60	65
1160	25c. As No. 1154	60	65
1161	50c. Type **235**	1·00	1·25
1162	50c. As No. 1150	1·00	1·25
1163	50c. As No. 1151	1·00	1·25
1164	50c. As No. 1152	1·00	1·25
1165	50c. As No. 1153	1·00	1·25
1166	50c. As No. 1154	1·00	1·25
1167	75c. Type **235**	1·50	1·60
1168	75c. As No. 1150	1·50	1·60
1169	75c. As No. 1151	1·50	1·60
1170	75c. As No. 1152	1·50	1·60
1171	75c. As No. 1153	1·50	1·60
1172	75c. As No. 1154	1·50	1·60
1173	80c. Type **235**	1·60	1·75
1174	80c. As No. 1150	1·60	1·75
1175	80c. As No. 1151	1·60	1·75
1176	80c. As No. 1152	1·60	1·75
1177	80c. As No. 1153	1·60	1·75
1178	80c. As No. 1154	1·60	1·75
1179	$1 Type **235**	1·75	1·90
1180	$1 As No. 1150	1·75	1·90
1181	$1 As No. 1151	1·75	1·90
1182	$1 As No. 1152	1·75	1·90
1183	$1 As No. 1153	1·75	1·90
1184	$1 As No. 1154	1·75	1·90

(b) Self-adhesive. Size 30×25 mm.

1185	20c. As Type **235**	55	65
1186	25c. As No. 1151	55	65
1187	25c. As No. 1152	55	65
1188	25c. As No. 1154	55	65

236 Land Crab

2008. Darwin Initiative. Indigenous Creatures. Multicoloured.

1189	20c. Type **236**	70	50
1190	25c. Needlecase Freshwater Pools	75	55
1191	75c. Little Cayman green anole	2·00	2·00
1192	80c. Cayman Brac ground boa	2·00	2·00
1193	$1 White-shouldered bat	2·25	2·50
MS1194	110×78 mm. $2 Caribbean reef squid	4·25	4·75

2008. Olympic Games, Beijing. As T **287** of Bahamas. Multicoloured.

1195	20c. Swimming – backstroke	70	55
1196	25c. Swimming – butterfly	75	60
1197	50c. Running	1·50	1·50
1198	75c. Hurdling	2·00	2·50

238 Father Christmas on board Sailing Ship

2008. Christmas. Unique Transportation. Multicoloured.

1202	25c. Type **238**	75	60
1203	75c. Father Christmas with horse and carriage laden with presents	2·25	2·00
1204	80c. Father Christmas in helicopter dropping presents by parachute	2·25	2·00
1205	$1 Father Christmas with racing car	2·75	2·75

239 Silver Thatch Palm

2009. Silver Thatch Palm. Multicoloured.

1206	25c. Type **239**	90	95
1207	25c. Rope strands	90	95
1208	25c. Twisting the three strands into rope ('Cobbing rope')	90	95
1209	25c. Basketware ('Thatch products')	90	95
1210	25c. Traditional home with silver thatch roof	90	95

Nos. 1206/10 were printed together, *se-tenant*, forming a composite design.

240 Hammock at Sunset

2009. Cayman Islands Scenes (2nd series). Multicoloured. (a) Ordinary gum.

1211	20c. Type **240**	45	55
1212	25c. Cayman Islands houses	55	60
1213	75c. Palm trees on beach (vert)	2·00	2·00
1214	80c. Cruise ships off Cayman Islands	2·00	2·00
1215	$1 Street with signpost (vert)	2·25	2·50
1216	$1.50 Inland landscape of rocks and scrub	4·25	4·50
MS1217	80×65 mm. $2 Iguana in road, Little Cayman	5·25	5·25

(b) Self-adhesive. Size 30×25 mm.

1218	20c. As Type **240**	55	60
1219	25c. As No. 1212	65	70

2009. International Year of Astronomy. 40th Anniv of First Moon Landing. A T **214** of Bermuda. Multicoloured.

1220	20c. Mars Rover, 2004	45	50
1221	25c. Space Transportation System 71 launch, 1995	50	55
1222	75c. Hubble Telescope	1·50	1·75
1223	$1 Apollo 11, 1969	2·25	2·50
1224	$1.50 International Space Station	3·25	3·50
MS1225	100×80 mm. $2 *Hadley Rille* (astronaut Jim Irwin and Lunar Rover) (Alan Bean) (39×59 mm). Wmk upright	3·75	4·00

241 Women's Hands signing Petition

2009. 'Equality through Democracy'. 50th Anniv of the Constitution and Women's Suffrage. Multicoloured.

1226	25c. Type **241**	60	60
1227	25c. Town Hall, George Town	60	60
1228	50c. Woman casting vote	1·25	1·25
MS1229	135×86 mm. Nos. 1226/8	2·50	2·50

242 10c. Santa in Hammock Stamp

2009. Christmas. Showing 1997 Christmas stamps. Multicoloured.

1230	25c. Type **242**	60	60
1231	75c. 30c. Santa with children on the Bluff stamp	1·50	1·75
1232	80c. 40c. Santa playing golf	1·60	2·00
1233	$1 Santa scuba diving stamp	2·25	2·50

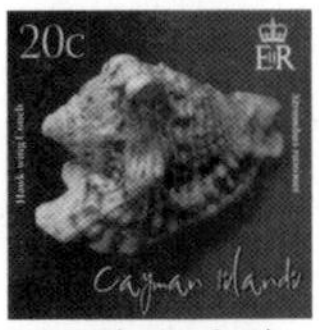

243 Hawk-wing Conch (*Strombus raninus*)

2010. Shells. Multicoloured.

(a) Ordinary gum

1234	20c. Type **243**	60	65
1235	25c. Ornate scallop (*Chlamys ornata*)	80	85
1236	60c. Chestnut turban (*Turbo castanea*)	1·50	1·60
1237	75c. Beautiful mitre (*Vexillum pulchellum*)	1·90	2·00
1238	80c. Four-toothed nerite (*Nerita versicolor gmelin*)	2·00	2·10
1239	$1.60 White-spotted marginella (*Marginella guttata*)	4·25	4·50
MS1240	94×64 mm. $3 Queen conch (*Strombus gigas*)	7·75	8·00

(b) Self-adhesive

1241	25c. As No. 1235	80	85
1242	75c. As No. 1237	1·90	2·00

244 Brownie, Rainbow and Guide Uniforms

2010. Centenary of Girlguiding. Multicoloured.

1243	20c. Type **244**	55	60
1244	25c. Camping	65	70
1245	50c. Parade of guides, 1930s	1·20	1·40
1246	80c. Badges of rainbows, brownies and guides	2·00	2·10

2011. Royal Wedding. Multicoloured.

1247	25c. Duke and Duchess of Cambridge kissing on Buckingham Palace balcony (vert)	80	85
1248	75c. Duke and Duchess of Cambridge waving from State Landau	1·90	2·00
1249	80c. Duke and Duchess of Cambridge at Westminster Abbey after wedding ceremony (vert)	2·00	2·10
1250	$2 Prince William, Miss Catherine Middleton and her father	4·50	5·00

245 Catching Turtles

2011. Catboats. Multicoloured.

(a) Ordinary paper

1251	20c. Type **245**	60	65
1252	25c. Building catboat	80	85
1253	25c. Sailing catboat around Cayman Brac's Bluff	80	85
1254	50c. Catboats racing regatta style	1·20	1·40
1255	$1.60 Unloading cargo from catboats	4·25	4·50
1256	$2 Sewing the sail	4·75	5·00

(b) Self-adhesive. Size 30×25 mm

1257	25c. As No. 1252	80	85

246 King James Bible

2011. Christmas. 400th Anniv of the King James Bible. Multicoloured.

1258	25c. Type **246**	90	95
1259	75c. King James I of Scotland (1566-1625) and VI of England (1603-25)	1·90	2·00
1260	80c. William Tyndale (translator)	2·10	2·25
1261	$1 Printing the King James Bible	2·50	2·75
1262	$1.60 Translators in the Jerusalem Chamber of Westminster Abbey for final editing	3·75	4·00

247 Almeria L. McLaughlin Tomlinson (1882-1974) (midwife)

2011. Pioneers. Multicoloured.

1263	20c. Type **247**	60	65
1264	25c. Captain Rayal B. Bodden (1885-1976) (shipwright and builder)	1·00	1·10
1265	75c. Irksie Leila Yates (1899-1996) (maternity nurse)	2·10	2·25
1266	$1.50 Major Joseph R. Walter (1890-1965) (Inspector of Police)	3·00	3·25

Pt. 12

CENTRAL AFRICAN EMPIRE

Central African Republic was renamed Central African Empire on 4 December 1976, when Pres. Bokassa became Emperor.

The country reverted to Central African Republic on his overthrow in 1979.

100 centimes = 1 franc.

1977. Various stamps of Central African Republic optd **EMPIRE CENTRAFRICAIN**.

439	**150**	3f. mult (postage)	55	50
444	**167**	10f. multicoloured	30	25
457	-	10f. red and blue (386)	30	25
459	**172**	10f. multicoloured	45	40
460	-	15f. multicoloured (391)	75	75
465	-	15f. brown, grn & bl (397)	30	25
445	-	20f. multicoloured (366)	45	40
461	-	20f. multicoloured (392)	55	55
446	-	25f. multicoloured (367)	35	30
451	-	25f. multicoloured (376)	35	30
449	**168**	30f. multicoloured	30	25
452	-	30f. multicoloured (377)	55	55
462	-	30f. multicoloured (393)	30	25
447	-	40f. multicoloured (370)	45	40
450	-	40f. multicoloured (373)	45	40
453	-	40f. multicoloured (378)	45	40
454	-	40f. multicoloured (380)	55	55
455	**170**	40f. multicoloured	45	40
456	-	40f. multicoloured (384)	40	25
458	-	40f. multicoloured (389)	75	75
482	-	40f. multicoloured (423)	40	25
466	-	50f. blue, brn & grn (398)	75	75
483	-	50f. mult (424) (air)	45	25
440	**163**	100f. multicoloured	1·70	1·60
441	**164**	100f. grn, red & brn	1·80	1·80
442	**165**	100f. brn, grn & blue	1·70	1·60
448	-	100f. multicoloured (371)	95	90
463	**173**	100f. red and blue	95	90
467	**178**	100f. multicoloured	95	90
468	**179**	100f. black and yellow	1·70	1·60
469	**180**	100f. purple, blue & grn	1·80	1·90
484	-	100f. multicoloured (425)	95	90
491	**185**	100f. multicoloured	1·80	1·90
464	**174**	200f. multicoloured	4·25	2·10
443	**166**	500f. red, green & brown	8·50	8·25

1977. "Apollo–Soyuz" Space Link. Nos. 410/**MS**415 of Central African Republic optd **EMPIRE CENTRAFRICAIN**.

470	**181**	40f. mult (postage)	50	25
471	-	50f. multicoloured	75	40
472	-	100f. multicoloured (air)	95	55
473	-	200f. multicoloured	1·90	90
474	-	300f. multicoloured	3·00	1·30
MS475		103×78 mm. 500f. multicoloured	5·25	3·50

1977. Air. Bicentenary of American Revolution. Nos. 416/**MS**421 of Central African Republic optd **EMPIRE CENTRAFRICAIN**.

476	**182**	100f. multicoloured	1·00	70
477	-	125f. multicoloured	1·40	1·10
478	-	150f. multicoloured	1·60	1·30
479	-	200f. multicoloured	2·30	1·80
480	-	250f. multicoloured	2·50	2·00
MS481		119×81 mm. 450f. multicoloured	5·25	5·25

1977. Winners of Winter Olympic Games, Innsbruck. Nos. 426/**MS**430 of Central African Republic optd **EMPIRE CENTRAFRICAIN**.

485		40f. mult (postage)	55	50
486		60f. multicoloured	75	65
487	**184**	100f. multicoloured (air)	1·00	80
488	-	200f. multicoloured	2·20	1·70
489	-	300f. multicoloured	3·25	2·40
MS490		103×78 mm. 500f. multicoloured	5·25	5·00

1977. "Viking" Space Mission. Nos. 433/**MS**438 of Central African Republic optd **EMPIRE CENTRAFRICAIN**.

492	**186**	40f. mult (postage)	55	50
493	-	60f. multicoloured	75	65
494	-	100f. multicoloured (air)	1·00	1·00
495	-	200f. multicoloured	2·30	2·20
496	-	300f. multicoloured	3·50	3·50
MS497		102×78 mm. 500f. multicoloured	5·25	5·00

189 Pierre and Marie Curie (Physics, 1903)

1977. Nobel Prize-winners. Multicoloured.

503		40f. Type **189** (postage)	1·00	40
504		60f. W. C. Rontgen (Physics, 1901)	90	45
505		100f. Rudyard Kipling (Literature, 1907) (air)	1·80	50
506		200f. Ernest Hemingway (Literature, 1954)	3·50	85
507		300f. L. Pirandello (Literature, 1934)	3·50	1·00
MS508		118×80 mm. 500f. Rabindranath Tagore (Literature, 1913)	5·25	1·90

190 Roman Temple and Italy 1933 3l. stamp

1977. *Graf Zeppelin* Flights. Multicoloured.

509	40f. Type **190** (postage)	85	25
510	60f. St. Basil's Cathedral, Moscow, and Russia 1930 40k. stamp	1·00	45
511	100f. North Pole and Germany 1931 "Polarfahrt" stamp (air)	1·40	40
512	200f. Museum of Science and Industry, Chicago, and Germany 1933 "Chicagofahrt" stamp	2·50	75
513	300f. Brandenburg Gate, Berlin, and German 1931 stamp	3·75	1·00
MS514	129×90 mm. 500f. Capitol, Washington, and US $1.30 stamp, 1930	5·50	2·20

191 Charles Lindbergh and *Spirit of St. Louis*

1977. History of Aviation. Multicoloured.

515	50f. Type **191**	50	25
516	60f. Alberto Santos-Dumont and *14 bis* biplane	75	25
517	100f. Louis Bleriot and Bleriot XI	1·40	45
518	200f. Roald Amundsen and Dornier Wal flying boat	2·10	60
519	300f. Concorde	4·00	1·40
MS520	117×91 mm. 500f. Lindbergh and his arrival in Paris	5·00	1·80

192 Lily

1977. Flowers. Multicoloured.

521	5f. Type **192**	45	30
522	10f. Hibiscus	90	70

193 Group of Africans and Rotary Emblem

1977. 20th Anniv of Bangui Rotary Club.

523	**193**	60f. multicoloured	3·50	1·80

194 Africans queueing beside Bible

1977. Bible Week.

524	**194**	40f. multicoloured	5·75	1·40

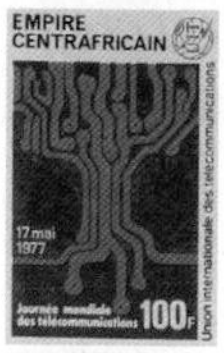

195 Printed Circuit

1977. World Telecommunications Day.

525	**195**	100f. orange, brown & blk	3·00	2·10

196 Doctor inoculating Child

1977. Air. World Health Day.

526	**196**	150f. multicoloured	3·50	1·80

197 Goalkeeper

1977. World Cup Football Championship (1978). Multicoloured.

527	50f. Type **197**	50	25
528	60f. Goalmouth melee	60	25
529	100f. Mid-field play	1·00	30
530	200f. World Cup poster	2·10	60
531	300f. Mario Jorge Lobo Zagalo (Argentine trainer) and Buenos Aires stadium	3·75	1·30
MS532	120×81 mm. 500f. Ferenc Puskas (Hungarian player)	6·25	2·20

198 Emperor Bokassa I

1977. Coronation of Emperor Bokassa.

533	**198**	40f. mult (postage)	35	15
534	**198**	60f. multicoloured	50	25
535	**198**	100f. multicoloured	1·00	55
536	**198**	150f. multicoloured	1·40	70
537	**198**	200f. mult (air)	1·90	85
538	**198**	300f. multicoloured	2·50	1·40
MS539		102×80 mm. 500f. Emperor Bokassa, inscription and furled flag (48×39 mm)	5·25	2·50

199 Bangui Telephone Exchange

1978. Opening of Automatic Telephone Exchange, Bangui. Multicoloured.

541	40f. Type **199**	45	25
542	60f. Bangui Telephone Exchange (different)	60	35

200 Bokassa Sports Palace

1978. Bokassa Sports Palace. Multicoloured.

543	40f. Type **200**	45	25
544	60f. Sports Palace (different)	60	35

201 *The Holy Family*

1978. 400th Birth Anniv of Rubens. Multicoloured.

545	60f. Type **201**	75	25
546	150f. *Marie de Medici*	1·30	45
547	200f. *The Artist's Sons*	2·00	65
548	300f. *Neptune* (horiz)	3·25	85
MS549	90×116 mm. 500f. *Marie de Medici* (different) (37×49 mm)	5·75	2·00

202 Black Rhinoceros

1978. Endangered Animals. Multicoloured.

550	40f. Type **202**	1·10	25
551	50f. Crocodile	1·70	30
552	60f. Leopard (vert)	1·90	45
553	100f. Giraffe (vert)	3·00	65
554	200f. African elephant	7·75	90
555	300f. Gorilla (vert)	9·25	1·50

203 Mail Coach and Satellite

1978. 100 Years of Progress in Posts and Telecommunications. Multicoloured.

556	40f. Type **203** (postage)	45	25
557	50f. Steam locomotive and space communications	1·80	85
558	60f. Paddle-steamer and ship-to-shore communications	55	25
559	80f. Renault car and "Pioneer" satellite	75	25
560	100f. Mail balloon and "Apollo"–"Soyuz" link-up (air)	1·00	40
561	200f. Seaplane *Comte da la Vaulx* and Concorde	1·80	70
MS562	104×70 mm. 500f. Tom-toms and Zeppelin (53×35 mm)	6·75	1·90

205 H.M.S. *Endeavour* under Repair (after W. Byrne)

1978. 250th Birth Anniv of Captain Cook. Multicoloured.

578	60f. Type **205**	75	25
579	80f. Cook on board *Endeavour* (vert)	1·00	40
580	200f. Landing party in New Hebrides	2·75	75
581	350f. Masked paddlers in canoe (after Webber)	4·50	1·50

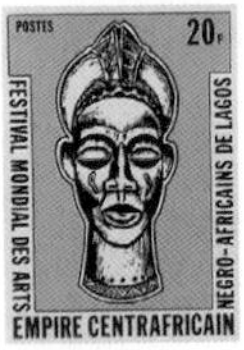

206 Ife Bronze Head

1978. Second World Festival of Negro Arts, Lagos.

582	**206**	20f. black and yellow	30	25
583	-	30f. black and blue	30	25
584	-	60f. multicoloured	70	40
585	-	100f. multicoloured	1·20	70

DESIGNS—VERT: 30f. Carved mask. HORIZ: 60f. Dancers; 100f. Dancers with musical instruments.

207 Clement Ader and *Avion III*

1978. Air. Aviation Pioneers. Multicoloured.

586	40f. Type **207**	50	25
587	50f. Wright Brothers and glider No. III	50	25
588	60f. Alcock, Brown and Vickers Vimy	60	40
589	100f. Sir Alan Cobham and De Havilland D.H.50	1·20	40
590	150f. Dr. Claude Dornier and Dornier Gs1 flying boat	1·80	70
MS591	117×80 mm. 500f. Wright Brothers and *Flyer*	5·50	1·80

208 *Self-portrait*

1978. 450th Death Anniv of Albrecht Durer (artist). Multicoloured.

592	60f. Type **208**	60	25
593	80f. *The Four Apostles*	1·00	25
594	200f. *The Virgin and Child*	2·40	90
595	350f. *The Emperor Maximilian I*	4·00	1·50

1978. Air. "Philexafrique" Stamp Exhibition, Gabon (1st issue) and International Stamp Fair, Essen. As T **237** of Benin. Multicoloured.

596	100f. Red crossbills and Mecklenberg-Schwerin 1856 ¼s. stamp	2·20	1·40
597	100f. Crocodile and Central African Republic 1960 500f. stamp	2·20	1·40

See also Nos. 647/8.

209 Third Mummiform Coffin

1978. Treasures of Tutankhamun. Multicoloured.

598	40f. Type **209**	70	30
599	60f. Tutankhamun and Ankhesenamun (back of gilt throne)	95	35
600	80f. Ecclesiastical throne	1·40	50
601	100f. Head of Tutankhamun (wooden statuette)	1·50	50
602	120f. Lion's head (funerary bedhead)	2·00	65
603	150f. Life-size statue of Tutankhamun	2·50	70
604	180f. Gilt throne	3·25	85
605	250f. Canopic coffin	4·00	1·10

210 Lenin speaking at the Smolny Institute

1978. 60th Anniv of Russian Revolution.

606	**210**	40f. multicoloured	50	30
607	-	60f. multicoloured	60	45
608	-	100f. black, grey and gold	1·00	50
609	-	150f. red, black and gold	1·90	80
610	-	200f. multicoloured	2·50	1·00
611	-	300f. multicoloured	3·25	1·50
MS612		78×110 mm. 500f. multicoloured	5·25	4·00

DESIGNS—VERT: 60f. Lenin addressing crowd in Red Square; 200f. Lenin in Smolny Institute; 300f. Lenin and banner; 500f. Cruiser *Aurora* and Order of Lenin. HORIZ: 100f. Lenin, Kurpskaya and family; 150f. Lenin, cruiser *Aurora*, banner and revolutionaries.

211 Catherine Bokassa

1978. First Anniv of Emperor Bokassa's Coronation. Multicoloured.

613	40f. Type **211** (postage)	50	25
614	60f. Emperor Bokassa	70	30
615	150f. The Emperor and Empress (horiz) (air)	1·70	75
MS616	Two sheets. (a) 101×82 mm. 250f. Coronation ceremony (horiz); (b) 76×100 mm. 1000f. Emperor and eagle	12·00	5·50

212 Rowland Hill, Letter-weighing Scale and Penny Black

1978. Death Centenary of Sir Rowland Hill (1st issue). Multicoloured.

617	40f. Type **212** (postage)	55	25
618	50f. Postman on bicycle and U.S. 5c. stamp, 1847	55	25
619	60f. Danish postman and Austrian newspaper stamp, 1856	80	35
620	80f. Postilion, mail coach and Geneva 5+5c. stamp, 1843	95	45
621	100f. Postman, mail train and Tuscan 3l. stamp, 1860 (air)	2·40	1·00
622	200f. Mail balloon and French 10c. stamp, 1850	1·70	70
MS623	81×85 mm. 500f. First Central African Republic stamps, 1959 (37×38 mm)	5·50	1·80

See also Nos. 671/**MS**675.

1978. Argentina's Victory in World Cup Football Championship. Nos. 527/31 optd **VAINQUEUR ARGENTINE**.

625	50f. Type **197**	55	35
626	60f. Goalmouth melee	60	40
627	100f. Midfield play	95	60
628	200f. World Cup poster	2·00	1·10
629	300f. Mario Jorge Lobo Zagalo and Buenos Aires Stadium	3·00	1·40
MS630	120×81 mm. 500f. multicoloured, optd **ARGENTINE-PAYS BAS 3-1/25 juin 1978**	5·25	5·25

214 Children painting and Dutch Master

1979. International Year of the Child (1st issue). Multicoloured.

631	40f. Type **214** (postage)	50	10
632	50f. Eskimo children and skier	65	20
633	60f. Benz automobile and children with toy car	85	25
634	80f. Satellite and children launching rocket	1·20	25
635	100f. Dornier Do-X flying boat and Chinese child flying kite (air)	1·30	45
636	200f. Hurdler and children playing leap-frog	2·50	70
MS637	109×79 mm. 500f. Albert Einstein and child with abacus (55×32 mm)	5·50	1·80

See also Nos. 666/70.

215 High Jump

1979. Pre-Olympic Year (1st issue). Multicoloured.

639	40f. Type **215** (postage)	50	10
640	50f. Cycling	55	20
641	60f. Weightlifting	65	25
642	80f. Judo	90	30
643	100f. Hurdles (air)	1·00	40
644	200f. Long jump	1·90	70
MS645	110×79 mm. 500f. Pole vault (55×37 mm)	5·00	1·70

See also Nos. 676/80 and 700/**MS**706.

216 Co-operation Monument, *Aurivillius arata* and Hibiscus

1979. "Philexafrique" Exhibition (2nd issue). Multicoloured.

647	60f. Type **216**	2·40	1·20
648	150f. Envelopes, van, canoeist and UPU emblem	4·25	2·30

217 School Teacher

1979. 50th Anniv of International Bureau of Education.

649	**217**	70f. multicoloured	85	45

218 "Madonna seated on a Bench" (woodcut)

1979. 450th Death Anniv (1978) of Albrecht Durer (artist) (2nd issue). Sheet 90×115 mm.

MS650	**218** 500f. green and lake	5·50	1·80

219 Chicken

1979. National Association of Farmers. Multicoloured.

651	10f. Type **219** (postage)	1·80	1·10
652	20f. Bullock	1·80	1·10
653	40f. Sheep	3·75	2·20
654	60f. Horse (air)	5·50	2·10

OFFICIAL STAMPS

1977. Official stamps of Central African Republic optd **EMPIRE CENTRAFRICAIN**.

O498	**O109**	5f. multicoloured	25	10
O499	**O109**	40f. multicoloured	45	25
O500	**O109**	100f. multicoloured	1·20	40
O501	**O109**	140f. multicoloured	1·50	80
O502	**O109**	200f. multicoloured	2·50	1·10

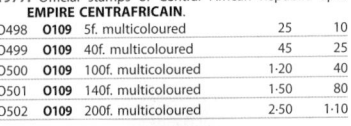

O204 Coat of Arms

1978

O564	**O204**	1f. multicoloured	10	10
O565	**O204**	2f. multicoloured	10	10
O566	**O204**	5f. multicoloured	10	10
O567	**O204**	10f. multicoloured	25	10
O568	**O204**	15f. multicoloured	25	10
O569	**O204**	20f. multicoloured	25	10
O570	**O204**	30f. multicoloured	45	25
O571	**O204**	40f. multicoloured	45	25
O572	**O204**	50f. multicoloured	70	55
O673	**O204**	60f. multicoloured	65	45
O574	**O204**	100f. multicoloured	1·10	90
O575	**O204**	130f. multicoloured	1·40	1·50
O576	**O204**	140f. multicoloured	1·70	1·30
O577	**O204**	200f. multicoloured	3·25	1·60

Pt. 12

CENTRAL AFRICAN REPUBLIC

Formerly Ubangi-Shari. An independent republic within the French Community.

100 centimes = 1 franc.

1 President Boganda

1959. Republic. First Anniv. Centres multicoloured. Frame colours given.

1	**1**	15f. blue	55	25
2	-	25f. red	55	25

DESIGN—HORIZ: 25f. As Type **1** but flag behind portrait.

1960. Tenth Anniv of African Technical Co-operation Commission. As T **62** of Cameroun.

3		50f. blue and green	1·80	95

3 *Dactyloceras widenmanni*

4 Abyssinian Roller

1960

4	-	50c. brn, red & turq (postage)	10	10
5	-	1f. myrtle, brown & violet	10	10
6	-	2f. myrtle, brown and green	10	20
7	-	3f. brown, red and olive	45	20
8	**3**	5f. brown and green	45	25
9	-	10f. blue, black and green	95	55
10	-	20f. red, black and green	2·30	80
12	-	50f. turq, red & green (air)	1·90	60
11	-	85f. red, black and green	7·25	1·70
13	**4**	100f. violet, brown & green	2·40	90
14	-	200f. multicoloured	4·50	2·20
15	-	250f. multicoloured	6·75	2·50
16	-	500f. brown, blue and green	13·00	5·25

BUTTERFLIES—As Type **3**: 50c., 3f. *Cymothoe sangaris*; 1f., 2f. *Charaxe mobilis*; 10f. *Charaxes ameliae*; 20f. *Charaxes zingha*; 85f. *Drurya antimachus*. BIRDS—As Type **4**: 50f. Great blue turaco; 200f. Green turaco; 250f. Red-faced lovebirds; 500f. African fish eagle.

See also Nos. 42/5.

1960. National Festival. No. 2 optd **FETE NATIONALE 1-12-1960.**

17		25f. multicoloured	1·40	1·30

1960. Air. Olympic Games. No. 276 of French Equatorial Africa optd with Olympic rings, **XVIIe OLYMPIADE 1960 REPUBLIQUE CENTRAFRICAINE** and surch 250F and bars.

18		250f. on 500f. blue, blk & grn	8·75	8·25

7 Pasteur Institute, Bangui

1961. Opening of Pasteur Institute, Bangui.

19	**7**	20f. multicoloured	1·00	80

8 U.N. Emblem, Map and Flag

1961. Admission into UNO.

20	**8**	15f. multicoloured	40	30
21	**8**	25f. multicoloured	50	30
22	**8**	85f. multicoloured	1·50	1·00

1961. National Festival. Optd with star and **FETE NATIONALE 1-12-01.**

23		25f. multicoloured	2·00	1·90

1962. Air. "Air Afrique" Airline. As T **69** of Cameroun.

24		50f. violet, brown and green	95	70

1962. Union of African States and Madagascar Conference, Bangui. Surch **U.A.M. CONFERENCE DE BANGUI 25-27 MARS 1962 50F.**

25		50f. on 85f. multicoloured	1·70	1·60

1962. Malaria Eradication. As T **70** of Cameroun.

26		25f.+5f. slate	1·10	1·10

12 Hurdling

1962. Sports.

27	**12**	20f. sep, yell & grn (postage)	45	30
28	-	50f. sepia, yellow and green	1·30	80
29	-	100f. sep, yell & grn (air)	2·20	1·50

DESIGNS—As Type **12**: 50f. Cycling. VERT: (26×47 mm): 100f. Pole-vaulting.

13 Pres. Dacko

1962

30	**13**	20f. multicoloured	35	20
31	**13**	25f. multicoloured	45	25

1962. First Anniv of Union of African and Malagasy States. As T **72** of Cameroun.

32		30f. green	1·20	95

15 Athlete

1962. Air. "Coupe des Tropiques" Games, Bangui.

33	**15**	100f. brown, turquoise & red	2·40	1·60

1963. Freedom from Hunger. As T **76** of Cameroun.

34		25f.+5f. turquoise, brn & bis	1·00	1·00

17 "National Army"

1963. Third Anniv of Proclamation of Republic.

35	**17**	20f. multicoloured	65	45

18 "Posts and Telecommunications"

1963. Air. African and Malagasy Posts and Telecommunications Union.

36	**18**	85f. multicoloured	1·80	90

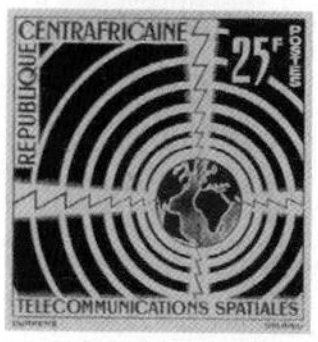

19 "Telecommunications"

1963. Space Telecommunications.

37	**19**	25f. green and purple	75	60
38	-	100f. green, orange & blue	1·80	1·60

DESIGN: 100f. Radio waves and globe.

20 "Young Pioneers"

1963. Young Pioneers.

39	**20**	30f. brown, blue & turquoise	85	50

21 Boali Falls

1963

40	**21**	30f. purple, green and blue	85	50

22 Map of Africa and Sun

1963. Air. "African Unity".

41	**22**	25f. ultramarine, yellow & bl	65	45

23 *Colotis evippe*

1963. Butterflies. Multicoloured.

42	1f. Type **23**	20	20
43	3f. *Papilio dardanus*	55	25
44	4f. *Papilio lormieri*	80	35
45	60f. *Papilio zalmoxis*	5·00	3·00

24 "Europafrique"

1963. Air. European–African Economic Convention.

46	**24**	50f. multicoloured	2·75	2·10

25 ABJ-6 Diesel Railcar

1963. Air. Bangui–Douala Railway Project.

47	-	20f. green, purple & brown	65	50
48	**25**	25f. chocolate, blue & brn	95	60
49	-	50f. violet, purple & brown	2·50	1·90
50	-	100f. purple, turquoise and brown	3·75	2·75
MS50a		190×98 mm. Nos. 47/50	8·00	8·00

DESIGNS: (Diesel rolling stock)—HORIZ: 20f. ABJ-6 railcar; 100f. Diesel locomotive. VERT: 50f. Series BB500 diesel shunter.

26 UNESCO Emblem, Scales of Justice and Tree

1963. 15th Anniv of Declaration of Human Rights.

51	**26**	25f. bistre, green and brown	85	60

27 Bangui Cathedral

1964. Air.

52	**27**	100f. brown, green & blue	2·00	1·10

28 Cleopatra, Temple of Kalabsha

1964. Air. Nubian Monuments Preservation.

53	**28**	25f.+10f. mauve, bl & grn	1·30	1·20
54	**28**	50f.+10f. brn, grn & turq	2·20	2·10
55	**28**	100f.+10f. pur, vio & grn	3·50	3·25

29 Radar Scanner

1964. Air. World Meteorological Day.

56	**29**	50f. violet, brown and blue	1·00	1·00

30 "Tree" and Sun Emblem

1964. International Quiet Sun Years.

57	**30**	25f. orange, ochre & turq	1·30	85

31 Map and African Heads of State

1964. Air. 5th Anniv of Equatorial African Heads of State Conference.

58	**31**	100f. multicoloured	1·80	90

32 Throwing the Javelin

1964. Air. Olympic Games, Tokyo.

59	**32**	25f. brown, green and blue	45	30
60	-	50f. red, black and green	95	55
61	-	100f. brown, blue and green	2·20	1·30
62	-	250f. black, green and red	6·50	3·00
MS62a		130×100 mm. Nos. 59/62	16·00	15·00

DESIGNS: 50f. Basketball; 100f. Running; 250f. Diving and swimming.

33 Pres. Kennedy

1964. Air. Pres. Kennedy Memorial Issue.

63	**33**	100f. brown, black & violet	2·40	1·70
MS63a 90×130 mm. No. 63 in block of four			10·50	10·00

34 African Child

1964. Child Welfare. Different portraits of children. As T **34**.

64	**34**	20f. brown, green & purple	45	25
65	-	25f. brown, blue and red	45	30
66	-	40f. brown, purple & green	60	45
67	-	50f. brown, green and red	80	60
MS67a 144×100 mm. Nos. 64/7			3·25	3·00

1964. French, African and Malagasy Co-operation. As T **88** of Cameroun.

68	25f. brown, red and green	85	50

35 Silhouettes of European and African

1964. National Unity.

69	**35**	25f. multicoloured	85	50

36 "Economic Co-operation"

1964. Air. "Europafrique".

70	**36**	50f. green, red and yellow	1·20	85

37 Handclasp

1965. Air. International Co-operation Year.

71	**37**	100f. multicoloured	1·80	90

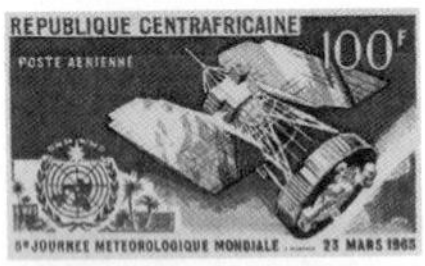
38 Weather Satellite

1965. Air. World Meteorological Day.

72	**38**	100f. blue and brown	1·80	90

39 Abraham Lincoln

1965. Air. Death Centenary of Abraham Lincoln.

73	**39**	100f. flesh, blue & green	1·80	90

40 Team of Oxen

1965. Harnessed Animals in Agriculture.

74	**40**	25f. red, brown and green	50	30
75	-	50f. purple, green and blue	95	55
76	-	85f. brown, green and blue	1·30	80
77	-	100f. multicoloured	1·70	90

DESIGNS: 50f. Ploughing with bullock; 85f. Ploughing with oxen; 100f. Oxen with hay cart.

41 Pouget-Maisonneuve Telegraph Instrument

1965. Centenary of ITU.

78	**41**	25f. blue, red & grn (post)	55	45
79	-	30f. lake and green	60	55
80	-	50f. red and violet	1·00	70
81	-	85f. blue and purple	1·80	1·20
82	-	100f. brown, blue & green (48½×27 mm) (air)	2·00	1·20

DESIGNS—VERT: 30f. Chappe's telegraph instrument; 50f. Doignon regulator for Hughes telegraph. HORIZ: 85f. Pouillet's telegraph apparatus; 100f. "Relay" satellite and ITU emblem.

42 Women and Loom ("To Clothe")

1965. "MESAN" Welfare Campaign. Designs depicting "Five Aims".

83	**42**	25f. green, brown and blue (postage)	45	30
84	-	50f. brown, blue and green	80	55
85	-	60f. brown, blue and green	1·00	65
86	-	85f. multicoloured	1·40	70
87	-	100f. blue, brown and green (48×27 mm) (air)	1·80	1·10

DESIGNS: 50f. Doctor examining child, and hospital ("To care for"); 60f. Student and school ("To instruct"); 85f. Women and child, and harvesting scene ("To nourish"); 100f. Village houses ("To house"). "MESAN—Mouvement Evolution Social Afrique Noire".

43 Coffee Plant, Hammer Grubs and *Epicampoptera strandi*

1965. Plant Protection.

88	**43**	2f. purple, red and green	30	10
89	-	3f. red, green and black	75	20
90	-	30f. purple, green and red	4·50	90

DESIGNS—HORIZ: 3f. Coffee plant, caterpillar and hawk-moth. VERT: 30f. Cotton plant caterpillar and rose-moth.

1965. Surch.

91		2f. on 3f. (No. 43)	4·25	4·00
92	**1**	5f. on 15f.	3·75	3·00
93	-	5f. on 85f. (No. 76)	35	30
94	**13**	10f. on 20f.	4·50	4·25
95	-	10f. on 100f. (No. 77)	55	55

45 Camp Fire

1965. Scouting.

96	**45**	25f. red, purple and blue	75	25
97	-	50f. brown and blue (Boy Scout)	1·30	65

46 U.N. and Campaign Emblems

1965. Freedom from Hunger.

98	**46**	50f. brown, blue and green	1·10	75

47 "Industry and Agriculture"

1965. Air. "Europafrique".

99	**47**	50f. multicoloured	1·00	75

48 Mercury (statue after Coysevox)

1965. Air. Fifth Anniv of Admission to UPU.

100	**48**	100f. black, blue & red	2·30	1·30

49 Father and Child

1965. Air. Red Cross.

101	**49**	50f. black, blue and red	1·20	55
102	-	100f. brown, green and red (Mother and Child)	2·50	1·20

50 Grading Diamonds

1966. National Diamond Industry.

103	**50**	25f. brown, violet and red	1·00	50

51 Mbaka Porter

1966. World Festival of Negro Arts, Dakar.

104	**51**	25f. multicoloured	85	50

52 WHO Building

1966. WHO Headquarters, Geneva. Inaug.

105	**52**	25f. violet, blue & yellow	85	50

53 *Eulophia cucullata*

1966. Flowers. Multicoloured.

106	2f. Type **53**	25	10
107	5f. *Lissochilus horsfalii*	45	10
108	10f. *Tridactyle bicaudata*	45	25
109	15f. *Polystachya*	95	50
110	20f. *Eulophia alta*	1·40	60
111	25f. *Microcelia macrorrhynchium*	2·00	95

54 Douglas DC-8F Aircraft and "Air Afrique" Emblem

1966. Air. Inaug of "DC-8" Air Services.

112	**54**	25f. multicoloured	85	45

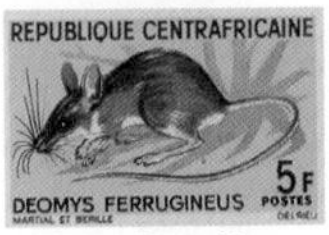
55 Congo Forest Mouse

1966. Rodents. Multicoloured.

113	5f. Type **55**	55	30
114	10f. Black-striped mouse	1·00	50
115	20f. Dollman's tree mouse	1·70	80

56 "Luna 9"

1966. Air. "Conquest of the Moon". Multicoloured.

116	130f. Type **56**	1·70	1·00
117	130f. "Surveyor"	1·70	1·00
118	200f. "From the Earth to the Moon" (Jules Verne)	3·25	1·80
MS119 132×160 mm. Nos. 116/18		8·25	7·75

57 Cernan

1966. Air. Astronauts. Multicoloured.

120	50f. Type **57**	1·10	60
121	50f. Popovich	1·10	60

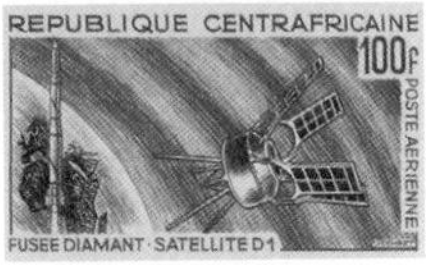
58 Satellite "D 1" and Rocket "Diamant"

1966. Air. Launching of Satellite "D 1".

122	**58**	100f. purple and brown	1·80	95

59 UNESCO Emblem

1966. 20th Anniv of UNESCO.

123	**59**	30f. multicoloured	60	45

60 Symbols of Industry and Agriculture

1966. Air. Europafrique.

124	**60**	50f. multicoloured	1·20	95

61 Pres. Bokassa

1967

125	**61**	30f. black, ochre & green	60	35

1967. Provisional Stamps. (a) Postage. No. 111 surch **XX** and value.

126	10f. on 25f. multicoloured	50	25

(b) Air. No. 112 with face value altered by obliteration of figure "2" in "25".

127	**54**	5f. multicoloured	45	25

63 Douglas DC-8 over Bangui M'Poko Airport

1967. Air.

128	**63**	100f. blue, green & brown	2·30	1·10

64 Aerial View of Fair

1967. Air. World Fair, Montreal.

129	**64**	100f. brown, ultram & bl	2·00	80

65 Central Market, Bangui

1967. Multicoloured.. Multicoloured..

130	30f. Type **65**	85	45
131	30f. Safari Hotel, Bangui	85	35

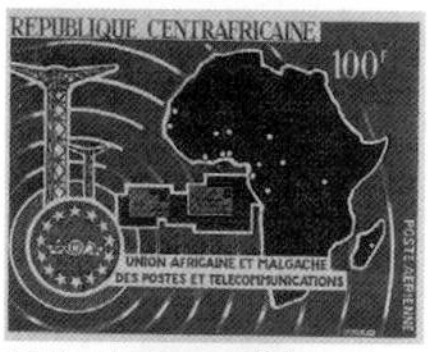
66 Map, Letters and Pylons

1967. Air. Fifth Anniv of African and Malagasy Posts and Telecommunications Union (UAMPT).

132	**66**	100f. purple, grn & red	2·00	85

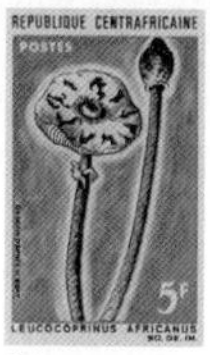
67 *Leucocoprinus africanus*

1967. Mushrooms. Multicoloured.

133	5f. Type **67**	5·25	60
134	10f. *Synpodia arborescens*	8·25	1·00
135	15f. *Phlebopus sudanicus*	9·25	1·30
136	30f. *Termitomyces schimperi*	26·00	3·25
137	50f. *Psalliota sebedulis*	42·00	5·00

68 Projector, Africans and Map

1967. "Radiovision" Service.

138	**68**	30f. blue, green and brown	85	50

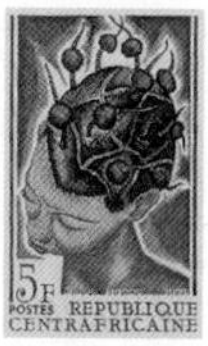
69 Coiffure

1967. Female Coiffures. Showing different hairstyles.

139	**69**	5f. brown and blue	30	15
140	-	10f. brown, choc & red	45	25
141	-	15f. brown, choc & grn	75	45
142	-	20f. brown, choc & orge	95	55
143	-	30f. brown, choc & purple	1·30	70

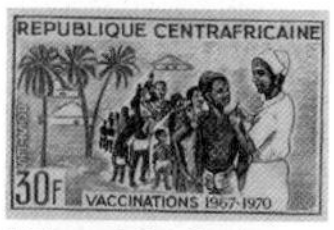
70 Inoculation Session

1967. Vaccination Programme, 1967–70.

144	**70**	30f. brown, green & red	85	60

71 Douglas DC-3

1967. Aircraft.

145	**71**	1f. grey, grn & brn (post)	10	10
146	-	2f. black, blue and purple	10	10
147	-	5f. black, green and blue	30	10
148	-	100f. brown, grn & bl (air)	2·00	85
149	-	200f. blue, brown and green	4·75	1·80
150	-	500f. slate, red and blue	12·50	4·75

DESIGNS—As T **71**: 2f. Beechcraft Baron; 5f. Douglas DC-4. 48×27 mm: 100f. Potez 25-TOE; 200f. Junkers 52/3m; 500f. Sud Aviation Caravelle.

72 Presidents Boganda and Bokassa

1967. Air. Ninth Anniv of Republic.

151	**72**	130f. multicoloured	2·00	1·30

73 Primitive Shelter, Toulou

1967. Sixth Pan-African Prehistory Congress, Dakar.

152	**73**	30f. blue, purple and red	75	40
153	-	50f. bistre, ochre & green	1·50	80
154	-	100f. purple, brown & blue	2·75	1·10
155	-	130f. red, green & brown	3·00	1·10

DESIGNS—VERT: 50f. Kwe perforated stone; 100f. Megaliths, Bouar. HORIZ: 130f. Rock drawings, Toulou.

74 Pres. Bokassa

1968. Air.

156	**74**	30f. multicoloured	85	50

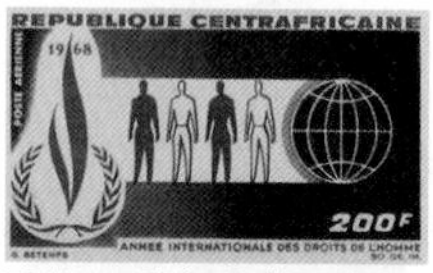
75 Human Rights Emblem, Human Figures and Globe

1968. Air. Human Rights Year.

157	**75**	200f. red, green and violet	3·50	1·70

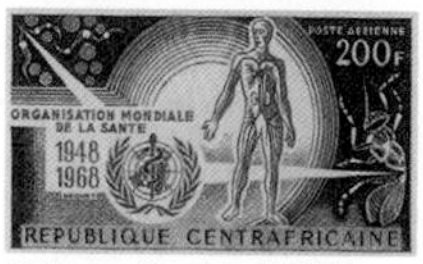
76 Human Figure and WHO Emblem

1968. Air. 20th Anniv of WHO.

158	**76**	200f. red, blue & brown	3·75	2·10

77 Alpine Skiing

1968. Air. Olympic Games, Grenoble and Mexico.

159	**77**	200f. brown, blue and red	5·00	3·25
160	-	200f. brown, blue and red	5·00	3·25

DESIGN: No. 160, Throwing the javelin.

78 Parachute-landing on Venus

1968. Air. "Venus 4". Exploration of planet Venus.

161	**78**	100f. blue, turquoise & green	1·80	95

79 Marie Curie and impaled Crab (of Cancer)

1968. Air. Marie Curie Commem.

162	**79**	100f. brown, violet & blue	2·40	1·20

80 Refinery and Tanker

1968. Inauguration of Petroleum Refinery, Port Gentil, Gabon.

163	**80**	30f. multicoloured	85	40

1968. Air. Surch. Nos. 165/6 are obliterated with digit.

164	**56**	5f. on 130f. (No. 116)	10	10
165	-	10f. (100f. No. 148)	30	10
166	-	20f. (200f. No. 149)	45	30
167	-	50f. on 130f. (No. 117)	1·00	60

82 "CD-8" Bulldozer

1968. Bokassa Project.

168	**82**	5f. brown, black & green	35	15
169	-	10f. black, brown & green	65	30
170	-	20f. green, yellow & brown	75	40
171	-	30f. blue, drab and brown	1·20	55
172	-	30f. red, blue and green	1·20	60

DESIGNS: 10f. Baoule cattle; 20f. Spinning-machine; 30f. (No. 171), Automatic looms; 30f. (No. 172), "D4-C" bulldozer.

83 Bangui Mosque

1968. Second Anniv of Bangui Mosque.

173	**83**	30f. flesh, green and blue	80	45

84 Za Throwing-knife

1968. Hunting Weapons.

174	**84**	10f. blue and bistre	45	25
175	-	20f. green, brown & blue	60	40
176	-	30f. green, orange & blue	95	45

DESIGNS: 20f. Kpinga-Gbengue throwing-knife; 30f. Mbano cross-bow.

85 *Ville de Bangui* (1958)

1968. River Craft.

177	**85**	10f. blue, green and purple (postage)	60	40
178	-	30f. brown, blue & green	1·10	55
179	-	50f. black, brown & grn	1·90	90
180	-	100f. brown, grn & bl (air)	2·40	1·10
181	-	130f. blue, green & purple	2·75	1·40

DESIGNS: 30f. *J. B. Gouandjia* (1968); 50f. *Lamblin* (1944). LARGER (48×27 mm): 100f. *Pie X* (Bangui, 1894); 130f. *Ballay* (Bangui, 1891).

86 *Madame de Sevigne* (French School, 17th century)

1968. Air. "Philexafrique" Stamp Exhibition, Abidjan, Ivory Coast (1969) (1st issue).

182	**86**	100f. multicoloured	3·00	2·50

87 President Bokassa, Cotton Plantation, and Ubangui Chari stamp of 1930

1969. Air. "Philexafrique" Stamp Exhibition, Abidjan, Ivory Coast (2nd issue).

183	**87**	50f. black, green & brown	1·80	1·70

88 "Holocerina angulata"

1969. Air. Butterflies. Multicoloured.

184	10f. Type **88**	75	30
185	20f. *Nudaurelia dione*	1·20	55
186	30f. *Eustera troglophylla* (vert)	2·75	85
187	50f. *Aurivillius aratus*	4·50	2·20
188	100f. *Epiphora albida*	7·50	3·50

89 Throwing the Javelin

1969. Sports. Multicoloured.

189	5f. Type **89** (postage)	20	10
190	10f. Start of race	30	15
191	15f. Football	45	20
192	50f. Boxing (air)	1·00	40

193		100f. Basketball	2·10	70

Nos. 192/3 are 48×28 mm.

90 Miner and Emblems

1969. 50th Anniv of I.L.O.

194	**90**	30f. multicoloured	90	40
195	**90**	50f. multicoloured	1·40	65

91 "Apollo 8" over Moon's Surface

1969. Air. Flight of "Apollo 8" Around Moon.

196	**91**	200f. multicoloured	3·50	1·80

92 Nuremberg Spire and Toys

1969. Air. International Toy Fair, Nuremberg.

197	**92**	100f. black, purple & grn	1·90	1·10

1969. Air. Birth Bicentenary of Napoleon Bonaparte. As T **144** of Cameroun. Multicoloured.

198	100f. *Napoleon as First Consul* (Girodet-Trioson) (vert)	2·30	1·40
199	130f. *Meeting of Napoleon and Francis II of Austria* (Gros)	3·25	1·60
200	200f. *Marriage of Napoleon and Marie-Louise* (Rouget)	4·75	3·00

93 President Bokassa in Military Uniform

1969

201	**93**	30f. multicoloured	60	30

1969. Tenth Anniv of ASECNA. As T **151** of Cameroun.

202	100f. blue	1·80	85

94 Pres. Bokassa, Flag and Map

1970. Air. Die-stamped on gold foil.

203	**94**	2000f. gold	37·00	35·00

95 Garayah

1970. Musical Instruments.

204	**95**	10f. brown, sepia & green	60	25
205	-	15f. brown and green	65	25
206	-	30f. brown, lake & yellow	1·00	50
207	-	50f. blue and red	1·50	55
208	-	130f. brown, olive & blue	5·00	1·30

DESIGNS—VERT: 130f. Gatta and Babylon. HORIZ: 15f. Ngombi; 30f. Xylophone; 50f. Nadla.

96 Flour Storage Depot

1970. Societie Industrielle Centrafricaine des Produits Alimentaires et Derives (SICPAD) Project. Multicoloured.

209	25f. Type **96**	11·50	80
210	50f. Mill machinery	24·00	1·60
211	100f. View of flour mill	36·00	2·50

97 F. D. Roosevelt (25th Death Anniv)

1970. Air. World Leaders. Multicoloured.

212	100f. Lenin (birth centenary)	3·50	1·50
213	100f. Type **97**	1·90	1·00

1970. New UPU Headquarters Building, Berne. As T **156** of Cameroun.

214	100f. vermilion, red and blue	1·70	75

1970. Air. Moon Landing of "Apollo 12". No. 196 optd **ATTERRISSAGE d'APOLLO 12 19 novembre 1969**.

215	**91**	200f. multicoloured	15·00	10·50

99 Pres. Bokassa

1970

216	**99**	30f. multicoloured	7·25	4·50
217	**99**	40f. multicoloured	8·25	4·75

100 Cheese Factory, Sarki **101** Silkworm

1970. "Operation Bokassa" Development Projects. Multicoloured.

218	5f. Type **100** (postage)	45	25
219	10f. M'Bali Ranch	5·50	4·00
220	20f. Zebu bull and herdsman (vert)	75	40
221	40f. Type **101**	2·20	70
222	140f. Type **101** (air)	2·20	90

102 African Dancer

1970. Air. "Knokphila 70" Stamp Exhibition, Knokke, Belgium. Multicoloured.

223	100f. Type **102**	1·80	60
224	100f. African produce	2·00	60

103 Footballer

1970. Air. World Cup Football Championship, Mexico.

225	**103**	200f. multicoloured	3·75	1·70

104 Central African Republic's Pavilion

1970. Air. "EXPO 70", Osaka, Japan.

226	**104**	200f. multicoloured	4·00	1·90

105 Dove and Cogwheel

1970. Air. 25th Anniv of UNO.

227	**105**	200f. black, yellow & bl	3·75	1·70

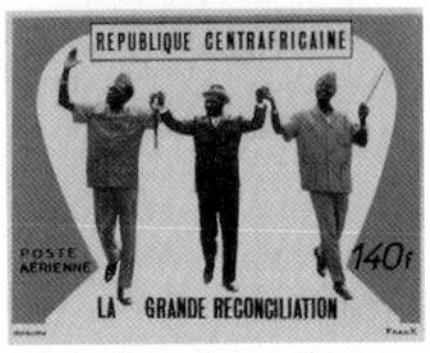

106 Presidents Mobutu, Bokassa and Tombalbaye

1970. Air. Reconciliation with Chad and Zaire.

228	**106**	140f. multicoloured	2·75	1·10

107 Scaly Francolin and Helmeted Guineafowl

1971. Wildlife. Multicoloured.

229	5f.+5f. Type **107**	4·75	2·20
230	10f.+5f. Common duiker and true achatina (snail)	6·25	3·00
231	20f.+5f. Hippopotamus, African elephant and tortoise in tug-of-war	7·75	3·25
232	30f.+10f. Tortoise and Senegal coucal	10·50	7·75
233	50f.+20f. Monkey and leopard	18·00	12·50

108 Lengue Dancer

1971. Traditional Dances. Multicoloured.

234	20f.+5f. Type **108**	55	25
235	40f.+10f. Lengue (diff)	95	45
236	100f.+40f. Teke	2·75	1·30
237	140f.+40f. Englabolo	3·25	1·60

110 Monteir's Mormyrid

1971. Fish. Multicoloured.

244	10f. Type **110**	35	25
245	20f. Trunk-nosed mormyrid	75	30
246	30f. Wilverth's mormyrid	1·20	65
247	40f. Elephant-nosed mormyrid	2·30	75
248	50f. Curve-nosed mormyrid	3·00	1·30

111 Satellite and Globe

1971. Air. World Telecommunications Day.

249	**111**	100f. multicoloured	1·90	90

112 Berberati Cathedral

1971. Consecration of Roman Catholic Cathedral, Berberati.

250	**112**	5f. multicoloured	45	20

113 Gen. De Gaulle

1971. First Death Anniv of De Gaulle.

251	**113**	100f. multicoloured	3·50	2·10

114 Lesser Bushbaby

1971. Animals: Primates. Multicoloured.

252	30f. Type **114**	85	65
253	40f. Western needle-clawed bushbaby	1·20	75
254	100f. Angwantibo (horiz)	2·75	1·70
255	150f. Potto (horiz)	4·75	2·50
256	200f. Red colobus (horiz)	6·50	3·75

1971. Air. Tenth Anniv of African and Malagasy Posts and Telecommunications Union. Similar to T **184** of Cameroun. Multicoloured.

257	100f. Headquarters and carved head	1·90	90

115 Shepard in Capsule

1971. Space Achievements. Multicoloured.

258	40f. Type **115**	55	40
259	40f. Gagarin in helmet	55	40
260	100f. Aldrin in Space	1·40	55
261	100f. Leonov in Space	1·40	55
262	200f. Armstrong on Moon	2·50	1·20
263	200f. "Lunokhod 1" on Moon	2·50	1·20

116 Crab Emblem

1971. Air. Anti-cancer Campaign.

264	**116**	100f. multicoloured	2·40	1·20

117 "Operation Bokassa"

1971. 12th Year of Independence.

265	**117**	40f. multicoloured	80	50

118 Racial Equality Year Emblem

1971. Racial Equality Year.

266	**118**	50f. multicoloured	80	50

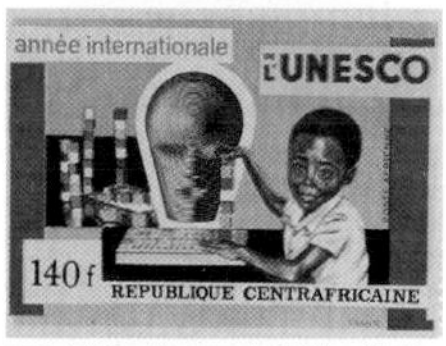

119 IEY Emblem and Child with Toy Bricks

1971. Air. 25th Anniv of UNESCO.

267	**119**	140f. multicoloured	1·90	85

120 African Children

1971. Air. 25th Anniv of UNICEF.

268	**120**	140f.+50f. multicoloured	3·00	1·80

121 Arms and Parade

1972. Bokassa Military School.

269	**121**	30f. multicoloured	80	50

122 Pres. G. Nasser

1972. Air. Nasser Commemoration.

270	**122**	100f. ochre, brown & red	2·10	95

123 Book Year Emblem

1972. International Book Year.

271	**123**	100f. gold, yellow & brn	3·00	1·30

124 Heart Emblem

1972. World Heart Month.

272	**124**	100f. red, black & yellow	1·80	95

125 First-Aid Post

1972. Red Cross Day.

273	**125**	150f. multicoloured	3·25	1·60

126 Global Emblem

1972. World Telecommunications Day.

274	**126**	50f. black, yellow & red	95	60

127 Boxing

1972. Air. Olympic Games, Munich.

275	**127**	100f. bistre and brown	1·70	1·10
276	-	100f. violet and green	1·70	1·10

MS277 130×100 mm. Designs as Nos. 275/6, but colours changed: 100f. emerald and purple; 100f. purple and brown 4·50 4·25

DESIGN—VERT: No. 276 Long jump.

128 Pres. Bokassa and Family

1972. Mothers' Day.

278	**128**	30f. multicoloured	60	40

129 Pres. Bokassa planting Cotton Bush

1972. "Operation Bokassa" Cotton Development.

279	**129**	40f. multicoloured	95	45

130 Savings Bank Building

1972. Opening of New Postal Cheques and Savings Bank Building.

280	**130**	30f. multicoloured	95	45

131 "Le Pacifique" Hotel

1972. "Operation Bokassa" Completion of "Le Pacifique" Hotel.

281	**131**	30f. blue, red and green	55	25

132 Giraffe and Monkeys

1972. Clock-faces from Central African HORCEN Factory. Multicoloured.

282	5f. Rhinoceros chasing African	30	25
283	10f. Camp fire and Native warriors	45	25
284	20f. Fishermen	45	30
285	30f. Type **132**	75	55
286	40f. Warriors fighting	1·20	70

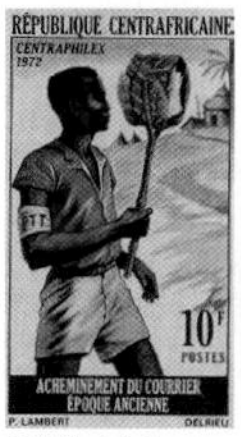

133 Postal Runner **134** Tiling's Postal Rocket, 1931

1972. "CENTRAPHILEX" Stamp Exhibition, Bangui.

287	**133**	10f. mult (postage)	30	20
288	-	20f. multicoloured	45	25
289	**134**	40f. orange, blue and slate (air)	70	45
290	-	50f. blue, slate & orange	80	70
291	-	150f. grey, orange & brn	2·30	1·50
292	-	200f. blue, orange & brn	3·25	2·30

MS293 201×100 mm. Nos. 289/92 8·75 8·50

DESIGNS—AS Type **133**: HORIZ: Protestant Youth Centre. As Type **134**: VERT: 50f. Douglas DC-3 and camel postman; 150f. "Sirio" satellite and rocket. HORIZ: 200f. "Intelsat 4" satellite and rocket.

135 University Buildings

1972. Inauguration of Bokassa University.

294	**135**	40f. grey, blue and red	80	45

136 Mail Van

1972. World UPU Day.

295	**136**	100f. multicoloured	2·00	80

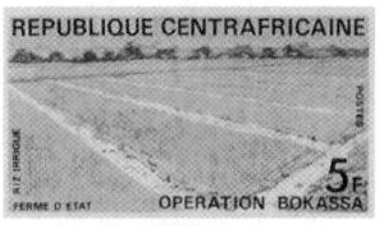

137 Paddy Field

1972. Bokassa Plan. State Farms. Multicoloured.

296	5f. Type **137**	65	20
297	25f. Rice cultivation	1·30	25

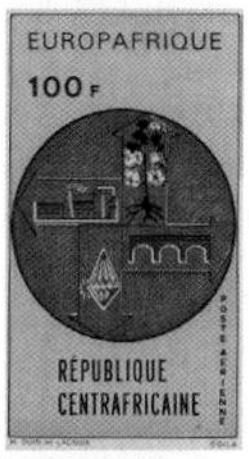

138 Four Linked Arrows

1972. Air. "Europafrique".

298	**138**	100f. multicoloured	1·60	85

1972. Air. Munich Olympic Gold Medal Winners. Nos. 275/6 optd as listed below.

299	**127**	100f. bistre and brown	1·60	95
300	-	100f. violet and green	1·60	95

MS301 130×100 mm. **MS**277 with opts as Nos. 299/300 3·75 3·50

OVERPRINTS: No. 299, **POIDS-MOYEN LEMECHEV MEDAILLE D'OR**. No. 300, **LONGUEUR WILLIAMS MEDAILLE D'OR**.

140 Hotel Swimming Pool

1972. Opening of Hotel St. Sylvestre.

302	**140**	30f. brown, turq & grn	45	30
303	-	40f. purple, green & blue	50	35

DESIGN: 40f. Facade of Hotel.

141 Landing Module and Lunar Rover on Moon

1972. Air. Moon Flight of "Apollo 16".

304	**141**	100f. green, blue & grey	1·60	80

142 *Virgin and Child* (F. Pesellino)

1972. Air. Christmas. Multicoloured.

305	100f. Type **142**	1·80	1·10
306	150f. *Adoration of the Child* (F. Lippi)	2·75	1·50

143 Learning to Write

1972. "Central African Mothers". Multicoloured.

307	5f. Type **143**	10	10
308	10f. Baby-care	30	10
309	15f. Dressing hair	40	25
310	20f. Learning to read	45	25
311	180f. Suckling baby	2·50	1·30
312	190f. Learning to walk	2·50	1·50

144 Louys (marathon), Athens, 1896

1972. Air. 75th Anniv of Revival of Olympic Games.

313	**144**	30f. purple, brown & grn	35	25
314	-	40f. green, blue & brown	45	25
315	-	50f. violet, blue and red	55	45
316	-	100f. purple, brn & grey	1·20	55
317	-	150f. black, blue & purple	1·70	1·30

DESIGNS: 40f. Barrelet (sculling), Paris, 1900; 50f. Prinstein (triple-jump), St. Louis, U.S.A., 1904; 100f. Taylor (400 m freestyle swimming), London, 1908; 150f. Johansson (Greco-Roman wrestling), Stockholm, 1912.

145 WHO Emblem, Doctor and Nurse

1973. Air. 25th Anniv of WHO.

318	**145**	100f. multicoloured	1·60	85

146 "Telecommunications"

1973. World Telecommunications Day.

319	**146**	200f. orange, blue & black	2·40	1·20

147 Harvesting

1973. Tenth Anniv of World Food Programme.

320	**147**	50f. multicoloured	80	50

148 *Garcinia punctata*

1973. "Flora". Multicoloured.

321	10f. Type **148**	45	20
322	20f. *Bertiera racemosa*	65	25
323	30f. *Coryanthe pachyceras*	90	50
324	40f. *Combretodendron africanum*	1·30	60
325	50f. *Xylopia villosa*	1·70	25

149 Pygmy Chameleon

1973

326	**149**	15f. multicoloured	1·50	40

150 *Mboyo Ndili*

1973. Caterpillars. Multicoloured.

327	3f. Type **150**	75	25
328	5f. *Piwili*	1·20	45
329	25f. *Loulia Konga*	2·50	65

1973. African Solidarity "Drought Relief". No. 321 surch **SECHERESSE SOLIDARITE AFRICAINE** and value.

330	**148**	100f. on 10f. mult	1·60	1·10

1973. UAMPT. As Type **216** of Cameroun.

331	100f. red, brown and olive	1·10	70

1973. Air. African Fortnight, Brussels. As T **217** of Cameroun.

332	100f. brown and violet	1·30	75

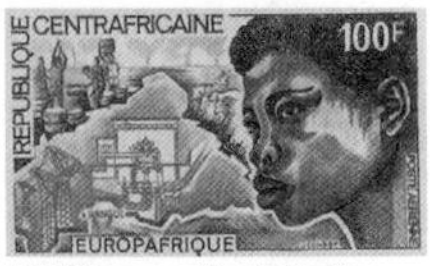

152 African and Symbolic Map

1973. Air. Europafrique.

333	**152**	100f. red, green & brown	1·60	85

153 Bird with Letter

1973. Air. World UPU Day.

334	**153**	200f. multicoloured	2·30	1·40

154 Weather Map

1973. Air. Centenary of IMO/WMO.

335	**154**	150f. multicoloured	2·40	1·00

155 Copernicus

1973. Air. 500th Birth Anniv of Copernicus.

336	**155**	100f. multicoloured	2·75	1·80

156 Pres. Bokassa

1973

337	**156**	1f. mult (postage)	10	10
338	**156**	2f. multicoloured	10	10
339	**156**	3f. multicoloured	10	10
340	**156**	5f. multicoloured	10	10
341	**156**	10f. multicoloured	35	10
342	**156**	15f. multicoloured	35	20
343	**156**	20f. multicoloured	45	25
344	**156**	30f. multicoloured	45	30
345	**156**	40f. multicoloured	60	35
346	-	50f. multicoloured (air)	65	35
347	-	100f. multicoloured	1·30	70

DESIGNS—SQUARE (35×35 mm): 50f. Pres. Bokassa facing left. VERT (26×47 mm): 100f. Pres. Bokassa in military uniform.

158 Launch

1973. Air. Moon Flight of "Apollo 17".

348	**158**	50f. red, green & brown	55	30
349	-	65f. green, red & purple	75	45
350	-	100f. blue, brown & red	1·20	70
351	-	150f. green, brown & red	1·70	85
352	-	200f. green, red and blue	2·20	1·30

DESIGNS—HORIZ: 65f. Surveying lunar surfaces; 100f. Descent on Moon. VERT: 150f. Astronauts on Moon's surface; 200f. Splashdown.

159 Interpol Emblem within "Eye"

1973. 50th Anniv of Interpol.

353	**159**	50f. multicoloured	80	55

160 St. Theresa

1973. Air. Birth Centenary of St. Theresa of Lisieux.

354	**160**	500f. blue and light blue	6·25	4·00

161 Main Entrance

1974. Opening of "Catherine Bokassa" Mother-and-Child Centre.

355	**161**	30f. brown, red and blue	35	25
356	-	40f. brown, blue and red	45	40

DESIGN: 40f. General view of Centre.

162 Cigarette-packing Machine

1974. "Centra" Cigarette Factory.

357	**162**	5f. purple, green & red	10	10
358	-	10f. blue, green & brown	35	20
359	-	30f. blue, green and red	45	25

DESIGNS: 10f. Administration block and factory building; 30f. Tobacco warehouse.

163 "Telecommunications"

1974. World Telecommunications Day.

360	**163**	100f. multicoloured	1·50	85

164 "Peoples of the World"

1974. World Population Year.

361	**164**	100f. green, red & brown	1·20	70

165 Mother and Baby

1974. 26th Anniv of WHO.

362	**165**	100f. brown, blue & grn	1·70	75

166 Letter and UPU Emblem

1974. Centenary of UPU.

363	**166**	500f. red, green & brown	7·00	4·25

167 Battle Scene

1974. "Activities of Forces' Veterans". Multicoloured.

364	10f. Type **167**	10	10
365	15f. "Today" (Peace-time activities)	20	10
366	20f. Planting rice	30	10
367	25f. Cattle-shed	35	20
368	30f. Workers hoeing	35	25
369	40f. Veterans' houses	55	25

1974. Tenth Anniv of Central African Customs and Economics Union. As Nos. 734/5 of Cameroun.

370	40f. multicoloured (postage)	60	35
371	100f. multicoloured (air)	1·30	80

168 Modern Building

1975. "OCAM City" Project.

372	**168**	30f. multicoloured	35	10
373	-	40f. multicoloured	45	25
374	-	50f. multicoloured	55	40
375	-	100f. multicoloured	1·00	55

DESIGNS: Nos. 373/5, Various views similar to Type **150**.

1975. "J. B. Bokassa Pilot Village Project". As T **168**, but inscr "VILLAGE PILOTE J. B. BOKASSA".

376	25f. multicoloured	30	10
377	30f. multicoloured	35	25
378	40f. multicoloured	45	30

DESIGNS: Nos. 376/8, Various views similar to Type **168**.

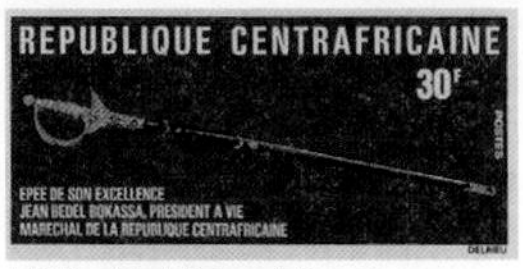

169 President Bokassa's Sword

1975. "Homage to President Bokassa". Multicoloured.

379	30f. Type **169** (postage)	45	30
380	40f. President Bokassa's baton	55	25
381	50f. Pres. Bokassa in uniform (vert, 36×49 mm) (air)	60	35
382	100f. Pres. Bokassa in cap and cape (vert, 36×49 mm)	1·30	55

170 Foreign Minister and Ministry

1975. Government Buildings. Multicoloured.

383	40f. Type **170**	55	35
384	40f. Television Centre (36×23 mm)	55	35

171 "No Entry"

1975. Road Signs.

385	**171**	5f. red and blue	10	10
386	-	10f. red and blue	10	10
387	-	20f. red and blue	30	10
388	-	30f. multicoloured	45	25
389	-	40f. multicoloured	75	30

SIGNS: 10f. "Stop"; 20f. "No stopping"; 30f. "School"; 40f. "Crossroads".

172 Kob

1975. Wild Animals. Multicoloured.

390	10f. Type **172**	45	10
391	15f. Warthog	90	25
392	20f. Waterbuck	1·20	25
393	30f. Lion	1·30	40

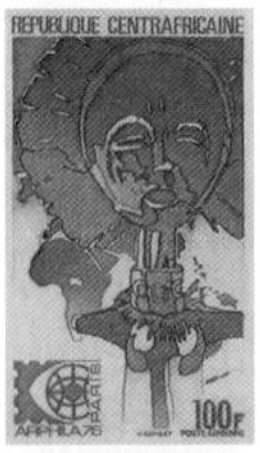

173 Carved Wooden Mask

1975. Air. "Arphila" International Stamp Exhibition. Paris.

394	**173**	100f. red, rose and blue	1·30	70

174 Dr. Schweitzer and Dug-out Canoe

1975. Air. Birth Centenary of Dr. Albert Schweitzer.

395	**174**	200f. black, blue & brown	3·75	2·00

175 Forest Scene

1975. Central African Woods.

396	**175**	10f. brown, green & red	10	10
397	-	15f. brown, green & blue	30	10
398	-	50f. blue, brown & green	55	25
399	-	100f. brown, blue & grn	1·20	60
400	-	150f. blue, brown & grn	1·60	1·00
401	-	200f. brown, red & green	2·10	1·40

DESIGNS—VERT: 15f. Cutting sapeles. HORIZ: 50f. Mobile crane; 100f. Log stack; 150f. Floating logs; 200f. Timber-sorting yard.

176 Women's Heads and Women Working

1975. International Women's Year.

402	**176**	40f. multicoloured	45	25
403	**176**	100f. multicoloured	1·30	65

177 River Vessel *Jean Bedel Bokassa*

1976. Air. Multicoloured.

404	30f. Type **177**	60	30
405	40f. Frontal view of *Jean Bedel Bokassa*	85	50

178 Co-operation Monument

1976. Air. Central African–French Co-operation and Visit of President Giscard d'Estaing. Multicoloured.

406	100f. Type **178**	1·30	85
407	200f. Flags and Presidents Giscard d'Estaing and Bokassa	2·75	1·40

179 Alexander Graham Bell

1976. Telephone Centenary.

408	**179**	100f. black and yellow	1·70	1·00

180 Telecommunications Satellite

1976. World Telecommunications Day.

409	**180**	100f. purple, blue & grn	1·70	1·10

181 Rocket on Launch-pad

1976. Apollo–Soyuz Space Link. Multicoloured.

410	40f. Type **181** (postage)	60	30
411	50f. Blast-off	75	40
412	100f. "Soyuz" in flight (air)	1·00	25
413	200f. "Apollo" in flight	1·90	65
414	300f. Crew meeting in space	3·00	1·00
MS415	103×78 mm. 500f. Space link	5·00	1·90

182 French Hussar

1976. Air. American Revolution Bicent. Multicoloured.

416	100f. Type **182**	85	40
417	125f. Black Watch soldier	1·20	50
418	150f. German Dragoons' officer	1·20	55
419	200f. British Grenadiers' officer	2·20	60
420	250f. American Ranger	2·50	95
MS421	119×81 mm. 450f. American dragoon	7·25	2·10

183 *Drurya antimachus*

1976. Butterflies. Multicoloured.

422	30f. Type **183** (postage)	5·25	1·10
423	40f. *Argema mittrei* (vert)	7·50	1·10
424	50f. *Acherontia atropos* and *Saturnia pyri* (air)	4·75	1·10
425	100f. *Papilio nireus* and *Heniocha marnois*	9·50	1·60

184 Dorothy Hamill of U.S.A. (figure skating)

1976. Medal Winners, Winter Olympic Games, Innsbruck. Multicoloured.

426	40f. Piero Gros of Italy (slalom) (horiz) (postage)	50	25
427	60f. Karl Schnabl and Toni Innauer of Austria (ski-jumping) (horiz)	75	40
428	100f. Type **184** (air)	95	45
429	200f. Alexandre Gorshkov and Ludmilla Pakhomova (figure-skating, pairs) (horiz)	1·90	75
430	300f. John Curry of Great Britain (figure-skating)	3·00	1·10
MS431	103×78 mm. 500f. Rosi Mittermaier of West Germany (skiing)	6·00	1·90

185 UPU Emblem, Letters, and Types of Mail Transport

1976. World UPU Day.

432	**185**	100f. multicoloured	1·60	90

186 Assembly of "Viking"

1976. "Viking" Space Mission to Mars. Multicoloured.

433	40f. Type **186** (postage)	50	25
434	60f. Launch of "Viking"	75	40
435	100f. Parachute descent on Mars (air)	95	45
436	200f. "Viking" on Mars (horiz)	1·90	70
437	300f. "Viking" operating gravel scoop	3·00	1·00
MS438	102×78 mm. 500f. "Viking" in flight (horiz)	5·00	1·90

220 Ski Jump

1979. Air. Winter Olympic Games, Lake Placid (1980). Multicoloured.

655	60f. Type **220**	60	25
656	100f. Downhill skiing	1·00	45
657	200f. Ice hockey	2·10	90
658	300f. Skiing (slalom)	3·00	1·40
MS659	103×77 mm. 500f. Two-man bobsleigh	5·50	1·80

Issues between 1977 and 1979 are listed under **CENTRAL AFRICAN EMPIRE**.

1979. "Apollo 11" Moon Landing. Tenth Anniv. Nos. 433/7 optd **ALUNISSAGE APOLLO XI JUILLET 1969** and lunar module.

660	**186**	40f. mult (postage)	50	30
661	-	60f. multicoloured	65	45
662	-	100f. multicoloured (air)	95	60
663	-	200f. multicoloured	1·80	95
664	-	300f. multicoloured	2·75	1·40
MS665		102×78 mm. 500f. multicoloured	5·50	5·00

222 *Thumbellina* (Andersen)

1979. International Year of the Child (2nd issue). Multicoloured.

666	30f. Type **222**	30	10
667	40f. *Sleeping Beauty* (horiz)	40	10
668	60f. *Hansel and Gretel*	55	25
669	200f. *The Match Girl* (horiz)	2·10	75
670	250f. *The Little Mermaid*	2·50	85

223 Steam Locomotive, U.S.A. Stamp and Hill

1979. Death Centenary of Sir Rowland Hill (2nd issue). Multicoloured.

671	60f. Type **223**	55	25
672	100f. Locomotive *Champion* (1882, U.S.A.), French stamp and Hill	1·00	35
673	150f. Steam locomotive, German stamp and Hill	1·70	55
674	250f. Steam locomotive, British stamp and Hill	2·75	1·10
MS675	115×78 mm. 500f. Locomotive, Central African Republic stamps and Hill	6·00	2·10

224 Basketball

1979. Olympic Games, Moscow (2nd issue). Basketball.

676	**224**	50f. multicoloured	45	10
677	-	125f. multicoloured	1·20	45
678	-	200f. multicoloured	2·00	60
679	-	300f. multicoloured	3·00	95
680	-	500f. multicoloured	4·50	1·50

DESIGNS: 125f. to 500f. Views of different basketball matches.

1980. Various stamps, including one unissued, of Central African Empire optd **REPUBLIQUE CENTRAFRICAINE**.

681	**192**	5f. multicoloured	20	20
682	-	10f. mult (No. 522)	20	25
683	-	20f. multicoloured (Balambo (stand))	20	10
684	**206**	20f. black and yellow	20	10
685	-	30f. black and blue (No. 583)	40	20

226 "Viking"

1980. Space Exploration. Multicoloured.

686	40f. Type **226** (postage)	45	10
687	50f. "Apollo"–"Soyuz" link	55	15
688	60f. "Voyager"	65	20
689	100f. European Space Agency	1·10	30
690	150f. Early satellites (air)	1·50	40
691	200f. Space shuttle	2·00	55
MS692	85×58 mm. 500f. Neil Armstrong (50×41 mm)	5·25	1·60

1980. Air. Winter Olympic Medal Winners. Nos. 655/8 optd as listed below.

693	**220**	60f. multicoloured	55	25
694	-	100f. multicoloured	95	45
695	-	200f. multicoloured	1·80	90
696	-	300f. multicoloured	2·75	1·40
MS697		103×77 mm. 500f. multicoloured	5·50	3·25

DESIGNS: 60f. **VAINQUEUR INNAVER AUTRICHE**; 100f. **VAINQUEUR MOSER-PROELL AUTRICHE**; 200f. **VAINQUEUR ETATS-UNIS**; 300f. **VAINQUEUR STENMARK SUEDE**; 500f. **VAINQUEURS / SCHAERER-BENZ / SUISSE**.

228 Telephone and Sun

1980. World Telecommunications Day. Multicoloured.

698	100f. Type **228**	1·00	60
699	150f. Telephone and sun (different)	1·50	85

229 Walking

1980. Olympic Games, Moscow (3rd issue). Multicoloured.

700	30f. Type **229** (postage)	40	10
701	40f. Women's relay	50	10
702	70f. Running	75	25
703	80f. Women's high jump	75	25
704	100f. Boxing (air)	95	25
705	150f. Hurdles	1·50	45
MS706	87×84 mm. 250f. Long jump (39×36 mm)	5·25	1·60

229a Fruit

1980

706a	**229a**	40f. multicoloured		

230 Agriculture

1980. European-African Co-operation. Multicoloured.

707	30f. Type **230** (postage)	35	10
708	40f. Industry	45	10
709	70f. Communications	80	25
710	100f. Building construction and rocket	1·40	40
711	150f. Meteorological satellite (air)	1·50	50
712	200f. Space shuttle	1·80	65
MS713	89×64 mm. 500f. Concorde (41×29 mm)	5·25	1·70

1980. Olympic Medal Winners. Nos. 676/80 optd.

717	50f. **MEDAILLE OR YOUGO-SLAVIE**	50	25
718	125f. **MEDAILLE OR URSS**	1·20	45
719	200f. **MEDAILLE OR URSS**	1·80	70
720	300f. **MEDAILLE ARGEN TITALIE**	3·00	1·10
721	500f. **MEDAILLE BRONZE URSS**	4·50	1·70

232 *Foligne Madonna* (detail)

1980. Christmas. Multicoloured.

722	60f. Type **232**	60	25
723	150f. *"irgin and Saints*	1·50	65
724	250f. *Conestabile Madonna*	2·75	1·10

1980. Fifth Anniv of African Posts and Telecommunications Union. As T **269** of Benin.

725	70f. multicoloured	75	40

233 Peruvian Football Team

1981. World Cup Football Championship, Spain (1982). Multicoloured.

726	10f. Type **233** (postage)	10	10
727	15f. Scottish team	20	10
728	20f. Mexican team	30	10
729	25f. Swedish team	30	10
730	30f. Austrian team	45	10
731	40f. Polish team	45	25
732	50f. French team	75	25
733	60f. Italian team	75	25
734	70f. West German team	95	35
735	80f. Brazilian team	95	40
736	100f. Dutch team (air)	95	25
737	200f. Spanish team	1·80	45
MS738	119×87 mm. 500f. Argentina team	6·00	1·70

234 *Fight between Jacob and the Angel*

1981. Air. 375th Birth Anniv of Rembrandt. Multicoloured.

739	60f. Type **234**	55	25
740	90f. *Christ in the Tempest*	95	25
741	150f. *Jeremiah mourning the Destruction of Jerusalem*	1·70	70
742	250f. *Anna accused by Tobit of Theft of a Goat*	2·75	80
MS743	104×80 mm. 500f. *Belshazzar's Feast* (horiz)	5·50	1·80

1981. Olympic Games Medal Winners. Nos. 700/**MS**706 optd.

744	30f. **50 K.M. MARCHE HARTWIG GAUDER–G.D.R.** (postage)	30	10
745	40f. **4×400 M. DAMES–U.R.S.S**	45	25
746	70f. **100 M. COURSE HOMMES ALAN WELLS–G.B.R**	75	30
747	80f. **SAUT EN HAUTEUR DAMES SARA SIMEONI–ITALIE**	75	45
748	100f. **BOXE–71 KG ARMANDO MARTINEZ–CUBA** (air)	1·00	35
749	150f. **110 M. HAIES HOMMES THOMAS MUNKELT–G.D.R**	1·50	65
MS750	87×84 mm. 250f. **SAUT LONGUEUR / LUTZ DOMBROWSKI–G.D.R**	5·50	5·00

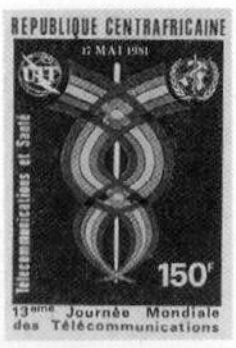

236 ITU and WHO Emblems and Ribbons forming Caduceus

1981. World Telecommunications Day.

751	**236**	150f. multicoloured	1·40	75

237 Boeing 747 carrying Space Shuttle "Enterprise"

1981. Conquest of Space. Multicoloured.

752	100f. "Apollo 15" and jeep on the Moon	95	40
753	150f. Type **237**	1·40	45
754	200f. Space Shuttle launch	1·80	65
755	300f. Space Shuttle performing experiment in space	3·00	1·00
MS756	103×78 mm. 500f. Space shuttle approaching landing strip	6·00	1·70

238 *Family of Acrobats with a Monkey*

1981. Birth Bicentenary of Pablo Picasso. Multicoloured.

757	40f. Type **238** (postage)	45	10
758	50f. *The Balcony*	75	25
759	80f. *The Artist's Son as Pierrot*	1·20	40
760	100f. *The Three Dancers*	1·70	45
761	150f. *Woman and Mirror with Self-portrait* (air)	2·10	50
762	200f. *Sleeping Woman, the Dream*	5·00	1·40
MS763	78×113 mm. 500f. *Portrait of Maria* (40×50 mm)	5·50	1·60

239 Tractor and Plough breaking Chain

1981. First Anniv of Zimbabwe's Independence.

764	**239**	100f. multicoloured	1·00	45
765	**239**	150f. multicoloured	1·40	60
766	**239**	200f. multicoloured	2·00	80

240 Prince Charles

1981. Royal Wedding (1st issue). Multicoloured.

767	75f. Type **240**	55	25
768	100f. Lady Diana Spencer	95	30
769	150f. St. Paul's Cathedral	1·40	65
770	175f. Couple and Prince's personal Standard	1·80	65
MS771	69×91 mm. 500f. Prince and Lady Diana	7·75	1·80

See also Nos. 772/**MS**778.

241 Lady Diana Spencer with Children

1981. Royal Wedding (2nd issue). Multicoloured.

772	40f. Type **241** (postage)	45	10
773	50f. Investiture of the Prince of Wales	55	25
774	80f. Lady Diana Spencer at Althorp House	75	25
775	100f. Prince Charles in naval uniform	1·20	40
776	150f. Prince of Wales's feathers (air)	2·30	55
777	200f. Highgrove House	3·50	1·00
MS778	120×70 mm. 500f. St. Paul's Cathedral (57×33 mm)	5·25	1·80

242 C. V. Rietschoten

1981. Navigators. Multicoloured.

779	40f. Type **242** (postage)	45	25
780	50f. M. Pajot	45	30
781	60f. L. Jaworski	65	45
782	80f. M. Birch	85	55
783	100f. O. Kersauson (air)	1·20	60
784	200f. Sir Francis Chichester	2·20	1·10
MS785	100×80 mm. 500f. A. Colas	6·00	1·60

243 Renault, 1906

1981. 75th Anniv of French Grand Prix Motor Race. Multicoloured.

786	20f. Type **243**	45	10
787	40f. Mercedes-Benz, 1937	45	10
788	50f. Matra-Ford, 1969	65	25
789	110f. Tazio Nuvolari	1·40	45
790	150f. Jackie Stewart	2·00	70
MS791	104×80 mm. 450f. Racing car, 1914	7·75	4·00

244 Emperor's Crown pierced by Bayonet

1981. Overthrow of the Empire. Multicoloured.

792	5f. Type **244**	10	10
793	10f. Type **244**	25	10
794	25f. Axe splitting crown, and angel holding map	30	10
795	60f. As 25f.	65	25
796	90f. Emperor Bokassa's statue being toppled and map of Republic	1·00	45
797	500f. As 90f.	4·50	2·00

245 FAO Emblem

1981. World Food Day.

798	**245**	90f. green, brown & yell	95	30
799	**245**	110f. green, brown & bl	1·10	45

246 Lizard

1981. Air. Reptiles. Multicoloured.

800	30f. Type **246**	80	20
801	60f. Snake	1·00	30
802	110f. Crocodile	1·80	50

247 Plumed Guineafowl ("Komba")

1981. Birds. Multicoloured.

803	50f. Type **247**	65	25
804	90f. Schlegel's francolin ("Dodoro")	1·30	25
805	140f. Black-headed bunting and ortolan bunting ("Kaya")	2·10	40

248 Bank Building

1981. Central African States' Bank.

806	**248**	90f. multicoloured	95	30
807	**248**	110f. multicoloured	1·10	45

249 *Madonna and Child* (Fra Angelico)

1981. Christmas. Various paintings showing Virgin and Child by named artists. Multicoloured.

808	50f. Type **249** (postage)	65	25
809	60f. Cosme-Tura	85	35
810	90f. Bramantino	1·30	50
811	110f. Memling	1·70	70
812	140f. Correge (air)	1·80	45
813	200f. Gentileschi	3·00	70
MS814	81×98 mm. 500f. *The Holy Family* (Cranach) (41×50 mm)	6·25	1·90

250 Scouts with Packs

1982. 75th Anniv of Boy Scout Movement. Multicoloured.

815	100f. Type **250**	1·10	45
816	150f. Three scouts (horiz)	1·60	60
817	200f. Scouts admiring mountain view (horiz)	2·30	85
818	300f. Scouts taking oath	3·25	1·40
MS819	84×113 mm. 500f. Lord Baden-Powell, scout and totem	5·75	1·70

251 African Elephant

1982. Animals. Multicoloured.

820	60f. Type **251** (postage)	70	10

821	90f. Giraffe	1·00	30
822	100f. Addax	1·20	40
823	110f. Okapi	1·40	55
824	300f. Mandrill (air)	3·00	70
825	500f. Lion	5·00	1·50
MS826	100×80 mm. 600f. Nile crocodile (47×38 mm)	6·50	1·80

252 *Grandfather Snowman*

1982. Norman Rockwell Illustrations. Multicoloured.

827	30f. Type **252**	30	10
828	60f. *Croquet Players*	80	25
829	110f. *Women talking*	1·20	45
830	150f. *Searching*	1·70	60

253 Vickers Valentia biplane, 1928

1982. Transport. Multicoloured.

831	5f. Astra Torres AT-16 airship, 1919 (postage)	10	10
832	10f. Beyer-Garrat 1 locomotive	10	10
833	20f. Bugatti *Royale* car, 1926	30	25
834	110f. Type **253**	1·30	45
835	300f. Nuclear-powered freighter *Savannah* (air)	3·75	70
836	500f. Space shuttle	5·25	1·50
MS837	100×81 mm. 600f. Man with winged horse (38×48 mm)	5·25	1·60

254 George Washington

1982. Anniversaries. Multicoloured.

838	200f. *Le Jardin de Bellevue* (E. Manet) (150th birth anniv) (horiz)	3·00	90
839	300f. Type **254** (250th birth anniv)	2·75	1·00
840	400f. Goethe (150th death anniv)	3·75	1·50
841	500f. Princess of Wales (21st Birthday)	4·50	2·30
MS842	80×104 mm. 500f. Princess of Wales (different)	5·25	1·60

255 Edward VII and Lady Diana Spencer with her Brother

1982. 21st Birthday of Princess of Wales. Multicoloured.

843	5f. George II and portrait of Lady Diana as child (postage)	10	10
844	10f. Type **255**	10	10
845	20f. Charles I and Lady Diana with guinea pig	30	10
846	110f. George V and Lady Diana as student in Switzerland	1·20	25
847	300f. Charles II and Lady Diana in skiing clothes (air)	3·00	70
848	500f. George IV and Lady Diana as nursery teacher	4·75	1·50
MS849	120×74 mm. 600f. Prince and Princess of Wales on wedding day (56×33 mm)	5·75	1·60

256 Football

1982. Olympic Games, Los Angeles. (1984). Multicoloured.

850	5f. Type **256** (postage)	10	10
851	10f. Boxing	10	10
852	20f. Running	30	10
853	110f. Hurdling	1·00	25
854	300f. Diving (air)	2·75	70
855	500f. Show jumping	4·50	1·50
MS856	80×108 mm. 600f. Basketball (38×56 mm)	5·50	1·70

257 Weather Satellite

1982. Space Resources. Multicoloured.

857	5f. Space shuttle and scientist (Food resources) (postage)	10	10
858	10f. Type **257**	10	10
859	20f. Space laboratory (Industrial use)	30	10
860	110f. Astronaut on Moon (Lunar resources)	1·00	25
861	300f. Satellite and energy map (Planetary energy) (air)	2·75	75
862	500f. Satellite and solar panels (Solar energy)	4·50	1·50
MS863	104×67 mm. 600f. Kohoutek, Halley's comet and satellites (Energy from comets)	5·50	1·60

1982. Birth of Prince William of Wales. Nos. 767/70 optd **NAISSANCE ROYALE 1982**.

864	240	75f. multicoloured	55	25
865	-	100f. multicoloured	75	45
866	-	150f. multicoloured	1·30	60
867	-	175f. multicoloured	1·90	85
MS868		69×91 mm. 500f. multicoloured	4·75	3·75

259 Pestle and Mortar, Chopping Board and Dish

1982. Utensils. Multicoloured.

869	5f. Basket of vegetables (horiz)	10	10
870	10f. As No. 869	10	10
871	25f. Flagon made from decorated gourd	30	10
872	60f. As No. 871	75	25
873	120f. Clay jars (horiz)	1·40	45
874	175f. Decorated bowls (horiz)	1·80	65
875	300f. Type **259**	3·75	1·30

260 Footballers

1982. World Cup Football Championship Results. Unissued stamps optd as T **260**. Multicoloured.

876	60f. **ITALIE 1er ALLEMAGNE 2e (R.F.A.)**	80	25
877	150f. **POLOGNE 3e**	1·60	60
878	300f. **FRANCE 4e**	3·25	1·30
MS879	104×81 mm. 500f. **ITALIE 1er**	5·25	1·60

261 Jean Tubind

1982. Painters. Multicoloured.

880	40f. Type **261**	55	25
881	70f. Pierre Ndarata and 10f. stamp	85	35
882	90f. As No. 881	1·10	45
883	140f. Type **261**	1·70	75

262 Globe and UPU Emblem

1982. UPU Day.

884	**262**	60f. violet, blue and red	55	25
885	**262**	120f. violet, yellow & red	1·20	50

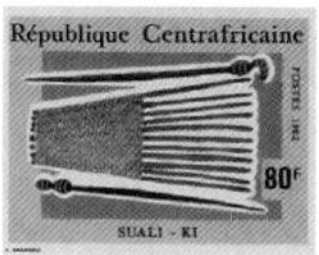

263 Hairpins and Comb

1983. Hair Accessories.

886	**263**	20f. multicoloured	10	10
887	**263**	30f. multicoloured	35	20
888	**263**	70f. multicoloured	65	30
889	**263**	80f. multicoloured	95	45
890	**263**	120f. multicoloured	1·30	50

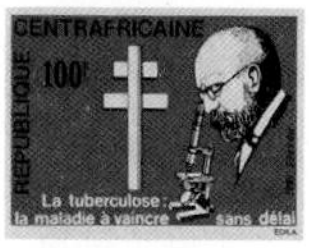

264 Koch and Microscope

1982. Centenary of Discovery of Tubercle Bacillus by Dr. Robert Koch.

891	**264**	100f. mauve and black	1·20	30
892	**264**	120f. red and black	1·50	50
893	**264**	175f. blue and black	2·00	80

265 Emblem

1982. Tenth Anniv of United Nations Environment Programme.

894	**265**	120f. blue, orange & blk	1·20	35
895	**265**	150f. blue, yellow & blk	1·30	55
896	**265**	300f. blue, green & black	2·75	1·10

266 Granary

1982

897	**266**	60f. multicoloured	55	25
898	**266**	80f. multicoloured	95	40
899	**266**	120f. multicoloured	1·30	60
900	**266**	200f. multicoloured	2·20	1·10

267 *The Beautiful Gardener*

1982. Air. Christmas. Paintings by Raphael. Multicoloured.

901	150f. Type **267**	2·00	45
902	500f. *The Holy Family*	5·00	1·50

268 Stylized Transmitter

1983. I.T.U. Delegates' Conference, Nairobi (1982).

903	**268**	100f. multicoloured	95	40
904	**268**	120f. multicoloured	1·30	55

269 Steinitz

1983. Chess Masters. Multicoloured.

905	5f. Type **269** (postage)	10	10
906	10f. Aaron Niemsovich	10	10
907	20f. Aleksandr Alekhine	30	10
908	110f. Botvinnik	1·40	25
909	300f. Boris Spassky (air)	3·50	80
910	500f. Bobby Fischer	5·00	1·40
MS911	116×72 mm. 600f. Korchnoi and Karpov (55×52 mm)	6·75	2·10

270 George Washington

1983. Celebrities. Multicoloured.

912	20f. Type **270** (postage)	10	10
913	110f. Pres. Tito of Yugoslavia	1·10	30
914	500f. Princess of Wales with Prince William (air)	5·00	1·60
MS915	120×70 mm. 600f. Prince and Princess of Wales with Prince William	5·00	3·00

271 Telephone, Satellite and Globe

1983. U.N. Decade for African Transport and Communications. Multicoloured.

916	5f. Type **271**	10	10
917	60f. Type **271**	75	25
918	120f. Radar screen and map of Africa	1·20	45
919	175f. As No. 918	1·70	60

272 Billy Hamilton and Bruno Pezzey

1983. World Cup Football Championship, Spain. Multicoloured.

920	5f. Type **272** (postage)	10	10
921	10f. Sergeij Borovski and Zbigniew Boniek	10	10
922	20f. Pierre Littbarski and Jesus Maria Zamora	35	25
923	110f. Zico and Alberto Pajsarella	1·30	30
924	300f. Paolo Rossi and Smolarek (air)	2·75	75
925	500f. Rummenigge and Alain Giresse	5·00	1·30
MS926	101×81 mm. 600f. Paolo Rossi and Karl Heinz Rummenigge	5·50	3·00

273 *Entombment*

1983. Easter. Paintings by Rembrandt. Multicoloured.

927	100f. Type **273**	95	45
928	300f. *Christ on the Cross*	2·75	1·30
929	400f. *Descent from the Cross*	3·75	1·80

274 J. and L. Robert and Colin Hullin's Balloon, 1784

1983. Air. Bicentenary of Manned Flight. Multicoloured.

930	65f. Type **274**	85	25
931	130f. John Wise and *Atlantic*, 1859	1·40	35
932	350f. *Ville d'Orleans*, Paris, 1870	3·75	1·10
933	400f. Modern advertising balloon	4·25	1·40
MS934	116×91 mm. 500f. Montgolfier balloon, 1783	6·00	1·60

275 Emile Levassor, Rene Panhard and Panhard-Levassor Car, 1895

1983. Car Manufacturers. Multicoloured.

935	10f. Type **275** (postage)	10	10
936	20f. Henry Ford and first Ford car, 1896	10	10
937	30f. Louis Renault and first Renault car, 1899	30	25
938	80f. Ettore Bugatti and Bugatti "Type 37", 1925	95	30
939	400f. Enzo Ferrari and Ferrari "815 Sport", 1940 (air)	4·25	1·00
940	500f. Ferdinand Porsche and Porsche "356 Coupe", 1951	4·75	1·20
MS941	77×88 mm. 600f. Karl Benz and first petrol-driven car, 1886	5·75	1·60

276 IMO Emblem

1983. 25th Anniv of Int Maritime Organization.

942	**276**	40f. blue, lt blue & turq	45	10
943	**276**	100f. multicoloured	95	45

277 Gymnastics

1983. Olympic Games, Los Angeles. Multicoloured.

944	5f. Type **277** (postage)	10	10
945	40f. Javelin	45	10
946	60f. High jump	60	25
947	120f. Fencing	1·50	30
948	200f. Cycling (air)	2·00	45
949	300f. Sailing	3·00	75
MS950	108×80 mm. 600f. Ball games (horiz 50×41 mm)	5·50	1·60

278 WCY Emblem and Satellite

1983. World Communications Year. Multicoloured.

951	50f. Type **278**	40	25
952	130f. WCY emblem and satellite (different)	1·30	50

279 Horse Jumping

1983. Air. Pre-Olympic Year. Multicoloured.

953	100f. Type **279**	95	40
954	200f. Dressage	2·00	80
955	300f. Jumping double jump	3·00	90
956	400f. Trotting	4·00	1·30
MS957	104×79 mm. 500f. Horse jumping (different)	5·75	1·60

280 Andre Kolingba

1983. Second Anniv of Military Committee for National Recovery.

958	**280**	65f. multicoloured	55	25
959	**280**	130f. multicoloured	1·40	40

281 Antenna, Bangui M'Poko Earth Station

1983. Bangui M'Poko Earth Station.

960	**281**	130f. multicoloured	1·40	60

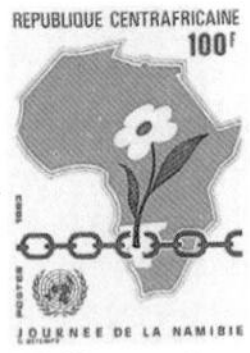

282 Flower and Broken Chain on Map of Africa

1983. Namibia Day.

961	**282**	100f. green, lt grn & red	1·30	45
962	**282**	200f. multicoloured	1·80	85

283 J. Montgolfier and Balloon

1983. Bicentenary of Manned Flight. Multicoloured.

963	50f. Type **283** (postage)	45	10
964	100f. J. Blanchard and Channel crossing, 1785	1·00	25
965	200f. Joseph Gay-Lussac and ascent to 4000 m, 1804	2·20	65
966	300f. Henri Giffard and steam-powered dirigible airship, 1852	3·00	1·00
967	400f. Santos-Dumont and airship *Ballon No. 6*, Paris, 1901 (air)	4·00	1·30
968	500f. A. Laquot and captive observation balloon, 1914	5·00	1·70
MS969	79×85 mm. 600f. J. Charles and hydrogen balloon and G. Tissandier and dirigible	6·00	1·60

284 "Global Communications"

1983. World Communications Year. UPU Day.

970	**284**	205f. multicoloured	2·00	1·00

285 Black Rhinoceros

1983. Endangered Animals. Multicoloured.

971	10f. Type **285** (postage)	40	10
972	40f. Two rhinoceros	1·10	20
973	70f. Black rhinoceros (different)	1·80	35
974	180f. Black rhinoceros and young	5·00	65
975	400f. Rangers attending sick rhinoceros (air)	5·25	1·20
976	500f. Wild animals and flag	6·50	1·40
MS977	111×75 mm. 600f. Cheetah (47×32 mm)	5·75	1·70

286 Handicapped Person and Old Man

1983. National Day of the Handicapped and Old.

978	**286**	65f. orange and mauve	55	30
979	**286**	130f. orange and blue	1·20	55
980	**286**	250f. orange and green	1·80	85

287 Fish Pond

1983. Fishery Resources. Multicoloured.

981	25f. Type **287**	20	10
982	65f. Net fishing	80	25
983	100f. Traditional fishing	1·00	45
984	130f. Butter catfish, eel and cichlids on plate	2·00	70
985	205f. Weir basket	2·40	75

288 *The Annunciation* (Leonardo da Vinci)

1984. Air. Christmas. Multicoloured.

986	130f. Type **288**	1·20	40
987	205f. *The Virgin of the Rocks* (Leonardo da Vinci)	2·00	55
988	350f. *Adoration of the Shepherds* (Rubens)	3·50	1·10
989	500f. *A. Goubeau before the Virgin* (Rubens)	4·75	1·40

289 Bush Fire

1984. Nature Protection. Multicoloured.

990	30f. Type **289**	2·10	40
991	130f. Soldiers protecting wildlife from hunters	3·00	1·00

290 Goethe and Scene from "Faust"

1984. Celebrities. Multicoloured.

992	50f. Type **290** (postage)	45	10
993	100f. Henri Dunant and battle scene	95	10
994	200f. Alfred Nobel	1·60	40
995	300f. Lord Baden-Powell and scout camp	2·50	70
996	400f. President Kennedy and first foot-print on Moon (air)	4·25	1·10
997	500f. Prince and Princess of Wales	4·75	1·30
MS998	101×72 mm. 600f. Prince and Princess of Wales	5·25	1·60

291 Fixed Bar

1984. Air. Olympic Games, Los Angeles. Gymnastics. Multicoloured.

999	65f. Type **291**	55	25
1000	100f. Parallel bars	1·00	25
1001	130f. Ribbon (horiz)	1·40	40
1002	205f. Cord	2·20	70
1003	350f. Hoop	3·75	1·10
MS1004	102×78 mm. 500f. Rhythmic team gymnastics (horiz)	5·25	1·60

292 *Madonna and Child* (Raphael)

1984. Paintings. Multicoloured.

1005	50f. Type **292** (postage)	50	10
1006	100f. *The Madonna of the Pear* (Durer)	1·00	20
1007	200f. *Aldobrandini Madonna* (Raphael)	2·20	50
1008	300f. *Madonna of the Pink* (Durer)	3·00	85
1009	400f. *Virgin and Child* (Correggio) (air)	4·00	1·60
1010	500f. *The Bohemian* (Modigliani)	5·50	2·10
MS1011	80×111 mm. 600f. *Madonna and Child on the Throne* (Raphael) (vert 29×58 mm)	6·00	1·60

293 *Le Pericles* (mail ship)

1984. Transport. Multicoloured. (a) Ships.

1012	65f. Type **293**	80	30
1013	120f. *Pereire* (steamer)	1·30	55
1014	250f. *Admella* (passenger steamer)	2·50	1·10
1015	400f. *Royal William* (paddle-steamer)	4·50	1·90
1016	500f. *Great Britain* (steam/sail)	5·50	2·50

(b) Locomotives.

1017	110f. CC-1500 ch	1·20	45
1018	240f. Series 210, 1968	2·50	95
1019	350f. 231-726, 1937	3·75	1·30
1020	440f. Pacific Series S3/6, 1908	5·00	1·50
1021	500f. Henschel 151 Series 45, 1937	5·75	3·25

Nos. 1017/21 each include an inset portrait of George Stephenson in the design.

294 Forest

1984. Forest Resources. Multicoloured.

1022	70f. Type **294**	85	30
1023	130f. Log cabin and timber	1·70	65

295 Weighing Baby and Emblem

1984. Infant Survival Campaign. Multicoloured.

1024	10f. Type **295**	10	10
1025	30f. Vaccinating baby	45	25
1026	65f. Feeding dehydrated baby	55	40
1027	100f. Mother, healthy baby and foodstuffs	1·10	60

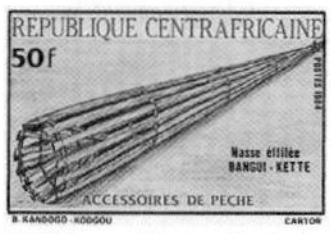

296 Bangui-Kette Conical Trap

1984. Fish Traps. Multicoloured.

1028	50f. Type **296**	75	30
1029	80f. Mbres fish trap	1·00	60
1030	150f. Bangui-Kette round fish trap	2·20	80

297 Galileo and "Ariane" Rocket

1984. Space Technology. Multicoloured.

1031	20f. Type **297** (postage)	30	10
1032	70f. Auguste Piccard and strato-sphere balloon *F.N.R.S.*	70	25
1033	150f. Hermann Oberth and satellite	1·50	50
1034	205f. Albert Einstein and "Giotto" satellite	2·00	65
1035	300f. Marie Curie and "Viking I" and "II" (air)	3·50	90
1036	500f. Dr. U. Merbold and "Navette" space laboratory	4·50	1·10
MS1037 75×59 mm. 600f. Neil Armstrong and "Apollo II" (41×34 mm)		5·25	1·60

298 *Leptoporus lignosus*

1984. Fungi. Multicoloured.

1038	5f. Type **298** (postage)	10	10
1039	10f. *Phlebopus sudanicus*	10	10
1040	40f. *Termitomyces letestui*	60	25
1041	130f. *Lepiota esculenta*	1·50	30
1042	300f. *Termitomyces aurantiacus* (air)	3·25	85
1043	500f. *Termitomyces robustus*	6·00	1·30
MS1044 68×90 mm. 600f. *Tricholoma lobayensis* (34×40 mm)		6·00	1·80

299 Hibiscus

1984. Flowers. Multicoloured.

1045	65f. Type **299**	90	45
1046	130f. Canna	1·60	75
1047	205f. Water Hyacinth	2·50	1·00

300 G. Boucher (speed skating)

1984. Winter Olympic Gold Medallists. Multicoloured.

1048	30f. Type **300** (postage)	30	10
1049	90f. W. Hoppe, R. Wetzig, D. Schauerhammer and A. Kirchner (bobsleigh)	95	30
1050	140f. P. Magoni (ladies' slalom)	1·40	45
1051	200f. J. Torvill and C. Dean (ice skating)	2·00	60
1052	400f. M. Nykanen (90 m ski jump) (air)	4·00	1·00
1053	400f. Russia (ice hockey)	4·75	1·30
MS1054 79×58 mm. 600f. W.D. Johnson (men's downhill skiing)		5·50	1·60

301 Workers sowing Cotton Seeds

1984. Economic Campaign. Multicoloured.

1055	25f. Type **301**	35	20
1056	40f. Selling cotton	55	45
1057	130f. Cotton market	1·60	65

302 Woman picking corn

1984. World Food Day.

1058	**302**	205f. multicoloured	2·50	1·00

303 Abraham Lincoln

1984. Celebrities. Multicoloured.

1059	50f. Type **303** (postage)	50	90
1060	90f. Auguste Piccard (undersea explorer)	95	30
1061	120f. Gottlieb Daimler (automobile designer)	1·50	45
1062	200f. Louis Bleriot (pilot)	2·30	60
1063	350f. A. Karpov (chess champion) (air)	3·75	90
1064	400f. Henri Dunant (founder of Red Cross)	4·25	1·10
MS1065 79×114 mm. 600f. Queen Elizabeth, the Queen Mother (85th birthday, 1985) (35×50 mm)		5·25	1·60

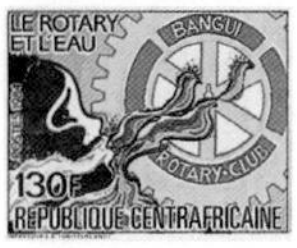

304 Profile, Water and Emblem

1984. Bangui Rotary Club and Water.

1066	**304**	130f. multicoloured	1·70	50
1067	**304**	205f. multicoloured	2·50	80

305 United States (4×400 m relay)

1985. Air Olympic Games Gold Medallists. Multicoloured.

1068	60f. Type **305**	55	20
1069	140f. E. Moses (400 m hurdles)	1·60	45
1070	300f. S. Aouita (5000 m)	3·50	90
1071	440f. D. Thompson (decathlon)	4·25	1·20
MS1072 102×76 mm. 500f. J. Cruz (800 metres) (horiz)		5·50	3·00

306 *Virgin and Infant Jesus* (Titian)

1985. Air. Christmas (1984). Multicoloured.

1073	130f. Type **306**	1·20	60
1074	350f. *Virgin with Rabbit*(Titian)	3·25	1·30
1075	400f. *Virgin and Child* (Titian)	3·75	1·50

307 Eastern Screech Owls

1985. Air. Birth Bicentenary of John J. Audubon (ornithologist) (1st issue). Multicoloured.

1076	60f. Type **307**	60	20
1077	110f. Mangrove cuckoo (vert)	1·20	50
1078	200f. Mourning doves (vert)	2·00	1·00
1079	500f. Wood ducks	5·25	2·20

See also Nos. 1099/1104.

1985. International Exhibitions. Nos. 1014/15, 1019/20 and **MS**1004 optd.

1083	250f. multicoloured (postage)	2·40	1·50
1084	350f. multicoloured	3·50	1·80
1085	400f. multicoloured	4·25	2·30
1086	440f. multicoloured	5·25	2·75
MS1087 102×78 mm. 500f. multicoloured (air)		4·75	4·50

DESIGNS: 250f. **ARGENTINA '85 BUENOS AIRES**; 350f. **TSUKUBA EXPO '85**; 400f **Italia '85 ROME** and emblem; 440f. **MOPHILA '85 HAMBOURG**; 500f. **OLYMPICPHILEX '85 LUSANNE** and emblem.

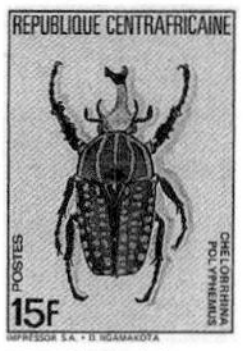

310 *Chelorrhina polyphemus*

1985. Beetles. Multicoloured.

1088	15f. Type **310**	1·70	25
1089	20f. *Fornasinius russus*	2·10	35
1090	25f. *Goliathus giganteus*	2·50	45
1091	65f. *Goliathus meleagris*	6·25	75

311 Olympic Games Poster and Stockholm

1985. "Olymphilex '85" Olympic Stamps Exhibition, Lausanne. Multicoloured.

1092	5f. Type **311** (postage)	15	10
1093	10f. Olympic Games poster and Paris	15	10
1094	20f. Olympic Games poster and London	30	15
1095	100f. Olympic Games poster and Tokyo	3·00	75
1096	400f. Olympic Games poster and Mexico (air)	4·00	90
1097	500f. Olympic Games poster and Munich	4·50	1·10
MS1098 107×68 mm. 600f. Baron Pierre de Coubertin (55×25 mm)		5·50	1·60

312 Blue Jay

1985. Birth Bicentenary of John J. Audubon (ornithologist) (2nd issue). Multicoloured.

1099	40f. Type **312** (postage)	65	15
1100	80f. Chuck Will's widow	1·00	20
1101	130f. Ivory-billed woodpecker	1·70	40
1102	250f. Collie's magpie-jay	2·75	60
1103	300f. Mangrove cuckoo (horiz) (air)	3·00	70
1104	500f. Barn swallow (horiz)	5·25	1·30
MS1105 69×103 mm. 600f. Pileated woodpeckers		6·25	1·70

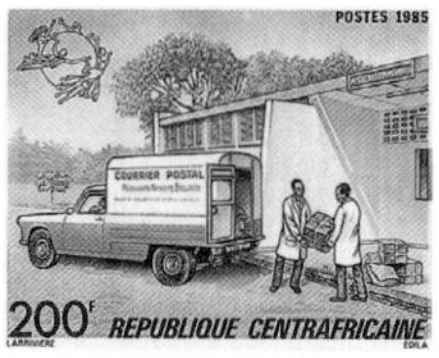

313 Delivering Post by Van

1985. "Philexafrique" Stamp Exhibition, Lome, Togo (1st issue). Multicoloured.

1106	200f. Type **313**	2·30	1·10
1107	200f. Scouts and flag	2·30	1·10

See also Nos. 1154/5.

314 Tiger and Rudyard Kipling

1985. Int Youth Year (1st issue). Multicoloured.

1108	100f. Type **314**	1·20	40
1109	200f. Men on horseback and Joseph Kessel	2·20	80
1110	300f. Submarine gripped by octopus and Jules Verne	2·75	1·20
1111	400f. Mississippi stern-wheeler, Huckleberry Finn and Mark Twain	3·75	1·70

See also Nos. 1163/**MS**1169.

315 Louis Pasteur

1985. Anniversaries. Multicoloured.

1112	150f. Type **315** (centenary of discovery of anti-rabies vaccine) (postage)	2·20	60
1113	200f. Henri Dunant (founder of Red Cross) and 125th anniv of Battle of Solferino (horiz)	2·50	80
1114	300f. Girl guides (75th anniv of Girl Guide Movement) (air)	2·20	1·20
1115	450f. Queen Elizabeth the Queen Mother (85th birthday)	4·00	2·00
1116	500f. Statue of Liberty (cent)	5·00	2·40

316 Pele and Footballers

1985. World Cup Football Championship, Mexico. Multicoloured.

1117	5f. Type **316** (postage)	10	10
1118	10f. Harald "Tony" Schumacher	10	10
1119	20f. Paolo Rossi	10	15
1120	350f. Kevin Keegan (wrongly inscr "Kervin")	3·25	1·00
1121	400f. Michel Platini (air)	4·00	1·00
1122	500f. Karl Heinz Rummenigge	4·50	1·20
MS1123 94×64 mm. 600f. Diego Armando Maradona		5·25	1·50

317 La Kotto Waterfalls

1985

1124	**317**	65f. multicoloured	95	35
1125	**317**	90f. multicoloured	1·10	45
1126	**317**	130f. multicoloured	1·70	75

318 Pope with Hand raised in Blessing

1985. Papal Visit. Multicoloured.

1127	65f. Type **318**	1·00	35
1128	130f. Pope John Paul II in Communion robes	1·90	75

319 Soldier using Ox-drawn Plough

1985. Economic Campaign. Multicoloured.

1129	5f. Type **319**	15	10
1130	60f. Soldier sowing cotton	60	30
1131	130f. Soldier sowing cotton (different)	1·30	50

320 As Young Girl with her Brother

1985. 85th Birthday of Queen Elizabeth the Queen Mother. Multicoloured.

1132	100f. Type **320** (postage)	80	25
1133	200f. Queen Mary with Duke and Duchess of York	1·90	45
1134	300f. Duchess of York inspecting Irish Guards	3·00	85
1135	350f. Duke and Duchess of York with the young Princesses	3·25	95
1136	400f. In the Golden State Coach at Coronation of King George VI (air)	4·00	1·00
1137	500f. At the service for her Silver Wedding	5·00	1·30
MS1138	75×87 mm. 600f. Holding Prince Charles at his christening	5·25	1·50

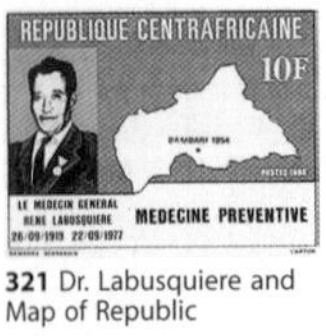

321 Dr. Labusquiere and Map of Republic

1985. Eighth Death Anniv of General Doctor Labusquiere.

1139	**321**	10f. multicoloured	15	10
1140	**321**	45f. multicoloured	45	25
1141	**321**	110f. multicoloured	95	50

322 Mail Van delivering Parcels to Local Post Office

1985. Postal Service. Multicoloured.

1142	15f. Type **322**	15	10
1143	60f. Van collecting mail from local post office	60	25
1144	150f. Vans at main post office	1·50	75

323 Gagarin, Korolev and Space Station Complex

1985. Space Research. Multicoloured.

1145	40f. Type **323** (postage)	30	10
1146	110f. Copernicus and "Cassini" space probe	1·00	40
1147	240f. Galileo and "Viking" orbiter	2·20	70
1148	300f. T. von Karman and astronaut recovering satellite	2·75	80
1149	450f. Percival Lowell and "Viking" space probe (air)	4·75	1·00
1150	500f. Dr. U. Merbold and "Columbus" space station	5·00	1·20
MS1151	96×68 mm. 600f. "Apollo II" capsule and astronaut	5·50	1·50

324 Damara Solar Energy Plant

1985

1152	**324**	65f. multicoloured	80	30
1153	**324**	130f. multicoloured	1·40	65

325 Ouaka Sugar Refinery

1985. "Philexafrique" Stamp Exhibition, Lome, Togo (2nd issue). Multicoloured.

1154	250f. Nature studies	3·50	1·60
1155	250f. Type **325**	3·50	1·60

326 Pres. Mitterrand, Gen. Kolingba and Flags

1985. Visit of President Mitterrand of France.

1156	**326**	65f. multicoloured	65	25
1157	**326**	130f. multicoloured	1·30	50
1158	**326**	160f. multicoloured	1·90	80

327 Map and U.N. Emblem

1985. 40th Anniv of UNO and 25th Anniv of Central African Republic Membership.

1159	**327**	140f. multicoloured	1·30	60

328 *Virgin and Angels* (Master of Burgo de Osma)

1985. Air. Christmas. Multicoloured.

1160	100f. Type **328**	1·00	35
1161	200f. *Nativity* (Louis Le Nain)	2·20	85
1162	400f. *Virgin and Child with Dove* (Piero di Cosimo)	4·00	1·60

329 Leonardo da Vinci and *Madonna of the Eyelet*

1985. Int Youth Year (2nd issue). Multicoloured.

1163	40f. Type **329** (postage)	55	10
1164	80f. Johann Sebastian Bach	95	25
1165	100f. Diego Velasquez and *St. John of Patmos*	1·20	40
1166	250f. Franz Schubert and illustration of *King of Aulnes*	2·50	60
1167	400f. Francisco Goya and *Vicente Osario de Moscoso* (air)	4·25	1·00
1168	500f. Wolfang Amadeus Mozart	4·75	1·20
MS1169	79×79 mm. 600f. Pablo Picasso and *Woman in Plumed Hat*	6·50	1·80

330 Halley and "Comet"

1985. Appearance of Halley's Comet (1st issue). Multicoloured.

1170	100f. Type **330** (postage)	75	25
1171	200f. Newton's telescope	1·80	45
1172	300f. Halley and Newton observing comet	2·75	80
1173	350f. American space probe and comet	3·25	1·00
1174	400f. Sun, Russian space probe and diagram of comet trajectory (air)	3·75	95
1175	500f. Infra-red picture of comet	4·75	1·20
MS1176	70×100 mm. 600f. American space probe, Earth, sun and comet	5·50	1·60

See also No. 1184/8.

331 Columbus with Globe

1986. 480th Death Anniv of Christopher Columbus (explorer). Multicoloured.

1177	90f. Type **331** (postage)	95	25
1178	110f. Receiving blessing	1·20	40
1179	240f. Crew going ashore in rowing boat	2·40	1·00
1180	300f. Columbus with American Indians	3·00	80
1181	400f. Ships at sea in storm (air)	4·25	1·60
1182	500f. Sun breaking through clouds over fleet	5·00	1·90
MS1183	71×100 mm. 600f. Columbus	5·25	1·50

332 Halley and Comet

1986. Air. Appearance of Halley's Comet (2nd issue). Multicoloured.

1184	110f. Type **332**	95	25
1185	130f. "Giotto" space probe	1·30	25
1186	200f. Comet and globe	2·00	55
1187	300f. "Vega" space probe	2·75	75
1188	400f. Space shuttle	4·00	1·00

1986. Nos. 874/5 surch.

1188a	-	30f. on 175f. multicoloured		
1188b	**259**	65f. on 300f. multicoloured		

333 Spiky Hair Style

1986. Traditional Hair Styles. Multicoloured.

1189	20f. Type **333**	35	10
1190	30f. Braids around head	40	20
1191	65f. Plaits	55	35
1192	160f. Braids from front to back of head	2·20	70

334 Communications

1986. Franco-Central African Week. Multicoloured.

1193	40f. Type **334**	45	15
1194	60f. Youth	55	25
1195	100f. Basket weaver (craft)	1·20	45
1196	130f. Cyclists (sport)	1·70	60

335 *Allamanda neriifolia*

1986. Flora and Fauna. Multicoloured.

1197	25f. Type **335** (postage)	30	15
1198	65f. Bongo (horiz)	85	25
1199	160f. *Plumieria acuminata*	1·80	40
1200	300f. Cheetah (horiz)	3·50	85
1201	400f. *Eulophia erthoplata* (air)	4·00	1·00
1202	500f. Leopard (horiz)	5·25	1·20
MS1203	100×69 mm. 600f. Giant eland and *Eulophia cucllata* (50×29)	5·50	1·70

336 Palm Tree and Bossongo Oil Refinery

1986. Centrapalm. Multicoloured.

1204	25f. Type **336**	30	20
1205	65f. Type **336**	75	45
1206	120f. Palm tree and Bossongo agro-industrial complex	1·30	75
1207	160f. As No. 1206	1·70	90

337 Pointer

1986. Dogs and Cats. Multicoloured.

1208	10f. Type **337** (postage)	20	15
1209	20f. Egyptian mau	45	25
1210	200f. Newfoundland	2·50	70
1211	300f. Borzoi (air)	3·25	70
1212	400f. Persian red	4·75	1·10
MS1213	95×60 mm. 500f. Spaniel and Burmese	5·50	1·60

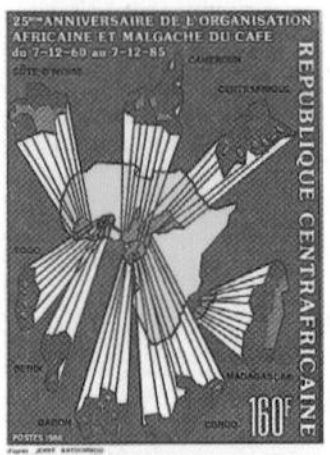

338 Map of Africa showing Member Countries

1986. 25th Anniv of African and Malagasy Coffee Producers Organization.

1214	**338**	160f. multicoloured	1·70	70

339 Trophy, Brazilian flag, L.-A. Muller and Socrates

1986. World Cup Football Championship, Mexico. Multicoloured.

1215	30f. Type **339** (postage)	30	15
1216	110f. Trophy, Belgian flag, V. Scifo and F. Ceulemans	1·00	45
1217	160f. Trophy, French flag, Y. Stopyra and M. Platini	1·50	55
1218	350f. Trophy, West German flag, A. Brehme and H. Schumacher	3·25	90
1219	450f. Trophy, Argentinian flag and Diego Maradona (air)	4·25	1·20
MS1220	110×68 mm. 500f. Hands holding trophy, H. Schumacher and J. L. Burruehaga (50×35 mm)	5·25	1·70

340 Judith Resnik and Astronaut

1986. Anniversaries and "Challenger" Astronauts Commemoration. Multicoloured.

MS1227	86×86 mm. 500f. "Challenger" crew (50×41 mm)	4·50	1·50
1221	15f. Type **340** (postage)	20	10
1222	25f. Frederic Bartholdi and torch (centenary of Statue of Liberty)	35	10
1223	70f. Elvis Presley (9th death anniv)	1·30	25
1224	300f. Ronald MacNair and man watching astronaut on screen	3·00	80
1226	450f. Christa McAulife and Shuttle lifting off (air)	4·25	1·50
1225	485f. on 70f. No. 1223	6·75	1·40

341 People around Globe within Emblem

1986. International Peace Year.

1228	**341**	160f. multicoloured	1·60	65

342 Globe, Douglas DC-10 and "25"

1986. 25th Anniv of Air Afrique.

1229	**342**	200f. multicoloured	1·80	85

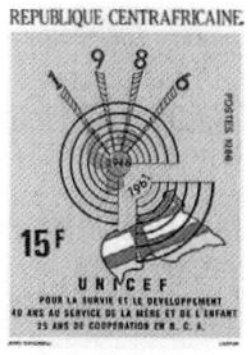

343 Emblem and Flag as Map

1986. UNICEF Child Survival Campaign. Multicoloured.

1230	15f. Type **343**	10	10
1231	130f. Doctor vaccinating child	1·30	60
1232	160f. Basket of fruit and boy holding fish on map	1·50	75

344 *Nativity* (detail, Giotto)

1986. Air. Christmas. Multicoloured.

1233	250f. Type **344**	2·30	1·10
1234	440f. *Adoration of the Magi* (detail, Sandro Botticelli) (vert)	4·25	1·60
1235	500f. *Nativity* (detail, Giotto) (different)	5·00	2·00

345 Transmission Mast, People with Radios and Baskets of Produce

1986. African Telecommunications Day. Telecommunications and Agriculture. Mult.

1236	170f. Type **345** (Rural Radio Agriculture Project)	1·90	95
1237	265f. Lorry, satellite, men using telephones and sacks of produce	2·75	1·40

346 Steam Locomotive Class *DH 2 Green Elephant* and Alfred de Glehn

1986. 150th Anniv of German Railways. Multicoloured.

1238	40f. Type **346** (postage)	50	10
1239	70f. Rudolf Diesel (engineer) and steam locomotive No. 1829 Rheingold	75	45
1240	160f. Electric locomotive Type 103 Rapide and Carl Golsdorf	1·90	55
1241	300f. Wilhelm Schmidt and Beyer-Garratt type steam locomotive	3·25	90
1242	400f. De Bousquet and compound locomotive Class 3500 (air)	4·00	1·20
MS1243	83×67 mm. 500f. Werner von Siemens (electrical engineer) and electric locomotive	5·00	1·50

347 Player returning Ball

1986. Air. Olympic Games, Seoul (1988) (1st issue). Tennis. Multicoloured.

1244	150f. Type **347**	1·70	55
1245	250f. Player serving (vert)	2·75	75
1246	440f. Right-handed player returning to left-handed player (vert)	4·25	1·40
1247	600f. Left-handed player returning to right-handed player	6·00	1·60

See also Nos. 1261/4, 1310/13 and 1315/18.

348 "Miranda" Satellite, Uranus, "Mariner II" and William Herschel (astronomer)

1987. Space Research. Multicoloured.

1248	25f. Type **348** (postage)	30	10
1249	65f. Mars Rover vehicle and Werner von Braun (rocket pioneer)	70	20
1250	160f. "Mariner II", Titan and Rudolf Hanel	1·50	40
1251	300f. Space ship "Hermes", space platform "Eureka" and Patrick Baudry	2·75	80
1252	400f. Halley's Comet, "Giotto" space probe and Dr. U. Keller (air)	3·50	1·10
1253	500f. European space station "Columbus", Wubbo Ockels and Ulf Merbold	4·50	1·20

349 Footballer and "Woman with Umbrella" Fountain

1987. Olympic Games, Barcelona (1992). Multicoloured.

1255	30f. Type **349** (postage)	35	15
1256	150f. Judo competitors and Barcelona Cathedral	1·30	50
1257	265f. Cyclist and Church of the Holy Family	2·50	80
1258	350f. Diver and Christopher Columbus's tomb (air)	3·25	1·00
1259	495f. Runner and human tower	4·75	1·50

350 Triple Jumping

1987. Air. Olympic Games, Seoul (1988) (2nd issue). Multicoloured.

1261	100f. Type **350**	95	35
1262	200f. High jumping (horiz)	1·80	75
1263	300f. Long jumping (horiz)	2·75	1·10
1264	400f. Pole vaulting	3·50	1·50
MS1265	104×86 mm. 500f. High jumping (different) (horiz)	4·50	2·50

351 Two-man Luge

1987. Winter Olympic Games, Calgary (1988) (1st issue). Multicoloured.

1266	20f. Type **351** (postage)	30	10
1267	140f. Cross-country skiing	1·40	55
1268	250f. Figure skating	2·30	70
1269	300f. Ice hockey (air)	2·75	90
1270	400f. Slalom	3·75	1·20
MS1271	130×77 mm. 500f. Downhill skiing	4·50	1·50

See also Nos. 1320/**MS**1324.

352 Peace Medal

1987. International Peace Year (1986).

1272	**352**	50f. brown, blue & blk	45	25
1273	**352**	160f. brown, grn & blk	1·50	1·30

1987. Tenth Death Anniv of Elvis Presley (singer). Nos. 1223 and 1225 optd **Elvis Presley 1977–1987**.

1274	70f. multicoloured	95	25
1275	485f. on 70f. multicoloured	5·75	1·70

354 Woman at Village Pump

1987. International Decade of Drinkable Water. Multicoloured.

1276	5f. Type **354**	33·00	
1277	10f. Woman at village pump (different)	33·00	
1278	200f. Three women at village pump	38·00	

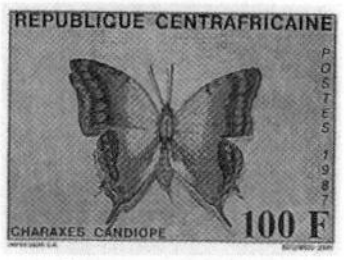

355 *Charaxes candiope*

1987. Butterflies. Multicoloured.

1279	100f. Type **355**	1·50	65
1280	120f. *Graphium leonidas*	2·00	75
1281	130f. *Charaxes brutus*	2·20	80
1282	160f. *Salamis aetiops*	2·50	1·00

356 Nola Football Team

1987. Campaign for Integration of Pygmies.

1283	**356**	90f. multicoloured	1·50	80
1284	**356**	160f. multicoloured	2·00	1·20

357 James Madison (U.S. President, 1809–17)

1987. Anniversaries and Celebrities. Multicoloured.

1285	40f. Type **357** (bicent of U.S. constitution) (postage)	45	15
1286	160f. Queen Elizabeth II and Prince Philip (40th wedding anniv)	1·50	25
1287	200f. Steffi Graf (tennis player)	2·00	55
1288	300f. Gary Kasparov (chess champion) and *The Chess Players* (after Honore Daumier) (air)	3·00	85
1289	400f. Boris Becker (tennis player)	3·75	1·30
MS1290	86×86 mm. 500f. Scene from *Orpheus* (opera) and Christoph Wilibald Gluck (composer, death bicent) (50×35 mm)	5·50	1·50

358 Brontosaurus

1988. Prehistoric Animals. Multicoloured.

1291	50f. Type **358**	50	15
1292	65f. Triceratops	65	20
1293	100f. Ankylosaurus	1·00	35
1294	160f. Stegosaurus	1·60	55
1295	200f. Tyrannosaurus rex (vert)	2·00	75
1296	240f. Corythosaurus (vert)	2·40	85
1297	300f. Allosaurus (vert)	3·00	1·10
1298	350f. Brachiosaurus (vert)	3·75	1·40

359 Pres. Kolingba vaccinating Baby

1988. 40th Anniv of WHO.

1299	**359**	70f. multicoloured	75	45
1300	**359**	120f. multicoloured	1·20	65

360 Carmine Bee Eater

1988. Scouts and Birds. Multicoloured.

1301	25f. Type **360** (postage)	30	15
1302	170f. Red-crowned bishop	1·50	60
1303	300f. Lesser pied kingfisher	3·00	1·40
1304	400f. Red-cheeked cordon-bleu (air)	2·75	1·60
1305	450f. Lizard buzzard	3·25	2·10
MS1306	90×70 mm. 500f. Splendid glossy starling	5·25	1·70

361 Schools replanting Campaign

1988. National Tree Day. Multicoloured.

1307	50f. Type **361**	45	25
1308	100f. Type **361**	95	60
1309	130f. Felling tree and planting saplings	1·50	75

362 1972 100f. Stamp and Beam Exercise

1988. Air. Olympic Games, Seoul (3rd issue). Gymnastics. Multicoloured.

1310	90f. Type **362**	95	35
1311	200f. 1964 50f. stamp and beam exercise (horiz)	1·80	65
1312	300f. 1964 100f. stamp and vault exercise (horiz)	2·75	1·10
1313	400f. 1964 250f. stamp and parallel bars exercise (horiz)	3·50	1·50
MS1314	105×85 mm. 500f. 1972 100f. stamp and ring exercise (horiz)	4·50	2·30

363 Running

1988. Olympic Games, Seoul (4th issue). Multicoloured.

1315	150f. Type **363** (postage)	1·50	25
1316	300f. Judo	2·75	80
1317	400f. Football (air)	3·00	1·00
1318	450f. Tennis	4·50	1·40
MS1319	70×100 mm. 500f. Boxing (horiz)	4·50	1·50

364 Cross-country Skiing

1988. Winter Olympic Games, Calgary (2nd issue). Multicoloured.

1320	170f. Type **364** (postage)	1·50	45
1321	350f. Ice hockey	3·00	80
1322	400f. Downhill skiing (air)	2·75	80
1323	450f. Slalom	3·75	1·20
MS1324	122×85 mm. 500f. Slalom (horiz)	4·50	1·40

1988. Nos. 1302/5 surch.

1325	30f. on 170f. mult (postage)	40	20
1326	70f. on 300f. mult	1·10	65
1327	160f. on 400f. mult (air)	1·90	1·00
1328	200f. on 450f. mult	2·75	1·40

366 Hospital and Grounds

1988. First Anniv of L'Amitie Hospital. Multicoloured.

1329	5f. Type **366**	45	25
1330	60f. Aerial view of hospital complex	95	55
1331	160f. Hospital entrance	1·50	80

367 Buildings Complex

1988. 30th Anniv of Republic. Multicoloured.

1332	65f. Family on map, flags and dove	50·00	
1334	240f. Type **367**	50·00	

368 Kristine Otto (East Germany)

1989. Olympic Games, Seoul, Gold Medal Winners. Multicoloured.

1335	150f. Type **368** (100 m butterfly and 100 m backstroke) (postage)	1·80	55
1336	240f. Matt Biondi (100 m freestyle)	2·75	80
1337	300f. Florence Griffith-Joyner (U.S.A.) (100 and 200 m sprints)	3·50	90
1338	450f. Pierre Durand (France) (show jumping) (air)	5·50	1·30
MS1339	98×68 mm. 600f. Carl Lewis (USA) (100m., 200m., long jump relay)	6·25	1·80

369 Hebmuller and Volkswagen Cabriolet, 1953

1989. Transport. Multicoloured.

1340	20f. Type **369** (postage)	30	10
1341	205f. Werner von Siemens and his first electric locomotive, 1879	2·00	70
1342	300f. Dennis Conner and *Stars and Stripes* (winner of Americas Cup yacht races)	2·75	80
1343	400f. Andre Citroen and "16 Six" car, 1955	3·75	1·40
1344	450f. Mare Seguin and Decauville Mallet locomotive, 1895 (air)	4·00	1·40
MS1345	80×75 mm. 750f. Duesenberg brothers and "J" Phaeton, 1929 (41×29 mm)	6·75	2·10

370 Allegory in Honour of Liberty

1989. Bicentenary of French Revolution and "Philexfrance 89" International Stamp Exhibition, Paris (1st issue). Multicoloured.

1346	200f. Type **370**	2·50	80
1347	300f. Declaration of Rights of Man	3·00	1·50
MS1348	113×80 mm. 500f. Demolition of the Bastille (51×40 mm)	5·00	3·25

See also Nos. 1366/**MS**1370.

371 Statue of Liberty at Night

1989. Centenary of Statue of Liberty. Multicoloured.

1349	150f. Type **371**	1·50	70
1350	150f. Maintenance worker	1·50	70
1351	150f. Close-up of face	1·50	80
1352	200f. Maintenance worker (different)	1·80	1·10
1353	200f. Colour party in front of statue	1·80	1·10
1354	200f. Close-up of head at night	1·80	1·10

373 "Apollo 11" Astronaut on Moon

1989. Air. 20th Anniv of First Manned Landing on Moon. Multicoloured.

1355	40f. Type **373**	35	20
1356	80f. "Apollo 15" astronaut and moon buggy	75	30
1357	130f. "Apollo 16" module landing in sea	1·50	55
1358	1000f. "Apollo 17" astronaut on Moon	9·00	2·75

374 Champagnat, Map and "Madonna and Child"

1989. Birth Bicentenary of Marcelino Champagnat (founder of Marist Brothers). Multicoloured.

1359	15f. Type **374**	10	10
1360	50f. Champagnat, cross, globe and emblem	45	25
1361	160f. Champagnat and flags (horiz)	1·60	1·20

375 Food Products

1989. Bambari Harvest Festival. Multicoloured.

1362	100f. Type **375**	1·00	60
1363	160f. Ploughing with oxen	1·60	75

376 Raising of Livestock

1989. World Food Day. Multicoloured.

1364	60f. Type **376**	55	40
1365	240f. Soldiers catching poachers	2·40	1·20

377 Gen. Kellermann and Battle of Valmy

1989. Bicentenary of French Revolution and "Philexfrance 89" International Stamp Exhibition, Paris (2nd issue). Multicoloured.

1366	160f. Type **377** (postage)	1·80	40
1367	200f. Gen. Dumouriez and Battle of Jemappes (wrongly inscr "JEMMAPES")	2·40	60
1368	500f. Gen. Pichegru and capture of Dutch fleet (air)	5·50	1·30
1369	600f. Gen. Hoche and Royalist landing at Quiberon	6·50	1·20
MS1370	160×107 mm. 1000f. Napoleon Bonaparte and Battle of Rivoli (60×50 mm)	14·50	3·75

378 Players and Trophy

1989. Victory in 1987 African Basketball Championships, Tunis (1st issue). Multicoloured.

1371	160f. Type **378**	1·50	70
1372	240f. National team with medals and trophy (horiz)	2·00	95
1373	500f. Type **378**	5·00	2·10

See also Nos. 1383/4.

379 Governor's Palace, 1906

1989. Centenary of Bangui. Multicoloured.

1374	100f. Type **379**	1·00	45
1375	160f. Bangui post office	1·70	95
1376	200f. A. Dosilie (founder of Bangui post office) (vert)	2·10	1·00
1377	1000f. Michel Dolisie and Chief Gbembo agreeing peace pact (vert)	9·75	4·50

380 Footballer and Palermo Cathedral Belltower

1989. World Cup Football Championship, Italy (1990) (1st issue). Multicoloured.

1378	20f. Type **380** (postage)	15	20
1379	160f. Footballer and St. Francis's church, Bologna	1·50	45
1380	200f. Footballer and Old Palace, Florence	2·00	70
1381	120f. Footballer and Church of Trinita dei Monti, Rome (air)	1·20	55
MS1382	83×84 mm. 1000f. Footballer and Milan cathedral (30×42 mm)	10·00	2·30

See also Nos. 1405/8.

381 Trophy and Map of Africa

1990. Victory in 1987 African Basketball Championships, Tunis (2nd issue).

1383	**381**	100f. multicoloured	95	45
1384	**381**	130f. multicoloured	1·30	70

382 Tree with Map as Foliage

1990. Inauguration (1989) of Forest Conservation Organization.

1385	**382**	160f. multicoloured	1·70	70

383 Speed Skating

1990. Winter Olympic Games, Albertville (1992). Multicoloured.

1386	10f. Type **383** (postage)	15	15
1387	60f. Cross-country skiing	55	40
1388	500f. Slalom skiing (air)	4·50	1·10
1389	750f. Ice dancing	6·75	1·60
MS1390	105×71 mm. 1000f. Skiing	8·75	2·10

384 *Euphaera eusemoides*

1990. Scouts and Butterflies. Multicoloured.

1391	25f. Type **384**	30	15
1392	65f. Becker's glider	55	25
1393	160f. *Pseudacraea clarki*	1·50	40
1394	250f. Giant charaxes	2·40	70
1395	300f. *Euphaedra gausape*	2·75	75
1396	500f. Red swallowtail	4·50	1·10
MS1397	131×103 mm. 1000f. *Euphaedra edwardsi*	9·50	2·20

385 Throwing the Javelin

1990. Olympic Games, Barcelona (1992). Multicoloured.

1398	10f. Type **385** (postage)	15	15
1399	40f. Running	40	25
1400	130f. Tennis	1·20	40
1401	240f. Hurdling (horiz)	2·20	55
1402	400f. Yachting (horiz) (air)	3·75	1·00
1403	500f. Football (horiz)	4·75	1·30
MS1404	95×68 mm. 1000f. Boxing (38×27 mm)	8·75	2·10

386 Footballers and Globe

1990. Air. World Cup Football Championship, Italy (2nd issue).

1405	**386**	5f. multicoloured	20	10
1406	-	30f. multicoloured	30	15
1407	-	500f. multicoloured	5·00	1·10
1408	-	1000f. multicoloured	8·75	2·10

DESIGNS: 30 to 1000f. Various footballing scenes.

387 Pres. Gorbachev of U.S.S.R., Map of Malta and Pres. Bush of U.S.A.

1990. Anniversaries and Events. Multicoloured.

1409	120f. Type **387** (summit conference, Malta) (postage)	95	25
1410	130f. Sir Rowland Hill and Penny Black (150th anniv of first postage stamps)	1·20	25
1411	160f. Galileo space probe and planet Jupiter	1·30	25
1412	200f. Pres. Gorbachev meeting Pope John Paul II, statue of Saturn and dove	1·80	40
1413	240f. Neil Armstrong and eagle (21st anniv of first manned landing on Moon)	2·20	55
1414	250f. Concorde, German experimental Maglev train and Rotary International emblem	2·40	70
1415	300f. Don Mattingly (baseball player) and New York Yankees club badge (air)	2·75	70
1416	500f. Charles de Gaulle (French statesman, birth centenary)	4·75	1·10
MS1417	82×112 mm. 1000f. Astronauts and rocket (35×50 mm)	8·75	2·10

388 AIDS Information on Radio, Television and Leaflets

1991. Anti-AIDS Campaign. Multicoloured.

1418	5f. Type **388**	25	10
1419	70f. Type **388**	1·00	50
1420	120f. Lecture on AIDS (vert)	1·50	75

389 Demonstrators

1991. Protection of Animals. Multicoloured.

1421	15f. Type **389**	40	10
1422	60f. Type **389**	1·50	35
1423	100f. Decrease in elephant population, 1945–2045 (vert)	2·20	50

390 Butter Catfish

1991. Fishes. Multicoloured.

1424	50f. Type **390**	85	25
1425	160f. Type **390**	2·00	80
1426	240f. Distichodus	3·00	1·40

391 President Kolingba

1992. Tenth Anniv (1991) of Assumption of Power by Military Committee under Andre Kolingba.

1427	**391**	160f. multicoloured	1·50	65

392 Count Ferdinand von Zeppelin (airship pioneer)

1992. Celebrities, Anniversaries and Events. Multicoloured.

1428	80f. Type **392** (75th death anniv) (postage)	80	20
1429	140f. Henri Dunant (founder of Red Cross)	1·50	45
1430	160f. Michael Schumacher (racing driver)	1·80	70
1431	350f. Brandenburg Gate (bicent) and Konrad Adenauer (German Federal Republic Chancellor) signing 1949 constitution	4·25	1·20
1432	500f. Pope John Paul II (tour of West Africa) (air)	5·50	1·20
1433	600f. Wolfgang Amadeus Mozart (composer, death bicent (1991))	6·50	1·40
MS1434	81×105 mm. 1000f. Christopher Columbus, *Santa Maria* and 15th-cent view of La Cartuja de las Cuevas (Expo' 92 World's Fair, Seville)	9·50	2·10

393 Dam

1993. River M'Bali Dam. Multicoloured.

1435	160f. Type **393**	1·50	70
1436	200f. People fishing near dam (self-sufficiency in food)	2·00	90

394 Compass Rose and Organization Emblem

1993. International Customs Day and 40th Anniv of Customs Co-operation Council.

1437	**394**	240f. multicoloured	2·30	1·40

395 Breastfeeding

1993. International Nutrition Conference, Rome (1992). Multicoloured.

1438	90f. Type **395**	75	40
1439	140f. Foodstuffs	1·30	70

396 Bangui University

1993

1440	**396**	100f. multicoloured	95	40

397 Masako Owada as Baby

1993. Wedding of Crown Prince Naruhito of Japan and Masako Owada. Multicoloured.

1441	50f. Type **397** (postage)	40	25
1442	65f. Prince Naruhito as child with parents	60	25
1443	160f. Masako Owada at Harvard University, U.S.A.	1·60	55
1444	450f. Prince Naruhito at Oxford University (air)	4·25	1·20
MS1445	184×83 mm. 750f. Prince Naruhito and Masako Owada	6·75	1·80

398 Presley singing *Heartbreak Hotel* (1956)

1993. 16th Death Anniv of Elvis Presley (entertainer). Multicoloured.

1446	200f. Type **398**	2·10	55
1447	300f. *Love Me Tender*, 1957	3·00	80
1448	400f. *Jailhouse Rock*, 1957	3·75	1·40
1449	600f. *Harum Scarum*, 1965 (air)	5·50	1·40
MS1450	98×69 mm. 1000f. Elvis performing (35×50 mm)	8·75	2·30

399 First World Cup Final, 1928, and Uruguay v. Argentina, 1930

1993. World Cup Football Championship, U.S.A. (1994). History of the World Cup. Multicoloured.

1451	40f. Type **399**	35	10
1452	50f. Italy v. Czechoslovakia, 1934, and Italy v. Hungary, 1938	45	10
1453	60f. Uruguay v. Brazil, 1950, and Germany v. Hungary, 1954	55	25
1454	80f. Brazil v. Sweden, 1958, and Brazil v. Czechoslovakia, 1962	75	25
1455	160f. England v. West Germany, 1966, and Brazil v. Italy, 1970	1·50	25
1456	200f. West Germany v. The Netherlands, 1974, and Argentina v. The Netherlands, 1978	1·80	40
1457	400f. Italy v. West Germany, 1982, and Argentina v. West Germany, 1986	3·50	70
1458	500f. West Germany v. Argentina, 1990, and 1994 Championship emblem and player	4·50	1·20
MS1459	101×85 mm. 1000f. West Germany and Argentina teams (59×29 mm)	8·75	2·10

400 Baron Pierre de Coubertin (founder of modern games)

1993. Centenary (1996) of Modern Olympic Games. Multicoloured.

1460	90f. Ancient Greek athlete	75	30
1461	90f. Type **400**	75	30
1462	90f. Charles Bennett (running), Paris, 1900	75	30
1463	90f. Etienne Desmarteau (stone throwing), St. Louis, 1904	75	30
1464	90f. Harry Porter (high jump), London, 1908	75	30
1465	90f. Patrick MacDonald (putting the shot), Stockholm, 1912	75	30
1466	90f. Coloured and black Olympic rings (1916)	75	30
1467	90f. Frank Loomis (400 m hurdles), Antwerp, 1920	75	30
1468	90f. Albert White (diving), Paris, 1924	95	35
1469	100f. El Ouafi (marathon), Amsterdam, 1928	95	35
1470	100f. Eddie Tolan (100 m), Los Angeles, 1932	95	35
1471	100f. Jesse Owens (100 m, long jump and 200 m hurdles), Berlin, 1936	95	35
1472	100f. Coloured and black Olympic rings (1940)	95	35
1473	100f. Coloured and black Olympic rings (1944)	95	35
1474	100f. Tapio Rautavaara (throwing the javelin), London, 1948	95	35
1475	100f. Jean Boiteux (400 m freestyle swimming), Helsinki, 1952	95	35
1476	100f. Petrus Kasterman (three-day equestrian event), Melbourne, 1956	95	35

1477	100f. Sante Gaiardoni (cycling), Rome, 1960	95	35
1478	160f. Anton Geesink (judo), Tokyo, 1964	1·50	45
1479	160f. Bob Beamon (long jump), Mexico, 1968	1·50	45
1480	160f. Mark Spitz (swimming), Munich, 1972	1·50	45
1481	160f. Nadia Comaneci (gymnastics (beam)), Montreal, 1976	1·50	45
1482	160f. Aleksandre Ditjatin (gymnastics (rings) and dressage), Moscow, 1980	1·50	45
1483	160f. J. F. Lamour (sabre), Los Angeles, 1984	1·50	45
1484	160f. Pierre Durand (show jumping), Seoul, 1988	1·50	45
1485	160f. Michael Jordan (basketball), Barcelona, 1992	1·50	45
1486	160f. Footballer and Games emblem, Atlanta, 1996	1·50	45

401 Man planting Sapling, and Animals

1993. Biodiversity. Multicoloured.

1487	100f. Type **401**	1·50	70
1488	130f. Man amongst flora and fauna (vert)	2·10	90

402 Woman selling Foodstuffs

1993. The Environment and Sustainable Development. Multicoloured.

1489	160f. Type **402**	1·50	70
1490	240f. Woman tending cooking pot	2·50	1·40

403 Saltoposuchus

1993. Prehistoric Animals. Multicoloured.

1491	25f. Type **403**	35	10
1492	25f. Rhamphorhynchus	35	10
1493	25f. Dimorphodon	35	10
1494	25f. Archaeopteryx	35	10
1495	30f. "Compsognathos longipes"	35	10
1496	30f. "Cryptocleidus oxoniensis"	35	10
1497	30f. Stegosaurus	35	10
1498	30f. Cetiosaurus	35	10
1499	50f. Brontosaurus	45	20
1500	50f. "Corythosaurus casuarius"	45	20
1501	50f. Styracosaurus	45	20
1502	50f. Gorgosaurus	45	20
1503	500f. Scolosaurus	4·75	1·00
1504	500f. Trachodon	4·75	1·00
1505	500f. Struthiomimus	4·75	1·00
1506	500f. "Tarbosaurus bataar"	4·75	1·00
MS1507	120×170 mm. 1000f. Tylosaur (50×59 mm) (air)	10·00	2·30

Nos. 1491/1506 were issued together, *se-tenant*, forming a composite design of a volcanic landscape.

404 Th. Haug (combined skiing, Chamonix, 1924)

1994. Winter Olympic Games, Lillehammer, Norway. Previous Medal Winners. Multicoloured.

1508	100f. Type **404**	1·00	25
1509	100f. J. Heaton (luge, St. Moritz, 1928)	1·00	25
1510	100f. B. Ruud (ski jumping, Lake Placid, 1932)	1·00	25
1511	100f. I. Ballangrud (speed skating, Garmisch-Partenkirchen, 1936)	1·00	25
1512	100f. G. Fraser (slalom, St. Moritz, 1948)	1·00	25
1513	100f. West German 4-man bobsleigh team (Oslo, 1952)	1·00	25
1514	100f. U.S.S.R. ice hockey team (Cortina d'Ampezzo, 1956)	1·00	25
1515	100f. J. Vuarnet (downhill skiing, Squaw Valley, 1960)	1·00	25
1516	200f. M. Goitschel (giant slalom, Innsbruck, 1964)	1·70	45
1517	200f. Jean-Claud Killy (special slalom, Grenoble, 1968)	1·70	45
1518	200f. U. Wehling (cross- country skiing, Sapporo, 1972)	1·70	45
1519	200f. Irina Rodnina and Aleksandr Zaitsev (figure skating, Innsbruck, 1976)	1·70	45
1520	200f. E. Heiden (speed skating, Lake Placid, 1980)	1·70	45
1521	200f. Katarina Witt (figure skating, Sarajevo, 1984)	1·70	45
1522	200f. J. Mueller (single luge, Calgary, 1988)	1·70	45
1523	200f. E. Grospiron (acrobatic skiing, Albertville, 1992)	1·70	45
1524	200f. Speed skiing, Lillehammer, 1994	1·70	45

405 *Ansellia africa*

1994. Flowers, Vegetables, Fruit and Fungi. Multicoloured.

1525	25f. Type **405**	10	10
1526	30f. Yams	30	10
1527	40f. Oranges	30	10
1528	50f. Termite mushroom	40	10
1529	60f. *Polystachia bella* (flower)	45	10
1530	65f. Manioc	55	10
1531	70f. Banana	55	10
1532	80f. *Synpodia arborescens* (wrongly inscr "Sympodia") (fungi)	75	10
1533	90f. *Aerangis rhodosticta* (flower)	75	10
1534	100f. Maize	85	10
1535	160f. Mango	1·40	25
1536	200f. *Phlebopus sudanicus* (fungi)	1·70	25
1537	300f. Coffee beans	2·75	45
1538	400f. Sweet potato	3·75	55
1539	500f. *Angraecum eburneum* (flower)	4·50	75
1540	600f. *Leucocoprinus africanus* (fungi)	5·25	90

Nos. 1525/40 were issued together, *se-tenant*, the backgrounds forming a composite design.

MILITARY FRANK STAMPS

1963. Optd FM. No. M1 also has the value obliterated with two bars. Centre multicoloured; frame colour given.

M35	1	(-) on 15f. blue	14·50
M36	1	15f. blue	15·00

OFFICIAL STAMPS

O41 Arms

1965

O78	**O41**	1f. multicoloured	10	10
O79	**O41**	2f. multicoloured	10	10
O80	**O41**	5f. multicoloured	10	10
O81	**O41**	10f. multicoloured	30	10
O82	**O41**	20f. multicoloured	50	25
O83	**O41**	30f. multicoloured	90	55
O84	**O41**	50f. multicoloured	1·00	80
O85	**O41**	100f. multicoloured	2·50	1·20
O86	**O41**	130f. multicoloured	4·00	2·30
O87	**O41**	200f. multicoloured	6·00	3·00

O109 Arms

1971

O238	**O109**	5f. multicoloured	10	10
O239	**O109**	30f. multicoloured	50	25
O240	**O109**	40f. multicoloured	85	25
O241	**O109**	100f. multicoloured	1·50	55
O242	**O109**	140f. multicoloured	2·20	80
O243	**O109**	200f. multicoloured	3·50	1·40

POSTAGE DUE STAMPS

D15 *Sternotomis gama* (Beetle)

1962. Beetles.

D33	50c. brown and turquoise	10	10
D34	50c. turquoise and brown	10	10
D35	1f. brown and green	20	20
D36	1f. green and brown	20	20
D37	2f. pink and black	25	25
D38	2f. green, black and pink	25	25
D39	5f. green and brown	45	40
D40	5f. green and brown	45	40
D41	10f. green, black and drab	75	75
D42	10f. drab, black and green	75	75
D43	25f. brown, black and green	2·00	1·90
D44	25f. brown, green and black	2·00	1·90

DESIGNS: No. D33, Type D **15**; D34, *Sternotomis virescens*; D35, *Augosoma centaurus*; D36, *Phosphorus virescens* and *Ceroplesis carabarica*; D37, *Ceroplesis S.P.*; D38, *Cetoine scaraboidae*; D39, *Cetoine scaraboidae*; D40, *Macrorhina S.P.*; D41, *Taurina longiceps*; D42, *Phryneta leprosa*; D43, *Monohamus griseoplagiatus*; D44, *Jambonus trifasciatus*.

D308 Giant Pangolin (*Manis gigantea*)

1985

D1080	**D308**	5f. multicoloured	40	35
D1081	**D308**	20f. multicoloured	70	70
D1082	**D308**	30f. multicoloured	80	80

APPENDIX

The following stamps have either been issued in excess of postal needs or have not been availble to the public in reasonable quantities at face value. Such stamps may later be given full listing if there is evidence of regular postal use.

All the stamps listed below are embossed on gold foil.

1977

Coronation of Emperor Bokassa. Air 2500f.

1978

100 Years of Progress in Posts and Telecommunications. Air 1500f.
Death Centenary of Sir Rowland Hill. Air 1500f.

1979

International Year of the Child. Air 1500f.
Olympic Games, Moscow. Air 1500f. ("The Discus-thrower")
Space Exploration. Air 1500f.

1980

Olympic Games, Moscow. Air 1500f. (Relay)
European-African Co-operation. Air 1500f.
World Cup Football Championship, Spain. Air 1500f.

1981

Olympic Games Medal Winners. 1980 Olympic Games issue optd. Air 1500f.
Birth Centenary of Pablo Picasso. Air 1500f.
Wedding of Prince of Wales. Air 1500f.
Navigators. Air 1500f.
Christmas. Air 1500f.

1982

Animals and Rotary International. Air 1500f.
Transport. Air 1500f.
21st Birthday of Princess of Wales. Air 1500f.
Olympic Games, Los Angeles.Air 1500f. (horiz)
Space Resources. Air 1500f.

1983

Chess Masters. Air 1500f.
World Cup Football Championship, Spain. Air 1500f.
Car Manufacturers. Air 1500f.
Olympic Games, Los Angeles. Air 1500f. (vert)
Bicentenary of manned flight. Air 1500f.

1984

Winter Olympic Gold Medalists. Air 1500f.
Celebrities. Air 1500f.

1985

85th Birthday of Queen Elizabeth the Queen Mother. Air 1500f.
Appearence of Halley's Comet. Air 1500f.
480th Death Anniv of Christopher Columbus. Air 1500f.

1988

Olympic Games, Seoul. Air 1500f.
Scouts and Birds. Air 1500f.

1989

Olympic Games, Seoul, Gold Medal Winner. Air 1500f.
Bicentenary of French Revolution. Air 1500f.
World Cup Football Championship, Italy. Air 1500f.

1990

Winter Olympic Games, Albertville (1992). Air 1500f.
Scouts and Butterflies. Air 1500f.
Birth Centenary of Charles de Gaulle. Air 1500f.

1993

Wedding of Crown Prince Naruhito of Japan and Masako Owada. Air 1500f.
16th Death Anniv of Elvis Presley. Air 1500f.
World Cup Football Championship, U.S.A. (1994). Air 1500f.
Visit of Pope John Paul II to Africa. Air 1500f.

1994

Winter Olympic Games, Lillehammer. Air 1500f.

Pt. 10

CENTRAL LITHUANIA

Became temporarily independent in 1918 and was subsequently absorbed by Poland.

100 fenigi = 1 mark.

POLISH OCCUPATION

1

1920. Imperf or perf.

1	1	25f. red	10	10
20	1	25f. green	20	30
2	1	1m. blue	10	10
21	1	1m. brown	20	30
3	1	2m. violet	15	15
22	1	2m. yellow	20	30

1920. Stamps of Lithuania of 1919 surch **SRODKOWA LITWA POCZTA**, new value and Arms of Poland and Lithuania. Perf.

4	5	2m. on 15s. violet	6·50	8·00
5	5	4m. on 10s. red	4·00	5·00
6	5	4m. on 20s. blue	6·00	8·00
7	5	4m. on 30s. orange	5·00	6·00
8	6	6m. on 50s. green	6·00	7·00
9	6	6m. on 60s. red and violet	6·00	8·00
10	6	6m. on 75s. red & yellow	6·00	8·00
11	7	10m. on 1a. red & grey	12·00	14·00
12	7	10m. on 3a. red & brown	£450	£550
13	7	10m. on 5a. red and green	£450	£550

3 Girl

1920. Imperf or perf. Inscr "LITWA SRODKOWA".

14	3	25f. grey	15	15
15	-	1m. orange	20	15
16	-	2m. red	40	50
17	-	4m. olive and yellow	60	75
18	-	6m. grey and red	1·00	1·25
19	-	10m. yellow and brown	1·50	2·00

DESIGNS: 1m. Warrior; 2m. Ostrabrama Gate, Vilnius; 4m. St. Stanislaus Cathedral and Tower, Vilnius; 6m. Rector's insignia; 10m. Gen. Zeligowski.

1921. Fund for Polish Participation in Plebiscite for Upper Silesia. Surch **NA SLASK** and new value. Imperf or perf.

23	1	25f.+2m. red	50	60
24	1	25f.+2m. green	50	60
25	1	1m.+2m. blue	60	80
26	1	1m.+2m. brown	60	80
27	1	2m.+2m. violet	70	1·10
28	1	2m.+2m. yellow	70	1·10

1921. Red Cross Fund. Nos. 16/17 surch with cross and value. Imperf or perf.

29	2m.+1m. red	50	65
30	4m.+1m. green and yellow	50	65

1921. White Cross Fund. As Nos. 16, 17 and 19, but with cross and value in white added. Imperf or perf.

31	2m.+1m. purple	30	30
32	4m.+1m. green and buff	30	30
33	10m.+2m. yellow and brown	30	30

13 St. Nicholas Cathedral

14 St. Stanislaus Cathedral

1921. Imperf or perf.

34	**13**	1m. yellow and slate	30	40
35	**14**	2m. green and red	30	40
36	-	3m. green	40	50
37	-	4m. brown	40	60
38	-	5m. brown	40	60
39	-	6m. buff and green	40	60
40	-	10m. buff and purple	60	80
41	-	20m. buff and brown	60	90

DESIGNS—HORIZ: 4m. Queen Jadwiga and King Wladislaw Jagiello; 6m. Poczobut Observatory, Vilnius University; 10m. Union of Lithuania and Poland, 1569; 20m. Kosciuszko and Mickiewicz. VERT: 3m. Arms (Eagle); 5m. Arms (Shield).

21 Entry into Vilnius

22 General Zeligowski

1921. First Anniv of Entry of Gen. Zeligowski into Vilnius. Imperf or perf.

42	**21**	100m. blue and bistre	1·75	1·75
43	**22**	150m. green and brown	2·25	2·25

24 Arms

1922. Opening of National Parliament. Inscr "SEJM—WILNIE". Imperf or perf.

44	-	10m. brown	1·50	1·75
45	**24**	25m. red and buff	1·75	1·90
46	-	50m. blue	2·75	3·00
47	-	75m. lilac	4·00	4·50

DESIGNS—HORIZ: 50m. National Assembly, Vilnius. VERT: 10m. Agriculture; 75m. Industry.

POSTAGE DUE STAMPS

D9 Government Offices

1921. Inscr "DOPLATA". Imperf or perf.

D23	**D9**	50f. red	50	60
D24	-	1m. green	50	60
D25	-	2m. purple	50	60
D26	-	3m. purple	75	90
D27	-	5m. purple	75	90
D28	-	20m. red	1·00	1·25

DESIGNS—HORIZ: 2m. Castle on Troki Island. VERT: 1m. Castle Hill, Vilnius; 3m. Ostrabrama Gate, Vilnius; 5m. St. Stanislaus Cathedral; 20m. (larger) St. Nicholas Cathedral.

Pt. 1

CEYLON

An island to the south of India formerly under British administration, then a self-governing Dominion. The island became a Republic within the Commonwealth on 22 May 1972 and was renamed Sri Lanka (q.v.).

1857. 12 pence = 1 shilling; 20 shillings = 1 pound.
1872. 100 cents = 1 rupee.

1

2

4

1857. Imperf.

17	**4**	½d. lilac	£180	£225
2	**1**	1d. blue	£1100	45·00
3	**1**	2d. green	£200	65·00
4	**2**	4d. red	£70000	£4500
5	**1**	5d. brown	£1600	£150
6	**1**	6d. brown	£2750	£140
7	**2**	8d. brown	£28000	£1500
8	**2**	9d. brown	£60000	£900
9	**1**	10d. orange	£900	£325
10	**1**	1s. violet	£5500	£200
11	**2**	1s.9d. green	£800	£800
12	**2**	2s. blue	£6500	£1300

The prices of these imperf stamps vary greatly according to condition. The above prices are for fine copies with four margins. Poor to medium specimens are worth much less.

1861. Perf.

48c	**4**	½d. lilac	50·00	50·00
49	**1**	1d. blue	£170	8·50
50	**1**	2d. green	£100	14·00
64b	**1**	2d. yellow	90·00	9·00
65b	**2**	4d. red	80·00	20·00
22	**1**	5d. brown	£120	8·00
66c	**1**	5d. green	55·00	50·00
67	**1**	6d. brown	£120	10·00
56	**2**	8d. brown	£130	65·00
69b	**2**	9d. brown	65·00	6·00
70b	**1**	10d. orange	80·00	17·00
71b	**1**	1s. violet	£140	11·00
72b	**2**	2s. blue	£150	15·00

8

1866. The 3d. has portrait in circle.

61	**8**	1d. blue	25·00	11·00
62	-	3d. red	90·00	50·00

9

10

30

1872. Various frames.

147	**9**	2c. green	2·75	15
256	**9**	2c. brown	4·75	30
122	**10**	4c. grey	45·00	1·50
148	**10**	4c. purple	5·50	30
149	**10**	4c. red	6·50	13·00
258	**10**	4c. yellow	3·75	3·50
150a	-	8c. yellow	5·00	10·00
126	-	16c. violet	£120	2·75
127	-	24c. green	70·00	2·25
128	-	32c. grey	£170	15·00
129	-	36c. blue	£190	28·00
130	-	48c. red	90·00	9·00
131	-	64c. brown	£300	75·00
132	-	96c. grey	£275	29·00
201	**30**	1r.12 red	29·00	29·00
138	**30**	2r.50 red	£800	£425
249	**30**	2r.50 purple on red	38·00	55·00

1882. Nos. 127 and 131 surch in words and figures.

142	**30**	16c. on 24c. green	38·00	9·00
143	**30**	20c. on 64c. brown	13·00	9·00

1885. As Nos. 148/132 surch Postage & Revenue and value in words.

178	5c. on 4c. red	25·00	4·75
179	5c. on 8c. yellow	85·00	11·00
180	5c. on 16c. violet	£160	16·00
154	5c. on 24c. green	£5500	£110
182	5c. on 24c. purple	-	£500
155	5c. on 32c. grey	65·00	15·00
156	5c. on 36c. blue	£300	13·00
157	5c. on 48c. red	£2250	60·00
158	5c. on 64c. brown	£130	12·00
159	5c. on 96c. grey	£550	70·00

1885. As Nos. 126/249 surch with new value in words.

184	10c. on 16c. violet	£12000	£1700
162	10c. on 24c. green	£500	£120
185	10c. on 24c. purple	16·00	9·50
163	10c. on 36c. blue	£450	£225
174	10c. on 64c. brown	90·00	£150
186	15c. on 16c. violet	14·00	11·00
165	20c. on 24c. green	75·00	25·00
166	20c. on 32c. grey	80·00	65·00
167	25c. on 32c. grey	24·00	7·00
168	28c. on 48c. red	40·00	10·00
169x	30c. on 36c. blue	15·00	10·00
170	56c. on 96c. grey	30·00	25·00
176	1r.12 on 2r.50 red	£110	45·00

1885. Surch **REVENUE AND POSTAGE 5 CENTS.**

187	5c. on 8c. lilac (as No. 150a)	25·00	1·50

1885. As Nos. 126/32 surch in words and figures.

188	10c. on 24c. purple	12·00	8·50
189	15c. on 16c. yellow	60·00	15·00
190	28c. on 32c. grey	27·00	2·50
191	30c. on 36c. olive	29·00	15·00
192	56c. on 96c. grey	50·00	17·00

1885. Surch **1 R. 12 C.**

193	1r.12 on 2r.50 red	60·00	£140

28

39

43

1886

245	**39**	3c. brown and green	6·00	45
257	**39**	3c. green	4·75	55
195	**28**	5c. purple	3·75	10
259	**39**	6c. red and black	2·75	45
260	**39**	12c. olive and red	5·00	9·00
196	**39**	15c. olive	8·50	2·25
261	**39**	15c. blue	8·00	1·25
198	**39**	25c. brown	6·00	1·75
199	**39**	28c. grey	24·00	1·40
247	**39**	30c. mauve and brown	4·75	3·25
262	**39**	75c. black and brown	9·50	9·50
263	**43**	1r.50 red	32·00	50·00
264	**43**	2r.25 blue	35·00	50·00

1887. Nos. 148/9 surch. A. Surch **TWO CENTS.**

202	**10**	2c. on 4c. purple	1·40	80
203	**10**	2c. on 4c. red	2·50	30

B. Surch **TWO.**

204	2c. on 4c. purple	1·00	30
205	2c. on 4c. red	8·00	20

C. Surch **2 Cents** and bar.

206	2c. on 4c. purple	80·00	32·00
207	2c. on 4c. red	4·00	75

D. **Surch Two** Cents and bar.

208	2c. on 4c. purple	65·00	28·00
209	2c. on 4c. red	2·50	1·10

E. Surch **2 Cents** without bar.

210	2c. on 4c. purple	65·00	38·00
211	2c. on 4c. red	14·00	1·00

1890. Surch **POSTAGE Five Cents REVENUE.**

233	**39**	5c. on 15c. olive	4·00	2·50

1891. Surch **FIFTEEN CENTS.**

239	15c. on 25c. brown	19·00	18·00
240	15c. on 28c. grey	20·00	9·00

1892. Surch **3 Cents** and bar.

241	**10**	3c. on 4c. purple	1·00	3·25
242	**10**	3c. on 4c. red	8·00	11·00
243	**39**	3c. on 28c. grey	6·50	6·00

1898. Surch **Six Cents.**

250	6c. on 15c. green	1·25	75

1898. Surch with new value.

254	**30**	1r.50 on 2r.50 grey	20·00	50·00
255	**30**	2r.25 on 2r.50 yellow	45·00	80·00

44

45

1903. Various frames.

277	**44**	2c. brown	1·75	10
278	**45**	3c. green (A)	1·50	15
293	**45**	3c. green (B)	1·00	75
279	**45**	4c. orange and blue	2·50	1·50
268	-	5c. purple	2·25	60
289	-	5c. purple	5·50	10
281	-	6c. red	4·25	15
291	-	6c. red	2·00	10
294	**45**	10c. olive and red	2·50	3·50
282	**45**	12c. olive and red	1·50	1·75
283	**45**	15c. blue	3·25	60
284	**45**	25c. brown	6·00	3·75
295	**45**	25c. grey	2·50	2·75
285	**45**	30c. violet and green	2·50	3·00
296	**45**	50c. brown	4·00	7·50
286	**45**	75c. blue and orange	5·25	8·00
297	**45**	1r. purple on yellow	8·00	12·00
287	**45**	1r.50 grey	29·00	11·00
298	**45**	2r. red on yellow	15·00	29·00
288	**45**	2r.25 brown and green	22·00	32·00
299	**45**	5r. black on green	42·00	85·00
300	**45**	10r. black on red	£120	£250

(A) has value in shaded tablet; (B) in white tablet as in Type **45**.

Nos. 268 and 281 have the value in words; Nos. 289 and 291 in figures.

52

1912

301	**52**	1c. brown	1·00	10
307a	**52**	2c. orange	30	20
339	**52**	3c. green	5·00	75
340	**52**	3c. grey	75	20
341	**52**	5c. purple	60	15
342	**52**	6c. red	2·75	75
343	**52**	6c. violet	2·25	15
345	**52**	9c. red on yellow	2·50	30
346	**52**	10c. olive	1·40	40
347a	**52**	12c. red	1·00	2·25
311a	**52**	15c. blue	1·75	1·25
349a	**52**	15c. green on yellow	4·50	1·00
350b	**52**	20c. blue	3·50	45
351	**52**	25c. yellow and blue	2·75	1·90
352	**52**	30c. green and violet	1·60	4·75
353	**52**	50c. black and red	2·00	80
315	**52**	1r. purple on yellow	5·00	4·25
355	**52**	2r. black and red on yellow	7·00	12·00
317	**52**	5r. black on green	19·00	40·00
318	**52**	10r. purple & blk on red	70·00	90·00
319	**52**	20r. black and red on blue	£150	£160

Large type, As Bermuda T **15**.

358	50r. purple	£650	£1100
359	100r. black	£2500	
360	100r. purple and blue	£1800	

1918. Optd **WAR STAMP**, No. 335 surch **ONE CENT** and bar also.

335	1c. on 5c. purple	50	40
330	2c. orange	20	40
332	3c. green	20	50
333	5c. purple	50	30

1918. Surch **ONE CENT** and bar.

337	1c. on 5c. purple	15	25

1926. Surch with new value and bar.

361	2c. on 3c. grey	2·50	1·00
362	5c. on 6c. violet	60	40

57

1927

363	**57**	1r. purple	2·50	1·25
364	**57**	2r. green and red	3·75	2·75
365	**57**	5r. green and purple	16·00	25·00
366	**57**	10r. green and orange	55·00	£120
367	**57**	20r. purple and blue	£200	£350

59 Adam's Peak

1935. King George V.

368	-	2c. black and red	30	40
369	**59**	3c. black and green	35	40
370	-	6c. black and blue	30	30
371	-	9c. green and orange	1·00	65
372	-	10c. black and purple	1·25	3·00
373	-	15c. brown and green	1·50	50
374	-	20c. black and blue	2·75	3·25
375	-	25c. blue and brown	1·40	1·25
376	-	30c. red and green	2·25	3·50
377	-	50c. black and violet	14·00	1·75
378	-	1r. violet and brown	35·00	25·00

DESIGNS—VERT: 2c. Tapping rubber; 6c. Colombo Harbour; 9c. Plucking tea; 20c. Coconut palms. HORIZ: 10c. Hill paddy (rice); 15c. River scene; 25c. Temple of the Tooth, Kandy; 30c. Ancient irrigation tank; 50c. Indian elephants; 1r. Trincomalee.

1935. Silver Jubilee. As T **13** of Antigua.

379	6c. blue and grey	75	30
380	9c. green and blue	75	2·75
381	20c. brown and blue	4·25	2·75
382	50c. grey and purple	5·25	16·00

1937. Coronation. As T **2** of Aden.

383	6c. red	65	1·00
384	9c. green	2·50	4·50
385	20c. blue	3·50	4·00

70 Sigiriya (Lion Rock)

1938. As 1935 issue but with portrait of King George VI, and "POSTAGE & REVENUE" omitted.

386b	-	2c. black and red	2·50	10
387d	59	3c. black and green	80	10
387f	-	5c. green and orange	30	10
388	-	6c. black and blue	30	10
389	70	10c. black and blue	3·25	20
390	-	15c. green and brown	2·00	20
391	-	20c. black and blue	3·25	20
392a	-	25c. blue and brown	4·25	20
393	-	30c. red and green	12·00	3·50
394e	-	50c. black and violet	6·00	20
395	-	1r. blue and brown	18·00	1·50
396	-	2r. black and red	15·00	4·00
396b	-	2r. black and violet	3·00	3·00

DESIGNS—VERT: 5c. Coconut palms; 20c. Plucking tea; 2r. Ancient guard-stone, Anuradhapura. Others, same as for corresponding values of 1935 issue.

1938. As T **57**, but head of King George VI to right.

397a	5r. green and purple	30·00	11·00

1940. Surch with new value and bars.

398	3c. on 6c. blk & bl (No. 388)	65	10
399	3c. on 20c. blk & bl (No. 391)	5·00	3·00

1946. Victory. As T **9** of Aden.

400	6c. blue	30	35
401	15c. brown	30	1·75

75 Parliament Building

1947. New Constitution.

402	75	6c. black and blue	20	15
403	-	10c. black, orange and red	25	40
404	-	15c. green and purple	25	80
405	-	25c. yellow and green	25	1·75

DESIGNS—VERT: 10c. Adam's Peak; 25c. Anuradhapura. HORIZ: 15c. Temple of the Tooth.

79 Lion Flag of Dominion

80 D. S. Senanayake

1949. First Anniv of Independence.

406	79	4c. red, yellow and brown	20	20
407	80	5c. brown and green	10	10
408	79	15c. red, yellow and orange	1·00	40
409	80	25c. brown and blue	15	1·00

No. 408 is larger, 28×22 mm.

82 Globe and Forms of Transport

1949. 75th Anniv of UPU. Inscr as in T **82**. Designs showing globe.

410	82	5c. brown and green	75	10
411	-	15c. black and red (horiz)	1·10	2·75
412	-	25c. black and blue (vert)	1·10	1·10

85 Kandyan Dancer

88 Sigiriya (Lion Rock)

90 Ruins at Madirigiriya

1950

413	85	4c. purple and red	15	10
414	-	5c. green	15	10
415	-	15c. green and violet	2·50	50
416	88	30c. red and yellow	30	70
417	-	75c. blue and orange	8·50	20
418	90	1r. blue and brown	1·75	30

DESIGNS—VERT (As Types **85** and **88**): 5c. Kiri Vehera, Polonnaruwa; 15c. Vesak orchid. (As Type **90**): 75c. Octagon Library, Temple of the Tooth.

94 Coconut Trees

99 Tea Plantation

1951

419	-	2c. brown and turquoise	10	1·25
420	-	3c. black and violet	10	1·00
421	-	6c. sepia and green	15	30
422	94	10c. green and grey	1·00	65
423	-	25c. orange and blue	20	20
424	-	35c. red and green	1·50	1·50
425	-	40c. brown	5·00	1·00
426	-	50c. slate	30	10
427	99	85c. black and turquoise	1·50	30
428	-	2r. blue and brown	9·00	1·25
429	-	5r. brown and orange	10·00	1·40
430	-	10r. brown and buff	60·00	23·00

DESIGNS—VERT (As Type **94**): 2c. Sambars, Ruhuna National Park; 3c. Ancient guardstone, Anuradhapura; 6c. Harvesting rice; 25c. Sigiriya fresco; 35c. Star orchid. (As Type **99**): 5r. Bas-relief, Anuradhapura; 10r. Harvesting rice. HORIZ (As Type **94**): 40c. Rubber plantation; 50c. Outrigger canoe. (As Type **99**): 2r. River Gal Dam.

103 Ceylon, Mace and Symbols of Progress

1952. Colombo Plan Exhibition.

431	103	5c. green	10	30
432	103	15c. blue	30	60

104 Queen Elizabeth II

1953. Coronation.

433	104	5c. green	1·50	10

105 Ceremonial Procession

1954. Royal Visit.

434	105	10c. blue	1·25	10

106 King Coconuts

1954

435	106	10c. orange, brown and buff	10	10

107 Farm Produce

1955. Royal Agricultural and Food Exhibition.

436	107	10c. brown and orange	10	10

108 Sir John Kotelawala and House of Representatives

1956. Prime Minister's 25 Years of Public Service.

437	108	10c. green	10	10

109 Arrival of Vijaya in Ceylon

110 Lampstand and Dharmachakra

1956. Buddha Jayanti. Inscr "2500".

438	109	3c. blue and grey	15	15
439	110	4c.+2c. yellow and blue	20	75
440	-	10c.+5c. red, yell & grey	20	1·00
441	-	15c. blue	25	10

DESIGNS—VERT: 10c. Hand of Peace and Dharmachakra. HORIZ: 15c. Dharmachakra encircling the globe.

113 Mail Transport

114 Stamp of 1857

1957. Stamp Centenary.

442	113	4c. red and turquoise	75	50
443	113	10c. red and blue	75	10
444	114	35c. brown, yellow and blue	30	50
445	114	85c. brown, yellow & grn	80	1·60

1958. Nos. 439/40 with premium obliterated with bars.

446	110	4c. yellow and blue	10	10
447	-	10c. red, yellow and grey	10	10

117 Kandyan Dancer

1958. As Nos. 413 and 419 etc, and 435, but with inscriptions changed as in T **117**.

448	2c. brown and turquoise	10	50
449	3c. black and violet	10	70
450	4c. purple and red	10	10
451	5c. green	10	1·60
452	6c. sepia and green	10	65
453	10c. orange, brown and buff	10	10
454	15c. green and violet	3·50	1·00
455	25c. orange and blue	20	10
456	30c. red and yellow	20	1·40
457	35c. red and green	4·00	30
459	50c. slate	30	10
460a	75c. blue and orange	9·50	3·00
461	85c. black and turquoise	3·75	10·00
462	1r. blue and brown	60	10
463	2r. blue and brown	3·50	30
464	5r. brown and orange	14·00	30
465	10r. brown and buff	14·00	1·00

118 "Human Rights"

1958. Tenth Anniv of Declaration of Human Rights.

466	118	10c. red, brown and purple	10	10
467	118	85c. red, turq & grn	30	55

119 Portraits of Founders and University Buildings

1959. Institution of Pirivena Universities.

468	119	10c. orange and blue	10	10

120 "Uprooted Tree"

1960. World Refugee Year.

469	120	4c. brown and gold	10	85
470	120	25c. violet and gold	10	15

121 S. W. R. D. Bandaranaike

1961. Prime Minister Bandaranaike Commemoration.

471	121	10c. blue and turquoise	10	10

See also Nos. 479 and 481.

122 Ceylon Scout Badge

1962. Golden Jubilee of Ceylon Boy Scouts Association.

472	122	35c. buff and blue	15	10

123 Campaign Emblem

1962. Malaria Eradication.

473	123	25c. red and drab	10	10

124 De Havilland Leopard Moth and Hawker Siddeley Comet 4

1963. 25th Anniv of Airmail Services.

474	124	50c. black and blue	50	50

125 "Produce" and Campaign Emblem

1963. Freedom from Hunger.

475	125	5c. red and blue	75	2·00
476	125	25c. brown and olive	3·00	30

ශත
2
சதம்

(126)

1963. No. 450 surch with T **126**.

477	2c. on 4c. purple and red	10	10

127 "Rural Life"

1963. Golden Jubilee of Ceylon Co-operative Movement (1962).

478	127	60c. red and black	2·00	50

1963. Design as T **121**, but smaller (21×26 mm) and with inscription rearranged at top.

479	10c. blue	10	10
481	10c. violet and grey	10	10

No. 481 has a decorative pattern at foot instead of the inscription.

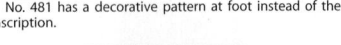

129 Terrain, Indian Elephant and Tree

1963. National Conservation Week.

480	**129**	5c. sepia and blue	60	40

131 Anagarika Dharmapala (Buddhist missionary)

1964. Birth Centenary of A. Dharmapala (founder of Maha Bodhi Society).

482	**131**	25c. sepia and yellow	10	10

135 D. S. Senanayake

143 Ceylon Jungle Fowl

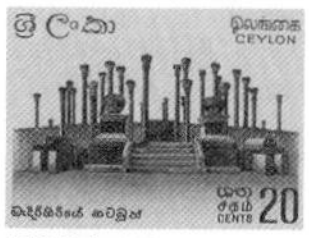
138 Ruins at Madirigiriya

1964

485	-	5c. multicoloured	2·00	1·00
486	**135**	10c. green	80	10
487	-	10c. green	10	10
488	-	15c. multicoloured	4·25	30
489	**138**	20c. purple and buff	20	25
494	**143**	60c. multicoloured	4·50	1·25
495	-	75c. multicoloured	3·00	70
497	-	1r. brown and green	1·00	30
499	-	5r. multicoloured	9·50	9·50
500	-	10r. multicoloured	26·00	3·00
MS500a		148×174 mm. As Nos. 485, 488, 494 and 495 (imperf)	7·00	14·00

DESIGNS—HORIZ (As Type **143**): 5c. Southern grackle ("Grackle"); 15c. Common peafowl ("Peacock"); 75c. Asian black-headed oriole ("Oriole"). (As Type **138**): 5r. Girls transplanting rice. VERT (As Type **135**): 10c. (No. 487) Similar portrait, but large head and smaller inscriptions. (21×35 mm): 1r. Tea plantation. (23×36 mm): 10r. Map of Ceylon.

150 Exhibition Buildings and Cogwheels

1964. Industrial Exhibition.

501		5c. multicoloured	10	75
502	**150**	5c. multicoloured	10	75

No. 501 is inscribed "INDUSTRIAL EXHIBITION" in Sinhala and Tamil, No. 502 in Sinhala and English.

151 Trains of 1864 and 1964

1964. Centenary of Ceylon Railways.

503	-	60c. blue, purple and green	2·75	40
504	**151**	60c. blue, purple and green	2·75	40

No. 503 is inscribed "RAILWAY CENTENARY" in Sinhala and Tamil, No. 504 in Sinhala and English.

152 ITU Emblem and Symbols

1965. Centenary of ITU.

505	**152**	2c. blue and red	1·00	1·10
506	**152**	30c. brown and red	3·00	45

153 ICY Emblem

1965. International Co-operation Year.

507	**153**	3c. blue and red	1·25	1·00
508	**153**	50c. black, red and gold	3·25	50

154 Town Hall, Colombo

1965. Centenary of Colombo Municipal Council.

509	**154**	25c. green and sepia	20	20

1965. No. 481 surch **5**.

510	5c. on 10c. violet and grey	10	2·00

157 Kandy and Council Crest

1966. Centenary of Kandy Municipal Council.

512	**157**	25c. multicoloured	20	20

158 WHO Building

1966. Inauguration of WHO Headquarters, Geneva.

513	**158**	4c. multicoloured	3·00	3·00
514	**158**	1r. multicoloured	7·50	1·50

159 Rice Paddy and Map of Ceylon

1966. International Rice Year. Multicoloured.

515	6c. Type **159**	20	75
516	30c. Rice paddy and globe	30	15

161 UNESCO Emblem

1966. 20th Anniv of UNESCO.

517	**161**	3c. multicoloured	2·75	3·75
518	**161**	50c. multicoloured	8·00	50

162 Water-resources Map

1966. International Hydrological Decade.

519	**162**	2c. brown, yellow and blue	30	85
520	**162**	2r. multicoloured	1·50	2·25

163 Devotees at Buddhist Temple

1967. Poya Holiday System. Multicoloured.

521	5c. Type **163**	15	60
522	20c. Mihintale	15	10
523	35c. Sacred Bo-tree, Anuradhapura	15	15
524	60c. Adam's Peak	15	10

167 Galle Fort and Clock Tower

1967. Centenary of Galle Municipal Council.

525	**167**	25c. multicoloured	70	20

168 Field Research

1967. Centenary of Ceylon Tea Industry. Multicoloured.

526	4c. Type **168**	60	80
527	40c. Tea-tasting equipment	1·75	1·50
528	50c. Leaves and bud	1·75	20
529	1r. Shipping tea	1·75	10

169 Elephant Ride

1967. International Tourist Year.

530	**169**	45c. multicoloured	2·25	80

1967. First National Stamp Exhibition. No. **MS**500a optd **FIRST NATIONAL STAMP EXHIBITION 1967**.

MS531	148×174 mm. Nos. 485, 488, 494/5. Imperf	7·00	9·00

170 Ranger, Jubilee Emblem and Flag

1967. Golden Jubilee of Ceylon Girl Guides' Association.

532	**170**	3c. multicoloured	50	20
533	**170**	25c. multicoloured	75	10

171 Colonel Olcott and Buddhist Flag

1967. 60th Death Anniv of Colonel Olcott (theosophist).

534	**171**	15c. multicoloured	30	20

172 Independence Hall

1968. 20th Anniv of Independence. Multicoloured.

535	5c. Type **172**	10	55
536	1r. Lion flag and sceptre	50	10

174 Sir D. B. Jayatilleke

1968. Birth Centenary of Sir Baron Jayatilleke (scholar and statesman).

537	**174**	25c. brown	10	10

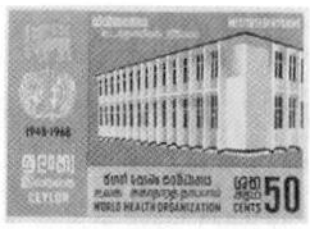
175 Institute of Hygiene

1968. 20th Anniv of World Health Organization.

538	**175**	50c. multicoloured	10	10

176 Vickers Super VC-10 over Terminal Building

1968. Opening of Colombo Airport.

539	**176**	60c. multicoloured	1·00	10

177 Open Koran and "1400"

1968. 1400th Anniv of Koran.

541	**177**	25c. multicoloured	10	10

178 Human Rights Emblem

1968. Human Rights Year.

542	**178**	2c. multicoloured	10	30
543	**178**	20c. multicoloured	10	10
544	**178**	40c. multicoloured	10	10
545	**178**	2r. multicoloured	80	4·75

179 All-Ceylon Buddhist Congress Headquarters

1968. Golden Jubilee of All-Ceylon Buddhist Congress.

546	**179**	5c. multicoloured	10	50

180 E. W. Perera (patriot)

1969. Perera Commemoration.

547	**180**	60c. brown	10	30

181 Symbols of Strength in Savings

1969. Silver Jubilee of National Savings Movement.

548	**181**	3c. multicoloured	10	30

182 Seat of Enlightenment under Sacred Bodhi Tree

1969. Vesak Day. Inscr "Wesak".

549	**182**	4c. multicoloured	10	50
550	-	6c. multicoloured	10	50
551	**182**	35c. multicoloured	10	10

DESIGN: 6c. Buduresmala (six-fold Buddha-rays).

184 A. E. Goonesinghe

1969. Goonesinghe Commemoration.

552	**184**	15c. multicoloured	10	10

185 ILO Emblem

1969. 50th Anniv of ILO.

553	**185**	5c. black and blue	10	10
554	**185**	25c. black and red	10	10

186 Convocation Hall, University of Ceylon

1969. Educational Centenary. Multicoloured.

555	4c. Type **186**	10	80
556	35c. Lamp of learning, globe and flags (horiz)	20	10
557	50c. Uranium atom	20	10
558	60c. Symbols of scientific education	30	10

188 Ath Pana (Elephant Lamp)

1969. Archaeological Centenary. Multicoloured.

559	6c. Type **188**	25	1·50
560	1r. Rock fortress of Sigiriya	25	10

190 Leopard

1970. Wild Life Conservation. Multicoloured.

561	5c. Water buffalo	1·25	1·25
562	15c. Slender loris	2·00	1·25
563	50c. Spotted deer	1·40	1·25
564	1r. Type **190**	1·40	1·75

191 Emblem and Symbols

1970. Asian Productivity Year.

565	**191**	60c. multicoloured	10	10

192 New UPU HQ Building

1970. New UPU Headquarters Building.

566	**192**	50c. orange, black and blue	50	10
567	**192**	1r.10 red, black and blue	4·50	40

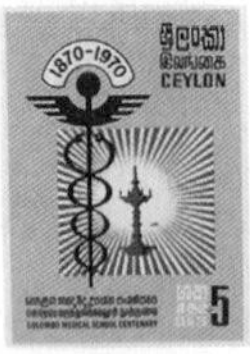

193 Oil Lamp and Caduceus

1970. Centenary of Colombo Medical School.

568	**193**	5c. multicoloured	1·25	80
569	**193**	45c. multicoloured	1·50	60

194 Victory March and S. W. R. D. Bandaranaike

1970. Establishment of United Front Government.

570	**194**	10c. multicoloured	10	10

195 U.N. Emblem and Dove of Peace

1970. 25th Anniv of United Nations.

571	**195**	2r. multicoloured	2·00	4·00

196 Keppetipola Dissawa

1970. 152nd Death Anniv of Keppetipola Dissawa (Kandyan patriot).

572	**196**	25c. multicoloured	10	10

197 Ola Leaf Manuscript

1970. International Education Year.

573	**197**	15c. multicoloured	2·75	1·25

198 C. H. de Soysa

1971. 135th Birth Anniv of C. H. de Soysa (philanthropist).

574	**198**	20c. multicoloured	15	50

199 D. E. H. Pedris (patriot)

1971. D. E. H. Pedris Commemoration.

575	**199**	25c. multicoloured	15	50

200 Lenin

1971. Lenin Commemoration.

576	**200**	40c. multicoloured	15	50

201 Ananda Rajakaruna

1971. Poets and Philosophers.

577	**201**	5c. blue	10	15
578	-	5c. brown	10	15
579	-	5c. orange	10	15
580	-	5c. blue	10	15
581	-	5c. brown	10	15

PORTRAITS: No. 578, Arumuga Navalar; 579, Rev. S. Mahinda; 580, Ananda Coomaraswamy; 581, Cumaratunga Munidasa.

1971. Surch in figures.

582	**182**	5c. on 4c. multicoloured	6·50	1·75
583	**186**	5c. on 4c. multicoloured	10	1·25
584	**194**	15c. on 10c. multicoloured	10	30
585	-	25c. on 6c. mult (No. 550)	30	60
586	**188**	25c. on 6c. multicoloured	30	2·25

203 Colombo Plan Emblem and Ceylon

1971. 20th Anniv of Colombo Plan.

587	**203**	20c. multicoloured	15	30

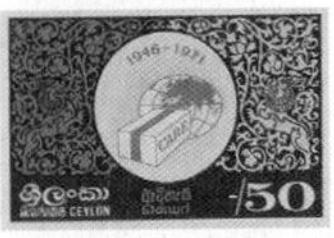

204 Globe and CARE Package

1971. 20th Anniv of Co-operative for American Relief Everywhere.

588	**204**	50c. blue, violet and lilac	35	30

205 WHO Emblem and Heart

1972. World Health Day.

589	**205**	25c. multicoloured	2·50	60

206 Map of Asia and U.N. Emblem

1972. 25th Anniv of ECAFE.

590	**206**	85c. multicoloured	4·75	2·75

OFFICIAL STAMPS

1895. Stamps of Queen Victoria optd **On Service**.

O11	**9**	2c. green	17·00	70
O18	**9**	2c. brown	10·00	60
O12	**39**	3c. brown and green	10·00	2·50
O19	**39**	3c. green	12·00	4·50
O13	**28**	5c. purple	5·00	30
O14	**39**	15c. olive	20·00	50
O20	**39**	15c. blue	25·00	60
O15	**39**	25c. brown	13·00	3·00
O16	**39**	30c. mauve and brown	13·00	60
O21	**39**	75c. black and brown	8·00	8·50
O17	**30**	1r.12 red	95·00	60·00

1903. Stamps of King Edward VII optd **On Service**.

O22	**44**	2c. brown	20·00	1·00
O23	**45**	3c. green	14·00	2·00
O24	-	5c. purple (No. 268)	28·00	1·50
O25	**45**	15c. blue	38·00	2·50
O26	**45**	25c. brown	35·00	18·00
O27	**45**	30c. violet and green	19·00	1·50

For later issues see **SRI LANKA**.

Pt. 6, Pt. 12

CHAD

Formerly a dependency of Ubangi-Shari. Became one of the separate colonies of Fr. Equatorial Africa in 1937. In 1958 became a republic within the French Community.

100 centimes = 1 franc.

1922. Stamps of Middle Congo, colours changed, optd **TCHAD**.

1	**1**	1c. pink and violet	60	6·75
2	**1**	2c. brown and pink	1·50	6·75
3	**1**	4c. blue and violet	2·10	7·25
4	**1**	5c. brown and green	3·00	7·75
5	**1**	10c. green and turquoise	5·25	8·50
6	**1**	15c. violet and pink	4·50	9·00
7	**1**	20c. green and violet	8·75	18·00
8	**2**	25c. brown and chocolate	10·50	34·00
9	**2**	30c. red	3·25	8·25
10	**2**	35c. blue and pink	3·75	11·00
11	**2**	40c. brown and green	3·75	11·50
12	**2**	45c. violet and green	3·75	11·00
13	**2**	50c. blue and light blue	3·00	11·00
14	**2**	60 on 75c. violet on pink	5·00	16·00
15	**2**	75c. pink and violet	4·00	10·50
16	**3**	1f. blue and pink	19·00	37·00
17	**3**	2f. blue and violet	24·00	60·00
18	**3**	5f. blue and brown	20·00	55·00

1924. Stamps of 1922 and similar stamps further optd **AFRIQUE EQUATORIALE FRANCAISE**.

19	**1**	1c. pink and violet	35	6·00
20	**1**	2c. brown and pink	25	6·25
21	**1**	4c. blue and violet	70	6·50
22	**1**	5c. brown and green	75	6·25
23	**1**	10c. green and turquoise	2·50	7·75
24	**1**	10c. red and grey	1·10	6·25
25	**1**	15c. violet and red	1·10	6·50
26	**1**	20c. green and violet	2·10	6·75
27	**2**	25c. brown and chocolate	2·10	6·75
28	**2**	30c. red	1·40	6·75
29	**2**	30c. grey and blue	95	6·25
30	**2**	30c. olive and green	2·10	8·25
31	**2**	35c. blue and pink	1·10	7·00
32	**2**	40c. brown and green	2·10	6·75
33	**2**	45c. violet and green	1·90	7·75
34	**2**	50c. blue and light blue	1·20	7·00
35	**2**	50c. green and purple	2·40	2·30
36	**2**	60 on 75c. violet on pink	85	7·25
37	**2**	65c. brown and blue	3·50	10·00
38	**2**	75c. pink and violet	1·40	5·50
39	**2**	75c. blue and light blue	2·20	5·75
40	**2**	75c. purple and brown	3·75	9·75
41	**2**	90c. carmine and red	6·25	25·00
42	**3**	1f. blue and pink	3·00	4·75
43	**3**	1f.10 green and blue	3·75	11·50
44	**3**	1f.25 brown and blue	13·50	28·00
45	**3**	1f.50 ultramarine and blue	6·00	28·00
46	**3**	1f.75 brown and mauve	55·00	95·00
47	**3**	2f. blue and violet	3·25	5·50
48	**3**	3f. mauve on pink	8·75	39·00
49	**3**	5f. blue and brown	3·75	7·25

1925. Stamps of Middle Congo optd **TCHAD** and **AFRIQUE EQUATORIALE FRANCAISE** and surch also.

50		65 on 1f. brown and green	2·75	8·50
51		85 on 1f. brown and green	2·75	8·50
52	**2**	90 on 75c. red and pink	2·30	8·75
53	**3**	1f.25 on 1f. blue & ultram	1·40	6·25
54	**3**	1f.50 on 1f. blue & ultram	3·00	8·75
55	**3**	3f. on 5f. brown and red	5·25	14·50
56	**3**	10f. on 5f. green and red	15·00	34·00
57a	**3**	20f. on 5f. violet & orange	24·00	43·00

1931. "Colonial Exhibition" key-types inscr "TCHAD".

58	**E**	40c. green	5·00	15·00
59	**F**	50c. mauve	5·00	15·00
60	**G**	90c. red	5·00	15·00
61	**H**	1f.50 blue	5·00	15·00

2 "Birth of the Republic"

1959. First Anniv of Republic.

62	**2**	15f. multicoloured	3·50	3·25
63	-	25f. lake and myrtle	75	50

DESIGN: 25f. Map and birds.

1960. Tenth African Technical Co-operation Commission. As T **62** of Cameroun.

64	50f. violet and purple	2·75	4·75

1960. Air. Olympic Games. No. 276 of French Equatorial Africa surch with Olympic rings and **XVIIe OLYMPIADE 1960 REPUBLIQUE DU TCHAD 250F.**

65	250f. on 500f. blue, black & grn	13·50	13·00

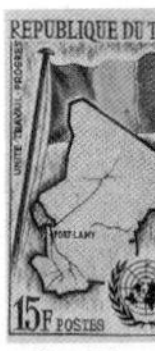

3 Flag, Map and U.N. Emblem

1961. Admission into U.N.

66	**3**	15f. multicoloured	65	25
67	**3**	25f. multicoloured	80	40
68	**3**	85f. multicoloured	2·40	1·10

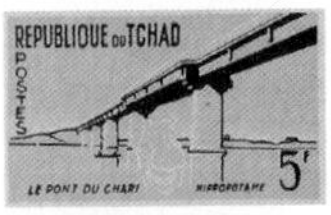

4 Shari Bridge and Hippopotamus

1961

69	-	50c. green and black	10	10
70	-	1f. green and black	10	10
71	-	2f. brown and black	10	10
72	-	3f. orange and green	10	10
73	-	4f. red and black	20	10
74	**4**	5f. lemon and black	20	20
75	-	10f. pink and black	40	25
76	-	15f. violet and black	80	30
77	-	20f. red and black	90	45
78	-	25f. blue and black	1·00	50
79	-	30f. blue and black	1·20	65
80	-	60f. yellow and black	2·30	1·00
81	-	85f. orange and black	2·50	1·20

DESIGNS (with animal silhouettes)—VERT: 50c. Biltine and Dorcas gazelle; 1f. Logone and elephant; 2f. Batha and lion; 3f. Salamat and buffalo; 4f. Ouaddai and greater kudu; 10f. Abtouyour and bullock; 15f. Bessada and Derby's eland; 20f. Tibesti and moufflon; 25f. Tikem Rocks and hartebeest; 30f. Kanem and cheetah; 60f. Borkou and oryx; 85f. Guelta D'Archei and addax.

5 Red Bishops

1961. Air.

82	**5**	50f. black, red and green	1·50	55
83	-	100f. multicoloured	4·50	1·30
84	-	200f. multicoloured	4·75	2·40
85	-	250f. blue, orange and green	10·00	4·25
86	-	500f. multicoloured	22·00	13·00

BIRDS: 100f. Scarlet-chested sunbird; 200f. African paradise flycatcher; 250f. Malachite kingfisher; 500f. Carmine bee eater.

1962. Air. "Air Afrique" Airline. As T **69** of Cameroun.

87		25f. blue, brown and black	1·00	40

1962. Malaria Eradication. As T **70** of Cameroun.

88		25f.+5f. orange	1·30	1·10

1962. Sports. As T **12** of Central African Republic. Multicoloured.

89		20f. Relay-racing (horiz) (postage)	75	60
90		50f. High-jumping (horiz)	1·80	95
91		100f. Throwing the discus (air)	3·75	1·90

The 100f. is 26×47 mm.

1962. First Anniv of Union of African and Malagasy States. As No. 328 of Cameroun.

92	**72**	30f. blue	1·30	70

1963. Freedom from Hunger. As T **76** of Cameroun.

93		25f.+5f. blue, brown & green	1·30	1·10

6 Pres. Tombalbaye

1963

94	**6**	20f. multicoloured	65	30
95	**6**	85f. multicoloured	1·70	80

1963. Air. African and Malagasy Posts and Telecommunications Union. As T **11** of Central African Republic.

96		85f. multicoloured	2·20	1·10

1963. Space Telecommunications, As Nos. 37/8 of Central African Republic.

97		25f. violet, emerald and green	85	55
98		100f. blue and pink	3·25	1·60

1963. Air. First Anniv of "Air Afrique" and Inauguration of "DC-8" Service. As T **11** of Congo Republic.

99		50f. multicoloured	2·40	1·10

1963. Air. European-African Economic Convention. As T **24** of Central African Republic.

100		50f. multicoloured	1·70	95

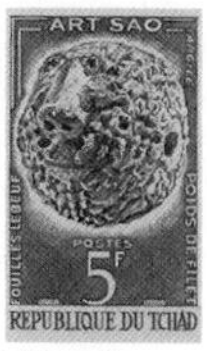

7 Carved Thread-weight

1963. Sao Art.

101	**7**	5f. orange and turquoise	20	10
102	-	15f. purple, slate and red	50	25
103	-	25f. brown and blue	1·00	70
104	-	60f. bronze and brown	2·50	1·00
105	-	80f. bronze and brown	3·00	1·30

DESIGNS: 15f. Ancestral mask; 25f. Ancestral statuette; 60f. Gazelle's-head pendant; 80f. Pectoral.

1963. 15th Anniv of Declaration of Human Rights. As Central African Republic T **26**.

106		25f. purple and green	1·00	55

8 Broussard Monoplane

1963. Air.

107	**8**	100f. blue, green & brown	3·75	1·80

9 Pottery

1964. Sao Handicrafts.

108	**9**	10f. black, orange & blue	40	25
109	-	30f. red, black and yellow	95	50
110	-	50f. black, red and green	1·50	75
111	-	85f. black, yellow & purple	2·30	1·10

DESIGNS: 30f. Canoe-building; 50f. Carpet-weaving; 85f. Blacksmith working iron.

10 Rameses II in War Chariot, Abu Simbel

1964. Air. Nubian Monuments Preservation Fund.

112	**10**	10f.+5f. violet, grn & red	90	55
113	**10**	25f.+5f. purple, grn & red	1·50	85
114	**10**	50f.+5f. turq, grn & red	3·00	1·90

1964. World Meteorological Day. As T **14** of Congo Republic.

115		50f. violet, blue and purple	1·30	75

11 Cotton

1964. Multicoloured.

116		20f. Type **11**	1·70	70
117		25f. Flamboyant tree	1·80	85

1964. Air. Fifth Anniv of Equatorial African Heads of State Conf. As T **31** of Central African Republic.

118		100f. multicoloured	2·40	1·10

12 Globe, Chimneys and Ears of Wheat

1964. Air. Europafrique.

119	**12**	50f. orange, purple & brn	1·70	85

13 Football

1964. Air. Olympic Games. Tokyo.

120	**13**	25f. green, lt green & brn	1·00	60
121	-	50f. brown, indigo & blue	1·80	1·00
122	-	100f. black, green and red	3·50	1·90
123	-	200f. black, bistre and red	6·25	3·50
MS123a		191×100 mm. Nos. 120/3	17·00	13·50

DESIGNS—VERT: 50f. Throwing the javelin; 100f. High-jumping. HORIZ: 200f. Running.

1964. Air. Pan-African and Malagasy Post and Telecommunications Congress, Cairo. As T **23** of Congo Republic.

124		25f. sepia, red and mauve	1·00	40

1964. French, African and Malagasy Co-operation. As T **88** of Cameroun.

125		25f. brown, blue and red	1·50	80

14 Pres. Kennedy

1964. Air. Pres. Kennedy Commem.

126	**14**	100f. multicoloured	2·50	1·80
MS126a		90×129 mm. No. 126 (×4)	12·00	9·75

15 National Guard

1964. Chad Army. Multicoloured.

127		20f. Type **15**	80	40
128		25f. Standard-bearer and troops of Land Forces	1·10	40

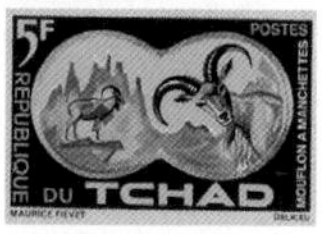

16 Barbary Sheep

1964. Fauna. Protection. Multicoloured.

129		5f. Type **16**	40	10
130		10f. Addax	70	30
131		20f. Scimitar oryx	1·30	45
132		25f. Giant eland (vert)	1·70	60
133		30f. Giraffe, African buffalo and lion (Zakouma Park)(vert)	2·30	75
134		85f. Greater kudu (vert)	5·00	1·50

17 Perforator of Olsen's Telegraph Apparatus

1965. I.T.U. Centenary.

135	**17**	30f. brown, red and green	90	40
136	-	60f. green, red and brown	1·50	75
137	-	100f. green, brown & red	2·40	1·10

DESIGNS—VERT: 60f. Milde's telephone. HORIZ: 100f. Distributor of Baudot's telegraph apparatus.

18 Badge and Mobile Gendarmes

1965. National Gendarmerie.

138	**18**	25f. multicoloured	90	50

19 ICY Emblem

1965. Air. International Co-operation Year.

139	**19**	100f. multicoloured	1·80	1·10

20 Abraham Lincoln

1965. Air. Death Centenary of Abraham Lincoln.

140	**20**	100f. multicoloured	2·50	1·30

21 Guitar

1965. Native Musical Instruments.

141	-	1f. brown & grn (postage)	10	10
142	**21**	2f. brown, purple and red	10	10
143	-	3f. lake, black and brown	10	10
144	-	15f. green, orange and red	1·00	30
145	-	60f. green and lake	2·00	1·40
146	-	100f. ultram, brn & bl (48½×27 mm) (air)	3·00	1·90

DESIGNS—VERT: 1f. Drum and seat; 3f. Shoulder drum; 60f. Harp. HORIZ: 15f. Viol; 100f. Xylophone.

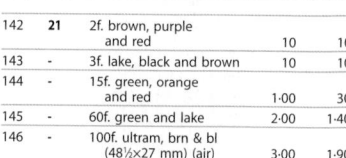

22 Sir Winston Churchill

1965. Air. Churchill Commemoration.

147	**22**	50f. black and green	1·50	85

23 Dr. Albert Schweitzer (philosopher and missionary) and "Appealing Hands"

1966. Air. Schweitzer Commemoration.

148	**23**	100f. multicoloured	3·00	1·50

24 Mask in Mortar

1966. World Festival of Negro Arts, Dakar.

149	**24**	15f. purple, bistre & blue	50	20
150	-	20f. brown, red and green	80	40
151	-	60f. purple, blue and red	1·90	90
152	-	80f. green, brown & violet	3·00	1·20

DESIGNS—Sao Art: 20f. Mask; 60f. Mask (different) (All from J. Courtin's excavations at Bouta Kebira); 80f. Armband (from INTSH excavations, Gawi).

1966. No. 94 surch.

153	**6**	25f. on 20f. multicoloured	90	55

26 WHO Building

1966. Inaug of WHO Headquarters, Geneva.

154	**26**	25f. blue, yellow and red	65	30
155	**26**	32f. blue, yellow & green	85	40

27 Caduceus and Map of Africa

1966. Central African Customs and Economic Union.

156	**27**	30f. multicoloured	90	50

28 Footballer

1966. World Cup Football Championship.

157	**28**	30f. red, green and emerald	80	40
158	-	60f. red, black and blue	1·60	75

DESIGN—VERT: 60f. Footballer (different).

29 Youths, Flag and Arms

1966. Youth Movement.

159	**29**	25f. multicoloured	90	50

30 Columns

1966. 20th Anniv of UNESCO.

160	**30**	32f. blue, violet and red	90	50

1966. Air. Inauguration of "DC-8" Air Services. As T **54** of Central African Republic.

161		30f. grey, black and green	90	40

31 Skull of Lake Chad Man ("Tchadanthropus uxoris")

1966. Archaeological Excavation.

162	**31**	30f. slate, yellow and red	2·40	1·10

32 White-throated Bee Eater

1966. Air. Birds. Multicoloured.

163	50f. Greater blue-eared glossy starling	1·60	70
164	100f. Type **32**	3·50	1·70
165	200f. African pigmy kingfisher	6·00	2·75
166	250f. Red-throated bee eater	7·75	3·00
167	500f. Little green bee eater	14·00	6·00

33 Battle-axe

1966. Prehistoric Implements.

168	**33**	25f. brown, blue and red	75	30
169	-	30f. black, brown & blue	1·00	50
170	-	85f. brown, red and blue	2·75	95
171	-	100f. brown, turq & sepia	3·25	1·40
MS172		129×99 mm. Nos. 168/71	13·00	9·25

DESIGNS: 30f. Arrowhead; 85f. Harpoon; 100f. Sandstone grindstone and pounder. From Tchad National Museum.

34 Congress Palace

1967. Air.

173	**34**	25f. multicoloured	90	40

35 Sportsmen and Dais on Map

1967. Sports Day.

174	**35**	25f. multicoloured	90	55

36 *Colotis protomedia klug*

1967. Butterflies. Multicoloured.

175	5f. Type **36**	1·40	40
176	10f. *Charaxes jasius epijasius L*	2·75	95
177	20f. *Junonia cebrene trim*	6·00	2·00
178	130f. *Danaida petiverana H.D.*	13·00	3·50

37 Lions Emblem

1967. Air. 50th Anniv of Lions International.

179	**37**	50f.+10f. multicoloured	1·80	95

38 Dagnaux's Breguet "19" Aircraft

1967. Air. First Anniv of Air Chad Airline.

180	**38**	25f. green, blue & brown	90	40
181	-	30f. indigo, green and blue	1·10	55
182	-	50f. brown, green & blue	2·10	1·20
183	-	100f. red, blue and green	3·75	1·60

DESIGNS: 30f. Latecoere "631" flying-boat; 50f. Douglas "DC-3"; 100f. Piper Cherokee "6".

1967. Air. Fifth Anniv of UAMPT. As T **66** of Central African Republic.

184		100f. brown, bistre & mve	2·40	1·10

39 H.Q. Building

1967. Opening of WHO Regional Headquarters, Brazzaville.

185	**39**	30f. multicoloured	90	50

40 Scouts and Jamboree Emblem

1967. World Scout Jamboree, Idaho. Multicoloured.

186	25f. Type **40**	80	30
187	32f. Scout and Jamboree emblem	1·10	40

41 Flour Mills

1967. Economic Development.

188	**41**	25f. slate, brown and blue	70	30
189	-	30f. blue, brown & green	90	50

DESIGN: 30f. Land reclamation, Lake Bol.

42 Woman and Harpist

1967. Bailloud Mission in the Ennedi. Rock paintings.

190		2f. choc, brn & red (post)	50	15
191		10f. red, brown and violet	1·20	40
192	**42**	15f. lake, brown and blue	1·60	40
193	-	20f. red, brown and green	3·00	1·10
194	-	25f. red, brown and blue	3·25	1·20
195	-	30f. lake, brown and blue	1·50	75
196	-	50f. lake, brown and green	2·40	1·20
197	-	100f. red, brn & grn (air)	6·75	2·10
198	-	125f. lake, brown & blue	8·00	3·00

DESIGNS: 2f. Archers; 10f. Male and female costumes; 20f. Funeral vigil; 25f. *Dispute*; 30f. Giraffes; 50f. Cameleer pursuing ostrich. (48×27 mm): 100f. Masked dancers; 125f. Hunters and hare.

43 Emblem of Rotary International

1968. Tenth Anniv of Rotary Club, Fort Lamy.

199	**43**	50f. multicoloured	1·30	75

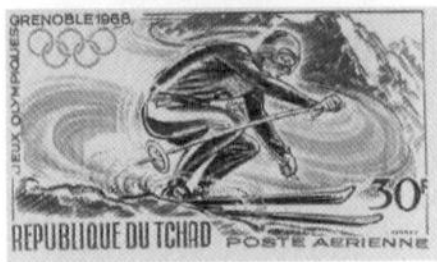

44 Downhill Skiing

1968. Air. Winter Olympic Games, Grenoble.

200	**44**	30f. brown, green & purple	1·20	60
201	-	100f. blue, green & turq	3·75	1·60

DESIGN—VERT: 100f. Ski-jumping.

45 Chancellor Adenauer

1968. Air. Adenauer Commemoration.

202	**45**	52f. brown, lilac and green	1·50	75
MS203		120×170 mm. No. 202×4	6·50	6·00

46 "Health Services"

1968. Air. Anniv of WHO.

204	**46**	25f. multicoloured	70	45
205	**46**	32f. multicoloured	90	45

47 Allegory of Irrigation

1968. International Hydrological Decade.

206	**47**	50f. blue, brown & green	1·20	50

48 *The Snake-charmer*

1968. Air. Paintings by Henri Rousseau. Multicoloured.

207	100f. Type **48**	3·75	2·10
208	130f. *The War* (49×35 mm)	5·75	3·00

49 College Building, Student and Emblem

1968. National College of Administration.

209	**49**	25f. purple, blue and red	75	30

50 Child writing and Blackboard

1968. Literacy Day.

210	**50**	60f. black, blue & brown	1·20	55

51 Harvesting Cotton

1968. Cotton Industry.

211	**51**	25f. purple, green & blue	80	30
212	-	30f. brown, blue & green	85	40

DESIGN—VERT: 30f. Loom, Fort Archambault Mill.

52 *Utetheisa pulchella*

1968. Butterflies and Moths. Multicoloured.

213	25f. Type **52**	4·00	90
214	30f. *Ophideres materna*	4·75	1·00
215	50f. *Gynanisa maja*	7·75	1·20
216	100f. *Epiphora bauhiniae*	9·50	2·40

53 Hurdling

1968. Air. Olympic Games, Mexico.

217	**53**	32f. chocolate, grn & brn	1·20	75
218	-	80f. purple, blue and red	3·00	1·40

DESIGN: 80f. Relay-racing.

54 Human Rights Emblem within Man

1968. Human Rights Year.

219	**54**	32f. red, green and blue	90	40

1969. Air. "Philexafrique" Stamp Exn, Abidjan, Ivory Coast (1st issue). As T **137** of Cameroun. Multicoloured.

220	100f. *The actor Wolf, called Bernard* (J. L. David)	4·25	3·75

1969. Air. "Philexafrique" Stamp Exn, Abidjan, Ivory Coast (2nd issue). As T **138** of Cameroun. Multicoloured.

221	50f. Moundangs dancers and Chad postage due stamp of 1930	2·75	2·50

55 G. Nachtigal and Tibesti landscape, 1869

1969. Air. Chad Explorers.

222	-	100f. violet, green & blue	2·75	1·10
223	**55**	100f. purple, blue & brown	2·75	1·10

DESIGN: No. 222, H. Barth (portrait) and aboard canoe, Lake Region, 1851.

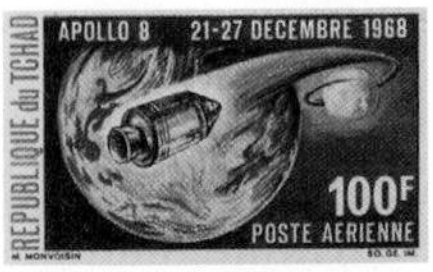

56 "Apollo 8" circling Moon

1969. Air. Flight of "Apollo 8" around the Moon.

224	**56**	100f. black, blue & orange	2·40	1·10

57 St. Bartholomew

1969. Jubilee Year of Catholic Church. Multicoloured.

225	50c. St. Paul	10	10
226	1f. St. Peter	10	10
227	2f. St. Thomas	10	10
228	5f. St. John the Evangelist	10	10
229	10f. Type **57**	15	10
230	20f. St. Matthew	35	15
231	25f. St. James the Less	40	20
232	30f. St. Andrew	55	30
233	40f. St. Jude	60	40
234	50f. St. James the Greater	75	40
235	85f. St. Philip	1·20	70
236	100f. St. Simon	1·20	80

58 Mahatma Gandhi

1969. Air. "Apostles of Peace".

237	**58**	50f. brown and green	1·50	75
238	-	50f. sepia and agate	1·50	75
239	-	50f. brown and pink	1·50	75
240	-	50f. brown and blue	1·50	75
MS241		120×160 mm. Nos. 237/40	6·75	6·50

DESIGNS: No. 238, President Kennedy; No. 239, Martin Luther King; No. 240, Robert F. Kennedy.

59 Motor Vehicles and ILO Emblem

1969. 50th Anniv of ILO.

242	**59**	32f. blue, purple & green	90	50

60 Cipolla, Baran and Sambo (pair with cox)

61 "African Woman" (Bezombes)

1969. "World Solidarity". Multicoloured. (a) Gold Medal Winners, Mexico Olympics.

243	1f. Type **60**	50	45
244	1f. R. Beamon (long-jump)	40	40
245	1f. I. Becker (women's pentathlon)	40	40
246	1f. C. Besson (women's 400 m)	40	40
247	1f. W. Davenport (110 m hurdles)	40	40
248	1f. K. Dibiasi (diving)	40	40
249	1f. R. Fosbury (high-jump)	40	40
250	1f. M. Gamoudi (5000 m)	40	40
251	1f. Great Britain (sailing)	40	40
252	1f. J. Guyon (cross-country riding)	40	40
253	1f. D. Hemery (400 m hurdles)	40	40
254	1f. S. Kato (gymnastics)	40	40
255	1f. B. Klinger (small bore rifle shooting)	40	40
256	1f. R. Matson (shot put)	40	40
257	1f. R. Matthes (100 m backstroke)	40	40
258	1f. D. Meyer (women's 200 m freestyle)	40	40
259	1f. Morelon and Trentin (tandem cycle)	40	40
260	1f. D. Rebillard (4000 m cycle pursuit)	40	40
261	1f. T. Smith (200 m)	40	40
262	1f. P. Trentin (1000 m cycle)	40	40
263	1f. F. Vianelli (196 km cycle race)	40	40
264	1f. West Germany (dressage)	40	40
265	1f. M. Wolke (welterweight boxing)	40	40
266	1f. Zimmermann and Esser (women's kayak pair)	40	40

(b) Paintings.

267	1f. Type **61**	40	40
268	1f. "Mother and Child" (Gauguin)	40	40
269	1f. "Holy Family" (Murillo) (horiz)	40	40
270	1f. "Adoration of the Kings" (Rubens)	40	40
271	1f. "Three Negroes" (Rubens)	40	40
272	1f. "Woman with Flowers" (Veneto)	40	40

62 Presidents Tombalbaye and Mobutu

1969. Air. First Anniv of Central African States Union.

273	**62**	1000f. gold, red and blue	30·00	29·00

This stamp is embossed in gold foil; colours of flags enamelled.

63 "Cochlospermum tinctorium"

1969. Flowers. Multicoloured.

274	1f. Type **63**	40	10
275	4f. *Parkia biglobosa*	65	20
276	10f. *Pancratium trianthum*	90	40
277	15f. *Ipomoea aquatica*	1·50	50

1969. Air. Birth Bicentenary of Napoleon Bonaparte. Multicoloured. As T **144** of Cameroun.

278	30f. *Napoleon visiting the Hotel des Invalides* (Veron-Bellecourt)	1·50	1·10
279	85f. *The Battle of Wagram* (H. Vernet)	3·00	1·50
280	130f. *The Battle of Austerlitz* (Gerard)	5·00	2·50

64 Frozen Carcases

1969. Frozen Meat Industry.

281	**64**	25f. red, green and orange	60	30
282	-	30f. brown, slate & green	75	40

DESIGN: 30f. Cattle and refrigerated abattoir, Farcha.

1969. Fifth Anniv of African Development Bank. As T **146** of Cameroun.

283	30f. brown, green and red	75	40

66 Astronaut and Lunar Module

1969. Air. First Man on the Moon. Embossed on gold foil.

289	**66**	1000f. gold	30·00	29·00

67 Nile Mouthbrooder

1969. Fishes.

290	**67**	2f. purple, grey and green	50	15
291	-	3f. grey, red and blue	75	25
292	-	5f. blue, yellow and ochre	1·10	35
293	-	20f. blue, green and red	3·50	90

FISHES: 3f. Deep-sided citharinid; 5f. Nile pufferfish; 20f. Lesser tigerfish.

1969. Tenth Anniv of ASECNA. As T **150** of Cameroun.

294	30f. orange	90	50

68 President Tombalbaye

1970. President Tombalbaye.

295	**68**	25f. multicoloured	75	30

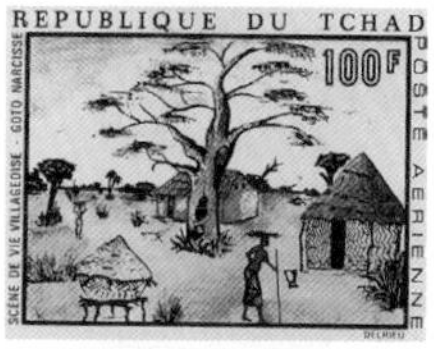

69 *Village Life* (G. Narcisse)

1970. Air. African Paintings. Multicoloured.

296	100f. Type **69**	3·50	1·50
297	250f. *Market Woman* (I. N'Diaye)	5·50	2·20
298	250f. *Flower-seller* (I. N'Diaye) (vert)	5·50	2·20

70 Lenin

1970. Birth Centenary of Lenin.

299	**70**	150f. black, cream & gold	4·25	1·90

1970. New U.P.U. Headquarters Building, Berne, As T **156** of Cameroun.

300	30f. brown, violet and red	90	50

71 Class and Torchbearers

1970. International Education Year.

301	**71**	100f. multicoloured	2·10	1·20

72 Osaka Print

1970. Air. World Fair "EXPO 70", Osaka, Japan.

302	**72**	50f. green, blue and red	90	55
303	-	100f. blue, green and red	1·50	75
304	-	125f. slate. brown & red	2·20	1·10

DESIGNS: 100f. Tower of the Sun; 125f. Osaka print (different).

1970. Air. "Apollo" Moon Flights. Nos. 164/6 surch with new value, and optd with various inscriptions and diagrams concerning space flights.

305	**32**	50f. on 100f. mult ("Apollo 11")	1·50	55
306	-	100f. on 200f. mult ("Apollo 12")	3·00	90
307	-	125f. on 250f. mult ("Apollo 13")	3·75	1·10

74 Meteorological Equipment and "Agriculture"

1970. World Meteorological Day.

308	**74**	50f. grey, green & orange	1·10	45

75 "DC-8-63" over Airport

1970. Air. "Air Afrique" DC-8 "Fort Lamy".

309	**75**	30f. multicoloured	1·20	60

76 Ahmed Mangue (Minister of Education)

1970. Ahmed Mangue (air crash victim) Commem.

310	**76**	100f. black, red and gold	1·80	75

77 Tanning

1970. Trades and Handicrafts.

311	**77**	1f. bistre, brown and blue	15	10
312	-	2f. brown, blue and green	20	10
313	-	3f. violet, brown & mauve	35	15
314	-	4f. brown, bistre & green	40	15
315	-	5f. brown, green and red	80	50

DESIGNS—VERT: 2f. Dyeing; 4f. Water-carrying. HORIZ: 3f. Milling palm-nuts for oil; 5f. Copper-founding.

78 U.N. Emblem and Dove

1970. 25th Anniv of United Nations.

316	**78**	32f. multicoloured	90	55

79 *The Visitation* (Venetian School, 15th cent)

1970. Air. Christmas. Multicoloured.

317	20f. Type **79**	80	50
318	25f. *The Nativity* (Venetian School, 15th cent)	1·20	55
319	30f. *Virgin and Child* (Veneziano)	1·40	75

80 Map and OCAM Building

1971. OCAM (Organization Commune Africaine et Malgache) Conference, Fort Lamy.

320	**80**	30f. multicoloured	90	50

81 Maritius "Post Office" 2d. of 1847

1971. Air. "PHILEXOCAM" Stamp Exhibition, Fort-Lamy.

321	**81**	10f. slate, brown & turq	55	30
322	-	20f. brown, black & turq	55	30
323	-	30f. brown, black and red	75	50
324	-	60f. black, brown & purple	1·20	60
325	-	80f. slate, brown and blue	1·80	1·10
326	-	100f. brown, slate & blue	2·20	1·50
MS327		160×130 mm. Nos. 321/6	8·75	8·25

DESIGNS—20f. Tuscany 3 lire of 1860; 30f. France 1f. of 1849; 30f., 60f. U.S.A. 10c. of 1847; 80f. Japan 5 sen of 1872; 100f. Saxony 3pf. of 1850.

82 Pres. Nasser

1971. Air. First Death Anniv of Gamal Abdel Nasser (Egypt).

328	**82**	75f. multicoloured	1·20	55

83 "Racial Harmony" Tree

1971. Racial Equality Year.

329	**83**	40f. red, green and blue	1·10	60

1971. Air. Reconciliation with Central African Republic and Zaire. As T 106 of Central African Republic.

330	100f. multicoloured	2·10	1·10

84 Map and Dish Aerial

1971. World Telecommunications Day.

331	**84**	5f. orge, red & bl (postage)	35	10
332	-	40f. green, brown & pur	95	40
333	-	50f. black, brown & red	1·10	60
334	-	125f. red, green & blue (air)	2·75	1·40

DESIGNS: 40f. Map and communications tower; 50f. Map and satellite. (48×27 mm): 125f. Map and telecommunications symbols.

85 Scouts by Camp-fire

1971. Air. World Scout Jamboree, Asagiri, Japan.

335	**85**	250f. multicoloured	5·75	2·75

86 Great Egret

1971. Air.

336	**86**	1000f. multicoloured	60·00	22·00

87 Ancient Marathon Race

1971. Air. 75th Anniv of Modern Olympic Games. Multicoloured.

337	40f. Type **87**	95	50
338	45f. Ancient stadium, Olympia	1·30	50
339	75f. Ancient wrestling	1·60	75
340	130f. Athens Stadium, 1896 Games	2·50	1·10

88 Sidney Bechet

1971. Air. Famous American Black Musicians. Multicoloured.

341	50f. Type **88**	2·00	85
342	75f. Duke Ellington	3·00	1·20
343	100f. Louis Armstrong	4·75	1·70

89 Gen. de Gaulle

1971. Air. First Death Anniv of De Gaulle.

344	-	200f. gold, blue and light blue	9·00	8·75
345	**89**	200f. gold, green & yellow	8·75	8·25
MS346		110×70 mm. Nos. 344/5 and central stamp-sized label with inscr	22·00	22·00

DESIGN: No. 344, Governor-General Felix Eboue.

1971. Air. Tenth Anniv of African and Malagasy Posts and Telecommunications Union. As T **184** of Cameroun. Multicoloured.

347	100f. Headquarters building and Sao carved animal head	1·80	1·10

90 Children's Heads

1971. 25th Anniv of UNICEF.

348	**90**	50f. blue, green & purple	1·20	55

On the above stamp, "24e" has been obliterated and "25e" inserted in the commemorative inscription.

91 Gorane Nangara Dancers

1971. Chad Dancers. Multicoloured.

349	10f. Type **91**	75	30
350	15f. Yondo initiates	1·10	45
351	30f. M'Boum (vert)	1·60	65
352	40f. Sara Kaba (vert)	2·40	90

93 Presidents Pompidou and Tombalbaye

1972. Visit of French President.

354	**93**	40f. multicoloured	1·90	85

94 Bobsleighing

1972. Air. Winter Olympic Games, Sapporo, Japan.

355	**94**	50f. red and blue	1·10	70
356	-	100f. green and purple	2·20	95

DESIGN: 100f. Slalom.

95 Human Heart

1972. World Heart Month.

357	**95**	100f. red, blue and violet	2·10	1·10

96 *Gorrizia dubiosa*

1972. Insects. Multicoloured.

358	1f. Type **96**	85	25
359	2f. *Argiope sector*	1·40	30
360	3f. *Nephila senegalense*	1·60	40
361	4f. *Oryctes boas*	2·75	55
362	5f. *Hemistigma albipunctata*	3·50	55
363	25f. *Dinothrombium tinctorium*	1·10	40
364	30f. *Bupreste sternocera H.*	1·70	45
365	40f. *Hyperechia bomboides*	2·10	50
366	50f. *Chrysis* (Hymenoptere)	2·50	70
367	100f. *Tithoes confinis* (Longicore)	4·25	1·20
368	130f. *Galeodes araba* (Solifuge)	7·00	1·90

1972. Air. UNESCO "Save Venice" Campaign. As T **191** of Cameroun. Multicoloured.

369	40f. "Harbour Panorama" (detail, Caffi)	1·80	70
370	45f. *Venice Panorama* (detail, Caffi) (horiz)	2·40	1·10
371	140f. *Grand Canal* (detail, Caffi)	4·75	2·10

97 Hurdling

1972. Olympic Games, Munich. Multicoloured.

372	50f. Type **97**	90	45
373	130f. Gymnastics	2·20	1·10
374	150f. Swimming	3·00	1·40
MS375	102×86 mm. 300f. Cycling	7·75	3·25

98 Alphonse Daudet and Scene from *Tartarin de Tarascon*

1972. Air. International Book Year.

376	**98**	100f. brown, red & purple	2·20	1·10

99 Dromedary

1972. Domestic Animals.

377	**99**	25f. brown and violet	1·30	30
378	-	30f. blue and mauve	1·70	40
379	-	40f. brown and green	2·40	55
380	-	45f. brown and blue	2·75	60

DESIGNS: 30f. Horse; 40f. Saluki hound; 45f. Goat.

100 "Luna 16" and Moon Probe

1972. Air. Russian Moon Exploration.

381	**100**	100f. violet, brown & blue	2·20	95
382	-	150f. brown, blue & purple	3·00	1·50

DESIGN—HORIZ: 150f. "Lunokhod 1" Moon vehicle.

101 Tobacco Production

1972. Economic Development.

383	**101**	40f. green, red & brown	80	40
384	-	50f. brown, green & blue	1·20	55

DESIGN: 50f. Ploughing with oxen.

102 Microscope, Cattle and Laboratory

1972. Air. 20th Anniv of Farcha Veterinary Laboratory.

385	**102**	75f. multicoloured	1·50	60

103 Massa Warrior

1972. Chad Warriors. Multicoloured.

386	15f. Type **103**	85	30
387	20f. Moudang archer	1·00	55

104 King Faisal and Pres. Tombalbaye

1972. Visit of King Faisal of Saudi Arabia. Multicoloured.

389	75f. King Faisal and Ka'aba, Mecca (air)	1·50	75
388	100f. Type **104** (postage)	2·75	1·30

105 Gen. Gowon, Pres. Tombalbaye and Map

1972. Visit of Gen. Gowon, Nigerian Head-of-State.

390	**105**	70f. multicoloured	1·10	50

106 *Madonna and Child* (G. Bellini)

1972. Air. Christmas. Paintings. Multicoloured.

391	40f. Type **106**	90	40

392		75f. *Virgin and Child* (bas-relief, Da Santivo, Dall' Occhio)	1·40	65
393		80f. *Nativity* (B. Angelico) (horiz)	2·10	80
394		90f. *Adoration of the Magi* (P. Perugino)	2·40	1·40

107 Commemorative Scroll

1972. 50th Anniv of U.S.S.R.

395	**107**	150f. multicoloured	2·20	85

108 High-jumping

1973. Second African Games, Lagos. Multicoloured.

396	50f. Type **108**	1·10	55
397	125f. Running	1·90	80
398	200f. Putting the shot	3·00	1·40
MS399	103×86 mm. 250f. Throwing the discus	4·25	2·75

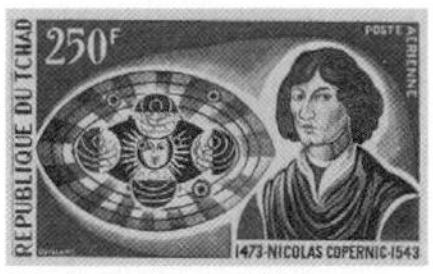
109 Copernicus and Planetary System Diagram

1973. Air. 500th Birth Anniv of Nicholas Copernicus.

400	**109**	250f. grey, brown & mve	6·00	2·50

1973. African Solidarity. "Drought Relief". No. 377 surch **SECHERESSE SOLIDARITE AFRICAINE 100F**.

401	**99**	100f. on 25f. brown & vio	2·40	1·10

1973. UAMPT. As Type **216** of Cameroun.

402	100f. green, red & brown	2·10	95

111 "Skylab" over Globe

1974. Air. "Skylab" Exploits.

403	**111**	100f. brown, red & blue	1·80	80
404	-	150f. turquoise, blue & brn	3·00	1·20

DESIGN: 150f. Close-up of "Skylab".

112 Chad Mother and Children

1974. First Anniv of Chad Red Cross.

405	**112**	30f.+10f. multicoloured	1·00	85

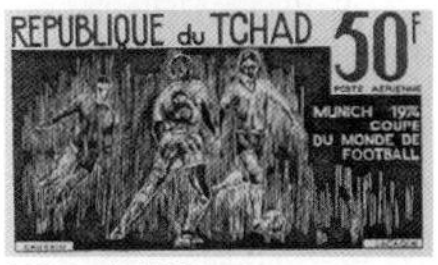
113 Football Players

1974. Air. World Cup Football Championship, West Germany.

406	**113**	50f. brown and red	75	60
407	-	125f. green and red (vert)	2·10	95
408	-	150f. red and green	2·75	1·50

DESIGNS: Nos. 407/8, Footballers in action similar to Type **113**.

114 Chad Family

1974. Air. World Population Year.

409	**114**	250f. brown, green & bl	4·50	2·40

115 U.P.C. Emblem and Mail Canoe

1974. Air. Centenary of U.P.U.

410	**115**	30f. brown, red & green	75	30
411	-	40f. black and blue	1·10	50
412	-	100f. blue, brown & blk	2·20	75
413	-	150f. violet, green & turq	3·00	1·10

DESIGNS—U.P.U. Emblem and: 40f. Electric train; 100f. Jet airliner; 150f. Satellite.

116 Rotary Emblem

1975. 70th Anniv of Rotary International.

414	**116**	50f. multicoloured	1·10	55

117 Heads of Women of Four Races

1975. Air. International Women's Year.

415	**117**	250f. multicoloured	5·25	2·50

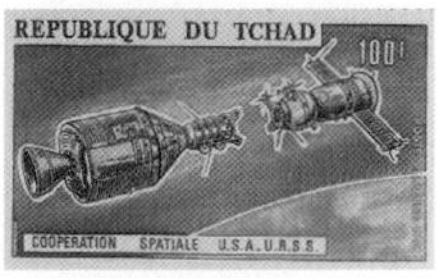
118 "Apollo" and "Soyuz" Spacecraft about to dock

1975. Air. "Apollo–Soyuz" Test Project.

416	**118**	100f. brown, blue & green	1·60	75
417	-	130f. brown, blue & green	2·10	1·00

DESIGN: 130f. "Apollo" and "Soyuz" spacecraft docked.

119 *Craterostigma plantagineum*

1975. Flowers. Multicoloured.

418	5f. Type **119**	30	10
419	10f. *Tapinanthus globiferus*	50	15
420	15f. *Commelina forsalaei* (vert)	75	20
421	20f. *Adenium obasum*	90	25
422	25f. *Hibiscus esulenus*	1·50	30
423	30f. *Hibiscus sabdariffa*	1·70	50
424	40f. *Kigelia africana*	2·40	75

120 Football

1975. Air. Olympic Games, Montreal (1976).

425	**120**	75f. green and red	1·10	55
426	-	100f. brown, blue & red	1·80	80
427	-	125f. blue and brown	2·10	1·20

DESIGNS: 100f. Throwing the discus; 125f. Running.

1975. Air. Successful Rendezvous of "Apollo–Soyuz" Mission. Optd **JONCTION 17 JUILLET 1975**.

428	**118**	100f. brown, blue & grn	1·70	95
429	-	130f. brown, blue & grn	2·30	1·50

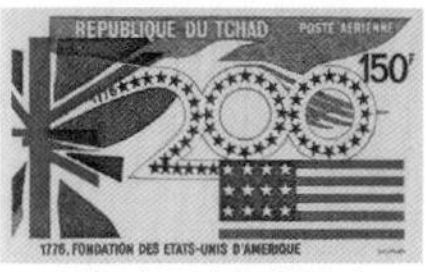
122 Stylized British and American Flags

1975. Air. Bicentenary of American Revolution.

430	**122**	150f. blue, red & brown	2·75	1·20

123 *Adoration of the Shepherds* (Murillo)

1975. Air. Christmas. Religious Paintings. Multicoloured.

431	40f. Type **123**	85	55
432	75f. *Adoration of the Shepherds* (G. de la Tour)	1·60	80
433	80f. *Virgin of the Bible* (R. van der Weyden) (vert)	1·80	80
434	100f. *Holy Family with the Lamb* (attrib. Raphael) (vert)	2·75	1·40

124 Alexander Graham Bell and Satellite

1976. Telephone Centenary.

435	**124**	100f. multicoloured	1·70	75
436	**124**	125f. multicoloured	2·50	1·10

125 U.S.S.R. (ice hockey)

1976. Winter Olympics. Medal-winners, Innsbruck. Multicoloured.

437	60f. Type **125** (postage)	95	50
438	90f. Ski-jumping (K. Schnabl, Austria)	1·40	50
439	250f. Bobsleighing (West Germany) (air)	3·25	1·10
440	300f. Speed-skating (J. E. Storholt, Norway)	4·00	1·50
MS441	103×78 mm. 500f. F. Klamner of Austria (downhill skiing)	6·50	2·75

These stamps were not issued without overprints.

126 Paul Revere (after Copley) and his Night Ride

1976. Air. Bicentenary of American Revolution.. Multicoloured.

442	100f. Type **126**	1·20	30
443	125f. Washington (after Stuart) and *Washington crossing the Delaware* (detail, Leutze)	1·50	50
444	150f. Lafayette offering his services to America	2·10	65
445	200f. Rochambeau and detail *Siege of Yorktown* (Couder)	2·40	95
446	250f. Franklin (after Duplessis) and *Declaration of Independence* (detail, Trumball)	3·75	1·10
MS447	103×78 mm. 400f. De Grasse (after Mauzaisse) and *Battle of Virginia Capes* (detail, Zveg)	6·50	2·75

127 Hurdles

1976. Olympic Games, Montreal. Multicoloured.

448	45f. Type **127** (postage)	90	30
449	100f. Boxing (air)	1·50	60
450	200f. Pole vaulting	2·75	90
451	300f. Putting the shot	3·75	1·20
MS452	103×77 mm. 500f. Sprint	6·50	2·75

128 Launch of "Viking"

1976. "Viking" landing on Mars. Multicoloured.

453	45f. Type **128** (postage)	60	30
454	90f. Trajectory of flight	1·50	50
455	100f. Descent to Mars (air)	1·10	45
456	200f. "Viking" in flight	2·40	65
457	250f. "Viking" on landing approach	3·00	1·10
MS458	114×89 mm. 450f. "Viking" on Mars	5·00	1·90

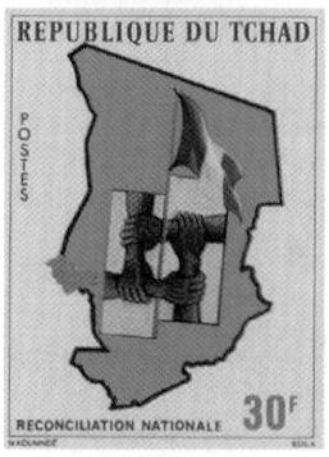
129 Flag and Clasped Hands on Map of Chad

1976. National Reconciliation. Multicoloured.

459	30f. Type **129**	65	30
460	60f. Type **129**	1·20	60
461	120f. Map, people and various occupations	2·75	1·20

130 Release of Political Prisoners

1976. First Anniv of April 1st Revolution. Multicoloured.

462	30f. Type **130**	35	20
463	60f. Officer-cadets on parade	85	55
464	120f. Type **130**	1·80	85

131 Concorde

1976. Air. Concorde's First Commercial Flight.

465	**131**	250f. blue, red & black	6·50	3·75

132 Gourd and Ladle

1976. Pyrograved Gourds.

466	**132**	30f. multicoloured	60	30
467	-	60f. multicoloured	95	45
468	-	120f. multicoloured	1·90	95

DESIGNS: 60f., 120f. Gourds with different decorations.

1976. Nobel Prizewinners. As T **189** of Central African Empire. Multicoloured.

469	45f. Robert Koch (Medicine, 1905)	1·50	55
470	90f. Anatole France (Literature, 1921)	1·80	80
471	100f. Albert Einstein (Physics, 1921) (air)	2·20	55
472	200f. Dag Hammarskjold (Peace, 1961)	2·75	80
473	300f. Dr. S. Tomonaga (Physics, 1965)	4·25	1·10
MS474	116×79 mm. 500f. Alexander Fleming (Medicine, 1945)	9·00	3·00

133 *The Nativity* (Hans Holbein)

1976. Air. Christmas. Multicoloured.

475	30f. *The Nativity* (Altdorfer)	60	30
476	60f. Type **133**	90	50
477	120f. *Adoration of the Shepherds* (Honthorst) (horiz)	1·60	95
478	150f. *Adoration of the Magi* (David) (horiz)	2·40	1·40

134 *Lesdiguieres Bridge*

1976. Air. Centenary of Impressionism. Paintings by Johan Bathold Jongkind. Multicoloured.

479	100f. Type **134**	1·90	1·10
480	120f. *Warship*	2·20	1·10

1977. Zeppelin Flights. As T **190** of Central African Empire. Multicoloured.

481	100f. Friedrichshafen and German 50pf. stamp, 1936 (postage)	2·10	1·70
482	125f. Polar scene and German 1m. stamp, 1931 (air)	2·00	60
483	150f. Chicago store and German 4m. stamp, 1933	3·25	75
484	175f. New York, London and German 2m. stamp, 1928	3·75	90
485	200f. New York and U.S. $2.60 stamp, 1930	4·00	1·40
MS486	130×92 mm. 500f. As No. 485	8·75	2·75

1977. Air. Tenth Anniv of International French Language Council. As T **204** of Benin.

487	100f. multicoloured	1·10	65

135 Simon Bolivar

1977. Great Personalities. Multicoloured.

488	150f. Type **135**	1·70	65
489	175f. Joseph J. Roberts	2·30	80
490	200f. Queen Wilhelmina	3·00	1·10
491	200f. General de Gaulle	3·50	1·30
493	250f. Coronation of Queen Elizabeth II (horiz)	3·75	1·50
492	325f. King Baudouin and Queen Fabiola	4·25	1·60

136 Queen Elizabeth II

1977. 25th Anniv of Queen Elizabeth II's Accession to Throne Multicoloured.

493a	250f. Type **136**	2·50	90
MS494	110×91 mm. 450f. Queen Elizabeth and Prince Philip	6·50	2·40

137 Lafayette and Arrival in America

1977. Air. Bicentenary of American Independence. Multicoloured.

495	100f. Type **137**	1·50	65
496	120f. Abraham Lincoln	1·90	80
497	150f. F. J. Madison	2·50	1·10

138 Radio Aerial, Sound Waves and Map

1977. Posts and Telecommunications Emblems.

498	-	30f. black and yellow	60	30
499	**138**	60f. multicoloured	90	40
500	-	120f. multicoloured	1·70	95

DESIGNS—HORIZ (47×26 mm): 30f. Posthorn and initials "ONPT". VERT (26×36 mm): 120f. Telecommunications skyline and initials "TIT".

139 Concorde

1977. Air. "North Atlantic"—Concorde and Lindbergh Commemorations.

501	**139**	100f. blue, red & lt blue	2·30	1·20
502	-	120f. brown, blue & grn	1·40	75
503	-	150f. violet, red & green	1·80	1·10
504	-	200f. orange, pur & brn	2·40	1·20
505	-	300f. blue, purple & blk	3·50	1·80

DESIGNS: 120f. to 300f. Various portraits of Lindbergh with *Spirit of St. Louis* against different backgrounds.

140 "Mariner 10"

1977. Air. Space Research.

506	**140**	100f. blue, olive & green	1·20	85
507	-	200f. brown, green & red	2·40	1·40
508	-	300f. brown, grn & bistre	3·50	1·80

DESIGNS: 200f. "Luna 21"; 300f. "Viking".

141 Running

1977. Air. Sports.

509	**141**	30f. brown, red & blue	40	25
510	-	60f. brown, blue & orge	90	50
511	-	120f. multicoloured	1·50	80
512	-	125f. mauve, violet & grn	2·10	1·00

DESIGNS: 60f. Volleyball; 120f. Football; 125f. Basketball.

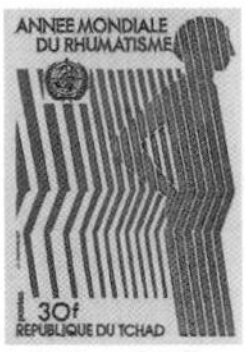

142 "Back Pain"

1977. World Rheumatism Year.

513	**142**	30f. red, green and violet	60	30
514	-	60f. red, violet and green	1·00	50
515	-	120f. blue, red & lt blue	1·70	1·00

DESIGNS—HORIZ: 60f. "Neck pain". VERT: 120f. "Knee pain".

1977. Air. First Commercial Paris–New York Flight of Concorde. Optd **PARIS NEW-YORK 22.11.77.**

516	**139**	100f. blue, red & lt blue	3·50	1·80

144 Saving a Goal

1977. World Football Cup Championship. Multicoloured.

517	40f. Type **144**	55	15
518	60f. Heading the ball	80	30
519	100f. Referee	1·50	50
520	200f. Foot kicking ball	3·00	95
521	300f. Pele (Brazilian player)	4·50	1·30
MS522	118×80 mm. 500f. Helmut Schoen and stadium	6·50	2·75

145 *Christ in the Manger* (detail)

1977. Air. Christmas. Paintings by Rubens. Multocoloured.

523	30f. Type **145**	75	35
524	60f. *Virgin and Child with Two Donors*	1·50	60
525	100f. *The Adoration of the Shepherds*	2·10	85
526	125f. *The Adoration of the Magi* (detail)	2·30	1·20

1978. Coronation of Queen Elizabeth II. No. 493 **MS**494 optd **ANNIVERSAIRE DU COURONNEMENT 1953–1978**.

527	250f. multicoloured	3·25	1·90
MS528	111×92 mm. 450f. multicoloured	6·75	4·00

147 Antoine de Saint-Exupery

1978. Air. History of Aviation. Multicoloured.

529	40f. Type **147**	75	30
530	50f. Wright Brothers and aircraft in flight	90	50
531	80f. Hugo Junkers	1·20	65
532	100f. Italo Balbo	1·70	85
533	120f. "Concorde"	2·00	1·00
MS534	104×98 mm. 500f. Wright Brothers and aircraft on ground	7·50	2·75

1978. Air. "Philexafrique" Stamp Exhibition, Gabon (1st issue), and International Stamp Fair, Essen. As T **237** of Benin. Multicoloured.

535	100f. Grey heron and Mecklenburg-Strelitz, ¼sgr. stamp, 1864	3·75	2·40
536	100f. Black rhinoceros and Chad 500f. stamp, 1961	3·75	2·40

148 *Portrait*

1978. 450th Death Anniv of Albrecht Durer (artist). Multicoloured.

537	60f. Type **148**	65	20
538	150f. *Jacob Muffel*	2·10	50
539	250f. *Young Girl*	3·25	95
540	350f. *Oswolt Krel*	5·00	1·20

149 *Helene Fourment*

1978. 400th Birth Anniv of Peter Paul Rubens (artist). Multicoloured.

541	60f. *Abraham and Melchisedek* (horiz)	95	20
542	120f. Type **149**	2·00	40
543	200f. *David and the Elders of Israel* (horiz)	3·00	95
544	300f. *Anne of Austria*	5·25	1·20
MS545	78×104 mm. 500f. *Marie de Medici*	7·25	2·75

150 Head and Unhealthy and Healthy Villages

1978. National Health Day.

546	**150**	60f. multicoloured	1·10	55

1978. World Cup Football Championship Finalists. Nos. 517/21 optd with teams and scores of past finals.

547	**144**	40f. multicoloured	55	30
548	-	60f. multicoloured	80	45
549	-	100f. multicoloured	1·60	75
550	-	200f. multicoloured	3·00	1·40
551	-	300f. multicoloured	4·50	2·20
MS552		118×80 mm. 500f. multicoloured	6·50	6·00

OPTS: 40f. **1962 BRESIL-TCHECOSLOVAQUE 3-1**; 60f. **1966 GRANDE BRETAGNE ALLEMAGNE (RFA) 4-2**; 100f. **1970 BRESIL-ITALIE 4-1**; 200f. **1974 ALLEMAGNE (RFA)-PAYS BAS 2-1**; 300f. **1978 ARGENTINE-PAYS BAS 3-1**; 500f. **ARGENTINE-PAYS BAS 3-1**.

152 Camel Riders, Satellites and UPU Emblem

1978. "Philexafrique 2" Exhibition, Libreville, Gabon (2nd issue).

553	**152**	60f. red, mauve & blue	3·00	1·70
554	-	150f. multicoloured	5·00	3·00

DESIGN: 150f. Mother and child, native village and hibiscus.

153 Sand Gazelle

1979. Endangered Animals. Multicoloured.

555	40f. Type **153**	1·40	25
556	50f. Addax	1·50	45
557	60f. Scimitar oryx	1·80	70
558	100f. Cheetah	3·00	1·20
559	150f. African ass	4·50	1·60
560	300f. Black rhinoceros	8·75	2·00

154 African Boy and Wall Painting

1979. International Year of the Child. Multicoloured.

561	65f. Type **154**	75	20
562	75f. Asian girl	90	40
563	100f. European child and doves	1·10	50
564	150f. African boys and drawing of boats	1·80	75
MS565	103×77 mm. 250f. Pencil and drawing of hands	3·50	1·70

155 *The Holy Family with There Hares* (woodcut)

1979. 450th Death Anniv (1978) of Albrecht Durer (artist). Sheet 90×115 mm.

MS566	**155** 500f. lake and brown	7·75	2·40

1979. Tenth Anniv of "Apollo 11" Moon Landing. Nos. 453/7 optd with lunar module and **ALUNISSAGE APOLLO XI JUILLET 1969**.

567	45f. Type **128** (postage)	65	30
568	90f. Trajectory of flight	1·20	50
569	100f. Descent on Mars (air)	1·20	70
570	200f. "Viking" in flight	2·30	1·20
571	250f. "Viking" on landing approach	3·00	1·60
MS572	114×89 mm. 450f. multicoloured	5·50	5·25

157 Hurdles

1979. Air. Olympic Games, Moscow 1980. Multicoloured.

573	15f. Type **157**	15	10
574	30f. Hockey	35	25
575	250f. Swimming	2·75	95
576	350f. Running	3·75	1·20
MS577	117×80 mm. 500f. Yachting	6·75	2·75

158 Reed Canoe and Austrian 10k. stamp, 1910

1979. Air. Death Centenary of Sir Rowland Hill. Multicoloured.

578	65f. Type **158**	90	10
579	100f. Sailing canoe and U.S. $1 stamp of 1894	1·50	50
580	200f. *Curacao* (paddle- steamer) and French 1f. stamp of 1853	2·75	85
581	300f. *Calypso* (liner) and Holstein 1¼s. stamp of 1864	3·25	1·10
MS582	103×91 mm. 500f. Liner and Chad 10c. Postage Due stamps of 1930	7·25	2·75

159 Slalom

1979. Winter Olympic Games, Lake Placid (1980). Multicoloured.

583	20f. Type **159**	35	10
584	40f. Biathlon	60	10
585	60f. Ski jump (horiz)	90	20
586	150f. Women's giant slalom	1·80	50
587	350f. Cross-country skiing (horiz)	3·50	1·20
588	500f. Downhill skiing (horiz)	5·25	1·80

160 Concorde and Map of Africa

1980. 20th Anniv of African Air Safety Organization (ASECNA).

589	**160** 15f. multicoloured	15	10
590	**160** 30f. multicoloured	35	15
591	**160** 60f. multicoloured	65	30

1981. Various stamps optd **POSTES 1981** or surch also.

592	**157** 30f. on 15f. multicoloured	1·30	85
593	- 30f. mult (No. 574)	1·30	85
594	**158** 60f. on 65f. multicoloured	2·40	1·60
595	- 60f. on 100f. mult (No. 579)	2·40	1·60

162 Footballer

1982. World Cup Football Championship, Spain. Multicoloured.

596	30f. Hungary (postage)	35	10
597	40f. Type **162**	55	10
598	50f. Algeria	55	30
599	60f. Argentina	65	40
600	80f. Brazil (air)	1·00	45
601	300f. West Germany	3·50	1·00
MS602	77×100 mm. 500f. Spain (38×48 mm)	6·50	2·20

DESIGNS: As T **162** but each value showing different team's footballer.

163 Lady Diana and her Brother (1967)

1982. 21st Birthday of Princess of Wales. Multicoloured.

603	30f. Lady Diana in christening robe (1961) (postage)	45	10
604	40f. Portrait of Lady Diana (1965)	50	15
605	50f. Type **163**	75	30
606	60f. Lady Diana and her pony (1975)	80	40
607	80f. Lady Diana in Switzerland (1977) (air)	1·00	40
608	300f. Lady Diana as nursery teacher (1980)	3·50	1·10
MS609	78×75 mm. 500f. Princess of Wales (39×36 mm)	6·00	1·90

164 West German Scouts

1982. 75th Anniv of Scout Movement. Multicoloured.

610	30f. Type **164** (postage)	55	10
611	40f. Upper Volta scouts	55	15
612	50f. Mali scouts and African dancers	75	30
613	60f. Scottish scout, piper and dancer	80	40
614	80f. Kuwait scouts (air)	1·00	40
615	300f. Chad cub scout	3·50	1·10
MS616	110×74 mm. 500f. Chad scouts (53×35 mm)	5·50	1·90

165 Judo

1982. Olympic Games, Los Angeles (1984) (1st issue). Multicoloured.

617	30f. Gymnastics (horse exercise) (postage)	35	10
618	40f. Show jumping	55	15
619	50f. Type **165**	55	30
620	60f. High jumping	65	40
621	80f. Hurdling (air)	1·00	40
622	300f. Gymnastics (floor exercise)	3·50	1·10
MS623	110×82 mm. 500f. Relay (56×38 mm)	5·50	1·90

See also Nos. 678/**MS**684 and 735/**MS**739.

1982. Birth of Prince William of Wales. Nos. 603/8 optd **21 JUIN 1982 WILLIAM ARTHUR PHILIP LOUIS PRINCE DE GALLES**.

624	30f. Type **163** (postage)	55	10
625	40f. Portrait of Lady Diana as a young girl	55	10
626	50f. Lady Diana and her brother	75	30
627	60f. Lady Diana with her pony	80	30
628	80f. Lady Diana in Switzerland (air)	90	30
629	300f. Lady Diana with children	3·50	1·30
MS630	78×75 mm. 500f. Portrait (39×36 mm)	5·50	2·75

167 Marco Tardelli (Italy) and Passarella (Argentine)

1983. World Cup Football Championship Results. Multicoloured.

631	30f. Type **167** (postage)	55	10
632	40f. Paolo Rossi (Italy) and Zico (Brazil)	55	15
633	50f. Pierre Littbarski (West Germany) and Platini (France)	75	30
634	60f. Gabriele Oriali (Italy) and Smolarek (Poland)	80	40
635	70f. Boniek (Poland) and Alain Giresse (France) (air)	90	40
636	300f. Bruno Conti (Italy) and Paul Breitner (West Germany)	3·25	1·10
MS637	110×79 mm. 500f. Rummenigge (West Germany) and Paolo Rossi (Italy) (56×32 mm)	6·25	2·30

168 Philidor and 19th-century European Rook

1982. Chess Grand Masters. Multicoloured.

638	30f. Type **168** (postage)	85	10
639	40f. Paul Morphy and 19th-century Chinese knight	1·00	15
640	50f. Howard Staunton and Lewis knight	1·30	30
641	60f. Jean-Paul Capablanca and African knight	1·40	40
642	80f. Boris Spassky and Staunton knight (air)	2·10	55
643	300f. Anatoly Karpov and 19th-century Chinese knight	4·25	1·10
MS644	98×80 mm. 500f. Victor Kortschnoi and modern chess pieces (53×35 mm)	9·50	2·75

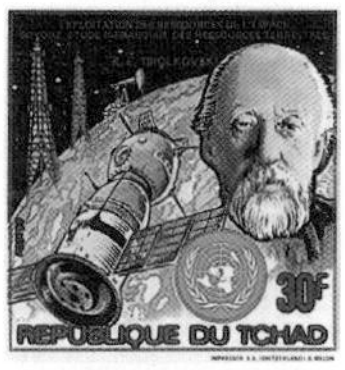

169 K. E. Tsiolkovski and "Soyuz"

1983. Exploitation of Space. Multicoloured.

645	30f. Type **169** (postage)	55	10
646	40f. R. H. Goddard and space telescope	55	15
647	50f. Korolev and ultra-violet telescope	75	30
648	60f. Von Braun and Space Shuttle	60	30
649	80f. Esnault Pelterie and "Ariane" rocket and "Symphonie" satellite (air)	1·00	40
650	300f. H. Oberth and construction of orbiting space station	3·50	1·10
MS651	85×85 mm. 500f. J.F.Kennedy and first man on the Moon (vert 41×50 mm)	6·25	2·30

170 Charles and Robert Balloon, 1783

1983. Air. Balloons. Multicoloured.

652	100f. Type **170**	85	25
653	200f. Blanchard balloon, Berlin, 1788	1·80	50
654	300f. Charles Green balloon, London, 1837 (horiz)	2·40	80
655	400f. Modern advertising airship (horiz)	3·00	1·00
MS656	79×98 mm. 500f. Montgolfiere balloon, 1783	6·50	2·30

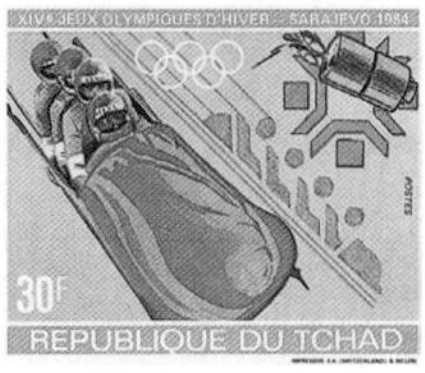

171 Bobsleigh

1983. Winter Olympic Games, Sarajevo. Multicoloured.

657	30f. Type **171** (postage)	55	10
658	40f. Speed skating	55	15
659	50f. Cross-country skiing	75	30
660	60f. Ice hockey	80	40
661	80f. Ski jump (air)	1·00	40
662	300f. Downhill skiing	3·50	1·10
MS663	100×80 mm. 500f. Ice dancing	5·50	2·20

172 Montgolfier Brothers and *Le Martia* Balloon, 1783

1983. Bicentenary of Manned Flight. Multicoloured.

664	25f. Type **172** (postage)	35	10
665	45f. Pilatre de Rozier and first manned flight, 1783	75	25
666	50f. Jacques Garnerin and balloon (first parachute descent, 1797)	75	30
667	60f. J. P. Blanchard and balloon at Chelsea, 1784	85	70
668	80f. H. Giffard and steam- powered dirigible, 1852 (air)	1·10	40
669	250f. Zeppelin and airship **L 21**, 1900	3·25	1·10
MS670	57×95 mm. 300f. Montgolfier Brothers and ascent of La Flesselles (41×38 mm)	6·25	1·90

173 Gottlieb Daimler, Karl Benz and Mercedes "Type S," 1927

1983. Car Manufacturers. Multicoloured.

671	25f. Type **173** (postage)	40	10
672	35f. Friedrich von Martini and Torpedo, Martini "Type GC 32", 1913	75	15
673	50f. Walter P. Chrysler and Chrysler "70", 1926	75	30
674	60f. Nicola Romeo and Alfa Romeo "6 C 1750 Grand Sport", 1929	85	40
675	80f. Stewart Rolls, Henry Royce and "Phantom II Continental", 1934 (air)	1·50	40
676	250f. Lord Shrewsbury and Talbot-Lago "Record", 1948	3·75	1·10
MS677	109×68 mm. 300f. Ettore Bugatti and Royale Coupe de Ville "41", 1926–33	4·25	1·60

174 Kayak

1983. Olympic Games, Los Angeles (2nd issue). Multicoloured.

678	25f. Type **174** (postage)	35	10
679	45f. Long jumping	75	15
680	50f. Boxing	75	30
681	60f. Discus-throwing	85	40
682	80f. Relay race (air)	1·10	40
683	350f. Horse jumping	3·75	1·10
MS684	90×93 mm. 500f. Gymnastics (horiz 50×41 mm)	5·00	1·60

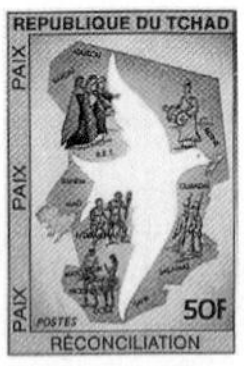

175 Dove on Map

1983. Peace and Reconciliation. Multicoloured.

685	50f. Type **175** (postage)	60	15
686	50f. Foodstuffs on map	60	15
687	50f. President Habre	80	20
688	60f. As No. 687	75	15
689	80f. Type **175**	85	30
690	80f. As No. 686	90	30
691	80f. As No. 687	1·20	30
692	100f. As No. 687	1·00	30
693	150f. Type **175** (air)	1·80	55
694	150f. As No. 686	1·80	55
695	200f. Type **175**	2·50	80
696	200f. As No. 686	2·50	80

1983. 15th World Scout Jamboree, Canada. Nos. 610/15 optd **XV WORLD JAMBOREE MONDIAL ALBERTA CANADA 1983**.

697	30f. multicoloured (postage)	35	10
698	40f. multicoloured	45	10
699	50f. multicoloured	55	20
700	60f. multicoloured	65	20
701	80f. multicoloured (air)	80	45
702	300f. multicoloured	3·25	1·60

1983. 60th Anniv of Int Chess Federation. Nos. 638/43 optd **60e ANNIVERSAIRE FEDERATION MONDIAL D'ECHECS 1924–1984**.

704	30f. multicoloured (postage)	1·00	10
705	40f. multicoloured	1·30	20
706	50f. multicoloured	1·70	30
707	60f. multicoloured	2·00	45
708	80f. multicoloured (air)	2·50	65
709	300f. multicoloured	5·00	2·20
MS710	98×80 mm. 500f. multicoloured	9·00	4·00

178 Chad Martyrs

1984. Celebrities. Multicoloured.

711	50f. Type **178** (postage)	60	15
712	200f. P. Harris and Rotary Headquarters, U.S.A.	2·20	50
713	300f. Alfred Nobel and will	3·75	90
714	350f. Raphael and *Virgin with the Infant and St. John the Baptist*	5·25	1·10
715	400f. Rembrandt and *The Holy Family* (air)	5·25	1·10
716	500f. Goethe and Scenes from *Faust*	6·50	1·40
MS717	78×86 mm. 600f. Rubens and *Helene Fourment and two of her Children*	7·75	2·40

179 Martyrs Memorial

1984. Martyrs Memorial.

718	**179**	50f. mult (postage)	60	10
719	**179**	80f. multicoloured	90	25
720	**179**	120f. multicoloured	1·20	40
721	**179**	200f. multicoloured (air)	2·40	75
722	**179**	250f. multicoloured	3·00	1·00

180 Durer and Painting

1984. Celebrities and Events. Multicoloured.

723	50f. Type **180** (postage)	1·10	10
724	200f. Henri Dunant and battle scene	2·40	50
725	300f. Early telephone and satellite receiving station, Goonhilly Downs	3·25	80
726	350f. President Kennedy and first foot-print on Moon	4·00	95
727	400f. Infra-red satellite picture (Europe–Africa co-operation) (air)	4·75	1·10
728	500f. Prince and Princess of Wales	5·50	1·40
MS729	60×110 mm. 600f. Wedding of Prince and Princess of Wales	6·50	1·90

181 "Communications"

1984. World Communications Year.

730	**181**	50f. mult (postage)	55	10
731	**181**	60f. multicoloured	75	15
732	**181**	70f. multicoloured	90	30
733	**181**	125f. multicoloured (air)	1·50	35
734	**181**	250f. multicoloured	2·75	1·10

182 Two-man Kayak

1984. Air. Olympic Games, Los Angeles (3rd issue). Multicoloured.

735	100f. Type **182**	1·10	45
736	200f. Kayaks (close-up)	2·20	85
737	300f. One-man kayak	2·75	1·30
738	400f. Coxed fours	3·75	1·70
MS739	104×80 mm. 500f. Coxless four	5·25	2·75

183 Class 13 Kitson Steam Locomotive

1984. Historic Transport. Multicoloured.

740	50f. Type **183** (postage)	95	25
741	200f. Sailing boat on Lake Chad	2·50	90
742	300f. Graf Zeppelin (airship)	4·75	1·40
743	350f. Six-wheel Renault automobile, 1930	4·50	1·70
744	400f. Bloch "120" airplane (air)	4·75	1·90
745	500f. Douglas "DC-8" airplane	5·75	2·30
MS746	84×109 mm. 600f. Ariane space rocket and "Intelsat V" communications satellite	6·75	4·00

184 African with broken Manacles

1984. Second Anniv of Entrance of Government Forces in N'Djamena.

747	**184**	50f. multicoloured	75	40

185 Pres. Hissein Habre

1984

748	**185**	125f. black, blue & yellow	1·80	75

186 British East Indiaman

1984. Transport. Multicoloured. (a) Ships.

749	90f. Type **186**	1·20	50
750	125f. *Vera Cruz* (steamer)	1·90	75
751	200f. *Carlisle Castle* (sail merchantman)	3·25	1·20
752	300f. *Britannia* (steamer)	4·50	1·60

(b) Locomotives.

753	100f. Series 701, 1885, France	1·60	45
754	150f. *Columbia*, 1888, Belgium	1·90	75
755	250f. Mediterranean locomotive, 1900, Italy	3·25	1·10
756	350f. MAV 114	4·50	1·70

187 Virgin and Child

1984. Christmas.

757	**187**	50f. brown and blue	60	20
758	**187**	60f. brown and orange	70	30
759	**187**	80f. brown and green	90	45
760	**187**	85f. brown and purple	60	40
761	**187**	100f. brown and orange	1·50	55
762	**187**	135f. brown and blue	1·60	85

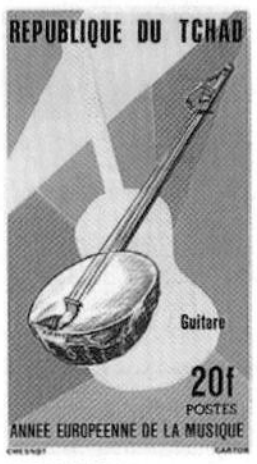

188 Guitars

1985. European Music Year. Multicoloured.

763	20f. Type **188**	30	10
764	25f. Harps	35	10
765	30f. Xylophones	40	20
766	50f. Drums	55	40
767	70f. As No. 766	90	45
768	80f. As No. 764	1·10	50
769	100f. Type **188**	1·50	70
770	250f. As No. 765	3·00	1·40

189 *Chlorophyllum molybdites*

1985. Fungi. Multicoloured.

771	25f. Type **189**	50	10
772	30f. *Tulostoma volvulatum*	70	10
773	50f. *Lentinus tuberregium*	90	40
774	70f. As No. 773	1·30	50
775	80f. *Podaxis pistillaris*	1·50	55
776	100f. Type **189**	2·20	85

190 Stylized Tree and Scout

1985. Air. "Philexafrique" Stamp Exhibition, Lome, Togo (1st issue). Multicoloured.

777	200f. Type **190**	3·00	2·30
778	200f. Fokker "27" airplane	3·00	2·30

See also Nos. 808/9.

191 Abraham Lincoln

1985. Celebrities. Multicoloured.

779	25f. Type **191** (postage)	35	10
780	45f. Henri Dunant (founder of Red Cross)	80	10
781	50f. Gottlieb Daimler (automobile designer)	85	20
782	60f. Louis Bleriot (pilot) (air)	1·00	30
783	80f. Paul Harris (founder of Rotary International)	1·10	50
784	350f. Auguste Piccard (undersea explorer)	5·00	1·70
MS785	78×75 mm. 600f. Anatoly Karpov (chess champion)	7·75	4·25

192 Figures within Geometric Pattern

1985. International Youth Year. Multicoloured.

786	70f. Type **192**	80	35
787	200f. Figures on ribbon around globe	2·00	1·20

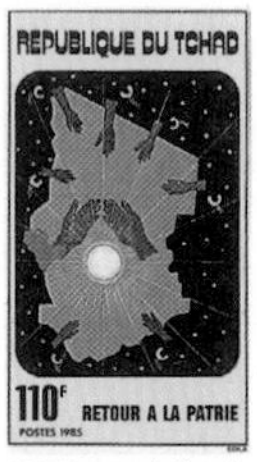

193 Sun and Hands breaking through Darkness

1985. Third Anniv of Entrance of Government Forces in N'DJamena. Multicoloured.

788	70f. Type **193**	85	40
789	70f. Claw attacking hand	85	40
790	70f. Pres. Hissein Habre (36×48 mm)	85	40
791	110f. Type **193**	1·50	85
792	110f. As No. 789	1·50	85
793	110f. As No. 790	1·50	85

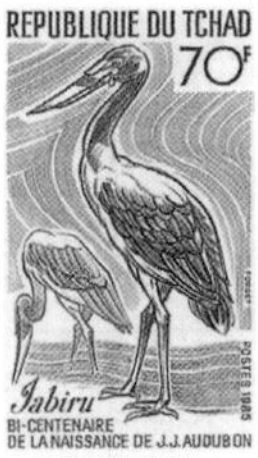

194 Saddle-bill Stork ("Jabiru")

1985. Birth Bicentenary of John J. Audubon (ornithologist).

794	**194**	70f. black, blue & brown	1·20	60
795	-	110f. olive, green & brown	1·70	85
796	-	150f. blue, red and olive	2·40	1·20

797	-	200f. dp blue, mauve & bl	3·25	1·80

MS798	129×100 mm. 500f. sepia, brown and olive	7·25	6·75

DESIGNS: 110f. Ostrich; 150f. Marabou stork; 200, 500f. Crested serpent eagle.

195 Fokker Friendship, Farman M.F.11 and Emblem

1985. Air. 25th Anniv of ASECNA (navigation agency). Multicoloured.

799	70f. Type **195**	90	45
800	110f. Fokker F.27 *Friendship* and *Spirit of St. Louis*	1·50	65
801	250f. Fokker "F.27" *Friendship* and Vickers Vimy	2·75	1·60

196 Sitatunga

1985. Mammals.

802	**196**	50f. brown, bl & dp brn	85	50
803	-	70f. brown, green and red	1·10	75
804	-	250f. multicoloured	3·75	2·30

MS805	130×100 mm. 500f. black, red and turquoise	6·50	5·75

DESIGNS—HORIZ:70f. Greater kudus; 500f. White rhinoceros. VERT: 250f. Bearded mouflons.

197 U.N. Emblem on Peace Dove and Girl with Flowers

1985. 40th Anniv of UNO and 25th Anniv of U.N. Membership.

806	**197**	200f. blue, red & brown	2·20	1·50
807	-	300f. blue, red & yellow	3·50	2·10

DESIGN: 300f. U.N. emblem as flower with peace doves forming stalk.

198 Girl with Posy, Youth Ceremony and IYY Emblem

1985. Air. "Philexafrique" Stamp Exhibition, Lome, Togo (2nd issue). Multicoloured.

808	250f. Type **198** (International Youth Year)	4·00	2·50
809	250f. Computer terminal, liner, airplane, diesel freight train, rocket and UPU emblem	4·00	2·50

199 Hugo

1985. Air. Death Centenary of Victor Hugo (writer).

810	**199**	70f. blue, sepia and brown	90	45
811	**199**	110f. brown, green & red	1·50	65
812	**199**	250f. black, red & orange	2·75	1·50
813	**199**	300f. purple, blue and red	4·25	1·80

200 Nativity

1985. Air. Christmas.

814	**200**	250f. multicoloured	3·00	1·20

201 Pictures of Visit on Map

1986. Visit of President to Interior.

815	**201**	100f. yellow, black & grn	1·40	70
816	**201**	170f. yellow, black & pink	2·50	1·10
817	**201**	200f. yellow, black & grn	2·75	1·70

1987. Various stamps surch.

822	**175**	100f. on 200f. mult (air)	70	55
823	-	100f. on 200f. mult (696)	60	60
824	-	100f. on 250f. mult (669)	70	55
825	-	100f. on 300f. mult (643)	40	30
826	-	100f. on 300f. mult (662)	40	30
827	**179**	170f. on 200f. mult	70	60
828	**181**	170f. on 250f. mult	1·10	90
818	-	170f. on 300f. mult (725) (postage)	70	60
829	-	170f. on 300f. mult (601)	70	60
830	-	170f. on 300f. mult (622)	70	60
819	-	230f. on 300f. blue, red and yellow (807)	1·00	85
820	-	240f. on 300f. mult (742)	1·00	85
831	-	240f. on 300f. mult (636)	1·00	90

203 Fada

1987. Liberation of Fada.

832	**203**	40f. multicoloured		

204 Boy suffering from Trachoma

1987. Lions Club Anti-trachoma Campaign. Multicoloured.

835	30f. Type **204**		
837	100f. Type **204**		
838	120f. Healthy boy and afflicted boys (horiz)		
840	200f. Doctor examining boy (horiz)		

205 400 m Hurdles

1988. Air. Olympic Games, Seoul. Multicoloured.

841	100f. Type **205**	1·20	45
842	170f. 5000 m (horiz)	1·90	80
843	200f. Long jump (horiz)	2·40	85
844	600f. Triple jump	6·50	2·75
MS845	105×80 mm. 750f. 10,000 metres	8·50	4·50

206 Barbary Sheep

1988. Endangered Animals. Barbary Sheep. Multicoloured.

846	25f. Type **206**	2·00	75
847	45f. Mother and lamb	2·50	85
848	70f. Two sheep	3·00	1·00
849	100f. Two adults with lamb	4·50	1·70

207 President and Crowd on Map

1989. "Liberation".

850	**207**	20f. multicoloured	30	10
851	**207**	25f. multicoloured	35	10
852	**207**	40f. multicoloured	55	20
853	**207**	100f. multicoloured	1·60	50
854	**207**	170f. multicoloured	2·20	1·10

208 Boy posting Letter

1989. World Post Day.

855	**208**	100f. multicoloured		
856	**208**	120f. multicoloured		
857	**208**	170f. multicoloured		
858	**208**	250f. multicoloured		

209 N'Djamena Cathedral and Pope with Crucifix

1990. Visit of Pope John Paul II. Multicoloured.

859	20f. Type **209**	45	10
860	80f. Cathedral and Pope (different)	1·10	55
861	100f. Type **209**	1·30	85
862	170f. As No. 860	2·20	1·60

210 Traditional Hairstyle

1990

863	**210**	100f. multicoloured	24·00	
864	**210**	120f. multicoloured	24·00	
865	**210**	170f. multicoloured	25·00	
866	**210**	250f. multicoloured	26·00	

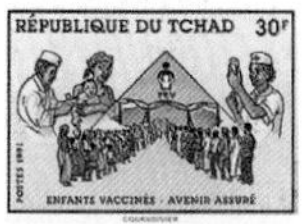

215 Queues and Nurse vaccinating Child

1991. "Child Vaccination—Assured Future".

880	**215**	30f. multicoloured	40	10
881	**215**	100f. multicoloured	1·10	75
882	**215**	170f. multicoloured	1·80	1·20
883	**215**	180f. multicoloured	2·00	1·30
884	**215**	200f. multicoloured	2·20	1·50

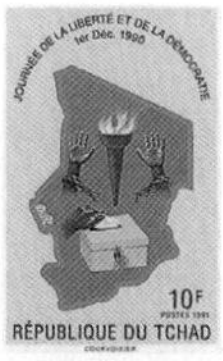

216 Torch, Hands with Broken Manacles and Ballot Box

1991. Day of Freedom and Democracy.

885	**216**	10f. multicoloured	10	10
886	**216**	20f. multicoloured	30	10
887	**216**	40f. multicoloured	50	30
888	**216**	70f. multicoloured	65	55
889	**216**	130f. multicoloured	1·40	1·20
890	**216**	200f. multicoloured	2·10	1·40

217 Mother and Child

1992. 20th Anniv of Medecins sans Frontieres (medical relief organization).

891	**217**	20f. multicoloured	30	10
892	**217**	45f. multicoloured	50	20
893	**217**	85f. multicoloured	1·10	60
894	**217**	170f. multicoloured	2·00	1·20
895	**217**	300f. multicoloured	3·25	2·10

218 Class

1992. Literacy Campaign.

896	**218**	25f. multicoloured	30	10
897	**218**	40f. multicoloured	50	20
898	**218**	70f. multicoloured	65	50
899	**218**	100f. multicoloured	1·00	70
900	**218**	180f. multicoloured	1·80	1·20
901	**218**	200f. multicoloured	2·20	1·50

219 Mother and Child, Globe and Cereals

1992. International Nutrition Conference, Rome.

902	**219**	10f. multicoloured	35	10
903	**219**	60f. multicoloured	80	45
904	**219**	120f. multicoloured	1·80	80
905	**219**	500f. multicoloured	5·00	3·00

219a Symbols of Literacy

1997. Development of Literacy.

905a	**219a**	150f. multicoloured	90	60
905b	**219a**	300f. multicoloured	1·80	1·20
905c	**219a**	475f. multicoloured	2·75	1·80

219b Hand over Symbols of Environment

1998. Protection of Ozone Layer.

905d	**219b**	150f. multicoloured	75	60
905e	**219b**	300f. multicoloured	1·80	1·20
905f	**219b**	475f. multicoloured	2·75	1·80
905g	**219b**	500f. multicoloured	3·00	2·00

220 Stone Heads, Easter Island

2000. Wonders of the World. Multicoloured.

906	50f. Type **220**	10	10
907	150f. Stonehenge	65	50
908	300f. Jericho	1·30	1·00
909	400f. Machu Picchu	1·80	1·40
910	500f. Valley of statues	2·20	1·70
911	700f. Chichen Itza	3·25	3·00
912	900f. Persepolis	4·00	3·00

221 Mastiff ("Matin Espagnol")

2000. Dogs. Multicoloured.

915	400f. Type **221**	1·40	55
916	500f. Kuvasz	1·70	65
917	700f. Beauceron	2·40	85
918	900f. Rough collie	3·00	1·20

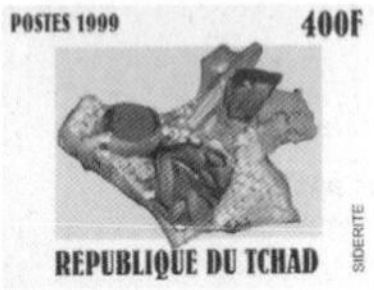

222 Siderite

2000. Minerals. Multicoloured.

921	400f. Type **222**	1·80	1·40
922	500f. Dolomite and quartz	2·20	1·70
923	700f. Azurite	3·25	2·30
924	900f. Calcite	4·00	3·00

223 Renault (1906)

2000. Vintage Cars. Multicoloured.

927	400f. Type **223**	1·80	1·40
928	500f. Pierce Arrow (1919)	2·20	1·70
929	700f. Citroen (1919)	3·25	2·30
930	900f. Ford (1928)	4·00	3·00

224 Green Locomotive 0-6-0

2000. Trains. Multicoloured.

933	400f. Type **224**	1·80	1·40
934	500f. Brown locomotive	2·20	1·70
935	700f. Blue locomotive	3·25	2·30
936	900f. Purple locomotive with red stripe	4·00	3·00

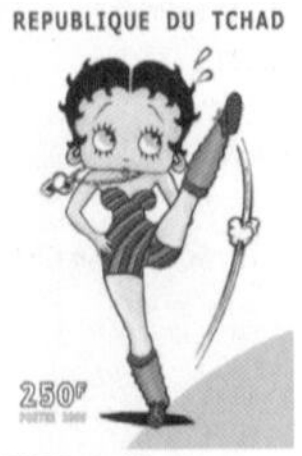

225 Betty Boop

2000. Betty Boop (cartoon character). Multicoloured.

937	250f. Type **225**	1·10	85
938	250f. As cheer leader	1·10	85
939	250f. Wearing fur coat	1·10	85
940	250f. At soda bar	1·10	85
941	250f. Wearing short leotard and leggings	1·10	85
942	250f. Wearing cap and shorts	1·10	85
943	250f. Wearing cap and leggings	1·10	85
944	250f. Seated	1·10	85
945	250f. Wearing ragged shorts and boots	1·10	85
MS946	89×140 mm. 1500f. Riding bicycle	7·00	5·25
MS947	140×94 mm. 2000f. Roller skating	8·75	6·50

Nos. 937/8 and 940/5 have a composite background design.

226 Larry and Curly

2000. Three Stooges (comedy act) (1st issue). Multicoloured.

948	250f. Type **226**	1·10	85
949	250f. As cowboys	1·10	85
950	250f. As cowboys on horseback	1·10	85
951	250f. Larry with raised arm	1·10	85
952	250f. Moe having hair pulled	1·10	85
953	250f. Moe holding hammer	1·10	85
954	250f. As cowboys, Curly kneeling	1·10	85
955	250f. Larry and Moe leading man by nose	1·10	85
956	250f. Moe and patient	1·10	85
MS957	130×92 mm. 1500f. As No. 956 (42×51 mm)	7·00	4·75
MS958	122×92 mm. 2000f. As No. 954 (42×51 mm)	8·75	6·50

See also Nos. 969/**MS**978.

227 Lucy

2000. *I love Lucy* (TV show starring Lucille Ball). Multicoloured.

959	225f. Type **227**	1·00	70
960	225f. Crouched wearing tutu	1·00	70
961	225f. Dressed as clown	1·00	70
962	225f. Wearing tutu and wings	1·00	70
963	225f. With leg raised	1·00	70
964	225f. Falling backwards	1·00	70
965	225f. With bent knees	1·00	70
966	225f. Wearing clown outfit being sprayed with water	1·00	70
967	225f. Wearing tutu with leg on barre	1·00	70
MS968	Two sheets, each 122×88 mm. (a) 1500f. As clown (51×36 mm). (b) 2000f. As clown jumping	17·00	12·50

228 Larry and Moe

2000. Three Stooges (comedy act) (2nd issue). Multicoloured.

969	300f. Type **228**	1·50	1·00
970	300f. Larry and Moe wearing suits holding diplomas	1·50	1·00
971	300f. Moe	1·50	1·00
972	300f. Larry	1·50	1·00
973	300f. Three Stooges	1·50	1·00
974	300f. Shemp facing left	1·50	1·00
975	300f. Shemp facing right	1·50	1·00
976	300f. Shemp and Larry	1·50	1·00
977	300f. Moe and Larry	1·50	1·00
MS978	Two sheets, each 130×92 mm. (a) 1500f. Moe as troubadour (42×51 mm). (b) 2000f. Larry holding fiddle (42×51 mm)	18·00	11·50

229 Emblem

2000. Centenary of Fort Lamy N'Djamena.

980	**229** 300f. multicoloured		
981	**229** 475f. multicoloured		

230 Giraffes (*Giraffa camelopardalis*)

2000. Fauna. Multicoloured.

982	150f. Type **230**	95	60
983	150f. Two giraffes	95	60
984	150f. Three giraffes	95	60
985	150f. Two giraffes (different)	95	60
986	200f. Gazelle (*Gazella granti*)	1·20	75
987	200f. Facing right	1·20	75
988	200f. Eating	1·20	75
989	200f. Drinking	1·20	75
990	250f. Addax (*Addax nasomaculatus*)	1·50	90
991	250f. Laying down	1·50	90
992	250f. Facing left	1·50	90
993	250f. Grazing	1·50	90
994	300f. Barbary sheep(*Ammotragus lervia*)	1·80	1·10
995	300f. Barbary sheep's head	1·80	1·10
996	300f. Facing left	1·80	1·10
997	300f. Facing front	1·80	1·10
998	375f. Black rhinoceros (*Diceros bicornis*)	2·10	1·40
999	375f. Facing right	2·10	1·40
1000	375f. Facing left	2·10	1·40
1001	375f. Amongst herbage	2·10	1·40
1002	400f. Leopard (*Panthera pardus*)	2·10	1·40
1003	400f. Laying down	2·10	1·40
1004	400f. Facing left	2·10	1·40
1005	400f. Leopard's head	2·10	1·40
1006	450f. Hippopotamus (*Hippopotamus amphibius*)	2·40	1·70
1007	450f. Two laying down	2·40	1·70
1008	450f. Group	2·40	1·70
1009	450f. Drinking	2·40	1·70
1010	450f. Gelada baboon (*Theropithecus gelada*)	2·40	1·70
1011	450f. Vervet monkey (*Cercopithecus aethiops*)	2·40	1·70
1012	450f. Olive baboon (Papio anubis)	2·40	1·70
1013	450f. Gelada baboon mother and baby	2·40	1·70
1014	475f. Scimitar-horned oryx (*Oryx dammah*)	2·75	1·90
1015	475f. Facing right	2·75	1·90
1016	475f. Grazing	2·75	1·90
1017	475f. Two scimitar-horned oryx	2·75	1·90
1018	500f. Two lions (*Panthera leo*)	2·75	1·90
1019	500f. Drinking	2·75	1·90
1020	500f. Mother and cub	2·75	1·90
1021	500f. Laying down	2·75	1·90
1022	600f. Elephant (Loxodonta africana)	3·25	2·10
1023	600f. Grazing	3·25	2·10
1024	600f. Facing front	3·25	2·10
1025	600f. Elephant's head	3·25	2·10
1026	750f. African buffalo cow and calf (*Syncerus caffer*)	4·00	2·50
1027	750f. African buffalo	4·00	2·50
1028	750f. Laying down	4·00	2·50
1029	750f. African buffalo's head	4·00	2·50
MS1030	Three sheets, each 130×90 mm. (a) 1000f. Two hippopotami (42×51 mm). (b) 1000f. Two rhinoceros (42×51 mm). (b) 1500f. Lion eating (42×51 mm)	19·00	14·50

Nos. 1031/50 and Types **231/40** are left for possible issues not yet seen.

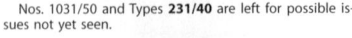

241 Family under Umbrella

2004. AIDS Prevention Campaign. Multicoloured.

1051	50f. Type **241**	40	25
1052	100f. Couple and 'PRUDENCE'	80	50
1053	150f. Doctor holding medicines	1·20	75
1054	300f. 'Prudence', 'Abstinence' and 'Fidelite'	2·30	2·00

Nos. 1055/1060 and Types **242/5** are left for possible issues not yet seen.

246 Opening the Valuve and Storage Tank

2004. First Anniv of Chad Oil Pipeline. Multicoloured.

1061	150f. Type **246**	80	40
1062	350f. Opening valve and two storage tanks	1·70	80
1063	400f. Opening valve and refinery	2·20	1·00
1064	500f. Opening valve and well head (vert)	2·75	1·30

Nos. 1065/70 and Types **247/50** are left for possible issues not yet seen.

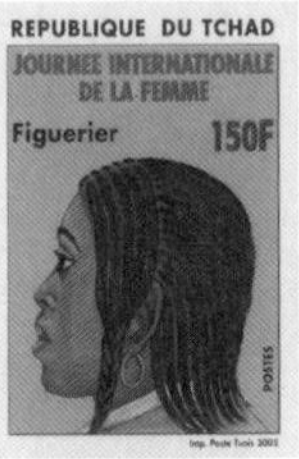

251 Figuerier

2005. International Women's Day Women's Hairstyles. Multicoloured.

1071	150f. Type **251**	90	45
1072	350f. Sakkindjala	1·80	80
1073	550f. Kileskou	2·40	1·20
1074	575f. Dabbou	3·00	1·50

MILITARY FRANK STAMPS

1965. No. 77 optd **F.M.**

M148	20f. red and black	£325	£325

M 24 Soldier with Standard

1966. No value indicated.

M149	**M 24** (–) multicoloured	2·00	3·50

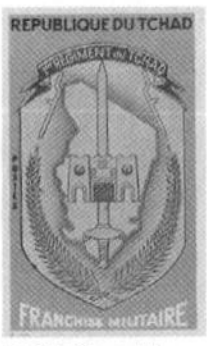

M 92 Shoulder Flash of 1st Regiment

1972. No value indicated.

M353	**M 92** (–) multicoloured	1·10	1·40

OFFICIAL STAMPS

O23 Flag and Map

1966. Flag in blue, yellow and red.

O148	**O23**	1f. blue	10	10
O149	**O23**	2f. grey	10	10
O150	**O23**	5f. black	10	10
O151	**O23**	10f. blue	10	10
O152	**O23**	25f. orange	35	10
O153	**O23**	30f. turquoise	45	30
O154	**O23**	40f. red	90	40
O155	**O23**	50f. purple	45	30
O156	**O23**	85f. green	1·10	50
O157	**O23**	100f. brown	2·00	65
O158	**O23**	200f. red	3·25	1·10

POSTAGE DUE STAMPS

1928. Postage Due type of France optd **TCHAD A. E. F.**

D58	**D11**	5c. blue	45	6·50
D59	**D11**	10c. brown	45	6·50
D60	**D11**	20c. olive	1·00	7·00
D61	**D11**	25c. red	1·60	7·25

D62	**D11**	30c. red	1·60	7·25
D63	**D11**	45c. green	1·60	8·50
D64	**D11**	50c. purple	1·70	8·75
D65	**D11**	60c. brown on cream	1·80	9·50
D66	**D11**	1f. red on cream	2·00	9·50
D67	**D11**	2f. red	2·75	15·00
D68	**D11**	3f. violet	2·30	10·50

D3 Village of Straw Huts

D 4 Pirogue on Lake Chad

1930

D69	**D3**	5c. olive and blue	60	7·25
D70	**D3**	10c. brown and red	1·00	7·50
D71	**D3**	20c. brown and green	2·30	8·00
D72	**D3**	25c. brown and blue	2·75	8·25
D73	**D3**	30c. green and brown	2·75	8·25
D74	**D3**	45c. olive and green	2·75	9·00
D75	**D3**	50c. brown & mauve	3·25	10·00
D76	**D3**	60c. black and lilac	3·75	13·00
D77	**D 4**	1f. black and brown	5·50	13·50
D78	**D 4**	2f. brown and mauve	5·25	21·00
D79	**D 4**	3f. brown and red	21·00	80·00

D6 Gonoa Hippopotamus

1962

D89	50c. bistre	10	10
D90	50c. brown	10	10
D91	1f. blue	10	10
D92	1f. green	10	10
D93	2f. red	10	10
D94	2f. red	10	10
D95	5f. myrtle	60	60
D96	5f. violet	60	60
D97	10f. brown	1·10	1·10
D98	10f. brown	1·10	1·10
D99	25f. purple	2·75	2·75
D100	25f. violet	2·75	2·75

DESIGNS (rock-paintings): No. D89, Type D **6**; D90, Gonoa kudu; D91, Two Gonoa antelopes; D92, Three Gonoa antelopes; D93, Gonoa antelope; D94, Tibestiram; D95, Tibestiox; D96, Oudingueur boar; D97, Gonoa elephant; D98, Gira-Gira rhinoceros; D99, Bardai warrior; D100, Gonoa masked archer. The two designs in each value are arranged in tete-beche pairs throughout the sheet.

D65 Kanem Puppet

1969. Native Puppets.

D284	**D65**	1f. brown, red & grn	10	10
D285	-	2f. brown, grn & red	10	10
D286	-	5f. green and brown	10	10
D287	-	10f. brown, pur & grn	20	20
D288	-	25f. brown, pur & grn	45	25

DESIGNS: 2f. Kotoko doll; 5f. Copper doll; 10f. Kotoko (diff); 25f. Guera doll.

APPENDIX

The following stamps have either been issued in excess of postal needs or have not been available to the public in reasonable quantities at face value. Such stamps may later be given full listing if there is evidence of regular postal use.

1970

"Apollo programme". Postage 40f.; Air 15, 25f.
Birth Bicent of Napoleon. Air. 10, 25, 32f.
World Cup Football Championship, Mexico. Air 5f.
World Cup. Previous Winners. 1, 4f., 5f.×2.
"Expo 70" World Fair, Osaka, Japan. Japanese Paintings. 50c., 1, 2f.
Christmas. Paintings. Postage 3, 25f.; Air 32f.
Past Olympic Venues. Postage 3, 8, 20f.; Air 10, 35f.

1971

Space Exploration. 8, 10, 35f.
Winter Olympic Games, Sapporo, Japan. Japanese Paintings. 50c., 1, 2f.
Kings and Queens of France. Postage 25f.×2, 30, 32, 35f., 40f.×2, 50f.×4, 60f.; Air 40, 50, 60, 70, 75, 80f., 100f.×5, 150f., 200f.×4.
150th Death Anniv of Napoleon. Air. 10f.
Famous Paintings. 1, 4, 5f.
Past Olympic Venues. Postage 15, 20f.; Air 25, 50f.
Winter Olympic Games, Sapporo, Japan. Optd on 1970 "Expo 70" issue 50c., 1, 2f.
Olympic Games Munich. World Cup Previous Winners issue (1970) optd **1f.**

1972

Moon Flight of "Apollo 15". Air 40, 80, 150, 250, 300, 500f.
"Soyuz 11" Disaster. Air 30, 50, 100, 200, 300, 400f.
Pres. Tombalbaye. Postage 30, 40f.; Air 70, 80f.
Winter Olympic Games, Sapporo, Japan. Postage 25, 75, 150f.; Air 130, 200f.
13th World Scout Jamboree, Asagiri, Japan (1971). Postage 30, 70, 80f.; Air 100, 120f.
Medal Winners, Sapporo Winter Olympics. Postage 25, 75, 100, 130f.; Air 150, 200f.
Olympic Games, Munich. Postage 20, 40, 60f.; Air 100, 120, 150f.
African Animals. Air 20, 30, 100, 130, 150f.
Medal Winners, Munich Olympics (1st series). Postage 10, 20, 40, 60f.; Air 150, 250f.
Medal Winners, Munich Olympics (2nd series). Gold frames, Postage 20, 30, 50f.; Air 150, 250f.

1973

Locomotives. 10, 40, 50, 150, 200f.
Domestic Animals (2nd issue). Postage 20, 30f.; Air 100, 130, 150f.
Horses. 20, 60, 100, 120f.
Airplanes. Air 5, 25, 70, 150, 200f.
Christmas. Postage 30, 40, 55f.; Air 60, 250f.

Other issues exist which were prepared by various agencies, but it is uncertain whether these were placed on sale in Chad. They include further values in the "Kings and Queens of France" series.

All the stamps below are on gold foil.

1982

World Cup Football Championship, Spain. Air 1500f.
21st Birthday of Princess of Wales. Air 1500f.
75th Anniv of Scout Movement. Air 1500f.
Olympic Games, Los Angeles. Air 1500f.
Birth of Prince William of Wales. 21st Birthday of Princess of Wales stamp optd. Air 1500f.

1983

World Cup Football Championship Results. Air 1500f.
Chess Grand Masters. Air 1500f.
Exploitation of Space. Air 1500f.
Winter Olympic Games, Sarajevo. Air 1500f.
Bicentary of Manned Flight. Air 1500f.
Olympic Games, Los Angeles. Air 1500f.

1993

30th Anniv of the Organisation for African Unity. 15f.; 30f.; 110f.; 190f.
Death Centenary of Victor Schoelcher. 55; 105; 125; 300f.

1994

Inauguration of Bank of Central African States 20; 30; 105; 190f.

1995

Traditional Grain Stores. 75; 150; 300; 450f.

1996

Fungi. 150; 170; 200; 350; 450; 800f.
Marilyn Monroe Commemoration. 170; 200; 300; 1000f.
Singers and Entertainers. 170; 350; 500; 700f.
The Beatles. 300f.×9.
John Lennon Commemoration. 100f.×9.
Elvis Presley Commemoration. 500f.×9.
Jacqueline Kennedy Commemoration. 200f.×9.
Marilyn Monroe Commemoration. 250f.×9.
Olympic Games, Nagano. 250f.×4; 300f.×4.
Sumo Wrestlers. 400f.×4.
Michael Schumacher. 700f.×4.
Rotary International. Ungulates. 170; 350; 500; 600f.
Rotary International. Ungulates. Overprinted for Calgary '96. 170; 350; 500; 600f.
World Cup Football Championships. 150f.; 250f.; 300f.; 600f.
Scouting. 200f.; 250f.; 300f.; 400f.; 450f.; 500f.
UNICEF. 150f.; 170f.; 400f.; 500f.;
Red Cross. 100f.; 350f.
Lions. 200f.; 800f.
Rotary International. 300f.; 700f.
Scouting. 250f.; 1000f.
John Lennon Commemoration. 400f.; 600f.
Elvis presley commemoration.200f.; 350f.; 500f.; 800f.

1997

Deng Xiaoping Commemoration. 75f.×6
Bruce Lee commemoration. 125f.×6.
Jacqueline Kennedy Commemoration. 150f.×9.
Traditional Housework. 50f.; 100f.; 150; 300; 450; 500f.
Diana, Princess of Wales. 250f.×9; 300f.×9; 450f.×9.
John f. Kennedy Commemoration. 250f.×9.
20th Death Anniv of Elvis Presley. 600f.×9.
Marilyn Monroe Commemoration. 500f.×9.
Aircraft. 150f.×6; 200f.×6; 250f.×6; 475f.×6.
150th Anniv of Swiss Railways. 350f.×6.
Trains. 600f.×6.

1998

Personalities. 100; 150; 300; 450; 475; 500; 600; 800; 1000f.
50th Anniv of Diplomatic relations with India. 150f.×3.
Dogs and Cats. 330f.×2; 450f.×2; 475f.×2; 500f.×2.
Wild Animals. 150f.×2; 550f.×2; 600f.×2.
Traditional Hairstyles. 50; 100; 150; 300; 400f.
Fauna. 150f.×6; 250f.×6; 300f.×12; 350f.×6.
Butterflies. 660f.×6
Ostrich. Surcharged. 300f.×4 on 220f.×4
Kofi Annan. 150f.×9.
American Railway Pioneers. 200f.×9.
Bela Lugosi Commemoration. 250f.×9.
Pope John Paul II. 300f.×9.
Ronald Reagan. 450f.×9.
John Glenn. 500f.×9.
Fossils and Pre-History. 150f.×9.
Dinosaurs. 400f.×6; 450f.×6.
Historical Vehicles. 50; 150; 200; 300; 400; 500f.
Winter Olympic Games, Nagano. 100f.; 170f.; 350f.; 750f.

1999

African Birds. 75; 150; 200; 300; 400; 475f.
Diana, Princess of Wales Commemoration. 250f.×9.
Football. 300f.×4; 400f.×4; 500f.×4.
Chess. 375f.×6; 500f.×6.
Betty Boop. 450f.×9.
Carl Benz Commemoration. 250f.×6.
Elvis Presley Commemoration. 300f.×9.
Napoleon Bonaparte. 300×6.
Pope John Paul II. 475f.×6.
Space Exploration. 500f.×6.

2001

Personalities. 200f.; 250f.; 300f.; 400f.; 500f.; 550f.; 600f.; 750f.; 800f.; 1000f.

2002

Tomb of Tutankamun. 3000f.×8

2003

Eagle. 3000f.
Yugi Gagarin Commemoration. 3000f.

2004

Personalities.300f.; 350f.; 400f.×2; 750f.×2; 1000f.×2

Pt. 1

CHAMBA

An Indian "convention" state of the Punjab.

12 pies = 1 anna; 16 annas = 1 rupee.

Stamps of India overprinted.

1886. Queen Victoria. Optd **CHAMBA STATE** in two lines.

1	**23**	½a. turquoise	2·00	2·00
2	-	1a. purple	3·50	3·50
4	-	1a.6p. brown	4·50	18·00
6	-	2a. blue	2·50	3·00
7	-	2a.6p. green	45·00	£140
9	-	3a. orange	3·00	7·00
11	-	4a. green (No. 96)	6·50	14·00
12	-	6a. brown (No. 80)	8·50	28·00
14	-	8a. mauve	10·00	16·00
16	-	12a. purple on red	7·50	20·00
17	-	1r. grey (No. 101)	65·00	£190
18	**37**	1r. green and red	13·00	23·00
19	**38**	2r. red and brown	£140	£500
20	**38**	3r. brown and green	£150	£450
21	**38**	5r. blue and violet	£170	£750

1900. Queen Victoria. Optd **CHAMBA STATE** in two lines.

22	**40**	3p. red	1·00	1·75
23	**40**	3p. grey	75	3·25
25	**23**	½a. green	90	2·75
26	-	1a. red	1·50	50
27	-	2a. lilac	15·00	45·00

1903. King Edward VII. Optd **CHAMBA STATE** in two lines.

28	**41**	3p. grey	25	2·00
30	-	½a. green (No. 122)	1·50	1·50
31	-	1a. red (No. 123)	2·75	1·75
33	-	2a. lilac	3·00	4·50
34	-	3a. orange	8·00	8·00
35	-	4a. olive	10·00	29·00
36	-	6a. bistre	6·00	30·00
37	-	8a. mauve	8·00	28·00
39	-	12a. purple on red	10·00	42·00
40	-	1r. green and red	11·00	29·00

1907. King Edward VII. Optd **CHAMBA STATE** in two lines.

41	½a. green (No. 149)	2·75	4·00
42	1a. red (No. 150)	2·75	4·75

1913. King George V. Optd **CHAMBA STATE** in two lines.

43	**55**	3p. grey	40	1·50
44	**56**	½a. green	2·50	2·75
45a	**57**	1a. red	2·50	5·00
55	**57**	1a. brown	3·50	7·50
56	**58**	1½a. brown (No. 163)	35·00	£170
57	**58**	1½a. brown (No. 165)	3·50	8·50
58	**58**	1½a. red	1·25	28·00
47	**59**	2a. purple	6·00	17·00
59	**61**	2a.6p. blue	90	6·00
60	**61**	2a.6p. orange	4·50	32·00
48	**62**	3a. orange	7·00	12·00
61	**62**	3a. blue	4·75	28·00
49	**63**	4a. olive	4·25	7·50
50	**64**	6a. bistre	6·50	11·00
51	**65**	8a. mauve	8·00	22·00
52	**66**	12a. red	5·50	17·00
53b	**67**	1r. brown and green	23·00	40·00

1921. No. 192 of India optd **CHAMBA**.

54	**57**	9p. on 1a. red	1·00	20·00

1927. Stamps of India (King George V) optd **CHAMBA STATE** in one line.

62	**55**	3p. grey	20	2·75
64	**80**	9p. green	8·50	30·00
63	**56**	½a. green	30	3·50
76	**79**	½a. green	1·10	15·00
65	**57**	1a. brown	2·50	2·50
77	**81**	1a. brown	2·75	1·75
66	**82**	1a.3p. mauve	2·25	8·00
67	**58**	1½a. red	8·50	9·50
68	**70**	2a. lilac	2·50	5·00
78	**59**	2a. red	1·40	28·00
69	**61**	2a.6p. orange	4·50	24·00
70	**62**	3a. blue	1·25	26·00
80	**62**	3a. red	3·50	18·00
71	**71**	4a. green	1·25	9·00
81	**63**	4a. olive	7·50	23·00
72	**64**	6a. bistre	30·00	£225
73	**65**	8a. mauve	1·75	14·00
74	**66**	12a. red	1·60	17·00
75	**67**	1r. brown and green	18·00	40·00

1938. Stamps of India (King George VI Nos. 247/64) optd **CHAMBA STATE.**

82	**91**	3p. slate	20·00	30·00
84	**91**	9p. green	14·00	48·00
83	**91**	½a. brown	2·75	22·00
85	**91**	1a. red	5·00	5·50
86	**92**	2a. red	12·00	28·00
87	-	2a.6p. violet	12·00	42·00
88	-	3a. green	13·00	38·00
89	-	3a.6p. blue	13·00	40·00
90	-	4a. brown	30·00	45·00
91	-	6a. green	40·00	£100
92	-	8a. violet	35·00	80·00
93	-	12a. red	27·00	85·00
94	**93**	1r. slate and brown	45·00	£100
95	**93**	2r. purple and brown	85·00	£425
96	**93**	5r. green and blue	£130	£650
97	**93**	10r. purple and red	£180	£1000
98	**93**	15r. brown and green	£170	£1400
99	**93**	25r. slate and purple	£275	£1500

1942. Stamps of India (King George VI) optd **CHAMBA.**
(a) On issue of 1938.

100	**91**	½a. brown	85·00	70·00
101	**91**	1a. red	£130	80·00
102	**93**	1r. slate and brown	24·00	75·00
103	**93**	2r. purple and brown	24·00	£325
104	**93**	5r. green and blue	45·00	£350
105	**93**	10r. purple and red	80·00	£600
106	**93**	15r. brown and green	£180	£1100
107	**93**	25r. slate and purple	£150	£1100

(b) On issue of 1940.

108	**100a**	3p. slate	2·25	8·00
110	**100a**	9p. green	1·25	25·00
109	**100a**	½a. mauve	1·00	8·00
111	**100a**	1a. red	2·75	6·00
112	**101**	1½a. violet	3·50	17·00
113	**101**	2a. red	13·00	20·00
114	**101**	3a. violet	27·00	65·00
115	**101**	3½a. blue	14·00	50·00
116	**102**	4a. brown	20·00	18·00
117	**102**	6a. green	21·00	48·00
118	**102**	8a. violet	24·00	65·00
119	**102**	12a. purple	27·00	75·00
120	-	14a. purple (No. 277)	18·00	3·00

OFFICIAL STAMPS

Stamps of India overprinted

1886. Queen Victoria. Optd **SERVICE CHAMBA STATE.**

O1	**23**	½a. turquoise	1·25	20
O3	-	1a. purple	3·50	20
O5	-	2a. blue	3·50	3·25
O7	-	3a. orange	2·50	17·00
O8	-	4a. green (No. 96)	5·00	10·00
O10	-	6a. brown (No. 80)	6·50	19·00
O13	-	8a. mauve	5·00	5·00
O14	-	12a. purple on red	13·00	60·00
O15	-	1r. grey (No. 101)	22·00	£225
O16	**37**	1r. green and red	7·00	55·00

1902. Queen Victoria. Optd **SERVICE CHAMBA STATE.**

O17	**40**	3p. grey	60	1·25
O18	**23**	½a. green	2·25	5·00
O20	-	1a. red	2·25	1·00
O21	-	2a. lilac	14·00	45·00

1903. King Edward VII. Optd **SERVICE CHAMBA STATE.**

O22	**41**	3p. grey	35	15
O24	**41**	½a. green (No. 122)	35	10
O25	**41**	1a. red (No. 123)	1·50	30
O27	-	2a. lilac	1·50	2·25
O28	-	4a. olive	3·50	23·00
O29	-	8a. mauve	11·00	24·00
O31	-	1r. green and red	2·00	18·00

1907. King Edward VII. Optd **SERVICE CHAMBA STATE.**

O32	½a. green (No. 149)	40	75
O33	1a. red (No. 150)	2·25	3·25

1913. King George V Official stamps optd **CHAMBA STATE.**

O34	**55**	3p. grey	20	40
O36	**56**	½a. green	20	60
O38	**57**	1a. red	20	10
O47	**57**	1a. brown	6·00	1·50

O40	**59**	2a. lilac (No. O83)	1·10	19·00
O41	**63**	4a. olive (No. O86)	1·10	24·00
O42	**65**	8a. mauve	2·00	28·00
O43	**67**	1r. brown and green	7·50	45·00

1914. King George V Postage stamps optd **SERVICE CHAMBA STATE**.

O44	**59**	2a. lilac (No. 166)	15·00	
O45	**63**	4a. olive (No. 210)	13·00	

1921. No O97 of India optd **CHAMBA**.

O46	**57**	9p. on 1a. red	20	10·00

1927. King George V Postage stamps optd **CHAMBA STATE SERVICE**.

O48	**55**	3p. grey	50	40
O50	**80**	9p. green	7·00	15·00
O49	**56**	½a. green	50	15
O61	**79**	½a. green	8·00	60
O51	**57**	1a. brown	30	10
O62	**81**	1a. brown	4·50	45
O52	**82**	1¼a. mauve	8·00	1·00
O53	**70**	2a. lilac	4·00	1·00
O63	**59**	2a. red	6·50	1·40
O54	**71**	4a. olive	2·25	3·75
O65	**63**	4a. green	11·00	10·00
O55	**65**	8a. mauve	12·00	15·00
O56	**66**	12a. red	6·50	32·00
O57	**67**	1r. brown and green	16·00	60·00
O60	**67**	1r. green and red	70·00	£375
O58	**67**	2r. red and orange	25·00	£325
O59	**67**	5r. blue and violet	45·00	£375

1938. King George VI Postage stamps of India optd **CHAMBA STATE SERVICE**.

O66	**91**	9p. green	45·00	85·00
O67	**91**	1a. red	50·00	9·00
O68	**93**	1r. slate and brown	£200	£800
O69	**93**	2r. purple and brown	42·00	£550
O70	**93**	5r. green and blue	60·00	£650
O71	**93**	10r. purple and red	85·00	£1100

1940. Official stamps of India optd **CHAMBA**.

O72	**O20**	3p. grey	70	1·40
O75	**O20**	9p. green	10·00	16·00
O73	**O20**	½a. brown	75·00	5·50
O74	**O20**	½a. purple	70	5·00
O76	**O20**	1a. red	2·00	3·25
O77	**O20**	1a.3p. brown	£130	24·00
O78	**O20**	1½a. violet	13·00	11·00
O79	**O20**	2a. orange	11·00	11·00
O80	**O20**	2½a. violet	7·00	29·00
O81	**O20**	4a. brown	11·00	24·00
O82w	**O20**	8a. violet	22·00	£100

1942. King George VI Postage stamps of India optd **CHAMBA SERVICE**.

O83	**93**	1r. slate and brown	20·00	£275
O84	**93**	2r. purple and brown	35·00	£375
O85	**93**	5r. green and blue	70·00	£600
O86	**93**	10r. purple and red	75·00	£1000

Pt. 1

CHARKHARI

A state of Central India. Now uses Indian stamps.

12 pies = 1 anna; 16 annas = 1 rupee.

1

1894. Imperf. No gum.

10	**1**	¼a. purple	1·75	2·50
6a	**1**	½a. purple	2·50	3·00
7a	**1**	1a. green	4·50	7·50
8a	**1**	2a. green	7·00	9·00
9a	**1**	4a. green	7·50	18·00

2

1909. Perf or imperf.

15a	**2**	1p. brown	5·00	38·00
16	**2**	1p. blue	1·00	55
32	**2**	1p. green	75·00	£350
33	**2**	1p. violet	22·00	£225
25	**2**	½a. red	3·25	1·60
34	**2**	½a. olive	2·50	16·00
35	**2**	½a. brown	6·00	28·00
36	**2**	½a. black	75·00	£300
18a	**2**	1a. green	3·75	1·75
40	**2**	1a. brown	13·00	29·00
41	**2**	1a. red	£180	90·00
19	**2**	2a. blue	3·25	3·25
43	**2**	2a. grey	75·00	£110
20	**2**	4a. green	4·25	5·50
44	**2**	4a. red	3·00	22·00
21	**2**	8a. red	7·50	23·00
22	**2**	1r. brown	13·00	50·00

4

1912. Imperf.

28	**4**	1p. violet	7·00	5·00

5

1922. Imperf.

29	**5**	1a. violet	90·00	£100

7 The Lake

1931. Perf.

45	-	½a. green	2·50	10
46	**7**	1a. sepia	1·60	10
47	-	2a. violet	1·75	10
48	-	4a. olive	2·00	15
49	-	8a. mauve	3·25	10
50	-	1r. green and red	4·00	20
51	-	2r. red and brown	6·50	25
52	-	3r. brown and green	22·00	40
53	-	5r. blue and lilac	9·50	50

DESIGNS—HORIZ: ½a. The Lake; 2a. Industrial school; 4a. Bird's-eye view of city; 8a. Fort; 1r. Guest House; 2r. Palace Gate; 3r. Temples at Rainpur; 5r. Goverdhan Temple.

1940. Nos. 21/2 surch.

54	**2**	½a. on 8a. red	45·00	£170
55	**2**	1a. on 1r. brown	£170	£550
56	**2**	"1 ANNA" on 1r. brown	£1700	£1200

Index